British National Bibliography

1981

The British National Bibliography has been published since 1950. The BNB Weekly Lists give new publications in classified subject order together with an author and title index. Indexes under authors and titles, and subjects for the month appear in the last issue of each month. Interim cumulations are published at four-monthly intervals, providing an up-to-date reference service to books published in Great Britain. Cumulations covering longer periods from 1950 are also available.

British National Bibliography

A Subject Catalogue of new British books received by the Copyright Receipt Office of the British Library, arranged according to the Dewey Decimal Classification and catalogued according to the Anglo-American Cataloguing Rules, with a full Author & Title Index, and a Subject Index

1981

Volume 1: Subject Catalogue

The British Library BIBLIOGRAPHIC SERVICES DIVISION

The British National Bibliography is compiled within
The British Library
BIBLIOGRAPHIC SERVICES DIVISION
2 Sheraton Street, London W1V 4BH
Telephone 01–636 1544
Telex 21462

ISBN 0–900220–95–3

ISSN 0007–1544

Annual subscription: Full printed service including cumulations and annual volume £210 (£265 overseas); full service including printed cumulations and an annual volume on microfiche £160 + £9 VAT. (£200 overseas)

British Library Cataloguing in Publication data
British national bibliography.—1981
1. Great Britain—Imprints
I. British Library. *Bibliographic Services Division*
015.41'03'05 Z2001

ISBN 0–900220–95–3
ISSN 0007–1544

Computer-controlled phototypesetting by Computaprint Ltd London
Printed in Great Britain at the University Press, Oxford

Preface

The objects of the British National Bibliography are to list every new work published in the British Isles, to describe each work in detail and to give the subject matter of each work as precisely as possible. These operations are undertaken by a staff of qualified librarians. The material catalogued is based upon the items received, under the Copyright Act, 1911, by the Copyright Receipt Office of the British Library. Every endeavour is made to ensure the accuracy of the information given.

A few classes of publications are intentionally excluded, they are:

a) Periodicals (except the first issue of a new periodical and the first issue of a periodical under a new title)

b) Music (listed separately in the *British Catalogue of Music*)

c) Maps

d) Certain Government publications*

e) Publications without a British imprint, except those published in the Republic of Ireland.†

Hints for tracing information

This bibliography is in three sections: in the first, or Classified Subject Catalogue, the entries are arranged according to the Dewey Decimal system of subject classification; in the second the entries are arranged alphabetically by authors, titles, editors, series, etc.; the third section, the Subject Index, is an alphabetical index of subjects appearing in the Classified Subject Catalogue. The fullest information about a book is given in the Classified Subject Catalogue, including the form of name used by the author in his books, the full title, edition, publisher, date of publication and the series as well as the number of pages, the kind of illustrations, the size, the International Standard Book Number and the price. A shorter entry is given in the Author & Title Index under the name of the author, including the short title, edition, publisher and price, the International Standard Book Number, Dewey Decimal Classification Number and BNB Number.

Authors, titles, editors, series, etc.

When the author of a book is known look under his name in the Author & Title Index. The information given there will be adequate for many purposes. If the fullest information about a book is required, refer to the entry in the Classified Subject Catalogue. This is easily found by means of the first reference number (the Dewey Decimal Classification Number) at the end of an entry in the Author & Title Index. The number is read as a decimal number. Thus, for example, the number 621 will be found after the number 598.2942 and before the number 621.384.

Books emanating from societies and other organisations are sometimes entered under the name of the society or organisation, while publications of governments are frequently entered under the name of the country or city for which they are responsible.

Books with diffuse or unknown authorship will be found entered under the first word of the title which is not an article.

Entries are made in the Author & Title Index under the titles of works, so that if the author is not known a work can be found by looking up its title in this Index.

If neither the author nor the title is known, it may still be possible to trace the work by means of the editor, illustrator, series, etc.

Subjects

One of the most important aspects of this bibliography is its exhaustive index to the subject matter of books. The Classified Subject Catalogue itself displays the works on a subject in such a way that the whole field of literature on that subject can be easily perused. The Subject Index lists all the subjects found in the Classified Subject Catalogue and shows by means of the class number (i.e. the Dewey Decimal Classification Number) where books on those subjects are listed in the Classified Subject Catalogue. For example, in the Subject Index under the word Africa is a full list of the places in the Classified Subject Catalogue where books in any way concerned with Africa may be found, thus:

Africa

Central Africa. Description & travel — *Illustrations*	916.7'04'0222
Common law countries. Commercial law — *Cases — Serials*	346.06'7'0264
East Africa. Birds	598.29676
Economic development — *Case studies*	330.96'0328
Freshwater gastropoda — *For medicine*	594'.3'096
North Africa — *Serials*	961'.048'05
Vertebrates. Cinematography — *Personal observations*	778.5'38596'0924

*Many titles published by Her Majesty's Stationery Office and included in its Selected Subscription Service to libraries are recorded in the British National Bibliography.

The following categories of very specialised material are ***not*** included in B.N.B.:

Parliamentary Papers
House of Lords Papers and Bills, House of Lords Parliamentary Debates; House of Commons Papers relating solely to the business of the House, House of Commons Parliamentary Debates, House of Commons Bills; Local Acts, Private Acts, Church Assembly Measures.

Non-Parliamentary Papers
Such routine administrative publications as:
Amendments, Appeals, Awards; Circulars; Defence Guides, Lists and Specifications; Examination Papers; Forms, Licences; Memoranda; Notices; Orders; Regulations; Returns; Tax Cases; Warrants.

†Government publications of the Republic of Ireland are not included.

BLAISE filing rules

Entries in all sections of the British National Biliography are ordered according to the *BLAISE filing rules*, published by the British Library, BLAISE, 2 Sheraton Street, London W1V 4BH.

Classification numbers

Entries in the British National Bibliography are classified by 19th edition of the Dewey Decimal Classification.

Bibliographic Descriptions

Entries in the Classified Subject Catalogue are prepared according to the requirements of the second edition of the Anglo-American Cataloguing Rules.

Publisher and place of publication

The place of publication is always given before the name of the publisher thus:

London : Harrap.

The address of a publisher is given in full in an entry if the address is not readily available elsewhere.
Where publisher and place of publication are not known, the abbreviations used are:

s.l.	sine loco—no place of publication.
s.n.	sine nomine—no publisher's name.

Collation

The collation is that part of the entry which describes the physical make-up of the book. The abbreviations used are:

v.	volumes.
p	pages. The preliminary pages, if they are separately numbered, are shown separately. For example, vii,222p. means seven preliminary pages are numbered with roman numerals and two hundred and twenty-two pages of text.
plates	pages not forming part of the main and preliminary sequences of pagination, generally containing illustrative matter, frequently numbered and sometimes on different paper.
ill	illustrations in the text or on plates.
col.ill	coloured illustrations.
facsims	facsimile reproductions.
geneal.table	genealogical table.
port	portrait.
cm	centimetres—used to give the height of a book.
pbk	paperback book.

International Standard Book Number

The International Standard Book Number (ISBN) relating to an individual book is given in the entry for that book in the Classified Subject Catalogue and in all related entries in the Author & Title Index. The International Standard Book Number consists of five parts; the initials ISBN; a country code; a publisher code; a title code and, finally, a 'check digit'. For example ISBN 0 406 55500 1 means:

ISBN - International Standard Book Number
0 - UK/US group of publishers
406 - Butterworth
55500 - specific title; An introduction to English legal history, by J. H. Baker
1 - the check digit (a device preventing incorrectly quoted numbers from being processed).

Prices

Prices given are those current at the time of appearance of an entry in the Weekly List.

Cataloguing in Publication (CIP)

When "CIP entry" appears in an annotation it indicates that the entry has been prepared from advance information supplied by the publisher and not from the book itself. CIP entries are revised when titles are published and deposited at the Copyright Receipt Office, and then bear the annotation "CIP rev."

An entry fully explained:

Derbyshire, Edward

Geomorphological processes / E. Derbyshire, K.J. Gregory, J.R. Hails. — London : Butterworths, 1981, c1979. — 312p :
ill,charts,maps ; 26cm. — (Studies in physical geography, ISSN 0142-6389)
Originally published: Folkestone : Dawson, 1979. — Bibliography: p290-305. — Includes index
ISBN 0-408-10735-9 (cased) : £12.50
ISBN 0-408-10739-1 (pbk) : £6.95
B81-11453

means

The main entry heading for this book is the first named author, Derbyshire, Edward. The title is: Geomorphological processes, and is written by E. Derbyshire, K.J. Gregory and J.R. Hails. It is published in London by Butterworths in 1981, and bears a copyright date of 1979. There are 312 pages, with illustrations, charts and maps, and the volume is approximately 26 cm. in height. This book is published as part of a series entitled Studies in physical geography which has the International Standard Serial Number (ISSN) 0142-6389. The title was originally published in Folkestone by Dawson in 1979 and includes a bibliography on pages 290–305 and an index. There are two International Standard Book Numbers (ISBN) for this book: the first one, 0-408-10735-9 is for the hardback (cased) edition, which was priced at £12.50 at the time of publication; the second, 0-408-10739-1 is for the paperback edition, which was priced at £6.95 at the time of publication. The catalogue record bears a BNB number of B81-11453

Outline of the Dewey Decimal Classification

000 Generalities

010 Bibliography
020 Library & Information Sciences
030 General Encyclopaedic Works
040
050 General Serial Publications
060 General Organizations & Museology
070 Journalism, Publishing, Newspapers
080 General Collections
090 Manuscripts & Book Rarities

100 Philosophy & Related Disciplines

110 Metaphysics
120 Epistemology, Causation, Humankind
130 Paranormal Phenomena & Arts
140 Specific Philosophical Viewpoints
150 Psychology
160 Logic
170 Ethics (Moral Philosophy)
180 Ancient, Medieval, Oriental
190 Modern Western Philosophy

200 Religion

210 Natural Religion
220 Bible
230 Christian Theology
240 Christian Moral & Devotional
250 Local Church & Religious Orders
260 Social & Ecclesiastical Theology
270 History & Geography of Church
280 Christian Denominations & Sects
290 Other & Comparative Religions

300 Social Sciences

310 Statistics
320 Political Science
330 Economics
340 Law
350 Public Administration
360 Social Problems & Services
370 Education
380 Commerce (Trade)
390 Customs, Etiquette, Folklore

400 Language

410 Linguistics
420 English & Anglo-Saxon Languages
430 Germanic Languages German
440 Romance Languages French
450 Italian, Romanian, Rhaeto-Romanic
460 Spanish & Portuguese Languages
470 Italic Languages Latin
480 Hellenic Languages Classical Greek
490 Other Languages

500 Pure Sciences

510 Mathematics
520 Astronomy & Allied Sciences
530 Physics
540 Chemistry & Allied Sciences
550 Science of Earth & Other Worlds
560 Palaeontology
570 Life Sciences
580 Botanical Sciences
590 Zoological Sciences

600 Technology (Applied Sciences)

610 Medical Sciences
620 Engineering & Allied Operations
630 Agriculture & Related Technologies
640 Home Economics & Family Living
650 Management & Auxiliary Services
660 Chemical & Related Technologies
670 Manufactures
680 Manufacture for Specific Uses
690 Buildings

700 The Arts

710 Civic & Landscape Art
720 Architecture
730 Plastic Arts Sculpture
740 Drawing, Decorative & Minor Arts
750 Painting & Paintings
760 Graphic Arts Prints
770 Photography & Photographs
780 Music
790 Recreational & Performing Arts

800 Literature (Belles-lettres)

810 American Literature in English
820 English & Anglo-Saxon Literatures
830 Literatures of Germanic Languages
840 Literatures of Romance Languages
850 Italian, Romanian, Rhaeto-Romanic
860 Spanish & Portuguese Literatures
870 Italic Literatures Latin
880 Hellenic Literatures Greek
890 Literatures of Other Languages

900 General Geography & History

910 General Geography Travel
920 General Biography & Genealogy
930 General History of Ancient World
940 General History of Europe
950 General History of Asia
960 General History of Africa
970 General History of North America
980 General History of South America
990 General History of Other Areas

Classified Subject Catalogue

001 — KNOWLEDGE

001 — Great Britain. Further education institutions & higher education institutions. Curriculum subjects: General studies

National Association of Teachers in Further and Higher Education. General studies / NATFHE. — London : National Association of Teachers in Further and Higher Education, 1980. — 11p ; 21cm
Cover title
£0.35 (£0.25 to members) (pbk) B81-08224

001 — Inquiry

Inquiry : a second level University course. — Milton Keynes : Open University Press
At head of title: The Open University
Units 1-3: Mapping inquiry. — 1981. — 118p : ill,facsims,ports ; 30cm. — (U202 ; 1-3)
Includes bibliographies. — Contents: Unit 1 : Beginning with examples - Unit 2 : Inquiry in an age of uncertainty - Unit 3 : The changing map of inquiry
ISBN 0-335-10065-1 (pbk) : Unpriced B81-15093

Inquiry : a second level University course. — Milton Keynes : Open University Press
At head of title: The Open University. — Bibliography: p27
Unit 4: Conjectures and their refutations / Jennifer Trusted. — 1981. — 29p : ill,ports ; 30cm. — (U202 ; 4)
ISBN 0-335-10066-x (pbk) : Unpriced B81-15092

Inquiry : a second level University course. — Milton Keynes : Open University Press
At head of title: The Open University
Units 5-6: Mathematical inquiry. — 1981. — 78p : ill,1facsim,ports ; 30cm. — (U202 ; 5-6)
Includes bibliographies. — Contents: Unit 5 : Mathematical reasoning - Unit 6 : Mathematical inquiry
ISBN 0-335-10067-8 (pbk) : Unpriced B81-15091

Inquiry : a second level University course. — [Milton Keynes] : [Open University Press]
At head of title: The Open University
Examples of inquiry / [edited by R.N.D. Martin]. — [1981]. — x,252p : ill,maps,ports ; 30cm. — (U202 ; E1)
Includes bibliographies
ISBN 0-335-10081-3 (pbk) : Unpriced B81-15094

001 — Knowledge

Machlup, Fritz. Knowledge and knowledge production / by Fritz Machlup. — Princeton ; Guildford : Princeton University Press, c1980. — xxix,272p ; 25cm. — (Knowledge ; v.1)
Includes index
£9.80 B81-11407

001′.012 — Classification, *ca 1630-ca 1860*

Knight, David, *1936 Nov.30-*. Ordering the world : a history of classifying man / David Knight. — London : Burnett in association with Deutsch, 1981. — 215p : ill ; 23cm
Includes index
ISBN 0-233-97293-5 : £7.95 : CIP rev. B80-18274

001.2 — SCHOLARSHIP AND LEARNING

001.2′092′4 — Scholarship. Casaubon, Meric — *Critical studies*

Spiller, Michael R. G.. Concerning natural experimental philosophie : Meric Casaubon and the Royal Society / by Michael R.G. Spiller. — The Hague ; London : Nijhoff, 1980. — 232p : 1 facsim ; 24cm. — (Archives internationales d'histoire des idées = International archives of the history of ideas ; 94)
Bibliography: p218-227. — Includes index. — Includes facsim of: A letter of Meric Casaubon to Peter du Moulin ... concerning natural experimental philosophie. Cambridge : W.Morden, 1669
ISBN 90-247-2414-7 : Unpriced B81-05824

001.2′092′4 — Scholarship. Erasmus — *Biographies*

Phillips, Margaret Mann. Erasmus and the northern Renaissance. — Rev. ed. — Woodbridge : Boydell and Brewer, Sept.1981. — [192]p
Previous ed.: London : Hodder & Stoughton, 1949
ISBN 0-85115-151-5 : £10.00 : CIP entry B81-22590

001.2′092′4 — Scholarship. Erasmus — *Critical studies*

Boyle, Marjorie O'Rourke. Christening pagan mysteries : Erasmus in pursuit of wisdom / Marjorie O'Rourke Boyle. — Toronto ; London : University of Toronto Press, c1981. — xiii,174p ; 24cm. — (Erasmus studies)
Bibliography: p163-169. — Includes index
ISBN 0-8020-5525-7 : £9.00 B81-34333

001.2′092′4 — Scotland. Scholarship. Buchanan, George, *1506-1582 — Biographies*

McFarlane, I. D.. Buchanan / I.D. McFarlane. — London : Duckworth, 1981. — xvii,574p[1] leaf of plates : 1port,geneal.tables ; 26cm
Bibliography: p544-552. — Includes index
ISBN 0-7156-0971-8 : £45.00 : CIP rev. B80-13172

001.3 — HUMANITIES

001.3 — Humanities

An Arts foundation course. — Milton Keynes : Open University Press
At head of title: The Open University
Units 1-2A: An introduction to the study of the humanities / prepared for the Course Team by Arthur Marwick ... [et al.]. — 1981. — 57p : ill,ports ; 30cm. — (A101 ; 1-2A)
ISBN 0-335-05428-5 (pbk) : Unpriced B81-11356

001.3′01′8 — Humanities. Concepts. Formation

Pawlowski, Tadeusz. Concept formation in the humanities and the social sciences / Tadeusz Pawlowski. — Dordrecht ; London : Reidel, c1980. — ix,229p ; 23cm. — (Synthese library, ISSN 0166-6991 ; v.144)
Bibliography: p221-224. — Includes index
ISBN 90-277-1096-1 : Unpriced
Also classified at 300′.1′8 B81-07830

001.3′028′54 — Humanities. Applications of digital computer systems

Computing in the humanities. — Lexington : Lexington Books, Sept.1981. — [416]p
ISBN 0-566-00490-9 : £15.00 : CIP entry B81-21560

Hockey, Susan M.. A guide to computer applications in the humanities / Susan Hockey. — London : Duckworth, 1980. — 248p : ill ; 23cm
Bibliography: p230-231. — Includes index
ISBN 0-7156-1315-4 (cased) : £28.00 : CIP rev.
ISBN 0-7156-1310-3 (pbk) : £8.50 B80-00502

001.3′05 — Humanities. Serials: British Academy. Proceedings of the British Academy — *Indexes*

Hope, Michael. Index to the Proceedings of the British Academy, Volumes 1-63 / compiled by Michael Hope. — London : Published for the British Academy by the Oxford University Press, 1980. — 85p ; 26cm
ISBN 0-19-725999-5 : Unpriced B81-15378

001.3'07'1142821 — Humanities. Information sources. Use by Ph.D. students — *Study examples: Ph.D. students at University of Sheffield*

Corkill, Cynthia M.. Doctoral students in humanities : a small-scale panel study of information needs & uses 1976-79 / Corkill, C., Mann, M., and Stone, S.. — Sheffield : Centre for Research on User Studies, University of Sheffield, 1981. — iv,66p ; 29cm. — (CRUS occasional paper, ISSN 0140-3834 ; 5) (BLR&DD report ; no.5637)
ISBN 0-906088-04-6 (pbk) : Unpriced
B81-31483

001.3'072041 — Great Britain. Humanities. Research. Use of information sources. Research projects financed by British Library. *Research and Development Department — Conference proceedings*

Humanities information research : proceedings of a seminar, Sheffield 1980 / edited by Sue Stone. — Sheffield : Centre for Research on User Studies, University of Sheffield, 1980. — vii,96p ; 30cm. — (CRUS occasional paper, ISSN 0140-3834 ; 4) (BLR & DD report ; no.5588)
ISBN 0-906088-03-8 (pbk) : Unpriced
B81-16201

001.3'0973 — United States. Humanities

Commission on the Humanities. The humanities in American life : report of the Commission on the Humanities. — Berkeley ; London : University of California Press, c1980. — xiii,192p : 1ill ; 23cm
Includes index
ISBN 0-520-04183-6 (cased) : £7.50
ISBN 0-520-04208-5 (pbk) : £2.10 B81-08145

001.4 — RESEARCH

001.4 — Evaluation — *Manuals*

Guba, Egon G.. Effective evaluation / Egon G. Guba, Yvonna S. Lincoln. — San Francisco ; London : Jossey-Bass, 1981. — xxi,423p ; 24cm. — (The Jossey-Bass higher education series) (The Jossey-Bass social and behavioral science series)
Bibliography: p383-410. — Includes index
ISBN 0-87589-493-3 : £14.35 B81-29473

001.4 — Man. Needs. Research

Research and human needs / edited by Augusto Forti and Paolo Bisogno. — Oxford : Pergamon, 1981. — vi,191p : ill ; 22cm
Bibliography: p185-191
ISBN 0-08-027417-x : £13.50 : CIP rev.
B81-16401

001.4'025'41 — Great Britain. Research organisations — *Directories — Serials*

United Kingdom research establishments / [Data Research Group]. — 1980. — Great Missenden : The Group, [1980]. — 58p
ISBN 0-86099-286-1 : [£23.00] B81-19414

001.4'025'42143 — Research by Polytechnic of North London — *Directories — Serials*

Polytechnic of North London. Research review / the Polytechnic of North London. — 1978-80. — London (Holloway Rd, N7 8DB) : The Polytechnic, [1980?]. — 98p
ISSN 0307-451x : Unpriced B81-32220

001.4'079 — Ireland *(Republic)*. **Research. Grants** — *Directories*

Whelan, Sara. Funding sources for research in Ireland / compiled by Sara Whelan. — Dublin (Shelbourne House, Shelbourne Rd., Dublin 4) : National Board for Science and Technology, [1981]. — 132p ; 22cm
Includes index
ISBN 0-86282-003-0 (pbk) : £1.00 B81-23160

001.4'0941 — Great Britain. Research. Role of government — *Conference proceedings*

Government and research : proceedings of the symposium held on 29th April 1980 at the rooms of the Royal Society, London SW1. — London (47 Belgrave Sq., SW1X 8QX) : Research and Development Society, c1980. — 101p : 2ill ; 21cm
Unpriced (pbk) B81-18401

001.4'09422'162 — Surrey. Guildford. Universities: University of Surrey. Research projects — *Lists — Serials*

University of Surrey. *Research Committee*. Register of research projects / compiled for the Research Committee by the Bureau of Industrial Liaison. — 1978-. — Guildford (University of Surrey, Guildford GU2 5XH) : University of Surrey Research Committee, 1978-. — v. ; 21cm
Issued every two years
ISSN 0261-0612 = Register of research projects - University of Surrey. Research Committee : £5.00 B81-16235

University of Surrey. *Research Committee*. Register of research projects / compiled for the Research Committee by the Bureau of Industrial Liaison. — 1980. — Guildford (University of Surrey, Guildford GU2 5XH) : University of Surrey Research Committee, [1980?]. — v,205p
ISSN 0261-0612 : £5.00 B81-16236

001.4'2 — Great Britain. Secondary schools. Curriculum subjects: Problem solving — *For teaching*

Fineran, K.. Problem solving / prepared by K. Fineran, contributions by K. Fineran ... [et al.]. — Hatfield (College La., Hatfield, Hertfordshire, AL10 9AA) : Association for Science Education, c1978. — 17 leaves : ill ; 30cm. — (Topic brief / LAMP Project ; no.13)
ISBN 0-902786-48-2 (pbk) : £0.50 B81-06377

001.4'2 — Problem solving

Adams, James L.. Conceptual blockbusting : a guide to better ideas / James L. Adams. — 2nd ed. — New York ; London : Norton, 1980, c1979. — xii,153p : ill,facsims ; 22cm
Previous ed.: Stanford, Calif. : Stanford Alumni Association, 1974. — Includes index
ISBN 0-393-01223-9 : £6.50
ISBN 0-393-95016-6 (pbk) : £2.50 B81-02450

VanGundy, Arthur B.. Techniques of structured problem solving / Arthur B. VanGundy. — New York ; London : Van Nostrand Reinhold, c1981. — xi,307p : ill ; 24cm
Bibliography: p295-300. — Includes index
ISBN 0-442-21223-2 : £14.20 B81-21176

001.4'2 — Research. Methodology

Drew, Clifford J.. Introduction to designing and conducting research / Clifford J. Drew. — 2nd ed. — St. Louis ; London : Mosby, 1980. — xi,356p : ill,forms ; 25cm
Previous ed.: published as Introduction to designing research and evaluation. 1976. — Includes bibliographies and index
ISBN 0-8016-1460-0 : £18.50 B81-08017

001.4'22 — Statistics — *For schools*

Moss, Peter, *1921-*. Numbers working : an introduction to the collection, presentation and interpretation of statistics and their use in decision-making / Peter Moss & Owen Perry. — Cambridge : Hobsons Press [for] CRAC, c1981. — 64p : ill ; 30cm
Cover title. — Originally published: 1976
ISBN 0-86021-419-2 (pbk) : Unpriced
B81-29886

001.4'222 — Surveys. Data. Collection — *For schools*

Car careers / [Schools Council Project on Statistical Education]. — Slough : Published for the Schools Council by Foulsham Educational, c1981. — 16p : ill ; 21cm + teachers' notes(16p : 1form ; 21cm). — (Statistics in your world. [Level 3])
ISBN 0-572-01079-6 (pbk) : Unpriced
ISBN 0-572-01106-7 (teachers' notes) : Unpriced B81-16722

001.4'222 — Surveys. Data. Collection. Statistical methods: Sampling

Yates, Frank. Sampling methods for censuses and surveys / Frank Yates. — 4th ed., rev. and enl. — London : Griffin, 1981. — xvi,458p : ill ; 25cm
Previous ed.: 1960. — Bibliography: p416-450. — Includes index
ISBN 0-85264-253-9 : £21.00
Also classified at 304.6'0723 B81-05944

001.4'224 — Data: Tables — *For schools*

Tidy tables / [Schools Council Project on Statistical Education]. — Slough : Published for the Schools Council by Foulsham Educational, c1980. — 16p : ill ; 21cm + teachers' notes(24p : ill ; 21cm). — (Statistics in your world. [Level 1])
ISBN 0-572-01067-2 (pbk) : Unpriced
ISBN 0-572-01094-x (teachers' notes) : Unpriced B81-16715

001.4'24 — Mathematical models. Applications of digital computer systems — *Conference proceedings*

Symposium on Computer-Assisted Analysis and Model Simplification *(1st : 1980 : University of Colorado)*. Computer-assisted analysis and model simplification / edited by Harvey J. Greenberg, John S. Maybee ; proceedings of the First Symposium on Computer-Assisted Analysis and Model Simplification, University of Colorado, Boulder, Colorado, March 28 1980. — New York ; London : Academic Press, 1981. — xii,522p : ill ; 24cm
Includes bibliographies
ISBN 0-12-299680-1 : £19.60 B81-37755

001.4'24 — Networks. Analysis

Phillips, Don T.. Fundamentals of network analysis / Don T. Phillips, Alberto Garcia-Diaz. — Englewood Cliffs ; London : Prentice-Hall, c1981. — xv,474p : ill ; 24cm. — (Prentice-Hall international series in industrial and systems engineering)
Includes bibliographies and index
ISBN 0-13-341552-x : £17.50 B81-17310

001.4'24 — Networks. Analysis. Algorithms

Kennington, Jeff L.. Algorithms for network programming / Jeff L. Kennington, Richard V. Helgason. — New York ; Chichester : Wiley, c1980. — xiii,291p : ill ; 24cm
Bibliography: p279-288. — Includes index
ISBN 0-471-06016-x : £12.60 B81-03206

Network models and associated applications / edited by D. Klingman and J.M. Mulvey ; [contributors] T.E. Baker ... [et al.]. — Amsterdam ; Oxford : North-Holland, 1981. — vii,176p : ill ; 24cm. — (Mathematical programming study ; 15)
Includes bibliographies
ISBN 0-444-86203-x (pbk) : Unpriced
B81-31126

001.4'24 — Operations research. Mathematical models

Schmidt, J. William. Foundations of analysis in operations research / J. William Schmidt, Robert P. Davis. — New York ; London : Academic Press, 1981. — xi,383p : ill ; 24cm. — (Operations research and industrial engineering)
ISBN 0-12-626850-9 : £18.00 B81-37705

001.4'24 — Operations research. Search theory — *Conference proceedings*

NATO Advanced Research Institute on Search Theory and Applications *(1979 : Praia Da Rocha)*. Search theory and applications / [proceedings of the NATO Advanced Research Institute on Search Theory and Applications held in Praia Da Rocha, Portugal, March 26-30, 1979] ; edited by K. Brian Haley and Lawrence D. Stone. — New York ; London : Published in cooperation with NATO Scientific Affairs Division [by] Plenum, c1980. — ixx,277p : ill,maps ; 26cm. — (NATO conference series. II Systems science ; v.8)
Includes bibliographies and index
ISBN 0-306-40562-8 : Unpriced B81-09916

001.4'24 — Operations research. Techniques

Conolly, Brian. Techniques in operational research / Brian Conolly. — Chichester (Market Cross House, Cooper St., Chichester, W. Sessux PO19 1EB) : Ellis Horwood. — (Ellis Horwood series in mathematics and its applications)
Vol.2: Models, search and randomization. — 1981. — 338p : ill ; 24cm
Includes index
ISBN 0-85312-240-7 : £21.50 : CIP rev.
ISBN 0-8351-2302-0 (Student ed) : Unpriced
B80-35594

001.4′24 — Problem solving. Applications of digital computer systems. Programming languages: Basic language

Koffman, Elliot B.. Problem solving and structured programming in BASIC / Elliot B. Koffman, Frank L. Friedman. — Reading, Mass. ; London : Addison-Wesley, c1979. — 395,[64]p : ill ; 24cm. — (Addison-Wesley series in computer science and information processing)
Includes index
ISBN 0-201-03888-9 (pbk) : £6.95 B81-40849

001.42′4 — Simulations. Applications of computer systems

Spriet, J. A.. Computer-aided modelling and simulation. — London : Academic Press, Dec.1981. — [486]p
ISBN 0-12-659050-8 : CIP entry B81-31349

001.4′24 — Simulations. Applications of digital computer systems. Programming languages: GPSS F language

Schmidt, B.. GPSS-Fortran / B. Schmidt. — Chichester : Wiley, c1980. — xiii,523p : ill ; 25cm. — (Wiley series in computing)
Bibliography: p519. — Includes index
ISBN 0-471-27881-5 : £13.00 : CIP rev.
B80-25026

001.4′33 — Surveys. Methodology

Backstrom, Charles H.. Survey research / Charles H. Backstrom, Gerald Hursh-César. — 2nd ed. — New York ; Chichester : Wiley, c1981. — xxvii,436p : ill,forms ; 24cm
Previous ed.: Chicago : Northwestern University Press, 1963. — Includes bibliographies and index
ISBN 0-471-02543-7 : £9.25 B81-37113

001.5 — CYBERNETICS AND RELATED DISCIPLINES

001.5 — Information systems — *Conference proceedings*

Jerusalem Conference on Information Technology *(3rd : 1978)*. Information technology : proceedings of the 3rd Jerusalem Conference on Information Technology (JCIT3) Jerusalem, August 3-9, 1978 / edited by Josef Moneta. — Amsterdam ; Oxford : North-Holland, 1978. — xviii,804p : ill ; 27cm
Includes index
ISBN 0-444-85192-5 : Unpriced B81-10116

001.5 — Information systems. Design

Methlie, Leif B.. Information systems design : concepts and methods : aspects of analysis and design of transaction processing systems / Leif B. Methlie. — Bergen : Universitetsforlaget ; Henley on Thames : Global Book [distributor], c1978. — xi,259p : ill,forms ; 22cm
Bibliography: p253-256. — Includes index
ISBN 82-00-05216-8 (pbk) : £11.10 B81-16083

001.5 — Non-human intelligence

Holroyd, Stuart. Alien intelligence / Stuart Holroyd. — London : Abacus, 1981, c1979. — xxii,227p,[16]p of plates : ill,ports ; 20cm
Originally published : Newton Abbot : David and Charles, 1979. — Bibliography: p219-222. — Includes index
ISBN 0-349-11709-8 (pbk) : £2.50 B81-12938

001.5 — Video based information systems — *Serials*

Videoinfo : video markets & technology news bulletin. — Vol.1, no.1 (July 1981)-. — Alton (PO Box 3, Newman La., Alton, Hants. GU34 2PG) : Microinfo Ltd, 1981-. — v. ; 30cm
Monthly
ISSN 0261-393x = Videoinfo : £65.00 per year
B81-39530

001.51 — Communication. Content analysis

Advances in content analysis / Karl Erik Rosengren editor. — Beverly Hilss ; London : Sage, c1981. — 283p : ill ; 23cm. — (Sage annual reviews of communication research vol.9)
Conference papers. — Includes bibliographies and index
ISBN 0-8039-1555-1 (cased) : Unpriced
ISBN 0-8039-1556-x (pbk) : £6.25 B81-14617

001.51 — Communication — *For schools*

Communicate! / [compiled by] John Foster, Pat O'Shea and Andrew Carter. — Basingstoke : Published by arrangement with BBC School Television by Macmillan Education, 1981. — 93p : ill,facsims,ports ; 30cm
ISBN 0-333-30562-0 (pbk) : £2.45 B81-23043

001.51 — Content analysis. Methodology

Krippendorff, Klaus. Content analysis : an introduction to its methodology / Klaus Krippendorff. — Beverly Hills ; London : Sage, c1980. — 191p : ill ; 23cm. — (The Sage CommText series ; 5)
Bibliography: p181-189
ISBN 0-8039-1497-0 (cased) : Unpriced
ISBN 0-8039-1498-9 (pbk) : Unpriced
B81-16679

001.51 — Information systems — *For British public administration — Serials*

CCTA news. — Issue no.1 (Mar. 1981)-. — [London] ([Riverwalk House, Millbank, SW1P 4RT]) : Central Computer and Telecommunications Agency, 1981-. — v. ; 30cm
Monthly. — Merger of: Government computer topics ; Microcomputer newsletter ; and, Standards bulletin (Central Computer and Telecommunications Agency)
ISSN 0260-857x = CCTA news : Unpriced
B81-38992

001.51 — Information systems — *For chartered surveyors*

An **Introduction** to information systems and technology. — [London] : [Royal Institution of Chartered Surveyors], [1980]. — 29p ; 30cm
Bibliography: p29
£2.40 (£2.00 to members) (pbk) B81-22241

001.51 — Information systems — *For management — Serials*

Information systems report : the management report for executives concerned with the marketing and application of office information technology products. — Vol.1, no.1-. — Luton (PO Box 66, Luton, Bedfordshire LU2 7JZ) : Valvelord, 1981-. — v. ; 30cm
Monthly
ISSN 0262-0936 = Information systems report : £78.00 per year B81-38190

001.51 — Man. Communication

Contexts of communication / Jean M. Civikly editor. — New York ; London : Holt, Rinehart and Winston, c1981. — ix,333p : ill ; 24cm
Includes bibliographies
ISBN 0-03-053536-0 (pbk) : £5.95 B81-11371

001.51 — Semiotics

Gillan, Garth. From sign to symbol. — Brighton : Harvester Press, Dec.1981. — [112]p
ISBN 0-7108-0343-5 : £15.95 : CIP entry
B81-31545

Todorov, Tzvetan. Theories of the symbol. — Oxford : Blackwell, Feb.1982. — [340]p
Translation of: Théories du symbole
ISBN 0-631-10511-5 : £15.00 : CIP entry
B81-38327

001.51′0246 — Communication — *For technicians*

Garland, Paul. Communication and general studies for technician students / Paul Garland and Geoffrey Jones. — London : McGraw-Hill
Bibliography: p187. — Includes index
ISBN 0-07-084637-5 : £3.95 B81-21328

001.51′02461 — Communication — *Manuals — For medicine*

Sourcebook on medical communication / [edited by] Robert C. Reeder. — St. Louis ; London : Mosby, 1981. — x,308p : ill,facsims,plans,forms ; 28cm
Conference papers. — Bibliography: p295-298. — Includes index
ISBN 0-8016-4177-2 (pbk) : £18.50 B81-40358

001.51′02462 — Communication — *Manuals — For engineering*

Communication and the technical professional / edited by Charles H. Vervalin. — Houston ; London : Gulf, c1981. — vi,138p : ill ; 28cm
ISBN 0-87201-133-x (pbk) : Unpriced
B81-26626

001.51′024658 — Communication — *For business studies*

Deverell, C. S. People and communication / by C.S. Deverell. — London : Gee, 1979. — 147p : ill ; 22cm. — (GeeBEC series of study books)
Bibliography: p144. - Includes index
ISBN 0-85258-170-x (pbk) : £2.95 B81-12566

001.51′03′21 — Communication — *Encyclopaedias*

Gill, David. The ABC of communication studies / David Gill, Debra Murray. — [High Wycombe] ([Bucks College of Higher Education, Queen Alexandra Rd., High Wycombe, Bucks.]) : [D. Gill], [1981]. — 19p : ill ; 30cm
Bibliography: p19
ISBN 0-9507558-0-x (pbk) : Unpriced
B81-23298

001.51′05 — Communication — *Serials*

Language & communication : an interdisciplinary journal. — Vol.1, no.1 (1981)-. — Oxford : Pergamon, 1981-. — v. ; 25cm
Three issues yearly
Unpriced
Primary classification 410′.5 B81-13320

001.51′072 — Man. Communication. Research. Applications of multivariate analysis

Multivariate techniques in human communication research / edited by Peter R. Monge, Joseph N. Cappella. — London : Academic Press, 1980. — xxiv,552p : ill ; 24cm. — (Human communication research series)
Includes bibliographies and index
ISBN 0-12-504450-x : £25.20 B81-16782

001.53 — Cybernetics

Rudall, B. H.. Computers and cybernetics. — Tunbridge Wells : Abacus, July 1981. — [200]p
ISBN 0-85626-173-4 : £16.00 : CIP entry
Primary classification 001.64 B81-13739

001.53′4 — Pattern recognition

Devijer, P.. Pattern recognition. — Hemel Hempstead : Prentice-Hall, Jan.1982. — [440]p
ISBN 0-13-654236-0 : £25.00 : CIP entry
B81-33846

001.53′4 — Pattern recognition. Applications of fuzzy sets

Bezdek, James C.. Pattern recognition with fuzzy objective function algorithms / James C. Bezdek. — New York ; London : Plenum, c1981. — xv,256p : ill ; 24cm. — (Advanced applications in pattern recognition)
Bibliography: p241-248. — Includes index
ISBN 0-306-40671-3 : Unpriced B81-37470

001.53′4 — Pattern recognition — *Conference proceedings*

Pattern recognition in practice : proceedings of an international workshop held in Amsterdam, May 21-23, 1980 / edited by Edzard S. Gelsema and Laveen N. Kanal. — Amsterdam ; Oxford : North-Holland, 1980. — xii,552p : ill ; 23cm
Includes index
ISBN 0-444-86115-7 : £32.39 B81-03391

001.53′5 — Artificial intelligence

The **Handbook** of artificial intelligence / edited by Avron Barr and Edward A. Feigenbaum. — London : Pitman, 1981
Originally published: Los Altos, Calif. : W. Kaufmann, 1981. — Text on lining papers. — Bibliography: p365-388. — Includes index
Vol.1. — xiv,409p : ill ; 24cm
ISBN 0-273-08540-9 : Unpriced B81-40392

Machine intelligence. — Maidenhead : Pergamon Infotech, c1981. — iv,407p : ill,ports ; 30cm. — (Infotech state of the art report. Series 9 ; no.3)
Editor: A. Bond. — Bibliography: p369-400. — Includes index
ISBN 0-08-028556-2 : Unpriced B81-37813

001.53'5 — Artificial intelligence — *Conference proceedings*
Artificial intelligence : proceedings of the Joint IBM/University of Newcastle upon Tyne Seminar held in the University Computing Laboratory, 2nd-5th September 1980 / edited by M.J. Elphick. — [Newcastle-upon-Tyne] : University of Newcastle upon Tyne Computing Laboratory, 1981. — xiii,166p : ill ; 30cm
Includes bibliographies
Unpriced (pbk) B81-40393

001.53'5 — Automata theory
Lewis, Harry R.. Elements of the theory of computation / Harry R. Lewis, Christos H. Papadimitriou. — Englewood Cliffs : Prentice-Hall, c1981. — xiv,466p : ill ; 24cm. — (Prentice-Hall software series)
Includes bibliographies and index
ISBN 0-13-273417-6 : £14.90 B81-22707

001.53'9 — Information theory
Pierce, John R.. An introduction to information theory : symbols, signals & noise / John R. Pierce. — 2nd, rev. ed. — New York : Dover ; London : Constable, 1980. — xii,305p : ill,music ; 22cm
Previous ed.: published as Symbols, signals and noise. New York : Harper, 1961 ; London : Hutchinson, 1962. — Includes index
ISBN 0-486-24061-4 (pbk) : £2.70 B81-23234

001.53'9 — Information theory — *Conference proceedings*
Topics in information theory / edited by I. Csiszár and P. Elias. — Amsterdam ; Oxford : North-Holland, [1977]. — 592p : ill ; 25cm. — (Colloquia mathematica Societatis Janos Bolyai ; 16)
Conference papers. — Includes bibliographies
ISBN 0-7204-0699-4 : Unpriced B81-12697

001.53'9 — Information theory. Text compression
Cooper, David, *1949-*. Review of variety generation techniques : consolidation report on variety generation research funded by the British Library Research and Development Department 1971-1980 / David Cooper, Michael F. Lynch. — Sheffield : Postgraduate School of Librarianship and Information Science, University of Sheffield, 1980. — xii,109leaves ; 30cm. — (Report ; no.5586)
Bibliography: leaves 76-84. - Includes index
Unpriced (pbk) B81-11460

001.54'2 — Speech
Goffman, Erving. Forms of talk / Erving Goffman. — Oxford : Blackwell, 1981. — 335p ; 24cm
Includes bibliographies and index
ISBN 0-631-12788-7 (cased) : £12.00 : CIP rev.
ISBN 0-631-12886-7 (pbk) : £4.95 B81-03697

001.54'2 — Speech — *For children*
Allington, Richard L.. Beginning to learn about talking. — Oxford : Blackwell, Aug.1981. — [32]p
ISBN 0-86256-040-3 : £2.50 : CIP entry B81-19114

001.54'2'05 — Speech — *Serials*
Nie .... — Vol.1, no.1 (Dec.1980)-. — Accrington (1 Stanley St., Accrington, Lancs.) : [s.n.], 1980-. — v. : ill ; 30cm
Irregular. — Text in English and Polish. — Description based on: Vol.2, no.1 (Jan.1981)
ISSN 0260-6852 = Nie ... : £5.00 per issue B81-09050

001.54'2'0712 — Secondary schools. Students. Speech skills. Teaching
Sarbaugh, L. E.. Teaching speech communication / L.E. Sarbaugh. — Columbus ; London : Merrill, c1979. — x,268p : ill ; 26cm
Bibliography: p259-260. - Includes index
ISBN 0-675-08300-1 : Unpriced B81-09017

001.54'2'072 — Oral communication. Research. Methodology
Tucker, Raymond K.. Research in speech communication / Raymond K. Tucker, Richard L. Weaver II, Cynthia Berryman-Fink. — Englewood Cliffs ; London : Prentice-Hall, c1981. — xv,334p : ill ; 24cm
Includes bibliographies and index
ISBN 0-13-774273-8 : £12.30 B81-23111

001.54'36 — Codes & ciphers — *For children*
Albert, Burton. Codes for kids / Burton Albert Jr. ; revised and expanded by Neil Grant ; illustrated by Jill McDonald. — Harmondsworth : Puffin, 1981, c1976. — 90p : ill ; 18cm
Originally published: Chicago : A. Whitman, 1976
ISBN 0-14-031367-2 (pbk) : £0.80 B81-33605

001.55'3'05 — Audio-visual aids — *Serials*
Electrosonic world : lighting control audio, audio visual. — No.1 (Sept. 1980)-. — London (815 Woolwich Rd, SE7 8LT) : Electrosonic Limited, 1980-. — v. : ill ; 42cm
Irregular
ISSN 0261-2666 = Electrosonic world : Unpriced B81-20327

001.56 — Graphic communication — *For schools*
Twyford, John. Graphic communication / John Twyford. — London : Batsford Academic and Educational, 1981. — 120p : ill ; 25cm
ISBN 0-7134-3388-4 (pbk) : £6.95 B81-15961

001.56 — Isotype system
Neurath, Otto. International picture language : a facsimile reprint of the (1936) English edition / Otto Neurath ; with a German translation by Marie Neurath = Internationale Bildersprache : ein Faksimile-Neudruck der englischen Ausgabe (1936) / Otto Neurath ; mit einer deutschen Übersetzung von Marie Neurath. — Reading (2 Earley Gate, Whiteknights, Reading RG6 2AU) : Department of Typography & Graphic Communication, University of Reading, 1980. — 70p : ill(some col.),facsims
Parallel English text and German translation. — Facsim of: edition published London : Kegan Paul, Trench, Trubner, 1936. — Bibliography: p68
ISBN 0-7049-0489-6 (pbk) : Unpriced B81-31215

001.6 — DATA PROCESSING

001.6 — Data processing
Lester, Graham C.. Data processing / by Graham C. Lester. — Stockport : Polytech, 1980. — 2v.(497p) : ill ; 22cm
Includes index
ISBN 0-85505-056-x (pbk)
ISBN 0-85505-057-8 (v.2) : £2.50 B81-39045

Lipschutz, Martin M.. Schaum's outline of theory and problems of data processing / by Martin M. Lipschutz and Seymour Lipschutz. — New York ; London : McGraw-Hill, c1981. — 218p : ill ; 28cm. — (Schaum's outline series)
Includes index
ISBN 0-07-037983-1 (pbk) : £4.75 B81-10343

001.6 — Data processing. Applications of cryptology
Konheim, Alan G.. Cryptography : a primer / Alan G. Konheim. — New York ; Chichester : Wiley, c1981. — xiv,432p : ill ; 24cm
Includes index
ISBN 0-471-08132-9 : £23.40 B81-30022

001.6'024658 — Data processing — *For management*
Oliver, E. C.. Data processing : an instructional manual for business and accounting students / E.C. Oliver and R.J. Chapman ; revised and with additional material by J. Allen. — 5th ed. — Winchester : D.P. Publications, 1981. — vii,323p : ill,facsims ; 22cm
Previous ed.: 1979. — Includes index
ISBN 0-905435-15-x (pbk) : Unpriced B81-19823

001.6'03 — Data processing — *Encyclopaedias*
Maynard, Jeff. Dictionary of data processing. — 2nd ed. — London : Butterworths, Jan.1982. — [270]p
Previous ed.: London : Newnes-Butterworths, 1975
ISBN 0-408-00591-2 : £12.00 : CIP entry B81-34162

001.6'05 — Data processing — *Serials*
The **Auerbach** annual ... best computer papers. — 1980. — New York ; Oxford : North-Holland Publishing Co., c1980. — 412p
ISBN 0-444-00447-5 : £24.91
ISSN 0092-6507 B81-20066

001.6'06'041 — Great Britain. Data processing. Organisations: Institute of Data Processing Management — *Serials*
Dp international / the Institute of Data Processing Management members' yearbook. — 1981. — London (86 Edgware Rd, W2 2YW) : Sterling Publications for IDPM, [1981]. — 308p
ISSN 0143-1102 : Unpriced B81-25011

001.6'07 — Data processing services. Personnel. Training — *Directories* — *Serials*
Directory of training. — 1982. — Henley-on-Thames (Enterprise House, Badgemore Park, Henley-on-Thames, Oxon RG9 4NR) : Badgemore Park Enterprises, Jan.1982. — [500]p
ISBN 0-9507655-0-3 : £30.00 : CIP entry B81-35898

001.63 — Automated information processing systems
Computer-based information systems / [the M352 Course Team]. — Milton Keynes : Open University Press. — (Mathematics : a third level course)
At head of title: The Open University
Block 4: Data management / prepared by the Course Team. — 1981. — 23p : ill,1facsim ; 30cm. — (M352 ; block 4)
Includes index
ISBN 0-335-14003-3 (pbk) : Unpriced B81-25371

001.64 — Computer sciences
Reeves, C. M.. Computer science : a career in modelling? : an inaugural lecture / by C.M. Reves ; given in the University of Keele on Wednesday 22nd October 1975. — [Keele] : [University of Keele], [1976]. — 17p : ill ; 22cm
£0.50 (pbk) B81-03289

001.64 — Computer systems
Slotnik, Daniel L.. Computers : their structure, use, and influence / Daniel L. Slotnick and Joan K. Slotnik. — Englewood Cliffs ; London : Prentice-Hall, c1979. — ix,438p,[2]p of plates : ill(some col.) ; 25cm. — (Prentice-Hall software series)
Includes index
ISBN 0-13-165068-8 : £12.30 B81-24400

001.64 — Computer systems. Design
Baer, Jean-Loup. Computer systems architecture / Jean-Loup Baer. — London : Pitman, 1980. — xiii,626p : ill ; 24cm
Includes bibliographies and index
ISBN 0-273-01474-9 : £13.95 B81-00679

Wise, Harold. Computer architecture / Harold Wise. — Glasgow : Blackie, 1981. — 80p : ill,forms ; 17x25cm. — (Basic computing science)
Bibliography: p77. — Includes index
ISBN 0-216-90859-0 (pbk) : £3.25 B81-21327

001.64 — Computer systems. Design — *Conference proceedings*
International Computing Symposium *(6th : 1981)*. Systems architecture : proceedings of the sixth ACM European regional conference. — Guildford : Westbury House, c1981. — x,515p : ill ; 24cm
At head of title: The International Computing Symposium. — Includes bibliographies and index
ISBN 0-86103-050-8 (pbk) : Unpriced B81-28524

001.64 — Computer systems. Design faults. Tolerances
Anderson, T.. Fault tolerance. — London : Prentice-Hall, Sept.1981. — [288]p
ISBN 0-13-308254-7 : £13.95 : CIP entry B81-25658

001.64 — Computer systems. Design. Human factors
Damodaran, Leela. Designing systems for people / Leela Damodaran, Alison Simpson, Paul Wilson. — Manchester : NCC Publications, 1980. — 193p : ill,forms ; 21cm
Bibliography: p183-187. - Includes index
ISBN 0-85012-242-2 (pbk) : £12.50 : CIP rev. B80-13663

001.64 — Computer systems. Evaluation — *Serials*

Computer performance. — Vol.1, no.1 (June 1980)-. — Guildford : IPC Science and Technology Press, 1980-. — v. : ill ; 30cm
Quarterly. — Also available on 98-frame A6 microfiche
ISSN 0143-9642 = Computer performance : £50.00 per year B81-02337

001.64 — Computer systems — *For schools*

Bishop, Peter. Comprehensive computer studies / Peter Bishop. — London : Edward Arnold, 1981. — iv,201p : ill,facsims ; 25cm
Includes index
ISBN 0-7131-0371-x (pbk) : £3.95 : CIP rev. B80-13173

Griffiths, Mike. Computers / Mike Griffiths. — London : Edward Arnold, 1981. — 16p : ill ; 30cm. — (Checkpoint ; 17)
ISBN 0-7131-0530-5 (pbk) : 0.98 B81-34989

001.64 — Digital computer systems

Chronicler. Fred learns about computers / The Chronicler, Lord High Keeper of the Royal Fredlandic Archives. — 2nd ed. — Plymouth : Macdonald & Evans, 1981. — 159p : ill ; 18cm
Previous ed.: Plymouth : Continua Productions, 1978. — Includes index
ISBN 0-7121-0636-7 (pbk) : £2.95 B81-32971

Couger, J. Daniel. First course in data processing with BASIC / J. Daniel Couger, Fred R. McFadden. — New York ; Chichester : Wiley, c1981. — xviii,443p : ill(some col.),maps,forms ; 28cm
Originally published: as A First course in data processing. 1977. — Ill on inside covers. — Includes index
ISBN 0-471-08046-2 (pbk) : £9.40 B81-16943

Couger, J. Daniel. First course in data processing with BASIC, COBOL, FORTRAN, RPG / J. Daniel Couger, Fred R. McFadden. — 2nd ed. — New York ; Chichester : Wiley, c1981. — xix,532p : ill(some col.),forms ; 28cm
Previous ed.: published as A first course in data processing. 1977. — Ill on lining papers. — Includes index
ISBN 0-471-05581-6 (pbk) : £13.60 B81-16946

Fry, T. F.. Computer appreciation. — 3rd ed. — London : Butterworths, Dec.1981. — [260]p
Previous ed.: London : Newnes-Butterworths, 1975
ISBN 0-408-00492-4 : £4.95 : CIP entry B81-31722

Fuori, William M.. Introduction to computer operations / William M. Fuori, Anthony D'Arco, Lawrence Orilia. — 2nd ed. — Englewood Cliffs ; London : Prentice-Hall, c1981. — xx,620p : ill,forms ; 25cm
Previous ed.: 1973. — Includes index
ISBN 0-13-480392-2 : £12.35 B81-17207

Introducing data processing. — Manchester : NCC Publications, 1980. — 237p : ill,forms ; 21cm
Bibliography: p223. - Includes index
ISBN 0-85012-245-7 (pbk) : £6.50 : CIP rev. B80-17507

Lester, Graham C.. Data processing / by Graham C. Lester. — Stockport : Polytech, 1980. — 506p : ill,forms ; 22cm
Includes index
ISBN 0-85505-044-6 (pbk) : £6.00 B81-22910

Rudall, B. H.. Computers and cybernetics. — Tunbridge Wells : Abacus, July 1981. — [200]p
ISBN 0-85626-173-4 : £16.00 : CIP entry
Also classified at 001.53 B81-13739

Unger, E. A.. Computer science fundamentals : an algorithmic approach via structured programming / E.A. Unger, Nasir Ahmed. — Columbus ; London : Merrill, c1979. — xii,387p : ill ; 26cm
Bibliography: p353-355. - Includes index
ISBN 0-675-08301-x : £11.95 B81-03330

Zwass, Vladimir. Introduction to computer science / Vladimir Zwass. — New York ; London : Barnes & Noble, c1981. — xiv,268p : ill ; 21cm. — (Barnes & Noble outline series ; Cos 193)
Text on inside covers. — Includes bibliographies and index
ISBN 0-06-460193-5 (pbk) : £3.95 B81-14521

001.64 — Digital computer systems. Applications

Sealey, G. B.. Development of computer-based systems / G.B. Sealey and P.R. Sealey. — Glasgow : Blackie, 1980. — vi,82p : ill,forms ; 17x25xcm. — (Basic computing science)
Includes index
ISBN 0-216-90858-2 (pbk) : £3.25 B81-19531

001.64 — Digital computer systems. Data transmission. Use of telephone systems — *Standards*

The **V-series** report : standard for data transmission by telephone. — 2nd ed. — Sandycove : Bootstrap Ltd., 1981. — ii,51leaves : ill ; 30cm
Previous ed.: 1981
ISBN 0-9507550-0-1 (pbk) : Unpriced B81-40295

001.64 — Digital computer systems. Development — *Forecasts*

The **Fifth** generation / [Infotech Limited]. — Maidenhead : Infotech, c1981. — iii,419p : ill,ports ; 30cm. — (Infotech state of the art report. Series 9 ; no.1)
Editor: J. Iliffe. — Bibliography: p387-407. — Includes index
ISBN 0-85539-710-1 : £195.00 B81-10035

001.64 — Digital computer systems. Effectiveness. Evaluation. Use of models

Sauer, Charles H.. Computer systems performance modeling / Charles H. Sauer, K. Mani Chandy. — Englewood Ciffs ; London : Prentice-Hall, c1981. — xiii,352p : ill ; 25cm. — (Prentice-Hall series in advances in computing science and technology)
Bibliography: p341-350. — Includes index
ISBN 0-13-165175-7 : £12.30 B81-16519

001.64 — Digital computer systems. Evaluation — *Conference proceedings*

ICPCI 78 *(Conference : Gardone Riviera)*. Performance of computer installations : evaluation and management : proceedings of the International Conference on the Performance of Computer Installations, ICPCI 78 June 22-23, 1978, Gardone Riviera, Lake Garda, Italy / [sponsoring organisations Consorzio interuniversitario lombardo per l'elaborazione automatica (Lombard Inter-University Computing Center) ... et al. with the cooperation of ACM SIGMETRICS-SIG on Measurement and Evaluation ... et al. ; conference sponsor Sperry Univac, Italy] ; edited by Domenico Ferrari. — Amsterdam ; Oxford : North-Holland, 1978. — viii,351p : ill ; 23cm
ISBN 0-444-85186-0 : Unpriced B81-15605

001.64 — Digital computer systems — *For business firms*

Price, Wilson T.. Introduction to computer data processing / Wilson T. Price. — 3rd ed. — New York ; London : Holt, Rinehart and Winston, c1981. — xiii,577p : ill(some col.) ; 25cm
Previous ed.: Hinsdale : Dryden Press, 1977. — Includes index
ISBN 0-03-056728-9 : £10.50 B81-22882

001.64 — Digital computer systems — *For schools*

Bishop, Peter, *1949-*. Introducing computers / Peter Bishop. — Walton-on-Thames : Nelson, 1981. — 154p : ill,forms,ports ; 25cm
Publisher's no.: NCN 3285-21-0
ISBN 0-17-431273-3 (pbk) : £2.95
ISBN 0-17-431274-1 (Teachers' book) : £1.95 B81-29118

Moss, John, *19---*. Introducing computing : a first course for schools / John Moss. — Purley : Input Two-Nine, 1979. — 101p,[8]p of plates : ill,1form ; 21cm
ISBN 0-905897-39-0 (pbk) : Unpriced B81-01871

001.64 — Digital computer systems. Multiprocessors

Satyanarayanan, M.. Multiprocessors : a comparative study / M. Satyanarayanan. — Englewood Cliffs ; London : Prentice-Hall, c1980. — vi,201p : ill ; 24cm
Includes bibliographies and index
ISBN 0-13-605154-5 : £14.00 B81-02996

001.64 — Digital computer systems. Parallel-processor systems

Hockney, R. W.. Parallel computers architecture, programming and algorithms. — Bristol : Adam Hilger, Oct.1981. — [450]p
ISBN 0-85274-422-6 : £20.00 : CIP entry B81-27428

001.64 — Digital computer systems. Systems analysis & design

Millington, D.. Systems analysis and design for computer applications. — Chichester : Ellis Horwood, June 1981. — [192]p. — (Ellis Horwood series in computers and their applications)
ISBN 0-85312-249-0 : £18.50 : CIP entry B81-12899

001.64 — Distributed automatic data processing systems

Lorin, Harold. Aspects of distributed computer systems / Harold Lorin. — New York ; Chichester : Wiley, c1980. — xiv,286p : ill ; 25cm
Bibliography: p277-283. - Includes index
ISBN 0-471-08114-0 : £14.70 B81-03886

Martin, James, *1933-*. Design and strategy for distributed data processing / James Martin. — Englewood Cliffs ; London : Prentice-Hall, c1981. — xiii,624p : ill(some col.) ; 25cm
Text and ill on lining papers. — Includes index
ISBN 0-13-201657-5 : £28.15 B81-40174

001.64 — Distributed digital computer systems

Booth, Grayce M.. The distributed system environment : some practical approaches / Grayce M. Booth. — New York ; London : McGraw-Hill, c1981. — ix,276p : ill,1map ; 24cm
Bibliography: p267-270. — Includes index
ISBN 0-07-006507-1 : £15.50 B81-26160

001.64 — Distributed digital computer systems — *For management*

Champine, George A.. Distributed computer systems : impact on management, design, and analysis / George A. Champine with Ronald D. Coop, Russell C. Heinselman. — Amsterdam ; Oxford : North-Holland, 1980. — xvi,380p : ill,maps ; 23cm
Bibliography: p341-369. — Includes index
ISBN 0-444-86109-2 : £13.85 B81-03204

001.64 — Distributed digital computer systems — *Serials*

The **coordinated** programme of research in distributed computing systems : annual report. — 77-78. — Swindon : Science Research Council, 1978-. — v. ; 30cm
Cover title: Distributed computing systems. — 'Issued by the Information Engineering Committee of the Science Research Council' — cover. — Description based on: Sept.79-Sept.80 issue
ISSN 0261-684x = Coordinated programme of research in distributed computing systems : Unpriced B81-33458

001.64 — Man. Communication. Use of computer systems — *Conference proceedings*

IFIP TC-6 International Symposium on Computer Message Systems *(1981 : Ottawa)*. Computer message systems : proceedings of the IFIP TC-6 International Symposium on Computer Message Systems, Ottawa, Canada, 6-8 April, 1981 / [sponsored by International Federation for Information Processing (IFIP)] ; [organized by IFIP TC-6 Working Group 6.5 International Computer Message Services] ; edited by Ronald P. Uhlig. — Amsterdam ; Oxford : North-Holland, 1981. — xi,465p : ill ; 23cm
Includes bibliographies
ISBN 0-444-86253-6 (corrected) : Unpriced B81-40178

001.64 — Man. Interactions with computer systems
Computing skills and the user interface / edited by M.J. Coombs and J.L. Alty. — London : Academic Press, 1981. — xii,499p : ill ; 24cm. — (Computers and people series ; 3)
Includes bibliographies and index
ISBN 0-12-186520-7 : £19.00 B81-23414

001.64 — Microprocessor systems
Aumiaux, M.. The use of microprocessors / M. Aumiaux ; translation by Anne Hutt. — Chichester : Wiley, c1980. — viii,198p : ill ; 24cm. — (Wiley series in computing)
Translation of: L'emploi des microprocesseurs. — Includes index
ISBN 0-471-27689-8 : £12.00 : CIP rev. B80-08570

001.64 — Microprocessor systems. Design
Bowen, B. A.. The logical design of multiple-microprocessor systems / B.A. Bowen and R.J.A. Buhr. — Englewood Cliffs ; London : Prentice-Hall, c1980. — xiv,310p : ill ; 25cm
Includes bibliographies and index
ISBN 0-13-539908-4 : £14.00 B81-01800

001.64 — Microprocessor systems — *Study examples: INTEL 8085 A*
Short, Kenneth L.. Microprocessors and programmed logic / Kenneth L. Short. — Englewood Cliffs ; London : Prentice-Hall, c1981. — xvi,528p : ill ; 25cm
Includes bibliographies and index
ISBN 0-13-581173-2 : £18.80 B81-09290

001.64 — United States. Computer industries & services. Contracts. Negotiation
Auer, Joseph. Computer contract negotiations / Joseph Auer, Charles Edison Harris. — New York ; London : Van Nostrand Reinhold, c1981. — ix,390p ; 26cm
Bibliography: p383. — Includes index
ISBN 0-442-20369-1 : £29.35 B81-37784

001.64'02341 — Great Britain. Computer industries — *Career guides — Serials*
New computer careers. — Issue 1 (14 Nov.1980)-. — Teddington (3A Church Rd, Teddington, Middlesex) : Teddington Publications, 1980-. — v. : ill ; 30cm
Fortnightly. — Continues: Computer careers (Ascot). — Description based on: Issue 2 (28 Nov.1980)
ISSN 0260-9150 = New computer careers : £9.00 per year B81-10556

001.64'02438 — Digital computer systems — *For commerce*
Walsh, Myles E.. Understanding computers : what managers and users need to know / Myles E. Walsh. — New York ; Chichester : Wiley, c1981. — xii,266p : ill,facsims,forms ; 24cm
Includes index
ISBN 0-471-08191-4 : £11.75 B81-16336

001.64'02461 — Digital computer systems — *For medicine*
Enlander, Derek. Computers in medicine : an introduction / Derek Enlander. — St. Louis ; London : Mosby, 1980. — xii,124p : ill,ports ; 24cm
Includes index
ISBN 0-8016-1525-9 (pbk) : £9.25 B81-05464

001.64'024657 — Digital computer systems — *For accountancy — Serials*
Guide to systems for practising accountants. — 1980/81-. — London (30 Islington Green, N1 8BJ) : Computer Guides Ltd., 1980-. — v. : ill ; 30cm. — (Computer guides — for the businessman)
Annual
ISSN 0260-9002 = Guide to systems for practising accountants : £24.00 B81-10256

001.64'024658 — Digital computer systems — *For management*
Bedell-Pearce, Keith. Computers : the essentials for senior management / by Keith Bedell-Pearce. — London : Financial Times, c1979. — 2v.(v,313p) ; 30cm. — (An International management report)
ISBN 0-903199-35-1 (spiral) : Unpriced
ISBN 0-903199-33-5 (v.1) : Unpriced
ISBN 0-903199-34-3 (v.2) : Unpriced B81-38063

001.64'024658 — Digital computer systems — *For small firms*
Shaw, Donald R.. Your small business computer : evaluating, selecting, financing, installing and operating the hardware and software that fits / Donald R. Shaw. — New York ; London : Van Nostrand Reinhold, c1981. — ix,256p : ill ; 24cm
Includes index
ISBN 0-442-27540-4 : £14.95 B81-00680

001.64'03'21 — Computer systems — *Encyclopaedias*
Prenis, John. [Running Press glossary of computer terms]. The language of computers / John Prenis. — [London] : W.H. Allen, 1981, c1977. — vii,[86]p : ill ; 20cm. — (A Star book)
Originally published: Philadelphia : Running Press, c1977
ISBN 0-352-30896-6 (pbk) : £1.50 B81-35607

001.64'04 — Atom microcomputer systems — *Manuals — For businessmen*
Phipps, John. Atom business / by John Phipps. — Epsom : Phipps, 1981. — 110p : ill ; 21cm
ISBN 0-9507302-1-1 (spiral) : Unpriced B81-36334

001.64'04 — Commodore PET microcomputer systems — *Manuals*
Dunn, Seamus. The PET personal computer for beginners / Seamus Dunn, Valerie Morgan. — Englewood Cliffs ; London : Prentice-Hall, c1981. — x,242p : ill ; 24cm
Bibliography: p234-236. — Includes index
ISBN 0-13-661835-9 (cased) : Unpriced : CIP rev.
ISBN 0-13-661827-8 (pbk) : £9.70 B81-22484

001.64'04 — HP1000 microcomputer systems — *Conference proceedings*
European HP1000 Users Conference *(1st : 1981 : Noordwijkerhout)*. HP1000 computer trends. — Chertsey : Reedbooks, Oct.1981. — [186]p
ISBN 0-906544-09-2 : £20.00 : CIP entry B81-30905

001.64'04 — INTEL 8080 & 8085 microprocessor systems, Motorola 6800 microprocessor systems & Zilog Z80 microprocessor systems
Coffron, James W.. Practical hardware details for 8080, 8085, Z80 and 6800 microprocessor systems / James W. Coffron. — Englewood Cliffs ; London : Prentice-Hall, c1981. — xvi,330p : ill ; 25cm. — (Prentice-Hall series in microprocessor technology)
Includes index
ISBN 0-13-691089-0 : £14.25 B81-17206

001.64'04 — Microcomputer systems
Bradbeer, Robin. The personal computer book. — 2nd ed. — Aldershot : Gower, Dec.1981. — [220]p
Previous ed.: 1980
ISBN 0-566-03423-9 (pbk) : £5.25 : CIP entry B81-34724

Lipovski, G. Jack. Microcomputer interfacing : principles and practices / G. Jack Lipovski. — Lexington : Lexington Books ; [Farnborough, Hants.] : Gower [distributor], 1981, c1980. — xix,426p : ill,facsims ; 24cm. — (Lexington Books series in computer science)
Includes index
ISBN 0-669-03619-6 : £15.00 B81-09605

Morgan, Eric. Microprocessors : a short introduction / witten by Eric Morgan. — London : Department of Industry, c1980. — 95p : ill(some col.) ; 30cm
£5.00 (pbk) B81-19487

001.64'04 — Microcomputer systems & microprocessor systems
Carter, L. R.. Microelectronics and microcomputers / L.R. Carter, E. Huzan ; illustrated by G. Hartfield Illustrators. — London : Teach Yourself Books, 1981. — vii,232p : ill ; 18cm. — (Teach yourself books)
Bibliography: p223-225. — Includes index
ISBN 0-340-26830-1 (pbk) : £1.95 : CIP rev. B81-23930

Introduction to microcomputers. — London : Pitman, Oct.1981. — [245]p
ISBN 0-273-01706-3 : £5.95 : CIP entry B81-28156

Shelley, John. Microfuture / John Shelley. — London : Pitman, 1981. — 70p : ill ; 25cm
Includes index
ISBN 0-273-01676-8 (pbk) : Unpriced B81-38673

Woollard, Barry G.. Microprocessors and microcomputers for engineering students and technicians / by Barry G. Woollard. — London : McGraw-Hill, c1981. — vii,269p : ill ; 23cm
Includes index
ISBN 0-07-084640-5 (pbk) : £4.95 B81-10374

001.64'04 — Microcomputer systems. Applications
Lane, J. E.. Microprocessors and information handling. — Manchester : NCC Publications, Sept.1981. — [60]p. — (Computing in the '80s ; 4)
ISBN 0-85012-334-8 (pbk) : £4.00 : CIP entry B81-28150

001.64'04 — Microcomputer systems — *For business practices*
Lucas, Pannell Jackson. Make a success of micro-computing in your business. — Hemel Hempstead (P.O. Box 81, Hemel Hempstead, Herts. HP1 1UR) : PasTest Service, Sept.1981. — [136]p
ISBN 0-906896-05-3 (pbk) : £4.95 : CIP entry B81-30277

001.64'04 — Microcomputer systems — *For hotel & catering industries*
Choosing a microcomputer : an introduction to microcomputers for the hotel and catering industry. — Wembley : HCITB, 1981. — 48p : ill ; 30cm
Unpriced (pbk) B81-33192

001.64'04 — Microcomputer systems — *Serials*
[Computing today *(London)***]**. Computing today. — No.1-4; Vol.1, no.1 (1979)-. — London (145 Charing Cross Rd, WC2H 0EE) : Modmags, 1978-. — v. : ill ; 29cm
Monthly. — No.1-4 issued as supplement to: Electronics today international (British edition). — Description based on: Vol.2, no.5 (July 1980)
ISSN 0142-7210 = Computing today (London) : £9.00 per year B81-00681

MNI : microcomputer news international : the monthly report on microprocessors, memories, peripherals and software. — Vol.5, no.1 (Mar.1981)-. — Lausanne : Elsevier Sequoia ; Oxford (256 Banbury Rd, Oxford OX2 7DH) : Elsevier International Bulletins, 1981-. — v. ; 30cm
Continues: Microcomputer analysis
ISSN 0560-8472 = MNI. Microcomputer news international : £95.00 per year B81-32707

001.64'04 — Microcomputer systems — *Study examples: MAVIS — For physically handicapped persons*
Schofield, Julia. Microcomputer-based aids for the disabled. — London : Heyden, Oct.1981. — [102]p. — (Monographs in informatics)
ISBN 0-85501-700-7 : £10.30 : CIP entry B81-30458

001.64'04 — Micromputer systems. Interfaces with peripheral equipment
Pasahow, Edward J.. Microcomputer interfacing : for electronics technicians / Edward J. Pasahow. — New York ; London : McGraw-Hill, c1981. — viii,221p : ill ; 28cm
Bibliography: p214. — Includes index
ISBN 0-07-048718-9 (pbk) : £7.65 B81-39820

001.64'04 — Microprocessor systems
Kimberley, Paul. Microprocessors : an introduction for the professional layman / Paul Kimberley. — Thame (103 High St., Thame, Oxon [OX9 3DZ]) : Hayes Kennedy, 1981. — vii,280p,8pof plates : ill ; 22cm
Bibliography: p277-280
ISBN 0-86269-000-5 (pbk) : £7.95 B81-16087

001.64′04 — Microprocessor systems *continuation*

Sinclair, Ian R.. Practical microprocessor systems. — Sevenoaks : Newnes, Dec.1981. — [144]p
ISBN 0-408-00496-7 (pbk) : £2.95 : CIP entry B81-31736

001.64′04 — Microprocessor systems — *Conference proceedings*

EUROMICRO Symposium on Microprocessing and Microprogramming *(6th : 1980 : London).* Microprocessor systems : software, firmware hardware : sixth EUROMICRO Symposium on Microprocessing and Microprogramming, September 16-18, 1980, London / edited by Mariagiovanna Sami ... [et al.] ; organized by EUROMICRO, with the support of the European Research Office, US Army, London ... [et al.] and the co-operation of E.C.I. (AFCET, AICA, BCS, GI, NTG, NGI), IEEE Computer Society, IEE PGC6. — Amsterdam ; Oxford : North-Holland, 1980. — 372p : ill ; 27cm
Includes bibliographies and index
ISBN 0-444-86098-3 : £20.56 B81-20823

Microprocessors in automation and communications : London, 27th-29th January 1981. — London : 99 Gower St., WC1E 6AZ : Institution of Electronic and Radio Engineers, c1980. — 284p : ill ; 30cm. — (Proceedings / Institution of Electronic and Radio Engineers)
Includes index
ISBN 0-903748-43-6 (pbk) : Unpriced B81-11341

Microsystems ′81 *(Conference : London).* Microsystems ′81 : proceedings of the 4th annual conference, Wembley Conference Centre, London, 11-13 March 1981. — Guildford, Surrey : Westbury House, 1981. — iv,124p : ill ; 24cm
ISBN 0-86103-046-x (pbk) : Unpriced B81-29209

001.64′04 — Microprocessor systems. Debugging

Ghani, Noordin. Microprocessor system debugging / Noordin Ghani and Edward Farrell. — Chichester : Research Studies, 1980. — xii,143p : ill ; 29cm. — (Electronic & electrical engineering research studies. Computer engineering series ; 1)
Includes index
ISBN 0-471-27860-2 (pbk) : Unpriced : CIP rev. B80-34383

001.64′04 — Microprocessor systems. Design. Use of 16-bit microprocessors & bit-slice microprocessors

McGlynn, Daniel R.. Modern microprocessor system design : sixteen-bit and bit-slice architecture / Daniel R. McGlynn. — New York ; Chichester : Wiley, c1980. — viii,295p,[2] folded leaves : ill ; 29cm
Bibliography: p283-284. - Includes index
ISBN 0-471-06492-0 : £11.75 B81-05431

001.64′04 — Microprocessor systems — *Encyclopaedias*

Chandor, Anthony. The Penguin dictionary of microprocessors / Anthony Chandor. — Harmondsworth : Penguin, 1981. — 183p ; 20cm. — (Penguin reference books)
ISBN 0-14-051100-8 (pbk) : £2.25 B81-11527

001.64′04 — Microprocessor systems — *For management*

Cooper, James Arlin. Microprocessor background for management personnel / James Arlin Cooper. — Englewood Cliffs ; London : Prentice-Hall, c1981. — xii,163p : ill ; 24cm
Includes bibliographies and index
ISBN 0-13-580829-4 : £9.70 B81-12513

Jones, W. S.. Micros for managers. — Stevenage : Peregrinus, Oct.1981. — [192]p
ISBN 0-906048-60-5 : £8.25 : CIP entry B81-27476

001.64′04 — Microprocessor systems. Hardware — *Technical data*

Towers, T. D.. Towers′ international microprocessor selector : specification data for the identification, selection and substitution of microprocessors / by T.D. Towers. — London : Foulsham, c1980. — xvi,244p ; 25cm
Bibliography: p232-236
ISBN 0-572-01037-0 (pbk) : £14.95 B81-03109

001.64′04 — Minicomputer systems

Parker, Yakup. Minicomputers : guidelines for first time users / Yakup Paker. — Tunbridge Wells : Abacus, 1980. — 250p : ill,1form ; 23cm
Bibliography: p211-230. - Includes index
ISBN 0-85626-184-x : Unpriced : CIP rev. B79-37111

001.64′04 — Minicomputer systems. Evaluation & selection — *For businessmen*

Knight, P. A.. Installing a small business computer. — Manchester : NCC Publications, Feb.1982. — [70]p
ISBN 0-85012-343-7 (pbk) : £8.00 : CIP entry B81-37593

001.64′04 — Motorola 6800 microprocessor systems

Greenfield, Joseph D.. Using microprocessors and microcomputers : the 6800 family / Joseph D. Greenfield, William C. Wray. — New York ; Chichester : Wiley, c1981. — xiv,460p : ill,1facsim ; 25cm. — (Electronic technology series)
Includes index
ISBN 0-471-02727-8 : £11.25 B81-11299

Simpson, Robert J.. Introduction to 6800/6802 microprocessor systems. — London : Newnes Technical Books, Feb.1982. — [240]p
ISBN 0-408-01179-3 : £6.50 : CIP entry B81-36377

001.64′04 — Personal computer systems

Lafferty, Peter. Personal computing. — London : Newnes Technical Books, Aug.1981. — [96]p. — (Questions & answers)
ISBN 0-408-00555-6 (pbk) : £1.95 : CIP entry B81-20608

001.64′04 — Small digital computer systems

Monds, Fabian. An introduction to mini & micro computers / by Fabian Monds and Robert McLaughlin. — Stevenage : Peregrinus, c1981. — x,133p : ill,forms ; 30cm
Includes index
ISBN 0-906048-48-6 (pbk) : Unpriced B81-15485

001.64′04 — Small digital computer systems — *Amateurs′ manuals*

Leventhal, Lance A.. Why do you need a personal computer? / Lance A. Leventhal, Irvin Stafford. — New York ; Chichester : Wiley, c1981. — x,278p : ill ; 26cm
Includes bibliographies and index
ISBN 0-471-04784-8 (pbk) : £3.40 B81-16949

001.64′04 — Tandy TRS-80 microcomputer systems — *Manuals*

Lord, Kenniston W.. Using the Radio Shack TRS-80 in your home / Kenniston W. Lord, Jr.. — New York ; London : Van Nostrand Reinhold, c1981. — x,457p : ill ; 24cm
Includes index
ISBN 0-442-25707-4 : £16.45 B81-29557

001.64′04′024658 — Minicomputer systems — *For businessmen*

Brown, Carol W.. The minicomputer simplified : an executive′s guide to the basics / Carol W. Brown. — New York : Free Press ; London : Collier Macmillan, c1980. — vii,213p ; 25cm
Bibliography: p205-207. - Includes index
ISBN 0-02-905130-4 : £6.95 B81-04515

001.64′05 — Computer systems — *Serials*

Advances in computers. — Vol.19. — New York ; London : Academic Press, 1980. — x,351p
ISBN 0-12-012119-0 : Unpriced
ISSN 0065-2468 B81-04938

001.64′07′1141 — Great Britain. Higher education institutions. Curriculum subjects: Computer sciences — *Conference proceedings*

Computer science and the education of computer scientists : proceedings of a symposium organised by the Institute of Mathematics and its Applications held in London in November 1974. — Southend-on-Sea (Maitland House, Warrior Sq., Southend-on-Sea, Essex SS1 2JY) : The Institute, c1975. — xi,58p : ill ; 20cm. — (Symposium proceedings series / Institute of Mathematics and its Applications ; no.9)
Unpriced (spiral) B81-13269

001.64′09 — Computer systems, *to 1975* — *Conference proceedings*

A History of computing in the twentieth century : a collection of essays / edited by N. Metropolis, J. Howlett, Gian-Carlo Rota. — New York ; London : Academic Press, 1980. — xix,659p : ill,1map,facsims,ports ; 24cm
Conference papers. — Includes bibliographies
ISBN 0-12-491650-3 : £16.60 B81-18017

001.64′09 — Computers, *to 1980*

Evans, Christopher. The making of the micro : a history of the computer / by Christopher Evans ; foreword by Tom Stonier. — London : Gollancz, 1981. — 118p : ill(some col.),ports ; 27cm
Bibliography: p118. - Includes index
ISBN 0-575-02913-7 : £5.95 B81-15238

001.64′0941 — Great Britain. Digital computer systems. Selection by government departments — *Manuals*

Assessment of project suitability for micro/mini/mainframe computers. — [London] : Central Computer and Telecommunications Agency, 1981. — [19]p ; 30cm
Cover title
ISBN 0-7115-0036-3 (pbk) : Unpriced B81-39443

001.64′2 — Computer systems. Programming — *Conference proceedings*

On the construction of programs / edited by R.M. McKeag and A.M. Macnaghten. — Cambridge : Cambridge University Press, 1980. — 422p : ill ; 24cm
Includes bibliographies and index
ISBN 0-521-23090-x : £10.00 : CIP rev. B80-25031

001.6′42 — Digital computer systems. Functional programming

Cody, William J.. Software manual for the elementary functions / William J. Cody, Jr. and William Waite. — Englewood Cliffs ; London : Prentice-Hall, c1980. — x,269p ; 24cm. — (Prentice-Hall series in computational mathematics)
Bibliography: p265-266
ISBN 0-13-822064-6 : £11.00 B81-01680

001.64′2 — Digital computer systems. On-line programming. Management

Abbott, Joe. On-line programming : a management guide / Joe Abbott. — Manchester : NCC Publications, 1981. — 64p ; 22cm
Includes index
ISBN 0-85012-295-3 (pbk) : £7.50 B81-23567

001.64′2 — Digital computer systems. Programming

Chantler, Alan. Programming techniques and practice. — Manchester : N.C.C. Publications, Sept.1981. — [250]p
ISBN 0-85012-338-0 : £9.50 : CIP entry B81-28137

Longworth, G.. Standards in programming. — Manchester : NCC Publications, Aug.1981. — [280]p
ISBN 0-85012-341-0 : £50.00 : CIP entry B81-21597

Pattis, Richard E.. Karel the robot : a gentle introduction to the art of programming / Richard E. Pattis. — New York ; Chichester : Wiley, c1981. — xiv,106p : ill ; 23cm
Includes index
ISBN 0-471-08928-1 (pbk) : £3.15 B81-21166

001.64′2 — Digital computer systems. Programming. Algorithms. Design. Applications of mathematics

Sellers, Peter H.. Combinatorial complexes : a mathematical theory of algorithms / Peter H. Sellers. — Dordrecht ; London : Reidel, c1979. — xv,184p : ill ; 23cm. — (Mathematics and its applications ; v.2)
Bibliography: p181. - Includes index
Unpriced B81-04160

001.64′2 — Digital computer systems. Programming — *Manuals*

Jackson, Brian, *19---*. Approaches to programming / Brian Jackson. — Glasgow : Blackie, 1981. — 104p : ill ; 17x25cm. — (Basic computing science)
Includes index
ISBN 0-216-90857-4 (pbk) : £3.60 B81-16145

Reynolds, John C.. The craft of programming. — Hemel Hempstead : Prentice-Hall, May, 1981. — [416]p
ISBN 0-13-188862-5 : £14.95 : CIP entry
B81-06602

001.64′2 — Digital computer systems. Programming. Techniques: Build Program Technique

Rice, John G.. Build program technique : a practical approach for the development of Automatic Software Generation Systems / John G. Rice. — New York ; Chichester : Wiley, c1981. — xiii,372p : ill ; 24cm
Includes bibliographies and index
ISBN 0-471-05278-7 : £21.00 B81-33070

001.64′2 — Digital computer systems. Programs. Flow analysis

Program flow analysis : theory and applications / [edited by] Steven S. Muchnick, Neil D. Jones. — Englewood Cliffs ; London : Prentice-Hall, c1981. — xvii,418p : ill ; 24cm. — (Prentice-Hall software series)
Bibliography: p394-407. — Includes index
Unpriced B81-36495

001.64′2 — Digital computer systems. Programs. Mathematics

Wand, Mitchell. Induction, recursion and programming / Mitchell Wand. — New York ; Oxford : North Holland, c1980. — xii,202p : ill ; 24cm
Bibliography: p190-194. - Includes index
ISBN 0-444-00322-3 : £13.92 B81-06506

001.64′2 — Digital computer systems. Programs. Testing

The **Correctness** problem in computer science. — London : Academic Press, Sept.1981. — [300]p
ISBN 0-12-122920-3 : CIP entry B81-23896

001.64′2 — Digital computer systems. Structured programming

Stevens, Wayne P.. Using structured design : how to make programs simple, changeable, flexible and reusable / Wayne P. Stevens. — New York ; Chichester : Wiley, c1981. — xvii,213p : ill ; 24cm
Bibliography: p209. - Includes index
ISBN 0-471-08198-1 : £13.40 B81-11304

001.64′2 — Microcomputer systems. Programming

Wakerly, John F.. Microcomputer architecture and programming / John F. Wakerly. — New York ; Chichester : Wiley, c1981. — xxviii,692p : ill ; 24cm
Includes index
ISBN 0-471-05232-9 : £15.50 B81-23986

001.64′2 — Microcomputer systems. Programs written in Basic language — *Collections*

Race, John. The alien, numbereater and other programs for personal computers / John Race. — London : Macmillan, 1981. — 86p : ill ; 25cm
Includes index
ISBN 0-333-28079-2 (pbk) : £3.50 B81-23008

001.64′2 — Microprogramming

Kraft, George D.. Microprogrammed control and reliable design of small computers / George D. Kraft, Wing N. Toy. — Englewood Cliffs ; London : Prentice-Hall, c1981. — xviii,428p : ill ; 24cm
Includes bibliographies and index
ISBN 0-13-581140-6 : £14.25 B81-16516

001.64′2 — Motorola MEK6800D2 microcomputer systems. Programming — *Manuals*

Leventhal, Lance A.. Microcomputer experimentation with the Motorola MEK6 800D2 / Lance A. Leventhal. — Englewood Cliffs ; London : Prentice-Hall, c1981. — x,438p : ill ; 24cm
Bibliography: p421-427. — Includes index
ISBN 0-13-580761-1 (pbk) : £11.00 B81-17173

001.64′2 — Programmable electronic calculators. Programming — *Manuals*

Weir, Maurice D.. Calculator clout : programming methods for your programmable / Maurice D. Weir. — Englewood Cliffs ; London : Prentice-Hall, c1981. — xv,235p : ill ; 24cm. — (A spectrum book)
Bibliography: p228-229. — Includes index
ISBN 0-13-110411-x (cased) : Unpriced
ISBN 0-13-110403-9 (pbk) : Unpriced
B81-36597

001.64′2 — Real time computer systems. Programming — *Conference proceedings*

Real time programming 1978 : proceedings of the IFAC/IFIP workshop Marishamm/Aland, Finland 19-21 June 1978 / edited by B. Cronhjort. — Oxford : Published for the International Federation of Automatic Control by Pergamon, 1979. — vii,129p : ill ; 21cm
Includes bibliographies and index
ISBN 0-08-024492-0 : £22.50 : CIP rev.
B79-34648

Real time programming 1980 : proceedings of the IFAC/IFIP workshop, Scholars Retz-hof, Leibintz, Austria, 14-16 April 1980 / [workshop supported by TC 5 (Computer Applications in Technology) of IFII ... et al.] ; edited by V.H. Haase. — Oxford : Published for the International Federation of Automatic Control by Pergamon, 1980. — x,131p : ill ; 31cm. — (IFAC proceedings series)
Includes bibliographies
ISBN 0-08-027305-x : £17.00 : CIP rev.
B80-30580

001.64′2 — Rockwell AIM 65 microcomputer systems. Programming — *Manuals*

Scanlon, Leo J.. AIM 65 : laboratory manual and study guide / Leo J. Scanlon. — New York ; Chichester : Wiley, c1981. — 179p : ill ; 28cm
ISBN 0-471-06488-2 (pbk) : £5.60 B81-18675

001.64′2 — Science of Cambridge Mk14 microcomputer systems. Programming

Williamson, Ian. Understanding microprocessors with the science of Cambridge Mk14 / Ian Williamson, Rodney Dale. — London : Macmillan, 1980. — v,209p : ill ; 21cm
ISBN 0-333-31075-6 (pbk) : £5.95 B81-02905

001.64′2 — Sinclair ZX81 microcomputer systems. Programming — *Manuals*

Toms, Trevor. The ZX81 pocket book / by Trevor Toms. — Epsom (3 Downs Ave., Epsom, Surrey KT18 5HQ) : Phipps Associates, 1981. — 136p : ill ; 21cm
ISBN 0-9507302-2-x (spiral) : Unpriced
B81-37101

001.64′2′0246213 — Digital computer systems. Programming — *For technicians*

Morland, R. S.. Computing : level II / R.S. Morland. — New York ; London : Van Nostrand Reinhold, 1980. — xi,153p : ill ; 25cm. — (Technical education courses) (Business education courses)
'Reference card for practical computing in BASIC' (1 folded sheet) as insert
ISBN 0-442-30335-1 (cased) : £9.50
ISBN 0-442-30337-8 (pbk) : £4.25 B81-08715

001.64′2′068 — Digital computer systems. Programming. Management

Metzger, Philip W.. Managing a programming project / Philip W. Metzger. — 2nd ed. — Englewood Cliffs ; London : Prentice-Hall, c1981. — xi,244p : ill ; 24cm
Previous ed.: 1973. — Bibliography: p239-241. — Includes index
ISBN 0-13-550772-3 : £14.90 B81-26099

001.64′24 — Acorn/BBC microcomputer systems. Programming languages: Basic language — *Manuals*

Cryer, Neil. BASIC programming on the Acorn/BBC microcomputer. — London : Prentice-Hall, Jan.1982. — [224]p
ISBN 0-13-066407-3 : £4.95 : CIP entry
B81-39228

001.64′24 — Apple II microcomputer systems. Programming languages: Pascal language — *Manuals*

Luehrmann, Arthur. Apple PASCAL : a hands-on-approach / Arthur Luehrmann, Herbert Peckham. — New York ; London : McGraw-Hill, c1981. — xiv,430p : ill ; 24cm
Text on inside cover. — Includes index
ISBN 0-07-049171-2 (spiral) : £10.50
B81-39975

001.64′24 — Commodore VIC microcomputer systems. Programming languages: Basic language — *Manuals*

Carter, L. R.. Learn computer programming with the Commodore VIC. — London : Hodder and Stoughton, Jan.1982. — [176]p
ISBN 0-340-28070-0 (pbk) : £1.95 : CIP entry
B81-35900

001.64′24 — Digital computer systems. Programming languages

McGettrick, Andrew D.. The definition of programming languages / Andrew D. McGettrick. — Cambridge : Cambridge University Press, 1980. — xii,268p : ill ; 24cm. — (Cambridge computer science texts ; 11)
Bibliography: p255-260. — Includes index
ISBN 0-521-22631-7 : £13.50 B81-05823

Tennent, R. D.. Principles of programming languages / R.D. Tennent. — Englewood Cliffs ; London : Prentice-Hall, c1981. — xiv,271p : ill ; 24cm. — (Prentice-Hall international series in computer science)
Bibliography: p249-252. — Includes index
ISBN 0-13-709873-1 : £12.95 B81-33265

001.64′24 — Digital computer systems. Programming languages: Ada language

Barnes, J. G. P.. Programming in Ada. — London : Addison-Wesley, Oct.1981. — [320]p. — (International computer science series)
ISBN 0-201-13793-3 : £14.95 : CIP entry
ISBN 0-201-13792-5 (pbk) : £7.95 B81-26783

Mayoh, Brian. Ada. — Chichester : Wiley, July 1981. — [450]p. — (Wiley series in computing)
ISBN 0-471-10025-0 : £20.00 : CIP entry
B81-15808

Pyle, I. C.. The ADA programming language : a guide for programmers / I.C. Pyle. — Englewood Cliffs ; London : Prentice-Hall, c1981. — x,293p : 24cm
ISBN 0-13-003921-7 (pbk) : £8.95 B81-26903

001.64′24 — Digital computer systems. Programming languages: Basic language

Carter, L. R.. Computer programming in BASIC / L.R. Carter, E. Huzan. — [Sevenoaks] : Teach Yourself, 1981. — x,163p : ill ; 18cm. — (Computer science series)
Includes index
ISBN 0-340-24882-3 (pbk) : £1.75 B81-16342

Heiserman, David L.. Programming in Basic for personal computers / David L. Heiserman. — Englewood Cliffs ; London : Prentice-Hall, c1981. — xii,333p : ill ; 23cm
Includes index
ISBN 0-13-730747-0 (cased) : Unpriced
ISBN 0-13-730739-x (pbk) : £5.15 B81-12519

Peckham, Herbert D.. BASIC : a hands-on method / Herbert D. Peckham. — 2nd ed. — New York ; London : McGraw-Hill, c1981. — xiv,306p : ill ; 24cm
Previous ed.: 1978. — Includes index
ISBN 0-07-049160-7 (spiral) : £9.25
B81-23994

001.64'24 — Digital computer systems. Programming languages: Basic language *continuation*

Sawatzky, Jasper J.. Programming in BASIC-PLUS / Jasper J. Sawatzky, Shu-Jen Chen. — New York ; Chichester : Wiley, c1981. — ix,273p : ill ; 28cm
Includes index
ISBN 0-471-07729-1 (pbk) : Unpriced B81-37491

001.64'24 — Digital computer systems. Programming languages: Basic language. Applications

Jones, Richard M. (Richard Moody). Instructor's guide to accompany Introduction to computer applications using BASIC / Richard M. Jones. — Boston, Mass. ; London : Allyn and Bacon, c1981. — iv,134,[54]p : ill ; 28cm
ISBN 0-205-07297-6 (pbk) : £1.00 B81-40099

Jones, Richard M. (Richard Moody). Introduction to computer applications using BASIC / Richard M. Jones. — Boston [Mass.] ; London : Allyn and Bacon, c1981. — xvi,444p : ill ; 28cm
Includes index
ISBN 0-205-07296-8 (pbk) : £8.50
ISBN 0-205-07349-2 (International student ed.) : Unpriced B81-26201

001.64'24 — Digital computer systems. Programming languages: Basic language — *Manuals*

Cope, Tonia. Computing using Basic. — Chichester : Ellis Horwood, Aug.1981. — [288] p. — (Ellis Horwood series in computers and their applications, ISSN 02711-6135)
ISBN 0-85312-289-x : £15.00 : CIP entry B81-26694

Daly, S.. An introduction to BASIC programming techniques / by S. Daly. — London : Babani, 1981. — 87p : ill ; 19cm. — (BP ; 86)
ISBN 0-85934-061-9 (pbk) : £1.95 : CIP rev. B81-13756

001.64'24 — Digital computer systems. Programming languages: Basic language — *Programmed instructions*

Finkel, LeRoy. Data file programming in BASIC / LeRoy Finkel and Jerald R. Brown. — New York ; Chichester : Wiley, c1981. — ix,338p : ill ; 26cm. — (A Self-teaching guide)
Includes index
ISBN 0-471-08333-x (pbk) : £6.75 B81-24883

001.64'24 — Digital computer systems. Programming languages: Cobol language

Brown, P. R.. COBOL control : possible United Kingdom measures for the improvement of COBOL portability. — Manchester : NCC Publications, Nov.1981. — [73]p
ISBN 0-85012-349-6 (pbk) : £6.50 : CIP entry B81-38827

COBOL reference summary. — Manchester : NCC Publications, 1981. — 100p : ill ; 21cm
Includes index
ISBN 0-85012-318-6 (pbk) : Unpriced : CIP rev. B81-12884

Parkin, Andrew, *1941-*. COBOL workbook : a self-study introduction to the COBOL programming language / Andrew Parkin. — London : Edward Arnold, 1981. — 76p : ill ; 25cm
Includes index
ISBN 0-7131-3438-0 (pbk) : £2.95 : CIP rev. B81-13867

001.64'24 — Digital computer systems. Programming languages: Cobol language — *Manuals*

Grauer, Robert T.. COBOL : a vehicle for information systems / Robert T. Grauer. — Englewood Cliffs ; London : Prentice-Hall, c1981. — xvi,432p : ill ; 25cm. — (Prentice-Hall software series)
Includes index
ISBN 0-13-139709-5 : £12.30 B81-16598

Grauer, Robert T.. A COBOL book of practice and reference / Robert T. Grauer. — Englewood Cliffs ; London : Prentice-Hall, c1981. — xvii,382p : ill ; 24cm. — (Prentice-Hall software series)
Includes index
ISBN 0-13-139725-7 (cased) : Unpriced
ISBN 0-13-139717-6 (pbk) : £10.35 B81-25464

Triance, J. M.. COBOL programming / J.M. Triance. — Manchester : NCC Publications, 1981. — 178p : ill,forms ; 30cm
Includes index
ISBN 0-85012-249-x (pbk) : Unpriced : CIP rev. B81-12896

001.64'24 — Digital computer systems. Programming languages — *Conference proceedings*

ACM SIGPLAN History of Programming Languages Conference *(1978 : Los Angeles)*. History of programming languages : [from the ACM SIGPLAN History of Programming Languages Conference, June 1-3, 1978] / edited by Richard L. Wexelblat. — New York ; London : Academic Press, 1981. — xxiii,758p : ill,facsims,ports ; 27cm. — (ACM monograph series)
Text and ill on lining papers. — Includes bibliographies and index
ISBN 0-12-745040-8 : £25.50 B81-35424

001.64'24 — Digital computer systems. Programming languages: Fortran 77 language

Ellis, T. M. R.. Structured FORTRAN : a FORTRAN 77 programming course / T.M.R. Ellis. — Rev. ed. — [Sheffield] : Computing Services, University of Sheffield, 1980. — v,121p ; 30cm
Previous ed.: 1980. — Includes index
ISBN 0-9506910-1-1 (pbk) : Unpriced B81-14295

Nanney, T. Ray. Computing : a problem-solving approach with FORTRAN 77 / T. Ray Nanney. — Englewood Cliffs ; London : Prentice-Hall, c1981. — xiv,530p : ill ; 25cm
Includes index
ISBN 0-13-165209-5 : £11.65 B81-24912

001.64'24 — Digital computer systems. Programming languages: Fortran IV & Fortran 77 languages — *Manuals*

Zwass, Vladimir. Programming in Fortran : structured programming with Fortran IV and Fortran 77 / Vladimir Zwass. — New York ; London : Barnes & Noble, 1981. — x,213p : ill ; 21cm. — (Barnes & Noble outline series ; cos 194)
Text on inside covers. — Bibliography: p208. - Includes index
ISBN 0-06-460194-3 (pbk) : £3.95 B81-13251

001.64'24 — Digital computer systems. Programming languages: Fortran IV language — *Programmed instructions*

Friedmann, Jehosua. Fortran IV / Jehosua Friedmann, Philip Greenberg, Alan M. Hoffberg. — 2nd ed. — New York ; Chichester : Wiley, c1981. — xii,499p : ill ; 26cm. — (A Self-teaching guide)
Previous ed.: 1975. — Includes index
ISBN 0-471-07771-2 (pbk) : £6.75 B81-18676

001.64'24 — Digital computer systems. Programming languages: Fortran language

Hill, Louis A.. Structured programming in FORTRAN / Louis A. Hill Jr.. — Englewood Cliffs ; London : Prentice-Hall, c1981. — xvi,526p : ill ; 24cm
Includes index
ISBN 0-13-854612-6 (pbk) : £11.15 B81-33266

Programming with FORTRAN 77 / J. Ashcroft ... [et al.]. — London : Granada, 1981. — 294p : ill ; 24cm
Includes index
ISBN 0-246-11573-4 (pbk) : £5.95 B81-24463

001.64'24 — Digital computer systems. Programming languages: Fortran language — *Programmed instructions — For business studies*

Martin, E. Wainright. FORTRAN for business students : a programmed instruction approach / E. Wainright Martin, William C. Perkins. — New York ; Chichester : Wiley, c1981. — xiv,811p : ill ; 28cm
Includes index
ISBN 0-471-04622-1 (pbk) : £12.15 B81-24882

001.64'24 — Digital computer systems. Programming languages. Grammar

Pagan, Frank G.. Formal specification of programming languages : a panoramic primer / Frank G. Pagan. — Englewood Cliffs ; London : Prentice-Hall, c1981. — x,245p : ill ; 24cm
Bibliography: p235-239. - Includes index
ISBN 0-13-329052-2 : £12.95 B81-17284

001.64'24 — Digital computer systems. Programming languages: Pascal language

Pascal : the language and its implementation / edited by D.W. Barron. — Chichester : Wiley, c1981. — ix,301p : ill ; 24cm. — (Wiley series in computing)
Includes index
ISBN 0-471-27835-1 : £12.50 B81-17090

Rohl, J. S.. Programming via Pascal / J.S. Rohl and H.J. Barrett. — Cambridge : Cambridge University Press, 1980. — xii,327p : ill ; 24cm. — (Cambridge computer science texts ; 12)
Includes index
ISBN 0-521-22628-7 (cased) : £12.50
ISBN 0-521-29583-1 (pbk) : £5.95 B81-00682

001.64'24 — Digital computer systems. Programming languages: Pascal language — *Manuals*

Atkinson, Laurence V.. Pascal programming / Laurence V. Atkinson. — Chichester : Wiley, c1980. — x,428p : ill ; 24cm. — (Wiley series in computing)
Includes index
ISBN 0-471-27773-8 (cased) : £16.50 : CIP rev.
ISBN 0-471-27774-6 (pbk) : £6.95 B80-13175

Kemp, R.. PASCAL for students. — London : E. Arnold, Nov.1981. — [256]p
ISBN 0-7131-3447-x (pbk) : £5.95 : CIP entry B81-30611

Welsh, Jim. Introduction to Pascal. — Rev. ed. — London : Prentice-Hall, Feb.1982. — [320]p
Previous ed.: 1979
ISBN 0-13-491530-5 (pbk) : £9.50 : CIP entry B81-35789

001.64'24 — Digital computer systems. Programming languages: Pascal language — *Manuals — For science*

Cooper, James W.. Introduction to Pascal for scientists / by James W. Cooper. — New York ; Chichester : Wiley, c1981. — xv,260p : ill ; 24cm
Includes index
ISBN 0-471-08785-8 : £12.50 B81-24220

001.64'24 — Digital computer systems. Programming languages: PL/C languages

Hughes, Joan K.. Structured programming using PL/C / Joan K. Hughes, Barbara J. La Pearl ; with programming assistance by L. David Jones. — New York ; Chichester : Wiley, c1981. — ix,414p : ill ; 28cm
Includes index
ISBN 0-471-04969-7 (pbk) : £11.50 B81-40149

001.64'24 — Digital computer systems. Programming languages. Standardisation

Progamming language standardisation / editors : I.D. Hill and B.L. Meek. — Chichester : Horwood, 1980. — 261p : ill ; 24cm. — (The Ellis Horwood series in computers and their applications ; [7])
Text on lining papers. — Includes index
ISBN 0-85312-188-5 : £18.50 : CIP rev. B80-18956

001.64'24 — Digital computer systems. Programming languages. Validation — *Conference proceedings*

Language implementation validation : proceedings of the two-day workshop held at the National Computing Centre, Manchester, England, 12 and 13 September 1979 / edited by D.J. Dwyer, D.I. Noble ; organized by Gesellschaft für Mathematik und Datenverarbeitung, Bureau d'orientation de la normalisation en informatique, National Computing Centre. — [Manchester] : The Centre, 1980. — 227,21p : ill ; 30cm
Includes one paper in French
ISBN 0-85012-324-0 (spiral) : Unpriced B81-27532

001.64'24 — Digital computer systems. Structured programming. Programming languages: Cobol language — *Manuals*

Grauer, Robert T.. Structured COBOL : a pragmatic approach / Robert T. Grauer, Marshal A. Crawford. — Englewood Cliffs ; London : Prentice-Hall, c1981. — xi,387p : ill ; 28cm
Includes index
ISBN 0-13-854455-7 (pbk) : £11.65 B81-25465

Popkin, Gary S.. Introductory structured COBOL programming / Gary S. Popkin. — New York ; London : D. Van Nostrand, 1981. — xv,471p : forms ; 24cm
Includes index
ISBN 0-442-23166-0 (pbk) : £12.70 B81-11437

001.64'24 — Digital computer systems. Structured programming. Programming languages: Fortran IV language & ANSI Fortran 77 language — *Programmed instructions*

Khailany, Asad. Business programming in Fortran IV and Ansi Fortran 77 : a structured approach / Asad Khailany. — Englewood Cliffs ; London : Prentice-Hall, 1981. — xvii,440p : ill ; 23cm
Includes index
ISBN 0-13-107607-8 (pbk) : Unpriced B81-32555

001.64'24 — Digital computer systems. Structured programs. Design

Ingevaldsson, Leif. JSP : a practical method of program design / Leif Ingevaldsson. — Lund : Studentlitteratur ; Bromley (Old Orchard, Bickley Rd., Bromley, Kent BR1 2NE) : Chartwell-Bratt, c1979. — 194p : ill ; 23cm
Translation of: JSP — en praktisk metod för programkonstruktion
ISBN 0-86238-011-1 (pbk) : Unpriced B81-38126

001.64'24 — Digital computer systems. Structured programs. Design. Techniques: Logical Construction of Systems

Gardner, Albert C.. Practical LCP. — London : McGraw-Hill, Aug.1981. — [256]p
ISBN 0-07-084561-1 (pbk) : £12.50 : CIP entry B81-15867

001.64'24 — Interactive computer systems. Programming languages

Kupka, I.. Conversational languages / I. Kupka and N. Wilsing. — Chichester : Wiley, 1980. — ix,117p : ill ; 24cm
Translation of: Dialogsprachen. — Bibliography: p110-113. - Includes index
ISBN 0-471-27778-9 : £9.45 : CIP rev. B80-25036

001.64'24 — Microcomputer systems. Programming languages: Basic language — *Manuals*

Gosling, P. E.. Program your microcomputer in BASIC / P.E. Gosling. — London : Macmillan, 1981. — 91p : ill ; 24cm
ISBN 0-333-28654-5 (pbk) : £3.95 B81-38729

001.64'24 — Radio Shack TRS-80 microcomputer systems. Programming languages: Basic language — *Manuals*

Zabinski, Michael P.. Introduction to trs-80 Level II BASIC and computer programming / Michael P. Zabinski. — Englewood Cliffs ; London : Prentice-Hall, 1980. — 186p : ill ; 28cm. — (A Reward book)
Includes index
ISBN 0-13-499970-3 (cased) : £9.70
ISBN 0-13-499962-2 (pbk) : £7.10 B81-09331

001.64'24 — Sinclair ZX80 microcomputer systems. Programming — *Manuals*

Norman, Robin. Learning BASIC with your Sinclair ZX80 / Robin Norman. — London : Newnes Technical, 1981. — 153p : ill ; 22cm. — (Newnes microcomputer books)
Includes index
ISBN 0-408-01101-7 (pbk) : £3.95 : CIP rev. B81-02652

Toms, Trevor. The ZX80 pocket book / by Trevor Toms. — Epsom : Phipps, 1980 (1981 [printing]). — 116p ; 21cm
ISBN 0-9507302-0-3 (spiral) : Unpriced B81-36333

001.64'24 — Tandy TRS-80 microcomputer systems. Programming languages: Basic language — *Manuals*

Inman, Don. More TRS-80 BASIC / Don Inman, Ramon Zamora and Bob Albrecht. — New York ; Chichester : Wiley, c1981. — vii,280p : ill ; 24cm. — (A Self-teaching guide)
Includes index
ISBN 0-471-08010-1 (pbk) : £6.75 B81-29268

001.64'25 — Computer systems. Software. Evaluation

Software metrics : an analysis and evaluation / Alan Perlis, Frederick Sayward, Mary Shaw, editors. — Cambridge, Mass. ; London : MIT, c1981. — lx,404p : ill ; 23cm. — (The MIT press series in computer science)
Bibliography: p271-399. — Includes index
ISBN 0-262-16083-8 : £17.50 B81-39760

001.64'25 — DEC-PDP-11 minicomputer systems. Software packages: SPSS — *Manuals*

SPSS-11 : the SPSS batch system for the DEC PDP-11 / series editors Norman H. Nie, C. Hadlai Hull ; contributors Graham Kimble ... [et al.]. — New York ; London : McGraw-Hill, c1980. — viii,165p ; 28cm
Bibliography: p161. — Includes index
ISBN 0-07-046537-1 (pbk) : £5.95 B81-10122

001.64'25 — Digital computer systems. Assembly languages: ASS 300 language

Ernst, Manfred. Programming with assembler language ASS 300 / Manfred Ernst and Walter Steigert. — Berlin : Siemens ; London : Heyden, c1980. — 316p : ill ; 25cm
Translation of: Programmierung mit der Assemblersprache ASS 300
ISBN 0-85501-274-9 (pbk) : £12.00 B81-38201

001.64'25 — Digital computer systems. Assembly programming

Peterson, James L.. Instructor's manual for Computer organization and assembly language programming / James L. Peterson. — New York ; London : Academic Press, [1980]. — 80p : 1ill ; 23cm
Cover title. — Bibliography: p19-20
ISBN 0-12-552252-5 (pbk) : £1.70 B81-06131

001.64'25 — Digital computer systems. Compilers. Writing — *Manuals*

Hunter, Robin. The design and construction of compilers. — Chichester : Wiley, Jan.1982. — [240]p. — (Wiley series in computing)
ISBN 0-471-28054-2 (cased) : £10.50 : CIP entry
ISBN 0-471-09979-1 (pbk) : £6.00 B81-34411

001.64'25 — Digital computer systems. Intel 8080 central processing units & Zilog Z-80 central processing units. Assembly languages — *Manuals*

Miller, Alan R.. The 8080/Z-80 assembly language : techniques for improved programming / Alan R. Miller. — New York ; Chichester : Wiley, c1981. — x,318p ; 26cm
Includes index
ISBN 0-471-08124-8 (pbk) : £6.75 B81-13962

001.64'25 — Digital computer systems. Job control languages

Query languages. — London : Heyden, May 1981. — [118]p. — (Monographs in informatics)
ISBN 0-85501-494-6 : £8.00 : CIP entry B81-14819

001.64'25 — Digital computer systems. Job control languages. Design

User-oriented command language : requirements and designs for a standard job control language / edited by K. Hopper. — London : Heyden on behalf of the British Computer Society, c1981. — xi,111p : ill ; 24cm. — (Monographs in informatics)
ISBN 0-85501-691-4 (pbk) : £10.50 B81-21160

001.64'25 — Digital computer systems. Programs. Decision tables

Welland, R.. Decision tables and computer programming. — London : Heyden, Sept.1981. — [250]p
ISBN 0-85501-708-2 : CIP entry B81-28274

001.64'25 — Digital computer systems. Software — *Conference proceedings*

Software engineering environments : proceedings of the symposium held in Lahnstein, Federal Republic of Germany June 16-20, 1980 / organized by Gesellschaft für Mathematik und Datenverarbeitung mbH Bonn, Institut für Software-Tecnhologie ; edited by Horst Hünke. — Amsterdam ; Oxford : North-Holland, 1981. — viii,410p : ill ; 24cm
Bibliography: p362-398. — Includes index
ISBN 0-444-86133-5 : £23.17 B81-09434

001.64'25 — Digital computer systems. Software. Design — *Conference proceedings*

Software Engineering Workshop *(1978 : Albany, etc.)*. Software engineering / [proceedings of the Software Engineering Workshop held in Albany, Troy, and Schenectady, New York from May 30-June 1, 1979] ; edited by Herbert Freeman, Philip M. Lewis II. — New York ; London : Academic Press, 1980. — x,244p : ill ; 24cm
Conference papers. — Includes bibliographies and index
ISBN 0-12-267160-0 : £11.80 B81-16620

001.64'25 — Digital computer systems. Software. Development & maintenance. Management

McClure, Carma L.. Managing software development and maintenance / Carma L. McClure. — New York ; London : Van Nostrand Reinhold, c1981. — x,203p : ill,forms ; 24cm
Bibliography: p197-199. — Includes index
ISBN 0-442-22569-5 : £12.70 B81-25379

001.64'25 — Digital computer systems. Software. Quality control

Cho, Chin-Kuei. An introduction to software quality control / Chin-Kuei Cho. — New York ; Chichester : Wiley, c1980. — xxii,445p : ill ; 24cm. — (Business data processing)
Includes index
ISBN 0-471-04704-x : £16.00 B81-04405

001.64'25 — Digital computer systems. Software. Reliability. Management

Walker, Michael G.. Managing software reliability : the paradigmatic approach / Michael G. Walker. — New York ; Oxford : North Holland, c1981. — ix,251p : ill,forms ; 24cm. — (North Holland series in systems and software development ; v.1)
Includes index
ISBN 0-444-00381-9 : £23.91 B81-08303

001.64'25 — Digital computer systems. Structured programming. Programming languages: Fortran language. Compilers: Watfiv-S

Cress, Paul. Structured FORTRAN with WATFIV-S / Paul Cress, Paul Dirksen, J. Wesley Graham. — Englewood Cliffs ; London : Prentice-Hall, c1980. — xi,403p : ill ; 24cm
Includes index
ISBN 0-13-854752-1 (pbk) : £8.40 B81-03724

001.64'25 — INTEL 8080 & 8085 microcomputer systems. Assembly languages — *Programmed instructions*

Fernandez, Judi N.. 8080/8085 Assembly Language programming / by Judi N. Fernandez, Ruth Ashley. — New York ; Chichester : Wiley, c1981. — xiv,303p : ill ; 26cm. — (A Self-teaching guide)
Includes index
ISBN 0-471-08009-8 (pbk) : £5.95 B81-24884

001.64'25 — Macro processors
Cole, A. J.. Macro processors. — 2nd ed. — Cambridge : Cambridge University Press, Nov.1981. — [256]p. — (Cambridge computer science texts ; 4)
Previous ed.: 1976
ISBN 0-521-24259-2 (cased) : £12.00 : CIP entry
ISBN 0-521-28560-7 (pbk) : £5.95 B81-32536

001.64'25 — Microcomputer systems. Operating systems
Lane, J. E.. Operating systems for microcomputers / J.E. Lane. — Manchester : NCC Publications, 1981. — 77p ; 22cm. — (Computing in the '80s)
Bibliography: p77
ISBN 0-85012-277-5 (pbk) : £3.50 B81-23568

001.64'25 — Microcomputer systems. Software packages
Lane, J. E.. Choosing programs for microcomputers / J.E. Lane. — Manchester : MCC Publications, 1980. — 138p ; 21cm
Bibliography: p129
ISBN 0-85012-255-4 (pbk) : £8.00 : CIP rev. B80-17511

001.64'25 — Microcomputer systems. Software — ***Serials***
Liverpool software gazette. — 1st ed. (Nov.1979)-. — Liverpool (14 Castle St., Liverpool L2 0TA) : Liverpool Software Gazette Ltd., 1979-. — v. : ill ; 27cm
Six issues yearly. — Description based on: 3rd ed. (Mar.1980)
£9.00 for 12 issues B81-05678

001.64'25 — Microprocessor systems. Software
Microprocessor software / [editor] Martin Whitbread. — Tunbridge Wells : Castle House Publications, 1980. — 150p : ill,1port ; 30cm. — (Topics in microprocessing ; bk.2)
Bibliography: p.143-145
ISBN 0-7194-0013-9 (pbk) : £9.50 : CIP rev. B80-08076

001.64'25 — Real time computer systems. Software. Design
Allworth, S. T.. Introduction to real-time software design / S.T. Allworth. — London : Macmillan, 1981. — x,140p : ill ; 25cm. — (Macmillan computer science series)
Bibliography: p129-131. - Includes index
ISBN 0-333-27135-1 (cased) : £12.00
ISBN 0-333-27137-8 (pbk) : Unpriced B81-22249

001.64'25 — TRS-80 microcomputer systems. Assembly programming — ***Manuals***
Howe, Hubert S.. TRS-80 assembly language / Hubert S. Howe, Jr. — Englewood Cliffs ; London : Prentice-Hall, c1981. — 186p : ill ; 24cm. — (A Spectrum book)
Bibliography: p186
ISBN 0-13-931139-4 (cased) : Unpriced
ISBN 0-13-931121-1 (pbk) : £6.45 B81-16649

001.64'25'0212 — Microcomputer systems. Software — ***Lists***
International microcomputer software directory. — [Romford] : Imprint Software, c1981. — ca.320p : 1form ; 29cm
Includes index
ISBN 0-907352-03-0 (pbk) : Unpriced B81-40365

001.64'25'0288 — Digital computer systems. Software. Maintenance
Glass, Robert L.. Software maintenance guidebook / Robert L. Glass, Ronald A. Noiseux. — Englewood Cliffs ; London : Prentice-Hall, c1981. — xi,193p : ill ; 24cm
Bibliography: p185-186. - Includes index
ISBN 0-13-821728-9 : £14.25 B81-25055

001.64'25'05 — Computer systems. Software packages — ***Lists — Serials***
International directory of software. — 1980-81-. — Bournemouth (430 Holdenhurst Rd, Bournemouth BH8 9AA) : CUYB Publications, c1980-. — v. : ill ; 29cm
Issued every two years. — Text in English, introductory material also in French and German. — Continues: CUYB directory of software
ISSN 0260-3438 = International directory of software : £36.00 B81-00683

001.64'4 — Microcomputer systems. Input-output systems
Lane, J. E.. Communicating with microcomputers / J.E. Lane. — Manchester : NCC Publications, 1981. — 66p : ill ; 22cm. — (Computing in the '80s)
Bibliography: p61
ISBN 0-85012-302-x (pbk) : £4.00 B81-38061

001.64'4 — Small digital computer systems. Peripheral equipment
Hohenstein, C. Louis. Computer peripherals for minicomputers, microprocessors, and personal computers / Louis Hohenstein. — New York ; London : McGraw-Hill, c1980. — viii,312p : ill ; 24cm
Includes index
ISBN 0-07-029451-8 : £11.70 B81-03040

001.64'4 — Small digital computer systems. Terminals — ***For business practices — Serials***
Guide to data communications and terminals for small systems. — 1980/81-. — London (30 Islington Green, N1 8BJ) : Computer Guides Ltd., 1980-. — v. : ill ; 30cm. — (Computer guides — for the businessman)
Annual
ISSN 0260-8995 = Guide to data communications and terminals for small systems : £24.00 B81-10255

001.64'404 — Computer systems. Networks
Gee, K. C. E.. Proprietary network architectures. — Manchester : NCC Publications, July 1981. — [280]p
ISBN 0-85012-327-5 : £75.00 : CIP entry B81-18051

Tanenbaum, Andrew S.. Computer networks / Andrew S. Tonenbaum. — Englewood Cliffs ; London : Prentice-Hall, c1981. — xv,517p : ill ; 25cm
Bibliography: p493-507. — Includes index
ISBN 0-13-165183-8 : £18.20 B81-17178

001.64'404 — Digital computer systems. Networks
Networks. — Maidenhead : Infotech, c1981. — iv,422p : ill,ports ; 31cm. — (Infotech state of the art report. Series 9 ; no.2)
Editor A.V. Stokes. — Bibliography: p395-416. — Includes index
ISBN 0-85539-720-9 : Unpriced B81-35530

001.64'404 — Digital computer systems. Networks. Data transmission
Protocols and techniques for data communication networks / Franklin F. Kuo, editor. — Englewood Cliffs ; London : Prentice-Hall, c1981. — xi,468p : ill ; 25cm. — (Prentice-Hall computer applications in electrical engineering series)
Includes bibliographies and index
ISBN 0-13-731729-8 : £19.45 B81-14677

001.64'404 — Digital computer systems. Networks. Data transmission — ***Conference proceedings***
IFIP(TC-6)/CSI Conference on Networks 80 ***(1981 : Bombay)***. Data communication and computer networks : proceedings of the IFIP (TC-6)/CSI Conference on Networks 80, Bombay, India, 4-6 February, 1981 / edited by S. Ramani. — Amsterdam ; Oxford : North-Holland, c1981. — viii,309p : ill,ports ; 27cm
Includes bibliographies
ISBN 0-444-86220-x : £19.67 B81-35336

001.64'404 — Digital computer systems. Networks. Data transmission. Control
Pužman, Josef. Communication control in computer networks / Josef Pužman, Radoslav Pořízek. — Chichester : Wiley, c1980. — 296p : ill ; 24cm. — (Wiley series in computing)
Published simultaneously in Czechoslovakia. — Bibliography: p273-286. - Includes index
ISBN 0-471-27894-7 : £13.20 : CIP rev. B81-06898

001.64'404 — Digital computer systems. Networks. Interlinking — ***Conference proceedings***
Interlinking of Computer Networks : proceedings of the NATO Advanced Study Institute held at Bonas, France, August 28 - September 8, 1978 / edited by Kenneth G. Beauchamp. — Dordrecht ; London : Reidel, published in cooperation with NATO Scientific Affairs Division, c1979. — x,475p : ill,maps,forms ; 25cm. — (NATO advanced study institutes series. Series C - Mathematical and physical science ; v.42)
Includes index
ISBN 90-277-0979-3 : Unpriced B81-16319

001.64'404 — On-line information systems. Development. Influence of users — ***Conference proceedings***
Eurim ***(3rd : 1978 : Munich)***. Eurim 3 : a European conference on the contribution of users to planning and policy making for information systems and networks / presented by Aslib in association with Association nationale de la recherche technique ... [et al.], 25-27 April 1978, Künstlerhaus, Munich, Germany ; proceedings edited by A. Dewe and J. Deunette. — London : Aslib, c1980. — 100p : ill ; 30cm
ISBN 0-85142-133-4 (pbk) : £8.40 (£7.00 to members) B81-08343

001.64'404 — Time-sharing computer systems: Dartmouth Time-sharing System
Bull, G. M.. The Dartmouth time-sharing system / Gordon M. Bull. — Chichester : Horwood, 1980. — 240p : ill ; 24cm. — (The Ellis Horwood series in computers and their applications ; [8])
Text on lining papers. — Includes index
ISBN 0-85312-253-9 : £18.50 : CIP rev. B80-22798

001.64'42 — Data dictionary systems: ICL data dictionary system
Using the ICL data dictionary : proceedings of the user group / edited by A.T. Windsor. — Orpington (9 Clareville Rd, Orpington, Kent BR5 1RU) : Shiva, c1980. — 153p : ill ; 24cm
ISBN 0-906812-06-2 (pbk) : £15.00 : CIP rev. B80-13176

001.64'42 — Data processing. Keyboarding — ***Manuals***
Hanson, Robert N.. Keyboarding : for information processing / Robert N. Hanson, D. Sue Rigby. — New York ; London : Gregg, c1981. — vi,90p : ill(some col.) ; 23cm
ISBN 0-07-026105-9 (spiral) : £4.95 B81-24318

001.64'42 — Digital computer systems. Data. Logging — ***Conference proceedings***
New frontiers in PLC data logging and microprocessors : international conference at the Polytechnic of Central London, 1.12.78 / [organized] by Engineers' digest, Automation & the Polytechnic of Central London. — [London] : [The Polytechnic], [1981?]. — 1v.(various foliations) : ill,forms ; 31cm
Unpriced (unbound) B81-26530

001.64'42 — Digital computer systems. Data. Structure
Bailey, Brian. Data structures / Brian Bailey. — Glasgow : Blackie, 1980. — 52p : ill ; 17x25cm. — (Basic computing science)
Includes index
ISBN 0-216-90856-6 (pbk) : £2.50 B81-00684

Pfaltz, John L.. Computer data structures / John L. Pfaltz. — Tokyo ; London : McGraw-Hill Kogakusha, c1977. — xi,446p : ill ; 21cm
Bibliography: p434-436. — Includes index
ISBN 0-07-085559-5 (pbk) : £5.75 B81-12106

001.64'42 — Digital computer systems. Storage devices
McKay, Charles W.. Experimenting with MSI, LSI, IO and modular memory systems / Charles W. McKay. — Englewood Cliffs ; London : Prentice-Hall, c1981. — xiii,272p : ill ; 25cm
Bibliography: p265-266. — Includes index
ISBN 0-13-295477-x : £12.95 B81-19648

001.64′42 — Distributed machine-readable files

Distributed data bases / edited by I.W. Draffan and F. Poole. — Cambridge : Cambridge University Press, 1980. — x,374p : ill ; 24cm
Based on an advanced course held at the Sheffield City Polytechnic in 1979. — Includes bibliographies
ISBN 0-521-23091-8 : £15.00 B81-14663

001.64′42 — Machine-readable files

Database achievements / edited by Geoffrey J. Baker. — London (322 St. John St., EC1 4QH) : A.P. Publications, 1979. — viii,128p : ill ; 21cm
Unpriced (pbk) B81-30106

Martin, James, *1933*. An end-user's guide to data base / James Martin. — Englewood Cliffs ; London : Prentice-Hall, c1981. — xi,144p,[1] folded leaf of plates : ill(some col.),1form ; 25cm. — (A James Martin book)
Includes bibliographies and index
ISBN 0-13-277129-2 : Unpriced B81-36493

001.64′42 — Machine-readable files — *Conference proceedings*

International Conference on Data Bases *(1980 : University of Aberdeen)*. Proceedings, International Conference on Data Bases, University of Aberdeen July 1980 / edited by S.M. Deen and P. Hammersley. — London : Heyden, c1981. — xii,288p : ill ; 24cm. — (The British Computer Society workshop series)
At head of title: Department of Computing Science, University of Aberdeen and The British Computer Society. — Includes bibliographies and index
ISBN 0-85501-495-4 (pbk) : Unpriced B81-38407

National Conference on Databases *(1st : 1981 : Cambridge)*. Databases. — London (4 Graham Lodge, Graham Rd., NW4 3DG) : Pentech Press, Oct.1981. — [250]p
Conference papers
ISBN 0-7273-0405-4 : £16.00 : CIP entry B81-28813

001.64′42 — Machine-readable files. Design

Hubbard, George U.. Computer-assisted data base design / George U. Hubbard. — New York ; London : Van Nostrand Reinhold, c1981. — xxi,285p : ill ; 24cm. — (Van Nostrand Reinhold data processing series)
Bibliography: p276-277. — Includes index
ISBN 0-442-23205-5 : £21.20 B81-39884

Inman, William H.. Effective data base design / William H. Inman. — Englewood Cliffs ; London : Prentice-Hall, c1981. — xi,228p : ill ; 25cm. — (Prentice-Hall series in data processing management)
Bibliography: p223-224. — Includes index
ISBN 0-13-241489-9 : £16.30 B81-16560

Vetter, M.. Database design methodology / M. Vetter, R.N. Maddison. — Englewood Cliffs ; London : Prentice-Hall, c1981. — xii,306p : ill ; 25cm
Includes bibliographies and index
ISBN 0-13-196535-2 : £13.95 : CIP rev. B79-33864

001.64′42 — Machine-readable files. Design & management

Atre, S.. Data base : structured techniques for design, performance, and management : with case studies / S. Atre. — New York ; Chichester : Wiley, c1980. — xvi,442p : ill ; 24cm. — (Business data processing)
Includes index
ISBN 0-471-05267-1 : £15.00 B81-02745

001.64′42 — Machine-readable files. Management

Flores, Ivan. Data base architecture / Ivan Flores. — New York ; London : Van Nostrand Reinhold, c1981. — xiv,396p : ill ; 24cm
Includes index
ISBN 0-442-22729-9 : £22.55 B81-39883

Mayne, Alan. Database management systems. — Manchester : NCC Publications, July 1981. — [200]p
ISBN 0-85012-323-2 (pbk) : CIP entry B81-18064

001.64′42 — Machine-readable files. Management. Application of programs written in Cobol language

Johnson, LeRoy F.. File techniques for data base organization in COBOL / LeRoy F. Johnson and Rodney H. Cooper. — Englewood Cliffs ; London : Prentice-Hall, c1981. — xvi,368p : ill ; 24cm
Bibliography: p361-364. - Includes index
ISBN 0-13-314039-3 : £12.95 B81-17303

001.64′42 — Machine-readable files — *Serials*

Advances in data base theory. — Vol.1-. — New York ; London : Plenum, 1981-. — v. ; 26cm
Unpriced B81-15069

001.64′42 — Sinclair ZX81 microcomputer systems. Programming languages: Basic language — *Manuals*

Norman, Robin. ZX81 Basic book. — London : Newnes Technical Books, Jan.1982. — [160]p
ISBN 0-408-01178-5 (pbk) : £4.95 : CIP entry B81-34577

001.64′42 — Small digital computer systems. Machine-readable files. Design

Martin, Daniel. Database design and implementation : on maxi- and mini-computers / Daniel Martin. — New York ; London : Van Nostrand Reinhold, 1980. — x,144p : ill ; 24cm
Translation of: Bases de données
ISBN 0-442-30429-3 (cased) : £9.50
ISBN 0-442-30430-7 (pbk) : Unpriced B81-08709

001.64′43 — Computer systems. Visual display terminals

Sippl, Charles J.. Video/Computers : how to select, mix and operate personal computers and home video systems / Charles J. Sippl and Fred Dahl. — Englewood Cliffs ; London : Prentice-Hall, c1981. — lx,246p : ill ; 24cm. — (A spectrum book)
Includes index
ISBN 0-13-941856-3 (cased) : Unpriced
ISBN 0-13-941849-0 (pbk) : £5.55 B81-36598

001.64′43 — Computer systems. Visual display terminals. Ergonomic aspects — *Conference proceedings*

An **edited** transcript of the one-day meeting on eyestrain and VDUs : December 15th 1978 / [organised by] the Ergonomics Society with the technical collaboration of the Applied Vision Association. — Loughborough (Mechanical Engineering Building, Loughborough University of Technology, Loughborough, Leics.) : Loughborough University of Technology, [1978?]. — x,58p : ill ; 30cm
Cover title
£4.50 (£3.50 to members of the Ergonomics Society) (pbk) B81-38886

Ergonomic aspects of visual display terminals : proceedings of the international workshop, Milan, March 1980 / edited by E. Grandjean and E. Vigliani. — London : Taylor & Francis, 1980. — x,300p,[1] leaf of plates : ill(some col.) ; 24cm
Includes bibliographies and index
ISBN 0-85066-211-7 : £18.00 : CIP rev. B80-32781

001.64′43 — Microcomputer systems. Graphic displays

Lane, J. E.. Graphics on microcomputers / J.E. Lane. — Manchester : NCC, 1981. — 59p : ill ; 21cm. — (Computing in the 80s)
ISBN 0-85012-333-x (pbk) : Unpriced : CIP rev. B81-16859

001.64′43 — Modems. Use

Scott, P. R. D.. Modems in data communications / P.R.D. Scott. — Manchester : NCC Publications, 1980. — 166p : ill ; 21cm
Includes index
ISBN 0-85012-243-0 (pbk) : £12.50 : CIP rev. B80-17512

001.9 — CONTROVERSIAL KNOWLEDGE

001.9 — Controversial & spurious knowledge

The **Directory** of possibilities / edited by Colin Wilson and John Grant. — Exeter : Webb & Bower, 1981. — 255p : ill,ports ; 24cm
Bibliography: p223-225. — Includes index
ISBN 0-906671-27-2 : £8.95 : CIP rev. B81-08941

001.9′3 — Curiosities

Däniken, Erich von. Signs of the gods? / Erich von Däniken ; translated by Michael Heron. — London : Corgi, 1981, c1980. — 256p : ill ; 18cm
Translation of: Prophet der Vergangenheit. — Originally published: London : Souvenir, 1980. — Bibliography: p253-256
ISBN 0-552-11716-1 (pbk) : £1.50 B81-32926

001.9′3 — Curiosities — *For children*

Baguley, Nigel. Strange but true / Nigel Baguley. — London : Harrap, 1981. — 39p : ill,ports ; 19cm. — (The Reporters series)
ISBN 0-245-53591-8 (pbk) : £0.80 B81-19676

001.9′3′0904 — Curiosities, *1900-1945* — *Readings from contemporary sources*

Man bites man : the scrapbook of an Edwardian eccentric / [collected by] George Ives ; edited by Paul Sieveking. — London : Landesman, c1980. — 160p : ill,facsims,ports ; 31cm
Includes index
ISBN 0-905150-15-5 : £6.50 B81-05433

Man bites man : the scrapbook of an Edwardian eccentric / [compiled by] George Ives ; edited by Paul Sieveking. — Harmondsworth : Penguin, 1981, c1980. — 160p : ill,chieflyfacsims,ports ; 29cm
Originally published: London : Landesman, 1980
ISBN 0-14-005960-1 (pbk) : £3.95 B81-40479

001.9′3′094281 — Yorkshire. Curiosities

Colbeck, Maurice. Queer goings on / by Maurice Colbeck ; illustrated by Albin Trowski. — Manchester : Whitethorn, 1979. — 96p : ill ; 21cm
ISBN 0-9506055-6-5 (pbk) : £1.85 B81-40630

001.9′4 — Mysteries

Allan, John, *1950-*. Mysteries : a book of beliefs / John Allan. — Tring : Lion, 1981. — 61p : ill (some col.) ; 29cm
Text and ill on lining papers
ISBN 0-85648-318-4 : £3.95 B81-23400

Berlitz, Charles. The Philadelphia experiment : project invisibility / Charles Berlitz and William Moore. — London : Souvenir Press, 1979. — 188p : ill,facsims,ports ; 23cm
Originally published: New York : Grosset & Dunlap, 1979. — Bibliography: p187-188
ISBN 0-285-62400-8 : £4.95 B81-13007

Mysteries of the world / general editor Christopher Pick. — [London] ([66b The Broadway, N.W.7]) : Lyric, [1980?]. — 160p : col.ill,col.maps,1col.facsim,ports(some col.) ; 31cm
Col. ill on lining papers. — Includes index
£5.95 B81-00685

001.9′4 — Mysteries — *For children*

Haining, Peter. The hell hound : and other true mysteries / Peter Haining ; illustrated by Philip Emms. — London : Armada, 1980. — 123p : ill ; 18cm
ISBN 0-00-691745-3 (pbk) : £0.75 B81-20393

Maynard, Christopher. The book of great mysteries / by Christopher Maynard. — Maidenhead : Purnell, 1981. — 117p : ill(some col.),col.maps,ports ; 29cm
Ill on lining papers
ISBN 0-361-05077-1 : Unpriced B81-37809

001.9′4 — Persons. Disappearance, *to 1978*

Begg, Paul. Into thin air : people who disappear / Paul Begg. — London : Sphere, 1981, c1979. — 186p ; 18cm
Originally published: Newton Abbot : David & Charles, 1979. — Bibliography. — Includes index
ISBN 0-7221-1549-0 (pbk) : £1.25 B81-23532

001.9′4′05 — Mysteries — *Serials*

The **Unexplained** : mysteries of mind space & time. — Vol.1, issue 1-. — London : Orbis, 1980-. — v. : ill ; 29cm
Weekly. — Description based on: Vol.1, issue 6
ISSN 0261-1961 = Unexplained : £30.00 per year B81-17465

001.9′4′09162 — Oceans. Mysteries, *to 1976 — For children*

Wall, Anthony. Sea mysteries / by Anthony Wall ; illustrated by Harry Bishop and Michael Atkinson ; edited by Jill Coleman. — London : Kingfisher, 1980. — 24p : col.ill ; 23cm. — (Kingfisher explorer books. Mysteries)
Originally published: London : Pan, 1980. — Bibliography: p24. — Includes index
ISBN 0-7063-6043-5 : £1.95 B81-04714

001.9′4′094237 — Cornwall. Mysteries

Williams, Michael, *1933-*. Cornish mysteries / Michael Williams. — Bodmin : Bossiney, 1980. — 104p : ill,ports ; 21cm
ISBN 0-906456-45-2 (pbk) : £1.50 B81-04566

001.9′4′094271 — Cheshire. Mysteries

Rickman, Philip. Mysterious Cheshire / by Philip Rickman. — Clapham, N. Yorkshire : Dalesman, 1980. — 63p : ill ; 22cm
Bibliography: p62-63
ISBN 0-85206-618-x (pbk) : £1.50 B81-13394

001.9′4′0942881 — Northumberland. Hexham. Mysteries

Screeton, Paul. Tales of the Hexham Heads / [by Paul Screeton]. — Hartlepool (5 Egton Drive, Seaton Carew, Hartlepool, Cleveland TS25 2AT) : Outlaw, [1981?]. — 16p ; 30cm
Bibliography: p16
£0.60 (unbound) B81-13963

001.9′4′0977 — North America. Great Lakes. Mysteries

Cochrane, Hugh F.. Gateway to oblivion / Hugh F. Cochrane. — London : W.H. Allen, 1981, c1980. — 183p,[8]p of plates : ill,1maps ; 18cm. — (A star book)
Originally published: Garden City, N.Y. : Doubleday ; London : W.H. Allen, 1980. — Bibliography: p175-176. - Includes index
ISBN 0-352-30811-7 (pbk) : £1.50 B81-17570

001.9′42 — Oxfordshire. Faringdon region. Extraterrestial beings. Claimed observations

Johnson, Frank, *1914-*. The Janos people : a close encounter of the fourth kind / Frank Johnson. — Sudbury : Spearman, 1980. — x,198p : ill,1map,plans,ports ; 23cm
Bibliography: p193-194. — Includes index
ISBN 0-85435-374-7 : £5.25 B81-03225

001.9′42 — Unidentified flying objects

Cathie, B. L.. Harmonic 695 : the UFO and anti-gravity / B.L. Cathie, P.N. Temm. — London : Sphere, 1980. — viii,204p,[8]p of plates : ill,maps,facsims ; 18cm
Originally published: Wellington, N.Z. : Reed, 1971. — Includes index
ISBN 0-7221-2279-9 (pbk) : £1.50 B81-00001

Cathie, B. L.. The pulse of the universe : Harmonic 288 / Bruce Cathie. — London : Sphere, 1981, c1977. — xix,214p : ill,maps,2plans ; 18cm
ISBN 0-7221-2280-2 (pbk) : £1.50 B81-20989

Story, Ronald. UFOs and the limits of science / Ronald D. Story with J. Richard Greenwell. — London : New English Library, 1981. — 245p,12p of plates : ill,maps,ports ; 23cm
Ill on lining papers
ISBN 0-450-04817-9 : £5.95 B81-15427

001.9′42 — Unidentified flying objects. Claimed observations by children

Bord, Janet. Are we being watched? : true UFO sightings by children around the world / Janet & Colin Bord. — London : Angus & Robertson, 1980. — 96p : ill ; 26cm
Bibliography: p96
ISBN 0-207-95898-x : £4.95 B81-09279

001.9′42′0321 — Unidentified flying objects — *Encyclopaedias*

Sachs, Margaret. The UFO encyclopedia / by Margaret Sachs. — [London] : Corgi, 1981, c1980. — 408p : ill,maps,1form,ports ; 24cm
Originally published: New York : Putnam, 1980. — Bibliography: p401-408
ISBN 0-552-98113-3 (pbk) : £4.95 B81-21403

001.9′42′0321 — Unidentified flying objects, *to 1978 — Encyclopaedias*

The **Encyclopedia** of UFOs / edited by Ronald D. Story ; J. Richard Greenwell, consulting editor. — London : New English Library, 1980. — x,440p,[8]p of plates : ill(some col.),maps,ports ; 29cm
Bibliography: p426-440
ISBN 0-450-04118-2 : £12.95 B81-01897

001.9′42′05 — Unidentified flying objects — *Serials*

The **Probe** report. — Vol.1, no.3 (Dec.1980)-. — Bristol (c/o 16 Marigold Walk, Ashton, Bristol BS3 2PD) : Probe, 1980-. — v. : ill ; 30cm
Quarterly. — Continues: Probe (Bristol). — Description based on: Vol.1, no.4 (Mar.1981)
ISSN 0260-8189 = Probe report : £1.00 per year B81-23153

Search (West) : UFO research group magazine. — No.1-. — [Melksham] ([c/o P.R. Vines, 120 Savernake Ave., Melksham, Wilts. SN12 7HQ]) : Search (West), [1980]-. — v. ; 30cm
Quarterly
ISSN 0260-8561 = Search West : £2.20 per year B81-34040

UFO insight. — Vol.1, no.1 (Nov.1978)-. — Crewe (2 Acer Ave., Crewe, Cheshire) : Federation U.F.O. Research, 1978-. — v. ; 29cm
Irregular
ISSN 0260-7506 = UFO insight : £1.80 for six issues B81-06707

001.9′42′072 — Unidentified flying objects. Investigation — *Manuals*

Randles, Jenny. UFO study : a handbook for enthusiasts / Jenny Randles. — London : Hale, 1981. — 271p,[8]p of plates : ill ; 23cm
Includes index
ISBN 0-7091-8864-1 : £7.95 B81-24556

001.9′42′0942713 — Cheshire. Middlewich region. Unidentified flying objects. Claimed observations, *1980*

Case history 210980/15/SRC-MAC / compiled by "Federation U.F.O. Research" ; edited by M.A. Tyrell. — Crewe (2 Acer Ave., Crewe, Cheshire) : [The Federation], [1981]. — 18p : ill,1map ; 30cm
Cover title: F.U.F.O.R. case history
Unpriced (pbk) B81-21736

001.9′42′0942962 — Dyfed. St Bride′s Bay region. Unidentified flying objects. Claimed observations, *1977*

Harold, Clive. The uninvited / Clive Harold ; abridged by J.R.C. and G.M. Yglesias. — Walton-on-Thames : Nelson, 1981. — 120p : 1map ; 19cm. — (Getaway)
Full ed.: London : Star Books, 1979
ISBN 0-17-432184-8 (pbk) : £0.95 B81-40036

001.9′42′0942962 — Dyfed. St. Bride′s Bay region. Unidentified flying objects. Claimed observations, *1977 - Reports, surveys*

Pugh, Randall. The Dyfed enigma. — Sevenoaks : Coronet Books, Aug.1981. — [192]p
Originally published: London : Faber, 1979
ISBN 0-340-26665-1 (pbk) : £1.50 : CIP entry B81-15819

001.9′42′0973 — United States. Unidentified flying objects. Claimed observations, *to 1979*

Fowler, Raymond E.. Casebook of a UFO investigator : a personal memoir / Raymond E. Fowler. — Englewood Cliffs ; London : Prentice-Hall, c1981. — 246p : ill ; 24cm
Bibliography: p235-238. — Includes index
ISBN 0-13-117432-0 (cased) : Unpriced
ISBN 0-13-117424-x (pbk) : £4.15 B81-28480

Gansberg, Judith M.. Direct encounters. — London : Hodder & Stoughton, Sept.1981. — [192]p. — (Coronet books)
Originally published: New York : Walker, 1980
ISBN 0-340-26685-6 (pbk) : £1.50 : CIP entry B81-22547

001.9′42′09789 — New Mexico. Unidentified flying objects. Claimed observations, *1947*

Berlitz, Charles. The Roswell incident / Charles Berlitz and William Moore. — London : Granada, 1980. — 176p,[16]p of plates : ill,maps,facsims,ports ; 22cm
Bibliography: p171-172. — Includes index
ISBN 0-246-11384-7 : £5.95 B81-40155

001.9′42′09791 — Arizona. Unidentified flying objects. Claimed observations, *1975*

Barry, Bill. Ultimate encounter : the true story of a UFO kidnapping / Bill Barry. — London : Corgi, 1981, c1978. — 205p ; 18cm
Originally published: New York : Pocket Books, 1978
ISBN 0-552-11619-x (pbk) : £1.25 B81-11571

001.9′42′0979493 — California. Tujunga Canyon. Unidentified flying objects. Claimed observations

Druffel, Ann. The Tujunga Canyon contacts / Ann Druffel & D. Scott Rogo. — Englewood Cliffs ; London : Prentice-Hall, c1980. — x,264p : ill,1map,1port ; 24cm
Includes index
ISBN 0-13-932541-7 : £7.65 B81-28473

001.9′44 — Loch Ness monster

Harmsworth, Anthony G.. The mysterious monsters of Loch Ness / by Anthony G. Harmsworth. — Huntingdon : Photo Precision, [1980]. — 32p : ill(some col.),1col.map,ports ; 24cm. — (Colourmaster International)
English text, French and German notes
ISBN 0-85933-201-2 (pbk) : Unpriced B81-30683

001.9′44 — Monsters — *For children*

Brett, Bernard. [Monsters]. A young person′s guide to monsters / Bernard Brett ; with illustrations by the author. — London : Granada, 1981, c1976. — 96p : ill ; 18cm. — (A Dragon book)
Originally published: Hove : Firefly, 1976
ISBN 0-583-30478-8 (pbk) : £0.85 B81-32914

001.94′4′094487 — France. Aude *(Department)*. **Rennes-le-Château. Curiosities & mysteries**

Baigent, Michael. The Holy Blood and the Holy Grail. — London : Cape, Jan.1982. — [432]p
ISBN 0-224-01735-7 : £8.50 : CIP entry B81-34555

001.9′5 — Fakes, *ca 1485-1978*

Salway, Lance. Forgers / Lance Salway. — Harmondsworth : Puffin, 1980, c1979. — 96p : ill,1map,facsims,ports ; 20cm
Originally published: Harmondsworth : Kestrel, 1979. — Bibliography: p91-92. - Includes index
ISBN 0-14-031114-9 (pbk) : £0.95 B81-00686

001.9′6 — Fallacies

Facts and fallacies : a book of definitive mistakes and misguided predictions / [compiled by] Chris Morgan and David Langford. — Exeter : Webb & Bower, 1981. — 176p ; 23cm
Includes index
ISBN 0-906671-25-6 : £5.95 B81-27034

Rosenbloom, Joseph. Bananas don′t grow on trees : a guide to popular misconceptions / Joseph Rosenbloom ; illustrations by Joyce Behr. — London : Pan, 1981, c1978. — 126p : ill ; 18cm. — (Piccolo books)
Originally published: New York : Sterling, 1978. — Includes index
ISBN 0-330-26290-4 (pbk) : £0.90 B81-15050

002 — THE BOOK

002′.075 — Books. Collecting — *Encyclopaedias*

Carter, John, *1905-1976*. ABC for book collectors / by John Carter. — 6th ed. / with corrections and additions by Nicolas Barker. — London : Granada, 1980. — 219p ; 21cm
Previous ed.: London : Hart-Davis, 1972. — Text on lining papers
ISBN 0-246-11352-9 : £7.50 B81-05700

002′.075 — Erotic books — *Collectors' guides*

Lewis, Roy Harley. The book browser's guide to erotica / Roy Harley Lewis. — Newton Abbot : David & Charles, c1981. — 199p : ill,facsims ; 23cm
Bibliography: p192-194. — Includes index
ISBN 0-7153-7949-6 : £8.95 : CIP rev.
B81-22511

002′.75 — Book collectors - *Directories - Serials*

The **International** directory of book collectors. — 1981-83. — Beckenham (117 Kent House Rd, Beckenham, Kent BR3 1JJ) : Trigon Press, Apr.1981. — 1v.
ISBN 0-904929-20-5 : £16.00 : CIP entry
B81-08932

003 — SYSTEMS

003 — Autopoiesis

Autopoiesis : a theory of living organization / edited by Milan Zeleny. — New York ; Oxford : North Holland, c1981. — xvii,314p : ill ; 24cm. — (The North Holland series in general systems research ; v.3)
Includes bibliographies and index
ISBN 0-444-00385-1 : £22.90 B81-23636

003 — Dynamical systems. Stability

Instabilities in dynamical systems : applications to celestial mechanics : proceedings of the NATO Advanced Study Institute held at Cortina D'Ampezzo, Italy, July 30-August 12, 1978 / edited by Victor G. Szebehely. — Dordrecht ; London : Reidel in cooperation with NATO Scientific Affairs Division, c1979. — xxiv,314p : ill,ports ; 25cm. — (NATO advanced study institutes series. Series C, mathematical and physical sciences ; v.47)
Includes bibliographies and index
ISBN 90-277-0973-4 : Unpriced B81-16613

003 — Dynamical systems theory — *For management*

System dynamics / edited by Augusto A. Legasto, Jr., Jay W. Forrester, James M. Lyneis. — Amsterdam ; Oxford : North-Holland, c1980. — ix,282p : ill ; 24cm. — (TIMS studies in the management sciences ; v.14)
Bibliography: p259-271
ISBN 0-444-85491-6 (pbk) : Unpriced
B81-13250

003 — Forecasting

Lewis, C. D.. Industrial and business forecasting methods. — London : Butterworth, Feb.1982. — [148]p
ISBN 0-408-00559-9 : £8.95 : CIP entry
B81-39222

003 — General systems theory

Bowler, T. Downing. General systems thinking : its scope and applicability / T. Downing Bowler. — New York ; Oxford : North-Holland, c1981. — xii,234p : ill ; 24cm. — (The North Holland series in general systems research ; v.4)
Includes index
ISBN 0-444-00420-3 : Unpriced B81-25605

Systems behaviour. — 3rd ed. — London : Harper and Row, Jan.1982. — [330]p
Previous ed.: 1976
ISBN 0-06-318211-4 (cased) : £12.00 : CIP entry
ISBN 0-06-318212-2 (pbk) : £5.95 B81-33971

003 — Large scale systems. Automatic control — *Conference proceedings*

Comparison of automatic control and operational research techniques applied to large systems analysis and control : IFAC/IFORS Symposium, Toulouse, France, 1979 / editors M.J. Pelegrin and J.H. Delmas. — Oxford : Pergamon, 1980. — ix,233p : ill ; 31cm
Papers in English or French. — Includes bibliographies and index
ISBN 0-08-024454-8 : £17.00 : CIP rev.
Also classified at 003 B80-18562

003 — Large scale systems. Resources. Management. Mathematical models

Suri, Rajan. Resource management concepts for large systems / by Rajan Suri. — Oxford : Pergamon, 1981. — 83p : ill ; 24cm. — (International series in modern applied mathematics and computer science ; v.3)
Bibliography: p75-77. — Includes index
ISBN 0-08-026473-5 : £7.00 : CIP rev.
B81-12372

003 — Large scale systems. Systems analysis. Applications of operations research — *Conference proceedings*

Comparison of automatic control and operational research techniques applied to large systems analysis and control : IFAC/IFORS Symposium, Toulouse, France, 1979 / editors M.J. Pelegrin and J.H. Delmas. — Oxford : Pergamon, 1980. — ix,233p : ill ; 31cm
Papers in English or French. — Includes bibliographies and index
ISBN 0-08-024454-8 : £17.00 : CIP rev.
Primary classification 003 B80-18562

003 — Large scale systems theory — *Conference proceedings*

Large scale systems theory and applications : proceedings of the IFAC Symposium, Toulouse, France, 24-26 June 1980 / edited by André Titli, Madan G. Singh. — Oxford : Published for the International Federation of Automatic Control by Pergamon, 1981. — xxxiii,614p : ill ; 31cm. — (IFAC proceedings series)
Includes bibliographies and index
ISBN 0-08-024484-x : £50.00 : CIP rev.
B80-18567

003 — Linear systems. Stability

Harris, C. J.. Stability of linear systems : some aspects of kinematic similarity / C.J. Harris and J.F. Miles. — London : Academic Press, 1980. — x,236p : ill ; 24cm. — (Mathematics in science and engineering ; v.153)
Bibliography: p220-231. — Includes index
ISBN 0-12-328250-0 : £9.80 B81-06564

003 — Nonlinear systems. Stability

Atherton, Derek P.. Stability of nonlinear systems / Derek P. Atherton. — Chichester : Research Studies Press, c1981. — xii,231p : ill ; 24cm. — (Electronic & electrical engineering research studies. Control theory and applications studies series ; 1)
Includes index
ISBN 0-471-27856-4 : £15.00 : CIP rev.
B80-28973

003 — Systems

Bennett, R. J.. Environmental systems : philosophy, analysis and control / R.J. Bennett and R.J. Chorley. — London : Methuen, 1978 (1980 [printing]). — xii,624p : ill ; 24cm. — (University paperbacks ; 695)
Bibliography: p566-598. — Includes index
ISBN 0-416-73580-0 (pbk) : £10.00 : CIP rev.
B79-37114

Systems organization : the management of complexity / [Systems Organization Course Team]. — Milton Keynes : Open University Press. — (Technology : a second level course)
At head of title: Open University
Block 1: Introduction to systems thinking and organization. — 1980. — 69p : ill ; 30cm. — (T243 ; block 1)
Bibliography: p69. — Contents: Units 1/2. Introduction to systems thinking and organization
ISBN 0-335-17030-7 (pbk) : Unpriced
B81-39321

Systems organization : the management of complexity / [Systems Organization Course Team]. — Milton Keynes : Open University Press. — (Technology : a second level course)
At head of title: Open University
Block 2: Subsystems : operations, people and groups. — 1980. — 31,43,39p : ill ; 30cm. — (T243 ; block 2)
Includes bibliographies. — Contents: Unit 3. The control model — Unit 4. Man the irrational animal — Unit 5. Beyond the control model
ISBN 0-335-17031-5 (pbk) : Unpriced B81-39322

Systems organization : the management of complexity / [Systems Organization Course Team]. — Milton Keynes : Open University Press. — (Technology : a second level course)
At head of title: Open University
Block 3: Organizations. — 1980. — 193p in various pagings : ill ; 30cm. — (T243 : block 3)
Includes bibliographies. — Contents: Unit 6. Organizations in practice — Unit 7. Organizational structures — Unit 8. Information — Unit 9. Organizational conflict
ISBN 0-335-17032-3 (pbk) : Unpriced
B81-39323

Systems organization : the management of complexity / [Systems Organization Course Team]. — Milton Keynes : Open University Press. — (Technology : a second level course)
At head of title: Open University
Block 4: Multiorganizations. — 1980. — 42,39p : ill ; 30cm. — (T243 ; block 4)
Includes bibliographies. — Contents: Unit 10. Multiorganizations — Units 11/12. Implementing values
ISBN 0-335-17033-1 (pbk) : Unpriced
B81-39324

Systems thinking : selected readings / edited by F.E. Emery. — Harmondsworth : Penguin Education. — (Penguin modern management readings)
Previous ed.: published in 1 vol. 1969. — Includes bibliographies and index
1. — 1981. — 429p : ill ; 20cm
ISBN 0-14-080395-5 (pbk) : £5.95 B81-16991

Systems thinking : selected readings / edited by F.E. Emery. — Harmondsworth : Penguin Education, 1981. — (Penguin modern management readings)
Previous ed.: published in 1 vol. 1969. — Includes bibliographies and index
2. — 477p : ill ; 20cm
ISBN 0-14-080396-3 (pbk) : £5.95 B81-16990

003 — Systems analysis

Daniels, Alan. Basic systems analysis. — London : Pitman, Nov.1981. — [270]p
ISBN 0-273-01731-4 : £5.95 : CIP entry
B81-30299

Medina, Barbara F.. Structured system analysis : a new technique / Barbara F. Medina. — New York ; London : Gordon and Breach Science, 1981. — xii,80p : ill ; 24cm
Bibliography: p77-80. — Includes index
ISBN 0-677-05570-6 : Unpriced B81-35179

003 — Systems. Dynamics. Mathematical models — *Conference proceedings*

International Conference on System Dynamics *(6th : 1980 : University of Paris-Dauphine)*. System dynamics and the analysis of change : proceedings of the 6th International Conference on System dynamics, University of Paris-Dauphine, November, 1980, organized by A.F.C.E.T. / edited by E. Paulré. — Amsterdam ; Oxford : North-Holland, c1981. — xii,382p : ill ; 24cm
ISBN 0-444-86251-x : £26.57 B81-39269

003 — Systems theory

Checkland, Peter. Systems thinking, systems practice / Peter Checkland. — Chichester : Wiley, c1981. — xiv,330p : ill ; 24cm
Bibliography: p299-311. - Includes index
ISBN 0-471-27911-0 : £11.95 : CIP rev.
B81-15940

003′.01′51635 — Systems theory. Applications of algebraic geometry — *Conference proceedings*

Geometrical methods for the theory of linear systems : proceedings of a NATO Advanced Study Institute and AMS Summer Seminar in Applied Mathematics, held at Harvard University, Cambridge, Mass., June 18-29 1979 / edited by Christopher I. Byrnes and Clyde F. Martin. — Dordrecht ; London : Reidel published in cooperation with NATO Scientific Affairs Division, c1980. — ix,317p : ill ; 25cm. — (NATO advanced study institutes series. Series C, Mathematical and physical sciences ; v.62)
Includes bibliographies and index
ISBN 90-277-1154-2 : Unpriced B81-05521

003'.0724 — Large scale systems. Mathematical models
Mahmoud, Magdi S.. Large scale systems modelling. — Oxford : Pergamon, Dec.1981. — [350]p. — (International series on system and control ; v.3)
ISBN 0-08-027313-0 : £25.00 : CIP entry B81-31355

003'.0724 — Systems. Mathematical models: Petri nets
Peterson, James L.. Petri net theory and the modeling of systems / James L. Peterson. — Englewood Cliffs ; London : Prentice-Hall, c1981. — x,290p : ill ; 24cm
Bibliography: p241-278. — Includes index
ISBN 0-13-661983-5 : £16.05 B81-27780

003'.0724 — Systems. Simulation. Applications of digital computer systems — *Conference proceedings*
UKSC Conference on Computer Simulation *(1981 : Harrogate)*. UKSC 81 : proceedings of the 1981 UKSC Conference on Computer Simulation, 13-15 May 1981, Old Swan Hotel, Harrogate, England / [Conference sponsored by United Kingdom Simulation Council (UKSC), The Society for Computer Simulation (SCS)]. — Guildford : Westury House, c1981. — xii,451p : ill ; 25cm
Includes index
ISBN 0-86103-051-6 : Unpriced B81-25566

010 — BIBLIOGRAPHY

010 — Bibliography
Harmon, Robert B.. Elements of bibliography : a simplified approach / Robert B. Harmon. — Metuchen, N.J. ; London : Scarecrow Press, 1981. — viii,253p ; 23cm
Bibliography: p204-222. — Includes index
ISBN 0-8108-1429-3 : £8.75 B81-36523

011 — BIBLIOGRAPHIES

011 — Books — *Lists*
The **Anti-book** list. — London : Hodder & Stoughton, Oct.1981. — [128]p
ISBN 0-340-27084-5 (cased) : £6.25 : CIP entry
ISBN 0-340-27447-6 (pbk) : £1.95 B81-25755

011'.02 — Middle schools. Libraries. Stock: Reference books — *Lists*
Guide to reference books for middle schools / Buckinghamshire County Library. — [Aylesbury] ([Walton St., Aylesbury, Bucks HP20 1UU]) : The Library, 1981. — 26p : ill ; 21cm
Cover title. — Includes index
ISBN 0-86059-113-1 (pbk) : £1.00 B81-25193

011'.02 — Reference books — *Lists*
Chandler, G.. How to find out. — 5th ed. — Oxford : Pergamon, Aug.1981. — [240]p
Previous ed.: 1974
ISBN 0-08-027433-1 : £10.00 : CIP entry B81-17514

Walford's concise guide to reference material / edited by A.J. Walford. — London : Library Association, 1981. — x,434p ; 25cm
Includes index
ISBN 0-85365-882-x : Unpriced : CIP rev. B81-07460

011'.02'024092 — Reference books — *Lists* — *For British public libraries* — *Serials*
The **top** 1,000 directories & annuals : a guide to the major titles used in British libraries. — 1981-. — Reading (8 Queen Victoria St., Reading, Berks. RG1 1TG) : Alan Armstrong, 1981-. — v. ; 30cm
Annual. — Continues: The Top 1,000 directories used in British libraries
ISSN 0262-0219 = Top 1,000 directories & annuals : £17.95 B81-38995

011'.29163 — Books in Gaelic, *1900-1973* — *Bibliographies*
Macleod, Donald John. Twentieth century publications in Scottish Gaelic / [compiled by] Donald John Macleod. — Edinburgh : Scottish Academic, 1980. — viii,188p ; 26cm
ISBN 0-7073-0266-8 : £12.50 B81-36809

011'.31 — Great Britain. Records. Repositories. Stock: Manuscripts: Acquisitions — *Lists* — *Serials*
Accessions to repositories and reports added to the National register of archives / the Royal Commission on Historical Manuscripts. — 1979. — London : H.M.S.O., 1980. — iv,76p
ISBN 0-11-440112-8 : £4.40
ISSN 0308-0986 B81-06298

011'.34 — Europe. Directories — *Lists*
Henderson, G. P. (George Poland). Current European directories : a guide to international, national, city and specialised directories and similar reference works for all countries of Europe - excluding Great Britain and Ireland = Répertoires des annuaires européennes = Handbuch der europäischen Adressbücher = Repertorio degli annuari europei = Catalogus van europese adresboeken = Repertorio de los anuarios europeos / G.P. Henderson. — Beckenham : CBD Research, 1981. — xix,413p ; 31cm
Introduction, text and index in English, French and German. — Previous ed.: 1969. — Includes index
ISBN 0-900246-30-8 : £45.00 B81-39861

011'.34 — House journals — *Lists* — *For libraries*
Smith, Adeline Mercer. Free magazines for libraries / Adeline Mercer Smith. — Jefferson, N.C. : McFarland ; Folkestone : distributed by Bailey & Swinfen, 1980. — xxi,258p ; 24cm
Includes index
ISBN 0-89950-021-8 : £13.55 B81-37032

011'.34'05 — Great Britain. Libraries. Stock: Serials — *Catalogues* — *Serials*
British union-catalogue of periodicals. New periodical titles / edited for the British Library. — 1980. — London : Butterworths, 1981. — [107]p in various pagings
ISBN 0-408-70861-1 : £25.00
ISSN 0007-1919 B81-29662

Serials in the British Library : together with locations and holdings of other British and Irish libraries. — No.1 (June 1981)-. — London : The British Library, Bibliographic Services Division, 1981-. — v. ; 30cm
Quarterly. — Continues: British union-catalogue of periodicals. New periodical titles
ISSN 0260-0005 = Serials in the British Library : £25.00 per year B81-20458

011'.36'05 — Microforms in print — *Lists* — *Serials*
Guide to microforms in print. Author, title. — 1980. — London : Mansell Publishing, c1980. — xxx,769p
ISBN 0-7201-1578-7 : £29.00 : CIP rev. B80-11706

Guide to microforms in print. Author-title. — 1981. — London : Mansell, Sept.1981. — [840]p
ISBN 0-7201-1638-4 : £40.00 : CIP entry
ISSN 0164-0747 B81-26689

Guide to microforms in print. Subject. — 1980. — London : Mansell Publishing, c1980. — xxxvi,1094p
ISBN 0-7201-1582-5 : £33.00 : CIP rev. B80-11707

Guide to microforms in print. Subject. — 1981. — London : Mansell Publishing, Sept.1981. — [1200]p
ISBN 0-7201-1639-2 : £43.00 : CIP entry B81-30272

011'.37 — Cinema films — *Filmographies*
Steinberg, Cobbett. Reel facts : the movie book of records / Cobbett Steinberg. — Rev. ed. — Harmondsworth : Penguin, 1981. — 587p ; 20cm
Previous ed.: New York : Vintage, 1978
ISBN 0-14-005335-2 (pbk) : £2.95 B81-21002

011'.37 — Cinema films — *Filmographies* — *Serials*
Annual index to motion picture credits / Academy of Motion Picture Arts and Sciences. — 1978-. — Westport ; London : Greenwood, [1979?]-. — v. ; 29cm
Two interim indices issued cumulating annually. — Continues: Screen achievement records bulletin. — Description based on: 1979 issue
Unpriced B81-11228

011'.37 — London. Hounslow *(London Borough)*. **Cinema films. Organisations: Rank Film Library. Stock: Cinema films available for hire** — *Catalogues* — *Serials*
Rank Film Library. Rank Film Library 16mm entertainment film catalogue. — 1981/2. — Brentford (Rank Audio Visual Ltd, P.O. Box 20, Great West Rd, Brentford, Middlesex TW8 9HR) : The Library, 1981. — 220p
£2.00 B81-30851

011'.37 — United States. 16mm cinema films based on books: Short films — *Lists*
Parlato, Salvatore J.. Films ex libris : literature in 16mm and video Salvatore J. Parlato, Jr. — Jefferson, N.C. : McFarland ; Folkestone : Distributed by Bailey & Swinfen, 1980. — xii,271p : ill ; 24cm
Includes index
ISBN 0-89950-006-4 : £12.75 B81-37668

011'.37 — United States. Cinema films: Educational films. Organisations: Consortium of University Film Centers. Libraries. Stock — *Lists* — *Serials*
Educational film locator of the Consortium of University Film Centers and R.R. Bowker Company. — 2nd ed. (1980). — New York ; London : Bowker, c1980. — xxxvii,2611p
ISBN 0-8352-1295-5 : Unpriced B81-20076

011'.38'028 — Sound recordings. Discographies. Compilation — *Manuals*
Rust, Brian. Brian Rust's guide to discography / Brian Rust. — Westport, Conn. ; London : Greenwood Press, 1980. — x,133p : facsims ; 25cm. — (Discographies ; no.4)
Bibliography: p89-103. — Includes index
ISBN 0-313-22086-7 : £12.95 B81-23471

011'.52 — Commission of the European Communities. Publications — *Lists*
Hopkins, Michael, *1945-*. Policy formation in the European Communities : a bibliographic guide to Community documentation 1958-1978 / Michael Hopkins. — London : Mansell, 1981. — xx,339p ; 24cm
Includes index
ISBN 0-7201-1597-3 : £24.50 B81-30026

011'.52 — European Community. Publications — *Lists*
Jeffries, John. A guide to official publications of the European Communities / John Jeffries. — 2nd ed. — London : Mansell, 1981. — xiv,318p ; 23cm
Previous ed.: 1978. — Bibliography: p284-287. — Includes index
ISBN 0-7201-1590-6 : £21.00 : CIP rev. B80-32792

011'.52 — European Community. Publications: Reports. Authors & chairmen, *to 1977* — *Lists*
Neilson, June. Reports of the European Communities 1952-1977 : an index to authors and chairmen / compiled by June Neilson. — London : Mansell, 1981. — xiv,561p ; 23cm
Includes index
ISBN 0-7201-1592-2 : £27.50 B81-29264

011'.62 — Children's books — *Bibliographies* — *For teaching*
A **Wider** heritage : a selection of books for children and young people in multicultural Britain / compiled by Ruth Ballin, Jean Bleach, Josie Levine. — London : National Book League, 1980. — 66p ; 21cm
ISBN 0-85353-344-x (pbk) : £1.80 (£1.50 to members) B81-04617

011′.62 — Children's books in Welsh — *Lists — Welsh texts*

Jones, Rhiannon Clifford. Llyfrau Cymraeg i blant / trefnwyd gan Rhiannon Clifford Jones. — [Caernarfon] (['Maesincla', Caernarfon, Gwynedd]) : Gwasanaeth Llyfrgell Gwynedd, 1980. — 42p ; 21cm
Includes index
£0.25 (pbk) B81-12264

011′.625054 — Children's books in English, *to 1945 — Chronologies*

Bingham, Jane. Fifteen centuries of children's literature : an annotated chronology of British and American works in historical context / Jane Bingham and Grayce Scholt. — Westport, Conn. ; London : Greenwood Press, 1980. — xlix,540p : ill,facsims ; 25cm
Bibliography: p407-418. — Includes index
ISBN 0-313-22164-2 : £21.95 B81-23599

011′.625054 — Children's reference books — *Lists*

Peterson, Carolyn Sue. Reference books for children / Carolyn Sue Peterson and Anne D. Fenton. — Metuchen ; London : Scarecrow, c1981. — viii,265p ; 23cm
Previous ed.: published as Reference books for elementary and junior high school libraries. 1975. — Includes index
ISBN 0-8108-1441-2 : £10.80 B81-38414

011′.625054′05 — Children's books — *Bibliographies — Serials*

Children's books of the year. — 1980. — London : Julia MacRea Books in association with the National Book League, 1981. — 160p
ISBN 0-86203-032-3 : £3.95 : CIP rev.
B81-14910

012 — BIBLIOGRAPHIES OF INDIVIDUALS

012 — West Yorkshire *(Metropolitan County).* **Leeds. Universities: University of Leeds.** *School of English.* **Walsh, William** — *Bibliographies*

William Walsh : professor of education, 1957-1972, professor of Commonwealth literature and Douglas Grant Fellow 1972-1981. — [Leeds] ([Leeds LS2 9JT]) : [The School of English, University of Leeds], 1981. — 11p ; 26cm
Limited ed. of 75 copies
Unpriced (pbk) B81-33746

013 — BIBLIOGRAPHIES OF SPECIFIC CLASSES OF WRITERS

013′.335 — Radical documents with British imprints — *Lists — Serials*

The **radical** bookseller. — No.1 (Oct.1980)-. — London (27 Clerkenwell Close, EC1R 0AT) : Radical Bookseller, 1980-. — v. : ill ; 30cm
Ten issues yearly. — With: Radical books of the month
ISSN 0144-1779 = Radical bookseller : £15.00 per year
Also classified at 380.1′45002′0941 B81-06779

015 — BIBLIOGRAPHIES OF WORKS FROM SPECIFIC PLACES

015′.41 — Great Britain. Official publications: Documents not published by Great Britain. *Her Majesty's Stationery Office - Lists - Serials*

Catalogue of British official publications not published by HMSO. — 1980. — Cambridge : Chadwyck-Healey, May 1981. — [256]p
ISBN 0-85964-101-5 : £80.00 : CIP entry
ISSN 0260-5619 B81-12904

015.41 — Serials with British imprints. Special reports — *Indexes — Serials*

Hunter, N. R.. Index to special reports in U.K. newspapers and selected periodicals / compiled by Neil Hunter. — 1978-80. — Hartlepool (10 MacDonald Place, Headland, Hartlepool, Cleveland TS24 0PZ) : Headland Press, c1981. — 53p
ISBN 0-906889-02-2 : £7.95 B81-29982

015.41 — Subscription books with subscription lists: Books with British imprints, *1617-1973 — Lists*

Book subscription lists : a revised guide. — [Newcastle upon Tyne] : Project for Historical Biobibliography, University of Newcastle upon Tyne. — (PHIBB ; 275)
4th supplement / [compiled by] Barbara White, Peter J. Wallis. — 1981. — 26p ; 21cm
Includes index
ISBN 0-7017-0027-0 (unbound) : Unpriced
B81-37420

015.41′03′05 — Books with British imprints — *Lists — Serials*

. British books in print. — 1980. — London : Whitaker, c1980. — 2v.
ISBN 0-85021-119-0 : Unpriced B81-09704

British national bibliography. — 1980. — London : British Library, Bibliographic Services Division, c1981. — 2v.
ISBN 0-900220-93-7 : £76.00 : CIP rev.
ISSN 0007-1544 B81-01852

Whitaker's cumulative book list. — Pt.218 (Jan.-Dec.1978). — London : Whitaker, c1979. — xxxv,860p
ISBN 0-85021-112-3 : £8.00
ISSN 0140-4229 B81-29431

015.41′034 — Serials with British imprints, *1800-1900.* **Criticism** — *Bibliographies*

Madden, Lionel. The nineteenth-century periodical press in Britain : a bibliography of modern studies 1901-1971 / [compiled by] Lionel Madden and Diana Dixon. — New York ; London : Garland, 1976. — xiv,280p ; 23cm. — (Garland reference library of the humanities ; v.53)
Includes index
ISBN 0-8240-9945-1 : Unpriced B81-31785

015.41′034′05 — Serials with British imprints — *Indexes — Serials*

British humanities index. — 1980. — London : Library Association, c1981. — 630,256p
ISBN 0-85365-744-0 : Unpriced
ISSN 0007-0815 B81-32666

015.41′034′05 — Serials with British imprints — *Lists — Serials*

Technical and specialist periodicals published in Britain. — [1980]. — London ([Hercules Rd, SE1 7DU]) : Central Office of Information, [c1981]. — 275p
Unpriced B81-24119

015.41′037′05 — Audiovisual materials with British imprints — *Lists — Serials*

British catalogue of audiovisual materials. Supplement. — 1980-. — London : The British Library, Bibliographic Services Division, 1980-. — v. ; 30cm
Supplement to: British catalogue of audiovisual materials
ISBN 0-900220-85-6 : £12.50 : CIP rev.
ISSN 0260-9746 = British catalogue of audiovisual materials. Supplement B80-30587

015.41′044 — Great Britain. Books. Organisations: National Book League. Exhibits: Books notable for design & production: Books with British imprints — *Catalogues — Serials*

British book design and production / the National Book League. — 1980. — London : National Book League, 1980. — 50p
ISBN 0-85353-355-5 : Unpriced
ISSN 0302-2846 B81-06717

015.41′053 — Great Britain. *Public Record Office.* **Stock: State papers domestic,** *to 1820 — Lists*

Great Britain. *State Paper Office*. Index to state papers, domestic supplementary. — London : Swift. — (Publications / List & Index Society ; v.178)
Pt.3: General papers, chiefly 1603-42 : (SP 46/61-70, 78-80, 82, 89, 127, 131, 164). — 1981. — 95p ; 33cm
Papers held at the Public Record Office, formerly held by the State Paper Office. — At head of title: List & Index Society
£5.50 (Subscribers only) B81-34273

Great Britain. *State Paper Office*. Index to state papers, domestic supplementary. — London : Swift. — (Publications / List & Index Society ; v.182)
Pt.7: Private papers, series III, 1511, 1563-1712 : (SP 46/44-46, 47, 50-56, 139). — 1981. — 163p ; 33cm
Papers now held at the Public Record Office, formerly held by the State Paper Office. — At head of title: List & Index Society
£7.15 (Subscribers only) B81-34274

015.41′053′05 — British government publications: Serials — *Lists — Serials*

Checklist of British official serial publications / the British Library Reference Division. — 11th ed. (1980). — London : British Library Reference Division Publications, c1980. — 102p
ISBN 0-904654-53-2 : Unpriced
ISSN 0084-8085 B81-06716

015.41′0532 — Great Britain. *Central Office of Information. Reference Services.* **Publications** — *Lists — Serials*

Great Britain. *Central Office of Information. Reference Services*. Catalogue of reference documents / prepared [by Reference Services, Publications Division, Central Office of Information] for British Information Services. — Jan.1981. — London ([Hercules Rd, SE1 7DU]) : [The Division], [1981]. — 8p
Unpriced B81-36535

015.41′0532′05 — British parliamentary papers — *Indexes — Serials*

Great Britain. *Parliament. House of Commons*. Sessional index for session .... — 25th and 26th Elizabeth II, 47th Parliament - 3rd Session. — London : H.M.S.O., 1977. — vi,196p
ISBN 0-10-260477-0 : £4.00 B81-06947

015.41′062 — Children's books: Books for children, to 12 years: Books with British imprints — *Bibliographies*

Wood, Anne, *1937-*. Children and books / by Anne Wood and Jean Russell. — 2nd ed. — [Billericay] ([17 Jacksons La., Billericay, Essex, CM11 1AH]) : Home and School Council, c1979. — 24p : ill ; 21cm
Cover title. — Previous ed.: 1973. — Bibliography: p15-24
ISBN 0-901181-32-3 (pbk) : £0.40 B81-08495

015.415′03′05 — Books with Irish imprints — *Bibliographies — Serials*

Irish publishing record. — 1980. — Dublin ([Belfield, Dublin 4]) : The Library, University College Dublin, c1981. — 167p
ISSN 0579-4056 : Unpriced B81-33470

015.415′031 — Ireland *(Republic).* **National libraries: National Library of Ireland. Stock: Irish manuscripts** — *Catalogues*

National Library of Ireland. Catalogue of Irish manuscripts in the National Library of Ireland. — Dublin : Dublin Institute for Advanced Studies
Fasc.6: Mss. G208-257 / Nessa Ní Shéaghdha. — 1980. — iii,83p ; 25cm
Unpriced (pbk) B81-23230

015.415′053 — Ireland *(Republic)* **government publications** — *Lists*

Maltby, Arthur. Irish offical publications : a guide to Republic of Ireland papers, with a breviate fo reports 1922-1972 / by Arthur Maltby and Brian McKenna. — Oxford : Pergamon, 1980. — xi,377p : ill,facsims ; 26cm. — (Guides to official publications ; v.7)
Includes index
ISBN 0-08-023703-7 : £22.50 B81-03425

015.421′07 — London. Camden *(London Borough).* **Universities. Libraries: University of London.** *Library.* **Stock: Theses accepted by University of London** — *Catalogues — Serials*

University of London. Theses and dissertations accepted for the degrees of M.Phil. and Ph.D. 1 October ... -30 September ... : arranged under boards of studies with an author index / University of London ; prepared by the University of London Library. — 1977-1978-. — London : The University, 1979-. — v. ; 21
Annual. — Continues: University of London. Theses and dissertations accepted for higher degrees 1 October ... -30 September .... — Description based on: 1978-1979 issue
£2.50 B81-27321

015.429'03'05 — Books with Welsh imprints — *Lists — Welsh texts — Serials*

Catalog llyfrau Cymraeg. — 1978. — Aberystwyth (Sgwâr y Frenhines, Aberystwyth, Dyfed) : Cyngor Lly'frau Cymraeg, [1978]. — 38p
Unpriced B81-10579

015.494'3 — Books with Swiss imprints: Books with Lausanne & books with Morges imprints, *1550-1600 — Bibliographies*

Draft bibliography of Lausanne & Morges imprints 1550-1600. — Oxford : [Bodleian Library], 1981. — iv,52p ; 21cm
Compiled by J.W. Jolliffe
Private circulation (pbk) B81-25898

015.52'053 — Japanese government publications

Kuroki, Tsutomu. An introduction to Japanese government publications / by Tsutomu Kuroki ; translated by Masako Kishi ; with an annotated bibliography by Chine Hayeshi. — Oxford : Pergamon, 1981. — x,204p ; 22cm. — (Guides to official publications ; v.10)
Translation of: Seifu kankobutsu gaisetsu. — Includes bibliographies and index
ISBN 0-08-024679-6 : £20.00 B81-22987

015.73 — Books in English: Books with American imprints *— Lists — Serials*

The **Publishers'** trade list annual. — 1980. — New York ; London : Bowker, c1980. — 6v.
ISBN 0-8352-1289-0 : Unpriced B81-00687

015.73'03 — Books in English: Books with American imprints: Books in print *— Lists — Serials*

Books in print. — 1980-1981. — New York ; London : Bowker, c1980. — 4v.
ISBN 0-8352-1300-5 : Unpriced B81-02800

015.73'03'05 — Books in English: Books with American imprints: Books in print *— Lists — Serials*

American book publishing record. Cumulative. — 1980. — New York ; London : Bowker, 1981. — 1264p
ISBN 0-8352-1367-6 : Unpriced
ISSN 0002-7707 B81-30847

Books in print. Supplement. — 1980-1981. — New York ; London : Bowker, c1981. — xv,3192p
ISBN 0-8352-1328-5 : Unpriced
ISSN 0000-0310 B81-31585

015.73'032'05 — Paperback books with American imprints: Books in print *— Lists — Serials*

Paperbound books in print. — Spring 1981. — New York ; London : Bowker, c1981. — 2v.(xv,4272p.)
ISBN 0-8352-1330-7 : Unpriced B81-32273

015.73'034 — Serials with American imprints — *Lists — For librarianship*

Marshall, Joan K.. Serials for libraries : an annotated guide to continuations, annuals, yearbooks, almanacs, transactions, proceedings, directories, services / compiled by Joan K. Marshall. — New York : Neal/Schuman ; Oxford : ABC-Clio, c1979 (1980 printing). — xv,494p ; 29cm
Includes index
ISBN 0-87436-280-6 : £27.50 B81-23352

015.73'053 — United States. Libraries. Stock: American government publications, *to 1956 — Author catalogues*

[National union catalogue pre-1956 imprints. *Selections*]. United States government publications : an author index representing pre-1956 holdings of American libraries reported to the National Union Catalogue in the Library of Congress. — London : Mansell, 1980. — 16v. ; 36cm
Originally published: as vols. 609-624. 1968. — Text on lining papers
ISBN 0-7201-1509-4 : £464.00 : CIP rev. B79-36129

015.73'062 — United States. Children's books: Paperback books with American imprints *— Lists — Serials*

Paperbound books for young people : preschool through grade 12. — 1st ed. — New York ; London : Bowker, 1979-. — v. ; 28cm
Description based on: 2nd ed.
Unpriced B81-09690

015.73'062'05 — Young persons' books in English: Books with American imprints: Books in print *— Lists — Serials*

Children's books in print. — 1980-1981. — New York ; London : Bowker, c1980. — 889p
ISBN 0-8352-1311-0 : Unpriced
ISSN 0069-3480 B81-15174

Subject guide to children's books in print. — 1980-1981. — New York ; London : Bowker, c1980. — 469p
ISBN 0-8352-1312-9 : Unpriced B81-18809

015.73'0625054 — Children's books in English: Books for children, to 13 years: Books with American imprints: Books in print *— Lists*

Best books for children : preschool through the middle grades. — 2nd ed. / edited by John T. Gillespie and Christine B. Gilbert. — New York ; London : Bowker, 1981. — xii,635p ; 27cm
Previous ed.: i.e. New ed. 1978. — Includes index
ISBN 0-8352-1332-3 : Unpriced B81-24187

015.73'0625055 — Books for secondary school students: Books with American imprints *— Lists*

Books for secondary school libraries / compiled by the Ad Hoc Library Committee of the National Association of Independent Schools. — 6th ed. — New York ; London : Bowker, 1981. — viii,844p ; 24cm
Previous ed.: 1976. — Includes index
ISBN 0-8352-1111-8 : Unpriced B81-20265

015.73'07 — School texts in print: School texts with American imprints *— Lists — Serials*

EL-HI textbooks in print. — 1981. — New York ; London : Bowker, c1981. — xi,769p
ISBN 0-8352-1357-9 : Unpriced B81-29046

015.94'053 — Australian government publications *— Lists*

Coxon, Howard. Australian official publications / by Howard Coxon. — Oxford : Pergamon, 1980. — xvi,211p,[1] leaf of plates : ill,facsims ; 26cm. — (Guides to official publications ; v.5)
Bibliography: p187-199. - Includes index
ISBN 0-08-023131-4 : £15.00 B81-03424

016 — BIBLIOGRAPHIES OF SPECIFIC SUBJECTS

016.00151 — Communication *— Abstracts — Serials*

Communication abstracts : an international information service. — Vol.1, no.1 (Mar.1978)-. — Beverly Hills ; London : Sage, with the cooperation of the School of Communications and Theater, Temple University, Philadelphia, Pennsylvania, 1978-. — v. ; 22cm
Quarterly
ISSN 0162-2811 = Communication abstracts : Unpriced B81-03845

016'.0015535 — Berkshire. Reading. Universities. Libraries: University of Reading. *Library.* **Exhibits: Documents associated with Isotype Movement** *— Catalogues*

Graphic communication through Isotype. — 2nd rev. ed. — Reading (2 Early Gate, Whiteknights, Reading) : Department of Typography & Graphic Communication, University of Reading, 1981. — 48p : ill ; 30cm
Previous ed.: 1975 '... published in connection with an exhibition recording the 50th anniversary of the foundation of the Gesellschafts- und Wirtschaftsmuseum in Wien, which was held in the Library of the University of Reading May to October 1975'. — Bibliography: p35-48
ISBN 0-7049-0480-2 (pbk) : Unpriced B81-37729

016'.00164'091724 — Developing countries. Digital computer systems *— Bibliographies*

Computers in developing countries : a bibliography / edited by S. Deighton. — London : Institution of Electrical Engineers, 1981. — [160]p ; 30cm
Includes index
£12.00 (spiral) B81-31765

016.00164'2 — Microcomputer systems. Programs *— Bibliographies*

Pritchard, Alan. Small computer program index. — Bushey (21 Beechcroft Rd, Bushey, Herts. WD2 2JU) : Allm Books, Jan.1982. — [120]p
ISBN 0-9506784-1-4 : £15.00 : CIP entry B81-34969

016'.0162 — Religion. Bibliographies: Serials *— Bibliographies*

Walsh, Michael J.. Religious bibliographies in serial literature : a guide / compiled by Michael J. Walsh with the help of John V. Howard, Graham P. Cornish, Robert J. Duckett ; on behalf of the Association of British Theological and Philosophical Libraries. — London : Mansell, 1981. — xxiv,216p ; 23cm
Includes index
ISBN 0-7201-1593-0 : £15.00 B81-24899

016'.016789912 — Music. Sound recordings. Discographies *— Lists*

Bibliography of discographies. — New York ; London : Bowker
Vol.2: Jazz / by Daniel Allen. — 1981. — xvi,239p ; 27cm
Includes index
ISBN 0-8352-1342-0 : Unpriced B81-37336

016'.0169415 — Ireland *— Bibliographies of bibliographies*

Eager, Alan R.. A guide to Irish bibliographical material : a bibliography of Irish bibliographies and sources of information / Alan R. Eager. — 2nd rev. and enl. ed. — London : Library Association, 1980. — xv,502p ; 26cm
Previous ed.: 1964. — Includes index
ISBN 0-85365-931-1 : Unpriced : CIP rev. B80-06257

016.02'05 — Librarianship & information science. Serials *— Bibliographies*

Sharp, J. R.. A select list of newsletters in the field of librarianship and information science / J.R. Sharp (compiler) and M. Mann (editor). — [London] : British Library ; Boston Spa, 1981. — 53p ; 30cm. — (British Library research & development reports, ISSN 0308-2385 ; no.5630)
ISBN 0-905984-72-2 (pbk) : Unpriced B81-34542

016.025 — Bibliometrics *— Bibliographies*

Pritchard, Alan. Bibliometrics : a bibliography and index / by Alan Pritchard in collaboration with Glenn R. Wittig. — Watford (4 Knutsford Ave., Watford, Herts. WD2 4EL) : ALLM Books
Vol.1: 1874-1959. — 1981. — 139p in various pagings ; 29cm
Includes index
ISBN 0-9506784-0-6 (pbk) : £5.00 B81-18204

016.025 — Bibliometrics *— Bibliographies — Serials*

Bibliometrics bulletin : a (mainly) bibliographic newsletter on bibliometrics. — No.1 (Mar.1981)-. — Watford (4 Knutsford Ave., Watford, Herts. WD2 4EL) : ALLM Books, 1981. — v. ; 30cm
ISSN 0260-9665 = Bibliometrics bulletin : Unpriced B81-33285

016.0251'1 — Libraries & information services. Financial aspects *— Bibliographies*

Cooper, Alan, *1948-*. Financial aspects of library and information services : a bibliography / Alan Cooper. — Loughborough : Centre for Library and Information Management, Department of Library and Information Studies, Loughborough University, c1980. — 117p : ill ; 30cm. — (Report / Centre for Library and Information Management Department of Library and Information Studies Loughborough University ; no.5) (Research and development reports / British Library, ISSN 0308-2385 ; 5573)
Includes index
ISBN 0-904924-23-8 (pbk) : £10.00 B81-11824

016.02′53 — Indexing — *Bibliographies*

Wellisch, Hans H.. Indexing and abstracting : an international bibliography / Hans H. Wellisch. — Santa Barbara ; Oxford : Published in cooperation with the American Society of Indexers and the Society of Indexers (U.K.) [by] ABC-Clio, c1980. — xxi,308p ; 29cm
Includes index
ISBN 0-87436-300-4 : £11.80
Also classified at 016.02′54′028 B81-12506

016.02′54′028 — Abstracting — *Bibliographies*

Wellisch, Hans H.. Indexing and abstracting : an international bibliography / Hans H. Wellisch. — Santa Barbara ; Oxford : Published in cooperation with the American Society of Indexers and the Society of Indexers (U.K.) [by] ABC-Clio, c1980. — xxi,308p ; 29cm
Includes index
ISBN 0-87436-300-4 : £11.80
Primary classification 016.02′53 B81-12506

016.0276′63 — Great Britain. Libraries. Services for handicapped persons — *Bibliographies*

Hay, Wendy. Library services to disabled people in Britain : an annotated bibliography, 1970-1981. — London : Library Association, Feb.1982. — [40]p
ISBN 0-85365-824-2 (pbk) : £7.00 : CIP entry
B81-39241

016.02′87 — Information sources — *Bibliographies*

A Literature guide to literature guides / Manchester Polytechnic Department of Library and Information Studies. — Manchester (Ormond Building, Manchester Polytechnic, All Saints, Manchester MI5 6BX) : The Department, 1980. — 57p ; 30cm. — (Occasional paper / Manchester Polytechnic Department of Library and Information Studies ; no.1)
£2.00 (pbk) B81-11478

016′.06 — Great Britain. National libraries: British Library. *Lending Division.* **Stock: Conference proceedings** — *Catalogues* — *Serials*

British Library. *Lending Division*. Index of conference proceedings received. Annual cumulation. — 1980. — Boston Spa : British Library Lending Division, c1981. — 847p
ISSN 0305-5183 : Unpriced B81-15171

016.1554 — Children. Development. Effects of parental deprivation — *Abstracts*

Akins, Faren R.. Parent-child separation : psychosocial effects on development : an abstracted bibliography / Faren R. Akins, Dianna L. Akins and Gillian S. Mace. — New York ; London : IFI/Plenum, c1981. — ix,356p ; 26cm
Includes index
ISBN 0-306-65196-3 : Unpriced B81-34708

016.1559 — Environmental psychology — *Bibliographies*

Wohlwill, Joachim F.. The physical environment and behavior : an annotated bibliography and guide to the literature / Joachim F. Wohlwill and Gerald D. Weisman. — New York ; London : Plenum, c1981. — ix,474p ; 24cm
Includes index
ISBN 0-306-40739-6 : Unpriced B81-25955

016.1559′37 — Bereaved children. Grief. Psychosocial aspects — *Bibliographies*

Mace, Gillian S.. The bereaved child : analysis, education and treatment : an abstracted bibliography / Gillian S. Mace, Faren R. Akins and Dianna L. Akins. — New York ; London : IFI/Plenum, 1981. — vii,284p ; 26cm. — (IFI data base library)
Includes index
ISBN 0-306-65197-1 : Unpriced B81-39084

016.192 — English philosophy. Wittgenstein, Ludwig — *Bibliographies*

Lapointe, François H.. Ludwig Wittgenstein : a comprehensive bibliography / compiled by François H. Lapointe. — Westport ; London : Greenwood Press, 1980. — ix,297p ; 25cm
Includes index
ISBN 0-313-22127-8 : Unpriced B81-05278

016.192 — London. Camden *(London Borough).* **Universities. Colleges. Libraries: University College, London.** *Library.* **Stock: Manuscripts of Bentham, Jeremy** — *Indexes*

University College, London. *Library*. The manuscripts of Jeremy Bentham : a chronological index to the collection in the Library of University College London / compiled by Douglas Long for the Bentham Committee, University College London ; based on the catalogue by A. Taylor Milne. — [London] : [The Library], [1981?]. — 90p ; 30cm
Cover title
Unpriced (pbk) B81-28323

016.193 — German philosophy. Hegel, Georg Wilhelm Friedrich — *Bibliographies*

Steinhauer, Kurt. Hegel bibliography : background material on the international reception of Hegel within the context of the history of philosophy / compiled by Kurt Steinhauer ; keyword index by Gitta Hausen = Hegel Bibliographie : Materialien zur Geschichte der internationalen Hegel-Rezeption und zur Philosophie-Geschichte / zusammengestellt von Kurt Steinhauer ; Stichwortregister von Gitta Hausen. — München ; London : Saur, 1980. — xvi,894p ; 25cm
Introduction and notes in English and German. — Includes index
ISBN 3-598-03184-x : Unpriced B81-12983

016.198′9 — Danish philosophy. Kierkegaard, Søren. Criticism — *Bibliographies*

Lapointe, François H.. Sören Kierkegaard and his critics : an international bibliography of criticism / compiled by François H. Lapointe. — Westport ; London : Greenwood Press, 1980. — viii,430p ; 25cm
Includes index
ISBN 0-313-22333-5 : £23.75 B81-23453

016.2 — Religion — *Bibliographies*

Cornish, G. P.. Theological & religious bibliographies (continuing Theological & religious index) / compiled by G.P. Cornish. — Harrogate (33 Mayfield Grove, Harrogate, N. Yorkshire) : Theological Abstracting and Bibliographical Services
Vol.3: Inter-action between modern drama and the church : a selective bibliography. — 1981. — [16]p ; 21cm
Cover title
£1.25 (pbk) B81-16177

016.2 — Religion. Books in print — *Lists* — *Serials*

Religious books and serials in print. — 1980-1981. — New York ; London : Bowker, c1980. — lxxiv,1326p
ISBN 0-8352-1306-4 : Unpriced
ISSN 0000-0612
Also classified at 016.2′005 B81-08786

016.2′005 — Religion. Serials in print — *Lists* — *Serials*

Religious books and serials in print. — 1980-1981. — New York ; London : Bowker, c1980. — lxxiv,1326p
ISBN 0-8352-1306-4 : Unpriced
ISSN 0000-0612
Primary classification 016.2 B81-08786

016.2216 — Bible. O.T.. Criticism — *Bibliographies* — *Serials*

[Book list *(Society for Old Testament Study)*]. Book list / the Society for Old Testament Study. — 1981. — Manchester (c/o Mr M.E.J. Richardson, Department of Near Eastern Studies, University of Manchester, Manchester M13 9PL) : The Society, c1981. — 151p
£5.50 (free to Society members only)
B81-31890

016.23′02 — Catholic Church. Christian doctrine. Thomas, *Aquinas, Saint.* **Criticism** — *Bibliographies*

Miethe, Terry L.. Thomistic bibliography, 1940-1978 / compiled by Terry L. Miethe and Vernon J. Bourke. — Westport ; London : Greenwood Press, 1980. — xxii,318p ; 25cm
Includes index
ISBN 0-313-21991-5 : £24.95 B81-23454

016.2618′3576 — Homosexuality. Attitudes of Christian church — *Bibliographies*

Horner, Tom, *1927-*. Homosexuality and the Judeo-Christian tradition : an annotated bibliograhy / Tom Horner. — Metuchen, N.J. ; London : American Theological Library Assn., 1981. — ix,131p ; 23cm. — (ATLA bibliography series ; no.5)
Includes index
ISBN 0-8108-1412-9 : £7.00 B81-26171

016.264′2 — Oxfordshire. Oxford. Universities. Libraries: Bodleian Library. Exhibits: Hymnals with British imprints — *Catalogues*

English hymns & hymn books : catalogue of an exhibition held in the Bodleian Library Oxford / by Robin Leaver with the assistance of Paul Morgan. — Oxford : The Bodleian Library, 1981. — viii,34p ; 21cm
ISBN 0-900177-81-0 (pbk) : Unpriced
B81-26827

016.266′36 — Anglican missions: Church Missionary Society. *Africa (Group 3) Committee.* **Archives** — *Lists*

Church Missionary Society. Catalogue of the papers of the missions of the Africa (Group 3) Committee / catalogued by Rosemary A. Keen. — London : Church Missionary Society
Vol.3: South and East Africa missions (South Africa, Kenya and Tanzania) 1836-1934. — 1981. — 49leaves ; 30cm
£2.00 (pbk) B81-38675

Church Missionary Society. Catalogue of the papers of the missions of the Africa (Group 3) Committee / catalogued by Rosemary A. Keen. — London : Church Missionary Society
Vol.4: East Africa Missions (Nyanza, Uganda and Ruanda) 1875-1934. — 1981. — 33leaves ; 30cm
£2.00 (pbk) B81-38676

Church Missionary Society. Catalogue of the papers of the missions of the Africa (Group 3) Committee / catalogued by Rosemary A. Keen. — London : Church Missionary Society
Vol.5: Egypt and Sudanese Missions (including Upper Nile) 1889-1934. — 1981. — 30leaves ; 30cm
£2.00 (pbk) B81-38677

016.269′2 — Christian church. Evangelism. Audiovisual materials — *Lists* — *Serials*

Training for evangelism : a survey of training materials available to local churches. — 1980/1981-. — London (146 Queen Victoria St., EC4V 4BX) : Nationwide Institute on Evangelism, [1981]-. — v. ; 22cm
Irregular
£0.40 B81-27322

016.271′00942 — Great Britain. *Public Record Office.* **Stock: State papers on dissolution of religious orders in England. Collections: Suppression Papers** — *Lists*

England and Wales. *Exchequer*. State papers domestic and foreign, Suppression Papers (SP5) : list and index / [Exchequer]. — London : Swift, 1981. — 30p ; 33cm. — (Publication / List & Index Society ; v.179)
Papers held in Public Record Office. — At head of title: List & Index Society. — Includes index
£4.00 (Subscribers only) B81-34883

016.285′242527 — Nottinghamshire. Nottingham. Universities. Libraries: University of Nottingham. *Manuscripts Department.* **Stock: Archives of United Reformed Church St. Andrews with Castle Gate** *(Church : Nottingham)* — *Catalogues*

University of Nottingham. *Manuscripts Department*. United Reformed Church St. Andrews with Castle Gate, Nottingham / [University of Nottingham Department of Manuscripts]. — Nottingham : The Department
Supplementary list. — [1980]. — 23p ; 30cm
£1.50 (unbound) B81-17276

016.297 — Islam — *Bibliographies — Serials*

New books quarterly on Islam & the Muslim world. — Vol.1, no.1 (Autumn 1980)-. — London (16 Grosvenor Cres., SW1 7EP) : Islamic Council of Europe, 1980-. — v. ; 22cm
Description based on: Vol.1, no.2 & 3 (Spring 1981)
ISSN 0144-994x = New books quarterly on Islam & the Muslim world : £4.00 per year
B81-37241

016.297'124 — Islam. Hadith — *Bibliographies*

Denffer, Ahmad von. Literature on hadith in European languages : a bibliography / Ahmad von Denffer. — Leicester (223 London Rd., Leicester) : Islamic Foundation, c1981. — 94p ; 21cm
Includes index
ISBN 0-86037-060-7 (pbk) : Unpriced
B81-18578

016.3 — Northern Ireland. Public libraries: SELB Library Service. Stock: Audiovisual aids on social sciences — *Catalogues*

SELB Library Service. Audio visual resources : history, economics, politics : a select list of materials available on loan from the SELB Library Service. — [Craigavon] ([Library Headquarters, Brownlow Rd., Legahory, Craigavon, County Armagh BT5 8DP]) : [The Library Service], [1980]. — 63p ; 30cm
Cover title
Unpriced (pbk)
Also classified at 016.9 B81-25043

016.3 — Social sciences — *Bibliographies — Serials*

A London bibliography of the social sciences. 15th supplement. — Vol.38 (1980). — London : Mansell, July 1981. — [912]p
ISBN 0-7201-1631-7 : £43.00 : CIP entry
ISSN 0076-051x B81-25698

016.3'005 — Great Britain. *Overseas Development Administration. Library.* **Stock: Serials** — *Catalogues — Serials*

Great Britain. *Overseas Development Administration. Library.* List of periodicals currently received / Overseas Development Administration Library. — June 1980. — [London] ([Eland House, Stag Place, SW1E 5DH]) : Overseas Development Administration, 1980. — 69p
Unpriced B81-06928

016.301 — Higher education institutions. Curriculum subjects: Sociology. Theories. Teaching aids: Audiovisual materials — *Lists*

Van Haeften, Kate. Media resources on sociological theory for lecturers / by Kate Van Haeften. — London : LLRS, 1981. — 13p ; 30cm
Includes index
ISBN 0-904264-55-6 (pbk) : Unpriced
B81-35529

016.301 — Massachusetts. Cambridge. Universities. Libraries: Harvard University. *Library.* **Stock: Anthropology** — *Catalogues*

Harvard University. *Library.* Geography and anthropology : classification schedules, classified listing by call number, chronological listing, author and title listing / Harvard University Library. — Cambridge, Mass. : The Library ; Cambridge, Mass. ; London : Distributed by Harvard University Press, 1979. — 270p ; 29cm. — (Widener Library shelflist ; 60)
ISBN 0-674-34855-9 : £21.00
Primary classification 016.91 B81-36591

016.302 — Social skills. Development — *Bibliographies — Serials*

Development of social skills. — Vol.1, no.1 (Jan.1981)-. — Sheffield : University of Sheffield Biomedical Information Service, 1981-. — v. ; 30cm
Monthly
ISSN 0260-5910 = Development of social skills : Unpriced B81-25008

016.3022'3 — Mass media. Social aspects — *Bibliographies*

Gordon, Thomas F.. Mass communication effects and processes : a comprehensive bibliography, 1950-1975 / Thomas F. Gordon and Mary Ellen Verna. — Beverly Hills ; London : Sage, c1978. — 229p ; 23cm
Includes index
ISBN 0-8039-0903-9 : £12.50 B81-12971

016.3034'82'091812 — Norfolk. Norwich. Universities. Libraries: University of East Anglia. *Library.* **Exhibits: Documents associated with relations between Western world & Russia,** *1780-1789 — Catalogues*

1780s: Russia Under Western Eyes *(Exhibition) (1981 : University of East Anglia).* The 1780s : Russia under Western eyes : 17 July-7 August 1981, Library Concourse, University of East Anglia, Norwich / exhibition devised and catalogue compiled by Anthony Cross. — [Norwich] ([School of Modern Languages and European History, University of East Anglia, Norwich NR4 7TJ]) : Study Group on Eighteenth-Century Russia, 1981. — 85p : ill,facsims,ports ; 24cm
Includes index
Unpriced (pbk)
Primary classification 016.3034'82'0947
B81-36640

016.3034'82'0947 — Norfolk. Norwich. Universities. Libraries: University of East Anglia. *Library.* **Exhibits: Documents associated with relations between Russia & Western world,** *1780-1789 — Catalogues*

1780s: Russia Under Western Eyes *(Exhibition) (1981 : University of East Anglia).* The 1780s : Russia under Western eyes : 17 July-7 August 1981, Library Concourse, University of East Anglia, Norwich / exhibition devised and catalogue compiled by Anthony Cross. — [Norwich] ([School of Modern Languages and European History, University of East Anglia, Norwich NR4 7TJ]) : Study Group on Eighteenth-Century Russia, 1981. — 85p : ill,facsims,ports ; 24cm
Includes index
Unpriced (pbk)
Also classified at 016.3034'82'091812
B81-36640

016.3036 — London. Southwark *(London Borough).* **Libraries: India Office Library and Records. Stock: Public records. Special subjects: Role of Gandhi, M. K. in civil disobedience in India: Lists**

India Office Library and Records. Gandhi and civil disobedience : documents in the India Office Records 1922-1946 / [compiled by] Amar Kaur Jasbir Singh. — London : India Office Library and Records, 1980. — v,62p : facsims,1port ; 30cm
Bibliography: p56-57. — Includes index
ISBN 0-903359-27-8 (pbk) : Unpriced
B81-39683

016.3046'6'0941 — Great Britain. Birth control, *1922-1931 — Bibliographies*

Doughan, David. Birth control : the equal knowledge campaign 1922-1931. — London (Calcutta House, Old Castle St., E1 7NT) : LLRS Publications, Oct.1981. — [23]p. — (Fawcett library papers ; no.3)
ISBN 0-904264-58-0 (pbk) : £2.50 : CIP entry
B81-31092

016.3048'8 — Latin America. Immigration, *1830-1950 — Bibliographies*

Bailey, Juan. Intercontinental migration to Latin America : a select bibliography / compiled by Juan Bailey and Freya Headlam. — London (31 Tavistock Sq., WC1H 9HA) : Institute of Latin American Studies, University of London, 1980. — 62p : 1map ; 26cm
Includes index
ISBN 0-901145-40-8 (pbk) : Unpriced
B81-05188

016.3052'6'08996073 — United States. Old persons: Negroes — *Bibliographies*

Davis, Lenwood G.. The Black aged in the United States : an annotated bibliography / Lenwood G. Davis. — Westport, Conn. ; London : Greenwood Press, 1980. — xviii,200p ; 25cm
Includes index
ISBN 0-313-22560-5 : £14.50 B81-23595

016.3054 — Women. Audiovisual materials — *Lists*

Nordquist, Joan. Audiovisuals for women / Joan Nordquist. — Jefferson, N.C. : McFarland ; Folkestone : distributed by Bailey & Swinfen, 1980. — viii,145p ; 24cm
Includes index
ISBN 0-89950-011-0 (cased) : Unpriced (pbk) : £7.15 B81-40125

016.3054 — Women. Bibliographies: BiblioFem — *Serials*

BiblioFem news. — No.1 (Oct.1979)-. — London : Calcutta House, Old Castle St., E1 7NT : City of London Polytechnic, Fawcett Library, 1979-. — v. ; 30cm
Irregular. — Issued as information sheet for subscribers to: BiblioFem. — Description based on: No.2 (May 1980)
ISSN 0260-0609 = BiblioFem news : Unpriced
B81-08574

016.3054'2 — Women. Ambitions. Psychosocial aspects — *Bibliographies*

Faunce, Patricia Spencer. Women and ambition : a bibliography / by Patricia Spencer Faunce. — Metuchen ; London : Scarecrow, 1980. — xxvii,695p ; 23cm
Includes index
ISBN 0-8108-1242-8 : £22.75 B81-01612

016.3054'2'09174927 — Arab countries. Society. Role of women, *1900-1979 — Bibliographies*

Meghdessian, Samira Rafidi. The status of the Arab woman : a select bibliography / compiled by Samira Rafidi Meghdessian under the auspices of the Institute for Women's Studies in the Arab World, Beirut University College, Lebanon. — London : Mansell, 1980. — 176p ; 23cm
Includes index
ISBN 0-7201-1517-5 : £14.00 : CIP rev.
B80-11708

016.3054'2'0954 — South Asia. Rural regions. Society. Role of women. Effects of economic development — *Bibliographies*

Nelson, Nici. Why has development neglected rural women? : a review of the South Asian literature / by Nici Nelson. — Oxford : Pergamon, 1979. — viii,108p,8p of plates : ill ; 22cm. — (Women in development ; vol.1) (Pergamon international library)
Bibliography: p79-103
ISBN 0-08-023377-5 (cased) : £10.50 : CIP rev.
B79-12712

016.3056'971'04 — Europe. Muslims. Research organisations: Research Programme on Muslims in Europe. Stock: Documents — *Lists — Serials*

Research Programme on Muslims in Europe. Recent acquisitions / Centre for the Study of Islam and Christian Muslim Relations, Research Programme on Muslims in Europe. — No.1 (Jan. 1980)-. — Birmingham (Selly Oak Colleges, Birmingham 29) : The Centre, 1980-. — v. ; 30cm
Irregular
ISSN 0260-034x = Recent acquisitions — Centre for the Study of Islam and Christian Muslim Relations. Research Programme on Muslims in Europe : Unpriced B81-02038

016.3058'96'024 — Negroes. Race relations. Garvey, Marcus — *Bibliographies*

Davis, Lenwood G.. Marcus Garvey : an annotated bibliography / compiled by Lenwood G. Davis and Janet L. Sims ; foreword by John Henrik Clarke. — Westport, Conn. ; London : Greenwood Press, 1980. — xvi,192p ; 25cm
Includes index
ISBN 0-313-22131-6 : £14.50 B81-24032

016.306 — Social anthropology — *Bibliographies — Serials*

International bibliography of social and cultural anthropology / prepared by the International Committee for Social Science Information and Documentation. — Vol.23 (1977). — London : Tavistock, 1981. — xli,569p. — (International bibliography of the social sciences)
ISBN 0-422-80860-1 : Unpriced B81-20457

016.306 — Social anthropology — *Bibliographies — Serials* *continuation*

International bibliography of social and cultural anthropology = Bibliographie internationale d'anthropologie sociale et culturelle. — Vol.24 (1978). — London : Tavistock, Nov.1981. — [560]p. — (International bibliography of the social sciences)
ISBN 0-422-80930-6 : £33.00 : CIP entry
ISSN 0085-2074 B81-30160

016.306'4 — Alcoholic drinks. Consumption by old persons — *Bibliographies*

Barnes, Grace M.. Alcohol and the elderly : a comprehensive bibliography / compiled by Grace M. Barnes, Ernest L. Abel and Charles A.S. Ernst. — Westport, Conn. ; London : Greenwood Press, 1980. — xvii,138p ; 24cm
Includes index
ISBN 0-313-22132-4 : £15.95 B81-23597

016.306'4 — Great Britain. Vacations. Organisations: Countrywide Holidays Association. Archives — *Lists*

Bassett, Philippa. A list of the historical records of the Countrywide Holidays Association / compiled by Philippa Bassett as part of a research project funded by the Social Science Research Council. — [Birmingham] : Centre for Urban and Regional Studies, 1980. — v,26p ; 30cm. — (Lists of historical records)
At head of title: Centre for Urban and Regional Studies, University of Birmingham and Institute of Agricultural History, University of Reading
Unpriced (pbk) B81-28415

016.306'4 — Vacations. Organisations: Holiday Fellowship. Archives — *Lists*

Bassett, Philippa. A list of the historical records of the Holiday Fellowship / compiled by Philippa Bassett as part of a research project funded by the Social Science Research Council. — [Birmingham] : Centre for Urban and Regional Studies, University of Birmingham, 1980. — viii,24p ; 30cm. — (Lists of historical records)
At head of title:Centre for Urban and Regional Studies, University of Birmingham and Institute of Agricultural History, University of Reading
Unpriced (pbk) B81-27670

016.3067 — Great Britain. Sexual liberation movements. Bibliographies, *1977-1978* — *Indexes*

Thomas, Mavis. Sexual politics in Britain during 1977 and 1978. — Brighton : Harvester Press Microform Publications, Dec.1981. — [30]p
ISBN 0-86257-007-7 (pbk) : £4.00 : CIP entry
B81-35903

016.3067'2'0941 — Great Britain. Rural regions. Social problems — *Bibliographies*

Neate, Simon. Rural deprivation : an annotated bibliography of economic and social problems in rural Britain / compiled, with an introduction, by Simon Neate. — Norwich : Geo Abstracts, c1981. — 81p ; 21cm. — (Geo Abstracts bibliography ; no.8)
Includes index
ISBN 0-86094-061-6 (pbk) : £2.85 B81-10364

016.3068 — Family life — *Abstracts — Serials*

Sage family studies abstracts. — Vol.1, no.1 (Feb. 1979)-. — Beverly Hills ; London : Sage, 1979. — v. ; 22cm
Quarterly
ISSN 0164-0283 = Sage family studies abstracts : Unpriced B81-03615

016.3068'0973 — United States. Families. Cinema films — *Lists*

Trojan, Judith. American family life films / [compiled by] Judith Trojan. — Metuchen ; London : Scarecrow, 1981. — lxxxiii,425p : ill ; 23cm
Includes index
ISBN 0-8108-1313-0 : £17.50 B81-17101

016.3077'6'09 — Urban regions. Social planning, *to 1979* — *Bibliographies*

Sutcliffe, Anthony. The history of urban and regional planning : an annotated bibliography / Anthony Sutcliffe. — London : Mansell, 1981. — ix,284p ; 23cm
Includes index
ISBN 0-7201-0901-9 : £12.95 : CIP rev.
Also classified at 016.3616'1'09 B80-18148

016.312'0942 — England. Repositories. Stock: Microfilms of census data of England, *1841-1871* — *Catalogues*

Gibson, J. S. W.. Census returns 1841, 1851, 1861, 1871 on microfilm : a directory to local holdings / compiled by J.S.W. Gibson. — 3rd ed. — Banbury (White Lion Walk, Banbury, Oxfordshire) : Gulliver and the Federation of Family History Societies, 1981. — 44p ; 21cm
Previous ed.: 1980
ISBN 0-906428-08-4 (pbk) : £1.20
ISBN 0-907099-05-x (Federation of Family History Soceities) B81-19724

016.314 — European Community statistical publications — *Indexes*

Ramsay, Anne. Eurostat index. — Edinburgh (6, Castle St., Edinburgh EH2 3AT) : Capital Planning Information, Oct.1981. — [120]p
ISBN 0-906011-15-9 (pbk) : £15.00 : CIP entry
B81-30628

016.318 — Great Britain. Libraries. Stock: Texts of Latin American censuses — *Catalogues*

Guide to Latin American and West Indian census material : a bibliography and union list. — [London] ([102 Euston St., NW1 2HA]) : SCONUL Advisory Committee on Latin American Materials, 1981
1: Venezuela / compiled by Ann E. Wade. — 30p ; 30cm
ISBN 0-9505324-1-x (unbound) : Unpriced
B81-32314

016.32 — Politics — *Bibliographies*

Holler, Frederick L. Information sources of political science / Frederick L. Holler. — 3rd ed. — Santa Barbara ; Oxford : ABC-Clio, c1981. — x,278p ; 29cm
Previous ed.: 1975. — Includes index
ISBN 0-87436-179-6 : £32.50 B81-12507

016.32 — Politics - *Bibliographies*

International bibliography of political science = Bibliographie internationale de science politique. — Vol.28, (1979). — London : Tavistock, June 1981. — [600]p. — (International bibliography of the social sciences = Bibliographie internationale des sciences sociales)
ISBN 0-422-80920-9 : £32.50 : CIP entry
B81-12339

016.32 — Politics — *Bibliographies — Serials*

International bibliography of political science / prepared by the International Committee for Social Science Information and Documentation. — Vol.26 (1977). — London : Tavistock, 1979. — lxix,359p. — (International bibliography of the social sciences)
ISBN 0-422-80840-7 : Unpriced B81-06561

016.3209'041 — British government publications: Reports. Chairmen — *Lists*

Richard, Stephen. British government publications : an index to chairmen of Committees and Commissions of Inquiry. — London : Library Association
Vol.1: 1800-1899. — Nov.1981. — [220]p
ISBN 0-85365-743-2 : £30.00 : CIP entry
B81-30438

Richard, Stephen. British government publications : an index to chairmen and authors. — London : Library Association
Vol.3: 1941-1978. — Nov.1981. — [162]p
ISBN 0-85365-753-x : £22.00 : CIP entry
B81-30430

016.320941 — Great Britain. Left-wing political movements — *Bibliographies — Serials*

The Left in Britain. — 1975 and 1976. — Brighton : Harvester Press Microform, 1981. — 95p
ISBN 0-86257-005-0 : Unpriced B81-15445

016.3271'74 — Disarmament. British writers, *1905-1978* — *Bibliographies*

Lloyd, Lorna. British writing on disarmament from 1914 to 1978 : a bibliography / Lorna Lloyd and Nicholas A. Sims. — London : Pinter, 1979. — 171p ; 23cm
Includes index
ISBN 0-903804-40-9 : £15.00 B81-11497

016.327417 — Ireland *(Republic).* **Foreign relations,** *1921-1978* — *Bibliographies*

Maguire, Maria. A bibliography of published works on Irish foreign relations 1921-1978 / compiled by Maria Maguire. — Dublin (19 Dawson St., Dublin 2) : Royal Irish Academy, 1981. — viii,136p ; 21cm
Cover title. — Includes index
ISBN 0-901714-15-1 (pbk) : Unpriced
B81-28720

016.331'01'12 — Industrial democracy — *Bibliographies*

Pettman, Barrie O.. Industrial democracy : a selected bibliography / by Barrie O. Pettman. — Bradford : M.C.B. Publications, c1979. — vii,95p ; 25cm. — (Bibliography / Institute of Scientific Business ; no.11)
Includes index
ISBN 0-905440-61-7 (pbk) : Unpriced
B81-19859

016.33111'91027 — Libraries. Manpower planning — *Bibliographies*

Mann, Margaret. Library manpower planning : a bibliographical review / Margaret Mann. — [London] : British Library, 1981 ; Boston Spa : British Library Lending Division [Distributor]. — iv,68p ; 30cm. — (British Library research & development reports, ISSN 0308-2385 ; 5614)
Includes index
ISBN 0-905984-66-8 (pbk) : Unpriced : CIP rev. B81-08848

016.3312'09485 — Sweden. Working conditions. Improvement — *Bibliographies*

Clifford, Brian, *1953-*. Quality of work life developments in Sweden : a review of the literature / by Brian Clifford. — London (26 King St., SW1Y 6RB) : [Department of Employment], Work Research Unit, 1980. — 55p ; 30cm. — (Information system literature review ; no.2)
Unpriced (unbound) B81-38930

016.3315'9 — Handicapped persons. Employment — *Bibliographies*

Simpson, Struan. Employment for handicapped people. — Chertsey : Reedbooks, Oct.1981. — [90]p
ISBN 0-906544-08-4 : £7.00 : CIP entry
B81-32537

016.33188'0941 — West Midlands *(Metropolitan County).* **Coventry. Universities. Libraries: University of Warwick.** *Library.* **Stock: Documents of British trade unions,** *to 1974* — *Catalogues*

Bennett, John, *1946-*. Trade union and related records / compiled by John Bennett ; edited by Richard Storey. — Rev. & enl. 2nd ed. — Coventry : University of Warwick, 1981. — 32p : 1facsim ; 21cm. — (Occasional publications / University of Warwick Library ; no.5)
ISBN 0-903220-09-1 (pbk) : Unpriced
B81-19609

016.3321'028'5 — Banking. Applications of digital computer systems — *Bibliographies*

Banking and finance : an annotated bibliography. — London : Heyden, Dec.1981. — [48]p. — (Use of computers for national development)
ISBN 0-85501-695-7 (pbk) : £4.00 : CIP entry
B81-40228

016.3332 — England. Common land. Preservation. Organisations: Commons, Open Spaces and Footpaths Preservation Society. Archives — *Lists*

Bassett, Philippa. A list of the historical records of the Commons, Open Spaces and Footpaths Preservation Society / compiled by Philippa Bassett as part of a research project funded by the Social Science Research Council. — [Birmingham] : Centre for Urban and Regional Studies, University of Birmingham, 1980. — vi,29p ; 30cm. — (Lists of historical records)
At head of title: Centre for Urban and Regional Studies, University of Birmingham and Institute of Agricultural History, University of Reading
Unpriced (pbk)
Also classified at 016.3881'2 B81-27741

016.3333'06'0411 — Scotland. Landowners. Organisations: Scottish Landowners Federation. Archives — *Lists*

Bassett, Philippa. A list of the historical records of the Scottish Landowners Federation / compiled by Philippa Bassett as part of a research project funded by the Social Science Research Council. — [Birmingham] : Centre for Urban and Regional Studies, University of Birmingham, 1980. — v,6p ; 30cm. — (Lists of historical records)
At head of title: Centre for Urban and Regional Studies, University of Birmingham and Institute of Agricultural History, University of Reading
Unpriced (pbk) B81-27682

016.3333'22'0942644 — Suffolk. Bury St Edmunds. Abbeys: Bury St Edmunds Abbey. Ecclesiastical estates. Archives — *Catalogues*

The **Archives** of the Abbey of Bury St Edmunds / edited by Rodney M. Thomson. — Woodbridge : Published for the Suffolk Records Society by Boydell, c1980. — ix, 173p : facsims ; 25cm. — (Suffolk charters)
Includes index
ISBN 0-85115-087-x : £15.00 : CIP rev.
B80-18968

016.3333'22'0942651 — Cambridgeshire. Peterborough. Abbeys: Peterborough Abbey. Cartularies & registers — *Lists*

Martin, Janet D.. The court and account rolls of Peterborough Abbey : a handlist / by Janet D. Martin. — [Leicester] : University of Leicester, History Department, 1980. — ix,51p ; 21cm. — (Occasional publication / University of Leicester, History Department, ISSN 0144-3739 ; no.2)
ISBN 0-906696-01-1 (pbk) : Unpriced
B81-19515

016.3333'23'0942525 — Nottinghamshire. Nottingham. Universities. Libraries: University of Nottingham. *Manuscripts Department.* **Stock: Archives of Manvers Estate, Thoresby,** *1737-1956* — *Lists*

University of Nottingham. *Manuscripts Department*. Manvers of Thoresby manuscripts c.1737-1956 / University of Nottingham Manuscripts Department. — [Nottingham] ([University Park, Nottingham NG7 2RD]) : [The Department], [1980]. — 25p ; 30cm
£1.50 (pbk) B81-08058

016.3337 — Great Britain. Education. Curriculum studies: Environmental studies. Teaching aids: Films — *Lists*

Williams, Gwyndaf. Urban and environmental studies : a film guide / Gwyndaf Williams. — Manchester (Manchester M13 9PL) : Department of Town and Country Planning, University of Manchester, 1980. — 81p ; 30cm. — (Occasional paper / Department of Town and Country Planning University of Manchester ; no.6)
Unpriced (pbk) B81-04818

016.3337'07 — Education. Curriculum subjects: Environmental studies — *Bibliographies*

Sterling, S. R.. Environmental education in theory and practice : an annotated bibliography / compiled by S.R. Sterling. — Reading (School of Education, University of Reading, London Rd, Reading RG1 5AQ) : Council for Environmental Education, c1980. — 12p ; 15x21cm
ISBN 0-906711-05-3 (pbk) : £0.30 B81-14742

016.3337'2'0604261 — Norfolk. Environment. Conservation. Organisations: Norfolk Naturalists' Trust. Archives — *Lists*

Bassett, Philippa. A list of the historical records of the Norfolk Naturalists' Trust / compiled by Philippa Bassett as part of a research project funded by the Social Science Research Council. — [Birmingham] : Centre for Urban and Regional Studies, 1980. — viii,7p ; 30cm. — (Lists of historical records)
At head of title: Centre For Urban and Regional Studies University of Birmingham and Institute of Agricultural History University of Reading
Unpriced (pbk) B81-27629

016.33376'16'06042 — England. Rural regions. Conservation. Organisations: Council for the Protection of Rural England. Archives — *Lists*

Bassett, Philippa. A list of the historical records of the Council for the Protection of Rural England / compiled by Philippa Bassett as part of a research project funded by the Social Science Research Council. — [Birmingham] : Centre for Urban and Regional Studies, 1980. — vl,58p ; 30cm. — (Lists of historical records)
At head of title: Centre For Urban and Regional Studies University of Birmingham and Institute of Agricultural History University of Reading
Unpriced (pbk) B81-27633

016.33377'15'0941 — Great Britain. *Departments of the Environment and Transport Library.* **Stock: Documents on redevelopment of urban regions in Great Britain** — *Catalogues*

Great Britain. *Departments of the Environment and Transport Library*. Urban renaissance : a select list of material located in the DOE/DTp Library / compiled by Jane Gardner. — London (2 Marsham St., SW1P 3EB) : Departments of the Environment and Transport, c1980. — 60p ; 30cm. — (Bibliography series / Headquarters Library, Department of the Environment, Department of Transport ; no.200)
ISBN 0-7184-0183-2 (pbk) : £1.95 B81-13151

016.33378 — Great Britain. *Departments of the Environment and Transport Library.* **Stock: Documents on open spaces in urban regions in Great Britain** — *Catalogues*

Great Britain. *Departments of the Environment and Transport Library*. Urban open spaces : a select list of material based on the DOE-DTp Library / compiled by Claire M. Lambert. — London (2 Marsham St., SW1P 3EB) : Departments of the Environment and Transport, c1980. — 52p ; 30cm. — (Bibliography series / Headquarters Library, Department of the Environment, Department of Transport ; 95B)
ISBN 0-7184-0182-4 (pbk) : £1.94 B81-13152

016.33379 — Energy resources — *Bibliographies* — *For teaching*

Higgins, Judith H.. Energy : a multimedia guide for children and young adults / Judith H. Higgins. — New York : Neal/Schuman ; Santa Barbara ; Oxford : ABC-Clio, c1979. — xiii,195p ; 24cm. — (Selection guide series ; 2)
Includes index
ISBN 0-87436-266-0 : £9.00 B81-23409

016.33391 — Natural resources: Water. Management & exploitation — *Bibliographies*

Jones, A. Neville. Land drainage, fisheries and aquatic environment bibliography : a literature source for the use of fisheries, recreation and amenity staff / A. Neville Jones. — [Brecon] ([Cambrian Way, Brecon, Powys LD3 7HP]) : Welsh Water Authority, 1980. — 20p ; 30cm
ISBN 0-86097-069-8 (pbk) : Unpriced
B81-19619

016.33391'0028'5 — Natural resources: Water. Management. Applications of digital computer systems — *Bibliographies*

Water resource management : an annotated bibliography. — London : Heyden, Dec.1981. — [48]p. — (Use of computers for national development)
ISBN 0-85501-693-0 (pbk) : £4.00 : CIP entry
B81-40231

016.334 — Cooperative movements — *Bibliographies* — *Serials*

Co-operative literature : accessions lists for the period ... / compiled by the librarians of the Co-operative College ... [et al.]. — 1979-. — [Oxford] ([31 St Giles, Oxford OX1 3LF]) : Plunkett Foundation for Co-operative Studies, c1980-. — v. ; 21cm
Annual
ISSN 0260-5260 = Co-operative literature : £2.00 B81-03262

016.334'0941 — Great Britain. Cooperatives — *Bibliographies*

Clarke, Peter, *1949-*. New co-operatives : a lightning tour of new literature / by Peter Clarke. — London (158 Buckingham Palace Rd., SW1W 9UB) : Co-operative Party, 1981. — 25p ; 21cm
Bibliography: p13-19
£0.40 (unbound) B81-40188

016.335'1'0941 — Great Britain. Labour movements, *to 1970* — *Bibliographies*

Smith, Harold, *1918-*. The British labour movement to 1970 : a bibliography / compiled by Harold Smith ; with a foreword by Asa Briggs. — London : Mansell, 1981. — xviii,250p ; 24cm
Includes index
ISBN 0-7201-0924-8 : £30.00 : CIP rev.
B80-22809

016.33641 — Great Britain. Public bodies. Finance — *Bibliographies* — *Serials*

Guide to public sector financial information / HM Treasury, Central Statistical Office. — No.1 (1979)-. — London : H.M.S.O., 1979-. — v. ; 25cm
Irregular
ISSN 0260-3292 = Guide to public sector financial information : £2.50 B81-06820

016.338'06 — Manufacturing industries. Applications of microprocessors — *Bibliographies*

Microprocessor applications in the manufacturing industry : a bibliography (1978-1979) / edited by P.J. Dayasena. — London : Institution of Electrical Engineers, 1981. — [94]p ; 30cm. — (Microprocessor application series)
Includes index
ISBN 0-85296-227-4 (spiral) : £10.00
B81-28300

016.3380941 — Great Britain. Industries — *Abstracts* — *Serials*

Reports index. — 1981. — Dorking : Business Surveys, [1981]. — 114p
Unpriced B81-09102

016.3381'06'0411 — Scotland. Agricultural industries. Organisations: National Farmers' Union of Scotland — *Archives* — *Lists*

Bassett, Philippa. A list of the historical records of the National Farmers' Union of Scotland / compiled by Philippa Bassett as part of a research project funded by the Social Science Research Council. — [Birmingham] : Centre for Urban and Regional Studies, University of Birmingham, 1980. — v,3leaves ; 30cm. — (Lists of historical records)
At head of title: Centre for Urban and Regional Studies, University of Birmingham and Institute of Agricultural History, University of Reading
Unpriced (pbk) B81-31792

016.3381'0941 — Great Britain. Agricultural industries. Theses accepted by universities, *1876-1978* — *Lists*

Morgan, Raine. Dissertations on British agrarian history : a select list of theses awarded higher degrees in British and foreign universities between 1876 and 1978 / by Raine Morgan. — [Reading] : University of Reading, 1981. — xxvi,170p ; 21cm. — (Institute of Agricultural History bibliographies in agricultural history ; no.2)
Bibliography: p137-138. — Includes index
ISBN 0-7049-0705-4 (pbk) : Unpriced
B81-28880

016.3381'7373 — International Coffee Organization. *Library.* **Stock** — *Catalogues* — *Serials*

International Coffee Organization. *Library*. International Coffee Organization Library monthly entries. — No.01 (July 1980)-. — London (22 Berners St., W1P 4DD) : The Organization, 1980-. — v. ; 30cm
Description based on: No.03 (Sept.1980)
ISSN 0144-6800 = International Coffee Organization Library monthly entries :
Unpriced B81-06534

016.3382′72′40941 — Great Britain. Coal industries — *Bibliographies*

Benson, John. Bibliography of the British coal industry. — Oxford : Oxford University Press for the National Coal Board, Nov.1981. — [760]p
ISBN 0-19-920120-x : £45.00 : CIP entry
B81-31194

016.3384′73621 — Health services. Economic aspects — *Bibliographies*

An **Annotated** bibliography of health economics : Western European sources / Adrian Griffiths ... [et al.]. — Oxford : Published for Sandoz Institute for Health and Socio-Economic Studies, Geneva by Martin Robertson, 1980. — xiii,332p ; 22cm
Includes index
ISBN 0-85520-246-7 : £25.00 B81-00688

016.3384′7669142 — Steel industries — *Abstracts — Serials*

Steel industry monitor. — Vol.1, no.1 (Jan. 1981)-. — London (1 Carlton House Terrace, SW1Y 5DB) : Metals Information, 1981-. — v. ; 30cm
Monthly
ISSN 0260-6399 = Steel industry monitor : £250.00 per year B81-24098

016.3384′7′677095492 — Great Britain *Foreign and Commonwealth Office.* **Libraries: India Office Library and Records. Stock: Documents on textile industries and trades in Dacca, Bangladesh,** *ca 1700-ca 1800:* **Documents in Bengali** - *Lists*

India Office Library and Records. Factory correspondence and other Bengali documents in the India Office Library and Records. — London : India Office Library and Records, May 1981. — 1v.. — (Oriental documents ; 4)
ISBN 0-903359-31-6 : CIP entry B81-07461

016.3384′7687 — Clothing industries & trades — *Bibliographies*

Select bibliography of clothing sources : compiled according to the structure of the Clothing Examinations of the Clothing and Footwear Institute. — [London] ([Albert Rd., Hendon, NW4 2JS]) : [The Institute], c1980. — 1v.(loose-leaf) ; 32cm
£12.00 (or £1.50 per section) B81-33114

016.3384′79142 — England. Tourism. Promotion. Organisations: English Tourist Board. Publications — *Lists — Serials*

English Tourist Board. *Planning and Research Services.* English Tourist Board research sources / prepared by the Planning & Research Services Branch of the English Tourist Board for general distribution. — Apr.1980-. — London (4 Grosvenor Gardens, SW1W 0DU) : The Board, 1980-. — v. ; 30cm
Annual
ISSN 0260-1540 = English Tourist Board research sources : Unpriced B81-06782

016.3385′44 — Economic forecasting — *Bibliographies*

Fildes, Robert. A bibliography of business and economic forecasting / Robert Fildes with David Dews and Syd Howell. — Farnborough, Hants. : Gower, c1981. — vi,424p ; 23cm
Includes index
ISBN 0-566-00280-9 : £25.00 B81-11606

016.3386′34 — Scotland. Highlands & Islands. Agricultural industries. Crofting — *Bibliographies*

Gold, John R.. The crofting system : a selected bibliography / John R. Gold, Margaret M. Gold. — [Oxford] ([c/o Geography Section, Faculty of Modern Studies, Headington, Oxford OX3 0BP]) : Oxford Polytechnic, 1979. — 33p ; 30cm. — (Discussion papers in geography / Oxford Polytechnic ; no.10)
Unpriced (pbk) B81-04832

016.3387′09427 — Northern England. Business firms, *to 1977 — Bibliographies*

Northern business histories : a bibliography / edited by D.J. Rowe. — London : Library Association, Reference, Special and Information Section, 1979. — viii,191p ; 31cm
Includes index
ISBN 0-85365-900-1 : £27.50 (£22.00 to members) B81-19797

016.3388′8 — Multinational companies — *Bibliographies — Serials*

Current TNC bibliography : [an indexing service to the literature on transnational corporations]. — 1980: 1(1)-. — Brighton (PO Box 450, Brighton, East Sussex BN1 8GR) : John L. Noyce, 1980. — v. ; 22cm
3-4 issues yearly
ISSN 0260-0447 = Current TNC bibliography : £23.00 per year B81-00689

016.34′0115 — Law. Social aspects — *Bibliographies — Serials*

Bibliography in socio-legal studies. — No.1-. — Oxford (Wolfson College, Oxford [OX2 6UD]) : Centre for Socio-legal Studies, 1980-. — v. ; 21cm
Irregular
ISSN 0144-9966 = Bibliography in socio-legal studies : Unpriced B81-07796

016.341′026441 — Great Britain. Treaties — *Indexes — Serials*

Index to Treaty series. — 1980. — London : H.M.S.O., 1981. — 31p. — (Treaty series ; no.97 (1980)) (Cmnd. ; 8176)
ISBN 0-10-181760-6 : £2.40 B81-25015

016.341′026441 — Great Britain. Treaties. Ratifications, accessions & withdrawals — *Lists*

Great Britain. *Foreign and Commonwealth Office*. First supplementary list of ratifications, accessions, withdrawals, etc. for 1981 : (in continuation of Treaty series no.96 (1980) Cmnd.8172) / presented to Parliament by the Secretary of State for Foreign and Commonwealth Affairs. — London : H.M.S.O., [1981]. — 28p ; 25cm. — (Treaty series ; no.34 (1981)) (Cmnd. ; 8276)
ISBN 0-10-182760-1 (unbound) : £2.40
B81-32950

016.341′026441 — Great Britain. Treaties. Ratifications, accessions & withdrawals — *Lists — Serials*

Supplementary list of ratifications, accessions, withdrawals, etc. for .... — 4th (1980). — London : H.M.S.O., 1981. — 24p. — (Cmnd. ; 8172)
ISBN 0-10-181720-7 : £2.10 B81-16245

016.341′094 — European Community. Law. Secondary legislation — *Indexes — Serials*

Secondary legislation of the European communities, subject list and table of effects / prepared for the Statutory Publications Office by the Departments of Industry and Trade Common Services : Libraries. — 1979. — London : H.M.S.O., 1980. — 142p
ISBN 0-11-330513-3 : £9.25 B81-00690

016.3426′2 — Contracts. Law — *Bibliographies — Serials*

Veljanovski, Čento G.. Contract analysis / by Cento G. Veljanovski. — Oxford (Wolfson College, Oxford) : Centre for Socio-Legal Studies, 1979. — [23]p ; 21cm. — (Bibliography in law & economics, ISSN 0143-4667 ; no.1)
ISBN 0-900296-97-6 (pbk) : Unpriced
B81-34801

016.344103′7869 — Great Britain. Buildings. Construction. Law - *Abstracts*

Harlow, P. A.. Contracts and building law. — Ascot : Chartered Institute of Building, June 1981
Vol.2. — 1v.
ISBN 0-906600-43-x (pbk) : CIP entry
B81-18063

016.344104′1 — Great Britain. Employment. Labour. Law — *Bibliographies*

Labour law in Great Britain and Ireland to 1978 : a companion volume to A bibliography of the literature on British and Irish labour law / B.A. Hepple ... [et al.]. — London : Sweet & Maxwell, 1981. — xxii,131p ; 25cm
Includes index
ISBN 0-421-28800-0 : Unpriced : CIP rev.
B81-08803

016.3441103′942 — Scotland. Rights of way. Organisations: Scottish Rights of Way Society. Archives — *Lists*

Bassett, Philippa. A list of the historical records of the Scottish Rights of Way Society Ltd / compiled by Philippa Bassett as part of a research project funded by the Social Science Research Council. — [Birmingham] : Centre for Urban and Regional Studies, University of Birmingham, 1980. — vi,23p ; 30cm. — (Lists of historical records)
At head of title: Centre for Urban and Regional Studies, University of Birmingham and Institute of Agricultural History, University of Reading
Unpriced (pbk) B81-27740

016.344203′96′0269 — Great Britain. *Public Record Office.* **Stock: Archives of Great Britain.** *Court of Admiralty — Lists*

Great Britain. *Public Record Office.* Revised catalogue of PRO lists and indexes : Kings Bench, Common Pleas, High Court of Admiralty. — London : Swift, 1981. — 80p ; 33cm. — (Publications / List & Index Society ; v.180)
At head of title : List & Index Society
£5.00 (Subscribers only)
Primary classification 016.344207′27
B81-36279

016.3442064′38 — Great Britain. *Public Record Office.* **Stock: Legal instruments: Deeds in archives of England and Wales.** *Office of Auditors of Land Revenue, to 1603.* **Collections: Ancient Deeds** — *Lists*

England and Wales. *Office of Auditors of Land Revenue.* List of ancient deeds Series E (L.R.14) / Exchequer, Office of Auditors of Land Revenue. — London : Swift, 1981. — 196p ; 33cm. — (Publications / List & Index Society ; v.181)
Papers held in the Public Record Office. — At head of title: List & Index Society
£7.90 (Subscribers only) B81-34673

016.344207′27 — Great Britain. *Public Record Office.* **Stock: Archives of Great Britain.** *Court of Queen's Bench* **& Great Britain.** *Court of Common Pleas — Lists*

Great Britain. *Public Record Office.* Revised catalogue of PRO lists and indexes : Kings Bench, Common Pleas, High Court of Admiralty. — London : Swift, 1981. — 80p ; 33cm. — (Publications / List & Index Society ; v.180)
At head of title : List & Index Society
£5.00 (Subscribers only)
Also classified at 016.344203′96′0269
B81-36279

016.34427′340822 — Greater Manchester *(Metropolitan County).* **Stockport** *(District).* **Public libraries: Stockport Metropolitan Borough Libraries.** *Library of Local Studies.* **Stock: Local acts of Stockport** *(District) — Catalogues*

Stockport Metropolitan Borough Libraries. *Library of Local Studies.* Local acts of Parliament / Metropolitan Borough of Stockport, Recreation and Culture Division, Department of Culture, Local Studies Library. — [Stockport] ([Central Library, Wellington Rd. South, Stockport SK1 3RS]) : [The Library], [1981]. — 25p ; 21cm. — (Handlist / Metropolitan Borough of Stockport, Recreation and Culture Division, Department of Culture, Local Studies Library ; no.13)
Cover title
ISBN 0-905164-45-8 (pbk) : Unpriced
B81-29546

016.3473′0092′4 — United States. Law. Darrow, Clarence — *Bibliographies*

Hunsberger, Willard D.. Clarence Darrow : a bibliography / by Willard D. Hunsberger. — Metuchen ; London : Scarecrow, 1981. — 215p,[1]leaf of plates : 1port ; 23cm
Includes index
ISBN 0-8108-1384-x : £8.75 B81-18274

016.352′0073′06042 — England. District councils. Organisations: Association of District Councils. Archives — *Lists*

Bassett, Philippa. A list of the historical records retained by the Association of District Councils / compiled by Philippa Basset[t] as part of a research project funded by the Social Science Research Council. — [Birmingham] : Centre for Urban and Regional Studies, University of Birmingham, 1980. — viii,5leaves ; 30cm. — (Lists of historical records)
At head of title: Centre for Urban and Regional Studies, University of Birmingham and Institute of Agricultural History, University of Reading
Unpriced (pbk) B81-27667

016.3520423′1 — Wiltshire. Parish records — *Lists*

Carter, Barbara J.. Location of documents for Wiltshire parishes / [compiled] by Barbara J. Carter. — Swindon (28 Okus Rd, Swindon, Wilts.) : B.J. Carter
Pt.1: Aldbourne to Bromham. — 1981. — [40]p ; 22cm
ISBN 0-9507586-0-4 (pbk) : £2.00 B81-32745

Carter, Barbara J. Location of documents for Wiltshire parishes / [compiled] by Barbara J. Carter. — Swindon (28 Okus Rd., Swindon, Wilts.) : B.J. Carter
Pt. 2: Broughton to Dinton. — 1981. — [80]p ; 22cm
ISBN 0-9507586-1-2 (pbk) : £2.00 B81-40276

016.3521′2 — England. Local authorities. Economic policies — *Bibliographies*

Evers, Clive. Local authority economic and employment policy and practice : an annotated bibliography / compiled by Clive Evers. — London : National Council for Voluntary Organisations, Information Dept., 1981. — 32p ; 30cm
Includes index
£1.00 (pbk) B81-28735

016.35441006 — Great Britain. *Civil Service Department*. Publications — *Lists — Serials*

Great Britain. *Civil Service Department*. Published by CSD. — 1968-1980. — London (Whitehall, SW1A 2AZ) : Central Management Library, Civil Service Department, 1981. — ii,23p
ISSN 0308-0803 : Unpriced B81-23136

016.355′02184 — Unconventional warfare, *1939-1980*. Bibliographies

Smith, Myron J.. The secret wars : a guide to sources in English / Myron J. Smith, Jr. — Santa Barbara ; Oxford : ABC-Clio. — (War/peace bibliography series ; 12)
Includes index
Vol.1: Intelligence, propaganda and psychological warfare, resistance movements and secret operations, 1939-1945 / with an historical introduction by Lyman B. Kirkpatrick, Jr. — c1980. — lxii,250p ; 24cm
ISBN 0-87436-271-7 : £17.25 B81-13386

Smith, Myron J.. The secret wars : a guide to sources in English / Myron J. Smith, Jr. — Santa Barbara ; Oxford : ABC-Clio. — (War/peace bibliography series ; 14)
Includes index
Vol.3: International terrorism, 1968-1980 / with a foreword and selected chronology by Lloyd W. Garrison. — c1980. — xxxvi,237p ; 24cm
ISBN 0-87436-304-7 : £16.90 B81-13387

016.359′00947 — Union of Soviet Socialist Republics. *Voenno-morskoĭ flot, 1941-1978 — Bibliographies*

Smith, Myron J.. The Soviet navy, 1941-1978 : a guide to sources in English / Myron J. Smith, Jr. — Santa Barbara ; Oxford : ABC-Clio, c1980. — xix,211p,[2]leaves of plates : 2ill ; 24cm. — (The War/peace bibliography series ; 9)
Includes index
ISBN 0-87436-265-2 : £16.50 B81-04049

016.361 — Ireland *(Republic)*. Voluntary welfare work. Organisations: National Social Service Council. Stock: Teaching aids: Non-book materials — *Catalogues*

National Social Service Council. Audio-visual training aids library. — Dublin (71 Lr Leeson St., Dublin 2) : National Social Service Council, 1980. — 47leaves ; 30cm
Unpriced (pbk) B81-08084

016.3616′1′09 — Regional planning, *to 1979 — Bibliographies*

Sutcliffe, Anthony. The history of urban and regional planning : an annotated bibliography / Anthony Sutcliffe. — London : Mansell, 1981. — ix,284p ; 23cm
Includes index
ISBN 0-7201-0901-9 : £12.95 : CIP rev.
Primary classification 016.3077′6′09 B80-18148

016.3622′92′088042 — Women. Alcoholism. Psychosocial aspects — *Bibliographies*

Chalfant, H. Paul. Social and behavioral aspects of female alcoholism : an annotated bibliography / compiled by H. Paul Chalfant and Brent S. Roper with the assistance of Carmen Rivera-Worley. — Westport, Conn. ; London : Greenwood Press, 1980. — xvi,145p ; 25cm
ISBN 0-313-20947-2 : £14.50 B81-23596

016.3624 — Handicapped persons — *Bibliographies*

A **Select** list of books to mark International Year of the Disabled 1981 / SELB Library Service. — [Armagh] ([1 Markethill Rd., Armagh, N. Ireland BT60 1NR]) : [The Service], [1981]. — 12p ; 22cm
Unpriced (pbk) B81-25415

016.3624′1 — Partially sighted persons — *Bibliographies*

Cameron, Agnes T.. Partial sight : bibliography on the living problems of partially sighted people. — 2nd ed. — Chertsey : Reedbooks for the Disabled Living Foundation, Nov.1981. — [120]p
ISBN 0-906544-07-6 (pbk) : CIP entry B81-39240

016.3628′2 — Single-parent families — *Bibliographies*

Schlesinger, Benjamin. The one-parent family : perspectives and annotated bibliography / Benjamin Schlesinger. — 4th ed. — Toronto ; London : University of Toronto Press, 1978 (1980 [printing]). — x,224p ; 24cm
Previous ed.: 1975. — Includes bibliographies and index
ISBN 0-8020-2335-5 : £7.50
Also classified at 362.8′2′097 B81-25471

016.3631′1 — Great Britain. *Health and Safety Executive*. Publications — *Lists — Serials*

Great Britain. *Health and Safety Executive*. Publications catalogue / Health and Safety Executive. — ′80. — London : H.M.S.O., 1980. — vi,185p
ISBN 0-11-883263-8 : £3.50 : CIP rev.
ISSN 0143-4047 B80-07197

016.3631′1′0941 — Great Britain. Industrial health & industrial safety — *Bibliographies*

Everall, Anne. Health and safety at work : a select bibliography : 2nd supplement / compiled by Anne Everall. — Birmingham (Paradise Circus, Birmingham B3 3HQ) : Science and Technology Department, Central Library, 1978. — 66p ; 30cm. — (Technical bibliographies / Birmingham Public Libraries, ISSN 0308-4191 ; 11b)
Unpriced (pbk) B81-15667

016.3631′2575 — Great Britain. Pedestrians. Road safety. Organisations: Pedestrians′ Association for Road Safety. Archives — *Lists*

Bassett, Philippa. List of the historical records of the Pedestrians′ Association for Road Safety / compiled by Philippa Bassett as part of a research project funded by the Social Science Research Council. — [Birmingham] : Centre for Urban and Regional Studies, University of Birmingham, 1980. — iv,5leaves ; 30cm. — (Lists of historical records)
At head of title: Centre for Urban and Regional Studies, University of Birmingham and Institute of Agricultural History, University of Reading
Unpriced (pbk) B81-27674

016.3636′9′06041 — Great Britain. Buildings of historical importance. Conservation. Organisations: Society for the Protection of Ancient Buildings. Archives — *Lists*

Bassett, Philippa. List of the historical records of the Society for the Protection of Ancient Buildings / compiled by Philippa Bassett as part of a research project funded by the Social Science Research Council. — [Birmingham] : Centre for Urban and Regional Studies, University of Birmingham, 1980. — xi,261p ; 30cm. — (Lists of historical records)
At head of title: Centre for Urban and Regional Studies, University of Birmingham and Institute of Agricultural History, University of Reading
Unpriced (pbk) B81-27676

016.3636′9′060411 — Scotland. Landscape conservation. Organisations: National Trust for Scotland. Archives — *Lists*

Bassett, Philippa. List of the historical records of the National Trust For Scotland / compiled by Philippa Bassett as part of a research project funded by the Social Science Research Council. — [Birmingham] : Centre for Urban and Regional Studies, 1980. — xl,97p ; 30cm. — (Lists of historical records)
At head of title: Centre For Urban and Regional Studies University of Birmingham and Institute of Agricultural History University of Reading
Unpriced (pbk)
Also classified at 016.72′09411 B81-27627

016.3637′392′06041 — Great Britain. Atmosphere. Pollution. Organisations: National Society for Clean Air. Archives — *Lists*

Bassett, Philippa. A list of the historical records retained by the National Society for Clean Air / compiled by Philippa Bassett as part of a research project funded by the Social Science Research Council. — [Birmingham] : Centre for Urban and Regional Studies, University of Birmingham, 1980. — x,18p ; 30cm. — (Lists of historical records)
At head of title: Centre for Urban and Regional Studies, University of Birmingham and Institute of Agricultural History, University of Reading
Unpriced (pbk) B81-27675

016.3641′524′0924 — United States. Kennedy, John F.. Assassination. Inquiry reports — *Indexes*

Meagher, Sylvia. Master index to the J.F.K. assassination investigations : the reports and supporting volumes of the House Select Committee on Assassinations and the Warren Commission / by Sylvia Meagher in collaboration with Gary Owens. — Metuchen ; London : Scarecrow, 1980. — xi,435p ; 23cm
ISBN 0-8108-1331-9 : £14.00 B81-04882

016.37 — Education — *Bibliographies*

Berry, Dorothea M.. A bibliographic guide to educational research / Dorothea M. Berry. — 2nd ed. — Metuchen ; London : Scarecrow, 1980. — lx,215p : ill ; 23cm
Previous ed.: 1975. — Includes index
ISBN 0-8108-1351-3 : £7.70 B81-03341

Clarke, John L.. Educational development : a select bibliography with particular reference to further and higher education / John L. Clarke. — London : Kogan Page, 1981. — 207p ; 23cm
ISBN 0-85038-346-3 : £12.00 B81-22199

016.37 — Education. Serial articles — *Indexes — Serials*

British education index. — Vol.16 (Jan.-Dec.1980). — London : The British Library, Bibliographic Services Division, c1981. — viii,304p
ISBN 0-900220-90-2 : Unpriced
ISSN 0007-0637 B81-28381

016.37 — United States. Education. Information & resources centres: Educational Resources Information Center. Stock — *Abstracts*

Drazan, Joseph Gerald. The unknown ERIC : a selection of documents for the general library / Joseph Gerald Drazan. — Metuchen ; London : Scarecrow, 1981. — vii,231p ; 23cm
Includes index
ISBN 0-8108-1402-1 : £8.75 B81-22832

016.37'0947 — Soviet Union. Edcuation. Documents on education in Soviet Union: Documents in English, ***1893-1978 — Lists***

Yoo, Yushin. Soviet education : an annotated bibliography and readers' guide to works in English, 1893-1978 / compiled by Yushin Yoo. — Westport ; London : Greenwood Press, 1980. — xvi,408p ; 25cm
Includes index
ISBN 0-313-22085-9 : £23.75 B81-23457

016.37191 — Physically handicapped school leavers ***— Bibliographies***

Tumim, Winifred. The disabled school-leaver : books for disabled school-leavers, their families, friends and employers / Winifred Tumim. — London : National Book League, 1981. — 46p : 1ill ; 21cm
Published in conjunction with a touring exhibition arranged by the National Book League
ISBN 0-85353-361-x (unbound) : £0.30 B81-29455

016.37314'25 — School leavers. Vocational preparation. Teaching aids ***— Lists***

Counselling and Careers Information Resource Centre. Games, kits, simulations / North East London Polytechnic, Livingstone House Library, Counselling and Careers Information Resource Centre. — 2nd ed. — [London] ([Livingstone House, Livingstone Rd., E15 2LJ]) : [The Library], [1980]. — [23] leaves ; 30cm
Cover title. — Previous ed.: 1978
Unpriced (pbk) B81-06785

016.374'012 — Dyfed. Aberystwyth. Schools of librarianship. Libraries: College of Librarianship, Wales. ***Library.*** **Stock: Books for adult literacy education** ***— Catalogues***

College of Librarianship, Wales. ***Library.*** Adult literacy : a catalogue of materials in the Library of the College of Librarianship Wales / compiled by Ann Clarke. — 2nd ed. / augm. and rev. by Mary Jones. — Aberystwyth (Aberystwyth, Dyfed SY23 3AS) : The College, 1979. — 78p ; 30cm. — (Occasional paper / College of Librarianship, Wales ; no.7)
Previous ed.: 1977. — Includes index
ISBN 0-904020-20-7 (unbound) : £1.00 B81-34894

016.374'941 — Great Britain. Adult education ***— Bibliographies***

Morrison, Charles M.. An annotated bibliography of adult education / by C.M. Morrison. — [Edinburgh] ([15 St John St., Edinburgh EH8 8JR]) : Scottish Council for Research in Education, [1980]. — 62 leaves ; 30cm
ISBN 0-901116-28-9 (pbk) : Unpriced B81-20051

016.378'1056'0973 — United States. Higher education institutions. Students. Admission. Use of positive discrimination ***— Bibliographies***

Swanson, Kathryn. Affirmative action and preferential admissions in higher education : an annotated bibliography / by Kathryn Swanson. — Metuchen ; London : Scarecrow, 1981. — viii,336p ; 23cm
Includes index
ISBN 0-8108-1411-0 : £12.25 B81-26608

016.378'173'0941 — Great Britain. Higher education. Audio-visual aids ***— Lists***

Audio-visual materials for higher education. — London : British Universities Film Council, Sept.1981
Previous ed.: 1979
Supplement. — [110]p
ISBN 0-901299-28-6 : £8.00 : CIP entry B81-24628

016.378'173'0941 — Great Britain. Higher education. Teaching aids: Audiovisual materials ***— Lists — Serials***

Higher Education Learning Programmes Information Service catalogue / British Universities Film Council. — 5th ed. (1978). — London (81, Dean St., W1V 6AA) : British Universities Film Council, c1978. — xv,142p
Also entitled: HELPIS catalogue
ISBN 0-901299-19-7 : £6.50 (£5.50 to BUFC members) B81-04915

Higher Education Learning Programmes Information Service catalogue / British Universities Film Council. — 6th ed. (1980-81). — London (81, Dean St., W1V 6AA) : The Council, 1980. — xiv,193p
ISBN 0-901299-26-x : £8.50 : CIP rev. B80-19549

016.3801'025 — Great Britain. National libraries: Science Reference Library. Stock: Serials containing directories of industries & trades ***— Catalogues***

Science Reference Library. Trade directories in journals : a list of those appearing within numbered parts of serials / British Library, Reference Division, Science Reference Library ; [compiled] by H. Rahman and G.S. Cooper. — 2nd ed. — London (25 Southampton Buildings, Chancery Lane, WC2A 1AW) : The Library, 1981. — 12p : ill ; 30cm
Cover title. — Previous ed.: 1980. — Includes index
ISBN 0-902914-62-6 (pbk) : Unpriced : CIP rev. B81-25863

016.381'456413'0072041 — Great Britain. Grocery trades. Research ***— Indexes — Serials***

. A Guide to current research / Institute of Grocery Distribution, Research Services. — 1979/80. — [Watford] ([Letchmore Heath, Watford WD2 8DQ]) : [The Institute], [1980]. — [184]p
ISSN 0308-9509 : £30.00 B81-06686

016.385'0942 — England. Railway services: Great Western Railway ***— Bibliographies***

Prytherch, R. J.. The Great Western Railway : and other services in the West country and South Wales : a bibliography of British books published 1950-1969 / compiled by R.J. Prytherch. — Leeds (8 Cork Exchange, Leeds LS1 7BP) : Viaduct Press, 1980. — [16]p ; 22cm
ISBN 0-907298-00-1 (pbk) : £1.80 B81-08233

016.3875 — Hampshire. Southampton. Public reference libraries: Southampton Reference Library. Stock: Documents on shipping ***— Catalogues***

Southampton Reference Library. Catalogue of the Maritime collection / Southampton Reference Library, Hampshire County Library ; compiled by Gill Joye. — Southampton ([Central Library, Civic Centre, Southampton SO9 4XP]) : Southampton Reference Library, 1981. — 239p ; 30cm
Includes index
£2.50 (spiral) B81-25067

016.3875'0941'34 — Edinburgh. Universities. Libraries: University of Edinburgh. ***Library.*** **Stock: Archives of Christian Salvesen Limited** ***— Catalogues***

List of the archives of Messrs. Christian Salvesen Ltd. deposited in Edinburgh University Library / Edinburgh University Library. — Edinburgh ([George Sq. Edinburgh EH8 9LT]) : [The Library], 1981. — 23p ; 22cm
Cover title
Unpriced (pbk) B81-34679

016.3881'2 — England. Footpaths. Preservation. Organisations: Commons, Open Spaces and Footpaths Preservation Society. Archives ***— Lists***

Bassett, Philippa. A list of the historical records of the Commons, Open Spaces and Footpaths Preservation Society / compiled by Philippa Bassett as part of a research project funded by the Social Science Research Council. — [Birmingham] : Centre for Urban and Regional Studies, University of Birmingham, 1980. — vi,29p ; 30cm. — (Lists of historical records)
At head of title: Centre for Urban and Regional Studies, University of Birmingham and Institute of Agricultural History, University of Reading
Unpriced (pbk)
Primary classification 016.3332 B81-27741

016.3881'3 — Great Britain. Roadsides. Improvement. Organisations: Roads Beautifying Association. Archives ***— Lists***

Bassett, Philippa. A list of the historical records of the Roads Beautifying Association / compiled by Philippa Bassett as part of a research project funded by the Social Science Research Council. — [Birmingham] : Centre for Urban and Regional Studies, University of Birmingham, 1980. — iv,12leaves ; 30cm. — (Lists of historical records)
At head of title: Centre for Urban and Regional Studies, University of Birmingham and Institute of Agricultural History, University of Reading
Unpriced (pbk) B81-27742

016.398'352 — Legends. Arthur, ***King — Bibliographies***

The **Arthurian** bibliography / edited by Cedric E. Pickford and Rex Last ; assistant editor Christine R. Barker. — Cambridge (240 Hills Road, Cambridge) : D.S. Brewer. — (Arthurian studies ; 3)
1: Author listing. — 1981. — 820p ; 24cm
ISBN 0-85991-069-5 : £35.00 : CIP rev. B81-15827

016.4 — Language ***— Bibliographies — Serials***

Linguistic bibliography for the year ... and supplement for previous years / Permanent International Committee of Linguistics. — 1977. — [Leiden] : Permanent International Committee of Linguists under the auspices of the International Council for Philosophy and Humanistic Studies ; The Hague ; London : Nijhof, 1980. — liv,834p
ISBN 90-247-2388-4 : Unpriced B81-09177

016.41'092'4 — Linguistics. Vočadlo, Otakar ***— Bibliographies***

Bradbrook, B. R.. Otakar Vočadlo (1895-1974) : professor of English, Charles University, Prague : biography and bibliography of his works / compiled and edited by B.R. Bradbrook from material provided in Czech by L. Vočadlová. — [Bangor, Gwynedd] ([School of Education, University College of North Wales, Lôn Pobty, Bangor, Gwynedd LL57 1DZ]) : [B. R. Bradbrook], 1980. — 32p,[1]leaf of plates ; 21cm
Cover title
Unpriced (pbk) B81-33237

016.413 — Non-European languages. Dictionaries ***— Lists***

Lennox-Kay, A. R. P.. Bailey's catalogue of dictionaries and grammars in the languages of the Orient, Africa, the Americas & Oceania / [compiled by A.R.P. & J.L. Lennox-Kay]. — Folkestone : Bailey & Swinfen, c1980. — 123p ; 21cm
Includes index
ISBN 0-561-00310-6 (pbk) : Unpriced
Also classified at 016.418 B81-17288

016.418 — Non-European languages. Grammar ***— Bibliographies***

Lennox-Kay, A. R. P.. Bailey's catalogue of dictionaries and grammars in the languages of the Orient, Africa, the Americas & Oceania / [compiled by A.R.P. & J.L. Lennox-Kay]. — Folkestone : Bailey & Swinfen, c1980. — 123p ; 21cm
Includes index
ISBN 0-561-00310-6 (pbk) : Unpriced
Primary classification 016.413 B81-17288

016.42 — English language ***— Bibliographies — Serials***

Annual bibliography of English language and literature for ... / Modern Humanities Research Association. — Vol.52 (1977). — London : The Association, 1980. — 757p
ISBN 0-900547-75-8 : Unpriced
ISSN 0066-3786
Also classified at 016.82 B81-16748

016.4284 — Reading ***- Bibliographies***

Friedlander, Janet. Early reading development. — London : Harper & Row, Sept.1981. — [384]p. — (Harper reference)
ISBN 0-06-318161-4 : £25.00 : CIP entry B81-20551

016.4284 — Reading — *Bibliographies — Serials*

Goodacre, Elizabeth J.. Reading research / Elizabeth J. Goodacre. — 1975. — Reading (University of Reading, School of Education, 29 Eastern Ave., Reading, Berks RG1 5RU) : Centre for the Teaching of Reading, [1976]. — 23p
ISBN 0-7049-0399-7 : Unpriced
ISSN 0307-4560 B81-06653

Goodacre, Elizabeth J.. Reading research / Elizabeth J. Goodacre. — 1976. — Reading (University of Reading, School of Education, 29 Eastern Ave., Reading, Berks RG1 5RU) : Centre for the Teaching of Reading, [1977]. — 19p
ISBN 0-7049-0557-4 : Unpriced
ISSN 0307-4560 B81-06652

Goodacre, Elizabeth J.. Reading research / Elizabeth J. Goodacre. — 1977. — Reading (University of Reading, School of Education, 29 Eastern Ave., Reading, Berks RG1 5RU) : Centre for the Teaching of Reading, [1977]. — 32p
ISBN 0-7049-0564-7 : Unpriced
ISSN 0307-4560 B81-06651

Goodacre, Elizabeth J.. Reading research / Elizabeth J. Goodacre. — 1978. — Reading (University of Reading, School of Education, 29 Eastern Ave., Reading, Berks RG1 5RU) : Centre for the Teaching of Reading, [1979]. — 24p
ISBN 0-7049-0726-7 : Unpriced
ISSN 0307-4560 B81-06650

016.4284'07'1 — Schools. Curriculum subjects: Reading. Teaching — *Bibliographies*

Moyle, Donald. Teaching reading : an annotated bibliography / compiled by Donald Moyle and Jean Ainslie. — 2nd ed. — London : National Book League, 1981. — 40p ; 21cm
Previous ed.: 1977
ISBN 0-85353-359-8 (pbk) : Unpriced : CIP rev. B81-07456

016.4286'2 — Books for illiterate adults: Books in English — *Bibliographies*

Take off - : a guide to books for students who are learning reading, writing, spelling, maths, life-skills, handwriting / compiled by Jenny Armour. — London : Library Association, 1980. — 180p : ill,1map ; 21cm
Includes index
ISBN 0-85365-673-8 (pbk) : £3.50 : CIP rev. B80-13321

016.43 — German language. Theses accepted by British universities — *Lists — Serials*

Theses in progress at British universities and other institutions of higher education and theses completed in ... with work published in ... and work due to be published in ... by members of the Conference of University Teachers of German in Great Britain and Ireland as known on 1 January ... / University of London, Institute of Germanic Studies. — [1980]-. — [London] ([29 Russell Square, WC1B 5DP]) : The Institute, c1980-. — v. ; 25cm. — (Library publication / Institute of Germanic Studies)
Annual. — Continues: Theses in progress at British universities and work due to be published by members of the Conference of University Teachers of German in Great Britain and Ireland
ISSN 0260-5031 = Theses in progress at British universities and other institutions of higher education : Unpriced
Primary classification 016.83 B81-06335

016.5 — Oxfordshire. Oxford. Universities. Libraries: Bodleian Library. Exhibits: Islamic manuscripts on science, *to 1600 — Catalogues*

Doctrina arabum : science and philosophy in medieval Islam & their transmission to Europe : an exhibition held at the Bodleian Library, Oxford, Spring-Summer 1981. — [Oxford] : [The Library], c1981. — 19p ; 15x22cm
Includes index
ISBN 0-900177-80-2 (pbk) : Unpriced B81-24909

016.5 — Science. Documents on science: Documents in English: Documents with American imprints: Documents in print — *Lists — Serials*

Scientific and technical books and serials in print . — 1981. — New York ; London : Bowker, c1980. — xxiii,2829p
ISBN 0-8352-1313-7 : Unpriced
ISSN 0000-054x
Also classified at 016.6 B81-16254

016.54'01'12 — Alchemy — *Bibliographies*

Pritchard, Alan. Alchemy : a bibliography of English-language writings : Alan Pritchard. — London : Routledge & Kegan Paul jointly with the Library Association, 1980. — vii,439p ; 24cm
Includes index
ISBN 0-7100-0472-9 : £30.00 : CIP rev. B80-09552

016.54'05 — Great Britain. National libraries: Science Reference Library. Stock: Serials on chemistry — *Catalogues*

Science Reference Library. Periodicals on chemistry held by the Science Reference Library / compiled by Christine L. de Hamel. — London : Science Reference Library, 1980. — ii,139p ; 30cm
ISBN 0-902914-59-6 (unbound) : £2.00 B81-17231

016.5412'8 — Molecules. Wave functions — *Bibliographies*

A **Bibliography** of ab initio molecular wave functions : supplement for 1978-80. — Oxford : Clarendon Press, Sept.1981. — [350]p. — (Oxford science research papers)
ISBN 0-19-855367-6 : £22.50 : CIP entry B81-21633

016.5413'63 — Phase diagrams — *Bibliographies*

Wisniak, Jaime. Phase diagrams : a literature source book / Jaime Wisniak. — Amsterdam ; Oxford : Elsevier, 1981. — 2v. ; 25cm. — (Physical sciences data ; 10)
ISBN 0-444-41981-0 : Unpriced : CIP rev.
ISBN 0-444-41980-2 (Pt.A) : Unpriced
ISBN 0-444-41984-5 (Pt.B) : Unpriced B81-32330

016.547 — Organic compounds. Documents on organic compounds - *Indexes*

Lewis, D. A.. Index of reviews in organic chemistry. — London : Royal Society of Chemistry, Apr.1981
1980 supplement to the second cumulative volume. — 1v.
ISBN 0-85186-549-6 (pbk) : CIP entry B81-05142

016.551 — Geology — *Bibliographies*

Ward, Dederick C.. Geologic reference sources : a subject and regional bibliography of publications and maps in the geological sciences. — 2nd ed. / Dederick C. Ward, Marjorie W. Wheeler & Robert A. Bier. — Metuchen, N.J. ; London : Scarecrow Press, 1981. — xxv,560p ; 23cm
Previous ed.: / by Dederick C. Ward, Marjorie W. Wheeler. Metuchen, N.J. : Scarecrow Press 1972. — Includes index
ISBN 0-8108-1428-5 : £21.00 B81-36520

016.5514'47 — Caves. Serial articles — *Lists — Serials*

Current titles in speleology. — No.13 (1980). — Crymych (Rhychydwr, Crymych, Dyfed SA41 3RB) : Anne Oldham, 1981. — xiv,221p
£5.00 B81-28710

016.5519 — Geology. Chemical analysis. Electron spin resonance spectroscopy — *Bibliographies*

Cubitt, John M.. A bibliography of electron spin resonance : applications in the earth sciences / by John M. Cubitt, Cynthia V. Burek. — Norwich : Geo Abstracts Ltd., c1980. — 64p ; 21cm. — (Geo Abstracts bibliography ; no.6)
Includes index
ISBN 0-86094-034-9 (pbk) : £2.50 B81-04420

016.55866 — Ecuador. Geological features — *Bibliographies*

Bristow, C. R.. An annotated bibliography of Ecuadorian geology / C.R. Bristow. — London : H.M.S.O., 1981. — 38p : 2maps ; 28cm. — (Overseas geology and mineral resources ; no.58)
Includes index
ISBN 0-11-884140-8 (pbk) : £5.25 B81-36470

016.574 — Natural environment. Manuscripts in repositories in Great Britain — *Catalogues*

Bridson, Gavin D. R.. Natural history manuscript resources in the British Isles / compiled by Gavin D.R. Bridson, Valerie C. Phillips and Anthony P. Harvey. — London : Mansell, 1980. — xxxiv,473p ; 29cm
Bibliography: pxv-xxi. - Includes index
ISBN 0-7201-1559-0 : £97.00 : CIP rev. B80-11711

016.574 — Natural environment. Research projects supported by Natural Environment Research Council — *Lists*

Natural Environment Research Council. Research grants awarded by the Natural Environment Research Council : current on 1st October 1980. — [Swindon] ([Polaris House, North Star Ave., Swindon, Wilts. SN2 1EU]) : The Council, 1980. — v,70p ; 30cm. — (The Natural Environment Research Council publications. Series D, ISSN 0309-6874 ; no.23)
Cover title
Unpriced (pbk) B81-13159

016.574 — Natural history. Documents on natural history, *1495-1900 — Lists*

Freeman, R. B.. British natural history books, 1495-1900 : a handlist / by R.B. Freeman. — Folkestone : Dawson, 1980. — 437p ; 23cm
Includes index
ISBN 0-7129-0971-0 : £20.00 : CIP rev. B80-07195

016.574 — Organisms. Field guides — *Lists*

Huckin, Dorothy. Flora and fauna of localities : a bibliography of books and articles dealing with the plant and animal life of specific countries and regions of the world / by Dorothy Huckin. — Biggleswade (8 Ashby Drive, Caldecote, Biggleswade, Beds. SG18 9DJ) : Clover, 1981
Vol.1: Great Britain & Europe. — 116p ; 21cm
£12.50(set of 2 vol.) (spiral) B81-31684

Huckin, Dorothy. Flora and fauna of localities : a bibliography of books and articles dealing with the plant and animal life of specific countries and regions of the world / by Dorothy Huckin. — Biggleswade (8 Ashby Drive, Caldecote, Biggleswade, Beds. SG18 9DJ) : Clover, 1981
Vol.2: Africa, America, Asia, Australia, & U.S.S.R.. — 158p ; 21cm
£12.50(set of 2 vol.) (spiral) B81-31685

016.574'028 — Biology. Use of ultrasonic waves — *Bibliographies*

Ultrasound in biomedicine. — Oxford : Pergamon, Dec.1981. — [712]p
ISBN 0-08-027374-2 : £41.70 : CIP entry
Also classified at 016.610'28 B81-32602

016.574'0724 — Haemic cells & lymphoid cells. Culture — *Bibliographies — Serials*

Haemic and lymphatic cell culture. — Vol.1, no.1 (Jan.1981)-. — Sheffield : University of Sheffield Biomedical Information Service, 1981-. — v. ; 30cm
Monthly
ISSN 0260-5880 = Haemic and lymphatic cell culture : Unpriced B81-25009

016.57419'258 — Organisms. Cytochromes — *Bibliographies — Serials*

Cytochromes. — Vol.1, no.1 (Jan.1981)-. — Sheffield : University of Sheffield Biomedical Information Service, 1981-. — v. ; 30cm
Monthly
ISSN 0260-1133 = Cytochromes : Unpriced B81-25010

016.5745'06'041 — Great Britain. Ecology. Organisations: British Ecological Society. Archives — *Lists*

Bassett, Philippa. A list of the historical records of the British Ecological Society / compiled by Philippa Bassett as part of a research project funded by the Social Science Research Council. — [Birmingham] : Centre for Urban and Regional Studies, 1980. — vii,7p ; 30cm. — (Lists of historical records)
At head of title: Centre for Urban and Regional Studies University of Birmingham and Institute of Agricultural History University of Reading
Unpriced (pbk) B81-27625

016.5745'26325 — Great Britain. Peat ecosystems — *Bibliographies*

Field, E. M.. Peatland ecology in the British Isles : a bibliogrphy / E.M. Field, D.A. Goode. — [Cambridge] : Institute of Terrestrial Ecology (National Environment Research Council) ; Banbury (Information and Library Services, Calthorpe House, Calthorpe St., Banbury, Oxon OX16 8EX) : Nature Conservancy Council, 1981. — vi,178p ; 31cm
Includes index
ISBN 0-86139-118-7 (spiral) : £4.00
B81-37630

016.5745'2636 — Great Britain. Coastal ecosystems & estuary ecosystems — *Bibliographies — Serials*

Estuaries and coastal waters of the British Isles. — No.4 (1980). — Plymouth (Citadel Hill, Plymouth, [Devon]) : Marine Biological Association of the United Kingdom, 1980. — vi,128p
ISSN 0261-0663 : Unpriced B81-21936

016.574941 — Great Britain. Coastal waters. Natural environment — *Bibliographies — Serials*

Estuaries and coastal waters of the British Isles : an annual bibliography of recent scientific papers / Library and Information Services, Marine Biological Association of the United Kingdom. — No.3 (1979)-. — Plymouth (Citadel Hill, Plymouth) : The Association, 1979-. — v. ; 30cm
Continues: Estuaries of the British Isles. — Description based on: No.5 (1981)
ISSN 0261-0663 = Esturaries and coastal waters of the British Isles : £6.50 B81-17476

016.5749427 — North-west England. Organisms — *Bibliographies*

Gray, L. C.. Environmental bibliography of North-West England / [compiled by L.C. Gray]. — Lancaster ([Bailrigg, Lancaster LA1 4YH]) : University of Lancaster Library, 1980. — iii,169p ; 30cm. — (University of Lancaster Library occasional papers ; no.10)
Includes index
ISBN 0-901699-73-x (pbk) : Unpriced
B81-14516

016.5749718 — Newfoundland. Organisms — *Bibliographies*

Laird, M.. Bibliography of the natural history of Newfoundland and Labrador / M. Laird. — London : Academic Press, 1980. — lxxi,376p : ill,maps ; 24cm
Maps on lining papers. — Bibliography: plxiv-lxxi. — Includes index
ISBN 0-12-434050-4 : £25.00 : CIP rev.
B79-35139

016.581 — Vascular plants — *Bibliographies — Serials*

The **Kew** record of taxonomic literature relating to vascular plants / Royal Botanic Gardens, Kew. — 1976. — London : H.M.S.O., 1981. — xv,385p
ISBN 0-11-241119-3 : Unpriced
ISSN 0307-2835 B81-24130

016.5811'13 — Plants. Water — *Bibliographies — Serials*

Water-in-plants bibliography. — Vol.5 (1979). — The Hague ; London : Junk, 1981. — vi,232p
ISBN 90-619-3905-4 : Unpriced B81-09276

016.5811'33 — Plants. Carbon. Assimilation — *Bibliographies — Serials*

Photosynthetic carbon assimilation. — Vol.1, no.1 (Jan.1981)-. — Sheffield (Sheffield S10 2TN) : University of Sheffield Biomedical Information Service, 1981-. — v. ; 30cm
Monthly
ISSN 0260-5899 = Photosynthetic carbon assimilation : Unpriced B81-30006

016.5816'4 — Plants. Industrial biology — *Bibliographies — Serials*

Plant biotechnology. — Vol.1, no.1 (Jan.1981)-. — Sheffield (Sheffield S10 2TN) : University of Sheffield Biomedical Information Service, 1981-. — v. ; 30cm
Monthly
ISSN 0260-5902 = Plant biotechnology : Unpriced B81-30007

016.59119'24 — Animals. Purines — *Bibliographies — Serials*

Purines. — Vol.1, no.1 (Jan.1981)-. — Sheffield (Sheffield S10 2TN) : University of Sheffield Biomedical Information Service, 1981-. — v. ; 30cm
Monthly
ISSN 0260-1141 = Purines : Unpriced
B81-30005

016.5951'46 — Earthworms — *Bibliographies*

Satchell, J. E.. A bibliography of earthworm research / J.E. Satchell, Kyla Martin. — Grange-over-Sands (Merlewood Research Station, Grange-over-Sands, Cumbria) : Institute of Terrestrial Ecology, 1981. — [188]p ; 30cm
Unpriced (spiral) B81-39477

016.6 — Technology — *Bibliographies — Serials*

CTI : current technology index. — Vol.1, no.1 (Jan. 1981)-. — London : Library Association Pub., 1981. — v. ; 30cm
Monthly. — Continues: British technology index
ISSN 0260-6593 = CTI. Current technology index : £140.00 per year B81-20300

016.6 — Technology. Documents on technology: Documents in English: Documents with American imprints: Documents in print — *Lists — Serials*

Scientific and technical books and serials in print . — 1981. — New York ; London : Bowker, c1980. — xxiii,2829p
ISBN 0-8352-1313-7 : Unpriced
ISSN 0000-054x
Primary classification 016.5 B81-16254

016.602'18 — Technology. British standards — *Lists — Serials*

British standards yearbook. — 1981. — London : British Standards Institution, [1980]. — 966p
ISBN 0-580-11479-1 : £14.00 B81-10263

016.608 — Great Britain. National libraries: Science Reference Library. Stock: Serials on industrial property — *Catalogues*

Barton, Helena M.. Industrial property literature : a directory of journals / Helena M. Barton. — London (25 Southampton Buildings, WC2A 1AW) : British Library, Science Reference Library, c1981. — 60p ; 30cm
ISBN 0-902914-58-8 (pbk) : Unpriced
B81-18823

016.608741 — British patents — *Abstracts — Serials*

Bulletin of inventions and summary of patent specifications. — Issue no.1 (1981)-. — London ([Flat 160, 19 Newport Court, WC2H 7JS) : Okikiolu Scientific and Industrial], 1981-. — ill ; 22cm
ISSN 0261-023x = Bulletin of inventions and summary of patent specifications : £2.00 per issue B81-14364

016.608741 — Expired British patents — *Lists — Serials*

Expired British patents & licences of right. — Vol.1, no.1 (Jan. 1981)-. — London (229 High Holborn, WC1V 7DA) : Scientific and Medical Information Services, 1981-. — v. ; 30cm
Monthly. — Description based on: Vol.1, no.4 (Apr. 1981)
ISSN 0260-4698 = Expired British patents & licences of right : Unpriced B81-38983

016.61 — Medicine. Educational films — *Lists*

Medical films 1980 : selected for their educational value. — London : Published by the British Life Assurance Trust for Health and Medical Education with the British Medical Association, c1980. — 2v.(242,xiip) ; 30cm + 2sheets(4sides)
'This catalogue contains films available from The BMA/BLAT Film Library and films distributed from other sources'. — Includes index
Unpriced (spiral) B81-14016

016.61 — Tyne and Wear *(Metropolitan County)*. **Newcastle upon Tyne. Universities. Libraries: University of Newcastle upon Tyne.** *Library*. **Stock: Documents on medicine. Collections: Pybus Collection** — *Catalogues*

University of Newcastle upon Tyne. *Library*. Catalogue of the Pybus collection : of medical books, letters and engravings 15th-20th centuries held in the University Library, Newcastle upon Tyne / compiled by Joan S. Emmerson. — Manchester : Published on behalf of the University Library, Newcastle upon Tyne by Manchester University Press, c1981. — xiv,270p : ill,facsims,1port ; 31cm
Bibliography: pxi-xii. — Includes index
ISBN 0-7190-1295-3 : £35.00 : CIP rev.
B81-12851

016.610'28 — Great Britain. National Libraries: Science Reference Library. Stock : Documents on medical equipment — *Catalogues*

Oates, Judith. Medical equipment. — London : British Library, Science Reference Library, Nov.1981. — [12]p. — (Guidelines / Science Reference Library)
ISBN 0-902914-64-2 (pbk) : CIP entry
B81-30884

016.610'28 — Medicine. Use of ultrasonic waves — *Bibliographies*

Ultrasound in biomedicine. — Oxford : Pergamon, Dec.1981. — [712]p
ISBN 0-08-027374-2 : £41.70 : CIP entry
Primary classification 016.574'028 B81-32602

016.61073'678 — Midwifery — *Bibliographies — Serials*

Royal College of Midwives. *Library*. Current awareness service : a list of recent literature on midwifery / compiled by Royal College of Midwives Library. — No.1 (Feb.1980)-. — London (15 Mansfield St., W1M 0BE) : The Library, 1980-. — v. ; 30cm
6 issues yearly
ISSN 0260-5848 = Current awareness service — Royal College of Midwives Library : £5.00 per year B81-04089

016.611'01816 — Man. Cells. Genetics — *Bibliographies — Serials*

Clinical cytogenetics. — Vol.1, no.1 (Jan.1981)-. — Sheffield (Sheffield S10 2TN) : University of Sheffield Biomedical Information Service, 1981-. — v. ; 30cm
Monthly
ISSN 0260-5872 = Clinical cytogenetics : Unpriced B81-38518

016.613'07 — Health education — *Bibliographies*

Chafetz. Health education : an annotated bibliography on lifestyle, behavior and health / Marion C. Chafetz. — New York ; London : Plenum, c1981. — 272p ; 24cm
Includes index
Unpriced B81-36113

016.613'0973 — United States. Man. Health — *Bibliographies*

Rees, Alan M.. The consumer health information source book / Alan M. Rees and Blanche A. Young. — New York ; London : Bowker, 1981. — xxi,450p ; 24cm. — (Consumer information series)
Includes index
ISBN 0-8352-1336-6 : Unpriced B81-24185

016.615'364 — Medicine. Drug therapy. Adrenocorticotrophic hormones — *Bibliographies — Serials*

ACTH & related peptides. — Jan.1981-. — Sheffield (Sheffield S10 2TN) : University of Sheffield Biomedical Information Service, 1981-. — v. ; 30cm
Monthly
ISSN 0260-1117 = ACTH & related peptides : Unpriced B81-38516

016.615'71 — Man. Adrenergic receptors — *Bibliographies — Serials*

Adrenergic receptors. — Jan.1981-. — Sheffield (Sheffield S10 2TN) : University of Sheffield Biomedical Information Service, 1981-. — v. ; 30cm
Monthly
ISSN 0260-1125 = Adrenergic receptors : Unpriced B81-38517

016.6159'2539224 — Man. Toxic effects of asbestos *— Bibliographies*

Berton, Alberta D.. Asbestosis : a comprehensive bibliography / compiled by Alberta D. Berton assisted by K. Bernice Odom. — New York ; London : IFI/Plenum in conjunction with Medical Documentation Service, c1980. — 393p ; 28cm. — (Biomedical information guides ; v.1)
ISBN 0-306-65176-9 : Unpriced B81-09834

016.616'00967'9 — Mozambique. Population. Diseases — *Bibliographies*

Cliff, Julie L.. Health in Mozambique : a select bibliography 1950-1980 / Julie L. Cliff. — London (34 Percy St., W1P 9FG) : Mozambique Angola and Guine Information Centre, 1980. — 29p leaves ; 30cm
Includes index
£2.50 (pbk) B81-04631

016.61607'543 — Man. Diagnosis. Ultrasonography *— Abstracts — Serials*

Clinical ultrasound review. — Vol.1-. — New York ; Chichester : Wiley, c1981-. — v. : ill ; 26cm
Annual
£20.00 B81-13034

016.6163'98 — Man. Obesity — *Bibliographies*

Smith, Anne, *1954-*. Obesity : a bibliography 1974-1979 / compiled and edited by Anne Smith ; advisers J.S. Garrow, J.T. Silverstone ; editorial assistance Candida Chaplin. — London (1 Falconberg Court, W1V 5FG) : Information Retrieval Ltd, c1980. — 340p ; 24cm
Includes index
ISBN 0-904147-17-7 : £22.50 B81-00691

016.6166'3 — Man. Incontinence — *Bibliographies*

Mandelstam, Dorothy. Incontinence. — Chertsey : Reedbooks, Oct.1981. — [104]p
ISBN 0-906544-06-8 (pbk) : £7.00 : CIP entry B81-30278

016.61689'14 — Medicine. Brief psychotherapy — *Bibliographies*

Mandel, Harvey P.. Short-term psychotherapy and brief treatment techniques : an annotated bibliography 1920-1980 / Harvey P. Mandel. — New York ; London : Plenum, c1981. — xxii,682p ; 24cm
Includes index
ISBN 0-306-40658-6 : Unpriced B81-29873

016.61699'2027 — Laboratory animals. Tumours. Transplantation. Research — *Bibliographies — Serials*

Research using transplanted tumours of laboratory animals : a cross referenced bibliography. — 13 (1976). — London (Burtonhole Lane, Mill Hill, NW7 1AD) : Registry and Information Service for Experimental Tumours, Research Data Unit, Imperial Cancer Research Fund, [1977]. — 202p
Unpriced B81-08180

Research using transplanted tumours of laboratory animals : a cross-referenced bibliography. — 15 (1978). — London (Burtonhole Lane, Mill Hill, NW7 1AD) : Registry and Information Service for Experimental Tumours, Research Data Unit, Imperial Cancer Research Fund, [1979]. — 245p
Unpriced B81-08179

016.6202'8 — Ultrasonic waves. Use — *Abstracts — Serials*

Ultrasound patents & papers. — Vol.1, no.1 (July 1980)-. — London (Kingsbourne House, 229 High Holborn, WC1V 7DA) : Scientific and Medical Information Services, 1980-. — v. : ill ; 30cm
Vol.1, no.1 preceded by a prepublication issue
ISSN 0260-4043 = Ultrasound patents & papers : Unpriced B81-02005

016.6213815'284 — Electronic equipment. Metal oxide semicomductor field effect transistors — *Bibliographies*

Agajanian, A. H.. MOSFET technologies : a comprehensive bibliography / compiled by A.H. Agajanian. — New York ; London : IFI / Plenum, c1980. — xii,377p ; 26cm. — (IFI data base library)
Includes index
ISBN 0-306-65193-9 : Unpriced B81-04108

016.621402'5 — Heat pumps — *Bibliographies*

Loyd, Stephen. The heat pump : an annotated bibliography with a survey of suppliers / Stephen Loyd. — Bracknell (Old Bracknell La., Bracknell, Berks. RG12 4AH) : BSRIA, 1981. — 106p ; 30cm. — (Bibliography / BSRIA ; LB 103/81)
Previous ed.: 1975
ISBN 0-86022-099-0 (pbk) : £9.00 B81-14572

016.62148 — Nuclear power — *Bibliographies*

Nuclear power and Sizewell 'B' / Suffolk County Library. — [Ipswich] ([Central Library, Northgate St., Ipswich IP1 3DE]) : [The Library], [1981]?. — [12]p ; 30cm
ISBN 0-86055-080-x (unbound) : £0.50 B81-34258

016.6241'84 — Temporary structures. Construction materials: Timber — *Bibliographies*

Timber in temporary works : an guide to available literature. — High Wycombe : Timber Research and Development Association, c1981. — xiv,107p ; 30cm
ISBN 0-901348-56-2 (spiral) : Unpriced B81-34550

016.627'54'0942827 — Nottinghamshire. Nottingham. Universities. Libraries: University of Nottingham. *Manuscripts Department.* **Stock: Archives of Hatfield Chase Corporation,** *1626-1973 — Lists*

University of Nottingham. *Manuscripts Department.* Hatfield Chase Corporation 2nd deposit 1626-1973. — [Nottingham] ([University Park, Nottingham NG7 2RD]) : [The Department], [1980]. — 53p ; 30cm
Unpriced (pbk) B81-08057

016.6285'3 — Industrial buildings. Air. Pollution. Control measures: Ventilation — *Bibliographies*

Loyd, Stephen. Industrial process ventilation : an annotated bibliography / Stephen Loyd. — Bracknell (Old Bracknell La., Bracknell, Berks. RG12 4AH) : Building Services Research and Information Association, 1979. — 79p ; 30cm. — (Bibliography / BSRIA ; LB107/79)
ISBN 0-86022-071-0 (pbk) : £6.00 (£2.00 to members) B81-21274

016.62913 — Great Britain. Aeronautical engineering. Organisations: Royal Aeronautical Society. Publications, *1897-1977 — Indexes*

Royal Aeronautical Society. Publications index 1897-1977 / The Royal Aeronautical Society ; compiled by Francis Maccabee. — London (4 Hamilton Place, W1V 0BQ) : The Society, 1979. — 560p ; 21cm
Unpriced (spiral) B81-23615

016.6292'53 — Great Britain. National libraries: British Library. *Science Reference Library.* **Stock: Documents on non-petrol motor fuels —** *Bibliographies*

British Library. *Science Reference Library.* Automobile fuels : the alternatives to petroleum : a guide to selected literature / The British Library, Science Reference Library. — Rev. ed. / [compiled by D.M. King and R.G. Goldfinch]. — [London] ([25 Southampton Buildings, Chancery La., WC2A 1AW]) : [SRL], 1980. — 12p ; 30cm. — (Guideline / British Library Science Reference Library)
ISBN 0-902914-56-1 (unbound) : Unpriced B81-08171

016.6298'92 — Industrial robots — *Bibliographies*

Farmer, Penny. Robotics bibliography 1970-1981 / Penny Farmer, Alan Gomersall. — Bedford : IFS, c1981. — xvii,190p ; 30cm
Includes index
ISBN 0-903608-19-7 (pbk) : Unpriced B81-40043

016.63 — Scotland. Agricultural colleges. Publications — *Lists*

Catalogue of Colleges publications. — Revised. — [Edinburgh] ([West Mains Rd., Edinburgh EH9 3JG]) : [East of Scotland Colleges of Agriculture], 1981. — 22p ; 21cm. — (Publication / The Scottish Agricultural Colleges, ISSN 0308-5708 ; no.26)
Originally published: 1975?
Unpriced (unbound) B81-31317

016.63'05 — Great Britain. National libraries: Science Reference Library. Stock : Serials on agriculture — *Catalogues*

Science Reference Library. Periodicals on agriculture held by the Science Reference Library. — London : Science Reference Library
Pt.1: Agricultural research and industry. — Nov.1981. — [80]p
ISBN 0-902914-66-9 (pbk) : CIP entry
ISBN 0-902914-65-0 (set) B81-32005

016.63'05 — Ireland *(Republic).* **Agriculture. Research organisations: Agricultural Institute. Libraries. Stock: Serials —** *Lists*

Agricultural InstituteLiosta na dtréimseachán i gcuid leabharlann An Fhorais Talúntais 1980 = List of journals received in the libraries of An Foras Talúntais 1980. — [Dublin] ([19 Sandymount Ave., Dublin 4]) : [An Foras Talúntais], 1980. — 62p ; 30cm
English text, Irish and English introduction
Unpriced (pbk) B81-24774

016.63'0941 — Great Britain. Agriculture, *1793-1839 — Bibliographies*

Fussell, G. E.. The old English farming books. — London (35 Palace Court, W2 4LS) : Pindar Press
Vol.3: 1793-1839. — Oct.1981. — [304]p
ISBN 0-907132-03-0 : £27.00 : CIP entry B81-27994

016.6315 — Crops. Nutrients: Boron — *Abstracts — Serials*

Boron in agriculture : a quarterly bulletin of abstracts. — Vol.1, no.1 (Oct. 1980)-. — Tring (M.B. House, Wigginton, Tring, Hertfordshire HP23 6ED) : Micronutrient Bureau, 1980-. — v. ; 30cm
Description based on: Vol.1, no.3 (Apr.1981)
ISSN 0261-5444 = Boron in agriculture : Unpriced B81-38188

016.6315 — Crops. Nutrients: Copper — *Astracts — Serials*

Copper in agriculture : a quarterly bulletin of abstracts. — Vol.1, no.1 (Oct.1980)-. — Tring (M.B. House, Wigginton, Tring, Herts. HP23 6ED) : Micronutrient Bureau, 1980-. — v. ; 30cm
ISSN 0261-5436 = Copper in agriculture : Unpriced B81-33950

016.6315 — Crops. Nutrients: Zinc — *Abstracts — Serials*

Zinc in agriculture : a quarterly bulletin of abstracts. — Vol.1, no.1 (Oct.1980)-. — Tring (M.B. House, Wigginton, Tring, Herts. HP23 6ED) : Micronutrient Bureau, 1980-. — v. ; 30cm
ISSN 0261-5452 = Zinc in agriculture : Unpriced B81-33714

016.6317 — Agricultural land. Irrigation — *Abstracts — Serials*

Irricab : current annotated bibliography of irrigation. — Vol.1 (1976)-. — Bet Dagan : International Irrigation Information Center ; Oxford : Distributed by Pergamon, 1976-. — v. ; 24cm
Quarterly. — Description based on: Vol.5, no.2 (Apr.1980)
Unpriced B81-03613

016.6318'1 — Fertilisers — *Abstracts — Serials*

World fertilizer news summary / [British Sulphur Information Service]. — Issue no.1 (Jan.1981)-. — London (25 Wilton Rd, SW1V 1NH) : British Sulphur Corporation, 1981-. — v. ; 30cm
Monthly. — Description based on: Issue no.3 (Mar.1981)
ISSN 0261-5789 = World fertilizer news summary : £45.00 per year B81-33277

016.6333'043 — Crops: Legumes. Pollination by insects — *Bibliographies*

Woyke, H. W.. Insect pollination of papilionaceae vegetable crops. — London : International Bee Research Association, Dec.1981. — 1v.. — (IBRA bibliography ; no.28)
ISBN 0-86098-096-0 : £4.00 : CIP entry
B81-30907

016.6349'56'06041 — Great Britain. Afforestation. Organisations: Men of the Trees. Archives — *Lists*

Bassett, Philippa. A list of the historical records of the Men of the Trees / compiled by Philippa Bassett as part of a research project funded by the Social Science Research Council. — [Birmingham] : Centre for Urban and Regional Studies, University of Birmingham, 1980. — iv,4leaves ; 30cm. — (Lists of historical records)
At head of title: Centre for Urban and Regional Studies, University of Birmingham and Institute of Agricultural History, University of Reading
Unpriced (pbk) B81-31791

016.635'61 — Pepos. Pollination by insects — *Bibliographies*

Woyke, H. W.. Insect pollination of Cucurbitaceae vegetable crops. — London : International Bee Research Association, Sept.1981. — 1v.. — (IBRA bibliography ; no.27)
ISBN 0-86098-095-2 : £6.00 : CIP entry
B81-25663

016'.636'1 — Livestock: Horses, ***1851-1967*** — *Bibliographies*

Grimshaw, Anne. Hippobibliography 1851-1967. — London : Library Association, Dec.1981. — [372]p
ISBN 0-85365-533-2 : £35.00 : CIP entry
B81-31725

016.6364 — Livestock: Pigs — *Abstracts — Serials*

Pig news and information. — Vol.1, no.1 (Mar. 1980)-. — Slough : Commonwealth Agricultural Bureaux, 1980-. — v. ; 30cm
Quarterly
ISSN 0143-9014 = Pig news and information : £25.00 per year B81-02009

016.6368 — Pets: Cats — *Bibliographies*

Tootill, Tina. Cat's tales : an annotated bibliograhy of 101 items about cats / by Tina Tootill. — Liverpool (101 Swanside Rd, Liverpool) : T. Tootill, 1981. — iii leaves, 29p : ill ; 22cm
Includes index
£1.00 (pbk) B81-25956

016.6399 — Great Britain. Nature conservation. Organisations: Nature Conservancy Council. Research projects — *Abstracts — Serials*

[Research reports digest *(Nature Conservancy Council)*]. Research reports digest / Nature Conservancy Council. — No.1 (June 1979)-. — Banbury (Calthorpe House, Calthorpe St., Banbury, Oxon OX16 8EX) : Nature Conservancy Council, Information & Library Services, 1979-. — v. ; 30cm
Two or three issues yearly. — Consists of summaries of reports published in the series: CST report
ISSN 0143-0386 = Research reports digest - Nature Conservancy Council : Free B81-04635

016.6399'06'01 — Animals. Conservation. Organisations: Fauna Preservation Society. Archives — *Lists*

Bassett, Philippa. A list of the historical records of the Fauna Preservation Society / compiled by Philippa Basset[t] as part of a research project funded by the Social Science Research Council. — [Birmingham] : Centre for Urban and Regional Studies, University of Birmingham, 1980. — vii,8leaves ; 30cm. — (Lists of historical records)
At head of title: Centre for Urban and Regional Studies, University of Birmingham and Institute of Agricultural History, University of Reading
Unpriced (pbk) B81-27685

016.6399'06'041 — Great Britain. Nature conservation. Organisations: Society for the Promotion of Nature Conservation. Archives — *Lists*

Bassett, Philippa. A list of the historical records of the Society for the Promotion of Nature Conservation / compiled by Philippa Bassett as part of a research project funded by the Social Science Research Council. — [Birmingham] : Centre for Urban and Regional Studies, University of Birmingham, 1980. — x,77p ; 30cm. — (Lists of historical records)
At head of title: Centre for Urban and Regional Studies, University of Birmingham and Institute of Agricultural History, University of Reading
Unpriced (pbk) B81-27679

016.6399'78'06041 — Great Britain. Birds. Conservation. Organisations: Royal Society for the Protection of Birds. Archives — *Lists*

Bassett, Philippa. A list of the historical records of the Royal Society for the Protection of Birds / compiled by Philippa Bassett as part of a research project funded by the Social Science Research Council. — [Birmingham] : Centre for Urban and Regional Studies, University of Birmingham, 1980. — ix,24p ; 30cm. — (Lists of historical records)
At head of title: Centre for Urban and Regional Studies, University of Birmingham and Institute of Agricultural History, University of Reading
Unpriced (pbk) B81-31790

016.6413'005 — Surrey. Leatherhead. Food. Research organisations. Libraries: Leatherhead Food R.A.. ***Library.*** **Stock: Serials** — *Catalogues*

Leatherhead Food R.A.. The Leatherhead Food R.A. library & information service guide. — [Leatherhead] ([Randalls Rd., Leatherhead, KT22 7RY]) : [Leatherhead Food R.A.], 1981. — 45p : ill ; 30cm
Unpriced (pbk)
Also classified at 026'.6413 B81-08439

016.6415'882 — Cookery. Use of microwave ovens — *Bibliographies*

Tooley, James B.. Microwave cooking : a bibliography / James B. Tooley. — London : Woodlands Avenue, Acton, W3 9DN : School of Library & Information Studies, Ealing College of Higher Education, c1981. — 14p ; 30cm. — (Ealing miscellany ; no.18)
£0.20 (unbound) B81-16693

016.647'94'02854 — Hotel industries. Applications of digital computer systems — *Bibliographies*

Tooley, James B.. Computers in the hotel and catering industry : a bibliography / prepared by James B. Tooley for the Catering Education Research Institute. — London (Ealing College of Higher Education, Woodlands Ave., Acton, W3 9DN) : Catering Education Research Institute, c1979. — 17p ; 21cm. — (Bibliography / CERI)
ISBN 0-906302-04-8 (pbk) : £0.50
Also classified at 016.647'95'02854 B81-05418

016.647'94'068 — Hotels. Management — *Bibliographies — Serials*

HCIMA quarterly bibliography of hotel and catering management. — Ed.1 (Apr.1980)-. — [London] ([191 Trinity Road, SW17 7HN]) : [Hotel Catering and Institutional Management Association], 1980-. — v. ; 30cm
ISSN 0144-7580 = HCIMA quarterly bibliography of hotel and catering management : £4.00
Also classified at 016.647'95'068 B81-02339

016.647'95'02854 — Catering industries. Applications of digital computer systems — *Bibliographies*

Tooley, James B.. Computers in the hotel and catering industry : a bibliography / prepared by James B. Tooley for the Catering Education Research Institute. — London (Ealing College of Higher Education, Woodlands Ave., Acton, W3 9DN) : Catering Education Research Institute, c1979. — 17p ; 21cm. — (Bibliography / CERI)
ISBN 0-906302-04-8 (pbk) : £0.50
Primary classification 016.647'94'02854
B81-05418

016.647'95'068 — Catering establishments. Management — *Bibliographies — Serials*

HCIMA quarterly bibliography of hotel and catering management. — Ed.1 (Apr.1980)-. — [London] ([191 Trinity Road, SW17 7HN]) : [Hotel Catering and Institutional Management Association], 1980-. — v. ; 30cm
ISSN 0144-7580 = HCIMA quarterly bibliography of hotel and catering management : £4.00
Primary classification 016.647'94'068
B81-02339

016.6517 — Business practices. Communicaton — *Bibliographies*

Walsh, Ruth M.. Business communications : an annotated bibliography / compiled and edited by Ruth M. Walsh and Stanley J. Birkin. — Westport, Conn. ; London : Greenwood Press, 1980. — ix,686p ; 25cm
ISBN 0-313-20923-5 : Unpriced B81-05297

016.658 — Management — *Abstracts — Serials*

Anbar yearbook. — 9. — Wembley : Anbar Publications, c1980. — [252]p in various pagings
Cover title: The Compleat Anbar
ISBN 0-900060-20-4 : Unpriced
ISSN 0307-0409 B81-20714

016.658 — Management. Theses accepted by British universities — *Lists — Serials*

Selected list of U.K. theses and dissertations in management studies. — 1979. — [Bradford] ([Richmond Rd, Bradford BD7 1DR]) : University of Bradford Library, [1980]. — ii,41p
ISSN 0140-7414 : Unpriced B81-04945

016.658'022'0941 — Great Britain. Small firms. Management — *Abstracts — Serials*

SBMA : Smaller business management abstracts. — Vol.1, no.1 (Oct.1980)-. — Wembley : Anbar in association with Institute of Small Business, London Business School, 1980-. — v. ; 21cm
Eight issued yearly
ISSN 0143-4780 = SBMA. Smaller business management abstracts : £38.00 per year
B81-06155

016.6583'82 — Great Britain. Safety representatives — *Bibliographies*

Merchant, Caroline. Safety representatives : a reading list / compiled by Caroline Merchant. — [London] : Health and Safety Executive, [1981]. — [4]p ; 30cm
ISBN 0-7176-0074-2 (unbound) : £0.75 : CIP rev. B81-13806

016.6588'3 — Great Britain. National libraries: Science Reference Library. Stock: Documents on market research — *Catalogues*

Science Reference Library. Market research and industry surveys. — London : British Library, Science Reference Library, Nov.1981. — [90]p
ISBN 0-902914-63-4 (pbk) : £8.00 : CIP entry
B81-34960

016.662'6 — Energy sources: Biomass — *Abstracts — Serials*

[Current awareness bulletin *(IEA Biomass Conversion Technical Information Service)*]. Current awareness bulletin / prepared by the Information Technology Group of the Institute for Industrial Research and Standards in conjunction with the National Board for Science and Technology [for the IEA Biomass Conversion Technical Information Service]. — No.5 (Jan. 1980)-. — Dublin (c/o [Miss Lorraine Segon] National Board for Science and Technology, Shelbourne House, Shelbourne Rd, Dublin 4) : The Service, 1980-. — v. ; 30cm
Continues: Current awareness bulletin (IEA Biomass Information Service). — Numbering irregular. — Description based on: No.2 (July 1980)
Unpriced B81-05351

016.667'9 — High solids coatings — *Bibliographies*

Chandler, R. H.. High solids coatings / by R.H. Chandler. — Braintree (P.O. Box 55, Braintree, Essex) : R.H. Chandler, 1980. — 86p : ill ; 28cm. — (Bibliographies in paint technology ; no.35)
Includes index
Unpriced (pbk) B81-03576

016.669'94 — Multicomponent alloys — *Bibliographies*

Prince, Alan. Multicomponent alloy constitution bibliography 1974-1977 / Alan Prince. — London : Metals Society, c1981. — xl,503p ; 24cm
ISBN 0-904357-35-x : Unpriced B81-25228

016.6713'6 — Rapidly quenched metals — *Bibliographies*

Suryanarayana, C.. Rapidly quenched metals : a bibliography, 1973-1979 / compiled by C. Suryanarayana. — New York ; London : IFI/Plenum, c1980. — ix,278p ; 26cm. — (IFI data base library)
Includes index
ISBN 0-306-65194-7 : Unpriced B81-04107

016.677 — Textiles. Manufacture — *Abstracts — Serials*

Textile digest / Shirley Institute. — Jan.1981-. — Manchester : The Institute, 1981-. — v. ; 30cm
Monthly. — Continues: Digest of English-language textile literature
ISSN 0260-4256 = Textile digest : £22.50 per year B81-17470

016.6888 — Packaging — *Abstracts — Serials*

International packaging abstracts / [compiled by the Information Section of Pira]. — Vol.1, no.1 (Jan. 1981)-. — Leatherhead (Randalls Rd, Leatherhead, Surrey KT22 7RU) : International Packaging Information Service under the direction of Institut für Lebensmitteltechnologie und Verpackung, International Food Information Service [and] Research Association for the Paper and Board, Printing and Packaging Industries, 1981-. — v. ; 21
Monthly. — Continues: Packaging abstracts
ISSN 0260-7409 = International packaging abstracts : £128.00 per year B81-20313

016.69 — Great Britain. Buildings. Construction. Research organisations: Building Research Establishment. Publications — *Lists — Serials*

Building Research Establishment. Information directory : current publications, films and services from the Building Research Establishment. — 1980. — [Watford] : The Establishment, 1980. — 56p
Unpriced B81-06822

016.7 — London. Kensington and Chelsea *(London Borough)*. **Museums. Libraries: Victoria and Albert Museum.** *Library*. **Stock: Microfilms** — *Catalogues*

Victoria and Albert Museum. *Library*. A bibliography of the microfilms in the National Art Library, Victoria and Albert Museum / compiled and catalogued by Michael E. Keen. — [London] ([South Kensington, S.W.7]) : The Museum, 1980. — 42p ; 30cm
Includes index
Unpriced (pbk) B81-11184

016.704'0396073 — United States. Visual arts. Negro artists, *1779-1979 — Bibliographies*

Davis, Lenwood G.. Black artists in the United States : an annotated bibliography of books, articles, and dissertations on black artists, 1779-1979 / Lenwood G. Davis and Janet L. Sims ; foreword by James E. Newton. — Newport ; London : Greenwood Press, 1980. — xiv,138p ; 25cm
Includes index
ISBN 0-313-22082-4 : Unpriced B81-06546

016.709 — Visual arts, *to 1977 — Bibliographies*

Arntzen, Etta. Guide to the literature of art history / Etta Arntzen, Robert Rainwater. — Chicago : American Library Association ; London : Art Book Co, 1980. — xviii,616p ; 29cm
Includes index
ISBN 0-905309-05-7 : £35.00 B81-23439

016.709'04 — Visual arts, *1870- — Bibliographies — Serials*

Art, design, photo. — 1976-1977. — Hemel Hempstead (43, South Hill Road, Hemel Hempstead, Herts. HP1 1JB) : Alexander Davis, 1980. — 314p
ISBN 0-903904-04-7 : Unpriced
ISSN 0306-817x B81-09703

016.709'04'6 — Visual arts, *1960-1980 — Bibliographies*

Bell, Doris L.. Contemporary art trends : 1960-1980 : a guide to sources / by Doris L. Bell. — Metuchen ; London : Scarecrow, 1981. — x,171p ; 23cm
Bibliography: p141-171
ISBN 0-8108-1445-5 : £8.80 B81-37817

016.711 — Higher education institutions. Curriculum subjects: Environment planning. Teaching aids: Audiovisual materials — *Lists*

Van Haeften, Kate. Media resources on town and country for lecturers / by Kate Van Haeften. — London (City of London Polytechnic, Calcutta House, Old Castle St., E1 7NT) : LLRS Publications, 1981. — i,29p ; 30cm
Includes index
ISBN 0-904264-54-8 (pbk) : £1.00 B81-23037

016.711'06'041 — Great Britain. Environment planning. Organisations: Royal Town Planning Institute. Archives — *Lists*

Bassett, Philippa. List of the historical records of the Royal Town Planning Institute / compiled by Philippa Bassett as part of a research project funded by the Social Science Research Council. — [Birmingham] : Centre for Urban and Regional Studies, 1980. — vii,6leaves ; 30cm. — (Lists of historical records)
At head of title: Centre For Urban and Regional Studies University of Birmingham and Institute of Agricultural History University of Reading
Unpriced (pbk) B81-27631

016.711'06'042 — England. Environment planning. Organisations: Town and Country Planning Association. Archives — *Lists*

Bassett, Philippa. A list of the historical records of the Town and Country Planning Association / compiled by Philippa Bassett as part of a research project funded by the Social Science Research Council. — [Birmingham] : Centre for Urban and Regional Studies, University of Birmingham, 1980. — x,16p ; 30cm. — (Lists of historical records)
At head of title: Centre for Urban and Regional Studies, University of Birmingham and Institute of Agricultural History, University of Reading
Unpriced (pbk) B81-27673

016.711'4'099471 — Canberra. Environment planning, *to 1976 — Bibliographies*

Johnson, Donald L.. Canberra and Walter Burley Griffin : a bibliography of 1876 to 1976 and a guide to published sources / Donald L. Johnson. — Melbourne ; Oxford : Oxford University Press, 1980. — 120p : ill,1port ; 22cm
ISBN 0-19-554203-7 (pbk) : £3.25
Also classified at 016.72'092'4 B81-04711

016.711'7'0285 — Transport. Planning. Applications of digital computer systems — *Bibliographies*

Transportation : an annotated bibliography. — London : Heyden, Dec.1981. — [48]p. — (Use of computers for national development)
ISBN 0-85501-696-5 (pbk) : £4.00 : CIP entry B81-40230

016.719'06'04278 — Cumbria. Lake District. Landscape conservation. Organisations: Friends of the Lake District. Archives — *Lists*

Bassett, Philippa. A list of the historical records retained by the Friends of the Lake District / compiled by Philippa Bassett as part of a research project funded by the Social Science Research Council. — [Birmingham] : Centre for Urban and Regional Studies, 1980. — x,48p ; 30cm. — (Lists of historical records)
At head of title: Centre For Urban and Regional Studies University of Birmingham and Institute of Agricultural History University of Reading
Unpriced (pbk) B81-27628

016.719'32'06042 — England. National parks. Organisations: Council for National Parks. Archives — *Lists*

Bassett, Philippa. A list of the historical records of the County Councils Association / compiled by Philippa Bassett as part of a research project funded by the Social Science Research Council. — [Birmingham] : Centre for Urban and Regional Studies, University of Birmingham, 1980. — v,4leaves ; 30cm. — (Lists of historical records)
At head of title: Centre for Urban and Regional Studies, University of Birmingham and Institute of Agricultural History, University of Reading
Unpriced (pbk) B81-27683

Bassett, Philippa. A list of the historical records of the Standing Committee on National Parks (now the Council for National Parks) / compiled by Philippa Bassett as part of a research project funded by the Social Science Research Council. — [Birmingham] : Centre for Urban and Regional Studies, 1980. — vi,5 leaves ; 30cm. — (Lists of historical records)
At head of title: Centre for Urban and Regional Studies, University of Birmingham and Institute of Agricultural History, University of Reading
Unpriced (pbk) B81-30796

016.72 — Architecture. Serials — *Indexes — Serials*

Architectural periodicals index. — Cumulative ed. — Vol.8 (Jan. to Dec.1980). — London : Published for the British Architectural Library at the Royal Institute of British Architects by RIBA Publications Limited, c1980. — 421p
£50.00 B81-29049

016.72'06'041 — Great Britain. Architectural design. Organisations: Royal Institute of British Architects. Archives — *Lists*

Bassett, Philippa. List of the historical records retained by the Royal Institute of British Architects / compiled by Philippa Bassett as part of a research project funded by the Social Science Research Council. — [Birmingham] : Centre for Urban and Regional Studies, University of Birmingham, 1980. — xiii,29p ; 30cm. — (Lists of historical records)
At head of title: Centre for Urban and Regional Studies, University of Birmingham and Institute of Agricultural History, University of Reading
Unpriced (pbk) B81-27671

016.72'092'4 — Architectural design. Griffin, Walter Burley — *Bibliographies*

Johnson, Donald L.. Canberra and Walter Burley Griffin : a bibliography of 1876 to 1976 and a guide to published sources / Donald L. Johnson. — Melbourne ; Oxford : Oxford University Press, 1980. — 120p : ill,1port ; 22cm
ISBN 0-19-554203-7 (pbk) : £3.25
Primary classification 016.711'4'099471 B81-04711

016.72′092′4 — Scotland. Architectural design. Mackintosh, Charles Rennie — *Bibliographies*

Dixon, Elizabeth. Charles Rennie Mackintosh : a selective bibliography / compiled by Elizabeth Dixon ; cover designed by Nigel Westbrook. — London (36 Bedford Sq., WC1B 3ES) : Architectural Association Library, 1981. — 22p : ill ; 30cm. — (AA Library bibliography (new series), ISSN 0308-9177 ; no.55)
£2.00 (pbk) B81-17838

016.720′941 — Great Britain. Architecture, *to 1980* — *Bibliographies*

Kamen, Ruth. British and Irish architectural history. — London : Architectural Press, Nov.1981. — [224]p
ISBN 0-85139-077-3 : £25.00 : CIP entry
B81-30416

016.72′09411 — Scotland. Buildings of historical importance. Organisations: National Trust for Scotland. Archives — *Lists*

Bassett, Philippa. List of the historical records of the National Trust For Scotland / compiled by Philippa Bassett as part of a research project funded by the Social Science Research Council. — [Birmingham] : Centre for Urban and Regional Studies, 1980. — xl,97p ; 30cm. — (Lists of historical records)
At head of title: Centre For Urban and Regional Studies University of Birmingham and Institute of Agricultural History University of Reading
Unpriced (pbk)
Primary classification 016.3636′9′060411
B81-27627

016.7249′1 — Architecture, *1900-1980* — *Bibliographies*

Sharp, Dennis. Sources of modern architecture : a critical bibliography / Dennis Sharp. — 2nd ed. (rev. and enl.). — London : Granada, 1981. — 192p : ill,facsims,ports ; 24cm
Previous ed.: London : Lund Humphries, 1967. — Includes index
ISBN 0-246-11218-2 : £15.75 B81-05423

016.73′092′4 — English sculptures. Moore, Henry, *1898-* — *Bibliographies*

Teague, Edward H.. Henry Moore : bibliography and reproductions index / by Edward H. Teague. — Jefferson, N.C. : McFarland ; Folkestone : distributed by Bailey & Swinfen, 1981. — v,165p,11p of plates : ill ; 24cm
Bibliography: p159-160. — Includes index
ISBN 0-89950-016-1 : £16.80 B81-37039

016.74164′09 — Illustrated books. Illustrations. Techniques, *to 1979* — *Bibliographies*

Brenni, Vito Joseph. Book illustration and decoration : a guide to research / compiled by Vito J. Brenni. — Westport, Conn. ; London : Greenwood Press, 1980. — viii,191p ; 25cm. — (Art reference collection, ISSN 0193-6867 ; no.1)
Includes index
ISBN 0-313-22340-8 : £17.75 B81-23472

016.7695 — Scotland. Youth hostelling. Organisations: Scottish Youth Hostels Association. Archives — *Lists*

Bassett, Philippa. List of the historical records of the Scottish Youth Hostels Association / compiled by Philippa Bassett as part of a research project funded by the Social Science Research Council. — [Birmingham] : Centre for Urban and Regional Studies, 1980. — vi,6leaves ; 30cm. — (Lists of historical records)
At head of title: Centre For Urban and Regional Studies University of Birmingham and Institute of Agricultural History University of Reading
Unpriced (pbk) B81-27630

016.77 — Photography. Documents on photography: Documents in German — *Lists*

Heidtmann, Frank. Die deutsche Photoliteratur 1839-1978 : Theorie-Technik, Bildleistungen : eine systematische Bibliographie der selbständigen deutschsprachigen Photoliteratur = German photographic literature 1839-1978 : theory-technology, visual : a classified bibliography of German-language photographic publications / Frank Heidtmann, Hans-Joachim Bresemann, Rolf H. Krauss. — München ; London (1 New Oxford St., WC1A 1NE) : Saur, 1980. — xxx,690p ; 22cm. — (Schriftenreihe der Deutschen Gesellschaft für Photographie ; Bd 1)
German text, German and English Preface, Contents, Introduction and chapter titles. — Includes index
ISBN 3-598-10026-4 : Unpriced B81-11752

016.771′09 — Photographic equipment, *1858-1980* — *Bibliographies*

Oldtimer Cameras Limited : catalogue 1858-1980. — [Borehamwood] (P.O. Box 28, 14 Gables Ave., Borehamwood, Herts., WD6 4SY) : Oldtimer Cameras, 1981?. — 4p,162columns ; 30cm
Unpriced (pbk) B81-10380

016.78 — Great Britain. National libraries: British Library. *Department of Printed Books.* **Stock: Musical scores** — *Catalogues*

British Library. The catalogue of printed music in the British Library to 1980. — London : Saur
1: A-Ander / [editor Laureen Baillie]. — 1981. — 404p ; 30cm
ISBN 0-85157-901-9 : Unpriced
ISBN 0-85157-900-0 (set) B81-32130

British Library. The catalogue of printed music in the British Library to 1980. — London : Saur
2: Ander-Bach, J. N. / [editor Laureen Baillie]. — 1981. — 424p ; 30cm
ISBN 0-85157-902-7 : Unpriced
ISBN 0-85157-900-0 (set) B81-32131

016.78 — Music & musical scores — *Bibliographies* — *Serials*

British catalogue of music. — 1979. — London : British Library Bibliographic Services Division, c1980. — 141p
ISBN 0-900220-82-1 : Unpriced
ISSN 0068-1407 B80-05766

British catalogue of music. — 1980. — London : The British Library, Bibliographic Services Division, c1981. — 128p
ISBN 0-900220-91-0 : £18.00
ISSN 0068-1407 B81-29667

016.78 — Music — *Bibliographies* — *German texts* — *Serials*

Bibliographie des Musikschrifttums / herausgegeben vom Staatlichen Institut für Musikforschung Preussischer Kulturbesitz. — 1974. — Mainz ; London : Schott, c1980. — xvi,513p
ISBN 3-7957-1474-5 : £27.00
ISSN 0340-2169 B81-35106

016.78 — Oxfordshire. Oxford. Universities. Colleges: Christ Church *(University of Oxford). Library.* **Stock: Music** — *Catalogues*

Bray, Roger. The music collection of Christ Church, Oxford. — Brighton : Harvester Press Microform Publications, Dec.1981. — [75]p
ISBN 0-86257-006-9 (pbk) : £4.50 : CIP entry
B81-35897

016.78′092′4 — Australia. Victoria. Melbourne. Museums: Grainger Museum. Stock: Documents associated with Delius, Frederick — *Catalogues*

Lowe, Rachel. A descriptive catalogue with checklists of the letters and related documents in the Delius collection of the Grainger Museum, University of Melbourne, Australia / Rachel Lowe. — London : Delius Trust ; London : Boosey & Hawkes [[distributor]], 1981, c1980. — v,233p : facsims,ports ; 26cm
Limited ed. of 500 numbered copies
ISBN 0-9502653-2-2 : £12.00 B81-18783

016.78′092′4 — Czechoslovak music. Dvořák, Antonín — *Catalogues*

Trufitt, Ian T.. Antonín Dvořák : complete catalogue of works / compiled by Ian T. Trufitt. — [Great Britain] : Dvořák Society of Great Britain, 1974. — 31 leaves ; 21cm
Unpriced (unbound) B81-09875

016.78′092′4 — English music. Rubbra, Edmund — *Catalogues*

Edmund Rubbra : an appreciation by Hugh Ottaway : together with a complete catalogue of compositions to May 1981. — Croydon (421A Brighton Rd., South Croydon, Surrey CR2 6YR) : Lengnick, [1981]. — 45p ; 22cm
£2.00 (pbk) B81-32539

016.7828′55 — Cinema films. Musical scores, *1908-1979* — *Lists*

Limbacher, James L.. Keeping score : film music 1972-1979 / James L. Limbacher. — Metuchen ; London : Scarecrow, 1981. — ix,510p ; 23cm
Bibliography: p6-7. — List of sound discs: p334-425
ISBN 0-8108-1390-4 : £15.75 B81-25965

016.7841′063 — Male voice choral music — *Lists*

Tortolano, William. Original music for men's voices : a selected bibliography / by William Tortolano. — 2nd ed. — Metuchen ; London : Scarecrow, 1981. — 201p ; 23cm
Previous ed.: 1973. — Bibliography: p155-156. — Includes index
ISBN 0-8108-1386-6 : £8.75 B81-22829

016.7845 — Popular songs in English — *Indexes*

Whitter, John. Song index : popular songs and where to find them / compiled by John Whitter and Ruth Watts. — London : Association of Assistant Librarians, 1981. — xvi,111p ; 22cm
Bibliography: pix-xvi
ISBN 0-900092-36-x : Unpriced B81-38471

016.7845′0092′4 — Pop music. Singing. Presley, Elvis. Criticism — *Bibliographies*

Whistler, John A.. Elvis Presley : reference guide and discography / John A. Whistler. — Metuchen, N.J. ; London : Scarecrow Press, 1981. — vii,258p ; 23cm
Includes index
ISBN 0-8108-1434-x : £10.75
Also classified at 016.7899′1245′00924
B81-36518

016.7845′4′009 — Rock music, *to 1978* — *Bibliographies*

Hoffmann, Frank. The literature of rock, 1954-1978 / by Frank Hoffmann. — Metuchen ; London : Scarecrow, 1981. — xi,337p : ports ; 23cm
Includes index
ISBN 0-8108-1371-8 : £12.25 B81-29219

016.78542 — Jazz — *Bibliographies*

Kennington, Don. The literature of jazz : a critical guide. — 2nd ed., revised / by Donald Kennington and Danny L. Read. — London : Library Association, 1980. — 236p ; 22cm
Previous ed.: 1970 / by Donald Kennington. — Includes bibliographies and index
ISBN 0-85365-663-0 (pbk) : Unpriced : CIP rev. B80-21279

016.7899′12 — Music. Savoy sound recordings — *Discographies*

Ruppli, Michel. The Savoy label : a discography / compiled by Michel Ruppli with assistance from Bob Porter. — Westport ; London : Greenwood Press, 1980. — xix,442p : ports ; 24cm. — (Discographies : no.2)
Includes index
ISBN 0-313-21199-x : Unpriced B81-07251

016.7899′12 — Music. Sound discs — *Discographies*

Gammond, Peter. Music on record. — Cambridge : Stephens
2: Big bands. — Oct.1981. — [192]p
ISBN 0-85059-495-2 : £8.95 : CIP entry
B81-30333

016.7899'12 — Music. Sound recordings — *Discographies*
Greenfield, Edward. The new Penguin guide to bargain records (and cassettes) / Edward Greenfield, Robert Layton, Ivan March ; edited by Ivan March. — Harmondsworth : Penguin, 1980. — xx,172p ; 20cm. — (Penguin handbooks)
ISBN 0-14-046474-3 (pbk) : £1.95 B81-00692

016.7899'12 — Music, *to ca 1750.* **Sound recordings. Discographies**
Croucher, Trevor. Early music discography. — London : Library Association, May 1981. — 2v.
ISBN 0-85365-613-4 (pbk) : £15.00 : CIP entry B81-04261

016.7899'12 — Music. V-Disc sound discs — *Discographies*
Sears, Richard S.. V-Discs : a history and discography / Richard S. Sears. — Westport, Conn. ; London : Greenwood Press, c1980. — xciii,1166p : facsims ; 23cm. — (Association for Recorded Sound Collections discographic reference series) (Discographies ; no.5)
ISBN 0-313-22207-x : £41.85 B81-23643

016.7899'12 — Pop music. Sound discs: British top fifty singles, *1970-1979* **—** *Discographies*
The **Guinness** book of hits of the 70's / Jo Rice ... [et al.]. — Enfield : Guinness Superlatives, c1980. — 23p : ports ; 21cm
ISBN 0-85112-217-5 (cased) : Unpriced : CIP rev.
ISBN 0-85112-205-1 (pbk) : £4.95 B80-09064

016.7899'12 — Popular music. Sound discs — *Discographies — Serials*
Music master. — 1981. — Hastings (1 De Cham Ave., Hastings, Sussex) : John Humphries, 1981. — 987p
ISBN 0-904520-11-0 : Unpriced
ISSN 0308-9347 B81-35807

016.7899'1228 — Theme music. Sound discs — *Discographies*
Preston, Mike. Tele-tunes : the book of TV and film music : television and film music on record / compiled by Mike Preston. — Kidderminster (78 Birchfield Rd., Kidderminster, Worcs. DY11 LPG) : Record Information Centre, 1979. — 108p ; 21cm
ISBN 0-906655-00-5 (pbk) : £2.50 B81-06019

016.7899'12281 — New York *(City).* **Broadway. Musical shows in English,** *to 1979.* **Long-playing sound discs —** *Discographies*
Hodgins, Gordon W. The Broadway musical : a complete LP discography / Gordon W. Hodgins. — Metuchen, N.J. ; London : Scarecrow, 1980. — v,183p ; 23cm
ISBN 0-8108-1343-2 : £7.00 B81-05284

016.7899'1245 — Pop music. Sound discs: British top fifty singles, *1952-1980* **—** *Discographies*
The **Guinness** book of British hit singles : (the Guinness book of records records). — [3rd ed.], Jo Rice ... [et al.]. — London : Guinness Superlatives, c1981. — 352p : ill(some col.),ports(some col.) ; 21cm
Previous ed.: 1979
ISBN 0-85112-224-8 (pbk) : £4.99 : CIP rev. B81-12848

016.7899'1245'00924 — Pop music. Singing. Presley, Elvis. Sound recordings — *Discographies*
Whistler, John A.. Elvis Presley : reference guide and discography / John A. Whistler. — Metuchen, N.J. ; London : Scarecrow Press, 1981. — vii,258p ; 23cm
Includes index
ISBN 0-8108-1434-x : £10.75
Primary classification 016.7845'0092'4 B81-36518

016.7899'12454 — Rock music. Sound recordings — *Discographies*
New rock record : a collectors' directory of rock albums and musicians / [edited by] Terry Hounsome & Tim Chambre. — This ed. — Poole : Blandford, 1981. — ix,526p ; 24cm
Previous ed.: i.e. [new] ed. published as Rock record, 1979. — Includes index
ISBN 0-7137-1117-5 (pbk) : £5.50 : CIP rev. B81-14861

016.7899'125'0924 — Music. Conducting. Boult, *Sir* **Adrian. Sound recordings —** *Discographies*
Sanders, Alan. Sir Adrian Boult : a discography / by Alan Sanders. — Harrow (177 Kenton Rd., Harrow, Middx. HA3 0HA) : General Gramophone, [1981]. — xv,37p : ports ; 22cm
Includes index
ISBN 0-902470-13-2 (pbk) : Unpriced B81-20827

016.7899'12542 — Jazz. Prestige sound recordings — *Discographies*
Ruppli, Michel. The Prestige label : a discography / compiled by Michel Ruppli with assistance from Bob Porter. — Westport, Conn. ; London : Greenwood Press, 1980. — xiii,377p ; 24cm. — (Discographies ; no.3)
Includes index
ISBN 0-313-22019-0 : Unpriced B81-07211

016.7899'12542 — Jazz. Sound discs — *Discographies — Serials*
[Collectors items *(Walton-on-Thames)***]**.
Collectors items. — [No.1] (Aug.1980)-. — Walton-on-Thames (10, Rydens Rd, Walton-on-Thames, Surrey) : J.A. Holley, 1980-. — v. ; 22cm
Six issues yearly
ISSN 0261-2550 = Collectors items (Walton-on-Thames) : £0.50 per issue B81-21349

016.7899'12542'0924 — Jazz. Morton, Jelly Roll. Sound discs — *Discographies*
Wright, Laurie. Mr. Jelly Lord / by Laurie Wright ; with special contributions by John H. Cowley ... [et al.]. — Chigwell (66 Fairview Drive, Chigwell, Essex IG7 6HS) : Storyville, c1980. — x,245p : ill,facsims,music,ports ; 21cm
Bibliography: p245. — Includes index
ISBN 0-902391-01-1 : £9.00 B81-01621

016.7899'12761'0924 — Popular music. Guitar playing. Weedon, Bert. Sound recordings — *Discographies*
Geddes, George T.. Mr Guitar : Bert Weedon / George T. Geddes. — Glasgow (102 Dorchester Ave., Glasgow G12 0EB) : G.T. Geddes, c1980. — 10p ; 21cm
Cover title
£0.40 (pbk) B81-02001

016.791'092'2 — United States. Entertainment industries. Serials: 'Variety'. Obituaries, *1905-1978* **—** *Indexes*
Perry, Jeb H.. Variety obits : an index to obituaries in variety, 1905-1978 / Jeb H. Perry. — Metuchen ; London : Scarecrow, 1980. — x,309p ; 23cm
ISBN 0-8108-1289-4 : £11.20 B81-22834

016.79143 — Cinema films — *Bibliographies*
Armour, Robert A.. Film : a reference guide / Robert A. Armour. — Westport, Conn. ; London : Greenwood Press, 1980. — xxiv,251p ; 25cm. — (American popular culture, ISSN 0193-6859)
Includes bibliographies and index
ISBN 0-313-22241-x : £19.50
Primary classification 791.43 B81-23593

016.79143 — Cinema films. Criticism — *Bibliographies*
Sheahan, Eileen. Moving pictures : an annotated guide to selected film literature with suggestions for the study of film / Eileen Sheahan. — South Brunswick : Barnes ; London : Yoseloff, c1979. — 146p ; 22cm
Includes index
ISBN 0-498-02296-x (cased) : £5.00
ISBN 0-498-02297-8 (pbk) : Unpriced B81-38083

016.79143'028'0922 — Cinema films. British actors & British actresses — *Filmographies*
Palmer, Scott. A who's who of British film actors / by Scott Palmer. — Metuchen ; London : Scarecrow, 1981. — 561p ; 23cm
ISBN 0-8108-1388-2 : £19.25 B81-35349

016.79143'52 — American film noir cinema films, *1940-1958* **—** *Filmographies*
Ottoson, Robert. A reference guide to the American film noir, 1940-1958 / Robert Ottoson. — Metuchen ; London : Scarecrow, 1981. — 285p : ill ; 23cm
Bibliography: p233-251. — Includes index
ISBN 0-8108-1363-7 : £10.50 B81-22837

016.79143'75 — Cinema films: Detective films. Criticism, *to 1979* **—** *Bibliographies*
Skene Melvin, David. Crime, detective, espionage, mystery, and thriller fiction and film : a comprehensive bibliography of critical writing through 1979 / compiled by David Skene Melvin and Ann Skene Melvin. — Westport ; London : Greenwood Press, 1980. — xx,367p ; 25cm
Includes index
ISBN 0-313-22062-x : £19.50
Primary classification 016.8093'872 B81-23455

016.79143'75 — Warner Brothers animated films — *Filmographies*
Friedwald, Will. The Warner Brothers cartoons / Will Friedwald, Jerry Beck. — Metuchen, N.J. ; London : Scarecrow Press, 1981. — xvi,271p ; 23cm
Includes index
ISBN 0-8108-1396-3 : £10.50 B81-29221

016.79145'5 — United States. Television programmes. Drama: Series, *1947-1959* **—** *Filmographies*
Gianakos, Larry James. Television drama series programming : a comprehensive chronicle, 1947-1959 / by Larry James Gianakos. — Metuchen ; London : Scarecrow Press, 1980. — xv,565p ; 23cm
Includes index
ISBN 0-8108-1330-0 : £20.65 B81-05092

016.792 — Theatre — *Bibliographies*
Redington, Christine. Select bibliography of drama and education. — [Rev.] ed. / compiled by Christine Redington and Kenneth Pickering. — London (30 Clareville St., SW7 5AW) : British Theatre Institute, 1980. — 19p ; 21cm. — (BTI bibliographic series ; no.3)
Previous ed.: / compiled by Kenneth Pickering with David A. Male. 1975
£3.00 (pbk)
Also classified at 016.792'07'1 B81-16269

016.792'028 — Public performances. Stage fright — *Bibliographies*
Tension in performance : a selective biliography. — Kingston, Surrey (Penrhyn Rd., Kingston, Surrey, KT1 2EE) : Learning Resources Publications Committee, Kingston Polytechnic, 1981. — [8]p ; 21cm
Cover title
Unpriced (pbk) B81-40646

016.792'07'1 — Schools. Activities: Drama — *Bibliographies*
Redington, Christine. Select bibliography of drama and education. — [Rev.] ed. / compiled by Christine Redington and Kenneth Pickering. — London (30 Clareville St., SW7 5AW) : British Theatre Institute, 1980. — 19p ; 21cm. — (BTI bibliographic series ; no.3)
Previous ed.: / compiled by Kenneth Pickering with David A. Male. 1975
£3.00 (pbk)
Primary classification 016.792 B81-16269

016.7933 — West Germany. Stuttgart. Libraries: Württembergische Landesbibliothek. Stock: Documents on dancing. Collections: Dance Collection of Doris Niles & Serge Leslie — *Catalogues*
Leslie, Serge. A bibliography of the dance collection of Doris Niles & Serge Leslie / annotated [compiled] by Serge Leslie
Pt.4: A-Z : mainly 20th century publications / with a preface by Sir Sacheverell Sitwell. — London : Dance Books, 1981. — 283p ; 23cm
Limited ed. of 525 copies (25 not for sale). — Includes index
ISBN 0-903102-56-0 : £9.95 B81-25085

016.796352 — Golf — *Bibliographies*
Kennington, Don. The sourcebook of golf / Don Kennington ; with an appendix on collecting golfiana by Sarah Baddiel. — [London] : Library Association, 1981. — 255p : ill ; 23cm
Bibliography: p207-210. — Includes index
ISBN 0-85365-584-7 : Unpriced : CIP rev. B81-14456

016.7965 — England. Youth hostelling. Organisations: Youth Hostels Association (England and Wales). Archives — *Lists*
Bassett, Philippa. List of the historical records of the Youth Hostels Association / compiled by Philippa Bassett as part of a research project funded by the Social Science Research Council. — [Birmingham] : Centre for Urban and Regional Studies, University of Birmingham, 1980. — vi,28p ; 30cm. — (Lists of historical records)
At head of title: Centre for Urban and Regional Studies, University of Birmingham and Institute of Agricultural History, University of Reading
Unpriced (pbk) B81-27672

016.7965'1'06041 — Great Britain. Recreations: Walking. Organisations: Ramblers' Association. Archives — *Lists*
Bassett, Philippa. List of the historical records of the Ramblers' Association / compiled by Philippa Bassett as part of a research project funded by the Social Science Research Council. — [Birmingham] : Centre for Urban and Regional Studies, University of Birmingham, 1980. — vi,25p ; 30cm. — (Lists of historical records)
At head of title: Centre for Urban and Regional Studies, University of Birmingham and Institute of Agricultural History, University of Reading
Unpriced (pbk) B81-27666

016.7965'22 — Cumbria. Lake District. Hill walking & rock climbing. Organisations. Libraries: Fell and Rock Climbing Club of the English Lake District. *Library*. Stock — *Catalogues*
Fell and Rock Climbing Club of the English Lake District. *Library*. Catalogue of the Library / the Fell & Rock Climbing Club of the English Lake District ; compiled by Muriel Files. — Lancaster : The Club
Additions : June 1975 to March 1979. — 1979. — vi,21p ; 26cm
Includes index
ISBN 0-85028-026-5 (pbk) : £0.65 B81-39029

016.7965'22 — Mountaineering — *Bibliographies*
Neate, W. R.. Mountaineering and its literature : a descriptive bibliography of selected works published in the English language, 1744-1976 / W.R. Neate. — Milnthorpe (Harmony Hall, Milnthorpe, Cumbria [LA7 7QE]) : Cicerone, 1978. — 165p : ill ; 25cm
Includes index
ISBN 0-902363-18-2 : £8.95 B81-03132

016.7966'06'041 — Great Britain. Cycling. Organisations: Cyclists' Touring Club. Archives — *Lists*
Bassett, Philippa. A list of the historical records of the Cyclists' Touring Club / compiled by Philippa Basset[t] as part of a research project funded by the Social Science Research Council. — [Birmingham] : Centre for Urban and Regional Studies, University of Birmingham, 1980. — ix,18p ; 30cm. — (Lists of historical records)
At head of title: Centre for Urban and Regional Studies, University of Birmingham and Institute of Agricultural History, University of Reading
Unpriced (pbk) B81-27684

016.7967'06'041 — Great Britain. Motoring. Organisations: Automobile Association. Archives — *Lists*
Bassett, Philippa. List of the historical records of the Automobile Association / compiled by Philippa Bassett as part of a research project funded by the Social Science Research Council. — [Birmingham] : Centre for Urban and Regional Studies, University of Birmingham, 1980. — vii,40p ; 30cm. — (Lists of historical records)
At head of title: Centre for Urban and Regional Studies, University of Birmingham and Institute of Agricultural History, University of Reading
Unpriced (pbk) B81-27668

016.7967'9 — Great Britain. Caravanning. Organisations: Caravan Club. Archives — *Lists*
Bassett, Philippa. A list of the historical records of the Caravan Club of Great Britain and Ireland / compiled by Philippa Bassett as part of a research project funded by the Social Science Research Council. — [Birmingham] : Centre for Urban and Regional Studies, University of Birmingham, 1980. — viii,5p ; 30cm. — (Lists of historical records)
At head of title: Centre for Urban and Regional Studies, University of Birmingham and Institute of Agricultural History, University of Reading
Unpriced (pbk) B81-27681

016.799'06'041 — Great Britain. Field sports. Organisations: British Field Sports Society. Archives — *Lists*
Bassett, Philippa. A list of the historical records of the British Field Sports Society / compiled by Philippa Bassett as part of a research project funded by the Social Science Research Council. — [Birmingham] : Centre for Urban and Regional Studies, 1980. — v,1leaves ; 30cm. — (Lists of historical records)
At head of title: Centre for Urban and Regional Studies University of Birmingham and Institute of Agricultural History University of Reading
Unpriced (pbk) B81-27626

016.8 — Northern Ireland. Public libraries: SELB Library Service. Stock: Audiovisual aids on literatures — *Catalogues*
SELB Library Service. Audio visual resources : literature : a select list of materials available on loan from the SELB Library Service. — [Craigavon] ([Library Headquarters, Brownlow Rd., Legahory, Craigavon, County Armagh BT65 8DB]) : [The Library Service], [1981]. — 54p ; 30cm
Cover title
Unpriced (pbk) B81-25042

016.808'0666021 — Technical writing — *Bibliographies*
Alred, Gerald J.. Business and technical writing : an annotated bibliography of books, 1880-1980 / Gerald J. Alred, Diana C. Reep, Mohan R. Limaye with the assistance of Michael A. Mikolajczak. — Metuchen ; London : Scarecrow, 1981. — ix,240p ; 23cm
Bibliography: p197-207. — Includes index
ISBN 0-8108-1397-1 : £8.75
Also classified at 016.808'066651021 B81-22830

016.808'066651021 — Business correspondence — *Bibliographies*
Alred, Gerald J.. Business and technical writing : an annotated bibliography of books, 1880-1980 / Gerald J. Alred, Diana C. Reep, Mohan R. Limaye with the assistance of Michael A. Mikolajczak. — Metuchen ; London : Scarecrow, 1981. — ix,240p ; 23cm
Bibliography: p197-207. — Includes index
ISBN 0-8108-1397-1 : £8.75
Primary classification 016.808'0666021 B81-22830

016.8083'876 — Science fiction, *to 1975* — *Bibliographies*
Barron, Neil. Anatomy of wonder : science fiction / Neil Barron. — New York ; London : Bowker, 1976. — xxi,471p ; 24cm. — (Bibliographic guides for contemporary collections)
Includes index
ISBN 0-8352-0884-2 : Unpriced B81-37954

016.80881 — Great Britain. Arts. Patronage. Organisations. Libraries: Arts Council of Great Britain. *Poetry Library*. Stock — *Catalogues*
Barker, Jonathan. Arts Council Poetry Library short catalogue. — 6th ed. — Manchester : Carcanet Press, Oct.1981. — [152]p
Previous ed.: 1969
ISBN 0-85635-394-9 (cased) : £5.95 : CIP entry
ISBN 0-85635-395-7 (pbk) : £2.95 B81-28132

016.809 — European literatures, *to 1980*. Works. Revisions. Criticism — *Bibliographies*
Madden, David. Writers' revisions : an annotated bibliography of articles and books about writers' revisions and their comments on the creative process / David Madden and Richard Powers. — Metuchen ; London : Scarecrow, 1981. — xiii,241p ; 23cm
Includes index
ISBN 0-8108-1375-0 : £9.45 B81-17094

016.809 — Literature. Marxist criticism — *Bibliographies*
Bullock, Chris. Guide to Marxist literary criticism / compiled by Chris Bullock and David Peck. — Brighton : Harvester, 1980. — xi,176p ; 22cm
Includes index
ISBN 0-7108-0003-7 : £16.50 B81-10585

016.8093'872 — Detective fiction in European languages. Criticism, *to 1979* — *Bibliographies*
Skene Melvin, David. Crime, detective, espionage, mystery, and thriller fiction and film : a comprehensive bibliography of critical writing through 1979 / compiled by David Skene Melvin and Ann Skene Melvin. — Westport ; London : Greenwood Press, 1980. — xx,367p ; 25cm
Includes index
ISBN 0-313-22062-x : £19.50
Also classified at 016.79143'75 B81-23455

016.809'924 — Literature. Plot outlines — *Indexes*
Kolar, Carol Koehmstedt. Plot summary index / compiled by Carol Koehmstedt Kolar. — 2nd ed., rev. and enlarged. — Metuchen ; London : Scarecrow, 1981. — xviii,526p ; 23cm
Previous ed.: S.l. : s.n., 19?. — Includes index
ISBN 0-8108-1392-0 : £17.50 B81-22838

016.8108'09729 — English literature. West Indian writers, *1945-* — *Bibliographies*
Derek Walcott and other Caribbean writers : a select annotated bibliography. — [Mold] ([Headquarters Library, County Civic Centre, Mold, Clwyd CH7 6NW]) : Gwasanaeth Llyfrgell Clwyd, [1980]. — [9]p ; 30cm
Cover title
ISBN 0-904444-54-6 (pbk) : Unpriced B81-04836

016.811'3 — Poetry in English. American writers. Whitman, Walt. Criticism — *Bibliographies*
Boswell, Jeanetta. Walt Whitman and the critics : a checklist of criticism, 1900-1978 / Jeanetta Boswell. — Methuen ; London : Scarecrow, 1980. — xiii,257p ; 23cm. — (The Scarecrow author bibliographies ; no.51)
Includes index
ISBN 0-8108-1355-6 : £10.15 B81-09563

016.811'54 — Poetry in English. American writers. Ginsberg, Allen — *Bibliographies*
Kraus, Michelle P.. Allen Ginsberg : an annotated bibliography, 1969-1977 / by Michelle P. Kraus. — Metuchen ; London : Scarecrow, 1980. — xxx,328p : ports ; 23cm. — (The Scarecrow author bibliographies ; no.46)
Includes index
ISBN 0-8108-1284-3 : £12.25 B81-02707

016.811'54'08 — Poetry in English. American writers, *1945-*. Poetry published in serials with American imprints — *Indexes* — *Serials*
Index of American periodical verse. — 1979. — Metuchen, N.J. ; London : Scarecrow Press ; [Folkestone] : [Distributed by Bailey and Swinfen], 1981. — ix,434p
ISBN 0-8108-1389-0 : £15.75
ISSN 0090-9130 B81-30850

016.812'52 — Drama in English. American writers. Hellman, Lillian — *Bibliographies*
Riordan, Mary Marguerite. Lillian Hellman : a bibliography : 1926-1978 / Mary Marguerite Riordan. — Metuchen ; London : Scarecrow, 1980. — xxxiv,210p : 1port ; 23cm. — (Scarecrow author bibliographies ; no.50)
Includes index
ISBN 0-8108-1320-3 : £8.75 B81-01613

016.813'081'083273 — Historical fiction in English. American writers, *to 1977.* Special subjects: United States, *to 1977* — *Bibliographies*

Dickinson, A. T.. Dickinson's American historical fiction. — 4th ed. / Virginia Brokaw Gerhardstein. — Metuchen ; London : Scarecrow, 1981. — xvi,312p ; 23cm
Previous ed.: 197-?. — Includes index
ISBN 0-8108-1361-0 : £10.50
ISBN 0-8108-1362-9 B81-16267

016.813'3 — Fiction in English. American writers. Melville, Herman. Criticism — *Bibliographies*

Boswell, Jeanetta. Herman Melville and the critics : a checklist of criticism, 1900-1978 / by Jeanetta Boswell. — Metuchen ; London : Scarecrow, 1981. — xi,247p ; 22cm. — (The Scarecrow author bibliographies ; no.53)
Includes index
ISBN 0-8108-1385-8 : £9.45 B81-22992

016.813'4 — Fiction in English. American writers. Alger, Horatio. Criticism — *Bibliographies*

Scharnhorst, Gary. Horatio Alger, Jr : an annotated bibliography of comment and criticism / by Gary Scharnhorst and Jack Bales ; with an inroduction by Herbert R. Mayes. — Metuchen ; London : Scarecrow, 1981. — xiii,179p ; 23cm. — (Scarecrow author bibliographies ; no.54)
Includes index
ISBN 0-8108-1387-4 : £8.40 B81-26234

016.813'4 — Fiction in English. American writers. James, Henry, *1843-1916.* Criticism — *Bibliographies*

Edel, Leon. A bibliography of Henry James. — 3rd ed. — Oxford : Clarendon, Oct.1981. — [448]p. — (Soho bibliographies)
Previous ed.: 1961
ISBN 0-19-818186-8 : £20.00 : CIP entry
B81-25845

016.813'52 — Fiction in English. American writers. Faulkner, William. Criticism — *Bibliographies*

Ricks, Beatrice. William Faulkner : a bibliography of secondary works / compiled by Beatrice Ricks. — Metuchen ; London : Scarecrow, 1981, c1980. — xxvii,657p ; 23cm. — (The Scarecrow author bibliographies ; no.49)
Includes index
ISBN 0-8108-1323-8 : £22.75 B81-22989

016.813'52 — Fiction in English. American writers. Fitzgerald, F. Scott. Criticism — *Bibliographies*

Stanley, Linda C.. The foreign critical reputation of F. Scott Fitzgerald : an analysis and annotated bibliography / Linda C. Stanley. — Westport, Conn. ; London : Greenwood Press, 1980. — xiii,276p ; 25cm
Includes index
ISBN 0-313-21444-1 : Unpriced B81-04152

016.813'52 — Fiction in English. American writers. Van Vechten, Carl — *Bibliographies*

Kellner, Bruce. A bibliography of the work of Carl van Vechten / compiled by Bruce Kellner. — Westport ; London : Greenwood Press, 1980. — xvii,258p,[31]p of plates : ill,facsims,ports ; 25cm
Includes index
ISBN 0-313-20767-4 : Unpriced B81-07411

016.813'52'09 — Fiction in English. American writers. Hemingway, Ernest & Steinbeck, John, *1902-1968.* Criticism. Theses accepted by American universities — *Abstracts*

Steinbeck and Hemingway : dissertation abstracts and research opportunities / edited and compiled by Tetsumaro Hayashi ; with an introduction by Warren French. — Metuchen ; London : Scarecrow, 1980. — xiv,228p ; 23cm
Includes index
ISBN 0-8108-1321-1 : £8.75 B81-06293

016.813'54 — Fiction in English. American writers. Kerouac, Jack. Criticism — *Bibliographies*

Milewski, Robert J.. Jack Kerouac : an annotated bibliography of secondary sources, 1944-1979 / by Robert J. Milewski with the assistance of John Z. Guzlowski and Linda Calendrillo. — Metuchen ; London : Scarecrow, 1981. — x,225p ; 23cm. — (The Scarecrow author bibliographies ; no.52)
Includes index
ISBN 0-8108-1378-5 : £8.75 B81-22991

016.813'54'0935203924 — Fiction in English. American writers, *1945-1980.* Special themes: Jews — *Bibliographies*

Blackman, Murray. A guide to Jewish themes in American fiction 1940-1980 / Murray Blackman. — Metuchen ; London : Scarecrow, 1981. — v,266p ; 23cm
Includes index
ISBN 0-8108-1380-7 : £10.50 B81-22831

016.818'309 — English literature. American writers. Thoreau, Henry David. Criticism — *Bibliographies*

Boswell, Jeanetta. Henry David Thoreau and the critics : a checklist of criticism 1900-1978 / by Jeanetta Boswell and Sarah Crouch. — Metuchen ; London : Scarecrow, 1981. — ix,204p ; 23cm. — (The Scarecrow author bibliographies ; no.56)
Includes index
ISBN 0-8108-1416-1 : £7.70 B81-32561

016.82 — English literature — *Bibliographies*

The **Shorter** new Cambridge bibliography of English literature / edited by George Watson. — Cambridge : Cambridge University Press, 1981. — xivp,1612 columns,[8]p ; 26cm
Includes index
ISBN 0-521-22600-7 : £40.00 : CIP rev.
B81-20537

016.82 — English literature — *Bibliographies — Serials*

Annual bibliography of English language and literature for ... / Modern Humanities Research Association. — Vol.52 (1977). — London : The Association, 1980. — 757p
ISBN 0-900547-75-8 : Unpriced
ISSN 0066-3786
Primary classification 016.42 B81-16748

016.8208 — English literature. Manuscripts — *Indexes*

Index of English literary manuscripts. — London : Mansell
Vol.4: 1800-1900
Part 1: Arnold-Gissing. — Nov.1981. — [900]p
ISBN 0-7201-1587-6 : £70.00 : CIP entry
ISBN 0-7201-0898-5 (set) B81-31081

016.8208'09411 — English literature. Scottish writers, *1945-* — *Bibliographies — Serials*

Annual bibliography of Scottish literature. — 1979. — Edinburgh (National Library of Scotland, George IV Bridge, Edinburgh EH1 1EW) : Scottish Group of the University, College and Research Section of the Library Association, [1980]. — 93p
ISSN 0307-9864 : Unpriced B81-12412

016.8208'0954 — English literature. Indian writers, *1947-* — *Bibliographies*

Commonwealth Institute. *Library & Resource Centre*. Indian literature in English : a checklist / [Commonwealth Institute Library & Resource Centre] ; compiled by Ronald J. Warwick. — London : Commonwealth Institute, 1979. — 86p ; 21cm. — (Checklists on Commonwealth literature, ISSN 0143-5477 ; no.5)
ISBN 0-900906-88-x (pbk) : £1.00 B81-36182

016.8209'352042 — English literature, *1660-1800.* Special subjects: Women. Criticism — *Bibliographies*

Backscheider, Paula. An annotated bibliography of twentieth-century critical studies of women and literature, 1660-1800 / Paula Backscheider, Felicity Nussbaum, Philip B. Anderson. — New York ; London : Garland, 1977. — x,287p ; 23cm. — (Garland reference library of the humanities ; v.64)
Includes index
ISBN 0-8240-9934-6 : Unpriced
Also classified at 016.8209'9287 B81-26168

016.8209'9287 — English literature. Women writers, *1660-1800.* Criticism — *Bibliographies*

Backscheider, Paula. An annotated bibliography of twentieth-century critical studies of women and literature, 1660-1800 / Paula Backscheider, Felicity Nussbaum, Philip B. Anderson. — New York ; London : Garland, 1977. — x,287p ; 23cm. — (Garland reference library of the humanities ; v.64)
Includes index
ISBN 0-8240-9934-6 : Unpriced
Primary classification 016.8209'352042
B81-26168

016.8209'9411 — English literature. Scottish writers, *to 1980.* Audiovisual materials — *Lists*

Crozier, Jo. Scottish literature / compiled by Jo Crozier. — [Glasgow] ([Dowanhill, 74 Victoria Cres. Rd., Glasgow G12 9JN]) : SCET Information Service. — (S.C.E.T. Information Service materiography ; no.1)
Includes index
Pt.1: Poetry and drama. — [1980]. — iii,52p ; 21cm
ISBN 0-86011-035-4 (pbk) : Unpriced
B81-17233

Crozier, Jo. Scottish literature / compiled by Jo Crozier. — [Glasgow] ([Dowanhill, 74 Victoria Cres. Rd. Glasgow G12 9JN]) : SCET Information service. — (S.C.E.T. Information Service materiography ; no.2)
Pt 2: Prose. — [1981]. — iii,51p ; 21cm
Includes index
ISBN 0-86011-038-9 (pbk) : Unpriced
B81-39273

016.821'008'09282 — Poetry in English, *ca 1500-ca 1970.* Secondary school anthologies — *Indexes*

Morris, Helen, *1909-*. Where's that poem? : an index of poems for children arranged by subject with a bibliography of books of poetry / Helen Morris. — Rev. and enl. ed. — Oxford : Blackwell, 1974 (1979 [printing]). — xi,287p ; 20cm
Previous ed. 1967. — Bibliography: p239-272. — Includes index
ISBN 0-631-11791-1 (pbk) : £4.95 B81-40017

016.821'009 — Poetry in English, *1570-1980.* Versification — *Bibliographies*

Brogan, T. V. F.. English versification, 1570-1980 : a reference guide with a global appendix / T.V.F. Brogan. — Baltimore ; London : Johns Hopkins University Press, c1981. — xxix,794p ; 24cm
Bibliography: p744-749. — Includes index
ISBN 0-8018-2541-5 : £28.50 B81-36456

016.821'7 — Poetry in English, *1800-1837* — *Bibliographies*

Keats, Shelley, Byron, Hunt, and their circles : a bibliography : July 1, 1962-December 31, 1974 / edited by Robert A. Hartley ; compiled by David Bonnell Green ... [el al.]. — Lincoln, [Neb.] ; London : University of Nebraska Press, c1978. — 487p ; 24cm
Includes index
ISBN 0-8032-0960-6 : Unpriced B81-10181

016.821'8 — Poetry in English. Mangan, James Clarence — *Bibliographies*

Chutto, Jacques. The James Clarence Mangan bibliography. — Dublin : Wolfhound Press, Oct.1981. — [200]p. — (Irish literary bibliographies ; 2)
ISBN 0-905473-48-5 : £20.00 : CIP entry
B81-30201

016.821'912 — Poetry in English. Housman, A. E. — *Bibliographies*

Sparrow, John. A.E. Housman. — New rev. ed. — Godalming (Foxbury Meadow, Godalming, Surrey) : St. Paul's Bibliographies, Sept.1981. — [72]p
Previous ed.: / by John Carter and John Sparrow. London : Hart-Davis, 1952
ISBN 0-906795-05-2 : £10.00 : CIP entry
B81-25896

016.821'914'08 — North-east England. Arts. Patronage. Organisations. Libraries: Northern Arts. *Poetry Library — Author catalogues — Serials*

Northern Arts. *Poetry Library*. Northern Arts Poetry Library catalogue. — [3rd ed.] (1980). — [Morpeth] ([County Central Library, The Willows, Morpeth, Northumberland NE61 1TA]). — 133p
ISSN 0307-6350 : £3.00 (£0.50 to members of the Library) B81-32700

016.822'914 — Drama in English. Behan, Brendan. Criticism — *Bibliographies*

Mikhail, E. H.. Brendan Behan : an annotated bibliography of criticism / E. H. Mikhail. — London : Macmillan, 1980. — xii,117p ; 23cm
Includes index
ISBN 0-333-27822-4 : £12.00 : CIP rev.
B80-13669

016.823'0872 — Detective fiction in English, ***to 1980.*** **Criticism —** ***Bibliographies***
Breen, Jon L.. What about murder? : a guide to books about mystery and detective fiction / by Jon L. Breen. — Metuchen ; London : Scarecrow, 1981. — xviii,157p ; 23cm
Includes index
ISBN 0-8108-1413-7 : £7.00 B81-26607

016.823'912 — Fiction in English. Doyle, ***Sir*** **Arthur Conan. Characters: Sherlock Holmes —** ***Bibliographies***
De Waal, Ronald Burt. The international Sherlock Holmes / by Ronald Burt De Waal. — Hamden : Archon ; London : Mansell, 1980. — 621p : 1ill ; 27cm
'A companion volume to The world bibliography of Sherlock Holmes and Dr. Watson'. — Includes index
ISBN 0-7201-1600-7 : £27.50 : CIP rev. B80-11716

016.823'912 — Fiction in English. Greene, Graham. Criticism — ***Bibliographies***
Cassis, A. F.. Graham Greene : an annotated bibliography of criticism / by A.F. Cassis. — Metuchen ; London : Scarecrow, 1981. — xx,401p ; 23cm. — (Scarecrow author bibliographies ; no.55)
Includes index
ISBN 0-8108-1418-8 : £15.75 B81-32562

016.823'912 — Fiction in English. Priestley, J. B. — ***Bibliographies***
Day, Alan Edwin. J.B. Priestley : an annotated bibliography / Alan Edwin Day ; with a foreword by J.B. Priestley. — Stroud (Mount Vernon, Butterow, Rodborough, Stroud, Glos. GL5 2LP) : Ian Hodgkins, 1980. — xi,360p ; 22cm
Includes index
ISBN 0-906460-04-2 : £40.00 B81-01971

016.823'912 — Fiction in English. Wallace, Edgar. First editions — ***Bibliographies***
Kiddle, Charles. A guide to the first editions of Edgar Wallace / Charles Kiddle. — Motcombe : Ivory Head Press, 1981. — 88p : ill,facsims ; 21cm
ISBN 0-903639-05-x (pbk) : Unpriced B81-40411

016.823'914'0809282 — Children's stories in English, ***1945-:*** **Books for young persons, 10-15 years —** ***Lists***
Best of the decade : outstanding fiction for young people 1970-1979 / Buckinghamshire County Library, School Library Service. — [Aylesbury] ([Walton St., Aylesbury, Bucks HP20 1UU]) : The Library, 1981. — 37p : ill ; 21cm
ISBN 0-86059-133-6 (pbk) : £1.00 B81-25192

016.823'914'0809282 — Childrens' stories in English, ***1945-.*** **Commonwealth writers —** ***Bibliographies***
Commonwealth Institute. *Library & Resource Centre.* Commonwealth childrens literature / [Commonwealth Institute Library & Resource Centre]. — London : Commonwealth Institute, 1979. — 56p : ill ; 15x21cm. — (Checklists on Commonwealth literature, ISSN 0143-5477 ; no.1)
ISBN 0-900906-86-3 (pbk) : £1.00 B81-36183

016.828'809 — English literature. Carroll, Lewis — ***Bibliographies***
Guiliano, Edward. Lewis Carroll : an annotated international bibliography 1960-77 / by Edward Guiliano. — Brighton : Harvester, 1981, c1980. — viii,253p ; 24cm
Originally published: Charlottesville : Published for the Bibliographic Society of the University of Virginia and the Lewis Carroll Society of North America by the University Press of Virginia, 1980. — Includes index
ISBN 0-7108-0008-8 (corrected) : £25.00 : CIP rev. B81-05166

016.828'91209 — Belfast. Universities. Libraries: Queen's University of Belfast. ***Library.*** **Stock: Documents associated with Waddell, Helen —** ***Catalogues***
Kelly, Mary T.. Papers of Helen Waddell (MS18) : a calendar / complied by Mary T. Kelly. — Belfast : Library, Queen's University, 1981. — 81p ; 30cm
At head of title: The Queen's University of Belfast. — Bibliography: p6. — Includes index
ISBN 0-85389-193-1 (pbk) : £2.00 B81-35565

016.829 — Old English literature — ***Bibliographies***
Greenfield, Stanley B.. A bibliography of publications on Old English literature to the end of 1972 / Stanley B. Greenfield and Fred C. Robinson. — Manchester : Manchester University Press, c1980. — xxii,437p ; 26cm
Includes index
ISBN 0-7190-0773-9 : £35.00 B81-18599

016.83 — German literature. Theses accepted by British universities — ***Lists — Serials***
Theses in progress at British universities and other institutions of higher education and theses completed in ... with work published in ... and work due to be published in ... by members of the Conference of University Teachers of German in Great Britain and Ireland as known on 1 January ... / University of London, Institute of Germanic Studies. — [1980]-. — [London] ([29 Russell Square, WC1B 5DP]) : The Institute, c1980-. — v. ; 25cm. — (Library publication / Institute of Germanic Studies)
Annual. — Continues: Theses in progress at British universities and work due to be published by members of the Conference of University Teachers of German in Great Britain and Ireland
ISSN 0260-5031 = Theses in progress at British universities and other institutions of higher education : Unpriced
Also classified at 016.43 B81-06335

016.841'1'080351 — Poetry in Old French. Special subjects: Tristan — ***Bibliographies***
Shirt, David J.. The old French poems : a bibliographical guide / by David J. Shirt. — London : Grant & Cutler, 1980. — 186p ; 23cm. — (Research bibliographies & checklists ; 28)
Includes index
ISBN 0-7293-0088-9 (pbk) : Unpriced B81-31761

016.843'914 — Fiction in French. Butor, Michel — ***Bibliographies***
Mason, Barbara, *1949-*. Michael Butor : a checklist / by Barbara Mason. — London : Grant & Cutler, 1979. — 98p ; 23cm. — (Research bibliographies & checklists ; 27)
ISBN 0-7293-0078-1 (pbk) : £4.80 B81-03220

016.862 — New York ***(City).*** **Public libraries: New York Public Library. Stock: Drama in Spanish. Comedias sueltas,** ***to 1833 — Catalogues***
Bergman, Hannah E.. A catalogue of comedias sueltas in the New York Public Library / by Hannah E. Bergman and Szilvia E. Szmuk. — London : Grant & Cutler. — (Research bibliographies & checklists ; 32.1)
ISBN 0-7293-0090-0 (pbk) : Unpriced B81-31763

016.863'62 — Fiction in Spanish. Pérez de Ayala, Ramón. Criticism — ***Bibliographies***
Best, Marigold. Ramón Pérez de Ayala : an annotated bibliography of criticism / Marigold Best. — London : Grant & Cutler, 1980. — 81p ; 23cm. — (Research bibliographies & checklists ; 33)
Includes index
ISBN 0-7293-0102-8 (pbk) : Unpriced B81-32435

016.88 — Massachusetts. Cambridge. Universities. Libraries: Harvard University. ***Library.*** **Stock: Greek literature —** ***Catalogues***
Harvard University. *Library.* Ancient Greek literature : classification schedules, classified listing by call number, chronological listing, author and title listing / Harvard University Library. — Cambridge, Mass. : The Library ; Cambridge, Mass. ; London : Distributed by Harvard University Press, 1979. — 638p ; 29cm. — (Widener Library shelflist ; 58)
ISBN 0-674-03310-8 : £38.50 B81-36592

016.8916'612 — Poetry in Welsh. Jones, Thomas Gwynn — ***Bibliographies — Welsh texts***
Roberts, D. Hywel E.. Llyfryddiaeth Thomas Gwynn Jones. — Cardiff : University of Wales Press, Sept.1981. — [337]p
ISBN 0-7083-0757-4 : £12.95 : CIP entry B81-23840

016.89171'3 — Poetry in Russian. Lermontov, M. ÎU.. German criticism & translations into German language — ***Bibliographies — Russian texts***
Dukmeĭer, Fr. M. Îu. Lermontov u nîemtsev / Fr. Dukmeĭer = Lermontov in Germany / F. Dukmeyer. — Letchworth : Prideaux, 1980. — 18p ; 21cm. — (Russian titles for the specialist, ISSN 0305-3741 ; no.221)
Russian text. — Russian title transliterated. — Added t.p. in Russian. — Originally published: S.-Peterburg : Imperatorskaîa Akademiîa Nauk, 1913. — Bibliography: p14-18
£1.20 (pbk) B81-04593

016.8956'08'004 — Japanese literature. Translation, ***1868-1978 — Bibliographies***
Modern Japanese literature in translation : a bibliography / compiled by The International House of Japan Library. — Tokyo : Kodansha International ; Oxford : Phaidon [distributor], c1979. — 311p ; 27cm
Includes index
ISBN 0-87011-339-9 : £7.95 B81-09337

016.9 — Historical events — ***Bibliographies — For secondary school teaching in Scotland***
C.S.Y.S. history bibliography. — [Glasgow] ([Jordanhill College of Education, 76 Southbrae Drive, Glasgow, G13 1PP]) : Scottish Curriculum Development Service, Glasgow Centre, 1980. — 104p ; 30cm
Previous ed.: 197-?
£1.60 (spiral) B81-08524

016.9 — Historical events. Theses accepted by British universities — ***Lists — Serials***
Historical research for university degrees in the United Kingdom. Part 1, Theses completed .... — List no.41 (1979). — London : University of London, Institute of Historical Research, 1980. — v,35p
ISBN 0-901179-62-0 : Unpriced
ISSN 0308-7417 B81-06834

Historical research for university degrees in the United Kingdom. Part 1, Theses completed ... — List no.42 (1980). — London : University of London, Institute of Historical Research, 1981. — v,35p
ISBN 0-901179-66-3 : Unpriced
ISSN 0308-7417 B81-29656

Historical research for university degrees in the United Kingdom. Part 2, Theses in porgress ... — List no.42 (1981). — London : University of London, Institute of Historical Research, 1981. — vi,158p
ISBN 0-901179-67-1 : Unpriced
ISSN 0308-7425 B81-29657

016.9 — Northern Ireland. Public libraries: SELB Library Service. Stock: Audiovisual aids on history — ***Catalogues***
SELB Library Service. Audio visual resources : history, economics, politics : a select list of materials available on loan from the SELB Library Service. — [Craigavon] ([Library Headquarters, Brownlow Rd., Legahory, Craigavon, County Armagh BT5 8DP]) : [The Library Service], [1980]. — 63p ; 30cm
Cover title
Unpriced (pbk)
Primary classification 016.3 B81-25043

016.907'2024 — Historiography. Offler, H. S. — ***Bibliographies***
A List of the historical writings 1936-1978 of Hilary Seton Offler : presented to him by his colleagues in the University of Durham on the occasion of his retirement from the chair of medieval history. — [Durham] : University of Durham, 1978. — 27p ; 21cm
Free distribution (pbk) B81-29538

016.907'2024 — Historiography. Toynbee, Arnold, ***1889-1975 — Bibliographies***
Morton, S. Fiona. A bibliography of Arnold J. Toynbee / compiled by S. Fiona Morton ; with a foreword by Veronica M. Toynbee. — Oxford : Oxford University Press, 1980. — xi,316p ; 27cm
Includes index
ISBN 0-19-215261-0 : £25.00 : CIP rev. B79-26833

016.907′2037 — Ancient Roman historiography — *Bibliographies*

The **Classical** world bibliography of Greek and Roman history / with a new introduction by Walter Donlan. — New York ; London : Garland, 1978. — xiii,234p ; 24cm. — (Garland reference library of the humanities ; v.94)
Facsim. of 14 articles originally published in the Classical world from 1954 to 1971
ISBN 0-8240-9879-x : Unpriced
Primary classification 016.907′2038 B81-08059

016.907′2038 — Ancient Greek historiography — *Bibliographies*

The **Classical** world bibliography of Greek and Roman history / with a new introduction by Walter Donlan. — New York ; London : Garland, 1978. — xiii,234p ; 24cm. — (Garland reference library of the humanities ; v.94)
Facsim. of 14 articles originally published in the Classical world from 1954 to 1971
ISBN 0-8240-9879-x : Unpriced
Also classified at 016.907′2037 B81-08059

016.909′0974927 — Arab countries. Serials — *Bibliographies*

Aman, Mohammed M.. Arab periodicals and serials : a subject bibliography / Mohammed M. Aman. — New York ; London : Garland, 1979. — x,252p ; 23cm. — (Garland reference libarary of social science ; v.57)
ISBN 0-8240-9816-1 : £33.00 B81-26232

016.90982′8 — Social conditions — *Abstracts — Serials*

[Feedback *(London)***]**. Feedback. — No.1 (Sept.1977)-. — London (1c Cambridge Terrace, Regents Park, NW1 4JL) : Returned Volunteer Action, 1977-. — v. ; 30cm
Irregular
ISSN 0260-9611 = Feedback (London) : Unpriced B81-11217

016.91 — Geography. Theses accepted by British higher education institutions — *Lists — Serials*

Geography departments of universities and polytechnics in the British Isles, theses in preparation, theses completed / Heads of Geography Departments Conference and Human Geography Committee, Social Science Research Council. — 1980-81. — Lampeter (c/o Professor P. Beaumont, Department of Geography, Saint David′s University College, Lampeter, Dyfed SA48 7ED) : [The Conference], [1981]. — 178p
£3.00 B81-31006

016.91 — Massachusetts. Cambridge. Universities. Libraries: Harvard University. *Library.* **Stock: Geography —** *Catalogues*

Harvard University. *Library.* Geography and anthropology : classification schedules, classified listing by call number, chronological listing, author and title listing / Harvard University Library. — Cambridge, Mass. : The Library ; Cambridge, Mass. ; London : Distributed by Harvard University Press, 1979. — 270p ; 29cm. — (Widener Library shelflist ; 60)
ISBN 0-674-34855-9 : £21.00
Also classified at 016.301 B81-36591

016.91′02′02 — Guidebooks — *Lists*

Heise, Jon O.. The travel book : guide to the travel guides / Jon O. Heise with Dennis O′Reilly. — New York ; London : Bowker, 1981. — xi,319p ; 24cm. — (Consumer information series)
Includes index
ISBN 0-8352-1337-4 : Unpriced B81-29719

016.9104 — Travel — *Bibliographies*

Anderson, Janice. Books and travellers / selected and annotated by Janice Anderson. — Wandsworth : National Book League, c1980. — 16p ; 21cm
ISBN 0-85353-354-7 (pbk) : £1.30 (£1.00 NBL members) B81-07759

016.910′6′041 — Great Britain. Geography. Organisations: Geographical Association. Archives — *Lists*

Bassett, Philippa. A list of the historical records of the Geographical Association / compiled by Philippa Bassett as part of a research project funded by the Social Science Research Council. — [Birmingham] : Centre for Urban and Regional Studies, 1980. — viii,5leaves ; 30cm. — (Lists of historical records)
At head of title: Centre For Urban and Regional Studies University of Birmingham and Institute of Agricultural History University of Reading
Unpriced (pbk) B81-27632

016.912′4225 — East & West Sussex. Archaeology. Organisations: Sussex Archaeological Society. Stock: Manuscript maps of East & West Sussex *— Catalogues*

Sussex Archaeological Society. A catalogue of manuscript maps in the custody of the Sussex Archaeological Society / compiled by K.W. Dickins. — Lewes (Barbican House, Lewes, East Sussex BN7 1YE) : Sussex Archaeological Society, 1981. — 68p ; 21cm. — (Sussex Archaeological occasional paper, ISSN 0143-8212 ; no.4)
ISBN 0-904973-01-8 (pbk) : Unpriced B81-26876

016.91421 — London. Geographical features — *Bibliographies*

Dolphin, Philippa. The London region. — London : Mansell, Oct.1981. — [368]p
ISBN 0-7201-1598-1 : £25.00 : CIP entry B81-27406

016.92 — Books with American imprints: Biographies, *1950-1980 — Lists*

Biographical books 1950-1980. — New York ; London : Bowker, c1980. — lix,1557p ; 29cm
ISBN 0-8352-1315-3 : £44.00 B81-07681

016.92 — Newspapers with British imprints. Colour supplements. Articles: Biographies — *Indexes*

Buckinghamshire County Library. Biographical references in the colour supplements (BRICS) : 1965- April 1981 / Buckinghamshire County Library. — [Aylesbury] : [The Library], [1981]. — [52]p ; 30cm
ISBN 0-86059-205-7 (unbound) : £1.00 B81-40180

016.92′0041 — British persons. Yorkshire records: East Riding records - *Indexes*

Cawley, A. P. D.. East Riding strays and strangers / compiled by A.P.D. Cawley. — [Beverley] ([23 The Woodlands, Beverley, N. Humberside HU1 8BI]) : East Yorkshire Family History Society, 1981. — 25p ; 21cm
Cover title
Unpriced (pbk)
Primary classification 016.92′004283 B81-19281

016.92′004283 — Yorkshire persons: East Riding persons. British records — *Indexes*

Cawley, A. P. D.. East Riding strays and strangers / compiled by A.P.D. Cawley. — [Beverley] ([23 The Woodlands, Beverley, N. Humberside HU1 8BI]) : East Yorkshire Family History Society, 1981. — 25p ; 21cm
Cover title
Unpriced (pbk)
Also classified at 016.92′0041 B81-19281

016.929′2′09415 — Ireland. Families. Genealogical aspects — *Bibliographies*

MacLysaght, Edward. Bibliography of Irish family history / Edward MacLysaght. — Dublin : Irish Academic Press, c1981. — 69p ; 20cm
ISBN 0-7165-0206-2 (unbound) : £1.50 B81-40905

016.929′2′09416 — Down *(County).* **North Down** *(District).* **Blackwood** *(Family) — Bibliographies*

Clandeboye : a reading guide. — [Ballynahinch] ([Library Headquarters, Windmill Hill, Ballynahinch, BT24 8DH]) : [Irish Section, South Eastern Education and Library Service], [1981]. — [29]p : ill,1coat of arms,facsims ; 30cm
Unpriced (unbound) B81-19329

016.929′2′0942 — England. Bath *(Marquesses of).* **Archives —** *Abstracts*

Bath *(Marquesses of).* Calendar of the manuscripts of the Most Honourable the Marquess of Bath preserved at Longleat, Wiltshire. — London : H.M.S.O.. — (Historical Manuscripts Commission [reports and calendars series] ; 58)
Vol.5: Talbot, Dudley and Devereux papers 1533-1659 / edited by G. Dyfnallt Owen. — 1980. — 376p ; 25cm
Includes index
ISBN 0-11-440092-x : Unpriced B81-15977

016.929′342 — England. Record repositories. Stock: Parish registers — *Lists*

Peach, E. O.. The third supplement to Original parish registers in record offices and libraries / [compiled by E.O. Peach]. — Matlock (Tawney House, Matlock, Derbyshire) : Local Population Studies in association with the SSRC Cambridge Group for the History Population and Social Structure, 1980. — 92p ; 22cm
ISBN 0-9503951-5-3 (pbk) : £3.75 (£2.50 to members of the LPS Society) B81-18612

016.929′342 — England. Repositories. Stock: Bishops′ transcripts of parish registers — *Catalogues*

Gibson, J. S. W.. Bishops transcripts and marriage licences : bonds and allegations : a guide to their location and indexes / compiled by J.S.W. Gibson. — Banbury (White Lion Walk, Banbury, Oxfordshire) : Gulliver and the Federation of Family History Societies, 1981. — 32p ; 21cm
ISBN 0-906428-09-2 (pbk) : £1.00
ISBN 0-907099-06-8 (Federation of Family History Societies)
Also classified at 016.929′342 B81-19719

016.929′342 — England. Repositories. Stock: Records of marriage licences — *Catalogues*

Gibson, J. S. W.. Bishops transcripts and marriage licences : bonds and allegations : a guide to their location and indexes / compiled by J.S.W. Gibson. — Banbury (White Lion Walk, Banbury, Oxfordshire) : Gulliver and the Federation of Family History Societies, 1981. — 32p ; 21cm
ISBN 0-906428-09-2 (pbk) : £1.00
ISBN 0-907099-06-8 (Federation of Family History Societies)
Primary classification 016.929′342 B81-19719

016.929′34249 — West Midlands *(Metropolitan County).* **Black Country. Parish registers —** *Lists*

Billington, Eric R.. Parish registers and churches of the West Midlands and Black Country : including district locations of churches, commencement date of registers and guide to their whereabouts / compiled by Eric R. Billington. — Birmingham (69 Hollydale Rd., Erdington, Birmingham B24 9LS) : Birmindex, 1980. — 17p ; 30cm
Bibliography: p9
Unpriced (pbk)
Also classified at 914.24′904858 B81-28881

016.929′34251 — Derbyshire. Matlock. Record repositories: Derbyshire Record Office. Stock: Derbyshire parish registers, *to 1837 — Catalogues*

Derbyshire Record Office. Anglican and nonconformist registers in the Derbyshire Record Office. — [Matlock] ([County Offices, Matlock, Derbyshire DE4 3AG]) : [Derbyshire Record Office], 1980. — 75 leaves ; 30cm
Bibliography: leaf 6
Unpriced (pbk) B81-12275

016.929′34257 — Oxfordshire. Parish registers — *Lists*

Harris, C. G.. Oxfordshire parish registers and bishop′s transcripts / C.G. Harris. — Oxford (90 Hockmore Tower, Cowley Centre, Oxford) : Oxfordshire Family History Society, 1981. — 23p : 1map ; 22cm
Cover title. — Text on inside covers
ISBN 0-905863-06-2 (pbk) : Unpriced B81-08078

016.929'34264 — Suffolk. Genealogical sources — *Lists*

Suffolk Record Office. A guide to genealogical sources in Suffolk / Suffolk Record Office. — Ipswich : Suffolk County Council, 1981. — [124]p ; 30cm
ISBN 0-86055-086-9 (pbk) : Unpriced
B81-39892

016.929'34296 — Dyfed. Parish registers — *Lists*

Parish registers / Dyfed County Council Archives. — [Carmarthen] ([County Record Office, County Hall, Carmarthen, Dyfed]) : [Dyfed County Council], [1980]. — [16]p ; 21cm
Cover title
Unpriced (pbk) B81-07538

016.9297'2 — Berkshire. Windsor. Castles: Windsor Castle. Stock: Archives of Stuart *(House of)*

Gain, Marion F.. The Stuart papers at Windsor / by Marion F. Gain. — London (10 Uphill Grove, NW7 4NJ) : Royal Stuart Society, 1981. — 18p ; 21cm. — (Royal Stuart papers, ISSN 0307-997x ; 17)
Unpriced (pbk) B81-20778

016.9301 — Massachusetts. Cambridge. Universities. Libraries: Harvard University. *Library.* **Stock: Archaeology —** *Catalogues*

Harvard University. *Library*. Archaeology : classification schedules, classified listing by call number, chronological listing, author and title listing / Harvard University Library. — Cambridge, Mass. : The Library ; Cambridge, Mass. ; London : Distributed by Harvard University Press, 1979. — 442p ; 29cm. — (Widener Library shelflist ; 56)
ISBN 0-674-04318-9 : £31.50 B81-36593

016.932'.007'2 — Egyptology - *Bibliographies - Serials*

Annual Egyptological bibliography = Bibliographie Egyptologique annuelle. — 1977. — Warminster : Aris & Phillips, Apr.1981. — [256]p
ISBN 0-85668-186-5 : £15.00 : CIP entry
B81-06067

016.9361 — Great Britain. Antiquities — *Bibliographies — Serials*

Archaeological bibliography for Great Britain and Ireland. — 1976. — London : Council for British Archaeology, c1981. — xiv,173p
Unpriced B81-29420

016.9361'01 — Great Britain. Megalithic monuments — *Bibliographies*

Graham, J. T. (Joseph Turnbull). British megaliths : a bibliographic guide / by J.T. Graham. — Hatfield (The Library, Hatfield Polytechnic, P.O. Box 110, Hatfield, AL10 9AD) : Hertis, c1981. — ixp,24columns ; 21cm
Cover title. — Includes index
ISBN 0-85267-143-1 (pbk) : £1.00 B81-17803

016.938 — Massachusetts. Cambridge. Universities. Libraries: Harvard University. *Library.* **Stock: Classical studies —** *Catalogues*

Harvard University. *Library*. Classical studies : classification schedules, classified listing by call number, chronological listing, author and title listing / Harvard University Library. — Cambridge, Mass. : The Library ; Cambridge, Mass. ; London : Distributed by Harvard University Press, 1979. — 215p ; 29cm. — (Widener Library shelflist ; 57)
ISBN 0-674-13461-3 : £17.50 B81-36594

016.94 — European Community countries. Social conditions. Research organisations: European Foundation for the Improvement of Living and Working Conditions. Publications — *Lists*

European Foundation for the Improvement of Living and Working Conditions. Publications of the European Foundation to May 1981 / European Foundation for the Improvement of Living and Working Conditions. — Shankill, Loughlinstown House, Shankill, Co. Dublin : [The Foundation], [1981]. — 9 leaves ; 28cm
Cover title
Unpriced (pbk) B81-09731

016.9403'73 — World War 1. Role of United States — *Bibliographies*

Schaffer, Ronald. The United States in World War I : a selected bibliography / Ronald Schaffer. — Santa Barbara ; Oxford : Clio, c1978. — xxix,224p ; 24cm. — (The War/peace bibliography series ; 7)
Includes index
ISBN 0-87436-274-1 : £13.25 B81-01618

016.94053 — Humberside. Hull. Record repositories: Kingston upon Hull Record Office. Stock: Documents on World War 2 — *Lists*

Oxley, G. W.. World War II / completed [i.e. compiled] by G.W. Oxley. — Kingston upon Hull ([Alfred Gelder St., Kingston upon Hull N. Humberside HU1 2AA]) : Kingston upon Hull City Council, 1980. — 11p ; 21cm. — (Subject guide / Kingston Upon Hull Record Office ; no.1)
Cover title
ISBN 0-904767-04-3 (pbk) : Unpriced
B81-15755

016.94055'8 — Great Britain. National libraries: British Library. *Lending Division.* **Stock: Serials published by European Community agencies —** *Catalogues*

British Library. *Lending Division*. Serial publications of the European Communities and its institutions held by the British Library Lending Division / [compiled by] G.P. Cornish. — 3rd ed. — Boston Spa : British Library Lending Division, [1979]. — 33p ; 30cm
Cover title. — Previous ed.: 1977. — Includes index
ISBN 0-85350-173-4 (pbk) : Unpriced
B81-16170

016.941 — Great Britain — *History — Bibliographies — Serials*

Annual bibliography of British and Irish history. — Publications of 1980. — Brighton : Harvester Press, Sept.1981. — 1v.
ISBN 0-7108-0361-3 : CIP entry B81-23879

016.94107'3'0924 — Great Britain. Politics. Burke, Edmund, *1729-1797 — Bibliographies*

Todd, William B.. A bibliography of Edmund Burke. — Godalming (Foxbury Meadow, Godalming, Surrey) : St. Paul's Bibliographies, Feb.1982. — [336]p. — (St. Paul's bibliographies ; 5)
Originally published: London : Hart-Davis, 1964
ISBN 0-906795-03-6 : £16.00 : CIP entry
B81-25895

016.941081'092'4 — Durham *(County).* **Durham. Universities: University of Durham.** *Department of Palaeography and Diplomatic.* **Stock: Documents associated with Grey, Maria Grey,** *Countess — Catalogues*

University of Durham. *Department of Palaeography and Diplomatic*. List of the papers of Maria 3rd Countess Grey. — [Durham] ([South Rd., Durham DH1 3LE]) : Department of Palaeography and Diplomatic, University of Durham, 1981. — 40 leaves ; 30cm
Unpriced (pbk) B81-22983

016.941082'092'4 — Great Britain. Churchill, Winston S. (Winston Spencer), *1874-1965.* **Works** *— Bibliographies*

Woods, Frederick. A bibliography of the works of Sir Winston Churchill KG, OM, CH / by Frederick Woods. — 2nd rev. ed. — Godalming (Foxbury Meadow, Godalming, Surrey) : St Paul's Bibliographies, 1979, c1975. — 406p,[5]p of plates : ill,1port ; 23cm. — (St Paul's bibliogrphies ; no.1)
Previous ed.: London : Kaye & Ward, 1969. — Includes index
ISBN 0-906795-00-1 : Unpriced : CIP rev.
B79-20583

016.9411085'8 — Scotland. Social conditions — *Bibliographies*

Public knowledge / [prepared by the Scottish Information Providers Group]. — Edinburgh (4 Queensferry St., Edinburgh EH2 4PA) : C.E.C., 1980. — 27,[9]p ; 30cm
Includes index
ISBN 0-907065-00-7 (pbk) : £1.00 B81-15691

016.9416'51 — Castlereagh *(District) — Bibliographies*

Castlereagh. — [Ballynahinch] ([Library Headquarters, Windmill Hill, Ballynahinch, BT24 8DH]) : [Irish Section, South Eastern Education and Library Service], [1980]. — [27]p : ill,1map,facsims ; 30cm
Unpriced (unbound) B81-18916

016.9416'54 — Ards *(District) — Bibliographies*

The **Ards** : a local history source list. — [Ballynahinch] ([Library Headquarters, Windmill Hill, Ballynahinch, BT24 8DH]) : [Irish Section, South Eastern Education and Library Service], [1980]. — [35]p : ill,1map,facsims ; 30cm ; unbound
Unpriced B81-18917

016.94202'1 — England. Norman Conquest — *Bibliographies*

The **Norman** Conquest : a booklist / [Hastings Public Library]. — 2nd ed. — [Lewes] ([44 St. Annes Cres., Lewes, East Sussex BN7 1SQ]) : East Sussex County Council, 1981. — 32p ; 21cm
Previous ed.: 1966
ISBN 0-86147-012-5 (pbk) : £1.00 B81-21910

016.94206'6'0924 — Cambridgeshire. Cambridge. Libraries: Pepys Library — *Catalogues*

Pepys Library. Catalogue of the Pepys Library at Magdalene College, Cambridge / [general editor Robert Latham]. — Woodbridge : Brewer
Vol.3: Prints and drawings
Pt.1: General / compiled by A.W. Aspital ; with a introduction by P.H. Hulton. — 1981. — xii,357p,[8]p of plates : facsims ; 31cm
Includes index
ISBN 0-85991-045-8 : £45.00 : CIP rev.
B80-13670

016.94206'6'0924 — Cambridgeshire. Cambridge. Universities. Colleges. Libraries: Magdalene College, *Cambridge. Library.* **Stock: Documents associated with Pepys, Samuel. Collections: Magdalene College,** *Cambridge. Pepys Library - Catalogues*

Magdalene College *(Cambridge)*. Catalogue of the Pepys Library at Magdalene College, Cambridge. — Woodbridge : Brewer, Sept.1981
Vol.5
Pt.2: Modern manuscripts. — [190]p
ISBN 0-85991-078-4 : £35.00 : CIP entry
B81-19204

016.942081'092'4 — Nottinghamshire. Nottingham. Universities. Libraries: University of Nottingham. *Manuscripts Department.* **Stock: Documents of Denison, John Evelyn —** *Catalogues*

University of Nottingham. *Manuscripts Department*. Papers of John Evelyn Denison Viscount Ossington 1827-1873 / University of Nottingham, Department of Manuscripts. — [Nottingham] : [The Department], [1981?]. — 25p ; 30cm
£1.50 (pbk) B81-37838

016.9422'1 — Surrey — *Bibliographies — Serials*

A **Current** bibliography of Surrey. — Vol.5 (1980). — [Dorking] ([West St., Dorking, Surrey RH4 1DE]) : Surrey County Library, 1981. — [32]p
ISSN 0140-0940 : Unpriced B81-31028

016.9422'5 — East & West Sussex — *Bibliographies — Serials*

Sussex bibliography / East Sussex County Library. — 1979. — Lewes : East Sussex County Library, [1980]. — 50p
ISBN 0-900348-87-9 : Unpriced
ISSN 0141-5093 B81-06719

016.9422'5'05 — East & West Sussex, *1500-1700 — Bibliographies*

Brent, Colin E.. Sussex in the 16th and 17th centuries : a bibliography / by Colin E. Brent, Anthony J. Fletcher and Timothy J. McCann. — 2nd ed. / John H. Farrant. — Brighton (Education Development Building, Falmer, Brighton, BN1 9RG) : Centre for Continuing Education, University of Sussex, 1980. — 52p ; 21cm. — (Occasional papers / University of Sussex Centre for Continuing Education, ISSN 0306-1108 ; no.2)
Previous ed.: 1974. — Includes index
ISBN 0-904242-12-9 (pbk) : £0.60 B81-05237

016.9423'13 — Wiltshire. Swindon, *1945-1980 — Bibliographies*

Scott, Colin, *1948-*. The expansion of Swindon, Wiltshire since 1945 : a bibliography / Colin Scott. — [London] ([Woodlands Avenue, Acton, W3 9DN]) : School of Library & Information Studies, Ealing College of Higher Education, [1981?]. — 17leaves ; 30cm. — (Ealing miscellany ; no.16)
Includes index
£0.20 (unbound) B81-16694

016.9425'4 — Leicestershire. Churches — *Bibliographies*

A **Bibliography** of Leicestershire churches / edited by David Parsons. — [Leicester] ([University Rd., Leicester, LE1 7RH]) : [Department of Adult Education, University of Leicester in association with Leicestershire Libraries and Information Service]
Part 1: The periodical sources. — 1978. — 60p ; 21cm
ISBN 0-901507-12-1 (pbk) : Unpriced
B81-15688

016.9425'7 — Oxfordshire, *to 1980 — Bibliographies*

Cordeaux, E. H.. A bibliography of printed works relating to Oxfordshire (excluding the University and City and Oxford) / by E. H. Cordeaux and D.H. Merry. — Oxford : At the Clarendon Press for the Oxford Historical Society
Supplementary vol. — 1981. — xxvii,289p ; 23cm. — (New series / Oxford Historical Society ; 28)
Includes index
Unpriced B81-36102

016.9428'1 — West Yorkshire *(Metropolitan County)*. **Wakefield. Records. Repositories: Wakefield Metropolitan District Libraries.** *Archives Department.* **Stock: Manuscripts —** *Catalogues*

Wakefield Metropolitan District Libraries. *Archives Department.* Wakefield District archives : a handlist for students. — Wakefield (Archives Dept., Library H.Q, Balne La., Wakefield, W. Yorkshire) : Wakefield Metropolitan District Libraries. — (Archives publication / Wakefield Metropolitan District Libraries ; no.3)
Part 1: Manuscripts relating to local social life. — [1981?]. — 10p ; 30cm
Cover title
ISBN 0-86169-004-4 (pbk) : Unpriced
B81-29256

016.94308'092'2 — Nottinghamshire. Nottingham. Universities. Libraries: University of Nottingham. *Manuscripts Department.* **Stock: Documents of Steinitz, Bernard & Steinitz, Irene —** *Catalogues*

University of Nottingham. *Manuscripts Department.* Steinitz papers 1899-1964 / University of Nottingham Manuscripts Department. — Nottingham : The Department, [1981]. — 79p : geneal.table ; 30cm
£2.50 (unbound) B81-17275

016.94404'1 — Great Britain. National libraries: British Library. *Department of Printed Books.* **Stock: Documents associated with political events in France,** *1789-1799 — Catalogues*

British Library. *Department of Printed Books.* French revolutionary collections in the British Library : list of the contents of the three special collections of pamphlets, journals and other works in the British Library, relating chiefly to the French Revolution / compiled by G.K. Fortescue. — 2nd ed. / revised and augmented by A.C. Brockhurst. — London : British Library, 1979. — 87p ; 24cm
Previous ed.: London : British Museum, 1899. — Includes index
ISBN 0-904654-21-4 (pbk) : £7.50 : CIP rev.
B79-16306

016.945'08 — Italy. Risorgimento, *1796-1870 — Bibliographies — Italian texts*

Bibliografia storica del Risorgimento Italiano 1796-1870 / Istituto Italiano di cultura nel Regno Unito, Biblioteca. — London (39 Belgrave Sq., SW1) : La Biblioteca, 1980. — 52p ; 21cm
Published in a limited edition of 500 copies
Unpriced (pbk) B81-11547

016.946'89 — Gibraltar — *Bibliographies*

Green, Muriel M.. A Gibraltar bibliography ... / by Muriel M. Green. — London (27 Russell Sq., WC1B 5DS) : University of London Institute of Commonwealth Studies, 1980. — vii,108p ; 29cm
Includes index
ISBN 0-902499-26-2 (pbk) : £3.00 B81-05057

016.947'00431 — Soviet Union. Germans, *1763-1976 — Bibliographies*

Long, James, *1942-*. The German-Russians : a bibliography of Russian materials : with introductory essay, annotations and locations of materials in major American and Soviet libraries / James Long. — Santa Barbara ; Oxford : Clio, 1979, c1978. — xl,136p ; 24cm
Includes index
ISBN 0-87436-282-2 : £9.96 B81-03086

016.947'41 — Great Britain. National libraries: British Library. *Reference Division.* **Stock: Documents on Estonia —** *Catalogues*

British Library. *Reference Division.* Catalogue of books and periodicals on Estonia in the British Library Reference Division / compiled by Salme Pruuden ; edited by Dalibor B. Chrástek, Christine G. Thomas. — London : British Library, 1981. — 309p ; 23cm. — (Garland reference library of social science ; v.71)
Includes index
ISBN 0-904654-48-6 : Unpriced
ISBN 0-8240-9553-7 (Garland) B81-24473

016.94897 — Finland - *Bibliographies*

Screen, J. E. O.. Finland. — Oxford : Clio, June 1981. — [244]p. — (World bibliographical series ; 31)
ISBN 0-903450-55-0 : £22.00 : CIP entry
B81-09471

016.9495 — Byzantine studies, *1892-1977 — Bibliographies*

Literature in various Byzantine disciplines, 1892-1977. — London : Mansell, Sept.1981. — (Dumbarton Oaks bibliographies)
Vol.1: Epigraphy. — [380]p
ISBN 0-7201-1586-8 : £60.00 : CIP entry
ISBN 0-7201-1586-8 (set) B81-21538

016.9495 — Greece — *Bibliographies*

Clogg, Mary Jo. Greece / Mary Jo Clogg, Richard Clogg, compilers. — Oxford : Clio, c1980. — xvii,224p : 1map ; 23cm. — (World bibliographical series ; v.17)
Includes index
ISBN 0-903450-30-5 : £21.00 : CIP rev.
B80-32806

016.9495 — Greece. Theses accepted by British Universities, *1874-1950 — Lists*

Koundouros, R.. On Greece : theses index in Britain (1874-1950) / compiled by R. Koundouros. — London (1A Holland Park, W.11) : Greek Press and Information Office, 1980. — 16p ; 21cm
Unpriced (pbk) B81-11416

016.952 — Great Britain. Libraries. Stock: Documents on local history of Japan: Documents in Japanese — *Lists*

Bunn, J. M.. A union list of Japanese local histories in British libraries. — Oxford : Bodleian Library, Nov.1981. — [400]p
ISBN 0-900177-83-7 (pbk) : £6.00: CIP entry
B81-30618

016.953'67 — Kuwait. Political agencies: British Political Agency *(Kuwait)*. **Stock: Documents on Kuwait: Documents in Arabic -** *Lists*

British Political Agency *(Kuwait)*. Arabic documents in the archives of the British Political Agency, Kuwait, 1904-1919. — London : India Office Library and Records, July 1981. — 1v.. — (British Academy oriental documents ; 5)
ISBN 0-903359-32-4 (pbk) : CIP entry
B81-15839

016.953'8 — Saudi Arabia, *to 1978 — Bibliographies*

Clements, Frank A.. Saudi Arabia / Frank A. Clements. — Oxford : Clio, c1979. — xiv,197p : 1map ; 23cm. — (World bibliographical series : v.5)
Includes index
ISBN 0-903450-15-1 : £16.75 : CIP rev.
B79-06196

016.95403'5 — India, *1908-1947*. **British parliamentary papers —** *Lists*

India Office Library and Records. A list and index of parliamentary papers relating to India 1908-1947 / India Office Library and Records ; [compiled by] John Sims. — London ([197 Blackfriars Rd., SE1 8NG]) : [India Office Library and Records], 1981. — ii,129p ; 30cm
Includes index
ISBN 0-903359-29-4 (pbk) : Unpriced
B81-19438

016.95403'5 — India. Britons. Social life, *ca 1900-1947*. **Interviews —** *Catalogues*

Plain tales from the Raj : a catalogue of the BBC recordings. — London : India Office Library and Records, Jan.1982. — 1v.
ISBN 0-903359-34-0 (pbk) : CIP entry
B81-33841

016.9549'3 — Sri Lanka — *Bibliographies*

A **Checklist** of recent publications from and about Sri Lanka / compiled and edited by Ronald Warwick & Virginia Tebbit ; book exhibition organised with the assistance of the Sri Lankan government and the Ceylon National Library Services Board by the Library and Resource Centre, Commonwealth Institute. — London : Commonwealth Institute, [1981]. — vi,80p ; 21cm
Published to accompany the Festival of Sri Lanka, 17 July-13 Sept. 1981
ISBN 0-900906-93-6 (pbk) : £2.50 B81-39682

016.9561 — Turkey — *Bibliographies*

Güçlü, Meral. Turkey. — Oxford : Clio Press, Oct.1981. — [320]p. — (World bibliographical series ; 27)
ISBN 0-903450-39-9 : £28.00 : CIP entry
B81-28122

016.95645 — Cyprus — *Bibliographies*

Kitromilides, Paschalis M.. Cyprus. — Oxford : Clio Press, Feb.1982. — [240]p. — (World bibliographical series ; 28)
ISBN 0-903450-40-2 : £25.00 : CIP entry
B81-36039

016.958'1 — London. Southwark *(London Borough)*. **Libraries: India Office Library and Records. Stock: Documents on Afghanistan,** *to 1950*. **Collections: India Office Records —** *Lists*

India Office Library and Records. A brief guide to sources for the study of Afghanistan in the India Office Records / India Office Library and Records ; [prepared by] Lesley Hall. — London ([197 Blackfriars., SE1 8NG]) : The Library, 1981. — v,60p : 1ill,1map ; 30cm
ISBN 0-903359-20-0 (pbk) : Unpriced : CIP rev. B81-15858

016.96 — Africa. Serials with African imprints — *Indexes — Serials*

Africa index to continental periodical literature. — No.3 (1978). — Oxford : Hans Zell Publishers on behalf of the Africa Bibliographic Centre, 1981. — 191p
ISBN 3-598-21820-6 : Unpriced
ISSN 0378-4797 B81-30843

016.9676'1 — Uganda — *Bibliographies*

Collison, Robert. Uganda / Robert L. Collison, compiler. — Oxford : Clio, c1981. — xxviii,159p : 1map ; 22cm. — (World bibliographical series ; v.11)
Includes index
ISBN 0-903450-17-8 : £18.00 : CIP rev.
B81-13753

016.968 — London. Libraries. Stock: Documents on South Africa — *Lists*

Willan, Brian. The Southern African Materials Project University of London 1973-1976 / compiled by Brian Willan ; edited by Patricia M. Larby. — London (27 Russell Sq., WC1B 5DS) : University of London Institute of Commonwealth Studies, 1980. — 98p ; 29cm
ISBN 0-902499-25-4 (corrected : pbk) : £3.00
B81-06217

016.9681'6 — Lesotho — *Bibliographies*

Willet, Shelagh M.. Lesotho : a comprehensive bibliography / Shelagh M. Willet, David P. Ambrose. — Oxford : Clio, c1980. — xlii,496p : 1map ; 23cm. — (World bibliographical series ; v.3)
Includes index
ISBN 0-903450-11-9 : £33.00 : CIP rev.
B80-04639

016.970004'96 — North America. Negroes — *Bibliographies*

Afro-American history : a bibliography / Dwight L. Smith editor. — Santa Barbara : ABC-Clio ; Oxford : EBC-Clio. — vii,394p ; 29cm
ISBN 0-87436-314-4 : £59.00 B81-23412

016.970004'97 — North American Indians & Eskimos. Biographies — *Bibliographies*

Brumble, H. David. An annotated bibliography of American Indian and Eskimo autobiographies / H. David Brumble III. — Lincoln, [Neb.] ; London : University of Nebraska Press, c1981. — 177p ; 24cm
Includes index
ISBN 0-8032-1175-9 : £7.15 B81-29541

016.970004'97 — Sioux, *to 1980* — *Bibliographies*

Marken, Jack W.. Bibliography of the Sioux / by Jack W. Marken and Herbert T. Hoover. — Metuchen ; London : Scarecrow, 1980. — xvi,370p ; 23cm. — (Native American bibliography series ; no.1)
Includes index
ISBN 0-8108-1356-4 : £12.25 B81-06801

016.97001 — Prehistoric American civilization — *Bibliographies*

Snow, Dean R.. Native American prehistory : a critical bibliography / Dean R. Snow. — Bloomington ; London : Indiana University Press for the Newberry Library, c1979. — xiv,75p : ill ; 21cm. — (Bibliographical series / Newberry Library Center for the History of the American Indian)
ISBN 0-253-33498-5 (pbk) : £2.40 B81-08304

016.97281 — Guatemala — *Bibliographies*

Franklin, Woodman B.. Guatemala. — Oxford : Clio Press, Dec.1981. — [170]p. — (World bibliographical series ; 9)
ISBN 0-903450-24-0 : £17.00 : CIP entry
B81-31542

016.97282 — Belize — *Bibliographies*

Woodward, Ralph Lee. Belize / Ralph Lee Woodward, Jr. compiler ; edited by Sheila R. Herstein. — Oxford : Clio, c1980. — xxii,229p,[1] leaf of plates : 1maps ; 23cm. — (World bibliographical series ; v.21)
Includes index
ISBN 0-903450-41-0 : £19.00 B81-03352

016.973 — United States — *Bibliographies*

Hernstein, Sheila. United States of America. — Oxford : Clio Press, Jan.1982. — [290]p. — (World bibliographical series ; 16)
ISBN 0-903450-29-1 : £30.00 : CIP entry
B81-34780

016.973'04 — United States. European immigrants — *Bibliographies*

Cordasco, Francesco. American ethnic groups : the European heritage : a bibliography of doctoral dissertations completed at American universities / by Francesco Cordasco and David N. Alloway. — Metuchen ; London : Scarecrow, 1981. — x,366p ; 23cm
Includes index
ISBN 0-8108-1405-6 : £12.25 B81-25959

016.9747 — New York *(State)* — *Bibliographies*

Lopez, Manuel D.. New York : a guide to information and reference sources / by Manuel D. Lopez. — Metuchen ; London : Scarecrow, 1980. — x,307p ; 23cm
Includes index
ISBN 0-8108-1326-2 : £12.25 B81-05084

016.98 — Latin America — *Bibliographies — Serials*

Handbook of Latin American studies. — No.41. — Austin ; London : University of Texas Press, 1979. — xvii,796p
ISBN 0-292-73013-6 : £35.75 B81-32261

016.981 — Brazil, *1500-1822* — *Bibliographies*

Dutra, Francis A.. A guide to the history of Brazil, 1500-1822 : the literature in English / Francis A. Dutra. — Santa Barbara ; Oxford : ABC-Clio, c1980. — xxviii,625p ; 24cm
Maps on lining papers. — Includes index
ISBN 0-87436-263-6 : £27.50 B81-12508

016.9931 — New Zealand — *Bibliographies*

Grover, Ray, *1931-*. New Zealand / Ray Grower, compiler. — Oxford : Clio, c1980. — xxxvii,254p : 2maps ; 23cm. — (World bibliographical series ; v.18)
Includes index
ISBN 0-903450-31-3 : £22.00 B81-13384

017 — SUBJECT CATALOGUES

017'.531 — Great Britain. *India Office. Library.* Stock: Manuscripts in Persian — *Subject catalogues*

India Office Library. Catalogue of Persian manuscripts in the India Office Library / Hermann Ethé. — London (197 Blackfriars Rd, SE1 8NG) : India Office Library & Records, 1980. — [384]p ; 30cm
Facsim. of: ed. originally published in 2 vols. Oxford, 1903-1937
ISBN 0-903359-25-1 (pbk) : Unpriced : CIP rev.
B80-26374

017'.537 — Scotland. Cinema films. Organisations: Scottish Film Archive. Stock — *Subject catalogues — For teaching*

Scottish Film Archive reference catalogue : films for education : 1979. — [Glasgow] ([74 Victoria Crescent Rd., Glasgow G12 9JN]) : Scottish Film Council, [1980]. — vi,79p : ill,2ports ; 26cm
Includes index
ISBN 0-86011-017-6 (spiral) : £1.00
B81-07272

018 — AUTHOR CATALOGUES

018'.1 — Great Britain. National libraries: British Library. *Department of Printed Books.* Stock — *Author catalogues*

British Library. The British Library catalogue of printed books to 1975 / [managing editor Jim Emmett]. — London : Bingley
71: Cotto-Crann. — 1980. — 522p ; 31cm
ISBN 0-85157-591-9 : Unpriced : CIP rev.
ISBN 0-85157-520-x (set) : Unpriced
B80-35607

British Library. The British Library general catalogue of printed books / [managing editor Jim Emmett]. — London : Saur
83: Dicti-Direc / [editor Judi Vernau]. — 1981. — 522p ; 31cm
ISBN 0-85157-603-6 : Unpriced
ISBN 0-85157-520-x (set) . Unpriced
B81-38449

British Library. The British Library general catalogue of printed books / [managing editor Jim Emmett]. — London : Saur
84: Direc-Dod / [editor Judi Vernau]. — 1981. — 522p ; 31cm
ISBN 0-85157-604-4 : Unpriced
ISBN 0-85157-520-x (set) : Unpriced
B81-38450

British Library. The British Library general catalogue of printed books / [managing editor Jim Emmett]. — London : Saur
85: Dod-Dopp / [editor Judi Vernau]. — 1981. — 522p ; 31cm
ISBN 0-85157-605-2 : Unpriced
ISBN 0-85157-520-x (set) : Unpriced
B81-38451

British Library. The British Library general catalogue of printed books / [managing editor Jim Emmett]. — London : Saur
86: Dopp-Drake / [editor Judi Vernau]. — 1981. — 522p ; 31cm
ISBN 0-85157-606-0 : Unpriced
ISBN 0-85157-520-x (set) : Unpriced
B81-38452

British Library. The British Library general catalogue of printed books / [managing editor Jim Emmett]. — London : Saur
87: Drake-Duboi / [editor Judi Vernau]. — 1981. — 522p ; 31cm
ISBN 0-85157-607-9 : Unpriced
ISBN 0-85157-520-x (set) : Unpriced
B81-38453

British Library. The British Library general catalogue of printed books / [managing editor Jim Emmett]. — London : Saur
88: Duboi-Dumas / [editor Judi Vernau]. — 1981. — 522p ; 31cm
ISBN 0-85157-608-7 : Unpriced
ISBN 0-85157-520-x (set) : Unpriced
B81-38448

British Library. The British Library general catalogue of printed books / [managing editor Jim Emmett]. — London : Saur
89: Dumas-Durha / [editor Judi Vernau]. — 1981. — 538p ; 31cm
ISBN 0-85157-609-5 : Unpriced : CIP rev.
ISBN 0-85157-520-x (set) : Unpriced
B81-30993

British Library. The British Library general catalogue of printed books / [managing editor Jim Emmett]. — London : Saur
90: Durha-East / [editor Judi Vernau]. — 1981. — 538p ; 31cm
ISBN 0-86291-001-3 : Unpriced : CIP rev.
ISBN 0-85157-520-x (set) : Unpriced
B81-30992

British Library. The British Library general catalogue of printed books / [managing editor Jim Emmett]. — London : Saur
91: East-Edito / [editor Judi Vernau]. — 1981. — 538p ; 31cm
ISBN 0-86291-002-1 : Unpriced : CIP rev.
ISBN 0-85157-520-x (set) : Unpriced
B81-30991

British Library. The British Library general catalogue of printed books / [managing editor Jim Emmett]. — London : Saur
92: Edizi-Einem / [editor Judi Vernau]. — 1981. — 538p ; 31cm
ISBN 0-86291-003-x : Unpriced : CIP rev.
ISBN 0-85157-520-x (set) : Unpriced
B81-30990

British Library. The British Library general catalogue of printed books to 1975 / [managing editor Jim Emmett]. — London : Bingley
69: Cook-Cordo. — 1980. — 522p ; 31cm
ISBN 0-85157-589-7 : Unpriced : CIP rev.
ISBN 0-85157-520-x (set) : Unpriced
B80-35608

British Library. The British Library general catalogue of printed books to 1975 / [managing editor Jim Emmett]. — London : Bingley
70: Cordo-Cotto. — 1980. — 522p ; 31cm
ISBN 0-85157-590-0 : Unpriced : CIP rev.
ISBN 0-85157-520-x (set) B80-35609

British Library. The British Library general catalogue of printed books to 1975 / [managing editor Jim Emmett]. — London : Bingley
72: Crab-Crace. — 1980. — 522p ; 21cm
ISBN 0-85157-592-7 : Unpriced : CIP rev.
ISBN 0-85157-520-x (set) : Unpriced
B80-35610

British Library. The British Library general catalogue of printed books to 1975 / [managing editor Jim Emmett]. — London : Bingley
75: Cviji-Dalry. — Saur, 1980. — 522p ; 31cm
ISBN 0-85157-595-1 : Unpriced
ISBN 0-85157-520-x B81-16688

018'.1 — Great Britain. National libraries: British Library. *Department of Printed Books.* **Stock —** *Author catalogues* *continuation*

British Library. The British Library general catalogue of printed books to 1975 / [managing editor Jim Emmett]. — London : Bingley
76: Dalry-Darby / [editor Judi Vernau]. — Saur, 1981. — 522p ; 31cm
ISBN 0-85157-596-x : Unpriced B81-16691

British Library. The British Library general catalogue of printed books to 1975 / [managing editor Jim Emmett]. — London : Bingley
77: Darby-Davie / [editor Judi Vernau]. — Saur, 1981. — 522p ; 31cm
ISBN 0-85157-597-8 : Unpriced B81-16690

British Library. The British Library general catalogue of printed books to 1975 / [managing editor Jim Emmett]. — London : Bingley
78: Davie-Decca / [editor Judi Vernau]. — Saur, 1981. — 522p ; 31cm
ISBN 0-85157-598-6 : Unpriced B81-16689

British Library. The British library general catalogue of printed books to 1975 / [managing editor Jim Emmett]. — London : Saur
79: Decca-Delic / [editor Judi Vernau]. — 1981. — 522p ; 31cm
ISBN 0-85157-599-4 : Unpriced
ISBN 0-85157-520-x (set) : Unpriced
B81-31474

British Library. The British library general catalogue of printed books to 1975 / [managing editor Jim Emmett]. — London : Saur
80: Delic-Dento / [editor Judi Vernau]. — 1981. — 522p ; 31cm
ISBN 0-85157-600-1 : Unpriced
ISBN 0-85157-520-x (set) : Unpriced
B81-31473

British Library. The British Library general catalogue of printed books to 1975 / [managing editor Jim Emmett]. — London : Saur
81: Dento-Deva / [editor Judi Vernau]. — 1981. — 522p ; 31cm
ISBN 0-85157-601-x : Unpriced
ISBN 0-85157-520-x (set) : Unpriced
B81-29002

British Library. The British Library general catalogue of printed books to 1975 / [managing editor Jim Emmett]. — London : Saur
82: Deva-Dicti / [editor Judi Vernau]. — 1981. — 522p ; 31cm
ISBN 0-85157-602-8 : Unpriced
ISBN 0-85157-520-x (set) : Unpriced
B81-29003

British Library. The British Library general catalogue of printed books to 1975. — London : Saur
93: Einem-Ellis. — Sept.1981. — [538]p
ISBN 0-86291-004-8 : £38.00 : CIP entry
B81-30989

British Library. The British Library general catalogue of printed books to 1975. — London : Saur
94: Ellis-Engla. — Sept.1981. — [538]p
ISBN 0-86291-005-6 : £38.00 : CIP entry
B81-30988

British Library. The British Library general catalogue of printed books to 1975. — London : Saur
95: England 1-492. — Oct.1981. — [492]p
ISBN 0-86291-007-2 : £38.00 : CIP entry
B81-30987

British Library. The British Library general catalogue of printed books to 1975. — London : Saur
96: England 493-985. — Sept.1981. — [493-985]p
ISBN 0-86291-008-0 : £38.00 : CIP entry
B81-30994

British Library. The British Library general catalogue of printed books to 1975. — London : Saur
101: Engla-Equiv. — Nov.1981. — [522]p
ISBN 0-86291-013-7 : £44.00 : CIP entry
B81-34720

British Library. The British Library general catalogue of printed books to 1975. — London : Saur
102: Equiv-Essex. — Nov.1981. — [522]p
ISBN 0-86291-014-5 : £44.00 : CIP entry
B81-34721

British Library. The British Library general catalogue of printed books to 1975. — London : Saur
103: Essex-Evans. — Nov.1981. — [522]p
ISBN 0-86291-015-3 : £44.00 : CIP entry
B81-34722

British Library. The British Library general catalogue of printed books to 1975. — London : Saur
104: Evans-Fabre. — Dec.1981. — [522]p
ISBN 0-86291-016-1 : £38.00 : CIP entry
B81-38849

British Library. The British Library general catalogue of printed books to 1975. — London : Saur
105. — Dec.1981. — [522]p
ISBN 0-86291-017-x : £38.00 : CIP entry
B81-38294

018'.1294811 — Great Britain. National libraries: British Library. *Department of Oriental Manuscripts and Printed Books.* **Stock: Books in Tamil** — *Catalogues*

British Library. *Department of Oriental Manuscripts and Printed Books.* Second supplementary catalogue of Tamil books in the British Library Department of Oriental Manuscripts and Printed Books / by Albertine Gaur. — London : British Library, Reference Division Publications, 1980. — xi,512p ; 29cm
Includes index
ISBN 0-904654-18-4 : Unpriced : CIP rev.
B79-04765

018'.131 — Great Britain. *Foreign and Commonwealth Office.* **Libraries: India Office Library and Records. Stock: Manuscripts in Sinhalese** - *Catalogues*

India Office Library and Records. Catalogue of the Sinhalese manuscripts in the India Office Library. — London : India Office Library & Records, Sept.1981. — 1v.
ISBN 0-903359-33-2 (pbk) : CIP entry
B81-20654

018'.131 — Great Britain. National libraries: British Library. *Department of Manuscripts.* **Stock: Manuscripts in Hebrew & manuscripts in Samaritan** — *Catalogues*

British Library. Catalogue of the Hebrew & Samaritan manuscripts in the British Museum (now in the British Library) / G. Margoliouth. — London : British Museum Publications for the British Library
Part 4: Introduction, indexes, brief description of accessions and addenda and corrigenda / by J. Leveen. — c1977. — xiii,208p ; 29cm
Facsim. of: ed. originally published London : s.n., 1935
ISBN 0-7141-0619-4 : Unpriced B81-36472

018'.131 — Great Britain. National libraries: British Library. Exhibits: English illuminated manuscripts, *ca 700-750* — *Catalogues*

Backhouse, Janet. Books from the age of Bede : the Bede Monastery Museum, Jarow 28th May-17th June, 1979 : The British Library, London, 22nd June-2nd September, 1979 / [catalogue by Janet Backhouse]. — [S.l.] : [s.n.], 1979 (Hebburn : Smith Bros). — [7]p ; 21cm
Unpriced (pbk)
Primary classification 018'.131 B81-39623

018'.131 — Great Britain. National libraries: British Library. *Reference Division.* **Stock: Manuscripts received 1951-1955** — *Catalogues*

British Library. Catalogue of additions to the manuscripts, 1951-1955. — London : British Library Reference Division, Jan.1982. — 2v.[(714p.)]
ISBN 0-904654-69-9 : CIP entry B81-34661

018'.131 — London. Camden *(London Borough).* **Universities. Colleges. Libraries: University of London.** *School of Oriental and African Studies. Library.* **Stock: Manuscripts in Arabic —** *Catalogues*

University of London. *School of Oriental and African Studies. Library.* Catalogue of the Arabic manuscripts in the library of the School of Oriental and African Studies University of London / by Adam Gacek. — London : School of Oriental and African Studies, 1981. — 305p,12p of plates : ill,facsims ; 21cm
Includes index
ISBN 0-7286-0088-9 (pbk) : £6.00 : CIP rev.
B81-19211

018'.131 — Netherlands. Leiden. Universities. Libraries: Rijksuniversiteit te Leiden. *Bibliotheek.* **Stock: Manuscripts in Arabic —** *Title catalogues*

Rijksuniversiteit te Leiden. *Bibliotheek.* Handlist of Arabic manuscripts in the library of the University of Leiden and other collections in the Netherlands / compiled by P. Voorhoeve. — 2nd enl. ed. — The Hague ; London : Leiden University Press, 1980. — xxiii,749p : ill,facsims ; 24cm. — (Codices manuscripti ; 7) (Bibliotheca universitatis Leidensis)
Previous ed.: 1957
ISBN 90-602-1471-4 (pbk) : Unpriced
B81-07806

018'.131 — Scotland. Central Region. Dunblane. Cathedrals. Libraries: Leighton Library. Stock: Manuscripts — *Catalogues*

Leighton Library. Catalogue of manuscripts / Leighton Library ; [compiled] by Gordon Willis. — Stirling (University Library, University of Stirling, Stirling FK9 4LA) : University of Stirling Bibliographical Society, c1981. — 42p,[12]p of plates : ill,facsims ; 21cm. — (Occasional publications / University of Stirling Bibliographical Society ; 1)
Includes index
ISBN 0-907250-00-9 (pbk) : £3.00 B81-23044

018'.131 — Tyne and Wear *(Metropolitan County).* **Jarrow. Museums: Bede Monastery Museum. Exhibits: English illuminated manuscripts,** *ca 700-750* — *Catalogues*

Backhouse, Janet. Books from the age of Bede : the Bede Monastery Museum, Jarow 28th May-17th June, 1979 : The British Library, London, 22nd June-2nd September, 1979 / [catalogue by Janet Backhouse]. — [S.l.] : [s.n.], 1979 (Hebburn : Smith Bros). — [7]p ; 21cm
Unpriced (pbk)
Also classified at 018'.131 B81-39623

018'.134 — Cambridgeshire. Cambridge. Universities. Libraries: University of Cambridge. *Library.* **Stock: Serials** — *Title catalogues — Serials*

University of Cambridge. *Library.* Current serials available in the University Library and in other libraries connected with the University. — 1980. — Cambridge : Published for the Library by Cambridge University Press, 1980. — 2v.
ISBN 0-521-23837-4 : £95.00
ISSN 0306-4174 B81-02958

018'.134 — Essex. Colchester. Universities. Libraries: University of Essex. *Library.* **Stock: Serials** — *Title catalogues — Serials*

University of Essex. *Library.* Current periodicals / University of Essex Library. — 1979-. — [Colchester] ([P.O. Box 24, Colchester CO4 3UA]) : The Library, 1979-. — v. ; 21cm
Irregular. — Continues: University of Essex. Library. Periodicals
ISSN 0260-9010 = Current periodicals — University of Essex Library : Unpriced
B81-10558

018'.142 — Oxfordshire. Oxford. Universities: University of Oxford. Libraries. Stock: Incunabula — *Author catalogues*

Rhodes, Dennis E. A catalogue of incunabula in all the libraries of Oxford University outside the Bodleian. — Oxford : Clarendon Press, Aug.1981. — [320]p
ISBN 0-19-818175-2 : £20.00 : CIP entry
B81-22549

018'.144 — England. Legal deposit libraries. Stock: Books with British imprints: Books published between 1701 & 1800 — *Author catalogues*

Eighteenth-century British books : an author union catalogue : extracted from the British Museum General Catalogue of Printed Books, the catalogues of the Bodleian Library and of the University Library, Cambridge / by F.J.G. Robinson ... [et al.]. — Folkestone : Dawson [for] Project for Historical Bibliography
Vol.1: A-C. — 1981. — xx,754p ; 30cm
Unpriced B81-38404

Eighteenth-century British books : an author union catalogue : extracted from the British Museum General Catalogue of Printed Books, the catalogues of the Bodleian Library and of the University Library, Cambridge / by F.J.G. Robinson ... [et al.]. — Folkestone : Dawson [for] Project for Historical Bibliography
Vol.2. — 1981. — xxi,716p ; 30cm
Unpriced B81-38405

Eighteenth-century British books : an author union catalogue : extracted from the British Museum General Catalogue of Printed Books, the catalogues of the Bodleian Library and of the University Library, Cambridge / by F.J.G. Robinson ... [et al.]. — Folkestone : Dawson [for] Project for Historical Bibliography
Vol.3: H-L. — 1981. — xvi,627p ; 1 ; 31cm
Unpriced B81-38403

018'.17 — Great Britain. National libraries: British Library. *Department of Printed Books.* **Stock: Erotic books. Collections: Private Case** — *Catalogues*

Kearney, Patrick J.. The Private Case : an annotated bibliography of the Private Case erotica collection in the British (Museum) Library / compiled by Patrick J. Kearney ; with an introduction by G. Legman. — London : Landesman, 1981. — 354p,[1]folded leaf : 1facsim ; 26cm
Limited ed. of 1,000 numbered copies. — Includes index
ISBN 0-905150-24-4 : £45.00 : CIP rev.
B81-04268

018'.262 — Dublin. Libraries: Marsh's Library. Exhibits: Young persons' books, *1700-1900* — *Catalogues*

Books for Children's Pleasure 1700-1840-1900 *(Exhibition) (1981 : Marsh's Library).* Books for children's pleasure 1700-1840-1900 : catalogue of an exhibition at Marsh's Library, July-December 1981 / [compiled by M. Pollard]. — [Dublin] ([College St., Dublin 2]) : [Library, Trinity College], [1981]. — 35p ; 24cm
Unpriced (pbk) B81-37103

020 — LIBRARY AND INFORMATION SCIENCES

020 — Comparative librarianship

Simsova, Sylva. A primer of comparative librarianship. — London : Bingley, Dec.1981. — [96]p
ISBN 0-85157-341-x : £6.50 : CIP entry
B81-31527

020 — Librarianship

Harrison, Colin. The basics of librarianship / Colin Harrison, Rosemary Oates. — London : Library Association, 1980. — 218p : ill,forms ; 22cm
Includes bibliographies and index
ISBN 0-85365-523-5 (pbk) : Unpriced : CIP rev. B80-19565

Swank, Raynard C.. A unifying influence : essays of Raynard Coe Swank / edited by David W. Heron ; with a foreword by Lawrence Clark Powell ; and an appreciation by J. Periam Danton. — Metuchen ; London : Scarecrow, 1981. — xvii,220p ; 23cm
ISBN 0-8108-1407-2 : £9.45 B81-25967

020 — Librarianship & information science. Applications of general systems theory

Smith, David, *1936-*. Systems thinking : in library and information management / David Smith. — New York ; London : Saur : Bingley, 1980. — 142p : ill ; 23cm
Includes index
ISBN 0-85157-333-9 : Unpriced : CIP rev.
B80-13678

020'.148 — Librarianship & information science — *Abbreviations*

Vaillancourt, Pauline M.. International directory of acronyms in library, information and computer sciences / Pauline M. Vaillancourt. — New York ; London : R.B. Bowker, 1980. — xi,518p ; 24cm
Includes index
ISBN 0-8352-1152-5 : £29.75 B81-02634

020'.25'73 — United States. Librarianship - *Directories - Serials*

LRMP ... : library resources market place. — 1980-. — New York ; London : Bowker, 1980-. — v. ; 28cm
Unpriced B81-09096

020'.5 — Information science. Applications of social sciences — *Serials*

Social science information studies. — Vol.1, no.1 (Oct.1980)-. — Sevenoaks : Butterworths, 1980-. — v. ; 25cm
Quarterly
ISSN 0143-6236 = Social science information studies : £30.00 per year
Also classified at 300'.5 B81-06533

020'.6 — Archives, librarianship & information science. Organisations — *Directories*

Fang, Josephine Riss. International guide to library, archival and information science associations / Josephine Riss Fang and Alice H. Songe. — 2nd ed. — New York ; London : Bowker, 1980. — xxv,448p ; 24cm
Previous ed.: 1976. — Bibliography: p382-387. - Includes index
ISBN 0-8352-1285-8 : £13.25 B81-03460

020'.621 — Librarianship. International organisations

Chandler, George. International and national library and information services. — Oxford : Pergamon, Jan.1982. — [230]p. — (Recent advances in library and information services ; v.2)
ISBN 0-08-025793-3 : £10.00 : CIP entry
Also classified at 027.5 B81-34467

020'.622'41 — Great Britain. Librarianship. Organisations: Library Association — *Serials*

Library Association. The Library Association year book. — 1981. — London : The Association, c1981. — A78,280p
ISBN 0-85365-892-7 : Unpriced
ISSN 0075-9066 B81-30860

020'.7 — Great Britain. Librarians. Professional education, *to 1980*

Bramley, Gerald. Apprentice to graduate. — London : Bingley, Oct.1981. — [216]p
ISBN 0-85157-343-6 : £9.50 : CIP entry
B81-24670

020'.7 — Librarians. Professional education. Courses - *Directories*

World guide to library schools and training courses in documentation. — 2nd ed. — London : Bingley, Sept.1981. — [540]p
Previous ed.: 1972
ISBN 0-85157-309-6 : £15.00 : CIP entry
B81-20190

020'.7'15 — Libraries. Personnel. Training

Casteleyn, Mary. Planning library training programmes / Mary Casteleyn. — London : Deutsch, 1981. — 175p ; 23cm. — (Grafton basic text)
Bibliography: p169-171. — Includes index
ISBN 0-233-97338-9 : £7.95 : CIP rev.
B81-13430

020'.72 — Librarianship. Research

Gilbert, John, *1940-*. Making library research results pay / John Gilbert and Nancy Fjällbrant. — Bradford : MCB, c1981. — 39p : ill ; 30cm
Bibliography: p38-39
ISBN 0-86176-069-7 (pbk) : Unpriced
B81-34849

020'.7'8 — Great Britain. Schools of librarianship. Teaching aids: Microcomputer systems

Tedd, Lucy A.. The teaching of online cataloguing and searching and the use of new technology in U.K. schools of librarianship and information science / Lucy A. Tedd. — [London] : British Library ; Boston Spa : Distributed by Publications, the British Library Lending Division, 1981. — viii,120p : 2forms ; 30cm. — (British Library research & development reports, ISSN 0308-2385 ; no.5616)
ISBN 0-905984-67-6 (pbk) : Unpriced : CIP rev.
Primary classification 025'.04 B81-10509

020'.92'2 — Librarianship — *Biographies*

Engelbarts, Rudolf. Librarian authors : a bibliography / [compiled by] Rudolf Engelbarts. — Jefferson, N.C. : McFarland ; Folkestone : Distributed by Bailey Bros. & Swinfen, 1981. — v,276p : ports ; 24cm
Includes index
ISBN 0-89950-007-2 : £17.55 B81-38760

020'.92'4 — United States. Librarianship. Lyle, Guy — *Biographies*

Lyle, Guy. Beyond my expectation : a personal chronicle / by Guy Lyle. — Metuchen ; London : Scarecrow, 1981. — vii,219p,[16]p of plates : ill,1facsim,ports ; 23cm
ISBN 0-8108-1426-9 : £10.00 B81-37818

020'.941 — Great Britain. Librarianship

Urquhart, Donald. The principles of librarianship / Donald Urquhart. — Leeds (15 First Ave., Bardsey, Leeds, LS17 9BE) : Wood Garth, 1981. — 98p ; 21cm
Includes index
ISBN 0-9507501-0-7 : £4.50 B81-30671

020'.941 — Great Britain. Librarianship & information science

The **Professional** development of the librarian and information worker / edited by Patricia Layzell Ward. — London : Aslib, c1980. — 332p : ill,facsims ; 26cm. — (Aslib reader series ; v.3)
Includes index
ISBN 0-85142-135-0 : Unpriced
ISBN 0-85142-136-9 (pbk) : Unpriced
B81-18360

020'.941 — Great Britain. Librarianship & information science — *Conference proceedings*

The **Nationwide** provision and use of information : ASLIB, IIS, LA joint conference, 15-19 September 1980, Sheffield proceedings. — London : Library Association, 1981. — 414p : ill,facsims ; 23cm
Includes index
ISBN 0-85365-563-4 (pbk) : Unpriced
B81-12096

020'.9427 — North-west England. Librarianship & information science. Serials: North western newsletter — *Indexes*

Bakewell, K. G. B.. North western newsletter : index, 1950-1975 / compiled by K.G.B. Bakewell and students of the School of Librarianship and Information Studies, Liverpool Polytechnic [for the] Library Association, North Western Branch and Association of Assistant Librarians, North West Division. — [Liverpool] ([Tithebarn St., Liverpool L2 2ER]) : [Liverpool Polytechnic, School of Librarianship and Information Studies], [1981]. — 65p ; 30cm. — (Occasional paper / Liverpool Polytechnic School of Librarianship and Information Studies ; 12)
Cover title
ISBN 0-901537-15-2 (pbk) : £2.00 B81-06720

020'.9669 — Africa south of the Sahara. Librarianship. Cultural factors — *Study regions: Nigeria*

Amadi, Adolphe O.. African libraries : Western tradition and colonial brainwashing / Adolphe O. Amadi. — Metuchen, N.J. ; London : Scarecrow Press, 1981. — xii,265p ; 23cm
Bibliography: p247-254. — Includes index
ISBN 0-8108-1409-9 : £9.80 B81-29220

020'.973 — United States. Librarianship — *Serials*

The **Bowker** annual of library & book trade information. — 26th ed. (1981). — New York ; London : Bowker, c1981
ISBN 0-8352-1343-9 : Unpriced
Also classified at 338.4'7686'0973 B81-33466

021 — LIBRARY RELATIONSHIPS

021′.0025′4283 — Libraries. Services *Humberside. Directories*

Library resources in Yorkshire and Humberside / Library Association Reference, Special and Information Section, Yorkshire and Humberside Group ; edited by Isabel R. Buxton. — London : Library Association Reference, Special and Information Section, c1980. — viii,96p : 1form ; 25cm
Includes index
ISBN 0-85365-982-6 (pbk) : Unpriced : CIP rev.
Primary classification 027′.0025′4283
B80-04641

021.2 — LIBRARIES AND COMMUNITY

021.2′8 — Great Britain. Public libraries. Community information services

Bowen, Judith. Report of a dissemination workshop to review progress and developments in community information services in the public library : Project no.SI/G/257 funded by British Library Research and Development Department / Judith Bowen, Ed Walley. — [Leeds] ([Calverley St., Leeds, LS1 3HE]) : Public Libraries Management Research Unit, School of Librarianship, Leeds Polytechnic, [1981]. — 53p in various pagings : ill,1form ; 30cm. — (British Library report ; no.5597)
ISBN 0-900738-23-5 (pbk) : £2.50 B81-16311

021.6 — LIBRARY COOPERATION AND NETWORKS

021.6′4′0254246 — Staffordshire. Libraries. Cooperation. Organisations: MISLIC — *Directories*

MISLIC. Directory of resources / compiled by a working party of MISLIC members. — 2nd ed. — Stafford (Staffordshire County Library H.Q., Friars Terrace, Stafford) : MISLIC, 1981. — [70]leaves ; 30cm
Previous ed.: 197-?. — Includes index
£2.00 (pbk) B81-13678

021.6′4′0941 — Great Britain. Libraries. Cooperation

Sewell, Philip H.. Resource sharing. — London : Deutsch, Nov.1981. — [175]p. — (André Deutsch Grafton series on library and information science)
ISBN 0-233-97342-7 : £6.95 : CIP entry
B81-28801

021.6′4′0941 — Great Britain. Libraries. Cooperation — *Conference proceedings*

Yelland, M.. Local library co-operation : its current state and future development / M. Yelland. — [London] : British Library ; Boston Spa : Distributed by Publications, British Library Lending Division, c1980. — iii,24p ; 30cm. — (The British Library research & development reports, ISSN 0308-2385 ; no.5578)
ISBN 0-905984-62-5 (spiral) : Unpriced
B81-09959

021.6′5′068 — United States. Libraries. Networks. Management

Rouse, William B.. Management of library networks : policy analysis, implementation and control / William B. Rouse and Sandra H. Rouse. — New York ; Chichester : Wiley, c1980. — xiv,288p : ill ; 24cm. — (Information sciences series)
Bibliography: p266-274. — Includes index
ISBN 0-471-05534-4 : £13.90 B81-04879

021.6′5′09417 — Ireland *(Republic).* **Libraries. Networks** — *Conference proceedings*

Applications of networking in Irish libraries : proceedings of a conference held on 13th March, 1980 in the Department of Library and Information Studies, University College, Belfield, Dublin 4 / edited by Michael Casey. — Dublin (Belfield, Dublin 4) : Dept. of Library and Information Studies, University College Dublin, 1980. — ii, 61p : ill ; 30cm. — (Occasional publication / University College Dublin. Department of Library and Information Studies ; no.1)
ISBN 0-901120-66-9 (pbk) : Unpriced
Primary classification 022′.9 B81-31395

021.7 — LIBRARY PROMOTION

021.7 — Great Britain. Public libraries. Public relations — *Manuals*

Usherwood, Bob. The visible library : practical public relations for public librarians / Bob Usherwood. — London : Library Association, 1981. — 207p : ill,facsims ; 23cm
Bibliography: p196-200. - Includes index
ISBN 0-85365-562-6 (pbk) : £8.75 (£7.00 to LA members) B81-19780

021.7 — Great Britain. Public libraries. Use. Promotion. Role of opinion leaders. Research. Methodology — *Study regions: Cheshire. Chester region — Sources of data: Children, 7-11 years*

Yorke, D. A.. Non-commercial channels of communication for a public library service / David Yorke. — [Manchester] ([P.O. Box 88, Sackville St., Manchester M60 1QD]) : University of Manchester Institute of Science and Technology, 1981. — 13leaves : ill,1form ; 30cm. — (BL R&D report ; 5641)
Unpriced (unbound) B81-27582

021.7 — Great Britain. Public libraries. Users. Organisations

Murison, W. J.. Public library users' consultative councils / W.J. Murison. — London : British Library, Research and Development Department, 1979. — vi,77p ; 30cm. — (British Library research & development reports, ISSN 0308-2385 ; no.5499)
ISBN 0-905984-42-0 (spiral) : £6.50
B81-14285

021.7 — Libraries. Public relations — *Manuals*

Kohn, Rita. You can do it : a PR skills manual for librarians / by Rita Kohn and Krysta Tepper. — Metuchen ; London : Scarecrow, 1981. — xii, : ill,forms ; 28cm
Bibliography: p223-225. - Includes index
ISBN 0-8108-1401-3 (pbk) : £8.75 B81-17104

021.7 — Libraries. Services. Marketing — *Conference proceedings*

Library Association. *London and Home Counties Branch. Conference (1980 : London).*
Marketing library services : papers read at the one-day Conference of the London and Home Counties Branch of the Library Association, held at Holborn Library, 7th May 1980, under the chairmanship of Mark Lunt, F.L.A. / edited by Vaughan Whibley. — [London] ([c/o V. Whibley, 65 Glentrammon Rd., Green Street Green, Orpington, Kent]) : The Library Association, London and Home Counties Branch, 1981. — 87p : ill ; 19cm
ISBN 0-902119-29-x (pbk) : £3.20 B81-27047

021.7 — London. Westminster *(London Borough).* **Public libraries: Westminster City Libraries. Stock: Books. Reading by adolescents. Promotion. Projects: Bookmaster scheme**

Westminster City Libraries. The 1980 Bookmaster scheme / Westminster City Libraries ; a report by Lorna Roberts. — [London] : Westminster City Libraries, 1980. — 61p : ill ; 30cm
ISBN 0-900802-04-9 (pbk) : £2.00 B81-06443

022.3 — LIBRARIES. BUILDINGS

022′.3342819 — Great Britain. National libraries: British Library. *Lending Division.* **Urquhart Building**

British Library. *Lending Division.* Extension to the Urquhart building / the British Library Lending Division. — [London] ([2 Sheraton St., W1]) : British Library Board, 1981. — [8]p : ill ; 21cm
Cover title
Unpriced (pbk) B81-39767

British Library. *Lending Division.* The Urquhart building / the British Library Lending Division. — [London] : [2 Sheraton St. W1] : British Library Board, 1981. — [12]p : ill,3plans ; 30cm
Cover title
Unpriced (pbk) B81-39766

022.9 — LIBRARIES. EQUIPMENT, FURNITURE, FURNISHINGS

022′.9 — Ireland *(Republic).* **Libraries. Applications of computer systems networks** — *Conference proceedings*

Applications of networking in Irish libraries : proceedings of a conference held on 13th March, 1980 in the Department of Library and Information Studies, University College, Belfield, Dublin 4 / edited by Michael Casey. — Dublin (Belfield, Dublin 4) : Dept. of Library and Information Studies, University College Dublin, 1980. — ii, 61p : ill ; 30cm. — (Occasional publication / University College Dublin. Department of Library and Information Studies ; no.1)
ISBN 0-901120-66-9 (pbk) : Unpriced
Also classified at 021.6′5′09417 B81-31395

023.2 — LIBRARY STAFF. PROFESSIONAL

023′.2′068 — United States. Professional librarians. Personnel management

Personnel policies in libraries / edited by Nancy Patton Van Zant. — New York : Neal-Schuman ; London : Mansell, c1980. — xxxvii,334p : ill,forms ; 24cm
Includes index
ISBN 0-918212-26-x : £10.50 B81-05387

025 — LIBRARY OPERATIONS

025 — Documentation

Progress in documentation : some themes and topics : a selection from the progress in documentation articles published in Journal of documentation, 1969-1979. — London : Aslib, c1981. — vii,245p : ill ; 25cm
ISBN 0-85142-140-7 (pbk) : Unpriced
B81-18258

025 — Great Britain. Information sources — *For mentally handicapped persons*

A-Z : your question answered. — New ed., no.16. — London (MENCAP National Centre, 123 Golden La., EC1Y 0RT) : National Society for Mentally Handicapped Children and Adults, c1981. — 51p ; 21cm. — (MENCAP information bulletin)
Previous ed.: 1979
ISBN 0-85537-061-0 (pbk) : £1.00
Primary classification 362.3′8′0941 B81-09420

025′.0028′54 — Great Britain. Libraries. Applications of digital computer systems — *Conference proceedings*

Books on-line : proceedings of a conference organised by the Working Party of Libraries and the Book Trade at Book House on 12th May 1981. — [London] : [Working Party on Library and Book Trade Relations], 1981. — i,86p : 1ill,ports ; 30cm
Original title: Library book funds ; 1978-80
ISBN 0-904572-05-6 (pbk) : Unpriced : CIP rev.
Primary classification 338.4′5686′0941
B79-15775

025′.0028′54 — Libraries. Automation. Management — *Conference proceedings*

The **management** of technical innovation in libraries : proceedings of a conference. — Loughborough : Centre for Library and Information Management, Department of Library and Information Studies, Loughborough University, c1981. — v,33p ; 30cm. — (British Library research & development reports, ISSN 0308-2385 ; 5639) (Report / Loughborough University of Technology. Centre for Library and Information Management, ISSN 0261-0302 ; no.8)
ISBN 0-904924-27-0 (pbk) : £2.00 B81-29600

025.04 — LIBRARIES. INFORMATION STORAGE AND RETRIEVAL SYSTEMS

025′.04 — Great Britain. Public libraries. On-line information retrieval services. Projects

On-line information in public libraries : a review of recent British Research / Nick Moore (editor). — [London] : British Library ; Boston Spa : Distributed by Publications [Section], British Library Lending Division, c1981. — v,64p ; 30cm. — (The British Library research & development reports, ISSN 0308-2385 ; no.5648)
Bibliography: p54-64
ISBN 0-905984-76-5 (pbk) : Unpriced
B81-40521

025'.04 — Great Britain. Schools of librarianship. Curriculum subjects: On-line information systems. Teaching

Tedd, Lucy A.. The teaching of online cataloguing and searching and the use of new technology in U.K. schools of librarianship and information science / Lucy A. Tedd. — [London] : British Library ; Boston Spa : Distributed by Publications, the British Library Lending Division, 1981. — viii,120p : 2forms ; 30cm. — (British Library research & development reports, ISSN 0308-2385 ; no.5616)
ISBN 0-905984-67-6 (pbk) : Unpriced : CIP rev.
Also classified at 020'.7'8 B81-10509

025'.04 — Information retrieval. Implications of video discs

Barrett, R.. Developments in optical disc technology and the implications for imformation storage and retrieval / R. Barrett. — [London] : British Library ; Boston Spa : Distributed by Publications, British Library Lending Division, 1981. — viii,72p : ill ; 30cm. — (British Library research & development reports, ISSN 0308-2385 ; no.5623)
ISBN 0-905984-71-4 (pbk) : Unpriced : CIP rev. B81-19151

025'.04 — Public libraries. On-line information retrieval services — *Conference proceedings*

On-line information retrieval : its role in the public library : proceedings of a One-day school, Thursday 31 May 1979 / East Midlands Branch of the Library Association. — Derby : The Branch, 1980. — 51p ; 30cm
Promotional literature in pocket
ISBN 0-85365-524-3 (pbk) : Unpriced
B81-29608

025'.04'025 — Great Britain. On-line information retrieval brokers — *Directories*

Deunette, J. B.. UK online search services / compiled by J.B. Deunette. — London : Published on behalf of the Online Information Centre [by] Aslib, c1981. — iv,88p ; 30cm
Includes index
ISBN 0-85142-141-5 (pbk) : £9.50 B81-27859

025'.04'025 — On-line bibliographic information retrieval services — *Directories*

Hall, J. L. (James Logan). Online bibliographic databases : an international directory. — 2nd ed., [compilers] James L. Hall, Marjorie J. Brown. — London : Aslib, 1981. — xxx,213p : ill ; 25cm
Previous ed.: published as On line bibliographic data bases directory / J.L. Hall. — Includes index
ISBN 0-85142-138-5 : Unpriced : CIP rev.
B80-32825

025'.04'05 — On-line information retrieval services — *Serials*

[Monitor *(Abingdon)***]**. Monitor : an analytical review of current events in the online and electronic publishing industry. — No.1 (Mar.1981)-. — Abingdon (Besselsleigh Rd, Abingdon, Oxford OX13 6LG) : Learned Information, 1981-. — v. ; 28cm
Monthly
ISSN 0260-6666 = Monitor (Abingdon) : Unpriced B81-32269

025'.04'0941 — Great Britain. Libraries. Information retrieval services. Great Britain. *Parliament. House of Commons. Education, Science and Arts Committee.* **Reports** — *Critical studies*

Great Britain. Information storage and retrieval in the British library service : observations by the government on the second and fourth reports from the Select Committee on Education, Science and Arts, session 1979-80. — London : H.M.S.O., [1981]. — 3p ; 25cm. — (Cmnd. ; 8237)
ISBN 0-10-182370-3 (unbound) : £1.10
B81-23181

025'.060013 — Humanities. Information retrieval. Techniques — *Questions & answers*

SantaVicca, Edmund F., *1947-*. Reference work in the humanities / Edmund F. SantaVicca. — Metuchen ; London : Scarecrow, 1980. — x,163p ; 23cm
ISBN 0-8108-1342-4 : £6.30 B81-08275

025'.060016425 — Digital computer systems. Software. Documentation

Harper, William L.. Data processing documentation : standards, procedures and applications / William L. Harper. — 2nd ed. — Englewood Cliffs ; London : Prentice Hall, c1980. — 303p : ill,forms,1port ; 29cm
Previous ed.: 1973. — Includes index
ISBN 0-13-196816-5 : £22.70 B81-16535

025'.0602 — Librarianship & information science. Research projects financed by British Library. *Research and Development Department.* **Information. Dissemination**

Singleton, A. K. J.. Preliminary studies in the dissemination of information research results / by Alan Singleton ; edited by John Martyn. — [London] : [Research and Development Department, British Library], 1981. — xii,123p : ill,forms ; 30cm. — (BL R & D report ; 5575)
Unpriced (pbk) B81-16326

025'.0633 — Economics. On-line information retrieval services

Houghton, Bernard. Non-bibliographic online databases : an investigation into their uses within the field of economics and business studies / B. Houghton and J.C. Wisdom. — [London] : British Library ; Boston Spa : Distributed by Publications, British Library Lending Division, 1981. — iii,23p : forms ; 30cm. — (British Library research & development reports, ISSN 0308-2385 ; no.5620)
ISBN 0-905984-70-6 (pbk) : Unpriced : CIP rev.
Also classified at 025'.06658 B81-14938

025'.063713'078 — Educational technology. Information. Information retrieval & dissemination — *Conference proceedings*

Symposium on Information Retrieval in Educational Technology *(1st : 1981 : Aberdeen)*.
Information retrieval in educational technology : conference proceedings of the first Symposium on Information Retrieval in Educational Technology, held at ETIC '81, Aberdeen, Scotland, 1st April, 1981 / edited by Elizabeth B. Duncan and Ray McAleese. — [Aberdeen] : [University of Aberdeen, University Teaching Centre], c1981. — 90p : ill ; 30cm
Includes bibliographies
ISBN 0-907258-01-8 (pbk) : £4.50 B81-40922

025'.0637312912'09411 — Scotland. School leavers. Data retrieval services using digital computer systems. Machine-readable files: Scottish Education Data Archive. Data

Collaborative research dictionary and questionnaires 1979 : documentation for the 1979 National School Leavers Survey, supplementing the Collaborative research dictionary 1977 and to be used in conjunction with it / by David Raffe ... [et al.]. — Edinburgh : Centre for Educational Sociology, University of Edinburgh, 1980. — 108,[108]p : forms ; 30cm
Unpriced (pbk) B81-29776

025'.0637312912'09411 — Scotland. School leavers. Data retrieval services using digital computer systems. Machine-readable files: Scottish Education Data Archive. Data on S.C.E. (H grade) qualified school leavers

Armstrong, Christine. Dictionary of variables for SCE H grade qualified school leavers in 1962, 1970 and 1972 / Christine Armstrong, Andrew McPherson. — Edinburgh (7 Buccleuch Pl., Edinburgh EH8 9LW) : University of Edinburgh, Centre for Educational Sociology, Scottish Education Data Archive, [1975?]. — 361,[2]leaves ; 30cm
Unpriced (pbk) B81-20366

025'.065 — Japan. Science. Information systems

Scientific information systems in Japan / edited by Hiroshi Inose. — Amsterdam ; Oxford : North-Holland, c1981. — ix,257p,[2]p of plates : ill(some col.),charts, 1map ; 27cm
ISBN 0-444-86151-3 : £22.98 B81-22445

025'.065'0941 — Great Britain. Science. Information. Communication & dissemination

Royal Society. A study of the scientific information system in the UK : supporting papers / Royal Society. — [London] : [British Library Research & Development Department], 1981. — 80p in various pagings ; 30cm. — (BL R & D report ; 5629)
Unpriced (pbk) B81-29229

025'.06613 — Great Britain. Health education. Information retrieval systems

Dub, Miriam E.. Information retrieval systems in health education : a project for the CNAA health education diploma course 1980 / Miriam E. Dub. — London (Borough Rd., SE1 0AA) : Polytechic of the South Bank, Department of Nursing and Community Health Studies, 1980. — 119p : ill,1facsim,1form ; 30cm
Cover title. — Includes bibliographies and index
ISBN 0-905267-14-1 (pbk) : £3.00 B81-16732

025'.0662'000285425 — Engineering. Applications of digital computer systems. Software. Documentation — *Standards*

Technical Documentation Standards for computer programs and computer-based systems used in engineering / prepared by the National Computing Centre Ltd ; advised by a panel set up by the Institution of Civil Engineers, the Institution of Mechanical Engineers. — Manchester : NCC Publications, 1981. — 1v.(loose-leaf) : ill ; 32cm
Includes index
ISBN 0-85012-247-3 (unbound) : £30.00
B81-23566

025'.0662131 — Great Britain. Ethnic minorities. Dissemination of information on electricity supply by electricity supply industries

Information on electricity for ethnic minorities / Electricity Consumers' Council. — London (119 Marylebone Rd., NW1 5PY) : The Council, 1980. — 21p : facsims ; 30cm. — (Discussion paper / Electricity Consumers' Council ; 4)
Unpriced (pbk) B81-34748

025'.06658 — Business studies. On-line information retrieval services

Houghton, Bernard. Non-bibliographic online databases : an investigation into their uses within the field of economics and business studies / B. Houghton and J.C. Wisdom. — [London] : British Library ; Boston Spa : Distributed by Publications, British Library Lending Division, 1981. — iii,23p : forms ; 30cm. — (British Library research & development reports, ISSN 0308-2385 ; no.5620)
ISBN 0-905984-70-6 (pbk) : Unpriced : CIP rev.
Primary classification 025'.0633 B81-14938

025'.067113'0941 — Information on environment planning. Cooperation between British district councils & county councils

Joint working on information : report of the Computer Panel of LAMSAC. — [London] : LAMSAC, [1980]. — 35p : col.ill ; 30cm
ISBN 0-85497-120-3 (pbk) : £3.00 B81-19880

025.1 — LIBRARY ADMINISTRATION

025.1 — Libraries. Management — *Conference proceedings*

Marketing the library. — Newcastle upon Tyne (c/o P.M. Judd, Newcastle upon Tyne Polytechnic Library, Ellison Building, Ellison Place, Newcastle upon Tyne NE1 8ST) : Association of Assistant Librarians, Northern Division, July 1981. — [130]p
Conference papers
ISBN 0-9506682-1-4 (pbk) : £4.00 : CIP entry
B81-23736

025.1'0973 — United States. Libraries. Management

Bailey, Martha J.. Supervisory and middle managers in libraries / Martha J. Bailey. — Metuchen ; London : Scarecrow, 1981. — viii,210p : ill ; 23cm
Includes bibliographies and index
ISBN 0-8108-1400-5 : £8.40 B81-13911

025.1'1 — Great Britain. Public libraries. Expenditure. Reduction

Barnes, Anne. Implementing budget cuts in the public library service, or, Through the mangle once again : a paper presented to the Library Association Public Libraries Group Week-end school in Bath in April 1980 / by Anne Barnes. — Penzance (Penzance Library, Morrab Rd., Penzance, Cornwall TR18 4EY) : Public Libraries Group of the Library Association, 1980. — 7p ; 22cm
ISBN 0-85365-823-4 (pbk) : £1.60 (£1.20 to members of the Group) B81-04712

025.1'1 — Libraries. Financial management. Zero-based budgeting

Chen, Ching-chih. Zero-base budgeting in library management : a manual for librarians / by Ching-chih Chen. — Pheonix : Oryx ; London : Mansell [distributor], 1980. — xiv,293p : ill,forms ; 29cm. — (A Neal-Schuman professional book)
Bibliography: p285-290. — Includes index
ISBN 0-7201-0831-4 : £12.75 : CIP rev. B80-10689

025.17 — Great Britain. Public records. Selection — *Inquiry reports*

Modern public records : selection and access : report of a committee appointed by the Lord Chancellor / Chairman Sir Duncan Wilson ; presented to Parliament by the Lord High Chancellor. — London : H.M.S.O., 1981. — xiii,256p,[1]leaf of plates : 1ill ; 25cm. — (Cmnd. ; 8204)
ISBN 0-10-182040-2 (pbk) : £8.10
Also classified at 323.44'5 B81-21676

025.17 — Libraries. Stock: Fiction

Atkinson, Frank, *1922-*. Fiction librarianship / Frank Atkinson. — London : Bingley, 1981. — 107p,[8]p of plates : ill,facsims ; 23cm. — (Outlines of modern librarianship)
Includes bibliographies and index
ISBN 0-85157-293-6 : Unpriced : CIP rev. B80-13679

025.17 — Printed ephemera. Collections. Organisation

Chinton, Alan. Printed ephemera : collection, organisation and access / Alan Clinton. — London : Bingley, c1981. — 125p ; 23cm
Includes index
ISBN 0-85157-337-1 : Unpriced : CIP rev. B81-08840

025.17'12'0942574 — Oxfordshire. Oxford. Universities: University of Oxford. Libraries. Stock: Manuscripts — *Festschriften*

Manuscripts at Oxford : an exhibition in memory of Richard William Hunt (1908-1979), Keeper of Western Manuscripts at the Bodleian Library Oxford, 1945-1975, on themes selected and described by some of his friends / edited by A.C. de la Mare & B.C. Barker-Benfield. — Oxford : Bodleian Library, 1980. — x,155p : ill,facsims,ports ; 31cm
Bibliography: p147-148. - Includes index
ISBN 0-900177-76-4 (pbk) : £9.00 B81-05917

025.17'14 — Archives. Administration

Jenkinson, *Sir* **Hilary.** Selected writings of Sir Hilary Jenkinson. — Gloucester : Alan Sutton, 1980. — 380p : ill,1port ; 23cm
Includes one chapter in French
ISBN 0-904387-52-6 : £12.00 : CIP rev. B80-21288

025.17'14 — Archives. Administration. Applications of digital computer systems

Cook, Michael, *1931-*. Archives and the computer / Michael Cook. — London : Butterworths, 1980. — 152p : ill,2forms ; 23cm
Bibliography: p137-145. - Includes index
ISBN 0-408-10734-0 : £12.50 : CIP rev. B80-20111

025.17'2 — Libraries. Stock: Press cuttings. Management — *Conference proceedings*

Howcroft, Bernard. Press cuttings / by Bernard Howcroft and Irene Wagner. — London ([c/o The Labour Party Library, The Labour Party, 144 Walworth Rd, SE17 1JT]) : International Co-operative Alliance, 1980. — 28p : ill ; 21cm. — (Co-operative library guide)
Conference papers
Unpriced B81-15348

025.17'32 — Libraries. Stock: Serials

Serials librarianship / edited by Ross Bourne. — London : Library Association, 1980. — xi,257p ; 22cm. — (Handbooks on library practice)
Includes index
ISBN 0-85365-631-2 (cased) : £10.00(£8.00 to members) : CIP rev.
ISBN 0-85365-721-1 (pbk) : £5.75 (£4.60 to members) B80-17521

025.17'6 — Libraries. Stock: Maps. Collections. Administration

Ristow, Walter W.. The emergence of maps in libraries / by Walter W. Ristow. — Hamden : Linnet ; London : Mansell, 1980. — 358p ; 24cm
ISBN 0-7201-1620-1 : £15.00 : CIP rev. B80-32814

025.17'7 — Librarianship. Use of photography

Waters, Alan. Photography & its use in library work / by Alan Waters. — Truro (11 Cryon View, Gloweth, Truro, Cornwall) : Branch and Mobile Libraries Group of the Library Association, 1981. — 52p : ill ; 21cm. — (Basic library guides ; 3)
ISBN 0-85365-764-5 (pbk) : Unpriced B81-38873

025.17'71 — Great Britain. Repositories holding photographs of developing countries — *Directories*

Where to find photos of the developing countries / edited and compiled by Adam Harvey. — Rev. ed. — London (128 Buckingham Palace Rd, SW1W 9SH) : Centre for World Development Education in association with CAFOD ... [et al.], 1980. — 57p ; 15x21cm
Previous ed.: 1978. — Includes index
Unpriced (pbk) B81-01986

025.17'71 — Libraries. Stock: Pictures. Collections. Administration

Picture librarianship / edited by Helen P. Harrison. — London : Library Association, 1981. — xii,542p : ill,facsims ; 22cm. — (Handbooks on library practice)
Bibliography: p494-517. — Includes index
ISBN 0-85365-912-5 (cased) : Unpriced : CIP rev.
ISBN 0-85365-693-2 (pbk) : Unpriced B81-10017

025.17'73 — Great Britain. Cinema films & television films. Collections — *Directories*

Researcher's guide to British film and television collections / editor Elizabeth Oliver. — [London] ([81 Dean Street, W1V 6AA]) : British Universities Film Council, c1981. — 176p : ill ; 25cm
Bibliography: p131-151. - Includes index
ISBN 0-901299-27-8 (pbk) : Unpriced B81-17750

025.17'9 — Great Britain. Public libraries. Stock: Large print books. Use

Bell, Lorna. The large print book and its user / Lorna J. Bell. — London : British National Bibliography Research Fund in association with the Library Association, 1980. — 326p : ill,forms ; 23cm. — (Library Association research publication ; no.22)
Bibliography: p322-324
ISBN 0-85365-632-0 (pbk) : £12.50 : CIP rev. B80-21289

025.17'96 — Great Britain. Libraries. Stock: Board games & toys. Provision

Hewitt, Jill. Toys and games in libraries / Jill Hewitt. — London : Library Association, 1981. — vii,85p : ill ; 21cm
Bibliography: p83-85
ISBN 0-85365-963-x (pbk) : Unpriced : CIP rev. B81-15800

025.1'9661 — Great Britain. Medical libraries. Administration

Medical librarianship / edited by Michael Carmel. — London : Library Association, 1981. — xi,359p ; 22cm. — (Handbook on library practice)
Includes index
ISBN 0-85365-502-2 (cased) : Unpriced
ISBN 0-85365-703-3 (pbk) : Unpriced B81-14706

025.1'974 — Public libraries. Administration

Stoakley, Roger. Presenting the library service. — London : Bingley, Jan.1982. — [112]p. — (Outlines of modern librarianship)
ISBN 0-85157-320-7 (pbk) : £6.25 : CIP entry B81-34572

025.1'977'0941 — Great Britain. Universities. Libraries. Administration

University librarianship / edited by John F. Stirling. — London : Library Association, 1981. — xv,229p : ill ; 23cm. — (Handbooks on library practice)
Includes index
ISBN 0-85365-621-5 : Unpriced : CIP rev. B81-04362

025.1'977'0973 — United States. Academic libraries. Management

College librarianship / edited by William Miller & D. Stephen Rockwood. — Metuchen ; London : Scarecrow, 1981. — v,284p : ill ; 25cm
Includes bibliographies
ISBN 0-8108-1383-1 : £10.50 B81-22833

025.1'978 — Schools. Libraries. Administration

Carroll, Frances Laverne. Recent advances in school librarianship / by Frances Laverne Carroll. — Oxford : Pergamon, 1981. — xiii,249p : forms ; 26cm. — (Recent advances in library and information services ; vol.1)
Includes index
ISBN 0-08-026084-5 : £12.50 : CIP rev. B81-13845

025.1'978'0941 — Great Britain. Schools. Libraries. Administration

Routines : managing a small school library / [School Library Association]. — Oxford : The Association, 1980. — 14p : ill ; 21cm. — (School Library Association guidelines ; 1)
Bibliography: p14
ISBN 0-900641-36-3 (pbk) : £1.30 (£0.90 to SLA members) B81-15753

025.2 — LIBRARY ACQUISITIONS

025.2 — United States. Academic libraries. Stock. Administration — *Case studies*

Cline, Hugh F.. Building library collections : policies and practices in academic libraries / Hugh F. Cline, Loraine T. Sinnott. — Lexington, Mass. : Lexington Books ; [Aldershot] : Gower [distributor], 1981. — xvi,170p : ill ; 24cm
Bibliography: p161-163. — Includes index
ISBN 0-669-04321-4 : £10.50 B81-39703

025.2'13'0973 — United States. Libraries. Stock. Censorship, *1950-1979*

Oboler, Eli M.. Defending intellectual freedom : the library and the censor / Eli M. Oboler. — Westport, Conn. ; London : Greenwood Press, 1980. — xix,246p ; 22cm. — (Contributions in librarianship and information science ; no.32)
Bibliography: p212-220. — Includes index
ISBN 0-313-21472-7 : £14.75 B81-23477

025.2'187441 — Great Britain. Public libraries. Stock: Books. Acquisition. Selection

Spiller, David. Book selection : an introduction to principles and practice / David Spiller. — 3rd ed. — New York : Saur ; London : Bingley, 1980. — 206p : 1facsim ; 23cm
Previous ed.: 1974. — Includes index
ISBN 0-85157-305-3 : £6.25 B80-17522

025.2'3 — Great Britain. Local authorities. Libraries. Book funds — *Statistics* — *Serials*

Library book funds / the Working Party on Library and Book Trade Relations. — 1980/82. — [Loughborough] ([c/o Department of Library and Information Studies, Loughborough University, Loughborough, Leicestershire LE11 3TU]) : The Working Party ; Huntingdon (12 Church St., Fenstanton, Huntingdon) : Distributed by Grasshopper Press, [1981?]. — [14]p
ISBN 0-904572-07-2 : Unpriced B81-24700

025.2'832 — Great Britain. Serials subscription agents

Singleton, Alan. The role of subscription agents / by Alan Singleton ; with a supplementary report on U.K. libraries, trade with agents by Alan Cooper. — Leicester (Leicester LE1 7RH) : Primary Communications Research Centre, University of Leicester, c1981. — 68p ; 21cm. — (BL (R&D) report ; no.5621) (Occasional papers / University of Leicester. Primary Communications Research Centre, ISSN 0144-6460)
ISBN 0-906083-17-6 (pbk) : Unpriced : CIP rev. B81-14408

025.3 — LIBRARIES. BIBLIOGRAPHIC ANALYSIS AND CONTROL

025.3 — Bibliographic control
Davinson, Donald. Bibliographic control / Donald Davinson. — 2nd ed. — London : Bingley, 1981. — 164p ; 23cm. — (Outlines of modern librarianship)
Previous ed.: 1975. — Includes index
ISBN 0-85157-319-3 : Unpriced : CIP rev.
B81-13759

025.3 — Documents. Cataloguing — *Conference proceedings*
International Conference on Cataloguing Principles *(1961 : Paris)***International** Conference on Cataloguing Principles, Paris, 9th-18th October, 1961 : report / edited by A.H. Chaplin and Dorothy Anderson. — London (c/o The British Library, Reference Division, Great Russell St., WC1B 3DG) : IFLA International Office for UBC, 1981, c1963. — viii,293p ; 21cm
At head of title: International Federation of Library Associations and Institutions. — Originally published: London (National Central Library, Malet Pl., WC1) : Organizing Committee of the International Conference on Cataloguing Principles, 1963. — Includes index
ISBN 0-903043-33-5 (pbk) : Unpriced
B81-33230

025.3 — Documents. Indexing
Rowley, Jennifer E.. Abstracting and indexing. — London : Bingley, Nov.1981. — [155]p. — (Outlines of modern librarianship)
ISBN 0-85157-336-3 : £7.50 : CIP entry
Primary classification 025.4'028 B81-30413

025.3 — Documents. Printed indexes. Production. Applications of digital computer systems. Software packages
Armstrong, C.. Software for printed indexes, a guide : part of a report to the British Library Research and Development Department for Project SI/G/243 / C. Armstrong. — London : ASLIB, [1981?]. — 98p : facsims ; 30cm. — (BL R & D report ; no.5622)
ISBN 0-85142-142-3 (pbk) : Unpriced
B81-34669

025.3 — Great Britain. Official publications. Bibliographic control
Richard, Stephen. Directory of British official publications. — London : Mansell, Oct.1981. — [400]p
ISBN 0-7201-1596-5 : £20.00 : CIP entry
B81-27392

025.3 — Libraries. Stock: Documents in non-Western languages. Cataloguing & classification
Cataloging and classification of non-Western material : concerns, issues and practices / edited by Mohammed M. Aman. — [Phoenix] : Oryx ; London ; Mansell [distributor], 1980. — 368p : ill ; 24cm. — (A Neal-Schuman professional book)
ISBN 0-912700-06-8 : £11.50 B81-05386

025.3'028'54 — Great Britain. National libraries: British Library. On-line information processing systems: BLAISE. Cataloguing systems: LOCAS — *Manuals*
LOCAS user manual. — London : The British Library, Bibliographic Services Division, Nov.1981. — 1v.
ISBN 0-900220-94-5 (unbound) : £25.00 (One copy free to LOCAS customers) : CIP entry
B81-34213

025.3'028'5442 — Documents. Cataloguing. Machine-readable files: MARC records. International exchange
International access to MARC records : a summary report with recommended text for a bilateral ageement for the international exchange of MARC records / prepared by the International MARC Network Study Steering Committee of the Conference of Directors of National Libraries ; approved by the Conference of Directors of National Libraries, August 1980. — London : IFLA International Office for UBC, 1980. — 7p ; 30cm. — (Occasional papers / The IFLA International Office for UBC, ISSN 0309-9202 ; no.7)
ISBN 0-903043-31-9 (unbound) : £2.00
B81-32374

025.3'028'5442 — Documents. Cataloguing. Machine-readable files: UK MARC records — *Manuals*
UK MARC manual. — 2nd ed. — London : British Library, Bibliographic Services Division, 1980. — 112p in various pagings ; 32cm
Previous ed.: 1975
ISBN 0-900220-84-8 (spiral) : £9.00
B81-19523

025.3'1'05 — Libraries. Catalogues — *Serials*
[Newsletter *(Bath University Programme of Catalogue Research)*]. Newsletter / Bath University Programme of Catalogue Research. — [No.1] (July 1978)- no.2 (April 1979). — Bath (The Library, University of Bath, Claverton Down, Bath BA2 7AY) : The Programme, 1978-1979. — 2v. ; 30cm
Continued by: Newsletter (Centre for Catalogue Research)
ISSN 0260-2598 = Newsletter — Bath University Programme of Catalogue Research : Free B81-02012

[Newsletter *(Centre for Catalogue Research)*]. Newsletter / Centre for Catalogue Research. — No.3 (Dec. 1979)-. — Bath (The Library, University of Bath, Claverton Down, Bath BA2 7AY) : The Centre, 1979-. — v. ; 30cm
Two issues yearly. — Continues : Newsletter (Bath University Programme of Catalogue Research)
ISSN 0144-5073 = Newsletter — Centre for Catalogue Research : Free B81-02013

025.3'13 — United States. Libraries. Card catalogues
The **Card** catalog : current issues : readings and selected bibliography / edited by Cynthia C. Ryans. — Metuchen ; London : Scarecrow, 1981. — xi,334p : ill ; 23cm
Includes bibliographies and index
ISBN 0-8108-1417-x : £12.80 B81-37819

025.3'17 — Great Britain. National libraries: British Library. Catalogues. Filing — *Rules*
BLAISE filing rules / British Library Filing Rules Committee. — London : British Library, c1980. — 34p ; 30cm
ISBN 0-900220-83-x (pbk) : £5.00 : CIP rev.
B80-13180

025.3'2 — Documents. Author & descriptive cataloguing. Rules: Anglo-American cataloguing rules. 2nd ed — *Conference proceedings*
Seminar on AACR2 : proceedings of a seminar organized by the Cataloguing and Indexing Group of the Library Association at the University of Nottingham, 20-22 April 1979 / edited by Graham Roe. — London : Library Association, 1980. — iv,92p ; 23cm
Includes index
ISBN 0-85365-593-6 (pbk) : £6.35 B81-05095

025.3'2 — Documents. Author & descriptive cataloguing. Rules: Anglo-American cataloguing rules. 2nd ed — *Samplers*
Slocum, Robert B.. Sample cataloguing forms : illustrations of solutions to problems of descriptions : (with particular reference to Chapters 1-13 of the Anglo-American Cataloguing Rules, second edition) / by Robert B. Slocum. — 3rd ed. — Metuchen ; London : Scarecrow, 1980. — vii,114p ; 29cm
Previous ed.: published as Sample cataloging forms, 1968. — Includes index
ISBN 0-8108-1364-5 : £7.70 B81-06243

025.3'2 — Documents. Author cataloguing & descriptive cataloguing — *Rules*
Gorman, Michael, *1941-*. The concise AACR2 : being a rewritten and simplified version of Anglo-American cataloguing rules, second edition / prepared by Michael Gorman. — Chicago : American Library Association ; London : Library Association, 1981. — ix,164p ; 23cm
Includes index
ISBN 0-85365-733-5 (pbk) : Unpriced : CIP rev. B81-17513

025.3'2 — Documents. Descriptive cataloguing
Downing, Mildred Harlow. Introduction to cataloging and classification / Mildred Harlow Downing. — 5th ed. — Jefferson, N.C. : McFarland ; Folkestone : Distributed by Bailey Bros. & Swinfen, 1981. — x,230p : 1ill,forms ; 24cm
Bibliography: p218-224. — Includes index
ISBN 0-89950-017-x : £11.95
Also classified at 025.4'2 B81-38761

025.3'2 — Monographs. Descriptive cataloguing. Rules: International Federation of Library Associations and Institutions. ISBD(M) — International standard bibliographic description for monographic publications — *Questions & answers*
Ravilious, C. P.. Manual of annotated ISBD(M) examples. — London (c/o British Library Reference Division, Gt. Russell St., WC1B 3DG) : IFLA International Office for UBC, Dec.1981. — [106]p
ISBN 0-903043-36-x (pbk) : £10.00 : CIP entry
B81-40232

025.3'22 — Catholic Church. *Liturgy and ritual* **Latin rites,** *1563-1980.* **Descriptive cataloguing. Uniform titles** — *Rules*
International Federation of Library Associations and Institutions. *Working Group on Uniform Headings for Liturgical Works.* List of uniform titles for liturgical works of the Latin rites of the Catholic Church. — 2nd ed. rev. — London (c/o The British Library, Reference Division, Great Russell St., WC1B 3DG) : IFLA International Office for UBC, Aug.1981. — [17]p
Previous ed.: 1975
ISBN 0-903043-35-1 (pbk) : £5.00 : CIP entry
B81-24625

025.3'22 — Documents. Author cataloguing. Rules: Anglo-American cataloguing rules. 2nd ed — *Algorithms*
Using AACR2 : a step-by-step algorithmic approach to part II of the Anglo-American Cataloguing Rules / Malcolm Shaw ... [et al.]. — London : Library Associaton, 1980. — viii,180p : ill,facsims ; 24cm
ISBN 0-85365-612-6 (cased) : £7.50 : CIP rev.
ISBN 0-85365-622-3 (pbk) : £4.75 B80-05767

025.3'434 — Great Britain. Local authorities. Planning departments. Publications. Bibliographic control
Nuttall, Barry S.. Organisation and control of local government planning documentation / Barry S. Nuttall. — Leeds (c/o Dr. S.J. Craig-Smith, Brunswick Terrace, Leeds LS2 8BU) : Planning Research Unit, School of Town Planning, [1980?]. — v,44p ; 30cm. — (Planning papers / Dept. of Town Planning. Leeds Polytechnic ; 23)
Unpriced (pbk) B81-31294

025.3'434 — United Nations. Official publications. Bibliographic control
Clews, John. Documentation of the UN system. — London : IFLA International Office for UBC, Sept.1981. — [26]p. — (The IFLA International Office for UBC occasional papers, ISSN 0309-9202 ; no.8)
ISBN 0-903043-34-3 (pbk) : £5.00 : CIP entry
B81-28108

025.3'488 — Musical scores. Descriptive cataloguing — *Rules*
ISBD (PM) : international standard bibliographic description for printed music / recommended by the Joint Working Group on the International Standard Bibliographic Description for Printed Music ; approved by the Standing Committee of the IFLA Section on Cataloguing and by the International Association of Music Libraries. — London : IFLA International Office for UBC, 1980. — ix,53p ; 30cm
ISBN 0-903043-26-2 (pbk) : £8.00 : CIP rev.
B80-17524

025.3′5′09421 — London. Universities: University of London. Libraries. Cooperative cataloguing systems: University of London. *Shared Cataloguing System — Serials*
[Catalyst *(London)*]. Catalyst : information from the University of London Shared Cataloguing System. — No.1 (Aug.1980)-. — London (LRCC Office, Senate House, Malet Street, WC1E 7HU) : [Library Resources Co-ordinating Committee], 1980-. — v. ; 33cm
Irregular
Unpriced B81-05176

025.4 — LIBRARIES. SUBJECT ANALYSIS AND CONTROL

025.4 — Documents. Classification
Foskett, A. C.. The subject approach to information. — 4th ed. — London : Bingley, Nov.1981. — [545]p
Previous ed.: 1977
ISBN 0-85157-313-4 (cased) : £13.50 : CIP entry
ISBN 0-85157-339-6 (pbk) : £9.50
Also classified at 025.4′7 B81-31076

025.4′028 — Documents. Abstracting
Rowley, Jennifer E.. Abstracting and indexing. — London : Bingley, Nov.1981. — [155]p. — (Outlines of modern librarianship)
ISBN 0-85157-336-3 : £7.50 : CIP entry
Also classified at 025.3 B81-30413

025.4′2 — Documents. Classification
Downing, Mildred Harlow. Introduction to cataloging and classification / Mildred Harlow Downing. — 5th ed. — Jefferson, N.C. : McFarland ; Folkestone : Distributed by Bailey Bros. & Swinfen, 1981. — x,230p : 1ill,forms ; 24cm
Bibliography: p218-224. — Includes index
ISBN 0-89950-017-x : £11.95
Primary classification 025.3′2 B81-38761

025.4′2′077 — Documents. Classification — *Programmed instructions*
Brown, A. G.. Introduction to subject indexing. — 2nd ed. — London : Bingley, Jan.1982. — [254]p
Previous ed.: 1976
ISBN 0-85157-331-2 : £8.75 : CIP entry
Primary classification 025.4′8′077 B81-38856

025.4′31 — Documents. Subject classification schemes: Dewey Decimal Classification - *Programmed texts*
Batty, C. D.. An introduction to the nineteenth edition of the Dewey Decimal Classification. — London : Bingley, Aug.1981. — [110]p
ISBN 0-85157-303-7 : £5.25 : CIP entry B81-18037

025.4′34 — Documents. Subject classification schemes: Bliss, Henry Evelyn. Bliss bibliographic classification — *Texts*
Bliss, Henry Evelyn. Bliss bibliographic classification. — 2nd ed. — London : Butterworths
Previous ed.: published as A bibliographic classification. New York : H.W. Wilson, 1940-1953. — Includes index
Class H: Anthropology, human biology, health sciences / J. Mills and Vanda Broughton with the assistance of Valerie Lang. — 1980. — xl,326p ; 29cm
ISBN 0-408-70828-x : Unpriced B81-10383

025.4′66381 — Livestock: Bees. Research organisations: International Bee Research Association. Stock: Illustrations — *Classification schedules*
International Bee Research Association. List of UDC numbers and subjects of files in the IBRA picture collection. — [Gerrards Cross] : International Bee Research Association, 1978. — 13leaves ; 31cm
ISBN 0-86098-017-0 (pbk) : £1.00 B81-10766

025.4′6796 — Sports. Documents on sports — *Classification schedules*
Wilmot, Carole E.. Classification/thesaurus for sport and physical recreation (and allied topics) / compiled by Carole E. Wilmot. — Development ed. — London : The Sports Council, c1981. — xii,185p ; 30cm
At head of title: The Sports Council
ISBN 0-906577-16-0 (pbk) : £50.00 B81-28721

025.4′680883876 — Libraries. Stock: Science fiction. Classification
Croghan, Antony. Science fiction and the universe of knowledge : the structure of an aesthetic form / by Antony Croghan. — London (91 Cranwich Rd., N16 5JP) : Coburgh Publications, 1981. — iv,47p ; 22cm
Includes index
£1.50 (pbk) B81-24765

025.4′7 — Documents. Subject indexing
Foskett, A. C.. The subject approach to information. — 4th ed. — London : Bingley, Nov.1981. — [545]p
Previous ed.: 1977
ISBN 0-85157-313-4 (cased) : £13.50 : CIP entry
ISBN 0-85157-339-6 (pbk) : £9.50
Primary classification 025.4 B81-31076

025.4′8′077 — Documents. Subject indexing — *Programmed instructions*
Brown, A. G.. Introduction to subject indexing. — 2nd ed. — London : Bingley, Jan.1982. — [254]p
Previous ed.: 1976
ISBN 0-85157-331-2 : £8.75 : CIP entry
Also classified at 025.4′2′077 B81-38856

025.4′82 — Documents. Subject indexing. Schemes: PRECIS
Ramsden, Michael J.. Precis : a workbook for students of librarianship / Michael J. Ramsden. — London : Bingley, 1981. — 152p ; 23cm. — (Outlines of modern librarianship)
ISBN 0-85157-334-7 : Unpriced : CIP rev. B80-21298

025.4′82 — Documents. Subject indexing. Schemes: PRECIS. Reactions of users
Peters, Helen Jane. User reactions to PRECIS indexes : final report for the period July 1980-June 1981 / Helen Jane Peters. — [Liverpool] : School of Librarianship and Information Studies, Faculty of Humanities and Social Studies, Liverpool Polytechnic, 1981. — i,77p : forms ; 30cm. — (BLRDD report ; 5659)
Report to the British Library Research and Development Department on Project SI/G/349. Project head K.G.B. Bakewell. — Includes index
ISBN 0-901537-16-0 (pbk) : £4.00 B81-41017

025.4′82 — Documents. Subject indexing. Translingual schemes. Projects: PRECIS/Translingual Project
Verdier, Veronica. Final report of the PRECIS/Translingual project / by Veronica Verdier. — [Wetherby] : [British Library], [1981]. — v,279,[18]p : ill,forms ; 30cm. — (British Library R & D report ; 5631)
Bibliography: p279
Unpriced (unbound) B81-25262

025.4′82 — Information science & librarianship. Documents on information science & documents on librarianship. Subject indexing. Intermediate lexicons. Research
Horsnell, Verina. Intermediate lexicon for information science : a feasibility study : final report / by Verina Horsnell. — London (207, Essex Rd., N1 3PN) : Polytechnic of North London School of Librarianship, 1974 (1981 [printing]). — viii,110p : 1ill,forms ; 30cm. — (Research report (old series) (Polytechnic of North London. School of Librarianship)) (Research report (old series) / Polytechnic of North London. School of Librarianship)
Includes bibliographies
ISBN 0-900639-08-3 (pbk) : £4.60 B81-34269

025.4′9 — Documents. Subject indexing. Thesauri. Construction — *Manuals*
Townley, Helen M.. Thesaurus-making : grow your own word-stock / Helen M. Townley and Ralph D. Gee. — London : Deutsch, 1980. — 206p ; 23cm
Bibliography: p195-201. — Includes index
ISBN 0-233-97225-0 : £7.95 : CIP rev. B80-23942

025.4′9 — Great Britain. *Parliament. House of Commons. Library.* **Stock —** *Thesauri*
Great Britain. *Parliament. House of Commons. Library*. The House of Commons Library thesaurus. — 1st working ed. — [London] : House of Commons Library ; Milton Keynes (Brick Close, Kiln Farm, Milton Keynes MK11 3EJ) : printed and produced by Scicon Computer Services, 1980. — 616p ; 34cm
£110.00 B81-29573

025.4′9 — Great Britain. Secondary schools. Libraries. Stock. Subject indexing. Subject headings — *Lists*
Swatridge, Colin. A list of subject headings for school and other libraries / Colin Swatridge. — Oxford : School Library Association, c1981. — xi,148p ; 24cm
ISBN 0-900641-37-1 : £6.00 (£4.50 to SLA members) B81-11599

025.4′953 — Physics — *Thesauri* **—** *Serials*
INSPEC thesaurus / Institution of Electrical Engineers. — 1981. — [London] : The Institution, c1980. — 462p in various pagings
ISBN 0-85296-225-8 : Unpriced
Also classified at 025.4′96213 B81-04805

025.4′96151 — Pharmacology — *Thesauri*
National abstracts thesaurus. — London (The London Hospital, Whitechapel Rd, E1 1BB) : Drug Information Pharmacists Group, 1981. — 98p ; 30cm
ISBN 0-907625-00-2 (pbk) : Unpriced B81-23214

025.4′96213 — Electrical engineering — *Thesauri* **—** *Serials*
INSPEC thesaurus / Institution of Electrical Engineers. — 1981. — [London] : The Institution, c1980. — 462p in various pagings
ISBN 0-85296-225-8 : Unpriced
Primary classification 025.4′953 B81-04805

025.4′9627 — Hydraulic engineering — *Thesauri*
The **Thesaurus** for fluid engineering. — Cranfield : BHRA Fluid Engineering, Aug.1981. — [128]p
ISBN 0-906085-57-8 (pbk) : £15.00 : CIP entry B81-25117

025.5 — LIBRARY SERVICES TO USERS

025.5 — Libraries. Stock. Classification. Guiding signs
Masson, André. The pictorial catalogue. — Oxford : Clarendon Press, Nov.1981. — [88]p
Translation of: Le catalogue figuratif
ISBN 0-19-818159-0 : £12.50 : CIP entry B81-30311

025.5′2 — Great Britain. Information services for Indian women — *Study regions: London. Ealing (London Borough). Southall*
Gundara, *Jaswinder*. Indian women in Britain : a study of information needs / by Jaswinder Gundara. — London (207 Essex Rd., N1 3PN) : Polytechnic of North London School of Librarianship, 1981. — viii,92p : 1map,forms ; 30cm. — (Occasional publication / Polytechnic of North London. School of Librarianship, ISSN 0144-2392)
Bibliography: p89-92
ISBN 0-900639-17-2 (pbk) : £3.25 B81-18431

025.5′2 — United States. Information broking services
White, Martin S.. Information broking services in U.S.A. / Martin S. White. — London (Management House, Parker St., WC2B 5PU) : NPM Information Services, 1980. — 30p ; 30cm. — (British Library R & D report ; 5624)
Unpriced (pbk) B81-20999

025.5′2′024097 — Great Britain. Information services — *For journalism — Directories — Serials*
[Contact *(East Grinstead)*]. Contact : the UK news contact directory. — 1980-81-. — East Grinstead (Windsor Court, East Grinstead House, East Grinstead, West Sussex RH19 1XA) : IPC Media Publications, c1980-. — v. ; 30cm
Annual
ISSN 0260-8936 = Contact (East Grinstead) : £25.00 B81-09076

025.5′2′02541 — Great Britain. Information services. Directories
Finer, Ruth. Survey of current directories : an update : report to British Library Research and Development Department on Project SI/OPA/094 / Ruth Finer. — [London] : [The Department], 1979. — 52leaves : ill,maps ; 30cm. — (BL R and D report ; 5615)
Unpriced (spiral) B81-16307

025.5′2′028 — Great Britain. Rural regions. Information services. Provision. Role of telecommunication services — *Study regions: Lincolnshire. East Lindsey (District)*
Clark, D.. Information services in rural areas : prospects for telecommunications access / D. Clark, K.I. Unwin. — Norwich : Geo Books, c1980. — x,122p : ill,maps,forms ; 24cm
Bibliography: p119-122
ISBN 0-86094-058-6 (pbk) : £7.95 B81-09226

025.5′2′05 — Information services — *Serials*
ICP : the journal of information products & services, U.K. edition. — Vol.1, no.1 (Autumn 1980)-. — Indianapolis ; London (2 Deanery St., Park La., W1Y 5LH) : International Computer Programs, 1980-. — v. : ill,ports ; 27cm
Quarterly
£10.00 per year B81-15150

025.5′2′068 — Information services. Management
White, Martin S.. Profit from information : a guide to the establishment, operation and use of an information consultancy / Martin S. White. — London : Deutsch in association with the Institute of Information Scientists, 1981. — xii,118p ; 23cm. — (Institute of Information Scientists monograph series)
Includes index
ISBN 0-233-97336-2 : £6.95 : CIP rev.
B81-13431

025.5′2′0941 — Great Britain. Information services for professional personnel. Provision
Wilkin, Anne. The information needs of practitioners : a review of the literature / prepared by Anne Wilkin for the British Library Research and Development Department. — [London] : University of London, 1981. — 284p on various pagings ; 30cm. — (BL R & D report ; 5611)
Bibliography: pR1-R18
Unpriced (pbk) B81-16328

025.52′0941 — Great Britain. Libraries. Reference services — *Conference proceedings*
Library Association. *Reference, Special and Information Section. Annual Study Group (29th : 1981 : Newcastle-upon-Tyne)*.
Proceedings of the 29th Annual Study Group, Newcastle-upon-Tyne, 10th-13th April 1981. — London (16 Springfield, Ovington, Northumberland NE42 6EH) : The Section, Oct.1981. — 1v.
ISBN 0-85365-864-1 (pbk) : £4.00 (£3.20 to members) : CIP entry B81-32088

025.5′2′0973 — United States. Information services
Maranjian, Lorig. Fee-based information services : a study of a growing industry / Lorig Maranjian and Richard W. Boss. — New York ; London : Bowker, 1980. — ix,199p : ill ; 24cm. — (Information management series ; 1)
Bibliography: p169-186. — Includes index
ISBN 0-8352-1287-4 : Unpriced B81-13977

025.5′24 — Bibliographic information retrieval. Requests. Relevance weighting
Jones, K. Sparck. Research on relevance weighting 1976-1979 / K. Sparck Jones, C.A. Webster. — Cambridge (Corn Exchange St., Cambridge CB2 3QG) : Computer Laboratory, University of Cambridge, c1980. — v,61,[116]p : ill : 30cm. — (British Library R & D report ; 5553)
Bibliography: pR1-R2
Unpriced (pbk) B81-11461

025.5′24 — Great Britain. National libraries: British Library. On-line information processing systems: BLAISE - *Manuals*
BLAISE mini manual. — 2nd ed. — London (2 Sheraton St., W1V 4BH) : British Library, Bibliographic Services Division, Apr.1981. — 1v.
Previous ed.: 1980
ISBN 0-900220-92-9 (spiral) : £5.00 : CIP entry B81-12364

025.5′24 — Hydraulic engineering. On-line information retrieval services: FLUIDEX
Guide to the FLUIDEX database. — Cranfield : BHRA Fluid Engineering, Oct.1981. — [64]p
ISBN 0-906085-62-4 (pbk) : £3.00 : CIP entry
B81-30980

025.5′24 — Information retrieval systems — *Conference proceedings*
Information retrieval research / edited by R.N. Oddy ... [et al.]. — London : Butterworths, 1981. — x,389p : ill ; 25cm
Conference papers. — Includes bibliographies and index
ISBN 0-408-10775-8 : Unpriced : CIP rev.
B81-13844

025.5′24 — Information retrieval systems. Evaluation
Information retrieval experiment / edited by Karen Sparck Jones. — London : Butterworths, 1981. — viii,352p : ill ; 24cm
Bibliography: p330-342. — Includes index
ISBN 0-408-10648-4 : Unpriced : CIP rev.
B81-16927

025.5′24 — Libraries. On-line bibliographic information retrieval — *Manuals*
Meadow, Charles T.. Basics of online searching / Charles T. Meadow, Pauline (Atherton) Cochrane. — New York ; Chichester : Wiley, c1981. — xiv,245p : ill,forms ; 26cm. — (Information sciences series)
Text on lining paper. — Includes bibliographies and index
ISBN 0-471-05283-3 : £10.00 B81-26329

025.5′24 — London. Universities. Information services using digital computer systems: University of London. *Central Information Services.* **On-line bibliographic information retrieval services. Provision. Role of travelling workshops**
Organisation and impact of a travelling workshop for on-line information retrieval in the University of London : final report to the British Library R. & D Department no.SI/G/186 / project head A. Vickery ; research assistants G. Pratt, D. Wiseman, G. Burgess. — London : CIS/LRCC, University of London, 1981. — 132p : ill,facsims,forms ; 30cm. — (BL R & D report ; 5612)
Unpriced (pbk) B81-16329

025.5′24 — On-line information retrieval systems — *For librarianship*
Online searching : an introduction / W.M. Henry ... [et al.]. — London : Butterworths, 1980. — 209p : ill,forms ; 24cm
Includes bibliographies and index
ISBN 0-408-10696-4 : £10.00 : CIP rev.
B80-08580

025.5′24 — On-line information retrieval. Techniques. Theories
Radecki, Tadeusz. Theoretical approaches to information retrieval / Tadeusz Radecki. — Sheffield : Postgraduate School of Librarianship and Information Science, University of Sheffield, 1981. — 206leaves in various foliations ; 30cm. — (British Library Research and Development Department report ; no.5651)
Unpriced (pbk) B81-34606

025.5′24′02854 — Libraries. On-line bibliographic information retrieval. Techniques. Teaching
Scott, Aldyth D.. Teaching and training for on-line work in libraries : interim report for the period June 1978-February 1979 : report to the British Library Research and Development Department on Project S1/G/270 / Aldyth D. Scott. — [Brighton] ([Falmer, Brighton BN1 9PH]) : School of Librarianship, Department of Communication and European Studies, Brighton Polytechnic, 1979. — iii,21leaves ; 30cm
Bibliography: leaf 21
Unpriced (pbk) B81-06529

025.5′24′0941 — Great Britain. Libraries. Bibliographic information retrieval services — *Inquiry reports*
Great Britain. *Parliament. House of Commons. Education, Science and Arts Committee.*
Fourth report from the Education, Science and Art Committee, session 1979-80 : information storage and retrieval in the British library service : together with the minutes of evidence and appendices. — London : H.M.S.O., [1980]. — xxix,158p ; 25cm. — (HC ; 767) (HC ; 409i-iv)
ISBN 0-10-027679-2 (pbk) : £6.80 B81-20361

025.5′25 — Current awareness bulletins. Evaluation — *Manuals*
Francis, G. M.. A manual for the evaluation of current awareness bulletins / G.M. Francis, C. Mullings, T.D. Wilson. — [London] : British Library ; Boston Spa : Distributed by Publications, The British Library Lending Division, 1981. — xii,276p : ill,forms ; 30cm
Includes index
ISBN 0-905984-60-9 (pbk) : Unpriced
B81-22301

025.5′6 — Libraries. Guiding signs
Reynolds, Linda. Signs and guiding for libraries / Linda Reynolds and Stephen Barrett. — London : Bingley, 1981. — 158p : ill,facsims ; 16x22cm
Bibliography: p155. — Includes index
ISBN 0-85157-312-6 : Unpriced : CIP rev.
B80-18987

025.5′6 — Libraries. Use
Wolf, Carolyn E.. Basic library skills : a short course / by Carolyn E. Wolf and Richard Wolf. — Jefferson, N.C. : McFarland ; Folkestone : Distributed by Bailey Bros. & Swinfen, 1981. — x,127p : ill,facsims ; 23cm
Includes bibliographies and index
ISBN 0-89950-018-8 (pbk) : £7.15 B81-38763

025.5′6 — Libraries. Use — *For children*
Rushton, Doris. How to use a library / by Doris Rushton ; illustrated by George W. Thompson. — London (30 Marsh Rd., Pinner, Middx.) : Peter Daffon Associates, 1980. — 96p : col.ill,1col.map ; 30cm. — (Read to learn series)
ISBN 0-906749-00-x (pbk) : £3.50 B81-06568

025.5′677′0941 — Great Britain. Higher education institutions. Libraries. Guidance for users. Role of travelling seminars. Projects: Travelling Workshops Experiment
The **Travelling** Workshops Experiment in library user education / D. Clark ... [et al.]. — Wetherby : British Library, 1981. — ix,259p ; 30cm. — (The British Library research & development reports, ISSN 0308-2385 ; 5602)
Bibliography: p179
ISBN 0-905984-63-3 (spiral) : Unpriced
B81-25182

025.5′678′0973 — United States. Schools. Libraries. Users. Education
Irving, Ann. Some impressions of library user education in U.S. schools : report of a visit in May 1981 / Ann Irving. — [Loughborough] : Department of Library and Information Studies, Loughborough University, 1981. — 15p : 1facsim ; 30cm. — (British Library L R & D report ; 5652)
Unpriced (pbk) B81-37947

025.5′8′0723 — Great Britain. Libraries. Use by readers. Surveys. Methodology
McGilvray, Alison. Readership surveys and local library co-operation / by Alison McGilvray. — [Stirling] : University of Stirling, 1980. — 13,[49]p : facsim,forms ; 30cm. — (British Library R & D report ; 5625)
Unpriced (pbk) B81-20998

025.6 — LIBRARY CIRCULATION SERVICES

025.6′2 — Great Britain. Libraries holding stock for inter-library loans through British Library. *Lending Division.* **Codes** — *Directories*
British Library. *Lending Division*. Amendments to the 1980 edition of the Directory of library codes / the British Library, Lending Division. — [Boston Spa] : [The Library], [1981]. — [11]p ; 30cm
Unpriced (unbound) B81-31133

025.6'2 — London & South-east England. Libraries. Stock. Inter-library loans. Road transport. Projects
Transport scheme for inter-library loans in London and the Home Counties : user's guide / [London & South Eastern Library Region (LASR)]. — London (33 Alfred Place, WC1E 7DP) : LASER, 1981. — 9p ; 30cm
Unpriced (unbound) B81-21759

025.6'2 — London. Universities: University of London. Libraries. Stock. Inter-library loans — *Conference proceedings*
Interlibrary Loan Seminar *(1979 : Senate House, University of London).* Interlibrary loan : papers given at the Interlibrary Loan Seminar held by the University of London Library Resources Co-ordinating Committee in November 1979 / University of London, Library Resources Co-ordinating Committee, Standing Advisory Panel on Interlibrary Loans. — [London] ([Senate House, Malet St., WC1E 7HU]) : [University of London Central Library Services], [1981?]. — 39p : 1ill ; 30cm
Includes bibliographies
Unpriced (pbk) B81-32388

025.7 — LIBRARIES. PHYSICAL PREPARATION OF MATERIAL FOR STORAGE

025.7 — Libraries. Stock: Books. Maintenance & repair
Mortimer, E. A.. Library books : their care and repair / E.A. Mortimer. — Rev. and enl. ed. — Hornchurch : Henry, 1980. — 56p : ill ; 25cm
Previous ed.: Auckland : University of Auckland, 1968. — Includes index
ISBN 0-86025-904-8 (pbk) : £1.75 B81-24378

026 — SPECIAL LIBRARIES

026 — Great Britain. National libraries: British Library. *Department of Printed Books.* **Stock: Special collections —** *Lists*
British Library. *Department of Printed Books.* Named special collections in the Department of Printed Books / compiled by Alison Gould. — London : British Library Reference Division, 1981. — 27p ; 21cm. — (Reader guide / Department of Printed Books, British Library ; no.9)
Includes index
Unpriced (pbk) B81-15679

026'.000941 — Great Britain. Special libraries. Information services. Use
Slater, Margaret. The neglected resource : non-usage of library-information services in industry and commerce / Margaret Slater. — London : Aslib, c1981. — 68p : 1facsim,1form ; 21cm. — (Aslib occasional publications ; no.25) (British Library research and development report ; no.25)
Bibliography: p67-68
ISBN 0-85142-145-8 (pbk) : £9.50 B81-36093

026'.000973 — United States. Special libraries
Special librarianship : a new reader / edited by Eugene B. Jackson. — Metuchen ; London : Scarecrow, 1980. — xiii,759p : ill ; 24cm
Includes index
ISBN 0-8108-1295-9 : £19.25 B81-05699

026'.0025'421 — London. Special libraries — *Directories — For students of City of London Polytechnic*
Libraries of London / City of London Polytechnic. — 4th ed. — [London] ([Calcutta House Precinct, Old Castle St., E1 7NT]) : [City of London Polytechnic], 1980. — 54p ; 17cm
Previous ed.: 1979. — Bibliography: p48. — Includes index
ISBN 0-904264-51-3 (pbk) : £1.00
Also classified at 027.4'025'421 B81-16051

026'.07 — Great Britain. National libraries: British Library. *Newspaper Library — Serials*
British Library Reference Division Newspaper Library newsletter. — No.1 [Autumn 1980]-. — London (Colindale Ave., NW9 5HE) : The Library, 1980-. — v. ; 30cm
Two issues yearly
ISSN 0144-9958 = British Library Reference Division Newspaper Library newsletter : Unpriced B81-11864

026'.33188'0942819 — West Yorkshire *(Metropolitan County).* **Leeds** *(District).* **Trade unions. Information services: TUCRIC,** *to 1979*
Dee, Marianne. TUCRIC : the first year / Marianne Dee and John Allred with assistance from the other TUCRIC workers. — Leeds (28 Park Place, Leeds, LS1 2SY) : Leeds Polytechnic School of Librarianship, 1980. — 25p ; 21cm
Cover title
ISBN 0-900738-24-3 (pbk) : £1.50
Also classified at 361'.06 B81-14094

026'.3337'0941 — Great Britain. Records on British environment. Repositories, *1970-1980*
Stewart, Jennifer D.. Environmental record centres : a decade of progress / Jennifer D. Stewart. — Duxford (Imperial War Museum, Duxford Airfield, Duxford, Cambs. CB2 4QR) : Museum Documentation Association, 1980. — v,38p : forms ; 30cm. — (MDA occasional paper, ISSN 0140-7198 ; 3)
At head of title: Museum Documentation Association. — Bibliography: p24-37
ISBN 0-905963-32-6 (spiral) : £2.25 (£1.50 to members of the Museum Documentation Association) B81-25547

026'.338 — Great Britain. Industries & trades. Information services using digital computer systems — *Directories*
The **Directory** of computerised business information / editor Douglas Tookey ; editorial consultant Peter Lansley. — Berkhamstead : Trade Research, 1979. — 146p ; 30cm
Includes index
ISBN 0-904783-08-1 (pbk) : £20.00 B81-21383

026'.34 — Law. Information services
Miskin, C.. Library and information services for the legal profession / C. Miskin. — [London] : British Library, 1981. — iv,60p ; 30cm. — (British Library research & development reports, ISSN 0308-2385 ; no.5633)
ISBN 0-905984-73-0 (pbk) : Unpriced B81-38999

026'.352041'072 — Great Britain. Local authorities. Information services. Requirements. Investigation — *Manuals*
Mullings, C.. A manual for the investigation of local government information needs / C. Mullings, G.M. Francis, T.D. Wilson. — [London] : British Library ; Boston Spa : Distributed by Publications, British Library Lending Division, 1981. — lx,162p : ill,forms ; 30cm. — (British Library research & development reports, ISSN 0308-2385 ; no.5585)
ISBN 0-905984-61-7 (spiral) : Unpriced B81-14600

026'.3616'094231 — Wiltshire. Public welfare services. Information services
Blake, William, *1945-*. Experimental information service in two statutory welfare agencies (Wiltshire) : final report : report to the British Library Research and Development Department on Project SI/9/206 / William Blake, Trevor Morkham, Alison Skinner. — Bath ([Claverton Down, Bath BA2 7AY]) : The Library, The University, 1980. — 3v. : ill,1map ; 30cm. — (Report ; no.5609)
Unpriced (spiral) B81-16313

026'.3719'0941 — Great Britain. Educationally disadvantaged persons. Information services: Centre for Information and Advice on Educational Disadvantage — *Serials*
Intercede : newsheet of the Centre for Information and Advice on Educational Disadvantage. — No.1 (1979) - no.5 (Summer 1980). — Manchester (11 Anson Rd, Manchester M14 5BY) : The Centre, 1979-1980. — 5v. : ill ; 30cm
Three issues yearly. — Description based on: no.5 (Summer 1980)
ISSN 0260-4019 = Intercede : Free B81-04450

026'.54'0941 — Great Britain. Chemistry. Information services: United Kingdom Chemical Information Service — *Serials*
UKCIS newsletter. — No.1 (Jan.1979)-. — Nottingham (The University, Nottingham NG7 2RD) : United Kingdom Chemical Information Service, 1979-. — v. ; 30cm
Quarterly. — Description based on: No.3 (Aug.79)
ISSN 0144-2570 = UKCIS newsletter : Free B81-04942

026'.61 — Great Britain. Medicine. Information services
. Information and the practice of medicine : report of the Medical Information Review Panel / [research officer] P.E. Cockerill. — Wetherby : British Library, 1981. — vii,34p ; 30cm. — (The British Library research & development reports, ISSN 0308-2385 ; 5605)
Appendices 1-5 and 7 on 1 microfiche in pocket
ISBN 0-905984-64-1 (pbk) : Unpriced B81-24251

026'.622'0941486 — Scotland. Dumfries and Galloway region. Wanlockhead. Libraries: Wanlockhead Miners' Library, *to 1979*
Crawford, John C.. The Society for Purchasing Books in Wanlockhead : 1756-1979 / John C. Crawford, Stuart James. — Glasgow : Scottish Library Association, 1981. — ix,57p : ill,1plan ; 21cm. — (Scottish library essay ; 1)
Bibliography: p50-52. — Includes index
ISBN 0-900649-25-9 (pbk) : Unpriced B81-32506

026'.6413 — Surrey. Leatherhead. Food. Research organisations. Libraries: Leatherhead Food R.A.. *Library.* **Services**
Leatherhead Food R.A.. The Leatherhead Food R.A. library & information service guide. — [Leatherhead] ([Randalls Rd., Leatherhead, KT22 7RY]) : [Leatherhead Food R.A.], 1981. — 45p : ill ; 30cm
Unpriced (pbk)
Primary classification 016.6413'005 B81-08439

026'.658 — Business firms. Information services & libraries
Campbell, Malcolm J.. Business information services. — London : Bingley, Aug.1981. — [170]p
ISBN 0-85157-321-5 : £8.50 : CIP entry B81-18084

026'.658 — Great Britain. National libraries: British Library. Information services on business
British Library. *Working Group on Business Information.* Business information : the role of the British Library : report of the British Library Working Group on Business Information 1980. — [London] : British Library, 1981. — 8p ; 21cm
Cover title
Unpriced (pbk) B81-40338

026'.711'094229 — Environment planning. Information services — *Study regions: Berkshire, 1976-1977*
Cater, Erlet. Patterns of information use in planning : a study of Oxfordshire and Berkshire (1976-1977) / Erlet Cater. — [Oxford] ([Gypsy Lane, Headington, Oxford OX3 0BP]) : [Oxford Polytechnic Department of Town Planning], [1979?]. — 54p : ill ; 30cm. — (Working paper / Oxford Polytechnic Department of Town Planning ; no.39)
Bibliography: p48-54
£2.10 (pbk)
Primary classification 026'.711'094257 B81-05183

026'.711'094257 — Environment planning. Information services — *Study regions: Oxfordshire, 1976-1977*
Cater, Erlet. Patterns of information use in planning : a study of Oxfordshire and Berkshire (1976-1977) / Erlet Cater. — [Oxford] ([Gypsy Lane, Headington, Oxford OX3 0BP]) : [Oxford Polytechnic Department of Town Planning], [1979?]. — 54p : ill ; 30cm. — (Working paper / Oxford Polytechnic Department of Town Planning ; no.39)
Bibliography: p48-54
£2.10 (pbk)
Also classified at 026'.711'094229 B81-05183

026'.72 — Great Britain. Architecture. Organisations. Libraries: Architectural Association. *Library, to 1979*

Architectural Association. The Architectural Association library / by Elizabeth Dixon. — London (34-36 Bedford Sq., WC1B 3ES) : The Association, 1981, c1979. — 64p : ill,facsisms,plans,ports ; 30cm
Originally published: in the Architectural Association annual review 1979. London : Diplomatic and Consular Year Book, 1979. — Includes index
ISBN 0-904503-04-6 (pbk) : Unpriced
B81-22354

026'.72 — Great Britain. Architecture. Organisations. Libraries: Architectural Association. *Slide Library*

Architectural Association. The Architectural Association slide library / by Andrew Higgott ; history by Marjorie Morrison. — London ([34-36 Bedford Sq., WC1B 3ES]) : The Association, c1980. — 62p : ill,ports ; 30cm
ISBN 0-904503-05-4 (pbk) : Unpriced
B81-22355

026'.78 — Great Britain. Libraries holding music — *Directories*

Penney, Barbara. Music in British libraries : a directory of resources. — 3rd ed. / compiled and edited by Barbara Penney. — London : Library Association, 1981. — 425p ; 23cm
Previous ed: compiled by Maureen W. Long, 1974. — Includes index
ISBN 0-85365-981-8 : Unpriced : CIP rev.
B81-12871

026'.82 — Oxfordshire. Oxford. Universities. Libraries: University of Oxford. *English Faculty Library, to 1979*

Harker, Jean. The historical development of the English Faculty Library, Oxford / Jean Harker. — London (Woodlands Avenue, Acton, W3 9DN) : School of Library & Information Studies, Ealing College of Higher Education, c1980. — 28p : 1map ; 30cm. — (Ealing miscellany ; no.17)
Bibliography: p28
£0.20 (unbound) B81-17160

026'.94276 — Lancashire. Public libraries: Lancashire Library. Local history collections. Provision — *Proposals*

Lancashire Library. Standards of provision for local studies : report and policy statement / the Lancashire Library. — Preston : Lancashire Library, 1981. — iii,20p : 30cm
ISBN 0-902228-41-2 (unbound) : Unpriced
B81-40214

026'.947 — Great Britain. Libraries holding documents on Eastern Europe & Soviet Union — *Directories*

Resources for Soviet, East European and Slavonic studies in British libraries / edited by Gregory Walker with the assistance of Jenny Brine. — Birmingham : Centre for Russian and East European Studies, University of Birmingham, 1981. — 240p ; 21cm
Includes index
ISBN 0-7044-0436-2 (pbk) : £5.00 B81-11832

026'.947 — Great Britain. National libraries. Stock: Documents on Eastern Europe — *Serials*

SCONUL. *Advisory Committee on Slavonic and East European Materials.*
SCONUL-ACOSEEM newsletter / Standing Conference of National and University Libraries, Advisory Committee on Slavonic and East European Materials. — No.19 (Apr.1980)-. — [London] ([c/o Dr. Screen, Library, School of Slavonic and East European Studies, University of London, Malet St., WC1]) : The Committee, 1980-. — v. ; 33cm
Three issues yearly. — Continues: SCONUL. Slavonic and East European Group. SCONUL-SEEG newsletter. — Description based on: No.20 (Aug.1980)
Unpriced
Also classified at 026'.947 B81-09192

026'.947 — Great Britain. Universities. Libraries. Stock: Documents on Eastern Europe — *Serials*

SCONUL. *Advisory Committee on Slavonic and East European Materials.*
SCONUL-ACOSEEM newsletter / Standing Conference of National and University Libraries, Advisory Committee on Slavonic and East European Materials. — No.19 (Apr.1980)-. — [London] ([c/o Dr. Screen, Library, School of Slavonic and East European Studies, University of London, Malet St., WC1]) : The Committee, 1980-. — v. ; 33cm
Three issues yearly. — Continues: SCONUL. Slavonic and East European Group. SCONUL-SEEG newsletter. — Description based on: No.20 (Aug.1980)
Unpriced
Primary classification 026'.947 B81-09192

026'.95 — Great Britain. Libraries. Stock: Documents associated with oriental countries — *Conference proceedings — Serials*

SCONUL. *Advisory Committee on Orientalist Materials*Report of the conference and annual meeting / SCONUL Advisory Committee on Oriental[ist] Materials. — 1980. — [S.l.] ([c/o University Library, Oriental Section, Elvet Hill, Durham DH1 3TH]) : [The Committee], c1980. — v. ; 30cm
Annual. — Continues: Report of the annual conference (SCONUL Group of Orientalist Libraries)
ISSN 0144-5812 = Report of the conference and annual meeting — SCONUL. Advisory Committee on Orientalist Materials : Unpriced
B81-25492

027 — LIBRARIES

027'.001'8 — Libraries. Performance. Assessment. Methodology

Blagden, John. Do we really need libraries? : an assessment of approaches to the evaluation of the performance of libraries / John Blagden. — New York : Saur ; London : Bingley, 1980. — 162p : 2ill ; 23cm
Bibliography: p147-157. - Includes index
ISBN 0-85157-308-8 : £7.75 : CIP rev.
B80-12201

027'.0025'41 — Great Britain. Libraries. *Directories*

Libraries in the United Kingdom and the Republic of Ireland. — 9th ed. — London : Library Association, July 1981. — [174]p
Previous ed.: 1979
ISBN 0-85365-803-x (pbk) : £9.50 : CIP entry
B81-14457

027'.0025'41 — Great Britain. Libraries - *Directories - Serials*

Libraries, museums and art galleries year book. — 1978-1979. — Cambridge : James Clarke, May 1981. — [272]p
ISBN 0-227-67835-4 : £23.00 : CIP entry
ISSN 0075-899x
Also classified at 069'.025'41 ; 708'.0025'41
B81-14963

027'.0025'411 — Scotland. Libraries. Services — *Directories — Serials*

Library resources in Scotland. — 1980-1981. — Glasgow : Scottish Library Association, 1981. — vii,149p
ISBN 0-900649-22-4 : £8.00 B81-13322

027'.0025'4283 — Yorkshire. Libraries. Services — *Directories*

Library resources in Yorkshire and Humberside / Library Association Reference, Special and Information Section, Yorkshire and Humberside Group ; edited by Isabel R. Buxton. — London : Library Association Reference, Special and Information Section, c1980. — viii,96p : 1form ; 25cm
Includes index
ISBN 0-85365-982-6 (pbk) : Unpriced : CIP rev.
Also classified at 021'.0025'4283 B80-04641

027.041 — Great Britain. Libraries. Performance. Comparison — *Feasibility studies*

Centre for Interfirm Comparison. Inter-library comparisons : report to the British Library on a feasibility study : July 1977 / by The Centre for Interfirm Comparison. — Colchester (8 West Stockwell St., Colchester, Essex CO1 1HN) : The Centre, 1981. — 21,[5]leaves : ill ; 30cm. — (BL R and D report ; 5608)
Unpriced (pbk) B81-13242

027.0411 — Scotland. Libraries, *1978-1980*

Scottish libraries 1978-1980 : a triennial review / compiled by Robert Craig. — Glasgow : Scottish Library Association, 1981. — 47p : ill,1plan ; 21cm
ISBN 0-900649-26-7 (pbk) : Unpriced
B81-30688

027.4 — PUBLIC LIBRARIES

027.4'025'421 — London. Public libraries — *Directories — For students of City of London Polytechnic*

Libraries of London / City of London Polytechnic. — 4th ed. — [London] ([Calcutta House Precinct, Old Castle St., E1 7NT]) : [City of London Polytechnic], 1980. — 54p ; 17cm
Previous ed.: 1979. — Bibliography: p48. — Includes index
ISBN 0-904264-51-3 (pbk) : £1.00
Primary classification 026'.0025'421 B81-16051

027.441 — Great Britain. Public libraries — *Comparative studies*

Centre for Interfirm Comparison. Inter-library comparisons. — London : British Library, Research & Development Dept., July 1981. — [136]p. — (British Library research & development report series, ISSN 0308-2385 ; 5638)
ISBN 0-905984-74-9 : £7.50 : CIP entry
B81-23891

027.441 — Great Britain. Public libraries — *Conference proceedings*

Public Library Authorities Conference *(1980 : Southport)*. Proceedings of the Public Library Authorities Conference 1980 : papers presented to the Public Library Authorities Conference at Southport, 6-9th October 1980. — Penzance (Penzance Library, Morrab Rd., Penzance, Cornwall TR18 3EY) : Public Libraries Group of the Library Association, 1980. — 66p ; 22cm
ISBN 0-85365-983-4 (pbk) : £4.95 B81-32345

027.441 — Great Britain. Public libraries. Effectiveness. Evaluation. Attitudes of librarians

Bird, Jean, *1946-*. Assessing effectiveness : a preliminary study of the views of public librarians, Septembert 1979-May 1980 / by Jean Bird. — London (207 Essex Rd., N1 3PN) : Polytechnic of North London, School of Librarianship, 1981. — 78p ; 30cm. — (Research report / Polytechnic of North London. School of Librarianship, ISSN 0143-8549 ; no.5) (British Library R & D reports ; 5632)
ISBN 0-900639-18-0 (pbk) : £3.00 B81-24078

027.441'0212 — Great Britain. Public libraries — *Statistics — Serials*

Public library statistics. Actuals / CIPFA Statistical Information Service. — 1979-80. — London : Chartered Institute of Public Finance and Accountancy, 1981. — 27p
ISSN 0309-6629 : £10.00 B81-26379

Public library statistics. Estimates / CIPFA Statistical Information Service. — 1980-81. — London : Chartered Institute of Public Finance and Accountancy, 1980. — 8p
ISSN 0307-0522 : £5.00 B81-06786

027.4423'7 — Cornwall. Small communities. Public libraries. Services. Organisation

Pybus, Ron L.. Library services to small communities : alternative solutions to a common problem / Ron L. Pybus. — Truro (c/o 11, Cryon View, Truro, Cornwall TR1 3JT) : Branch and Mobile Libraries Group of the Library Association, 1981. — 12p ; 21cm. — (Occasional papers / Libraries Group of the Library Association ; no.11)
Text on inside back cover
ISBN 0-85365-604-5 (pbk) : £1.30 (£1.00 to Group members) B81-15682

027.4423'8 — Somerset. Public libraries. Services — *Inquiry reports*

Public library services points in Somerset : an appraisal report to the Libraries, Museums and Records Committee of Somerset County Council, 4th June, 1980 / Roger Stoakley. — Bridgwater (Mount St., Bridgwater, Somerset TA6 3ES) : Somerset County Library, 1980. — 28p,[4]fold.leaves of plates : 4maps ; 30cm
ISBN 0-86183-014-8 (pbk) : £1.00 B81-29513

027.473 — United States. Public libraries. Services — *Conference proceedings*

The **Changing** role of public libraries : background papers from the White House Conference / compiled by Whitney North Seymour, Jr. — Metuchen ; London : Scarecrow, 1980. — 270p in various pagings ; 23cm
Bibliography: p269-270
ISBN 0-8108-1333-5 : £10.50 B81-07677

027.5 — GOVERNMENT LIBRARIES

027.5 — National libraries

Chandler, George. International and national library and information services. — Oxford : Pergamon, Jan.1982. — [230]p. — (Recent advances in library and information services ; v.2)
ISBN 0-08-025793-3 : £10.00 : CIP entry
Primary classification 020'.621 B81-34467

027.5'025'42 — England. Record repositories — *Directories*

Gibson, Jeremy. Record offices : how to find them / Jeremy Gibson and Pamela Peskett. — Plymouth (96 Beaumont St. Milehouse, Plymouth, Devon PL2 3AQ) : Federation of Family History Societies, 1981. — 40p : chiefly maps ; 21cm
Text, map on inside covers
ISBN 0-907099-10-6 (pbk) : Unpriced
B81-39996

027.541 — Great Britain. ***Parliament.*** **Information services & libraries**

Englefield, Dermot J. T.. Parliament and information : the Westminster scene / Dermot Englefield. — London : Library Association, 1981. — vii,132p : 2plans ; 24cm
Includes index
ISBN 0-85365-570-7 (cased) : Unpriced
ISBN 0-85365-993-1 (pbk) : Unpriced
B81-10859

027.541 — Great Britain. ***Public Record Office*** — *Serials*

Great Britain. *Public Record Office*. The ... annual report of the Keeper of Public Records on the Work of the Public Record Office. — 21st (1979). — London : H.M.S.O., 1980. — iii,36p
ISBN 0-10-028019-6 : £3.20 B81-19701

027.5417'022'2 — Ireland ***(Republic).*** **National libraries: National Library of Ireland,** ***to 1979*** — *Illustrations*

Illustrations to the history of the National Library of Ireland. — Dublin ([G.P.O. Arcade, Dublin]) : Stationery Office, 1979. — 32p : ill,1map,ports ; 13x18cm. — (Centenary series ; no.1)
£0.50 (pbk) B81-07501

027.6 — LIBRARIES FOR SPECIAL GROUPS AND SPECIFIC ORGANISATIONS

027.6'22 — Great Britain. Public libraries. Services to day centres for old persons — *Case studies*

Do books still matter? : the library and information needs of the elderly in community day centres : report on a one year project / funded jointly by the Beth Johnson Foundation and the Manpower Services Commission, February 1977-February 1980 ; Michael Simes ... [et al.]. — [Leeds] ([Calverley St., Leeds, LS1 3HE]) : Public Libraries Management Research Unit, School of Librarianship, Leeds Polytechnic, 1980. — 165p : ill,facsims,1form ; 30cm
Cover title. — Bibliography: p108-111
ISBN 0-900738-22-7 (pbk) : £10.00 B81-14476

027.62'5 — Great Britain. Libraries. Services for handicapped children

Marshall, Margaret R.. Libraries and the handicapped child / Margaret R. Marshall. — London : Deutsch, 1981. — 205p ; 23cm
Includes bibliographies and index
ISBN 0-233-97299-4 : £8.95 : CIP rev.
B80-23944

027.62'5 — Libraries. Stock: Children's books — *Conference proceedings*

University of Chicago. *Graduate Library School. Conference (41st : 1980 : Chicago)*. Children in libraries : patterns of access to materials and services in school and public libraries : proceedings of the forty-first Conference of the Graduate Library School, May 16-17, 1980 / edited by Zena Sutherland. — Chicago ; London : University of Chicago Press, c1981. — 89p ; 24cm. — (The University of Chicago studies in library science)
Originally published: in Library quarterly. Vol.51 no.1, Jan.1981
ISBN 0-226-78063-5 : £7.00 B81-38906

027.62'6 — Libraries. Services for slow reading adolescents

High low handbook : books, materials, and services for the teenage problem reader / compiled and edited by Ellen V. Libretto. — New York ; London : Bowker, 1981. — xvi,210p : ill ; 24cm. — (Serving special populations series)
Includes bibliographies and index
ISBN 0-8352-1340-4 : Unpriced B81-39042

027.6'3 — Great Britain. Public libraries. Services for disadvantaged persons — *Conference proceedings*

Serving all the community : Library services to the disadvantaged : a collection of papers presented at a seminar organised by the South Western Branch of the Library Association and held at the Rozel Hotel, Weston-super-Mare, November 11th-13th, 1979 / compiled and edited by John Loosley. — Weston-super-Mare : Library Association, South Western Branch, c1981. — 52p ; 30cm
Cover title
ISBN 0-85365-544-8 (pbk) : £7.00 B81-18448

027.6'3 — London. Libraries. Services. Requirements of native language schools

Elliott, Pirkko. Library needs of children attending self-help mother-tongue schools in London / by Pirkko Elliott. — London : School of Librarianship, the Polytechnic of North London, 1981. — 118p : ill ; 30cm. — (Research report / Polytechnic of North London. School of Librarianship, ISSN 0143-8549 ; no.6)
Cover title: Library needs of mother-tongue schools in London. — Bibliography: p71-72. — Includes index
ISBN 0-900639-19-9 (pbk) : £3.40 B81-29953

027.6'3 — United States. Libraries. Services for Hispanic Americans

Haro, Robert P.. Developing library and information services for Americans of Hispanic origin / by Robert P. Haro. — Metuchen ; London : Scarecrow, 1981. — xvi,286p ; 23cm
Bibliography: p245-261. — Includes index
ISBN 0-8108-1394-7 : £12.25 B81-29217

027.6'62'0942 — Great Britain. Hospitals. Libraries

Hospital libraries and work with the disabled in the community. — 3rd ed. — London : Library Association, Oct.1981. — [240]p
Previous ed.: 1973
ISBN 0-85365-723-8 : £12.50 : CIP entry
B81-27997

027.6'63 — Libraries. Services for mentally handicapped persons

Pearlman, Della. No choice : library services for the mentally handicapped. — London : Library Association, Dec.1981. — [96]p
ISBN 0-85365-543-x (pbk) : £9.00 : CIP entry
B81-31508

027.6'65 — South Yorkshire ***(Metropolitan County).*** **Hatfield. Borstals. Libraries: Hatfield Borstal.** *Library*

Hatfield Borstal : a survey of library provision to trainees, February '81. — Doncaster : Doncaster Library Service, c1981. — 15p : 2plans ; 22cm
ISBN 0-906976-02-2 (pbk) : £1.00 B81-34693

027.6'65'0942 — England. Prisons. Libraries. Standards — *Proposals*

Prison libraries : Library Association guidelines for library provision in prison department establishment. — London : Library Association, 1981. — 63p : 1ill ; 21cm
Bibliography: p62-63
ISBN 0-85365-614-2 (pbk) : Unpriced : CIP rev. B81-08860

027.7 — COLLEGE AND UNIVERSITY LIBRARIES

027.7'06'041 — Great Britain. Academic libraries. Organisations: Library Association. ***University, College and Research Section*** — *Serials*

[Newsletter *(Library Association. University, College and Research Section)*]. Newsletter / University, College and Research Section of the Library Association. — No.1 (June 1980)-. — Newcastle upon Tyne (c/o A.C. McDonald, University Library, Newcastle upon Tyne NE1 7RU) : The Section, 1980-. — v. ; 30cm
Three issues yearly
ISSN 0144-056x = Newsletter — University, College and Research Section of the Library Association : Free to Section members only
B81-06780

027.7'068 — United States. Academic libraries. Management. Evaluation. Research projects: Management Review and Analysis Program

Johnson, Edward R.. Organization development for academic libraries : an evaluation of the Management Review and Analysis Program / Edward R. Johnson and Stuart H. Mann. — Westport ; London : Greenwood Press, 1980. — 199p : ill,1facsim,forms ; 22cm. — (Contributions in librarianship and information science ; no.28)
Bibliography: p187-193. - Includes index
ISBN 0-313-21373-9 : Unpriced B81-05482

027.7'09 — Universities. Libraries, ***to 1979***

University library history : an international review / edited by James Thompson. — New York : Saur ; London : Bingley, 1980. — vi,330p,[9]p of plates : ill ; 23cm
Includes index
ISBN 0-85157-304-5 : £14.75 : CIP rev.
B80-11719

027.7'0941 — Great Britain. Higher education institutions. Libraries

Roe, Ernest. Academics, librarians, resource management and resource use : a preliminary study / Ernest Roe. — London : British Library, 1981. — vi,83p ; 30cm. — (British Library research and development reports, ISSN 0308-2385 ; no.5649)
Includes bibliographies
ISBN 0-905984-77-3 (pbk) : Unpriced
B81-38998

027.7'0973 — United States. Academic libraries — *Conference proceedings*

Essays from the New England Academic Librarians' Writing Seminar / edited by Norman D. Stevens. — Metuchen ; London : Scarecrow, 1980. — vi,224p ; 23cm
Bibliography: p194-196
ISBN 0-8108-1365-3 : £8.75 B81-17100

027.7'0995'3 — Papua New Guinea. Universities. Libraries. Development

Baker, Leigh R.. Development of university libraries in Papua New Guinea / by Leigh R. Baker. — Metuchen, N.J. ; London : Scarecrow Press, 1981. — xi,399p : ill,maps ; 23cm
Bibliography: p354-378. - Includes index
ISBN 0-8108-1393-9 : £14.00 B81-29226

027.7424'96'09 — West Midlands ***(Metropolitan County).*** **Birmingham. Universities. Libraries: University of Birmingham.** ***Library, to 1980***

Evans, Hywel Berwyn. The library over a hundred years (1880-1980) / by Hywel Berwyn Evans. — [Birmingham] : University of Birmingham, 1981. — 10p : ill ; 22cm
Cover title
ISBN 0-7044-0555-5 (pbk) : £0.50 B81-29569

027.7425'74'09 — Oxfordshire. Oxford. Universities. Libraries: Bodleian Library, *1700-1800*

Noel-Tod, Alex. The Bodleian Library in the eighteenth century with reference to Oxford college libraries and the Radcliffe Library / Alex Noel-Tod. — [Aberystwyth] ([Llanbadarn Fawr, Aberystwyth, Dyfed SY23 3AS]) : College of Librarianship Wales, 1980. — 42p,[2]leaves of plates : 2ill,2plans ; 30cm
Bibliography: p35-37
ISBN 0-904020-35-5 (pbk) : £1.50 B81-06114

027.7425'74'09 — Oxfordshire. Oxford. Universities. Libraries: Bodleian Library, *1845-1945*

Bodleian Library. History of the Bodleian Library 1845-1945 / by Sir Edmund Craster. — Oxford : The Library, 1981. — xi,371p,[12]p of plates : ill,2facsims,3plans,ports ; 24cm
Originally published: Oxford : O.U.P., 1952
ISBN 0-900177-79-9 : Unpriced B81-24911

027.7425'95 — Buckinghamshire. High Wycombe. Colleges of higher education. Libraries: Buckinghamshire College of Higher Education. *Library — Visitors' guides*

Buckinghamshire College of Higher Education. Library guide / Bucks College of Higher Education, High Wycombe. — High Wycombe (Queen Alexandra Rd., High Wycombe, Bucks. HP11 2JZ) : [The College], [1981?]. — 4p ; 21cm
Cover title
ISBN 0-86059-163-8 (pbk) : Unpriced B81-25601

027.7426'59 — Cambridgeshire. Cambridge. Universities. Colleges. Libraries: Emmanuel College. *Library, to 1980*

Emmanuel College. *Library*. A brief history of Emmanuel College Library / Frank Stubbings. — [Cambridge] ([Cambridge CB2 3AP]) : [Emmanuel College Library], 1981. — 21p,8p of plates : ill,2facsims ; 21cm
Text on inside cover. — Bibliography: p21
Unpriced (pbk) B81-34973

027.7426'59 — Cambridgeshire. Cambridge. Universities. Colleges. Libraries: University of Cambridge. *Trinity College. Library, to 1695*

Gaskell, Philip. Trinity College Library : the first 150 years / Philip Gaskell. — Cambridge : Cambridge University Press, 1980. — xix,275p : ill,facsims,plans ; 24cm. — (The Sandars Lectures ; 1978-9)
Includes index
ISBN 0-521-23100-0 : £30.00 B81-08072

027.8 — SCHOOL LIBRARIES

027.8'06'041 — Great Britain. Schools. Libraries. Organisations: Library Association. *School Libraries Group — Serials*

[**News** *(Library Association. School Libraries Group)*]. News / Library Association, School Libraries Group. — Issue no.1 (Winter 1980)-. — London (c/o 1 Skelgill Rd, SW15) : The Group, 1980-. — v. ; 23cm
Two issues yearly. — Description based on: Issue no.2 (Summer 1980)
ISSN 0261-1678 = News - Library Association School Libraries Group : £2.00 per year (free to members) B81-21925

027.8'068 — Great Britain. Schools. Libraries. Administration — *Proposals*

School Library Association. The way ahead : the organization and staffing of libraries and learning resources in schools in the 1980s. — Oxford : School Library Association, 1980. — 28p : ill ; 21cm
ISBN 0-900641-38-x (pbk) : £1.30 (£0.90 to members) B81-09270

027.8'0971 — Canada. Schools. Libraries. Organisations

Kogon, Marilyn H.. Organizing the school library : a Canadian handbook / Marilyn H. Kogon and George Whalen ; foreword by Doris Pauline Fennell. — Toronto ; London : McGraw-Hill Ryerson, c1980. — xviii,268p : ill,facsims,forms ; 24cm
Bibliography: p247. — Includes index
ISBN 0-07-077833-7 : £12.25 B81-01529

027.8'0973 — United States. Schools. Libraries. Cooperation with public libraries

Woolard, Wilman Lee Broughton. Combined school/public libraries : a survey with conclusions and recommendations / Wilma Lee Broughton Woolard. — Metuchen ; London : Scarecrow, 1980. — xix,184p : forms ; 23cm
Bibliography: p83-102. - Includes index
ISBN 0-8108-1335-1 : £7.70 B81-09373

028.1 — BOOK REVIEWS

028.1'05 — Books in English — *Reviews — Serials*

Book choice. — No.1 (Jan.1981)-. — London (Park Lane Hotel, Piccadilly W1Y 8BX) : [Gradegate], 1981-. — v. : ill ; 28cm
Monthly. — Description based on: No.2 (Feb.1981)
ISSN 0261-4227 = Book choice : £8.50 per year B81-26589

The **Library** journal book review. — 1980. — New York ; London : Bowker, 1981. — vii,789p
ISBN 0-8352-1344-7 : Unpriced B81-33307

028.1'37 — Videorecordings — *Reviews — Serials*

Video review. — Dec.1980-. — Sutton : IPC Business Press, 1980-. — v. : ill,ports ; 30cm
Monthly
ISSN 0261-3263 = Video review : £10.00 per year
Primary classification 621.388 B81-25475

Video today. — Oct.1980-. — London : Modmags ; London : Argus Press Sales & Distribution [distributor], 1980-. — v. : ill (some col.),ports ; 29cm
Monthly
ISSN 0144-6010 = Video today : £10.00 per year
Primary classification 621.388 B81-25476

028.1'38 — Sound cassette tape recordings. Reviews — *Serials — For librarianship*

Cassette scrutiny : a journal for librarians & library users. — Jan. 1981-. — London (Woodlands Ave., Acton W3 9DN) : Ealing College of Higher Education, School of Library and Information Studies, 1981-. — v. ; 30cm
Monthly
£12.00 per year B81-13091

028.1'62'05 — Children's books — *Reviews*

Sutherland, Zena. The best in children's books : the University of Chicago guide to children's literature 1973-1978 / written and edited by Zena Sutherland. — Chicago ; London : University of Chicago Press, 1980. — xii,547p ; 24cm
Includes index
ISBN 0-226-78059-7 : £10.50 B81-01881

028.5 — READING AND USE OF OTHER INFORMATION MEDIA BY CHILDREN AND YOUNG ADULTS

028.5 — Children's books

The **Signal** approach to children's books : a collection / edited by Nancy Chambers. — Harmondsworth : Kestrel, 1980. — 352p : ill ; 23cm
Includes index
ISBN 0-7226-5641-6 : £12.50 B81-02217

028.5 — Children's books — *Critical studies*

Tucker, Nicholas. The child and the book : a psychological and literary exploration / Nicholas Tucker. — Cambridge : Cambridge University Press, 1981. — ix,259p ; 23cm
Bibliography: p244-251. — Includes index
ISBN 0-521-23251-1 : £15.00 B81-15335

028.5 — Children's books in English

Darton, F. J. Harvey. Children's books in England. — 3rd ed. — Cambridge : Cambridge University Press, Dec.1981. — [398]p
Previous ed.: 1958
ISBN 0-521-24020-4 : £12.95 : CIP entry B81-37003

028.5 — Children's books — *Serials*

[**Bookmark** *(Edinburgh)*]. Bookmark. — 1 (May 1978)-. — [Edinburgh] ([Holyrood Rd., Edinburgh EH8 8AQ]) : English Department, Moray House College of Education], 1978-. — v. : ill ; 21x30cm
Three issues yearly. — Description based on: 6 (Spring 1980)
ISSN 0260-0315 = Bookmark (Edinburgh) : £2.00 per year

028.5'34 — Ontario. Toronto. Public libraries. Stock: Illustrated children's books: Books with English imprints, *to 1910.* **Collections: Osborne Collection of Early Children's Books**

English illustrated books for children : a descriptive companion to a selection from the Osborne Collection / edited by Margaret Crawford Maloney. — Tokyo : Holp Shuppan ; London : Bodley Head, 1981. — 88p : ill(some col.) ; 22cm
Originally published: Tokyo : Holp Shuppan, 1979. — In slip-case. — Includes index
ISBN 0-370-30371-7 : Unpriced B81-33244

028.5'5 — Reading — *For children*

Allington, Richard L.. Beginning to learn about reading. — Oxford : Blackwell, Aug.1981. — [32]p
ISBN 0-86256-041-1 : £2.50 : CIP entry B81-19155

028.7 — USE OF BOOKS AND OTHER MEDIA AS SOURCES OF INFORMATION

028.7 — Reference books — *Questions & answers*

Taylor, Margaret T.. Basic reference sources : a self-study manual / Margaret T. Taylor and Ronald R. Powell. — 2nd ed. — Metuchen, N.J. ; London : Scarecrow Press, 1981. — xvi,299p ; 28cm
Previous ed.: 1973. — Includes index
ISBN 0-8108-1410-2 (pbk) : £9.45 B81-29227

028.7 — Reference books. Use — *For illiterate adults*

Using your reference skills / [compiled by Linda Storey]. — Leeds (Leeds Adult Literacy Scheme, 27 Harrogate Rd., Leeds 7) : Printed Resources Unit for Continuing Education, c1979. — 31p : ill,2maps,facsims,1form ; 21cm
Cover title
Unpriced (pbk) B81-15719

028.7 — Reference books. Use — *For schools*

Weston, Paul. Look up, find out. — London : Bell & Hyman, Sept.1981. — [64]p
ISBN 0-7135-1266-0 (pbk) : £1.75 : CIP entry B81-23751

028.9 — READING INTERESTS AND HABITS

028'.9 — Fiction in English. American writers. Hemingway, Ernest. Reading habits, *1910-1940*

Reynolds, Michael S.. Hemingway's reading 1910-1940 : an inventory / Michael S. Reynolds. — Princeton ; Guildford : Princeton University Press, c1981. — x,236p ; 24cm
Includes index
ISBN 0-691-06447-4 : £9.80 B81-16141

028'.9'0899510421 — London. Chinese immigrants. Reading habits — *For librarianship*

Simsova, Sylva. The library needs of the Chinese in London : interim report / Sylva Simsova, Wey Tze Chin. — London (207 Essex Rd., Islington, N1 3PN) : School of Librarianship, Polytechnic of North London, 1981. — 104p in various pagings : maps ; 30cm. — (Report ; no.5634)
English and Chinese text
Unpriced (spiral) B81-24249

031 — AMERICAN ENCYCLOPAEDIAS

031 — Children's encyclopaedias in English: American encyclopaedias — *Texts*

Childcraft : the how and why library / [editorial director William H. Nault]. — Chicago ; London : World-Book-Childcraft International, c1979. — 15v. : ill(some col.),col.maps,music,facsims,ports(some col.) ; 26cm
Includes bibliographies and index
ISBN 0-7166-0179-6 : Unpriced B81-11841

031′.02 — Miscellaneous facts — *American collections*

Asimov, Isaac. The book of facts. — London : Hodder & Stoughton. — (Coronet books)
Originally published: 1980
Vol.2. — Dec.1981. — [336]p
ISBN 0-340-27268-6 : £1.50 : CIP entry
B81-31467

Asimov, Isaac. Isaac Asimov's book of facts. — London : Hodder and Stoughton, Apr.1981
Originally published: New York : Red Dembner Enterprises Corp., 1979 ; London : Hodder and Stoughton, 1980
Vol.1. — [560]p
ISBN 0-340-26218-4 (pbk) : £1.25 : CIP entry
B81-02650

May, John, *1950-*. Curious facts / John May with Michael Marten ... [et al.]. — London : Secker & Warburg, 1981, c1980. — xi,319p ; 24cm
Originally published: New York : Holt, Rinehart and Winston, 1980. — Includes index
ISBN 0-436-27438-8 (cased) : £7.95
ISBN 0-436-27439-6 (pbk) : £2.95 B81-10621

The **People's** almanac presents the book of lists 2 / by Irving Wallace ... [et al.]. — London : Corgi, 1981, c1980. — xx,529p : ill,1map,ports ; 18cm
Originally published: London: Elm Tree, 1980. — Includes index
ISBN 0-552-11681-5 (pbk) : £1.95 B81-27822

Storer, Doug. Encyclopedia of amazing but true facts / Doug Storer. — New York : Sterling ; London : Oak Tree, c1980. — 448p : ill,ports ; 22cm
Includes index
ISBN 0-7061-2692-0 : £5.95 B81-00693

032 — ENGLISH ENCYCLOPAEDIAS

032 — Children's encyclopaedias in English — *Texts*

Explorer encyclopedia / edited by Bill Bruce ; contributors Michael Chinery ... [et al.]. — London : Watts, 1981. — 223p : ill(some col.),maps(some col.),col.ports ; 23cm
Includes index
ISBN 0-85166-940-9 : £4.99 B81-34681

Ten Kate, Lynn. My favourite encyclopedia / Lynn ten Kate. — London : Hamlyn, 1981. — 70p : col.ill ; 33cm
Includes index
ISBN 0-600-33202-0 : £2.75 B81-32359

032 — Encyclopaedias in English — *Texts*

Collins double book encyclopedia & dictionary : with 293 colour photographs. — Rev. ed. — London : Collins, 1981. — 575,444p,[32]p of plates : ill(some col.),maps,ports ; 22cm
Previous ed.: 1968
ISBN 0-00-434337-9 : £6.95
Primary classification 423 B81-39289

Collins family encyclopedia. — London : Collins, 1981. — 506p : ill,maps ; 19cm
' ... based on and abridged from Collins concise encyclopedia' — title pager verso
ISBN 0-00-434320-4 : £3.95 B81-39550

The **Macmillan** encyclopedia / [editor Alan Isaacs]. — London : Macmillan, 1981. — 1336p,[32]p of plates : ill(some col.),charts,maps(some col.),plans,ports ; 26cm
Charts on lining papers
ISBN 0-333-27860-7 : £14.95 B81-27012

The **New** Caxton encyclopedia. — [5th ed.] / [editor Graham Clarke]. — London : Caxton, c1979. — 20v. : ill(some col.),col.charts,col.maps,facsims(some col.),col.plans,ports(some col.) ; 31cm
Previous ed.: / edited by Bernard A. Workman, 1977. — Includes index
ISBN 0-7014-0056-0 : £485.00 (£260.00 to educational institutions) B81-00694

032′.02 — English encyclopaedias. Books of miscellaneous facts — *Texts*

Pile, Stephen, *1949-*. The book of heroic failures : the official handbook of the Not Terribly Good Club of Great Britain / by Stephen Pile ; with cartoons by Bill Tidy. — London : Futura, 1980, c1979. — 216p : ill ; 18cm
Originally published: London : Routledge and Kegan Paul, 1979
ISBN 0-7088-1908-7 (pbk) : £0.95 B81-00003

032′.02 — Miscellaneous facts — *Collections*

The **Book** of comparisons of distance, size, area, volume, mass, weight, density, energy, temperature, time, speed and number throughout the universe / by the Diagram Group. — London : Sidgwick & Jackson in association with Penguin, 1980. — 240p : ill(some col.),charts (some col.), maps(some col.),facsims,ports ; 29cm
Includes index
ISBN 0-283-98617-4 : £6.95 B81-04919

Davies, Hunter. Book of British lists / Hunter Davies. — Feltham : Hamlyn, 1980. — xvii,222p ; 18cm
ISBN 0-600-20267-4 (pbk) : £1.25 B81-04920

032′.02 — Miscellaneous facts — *Collections — For children*

Boys' handbook. — London : Octopus, 1981. — 252p : ill,charts,maps,ports ; 22cm
Includes index
ISBN 0-7064-1545-0 : £1.99 B81-20281

The **Girls'** handbook. — London : Octopus, 1981. — 252p : ill,1chart,maps,ports ; 22cm
Includes index
ISBN 0-7064-1546-9 : £1.99 B81-20280

032′.02 — Persons — *Records of achievement*

The **Guinness** book of amazing people / edited by Shirley Greenway ; illustrated with photographs. — [London] : Piccolo, 1981. — 96p : ill,ports ; 20cm. — (Piccolo young Guinness series)
ISBN 0-330-26451-6 (pbk) : £0.95 B81-27063

032′.02 — Records of achievement — *Collections*

Russell, Alan. More record breakers / Alan Russell. — London : British Broadcasting Corporation, 1980. — 78p : ill(some col.),facsims,col.maps,music,ports ; 27cm
Text on inside cover
ISBN 0-563-17846-9 : £3.50 B81-04474

032′.02 — Records of achievement — *Collections — For children*

Cunningham, Bronnie. Cunningham's little red record book / Bronnie Cunningham ; illustrated by Rowan Barnes-Murphy. — Harmondsworth : Puffin, 1981. — 191p : ill ; 19cm
Text on inside cover
ISBN 0-14-031334-6 (pbk) : £0.95 B81-21036

032′.02 — Records of achievement — *Collections — Serials*

Guinness book of records. — Ed.27 (1981). — Enfield : Guinness Superlatives, c1980. — 349p
ISBN 0-900424-98-2 : Unpriced
ISSN 0300-1679 B81-03513

Guinness book of records. — 28th ed. (1982). — Enfield : Guinness Superlatives, Oct.1981. — [352]p
ISBN 0-85112-232-9 : £4.99 : CIP entry
B81-24647

032′.02 — Speed — *Records of achievement*

The **Guinness** book of fastest and slowest / edited by Shirley Greenway ; illustrated with photographs. — [London] : Piccolo, 1981. — 95p : ill,ports ; 20cm. — (Piccolo young Guinness series)
ISBN 0-330-26452-4 (pbk) : £0.95 B81-23560

032′.02′05 — Miscellaneous facts — *Collections — Serials*

[Whitaker's almanack]. An almanack ... established 1868 by Joseph Whitaker. — Library ed.. — 1979. — London : Whitaker, 1978. — xii,1220p
ISBN 0-85021-108-5 : £7.50
ISBN 0-85021-106-9 (cloth ed.) : £5.75
ISBN 0-85021-107-7 (pbk) : £2.80
ISSN 0083-9256 B81-29445

[Whitaker's almanack]. An almanack ... established 1868 by Joseph Whitaker. — Library ed.. — 1980. — London : Whitaker, 1979. — xvi,1220p
ISBN 0-85021-116-6 : £9.00
ISBN 0-85021-114-x (cloth ed.) : £6.80
ISBN 0-85021-115-8 (pbk) : £3.20
ISSN 0083-9256 B81-29446

[Whitaker's almanack]. An almanack ... established 1868 by Joseph Whitaker. — Library ed.. — 1981. — London : Whitaker, 1980. — xvi,1196p
ISBN 0-85021-123-9 : £11.00
ISBN 0-85021-121-2 (cloth ed.) : £8.20
ISBN 0-85021-122-0 (pbk) : £3.90 B81-29447

039 — ENCYCLOPAEDIAS IN MINOR EUROPEAN AND NON-EUROPEAN LANGUAGES

039′.9166 — Children's encyclopaedias in Welsh — *Texts*

Jones, D. Gwyn. Chwilota / D. Gwyn Jones. — [Caerdydd] : Gwasg Prifysgol Cymru
Cyfrol 3. — 1981. — vii,133p : ill(some col.),col.maps,1plan,ports ; 31cm
ISBN 0-7083-0802-3 : Unpriced : CIP rev.
B81-10462

050 — GENERAL SERIAL PUBLICATIONS AND THEIR INDEXES

050′.25 — Serials — *Directories — Serials*

Willing's press guide. — 107th annual ed. (1981). — East Grinstead : Thomas Skinner Directories, 1981. — 932p
ISBN 0-611-00648-0 : Unpriced
ISSN 0000-0213
Also classified at 070′.025 B81-22402

052 — ENGLISH SERIALS

052 — Children's serials in English — *Texts*

[The Egg *(Junior Puffin Club)***]**. The Egg : the magazine of the Junior Puffin Club. — Vol.1, no.1 (Autumn 1978)-. — Harmondsworth (Penguin Books, Bath Rd, Harmondsworth, Middx) : The Club, 1978-. — v. : ill ; 20cm
Quarterly
ISSN 0142-3207 = Egg (Junior Puffin Club) : Free to Club members B81-33720

052 — General serials in English — *Texts*

Creative mind : arts and phenomena. — 1-. — Liverpool (26 Linnet La., Liverpool L17 3BQ) : Creative Mind, 1978-. — v. : ill,ports ; 31cm
Quarterly. — Description based on: 5
ISSN 0260-8278 = Creative mind : £1.60 per year B81-09025

First class : the official magazine for the International Airline Passengers Association Inc. — [No.1]-. — London (c/o Suzanne Fields and Associates, 2nd Floor, 34 Brook St, W1) : Rolmaston, [1981]-. — v. : ill,ports ; 30cm
Six issues yearly
ISSN 0261-2771 = First class : £1.00 per issue
B81-33731

[Foresight *(Hastings)***]Foresight** : large print newspaper. — No.1 (Nov. 14th 1980)-. — Hastings (15, Sussex Chambers, Havelock Rd., Hastings, East Sussex TW34 1DE) : Fairlight Publications, 1980-. — v. ; 39cm
Weekly
ISSN 0261-0442 = Foresight (Hastings) : £13.00 per year B81-15449

052 — General serials in English — *Texts continuation*

Greater London living : incorporating Jobs weekly. — Apr.25-. — London (11 St Bride St., EC4) : Jobs Weekly, [1981]-. — v. : ill,ports ; 29cm
Weekly. — Continues: Jobs weekly
ISSN 0261-6750 = Greater London living : £0.20 B81-32703

The **Irish** woman : [the official journal of the Irish Countrywomen's Association]. — Vol.1, no.1 (Sept.1978)-. — Dublin (48 North Great George's St., Dublin 1) : GP Pub., 1978-. — v. : ill(some col.),ports ; 29cm
Description based on: Vol.2, no.1 (Sept.1979)
£0.40 B81-00695

Life and leisure monthly. — Vol.1, no.1 (May/June 1980)-. — Worksop (33 Bridge St., Worksop S80 1DD) : Sissons, 1980-. — v. : ill ; 28cm. — (Worksop guardian series)
ISSN 0143-988x = Life and leisure monthly : £0.12 per issue B81-00696

One earth image. — [Vol.1, issue 1] (Feb./Mar.1980)-v.1, issue 3 (June/July 1980). — Forres : Findhorn Foundation, 1980-1980. — 3v. : ill ; 30cm
Six issues yearly. — Continued by: One earth (1980). — Merger of: Open letter ; and, One earth (1975)
ISSN 0143-8247 = One earth image : £4.50 per year B81-00697

Period piece & paperback : a bimonthly review of books, leisure & the arts - past, present & future. —.Vol.1, no.1 (Oct.1979)-. — Bournemouth (26 Ashley Rd, Boscombe, Bournemouth) : Boscombe Books, 1979-. — v. : ill ; 21cm
Description based on: Vol.1, no.5 (Nov.1980)
£2.50 per year B81-06103

052 — General serials in English — *Texts — Facsimiles*

The **Adventurer** / edited with introductory notes by Donald D. Eddy. — New York ; London : Garland, 1978. — 2v. ; 29cm. — (Samuel Johnson & periodical literature ; 3)
Facsim of: Bi-weekly issues published: London : S.n., 1753-1754
ISBN 0-8240-3428-7 : Unpriced B81-33589

The **Literary** magazine / edited with introductory notes by Donald D. Eddy. — New York ; London : Garland, 1978. — 3v. : ill(some col.),maps,music ; 23cm. — (Samuel Johnson & periodical literature)
Facsim of: monthly issues published: London : s.n., 1756-1758. — Includes index
ISBN 0-8240-3430-9 : £144.00 B81-15059

The **Rambler** / edited with introductory notes by Donald D. Eddy. — New York ; London : Garland, 1978. — 2v.(1244p) ; 26cm. — (Samuel Johnson & periodical literature ; 1)
Facsim of: Bi-weekly issues published: London : S.n., 1750-1752
ISBN 0-8240-3426-0 : Unpriced B81-33588

The **Student,** or, The Oxford and Cambridge monthly miscellany / edited with introductory notes by Donald D. Eddy. — New York ; London : Garland, 1979. — 2v. : ill ; 23cm. — (Samuel Johnson & periodical literature ; 2)
Facsim of: monthly issues published: Oxford : S.n., 1750-1751. — Includes index
ISBN 0-8240-3427-9 : Unpriced B81-33587

The **Test**. bound with The Con-test / edited with introductory notes by Donald D. Eddy. — New York ; London : Garland, 1979. — 204,288p ; 29cm. — (Samuel Johnson & periodical literature ; 6)
Facsim of: Weekly issues published: London : S.n., 1758
ISBN 0-8240-3431-7 : Unpriced B81-33590

The **Universal** Visiter / edited with introductory notes by Donald D. Eddy. — New York ; London : Garland, 1979. — vii,580p,[1]folded leaf of plates : ill,music,1plan ; 23cm. — (Samuel Johnson & periodical literature ; 4)
Facsim of: monthly issues published: London : S.n., 1756
ISBN 0-8240-3429-5 : Unpriced B81-33586

052 — Periodicals with British imprints, *1830-1900 — Critical studies*

The **Victorian** periodical press. — Leicester : Leicester University Press, Feb.1982. — [400]p
ISBN 0-7185-1190-5 : £30.00 : CIP entry B81-35852

052 — Serials for girls — *Texts*

[Girl *(London : 1981)***]**. Girl. — No.1 (14th Feb.1981)-. — London : IPC Magazines, 1981-. — v. : chiefly ill ; 30cm
Weekly
ISSN 0261-6726 = Girl (London. 1981) : £0.20 per issue B81-32254

055 — ITALIAN, ROMANIAN, RHAETO-ROMANIC SERIALS

055′.91 — General serials in Romanian — *Texts*

Orizonturi Românești. — [Anul 1, nr.1 (1978)]-. — [London] ([c/o Rev. C. Alecse, St. Dunstan's in the West, 184A Fleet St., EC4]) : [Biserica Ortodoxă Romană din Londra], 1978. — v. ; 21cm
Irregular
ISSN 0144-7807 = Orizonturi Românești : Unpriced B81-25007

059 — SERIALS IN MINOR EUROPEAN AND NON-EUROPEAN LANGUAGES

059′.91439 — Serials for Pakistani immigrants in West Midlands *(Metropolitan County):* **Serials for Pakistani immigrants in Birmingham: Serials in Urdu** — *Texts*

A z̲ ān. — Vol.1, no.1 (Rajab 1400 [June 1980])-. — [Birmingham] ([187 Anderton Rd, Birmingham B11 1ND]) : [Idara ′A z̲ ān′], 1980-. — v. ; 26cm
Monthly
ISSN 0261-1007 = Azan : Unpriced B81-38510

059′.927 — General serials in Arabic — *Texts*

[Al Majalla *(London)***]**. Al Majalla : the international magazine of the Arabs : a weekly political news magazine. — as-Sanah at ūlā, al ′Adad 1. (as Sabt16-22 Šubāt 1980-) = 29 Rabī ′al-awwal- 6 Rabī aṯ-ṯānī 1400 A.H. (Feb. 16-22, 1980-). — London (6 Gough Square, Fleet St., EC4A 3DJ) : Saudi Research and Marketing (UK), 1980-. — ill,ports
Weekly
ISSN 0261-0876 = Al Majalla (London) : £1.00 B81-20343

059′.9435 — Serials for Muslims: Serials in Turkish: Serials with British imprints — *Texts*

Cemaat. — Sayi 1 (Rabi′ul - Ahir 1400 [Mart 1980])-. — London (219 Whitechapel Rd, E1) : Ingiltere Türk İslam Derneği, 1980-. — v. : ill ; 35cm
Monthly
ISSN 0261-5940 = Cemaat : Unpriced B81-31563

059′.9999 — General serials in Volapük language — *Texts*

Vög Volapüka. — Nüml (d. 31id Mazüla 1979)-. — [Scunthorpe] (c/o Mr R. Midgley, 24 Staniwell Rise, Scunthorpe, South Humberside]) : [s.n.], 1979-. — v. : ill ; 21cm
Monthly
ISSN 0260-6623 = Vög Volapüka : £0.15 per issue B81-05634

060 — GENERAL ORGANISATIONS

060 — Conferences & exhibitions — *Serials*

Conferences & exhibitions international : the international market leader in meetings, exhibitions and incentives. — June 1980-. — London (146A Queen Victoria St., EC4V 5DQ) : Conferences & Exhibitions Publications for International Trade Publications, 1980-. — v. : ill ; 29cm
Monthly. — Continues: Conferences & exhibitions (1974). — Description based on: Dec.1980
ISSN 0260-8316 = Conferences & exhibitions international : £8.50 per year B81-09212

060 — Learned institution — *Directories — Serials*

The **World** of learning. — 31st ed. (1980-81). — London : Europa, c1980. — 2v.
ISBN 0-905118-52-9 : Unpriced
ISSN 0084-2117 B81-09114

060 — Learned institutions — *Directories — Serials*

The **World** of learning. — 32nd ed. (1981-82). — London : Europa, Jan.1982. — 2v.([11042]p)
ISBN 0-905118-70-7 : CIP entry
ISSN 0084-2117 B81-34566

060′.148 — Organisations. Names — *Abbreviations*

Buttress, F. A.. World guide to abbreviations of organizations / F.A. Buttress. — 6th ed. — Glasgow : Leonard Hill, 1981. — vii,464p ; 26cm
Previous ed.: 1974
ISBN 0-249-44159-4 : £40.00 : CIP rev. B80-23950

G of A : a glossary of abbreviations used in the UK chemical industry. — London (Alembic House, 93 Albert Embankment, SE1 7TU) : Chemical Industries Association, [1981]. — 27p ; 30cm
Unpriced (pbk) B81-12032

061′.4795 — New York *(State).* **Chautauqua. Cultural institutions: Chautauqua Institution,** *to 1973*

Morrison, Theodore. Chautauqua : a center for education religion and the arts in America / Theodore Morrison ; drawings by Jane E. Nelson. — Chicago ; London : University of Chicago Press, 1974 (1975 [printing]). — viii,351p : ill,1map,facsims,ports ; 22x20cm
Bibliography: p339-341. — Includes index
ISBN 0-226-54063-4 (pbk) : £4.90 B81-38563

061′.53′08996 — United States. Negroes. Learned institutions: American Negro Academy, *to 1928*

Moss, Alfred A.. The American Negro Academy : voice of the talented tenth / Alfred A. Moss, Jr.. — Baton Rouge ; London : Louisiana State University Press, c1981. — 327p,[10]p of plates ; 24cm
Bibliography: p305-318. — Includes index
ISBN 0-8071-0699-2 (cased) : £18.00
ISBN 0-8071-0782-4 (pbk) : £7.75 B81-24852

062 — Great Britain. Irish organisations — *Directories — Serials*

Irish in Britain directory. — 1979-. — London (9 Brondesbury Rd, Kilburn, NW6 6BX) : Brent Irish Advisory Service, 1979-. — v. ; 30cm
Annual. — Description based on: 1980 issue
ISSN 0260-650x = Irish in Britain directory : £0.50 B81-06682

062 — Great Britain. Organisations — *For lawyers*

The **Fourmat** legal directory / general editor Theodore Ruoff. — London : Fourmat, 1981. — 285p ; 22cm
Includes index
ISBN 0-906840-41-4 (spiral) : £11.50
Also classified at 344.207′1′025 B81-26310

062′.539 — Lincolnshire. Spalding. Learned societies: Spalding Gentlemen's Society, *1712-1755 — Minutes*

Spalding Gentleman's Society. The minute-books of the Spalding Gentleman's Society 1712-1755 / selected and introduced by Dorothy M. Owen with the help of S.W. Woodward. — [Lincoln] ([21 Queensway, Lincoln]) : Lincoln Record Society, 1981. — xvii,53p : facsims ; 34cm. — (The Publications of the Lincoln Record Society ; v.73)
Bibliography: p53. — Includes index
Unpriced B81-13978

062′.7665 — Lancashire. Preston. Societies — *Directories — Serials*

Directory of local societies in the Preston district / Lancashire Library, Preston District Libraries. — Jan.1981-. — Preston (District Central Library, Market Sq., Preston PR1 2PP) : Preston District Libraries, 1981-. — v.
Issued every two years
ISSN 0261-2070 = Directory of local societies in the Preston district : Unpriced B81-20439

062'.9134 — Scotland. Learned societies: Royal Society of Edinburgh. Fellows, *to 1832 — Biographies*

Scotland's cultural heritage. — Edinburgh : [University of Edinburgh]
Vol.1: One hundred medical and scientific fellows of The Royal Society of Edinburgh, elected from 1783-1832 : an illustrated catalogue containing brief biographical sketches ... / compiled by Evelyn Collinson ... [et al.] ; edited by Sheila Devlin-Thorp. — 1981. — [112]p : ill,ports ; 30cm
Unpriced (pbk) B81-39562

062'.91443 — Scotland. Strathclyde Region. Glasgow. Voluntary organisations *— Directories — Serials*

Glasgow directory of voluntary organisations. — [No.1]-. — Glasgow (234 West Regent St., Glasgow G2 4DZ) : Glasgow Council for Voluntary Service, 1980-. — v. : ill ; 25cm
Irregular
ISSN 0143-7429 = Glasgow directory of voluntary organisations : Unpriced B81-33935

062'.917 — Ireland *(Republic).* **Learned institutions: Royal Irish Academy** *— Directories — Serials*

Royal Irish Academy. List of the council and officers, members, honorary members and Cunningham medallists / Royal Irish Academy. — 1981. — Dublin : The Academy, 1981. — 40p
Cover title: List of members (Royal Irish Academy)
Unpriced B81-21342

062'.91835 — Dublin. Organisations: Royal Dublin Society, *to 1981*

Royal Dublin Society. RDS : the Royal Dublin Society 1731-1981 / edited by James Meenan and Desmond Clarke. — Dublin : Gill and Macmillan, 1981. — 288p : ill,1map,facsims,1plan,ports ; 25cm
Includes index
ISBN 0-7171-1125-3 : Unpriced B81-36878

068'.171241 — Commonwealth organisations *— Directories*

Commonwealth organisations : a handbook of official and unofficial organisations active in the Commonwealth / [compiled by the Information Division, Commonwealth Secretariat]. — 2nd ed. — London : Commonwealth Secretariat, 1979. — Vii,65p ; 21cm
Previous ed.: 1977. — Bibliography: p107-108. — Includes index
ISBN 0-85092-164-3 (pbk) : £2.00 B81-15355

068'.4 — Europe. Associations *— Directories*

Directory of European associations = Répertoire des associations européennes = Handbuch der europäischen Verbände. — Beckenham : CBD
Part 1: National industrial, trade & professional associations = Partie 1: Associations nationales dans l'industrie, le commerce et les professions = Teil 1: Nationale Verbände im Bereich der gewerblichen Wirtschaft und der Berufe / editor I.G. Anderson. — Ed.3. — 1981. — lxix,540p ; 31cm
Includes introduction in English, French, German, Italian, Dutch and Spanish ; subject index in English, French and German. — Previous ed.: 1976. — Text on lining papers. — Includes index
ISBN 0-900246-35-9 : Unpriced B81-22229

068'.4'05 — Europe. International organisations *— Serials*

Annuaire Européen. — Vol.25 (1977). — La Haye ; Londres : Marinus Nijhoff sous les auspices du Conseil de l'Europe, 1979. — xvii,693p
ISBN 90-247-2161-x : £33.45 B81-13196

Annuaire Européen. — Vol.26 (1978). — La Haye ; Londres : Martinus Nijhoff sous les auspices du Conseil de l'Europe, 1980. — xix,696p
ISBN 90-247-2298-5 : Unpriced B81-11220

068'.94 — Australia. Voluntary organisations. Political aspects
Scott, David. The social and political uses of voluntary organisations in Australia. — London : Allen & Unwin, Jan.1982. — [170]p
ISBN 0-08-686251-0 (cased) : £10.95 : CIP entry
ISBN 0-08-686259-6 (pbk) : £4.95 B81-33755

069 — MUSEUMS

069 — Museums. Information processing
Orna, Elizabeth. Information handling in museums / Elizabeth Orna and Charles Pettitt. — New York : Saur ; London : Bingley, 1980. — 190p : ill ; 23cm
Bibliography: p181-183. — Includes index
ISBN 0-85157-300-2 : Unpriced : CIP rev.
ISBN 0-89664-440-5 (U.S.) B80-09068

069'.022'2 — Museums *— Illustrations — For children*
Adams, Pam. The Child's Play Museum / curator P. Adams. — [Swindon] : Child's Play, c1979. — [20]p : chiefly col.ill ; 19cm
ISBN 0-85953-094-9 : Unpriced B81-32885

069'.025'41 — Great Britain. Museums *- Directories - Serials*
Libraries, museums and art galleries year book. — 1978-1979. — Cambridge : James Clarke, May 1981. — [272]p
ISBN 0-227-67835-4 : £23.00 : CIP entry
ISSN 0075-899x
Primary classification 027'.0025'41 B81-14963

069'.025'41 — Great Britain. Museums *— Directories — Serials*
Museums and art galleries in Great Britain and Ireland. — 1981. — Dunstable : ABC Historic Publications, [1980?]. — 115p
ISBN 0-900486-30-9 : £1.00
ISSN 0141-6723 B81-04056

069'.025'411 — Scotland. Museums *— Directories — For teachers*
Museum education in Scotland : a directory / The Council for Museums and Galleries in Scotland, Scottish Education Department Department. — Edinburgh : H.M.S.O., 1981. — 143p : ill,maps ; 25cm
Bibliography: p135-137. - Includes index
ISBN 0-11-491734-5 (pbk) : £3.25 B81-22223

069'.06'0421 — London. Museum. Organisations: London Federation of Museum and Art Galleries *— Serials*
[Newsletter *(London Federation of Museums and Art Galleries)*]. Newsletter / the London Federation of Museums and Art Galleries. — No.1 (Nov.1979)-. — [London] ([c/o J. Daniels, Geffrye Museum, Kingsland Rd, E2 2EA]) : The Federation, 1979-. — v. ; 30cm
Two issues yearly. — Description based on: No.3 (Dec.1980)
ISSN 0260-7743 = Newsletter - London Federation of Museums and Art Galleries : Free to members of the Federation only B81-09217

069'.06'0427 — North-west England. Museums. Organisations: North Western Museum and Art Gallery Service *— Serials*
North Western Museum and Art Gallery Service. Annual report / North Western Museum and Art Gallery Service. — 1979-80. — [Blackburn] ([Griffin Lodge, Griffin Park, Cavendish Place, Blackburn BB2 2PN]) : The Service, [1980]. — 64p
Unpriced B81-10569

069'.0941 — Great Britain. Museums *— Conference proceedings*
Conference 1980 proceedings : the care and maintenance of collections : challenges and constraints / Museums Association. — London : The Association, [1980?]. — 27p ; 30cm
Cover title
Unpriced (unbound) B81-14517

069'.09413'4 — Edinburgh. Museums: National Museum of Antiquities of Scotland *— Serials*
National Museum of Antiquities of Scotland. Report by the Board of Trustees : 1st April ... to 31st March ... / The National Museum of Antiquities of Scotland. — 1979-80. — Edinburgh : H.M.S.O., 1980. — 43p
ISBN 0-11-491701-9 : £3.00 B81-09112

069'.09413'4 — Edinburgh. Museums: Royal Scottish Museum *— Serials*

Royal Scottish Museum. The Royal Scottish Museum Triennial report. — 1977-78-79. — [Edinburgh] ([Chambers St., Edinburgh]) : [The Museum], [1980]. — 71p
ISSN 0144-2961 : Unpriced B81-04595

069'.09416'53 — North Down *(District).* **Holywood. Museums: Ulster Folk and Transport Museum** *— Serials*

Ulster Folk and Transport Museum. Year book ... incorporating annual report and accounts / Ulster Folk and Transport Museum. — 1978-79. — Holywood, County Down (Cultra Manor, Holywood, County Down BT18 QEU) : The Museum, 1980. — iv,51p
£2.00 B81-06930

069'.09421'42 — London. Camden *(London Borough).* **Museums: British Museum,** *1975-1978*

British Museum. *Trustees.* Report of the Trustees 1975-1978. — London : Published for The Trustees of the British Museum by British Museum Publications, c1978. — 57p,[8]p of plates : ill,ports ; 25cm
At head of title: The British Museum. — Includes index
ISBN 0-7141-0094-3 (pbk) : £1.50 B81-34095

069'.09421'42 — London. Camden *(London Borough).* **Museums: British Museum. Stock** *— Serials*

The **British** Museum yearbook. — 3. — London : British Museum Publications for the Trustees, 1979. — 249p
ISBN 0-7141-0088-9 : £10.00 : CIP rev. B78-40595

The **British** Museum Yearbook. — 4. — London : British Museum Publications for the Trustees, c1980. — 247p
ISBN 0-7141-2004-9 : £16.00 : CIP rev. B80-07648

069'.09421'42 — London. Camden *(London Borough).* **Museums: British Museum,** *to 1980*

Caygill, Marjorie L.. The story of the British Museum. — London : British Museum Publications, May 1981. — [64]p
ISBN 0-7141-8039-4 (pbk) : £3.50 : CIP entry B81-04206

069'.09421'42 — London. Camden *(London Borough).* **Museums: British Museum** *- Visitors' guides*

British Museum. British Museum guide and map. — London : British Museum Publications, July 1981. — 1v.
ISBN 0-7141-2011-1 (pbk) : £1.00 : CIP entry B81-14444

069'.09422 — South-east England. Museums *— Lists*

Museums in the South East. — [Milton Keynes] ([34 Burners La., Kiln Farm, Milton Keynes]) : [Area Museums Service for South Eastern England], [198-?]. — 12p ; 30cm
Unpriced (unbound) B81-36886

069'.09422'62 — West Sussex. Chichester. Museums: Chichester District Museum, *to 1978*

The **Chichester** Museum / [researched and designed by members of the Chichester WEA local history workshop class]. — [Chichester] ([29 Little London, Chichester PO19 1PB]) : Chichester District Museum, [1979?]. — [8]p : ill,1port ; 21cm
£0.15 (unbound) B81-37218

069'.09423'37 — Dorset. Poole. Museums *— Visitors' guides*

3 museums in Poole / [photography by Poole Museums Service]. — [Poole] ([Guildhall Museum, Market Place, Poole, Dorset]) : [Poole Museums Service], [1980]. — 23p : ill (some col.),facsims ; 22cm
Unpriced (unbound) B81-25912

069′.09423′93 — Avon. Bristol. Museums: St Nicholas′ Church & City Museum ***(Bristol), to 1975***

Little, Bryan. St. Nicholas′ Church & City Museum : a guide to the building and its history / by Bryan Little. — Bristol ([Queens Rd., Bristol BS8 1RL]) : City of Bristol Museum & Art Gallery, 1980. — 21p : ill,1map ; 22cm
Text, map on inside covers
ISBN 0-900199-11-3 (pbk) : Unpriced
B81-32332

069′.09426′18 — Norfolk. Martham. Museums: Countryside Collection — ***Visitors′ guides***

Countryside Collection. Countryside Collection. — Derby : English Life, c1981. — 16p : ill ; 24cm
Cover title. — Ill on inside covers
ISBN 0-85101-183-7 (pbk) : Unpriced
B81-37994

069′.09429′25 — Gwynedd. Llanberis. Visitor centres — ***Proposals***

Proposal for an environmental centre in Snowdonia / National Museum of Wales. — [Cardiff] : [The Museum], [1977?]. — 14p : ill,maps(some col.) ; 21x30cm
Cover title. — Text, maps on covers
Unpriced (pbk) B81-28865

069.1′09422 — South-east England. Museums. Organisations: Area Museums Service for South Eastern England. Services

Area Museums Service for South Eastern England. Services for museums / Area Museums Service for SE England. — Milton Keynes (34 Burners La., Kiln Farm, Milton Keynes MK11 3HB) : The Service, [1981]. — [8]p : ill ; 30cm + 1sheet(30cm)
Unpriced B81-37400

069.1′5′0941 — Great Britain. Education. Role of museums — ***Serials***

Journal of education in museums. — No.1 (Sept. 1980)-. — [Oldham] ([c/o Dr M. Blanch, Oldham Museum and Art Galleries, Union St., Oldham]) : [Group for Educational Services in Museums], 1980-. — v. : ill ; 30cm
Annual
ISSN 0260-9126 = Journal of education in museums : Unpriced B81-20318

069.5′2 — Museums. Stock: Costume. Documentation systems: MDA system — ***Manuals***

Costume card instructions. — Duxford (Imperial War Museum, Duxford Airfield, Duxford, Cambs. CB2 4QR) : Museum Documentation Association, 1981. — iii,76p : ill,forms ; 30cm. — (Museum documentation system)
Previous ed.: published as Museum documentation system, costume card instructions. 1979. — Three record sheets in pocket. — Bibliography: p51
ISBN 0-905963-33-4 (spiral) : Unpriced
B81-25279

069.5′2 — Museums. Stock. Documentation. Applications of digital computer systems. Software packages: GOS

Porter, M. F.. GOS reference manual / by M.F. Porter. — Duxford (Imperial War Museum, Duxford Airfield, Duxford, Cambridgeshire, CB2 4QR) : Museum Documentation Association, 1981. — vi,214p ; 30cm
Includes index
ISBN 0-905963-27-x (pbk) : Unpriced
B81-29203

069.5′2 — Museums. Stock. Documentation. Applications of digital computer systems. Software packages: GOS — ***Serials***

GOS information. — Vol.1, no.1 (Apr.1980)-. — Duxford, Cambs. (Imperial War Museum, Duxford Airfield, Duxford, Cambridgeshire CB2 4QR) : Museum Documentation Association, 1980-. — v. ; 30cm
Quarterly. — Published for: GOS User Group
ISSN 0143-862x = GOS information : Free
B81-06291

069.5′2 — Museums. Stock. Documentation systems: MDA system — ***Manuals***

Practical museum documentation / Museum Documentation Association. — Duxford (Imperial War Museum, Duxford Airfield, Duxford, Cambs. CB2 4QR) : The Association, 1980. — vii,148p : forms ; 30cm. — (Museum documentation system)
Bibliography: p134-140. — Includes index
ISBN 0-905963-23-7 (spiral) : Unpriced
B81-09259

069.5′2 — South Glamorgan. St Fagans. Museums: Welsh Folk Museum. Exhibits — ***Classification schedules***

Welsh Folk Museum. Classification of objects in the Welsh Folk Museum collections. — Cardiff : The Museum, 1980. — iii,42p ; 30cm
Cover title. — Bibliography: piii,. — Includes index
ISBN 0-85485-047-3 (pbk) : £1.50 B81-07992

069.5′2′0218 — Museums. Stock. Documentation. Standards

Light, Richard B.. International museum data standards and experiments in data transfer / Richard B. Light and D. Andrew Roberts. — Duxford (Imperial War Museum, Duxford Airfield, Duxford, Cambs. CB2 4QR) : Museum Documentation Association, 1981. — vi,106p ; 30cm. — (MDA occasional paper, ISSN 0140-7198 ; 5)
At head of title: Museum Documentation Association
ISBN 0-905963-36-9 (spiral) : £7.50 (£5.50 to members of the Museum Documentation Association) B81-25548

069.5′3 — Great Britain. Artefacts. Conservation — ***Conference proceedings***

Conservation, archaeology & museums / editor Suzanne Keene ; contributors Peter Addyman...[et al]. — London (Conservation Dept., Tate Gallery, Millbank SW1 4RG) : United Kingdom Institute for Conservation, 1980. — 20p : ill ; 30cm. — (Occasional papers / United Kingdom Institute for Conservation ; no.1)
ISBN 0-9504155-1-0 (pbk) : £1.50 B81-31396

069.5′3 — Museums. Showcases. Design

Turner, I. K.. Museum showcases : a design brief / I.K. Turner. — London : British Museum, 1980. — x,94p : ill ; 30cm. — (Occasional paper / British Museum, ISSN 0142-4815 ; no.29)
Bibliography: p90-94
ISBN 0-86159-028-7 (pbk) : Unpriced
B81-13639

069.5′3 — Repositories. Stock. Conservation

International Conference on the Conservation of Library and Archive Materials and the Graphic Arts ***(1980 : Cambridge)***. Abstracts & preprints : Cambridge 1980 / International Conference on the Conservation of Library and Archive Materials and the Graphic Arts ; sponsored jointly by the Society of Archivists and the Institute of PaperConservation ; editor Guy Petherbridge. — London (P.O. Box 17, WC1N 2PE) : Institute of Paper Conservation, c1980. — 209p : ill ; 30cm
Spine title: The conservation of library and archive materials and the graphic arts
ISBN 0-9507268-0-x (pbk) : Unpriced
ISBN 0-902886-04-5 (Society of Archivists)
B81-05332

069.5′3′060411 — Scotland. Art objects. Conservation. Organisations: Scottish Society for the Conservation and Restoration of Historic and Artistic Works — ***Serials***

[Newsletter ***(Scottish Society for the Conservation and Restoration of Historic and Artistic Works)***]. Newsletter / The Scottish Society for the Conservation and Restoration of Historic and Artistic Works. — No.29 (Sept.1980)?-. — Glasgow (c/o Ms A. Fraser, Camphill House, Queens Park, Glasgow G41 2EW) : The Society, 1980-. — v. ; 30cm
Eight issues yearly. — Continues: SSCR newsletter
ISSN 0260-5597 = Newsletter - Scottish Society for the Conservation and Restoration of Historic and Artistic Works : Unpriced
B81-06922

069′.9306′05 — Museums. Ethnographic collections — ***Serials***

[Newsletter ***(Museum Ethnographers′ Group)***]. Newsletter / Museum Ethnographers′ Group. — No.1 (July 1976)-. — [London] ([c/o Mrs M. Wood, Horniman Museum, London Rd, SE23]) : The Group, 1976-. — v. : ill ; 30cm
Two issues yearly. — Description based on: No.9 (Mar.1980)
ISSN 0260-0366 = Newsletter - Museum Ethnographers′ Group : £1.00 per issue
B81-02340

070 — JOURNALISM, PUBLISHING, NEWSPAPERS

070 — Journalism — ***Manuals***

Brearey, Peter. Never say scoop : (or how to look good with your local editor) / Peter Brearey. — Cleckheaton (66 High St., Cleckheaton BD19 3PX) : Kirklees Monographs, c1981. — 12p ; 28cm
£1.00 (pbk) B81-23976

070′.023′41 — Great Britain. Journalism — ***Career guides***

Medina, Peter. Careers in journalism / Peter Medina. — London : Kogan Page, 1981. — 96p ; 19cm
ISBN 0-85038-439-7 (cased) : £5.95
ISBN 0-85038-442-7 (pbk) : £2.50 B81-23699

070′.025 — Newspapers — ***Directories — Serials***

Willing′s press guide. — 107th annual ed. (1981). — East Grinstead : Thomas Skinner Directories, 1981. — 932p
ISBN 0-611-00648-0 : Unpriced
ISSN 0000-0213
Primary classification 050′.25 B81-22402

070.1 — NEWS MEDIA

070.1′72 — Community newspapers. Production — ***Manuals***

Corbett, Bernard J.. The theory and practice of producing your own community paper / Bernard J. Corbett. — Manchester (36 Thornleigh Rd., Off Hart Rd., Fallowfield, Manchester M14 7AN) : [B.J. Corbett], [c1981]. — [14]leaves ; 21cm
Unpriced (unbound) B81-19447

070.1′9 — Television programmes: News programmes. Journalism

Tyrrell, Robert. The work of the television journalist / by Robert Tyrrell. — 2nd ed. — London : Focal, 1981. — viii,180p : ill ; 24cm. — (Library of film and television practice)
Previous ed.: 1972. — Includes index
ISBN 0-240-51051-8 : £9.95 : CIP rev.
B80-09069

070.1′9′0973 — United States. Radio & television programmes: News programmes. Journalism

Hunter, Julius K.. Broadcast news : the inside out / Julius K. Hunter, Lynne S. Gross. — St. Louis ; London : Mosby, 1980. — xii,363p : ill,plans,forms,ports ; 25cm
Includes index
ISBN 0-8016-2319-7 : Unpriced B81-08541

070.4 — JOURNALISM. TECHNIQUES AND TYPES

070.4′1′076 — Newspapers. Editing. Techniques — ***Questions & answers***

Hollstein, Milton. Editing with understanding : a text book and workbook / Milton Hollstein, Larry Kurtz. — New York : Macmillan ; London : Collier Macmillan, c1981. — viii,342p ; 28cm
Includes bibliographies and index
ISBN 0-02-356290-0 (pbk) : £9.50 B81-33452

070.4′1′09224 — Newspapers with British imprints: Guardian. Editors. Hetherington, Alastair, ***1956-1975 — Biographies***

Hetherington, Alastair. Guardian years. — London : Chatto & Windus, Sept.1981. — [288]p
ISBN 0-7011-2552-7 : £12.50 : CIP entry
B81-23843

070.4'12'0941 — Great Britain. Newspapers. Editorial policies. Influence of newspaper advertising
Simpson, D. H. (David Hugh). Commercialisation of the regional press : the development of monopoly, profit and control / D.H.nSimpson. — Aldershot : Gower, c1981. — xv,224p : ill ; 23cm
Bibliography: p217-224
ISBN 0-566-00441-0 : Unpriced B81-36328

070.4'3 — United States. Journalism. Investigative reporting
Mollenhoff, Clark R.. Investigative reporting : from courthouse to White House / Clark R. Mollenhoff. — New York : Macmillan ; London : Collier Macmillan, c1981. — xxii,381p ; 24cm
Bibliography: p370-372. — Includes index
ISBN 0-02-381870-0 (pbk) : £7.95 B81-29326

070.4'3'0973 — United States. Journalism. Reporting — *Manuals*
Schulte, Henry H.. Reporting public affairs / Henry H. Schulte. — New York : Macmillan ; London : Collier Macmillan, c1981. — xiii,445p : ill,forms ; 24cm
Includes bibliographies and index
ISBN 0-02-408040-3 : £10.50 B81-36124

070.4'3'0973 — United States. News. Reporting
Tuchman, Gaye. Making news : a study in the construction of reality / Gaye Tuchman. — New York : Free Press ; London : Collier Macmillan, c1978. — xi,244p : ill ; 22cm
Bibliography: p218-230. — Includes index
ISBN 0-02-932930-2 : £9.75 B81-02675

070.4'33'092'4 — Foreign correspondents, *1950-1978 — Personal observations*
Behr, Edward. Anyone here been raped and speaks Englisn. — London : New English Library, Feb.1982. — [256]p
Originally published: New York : Viking Press, 1978 ; London : H. Hamilton, 1981
ISBN 0-450-05360-1 (pbk) : £1.75 : CIP entry B81-36205

Behr, Edward. [Bearings]. Anyone here been raped and speaks English? : a foreign correspondent's life behind the lines / Edward Behr. — London : Hamilton, 1981, c1978. — xvii,316p ; 23cm
Originally published: New York : Viking Press, 1978
ISBN 0-241-10529-3 : £7.95 B81-04653

070.4'493058'00941 — Great Britain. Race. Reporting by newspapers
Read all about it / [edited by Bob Baker et al.]. — Birmingham (1 Finch Rd., Lozells, Birmingham B19 1HS) : AFFOR, 1980. — 31p : ill,facsims,ports ; 26cm
Bibliography: p31
ISBN 0-907127-02-9 (pbk) : £1.25 B81-22239

070.4'4933 — Economic conditions. Newspapers: Financial times. Journalists: Subject specialists — *Directories*
Financial Times : journalists available for broadcasting & public speaking. — [London] ([10 Cannon St., EC4P 4BY]) : [Press & PR Manager Financial Times], [1981]. — 22p ; 30cm
Cover title
Unpriced (pbk) B81-16729

070.4'4963 — Great Britain. Agriculture. Journalism. Organisations: Guild of Agricultural Journalists — *Directories — Serials*
Guild of Agricultural Journalists. Year book / Guild of Agricultural Journalists. — 24th ed. (1981). — London (79 Great Titchfield St., WIP 7FN) : Graham Cherry Organisation, c1981. — 108p
Unpriced B81-35125

070.4'49796352'0924 — Golf. Reporting. Ward-Thomas, Pat — *Biographies*
Ward-Thomas, Pat. Not only golf. — London : Hodder & Stoughton, Nov.1981. — [224]p
ISBN 0-340-26756-9 : £7.95 : CIP entry B81-30128

070.4'497967 — Great Britain. Motoring. Journalism. Organisations: Guild of Motoring Writers — *Directories — Serials*
Guild of Motoring Writers. Guild of Motoring Writers' year book. — 1980-81. — Woking (Fairfield, Pyrford Woods, Woking, Surrey GU22 8QT) : The Guild, c1980. — 375p
£12.50 B81-06693

Guild of Motoring Writers. Guild of Motoring Writers' year book. — 1981-82. — Woking (c/o Jean Peters, Fairfield, Pyrford Woods, Woking, Surrey GU22 8QT) : The Guild, c1981. — 400p
ISBN 0-907434-00-2 : £17.50 B81-25032

070.4'49961204 — Libya. Reporting by Western news media
Abbas, Zainab. Responsible reporting? : Libya in the Western press / [Zainab Abbas, Nicholas Hyman]. — Jersey : Highclere, [1981]. — 94p ; 20cm
£1.00 (pbk) B81-24183

070.5 — PUBLISHING

070.5 — Books with British imprints. Machine-readable code numbers — *Technical data*
Machine readable codes for the book trade : technical specification and operating manual / by the Machine Readable Codes Joint Working Party. — London : Publishers Association, [c1981]. — 1v.(loose-leaf) : ill ; 32cm
ISBN 0-85386-070-x : Unpriced B81-38784

070.5 — Ireland, Isle of Man & Scotland. Law. Documents on law. Publishing
Law publishing and legal information. — London : Sweet & Maxwell, Nov.1981. — [185]p
ISBN 0-421-28930-9 (pbk) : £13.95 : CIP entry B81-30511

070.5 — Printing & publishing — *Amateurs' manuals*
Cohen, Colin. Print it!. — London : Kaye and Ward, July 1981. — [128]p
ISBN 0-7182-1256-8 (pbk) : £3.95 : CIP entry B81-19200

070.5 — Publishing. Technological innovation — *Conference proceedings*
EURIM4 *(Conference : 1980 : Brussels).* EURIM4 : a European conference on innovation in primary publication : impact on producers and users / presented by Aslib in association with Association nationale de la recherche technique ... [et al.], 23-26 March 1980, Palais des Congrès, Brussels, Belgium ; proceedings edited by L.J. Anthony. — London : Aslib, c1980. — 112p ; 30cm
ISBN 0-85142-139-3 (pbk) : £9.00 (£7.50 to members) B81-31222

070.5'068'8 — Great Britain. Marketing by book publishing industries. Book publishing industries. Small firms — *Manuals*
Smith, Keith, *1946-*. Marketing for small publishers / Keith Smith ; illustrations by Judy Farrar. — London (15 Wilkin St., NW5 3NG) : Inter-Action Inprint in association with the Institute for Social Enterprise, 1980. — viii,128p : ill,forms ; 21cm
Bibliography: p103-112. — Includes index
ISBN 0-904571-34-3 (pbk) : £3.50 B81-07887

070.5'092'4 — Great Britain. Publishing. Hamilton, Hamish — *Festschriften*
Jamie : an 80th birthday tribute from his friends, 15 November 1980. — [London] : Hamish Hamilton, [1980]. — 90p,[1]leaf of plates : 1col.port ; 23cm
Includes two chapters in French. — Limited ed. of 500 numbered copies of which the first 10 are leather bound
Unpriced B81-27700

070.5'092'4 — Wales. Printing & publishing. Jones, Thomas, *1648-1713 — Biographies — Welsh texts*
Jenkins, Geraint H.. Thomas Jones yr almanaciwr 1648-1713 / gan Geraint H. Jenkins. — Caerdydd : Gwasg Prifysgol Cymru, 1980. — ix,162p : 1ill,2maps,facsims,2ports ; 22cm
Bibliography: p138-154. - Includes index
ISBN 0-7083-0770-1 : £8.95 : CIP rev. B80-08582

070.5'0941 — Great Britain. Books. Publishing, *ca 1900-1979*
Lane, Michael, *1941-*. Books and publishers : commerce against culture in postwar Britain / Michael Lane with Jeremy Booth. — Lexington : Lexington Books ; [Farnborough, Hants.] : Gower [distributor], 1980. — ix,148p : ill ; 24cm
Bibliography: p133-141. — Includes index
ISBN 0-669-03383-9 : £9.50 B81-07057

070.5'0973 — United States. Publishing — *History*
Tebbel, John. A history of book publishing in the United States / John Tebbel. — New York ; London : Bowker
Vol.4: The great change, 1940-1980. — 1981. — xi,830p ; 26cm
Includes index
ISBN 0-8352-0499-5 : Unpriced B81-39043

070.5'2 — Great Britain. Academic journals. Publishing. Cooperation between learned societies & publishing industries
Singleton, A. K. J.. Learned societies, journals and collaboration with publishers / Alan Singleton. — Leicester : Primary Communications Research Centre, University of Leicester, c1980. — vi,164p : ill,1form ; 30cm. — (A Primary Communications Research publication, ISSN 0141-0261) (BL (R&D) report ; no.5565)
ISBN 0-906083-14-1 (spiral) : Unpriced : CIP rev. B80-26403

070.5'2 — Serials. Publishing by learned societies. Cooperation between learned societies & publishers
Singleton, A. K. J.. Societies and publishers : hints on collaboration in journal publishing / Alan Singleton. — Leicester : Primary Communications Research Centre, University of Leicester, c1980. — ii,52p ; 21cm. — (Aids to scholarly communication, ISSN 0142-7288) (BL R and D report ; no.5563)
Includes index
ISBN 0-906083-13-3 (pbk) : £2.40 : CIP rev. B80-21303

070.5'79 — Poetry. Publishing — *Practical information — For poets*
Hidden, Norman. How to get your poems accepted : a guide for poets / by Norman Hidden. — London : Workshop Press, c1981. — 59p ; 21cm. — (The Poet's guide ; no.2)
ISBN 0-902705-43-1 (pbk) : £2.70 B81-34249

070.5'795'0941 — Great Britain. Micropublishing
Davies, M. K.. Micropublishing today : an outline of some current micropublishing applications in the United Kingdom / prepared by M.K. Davies. — Bicester (Telford Rd., Bicester, Oxford, OX6 0UP) : Bell & Howell Micromedia Division, [1981?]. — [12]p : ill ; 15x21cm
Unpriced (unbound) B81-27837

070.5'94 — United States. Non-fiction: Academic books. Marketing — *Manuals*
Bodian, Nat G.. Book marketing handbook : tips and techniques for the sale and promotion of scientific, technical, professional, and scholarly books and journals / Nat G. Bodian. — New York ; London : Bowker, 1980. — xxvii,482p : ill,1map,facsims,1plan,forms ; 27cm
Includes index
ISBN 0-8352-1286-6 : £27.50 B81-05279

070.5'95 — European Community. Publications. Dissemination
Hopkins, Michael, *1945-*. Publications, documentation and means for their dissemination in the Commission of the European Communities / M. Hopkins. — [London] : British Library ; Boston Spa : Distributed by Publications, British Library Lending Division, 1981. — iv,28p ; 30cm. — (British Library research & development reports, ISSN 0308-2385 ; no.5618)
ISBN 0-905984-69-2 (pbk) : Unpriced B81-34605

070.5'95 — Government publications
Government publications. — Oxford : Pergamon, June 1981. — [684]p. — (Guides to official publications ; v.8)
ISBN 0-08-025216-8 : £42.00 : CIP entry B81-10428

070.9 — NEWSPAPERS AND JOURNALISM. HISTORICAL TREATMENT

070′.92′4 — Australia. Journalism. Burchett, Wilfred — *Biographies*

Burchett, Wilfred. At the barricades / Wilfred Burchett ; with an introduction by Harrison E. Salisbury. — London : Quartet, 1980. — x,341p ; 25cm
Includes index
ISBN 0-7043-2214-5 : £10.95 B81-25252

070′.92′4 — Australia. Journalism. James, Clive, *to 1961 — Biographies*

James, Clive. Unreliable memoirs / Clive James. — London : Pan, 1981, c1980. — 174p ; 20cm. — (Picador)
Originally published: London : Cape, 1980
ISBN 0-330-26463-x (pbk) : £1.50 B81-38106

James, Clive. Unreliable memoirs / Clive James. — Large print ed. — Bath : Chivers, 1981, c1980. — xii,306p ; 23cm. — (A New Portway large print book)
Originally published: London : Cape, 1980
ISBN 0-85119-134-7 : £5.30 : CIP rev.
B81-20112

070′.92′4 — Great Britain. Journalism. Lambert, Derek — *Biographies*

Lambert, Derek. And I quote / Derek Lambert. — London : Arlington, 1980. — 212p ; 23cm
ISBN 0-85140-503-7 : £5.95 : CIP rev.
B80-11724

Lambert, Derek. Unquote. — London : Arlington, Oct.1981. — [224]p
ISBN 0-85140-543-6 : £6.50 : CIP entry
B81-30315

070′.92′4 — Journalism. Muggeridge, Malcolm — *Biographies*

Hunter, Ian, *1945-*. Malcolm Muggeridge : a life / by Ian Hunter. — London : Collins, 1980. — 270p,[12]p of plates : ports ; 24cm
Bibliography: p257-258. — Includes index
ISBN 0-00-216538-4 : £6.95 B81-00004

Muggeridge, Malcolm. Chronicles of wasted time / Malcolm Muggeridge. — London : Fontana
Pt.1: The green stick. — 1975, c1972 (1981 [printing]). — 316p ; 18cm
Originally published: London: Collins, 1972. — Includes index
ISBN 0-00-636191-9 (pbk) : £1.75 B81-13382

Muggeridge, Malcolm. Chronicles of wasted time / Malcolm Muggeridge. — London : Fontana
Pt.2: The infernal grove. — 1975, c1973 (1981 [printing]). — 313p ; 18cm
Originally published: London : Collins, 1973. — Includes index
ISBN 0-00-636192-7 (pbk) : £1.75 B81-13381

070′.92′4 — Journalism. Muggeridge, Malcolm — *Correspondence, diaries, etc.*

Muggeridge, Malcolm. Like it was : the diaries of Malcolm Muggeridge / selected and edited by John Bright-Holmes. — London : Collins, 1981. — 560p ; 24cm
Includes index
ISBN 0-00-216468-x : £9.95 B81-16795

071/079 — NEWSPAPERS AND JOURNALISM. GEOGRAPHICAL TREATMENT

071′.3 — United States. Journalism — *Manuals*

Harriss, Julian. The complete reporter : fundamentals of news gathering, writing and editing : complete with exercises / Julian Harriss, Kelly Leiter and Stanley Johnson. — 4th ed. — New York : Macmillan ; London : Collier Macmillan, c1981. — xv,499p : ill,facsims ; 26cm
Previous ed.: New York : Macmillan, 1977. — Bibliography: p488-492. — Includes index
ISBN 0-02-350600-8 (pbk) : £8.95 B81-36164

072 — England. Popular press, *1855-1914*

Lee, Alan J.. The origins of the popular press in England : 1855-1914 / Alan J. Lee. — London : Croom Helm, 1976 (1980 [printing]). — 310p,7p of plates : maps ; 22cm
Bibliography: p234-241. - Includes index
ISBN 0-7099-0361-8 (pbk) : £7.50 B81-07143

072 — Great Britain. Evening newspapers, *to 1981*

Clark, Peter A.. Sixteen million readers. — Eastbourne : Holt, Rinehart & Winston, Sept.1981. — [96]p
ISBN 0-03-910296-3 : £15.00 : CIP entry
B81-20528

072 — Great Britain. Press — *Minority Press Group viewpoints*

Whitaker, Brian. News limited : why you can′t read all about it / Brian Whitaker ; preface by Tom Hopkinson. — London (9 Poland St., W1V 3DG) : Minority Press Group, 1981. — 176p : ill,ports ; 22cm. — (Minority Press Group series ; no.5)
ISBN 0-906890-04-7 (cased) : £9.50
ISBN 0-906890-03-9 (pbk) : £3.25 B81-28535

072 — Great Britain. Press. Relations with Conservative Party — *International Marxist Group viewpoints*

Sheridan, Geoffrey. The Tory Press and how to fight it / by Geoffrey Sheridan. — London (328 Upper St. N.1) : Media Workers, International Marxist Group, [1980]. — 11p : ill,facsims ; 21cm. — (A Socialist challenge pamphlet)
£0.10 (unbound) B81-34770

072 — Great Britain. Radical press

Aubrey, Crispin. Here is the other news : challenges to the local commercial press / [by Crispin Aubrey, Charles Landry, Dave Morley]. — London (9 Poland St., W2V 3DG) : Minority Press Group, 1980. — 80p : ill,facsims ; 21cm. — (Minority Press Group series ; no.1)
ISBN 0-906890-00-4 (pbk) : £1.25
ISBN 0-906890-05-5 (library ed.) : Unpriced
B81-22203

072′.025 — Newspapers with British imprints — *Directories — Serials*

Benn′s press directory. Volume 1, UK. — 129th ed. (1981). — Tunbridge Wells : Benn, c1981. — 532p
ISBN 0-510-49025-5 : £30.00
ISSN 0141-1772
Primary classification 338.7′61070572′02541
B81-30743

072′.1 — National newspapers with London imprints: Daily mirror, *to 1980*

Allen, Robert, *1949-*. Daily mirror / Robert Allen & John Frost. — Cambridge : Stephens, 1981. — 88p : ill,facsims,ports ; 25cm. — (World press)
Facsims on lining papers
ISBN 0-85059-491-x : £4.95 : CIP rev.
B81-03180

072′.1 — Newspapers for Muslims: Newspapers with London imprints: Newspapers in Urdu — *Texts*

Inqilāb. — Vol.1, no.1 (6 June 1980)-. — London (16 Brushfield St., E1) : U. Khalid, 1980-. — v. : ill,ports ; 40cm
Weekly. — Text in English and Urdu. — Also entitled: Inqlab. — Description based on: Vol.1, no.5 (4 to 10 July 1980)
ISSN 0260-2210 = Inqlab : £14.00 per year
B81-33730

072′.1 — Newspapers with London imprints: Newspapers in Chinese — *Texts*

[Xing dao ri bao *(European edition)***]**. Xing dao ri bao. — European ed. — No.1 (20 Aug. 1976)-. — London (31 Frith St., W1V 5TL) : Sing Tao Newspapers, 1976-. — v. : ill ; 60cm
Daily. — Parent edition published in Hong Kong ; other regional editions also published. — Description based on: No.1366 (7 July 1980)
£0.15 per issue B81-00698

072′.91312 — Scotland. Central Region. Stirling. Newspapers: Stirling journal & advertiser — *Indexes*

The **Stirling** Journal & Advertiser : a local index. — Stirling ([Stirling, FK9 4LA]) : University of Stirling
Vol.3: 1920-1970. — 1981. — 202p ; 30cm
ISBN 0-901636-29-0 (pbk) : Unpriced
B81-16559

072′.91443 — Newspapers with Scottish imprints: Newspapers with Strathclyde Region imprints: Newspapers with Glasgow imprints — *Texts*

Sunday standard. — No.1 (Sunday Apr.26 1981)-. — Glasgow (195 Albion St., Glasgow G1 1QP) : George Outram, 1981-. — v. : ill,ports ; 60cm
Weekly
ISSN 0261-6068 = Sunday standard : £0.22
B81-32293

072′.91486 — Scotland. Dumfries and Galloway Region. Newspapers: Dumfries and Galloway Standard and Advertiser, *to 1979 — Indexes*

A **Local** index of the Dumfries and Galloway Standard and Advertiser and its predecessors over 200 years. — Dumfries (35 Rosemount St., Dumfries) : James Urquhart
Ill on inside cover
Vol.2: The Dumfries Weekly Journal, 1777-1833, addendum, The Dumfries Times, 1833-1842, the Dumfries Standard, 1843-1860 / [general editor James Urquhart]. — 1981. — xvii,251p : ill,coats of arms,facsims ; 30cm
ISBN 0-9507033-1-1 (pbk) : Unpriced
B81-29344

072′.929 — Newspapers with Welsh imprints: Newspapers in Welsh. Publishing, *to 1980 — Welsh texts*

Lloyd, D. Tecwyn. Gysfenu i′r Wasg gynt / D. Tecwyn Lloyd. — Llundain [London] : Corfforaeth Ddarlledu Brydeinig, 1980. — 34p ; 19cm. — (Darlith radio blynyddol / BBC Cymru)
″Darlledwyd ar Radio Cymru, Tachwedd 23 am 7.30pm″
ISBN 0-563-17922-8 (pbk) : £0.75 B81-06469

080 — GENERAL COLLECTIONS

080 — Graffiti — *Illustrations*

Graffiti 2 : the walls of the world : more great graffiti of our times / collected and introduced by Roger Kilroy ; illustrated by McLachlan. — London : Corgi, 1980. — 96p : ill ; 20cm
ISBN 0-552-98116-8 (pbk) : £1.00 B81-02618

080 — Quotations, *1900-1980 — Anthologies — English texts*

Cohen, J. M.. The Penguin dictionary of modern quotations / J.M. and M.J. Cohen. — 2nd ed. — Harmondsworth : Penguin, 1980 (1981 [printing]). — 496p ; 20cm
Previous ed.: 1971. — Includes index
ISBN 0-14-051038-9 (pbk) : £2.50 B81-30953

080 — Quotations, *to 1979 — Anthologies — English texts*

Dictionary of quotations / edited by Jonathan Hunt. — London : Hamlyn, 1979 (1981 [printing]). — 194p ; 22cm
Includes index
ISBN 0-600-33214-4 : £5.00 B81-25455

080 — Quotations, *to 1979 — Anthologies — Polyglot texts*

Dictionary of foreign quotations / compiled by Robert and Mary Collison. — London : Macmillan, 1980. — vii,407p ; 24cm
Includes index
ISBN 0-333-27238-2 : £15.00 B81-03783

080 — Quotations, to 1980 — *Anthologies — English texts*

[The Quote - unquote book of love, death and the universe]. Quote - unquote 2. — London : Allen & Unwin, Jan.1982. — [160]p
Originally published: as The quote - unquote book of love, death and the universe. 1980
ISBN 0-04-827031-8 (pbk) : £1.50 : CIP entry
B81-33899

080 — Quotations, *to ca 1970 — Anthologies — English texts*

Familiar quotations : a collection of passages, phrases and proverbs traced to their sources in ancient and modern literature / [compiled by] John Bartlett. — 15th and 125th anniversary ed. rev. and enl. / edited by Emily Morison Beck. — London : Macmillan, 1980. — lviii,1540p ; 26cm
Previous ed.: Boston, Mass. : Little, Brown, 1968 ; London : Macmillan, 1977. — Includes index
ISBN 0-333-30917-0 : £15.00 B81-08081

081 — General essays in English. American writers: Journalists *— Anthologies*

The **New** journalism / [edited by] Tom Wolfe ; with an anthology edited by Tom Wolfe and E.W. Johnson. — London : Pan, 1975, c1973 (1980 printing). — 430p ; 20cm. — (Picador)
Originally published: New York : Harper and Row, 1973
ISBN 0-330-24315-2 (pbk) : £2.50 B81-00699

081 — General essays in English. American writers *— Texts*

Brautigan, Richard. The Tokyo-Montana express / Richard Brautigan. — London : Cape, 1981, c1980. — xiv,258p : ill ; 21cm
Originally published: New York : Delacorte Press/Seymour Lawrence, 1980
ISBN 0-224-01907-4 : £6.50 B81-18852

Didion, Joan. The white album / Joan Didion. — Harmondsworth : Penguin, 1981, c1979. — 222p ; 20cm
Originally published: New York : Simon & Schuster ; London : Weidenfeld & Nicolson, 1979
ISBN 0-14-005678-5 (pbk) : £1.95 B81-15395

Morowitz, Harold J.. The wine of life : and other essays on societies, energy & living things / Harold J. Morowitz. — London : Abacus, 1981, c1979. — 265p ; 20cm
Originally published: New York : St. Martin's Press, 1979
ISBN 0-349-12386-1 (pbk) : £1.95 B81-23336

Morris, Wright. A bill of rites, a bill of wrongs, a bill of goods / Wright Morris. — Lincoln [Neb.] ; London : University of Nebraska Press, 1980, c1968. — 176p ; 21cm
Originally published: New York : New American Library, 1968
ISBN 0-8032-3065-6 (cased) : Unpriced
ISBN 0-8032-8107-2 (pbk) : Unpriced
B81-12668

Wolfe, Tom. The kandy-kolored tangerine-flake streamline baby / Tom Wolfe. — [London] : Picador, 1981, c1965. — 248p ; 20
Originally published: New York : Farrar, Strauss, 1965 ; London : Cape, 1966
ISBN 0-330-26525-3 (pbk) : £2.25 B81-37347

081 — General essays in English. Trinidadian writers *— Texts*

Naipaul, V. S.. The overcrowded barracoon : and other articles / V.S. Naipaul. — Harmondsworth : Penguin, 1976, c1972 (1981 [printing]). — 308p ; 20cm
Originally published: London : Deutsch, 1972
ISBN 0-14-004128-1 (pbk) : £2.95 B81-35609

081 — Newspapers with American imprints. Pulitzer Prize winning items, *1959-1980 — Collections*

The **Pulitzer** prize story II : award-winning news stories, columns, editorials, cartoons, and news pictures, 1959-1980 / edited, with commentaries by John Hohenberg. — New York ; Guildford : Columbia University Press, 1980. — xviii,375p : ill,ports ; 24cm
Includes index
ISBN 0-231-04978-1 : £9.40 B81-09658

082 — Boys' annuals in English *— Texts*

Action annual. — 1981. — London : IPC Magazines, c1980. — 127p
ISBN 0-85037-513-4 : £1.50 B81-06848

Hotspur book for boys. — 1981. — London : D.C. Thomson, c1980. — 127p
£1.35 B81-04904

Lion annual. — 1981. — London : IPC Magazines, [1980?]. — 95p
ISBN 0-85037-543-6 : £1.50 B81-06849

Tiger annual. — 1981. — London : IPC Magazines, c1980. — 127p
ISBN 0-85037-583-5 : £1.80 B81-06850

Tornado annual. — 1981. — London : IPC Magazines, c1980. — 126p
ISBN 0-85037-631-9 : £1.80 B81-05815

Valiant annual. — 1981. — London : IPC Magazines, c1980. — 127p
ISBN 0-85037-590-8 : £1.80 B81-05813

082 — Children's annuals in English *— Texts*

2000 AD annual. — 1981. — London : IPC Magazines, c1980. — 126p
ISBN 0-85037-512-6 : £1.50 B81-03461

Baby's own annual. — 1981. — London : IPC Magazines, c1980. — 47p
ISBN 0-85037-630-0 : £2.40 B81-03464

The **Beezer** book. — 1981. — London : D.C. Thomson, c1980. — [88]p
£1.35 B81-00700

The **Beryl** book. — 1981-. — London : D.C. Thompson, 1980-. — v. : chiefly ill ; 28cm
Issued every two years. — Continues: Beryl the peril (1958)
£1.20 B81-05792

Bimbo book. — 1981. — Dundee : D.C. Thomson, c1980. — [56]p
ISBN 0-85116-190-1 : £1.20 B81-00701

Blue Peter. — 18th book. — London : British Broadcasting Corporation, c1981. — 77p
ISBN 0-563-17938-4 : £1.95 B81-35981

Buster book. — 1981. — London : IPC Magazines, c1980. — 127p
ISBN 0-85037-521-5 : £1.50 B81-06853

Cheeky annual. — 1981. — London : IPC Magazines, c1980. — 122p
ISBN 0-85037-522-3 : £1.50 B81-05948

Cor!! comic annual. — 1981. — London : IPC Magazines, c1980. — 126p
ISBN 0-85037-523-1 : £1.50 B81-03876

The **Daily** Mirror book for boys and girls. — 1981. — London : IPC Magazines, c1980. — 127p
ISBN 0-85037-601-7 : £2.20 B81-03883

Dickory dock annual. — 1981. — London : IPC Magazines, c1980. — 79p
ISBN 0-85037-620-3 : £1.80 B81-06852

Disney time annual. — 1981. — London : IPC Magazines, c1980. — 79p
ISBN 0-85037-530-4 : £2.40
ISSN 0140-7171 B81-10278

Disneyland annual. — 1981. — London : IPC Magazines, c1980. — 69p
ISBN 0-85037-524-x : £2.20 B81-03885

Jack and Jill book. — 1981. — London : IPC Magazines, c1980. — 78p
ISBN 0-85037-533-9 : £1.80 B81-06851

Jackpot annual. — 1981. — London : IPC Magazines, c1980. — 127p
ISBN 0-85037-603-3 : £1.50 B81-03877

Knockout annual. — 1981. — London : IPC Magazines, c1980. — 127p
ISBN 0-85037-541-x : £1.80 B81-06855

Krazy annual. — 1981. — London : IPC Magazines, c1980. — 127p
ISBN 0-85037-542-8 : £1.50
ISSN 0140-718x B81-03882

Little star. — 1981. — Dundee : D.C. Thomson, c1980. — [56]p
ISBN 0-85116-192-8 : £1.20 B81-00702

Look-in television annual. — [1978]. — London : Independent Television Books, c1977. — 77p
ISBN 0-900727-53-5 : £1.20 B81-00703

Look-in television annual. — [1979]. — London : Independent Television Books, c1978. — 77p
ISBN 0-900727-65-9 : £1.35 B81-00704

Look-in television annual. — [1980]. — London : Independent Television Books, c1979. — 76p
ISBN 0-900727-67-5 : £1.45 B81-00705

Monster fun annual. — 1981. — London : IPC Magazines, c1980. — 127p
ISBN 0-85037-554-1 : £1.80 B81-03866

Mr. Men annual. — No.2. — London : Thurman, c1980. — 62p
ISBN 0-85985-153-2 : £1.95 B81-01820

Playhour annual. — 1981. — London : IPC Magazines, c1980. — 79p
ISBN 0-85037-563-0 : £1.80 B81-03880

Shiver and Shake annual. — 1981. — London : IPC Magazines, c1980. — 126p
ISBN 0-85037-574-6 : £1.50 B81-03879

Teddy bear annual. — 1981. — London : IPC Magazines, c1980. — 79p
ISBN 0-85037-614-9 : £2.20 B81-03463

The **Topper** and Sparky fun book. — 1981. — London : D.C. Thomson, c1980. — [80]p
£1.35 B81-00706

Walt Disney's Mickey Mouse annual. — 1981. — London : IPC Magazines, c1980. — 79p
ISBN 0-85037-552-5 : £2.40 B81-03878

Whizzer and Chips annual. — 1981. — London : IPC Magazines, c1980. — 126p
ISBN 0-85037-592-4 : £1.50 B81-06854

Whoopee! annual. — 1981. — London : IPC Magazines, c1980. — 126p
ISBN 0-85037-593-2 : £1.50 B81-03881

The **Wonderful** world of Disney annual. — 1981. — London : IPC Magazines, c1980. — 79p
ISBN 0-85037-594-0 : £2.40 B81-03884

082 — Children's anthologies in English *— Texts*

Murray, Philippa. Links / Philippa Murray, Alison Sinclair and Susan Quilliam. — Welwyn : Nisbet, 1981. — 96p : ill(some col.) ; 21cm
ISBN 0-7202-1016-x (pbk) : Unpriced
B81-37189

Murray, Philippa. Treasures / Philippa Murray, Alison Sinclair and Susan Quilliam. — Welwyn : Nisbet, 1981. — 96p : ill(some col.) ; 21cm
ISBN 0-7202-1015-1 (pbk) : Unpriced
B81-37190

082 — General essays in English *— Texts*

Cameron, James. The best of Cameron. — London : New English Library, Nov.1981. — [368]p
ISBN 0-450-04881-0 : £7.95 : CIP entry
B81-32009

Coleridge, Nicholas. Tunnel vision. — London : Quartet, Sept.1981. — [192]p
ISBN 0-7043-2295-1 (cased) : £8.95 : CIP entry
ISBN 0-7043-3391-0 (pbk) : £2.95 B81-28146

082 — General essays in English — *Texts continuation*

Hope, S. G.. Reflections of the London, Midland & Scottish Railway ; &, Cameos of life / [S.G. Hope]. — Macclesfield (No.2 Bungalow, Macclesfield Marina, Macclesfield, Cheshire) : S.G. Hope, 1980. — 75p : ill ; 21cm
£1.75 (pbk)
Primary classification 385'.0941 B81-23171

Hope-Wallace, Philip. Words and music : a selection from the criticism and occasional pieces of Philip Hope-Wallace / made by Jaqueline Hope-Wallace ; introduction by C.V. Wedgwood. — London : Collins, 1981. — 279p : 1port ; 23cm
Includes index
ISBN 0-00-216309-8 : £9.95 : CIP rev.
B81-24588

Kane, Vincent. The lighter side / Vincent Kane ; illustrated by Michael ffolkes. — London : Unwin Paperbacks, 1980. — 143p : ill ; 18cm
ISBN 0-04-827024-5 (pbk) : £1.75 : CIP rev.
B80-18153

Koestler, Arthur. Kaleidoscope. — Danube ed. — London : Hutchinson, Oct.1981. — 1v.
ISBN 0-09-145950-8 : £9.95 : CIP entry
B81-26768

Levin, Bernard. Taking sides / Bernard Levin. — London : Pan, 1980, c1979. — 272p ; 18cm
Originally published: London : Cape, 1979. — Includes index
ISBN 0-330-26203-3 (pbk) : £1.95 B81-00707

Madan, Geoffrey. Geoffrey Madan's notebooks. — Oxford : Oxford University Press, Sept.1981. — [144]p
ISBN 0-19-215870-8 : £6.95 : CIP entry
B81-22469

Magnusson, Magnus. Magnus on the move / Magnus Magnusson. — Edinburgh : Macdonald, c1980. — 168p : ill,1facsim,ports ; 24cm
ISBN 0-904265-40-4 : £6.95 B81-03036

More, *Sir* Thomas, *Saint*. The complete works of St. Thomas More. — New Haven ; London : Yale University Press. — 1979
Vol.9 / edited by J.B. Trap. — xciii,461p,[9]p of plates : ill,facsims,ports ; 24cm
Includes index
ISBN 0-300-02067-8 : £23.65 B81-07852

Oakeshott, Michael. Rationalism in politics : and other essays / Michael Oakeshott. — London : Methuen, 1981, c1962. — 333p ; 22cm
ISBN 0-416-69950-2 (pbk) : £4.50 : CIP rev.
B81-13468

Parkinson, Michael. Parkinson's lore. — London (8 Cork St., W1X 2HA) : Pavilion Books, Oct.1981. — [160]p
ISBN 0-907516-05-x : £5.95 : CIP entry
B81-25740

Ridge, Antonia. By special request / Antonia Ridge. — Large print ed. — Leicester : Ulverscroft, 1981, c1958. — 234p ; 23cm. — (Ulverscroft large print series)
Originally published: London : Faber, 1958
ISBN 0-7089-0573-0 : £5.00 B81-12614

Sparrow, John. Words on the air / John Sparrow. — London : Collins, 1981. — 263p ; 22cm
ISBN 0-00-216876-6 : £7.95 B81-28967

Symons, Julian. Critical observations. — London : Faber, Nov.1981. — [120]p
ISBN 0-571-11688-4 : £9.75 : CIP entry
B81-31277

Taylor, A. J. P.. Politicians, socialism and historians / by A.J.P. Taylor. — London : Hamilton, 1980. — 259p ; 23cm
Includes index
ISBN 0-241-10486-6 : £12.50 B81-00708

Toynbee, Polly. The way we live now. — London : Eyre Methuen, Oct.1981. — [160]p
ISBN 0-413-49090-4 : £6.50 : CIP entry
B81-25308

Visions of paradise. — London : Hodder & Stoughton, Oct.1981. — [242]p
ISBN 0-340-27220-1 : £8.50 : CIP entry
B81-27391

Worsthorne, Peregrine. Peregrinations : selected pieces / by Peregrine Worsthorne. — London : Weidenfeld and Nicolson, c1980. — 277p ; 23cm
ISBN 0-297-77807-2 : £9.95 B81-00709

082 — General knowledge — *For children*

Cassell discovery books. — London : Cassell
Cover title
Set 1: Transport / A. Ramsay. — 1981. — 4v. : ill,1map,ports ; 19cm
Includes index
ISBN 0-304-30272-4 (pbk) : Unpriced
ISBN 0-304-30829-3 (Railways) : Unpriced
ISBN 0-304-30830-7 (Motor cars) : Unpriced
ISBN 0-304-30831-5 (Ships) : Unpriced
ISBN 0-304-30832-3 (Flight) : Unpriced
B81-20752

Cassell discovery books. — London : Cassell
Cover title
Set 2: Hobbies / A. Ramsay. — 1981. — 4v. : ill,ports ; 19cm
Includes index
ISBN 0-304-30273-2 (pbk) : Unpriced
ISBN 0-304-30833-1 (Motorcycling) : Unpriced
ISBN 0-304-30834-x (Angling) : Unpriced
ISBN 0-304-30835-8 (Collecting) : Unpriced
ISBN 0-304-30836-6 (Pop music) : Unpriced
B81-20751

Cassell discovery books. — London : Cassell
Cover title
Set 3: Magic & mystery / D.S. & A.L. Higgins. — 1981. — 4v. : ill,maps,ports ; 19cm
Includes index
ISBN 0-304-30275-9 (pbk) : Unpriced
ISBN 0-304-30837-4 (The Bermuda triangle) : Unpriced
ISBN 0-304-30838-2 (UFOs) : Unpriced
ISBN 0-304-30839-0 (Vampires & werewolves) : Unpriced
ISBN 0-304-30840-4 (Ghosts) : Unpriced
B81-20750

The **Children's** book of questions & answers / edited by Anthony Addison. — London : Octopus, 1977, c1974 (1981 [printing]). — 480p : ill(some col.),maps(some col.) ; 29cm
Includes index
ISBN 0-7064-0620-6 : £3.99 B81-31908

Explorer encyclopedia / edited by Bill Bruce ; contributors Michael Chinery ... [et al.]. — London : Pan, 1981. — 223p : col.ill,charts,maps(some col.) ; 22cm. — (A Piccolo explorer book)
Includes index
ISBN 0-330-26362-5 (pbk) : £2.95 B81-19705

Kerr, David, *1940-*. Junior mirror / by David Kerr. — [London] : [Mirror Books], [1981]. — 26p : ill(some col.),ports ; 36cm. — (A Daily mirror junior special)
£0.50 (unbound) B81-35185

My first fun to learn book. — Maidenhead : Purnell, 1981. — [28]p : chiefly col.ill ; 25cm
ISBN 0-361-05073-9 : £1.99 B81-19312

082 — General knowledge — *Questions & answers — For schools*

Deadman, Ronald. Check up tests in general knowledge / Ronald Deadman and Peter Pile. — London : Macmillan Education
[Pupil's book]. — 1981. — 47p : ill ; 26cm
ISBN 0-333-31840-4 (pbk) : £0.65 B81-31846

Deadman, Ronald. Check up tests in general knowledge / Ronald Deadman and Peter Pile. — London : Macmillan Education
[Teacher's book]. — 1981. — 53p : ill ; 26cm
Text on inside covers
ISBN 0-333-31841-2 (spiral) : £1.95 B81-39091

082 — Girls' annuals in English — *Texts*

Blue jeans annual. — 1981. — London : D.C. Thomson, c1980. — 93p
ISBN 0-85116-183-9 : £1.50 B81-03081

The **Brownie** annual. — 1982. — Manchester : World International Publishing [for] the Girl Guides Association, c1981. — 63p
ISBN 0-7235-6625-9 : Unpriced B81-33472

Bunty for girls. — 1981. — London : D.C. Thomson, c1980. — 125p
£1.35 B81-03270

Debbie for girls. — 1981. — London : D.C. Thomson, c1980. — [120]p
ISBN 0-85116-178-2 : £1.35 B81-03118

Diana for girls. — 1981. — Dundee : D.C. Thomson, c1980. — 125p
ISBN 0-85116-181-2 : £1.40 B81-03119

Fab 208 annual. — 1981. — London : IPC Magazines, c1980. — 77p
ISBN 0-85037-532-0 : £2.00 B81-07503

The **Girl** Guide annual. — 1982. — Manchester : World International Publishing [for] the Girl Guides Association, c1981. — 63p
ISBN 0-7235-6623-2 : Unpriced B81-33471

Jackie annual. — 1981. — London : D.C. Thomson, c1980. — 93p
ISBN 0-85116-198-7 : £1.50 B81-03122

Jinty annual. — 1981. — London : IPC Magazines, c1980. — 143p
ISBN 0-85037-534-7 : £1.80 B81-03868

Judy for girls. — 1981. — London : D.C. Thomson, c1980. — [104]p
£1.35 B81-03268

June book. — 1981. — London : IPC Magazines, c1980. — 93p
ISBN 0-85037-540-1 : £2.00 B81-03871

Mandy. Stories for girls. — 1981. — London : D.C. Thomson, c1980. — 127p
£1.35 B81-03269

Mates annual. — 1981. — London : IPC Magazines, c1980. — 126p
ISBN 0-85037-551-7 : £2.00 B81-03874

Misty annual. — 1981. — London : IPC Magazines, c1980. — 143p
ISBN 0-85037-553-3 : £1.80 B81-03873

My guy annual. — 1981. — London : IPC Magazines, c1980. — 126p
ISBN 0-85037-560-6 : £2.00 B81-03867

Oh boy! annual. — 1981. — London : IPC Magazines, c1980. — 127p
ISBN 0-85037-561-4 : £2.00
ISSN 0140-7112 B81-03462

Penny annual. — 1981. — London : IPC Magazines, c1980. — 95p
ISBN 0-85037-604-1 : £1.50 B81-05814

Pink annual. — 1981. — London : IPC Magazines, c1980. — 127p
ISBN 0-85037-562-2 : £2.00 B81-03870

Princess Tina annual. — 1981. — London : IPC Magazines, c1980. — 94p
ISBN 0-85037-611-4 : £2.20 B81-03869

School friend annual. — 1981. — London : IPC Magazines, c1980. — 94p
ISBN 0-85037-600-9 : £2.20 B81-03872

Tammy annual. — 1981. — London : IPC Magazines, c1980. — 142p
ISBN 0-85037-582-7 : £1.50 B81-06734

082 — Girls' annuals in English — *Texts continuation*

Twinkle. — 1981. — Dundee : D.C. Thomson, c1980. — [60]p
ISBN 0-85116-191-x : Unpriced B81-03121

082 — Graffiti — *Illustrations — For children*

Birch, Therese. Therese Birch's jelly bone graffiti book. — London (3 Fitzroy Sq., W1P 6JD) : Sparrow, 1980. — [94]p : col.ill ; 18cm
ISBN 0-09-924090-4 (pbk) : £0.85 B81-00710

082 — Graffiti in English — *Anthologies*

Rees, NigelGraffiti 3 / [compiled by] Nigel Rees. — London : Unwin Paperbacks, 1981. — 144p : ill ; 18cm
ISBN 0-04-827030-x (pbk) : £1.25 : CIP rev. B81-13439

082 — Quotations in English, *to 1980 — Anthologies*

Eavesdropping / edited by Nigel Rees ; illustrated by Chris Winn. — London : Unwin Paperbacks, 1981. — 144p : ill ; 18cm
ISBN 0-04-827044-x (pbk) : £1.25 : CIP rev. B81-20117

082'.05 — General essays in English — *Anthologies — Serials*

The **Bedside** 'Guardian'. — 29. — London : Collins, 1980. — 247p
ISBN 0-00-216285-7 : £5.95 B81-12436

The **Bedside** Guardian. — 30. — London : Collins, Nov.1981. — [250]p
ISBN 0-00-216356-x : £6.95 : CIP entry B81-28762

The **Sunday** Times bedside book. — 2. — London : André Deutsch, 1980. — 256p
ISBN 0-233-97298-6 : £6.50 B81-08245

082'.05 — General knowledge — *For children — Serials*

The **Look** and learn book. — 1981. — London : IPC Magazines, 1980. — 126p
ISBN 0-85037-544-4 : £2.40 B81-20411

The **New** look and learn with world of knowledge . — No.983 (10th Jan.1981)-. — London : IPC Magazines, 1981-. — v. : ill ; 30cm
Weekly. — Merger of: Look and learn ; and, World of knowledge
ISSN 0261-5738 = New look and learn with world of knowledge : £0.40 per issue B81-32191

087'.85 — General essays in Polish — *Texts*

Mirewicz, Jerzy. Spotkania i dialogi / Jerzi Mirewicz. — Londyn ([182 Walm La., NW2 3AX]) : Księża Jezuici, 1980. — 131p ; 21cm
£4.00 (pbk) B81-14728

Trojanowski, Wojciech. Ach, jaka szkoda - / Wojciech Trojanowski. — London : Veritas, 1980. — 350p,[18]p of plates : ill,ports ; 20cm. — (Serrii czerwonej Biblioteki Polskiej ; tom 94)
Unpriced B81-09362

Wieniewski, Ignacy. Pisma wybrane / Ignacy Wieniewski ; z przedmową Wita Tarnawskiego. — Londyn : Oficyna poetów i malarzy, 1980. — 218p,[1] leaf of plates : 1port ; 22cm
£4.50 (pbk) B81-00711

089'.9166 — General essays in Welsh — *Texts*

Payne, Ffransis G.. Cwysau : casgliad o erthyglau ac ysgrifau / Ffransis G. Payne. — Llandysul : Gwasg Gomer, 1980. — 170p ; 22cm
ISBN 0-85088-693-7 : £3.75 B81-02758

090 — RARE BOOKS

090 — Antiquarian books & manuscripts — *Festschriften*

Fine books and book collecting. — Leamington Spa : James Hall, Oct.1981. — [88]p
ISBN 0-907471-03-x : £15.00 : CIP entry B81-24615

091 — MANUSCRIPTS

091 — English illuminated manuscripts: Bible. N.T. Gospels. *Latin. Durham Cathedral. Library. Manuscript. AII 17 — Illustrations*

[Bible. N.T.. Gospels. *Latin. Durham Cathedral. Library. Manuscript. A II 17. ca.675-725*]. The Durham Gospels : together with fragments of a gospel book in uncial / Durham, Cathedral Library, MS A. II 17 ; edited by Christopher D. Verey, T. Julian Brown, Elizabeth Coatsworth ; with an appendix by Roger Powell. — Copenhagen : Rosenkilde and Bagger ; London : Allen & Unwin, 1980. — 110,111[i.e.222]p,vii leaves of plates(1folded) : ill ; 47cm. — (Early English manuscripts in facsimile ; v.20)
Latin text, English introduction and notes
Unpriced (pbk) B81-10104

091 — English illuminated manuscripts: Bible. N.T. Gospels. *Latin. Lindisfarne Gospels — Critical studies*

Backhouse, Janet. The Lindisfarne Gospels / Janet Backhouse. — Oxford : Phaidon in association with the British Library, 1981. — 96p : ill(some col.),facsims ; 29cm
ISBN 0-7148-2148-9 : £9.95 : CIP rev. B81-25856

091 — Irish illuminated manuscripts in Latin: Book of Kells — *Illustrations*

[Book of Kells. *Selections*]. The Book of Kells : forty-eight pages and details in colour from the manuscript in Trinity College, Dublin / selected and introduced by Peter Brown. — London : Thames and Hudson, 1980. — 96p : ill(some col.),2maps,facsims(some col.) ; 26cm
Bibliography: p96
ISBN 0-500-23326-8 : £8.50 B81-06560

091 — Papyri in Coptic & Greek — *Texts with commentaries — Festschriften*

Papyri : Greek & Egyptian / edited by various hands in honour of Eric Gardner Turner on the occasion of his seventieth birthday. — London : Published for the British Academy by the Egypt Exploration Society, 1981. — xx,236p,xx leaves of plates(3 folded) : facsims,geneal.tables ; 26cm. — (Graeco-Roman memoirs, ISSN 0306-9222 ; no.68)
Includes papers in French, German and Italian, and texts in Greek and Coptic. — List of works: pxiii-xx. — Includes index
ISBN 0-85698-082-x : Unpriced B81-16787

091 — Papyri in Greek — *Critical studies*

Turner, E. G.. Greek papyri : an introduction / E.G. Turner. — Oxford : Clarendon, 1980, c1968. — xii,225p,viiip of plates : ill,2maps ; 22cm
Bibliography: p154-179. — Includes index
ISBN 0-19-814841-0 (pbk) : £7.50 : CIP rev. B80-21306

091'.0954'07402142 — Great Britain. National libraries: British Library. *Department of Oriental Manuscripts and Printed Books.* **Exhibits: Indian manuscripts** — *Critical studies*

Indian manuscripts : an introduction to the permanent exhibition. — [London] : British Library, Dept. of Oriental Manuscripts and Printed Books, c1977. — 1sheet ; 30x22cm
Unpriced B81-39891

094 — BOOKS NOTABLE FOR PRINTING

094 — Books printed by Kelmscott Press: Works of Geoffrey Chaucer now newly imprinted - *Critical studies*

Robinson, Duncan. William Morris, Edward Burne-Jones and the Kelmscott Chaucer. — London : Gordon Fraser, July 1981. — [160]p
ISBN 0-86092-038-0 : £30.00 : CIP entry B81-14439

095 — BOOKS NOTABLE FOR BINDINGS

095'.092'2 — Cambridgeshire. Cambridge. Museums: Fitzwilliam Museum. Exhibits: Books. English hand bindings. Cockerell, Sydney Morris & Tebbutt, Joan Rix — *Catalogues*

Cockerell, Sydney Morris. Thirty recent bindings / Sydney Morris Cockerell & Joan Rix Tebbutt ; with an introduction by Sir Harry Barnes. — Pitlochry (Frenich, Foss, Bitlochry, Perthshire PH16 5NG) : Duval, [1981?]. — 23p,[50]p of plates (some folded) : ill ; 21x24cm
Published to accompany an exhibition at the Fitzwilliam Museum, Cambridge, 1981
Unpriced (pbk) B81-15401

100 — PHILOSOPHY AND RELATED DISCIPLINES

100 — Comparative philosophy

Corbin, Henry. The concept of comparative philosophy / Henry Corbin ; translated from the French by Peter Russell. — Ipswich (3 Cambridge Drive, Ipswich 1P2 9EP) : Golgonooza, c1981. — 32p ; 23cm
£1.80 (pbk) B81-18981

100 — Philosophy — *Critical studies*

Ayer, A. J.. The central questions of philosophy / A.J. Ayer. — Harmondsworth : Penguin, 1976, c1973 (1981 [printing]). — x,243p ; 18cm. — (Pelican books)
Originally published: London : Weidenfeld & Nicolson, 1973. — Includes index
ISBN 0-14-021982-x (pbk) : £1.95 B81-25447

Christian, James L.. Philosophy : an introduction to the art of wondering / James L. Christian. — 3rd ed. — New York ; London : Holt, Rinehart and Winston, c1981. — xx,597p : ill,charts,facsims,ports ; 26cm
Previous ed.: 1977. — Includes bibliographies and index
ISBN 0-03-047416-7 : £11.95 B81-22861

Engel, S. Morris. The study of philosophy : an introduction / S. Morris Engel. — New York ; London : Holt, Rinehart and Winston, c1981. — xi,340p : ill,1map,facsims,ports ; 25cm
Includes bibliographies and index
ISBN 0-03-047511-2 : £10.95 B81-23097

Ewing, A. C.. The fundamental questions of philosophy / by A.C. Ewing. — London : Routledge & Kegan Paul, 1980, c1951. — 260p ; 22cm
Bibliography: p252-255. — Includes index
ISBN 0-7100-0586-5 (pbk) : £2.95 B81-00712

Philosophical problems. — Milton Keynes : Open University Press. — (Arts : a third level course)
At head of title: The Open University
Units 1-2: Body and mind / prepared for the Course Team by Oswald Hanfling. — 1980. — 63p : ports ; 30cm. — (A313 ; 1-2)
Bibliography: p62-63
ISBN 0-335-11015-0 (pbk) : Unpriced B81-13181

Philosophical problems. — Milton Keynes : Open University Press. — (Arts : a third level course)
At head of title: The Open University
Unit 9: Formal logic : a workbook / prepared for the Course Team by Rosalind Hursthouse, Janet Radcliffe Richards, Tom Sorell. — 1980. — 68p : ill ; 30cm. — (A313 ; 9)
Bibliography: p68
ISBN 0-335-11019-3 (pbk) : Unpriced B81-13180

Philosophical problems. — Milton Keynes : Open University Press. — (Arts : a third level course)
At head of cover title: The Open University
Units 17-18: Proof and the existence of God / prepared for the Course Team by Stuart Brown. — New rev. ed.. — 1980. — 50p : ports ; 30cm. — (A313 ; 17-18)
Previous ed.: published as A 303, units 7-8. 1973. — Bibliography: p50
ISBN 0-335-11023-1 (pbk) : Unpriced B81-27592

100 — Philosophy — *Critical studies* *continuation*

Philosophical problems. — Milton Keynes : Open University Press. — (Arts : a third level course)
At head of title: The Open University
Units 19-20: Knowledge / prepared for the Course Team by Tom Sorell. — 1981. — 79p : ill ; 30cm. — (A313 ; 19-20)
Bibliography: p75-76
ISBN 0-335-11024-x (pbk) : Unpriced
B81-25375

Popkin, Richard H.. Philosophy made simple / Richard H. Popkin, and Avrum Stroll ; advisory editor A.V. Kelly. — London : Heinemann, 1981. — xviii,302p ; 22cm. — (Made simple books)
Originally published: New York : Made Simple Books, 1956 ; London : W.H. Allen, 1969. — Bibliography: p295-296. — Includes index
ISBN 0-434-98452-3 (pbk) : £2.75 B81-23213

100 — Philosophy — *Texts — Festschriften*

Philosophical subjects : essays presented to P.F. Strawson / edited by Zak van Straaten. — Oxford : Clarendon Press, 1980. — vii,302p ; 23cm
Bibliography: p297-300. - Includes index
ISBN 0-19-824603-x : £12.00 B81-02997

102'.42 — Philosophy — *For christian theology*

Brümmer, Vincent. Theology and philosophical inquiry : an introduction / Vincent Brümmer. — London : Macmillan, 1981. — 306p : ill ; 23cm
Includes index
ISBN 0-333-31030-6 (cased) : £13.00
ISBN 0-333-31031-4 (pbk) : Unpriced
B81-39952

109 — Philosophy, *to 1978 — Comparative studies*

Copleston, Frederick. Philosophies and cultures / Frederick C. Copleston. — Oxford : Oxford University Press, 1980. — x,198p ; 23cm
Bibliography: p180-189. - Includes index
ISBN 0-19-213960-6 : £5.50 : CIP rev.
B80-12708

109 — Philosophy, *to 1980 — Texts — Collections*

The **Human** search : an introduction to philosophy / edited by John Lachs, Charles E. Scott. — New York ; Oxford : Oxford University Press, 1981. — xv,496p ; 23cm
ISBN 0-19-502675-6 (pbk) : £7.50 B81-32569

109'.033 — Philosophy *related to* **economics,** *1750-ca 1850*

Fischer, Norman. Economy and self : philosophy and economics from the mercantilists to Marx / Norman Fischer. — Westport ; London : Greenwood Press, 1979. — x,264p ; 22cm. — (Contributions in economics and economic history ; no.24)
Bibliography: p251-259. — Includes index
ISBN 0-313-20888-3 : £14.75
Primary classification 330.1 B81-11081

110 — METAPHYSICS

110 — Archetypes

Zolla, Elemire. Archetypes / by Elemire Zolla. — London : Allen & Unwin, 1981. — viii,140p ; 23cm
ISBN 0-04-111007-2 : £8.50 B81-17265

110 — Metaphysics

Anscombe, G. E. M.. Metaphysics and the philosophy of mind / [G.E.M. Anscombe]. — Oxford : Blackwell, 1981. — x,239p : ill ; 24cm. — (The Collected philosophical papers of G.E.M. Anscombe ; v.2)
Includes index
ISBN 0-631-12932-4 : £15.00
Also classified at 128'.2 B81-40049

Aristotle. [Metaphysics. English]. Aristotle's metaphysics. — Oxford : Clarendon Press. — (Clarendon Aristotle series)
Translated from the Greek
Books [Gamma], [Delta], and [Epsilon] / translated with notes by Christopher Kirwan. — 1971 (1980 [printing]). — vi,206p ; 21cm
Bibliography: p201-202. — Includes index
ISBN 0-19-872028-9 (pbk) : £6.95 : CIP rev.
B80-02294

Brentano, Franz. The theory of categories / by Franz Brentano ; translated by Roderick M. Chisholm and Norbert Guterman. — The Hague ; London : Nijhoff, 1981. — ix,275p : 1port ; 25cm. — (Melbourne international philosophy series ; v.8)
Translation of: Kategorienlehre. — Includes index
ISBN 90-247-2302-7 : Unpriced B81-17110

Oliver, Harold H.. A relational metaphysic / by Harold H. Oliver. — The Hague ; London : Nijhoff, 1981. — xiv,228p ; 25cm. — (Studies in philosophy and religion)
Bibliography: p209-215. — Includes index
ISBN 90-247-2457-0 : Unpriced B81-36724

110'.92'4 — Metaphysics. Theories of Kant, Immanuel

Findlay, J. N.. Kant and the transcendental object : a hermeneutic study / by J.N. Findlay. — Oxford : Clarendon, 1981. — xxiv,392p ; 22cm
Includes index
ISBN 0-19-824638-2 : £17.50 B81-36152

110'.92'4 — Metaphysics. Theories of Leibniz, Gottfried Wilhelm

Rescher, Nicholas. Leibniz's metaphysics of nature : a group of essays / Nicholas Rescher. — Dordrecht ; London : Reidel, c1981. — xiv,126p ; 23cm. — (The University of Western Ontario series in philosophy of science ; v.18)
Includes index
ISBN 90-277-1252-2 (cased) : Unpriced
ISBN 90-277-1253-0 (pbk) : Unpriced
B81-33339

111 — ONTOLOGY

111 — Identity — *Philosophical perspectives*

Noonan, Harold W.. Objects and identity : an examination of the relative identity thesis and its consequences / by Harold W. Noonan. — The Hague ; London : Nijhoff, 1980. — xiv,176p : 3ill ; 25cm. — (Melbourne international philosophy series ; v.6)
Bibliography: p172-173. - Includes index
ISBN 90-247-2292-6 : Unpriced B81-01778

111 — Ontology — *Phenomenological viewpoints — Conference proceedings*

The **Great** chain of being and Italian phenomenology / edited by Angela Ales Bello. — Dordrecht ; London : Reidel, c1981. — xvii,347p : ports ; 23cm. — (Analecta Husserliana ; v.11)
Includes contributions in French and German. — Bibliography: p36-37. — Includes index
ISBN 90-277-1071-6
Primary classification 142'.7 B81-37020

111'.092'4 — Ontology. Theories of Frege, Gottlob

Kluge, Eike-Henner W.. The metaphysics of Gottlob Frege : an essay in ontological reconstruction / by E.-H. W. Kluge. — The Hague ; London : Nijhoff, 1980. — 296p ; 25cm. — (Martinus Nijhoff philosophy library ; v.5)
Includes index
ISBN 90-247-2422-8 : Unpriced B81-04652

111'.1 — Existence — *Philosophical perspectives*

Williams, C. J. F.. What is existence?. — Oxford : Clarendon Press, July 1981. — [380]p. — (Clarendon library of logic and philosophy)
ISBN 0-19-824429-0 : £17.50 : CIP entry
B81-13802

111'.1 — Man. Existence — *Philosophical perspectives*

Levinas, Emmanuel. Otherwise than being, or, Beyond essence / by Emmanuel Levinas ; translated by Alphonso Lingis. — The Hague ; London : Nijhoff, 1981. — xlii,200p ; 25cm. — (Martinus Nijhoff philosophy texts ; v.3)
Translation of: Autrement qu'être. 2e éd
ISBN 90-247-2374-4 : Unpriced B81-36720

111'.1 — Non-existent objects — *Philosophical perspectives*

Parsons, Terence. Nonexistent objects / Terence Parsons. — New Haven ; London : Yale University Press, c1980. — xiii,258p : ill ; 22cm
Bibliography: p247-254. - Includes index
ISBN 0-300-02404-5 : £12.00 B81-05024

111'.2'0924 — Universals & particulars. Theories of Aristotle

Lloyd, A. C.. Form and universal in Aristotle / by A.C. Lloyd. — Liverpool (School of Classics, Abercromby Sq., Liverpool L69 3BX) : Cairns, c1981. — vi,89p ; 21cm. — (ARCA classical and medieval texts, papers and monographs, ISSN 0309-5561 ; v)
Bibliography: p77-82. — Includes index
ISBN 0-905205-05-7 (pbk) : £5.00 B81-16126

111'.85 — Aesthetics

Gombrich, E. H.. Nature and art as needs of the mind : the fourth Leverhulme Memorial Lecture delivered 23 February, 1981 in the University of Liverpool / Ernst Gombrich. — Liverpool : Liverpool University Press, 1981. — 24p ; 21cm
ISBN 0-85323-354-3 (pbk) : £0.75 B81-40714

111'.85'0922 — Aesthetics. Theories of Kant, Immanuel; Hegel, Georg Wilhelm Friedrich & Schopenhauer, Arthur

Knox, Israel. The aesthetic theories of Kant, Hegel, and Schopenhauer / by Israel Knox. — [Atlantic Highlands] : Humanities Press ; [Brighton] : Harvester Press, 1978, c1958. — xi,219p ; 24cm
Originally published: New York : Columbia University Press, 1936 ; London : Thames & Hudson, 1958. — Bibliography: p195-207. — Includes index
ISBN 0-85527-207-4 : Unpriced B81-27886

111'.85'0947 — Aesthetics. Soviet theories, *1945-1978*

Swiderski, Edward M.. The philosophical foundations of Soviet aesthetics : theories and controversies in the post-war years / Edward M. Swiderski. — Dordrecht ; London : Reidel, c1979. — xviii,225p ; 23cm. — (Sovietica ; v.42)
Bibliography: p210-219. — Includes index
ISBN 90-277-0980-7 : Unpriced B81-16283

113 — METAPHYSICS. COSMOLOGY

113 — Cosmology. Theories, *to 1980*

Cronin, Vincent. The view from planet Earth. — London : Collins, Oct.1981. — [368]p
ISBN 0-00-211397-x : £9.00 : CIP entry
B81-25105

113 — Nature, *ca 1500-ca 1700 — Philosophical perspectives*

Merchant, Carolyn. The death of nature. — London : Wildwood House, Sept.1981. — [368]p
ISBN 0-7045-3049-x : £6.95 : CIP entry
B81-23793

113'.8 — Life. Origin — *Philosophical perspectives — Polish texts*

Kucia, Thaddaeus. Filozofia biogenezy = (Philosophy of biogenesis) / Thaddaeus Kucia. — London : Veritas Foundation, c1981. — 199p ; 22cm
Polish text, English table of contents. — Bibliography: p1-196
Unpriced (pbk) B81-21025

115 — METAPHYSICS. TIME

115 — Time — *Philosophical perspectives*

Mellor, D. H.. Real time. — Cambridge : Cambridge University Press, Oct.1981. — [203]p
ISBN 0-521-24133-2 : £17.50 : CIP entry
B81-31280

Whitrow, G. J.. The natural philosophy of time. — 2nd ed. — Oxford : Clarendon Press, Nov.1981. — [400]p
Previous ed.: London : Nelson, 1961
ISBN 0-19-858215-3 (pbk) : £7.95 : CIP entry
B81-31193

115 — Time — *Philosophical perspectives — Festschriften*

Time and cause : essays presented to Richard Taylor / edited by Peter Van Inwagen. — Dordrecht ; London : Reidel, c1980. — x,313p : ill,1port ; 23cm. — (Philosophical studies series in philosophy ; v.19)
Bibliography: p301-306. — Includes index
ISBN 90-277-1048-1 : Unpriced
Also classified at 122 B81-06980

116 — METAPHYSICS. EVOLUTION

116 — Evolution — *Philosophical perspectives*

Bateson, Gregory. Mind and nature : a necessary unity / Gregory Bateson. — [London] : Fontana, 1980, c1979. — 251p : ill,1facsim ; 18cm
Originally published: New York : Dutton ; London : Wildwood, 1979. — Includes index
ISBN 0-00-635752-0 (pbk) : £1.95 B81-05243

Good, Ronald. The philosophy of evolution / Ronald Good. — Wimborne (Stanbridge, Wimborne, Dorset) : Dovecote Press, 1981. — 182p ; 23cm
Includes index
ISBN 0-9503518-6-5 : £8.50 B81-21429

The **Philosophy** of evolution. — Brighton : Harvester, Sept.1981. — [288]p. — (Studies in philosophy ; no.26)
ISBN 0-7108-0072-x : £20.00 : CIP entry
B81-22602

121 — EPISTEMOLOGY

121 — Epistemology — *Conference proceedings*

Justification and knowledge : new studies in epistemology / edited by George S. Pappas. — Dordrecht ; London : Reidel, c1979. — xv,218p : ill ; 23cm. — (Philosophical studies series in philosophy ; v.17)
Conference papers. — Bibliography: p182-211. - Includes index
ISBN 90-277-1023-6 : Unpriced B81-06137

121 — Epistemology. Kant, Immanuel. Kritik der reinen Vernunft — *Critical studies*

Cassirer, H. W.. Kant's first Critique : an appraisal of the permanent significance of Kant's Critique of pure reason / by H.W. Cassirer. — London : Harvester by arrangement with Allen & Unwin, 1978. — 367p ; 23cm. — (Muirhead library of philosophy)
Originally published: London : Allen & Unwin, 1954. — Includes index
ISBN 0-85527-904-4 : £8.50 B81-07110

121 — Epistemology. Transcendentalism

Transcendental arguments and science : essays in epistemology / edited by Peter Bieri, Rolf-P. Horstmann and Lorenz Krüger. — Dordrecht ; London : Reidel, 1979. — vii,314p ; 23cm. — (Synthese library ; v.133)
Conference papers. — Includes index
ISBN 90-277-0963-7 (cased) : Unpriced
ISBN 90-277-0964-5 (pbk) : Unpriced
B81-16290

121 — Intentionality — *Philosophical perspectives*

Chisholm, Roderick M.. The first person : an essay on reference and intentionality / Roderick M. Chisholm. — Brighton : Harvester, 1981. — 135p ; 23cm. — (The Benefactors' lectures 1979 / Royal Institute of Philosophy)
Includes index
ISBN 0-7108-0077-0 : £16.50 : CIP rev.
B81-02383

Thought and object. — Oxford : Clarendon Press, Jan.1982. — [320]p
ISBN 0-19-824606-4 : £16.00 : CIP entry
B81-34387

121 — Knowledge. Justification

Swain, Marshall. Reasons and knowledge / Marshall Swain. — Ithaca ; London : Cornell University Press, 1981. — 243p ; 23cm
Includes index
ISBN 0-8014-1378-8 : £13.50 B81-36451

121 — Knowledge — *Philosophical perspectives*

Berkeley, George. The principles of human knowledge ; Three dialogues between Hylas and Philonous / George Berkeley ; edited with an introduction by G.J. Warnock. — [London] : Collins, 1962 (1981 [printing]). — 288p ; 18cm
Originally published: London : Jacob Tonson, 1734. — Bibliography: p279-281. — Includes index
ISBN 0-00-636400-4 (pbk) : £1.75 B81-25619

Ginet, Carl. Knowledge, perception, and memory / Carl Ginet. — Dordrecht ; London : Reidel, c1975. — viii,212p ; 23cm. — (Philosophical studies series in philosophy ; v.5)
Bibliography: p205-207. - Includes index
ISBN 90-277-0574-7 (cased) : Unpriced
ISBN 90-277-1191-7 (pbk) : Unpriced
B81-13649

Locke, John. An essay concerning human understanding / John Locke. — [Abridge ed.] / abridged and edited with an introduction by A.D. Woozley. — [London] : Fount, 1964 (1980 [printing]). — 475p ; 18cm
Originally published: London : Fontana, 1964. — Bibliography: p463-464. - Includes index
ISBN 0-00-646149-2 (pbk) : £2.75 B81-07248

121 — Knowledge. Philosophical perspectives. Theories of Marxists

Ruben, David-Hillel. Marxism and materialism : a study in Marxist theory of knowledge / David-Hillel Ruben. — New and rev.ed. — Brighton : Harvester, 1979. — x,223p ; 23cm
Previous ed.: 1977. — Includes index
ISBN 0-85527-766-1 : £14.50 : CIP rev.
ISBN 0-85527-776-9 (pbk) : £5.50 B78-38176

121'.092'4 — Knowledge. Philosophical perspectives. Theories of Piaget, Jean

Piaget, philosophy and the human sciences / edited by Hugh J. Silverman. — New Jersey : Humanities ; Brighton : Harvester, c1980. — xi,174p : ill ; 23cm
Includes index
ISBN 0-85527-895-1 : £18.95 : CIP rev.
B80-04049

121'.2 — Possibility — *Philosophical perspectives*

Reforging the great chain of being : studies of the history of modal theories / edited by Simo Knuuttila. — Dordrecht ; London : Reidel, c1981. — xiv,320p ; 23cm. — (Synthese historical library ; v.20)
Includes bibliographies and index
ISBN 90-277-1125-9 : Unpriced B81-03893

121'.3 — Knowledge. Acquisition. Role of human cognition & perception

Dretske, Fred I.. Knowledge and the flow of information / Fred I. Dretske. — Oxford : Blackwell, 1981. — xiv,273p : ill ; 25cm
Includes index
ISBN 0-631-12765-8 : £12.00 B81-39948

121'.3 — Man. Perception — *Philosophical perspectives*

Dicker, Georges. Perceptual knowledge : an analytical and historical study / Georges Dicker. — Dordrecht ; London : Reidel, c1980. — ix,226p ; 23cm. — (Philosophical studies series in philosophy ; v.22)
Bibliography: p216-219. — Includes index
ISBN 90-277-1130-5 : Unpriced B81-03520

Fodor, Jerry A.. Representations : philosophical essays on the foundations of cognitive science / Jerry A. Fodor. — Brighton : Harvester, 1981. — ix,343p ; 25cm
Bibliography: p335-339. — Includes index
ISBN 0-85527-977-x : £22.50 : CIP rev.
Also classified at 153.4 B81-16892

121'.4 — Empirical knowledge

Russell, Bertrand. An inquiry into meaning and truth : the William James Lectures for 1940, delivered at Harvard University / by Bertrand Russell. — London : Unwin Paperbacks, 1980. — 352p : ill ; 20cm
Originally published: London : Allen and Unwin, 1940. — Bibliography: p4. - Includes index
ISBN 0-04-121019-0 (pbk) : £2.50 : CIP rev.
B79-33887

121'.5 — Knowledge. Scepticism — *Philosophical perspectives*

Cornman, James W.. Skepticiam, justification and explanation / James W. Cornman ; with a bibliographic essay by Walter N. Gregory. — Dordrecht ; London : Reidel, c1980. — xxix,341p : 1port ; 23cm. — (Philosophical studies series in philosophy ; v.18)
Bibliography: p315-328. - Includes index
ISBN 90-277-1041-4 : Unpriced B81-06009

Klein, Peter D.. Certainty. — Brighton : Harvester Press, Dec.1981. — [244]p
ISBN 0-7108-0369-9 : £20.00 : CIP entry
B81-32056

121'.6 — Belief *related to* **science** — *Early works*

Darwin to Einstein : primary sources on science and belief / edited by Noel G. Coley and Vance M.D. Hall. — Harlow : Longman in association with The Open University Press, 1980. — ix,358p : ill ; 23cm. — (Open University set book)
Includes index
ISBN 0-582-49158-4 (cased) : Unpriced : CIP rev.
ISBN 0-582-49159-2 (pbk) : £5.95
Also classified at 500 B80-25084

121'.6 — Belief. Relations with science. Theories, *ca 1800-ca 1930*

Darwin to Einstein : historical studies on science and belief / edited by Colin Chant and John Fauvel at the Open University. — Harlow : Longman in association with The Open University Press, 1980. — x,335p : ill ; 23cm
Includes index
ISBN 0-582-49156-8 (cased) : Unpriced : CIP rev.
ISBN 0-582-49157-6 (pbk) : £5.65
Also classified at 501 B80-25083

Science and belief : from Darwin to Einstein. — Milton Keynes : Open University Press. — (Arts : a third level course)
At head of title: The Open University
Block 1 (Unit 1): Beliefs in science : an introduction / prepared for the Course Team by James R. Moore. — 1981. — 44p : ill,ports ; 30cm. — (A381 ; block 1(1))
Bibliography: p42-44
ISBN 0-335-11000-2 (pbk) : Unpriced
Also classified at 501 B81-27594

Science and belief : from Darwin to Einstein. — Milton Keynes : Open University Press. — (Arts : a third level course)
At head of title: The Open University
Block 2: Science and metaphysics in Victorian Britain / prepared for the Course Team by James R. Moore ... [et al.]. — 1981. — 73p : ill,facsim,ports ; 30cm. — (A381 ; block II (2,3))
Includes bibliographies. — Contents: Unit 2: The metaphysics of evolution - Unit 3: Scientists and the spiritual world
ISBN 0-335-11001-0 (pbk) : Unpriced
Also classified at 501 B81-13179

Science and belief : from Darwin to Einstein. — Milton Keynes : Open University Press. — (Arts : a third level course)
At head of title: The Open University
Block 3: Time, chance and thermodynamics / prepared for the Course Team by Colin A. Russell. — 1981. — 74p : ill,ports ; 30cm. — (A381 ; block 3)
Includes bibliographies. — Contents: Unit 4 : Thermodynamics and time — Unit 5 : Thermodynamics and chance
ISBN 0-335-11002-9 (pbk) : Unpriced
Also classified at 501 B81-27593

121'.6 — Inquiry — *Philosophical perspectives*

Rescher, Nicholas. Empirical inquiry. — London : Athlone Press, Feb.1982. — [285]p
ISBN 0-485-30009-5 : £15.00 : CIP entry
B81-36219

121'.68 — Hermeneutics

Gadamer, Hans-Georg. Truth and method / Hans-Georg Gadamer. — 2nd ed. — London : Sheed and Ward, c1979 (1981 [printing]). — xxvi,552p ; 22cm
Translation of: Wahrheit und Methode. 2nd Aufl. — Includes index
ISBN 0-7220-9215-6 (pbk) : £13.50 B81-40908

Ricoeur, Paul. Hermeneutics and the human sciences. — Cambridge : Cambridge University Press, Feb.1982. — [314]p
ISBN 0-521-23497-2 (cased) : £20.00 : CIP entry
ISBN 0-521-28002-8 (pbk) : £6.95 B81-35921

121′.8 — Values — *Philosophical perspectives*
Kraft, Victor. Foundations for a scientific analysis of value / Victor Kraft ; edited by Henk L. Mulder ; translated by Elizabeth Hughes Schneewind ; with an introduction by Ernst Topitsch. — Dordrecht ; London : Reidel, c1981. — xvii,195p : 1port ; 23cm. — (Vienna Circle collection ; v.15)
Translation of: Die Grundlagen einer wissenschaftlichen Wertlehre. 2nd ed. 1951. — Bibliography: p188-191. — Includes index
ISBN 90-277-1211-5 (cased) : Unpriced
ISBN 90-277-1212-3 (pbk) : Unpriced B81-33273

122 — CAUSATION

122 — Causation — *Philosophical perspectives — Festschriften*
Time and cause : essays presented to Richard Taylor / edited by Peter Van Inwagen. — Dordrecht ; London : Reidel, c1980. — x,313p : ill,1port ; 23cm. — (Philosophical studies series in philosophy ; v.19)
Bibliography: p301-306. — Includes index
ISBN 90-277-1048-1 : Unpriced
Primary classification 115 B81-06980

122 — Karma
Karma and rebirth in classical Indian traditions / Wendy Doniger O'Flaherty editor. — Berkeley ; London : University of California Press, c1980. — xxv,342p : ill ; 25cm
Bibliography: p319-329. — Includes index
ISBN 0-520-03923-8 : £16.50 B81-11248

126 — THE SELF

126 — Man. Consciousness — *Philosophical perspectives*
Brentano, Franz. Sensory and noetic consciousness : psychology from an empirical standpoint III / Franz Brentano ; edited by Oskar Kraus ; English edition by Linda L. McAlister ; translated by Margarete Schättle and Linda L. McAlister. — London : Routledge & Kegan Paul, 1981. — xxv,139p ; 23cm. — (International library of philosophy and scientific method)
Translation of: Vom sinnlichen und noetischen Bewußtsein (Psychologie III). — Includes index
ISBN 0-7100-0404-4 : £8.50 : CIP rev. B80-08583

126 — Man. Identity — *Philosophical perspectives*
Madell, Geoffrey. The identity of the self / Geoffrey Madell. — Edinburgh : Edinburgh University Press, c1981. — vi,148p : ill ; 19cm
Includes index
ISBN 0-85224-422-3 : £7.50 B81-36326

126 — Man. Self-consciousness — *Russian texts*
Gershenzon, M.. Tvorcheskoe samosoznanie = Creative self-conciousness / M. Gershenzon. — Letchworth : Prideaux, 1980. — 29p ; 21cm. — (Russian titles for the specialist, ISSN 0305-3741 ; no.224)
Originally published: Moscow : s.n., 1909
£0.90 (pbk) B81-14003

126′.092′4 — Self. Theories of Kierkegaard, Søren
Kierkegaard's truth : the disclosure of the self / editor Joseph H. Smith. — New Haven ; London : Yale University Press, c1981. — xvii,438p ; 22cm. — (Psychiatry and the humanities ; v.5)
Includes index
ISBN 0-300-02621-8 : £25.55 : CIP rev. B81-22686

128 — HUMANKIND

128 — Man
Falconar, A. E. I.. Gardens of meditation / A.E.I. Falconar. — Gerrards Cross : Colin Smythe, 1980. — 124p ; 22cm
Bibliography: p121-122. — Includes index
ISBN 0-86140-057-7 : Unpriced B81-32774

The King's son : readings in the traditional psychologies and contemporary thought on man / edited by Robert Cecil. — London : Published by the Octagon Press for the Institute for Cultural Research, 1980, c1981. — xxvi,181p ; 23cm
Includes index
ISBN 0-900860-88-x : £7.50 B81-26899

128 — Man. Mind, body & soul
Bailey, Alice A.. The soul and its mechanism : the problem of psychology / by Alice A. Bailey. — New York ; London : Lucis, 1930, c1965 (1976 printing). — 165p ; 19cm
Bibliography: p158-160. — Includes index
Unpriced (pbk) B81-37048

128 — Man. Mind, body & soul — *Philosophical perspectives — French texts*
Peursen, C. A. van. Le corp - l'âme - l'esprit : introduction à une anthropologie phénoménologique / C.A. van Peursen ; [traduit de Néerlandais par Marie Claes]. — La Haye ; Londres [London] : Nijhoff, 1979. — 174p ; 23cm
Translation of: Lichaam - zeil - geest
ISBN 90-247-2176-8 (pbk) : Unpriced B81-07024

128 — Man — *Phenomenological viewpoints — French texts*
Levinas, Emmanuel. Totalité et infini : essai sur l'extériorité / Emmanuel Levinas. — 4th ed. — La Haye [The Hague] ; Londres : Nijhoff, 1971, c1961 (1980 [printing]). — xviii,284p ; 25cm. — (Phaenomenologica ; 8)
Previous ed.: 1968
ISBN 90-247-5105-5 : Unpriced B81-16021

128 — Man — *Philosophical perspectives*
Samson, Frederic. Concepts of man / Frederic Samson. — London (Kensington Gore, SW7 2EU) : Royal College of Art, 1979. — 12p ; 30cm. — (RCA papers, ISSN 0141-1365 ; no.7)
Bibliography: p12
ISBN 0-902490-35-4 (pbk) : Unpriced B81-19443

128′.092′4 — Man. Theories of Cabanis, Pierre-Jean-Georges
Staum, Martin S.. Cabanis : Enlightenment and medical philosophy in the French Revolution / Martin S. Staum. — Princeton ; Guildford : Princeton University Press, c1980. — xi,430p ; 23cm
Bibliography: p383-417. - Includes index
ISBN 0-691-05301-4 : £45.40 B81-00713

128′.1 — Greek language. Words: Psyche. Meaning
Claus, David B.. Toward the soul : an inquiry into the meaning of 'psyche' before Plato / David B. Claus. — New Haven ; London : Yale University Press, c1981. — 200p ; 25cm
Bibliography: p185-191. — Includes index
ISBN 0-300-02096-1 : £12.55 : CIP rev. B81-22692

128′.1 — Man. Soul — *Philosophical perspectives*
Critchlow, Keith. The soul as sphere & androgyne / Keith Critchlow. — Ipswich : Golgonooza Press, c1980. — 34p : ill ; 24cm
£2.40 (pbk) B81-05488

128′.2 — Man. Mind *related to* **body**
Body and mind : past, present and future / edited by R.W. Rieber. — New York ; London : Academic Press, 1980. — xiv,261p : ill ; 24cm
Includes bibliographies and index
ISBN 0-12-588260-2 : £11.00 B81-01582

128′.2 — Man. Mind *related to* **brain**
Taylor, Gordon Rattray. The natural history of the mind : an exploration / Gordon Rattray Taylor. — London : Granada, 1980, c1979. — x,370p ; 20cm. — (A Paladin book)
Originally published: London : Secker and Warburg, 1979. — Bibliography: p341-357. — Includes index
ISBN 0-586-08386-3 (pbk) : £2.50
Also classified at 612′.82 B81-02750

128′.2 — Mind — *Philosophical perspectives*
Anscombe, G. E. M.. Metaphysics and the philosophy of mind / [G.E.M. Anscombe]. — Oxford : Blackwell, 1981. — x,239p : ill ; 24cm. — (The Collected philosophical papers of G.E.M. Anscombe ; v.2)
Includes index
ISBN 0-631-12932-4 : £15.00
Primary classification 110 B81-40049

Armstrong, D. M.. The nature of mind / D.M. Armstrong. — Brighton : Harvester, 1981, c1980. — x,175p ; 22cm
Originally published: St Louia, Queensland : University of Queensland Press, 1980. — Bibliography: p166-168. - Includes index
ISBN 0-7108-0027-4 : £12.50 : CIP rev. B81-10589

Boden, Margaret A.. Minds and mechanisms : philosophical psychology and computational models / Margaret A. Boden. — Brighton : Harvester, 1981. — 311p : ill ; 22cm. — (Harvester studies in cognitive science ; 16)
Bibliography: p309-311
ISBN 0-7108-0005-3 : £20.00 : CIP rev. B80-12207

128′.2 — Philosophical psychology
Loar, Brian. Mind and meaning. — Cambridge : Cambridge University Press, Dec.1981. — [268]p. — (Cambridge studies in philosophy)
ISBN 0-521-22959-6 : £22.00 : CIP entry
Also classified at 401′.9 B81-37004

128′.2′09 — Mind. Theories, *to 1980*
Gregory, R. L.. Mind in science : a history of explanations in psychology and physics / Richard L. Gregory. — London : Weidenfeld and Nicolson, c1981. — xxvi,641p : ill ; 24cm
Bibliography: p605-626. — Includes index
ISBN 0-297-77825-0 : £18.50 B81-38269

128′.3 — Happiness. Evolutionary aspects
Attenborough, David. Happiness / David Attenborough. — [Birmingham] : [University of Birmingham], [1981]. — 8p : ports ; 21cm. — (The 1980 Baggs memorial lecture)
Cover title
ISBN 0-7044-0520-2 (pbk) : Unpriced B81-28991

128′.3 — Love — *Philosophical perspectives*
Francis, Chris. Love and peace / Chris Francis. — Bognor Regis : New Horizon, c1979. — 132,[16]p ; 22cm
ISBN 0-86116-171-8 : £3.25
Also classified at 327.1′72′01 B81-21775

128′.3 — Man. Mind. Relationship with body — *Study examples: Memory — Philosophical perspectives*
Bergson, Henri. Matter and memory / Henri Bergson ; authorised translation by Nancy Margaret Paul and W. Scott Palmer. — London : Allen & Unwin, 1978. — xxiv,339p : ill ; 23cm. — (Muirhead library of philosophy)
Translation of: Matière et mémoire. — Originally published: London : Swan Sonnenschein, 1911. — Includes index
ISBN 0-85527-914-1 : £10.50 B81-04402

128′.4 — Interpersonal relationships — *Philosophical perspectives*
Berenson, F. M.. Understanding persons : personal and impersonal relationships / F.M. Berenson. — Brighton : Harvester, 1981. — 198p ; 23cm. — (Harvester studies in philosophy ; 22)
Bibliography: p191-193. — Includes index
ISBN 0-85527-463-8 : £18.95 B81-19690

128′.4 — Man. Actions — *Phenomenological viewpoints*
John Paul II, *Pope*. The acting person / Karol Wojtyla ; translated from the Polish by Andrzej Potocki ; this definitive text of the work established in collaboration with the author by Anna-Teresa Tymieniecka. — Dordrecht ; London : Reidel, c1979. — xxiii,367p : 2facsims,1port ; 23cm. — (Analecta Husserliana ; v.10)
Translation and revision of: Osoba i Czyn. — Includes index
ISBN 90-277-0985-8 (cased) : Unpriced
ISBN 90-277-0969-6 (library ed) B81-15259

128′.4 — Man. Actions — *Philosophical perspectives — Conference proceedings*

Winnipeg Conference on Human Action *(1975)*. Action theory : proceedings of the Winnipeg Conference on Human Action, held at Winnipeg, Manitoba, Canada, 9-11 May 1975 / edited by Myles Brand and Douglas Walton. — Dordrecht ; London : Reidel, c1980. — vi,345p ; 23cm. — (Synthese library ; v.97)
Includes index
ISBN 90-277-0671-9 (cased) : Unpriced
ISBN 90-277-1188-7 (pbk) : Unpriced
B81-13652

128′.4 — Man. Nature

Amor, J. B. G.. Everybody is an idiot / J.B.G. Amor. — London ([370A Green Lanes, N13]) : [Topset Typographers], 1980. — 107p : 1ill ; 18cm
Includes index
ISBN 0-9507354-0-x (pbk) : £1.50 B81-19784

Midgley, Mary. Beast and man : the roots of human nature / Mary Midgley. — London : Methuen, 1980, c1978. — xxii,377p ; 22cm ; pbk. — (University paperbacks)
Originally published: Ithaca : Cornell University Press, 1978 ; Hassocks : Harvester, 1979. — Bibliography: p365-369. — Includes index
ISBN 0-416-73250-x : £4.50 : CIP rev.
B79-34658

128′.4 — Man. Nature — *Anthroposophical viewpoints*

Steiner, Rudolf. The being of man and his future evolution : nine lectures given in Berlin from November 2nd 1908 to June 17th 1909 / Rudolf Steiner ; translated by Pauline Wehrle. — London : Steiner, 1981. — 148p ; 23cm
Translation from the German
ISBN 0-85440-402-3 (cased) : £7.50
ISBN 0-85440-405-8 (pbk) : £4.95 B81-35610

Trevelyan, George. Operation redemption : a vision of hope in an age of turmoil / by George Trevelyan. — Wellingborough : Turnstone, 1981. — 160p ; 22cm
Bibliography: p158-159
ISBN 0-85500-150-x (pbk) : £3.50 : CIP rev.
B81-00714

128′.4 — Man. Nature. Theories, *to 1980 — Readings from contemporary sources*

The **Study** of human nature : readings / selected, edited, and introduced by Leslie Stevenson. — New York ; Oxford : Oxford University Press, 1981. — xi,333p ; 23cm
Bibliography: p331-333
ISBN 0-19-502827-9 (pbk) : £5.95 B81-22125

128′.5 — Life — *Philosophical perspectives*

Fowles, John. The Aristos / John Fowles. — Rev. ed. — London : Triad, 1981, c1980. — 206p ; 18cm
Previous ed.: London : Cape, 1964
ISBN 0-586-05377-8 (pbk) : £1.50 B81-32919

The **Meaning** of life / edited by E.D. Klemke. — New York ; Oxford : Oxford University Press, 1981. — xii,269p ; 23cm
Bibliography: p267-269
ISBN 0-19-502871-6 (pbk) : £4.50 B81-25974

129 — ORIGIN AND DESTINY OF INDIVIDUAL SOULS

129 — Immortality — *Philosophical perspectives*

Feuerbach, Ludwig. Thoughts on death and immortality : from the papers of a thinker, along with an appendix of theological-satirical epigrams, edited by one of his friends / Ludwig Feuerbach ; translated with introduction and notes by James A. Massey. — Berkeley ; London : University of California Press, c1980. — xliii,261p ; 24cm
Translation of: Gedanken über Tod und Unsterblichkeit
ISBN 0-520-04051-1 : £15.50 B81-34329

131 — PARAPSYCHOLOGICAL AND OCCULT TECHNIQUES FOR ACHIEVEMENT OF WELL-BEING, HAPPINESS, SUCCESS

131 — Meditation

White Eagle *(Spirit)*. The still voice. — Liss : White Eagle Publishing Trust, Sept.1981. — [128]p
ISBN 0-85487-049-0 : £2.50 : CIP entry
B81-21591

131 — Personal success. Parapsychological aspects

McNeil, Sandra. Psi-kinetic power. — Wellingborough : Excalibur, Nov.1981. — [256]p
ISBN 0-85454-081-4 (pbk) : £3.50 : CIP entry
B81-30425

133 — PARAPSYCHOLOGY AND OCCULTISM

133 — Candles. Burning. Occult aspects

Vinci, Leo. The book of practical candle magic. — Wellingborough : Aquarian Press, Sept.1981. — [128]p
ISBN 0-85030-271-4 (pbk) : £2.95 : CIP entry
B81-20532

133 — Education. Occult aspects

Bailey, Alice A.. Education in the new age / by Alice A. Bailey. — New York ; London : Lucis, c1954 (1974 printing). — 174p ; 20cm
Includes index
Unpriced (pbk) B81-37853

133 — Evolution. Occult aspects

Bailey, Alice A.. The consciousness of the atom / by Alice A. Bailey. — New York ; London : Lucis, c1961 (1974 printing). — 163p ; 20cm
Originally published: 1922. — Includes index
Unpriced (pbk) B81-37854

133 — Gemstones. Occult aspects

Uyldert, Mellie. The magic of precious stones. — Wellingborough : Turnstone Press, Oct.1981. — [160]p
Translation of: Verborgen krachten der edelstenen
ISBN 0-85500-138-0 (pbk) : £3.95 : CIP entry
B81-27427

133 — Glamour. Occult aspects

Bailey, Alice A.. Glamour : a world problem / by Alice A. Bailey. — New York ; London : Lucis, c1978. — xi,290p ; 20cm
Originally published: 1950. — Includes index
Unpriced (pbk) B81-37859

133 — Life. Occult aspects

Bailey, Alice A.. A treatise on the seven rays / by Alice A. Bailey. — New York ; London : Lucis, 1936-1960 (1972-1979 printing). — 5v. : ill ; 24cm
Also available in paperback. — Includes index. — Contents: Vol.1 Esoteric psychology (part 1) — Vol.2 Esoteric psychology (part 2) — Vol.3 Esoteric astrology — Vol.4 — Esoteric healing — Vol.5 Rays and initiations
Unpriced B81-37860

Pandit, M. P.. Occult lines behind life / M.P. Pandit. — Pomona, Calif. : Auromere ; London : Fudge [distributor], 1979. — 100p ; 22cm
ISBN 0-89744-001-3 (pbk) : £1.95 B81-05528

133 — Man. Influence of cosmic forces

Sturzaker, James. The cosmic breath / James Sturzaker. — London (25 Circle Gardens, SW19 3JX) : Metatron, 1981. — 86p ; 19cm
ISBN 0-9506168-1-8 (pbk) : Unpriced
B81-18382

133 — Man. Mind. Occult aspects

Gooch, Stan. The double helix of the mind / by Stan Gooch. — London : Wildwood, 1980. — 250p : ill ; 23cm
Bibliography: p242-246. — Includes index
ISBN 0-7045-3037-6 : £7.95 B81-36678

133 — Man. Occult aspects

Bennett, J. G.. Transformation / J.G. Bennett. — Sherborne : Coombe Springs, 1978. — viii,198p ; 21cm
ISBN 0-900306-51-3 (pbk) : £2.50 B81-00715

133 — Occult practices — *Amateurs' manuals*

Green, Marian. The paths of magic / Marian Green. — [London] ([BCM-SCL Quest, WC1V 6XX]) : [M. Green], [c1980]. — 36p : ill ; 26cm
Cover title. — Bibliography: p36
£1.00 (pbk) B81-00716

133 — Occultism

Butler, W. E.. Apprenticed to magic. — Wellingborough : Aquarian Press, Aug.1981. — [112]p
Originally published: 1962
ISBN 0-85030-284-6 (pbk) : £2.95 : CIP entry
B81-22608

Fludd, Robert. Mosaical philosophy : grounded upon the essential truth or eternal sapience / written first in Latin, and afterwards thus rendered into English by Robert Fludd ; edited by Adam McLean. — Edinburgh (12 Antigua St., Edinburgh) : [A. McLean], c1979. — 125p : ill,1port ; 22cm. — (Magnum opus hermetic sourceworks ; no.2)
Translation of: Philosophia Moysaica. — Originally published: London : Humphrey Moseley, 1659. — Limited ed. of 250 copies. — Bibliography: p125
Unpriced B81-34438

Fortune, Dion. Practical occultism in daily life / by Dion Fortune. — Wellingborough : Aquarian Press, 1976 (1980 [printing]). — 64p ; 22cm
Originally published: London : Williams & Norgate, 1935
ISBN 0-85030-133-5 (pbk) : £1.95 B81-01713

Grant, Kenneth. Outside the circles of time / Kenneth Grant. — London : Muller, 1980. — xii,316p,[16]p of plates : ill ; 23cm
Bibliography: p299-305. - Includes index
ISBN 0-584-10468-5 : £10.95 B81-00717

Khunrath, Heinrich. The amphitheatre engravings of Heinrich Khunrath / translated by Patricia Tahil ; edited by Adam McLean. — Edinburgh (12 Antigua St., Edinburgh) : [A. McLean], c1980. — 95p,[9]folded leaves of plates : ill,1facsim,1ports ; 22cm. — (Magnum opus hermetic sourceworks ; no.7)
Translation of: Amphitheatrum sapientiae aeternae solius verae Christiano-Kabalisticum, divino-magicum nec non physico-chymicum, tertriunum Catholicon. — Limited ed. of 250 copies. — Includes commentaries on the text by De Guaita, Craven, Arndt and McLean
Unpriced B81-34439

Norvell. Amazing secrets of the mystic East : how to control the hidden forces of the universe / by Norvell. — Wellingborough : Thomas, 1981, c1980. — 227p : ill ; 22cm
Originally published: West Nyack : Parker, 1980
ISBN 0-85454-075-x (pbk) : £3.50 B81-08529

Van Buren, Elizabeth. Lord of the flame / Elizabeth Van Buren. — Sudbury : Spearman, 1981. — 285p : ill,maps ; 23cm
ISBN 0-85435-424-7 : £6.95 B81-36506

Yeats, W. B.. A vision / by W.B. Yeats. — Reissued with corrections. — London : Macmillan, 1962 (1981 [printing]). — vii,305p : ill ; 23cm
ISBN 0-333-07689-3 (cased) : Unpriced
ISBN 0-333-30980-4 (pbk) : £3.95 B81-26182

133 — Occultism — *Correspondence, diaries, etc.*

Lévi, Éliphas. Letters to a disciple : letters from Eliphas Lévi Zahed to Baron Nicolas-Joseph Spedalieri on magic, numerology and the Tarot / Eliphas Lévi ; introduction by Christopher McIntosh. — Wellingborough : Aquarian Press, 1980. — 128p : ill ; 22cm
Originally published: in Lucifer, 1894-1895
ISBN 0-85030-222-6 (pbk) : £2.95 : CIP rev.
B80-06268

133 — Occultism. Meditation

Bailey, Alice A.. From intellect to intuition / by Alice A. Bailey. — New York ; London : Lucis, 1960 (1978 printing). — vii,275p ; 19cm
Originally published: 1932. — Includes index
Unpriced (pbk) B81-37858

133 — Occultism. Meditation *continuation*

Letters on occult meditation / revised and edited by Alice A. Bailey. — New York ; London : Lucis, 1922, c1978 (1978 printing). — 375p : ill ; 20cm
Includes index
Unpriced (pbk) B81-37043

133 — Paranormal phenomena

Gooch, Stan. The secret life of humans / Stan Gooch. — London : Dent, 1981. — 225p : ill ; 25cm
Bibliography: p211-216. — Includes index
ISBN 0-460-04527-x : £7.95 : CIP rev.
B81-06876

Taylor, John, *1931-*. Science and the supernatural / John Taylor. — London : Granada, 1981, c1980. — 192p ; 20cm. — (A Paladin book)
Originally published: London : Temple Smith, 1980. — Bibliography: p182-185. — Includes index
ISBN 0-586-08367-7 (pbk) : £1.95 B81-31391

133 — Paranormal phenomena — *Stories, anecdotes*

Weekend book of ghosts and horror / edited by Richard Whittington-Egan. — London : Published by Harmsworth Publications for Associated Newspapers Ltd, c1981. — 128p : ill,ports ; 22cm
ISBN 0-85144-178-5 (pbk) : £1.00
Also classified at 364.1′523′09 B81-24182

133 — Parapsychology

Alcock, James E.. Parapsychology, science or magic. — Oxford : Pergamon, Apr.1981. — [280]p. — (Foundations and philosophy of science and technology series) (Pergamon international library)
ISBN 0-08-025773-9 : £23.00 : CIP entry
ISBN 0-08-025772-0 (pbk) : £11.50 B81-02083

133 — Parapsychology — *Conference proceedings — Serials*

Research in parapsychology. — 1979. — Metuchen, N.J. ; London : Scarecrow Press, 1980. — vi,232p
ISBN 0-8108-1327-0 : Unpriced
ISSN 0093-4798 B81-21940

133 — Plants. Occult aspects

Warburton, Diana. Magiculture / Diana Warburton ; with chapter page woodcuts by the author. — Dorchester : Prism, 1980. — 80p : ill ; 20cm
ISBN 0-904727-98-x : £3.95 B81-00718

133 — Universe. Occult aspects

Bailey, Alice A.. A treatise on cosmic fire / by Alice A. Bailey. — New York ; London : Lucis, c1962 (1977 printing). — xxvi,1367p ; 19cm
Originally published: 1925. — Includes index
Unpriced (pbk) B81-37857

133 — World. Occult aspects

Bailey, Alice A.. The externalisation of the hierarchy / by Alice A. Bailey. — New York ; London : Lucis, 1957 (1976 printing). — vii,744p ; 20cm
Includes index
Unpriced (pbk) B81-37041

133′.022′2 — Paranormal phenomena — *Illustrations*

Rickard, Robert. Photographs of the unknown / Robert Rickard, Richard Kelly. — London : New English Library, 1981, c1980. — 144p : ill (some col.),ports(some col.) ; 30cm
ISBN 0-450-04991-4 (pbk) : £4.95 B81-21367

133′.03′21 — Occultism — *Encyclopaedias*

Gettings, Fred. Dictionary of occult, hermetic and alchemical sigils / Fred Gettings. — London : Routledge & Kegan Paul, 1981. — 410p : ill ; 26cm
Bibliography: p293-312. - Includes index
ISBN 0-7100-0095-2 : £15.95 : CIP rev.
B81-08815

133′.03′21 — Paranormal phenomena — *Encyclopaedias*

Knight, Jan. A-Z of ghosts and the supernatural / Jan Knight ; illustrated by Valerie Littlewood. — [Leeds] : Pepper, 1980. — 128p : ill ; 21cm
ISBN 0-560-74509-5 : £3.95 B81-02792

133′.05 — Occultism — *Serials*

[Griffin *(Wakefield)***].** Griffin. — Vol.1, no.1 (Oct.-Nov.1980)-. — Wakefield (c/o G.B. Savage, 2 Prospect Building, East Ardsley, Wakefield, West Yorkshire) : Griffin Enterprises, 1980-. — v. : ill ; 33cm
Eight issues yearly
ISSN 0261-2003 = Griffin (Wakefield) : 5.50 per year B81-20090

Prediction annual. — 1981. — Croydon : Link House Magazines on behalf of Link House Publications, 1980. — 100p
ISSN 0079-4953 : £1.20 B81-03290

133′.05 — Paranormal phenomena — *Serials*

Alpha. — Issue 1 (Mar./Apr.1979)-issue 9 (Oct.1980). — Fleet (20 Regent St., Fleet, Hants GU13 9NR) : Pendulum Publishing, 1979-1980. — 9v. : ill,ports ; 30cm
Six issues yearly
£5.90 per year B81-38511

133′.09 — Occultism, *to 1980*

Maple, Eric. Old wives′ tales / Eric Maple ; with illustrations by Valerie Croker. — London : Hale, 1981. — 190p : ill ; 23cm
Bibliography: p175-177. — Includes index
ISBN 0-7091-8585-5 : £6.95 B81-10854

133′.09 — Paranormal phenomena, *to 1914*

Inglis, Brian. Natural and supernatural : a history of the paranormal from earliest times to 1914 / Brian Inglis. — London : Abacus, 1979, c1977. — xviii,579p ; 18cm
Originally published: London : Hodder and Stoughton, 1977. — Bibliography: p533-556. — Includes index
ISBN 0-349-11826-4 (pbk) : £2.95 B81-03482

133′.09′04 — Occultism, *1900-1982*

Webb, James. The occult establishment. — Glasgow (20 Park Circus, Glasgow G3 6BE) : Richard Drew, Nov.1981. — [544]p
Originally published: La Salle, Ill. : Open Court Publishing Co., 1976
ISBN 0-904002-82-9 : £9.50 : CIP entry
B81-30891

133′.092′2 — Paranormal phenomena — *Personal observations — Collections*

I′ve seen a ghost : true stories from show business / [compiled by] Richard Davis. — London : Granada, 1980, c1979. — 158p : ill ; 18cm. — (A Dragon book)
Originally published: London : Hutchinson, 1979
ISBN 0-583-30426-5 (pbk) : £0.95 B81-29278

133′.092′4 — Occultism. Crowley, Aleister — *Correspondence, diaries, etc.*

Crowley, Aleister. The magical diaries of To Mega Therion : the Beast 666 : logos aionos Thelema 1923 / Aleister Crowley ; edited by Stephen Skinner. — St. Helier, Jersey : Spearman, 1979. — 251p ; 26cm
Includes index
ISBN 0-85978-022-8 : £11.25 B81-09222

133′.092′4 — Paranormal phenomena — *Personal observations*

Bentine, Michael. The door marked summer / Michael Bentine ; foreword by E.R. Laithwaite. — London : Granada, 1981. — 294p ; 25cm
ISBN 0-246-11405-3 : £6.95 B81-39467

Moss, Thelma. The body electric : a personal journey into the mysteries of parapsychological research, bioenergy and kirlian photography / Thelma Moss. — London : Granada, 1981. — 256p,[8]p of plates : ill ; 20cm. — (A Paladin book)
Includes index
ISBN 0-586-08383-9 (pbk) : £2.25 B81-38227

133′.09412′23 — Scotland. Grampian Region. Findhorn. Occult communities: Findhorn Foundation

Faces of Findhorn : images of a planetary family / by the Findhorn Community ; [compiled and edited by Edwin Maynard]. — Forres : Findhorn Publications, c1980. — ix,177p : ill,ports ; 24cm
ISBN 0-905249-46-1 (cased) : Unpriced
ISBN 0-905249-48-8 (pbk) : £4.95 B81-40508

133′.09425′3 — Lincolnshire. Paranormal phenomena — *Serials*

Lincolnshire dragon. — No.1 (Mar.1980)-. — Boston, Lincs. (c/o A. Pickering, 16 Packhorse Lane, Swineshead, Boston, Lincs. PE20 3JE) : Lincolnshire Earth Mysteries Research, 1980-. — v. ; 30cm
Quarterly
ISSN 0260-0374 = Lincolnshire dragon : Free to members only B81-04590

133.1 — GHOSTS

133.1 — Ghosts

The **Folklore** of ghosts. — Woodbridge : Brewer, Oct.1981. — [224]p. — (Mistletoe series ; v.15)
ISBN 0-85991-079-2 : £15.00 : CIP entry
B81-30472

133.1 — Ghosts — *Case studies — For children*

Chambers, Aidan. Great ghosts of the world / Aidan Chambers ; text illustrations by Peter Edwards. — London : Severn House, 1981, c1974. — 137p : ill ; 21cm
Originally published: London : Pan, 1974
ISBN 0-7278-0664-5 : £4.25 B81-09015

133.1 — Ghosts — *For children*

Lambert, David, *1932-*. Ghosts / by David Lambert ; illustrated by Harry Bishop ; edited Jacqui Bailey. — London : Pan, 1981. — [24]p : col.ill,2col.ports ; 22cm. — (A Piccolo explorer book. Mysteries)
Bibliography: p[24]. — Includes index
ISBN 0-330-26356-0 (pbk) : £0.75 B81-07883

Lambert, David, *1932-*. Ghosts / by David Lambert ; illustrated by Harry Bishop. — London : Kingfisher, 1981. — [24]p : col.ill,col.ports ; 23cm. — (Kingfisher explorer books. Mysteries)
Bibliography p[24]. - Includes index
ISBN 0-7063-6103-2 : £1.95 B81-26673

133.1′072 — Ghosts. Investigation — *Manuals — For children*

Underwood, Peter. A ghost hunter′s handbook / Peter Underwood. — London : Sparrow, 1980. — 96p : ill,facsims ; 18cm
Bibliography: p96
ISBN 0-09-924080-7 (pbk) : £0.85 B81-04584

133.1′0941 — Great Britain. Ghosts — *Case studies*

Green, Andrew. Ghosts of today / Andrew Green. — London : Kaye & Ward, 1980. — xx,209p : ill,ports ; 20cm
Bibliography: p209
ISBN 0-7182-1255-x : £5.25 B81-01563

133.1′09422′7 — Southern Hampshire. Ghosts

Chilcott-Monk, J. P.. Ghosts of south Hampshire and beyond / J.P. Chilcott-Monk ; pen and ink illustrations — A. Ernest Monk. — Southampton : G.F. Wilson, 1980. — xiv,80p : ill,maps ; 22cm. — (Ghosts of Hampshire and beyond ; 1)
Maps on inside covers
ISBN 0-900810-23-8 (pbk) : Unpriced
B81-23562

133.1′09424′17 — England. Cotswolds. Ghosts

Brooks, John, *1939-*. Ghosts and witches of the Cotswolds / by J.A. Brooks. — Norwich : Jarrold Colour, c1981. — 144p : ill,facsims,ports ; 21cm
Includes index
ISBN 0-85306-914-x (pbk) : Unpriced
B81-26968

133.1'09427'36 — Greater Manchester *(Metropolitan County).* **Leigh. Ghosts** — *Stories, anecdotes*

Ward, Cyril. Ghosts of Leigh / by Cyril Ward ; illustrated by students of Butts C.E. Junior School. — Leigh (c/o Leigh Library, Leigh, Lancs. WN7 2EB) : Leigh Local History Society, 1980. — 32p : ill ; 14x22cm. — (Publication / Leigh Local History Society ; no.8)
£0.75 (pbk) B81-32493

133.1'2942189 — London. Enfield *(London Borough).* **Poltergeists** — *Case studies*

Playfair, Guy Lyon. This house is haunted : an investigation of the Enfield poltergeist / by Guy Lyon Playfair. — London : Souvenir, 1980. — 288p,[16]p of plates : ill,ports ; 23cm
Bibliography: p287-288
ISBN 0-285-62443-1 : £6.95 : CIP rev. B80-05187

Playfair, Guy Lyon. This house is haunted : the investigation of the Enfield poltergeist / Guy Lyon Playfair. — London : Sphere, 1981, c1980. — xi,275p,[8]p of plates : ill,facsims,ports ; 18cm
Originally published: London : Souvenir Press, 1980
ISBN 0-7221-6908-6 (pbk) : £1.50 B81-23338

133.1'29426715 — Essex. Borley. Rectories: Borley Rectory. Ghosts. Claimed observations, *1930-1945*

Price, Harry, *1881-1948*. The end of Borley Rectory / Harry Price. — Bath : Chivers, 1980. — 358p,[16]leaves of plates : ill,facsims,plans ; 23cm. — (A New Portway book)
Originally published: London : Harrap, 1946. — Bibliography: p341-347. - Includes index
ISBN 0-85594-074-3 : £5.95 B81-08755

133.1'29426723 — Essex. Dedham. Ghosts — *Personal observations*

Palmer, Terry. The ghost at my shoulder / Terry Palmer. — [London] : Corgi, 1981. — 192p : 2maps ; 18cm
Bibliography: p192
ISBN 0-552-11692-0 (pbk) : £1.00 B81-24307

133.1'4 — Poltergeists

Wilson, Colin. Poltergeist. — London : New English Library, Nov.1981. — [384]p
ISBN 0-450-04880-2 : £7.95 : CIP entry B81-32010

133.3 — DIVINATORY ARTS

133.3 — Political events, *ca 1995.* **Prophecies: Nostradamus. Vrayes centuries** — *Critical studies*

Noorbergen, Rene. Invitation to a holocaust : Nostradamus forecasts World War III / Rene Noorbergen ; research by Joey Jochmans. — London : New English Library, 1981. — 200p : maps,1port ; 23cm
Includes quatrains in French by Nostradamus and the English translation. — Port on lining papers. — Bibliography: p199-200
ISBN 0-450-04751-2 : £5.95 B81-27008

133.3 — Prophecies, *1555-1566* — *Texts with commentaries*

Houghton-Brown, Geoffrey. British history according to the oracles of Nostradamus 1549-1945 / by Geoffrey Houghton-Brown. — [London] ([29 Thurloe Sq., S.W.7.]) : [G. Houghton-Brown]. — 96p ; 21cm
Unpriced (pbk) B81-21432

Houghton-Brown, Geoffrey. The future according to the oracles of Nostradamus 1981-1999 / by Geoffrey Houghton-Brown. — [London] ([29 Thurloe Sq., S.W.7]) : [G. Houghton-Brown], c1980. — 22p ; 21cm
Unpriced (pbk) B81-21433

133.3 — Prophecies, *1568* — *Texts*

Nostradamus. The prophecies of Nostradamus / translated, edited and introduced by Erika Cheetham. — Rev. ed. — London : Corgi, 1981, c1973. — 478p ; 18cm
Parallel Middle French text with English translation. — Previous ed.: London : Spearman 1974
ISBN 0-552-11567-3 (pbk) : £1.75 B81-27825

133.3 — Psychic phenomena: Divination

Divination and oracles / edited by Michael Loewe and Carmen Blacker ; with contributions by Lama Chime Radha ... [et al.]. — London : Allen & Unwin, 1981. — 244p,8p of plates : ill ; 23cm
Includes index
ISBN 0-04-291016-1 : Unpriced : CIP rev. B81-02349

133.3'09 — Predictions, *to 1979*

Fisher, Joe. Predictions / by Joe Fisher ; with illustrations compiled by Peter Commins. — London : Sidgwick & Jackson, 1981, c1980. — 224p : ill,maps,ports ; 25cm. — (A Jonathan-James book)
Originally published: New York : Van Nostrand Reinhold, 1980. — Bibliography: p219-222
ISBN 0-283-98726-x : £7.95 B81-17735

133.3'09'034 — Predictions, *1800-1945*

Morgan, Chris. The shape of futures past : the story of prediction / Chris Morgan. — Exeter : Webb & Bower ; Leicester : WHS Distributors, 1980. — 208p : ill,1map ; 24cm
Bibliography: p202-203. — Includes index
ISBN 0-906671-15-9 (pbk) : £5.95 : CIP rev. B80-18996

133.3'092'4 — Prophecies. Hermann, John — *Biographies*

Hermann, John. Signs / by John Hermann. — London : Regency Press, c1980. — 121p ; 23cm
ISBN 0-7212-0650-6 : £4.00 B81-06184

133.3'23 — Radiaesthesia

Eerenbeemt, Noud van den. The pendulum, crystal ball and magic mirror. — Wellingborough : Aquarian Press, Feb.1982. — [64]p
Translation of: Pendel-, kristal- en speigelmagic
ISBN 0-85030-270-6 (pbk) : £2.95 : CIP entry B81-35840

133.3'23 — Radiaesthesia. Use of pendulums

Nielsen, Greg. Pendulum power : a mystery you can see, a power you can feel / by Greg Nielsen and Joseph Polansky. — Wellingborough ([Denington Estate], Wellingborough, Northants. [NN8 2RQ]) : Excalibur, 1981, c1977. — 128p : ill,1map ; 22cm
Originally published: New York : Destiny Books, 1977. — Bibliography: p124-128
ISBN 0-85454-077-6 (pbk) : £2.95 : CIP rev. B81-13742

133.3'24'028 — Fortune-telling. Techniques — *Manuals*

Cheiro. The Cheiro book of fate and fortune. — London : Hamlyn Paperbacks, 1980, c1971. — 339p : ill ; 18cm
Originally published: London : Barrie & Jenkins, 1971
ISBN 0-600-32034-0 (pbk) : £1.50 B81-02865

133.3'2424 — Tarot cards

Woudhuysen, Jan. Tarotmania / Jan Woudhuysen. — London : Sphere, 1981, c1979. — 223p : ill ; 18cm
Originally published: London : Wildwood House, 1979. — Bibliography: p222-223
ISBN 0-7221-9314-9 (pbk) : £1.40 B81-14595

133.3'2424 — Tarot cards. Cabalistic interpretations

Wirth, Oswald. Introduction to the study of the Tarot. — Wellingborough : Aquarian Press, July 1981. — [64]p
Translation of: L'Etude du Tarot
ISBN 0-85030-263-3 (pbk) : £2.25 : CIP entry B81-14901

133.3'3 — Man. Problem solving. Use of I Ching

Norvell. Miracle power of the I Ching / by Norvell. — Wellingborough (Wellingborough, Northants.) : Excalibur, 1981, c1980. — 204p ; 22cm
Originally published: West Nyack, N.Y. : Parker, 1980
ISBN 0-85454-080-6 (pbk) : £2.95 B81-29251

133.3'33 — Antiquities: Geomantic aspects — *Serials*

Ancient mysteries : the journal of geomancy lost knowledge and ancient enigmas. — Vol.4, no.4 = no.16 (Autumn 1980)-. — Cambridge (142, Pheasant Rise, Bar Hill, Cambridge CB3 8SD) : Institute of Geomantic Research, 1980-. — v. : ill ; 21cm
Quarterly. — Continues: Journal of geomancy
£3.75 per year B81-04902

133.3'33 — Cambridgeshire. Wandlebury. Antiquities. Geomantic aspects

Pennick, Nigel. Wandlebury mysteries / by Nigel Pennick. — Cambridge (142 Pheasant Rise, Bar Hill, Cambridge CB3 8SD) : Cambridgeshire Ancient Mysteries Group, [1981?]. — 10p : ill,1map ; 21cm. — (Occasional paper / Cambridgeshire Ancient Mysteries Group)
Unpriced (unbound) B81-27612

133.3'33 — Measurement. Geomantic aspects

Macleod, Donald, *1927-*. Theory of measurement / Donald Macleod. — Bognor Regis : New Horizon, c1980. — 89p : ill ; 21cm
ISBN 0-86116-150-5 : £3.50 B81-21730

133.3'33 — South-east England. Antiquities. Geomantic aspects — *Serials*

Quicksilver messenger : the South-east magazine of earth mysteries. — No.1 (1980)-. — Hove (26a, Wilbury Ave., Hove, Sussex) : C. Ashton Quicksilver Messenger, 1980-. — v. : ill ; 30cm
Irregular. — Description based on: No.2 (Autumn 1980)
ISSN 0260-7484 = Quicksilver messenger : £3.20 B81-13697

133.3'33 — West Germany. Osterholz. Prehistoric earthwork structures. Siting & construction. Geomantic aspects

Heinsch, Josef. Prechristian geomancy / Josef Heinsch ; translated by Michael Behrend. — Cambridge (142 Pheasant Rise, Bar Hill Cambridge CB3 85D) : Cambridgeshire Ancient Mysteries Group, [1981?]. — [8]p : ill ; 22cm. — (Occasional paper / Cambridgeshire Ancient Mysteries Group)
Translation from the German
Unpriced (unbound) B81-27611

133.3'35 — Numerology

Phillips, David A.. Secrets of the inner self : the complete book of numerology / David A. Phillips. — London : Angus & Robertson, 1980. — xiii,176p : ill ; 23cm
ISBN 0-207-14154-1 : £3.95 B81-08460

133.3'35 — Pyramidology

Toth, Max. Pyramid power : the secret energy of the ancients revealed / by Max Toth and Greg Nielsen. — Wellingborough ([Denington Estate], Wellingborough, Northants. [NN8 2RQ]) : Excalibur, 1981, c1976. — 207p : ill,maps,plans ; 22cm
Originally published: New York : Destiny Books, 1974. — Bibliography: p195-201. — Includes index
ISBN 0-85454-079-2 (pbk) : £3.75 : CIP rev. B81-13749

133.3'35 — Pyramids. Psychic powers

Gray-Cobb, Geoff. Secrets from beyond the Pyramids. — Wellingborough : Excalibur, Feb.1982. — [224]p
ISBN 0-85454-076-8 (pbk) : £3.50 : CIP entry B81-36970

133.4 — MAGIC, WITCHCRAFT, DEMONOLOGY

133.4'0932 — Ancient Egyptian magic

Farr, Florence. Egyptian magic : occult mysteries in Ancient Egypt. — Wellingborough : Aquarian Press, Feb.1982. — [96]p
ISBN 0-85030-277-3 (pbk) : £2.95 : CIP entry B81-36971

133.4′22′0924 — British Columbia. Victoria. Satanism, *ca 1955 — Childhood reminiscences*

Smith, Michelle. Michelle remembers / Michelle Smith and Lawrence Pazder. — London : Joseph, 1981, c1980. — 308p,[16]p of plates : ill,ports ; 23cm
Originally published: New York : Congdon & Lattes, c1980
ISBN 0-7181-1992-4 : £6.95 B81-08489

133.4′26′0926 — England. Man. Demonic possession, *1589-1599 — Case studies*

Walker, D. P.. Unclean spirits : possession and exorcism in France and England in the late sixteenth and early seventeenth centuries / D.P. Walker. — London : Scolar, 1981. — 116p ; 25cm
Includes index
ISBN 0-85967-620-x : £9.95 : CIP rev.
Also classified at 133.4′26′0926 B80-32841

133.4′26′0926 — France. Man. Demonic possession, *1566-1599 — Case studies*

Walker, D. P.. Unclean spirits : possession and exorcism in France and England in the late sixteenth and early seventeenth centuries / D.P. Walker. — London : Scolar, 1981. — 116p ; 25cm
Includes index
ISBN 0-85967-620-x : £9.95 : CIP rev.
Primary classification 133.4′26′0926 B80-32841

133.4′3 — Magic & witchcraft

Crowther, Patricia. Lid off the cauldron : a handbook for witches / Patricia Crowther. — London : Fredrick Muller, 1981. — 156p,[8]p of plates : ill,2ports ; 23cm
Bibliography: p151-152. — Includes index
ISBN 0-584-10421-9 : £6.95 : CIP rev.
B81-06608

133.4′3 — Magic. Rituals

Regardie, Israel. Ceremonial magic : a guide to the mechanisms of ritual / by Israel Regardie. — Wellingborough : Aquarian Press, 1980. — 127p : ill ; 22cm
ISBN 0-85030-237-4 (pbk) : £2.95 : CIP rev.
B80-22834

133.4′3 — White magic — *Manuals*

Bailey, Alice A.. A treatise on white magic : or The way of the disciple / by Alice A. Bailey. — New York ; London ([Suite 54, 3 Whitehall Court SW14 2EF]) : Lucis, 1934, c1979 (1979 printing). — xiv,705p ; 24cm
Also available as a paperback. — Includes index
Unpriced B81-37024

133.4′3 — Witches — *For children*

Jack, Adrienne. Witches and witchcraft / by Adrienne Jack ; illustrated by Esme Eve. — London : Watts, c1980. — 48p : col.ill ; 22cm. — (An Easy-read fact book)
Includes index
ISBN 0-85166-801-1 : £2.99 B81-04470

133.4′3′0922 — Witches — *Biographies*

Ericson, Eric. The world, the flesh, the Devil : a biographical dictionary of witches / Eric Ericson. — London : New English Library, 1981. — 285p,[16]p of plates : ports ; 23cm
ISBN 0-450-04726-1 : £6.95 B81-27009

133.4′3′0924 — United States. Witchcraft — *Personal observations — Correspondence, diaries, etc.*

Jay′s journal / edited by Beatrice Sparks. — [London] : Corgi, 1981, c1979. — 170p ; 18cm
Originally published: New York : Times Books, 1979
ISBN 0-552-11603-3 (pbk) : £1.25 B81-08449

133.4′3′0934 — Ancient India. Magic

Stutley, Margaret. Ancient Indian magic and folklore : an introduction : Margaret Stutley. — London : Routledge & Kegan Paul, 1980. — xiii,190p,[8]p of plates : ill ; 23cm
Bibliography: p171-178. - Includes index
ISBN 0-7100-0388-9 : £6.50 : CIP rev.
B80-11298

133.4′3′0941 — Great Britain. Witchcraft — *For children*

Finlay, Winifred. Tales of sorcery and witchcraft / Winifred Finlay ; illustrated by Laszlo Acs. — London : Kaye & Ward, 1980. — 127p : ill ; 23cm
ISBN 0-7182-1249-5 : £4.50 B81-02304

133.4′3′09415 — Ireland. Witchcraft

Seymour, St. John D.. Irish witchcraft and demonology. — Kilkenny : Roberts Books, Dec.1981. — [288]p
Originally published: Dublin : Hodges, Figgis & Co., 1913
ISBN 0-907561-04-7 (pbk) : CIP entry
B81-34219

133.4′3′0942 — England. Witchcraft, *to 1951*

Hole, Christina. [Witchcraft in England]. Witchcraft in Britain / Christina Hole ; drawings by Mervyn Peake. — London : Paladin : Granada, 1979, c1977. — 203p : ill ; 20cm
Originally published: London : Batsford, 1977. — Bibliography: p183-186. — Includes index
ISBN 0-586-08333-2 (pbk) : £1.50 B81-01655

133.4′3′09426 — East Anglia. Witchcraft, *1600-1700*

Gardiner, Tom. Broomstick over Essex and East Anglia : an introduction to witchcraft in the eastern counties during the seventeenth century / by Tom Gardiner. — Hornchurch : Henry, 1981. — 59p : ill ; 22cm
Bibliography: p59. — Includes index
ISBN 0-86025-851-3 : £3.45 : CIP rev.
B81-08859

133.4′3′0979461 — California. San Francisco. Witchcraft — *Rites*

Starhawk. The spiral dance : a rebirth of the ancient religion of the great Goddess / Starhawk. — San Francisco ; London : Harper & Row, c1979. — vi,218p : ill ; 24cm
Bibliography: p214-218
ISBN 0-06-067535-7 (pbk) : £5.95 B81-35441

133.4′4 — Holy Grail. Occult aspects

Ravenscroft, Trevor. The cup of destiny : the quest for the grail / Trevor Ravenscroft. — London : Rider, 1981. — 194p : 1ill ; 22cm
ISBN 0-09-144641-4 (pbk) : £4.95 B81-21414

133.4′4 — Talismans — *Manuals*

Regardie, Israel. How to make and use talismans / by Israel Regardie. — Rev. and reset. — Wellingborough : Aquarian Press, 1981. — 62p : ill ; 22cm
Previous ed.: 1972. — Bibliography: p63
ISBN 0-85030-209-9 (pbk) : £2.25 : CIP rev.
B81-07430

133.5 — ASTROLOGY

133.5 — Astrological predictions. Use of plants

Sheridan, Jo. The floral oracle / Jo Sheridan. — London : Granada, 1980. — 256p : ill ; 18cm. — (A Mayflower book)
Bibliography: p254-256
ISBN 0-583-12870-x (pbk) : £1.50 B81-02915

133.5 — Astrology

Alexander, John, *1952-*. The astrology cycle / John Alexander. — Pyrford (23 Warren Farm, Pyrford, Surrey. GU22 8AF) : Imp, 1981. — 77p : ill ; 22cm
ISBN 0-906756-00-6 (pbk) : £2.25 B81-26853

Baker, Douglas, *1922-*. The theory, interpretation and practice of esoteric astrology / by Douglas Baker. — Essendon (′Little Elephant′, Essendon, Herts.) : D. Baker. — (The seven pillars of ancient wisdom ; v.4)
Part 1. — c1975. — 434p : ill(some col.) ; 29cm
Includes index
ISBN 0-906006-01-5 (pbk) : Unpriced
B81-08404

Baker, Douglas, *1922-*. The theory, interpretation and practice of esoteric astrology / by Douglas Baker. — Essendon (′Little Elephant′, Essendon, Herts.) : D. Baker. — (The seven pillars of ancient wisdom ; v.5)
Part 2. — c1978. — 242,37p : ill(some col.),maps(some col.),ports(some col.) ; 29cm
Includes index
ISBN 0-906006-12-0 (pbk) : Unpriced
B81-08405

Eysenck, H. J.. Astrology : science or superstition. — London : Maurice Temple Smith, Jan.1982. — [288]p
ISBN 0-85117-214-8 : £9.00 : CIP entry
B81-33833

Gauquelin, Michel. Dreams and illusions of astrology / Michel Gauquelin. — London : Glover & Blair, 1980, c1979. — xiv,181p ; 23cm
Translation of: Songes et mensonges de l′astrologie. — This translation originally published: New York : Prometheus, 1979
ISBN 0-906681-04-9 : £9.95 B81-10817

Parker, Derek. The compleat astrologer : the practical encyclopaedia of astrological science ... / by Derek and Julia Parker. — London : Mitchell Beazley, 1971 (1979 [printing]). — 256p : col.ill,charts,maps,ports ; 30cm
Includes index
Unpriced (corrected : cased)
ISBN 0-85533-064-3 (pbk) : £4.95 B81-15434

Rathgeb, Marlene Masini. Success signs. — London : New English Library, Feb.1982. — [256]p
Originally published: New York : St Martin′s Press, 1981
ISBN 0-450-05353-9 (pbk) : £2.25 : CIP entry
B81-37582

133.5 — Man. Personality. Astrological aspects

Gauquelin, Michel. The spheres of destiny : your personality and the planets / Michael Gauquelin. — [London] : Corgi, 1981, c1980. — 256p : ill ; 18cm
Originally published: London : Dent, 1980. — Bibliography: p251. — Includes index
ISBN 0-552-11636-x (pbk) : £1.50 B81-17049

133.5 — Meditation. Astrological aspects

Hodgson, Joan. Planetary harmonies : an astrological book of meditation / Joan Hodgson ; illustrated by Margaret Clarke. — Liss : White Eagle Publishing Trust, 1980. — 151p : ill(some col.) ; 23cm
Includes index
ISBN 0-85487-047-4 : £5.50 : CIP rev.
B80-21318

133.5′0240431 — Astrology — *For parents*

Astrop, John. Sun child moon child : how to make the most of your relationship with your child / John Astrop ; with cartoons by the author. — London : Pan, 1981. — 268p : ill ; 18cm
ISBN 0-330-26283-1 (pbk) : £1.50 B81-14116

133.5′03′21 — Astrology — *Encyclopaedias*

Fleming-Mitchell, Leslie. [Running Press glossary of astrology terms]. The language of astrology / Leslie Fleming-Mitchell. — [London] : W.H. Allen, 1981, c1977. — [102]p ; 20cm. — (A Star book)
Originally published: Philadelphia : Running Press, c1977
ISBN 0-352-30950-4 (pbk) : £1.50 B81-35605

133.5′05 — Astrological predictions — *Serials*

Raphael′s astrological almanac. — 1981. — Slough : W. Foulsham, c1980. — 113p
ISBN 0-572-01125-3 : £0.95
ISSN 0305-1463 B81-00719

133.5′09 — Astrology, *to 1979*

Pattie, T. S.. Astrology : as illustrated in the collections of the British Library and the British Museum / T.S. Pattie. — London : British Library, c1980. — 36p : ill,facsims (some col.) ; 24cm
Text and illustration on inside cover
ISBN 0-904654-49-4 (pbk) : £1.50 : CIP rev.
B80-32842

133.5'0951 — Chinese astrology

Pushong, Carlyle A.. The Chinese animal zodiac / by Carlyle A. Pushong ; foreword by Roger Elliot. — London : Regency Press, c1980. — 92p : ill,ports ; 23cm
Bibliography: p91-92
£3.00 B81-12631

Wilhelm, Hans. Hans Wilhelm's Chinese horoscopes. — London : Pan, 1980. — 205p : ill ; 20cm
ISBN 0-330-26209-2 (pbk) : £1.25 B81-03310

133.5'2 — Signs of the zodiac

Katina. Astrology / Katina. — London (36 Park St., W1Y 4DE) : Park Lane Press, 1981. — 80p : col.ill ; 28cm
Includes index
£0.99 (pbk) B81-31878

133.5'2 — Signs of the zodiac — *For cat owners*

Fairchild, William. Astrology for cats : your cat's moon sign and how to live with it / William Fairchild ; illustrations by Lalla Ward. — London : Elm Tree, 1980. — 96p : ill ; 21cm
ISBN 0-241-10485-8 : £3.95 B81-00005

Leman, Martin. Martin Leman's starcats. — London : Pelham, 1980. — [28]p : col.ill,1col.port ; 26cm
Ill on lining papers
ISBN 0-7207-1232-7 : £3.95 B81-00006

133.5'3 — Astrology. Aspects

Lee, Jason. Modern aspects / by Jason Lee (J.E. Sunley). — Grimsby (42 Worlaby Rd., Grimsby, S. Humberside DN33 3JT) : J. Lee, 1980. — 132p : ill ; 30cm
ISBN 0-906947-03-0 (pbk) : £1.50 B81-05563

133.5'3 — Saturn. Astrological aspects

Lutin, Michael. Saturn signs : a new astrological approach to transforming your fears and anxieties into success / Micheal Lutin. — London : Sphere, 1980, c1979. — xiii,221p : ill ; 18cm
Originally published: New York : Delacorte Press, c1979
ISBN 0-7221-5651-0 (pbk) : £1.25 B81-14592

133.5'4 — Astrological predictions — *Horoscopes*

Acora, *Gypsy*. Your date with destiny / Gypsy Acora. — St. Teath : Bossiney, c1981. — 48p : ill,ports ; 21cm
Cover title
ISBN 0-906456-50-9 (pbk) : £0.50 B81-19626

133.5'4 — Astrological predictions. Horoscopes

Evans, Colin, *b.1894-*. The new Waite's compendium of natal astrology : with ephemeris for 1880-1990 and universal table of house / by Colin Evans. — Rev. ed / revised and brought up to date by Brian E.F. Gardener. — London : Routledge & Kegan Paul, 1981. — xiv,262p ; 22cm
Previous ed.: 1971
ISBN 0-7100-0882-1 (pbk) : £2.95 : CIP rev.
B81-08842

133.5'4 — Astrological predictions — *Horoscopes*

King, Teri. Libra 1982 : Teri King's complete horoscope for all those whose birthdays fall between 24 September and 23 October. — London : Pan Astral, 1981. — 91p : ill ; 18cm. — (Teri King's Pan Astral horoscopes)
ISBN 0-330-26392-7 (pbk) : £0.80 B81-39003

Petrie, Ann. Everything you ever wanted to know about astrology but thought you shouldn't ask. — London : Eyre Methuen, July 1981. — [192]p
ISBN 0-413-48360-6 : £6.50 : CIP entry
B81-13870

133.5'4 — Astrological predictions. Horoscopes. Interpretation - *Manuals*

Freeman, Martin. How to interpret a birth chart. — Wellingborough : Aquarian Press, Aug.1981. — [128]p
ISBN 0-85030-249-8 (pbk) : £2.95 : CIP entry
B81-19181

133.5'4'05 — Astrological predictions — *Horoscopes — Serials*

The **Mitchell** Beazley astrologer's pocket almanac . Pisces, February 19th-March 20th. — 1981-. — London : Mitchell Beazley, 1980-. — v. : ill ; 20cm
Annual. — Description based on: 1982
ISSN 0262-2114 = Mitchell Beazley astrologer's pocket almanac. Pisces, February 19th-March 20th : £2.95 B81-39497

The **Mitchell** Beazley astrologer's pocket almanac . Aquarius, January 21st-February 18th. — 1981-. — London : Mitchell Beazley, 1980-. — v. : ill ; 20cm
Annual. — Description based on: 1982
ISSN 0262-2025 = Mitchell Beazley astrologer's pocket almanac. Aquarius, January 21st-February 18th : £2.95 B81-39496

The **Mitchell** Beazley astrologer's pocket almanac . Aries, March 21st-April 20th. — 1981-. — London : Mitchell Beazley, 1980-. — v. : ill ; 20cm
Annual. — Description based on: 1982
ISSN 0262-2017 = Mitchell Beazley astrologer's pocket almanac. Aries, March 21st-April 20th : £2.95 B81-39498

The **Mitchell** Beazley astrologer's pocket almanac . Taurus, April 21st-May 21st. — 1981-. — London : Mitchell Beazley, 1980-. — v. : ill ; 20cm
Annual. — Description based on: 1982
ISSN 0262-2084 = Mitchell Beazley astrologer's pocket almanac. Taurus, April 21st-May 21st : £2.95 B81-39499

The **Mitchell** Beazley astrologer's pocket almanac . Capricorn, December 22nd-January 20th. — 1981-. — London : Mitchell Beazley, 1980-. — v. : ill ; 20cm
Annual. — Description based on: 1982
ISSN 0262-2076 = Mitchell Beazley astrologer's pocket almanac. Capricorn, December 22nd-January 20th : £2.95
B81-39507

The **Mitchell** Beazley astrologer's pocket almanac . Gemini, May 22nd-June 21st. — 1981-. — London : Mitchell Beazley, 1980-. — v. : ill ; 20cm
Annual. — Description based on: 1982
ISSN 0262-2033 = Mitchell Beazley astrologer's pocket almanac. Gemini, May 22nd-June 21st : £2.95 B81-39500

The **Mitchell** Beazley astrologer's pocket almanac . Cancer, June 22nd-July 22nd. — 1981-. — London : Mitchell Beazley, 1980-. — v. : ill ; 20cm
Annual. — Description based on: 1982
ISSN 0262-205x = Mitchell Beazley astrologer's pocket almanac. Cancer, June 22nd-July 22nd : £2.95 B81-39501

The **Mitchell** Beazley astrologer's pocket almanac . Leo, July 23rd-August 23rd. — 1981-. — London : Mitchell Beazley, 1980-. — v. : ill ; 20cm
Annual. — Description based on: 1982
ISSN 0262-2009 = Mitchell Beazley astrologer's pocket almanac. Leo, July 23rd-August 23rd : £2.95 B81-39502

The **Mitchell** Beazley astrologer's pocket almanac . Libra, September 23rd-October 23rd. — 1981-. — London : Mitchell Beazley, 1980-. — v. : ill ; 20cm
Annual. — Description based on: 1982
ISSN 0262-2041 = Mitchell Beazley astrologer's pocket almanac. Libra, September 23rd-October 23rd : £2.95 B81-39504

The **Mitchell** Beazley astrologer's pocket almanac . Sagittarius, November 24th-December 21st. — 1981-. — London : Mitchell Beazley, 1980-. — v. : ill ; 20cm
Annual. — Description based on: 1982
ISSN 0262-2106 = Mitchell Beazley astrologer's pocket almanac. Sagittarius, November 24th-December 21st : £2.95
B81-39506

The **Mitchell** Beazley astrologer's pocket almanac . Virgo, August 24th-September 22nd. — 1981-. — London : Mitchell Beazley, 1980-. — v. : ill ; 20cm
Annual. — Description based on: 1982
ISSN 0262-2068 = Mitchell Beazley astrologer's pocket almanac. Virgo, August 24th-September 22nd : £2.95 B81-39503

The **Mitchell** Beazley astrologer's pocket almanac . Scorpio, October 24th-November 22nd. — 1981-. — London : Mitchell Beazley, 1980-. — v. : ill ; 20cm
Annual. — Description based on: 1982
ISSN 0262-2092 = Mitchell Beazley astrologer's pocket almanac. Scorpio, October 24th-November 22nd : £2.95 B81-39505

133.5'42 — Astrological predictions. Horoscopes. Casting — *Manuals*

Filbey, John. Natal charting : how to master the techniques of birth control construction / by John Filbey. — Wellingborough : Aquarian Press, 1981. — 191p : ill,charts,1map ; 22cm. — (An Aquarian astrology handbook)
Bibliography: p154-156. — Includes index
ISBN 0-85030-268-4 (cased) : Unpriced
ISBN 0-85030-246-3 (pbk) : £3.75 B81-14775

133.5'8129 — Reincarnation. Astrological aspects

Elliot, Roger. Who were you? / Roger Elliot. — London : Granada, 1981. — 240p ; 18cm. — (A Mayflower book)
ISBN 0-583-13442-4 (pbk) : £1.50 B81-18945

133.5'8302 — Interpersonal relationships. Astrological predictions — *Texts*

Hunt, Diana. You, your stars and your partner / by Diana Hunt. — London : W.H. Allen, 1981, c1969. — 230p ; 18cm. — (A Star book)
Originally published: London : Macdonald, 1969
ISBN 0-352-30942-3 (pbk) : £1.50 B81-35759

133.5'8332024 — Personal finance — *Horoscopes*

Davies, Frederick. Money signs / Frederick Davies and Paul Bannister. — London : Star, 1981. — 213p ; 18cm
ISBN 0-352-30809-5 (pbk) : £1.60 B81-40366

133.5'8613 — Man. Health. Astrological aspects

Geddes, Sheila. Astrology and health / by Sheila Geddes. — Wellingborough : Aquarian Press, 1981. — 128p ; 22cm. — (An Aquarian astrology handbook)
Includes index
ISBN 0-85030-267-6 (cased) : Unpriced
ISBN 0-85030-248-x (pbk) : £2.95 B81-14773

133.6 — PALMISTRY

133.6 — Palmistry — *Manuals*

Brandon-Jones, David. Practical palmistry / David Brandon-Jones. — London : Rider, 1981. — 268p : ill ; 23cm
Bibliography: p265
ISBN 0-09-144830-1 (cased) : £8.95 : CIP rev.
ISBN 0-09-144831-x (pbk) : £5.95 B81-14377

Mir Bashir. The art of hand analysis / Mir Bashir. — London : Muller, 1973 (1981 [printing]). — 258p : ill,facsims ; 22cm
Includes index
ISBN 0-584-11001-4 (pbk) : £3.85 B81-39181

West, Peter, *1939-*. Life lines : an introduction to palmistry / by Peter West. — Wellingborough : Aquarian, 1981. — 127p : ill ; 22cm
Bibliography: p125. - Includes index
ISBN 0-85030-269-2 (cased) : £6.50 : CIP rev.
ISBN 0-85030-252-8 (pbk) : £2.95 B81-00007

133.6 — Sex relations. Prediction. Use of palmistry

Brandon-Jones, David. The palmistry of love / David Brandon-Jones and Veronica Bennett. — London : Arrow, 1980. — 216p : ill ; 18cm
Includes index
ISBN 0-09-923740-7 (pbk) : £1.50 B81-05099

133.8 — PSYCHIC PHENOMENA

133.8 — Psychic phenomena

Bartlett, Laile E.. Psi trek : a world-wide investigation into the lives of psychic people and the researchers who test such phenomena as healing, prophecy, dowsing, ghosts, and life after death / Laile E. Bartlett. — New York ; London : McGraw-Hill, c1981. — xi,337p ; 24cm
Bibliography: p325-332. — Includes index
ISBN 0-07-003915-1 : £9.50 B81-31768

Lamont, Stewart. Is anybody there? / Stewart Lamont. — Edinburgh : Mainstream, c1980. — 143p ; 23cm
ISBN 0-906391-11-3 : £6.50 B81-07186

133.8 — Psychic phenomena — *Christian viewpoints*

An **Introduction** to psychic awareness. — [London] ([Abchurch La., E.C.4]) : Churches' Fellowship for Psychical & Spiritual Studies, [1980?]. — 16p ; 19cm + Supplement(6leaves : 21cm)
Cover title. — Bibliography: p16
£0.20 (pbk) B81-32465

133.8 — Psychic phenomena: Coincidences — *Case studies*

Vaughan, Alan. Incredible coincidence : the baffling world of synchronicity / Alan Vaughan. — [London] : Corgi, 1981, c1979. — 282p ; 18cm
Originally published: United States : S.n., 1979. — Bibliography: p276-277. - Includes index
ISBN 0-552-11670-x (pbk) : £1.45 B81-21393

133.8 — Psychic powers

Warne, H. C. S.. Your life has purpose / H.C.S. Warne. — Bognor Regis : New Horizon, c1979. — 121p : ill ; 21cm
Bibliography: p121
ISBN 0-86116-054-1 : £3.25 B81-21808

133.8 — Psychic powers. Development — *Manuals*

Burns, Jean. Your innate psychic powers / Jean Burns. — London : Sphere, 1981. — ix,276p ; 18cm
Includes index
ISBN 0-7221-2085-0 (pbk) : £1.50 B81-10057

133.8'072 — Psychic phenomena. Research, *1920-1940*

Mauskopf, Seymour H.. The elusive science : origins of experimental psychical research / Seymour H. Mauskopf and Michael R. McVaugh ; afterword by J.B. and L.E. Rhine. — Baltimore ; London : Johns Hopkins University Press, c1980. — xvi,368p : ill,1facsim,ports ; 24cm
Includes index
ISBN 0-8018-2331-5 : £14.75 B81-21086

133.8'0722 — Extrasensory perception — *Case studies*

Rhine, Louisa E.. The invisible picture : a study of psychic experiences / Louisa E. Rhine. — Jefferson, N.C. : McFarland ; Folkestone : distributed by Bailey & Swinfen, 1981. — viii,267p ; 24cm
Bibliography: p259-261. — Includes index
ISBN 0-89950-015-3 : £12.75 B81-37038

133.8'092'4 — Extrasensory perception & psychokinesis. Kiyota, Masuaki

Uphoff, Walter. Mind over matter : implications of Masuaki Kiyota's PK feats with metal and film for healing, physics, psychiatry, war & peace et cetera / Walter and Mary Jo Uphoff ; foreword by Berthold E. Schwarz. — Oregon, Wis. : New Frontiers Center ; Gerrards Cross : Smythe, 1980. — xvi,256p : ill,facsims,ports ; 23cm
Bibliography: p248-249. — Includes index
ISBN 0-86140-079-8 (cased) : £4.95
ISBN 0-86140-062-3 (pbk) : £3.25 B81-04964

133.8'092'4 — Psychic phenomena — *Personal observations*

Barham, Allan. Strange to relate / Allan Barham. — Bognor Regis : New Horizon, c1980. — 141p,[6]p of plates : ill ; 22cm
Bibliography: p137. — Includes index
ISBN 0-86116-349-4 : £4.25 B81-21704

133.8'2 — Telepathy

Bailey, Alice A.. Telepathy : and the etheric vehicle / by Alice A. Bailey. — New York ; London : Lucis, c1978 (1980 printing). — xi,219p : ill ; 19cm
Originally published: 1950. — Includes index
Unpriced (pbk) B81-37856

133.8'8 — Metals. Bending. Use of psychic powers

Hasted, J. B.. The metal-benders / John Hasted. — London : Routledge & Kegan Paul, 1981. — xii,279p : ill ; 23cm
Includes index
ISBN 0-7100-0597-0 : £9.75 B81-11640

133.9 — SPIRITUALISM

133.9 — Psychic phenomena: Reincarnation

Brennan, J. H.. Reincarnation. — 2nd ed. — Wellingborough : Aquarian Press, Aug.1981. — [96]p
Previous ed.: 1971
ISBN 0-85030-275-7 (pbk) : £0.95 : CIP entry B81-15924

133.9 — Spiritualism

Austin, Fred. A conception of life / [Fred Austin]. — [London] (73 Cromwell Rd., Wimbledon, SW19 8LF) : F. Austin, [1980]. — 32p ; 26cm
Unpriced (pbk) B81-20391

133.9'01'3 — Future life — *Christian viewpoints*

Perry, Michael. Spiritual implications of survival / Michael Perry. — London (St. Mary Abchurch, EC4N 7BA) : The Churches' Fellowship for Psychical and Spiritual Studies, 1979. — 16p ; 21cm. — (Christian parapsychology papers ; no.2)
Cover title
ISBN 0-906326-02-8 (pbk) : £0.40 B81-18610

133.9'01'3 — Future life — *Personal observations*

Doyle, *Sir* Arthur Conan *(Spirit)*. The return of Arthur Conan Doyle / edited by Ivan Cooke. — 4th ed. — Liss ([New Lands], Liss, Hampshire) : White Eagle Publishing Trust, 1980, c1975. — viii,204p : ill,1facsim,ports ; 23cm
Previous ed.: 1975. — Includes index
ISBN 0-85487-045-8 : £4.95 : CIP rev. B80-04052

133.9'01'3 — Future life — *Spiritualist viewpoints*

Guirdham, Arthur. Paradise found : reflections on psychic survival / by Arthur Guirdham. — Wellingborough : Turnstone, c1980. — 224p ; 23cm
ISBN 0-85500-128-3 (cased) : £7.50
ISBN 0-85500-135-6 (pbk) : £4.50 B81-13017

133.9'01'3 — Psychic phenomena: Reincarnation

Walker, Benjamin. Masks of the soul : the facts behind reincarnation / by Benjamin Walker. — Wellingborough : Aquarian Press, 1981. — 160p ; 22cm
Bibliography: p145-156. — Includes index
ISBN 0-85030-259-5 (cased) : Unpriced
ISBN 0-85030-258-7 (pbk) : £2.95 B81-25174

133.9'01'3 — Psychic phenomena: Reincarnation — *Case studies*

Moss, Peter, *1921-*. Encounters with the past : how man can experience and relive history / Peter Mass with Jos Keeton. — Harmondsworth : Penguin, 1981, c1979. — 233p,[8]p of plates : 8ports ; 18cm
Originally published: London : Sidgwick and Jackson, 1979. — Includes index
ISBN 0-14-005587-8 (pbk) : £1.50 B81-11532

Wilson, Ian, *1941-*. Mind out of time? : reincarnation claims investigated / by Ian Wilson. — London : Gollancz, 1981. — 283p,16p of plates : ill,facsims,ports ; 23cm
Includes index
ISBN 0-575-02968-4 : £6.95 B81-26880

133.9'1'0924 — Spiritualism. Mediums: Harris, Alec — *Biographies*

Harris, Louie. They walked among us / by Louie Harris. — London : Psychic, 1980. — 121p ; 20cm
ISBN 0-85384-055-5 : £4.50 B81-12757

133.9'1'0924 — Spiritualism. Mediums: Lever, Marshall N. — *Biographies*

Lever, Marshall N.. The search for the hidden door / by Marshall N. Lever. — London (44 Hertford St., W1Y 7TF) : Enchantment Unlimited, c1981. — 147p : ill ; 22cm
Unpriced (pbk) B81-16575

133.9'1'0924 — Spiritualism. Mediums: Stokes, Doris - *Biographies*

Stokes, Doris. More voices in my ear. — Henley-on-Thames : A. Ellis, July 1981. — [224]p
ISBN 0-85628-105-0 : £6.50 : CIP entry B81-14913

133.9'3 — Ouija boards

Covina, Gina. The ouija book / Gina Covina. — London : Hale, 1981, c1979. — 158p : ill,ports ; 23cm
Originally published: New York : Simon and Schuster, 1979
ISBN 0-7091-8983-4 : £6.50 B81-40933

133.9'3 — Spiritualism. Automatic writing — *Texts*

Akehurst, Ken. Everyone's guide to the hereafter / Ken Akehurst ; transmitted by G.M. Roberts. — Suffolk : Spearman, 1981. — ix,114p ; 20cm
ISBN 0-85435-414-x (pbk) : £2.25 B81-40323

Phylos, *the Thibetan (Spirit)*. A dweller on two planets or the dividing of the way / by Phylos the Thibetan ; [through the hand of Frederick S. Oliver]. — San Francisco ; London : Harper & Row, c1974. — 423p,[7]leaves of plates : ill,1map,1port ; 21cm
Originally published: Los Angeles : Baumgardt, [ca.1900]
ISBN 0-06-066565-3 (pbk) : £3.50 B81-28454

133.9'3 — Spiritualism. Communication — *Personal observations*

Stevenson, Victoria. The triumph of love / Victoria Stevenson. — London : Arlington, 1980. — 150p ; 21cm
ISBN 0-85140-499-5 : £4.95 : CIP rev. B80-04053

133.9'3 — Spiritualism. Communication. Special subjects: Aviation. Mysteries, *1928-1930*

Fuller, John G.. The airmen who would not die / John G. Fuller. — [London] : Corgi, 1981, c1979. — 430p ; 18cm
Originally published: New York : Putnam, 1978 ; London : Souvenir, 1979. — Includes index
ISBN 0-552-11591-6 (pbk) : £1.50 B81-08452

133.9'3 — Spiritualism. Communication — *Texts*

Cleeve, Brian. The house on the rock / Brian Cleeve. — London : Watkins, 1980. — 266p ; 21cm
ISBN 0-7224-0178-7 (pbk) : £2.70 B81-10200

Eyre, Margery. The sacred mirror : a spiritual diary / Margery Eyre ; edited by Elizabeth Gaythorpe. — Gerrards Cross : Smythe, 1980. — 94p ; 23cm
ISBN 0-86140-068-2 : £3.95 : CIP rev. B80-17533

Wallace, Mary Bruce. The thinning of the veil : a record of psychic experience / Mary Bruce Wallace. — Rev. ed. — St. Helier : Spearman, 1981. — xix,155p ; 21cm
Previous ed.: 1919
ISBN 0-85978-076-7 (cased) : £3.50
ISBN 0-85978-081-3 (pbk) : Unpriced B81-40326

135 — DREAMS AND THE MYSTIC TRADITIONS

135'.3 — Dreams — *Personal observations*

Saint-Denys, Hervey de. Dreams and how to guide them. — London : Duckworth, Oct.1981. — [172]p
Translation of: Les rêves et les moyens de les diriger
ISBN 0-7156-1584-x : £18.00 : CIP entry B81-28165

135'.4 — Cabala

Lévi, Éliphas. The book of splendours. — Wellingborough : Aquarian Press, Sept.1981. — [192]p
Translation of: Le livre des splendeurs. — Originally published: 1973
ISBN 0-85030-245-5 (pbk) : £3.50 : CIP entry B81-20472

Lévi, Éliphas. The great secret. — Wellingborough : Aquarian Press, Sept.1981. — [192]p
Translation of: Le grand arcane. — Originally published: Wellingborough : Thorsons, 1975
ISBN 0-85030-243-9 (pbk) : £3.50 : CIP entry B81-20471

Richardson, Alan. An introduction to the mystical Qabalah. — 2nd ed. — Wellingborough : Aquarian, Aug.1981. — [96]p
Previous ed.: 1974
ISBN 0-85030-264-1 (pbk) : £0.95 : CIP entry B81-24677

137 — ANALYTIC AND DIVINATORY GRAPHOLOGY

137 — Graphology — *Manuals*

Hill, Barbara. Graphology / by Barbara Hill. — London : Hale, 1981. — 144p : ill,facsims ; 23cm
Bibliography: p144
ISBN 0-7091-8363-1 : £6.25 B81-14693

Marne, Patricia. Graphology / Patricia Marne. — London : Hodder and Stoughton, 1980. — 169p : facsims ; 20cm. — (Teach yourself books)
Bibliography: p169. — Includes index
ISBN 0-340-24792-4 (pbk) : £1.50 : CIP rev. B80-23961

137 — Graphology - *Manuals*

West, Peter, *19---*. Graphology. — Wellingborough : Aquarian Press, Aug.1981. — [96]p
ISBN 0-85030-260-9 (pbk) : £0.95 : CIP entry B81-18093

140 — PHILOSOPHICAL VIEWPOINTS

141'.3'097403 — New England. Social movements. Transcendentalism, *1830-1850*

Rose, Ann C.. Transcendentalism as a social movement, 1830-1850. — London : Yale University Press, Nov.1981. — [272]p
ISBN 0-300-02587-4 : £15.75 : CIP entry B81-35028

142'.7 — Phenomenology — *Conference proceedings*

The **Great** chain of being and Italian phenomenology / edited by Angela Ales Bello. — Dordrecht ; London : Reidel, c1981. — xvii,347p : ports ; 23cm. — (Analecta Husserliana ; v.11)
Includes contributions in French and German. — Bibliography: p36-37. — Includes index
ISBN 90-277-1071-6
Also classified at 111 B81-37020

142'.7 — Phenomenology — *German texts*

Boehm, Rudolf. Vom Gesichtspunkt der Phänomenologie / Rudolf Boehm. — The Hague ; London : Nijhoff. — (Phaenomenologica ; 83)
2 Bd.: Studien zur Phänomenologie der Epoché. — 1981. — viii,262p ; 25cm
Includes index
ISBN 90-247-2415-5 : Unpriced B81-29285

142'.78 — Existentialism

Wilson, Colin, *1931-*. [Introduction to the new existentialism]. The new existentialism / Colin Wilson. — London : Wildwood House, 1980, c1966 300 188p, 20cm [pbk]
Originally published: London : Hutchinson, 1966. — Includes index
ISBN 0-7045-0415-4 : £3.95 B81-00720

144 — Humanism

Holmes, Harry. Our sweetest song / Harry Holmes. — Bognor Regis : New Horizon, c1981. — 223p ; 21cm
Bibliography: p221-223. - Includes index
ISBN 0-86116-477-6 : £5.75 B81-23367

144'.3 — Philosophy. Pragmatism — *Festschriften*

Prospects for pragmatism : essays in memory of F.P. Ramsey / edited by D.H. Mellor. — Cambridge : Cambridge University Press, 1980. — xiii,261p : 1port ; 24cm
Includes bibliographies and index
ISBN 0-521-22548-5 : £15.00 : CIP rev. B80-32851

145 — Ideologies

Ruddock, Ralph. Ideologies : five exploratory lectures / Ralph Ruddock. — Manchester (The University, Manchester M13 9PL) : Department of Adult and Higher Education, University of Manchester, c1981. — viii,81p : ill ; 22cm. — (Manchester monographs ; 15)
Bibliography: p80-81
ISBN 0-903717-24-7 (pbk) : Unpriced B81-22902

145 — Ideology

Béteille, André. Ideologies and intellectuals / André Béteille. — Delhi ; Oxford : Oxford University Press, 1980. — iii,51p ; 22cm
ISBN 0-19-561306-6 (pbk) : £1.25
Also classified at 305.5'5 B81-38591

Therborn, Göran. The ideology of power and the power of ideology / Göran Therborn. — London : NLB, c1980. — ix,133p : 1ill ; 22cm
ISBN 0-86091-034-2 (cased) : £6.00 : CIP rev.
ISBN 0-86091-731-2 (pbk) : £2.50 B80-18997

146'.42'09 — Logical positivism, *ca 1900- ca 1955*

Hanfling, Oswald. Logical positivism / Oswald Hanfling. — Oxford : Blackwell, 1981. — 181p ; 23cm
Bibliography: p173-176. — Includes index
ISBN 0-631-10861-0 (cased) : £14.00
ISBN 0-631-12853-0 (pbk) : £5.50 B81-29693

146'.44 — Empiricism

Challenges to empiricism / edited by Harold Morick ; [contributors] Rudolf Carnap ... [et al.]. — London : Methuen, 1980. — 329p : ill ; 24cm
Originally published: Belmont : Wadsworth, 1972. — Bibliography: p319-326
ISBN 0-416-74610-1 (cased) : £9.00
ISBN 0-416-74620-9 (pbk) : £4.50 B81-06112

148 — Great Britain. Liberals. Influence of socialism, *ca 1860-ca 1960*

Clarke, Peter. Liberals and social democrats. — Cambridge : Cambridge University Press, Dec.1981. — [360]p
Originally published: 1978
ISBN 0-521-28651-4 (pbk) : £7.95 : CIP entry B81-31606

149'.3 — Mysticism

Wainright, William J.. Mysticism. — Brighton : Harvester Press, Sept.1981. — [256]p
ISBN 0-7108-0062-2 : CIP entry B81-27953

149'.8 — Nihilism — *Russian texts*

Frank, S. L.. Étika nigilizma = The ethics of nihilism / S.L. Frank. — Letchworth : Prideaux, 1980. — 38p ; 21cm. — (Russian titles for the specialist, ISSN 0305-3741 ; no.225)
Originally published: Moscow : s.n., 1909
£0.90 (pbk) B81-14005

149'.94'0942 — English linguistic philosophy, *1920-1960 — Critical studies*

Mundle, C. W. K.. A critique of linguistic philosophy : with second thoughts — an epilogue after ten years / C.W.K. Mundle ; foreword by P.L. Heath. — 2nd, rev. ed. — London : Glover & Blair, 1979. — 282p ; 23cm
Previous ed. published: Oxford : Oxford University Press, 1970. — Includes index
ISBN 0-906681-02-2 : £9.50 B81-10818

149'.943 — Ordinary language philosophy

Ordinary language : essays in philosophical method / edited by V.C. Chappell. — New York : Dover ; London : Constable, 1981, c1964. — vi,115p ; 21cm
Originally published: Englewood Cliffs : Prentice-Hall, 1964. — Bibliography: p113-115
ISBN 0-486-24082-7 (pbk) : £1.90 B81-39070

149'.943 — Philosophical logic

Davies, Martin, *1950-*. Meaning, quantification, necessity : themes in philosophical logic / Martin Davies. — London : Routledge & Kegan Paul, 1981. — xii,282p ; 23cm. — (International library of philosophy)
Bibliography: p269-277. — Includes index
ISBN 0-7100-0759-0 : £14.95 : CIP rev. B81-14816

Martin, R. M.. Pragmatics, truth, and language / R.M. Martin. — Dordrecht ; London : Reidel, c1979. — xv,310p ; 23cm. — (Boston studies in the philosophy of science ; v.38)
Includes index
ISBN 90-277-0992-0 (cased) : Unpriced
ISBN 90-277-0993-9 (pbk) : Unpriced B81-03470

Wittgenstein, Ludwig. Tractatus logico-philosophicus / by Ludwig Wittgenstein ; [translated from the German by C.K. Ogden] ; with an introduction by Bertrand Russell. — London : Routledge & Kegan Paul, 1955 (1981 [printing]). — 207p ; 22cm. — (International library of psychology, philosophy and scientific method)
Translation of: Logisch-Philosophische Abhandlung. — Parallel German text and English translation. — Originally published: 1922. — Includes index
ISBN 0-7100-3004-5 (cased) : Unpriced
ISBN 0-7100-3004-5 (pbk) : £3.50 B81-37620

149'.943 — Philosophical logic. Husserl, Edmund. Logische Untersuchungen — *Critical studies*

Mensch, James R.. The question of Being in Husserl's Logical investigations / James R. Mensch. — The Hague ; London : Nijhoff, 1981. — 211p ; 25cm. — (Phaenomenologica ; 81)
Bibliography: p207-208. — Includes index
ISBN 90-247-2413-9 : Unpriced B81-21178

149'.943 — Philosophical logic. Wittgenstein, Ludwig. Tractatus logico-philosophicus — *Critical studies*

Mounce, H. O.. Wittgenstein's Tractatus : an introduction / H.O. Mounce. — Oxford : Blackwell, 1981. — 136p ; 22cm
Includes index
ISBN 0-631-12556-6 (cased) : £12.00
ISBN 0-631-12707-0 (pbk) : £4.50 B81-39946

149'.943 — Statements. Reference — *Philosophical perspectives*

Geach, P. T.. Reference and generality : an examination of some medieval and modern theories / by Peter Thomas Geach. — 3rd ed. — Ithaca ; London : Cornell University Press, 1980. — 231p : 1ports ; 23cm. — (Contemporary philosophy)
Previous ed.: i.e. Emended ed.: 1968. — Bibliography: p221-222. - Includes index
ISBN 0-8014-1315-x : £11.75 B81-07046

149'.946 — Natural language. Reference — *Philosophical perspectives*

Devitt, Michael. Designation / Michael Devitt. — New York ; Guildford : Columbia University Press, 1981. — xiii,311p ; 22cm
Bibliography: p295-303. — Includes index
ISBN 0-231-05126-3 : £16.10 B81-27080

149'.96 — Stylistics. Structuralism. Theories

Taylor, Talbot J.. Linguistic theory and structural stylistics / by Talbot J. Taylor. — Oxford : Pergamon, 1981, c1980. — vii,111p : 2ill ; 24cm. — (Language & communication library ; v.2)
Bibliography: p108-109. - Includes index
ISBN 0-08-025821-2 : £7.50 : CIP rev. B80-26429

150 — PSYCHOLOGY

150 — Man. Achievement

Cooper, Wendy. Human potential : the limits and beyond / Wendy Cooper and Tom Smith. — Newton Abbot : David and Charles, c1981. — 223p ; 24cm
ISBN 0-7153-7925-9 : £8.50 B81-13390

150 — Man. Behaviour

Bach, Charlotte M.. An outline of human ethology : extracts from an unpublished work / by Charlotte M. Bach ; edited by Bob Mellors. — [London] ([c/o 5 Caledonian Rd., N.1]) : [Another Orbit Press]
1: In the beginning. — [1981?]. — 11p ; 22cm
Cover title
£0.50 (pbk) B81-17793

Bach, Charlotte M.. An outline of human ethology : extracts from an unpublished work / by Charlotte M. Bach ; edited by Bob Mellors. — [London] ([c/o 5 Caledonian Rd., N.1]) : [Another Orbit Press]
2: The meaning of sexual deviation. — [1981?]. — 11p ; 21cm
Cover title
£0.50 (pbk) B81-17790

Bach, Charlotte M.. An outline of human ethology : extracts from an unpublished work / by Charlotte M. Bach ; edited by Bob Mellors. — [London] ([c/o 5 Caledonian Rd., N.1]) : [Another Orbit Press]
3: Interviewing sexual deviants. — [1981?]. — 11p ; 22cm
Cover title
£0.50 (pbk) B81-17791

Bach, Charlotte M.. An outline of human ethology : extracts from an unpublished work / by Charlotte M. Bach ; edited by Bob Mellors. — [London] ([c/o 5 Caledonian Rd., N.1]) : [Another Orbit Press]
4: Homosexuals and the gas chambers. — 15p ; 21cm
Cover title
£0.50 (pbk) B81-17792

Baldwin, John D.. Behavior principles in everyday life / John D. Baldwin, Janice I. Baldwin. — Englewood Cliffs ; London : Prentice-Hall, c1981. — x,326p : ill ; 24cm
Bibliography: p299-311. - Includes index
ISBN 0-13-072751-2 (pbk) : £9.70 B81-17277

150 — Man. Mind. Relationship with body. Psychobiological aspects

Dychtwald, Ken. Bodymind / by Ken Dychtwald ; with illustrations by Juan Barberis and Jad King. — London : Wildwood House, 1978, c1977 (1979 [printing]). — xvi,298p : ill ; 21cm
Originally published: New York : Pantheon, 1977 ; London : Wildwood House, 1978. — Bibliography: p277-289. - Includes index
ISBN 0-7045-0329-8 (pbk) : £3.95 B81-06458

150 — Psychology

Colman, Andrew M.. What is psychology? / Andrew M. Colman ; illustrated by Angela Chorley. — London : Kogan Page, 1981. — 207p : ill ; 19cm
Includes bibliographies and index
ISBN 0-85038-379-x (cased) : £6.95 : CIP rev.
ISBN 0-85038-413-3 (pbk) : £3.50 B80-29016

Eysenck, H. J.. Mindwatching / Hans & Michael Eysenck. — London : Joseph, 1981. — 223p : ill(some col.),ports(some col.) ; 26cm
Bibliography: p220-221. — Includes index
ISBN 0-7181-1937-1 : £10.50 B81-16663

Introduction to psychology. — Milton Keynes : Open University Press. — (Social sciences : a second level course)
At head of title: The Open University
Block 2: Psychology of the person. — 1981. — 88p : ill ; 30cm. — (DS262 ; 2,4)
Includes bibliographies and index. — Contents: Unit 2: Psychodynamics - Unit 4: Dimensions of personality
ISBN 0-335-12041-5 (pbk) : Unpriced
B81-11457

Introduction to psychology. — Milton Keynes : Open University Press. — (Social sciences : a second level course)
At head of title: The Open University
Block 3: Psychological processes. — 1981. — 103p : ill ; 30cm. — (DS262 ; 3, 10)
Includes bibliographies and index. — Contents: Unit 3: Learning and conditioning - Unit 10: Memory
ISBN 0-335-12043-1 (pbk) : Unpriced
B81-11347

Introduction to psychology. — Milton Keynes : Open University Press. — (Social sciences : a second level course)
At head of title: The Open University Methodology handbook / prepared for the course team by Judith Greene and Manuela d'Oliviera. — 1981. — 104p : ill ; 30cm. — (DS262 ; MH)
Includes index
ISBN 0-335-12047-4 (pbk) : Unpriced
B81-11458

Invitation to psychology / John P. Houston ... [et al.]. — New York ; London : Academic Press. — xx,679,[66]p : ill(some col.),facsims,ports ; 27cm
Includes bibliographies and index
ISBN 0-12-356860-9 : £11.20 B81-16577

Kristal, Leonard. Understanding psychology : a personal perspective / Leonard Kristal. — London : Harper & Row, 1979. — 128p : ill (some col.) ; 25cm. — (The life cycle series)
Bibliography: p125. — Includes index
ISBN 0-06-318110-x (cased) : Unpriced
ISBN 0-06-318109-6 (pbk) : £2.25 B81-01790

Lugo, James O.. Living psychology / James O. Lugo and Gerald L. Hershey. — 3rd ed. / prepared by James O. Lugo. — New York : Macmillan ; London : Collier Macmillan, c1981. — xii,564p : ill(some col.),ports ; 24cm
Previous ed.: 1976. — Includes bibliographies and index
ISBN 0-02-372250-9 : £12.50 B81-33396

Osborne, Kate. Alternative perspectives for a psychology of the person / Kate Osborne & David Cope. — Cardiff (c/o R. Slater, Department of Applied Psychology, UWIST, Llwyn-y-Grant, Penylan, Cardiff CF3 7UX) : [UWIST Department of Applied Psychology], 1978. — 24p ; 30cm. — (Occasional paper / UWIST Department of Applied Psychology ; no.7)
Conference paper. — Bibliography: p23-24
£0.50 (spiral) B81-24795

Psychology / John M. Darley ... [et al.]. — Englewood Cliffs ; London : Prentice-Hall, c1981. — xvi,652,[4]p of plates : ill(some col.),ports ; 27cm
Bibliography: p614-633. — Includes index
ISBN 0-13-733154-1 : £12.30 B81-17215

Psychology for today / contributing editor Bill Gillham. — [Sevenoaks] : Teach Yourself, 1981. — 306p : ill ; 18cm. — (Care and welfare)
Includes bibliographies and index
ISBN 0-340-25107-7 (pbk) : £2.50 : CIP rev.
B81-04218

Rathus, Spencer A.. Psychology / Spencer A. Rathus. — New York ; London : Holt, Rinehart and Winston, c1981. — xxix,720,R21p : ill(some col.),ports ; 25cm
Ill on lining papers. — Bibliography: pR1-R21. - Includes index
ISBN 0-03-057894-9 : £11.25 B81-23091

The **Structure** of psychology : an introductory text / edited by C.I. Howarth and W.E.C. Gillham. — London : Allen & Unwin, 1981. — 752p : ill,maps
Bibliography: p697-737. - Includes index
ISBN 0-04-150071-7 (cased) : Unpriced : CIP rev. B80-13182

Understanding psychology / C.B. Dobson ... [et al.]. — London : Weidenfeld and Nicolson, c1981. — xiii,482p : ill ; 23cm
Bibliography: p446-467. - Includes index
ISBN 0-297-77871-4 (cased) : £13.50
ISBN 0-297-77872-2 (pbk) : £6.95 B81-19319

150 — Psychology — *Anthropological perspectives*

Indigenous psychologies : the anthropology of the self / edited by Paul Heelas and Andrew Lock. — London : Academic Press, 1981. — xviii,322p : ill ; 24cm. — (Language, thought, and culture)
Includes bibliographies and index
ISBN 0-12-336480-9 : £12.20 : CIP rev.
B81-03679

150'.1 — Psychology. Mechanist theories. Implications of incompleteness theorems in metamathematics

Webb, Judson Chambers. Mechanism, mentalism, and metamathematics : an essay on finitism / Judson Chambers Webb. — Dordrecht ; London : Reidel, c1980. — xiii,277p : ill ; 23cm. — (Synthese library ; v.137)
Bibliography: p248-263. — Includes index
ISBN 90-277-1046-5 : Unpriced
Primary classification 510'.1 B81-07824

150'.1 — Psychology — *Philosophical perspectives*

Cosgrove, Mark P.. Psychology gone awry : four world views in psychology. — Rev. ed.. — Leicester : Inter-Varsity Press, Feb.1982. — [144]p
Previous ed.: 1979
ISBN 0-85110-432-0 (pbk) : £1.95 : CIP entry
B81-40265

150'.1 — Psychology. Reasoning

Bell, Philip Brian. Reasoning and argument in psychology / Philip Brian Bell, Phillip James Staines. — London : Routledge & Kegan Paul, 1981, c1979. — 217p ; 22cm
Originally published: Kensington, N.S.W. : New South Wales University Press, 1979. — Bibliography: p209-211. — Includes index
ISBN 0-7100-0712-4 (pbk) : £4.95 : CIP rev.
B80-34429

150'.1 — Psychology. Theories

Wolman, Benjamin B.. Contemporary theories and systems in psychology / Benjamin B. Wolman in collaboration with Susan Knapp. — 2nd ed., expanded and rev. — New York ; London : Plenum, c1981. — xii,639p ; 26cm
Previous ed.: New York : Harper ; London : H. Hamilton, 1960. — Bibliography: p589-625. — Includes index
ISBN 0-306-40515-6 : Unpriced B81-15037

150'.1 — Psychology. Theories, *ca 1800-1979*

Psychology : theoretical-historical perspectives / edited by R.W. Rieber, Kurt Salzinger. — New York ; London : Academic Press, 1980. — xiv,364p : ill,facsims,ports ; 24cm
Includes bibliographies and index
ISBN 0-12-588265-3 : £11.80 B81-05701

150'.1 — Psychology. Theories. Construction & testing

Hyland, Michael. Introduction to theoretical psychology / Michael Hyland. — London : Macmillan, 1981. — viii,147p : ill ; 23cm
Bibliography: p140-147
ISBN 0-333-25826-6 (cased) : £10.00 : CIP rev.
ISBN 0-333-25827-4 (pbk) : Unpriced
B80-10928

150'.1 — Psychology. Theories, *to 1970*

Wilson, Colin. New pathways in psychology : Maslow and the post-Freudian revolution / by Colin Wilson. — London : Gollancz, 1972 (1979 printing). — 288p ; 22cm
Bibliography: p243-274. — Includes index
ISBN 0-575-02796-7 (pbk) : £3.95 B81-19795

150'.1'51 — Man. Behaviour. Mathematical aspects

Atkin, Ron. Multidimensional man / Ron Atkin. — Harmondsworth : Penguin, 1981. — 199p,[8]p of plates : ill,1map ; 20cm
Bibliography: p199
ISBN 0-14-005478-2 (pbk) : £2.95 B81-05558

150.19 — Psychology. Systems

Wolman, Benjamin B.. Contemporary theories and systems in psychology. — 2nd ed. / expanded and rev. Benjamin B. Wolman in collaboration with Susan Knapp. — New York ; London : Plenum, c1981. — xii,639p ; 25cm
Previous ed.: New York : Harper, 1960. — Bibliography: p589-625. — Includes index
ISBN 0-306-40530-x (pbk) : Unpriced
B81-16799

150.19'09 — Psychology. Systems, *to 1979*

Schultz, Duane P.. A history of modern psychology / Duane Schultz. — 3rd ed. — New York ; London : Academic Press, c1981. — xv,416p : ill,ports ; 25cm
Previous ed.: 1975. — Includes bibliographies and index
ISBN 0-12-633060-3 : £10.80 B81-19324

150.19′2 — Humanistic psychology

Humanistic psychology : concepts and criticisms / edited by Joseph R. Royce and Leendert P. Mos. — New York ; London : Plenum, c1981. — xx,311p ; 24cm
Includes bibliographies and index
ISBN 0-306-40596-2 : Unpriced B81-35256

150.19′32 — Psychodynamics

Bridger, Harold. Consultative work with communities and organisations towards a psychodynamic image of man. — Aberdeen : Aberdeen University Press, June 1981. — [42] p. — (The Malcolm Miller lecture, ISSN 0144-1663 ; 1980)
ISBN 0-08-025751-8 (pbk) : £1.25 : CIP entry B81-14783

150.19′43 — Behaviourism

Rachlin, Howard. Behaviorism in everday life / Howard Rachlin. — Englewood Cliffs ; London : Prentice-Hall, c1980. — 186p : ill ; 21cm. — (The Psychology in action series) (A Spectrum book)
Includes index
ISBN 0-13-074583-9 (cased) : Unpriced
ISBN 0-13-074575-8 (pbk) : £3.50 B81-14102

150.19′5 — Psychoanalysis

Farrell, B. A.. The standing of psychoanalysis / B.A. Farrell. — Oxford : Oxford University Press, 1981. — 240p ; 21cm. — (OPUS)
Includes index
ISBN 0-19-219133-0 (cased) : £5.95
ISBN 0-19-289120-0 (pbk) : £3.95 B81-18586

Ferenczi, Sándor. Final contributions to the problems & methods of psycho-analysis / by Sándor Ferenczi ; edited by Michael Balint ; translated by Eric Masbacher and others. — London (58 Gloucester Rd., S.W.7.) : Maresfield Reprints, 1980, c1975. — 447p ; 22cm
Originally published: London : Hogarth, 1955. — Bibliography: p377-386. — Includes index
ISBN 0-9507146-2-3 : £9.00 B81-00721

Ferenczi, Sándor. Further contributions to the theory and technique of psycho-analysis / by Sándor Ferenczi ; compiled by John Rickman ; authorised translation by Jane Isabel Suttie and others. — London (58 Gloucester Rd., S.W.7) : Maresfield Reprints, 1980, c1926. — 480p ; 22cm
Originally published: London : Institute of Psycho-Analysis, 1926. — Bibliography: p451-469. - Includes index
ISBN 0-9507146-1-5 : £9.00 B81-00722

Fine, Rueben. The psychoanalytic vision / Reuben Fine. — New York : Free Press ; London : Collier Macmillan, c1981. — xiv,577p ; 25cm
Bibliography: p538-563. — Includes index
ISBN 0-02-910270-7 : £12.50 B81-39027

Loewald, Hans W.. Papers on psychoanalysis / Hans W. Loewald. — New Haven ; London : Yale University Press, c1980. — ix,434p ; 25cm
Includes index
ISBN 0-300-02406-1 : £15.75 : CIP rev. B80-29018

Pontalis, J.-B.. Frontiers in psychoanalysis : between the dream and psychic pain / by J.-B. Pontalis ; translated by Catherine Cullen and Philip Cullen ; with an introduction by M. Masud R. Khan. — London : Hogarth and the Institute of Psycho-Analysis, 1981. — 224p ; 23cm. — (The International Psycho-analytical library ; no.111)
Translation of: Entre le rêve et la douleur. — Bibliography: p214-218. — Includes index
ISBN 0-7012-0453-2 : £12.50 : CIP rev. B81-08847

Schafer, Roy. A new language for psychoanalysis. — London : Yale University Press, Oct.1981. — [416]p
ISBN 0-300-02761-3 : £6.95 : CIP entry B81-31942

150.19′5 — Psychoanalysis. Role of language

The **Talking** cure : essays in psychoanalysis and language / edited by Colin MacCabe. — London : Macmillan, 1981. — xiii,230p : ill ; 23cm. — (Language, discourse, society series)
Conference papers. — Bibliography: p218-223. - Includes index
ISBN 0-333-23560-6 : £20.00 : CIP rev. B80-08585

150.19′5 — Psychoanalysis. Theories of Lacan, Jacques

Returning to Freud : clinical psychoanalysis in the school of Lacan / edited and translated by Stuart Schneiderman ; contributors Jean Clavreul ... [et al.]. — New Haven ; London : Yale University Press, c1980. — viii,265p : 1ill ; 24cm
Includes index
ISBN 0-300-02476-2 : £12.60 B81-05559

150.19′52 — Psychoanalysis. Freud, Sigmund — *Biographies*

Jones, Ernest, *1879-1958*. The life and work of Sigmund Freud / Ernest Jones ; edited and abridged by Lionel Trilling and Steven Marcus ; with an introduction by Lionel Trilling. — Abridged ed. — Harmondsworth : Penguin in associaton with Hogarth, 1964, c1961 (1981 [printing]). — 670p,12p of plates : ill,ports ; 20cm. — (Pelican books)
Originally published: New York : Basic Books, 1961 ; London : Hogarth, 1962. — Includes index
ISBN 0-14-020661-2 (pbk) : £4.95 B81-15433

Sulloway, Frank J.. Freud, biologist of the mind : beyond the psychoanalytic legend / Frank J. Sulloway. — [London] : Fontana, 1980, c1979. — xxvi,612p : ports ; 20cm
Originally published: New York : Basic Books ; London : Burnett Books, 1979. — Bibliography : p519-575. — Includes index
ISBN 0-00-635784-9 (pbk) : £4.95 B81-00008

150.19′52 — Psychoanalysis. Freud, Sigmund — *Critical studies*

Breger, Louis. Freud's unfinished journey : conventional and critical perspectives in psychoanalytic theory / Louis Breger. — London : Routledge & Kegan Paul, 1981. — vi,145p ; 23cm
Bibliography: p138-142 — Includes index
ISBN 0-7100-0613-6 : £8.50 : CIP rev. B81-08844

Freud / a collection of critical essays ; edited by Perry Meisel. — Englewood Cliffs ; London : Prentice-Hall, c1981. — ix,240p ; 21cm. — (Twentieth century views) (A Spectrum book)
Bibliography: p237-240
ISBN 0-13-331405-7 (cased) : Unpriced
ISBN 0-13-331397-2 (pbk) : £3.85 B81-22760

Fromm, Erich. Greatness and limitations of Freud's thought / Erich Fromm. — London : Cape, 1980. — xi,147p ; 22cm
Translation of: Sigmund Freuds Psychoanalyse, Grösse und Grenzen. — Bibliography: p139-141. - Includes index
ISBN 0-224-01875-2 : £4.95 B81-00723

150.19′52 — Psychoanalysis. Freudian system — *Early works*

Ferenczi, Sándor. [Contributions to psycho-analysis]. First contributions to psycho-analysis / by Sándor Ferenczi ; authorised translation by Ernest Jones. — London (58 Gloucester Rd., S.W.7) : Maresfield Reprints, 1980. — 337p ; 22cm
Originally published: as Contributions to psycho-analysis Boston, Mass : Badger, 1916 and as First contributions to psycho-analysis London : Hogarth, 1952. — Includes index
ISBN 0-9507146-0-7 : £9.00 B81-04116

150.19′52 — Psychoanalysis. Freudian system. Testing

Kline, Paul. Fact and fantasy in Freudian theory. — 2nd ed. — London : Methuen, Dec.1981. — [450]p
Previous ed.: 1972
ISBN 0-416-72640-2 : £19.50 : CIP entry B81-31747

150.19′52 — Psychoanalysis. Theories of Freud, Sigmund

Freud, Sigmund. Two short accounts of psycho-analysis / Sigmund Freud ; translated and edited by James Strachey. — Harmondsworth : Penguin, 1962 (1981 [printing]). — 175p ; 19cm. — (Pelican handbooks)
Bibliography: p171-172. — Includes index. — Contents: Five lectures on psycho-analysis. Translation of: Über Psychoanalyse - The question of lay analysis. Translation of: Die Frage der Laienanalyse
ISBN 0-14-020571-3 (pbk) : £1.95 B81-21037

150.19′52 — Psychoanalysis. Theories of Freud, Sigmund. Compared with psychological aspects of poetry of Blake, William

George, Diana Hume. Blake and Freud / Diana Hume George. — Ithaca ; London : Cornell University Press, 1980. — 253p : ill ; 23cm
Includes index
ISBN 0-8014-1286-2 : £9.00
Primary classification 821′.7 B81-06791

150.19′52′0924 — Psychology. Reich, Wilhelm — *Biographies*

Wilson, Colin, *1931-*. The quest for Wilhelm Reich / Colin Wilson. — London : Granada, 1981. — xiv,306p ; 24cm
Bibliography: p295-297. — Includes index
ISBN 0-246-11093-7 : £9.95 B81-10649

150.19′53 — Psychology. Adler, Alfred

McDermot, Violet. The social vision of Alfred Adler / Violet Macdermot. — Ditchling (1 Dymocks Manor, East End La., Ditchling, Sussex) : New Atlantis Foundation, 1980. — 19p ; 22cm. — (Foundation lecture / New Atlantis Foundation ; 20)
Bibliography: p19
Unpriced (pbk) B81-15750

150.19′54 — Psychoanalysis. Jungian system

Analytical psychology : a modern science. — London : Academic Press, 1980, c1973. — x,209p,[4]p of plates : 4ill ; 12cm. — (The Library of analytical psychology ; v.1)
Originally published: London : Heinemann Medical, 1973. — Includes bibliographies and index
ISBN 0-12-262161-1 : £8.00 B81-07052

150.19′54′05 — Psychoanalysis. Jungian system — *Serials*

Harvest : journal for Jungian studies. — No.22 (1976). — London (60 Stanhope Gardens, SW7 5RF) : Analytical Psychology Club, 1976. — 158p
Unpriced B81-32414

Harvest : journal for Jungian studies. — No.23 (1977). — London (60 Stanhope Gardens, SW7 5RF) : Analytical Psychology Club, 1977. — 168p
Unpriced B81-32415

Harvest : journal for Jungian studies. — No.24 (1978). — London (60 Stanhope Gardens, SW7 5RF) : Analytical Psychology Club, 1978. — 189p
Unpriced B81-32416

Harvest : journal for Jungian studies. — No.25 (1979). — London (60 Stanhope Gardens, SW7 5RF) : Analytical Psychology Club, 1979. — 102p
Unpriced B81-32417

Harvest : journal for Jungian studies. — No.26 (1980). — London (60 Stanhope Gardens, SW7 5RF) : Analytical Psychology Club, 1980. — 119p
Unpriced B81-32418

150′.243318 — Psychology — *For trade unionism*

Cooper, Cary L.. Psychology and management : a text for managers and trade unionists / Cary L. Cooper. — London : Macmillan, 1981. — xii,305p : ill ; 26cm. — (Psychology for professional groups)
Includes bibliographies and index
ISBN 0-333-31856-0 (cased) : Unpriced
ISBN 0-333-31875-7 (pbk) : £12.95
Also classified at 150′.24658 B81-31312

150'.2436 — Psychology — *For counselling*
Nelson-Jones, Richard. The theory and practice of counselling psychology. — Eastbourne : Holt, Rinehart and Winston, Jan.1982. — [450]p
ISBN 0-03-910350-1 : £6.95 : CIP entry B81-34486

150'.24362 — Psychology — *For welfare work*
Psychology for social workers / [edited by] Martin Herbert. — London : Macmillan, 1981. — xii,352p : ill ; 26cm. — (Psychology for professional groups)
Includes bibliographies and index
ISBN 0-333-31866-8 : £12.50
ISBN 0-333-31878-1 (pbk) : Unpriced B81-30680

150'.24372 — Psychology — *For teaching*
Psychology for teachers / [edited by] David Fontana. — London : Macmillan, 1981. — xii,402p : ill ; 26cm. — (Psychology for professional groups)
Includes bibliographies and index
ISBN 0-333-31858-7 (cased) : £12.50
ISBN 0-333-31880-3 (pbk) : Unpriced B81-30675

150'.2461 — Psychology — *For medicine*
Weinman, John. An outline of psychology as applied to medicine / John Weinman. — Bristol : John Wright, 1981. — xii,274p : ill ; 22cm pbk
Bibliography: p259-265. — Includes index
ISBN 0-7236-0591-2 : £5.00 : CIP rev. B81-03708

150'.24613 — Psychology — *For nursing*
Altschul, A.. Psychology for nurses. — 5th ed. / Annie Altschul, Helen C. Sinclair. — London : Baillière Tindall, 1981. — ix,373p : ill ; 18cm. — (Nurses' aids series)
Previous ed.: 1975. — Includes bibliographies and index
ISBN 0-7020-0848-6 (pbk) : Unpriced B81-24913

150'.24658 — Psychology — *For management*
Cooper, Cary L.. Psychology and management : a text for managers and trade unionists / Cary L. Cooper. — London : Macmillan, 1981. — xii,305p : ill ; 26cm. — (Psychology for professional groups)
Includes bibliographies and index
ISBN 0-333-31856-0 (cased) : Unpriced
ISBN 0-333-31875-7 (pbk) : £12.95
Primary classification 150'.243318 B81-31312

150'.28'7 — Man. Psychological assessment
Advances in psychological assessment / Paul McReynolds editor. — San Francisco ; London : Jossey-Bass. — (Jossey-Bass social and behavioral science series)
Vol.4. — 1978, c1977. — xiv,597p : ill ; 24cm
Includes bibliographies and index
ISBN 0-87589-355-4 : Unpriced B81-33104

150'.28'7 — Psychology. Measurement
Ghiselli, Edwin E.. Measurement theory for the behavioral sciences / Edwin E. Ghiselli, John P. Campbell, Sheldon Zedeck. — Oxford : W.H. Freeman, c1981. — xv,494p : ill ; 24cm. — (A Series of books in psychology)
Includes bibliographies and index
ISBN 0-7167-1048-x (cased) : £18.70
ISBN 0-7167-1252-0 (pbk) : £11.70 B81-36486

150'.3 — Man. Behaviour — *Encyclopaedias*
Statt, David. A dictionary of human behaviour. — London : Harper & Row, Sept.1981. — [160]p. — (Harper reference)
ISBN 0-06-318191-6 : £5.95 : CIP entry B81-22569

150'.3'21 — Man. Psychological problems — *Encyclopaedias*
Bugelski, B. Richard. The handbook of practical psychology / B. Richard Bugelski, Anthony M. Graziano. — Englewood Cliffs ; London : Prentice-Hall, c1981. — vi,296p ; 23cm. — (A Spectrum book)
Includes index
ISBN 0-13-380600-6 (cased) : Unpriced
ISBN 0-13-380592-1 (pbk) : £4.50 B81-12527

150'.3'21 — Psychology — *Encyclopaedias*
ABC of psychology / general editor Leonard Kristal ; associate editors Michael Argyle ... [et al.]. — London : Michael Joseph, 1981. — 253p : ill,ports ; 22cm
ISBN 0-7181-2060-4 : £7.95 B81-36288

150'.5 — Psychology — *Serials*
Psychology USSR : selected papers from Voprosy psikhologii ... — Vol.1, no.1 (1981)-. — Oxford : Pergamon, 1981-. — v. : ill ; 25cm
Translation of: Voprosy psikhologii
ISSN 0160-7901 = Psychology USSR : Unpriced B81-36541

Review of personality and social psychology. — 1-. — Beverly Hills ; London : Sage in co-operation with the Society for Personality and Social Psychology, 1980-. — v. ; 22cm
Annual
Unpriced B81-20320

150'.7'1141 — Great Britain. Higher education institutions. Curriculum subjects: Psychology. Postgraduate courses — *Directories* — *Serials*
Compendium of postgraduate studies in psychology / produced by the Department of Psychology, University of Surrey, Guildford on the initiative of the Heads of Psychology Departments Committee. — 1977-. — [Guildford] ([Guildford, Surrey GU2 5XH]) : [The Department], 1977-. — v. ; 30cm
Annual. — Cover title: Compendium of U.K. postgraduate studies in psychology. — Spine title: U.K. postgraduate studies in psychology. — Description based on: 5th ed. (1981)
ISSN 0261-6521 = Compendium of postgraduate studies in psychology : £4.20 B81-33719

150'.72 — Psychology. Research
Wallis, D.. Reflections on psychological research / D. Wallis. — Cardiff (c/o R. Slater, Department of Applied Psychology, UWIST, Llwyn-y-Grant, Penylan, Cardiff CF3 7UX) : [UWIST Department of Applied Psychology], 1979. — 9p ; 30cm. — (Occasional paper / UWIST Department of Applied Psychology ; no.8)
Conference paper
£0.50 (spiral) B81-24796

150'.724 — Experimental psychology
Conrad, Eva. Introduction to experimental psychology / Eva Conrad, Terry Maul. — New York ; Chichester : Wiley, c1981. — xiii,542p : ill ; 25cm
Bibliography: p517-533. — Includes index
ISBN 0-471-06005-4 : £11.55 B81-30790

Robinson, Paul W.. Fundamentals of experimental psychology / Paul W. Robinson. — 2nd ed. — Englewood Cliffs ; London : Prentice-Hall, c1981. — xv,415p : ill ; 25cm
Previous ed.: 1976. — Bibliography: p403-406. — Includes index
ISBN 0-13-339135-3 : £12.95 B81-22726

150'.724 — Experimental psychology. Applications of real time computer systems
Bird, R. J.. The computer in experimental psychology / R.J. Bird. — London : Academic Press, 1981. — xi,243p : ill ; 24cm. — (Computers and people series)
Bibliography: p225-227. — Includes index
ISBN 0-12-099760-6 : £16.40 B81-33158

150'.724 — Psychology. Experiments. Applications of digital computer systems
Hale, David, *1944-*. Psychology laboratory computing : a report of a study group on possible SSRC initiatives to aid psychology laboratory computing made to the Computing Committee of the Social Science Research Council / David Hale, Thomas Green, Roger Henry. — London : The Council, 1981. — 77p ; 30cm
Bibliography: p66-69
ISBN 0-86226-085-x (pbk) : £3.50 B81-20819

150'.724 — Psychology. Experiments. Design & statistical analysis
Burns, R. B.. Experimental psychology : research methods and statistics / R.B. Burns, C.B. Dobson. — Lancaster : MTP, 1981. — xi,439p : ill ; 22cm
Includes index
ISBN 0-85200-369-2 (pbk) : £5.95 B81-06249

150'.724 — Psychology. Experiments. Effects of experimenters
Farr, R. M.. On the social significance of artifacts in experimenting / R.M. Farr. — Cardiff (c/o R. Slater, Department of Applied Psychology, UWIST, Llwyn-y-Grant, Penylan, Cardiff CF3 7UX) : [UWIST Department of Applied Psychology], 1977. — 14p ; 30cm. — (Occasional paper / UWIST Department of Applied Psychology ; no.4)
Bibliography: p12-14
£0.50 (unbound) B81-24798

150'.76 — Psychology — *Questions & answers*
Benassi, Victor. Test booklet for essentials of psychology : Houston — Bee — Hatfield — Rimm / Victor Benassi, Martin Lobdell. — New York ; London : Academic Press, c1981. — v,258p : ill ; 26cm
ISBN 0-12-356855-2 (pbk) : £2.00 B81-39787

150'.9 — Psychology, *to 1980*
O'Neil, W. M.. The beginnings of modern psychology. — 2nd ed. — Brighton : Harvester Press, Jan.1982. — [192]p
Previous ed.: Harmondsworth : Penguin, 1968
ISBN 0-7108-0334-6 (cased) : £14.95 : CIP entry
ISBN 0-7108-0329-x (pbk) : £3.95 B81-33847

Robinson, Daniel N.. An intellectual history of psychology / Daniel N. Robinson. — Rev. ed. — New York : Macmillan ; London : Collier Macmillan, c1981. — xi,484p ; 25cm
Previous ed.: 1976. — Bibliography: p461-471. — Includes index
ISBN 0-02-402480-5 : £13.95 B81-29332

150'.917'671 — Islamic countries. Psychologists. Role
Badri, Malik B.. The dilemma of Muslim psychologists / Malik B. Badri. — London : MWH London, 1979. — xi,131p : ill ; 18cm
Bibliography: p124-126. - Includes index
ISBN 0-906194-05-9 (pbk) : £1.60 B81-05102

150'.92'4 — Experimental psychology. Cattell, James McKeen — *Correspondence, diaries, etc.*
Cattell, James McKeen. An education in psychology : James McKeen Cattell's journal and letters from Germany and England 1880-1888 / selected and edited by Michael M. Sokal. — Cambridge, Mass. ; London : MIT, c1981. — xxxvii,372p : ill,map,facsims,ports ; 24cm
Bibliography: pxxiv-xxvii. - Includes index
ISBN 0-262-19185-7 : £18.60 B81-21254

150'.92'4 — Psychology. Eysenck, H. J. — *Biographies*
Gibson, H. B.. Hans Eysenck : the man and his work / H.B. Gibson. — London : Owen, 1981. — 275p,[8]p of plates : ill,ports ; 23cm
Bibliography: p263-266. - Includes index
ISBN 0-7206-0566-0 : £11.95 B81-17365

150'.92'4 — Psychology. Wolff, Charlotte — *Biographies*
Wolff, Charlotte. Hindsight / Charlotte Wolff. — London : Quartet, 1980. — viii,312p,[8]p of plates : ill,1map,1facsim,ports ; 24cm
Includes index
ISBN 0-7043-2253-6 : £8.95 B81-03791

150'.973 — United States. Psychology. Social aspects
Sarason, Seymour B.. Psychology misdirected / Seymour B. Sarason. — New York : Free Press ; London : Collier Macmillan, c1981. — xiii,192p ; 25cm
Bibliography: p185-188. — Includes index
ISBN 0-02-928100-8 : £10.50 B81-38655

152 — PHYSIOLOGICAL PSYCHOLOGY

152 — Man. Behaviour. Physiological aspects
Carlson, Neil R.. Instructor's manual to accompany Physiology of behavior. 2nd ed. / prepared by Neil R. Carlson, Paula Condon, and Anne E. Powell. — Boston, Mass. ; London : Allyn and Bacon, c1981. — 169p ; 24cm
ISBN 0-205-07263-1 (pbk) : Unpriced B81-18239

152 — Man. Behaviour. Physiological aspects *continuation*

Carlson, Neil R.. Physiology of behavior / Neil R. Carlson. — 2nd ed. — Boston [Mass.] ; London : Allyn and Bacon, c1980. — xiii,747p : ill ; 25cm
Previous ed.: 1977. — Bibliography: p707-728. - Includes index
ISBN 0-205-07262-3 : Unpriced
ISBN 0-205-07291-7 (international student ed.) : Unpriced B81-18900

Levitt, Robert A.. Physiological psychology / Robert A. Levitt. — New York ; London : Holt, Rinehart and Winston, c1981. — xiii,594p : ill ; 25cm
Bibliography: p515-568. — Includes index
ISBN 0-03-055206-0 : £13.50 B81-22878

152 — Psychophysiology

Stern, Robert M. (Robert Morris). Psychophysiological recording / Robert M. Stern, William J. Ray, Christopher M. Davis. — New York ; Oxford : Oxford University Press, 1980. — xii,238p : ill ; 23cm
Includes bibliographies and index
ISBN 0-19-502696-9 (pbk) : £5.75 B81-01635

152 — Vigilance. Psychological aspects

Davies, D. R.. The psychology of vigilance. — London : Academic Press, Feb.1982. — [300]p
ISBN 0-12-206180-2 : CIP entry B81-35916

152'.05 — Man. Behaviour. Physiological aspects — *Serials*

Progress in psychobiology and physiological psychology. — Vol.9. — New York ; London : Academic Press, 1980. — xiv,373p
ISBN 0-12-542109-5 : Unpriced
ISSN 0363-0951 B81-04936

152.1 — PSYCHOLOGY. SENSORY PERCEPTION

152.1 — Man. Sensory perception

Intersensory perception and sensory integration / edited by Richard D. Walk and Herbert L. Pick, Jr. — New York ; London : Plenum, c1981. — xxi,415p : ill ; 24cm. — (Perception and perceptual development ; v.2)
Includes bibliographies and index
ISBN 0-306-40610-1 : Unpriced B81-31782

152.1'4 — Learning. Role of visual perception

Sless, David. Learning and visual communication. — London : Croom Helm, Sept.1981. — [192] p. — (New patterns of learning series)
ISBN 0-7099-2319-8 : £11.50 : CIP entry B81-22596

152.1'4 — Man. Visual perception

Fineman, Mark. The inquisitive eye / Mark Fineman. — New York ; Oxford : Oxford University Press, 1981. — 171p,[4]p of plates : ill(some col.) ; 24cm
Bibliography: p159-167. — Includes index
ISBN 0-19-502773-6 (pbk) : £6.25 B81-38072

Haber, Ralph Norman. The psychology of visual perception / Ralph Norman Haber, Maurice Hershenson. — 2nd ed. — New York ; London : Holt, Rinehart and Winston, c1980. — ix,431p,[4]p of plates : ill(some col.) ; 25cm
Previous ed.: 1973. — Bibliography: p408-421. — Includes index
ISBN 0-03-020276-0 : £10.50 B81-00724

152.1'4 — Man. Visual perception. Psychological aspects

Perceiving and remembering faces. — London : Academic Press, Oct.1981. — [300]p
ISBN 0-12-206220-5 : CIP entry B81-26771

152.1'4'02474 — Man. Visual perception — *For design*

Thiel, Philip. Visual awareness and design : an introductory program in conceptual awareness, perceptual sensitivity, and basic design skills / Philip Thiel. — Seattle ; London : University of Washington Press, c1981. — 287p : ill ; 29cm
Bibliography: p273-277
ISBN 0-295-95712-3 (cased) : £22.75
ISBN 0-295-95786-7 (pbk) : £12.65 B81-29537

152.1'4'02477 — Man. Visual perception — *For photography*

Stroebel, Leslie. Visual concepts for photographers / Leslie Stroebel, Hollis Todd and Richard Zakia. — London : Focal, 1980. — 350p : ill(some col.) ; 25cm
Bibliography : p337-343. — Includes index
ISBN 0-240-51025-9 : £14.95 : CIP rev. B79-25556

152.1'4'0724 — Man. Visual perception. Mathematical models

Caelli, Terry. Visual perception : theory and practice / by Terry Caelli. — Oxford : Pergamon, 1981. — x,197p : ill ; 26cm. — (Pergamon international library)
Includes bibliographies and index
ISBN 0-08-024420-3 (cased) : £17.50
ISBN 0-08-024419-x (pbk) : £8.50 B81-19102

152.1'42 — Man. Spatial ability

Spatial representation and behavior across the life span : theory and application / edited by Lynn S. Liben, Arthur H. Patterson, Nora Newcombe. — New York ; London : Academic Press, 1981. — xv,404p : ill ; 24cm. — (Developmental psychology series)
Includes bibliographies and index
ISBN 0-12-447980-4 : £15.40 B81-17423

152.1'423 — Man. Visual perception. Pattern recognition. Cultural factors

Deręgowski, J. B.. Illusions, patterns and pictures : a cross-cultural perspective / J.B. Deręgowski. — London : Academic Press, 1980. — xii,219p : ill,1coat of arms ; 24cm. — (Academic Press series in cognition an perception)
Bibliography: p203-215. - Includes index
ISBN 0-12-210750-0 : £14.80 : CIP rev. B80-20135

152.1'423 — Pictures. Perception by man

The **Perception** of pictures / edited by Margaret A. Hagen. — New York ; London : Academic Press, 1980. — (Academic Press series in cognition and perception)
Vol.1: Alberti's window : the projective model of pictorial information / with a foreword by James J. Gibson. — xxx,293p : ill ; 24cm
Includes bibliographies and index
ISBN 0-12-313601-6 : £15.20 B81-38492

The **Perception** of pictures / edited by Margaret A. Hagen. — New York ; London : Academic Press. — (Academic Press series in cognition and perception)
Vol.2: Dürer's devices : beyond the projective model of pictures / with a foreword by Rudolph Arnheim. — 1980. — xiii,356p : ill ; 24cm
Includes bibliographies and index
ISBN 0-12-313602-4 : £22.40 B81-14559

152.1'824 — Man. Pain. Toleration

Miller, Miriam. How to live with pain / by Miriam Miller. — Romford : Fowler, c1980. — 136p ; 19cm
ISBN 0-85243-363-8 (pbk) : £2.95 B81-38079

152.1'88 — Man. Biofeedback

Stern, Robert M. (Robert Morris). Biofeedback : potential and limits / Robert M. Stern, William J. Ray. — Lincoln [Neb.] ; London : University of Nebraska Press, 1980, c1977. — viii,197p : ill ; 21cm. — (Bison books in clinical psychology)
Originally published: Homewood, Ill. : Dow Jones-Irwin, 1977. — Includes index
ISBN 0-8032-9114-0 (pbk) : £2.40 B81-12002

152.3 — PSYCHOLOGY. MOVEMENTS AND MOTOR FUNCTIONS

152.3 — Man. Perceptuo-motor skills

Human skills / edited by Dennis H. Holding. — Chichester : Wiley, c1981. — xi,303p : ill ; 24cm. — (Wiley series on studies in human performance)
Bibliography: p269-299. — Includes index
ISBN 0-471-27838-6 : £14.50 : CIP rev. B81-00009

152.3'028'7 — Man. Motor activities. Neuropsychological aspects. Tests: Halstead-Reitan Neuropsychological Test Battery. Interpretation — *Manuals*

Interpretation of the Halstead-Reitan neuropsychological test battery : a casebook approach / Charles J. Golden ... [et al.]. — New York ; London : Grune & Stratton, c1981. — ix,401p : ill ; 24cm
Bibliography: p383-389. - Includes index
ISBN 0-8089-1298-4 : £15.00 B81-15013

152.4 — PSYCHOLOGY. EMOTIONS AND FEELINGS

152.4 — Love. Evolutionary aspects

Mellen, Sydney L. W.. The evolution of love / Sydney L.W. Mellen. — Oxford : W.H. Freeman, c1981. — x,312p ; 22cm
Bibliography: p292-306. — Includes index
ISBN 0-7167-1271-7 (cased) : £8.50
ISBN 0-7167-1272-5 (pbk) : Unpriced B81-36483

152.4 — Love. Psychological aspects — *Personal observations*

Garbo, Norman. To love again : a true story / Norman Garbo. — London : W.H. Allen, 1981, c1977. — 262p ; 21cm
Originally published: New York : McGraw-Hill, c1977
ISBN 0-491-02644-7 : £6.95 B81-17290

152.4 — Love. Psychosocial aspects

Pope, Kenneth S.. On love and loving / Kenneth S. Pope and Associates. — San Francisco ; London : Jossey-Bass, 1980. — xix,377p ; 24cm. — (The Jossey-Bass social and behavioral science series)
Bibliography: p336-366. — Includes index
ISBN 0-87589-479-8 : £13.55 B81-07328

152.4 — Love. Psychosocial aspects — *Feminist viewpoints*

Tweedie, Jill. In the name of love / Jill Tweedie. — London : Granada, 1980, c1979. — 223p ; 20cm. — (A Paladin book)
Originally published: London : Cape, 1979. — Bibliography: p213-215. - Includes index
ISBN 0-586-08348-0 (pbk) : £1.50 B81-00725

152.4 — Man. Anxiety *related to* **Christian doctrine of original sin** — *Philosophical perspectives*

Kierkegaard, Søren. The concept of anxiety : a simple psychologically orienting deliberation on the dogmatic issue of hereditary sin / by Soren Kierkegaard ; edited and translated with introduction and notes by Reidar Thomte in collaboration with Albert B. Anderson. — Princeton ; Guildford : Princeton University Press, c1980. — xviii,273p : 1facsim ; 22cm. — (Kierkegaard's writings ; 8)
Translation of: Begrebet angest. — Bibliography: p257. - Includes index
ISBN 0-691-07244-2 : £10.20
Primary classification 233'.14 B81-06740

152.4 — Man. Despair *related to* **Christian doctrine of sin** — *Philosophical perspectives*

Kierkegaard, Søren. The sickness unto death : a Christian psychological exposition for upbuilding and awakening / by Søren Kierkegaard ; edited and translated with introduction and notes by Howard V. Hong and Edna H. Hong. — Princeton ; Guildford : Princeton University Press, c1980. — xxiii,201p ; 23cm. — (Kierkegaard's writings ; 19)
Translation of: Sygdommen til doden. — Bibliography: p183. - Includes index
ISBN 0-691-07247-7 : £9.10
Primary classification 241'.3 B81-06741

152.4 — Man. Emotions & feelings — *For children*

Allington, Richard. Feelings / by Richard Allington and Kathleen Krull ; illustrated by Brian Cody. — Oxford : Blackwell Raintree, 1981. — 32p : col.ill ; 24cm. — (Beginning to learn about)
Originally published: / by Richard L. Allington and Kathleen Cowles. Milwaukee : Raintree Children's, 1980
ISBN 0-86256-019-5 : £2.50
ISBN 0-8265-6019-5 B81-28666

152.4 — Man. Fear

Tuan, Yi-fu. Landscapes of fear / Yi-fu Tuan. — Oxford : Blackwell, 1980, c1979. — 262p ; 25cm
Originally published: New York : Pantheon Books, c1979. — Includes index
ISBN 0-631-12821-2 : £10.00 : CIP rev.
B79-37141

152.4 — Transcendental experiences

Neher, Andrew. The psychology of transcendence / Andrew Neher. — Englewood Cliffs ; London : Prentice-Hall, c1980. — 361p : ill ; 21cm. — (Transpersonal books) (A Spectrum book)
Bibliography: p299-338. — Includes index
ISBN 0-13-736652-3 (cased) : Unpriced
ISBN 0-13-736645-0 (pbk) : £5.15 B81-14105

152.4'028'7 — Man. Emotions. Testing — *Manuals*

Markert, Christopher. Test your emotions / by Christopher Markert. — Wellingborough : Thomas, 1980. — 64p : ill ; 18cm
ISBN 0-85454-073-3 (pbk) : £0.70 B81-02712

152.8 — PSYCHOPHYSICS

152.8 — Psychological tests

Jensen, Arthur P.. Straight talk about mental tests. — London : Methuen, July 1981. — [320]p
ISBN 0-416-32300-6 : £8.95 : CIP entry
B81-14866

152.8'3 — Man. Reaction times

Reaction times / edited by A.T. Welford ; with contributions by J.M.T. Brebner ... [et al.]. — London : Academic Press, 1980. — ix,418p : ill ; 24cm
Includes bibliographies and index
ISBN 0-12-742880-1 : £27.80 : CIP rev.
B80-18156

153 — PSYCHOLOGY. INTELLIGENCE, INTELLECTUAL AND CONSCIOUS MENTAL PROCESSES

153 — Man. Consciousness

Aspects of consciousness / edited by Geoffrey Underwood and Robin Stevens. — New York ; London : Academic Press
Vol.2: Structural issues. — 1981. — xi,246p : ill ; 24cm
Includes bibliographies and index
ISBN 0-12-708802-4 : £15.00 : CIP rev.
B81-08936

The **metaphors** of consciousness / edited Ronald S. Valle and Rolf von Eckartsberg. — New York ; London : Plenum, c1981. — xxii,521p : ill ; 24cm
Includes bibliographies and index
ISBN 0-306-40520-2 : Unpriced B81-26012

Miller, Robert. Meaning and purpose in the intact brain. — Oxford : Oxford University Press, Oct.1981. — [275]p
ISBN 0-19-857579-3 : £20.00 : CIP entry
B81-26751

153 — Man. Consciousness. Psychological aspects

Nicoll, Maurice. Living time and the integration of the life / Maurice Nicoll. — London : Watkins, c1981. — viii,252p : ill ; 22cm
Originally published: London : Vincent Stuart, 1952. — Bibliography: p247. - Includes index
ISBN 0-7224-0146-9 (pbk) : £3.95 B81-20966

153 — Man. Mental processes

Bruner, Jerome S.. Beyond the information given : studies in the psychology of knowing / Jerome S. Bruner ; contributors with Jerome S. Bruner, George Austin ... [et al.] ; selected, edited and introduced by Jeremy M. Anglin. — London : Allen & Unwin, 1974, c1976 (1980 [printing]). — xxxiv,502p : ill ; 24cm
Originally published: New York : Norton, 1973 ; London : Allen and Unwin, 1974. — Bibliography: p481-490. - Includes index
ISBN 0-04-150076-8 (pbk) : £5.95 B81-12776

Wisberg, Robert W.. Memory, thought, and behaviour / Robert W. Weisberg. — New York ; Oxford : Oxford University Press, 1980. — xx,458p : ill ; 23cm
Bibliography: p422-441. — Includes index
ISBN 0-19-502583-0 (pbk) : £8.95 B81-01975

153 — Man. Mental processes. Effects of sleep

Sleep, dreams and memory / edited by William Fishbein. — Lancaster : MTP Press, c1981. — 255p : ill,1port ; 24cm. — (Advances in sleep research ; v.6)
Includes bibliographies and index
ISBN 0-85200-543-1 : £15.50 B81-24024

153 — Self-deception

Haight, M. R.. A study of self-deception / M.R. Haight. — Brighton : Harvester, 1980. — xii,163p ; 23cm
Bibliography: p157-158. — Includes index
ISBN 0-85527-918-4 : £16.50 B81-01666

153.1 — PSYCHOLOGY. MEMORY AND LEARNING

153.1 — Man. Learning & memory

Houston, John P.. Fundamentals of learning and memory / John P. Houston. — 2nd ed., International ed. — New York ; London : Academic Press, c1981. — xvii,639p : ill ; 24cm
Previous ed.: pubished as Fundamentals of learning. 1976. — Bibliography: p562-621. — Includes index
ISBN 0-12-356830-7 (pbk) : Unpriced
B81-29821

153.1'2 — Man. Memory

Wingfield, Arthur. The psychology of human memory / Arthur Wingfield, Dennis L. Byrnes. — International ed. — New York ; London : Academic Press, c1981. — xiv,429p : ill ; 24cm
Bibliography: p381-410. — Includes index
ISBN 0-12-759630-5 (pbk) : Unpriced
B81-23231

153.1'2 — Man. Memory. Theories

Wingfield, Arthur. The psychology of human memory / Arthur Wingfield, Dennis L. Byrnes. — New York ; London : Academic Press, c1981. — xiv,429p : ill ; 24cm
Bibliography: p381-410. — Includes index
ISBN 0-12-759650-x (pbk) : £6.20 B81-35421

153.1'5 — Learning

Wittig, Arno F.. Schaum's outline of theory and problems of psychology of learning / by Arno F. Wittig. — New York ; London : McGraw-Hill, c1981. — 326p : ill ; 28cm. — (Schaum's outline series)
Includes index
ISBN 0-07-071192-5 (pbk) : £4.95 B81-02495

153.1'5 — Learning by man

Language and learning : the debate between Jean Piaget and Noam Chomsky / edited by Massimo Piattelli-Palmarini. — London : Routledge & Kegan Paul, 1980. — xxxvi,409p ; 25cm
Includes index
ISBN 0-7100-0438-9 : £9.75 B81-07236

153.1'5 — Learning by man. Psychological aspects

Bower, Gordon H.. Theories of learning / Gordon H. Bower, Ernest R. Hilgard. — 5th ed. — Englewood Cliffs ; London : Prentice-Hall, c1981. — vi,647p : ill ; 25cm. — (The Century psychology series)
Authors' names in reverse order in 3rd and 4th eds. — Previous ed.: 1975. — Bibliography: p578-625. — Includes index
ISBN 0-13-914432-3 : £13.60 B81-22722

153.1'5'05 — Learning by man — *Serials*

The **Psychology** of learning and motivation. — Vol.14 (1980). — New York ; London : Academic Press, c1980. — xiv,367p
ISBN 0-12-543314-x : £23.40
ISSN 0079-7421
Also classified at 153.8'05 B81-16838

153.1'5'076 — Learning — *Questions & answers*

Thompson, Myrthalyne C.. Instructor's manual for Fundamentals of learning [by] John P. Houston / Myrthalyne C. Thompson. — New York ; London : Academic Press, [1981]. — i,54p ; 23cm
Bibliography: p47-54
ISBN 0-12-356852-8 (unbound) : £1.40
B81-18183

153.1'52 — Man. Steady-state operant behaviour. Research. Quantitative methods — *Conference proceedings*

International Symposium on Recent Developments in the Quantification of Steady-State Operant Behaviour *(1980 : Manchester)*. Quantification of steady-state operant behaviour : proceedings of the International Symposium on Recent Developments in the Quantification of Steady-State Operant Behaviour held at Owens Park, Manchester, on 22nd - 25th July, 1980 / edited by C.M. Bradshaw, E. Szabadi and C.F. Lowe. — Amsterdam ; Oxford : Elsevier/North-Holland, 1981. — xiii,498p : ill ; 25cm
Includes index
ISBN 0-444-80298-3 : £30.97 B81-05082

153.3 — PSYCHOLOGY. IMAGINATION AND IMAGERY

153.3'094 — Imagination. Theories of Western European writers, *1700-1850*

Engell, James. The creative imagination : enlightenment to romanticism / James Engell. — Cambridge, Mass. ; London : Harvard University Press, 1981. — xix,416p ; 25cm
Bibliography: p369-379. - Includes index
ISBN 0-674-17572-7 : £9.60 B81-28254

153.3'2 — Geographical features. Mental images

Haynes, Robin M.. Geographical images and mental maps / Robin M. Haynes. — Basingstoke : Macmillan Education, 1981, c1980. — v,38p : ill,maps ; 22cm. — (Aspects of geography)
Bibliography: p38
ISBN 0-333-28680-4 (pbk) : £1.30 : CIP rev.
B80-12213

153.3'2 — Mental images

Kosslyn, Stephen Michael. Image and mind / Stephen Michael Kosslyn. — Cambridge, Mass. ; London : Harvard University Press, 1980. — xv,500p : ill,1map ; 24cm
Bibliography: p480-494. — Includes index
ISBN 0-674-44365-9 : £12.00 B81-08332

153.4 — PSYCHOLOGY. COGNITION

153.4 — Man. Cognition — *Philosophical perspectives*

Fodor, Jerry A.. Representations : philosophical essays on the foundations of cognitive science / Jerry A. Fodor. — Brighton : Harvester, 1981. — ix,343p ; 25cm
Bibliography: p335-339. — Includes index
ISBN 0-85527-977-x : £22.50 : CIP rev.
Primary classification 121'.3 B81-16892

Wilson, Kellogg V.. From associations to structure : the course of cognition / Kellogg V. Wilson. — Amsterdam ; Oxford : North-Holland, 1980. — xvi,338p : ill ; 23cm. — (Advances in psychology ; 6)
Bibliography: p305-334. — Includes index
ISBN 0-444-86043-6 : £16.05 B81-02052

153.4 — Man. Cognition. Role of memory

Cognition and memory / edited by F. Klix and J. Hoffman. — Amsterdam ; Oxford : North-Holland, 1980. — 306p : ill ; 23cm. — (Advances in psychology ; 5)
Conference papers. — Includes bibliographies
ISBN 0-444-86041-x : Unpriced B81-11699

153.4 — Man. Cognition. Theories

Cognitive theories in social psychology : papers from Advances in experimental social psychology / edited by Leonard Berkowitz ; contributors Norman H. Anderson ... [et al.]. — New York ; London : Academic Press, 1978. — xv,528p : ill ; 23cm
Includes bibliographies and index
ISBN 0-12-091850-1 (pbk) : £9.80 B81-11266

153.4 — Man. Cognition. Theories
continuation

Mayer, Richard E.. The promise of cognitive psychology / Richard E. Mayer. — Oxford : W.H. Freeman, c1981. — xiv,120p : ill ; 24cm. — (A Series of books in psychology)
Bibliography: p108-115. — Includes index
ISBN 0-7167-1275-x (cased) : £8.00
ISBN 0-7167-1276-8 (pbk) : £3.70 B81-36490

153.4′09 — Man. Cognition. Theories, *to 1979 — Critical studies*

Cohen, John, *1911-*. The lineaments of mind in historical perspective / by John Cohen. — Oxford : W.H. Freeman, c1980. — xv,325p ; 24cm
Includes index
ISBN 0-7167-1175-3 : £13.50 B81-04027

153.4′2 — Thought processes. Contradiction

Piaget, Jean. Experiments in contradiction / Jean Piaget ; translated by Derek Coltman. — Chicago ; London : Universiy of Chicago Press, 1980. — xviii,310p ; 24cm
Translation of: Recherches sur la contradiction
ISBN 0-226-66779-0 : £13.20 B81-21064

153.4′2 — Thought processes. Cultural factors

Hofstede, Geert. Culture′s consequences : international differences in work-related values / Geert Hofstede. — Beverly Hills ; London : Sage, c1980. — 475p : ill ; 24cm. — (Cross-cultural research and methodology series ; v.5)
Bibliography: p427-454. — Includes index
ISBN 0-8039-1444-x : £18.72 B81-14023

153.4′2 — Thought processes — *For children*

Allington, Richard L.. Beginning to learn about thinking. — Oxford : Blackwell, Aug.1981. — [32]p
ISBN 0-86256-042-x : £2.50 : CIP entry
B81-19156

153.4′2 — Thought processes *related to* **learning**

McPeck, John E.. Thinking skills and education. — Oxford : Martin Robertson, May 1981. — [176]p. — (Issues and ideas in education)
ISBN 0-85520-383-8 (cased) : £12.50 : CIP entry
ISBN 0-85520-384-6 (pbk) : £3.75 B81-04291

153.4′2′072 — Man. Thought processes. Comparative studies. Methodology

Cole, Michael, *1938-*. Comparative studies of how people think : an introduction / Michael Cole and Barbara Means. — Cambridge, Mass. ; London : Harvard University Press, 1981. — 208p : ill ; 22cm
Bibliography: p183-193. — Includes index
ISBN 0-674-15260-3 : £9.00 B81-38137

153.4′3 — Man. Problem solving. Role of visual imagery. Psychological aspects

Kaufmann, Geir. Visual imagery and its relation to problem solving : a theoretical and experimental inquiry / Geir Kaufmann. — Bergen : Universitetsforlaget ; Henley on Thames : Global Book Resources [[distributor]], 1979. — 144p : ill ; 22cm
Bibliography: p83-89. — Includes index
ISBN 82-00-01788-5 (pbk) : £7.00 B81-03923

153.4′4 — Man. Intuition

Bastick, Tony. Intuition. — Chichester : Wiley, Jan.1982. — [500]p
ISBN 0-471-27992-7 : £25.00 : CIP entry
B81-34478

153.6 — PSYCHOLOGY. COMMUNICATION

153.6 — Adults. Oral communication with children — *Conference proceedings*

Adult-child conversation / edited by Peter French and Margaret Maclure. — London : Croom Helm, c1981. — 310p : ill ; 23cm
Conference papers. — Includes bibliographies and index
ISBN 0-7099-0069-4 : £14.95 : CIP rev.
B80-08178

153.7 — PSYCHOLOGY. PERCEPTUAL PROCESSES

153.7 — Man. Perception

Michaels, Claire F.. Direct perception / Claire F. Michaels, Claudia Carello. — Englewood Cliffs ; London : Prentice-Hall, c1981. — viii,200p : ill ; 24cm
Bibliography: p189-196. — Includes index
ISBN 0-13-214791-2 : £12.60 B81-28422

153.7 — Material objects. Perception by man. Psychological aspects

Lian, Arild. The psychological study of object perception : examination of methodological problems and a critique of main research approaches / Arild Lian. — London : Academic Press, 1981. — x,205p : ill ; 24cm
Bibliography: p196-201. - Includes index
ISBN 0-12-447850-6 : £11.80 B81-22426

153.7 — Reality. Perception by man. Effects of literature & language

Martin, Graham Dunstan. The architecture of experience : a discussion of the role of language and literature in the construction of the world / Graham Dunstan Martin. — Edinburgh : Edinburgh University Press, c1981. — vi,201p ; 23cm
Bibliography: p188-196. — Includes index
ISBN 0-85224-409-6 : £12.00 B81-40718

153.7 — Reality. Perception by man — *Polish texts*

Krzyżanowski, Marian. Anatomia rzeczywistości / Marian Krzyżanowski. — Londyn : Oficyna Poetów i Malarzy, 1980. — 69p ; 21cm
£1.80 (pbk) B81-06085

153.7 — Risks. Perception by man

Green, C. H.. Through a glass darkly : perceiving perceived risks to health and safety / C.H. Green, R.A. Brown ; prepared for the Workshop on Perceived Risk, Eugene, Oregon, December 1980. — Dundee (Perth Rd., Dundee DD1 4HT) : Duncan of Jordanstone College of Art, University of Dundee, c1980. — 169p : ill ; 30cm
Unpriced (pbk) B81-36691

153.7′36 — Man. Subliminal perception

Dixon, Norman F.. Preconscious processing. — Chichester : Wiley, Oct.1981. — [320]p
ISBN 0-471-27982-x : £12.50 : CIP entry
B81-28015

153.7′36 — Universals. Perception by man — *Study regions: Africa — Conference proceedings*

Universals of human thought : some African evidence / edited by Barbara Lloyd, John Gay. — Cambridge : Cambridge University Press, 1981. — xxiii,273p : ill,maps,plans ; 24cm
Conference papers. — Includes bibliographies and index
ISBN 0-521-22953-7 (cased) : £20.00 : CIP rev.
ISBN 0-521-29818-0 (pbk) : £6.50 B80-25097

153.7′52 — Space. Perception by man

Sack, Robert David. Conceptions of space in social thought : a geographic perspective / Robert David Sack. — London : Macmillan, 1980. — ix,231p : ill,2ports ; 23cm. — (Critical human geography)
Includes index
ISBN 0-333-28683-9 (cased) : £5.95 : CIP rev.
ISBN 0-333-28684-7 (pbk) : Unpriced
B80-09073

Tuan, Yi-Fu. Space and place : the perspective of experience / Yi-Fu Tuan. — London : Edward Arnold, 1977, (1979 [printing]). — vi,235p : ill,maps,plans ; 23cm
Originally published: Minneapolis : University of Minnesota Press, 1977. — Includes index
ISBN 0-7131-6221-x (pbk) : £5.95 B81-10517

153.8 — PSYCHOLOGY. VOLITION

153.8 — Man. Development. Role of social motivation

Veroff, Joseph. Social incentives : a life-span developmental approach / Joseph Veroff, Joanne B. Veroff. — New York ; London : Academic Press, 1980. — xiv,311p ; 24cm
Bibliography: p291-303. — Includes index
ISBN 0-12-718750-2 : £13.00 B81-02842

153.8 — Man. Motivation

Advances in intrinsic motivation and aesthetics / edited by Hy I. Day. — New York ; London : Plenum, c1981. — xii,503p : ill ; 24cm
Includes bibliographies and index
ISBN 0-306-40606-3 : Unpriced
Also classified at 700′.1′9 B81-32645

Apter, Michael J.. The experience of motivation. — London : Academic Press, Feb.1982. — [420]p
ISBN 0-12-058920-6 : CIP entry B81-36036

153.8 — Man. Motivation — *Conference proceedings*

Analysis of motivational processes / edited by Frederick M. Toates, Timothy R. Halliday. — London : Academic Press, 1980. — x,363p : ill ; 24cm
Conference papers. — Includes bibliographies and index
ISBN 0-12-692260-8 : £16.60 : CIP rev.
B80-30675

153.8 — Man. Motivation. Role of cognition

Eckblad, Gudrun. Scheme theory : a conceptual framework for cognitive-motivational processes / Gudrun Eckblad. — London : Academic Press, 1981. — v,131p : ill ; 24cm
Bibliography: p120-127. — Includes index
ISBN 0-12-229550-1 : £13.00 B81-22392

153.8′05 — Man. Motivation — *Conference proceedings — Serials*

Nebraska Symposium on Motivation *(1979)*. Nebraska Symposium on Motivation. — 1979. — Lincoln [Neb.] ; London : University of Nebraska Press, 1980. — xii,365p ; 24cm. — (Current theory and research in motivation ; v.27)
Includes bibliographies and index
ISBN 0-8032-2313-7 (cased) : £12.00
ISSN 0146-7875 B81-23127

Nebraska Symposium on Motivation *(1980)*. Nebraska Symposium on Motivation. — 1980. — Lincoln [Neb.] ; London : University of Nebraska Press, 1981. — xv,249p. — (Current theory and research in motivation ; v.28)
ISBN 0-8032-0620-8 : £10.70
ISSN 0146-7875 B81-31040

153.8′05 — Man. Motivation — *Serials*

The **Psychology** of learning and motivation. — Vol.14 (1980). — New York ; London : Academic Press, c1980. — xiv,367p
ISBN 0-12-543314-x : £23.40
ISSN 0079-7421
Primary classification 153.1′5′05 B81-16838

153.8′3 — Decision making. Psychological aspects

Hogarth, Robin M.. Judgement and choice : the psychology of decision / Robin M. Hogarth. — Chichester : Wiley, c1980. — xi,250p : ill ; 24cm
Bibliography: p232-246. - Includes index
ISBN 0-471-27744-4 : £8.00 : CIP rev.
B80-13183

153.8′5 — Man. Behaviour modification

Applications of conditioning theory / edited by Graham Davey. — London : Methuen, 1981. — xviii,222p : ill ; 22cm. — (Psychology in progress)
Includes bibliographies and index
ISBN 0-416-73560-6 (cased) : Unpriced : CIP rev.
ISBN 0-416-73570-3 (pbk) : Unpriced
B81-23770

Kalish, Harry I.. From behavioral science to behavior modification / Harry I. Kalish. — New York ; London : McGraw-Hill, c1981. — xii,436p : ill ; 25cm
Bibliography: p393-417. - Includes index
ISBN 0-07-033245-2 : £16.50 B81-09936

Progress in behavior modification / edited by Michael Hersen, Richard M. Eisler, Peter M. Miller. — New York ; London : Academic Press. — xv,297p : ill ; 24cm
Includes bibliographies and index
ISBN 0-12-535611-0 : £21.80 B81-39567

153.8′5′05 — Man. Behaviour modification — *Serials*
[Behavior modification *(Beverly Hills)*]. Behavior modification. — Vol.1, no.1 (Jan.1977)-. — Beverly Hills ; London : Sage, 1977-. — v. : ill ; 22cm
Quarterly
ISSN 0145-4455 = Behavior modification : Unpriced B81-03261

153.9 — PSYCHOLOGY. INTELLIGENCE AND APTITUDES

153.9 — Man. Intelligence
Davies, Don D.. The unique animal. — London (121 Bouverie Rd, N16 0AA) : Prytaneum Press, Nov.1981. — [336]p
ISBN 0-907152-02-3 (cased) : £12.95 : CIP entry
ISBN 0-907152-01-5 (pbk) : £6.95 B81-28564

153.9 — Man. Intelligence & ability. Theories — *German texts*
Werder, Hans. Zum Problem der Begabung und Intelligenz / Hans Werder. — Basel ; London : Karger, c1980. — 193p ; 23cm. — (Psychologische Praxis ; Bd.55)
Bibliography: p174 193
ISBN 3-8055-1123-x (pbk) : £8.50 B81-04579

153.9 — Man. Intelligence — *Conference proceedings*
Nato Conference on Intelligence and Learning *(1979 : York)*. Intelligence and learning / [proceedings of a Nato Conference on Intelligence and Learning held July 16-20, 1979, in York] ; edited by Morton P. Friedman, J.P. Das and Neil O'Connor. — New York ; London : Published in cooperation with Nato Scientific Affairs Division by Plenum, c1981. — xii,624p : ill ; 26cm. — (Nato conference series. 111, Human factors ; v.14)
Includes bibliographies and index
ISBN 0-306-40643-8 : Unpriced B81-35257

153.9′2 — Man. Intelligence. Environmental factors *compared with* **genetic factors**
Eysenck, H. J.. Intelligence : the battle for the mind / H.J. Eysenck versus Leon Kamin. — London : Pan, 1981. — 192p : ill,1map,ports ; 20cm. — (Pan psychology)
Bibliography: p182-187. - Includes index
ISBN 0-330-26399-4 (pbk) : £2.95 B81-09726

Eysenck, H. J.. Intelligence : the battle for the mind / H.J. Eysenck versus Leon Kamin. — London : Macmillan, 1981. — 192p : ill,1map,ports ; 21cm
Bibliography: p182-187. — Includes index
ISBN 0-333-31279-1 : £12.00
ISBN 0-330-36399-4 (Pan) : Unpriced B81-18855

153.9′3 — Man. Intelligence. Measurement. Social aspects
Evans, Brian. IQ and mental testing : an unnatural science and its social history / Brian Evans and Bernard Waites. — London : Macmillan, 1981. — x,228p : ill ; 23cm. — (Critical social studies)
Includes index
ISBN 0-333-25648-4 (cased) : Unpriced : CIP rev.
ISBN 0-333-25649-2 (pbk) : Unpriced B80-20144

153.9′33 — Intelligence tests. Performance of small groups. Effects of members' beliefs about performance in previous tests
Davis, Don D.. Induced task competence : and effects on problem solving behaviour / by Don D. Davis. — London (121 Bouverie Rd., N16 0AA) : Prytaneum, 1980. — 39p ; 21cm
Bibliography: p37-38
ISBN 0-907152-00-7 (pbk) : £1.50 B81-05652

153.9′4 — Careers. Choice. Aptitude tests
Barrett, James. Test your own aptitude : how to find your true job potential / James Barrett and Geoffrey Williams. — London : Futura, 1980. — 122p : ill ; 18cm
Originally published: London : Page, 1980
ISBN 0-7088-1925-7 (pbk) : £0.95 B81-00010

154.3 — PSYCHOLOGY. SECONDARY CONSCIOUSNESS

154.3 — Daydreaming
Singer, Jerome L.. Daydreaming and fantasy / Jerome L. Singer. — Oxford : Oxford University Press, 1981, c1975. — vi,281p ; 20cm. — (Oxford paperbacks)
Originally published: New York : Harper and Row, 1975 ; London : Allen and Unwin, 1976. — Bibliography: p263-269. — Includes index
ISBN 0-19-281305-6 (pbk) : £2.95 : CIP rev. B81-15803

154.6 — PSYCHOLOGY. SLEEP PHENOMENA

154.6′34 — Dreams. Interpretation
Dunne, J. W.. An experiment with time / by J.W. Dunne. — Rev. ed. / introduction by Brian Inglis. — London : Macmillan, 1981. — xvii,288p : ill ; 20cm. — (Papermac)
Originally published: London : Faber, 1934. — Includes index
ISBN 0-333-31232-5 (pbk) : £3.50 B81-38642

154.6′34 — Dreams — *Psychoanalytical perspectives*
Rycroft, Charles. The innocence of dreams. — Oxford : Oxford University Press, Oct.1981. — [192]p
Originally published: London : Hogarth, 1979
ISBN 0-19-281315-3 (pbk) : £2.25 : CIP entry B81-25792

154.7 — HYPNOTISM

154.7 — Hypnotism
Erickson, Milton H.. Hypnotic alteration of sensory, perceptual and psychophysical processes / by Milton H. Erickson. — New York : Irvington ; New York ; London : Halsted [distributor], c1980. — xii,367p : 2ports ; 24cm. — (The Collected papers of Milton H. Erickson on hypnosis ; v.2)
Bibliography: p355-358. — Includes index
ISBN 0-470-26722-4 : £16.00 B81-03545

Erickson, Milton H.. The nature of hypnosis and suggestion / by Milton H. Erickson. — New York : Irvington ; New York ; London : Halsted [distributor], c1980. — xi,570p : 2ports ; 24cm. — (The Collected papers of Milton H. Erickson on hypnosis ; vol.1)
Bibliography: p556-560. — Includes index
ISBN 0-470-26721-6 : £18.75 B81-03544

Udolf, Roy. Handbook of hypnosis for professionals / Roy Udolf. — New York ; London : Van Nostrand Reinhold, c1981. — xiv,366p : ill ; 24cm
Includes bibliographies and index
ISBN 0-442-28881-6 : £18.40 B81-03542

Wagner, Clarence J.. How to be a hypnotist : hypnosis and its phenomenological aspects / by Clarence J. Wegner. — Bideford (64 High St., Bideford, Devon) : Supreme Magic, c1981. — 60p : ill ; 25cm
Unpriced (pbk) B81-40592

154.7′6 — Hypnotism. Induction. Relaxation
Edmonston, William E.. Hypnosis and relaxation : modern verification of an old equation / William E. Edmonston, Jr.. — New York ; Chichester : Wiley, c1981. — xiii,255p : ill ; 24cm. — (Wiley series on personality processes)
Bibliography: p222-243. - Includes index
ISBN 0-471-05903-x : £13.25 B81-16320

154.7′6 — Self-hypnotism — *Manuals*
Hariman, Jusuf. How to use the power of self-hypnosis. — Wellingborough : Thorsons, Dec.1981. — [128]p
ISBN 0-7225-0728-3 (pbk) : CIP entry B81-31536

154.7′72 — Hypnotism. Special subjects: Occultism
Follas, Lawrence. Hypnosis and the higher self / by Lawrence Follas. — London : Regency Press, c1980. — 186p : 1ill,facsims ; 23cm
Includes index
ISBN 0-7212-0581-x : £4.00 B81-05770

155 — DIFFERENTIAL AND GENETIC PSYCHOLOGY

155 — Developmental psychology
LaBarba, Richard C.. Foundations of developmental psychology / Richard C. LaBarba. — International ed. — New York ; London : Academic Press, c1981. — xiv,545p : ill,ports ; 24cm
Includes bibliographies and index
ISBN 0-12-432330-8 (pbk) : £8.00 B81-19325

LaBarba, Richard C.. Foundations of developmental psychology / Richard C. LaBarba. — New York ; London : Academic Press, c1981. — xiv,545p : ill ; 25cm
Includes bibliographies and index
ISBN 0-12-432350-2 : £10.80 B81-29771

Liebert, Robert M.. Developmental psychology. — 3rd ed. / Robert M. Liebert, Rita Wicks-Nelson. — Englewood Cliffs ; London : Prentice-Hall, c1981. — xii,655p : ill,1form,ports ; 25cm
Previous ed.: 1977. — Bibliography: p593-627. — Includes index
ISBN 0-13-208256-x : £12.95 B81-17214

155 — Exceptional persons
Telford, Charles W.. The exceptional individual / Charles W. Telford, James M. Sawrey. — 4th ed.. — Englewood Cliffs ; London : Prentice-Hall, c1981. — xi,532p : ill ; 25cm
Previous ed.: 1977. — Includes bibliographies and index
ISBN 0-13-293878-2 : £12.30 B81-17286

155 — Man. Behaviour. Development. Psychological aspects
Brain and behavioural development. — Glasgow : Surrey University Press, Nov.1981. — [276]p
ISBN 0-903384-27-2 : £27.50 : CIP entry B81-30372

155 — Man. Development
Constancy and change in human development / Orville G. Brim, Jr., Jerome Kagan editors. — Cambridge, Mass. ; London : Harvard University Press, 1980. — vi,754p : ill ; 25cm
Includes bibliographies and index
ISBN 0-674-16625-6 : £16.50 B81-02625

Kahn, Jack. Human growth and the development of personality / foreword by G.M Carstairs. — 3rd ed. / by Jack Kahn and Susan Elinor Wright. — Oxford : Pergamon, 1980. — xxiii,227p ; 26cm. — (Social work series) (Pergamon international library)
Previous ed.: / by Jack Kahn. 1971. — Bibliography: p215-219. - Includes index
ISBN 0-08-023383-x (cased) : £14.95 : CIP rev.
ISBN 0-08-023382-1 (pbk) : £6.95 B80-12214

Maturation and development : biological and psychological perspectives / edited by Kevin J. Connolly and Heinz F. R. Prechtl. — [S.l.] : Spastics International Medical ; London : Heinemann Medical [distributor], 1981. — xii,326p : ill ; 25cm. — (Clinics in developmental medicine ; no.77/78)
Includes bibliographies and index
ISBN 0-433-06415-3 : Unpriced B81-36156

Papalia, Diane E.. Human development / Diane E. Papalia, Sally Wendkos Olds. — 2nd ed. — New York ; London : McGraw-Hill, c1981. — xii,671p : ill ; 25cm
Previous ed.: 1978. — Bibliography: p603-649. — Includes index
ISBN 0-07-048391-4 : £13.25 B81-23721

Rapoport, Rhona. Growing through life / Rhona Rapoport and Robert Rapoport. — London : Harper & Row, 1980. — 128p : ill(some col.) ; 24cm ; cased. — (The Life cycle series)
Includes index
ISBN 0-06-318126-6 : £4.95
ISBN 0-06-318127-4 (pbk) : £2.25 B81-02595

155 — Man. Psychological development
Hunt, Sonja M.. Individual development and social experience / Sonja Hunt, Jennifer Hilton. — Rev. ed. — London : Allen & Unwin, 1981. — 288p : ill ; 22cm
Previous ed.: 1975. — Includes index
ISBN 0-04-150077-6 (pbk) : £4.95 B81-11360

155′.01 — Man. Psychological development. Theories, *1900-1980*

Salkind, Neil J.. Theories of human development / Neil J. Salkind. — New York ; London : D. Van Nostrand, c1981. — ix,273p : ill ; 24cm
Bibliography: p261-266. — Includes index
ISBN 0-442-25859-3 : £10.45 B81-10056

155′.0724 — Man. Psychological development. Models

Development models of thinking / edited by Rainer H. Kluwe, Hans Spada. — New York ; London : Academic Press, 1980. — xvi,304p : ill ; 24cm. — (Developmental psychology series)
Conference papers. — Includes bibliographies and index
ISBN 0-12-416450-1 : £15.00 B81-05261

155.2 — INDIVIDUAL PSYCHOLOGY, PERSONALITY

155.2 — Individuality

Lambert, Kenneth. Analysis repair and individuation. — London : Academic Press, June 1981. — [240]p. — (The library of analytical psychology ; v.5)
ISBN 0-12-434640-5 : CIP entry B81-11934

155.2 — Man. Behaviour. Personal construct theory. Repertory grid technique — *For business firms*

Stewart, Valerie. Business applications of repertory grid / Valerie Stewart, Andrew Stewart with Nickie Fonda. — London : McCraw-Hill, c1981. — viii,211p : ill ; 24cm
Bibliography: p209-210. — Includes index
ISBN 0-07-084549-2 : £11.95 B81-27881

155.2 — Man. Behaviour. Reversal theory — *Conference proceedings*

Reversal theory and personality / edited by Michael J. Apter and Cyril Rushton. — Wiltshire (c/o Psychology Department, University College Cardiff, P.O. Box 78, Cardiff CF1 1XL) : South-West Inter-Clinic Conference, 1981. — 59p : ill, ; 22cm
ISBN 0-9507527-0-3 (unbound) : Unpriced B81-38880

155.2 — Man. Behaviour. Self-determination

Deci, Edward L.. The psychology of self-determination / Edward L. Deci. — Lexington, Mass. : Lexington Books, c1980 ; [Aldershot] : Gower [distributor], 1981. — x, 240p : ill ; 24cm
Bibliography: p219-230. — Includes index
ISBN 0-669-04045-2 : Unpriced B81-28860

155.2 — Man. Personality. Personal construct theory

Personal construct psychology : psychotherapy and personality / edited by A.W. Landfield, L.M. Leitner. — New York ; Chichester : Wiley, c1980. — xviii,330p : ill,forms ; 24cm. — (Wiley series on personality processes)
Includes bibliographies and index
ISBN 0-471-05859-9 : £15.00 B81-10641

Recent advances in personal construct technology / edited by Mildred L.G. Shaw. — London : Academic Press, 1981. — xii,252p : ill ; 26cm. — (Computers and people series)
Includes bibliographies
ISBN 0-12-639260-9 : £12.00 : CIP rev. B81-12360

155.2 — Personality

Byrne, Donn, *1931-*. An introduction to personality. — 3rd ed. / Donn Byrne, Kathryn Kelley. — Englewood Cliffs ; London : Prentice-Hall, c1981. — xiv,591p : ill,1port ; 25cm
Previous ed.: 197-. — Bibliography: p546-581. — Includes index
ISBN 0-13-491605-0 : £12.30 B81-17172

Further explorations in personality / edited by A.I. Rabin ... [et al.]. — New York ; Chichester : Wiley, c1981. — xvi,281p ; 24cm. — (Wiley series on personality processes)
Includes bibliographies and index
ISBN 0-471-07721-6 : £13.00 B81-10646

Mischel, Walter. Introduction to personality / Walter Mischel. — 3rd ed. — New York ; London : Holt, Rinehart and Winston, c1981. — xii,623p : ill ; 25cm
Previous ed.: 1976. — Bibliography: p537-582. — Includes index
ISBN 0-03-056998-2 : £14.95 B81-22858

Murray, Henry A.. Endeavors in psychology : selections from the personology of Henry A. Murray / edited by Edwin S. Shneidman. — New York ; London : Harper & Row, c1981. — vi,641p : 1port ; 25cm
Bibliography: p617-623. — Includes index
ISBN 0-06-014039-9 : £9.50 B81-29830

Samuel, William. Personality : searching for the sources of human behavior / William Samuel. — New York ; London : McGraw-Hill, c1981. — xiv,474p : ill,ports ; 25cm
Text on lining papers. — Bibliography: p403-441. — Includes index
ISBN 0-07-054520-0 : £13.25 B81-23710

Storr, Anthony. The integrity of the personality / Anthony Storr. — Harmondsworth : Penguin, 1963, 1960 (1981 [printing]). — 185p ; 20cm. — (Pelican books)
Originally published: London : Heinemann Medical, 1960. — Includes index
ISBN 0-14-020603-5 (pbk) : £2.75 B81-40438

155.2 — Personality — *Festschriften*

Dimensions of personality : papers in honour of H.J. Eysenck / edited by Richard Lynn. — Oxford : Pergamon, 1981. — ix,389p,[1]folded leaf of plates : ill ; 26cm
Includes bibliographies and index
ISBN 0-08-024294-4 : £28.50 : CIP rev. B81-05168

155.2 — Personality. Theories

Hjelle, Larry A.. Personality theories : based assumptions, research, and applications / Larry A. Hjelle, Daniel J. Ziegler. — 2nd ed. — New York ; London : McGraw-Hill, c1981. — xviii,494p : ill ; 25cm. — (McGraw-Hill series in psychology)
Previous ed.: 1976. — Includes bibliographies and index
ISBN 0-07-029063-6 : £14.95 B81-12762

Massey, Robert F.. Personality theories : comparisons and syntheses / Robert F. Massey. — New York ; London : D. Van Nostrand, c1981. — 577p : ill ; 24cm
Bibliography: p533-549. — Includes index
ISBN 0-442-23892-4 : £14.95 B81-26429

Personality : theory, measurement and research / edited by Fay Fransella. — London : Methuen, 1981. — 256p ; 22cm. — (Psychology in progress)
Bibliography: p223-245. — Includes index
ISBN 0-416-72770-0 (cased) : Unpriced : CIP rev.
ISBN 0-416-72780-8 (pbk) : £7.45 B81-02101

155.2 — Personality. Theories. Psychophysiological aspects

Mangan, G. L.. The biology of human conduct. — Oxford : Pergamon, Dec.1981. — [470]p. — (International series in experimental psychology ; v.25)
ISBN 0-08-026781-5 : £30.00 : CIP entry B81-31719

155.2 — Self — *Psychological perspectives*

Dempsey, Peter J. R.. The self, some aspects of a significant concept / P.J.R. Dempsey. — Cardiff (c/o R. Slater, Department of Applied Psychology, UWIST, Llwyn-y-Grant, Penylan, Cardiff CF3 7UX) : [UWIST Department of Applied Psychology], 1977. — 9p ; 30cm. — (Occasional paper / UWIST Department of Applied Psychology ; no.2)
£0.50 (spiral) B81-24803

155.2′072 — Personality. Research

Fiske, Donald W.. Strategies for personality research / Donald W. Fiske. — San Francisco ; London : Jossey-Bass, 1978. — xxii,448p ; 24cm. — (The Jossey-Bass social and behavioral science series)
Bibliography: p407-435. — Includes index
ISBN 0-87589-373-2 : £12.80 B81-15104

155.2′32 — Man. Helplessness. Psychological aspects

Human helplessness : theory and applications / edited by Judy Garber, Martin E.P. Seligman. — New York ; London : Academic Press, 1980. — xvii,402p : ill ; 24cm
Bibliography: p241-375. — Includes index
ISBN 0-12-275050-0 : £10.40 B81-21833

155.2′32 — Man. Hostility. Psychological aspects

Saul, Leon J.. The childhood emotional pattern and human hostility / Leon J. Saul. — New York ; London : Van Nostrand Reinhold, c1980. — xiii,322p : ill ; 24cm
Bibliography: p295-318. — Includes index
ISBN 0-442-23993-9 : £12.70 B81-02859

155.2′34 — Man. Moral development. Sociobiological aspects — *Conference proceedings*

Morality as a biological phenomenon : the presuppositions of sociobiological research / edited by Gunther S. Stent. — Rev. ed. — Berkeley ; London : University of California Press, c1980. — vi,295p : ill ; 23cm
Conference papers. — Previous ed.: Berlin : Abakon-Verlagsgesellschaft, 1978. — Includes bibliographies and index
ISBN 0-520-04028-7 : £12.00 B81-34337

155.2′34 — Moral development — *Philosophical perspectives*

Kohlberg, Lawrence. The philosophy of moral development : moral stages and the idea of justice / Lawrence Kohlberg. — San Francisco ; London : Harper & Row, c1981. — xxxv,441p ; 22cm. — (Essays on moral development ; vol.1)
Bibliography: p413-428. — Includes index
ISBN 0-06-064760-4 : Unpriced B81-39880

155.2′8 — Personality. Assessment

Klein, Mavis. How to choose a mate / Mavis Klein. — London : Boyars, 1981. — 160p : ill ; 23cm
ISBN 0-7145-2727-0 : £5.95
Primary classification 306.8′7 B81-08398

155.2′83 — Personality. Assessment. Minnesota Multiphasic Personality Inventory

Greene, Roger L.. The MMPI : n an interpretive manual / by Roger L. Greene. — New York ; London : Grune & Stratton, c1980. — xi,306p : ill ; 27cm
Includes bibliographies and index
ISBN 0-8089-1279-8 : £11.80 B81-10940

155.3 — SEX PSYCHOLOGY

155.3 — Man. Sexual attraction

The **Bases** of human sexual attraction / edited by Mark Cook. — London : Academic Press, 1981. — x,300p : ill ; 24cm
Includes bibliographies and index
ISBN 0-12-187220-3 : £12.40 : CIP rev. B81-11929

155.3 — Man. Sexual behaviour. Psychosocial aspects

Eysenck, H. J.. The psychology of sex / H.J. Eysenck and Glenn Wilson. — London : New English Library, 1981, c1979. — 208p : ill ; 18cm
Originally published: London : Dent, 1979. — Includes bibliographies and index
ISBN 0-450-05104-8 (pbk) : £1.50 B81-17197

155.3′3 — Men. Sexual fantasies *compared with* **sexual fantasies of women**

May, Robert, *1940-*. Sex and fantasy : patterns of male and female development / Robert May. — New York ; London : Norton, c1980. — xi,226p : 1ill ; 22cm
Includes index
ISBN 0-393-01316-2 : £7.50 B81-04785

155.3′32 — Men. Sexual fantasies — *Collections*

Friday, Nancy. Men in love : men′s sexual fantasies : the triumph of love over rage / Nancy Friday. — London : Arrow, 1980. — x,527p ; 18cm
Originally published: New York : Delacorte ; London : Hutchinson, 1980
ISBN 0-09-924970-7 (pbk) : £1.75 B81-04019

155.3′33 — Feminine principle — *Jungian viewpoints*

Hall, Nor. The moon and the virgin : reflections on the archetypal feminine / Nor Hall. — London : Woman's Press, 1980. — xvii,284p : ill ; 21cm
Originally published: New York : Harper and Row, 1980. — Bibliography: p264-272. — Includes index
ISBN 0-7043-3862-9 (pbk) : £3.95 B81-01704

155.3′33 — Women. Sexuality — *Psychoanalytical perspectives*

Chasseguet-Smirgel, Janine. Female sexuality : new psychoanalytic views / by Janine Chasseguet-Smirgel with C. F. Luquet-Parat ... [et al.] ; foreword by Frederick Wyatt ; introduction to British edition by Susan Lipshitz. — London : Virago, 1981. — xviii,220p ; 21cm
Translation of: Recherches psychanalytiques nouvelles sur la sexualité féminine
ISBN 0-86068-148-3 (cased) : Unpriced
ISBN 0-86068-149-1 (pbk) : £4.95 B81-06931

155.3′4 — Incest. Psychological aspects

Forward, Susan. Betrayal of innocence : incest and its devastation / Susan Forward and Craig Buck ; with an introduction by John Gordon. — Rev. ed. — Harmondsworth : Penguin, 1981. — xiv,154p ; 20cm. — (A Pelican book)
Previous ed.: Los Angeles : J.P. Tarcher, 1978
ISBN 0-14-022287-1 (pbk) : £1.95 B81-11533

Fox, Robin. The red lamp of incest / Robin Fox. — London : Hutchinson, 1980. — xi,271p : ill ; 22cm
Includes index
ISBN 0-09-144080-7 : £7.95 B81-01972

155.4 — CHILD PSYCHOLOGY

155.4 — Africa. Children. Influence of environment

The **African** child and his environment / editors R. Ogbonna Ohuche, Barnabas Otaala for the Science Education Programme for Africa (SEPA), with the assistance of the United Nations Environment Programme (UNEP). — Oxford : Published for the United Nations Environment Programme by Pergamon, 1981. — vi,97p,[4]p of plates : ill ; 22cm. — (UNEP studies ; v.3)
Bibliography: p88-97
ISBN 0-08-025671-6 : £6.25 : CIP rev.
B79-37144

155.4 — Children. Behaviour. Development

Hofer, Myron A.. The roots of human behavior : an introduction to the psychobiology of early development / Myron A. Hofer. — Oxford : W.H. Freeman, c1981 — xiii,331p : ill ; 25cm
Includes bibliographies and index
ISBN 0-7167-1277-6 : £14.10
ISBN 0-7167-1278-4 (pbk) : £6.70 B81-37380

155.4 — Children. Development

Askew, Susan. Growing and changing. — London : Edward Arnold, Sept.1981. — [128]p
ISBN 0-7131-0567-4 (pbk) : £2.25 : CIP entry
B81-22488

Bee, Helen. The developing child / Helen Bee. — 3rd ed. — New York ; London : Harper & Row, c1981. — xxiv,531p : ill(some col.) ; 24cm
Previous ed.: 1978. — Bibliography: p496-517. - Includes index
ISBN 0-06-040579-1 : Unpriced
ISBN 0-06-350134-1 (pbk) : £6.50 B81-15985

Brierley, John. Children's well-being / John Brierley. — [Windsor] : NFER, [1980]. — 171p : ill ; 22cm
Includes index
ISBN 0-85633-218-6 (pbk) : £6.75 B81-00011

Helms, Donald B.. Exploring child behaviour / Donald B. Helms, Jeffrey S. Turner. — 2nd ed. — New York ; London : Holt, Rinehart and Winston, c1981. — xvi,539p : ill(some col.) ; 25cm
Previous ed.: Philadelphia : Saunders, 1976. — Text on lining papers. — Bibliography: p479-508. — Includes index
ISBN 0-03-057746-2 : £11.95 B81-22873

Murphy, Lois Barclay. Vulnerability, coping, and growth : from infancy to adolescence / Lois Barclay Murphy and Alice E. Moriarty. — New Haven ; London : Yale University Press, c1976 (1978 [printing]). — xxiii,460p : ill ; 24cm
Bibliography: p435-452. — Includes index
ISBN 0-300-01901-7 (cased) : Unpriced
ISBN 0-300-02355-3 (pbk) : £5.65 B81-19314

The **Process** of child development / edited by Peter B. Neubauer. — New York : New American Library ; London : New English Library, 1976. — vi,361p : ill ; 21cm. — (A Meridian book)
Includes bibliographies
Unpriced (pbk) B81-18944

Segal, Julius. A child's journey : forces that shape the lives of our young / Julius Segal and Herbert Yahraes. — Harmondsworth : Penguin, 1981, c1978. — xiv,354p : ill ; 21cm. — (Penguin education)
Originally published: New York, London : McGraw-Hill, 1978. — Bibliography: p315-336. — Includes index
ISBN 0-14-080432-3 (pbk) : £4.95 B81-37207

Tudor, Mary, *19---*. Child development / Mary Tudor ; advisors Margaret E. Armstrong, Marie Scott Brown, Sally M. O'Neil. — New York ; London : McGraw-Hill, c1981. — xviii,537p : ill ; 25cm
Includes bibliographies and index
ISBN 0-07-065412-3 : £16.25 B81-23728

White, Sheldon. Childhood : pathways of discovery / Sheldon White and Barbara Notkin White. — London : Harper & Row, 1980. — 128p : ill(some col.) ; 24cm. — (The Life cycle series)
Includes index
ISBN 0-06-318124-x (cased) : £4.95
ISBN 0-06-318125-8 (pbk) : £2.25 B81-01678

155.4 — Children. Development. Assessment. Methodology

Nadelman, Lorraine. Research manual in child development / Lorraine Nadelman. — New York ; London : Harper & Row, c1982. — viii,471p : ill ; 28cm
Includes bibliographies and index
ISBN 0-06-044715-x (pbk) : £7.25 B81-38373

155.4 — Children. Development — *Psychoanalytical perspectives*

Hoffer, Willi. Early development and education of the child / by Willi Hoffer ; edited by Marjorie Brierley ; with a foreword by Anna Freud. — London : Hogarth, 1981. — xvi,220p ; 23cm. — (The international psycho-analytical library ; no.102)
Bibliography: p207-214. — Includes index
ISBN 0-7012-0404-4 : £12.00 : CIP rev.
Also classified at 370.15 B81-12844

155.4 — Children. Development. Role of interpersonal relationships with fathers

Parke, Ross D.. Fathering / Ross D. Parke. — [London] : Fontana, 1981. — 156p ; 19cm. — (The Developing child)
Bibliography: p149-150. - Includes index
ISBN 0-00-636057-2 (pbk) : £1.75 B81-21060

155.4 — Children. Emotional problems — *Encyclopaedias — For parents*

Crabtree, Tom. An A-Z of children's emotional problems / Tom Crabtree. — London : Elm Tree, 1981. — viii,276p ; 23cm
ISBN 0-241-10581-1 : £8.95 : CIP rev.
B81-12354

155.4 — Children. Psychological development

Wood, Margaret E.. The development of personality and behaviour in children / Margaret E. Wood. — London : Harrap, 1981. — 294p ; 22cm
Bibliography: p266-282. — Includes index
ISBN 0-245-53693-0 (pbk) : £5.50 B81-29247

155.4 — Children. Psychological development. Effects of maternal deprivation

Rutter, Michael. Maternal deprivation reassessed / Michael Rutter. — 2nd ed. — Harmondsworth : Penguin, 1981. — 285p ; 18cm. — (Penguin modern psychology) (Penguin education)
Previous ed.: 1972. — Bibliography: p219-272. - Includes index
ISBN 0-18-080561-3 (pbk) : £1.95 B81-20664

155.4 — Children. Psychology

Contemporary readings in child psychology / [edited by] E. Mavis Hetherington, Ross D. Parke. — 2nd ed. — New York ; London : McGraw-Hill, c1981. — xviii,419p : ill ; 24cm
Previous ed.: 1977. — Includes bibliographies
ISBN 0-07-028426-1 (pbk) : £9.50 B81-23445

155.4 — Young persons, 3-18 years. Development

Sahler, Olle Jane Z.. The child from three to eighteen / Olle Jane Z. Sahler, Elizabeth R. McAnarney. — St. Louis ; London : Mosby, 1981. — xv,233p : ill ; 24cm
Bibliography: p200-225. — Includes index
ISBN 0-8016-4290-6 (pbk) : £11.00 B81-31155

155.4 — Young persons. Development

Angrilli, Albert. Child psychology / Albert Angrilli and Lucile Helfat. — New York ; London : Barnes & Noble, c1981. — viii,180p ; 21cm. — (The Barnes & Noble outline series ; COS 189)
Bibliography: p163-170. — Includes index
ISBN 0-06-460189-7 (pbk) : £2.50 B81-30808

155.4 — Young persons. Psychological development

Readings in child and adolescent psychology : contemporary perspectives / edited by Paul Henry Mussen, John Janeway Conger, Jerome Kagan. — New York ; London : Harper & Row, c1980. — xii,280p : ill,1port ; 28cm. — (Harper & Row's contemporary perspectives reader series)
Includes bibliographies
ISBN 0-06-041888-5 (pbk) : £5.50 B81-00726

155.4 — Young persons, to 18 years. Development

Zaichkowsky, Leonard D.. Growth and development : the child and physical activity / Leonard D. Zaichkowsky, Linda B. Zaichkowsky, Thomas J. Martinek. — St. Louis ; London : Mosby, 1980. — x,277p : ill ; 26cm
Includes bibliographies and index
ISBN 0-8016-5663-x (pbk) : £7.95 B81-08043

155.4′01 — Children. Psychological development. Theories

Baldwin, Alfred L.. Theories of child development / Alfred L. Baldwin. — 2nd ed. — New York ; Chichester : Wiley, c1980. — xiv,582p : ill ; 24cm
Previous ed.: 1967. — Bibliography: p559-570. — Includes index
ISBN 0-471-04583-7 : £12.45 B81-19834

155.4′072 — Children. Development. Research. Methodology

Hindley, C. B.. Conceptual and methodological issues in the study of child development : an inaugural lecture delivered at the University of London Institute of Education on Thursday, 8 November 1979 / C.B. Hindley. — London : University of London, Institute of Education, 1980. — 36p : ill ; 21cm
Bibliography: p31-36
ISBN 0-85473-097-4 (pbk) : £0.90 B81-07760

155.4′12 — Children. Sensory perception. Development — *For teaching*

Tansley, A. E.. Perceptual training / A.E. Tansley. — Leeds : E.J. Arnold, 1980. — 56p : ill,1form ; 21cm. — (Educational development programmes)
ISBN 0-560-00117-7 (pbk) : £2.20 B81-04728

155.4′13 — Children. Cognition. Role of language

Children thinking through language. — London : Edward Arnold, Feb.1982. — [224]p
ISBN 0-7131-6352-6 (pbk) : £5.95 : CIP entry
B81-37563

155.4'13 — Children. Cognitive development
Cognition, development and instruction / edited by John R. Kirby, John B. Biggs. — New York ; London : Academic Press, 1980. — xii,217p : ill ; 24cm
Conference papers. — Includes bibliographies and index
ISBN 0-12-409550-x : £10.80 B81-06508

155.4'13 — Children. Cognitive development. Social factors
Social cognition. — Brighton : Harvester Press, Nov.1981. — [272]p. — (The Developing body and mind ; 2)
ISBN 0-7108-0095-9 : CIP entry B81-30602

155.4'13 — Children. Cognitive development. Theories of Piaget, Jean
ElKind, David. Children and adolescents : interpretive essays on Jean Piaget / David ElKind. — 3rd ed. — New York ; Oxford : Oxford University Press, 1981. — xv,250p : ill ; 22cm
Previous ed.: 1974. — Bibliography: p241-250
ISBN 0-19-502820-1 (cased) : Unpriced
ISBN 0-19-502821-x (pbk) : £3.50 B81-32538

Jean Piaget : consensus and controversy. — Eastbourne : Holt, Rinehart and Winston, Jan.1982. — [500]p. — (Praeger special studies)
ISBN 0-03-910352-8 : £12.95 : CIP entry B81-33925

Pulaski, Mary Ann Spencer. Understanding Piaget : an introduction to children's cognitive development / Mary Ann Spencer Pulaski. — Rev. and expanded ed. — New York ; London : Harper & Row, c1980. — xvii,248p : ill,1port ; 22cm
Previous ed.: 1971. — Bibliography: p237-242. — Includes index
ISBN 0-06-013454-2 : £7.50 B81-03521

Singer, Dorothy G.. A Piaget primer : how a child thinks / Dorothy G. Singer & Tracey A. Revenson. — New York ; London : New American Library, 1978. — x,148p : ill,facsims ; 21cm. — (A Plume book)
Bibliography: p135-143. - Includes index
ISBN 0-452-25189-3 (pbk) : Unpriced B81-18919

Vuyk, Rita. Overview and critique of Piaget's genetic epistemology 1965-1980 / Rita Vuyk. — London : Academic Press, 1981. — 2v.(xix,537p) ; 24cm
Includes bibliographies and index
ISBN 0-12-728501-6 : Unpriced
ISBN 0-12-728502-4 (v.2) : £14.80 B81-17589

Wadsworth, Barry J.. Piaget's theory of cognitive development : an introduction for students of psychology and education / Barry J. Wadsworth ; with drawings by the author. — 2nd ed. — New York ; London : Longman, c1979. — xvi,189p : ill ; 21cm
Previous ed.: 1977. — Bibliography: p182-186. — Includes index
ISBN 0-582-28124-5 (pbk) : £3.50 B81-33744

155.4'13 — Children. Cognitive development. Theories of Piaget, Jean — *Critical studies*
Infancy and epistemology. — Brighton : Harvester Press, Sept.1981. — [416]p. — (The Developing body and mind series ; no.1)
ISBN 0-85527-497-2 : CIP entry B81-23847

155.4'13 — Children. Development. Role of acquisition of communication skills
Communication in development. — London : Academic Press, July 1981. — [250]p. — (European monographs in social psychology series ; no.24)
ISBN 0-12-590140-2 : CIP entry B81-13424

155.4'13 — Children. Intelligence. Measurement
Sattler, Jerome M.. Assessment of children's intelligence and special abilities / Jerome M. Sattler. — 2nd ed. — Boston, Mass. ; London : Allyn and Bacon, c1982. — xxiv,722p : ill,forms ; 25cm
Previous ed.: i.e. rev. ed. published as Assessment of children's intelligence, Philadelphia : London : Saunders, 1977. — Bibliography: p647-699. — Includes index
ISBN 0-205-07362-x : Unpriced B81-40647

155.4'13 — Children. Probabilistic thought processes. Acquisition. Role of intuition
Fischbein, E.. The intuitive sources of probabilistic thinking in children / E. Fischbein. — Dordrecht ; London : Reidel, c1975. — x,204p : ill ; 23cm. — (Synthese library : v.85)
Translation of: Le concept de probabilité chez l'enfant. — Includes bibliographies and index
ISBN 90-277-0626-3 (cased) : Unpriced
ISBN 90-277-1190-9 (pbk) : Unpriced B81-07246

155.4'13 — Children. Thought processes. Role of philosophy
Matthews, Gareth B.. Philosophy and the young child / Gareth B. Matthews. — Cambridge, Mass. ; London : Harvard University Press, 1980. — viii,115p ; 22cm
Includes index
ISBN 0-674-66605-4 : £6.00 B81-09354

155.4'13 — Children, to 5 years. Egocentrism — *Conference proceedings*
Are young children egocentric? / edited by M.V. Cox. — London : Batsford, 1980. — 154p : ill ; 23cm
Conference papers. — Includes bibliographies and index
ISBN 0-7134-3720-0 : £11.00 : CIP rev. B80-13184

155.4'13 — Concepts: Conservation. Acquisition by children
Pinard, Adrien. The conservation of conservation : the child's acquisition of a fundamental concept / Adrien Pinard ; translated by Helga Feider. — Chicago ; London : University of Chicago Press, 1981. — xii,199p ; 22cm
Bibliography: p181-194. — Includes index
ISBN 0-226-66834-7 (pbk) : £8.40 B81-39825

155.4'13 — Drawings by children, 1-6 years. Interpretation
Strauss, Michaela. Understanding children's drawings : the path to manhood / Michaela Strauss ; with notes on the study of man by Wolfgang Schad ; translated by Pauline Wehrle. — London : Steiner, 1978. — 95p : ill (some col.) ; 21x23cm
Translation of: Von der Zeichensprache des kleinen Kindes. — Bibliography: p92-93
ISBN 0-85440-330-2 : £3.95 B81-04073

155.4'13 — Man. Musical ability. Psychological aspects
Shuter-Dyson, Rosamund. The psychology of musical ability. — 2nd ed. — London : Methuen, Nov.1981. — [384]p
Previous ed.: 1968
ISBN 0-416-71300-9 : £15.00 : CIP entry B81-30459

155.4'13 — Speech. Perception by children
Child phonology / edited by Grace H. Yeni-Komshian, James F. Kavanagh, Charles A. Ferguson. — New York ; London : Academic Press. — (Perspectives in neurolinguistics, neuropsychology, and psycholinguistics)
Vol.2: Perception. — 1980. — xiv,254p : ill ; 24cm
Conference papers. — Includes bibliographies and index
ISBN 0-12-770602-x : £13.60 B81-19395

155.4'13 — Young persons, to 18 years. Cognitive development
Cognitive development : language and thinking from birth to adolescence / [the E362 Course Team]. — Milton Keynes : Open University Press. — (Educational studies : a third level course)
At head of title: The Open University
Project guide. — 1979. — 15p ; 30cm. — (E362 ; PG)
ISBN 0-335-06854-5 (unbound) : Unpriced B81-14714

155.4'18 — Children, 2-5 years. Development. Role of play
Riggs, Maida L.. Jump to joy : helping children grow through active play / Maida L. Riggs ; photographs by University of Massachusetts Photo Center and Cynthia Buck. — Englewood CliffsLondon. — xi,164p : ill ; 24cm. — (A Spectrum book)
Includes bibliographies and index
ISBN 0-13-512343-7 (cased) : £8.40
ISBN 0-13-512335-6 (pbk) : £4.50 B81-07234

155.4'18 — Children. Cognitive development *related to* **social development** — *Conference proceedings*
Social cognitive development : frontiers and possible futures / based on seminars sponsored by the Committee on Social and Affective Development during Childhood of the Social Science Research Council ; edited by John H. Flavell and Lee Ross. — Cambridge : Cambridge University Press, 1981. — ix,322p : ill ; 24cm. — (Cambridge studies in social and emotional development)
Includes bibliographies and index
ISBN 0-521-23687-8 (cased) : £20.00
ISBN 0-521-28156-3 (pbk) : £6.95 B81-32627

155.4'18 — Children. Development. Effects of television
Large, Martin. Who's bringing them up? : television and child development / Martin Large. — Gloucester (25 Reservoir Rd., Gloucester GL4 9RW) : M. Large for the TV Action Group, 1980. — 136p ; 23cm
ISBN 0-9507062-0-5 (cased) : £5.95
ISBN 0-9507062-1-3 (pbk) : £2.95 B81-05259

155.4'18 — Children. Friendship. Psychosocial aspects
The **Development** of children's friendships / edited by Steven R. Asher and John M. Gottman. — Cambridge : Cambridge University Press, 1981. — xiv,347p ; 24cm. — (Cambridge studies in social and emotional development)
Includes bibliographies and index
ISBN 0-521-23103-5 (cased) : £20.00
ISBN 0-521-29806-7 (pbk) : £7.50 B81-32624

155.4'18 — Children. Interpersonal relationships with mothers. Psychological aspects
Bowlby, John. Attachment and loss / John Bowlby. — Harmondsworth : Penguin, 1971-1975, c1969-1980 (1981 [printing]). — 3v. ; 20cm. — (Penguin education)
Originally published: London : Hogarth, 1969-1980. — Includes bibliographies and indexs
ISBN 0-14-080306-8 (pbk) : Unpriced
ISBN 0-14-080307-6 (v.2) : £4.95 B81-40475

155.4'18 — Children. Personality. Development — *Serials*
Advances in child development and behavior. — Vol.15. — New York ; London : Academic Press, 1980. — x,263p
ISBN 0-12-009715-x : Unpriced
ISSN 0065-2407 B81-20709

155.4'18 — Normal children. Communication skills. Development *compared with* **communication development in mentally retarded children**
Communicating with normal and retarded children / edited by W.I. Fraser and R. Grieve. — Bristol : John Wright, 1981. — xv,189p : ill ; 22cm
Includes bibliographies and index
ISBN 0-7236-0572-6 (pbk) : Unpriced
Primary classification 155.4'528 B81-20005

155.4'18 — United States. Children. Psychological development. Role of competition & cooperation
Pepitone, Emmy A.. Children in cooperation and competition : toward a developmental social psychology / Emmy A. Pepitone. — Lexington : Lexington, c1980 ; Farnborough, Hants. : Gower [distributor], 1981. — xxiv,454p : ill ; 24cm
Bibliography: p413-439. — Includes index
ISBN 0-669-02842-8 : £17.50 B81-14054

155.4'22 — Babies. Development
Richards, Martin. Infancy : world of the newborn / Martin Richards. — London : Harper & Row, 1980. — 128p : ill(some col.) ; 24cm. — (The Life cycle series)
Includes index
ISBN 0-06-318122-3 : £4.95
ISBN 0-06-318123-1 (pbk) : £2.25 B81-01922

155.4'22 — Babies. Development *continuation*

Rubin, Richard R.. Your toddler : ages one and two / text by Richard R. Rubin, John J. Fisher III, Susan G. Doering ; photographs by Bill Parsons. — New York ; [London] : Collier, 1980. — ix,308p : ill ; 27cm. — (Johnson & Johnson child development publications)
Bibliography: p301. — Includes index
ISBN 0-02-043920-2 (pbk) : £6.95 B81-20733

155.4'22 — Children, to 3 years. Development — *For parents*

McCall, Robert B.. Babies : the first three years of life / Robert B. McCall. — London : Macmillan, 1980, c1979. — xi,170p : ill ; 22cm
Originally published: Cambridge, Mass : Harvard University Press, 1979. — Includes index
ISBN 0-333-30650-3 (pbk) : £2.95 : CIP rev. B80-21328

155.4'22 — Children, to 5 years. Development

Illingworth, Ronald S.. Your child's development in the first five years / Ronald S. Illingworth. — Edinburgh : Churchill Livingstone, 1981. — 72p ; 19cm. — (A Churchill Livingstone patient handbook)
ISBN 0-443-02237-2 (pbk) : £1.20 : CIP rev. B80-17537

155.4'22 — Children, to 5 years. Development. Assessment

Powell, Marcene Lee. Assessment and management of developmental changes and problems in children / Marcene Lee Powell ; chapter 9 contributed by Peggy L. Pipes ; original photographs by Janis K. Smith ; original drawings by Mary K. Shrader ; original cover by Greg Owen. — 2nd ed. — St. Louis ; London : Mosby, 1981. — x,344p : ill ; 26cm
Previous ed.: published as Assessment and management of developmental changes in children. 1976. — Includes bibliographies and index
ISBN 0-8016-1520-8 (pbk) : £9.25
Also classified at 649'.64 B81-25462

155.4'22 — Children, to 5 years. Development — *For parents*

Shapiro, Jean. Good Housekeeping baby & child record book / Jean Shapiro. — London : Ebury Press, 1981. — 160p : ill,forms ; 20cm
ISBN 0-85223-185-7 : £3.95 B81-22015

155.4'22 — Children, to 5 years. Development — *For parents of hearing disordered children*

Child development / Christine Fulbeck ... [et al.] ; illustrations by Vivien Cripps. — London (45 Hereford Rd., W2 5AH) : National Deaf Children's Society, c1981. — 32p : ill ; 21cm
Includes index
£0.35 (pbk) B81-37775

155.4'22 — Children, to 5 years. Mental development. Stimulation — *For parents*

Lewis, David, *1942-*. How to be a gifted parent : realize your child's full potential / David Lewis. — London : Pan, 1981, c1979. — 255p,[4]p of plates : ill ; 18cm
Originally published: London : Souvenir, 1979. — Bibliography: p253-255
ISBN 0-330-26257-2 (pbk) : £1.95 B81-09722

155.4'22 — Children, to 5 years. Psychology

Gillham, Bill. Child psychology. — London : Hodder and Stoughton, Jan.1982. — [144]p. — (Teach yourself books)
ISBN 0-340-25112-3 (pbk) : £1.50 : CIP entry B81-33984

155.4'22 — Premature babies. Psychological development

Preterm birth and psychological development / edited by Sarah L. Friedman, Marian Sigman. — New York ; London : Academic Press, 1981. — xix,438p : ill ; 24cm. — (Developmental psychology series)
Includes bibliographies and index
ISBN 0-12-267880-x : £19.20 B81-19327

155.4'23 — Children, 3-5 years. Behaviour. Effects of playgroups

Smith, Peter K.. The ecology of preschool behaviour / Peter K. Smith and Kevin J. Connolly. — Cambridge : Cambridge University Press, 1980. — xii,383p : ill ; 24cm
Bibliography: p363-376. - Includes index
ISBN 0-521-22331-8 : £25.00 : CIP rev. B80-38734

155.4'23 — Children, 3-5 years. Communication. Development

Lloyd, P.. Information and meaning in child communication. — London : Academic Press, Dec.1981. — [200]p
ISBN 0-12-453520-8 : CIP entry B81-31342

155.4'23 — Children, 3 to 5 years. Development. Assessment. Tests

Bate, Margaret. Review of tests and assessments in early education (3-5 years) / Margaret Bate, Marjorie Smith and Jeannette James ; revised by Jeannette James. — Windsor : NFER-Nelson, [1981?]. — 123p ; 30cm
Bibliography: p117-120
ISBN 0-85633-198-8 (pbk) : £3.95 B81-25400

155.4'23 — Children, 5 years. Development. Assessment. Tests

Curtis, Audrey. Early learning : assessment and development / Audrey Curtis and Mary Wignall. — London : Macmillan Education, 1981. — 1v.(looseleaf) : ill ; 31cm
ISBN 0-333-30587-6 : £9.50 B81-39090

155.4'24 — Children, 6-12 years. Intellectual development — *For parents*

Lewis, David, *1942-*. You can teach your child intelligence / by David Lewis. — London : Souvenir, 1981. — 271p : ill ; 23cm
Bibliography: p263-268. — Includes index
ISBN 0-285-62479-2 : £6.95 B81-36742

155.4'43 — Birth order. Psychological aspects

König, Karl. Brothers and sisters : a study in child psychology / Karl König. — 4th ed. — Edinburgh : Floris, 1980. — 91p ; 22cm
Previous ed.: i.e. 2nd ed. New York : Anthrosophic Press, 1970. — Includes index
ISBN 0-903540-38-x (pbk) : £3.50 : CIP rev. B80-02298

155.4'43 — Children. Interpersonal relationships with siblings

Dunn, Judy. Siblings. — London : Grant McIntyre, Feb.1982. — [240]p
ISBN 0-86216-045-6 (cased) : £12.95 : CIP entry
ISBN 0-86216-078-2 (pbk) : £5.95 B81-36042

155.4'44 — Identical twins. Behaviour. Development. Environmental factors

Watson, Peter. Twins. — London : Hutchinson, June 1981. — [176]p
ISBN 0-09-145330-5 : £6.95 : CIP entry B81-12320

155.4'5 — Exceptional children. Development

The **Uncommon** child / edited by Michael Lewis and Leonard A. Rosenblum. — New York ; London : Plenum, c1981. — xii,342p : ill ; 24cm. — (Genesis of behavior ; v.3)
Conference papers. — Includes bibliographies and index
ISBN 0-306-40499-0 : Unpriced B81-17153

155.4'51 — Handicapped children, to 10 years. Development

Chazan, Maurice. The early years. — Milton Keynes : Open University Press, Feb.1982. — [128]p. — (Children with special needs)
ISBN 0-335-10050-3 (cased) : £11.95 : CIP entry
ISBN 0-335-10052-x (pbk) : £4.95 B81-36982

155.4'511 — Visually handicapped children. Perception — *Interviews* — *For children*

Bergman, Thomas. Fingers that see : there should be a mirror where you can feel what you look like / Thomas Bergman ; translated by Irene D. Morris. — Harmondsworth : Kestrel Books, 1981. — [47]p : ill,ports ; 25cm
Translation of: Fingrar som ser
ISBN 0-7226-5679-3 : £4.25 B81-11807

155.4'512'0973 — United States. Deaf children. Development

Meadow, Kathryn P.. Deafness and child development / Kathryn P. Meadow. — London : Edward Arnold, 1980. — x,236p : ill ; 22cm
Bibliography: p199-227. - Includes index
ISBN 0-7131-6325-9 : £8.95 : CIP rev. B80-18577

155.4'528 — Mentally retarded children. Communication skills. Development *compared with* **communication development in normal children**

Communicating with normal and retarded children / edited by W.I. Fraser and R. Grieve. — Bristol : John Wright, 1981. — xv,189p : ill ; 22cm
Includes bibliographies and index
ISBN 0-7236-0572-6 (pbk) : Unpriced
Also classified at 155.4'18 B81-20005

155.4'55'0240431 — Gifted children. Development — *For parents*

Perino, Sheila C.. Parenting the gifted : developing the promise / Sheila C. Perino, Joseph Perino. — New York ; London : Bowker, 1981. — viii,214p : forms ; 24cm. — (Serving special populations series)
Bibliography: p199-207. — Includes index
ISBN 0-8352-1354-4 (cased) : Unpriced
ISBN 0-8352-1408-7 (pbk) : Unpriced B81-39044

155.4'55092'6 — Gifted children. Development — *Case studies*

Deakin, Michael. The children on the hill. — London : Quartet Books, Feb.1982. — [120]p
Originally published: London : Deutsch, 1972
ISBN 0-7043-3086-5 (pbk) : £1.95 : CIP entry B81-40248

155.4'567 — France. Aveyron. Feral children: Victor, *of Aveyron*

Shattuck, Roger. The forbidden experiment. — London : Quartet Books, Oct.1981. — [240]p
Originally published: London : Secker and Warburg, 1980
ISBN 0-7043-3383-x (pbk) : £3.50 : CIP entry B81-28117

155.4'579915 — Central Australia. Australian aboriginal children. Cognitive development. Cultural factors - *Comparative studies*

Seagrim, Gavin. Furnishing the mind : a comparative study of cognitive development in Central Australian Aborigines / Gavin Seagrim, Robin Lendon. — Sydney ; London : Academic Press, 1980. — xii,242p : ill,2maps ; 24cm. — (Behavioural development ; 1)
Bibliography: p223-232. - Includes index
ISBN 0-12-634340-3 : £16.80 B81-17262

155.5 — PSYCHOLOGY OF ADOLESCENTS

155.5 — Adolescents. Psychological development

Haviland, Jeannette M.. Adolescent development in contemporary society / Jeannette M. Haviland, Hollis S. Scarborough. — New York ; London : Van Nostrand, c1981. — xvii,337p : ill,ports ; 24cm
Includes bibliographies and index
ISBN 0-442-25862-3 : Unpriced B81-26037

155.5 — Great Britain. Undergraduates. Personality. Assessment. Eysenck Personality Inventory — *Study examples: University of Birmingham. Undergraduates*

Wa'nkowski, J. A.. Personality dimensions of students and some educational implications of Eysenck's theory of extraversion and neuroticism / J.A. Wa'nkowski. — 2nd ed. — Birmingham : University of Birmingham Educational Counselling Service, 1978. — ii,66,leaves ; 30cm. — (Research report / Universtiy of Birmingham Educational Survey)
Previous ed.: 1970
ISBN 0-7044-0309-9 (spiral) : £1.50 B81-09443

155.5 — Israel. Adolescents. Sexual behaviour
Antonovsky, Helen F.. Adolescent sexuality : a study of attitudes and behavior / Helen F. Antonovsky with Sophie Kav-venaki ... [et al.]. — Lexington, Mass. : Lexington Books, c1980 ; [Aldershot] : Gower [distributor], 1981. — xii,162p ; 24cm
Bibliography: p153-159. — Includes index
ISBN 0-669-04030-4 : £11.50 B81-33348

155.5′32 — Massachusetts. Boston. Italian immigrant adolescent boys. Development — *Comparative studies*
Young, Harben Boutourline. Puberty to manhood in Italy and America / Harben Boutourline Young, Lucy Rau Ferguson. — New York ; London : Academic Press, 1981. — xiii,283p : ill ; 24cm. — (Developmental psychology series)
Bibliography: p267-276. — Includes index
ISBN 0-12-773150-4 : £14.60
Also classified at 155.5′32′0945632 ; 155.5′32′0945823 B81-22393

155.5′32′0945632 — Italy. Rome. Adolescent boys. Development — *Comparative studies*
Young, Harben Boutourline. Puberty to manhood in Italy and America / Harben Boutourline Young, Lucy Rau Ferguson. — New York ; London : Academic Press, 1981. — xiii,283p : ill ; 24cm. — (Developmental psychology series)
Bibliography: p267-276. — Includes index
ISBN 0-12-773150-4 : £14.60
Primary classification 155.5′32 B81-22393

155.5′32′0945823 — Italy. Palermo. Adolescent boys. Development — *Comparative studies*
Young, Harben Boutourline. Puberty to manhood in Italy and America / Harben Boutourline Young, Lucy Rau Ferguson. — New York ; London : Academic Press, 1981. — xiii,283p : ill ; 24cm. — (Developmental psychology series)
Bibliography: p267-276. — Includes index
ISBN 0-12-773150-4 : £14.60
Primary classification 155.5′32 B81-22393

155.6 — PSYCHOLOGY OF ADULTS

155.6 — Adults. Development
Allman, Paula. Adult development : an overview of recent research / by Paula Allman. — Nottingham (14 Shakespeare St, Nottingham) : Department of Adult Education, University of Nottingham, [1981?]. — iii,42p ; 21cm. — (Adults : psychological and educational perspectives ; 1)
Bibliography: p32-42
ISBN 0-902031-46-5 (pbk) : £1.25 B81-25242

155.6 — Adults. Development & ageing
Hultsch, David F.. Adult development and aging : a life-span perspective / David F. Hultsch, Francine Deutsch. — New York ; London : McGraw-Hill, c1981. — xiv,431p : ill ; 24cm
Bibliography: p377-399. - Includes index
ISBN 0-07-031156-0 : £15.25 B81-19471

Kimmel, Douglas C.. Adulthood and aging : an interdisciplinary, development view / Douglas C. Kimmel. — 2nd ed. — New York ; Chichester : Wiley, c1980. — xiii,574p : ill ; 24cm
Previous ed.: 1974. — Includes bibliographies and index
ISBN 0-471-05229-9 : £10.25 B81-18978

155.6 — Adults. Psychological development
Colarusso, Calvin A.. Adult development : a new dimension in psychodynamic theory and practice / Calvin A. Colarusso and Robert A. Nemiroff. — New York ; London : Plenum Press, c1981. — xxx,290p : ill ; 24cm. — (Critical issues in psychiatry)
Includes bibliographies and index
ISBN 0-306-40619-5 : Unpriced B81-37958

155.6′092′4 — Adults. Psychological development — *Study examples: Jung, C. G.*
Staude, John-Raphael. The adult development of C.G. Jung / John-Raphael Staude. — London : Routledge & Kegan Paul, 1981. — xxiv,134p : 2ill ; 22cm
Bibliography: p125-130. — Includes index
ISBN 0-7100-0749-3 : £7.50 : CIP rev. B81-14879

155.6′32 — Men. Personality — *For women*
Hoffman, Susanna M.. The classified man : twenty-two types of men (and what to do about them) / Susanna M. Hoffman. — London : Sphere, 1981, c1980. — xviii,363p : 1ill,1form ; 18cm
Originally published: New York : Coward, McCann & Geoghegan, 1980
ISBN 0-7221-4603-5 (pbk) : £1.50 B81-28980

155.6′33 — Women. Emotional problems
Kurtz, Irma. Crises : a guide to your emotions / Irma Kurtz. — London : Ebury, 1981. — 146p ; 23cm
ISBN 0-85223-210-1 : £4.95 B81-40914

155.6′33 — Women. Psychology
Rohrbaugh, Joanna Bunker. Women : psychology′s puzzle / Joanna Bunker Rohrbaugh. — [London] : Abacus, 1981, c1979. — xvi,503p ; 20cm
Originally published: New York : Basic, 1979 Brighton : Harvester, 1980. — Bibliography: p469-491. — Includes index
ISBN 0-349-12943-6 (pbk) : £2.95 B81-39877

155.6′46 — Parents of hearing disordered children. Psychological aspects
You and your hearing impaired child / Kim McArthur ... [et al.]. — London (45 Hereford Rd., W2 5AH) : National Deaf Children′s Society, c1981. — 4p ; 21cm
£0.10 (pbk) B81-37776

155.67 — Man. Ageing. Psychobiological aspects — *Conference proceedings*
Luxembourg Conference on the Psychobiology of Aging *(1st : 1979 : Walferdange)*. The psychobiology of aging : problems and perspectives : proceedings of the First Luxembourg Conference on the Psychobiology of Aging held in Walferdange, Luxembourg on May 24-25, 1979 / editor Donald G. Stein. — New York ; Oxford : Elsevier/North-Holland, c1980. — 446p : ill ; 24cm
Includes bibliographies and index
ISBN 0-444-00391-6 : £23.91 B81-07306

155.67 — Man. Intellectual skills. Effects of ageing
Age, learning ability, and intelligence / edited by Richard L. Sprott. — New York ; London : Van Nostrand Reinhold, c1980. — xi,170p : ill ; 24cm
Includes bibliographies and index
ISBN 0-442-27895-0 : £11.25 B81-08309

155.67 — Old persons. Sexual behaviour
Croft, L. H.. Sexuality in later life. — Bristol : Wright, Jan.1982. — [298]p
ISBN 0-7236-7002-1 : £14.75 : CIP entry B81-34778

155.7 — EVOLUTIONAL PSYCHOLOGY

155.7 — Man. Behaviour. Genetic aspects — *Conference proceedings*
European Society of Human Genetics. *Symposium (1981 : University of Zürich)*. Human behaviour and genetics : proceedings of the Symposium of the European Society of Human Genetics held at the University of Zurich, Switzerland, March 26-28, 1981 / editors Werner Schmid and Johannes Nielsen. — Amsterdam ; Oxford : Elsevier/North-Holland Biomedical, 1981. — viii,253p : ill ; 25cm
Includes index
ISBN 0-444-80357-2 : £24.11 B81-35335

155.7 — Man. Behaviour. Genetic factors
Lumsden, Charles J.. Genes, mind and culture : the coevolutionary process / Charles J. Lumsden and Edward O. Wilson. — Cambridge, Mass. ; London : Harvard University Press, 1981. — xii,428p : ill ; 25cm
Bibliography: p385-415. — Includes index
ISBN 0-674-34475-8 : £12.00 B81-38132

Wells, Brian W. P.. Personality and heredity : an introduction to psychogenetics / Brian W.P. Wells. — London : Longman, 1980. — xi,223p ; 20cm
Bibliography: p210-217. - Includes index
ISBN 0-582-29545-9 (pbk) : £5.50 : CIP rev. B80-20149

155.8 — ETHNOPSYCHOLOGY AND NATIONAL PSYCHOLOGY

155.8 — Cross-cultural psychology
Handbook of cross-cultural psychology. — Boston [Mass.] ; London : Allyn and Bacon
Vol.4: Developmental psychology / edited by Harry C. Triandis, Alastair Heron. — c1981. — xx,492p : ill ; 25cm
Includes bibliographies and index
ISBN 0-205-06500-7 : Unpriced B81-30693

Studies in cross-cultural psychology. — London : Academic Press
Includes bibliographies and index
Vol.2 / edited by Neil Warren. — 1980. — xvii,357p : ill ; 24cm
ISBN 0-12-609202-8 : £24.00 : CIP rev. B80-10930

155.9 — ENVIRONMENTAL PSYCHOLOGY

155.9 — Environmental psychology
Personality and the environment / edited by Kenneth H. Craik and George E. McKechnie. — Beverly Hills ; London : Sage, 1978. — 128p : ill ; 22cm. — (Sage contemporary social science issues ; 42)
Includes bibliographies
ISBN 0-8039-1023-1 (pbk) : Unpriced B81-11330

155.9 — Man. Behaviour. Influence of money
Goldberg, Herb. Money madness : the psychology of saving, spending, loving, and hating money / Herb Goldberg and Robert T. Lewis. — London : Springwood, 1979, c1978. — 264p ; 22cm
Originally published: New York : Morrow, 1978. — Includes index
ISBN 0-905947-19-3 : £4.95 B81-01625

155.9′05 — Environmental psychology — *Serials*
Journal of environmental psychology. — [Vol.1, no.1 (Mar.1981)]-. — London : Academic Press, 1981-. — v. : ill ; 25cm
Quarterly
ISSN 0272-4944 : £19.50 per year B81-28389

155.9092′472 — Environmental psychology - *For architects*
Brebner, John. Environmental psychology for architects. — London : Applied Science, May 1981. — [224]p. — (Architectural science series)
ISBN 0-85334-969-x : £18.00 : CIP entry B81-08851

155.9′1 — Man. Effects of moon
Lieber, Arnold L.. The lunar effect / Arnold L. Lieber ; produced by Jerome Agel. — London : Corgi, 1979, c1980. — 174p : ill ; 18cm
Originally published: Garden City : Anchor Press, 1978. — Bibliography: p155-163. - Includes index
ISBN 0-552-11048-5 (pbk) : £0.85 B81-09544

155.9′16 — Adults. Effects of childhood cancer. Psychosocial aspects
Koocher, Gerald P.. The Damocles syndrome : psychosocial consequences of surviving childhood cancer / Gerald P. Koocher and John E. O′Malley. — New York ; London : McGraw-Hill, c1981. — xx,219p : ill ; 24cm
Bibliography: p191-199. — Includes index
ISBN 0-07-035340-9 : £12.95 B81-27522

155.9′35 — Man. Behaviour. Effects of fires
Fires and human behaviour / edited by David Canter. — Chichester : Wiley, c1980. — xvii,338p : ill,plans ; 24cm
Includes bibliographies and index
ISBN 0-471-27709-6 : £15.00 : CIP rev. B80-21330

155.9′35 — West Virginia. Buffalo Creek. Inhabitants. Long-term effects of floods, *1972*. Psychosocial aspects
Gleser, Goldine C.. Prolonged psychosocial effects of disaster : a study of Buffalo Creek / Goldine C. Gleser, Bonnie L. Green, Carolyn Winget. — New York ; London : Academic Press, c1981. — x,176p : ill ; 24cm. — (Personality and psychopathology)
Bibliography: p157-161. — Includes index
ISBN 0-12-286260-0 : £12.60 B81-39579

155.9′37 — Bereaved persons. Grief

Acute grief : counselling the bereaved / Otto S. Margolis ... [et al.], editors with the editorial assistance of Lillian G. Kutscher. — New York ; Guildford : Columbia University Press, 1981. — xii,276p ; 24cm. — (Foundation of Thanatology series)
Includes bibliographies and index
ISBN 0-231-04586-7 : £14.25 B81-24018

155.9′37 — Bereavement. Psychological aspects

Dunlop, Richard S.. Helping the bereaved / Richard S. Dunlop. — Bowie, Md. ; [London] : Charles Press, c1978. — xii,188p ; 21cm
Bibliography: p171-181. — Includes index
ISBN 0-913486-91-4 (pbk) : £6.45
Also classified at 155.9′37 B81-24925

Pincus, Lily. Death and the family : the importance of mourning / by Lily Pincus. — London : Faber, 1976, c1974 (1981 [printing]). — ix,278p ; 20cm
Originally published: New York : Pantheon, 1975
ISBN 0-571-11735-x (pbk) : £2.95 B81-13042

155.9′37 — Death. Psychological aspects

Kastenbaum, Robert. Death, society and human experience / Robert J. Kastenbaum. — 2nd ed. — St. Louis ; London : Mosby, 1981. — xi,316p : ill,forms ; 24cm
Previous ed.: 1977. — Bibliography: p307-308. — Includes index
ISBN 0-8016-2640-4 (pbk) : £9.75 B81-40360

155.9′37 — Death. Psychological aspects — *Conference proceedings*

Death and dying. — Tunbridge Wells : Pitman Medical, Sept.1981. — [200]p
Conference papers
ISBN 0-272-79606-9 (pbk) : £15.00 : CIP entry B81-23887

155.9′37 — Grief

Tatelbaum, Judy. The courage to grieve / by Judy Tatelbaum. — London : Heinemann, 1981, c1980. — viii,173p ; 22cm
Bibliography: p167-169. — Includes index
ISBN 0-434-75650-4 (pbk) : £2.95 B81-35369

155.9′37 — Man. Dying. Psychological aspects

Dunlop, Richard S.. Helping the bereaved / Richard S. Dunlop. — Bowie, Md. ; [London] : Charles Press, c1978. — xii,188p ; 21cm
Bibliography: p171-181. — Includes index
ISBN 0-913486-91-4 (pbk) : £6.45
Primary classification 155.9′37 B81-24925

155.9′37 — United States. Death. Attitudes of children — *For teaching*

If I die & when I do : exploring death with young people / [compiled by] Franki Sternberg, Barbara Sternberg. — Englewood Cliffs ; London : Prentice-Hall, c1980. — xii,227p : ill ; 24cm. — (Transformation series) (A Spectrum book)
Bibliography: p225-227
ISBN 0-13-450668-5 (cased) : £7.75
ISBN 0-13-450650-2 (pbk) : £3.85 B81-07886

155.9′62 — Long-term imprisonment. Psychological aspects — *Sources of data: Durham Prison. E-wing*

Cohen, Stanley, *1928-*. Psychological survival : the experience of long-term imprisonment / Stanley Cohen and Laurie Taylor. — 2nd ed. — Harmondsworth : Penguin, 1981. — 239p : 2ill ; 19cm. — (Pelican books)
Previous ed.: 1972. — Bibliography: p230-239
ISBN 0-14-021657-x (pbk) : £2.25 B81-08754

156.2 — ANIMAL PSYCHOLOGY. PHYSIOLOGICAL PSYCHOLOGY

156′.2′05 — Psychobiology — *Serials*

Psychobiology and psychopathology. — Vol.1-. — Pacific Grove, Calif. : Boxwood Press ; Amsterdam ; Oxford : [Distributed by] Elsevier/North-Holland Biomedical Press, 1981-. — v. : ill ; 24cm
Unpriced
Also classified at 616.89′07′05 B81-39508

156.3 — ANIMAL PSYCHOLOGY. INTELLIGENCE AND INTELLECTUAL PROCESSES

156′.315 — Learning by animals. Autoshaping. Theories

Autoshaping and conditioning theory / edited by C.M. Locurto, H.S. Terrace, John Gibbon. — New York ; London : Academic Press, c1981. — xii,313p : ill ; 24cm
Includes bibliographies and index
ISBN 0-12-454480-0 : £16.80 B81-17706

156′.315 — Learning by animals. Conditioning

Dickinson, Anthony. Contemporary animal learning theory / Anthony Dickinson. — Cambridge : Cambridge University Press, 1980. — xi,177p : ill ; 23cm. — (Problems in the behavioural sciences)
Bibliography: p169-173. - Includes index
ISBN 0-521-23469-7 (cased) : £12.50
ISBN 0-521-29962-4 (pbk) : Unpriced B81-08186

156′.3152 — Learning by animals. Reinforcement. Role of electrical stimulation of brain

Biology of reinforcement : facets of brain-stimulation reward / edited by Aryeh Routtenberg. — New York ; London : Academic, 1980. — xiii,174p : ill ; 24cm. — (Behavioral biology)
Includes bibliographies and index
ISBN 0-12-599350-1 : £9.00 B81-04621

157 — ABNORMAL PSYCHOLOGY

157 — Abnormal psychology

Martin, Barclay. Abnormal psychology : clinical and scientific perspectives. — 2nd ed. / Barclay Martin. — New York ; London : Holt, Rinehart and Winston, c1981. — xiv,578p : ill (some col.),ports ; 25cm
Previous ed.: / Barclay Martin et al. 1977. — Text on lining papers. — Bibliography: p533-565. — Includes index
ISBN 0-03-050721-9 : £11.50 B81-05618

White, Robert W.. The abnormal personality / Robert W. White, Norman F. Watt. — 5th ed. — New York ; Chichester : Wiley, c1981. — xiii,793p : ill,ports ; 25cm
Previous ed.: New York : Ronald Press, 1973. — Bibliography: p677-732. — Includes index
ISBN 0-471-04599-3 : £11.90 B81-12959

157′.6 — Drug abuse. Psychological factors

Drugs and suicide : when other coping strategies fail / Dan J. Lettieri, editor. — Beverly Hills ; London : Sage, c1978. — 303p : ill,forms ; 23cm. — (Sage annual reviews of drug and alcohol abuse ; v.2)
Includes bibliographies and index
ISBN 0-8039-1037-1 : £12.50
ISBN 0-8039-1038-x (pbk) : Unpriced
Also classified at 157′.7 B81-18358

157′.7 — Suicide. Psychological factors

Drugs and suicide : when other coping strategies fail / Dan J. Lettieri, editor. — Beverly Hills ; London : Sage, c1978. — 303p : ill,forms ; 23cm. — (Sage annual reviews of drug and alcohol abuse ; v.2)
Includes bibliographies and index
ISBN 0-8039-1037-1 : £12.50
ISBN 0-8039-1038-x (pbk) : Unpriced
Primary classification 157′.6 B81-18358

157.9 — CLINICAL PSYCHOLOGY

157′.9 — Clinical psychology

Vingoe, Frank James. Clinical psychology and medicine : an interdisciplinary approach / Frank James Vingoe with contributions by Ian Taylor. — Oxford : Oxford University Press, 1981. — xiii,451p : ill ; 24cm. — (Oxford medical publications)
Bibliography: p363-410. — Includes index
ISBN 0-19-261219-0 (pbk) : £14.00 B81-23577

157′.9′05 — Clinical psychology — *Serials*

The British journal of clinical psychology. — Vol.20, pt.1 (Feb.1981)-. — Leicester (48 Princess Rd East, Leicester LE1 7DR) : The British Psychological Society, 1981-. — v. ; 25cm
Quarterly. — Continues in part: British journal of social and clinical psychology
ISSN 0144-6657 = British journal of clinical psychology : £45.00 per year B81-20453

158 — APPLIED PSYCHOLOGY

158′.092′4 — Applied psychology — *Personal observations*

Wallis, D.. Applied psychology in UWIST / D. Wallis. — Cardiff (c/o R. Slater, Department of Applied Psychology, UWIST, Llwyn-y-Grant, Penylan, Cardiff CF3 7UX) : [UWIST Department of Applied Psychology], 1977. — 7p ; 30cm. — (Occasional paper / UWIST Department of Applied Psychology ; no.1)
Bibliography: p7
£0.50 (spiral) B81-24804

158′.0973 — United States. Applied psychology, *to 1980*

Napoli, Donald S.. Architects of adjustment : the history of the psychological profession in the United States / Donald S. Napoli. — Port Washington ; London : National University Publications : Kennikat, 1981. — 176p ; cm. — (Series in American studies)
Bibliography: p157-164. — Includes index
ISBN 0-8046-9269-6 : £17.00 B81-21849

158′.1 — Man. Mind. Self-development — *Manuals*

Buzan, Tony. Make the most of your mind / Tony Buzan ; illustrated by Richard Fowler. — London : Pan, 1981, c1977. — 159p : ill,1port ; 18cm. — (Pan information)
Originally published: s.l. : Colt Books, 1977. — Bibliography: p156-157. - Includes index
ISBN 0-330-26230-0 (pbk) : £1.00 B81-05644

158′.1 — Personal success — *Manuals*

Hill, Napoleon. Success through a positive mental attitude / by Napoleon Hill and W. Clement Stone. — Wellingborough : Thomas, 1961, c1960 (1979 [printing]). — 315p : forms ; 22cm
Originally published: Englewood Cliffs : Prentice Hall, 1960. — Bibliography: p302-303. - Includes index
ISBN 0-85454-061-x (pbk) : £3.50 B81-00727

Morrisey, George L.. Getting your act together : goal setting for fun, health and profit / George L. Morrisey. — New York ; Chichester : Wiley, c1980. — xiii,160p : ill,forms ; 23cm
Bibliography: p147-153
ISBN 0-471-08185-x (pbk) : £4.00 B81-06362

158′.1 — Self-assertion — *Manuals*

Shaw, Malcolm E.. Making it, assertively / Malcolm E. Shaw, Emmett Wallace, Frances N. LaBella. — Englewood Cliffs ; London : Prentice-Hall, c1980. — 164p : ill ; 21cm. — (A Spectrum book)
Bibliography: p163-164
ISBN 0-13-545897-8 (cased) : Unpriced
ISBN 0-13-545889-7 (pbk) : £3.20 B81-14099

158′.1 — Self-assertion — *Manuals* — *For dentistry*

Morton, Judy C.. Building assertive skills / Judy C. Morton, Cheryl A. Richey, Michele Kellett. — St. Louis ; London : Mosby, 1981. — xii,283p : ill,forms ; 24cm
Bibliography: p251-253. - Includes index
ISBN 0-8016-3520-9 (pbk) : £9.25 B81-14991

158′.1 — Self-development — *Manuals*

Dyer, Wayne W.. The sky′s the limit / Wayne Dyer. — London : Granada, 1981. — 382p : 1ill ; 24cm
Originally published: New York : Simon and Schuster, 1980
ISBN 0-246-11569-6 : £5.95 B81-12139

Hampshire, Sheila. How to realize your potential / Sheila Hampshire, Tom Jaap. — London : Institute of Personnel Management, 1981. — xii,145p : 1ill ; 19cm. — (Management paperbacks)
ISBN 0-85292-278-7 (pbk) : £1.95 : CIP rev. B81-12893

158′.1 — Self-discovery

Harding, D. E.. The science of the 1st person / D.E. Harding. — Ipswich (Nacton, Ipswich) : Shollond Publications, 1974. — 48p,[1]folded leaf : ill ; 25cm
Unpriced (pbk) B81-37791

158'.1 — Self-realisation

Kopp, Sheldon. Mirror, mask, and shadow : the risk and rewards of self-acceptance / Sheldon Kopp. — New York : Macmillan ; London : Collier Macmillan, c1980. — ix,198p ; 25cm
ISBN 0-02-566460-3 : £5.95 B81-19593

158'.1 — Self-realisation — *Manuals*

Clark, Rebecca. Macro-mind power / by Rebecca Clark. — Wellingborough : Thomas, 1980, c1978. — 239p : ill ; 22cm
Originally published: West Nyack : Parker, 1978
ISBN 0-85454-072-5 (pbk) : £3.50 B81-01714

Jodjana, Raden Ayou. A book of self re-education : the structure and functions of the human body as an instrument of expression / Raden Ayou Jodjana. — Romford : L. N. Fowler, c1981. — 200p,[8]p of plates : ill,ports ; 28cm
ISBN 0-85243-364-6 (pbk) : Unpriced B81-28957

Ostrander, Sheila. Superlearning / Sheila Ostrander and Lynn Schroeder with Nancy Ostrander. — London : Sphere, 1981, c1979. — 349p ; 18cm
Originally published: New York : Delacorte ; London : Souvenir, 1979. — Bibliography: p317-329. - Includes index
ISBN 0-7221-6557-9 (pbk) : £1.75 B81-12764

158'.1 — Self-realisation - *Manuals*

Rainwater, Janette. You're in charge!. — Wellingborough : Turnstone Press, Aug.1981. — [224]p
ISBN 0-85500-156-9 (pbk) : £3.75 : CIP entry B81-18162

158'.1 — Self-realisation — *Manuals*

Stevens, Cliff R.. How to attain anything you want through mind visualisations! : a basic course in achieving goals through the simplest occult method known - visualisations / Cliff R. Stevens. — Folkestone (16 Turketal Rd, Folkestone, Kent) : Finbarr Book Promotions, c1980. — [24]p : facsims ; 23cm
Unpriced (pbk) B81-12688

158'.1 — Self-realisation — *Spiritualist viewpoints*

Joseph, C. A.. Who am I? I am that I am / by C.A. Joseph. — London : Regency, c1980. — 116p ; 23cm
ISBN 0-7212-0620-4 : £5.00 B81-05871

158'.1 — Self-realisation. Use of suggestion

Cullinan, James F.. How to change yourself and your life - without will power or effort! / James F. Cullinan. — Folkstone (13 Turketel Rd., Folkestone, Kent) : Finbarr, c1980. — 94p ; 22cm
Unpriced (pbk) B81-04093

158'.12 — Meditation

Baker, Douglas, *1922-*. The jewel in the lotus / by Douglas Baker. — [Essendon] ([Little Elephant, Essendon, Herts.]) : [D. Baker], c1975. — 278p : ill(some col.),1coat of arms,ports ; 29cm. — (The seven pillars of ancient wisdom ; v.1)
Includes index
Unpriced (pbk) B81-32878

158'.12 — Meditation, *to 1980*

Johnson, Willard. Riding the ox home : a history of meditation. — London : Rider, Nov.1981. — [240]p
ISBN 0-09-146291-6 (pbk) : £4.95 : CIP entry B81-30343

158'.2 — Adults. Interpersonal relationships. Emotional problems. Self treatment: Behaviour modification. Techniques

Philips, Debora. How to fall out of love / Debora Phillips with Robert Judd. — London : Macdonald Futura, 1981, c1978. — 191p ; 18cm
Originally published: Boston : Houghton Mifflin, 1978. — Includes index
ISBN 0-7088-1986-9 (pbk) : £1.25 B81-17431

158'.2 — Interpersonal relationships. Communication — *Manuals*

Pace, R. Wayne. Techniques for effective communication / R. Wayne Pace, Brent D. Peterson, M. Dallas Burnett. — Reading, Mass. ; London : Addison-Wesley, c1979. — xv,329p : ill ; 24cm
Includes bibliographies and index
ISBN 0-201-05703-4 (pbk) : £7.70 B81-21356

158'.2 — Interpersonal relationships. Communication. Psychological aspects

Christie, Bruce. Face to file communication. — Chichester : Wiley, July 1981. — [250]p. — (Wiley series in information processing)
ISBN 0-471-27939-0 : £10.00 : CIP entry B81-14986

158'.2 — Interpersonal relationships — *Manuals*

Johnson, David W.. Reaching out : interpersonal effectiveness and self-actualization / David W. Johnson. — 2nd ed. — Englewood Cliffs ; London : Prentice-Hall, c1981. — xi,308p : ill,forms ; 24cm
Previous ed.: 1972. — Bibliography: p301-302. — Includes index
ISBN 0-13-753327-6 (cased) : Unpriced
ISBN 0-13-753319-5 (pbk) : £7.10 B81-16648

158'.2 — Interpersonal relationships. Verbal communication. Psychological aspects

Elgin, Suzette Haden. The gentle art of verbal self-defense / Suzette Haden Elgin. — Englewood Cliffs ; London : Prentice-Hall, c1980. — ix,310p : ill ; 21cm. — (A spectrum book)
Includes bibliographies and index
ISBN 0-13-351098-0 (cased) : £8.40
ISBN 0-13-351080-8 (pbk) : £3.85 B81-06466

158'.2 — Man. Shyness. Alleviation — *Manuals*

Zimbardo, Philip G.. Shyness : what it is, what to do about it / Philip G. Zimbardo. — London : Pan, 1981, c1977. — 315p : ill ; 18cm
Originally published: Reading, Mass. ; London : Addison-Wesley, 1977. — Bibliography: p276-298. — Includes index
ISBN 0-330-26409-5 (pbk) : £1.95 B81-39007

158'.2 — Transactional analysis — *For management*

Barker, Dave. Transactional analysis : a basic introduction for the manager / Dave Barker and Keri Phillips. — Horsham (Horsham, W. Sussex RH12 4TD) : Roffey Park College, [1980?]. — 34p : ill ; 21cm
Bibliography: p32-34
ISBN 0-907416-00-4 (pbk) : Unpriced B81-31114

158'.27 — Emergencies. Intervention by bystanders. Psychological aspects

Emergency intervention / Jane Allyn Piliavin ... [et al.]. — New York ; London : Academic Press, 1981. — xiv,293p : ill ; 24cm
Bibliography: p261-280. — Includes index
ISBN 0-12-556450-3 : £12.20 B81-33161

158'.7 — Industrial psychology

McCormick, Ernest J.. Industrial psychology. — 7th ed. / Ernest J. McCormick, Daniel R. Ilgen. — London : Allen & Unwin, 1981, c1980. — xv,464p : ill,forms ; 24cm
Previous ed.: 1975. — Includes bibliographies and index
ISBN 0-04-150078-4 (pbk) : £8.95 : CIP rev. B81-12836

158'.7 — Industrial psychology — *Conference proceedings*

Virginia Tech symposium on applied behavioral science / edited by Joseph A Sgro. — Lexington, Mass. : Lexington Books ; [Aldershot] : Gower [distributor]
Vol.1. — 1981. — xii,303p : ill ; 24cm
Includes bibliographies and index
ISBN 0-669-04332-x : £18.00 B81-39695

158.7 — Industries. Machine operators. Stress. Effects of machine-pacing

Machine pacing and occupational stress. — London : Taylor & Francis, Nov.1981. — [370]p
Conference papers
ISBN 0-85066-225-7 : £18.00 : CIP entry B81-30886

158.7 — Man. Organisational behaviour

Davis, Keith. Human behavior at work : organizational behaviour / Keith Davis. — 6th ed. — New York ; London : McGraw-Hill, c1981. — xviii,583p : col.ill,facsims ; 25cm. — (McGraw-Hill series in management)
Previous ed.: 1976. — Includes index
ISBN 0-07-015516-x : £13.25 B81-23960

Naylor, James C.. A theory of behavior in organizations / James C. Naylor, Robert D. Pritchard, Daniel R. Ilgen. — New York ; London : Academic Press, 1980. — xii,299p : ill ; 24cm
Ill on lining papers. — Bibliography: p277-283. — Includes index
ISBN 0-12-514450-4 : £13.60 B81-22157

The **Theory** and practice of organizational psychology. — London : Academic Press, Feb.1982. — [220]p. — (Organizational and occupational psychology)
ISBN 0-12-518040-3 : CIP entry B81-36060

158.7 — Managers. Stress

Cole, Donald W.. Professional suicide : a survival kit for you and your job / Donald W. Cole. — New York ; London : McGraw-Hill, c1981. — xvi,232p : ill ; 21cm
Bibliography: p215-220. - Includes index
ISBN 0-07-011697-0 : £9.50 B81-10371

158.7 — Personnel. Stress

Macdonald. The stresses of work / McDonald and Doyle. — Walton-on-Thames : Nelson, 1981. — x,82p : ill ; 22cm. — (Health and Safety in the workplace)
Bibliography: p79
ISBN 0-17-771070-5 : £1.40 B81-15351

158.7 — Personnel. Stress — *Case studies*

Coping with stress at work. — Farnborough : Gower, Nov.1981. — [260]p
ISBN 0-566-02338-5 : £12.50 : CIP entry B81-30967

158.7 — Personnel. Stress. Psychophysiological aspects

Stress, work design, and productivity. — Chichester : Wiley, Jan.1982. — [256]p. — (Wiley series on studies in occupational stress)
ISBN 0-471-28044-5 : £12.50 : CIP entry B81-33799

158.7 — White-collar personnel. Stress

White collar and professional stress / edited by Cary L. Cooper and Judi Marshall. — Chichester : Wiley, c1980. — xiii,257p ; 24cm. — (Wiley series on studies in occupational stress)
Includes bibliographies and index
ISBN 0-471-27760-6 : £13.50 : CIP rev. B80-30689

158.7'076 — Industrial psychology — *Questions & answers*

Dambrot, Faye. Test items to accompany second edition People, work, and organizations : an introduction to industrial and organizational psychology, Bernard M. Bass, Gerald V. Barrett / prepared by Faye Dambrot. — Boston, Mass. ; London : Allyn and Bacon, c1981. — 142p ; 24cm
Unpriced (pbk) B81-11244

158.7'094 — Europe. Industrial psychology

Wolff, Charles J. de. Conflicts and contradictions : work psychologists in Europe / Charles J. De Wolff, Sylvia Shimmin and Maurice De Montmollin with contributions from Marian Dobrzyński ... [et al.]. — London : Academic Press, 1981. — xii,196p ; 24cm. — (Organizational and occupational psychology)
Includes bibliographies and index
ISBN 0-12-214650-6 : Unpriced B81-29788

158.7'0973 — United States. Man. Organisational behaviour — *For management*

Milton, Charles R.. Human behavior in organizations : three levels of behavior / Charles R. Milton. — Englewood Cliffs ; London : Prentice-Hall, c1981. — vi,506p : ill ; 25cm
Includes index
ISBN 0-13-444596-1 : £13.60 B81-25336

160 — LOGIC

160 — Conditional propositions

Ifs : conditionals, belief, decision, chance, and time / edited by William L. Harper, Robert Stalnaker and Glenn Pearce. — Dordrecht ; London : Reidel ; London : Distributed by Kluwer Academic, c1981. — x,345p : ill ; 23cm. — (The University of Western Ontario series in philosophy of science ; v.15)
Includes bibliographies and index
ISBN 90-277-1184-4 (cased) : Unpriced
ISBN 90-277-1220-4 (pbk) : Unpriced
B81-12049

Nute, Donald. Topics in conditional logic / Donald Nute. — Dordrecht ; London : Reidel, c1980. — x,164p : ill ; 23cm. — (Philosophical studies series in philosophy ; v.20)
Bibliography: p157-158. - Includes index
ISBN 90-277-1049-x : Unpriced B81-06499

160 — Deontic logic

Deontic logic : introductory and systematic readings / edited by Risto Hilpinen. — Dordrecht ; London : Reidel, 1971 (1981 [printing]). — xvii,183p ; 23cm. — (A Pallas paperback ; 20)
Includes bibliographies and index
ISBN 90-277-1302-2 (pbk) : Unpriced
B81-38410

160 — Logic

Barry, Vincent E.. Practical logic / Vincent E. Barry. — 2nd ed. — New York ; London : Holt, Rinehart and Winston, c1980. — xiv,476p : ill ; 24cm
Includes bibliographies and index
ISBN 0-03-056836-6 : £8.95 B81-17695

Coleridge, Samuel Taylor. Logic / [Samuel Taylor Coleridge] ; edited by J.R. de J. Jackson. — London : Routledge & Kegan Paul, c1981. — lxvii,420p,4leaves of plates : ill,facsims ; 23cm. — (The collected works of Samuel Taylor Coleridge ; 13) (Bollinger series ; LXXV)
Bibliography: pxv-xviii. — Includes index
ISBN 0-7100-0254-8 : £20.00 : CIP rev.
B79-18912

Jeffrey, Richard C.. Formal logic : its scope and limits / Richard Jeffrey. — 2nd ed. — New York ; London : McGraw-Hill, c1981. — xiv,198p : ill ; 24cm
Previous ed.: 1967. — Bibliography: p189-191. — Includes index
ISBN 0-07-032321-6 : £12.55 B81-39718

O'Connor, D. J. (Daniel John). Elementary logic / D.J. O'Connor and Betty Powell. — Sevenoaks : Teach Yourself, 1980. — 273p : ill ; 18cm. — (Teach yourself books)
Bibliography: p269-270. — Includes index
ISBN 0-340-25824-1 (pbk) : £2.50 : CIP rev.
B80-13188

160 — Logic. Aristotle. De interpretatione — *Commentaries*

al-Fārābī, Abū Naṣr Muḥammad ibn Muḥammad. al-Farabi's commentary and short treatise on Aristotle's De interpretatione / translated with an introduction and notes by F.W. Zimmermann. — London : Published for the British Academy by the Oxford University Press, 1981. — clii,287p ; 26cm. — (Classical and medieval logic texts ; 3)
Translation from the Arabic. — Bibliography: pxvii-xx. — Includes index
ISBN 0-19-725959-6 : £58.00 B81-38683

160 — Logic. Definite articles — *Philosophical perspectives*

Barth, E. M.. The logic of the articles in traditional philosophy : a contribution to the study of conceptual structures / E.M. Barth ; [translated from the Dutch by E.M. Barth and T.C. Potts]. — Dordrecht ; London : Reidel, c1974. — xxv,533p ; 23cm. — (Synthese historical library ; v.10)
Translation of: De logica van de lidwoorden in de traditionele filosofie. — Bibliography: p482-501. - Includes index
ISBN 90-277-0350-7 (cased) : Unpriced
ISBN 90-277-1187-9 (pbk) : Unpriced
B81-15256

160 — Logic — *Philosophical perspectives*

Haack, Susan. Philosophy of logics / Susan Haack. — Cambridge : Cambridge University Press, 1978. — xvi,276p ; 24cm
Bibliography: p255-265. — Includes index
ISBN 0-521-21988-4 (cased) : £17.50
ISBN 0-521-29329-4 (pbk) : Unpriced
B81-25939

Putnam, Hilary. Reason, truth and history. — Cambridge : Cambridge University Press, Dec.1981. — [224]p
ISBN 0-521-23035-7 (cased) : £15.00 : CIP entry
ISBN 0-521-29776-1 (pbk) : £4.95 B81-32534

160 — Logic. Propositions — *Early works*

William, *of Ockham*. [Summa logicae. Pt.2. English]. Ockham's theory of propositions : part II of the Summa logicae / translated by Alfred J. Greddoso and Henry Schuurman ; introduction by Alfred J. Freddoso. — Notre Dame ; London : London : University of Notre Dame Press, c1980. — viii,212p ; 24cm
Bibliography: p75-76. — Includes index
ISBN 0-268-01495-7 : £10.30 B81-32348

160 — Logic — *Welsh texts*

Evans, Donald M.. Ymresymu i'r newyddian (Ranh 11) / gan Donald M. Evans ; cyfieithwyd gan Robin Bateman a Meredydd Evans. — Caerdydd (38 Heol y Parc, Caerdydd) : Adron Efrydiau Allanol, Coleg y Brifysgol, 1979. — 76p ; 22cm. — (Cyfres Heol y Parc ; Rhif 6)
Unpriced (pbk)
B81-07497

Palmer, Humphrey. Ymresymu i'r newyddian / gan Humphrey Palmer ; cyfieithwyd gan Robin Bateman a Meredydd Evans. — Caerdydd (38 Heol y Parc, Caerdydd) : Adran Efrydiau Allanol, Coleg y Brifysgol, 1979. — 63[i.e.78]p : ill ; 21cm. — (Cyfres Heol y Parc ; Rhif 4)
Unpriced (pbk) B81-07496

160 — Logical thought

Barker, Evelyn M.. Everyday reasoning / Evelyn M. Barker. — Englewood Cliffs ; London : Prentice-Hall, c1981. — xiii,272p : ill ; 23cm
Includes index
ISBN 0-13-293407-8 (pbk) : £5.80 B81-17174

Runkle, Gerald. Good thinking : an introduction to logic / Geral Runkle. — 2nd ed. — New York ; London : Holt, Rinehart and Winston, c1981. — xvii,413p : ill ; 24cm
Previous ed.: 1978. — Includes index
ISBN 0-03-058161-3 (pbk) : £7.95 B81-22975

160 — Man. Actions. Role of reasoning — *Philosophical perspectives*

Körner, Stephen. Experience and conduct : a philosophical enquiry into practical thinking / Stephen Körner. — Cambridge : Cambridge University Press, 1976 (1980 [printing]). — ix,268p ; 23cm
Bibliography: p262-263. — Includes index
ISBN 0-521-29943-8 (pbk) : £5.95 B81-00728

Milligan, David, *1930-*. Reasoning and the explanation of actions / David Milligan. — Brighton : Harvester, 1980. — xi,194p ; 23cm. — ([Studies in philosophy ; no.23])
Includes index
ISBN 0-85527-433-6 : £18.95 : CIP rev.
B80-21336

160 — Modal logic. Common nouns

Gupta, Anil. The logic of common nouns : an investigation in quantified modal logic / Anil Gupta. — New Haven ; London : Yale University Press, 1980. — xi,142p : ill ; 22cm
Bibliography: p137-139. — Includes index
ISBN 0-300-02346-4 : £9.50 : CIP rev.
B80-21337

160 — Propositional logical thought — *Philosophical perspectives*

Gochet, Paul. Outline of a nominalist theory of propositions : an essay in the theory of meaning and the philosophy of logic / Paul Gochet. — Dordrecht ; London : Reidel, c1980. — xii,205p : ill ; 23cm. — (Synthese library ; v.98)
Translation and revised version of: Esquisse d'une théorie nominaliste de la proposition. — Includes index
ISBN 90-277-1031-7 : Unpriced B81-05026

160'.244 — Logic — *For linguistics*

McCawley, James D.. Everything that linguists have always wanted to know about logic* *but were ashamed to ask / James D. McCawley. — Oxford : Basil Blackwell, 1981. — xv,508p ; 24cm
Bibliography: p488-498. - Includes index
ISBN 0-631-12614-7 : Unpriced : CIP rev.
B80-23970

160'.244 — Logic — *For linguistics — Encyclopaedias*

Dictionary of logic : as applied in the study of language : concepts-methods-theories / edited by Witold Marciszewski. — The Hague ; London : Nijhoff, 1981. — xiv,436p : ill ; 25cm. — (Nijhoff international philosophy series ; v.9)
Bibliography: p406-414. — Includes index
ISBN 90-247-2123-7 : Unpriced B81-36723

160'.9 — Logic — *History — Serials*

History and philosophy of logic. — Vol.1 (1980)-. — Tunbridge Wells : Abacus, 1980-. — v. ; 24cm
Annual
ISSN 0144-5340 = History and philosophy of logic : Unpriced B81-09133

161 — Inductive inference — *Philosophical perspectives*

Rescher, Nicholas. Induction : an essay on the justification of inductive reasoning / Nicholas Rescher. — Oxford : Blackwell, 1980. — xii,225p : ill ; 23cm
Includes index
ISBN 0-631-10341-4 : £16.50 : CIP rev.
B80-09954

165 — Logic. Paradoxes — *Philosophical perspectives*

Pierre, *d'Ailly, Cardinal*. [Conceptus et insolubilia. English]. Peter of Ailly : concepts and insolubles : an annotated translation / by Paul Vincent Spade. — Dordrecht ; London : Reidel, c1980. — xiii,193p ; 23cm. — (Synthese historical library ; v.19)
Translation of: Conceptus et insolubilia. — Bibliography: p162-168. - Includes index
ISBN 90-277-1079-1 : Unpriced B81 07287

165 — Metaphysics. Aristotle. 'Metaphysics'. Concepts: Contradiction

Dancy, R. M.. Sense and contradiction : a study in Aristotle / R.M. Dancy. — Dordrecht ; London : Reidel, c1975. — xii,184p ; 23cm. — (Synthese historical library ; v.14)
Includes an appendix of Greek text and parallel English translation. — Bibliography: p166-174. - Includes index
ISBN 90-277-0565-8 (cased) : Unpriced
ISBN 90-277-1189-5 (pbk) : Unpriced
B81-06502

168 — Argument

Jensen, J. Vernon. Argumentation : reasoning in communication / J. Vernon Jensen. — New York ; London : Van Nostrand, c1981. — xiii,347p : ill ; 25cm
Bibliography: p327-340. - Includes index
ISBN 0-442-25396-6 : £11.95 B81-17148

170 — ETHICS

170 — Ethics

Anscombe, G. E. M.. Ethics, religion and politics / [G.E.M. Anscombe]. — Oxford : Blackwell, 1981. — ix,161p ; 24cm. — (The collected philosophical papers of G.E.M. Anscombe ; v.3)
Includes index
ISBN 0-631-12942-1 : £12.00 B81-40051

170 — Ethics *continuation*

Aristotle. [Ethics. English]. The Nicomachean ethics / Aristotle ; translated with commentaries and glossary by Hippocrates G. Apostle. — Dordrecht ; London : Reidel, c1980. — 372p ; 23cm. — (Synthese historical library ; v.13)
Originally published: 1975. — Includes index
ISBN 90-277-1150-x (pbk) B81-07774

Barth, Karl. Ethics / Karl Barth ; edited by Dietrich Braun ; translated by Geoffrey W. Bromiley. — Edinburgh : T.T. Clark, 1981. — x,534p ; 24cm
Translation of: Ethik. — Includes index
ISBN 0-567-09319-0 : £17.50 B81-36251

Edel, Abraham. Exploring fact and value / Abraham Edal. — New Brunswick ; London : Transaction, c1980. — xxii,369p ; 24cm. — (Science, ideology and value ; vol.2)
Includes index
ISBN 0-87855-229-4 : £10.00 B81-14484

Fagothey, Austin. Fagothey's right and reason : ethics in theory and practice. — 7th ed. / revised by Milton A. Gonsalves. — St. Louis ; London : Mosby, 1981. — xiv,574p ; 24cm
Previous ed.: 1976. — Bibliography: p528-557. — Includes index
ISBN 0-8016-1541-0 (pbk) : £14.00 B81-33040

Grassian, Victor. Moral reasoning : ethical theory and some contemporary moral problems / Victor Grassian. — Englewood Cliffs ; London : Prentice-Hall, c1981. — xv,432p ; 23cm
Includes bibliographies and index
ISBN 0-13-600759-7 (pbk) : £7.10 B81-14477

Hare, R. M.. Moral thinking. — Oxford : Clarendon Press, Dec.1981. — [220]p
ISBN 0-19-824659-5 (cased) : £11.00 : CIP entry
ISBN 0-19-824660-9 (pbk) : £3.95 B81-31452

Meynell, Hugo A.. Freud, Marx and morals / Hugo Meynell. — London : Macmillan, 1981. — xi,209p ; 23cm. — (New studies in practical philosophy)
Includes index
ISBN 0-333-29521-8 : £18.00 : CIP rev.
B80-23971

Midgley, Mary. Heart and mind. — Brighton : Harvester Press, Sept.1981. — [192]p
ISBN 0-7108-0048-7 : £20.00 : CIP entry
B81-23884

Morality and moral controversies / edited by John Arthur. — Englewood Cliffs ; London : Prentice-Hall, c1981. — xiv,497p ; 23cm
Includes bibliographies
ISBN 0-13-601278-7 (pbk) : £7.10 B81-14478

170 — Ethics. Aristotle. 'Ethics' — *Critical studies*

Essays on Aristotle's ethics / edited by Amélie Oksenberg Rorty. — Berkeley ; London : University of California Press, c1980. — viii,438p ; 24cm. — (Major thinkers series ; 2)
ISBN 0-520-03773-1 : £19.50 B81-34460

170 — Ethics. Aristotle. Eudemian ethics — *Texts with commentaries*

Aristotle. [Ethics. English]. Aristotle's Eudemian ethics, Books I, II, and VIII. — Oxford : Clarendon Press, Dec.1981. — [250]p. — (Clarendon Aristotle series)
ISBN 0-19-872060-2 (cased) : £11.50 : CIP entry
ISBN 0-19-872061-0 (pbk) : £6.25 B81-31457

170 — Ethics. Implications of sociobiology

Singer, Peter, *1946-*. The expanding circle : ethics and sociobiology / Peter Singer. — Oxford : Clarendon Press, 1981. — xii,190p ; 22cm
Includes index
ISBN 0-19-824646-3 : £6.95 B81-36259

170 — Ethics. Reasoning

Ewin, R. E.. Co-operation and human values : a study of moral reasoning / R.E. Ewin. — Brighton : Harvester, 1981. — 216p ; 23cm. — (Harvester studies in philosophy ; [no.29])
Includes index
ISBN 0-85527-393-3 : £18.95 : CIP rev.
B81-24589

170 — Ethics. Universalizability

Rabinowicz Włodzimierz. Universalizability : a study in morals and metaphysics / Włodzimierz Rabinowicz. — Dordrecht ; London : Reidel, c1979. — 190p ; 23cm. — (Synthese library ; v.41)
Bibliography: p179-180. - Includes index
ISBN 90-277-1020-1 : Unpriced B81-07878

170 — Moral philosophy

Raphael, D. D.. Moral philosophy / D.D. Raphael. — Oxford : Oxford University Press, 1981. — 120p ; 21cm. — (OPUS)
Bibliography: p116-117. — Includes index
ISBN 0-19-219149-7 (cased) : £5.95 : CIP rev.
ISBN 0-19-289136-7 (pbk) : Unpriced
B81-22479

170 — Promises. Ethical aspects

Atiyah, P. S.. Promises, morals, and law / by P.S. Atiyah. — Oxford : Clarendon Press, 1981. — 218p ; 23cm
Includes index
ISBN 0-19-825377-x : £14.00 : CIP rev.
B81-07925

170'.2'0223 — Adolescents. Personal conduct. Ethics — *Topics for discussion groups*

Brown, Brian. Club chats : discussion starters for young people / arranged and devised by Brian Brown. — London : Chester House, 1976. — 35p ; 19cm
ISBN 0-7150-0062-4 (pbk) : Unpriced
B81-20957

170'.7'1173 — United States. Higher education institutions. Curriculum subjects: Ethics. Teaching

Ethics teaching in higher education / edited by Daniel Callahan and Sissela Bok. — New York ; London : Plenum, c1980. — xvi,315p ; 24cm. — (The Hastings Center series in ethics)
Bibliography: p303-311. — Includes index
ISBN 0-306-40522-9 : Unpriced B81-02410

170'.9 — Ethics. Theories, *to 1979*

Grayeff, Felix. A short treatise on ethics / Felix Grayeff. — London : Duckworth, 1980. — vi,89p ; 23cm
Includes index
ISBN 0-7156-1494-0 : £8.95 B81-01911

170'.9 — Ethics. Theories, *to 1980*

MacIntyre, Alasdair. After virtue : a study in moral theory / Alasdair MacIntyre. — London : Duckworth, 1981. — ix,252p ; 25cm
Bibliography: p246-248. — Includes index
ISBN 0-7156-0933-5 : £24.00 B81-27077

170'.92'4 — Ethics. Theories of Kant, Immanuel

Pelegrinis, T. N.. Kant's conceptions of the categorical imperative and the will / by T.N. Pelegrinis. — London : Zeno, 1980. — xv,221p ; 23cm
Includes index
ISBN 0-7228-0020-7 : £12.50 : CIP rev.
B80-07653

Rotenstreich, Nathan. Practice and realization : studies in Kant's moral philosophy / by Nathan Rotenstreich. — The Hague ; London : Nijhoff, 1979. — 153p ; 25cm
Includes index
ISBN 90-247-2112-1 : Unpriced B81-15710

170'.92'4 — Moral philosophy. Adler, Felix — *Biographies*

Friess, Horace L.. Felix Adler and ethical culture : memories and studies / Horace L. Friess ; edited by Fannia Weingartner. — New York ; Guildford, Surrey : Columbia University Press, 1981. — xi,272p,[13]p of plates : ports ; 21cm
Bibliography: p264-266. — Includes index
ISBN 0-231-05184-0 (cased) : £16.30
ISBN 0-231-05185-9 (pbk) : Unpriced
B81-38084

171 — ETHICS. SYSTEMS AND DOCTRINES

171'.6'09021 — Conscience — *Philosophical perspectives, 1100-1300*

Potts, Timothy C.. Conscience in medieval philosophy / Timothy C. Potts. — Cambridge : Cambridge University Press, 1980. — 152p ; 23cm
Includes passages translated from the Latin. — Bibliography: p145. - Includes index
ISBN 0-521-23287-2 : £10.50 B81-03790

172 — POLITICAL ETHICS

172 — Politics. Manipulative behaviour. Ethical aspects

Goodin, Robert E.. Manipulatory politics / Robert E. Goodin. — New Haven ; London : Yale University Press, c1980. — x,250p ; 22cm
Includes index
ISBN 0-300-02463-0 : £11.30 : CIP rev.
B80-21340

172'.0973 — United States. Cities. Politics. Ethical aspects

Arkes, Hadley. The philosopher in the city : the moral dimensions of urban politics / Hadley Arkes. — Princeton ; Guildford : Princeton University Press, c1981. — xiv,465p ; 24cm
Includes index
ISBN 0-691-09356-3 (cased) : £15.30
ISBN 0-691-02822-2 (pbk) : £3.90 B81-24176

172'.1 — Theft. Ethics — *Illustrations — For schools*

Smith, Gillian Crampton. Losers, weepers / [Gillian Crampton Smith and Sarah Curtis]. — [London] : [Longman], c1981. — 1portfolio(10 parts) : ill ; 30cm + Teachers' notes(folded sheet:[6]p:ill:30cm). — (Longman thinkstrips)
ISBN 0-582-22302-4 : Unpriced B81-09441

172'.2 — Equality & freedom. Ethical aspects

Charvet, John. A critique of freedom and equality / John Charvet. — Cambridge : Cambridge University Press, 1981. — vii,203p ; 23cm. — (Cambridge studies in the history and theory of politics)
Includes index
ISBN 0-521-23727-0 : £17.50 : CIP rev.
B81-19157

172'.4 — International relations. Ethical aspects — *Festschriften*

Explorations in ethics and international relations. — London : Croom Helm, Sept.1981. — [224]p
ISBN 0-7099-2300-7 : £10.95 : CIP entry
B81-21505

172'.4'0973 — United States. Foreign relations, *1800-1977*. Ethical aspects

Thompson, Kenneth W.. Morality and foreign policy / Kenneth W. Thompson. — Baton Rouge ; London : Louisiana State University Press, c1980. — xiii,197p ; 24cm
Includes index
ISBN 0-8071-0656-9 : £10.80 B81-01944

174 — PROFESSIONAL AND OCCUPATIONAL ETHICS

174 — Professional conduct. Ethics

Goldman, Alan H.. The moral foundations of professional ethics / Alan H. Goldman. — Totowa : Rowman and Littlefield ; London : Prior [distributor], 1980. — 305p ; 22cm. — (Philosophy and society)
Includes index
ISBN 0-8476-6274-8 : £11.50 B81-09600

174'.2 — Medicine. Ethical aspects

Kennedy, Ian. The unmasking of medicine / Ian Kennedy. — London : Allen & Unwin, 1981. — xiii,189p ; 23cm
Bibliography: p169-182. — Includes index
ISBN 0-04-610016-4 : Unpriced : CIP rev.
B81-15874

174'.2 — Medicine. Ethics

Purtilo, Ruth. Ethical dimensions in the health professions / Ruth B. Purtilo, Christine K. Cassel. — Philadelphia ; London : Saunders, 1981. — xv,224p : ill ; 23cm
Includes index
ISBN 0-7216-7411-9 (pbk) : £6.95 B81-32373

174'.2 — Medicine. Ethics — *Philosophical perspectives*

Pellegrino, Edmund D.. A philosophical basis of medical practice : towards a philosophy and ethic of the healing professions / Edmund D. Pellegrino, David C. Thomasma. — New York ; Oxford : Oxford University Press, 1981. — xvii,341p : ill ; 22cm
Includes index
ISBN 0-19-502790-6 B81-18953

174'.2 — Medicine. Nursing. Ethics

Fromer, Margot Joan. Ethical issues in health care / Margot Joan Fromer. — St. Louis ; London : Mosby, 1981. — xiii,420p ; 24cm
Includes index
ISBN 0-8016-1728-6 (pbk) : £10.50 B81-24288

174'.2 — Medicine. Psychiatry. Ethics

Psychiatric ethics / edited by Sidney Bloch and Paul Chodoff. — Oxford : Oxford University Press, 1981. — viii,365p : 2ill ; 25cm
Includes index
ISBN 0-19-261182-8 : £12.50 : CIP rev. B81-13446

174'.2'0321 — Medicine. Ethics — *Encyclopaedias*

Dictionary of medical ethics / edited by A.S. Duncan, G.R. Dunstan and R.B. Welbourn. — Rev. and enl. ed. — London : Darton, Longman & Todd, 1981. — xxxi,459p : ill ; 23cm
Previous ed.: 1977. — Includes bibliographies
ISBN 0-232-51492-5 : £12.50 : CIP rev. B80-17539

174'.2'0941 — Great Britain. Medicine. Ethics

British Medical Association. The handbook of medical ethics / [British Medical Association]. — London : The Association, c1981. — 104p ; 22cm
Previous ed.: 1980. — Bibliography: p90-92. — Includes index
ISBN 0-7279-0077-3 (pbk) : Unpriced B81-30084

174'.24 — United States. Euthanasia. Ethical aspects

Kluge, Eike-Henner W.. The ethics of deliberate death / Eike-Henner W. Kluge. — Port Washington ; London : Kennikat, 1981. — 154p ; 22cm. — (Multi-disciplinary studies in the law)
Bibliography: p145-150. — Includes index
ISBN 0-8046-9260-2 : £14.85 B81-16278

174'.28 — Man. Behaviour modification. Ethical aspects

Stoltz, Stephanie B.. Ethical issues in behaviour modification / Stephanie B. Stoltz and associates ; foreword by Albert Bandura. — San Francisco ; London : Jossey-Bass, 1978. — xxii,200p ; 24cm. — (The Jossey-Bass social and behavioral science series)
Bibliography: p183-194. — Includes index
ISBN 0-87589-368-6 : £9.60 B81-15106

174'.4 — Business enterprise. Ethics

Adair, John, *1934-*. Management and morality : the problems and opportunities of social capitalism / John Adair. — Farnborough, Hants. : Gower, 1980. — 189p : 1ill ; 23cm
Originally published: Newton Abbot : David and Charles, 1974
ISBN 0-566-02241-9 : £9.50 : CIP rev. B80-18579

Evans, William A.. Management ethics : an intercultural perspective / William A. Evans. — Boston, Mass. ; London : Nijhoff, c1981. — xvi,224p ; 24cm. — (Dimensions of international business)
Includes index
ISBN 0-89838-055-3 : Unpriced B81-38693

174'.4 — United States. Personnel. Implications of conduct of organisations. Ethical aspects — *Case studies*

Whistle blowing! : loyalty and dissent in the corporation / edited with an introduction and conclusion by Alan F. Westin with the assistance of Henry I. Kurtz and Albert Robbins. — New York ; London : McGraw-Hill, c1981. — x,181p ; 24cm
Bibliography: p169-173. — Includes index
ISBN 0-07-069483-4 : £8.95 B81-05611

174'.4'0973 — United States. Business enterprise. Ethics, *1840-1914*

Englebourg, Saul. Power and morality : American business ethics 1840-1914 / Saul Engelbourg. — Westport, Conn. ; London : Greenwood Press, 1980. — xvi,181p ; 22cm. — (Contributions in economics and economic history ; no.28)
Bibliography: p167-173. — Includes index
ISBN 0-313-20871-9 : Unpriced B81-05623

174'.9301 — Social sciences. Research, *1800-1978.* **Ethical aspects**

Barnes, J. A. (John Arundel). Who should know what? : social science, privacy and ethics / J.A. Barnes. — Cambridge : Cambridge University Press, 1980, c1979. — 232p ; 19cm
Originally published: Harmondsworth : Penguin, 1979. — Bibliography: p189-222. — Includes index
ISBN 0-521-23359-3 (cased) : £7.50
ISBN 0-521-29934-9 (pbk) : Unpriced B81-25186

174'.9362 — United States. Socially disadvantaged children. Care. Ethical aspects

Mearig, Judith S.. Working for children / Judith S. Mearig and associates. — San Francisco ; London : Jossey Bass, 1978. — xvii,348p ; 24cm. — (The Jossey-Bass social and behavioral science series)
Bibliography: p327-342. — Includes index
ISBN 0-87589-367-8 : £12.00 B81-16436

174'.9574 — Biology. Ethical aspects

Roberts, Catherine, *1917-*. Science, animals, and evolution : reflections on some unrealized potentials of biology and medicine / Catherine Roberts ; foreword by Arthur M. Young. — Westport ; London : Greenwood Press, 1980. — xv,221p ; 22cm. — (Contributions in philosophy, ISSN 0084-926x ; no.14)
Bibliography: p209-213. - Includes index
ISBN 0-313-21479-4 : Unpriced B81-05746

176 — ETHICS OF SEX AND REPRODUCTION

176 — United States. Mentally retarded persons. Sterilisation. Ethical aspects

Mental retardation and sterilization : a problem of competency and paternalism / edited by Ruth Macklin and Willard Gaylin. — New York ; London : Plenum, c1981. — xxvii,247p ; 22cm. — (The Hastings Center series in ethics)
Bibliography: p195-199. — Includes index
ISBN 0-306-40689-6 : Unpriced B81-38017

179 — MISCELLANEOUS ETHICAL NORMS

179 — Justice — *Philosophical perspectives*

Galston, William A.. Justice and the human good / William A. Galston. — Chicago ; London : University of Chicago Press, 1980. — xii,324p : ill ; 24cm
Bibliography: p303-312. - Includes index
ISBN 0-226-27963-4 : £15.00 B81-00729

Sterba, James P.. The demands of justice / James P. Sterba. — Notre Dame ; London : University of Notre Dame Press, c1980. — xii,164p ; 21cm
Includes index
ISBN 0-268-00848-5 (pbk) : £3.90 B81-29580

179.3 — ETHICS. TREATMENT OF ANIMALS

179'.3 — Animals. Treatment by man. Ethics

Salt, Henry S.. Animals' rights : considered in relation to social progress / Henry S. Salt ; preface by Peter Singer. — London : Centaur, c1980. — xvi,240p ; 21cm
Facsim of: 1st ed. London : G. Bell, 1892. — Bibliography: p170-218
ISBN 0-900000-98-8 : £7.50 B81-07070

179'.3 — Cruelty to animals

Dawkins, Marian Stamp. Animal suffering : the science of animal welfare / Marian Stamp Dawkins. — London : Chapman and Hall, 1980. — viii,149p ; 21cm
Bibliography: p131-144. — Includes index
ISBN 0-412-22580-8 (cased) : £7.50 : CIP rev.
ISBN 0-412-22590-6 (pbk) : £3.95 B80-25108

Yorke, Vera. The Church's supreme disgrace / Vera Yorke. — Bognor Regis : New Horizon, c1980. — xvi,228p ; 21cm
ISBN 0-86116-220-x : £4.50 B81-21803

179'.3 — Great Britain. Food animals. Exporting. Ethical aspects

Illgotten gains : facts and figures for the fight against the trade in live food animals for export / produced by Protect Our Livestock Group. — [Cheltenham] ([The Court House, Newcourt Rd, Charlton Kings, Gloucestershire GL53 9AZ]) : [The Group], [1980]. — [12]p : ill ; 21cm
Unpriced (pbk) B81-24742

179'.3'05 — Animals. Cruelty by man — *Serials*

Flesh and blood. — Issue 1-. — Stevenage (PO Box 32, Stevenage, Herts. [SG1 3SD]) : [Caroline Publications], 1980-. — v. : ill ; 21cm
Irregular
ISSN 0261-8044 = Flesh and blood : £3.00 for 4 issues B81-33723

179'.3'05 — Animals. Treatment by man. Ethics — *Serials*

The **Beast** : the magazine that bites back. — No.1 (June-July 1979)-. — London (2 Blenheim Cres., W11 1NN) : Clanose, 1979-. — v. : ill,ports ; 28cm
Six issues yearly (1979), quarterly (1980-)
£3.25 per year B81-05350

179'.3'0941 — Great Britain. Animals. Attitudes of society, *1800-1900*

Turner, James, *1946-*. Reckoning with the beast : animals, pain and humanity in the Victorian mind / James Turner. — Baltimore ; London : Johns Hopkins University Press, c1980. — xii,190p : ill ; 24cm. — (The Johns Hopkins University studies in historical and political science. 98th series ; 2)
Includes index
ISBN 0-8018-2399-4 : £7.50
Also classified at 179'.3'0973 B81-11317

179'.3'0973 — United States. Animals. Attitudes of society, *1800-1900*

Turner, James, *1946-*. Reckoning with the beast : animals, pain and humanity in the Victorian mind / James Turner. — Baltimore ; London : Johns Hopkins University Press, c1980. — xii,190p : ill ; 24cm. — (The Johns Hopkins University studies in historical and political science. 98th series ; 2)
Includes index
ISBN 0-8018-2399-4 : £7.50
Primary classification 179'.3'0941 B81-11317

179.4 — ETHICS. EXPERIMENTATION ON ANIMALS

179'.4 — Science. Research. Use of laboratory animals — *Anti-vivisection viewpoints*

Smith, Colin, *1941-*. The moral and social aspects of vivisection : the following speech was delivered at a symposium organised by the South African Association Against Painful Experiments on Animals, Johannesburg, Republic of South Africa at the Rand Afrikaans University, Johannesburg on 10th April, 1981 / by Colin Smith. — London (51 Harley St., W1N 1DD) : International Association Against Painful Experiments on Animals, [1981]. — 12p : ill ; 22cm
Unpriced (pbk) B81-25551

179'.4 — Scotland. Anti-vivisection movements: Scottish Anti-Vivisection Society — *Serials*

Scottish Anti-Vivisection Society. Newsletter / Scottish Anti-Vivisection Society. — No.1 (Feb.1981)-. — Glasgow (121 West Regent St., Glasgow G2 2SD) : The Society, 1981-. — v. ; 30cm
Quarterly
ISSN 0261-2089 = Newsletter - Scottish Anti-Vivisection Society : Free to Society members B81-20440

179.6 — ETHICS. COURAGE AND COWARDICE

179′.6 — Great Britain. Heroism. Awards. Organisations: Carnegie Hero Fund Trust — *Serials*

Carnegie Hero Fund Trust. Report of the Carnegie Hero Fund Trust. — 1974. — Dunfermline (Abbey Park House, Dunfermline) : The Trust, [1975]. — 39p in various paging
Unpriced B81-09107

Carnegie Hero Fund Trust. Report of the Carnegie Hero Fund Trust. — 1975. — Dunfermline (Abbey Park House, Dunfermline) : The Trust, [1976]. — 38p in various paging
Unpriced B81-09106

Carnegie Hero Fund Trust. Report of the Carnegie Hero Fund Trust. — 1976. — Dunfermline (Abbey Park House, Dunfermline) : The Trust, [1977]. — 46p in various paging
Unpriced B81-09108

Carnegie Hero Fund Trust. Report of the Carnegie Hero Fund Trust. — 1977. — Dunfermline (Abbey Park House, Dunfermline) : The Trust, [1978]. — 31p in various paging
Unpriced B81-09109

Carnegie Hero Fund Trust. Report of the Carnegie Hero Fund Trust. — 1978. — Dunfermline (Abbey Park House, Dunfermline) : The Trust, [1979]. — 43p
Unpriced B81-09110

Carnegie Hero Fund Trust. Report of the Carnegie Hero Fund Trust. — 1979. — Dunfermline (Abbey Park House, Dunfermline) : The Trust, [1980]. — 36p
Unpriced B81-09111

179.7 — ETHICS. RESPECT AND DISRESPECT FOR HUMAN LIFE

179′.7 — Suicide — *Philosophical perspectives*

Suicide : the philosophical issues / edited by M. Pabst Battin and David J. Mayo. — London : P. Owen, 1981, c1980. — viii,292p ; 23cm
Originally published: New York : St. Martin's Press, 1980
ISBN 0-7206-0579-2 : £9.95 B81-26052

179′.76 — Abortion. Ethical aspects

Sumner, L. W.. Abortion and moral theory / L.W. Sumner. — Princeton ; Guildford : Princeton University Press, c1981. — x,246p ; 23cm
Bibliography: p229-239. — Includes index
ISBN 0-691-07262-0 (cased) : £9.20
ISBN 0-691-02017-5 (pbk) : £2.75 B81-26013

180 — ANCIENT, MEDIEVAL, ORIENTAL PHILOSOPHY

180′.937 — Ancient Roman philosophy. Boethius — *Critical studies*

Chadwick, Henry. Boethius. — Oxford : Clarendon Press, Nov.1981. — [272]p
ISBN 0-19-826447-x : £15.00 : CIP entry
B81-30543

180′.938 — Ancient Greek philosophy, *to ca 200 — Critical studies*

Guthrie, W. K. C.. A history of Greek philosophy / by W.K.C. Guthrie. — Cambridge : Cambridge University Press
Vol.6: Aristotle an encounter. — 1981. — xvi,456p : ill ; 24cm
Bibliography: p401-424. — Includes index
ISBN 0-521-23573-1 : £30.00 : CIP rev.
B81-25882

180′.938 — Classical philosophy — *Critical studies*

Armstrong, A. H.. An introduction to ancient philosophy. — 3rd ed. — London : Methuen, Oct.1981. — [260]p
Originally published: 1965
ISBN 0-416-69310-5 (pbk) : £4.25 : CIP entry
B81-28834

Strauss, Leo. The city and man / Leo Strauss. — Chicago ; London : University of Chicago Press, 1978, c1964. — 245p ; 23cm
Originally published: Chicago : Rand McNally, 1964. — Includes index
ISBN 0-226-77701-4 (pbk) : £3.50 B81-38564

181 — ORIENTAL PHILOSOPHY

181 — Asian philosophy — *Critical studies*

Asian philosophy today / edited by Dale Riepe. — New York ; London : Gordon and Breach, c1981. — xvii,303p ; 23cm
Includes bibliographies and index
ISBN 0-677-15490-9 : Unpriced B81-28886

181′.04392 — Mahayana Buddhist philosophy. Madhyamika school — *Critical studies*

Murti, T. R. V.. The central philosophy of Buddhism : a study of the M a dhyamika system / T.R.V. Murti. — 2nd ed. — London : Unwin, 1960 (1980[printing]). — xii,372p ; 20cm. — (Mandala books)
Previous ed.: London : Allen and Unwin, 1955. — Bibliography: pxii. - Includes index
ISBN 0-04-294108-3 (pbk) : £2.95 : CIP rev.
B79-35155

181′.06 — Jewish philosophy, *to 1980 — Critical studies*

Altmann, Alexander. Essays in Jewish intellectual history / Alexander Altmann. — Hanover, N. H. ; London : Published for Brandeis University Press by University Press of New England, 1981. — x,324p ; 24cm
Includes index
ISBN 0-87451-192-5 : £12.50 B81-39839

181′.11 — Chinese philosophy — *Texts with commentaries*

Graham, A. C.. Chuang-tzŭ, textual notes to a partial translation. — London : University of London, School of Oriental and African Studies, Nov.1981. — [77]p
ISBN 0-7286-0089-7 (pbk) : £3.00 : CIP entry
B81-30590

Zhuang Zi. Chuang Tzŭ : Taoist philosopher and Chinese mystic / translated from Chinese by Herbert A. Giles. — 2nd ed. — London : Unwin Paperbacks, 1926 (1980 [printing]). — 335p ; 20cm. — (Mandala books)
Translation of: Zhuang Zi. — Previous ed.: London : Quaritch, 1889. — Includes index
ISBN 0-04-299009-2 (pbk) : £2.50 : CIP rev.
B81-05582

Zhuang Zi. Chuang-tzŭ. — London : Allen & Unwin, Nov.1981. — [240]p
ISBN 0-04-299010-6 : £9.75 : CIP entry
B81-28778

181′.45 — Transcendental meditation

Campbell, Anthony. Seven states of consciousness : a vision of possibilities suggested by the teaching of Maharishi Mahesh Yogi / by Anthony Campbell. — London : Gollancz, 1973 (1980 [printing]). — 175p : ill,1port ; 22cm
Bibliography: p175
ISBN 0-575-02926-9 (pbk) : £2.95 B81-32364

181′.45 — Yoga

Gent, John. Yoga seeker / by John Gent. — Mansfield (136 Oak Tree La., Mansfield, Notts.) : J. Gent
Action plan 3: The mysteries of oriental yoga. — 1981. — 14p : 2ill ; 21cm
Unpriced (unbound) B81-36793

Gent, John. Yoga seeker / by John Gent. — Mansfield (136 Oak Tree La., Mansfield Notts.) : J. Gent
Action plan 2 : health, happiness and perfection. — 1980. — 14p : ill ; 21cm
Text on covers
£0.40 (pbk) B81-17888

Gopi Krishna. The secret of yoga / by Gopi Krishna. — Wellingborough : Turnstone, 1981, c1972. — 210p ; 22cm
Originally published: New York : Harper, 1972 ; London : Turnstone, 1973
ISBN 0-85500-102-x (pbk) : £3.75 : CIP rev.
B81-06878

Varenne, Jean. Yoga : and the Hindu tradition / Jean Varenne ; translated from the French by Derek Coltman. — Chicago ; London : University of Chicago Press, 1976. — x,253p : ill ; 23cm. — (A Phoenix book)
Translation of: Yoga et la tradition hindoue. — Bibliography: p237-240. — Includes index
ISBN 0-226-85114-1 (cased) : Unpriced
ISBN 0-226-85116-8 (pbk) : £3.85 B81-38151

181′.45 — Yoga - *Manuals*

Hoare, Sophy. Start yoga. — London : Paul, July 1981. — [144]p
ISBN 0-09-145410-7 (cased) : £6.50 : CIP entry
ISBN 0-09-145411-5 (pbk) : £3.95 B81-13440

181′.452 — Yoga. Patanjali. Yoga sutras. Commentaries: Vyāsa. Vyāsa-bhāsya — *Commentaries*

Śaṅkarācārya. Śaṅkara on the Yoga-sūtra-s. — London : Routledge & Kegan Paul
Vol.1: Samādhi : the Vivaraṇa sub-commentary to Vyāsabhāṣya on the Yoga-sūtra-s of Pantañjali Samādhi-pāda / [translated by] Trevor Leggett. — 1981. — xxxii,178p ; 24cm
Translation of: Patañjalayogasūtrabhāṣyavivaraṇa
ISBN 0-7100-0826-0 : £12.50 B81-38462

181′.452 — Yoga. Patanjali. Yoga sutras — *Texts with commentaries*

Bailey, Alice A.. The light of the soul : its science and effect : a paraphrase of the Yoga sutras of Patanjali : with commentary / by Alice A. Bailey. — New York ; London : Lucis, 1927, c1955 (1978 printing). — xvii,458p ; 20cm
Bibliography: pxvii. — Includes index
Unpriced (pbk) B81-37044

181′.482 — Advaita vedanta

Klein, Jean. Neither this nor that I am / Jean Klein ; translator Mary Mann. — London : Watkins, c1981. — x,138p ; 21cm
Translation from the French
ISBN 0-7224-0189-2 (pbk) : £3.95 : CIP rev.
B81-05136

181′.482 — Shankara vedanta

Śaṅkarācārya. The crest jewel of wisdom. — Dulverton : Watkins, Oct.1981. — [116]p
ISBN 0-7224-0191-4 (pbk) : £3.50 : CIP entry
B81-27431

182 — PRE-SOCRATIC PHILOSOPHY

182′.4 — Ancient Greek philosophy. Heraclitus — *Texts*

Heraclitus. The art and thought of Heraclitus : an edition of the fragments with translation and commentary / Charles H. Kahn. — Cambridge : Cambridge University Press, 1979 (1981 [printing]). — xiv,354p ; 23cm
Parallel Greek text and English translation, English commentary and notes. — Bibliography: pxii-xiv. — Includes index
ISBN 0-521-28645-x (pbk) : £7.50 : CIP rev.
B81-21575

182′.5 — Ancient Greek philosophy. Empedocles — *Texts*

Empedocles. Empedocles, the extant fragments. — London : Yale University Press, Sept.1981. — [416]p
ISBN 0-300-02475-4 : £28.00 : CIP entry
B81-30246

183 — SOPHISTIC, SOCRATIC AND RELATED GREEK PHILOSOPHIES

183′.1 — Ancient Greek philosophy. Sophism — *Critical studies*

Kerferd, G. B.. The sophistic movement / G.B. Kerferd. — Cambridge : Cambridge University Press, 1981. — vii,184p ; 23cm
Bibliography: p177-179. — Includes index
ISBN 0-521-23936-2 (cased) : £14.00 : CIP rev.
ISBN 0-521-28357-4 (pbk) : £4.95 B81-20615

184 — PLATONIC PHILOSOPHY

184 — Ancient Greek philosophy. Heraclides of Pontus — *Critical studies*

Gottschalk, H. B.. Heraclides of Pontus / by H.B. Gottschalk. — Oxford : Clarendon, 1980. — x,178p ; 23cm
Bibliography: p163-170. - Includes index
ISBN 0-19-814021-5 : £12.50 : CIP rev. B80-18159

184 — Ancient Greek philosophy. Plato — *Critical studies*

Grube, G. M. A.. Plato's thought / G.M.A. Grube ; with new introduction, bibliographic essay and bibliography by Donald J. Zeyl. — London : Athlone, 1980. — xxi,346p ; 21cm
Originally published: London : Methuen, 1935. — Includes bibliographies and index
ISBN 0-485-11211-6 (cased) : £8.50
ISBN 0-485-12034-8 (pbk) : £4.25 B81-01934

184 — Ancient Greek philosophy. Plato — *Esperanto texts*

Plato. Apologio de Sokrato ; Kay, Kritono / Platono ; elhelenigis Albert Goodheir. — Glasgow : Kardo, 1981. — 51p ; 21cm
Translation from the Greek
ISBN 0-905149-15-7 (pbk) : £2.40 B81-20960

185 — ARISTOTELIAN PHILOSOPHY

185 — Ancient Greek philosophy. Aristotle — *Critical studies*

Ackrill, J. L.. Aristotle the philosopher / J.L. Ackrill. — Oxford : Oxford University Press, 1981. — 160p ; 21cm. — (OPUS)
Bibliography : p156-158. — Includes index
ISBN 0-19-219131-4 (cased) : £6.95
ISBN 0-19-289118-9 (pbk) : £2.95 B81-36517

189 — MEDIAEVAL WESTERN PHILOSOPHY

189 — Ancient Roman philosophy. Boethius — *Critical studies*

Boethius. — Oxford : Basil Blackwell, Sept.1981. — [432]p
ISBN 0-631-11141-7 : £25.00 : CIP entry B81-21475

189 — European philosophy, *780-950*

Marenbon, John. From the circle of Alcuin to the School of Auxerre : logic, theology and philosophy in the early middle ages / John Marenbon. — Cambridge : Cambridge University Press, 1981. — ix,219p ; 23cm. — (Cambridge studies in medieval life and thought. 3rd series ; v.15)
Bibliography: p207-214. — Includes index
ISBN 0-521-23428-x : £22.50 : CIP rev. B81-15856

189 — European thought, *ca 1100-1384*

Smalley, Beryl. Studies in medieval thought and learning from Abelard to Wyclif. — London (35 Gloucester Ave., NW1 7AX) : Hambledon Press, Dec.1981. — [455]p. — (History series ; 6)
ISBN 0-9506882-6-6 : £25.00 : CIP entry B81-31521

189 — Western philosophy, *400-1600* — *Latin-English parallel texts*

Eriugena, Johannes Scottus. [Periphyseon]. Iohannis Scotti Eriugenae Periphyseon (De diuisione naturae) / edited by I.P. Sheldon-Williams with the collaboration of Ludwig Bieler. — Dublin : Dublin Institute for Advanced Studies. — (Scriptores Latini Hiberniae ; v.11)
Liber 3. — 1981. — vii,324p ; 26cm
Parallel Latin text and English translation, English introduction and notes
Unpriced B81-23226

189'.2 — Christian philosophy, *to 400* — *Critical studies*

Osborn, Eric. The beginning of Christian philosophy / Eric Osborn. — Cambridge : Cambridge University Press, 1981. — xiv,321p ; 23cm
Bibliography: p289-304. — Includes index
ISBN 0-521-23179-5 : £24.00 B81-38977

189'.4 — Scholastic philosophy — *Critical studies*

Piltz, Anders. The world of medieval learning / Anders Piltz ; translated into English by David Jones. — Oxford : Basil Blackwell, 1981. — x,299p : ill,1map,facsims ; 26cm
Translation of: Medeltidens lärda värld. — Includes index
ISBN 0-631-12712-7 : £15.00 : CIP rev. B80-20496

190 — MODERN WESTERN PHILOSOPHY

190 — Analytic philosophy, *1900-1978* — *Critical studies*

Barth, E. M.. Perspectives on analytic philosophy / E.M. Barth. — Amsterdam ; Oxford : North-Holland Publishing Co., 1979. — 47p ; 24cm. — (Mededelingen der Koninklijke Nederlandse Akademie van Wetenschappen, Afd. Letterkunde. Nieuwe reeks ; d.42, no.2)
Pages also numbered 35-75. — Bibliography: p45-47
ISBN 0-7204-8484-7 (pbk) : Unpriced B81-37788

190 — Western philosophy — *Texts*

Fundamental problems in philosophy / edited by Oswald Hanfling at the Open University. — 2nd ed. — Oxford : Blackwell in association with the Open University Press, 1980. — 326p ; 23cm
Previous ed.: 1972. — Includes index
ISBN 0-631-12713-5 (cased) : £15.00 : CIP rev.
ISBN 0-631-12733-2 (pbk) : £6.95 B80-20122

Johnson, Oliver A.. The individual and the universe : an introduction to philosophy / Oliver A. Johnson. — New York ; London : Holt, Rinehart and Winston, c1981. — xiii,407p ; 24cm
Includes bibliographies and index
ISBN 0-03-056888-9 : £8.95 B81-22996

190'.3'21 — Western philosophy — *Encyclopaedias*

Angeles, Peter A.. A dictionary of philosophy / Peter A. Angeles. — London : Harper & Row, c1981. — ix,326p ; 22cm
ISBN 0-06-463461-2 : £6.95 B81-27782

190'5 — European thought — *History* — *Serials*

History of European ideas. — Vol.1, no.1 (1980)-. — Oxford : Pergamon Press, 1980-. — v. ; 26cm
Quarterly. — Text in English and French
Unpriced B81-08267

190'.9 — Western philosophy, *1630-1980* — *Critical studies*

Scruton, Roger. From Descartes to Wittgenstein : a short history of modern philosophy / Roger Scruton. — London : Routledge & Kegan Paul, 1981. — vi,298p ; 23cm
Bibliography: p285-293. — Includes index
ISBN 0-7100-0798-1 : £9.50 : CIP rev. B81-13726

190'.9'03 — European thought, *1789-1980*

Stromberg, Roland N.. European intellectual history since 1789 / Roland N. Stromberg. — Englewood Cliffs ; London : Prentice-Hall, c1981. — xii,386p : ill,ports ; 23cm
Previous ed.: 1975. — Bibliography: p349-375. — Includes index
ISBN 0-13-291955-9 (pbk) : £9.70 B81-12670

190'.9'031 — European philosophy, *1500-1600*

Schmitt, Charles B.. Studies in Renaissance philosophy and science / Charles B. Schmitt. — London : Variorum Reprints, 1981. — 342p in various pagings : ill,1port ; 24cm. — (Collected studies series ; CS146)
Includes 1 paper in Italian and 1 in French. — Includes index
ISBN 0-86078-093-7 : £24.00 : CIP rev.
Also classified at 509'.4 B81-21551

190'.9'033 — European thought, *1715-1796*

The **Enlightenment** in national context / edited by Roy Porter and Mikuláš Teich. — Cambridge : Cambridge University Press, 1981. — xii,275p ; 24cm
Bibliography: p260-267. — Includes index
ISBN 0-521-23757-2 (cased) : £19.50 : CIP rev.
ISBN 0-521-28212-8 (pbk) : £6.95 B81-22687

190'.9'04 — Analytic philosophy, *1900-1980* — *Critical studies*

Munitz, Milton K.. Contemporary analytic philosophy / Milton K. Munitz. — New York : Macmillan ; London : Collier Macmillan, c1981. — viii,434p ; 24cm
Bibliography: p413-427. — Includes index
ISBN 0-02-384840-5 (pbk) : £9.50 B81-29328

190'.9'04 — Western philosophy. Theories, *1889-1954*

Levi, Albert Wiliam. Philosophy and the modern world / by Albert William Levi. — Chicago ; London : University of Chicago Press, 1977, c1959. — xiv,591p ; 23cm
Originally published: Bloomington : Indiana University Press, 1959. — Includes index
ISBN 0-226-47391-0 (pbk) : £11.20 B81-38145

190'.9'042 — European philosophy, *ca 1920-ca 1935* — *Texts* — *Collections*

Essential readings in logical positivism / edited by Oswald Hanfling. — Oxford : Basil Blackwell, 1981. — 248p ; 22cm
Bibliography: p243-246. — Includes index
ISBN 0-631-12566-3 (pbk) : £5.95 B81-31927

191 — American philosophy. Lehrer, Keith — *Critical studies*

Keith Lehrer / edited by Padu J. Boghan. — Dordrecht ; London : Reidel, c1981. — x,260p : ill,1port ; 23cm. — (Profiles ; v.2)
Bibliography: p245-255. - Includes index
ISBN 90-277-1172-0 (cased) : Unpriced
ISBN 90-277-1173-9 (pbk) : Unpriced B81-10821

191 — American philosophy. Rescher, Nicholas — *Critical studies*

The **Philosophy** of Nicholas Rescher : discussion and replies / edited by Ernest Sosa with the advice and assistance of the Editorial Committee, L. Jonathan Cohen ... [et al.]. — Dordrecht ; London : Reidel, c1979. — xi,236p : 1port ; 23cm. — (Philosophical studies series in philosophy ; v.15)
Bibliography: p209-227. - Includes index
ISBN 90-277-0962-9 : Unpriced B81-04400

191 — American philosophy — *Texts*

Feigl, Herbert. Inquiries and provocations : selected writings 1929-1974 / Herbert Feigl ; edited by Robert S. Cohen. — Dordrecht ; London : Reidel, c1981. — xii,453p : 2ports ; 23cm. — (Vienna Circle collection ; v.14)
Bibliography: p422-446. - Includes index
ISBN 90-277-1101-1 (cased) : Unpriced
ISBN 90-277-1102-x (pbk) : Unpriced B81-15252

James, William. The writings of William James : a comprehensive edition : including an annotated bibliography updated through 1977 / edited with an introduction and new preface, by John J. McDermott. — Chicago ; London : University of Chicago Press, 1977. — liv,858p : ill ; 21cm. — (A Phoenix book)
Originally published: New York : Random House, 1967. — Bibliography: p811-858
ISBN 0-226-39188-4 (pbk) : £7.70 B81-38150

Mates, Benson. Skeptical essays / Benson Mates. — Chicago ; London : University of Chicago Press, 1981. — xi,176p ; 24cm
Includes index
ISBN 0-226-50986-9 : £10.20 B81-29779

Nozick, Robert. Philosophical explanations. — Oxford : Clarendon Press, Oct.1981. — [720]p
ISBN 0-19-824672-2 : £15.00 : CIP entry B81-26718

191 — American philosophy — *Texts* — *Festschriften*

Analysis and metaphysics : essays in honor of R.M. Chisholm / edited by Keith Lehrer. — Dordrecht ; London : Reidel, c1975. — x,317p : 1port ; 23cm. — (Philosophical studies series in philosophy ; v.4)
Includes index
ISBN 90-277-0571-2 (cased) : Unpriced
ISBN 90-277-1193-3 (pbk) : Unpriced B81-13648

191 — American philosophy — *Texts — Festschriften* *continuation*

Body, mind, and method : essays in honor of Virgil C. Aldrich / edited by Donald F. Gustafson and Bangs L. Tapscott. — Dordrecht ; London : Reidel, c1979. — xiii,307p : ill,1port ; 23cm. — (Synthese library ; v.138)
Bibliography: p297-300. - Includes index
ISBN 90-277-1013-9 : Unpriced B81-06113

192 — English philosophy. Bacon, Francis, *Viscount St. Albans - Biographies*

Fuller, Jean Overton. Francis Bacon. — London : East-West, Apr.1981. — [400]p
ISBN 0-85692-069-x : £10.00 : CIP entry B81-06885

192 — English philosophy. Bacon, Francis, *Viscount St. Albans — Critical studies*

Quinton, Anthony. Francis Bacon / Anthony Quinton. — Oxford : Oxford University Press, 1980. — 90p ; 19cm. — (Past masters)
Bibliography: p86-87. — Includes index
ISBN 0-19-287525-6 (cased) : £4.50 : CIP rev.
ISBN 0-19-287524-8 (pbk) : £0.95 B80-13190

192 — English philosophy. Bentham, Jeremy - *Correspondence, diaries, etc*

Bentham, Jeremy. The correspondence of Jeremy Bentham. — London : Athlone Press, May 1981. — (The collected works of Jeremy Bentham)
Vol.4: October 1788 to December 1793. — [564]p
ISBN 0-485-13204-4 : £45.00 (vols.4 & 5 £90.00) : CIP entry B81-08809

192 — English philosophy. Bentham, Jeremy - *Correspondence, diaries, etc.*

Bentham, Jeremy. The correspondence of Jeremy Bentham. — London : Athlone Press, May 1981. — (The collected works of Jeremy Bentham)
Vol.5: January 1794 to December 1797. — [470]p
ISBN 0-485-13205-2 : £40.00 (vols 4 & 5 £90.00) : CIP entry B81-08810

192 — English philosophy. Glanvill, Joseph — *Critical studies*

Talmor, Sascha. Glanvill : the uses and abuses of scepticism / by Sascha Talmor. — Oxford : Pergamon, 1981. — xv,102p,[1]leaf of plates : 1port ; 22cm
Bibliography: p96-99. — Includes index
ISBN 0-08-027407-2 : £12.50 : CIP rev. B81-03815

192 — English philosophy. Locke, John — *Correspondence, diaries, etc.*

Locke, John. The correspondence of John Locke / edited by E.S. de Beer. — Oxford : Clarendon. — (The Clarendon edition of the works of John Locke. The correspondence)
Vol.6: Letters nos. 2199-2664. — 1981. — vii,798p ; 23cm
Includes letters in English, French and Latin. — Includes index
ISBN 0-19-824563-7 : £42.50 : CIP rev. B80-19005

Locke, John. The correspondence of John Locke. — Oxford : Clarendon. — (The Clarendon edition of the works of John Locke. The correspondence)
Vol.7: Letters nos.2665-3286. — Nov.1981. — [808]p
ISBN 0-19-824564-5 : £45.00 : CIP entry B81-30529

192 — English philosophy. Moore, G. E. — *Biographies*

Levy, Paul, *1941-*. Moore : G.E. Moore and the Cambridge Apostles / Paul Levy. — Oxford : Oxford University Press, 1981, c1979. — xv,335p,[8]p of plates : ports ; 21cm
Originally published: London : Weidenfeld and Nicolson, 1979. — Bibliography: p320-322. — Includes index
ISBN 0-19-281313-7 (pbk) : £3.95 : CIP rev. B81-00730

192 — English philosophy. Russell, Bertrand — *Biographies*

Clark, Ronald. Bertrand Russell : and his world / Ronald Clark. — [London] : Thames and Hudson, c1981. — 127p : ill,facsims,ports ; 24cm
Bibliography: p117. — Includes index
ISBN 0-500-13070-1 : £5.95 B81-29211

192 — English philosophy. Russell, Bertrand. Effects of World War 1

Vellacott, Jo. Bertrand Russell : and the pacifists in the First World War / Jo Vellacott. — Brighton : Harvester, 1980. — ix,326p ; 24cm
Bibliography: p.301-311. - Includes index
ISBN 0-7108-0050-9 : £28.50 : CIP rev. B81-07742

192 — English philosophy. Ryle, Gilbert — *Critical studies*

Lyons, William. Gilbert Ryle : an introduction to his philosophy / William Lyons. — Brighton : Harvester, 1980. — xi,215p ; 23cm. — ([Studies in philosophy] ; [no.21])
Bibliography: p202-209. - Inlcudes index
ISBN 0-85527-477-8 : £18.95 : CIP rev. B80-21341

192 — English philosophy — *Texts*

Anscombe, G. E. M.. From Parmenides to Wittgenstein / [G.E.M. Anscombe]. — Oxford : Blackwell, 1981. — xi,141p ; 24cm. — (The Collected philosophical papers of G.E.M. Anscombe ; v.1)
Includes index
ISBN 0-631-12922-7 : £10.00 B81-39947

Bealer, George. Quality and concept. — Oxford : Clarendon Press, Dec.1981. — [360]p. — (Clarendon library of logic and philosophy)
ISBN 0-19-824428-2 : £20.00 : CIP entry B81-31451

Berlin, Isaiah. Against the current : essays in the history of ideas / Isaiah Berlin ; edited and with a bibliography by Henry Hardy ; with an introduction by Roger Hausheèr. — Oxford : Oxford University Press, 1981, c1979. — liii,394p ; 20cm
Originally published: London : Hogarth Press, 1979. — Bibliography: p356-373. — Includes index
ISBN 0-19-283028-7 (pbk) : £3.95 : CIP rev. B81-11973

The **Cambridge** Platonists / edited by C.A. Patrides. — Cambridge : Cambridge University Press, 1980, c1969. — xxxii,343p : 1port ; 23cm
Originally published: London : Edward Arnold, 1969. — Includes index
ISBN 0-521-23417-4 (cased) : £17.50
ISBN 0-521-29942-x (pbk) : £5.50 B81-02791

Koestler, Arthur. Bricks to Babel : selected writings with comments by the author / Arthur Koestler. — London : Hutchinson, 1980. — 697p : ill ; 25cm
Bibliography: p687-688. — Includes index
ISBN 0-09-143670-2 : £12.50 : CIP rev.
Also classified at 823'.9'1[F] B80-22862

Williams, Bernard. Moral luck : philosophical papers 1973-1980. — Cambridge : Cambridge University Press, Nov.1981. — [192]p
ISBN 0-521-24372-6 (cased) : £16.50 : CIP entry
ISBN 0-521-28691-3 (pbk) : £5.95 B81-34006

Wittgenstein, Ludwig. Culture and value / Ludwig Wittgenstein ; edited by G.H. von Wright in collaboration with Heikki Nyman. — [Amended 2nd ed. with English translation] / translated by Peter Winch. — Oxford : Blackwell, 1980. — 94p ; 23cm
Parallel German text and English translation. — First t.p. in German. — Previous ed.: i.e. 2nd ed., published as Vermischte Bemerkungen: Frankfurt am Main : Suhrkamp, 1978. — Includes index
ISBN 0-631-12752-6 : £9.50 : CIP rev. B80-09959

Wittgenstein, Ludwig. Zettel / Ludwig Wittgenstein ; edited by G.E.M. Anscombe and G.H. von Wright ; translated by G.E.M. Anscombe. — 2nd ed. — Oxford : Blackwell, 1981. — v,138p ; 22cm. — (An Open University set book)
Translation of: Zettel. — Previous ed.: 1967. — Includes index
ISBN 0-631-12813-1 (cased) : £12.00
ISBN 0-631-12823-9 (pbk) : £4.95 B81-11471

192 — English philosophy — *Texts — Facsimiles*

Culverwel, Nathanael. An elegant and learned discourse of the light of nature, with other treatises : including Spiritual opticks, 1652 / Nathanael Culverwel. — New York ; London : Garland, 1978. — 212p ; 23cm. — (British philosophers and theologians of the 17th & 18th centuries)
Facsimile of: ed. printed by T.R. and E.M. for John Rothwell, London, 1652
ISBN 0-8240-1769-2 : Unpriced B81-27504

192 — English philosophy. Wittgenstein, Ludwig — *Critical studies*

Wittgenstein : to follow a rule / edited by Steven H. Holtzman and Christopher M. Leich. — London : Routledge & Kegan Paul, 1981. — xiii,250p ; 23cm. — (International library of philosophy)
Conference papers. — Includes index
ISBN 0-7100-0760-4 : £12.50 : CIP rev. B81-15934

Wittgenstein and his times. — Oxford : Blackwell, June 1981. — [144]p
ISBN 0-631-11161-1 : £7.95 : CIP entry B81-10483

192 — English philosophy. Wittgenstein, Ludwig — *Critical studies — Conference proceedings*

Perspectives on the philosophy of Wittgenstein. — Oxford : Blackwell, Sept.1981. — [256]p
Conference papers
ISBN 0-631-19550-5 : £9.50 : CIP entry B81-22617

192 — English philosophy. Wittgenstein, Ludwig — *Personal observations — Collections*

Ludwig Wittgenstein : personal recollections / edited by Rush Rhees. — Oxford : Blackwell, 1981. — x,235p ; 22cm
Includes index
ISBN 0-631-19600-5 : £9.95 B81-40050

192 — Irish philosophy — *Texts*

Boyle, Robert, *1627-1691.* Selected philosophical papers of Robert Boyle / edited with an introduction by M.A. Stewart. — Manchester : Manchester University Press, 1979. — xxxi,256p : ill ; 23cm. — (Philosophical classics)
Includes index
ISBN 0-7190-0681-3 : £12.00 : CIP rev. B79-20618

192 — Scottish philosophy, *1700-1840 — Critical studies*

Davie, George E.. The Scottish Enlightenment / George E. Davie. — London : Historical Association, c1981. — 36p ; 22cm. — (General series / Historical Association ; 99)
Bibliography: p35-36
ISBN 0-85278-238-1 (pbk) : Unpriced B81-32841

192 — Scottish philosophy. Hume, David — *Critical studies*

Passmore, John. Hume's intentions / John Passmore. — 3rd ed. — London : Duckworth, 1980. — x,183p ; 23cm
Previous ed.: 1968. — Bibliography: p.x. - Includes index
ISBN 0-7156-0918-1 : £15.00 : CIP rev. B80-00535

Stroud, Barry. Hume / Barry Stroud. — London : Routledge & Kegan Paul, 1977 (1981 printing). — xii,280p ; 24cm. — (The Arguments of the philosophers)
Bibliography: p271-276. — Includes index
ISBN 0-7100-0667-5 (pbk) : £5.95 B81-32467

192 — Scottish philosophy. McCosh, James — *Biographies*

Hoeveler, J. David. James McCosh and the Scottish intellectual tradition : from Glasgow to Princeton / J. David Hoeveler, Jr. — Princeton ; Guildford : Princeton University Press, c1981. — xiv,374p : ports ; 25cm
Bibliography: p351-359. — Includes index
ISBN 0-691-04670-0 : £13.70 B81-25264

192 — Scottish philosophy — *Texts*

Porteous, James A. A.. Man and the universe : the great questions / by James A.A. Porteous. — Dollar ([Park House, Dollar, FK17 7DW]) : [J.A.A. Porteous], 1981. — xiv,154p ; 21cm
Includes index
£6.95 B81-20919

193 — Austrian philosophy. Meinong, Alexius — *Critical studies*

Lindenfeld, David F.. The transformation of positivism : Alexius Meinong and European thought, 1880-1920 / David F. Lindenfeld. — Berkeley ; London : University of California Press, c1980. — xii,301p : 2ill ; 24cm
Bibliography: p271-292. — Includes index
ISBN 0-520-03994-7 : £15.00 B81-27268

193 — Europe. Hegelianism, *1805-1841*

Toews, John Edward. Hegelianism : The path toward dialectical humanism, 1805-1841 / John Edward Toews. — Cambridge : Cambridge University Press, 1980. — x,450p ; 24cm
Bibliography: p417-438. — Includes index
ISBN 0-521-23048-9 : £25.00 B81-16424

193 — German philosophy, *1945-1980 — Critical studies*

Bubner, Rüdiger. Modern German philosophy. — Cambridge : Cambridge University Press, Oct.1981. — [223]p
ISBN 0-521-22908-1 (cased) : £18.50 : CIP entry
ISBN 0-521-29711-7 (pbk) : £5.95 B81-31281

193 — German philosophy. Cassirer, Ernst, *1914-1933 — Critical studies*

Lipton, David R.. Ernst Cassirer : the dilemma of a liberal intellectual in Germany 1914-1933 / David R. Lipton. — Toronto ; London : University of Toronto Press, c1978. — xi,212p ; 24cm
Bibliography: p197-207. — Includes index
ISBN 0-8020-5408-0 : £10.50 B81-26262

193 — German philosophy. Hegel, Georg Wilhelm Friedrich — *Critical studies*

Lamb, David, *1942-*. Hegel : from foundation to system / by David Lamb. — The Hague ; London : Nijhoff, 1980. — xviii,234p ; 25cm. — (Martinus Nijhoff philosophy library ; v.1)
Bibliography: p229. — Includes index
ISBN 90-247-2359-0 : Unpriced B81-02807

Taylor, Mark C.. Journeys to selfhood : Hegel & Kierkegaard / Mark C. Taylor. — Berkeley ; London : University of California Press, c1980. — viii,298p ; 24cm
Bibliography: p277-290. — Includes index
ISBN 0-520-04167-4 : £12.50
Also classified at 198'.9 B81-27269

193 — German philosophy. Heidegger, Martin — *Critical studies*

Waterhouse, Roger. A Heidegger critique : a critical examination of the existential phenomenology of Martin Heidegger / Roger Waterhouse. — Brighton : Harvester, 1981. — xi,239p ; 23cm. — (Harvester philosophy now ; 15)
Bibliography: p217-221. — Includes index
ISBN 0-7108-0020-7 : £18.95 : CIP rev. B81-00731

193 — German philosophy. Husserl, Edmund — *Critical studies*

Landgrebe, Ludwig. The phenomenology of Edmund Hersserl : six essays / Ludwig Landgrebe ; edited with an introduction by Donn Welton. — Ithaca ; London : Cornell University Press, 1981. — 205p ; 22cm
Translations from the German. — Includes index
ISBN 0-8014-1177-7 : £13.75 B81-39762

193 — German philosophy. Jaspers, Karl — *Critical studies*

Olson, Alan M.. Transcendence and hermeneutics : an interpretation of the philosophy of Karl Jaspers / by Alan M. Olson. — The Hague ; London : Nijhoff, 1979. — xxiii,198p : 1ill ; 25cm. — (Studies in philosophy and religion ; v.2)
Bibliography: p193-195. - Includes index
ISBN 90-247-2092-3 : Unpriced B81-05859

193 — German philosophy. Leibniz, Gottfried Wilhelm von — *Critical studies*

Leibniz : metaphysics and philosophy of science. — Oxford : Oxford University Press, Dec.1981. — [200]p. — (Oxford readings in philosophy)
ISBN 0-19-875050-1 (pbk) : £3.95 : CIP entry B81-31458

193 — German philosophy. Marx, Karl — *Critical studies*

Wood, Allen W.. Karl Marx / Allen W. Wood. — London : Routledge & Kegan Paul, 1981. — 282p ; 25cm. — (The Arguments of the philosophers)
Bibliography: p270-275. - Includes index
ISBN 0-7100-0672-1 : £13.50 B81-07136

193 — German philosophy. Nietzsche, Friedrich — *Biographies*

Hayman, Ronald. Nietzsche : a critical life / Ronald Hayman. — London : Quartet, 1981, c1980. — xxiii,424p,[8]p of plates : ill,2facsims,ports ; 21cm
Originally published: London : Weidenfeld and Nicolson, 1980. — Bibliography: p403-410. — Includes index
ISBN 0-7043-3363-5 (pbk) : £4.95 : CIP rev. B81-14420

193 — German philosophy. Nietzsche, Friedrich — *Critical studies*

Heidegger, Martin. Nietzsche / Martin Heidegger ; translated from the German, with notes and analysis, by David Farrell Krell. — London : Routledge & Kegan Paul
Translation of: Nietzsche
Vol.1: The will to power as art. — 1981, c1979. — xvi,263p : 2facsims ; 23cm
ISBN 0-7100-0744-2 : £11.50 : CIP rev. B80-27767

Stern, J. P.. A study of Nietzsche. — Cambridge : Cambridge University Press, Dec.1981. — [220]p. — (Major European authors)
Originally published: 1979
ISBN 0-521-28380-9 (pbk) : £6.95 : CIP entry B81-32595

193 — German philosophy. Rosenzweig, Franz. Stern der Erlosung — *Critical studies*

Freund, Else-Rahel. Franz Rosenzweig's philosophy of existence : an analysis of the Star of redemption / by Else-Rahel Freund ; [translated into English from the German revised edition by Stephen L. Weinstein and Robert Israel] ; [edited by Paul R. Mendes-Flohr]. — The Hague ; London : Nijhoff, 1979. — viii,189p ; 25cm. — (Studies in philosophy and religion ; v.1)
Translation of: Die Existenzphilosophie Franz Rosenzweig. 2 durchgesehene Aufl.
ISBN 90-247-2091-5 : Unpriced B81-17097

193 — German philosophy. Schopenhauer, Arthur *— Critical studies*

Hamlyn, D. W.. Schopenhauer : the arguments of the philosophers / D.W. Hamlyn. — London : Routledge & Kegan Paul, 1980. — viii,181p ; 24cm. — (The Arguments of the philosophers)
Bibliography: p174-176. — Includes index
ISBN 0-7100-0522-9 : £9.75 : CIP rev. B80-26458

Schopenhauer : his philosophical achievement : edited by Michael Fox. — Brighton : Harvester, 1980. — xvii,276p ; 24cm
Bibliography: p262-268. -Includes index
ISBN 0-85527-788-2 : £25.00 : CIP rev. B80-09960

193 — German philosophy — *Texts*

Eckhart, *Meister*. Sermons & treatises. — Dulverton : Watkins
Translation of: Meister Eckhart, die deutschen Werke
Vol.2. — Oct.1981. — 1v.
ISBN 0-7224-0190-6 (pbk) : £7.00 : CIP entry B81-26699

Hegel, Georg Wilhelm Friedrich. Die Berliner Phänomenologie / G.W.F. Hegel ; Herausgegeben und Übersetzt mit einer Einleitung und Erläuterungen von M.J. Petry = The Berlin phenomenology / G.W.F. Hegel ; edited and translated with an introduction and explanatory notes by M.J. Petry. — Dordrecht ; London : Reidel, c1981. — cx,210p ; 25cm
Parallel German text and English translation, English introduction and notes. — Bibliography: pcix-cx. — Includes index
ISBN 90-277-1205-0 (cased) : Unpriced
ISBN 90-277-1208-5 (pbk) : Unpriced B81-27811

Leibniz, Gottfried Wilhelm. New essays on human understanding / G.W. Leibniz ; translated and edited by Peter Remnant and Jonathan Bennett. — Cambridge : Cambridge University Press, 1981. — xcvi,[404]p : 1facsim ; 24cm
Translation of: Nouveaux essais sur l'entendement humain. — Bibliography plxxxi-lxxxiii. — Includes index
ISBN 0-521-23147-7 (cased) : £28.00 : CIP rev.
ISBN 0-521-29836-9 (pbk) : £10.50 B81-07914

193 — Ideology. Theories of Marx, Karl

Parekh, Bhikhu. Marx's theory of ideology. — London : Croom Helm, Aug.1981. — [272]p
ISBN 0-7099-0045-7 : £13.95 : CIP entry B81-16372

193 — Philosophy. Idealism. Theories of Kant, Immanuel

Buroker, Jill Vance. Space and incongruence : the origin of Kant's idealism / Jill Vance Buroker. — Dordrecht ; London : Reidel, 1981. — vii,143p ; 23cm. — (Synthese historical library ; v.21)
Bibliography: p135-138. — Includes index
ISBN 90-277-1203-4 : Unpriced B81-23227

194 — French philosophy, *1933-1978 — Critical studies*

Descombes, Vincent. Modern French philosophy / Vincent Descombes ; translated by L. Scott-Fox and J.M. Harding. — Cambridge : Cambridge University Press, 1980. — xii,192p ; 23cm
Translation of: Le même et l'autre. — Includes index
ISBN 0-521-22837-9 (cased) : £14.50
ISBN 0-521-29672-2 (pbk) : £4.50 B81-09918

194 — French philosophy. Condillac, Étienne Bonnot de. Traité des systèmes — *Critical studies*

Hine, Ellen McNiven. A critical study of Condillac's Traité des systèmes / by Ellen McNiven Hine. — The Hague ; London : Nijhoff, 1979. — 226p ; 25cm. — (Archives internationales d'histoire des idées = International archives of the history of ideas ; 93)
Bibliography: p210-222. — Includes index
ISBN 90-247-2120-2 : Unpriced B81-07111

194 — French philosophy. Derrida, Jacques — *Critical studies*

Hartman, Geoffrey H.. Saving the text : literature, Derrida, philosophy / Geoffrey H. Hartman. — Baltimore ; London : Johns Hopkins University Press, c1981. — xxvii,184p : ill,facsims ; 24cm
Bibliography: p168-175. — Includes index
ISBN 0-8012-4524-9 : £7.75 B81-34335

194 — French philosophy. Foucault, Michel — *Critical studies*

Sheridan, Alan. Michel Foucault : the will to truth / Alan Sheridan. — London : Tavistock, 1980. — x,243p ; 21cm
Bibliography: p227-234. — Includes index
ISBN 0-422-77350-6 (cased) : £10.50
ISBN 0-422-76570-8 (pbk) : £4.50 B81-00732

194 — French philosophy. Rousseau, Jean-Jacques — *Correspondence, diaries, etc.* — *French texts*

Rousseau, Jean-Jacques. Correspondance complète de Jean Jacques Rousseau. — Éd. critique / établie et annotée par R.A. Leigh. — Oxford (Taylor Institution, [St. Giles, Oxford OX1 3NA]) : Voltaire Foundation
French text
T.37: Janvier 1769-avril 1770. — 1980. — xxiv,399p,[4]leaves of plates : facsims ; 24cm
Includes index
ISBN 0-7294-0262-2 : £32.00 B81-19375

194 — French philosophy. Rousseau, Jean-Jacques — *Critical studies* — *Festschriften*

Reappraisals of Rousseau : studies in honour of R.A. Leigh / Simon Harvey ... [et al.] editors. — Manchester : Manchester University Press, 1980. — viii,312p : 1port ; 23cm
Papers in French or English
ISBN 0-7190-0779-8 : £22.50 : CIP rev.
B80-04061

194 — French philosophy — *Texts*

Derrida, Jacques. Dissemination. — London : Athlone Press, Oct.1981. — [448]p
Translation of: Dissemination
ISBN 0-485-30005-2 : £20.00 : CIP entry
B81-28162

Derrida, Jacques. Writing and difference / Jacques Derrida ; [translated with an introduction and additional notes, by Alan Bass]. — London : Routledge & Kegan Paul, 1978 (1981 [printing]). — xx,342p ; 24cm
Translation of: L'écriture et la différence. — Bibliography: p341-342
ISBN 0-7100-0900-3 (pbk) : £4.95 B81-40821

Levinas, Emmanuel. Totality and infinity : an essay on exteriority / by Emmanuel Levinas ; translated by Alphonso Lingis. — The Hague ; London : Nijhoff, 1969 (1979 printing). — 307p ; 25cm. — (Martinus Nijhoff philosophy texts ; v.1)
Translation of: Totalité et infini
ISBN 90-247-2288-8 : Unpriced B81-13008

Vaysse, Jean. Toward awakening : an approach to the teaching left by Gurdjieff / Jean Vaysse. — London : Routledge & Kegan Paul, 1980. — v,170p ; 22cm
ISBN 0-7100-0715-9 (pbk) : £3.75 : CIP rev.
B80-20158

194 — French philosophy - *Texts - Correspondence, diaries, etc.*

Descartes, René. Philosophical letters. — Oxford : Blackwell, Aug.1981. — [288]p
These translations originally published: Oxford : Clarendon Press, 1970
ISBN 0-631-12818-2 (pbk) : £7.00 : CIP entry
B81-16930

194 — Structuralism. Theories of Lévi-Strauss, Claude

Clarke, Simon. The foundations of structuralism : a critique of Lévi-Strauss and the Structuralist movement / Simon Clarke. — [Brighton] : Harvester Press, 1981. — viii,264p ; 23cm. — ([Studies in philosophy ; no.17])
Bibliography: p255-264
ISBN 0-85527-978-8 : £20.00 B81-23066

195 — Italian philosophy. Ficino, Marsilio - *Correspondence, diaries, etc*

Ficino, Marsilio[Epistolae. *English*]. The letters of Marsilio Ficino. — London : Shepheard-Walwyn, July 1981
Vol.3. — [176]p
ISBN 0-85683-045-3 : £8.00 : CIP entry
B81-14449

195 — Italian philosophy. Gramsci, Antonio — *Critical studies*

Nemeth, Thomas. Gramsci's philosophy : a critical study / Thomas Nemeth. — Brighton : Harvester, 1980. — 206p ; 23cm. — ([Marxist theory and contemporary capitalism ; no.27])
Bibliography: p197-203. - Includes index
ISBN 0-85527-997-4 : £20.00 B81-04399

195 — Italian philosophy. Vico, Giambattista — *Critical studies*

Verene, Donald Phillip. Vico's science of imagination / Donald Phillip Verene. — Ithaca ; London : Cornell University Press, 1981. — 227p : 1facsim ; 22cm
Bibliography: p223-224. — Includes index
ISBN 0-8014-1391-5 : £13.75 B81-39763

196'.1 — Spain. Krausist movement, *to 1874*

López-Morillas, Juan. The Krausist movement and ideological change in Spain, 1854-1874 / Juan López-Morillas ; translated by Frances M. López-Morillas. — Cambridge : Cambridge University Press, 1981. — xix,152p ; 24cm. — (Cambridge Iberian and Latin American studies)
Translation of: El Krausismo español. 2nd ed. — Bibliography: p147-148. —Includes index
ISBN 0-521-23256-2 : £17.50 : CIP rev.
B81-10445

197'.2 — Russian philosophy. Gurdjieff, G. I. — *Critical studies*

Reyner, J. H.. Gurdjieff in action / J.H. Reyner. — London : Allen & Unwin, 1980. — ix,117p : ill ; 23cm
Bibliography: p113. - Includes index
ISBN 0-04-294117-2 : £5.50 : CIP rev.
B80-26459

Waldberg, Michel. Gurdjieff : an approach to his ideas / Michel Waldberg ; translated by Steve Cox. — London : Routledge & Kegan Paul, 1981. — xiii,158p : ill ; 22cm
Translation of: Gurdjieff. — Bibliography: p158
ISBN 0-7100-0811-2 (pbk) : £3.95 : CIP rev.
B81-13743

Walker, Kenneth, *1882-1966*. [A study of Gurdjieff's teaching]. Gurdjieff : a study of his teaching / Kenneth Walker. — London : Unwin Paperbacks, 1979, c1957. — 221p : ill ; 20cm. — (Mandala books)
Originally published: as A study of Gurdjieff's teaching. London : Cape, 1957. — Bibliography: p217. - Includes index
ISBN 0-04-294106-7 (pbk) : £2.50 : CIP rev.
B79-30490

197'.2 — Russian philosophy. Ouspensky, P. D. — *Biographies*

Reyner, J. H.. Ouspensky : the unsung genius / J.H. Reyner. — London : Allen & Unwin, 1981. — 115p : ill ; 23cm
Bibliography: p114
ISBN 0-04-294122-9 : Unpriced : CIP rev.
B81-19126

197'.2 — Russian philosophy — *Texts*

Gurdjieff, George. Life is real only then, when 'I am' / Gurdjieff. — 2nd ed. — London : Routledge & Kegan Paul, 1981, c1978. — xiv,177p : 1port ; 22cm. — (All and everything. 3rd series)
Translated from the Russian and Armenian. — Previous ed.: New York : privately printed by Dutton for Triangle, 1975
ISBN 0-7100-0887-2 : £6.95 B81-22935

Ouspensky, P. D.. Tertium Organum : the third canon of thought : a key to the enigmas of the world / P.D. Ouspensky ; revised translation by E. Kadloubovsky and the authors ; first translated from the Russian by Nicholas Bessaraboff and Claude Bragdon. — London : Routledge & Kegan Paul, 1981. — xvi,298p : ill ; 24cm
Translation of: Tertium Organum. — Includes index
ISBN 0-7100-0671-3 : £11.50 B81-10683

198'.9 — Danish philosophy. Kierkegaard, Søren. Correspondence & diaries — *Critical studies*

Fenger, Henning. Kierkegaard, the myths and their origins : studies in the Kierkegaardian papers and letters / Henning Fenger ; translated from the Danish by George C. Schoolfield. — New Haven ; London : Yale University Press, c1980. — xiv,233p ; 22cm
Translation of: Kierkegaard-myter og Kierkegaard-kilder. — Bibliography: p221-228. - Includes index
ISBN 0-300-02462-2 : £11.00 B81-06739

198'.9 — Danish philosophy. Kierkegaard, Søren — *Critical studies*

Taylor, Mark C.. Journeys to selfhood : Hegel & Kierkegaard / Mark C. Taylor. — Berkeley ; London : University of California Press, c1980. — viii,298p ; 24cm
Bibliography: p277-290. — Includes index
ISBN 0-520-04167-4 : £12.50
Primary classification 193 B81-27269

199'.492 — Dutch philosophy — *Texts*

Erasmus, Desiderius. Opera omnia Desiderii Erasmi Roterodami : recognita et adnotatione critica instructa notisque illustrata. — Amsterdam ; Oxford : North-Holland
Part 2
Vol.5. — 1981. — viii,345p : ill,facsims,port ; 27cm
ISBN 0-444-86189-0 : Unpriced
ISBN 0-444-86191-2 (set) : Unpriced
B81-39205

200 — RELIGION, CHRISTIANITY

200 — Children. Questions. Special subjects: Christianity. Answering — *Manuals* — *For parents*

Hughes, Jeremie. Questions children ask / Jeremie Hughes. — Tring : Lion, 1981. — 109p ; 18cm
Bibliography: p108-109
ISBN 0-85648-323-0 (pbk) : £1.50 B81-19672

200 — Christianity

Carter, Sydney. Dance in the dark / Sydney Carter. — London : Collins : Fount, 1980. — 158p : ill ; 19cm
ISBN 0-00-625866-2 (pbk) : £1.50 B81-02041

Chudley, Albert. The listening crowd / by Albert Chudley. — Fairford (61 Aldsworth Close, Fairford, Glos.) : John Chudley, 1980. — vi,57p ; 22cm
Unpriced (pbk) B81-06950

Dyer, R. J.. The friendly universe / R.J. Dyer. — Bognor Regis : New Horizon, c1980. — 31p ; 22cm
ISBN 0-86116-198-x : £5.75 B81-22433

Green, Michael, *1930-*. What is Christianity? / Michael Green. — Tring : Lion Publishing, 1981. — 59p : ill(some col.) ; 29cm
Ill on lining papers
ISBN 0-85648-251-x : £4.95 B81-40224

Lewis, C. S.. Christian reflections / C.S. Lewis ; edited by Walter Hooper. — [London] : Collins : Fount Paperbacks, 1981, c1980. — 219p ; 18cm
Originally published: London : Bles, 1967
ISBN 0-00-625870-0 (pbk) : £1.50 B81-12011

Priestland, Gerald. Yours faithfully : collected radio talks / Gerald Priestland. — London : Collins
Vol.2. — 1981. — 172p ; 18cm
ISBN 0-00-626102-7 (pbk) : £1.25 B81-10853

Wilson, Bruce. The human journey : Christianity and modern consciousness / Bruce Wilson. — Sutherland, N.S.W. : Albatross Books ; Tring : Lion, c1980. — 318p : ill ; 18cm. — (An Albatross book)
ISBN 0-85648-333-8 (pbk) : £1.95 B81-09900

200 — Christianity *compared with* **Buddhism** — *Philosophical perspectives*

Smart, Ninian. Beyond ideology. — London : Collins, Sept.1981. — [350]p
ISBN 0-00-215846-9 : £7.95 : CIP entry
Also classified at 294.3 B81-20622

200 — Christianity *compared with* **Hinduism**

Panikkar, Raimundo. The unknown Christ of Hinduism : towards an ecumenical Christophany / Raimundo Panikkar. — Rev. and enl. ed. — London : Darton, Longman & Todd, c1981. — xii,195p ; 22cm
Previous ed.: 1965. — Bibliography: p170-182. - Includes index
ISBN 0-232-51496-8 (pbk) : £5.95 : CIP rev.
Primary classification 294.5 B80-24024

200 — Christianity — *Conference proceedings*

Lausanne Consultation on Gospel and Culture *(1978 : Willowbank, Bermuda).* Down to earth : studies in Christianity and culture : the papers of the Lausanne Consultation on Gospel and Culture / edited by John Stott and Robert T. Coote. — London : Hodder and Stoughton, 1981. — x,342p : ill ; 21cm
ISBN 0-340-23263-3 (pbk) : £4.95 B81-33131

200 — Christianity — *For African students*

Teacher's handbook for Developing in Christ. Course one : Christ and my humanity (units 1 to 13) / prepared by teachers throughout Africa and written at The AMECEA Pastoral Institute. — London : Chapman, 1981. — 198p : ill ; 25cm
ISBN 0-225-66298-1 (pbk) : £5.85 : CIP rev. B81-08868

200 — Christianity - *For African students - For schools*

Developing in Christ. — London : Chapman, Oct.1981
Course 2: Teacher's handbook. — [198]p
ISBN 0-225-66299-x (pbk) : £5.50 : CIP entry B81-08867

200 — Christianity *related to* **Ancient Greek myths**

Capel, Evelyn Francis. The making of Christianity and the Greek spirit / Evelyn Francis Capel. — Edinburgh : Floris, 1980. — 125p ; 22cm
ISBN 0-903540-37-1 (pbk) : £4.95 : CIP rev.
Primary classification 292'.13 B80-17543

200 — Christianity *related to* **Buddhism**

Johnston, William, *1925-*. The mirror mind : spirituality and transformation / William Johnston. — London : Collins, 1981. — x,181p : ill ; 22cm
Includes index
ISBN 0-00-215531-1 : £5.95
Also classified at 294.3 B81-32310

200 — Christianity *related to* **Islam**

Dialogue between Christians and Muslims. — Leicester (223 London Rd., Leicester LE2 1ZE) : Islamic Foundation. — (Documents on Christianity and Christian Muslim relations ; no.1)
3: Dialogue between Christians and Muslims : statements and resolutions / edited by Ahmad von Denffer. — 1980. — 45p ; 30cm
ISBN 0-86037-062-3 (pbk) : Unpriced
Also classified at 297 B81-16790

200 — Christianity — *Topics for discussion groups*

Leigh, Moira. Teenagers talking again / Moira Leigh. — Pinner (125 Waxwell La., Pinner, Middx. HA5 3ER) : Grail, c1980. — 32p : ill ; 25cm
ISBN 0-901829-55-2 (pbk) : £1.20 B81-07231

200 — Religion

Zaehner, R. C.. The city within the heart / R.C. Zaehner. — London : Unwin Paperbacks, 1980. — 153p ; 20cm. — (Mandala books)
Includes index
ISBN 0-04-200033-5 (pbk) : £2.50 : CIP rev. B79-33903

200 — Religion — *For schools*

Bruce, Ray. Beginning religion. — London : Edward Arnold, Sept.1981. — [96]p
ISBN 0-7131-0571-2 (pbk) : £2.00 : CIP entry B81-22487

200 — Religion - *For schools*

Collinson, Celia. Believers. — London : Edward Arnold, June 1981. — [128]p
ISBN 0-7131-0525-9 (pbk) : £1.95 : CIP entry B81-14835

200 — Religions

Hopfe, Lewis M.. Religions of the world / Lewis M. Hopfe. — 2nd ed. — Encino : Glencoe Publishing ; London : Collier Macmillan, 1979. — xiii,368p : ill,1 map,ports ; 23cm
Previous ed.: 1976. — Text on inside cover. — Includes bibliographies and index
ISBN 0-02-474820-x (pbk) : £6.25 B81-03471

Langley, Myrtle S.. Religions : a book of beliefs / Myrtle Langley. — Tring : Lion, 1981. — 61p : ill(some col.),maps ; 29cm
Text and ill on lining papers
ISBN 0-85648-319-2 : £3.95 B81-23407

200 — Religions — *For schools*

Cole, W. Owen. Five religions in the twentieth century / W. Owen Cole. — Amersham : Hulton, 1981. — 254p : ill,maps,facsims,plans,ports,1geneal.table ; 24cm
Includes bibliographies and index
ISBN 0-7175-0883-8 (pbk) : £2.85 B81-19538

200'.1 — Religion. Faith — *Philosophical perspectives*

Evans, Donald, *1927-*. Faith, authenticity, and morality / Donald Evans. — Edinburgh (33 Montgomery St., Edinburgh EH7 5JX) : Handsel, 1980. — xiii,298p : 3ill ; 24cm
Includes index
ISBN 0-905312-12-0 : Unpriced B81-00733

Swinburne, Richard. Faith and reason. — Oxford : Oxford University Press, Dec.1981. — [264]p
ISBN 0-19-824663-3 : £16.00 : CIP entry B81-31453

200'.1 — Religion — *Philosophical perspectives*

Thakur, Shivesh Chandra. Religion and rational choice / Shivesh Chandra Thakur. — London : Macmillan, 1981. — 122p ; 23cm
Includes index
ISBN 0-333-27419-9 : £15.00 B81-38718

200'.1 — Religious beliefs. Development

Slater, Peter, *1934-*. The dynamics of religion : continuity and change in patterns of faith / Peter Slater. — London : SCM, 1979, c1978. — xiv,206p : ill ; 22cm
Originally published: San Francisco : Harper and Row, 1978. — Bibliography: p201-202. — Includes index
ISBN 0-334-00342-3 (pbk) : £3.95 B81-06176

200'.14 — Religions. Terminology

Bishop, Peter D.. Words in world religions / Peter D. Bishop. — London : SCM Press, 1979. — viii,152p ; 22cm
Includes bibliographies and index
ISBN 0-334-01804-8 (pbk) : £2.95 B81-15619

200'.1'4 — Religious language. Secularisation

Fenn, Richard K.. Liturgies and trials. — Oxford : Blackwell, Sept.1981. — [208]p
ISBN 0-631 12786-0 : £9.50 : CIP entry B81-22628

200'.7'1041 — Great Britain. Schools. Curriculum subjects: Religion

New movements in religious education / edited by Ninian Smart & Donald Horder. — London : Temple Smith, 1975 (1980 [printing]). — 271p ; 22cm
Bibliography: p269
ISBN 0-85117-144-3 (pbk) : £4.50 B81-05802

200'.7'1042177 — London. Bexley *(London Borough).* **Schools. Curriculum subjects: Religious education**

Bexley. *Directorate of Education*. Agreed syllabus for religious education / Bexley London Borough. — Crayford (Town Hall, Crayford [DA1 4EN]) : Directorate of Education, [1981]. — [16]p ; 21cm
ISBN 0-9507491-0-9 (pbk) : Unpriced B81-29937

200'.7'104226 — West Sussex. Schools. Curriculum subjects: Religion. Syllabuses: Agreed Syllabus

Wilson-Voke, Maurice. The debate on the agreed syllabus of religious education in West Sussex 1979-1980 / Maurice Wilson-Voke. — Chichester (Larkspur, Cambrai Ave., Chichester PO19 2LB) : M. Wilson-Voke, 1981. — 42p : 2ill ; 21cm
ISBN 0-9507413-0-2 (pbk) : Unpriced B81-10661

200'.7'104226 — West Sussex. Schools. Curriculum subjects: Religion. Syllabuses. Controversies, *1979-1981*

Wilson-Voke, Maurice. The debate on religious education in West Sussex, 1979-1981 : a retrospective view / Maurice Wilson-Voke. — [Chichester] ([Larkspur, Cambrai Ave., Chichester, W. Sussex PO19 2LB]) : [M. Wilson-Voke], [1981]. — 4leaves ; 29cm
Unpriced (unbound) B81-16113

200'.92'4 — Religion. Theories of Harmann, Johann Georg

German, Terence J.. Harmann on language and religion. — Oxford : Oxford University Press, Oct.1981. — [216]p. — (Oxford theological monographs)
ISBN 0-19-826717-7 : £12.50 : CIP entry
Also classified at 400'.92'4 B81-26752

200'.92'4 — Religion. Theories of Marx, Karl

Ling, Trevor. Karl Marx and religion : in Europe and India / Trevor Ling. — London : Macmillan, 1980. — viii,168p ; 23cm
Includes index
ISBN 0-333-27683-3 (cased) : £9.00 : CIP rev.
ISBN 0-333-27684-1 (pbk) : £3.95 B80-00032

200'.94 — Western Europe. Religion, *1789-1970*

McLeod, Hugh. Religion and the people of Western Europe 1789-1970. — Oxford : Oxford University Press, Sept.1981. — [160]p. — (OPUS)
ISBN 0-19-289101-4 (cased) : £6.50 : CIP entry
ISBN 0-19-215832-5 (pbk) : £3.95 B81-22609

200'.9931 — New Zealand. Religions

Colless, Brian. Religion in New Zealand society / Brian Colless & Peter Donovan. — Edinburgh : T. & T. Clark, 1980. — 215p ; 22cm
Bibliography: p195-203. — Includes index
ISBN 0-567-09303-4 : £6.95 B81-02296

202 — CHRISTIANITY. MISCELLANY

202'.4372 — Christianity — *For primary school teaching in Nigeria*

All God's children : religious knowledge for primary schools / Northern Education Advisory Council. — London : Evans
Bk.4. — 1981. — viii,168p : ill ; 22cm
ISBN 0-237-50436-7 (pbk) : Unpriced B81-23538

All God's children : religious knowledge for primary schools / Northern Education Advisory Council. — London : Evans
Bk.6. — 1981. — 184p : ill,maps ; 22cm
ISBN 0-237-50627-0 (pbk) : Unpriced B81-37701

205 — CHRISTIANITY. SERIALS

205 — Christianity — *For students* — *Serials*

Cubit : the Christian magazine for students. — Autumn 1980-. — Leicester (38 De Montfort St., Leicester LE1 7GP) : Universities and Colleges Christian Fellowship, 1980-. — v. : ill ; 31cm
Three issues yearly. — Contintues: CU news
ISSN 0260-2202 = Cubit : £0.25 per issue B81-09026

205 — Christianity — *Serials*

The **Scottish** Evangelical Theology Society bulletin. — No.1-. — [Mallaig] ([c/o A. McGowan, The Manse, Mallaig, Inverness-shire]) : [The Society], [1981-]. — v. ; 21cm
Continues: Scottish Tyndale bulletin
ISSN 0262-1053 = Scottish Evangelical Theology Society bulletin : Unpriced B81-39742

205 — Christianity — *Serials* — *For families*

[Family *(London : 1980)*]. Family. — Sept.1980-. — London : Family Christian Ministries, 1980-. — v. : ill ; 28cm
Monthly. — Absorbed: Life of faith monthly, 1980
ISSN 0144-7696 = Family (London. 1980) : £7.38 per year B81-03296

207 — CHRISTIANITY. STUDY AND TEACHING

207 — Christian religious education

Groome, Thomas H.. Christian religious education : sharing our story and vision / Thomas H. Groome. — San Francisco ; London : Harper & Row, 1980. — xvii,296p ; 25cm
Bibliography: p279-290. — Includes index
ISBN 0-06-063491-x : £6.95 B81-30798

Sutcliffe, J. M.. Learning and teaching together / by John M. Sutcliffe. — London : Chester House, 1980. — 128p : ill ; 22cm
ISBN 0-7150-0078-0 (pbk) : Unpriced B81-20878

207 — Christian religious education — *Serials*

Theological education today. — Vo.6, no.1 (Feb.1976)-. — Castel : World Evangelical Fellowship Theological Commission, 1976-. — v. ; 21cm
Quarterly. — Continues: Programming
ISSN 0260-3721 = Theological education today : Unpriced B81-06703

207'.041 — Great Britain. Children. Christian religious education — *Inquiry reports*

Understanding Christian nurture / British Council of Churches. — [London] : The Council, 1981. — viii,104p ; 21cm
Text on inside cover
ISBN 0-85169-085-8 (pbk) : £3.00 B81-40687

207'.041 — Great Britain. Education. Curriculum subjects: Christianity — *Serials*

[Crosscurrent *(London)*]Crosscurrent. — No.1 (Jan.1980)-. — London (Church House, Dean's Yard, Westminster SW1P 3NZ) : National Society in conjunction with the General Synod Board of Education, 1980-. — v. : ill ; 30cm
Three issues yearly
ISSN 0260-6313 = Crosscurrent (London) : £1.00 per year (free to Society members) B81-04497

207'.1 — Schools. Christian religious education. Activities — *For Christian students* — *Serials*

IS annual / [Inter-School Christian Fellowship]. — [No. 1]-. — London (130 City Rd, EC1V 2NJ) : ISCF, 1980-. — v. : ill ; 30cm
Continues: IS magazine
ISSN 0261-1325 = IS annual : £0.40 B81-15289

207'.122 — Catholic secondary schools. Religious education. Teaching

George, Barbara. How can you teach religion?! : suggestion for R.E. in secondary schools / Barbara George. — Leigh-on-Sea : Mayhew, c1978. — 283p : ill ; 21cm
ISBN 0-905725-47-6 (pbk) : £3.75 B81-40406

207'.41 — Great Britain. Schools. Christian religious education — *For teaching*

Enrichment / editor Danny Sullivan. — London : Christian Education Movement, c1981. — 32p : ill ; 26cm. — (CEM primary resource for religious education, ISSN 0308-4523)
Unpriced (pbk) B81-12449

207'.42961 — Dyfed. Lampeter. Theological colleges: Saint David's University College. Organisation structure, *to 1971*

Thomas, J. R. Lloyd. Moth or phoenix? : St. Davids College and the University of Wales and the University Grants Committee / J.R. Lloyd Thomas. — [Llandysul] : Gomer, 1980. — 197p,[4]p of plates : ill ; 22cm
Includes index
ISBN 0-85088-503-5 : £3.50 B81-05285

207'.4933 — Belgium. Louvain. Theological colleges: St Anthony's College, *to 1977*

Conlan, Patrick. St Anthony's College of the Irish Franciscans Louvain : 1927-1977, 1607-1977. — Dublin (4 Merchant's Quay, Dublin 8) : Assisi Press, c1977. — 60p : ill,1plan,ports ; 21cm
Cover title. — Author: Patrick Conlan. — Plan on inside cover. — Bibliography: p56
£0.60 (pbk) B81-25921

207'.6 — Africa. Christian religious education

Megill, Esther L.. Education in the African church / Esther L. Megill. — Rev. ed. — London : Geoffrey Chapman, 1981. — 222p ; 22cm
Previous ed.: 1976. — Bibliography: p213-222
ISBN 0-225-66280-9 (pbk) : Unpriced : CIP rev. B80-35632

209 — CHRISTIANITY. HISTORICAL AND GEOGRAPHICAL TREATMENT

209 — Christianity, *to 1970*

Wilken, Robert L.. The myth of Christian beginnings / Robert L. Wilken. — London : SCM, 1979, c1971. — x,218p ; 22cm
Originally published: Garden City, N.Y. : Doubleday, 1971
ISBN 0-334-01064-0 (pbk) : £2.95 B81-03634

209 — Christianity, *to 1980*

The **Christian** world : a social and cultural history of Christianity / texts by Geoffrey Barraclough ... [et al.] ; edited by Geoffrey Barraclough. — London : Thames and Hudson, c1981. — 328p : ill(some col.),maps,facsims,ports(some col.)
Ill on lining papers. — Bibliography: p313-317. — Includes index
ISBN 0-500-25076-6 : £16.00 B81-40184

Dowley, Tim. The story of Christianity / Tim Dowley. — Tring : Lion, 1981. — 63p : ill (some col.),1col.map,1facsim,ports ; 29cm
Ill on lining papers
ISBN 0-85648-245-5 : £3.95 B81-14734

209'.2'2 — Christians, *1839-1968* — *Biographies* — *For children*

Tallach, John. They shall be mine / John Tallach ; illustrated by Lawrence Littleton Evans. — Edinburgh : Banner of Truth Trust, 1981. — 128p : ill ; 22cm
Bibliography: p127-128
ISBN 0-85151-320-4 (pbk) : £1.95 B81-36441

209'.2'2 — Christians, *1900-1980* — *Biographies*

Jessey, Cornelia. Profiles in hope / Cornelia Jessey. — Dublin : Veritas Publications, 1978. — 173p ; 19cm
ISBN 0-905092-22-8 (pbk) : £1.70 B81-06179

209'.2'2 — Great Britain. Christians, *1150-1970* — *Biographies*

Davis, H. Colin. Twelve good men and true / H. Colin Davis. — London : British Broadcasting Corporation, 1981. — 96p : 1ill,ports ; 20cm
ISBN 0-563-17898-1 (pbk) : £2.25 B81-18261

209'.2'4 — Christianity. Theories of Kierkegaard, Søren

Elrod, John W.. Kierkegaard and Christendom / John W. Elrod. — Princeton ; Guildford : Princeton University Press, c1981. — xxiv,320p ; 23cm
Bibliography: pxxii-xxiv. — Includes index
ISBN 0-691-07261-2 : £13.20 B81-28434

209'.2'4 — Theology. Barth, Karl — *Correspondence, diaries, etc*

Barth, Karl. Letters 1961-1968 / Karl Barth ; edited by Jürgen Fangmeier and Hinrich Stoevesandt ; translated and edited by Geoffrey W. Bromiley. — Edinburgh : T. & T. Clark, 1981. — xv,382p ; 24cm
Translation of: Karl Barth : Briefe, 1961-1968. — Originally published: Grand Rapids : Eerdmans, 1981. — Includes index
ISBN 0-567-09321-2 : £8.95 B81-28261

209'.361 — Great Britain. Christianity, *to 500*

Thomas, Charles, *1928-*. Christianity in Roman Britain to AD 500 / Charles Thomas. — London : Batsford Academic and Educational, c1981. — 408p,8p of plates : ill,maps,plans ; 24cm
Bibliography: p356-356. - Includes index
ISBN 0-7134-1442-1 : £14.95 B81-10720

209'.427'8 — Cumbria. Christianity, *to 1980*

Widdup, Henry L.. The story of Christianity in Cumbria : a geographical appraisal / by Henry L. Widdup ; with a foreword by the Lord Bishop of Carlisle. — Kendal ([28 Highgate, Kendal, Cumbria]) : Titus Wilson, 1981. — xi,146p : ill,maps ; 21cm
Bibliography: p140-141. - Includes index
ISBN 0-900811-13-7 (pbk) : Unpriced B81-11331

209'.66 — West Africa. Christianity, *to 1978*

The **History** of Chistianity in West Africa / edited and introduced by O.U. Kalu. — London : Longman, 1980. — 378p : 1map ; 22cm
Includes index
ISBN 0-582-64693-6 (cased) : Unpriced : CIP rev.
ISBN 0-582-60359-5 (pbk) : unpriced B79-36155

210 — NATURAL THEOLOGY

211'.6'06041 — Great Britain. Secularism. Organisations: National Secular Society — *Serials*

National Secular Society. Annual report / National Secular Society Ltd.. — 1979-80. — London (702 Holloway Rd, N19 3NL) : The Society, [1980]. — 13p
Unpriced B81-10251

212'.1 — God. Existence

Scully, David. God and reason : a survey of the arguments / by David Scully. — London (2 Chester House, Pages La., N10 1PR) : Christian Education Movement, c1980. — 72p : 1ill ; 22cm. — (CEM student theology series)
ISBN 0-905022-66-1 (pbk) : Unpriced B81-05810

212'.1 — God. Existence - *Philosophical perspectives*

Ward, Keith. Rational theology and the creativity of God. — Oxford : Blackwell, July 1981. — [176]p
ISBN 0-631-12597-3 : £9.95 : CIP entry B81-14877

213 — Evolution. Theories — *Christian viewpoints*

Andrews, E. H.. God, science & evolution / E.H. Andrews. — Welwyn : Evangelical Press, 1980. — 129p ; 22cm
ISBN 0-85234-146-6 (pbk) : £1.75 B81-23047

215 — Religion, *related to* **science**

Burhoe, Ralph Wendell. Toward a scientific theology. — Belfast : Christian Journals, Apr.1981. — [228]p
ISBN 0-904302-70-9 : £5.95 : CIP entry B81-07452

215 — Religion *related to* **science**

Nebelsick, Harold P.. Theology and science in mutual modification. — Belfast : Christian Journals, Dec.1981. — [192]p. — (Theology and scientific culture ; v.2)
ISBN 0-904302-76-8 : £9.50 : CIP entry B81-36989

Roy, Rustum. Experimenting with truth : the fusion of religion with technology, needed for humanity's survival / Rustum Roy. — Oxford : Pergamon, 1981. — xiii,200p : ill ; 24cm. — (Pergamon international library) (The Hibbert lectures for 1979)
Includes index
ISBN 0-08-025820-4 (cased) : Unpriced : CIP rev.
ISBN 0-08-025819-0 (pbk) : £6.00 B80-26460

220 — BIBLE

220 — Bible. Aphorisms - *Critical studies*

Williams, James G.. Those who ponder proverbs : aphoristic thinking and Biblical literature. — Sheffield (24 Tapton Crescent Rd, Sheffield S10 5DA) : Almond Press, June 1981. — [128]p. — (Bible and literature series, ISSN 0206-4493 ; 2)
ISBN 0-907459-02-1 (cased) : £14.95 : CIP entry
ISBN 0-907459-03-x (pbk) : £5.95 B81-11953

220 — Bible — *Topics for discussion groups*

Christ every day : Christian Endeavour topics. — [Royal Leamington Spa] ([18 Leam Terrace, Royal Leamington Spa, Warwickshire CV31 1BB]) : Christian Endeavour Union of Great Britain and Ireland, [1981]. — 63p ; 19cm. — (General topic book)
For young people's, young adults' and senior C.E. grades. — Cover title
£1.20 (pbk) B81-40522

Christ every day : Christian Endeavour topics. — [Royal Leamington Spa] ([18 Leam Terrace, Royal Leamington Spa, Warwickshire CV31 1BB]) : Christian Endeavour Union of Great Britain and Ireland, [1981]. — 66p : ill ; 19cm. — (Junior topic book)
For junior C.E. grades. — Cover title
Unpriced (pbk) B81-40525

"**Rise** up & build". — [Royal Leamington Spa] ([18 Leam Terrace, Royal Leamington Spa, Warwickshire CV31 1BB]) : Christian Endeavour Union of Great Britain and Ireland, [1981]. — 62p : ill ; 19cm. — (Junior topic book)
For junior C.E. grades. — Cover title
Unpriced (pbk) B81-40526

"**Rise** up & build". — [Royal Leamington Spa] ([18 Leam Terrace, Royal Leamington Spa, Warwickshire CV31 1BB]) : Christian Endeavour Union of Great Britain and Ireland, [1981]. — 69p ; 19cm. — (General topic book)
For young people's, young adults' and senior C.E. grades. — Cover title. — Includes index
Unpriced (pbk) B81-40527

220 — Bible — *Topics for discussion groups — For children*

Jesus Christ : the way, the truth and the life : Christian Endeavour junior topics. — [Royal Leamington Spa] ([18 Leam Terrace, Royal Leamington Spa, Warwickshire CV31 1BB]) : Christian Endeavour Union of Great Britain and Ireland, [1981]. — 53p : ill ; 19cm. — (Junior topic book)
For junior C.E. grades. — Cover title
Unpriced (pbk) B81-40523

Jesus Christ : the way, the truth and the life : Christian Endeavour general topics. — [Royal Leamington Spa] ([18 Leam Terrace, Royal Leamington Spa, Warwickshire CV31 1BB]) : Christian Endeavour Union of Great Britain and Ireland, [1981]. — 56p : ill,1map ; 18cm. — (General topic book)
For young people's, young adults' and senior C.E. guides. — Cover title
Unpriced (pbk) B81-40524

220 — Society. Role of Bible

The **Bible** in perspective. — London : Bible Society, 1981. — 82p ; 18cm
" ... text of this book was originally given as the Olivier Beguin Memorial Lectures for the years 1978, 1979, 1976 and 1975 respectively ..." — title page verso
ISBN 0-564-07052-1 (pbk) : Unpriced
B81-35171

220'.014 — Bible. Language. Semantics

Gibson, Arthur. Biblical semantic logic : a preliminary analysis / Arthur Gibson. — Oxford : Blackwell, 1981. — xi,244p ; 24cm
Includes index
ISBN 0-631-12515-9 : £12.00 B81-39957

220'.014 — Bible. Words — *Dictionaries*

Turner, Nigel. Christian words / by Nigel Turner. — Edinburgh : Clark, 1980. — xvii,513p ; 23cm
English text, index in Greek. — Includes index
ISBN 0-567-09301-8 : Unpriced B81-07016

Vine, W. E.. Expository dictionary of Old and New Testament words. — London : Marshall Morgan & Scott, Sept.1981. — [1504]p
ISBN 0-551-00913-6 : £13.95 : CIP entry
B81-28339

220'.06'01 — Bible societies: Trinitarian Bible Society, *to 1981*

Brown, Andrew J.. The word of God among all nations : a brief history of the Trinitarian Bible Society 1831-1981 / Andrew J. Brown. — London (217 Kingston Rd., SW19 3NN) : The Society, 1981. — xi,162p,[15]p of plates : ill,ports ; 22cm
Bibliography: p150. — Includes index
Unpriced (pbk) B81-26857

220'.07 — Bible study

Basics : introduction to Bible reading and prayer. — Rev.. — London : Scripture Union, 1980, c1964. — 16p : ill ; 15cm
Previous ed.: i.e. rev. ed. 1970
ISBN 0-85421-042-3 (pbk) : Unpriced
Also classified at 248.3'2 B81-17201

Sherrill, John. My friend, the Bible / John Sherrill. — London : Hodder and Stoughton, 1979, c1978 (1981 [printing]). — 155p ; 18cm. — (Hodder Christian paperbacks)
Originally published: Lincoln, Va : Chosen Books, 1978
ISBN 0-340-26708-9 (pbk) : £1.50 B81-17846

220'.076 — Bible — *Questions & answers*

Chapman, Roy, *1930-*. Bible quizzes / compiled by Roy Chapman. — Redhill : National Christian Education Council, 1981. — 32p ; 21cm
ISBN 0-7197-0294-1 (pbk) : £0.70 B81-29162

Parker, R. G. The God whom we worship : a home study course of three lessons based on the Holy Bible / prepared by R.G. Parker. — Birmingham (47 Woodbridge Rd., Mosley, Birmingham B13 9DZ) : R.G. Parker, [1981?]. — 7leaves ; 30cm
Unpriced (unbound) B81-40300

220.1'3 — Bible. Inspiration

Abraham, William J.. The divine inspiration of Holy Scripture / William J. Abraham. — Oxford : Oxford University Press, 1981. — 126p ; 22cm
Includes index
ISBN 0-19-826659-6 : £9.50 : CIP rev.
B81-25664

220.1'3 — Bible. Inspiration & authority

Anderson, Norman. God's word for God's world / Norman Anderson. — London : Hodder and Stoughton, 1981. — 144p ; 20cm. — (Ecclesia books)
Includes index
ISBN 0-340-26569-8 (pbk) : £3.25 : CIP rev.
B81-12353

220.3'21 — Bible — *Encyclopaedias*

The **Illustrated** Bible dictionary / revision editor N. Hillyer ; consulting editors F.F. Bruce ... [et al.] ; additional consulting editors for the revised edition D. Guthrie, A.R. Millard ; consulting editor for illustrations A.R. Millard, J.P. Kane, K.A. Kitchen. — Leicester : Inter-Varsity, 1980. — 3v.(xvi,1728p) : ill(some col.),maps(some col.),facsims(some col.),plans (some col.),geneal.tables(some col.) ; 26cm
Includes bibliographies and index
ISBN 0-85110-627-7 : £41.85
ISBN 0-85110-628-5 (v.2) : £13.95
ISBN 0-85110-629-3 (v.3) : £13.95 B81-09241

220.5 — Bible. Translation

Sheehan, Bob. Which version now? / by Bob Sheehan. — Haywards Heath (5 Fairford Close, Haywards Heath, Sussex RH16 3EF) : Carey, [1981?]. — 32p ; 22cm
Cover title
£0.80 (pbk) B81-17938

220.5'2 — Bible. *English. New International. Selections — Texts*

[**Bible**. *English. New International. Selections. 1980*]. God / [selections by Norman Warren] ; [photographs by Gordon Gray and Gill Rennie]. — London : Ark, 1980. — [24]p : col.ill ; 10cm. — (Basics)
Cover title
ISBN 0-86201-063-2 (pbk) : £0.25 B81-08003

[**Bible**. *English. New International. Selections. 1980*]. Jesus Christ / [selections by Norman Warren] ; [photographs by Gordon Gray and Gill Rennie]. — London : Ark, 1980. — [24]p : col.ill ; 10cm. — (Basics)
Cover title
ISBN 0-86201-064-0 (pbk) : £0.25 B81-08000

[**Bible**. *English. New International. Selections. 1980*]. The Holy Spirit / [selections by Norman Warren] ; [photographs by Gordon Gray and Gill Rennie]. — London : Ark, 1980. — [24]p : col.ill ; 10cm. — (Basics)
Cover title
ISBN 0-86201-065-9 (pbk) : £0.25 B81-07997

[**Bible**. *English. New International. Selections. 1980*]. Man / [selections by Norman Warren] ; [photographs by Gordon Gray and Gill Rennie]. — London : Ark, 1980. — [24]p : col.ill ; 10cm. — (Basics)
Cover title
ISBN 0-86201-066-7 (pbk) : £0.25 B81-07998

[**Bible**. *English. New International. Selections. 1980*]. Salvation / [selections by Norman Warren] ; [photographs by Gordon Gray and Gill Rennie]. — London : Ark, 1980. — [24]p : col.ill ; 10cm. — (Basics)
Cover title
ISBN 0-86201-067-5 (pbk) : £0.25 B81-07999

[**Bible**. *English. New International. Selections. 1980*]. Forgiveness / [selections by Norman Warren] ; [photographs by Gordon Gray and Gill Rennie]. — London : Ark, 1980. — [24]p : col.ill ; 10cm. — (Basics)
Cover title
ISBN 0-86201-068-3 (pbk) : £0.25 B81-08002

[**Bible**. *English. New International. Selections. 1980*]. The church / [selections by Norman Warren] ; [photographs by Gordon Gray and Gill Rennie]. — London : Ark, 1980. — [24]p : col.ill ; 10cm. — (Basics)
Cover title
ISBN 0-86201-069-1 (pbk) : £0.25 B81-08001

[**Bible**. *English. New International. Selections. 1980*]. The Bible / [selections by Norman Warren] ; [photographs by Gordon Gray and Gill Rennie]. — London : Ark, 1980. — [24]p : col.ill ; 10cm. — (Basics)
Cover title
ISBN 0-86201-070-5 (pbk) : £0.25 B81-07996

The **Gift** of joy / [readings selected by Simon Jenkins]. — [London] : Ark, 1981. — [24]p : col.ill ; 19cm
Cover title
ISBN 0-86201-074-8 (pbk) : £0.50 B81-17256

The **Gift** of love / [readings selected by Simon Jenkins]. — [London] : Ark, 1981. — [24]p : col.ill ; 19cm
Cover title
ISBN 0-86201-073-x (pbk) : £0.50 B81-17253

The **Gift** of patience / [readings selected by Simon Jenkins]. — [London] : Ark, 1981. — [24]p : col.ill ; 19cm
Cover title
ISBN 0-86201-076-4 (pbk) : £0.50 B81-17255

The **Gift** of peace / [readings selected by Simon Jenkins]. — [London] : Ark, 1981. — [24]p : col.ill ; 19cm
Cover title
ISBN 0-86201-075-6 (pbk) : £0.50 B81-17254

220.5'2 — Bible. *English. New International — Texts*

[**Bible**. *English. New International. 1981*]. The Holy Bible : New International Version. — London : Hodder & Stoughton, Nov.1981. — [1182]p
ISBN 0-340-27818-8 (pbk) : £3.75 : CIP entry
B81-31159

220.5'2 — Bible. *English. Selections — Texts*

[**Bible**. *English. Selections. 1981*]. Selected Bible readings : for use in open-air meetings and visitation. — London : Salvationist, 1981. — 161p ; 12cm
Unpriced (pbk) B81-24376

220.5′2 — Bible. *English. Today′s English — Texts*

[Bible. *English. Today′s English. 1978*]**Good** News Bible : Today′s English version. — British usage ed., Unillustrated ed. — London : Bible Societies, 1978. — 372p : ill ; 22cm
Map on lining papers
ISBN 0-564-00501-0 : Unpriced
ISBN 0-00-512646-0 (Collins) B81-38348

[Bible. *English. Today′s English. 1979*]. Good News Bible : Today′s English version. — Special ed. — London : Bible Society, c1979. — 1280p : ill(some col.),col.maps,plans ; 24cm
Includes index
ISBN 0-564-00691-2 (cased) : £8.95
ISBN 0-564-00681-5 (pbk) : £4.95 B81-11077

220.5′201 — Bible. *English. Geneva — Critical studies*

Lupton, Lewis. A history of the Geneva Bible / Lewis Lupton. — London (2 Milnthorpe Rd., W.4 3DX) : The Olive Tree
Includes Welsh epilogue
Vol.13: Index. — 1981. — 192p : ill,maps,facsims,ports ; 23cm
Limited ed. of autographed copies. — Ill text on lining papers
£13.11 B81-12087

220.5′2033 — Bible. *English. Authorized — Concordances*

Strong, James, *1822-1894*. Strong′s concordance of the Bible / by James Strong. — Popular ed. — London : Pickering & Inglis, 1980. — 770p ; 24cm
Full ed. published in 4 vols. as: The exhaustive concordance of the Bible. London : Hodder and Stoughton, 1894
ISBN 0-7208-0478-7 : £6.50 B81-08584

220.6 — Bible — *Critical studies*

Bewes, Richard. The Bible / [Richard Bewes, Robert Hicks]. — [London] : Scripture Union, 1981. — [24]p : col.ill ; 17cm. — (Explaining Bible truth)
Cover title. — Text on inside covers
ISBN 0-85421-911-0 (pbk) : £0.40 B81-24505

Cryer, Neville B.. What is the Bible? / by Neville B. Cryer. — London : Mowbray, 1981. — 32p ; 15cm. — (Enquirer′s library)
Bibliography: p32
ISBN 0-264-66722-0 (pbk) : £0.60 B81-17907

Ways of reading the Bible / edited by Michael Wadsworth. — Brighton : Harvester, 1981. — viii,224p ; 25cm
Includes index
ISBN 0-85527-537-5 : £18.95 : CIP rev.
B80-21346

Welch, Charles H.. Dispensational truth : or the place of Israel and the Church in the purpose of the ages / by Charles H. Welch. — 4th (rev.) ed. — London : Berean Publishing Trust, 1981. — 263p ; 23cm
Previous ed.: 1959. — Includes index
ISBN 0-85156-082-2 : Unpriced B81-10059

Wilson, C. Vincent. The Westminster concise handbook for the Bible / by C. Vincent Wilson. — Amersham : Hulton Educational, 1981, c1979. — 91p,xvip of plates : col.maps ; 23cm
Originally published: Philadelphia : Westminster Press, 1979. — Includes index
ISBN 0-7175-0879-x (pbk) : £2.10 B81-20009

220.6 — Bible — *Critical studies — For schools*

Hughes, Gerald. Introducing the Bible / Gerald Hughes and Stephen Travis. — Tring : Lion, c1981. — 128p : ill(some col.),col.maps ; 25cm
Ill on lining papers. — Also available as 4 separate booklets
ISBN 0-85648-162-9 : £5.95 B81-17010

220.6 — Bible — *Expositions*

The **Bible** now : its nature, meaning and use today / edited by Paul Burns & John Cumming. — Dublin : Gill and Macmillan, 1981. — 208p ; 22cm
Bibliography: p200-204
ISBN 0-7171-1110-5 (pbk) : £5.95 B81-22197

Mathews, Oliver. The Bible. — Edinburgh : Floris, Sept.1981. — [128]p
ISBN 0-903540-47-9 (pbk) : £5.75 : CIP entry
B81-20563

Patey, Edward H.. Open the book : a practical introduction to Bible study / by Edward H. Patey. — London : Mowbray, 1981. — vi,121p ; 18cm
Bibliography: p120-121
ISBN 0-264-66595-3 (pbk) : £1.50 B81-07805

220.6 — Bible — *Expositions — Conference proceedings*

The **People** and the King / from Donald English ... [et al.] ; edited by David Porter. — Bromley : STL [for] Keswick Convention Council, [1980]. — 189p ; 18cm
ISBN 0-903843-43-9 (pbk) : £1.75 B81-07028

220.6 — Bible. Interpretation

Grollenberg, Lucas. A Bible for our time / Lucas Grollenberg ; [translated by John Bowden from the Dutch]. — London : SCM, 1979. — vi,153p ; 20cm
Translation of: Modern bijbellezen
ISBN 0-334-00108-0 (pbk) : £2.50 B81-01642

220.6′01 — Bible. Hermeneutics

Balchin, John. Let the Bible speak / John F. Balchin. — Leicester : Inter-Varsity, 1981. — 96p ; 18cm
ISBN 0-85110-419-3 (pbk) : Unpriced
B81-26604

Schillebeeckx, Edward. The understanding of faith : interpretation and criticism / Edward Schillebeeckx. — London : Sheed and Ward, 1974 (1981 [printing]). — xiii,176p ; 22cm
Translation of: Geloofsverstaan. — Includes index
ISBN 0-7220-9313-6 (pbk) : £6.50 B81-40811

220.7 — Bible — *Commentaries — Welsh texts*

Bara′r bywyd : darlleniadau Beiblaidd dyddiol. — Pen-y-bont ar Ogwr [Bridgend] ([Bryntirion, Bridgend, M.Glam. CF31 4DX) : Gwasg Efengylaidd Cymru, 1980
Rhif 4: Rhufeiniaid / Gywn Davies. — 63p ; 19cm
ISBN 0-900898-55-0 (pbk) : £0.65 B81-07338

Bara′r bywyd : darlleniadau Beiblaidd dyddiol. — Pen-y-bont ar Ogwr [Bridgend] ([′Bryntirion′, Bridgend, M.Glam. CF31 4DX]) : Gwasg Efengylaidd Cymru, 1980
Rhif 5: Llyfr Job / Goronwy P. Owen. — 64p ; 19cm
ISBN 0-900898-56-9 (pbk) : £0.65 B81-07339

Bara′r bywyd : darlleniadau Beiblaidd dyddiol. — Pen-y-bont ar Ogwr [Bridgend] ([Bryntirion, Bridgend, M. Glam. CF31 4DX]) : Gwasg Efengylaidd Cymru
Rhif 6: Joel-Haggai / Gwyn Davies. — 1981. — 64p ; 19cm
ISBN 0-900898-57-7 (pbk) : £0.65 B81-17111

Bara′r bywyd : darlleniadau Beiblaidd dyddiol. — Pen-y-bont ar Ogwr [Bridgend] ([′Bryntirion′, Bridgend, M. Glam. CF31 4DX]) : Gwasg Efengylaidd Cymru
Rhif 7: 1 & 2 Corinthiaid / Emyr Roberts. — 1981. — 64p ; 19cm
ISBN 0-900898-60-7 (pbk) : £0.85 B81-24025

Bara′r bywyd : darlleniadau Beiblaidd dyddiol. — Pen-y-bont-ar Ogwr [Bridgend] ([′Bryntirion′, Bridgend, M. Glam. CF31 4DX]) : Gwasg Efengylaidd Cymru
Rhif 8: Llyf Josua / Edmund Owen. — 1981. — 63p ; 19cm
ISBN 0-900898-61-5 (pbk) : £0.85 B81-24026

220.7′7 — Bible — *Texts with commentaries*

The **Expositor′s** Bible commentary : with the New International Version of the Holy Bible / general editor Frank E. Gaebelein ; associate editor J.D. Douglas. — London : Pickering & Inglis
Vol.9: (John-Acts). — c1981. — xvi,573p ; 24cm
ISBN 0-7208-0475-2 : £12.50 B81-24476

220.8′3053 — Bible. Special themes: Sex roles

Hurley, James B.. Man and woman in biblical perspective : a study in role relationships and authority / James B. Hurley. — Leicester : Inter-Varsity, 1981. — 288p ; 22cm
Bibliography: p272-280. — Includes index
ISBN 0-85111-570-5 (pbk) : Unpriced
B81-26605

220.8′3054 — Bible. Special subjects: Women

Stagg, Evelyn. Woman in the world of Jesus / Evelyn and Frank Stagg. — Edinburgh : Saint Andrew, c1980. — 292p ; 21cm
Bibliography: p271-277. — Includes index
ISBN 0-7152-0431-9 (pbk) : £3.95 B81-17800

220.8′30556 — Bible. Special subjects: Poverty & wealth

Boerma, Conrad. Rich man, poor man, — and the Bible / Conrad Boerma. — London : SCM, 1979. — v,106p ; 20cm
Translation of: Kan ook een rijke zalig worden. — Includes index
ISBN 0-334-01419-0 (pbk) : £2.25 B81-40982

220.8′3068 — Bible. Special subjects: Marriage

Bromiley, Geoffrey W.. God and marriage / by Geoffrey W. Bromiley. — Edinburgh : T. & T. Clark, 1981, c1980. — 88p ; 21cm
Originally published: Grand Rapids : Eerdmans, 1980. — Includes index
ISBN 0-567-29104-9 (pbk) : £1.95 B81-17736

220.8′551554 — Bible. Special subjects: Storms

Double, Don. What to do in a storm / by Don Double. — St. Austell (32a Fore St., St. Austell, Cornwall PL25 5EP) : Good News Crusade, 1979. — [12]p : 1port ; 21cm
Text, port on cover
ISBN 0-903437-11-2 (pbk) : £0.20 B81-31905

220.8′95694 — Bible. Prophecies. Special subjects: Israel

Welch, Charles H.. The Eastern question, or, Israel and Egypt in prophecy / by Charles H. Welch. — London : Berean Publishing, 1957 (1980 [printing]). — 25p ; 21cm
ISBN 0-85156-080-6 (pbk) : Unpriced
Also classified at 220.8′962 B81-07847

220.8′962 — Bible. Prophecies. Special subjects: Egypt

Welch, Charles H.. The Eastern question, or, Israel and Egypt in prophecy / by Charles H. Welch. — London : Berean Publishing, 1957 (1980 [printing]). — 25p ; 21cm
ISBN 0-85156-080-6 (pbk) : Unpriced
Primary classification 220.8′95694 B81-07847

220.9 — BIBLICAL GEOGRAPHY AND HISTORY

220.9′1′0222 — Middle East. Places associated with Bible — *Illustrations*

Alexander, David, *1937-*. The Lion photo-guide to the Bible / [photographs and notes by David Alexander]. — New ed. / revised and expanded by Robin Keeley. — Tring : Lion, 1981. — 285p : ill(some col.),maps ; 24cm
Previous ed.: published in 2 vols. as : Photo-guide to the New Testament, 1972 ; Photoguide to the Old Testament 1973
ISBN 0-85648-430-x : £6.95 B81-38402

220.9′2 — Bible. Characters — *Encyclopaedias*

Coggins, Richard. Who′s who in the Bible / Richard Coggins. — London : Batsford, 1981. — 232p : 1map ; 24cm
Map on lining papers
ISBN 0-7134-0144-3 : £6.95 B81-10723

220.9′2′076 — Bible. Characters — *Questions & answers*

Reynolds, Erma. Bible people quiz book / Erma Reynolds. — London : Pickering & Inglis, 1981, c1979. — [80]p ; 18cm
Originally published: Grand Rapids : Baker Book House, 1979
ISBN 0-7208-0477-9 (pbk) : £1.30 B81-15581

220.9′5 — Ancient Middle East, *to ca 70.* **Historical sources: Bible**

Atlas of Bible times. — Tring : Lion Publishing, 1981, c1978. — [68]p : ill(some col.),col.maps ; 25cm. — (A lion book)
Originally published: in the Lion Encyclopedia of the Bible, pts. 9-10
ISBN 0-85648-436-9 : £2.95
ISBN 0-86760-346-1 (Australia) B81-40705

220.9′5 — Ancient Middle East, *to ca 70.* **Historical sources: Bible** — *For children*

Rowland-Entwistle, Theodore. The illustrated atlas of the Bible lands / [author Theodore Rowland-Entwistle] ; [editor Adrian Sington] ; [adviser John Ferguson] ; [maps by Tony Payne]. — Harlow : Longman, 1981. — 45p : col.ill,col.maps,2geneal.tables ; 33cm
Includes index
ISBN 0-582-39129-6 : £4.25 B81-40298

220.9′505 — Bible — *Stories for children*

Alexander, Pat. The Lion children's Bible : stories from the Old and New Testaments / retold by Pat Alexander ; illustrated by Lyndon Evans. — Tring : Lion, 1981. — 256p : col.ill ; 22cm
ISBN 0-85648-288-9 : £4.95 B81-13326

Alexander, Pat. The Puffin children's Bible : stories from the Old and New Testament / retold by Pat Alexander ; illustrated by Lyndon Evans. — Harmondsworth : Puffin, 1981. — 256p : col.ill ; 21cm
ISBN 0-14-031397-4 (pbk) : £2.50 B81-25348

The **Bible** story. — Redhill : National Christian Education Council
Book 7: Men of vision / Hazel Snashall ; artwork by Anne Farncombe. — 1981. — 32p : col.ill,col.maps ; 23cm
ISBN 0-7197-0285-2 (pbk) : Unpriced B81-33570

The **Bible** story. — Redhill : National Christian Education Council
Book 8: The early Church / Hazel Snashall ; artwork by Anne Farncombe. — 1981. — 32p : col.ill,col.maps ; 23cm
ISBN 0-7197-0286-0 (pbk) : Unpriced B81-33571

Bruce, F. F.. A first Bible history atlas. — Exeter : Paternoster, Nov.1981. — [96]p
ISBN 0-85364-312-1 : £4.95 : CIP entry B81-30424

Bull, Norman J.. 100 Bible stories / retold by Norman J. Bull ; illustrated by Val Biro. — London : Hamlyn, 1980. — 172p : col.ill,col.maps ; 22cm
Maps on lining papers
ISBN 0-600-31580-0 : £2.50 B81-01862

Hunt, Patricia. Bible stories. — London : Ward Lock, Sept.1981. — [256]p
ISBN 0-7063-5805-8 : £5.95 : CIP entry B81-25872

221 — OLD TESTAMENT

221′.076 — Bible. O.T. — *Questions & answers — For West African students*

Coutts, John. Revision guide : Bible knowledge, Old Testament / John Coutts. — Harlow : Longman, 1981. — xii,98p : ill,maps ; 22cm. — (Study for success)
ISBN 0-582-65070-4 (pbk) : £1.05 B81-38176

221.1′5 — Bible. O.T.. Prophecies. Failure. Responses. Psychological aspects

Carroll, Robert P.. When prophecy failed : reactions and responses to failure in the Old Testament prophetic traditions / Robert P. Carroll. — London : SCM, 1979. — 250p ; 23cm
Bibliography: p245-247. — Includes index
ISBN 0-334-01789-0 : £7.50 B81-11588

221.1′509′505 — Bible. O.T. Prophecies — *Stories for children*

Kent, David. The time of the prophets. — London (Elsley Court, 20 Great Titchfield St., W1P 7AD) : Kingfisher, Oct.1981. — [24]p. — (Kingfisher explorer books. Bible stories)
ISBN 0-86272-020-6 : £1.95 : CIP entry B81-27974

221.3′21 — Bible. N.T. — *Encyclopaedias*

Léon-Dufour, Xavier. Dictionary of the New Testament / Xavier Léon-Dufour ; translated from the second (revised) French edition by Terrence Prendergast. — London : Geoffrey Chapman, 1980. — 458p : ill,maps ; 24cm
Translation of: Dictionnaire du Nouveau Testament. — Originally published: New York : Harper & Row, 1980. — Includes index
ISBN 0-225-66253-1 : Unpriced B81-14669

221.6 — Bible. O.T. — *Critical studies*

Childs, Brevard S.. Introduction to the Old Testament as scripture / Brevard S. Childs. — London : SCM Press, 1979. — 688p ; 23cm
Includes bibliographies and index
ISBN 0-334-00710-0 : £17.50 B81-15618

West, James King. Introduction to the Old Testament / James King West. — 2nd ed. — New York : Macmillan ; London : Collier Macmillan, c1981. — xxvii,609p : ill,maps ; 24cm
Previous ed.: 1971. — Bibliography: p543-557. — Includes index
ISBN 0-02-425920-9 : £12.50 B81-36119

221.6 — Bible. O.T. — *Expositions*

Doorly, John W.. Talks given by John W. Doorly on the science of the Bible : (between January 4th and March 8th, 1949). — London : Foundational Book Co
Originally published: as 10 separate reports. 1949
vol.6, nos 48-57: I and II Kings. — 1981. — 293p ; 23cm
Unpriced B81-34980

221.6 — Bible. O.T — *Expositions*

Treasure, Geoff. The book that Jesus read / Geoff Treasure. — Leicester : Inter-Varsity, 1981. — 128p : ill,2maps ; 18cm
ISBN 0-85110-423-1 (pbk) : Unpriced B81-26606

221.6 — Bible. O.T. Theology

Dyrness, William. Themes in Old Testament theology / William Dyrness. — Exeter : Paternoster, c1979. — 252p ; 21cm
Bibliography: p243-248. - Includes index
ISBN 0-85364-297-4 (pbk) : £3.00 : CIP rev. B80-17544

Goldingay, John. Approaches to Old Testament interpretation. — Leicester : Inter-Varsity Press, Oct.1981. — [176]p. — (Issues in contemporary theology)
ISBN 0-85111-404-0 (pbk) : £3.50 : CIP entry B81-24674

221.6′01 — Bible. O.T.. Hermeneutics, *1870-1980*

Nicholson, Ernest W.. Interpreting the Old Testament : a century of the Oriel Professorship / by Ernest Nicholson. — Oxford : Clarendon Press, 1981. — 24p ; 22cm. — (Inaugural lecture / University of Oxford)
ISBN 0-19-951533-6 (pbk) : £1.95 : CIP rev. B81-21651

221.6′6 — Bible. O.T. Irony - *Critical studies*

Good, Edwin M.. Irony in the Old Testament. — 2nd ed. — Sheffield : Almond Press, June 1981. — [256]p. — (Bible and literature series, ISSN 0260-4493 ; 3)
ISBN 0-907459-05-6 (pbk) : £5.95 : CIP entry B81-12376

221.8′1 — Bible. O.T. Special subjects: Wisdom — *Critical studies*

Morgan, Donn F.. Wisdom in the Old Testament traditions. — Oxford : Blackwell, Oct.1981. — [180]p
ISBN 0-631-12948-0 : £12.00 : CIP entry B81-26703

221.9′22 — Bible. O.T. — *Biographies*

Comay, Joan. Who's who in the Old Testament together with the Apocrypha. — London : Hodder & Stoughton, Feb.1982. — [432]p. — (Teach yourself books)
Originally published: London : Weidenfeld & Nicolson, 1971
ISBN 0-340-27176-0 (pbk) : £2.95 : CIP entry B81-36355

221.9′22 — Bible. O.T. Prophets — *Devotional works*

Duncan, George B.. A preacher among the prophets. — London : Hodder & Stoughton, Sept.1981. — [192]p
ISBN 0-340-26356-3 (pbk) : £1.95 : CIP entry B81-23954

221.9′22 — Bible. O.T. Prophets. Role — *Sociological perspectives*

Petersen, David L.. The roles of Israel's prophets. — Sheffield : JSOT Press, Sept.1981. — [130]p. — (Journal for the study of the Old Testament. Supplement series, ISSN 0309-0787 ; 17)
ISBN 0-905774-32-9 (cased) : £12.00 : CIP entry
ISBN 0-905774-34-5 (pbk) : £6.95 B81-21594

221.9′3 — Bible. O.T. Historicity. Archaeological sources

Tullock, John. The Old Testament story / John Tullock. — Englewood Cliffs ; London : Prentice Hall, c1981. — xiii,433p : ill,maps,1plan ; 25cm
Includes bibliographies and index
ISBN 0-13-633941-7 : £10.35 B81-16537

221.9′5 — Israel, *to ca B.C.500 — Sources of data: Bible. O.T. — For schools*

Hughes, Gerald. The growth of the kingdom / Gerald Hughes and Stephen Travis. — Tring : Lion Publishing, 1981. — p33-34 : ill(some col.),maps ; 25cm. — (Introducing the Bible ; 2)
Cover title
ISBN 0-85648-264-1 (pbk) : £1.25 B81-16686

221.9′505 — Bible. O. T. — *Stories, anecdotes*

Dickinson, Peter, *1927-*. City of gold and other stories from the Old Testament / retold by Peter Dickinson ; illustrated by Michael Foreman. — London : Gollancz, 1980. — 188p : ill(some col.) ; 25cm
ISBN 0-575-02883-1 : £5.95 B81-03212

221.9′505 — Bible. O.T. — *Stories for children*

Hannon, Ruth. Children's Bible stories : from the Old Testament / retold by Ruth Hannon ; illustrated by Joe Giordano. — London : Dean, 1980, c1978. — 45p : col.ill ; 27cm. — (A New gold medal book)
Originally published: New York : Gold Press, 1978
ISBN 0-603-00202-1 : £1.25 B81-32158

Kent, David. The desert people. — London (Elsley Court, 20 Great Titchfield St., W1P 7AD) : Kingfisher, Oct.1981. — [24]p. — (Kingfisher explorer books. Bible stories)
ISBN 0-86272-017-6 : £1.95 : CIP entry B81-28039

Priestley, J. G.. The Old Testament / J.G. Priestley. — Exeter : Religious Education Press, 1981. — 162p : ill ; 22cm. — (Bible stories for today)
ISBN 0-08-025598-1 (cased) : £2.95
ISBN 0-08-025597-3 (pbk) : £2.25 B81-25360

222′.06 — Bible. O.T. Historical books — *Critical studies*

Nelson, Richard D.. The double redaction of the Deuteronomistic history. — Sheffield : JSOT Press, Dec.1981. — [176]p. — (Journal for the study of the Old Testament supplement series ; 18)
ISBN 0-905774-33-7 (cased) : £12.00 (subscription rate £7.95) : CIP entry
ISBN 0-905774-34-3 (pbk) : £7.50 (subscription rate £4.95) B81-35893

222'.09505 — Bible. O.T. Historical books — *Stories for children*

Kent, David. Escape from Egypt / by David Kent ; illustrated by Harry Bishop and Roger Payne. — London : Pan, 1981. — 23p : col.ill ; 23cm. — (Bible stories) (A Piccolo explorer book)
Includes index
ISBN 0-330-26495-8 (pbk) : £0.85 B81-38705

222'.1052 — Bible. O.T. Pentateuch. Paraphrases — *Texts*

Ward, Keith, *1938-*. The promise / Keith Ward. — London : SPCK, 1980. — xi,282p : maps,geneal.tables ; 20cm
Adaptation of the first five books of the Hebrew Bible
ISBN 0-281-03748-5 (pbk) : £3.95 B81-01686

222'.107 — Bible. O.T. Pentateuch — *Commentaries*

Goldsmith, Martin. Leviticus — Deuteronomy / M. Goldsmith. — London : Ark, 1981. — 126p : 3maps ; 21cm. — (Bible study commentary)
ISBN 0-86201-085-3 (pbk) : Unpriced
Also classified at 222'.1307 ; 222'.1407 ; 222'.1507 B81-32447

222'.11'00207 — Bible. O.T. Genesis. Noah's Ark — *Cartoons*

Steinmann, Friedel. Noah / Friedel Steinmann and Dieter Kohl ; [translated by Su Box and lettered by Bob Bond]. — Tring : Lion, 1979. — 63p : ill ; 17cm
Tranlation of: Noah. Eine alte Geschichte neu erzählt
ISBN 0-85648-165-3 (pbk) : £0.50 B81-39198

222'.11'005 — Bible. O.T. Genesis. Creation — *Serials*

Biblical creation : journal of the Biblical Creation Society. — [No.1] (Oct.1978)-no.4 (Nov.1979) ; Vol.2, no.5 (Feb.1980)-. — Glasgow (c/o The Secretary, 51 Cloan Cres., Bishopbriggs, Glasgow G64 2HN) : The Society, 1978-. — v. ; 21cm
Three issues yearly
ISSN 0260-9460 = Biblical creation : £1.35 per year B81-14367

222'.1101 — Bible. O.T. Genesis. Creation. Historicity

In the beginning - : a symposium on the Bible and creation / edited by N.M. de S. Cameron. — Glasgow (51 Cloan Cres., Bishopbriggs, Glasgow) : Biblical Creation Society, 1980. — 48p ; 22cm
£0.70 (pbk) B81-09845

222'.1107 — Bible. O.T. Genesis — *Commentaries*

Cundall, Arthur E.. Genesis and Exodus / A.E. Cundall. — London : Ark, 1981. — 126p : maps,1plan ; 21cm. — (Bible study commentary)
ISBN 0-86201-083-7 (pbk) : Unpriced
Also classified at 222'.1207 B81-32449

222'.1107 — Bible. O.T. Genesis I-XI — *Commentaries*

Knight, George A. F.. Theology in pictures : a commentary on Genesis chapters one to eleven / George A.F. Knight. — Edinburgh : Handsel, 1981. — xiii,123p ; 22cm
ISBN 0-905312-06-6 (pbk) : £3.95 B81-38959

222'.1107 — Bible. O.T. Genesis XII-XXIII — *Commentaries*

Wallace, Ronald S.. Abraham : Genesis 12-23 / Ronald S. Wallace. — London : Triangle, 1981. — 145p ; 18cm. — (The Bible for every day)
ISBN 0-281-03808-2 (pbk) : £1.85 B81-26885

222'.11077 — Bible. O.T. Genesis — *Texts with commentaries*

Asimov, Isaac. In the beginning / Isaac Asimov. — London : New English Library, 1981. — 234p ; 23cm
Includes index
ISBN 0-450-04867-5 : £6.95 B81-34987

Gibson, John C. L.. Genesis / John C.L. Gibson. — Edinburgh : Saint Andrew. — (The Daily study Bible)
Vol.1. — c1981. — ix,214p : ill,2maps ; 19cm
Bibliography: p213-214
ISBN 0-7152-0465-3 (pbk) : £2.95 B81-37149

222'.11'0922 — Bible. O.T. Genesis. Patriarchs

Essays on the patriarchal narratives / edited by A.R. Millard & D.J. Wiseman. — Leicester : Inter-Varsity, 1980. — 223p ; 23cm
Bibliography: p207-212. - Includes index
ISBN 0-85111-743-0 : £6.95 : CIP rev. B80-23978

222'.11'0924 — Bible. O.T. Genesis. Joseph — *Stories for children*

Robertson, Jenny. Joseph / text by Jenny Robertson ; illustrations by Alan Parry. — London : Scripture Union, 1981. — [28]p : col.ill ; 27cm. — (A Ladybird Bible book ; 4)
Text, ill on lining papers
ISBN 0-85421-900-5
ISBN 0-7214-0575-4 (Ladybird) B81-16285

222'.110924 — Bible. O.T. Genesis. Mark of Cain

Mellinkoff, Ruth. The mark of Cain / Ruth Mellinkoff. — Berkeley ; London : University of California Press, 1981. — xiii,151p,22p of plates : ill ; 21cm. — (Quantum books)
Bibliography: p133-142. — Includes index
ISBN 0-520-03969-6 : £7.75 B81-27265

222'.11'0924 — Christian life. Faith — *Study examples: Abraham*

Lane, Denis. A man and his God / Denis Lane. — Welwyn : Evangelical, 1981. — 160p ; 18cm
ISBN 0-85234-155-5 (pbk) : Unpriced B81-26828

222'.1109505 — Bible. O.T. Genesis. Creation — *Stories for children*

Reed, Allison. Genesis / Allison Reed. — [London] : Abelard-Schuman, 1981. — [28]p : col.ill ; 29cm
Ill on lining papers
ISBN 0-200-72735-4 : £4.95 : CIP rev. B81-00012

222'.1109505 — Bible. O.T. Genesis — *Stories for children*

Doney, Meryl. Stories from Genesis / [retold by Meryl and Malcolm Doney]. — London : Hutchinson, 1981. — 45p : col.ill,1col.map ; 29cm. — (Living stories from the Bible)
Map on lining papers. — Includes index
ISBN 0-09-144320-2 : £3.25 : CIP rev. B81-04247

Kent, David. The desert people / David Kent illustrated ; by Harry Bishop. — London : Pan, 1981. — 22p : col.ill ; 23cm. — (Bible stories) (A Piccolo explorer book)
Includes index
ISBN 0-330-26494-x (pbk) : £0.85 B81-36694

222'1206 — Bible. O.T. Exodus — *Expositions*

Todd, William. New light on Exodus : the narrative explained against its geographical, historical and social background / by William Todd. — London (61 Lilford Rd, S.E.5) : Furnival, 1980. — 211p : 1geneal.table,maps ; 25cm
Includes index
Unpriced B81-02018

222'.1206 — Bible. O.T. Exodus. Special subjects: Tabernacle

Ferguson, J. L.. The parable of the Tabernacle / by J.L. Ferguson. — Bromley (6 Georgian Close, Bromley, Kent BR2 7RA) : Hayes Press, [1981?]. — 99p,viiip of plates : col.ill,1plan ; 21cm
Unpriced (pbk) B81-38091

222'.1207 — Bible. O.T. Exodus — *Commentaries*

Childs, Brevard S.. Exodus : a commentary / Brevard S. Childs. — London : SCM, 1974 (1979 [printing]). — xxv,659p ; 22cm. — (Old Testament library)
Bibliography: pxxi-xxv. — Includes index
ISBN 0-334-00433-0 (pbk) : £8.50 B81-05950

Cundall, Arthur E.. Genesis and Exodus / A.E. Cundall. — London : Ark, 1981. — 126p : maps,1plan ; 21cm. — (Bible study commentary)
ISBN 0-86201-083-7 (pbk) : Unpriced
Primary classification 222'.1107 B81-32449

222'.1209'05 — Bible. O.T. Exodus. Moses — *Stories for children*

Kent, David. The escape from Egypt. — London (Elsley Court, 20 Great Titchfield St., W1P 7AD) : Kingfisher, Oct.1981. — [24]p. — (Kingfisher explorer books. Bible stories)
ISBN 0-86272-018-4 : £1.95 : CIP entry B81-27976

222'.12'0924 — Bible. O.T. Exodus. Moses *(Prophet) — Stories for children*

Robertson, Jenny. Moses and Joshua / text by Jenny Robertson ; illustrations by Alan Parry. — London : Scripture Union, 1981. — [28]p : col.ill ; 27cm. — (A Ladybird Bible book ; 6)
ISBN 0-85421-902-1 : £0.95
Also classified at 222'.2'0924 B81-16284

Robertson, Jenny. Moses the prince / text by Jenny Robertson ; illustrations by Alan Parry. — London : Scripture Union, 1981. — [28]p : col.ill ; 27cm. — (A Ladybird Bible book ; 5)
Text, ill on lining papers
ISBN 0-85421-901-3 : £0.95 B81-16286

222'.1307 — Bible. O.T. Leviticus — *Commentaries*

Goldsmith, Martin. Leviticus — Deuteronomy / M. Goldsmith. — London : Ark, 1981. — 126p : 3maps ; 21cm. — (Bible study commentary)
ISBN 0-86201-085-3 (pbk) : Unpriced
Primary classification 222'.107 B81-32447

222'.13077 — Bible. O.T. Leviticus — *Texts with commentaries*

Knight, George A. F.. Leviticus / G.A.F. Knight. — Edinburgh : Saint Andrew, c1981. — viii,173p ; 19cm. — (The Daily study Bible)
Bibliography: p173
ISBN 0-7152-0479-3 (pbk) : £2.95 B81-37148

222'.1407 — Bible. O.T. Numbers — *Commentaries*

Goldsmith, Martin. Leviticus — Deuteronomy / M. Goldsmith. — London : Ark, 1981. — 126p : 3maps ; 21cm. — (Bible study commentary)
ISBN 0-86201-085-3 (pbk) : Unpriced
Primary classification 222'.107 B81-32447

222'.1507 — Bible. O.T. Deuteronomy — *Commentaries*

Goldsmith, Martin. Leviticus — Deuteronomy / M. Goldsmith. — London : Ark, 1981. — 126p : 3maps ; 21cm. — (Bible study commentary)
ISBN 0-86201-085-3 (pbk) : Unpriced
Primary classification 222'.107 B81-32447

222'.1606 — Ten Commandments — *Expositions*

Blanch, Stuart Y.. The Ten Commandments / Stuart Blanch. — London : Hodder and Stoughton, c1981. — 137p ; 18cm. — (Hodder Christian paperbacks)
ISBN 0-340-27149-3 (pbk) : £1.50 : CIP rev. B81-18027

Purcell, William. No other Gods : a modern meditation on the Commandments / William Purcell. — Rev. and updated ed. — London : Mowbray, 1981. — 121p ; 18cm. — (Mowbray's popular Christian paperbacks)
Previous ed.: published as The plain man looks at the Commandments. London : Collins, 1966
ISBN 0-264-66730-1 (pbk) : £1.50 B81-36805

222'.204 — Bible. O.T. Josua — *Textual criticisms*

Auld, A. Graeme. Joshua, Moses and the land : Tetrateuch-Pentateuch-Hexateuch in a generation since 1938 / by A. Graeme Auld. — Edinburgh : Clark, 1980. — vii,144p ; 23cm
Bibliography: p121-126. - Includes index
ISBN 0-567-09306-9 : £7.95 B81-13661

222'.2'0924 — Bible. O.T. Joshua. Joshua — *Stories for children*
Robertson, Jenny. Moses and Joshua / text by Jenny Robertson ; illustrations by Alan Parry. — London : Scripture Union, 1981. — [28]p : col.ill ; 27cm. — (A Ladybird Bible book ; 6)
ISBN 0-85421-902-1 : £0.95
Primary classification 222'.12'0924 B81-16284

222'.406 — Bible. O.T. Samuel — *Study outlines*
Smith, D. B. P.. Outline studies in the books of Samuel / D.B.P. Smith. — Birmingham (5 Pakenham Rd., Edgbaston, Birmingham B15 2NN) : Birmingham Bible Institute, c1980. — [36]p ; 22cm
Unpriced (pbk) B81-12747

222'.509'505 — Bible. O.T. Kings — *Stories for children*
Kent, David. The kings of Israel. — London (Elsley Court, 20 Great Titchfield St., W1P 7AD) : Kingfisher, Oct.1981. — [24]p. — (Kingfisher explorer books. Bible stories)
ISBN 0-86272-019-2 : £1.95 : CIP entry
B81-28079

222'.509505 — Bible. O.T. Kings - *Stories for children*
Watkins, Peter. The shepherd and the giant. — London : Julia MacRae Books, Sept.1981. — [48]p. — (Blackbird series)
ISBN 0-86203-054-4 : £2.75 : CIP entry
B81-20173

222'.5306 — Bible. O.T. Kings, 1st — *Study outlines*
Smith, D. B. P.. Outline studies in the book of I Kings / D.B.P. Smith. — Birmingham (8 Pakenham Rd., Edgbaston, Birmingham B15 2NE) : Quernmore Books, c1981. — 59p ; 21cm
Bibliography: p58-59
Unpriced (pbk) B81-12748

222'.90924 — Bible. O.T. Esther. Characters: Esther
Duff, Mildred. Esther the queen / by Mildred Duff. — Ossett (44 Queen's Drive, Ossett, W. Yorks., WF5 0ND) : Zoar, 1974. — 79p,[4]p of plates : ill,1plan ; 19cm
ISBN 0-904435-06-7 : £2.00 B81-31298

223'.107 — Bible. O.T. Job — *Commentaries — Welsh texts*
Williams, J. Tudno. Problem dioddefaint a Llyfr Job / J. Tudno Williams. — [Caernarfon?] : Gwasg Pantycelyn, c1980. — 132p ; 18cm
Bibliography: p130-132
Unpriced (pbk) B81-04092

223'.2044 — Bible. O.T. Psalms. *English and Hebrew — Texts*
[Bible. O.T.. Psalms. *English and Hebrew. 1980*].
A new-old rendering of the Psalms / by Solomon Schonfeld. — London (5 The Bishops Ave. N.2) : Uniby Press, 1980. — 288p : 1ill,facsims ; 21cm
English translations with photocopies of the original Hebrew texts
Unpriced B81-15275

223'.205209 — Bible. O.T. Psalms. *English. Frost and others — Texts*
The **ASB** Psalter and Canticles : set to Anglican chants / edited by Lionel Dakers and Cyril Taylor. — London : Collins, 1981. — 205p : music ; 26cm
Includes index
ISBN 0-00-599680-5 : Unpriced B81-32507

223'.2059166 — Bible. O.T. Psalms. *Welsh. Authorized. Selections — Texts*
[Bible. O.T. Psalms. *Welsh. Authorised. Selections. 1979*]. Detholion o'r Salmau / [golygwyd gan] Theo Roberts. — [Gaerwen] (['Heulfre', Stad Garnedd, Star, Gaerwen, Gwynedd]) : T. Roberts, 1979. — 69p ; 19cm
Unpriced (pbk) B81-04091

223'.206 — Bible. O.T. Psalms — *Expositions*
Redford, John. The Psalms : an introduction / by John Redford. — Godalming ([Ladywell Convent, Ashstead Lane], Godalming, Surrey [GU7 1ST]) : Ladywell Press, 1981. — 27p ; 30cm
£2.50 (pbk) B81-22388

223'.207 — Bible. O.T. Psalms - *Commentaries*
Anderson, A. A.. Psalms. — London : Marshall, Morgan & Scott, July 1981. — (The New Century Bible commentary)
Vol.1: (Psalms 1-72). — [527]p
ISBN 0-551-00846-6 (pbk) : £6.95 : CIP entry
B81-18167

Anderson, A. A.. Psalms. — London : Marshall, Morgan & Scott, July 1981. — (The New Century Bible commentary)
Vol.2: (Psalms 73-150). — [446]p
ISBN 0-551-00847-4 (pbk) : £5.95 : CIP entry
B81-18168

223'.8077 — Bible. O.T. Ecclesiastes — *Texts with commentaries*
Bridges, Charles. [An Exposition of the Book of Ecclesiastes]. A Commentary on Ecclesiastes / Charles Bridges. — Edinburgh : Banner of Truth Trust, 1961 (1981 [printing]). — xvi,319p : ill ; 20cm. — ([The Geneva series of commentaries])
Facsim of: 1st ed., London : Seeley, Jackson & Halliday, 1860. — Ill on lining papers. — Includes index
ISBN 0-85151-322-0 : £3.95 B81-36443

224'.1'06 — Bible. O.T. Isaiah. Special subjects: Ethics - *Critical studies*
Davies, Eryl W.. Prophecy and ethics. — Sheffield : JSOT Press, July 1981. — [170]p. — (Journal for the Study of the Old Testament. Supplement series ; 16)
ISBN 0-905774-26-4 : £6.50 : CIP entry
B81-14400

224'.206 — Bible. O.T. Jeremiah — *Expositions*
Maria, *Mother, b.1912*. Jeremiah : prophet of God / Mother Maria ; edited by Mother Thekla. — Whitby (Normanby, Whitby, N. Yorkshire YO22 4PS) : Greek Orthodox Monastery of the Assumption, c1981. — 173p ; 22cm. — (Library of Orthodox thinking)
Includes the text newly translated from Hebrew of the Book of Jeremiah
ISBN 0-903455-25-0 (pbk) : £6.50 B81-29532

224'.406'8 — Bible. O.T. Ezekial. Cabalistic interpretations
Lévi, Eliphas. The mysteries of the Qabalah, or, The occult agreement of the two testaments. — Wellingborough : Aquarian Press, Dec.1981. — [286]p
Translation of: Les mystères de la Kabbale. — Originally published: 1974
ISBN 0-85030-274-9 (pbk) : £4.95 : CIP entry
Also classified at 228'.06'8 B81-32054

224'.5077 — Bible. O.T. Daniel — *Texts with commentaries*
Russell, D. S.. Daniel / D.S. Russell. — Edinburgh : Saint Andrew, c1981. — x,234p ; 19cm. — (The Daily study Bible)
Bibliography: p233-234
ISBN 0-7152-0464-5 (pbk) : £2.95 B81-37150

224'.6'06 — Bible. O.T. Hosea — *Expositions*
Kidner, Derek. Love to the loveless : the story and message of Hosea. — London : Inter-Varsity Press, Oct.1981. — [128]p. — (The Bible speaks today)
ISBN 0-85110-703-6 (pbk) : £1.50 : CIP entry
B81-24676

224'.92'00207 — Bible. O.T. Jonah — *Cartoons*
Steinmann, Friedel. Jonah / Friedel Steinmann and Dieter Kohl ; [translated by Su Box and lettered by Bob Bond]. — Tring : Lion, 1979. — 62p : ill ; 17cm
Translation of: Jona. Eine alte Geschichte neu erzählt
ISBN 0-85648-164-5 (pbk) : £0.50 B81-39197

224'.9206 — Bible. O.T. Jonah — *Expositions*
Ferguson, Sinclair B.. Man overboard! : the story of Jonah / Sinclair B. Ferguson. — London : Pickering & Inglis, c1981. — 107p ; 21cm
ISBN 0-7208-0493-0 (pbk) : £2.25 B81-31939

225 — NEW TESTAMENT

225 — Bible. N.T — *Critical studies*
Moule, C. F. D.. The birth of the New Testament. — 3rd ed. — London : A. & C. Black, Apr.1981. — [352]p. — (Black's New Testament commentaries)
Previous ed.: 1966
ISBN 0-7136-2132-x : CIP entry
ISBN 0-7136-2133-8 (pbk) : Unpriced
B81-02119

225 — Bible. N.T. Theology — *Encyclopaedias*
The **New** international dictionary of New Testament theology. — 2nd ed. — Exeter : Paternoster Press, Aug.1981
Translation of: Theologisches Begriffslexikon zum Neuen Testament
Vol.2. — [1058]p
Previous ed.: 1976
ISBN 0-85364-331-8 : £26.00 : CIP entry
B81-23902

The **New** international dictionary of New Testament theology. — 2nd ed. — Exeter : Paternoster Press, Aug.1981
Translation of: Theologisches Begriffslexikon zum Neuen Testament
Vol.3. — [1514]p
Previous ed.: 1978
ISBN 0-85364-332-6 : £32.00 : CIP entry
B81-23903

225.4'8'0321 — Bible. N.T. *Greek.* **Words —** *Dictionaries*
Metzger, Bruce M.. Lexical aids for students of New Testament Greek / Bruce M. Metzger. — New ed. — Oxford : Blackwell, 1980, c1969. — xi,100p : 1ill ; 22cm
Previous ed.: Princeton, N.J. : Bruce M. Metzger, 1969. — Includes index
ISBN 0-631-12605-8 (pbk) : £2.95 : CIP rev.
B80-32875

225.4'8'0924 — Bible. N.T. *Greek.* **Manuscripts. Textual criticism. Tischendorf, Constantin**
Black, Matthew. Constantin von Tischendorf and the Greek New Testament / Matthew Black and Robert Davidson. — [Glasgow] : University of Glasgow Press, 1981. — 91p ; 25cm
ISBN 0-85261-164-1 (pbk) : Unpriced
B81-20780

225.5'2 — Bible. N.T. *English. Today's English — Texts*
[Bible. N.T.. *English. Today's English. 1976*]
Good News New Testament : Today's English version. — London : Bible Societies, 1976. — iv,695p : ill,maps ; 18cm
ISBN 0-564-04081-9 (pbk) : £0.95
ISBN 0-00-512642-8 (Collins) B81-35168

225.6 — Bible. N.T. — *Critical studies*
Tremmel, William Calloley. The twenty-seven books that changed the world : a guide to reading the New Testament / William Calloley Tremmel. — New York ; London : Holt, Rinehart and Winston, c1981. — xii,272p : 2maps ; 24cm
Includes bibliographies and index
ISBN 0-03-052631-0 (pbk) : £7.95 B81-23055

225.6 — Bible. N.T. — *Expositions*
Guthrie, Donald. New testament theology / Donald Guthrie. — Leicester : Inter-Varsity, 1981. — 1064p ; 25cm
Bibliography: p983-1019. — Includes index
ISBN 0-85111-742-2 : £14.95 B81-36327

225.6 — Bible N.T. — *Expositions*
Hoskyns, *Sir* **Edwyn**. Crucifixion-resurrection : the pattern of the theology and ethics of the New Testament / Edwyn Clement Hoskyns & Francis Noel Davey ; edited with a biographical introduction by Gordon S. Wakefield. — London : SPCK, 1981. — xvi,383p,[4]p of plates : ports ; 23cm
Bibliography: p369-374. — Includes index
ISBN 0-281-03705-1 : £21.00 B81-40629

225.6 — Bible. N.T — *Expositions*
Schillebeeckx, Edward. Christ : the Christian experience in the modern world / Edward Schillebeeckx ; [translated by John Bowden]. — London : S.C.M., 1980. — 925p ; 24cm
Translation of: Gerechtigheid en liefde. — Bibliography: p938-912. — Includes index
ISBN 0-334-00173-0 : £19.50 B81-22769

225.7 — Bible. N.T. — *Commentaries*

Harvey, A. E.. Companion to the New Testament : the New English Bible / by A.E. Harvey. — [Oxford] : Oxford University Press, 1970 (1979 [printing]). — vii,850p : maps ; 24cm
Includes index
ISBN 0-19-826160-8 (cased) : £15.00
ISBN 0-19-213229-6 (pbk) : £6.95
ISBN 0-521-07705-2 (Cambridge University Press) B81-39939

225.9′22 — Bible. N.T. — *Biographies*

Brownrigg, Ronald. Who's who in the New Testament. — London : Hodder & Stoughton, Feb.1982. — [320]p. — (Teach yourself books)
Originally published: London : Weidenfeld & Nicolson, 1971
ISBN 0-340-27177-9 (pbk) : £2.95 : CIP entry B81-36356

225.9′24 — Bible. New Testament. Peter, *the Apostle, Saint*

Jeffery, Colin. Saint Peter / by Colin Jeffery and Paul Dunn ; illustrations by Janet Wicox. — London : Catholic Truth Society, 1981. — [16]p : col.ill ; 19cm
ISBN 0-85183-370-5 (pbk) : £0.50 B81-24330

225.9′24 — Bible. N.T.. Paul, *the Apostle, Saint*

Bruce, F. F.. Paul : apostle of the free spirit / F.F. Bruce. — [Rev. ed.]. — Exeter : Paternoster, [1981], c1977. — 510p,[16]p of plates : ill,1col.map ; 24cm
Previous ed.: 1977. — Map on lining papers. — Bibliography: p476-479. — Includes index
ISBN 0-85364-307-5 (cased)
ISBN 0-85364-308-3 (pbk) : Unpriced B81-18365

225.9′24 — Bible. N.T.. Paul, *the Apostle, Saint — Biographies*

Montefiore, Hugh. Paul the Apostle / Hugh Montefiore. — London : Fount, 1981. — 124p ; 18cm
ISBN 0-00-626389-5 (pbk) : £1.50 B81-38281

Pollock, John, *1923-*. The apostle : a life of Paul / by John Pollock. — Tring : Lion, 1981, c1969. — xii,244p ; 18cm
Originally published: London : Hodder & Stoughton, 1969
ISBN 0-85648-356-7 (pbk) : £1.75 B81-18731

225.9′24 — Bible. N.T.. Paul, *the Apostle, Saint.* **Chronology**

Jewett, Robert. [A chronology of Paul's life]. Dating Paul's life / Robert Jewett. — London : SCM, 1979. — viii,160p ; 22cm
Originally published: Philadelphia : Fortress Press, c1979. — Includes index
ISBN 0-334-00299-0 (pbk) : £3.95 B81-10052

225.9′24 — Bible. N.T.. Paul, *the Apostle, Saint — Festschriften*

Pauline studies : essays presented to Professor F.F. Bruce on his 70th birthday / edited by Donald A. Hagner and Murray J. Harris. — Exeter : Paternoster, c1980. — xli,293p : 1port ; 24cm
Bibliography: pxxii-xxxvi. - Includes index
ISBN 0-85364-271-0 : £10.00
Also classified at 227′.06 B81-06744

225.9′3 — Bible. N.T.. Historicity. Archaeological sourcecs

Finegan, Jack. The archeology of the New Testament : the Mediterranean world of the early Christian apostles / Jack Finegan. — Boulder : Westview Press ; London : Croom Helm, 1981. — xxxii,250p : ill,maps,ports ; 26cm
Includes index
ISBN 0-7099-1006-1 : £19.95 B81-41020

225.9′3 — Western Turkey. New Testament cities. Archaeological investigation

Yamauchi, Edwin M.. The archaeology of New Testament cities in Western Asia Minor / Edwin M. Yamauchi. — London : Pickering & Inglis, 1980. — 180p : ill,maps,plans ; 22cm
Bibliography: p167-169. — Includes index
ISBN 0-7208-0482-5 (pbk) : £3.95 B81-08970

225.9′5 — Christianity — *Sources of data: Bible. N.T. — For schools*

Hughes, Gerald. The birth of Christianity / Gerald Hughes and Stephen Travis. — Tring : Lion Publishing, 1981. — p97-128 : ill(some col.),col.maps ; 25cm. — (Introducing the Bible ; 4)
Cover title
ISBN 0-85648-266-8 (pbk) : £1.25 B81-16684

225.9′505 — Bible. N.T. — *Stories for children*

Bull, Norman J.. 100 New Testament stories / retold by Norman J. Bull ; illustrated by Val Biro. — London : Hamlyn, 1981. — 156p : col.ill,2col.maps,1col.plan ; 22cm
Maps, plans on lining papers
ISBN 0-600-36493-3 : £2.95 B81-34603

Kent, David. The last journey. — London (Elsley Court, 20 Great Titchfield St., W1P 7AD) : Kingfisher, Oct.1981. — [24]p. — (Kingfisher explorer books. Bible stories)
ISBN 0-86272-022-2 : £1.95 : CIP entry B81-27975

Priestley, J. G.. The New Testament / J.G. Priestley. — Exeter : Religious Education Press, 1981. — 155p : ill ; 22cm. — (Bible stories for today)
ISBN 0-08-025600-7 (cased) : £2.95
ISBN 0-08-025599-x (pbk) : £2.25 B81-25346

Robertson, Jenny. The Ladybird New Testament / text by Jenny Robertson ; based on the God's story script by Oliver Hunkin in association with Yorkshire Television ; illustrated by Alan Parry. — Loughborough : Ladybird, 1981. — 153p : col.ill,2col.maps ; 24cm
Col.maps on lining papers
ISBN 0-7214-7518-3 : £3.95
ISBN 0-85421-904-8 (Scripture Union) B81-19460

225.9′505 — Bible. N.T. — *Stories for children — Illustrations*

Sibley, Brian. Picture Bible : New Testament / text Brian Sibley ; illustrations John Pickering ... — London : Ark, c1981. — 143p : col.ill,col.maps ; 31cm
ISBN 0-86201-109-4 : £3.95 B81-28466

226′.01 — Bible. N.T. Gospels. Authenticity. Attitudes of Muslims

Wijngaards, John N. M.. Objections to the Gospels / John Wijngaards. — London : Catholic Truth Society, 1981. — 14p ; 19cm
ISBN 0-85183-424-8 (pbk) : £0.30 B81-36150

226′.01 — Bible. N.T. Gospels. Historicity

Gospel perspectives : studies of history and tradition in the four gospels / edited by R.T. France and David Wenham. — Sheffield : JSOT Press
Vol.2. — c1981. — 375p : ill ; 23cm
ISBN 0-905774-31-0 : Unpriced B81-26074

Staudinger, Hugo. The trustworthiness of the gospels / Hugo Staudinger ; translated by Robin T. Hammond. — Edinburgh (33 Montgomery Street, Edinburgh) : Handsel Press, 1981. — ix,106p ; 22cm
Translation of: Die historische Glaubwürdigkeit der Evangelien
ISBN 0-905312-15-5 : £6.50 B81-38973

226′.052 — Bible. N.T. Gospels. *English. Selections — Texts*

[Bible. N.T.. Gospels. *English. Selections. 1981*]. The good news : the life of Jesus told in the words of the evangelists / and illustrated by Franco Vasini ; the scripture texts are taken from a translation of the New Testament by John Bligh. — Slough : St Paul, c1981. — 186p : col.ill ; 26cm
Illustrations originally published with Italian text as 'Il vangelo'
ISBN 0-85439-190-8 : £7.50 B81-39177

226′.06 — Bible. N.T. Gospels. Influence of Jewish law

Walls, Roland. Law and gospel / by Roland Walls. — Oxford (Convent of the Incarnation, Fairacres, Oxford OX4 1TB) : SLG, c1980. — iii,38p ; 21cm. — (Fairacres publications, ISSN 0307-1405 ; no.77)
ISBN 0-7283-0087-7 (pbk) : £0.75 B81-33234

226′.06 — Bible. N.T. Gospels - *Psychological perspectives*

Nicoll, Maurice. The mark. — London : Watkins, Apr.1981. — 1v.
ISBN 0-7224-0195-7 (pbk) : CIP entry B81-05140

226′.09505 — Bible. N.T. Gospels — *Stories for children*

Ashley, Elizabeth. Wonderful stories Jesus told / stories retold by Elizabeth Ashley ; illustrated by Gerritt Vandersyde. — London : Dean, c1968 (1980 [printing]). — [28]p : col.ill ; 32cm. — (An Everyday picture book)
ISBN 0-603-00212-9 : £1.25 B81-32154

226′.2′0076 — Bible. N.T. Matthew — *Questions & answers — For schools*

Harris, J. G.. St Matthew / J.G. Harris. — Walton-on-Thames : Celtic Revision Aids, 1981. — 122p ; 19cm. — (New Testament studies, O level)
ISBN 0-17-751326-8 (pbk) : £1.25 B81-15511

226′.2077 — Bible. N.T. Matthew. *English - Texts with commentaries*

Beare, Francis Wright. The Gospel according to Matthew. — Oxford : Blackwell, June 1981. — [576]p
ISBN 0-631-12528-0 : £25.00 : CIP entry B81-14416

226′.2077 — Bible. N.T. Matthew — *Texts with commentaries*

Dickson, David, *1583-1663*. A brief exposition of the Evangel of Jesus Christ according to Matthew / David Dickson. — Edinburgh : Banner of Truth Trust, 1981. — x,416p : ill ; 22cm. — ([The Geneva series of commentaries])
Originally published: London : For Ralph Smith, 1647. — Ill on lining papers
ISBN 0-85151-319-0 : £5.95 B81-36444

226′.20924 — Bible. N.T. Matthew. Matthew, *Saint — Stories for children*

Lewis, David, *1932-*. The greedy tax man / [retold by David Lewis ; illustrated Alan Parry]. — London : Scripture Union, c1979. — [20]p : chiefly col.ill ; 16cm. — (Follow the leader)
Text, ill. on inside covers
ISBN 0-85421-772-x (pbk) : £0.40 B81-38970

226′.3′0076 — Bible. N.T. Mark — *Questions & answers — For schools*

Harris, J. G.. St Mark / J.G. Harris. — Walton-on-Thames : Celtic Revision Aids, 1981. — 118p ; 19cm. — (New Testament studies, O level)
ISBN 0-17-751327-6 (pbk) : £1.25 B81-15509

226′.3052 — Bible. N.T. Mark. *English — Texts*

[Bible. N.T.. Mark. *English. Selections. 1980*]. The passion of our Lord according to Saint Mark / arranged as a liturgical devotion by E. Milner-White ; and set to music by Charles Wood. — Croydon : Royal School of Church Music, [1980?]. — 7p ; 21cm
Cover title
Unpriced (unbound) B81-12142

226′.3059163 — Bible. N.T. Mark. *Gaelic — Texts*

[Bible. N.T.. Mark. *Gaelic. Today's Gaelic. 1980*] . An Deagh sgeul aig Marcus : Soisguel Mharcuis ann an Gàidhlig an là an diugh. — Edinburgh (7 Hampton Terrace, Edinburgh EH12 5XU) : Comann-Bhìoball Dùthchail na h-Alba, 1980. — 52p : ill,1map ; 18cm
Unpriced (pbk) B81-10860

226′.4′0076 — Bible. N.T. Luke — *Questions & answers — For schools*

Harris, J. G.. St Luke / J.G. Harris. — Walton-on-Thames : Celtic Revision Aids, 1981. — 120p ; 19cm. — (New Testament studies, O level)
ISBN 0-17-751328-4 (pbk) : £1.25 B81-15508

226′.4′07 — Bible. N.T. Luke — *Commentaries*

Barrell, E. V.. An introduction to St Luke. — London : Murray, Feb.1982. — [224]p
ISBN 0-7195-3903-x (pbk) : £2.25 : CIP entry B81-35851

226'.407 — Bible. N.T. Luke — *Commentaries*
Ellis, E. Earle. The Gospel of Luke. — London : Marshall, Morgan & Scott, July 1981. — [324] p. — (The New Century Bible commentary)
ISBN 0-551-00849-0 (pbk) : £4.95 : CIP entry B81-20643

226'.5'0076 — Bible. N.T. John — *Questions & answers — For schools*
Harris, J. G.. St John / J.G. Harris. — Walton-on-Thames : Celtic Revision Aids, 1981. — 120p ; 19cm. — (New Testament studies, O level)
ISBN 0-17-751329-2 (pbk) : £1.25 B81-15507

226'.506 — Bible. N.T. John — *Expositions*
Morrice, William G.. The new beginning : studies in the fourth Gospel / by William G. Morrice. — Edinburgh : St. Andrew Press, 1981. — 82p ; 18cm
ISBN 0-7152-0463-7 (pbk) : £1.75 B81-24175

Painter, John. John : witness and theologian / John Painter ; foreword by C.K. Barrett. — 2nd ed. — London : SPCK, 1979. — xv,160p ; 20cm
Previous ed.: 1975. — Bibliography: p143-147. - Includes index
ISBN 0-281-03684-5 (pbk) : £3.50 B81-11511

Ramsey, Michael. Lent with St. John / Michael Ramsey. — London : SPCK, 1980. — 47p ; 21cm
ISBN 0-281-03747-7 (pbk) : Unpriced B81-26351

226'.5066 — Bible. N.T. John. Authorship
Cooke, Greville. Who wrote the Fourth Gospel? : a short summary of the evidence / Greville Cooke. — Bognor Regis : New Horizon, c1981. — 104p ; 22cm
ISBN 0-86116-772-4 : £3.75 B81-33392

226'.507 — Bible. N.T. John — *Commentaries*
Hill, J. R.. John / J.R. Hill. — London : Ark, 1981. — 112p : 1map ; 21cm. — (Bible study commentary)
ISBN 0-86201-084-5 (pbk) : Unpriced B81-32448

Lindars, Barnabas. The Gospel of John. — London : Marshall, Morgan & Scott, July 1981. — [648]p. — (The New Century Bible commentary)
ISBN 0-551-00848-2 (pbk) : £7.95 : CIP entry B81-20647

226'.6'0076 — Bible. N.T. Acts — *Questions & answers — For schools*
Harris, J. G.. Acts of the Apostles / J.G. Harris. — Walton-on-Thames : Celtic Revision Aids, 1981. — 121p ; 19cm : 1map. — (New Testament studies, O level)
ISBN 0-17-751330-6 (pbk) : £1.25 B81-15510

226'.606 — Bible. N.T. Acts — *Expositions*
Bewes, Richard. The Church reaches out : a study of church growth from the Acts of the Apostles / by Richard Bewes. — London : Mowbray, 1981. — xi,110p ; 18cm. — (Mowbray's popular Christian paperbacks)
ISBN 0-264-66753-0 (pbk) : £1.50 B81-22951

226'.6'09505 — Bible. N.T. Acts - *Stories for children*
Jones, Roger. Saints alive!. — Redhill : National Christian Education Council, May 1981. — [64]p
ISBN 0-7197-0292-5 (pbk) : £3.00 : CIP entry B81-06047

226'.709505 — Jesus Christ. Miracles: Calming of waves — *Stories for children*
Lewis, David, *1932-*. The frightened fisherman / [retold by David Lewis ; illustrated by Alan Parry]. — London : Scripture Union, c1979. — [20]p : chiefly col.ill ; 16cm. — (Follow the leader)
Text, ill. on inside covers
ISBN 0-85421-775-4 (pbk) : £0.40 B81-38967

226'.709505 — Jesus Christ. Miracles: Centurion's servant — *Stories for children*
Lewis, David, *1932-*. The kind captain / [retold by David Lewis ; illustrated by Alan Parry]. — London : Scripture Union, c1979. — [20]p : chiefly col.ill ; 16cm. — (Follow the leader)
Text, ill. on inside covers
ISBN 0-85421-773-8 (pbk) : £0.40 B81-38968

226'.709505 — Jesus Christ. Miracles: Feeding of the five thousand — *Stories for children*
Lewis, David, *1932-*. The hungry crowd / [retold by David Lewis ; illustrated by Alan Parry]. — London : Scripture Union, c1979. — [20]p : chiefly col.ill ; 16cm. — (Follow the leader)
Text, ill. on inside covers
ISBN 0-85421-774-6 (pbk) : £0.40 B81-38969

226'.709'505 — Jesus Christ. Miracles — *Stories for children*
Kent, David. Miracles and parables. — London (Elsley Court, 20 Great Titchfield St., W1P 7AD) : Kingfisher, Oct.1981. — [24]p. — (Kingfisher explorer books. Bible stories)
ISBN 0-86272-021-4 : £1.95 : CIP entry
Also classified at 226'.809'505 B81-27977

226'.8'0076 — Bible. N.T.. Parables — *Questions & answers*
Parker, R. G. Secrets : of living God's way : a home study course of twelve lessons based on the Parables of the Lord Jesus Christ / prepared by R.G. Parker. — Birmingham (47 Woodbridge Rd., Mosley, Birmingham B13 9DZ) : R.G. Parker, [1981?]. — [14]leaves ; 30cm
Unpriced (unbound) B81-40299

226'.806 — Bible. N.T.. Parables — *Expositions*
Flood, Edmund. More parables for now / Edmund Flood ; illustrated by Penelope Burns. — London : Darton, Longman and Todd, 1981. — 102p : ill ; 22cm
ISBN 0-232-51532-8 (pbk) : £2.50 : CIP rev. B81-19147

Flood, Edmund. Parables for now / Edmund Flood ; illustrated by Penelope Burns. — London : Darton, Longman and Todd, 1981. — 98p : ill ; 22cm
ISBN 0-232-51517-4 (pbk) : £2.50 : CIP rev. B81-19148

226'.806 — Bible. N.T.. Parables: Prodigal Son — *Expositions*
Meek, N. T.. The search for satisfaction / [N.T. Meek]. — Ilford (22 Christchurch Rd., Ilford, Essex IG1 4QY) : F.C. Mutton, [1981]. — 9p ; 20cm
Unpriced (unbound) B81-32928

226'.8'06 — Bible. N.T. Parables - *Psychological perspectives*
Nicoll, Maurice. The new man. — London : Watkins, Apr.1981. — 1v.
ISBN 0-7224-0194-9 (pbk) : CIP entry B81-05139

226'.8077 — Bible N.T.. Parables — *Texts with commentaries*
Boucher, Madeleine I.. The parables / Madeleine I. Boucher. — Dublin : Veritas, c1981. — 159p : ill ; 21cm. — (New Testament message ; v.7)
Bibliography: p158-159
ISBN 0-89453-130-1 (pbk) : Unpriced B81-40457

226'.809505 — Bible. N.T. Parables: Prodigal son — *Stories for children*
Doney, Meryl. The loving Father : parables of Jesus in cartoon / words by Meryl Doney ; pictures by Graham Round. — Tring : Lion Publishing, 1979 (1981 [printing]). — [16]p : chiefly col.ill ; 19cm. — (Little Lions)
ISBN 0-85648-118-1 (pbk) : £0.35 B81-27004

226'.809505 — Bible. N.T. Parables — *Stories for children*
Doney, Meryl. Jesus the teacher / [retold by Meryl and Malcolm Doney]. — London : Hutchinson, 1981. — 45p : col.ill,col.maps ; 29cm. — (Living stories from the Bible)
Ill, maps on lining papers. — Includes index
ISBN 0-09-144330-x : £3.25 : CIP rev. B81-04255

226'.809'505 — Bible. N.T. Parables — *Stories for children*
Kent, David. Miracles and parables. — London (Elsley Court, 20 Great Titchfield St., W1P 7AD) : Kingfisher, Oct.1981. — [24]p. — (Kingfisher explorer books. Bible stories)
ISBN 0-86272-021-4 : £1.95 : CIP entry
Primary classification 226'.709'505 B81-27977

226'.809505 — Bible. N.T.. Parables — *Stories for children. Illustrations*
Mullen, Peter. The parables of Jesus in pictures / written by Peter Mullen, drawn by Martin Pitts. — London : Edward Arnold, 1981. — 80p : ill ; 25cm
ISBN 0-7131-0583-6 (pbk) : £1.75 : CIP rev. B81-08935

226'.8106 — Bible. N.T. Thessalonians 1 II — *Expositions*
Brown, T. H.. Not in vain / by T.H. Brown. — Chelmsford (1 Donald Way, Chelmsford, Essex CM2 9JB) : Bible Spreading Union, 1980?. — 14p ; 22cm
Unpriced (pbk) B81-08089

226'.9306 — Beatitudes — *Expositions*
Hutchison, Harry. 'Well, I'm blessed!' : devotional studies in the beatitudes / Harry Hutchison. — London : Eyre & Spottiswoode, 1981. — 130p ; 18cm
Includes index
ISBN 0-413-80160-8 (pbk) : £1.95 B81-19738

227'.06 — Bible. N.T. Epistles of Paul — *Expositions*
Beker, J. Christiaan. Paul the Apostle : the triumph of God in life and thought / J. Christaan Beker. — Edinburgh : Clark, 1980. — xi,452p ; 24cm
Bibliography: p399-418. - Includes index
ISBN 0-567-09309-3 : £11.95 B81-06737

Loane, Marcus L.. Grace and the Gentiles : expository studies in six Pauline Letters / by Marcus L. Loane. — Edinburgh : Banner of Truth Trust, 1981. — ix,149p ; 22cm
ISBN 0-85151-327-1 (pbk) : £2.50 B81-36445

Summenhart, Heinrich. Ain hüpsche frag = A polite inquiry / Heinrich Summenhart ; translated with an introduction and notes by Helga Robinson-Hammerstein. — Dublin ([College St., Dublin 3]) : The Friends of the Library, Trinity College, 1980. — [9]p : ill ; 21cm
German text, English translation. — Facsim of: ed. published Augsburg : Melciro Ramminger, 1524. — English translation (17p) in pocket
ISBN 0-904720-04-7 (pbk) : Unpriced B81-30098

227'.06 — Bible. N.T. Epistles of Paul — *Expositions — Festschriften*
Pauline studies : essays presented to Professor F.F. Bruce on his 70th birthday / edited by Donald A. Hagner and Murray J. Harris. — Exeter : Paternoster, c1980. — xli,293p : 1port ; 24cm
Bibliography: pxxii-xxxvi. - Includes index
ISBN 0-85364-271-0 : £10.00
Primary classification 225.9'24 B81-06744

227'.066 — Bible. N.T. Pastoral epistles. Authorship
Wilson, Stephen G.. Luke and the Pastoral Epistles / Stephen G. Wilson. — London : SPCK, 1979. — xii,162p ; 23cm
Includes index
ISBN 0-281-03676-4 : £8.50 B81-09249

227'.07 — Bible. N.T. Epistles of Paul — *Commentaries*
Cundy, Ian. Ephesians — 2 Thessalonians / Ian Cundy. — London : Ark, 1981. — 128p : maps ; 21cm. — (Bible study commentary)
ISBN 0-86201-086-1 (pbk) : Unpriced B81-32446

227'.1077 — Bible. N.T. Romans — *Texts with commentaries*
Hendriksen, William. Romans / William Hendriksen. — Edinburgh : Banner of Truth Trust. — (New Testament commentary)
Vol.1: Chs 1-8. — 1980. — ix,302p ; 23cm
Bibliography: p302
ISBN 0-85151-324-7 : £5.25 B81-09774

227'.205203 — Bible. N.T. Corinthians, 1st XIII. *English. Authorized — Texts*

[Bible. N.T. Corinthians, 1st XIII. *English. Authorized. 1981*]**St.** Paul's Cathedral Royal Wedding : the twenty-ninth July 1981. — Esher (Edward Burrett, Full Point, New Rd., Esher, Surrey KT10 9PG) : Penmiel Press, 1981. — [9]p ; 27cm
Limited ed. of 100 numbered copies. — The text of the lesson read during the Royal Wedding Service
£10.00 (unbound) B81-40317

227'.407 — Bible. N.T. Galatians — *Commentaries*

Metcalfe, John, *1932-*. Of God or man? : light from Galatians / John Metcalfe. — Pen : Metcalfe, 1980. — 178p ; 20cm
ISBN 0-9506366-3-0 (pbk) : Unpriced B81-07060

227'.5077 — Bible. N.T. Ephesians — *Texts with commentaries*

Carr, A. John. The emerging Church : in Ephesians / A. John Carr ; foreword by Roland Walls. — Dundee (58 Constitution St., Dundee, DDE 6NE) : Charis, 1980. — viii,199p ; 20cm
ISBN 0-9507339-0-3 (pbk) : £1.95 B81-05719

Swain, Lionel. Ephesians / Lionel Swain. — Dublin : Veritas Publications, c1980. — xii,114p ; 21cm. — (New Testament message ; v. 13)
Bibliography: p114
ISBN 0-86217-031-1 (pbk) : Unpriced B81-21992

227'.606 — Bible. N.T. Philippians — *Expositions*

Duncan, George B.. Sustained by joy : studies in Philippians / George B. Duncan. — London : Pickering & Inglis, c1980. — 123p ; 19cm
"Most of the material in this book was previously issued under the title The Life of Continual Rejoicing" — T. p. verso
ISBN 0-7208-0469-8 (pbk) : £1.60 B81-03934

227'.707 — Bible. N.T. Colossians — *Commentaries*

Rogers, Patrick V.. Colossians / Patrick V. Rogers. — Dublin : Veritas, c1980. — xxii,98p : ill ; 21cm. — (New Testament message ; v.15)
Bibliography: p95-98
ISBN 0-86217-032-x (pbk) : Unpriced B81-20885

227'.87077 — Bible. N.T. Hebrews — *Texts with commentaries*

Casey, Juliana. Hebrews / Juliana Casey. — Dublin : Veritas, c980. — xvii,101p ; 21cm. — (New Testament message ; v.18)
Bibliography: p100-101
ISBN 0-86217-033-8 (pbk) : Unpriced B81-22131

227'.91077 — Bible. N.T. Epistle of James — *Texts with commentaries*

Kugelman, Richard. James & Jude / Richard Kugelman. — Dublin : Veritas Publications, c1980. — viii,114p ; 21cm. — (New Testament message ; v.19)
Bibliography: p111-114
ISBN 0-89453-142-5 (pbk) : Unpriced
Also classified at 227'.97077 B81-21991

Laws, Sophie. A commentary on the epistle of James / Sophie Laws. — London : A. and C. Black, 1980. — x,273p ; 22cm. — (Black's New Testament commentaries)
Includes index
ISBN 0-7136-2075-7 (cased) : £6.95 : CIP rev.
ISBN 0-7136-2041-2 (pbk) : £5.95 B80-05781

227'.97077 — Bible. N.T. Epistle of Jude — *Texts with commentaries*

Kugelman, Richard. James & Jude / Richard Kugelman. — Dublin : Veritas Publications, c1980. — viii,114p ; 21cm. — (New Testament message ; v.19)
Bibliography: p111-114
ISBN 0-89453-142-5 (pbk) : Unpriced
Primary classification 227'.91077 B81-21991

228'.06 — Bible. N.T. Revelation — *Anthroposophical viewpoints*

Bock, Emil. The Apocalypse of Saint John / Emil Bock ; [translated by Alfred Heidenreich]. — Edinburgh : Floris, 1981, c1957. — 189p ; 22cm
Translation of: Apokalypse. — Originally published: London : Christian Community Press, 1957
ISBN 0-903540-42-8 (pbk) : £5.95 : CIP rev. B80-12718

228'.06 — Bible. N.T. Revelation — *Expositions*

Lawrence, D. H.. Apocalypse / D.H. Lawrence ; with an introduction by Richard Aldington. — Harmondsworth : Penguin in association with William Heinemann Ltd., 1974, c1932 (1981 [printing]). — xxvi,125p ; 18cm
Originally published: New York : Viking Press ; London : Martin Secker, 1932
ISBN 0-14-003856-6 (pbk) : £0.95 B81-30954

228'.06'8 — Bible. N.T. Revelation. Cabalistic interpretations

Lévi, Eliphas. The mysteries of the Qabalah, or, The occult agreement of the two testaments. — Wellingborough : Aquarian Press, Dec.1981. — [286]p
Translation of: Les mystères de la Kabbale. — Originally published: 1974
ISBN 0-85030-274-9 (pbk) : £4.95 : CIP entry
Primary classification 224'.406'8 B81-32054

230 — CHRISTIAN THEOLOGY, CHRISTIAN DOCTRINE

230 — Christian doctrine

Allan, John, *1950-*. Sure thing : how to be a Christian and know you're on solid ground / John Allan. — Eastbourne : Kingsway, 1981. — 64p ; 18cm
ISBN 0-86065-120-7 (pbk) : £0.95 B81-26969

Blamires, Harry. [The faith and modern error]. The secularist heresy : the erosion of the Gospel in the twentieth century / Harry Blamires. — London : SPCK, 1956 (1981 [printing]). — 155p ; 21cm
ISBN 0-281-03804-x (pbk) : £2.95 B81-06185

Cassidy, Michael. Christianity for the open-minded : an invitation to doubters / Michael Cassidy. — Leicester : Inter-Varsity Press, 1980, c1978. — 48p ; 13cm. — (An IVP Christian way booklet)
Originally published: Downers Grove : Inter-Varsity Christian Fellowship, 1978. — Bibliography: p47-48
ISBN 0-85110-133-x (pbk) : £0.30 : CIP rev. B80-21352

Eddison, John. What Christians believe / John Eddison. — London : Hodder and Stoughton, 1981. — 142p ; 18cm
ISBN 0-340-26361-x (pbk) : £1.50 B81-17917

Ferguson, Sinclair B.. The Christian life : a doctrinal introduction / Sinclair B. Ferguson. — London : Hodder and Stoughton, 1981. — xii,179p ; 20cm. — (Ecclesia books)
ISBN 0-340-26571-x (pbk) : £3.75 : CIP rev. B81-06034

Hanson, Anthony Tyrrell. Reasonable belief : a survey of the Christian faith / A.T. Hanson and R.P.C. Hanson. — Oxford : Oxford University Press, 1980. — xii,283p ; 22cm
Bibliography: p266-272. - Includes index
ISBN 0-19-213235-0 (cased) : £8.50 : CIP rev.
ISBN 0-19-213238-5 (pbk) : £3.95 B80-18583

Harries, Richard. Being a Christian / by Richard Harries. — London : Mowbray, 1981. — xii,159p ; 18cm. — (Mowbray's popular Christian paperbacks)
ISBN 0-264-66561-9 (pbk) : £1.75 B81-20855

Hinchliff, Peter. The human potential : Christian faith as an approach to the everyday reality of this world / Peter Hinchliff and David Young ; foreword by the Archbishop of Canterbury. — London : Darton, Longman and Todd, 1981. — 162p ; 22cm
Includes index
ISBN 0-232-51501-8 (pbk) : £4.50 B81-23382

International church index : (doctrinal) / edited by Roy A. Facey. — [Plymouth] ([P.O. Box 52, Plymouth PL1 1XN]) : Index Publications, c1981. — 243p : ill ; 21cm
Cover title
ISBN 0-907578-00-4 (pbk) : £2.75 B81-26149

Lang-Sims, Lois. The Christian mystery : an exposition of esoteric Christianity / by Lois Lang-Sims. — London : Allen & Unwin, 1980. — 147p ; 23cm
ISBN 0-04-200038-6 : Unpriced : CIP rev. B80-26469

Little, Paul E.. Paul Little's why & what book. — Wheaton, Ill. ; Amersham-on-the-Hill : Victor, c1980. — 255p : ports ; 24cm
Includes bibliographies. — Contents: Know why you believe. Originally published: Wheaton, Ill. : Scripture Press, 1967 - Know what you believe. Originally published: Wheaton, Ill. : Scripture Press, 1970
ISBN 0-88207-814-3 : Unpriced B81-11402

Packer, J. I.. God's words. — Leicester : Inter-Varsity Press, Nov.1981. — [208]p
ISBN 0-85110-434-7 (pbk) : £1.75 : CIP entry B81-30614

Thurian, Max. Our faith : basic Christian belief / Max Thurian ; translated by Emily Chisholm. — Taize : Presses de Taize ; Leighton Buzzard : Faith Press, 1978. — 219p ; 18cm
£3.25 (pbk) B81-10528

Tozer, A. W.. A treasury of A.W. Tozer : a collection of Tozer favourites / introduced by Warren W. Wiersbe. — Bromley : STL Books, 1981, c1980. — 296p ; 18cm
Originally published: Grand Rapids, Mich. : Baker Book House, c1980
ISBN 0-903843-44-7 (pbk) : Unpriced B81-21358

Urquhart, Colin. In Christ Jesus. — London : Hodder & Stoughton, Nov.1981. — [224]p
ISBN 0-340-27601-0 (pbk) : £1.75 : CIP entry B81-30127

230 — Christian doctrine — *Welsh texts*

Roberts, Emyr. Y ffydd a roddwyd / Emyr Robert. — 2 argraffiad. — Pen-y-bont ar Ogwr [Bridgend] ('Bryntirion', Bridgend, M. Glamorgan CF31 4DX) : Gwasg Efengylaidd Cymru, 1980. — 61p ; 18cm
Previous ed.: 1957
ISBN 0-900898-46-1 (pbk) : £0.9k B81-10823

230 — Christian theology

Ebeling, Gerhard. The study of theology / Gerhard Ebeling ; translated by Duane A. Priebe. — London : Collins, 1979. — x,196p ; 24cm
Translation of: Studium der Theologie. — Bibliography: p172-196
ISBN 0-00-215780-2 : £7.95 B81-12046

230 — Christian theology — *Philosophical perspectives — Festschriften*

The **Philosophical** frontiers of Christian theology. — Cambridge : Cambridge University Press, Feb.1982. — [240]p
ISBN 0-521-24012-3 : £15.00 : CIP entry B81-39210

230 — Lollards. Christian doctrine — *Readings from contemporary sources*

Selections from English Wycliffite writings / edited with an introduction, notes and glossary by Anne Hudson. — Cambridge : Cambridge University Press, 1981, c1978. — x,234p ; 24cm
Bibliography: p231-234. — Includes index
ISBN 0-521-28258-6 (pbk) : £7.95 B81-15332

230'.014 — Christian theology. Implications of transformational-generative linguistics

Lawrence, Irene, *1942-*. Linguistics and theology : the significance of Noam Chomsky for theological construction / Irene Lawrence. — Metuchen ; London : Scarecrow, 1980. — xv,196p : ill ; 23cm. — (ATLA monograph series ; no.16)
Bibliography: p176-188. - Includes index
ISBN 0-8108-1347-5 : £8.75 B81-17379

230'.014 — Christian theology. Use of metaphor

Rikhof, Herwi. The concept of Church : a methodological inquiry into the use of metaphors in ecclesiology / Herwi Rikhof. — London : Sheed and Ward, 1981. — xvi,304p ; 23cm
Bibliography: p279-296. — Includes index
ISBN 0-7220-2618-8 : £19.50 : CIP rev. B81-18165

230'.044'09031 — Protestant churches. Christian doctrine, *1500-1600*

Reardon, Bernard M. G.. Religious thought in the Reformation / Bernard M.G. Reardon. — London : Longman, 1981. — xv,349p ; 22cm
Bibliography: p330-340. — Includes index
ISBN 0-582-49030-8 (cased) : Unpriced : CIP rev. B81-03159

230'.05 — Christian doctrine — *For Indian immigrants — Serials*

The **Lord** is near : English issue of Nere. — 1-2-. — Smethwick (c/o The Editor, 163 Dibble Rd, Smethwick, Warley, W. Midlands B67 7PT) : [S.n.], 1978-. — v. ; 30cm
Annual. — English edition of: Prabhū neṛe hai
ISSN 0262-0367 = The Lord is near : Unpriced B81-36005

230'.05 — Christian doctrine — *Gujarati texts — Serials*

Kariba. — 1-. — Smethwick (c/o The Editor, 163 Dibble Rd, Warley, Smethwick, West Midlands B67 7PT) : [S.n.], 1979-. — v. ; 30cm
Irregular
ISSN 0262-0391 = Kariba : Unpriced B81-36006

230'.05 — Christian doctrine — *Punjabi texts — Serials*

Prabhū neṛe hai. — No.1-. — [Smethwick] ([c/o The Editor, 163 Dibble Rd, Smethwick, Warley, West Midlands B67 7PT]) : [S.n.], [1977]-. — v. ; 30cm
Two issues yearly
ISSN 0262-0375 = Prabhū neṛe hai : Unpriced B81-36004

230'.05 — Christian doctrine — *Serials*

Tyndale bulletin. — 31 (1980). — Nottingham (Norton St., Nottingham NG7 3HR) : Inter-Varsity Press, 1980. — 170p
ISBN 0-85111-075-4 : Unpriced B81-20302

230'.05 — Christian doctrine — *Serials — Welsh texts*

Ysgrifau diwinyddol. — 1-. — Pen-y-bont ar Ogwr [Bridgend] (Bryntirion, Pen-y-bont ar Ogwr, Morgannwg Ganol CF31 4DX) : Gwasg Efengylaidd Cymru, 1979-. — v. ; 21cm
Annual. — Continues: Bwletin diwinyddol
ISSN 0143-0092 = Ysgrifau diwinyddol : £2.00 B81-09184

230'.07'12 — Secondary schools. Curriculum subjects: Christian doctrine — *For teaching*

Mullen, Peter. Thinking about religion / Peter Mullen. — London : Edward Arnold, 1980. — vi,90p : 1ill ; 22cm
Bibliography: p89-90
ISBN 0-7131-0468-6 (pbk) : £1.95 : CIP rev. B80-20170

230'.09 — Christian theology. Influence of scientific theories, *to 1979*

Torrance, Thomas F.. The ground and grammar of theology / Thomas F. Torrance. — Belfast : Christian Journals, 1980. — xii,180p ; 23cm
Includes index
ISBN 0-904302-59-8 : £5.95 B81-06960

230'.09'015 — Christian doctrine *related to* **Dead Sea scrolls,** *to ca 100*

Allegro, John M.. The Dead Sea scrolls and the Christian myth / John M. Allegro. — London : Abacus, 1981, c1979. — 248p,[8]p of plates : ill ; 20cm
Originally published: Newton Abbot : David and Charles, 1979. — Includes index
ISBN 0-349-10069-1 (pbk) : £2.50
Primary classification 296.1'55 B81-12945

230'.11 — Christian theology. Neoplatonism, *to ca 450 — Festchiften*

. Neoplatonism and early Christian thought : essays in honour of A.H. Armstrong / edited by H.J. Blumenthal and R.A. Markus. — London : Variorum Publications, 1981. — x,256p ; 24cm
Includes index
ISBN 0-86078-085-6 : £18.00 : CIP rev. B81-21631

230'.193 — Syrian Orthodox Church. Christian doctrine

Joseph, Rebecca. Spirit, prayers, faith and Bible / Rebecca Joseph. — Bognor Regis : New Horizon, c1981. — 123p ; 21cm
ISBN 0-86116-452-0 : £5.25 B81-33406

230'.2 — Catholic Church. Christian doctrine

John Paul II, *Pope*. Letter of the Holy Father Pope John Paul II to the Bishops of the Catholic Church for the 1600th anniversary of the First Council of Constaninople and the 1550th aniversary of the Council of Ephesus. — London : Catholic Truth Society, 1981. — 22p ; 19cm
ISBN 0-85183-421-3 (pbk) : £0.45 B81-24333

O'Collins, Gerald. Fundamental theology / Gerald O'Collins. — London : Darton, Longman & Todd, c1981. — 283p ; 23cm
Includes index
ISBN 0-232-51522-0 (pbk) : £5.95 B81-23355

Rahner, Karl. Our Christian faith : answers for the future / Karl Rahner & Karl-Heinz Weger ; [translated by Francis McDonagh]. — London : Burns & Oates, 1980. — xi,179p ; 21cm
Translation of: Was sollen wir noch glauben?
ISBN 0-86012-108-9 (pbk) : £3.95 B81-18624

Rahner, Karl. Theological investigations / by Karl Rahner. — London : Darton, Longman and Todd
Translation of the second part of: Schriften zur Theologie, XII
Vol.XVII: Jesus, man and the church. — 1981. — 260p ; 23cm
Includes index
ISBN 0-232-51401-1 : £14.50 B81-23415

Rahner, Karl. Theological investigations. — London : Darton, Longman & Todd
Translation of: Schriften zur Theologie
Vol.20: Concern for the church. — Jan.1982. — [224]p
ISBN 0-232-51538-7 : £14.50 : CIP entry B81-34407

Thomas, *Aquinas, Saint*. Summa theologiæ / St. Thomas Aquinas ; Latin text and English translation, introductions, notes, appendices and glossaries. — London : Blackfriars in conjunction with Eyre & Spottiswoode
[Vol.61]: [General index : an index to the English text, Volumes 1-60, the questions, articles, terms, and the authors cited] / [T.C. O'Brien]. — 1980. — 383p ; 23cm
ISBN 0-413-35610-8 : £9.95 B81-29004

230'.2 — Catholic Church. Christian doctrine. Change

Lash, Nicholas. Change in focus : a study of doctrinal change and continuity / Nicholas Lash. — London : Sheed and Ward, 1973 (1981 [printing]). — ix,198p ; 22cm. — (Stagbooks)
Bibliography: p183-191. — Includes index
ISBN 0-7220-1712-x (pbk) : £6.50 B81-40812

230'.2 — Catholic Church. Christian doctrine — *Polish texts*

Catholic Church. *Pope (1978- : John Paul II)*. [Dives in misericordia. Polish]. Encyklika Dives in misericordia = O Bozym mitosierdziu / Jan Paweł II. — London : Veritas, [1980]. — 88p ; 19cm
Translation from the Latin
Unpriced (pbk) B81-15331

Thomas, *Aquinas, Saint*. [Summa theologiae. Polish]. Suma teologiczna / św. Tomasz z Akwinu. — London : Veritas Foundation Publication Centre
T.6: Człowiek
Część 1 ... / przełożył i objaśnieniami zaopatrzył o. Pius Bełch ... — 1980. — 296p,[2]p of plates : ports ; 20cm. — (Biblioteka polska. Seria tomistyczna ; t.24)
Translation of: Summa theologiae. Vol.1 : 75-84
Unpriced B81-19525

Thomas, *Aquinas, Saint*. [Summa theologiae. Polish]. Suma teologiczna / św. Tomasz z Akwinu. — London : Veritas Foundation Publication Centre
T.7: Człowiek
Część 2 ... / przełożył i objaśnieniami zaopatrzył o Pius Bełch ... — 1980. — 389p ; 20cm. — (Biblioteka polska. Seria tomistyczna ; t.25)
Translation of: Summa theologiae. Vol.1 : 85-102
Unpriced B81-19524

230'.2'05 — Catholic Church. Christian doctrine — *Serials*

Milltown studies. — [No.?]1 (1977)-. — Dublin (Milltown Park, Dublin 6) : Milltown Institute of Theology & Philosophy, 1977-. — v. ; 20cm
Two issues yearly. — Description based on: No.5 (Spring 1980)
£2.00 per year B81-04543

230'.2'0924 — Catholic Church. Apologetics. Rahner, Karl — *Critical studies*

Bacik, James J.. Apologetics and the eclipse of mystery : mystagogy according to Karl Rahner / James J. Bacik. — Notre Dame ; London : University of Notre Dame Press, c1980. — xvi,166p ; 24cm
Bibliography: p143-159. - Includes index
ISBN 0-268-00592-3 : £9.00 B81-03046

230'.2'0924 — Catholic Church. Christian doctrine. Küng, Hans — *Biographies*

Nowell, Robert. A passion for truth : Hans Küng : a biography / Robert Nowell. — London : Collins, 1981. — 377p ; 22cm
Bibliography: p8-9. - Includes index
ISBN 0-00-215056-5 : £9.95 B81-05670

230'.2'0924 — Catholic Church. Christian doctrine. Theories of Rahner, Karl

Weger, Karl-Heinz. Karl Rahner : an introduction to his theology / Karl-Heinz Weger ; [translated by David Smith]. — London : Burns & Oates, 1980. — viii,200p ; 22cm
Translation of: Karl Rahner
ISBN 0-86012-094-5 : £7.95 B81-02976

230'.3 — Church of England. Apologetics — *Early works*

Hooker, Richard, *1553 or 4-1600*. [Of the lawes of ecclesiasticall politie. Books 6-8]. Of the laws of ecclesiastical polity / Richard Hooker. — Cambridge [Mass.] ; London : Belknap Press
Books 6,7,8 / P.G. Stanwood, editor. — 1981. — lxxvii,644p : ill,facsims ; 25cm. — (The Folger Library edition of the works of Richard Hooker ; v.3)
Books 6 and 8 originally published: 1648. Book 7 originally published: 1662
ISBN 0-674-63210-9 : £45.50 B81-40032

230'.3 — Church of England. Christian doctrine

Cooke, Greville. The heresies of orthodoxy / Greville Cooke. — Bognor Regis : New Horizon, c1980. — 243p ; 21cm
ISBN 0-86116-352-4 : £5.25 B81-21773

230'.3 — Church of England. Christian doctrine — *Facsimiles*

Sibbes, Richard. Works of Richard Sibbes. — Edinburgh : Banner of Truth Trust
Facsim of: 1st ed., Edinburgh : J. Nichol, 1862-64
Vol.3: An exposition of 2nd Corinthians, Chapter One / edited by Alexander B. Grosart. — 1981. — 543p ; 23cm
ISBN 0-85151-329-8 : £5.95 B81-36440

230'.4 — Continental Protestant churches. Christian doctrine

Barth, Karl. The Christian life : Church dogmatics IV, 4 lecture fragments / by Karl Barth ; translated by Geoffrey W. Bromiley. — Edinburgh : T. & T. Clark, 1981. — xv,310p ; 24cm
Translation of: Das christliche Leben. — Originally published: Grand Rapids : Eerdmans, 1981. — Includes index
ISBN 0-567-09320-4 : £9.75 B81-28263

230'.42 — England. Calvinism, *to 1649*

Kendall, R. T.. Calvin and English Calvinism to 1649 / R.T. Kendall. — Oxford : Oxford University Press, c1979 (1981 [printing]). — xii,238p ; 22cm. — (Oxford theological monographs)
Bibliography: p214-226. - Includes index
ISBN 0-19-826720-7 (pbk) : £5.50 B81-17764

230'.42 — Reformed churches. Christian doctrine

De Witt, John Richard. What is the Reformed faith? / John Richard de Witt. — Edinburgh : Banner of Truth Trust, 1981. — 24p ; 19cm
ISBN 0-85151-326-3 (pbk) : £0.50 B81-36439

230'.52 — Church of Scotland. Christian doctrine — *Interviews*

Barclay, William, *1907-1978*. Arguing about Christianity / seven discussions between William Barclay and Iain Reid. — Edinburgh : Saint Andrew Press, 1980. — viii,70p ; 18cm
ISBN 0-7152-0427-0 (pbk) : £1.30 B81-05570

230'.673 — Seventh-Day Adventists. Christian doctrine

Ball, Bryan W.. The English connection. — Cambridge : James Clarke, June 1981. — 1v.
ISBN 0-227-67844-3 : £7.50 : CIP entry B81-15860

230'.75'0924 — Methodist Church. Christian doctrine. Theories of Reynolds, Anna

Albin, Thomas R.. Full salvation : the spirituality of Anna Reynalds of Truro 1775-1840 / Thomas R. Albin. — [Cornwall] : [Cornish Methodist Historical Association], 1981. — 28p ; 21cm. — (Cornish Methodist Historical Association occasional publication ; no.17)
£0.80 (pbk) B81-29561

230'.95 — Church of Christ, Scientist. Christian doctrine. Scientific translation

Morgan, John L.. Scientific translation : an exploration of the spiritual meaning and implications of the Scientific translation of immortal mind, and the Scientific translation of mortal mind, which are found in Science and health with key to the Scriptures, by Mary Baker Eddy / by John L. Morgan. — Revision. — Saffron Walden : Elmdon, c1981. — xii,149p ; 21cm
Previous ed.: published as The two translations. 1957
ISBN 0-900471-13-1 (pbk) : Unpriced B81-40182

230'.96 — Society of Friends. Christian doctrine

Fox, George, *1624-1691*. Wait in the light : the spirituality of George Fox : a selection of the writings of George Fox and early Friends / with introductions by John Lampen. — London : Quaker Home Service, 1981. — 118p ; 19cm
ISBN 0-85245-155-5 (pbk) : £2.50 B81-24373

Penn, William. No cross, no crown : a discourse showing the nature and discipline of the holy cross of Christ and that the denial of self and daily bearing of Christ's cross is the alone way to the rest and kingdom of God / by William Penn. — York : Sessions, 1981. — xxx,469p : 1facsim ; 19cm
Text of 2nd ed., corr. and much enl., 1682. — Bibliography: pxvii. — Includes index
ISBN 0-900657-57-x (cased) : Unpriced
ISBN 0-900657-58-8 (pbk) : Unpriced B81-19280

230'.99 — Brethren. Christian doctrine

Byng, C. R.. Faithfulness : meetings in Indianapolis, November 1977 / C.R. Byng. — London (50 Red Post Hill, SE24 9JQ) : E.C. Burr, [1981?]. — 156p ; 17cm
£1.40 (pbk) B81-19581

McCallum, S. The mediatorial economy : meetings in Macduff, June 1974 / S. McCallum. — London (50 Red Post Hill, SE24 9JQ) : E.C. Burr, [1974]. — 119p ; 17cm
£1.40 (pbk) B81-18826

Symington, J. H.. The blessing of Abraham and the burnt-offering : Regina & Detroit, May 1981 / J.H. Symington ; editor Wilbert J. Seed. — St. Vincent, Minn. ; Kingston [upon Thames] (Kingston, Surrey, KT1 4DX) : Bible & Gospel Trust, 1981. — 325p ; 16cm. — (JHS ; v.90)
Unpriced (pbk) B81-40449

Symington, J. H.. The covenant of salt, 2 Chronicles 13: 5 : Chicago & Neche, July 1980 / J.H. Symington. — Kingston, Surrey : Bible & Gospel Trust, c1980. — 245p ; 16cm. — (JHS ; v.80)
Private circulation (pbk) B81-32761

Symington, J. H.. Have we found the narrow way? : New York & Hamilton, November 1980 / J.H. Symington. — Kingston ([2 Upper Teddington Rd., Kingston-upon-Thames] Surrey KT1 4DX) : Bible and Gospel Trust, 1980. — 288p ; 16cm. — (JHS ; v.85)
Unpriced (pbk) B81-12095

Symington, J. H.. John's baptism and the counsel of God : Perth, Sydney, Auckland & elsewhere, September & October 1980 / J.H. Symington. — Kingston ([2 Upper Teddington Rd., Kingston-upon-Thames] Surrey KT1 4DX) : Bible and Gospel Trust, 1980. — 389p ; 16cm. — (JHS ; v.84)
Unpriced (pbk) B81-12093

Symington, J. H.. Leprosy - cleansed or fixed? : Vancouver & Winnipeg, June 1981 / J.H. Symington ; editor Wilbert J. Seed. — St. Vincent, Minn. ; Kingston [upon Thames] (Kingston, Surrey KT1 4DX) : Bible & Gospel Trust, 1981. — 262p ; 16cm. — (JHS ; v.92)
Unpriced (pbk) B81-40451

Symington, J. H.. Ministry of J.H. Symington : 1970-71. — Kingston, Surrey : Bible & Gospel Trust, c1980. — 257p ; 16cm. — (JHS ; v.75)
Unpriced (pbk) B81-32756

Symington, J. H.. Ministry of J.H. Symington : 1973. — Kingston, Surrey : Bible & Gospel Trust, c1980. — 345p ; 16cm. — (JHS ; v.81)
Private circulation (pbk) B81-32757

Symington, J. H.. Ministry of J.H. Symington : 1972. — Kingston, Surrey : Bible & Gospel Trust, c1980. — 337p ; 16cm. — (JHS ; v.76)
Unpriced (pbk) B81-32758

Symington, J. H.. Ministry of J.H. Symington 1973-74. — Kingston ([2 Upper Teddington Rd., Kingston-upon-Thames] Surrey KT1 4DX) : Bible & Gospel Trust, c1980. — 343p ; 16cm. — (JHS ; v.83)
Unpriced (pbk) B81-12092

Symington, J. H.. Ministry of J.H. Symington 1974-75 / [H. Magahy, editor]. — Kingston [upon Thames] (Kingston, Surrey KT1 4DX) : Bible & Gospel Trust, c1981. — 362p ; 16cm. — (JHS ; v.91)
Unpriced (pbk) B81-40450

Symington, J. H.. The new creation's stainless joy : Westfield & Chicago, April 1981 / J.H. Symington. — Kingston : Bible & Gospel Trust, 1981. — 289p ; 16cm. — (JHS ; vol.89)
Unpriced (pbk) B81-32566

Symington, J. H.. Once darkness but now light in the Lord : Victoria & Minneapolis, March 1981 / J.H. Symington. — Kingston : Bible & Gospel Trust, 1981. — 326p ; 16cm. — (JHS ; vol.88)
Unpriced (pbk) B81-32565

Symington, J. H.. Paul next to Christ : Victoria & Winnipeg, May 1980 / J.H. Symington. — Kingston, Surrey : Bible & Gospel Trust, c1980. — 131p ; 16cm. — (JHS ; v.78)
Unpriced (pbk) B81-32760

Symington, J. H.. The power of the Son's voice : San Francisco & Woodlands, December 1980 / J.H. Symington. — Kington : [2 Upper Teddington Rd., Kinston-upon-Thames] Surrey KT1 4DX : Bible and Gospel Trust, 1981. — 242p ; 16cm. — (JHS ; v.86)
Unpriced (pbk) B81-12094

Symington, J. H.. Repent and believe in the glad tidings : Neche, July 1981 / J.H. Symington ; editor Wilbert J. Seed. — St. Vincent, Minn. ; Kingston [upon Thames] (Kingston, Surrey KT1 4DX) : Bible & Gospel Trust, 1981. — 185p ; 16cm. — (JHS ; v.93)
Unpriced (pbk) B81-40452

Symington, J. H.. The thing as it is : Rochester & Minneapolis, August 1980 / J.H. Symington. — Kingston, Surrey : Bible & Gospel Trust, c1980. — 233p ; 16cm. — (JHS ; v.82)
Private circulation (pbk) B81-32762

Symington, J. H.. The unconquerable daughter of Zion : Bristol, Endbach & elsewhere, June 1980 / J. H. Symington. — Kingston, Surrey : Bible & Gospel Trust, 1980. — 238p ; 16cm. — (JHS ; v.79)
Unpriced (pbk) B81-36114

Symington, J. H.. The value of Paul's concern : Bristol, Coventry & elsewhere, January & February 1981 / J.H. Symington. — Kingston : Bible and Gospel Trust, 1981. — 439p ; 16cm. — (JHS ; vol.87)
Unpriced (pbk) B81-32564

Symington, J. H.. The washing of water by the word : Coventry, Redbridge & elsewhere, April 1980 / J.H. Symington. — Kingston, Surrey : Bible & Gospel Trust, c1980. — 155p ; 16cm. — (JHS ; v.77)
Unpriced (pbk) B81-32759

Welch, A. J. E.. The Priest and the Prophet : meetings in Indianapolis November 1978 / A.J.E. Welch. — London (50 Red Post Hill, SE24 9JQ) : E.C. Burr, [1978?]. — 120p ; 17cm
£1.40 (pbk) B81-24948

230'.99 — Spiritualist churches. Christian doctrine

Chang Wei *(Spirit)*. The truth of life : teachings of the Lord Chang Wei. — London : Regency, c1980. — 162p ; 23cm
ISBN 0-7212-0615-8 : £3.00 B81-06178

231 — CHRISTIAN DOCTRINE. GOD

231 — Bible. Special subjects: Christian doctrine. God — *Expositions*

Wood, A. Skevington. I want to know what the Bible says about God / A. Skevington Wood. — Eastbourne : Kingsway, 1980. — 111p ; 20cm
Bibliography: p108. - Includes index
ISBN 0-86065-040-5 (pbk) : £2.50 B81-04468

231 — Christian doctrine. God

Bewes, Richard. God / [Richard Bewes, Robert Hicks]. — [London] : Scripture Union, 1981. — [24]p : col.ill ; 17cm. — (Explaining Bible truth)
Cover title. — Text on inside covers
ISBN 0-85421-912-9 (pbk) : £0.40 B81-24503

Goldsmith, Joel S.. The Mystical 'I' / Joel S. Goldsmith ; edited by Lorraine Sinkler. — London : Unwin Paperbacks, 1981, c1971. — 145p ; 20cm. — (Mandala Books)
Originally published: New York : Harper and Row, 1971 ; London : Allen & Unwin, 1972
ISBN 0-04-200036-x (pbk) : £2.50 B81-24564

231'.3 — Bible. Special subjects: Christian doctrine. Holy Spirit — *Expositions*

Allen, Stuart. The doctrine of the Holy Spirit / by Stuart Allen. — London : Berean Publishing, c1980. — 35p ; 22cm
ISBN 0-85156-078-4 (pbk) : £0.50 B81-07848

231′.3 — Christian doctrine. Holy Spirit

Bewes, Richard. The Holy Spirit / [Richard Bewes, Robert Hicks]. — [London] : Scripture Union, 1981. — [24]p : col.ill ; 17cm. — (Explaining Bible truth)
Cover title. — Text on inside covers
ISBN 0-85421-914-5 (pbk) : £0.40 B81-24509

Rosato, Philip J.. The spirit as Lord : the pneumatology of Karl Barth / Philip J. Rosato. — Edinburgh : T. & T. Clark, 1981. — x,228p : ill ; 23cm
Includes index
ISBN 0-567-09305-0 : £8.95 B81-29180

231.7′2 — Bible. Special subjects: Christian doctrine. Kingdom of God

Chantry, Walter J.. God′s righteous kingdom : focusing on the law′s connection with the gospel / Walter J. Chantry. — Edinburgh : Banner of Truth Trust, 1980. — 151p ; 18cm
Bibliography: p151
ISBN 0-85151-310-7 (pbk) : £1.50 B81-05839

231.7′2 — Bible. Special subjects: Christian doctrine. Kingdom of God — *Expositions*

Allen, Stuart. The Kingdom of God in heaven and on earth : a study of the Kingdom of God throughout the Bible / by Stuart Allen. — London : Berean Publishing Trust, 1981. — 147p : 1map ; 22cm
Includes index
ISBN 0-85156-083-0 (pbk) : Unpriced B81-13053

Ladd, George Eldon. The presence of the future : the eschatology of biblical realism / George Eldon Ladd. — [2nd ed.]. — London : SPCK, 1980, c1974. — xiv,370p ; 21cm
Originally published: Grand Rapids : Eerdmans, 1974. — Bibliography: p341-355. - Includes index
ISBN 0-8028-1531-6 (pbk) : £4.95 B81-05864

231.7′45 — Christian doctrine. Prophecy

Gill, Robin. Prophecy and praxis. — London : Marshall Morgan & Scott, Nov.1981. — [144] p. — (Contemporary Christian studies)
ISBN 0-551-00918-7 (pbk) : £5.95 : CIP entry B81-34215

231.7′65 — Universe. Origins — *Christian viewpoints*

Jaki, Stanley L.. Cosmos and creater / by Stanley L. Jaki. — Edinburgh : Scottish Academic Press, 1980. — xii,168p ; 22cm
Includes index
ISBN 0-7073-0285-4 : £6.75 B81-19599

231′.8 — Bible. N.T. Special subjects: Suffering

Suffering and martyrdom in the New Testament. — Cambridge : Cambridge University Press, June 1981. — [240]p
ISBN 0-521-23482-4 : £17.50 : CIP entry
Also classified at 272′.1 B81-19191

231′.8 — Suffering — *Christian viewpoints*

Graham, Billy. Till Armageddon : a perspective on suffering / Billy Graham. — London : Hodder and Stoughton, 1981. — 224p ; 23cm
Includes index
ISBN 0-340-26634-1 (cased) : Unpriced : CIP rev.
ISBN 0-340-27210-4 (pbk) : £3.50 B81-13833

Greenwood, Hilda. Triumphant suffering / Hilda Greenwood. — Bognor Regis : New Horizon, c1980. — 52p ; 20cm
ISBN 0-86116-640-x (pbk) : £1.25 B81-12717

Israel, Martin. The pain that heals : the place of suffering in the growth of the person / Martin Israel. — London : Hodder and Stoughton, 1981. — 192p ; 22cm. — (Ecclesia books)
ISBN 0-340-26411-x (pbk) : £4.95 B81-12469

Sinclair, Max. Halfway to heaven. — London : Hodder & Stoughton, Oct.1981. — [160]p
ISBN 0-340-26336-9 (pbk) : £1.75 : CIP entry B81-25749

232 — JESUS CHRIST

232 — Bible. N.T. Gospels. Special subjects: Jesus Christ

Middlebrook, Douglas. A humanist′s Jesus / Douglas Middlebrook. — Adelaide : New Word ; London (93 Talfourd Rd., S.E.15) : Distributed by W. Slade, c1979. — 407p ; 22cm
ISBN 0-9595850-2-8 (pbk) : £3.00 B81-17642

232 — Bible. N.T. Gospels. Special subjects: Jesus Christ. Names: Son of Man. Derivation

Higgins, A. J. B.. The Son of Man in the teaching of Jesus / A.J.B. Higgins. — Cambridge : Cambridge University Press, 1980. — x,177p ; 23cm. — (Monograph series / Society for New Testament Studies ; 39)
Bibliography: p159-168. — Includes index
ISBN 0-521-22363-6 : £10.50 : CIP rev. B80-25125

232 — Bible. N.T.. Special subjects: Jesus Christ

Davies, Chris. Jesus, one of us : Bible studies on the person of Jesus Christ / Chris Davies, Brede Kristensen and Ada Lum. — [Rev. ed.]. — Leicester : Inter-Varsity, 1981. — 128p ; 17x23cm
Previous ed.: 1976. — Bibliography: p10
ISBN 0-85110-413-4 (pbk) : £1.95 : CIP rev. B80-21357

Meyer, Ben F.. The aims of Jesus / Ben F. Meyer. — London : SCM, 1979. — 335p ; 23cm
Includes index
ISBN 0-334-00027-0 : £9.50 B81-06956

232 — Jesus Christ

The **Alpha-omega** diagram. — [Plymouth] ([47 Lower Park Drive, Staddiscombe, Plymouth PL9 9DA]) : Joshuan, c1981. — [4]p : ill ; 21cm
Unpriced (unbound) B81-29501

Bewes, Richard. Jesus Christ / [Richard Bewes, Robert Hicks]. — [London] : Scripture Union, 1981. — [24]p : col.ill ; 17cm. — (Explaining Bible truth)
Cover title. — Text on inside covers
ISBN 0-85421-913-7 (pbk) : £0.40 B81-24502

Marsh, John, *1904-*. Jesus in his lifetime / John Marsh. — London : Sidgwick & Jackson, 1981. — 262p ; 24cm
Bibliography: p255. - Includes index
ISBN 0-283-98638-7 : £10.00 B81-17650

232 — Jesus Christ — *Anthroposophical viewpoints*

Stewart, Desmond. The foreigner. — London : H. Hamilton, Oct.1981. — [204]p
ISBN 0-241-10686-9 : £10.95 : CIP entry B81-26779

232 — Jesus Christ *compared with* **characters in drama in European languages,** *1884-1961*

Ditsky, John. The onstage Christ : studies in the persistence of a theme / by John Ditsky. — London : Vision, 1980. — 188p ; 23cm. — (Vision critical studies)
Includes index
ISBN 0-85478-284-2 : £9.95
Primary classification 809.2′927 B81-02713

232 — Jesus Christ. Influence of Judaism

Riches, John. Jesus and transformation of Judaism / John Riches. — London : Darton, Longman & Todd, 1980. — x,254p ; 23cm
Bibliography: p227-235. - Includes index
ISBN 0-232-51448-8 : £12.95 : CIP rev. B80-18585

232 — Jesus Christ — *Muslim viewpoints*

′Ata ur-Rahim, Muhammad. Jesus : a prophet of Islam / Muhammad ′Ata ur-Rahim. — 2nd ed. — London : MWH, c1979. — 244p ; 22cm
Previous ed.: 1977. — Bibliography: p237-244
ISBN 0-906194-08-3 (pbk) : £1.95 B81-38690

232′.09 — Christian doctrine. Jesus Christ, *to 1980*

Lewis, Hywel D.. Jesus in the faith of Christians / Hywel D. Lewis. — London : Macmillan, 1981. — viii,144p ; 23cm
Includes index
ISBN 0-333-29105-0 : £15.00 B81-38731

232′.092′4 — Christian doctrine. Jesus Christ. Theories of Newman, John Henry

Strange, Roderick. Newman and the Gospel of Christ / Roderick Strange. — Oxford : Oxford University Press, c1981. — xv,179p ; 22cm. — (Oxford theological monographs)
Bibliography: p168-175. — Includes index
ISBN 0-19-826718-5 : £12.50 : CIP rev. B81-06027

232′.092′4 — Christian doctrine. Jesus Christ. Theories of Origen *compared with* **theories of Teilhard de Chardin, Pierre**

Lyons, J. A.. The Cosmic Christ in Origen and Teilhard de Chardin. — Oxford : Oxford University Press, Jan.1982. — [256]p. — (Oxford theological monographs)
ISBN 0-19-826721-5 : £12.50 : CIP entry B81-34381

232′.1 — Jesus Christ. Incarnation

Haughton, Rosemary. The passionate God / Rosemary Haughton. — London : Darton, Longman and Todd, 1981. — 344p ; 23cm
Bibliography: p336-337. — Includes index
ISBN 0-232-51515-8 : £12.95 : CIP rev.
Primary classification 232′.5 B81-19188

Incarnation and myth : the debate continued / edited by Michael Goulder. — London : SCM, 1979. — xi,257p ; 22cm
Includes index
ISBN 0-334-00660-0 (pbk) : £3.50 B81-27862

232′.1 — Jesus Christ. Incarnation — *Conference proceedings*

The **Incarnation** : ecumenical studies in the Nicene-Constantinopolitan Creed A.D. 381 / edited by Thomas F. Torrance. — Edinburgh (33 Montgomery St., Edinburgh) : Handsel, 1981. — xxii,180p ; 23cm
Conference papers. — Includes index
ISBN 0-905312-14-7 : £6.50 B81-37118

232′.1 — Jesus Christ. Incarnation — *Society of Friends viewpoints*

Richards, Gerald. On being incarnate : a Quaker view / by Gerald Richards. — [Sutton] (12 Boston Court, Christchurch Park, Sutton, Surrey SM2 5TJ) : Open Letter Movement, 1979. — 60p : ill ; 21cm
£1.50 (pbk) B81-36335

232′.3 — Christian doctrine. Atonement

Wallace, Ronald. The atoning death of Christ. — London : Marshall, Morgan & Scott, July 1981. — [160]p. — (Foundations for faith)
ISBN 0-551-00855-5 (pbk) : £4.95 : CIP entry B81-20597

232′.5 — Jesus Christ. Resurrection

Haughton, Rosemary. The passionate God / Rosemary Haughton. — London : Darton, Longman and Todd, 1981. — 344p ; 23cm
Bibliography: p336-337. — Includes index
ISBN 0-232-51515-8 : £12.95 : CIP rev.
Also classified at 232′.1 B81-19188

O′Collins, Gerald. The Easter Jesus / Gerald O′Collins. — New ed. — London : Darton, Longman & Todd, 1980. — xxi,142p ; 22cm
Previous ed.: 1973. — Bibliography: p139-140. — Includes index
ISBN 0-232-51500-x (pbk) : £3.45 : CIP rev. B80-23981

232′.6 — Jesus Christ. Second coming

Bewes, Richard. The last things / [Richard Bewes, Robert Hicks]. — [London] : Scripture Union, 1981. — [24]p : col.ill ; 17cm. — (Explaining Bible truth)
Cover title. — Text on inside covers
ISBN 0-85421-919-6 (pbk) : £0.40 B81-24504

Fenn, Francis. Christ will come again / by Francis Fenn. — London : Catholic Truth Society, 1981. — 12p ; 19cm
ISBN 0-85183-427-2 (pbk) : £0.35 B81-36148

Travis, Stephen. I believe in the second coming of Jesus. — London : Hodder & Stoughton, Feb.1982. — [256]p
ISBN 0-340-27164-7 (pbk) : £4.95 : CIP entry B81-36354

232′.6 — Jesus Christ. Second coming *continuation*

Travis, Stephen. The Jesus hope / Stephen Travis. — Leicester : Inter-Varsity, 1980, c1974. — 128p ; 18cm
Originally published: London : Word Books, 1974. — Includes bibliographies
ISBN 0-85110-421-5 (pbk) : Unpriced : CIP rev. B80-21359

232′.6 — Jesus Christ. Second coming — *Occult viewpoints*

Bailey, Alice A.. The reappearance of the Christ / by Alice A. Bailey. — New York ; London : Lucis, 1948, c1976 (1979 printing). — 208p ; 20cm
Includes index
Unpriced (pbk) B81-37042

232′.8 — Jesus Christ. Divinity

Moore, Sebastian. The fire and the rose are one / Sebastian Moore. — London : Darton, Longman & Todd, 1980. — xv,158p ; 21cm
Originally published: New York : Seabury Press, 1980
ISBN 0-232-51471-2 (pbk) : £4.95 : CIP rev. B80-21360

232.9′01 — Jesus Christ. Life — *Anthroposophical viewpoints*

Bock, Emil. The three years / Emil Bock ; [translated by Alfred Heidenreich]. — Edinburgh : Floris, 1980, c1955. — 285p ; 22cm
Translation of: Die drei Jahre. — Originally published: London : Christian Community Press, 1955
ISBN 0-903540-41-x (pbk) : £5.95 : CIP rev. B80-12230

232.9′01 — Jesus Christ. Life — *Occult viewpoints*

Bailey, Alice A.. From Bethlehem to Calvary : the initiations of Jesus / by Alice A. Bailey. — New York ; London : Lucis, 1937, c1965 (1976 printing). — ix,292p ; 19cm
Unpriced (pbk) B81-37047

232.9′01 — Jesus Christ. Life — *Stories for children*

Ashley, Elizabeth. Day by day stories of Jesus / stories by Elizabeth Ashley ; illustrated by C. E. Caney. — London : Dean, 1980, c1967. — [28]p : col.ill ; 20cm
ISBN 0-603-00214-5 : £0.75 B81-10836

Bull, Norman J.. My little book of Jesus / Norman Bull ; [illustrations by Victor Ambrus]. — London : Hamlyn, 1981. — 42p : col.ill ; 16cm
ISBN 0-600-36484-4 : £0.99 B81-19952

Gosling, Angela. The other kingdom : a life of Jesus for children / by Angela Gosling ; with illustrations by Annabel Sebag-Montefiore. — Wetherden Sd Mutton Hall, Wetherden, Suffolk : [Dove], c1980. — viii,111p : ill,maps,1plan ; 23cm
ISBN 0-9507106-0-1 (cased) : £4.60
ISBN 0-9507106-1-x (pbk) : £3.60 B81-24047

Williams-Ellis, Virginia. Day by day stories about Jesus / written by Virginia Williams-Ellis ; illustrated by C.E. Cancy. — London : Dean, c1980. — [28]p : col.ill ; 20cm
ISBN 0-603-00215-3 : £0.75 B81-10835

232.9′08 — Jesus Christ. Life. Historicity

Harvey, A. E.. Jesus and the constraints of history. — London : Duckworth, Feb.1982. — [192]p. — (The Bampton lectures ; 1981)
ISBN 0-7156-1597-1 (cased) : £18.00 : CIP entry
ISBN 0-7156-1598-x (pbk) : £5.95 B81-36394

232.91 — Mary, *Mother of Jesus Christ — Devotional works*

Nassan, Maurice. Meditating of Mary / Maurice Nassan. — London : Catholic Truth Society, [1981]. — 32p ; 17cm
ISBN 0-85183-406-x (pbk) : £0.40 B81-24332

232.9′21 — Jesus Christ. Nativity — *Dramatisations — For schools*

Meade, Dorothy M.. A bairn is born : and other Nativity plays for juniors / by Dorothy M. Meade. — London : Published for the General Synod Board of Education by CIO Publishing, c1980. — viii,80p ; 21cm
Bibliography: p80
ISBN 0-7151-0391-1 (pbk) : £2.00 B81-04140

232.9′21 — Jesus Christ. Nativity — *Stories for children*

The **Christmas** story / [illustrated by Borje Svensson]. — London : Chatto & Windus, c1981. — [12]p : col.ill ; 18cm. — (A Peepshow book)
ISBN 0-7011-2566-7 : £2.25 B81-36089

232.9′5 — Jesus Christ. Entry into Jerusalem — *Stories, anecdotes*

Engel, Leopold. The entry into Jerusalem / conveyed through Leopold Engel. — Camberley (4 Bramcote, Camberley, Surrey, GU15 1SJ) : Parousia, c1980. — 24p ; 15x21cm
ISBN 0-906712-08-4 (pbk) : Unpriced B81-15746

232.9′57 — Bible. N.T. Special subjects: Jesus Christ. Last Supper

Marshall, I. Howard. Last Supper and Lord′s Supper / by I. Howard Marshall. — Exeter : Paternoster, c1980. — 191p ; 22cm
Includes index
ISBN 0-85364-306-7 (cased) : Unpriced : CIP rev.
ISBN 0-85364-313-x (pbk£4.20)
Also classified at 234′.163 B80-27789

232.9′6 — Catholics. Christian life. Prayer. Stations of the Cross — *Devotional works*

Cullen, Peter. The Stations of the Cross book / Peter Cullen ; [illustrations, the Benedictine Nuns]. — Great Wakering (Mayhew-McCrimmon), 1981. — [36]p : ill ; 15cm
ISBN 0-85597-304-8 (pbk) : £0.55 B81-26145

232.9′6 — Jesus Christ. Passion, death & resurrection

Benesch, Friedrich. Easter / Friedrich Benesch ; [translated by Robin and Sibylle Alexander]. — Edinburgh : Floris, 1981, c1978. — 79p ; 18cm
Translation of: Ostern
ISBN 0-903540-44-4 (pbk) : £2.25 B81-24020

Calvin, Jean. [The deity of Christ]. Sermons on the saving work of Christ / John Calvin ; selected and translated by Leroy Nixon. — Welwyn : Evangelical Press, 1980. — 302p : 1port ; 22cm
Translation from the French. — Originally published: Grand Rapids : Eerdmans, 1950
ISBN 0-85234-149-0 (pbk) : £3.25 B81-23050

232.9′6 — Jesus Christ. Passion — *Devotional works*

More, *Sir* **Thomas,** *Saint*. The Tower works : devotional writings / St. Thomas More ; edited by Garry E. Haupt. — New Haven ; London : Yale University Press, 1980. — xxvii,322p : 1ill ; 21cm. — (The Yale edition of the works of St. Thomas More. Selected works)
Bibliography: pxxv-xxvii. - Includes index
ISBN 0-300-02265-4 : £18.00 : CIP rev. B80-21358

232.9′62 — Jesus Christ. Trial

Brandon, S. G. F.. The trial of Jesus of Nazareth / S.G.F. Brandon. — London : Batsford, 1968 (1981 [printing]). — 223p,[15]p of plates : ill,1plan ; 23cm
Bibliography: p204-210. — Includes index
ISBN 0-7134-1250-x : £12.50 B81-24323

232.9′66 — Jesus Christ. Relics: Holy Shroud of Turin

Sox, H. David. The image on the Shroud : is the Turin Shroud a forgery? / H. David Sox. — London : Unwin Paperbacks, 1981. — x,175p,[8]p of plates : ill,ports ; 20cm. — (Mandala books)
ISBN 0-04-200039-4 (pbk) : £1.95 B81-08453

232.9′7 — Jesus Christ. Resurrection. Historical sources: Bible. N.T. Gospels

Butler, Samuel, *1835-1902*. Samuel Butler on the resurrection / edited and introduced by Robert Johnstone ; with an appendix by W.B. Primrose. — Gerrards Cross : Smythe, 1980. — 64p ; 23cm
ISBN 0-901072-59-1 : £3.95 : CIP rev. B80-11735

233 — CHRISTIAN DOCTRINE. HUMANKIND

233 — Christian doctrine. Man

Gilbert, G. W. H.. What is man? / G.W.H. Gilbert. — Bognor Regis : New Horizon, c1979. — 358p ; 22cm
ISBN 0-86116-391-5 : £4.25 B81-21774

Hillyard, Albert H.. The green leaves of the spirit : of things past, things present and things to come / by Albert H. Hillyard. — London : Greater World Association, 1981. — xliii,536p : 1ill ; 23cm
ISBN 0-900413-30-1 : £7.95 B81-28942

233′.1 — Christian doctrine. Creation

Torrance, Thomas F.. Divine and contingent order. — Oxford : Oxford University Press, Sept.1981. — [144]p
ISBN 0-19-826658-8 : £9.50 : CIP entry B81-21609

233′.11 — Christian doctrine. Creation — *For children*

God save me - / [illustrations by D′reen Neeves]. — Tring : Lion Publishing, c1981. — [12]p : col.ill ; 17cm. — (Lion board books)
ISBN 0-85648-354-0 : £0.65 B81-38474

233′.14 — Christian doctrine. Original sin *related to* **human anxiety** — *Philosophical perspectives*

Kierkegaard, Søren. The concept of anxiety : a simple psychologically orienting deliberation on the dogmatic issue of hereditary sin / by Soren Kierkegaard ; edited and translated with introduction and notes by Reidar Thomte in collaboration with Albert B. Anderson. — Princeton ; Guildford : Princeton University Press, c1980. — xviii,273p : 1facsim ; 22cm. — (Kierkegaard′s writings ; 8)
Translation of: Begrebet angest. — Bibliography: p257. - Includes index
ISBN 0-691-07244-2 : £10.20
Also classified at 152.4 B81-06740

234 — CHRISTIAN DOCTRINE. SALVATION AND GRACE

234 — Bible. N.T. Matthew. Special subjects: Righteousness — *Critical studies*

Przybylski, Benno. Righteousness in Matthew and his world of thought / Benno Przybylski. — Cambridge : Cambridge University Press, 1980. — xiii,184p ; 23cm. — (Monograph series / Society for New Testament Studies ; 41)
Bibliography: p160-170. — Includes index
ISBN 0-521-22566-3 : £9.50 : CIP rev. B80-29059

234 — Bible. Special subjects: Christian doctrine. Salvation — *Expositions*

Cotterell, Peter. Personal salvation / Peter Cotterell. — Eastbourne : Kingsway, 1980. — 127p ; 20cm. — (I want to know) (Kingsway Bible teaching series)
Bibliography: p123. - Includes index
ISBN 0-86065-038-3 (pbk) : £2.50 B81-06436

234 — Christian doctrine. Holiness

Armstrong, John, *19---*. The idea of holiness and the humane response : a study of the concept of holiness and its social consequence / John Armstrong. — London : Allen & Unwin, 1981. — 177p ; 23cm
ISBN 0-04-200042-4 : £7.50 : CIP rev. B81-02081

Nicholl, Donald. Holiness / Donald Nicholl. — London : Darton, Longman and Todd, 1981. — 158p ; 22cm
Includes index
ISBN 0-232-51497-6 (pbk) : £3.99 : CIP rev. B80-22875

234 — Christian doctrine. Sacrifice — *Anthropological perspectives — Conference proceedings*

Sacrifice / edited by M.F.C. Bourdillon, Meyer Fortes. — London : Academic Press for the Royal Anthropological Institute of Great Britain and Ireland, 1980. — xix,147p ; 24cm
Conference papers. — Bibliography: p137-143. — Includes index
ISBN 0-12-119040-4 : £7.80 : CIP rev.
B80-07221

234 — Christian doctrine. Salvation

Bewes, Richard. Salvation / [Richard Bewes, Robert Hicks]. — [London] : Scripture Union, 1981. — [24]p : col.ill ; 17cm. — (Explaining Bible truth)
Cover title. — Text on inside covers
ISBN 0-85421-916-1 (pbk) : £0.40 B81-24508

Caussade, Jean-Pierre de. The sacrament of the present moment / Jean-Pierre De Caussade ; translated by Kitty Muggeridge. — London : Collins : Fount Paperbacks, 1981. — 128p ; 18cm
Translation of: L'Abandon à la providence divine
ISBN 0-00-625545-0 (pbk) : £1.25 B81-11058

234'.1 — Christian doctrine. Grace

Pittenger, Norman. Abounding grace : a meditative and devotional study / by Norman Pittenger. — London : Mowbray, 1981. — vii,88p ; 18cm
ISBN 0-264-66789-1 (pbk) : £1.50 B81-29385

234'.163 — Bible. N.T. Special subjects: Christian doctrine. Eucharist

Marshall, I. Howard. Last Supper and Lord's Supper / by I. Howard Marshall. — Exeter : Paternoster, c1980. — 191p ; 22cm
Includes index
ISBN 0-85364-306-7 (cased) : Unpriced : CIP rev.
ISBN 0-85364-313-x (pbk£4.20)
Primary classification 232.9'57 B80-27789

234'.2 — Christian doctrine. Faith

Kendall, R. T.. Who by faith / R.T. Kendall. — London : Hodder and Stoughton, 1981. — vii,226p ; 18cm. — (Hodder Christian paperbacks)
Includes index
ISBN 0-340-26362-8 (pbk) : £1.95 B81-12286

Pinnock, Clark H.. Reason enough : a case for the Christian faith / Clark H. Pinnock. — Exeter : Paternoster, c1980. — 126p ; 21cm
Originally published: Downers Grove, Ill. : InterVarsity Press, 1980
ISBN 0-85364-296-6 (pbk) : £1.60 : CIP rev.
B80-09084

Roseveare, Helen. Living faith / by Helen M. Roseveare. — London : Hodder and Stoughton, 1980. — 187p ; 18cm. — (Hodder Christian paperbacks)
ISBN 0-340-25711-3 (pbk) : £1.50 : CIP rev.
B80-10936

Theissen, Gerd. On having a critical faith / Gerd Theissen. — London : SCM Press, 1979. — viii,101p ; 22cm
Translation of: Argumente für einen kritischen Glauben
ISBN 0-334-01180-9 (pbk) : £2.95 B81-17926

234'.2 — Christian doctrine. Hope

Rooney, John. Thinking about hope / John Rooney. — London : Catholic Truth Society, 1981. — 10p ; 16cm
ISBN 0-85183-400-0 (pbk) : £0.25 B81-14339

234'.4 — Christian doctrine. Regeneration — *Early works — Facsimiles*

Charnock, Stephen. The doctrine of regeneration / Stephen Charnock. — Welwyn : Evangelical Press, 1980. — 306p ; 18cm
Originally published: S.l. : S.n., 1840
Unpriced (pbk) B81-23046

234'.7 — Christian doctrine. Justification

The **Great** acquittal : justification by faith and current Christian thought / Tom Wright ... [et al.] ; edited Gavin Reid. — London : Fount Paperbacks, 1980. — 125p ; 18cm
ISBN 0-00-626111-6 (pbk) : £1.50 B81-06136

235 — CHRISTIAN DOCTRINE. SPIRITUAL BEINGS

235'.2 — Christian church. Saints. Veneration, *to 1980*

Perham, Michael. The communion of saints : an examination of the place of the Christian dead in the belief, worship, and calendars of the church / Michael Perham. — London : c/o St. Andrew's Vicarage, St. Andrew St., EC4 3AB : Alcuin Club, 1980. — xiv,177p ; 22cm. — (Alcuin Club collections ; no.62)
Bibliography: p169-170. - Includes index
ISBN 0-281-03794-9 (pbk) : £6.95 B81-06010

235'.3 — Christian doctrine. Angels

Graham, Billy. Angels : God's secret agents / Billy Graham. — London : Hodder and Stoughton, 1976, c1975 (1981 [printing]). — 15p ; 18cm. — (Hodder Christian paperbacks)
Originally published: Garden City, N.Y. : Doubleday, 1975
ISBN 0-340-21670-0 (pbk) : £1.25 B81-39134

235'.3 — Christian doctrine. Angels & principalities. Theories of Paul, *the Apostle, Saint*

Carr, Wesley. Angels and principalities. — Cambridge : Cambridge University Press, Nov.1981. — [256]p. — (Society for New Testament Studies monograph series ; 42)
ISBN 0-521-23429-8 : £13.50 : CIP entry
B81-32013

235'.47 — Bible. Special subjects: Christian doctrine. Satan — *Expositions*

Green, Michael, *1930*. I believe in Satan's downfall / Michael Green. — London : Hodder and Stoughton, 1981. — 254p ; 22cm
ISBN 0-340-26568-x (pbk) : £5.50 : CIP rev.
B81-19196

236 — CHRISTIAN DOCTRINE. ESCHATOLOGY

236 — Christian doctrine. Eschatology

Moltmann, Jürgen. The future of creation / Jürgen Moltmann. — London : SCM Press, 1979. — 198p ; 23cm
Translation of: Zukunft der Schöpfung. — Includes index
ISBN 0-334-00514-0 : £6.95 B81-17959

236'.09'02 — Christian doctrine. Eschatology. Theories, *ca 1150-ca 1650 — Festschriften*

Prophecy and millenarianism : essays in honour of Marjorie Reeves / edited by Ann Williams. — Harlow : Longman, 1980. — x,355p,1 leaf of plates : ill,1port ; 24cm
Includes a chapter in Latin. — Includes bibliographies
ISBN 0-582-36136-2 : £25.00 : CIP rev.
B80-34464

236'.1 — Death. Attitudes of Puritans of New England, *to ca 1750*

Stannard, David E.. The puritan way of death : a study in religion, culture, and social change / David E. Stannard. — Oxford : Oxford University Press, 1979, c1977. — x,236p : ill ; 21cm
Originally published: New York : Oxford University Press, 1977. — Includes index
ISBN 0-19-502521-0 (pbk) : £2.95 B81-10792

236'.2 — Christian doctrine. Future life

Rawlings, Maurice. Beyond death's door / Maurice Rawlings. — London : Sheldon, 1979, c1978 (1980 [printing]). — xiv,172p : ill ; 22cm
Originally published: Nashville : Nelson, 1978. — Bibliography: p161-164
ISBN 0-85969-169-1 (pbk) : £2.50 B81-03348

Winter, David. Hereafter : is there life beyond death? / by David Winter. — Rev. ed.. — London : Mowbray, 1981. — 96p ; 18cm
Previous ed.: London : Hodder & Stoughton, 1972. — Bibliography: p96
ISBN 0-264-66729-8 (pbk) : £1.50 B81-28999

236'.24 — Bible. N.T. Epistles of Paul. Special subjects: Christian doctrine. Heaven *related to* **Christian transcendental experiences**

Lincoln, Andrew T. Paradise now and not yet : studies in the role of the heavenly dimension in Paul's thought with special reference to his eschatology / Andrew T. Lincoln. — Cambridge : Cambridge University Press, 1981. — xiii,277p ; 23cm. — (Monograph series / Society for New Testament Studies ; 43)
Bibliography: p240-254. — Includes index
ISBN 0-521-22944-8 : £15.00 : CIP rev.
Also classified at 248.2 B81-30223

236'.8 — Bible. N.T. Gospels. Special subjects. Resurrection of the dead — *French texts*

Rochais, Gérard. Les récits de résurrection des morts dans le Nouveau Testament / Gérard Rochaís. — Cambridge : Cambridge University Press, 1981. — xv,252p : ill ; 23cm. — (Monograph series / Society for New Testament Studies ; 40)
Bibliography p235-243. — Includes index
ISBN 0-521-22381-4 : £15.00 : CIP rev.
B80-29060

236'.8 — Christian doctrine. Resurrection of the dead

Williams, H. A.. True resurrection / H.A. Williams. — London : Mitchell Beazley, 1979, c1972. — x,182p ; 22cm
ISBN 0-85533-163-1 (pbk) : £2.50 B81-05841

238 — CHRISTIAN DOCTRINE. CREEDS, CONFESSIONS OF FAITH, COVENANTS, CATECHISMS

238'.1 — Christian church. Creeds, *to ca 810*

Kelly, J. N. D.. Early Christian creeds. — 3rd ed. — London : Longman, Dec.1981. — [464]p
Previous ed.: 1960
ISBN 0-582-49219-x (pbk) : £6.95 : CIP entry
B81-30889

238'.11 — Apostles' Creed — *Expositions*

Harned, David Baily. Creed and personal identity : the meaning of the Apostles' Creed / David Baily Harned. — Edinburgh (33 Montgomery St., Edinburgh EH 7 5JX) : Handsel, 1981. — 120p ; 23cm
ISBN 0-905312-16-3 : Unpriced B81-16264

238'.142 — Nicene Creed. Filioque — *Critical studies*

Spirit of God, spirit of Christ : ecumenical reflections of the filioque controversy / [edited by Lukas Vischer]. — London : SPCK, c1981. — vi,186p ; 22cm. — (Faith and order paper ; no.103)
Conference papers
ISBN 0-281-03820-1 (pbk) : £6.50 B81-25911

238'.142 — Nicene Creed — *Topics for discussion groups — For Church of Scotland*

The **Nicene** Creed : a study guide / edited by V.C. Pogue. — [Edinburgh] : Department of Education, Church of Scotland, 1981. — iv,27p ; 20cm
ISBN 0-86153-034-9 (pbk) : £0.20 B81-17766

241 — CHRISTIANITY. MORAL THEOLOGY

241 — Christian ethics

Gustafson, James M.. Theology and ethics. — Oxford : Blackwell
Vol.1. — Oct.1981. — [384]p
ISBN 0-631-12945-6 : £15.00 : CIP entry
B81-28022

Hebblethwaite, Brian. The adequacy of Christian ethics. — London : Marshall Morgan & Scott, Nov.1981. — [144]p. — (Contemporary Christian studies)
ISBN 0-551-00919-5 (pbk) : £5.95 : CIP entry
B81-34214

Oppenheimer, Helen. The character of Christian morality / by Helen Oppenheimer. — 2nd ed. — Leighton Buzzard : Faith Press, 1974. — 102p ; 19cm
Previous ed.: 1965. — Includes index
ISBN 0-7164-0003-0 (pbk) : £1.25 B81-09898

241 — Christian ethics — *For schools*

Chignell, M. A.. Perspectives : a handbook of Christian responsibility. — London : Edward Arnold, Dec.1981. — [224]p
ISBN 0-7131-0614-x (pbk) : £3.25 : CIP entry B81-31552

241 — Christian social ethics

Preston, Ronald H.. The question of a just, participatory and sustainable society / by R.H. Preston. — Manchester : John Rylands University Library of Manchester, 1980. — p95-117 ; 25cm
£1.25 (pbk) B81-35539

241'.03'21 — Christian ethics — *Encyclopaedias*

Concise dictionary of Christian ethics / edited by Bernhard Stoeckle with contributions by J. Dominian, Anton Vögtle, Laurence Bright and others. — London : Burns & Oates, 1979. — x,2854p ; 24cm
Translation of: Wörterbuch christlicher Ethik
ISBN 0-86012-050-3 : £9.95 B81-14234

241'.042 — Catholic ethics

Häring, Bernard. Free and faithful in Christ : moral theology for priests and laity / Bernard Häring. — Slough : St Paul Publications
Vol.3: Light to the world, salt for the earth. — 1981. — xiv,437p ; 23cm
Includes index
ISBN 0-85439-172-x : £9.00 B81-17154

Mahoney, John. Seeking the Spirit : essays in moral and pastoral theology / John Mahoney. — London : Sheed and Ward, c1981. — 256p ; 23cm
Includes index
ISBN 0-7220-7923-0 : £17.50 B81-27702

241'.3 — Christian doctrine. Sin *related to* **human despair** — *Philosophical perspectives*

Kierkegaard, Søren. The sickness unto death : a Christian psychological exposition for upbuilding and awakening / by Søren Kierkegaard ; edited and translated with introduction and notes by Howard V. Hong and Edna H. Hong. — Princeton ; Guildford : Princeton University Press, c1980. — xxiii,201p ; 23cm. — (Kierkegaard's writings ; 19)
Translation of: Sygdommen til doden. — Bibliography: p183. - Includes index
ISBN 0-691-07247-7 : £9.10
Also classified at 152.4 B81-06741

241'.4 — Catholics. Christian life. Charity

Lubich, Chiara. Charity / Chiara Lubich. — London : New City, 1981. — 64p ; 19cm
Translation of: La carità come ideale
ISBN 0-904287-15-7 (pbk) : £1.60 B81-32612

241'.4 — Christian ethics. Self-love. Theories of Augustine, *Saint, Bishop of Hippo*

O'Donovan, Oliver. The problem of self-love in St. Augustine / Oliver O'Donovan. — New Haven ; London : Yale University Press, c1980. — viii,221p ; 22cm
Bibliography: p201-207. - Includes index
ISBN 0-300-02468-1 : £8.80 B81-08158

241'.64'2 — Medicine. Ethics — *Christian viewpoints*

Braine, David. Medical ethics and human life. — Aberdeen (99 High St., Old Aberdeen, Aberdeen) : Palladio Press, Jan.1982. — [30]p
ISBN 0-905292-01-4 (pbk) : £0.50 : CIP entry B81-39233

241'.6424 — Euthanasia — *Christian viewpoints*

Wilcockson, Stephen A.. Last rights : Christian perspectives on euthanasia. — Bramcote : Grove Books, 1981. — 20p ; 22cm. — (Grove booklet on ethics, ISSN 0305-4241 ; no.42)
ISBN 0-907536-04-2 (pbk) : £0.60 B81-37414

241'.644 — Finance. Ethics — *Christian viewpoints*

Ethics in the world of finance / edited by Ralph Hopps. — London : Chester House, 1979. — 87p : ill ; 19cm
ISBN 0-7150-0077-2 (pbk) : £1.50 B81-20877

241'.66 — Sex relations. Ethics — *Catholic viewpoints*

John Paul II, *Pope*. Love and responsibility / Karol Wojtyla (Pope John Paul II) ; translated by H.T. Willets. — London : Collins, 1981. — 319p ; 22cm
Translation of: Milosc i odpowiedzialnosc. — Includes index
ISBN 0-00-215476-5 : £9.95 B81-35659

241'.681'060415 — Ireland. Catholic temperance movements: Pioneer Total Abstinence Association of the Sacred Heart — *Serials*

New pioneer. — Vol.33, no.8 (Sept.1980)-. — Dublin (27 Upr. Sherrard St., Dublin 1) : Pioneer Total Abstinence Association of the Sacred Heart, 1980-. — v. : ill ; 29cm
Monthly. — Continues: Pioneer (Dublin : 1948)
£5.50 per year B81-04634

242 — CHRISTIANITY. DEVOTIONAL LITERATURE

242 — Anglicans. Christian life — *Devotional works*

Marshall, Michael, *1936-*. Pilgrimage and promise / Michael Marshall ; with a foreword by the Archbishop of Canterbury. — London : Fount Paperbacks in association with Faith Press, 1981. — 157p ; 18cm
ISBN 0-00-626067-5 (pbk) : £1.25 B81-12571

Stevens, Margaret. In life eternal : a preparation for Holy Communion / by Margaret Stevens. — Rev. ed. — London : Mowbray, 1980. — 207p ; 18cm
Previous ed.: Southend : Mayhew-McCrimmon, 1972. — Includes index
ISBN 0-264-66758-1 (pbk) : £1.95 B81-06181

242 — Carmelites. Christian life — *Meditations*

Laurent, *Frère*. The practice of the presence of God. — London : Hodder & Stoughton, Jan.1982. — [64]p
Translation of: La pratique de la présence de Dieu
ISBN 0-340-26937-5 (pbk) : £1.50 : CIP entry B81-33985

242 — Catholics. Christian life — *Devotional works*

Camara, Helder. A thousand reasons for living / Helder Camara ; edited by José de Broucker ; translated by Alan Neame. — London : Darton, Longman and Todd, 1981. — 118p ; 20cm
Translation of: Mille raisons pour vivre
ISBN 0-232-51521-2 (pbk) : £2.25 : CIP rev. B81-11954

Carretto, Carlo. The God who comes / Carlo Carretto ; translated by Rose Mary Hancock. — London : Darton, Longman & Todd, 1974 (1981 [printing]). — xxi,232p ; 20cm
Translation of: Il Dio che viene
ISBN 0-232-51529-8 (pbk) : £3.95 B81-23354

Seasons. — Liverpool (4 Hope Place, Liverpool L1 9BG) : Sisters of Notre Dame, [1980]. — [36]p : col.ill ; 13cm
Cover title
Unpriced (pbk) B81-11342

242 — Catholics. Christian life. Teresa, *of Avila, Saint.* **Castillo interior** — *Commentaries*

Burrows, Ruth. Interior castle explored : St. Teresa's teaching on the life of deep union with God / Ruth Burrows. — London : Sheed and Ward, 1981. — 122p ; 20cm
ISBN 0-7220-4418-6 (pbk) : £4.00 B81-15728

242 — Children. Interpersonal relationships with adults — *Christian viewpoints — Devotional works*

Schaffer, Ulrich. For the love of children : meditations on growing up with children / by Ulrich Schaffer. — Tring : Lion Publishing, 1980, c1979. — viii,94p : ill ; 20cm. — (An Aslan Lion paperback)
Originally published: New York : Harper & Row, 1980
ISBN 0-85648-317-6 (pbk) : £1.50 B81-05518

242 — Christian life — *Devotional works*

The **Bridge** is love. — London : Darton, Longman and Todd, Nov.1981. — [144]p
ISBN 0-232-51541-7 : £4.95 : CIP entry B81-33635

Love is my meaning : an anthology of assurance / collected by Elizabeth Basset. — London : Darton, Longman and Todd, 1973 (1980 [printing]). — 272p ; 23cm
Includes index
ISBN 0-232-51341-4 : £7.95 B81-11790

Maliński, Mieczysław. Our daily bread / M. Maliński ; [translated by Francis McDonagh]. — London : Burns & Oates, 1979. — 142p ; 22cm
Translation of: Nasz chleb powszedni. — Originally published: New York : Seabury, 1979
ISBN 0-86012-073-2 (pbk) : £2.95 B81-11791

Tate, Maurice, *1933-*. Over the mountain, through the valley : meditations for holiday reading / Maurice and Dorothy Tate. — Ilfracombe : Stockwell, 1981. — 37p ; 19cm
ISBN 0-7223-1435-3 (pbk) : £1.81 B81-05954

Traherne, Thomas. Centuries / Thomas Traherne. — London : Mowbray, 1960 (1975 [printing]). — xix,228p ; 20cm
ISBN 0-7164-0165-7 : £3.50 B81-17134

Valle, Francisca Javiera del. About the Holy Spirit / Francisca Javiera del Valle. — Houston : Lumen Christi ; Dublin (Kill Lane, Blackrock, Co. Dublin) : Four Courts, [1981?]. — 116p : ill ; 22cm
Translation of: Decenario del Espiritu Santo
ISBN 0-906127-43-2 (pbk cased) : Unpriced
ISBN 0-906127-44-0 (pbk) : Unpriced B81-31753

242 — Christian life. Mysticism — *Devotional works*

Thomas, *à Kempis*. [De imitatione Christi. English]. The imitation of Christ / by Thomas à Kempis ; translated by John Rooney. — London : Catholic Truth Society, [1981?]. — xiv,200p ; 18cm
ISBN 0-85183-230-x : Unpriced B81-37959

242 — Franciscans. Christian life — *Devotional works*

Bonaventure, *Saint*. [Itinerarium mentis in deum. English]. The soul's journey into God ; The tree of life ; The life of St. Francis / Bonaventure ; translation and introduction by Ewert Cousins ; prefaces by Ignatius Brady. — London : SPCK, c1978. — 353p ; 23cm. — (The Classics of Western spirituality)
Originally published: New York : Paulist Press, 1978. — Bibliography: p329-333. - Includes index
ISBN 0-281-03650-0 (pbk) : £6.50
Also classified at 271'.3'024 B81-06017

242 — Russkaia pravoslavnaia tserkov. Christian life — *Devotional works*

A **Treasury** of Russian spirituality / edited by G.P. Fedotov. — London : Sheed and Ward, 1950 (1981 [printing]). — 501p ; 22cm
Translation from the Russian. — Bibliography: p500-501
ISBN 0-7220-9214-8 (pbk) : £11.00 B81-40906

242'.2 — Adolescents. Christian life — *Daily readings*

Discovering the Bible. — Redhill : International Bible Reading Association
Part 3. — c1981. — 191p ; 18cm
ISBN 0-7197-0304-2 (pbk) : Unpriced B81-40984

242'.2 — Catholics. Christian life — *Daily readings*

John Paul, *II, Pope*. Through the year with Pope John Paul II / compiled and edited by Tony Castle. — London : Hodder and Stoughton, 1981. — 252p ; 24cm
ISBN 0-340-26359-8 : £6.95 : CIP rev. B81-23923

242′.2 — Christian life — *Daily readings*

Butler, John, *1928-*. Take Him at his word : an introduction to reading and understanding the Bible / John Butler. — Glasgow (Scripture Union Scotland, 280 St. Vincent St., Glasgow G2 5RT) : Tell Publishing, 1979. — 32p : 1ill ; 22cm
£0.40 (pbk) B81-40842

Crawford, Michael, *1937-*. A shot in the light : reflections day by day / Michael Crawford. — Guildford : Lutterworth, 1981. — 91p ; 19cm
Includes index
ISBN 0-7188-2503-9 (pbk) : £1.50 B81-24212

Daily thoughts from Keswick / selected and edited by Herbert F. Stevenson. — London : Hodder and Stoughton, 1980. — 381p ; 18cm
Includes index
ISBN 0-340-25883-7 (pbk) : £2.25 : CIP rev. B80-13692

A **Diary** of readings / [compiled] by John Baillie. — Oxford : Oxford University Press, 1955 (1981 [printing]). — ix,385p ; 20cm
Bibliography: p367-382. — Includes index
ISBN 0-19-283030-9 (pbk) : £2.95 B81-23527

Knight, Trevor F.. Beginning as a Christian / Trevor F. Knight. — Wrexham ('Woodlands', Gwersyllt, Wrexham, Clwyd) : National Young Life Campaign, [1981]. — 31p ; 19cm
£0.30 (19cm) B81-35754

Ramsey, Michael. Through the year with Michael Ramsey : devotional readings for every day / edited by Margaret Duggan. — London (SPCK, Holy Trinity Church, Marylebone Rd., NW1 4DU) : Triangle, 1981, c1975. — 253p ; 18cm
Originally published: London : Hodder and Stoughton, 1975
ISBN 0-281-03816-3 (pbk) : £1.75 B81-39127

Strong, Patience. Bedside book : daily readings in prose and verse / by Patience Strong. — Long Preston : Magna Print Books, 1981, c1953. — 258p ; 23cm
Originally published: London : Muller, 1953. — Published in large print
ISBN 0-86009-334-4 : £4.95 : CIP rev. B81-16906

Ten Boom, Corrie. This day is the Lord's. — London : Hodder & Stoughton, Sept.1981. — [192]p
Originally published: 1980
ISBN 0-340-27158-2 (pbk) : £1.50 : CIP entry B81-22454

242′.2 — Christian life — *Daily readings — For married couples*

Ellis, Charles H.. Heirs together of life / Charles H. and Norma R. Ellis. — Edinburgh : The Banner of Truth Trust, 1980. — 275p ; 18cm
ISBN 0-85151-311-5 (pbk) : £1.95 B81-06438

242′.2 — Church of Scotland. Christian life — *Daily readings*

Hewat, Elizabeth G. K.. Thine own secret stair : suggestions for a month's private prayer / Elizabeth G.K. Hewat. — [3rd ed.]. — Edinburgh : Saint Andrew Press, [c1981]. — 79p ; 19cm
Previous ed.: 1971
ISBN 0-7152-0469-6 (pbk) : £0.95 B81-26260

242′.2′05 — Christian life — *Daily readings — Serials*

Gay, Francis. The friendship book of Francis Gay. — 1981. — London : D.C. Thomson, c1980. — [188]p
ISBN 0-85116-197-9 : £1.05 B81-02481

Pause for?. — 1982-. — London : Stainer & Bell, 1981-. — v. ; 14cm
Annual
ISSN 0261-2577 = Pause for? : £1.95 B81-24683

242′.2′05 — Christian life. Family worship — *Daily readings — Serials*

Family prayers / Scripture Union. — 1981. — London : The Union, 1980. — 192p
ISBN 0-85421-892-0 : £2.00 B81-00734

242′.3 — Church year — *Devotional works*

Preston, Geoffrey. Hallowing the time : meditations on the cycle of the Christian liturgy / Geoffrey Preston ; texts prepared by Aidan Nichols. — London : Darton, Longman & Todd, 1980. — x,163p ; 22cm
ISBN 0-232-51481-x (pbk) : £4.50 B81-11794

242′.34 — Christian life — *Daily readings — For Lent*

Coggan, Donald. The name above all names / Donald Coggan. — London : SPCK, 1981. — 48p ; 21cm
ISBN 0-281-03803-1 (pbk) : Unpriced B81-01134

242′.35 — Holy Week — *Devotional works*

Gray, Alastair H.. Triumphant Jesus : the triumphs of Jesus from Palm Sunday to Easter / Alastair H. Gray. — [Methil] ([Methil, Fife]) : Methil Parish Church, 1980. — 8p ; 22cm
Cover title. — Text on inside cover
Unpriced (pbk) B81-08056

242′.4 — Physically handicapped persons. Christian life — *Devotional works*

Mayfield, Pat. 'I take my stand sitting down Lord' : meditations / by Pat Mayfield. — Ilkeston : Moorley's Bible & Bookshop, [1981]. — 32p ; 21cm
ISBN 0-86071-127-7 (pbk) : £0.55 B81-34823

242′.5 — Bible. O.T. Psalms — *Devotional works*

Campbell, Murdoch. From grace to glory : meditations on the Book of Psalms / Murdoch Campbell. — Edinburgh : Banner of Truth Trust, 1970 (1979 [printing]). — 206p ; 18cm
ISBN 0-85151-028-0 (pbk) : £1.50 B81-39935

McNeil, Brian. Christ in the Psalms / Brian McNeil. — Dublin : Veritas Publications, 1980. — xiii,90p ; 18cm
ISBN 0-905092-87-2 (pbk) : Unpriced B81-06297

242′.5 — Christian life. Prayers: Bible. N.T. Gospels — *Collections*

The **Gospels** for prayer / compiled by John C. Edwards. — London : Catholic Truth Society, 1981. — 201p ; 19cm
ISBN 0-85183-356-x (pbk) : £4.50 B81-22101

242′.62 — Christian life — *Devotional works — For children*

White, R. E. O.. 52 more stories for children / R.E.O. White. — London : Pickering & Inglis, c1981. — 192p : ill ; 19cm
ISBN 0-7208-0473-6 (pbk) : £2.25 B81-32061

242′.74 — Catholics. Christian life. Prayer. Rosary. Prayers — *Collections*

Our Lady's psalter : 150 texts for the 150 Hail Mary's in the rosary / edited by Raymund Devas. — London : Catholic Truth Society, 1980. — 35p ; 17cm
ISBN 0-85183-403-5 (pbk) : £0.40 B81-12454

242′.8 — Christian life. Prayers — *Collections*

Baillie, John. A diary of private prayer / John Baillie. — Oxford : Oxford University Press, 1980. — 135p ; 20cm
Originally published: 1936
ISBN 0-19-283031-7 (pbk) : £1.95 : CIP rev. B80-25131

George, Rosa. A pocket book of prayers for anytime / by Rosa George. — Great Wakering : Mayhew-McCrimmon, 1980. — 32p : ill ; 15cm
ISBN 0-85597-303-x (pbk) : £0.45 B81-07630

The **Illustrated** family prayer book / edited by Tony Jasper. — London : Muller, 1981. — 160p : ill(some col.) ; 26cm
Includes index
ISBN 0-584-97071-4 : £6.95 B81-11578

Konstant, David. Jesus Christ the way, the truth, the life : daily prayer book / David Konstant. — London : Collins, 1981. — 175p : ill ; 19cm
ISBN 0-00-599676-7 (cased) : £3.50
ISBN 0-00-599681-3 (pbk) : £2.50 B81-22309

Praise : prayers from Taize : extracts from Praise in all our days for personal or corporate prayer / [Communauté de Taize] ; [translated from the French by Emily Chisholm]. — London : Mowbray, 1980, c1976. — 46p ; 18cm
Originally published: Leighton Buzzard : Faith Press, 1977
ISBN 0-264-66589-9 (pbk) : £1.25 B81-13061

Topping, Frank. Pause for thought with Frank Topping : including Lord of the morning, Lord of my days, Lord of the evening / illustrations by Noeline Kelly. — Guildford, Surrey : Lutterworth, 1981. — 240p : ill ; 21cm
Includes index
ISBN 0-7188-2524-1 : £5.95 B81-31212

242′.802 — Catholics. Christian life. Prayers — *Collections*

A **treasury** of Catholic prayer / compiled by Michael Buckley ; illustrated by Michael Green. — Leigh-on-Sea : Kevin Mayhew, 1979. — 127p : col.ill ; 18cm
ISBN 0-905725-75-1 (pbk) : Unpriced B81-39865

242′.802 — Catholics. Christian life. Prayers — *Collections — Polish texts*

Faustyna, *siostra*. Koronka nowenna litania do mi l osierdzia bozego / wed l ug s. Faustyny. — Brighton (5 Hanover Terrace) : Collegium Marianum, 1981. — 16p ; 15cm
Unpriced (unbound) B81-28538

Żal doskonały : czyli sposób wzbudzenia żalu za grzechy popełnione. — Brighton (5 Hanover Terrace) : Collegium Marianum, 1980. — 16p : 1ill ; 17cm
Unpriced (unbound) B81-28539

242′.803 — Anglicans. Christian life. Prayer — *Prayer books*

Dutton, A. M.. Corporate worship / A.M. Dutton. — Bognor Regis : New Horizon, c1978. — 29p ; 21cm
Includes index
ISBN 0-86116-034-7 : £2.95 B81-21824

242′.803 — Anglicans. Christian life. Prayers — *Collections*

Front line praying. — London : Bible Reading Fellowship, Sept.1981. — [208]p
ISBN 0-900164-56-5 (pbk) : £2.25 : CIP entry B81-30302

242′.803′05 — Anglicans. Christian life — *Prayers & readings — Serials*

[Fellowship in prayer *(London)***]**. Fellowship in prayer / National Society (Church of England) for Promoting Religious Education. — [No.1] [197—]-. — London : Church House, Dean's Yard, Westminster SW1P 3NZ : The Society, [197—]-. — v. ; 14cm
Three issues yearly. — Description based on: Autumn 1979 issue
ISSN 0260-7921 = Fellowship in prayer (London) : Unpriced B81-06921

242′.82 — Children. Christian life. Prayers — *Collections*

Children's prayers : from around the world. — Tring : Lion, 1981. — 42p : col.ill ; 22cm
ISBN 0-85648-353-2 : £2.50 B81-40662

Cox, Lilian. Good morning, God : prayers and verses for young children / by Lilian Cox. — Redhill : National Christian Education Council, 1981. — 24p ; 19cm
ISBN 0-7197-0288-7 (pbk) : £0.60 B81-29293

Cox, Lilian. My private prayers : a personal book of prayer-help for boys and girls / by Lilian Cox. — Redhill : National Christian Education Council, 1981. — 24p ; 19cm
ISBN 0-7197-0289-5 (pbk) : £0.60 B81-29291

Cox, Lilian. What next, Lord? : prayers and meditations for growing Christians / by Lilian Cox. — Redhill : National Christian Education Council, c1981. — 24p ; 19cm
ISBN 0-7197-0290-9 (pbk) : £0.60 B81-29292

242'.82 — Children. Christian life. Prayers — *Collections* *continuation*

Gaze, Gillian. Prayers for special days / illustrated by Gillian Gaze. — Tring : Lion Publishing, 1978 (1981 [printing]). — [16]p : chiefly col.ill ; 19cm. — (Little Lions)
ISBN 0-85648-112-2 (pbk) : £0.35 B81-27003

Grahame Johnstone, Janet. A child's book of prayers / illustrated by Janet & Anne Grahame Johnstone. — London : Dean, c1968 (1980 [printing]). — [18]p : col.ill ; 32cm. — (An Everyday picture book)
ISBN 0-603-00213-7 : £1.25 B81-32155

Marshall-Taylor, Geoffrey. Let's pray together! / by Geoffrey Marshall-Taylor ; illustrated by George W. Thompson. — London : Collins, 1981. — 63p : col.ill ; 27cm
Text, ill on lining papers
ISBN 0-00-599663-5 : Unpriced B81-26061

Prayers for everyone. — Tring : Lion Publishing, 1981. — [16]p : col.ill ; 19cm. — (Little Lions)
ISBN 0-85648-374-5 (pbk) : £0.35 B81-37012

Prayers for home and school. — Tring : Lion Publishing, 1981. — [16]p : col.ill ; 19cm. — (Little Lions)
ISBN 0-85648-375-3 (pbk) : £0.35 B81-37015

Seymour, Peter. Our wonderful world / written by Peter Seymour ; designed and illustrated by Gordon Stowell. — [Tring] : [Lion Publishing], [c1981]. — 4v. : col.ill ; 10cm
Boxed set. — Contents: Friends are all around us — Lovely things to look for — We can be happy — Every day is different
ISBN 0-85648-405-9 : £1.95
ISBN 0-85648-404-4
ISBN 0-85648-402-4
ISBN 0-85648-403-2 B81-37010

Thank you for the world. — Tring : Lion Publishing, 1981. — [16]p : col.ill ; 19cm. — (Little Lions)
ISBN 0-85648-377-x (pbk) : £0.35 B81-37013

Thank you prayers. — Tring : Lion Publishing, 1981. — [16]p : col.ill ; 19cm. — (Little Lions)
ISBN 0-85648-376-1 (pbk) : £0.35 B81-37014

242'.82 — Cub scouts. Christian life. Prayers — *Collections*

Dear God — thank you for traffik wardens : a collection of prayers / written by the Cubs of the Eleventh Newham West Scout Group. — London (4 Hartsworth Close, E13 0TD) : The Group, 1980. — 32p ; 18cm
Limited ed. of 500 copies
Unpriced (pbk) B81-08950

242'.8'2 — Primary schools. Students. Christian life. Prayer — *Prayer books — For teaching*

Pearson, Muriel. A time for prayer. — London : Edward Arnold, Dec.1981. — [48]p
ISBN 0-7131-0604-2 (pbk) : £2.00 : CIP entry B81-31551

242'.843 — Women. Christian life. Prayers — *Collections*

Holmes, Marjorie. I've got to talk to somebody, God : a woman's conversations with God / Marjorie Holmes. — London : Hodder and Stoughton, c1969 (1981 [printing]). — 127p ; 18cm. — (Hodder Christian paperbacks)
Originally published: Garden City, N.Y. : Doubleday, 1969
ISBN 0-340-10636-0 (pbk) : £1.50 B81-39135

245 — CHRISTIANITY. HYMNS WITHOUT MUSIC

245'.51 — Hymns in Italian. Francis, *of Assisi, Saint.* **Cantico di frate sole —** *Critical studies*

Doyle, Eric. St. Francis and the song of brotherhood / Eric Doyle. — London : Allen & Unwin, 1980. — 205p : 1ill,music ; 23cm
Bibliography: p205
ISBN 0-04-922031-4 : £8.50 : CIP rev. B80-18162

246 — ART IN CHRISTIANITY

246'.558 — Christian church. Art objects: Bury Saint Edmunds Cross. Acquisition

Hoving, Thomas. King of the confessors. — London : Hamish Hamilton, Nov.1981. — [384]p
ISBN 0-241-10674-5 : £9.95 : CIP entry B81-30219

246'.95'05 — Churches. Architectural features. Liturgical aspects — *Serials*

[Research bulletin *(University of Birmingham Institute for the Study of Worship and Religious Architecture)*]. Research bulletin / University of Birmingham Institute for the Study of Worship and Religious Architecture. — 1981. — [Birmingham] : University of Birmingham, [1981?]. — 119p
ISBN 0-7044-0512-1 : Unpriced
ISSN 0305-2206 B81-15287

247 — CHURCH FURNISHINGS AND RELATED ARTICLES

247'.09423'93 — Avon. Bristol. Churches. Furnishings

Little, Bryan. Church treasures in Bristol / by Bryan Little. — Bristol (14 Dowry Sq., Bristol 8) : published for the City of Bristol by Redcliffe, 1979. — 40p : ill,2coatsofarms ; 22cm. — (The Bristol series)
Includes index
ISBN 0-905459-12-1 (pbk) : £1.00 B81-07108

248 — CHRISTIAN EXPERIENCE, PRACTICE, LIFE

248 — Christian life — *For African students — For schools*

Christian living today. — London : Chapman, Oct.1981. — [336]p
ISBN 0-225-66307-4 (pbk) : £7.50 : CIP entry B81-26705

248 — Man. Stress — *Christian viewpoints*

McPheat, W. Scott. Coping with life. — London : Hodder & Stoughton, Jan.1982. — [144]p
ISBN 0-340-27471-9 (pbk) : £1.50 : CIP entry B81-34122

248.2 — Bible. N.T. Epistles of Paul. Special subjects: Christian life. Transcendental experiences *related to* **Christian doctrine of heaven**

Lincoln, Andrew T. Paradise now and not yet : studies in the role of the heavenly dimension in Paul's thought with special reference to his eschatology / Andrew T. Lincoln. — Cambridge : Cambridge University Press, 1981. — xiii,277p ; 23cm. — (Monograph series / Society for New Testament Studies ; 43)
Bibliography: p240-254. — Includes index
ISBN 0-521-22944-8 : £15.00 : CIP rev.
Primary classification 236'.24 B81-30223

248.2'2 — Christian life. Mysticism

Cameron, Clare. Mystic of nature : selections from the writings of Clare Cameron / with a foreword by Martin Israel. — London : Skilton & Shaw, c1980. — vii,120p ; 22cm
ISBN 0-7050-0099-0 (pbk) : £3.50 B81-05616

248.2'2'01 — Christian life. Mysticism. Theories, *to ca 260*

Louth, Andrew. The origins of the Christian mystical tradition from Plato to Denys. — Oxford : Clarendon Press, Apr.1981. — [192]p
ISBN 0-19-826655-3 : £12.50 : CIP entry B81-00735

248.2'2'0942 — England. Christian life. Mysticism, *1300-1416*

Riehle, Wolfgang. The Middle English mystics / Wolfgang Riehle ; translated by Bernard Standring. — London : Routledge & Kegan Paul, 1981. — xvi,244p ; 23cm
Translation of: Studien zur englischen Mystik des Mittelalters unter besonderer Berücksichtigung ihrer Metaphorik. — Bibliography: p217-231. — Includes index
ISBN 0-7100-0612-8 : £12.95 : CIP rev. B81-08812

248.2'2'0942 — England. Christian life. Mysticism, *ca 1300-ca 1400 — Conference proceedings*

The **medieval** mystical tradition in England : papers read at the Exeter symposium, July 1980 / edited by Marion Glasscoe. — [Exeter] : University of Exeter, 1980. — v,249p ; 21cm. — (Exeter medieval English texts and studies)
ISBN 0-85989-141-0 (corrected : pbk) : £4.50 B81-07550

248.2'46 — Algeria. Christianity. Conversion of Muslims — *Personal observations*

Marsh, C. R.. The challenge of Islam / C.R. Marsh. — London : Ark, 1980. — 173p ; 18cm
ISBN 0-86201-082-9 (pbk) : £1.95 B81-01720

248.2'46 — Christianity. Conversion of Jews

Ball, Hermann. Thirza : or the power of the cross / [translated] from the German by Elizabeth Maria Lloyd ; edited by P.M. Rowell. — [New] ed.. — Ossett (44 Queen's Drive, Ossett, W. Yorkshire, WF5 0ND) : Gospel Tidings Publications, 1978. — 32p ; 21cm
Translation of: Thirza, oder die Anziehungskraft des Kreuzes. — Author: Hermann Ball. — Previous ed.: S.l. : S.H. Jarvis, 1914
ISBN 0-904731-04-9 (pbk) : £0.50 B81-31858

248'.246 — Christianity. Conversion of Muslims — *Manuals*

Marsh, C. R.. Share your faith with a Muslim / Charles Marsh. — Bromley : S.T.L., 1980, c1975. — 96p ; 18cm
Originally published: Chicago : Moody Bible Institute, 1975
ISBN 0-903843-34-x (pbk) : £0.95 B81-01969

248.2'46 — Christianity. Conversion of Muslims — *Personal observations — Collections*

Jesus — more than a prophet. — Leicester : Inter-Varsity Press, Nov.1981. — [64]p
ISBN 0-85110-422-3 (pbk) : £0.95 : CIP entry B81-30613

248.2'46 — Christianity. Conversion of non-Christians — *Personal observations*

Griffin, Emilie. How God became real : an experience of conversion / Emilie Griffin. — London : Sheldon, 1981, c1980. — 189p ; 22cm
Originally published: Garden City, N.Y. : Doubleday, 1980. — Bibliography: p181-186. - Includes index
ISBN 0-85969-333-3 (pbk) : £4.95 B81-18580

248.2'46 — Christianity. Conversion of Vikings, *800-1050*

Rohan, Michael Scott. The hammer and the cross / Michael Scott Rohan & Allan J. Scott. — Oxford (107 Marlborough Rd., Oxford) : Alder, 1980. — 64p : ill,col.maps ; 25cm
ISBN 0-907162-00-2 (pbk) : £2.95 B81-07244

248.2'46 — Europe. Christianity. Conversion of Jews. Wurmbrand, Judy — *Biographies*

Wurmbrand, Judy. Escape from the grip. — London : Hodder & Stoughton, Jan.1982. — [128]p
ISBN 0-340-27150-7 (pbk) : £1.50 : CIP entry B81-34651

248.2'9 — Christian life. Baptism in the Holy Spirit

Windward, Stephen F.. Fruit of the Spirit / Stephen F. Windward. — Leicester : Inter-Varsity, 1981. — 208p ; 18cm
ISBN 0-85110-430-4 (pbk) : Unpriced : CIP rev. B81-13509

248.2'9 — Christian life. Stigmata

Harrison, Ted. The marks of the cross : the story of Ethel Chapman and the stigmata / Ted Harrison. — London : Darton, Longman and Todd, 1981. — x,86p ; 22cm
ISBN 0-232-51513-1 (pbk) : £2.25 B81-23381

248.2'9 — Pentecostal churches. Christian life. Speaking in tongues
Williams, Cyril G.. Tongues of the spirit : a study of pentecostal glossolalia and related phenomena / Cyril G. Williams. — Cardiff : University of Wales Press, 1981. — xiii,276p ; 23cm
Bibliography: p241-268. - Includes index
ISBN 0-7083-0758-2 : £15.95 : CIP rev. B80-07664

248.3 — Christian life. Praise
Prime, Derek. Created to praise / by Derek Prime. — London : Hodder and Stoughton, 1981. — 125p ; 18cm. — (Hodder Christian paperbacks)
ISBN 0-340-26146-3 (pbk) : £1.50 B81-03001

248.3'2 — Anglicans. Christian life. Prayer
Mary Clare, *Mother*. Encountering the depths / Mother Mary Clare ; edited by Ralph Townsend ; foreword by Michael Ramsay. — London : Darton, Longman and Todd, 1981. — xi,81p ; 20cm
ISBN 0-232-51510-7 (pbk) : £1.99 B81-11788

248.3'2 — Bible. Special subjects: Prayer — *Expositions*
Appleton, George. Praying with the Bible. — London : Bible Reading Fellowship, Oct.1981. — [72]p
ISBN 0-900164-57-3 : £1.25 : CIP entry B81-30977

248.3'2 — Catholics. Christian life. Prayer
Metz, Johann Baptist. The courage to pray / Johann Baptist Metz & Karl Rahner. — London : Burns & Oates, 1980. — vi,87p ; 21cm
Translation of: Ermutigung zum Gebet
ISBN 0-86012-107-0 (pbk) : £2.50 B81-18621

248.3'2 — Christian life. Prayer
Bloom, Anthony. Courage to pray / Metropolitan Anthony and Georges Lefebvre ; translated by Dinah Livingstone. — London : Darton, Longman & Todd, 1973 (1981 [printing]). — 122p ; 20cm
Translation of: La prière
ISBN 0-232-51533-6 (pbk) : £2.25 B81-23366

Byrom, John, *1920-*. Prayer, the passion of love / John Byrom. — Oxford (Convent of the Incarnation, Fairacres, Oxford OX4 1TB) : SLG Press, c1981. — 32p ; 21cm. — (Fairacres publication, ISSN 0307-1405 ; 79)
Bibliography: p32
ISBN 0-7283-0090-7 (pbk) : £0.50 B81-23283

Hollings, Michael. Hearts not garments. — London : Darton, Longman & Todd, Jan.1982. — [96]p
ISBN 0-232-51539-5 (pbk) : £2.25 : CIP entry B81-37527

Murphy, Columcille. First steps in contemplative prayer / Colmcille Murphy [i.e. Columcille]. — London : Sheed and Ward, 1981. — ix,117p ; 20cm
ISBN 0-7220-3515-2 (pbk) : £4.50 B81-29366

248.3'2 — Christian life. Prayer. Inspiration, *ca 400-1970 — Case studies*
Gibbard, Mark. Guides to hidden springs : a history of Christian spirituality through the lives of some of its witnesses / Mark Gibbard. — London : SCM, 1980, c1979. — 94p ; 20cm
Bibliography: p91-94
ISBN 0-334-00562-0 (pbk) : £1.50 B81-06361

248.3'2 — Christian life. Prayer — *Manuals*
Basics : introduction to Bible reading and prayer. — Rev.. — London : Scripture Union, 1980, c1964. — 16p : ill ; 15cm
Previous ed.: i.e. rev. ed. 1970
ISBN 0-85421-042-3 (pbk) : Unpriced
Primary classification 220'.07 B81-17201

Malz, Betty. Prayers that are answered / Betty Malz. — London : Hodder and Stoughton, 1980. — 160p ; 18cm. — (Hodder Christian paperbacks)
ISBN 0-340-25839-x (pbk) : £1.40 : CIP rev. B80-23990

Topping, Frank. Working at prayer / by Frank Topping ; illustrations by Noeline Kelly. — Guildford : Lutterworth, 1981. — 79p : ill ; 20cm
ISBN 0-7188-2504-7 (pbk) : £1.95 B81-18398

Turnbull, Michael, *1935-*. Learning to pray / by Michael Turnbull. — London : Mowbray, 1981. — 32p ; 15cm. — (Enquirer's library)
Bibliography: p32
ISBN 0-264-66723-9 (pbk) : £0.60 B81-17906

248.3'2 — Christian life. Prayer. Silence
Edmée, *Sister*. Silence in prayer and action : two talks given to priests for a quiet day at Fairacres / Sister Edmée. — Fairacres (Convent of the Incarnation, Fairacres, Oxford OX4 1TB) : SLG Press, c1981. — 15p ; 21cm
Originally published: in Fairacres Chronicle, vol.13, no.1, Winter 1980
ISBN 0-7283-0088-5 (pbk) : £0.30 B81-18714

248.3'2 — Orthodox Eastern churches. Christian life. Prayer — *Early works*
The **Philokalia**. — London : Faber
Vol.2. — Oct.1981. — [408]p
ISBN 0-571-11725-2 : £12.50 : CIP entry B81-25326

248.3'2'088042 — Scotland. Women. Christian life. Prayers
The **day** Thou gavest - : the World Day of Prayer 1930 - Scotland - 1980. — [Edinburgh] ([121 George St., Edinburgh]) : Scottish Committee of the World Day of Prayer, 1980. — 32p : ill(some col.),1col.map,ports(some col.) ; 21cm
Cover title
Unpriced (pbk) B81-08474

248.3'4 — Christian life. Contemplation
Coulson, Robert. On course in contemplation / [Robert Coulson] ; [edited by Martin Tunnicliffe]. — Holmfirth (St. John's Vicarage, Upper Thong La., Holmfirth, Huddersfield HD7 1BQ) : Revd. Peter Dodson, [1981]. — 51p ; 20cm
ISBN 0-9503505-2-4 (pbk) : Unpriced B81-37423

Happold, F. C.. The journey inwards : a simple introduction to the practice of contemplative meditation by normal people / F.C. Happold. — London : Darton, Longman & Todd, 1968 (1981 [printing]). — 142p : ill ; 20cm
Bibliography: p137-142
ISBN 0-232-51523-9 (pbk) : £3.75 B81-23358

248.3'4 — Christian life. Meditation
Carretto, Carlo. The desert in the city / Carlo Carretto ; translated by Barbara Wall. — London : Collins, 1979. — 106p ; 18cm. — (Fount paperbacks)
Translation of: Il deserto nella città
ISBN 0-00-626349-6 (pbk) : £1.25 B81-40135

Main, John. Word into silence / John Main. — London : Darton, Longman & Todd, c1980. — xiii,82p ; 20cm
Bibliography: p80-82
ISBN 0-232-51499-2 (pbk) : £1.99 : CIP rev. B80-21367

248.3'4 — Christian life. Meditation — *Manuals*
Andere, Mary. - and the meditation of my heart- / Mary Andere. — London : Mothers' Union, [1981]?. — 15p ; 21cm
Cover title
£0.50 (pbk) B81-39587

Goldsmith, Joel S.. Living the infinite way / Joel S. Goldsmith. — London : Unwin Paperbacks, 1981, c1954. — 82p ; 20cm. — (Mandala Books)
Originally published: London : Allen & Unwin, 1954
ISBN 0-04-200040-8 (pbk) : £2.50 B81-24561

248.3'4 — Christian life. Meditation. Role of hatha-yoga
Amaldas, Brahmachari. Yoga and contemplation. — London : Darton Longman & Todd, June 1981. — [160]p
ISBN 0-232-51530-1 : £3.95 : CIP entry B81-11923

248.4 — Bereaved persons. Grief — *Christian viewpoints*
Kyle, William. Out of the dark valley : on loss and grief / William Kyle. — London : Mothers' Union, [1981]?. — 8p ; 19cm
Cover title
ISBN 0-85943-033-2 (pbk) : £0.35 B81-39588

248.4 — Catholics. Christian life. Love — *Devotional works*
Lubich, Chiara. Knowing how to lose / Chiara Lubich. — London : New City, 1981. — 149p ; 16cm
Translation of: Saper perdere
ISBN 0-904287-16-5 (pbk) : £2.00 B81-32611

248.4 — Christian life
Adams, Richard, *1940-*. Dear God - Dear George - / Richard Adams ; drawings by Frank Finch. — London : Epworth, 1980. — 111p : ill ; 20cm
ISBN 0-7162-0348-0 (pbk) : £1.75 B81-02261

Bagg, Douglas Gordon. The philosophy of life : a layman's Sunday addresses / Douglas Gordon Bagg. — Bognor Regis : New Horizon, 1981. — 71p ; 21cm
ISBN 0-86116-588-8 : £3.50 B81-40187

Bewes, Richard. The Christian / [Richard Bewes, Robert Hicks]. — [London] : Scripture Union, 1981. — [24]p : col.ill ; 17cm. — (Explaining Bible truth)
Cover title. — Text on inside covers
ISBN 0-85421-917-x (pbk) : £0.40 B81-24506

Bewes, Richard. Man / [Richard Bewes, Robert Hicks]. — [London] : Scripture Union, 1981. — [24]p : col.ill ; 17cm. — (Explaining Bible truth)
Cover title. — Text on inside covers
ISBN 0-85421-915-3 (pbk) : £0.40 B81-24507

Blaiklock, E. M.. Still a Christian / by E.M. Blaiklock. — London : Hodder and Stougthon, 1980. — 118p ; 18cm. — (Hodder Christian paperbacks)
ISBN 0-340-25995-7 (pbk) : £1.40 : CIP rev. B80-23986

Clark, Kelly James. Quiet times for Christian growth. — Leicester : Inter-Varsity Press, June 1981. — [32]p
ISBN 0-85110-245-x (pbk) : £0.50 : CIP entry B81-10498

Cliffe, Albert E.. Let go and let God : steps in victorious living / by Albert E. Cliffe. — 9th ed. — Evesham : James, 1981. — 137p ; 19cm
Previous ed.: 1972
ISBN 0-85305-233-6 (pbk) : £2.65 B81-25562

Comrie, Alexander. The abc of faith / by Alexander Comrie ; translated from the Dutch by J. Marcus Banfield. — Ossett (44 Queen's Drive, Ossett, W. Yorkshire, WF5 0ND) : Zoar, c1978. — xix,182p[3]p of plates : col.ill,1col.port ; 19cm
ISBN 0-904435-33-4 : £4.50 B81-31853

Duncan, George B.. Week by week : with George Duncan. — London : Pickering & Inglis, 1981. — 127p,[12]p of plates : col.ill,1col.port. ; 18cm
ISBN 0-7208-0489-2 (pbk) : £2.50 B81-28892

Erasmus. Enchiridion militis Christiani. — Oxford : Oxford University Press for the Early English Text Society, June 1981. — [440]p
ISBN 0-19-722284-6 : £12.00 : CIP entry B81-15938

Fewtrell, Sheila. Pathfinder and the pioneer spirit / Sheila Fewtrell. — Bognor Regis : New Horizon, c1979. — 100p ; 21cm
ISBN 0-86116-104-1 : £2.95 B81-21715

Harvey, E. F.. The new birth : selections from the book The new creation of the revealed religion series / by E.F. & L. Harvey & N. Woodhouse. — Stoke-on-Trent (247 Newcastle St., Burslem, Stoke-on-Trent, ST6 3QW) : M.O.V.E., 1981. — 19p : 1port ; 21cm
Unpriced (pbk) B81-33246

248.4 — Christian life *continuation*

Hughes, Selwyn. How to live the Christian life / Selwyn Hughes. — Rev. and extended ed. — Eastbourne : Kingsway, 1981. — 151p ; 18cm
Previous ed.: s.l. : Crusade Productions, 1974
ISBN 0-86065-149-5 (pbk) : £1.00 B81-33432

Keller, W. Phillip. A gardener looks at the fruits of the spirit / W. Phillip Keller. — London : Pickering & Inglis, c1979. — 187p ; 21cm
Originally published: Waco, Tex. : Word Books, 1979
ISBN 0-7208-0465-5 (pbk) : £2.25 B81-00736

McInnes, John, *1938-*. The new pilgrims : living Christians in the technological society / John McInnes. — Sutherland, N.S.W. : Albatross Books ; Tring : Lion, c1980. — 235p ; 18cm. — (An Albatross book)
ISBN 0-85648-328-1 (pbk) : £1.95 B81-09899

The **Path** to holiness : revealed by the Lord. — Camberley (4 Bramcote, Camberley, Surrey, GU15 1SJ) : Parousia, 1980. — 38p ; 18cm
Translated from the German
ISBN 0-906712-07-6 (pbk) : Unpriced B81-15747

Poonen, Zac. Beauty for ashes : the Christ-life for the self-life / Zac Poonen. — Eastbourne : Kingsway, 1980. — 93p ; 18cm
Originally published: India : Gospel Literature Service, 1973?
ISBN 0-86065-104-5 (pbk) : £1.00 B81-05562

Schaeffer, Francis A.. True spirituality / Francis Schaeffer. — Bromley (P.O. Box 48, Bromley, Kent) : STL Books, 1979, c1971. — 180p ; 18cm
Originally published: London : Hodder & Stoughton, 1972
ISBN 0-903843-25-0 (pbk) : £1.25 B81-37987

Secker, William. The nonsuch professor in his meridian splendour, or, The singular actions of sanctified Christians : laid open in seven sermons, at All-Hallow's Church, London Wall / by William Secker. — Ossett (44 Queen's Drive, Ossett, W. Yorks., WF5 0ND) : Zoar, [1981?]. — 150p ; 20cm
Originally published: London : M.S., for T. Parkhurst, 1660
£2.00 B81-31296

Shallis, Ralph. From now on - / Ralph Shallis. — Bromley : STL, 1978, c1973 (1980 [printing]). — 157p ; 18cm
Translation of: Si tu veux aller loin
ISBN 0-903843-17-x (pbk) : £0.95 B81-11494

Slack, Marjorie. Our young innocents / Marjorie Slack. — Bognor Regis : New Horizon, c1981. — 36p ; 21cm
ISBN 0-86116-434-2 : £2.95 B81-34843

Sugden, Chris. Radical discipleship. — London : Marshall Morgan & Scott, May 1981. — [160] p. — (Marshalls paperbacks)
ISBN 0-551-00901-2 (pbk) : £1.50 : CIP entry B81-12885

Tozer, A. W.. God tells the man who cares / A.W. Tozer. — Bromley : STL Books, 1980. — 172p ; 18cm
ISBN 0-903843-36-6 (pbk) : Unpriced B81-21357

Urch, Elizabeth. Ladders up to heaven / by Elizabeth Urch. — Evesham : Arthur James
Pt.3: Sorrow. — 1981. — 71p : music ; 20cm
Includes index
ISBN 0-85305-232-8 (pbk) : £2.25 : CIP rev. B81-08854

Wallis, Arthur. The radical Christian / Arthur Wallis. — Eastbourne : Kingsway, 1981. — 191p : 1map ; 18cm
ISBN 0-86065-162-2 (pbk) : £1.75 B81-33430

Watson, David, *1933-*. [How to win the war]. Hidden warfare / David Watson. — Rev. ed. / [revised by Mel Lorentzen]. — Bromley : STL, 1980. — 151p : ill ; 18cm
Previous ed.: published as God's freedom fighters. United States : Movements Books, 1972
ISBN 0-903843-39-0 (pbk) : £1.40 B81-06135

Watson, David, *1933-*. In search of God / David C.K. Watson. — 2nd ed. — London : Falcon, 1979. — 128p ; 18cm
Previous ed.: London : Church Pastoral-Aid Society, 1974. — Bibliography: p128
ISBN 0-85491-557-5 (pbk) : Unpriced B81-11835

Young, Samuel Chien-Sheng. Law, love, and life : first quarter 1982 / lesson author Samuel Chien-Sheng Young. [The glory of God] : [second quarter 1982] / [lesson author J. Ivan Crawford]. — Grantham : Stanborough, [1981]. — 190p : ill,1map ; 21cm. — (Sabbath school lessons)
Unpriced (pbk) B81-35305

248.4 — Christian life — *Correspondence, diaries, etc*

Carmichael, Amy. Candles in the dark : letters of Amy Carmichael. — London (Holy Trinity Church, Marylebone Rd., NW1 4DU) : Triangle, 1981. — x,115p ; 19cm. — (A Dohnavur book)
ISBN 0-281-03814-7 (pbk) : £1.50 B81-33023

Laurent, *Frère*. The practice of the presence of God : being conversations and letters / of Brother Lawrence. — London : Mowbray, 1914 (1980 [printing]). — iv,65p ; 15cm
Translation of: La pratique de la présence de Dieu
ISBN 0-264-66742-5 : Unpriced
ISBN 0-264-66743-3 (special binding) : Unpriced B81-18784

248.4 — Christian life. Duty — *Early works — Facsimiles*

Chubb, Thomas, *1679-1747*. The comparative excellence and obligation of moral and positive duties, 1730 ; and, A discourse concerning reason, 1731 / Thomas Chubb. — New York ; London : Garland, 1978. — 85,83p ; 23cm. — (British philosophers and theologians of the 17th & 18th centuries)
Facsims. of: edition published London : J. Roberts, 1730
ISBN 0-8240-1760-9 : Unpriced
Also classified at 248.4 B81-28429

248.4 — Christian life. Faith

Brandon, Owen. Give me faith / by Owen Brandon. — [Sevenoaks] : [Hodder and Stoughton], [1981]. — 12p ; 21cm
Cover title
£0.12 (pbk) B81-24002

248.4 — Christian life — *For confirmation candidates*

Johnson, Harold. Confirmed in faith / Harold Johnson. — Ilkeston : Moorley's, [1981?]. — 47p ; 21cm
ISBN 0-86071-119-6 (pbk) : £0.75 B81-25251

248.4 — Christian life — *For schools*

Vision 3 / compiled by Ian Wragg, David Day, Peter White ; with drawings by David Barlow. — Guildford (Luke House, Farnham Rd., Guildford, Surrey) : Lutterworth Educational, 1981. — 1portfolio : ill,1map,2ports ; 31cm
ISBN 0-7188-2267-6 : Unpriced B81-32317

Vision 4 / compiled by Ian Wragg, David Day, Peter White ; with drawings by David Barlow. — Guildford (Luke House, Farnham Rd., Guildford, Surrey) : Lutterworth Educational, 1981. — 1portfolio : ill ; 31cm
ISBN 0-7188-2268-4 : Unpriced B81-32318

248.4 — Christian life — *For slow learning adolescents*

Question marks / [prepared and edited by Brenda Lealman in collaboration with Alan Brown]. — [London] : Christian Education Movement, [1981?]. — 18p : chiefly ill ; 21cm. — (Doing & being)
ISBN 0-905022-69-6 (pbk) : Unpriced B81-27039

Question marks / [prepared and edited by Brenda Lealman in collaboration with Alan Brown]. — London : Christian Education Movement. — (Doing and being)
Four folded sheets as insert
Teacher's book. — c1981. — 11p : ill ; 21cm
ISBN 0-905022-70-x (pbk) : Unpriced B81-27038

248.4 — Christian life. Forgiveness

O'Mahony, Gerald. The gift of forgiveness / by Gerald O'Mahony. — London : Catholic Truth Society, 1981. — 46p ; 19cm
Revised version of: Seventy times seven. Great Wakering : Mayhew-McCrimmon, 1977
ISBN 0-85183-369-1 (pbk) : £0.65 B81-14121

248.4 — Christian life. Guidance

Brandon, Owen. You can trust God for He cares / by Owen Brandon. — [Sevenoaks] : [Hodder and Stoughton], [1981?]. — 10p ; 21cm
Cover title
£1.10 (pbk) B81-24007

248.4 — Christian life. Hospitality

Mains, Karen. Open heart open home : how to find joy through sharing your home with others / Karen Mains. — London : Pickering & Inglis, 1981, c1976. — 199p ; 21cm
Originally published: Elgin : D.C. Cook, 1976
ISBN 0-7208-0479-5 (pbk) : £2.50 B81-15582

248.4 — Christian life. Humility

Templeton, John M.. The humble approach : scientists discover God / John M. Templeton. — London : Collins, 1981. — xxvi,248p,[8]p of plates : ports ; 22cm
Bibliography: p133-248
ISBN 0-00-211398-8 : £7.50 B81-19505

248.4 — Christian life. Listening

Mitton, Michael. The wisdom to listen / by Michael Mitton. — Bramcote : Grove, 1981. — 25p ; 22cm. — (Grove pastoral series, ISSN 0144-171x ; no.5)
ISBN 0-905422-96-1 (pbk) : £0.60 B81-16971

248.4 — Christian life. Love

Duncan, Denis. Love : the word that heals / [Denis Duncan]. — Evesham : James, 1981. — 117p : ill ; 20cm. — (Amulree paperbacks ; no.4)
ISBN 0-85305-231-x (pbk) : £3.95 : CIP rev. B81-11969

248.4 — Christian life. Love — *For children*

God loves me / [illustrations by Mick Wells]. — Tring : Lion Publishing, c1981. — [12]p : col.ill ; 17cm. — (Lion board books)
ISBN 0-85648-355-9 : £0.65 B81-38472

248.4 — Christian life. Love — *For Christian communities*

O'Donnell, Desmond. Growing in love together : a programme for developing basic community or covenant groups / Desmond O'Donnell. — Dublin (St Saviour's, Dublin 1) : Dominican Publications, c1980. — 1portfolio ; 23cm
Originally published: Hurstville, N.S.W. : Oblate Community, 1979
Unpriced B81-22849

248.4 — Christian life — *Personal observations*

Brown, Elaine. The secret of life / Elaine Brown. — Tring : Lion, 1981. — 128p ; 18cm
ISBN 0-85648-334-6 (pbk) : £1.50 B81-19669

Buckingham, Jamie. Where eagles soar / Jamie Buckingham. — Eastbourne : Kingsway, 1980. — 214p ; 18cm
Originally published: Lincoln, Va.: Chosen Books, 1980
ISBN 0-86065-097-9 (pbk) : £1.35 B81-01719

Bull, Geoffrey T.. The sky is red / Geoffrey T. Bull. — London : Pickering & Inglis, 1981, c1965. — 252p ; 19cm
Originally published: London : Hodder & Stoughton, 1965
ISBN 0-7208-0480-9 (pbk) : £1.95 B81-15586

Grace, M. P.. The devil : his due / M.P. Grace. — Bognor Regis : New Horizon, c1981. — 130p,[14]leaves of plates : ill ; 21cm
ISBN 0-86116-659-0 : £5.25 B81-21732

248.4 — Christian life — *Personal observations continuation*

Greenwood, Hilda. Triumphant suffering / Hilda Greenwood. — Bognor Regis : New Horizon, c1980. — 52p ; 21cm
ISBN 0-86116-395-8 : £3.50 B81-21731

Jessop, A.. My glimpse into eternity / by A. Jessop ; illustrated by Sister M. Petrona. — [Manchester?] ([c/o The Alexian Brothers Nursing Home, St. Mary's Rd., Moston, Manchester 10]) : Dove Publications, [1981?]. — [46]p : ill ; 21cm
Unpriced (pbk) B81-17047

Lemon, Fred. Breakthrough. — London : Marshall Morgan & Scott, Oct.1981. — [160]p. — (Marshalls paperbacks)
ISBN 0-551-00920-9 (pbk) : £1.50 : CIP entry B81-30640

Marshall, Catherine. Meeting God at every turn. — London : Hodder & Stoughton, Sept.1981. — [256]p
ISBN 0-340-27155-8 : £5.95 : CIP entry B81-22495

Peale, Norman Vincent. The positive power of Jesus Christ / by Norman Vincent Peale. — London : Hodder and Stoughton, 1980. — 266p ; 22cm
ISBN 0-340-25838-1 : £5.95 : CIP rev. B80-13696

Peale, Norman Vincent. The positive power of Jesus Christ. — London : Hodder & Stoughton, Nov.1981. — [272]p
Originally published: 1980
ISBN 0-340-27156-6 (pbk) : £1.75 : CIP entry B81-31264

Rice, L. F.. Grains of Rice / L.F. Rice. — Bognor Regis : New Horizon, c1981. — 94p,[4]p of plates : ill ; 21cm
ISBN 0-86116-682-5 : £3.75 B81-40189

Ritter, Sue. I'm a Christian but — / Sue Ritter. — Eastbourne : Kingsway, 1980. — 121p : ill ; 18cm
ISBN 0-86065-081-2 (pbk) : £1.35 B81-01816

Snowden, Rita F.. I believe here and now / Rita F. Snowden. — [London] : Collins, 1981. — 155p ; 18cm
ISBN 0-00-625937-5 (pbk) : £1.25 B81-12013

Wraight, Pat. On to the summit : the Len Moules story / Pat Wraight. — Eastbourne : Kingsway, 1981. — 189p ; 18cm
ISBN 0-86065-115-0 (pbk) : £1.75 B81-19845

248.4 — Christian life. Role of reason — *Early works — Facsimiles*

Chubb, Thomas, *1679-1747*. The comparative excellence and obligation of moral and positive duties, 1730 ; and, A discourse concerning reason, 1731 / Thomas Chubb. — New York ; London : Garland, 1978. — 85,83p ; 23cm. — (British philosophers and theologians of the 17th & 18th centuries)
Facsims. of: edition published London : J. Roberts, 1730
ISBN 0-8240-1760-9 : Unpriced
Primary classification 248.4 B81-28429

248.4 — Christians. Personal problems. Solutions

Yancey, Philip. [Unhappy secrets of the Christian life]. Growing pains in the Christian life / Philip Yancey & Tim Stafford. — London : Pickering & Inglis, 1980, c1979. — 143p ; 18cm
Originally published: Grand Rapids : Zondervan Publishing House, c1979
ISBN 0-7208-0452-3 (pbk) : £1.95 B81-01752

248.4 — Grief — *Christian viewpoints — Personal observations — Collections*

Johnson, Margaret. Beyond heartache / Margaret Johnson. — Eastbourne : Kingsway, 1980, c1979. — 191p ; 18cm
Originally published: Grand Rapids : Zondervan, 1979
ISBN 0-86065-098-7 (pbk) : £1.35 B81-01963

248.4 — Lonely persons. Christian life — *Personal observations*

Cruz, Nicky. Lonely, but never alone / Nicky Cruz with Madalene Harris. — London : Pickering & Inglis, 1981. — 166p ; 19cm
ISBN 0-7208-0492-2 (pbk) : £1.60 B81-22422

248.4 — Man. Dying — *Christian viewpoints*

Casson, James H.. Dying : the greatest adventure of my life / James H. Casson. — London : Christian Medical Fellowship, 1980. — 40p ; 18cm
ISBN 0-906747-05-8 (pbk) : £0.60 B81-31113

248.4 — Single persons. Christian life

Gillett, David. A place in the family : being a single person in the local church / by David Gillett and Anne Long and Ruth Fowke. — Bramcote : Grove, 1981. — 24p ; 22cm. — (Grove pastoral series, ISSN 0144-171x ; no.6)
Text on inside cover. — Bibliography: p3
ISBN 0-907536-02-6 (pbk) : £0.60 B81-32437

248.4 — Single persons. Social life — *Christian viewpoints*

Stephenson, Elspeth. Enjoying being single / by Elspeth Stephenson. — Tring : Lion, 1981. — 70p ; 18cm
ISBN 0-85648-359-1 (pbk) : £1.00 B81-23529

248.4'05 — Christian life — *Serials — For schools*

Teen-search. — 1 (Winter)-. — Southall (32 Ellison Gardens, Southall, Middlesex UB2 4EW) : Go Teach Publications, 1981-. — v. : ill,ports ; 30cm
Quarterly
ISSN 0261-2860 : £1.20 per year B81-27907

248.4'09598 — Indonesia. Christian life — *Stories, anecdotes*

Kirk, Margaret. God was a stranger / Margaret Kirk. — Sevenoaks : OMF, 1980. — 120p ; 19cm
ISBN 0-85363-130-1 (pbk) : £0.90 B81-06011

248.4'6 — Palestine. Christian pilgrimages to Jerusalem, *312-460*

Hunt, E. D.. Holy Land pilgrimage in the later Roman Empire AD312-460. — Oxford : Clarendon Press, Jan.1982. — [290]p
ISBN 0-19-826438-0 : £15.00 : CIP entry B81-34386

248.4'63'094478 — France. Christian pilgrimages to Lourdes, *1978 — Personal observations — Polish texts*

Nietyksza, Wacław. Pamietnik pielgrzyma do Lourdes / Wacław Nietyksza. — London : Veritas Foundation, c1981. — 31p,[4]p of plates : ill, ; 19cm
Ill and map on inside covers
Unpriced (pbk) B81-21029

248.4'63'094478 — France. Christian pilgrimages to Lourdes, *to 1979*

Marnham, Patrick. Lourdes : a modern pilgrimage / Patrick Marnham. — London : Granada, 1981, c1980. — 285p, [8]p of plates : ill,ports ; 18cm. — (A Panther book)
Originally published: London : Heinemann. 1980. — Bibliography: p275-276. — Includes index
ISBN 0-586-05449-9 (pbk) : £1.95 B81-31390

248.4'7 — Christian life. Donation

Berrie, W. W. Badger. A theology of generosity : principles and practice of giving based on Bible teaching / W.W. Badger Berrie ; foreword by the Bishop of Warrington. — London : Mowbray, 1981. — 39p ; 22cm
ISBN 0-264-66772-7 (pbk) : £1.25 B81-15695

248.4'7 — Desert Fathers. Christian life. Asceticism

[Apophthegmata Patrum. *English***]**. The sayings of the Desert Fathers : the alphabetical collection / translated by Benedicta Ward ; foreword by Metropolitan Anthony. — Rev. ed. — London : Mowbray, 1981. — xxi,269p ; 22cm
Previous ed.: 1975. — Bibliography: p254-257. — Includes index
ISBN 0-264-66350-0 (pbk) : £4.95 : CIP rev. B81-16847

248.4'7 — Personal life styles. Simplicity — *Evangelical viewpoints*

Lifestyle in the eighties : an evangelical commitment to simple lifestyle. — Exeter : Paternoster Press, Nov.1981. — [256]p
ISBN 0-85364-327-x (pbk) : £5.00 : CIP entry B81-31079

248.4'811 — Desert Fathers. Christian life

Nouwen, Henri J. M.. The way of the heart : desert spirituality and contemporary ministry / Henri J.M. Nouwen. — London : Darton, Longman and Todd, 1981. — 96p ; 20cm
ISBN 0-232-51525-5 (pbk) : £1.95 : CIP rev. B81-10442

248.4'82 — Catholic lay fraternities. Christian life — *Manuals*

Handbook of the Lay Fraternities of Charles De Foucauld. — [London] ([34 Kidbrooke Gardens, SE3 0PD]) : The Lay Fraternities, c1981. — 47p ; 16cm
Cover title
Unpriced (pbk) B81-27151

248.4'82 — Catholics. Christian life

Kenny, Mary. Why Christianity works / Mary Kenny. — London : Joseph, 1981. — 220p ; 23cm
Bibliography: p211-216. — Includes index
ISBN 0-7181-1874-x : £6.95 B81-09897

Myers, Rawley. Be a better Christian : following Christ in the footsteps of Thomas Merton / by Rawley Myers. — London : Catholic Truth Society, [1981]. — 12p ; 17cm
Text on inside covers
ISBN 0-85183-218-0 (pbk) : £0.20 B81-39676

Ó Murchú, Diarmuid. The seed must die - : religious life - survival or extinction? / Diarmuid Ó Murchú. — Dublin : Veritas Publications, 1980. — x,150p ; 22cm
Bibliography: p143-145. - Includes index
ISBN 0-86217-040-0 (pbk) : Unpriced B81-19718

Orione, Luigi. The restless apostle. — London : Darton, Longman & Todd, Nov.1981. — [128]p
Translated from the Italian
ISBN 0-232-51547-6 (pbk) : £3.75 : CIP entry B81-30509

Roger, *of Taizé, Brother*. Violent for peace / by Brother Roger of Taizé. — Rev. ed. / [translated by Emily Chisholm and the Taizé Community]. — London : Mowbray, 1981. — 91p ; 18cm. — (Mowbray's popular Christian paperbacks)
Translation of: Violence des pacifiques. — Previous ed.: London : Darton, Longman & Todd, 1970
ISBN 0-264-66751-4 (pbk) : £1.50 B81-39658

248.4'82 — Catholics. Christian life — *Childhood reminiscences*

McCarthy, Mary, *1912-*. Memories of a Catholic girlhood / Mary McCarthy. — Harmondsworth : Penguin, 1963, c1957 (1981 [printing]). — 208p ; 20cm
Originally published: New York : Harcourt, Brace ; London : Heinemann, 1957
ISBN 0-14-001938-3 (pbk) : £2.50 B81-30949

248.4'82 — Catholics. Christian life — *Early works*

Teresa, *of Avila, Saint*. The interior castle / Teresa of Avila ; translation by Kieran Kavanaugh and Otilio Rodriguez ; introduction by Kieran Kavanaugh ; preface by Raimundo Panikkar. — London : SPCK, 1979. — xix,225p ; 23cm. — (The Classics of Western spirituality)
Translation of: Les moradas. — Bibliography: p214-216. — Includes index
ISBN 0-281-03711-6 (pbk) : £6.50 B81-23045

248.4'82 — Catholics. Christian life — *For schools*

Clemson, Josephine. Living and belonging / Josephine Clemson. — Catholic ed. — Walton-on-Thames : Nelson, 1981. — 63p : ill,ports ; 25cm. — (Living plus ; bk.1)
Previous ed.: 1977. — Bibliography: p63
ISBN 0-17-437025-3 (pbk) : £1.70 B81-16793

248.4′82 — Catholics. Christian life — *For schools continuation*

Clemson, Josephine. Living and sharing / Josephine Clemson. — Catholic ed. — Walton-on-Thames : Nelson, 1981. — iv,60p : ill,ports ; 25cm. — (Living plus ; Bk.2)
ISBN 0-17-437024-5 (pbk) : £1.60 B81-26559

248.4′8206 — Catholics: Handicapped persons. Christian life

All people together : a statement of the Roman Catholic Bishops of England and Wales. — Abbots Langley : Catholic Information Services ; London (St. Mary of the Angels, Moorhouse Rd., W2 5DJ) : Distributed by CSP Studies, 1981. — 16p : ill ; 21cm
Ill on inside covers
£0.30 (pbk) B81-16440

248.4′82094 — Catholic religious communities. Christian life

Moloney, Francis J.. Free to love : poverty — chastity — obedience / Francis J. Moloney. — London : Darton, Longman and Todd, 1981. — xiv,96p ; 22cm
Bibliography: p91-92. — Includes index
ISBN 0-232-51518-2 (pbk) : £2.95 : CIP rev. B81-04244

248.4′83 — Anglicans. Christian life

Law, William. William Law : a serious call to a devout, and holy life ; the spirit of love / edited from the first editions by Paul G. Stanwood ; introduction by Austin Warren and Paul G. Stanwood ; preface by John Booty. — London : SPCK, c1978. — x,526p ; 23cm. — (The Classics of Western spirituality)
Originally published: New York : Paulist Press, 1978. — Bibliography: p499-500. — Includes index
ISBN 0-281-03649-7 (pbk) : £7.50 B81-12496

248.4′83 — Anglicans. Christian life. Conflict

Williams, H. A.. Tensions : necessary conflicts in life and love / H.A. Williams. — London : Mitchell Beazley, 1979, c1976. — 120p ; 22cm
ISBN 0-85533-164-x (pbk) : £2.50 B81-05845

248.4′841 — Lutherans. Christian life

Christenson, Larry. Back to square one / Larry Christenson. — Eastbourne : Kingsway, 1980, c1979. — 155p ; 18cm
Originally published: Minneapolis : Bethany Fellowship, c1979
ISBN 0-86065-096-0 (pbk) : £1.35 B81-00737

248.4′865 — Church of the Brethren. Christian life

Gish, Art. Living in Christian community : a personal manifesto / Art Gish. — Sutherland, N.S.W. : Albatross Books ; Tring : Lion, c1979. — 379p : ill ; 18cm. — (An Albatross book)
Originally published: Scottdale, Pa : Herald Press, 1979. — Bibliography: p371-373. - Includes index
ISBN 0-85648-307-9 (pbk) : £2.95 B81-10586

248.4′896 — Quakers. Christian life

Foster, Richard J.. Celebration of discipline : the path to spiritual growth / Richard J. Foster. — London : Hodder & Stoughton, 1980, c1978. — 179p ; 18cm. — (Hodder Christian paperbacks)
Originally published: New York ; London : Harper and Row, 1978
ISBN 0-340-25992-2 (pbk) : £1.50 : CIP rev. B80-19596

Marsden, Lorna M.. A discipline of waiting : and other essays / by Lorna M. Marsden ; with an introduction by Gerald Priestland. — Sutton (12 Boston Court, Christchurch Park, Sutton, Surrey SM2 5TJ) : Published for the Open Letter Movement by R. Allen, [1978?]. — 40p ; 22cm
Unpriced (unbound) B81-36339

Marsden, Lorna M.. From the frontier / Lorna M. Marsden. — London (12 Boston Court, Christchurch Park, Sutton, Surrey SM2 5TJ) : Open Letter Movement, 1981. — 60p ; 21cm
Unpriced (pbk) B81-36338

248.4′899 — Salvation Army. Christian life

Brown, Jean, *1916-*. Excursions in thought / by Jean Brown. — London : Salvationist, 1980. — 90p ; 22cm
ISBN 0-85412-360-1 (pbk) : Unpriced B81-24375

248′.5 — Bible. N.T. Mark. Special subjects: Discipleship — *Textual criticisms*

Best, Ernest. Following Jesus : discipleship in the Gospel of Mark / Ernest Best. — Sheffield : JSOT, 1981. — 283p ; 23cm. — (Journal for the study of the New Testament supplement series ; 4)
Bibliography: p254-273. - Includes index
ISBN 0-905774-28-0 : Unpriced
ISBN 0-905774-29-9 (pbk) B81-19576

248′.5 — Christian church. Children, 9-14 years. Personal evangelism

Prince, John. Early harvest : leading a child to Christ / John Prince. — 2nd ed. — [London] : Falcon, 1978. — 47p ; 20cm
Previous ed.: 1976. — Bibliography: p46-47
ISBN 0-85491-858-2 (pbk) : Unpriced B81-17802

248′.5 — Christian church. Personal evangelism

Watson, David, *1933-*. Discipleship. — London : Hodder & Stoughton, Nov.1981. — [288]p
ISBN 0-340-26572-8 (pbk) : £3.95 : CIP entry B81-30134

248′.5 — Christian church. Personal evangelism. Follow-up — *Manuals*

Smith, Ron, *1924-*. The ABC of follow up / Ron Smith. — Bromley : STL Books, c1974 (1979 printing). — 142p ; 19cm
ISBN 0-903843-07-2 (pbk) : Unpriced B81-10054

248′.5 — Christian church. Personal evangelism — *Manuals*

Smith, Ron, *1924-*. The ABC of personal evangelism / Ron Smith. — Bromley : STL Books, c1974 (1979 printing). — 127p ; 19cm
ISBN 0-903843-05-6 (pbk) : Unpriced B81-19966

248′.5 — Christian church. Personal evangelism. Visiting — *Manuals*

Smith, Ron, *1924-*. The ABC of door to door visitation / Ron Smith. — Bromley : STL Books, c1974 (1979 printing). — 172p ; 19cm
ISBN 0-903843-06-4 (pbk) : Unpriced B81-10055

248′.6 — Christian church. Stewardship

Pulleng, A.. The stewardship of money / by A. Pulleng. — Rev. and repr. — Bath (1 Widcombe Cres., Bath [BA2 6AQ]) : Echoes of Service, 1979. — 1folded sheet(7p) ; 19cm
Previous ed.: 197-
Unpriced (unbound) B81-17868

248.8′2 — Children. Christian life. Role of parents

Martineau, Andrea. What can I tell my child about God? / by Andrea Martineau. — London : Mowbray, 1981. — 32p ; 15cm. — (Enquirer′s library)
Bibliography: p31-32
ISBN 0-264-66747-6 (pbk) : £0.60 B81-17902

248.8′2 — Children, to 7 years. Christian life — *For parents*

O′Mahoney, Gerald. Your child & God : the first seven years / Gerald O′Mahony. — Great Wakering : Mayhew-McCrimmon, 1979. — 104p ; 18cm
ISBN 0-85597-285-8 (pbk) : £1.40 B81-09572

248.8′2 — Christian life. Questions by children — *For parents*

Pigrem, Tim. The questions they ask! / Tim Pigrem. — London : Mothers′ Union, [1981]?. — 7p ; 21cm
Cover title
ISBN 0-85943-032-4 (pbk) : £0.40 B81-39586

248.8′43′2 — Single women. Emotional problems — *Christian viewpoints*

Andrews, Gini. Your half of the apple : God & the single girl / Gini Andrews ; foreword by Francis Schaeffer. — Bromley (P.O. Box 48, Bromley, Kent) : STL Productions, 1978, c1972. — 157p ; 18cm
Originally published: Grand Rapids : Zondervan, 1972 ; London : Lakeland, 1973
£1.25 (pbk) B81-11130

248.8′6 — Bereavement — *Catholic viewpoints*

Matthew, *Monk*. Comfort for the bereaved / [by Monk Matthew]. — London : Catholic Truth Society, 1980. — 16p ; 19cm
Cover title
ISBN 0-85183-362-4 (pbk) : £0.35 B81-08329

248.8′6 — Bereavement. Personal adjustment — *Christian viewpoints*

Purcell, William. Bereavement / by William Purcell. — London : Mowbray, 1981. — 32p ; 15cm. — (Enquirer′s library)
Bibliography: p32
ISBN 0-264-66727-1 (pbk) : £0.60 B81-17904

248.8′6 — Man. Depression — *Christian viewpoints*

Chave-Jones, Myra. Coping with depression / Myra Chave-Jones. — Tring : Lion, 1981. — 80p ; 18cm
ISBN 0-86760-282-1 (pbk) : £1.00 B81-23337

248.8′8 — Christian teachers. Commitment

Watkins, D. Alun. Stress and commitment for the Christian teacher / D. Alun Watkins. — Cardiff (23 St Edwen Gardens, Cardiff CF4 4J2) : Association of Christian Teachers of Wales, 1980. — [11]p ; 20cm
ISBN 0-907193-02-1 (pbk) : £0.35 B81-29282

248.8′8 — Prussian military forces. Deserters. Christian life — *Personal observations*

The **fugitive** : a true and faithful account of the amazing experiences and eventual conversion of a Prussian deserter / noted down from his own verbal relation and put in book form by J. de Liefde ; and translated in English by Marcus Banfield. — Ossett (44 Queen′s Drive, Ossett, W. Yorks., WF5 0ND) : Zoar, [1981?]. — 58p ; 19cm
Translated from the Dutch
ISBN 0-904435-11-3 (pbk) : £0.65 B81-31299

248.8′94 — Contemplative religious orders. Christian life

Merton, Thomas. Contemplation in a world of action / Thomas Merton ; introduction by Jean Leclercq. — London : Unwin Paperbacks, 1980. — xxviii,384p ; 20cm. — (A mandala book)
Originally published: Garden City, N.Y. : Doubleday ; London : Allen & Unwin, 1971
ISBN 0-04-248011-6 (pbk) : £3.25 : CIP rev. B80-13200

248.8′943 — Catholic Church. Nuns. Christian life — *Personal observations*

Armstrong, Karen. Through the narrow gate / Karen Armstrong. — London : Macmillan, 1981. — 285p ; 23cm
ISBN 0-333-31136-1 : £6.95 B81-24093

249 — CHRISTIAN OBSERVANCES IN FAMILY LIFE

249 — Catholics. Families. Christian life

Lyons, Teresa M.. The family business / Teresa M. Lyons. — Dublin : Veritas Publications, 1980. — vii,90p : ill ; 19cm
ISBN 0-86217-036-2 (pbk) : £1.75 B81-10305

251 — CHRISTIAN CHURCH. PREACHING

251 — Christian church. Preaching

Steel, David, *1910-*. Preaching : through the year / David Steel. — Edinburgh : St Andrew Press, 1980. — 170p ; 21cm
ISBN 0-7152-0457-2 (pbk) : £3.50 B81-11057

Stort, John R. W.. I believe in preaching. — London : Hodder & Stoughton, Feb.1982. — [256]p. — (Ecclesia books)
ISBN 0-340-27564-2 : £5.50 : CIP entry B81-36364

251 — Christian church. Preaching — *Manuals*
The **Living** word. — Alton : Redemptorist
Cycle 'A'. — c1981
Part 4 / contributors John Trenchard (general editor) ... [et al.]. — [64]p ; 21cm
ISBN 0-85231-046-3 (pbk) : Unpriced B81-40114

Lloyds-Jones, D. M.. Preaching and preachers / by D. Martyn Lloyd-Jones. — New ed. — London : Hodder and Stoughton, 1981. — 325p ; 22cm. — (Ecclesia books)
Previous ed.: 1971
£4.95 (pbk) B81-36527

251 — Church of England. Weddings. Preaching — *Manuals*
Bunting, Ian. Preaching at weddings / by Ian Bunting. — Bramcote : Grove, 1980. — 25p ; 22cm. — (Grove worship series, ISSN 0144-1728 ; no.74)
ISBN 0-905422-89-9 (pbk) : £0.60 B81-05641

251'.02 — Church of England. Sermons — *Sermon outlines — For church year — Serials*
Preaching through the Christian year. — 8. — London : Mowbray, 1981. — v,122p
ISBN 0-264-66598-8 : £3.50 B81-27918

251'.02'05 — Christian church. Sermons — *Sermon outlines — Serials*
The **Ministers** manual. — 56th annual issue (1981 ed.). — San Francisco ; Cambridge : Harper & Row, c1980. — vii,280p
ISBN 0-06-069026-7 : Unpriced B81-00738

251'.02'05 — Church of England. Sermons — *Sermon outlines — Serials*
The **Church** pulpit year book. — 1981. — London : Chansitor Publications, [1980]. — vi,300p
£4.50 B81-09087

The **Church** pulpit year book. — 1980. — London : Chansitor Publications, [1980]. — vi,307p
£4.50 B81-12434

252 — CHRISTIAN CHURCH. SERMONS

252'.00944 — France. Christian church. Sermons, *1000-1500 — Texts*
Bozon, Nicholas. Nine verse sermons. — Oxford (c/o Hon. Treasurer, Magdalen College, Oxford OX1 4AU) : Society for the Study of Mediaeval Languages and Literature, Nov.1981. — [99]p. — (Medium Aevum monographs. New series ; 11)
ISBN 0-907570-01-1 (pbk) : £4.50 : CIP entry B81-32587

252'.02 — Catholic Church. Sermons — *Texts — For church year*
The **Living** word. — Alton : Redemptorist, c1981
Cycle 'A'
Part 2 / contributors John Trenchard (general editor) ... [et al.]. — c1981. — [32]p ; 21cm
Bibliography: p[4]
ISBN 0-85231-044-7 (pbk) : Unpriced B81-11398

The **Living** word. — Alton : Redemptorist
Cycle 'A'
Part 3 / contributors John Trenchard (general editor) ... [et al.]. — c1981. — [64]p ; 21cm
ISBN 0-85231-046-3 (pbk) : Unpriced B81-24928

252'.03 — Church of England. Sermons — *Texts*
Coggan, Donald. Sure foundation / by Donald Coggan. — London : Hodder and Stoughton, 1981. — 319p ; 22cm. — (Ecclesia books)
ISBN 0-340-26357-1 (pbk) : £5.95 B81-17945

252'.03 — Church of England. Sermons — *Texts — Facsimiles*
Clarke, Samuel. [The works of Samuel Clarke]. The works, 1738 / Samuel Clarke. — New York ; London : Garland, 1978. — 4v. : 1port ; 29cm. — (British philosophers and theologians of the 17th & 18th centuries)
Facsim. of: edition published London : J. & P. Knapton, 1738
ISBN 0-8240-1762-5 : Unpriced B81-25528

252'.04 — Continental Protestant churches. Sermons — *Collections*
Barth, Karl. Come Holy Spirit : sermons / by Karl Barth and Eduard Thurneysen ; English translation by George W. Richards, Elmer G. Homrighausen, Karl J. Ernst ; translation read and approved by Karl Barth. — London : Mowbrays, 1978, c1933. — 287p ; 18cm
Translation of: Komm Schöpfer Geist. — Originally published: New York : Round Table Press, 1933
ISBN 0-264-66515-5 (pbk) : £1.75 B81-09921

252'.052 — Church of Scotland. Sermons — *Texts*
Burns, William C.. Revival sermons : notes of addresses / by William C. Burns ; edited by M.F. Barbour. — Edinburgh : Banner of Truth Trust, 1980. — 205p ; 18cm
Originally published: London : Nisbet, 1869
ISBN 0-85151-316-6 (pbk) : £1.75 B81-09849

252'.06 — Baptist churches. Sermons — *Texts*
Delves, Stanley. Forest Fold pulpit : sermons of Stanley Delves of Crowborough. — [Crowborough] ([c/o Secretary to the Trustees, Forest Fold Chapel, London Rd., Crowborough, E. Sussex]) : Stanley Delves Trust, 1980. — v,148p.[3]p of plates : ill,1port ; 19cm
ISBN 0-904435-38-5 : £4.50 B81-31297

252'.53 — Christian church. Children's sermons — *Texts*
Morrison, Edith M.. Trains and railways : story-object lessons / Edith M. Morrison ; [illustrations by B. Webley]. — Ilkeston : Moorley's Bible and Bookshop, c1980. — 72p : ill,1map ; 21cm
ISBN 0-86071-104-8 (pbk) : £0.80 B81-11397

253 — CHRISTIAN CHURCH. CLERGY AND PASTORAL WORK

253 — Baptist churches. New members. Care
Buckingham, Derek. Caring for new Christians / Derek Buckingham. — Ilkeston : Published on behalf of Mainstream by Moorleys, c1980. — 31p ; 20cm
ISBN 0-86071-114-5 (pbk) : £0.45 B81-10949

253 — Christian church. Pastoral work
Campbell, Alastair V.. Rediscovering pastoral care / Alastair V. Campbell. — London : Darton, Longman & Todd, 1981. — xii,124p ; 22cm
Includes index
ISBN 0-232-51472-0 (pbk) : £3.95 : CIP rev. B81-06056

253 — Church of England. Clergy. Pastoral role
Leonard, Graham. God alive : priorities in pastoral theology / Graham Leonard. — London : Darton, Longman and Todd, 1981. — viii,88p ; 22cm
Includes index
ISBN 0-232-51503-4 (pbk) : £2.50 B81-35515

253 — Great Britain. Christian church. Parish work
Gibbs, Eddie. I believe in church growth. — London : Hodder & Stoughton, Sept.1981. — [480]p. — ('I believe' series)
ISBN 0-340-26352-0 : £5.95 : CIP entry B81-22492

253.5 — Christian church. Pastoral work. Counselling
Hughes, Selwyn. A friend in need : how to help people through their problems / Selwyn Hughes. — Eastbourne : Kingsway, 1981. — 192p ; 18cm
Includes index
ISBN 0-86065-116-9 (pbk) : £1.75 B81-19844

Lake, Frank. Tight corners in pastoral counselling. — London : Darton, Longman & Todd, Apr.1981. — [144]p
ISBN 0-232-51309-0 (pbk) : £3.95 : CIP entry B81-11957

253.7 — Great Britain. Weekend holidaymakers. Evangelism by Christian church
Making known the good news to weekend leisure seekers / [compiled by David Gregg]. — London (146 Queen Victoria St., EC4V 4BX) : Nationwide Initiative in Evangelism, [1980]. — 10p ; 22cm. — (Discussion paper / Nationwide Initiative in Evangelism ; no.4)
£0.75 (£4.00 for 10 copies) (pbk) B81-20898

253.7'0880624 — Great Britain. Urban regions. Poor persons. Evangelism by Christian church
Making known the good news to the urban poor / [compiled by Colin Marchant]. — London (146 Queen Victoria St., EC4V 4BX) : Nationwide Initiative in Evangelism, [1980]. — 11p ; 21cm. — (Discussion paper / Nationwide Initiative in Evangelism ; no.2)
£0.75 (£5.00 for 10 copies) (pbk) B81-20897

253.7'0880694 — Great Britain. Disadvantaged young persons. Evangelism by Christian church
Making known the good news to young people at risk / [compiled by Michael Eastman]. — London (146 Queen Victoria St., EC4V 4BX) : Nationwide Initiative in Evangelism, [1980]. — 18p ; 22cm. — (Discussion paper / Nationwide Initiative in Evangelism ; no.3)
Bibliography: p16-17
£0.75 (£5.00 for 10 copies) (pbk) B81-20895

253.7'6 — Great Britain. Local authority housing. Tenants. Evangelism by Christian church
Making known the good news to the residents of council housing estates / [compiled by Lewis Misselbrook]. — London (146 Queen Victoria St., EC4V 4BX) : Nationwide Initiative in Evangelism, [1980]. — 23p ; 22cm. — (Discussion paper / Nationwide Initiative in Evangelism ; no.1)
£0.75 (£6.00 for 10 copies) (pbk) B81-20896

254 — CHRISTIAN CHURCH. PARISH WORK. ORGANISATION

254'.7 — Catholic Church. *Diocese of Przemyśl.* **Churches. Construction,** *1974-1978.* **Political aspects** — *Polish texts*
Boniecki, Adam. Budowa Kościołów : w diecezji przemyskiej / Adam Boniecki. — London (26 Pont St., S.W.1) : Spotkania, [1980]. — 147p : ill ; 22cm. — (Biblioteka Spotkań)
Unpriced (pbk) B81-30667

254'.7 — Great Britain. Multiracial communities. Use of church buildings
Carver, Gillian. A place to meet : the use of church property and the new religious minorities in Britain : a report prepared for the Community and Race Relations Unit, Division of Community Affairs, British Council of Churches 1978 / by Gillian Carver. — London : Community and Race Relations Unit, British Council of Churches, 1978?. — 39p ; 21cm
£0.50 (pbk) B81-10789

254.8 — Cambridgeshire. Brampton. Tithe apportionments, *1839 — Texts*
The **Brampton** Tithe Award. — Eastbourne ([24 Benbow Ave., Eastbourne, BN23 6EB]) : N.C. Beck, [1980]. — [12]leaves,[5]leaves of plates : maps ; 21x34cm
£1.00 (pbk) B81-10390

254.8 — Church of England. Parishes. Financial management — *Manuals*
Carter, Phyllis. A handbook of parish finance / by Phyllis Carter and Michael Perry. — London : Mowbray, 1981. — vii,152p ; 19cm. — (Mowbray parish handbooks)
Bibliography: p145-146. — Includes index
ISBN 0-264-66414-0 (pbk) : £3.50 B81-11483

254.8 — England. Tithes. Redemption — *Accounts — Serials*
Tithe Act 1936, accounts. — 1978-80. — London : H.M.S.O., 1981. — 5p
ISBN 0-10-219681-8 : £1.10 B81-26593

254'.8 — France. Tithe apportionments, *ca 1400-ca 1800*
Le Roy Ladurie, Emmanuel. Tithe and agrarian history from the fourteenth to the nineteenth centuries. — Cambridge : Cambridge University Press, Feb.1982. — [207]p
ISBN 0-521-23974-5 : £17.50 : CIP entry B81-39256

254.8 — Suffolk. Boxford. Churchwardens. Accounts, *1529-1561*

Boxford churchwardens' accounts 1529-1561. — Woodbridge : Boydell Press, Nov.1981. — [144]p. — (Suffolk Records Society ; v.23)
ISBN 0-85115-160-4 : £12.00 : CIP entry
B81-33648

254.8 — West Midlands *(Metropolitan county).* **Brierley Hill. Methodist Church: Bank Street Wesleyan Methodist Chapel,** *1833-1884*

Burial entries & pew rents from the account book, 1833-1884 / Bank Street Wesleyan Methodist Chapel, Brierley Hill, Staffordshire ; extracted by Peter D. Bloore. — Sedgley (21 Larkswood Drive, Sedgley, W. Midlands DY3 3QU) : Birmingham and Midland Society for Genealogy and Heraldry, 1980. — 46p : facsims ; 22cm
ISBN 0-905105-44-3 (pbk) : £1.00 B81-09570

255 — CHRISTIANITY. RELIGIOUS CONGREGATIONS AND ORDERS

255 — Christianity. Monasticism

Contemporary monasticism / Jean Leclercq ... [et al.]. — Fairacres : Convent of the Incarnation, Fairacres, Oxford OX4 1TB, c1981. — vi,41p : ill,ports ; 21cm
Cover title
ISBN 0-7283-0089-3 (pbk) : £0.75 B81-28273

255'.1 — Benedictines

Hume, George Basil. In praise of Benedict / George Basil Hume. — London (Hodder and Stoughton), 1981. — 93p ; 18cm. — (Hodder Christian paperbacks)
ISBN 0-340-26410-1 (pbk) : £1.00 B81-10529

255'.1'00941 — Great Britain. Benedictines — *Serials*

English Congregation of the Order of St. Benedict. The Benedictine yearbook. — 1981. — York (c/o Ampleforth Abbey, York YO6 4EN) : [English Congregation of the Order of St. Benedict], [1980]. — 162p
ISSN 0522-8883 : £0.40 B81-03291

255'.106 — Benedictines. Community life. Benedict, *Saint.* **Regula —** *Critical studies*

MacGinty, Gerard. The Rule of Benedict : themes, texts, thoughts / Gerard MacGinty. — Dublin : Dominican, 1980. — 166p ; 16cm
Includes index
ISBN 0-9504797-9-9 (pbk) : Unpriced
B81-26027

255'.106 — Benedictines. Community life. Benedict, *Saint.* **Regula —** *Expositions*

Baker, Augustine. The substance of the rule of St Bennet / by Augustine Baker ; transcribed and edited by the Benedictines of Stanbrook from a manuscript copied in 1650 by Leander Prichard. — Worcester ([Callow End, Worcester WR2 4TD]) : Stanbrook Abbey, 1981. — vi,51p ; 22cm
Transcript of Downside Library MS. 26595. — Includes index
Unpriced (pbk) B81-38955

255'.8 — Church of England. Monks. Community life

Walker, Lionel Marshall. Brothers of habit : life in a monastery / by Lionel Marshall Walker. — London : Hale, 1981. — 192p ; 23cm
ISBN 0-7091-9144-8 : £6.95 B81-31663

259 — CHRISTIAN CHURCH. PAROCHIAL ACTIVITIES

259 — Christian religious groups. Activities — *For parish priests*

Mallison, John. Creative ideas : for small groups in the Christian community / John Mallison (and a small group). — London : SU Specialist Publications, 1981, c1978. — 249p : ill ; 21cm. — (Abridged small group series ; no.2)
Originally published: West Ryde, N.S.W. : Renewal Publications, 1978. — Includes bibliographies
ISBN 0-85421-906-4 (pbk) : £2.95 B81-28934

259 — Christian religious groups. Organisation — *For parish priests*

Mallison, John. Building small groups : in the Christian community / John Mallison (and a small group). — London : SU Specialist Publications, 1981, c1978. — 238p : ill ; 21cm. — (Abridged small group series ; no.1)
Originally published: West Ryde, N.S.W. : Renewal Publications, 1978. — Bibliography: p226-236
ISBN 0-85421-905-6 (pbk) : £2.95 B81-28935

259'.2'0941 — Great Britain. Christian church. Pastoral work with young persons

Young people and the church : the report of a working party set up by the British Council of Churches Youth Unit. — London : British Council of Churches, c1981. — 94p : ill ; 21cm
ISBN 0-85169-084-x (pbk) : £1.00 B81-19008

259'.2'0941 — Great Britain. Methodist Church. Pastoral work with young persons

Time for talking : youth work as an expression of the Gospel / prepared from the consultations of the MAYC Development Group ; Martin Caldwell ... [et al.] ; edited and introduced by David J. Winwood. — London (2 Chester House, Pages La., N10 1PR) : Methodist Association of Youth Clubs, 1980. — 43p ; 21x18cm
ISBN 0-7192-0138-1 (pbk) : £1.50 B81-20830

259'.22 — Christian activities for children

Sing, say and move / compiled by Jill McWilliam. — London : Scripture Union, 1981. — 125p : ill,music ; 21cm
ISBN 0-85421-909-9 (pbk) : Unpriced
B81-17199

259'.3'0942 — Church of England. Parish work with old persons. Evangelism

Notes on the discussion which took place at the NIE National Assembly, held in Nottingham in September, 1980, on making known the Good News to senior citizens / compiled by Oliver Wright Holmes. — London (146 Queen Victoria St., EC4V 4BX) : Nationwide Initiative in Evangelism, [1981?]. — 5p : 1form ; 22cm
Cover title. — At head of title: Nationwide Initiative in Evangelism
£0.75 (£4.00 for 10 copies) (pbk) B81-20829

259'.5'0924 — West Midlands œi (Metropolitan County). Birmingham. Christian church. Pastoral work with deviants — *Personal observations*

Moore, Walter. Set me free / Walter Morre. — London : Pickering & Inglis, c1980. — 188p ; 19cm
ISBN 0-7208-0467-1 (pbk) : £1.95 B81-08281

260 — CHRISTIANITY. SOCIAL AND ECCLESIASTICAL THEOLOGY

260 — Bible. N.T. Epistles of Paul. Special subjects: Christian church

Banks, Robert, *1939-*. Paul's idea of community : the early house churches in their historical setting / Robert Banks. — Exeter : Paternoster, c1980. — 208p ; 23cm
Bibliography: p199-204
ISBN 0-85364-251-6 (cased) : £7.60 : CIP rev.
ISBN 0-85364-244-7 (pbk) : Unpriced
B79-31502

260 — Christian church

Bewes, Richard. The Church / [Richard Bewes, Robert Hicks]. — [London] : Scripture Union, 1981. — [24]p : col.ill ; 17cm. — (Explaining Bible truth)
Cover title. — Text on inside covers
ISBN 0-85421-918-8 (pbk) : £0.40 B81-24510

260 — Christian church. Fellowship

Poonen, Zac. One body in Christ : the meaning of Christian fellowship / Zac Poonen. — Eastbourne : Kingsway, 1980, c1974. — 64p ; 18cm
Originally published: Bombay : Gospel Literature Service, 1974
ISBN 0-86065-105-3 (pbk) : £0.75 B81-07981

261 — CHRISTIANITY. SOCIAL THEOLOGY

261 — Authority — *Christian viewpoints*

Dominian, Jack. Authority. — London : Darton, Longman & Todd, Oct.1981. — [128]p
Originally published: London : Burns & Oates, 1976
ISBN 0-232-51552-2 (pbk) : £2.95 : CIP entry
B81-31178

261 — Education — *Christian viewpoints*

May, Philip R. Which way to teach?. — Leicester : Inter-Varsity Press, Sept.1981. — [192]p
ISBN 0-85110-428-2 (pbk) : £1.65 : CIP entry
B81-22554

261 — Education. Role of non-Christians — *Christian viewpoints*

Elias, J. Hefin. The battle for ascendancy in education : the source and strength of anti-Christian elements in education today / J. Hefin Elias. — Cardiff (23, St. Edwen Gdns., Cardiff CF4 4JZ) : Association of Christian Teachers of Wales, 1981. — 34p ; 20cm
ISBN 0-907517-00-5 (pbk) : £0.75 B81-29624

261 — England. Schools. Authority — *Christian viewpoints*

Francis, Alan F. The place of authority in education / Alan F. Francis. — Cardiff (23 St. Edwen Gardens, Cardiff CF4 4JZ) : Association of Christian Teachers of Wales, 1976 (1980 [printing]). — [10]p ; 22cm
Annual lecture of the Association of Christian Teachers of Wales, delivered at Bryntirion, Bridgend, on September 27th 1975
ISBN 0-907193-01-3 (pbk) : £0.35 B81-08075

261 — England. Schools — *Christian viewpoints*

Martin, C. G. Have schools lost their way? / by Charles Martin. — Bramcote : Grove, 1980. — 25p ; 22cm. — (Grove pastoral series, ISSN 0144-171x ; no.4)
ISBN 0-905422-92-9 (pbk) : £0.50 B81-06272

261 — Future — *Christian viewpoints — For adolescents*

Sullivan, Danny. Look into the future / [written and compiled by Danny Sullivan]. — London (2 Chester House, Pages La., N19 1PR) : The Christian Education Movement, 1981. — 35p : ill ; 25cm
Cover title
ISBN 0-905022-68-8 (pbk) : Unpriced
B81-12029

261 — Great Britain. Education — *Christian viewpoints — Serials*

[Focus on education *(London : 1980)*]. Focus on education / Education and Society, Division of Community Affairs, British Council of Churches. — No.1 (Autumn 1980)-. — London : The Division, 1980-. — v. ; 21cm
Three issues yearly
ISSN 0260-8960 = Focus on education (London. 1980) : Unpriced B81-09047

261 — Great Britain. Education. Policies of government — *Christian viewpoints*

Brown, Douglas A. What is the government doing to our schools? : the Education Bill and its implications / by Douglas A. Brown. — London : Methodist Church Division of Education and Youth, c1980. — ii,18p ; 21cm
Bibliography: p17-18
ISBN 0-7192-0137-3 (pbk) : £0.50 B81-20881

261 — Society — *Christian viewpoints*

Dobbs, Geoffrey. What is social credit? / by Geoffrey Dobbs. — Sudbury : Bloomfield, c1981. — 24p ; 21cm
ISBN 0-904656-05-5 (pbk) : Unpriced
B81-37471

261.1 — Poland. Christian social movements: Odrodzenia, *to 1926 — Polish texts*

Kaczorowski, Stefan. Historia działalność i tradycje "odrodzenia" / Stefan Kaczorowski. — Londyn (27 Hamilton Rd., Bedford Park, W4 1AL) : Odnowa, 1980. — 62p ; 21cm. — (Zeszyty chrześcijańsko - społeczne ; zesz.2)
ISBN 0-903705-29-x (pbk) : £1.50 B81-21398

261.1 — Society. Role of Christian church

The **Growing** church (personal renewal). — Poole (57, Dorcester Rd, Lytchett Minster, Poole, Dorset BH16 6JE) : Post Green Press, c1981. — 144p ; 22cm. — (Bases for Christian renewal and growth ; book 3)
Bibliography: p141-144
ISBN 0-906309-18-2 (spiral) : Unpriced
B81-37995

Leech, Kenneth, *1939-*. The social God / Kenneth Leech. — London : Sheldon, 1981. — viii,167p ; 22cm
Includes index
ISBN 0-85969-342-2 (pbk) : £4.95 B81-25425

The **Living** Church : (a pastoral community) : Post Green leadership training course materials compiled and edited for individual or group study / contributing editors Faith Lees ... [et al.]. — Poole (57 Dorchester Rd, Lytchett Minster, Poole, Dorset BH16 6JE) : Post Green
Book 1: Bases for Christian renewal and growth. — Poole (57 Dorchester Rd, Lytchett Minster, Poole, Dorset BH16 6JE) : Post Green. — 146p ; 21cm
ISBN 0-906309-16-6 (spiral) : Unpriced
B81-06330

261.1 — Society. Role of Christian church *related to* **Marxism**

Bockmühl, Klaus. The challenge of Marxism : a Christian response / Klaus Bockmüehl. — Leicester : Inter-Varsity Press, 1980. — 187p ; 18cm
Translation of: Herausforderungen des Marxismus. — Includes index
ISBN 0-85110-417-7 (pbk) : £1.95 : CIP rev.
Also classified at 335.4 B80-21370

261.1 — Society. Role of Christianity

Blamires, Harry. Where do we stand? : an examination of the Christian's position in the modern world / Harry Blamires. — London : SPCK, 1980. — xi,158p ; 22cm
Originally published: Ann Arbor : Servant Books, 1980
ISBN 0-281-03766-3 : £3.95 B81-01638

261.1'0942 — England. Society. Role of Church of England

Living the faith : a call to the Church / edited by Kathleen Jones. — Oxford : Oxford University Press, 1980. — 152p ; 21cm
Bibliography: p151-152
ISBN 0-19-213233-4 (cased) : £5.95 : CIP rev.
ISBN 0-19-213239-3 (pbk) : Unpriced
B80-06768

261.1'0973 — United States. Society. Role of Christian church, *1960-1970*

Betsworth, Roger G. The radical movement of the 1960's / by Roger G. Betsworth. — Metuchen, N.J. ; London : Scarecrow Press and American Theological Library Association, 1980. — viii,363p ; 23cm. — (ATLA monograph series ; no.14)
Bibliography: p335-357. - Includes index
ISBN 0-8108-1307-6 : £12.25 B81-03953

261.1'0973 — United States. Society. Role of Christian church *compared with* **role of communist ideology in society in Soviet Union**

Henry, Maureen. The intoxication of power : an analysis of civil religion in relation to ideology / Maureen Henry. — Dordrecht ; London : Reidel, c1979. — xiii,231p ; 23cm. — (Sovietica ; v.43)
Includes index
ISBN 90-277-1027-9 : Unpriced
Also classified at 306'.2 B81-06237

261.2'0941 — Great Britain. Christian church. Relations with other religions

British Council of Churches. *Committee for Relations with People of Other Faiths.* Relations with people of other faiths : guidelines on dialogue in Britain / Committee for Relations with People of Other Faiths. — London : British Council of Churches, 1981. — 24p ; 21cm
ISBN 0-85169-088-2 (unbound) : £0.35
B81-28894

261.2'6 — Catholics. Relations with Jews — *Catholic viewpoints*

Catholic-Jewish relations : official documents and pastoral guidelines. — London : Catholic Truth Society, 1981. — 18p ; 19cm
ISBN 0-85183-405-1 (pbk) : £0.30
Also classified at 296.3'872 B81-19726

261.2'6 — Jews. Attitudes of Catholic Church

[**Über das Verhältnis der Kirche zum Judentum**. *English*]The **Church** and the Jews : declaration of the German bishops / [translated by Phil Jenkins]. — London : Catholic Truth Society, 1980. — 30p ; 19cm
Translation of: Über das Verhältnis der Kirche zum Judentum
ISBN 0-85183-381-0 (pbk) : £0.45 B81-07399

261.2'7 — Christianity. Relations with Islam — *Muslim viewpoints*

Denffer, Ahmad von. Some reflections on dialogue between Christians and Muslims / Ahmad von Denffer. — Leicester (223 London Rd., Leicester, LE2 1ZE) : The Islamic Foundation, c1980. — 22p ; 30cm. — (Seminar papers / Islamic Foundation ; 10)
ISBN 0-86037-084-4 (pbk) : Unpriced
Primary classification 297'.1972 B81-18607

261.5'15 — Man. Development — *Christian viewpoints*

Hoffman, George. Development — in all its fullness / by George Hoffman. — [S.l.] : G.C. Hoffman, [1980?]. — [6]p ; 30cm
Unpriced (unbound) B81-36900

261.5'15 — Psychology — *Christian viewpoints*

Rushforth, Winifred. Something is happening : spiritual awareness and depth psychology in the new age / by Winifred Rushforth. — Wellingborough : Turnstone, 1981. — 160p ; 22cm
ISBN 0-85500-149-6 (pbk) : £3.50 B81-17836

261.5'5 — Earth — *Christian viewpoints — For children*

Taysom, Laura. The earth / [Laura Taysom]. — London : Ark, [1980?]. — [16]p : col.ill ; 21cm. — (Know about nature series)
Cover title
ISBN 0-86201-051-9 (pbk) : £0.50 B81-04745

261.5'5 — Mountains — *Christian viewpoints — For children*

Taysom, Laura. Mountains / [Laura Taysom]. — London : Ark, [1980?]. — [16]p : col.ill ; 21cm. — (Know about nature series)
Cover title
ISBN 0-86201-053-5 (pbk) : £0.50 B81-04744

261.5'5 — Oceans — *Christian viewpoints — For children*

Taysom, Laura. The sea / [Laura Taysom]. — London : Ark, [1980?]. — [16]p : col.ill,1col.map ; 21cm. — (Know about nature series)
Cover title
ISBN 0-86201-052-7 (pbk) : £0.50 B81-07729

261.5'5 — Stars — *Christian viewpoints — For children*

Lee, Allan. Stars / [Allan Lee]. — London : Ark, [1980]. — [16]p : col.ill,1col.chart ; 22cm. — (Know about nature series)
Cover title
ISBN 0-86201-054-3 (pbk) : £0.50 B81-07730

261.5'6 — Medicine — *Christian viewpoints*

Medicine and the Christian mind / edited by J.A. Vale. — 2nd ed. — London : Christian Medical Fellowship, 1980. — 177p ; 18cm
Previous ed.: 1975
ISBN 0-85111-971-9 (pbk) : £1.75 B81-01766

261.5'6 — Psychotherapy — *Christian viewpoints*

Cox, David, *1920-*. Two faiths or one / by David Cox. — London : Guild of Pastoral Psychology, [1981?]. — 31p ; 19cm. — (Guild lecture ; no.204)
£0.75 (pbk) B81-40400

261.5'7 — Television programmes & cinema films — *Catholic viewpoints*

Mitchell, Keith, *1924-*. The magic box and the silver screen : a Christian approach to television and cinema / Keith Mitchell. — London : Catholic Truth Society, 1981. — 18p ; 19cm
ISBN 0-85183-433-7 (pbk) : £0.50 B81-40839

261.7 — Christian political theology

Agenda for prophets : towards a political theology for Britain / edited by Rex Ambler and David Haslam. — London : Bowerdean, 1980. — 176p ; 22cm
ISBN 0-906097-09-6 (pbk) : £2.95 B81-10306

261.7 — Great Britain. Politics. Role of Church of England

Church of England. *Board for Social Responsibility.* The Church of England and politics : reflections on Christian social engagement : a report / by the Board for Social Responsibility. — [London] ([Church House, Dean's Yard, SW1P 3NZ]) : General Synod, [1980]. — iii,131p ; 231cm
£2.00 (pbk) B81-07373

Ecclestone, Giles. The Church of England and politics / G.S. Ecclestone. — London : CIO, 1981. — iv,68p ; 21cm
Bibliography: p68
ISBN 0-7151-6557-7 (pbk) : £2.50 B81-25416

261.7 — Human rights — *Catholic viewpoints*

John XXIII, *Pope*. Pacem in terris : encyclical letter of Pope John XXIII on human rights and duties : a new translation and commentary / by Henry Waterhouse. — London : Catholic Truth Society, 1980. — 51p ; 21cm
ISBN 0-85183-372-1 (pbk) : £1.10 B81-10408

261.7 — Marxism — *Christian viewpoints*

Lash, Nicholas. A matter of hope. — London : Darton, Longman & Todd, Oct.1981. — [384]p
ISBN 0-232-51494-1 : £12.00 : CIP entry
B81-26790

261.7 — South Africa. Apartheid. Policies of government, *1978-1980 — South African Council of Churches viewpoints*

Tutu, Desmond. Bishop Desmond Tutu : the voice of one crying in the wilderness. — Oxford : Mowbray, Feb.1982. — [144]p. — (Mowbray's emerging church series)
ISBN 0-264-66827-8 (pbk) : £2.25 : CIP entry
B81-40257

261.8 — Developing countries. Rural regions. Economic development. Role of Christian church

Batchelor, Peter. People in rural development. — Exeter : Paternoster Press, Oct.1981. — [160]p
ISBN 0-85364-310-5 (pbk) : £3.40 : CIP entry
B81-28184

261.8 — Social development. Role of Christian church — *Evangelical viewpoints — Conference proceedings*

Evangelicals and development. — Exeter : Paternoster Press, Nov.1981. — [144]p. — (Contemporary issues in social ethics ; 2)
Conference papers
ISBN 0-85364-329-6 (pbk) : £3.40 : CIP entry
B81-30286

261.8'3 — Abortion — *Evangelical Presbyterian Church viewpoints*

Abortion : a matter of life and death / report of the Public Morals Committee of the Evangelical Presbyterian Church. — Belfast ([Evangelical Bookshop, 15 College Square East, Belfast BT1 6DD]) : Public Morals Committee of the Evangelical Presbyterian Church, 1981. — [16]p ; 21cm
Cover title
Unpriced (pbk) B81-28456

261.8'3 — Great Britain. Cigarette smoking, consumption of alcoholic drinks & drug abuse — *Christian viewpoints — Serials*

COAD words : the newssheet of the Churches Council on Alcohol and Drugs. — No.1, 1980-. — London (4 Southampton Row, WC1B 4AA) : The Council, 1980-. — v. ; 21cm
Quarterly. — Merger of: Fact finder (Temperance Council of the Christian Churches); and, Focus on drink and gambling
ISSN 0260-6429 = COAD words : Unpriced B81-06704

261.8'32292 — Alcoholism — *Christian viewpoints*

Drummond, Terry. Alcoholism / Terry Drummond. — London : Mowbray, 1981. — 32p ; 15cm. — (Enquirer's library)
Bibliography: p29
ISBN 0-264-66724-7 (pbk) : £0.60 B81-17903

261.8'32292'05 — Alcoholic drinks — *UK Band of Hope Union viewpoints — Serials*

[Chronicle digest *(UK Band of Hope Union)***].** Chronicle digest / U.K. Band of Hope Union. — 1-. — London (45 Great Peter St., SW1P 3LT) : Hope Press Publications, [1981]-. — v. : ill ; 30cm
Quarterly. — Continues: Chronicle (UK Band of Hope Union)
ISSN 0262-0715 = Chronicle digest - U.K. Band of Hope Union : Unpriced B81-38200

261.8'33 — Crime & punishment — *Christian viewpoints*

Crime and the responsible community / editors John Stott and Nick Miller. — London : Hodder and Stoughton, 1980. — 191p ; 22cm. — (London lectures in contemporary Christianity) (Ecclesia books)
ISBN 0-340-25323-1 (pbk) : £4.50 : CIP rev. B80-09979

261.8'33174 — Pornography — *Christian viewpoints*

Court, John H.. Pornography : a Christian critique / John H. Court. — Downes Grove InterVarsity ; Exeter : Paternoster, 1980. — 96p ; 21cm. — (Outreach and identity ; no.5)
ISBN 0-85364-293-1 (pbk) : £1.50 : CIP rev. B80-17550

261.8'3423 — Adolescents. Development — *Christian viewpoints — For parents*

Batchelor, Mary. Bringing up a family / Mary Batchelor. — Tring : Lion Publishing, c1981. — (A Lion guide)
10-18 years. — 80p : ill ; 21cm
ISBN 0-85648-308-7 (pbk) : £1.75 B81-27002

261.8'3423 — Adolescents. Interpersonal relationships — *Christian viewpoints*

Hopkinson, Anne. Teenager : how to get on with other people / by Anne Hopkinson and Anne Baldwin. — London : Mothers' Union, [1981?]. — [16]p : ill ; 30cm
ISBN 0-85943-028-6 (unbound) : £0.45 B81-39548

261.8'3423 — Children, to 9 years. Development — *Christian viewpoints — For parents*

Batchelor, Mary. Bringing up a family / Mary Batchelor. — Tring : Lion Publishing, c1981. — (A Lion guide)
0-9 years. — 80p : ill ; 21cm
ISBN 0-85648-246-3 (pbk) : £1.75 B81-27001

261.8'3426 — Old persons. Social aspects — *Catholic viewpoints*

Hobman, David. Ageing in today's world / by David Hobman. — London : Catholic Truth Society, 1981. — 13p ; 19cm
ISBN 0-85183-425-6 (pbk) : £0.30 B81-36641

261.8'343 — Masculinity — *Christian viewpoints*

Elliot, Elisabeth. The mark of a man. — London : Hodder & Stoughton, Oct.1981. — [176]p
ISBN 0-340-27566-9 (pbk) : £1.95 : CIP entry B81-25753

261.8'3442 — Society. Role of women — *Christian viewpoints*

Rogers, Dale Evans. Woman / Dale Evans Rogers with Carole C. Carlson. — London : Hodder and Stoughton, 1981, c1980. — 127p ; 18cm. — (Hodder Christian paperbacks)
Originally published: Old Tappan, N.J. : F.H. Revell, 1980
ISBN 0-340-25991-4 (pbk) : £1.25 B81-10619

261.8'357 — Sex relations — *Catholic viewpoints*

Macnamara, Angela. Living and loving / Angela Macnamara. — 2nd ed. — Dublin : Veritas Publications, 1980. — 41p ; 19cm
Previous ed.: Dublin : Catholic Trust Society of Ireland, 1969
Unpriced (pbk) B81-11129

261.8'357 — Sex relations — *Christian viewpoints*

God's yes to sexuality : towards a Christian understanding of sex, sexism and sexuality : the report of a working group appointed by the British Council of Churches / edited by Rachel Moss. — London : Collins : Fount Paperbacks, 1981. — 189p ; 18cm
Bibliography: p177-187
ISBN 0-00-626341-0 (pbk) : £1.75 B81-12015

261.8'3576 — Homosexuality — *Gay Christian Movement viewpoints*

Cotter, Jim. Good fruits / Jim Cotter. — Watford (1 Kingswood Rd., Watford, Herts. WD2 6EE) : J. Cotter, 1981. — 80p ; 21cm
ISBN 0-9507625-0-4 (pbk) : £1.75 B81-39472

261.8'358 — Marriage — *Christian viewpoints*

Dominian, Jack. Marriage, faith and love. — London : Darton, Longman & Todd, Sept.1981. — [288]p
ISBN 0-232-51548-4 : £7.50 : CIP entry B81-28207

Foley, Michael. Preparation for married life. — London : Darton, Longman & Todd, Oct.1981. — [96]p
ISBN 0-232-51544-1 : £1.95 : CIP entry B81-26792

Huggett, Joyce. Two into one?. — Leicester : Inter-Varsity Press, Sept.1981. — [128]p
ISBN 0-85110-424-x (pbk) : £1.40 : CIP entry B81-20135

Kasper, Walter. Theology of Christian marriage / Walter Kasper ; [translated by David Smith]. — London : Burns & Oates, 1980. — vi,102p ; 22cm
Translation of: Zur Theologie der christlichen Ehe
ISBN 0-86012-079-1 : £6.50 B81-00739

Marriage and the local church : an open letter from the British Council of Churches to local churches. — London : Division of Community Affairs, British Council of Churches, [1981]. — 24p ; 21cm
Bibliography: p22
Unpriced (pbk) B81-17742

Reid, Gavin. Starting out together : a book for those considering marriage / Gavin Reid. — London : Hodder and Stoughton, 1981. — 123p : ill ; 18cm. — (Hodder Christian paperbacks)
ISBN 0-340-26567-1 (pbk) : £1.25 : CIP rev. B81-01850

Warren, Ann. Marriage in the balance / Ann Warren. — Eastbourne : Kingsway, 1981. — 63p ; 18cm
ISBN 0-86065-121-5 (pbk) : £0.95 B81-26940

261.8'358 — Marriage. Preparation — *Christian viewpoints*

Preparing for marriage : a British Council of Churches folder of information and ideas for ministers and clergy counselling couples before marriage. — London : Division of Community Affairs, British Council of Churches, [1980]. — 36p in various pagings ; 30cm
Bibliography: p[35-36]
£1.00 (pbk) B81-17744

261.8'3587 — Family life. Role of husbands — *Christian viewpoints*

Dobson, James C.. Straight talk to men and their wives / James C. Dobson. — London : Hodder and Stoughton, 1981, c1980. — 217p : ill,1port ; 18cm. — (Hodder Christian paperbacks)
Originally published: Waco, Tex. : Word Books, 1980
ISBN 0-340-26425-x (pbk) : £1.75 : CIP rev. B81-02369

261.8'3587 — Married couples. Interpersonal relationships — *Christian viewpoints*

Noble, John, *1937-*. Hide and sex : love, marriage and the family / John Noble. — Rev. ed. — Eastbourne : Kingsway, 1981. — 119p : ill ; 18cm
Previous ed.: published as The battle of the sexes. Romford : J. Noble, 1978
ISBN 0-86065-127-4 (pbk) : £1.35 B81-26939

261.8'3587 — Motherhood — *Christian viewpoints — Stories, anecdotes*

Short, Katharine. Reflections : a book for mums / Katharine Short. — Tring : Lion, 1981. — 62p : ill(some col.) ; 22cm
Ill on lining paper
ISBN 0-85648-340-0 : £1.95 B81-40664

261.8'3587 — Parenthood — *Christian viewpoints*

Davies, Jane. The price of loving : a parent's emotions and beliefs / by Jane Davies. — London : Mowbray, 1981. — v,106p ; 18cm. — (Mowbray's popular Christian paperbacks)
ISBN 0-264-66566-x (pbk) : £1.50 B81-28890

261.8'3587 — Young married couples. Interpersonal relationships. Love — *Christian viewpoints*

Stroud, Marion. The gift of love / text written and compiled by Marion Stroud ; produced in conjunction with Tony Stone Photolibrary. — Tring : Lion, 1981. — [57]p : col.ill ; 25cm
ISBN 0-85648-341-9 : £4.95 B81-34674

261.8'36 — Environment. Conservation — *Christian viewpoints*

Elsdon, Ron. Bent world : science, the Bible, and the environment / Ron Elsdon. — Leicester : Inter-Varsity, 1981. — 170p ; 20cm
Includes index
ISBN 0-85111-318-4 (pbk) : Unpriced B81-26886

261.8'5 — Capital investment by Christians

O'Mahony, Patrick J.. Money : the Christian dilemma / Patrick J. O'Mahony. — London : Catholic Truth Society, 1981. — 14p ; 19cm
ISBN 0-85183-416-7 (pbk) : £0.30 B81-27606

261.8'5 — Capitalism *related to* **Protestant ethics. Theories of Weber, Max**

Marshall, Gordon. In search of the spirit of capitalism. — London : Hutchinson Education, Nov.1981. — [240]p
ISBN 0-09-145650-9 (pbk) : £12.00 : CIP entry
ISBN 0-09-145651-7 (pbk) : £4.95 B81-28842

261.8'5 — Great Britain. Consumer goods. Demand. Social aspects — *Christian viewpoints*

The **Consumer** goods society. — London : British Council of Churches, 1978. — 32p : 1ill ; 21cm
£0.95 (pbk) B81-19342

261.8'5 — Great Britain. Industrial relations. Strikes — *Christian viewpoints*

Winters of discontent : industrial conflict : a Christian perspective : the report of a working party under the chairmanship of Ronald H. Preston / foreword by Simon Phipps. — London : CIO, [1981?]. — 51p ; 21cm
Bibliography: p49-50
ISBN 0-7151-6558-5 (pbk) : £1.75 B81-25414

261.8'5 — Ownership — *Christian viewpoints*

Mine and thine, ours and theirs : an anthology on ownership in the Christian tradition / [compiled] by Thomas Cullinan. — London : Catholic Truth Society, 1979. — 50p : ill ; 19cm
£0.80 (pbk) B81-14048

261.8'5'0941 — Great Britain. Economic conditions — *Christian viewpoints*

The **Consumer** goods society. — London : British Council of Churches, 1978. — 32p : 1ill ; 21cm
£0.95 (pbk) B81-17725

261.8′73 — Peace — *Christian viewpoints*

Matheson, Peter. Profile of love : towards a theology of the just peace / Peter Matheson. — Belfast : Christian Journals, 1979. — 156p ; 18cm
ISBN 0-904302-47-4 (pbk) : £1.50 B81-07278

261.8′73 — Peacemaking — *Society of Friends viewpoints*

Curle, Adam. True justice : Quaker peace makers and peace making / by Adam Curle. — London : Quaker Home Service, 1981. — 106p : ill ; 19cm. — (Swarthmore lecture ; 1981)
Bibliography: p 103-106
ISBN 0-85245-156-3 (pbk) : £1.90 B81-26300

261.8′73 — Revolution — *Christian viewpoints*

Kingdon, David, *1934-*. A gospel of violence? / by David Kingdon. — Haywards Heath (5 Fairford Close, Haywards Heath, Sussex RH16 3EF) : Carey, [1981?]. — 15p ; 22cm
£0.50 (pbk) B81-17940

262 — CHRISTIAN CHURCH. GOVERNMENT AND ORGANISATION

262 — Church of England. Finance, *1978-1981*

. A giving Church? : a report on the finances of the Church of England 1978-1981 / prepared on behalf of the Central Board of Finance and the Church Commissioners [by the Joint Liaison Committee of the Central Board of Finance and The Church Commissioners]. — London : CIO, 1980. — 32p : col.ill ; 21cm
ISBN 0-7151-8053-3 (pbk) : £0.85 B81-07398

262 — Church of England. Financial management. Organisations: Church Commissioners for England — *Serials*

Church Commissioners for England. Report and accounts / the Church Commissioners for England. — 1980. — London (1 Millbank, Westminster, SW1P 3JZ) : The Commissioners, [1981]. — 44p
ISSN 0309-0663 : Unpriced B81-32430

262′.0011 — Ecumenism

Moss, Vladimir. The truth is one / Vladimir Moss. — Old Woking : Gresham Books, 1979. — 36p : ill,1port ; 21cm
ISBN 0-905418-45-x (pbk) : £1.25 B81-05726

Roger, *of Taizé, Brother*. The dynamic of the provisional / by Brother Roger of Taizé ; [translated by Emily Chisholm and the Taizé Community]. — Rev. ed. — London : Mowbray, 1981. — 80p ; 18cm. — (Mowbray′s popular Christian paperbacks)
Translation of: Dynamique du provisoire. — Previous ed.: published as The power of the provisional. London : Hodder and Stoughton, 1969
ISBN 0-264-66765-4 (pbk) : £1.50 B81-32874

262′.001′7 — Christian church. Renewal

Cotterell, Peter. Church alive!. — Leicester : Inter-Varsity Press, Sept.1981. — [112]p
ISBN 0-85110-431-2 (pbk) : £1.25 : CIP entry B81-20134

262′.0017 — Christian church. Renewal

Pulkingham, Graham. Renewal : an emerging pattern / Graham Pulkingham and others ; edited by Jeanne Hinton. — Poole : Celebration Publishing, 1980. — 190p : ill ; 21cm
ISBN 0-906309-10-7 (pbk) : £3.75 : CIP rev. B80-04666

Walker, Tom. Renew us by your Spirit. — London : Hodder & Stoughton, Feb.1982. — [128]p
ISBN 0-340-26601-5 (pbk) : £1.50 : CIP entry B81-36350

Wood, A. Skevington. [And with fire]. Baptised with fire : God promises revival / A. Skevington Wood. — London : Pickering & Inglis, 1981. — 176p ; 21cm
ISBN 0-7208-0484-1 (pbk) : £2.95 B81-15587

262′.0017 — Christian church. Renewal. Charismatic aspects

Lillie, David. Beyond charisma / by David Lillie. — Exeter : Paternoster, c1981. — 127p : 1ill ; 22cm
Bibliography: pxi
ISBN 0-85364-325-3 (pbk) : £2.50 : CIP rev. B81-11976

262′.0025′4 — Europe. English speaking churches — *Directories*

English speaking churches : a directory of churches in Europe, North Africa & the Middle East. — [New ed.]. — London (175 Tower Bridge Rd., SE1 2AQ) : Intercontinental Church Society, 1981. — 48p : maps ; 16cm
Cover title. — Previous ed.: 1978
£0.50 (pbk)
Also classified at 262′.0025′61 B81-19541

262′.0025′61 — North Africa. English speaking churches — *Directories*

English speaking churches : a directory of churches in Europe, North Africa & the Middle East. — [New ed.]. — London (175 Tower Bridge Rd., SE1 2AQ) : Intercontinental Church Society, 1981. — 48p : maps ; 16cm
Cover title. — Previous ed.: 1978
£0.50 (pbk)
Primary classification 262′.0025′4 B81-19541

262′.02 — Catholic Church. Hierarchy

Lubich, Chiara. Servants of all / Chiara Lubich. — London (57 Twyford Ave., W3 9PZ) : New City, 1979. — 111p ; 19cm
Translation of: Uomini al servizio di tutti
ISBN 0-904287-12-2 (pbk) : Unpriced B81-02766

262′.02411 — Scotland. Christian church. Organisation structure, *1100-1198* — *Readings from contemporary sources*

Scotia Pontificia. — Oxford : Clarendon Press, Nov.1981. — [260]p
ISBN 0-19-822433-8 : £30.00 : CIP entry B81-28851

262′.0242164′05 — Catholic Church. *Archdiocese of Southwark — Directories — Serials*

Catholic Church. *Archdiocese of Southwark.* Metropolitan see of Southwark Catholic directory. — 1981. — [Purley] ([Rudwell Hill Rd., Purley, Surrey CR2 2XB]) : Southwark Catholic Children′s Society, [1980]. — 139p
£0.75 B81-09090

262′.024225 — Catholic Church. *Diocese of Arundel and Brighton — Serials*

Catholic Church. *Diocese of Arundel and Brighton.* Arundel-Brighton diocesan directory. — 1981. — Chichester (Bishops House, Upper Drive, Hove, East Sussex BN3 6NE) : [The Diocese], [1980?]. — 131p
£0.75p B81-10275

262′.02428 — Catholic Church. *Diocese of Hexham and Newcastle — Directories — Serials*

Catholic Church. *Diocese of Hexham and Newcastle.* The Northern Catholic calendar for use in the Diocese of Hexham and Newcastle. — 1978. — Alnwick (c/o Rev. W.J. Nicholson, St. Mary′s, Whittingham, Alnwick, Northumberland NE66 4SY) : [The Diocese], [1977]. — 181p
£0.30 B81-29639

Catholic Church. *Diocese of Hexham and Newcastle.* The Northern Catholic calendar for use in the Diocese of Hexham and Newcastle. — 1979. — Alnwick (c/o Rev. W.J. Nicholson, St. Mary′s, Whittingham, Alnwick, Northumberland NE66 4SY) : [The Diocese], [1978]. — 150p
£0.30 B81-29640

Catholic Church. *Diocese of Hexham and Newcastle.* The Northern Catholic calendar for use in the Diocese of Hexham and Newcastle. — 1980. — Alnwick (c/o Rev. W.J. Nicholson, St. Mary′s, Whittingham, Alnwick, Northumberland NE66 4SY) : [The Diocese], [1979]. — 156p
£0.30 B81-29642

Catholic Church. *Diocese of Hexham and Newcastle.* The Northern Catholic calendar for use in the Diocese of Hexham and Newcastle. — 1981. — Alnwick (c/o Rev. W.J. Nicholson, St. Mary′s, Whittingham, Alnwick, Northumberland NE66 4SY) : [The Diocese], [1980]. — 165p
£0.40 B81-29641

262′.03411′025 — Episcopal Church in Scotland — *Directories — Serials*

Episcopal Church in Scotland. Year book : year book and directory of the Scottish Episcopal Church. — 1976-77-. — Inverness (St Ninian′s House, Glenurquhart, Inverness IV3 6TN) : S.E.C., 1976-. — v. ; 23cm
Continues: Scottish Episcopal Church yearbook and directory. — Description based on: 1980-81
ISSN 0260-0617 = Year book and directory of the Scottish Episcopal Church : Unpriced B81-06685

262′.03411′05 — Episcopal Church in Scotland — *Directories — Serials*

Episcopal Church in Scotland. Year book : year book and directory of the Scottish Episcopal Church. — 1981-82. — Inverness (St Ninian′s House, Glenurquhart, Inverness IV3 6TN) : S.E.C., [1981]. — 157p
ISSN 0260-0617 : Unpriced B81-30845

262′.03415′05 — Church of Ireland. Administration — *Serials*

Church of Ireland. *General Synod.* Journal of the second ordinary session of the ... General Synod of the Church of Ireland ... — 37th (1980). — [Dublin] ([Church of Ireland House, Church Ave., Rathmines, Dublin 6]) : The General Synod, [1980?]. — xcvii,322p
Unpriced B81-25480

262′.0342 — Church of England, *1500-1800.* **Economic aspects**

Princes & paupers in the English church 1500-1800 / edited by Rosemary O′Day and Felicity Heal. — Leicester : Leicester University Press, 1981. — 283p : 1ill,1map ; 23cm
Includes index
ISBN 0-7185-1178-6 : £13.00 : CIP rev. B81-04365

262′.0342 — Church of England. Administration — *Practical information — For parochial church councils*

MacMorran, Kenneth M.. A handbook for churchwardens and parochial church councillors / by Kenneth M. MacMorran and Kenneth J.T. Elphinstone. — New ed. / with introduction by E. Garth Moore. — London : Mowbray, 1980. — 178p ; 19cm
Previous ed.: 1979. — Includes index
ISBN 0-264-66720-4 (pbk) : £3.50 B81-33602

262′.03421′05 — Church of England. *Diocese of London — Directories — Serials*

Church of England. *Diocese of London.* London Diocese book. — 1981. — London (30, Causton St., SW1P JAU) : London Diocesan House, [1981?]. — vi,202p
ISBN 0-901338-11-7 : £2.00
ISSN 0306-1515 B81-15084

262′.03422323 — Church of England. *Diocese of Rochester — Serials*

Church of England. *Diocese of Rochester.* Rochester diocesan directory. — 1980-81. — Canterbury (11, Best La., Canterbury) : Elvy & Gibbs, 1980. — 124p : ill
ISSN 0305-1994 : Unpriced B81-00013

262′.0342234′05 — Church of England. *Diocese of Canterbury — Serials*

Church of England. *Diocese of Canterbury.* Canterbury Diocesan news service. — No.1 (Dec. 1980)-. — Canterbury (Diocesan House, Lady Wootton′s Green, Canterbury, Kent) : The Diocese, 1980-. — v. ; 30cm
Monthly. — Continues: Church of England. Diocese of Canterbury. Canterbury Diocesan notes. — Description based on: No.2 (Jan. 1981)
ISSN 0260-9924 = Canterbury Diocesan news service : Unpriced B81-12396

262'.0342262 — Church of England. *Diocese of Chichester — Directories — Serials*
Church of England. *Diocese of Chichester*The **Chichester** diocesan directory. — 1980-81. — Chichester (Diocesan Church House, Chichester) : Published by the authority of the Lord Bishop, [1980]. — 246p
ISSN 0305-7003 : £1.75 B81-06699

262'.03422735'05 — Church of England. *Diocese of Winchester — Directories — Serials*
Church of England. *Diocese of Winchester.* Winchester diocesan directory. — 1981. — [Winchester] ([Church House, 9 The Close, Winchester SO23 9LS]) : The Diocese, [1981]. — 99p
£2.00 B81-34062

262'.0342378 — Church of England. *Diocese of Truro — Directories — Serials*
Church of England. *Diocese of Truro.* Truro diocesan directory. — AD 1981. — Truro (c/o S.P.C.K., [Quay St., Truro, Cornwall]) : [Diocese of Truro], [1980]. — 73p
£1.00 B81-09029

262'.034238 — Church of England. *Diocese of Bath and Wells — Directories — Serials*
Church of England. *Diocese of Bath and Wells* **Bath** and Wells diocesan directory. — 1980/81. — Wells (The Old Deanery, Wells BA52UG) : The Diocesan Board of Finance, [1980]. — 160p
ISSN 0305-5485 : £2.00 B81-10311

262'.0342414'05 — Church of England. *Diocese of Gloucester — Directories — Serials*
Church of England. *Diocese of Gloucester.* Gloucester diocesan year book. — 1981. — Gloucester (Church House, College Green, Gloucester GL1 2LY) : [The Diocese], [1981?]. — 104p
Unpriced B81-32193

262'.0342468 — Church of England. *Diocese of Lichfield — Directories — Serials*
Church of England. *Diocese of Lichfield.* Lichfield diocesan directory. — 118th issue (1981). — Lichfield (St Mary's House, Lichfield WS13 7LD) : Lichfield Diocesan Board of Finance, [1981?]. — 160p
ISSN 0306-1507 : £3.00 B81-21343

262'.0342524 — Church of England. *Diocese of Southwell — Directories — Serials*
Church of England. *Diocese of Southwell.* The Southwell diocesan yearbook. — 1981. — [Southwell] ([Durham House, Westgate, Southwell, Notts. NG2 0JL]) : [The Diocese], [1981]. — 192p
ISSN 0308-860x : £1.50 B81-15162

262'.0342574'05 — Church of England. *Diocese of Oxford — Directories — Serils*
Church of England. *Diocese of Oxford.* The Oxford diocesan year book. — 1981. — Oxford (Diocesan Church House, North Hinksey, Oxford) : [The Diocese], 1980. — 159p,x p
£3.50 B81-09078

262'.0342585'05 — Church of England. *Diocese of St. Albans — Directories — Serials*
Church of England. *Diocese of St. Albans.* Directory / the Diocese of St. Albans. — 1980-81. — St. Albans (Holywell Lodge, 41, Holywell Hill, St. Albans AL1 1HE) : [The Diocese], [1980?]. — vi,154p
Unpriced B81-04542

262'.0342615'05 — Church of England. *Diocese of Norwich — Directories — Serials*
Church of England. *Diocese of Norwich.* Norwich Diocesan directory. — 121st issue (1981). — Norwich (44 Bethel St., Norwich, NR2 1NR) : G.W.D. Winkley, [1981]. — 158p
£2.50 B81-16742

262'.0342651'05 — Church of England. *Diocese of Peterborough — Serials*
Church of England. *Diocese of Peterborough.* Peterborough diocesan directory. — 1981. — [Peterborough] (Diocesan Office, The Palace, Peterborough PE1 1YA]) : The Diocese, [1980]. — 110p
£2.50 B81-10583

262'.0342815 — Church of England. *Diocese of Wakefield — Directories — Serials*
Church of England. *Diocese of Wakefield.* Wakefield diocesan directory. — [No.1]-. — Wakefield (1 South Parade, Wakefield WF1 1LP) : Wakefield Diocesan Board of Finance, [1980]-. — v. ; 21cm
Irregular. — Continues: Directory (Church of England. Diocese of Wakefield)
ISSN 0260-9495 = Wakefield diocesan directory : £2.00 (£1.00 to parishes) B81-14354

262'.0342817 — Church of England. *Diocese of Bradford — Directories — Serials*
Church of England. *Diocese of Bradford.* Diocese of Bradford directory. — 1981. — [Bradford?] ([c/o R. Anderton, Stott Hill, Bradford BD1 4ET]) : The Diocese, [1980?]. — 86p
ISSN 0305-5256 : £1.00 B81-03863

262'.0342987 — Church in Wales. *Diocese of Llandaff — Serials*
Church in Wales. *Diocese of Llandaff.* The Llandaff diocesan handbook for .... — 1978. — Newport, Gwent : Johns, [1978?]. — 151p
ISSN 0305-4748 : £0.50p B81-10276

Church in Wales. *Diocese of Llandaff.* The Llandaff diocesan handbook for .... — 1980-82. — Newport, Gwent : R.H. Johns, 1980. — 136p
ISSN 0305-4748 : Unpriced B81-03865

262'.0429'05 — Catholic Church. *Archdiocese of Cardiff* **& Catholic Church.** *Diocese of Menevia — Serials*
Catholic Church. *Archdiocese of Cardiff***Directory** and year book for the Archdiocese of Cardiff and the Diocese of Menevia. — 1981. — [Cardiff] ([Archbiship's House, Whitchurch, Cardiff CF4 2XN) : [published by the authority of the Archbishop of Cardiff] ; [Wrexham] : [published by the authority of the Bishop of Menevia], [1981]. — 210p
£0.50 B81-13698

262'.052411'05 — Free Church of Scotland — *Directories — Serials*
Free Church of Scotland. Year book / the Free Church of Scotland. — 1981. — Edinburgh (The Mound, Edinburgh [EH1 2LS]) : Knox Press (Edinburgh), [1981]. — 67p
£0.45 B81-31005

262'.052411'05 — United Free Church of Scotland — *Directories — Serials*
United Free Church of Scotland. The handbook of the United Free Church of Scotland. — 1981. — Glasgow (11 Newton Place, Glasgow G3 7PR) : The Church, [1981]. — 52p
£1.00 B81-32278

262'.058429'05 — Union of Welsh Independents — *Directories — Welsh texts — Serials*
Union of Welsh Independents[Blwyddiadur *(Union of Welsh Independents)***].** Blwyddiadur / Undeb yr Annibynwyr Cymraeg. — Cyfrol 79 (1981). — Abertawe [Swansea] (11 Heol San Helen, Abertawe, SA1 4AL) : Tŷ John Perry, [1980?]. — 147p
ISBN 0-903701-16-2 : Unpriced B81-20425

262'.06141 — Great Britain. Baptist Union of Great Britain and Ireland. Administration
Bacon, Fred. Church administration : a guide for Baptist ministers and church officers / by Fred Bacon. — Bristol (8 Heath Rd., Downend, Bristol [BS16 6HA]) : Bristol and District Association of Baptist Churches, c1981. — 187p : ill,1plan,forms ; 21cm
Bibliography: p181-182. — Includes index
ISBN 0-9507449-0-5 (pbk) : £2.20 B81-25245

262'.06141'05 — Baptist Union of Great Britain and Ireland — *Directories — Serials*
Baptist Union of Great Britain and Ireland. The Baptist Union directory for ... / edited and published under the direction of the Council of the Baptist Union of Great Britain and Ireland. — 1980-81. — London (4 Southampton Row, WC1B 4AB) : The Union, [1981?]. — 307p
£3.75 B81-18806

262'.0841'05 — Great Britain. Unitarian Churches — *Directories — Serials*
General Assembly of Unitarian and Free Christian Churches. Directory / the General Assembly of Unitarian and Free Christian Churches. — 1981. — London (Unitarian Headquarters, Essex Hall, 1-6 Essex St., Strand, WC2R 3HY) : The Assembly, [1981?]. — 86p
Unpriced B81-08758

262'.09341 — Great Britain. Reorganised Church of Jesus Christ of Latter Day Saints — *Directories*
Reorganised Church of Jesus Christ of Latter Day Saints. British Isles region directory 1981 / Reorganised Church of Jesus Christ of Latter Day Saints. — [Birmingham] ([769 Yardley Wood Rd., Billesley, Birmingham B13 0PT]) : The Church, [1981]. — 50leaves ; 34cm
Cover title
Unpriced (pbk) B81-37984

262'.09641'05 — Great Britain. Society of Friends — *Directories — Serials*
Book of meetings / Religious Society of Friends. — 1981. — London : c/o Friends Book Centre, Friends House, Euston Rd, NW1 2BJ : London Yearly Meeting, [1980?]. — 229
£1.50 B81-09708

262'.13 — Papacy — *Grand Orange Lodge of England viewpoints*
The **Pope** cannot be welcomed to Britain because —. — Liverpool (c/o The Grand Secretary, Provincial Headquarters, 108 Everton Rd., Liverpool L6 2EN) : Grand Orange Lodge of England, [1981?]. — [24]p ; 21x10cm
Unpriced (unbound) B81-32977

262'.13'09024 — Papacy. Authority, *1417-1517*
Thomson, John A. F.. Popes and princes, 1417-1517 : politics and polity in the late medieval Church / John A.F. Thomson. — London : Allen & Unwin, 1980. — xvii,252p ; 23cm. — (Early modern Europe today)
Bibliography: p218-236. — Includes index
ISBN 0-04-901027-1 : £12.50 : CIP rev.
B80-18163

262'.13'09033 — Papacy. Effects of political events in Europe, *1700-1830*
Chadwick, Owen. The Popes and European revolution / Owen Chadwick. — Oxford : Clarendon, 1981. — ix,646p ; 24cm. — (Oxford history of the Christian Church)
Bibliography: p614-631. - Includes index
ISBN 0-19-826919-6 : £28.00 B81-17581

262'.13'0904 — Papacy, *1878-1980*
Murphy, Francis Xavier. The papacy today / Francis Xavier Murphy. — London : Weidenfeld and Nicolson, c1981. — viii,269p ; 22cm
Bibliography: p259-260. — Includes index
ISBN 0-297-77857-9 : £8.95 B81-26470

262'.136 — Papal legates
Oliveri, Mario. The representatives : the real nature and function of papal legates / Mario Oliveri ; preface Giovanni Benelli ; postscript Salvatore Pappalardo. — Gerrards Cross ([Van Duren House, Oxford Rd, P.O. Box 6] Gerrards Cross, Bucks. SL9 7AE) : Van Duren, 1980. — 192p ; 23cm
Bibliography: p171-183. - Includes index
ISBN 0-905715-15-2 : £7.95 : CIP rev.
B80-21376

262'.14 — Christian church. Shared ministry
Metcalfe, Ronald. Sharing Christian ministry / Ronald Metcalfe. — London : Mowbray, 1981. — ix,113p ; 22cm
Bibliography: p113
ISBN 0-264-66756-5 (pbk) : £3.75 B81-17894

262'.14 — England. Christian church. Group ministry
Hammersley, John. TAP handbook for teams and groups / by John Hammersley. — London : British Council of Churches, c1981. — 119p ; 21cm
Bibliography: p107-110. - Includes index
Unpriced (pbk) B81-19338

262'.14 — England. Industrial regions. Christian Church. Ministry — *Personal observations*

Arnott, Anne. The unexpected call. — London : Hodder & Stoughton, Oct.1981. — [160]p
ISBN 0-340-26360-1 (pbk) : £1.75 : CIP entry
B81-24620

262'.14 — Great Britain. Christian church. Group ministry. Organisation — *Case studies*

Hammersley, John. TAP handbook for teams and groups / by John Hammersley. — London : British Council of Churches, c1981. — 119p ; 21cm
Bibliography: p107-110. - Includes index
Unpriced (pbk) B81-17724

262'.14 — United States. Southern states. Protestant churches. Clergy. Role, *1800-1860*

Loveland, Anne C.. Southern evangelicals and the social order : 1800-1860 / Anne C. Loveland. — Baton Rouge ; London : Louisiana State University Press, c1980. — x,293p ; 23cm
Bibliography: p267-285. - Includes index
ISBN 0-8071-0783-2 (pbk) : £7.75 B81-07554

262'.1426 — Africa. Catholic Church. Married auxiliary clergy

Hickey, Raymond. Africa : the case for an auxiliary priesthood / Raymond Hickey. — London : Geoffrey Chapman, c1980. — 143p : maps ; 22cm
Bibliography: p133-143
ISBN 0-225-66275-2 (pbk) : Unpriced : CIP rev. B80-06769

262'.143 — Church of England. Ministry

Church of England. *Ministry Co-ordinating Group*. The Church's ministry : a survey, November 1980 : a report / by the Ministry Co-ordinating Group. — [London] : Published for the General Synod of the Church of England by CIO, 1980. — 63p : 1ill ; 21cm
£1.10 (pbk) B81-07371

Martineau, Robert. The office and work of a priest / by Robert Martineau. — Rev. ed. — London : Mowbrays, 1981. — ix,143p ; 21cm
Previous ed.: 1972
ISBN 0-264-66528-7 (pbk) : £3.50 B81-29387

To a rebellious house? : report of the Church of England's Partners in Mission Consultation. — London : CIO Publishing, c1981. — 57p ; 21cm
£1.20 (pbk) B81-39677

262'.14342 — Church of England. Clergy. Deployment

Deployment for mission : study and discussion of Deployment of the clergy : the report of the House of Bishops' Working Group, General Synod GS205 / chairman Donald A. Tytler ; editor Edward S. Kessler. — Sheffield (210 Abbeyfield Rd., Sheffield S4 7AZ) : Urban Theology Unit, [1975?]. — 20p ; 30cm
£0.25 (pbk) B81-18002

262'.14342 — Church of England. Deaconesses, *to 1980*

Grierson, Janet. The deaconess / Janet Grierson. — London : C10, 1981. — viii,144p ; 21cm
Bibliography: p133-135. — Includes index
ISBN 0-7151-2538-9 (pbk) : £3.50 B81-23270

262'.14342446 — Hereford and Worcester. Hereford. Cathedrals. Clergy. Colleges: College of Vicars Choral, *to 1937*

Barrett, Philip. The college of vicars choral at Hereford Cathedral / by Philip Barrett. — [Hereford] ([c/o Hon. Secretary, 13 Elgar Ave, Hereford HR1 1TY]) : Friends of Hereford Cathedral, 1980. — 33p,[4]p of plates : ill,1port ; 22cm
£0.80 (pbk) B81-16591

262'.22 — Church of England. *Archdeaconry of Stafford*. **Parishes,** *1829-1841* — *Early works*

Visitations of the Archdeaconry of Stafford 1829-1841 / [prepared by the Staffordshire Record Society] ; edited by David Robinson. — London : H.M.S.O., 1980. — xxxvii,150p[2] leaves of plates : 1map,1port ; 26cm. — (Collections for a history of Staffordshire. Series 4 ; v.10) (Joint publications series / Royal Commission on Historical Manuscripts ; no.25)
Bibliography: pvii-viii. - Includes index
ISBN 0-11-440066-0 : Unpriced B81-11345

262'.52 — Catholic Church. Vatican Council *(2nd : 1962-1965)*

Butler, B. C.. The theology of Vatican II / Christopher Butler. — Rev. and enl. ed. — London : Darton, Longman & Todd, 1981. — x,230p ; 22cm
Previous ed.: 1967. — Includes index
ISBN 0-232-51520-4 (pbk) : £6.95 B81-23514

262'.72 — Christian church. Unity

Allchin, A. M.. Dynamics of tradition. — London : Darton Longman & Todd, July 1981. — [176]p
ISBN 0-232-51516-6 (pbk) : £4.50 : CIP entry
B81-13490

262'.72 — Great Britain. Christian church. Unity — *Proposals*

Essays on the Covenant / by participants in the Churches' Council for Covenanting. — London : Division of Ecumenical Affairs of the British Council of Churches, [1980]. — 75p ; 21cm
Cover title
ISBN 0-85169-081-5 (pbk) : £1.50 B81-09846

262'.77 — Christian church. Nature. Body of Christ

Brand, Paul. Fearfully and wonderfully made / Paul Brand and Philip Yancey ; illustrated by Charles Shaw. — London : Hodder and Stoughton, 1981, c1980. — 210p : ill ; 18cm
Originally published: Grand Rapids : Zondervan, c1980. — Bibliography: p209-210
ISBN 0-340-25955-8 (pbk) : £1.75 B81-12284

262'.8 — Christian church. Authority

Küng, Hans. The church maintained in truth : a theological meditation / Hans Küng. — London : SCM, 1980. — 87p ; 22cm
Translation of: Kirche, gehalten in der Wahrheit?
ISBN 0-334-01939-7 (pbk) : £2.95 B81-29634

263 — CHRISTIANITY. DAYS, TIMES, PLACES OF RELIGIOUS OBSERVANCE

263'.042417 — Ireland *(Republic)*. **Shrines: Wells**

Logan, Patrick. The holy wells of Ireland / Patrick Logan ; illustrated by Jim O'Callaghan. — Gerrards Cross : Smythe, 1980. — 170p : ill ; 23cm
Includes index
ISBN 0-86140-026-7 (cased) : Unpriced : CIP rev.
ISBN 0-86140-046-1 (pbk) : Unpriced
B80-30754

263'.04242612 — Norfolk. Walsingham. Shrines: Shrine of Our Lady of Walsingham *(Catholic), to 1958* — *Illustrations*

Walsingham : in times past / [compiled by] Peter Rollings. — Chorley : Countryside, c1981. — 48p : ill,ports ; 22x20cm
ISBN 0-86157-046-4 (pbk) : £2.00 B81-21243

263'.4 — Catholic Church. Sunday. Observance

Fenn, Francis. Sunday / Francis Fenn. — London : Catholic Truth Society, 1981. — 12p ; 19cm
ISBN 0-85183-404-3 (pbk) : £0.30 B81-28301

263'.4'0941 — Great Britain. Sunday. Observance, *1500-1914*

Wigley, John. The rise and fall of the Victorian Sunday / John Wigley. — Manchester : Manchester University Press, c1980. — 216p ; 23cm
Includes index
ISBN 0-7190-0794-1 : £14.50 : CIP rev.
B80-08097

263'.93 — Easter. Christian activities for children

Together for Holy Week : a resource anthology. — London : C10 for the General Synod Board of Education, 1981. — 115p : ill,music ; 21cm
ISBN 0-7151-0393-8 (pbk) : £2.75 B81-16478

264 — CHRISTIAN CHURCH. PUBLIC WORSHIP

264 — Christian church. Group worship. Activities — *Manuals*

Hodgetts, Colin. Exploring worship : a group study guide / by Colin Hodgetts. — London : Mowbray, 1980. — vi,153p : ill,music ; 18cm. — (Mowbray's popular Christian paperbacks)
ISBN 0-264-66460-4 (pbk) : £1.75 B81-04577

264 — Christian church. Public worship

Anderson, Jock. Worship the Lord / Jock Anderson. — Leicester : Inter-Varsity Press, 1980. — 160p ; 18cm
Bibliography: p159-160
ISBN 0-85110-418-5 (pbk) : £1.75 : CIP rev.
B80-21377

264 — Christian church. Public worship. Activities: Folk arts

Barker, Martha Keys. Building worship together. — Poole : Celebration, Sept.1981. — [128]p
ISBN 0-906309-21-2 (pbk) : £1.35 : CIP entry
B81-28131

264 — Christian church. Public worship. Leadership

Buchanan, Colin, *1934-*. Leading worship / by Colin Buchanan. — Bramcote : Grove, c1981. — 25p ; 22cm. — (Grove worship series, ISSN 0144-1728 ; no.76)
ISBN 0-907536-00-x (pbk) : £0.60 B81-27517

264 — Christian church. Public worship. Symbolism

Symbolism and the liturgy / edited by Kenneth W. Stevenson. — Bramcote : Grove Books. — (Grove liturgical study, ISSN 0306-0608 ; no.26)
Conference papers
II: The Anglican and Methodist contributors. — c1981. — 33p ; 21cm
ISBN 0-907536-03-4 (pbk) : £1.25 B81-33333

264 — Christian church. Worship

New directions in worship : an account of developments in all-age worship and education / edited by Wilfred Tooley. — London : Methodist Church, Division of Education and Youth, 1981. — 107p ; 22cm
ISBN 0-7192-0146-2 (pbk) : Unpriced
B81-36797

264 — Christian church. Worship — *For schools*

Wilkinson, Frances. Christian worship / [written by Frances Wilkinson and Zoe Jenkins]. — London (2 Chester House, Pages La., N10 1PR) : Christian Education Movement, [c1981]. — [16]p : ill,music ; 22cm. — (CEM ask about religion)
ISBN 0-905022-73-4 (unbound) : Unpriced
B81-27158

264 — Great Britain. Protestant churches. Harvest festivals. Public worship — *Rites*

Celebrating harvest : festival services / compiled by Donald Hilton. — Redhill : National Christian Education Council, c1981. — 32p : ill,1map,music ; 21cm
ISBN 0-7197-0293-3 (pbk) : £0.80 B81-29164

264 — Nonconformist churches. Public worship — *For lay preaching*

Jones, Richard G.. Groundwork of worship and preaching / Richard G. Jones. — London : Epworth, 1980. — 243p ; 22cm
Bibliography: p233-236. - Includes index
ISBN 0-7162-0355-3 (pbk) : £4.00 B81-03078

264'.012 — Christian church. Public worship, *to 300*

Bradshaw, Paul F.. Daily prayer in the early Church : a study of the origin and early development of the divine office / Paul F. Bradshaw. — London : Published for the Alcuin Club by SPCK, 1981. — x,191p ; 22cm. — (Alcuin Club collections ; no.63)
Bibliography: p176-178. — Includes index
ISBN 0-281-03827-9 (pbk) : £6.95 B81-39471

264'.01409 — Christian church, *300-500*. Baptism. Preparation of converts — *Rites*

Field, Anne, *1924-*. New life / Anne Field. — London : Mowbray, 1980, c1978. — 210p ; 18cm. — (Mowbray's popular Christian paperbacks)
Originally published: Ann Arbor : Servant Publications, 1978. — Bibliography: p201-203
ISBN 0-264-66731-x (pbk) : £1.95 B81-06256

264'.019 — Orthodox Eastern Church. Public worship. Octoechos — *Rites*

Octoechos / translated by Archimandrite Lazarus. — Fakenham (Dunton, Fakenham, Norfolk) : Monastery of Saint Seraphim of Sarov
Cover title
First tone. — c1981. — 23p ; 22cm
ISBN 0-907410-14-6 (pbk) : Unpriced
ISBN 0-907410-13-8 (8 tone set) : Unpriced
B81-31673

264'.019 — Orthodox Eastern Church. Public worship. Troparia & kontakia — *Collections*

The **Menaion**. — Fakenham (Dunton, Fakenham, Norfolk) : Monastery of Saint Seraphim of Sarov
ISBN 0-907410-11-1 (pbk) : Unpriced
ISBN 0-907410-00-6 (12v.set) : Unpriced
B81-31659

The **Menaion** : Troparia and Kontakia. — Fakenham (Dunton, Fakenham, Norfolk) : Monastery of Saint Seraphim of Sarov, c1981
April. — 19p ; 22cm
Cover title
ISBN 0-907410-08-1 (pbk) : Unpriced
ISBN 0-907410-00-6 (set) : Unpriced
B81-23733

The **Menaion** : Troparia and Kontakia. — Fakenham (Dunton, Fakenham, Norfolk) : Monastery of Saint Seraphim of Sarov, c1981
Cover title
August. — 24p ; 22cm
ISBN 0-907410-12-x (pbk) : Unpriced
ISBN 0-907410-00-6 (set) : Unpriced
B81-37125

The **Menaion** : Troparia and Kontakia. — Fakenham (Dunton, Fakenham, Norfolk) : Monastery of Saint Seraphim of Sarov, [c1981?]
February. — 24p ; 22cm
Cover title
ISBN 0-907410-06-5 (pbk) : Unpriced
ISBN 0-907410-00-6 (set) : Unpriced
B81-23732

The **Menaion** : Troparia and Kontakia. — Fakenham (Dunton, Fakenham, Norfolk) : Monastery of Saint Seraphim of Sarov, c1981
June. — 20p ; 22cm
Cover title
ISBN 0-907410-10-3 (pbk) : Unpriced (set) : Unpriced B81-26623

The **Menaion** : Troparia and Kontakia. — Fakenham (Dunton, Fakenham, Norfolk) : Monastery of Saint Seraphim of Sarov, c1981
Cover title
March. — 22p ; 22cm
ISBN 0-907410-07-3 (pbk) : Unpriced
ISBN 0-907410-00-6 (set) : unpriced
B81-37076

The **Menaion** : Troparia and Kontakia. — Fakenham (Dunton, Fakenham, Norfolk) : Monastery of Saint Seraphim of Sarov, c1981
May. — 26p ; 22cm
Cover title
ISBN 0-907410-09-x (pbk) : Unpriced
ISBN 0-907410-00-6 (set) : Unpriced
B81-23734

264'.019 — Orthodox Eastern churches. Holy Week services

Zander, Valentina. Christ - the new Passover : on the services of Holy week and Easter in the Orthodox church / by Valentina Zander ; translated by Anna Garrett and Pegeen O'Flaherty. — London (34 Upper Addison Gardens W14 8AT) : Russian Orthodox Diocese of Sourozh, c1980. — 30p : ill ; 22cm
Translated from the Russian
Unpriced (pbk) B81-18625

264'.0193 — Ekklēsia tēs Hellados. Public worship — *Rites*

Ekklēsia tēs Hellados. [Leitoyria toy Hagioy Iannoy toy Chrysostomoy]. The Liturgy of the Orthodox Church / translated and interpreted from the original Greek texts by Athenagoras Kokkinakis = E Leitoyria tes Orthodoxoy Ekklēsias / metaphrastheisa Kai hermēneytheisa ek toy Hellēnikoy Keimenoy hypo Athēnagoroy Kokkinakē. — London : Mowbrays, c1979 (1980 [printing]). — 261p ; 20cm
Parallel Greek and English translation
ISBN 0-264-66410-8 : £5.50 B81-13023

264'.02 — Catholic Church. Public worship

Boylan, Anthony B.. Living liturgy : a report to the Bishops of England and Wales / prepared by Anthony B. Boylan. — Slough : St. Paul Publications, 1981. — 67p ; 22cm
Report commissioned by the Bishops' Conference
ISBN 0-85439-195-9 (pbk) : £1.50 B81-30041

264'.02 — Catholic Church. Public worship. Lectionaries — *Commentaries*

Fitzsimmons, John H.. Guide to the Lectionary / John H. Fitzsimmons. — Great Wakering : Mayhew-McCrimmon, 1981. — 108p ; 21cm
ISBN 0-85597-314-5 (pbk) : £2.50 B81-38887

264'.02 — Catholic Church. Public worship. Reform

Boylan, Anthony B.. The content of liturgical formation : a paper / prepared by Anthony B. Boylan. — [London] ([42 Francis St., S.W.1.]) : Liturgy Commission, 1980. — 22p ; 21cm
£0.20 (unbound) B81-11359

264'.02'00942 — England. Catholic Church. Public worship. Reform — *Proposals*

Boylan, Anthony B.. Living liturgy : a report to the bishops of England and Wales / prepared by Anthony B. Boylan. — [Slough] : St. Paul Publications, [1981]. — 66p ; 22cm
Unpriced (pbk) B81-32541

264'.0201 — Catholic Church. Funerals. Prayers

Fenn, Francis. Praying for the dead / Francis Fenn. — London : Catholic Truth Society, 1980. — 13p ; 17cm
ISBN 0-85183-379-9 (pbk) : £0.30 B81-07802

264'.02036 — Catholic Church. Eucharist

Catholic Church. *Bishops' Conference of England and Wales. Liturgy Commission*. The Parish Mass : a resource book for clergy, religious and laity / prepared by the Liturgical Commission of the Bishops' Conference of England and Wales ; [artwork: Martin Hayes]. — London : Catholic Truth Society, 1981. — vii,102p : ill ; 19cm + Study programme([8]p; 23cm)
Includes index
ISBN 0-85183-407-8 (pbk) : £1.95 B81-24331

Sands, Ernest. Living liturgy : a companion to the Mass for Sundays and major feasts / Ernest Sands. — Leigh-on-Sea : Mayhew
Vol.1: The Matthew cycle of year A. — 1978, c1977. — 135p : music ; 22cm
ISBN 0-905725-49-2 (pbk) : £2.75 B81-40092

Sands, Ernest. Living liturgy : a companion to the Mass for Sunday and major feasts / Ernest Sands. — Leigh-on-Sea : Mayhew
Vol.2: The Mark cycle of year B. — 1979. — 149p : music ; 22cm
ISBN 0-905725-65-4 (pbk) : £3.00 B81-40093

264'.02036 — Catholic Church. Eucharist — *For children*

Bradley, Margaret. My first Holy Communion — soon / by Margaret Bradley ; [illustrated by Arthur Baker]. — Leigh-on-Sea : Mayhew, 1978. — 31p : col.ill ; 21cm
ISBN 0-905725-46-8 (unbound) : £0.40
B81-40183

Bradley, Margaret. My Mass book / by Margaret Bradley ; illustrated by Arthur Baker. — Leigh-on-Sea : Mayhew, 1979. — 31p : col.ill ; 18cm
ISBN 0-905725-72-7 (pbk) : Unpriced
B81-40094

Bradley, Margaret. What's the Mass about? / Margaret Bradley ; [illustrated by Arthur Baker]. — Leigh-on-Sea : Mayhew, 1977. — 16p : ill ; 30cm
Cover title
ISBN 0-905725-32-8 (pbk) : £0.70 B81-40185

A **gift** from my Heavenly Father : first communion workbook. — London : Catholic Truth Society, 1981. — 32p : ill ; 21x30cm
Cover title. — Text on inside covers
£0.85 (pbk) B81-34093

Simon, Madeleine. 'I am the way' : a way always leads somewhere : Jesus leads us to God our Father / text by Madeleine Simon ; drawings by Paul Chilvers. — Great Wakering : Mayhew-McCrimmon, c1981. — 24p : ill ; 15x21cm. — (Come to me series ; 4)
ISBN 0-85597-131-2 (pbk) : £0.60 B81-36860

Simon, Madeleine. Jesus says: 'Love each other' / text by Madeleine Simon ; drawings by Paul Chilvers. — Great Wakering : Mayhew-McCrimmon, c1981. — 23p : ill ; 15x21cm. — (Come to me series ; 2)
ISBN 0-85597-132-0 (pbk) : £0.60 B81-36858

Simon, Madeleine. 'This is me' / text by Madeleine Simon ; drawings by Paul Chilvers. — Great Wakering : Mayhew-McCrimmon, c1981. — 24p : ill(some col.) ; 15x21cm. — (Come to me series ; 3)
ISBN 0-85597-312-9 (pbk) : £0.60 B81-36859

264'.02036 — Catholic Church. Eucharist — *For parents & teaching*

Simon, Madeleine. Come to me : a practical course for preparing young children for their first sharing in the sacraments of penance and the eucharist / Madeleine Simon. — Great Wakering : Mayhew-McCrimmon, 1981. — 56p ; 21cm. — (Come to me series)
ISBN 0-85597-313-7 (pbk) : £0.90
Also classified at 265'.6 B81-36861

264'.02036 — Catholic Church. Eucharist — *Protestant viewpoints*

Trumper, Peter. The mass : should a Christian attend it? / by Peter Trumper. — London (184 Fleet St., EC4A 2HJ) : Protestant Truth Society, c1980. — 16p ; 17cm
Cover title
ISBN 0-900603-06-2 (pbk) : £0.30 B81-21993

264'.02036 — Catholic Church. Eucharist. Transubstantiation

Schillebeeckx, Edward. The Eucharist / Edward Schillebeeckx. — London : Sheed and Ward, 1968 (1980 [printing]). — 160p ; 20cm. — (Stagbooks)
Translation of: Christus' tegenwoordigheid in de eucharistie
ISBN 0-7220-7747-5 (pbk) : £3.75 B81-07189

264'.021 — Catholic Church. Public worship. Psalters & books of hours. Calendars, *1100-1500*

Pickering, F. P.. The calendar pages of medieval service books : an introductory note for art historians / by F. P. Pickering. — [Reading] : Reading Medieval Studies Graduate Centre for Medieval Studies, University of Reading, c1980. — 41p ; 21cm. — (Reading medieval studies. Monograph ; no.1)
ISBN 0-7049-0775-5 (pbk) : Unpriced
B81-15097

264'.023 — Catholic Church. Eucharist. Mentally handicapped children's services — *Rites*

Clifford, Stephanie. Invitation to Communion : a first Holy Communion programme for mentally handicapped children / by Stephanie Clifford. — Leigh-on-Sea : Mayhew, 1980. — 96p : ill ; 22cm
ISBN 0-86209-041-5 (pbk) : Unpriced
B81-40407

264'.025 — Catholic Church. Sunday worship — *Rites — Serials*

Living Sunday. — Issue 1 (1980/81)-. — Bedford (118 Bromham Rd, Bedford MK40 2QR) : St Mary's RE Centre, 1980-. — v. ; 30cm
Six issues yearly. — Description based on: Issue 3 (1980/81)
ISSN 0261-3514 = Living Sunday : £2.00 per issue B81-24125

264'.0274 — Catholic Church. Churches. Dedication — *Rites*

Catholic Church. [Dedication rite]. Dedication of a church and an altar : approved for interim use by the Standing Committee of the Bishops' Conference of England and Wales. — [London] : Catholic Truth Society, c1978. — v,143p ; 28cm
Text translated from the Latin. — Includes appendices in Latin with English translations
Unpriced (pbk) B81-36191

264'.03 — Church of England. Liturgy and ritual. Book of Common Prayer

No alternative : the prayer book controversy. — Oxford : Blackwell, Nov.1981. — [176]p
ISBN 0-631-12974-x (cased) : £7.95 : CIP entry
ISBN 0-631-12975-8 (pbk) : £3.50 B81-31228

264'.03 — Church of England. Public worship. Family services

Stevenson, Kenneth W.. Family services / Kenneth Stevenson. — London : S.P.C.K. for Alcuin Club, 1981. — ix,45p ; 22cm. — (Alcuin Club manuals ; no.3)
ISBN 0-281-03826-0 (pbk) : £1.95 B81-40447

264'.03 — Church of England. Public worship. Hymns. Words — *Anthologies*

. Favourite hymns / compiled and illustrated by Patricia Machin. — London : Collins, 1981. — 26p : col.ill,music ; 33cm
ISBN 0-00-215249-5 : £5.95 : CIP rev. B81-20150

264'.03 — Church of England. Public worship — *Rites*

Church of England. [Alternative Service Book]. Alternative Service Book. — London : Hodder & Stoughton, Nov.1981. — [1296]p
ISBN 0-340-27562-6 : £11.95 : CIP entry
ISBN 0-340-27563-4 (Bonded leather ed.) : £13.95 B81-30135

264'.03 — Church of England. Public worship. Rituals: Church of England. Alternative Service book — *Critical studies*

Getting to know your ASB 1980 : a parish study course with points for discussion / compiled by Jean Mayland. — London : Mowbray, 1981. — 32p ; 21cm
Bibliography: p32
ISBN 0-264-66822-7 (pbk) : £1.00 B81-36804

264'.03 — Church of England. Ritualism. Lowder, Charles — *Biographies*

Ellsworth, L. E.. Charles Lowder and the Ritualist Movement. — London : Darton, Longman & Todd, Nov.1981. — [208]p
ISBN 0-232-51535-2 : £9.95 : CIP entry B81-28815

264'.0301 — Church of England. Public worship. Prayers of intercession

Vasey, Michael. Intercessions in worship / by Michael Vasey. — Bramcote : Grove Books, 1981. — 24p : music ; 21cm. — (Grove worship series, ISSN 0144-1728 ; no.77)
Music on inside cover
ISBN 0-907536-05-0 (pbk) : £0.60 B81-37415

264'.0302 — Church of England. Public worship. Rituals: Church of England. Alternative Service book. Music

Music and the Alternative service book : a practical guide / edited by Lionel Dakers. — Croydon (Addington Palace, Croydon, CR9 5AD) : Addington Press, 1980. — 47p : music ; 21cm
ISBN 0-906851-05-x (pbk) : £1.50 B81-04618

264'.03036 — Church of England. Eucharist

A **Communicant's** manual : with preparatory notes on the Holy Communion, a guide through the Rite A Service from the Alternative Service Book 1980, an introduction to the Christian life, and an anthology of modern prayers for each day of the week / compiled by William Purcell ; foreword by the Archbishop of York, Stuart Blanch. — London : Mowbray, 1981. — 32p ; 17cm
Bibliography: p32
ISBN 0-264-66736-0 (pbk) : £0.75 B81-11695

Todd, Norman. Four celebrations : a teaching course on the Eucharist within the Eucharist / by Norman Todd and Michael Kindred. — London : CIO, 1981. — 27p ; 21cm
ISBN 0-7151-0394-6 (pbk) : £1.30 B81-23271

264'.031 — Church of England. Public worship. Hymns — *Calendars*

A **Hymn** guide for the Sunday themes of the new lectionary / compiled by a group of members from York diocese ; with an introduction by Ronald Jasper. — London : Mowbray, 1981. — vii,48p ; 21 cm
ISBN 0-264-66768-9 (pbk) : £1.75 B81-09923

Leaver, Robin. Hymns with the new lectionary / by Robin Leaver. — Bramcote : Grove Books, c1980. — 184p ; 22cm
Bibliography: p3-5. — Includes index
ISBN 0-905422-90-2 (pbk) : £3.50 B81-29026

264'.035 — Anglican churches. Eucharist. Prayers of intercession — *Collections* — *For church year*

Hockley, Raymond. Intercessions at Holy Communion on themes for the church's year / by Raymond Hockley. — London : Mowbray, 1981. — 61p ; 21cm
Includes index
ISBN 0-264-66769-7 (pbk) : £1.75 B81-09920

264'.035 — Church of England. Eucharist. Activities for children

Share the Word / by the Wadderton Group. — [London] : CIO
2. — Rev. — 1980. — viii,159p : ill ; 21cm
Previous ed.: 1977
ISBN 0-7151-0392-x (pbk) : £3.25 B81-23272

264'.035 — Church of England. Eucharist — *Rites* — *For children*

Church of England. [Holy Communion (Rite A)]. The Lord is here! : A Communion book using the Order for Holy Communion Rite A from Alternative Service Book 1980 / arranged by Paul Jenkins and Leslie Francis ; pictures by Clare Beaton. — Rev. ed. — London : Collins, 1981. — 60p : col.ill ; 15cm
Previous ed.: 1978
ISBN 0-00-599685-6 (pbk) : Unpriced B81-40458

Church of England. [Holy Communion (Rite A)]. Children's Communion book : Rite A : adapted from The alternative service book 1980 / [illustrations by Charles Bannerman]. — Oxford : Mowbray, 1981. — 24p : col.ill ; 22cm
Cover title. — Text, ill on inside covers
ISBN 0-264-66373-x (pbk) : £1.00 B81-38946

264'.035 — Church of England. Initiation — *Rites*

Church of England. [Initiation services (Ser.3)]. Initiation services. — Cambridge : Cambridge University Press, c1979. — 70p ; 17cm. — (Alternative services. Series 3)
Cover title
£0.55 (pbk) B81-19749

264'.035 — Church of England. Marriage — *Rites*

Church of England. [Marriage Service (Series 1 and 3)]. The marriage service with music. — Words ed. — Croydon : Royal School of Church Music, [1981?]. — 24p ; 21cm
ISBN 0-85402-127-2 (pbk) : £0.35 B81-27142

264'.038 — Church of England. Public worship. Psalters. English versions. Translation & use

Frost, David L.. Making the Liturgical psalter / by David Frost. — Bramcote : Grove Books, 1981. — 39p ; 22cm. — (The Morpeth lectures ; 1980) (Grove liturgical study, ISSN 0306-0608 ; no.25)
ISBN 0-905422-98-8 (pbk) : £1.25 B81-27583

264'.052 — Church of Scotland. Public worship. Innovation

New ways to worship / [written and compiled for the Committee on Public Worship and Aids to Devotion by David Beckett et al.]. — Edinburgh : St. Andrew Press, 1980. — v,125p ; 18cm
Bibliography: p122-124. — Includes index
ISBN 0-7152-0454-8 (pbk) : £1,75 B81-06991

264'.052036 — Presbyterian Church of Wales. Eucharist — *For confirmation candidates* — *Welsh texts*

Jones, Glyn Tudwal. Cymorth cyn cymuno : llyfryn cyfarwyddyd i'r Cristion ifanc / Glyn Tudwal Jones. — Abertawe : Penry, 1981. — 84p ; 19cm
Bibliography: p83-84
ISBN 0-903701-38-3 (pbk) : £1.50 B81-15186

264'.0523202 — United Reformed Church. Public worship. Hymnals: New church praise — *Commentaries*

Cutts, Peter. New church praise commentary / by Peter Cutts. — London : Church Life Department, The United Reformed Church, 1981. — [32]p ; 21cm
ISBN 0-902256-47-5 (pbk) : £0.65 B81-27607

264'.0523202 — United Reformed Church. Public worship. Hymns. Words — *Anthologies*

Linden praise : supplementary hymns of the United Reformed Church. — Bognor Regis (Linden Rd., Bognor Regis) : [The Church], [1981?]. — 37p ; 22cm
Cover title
Unpriced (pbk) B81-29357

264'.05802 — Union of Welsh Independents. Public worship. Hymns — *Collections* — *For children* — *Welsh texts*

Caniedydd yr ifanc. — 2 argraffiad. Sol-ffa. — Abertawe : Penry, 1980. — xxiv,220p : music ; 19cm
Previous ed.: 1980. — Includes index
ISBN 0-903701-23-5 : Unpriced B81-15185

264'.1 — Asia. Christian medical missions: BMMF International. Prayers of intercession. Intentions — *Calendars* — *Serials*

BMMF International. Prayer calendar / BMMF International. — 1980. — London : BMMF International, [1980]. — [48]p
£0.60 B81-35122

BMMF International. Prayer calendar / BMMF International. — 1981. — London : BMMF International, [1981]. — 52p
£0.75 B81-31898

264'.1 — Social conditions. Prayers of intercession. Intentions

Johnstone, P. J.. Operation world : a handbook for world intercession / P.J. Johnstone. — 2nd British ed. — Bromley : STL Publications, 1979. — 272p : maps ; 23cm
Previous ed.: 1978. — Includes index
ISBN 0-903843-09-9 (cased) : £3.95
ISBN 0-903843-08-0 (pbk) : £1.95 B81-02883

264'.2 — Christian church. Public worship. English hymns, *to 1981*

Routley, Erik. English hymns and their tunes : a survey / by Erik Routley. — London (7 Little Cloister, Westminster Abbey, SW1P 3PL) : Hymn Society of Great Britain and Ireland, [1981]. — 23p ; 21cm
Cover title
Unpriced (pbk) B81-40704

264'.2 — Christian church. Public worship. Hymns — *Critical studies*

Colquhoun, Frank. Hymns that live : their meaning and message / by Frank Colquhoun. — London : Hodder and Stoughton, 1980. — 320p ; 18cm. — (Hodder Christian paperbacks)
Includes index
ISBN 0-340-25724-5 (pbk) : £2.25 : CIP rev. B80-10942

264'.2 — Christian church. Public worship. Hymns. Sources: Bible. O.T. Psalms

The **Psalms** : their use and performance today / edited by Lionel Dakers. — Croydon : Royal School of Church Music, c1980. — 55p : ill ; 22cm. — (RSCM handbook ; no.5)
Bibliography: p52-55
ISBN 0-85402-088-8 (pbk) : Unpriced B81-12088

264'.2 — Christian church. Public worship. Hymns, *to 1000.* **Special subjects: Mary,** *Mother of Jesus Christ.* **Words** — *Anthologies*

In praise of Mary : hymns from the first millennium of the Eastern and Western Churches / [texts selected by Costante Berselli and Giorgio Gharib] ; [translated from the Italian by Phil Jenkins]. — Slough : St. Paul, 1981. — 110p : col.ill ; 25cm
Translated from the Italian. — Includes index
ISBN 0-85439-187-8 : £8.00 B81-25431

264'.2 — Christian church. Public worship. Hymns. Words — *Anthologies*

Alexander's hymns. — Large print ed. — London : Marshall Morgan & Scott
3. — Sept.1981. — [160]p
ISBN 0-551-00911-x (pbk) : £1.60 : CIP entry B81-28334

Cry Hosanna / edited by Betty Pulkingham, Mimi Farra. — Words ed. — London : Hodder and Stoughton, c1981. — 143p : 2ill ; 18cm
Includes index
ISBN 0-340-25993-0 (pbk) : £1.15 B81-25511

'Hill Top' choruses : 30 new songs to inspire. — Ilkeston : Moorley's, [1981?]. — [12]p ; 22cm
Cover title
ISBN 0-86071-118-8 (pbk) : £0.10 B81-25074

Hymns as poetry / edited by Samuel Carr ; preface by John Betjeman. — London : Batsford, 1980. — 124p : ill(some col.),1col.facsim ; 23cm
Ill on lining papers. — Includes index
ISBN 0-7134-3447-3 : £5.95 B81-00740

The **Richest** legacy : the Eucharistic hymns of John and Charles Wesley / selected and edited by Jack R. Burton. — [Norwich] ([11 Colegate, Norwich]) : J.R. Burton, [1981]. — [114]p : ill,music ; 21cm
Includes index
£2.00 B81-21071

Songs of fellowhip. — Words ed. — Eastbourne : Kingsway, 1981. — [32]p ; 22cm
Includes index
ISBN 0-86065-118-5 (pbk) : £0.45 B81-33427

264'.2 — Christian church. Public worship. Hymns. Words — *Anthologies* — *Welsh texts*

Nicholas, W. Rhys. Cerddi mawl : emynau, carolau a salmau W. Rhys Nicholas. — Abertawe : Penry, 1980. — 103p ; 22cm
ISBN 0-903701-37-5 : £2.50 B81-15193

264'.2 — Christian church. Public worship. Hymns. Words — *Texts* — *For children*

Away in a manger / illustrated by Gordon Stowell. — Rev. ed. — Oxford : Mowbray, 1977 (1981 [printing]). — [24]p : chiefly col.ill ; 15cm. — (Glow-worm books)
Text, ill on inside covers
ISBN 0-264-66442-6 (pbk) : Unpriced B81-39844

Farjeon, Eleanor. Morning has broken / words by Eleanor Farjeon ; illustrated by Gordon Stowell. — Oxford : Mowbray, 1981. — [24]p : chiefly col.ill ; 15cm. — (Glow-worm books)
Text, ill on inside covers
ISBN 0-264-66782-4 (pbk) : Unpriced B81-39842

Howard, Brian, *1949-.* The butterfly song / words by Brian Howard ; illustrated by Gordon Stowell. — Oxford : Mowbray, 1981. — [24]p : chiefly col.ill ; 15cm. — (Glow-worm books)
Text, ill on inside covers
ISBN 0-264-66780-8 (pbk) : Unpriced B81-39843

264'.2'0924 — Christian church. Public worship. Hymns. Words. Newton, John — *Biographies*

Pollock, John, *1923-.* Amazing grace : John Newton's story / by John Pollock. — London : Hodder and Stoughton, 1981. — 190p ; 18cm
Bibliography: p183-184. - Includes index
ISBN 0-340-26209-5 (pbk) : £1.95 B81-06750

264'.34 — Christian church. Eucharist. Lectionaries — *Commentaries*

This is the word of the Lord. — Oxford : Oxford University Press
Year B: The year of Mark. — Oct.1981. — [176]p
ISBN 0-19-826662-6 (pbk) : £2.95 : CIP entry B81-26742

264'.36 — Bible. Special subjects: Eucharist

Brandon, Owen. Bible teaching about the Lord's supper / compiled by Owen Brandon. — [Sevenoaks] : [Hodder and Stoughton], [1981]. — 12p ; 21cm
£0.10 (pbk) B81-24003

264'.36 — Christian church. Eucharist

Pellatt, J.. The Lord's supper : as the expression of Christian fellowship and that which leads to assembly privilege / J. Pellatt. — Ilford (22 Christchurch Rd., Ilford, Essex IG1 4QY) : F.C. Mutton, [1981?]. — 18p ; 15cm
Unpriced (unbound) B81-40179

264'.36 — Christian church. Eucharist. Eucharistic prayers — *Rites* — *Early works*

Addai and Mari : the anaphora of the apostles : a text for students / with introduction, translation and commentary by Bryan D. Spinks. — Bramcote : Grove, 1980. — 33p ; 21cm. — (Grove liturgical study, ISSN 0306-0608 ; no.24)
Translation from the Syriac. — Bibliography: p32-33
ISBN 0-905422-93-7 (pbk) : £1.00 B81-13149

264'.36 — Christian church. Eucharist — *Roman Catholic/Methodist Committee viewpoints*

Eucharist, ministry, authority : statements agreed by Roman Catholics and Methodists. — Abbots Langley (74 Gallows La., Abbots Langley, Herts. WD5 0BZ) : Published by Catholic Information Services on behalf of the Roman Catholic/Methodist Committee, [1981?]. — 26p ; 21cm
Unpriced (unbound) B81-32542

264'.36'09 — Christian church. Eucharist, *to 1980*

Bridge, Donald. The meal that unites? / Donald Bridge and David Phypers. — London : Hodder and Stoughton, 1981. — 191p ; 20cm. — (Ecclesia books)
Bibliography: p187-190. - Includes index
ISBN 0-340-26633-3 (pbk) : £3.25 : CIP rev. B81-11913

265 — CHRISTIAN RITES, CEREMONIES, ORDINANCES

265 — Christian Community *(1922-).* **Sacraments**

Capel, Evelyn Francis. Seven sacraments in the Christian community / Evelyn Francis Capel. — 3rd ed. — Edinburgh : Floris, 1981. — 122p ; 18cm
Previous ed.: 1966
ISBN 0-903540-35-5 (pbk) : Unpriced B81-24009

265'.1 — Catholic Church. Initiation

Searle, Mark. Christening : the making of Christians / Mark Searle. — Leigh-on-Sea : Kevin Mayhew, c1980. — x,165p ; 23cm
Includes index
ISBN 0-8146-1183-4 (pbk) : £4.00 B81-40222

265'.1 — Christian church. Baptism

Whitaker, E. C.. The baptismal liturgy / E.C. Whitaker. — 2nd ed. — London : SPCK, 1981. — v,106p ; 20cm
Previous ed.: London : Faith, 1965. — Bibliography: p93-101. - Includes index
ISBN 0-281-03809-0 (pbk) : £2.95 B81-20781

265'.1 — Christian church. Initiation

Newman, David, *1954-.* What we are about to receive : the Holy Spirit in initiation and experience / by David Newman. — Bramcote : Grove, 1981. — 25p ; 22cm. — (Grove pastoral series, ISSN 0144-171x ; no.7)
Text on inside cover
ISBN 0-907536-07-7 (pbk) : £0.60 B81-39596

265'.2 — Catholic Church. Confirmation — *For children*

Bradley, Margaret. My Confirmation — soon / by Margaret Bradley ; [illustrated by Arthur Baker]. — Leigh-on-Sea : Mayhew, 1977. — 26p : col.ill ; 21cm
ISBN 0-905725-42-5 (unbound) : £0.35 B81-40181

265'.2 — Catholic Church. Confirmation — *For schools*

Growth in the Holy Spirit : education for confirmation / prepared by Westminster Religious Education Centre ; foreword by David Konstant. — Wheathampstead : Published on behalf of Westminster Religious Education Centre by Anthony Clarke, 1981. — 43p ; 25cm
ISBN 0-85650-060-7 (pbk) : £2.45 B81-37425

McCallen, A. J.. My Confirmation : a workbook to accompany More like Christ / A. J. McCallen. — London : Collins, 1981. — 64p : ill,1port ; 25cm
ISBN 0-00-599677-5 (pbk) : Unpriced B81-22311

265'.6 — Catholic Church. Sacraments: Penance — *For children*

I love my Heavenly Father : first confession workbook. — [London] : [Catholic Truth Society], [1981]. — 22p : ill ; 21x30cm
Cover title. — Text on inside back cover
ISBN 0-85183-419-1 (pbk) : £0.65 B81-31980

Simon, Madeleine. 'I love you' / text by Madeleine Simon ; drawings by Paul Chilvers. — Great Wakering : Mayhew-McCrimmon, c1981. — 24p : ill ; 15x20cm. — (Come to me series ; 1)
ISBN 0-85597-311-0 (pbk) : £0.60 B81-36862

265'.6 — Catholic Church. Sacraments: Penance — *For parents & teaching*

Simon, Madeleine. Come to me : a practical course for preparing young children for their first sharing in the sacraments of penance and the eucharist / Madeleine Simon. — Great Wakering : Mayhew-McCrimmon, 1981. — 56p ; 21cm. — (Come to me series)
ISBN 0-85597-313-7 (pbk) : £0.90
Primary classification 264'.02036 B81-36861

265'.66 — Catholic Church. Indulgences

Sessolo, Giovanni. Indulgences / Giovanni Sessolo. — London : Catholic Truth Society, 1980. — 47p ; 19cm
Translation of: Indulgenze a fervore di carità. — Do 524
ISBN 0-85183-367-5 (pbk) : £0.75 B81-09223

265'.82 — Bible. Special subjects: Ministry of healing

Martin, Trevor. Kingdom healing. — London : Marshall Morgan & Scott, May 1981. — [160] p. — (Marshalls paperbacks)
ISBN 0-551-00902-0 (pbk) : £1.50 : CIP entry B81-12886

265'.82 — Church of England. Ministry of healing, *to 1980*

Maddocks, Morris. The Christian healing ministry / Morris Maddocks. — London : SPCK, 1981. — 243p ; 22cm
Bibliography: p231-234. — Includes index
ISBN 0-281-03760-4 (pbk) : £4.95 B81-06973

265'.94'0924 — Christian church. Exorcism. Omand, Donald

Alexander, Marc. [To anger the devil]. The devil hunter : an account of the work of exorcist extraordinary the Reverend Dr Donald Omand / Marc Alexander ; introduction by Colin Wilson. — London : Sphere, 1981, c1978. — 192p,[8]p of plates : ill,ports ; 18cm
Originally published: St Helens : Neville Spearman (Jersey) Ltd., 1978
ISBN 0-7221-1111-8 (pbk) : £1.50 B81-09818

266 — CHRISTIAN MISSIONS

266 — Christian missions

Cotterell, Peter. The eleventh commandment. — Leicester : Inter-Varsity Press, Nov.1981. — [256]p
ISBN 0-85110-705-2 (pbk) : £4.75 : CIP entry B81-30569

266 — Christian missions — *Conference proceedings*
World missions in the eighties / Michael Griffiths and others ; edited by Dave Foster. — Bromley : S.T.L., c1980. — 160p ; 18cm
Conference papers. — Bibliography: p160
ISBN 0-903843-42-0 (pbk) : £1.40 B81-07405

266 — Good News Crusade — *Serials*
Good News Crusade. Crusade news / Good News Crusade. — 1977 issue-. — St. Austell (32a Fore St., St. Austell, Cornwall PL25 5EP) : The Crusade, 1977-. — v. : ill,ports ; 42cm
Annual. — Absorbed: Good News Crusade. Overseas outreach. 1980. — Supplement to: Ripened grain
ISSN 0140-119x = Crusade news : Unpriced B81-13687

266'.0092'2 — China. Christian missions. French & Italian missionaries. Correspondence, *1844-1865 — Commentaries*
Lowe, Robson. From China and Tibet : a commentary on letters written by missionaries working in the interior, 1844-1865 / by Robson Lowe. — London : Pall Mall Stamp Co. for Robson Lowe, [1981]. — 20p : maps,facsims ; 22cm
ISBN 0-85397-240-0 (unbound) : £2.00 B81-33239

266'.0092'2 — Christian missions. Missionaries
Tatford, Frederick A.. The living flame / by Fredk. A. Tatford. — Bath (1 Widcombe Cres., Bath BA2 6AQ) : Echoes of Service, 1980. — viii,68p,[8]p of plates : ill,ports ; 22cm
Bibliography: p67-68
Unpriced (pbk) B81-17863

266'.0092'2 — Developing countries. Catholic missions. Irish missionaries, *ca 1870-1975 — Biographies*
Keaney, Marian. They brought the good news : modern Irish missionaries / Marian Keaney. — Dublin : Veritas, 1980. — 146p : ill,ports ; 21cm
ISBN 0-86217-006-0 : Unpriced B81-39678

266'.0092'2 — Western Europe. Anglo-Saxon Christian missions, *650-750 — Biographies*
The **Anglo-Saxon** missionaries in Germany : being the lives of SS. Willibrord, Boniface, Sturm, Leoba and Lebuin, together with the Hodeporicon of St. Willibald and a selection from the correspondence of St. Boniface / translated and edited by C.H. Talbot. — London : Sheed and Ward, 1954 (1981 [printing]). — xx,234p ; 22cm. — (Spiritual masters)
Translation from the Latin
ISBN 0-7220-1012-5 (pbk) : £7.50 B81-33220

266'.0092'4 — Brazil. Ponta Porã region. Christian missions — *Personal observations*
Taylor, Audrey. For me, with love : cameos from Armadillo Water / Audrey Taylor ; drawings by David Poole. — Eastbourne : Kingsway, 1981. — 96p : ill,2maps,port ; 18cm
ISBN 0-86065-148-7 (pbk) : £1.35 B81-33426

266'.0092'4 — Central Africa. Christian missions. Arnot, Frederick Stanley — *Biographies*
Tatford, Frederick A.. Frederick Stanley Arnot / by Fredk A. Tatford. — [Bath] ([1 Widcombe Cres., Bath, Avon BA2 6AQ]) : [Echoes of Service], 1981. — [18]p : ill,maps,1port ; 19cm
Unpriced (pbk) B81-27571

266'.0092'4 — China. Christian missions, *1970-1980 — Personal observations*
David, *Brother*. God's smuggler to China / Brother David with Dan Wooding and Sara Bruce. — London : Hodder & Stoughton, c1981. — xiv,304p ; 18cm. — (Hodder Christian paperbacks)
ISBN 0-340-26570-1 (pbk) : £1.50 : CIP rev. B81-08884

266'.0092'4 — China. Christian missions. Aylward, Gladys — *Biographies*
Burgess, Alan. The small woman / Alan Burgess. — London : Pan, 1959 (1981 printing). — 266p,[8]p of plates : ill,2maps,ports ; 18cm
Originally published: London : Evans, 1957
ISBN 0-330-10196-x (pbk) : £1.50 B81-38169

266'.0092'4 — China. Christian missions. Liddell, Eric — *Biographies*
Magnusson, Sally. The flying Scotsman / Sally Magnusson. — London : Quartet, 1981. — 191p,[8]p of plates : 1facsim,ports
ISBN 0-7043-3379-1 (pbk) : £2.50 B81-18231

266'.0092'4 — China. Christian missions. Taylor, Hudson — *Biographies*
Broomhall, A. J.. Hudson Taylor & China's open century / A.J. Broomhall. — Sevenoaks : Hodder and Stoughton, 1981. — (Hodder Christian paperbacks)
Bibliography: p411-416. — Includes index
Bk. 1: Barbarians at the gates. — 432p ; 18cm
ISBN 0-340-26210-9 (pbk) : £2.50 B81-11097

Broomhall, H. J.. Hudson Taylor and China's open century. — London : Hodder & Stoughton
Bk.2. — Nov.1981. — [432]p
ISBN 0-340-27561-8 (pbk) : £3.25 : CIP entry B81-31157

266'.0092'4 — Christian missions. Paton, William — *Biographies*
Jackson, Eleanor M.. Red tape and the Gospel : a study of the significance of the ecumenical missionary struggle of William Paton (1886-1943) / by Eleanor M. Jackson. — Birmingham (318 Summer La., Newtown, Birmingham, B19 3RL) : Published for the Paton family by Phlogiston in association with the Selly Oak Colleges, Birmingham, c1980. — 409p,[1]leaf of plates : ill,1port ; 26cm
Includes index
ISBN 0-906954-01-0 : £15.00 B81-10198

266'.0092'4 — Ecuador. Christian missions. Elliot, Jim — *Biographies*
Elliot, Elisabeth. Shadow of the Almighty : the life and testimony of Jim Elliot / by Elisabeth Elliot. — Bromley : STL Books, 1979, c1958 (1981 [printing]). — 256p ; 18cm
Originally published: New York : Harper, 1958 ; London : Hodder and Stoughton, 1959
ISBN 0-903843-03-x (pbk) : Unpriced B81-33120

266'.0092'4 — Hong Kong. Christian missions, *1963-1979 — Personal observations*
Pullinger, Jackie. Chasing the dragon / by Jackie Pullinger with Andrew Quicke. — London : Hodder and Stoughton, 1980. — 238p ; 18cm
ISBN 0-340-25760-1 (pbk) : £1.50 : CIP rev. B80-13699

266'.0092'4 — India. Christian missions. Carmichael, Amy — *Biographies*
Houghton, Frank. Amy Carmichael of Dohnavur : the story of a lover and her beloved / by Frank Houghton. — London : SPCK, 1953 (1981 printing). — xiii,390p ; 22cm
Includes index
ISBN 0-281-03828-7 (pbk) : £4.95 B81-26446

266'.0092'4 — India. Christian missions. Groves, A. N. — *Biographies*
Tatford, Frederick A.. A.N. Groves : the father of faith missions / by Fredk. A. Tatford. — Bath (1 Widcombe Cres., Bath, Avon BA2 6AQ) : Echoes of Service, 1979. — [10]p : ill,1map,ports ; 22cm
Unpriced (unbound) B81-17885

266'.0092'4 — Italy. Christian missions. Beckwith, J. C. — *Biographies*
Ashdown, A. George. The general with a wooden leg : the life and labours of General John Charles Beckwith among the Waldensians / by A. George Ashdown. — Bognor Regis : New Horizon, c1980. — 50p,[6]p of plates : ill ; 21cm
Bibliography: p49
ISBN 0-86116-204-8 : £3.50 B81-21834

266'.00953'6 — Arabia. Gulf States. Christian missions
Denffer, Ahmad von. Christian presence in the Gulf region / Ahmad von Denffer. — Leicester : Islamic Foundation, c1981. — 28p ; 30cm. — (Situation report / Islamic Foundation ; no.4)
English text, English and Arabic introduction
ISBN 0-86037-089-5 (pbk) : Unpriced B81-34742

266'.009593 — Thailand. Christian missions: Overseas Missionary Fellowship, *to 1978*
Dawn wind. — Sevenoaks (Belmont, The Vine, Sevenoaks, Kent TN13 3T2) : Overseas Missionary Fellowship, 1980. — 103p : ill,maps ; 19x22cm
Bibliography: p103
ISBN 0-85363-133-6 (pbk) : £1.20 B81-07049

266'.00966 — West Africa. Christian missions to Fulani, *1960-1980 — Islamic viewpoints*
Denffer, Ahmad von. The Fulani evangelisation-scheme in West-Africa / Ahmad von Denffer. — Leicester (223 London Rd., Leicester LE2 1ZE) : The Islamic Foundation, c1980. — 27p,[3]p of plates : ill,1map ; 30cm. — (Situation report / Islamic Foundation ; no.1)
English text, English and Arabic introduction
ISBN 0-86037-074-7 (pbk) B81-15223

266'.009744 — Massachusetts. Christian missions to North American Indians, *ca 1670 — Early works*
Eliot, John, *1604-1690*. [Indian dialogues]. John Eliot's Indian dialogues : a study in cultural interaction / edited by Henry W. Bowden and James P. Ronda. — Westport, Conn. ; London : Greenwood Press, 1980. — 173p : 2facsims ; 22cm. — (Contributions in American history ; no.88)
Originally published: Cambridge, Mass. : Marmaduke Johnson, 1671. — Bibliography: p167-169. — Includes index
ISBN 0-313-21031-4 : £14.75 B81-24014

266'.00982 — Argentina. Christian missions
Sinclair, Maurice. Green finger of God / by Maurice Sinclair ; foreword by Samuel Escobar. — Exeter : Paternoster, c1980. — 121p : 1map ; 22cm
ISBN 0-85364-273-7 (pbk) : £2.60 : CIP rev. B80-07668

266'.009866'4 — Ecuador. Napo-Pastaza. Christian missions to Aucas, *1956-1981*
Hefley, James. Unstilled voices. — London : Hodder & Stoughton, Jan.1982. — [240]p
ISBN 0-340-27284-8 (pbk) : £1.95 : CIP entry B81-34650

266'.023'410510922 — China. Christian missions: China Inland Mission. Women missionaries — *Biographies*
Thompson, Phyllis. Each at her post : six women of the China Inland Mission. — London : Hodder & Stoughton, Feb.1982. — [128]p
ISBN 0-340-26933-2 (pbk) : £1.50 : CIP entry B81-36353

266'.023'730866 — Ecuador. American Christian missions
Elliot, Elisabeth. Through the gates of splendour / by Elisabeth Elliot. — Bromley : ST2, 1980, c1957. — 191p : 1map ; 18cm
Originally published: New York : Harper ; London : Hodder, 1957
ISBN 0-903843-31-5 (pbk) : £1.25 B81-05560

266'.2'0922 — England. Jesuit missions. Campion, Edmund, *Saint* **& Persons, Robert**
Reynolds, E. E.. Campion and Parsons : the Jesuit mission of 1580-1 / E.E. Reynolds. — London : Sheed and Ward, 1980. — x,226p ; 23cm
Includes index
ISBN 0-7220-1412-0 : £15.00 B81-05324

266'.2'0924 — China. Jesuit missions. Schall, Adam — *Biographies*
Brinkworth, Guy. Adam Schall : missionary and mandarin / [author Guy Brinkworth]. — London : Catholic Trust Society, 1981. — 16p ; 17cm
Cover title
ISBN 0-85183-417-5 (pbk) : £0.40 B81-31970

266'.2'0924 — India *(Republic)*. **Catholic missions. Teresa,** *Mother — Biographies — For children*
Sebba, Anne. Mother Teresa. — London : MacRae, Feb.1982. — [48]p. — (Blackbird books)
ISBN 0-86203-064-1 : £2.75 : CIP entry B81-36045

266'.25414 — India *(Republic)*. Calcutta. Missionaries of Charity

Rae, Daphne. Love until it hurts / Daphne Rae. — London : Hodder and Stoughton, 1981. — 53p : ill(some col.) ; 25cm
ISBN 0-340-26311-3 (pbk) : £2.95 B81-30059

266'.26662 — Liberia. Catholic missions, *to 1950*

Hogan, Edmund M.. Catholic missionaries and Liberia : a study of Christian enterprise in West Africa, 1842-1950 / Edmund M. Hogan. — Cork : Cork University Press, 1981. — xiv,268p,[4]p of plates : 6maps,ports ; 21cm
Bibliography: p241-260. — Includes index
ISBN 0-902561-19-7 : £12.00 B81-29267

266'.3 — Anglican missions: Church Missionary Society, *1841-1872*

Yates, T. E.. Venn and Victorian bishops abroad : the missionary policies of Henry Venn and their repercussions upon the Anglican Episcopate of the colonial period 1841-1872 / T.E. Yates. — Uppsala : Swedish Institute of Miss[i]onary Research ; London : SPCK, 1978. — 212p ; 23cm. — (Studia missionalia Upsaliensia ; 33)
Bibliography: p203-208. — Includes index
ISBN 0-281-03687-x (pbk) : £3.50 B81-05722

266'.3 — Anglican missions: United Society for the Propagation of the Gospel — *Serials*

USPG year book. — 1979/80-. — London : United Society for the Propagation of the Gospel, [1980]-. — v. ; 30cm
Continues: USPG yearbook
ISSN 0144-9508 = USPG yearbook : £0.25
B81-04755

266'.3'0924 — Anglican missions: Church Missionary Society. Warren, Max — *Biographies*

Dillistone, F. W.. Into all the world : a biography of Max Warren / by F. W. Dillistone. — London : Hodder and Stoughton, 1980. — 251p ; 24cm
Bibliography: p243. - Includes index
ISBN 0-340-25479-3 : £8.25 : CIP rev.
B80-08098

266'.61 — Baptist missions: Baptist Missionary Society — *Serials*

Baptist Missionary Society. Prayer guide / Baptist Missionary Society. — 1979. — London (93 Gloucester Place, W1H 4AA) : The Society, [1978?]. — 64p
£0.30 B81-00741

266'.6181 — Brazil. Baptist missions: Baptist Missionary Society, *to 1980*

25 years in Brazil. — London (93 Gloucester Place, W1H 4AA) : Baptist Missionary Society, [1981?]. — [16]p : ill,1map,ports ; 23cm
Unpriced (unbound) B81-25359

266'.7'05 — Methodist missions — *Serials* — *For Christian religious education*

[Pacemaker *(London : 1980)*]. Pacemaker. — 1-. — London : [Methodist Church Division of Education and Youth in association with the Overseas Division], [1980]-. — v. : ill ; 30cm
Three issues yearly. — Description based on: 3
ISSN 0260-3586 = Pacemaker (London. 1980) : Free B81-05305

266'.7'0922 — China. Hunan. Methodist missions. Stanfield, John & Stanfield, May — *Biographies*

Stanfield, John. From Manchu to Mao / by John and May Stanfield ; edited by Margaret Thom. — London : Epworth, 1980. — 114p,[8]p of plates : ill,maps,ports ; 22cm
ISBN 0-7162-0361-8 (pbk) : £3.25 B81-07023

266'.96'0924 — China. Society of Friends missions. Silcock, Margaret — *Biographies*

Coutts, Anne. Meggie : the life of Margaret Silcock / Anne Coutts. — London : Quaker Peace & Service, 1980. — 32p : 1ill,1facsim,ports ; 21cm
Ports on back cover
ISBN 0-901689-12-2 (pbk) : £0.75 B81-06974

266'.99 — Brethren missions - *Directories* - *Serials*

Echoes daily prayer guide. — 1981. — Bath (1 Widcombe Cres., Bath, Avon BA2 6AQ) : Echoes of Service, [1980]. — 64p
£0.60 B81-16741

267 — CHRISTIAN ASSOCIATIONS FOR RELIGIOUS WORK

267 — Christian communities. Organisation — *Manuals*

O'Halloran, Jim. Living cells : building basic Christian community / Jim O'Halloran. — Dublin (St. Saviour's, Dublin 1, [Eire]) : Dominican Publications, 1980. — 70p : ill ; 16cm
Bibliography: p67-70
ISBN 0-9504797-7-2 (pbk) : Unpriced
B81-21360

267'.025'41 — Great Britain. Christian religious communities — *Directories*

A **Directory** of Christian communities and groups . — [Birmingham] ([c/o Westhill College, Wesley Park Rd, Selly Oak, Birmingham B29 6LL]) : [Community Resources Centre], [c1980]. — iv,101p ; 21cm
Includes index
£1.75 (pbk) B81-06199

267'.0973 — United States. Christian religious communities: Communes, *ca 1790-1890* — *Case studies*

Foster, Lawrence. Religion and sexuality : three American communal experiments of the nineteenth century / Lawrence Foster. — New York ; Oxford : Oxford University Press, 1981. — xi,363p ; 24cm
Bibliography: p341-352. — Includes index
ISBN 0-19-502794-9 : £12.00 B81-32474

267'.13 — Christian organisations: Toc H

Prideaux-Brune, Ken. A ticket for a journey : some thoughts on Toc H today / by Ken Prideaux-Brune. — Wendover (1 Forest Close, Wendover, Bucks. HP33 6BT) : Toc H, c1977. — 48p ; 21cm
£0.10 (pbk) B81-21242

267'.13 — Christian organisations: Toc H, *to 1980*

The **Way** of friendship : a Toc H anthology / compiled by Tom Gulliver. — Wendover (1 Forest Close, Wendover, Bucks. HP22 6BT) : Toc H, c1980. — 132p ; 21cm
Includes index
£2.00 (pbk) B81-21241

267'.13'0924 — New Zealand. Maungapohatu. Maori Christian religious communities. Rua Kenana

Binney, Judith. Mihaia : the prophet Rua Kenana and his Community at Maungapohatu / Judith Binney, Gillian Chaplin, Craig Wallace. — Wellington, N.Z ; Oxford : Oxford University Press, 1979. — 208p : ill(some col.),maps,facsims,ports,geneal.tables ; 29cm
Includes index
ISBN 0-19-558042-7 (cased) : Unpriced
ISBN 0-19-558052-4 (pbk) : £9.50 B81-17776

267'.15'05 — Salvation Army — *Serials*

Salvation Army. The Salvation Army year book. — 1981. — London : Salvationist Publishing and Supplies, 1981. — 283p
ISBN 0-85412-367-9 : Unpriced
ISSN 0080-567x B81-24121

267'.15'0924 — Salvation Army. Booth, Kate — *Biographies*

Scott, Carolyn. The heavenly witch : the story of the Maréchale / by Carolyn Scott. — London : Hamilton, 1981. — 260p,[8]p of plates : ill,ports ; 23cm
Bibliography: p251. — Includes index
ISBN 0-241-10412-2 : £12.50 : CIP rev.
B81-02364

267'.15'0942813 — West Yorkshire *(Metropolitan County)*. Batley. Salvation Army. *Batley Castle Corps, to 1981*

Salvation Army. *Batley Castle Corps*. A century in Batley : 1881 Batley Castle 1981, The Salvation Army / the Salvation Army. — Batley (48 Trafalgar St., Batley WF17 7HA) : Published for the Batley Castle Centenary Committee by Harry Hayes, c1981. — 26p : ill,facsim,ports ; 30cm
Unpriced (pbk) B81-34988

267'.15'0942843 — North Yorkshire. York. Salvation Army. *York Citadel Corps, to 1981*

York Salvation Army 1881-1981. — [York] ([c/o Press Officer, 17 Holly Tree Croft, Dunnington, York, Y01 5RG]) : [York Citadel Corps, Salvation Army], [1981]. — 58p : ill,ports ; 25cm
Cover title. — Compiled by R. Hawkshaw. — Bibliography: p58
£1.25 (pbk) B81-34984

267'.16 — Moral Re-Armament

Cook, Sydney. The black and white book : a handbook of revolution / Sydney Cook, Garth Lean. — London : Grosvenor, 1979. — 72p ; 13cm
Originally published: London : Blandford Press, 1972
ISBN 0-901269-44-1 (pbk) : £0.45 B81-11584

Surur, Mohammed Ahmed. Moral Re-armament and the modern world / Mohammed Ahmed Surur. — London : Grosvenor, 1980. — [24]p ; 16cm
Parallel English and Arabic text. — Originally published: Cairo : Alameya, 197-?
ISBN 0-901269-55-7 (pbk) : Unpriced
B81-37067

267'.182 — Catholic organisations: Society of St Vincent de Paul

Chouard, Pierre. Society of St Vincent de Paul in the modern world / [Pierre Chouard]. — Dublin (18 Nicholas St., Dublin 8) : The Society, [1981]. — 15p ; 21cm
Unpriced (unbound) B81-24001

267'.182 — Catholic organisations: Society of St Vincent de Paul — *Regulations*

Society of St Vincent de Paul. The rule of the Society of St Vincent de Paul : with the declaration and commentary. — Dublin (18 Nicholas St., Dublin 8) : Council of Ireland, The Society, [1976]. — vii,50p ; 21cm
Commentary by the Council of Ireland, Society of St Vincent de Paul
Unpriced (pbk) B81-24000

267'.182'0924 — Catholic organisations: Opus Dei. Escrivá de Balaguer, Josemaría — *Serials*

[Newsletter *(Opus Dei)*]. Newsletter. — No.1-. — London (6 Orme Court, W2 4RL) : Office of Vice Postulation of Opus Dei in Britain, 1977-. — v. : ill,ports ; 24cm
Irregular
ISSN 0260-6569 = Newsletter (Opus Dei) : Unpriced B81-08762

267'.182'0924 — Catholic organisations: Society of St Vincent de Paul. Ozanam, Frédéric — *Biographies*

Murphy, Michael P.. The Frederic Ozanam story / by Michael P. Murphy. — [Dublin] ([18 Nicholas St., Dublin 8]) : Society of St Vincent de Paul, [1981]. — 17p ; 19cm
Text on inside cover. — Bibliography: p17
Unpriced (pbk) B81-25147

267'.23'0924 — France. Taizé. Men's religious communities: Communauté de Taizé. Roger, *of Taizé, Brother* — *Correspondence, diaries, etc.*

Roger, *of Taizé, Brother*. The wonder of a love (Etonnement d'un amour) : journal 1974-1976 / Brother Roger of Taizé ; [translated by Emily Chisholm and the Taizé Community]. — London : Mowbray, 1981. — 108p ; 18cm. — (Mowbray's popular Christian paperbacks)
Translation of: Etonnement d'un amour
ISBN 0-264-66587-2 (pbk) : £1.50 B81-25963

267'.43'0942219 — Surrey. Farncombe. Women's Christian religious communities: Farncombe Community, *to 1973*

Graham, Carol. Record of the Farncombe Community 1960-1973 / Carol Graham. — Godalming ([Ladywell Convent, Ashtead Lane], Godalming, Surrey [GU7 1ST]) : Ladywell Press, [1981?]. — 24p ; 22cm
Cover title
Unpriced (pbk) B81-22349

267'.627541 — Great Britain. Methodist youth groups for children, 7-13 years: Shell Groups. Organisation — *Manuals*
Morgan, John, *1932-*. Shell Groups : a handbook for those working with 7-13s in weekday groups / [John Morgan]. — London : Methodist Church Division of Education and Youth, 1980. — 40p : ill ; 30cm
£1.00 B81-20981

268 — CHRISTIANITY. RELIGIOUS TRAINING AND INSTRUCTION

268 — Christian religious education. Role of Sunday schools
Reid, Ivan. Sunday schools : a suitable case for treatment / by Ivan Reid. — London : Chester House, 1980. — 40p ; 19cm
ISBN 0-7150-0080-2 (pbk) : £1.00 B81-20849

268'.092'4 — England. Sunday schools. Raikes, Robert, *1735-1811* — *Biographies* — *For children*
Hayden, Eric W. (Eric William). The adventures of Bobby Wildgoose / E.W. Hayden. — Bognor Regis : New Horizon, c1980. — 25p : ill,1map,1port ; 20cm
ISBN 0-86116-515-2 (pbk) : £1.50 B81-26189

268'.432 — Children, 10-13 years. Christian religious education — *For Sunday school teaching*
Baumohl, Anton. Ten plus : a handbook for teachers and leaders working with tens to thirteens in the church / by Anton Baumohl. — London : Scripture Union, 1981. — 160p : ill ; 21cm
ISBN 0-85421-903-x (pbk) : £1.95 B81-20791

268'.432 — Christian religious education — *For Church of Scotland Sunday school teaching*
Children of the way : a programme for Sunday School. — Edinburgh : Saint Andrew Press
Bk. 4 : for children of ages 8 and 9 / editor David P. Munro. — 1981. — 3v. : ill,2maps,1port ; 30cm
ISBN 0-7152-0475-9 (pbk) : £2.80
ISBN 0-7152-0476-7 (bk.4 : Term 2)
ISBN 0-7152-0477-5 (bk.4 : Term 3)
B81-17807

268'.432 — Christian religious education — *For Sunday school teaching*
Children of the way : a programme for Sunday school. — Edinburgh : Saint Andrew Press
Bk.6 / editor D.P. Munro. — 1981. — 3v. : ill,map,music ; 30cm
ISBN 0-7152-0466-1 (pbk) : £2.80
ISBN 0-7152-0467-x (Term 2)
ISBN 0-7152-0468-8 (Term 3) B81-20884

268'.432 — Religious education — *For Sunday school teaching*
Welcome -. — London : Methodist Church Division of Education and Youth, [1981?]. — 31p : ill ; 15x21cm
Cover title
ISBN 0-7192-0144-6 (pbk) : Unpriced
B81-20883

268'.6 — Catholic Church. Christian doctrine. Catechetics
A Catechist's handbook : adapted from Sharing the light of faith, the national catechetical directory for Catholics of the United States. — London : Catholic Truth Society, 1980. — xi,210p ; 19cm
Includes index
ISBN 0-85183-364-0 (pbk) B81-07397

269 — CHRISTIANITY. SPIRITUAL RENEWAL

269 — Christian life. Spiritual renewal
Tozer, A. W.. The divine conquest / A.W. Tozer. — Bromley : STL Books, 1979, c1950. — 128p ; 18cm
Originally published: New York : Revell, 1950
ISBN 0-903843-04-8 (pbk) : £1.20 B81-33346

269'.2 — Christian church. Evangelism
The Debate on evangelism : a study pamphlet. — London (146 Queen Victoria St., EC4V 4BX) : Nationwide Initiative in Evangelism, [1980?]. — 12p ; 21cm
Cover title
£0.25 (pbk) B81-20976

English, Donald. Closing address : delivered at the NIE National Assembly at Nottingham in September 1980 / by Donald English. — London (146 Queen Victoria St., EC4V 4BX) : Nationwide Initiative in Evangelism, [1981?]. — 7p ; 22cm
At head of title: Nationwide Initiative in Evangelism
£0.75 (£4.00 for 10 copies) (unbound)
B81-20825

Evangelism : convergence and divergence. — London (146 Queen Victoria St., EC4V 4BX) : Nationwide Initiative in Evangelism, 1980. — 39p ; 21cm
Cover title
£1.50 (pbk) B81-20977

McPhee, Arthur. Friendship evangelism / Arthur McPhee. — Eastbourne : Kingsway, 1980, c1978. — 149p ; 18cm
Originally published: Grand Rapids, Mich. : Zondervan, 1978
ISBN 0-86065-099-5 (pbk) : £1.35 B81-02268

269'.2 — Young persons. Evangelism by Salvation Army
Youth quest '81 : alive in Christ. — [London] ([c/o 117-121 Judd Street, WC1H 9NN]) : Arnold Brown, General of the Salvation Army, 1981. — 7p : ill(some col.),1col.map,ports(some col.) ; 32cm. — (An international war cry publication)
Unpriced (unbound) B81-29567

269'.2'05 — Christian church. Evangelism — *Serials*
WEF communications report / World Evangelical Fellowship. — Vol.1, issue 1 (1977)-. — Castel (Les Enurais de Bas, Castel, Guernsey, Channel Islands) : J. Langlois for the World Evangelical Fellowship Communications Commission, 1977-. — v. ; 30cm
Irregular. — Description based on: Vol.4, issue 2 (Apr.1980)
ISSN 0260-3691 = WEF communications report : Unpriced B81-15077

269'.2'060411 — Scotland. Christian church. Evangelism. Organisations: Scottish Evangelistic Council, *to 1980*
Scottish Evangelistic Council. Fifty years of evangelical witness : throughout Scotland 1930-1980 / by Scottish Evangelistic Council. — Glasgow (11 Bothwell St., Glasgow G2 6LY) : The Council, [1980?]. — 19p : ports ; 22cm
Cover title
£0.25 (pbk) B81-21159

269'.2'09034 — Christian church. Evangelism, *1806-1880*
Alexander, J. H.. More than notion / by J.H. Alexander ; illustrated by L.F. Lupton. — 2nd ed. — Ossett (44 Queen's Drive, Ossett, W. Yorkshire, WF5 0ND) : Zoar, 1976. — 284p : ill,1map,1geneal.table ; 19cm
Originally published: [London] : Fauconberg, 1965. — Previous ed.: 1964. — Map and genealogical table on inside covers. — Includes index
ISBN 0-904435-17-2 (pbk) : £2.00 B81-31855

269'.2'0924 — Christian church. Evangelism. Cooper, Howard — *Biographies*
Cooper, Howard. Miracles in Sin City / by Howard Cooper with Dan Wooding. — Evesham : James, 1981. — 171p ; 22cm
ISBN 0-85305-234-4 (pbk) : £1.95 : CIP rev.
B81-14465

269'.2'0924 — Christian church. Evangelism. Double, Don
Thomson, Eileen F. M.. It's a wonderful new life! : the Don Double story / Eileen F.M. Thomson. — Eastbourne : Kingsway, 1981. — 192p ; 18cm
ISBN 0-86065-141-x (pbk) : £1.75 B81-27487

269'.2'0924 — Christian church. Evangelism. Laird, John — *Biographies*
Laird, John. No mere chance / John Laird. — London : Hodder and Stoughton, c1981. — 191p ; 22cm. — (Ecclesia books)
ISBN 0-340-26966-9 (pbk) : £5.50 : CIP rev.
B81-18032

269'.2'0924 — Christian church. Evangelism — *Personal observations*
Hews, Francis. Spoils won in the day of battle / by Francis Hews. — Ossett (44 Queen's Drive, Ossett, W. Yorkshire, WF5 0ND) : Gospel Tidings Publications, [1981?]. — 108p,[4]leaves of plates : ill,2maps ; 19cm
Originally published: Biggleswade ('Sandiacres', Potton Rd., Biggleswade, Beds.) : E.J. Woodcraft, [1981?]. — Maps on lining papers
£1.50 B81-31854

269'.2'0924 — Great Britain. Christian church. Evangelism. Organisations: Open-Air Mission — *Personal observations*
Jealous, Ernest W.. "How can these things be?" : further chapters from the continuing saga of the Open-Air mission's ministry in Great Britain / Ernest W. Jealous. — London (19 John St., WC1N 2DL) : Open-Air Mission, [1981]. — 48p ; 18cm
Unpriced (pbk) B81-26001

269'.2'0924 — Latin America. Christian church. Evangelism. Palau, Luis — *Biographies*
Palau, Luis. The Luis Palau story : an autobiography / as told to Jerry B. Jenkins. — London : Pickering, 1981. — 176p : ill,ports ; 21cm
Originally published: Old Tappan, N.J. : Revell, 1980. — Bibliography: p176
ISBN 0-7208-0490-6 (cased) : £4.50
ISBN 0-7208-0491-4 (pbk) : Unpriced
B81-16080

269'.2'0941 — Great Britain. Christian church. Evangelism. Jackopson, Vic — *Biographies*
Jackopson, Vic. From prison to pulpit. — London : Marshall Morgan & Scott, Sept.1981. — [128]p. — (Marshalls paperbacks)
ISBN 0-551-00916-0 (pbk) : £1.25 : CIP entry
B81-27904

269'.2'09676 — East Africa. Christian church. Revivals, *1928-1965* — *Personal observations*
Church, J. E.. Quest for the highest : an autobiographical account of the East African revival. — Exeter : Paternoster Press, Sept.1981. — [272]p
ISBN 0-85364-328-8 (pbk) : £4.80 : CIP entry
B81-22691

269'.24 — Christian church. Revivals
Ravenhill, Leonard. Why revival tarries / Leonard Ravenhill. — 2nd ed. — Bromley : STL Books, 1979. — 139p ; 19cm
Previous ed.: 1972
ISBN 0-903843-24-2 (pbk) : £1.15 B81-09254

269'.24 — United States. Methodist churches. Revivals, *1835-1885*
Dieter, Melvin Easterday. The holiness revival of the nineteenth century / by Melvin Easterday Dieter. — Metuchen, N.J. ; London : Scarecrow, 1980. — x,356p ; 23cm. — (Studies in evangelicalism ; no.1)
Bibliography: p296-344. - Includes index
ISBN 0-8108-1328-9 : £12.25 B81-04786

269'.24'0943 — Central Europe. Christian church. Revivals, *ca 1700-ca 1750*
Ward, W. R. (William Reginald). Power and piety : the origins of religious revival in the early eighteenth century / by W.R. Ward. — Manchester : John Rylands University Library of Manchester, 1980. — p231-252 ; 25cm
£1.25 (pbk) B81-35545

270 — CHRISTIAN CHURCH. HISTORICAL AND GEOGRAPHICAL TREATMENT

270 — Christian church, *325-1965*
Copestake, Reginald H.. How the church grew / by Reginald H. Copestake. — London : Mowbray, 1981. — 32p ; 15cm. — (Enquirer's library)
Bibliography: p31-32
ISBN 0-264-66755-7 (pbk) : £0.60 B81-17905

270 — Christian church, *ca 600-1500*
Boyle, Leonard E.. Pastoral care, clerical education and canon law, 1200-1400 / Leonard E. Boyle. — London : Variorum Reprints, 1981. — 361p in various pagings : 1facsim ; 24cm. — (Collected studies series ; 135)
Includes index
ISBN 0-86078-081-3 : £22.00 B81-15563

270 — Christian church. Growth — *Festschriften*
Grow or die : essays on church growth to mark the 900th anniversary of Winchester Cathedral / edited by Alexander Wedderspoon. — London : SPCK, 1981. — ix,141p ; 22cm
ISBN 0-281-03789-2 (pbk) : £3.95 B81-27896

270 — Christian church — *History*
History of the Church / edited by Hubert Jedin and John Dolan. — London : Burns & Oates
Vol.2: The Imperial Church from Constantine to the early Middle Ages / by Karl Baus ... [et al.] ; translated by Anselm Biggs. — 1980. — xvii,846p ; 24cm
Translation of: Handbuch der Kirchengeschichte. Bd.2. — Bibliography: p763-821. — Includes index
ISBN 0-86012-084-8 : Unpriced B81-25422

History of the Church / edited by Hubert Jedin and John Dolan. — London : Burns & Oates
Vol.7: The Church between revolution and restoration / by Roger Aubert ... [et al.] ; translated by Peter Becker. — 1981. — xx,426p ; 24cm
Translation of: Handbuch der Kirchengeschichte. Bd.6/1, 2. Aufl.. — Bibliography: p353-407. — Includes index
ISBN 0-86012-089-9 : Unpriced B81-25421

270 — Christian church, *to 1980* — *For schools*
What is the Christian Church? / [Schools Council Religious Education in Secondary Schools Project]. — St. Albans : Hart-Davis Educational, 1981. — 56p : ill(some col.),2col.maps,facsims,1col.plan,ports ; 30cm. — (Journeys into religion)
ISBN 0-247-12969-0 (unbound) : £1.50 B81-24467

270 — Desert Fathers — *Biographies* — *Early works*
[Historia monachorum in Aegypto. *English***]**. The lives of the desert fathers / translated by Norman Russell ; introduction by Benedicta Ward. — London : Mowbray, 1981, c1980. — 181p : 1map ; 23cm
Translation of: Historia monachorum in Aegypto. — Bibliography: p162-164.
Includes index
ISBN 0-264-66581-3 (cased) : £8.50 : CIP rev.
ISBN 0-264-66428-0 (pbk) : Unpriced B81-04262

270 — Saints — *Biographies*
Clarke, C. P. S.. Every man's book of saints : following the ASB Calendar / C.P.S. Clarke's original text revised and supplemented by Brother Kenneth. — London : Mowbray, 1981. — iii,188p ; 20cm
Includes index
ISBN 0-264-66556-2 (pbk) : £4.50 B81-40161

Williams, Caroline. Saints : their cults and origins / Caroline Williams. — London : Bergstrom, c1980. — 112p : ill(some col.) ; 21cm
Includes index
ISBN 0-903767-33-3 (cased) : £7.95
ISBN 0-903767-28-7 (pbk) : £4.95 B81-01672

270 — Saints — *Biographies* — *Early works*
Lives of the saints / translated with an introduction by J.F. Webb. — Harmondsworth : Penguin, 1965 (1981 [printing]). — 206p ; 18cm. — (Penguin classics)
Contents: The Voyage of St Brendan - Life of Cuthbert / Bede - Life of Wilfred / Eddins Stephenus
ISBN 0-14-044153-0 (pbk) : £1.50 B81-21028

270 — Saints — *Biographies* — *For children*
Ross Williamson, Hugh. [Sixty saints of Christendom]. A children's book of saints / by Hugh Ross Williamson ; illustrated by Sheila Connelly. — London : Harrap, 1960 (1981 [printing]). — 239p : ill ; 23cm
ISBN 0-245-53769-4 : £4.95 B81-28411

270.1 — Christian church, *to 337*
Bulloch, James. Pilate to Constantine / by James Bulloch. — Edinburgh : Saint Andrew Press, 1981. — v,350p ; 20cm
Bibliography: p335-342. — Includes index
ISBN 0-7152-0460-2 (cased) : Unpriced : CIP rev.
ISBN 0-7152-0453-x (pbk) : £3.50 B81-28228

270.1 — Christian church, *to 451*
Copestake, Reginald H.. How the Church began / Reginald H. Copestake. — London : Mowbray, 1981. — 32p ; 15cm. — (Enquirer's library)
Bibliography: p32
ISBN 0-264-66754-9 (pbk) : £0.60 B81-17908

270.1 — Christian church, *to ca 70* — *Irish texts*
Ó Duáin, Odhrán. An eaglais og / Odhrán Ó Duáin. — Baile Átha Cliath [i.e. Dublin] (29 Sráid Uí Chonaill Íoch Baile Átha Cliath 1) : Foilseacháin Náisiúnta, 1980. — 131p,[4]p of plates : ill,2col.maps ; 20cm
Maps on lining papers
£2.50 B81-27084

270.1'092'4 — Christian church. Catherine, *of Alexandria, Saint* — *Biographies* — *Early works*
[Bodleian Library. Manuscript. MS Bodley 34]. Seinte Katerine : re-edited from MS Bodley 34 and other manuscripts / S.R.T.O. d'Ardenne and E.J. Dobson. — Oxford : Published for the Early English Text Society by the Oxford University Press, 1981. — xlix,347p,[2]leaves of plates : 2facsims ; 23cm. — (Early English Text Society. S.S. ; 7)
Text in English, Middle English and Latin. — Includes index
ISBN 0-19-722407-5 : £17.50 : CIP rev. B81-16395

270.2'092'4 — Christian church. Augustine, *Saint, Bishop of Hippo* — *Biographies*
Bentley-Taylor, David. Augustine : wayward genius / by David Bentley-Taylor. — London : Hodder and Stoughton, 1980. — 272p ; 18cm. — (Hodder Christian paperbacks)
Includes index
ISBN 0-340-25834-9 (pbk) : £1.95 : CIP rev. B80-24004

270.2'092'4 — Christian church. Piran, *Saint* — *Biographies*
Webb, Brian, *19---*. Kemysk Sen Perran = A St Piran miscellany / by Brian Webb. — Kernewek : Cowethas an yeth, 1981. — 19p : ill ; 21cm
English and Cornish text
Unpriced (pbk) B81-20972

270.3'092'4 — Christian church. Wistan, *Saint.* **Local associations: England. Midlands**
Weston, Stephen, *1948-*. St. Wistan : our local saint : his connection with Wistow, Wigston Magna, Repton, Bretby and Evesham / by Stephen Weston. — [Leicester] ([32 Burleigh Ave., Wigston Magna, Leicester]) : S. Weston, [1981?]. — iii,32p ; 21cm
Bibliography: p32
£1.00 (pbk) B81-11362

270.6 — Christian church, *ca 1500-ca 1700*
Birkin, John L.. The Sardis Church age : reformation or restoration / [John L. Birkin]. — [Caerphilly] ([40 Alexander Court, Lansbury Park, Caerphilly, M. Glam, CF8 1RJ]) : [J.L. Birkin], [c1981]. — iv,59p ; 21cm. — (A Study in the restoration of the Church ; no.8)
Cover title. — At head of title: The mystery of God shall be finished
£0.90 (pbk) B81-32619

270.6'092'4 — Christian church. Luther, Martin — *Biographies*
Todd, John M.. Luther. — London : H. Hamilton, Feb.1982. — [288]p
ISBN 0-241-10703-2 : £15.00 : CIP entry B81-35793

270.8'2 — Christian church. Ecumenical movement
Brockett, Lorna J. M.. The development of the ecumenical movement / by Lorna J.M. Brockett. — [London] ([2 Chester House, Pages La., N10 1PR]) : Christian Education Movement in collaboration with the Roehampton Institute of Higher Education, [1981]. — 58p ; 21cm. — (CEM student theology series)
Bibliography: p57-58
ISBN 0-905022-71-8 (pbk) : Unpriced B81-26138

270.8'28 — Christian church. Charismatic movement
Rahner, Karl. The spirit in the Church / Karl Rahner. — London : Burns & Oates, 1979. — 104p ; 22cm
Translation of: Erfahrung des Geistes
ISBN 0-86012-068-6 (pbk) : £2.25 B81-16086

270.8'28 — Great Britain. Christian church. Ecumenical movement — *British Council of Churches viewpoints*
Unity - why not yet? : a guide to the present situation in the search for Christian unity in Britain / by members of the Board of the Division of Ecumenical Affairs, British Council of Churches. — [London] : The Division, 1980. — 48p ; 21cm
ISBN 0-85169-080-7 (pbk) : £1.75 B81-09844

271 — CHRISTIAN CHURCH HISTORY. RELIGIOUS CONGREGATIONS AND ORDERS

271'.0092'4 — Greece. Mount Athos. Monasteries. Community life — *Personal observations* — *Correspondence, diaries, etc.*
Pennington, M. Basil. O holy mountain! : journal of a retreat on Mount Athos / M. Basil Pennington. — London : Chapman, c1979. — xx,291p : ill,1map ; 23cm
ISBN 0-225-66271-x : £7.50 : CIP rev. B80-06766

271'.1'024 — Benedictines. Benedict, *Saint* — *Biographies*
O'Donovan, Patrick. Benedict of Nursia / Patrick O'Donovan ; colour photographs by Helmut Nils Loose. — London : Collins, 1980. — 45p,[50]p of plates : col.ill ; 25cm
Translation of: Benedikt von Nursia. — Includes index
ISBN 0-00-216193-1 : £5.95 B81-01793

271'.1'041 — Great Britain. Benedictines, *to 1980*
British LibraryThe Benedictines in Britain. — London : British Library, c1980. — 111p,[4]p of plates : ill(some col.),facsims,ports ; 24cm. — (British Library series ; no.3)
Published to accompany an exhibition at the British Library, 1980. — Bibliography: p103
ISBN 0-904654-47-8 (cased) : £6.95 : CIP rev.
ISBN 0-904654-43-5 (pbk) : 3.75 B80-09062

271'.1'044361 — France. Paris. Abbeys. St. Germain des Prés. Community life, *1600-1700*
Ultee, Maarten. The abbey of St Germain des Prés in the seventeenth century. — London : Yale University Press, Oct.1981. — [224]p
ISBN 0-300-02562-9 : £14.00 : CIP entry B81-32085

271'.12'024 — Cistercians. Tansi, Michael Iwene — *Biographies*
Isichei, Elizabeth. Entirely for God : the life of Michael Iwene Tansi / Elizabeth Isichei. — London : Macmillan, 1980. — xii,132p,[4]p of plates : ill,ports ; 22cm
Includes index
ISBN 0-333-28504-2 (pbk) : £1.60 B81-24204

271'.125'024 — Trappists. Merton, Thomas — *Biographies*
Furlong, Monica. Merton : a biography / Monica Furlong. — London : Collins, 1980. — xx,342p,[8]p of plates : ill,ports ; 22cm
Includes index
ISBN 0-00-211867-x (corrected) : £6.95 B81-04719

271'.3'024 — Franciscans. Francis, *of Assisi, Saint*
The Francis book : 800 years with the Saint from Assisi / compiled and edited by Roy M. Gasnick. — New York : Collier ; London : Collier Macmillan, c1980. — x,211p : ill ; 29cm
ISBN 0-02-542760-1 (cased) : Unpriced
ISBN 0-02-003200-5 (pbk) : £4.95 B81-38657

271'.3'024 — Franciscans. Francis, *of Assisi, Saint — Biographies — Early works*
Bonaventure, *Saint.* [Itinerarium mentis in deum. English]. The soul's journey into God ; The tree of life ; The life of St. Francis / Bonaventure ; translation and introduction by Ewert Cousins ; prefaces by Ignatius Brady. — London : SPCK, c1978. — 353p ; 23cm. — (The Classics of Western spirituality)
Originally published: New York : Paulist Press, 1978. — Bibliography: p329-333. - Includes index
ISBN 0-281-03650-0 (pbk) : £6.50
Primary classification 242 B81-06017

271'.3'024 — Franciscans. Paschal, *Brother — Biographies*
Conlan, Patrick. A true Franciscan — Br Paschal / Patrick Conlan. — [S.l.] : [S.n.] ; Gormanston (Franciscan College, Gormanston, Co. Meath) : Distributed by P. Lane, c1978. — 64p : ill,ports ; 21cm
Text on inside covers
£0.40 (pbk) B81-25917

271'.38 — Order of Secular Franciscans, *to 1980*
Conlan, Patrick. Secular Franciscans down the ages : a brief history of the Third Order from the time of Saint Francis in Ireland and in the world / Patrick Conlan. — Ennis (c/o Franciscan Friary Ennis, Co. Clare) : Secular Franciscans, c1979. — 28p : ill,1map,1facsim,ports ; 21cm
Map on cover
£0.50 (pbk) B81-25208

271'.4'042 — England. Augustinians. Distribution, *to 1540*
Robinson, David M. (David Martin). The geography of Augustinian settlement in medieval England and Wales / David M. Robinson. — Oxford : B.A.R., 1980. — 2v.(xx,547p) : ill,maps ; 30cm. — (BAR. British series, ISSN 0143-3032 ; 80)
Bibliography: p519-534. — Includes index
ISBN 0-86054-093-6 (pbk) : £17.00 B81-36638

271'.53 — Jesuits, *to 1980*
Aveling, J. C. H.. The Jesuits / J.C.H. Aveling. — London : Blond & Briggs, 1981. — 390p,[1] leaf of plates : 1port ; 24cm
Bibliography: p373-384. — Includes index
ISBN 0-85634-110-x : £16.95 B81-14298

271'.62'024 — Passionists. Spencer, *Father — Biographies*
Walsh, Brendan. Father Spencer / Brendan Walsh. — London : Catholic Truth Society, 1981. — 12p ; 18cm
ISBN 0-85183-432-9 (pbk) : £0.30 B81-31971

271'.7 — Salvatorians, *to 1981*
First hundred years : Society of the Divine Saviour 1881-1981 / Salvatorians. — [Abbots Langley] ([c/o Fr. Edmund Lanning, Breakspear College, Abbots Langley, Watford, Herts. WD5 3DT]) : [Salvatorians], [1981]. — 20p : ill(some col.),maps,ports ; 22cm
Cover title. — Ill on inside covers
Unpriced (pbk) B81-29503

271'.79 — Knights of Malta, *to 1971*
Bradford, Ernle. The shield and the sword : the Knights of St. John / Ernle Bradford. — London : Hodder and Stoughton, 1981, c1972. — 245p : ill,maps,ports ; 22cm
Bibliography: p233-234. — Includes index
ISBN 0-340-27127-2 (pbk) : £4.95 : CIP rev. B81-13854

271'.79 — Templars *(Order of chivalry), to 1314*
Howarth, Stephen. The Knights Templar. — London : Collins, Jan.1982. — [256]p
ISBN 0-00-216452-3 : £8.95 : CIP entry B81-33974

271'.8 — Egypt. Sinai. Monasteries: Monastery of Saint Catherine
Galey, John. Sinai : and the monastery of St. Catherine / John Galey ; introduction George H. Forsyth, Kurt Weitzmann. — London : Chatto & Windus, c1980. — 191p : col.ill,1map,col.facsims,2plans,col.ports ; 32cm
Translation of: Sinai. — Includes index
ISBN 0-7011-2547-0 : £16.00 : CIP rev. B80-24007

271'.97 — Faithful Companions of Jesus. Houet, *Madame d' — Biographies*
McCarren, Mary Campion. Faithful companion of Jesus : venerable Marie Madeleine Victoire de Bengy, Viscountess de Bonnault d'Houet 1781-1858, founderess of the Society of Sisters Faithful Companions of Jesus / by Mary Campion McCarren. — London : Catholic Truth Society, 1981. — 44p : 1map ; 19cm. — (CTS pamphlets ; B531)
ISBN 0-85183-401-9 (pbk) : £0.45 B81-19556

271'.97 — Zgromadznie Sióstr Matki Bożej Miłosierdzia. Faustyna, *Sióstr — Biographies — Polish texts*
Cegiełka, Franciszek Antoni. Siostra Faustyna : szafarka miłosierdzia bożego / Franciszek Antoni Cegiełka. — 2-gie wyd.. — London : Veritas, 1980. — 334p,[4]p of plates : ill,1port ; 19cm
Previous ed.: 1954
Unpriced (pbk) B81-17171

271'.971'024 — Carmelites. Teresa, *of Avila, Saint — Biographies*
Gallagher, John, *1911-.* Teresa of Avila / by John Gallagher. — London : Catholic Truth Society, 1981. — 16p ; 19cm
ISBN 0-85183-422-1 (pbk) : £0.35 B81-33113

271'.971'024 — Carmelites. Teresa, *of Avila, Saint — Correspondence, diaries, etc.*
Teresa, *of Avila, Saint.* The letters of St Teresa of Jesus / translated by E. Allison Peers. — London : Sheed and Ward, 1980. — 2v.(xiii,1006p) ; 22cm
Originally published: London : Burns, Oates & Washbourne, 1951. — Bibliography: pxiii. - Includes index
ISBN 0-7220-4921-8 (pbk) : £15.00 B81-07877

271'.971'024 — Carmelites. Thérèse, *de Lisieux, Saint — Biographies*
Hollings, Michael. Thérèse of Lisieux / Michael Hollings ; photographs by Helmut Nils Loose. — London : Collins, 1981. — 62p,[44]p of plates : ill(some col.),facsims,ports ; 24cm
ISBN 0-00-216798-0 : £6.95 B81-20790

271'.98 — Community of the Holy Rood, *to 1980*
Jean, *Sister.* God thorn / Sister Jean. — Bognor Regis : New Horizon, c1981. — 63p ; 21cm
ISBN 0-86116-560-8 : £3.95 B81-21896

272 — CHRISTIAN CHURCH HISTORY. PERSECUTIONS

272'.1 — Bible. N.T. Special subjects: Martyrdom
Suffering and martyrdom in the New Testament. — Cambridge : Cambridge University Press, June 1981. — [240]p
ISBN 0-521-23482-4 : £17.50 : CIP entry
Primary classification 231'.8 B81-19191

272'.1 — Christian Church. Persecution, *to 313*
Workman, Herbert B.. Persecution in the early Church / by Herbert B. Workman ; with a foreword by Michael Bourdeaux. — Oxford : Oxford University Press, 1980. — v,145p ; 20cm
Originally published: London : Kelly, 1906. — Bibliography: p144-145
ISBN 0-19-283025-2 (pbk) : £1.95 : CIP rev. B80-00559

272'.2 — Inquisition, *to 1542*
Hamilton, Bernard. The Medieval Inquisition / Bernard Hamilton. — London : Edward Arnold, 1981. — 111p : 1maps ; 22cm
Bibliography: p100-105. - Includes index
ISBN 0-7131-6251-1 (pbk) : £3.95 B81-16701

272'.6'0922 — England. Protestants: Martyrs, *1555-1556 — Biographies*
Ryle, J. C.. Five English reformers / J.C. Ryle. — Rev. ed. — Edinburgh : Banner of Truth Trust, 1981. — 156p ; 18cm
Previous ed.: 1960
ISBN 0-85151-138-4 (pbk) : £1.50 B81-36442

272'.8 — Scotland. Witches. Persecution, *1590-1700*
Larner, Christina. Enemies of God : the witch-hunt in Scotland / Christina Larner ; with a foreword by Norman Cohn. — London : Chatto & Windus, 1981. — x,244p : ill,maps ; 23cm
Bibliography: p229-235. — Includes index
ISBN 0-7011-2424-5 : £12.95 : CIP rev. B81-07440

272'.9 — Soviet Union. Christian Church. Persecution *— Personal observations — Collections*
Hartfeld, Hermann. Faith despite the KGB / Hermann Hartfeld. — London : Pickering & Inglis, 1981. — 248p ; 19cm
Translation of: Glaube trotz KGB. — Originally published: Chappaqua : Christian Herald, 1980
ISBN 0-7208-0499-x (pbk) : £2.50 B81-36922

273 — CHRISTIAN CHURCH HISTORY. DOCTRINAL CONTROVERSIES AND HERESIES

273'.4 — Christian church. Arian heresy. Role of Eusebius, *Bishop of Caesarea*
Luibhéid, Colm. Eusebius of Caesarea and the Arian crisis / Colm Luibheid. — Dublin : Irish Academic Press, c1978. — 128p ; 23cm
ISBN 0-7165-2277-2 : £8.50 B81-05009

273'.6'094 — Western Europe. Christian church. Heresies, *ca 900-1500 — Readings from contemporary sources*
Heresy and authority in medieval Europe : documents in translation / edited, with an introduction, by Edward Peters. — London : Scolar Press, 1980. — viii,312p ; 24cm
Translations from Latin. — Originally published: Philadelphia : University of Pennsylvania Press, 1980. — Bibliography: p9-11
ISBN 0-85967-621-8 : £12.50 : CIP rev. B80-17553

274 — CHRISTIAN CHURCH. EUROPE

274 — Europe. Christian church. Radical movements, *1500-1760*
Mullett, Michael A.. Radical religious movements in early modern Europe / Michael A. Mullett. — London : Allen & Unwin, 1980. — xxiii,193p ; 23cm. — (Early modern Europe today)
Bibliography: p153-186. — Includes index
ISBN 0-04-901028-x : £10.00 : CIP rev. B80-18164

274'.04 — Europe. Christian church, *1124-1521*
From the high Middle Ages to the eve of the Reformation / by Hans-Georg Beck ... [et al.] ; translated by Anselm Biggs. — London : Burns & Oates, 1980. — xxiv,776p ; 25cm. — (History of the Church ; v.4)
Translation of: Vom kirchlichen Hochmittelalter bis zum Vorabend der Reformation. — Bibliography: p627-748. - Includes index
ISBN 0-86012-086-4 : £25.00 B81-09616

274'.05 — Europe. Christian church, *1250-1550*
Ozment, Steven E.. The age of reform. — London : Yale University Press, Nov.1981. — [472]p
ISBN 0-300-02760-5 (pbk) : £6.25 : CIP entry B81-34957

274'.0828 — Europe. Christian church. Ecumenical movement *— Conference proceedings*
Conference of European Churches. *Assembly (8th : 1979 : Crete).* Unity in the spirit : diversity in the churches / the report of the Conference of European Churches, Assembly VIII, 18th-25th October 1979, Crete. — Geneva : The Conference ; Edinburgh : Saint Andrew Press [distributor], [1979?]. — 337p ; 24cm
ISBN 2-88070-003-5 (pbk) : Unpriced B81-13327

274.1'06'0922 — Great Britain. Christian church. Reformation — *Biographies*

Coxon, Francis. Christian worthies / by Francis Coxon. — Ossett (44 Queens Drive, Ossett, W. Yorks. WF5 0ND) : Zoar Publications. — 262p : ill,ports ; 22cm
ISBN 0-904435-39-3 : £7.50 B81-31783

274.1'0828 — Great Britain. Christian church. Community churches — *Case studies — For children*

Palmer, Gwen. Visiting a Community church / Gwen Palmer ; photography Keith Huggett ; illustration-design Judy Billson. — Guildford : Lutterworth Educational, 1981. — 60p : 1plan ; 21cm
Bibliography: p48. — Includes index
ISBN 0-7188-2471-7 (pbk) : £1.60 B81-14302

274.1'0828'05 — Great Britain. Christian church. Evangelicalism — *Serials*

Ship of fools. — 1-. — London (17a Grosvenor Rd, W7 1HP) : [Fool Press], [1977]-. — v. : ill ; 21cm
Three issues yearly. — Description based on: 5
ISSN 0260-292x = Ship of fools : £2.20 per year B81-04437

274.15 — Ireland. Saints

Montague, Patrick. The saints and martyrs of Ireland. — Gerrards Cross : Colin Smythe, Sept.1981. — [160]p
ISBN 0-86140-106-9 (cased) : £6.50 : CIP entry
ISBN 0-86140-107-7 (pbk) : £2.50 B81-21592

274.2 — England. Christian church, *871-1204 — Readings from contemporary sources*

Councils & synods with other documents relating to the English church. — Oxford : Clarendon Press
1: 871-1204. — Oct.1981. — [1230]p
ISBN 0-19-822394-3 : £48.00 : CIP entry B81-25745

274.2 — England. Christian church, *to 1540*

Edwards, David L.. Christian England : its story to the Reformation / David L. Edwards. — London : Collins, 1981. — 351p : ill ; 24cm
Includes bibliographies and index
ISBN 0-00-215212-6 : £7.95 B81-05041

274.2'02 — England. Christian church, *634-780*

Gallyon, Margaret. The early church in Wessex and Mercia / by Margaret Gallyon. — Lavenham : Terence Dalton, 1980. — x,110p,[8]p of plates : ill,1map,2facsims ; 23cm
Map on lining papers. — Bibliography: p108. - Inlcudes index
ISBN 0-900963-58-1 : £4.95 B81-05640

274.25'305 — Lincolnshire. Christian church, *1100-1500*

Owen, Dorothy M.. Church and society in medieval Lincolnshire / by Dorothy M. Owen. — Lincoln (47 Newland, Lincoln) : History of Lincolnshire Committee for the Society of Lincolnshire History and Archaeology, 1971, (1981 [printing]). — xxii,170p,[9]p of plates : ill,maps,2facsims ; 23cm. — (History of Lincolnshire ; v.5)
Bibliography: pxvii-xx. — Includes index
ISBN 0-902668-13-7 (pbk) : £5.95 B81-32747

274.25'4202 — Leicestershire. Leicester region. Christian church, *653-814*

Bailey, Richard N.. The early Christian church in Leicester and its region / by Richard N. Bailey. — [Leicester] : University of Leicester, Department of Adult Education, 1980. — 25p ; 22cm. — (Vaughan paper, ISSN 0308-9258 ; no.25)
ISBN 0-901507-18-0 (pbk) : Unpriced B81-05876

274.26'0092'2 — East Anglia. Fens. Saints, *650-1076*

Bevis, Trevor A.. Fenland saints and shrines and associated places / Trevor Bevis. — March (150 Burrowmoor Rd., March, Cambs., PE15 9SS) : T.A. Bevis, c1981. — 22p : ill,1map ; 21cm
ISBN 0-901680-15-x (pbk) : £1.50 B81-37989

274.3'06 — Germany. Christian church. Reformation — *German texts — Early works — Facsimiles*

Luther, Martin. Martin Luther Eyn Ratschlag 1526 = Martin Luther's Counsel 1526 / translation, with an introduction and notes by Helga Robinson-Hammerstein. — Dublin (College St., Dublin 2) : The Friends of the Library, Trinity College, 1980. — [9]p ; 21cm
German text, English translation. — Facsim of: ed. published Augsburg : s.n., 1526. — English translation (11p) in pocket
ISBN 0-904720-03-9 (pbk) : Unpriced B81-15177

274.3'06 — Germany. Christian church. Reformation. Role of propaganda

Scribner, R. W.. For the sake of simple folk : popular propaganda for the German Reformation. — Cambridge : Cambridge University Press, Nov.1981. — [298]p. — (Cambridge studies in oral and literate culture ; 2)
ISBN 0-521-24192-8 : £25.00 : CIP entry B81-31259

274.3'06 — Germany. Christian church. Reformation, *to 1540*

Oberman, Heiko Augustinus. Masters of the Reformation : the emergence of a new intellectual climate in Europe / Heiko Augustinus Oberman ; translated by Dennis Martin. — Cambridge : Cambridge University Press, 1981. — xiii,369 : 1map ; 24cm
Rev. and abridged translation of: Werden und Wertung der Reformation. — Bibliography: p307-348. — Includes index
ISBN 0-521-23098-5 : £22.50 B81-25536

274.3'06'0922 — Germany. Christian church. Reformation, *1560-1600 — Biographies*

Shapers of religious traditions in Germany, Switzerland, and Poland, 1560-1600 / edited with an introduction by Jill Raitt ; foreword by Robert M. Kingdon. — New Haven ; London : Yale University Press, c1981. — xx,224p ; 25cm
Includes index
ISBN 0-300-02457-6 : £15.75 : CIP rev.
Also classified at 274.94'06'0922 ; 274.38'06'0922 B81-23798

274.3'0823 — Germany. Christian church, *1933-1945 — Readings from contemporary sources*

The **Third** Reich and the Christian Churches / edited by Peter Matheson. — Edinburgh : T. & T. Clark, 1981. — viii,103p ; 21cm
Translations from the German
ISBN 0-567-29105-7 (pbk) : £2.95 B81-28262

274.38'06'0922 — Poland. Christian church. Reformation, *1560-1600 — Biographies*

Shapers of religious traditions in Germany, Switzerland, and Poland, 1560-1600 / edited with an introduction by Jill Raitt ; foreword by Robert M. Kingdon. — New Haven ; London : Yale University Press, c1981. — xx,224p ; 25cm
Includes index
ISBN 0-300-02457-6 : £15.75 : CIP rev.
Primary classification 274.3'06'0922 B81-23798

274.94'06'0922 — Switzerland. Christian church. Reformation, *1560-1600 — Biographies*

Shapers of religious traditions in Germany, Switzerland, and Poland, 1560-1600 / edited with an introduction by Jill Raitt ; foreword by Robert M. Kingdon. — New Haven ; London : Yale University Press, c1981. — xx,224p ; 25cm
Includes index
ISBN 0-300-02457-6 : £15.75 : CIP rev.
Primary classification 274.3'06'0922 B81-23798

275 — CHRISTIAN CHURCH. ASIA

275.19'0828 — Korea. Christian church *expounded by* **Bible. N.T. Matthew**

Pattisson, Peter R. M.. Crisis unawares : a doctor examines the Korean church / Peter R.M. Pattisson. — Sevenoaks : O.M.F. Books, 1981. — 270p : 1map ; 21cm
ISBN 0-85363-135-2 (pbk) : Unpriced B81-25568

277 — CHRISTIAN CHURCH. NORTH AMERICA

277.88'081 — Colorado. Gold mining communities. Christian church. Role, *1858-1870*

Cochran, Alice Cowan. Miners, merchants, and missionaries : the roles of missionaries and pioneer churches in the Colorado gold rush and its aftermath, 1858-1870 / by Alice Cowan Cochran. — Metuchen ; London : Scarecrow, 1980. — xi,287p ; 23cm. — (ATLA monograph series ; no.15)
Bibliography: p248-276. — Includes index
ISBN 0-8108-1325-4 : £10.50 B81-09568

280 — CHRISTIAN CHURCH. DENOMINATIONS AND SECTS

280'.092'4 — Christian church. Elliot, Elisabeth — *Biographies*

Elliot, Elisabeth. Love has a price tag / Elizabeth Elliot. — London : Pickering & Inglis, 1980, c1979. — vii,148p ; 21cm
Originally published: Chappaqua : Christian Herald Books, 1979
ISBN 0-7208-0466-3 (pbk) : £1.95 B81-01769

280'.092'4 — Christian church. Malz, Betty — *Biographies*

Malz, Betty. My glimpse of eternity. — London : Hodder & Stoughton, Feb.1982. — [128]p
ISBN 0-340-22816-4 (pbk) : £1.50 : CIP entry B81-35688

280'.2 — Catholic churches. Holy fools

Saward, John. Perfect fools : folly for Christ's sake in Catholic and orthodox spirituality / John Saward. — Oxford : Oxford University Press, 1980. — xii,247p ; 23cm
Includes index
ISBN 0-19-213230-x : £9.95 : CIP rev. B80-12720

280'.4 — East Sussex. Eastbourne. Nonconformist churches. Cavendish Place Chapel *(Eastbourne), to 1979*

Cavendish Place Chapel *(Eastbourne)*. In season out of season : the story of Cavendish Place Chapel Eastbourne / compiled and written by B.B. Knopp, ; cover sketch by Ruth Tourle. — [Eastbourne] ([c/o 66 Royal Sussex Crescent, Eastbourne BN20 8RH]) : [The Chapel], 1980. — 28p : ports ; 21cm
Unpriced (pbk) B81-14025

281 — CHRISTIAN CHURCH. PRIMITIVE AND ORIENTAL CHURCHES

281.9'09'02 — Orthodox Eastern churches, *to 1400 — French texts*

Gouillard, Jean. La vie religieuse à Byzance / Jean Gouillard. — London : Variorum Reprints, 1981. — 363p in various pagings : 1port ; 24cm. — (Collected studies series ; 131)
Includes index
ISBN 0-86078-077-5 : £22.00 B81-15564

281.9'092'2 — Great Britain. Orthodox Eastern churches. Saints — *Biographies*

Bond, Andrew. Saints of the British Isles / Andrew Bond and Nicolas Mabin. — Bognor Regis : New Horizon, c1980. — 157p,[6]p of plates : ill ; 22cm
Bibliography: p154-155
ISBN 0-86116-540-3 : £4.25 B81-21710

281.9'092'4 — Russkaia pravoslavnaia 'tserkov'. Skobtsova, Maria — *Biographies*

Hackel, Sergei. [One of great price]. Pearl of great price. — London : Darton, Longman & Todd, Nov.1981. — [176]p
Originally published: 1965
ISBN 0-232-51540-9 (pbk) : £3.75 : CIP entry B81-30268

281.9'3 — Syrian Orthodox Church, *to 1980*

Joseph, Rebecca. The sceptre of Jacob / Rebecca Joseph. — Bognor Regis : New Horizon, c1979. — 99p : 2ill ; 21cm
ISBN 0-86116-290-0 : £2.50
ISBN 0-86116-159-9 B81-27642

281.9′41′05 — Great Britain. Orthodox Eastern churches — *History — Serials*
Ekklēsia kai thèologia : ekklēsiastikē kai thèologikē èpètēris tēs Hièras Archièpiskopēs Thyatèirōn kai Mègalēs Brètannias. — T.1 (1980)-. — London (Thyateira House, 5 Craven Hill, W2) : [Archbishopric of Thyateira and Great Britain], 1980-. — v. ; 24cm
Annual. — Text in Greek and English
ISSN 0260-5678 = Ekklēsia kai thèologia : £10.00 B81-06678

281.9′41′05 — Great Britain. Orthodox Eastern churches — *Serials*
Orthodoxy in Britain. — No.1-. — [London] ([243 Regent St., WIR 8PN]) : [Saint George Orthodox Information Service], [197-?]-. — v. ; 27cm
Irregular. — Description based on: No.2
ISSN 0260-0692 = Orthodoxy in Britain : Unpriced B81-06142

281.9′421′05 — Russkaīa pravoslavnaīa ts͡erkov. *London Russian Orthodox Parish.* **Parish life** — *Serials*
[The Shepherd *(London : 1980)***]The Shepherd** : pastoral letter of the London Russian Orthodox Parish. — No.1 (Sunday 2nd/15th June 1980)-. — London (14 St. Dunstan′s Rd, Barons Court, W6) : [Parish of Saint Gregory the Dialogist], 1980-. — v. ; 30cm
Fortnightly
Unpriced B81-04870

282 — CATHOLIC CHURCH

282 — Catholic Church
Bogan, Robert. 4,000,000,000 / [a summary by Robert Bogan of the Encyclical Redemptor Hominis of His Holiness Pope John Paul II]. — London : Catholic Truth Society, [1980?]. — 24p ; 21cm
ISBN 0-85183-271-7 (pbk) : £0.30 B81-09345

Coomaraswamy, Rama P.. The destruction of the Christian tradition. — London : Perennial Books ; Wellingborough : Thorsons [distributor], May 1981. — [228]p
ISBN 0-900588-20-9 (pbk) : £6.95 : CIP entry B81-12310

Newman, Jeremiah. Balance in the Church / Jeremiah Newman. — [Dublin] ([3 Serpentine Ave., Dublin 4]) : Four Courts Press, 1980. — 75p ; 22cm
ISBN 0-906127-39-4 : £5.00 B81-02486

Nichols, Peter, *1928-*. The Pope′s divisions : the Roman Catholic Church today / Peter Nichols. — London : Faber, 1981. — 382p ; 24cm
Includes index
ISBN 0-571-11740-6 : £10.00 B81-13038

Schillebeeckx, Edward. The mission of the church / Edward Schillebeeckx. — London : Sheed and Ward, 1973 (1981 [printing]). — vii,244p ; 22cm
Translation of: De zending van de kerk. — Includes index
ISBN 0-7220-5511-0 (pbk) : £7.50 B81-15727

282 — Catholic Church. Relations with Church of England, *1530-1973*
Pawley, Bernard. Rome and Canterbury through four centuries. — Updated and rev. ed. — London : Mowbray, Nov.1981. — [416]p
Previous ed.: 1974
ISBN 0-264-66415-9 (pbk) : £4.75 : CIP entry
Also classified at 283′.42 B81-30186

282′.03′21 — Catholic Church — *Encyclopaedias*
Hardon, John A.. Modern Catholic dictionary / John A. Hardon. — London : Hale, 1981, c1980. — xiii,619p ; 24cm
ISBN 0-7091-9381-5 : £10.95 B81-40934

282′.05 — Catholic Church. Archives — *Serials*
Catholic archives : the journal of the Catholic Archives Society. — No.1 (1981)-. — [Oxford] ([c/o Miss M. Kuhn-Regnier, 4 Polstead Rd, Oxford OX2 6TN]) : The society, [1981]-. — v. : ill,ports ; 21cm
Annual
ISSN 0261-4316 = Catholic archives : £2.00 per year B81-37246

282′.05 — Catholic Church — *Conference proceedings — Serials*
National Conference of Priests. Report of ... National Conference of Priests. — 11th 1980. — [s.l.] : The Conference, [1980]. — 12p
Unpriced B81-09185

282′.09 — Catholic Church. Relations with Anglican churches, *to 1980*
De Satgé, John. Peter and the single Church / John de Satgé. — London : S.P.C.K., 1981. — x,182p ; 22cm
Includes index
ISBN 0-281-03819-8 (pbk) : £4.95
Also classified at 283′.09 B81-35517

282′.092′2 — Popes — *Biographies*
Walsh, Brendan. The Popes from St Peter to John Paul II / revised by Brendan Walsh. — London : Catholic Truth Society, 1979. — 27p ; 19cm
ISBN 0-85183-220-2 (pbk) : £0.35 B81-39018

282′.092′4 — Catholic Church. Bea, Augustin — *Biographies*
Purdy, W. A.. Cardinal Bea / by William Purdy. — London : Catholic Truth Society, 1981. — 17p ; 17cm
ISBN 0-85183-430-2 (pbk) : Unpriced B81-36476

282′.092′4 — Catholic Church. Catherine, *of Siena, Saint — Biographies*
Maris Stella, *Sister*. Catherine : reflections and prayers / Sister Maris Stella OP. — Dublin (St Saviour′s, Dublin 1) : Dominican Publications, [1981?]. — vii,37p ; 16cm
ISBN 0-907271-05-7 (pbk) : Unpriced B81-26316

282′.092′4 — Catholic Church. Challoner, Richard — *Biographies*
Challoner and his church. — London : Darton, Longman & Todd, Oct.1981. — [192]p
ISBN 0-232-51527-1 : £10.00 : CIP entry B81-26791

282′.092′4 — Catholic Church. FitzRalph, Richard — *Biographies*
Walsh, Katherine. A fourteenth-century scholar and primate : Richard FitzRalph in Oxford, Avignon and Armagh / by Katherine Walsh. — Oxford : Clarendon, 1981. — xviii,518p,[1] leaf of plates : 1facsim ; 23cm
Bibliography: p476-499. — Includes index
ISBN 0-19-822637-3 : £25.00 : CIP rev. B81-20540

282′.092′4 — Catholic Church. Innocent III, *Pope — Biographies*
Tillmann, Helene. Pope Innocent III / by Helene Tillmann ; translated by Walter Sax. — Amsterdam ; Oxford : North-Holland, 1980. — xviii,374p ; 23cm. — (Europe in the Middle Ages ; v.12)
Translation of: Papst Innocenz III. — Bibliography: pxi-xviii. — Includes index
ISBN 0-444-85137-2 : Unpriced B81-39352

282′.092′4 — Catholic Church. John Paul II, *Pope, 1979-1980 — Polish texts*
Nowakowski, Tadeusz. Reporter Papieża / Tadeusz Nowakowski. — Londyn : Polska Fundacja Kulturalna, 1980. — 248p : 1port ; 22cm
Unpriced (pbk) B81-11512

282′.092′4 -- Catholic Church. John Paul II, *Pope, 1980 — Biographies*
Hebblethwaite, Peter. The papal year / Peter Hebblethwaite. — London : Chapman, 1981. — 127p : ill,ports ; 25cm
ISBN 0-225-66297-3 (pbk) : Unpriced : CIP rev. B80-30751

282′.092′4 — Catholic Church. John Paul II, *Pope — Biographies*
Maliński, Mieczysław. Pope John Paul II : the life of my friend Karol Wojtyla / by M. Malinski ; translated by P.S. Falla. — London : Burns & Oates, 1979. — 283p,[11]p of plates : ill,1facsim, ports ; 23cm
Translation from the Polish. — Includes index
ISBN 0-86012-074-0 : £6.95 B81-03892

282′.092′4 — Catholic Church. Pio, *Padre — Biographies*
Ingoldsby, Mary F.. Padre Pio : his life and mission / Mary F. Ingoldsby. — Dublin : Veritas, 1978. — xvi,175p ; 22cm
ISBN 0-905092-64-3 (pbk) : £2.50 B81-02805

O′Donovan, Patrick. Padre Pio / [by Patrick O′Donovan]. — London : Catholic Truth Society, 1979. — 11p : col.ill,1col.port ; 19cm
£0.25 (pbk) B81-40658

282′.092′4 — Catholic Church. Postgate, Nicholas, *1599?-1679 — Biographies*
Hamilton, Elizabeth, *1906-*. The priest of the moors : reflections on Nicholas Postgate / Elizabeth Hamilton ; foreword by Cardinal Hume. — London : Darton, Longman & Todd, 1980. — x,86p,[4]p of plates : ill, ; 20cm 1map,1facsim
Includes index
ISBN 0-232-51498-4 (pbk) : £2.60 B81-12104

282′.092′4 — Catholic Church. Southworth, John, *Saint — Biographies*
Anstruther, Godfrey. Saint John Southworth : priest and martyr / Godfrey Anstruther. — London : Catholic Truth Society, 1981. — 14p ; 19cm
ISBN 0-85183-393-4 (pbk) : £0.25 B81-15176

282′.092′4 — Catholic Church. Teilhard de Chardin, Pierre. Works — *Critical studies*
Faricy, Robert. All things in Christ : Teilhard de Chardin′s spitituality / Robert Faricy. — London : Collins : Fount, 1981. — 126p ; 20cm
Bibliography: p110-112
ISBN 0-00-626351-8 (pbk) : £2.50 B81-17814

282′.092′4 — El Salvador. San Salvador. Catholic Church. Romero, Oscar Arnulfo. Assassination
Keogh, Dermot. Romero : El Salvador′s martyr : a study of the tragedy of El Salvador / Dermot Keogh. — Dublin (St Saviour′s, Dublin 1) : Dominican Publications, 1981. — v,160p : ill,2maps ; 19cm
Bibliography: p148-150
ISBN 0-907271-03-0 (pbk) : Unpriced B81-26317

282′.092′4 — England. Catholic Church. Newman, John Henry — *Biographies*
Dessain, Charles Stephen. John Henry Newman / Charles Stephen Dessain. — 3rd ed. — Oxford : Oxford University Press, 1980. — xii,180p ; 20cm. — (Oxford paperbacks. Religion)
Previous ed.: London : A. & C. Black, 1971. — Bibliography: p170-176. — Includes index
ISBN 0-19-281306-4 (pbk) : £2.95 B81-08131

282′.092′4 — England. Catholic Church. Roger, *Bishop of Worcester — Biographies*
Cheney, Mary G.. Roger, Bishop of Worcester 1164-1179 / Mary G. Cheney. — Oxford : Clarendon Press, 1980. — xvi,397p,[2]p of plates : 1 ill,1facsim ; 23cm. — (Oxford historical monographs)
Includes the texts in Latin of documents issued by Bishop Roger. — Bibliography: pix-xvi. — Includes index
ISBN 0-19-821879-6 : £20.00 B81-17788

282′.092′4 — England. Catholic Church. Tyrrell, George — *Correspondence, diaries, etc*
Tyrrell, George. Letters from a ″modernist″ : the letters of George Tyrrell to Wilfred Ward, 1893-1908 / introduced and annotated by Mary Jo Weaver. — Shepherdstown : Patmos ; London : Sheed and Ward, c1981. — xxxiv,192p ; 23cm
Bibliography: p172-185. — Includes index
ISBN 0-7220-4917-x : £17.50 B81-27704

282′.092′4 — England. Catholic Church. White, Antonia — *Correspondence, diaries, etc*
White, Antonia. The hound and the falcon : the story of a reconversion to the Catholic faith / Antonia White ; new introduction by Sara Maitland. — London : Virago, 1980. — xx,171p ; 20cm
Originally published: London : Longmans, 1965
ISBN 0-86068-172-6 (pbk) : £2.50 B81-01812

282′.092′4 — Italy. Catholic Church. Orione, Luigi — *Biographies*

Don Orione : father of the poor. — London : Catholic Truth Society, 1981. — 16p ; 17cm
Cover title
£0.30 (pbk) B81-20013

282′.41 — Great Britain. Catholic Church — *Case studies — For children*

Sullivan, Danny. Visiting a Roman Catholic church / Danny Sullivan ; photography Ken Dover ; illustration-design Judy Billson. — Guildford : Lutterworth Educational, 1981. — 58p : ill,ports ; 21cm
Bibliography: p56. — Includes index
ISBN 0-7188-2470-9 (pbk) : £1.60 B81-14304

282′.415 — Ireland. Catholic Church, *1721-1739.* **Documents** — *Collections*

Fottrell, John. The Fottrell papers 1721-39 : an edition of the papers found on the person of Fr John Fottrell, Provincial of the Dominicans in Ireland, at his arrest in 1739 / by Hugh Fenning. — [Belfast] ([66 Balmoral Ave., Belfast 9]) : PRONI, 1980. — xx,137p : ill,facsims ; 31cm
Parallel Latin text, English translation
ISBN 0-905691-05-9 : £7.00 B81-10676

282′.42 — England. Catholic Church — *Conference proceedings*

National Pastoral Congress *(1980 : Liverpool).* Liverpool 1980 : official report of the National Pastoral Congress. — Slough : St. Paul Publications, 1981. — xviii,409p ; 23cm
Includes index
ISBN 0-85439-186-x : £9.00 B81-21903

282′.42 — England. Catholic Church — *Topics for discussion groups*

Pratt, Ianthe. Becoming the Easter people : discussion outlines / by Ianthe and Oliver Pratt. — London : Catholic Truth Society, 1981. — 32p ; 19cm
ISBN 0-85183-396-9 (pbk) : £0.40 B81-12455

282′.42 — England. Catholics. Opinions, *1974-1979*

Hornsby-Smith, Michael P.. Roman Catholic opinion : a study of Roman Catholics in England and Wales in the 1970s : final report / Michael P. Hornsby-Smith and Raymond M. Lee. — [Guilford] : University of Surrey, Department of Sociology, 1979. — iii,244p : ill,forms ; 30cm
Cover title. — Bibliography: p135-141
Unpriced (spiral) B81-13284

282′.42133 — London. Hammersmith and Fulham *(London Borough).* **Catholic religious institutions,** *1609-1979*

Evinson, Denis. Pope's Corner : an historical survey of the Roman Catholic institutions in the London Borough of Hammersmith and Fulham / by Denis Evinson. — London (c/o Fulham Library, 598 Fulham Rd., SW6 5NX) : Fulham and Hammersmith Historical Society, 1980. — ii,75p,[8]p of plates : ill,ports ; 21cm
Includes index
Unpriced (pbk)
Also classified at 377′.8242133 B81-05308

282′.42543 — Leicestershire. South Wigston. Catholic Church. St. Mary's *(Church : South Wigston), 1880-1980*

Kelly, Peter, *1940 Jan. 18-.* The Catholic Church in South Wigston, 1880-1980 / by Peter Kelly ; edited by Ray Eaton. — South Wigston ([Countesthorpe Rd., South Wigston, Leicester]) : St Mary's Parish, 1980. — 47p : ill,ports ; 22cm
ISBN 0-9507130-0-7 (pbk) : £1.00 B81-07187

282′.4276 — Lancashire. Catholic Church, *to 1980*

Hilton, J. A. (John Anthony), *1941-.* Catholic Lancashire : an historical guide / by J.A. Hilton. — Wigan (102 Algernon St., Hindley, Wigan) : North West Catholic History Society, 1981. — 27p ; 20cm
Unpriced (pbk) B81-34820

282′.42987 — Catholic Church. *Diocese of Llandaff, to 1132 — Early works — Latin texts*

[Book of Llan Dâv]. The text of the Book of Llan Dâv : reproduced from the Gwysaney Manuscript / by J. Gwenogvryn Evans ; with the co-operation of John Rhys. — Aberystwyth : National Library of Wales, 1979. — li,428p,[14]leaves of plates (13 folded) : 1ill,facsims ; 26cm
Latin and Welsh text, English preface. — Facsim of: edition published Oxford : J.G. Evans, 1893. — Includes index
£10.00 B81-13130

282′.46 — Spain. Catholic Church, *1575-1580*

Christian, William A. (William Armistead), *1944-.* Local religion in sixteenth-century Spain / William A. Christian, Jr. — Princeton ; Guildford : Princeton University Press, c1981. — viii,283p : ill,1map,facsims ; 23cm
Includes index
ISBN 0-691-05306-5 : £10.30 B81-26836

282′.5691 — Syria. Catholic Church, *1098-1291*

Hamilton, Bernard. The Latin Church in the Crusader states : the secular church / Bernard Hamilton. — London : Variorum, 1980. — x,409p : 2maps ; 24cm
Bibliography: p379-392. - Includes index
ISBN 0-86078-072-4 : £18.00 : CIP rev.
B80-13206

282′.775 — Wisconsin. Catholic Church. Role of Polish immigrants, *1896-1918*

Kuzniewski, Anthony J.. Faith and fatherland : the Polish Church war in Wisconsin, 1896-1918 / Anthony J. Kuzniewski. — Notre Dame ; London : University of Notre Dame Press, c1980. — xii,171p,[8]p of plates : ill,ports ; 24cm. — (Notre Dame studies in American Catholicism ; no.3)
Bibliography: p154-160. — Includes index
ISBN 0-268-00948-1 : £7.80 B81-25634

282′.8 — Latin America. Catholic Church

Kirby, Peadar. Lessons in liberation : the Church in Latin America / Peadar Kirby. — Dublin (St Saviour's, Dublin 1) : Dominican Publications, 1981. — 128p : ill,maps ; 22cm
Bibliography: p121-122. — Includes index
ISBN 0-907271-04-9 (pbk) : Unpriced
B81-26068

282′.81 — Brazil. Catholic Church — *Interviews*

Camara, Helder. The impossible dream : the spirituality of Dom Helder Camara / [interviewed] by Mary Hall. — Belfast : Christian Journals Ltd., 1979. — 96p ; 21cm
ISBN 0-904302-34-2 (pbk) : £2.60 B81-03661

282′.861 — Colombia. Catholic Church. Political aspects

Levine, Daniel H.. Religion and politics in Latin America : the Catholic Church in Venezuela and Colombia / Daniel H. Levine. — Princeton ; Guildford : Princeton University Press, c1981. — xii,342p ; 25cm
Bibliography: p317-335. — Includes index
ISBN 0-691-07624-3 : £12.60
ISBN 0-691-02200-3 (pbk) : £3.90
Also classified at 282′.87 B81-26188

282′.87 — Venezuela. Catholic Church. Political aspects

Levine, Daniel H.. Religion and politics in Latin America : the Catholic Church in Venezuela and Colombia / Daniel H. Levine. — Princeton ; Guildford : Princeton University Press, c1981. — xii,342p ; 25cm
Bibliography: p317-335. — Includes index
ISBN 0-691-07624-3 : £12.60
ISBN 0-691-02200-3 (pbk) : £3.90
Primary classification 282′.861 B81-26188

283 — ANGLICAN CHURCHES

283′.09 — Anglican churches. Relations with Catholic Church, *to 1980*

De Satgé, John. Peter and the single Church / John de Satgé. — London : S.P.C.K., 1981. — x,182p ; 22cm
Includes index
ISBN 0-281-03819-8 (pbk) : £4.95
Primary classification 282′.09 B81-35517

283′.092′2 — Church of England. Eccentric clergy, *1380-1945 — Biographies*

Hart, A. Tindall. Some clerical oddities in the Church of England from medieval to modern times / A. Tindal Hart. — Bognor Regis : New Horizon, c1980. — 323p,[6]p of plates : ill,ports ; 22cm
Bibliography: p286-303. — Includes index
ISBN 0-86116-208-0 : £6.75 B81-21709

283′.092′4 — Anglican churches — *Personal observations*

Smith, John Gurney. Reflections (of a lay preacher) / John Gurney Smith. — Bognor Regis : New Horizon, c1979. — 23lp ; 21cm
ISBN 0-86116-109-2 : £3.90 B81-21722

283′.092′4 — Church of England. Brontë, Patrick — *Biographies*

Lock, John. A man of sorrow : the life, letters and times of the Rev. Patrick Brontë 1777-1861 / by John Lock and W.T. Dixon ; foreword by the Archbishop of Canterbury (formerly the Archbishop of York). — [2nd ed.]. — London (37 Connaught St., W.2) : Hodgkins, 1979. — xiv,566p,[16]p of plates : ill,1facsim,ports ; 24cm
Previous ed.: London : Nelson, 1965. — Bibliography: p541-549. - Includes index
ISBN 0-906460-01-8 : Unpriced : CIP rev.
B78-35858

283′.092′4 — Church of England. Brown, Leslie, *1912- — Biographies*

Brown, Leslie, *1912-.* Three worlds: one Word : account of a mission / Leslie Brown. — London : Collings, 1981. — x,267p,[1]leaf of plates : 1port ; 23cm
Includes index
ISBN 0-86036-146-2 : £10.50 B81-22126

283′.092′4 — Church of England. Darby, Jonathan — *Biographies*

Armstrong, Robert, *1940-.* The Beachy Head light / by Robert Armstrong. — [Eastbourne] ([20 Pevensey Rd, Eastbourne, E. Sussex]) : [Sound Forum], [1979]. — [34]p : 1ill ; 19cm
£0.35 (unbound)
Also classified at 623.89′42′0942258
B81-06212

283′.092′4 — Church of England. Hodges, Percy — *Biographies*

Hodges, Percy. The end of a golden string : a memoir of a full life / Percy Hodges. — Bognor Regis : New Horizon, c1978. — 129p,[3]leaves of plates : ill ; 21cm
ISBN 0-86116-019-3 : £3.50 B81-21727

283′.092′4 — Church of England. Honywood, Michael — *Biographies*

Sprawley, J. H.. Michael Honywood : Dean of Lincoln (1660-81) : a story of the English Church in critical times / by J.H. Sprawley. — Rev. ed., Repr. with corrections. — [Lincoln] : Honywood Press, 1981, c1950. — 28p : ill,2facsims,1port ; 22cm
Previous ed.: Lincoln : The Friends of Lincoln Cathedral, 1950. — Bibliography: p28
ISBN 0-9505083-1-4 (pbk) : Unpriced
B81-40218

283′.092′4 — Church of England. Lightfoot, J. B. — *Biographies*

Robinson, John A. T.. Joseph Barber Lightfoot : delivered in the Prior's Hall at Durham, 12 March 1981 / John A.T. Robinson. — [Durham] (Durham Cathedral, [Durham]) : Dean and Chapter of Durham, c1981. — 19p : 1port ; 21cm. — (Durham Cathedral lecture ; 1981)
ISBN 0-907078-12-5 (pbk) : Unpriced
B81-24033

283′.092′4 — Church of England. Mortimer, R. C. — *Biographies*

Skinner, B. G.. Robert Exon / B.G. Skinner. — Bognor Regis : New Horizon, c1979. — 190p,[4]p of plates : ports ; 22cm
ISBN 0-86116-136-x : £4.00 B81-39476

283′.092′4 — Church of England. Osman, George — *Biographies*

Osman, George. Called to the priesthood / George Osman. — Bognor Regis : New Horizon, c1981. — 45p ; 21cm
ISBN 0-86116-714-7 : £3.25 B81-33403

283'.092'4 — West Africa. Church of England. Crowther, Samuel — *Biographies — For schools*

Sweetman, David. Bishop Crowther / David Sweetman. — London : Longman, 1981. — 52p : ill,1map ; 20cm. — (Makers of African history)
ISBN 0-582-60378-1 (pbk) : £0.65 B81-40198

283'.3 — Free Church of England — *Serials*

Free Church of England. Year book / the Free Church of England otherwise called the Reformed Episcopal Church. — 1980-81. — Swindon (28 Sedgebrook, Liden, Swindon SN3 6EY) : The Church, [1980]. — [62]p
Unpriced B81-09035

283'.41 — Great Britain. Anglican churches — *Case studies — For children*

Tompkins, Susan E.. Visiting an Anglican church / Susan Tompkins ; photography Nick Lockett ; illustration-design Judy Billson. — Guildford : Lutterworth Educational, 1981. — 60p : ill,1plan ; 21cm
Bibliography: p58. — Includes index
ISBN 0-7188-2469-5 (pbk) : £1.60 B81-14301

283'.415 — Church of Ireland

McAdoo, Henry R.. The identity of the Church of Ireland / H.R. McAdoo. — [Dublin] : [H. McAdoo], c1980. — [12]p ; 21cm
Cover title
Unpriced (pbk) B81-12611

283'.42 — Church of England. Relations with Catholic Church, *1530-1973*

Pawley, Bernard. Rome and Canterbury through four centuries. — Updated and rev. ed. — London : Mowbray, Nov.1981. — [416]p
Previous ed.: 1974
ISBN 0-264-66415-9 (pbk) : £4.75 : CIP entry
Primary classification 282 B81-30186

283'.42 — Church of England, *to 1979*

Barrow, Andrew. The flesh is weak : an intimate history of the Church of England / by Andrew Barrow. — London : Hamilton, 1980. — ix,254p : ill,ports ; 24cm
Ill on lining papers. — Bibliography: p235-236. — Includes index
ISBN 0-241-10234-0 : £10.95 : CIP rev.
B80-24016

283'.42'05 — Church of England — *Serials*

Church of England. The Church of England year book. — 97th ed. (1981). — London : Church Information Office, 1981. — xxxii,432p
ISBN 0-7151-8054-1 : £7.50
ISSN 0069-3987 B81-20433

Cross+way. — No.1-. — London (186 Kennington Park Rd, SE11 4BT) : Church Society, 1980-. — v. : ill,ports ; 30cm
Quarterly. — Description based on: No.3
ISSN 0261-8915 = Cross+way : £0.40 per issue B81-35094

283'.42142 — London. Camden *(London Borough).* **West Hampstead. Church of England. Emmanuel Church** *(West End, Hampstead), to 1980*

Tucker, Jennifer. Emmanuel Church West End, Hampstead : a complete history / Jennifer Tucker. — [London] ([2 Hillcrest Cres., Shoot Up Hill, NW2 3PG]) : J. Tucker, c1981. — 93p : ill,1plan,ports ; 21cm
£2.50 (pbk) B81-34913

283'.422162 — Surrey. Guildford. Church of England. St. Nicholas' *(Church : Guildford), to 1979*

Taylor, Brian, *1929-*. The lower church : a history of St Nicolas' Guildford / Brain Taylor. — Guildford ([The Rectory, Flower Walk, Guildford GU2 5EP]) : [B. Taylor], 1980. — 79p : ill,ports ; 30cm
Unpriced (pbk) B81-06104

283'.42493 — West Midlands *(Metropolitan County).* **Dudley. Church of England. Parish life,** *1618-1725 — Early works*

Roper, John S.. The Dudley churchwarden's book 1618-1725 / J.S. Roper. — [Sedgley] ([21 Larkswood Drive, Sedgley, W. Midlands DY3 3UQ]) : [Birmingham & Midland Society for Genealogy & Heraldry], 1980. — 185,9p : ill ; 29cm
Includes index
ISBN 0-905105-51-6 (pbk) : Unpriced
B81-38779

283'.42821 — Church of England. *Diocese of Sheffield.* **Parish life,** *1914-1979*

Walton, Mary. A history of the Diocese of Sheffield 1914-1979 / by Mary Walton. — Sheffield : Diocesan Board of Finance, 1981. — xi,172p,[4]p of plates : 1map,ports ; 22cm
Includes index
ISBN 0-9502235-2-2 (pbk) : £3.75 B81-40279

283'.42869 — Durham *(County).* **West Pelton. Church of England. St. Paul's Church** *(West Pelton)*

Stephenson, Christine. St. Paul's Church, West Pelton 1870-1980 / Christine Stephenson. — [Stanley] ([West Pelton Vicarage, Stanley, Co. Durham, DH9 GRT]) : [D. Murphy], [1980]. — 37p ; 21cm
Cover title
£1.00 (pbk) B81-07834

283'.42876 — Church of England. *Diocese of Newcastle.* **Parish life,** *1882-1982*

A **Social** history of the Diocese of Newcastle 1882-1982 / edited by W.S.F. Pickering ; foreword by Alec Vidler. — Stocksfield : Oriel Press, 1981. — xiv,338p,16p of plates : ill,1map,ports ; 23cm
Bibliography: p326-330. — Includes index
ISBN 0-85362-189-6 : £12.00 B81-33410

284 — PROTESTANT DENOMINATIONS OF CONTINENTAL ORIGIN

284.1'092'4 — Lutheran churches. Luther, Martin — *Biographies*

Haile, H. G.. Luther : a biography / H.G. Haile. — London : Sheldon, 1981, c1980. — 422p : 1col.map ; 23cm
Originally published: Garden City, N.Y. : Doubleday, 1980. — Map on lining papers. — Includes index
ISBN 0-85969-330-9 : £9.95 B81-27159

284.1'092'4 — Tanzania. Bukoba. Lutheran churches, *1940-1964 — Personal observations*

Sundkler, Bengt. Bara Bukoba : church and community in Tanzania / by Bengt Sundkler. — London : C. Hurst, c1980. — ix,229p[8]p of plates : ill,1map,ports ; 23cm
Translation of: Bara Bukoba. — Bibliography: p222-224. - Includes index
ISBN 0-905838-30-0 : £11.50 B81-06015

284'.2'0924 — Reformed churches. Calvin, Jean — *Correspondence, diaries, etc.*

Calvin, Jean. Letters of John Calvin : selected from the Bonnet edition with an introductory biographical sketch. — Edinburgh : Banner of Truth Trust, 1980. — 261p ; 18cm
Translations from the French
ISBN 0-85151-323-9 (pbk) : £1.95 B81-06721

284'.8 — Old Roman Catholic Church — *Serials*

ORC notes : official journal of the Old Roman Catholic Church. — June 1979-. — Beckenham (Our Lady's Priory, 10 Barnmead Rd, Beckenham, Kent) : F. Linale, 1979-. — v. ; 26cm
Issued every six weeks. — Continues in part: Spearhead (Beckenham)
ISSN 0144-9117 = ORC notes : Free B81-04088

285.2 — PRESBYTERIAN CHURCHES OF BRITISH COMMONWEALTH ORIGIN

285'.2'0922 — Scotland. Borders Region. Peebles. Church of Scotland. Leckie *(Family)*

Scott, Sheila A.. Children of the manse : the family of the Reverend Thomas Leckie of Peebles / [compiled by Sheila Scott]. — Peebles ([43 Rosetta Rd., Peebles EH45 8HH]) : S. Scott, 1980. — 12p : 2ill,ports ; 22cm
Cover title
£0.30 (pbk) B81-10951

285'.2'0924 — Church of Scotland. Wright, Ronald Selby — *Biographies*

Wright, Ronald Selby. Another home / by Ronald Selby Wright. — Edinburgh : Blackwood, 1980. — xii,283p,25p of plates : ill,ports ; 23cm
Includes index
ISBN 0-85158-139-0 : £5.00 B81-05213

285'.2'0924 — Edinburgh. Universities. Colleges: University of Edinburgh. *New College.* **Exhibits: Items associated with Chalmers, Thomas** — *Catalogues*

Thomas Chalmers bicentenary exhibition : New College, Edinburgh 1980. — [Edinburgh] ([Mound Place, Edinburgh EH21 2LU]) : New College (University of Edinburgh), [1980]. — 26leaves ; 22cm
Catalogue of the exhibition
£0.25 (pbk) B81-32801

285'.2'0924 — Presbyterian Church in Ireland. Cooke, Henry — *Biographies*

Holmes, Finlay. Henry Cooke. — Belfast : Christian Journals Ltd, Dec.1981. — [220]p
ISBN 0-904302-75-x : £9.95 : CIP entry
B81-34223

285'.232'05 — United Reformed Church — *Serials*

United Reformed Church. The United Reformed Churh year book. — 1981. — London : 86, Travistock Place, WC1H 9RT : The Church, [1980]. — iv,276p
ISBN 0-902256-46-7
ISSN 0069-8849 B81-05990

285'.232'0924 — United Reformed Church. Quick, Frank Ernest — *Biographies*

Quick, Frank Ernest. One man in his time : an autobiography of Frank Ernest Quick : 1896 to God knows. — Plymouth (7 Launceston Close, Plymouth) : F.E. Quick, 1981. — 182,xiip : ill,1facsim,ports ; 21cm
Unpriced (pbk) B81-26134

285'.2411'05 — Church of Scotland — *Serials*

Church of Scotland. Year-book / the Church of Scotland. — 1981. — Edinburgh : Saint Andrew Press for the Church of Scotland Department of Publicity and Publication, [1981]. — 418p
ISBN 0 86153-032-2 : £5.50 B81-30863

285'.24114 — Scotland. Western Isles. Isle of Lewis. Free Church of Scotland, *1843-1900 — Gaelic texts*

MacGilliosa, Dòmhnall. An Eaglais Shaor ann an Leédhas, 1843-1900 / Dòmhnall MacGilliosa. — Dun Eideann [Edinburgh] (15 North Bank Street, Edinburgh) : Clò Knox, 1981. — 134p,[6]leaves of plates : ports ; 23cm
Gaelic text, with 4 Chapters in English. — Includes index
Unpriced B81-13141

285'.241172 — Scotland. Highland Region. Ross and Cromarty *(District).* **Church of Scotland. Parish life,** *to 1884 — Early works*

Kennedy, John, *1819-1884*. The days of the fathers in Ross-shire / John Kennedy. — Inverness (Henderson Rd., Inverness 1V1 1SP) : Christian Focus, 1979. — 215p,[4]p of plates : ill,1port ; 23cm
Originally published: Toronto : J. Campbell & Son, 1867. 4th ed
ISBN 0-906731-00-3 : £3.75 B81-12292

285'.24128 — Scotland. Tayside Region. Kenmore. Church of Scotland. Kirk of Kenmore, *to 1979*

Kirk of Kenmore 1579-1979. — [Kenmore] ([Kenmore, Tayside]) : [Kenmore Kirk Session], [c1979]. — 28p : ill(some col.),col.ports ; 21cm
Cover title
£1.00 (pbk) B81-09806

285′.24134 — Edinburgh. Leith. Free Church of Scotland. Inverleith Church, *to 1981*

Fraser, Alexander, *19---.* Inverleith Church 1881-1981 / Alexander Fraser. — Edinburgh ([c/o Inverleith Church, Ferry Rd, Edinburgh]) : [A. Fraser?], [1981?]. — vi,95p : ill,2maps,ports ; 22cm
Unpriced (pbk) B81-37073

285′.24135 — Scotland. Lothian Region. West Calder. Church of Scotland. West Kirk of Calder, *to 1980*

Williamson, J. C.. West Kirk of Calder, West Calder : a short history written for the celebration of 100 years of worship in the present building, 7th September 1880-1980 / [by J.C. Williamson]. — [Scotland] : s.n., 1980 (West Calder : Clarkson) (Young St., West Calder, Midlothian). — 6p : ill,1port ; 21cm
Cover title
Unpriced (pbk) B81-09244

285′.241443 — Scotland. Strathclyde Region. Glasgow. Church of Scotland. St. Andrew's East *(Church : Glasgow), to 1979*

St. Andrew's East, Church of Scotland : 1899-1979. — [Glasgow] : [The Church?], [1979?]. — [24]p : 1ill,ports
Cover title
£0.50 (pbk) B81-37709

285′.241464 — Scotland. Strathclyde Region. Mauchline. Church of Scotland. Mauchline Parish Church, *to 1980*

Morrice, Charles S.. A brief history of Mauchline Parish Church / Charles S. Morrice. — [Mauchline] ([97 Loundoun St., Mauchline, Ayrshire, KA5 5BQ]) : [The Church], [1981]. — 32p : ill,ports ; 24cm
Cover title
£0.75 (pbk) B81-08437

285′.242195 — London. Kingston upon Thames *(London Borough).* **New Malden. United Reformed Church. United Reformed Church, New Malden,** *to 1979*

United Reformed Church, New Malden. The first 100 years / [research, compiled, and edited by Geraldine Swain] ; [illustrations by Bruce Rowling]. — New Malden (23 Cromwell Ave., New Malden, Surrey KT3 6DN) : United Reformed Church, New Malden, 1981. — 60p : ill,maps,plans,ports ; 22cm
Maps on inside covers
Unpriced (pbk) B81-18600

285′.2427 — United Reformed Church. *Province 2 North Western — Serials*

United Reformed Church. *Province 2 North Western.* The United Reformed Church, North Western Province year book. — 1981-82. — [Manchester] ([244 Deansgate, Manchester M3 4BQ]) : [The Province], [1981?]. — 34p
Unpriced B81-36553

285′.24281′05 — United Reformed Church. *Yorkshire Province — Serials*

United Reformed Church. *Yorkshire Province.* Provincial handbook / the United Reformed Church, Yorkshire Province. — 1981-82. — Leeds (43 Hunslet La., Salem Place, Leeds LS10 1JW) : The Province, [1981]. — 39p
Unpriced B81-32663

285′.2429′05 — Presbyterian Church of Wales — *Serials*

Presbyterian Church of Wales. Y Blwyddiadur / Eglwys Methodistaid Calfinaidd Cymru. — Cyfrol 84 (1981). — Caernarfon ([Heol Ddewi, Caernarfon LL55 1ER]) : Cyhoeddedig dros y Gymanfa Gyffredinol gan Y Llyfrfa, [1981?]. — 265p
Unpriced B81-16812

285′.242921 — Gwynedd. Ynys Môn. Penygarnedd. Presbyterian Church of Wales, *1876-1976 — Welsh texts*

Hanes yr achos yn Mhenygarnedd 1782-1976 : ar achlysur dathlu canmlwyddiant adeiladu y capel presennol 1876-1976. — [S.l.] : [s.n.], [1976] (Llangefni) (Swyddfa'r Ffowndri, Llangefni, Ynys Môn, Gwynedd) (W.O. Jones). — 60p,[12]p of plates : ill,facsims,ports ; 22cm
Cover title
Unpriced (pbk) B81-09334

285′.242982 — West Glamorgan. Swansea. United Reformed Church. Hill United Reformed Church *(Swansea), to 1980*

Yonge, Stanley. The story of Hill Chapel Swansea 1881-1981 / by Stanley Yonge. — Swansea (c/o The Secretary, 5, The Promenade, Swansea SA1 6EA) : Hill United Reformed Church, [1981]. — 32p : ill,ports ; 21cm
£1.00 (pbk) B81-10809

285.8 — CONGREGATIONAL CHURCHES

285.8′092′4 — New England. Congregational churches. Hooker, Thomas. Works — *Critical studies*

Bush, Sargent. The writings of Thomas Hooker : spiritual adventure in two worlds / Sargent Bush, Jr. — Madison ; London : University of Wisconsin Press, 1980. — x,387p ; 24cm
Bibliography: p373-375. — Includes index
ISBN 0-299-08070-6 : £10.05 B81-02685

285.8′092′4 — Union of Welsh Independents. Peregrine, T. J. — *Biographies — Welsh texts*

Hyd hanner dydd : cyfrol deyrnged i'r diweddar Barchedig T.J. Peregrine / golygyddion Emlyn G. Jenkins a Gerallt Jones. — Abertawe : Tŷ John Penry, 1980. — 83p,[4]p of plates : ill,ports ; 22cm
ISBN 0-903701-31-6 : £2.50 B81-09335

285.8′092′4 — Union of Welsh Independents. Rees, J. Derfel — *Biographies — Welsh texts*

Rees, J. Derfel. Blas ar fyw / J. Derfel Rees. — Abertawe : Penry, 1980. — 133p ; 22cm
ISBN 0-903701-36-7 (pbk) : £2.85 B81-15184

285.8′411′05 — Congregational Union of Scotland — *Serials*

Congregational Union of Scotland. Year book of the Congregational Union of Scotland. — 1981. — Glasgow : The Union, [1981?]. — 155p
Unpriced B81-17475

285.8′42967 — Dyfed. Llanelli. Union of Welsh Independents. Capel Als, *1780-1980 — Welsh texts*

Capel Als 1780-1980 / golygydd Maurice Loader. — Abertawe : Penry, 1980. — 137p,[5]p of plates : ill,1map,ports ; 19cm
Bibliography: p134-137
ISBN 0-903701-32-4 (cased) : £3.50
ISBN 0-903701-35-9 (pbk) : Unpriced B81-10285

286 — BAPTIST CHURCHES

286′.1′0924 — England. Baptist churches. Winzer, John — *Biographies*

Newman, S.. John Winzer, 1788-1868 / by S. Newman. — Ossett (44 Queen's Drive, Ossett, W. Yorkshire, WF5 3ND) : Zoar, [1981?]. — 96p,[4]p of plates : ill(some col.) ; 18cm
ISBN 0-904435-07-5 : Unpriced B81-31983

286′.1′0924 — London. Baptist churches. Windridge, Fred — *Biographies*

Windridge, Fred. His great goodness : being the life of the late Fred Windridge, for 45 years the beloved pastor of Providence Strict Baptist Chapel, London, 1916-1961 : together with eight sermons and the second edition of The harp of Zion / compiled by his daughter ; preface by L.S.B. Hyde. — Watford (12 Grosvenor Rd., Watford, Herts., WD1 2QT) : Olive Perks, [1981?]. — 398p,[7]p of plates : ill,ports ; 20cm
£4.75 B81-31300

286′.141 — Great Britain. Baptist churches

McBain, Douglas. No gentle breeze : Baptist churchmanship and the winds of change / Douglas McBain. — Ilkeston : Published on behalf of Mainstream by Moorley's Bible & Bookshop, c1981. — 32p ; 22cm
ISBN 0-86071-131-5 (pbk) : Unpriced B81-34822

286′.1411′05 — Baptist Union of Scotland — *Serials*

Baptist Union of Scotland. The Scottish Baptist year book for ... / edited and published under the direction of the Council of the Baptist Union of Scotland. — 1981. — Glasgow (14 Aytoun Rd, Glasgow G41 5RT) : The Union, [1981]. — 163p
Unpriced B81-23494

286′.142 — England. Baptist churches

Beasley-Murray, Paul. Turning the tide : an assessment of Baptist Church growth in England / Paul Beasley-Murray and Alan Wilkinson. — London : Bible Society, c1981. — 110p : ill(some col.),form ; 22cm
Bibliography: p89-91
ISBN 0-564-07062-9 (pbk) : Unpriced B81-35170

286′.1422352 — Kent. Eythorne. Baptist churches: Eythorne Baptist Church, *to ca 1980*

Clark, W. Philip. Eythorne : our Baptist heritage / by W. Philip Clark. — [Sandwich] (['Ashley', High Street, Eastry, Sandwich, Kent CT13 0HE]) : W. Philip Clark, [1981]. — 92p : ill,facsims ; 22cm
£2.25 (pbk) B81-37976

286′.1425′05 — East Midland Baptist Association — *Serials*

East Midland Baptist Association. Year book / the East Midland Baptist Association. — 1980-81. — [Leicester] ([c/o 249 Queens Rd., Leicester LE2 3FP]) : [The Association], [1980]. — 66p
£0.50 B81-08273

286.7 — ADVENTIST CHURCHES

286.7′3 — Seventh-day Adventist Church — *Serials*

[Focus *(Grantham)***].** Focus : on the world's least read best-seller. — Vol.1, no.1-. — Grantham : Stanborough Press, [1979]-. — v. : ill ; 28cm
Quarterly. — Subtitle varies. — Publication of: the Seventh-day Adventist Church. — Numbering discontinued after Vol.1, no.2
ISSN 0143-7925 = Focus (Grantham) : £0.10 per issue B81-02812

287 — METHODIST CHURCHES

287′.092′4 — Methodist churches. Wesley, John — *Biographies*

Tuttle, Robert G.. John Wesley : his life and theology / Robert G. Tuttle, Jr. — Exeter : Paternoster, c1979. — 368p,[8]p of plates : ill,maps,facsims,1plan,ports ; 23cm
Originally published: Grand Rapids : Zondervan, 1978. — Includes bibliographies and index
ISBN 0-85364-256-7 : £6.50 B81-16631

287′.092′4 — Methodist churches. Wesley, John — *Correspondence, diaries, etc*

Wesley, John. John Wesley's England : a 19th-century pictorial history based on an 18th-century journal / compiled by Richard Bewes. — London : Hodder and Stoughton, 1981. — [124]p : ill,1map,coat of arms,ports ; 21x28cm
ISBN 0-340-25843-8 (cased) : £8.95 : CIP rev.
ISBN 0-340-25747-4 (pbk) : £5.95
Primary classification 914.2′0472 B80-20031

287′.141′05 — Methodist Church — *Serials*

Methodist Church. The Minutes of the annual conference ... and church year book / the Methodist Church. — [1980]. — London ([1, Central Buildings, Matthew Parker St., SW1]) : Methodist Church Office, c1980. — 287p
Unpriced B81-04544

287′.142371 — Cornwall. Bodmin. Methodist Church. Bodmin Methodist Society, *to 1828*

Podmore, C. J.. Bodmin Methodist Society 1769-1828 / by C.J. Podmore. — Bodmin (11 Sandra Way, Bodmin) : C.J. Podmore, 1980. — 15p ; 21cm
Cover title
£0.50 (pbk) B81-10815

287'.1425'05 — England. East Midlands. Methodist Church — *History — Serials*

[Heritage *(Wesley Historical Society. East Midlands Branch)***].** Heritage : Journal of the East Midlands Branch of the Wesley Historical society. — Vol.1, no.1 (June 1980)-. — Loughborough (c/o Rev. Sidney Richardson, 15 Coniston Cres., Loughborough, Leics.) : The Branch, 1980-. — v. : ill ; 22cm
ISSN 0260-4957 = Heritage (Wesley Historical Society, East Midlands Branch) : £0.40 per issue (free to members) B81-06290

287'.5'088055 — Methodist Church. Persons, 18-30 years

Winwood, David J.. Before it's too late : including report to Methodist Conference : young adults / David J. Winwood. — London : Methodist Division of Education and Youth, 1980. — 27p ; 21cm
ISBN 0-7192-0142-x (pbk) : Unpriced B81-20879

287'.54174 — Galway *(County)***. Methodist churches,** *to 1978*

Cooney, D. A. Levistone. Methodism in Galway / Dudley Levistone Cooney. — [Cloughjordan] ([The Manse, Cloughjordan, Co. Tipperary]) : [The Methodist Church in Ireland, North Tipperary Circuit], [1978]. — 38p : ill,1map ; 21cm
£0.50 (pbk) B81-26465

287'.54192 — Northern Tipperary *(County)***. Methodist churches,** *to 1974*

Cooney, D. A. Levistone. The Ormond Methodists : a history of Methodism in the Cloughjordan and Borrisokane circuit / [D.A. Levistone Cooney]. — [Cloughjordan] ([The Manse, Cloughjordan, Co. Tipperary]) : [The Methodist Church in Ireland, North Tipperary Circuit], [c1975]. — 23p ; 21cm
£0.50 (pbk) B81-26466

287'.542262 — West Sussex. Midhurst. Methodist Church. Midhurst Methodist Church, *to 1979*

Breame, Ella M.. Methodism in the Western Weald : featuring Midhurst Methodist Church on its 75th anniversary / by Ella M. Breame. — [Midhurst] ([Midhurst, W. Sussex]) : The Church, [1981?]. — 51p,[4]p of plates : ill,1map,ports ; 21cm
Bibliography: p50
ISBN 0-9506622-0-8 (pbk) : £0.80 B81-10741

287'.542489 — Warwickshire. Shipston-on-Stour. Methodist Church. Shipston-on-Stour Methodist Church, *to 1981*

Drinkwater, P.. An history of Methodism in Shipston-on-Stour / by P. Drinkwater & F.W. Mayo. — Shipston-on-Stour (56, Church St, Shipston-on-Stour, Warwickshire) : P. Drinkwater, 1981. — 8p ; 24cm
Limited ed. of 250 numbered copies
Unpriced (pbk) B81-21748

287'.542554 — Northamptonshire. Warmington. Methodist churches. Warmington Methodist Church, *to 1981*

Centenary, Warmington Methodist Church, 1881-1981 / [compiled by J.F. Paterson]. — [Peterborough] ([c/o J. Goodridge, 73B, London Rd., Peterborough]) : [Warmington Methodist Church], [1981]. — 32p ; 30cm
Unpriced (pbk) B81-34516

287'.54278 — Cumbria. Methodist churches, *to 1932*

Burgess, John, *1949-*. A history of Cumbrian Methodism / John Burgess. — Kendal ([28 Highgate, Kendal, Cumbria]) : Titus Wilson, 1980. — 168p ; 22cm
Bibliography: p153-159. - Includes index
ISBN 0-900811-10-2 (pbk) : Unpriced B81-12972

287'.542873 — Tyne and Wear *(Metropolitan County)***. Ryton. Methodist churches. Ryton Methodist Church,** *to 1981*

Rippeth, N. G.. A celebration of one hundred years of Methodist worship at Ryton Lanehead Church : Lanehead Wesleyan Chapel 1881, Ryton Methodist Church 1981. — [Tyne and Wear] ([11 The Ridge, Ryton, Tyne and Wear NE40 3LN]) : [N.G. Rippeth], 1981. — 16p : ill,ports ; 24cm
Text on inside covers. — Cover title. — Author: N.G. Rippeth
£1.00 (pbk) B81-26328

287'.633'0924 — United States. Southern states. Methodist Episcopal Church. Candler, Warren A. — *Biographies*

Bauman, Mark K.. Warren Akin Candler : the conservative as idealist : Jesse Lee prize essay of the Commission on Archives and History, The United Methodist Church / by Mark K. Bauman. — Metuchen ; London : Scarecrow, 1981. — x,278p : 1port ; 23cm
Bibliography: p260-266. — Includes index
ISBN 0-8108-1368-8 : £11.20 B81-17719

288 — UNITARIAN CHURCHES

288 — Unitarianism

Hostler, John. Unitarianism / John Hostler. — [London] ([14 Gordon]) : Hibbert Trust, 1981. — viii,84p ; 19cm
Bibliography: p84
ISBN 0-9507535-0-5 (pbk) : £2.25 B81-27043

288'.42163 — London. Lewisham *(London Borough)***. Lewisham. Unitarian churches. Lewisham Unitarian Meeting,** *to 1980*

Lewisham Unitarian Meeting. A history of Lewisham Unitarian Meeting / by Wilfrid E. Reeve. — London (41 Bromley Rd., SE6 2TS) : The Meeting, 1981. — 15p : 1ill ; 21cm
Cover title. — Text, ill on covers
£0.50 (pbk) B81-29890

289.3 — CHURCH OF JESUS CHRIST OF LATTER-DAY SAINTS

289.3 — Mormonism

McCormick, W. J. McK.. Finding Mormons for Christ : a basic witnessing aid / by Jim McCormick. — Belfast : J. McCormick ; Edinburgh (28 George IV Bridge, Edinburgh EH1 1ES) : Distributors B. McCall Barbour, 1981. — 48p : ill,facsims,ports ; 21cm
Port., text on inside covers
Unpriced (pbk) B81-11831

289.3'73 — United States. Church of Jesus Christ of Latter-day Saints, *1820-1890*

Hansen, Klaus J.. Mormonism and the American experience / Klaus J. Hansen. — Chicago ; London : University of Chicago Press, c1981. — xviii,257p ; 22cm. — (Chicago history of American religion)
Bibliography: p245-249. — Includes index
ISBN 0-226-31552-5 : £9.00 B81-28264

289.4 — NEW CHURCH

289.4'05 — New Church — *Serials*

Year book ... of the General Conference of the New Church. — 1980-81. — London (20 Bloomsbury Way WC1A 2TH) : General Conference of the New Church, 1980. — 88p
£1.20 B81-10658

289.5 — CHURCH OF CHRIST, SCIENTIST

289.5'73 — United States. Church of Christ, Scientist, *1862-1894*

Eddy, Mary Baker. Mary Baker Eddy's six days of revelation / compiled by Richard Oakes showing the development of Christian Science from Let there be light to Let us make man in our image and using 1862-94 as a timed illustration of that which is timeless. — [Horsham] ([Japhet's Ark, Brooks Green, Horsham, W. Sussex RH13 8QR]) : Christian Science Research Library, c1981. — 561p ; 25cm
ISBN 0-9507286-0-8 : Unpriced B81-29189

289.6 — SOCIETY OF FRIENDS

289.6'092'4 — Society of Friends. Harvey, William Fryer — *Biographies*

Fryer, Charles. William Fryer Harvey : 1885-1937 : a friend with a difference / by Charles Fryer. — York : Sessions, [1981?]. — 59p,[2]p of plates : ports,2geneal.tables ; 22cm
ISBN 0-900657-61-8 (pbk) : Unpriced B81-26443

289.8 — SHAKERS

289'.8'0924 — Pennsylvania. Philadelphia. Shakers: Philadelphia Shaker Community. Jackson, Rebecca — *Biographies*

Williams, Richard E.. Called and chosen : the story of Mother Rebecca Jackson and the Philadelphia Shakers / Richard E. Williams ; edited by Cheryl Dorschner. — Metuchen ; London : Scarecrow, 1981. — xiii,179p : ill,facsims,ports ; 23cm. — (ATLA monograph series ; no.17)
Bibliography: p173-175. - Includes index
ISBN 0-8108-1382-3 : £7.70 B81-19367

289.9 — ASSEMBLIES OF GOD, BRETHREN, PENTECOSTAL CHURCHES, ETC

289.9 — British-Israel movement — *Serials*

[The Message *(London : 1981)***].** The Message : to the Anglo-Saxon & Celtic peoples : incorporating The National message. — Vol.1, no.1-. — London : Covenant Books, 1981-. — v. : maps ; 22cm
Monthly. — Official journal of: British Israel World Federation. — Continues: The National message (London). — Description based on: Vol.1, no.2
ISSN 0261-7404 = Message to the Anglo-Saxon & Celtic peoples : Unpriced B81-32794

289.9 — Children of God — *Personal observations*

McManus, Una. Not for a million dollars / Una McManus and John Charles Cooper. — Eastbourne : Kingsway, 1981, c1980. — 160p ; 18cm
Originally published: Nashville, Tenn.: Impact, 1980
ISBN 0-86065-128-2 (pbk) : £1.65 B81-27484

289.9 — Christian Community *(1922-)* — *Serials*

The **threshing** floor : a paper for religious renewal / published by the Christian Community. — Sept.1980-. — Edinburgh : Floris, 1980-. — v. : ill ; 30cm
Monthly. — Continues: Christian community (Shrewsbury)
ISSN 0260-4892 = Threshing floor : £7.50 per year B81-05404

289.9 — England. Brethren

Brown, Graham, *1938-*. The Brethren today : a factual survey / Graham Brown and Brian Mills. — Exeter : Paternoster, c1980. — 72p : ill,forms ; 21cm
ISBN 0-85364-324-5 (pbk) : £1.60 B81-05473

289.9 — Great Britain. Brethren, *to 1978*

Ellison, H. L.. The household church / by H.L. Ellison. — 2nd rev. ed. — Exeter : Paternoster, 1979. — 117p ; 18cm. — (Paternoster pocket book ; no.4)
Previous ed.: 1963
ISBN 0-85364-239-7 (pbk) : £1.50 : CIP rev. B79-32255

289.9 — People's Temple, *to 1978*

Naipaul, Shiva. Black and white / by Shiva Naipaul. — London : Hamilton, 1980. — 215p ; 24cm
ISBN 0-241-10337-1 : £8.50 : CIP rev. B80-18595

291 — COMPARATIVE RELIGION

291 — Comparative religion

Smith, Wilfred Cantwell. Towards a world theology : faith and the comparative history of religion / Wilfred Cantwell Smith. — London : Macmillan, 1981. — vi,206p ; 23cm. — (Library of philosophy and religion)
Includes index
ISBN 0-333-27605-1 : £15.00 : CIP rev. B80-13207

291 — Religious cults

Burrell, Maurice C.. The challenge of the cults / Maurice C. Burrell. — Leicester : Inter-Varsity, 1981. — 160p ; 18cm
ISBN 0-85110-420-7 (pbk) : £1.60 B81-15720

291'.07'1142733 — Greater Manchester *(Metropolitan County)*. Manchester. Universities: University of Manchester. Curriculum subjects: Comparative religion, *1904-1979*

Sharpe, Eric J.. Comparative religion at the University of Manchester, 1904-1979 / by Eric J. Sharpe. — Manchester : John Rylands University Library of Manchester, 1980. — p144-170 ; 25cm
£1.35 (pbk) B81-35543

291'.09'01 — Religious cults, *to ca 300* — *For schools*

Yamauchi, Edwin M.. Myths and cults / Edwin Yamauchi. — Tring : Lion Publishing, 1981. — p33-64 : ill(some col.),col.maps,ports(some col.) ; 25cm. — (The World of the first Christians ; 2)
Cover title
ISBN 0-85648-268-4 (pbk) : £1.25 B81-16682

291'.09'034 — Religious cults, *1850-1980*

Butterworth, John, *1953-*. Cults : and new faiths : a book of beliefs / John Butterworth. — Tring : Lion, 1981. — 61p : ill(some col.),ports ; 29cm
Text and ill on lining papers
ISBN 0-85648-249-8 : £3.95 B81-23399

291.1'3 — Indo-European myths. Characters. Camillus, Marcus Furius — *Critical studies*

Dumézil, Georges. Camillus : a study of Indo-European religion as Roman history / by Georges Dumézil ; edited with an introduction by Udo Strutynski ; translations by Annette Aronowicz and Josette Bryson. — Berkeley ; London : University of California Press, c1980. — xii,269p ; 23cm
Bibliography: p257-261. — Includes index
ISBN 0-520-02841-4 : £10.20 B81-12209

291.1'3 — Myths. Interpretation

Myth, symbol, and reality / edited by Alan M. Olson. — Notre Dame ; London : University of Notre Dame Press, c1980. — xiv,189p ; 24cm. — (Boston University studies in philosophy and religion ; v.1)
Includes index
ISBN 0-268-01346-2 : £9.00 B81-05743

291.1'3'0321 — Mythology — *Encyclopaedias*

Cotterell, Arthur. A dictionary of world mythology / Arthur Cotterell. — London : Book Club Associates, 1979. — 256p : ill,maps, ports ; 24cm
Bibliography: p246-249. — Includes index
Unpriced B81-39121

291.1'3'0321 — Myths — *Encyclopaedias*

Hendricks, Rhoda A.. [Mythologies of the world]. A dictionary of mythologies / compiled by Rhoda A. Hendricks. — London : Granada, 1981, c1979. — xviii,217p : geneal.table ; 20cm. — (A Paladin book)
Originally published: Garden City, N.Y. : Doubleday, 1979. — Bibliography: p217
ISBN 0-586-08347-2 (pbk) : £1.95 B81-11464

291.1'7 — Civilization. Evolution. Spiritual aspects

Bailey, Alice A.. The destiny of the nations / by Alice A. Bailey. — New York ; London : Lucis, 1949 (1974 printing). — vi,161p ; 20cm
Includes index
Unpriced (pbk) B81-37046

291.1'78357 — Sex. Attitudes of religions — *Comparative studies*

Parrinder, Geoffrey. Sex in the world's religions / Geoffrey Parrinder. — London : Sheldon, 1980. — 263p ; 23cm
Bibliography: p249-254. - Includes index
ISBN 0-85969-294-9 : £10.00 B81-06752

291.2 — Religious cults. Doctrines

Robertson, Irvine. What the cults believe / by Irvine Robertson. — 2nd ed. rev. — London : Pickering & Inglis, 1981, c1979. — 154p ; 21cm
Previous ed.: Chicago : Moody Press, 1966. — Bibliography: p149-154
ISBN 0-7208-0487-6 (pbk) : £2.25 B81-15580

291.2'12 — Cats. Worship, *to 1980*

St. George, E. A.. Ancient and modern cat worship / E.A. St. George. — London (38, Woodfield Ave., W5 1PA) : Spook Enterprises, c1981. — 20p ; 26cm
£0.40 (pbk) B81-34821

291.2'12 — Great Britain. Non-Christian religions. Sun cults

Toulson, Shirley. The winter solstice. — London : Jill Norman & Hobhouse, Nov.1981. — [160]p
ISBN 0-906908-25-6 : £7.50 : CIP entry B81-30620

291.2'15 — Angels

Wilson, Peter Lambourn. Angels / Peter Lambourn Wilson. — London : Thames and Hudson, c1980. — 200p : ill(some col.) ; 28cm
Bibliography: p194-196. — Includes index
ISBN 0-500-11017-4 : £12.00 B81-02293

291.2'15 — Religions. Spirits — *Anthroposophical viewpoints*

Bittleston, Adam. Our spiritual companions : from angels and archangels to cherubim and seraphim / Adam Bittleston. — Edinburgh : Floris, 1980. — 125p ; 23cm
ISBN 0-903540-39-8 : £6.50 B81-24028

291.2'16 — Devils — *For children*

Maple, Eric. Devils and demons / by Eric Maple ; illustrated by Steve Weston, Geoff Taylor and Harry Bishop ; edited by Jacqui Bailey. — London : Pan, 1981. — [24]p : col.ill,4col.ports ; 22cm. — (A Piccolo explorer book. Mysteries)
Bibliography: p[24]. — Includes index
ISBN 0-330-26357-9 (pbk) : £0.75 B81-07882

Maple, Eric. Devils and demons / by Eric Maple ; illustrated by Steve Weston, Geoff Taylor and Harry Bishop. — London : Kingfisher, 1981. — [24]p : col.ill,col.ports ; 23cm. — (Kingfisher explorer books. Mysteries)
Bibliography: p[24]. — Includes index
ISBN 0-7063-6104-0 : £1.95 B81-26672

291.2'37 — Reincarnation

Christie-Murray, David. Reincarnation : ancient beliefs and modern evidence / David Christie-Murray. — Newton Abbot : David & Charles, c1981. — 287p ; 23cm
Bibliography: p267-274. — Includes index
ISBN 0-7153-7861-9 : £10.50 B81-08706

291.2'4 — Myths. Special subjects: Creation

Primal myths : creating the world / [compiled by] Barbara C. Sproul. — London : Rider, 1980, c1979. — 373p ; 21cm
Originally published: San Francisco : Harper & Row, 1979. — Includes index
ISBN 0-09-143441-6 (pbk) : £5.50 : CIP rev. B80-12726

291.3'4 — Human sacrifices, *to 1980*

Davies, Nigel. Human sacrifice : in history and today / Nigel Davies. — London : Macmillan, c1981. — 320p : ill ; 25cm
Originally published: New York : Morrow, 1981. — Bibliography: p297-309. — Includes index
ISBN 0-333-22384-5 : £7.95 B81-28616

291.3'5 — Religious buildings

Mirsky, Jeannette. Houses of God / by Jeannette Mirsky. — Chicago ; London : University of Chicago Press, 1976, c1965. — 235p : ill ; 23cm. — (A Phoenix book)
Originally published: New York : Viking Press, 1965. — Includes index
ISBN 0-226-53184-8 (pbk) : £5.60 B81-38149

291.3'5'09362 — England. Religious buildings, *43-410*

Temples, churches and religion : recent research in Roman Britain : with a gazetteer of Romano-Celtic temples in continental Europe / edited by Warwick Rodwell. — Oxford : B.A.R., 1980. — 2v(585p) : ill,maps,plans ; 30cm. — (BAR. British series, ISSN 0143-3032 ; 77)
Includes bibliographies
ISBN 0-86054-085-5 (pbk) : £18.00 B81-17267

291.3'6 — Religious festivals

Butler, D. G.. Rejoicing in our midst : religious festivals round the world / D.G. Butler. — London : Edward Arnold, 1980. — 105p : ill ; 22cm
ISBN 0-7131-0478-3 (pbk) : £1.95 : CIP rev. B80-18165

291.3'6 — Religious festivals — *For children*

Joy, Margaret. Highdays and holidays. — London : Faber, Oct.1981. — [128]p
ISBN 0-571-11771-6 : £4.50 : CIP entry B81-28056

291.4 — India. Religious life — *Personal observations*

Pullar, Philippa. The shortest journey. — London : Hamish Hamilton, Oct.1981. — [256]p
ISBN 0-241-10685-0 : £9.95 : CIP entry B81-24614

291.4'2 — India. Religious life. Mysticism — *Personal observations*

Belfrage, Sally. Flowers of emptiness. — London : Women's Press, Nov.1981. — [256]p
ISBN 0-7043-3875-0 (pbk) : £3.95 : CIP entry B81-30352

291.4'2 — Religious experiences — *Interviews*

Living the questions : studies in the childhood & religious experience / edited and introduced by Edward Robinson. — Oxford (Oxford [OX1 3TD]) : Religious Experience Research Unit, Manchester College, c1978. — 164p ; 21cm
£2.00 (pbk) B81-05974

291.4'2 — Religious life. Mysticism

Johnston, William, *1925-*. The inner eye of love : mysticism and religion / William Johnston. — London : Collins : Fount Paperbacks, 1981, c1978. — 208p : ill ; 20cm
Originally published: London : Collins, 1978. — Bibliography: p197-198. — Includes index
ISBN 0-00-626300-3 (pbk) : £1.75 B81-11059

291.4'3 — Prayer — *Philosophical perspectives*

Phillips, D. Z.. The concept of prayer / D.Z. Phillips. — Oxford : Blackwell, 1981. — vii,167p ; 22cm
Originally published: London : Routledge and Kegan Paul, 1965. — Bibliography: p161-164. - Includes index
ISBN 0-631-12613-9 (pbk) : £4.50 : CIP rev. B80-13697

291.4'3 — Religious life. Contemplation *related to* human actions - *Conference proceedings*

Contemplation and action in world religions : selected papers from the Rothko Chapel colloquium 'Traditional modes of contemplation and action' / edited by Yusuf Ibish and Ileana Marculescu. — [Houston] : Rothko Chapel ; Seattle ; London : Distributed by University of Washington Press, c1978. — 274p ; 22cm
ISBN 0-295-95634-8 : Unpriced B81-11755

291.4'3 — Religious life. Prayers — *Collections*

Sing me the song of my world / [compiled by] Drutmar Cremer ; English adaptation by Sister Benedict Davies. — Slough : St Paul, 1981. — 191p ; 21cm
Translation of: Sing mir das Lied meiner Erde
ISBN 0-85439-191-6 (pbk) : £3.95 B81-39176

291.4'3 — Worship — *For schools*

Rankin, John. Looking at worship / written by John Rankin ; drawings by Edwin Beecroft. — Guildford : Lutterworth, c1981. — 1portfolio (14 parts) : ill ; 15x21cm + Teacher's guide ([4]p : 15x21cm)
ISBN 0-7188-2442-3 : Unpriced B81-10782

291.4'4 — Tibet. Religious life. Discipleship

Bailey, Alice A.. Discipleship in the new age / by Alice A. Bailey. — New York ; London : Lucis, 1944-1955 (1976-1979 printing). — 2v. ; 20cm
Includes index
Unpriced (pbk) B81-36838

292 — CLASSICAL RELIGIONS

292′.07 — Ancient Roman religion

MacMullen, Ramsay. Paganism in the Roman Empire / Ramsay MacMullen. — New Haven ; London : Yale University Press, c1981. — xiii,241p : ill,1map ; 25cm
Bibliography: p207-234. — Includes index
ISBN 0-300-02655-2 : £16.10 B81-34090

292′.13 — Ancient Greek myths — *Anthologies*

Graves, Robert. Greek myths / Robert Graves. — Ill ed. / [selected by John Buchanan-Brown]. — London : Cassell, 1981. — 224p : ill(some col.) ; 26cm
Previous ed.: 1958. — Includes index
ISBN 0-304-30720-3 : £9.95 B81-34633

292′.13 — Ancient Greek myths *related to* **Christianity**

Capel, Evelyn Francis. The making of Christianity and the Greek spirit / Evelyn Francis Capel. — Edinburgh : Floris, 1980. — 125p ; 22cm
ISBN 0-903540-37-1 (pbk) : £4.95 : CIP rev.
Also classified at 200 B80-17543

292′.13 — Ancient Greek myths. Special subjects: Signs of the zodiac — *For children*

Vautier, Ghislaine. The shining stars : Greek legends of the zodiac / by Ghislaine Vautier ; adapted by Kenneth McLeish ; illustrated by Jacqueline Benzençon. — Cambridge : Cambridge University Press, 1981. — [32]p : col.ill,charts ; 22x29cm
Translation of: Quand brillent les étoiles
ISBN 0-521-23886-2 : £4.95 B81-30024

292′.13 — Ancient Greek myths — *Structuralist perspectives*

Myth, religion and society. — Cambridge : Cambridge University Press, Feb.1982. — [322]p
ISBN 0-521-22780-1 : £20.00 : CIP entry
ISBN 0-521-29640-4 (pbk) : £6.95 B81-40270

292′.3 — Ancient Rome. Religious cults, *1-500*

Godwin, Joscelyn. Mystery religions : in the ancient world / Joscelyn Godwin. — London : Thames and Hudson, c1981. — 176p : ill ; 25cm
Bibliography: p172. — Includes index
ISBN 0-500-11019-0 : £10.00 B81-27860

292′.36 — Ancient Roman religious festivals

Scullard, H. H.. Festivals and ceremonies of the Roman Republic / H.H. Scullard. — London : Thames and Hudson, c1981. — 288p : ill ; 23cm. — (Aspects of Greek and Roman life)
Bibliography: p238. — Includes index
ISBN 0-500-40041-5 : £12.00 B81-27513

292′.37 — Ancient Greek myths. Symbolism

Diel, Paul. Symbolism in Greek mythology : human desire and its transformations / Paul Diel ; preface by Gaston Bachelard ; translated from the French by Vincent Stuart, Micheline Stuart and Rebecca Folkman. — Boulder ; London : Shambhala, 1980. — xx,218p ; 23cm
Translation of: Le symbolisme dans la mythologie qrecque
ISBN 0-87773-178-0 : £9.75 B81-15974

292′.38 — Ancient Greek religion. Eleusinian mysteries

D′Alviella, Goblet. The mysteries of Eleusis : the secret rites and rituals of the classical Greek mystery tradition / Goblet D′Alviella ; translated from the Dutch by Transcript. — Wellingborough : Aquarian, 1981. — 128p : ill ; 22cm
Translation of: Eleusinia. — Includes index
ISBN 0-85030-256-0 : £3.50 B81-29184

293 — GERMANIC NON-CHRISTIAN RELIGIONS

293′.0942 — England. Anglo-Saxon religion

Owen, Gale R.. Rites and religions of the Anglo-Saxons / Gale R. Owen. — Newton Abbot : David & Charles, c1981. — 216p : ill,maps ; 24cm
Bibliography: p206-211. — Includes index
ISBN 0-7153-7759-0 : £12.50 : CIP rev.
B81-14954

293′.13 — Norse myths — *Anthologies*

Crossley-Holland, Kevin. The Norse myths / introduced and retold by Kevin Crossley-Holland. — London : Deutsch, 1980. — xli,276p : ill ; 25cm
Ill and text on lining papers. — Bibliography: p254-261. - Includes index
ISBN 0-233-97271-4 : £8.95 : CIP rev.
B80-18167

294 — RELIGIONS OF INDIC ORIGIN

294 — Proto-Indo-Iranians. Religious beliefs *compared with* **religious beliefs of East African Nilotes**

Lincoln, Bruce. Priests, warriors, and cattle : a study in the ecology of religions / Bruce Lincoln. — Berkeley ; London : University of California Press, c1981. — xiii,242p : ill ; 24cm. — (Hermeneutics ; 10)
Bibliography: p185-215. — Includes index
ISBN 0-520-03880-0 : £19.50
Primary classification 299′.68 B81-27496

294.3 — BUDDHISM

294.3 — Buddhism

Pallis, Marco. A Buddhist spectrum / by Marco Pallis. — London : Allen & Unwin, 1980. — ix,163p ; 23cm
ISBN 0-04-294116-4 : £7.50 : CIP rev.
B80-20196

Ross, Nancy Wilson. Buddhism : a way of life and thought / Nancy Wilson Ross. — London : Collins, 1981, c1980. — xi,208p : ill,1map ; 24cm
Originally published: New York : Knopf, 1980. — Bibliography: p193-197. - Includes index
ISBN 0-00-215055-7 (pbk) : £4.95 B81-12641

294.3 — Buddhism *compared with* **Christianity** — *Philosophical perspectives*

Smart, Ninian. Beyond ideology. — London : Collins, Sept.1981. — [350]p
ISBN 0-00-215846-9 : £7.95 : CIP entry
Primary classification 200 B81-20622

294.3 — Buddhism — *Festschriften*

Buddhist studies in honour of Walpola Rahula / editorial committee Somaratna Balasooriya ... [et al.]. — London : Fraser, 1980. — xiii,293p : port ; 25cm
Bibliography: pxi-xiii
ISBN 0-86092-030-5 : £20.00 : CIP rev.
B79-26936

294.3 — Buddhism — *For schools*

Buddhism. — St Albans : Hart-Davis Educational, 1981. — 48p : ill(some col.),1col.map,1port ; 30cm. — (Journeys into religion)
ISBN 0-247-12962-3 (pbk) : Unpriced
B81-12222

294.3 — Buddhism *related to* **Christianity**

Johnston, William, *1925-*. The mirror mind : spirituality and transformation / William Johnston. — London : Collins, 1981. — x,181p : ill ; 22cm
Includes index
ISBN 0-00-215531-1 : £5.95
Primary classification 200 B81-32310

294.3′05 — Buddhism — *Serials*

Western Buddhist : Magazine of the Scientific Buddhist Association. — London (30 Hollingbourne Gardens, Ealing. WE13 8EN) : The Association, 1979-. — v. ; 26cm
Three issues yearly
ISSN 0144-9818 = Western Buddhist : £2.55 per year B81-03582

294.3′09 — Buddhism, *to 1978*

Conze, Edward. A short history of Buddhism / Edward Conze. — London : Allen & Unwin, 1980. — 135p : ill ; 23cm
Originally published: Bombay : Chetana, 1960. — Bibliography: p133-135
ISBN 0-04-294109-1 : Unpriced : CIP rev.
B79-30512

294.3′443 — Buddhist life. Meditation — *Manuals*

Khantipalo, Bhikkhu. Calm and insight : a Buddhist manual for meditators / Bhikkhu Khantipalo. — London : Curzon, 1981, c1980. — viii,152p : 1ill ; 22cm
ISBN 0-7007-0141-9 (pbk) : £3.00 : CIP rev.
B81-10460

294.3′443 — Tibetan Buddhist life — *Devotional works*

The **Rain** of wisdom : the essence of the ocean of true meaning, bringing the rain of wisdom, the spontaneous self-liberation, the blazing great bliss, the quick path to realization of the supreme siddhi : the vajra songs of the Kagyü gurus / translated by the Nālandā Translation Committee under the direction of Chögyam Trungpa. — Boulder ; London : Shambhala, 1980. — xxiii,384p ; 24cm
Translation from the Tibetan. — Includes index
ISBN 0-87773-196-9 (cased) : Unpriced
ISBN 0-87773-197-7 (pbk) : £7.95 B81-25969

294.3′443 — Tibetan Tantric Buddhist life. Meditation. Mantras

Tsoṅ-kha-pa Blo-bzaṅ-grags-pa. The yoga of Tibet : the great exposition of secret Mantra 2 and 3 / Tsong-ka-pa ; translated and edited by Jeffrey Hopkins ; associate editors for Tsong-ka-pa′s text Lati Rinbochay and Denma Locho Rinbochay ; assistant editor Elizabeth Napper ; introduced by His Holiness Tenzin Gyatso, the fourteenth Dalai Lama. — London : Allen & Unwin, 1981. — xii,274p : ill ; 22cm. — (The Wisdom of Tibet series ; 4)
Translation from the Tibetan. — Bibliography: p253-259. — Includes index
ISBN 0-04-294118-0 (cased) : £10.95
ISBN 0-04-294119-9 (pbk) : £5.95 B81-22089

294.3′443 — Vipaśyanā

Ginsberg, Mitchell. The far shore : Vispassanā, the practice of insight / by Mitchell Ginsberg. — London : Regency Press, c1980. — 100p : ill ; 23cm
Ill on lining papers
ISBN 0-7212-0577-1 : £3.00 B81-05960

294.3′443 — Zen Buddhist life. Meditation — *Manuals*

Samendra, Anand. The you book / Swami Anand Somendra. — [London] ([14 Mornington Crescent, NW1]) : Alchemy, 1981. — 171p : ill ; 21x31cm
Limited ed. of 500 copies
Unpriced (spiral) B81-29035

294.3′61 — China. Buddhism. Zhu hong

Yü, Chün-fang. The renewal of Buddhism in China : Chu-hung and the late Ming synthesis / Chün-fang Yü. — New York ; Guildford : Columbia University Press, 1981. — xvi,353p : ill ; 24cm. — (Buddhist studies and translations) (IASWR series)
Bibliography: p327-343. — Includes index
ISBN 0-231-04972-2 : £13.80 B81-15694

294.3′657′094288 — Northumberland. Carrshield. Zen Buddhist religious communities: Throssel Hole Priory — *Practical information*

Throssel Hole Priory : guest information. — Hexham (Carrshield, Hexham, Northumberland NE47 8AL) : Throssel Hole Priory, 1981. — 23p : ill,1map,ports ; 21cm
Cover title. — Text on inside covers
Unpriced (pbk) B81-37480

294.3′657′0952 — Japan. Rinzai Zen Buddhist monasteries, *1100-1600*

Collcutt, Martin. Five mountains : the Rinzai Zen monastic institution in Medieval Japan / Martin Collcutt. — Cambridge, Mass. ; London : Council on East Asian Studies, Harvard University Press, 1981. — xxi,399p : ill,facsims,plans,ports ; 24cm. — (Harvard East Asian monographs ; 85)
Bibliography: p335-359. — Includes index
ISBN 0-674-30497-7 : £14.00 B81-39826

294.3'82 — Theravada Buddhism. Scriptures — *Texts*

Bailey, H. W.. Khotanese Buddhist texts. — Rev. ed. — Cambridge : Cambridge University Press, Oct.1981. — [168]p. — (University of Cambridge oriental publications ; no.31)
Previous ed.: London : Taylor's Foreign Press, 1951
ISBN 0-521-23717-3 : £27.50 : CIP entry
B81-30496

294.3'822 — Buddhism. Vinayapitaka — *Commentaries — Pali texts*

Buddhaghosa. Samantapāsādikā : Buddhaghosa's commentary on the Vinaya Piṭka / edited by J. Takakusu and Makoto Nagai assisted by Kogen Mizuno. — London : Pali Text Society ; London : Distributed by Routledge & Kegan Paul. — (Text series ; no.115)
Vol.7. — 1947 (1981 [printing]). — p1302-1416 ; 23cm
ISBN 0-7100-0663-2 : Unpriced B81-40109

294.3'823 — Buddhism. Suttapitaka. *English. Selections — Texts*

[Suttapitaka. *English. Selections*]**The Buddha's** philosophy of man : early Indian Buddhist dialogues / arranged and edited by Trevor Ling. — London : Everyman, 1981. — xxvi,229p : 1map ; 19cm
Bibliography: p221-222. — Includes index
ISBN 0-460-01247-9 (pbk) : £2.50 : CIP rev.
B81-22629

294.3'92 — Mahayana Buddhism

Suzuki, Beatrice Lane. Mahayana Buddhism / Beatrice Lane Suzuki ; with an introduction by D.T. Suzuki ; and a foreword by Christmas Humphreys. — 4th ed. — London : Allen & Unwin, 1981. — xii,131p ; 23cm
Previous ed.: 1959. — Bibliography: p124-126
ISBN 0-04-294121-0 : Unpriced : CIP rev.
B81-15890

294.3'923 — Tibetan Buddhism

Tucci, Giuseppe. The religions of Tibet / Giuseppe Tucci ; translated from the German and Italian by Geoffrey Samuel. — London : Routledge & Kegan Paul, 1980. — xii,340p : ill,maps ; 23cm
Translation of: a selection from Die Religionen Tibets und der Mongolei. — Includes a chapter on Tibetan folk religion. — Bibliography: p275-287. — Includes index
ISBN 0-7100-0204-1 : £8.95 : CIP rev.
B79-22164

294.3'927 — Zen Buddhism

Dürckheim, Karlfried, *Graf von*. Hara : the vital centre of man / Karlfried Graf Von Dürckheim ; translated from the German by Sylvia-Monica Von Kospoth in collaboration with Estelle R. Healey. — London : Unwin Paperbacks, 1977 (1980 [printing]). — 208p,8p of plates : ill ; 20cm. — (Mandala books)
Translation of: Hara. — Originally published: London : Allan and Unwin, 1962
ISBN 0-04-290011-5 (pbk) : £2.25 B81-05973

294.5 — HINDUISM

294.5 — Hindu literature in Sanskrit, *ca B.C.500-ca A.D.800*

Masson, J. Moussaieff. The oceanic feeling : the origins of religious sentiments in ancient India / by J. Moussaieff Masson. — Dordrecht ; London : Reidel, c1980. — xv,213p ; 24cm. — ([Studies of classical India] ; v.3)
Bibliography: p143-207. - Includes index
ISBN 90-277-1050-3 : Unpriced B81-06109

294.5 — Hinduism

Chaudhuri, Nirad C.. Hinduism : a religion to live by / Nirad C. Chaudhuri. — Oxford : Oxford University Press, 1980, c1979. — xii,340p ; 21cm
Originally published: London : Chatto and Windus, 1979. — Bibliography: p331-332. — Includes index
ISBN 0-19-283033-3 (pbk) : £3.50 B81-15671

294.5 — Hinduism *compared with* **Christianity**

Panikkar, Raimundo. The unknown Christ of Hinduism : towards an ecumenical Christophany / Raimundo Panikkar. — Rev. and enl. ed. — London : Darton, Longman & Todd, c1981. — xii,195p ; 22cm
Previous ed.: 1965. — Bibliography: p170-182. - Includes index
ISBN 0-232-51496-8 (pbk) : £5.95 : CIP rev.
Also classified at 200 B80-24024

294.5 — Hinduism. Deva, Amrito, *Swami — Biographies*

Deva, Amrito, *Swami*. Coming home. — London : Wildwood House, Oct.1981. — [208]p
ISBN 0-7045-3053-8 : £7.95 : CIP entry
B81-28063

294.5'13 — Hindu myths. Śiva — *Anthologies*

Kramrisch, Stella. The presence of Śiva / Stella Kramrisch ; photography by Praful C. Patel. — Princeton ; Guildford : Princeton University press in cooperation with the Philadelphia Museum of Art, c1981. — x,514p,32leaves of plates : ill ; 24cm
Bibliography: p489-514. — Includes index
ISBN 0-691-03964-x (cased) : £21.80
ISBN 0-691-10115-9 (pbk: limited ed.) : £9.60
B81-28433

294.5'2 — International Society for Krishna Consciousness doctrine — *Interviews*

Lennon, John. Search for liberation : featuring a conversation between John Lennon and Swami Bhaktivedanta : Lennon '69. — Los Angeles ; London (Chaitanya College at Croome Court, Severn Stoke, Worcester WR8 9DW) : Bhaktivedanta Book Trust, 1981. — viii,66p : 1facsim,ports ; 18cm
ISBN 0-89213-109-8 (pbk) : Unpriced
B81-28329

294.5'37'0954 — India *(Republic)*. **Hinduism. Symbolism**

Sahi, Jyoti. The child and the serpent : reflections on popular Indian symbols / Jyoti Sahi. — London : Routledge & Kegan Paul, 1980. — xiv,218p : ill ; 24cm
Bibliography: p211-213. — Includes index
ISBN 0-7100-0704-3 (pbk) : £6.95 : CIP rev.
B80-26500

294.5'4 — Leela

Johari, Harish. Leela : game of knowledge / Harish Johari. — London : Routledge & Kegan Paul, 1980. — x,150p : ill ; 21cm
Translation of: Leela. — One folded sheet in pocket. — Bibliography: p150
ISBN 0-7100-0689-6 (pbk) : £6.95 : CIP rev.
B80-21391

294.5'43 — Rajneesh meditation centres — *Serials*

Rajneesh Buddhafield European newsletter. — Issue no.4-. — London (10a Belmont St., NW1 8HH) : Rajneesh Buddhafield European Newsletter, [1981]-. — v. : ill,ports ; 42cm
Monthly. — Continues: Sannyas news
ISSN 0261-8834 = Rajneesh Buddhafield European newsletter : £3.50 for 6 issues
B81-35446

294.5'65 — Friends of Lord Krishna — *Serials*

FOLK magazine : a quarterly journal for the Friends of Lord Krishna / The International Society for Krishna Consciousness. Great Britain. — Severn Stoke (Chaitanya College at Croome Court, Severn Stoke, Worcester, WR8 9DW) : The Friends, 1980-. — v. : ill,ports ; 28cm
Quarterly
ISSN 0260-938x = FOLK magazine : Unpriced B81-15148

294.5'65 — India. Hindu ashrams — *Practical information*

Murray, Muz. Seeking the Master : a guide to the ashrams of India / Muz Murray. — Jersey : Spearman, 1980. — 416p : ill,maps,ports ; 20cm
ISBN 0-85978-061-9 (cased) : £6.50
ISBN 0-85978-071-6 (pbk) : Unpriced
B81-05971

294.5'7 — India *(Republic)*. **Goshalas & pinjrapoles**

Lodrick, Deryck O.. Sacred cows, sacred places : origins and survivals of animal homes in India / Deryck O. Lodrick. — Berkeley ; London : University of California Press, c1981. — xii,307p : ill,maps ; 23cm
Bibliography: p271-293. — Includes index
ISBN 0-520-04109-7 : £20.00 B81-39757

294.5'9212 — Hinduism. Vedas. Ṛgveda. Literary aspects

Johnson, Willard. Poetry and speculation of the Ṛg Veda / Willard Johnson. — Berkeley ; London : University of California Press, c1980. — xxviii,192p : ill ; 23cm. — (Hermeneutics)
Bibliography: p181-183. — Includes index
ISBN 0-520-02560-1 : £11.00 B81-27567

294.5'9212 — Hinduism. Vedas. Rgveda — *Texts*

[Vedas. Rgveda. *English. Selections*]. The Rig veda : an anthology : one hundred and eight hymns / selected, translated and annotated by Wendy Doniger O'Flaherty. — Harmondsworth : Penguin, 1981. — 343p ; 18cm. — (Penguin classics)
Translated from the Sanskrit. — Bibliography: p301-320. — Includes index
ISBN 0-14-044402-5 (pbk) : £2.25 B81-40169

294.6 — SIKHISM

294.6'35 — Great Britain. Sikh temples — *Case studies — For children*

Babraa, Davinder Kaur. Visiting a Sikh temple / Davinder Kaur Babraa. — Guildford : Lutterworth Educational, 1981. — 59p : ill,1facsim,plans ; 21cm
Bibliography: p55. — Includes index
ISBN 0-7188-2472-5 (pbk) : £1.60 B81-14303

295 — ZOROASTRIANISM

295'.38 — Zoroastrianism. Rituals — *Middle Persian texts*

Erbadistān ud Nirangistān : facsimile edition of the manuscript TD : dedicated to the pious memory of Erbad Tahmurasp Dinshahji Anklesaria (1842-1903 A.C.) / edited by Firoze M. Kotwal, James W. Boyd. — Cambridge, Mass. ; London : Harvard University Press, c1980. — 12,131p ; 24cm. — (Harvard Iranian series ; v.3)
Persian text, English introduction and notes. — Facsim of: 17th century Middle Persian (Pahlavi) manuscript
ISBN 0-674-26040-6 (pbk) : £11.20 B81-38897

296 — JUDAISM

296 — Jewish myths — *Critical studies*

Goldstein, David, *1933-*. Jewish folklore and legend / David Goldstein. — London : Hamlyn, c1980. — 176p : ill,facsims,2maps ; 23cm
Bibliography: p170-172. - Includes index
ISBN 0-600-36365-1 : £6.00 B81-04021

296 — Judaism

Unterman, Alan. Jews : their religious beliefs and practices / Alan Unterman. — Boston, Mass. ; London : Routledge & Kegan Paul, 1981. — xiii,272p ; 23cm. — (Library of religious beliefs and practices)
Bibliography: p257-262. — Includes index
ISBN 0-7100-0743-4 (cased) : £10.50 : CIP rev.
ISBN 0-7100-0842-2 (pbk) : £6.50 B81-13717

296'.09'01 — Judaism, *to 100*

Stone, Michael E.. Scriptures, sects and visions. — Oxford : Blackwell, Jan.1982. — [160]p
Originally published: Petersham, N.S.W. : Maitland Publications, 1980
ISBN 0-631-13008-x : £7.95 : CIP entry
B81-34784

296'.09417 — Ireland *(Republic)*. **Judaism —** *Serials*

Irish-Jewish year book. — No.29 (5740) = 1979/80. — Dublin ([9 Crannagh Park, Dublin 14]) : Chief Rabbinate of Ireland, [1979]. — 88p
Unpriced B81-20063

296′.09417 — Ireland *(Republic)*. **Judaism** — *Serials* *continuation*
Irish-Jewish year book. — No.30 (5741) = 1980/81. — Dublin (9, Crannagh Park, Dublin 14) : [Chief Rabbinate of Ireland], [1980]. — [81]p
Unpriced B81-20064

296.1′276′00924 — Judaism. Aggadah. Theories of Isaac ben Jedaiah
Saperstein, Marc. Decoding the rabbis : a thirteenth-century commentary on the aggadah / Marc Saperstein. — Cambridge, Mass. ; London : Harvard University Press, 1980. — ix,289p ; 24cm. — (Harvard Judaic monographs ; 3)
Includes index
ISBN 0-674-19445-4 : £10.50 B81-12227

296.1′55 — Dead Sea scrolls *related to* **Christian doctrine**, *to ca 100*
Allegro, John M.. The Dead Sea scrolls and the Christian myth / John M. Allegro. — London : Abacus, 1981, c1979. — 248p,[8]p of plates : ill ; 20cm
Originally published: Newton Abbot : David and Charles, 1979. — Includes index
ISBN 0-349-10069-1 (pbk) : £2.50
Also classified at 230′.09′015 B81-12945

296.3 — Jewish doctrine
Kook, Abraham Isaac. Abraham Isaac Kook : the lights of penitence, the moral principles, lights of holiness, essays letters and poems / translation and introduction by Ben Zion Bokser ; preface by Jacob Agus and Rivka Schatz. — London : SPCK, 1979, c1978. — xxviii,415p,[1]leaf of plates : 1port ; 23cm. — (The Classics of Western spirituality)
Originally published: New York : Paulit Press, 1978. — Bibliography: p389-392. — Includes index
ISBN 0-281-03652-7 (pbk) : £6.95 B81-09792

296.3′872 — Jews. Relations with Catholics — *Catholic viewpoints*
Catholic-Jewish relations : official documents and pastoral guidelines. — London : Catholic Truth Society, 1981. — 18p ; 19cm
ISBN 0-85183-405-1 (pbk) : £0.30
Primary classification 261.2′6 B81-19726

296.3′8783576 — Homosexuality. Attitudes of Judaism
Blues, Lionel. Godly and gay : the fourth Michael Harding memorial address / by Lionel Blue. — London (BM Box 6914, WC1N 3XX) : Gay Christian Movement, c1981. — 15p ; 21cm
Unpriced (pbk) B81-37950

296.4′0933 — Ancient Israel. Judaism. Public worship *expounded by* **Bible. O.T.. Prophecies**
Eaton, J. H.. Vision in worship : the relation of prophecy and liturgy in the Old Testament / J.H. Eaton. — London : SPCK, 1981. — ix,115p ; 22cm
Bibliography: p111-112. — Includes index
ISBN 0-281-03800-7 (pbk) : £4.95 B81-27164

296.4′37 — Judaism. Passover services — *Rites — Hebrew-English parallel texts*
[Haggadah]. Passover Haggadah. — [London] ([109, Whitfield St., W.1]) : Union of Liberal and Progressive Synagogues, 1981. — ix,70p : col.ill ; 25cm
Parallel Hebrew text and English translation
ISBN 0-900521-06-6 (pbk) : Unpriced B81-24924

296.6′1′0924 — Judaism. Rabbis: Hirschell, Solomon — *Biographies*
Simons, Hyman A.. Forty years a Chief Rabbi : the life and times of Solomon Hirschell / Hyman A. Simons. — London : Robson, 1980. — 156p : 1facsim ; 23cm
ISBN 0-86051-090-5 : £6.25 : CIP rev. B79-35673

296.8′33 — Judaism. Cabala & hasidism. Teachers. Interpersonal relationships with students. Psychotherapeutic aspects
Mystics and medics : a comparison of mystical and psychotherapeutic encounters / edited by Reuven P. Bulka. — New York ; London : Human Sciences Press, 1979. — 120p ; 23cm
Includes bibliographies
ISBN 0-87705-377-4 (pbk) : £8.00 B81-39458

297 — ISLAM

297 — Islam
Goldziher, Ignaz. Introduction to Islamic theology and law / by Ignaz Goldziher ; translated by Andras and Ruth Hamori ; with an introduction and additional notes by Bernard Lewis. — Princeton ; Guildford : Princeton University Press, c1981. — xv,302p ; 25cm. — (Modern classics in Near Eastern studies)
Translation of: Vorlesungen über den Islam. — Bibliography: p269-295. — Includes index
ISBN 0-691-07257-4 (cased) : £12.50
ISBN 0-691-10099-3 (pbk) : £5.55 B81-18564

Hamidullah, Muhammad. Introduction to Islam / [Muhammad Hamidullah]. — 5th enl. ed. — Luton : Apex, 1980. — 348,vip,[3]leaves of plates(2folded) : ill,maps ; 22cm. — (Centre culturel islamique Paris series ; no.1/a)
Includes appendices in Arabic and English translation. — Also available in French, Turkish, German, Arabic, Africaans, Yugoslav, Tamil, Indonesian. — Previous ed.: Lahore : Sh. Muhammad Ashraf, 1974. — Bibliography: p328. — Includes index
ISBN 2-901049-05-2 (pbk) : Unpriced B81-26881

Ibn al-'Arabī, *Muḥyī al-Dīn*. The seals of wisdom / Muhyiddin Ibn al-Arabi ; [translated by 'Aisha 'Abdal-Rahman at-Tarjumana]. — Norwich : Diwan, c1980. — 207p ; 23cm
Translation of: Fuṣūṣ al-ḥikam
£5.95 B81-30707

Rahman, Afzalur. Islam : ideology and the way of life / Afzalur Rahman. — London (78 Gillespie Rd, N5 1LN) : Muslim Schools Trust, 1980. — 409p ; 22cm
ISBN 0-907052-05-3 (cased) : Unpriced
ISBN 0-907052-04-5 (pbk) : Unpriced B81-30092

Roberts, D. S.. Islam : a Westerner′s guide / D.S. Roberts. — London : Kogan Page, 1981. — 192p : maps ; 23cm
Bibliography: p192
ISBN 0-85038-345-5 : £8.25 B81-38903

297 — Islam — *For children*
Denffer, Ahmad von. Islam for children / Ahmad von Denffer ; [translator: Hatifah von Denffer] ; [illustrator: Arshad Gamiet]. — Leicester (223 London Rd., Leicester, LE2 1ZE) : Islamic Foundation, c1981. — 176p : ill ; 21cm. — (Muslim children′s library)
Translation of: Islam für Kinder
ISBN 0-86037-085-2 (pbk) : Unpriced B81-18383

Sarwar, Ghulam. Islam for younger people / Ghulam Sarwar. — London (130 Stroud Green Rd, London) : Muslim Educational Trust, 1981. — 64p : ill(some col.) ; 21cm
Bibliography: p64
ISBN 0-907261-02-7 (pbk) : £1.25 : CIP rev. B81-18169

297 — Islam — *For schools*
Thompson, Jan. Islamic belief and practice. — London : Edward Arnold, Oct.1981. — [80]p
ISBN 0-7131-0586-0 (pbk) : £1.75 : CIP entry B81-28032

297 — Islam *related to* **Christianity**
Dialogue between Christians and Muslims. — Leicester (223 London Rd., Leicester LE2 1ZE) : Islamic Foundation. — (Documents on Christianity and Christian Muslim relations ; no.1)
3: Dialogue between Christians and Muslims : statements and resolutions / edited by Ahmad von Denffer. — 1980. — 45p ; 30cm
ISBN 0-86037-062-3 (pbk) : Unpriced
Primary classification 200 B81-16790

297′.09181′2 — Western world. Islam
Murad, Khurram. Islamic movement in the West : reflections on some issues / Khurram Murad. — Leicester (223, London Rd, Leicester LE2 1ZE) : Islamic Foundation, 1981. — 29p ; 30cm
ISBN 0-86037-093-3 (pbk) : Unpriced B81-34683

297′.0966 — West Africa. Islam, *ca 700-1980*
Clarke, Peter B.. West Africa and Islam. — London : Edward Arnold, Feb.1982. — [256]p
ISBN 0-7131-8029-3 (pbk) : £3.50 : CIP entry B81-37564

297′.09669 — Nigeria. Islam
Lindsay, ′Abd al-Mumin. Nigeria : the subversion of Islam / ′Abd al-Mumin Lindsay. — Norwich (52 Colegate, Norwich NR3 1DD) : Diwan, c1978. — 41p : ill,1map ; 18cm. — (The Darqawi Institute papers)
ISBN 0-906512-04-2 (pbk) : £1.00 B81-20793

297′.122 — Islam. Koran — *Stories for children*
The **First** man on earth : the story of Adam and Hawwa / illustrations by Afsar Siddiqui. — London : MWH London, c1979. — [24]p : col.ill ; 21cm
ISBN 0-906194-10-5 (pbk) : £0.65 B81-36437

297′.122′0922 — Islam. Koran. Pre-Islamic prophets — *Biographies — For Muslim children*
Ashraf, Syed Ali. The prophets / Syed Ali Ashraf. — Sevenoaks : Hodder & Stoughton [for the] Union of Muslim Organisations, c1980. — vi,58p : ill(some col.) ; 26cm
ISBN 0-340-24837-8 (cased) : £3.75 : CIP rev.
ISBN 0-340-24840-8 (pbk) : £2.50
Also classified at 297′.124′00922 B80-08607

297′.1224 — Islam. Koran — *Arabic-English parallel texts*
[Koran. *Arabic. 1981*]. The Quran. — 3rd ed., rev. and reset. — London : Curzon Press, Dec.1981. — [736]p
Previous ed.: 1975
ISBN 0-7007-0148-6 : £6.50 : CIP entry B81-39227

297′.1225′21 — Islam. Koran — *Texts*
[Koran. *English. 1955*]. The Koran interpreted / by Arthur J. Arberry. — London : Allen & Unwin, 1955 (1980 [printing]). — 367p ; 23cm
Originally published: in 2 vols.. — Includes index
ISBN 0-04-297040-7 : Unpriced B81-08174

297′.1226 — Islam. Koran — *Expositions*
as-Sufi, 'Abd al-Qadir. Indications from signs / 'Abd al-Qadir as-Sufi. — Norwich : Iqra Communications, c1979. — 58p ; 18cm
Unpriced (pbk) B81-26946

Qutb, Sayyid. In the shade of the Qur′ān / Sayyid Qutb ; translated by M. Adil Salahi, Ashur A. Shamis. — London : MWH
Vol.30. — c1979. — xvii,366p : ill ; 22cm
Translation of the Arabic. ′Surah′ also in Arabic
ISBN 0-906194-06-7 (cased) : Unpriced
ISBN 0-906194-07-5 (pbk) : £3.00
ISBN 0-906194-15-6 (set(cased)) : unpriced
ISBN 0-906194-16-4 (set(pbk)) : unpriced B81-38688

297′.1226 — Islam. Koran - *Expositions - For schools*
Doi, A. Rahman I.. Introduction to the Qur′an. — London : Hodder & Stoughton, May 1981. — [128]p
ISBN 0-340-26705-4 (pbk) : £3.00 : CIP entry B81-13581

297′.124 — Islam. Hadith — *Critical studies*
Hamidullah, Muhammad. Sahifah Hammam Ibn Munabbi : the earliest extant work on the Hadith : comprising as Sahifah as—Sahihah of Aleu—Hurairah (d.58H./677) prepared for his pupil Hammam ibn Munabbih d.101H./719), together with an introduction to the history of the early compilation of the Hadith / by Muhammad Hamidullah ; translated into English by Muhammad Rahimuddin. — 10th rev. and enl. ed. — Luton : Apex, 1979. — 158,xviiip,[2]leaves of plates : ill,2facsims ; 22cm. — (Publication of Centre culturel islamique Paris ; no.2/c)
Includes the text in Arabic. — Previous ed.: Paris : Centre culturel islamique 1961. — Bibliography: pi-iii. — Includes index
ISBN 2-901049-06-0 (pbk) : Unpriced B81-26882

297'.124'00922 — Islam. Hadith. Pre-Islamic prophets — *Biographies — For Muslim children*

Ashraf, Syed Ali. The prophets / Syed Ali Ashraf. — Sevenoaks : Hodder & Stoughton [for the] Union of Muslim Organisations, c1980. — vi,58p : ill(some col.) ; 26cm
ISBN 0-340-24837-8 (cased) : £3.75 : CIP rev.
ISBN 0-340-24840-8 (pbk) : £2.50
Primary classification 297'.122'0922 B80-08607

297'.1240521 — Islam. Hadith — *Collections*

40 hadith / [collected by] Imam an-Nawawi. — Norwich (52A Colegate, Norwich NR3 1DD) : Diwan Press, [1981?]. — [28]p ; 22cm
Unpriced (pbk) B81-27049

297'.12406 — Islam. Hadith — *For Nigerian students — For schools*

Doi, A. Rahman I.. Introduction to the Hadith. — London : Hodder & Stoughton, Aug.1981. — [144]p
ISBN 0-340-26706-2 (pbk) : £1.75 : CIP entry B81-21650

297'.1972 — Islam. Relations with Christianity — *Muslim viewpoints*

Denffer, Ahmad von. Some reflections on dialogue between Christians and Muslims / Ahmad von Denffer. — Leicester (223 London Rd., Leicester, LE2 1ZE) : The Islamic Foundation, c1980. — 22p ; 30cm. — (Seminar papers / Islamic Foundation ; 10)
ISBN 0-86037-084-4 (pbk) : Unpriced
Also classified at 261.2'7 B81-18607

297'.1977 — Islam. Political aspects

as-Sufi, 'Abd al-Qadir. Resurgent Islam : 1400 Hijra / 'Abd al-Qadir as-Sufi. — Norwich : Diwan, c1979. — 56p : 2facsims ; 21cm
Bibliography: p52
£1.50 (pbk) B81-26947

Islam and power / edited by Alexander S. Cudsi and Ali E. Hillal Dessouki. — London : Croom Helm, c1981. — 204p ; 23cm. — (Croom Helm series on the Arab world)
Includes index
ISBN 0-7099-0710-9 : £11.95 : CIP rev. B81-14927

297'.1977 — Islam. Revival. Political aspects

Dodd, C. H. (Clement Henry). The revival of Islam and the modern nation state / by C.H. Dodd. — [Hull] : University of Hull, Department of Politics, 1981. — 16 leaves ; 30cm. — (Hull papers in politics, ISSN 0142-7377 ; no.23)
Unpriced (unbound) B81-23288

297'.1977 — Politics. Role of Islam

The **Islamic** revolution : achievements, obstacles & goals / Kalim Siddiqui ... [et al.]. — London (3 Endsleigh St., WC1H 0DS) : Open Press in association with The Muslim Institute, 1400, 1980. — 48p ; 21cm
ISBN 0-905081-07-2 (pbk) : £1.50 : CIP rev. B80-22899

The **Politics** of Islamic reassertion / edited by Mohammed Ayoob. — London : Croom Helm, c1981. — 298p ; 23cm
Includes index
ISBN 0-7099-0339-1 : £12.95 : CIP rev. B81-05127

297'.2 — Islamic doctrine

Ibn al'Arabī, *Muḥyī al-Dīn*. The bezels of wisdom / Ibn al'Arabi ; translation and introduction by R.W.J. Austin ; preface by Titus Burckhardt. — London : SPCK, 1980. — xviii,302p ; 23cm. — (The Classics of Western spirituality)
Translation of: Fuṣūṣ al-ḥikam. — Bibliography: p285-287. — Includes index
ISBN 0-281-03785-x (pbk) : £7.50 B81-36650

297'.2 — Sufi doctrine

Dougan, Abdullah. The quest / Abdullah Dougan. — Auckland ; East Grinstead (31 Old Convent, Moat Rd., East Grinstead, W. Sussex RH19 3RS) : Gnostic Press
Pt.1: Ideas. — 1981. — 607p ; 24cm
ISBN 0-9597566-1-2 : Unpriced B81-38268

Waliullah, *Shah*. Sufism and the Islamic tradition : the Lamahat and Sata'at of Shah Waliullah / translated by G.N. Jalbani and edited by D.B. Fry. — London : Octagon, 1980. — 127p ; 23cm
Translation from the Persian
ISBN 0-900860-81-2 : £10.00 B81-11255

297'.20413 — Malikite Islamic doctrine - *For West African students - For schools*

Doi, A. Rahman I.. The cardinal principles of Islam (according to the Maliki system). — Sevenoaks : Hodder & Stoughton, May 1981. — [192]p
ISBN 0-340-26704-6 (pbk) : £3.00 : CIP entry B81-07475

297'.2'07 — Islamic doctrine. Literary sources, *622-902*

Cook, M. A. (Michael Allan). Early Muslim dogma : a source-critical study / Michael Cook. — Cambridge : Cambridge University Press, 1981. — xi,242p : ill ; 23cm
Includes appendix in Arabic. — Includes index
ISBN 0-521-23379-8 : £19.50 : CIP rev. B81-07439

297'.211'0924 — Islamic doctrine. God. Theories of Iqbal, *Sir* **Muhammad,** *1877-1938*

Raschid, M. S.. Iqbal's concept of God / M.S. Raschid. — London : Kegan Paul International, 1981. — xiv,124p : 1port ; 23cm
Bibliography: p117-120. — Includes index
ISBN 0-7103-0004-2 : £10.50 : CIP rev. B81-13705

297'.4 — Sufism

Jāmī. Lawā'iḥ : a treatise on Ṣūfism / by Nūr-ud-dīn 'Abd-ur-Raḥmān Jāmī ... ; with a translation by E.H. Whinfield & Mīrzā Muhammad Kazvīnī ; and preface on the influence of Greek philosophy upon Ṣūfism. — 2nd ed. / new introduction by Seyyed Hossein Nasr, Repr. with additions and corrections. — London : Theosophical Publishing, 1978. — xxvii,61,[54]p ; 20cm
Text in English and Persian. — Originally published: as Oriental Translation Fund. New Series. v.16. London : Oriental Translation Fund, 1914
ISBN 0-7229-5135-3 (cased) : Unpriced
ISBN 0-7229-5136-1 (pbk) : £3.50 B81-39934

Lings, Martin. What is Sufism / Martin Lings. — 2nd ed. — London : Unwin Paperbacks, 1981. — 139p ; 20cm
Previous ed.: London : Allen & Unwin, 1975. — Includes index
ISBN 0-04-297039-3 (pbk) : £2.50 : CIP rev. B81-00014

The **Sufi** mystery / edited by Nathaniel P. Archer. — London : Octagon, c1980. — 218p ; 23cm
ISBN 0-900860-79-0 : Unpriced B81-07241

297'.4 — Sufism — *Arabic texts*

'Isā, 'Abd al-Qādir. Haqā'iq 'an al taṣawuf / Shayleh 'Abd al-Qādir 'Isā. — Norwich : Diwan, [1981?]. — 704p : ill,facsims ; 25cm
Unpriced (pbk) B81-27829

297'.4 — Sufism — *Early works*

Obadyāh b. Abraham b. Moses Maimonides. [Al-Maqāla al-hawdiyya. English]. The treatise of the pool = Al-Maqāla al-Hawdiyya / Obadyāh b. Abraham b. Moses Maimonides ; edited for the first time from a manuscript in the Bodleian Library, Oxford and Genizah fragments with a translation and notes by Paul Fenton ; with a preface by Georges Vajda. — London : Octagon, 1981. — 146,[30]p of plates : ill ; 23cm
Translation of: Al-Maqāla al-hawdiyya. — Parallel Judaeo-Arabic and English text, preface in French. — Bibliography: p140-146
ISBN 0-900860-87-1 : £10.00 B81-39290

297'.4'0955 — Iran. Sufism

Corbin, Henry. The man of light in Iranian Sufism / Henry Corbin ; translated from the French by Nancy Pearson. — Boulder ; London : Shambhala, 1978. — 174p ; 22cm
Translation of: L'Homme de lumière dans le soufisme iranien. — Bibliography: p161-162. — Includes index
ISBN 0-394-73441-6 (pbk) : £5.95 B81-36157

297'.43 — Islamic life. Prayer

Rahman, Afzalur. Prayer : its significance and benefits / Afzalur Rahman. — London (78 Gillespie Rd, N5 1LN) : Muslim Schools Trust, 1979. — 302p ; 21cm
ISBN 0-907052-00-2 (pbk) : £3.30 B81-30094

297'.446 — Islamic life. Salutations — *For children*

Kayani, M. S.. Assalamu alaikum = Peace be with you / [writer and researcher M.S. Kayani]. — Leicester (223 London Rd., Leicester) : Islamic Foundation, c1981. — 28p : col.ill ; 21cm. — (Muslim children's library)
ISBN 0-86037-076-3 (pbk) : Unpriced B81-14729

Kayani, M. S.. Love all creatures / [writer and researcher M. S. Kayani]. — Leicester 223 London Rd., Leicester : Islamic Foundation, 1981. — 36p : col.ill ; 21cm. — (Muslim children's library)
ISBN 0-86037-077-1 (pbk) : Unpriced B81-14730

297'.5 — Economics. Islamic ethics

Naqvi, Syed Nawab Haider. Ethics and economics : an Islamic synthesis / Syed Nawab Haider Naqvi. — Leicester : Islamic Foundation, c1981. — 176p ; 22cm. — (Islamic economic series ; 2)
Includes index
ISBN 0-86037-079-8 (cased) : Unpriced
ISBN 0-86037-080-1 (pbk) : Unpriced B81-18851

297'.63 — Islam. Muhammad *(Prophet)* — *Biographies*

Rahman, Afzalur. Muhammad : blessing for mankind / Afzalur Rahman. — London (78 Gillespie Rd, N5 1LN) : Muslim Schools Trust, 1979. — vi,337p ; 22cm
ISBN 0-907052-01-0 (pbk) : £3.80 B81-30093

Rahman, Afzalur. Muhammad. — London (78 Gillespie Rd, N5 1LN) : Muslim Schools Trust, Dec.1981. — [300]p
ISBN 0-907052-11-8 (cased) : £5.00 : CIP entry
ISBN 0-907052-10-x (pbk) : £3.00 B81-31520

Zafrulla Khan, Muhammad. Muhammad : seal of the prophets / Muhammad Zafrulla Khan. — London : Routledge & Kegan Paul, 1980. — viii,289p ; 22cm
Biblioghraphy p284. — Includes index
ISBN 0-7100-0610-1 (pbk) : £4.95 : CIP rev. B80-20201

297'.63 — Islam. Muhammad *(Prophet)* — *Stories for children*

Kayani, M. S.. A great friend of children / [writer and researcher M.S. Kayani]. — Leicester (223 London Rd., Leicester) : Islamic Foundation, c1981. — 38p : col.ill ; 21cm. — (Muslim children's library)
ISBN 0-86037-078-x (pbk) : Unpriced B81-14731

Tarantino, Mardijah Aldrich. Marvellous stories from the life of Muhammad. — Leicester (223 London Road, Leicester LE2 12E) : Islamic Foundation, Feb.1982. — [128]p. — (Muslim children's library)
ISBN 0-86037-103-4 (pbk) : £1.95 : CIP entry B81-39250

297'.63 — Islam. Muhammad *(Prophet)*. **Teachings**

Rahman, Afzalur. Muhammad : the educator of mankind / Afzalur Rahman. — London (78 Gillespie Rd., N5 1LN) : Muslim Schools Trust, 1980. — vi,473p ; 22cm
ISBN 0-907052-09-6 (cased) : Unpriced
ISBN 0-907052-08-8 (pbk) : Unpriced B81-34264

297'.89 — Bahaism

Báb, 'Al ī Muhammad Sh ī r ā z ī. Inspiring the heart / selections from the writings of the Báb, Bahá'u'lláh and 'Abdu'l-Bahá. — London : Bahá'í Publishing Trust, [1981?]. — 200p ; 20cm
Includes index. — Publisher's no. B189
ISBN 0-900125-45-4 (corrected) : Unpriced B81-20910

297'.89 — Bahaism — *Correspondence, diaries, etc*
Shoghi, *effendi*. The unfolding destiny of the British Bahá'í community : the messages from the Guardian of the Bahá'í faith to the Bahá'ís of the British Isles. — London : Bahá'í Publishing Trust, 1981. — xviii,529p,[1]leaf of plates : ill(some col.),facsims,2ports ; 23cm
Letters and cables of Shoghi Effendi Rabbani. — Includes index. — Publisher's No.B169
ISBN 0-900125-43-8 : Unpriced B81-17861

297'.89'07 — Children. Bahai religious education — *For parents*
Nakhjavání, Bahíyyih. When we grow up / Bahíyyih Nakhjavání. — Oxford : Ronald, c1979 (1980 [printing]). — 112p ; 20cm
Bibliography: p110-112
ISBN 0-85398-085-3 (cased) : £2.65
ISBN 0-85398-086-1 (pbk) : Unpriced B81-11586

297'.89'09 — Bahaism, *to 1944*
The **Bábí** and Bahá'í religions 1844-1944 : some contemporary Western accounts / edited by Moojan Momen. — Oxford : Ronald, c1981. — xxx,572p,[16]p of plates : ill,2maps,1facsim,ports ; 24cm
Bibliography: p532-542. — Includes index
ISBN 0-85398-102-7 : £12.00 B81-37431

297'.8917 — Education — *Bahai viewpoints*
Rost, H. T. D.. The brilliant stars : the Bahá'í Faith and the education of children / H.T.D. Rost. — Oxford : Ronald, c1979. — ix,182p ; 22cm
Bibliography: p178-182
ISBN 0-85398-082-9 (cased) : £3.85 B81-11642

297'.8923 — Bahaist doctrine. Death
Death the messenger of joy / [compiled by] Madeleine Hellaby. — London : Bahá'í Publishing Trust, c1980. — 34p ; 22cm
A compilation of the writings of Bahá'u'lláh and Abdu'l-Bahá
ISBN 0-900125-42-x (pbk) : Unpriced B81-07754

297'.8943 — Bahaism — *Devotional works*
A **Compilation** on the importance of prayer, meditation and the devotional attitude / compiled by the Research Department of the Universal House of Justice. — Oakham : Bahai, 1980. — 20p : ill ; 21cm
Unpriced (pbk) B81-17795

299.1/4 — NON-CHRISTIAN RELIGIONS. INDO-EUROPEAN, SEMITIC, HAMITIC, URAL-ALTAIC

299'.162 — Irish myths — *Anthologies*
Early Irish myths and sagas / translated with an introduction and notes by Jeffrey Gantz. — Harmondsworth : Penguin, 1981. — vi,280p ; 18cm. — (Penguin classics)
Bibliography: p28-31. — Includes index
ISBN 0-14-044397-5 (pbk) : £1.95 B81-40009

299'.31 — Ancient Egyptian religion. Symbolism — *Encyclopaedias*
Lurker, Manfred. The gods and symbols of ancient Egypt : an illustrated dictionary / Manfred Lurker. — London : Thames and Hudson, c1980. — 142p : ill,1map ; 25cm
Translation of: Götter und Symbole der alten Ägypter. — Bibliography: p136-137. - Includes index
ISBN 0-500-11018-2 : £8.95 B81-05419

299.5 — NON-CHRISTIAN RELIGIONS OF EAST AND SOUTHEAST ASIAN ORIGIN

299'.512 — Confucianism
Dawson, Raymond. Confucius / Raymond Dawson. — Oxford : Oxford University Press, 1981. — viii,95p ; 19cm. — (Past masters)
Bibliography: p91-92. — Includes index
ISBN 0-19-287537-x (cased) : Unpriced : CIP rev.
ISBN 0-19-287536-1 (pbk) : £1.25 B81-25789

299'.514 — Taoism
Cooper, J. C.. Yin and Yang. — Wellingborough : Aquarian Press, Oct.1981. — [128]p
ISBN 0-85030-265-x (pbk) : £3.50 : CIP entry B81-27971

Liu, Da. The Tao and Chinese culture / Da Liu. — London : Routledge & Kegan Paul, 1981, c1979. — vii,168p ; 22cm
Originally published: New York : Schocken Books, 1979. — Includes index
ISBN 0-7100-0841-4 (pbk) : £3.95 : CIP rev. B81-25670

299.6 — NON-CHRISTIAN RELIGIONS OF BLACK AFRICAN AND NEGRO ORIGIN

299'.68 — East Africa. Nilotes. Religious beliefs *compared with* **religious beliefs of Proto-Indo-Iranians**
Lincoln, Bruce. Priests, warriors, and cattle : a study in the ecology of religions / Bruce Lincoln. — Berkeley ; London : University of California Press, c1981. — xiii,242p : ill ; 24cm. — (Hermeneutics ; 10)
Bibliography: p185-215. — Includes index
ISBN 0-520-03880-0 : £19.50
Also classified at 294 B81-27496

299'.683 — Nigeria. Igbo. Religious beliefs
Metuh, Emehie Ikenga. God and man in African religion. — London : Geoffrey Chapman, July 1981. — [198]p
ISBN 0-225-66279-5 (pbk) : £4.50 : CIP entry B81-14468

299'.683 — North-western Tanzania. Zinza. Religious beliefs
Bjerke, Svein. Religion and misfortune : the Bacwezi complex and the other spirit cults of the Zinza of Northwestern Tanzania / Svein Bjerke. — Oslo : Universitetsforlaget ; London : Global Book Resources [distributor], c1981. — vii,318p : ill,maps ; 22cm
Bibliography: p314-318. — Includes index
ISBN 82-00-05681-3 (pbk) : £13.85 B81-33596

299.7 — NON-CHRISTIAN RELIGIONS OF NORTH AMERICAN INDIAN ORIGIN

299'.72 — Karok myths — *Anthologies*
Kroeber, A. L.. Karok myths / A.L. Kroeber, E.W. Gifford ; edited by Grace Buzaljko ; foreword by Theodora Kroeber ; folkloristic commentary by Alan Dundes ; linguistic index by William Bright. — Berkeley ; London : University of California Press, c1980. — xlix,380p : 1map,ports ; 24cm
Bibliography p331-335. — Includes index
ISBN 0-520-03870-3 : £15.00 B81-06993

299'.72 — Myths — *Study examples: American Indian myths*
Lévi-Strauss, Claude. The naked man / Claude Lévi-Strauss ; translated from the French by John and Doreen Weightman. — London : Cape, 1981. — 746p : ill,maps ; 24cm. — (Introduction to a science of mythology ; 4)
Bibliography: p696-713. — Includes index
ISBN 0-224-01535-4 : £17.50 : CIP rev. B80-20202

299'.72 — North American Indian myths — *Anthologies*
Where is the eagle? / [compiled by] William E. Coffer (Koi Hosh). — New York ; London : Van Nostrand Reinhold, c1981. — xvii,271p,[13]leaves of plates : ill ; 24cm
Includes index
ISBN 0-442-26163-2 : £12.70 B81-25377

299'.75 — Mexico. Yacqui. Shamanism — *Personal observations*
Castaneda, Carlos. The eagle's gift / by Carlos Castaneda. — London : Hodder and Stoughton, 1981. — 316p ; 22cm
ISBN 0-340-25882-9 : £6.95 B81-29746

299'.78 — Mexico. Aztecs. Religious beliefs
Brundage, Burr Cartwright. The fifth sun : Aztec gods, Aztec world / by Burr Cartwright Brundage ; illustrated by Roy E. Anderson. — Austin ; London : University of Texas Press, 1979. — xiii,269p : ill ; 24cm. — (The Texas Pan American series)
Bibliography: p251-258. - Includes index
ISBN 0-292-72427-6 : £9.00 B81-19748

299.9 — NON-CHRISTIAN RELIGIONS OF AUSTRONESIAN, OCEANIC, MISCELLANEOUS ORIGIN

299'.93 — Cosmic Religion
Rommayne, P. D.. Christ's gospel is the cosmic religion / P.D. Rommayne. — London (43 New Oxford St., WC1A 1BH) : P.D. Rommayne, [1981?]. — 32p ; 15cm
Unpriced (pbk) B81-17901

299'.934'09 — Theosophy, *to 1980*
Campbell, Bruce F.. Ancient wisdom revived : a history of the Theosophical movement / Bruce F. Campbell. — Berkeley ; London : University of California Press, c1980. — x,249p,[2]p of plates : 1ill,ports ; 23cm
Bibliography: p227-241. — Includes index
ISBN 0-520-03968-8 : £7.75 B81-01899

299'.936'05 — Scientology — *Serials*
[Communication! *(East Grinstead)***]**.
Communication! : the Saint Hill Foundation magazine : incorporating Change!. — Vol.1, issue 1-. — East Grinstead (St. Hill Manor, East Grinstead, West Sussex RH19 4JY) : Saint Hill Foundation and Dianetics Information Centre, c1980-. — v. : ill ; 21cm
Twenty-four issues yearly. — Continues: Change (East Grinstead)
ISSN 0260-6011 = Communication! (East Grinstead) : Unpriced B81-06477

300 — SOCIAL SCIENCES

300 — Behavioural sciences - *Conference proceedings*
The **Behavioural** sciences and industrial relations. — Farnborough, Hants. : Gower, July 1981. — [208]p
Conference papers
ISBN 0-566-00383-x : £10.00 : CIP entry
Also classified at 331 B81-14874

300 — Inequality
Green, Philip. The pursuit of inequality. — Oxford : Robertson, June 1981. — [336]p
ISBN 0-85520-446-x : £10.00 : CIP entry B81-10014

300 — Social sciences
Schusky, Ernest L.. Introduction to social science / Ernest Schusky. — Englewood Cliffs ; London : Prentice-Hall, c1981. — xiii,512p : ill,facsims,map,ports ; 24cm
Bibliography: p495-500. — Includes index
ISBN 0-13-496703-8 (pbk) : £11.85 B81-33127

300 — Social sciences. Applications of general systems theory
Hanken, A. F. G.. Social systems and learning systems / A.F.G. Hanken, H.A. Reuver. — Boston ; London : Nijhoff, c1981. — x,246p : ill ; 24cm. — (Frontiers in systems research ; v.4)
Bibliography: p229-236. — Includes index
ISBN 0-89838-050-2 : Unpriced B81-29761

300 — Social sciences. Evaluation
House, Ernest R.. Evaluating with validity / Ernest R. House. — Beverly Hills ; London : Sage, 1980. — 295p : ill ; 22cm
Bibliography: p287-294
ISBN 0-8039-1438-5 (cased) : Unpriced
ISBN 0-8039-1439-3 (pbk) : £6.25 B81-18613

300 — Social sciences. Explanation
Garfinkel, Alan. Forms of explanation : rethinking the questions in social theory / Alan Garfinkel. — New Haven ; London : Yale University Press, c1981. — xi,186p ; 22cm
Includes index
ISBN 0-300-02136-4 : £10.00 B81-18211

Turner, Stephen P.. Sociological explanation as translation / Stephen P. Turner. — Cambridge : Cambridge University Press, 1980. — x,110p ; 24cm. — (The Arnold and Caroline Rose monograph series of the American Sociological Association)
Bibliography: p103-105. — Includes index
ISBN 0-521-23030-6 (cased) : £9.00
ISBN 0-521-29773-7 (pbk) : £2.95 B81-25185

300 — Social sciences — *Festschriften*

Social science - for what? : festschrift for Johan Galtung / Hans-Henrik Holm and Erik Rudeng (eds.). — Oslo : Universitetsforlaget ; London : Global [distributor], c1980. — 223p : ill,1port ; 23cm
Includes one essay in French, one in German and one poem in Italian
ISBN 82-00-05521-3 : Unpriced B81-03029

300 — Society. Role of social sciences

MacRae, Duncan. The social function of social science. — London : Yale University Press, Apr.1981. — [367]p
Originally published: 1976
ISBN 0-300-02670-6 (pbk) : £5.00 : CIP entry B81-10005

300′.1 — Philosophy of social sciences. Theories — *Comparative studies*

Thompson, John B.. Critical hermeneutics : a study in the thought of Paul Ricoeur and Jürgen Habermas / John B. Thompson. — Cambridge : Cambridge University Press, 1981. — ix, 257p : ill ; 24cm
Bibliography: p241-251. — Includes index
ISBN 0-521-23932-x : £17.50 : CIP rev. B81-20614

300′.1 — Philosophy of social sciences. Theories of Marx, Karl & Wittgenstein, Ludwig

Rubinstein, David. Marx and Wittgenstein : social praxis and social explanation / David Rubinstein. — London : Routledge & Kegan Paul, 1981. — 231p ; 23cm
Bibliography: p220.228. — Includes index
ISBN 0-7100-0688-8 : £12.50 B81-25331

300′.1 — Social sciences — *Philosophical perspectives*

Macdonald, Graham. Semantics and social science / Graham Macdonald, Philip Pettit. — London : Routledge & Kegan Paul, 1981. — 194p ; 23cm
Bibliography: p186-190. — Includes index
ISBN 0-7100-0783-3 (cased) : £8.95 : CIP rev.
ISBN 0-7100-0784-1 (pbk) : £4.95 B81-13727

300′.1 — Social sciences - ***Philosophical perspectives***

Van Parijs, Philippe. Evolutionary exploration in the social sciences. — London : Tavistock, July 1981. — [288]p
ISBN 0-422-77860-5 : £14.50 : CIP entry B81-13469

300′.1 — Social sciences. Theories

Bergner, Jeffrey T.. The origin of formalism in social science / Jeffrey T. Bergner. — Chicago ; London : University of Chicago Press, 1981. — xi,162p ; 23cm
Includes index
ISBN 0-226-04362-2 : £9.60 B81-28350

300′.1 — Social sciences. Yugoslav theories

Praxis : Yugoslav essays in the philosophy and methodology of the social sciences : with the cumulative index to the international edition of Praxis, 1965-1974 / translated by Joan Coddington, David Rougé and others ; edited by Mihailo Marković and Gajo Petrović. — Dordrecht ; London : Reidel, c1979. — xxxvii,403p ; 23cm. — (Synthese library, ISSN 0166-6991 ; v.134) (Boston studies in the philosophy of science ; v.26)
Translated from the Serbo-Croation (roman). — Includes index
ISBN 90-277-0727-8 (cased) : Unpriced
ISBN 90-277-0968-8 (pbk) : Unpriced B81-07831

300.1 — Western Europe. Society — *Philosophical perspectives*

Fink, Hans. Social philosophy. — London : Methuen, Oct.1981. — [114]p
ISBN 0-416-71990-2 (cased) : £6.00 : CIP entry
ISBN 0-416-72000-5 (pbk) : £2.75 B81-28082

300′.1′5192 — Social sciences. Probabilities & statistical mathematics

Bartholomew, David J.. Mathematical methods in social science / David J. Bartholomew. — Chichester : Wiley, c1981. — ix,153p ; 24cm. — (Handbook of applicable mathematics ; [guidebook 1])
Bibliography: p144-148. — Includes index
ISBN 0-471-27932-3 (cased) : £10.50
ISBN 0-471-27933-1 (pbk) : Unpriced B81-35742

300′.1′51953 — Behavioural sciences. Cluster analysis

Mezzich, Juan E.. Taxonomy and behavioral science : comparative performance of grouping methods / Juan E. Mezzich and Herbert Solomon. — London : Academic Press, 1980. — xiv,178p : ill ; 24cm. — (Quantitative studies in social relations)
Bibliography: p170-175. - Includes index
ISBN 0-12-493340-8 : £10.80 : CIP rev. B80-18168

300′.1′51953 — Social sciences. Causal analysis

Birnbaum, Ian. An introduction to causal analysis in sociology / Ian Birnbaum. — London : Macmillan, 1981. — x,167p : ill ; 23cm
Bibliography: p160-163. — Includes index
ISBN 0-333-26111-9 (cased) : £15.00 : CIP rev.
ISBN 0-333-26112-7 (pbk) : Unpriced B80-20207

300′.1′8 — Social sciences. Concepts. Formation

Pawlowski, Tadeusz. Concept formation in the humanities and the social sciences / Tadeusz Pawlowski. — Dordrecht ; London : Reidel, c1980. — ix,229p ; 23cm. — (Synthese library, ISSN 0166-6991 ; v.144)
Bibliography: p221-224. — Includes index
ISBN 90-277-1096-1 : Unpriced
Primary classification 001.3′01′8 B81-07830

300′.1′8 — Social sciences. Methodology

Nowak, Stefan. Understanding and prediction : essays in the methodology of social and behavioral theories / Stefan Nowak. — Dordrecht ; London : Reidel, c1976. — xix,482p : ill ; 23cm. — (Synthese library ; v.94)
Includes bibliographies and index
ISBN 90-277-0558-5 (cased) : Unpriced
ISBN 90-277-1199-2 (pbk) : Unpriced B81-13654

300′.2′461 — Nigeria. Behavioural sciences — *For medicine*

Erinosho, Olayiwola A.. Behavioural science for nursing and medical students in Nigeria. — London : Allen & Unwin, Oct.1981. — [96]p
ISBN 0-04-362047-7 (pbk) : £3.50 : CIP entry B81-24599

300′.28′5425 — Social sciences. Software packages: SPSS — *Manuals*

SPSS update : new procedure and facilities for releases 7 and 8 / contributors ViAnn Beadle ... [et al.]. — New York ; London : McGraw-Hill, c1979. — x,172p ; 28cm
Companion volume to SPSS: statistical package for the social sciences / edited by Norman H. Nie et al.. — Includes index
ISBN 0-07-046534-7 (pbk) : Unpriced B81-10339

SPSS update 7-9 : new procedures and facilities for releases 7-9 / series editors C. Hadlai Hull, Norman H. Nie. — New York ; London : McGraw-Hill, c1981. — xxi,402p : ill ; 28cm
Includes index
ISBN 0-07-046542-8 (pbk) : £6.95 B81-36315

300′.28′7 — Social sciences. Measurement. Mathematics

Carley, Michael. Social measurement and social indicators. — London : Allen and Unwin, Apr.1981. — [208]p. — (Contemporary social research series ; 1)
ISBN 0-04-310009-0 : £12.95 : CIP entry
Primary classification 361.6′12 B81-00058

300′.5 — Social sciences. Applications of information science — *Serials*

Social science information studies. — Vol.1, no.1 (Oct.1980)-. — Sevenoaks : Butterworths, 1980-. — v. ; 25cm
Quarterly
ISSN 0143-6236 = Social science information studies : £30.00 per year
Primary classification 020′.5 B81-06533

300′.7 — Social sciences. Information sources

Li, Tze-chung. Social science reference sources : a practical guide / Tze-chung Li. — Westport, Conn. ; London : Greenwood Press, 1980. — xvi,315p ; 25cm. — (Contributions in librarianship and information science ; no.30)
Includes index
ISBN 0-313-21473-5 : Unpriced B81-05963

300′.7′1 — Schools. Curriculum subjects: Social studies. Teaching

UNESCO Handbook for the teaching of social studies / edited by Howard D. Mehlinger. — London : Croom Helm, 1981. — 409p : ill ; 22cm
Includes index
ISBN 0-7099-1720-1 (pbk) : £9.95 : CIP rev. B81-12827

300′.7′1017671 — Islamic countries. Educational institutions. Curriculum subjects: Social sciences. Teaching — *Islamic viewpoints*

Social and natural sciences : the Islamic perspective / edited by Isma′il R. Al-Faruqi and Abdullah Omar Nasseef. — [London] : Hodder and Stoughton, 1981. — viii,177p ; 24cm. — (Islamic education series)
Conference papers
ISBN 0-340-23613-2 : £6.95 : CIP rev.
Also classified at 507′.1017671 B80-11317

300′.7′12411 — Scotland. Secondary schools. Curriculum subjects: Social studies

Harvey, Colin. Welfare studies in the school curriculum / by Colin Harvey. — Milngavie (163 Mugdock Rd., Milngavie, Dunbartonshire G62 6BR) : Heatherbank Press for the Museum of Social Work, 1980. — ii,17leaves ; 31cm. — (Occasional paper / Museum of Social Work ; no.2)
Cover title. — Text on inside covers
ISBN 0-905192-23-0 (spiral) : £1.50 B81-29257

300′.7′1273 — United States. Middle schools. Curriculum subjects: Social studies. Teaching

Kenworthy, Leonard S.. Social studies for the eighties : in elementary and middle schools / Leonard S. Kenworthy. — 3rd ed. — New York ; Chichester : Wiley, c1981. — xiv,541p : ill ; 24cm
Previous ed.: published as Social studies for the seventies. Lexington, Mass. : Xerox College Pub., 1973. — Includes bibliographies and index
ISBN 0-471-05983-8 (pbk) : £8.90
Primary classification 372.8′3044′0973 B81-21167

300′.7′15 — Adult education. Curriculum subjects: Social sciences

Harrison, J. (John). Catching the colour of life : literature, sociology and the teaching of adult / J. Harrison ; with an end paper by W. Forster. — Leicester : Department of Adult Education, University of Leicester, 1980. — 35p ; 21cm. — (Vaughan paper, ISSN 0308-9258 ; no.24)
Cover title. — Bibliography: p35
ISBN 0-901507-15-6 (pbk) : £0.50 B81-13227

300′.72 — Behavioural sciences. Research. Methodology

Sommer, Robert. A practical guide to behavioral research : tools and techniques / Robert Sommer and Barbara B. Sommer. — New York ; Oxford : Oxford University Press, 1980. — vi,256p : ill ; 24cm
Includes bibliographies and index
ISBN 0-19-502691-8 (cased) : £9.50
ISBN 0-19-502692-6 (pbk) : £5.95 B81-00742

300′.72 — Social sciences. Research

Shipman, M. D.. The limitations of social research / Marten Shipman. — 2nd ed. — London : Longman, 1981. — xiii,210p ; 20cm. — (Aspects of modern sociology. Social research)
Previous ed.: 1972. — Includes index
ISBN 0-582-29526-2 (pbk) : £3.95 B81-32863

300'.72 — Social sciences. Research. Data. Collection

Ackroyd, Stephen. Data collection in context / Stephen Ackroyd and John A. Hughes. — London : Longman, [1981]. — 155p ; 20cm. — (Aspects of modern sociology. Social research)
Includes index
ISBN 0-582-48015-9 (pbk) : £2.95 B81-40146

300'.72 — Social sciences. Research. Methodology

Argyris, Chris. Inner contradictions of rigorous research / Chris Argyris. — New York ; London : Academic Press, 1980. — xl,203p : ill ; 24cm. — (Organizational and occupational psychology)
Bibliography: p189-196. — Includes index
ISBN 0-12-060150-8 : £9.00 B81-07214

Human inquiry : a sourcebook of new paradigm research / edited by Peter Reason and John Rowan. — Chichester : Wiley, c1981. — xxiv,530p : ill ; 24cm
Bibliography: p493-512. — Includes index
ISBN 0-471-27935-8 (cased) : £24.50
ISBN 0-471-27936-6 (pbk) : Unpriced B81-35615

Labovitz, Sanford. Introduction to social research / Sanford Labovitz, Robert Hagedorn. — 3rd ed. — New York ; London : McGraw-Hill, c1981. — xii,160p : ill ; 21cm
Previous ed.: 1976. — Includes bibliographies and index
ISBN 0-07-035777-3 (pbk) : £6.95 B81-19482

Smith, H. W.. Strategies of social research : the methodological imagination / H.W. Smith. — 2nd ed. — Englewood Cliffs ; London : Prentice-Hall, c1981. — xvii,509p : ill ; 24cm. — (Prentice-Hall methods of social science series)
Previous ed.: 1975. — Bibliography: p472-496. — Includes index
ISBN 0-13-851154-3 : £12.30 B81-12956

300'.72 — Social sciences. Research — *Philosophical perspectives*

Hughes, John A.. The philosophy of social research / John Hughes. — London : Longman, 1980. — 138p ; 20cm. — (Aspects of modern sociology. Social research)
Includes index
ISBN 0-582-49032-4 (pbk) : £3.95 B81-06309

300'.72 — Social sciences. Research. Use of speech — *Conference proceedings*

Uttering, muttering : collecting, using and reporting talk for social and educational research / edited by Clem Adelman. — London : Grant McIntyre, 1981. — 237p : ill ; 21cm
Includes bibliographies and index
ISBN 0-86216-042-1 (cased) : Unpriced : CIP rev.
ISBN 0-86216-043-x (pbk) : £4.95 B81-04277

300'.72041 — Great Britain. *Joint SRC/SSRC Committee — Serials*

Great Britain Joint SRC-SSRC Committee. Annual report / Joint SRC-SSRC Committee. — 1979-1980. — [Swindon] ([PO Box 18, North Star Ave, Swindon, Wilts., SN2 1ET]) : [The Committee], [1981?]. — 30p
Unpriced B81-15086

300'.72041 — Great Britain. *Social Science Research Council. Postgraduate Training Board — Statistics*

Great Britain. *Social Science Research Council*. A review of SSRC support for postgraduate training / Social Science Research Council. — London : The Council, 1980. — 45p ; 30cm
ISBN 0-86226-050-7 (pbk) : Unpriced B81-07874

300'.72041 — Great Britain. *Social Science Research Council — Serials*

Great Britain. *Social Science Research Council*. Report of the Social Science Research Council, April ... — March .... — 1979-1980. — London : H.M.S.O., 1980. — 58p
ISBN 0-10-202181-3 : £3.60 B81-09062

300'.7'2041 — Social sciences. Research in British Institutions — *Directories*

Research in British universities, polytechnics and colleges : Vol.2, Biological sciences. — 2nd ed. (1981). — Boston Spa (RBUPC Office, British Library Lending Division, Boston Spa, Wetherby, W.Yorks., LS23 7B9) : British Library, June 1981. — [655]p
ISBN 0-900220-88-0 (pbk) : £20.00 : CIP entry
ISSN 0143-0734
Primary classification 507'.2041 B81-13546

300'.72041 — Social sciences. Research in British institutions — *Directories — Serials*

Research in British universities, polytechnics and colleges. Vol.3, Social sciences. — 2nd ed. (1981). — Wetherby : British Library Lending Division, RBUPC Office, Aug.1981. — [450]p
ISBN 0-900220-89-9 (pbk) : £20.00 : CIP entry
ISSN 0143-0742 B81-25109

300'.72041 — Social sciences. Research projects supported by Great Britain. *Social Science Research Council — Directories — Serials*

Research supported by the Social Science Research Council. — 1980. — London : Social Science Research Council, 1980. — vi,532p
ISBN 0-86226-025-6 : £4.00 B81-03566

300'.720415 — Social sciences. Research in Irish institutions — *Lists*

Register of research projects in the social sciences in progress in Ireland November 1977 / [compiled by Maria Whelan]. — Dublin (4 Burlington Rd., Dublin 4) : Economic and Social Research Institute, c1977. — ii,39leaves ; 25cm
Cover title
£0.75 (pbk) B81-24918

300'.723 — Social sciences. Field studies. Methodology

Fiedler, Judith. Field research : a manual for logistics and management of scientific studies in natural settings / Judith Fiedler. — San Francisco ; London : Jossey-Bass, 1978. — 188p : ill,forms ; 24cm. — (The Jossey-Bass social and behavioral science series)
Bibliography: p177-185. — Includes index
ISBN 0-87589-381-3 : £9.60 B81-15105

300'.724 — Social sciences. Stochastic models

Bartholomew, D. J.. Stochastic models for social processes. — 3rd ed. — Chichester : Wiley, Jan.1982. — [384]p. — (Wiley series in probability and mathematical statistics)
Previous ed.: 1973
ISBN 0-471-28040-2 (cased) : £18.00 : CIP entry
ISBN 0-471-09978-3 (pbk) : £8.95 B81-33798

300'.9'04 — Behavioural sciences, *1900-1980.* **Influence of theories of human behaviour of Freud, Sigmund**

Lewis, Helen Block. Freud and modern psychology / Helen Block Lewis. — New York ; London : Plenum. — (Emotions, personality, and psychotherapy)
Vol.1: The emotional basis of mental illness. — c1981. — ix,247p ; 24cm
Bibliography: p229-240. — Includes index
ISBN 0-306-40525-3 : Unpriced B81-18199

300'.973 — Society. Theories of American writers, *1948-1951*

Neurotica : 1948-1951 / introduction by John Clellon Holmes. — London : Landesman, 1981. — 544p in various pagings : ill ; 24cm
Facsimile reprints
ISBN 0-905150-26-0 : £15.00 : CIP rev.
Primary classification 301'.0973 B81-06051

301 — SOCIOLOGY

301 — Ethnomethodology

Leiter, Kenneth. A primer on ethnomethodology / Kenneth Leiter. — New York ; Oxford : Oxford University Press, 1980. — viii,252p ; 21cm
Bibliography: p241-247. - Includes index
ISBN 0-19-502628-4 (cased) : Unpriced
ISBN 0-19-502629-2 (pbk) : £3.25 B81-00743

301 — Social sciences. Causation

Addison, John T.. Causation, social science and Sir John Hicks / by John T. Addison, John Burton and Thomas S. Torrance. — [Aberdeen] : [University of Aberdeen Department of Political Economy], [1980]. — 17leaves ; 30cm. — (Discussion paper / University of Aberdeen Department of Political Economy ; 80-11)
Bibliography: leaf 17
£1.00 (pbk) B81-05304

301 — Social systems. Sociopolitical aspects

Bienkowski, Wladislaw. Theory and reality. — London : Allison and Busby, June 1980. — [272]p
ISBN 0-85031-401-1 (cased) : £13.95 : CIP entry
ISBN 0-85031-402-x (pbk) : £4.95 B81-13516

301 — Society

Pareto, Vilfredo. The other Pareto / edited by Placido Bucolo ; translated by Placido and Gillian Bucolo ; with a preface by Ronald Fletcher. — London : Scolar, 1980. — xiv,308p : 2ports,1geneal.table ; 23cm
Bibliography: p304-305. — Includes index
ISBN 0-85967-516-5 : £15.00 : CIP rev. B80-04672

301 — Society — *African viewpoints*

Contemporary black thought : alternative analyses in social and behavioral science / edited by Molefi Kete Asante and Abdulai S. Vandi. — Beverly Hills ; London : Sage, c1980. — 302p : ill,1map ; 22cm. — (Sage focus editions ; no.26)
Includes bibliographies and index
ISBN 0-8039-1500-4 (cased) : £11.25
ISBN 0-8039-1501-2 (pbk) : £6.25 B81-05576

301 — Society — *Anarchist viewpoints*

Chegeche. The world-wide vandal squad / Chegeche. — [Portsmouth] ([18 Waverley Rd., Southsea, Porthmouth, Hants.]) : [M. Charlton], [1981]. — 14p ; 21cm. — (A Childish pamphlet)
Unpriced (pbk) B81-35502

301 — Society — *Feminist viewpoints*

Tweedie, Jill, *1936-*. It's only me : pieces from a column / Jill Tweedie ; illustrated by Posy Simmonds. — London : Robson, 1980. — 320p : ill ; 23cm
Includes index
ISBN 0-86051-123-5 : £6.95 : CIP rev. B80-19034

301 — Society — *For Nigerian students*

Ogunniyi, 'Dayo. Our origins and associations / 'Dayo Ogunniyi. — London : Evans. — (Social studies for schools and colleges ; 3)
Teachers' book. — 1981. — 70p ; 22cm
ISBN 0-237-50454-5 (pbk) : Unpriced B81-13972

301 — Society - *For schools*

Nobbs, Jack. Modern society. — 2nd ed. — London : Allen & Unwin, Sept.1981. — [208]p
Previous ed.: 1976
ISBN 0-04-301134-9 (pbk) : £3.95 : CIP entry B81-20094

301 — Society — *Muslim viewpoints*

Husaini, S. Wagar Ahmed. Islamic environmental systems engineering : a systems study of environmental engineering, and the law, politics, education, economics and sociology of science and culture of Islam / S. Wagar Ahmed Husaini. — London : Macmillan, 1980. — xi,239p ; 23cm
Bibliography: p215-229. - Includes index
ISBN 0-333-26138-0 (cased) : £12.50
ISBN 0-333-26139-0 (pbk) : £4.95 B81-05579

301 — Society. Psychoanalytical perspectives

Endleman, Robert. Psyche and society : explorations in psychoanalytic sociology / Robert Endleman. — New York ; Guildford : Columbia University Press, 1981. — xiii,465p ; 24cm
Bibliography: p421-447. — Includes index
ISBN 0-231-04992-7 : £21.50 B81-37751

301 — Society - *Sociological perspectives*

Springborg, Patricia. The problem of human needs and the critique of civilisation. — London : Allen & Unwin, Sept.1981. — [320]p
ISBN 0-04-301133-0 : £18.00 : CIP entry
B81-20148

301 — Society. Theories

Choue, Young Seek. Oughtopia / by Young Seek Choue. — Oxford : Pergamon, 1981. — 213p ; 22 cm
Originally published: Seoul : Kyung Hee University Press, 1979. — Includes index
ISBN 0-08-024534-x : £8.75 B81-25339

Gamble, Andrew. An introduction to modern social and political thought / Andrew Gamble. — London : Macmillan, 1981. — vii,264p ; 23cm
Bibliography: p232-237. — Includes index
ISBN 0-333-27028-2 (cased) : Unpriced (pbk) : Unpriced
Primary classification 320'.01 B81-40661

301 — Sociology

Bell, Daniel. [The winding passage]. Sociological journeys : essays 1960-1980 / Daniel Bell. — London : Heinemann, 1980. — xxiv,370p ; 25cm
Originally published: Cambridge, Mass. : Abt, 1980. — Includes index
ISBN 0-435-82069-9 : £12.50 : CIP rev.
B80-25162

Boudon, Raymond. The crisis in sociology : problems of sociological epistemology / Raymond Boudon ; translated by Howard H. Davis. — London : Macmillan, 1980. — vii,285p ; 23cm
Translation of: La crise de la sociologie. — Includes index
ISBN 0-333-23528-2 : £20.00 : CIP rev.
B80-20213

Boudon, Raymond. The logic of social action : an introduction to sociological analysis / Raymond Boudon ; translated by David Silverman with the assistance of Gillian Silverman. — London : Routledge & Kegan Paul, 1981. — xviii,190p : ill ; 23cm
Translation of: La logique du social. — Includes index
ISBN 0-7100-0857-0 (cased) : £8.25 : CIP rev.
ISBN 0-7100-0858-9 (pbk) : £3.95 B81-28114

Broom, Leonard. Sociology : a text with adapted readings. — 7th ed. / Leonard Broom, Philip Selznick, Dorothy Broom Darroch. — New York ; London : Harper & Row, 1981. — xv,622p : ill(some col.),maps(some col.),ports ; 24cm
Previous ed.: 1977. — Bibliography: p579-596. — Includes index
ISBN 0-06-040991-6 : £12.25
ISBN 0-06-350239-9 (pbk) : £6.95 B81-26054

Culture, ideology and social process. — London : Batsford, Nov.1981. — [288]p
ISBN 0-7134-4313-8 (cased) : £17.50 : CIP entry
ISBN 0-7134-4314-6 (pbk) : £6.95 B81-30386

Fletcher, Ronald. Sociology : the study of social systems / Ronald Fletcher. — London : Batsford Academic and Educational, 1981. — 240p ; 23cm
Bibliography: p219-232. - Includes index
ISBN 0-7134-2528-8 : £12.95 B81-15968

Fundamentals of sociology / edited by Patrick McNeill and Charles Townley. — London : Hutchinson, 1981. — 367p : ill ; 24cm
Bibliography: p345-357. — Includes index
ISBN 0-09-144771-2 (pbk) : Unpriced : CIP rev. B81-03359

The **Future** of the sociological classics. — London : Allen & Unwin, Nov.1981. — [224]p
ISBN 0-04-301136-5 (cased) : £11.95 : CIP entry
ISBN 0-04-301137-3 (pbk) : £5.50 B81-28777

An **Introduction** to sociology. — Milton Keynes : Open University Press. — (Social sciences : a second level course)
At head of title: The Open University
Block 1: Individual and culture
Study section 3: Society and culture / prepared for the course team by Robert Bocock. — 1981. — 26p : ill ; 30cm. — (D207 ; block 1, study section 3)
Bibliography: p24-25
ISBN 0-335-12002-4 (pbk) : Unpriced
B81-10751

An **Introduction** to sociology. — Milton Keynes : Open University Press. — (Social sciences : a second level course)
At head of title: The Open University
Block 1: Individual and culture
Study section 5: Socialization, culture and Freud / prepared for the course team by Robert Bocock. — 1981. — 47p : ill,ports ; 30cm. — (D207 ; block 1, study section 5)
Bibliography: p44-47
ISBN 0-335-12004-0 (pbk) : Unpriced
B81-10746

An **Introduction** to sociology. — Milton Keynes : Open University Press. — (Social sciences : a second level course)
At head of title: The Open University
Block 1: Individual and culture
Study section 6: Self in social context / prepared for the course team by Ray Holland. — 1981. — 42p : ill,2ports ; 30cm. — (D207 ; block 1, study section 6)
Bibliography: p39-40
ISBN 0-335-12005-9 (pbk) : Unpriced
B81-10747

An **Introduction** to sociology. — Milton Keynes : Open University Press. — (Social sciences : a second level course)
At head of title: The Open University
Block 1: Individual and culture
Study section 7: Socialization : conformity and opposition / prepared for the course team by Arthur Brittan. — 1980. — 45p : ill ; 30cm. — (D207 ; block 1, study section 7)
Bibliography: p44-45
ISBN 0-335-12006-7 (pbk) : Unpriced
B81-10748

An **Introduction** to sociology. — Milton Keynes : Open University Press. — (Social sciences : a second level course)
At head of title: The Open University
Block 1: Individual and culture
Study section 8: Changes in Western culture's sexual moralities / prepared for the course team by Robert Bocock. — 1980. — 31p : ill ; 30cm. — (D207 ; block 1, study section 8)
Bibliography: p29-30
ISBN 0-335-12007-5 (pbk) : Unpriced
B81-10745

An **Introduction** to sociology. — Milton Keynes : Open University Press. — (Social sciences : a second level course)
At head of title: The Open University
Block 1: Individual and culture
Study section 9: Sociologies of crime and deviance / prepared for the course team by Mike Fitzgerald. — 1980. — 37p : ill,3maps ; 30cm. — (D207 ; block 1, study section 9)
Bibliography: p36-37
ISBN 0-335-12008-3 (pbk) : Unpriced
B81-10749

An **Introduction** to sociology. — Milton Keynes : Open University Press. — (Social sciences : a second level course)
At head of title: The Open University
[Block 1]: [Individual and culture]
Introduction : preface to the course and study guide to block 1. — 1980. — 27p ; 30cm. — (D207 ; block 1, study section 1)
Includes bibliographies
ISBN 0-335-12000-8 (pbk) : Unpriced
B81-10750

An **Introduction** to sociology. — Milton Keynes : Open University Press. — (Social sciences : a second level course)
At head of title: The Open University
Block 2: Class and structure
Study section 11: Class and stratification / prepared for the Course Team by Alan Waton. — 1980. — 32p : ill,ports ; 30cm. — (D207 ; block 2, study section 11)
Bibliography: p30-31
ISBN 0-335-12010-5 (pbk) : Unpriced
B81-27797

An **Introduction** to sociology. — Milton Keynes : Open University Press. — (Social sciences : a second level course)
At head of title: The Open University
Block 2: Class and structure
Study section 12: Class and politics in Marxist theory / prepared for the course team by Tony Bennett. — 1981. — 49p : ill,1facsim ; 30cm. — (D207 ; block 2, study section 12)
Bibliography: p48-49
ISBN 0-335-12011-3 (pbk) : Unpriced
B81-27798

An **Introduction** to sociology. — Milton Keynes : Open University Press. — (Social sciences : a second level course)
At head of title: The Open University
Block 2: Class and structure
Study section 14: Class, race and immigration / prepared for the course team by Peter Braham. — 1980. — 50p : ill ; 30cm. — (D207 ; block 2, study section 14)
Bibliography: p47-49
ISBN 0-335-12013-x (pbk) : Unpriced
B81-27796

Introductory sociology / Tony Bilton ... [et al.]. — London : Macmillan, 1981. — xxi,771p : ill ; 23cm. — (Comtemporary social theory)
Includes bibliographies and index
ISBN 0-333-28204-3 (cased) : Unpriced
ISBN 0-333-28205-1 (pbk) : Unpriced
B81-37609

McKee, James B.. Sociology : the study of society / James B. McKee. — New York ; London : Holt, Rinehart and Winston, c1981. — xiii,509p : ill(some col.) ; 25cm
Includes bibliographies and index
ISBN 0-03-041851-8 : £11.50 B81-23052

Ritzer, George. Toward an integrated sociological paradigm : the search for an exemplar and an image of the subject matter / George Ritzer. — Boston, Mass. ; London : Allyn and Bacon, c1981. — viii,255p : ill ; 25cm
Bibliography: p239-248. — Includes index
ISBN 0-205-07317-4 : Unpriced B81-26213

Selfe, P. L.. Sociology : an introductory course / P.L. Selfe. — 2nd ed. — Walton-on-Thames : Nelson, 1981. — 312p : ill,forms,ports ; 22cm
Previous ed.: 1975. — Bibliography: p307-308. — Includes index
ISBN 0-17-448116-0 (pbk) : £2.95 B81-15317

Society and the social sciences. — London : Routledge & Kegan Paul, Nov.1981. — [446]p
ISBN 0-7100-0943-7 (pbk) : £2.15 : CIP entry
B81-30601

The **uses** of controversy in sociology / edited by Lewis A. Coser and Otto N. Larsen. — New York : Free Press ; London : Collier Macmillan, c1976. — xvi,398p : ill ; 24cm
Bibliography: p343-386. — Includes index
ISBN 0-02-906830-4 : £11.95 B81-26618

Weigert, Andrew J.. Sociology of everyday life / Andrew J. Weigert. — New York ; London : Longman, c1981. — xviii,318p ; 23cm
Bibliography: p299-311. — Includes index
ISBN 0-582-28199-7 (pbk) : £6.95 B81-29373

Zeitlin, Irving M.. The social condition of humanity : an introduction to sociology / Irving M. Zeitlin. — New York ; Oxford : Oxford University Press, 1981. — xi,413p ; 24cm
Bibliography: p395-406. — Includes index
ISBN 0-19-502734-5 (pbk) : £7.50 B81-25970

301 — Sociology — *Conference proceedings*

British Sociological Association. *Conference (1980 : University of Lancaster).* Development and diversity : British sociology, 1950-1980 : transactions of the Annual Conference of the British Sociological Association held at the University of Lancaster, April 8th-11th 1980 / collated and edited by Philip Abrams and Paula Lewthwaite. — [London] ([10 Portugal Street, WC2A 2HD]) : British Sociological Association, [1980]. — 3v.(1217(i.e. 609)leaves) ; 22x30cm
Includes bibliographies
ISBN 0-904569-03-9 (pbk) : Unpriced
ISBN 0-904569-04-7 (v.1) : Unpriced
ISBN 0-904569-05-5 (v.2) : Unpriced
ISBN 0-904569-06-3 (v.3) : Unpriced
B81-29032

301 — Sociology. Cybernetics aspects

Aulin-Ahmavaara, Arvid. The cybernetic laws of social progress. — Oxford : Pergamon, Dec.1981. — [220]p. — (Systems science and world order library) (Pergamon international library)
ISBN 0-08-025782-8 : £18.75 : CIP entry
B81-31804

301 — Sociology — *For schools*

Lines, C. J.. Exploring society / authors Clifford Lines, Laurie Bolwell. — London : Macdonald Educational, c1981. — 48p : ill(some col.),maps,1facsim,ports ; 22cm. — (Town and around)
Text on inside covers
ISBN 0-356-07193-6 (pbk) : Unpriced
B81-26253

O'Donnell, Mike. A new introduction to sociology / Mike O'Donnell ; foreword by Tony Marks. — London : Harrap, 1981. — x,611p : ill ; 22cm
Bibliography: p595-598. — Includes index
ISBN 0-245-53647-7 (pbk) : £5.50 B81-29671

301 — Sociology - *For schools*

Perspectives in sociology / edited by E.C. Cuff and G.C.F. Payne ; contributors E.C. Cuff ... [et al.]. — London : Allen & Unwin, 1979 (1980 [printing]). — xi,205p ; 22cm
Bibliography: p194-198. - Includes index
ISBN 0-04-301091-1 (cased) : £6.50 : CIP rev.
ISBN 0-04-301092-x (pbk) : £2.95 B78-39480

301 — Sociology — *For schools*

Taylor, James P.. Focus on life / James P. Taylor. — London : Murray, c1981. — ix,86p : ill,1port ; 22cm
ISBN 0-7195-3800-9 (pbk) : £1.30 B81-16164

301'.01 — Society. Theories, *to ca 1959*

Campbell, Tom. Seven theories of human society. — Oxford : Clarendon Press, July 1981. — [266]p
ISBN 0-19-876104-x (cased) : £14.00 : CIP entry
ISBN 0-19-876105-8 (pbk) : £4.95 B81-18166

301'.01 — Sociology. Action theory

Parsons, Talcott. Action theory and the human condition / Talcott Parsons. — New York : Free Press ; London : Collier Macmillan, c1978. — xi,464p : ill ; 25cm
Bibliography: p434-450. - Includes index
ISBN 0-02-923990-7 : £9.95 B81-08602

301'.01 — Sociology. Critical theory

Feenberg, Andrew. Lukács, Marx and the sources of critical theory / Andrew Feenberg. — Oxford : Robertson, 1981. — xiv,286p ; 22cm
Includes index
ISBN 0-85520-427-3 : £15.00 : CIP rev.
B81-10013

Friedman, George. The political philosophy of the Frankfurt School / George Friedman. — Ithaca ; London : Cornell University Press, 1981. — 312p ; 23cm
Bibliography: p303-307. - Includes index
ISBN 0-8014-1279-x : £9.50 B81-12771

Geuss, Raymond. The idea of a critical theory. — Cambridge : Cambridge University Press, Nov.1981. — [100]p. — (Modern European philosophy)
ISBN 0-521-24072-7 (cased) : £10.00 : CIP entry
ISBN 0-521-28422-8 (pbk) : £3.75 B81-32524

Held, David. Introduction to critical theory : Horkheimer to Habermas / David Held. — London : Hutchinson, 1980. — 511p ; 23cm
Bibliography: p483-499. — Includes index
ISBN 0-09-138940-2 (cased) : £13.95 : CIP rev.
ISBN 0-09-138941-0 (pbk) : £5.95 B80-13209

Keat, Russell. The politics of social theory : Habermas, Freud and the critique of positivism / Russell Keat. — Oxford : Blackwell, 1981. — ix,245p ; 22cm
Bibliography: p224-233. — Includes index
ISBN 0-631-12598-1 (cased) : £12.50 : CIP rev.
ISBN 0-631-12779-8 (pbk) : £4.95 B81-14826

301'.01 — Sociology. Theories

Abrahamson, Mark. Sociological theory : an introduction to concepts, issues and research / Mark Abrahamson. — Englewood Cliffs ; London : Prentice-Hall, c1981. — viii,280p : ill ; 24cm
Bibliography: p269-276. — Includes index
ISBN 0-13-820803-4 : £11.00 B81-12675

Johnson, Doyle Paul. Sociological theory : classical founders and contemporary perspectives / Doyle Paul Johnson. — New York ; Chichester : Wiley, c1981. — xvii,597p : ill ; 24cm
Bibliography: p568-580. — Includes index
ISBN 0-471-02915-7 : £9.30 B81-16452

Kinloch, Graham C.. Ideology and contemporary sociological theory / Graham C. Kinloch. — Englewood Cliffs ; London : Prentice-Hall, c1981. — xii,194p ; 24cm. — (Prentice-Hall series in sociology)
Bibliography: p182-187. - Includes index
ISBN 0-13-450601-4 : £10.35 B81-14674

Luckmann, Thomas. Life-world and social realities. — London : Heinemann Educational, Nov.1981. — [224]p
Translation of: Lebenswelt und Gesellschaft
ISBN 0-435-82550-x : £13.50 : CIP entry
B81-30307

Mennell, Stephen. Sociological theory : uses and unities / Stephen Mennell. — 2nd ed. — Walton-on-Thames : Nelson, 1980. — xi,191p : ill ; 23cm
Previous ed.: 1974. — Bibliography: p173-186. — Includes index
ISBN 0-17-711131-3 (cased) : £8.50
ISBN 0-17-712125-4 (pbk) : £4.50 B81-00015

301'.01 — Sociology. Theories, *to 1947*

Zeitlin, Irving M.. Ideology and the development of sociological theory / Irving M. Zeitlin. — 2nd ed. — Englewood Cliffs ; London : Prentice-Hall, c1981. — vi,330p ; 24cm. — (Prentice-Hall sociology series)
Previous ed.: 1968. — Includes index
ISBN 0-13-449769-4 : £11.65 B81-22713

301'.01'8 — Sociology. Methodology

Polish essays in the methodology of the social sciences / edited by Jerzy J. Wiatr. — Dordrecht ; London : Reidel, c1979. — xiii,260p ; 23cm. — (Boston studies in the philosophy of science ; v.29) (Synthese library ; v.131)
Includes index
ISBN 90-277-0723-5 : Unpriced
ISBN 90-277-0956-4 (pbk) : unpriced
B81-15269

Understanding and social inquiry / edited by Fred R. Dallmayr and Thomas A. McCarthy. — Notre Dame ; London : University of Notre Dame Press, c1977. — vi,365p : 1ill ; 24cm
Bibliography: p364-365
ISBN 0-268-01912-6 (cased) : £10.20
B81-05970

301'.01'8 — Sociology. Methodology — *Serials*

Sociological methodology. — 1980. — San Francisco ; London : Jossey-Bass, 1979. — xxi,576p. — (The Jossey-Bass social and behavioural series)
ISBN 0-87589-431-3 : Unpriced
ISSN 0081-1750 B81-01669

301'.02461 — Sociology — *For medicine*

Sociology as applied to medicine. — London : Baillière Tindall, Feb.1982. — [192]p. — (Concise medical textbooks)
ISBN 0-7020-0899-0 (pbk) : £5.50 : CIP entry
B81-35817

301'.05 — Society — *Libertarian viewpoints — Serials*

[Free life *(1979)*]. Free life : the journal of the Libertarian Alliance. — Vol.1, no.1 (winter 1979)-. — London (c/o 40 Floral Street, WC2) : Libertarian Alliance, 1979-. — v. : ill ; 21cm
Quarterly
£5.00 per year B81-04758

301'.05 — Sociology — *Reviews — Serials*

Reviewing sociology : a review journal from the School of Sociological Studies / City of Birmingham Polytechnic, Department of Sociology & Applied Social Studies. — Issue No.1 (Autumn 1979)-. — Birmingham ([City of Birmingham Polytechnic, C Block, Perry Bar, Birmingham B42 2SU]) : The School, 1979-. — v. ; 30cm
Three issues yearly. — Cumulative index in each issue from Issue no.2
ISSN 0261-0272 : Unpriced B81-29399

301'.05 — Sociology — *Serials*

The **International** journal of sociology and social policy. — Vol.1, no.1(1981)-. — Hull (Enholmes Hall, Patrington, Hull HU12 0PR) : Barmarick Publications, 1981-. — v. ; 22cm
Continues: Scottish journal of sociology
ISSN 0144-333x = International journal of sociology and social policy : Unpriced
B81-32413

301'.07'1 — Schools. Curriculum subjects: Social studies. Planning

Kissock, Craig. Curriculum planning for social studies teaching : a cross-cultural approach / Craig Kissock. — Chichester : Wiley, c1981. — ix,148p : ill,forms ; 24cm
Bibliography: p145-146. — Includes index
ISBN 0-471-27868-8 (cased) : £10.00 : CIP rev.
ISBN 0-471-27866-1 (pbk) : £4.75 B81-13585

301'.072 — Sociology. Research. Methodology

Selltiz, Claire. Selltiz, Wrightsman and Cook's Research methods in social relations. — 4th ed. / Louise H. Kidder. — New York ; London : Published for the Society for the Psychological Study of Social Issues (SPSSI) [by] Holt, Rinehart and Winston, [c1981]. — xii,483p : ill,1form ; 25cm
Previous ed.: 1976. — Bibliography: p451-469. — Includes index
ISBN 0-03-043566-8 : £12.95 B81-22876

Sociological methods : a sourcebook / [compiled by] Norman K. Denzin. — 2nd ed. — New York ; London : McGraw-Hill, c1978. — xii,434p : ill ; 24cm
Previous ed.: Chicago : Aldine ; London : Butterworths, 1970. — Includes bibliographies and index
ISBN 0-07-016366-9 (pbk) : £13.75 B81-10237

301'.072041 — Great Britain. Sociology. Research

Sociology and social research / Geoff Payne ... [et al.]. — London : Routledge & Kegan Paul, 1981. — xi,321p ; 23cm. — (International library of sociology)
Bibliography: p296-309. — Includes index
ISBN 0-7100-0626-8 : £14.50 : CIP rev.
B81-06899

301'.0724 — Social systems. Mathematical models

Hanken, A. F. G.. Cybernetics and society : an analysis of social systems / A.F.G. Hanken. — Tunbridge Wells : Abacus, 1981. — x,136p : ill ; 24cm. — (Cybernetics and systems series ; 6)
Includes index
ISBN 0-85626-168-8 : Unpriced : CIP rev.
B80-21399

301'.09 — Anthropology, *to 1978*

Evans-Pritchard, *Sir* **Edward**. A history of anthropological thought / Sir Edward Evans-Pritchard ; edited by André Singer ; with an introduction by Ernest Gellner. — London : Faber, 1981. — xxxvi,218p ; 22cm
Bibliography: p205-209. — Includes index
ISBN 0-571-11712-0 : £10.50 : CIP rev. B81-09502

301'.092'2 — Anthropology — *Biographies*

Totems and teachers : perspectives on the history of anthropology / Sydel Silverman editor. — New York ; Guildford : Columbia University Press, 1981. — xv,322p : ports ; 24cm
Bibliography: p299-311. - Includes index
ISBN 0-231-05086-0 : £12.40
ISBN 0-231-05087-9 (pbk) : £4.40 B81-11373

301'.092'4 — Society. Theories of Marcuse, Herbert

Geoghegan, Vincent. Reason and eros : the social theory of Herbert Marcuse / Vincent Geoghegan. — London : Pluto, 1981. — 122p ; 20cm. — (Pluto ideas in progress)
Bibliography: p113-119. - Includes index
ISBN 0-86104-335-9 (pbk) : £2.95 B81-16703

Schoolman, Morton. The imaginary witness : the critical theory of Herbert Marcuse / Morton Schoolman. — New York ; [London] : Free Press, c1980. — xv,399p ; 25cm
Bibliography: p359-393. — Includes index
ISBN 0-02-928040-0 : £12.50 B81-26023

301.092'4 — Sociology - *Biographies*

Hall, John A.. Diagnoses of our time. — London : Heinemann Educational, June 1981. — [320]p
ISBN 0-435-82402-3 : £14.00 : CIP entry B81-12344

301'.092'4 — Sociology. Theories of Goldmann, Lucien

Evans, Mary, *1946-*. Lucien Goldmann : an introduction / Mary Evans. — Brighton : Harvester, 1981. — 165p ; 23cm
Bibliography: p158-165
ISBN 0-7108-0067-3 : £15.95 B81-36254

301'.092'4 — Sociology. Theories of Hegel, Georg Wilhelm Friedrich

Rose, Gillian. Hegel contra sociology / Gillian Rose. — London : Athlone, 1981. — 261p ; 22cm
Bibliography: p249-258. — Includes index
ISBN 0-485-11214-0 (cased) : Unpriced
ISBN 0-485-12036-4 (pbk) : £6.95 B81-26662

301'.092'4 — Sociology. Theories of Marx, Karl

Modern interpretations of Marx / edited with an introduction by Tom Bottomore. — Oxford : Blackwell, 1981. — 218p ; 23cm
Bibliography: p202-206. — Includes index
ISBN 0-631-18040-0 (cased) : £12.00
ISBN 0-631-12708-9 (pbk) : £4.95 B81-24179

301'.092'4 — Sociology. Theories of Simmel, Georg

Frisby, David. Sociological impressionism : a reassessment of Georg Simmel's social theory / David Frisby. — London : Heinemann, 1981. — xi,190p ; 23cm
Bibliography: p187. — Includes index
ISBN 0-435-82320-5 : £16.00 B81-32308

301'.092'4 — Sociology. Theories of Weber, Max

Turner, Bryan S.. For Weber : essays on the sociology of fate / Bryan S. Turner. — Boston, Mass. ; London : Routledge & Kegan Paul, 1981. — x408p : ill ; 22cm
Bibliography: p369-397. — Includes index
ISBN 0-7100-0780-9 : £13.95 : CIP rev. B81-12811

301'.0941 — Great Britain — *Sociological perspectives*

Noble, Trevor. Structure and change in modern Britain. — London : Batsford, Oct.1981. — [384]p
ISBN 0-7134-3691-3 (pbk) : £7.50 : CIP entry B81-27936

301'.0941 — Great Britain. Sociology, *1950-1980*

Practice and progress : British sociology 1950-1980. — London : Allen & Unwin, Sept.1981. — [240]p
ISBN 0-04-301131-4 (cased) : £12.50 : CIP entry
ISBN 0-04-301132-2 (pbk) : £4.95 B81-20149

301'.0941 — Great Britain. Sociology, *1960-1979*

Eldridge, J. E. T.. Recent British sociology / John Eldridge. — London : Macmillan, 1980. — 276p : ill ; 25cm
Bibliography: p219-276
ISBN 0-333-26639-0 (cased) : £15.00 B81-23020

301'.0941 — Great Britain. Sociology. Influence of theories of evolution of Darwin, Charles

Jones, Greta. Social Darwinism and English thought : the interaction between biological and social theory / Greta Jones. — Brighton : Harvester, c1980. — xiv,234p ; 23cm. — ([Studies in philosophy] ; [no.20])
Bibliography: p196-217. - Includes index
ISBN 0-85527-811-0 : £22.50 B81-20055

301'.0942 — Society. Theories of English Christian conservatives, *ca 1900-1980*

Cowling, Maurice. Religion and public doctrine in modern England / Maurice Cowling. — Cambridge : Cambridge University Press, 1980. — xxiv,475p ; 23cm. — (Cambridge studies in the history and theory of politics)
Bibliography: p469. - Includes index
ISBN 0-521-23289-9 : £20.00 B81-06020

301'.0944 — France. Sociology, *1968-1980*

French sociology : rupture and renewal since 1968 / edited with an introduction by Charles C. Lemert. — New York ; Guildford : Columbia University Press, 1981. — xi,445p ; 24cm
Includes index
ISBN 0-231-04698-7 (cased) : £15.50
ISBN 0-231-04699-5 (pbk) : £5.95 B81-25645

301'.0973 — American culture, *1948-1951.* **Psychosexual aspects** — *Readings from contemporary sources*

Neurotica : 1948-1951 / introduction by John Clellon Holmes. — London : Landesman, 1981. — 544p in various pagings : ill ; 24cm
Facsimile reprints
ISBN 0-905150-26-0 : £15.00 : CIP rev.
Also classified at 300'.973 B81-06051

301'.0973 — United States. Sociology

Gordon, Leonard. Sociology and American social issues / Leonard Gordon with Patricia Atchison Harvey. — Dallas ; London : Houghton Mifflin, c1978. — xvii,548p : ill (some col.),col.maps,forms,ports ; 24cm
Includes bibliographies and index
ISBN 0-395-25369-1 : £13.50 B81-00744

301'.0973 — United States. Sociology. Theories, *ca 1890-1940*

Lewis, J. David. American sociology and pragmatism : Mead, Chicago sociology and symbolic interaction / J. David Lewis and Richard L. Smith. — Chicago ; London : University of Chicago Press, 1980. — xx,356p : 1ill ; 24cm
Bibliography: p312-344. - Includes index
ISBN 0-226-47697-9 : £12.50 B81-16993

301.31 — Environment

The Way things work book of nature : an illustrated encyclopedia of man & nature / [translated by John Cuthbert-Brown]. — London : Allen & Unwin, 1981. — xiii,525p : ill(some col.),maps(some col.) ; 25cm
Translation of: Wie funktioniert das?. — Includes index
ISBN 0-04-500027-1 : Unpriced B81-11316

302 — SOCIAL INTERACTION

302 — Great Britain. Social skills — *For school leavers*

Joyce, Stephen. New horizons / Stephen Joyce. — Glasgow : Collins
2: Decisions. — 1981. — 32p : ill ; 23cm
ISBN 0-00-327881-6 (pbk) : £0.65 B81-34244

302 — Interpersonal relationships

Gathorne-Hardy, Jonathan. Marriage, love, sex and divorce. — London : Cape, Oct.1981. — [320]p
ISBN 0-224-01602-4 : £7.50 : CIP entry B81-27340

. Impoving interpersonal relations. — Farnborough, Hants. : Gower [May 1981]. — [150]p
ISBN 0-566-02277-x : £12.50 : CIP entry B81-07913

Lake, Tony. Relationships / Tony Lake. — London : Joseph, 1981. — 320p : ill(some col.) ; 26cm
Includes index
ISBN 0-7181-1967-3 : £12.95 B81-37937

Personal relationships / editors Steve Duck and Robin Gilmour. — London : Academic Press
1: Studying personal relationships. — 1981. — xvii,253p : ill ; 24cm
Bibliography: p215-239. — Includes index
ISBN 0-12-222801-4 : £9.80 : CIP rev. B80-26512

Personal relationships / editors Steve Duck and Robin Gilmour. — London : Academic Press
2: Developing personal relationships. — 1981. — xv,288p : ill ; 24cm
Bibliography: p247-276. - Includes index
ISBN 0-12-222802-2 : £9.80 : CIP rev. B80-26513

Personal relationships. — London : Academic Press, Aug.1981
Vol.3: Personal relationships in disorder. — [250]p
ISBN 0-12-222803-0 : CIP entry B81-22558

302 — Man. Actions. Sociobiological aspects

Reynolds, Vernon. The biology of human action / Vernon Reynolds. — 2nd ed.. — Oxford : W.H. Freeman, 1980. — xxiv,303p : ill ; 24cm
Previous ed.: 1976. — Bibliography: p278-291. — Includes index
ISBN 0-7167-1239-3 (cased) : £9.00
ISBN 0-7167-1240-7 (pbk) : £4.50 B81-07894

302 — Man. Competition

Ong, Walter J.. Fighting for life : contest, sexuality, and consciousness / Walter J. Ong. — Ithaca ; London : Cornell University Press, 1981. — 231p ; 23cm
Bibliography: p211-222. — Includes index
ISBN 0-8014-1342-7 : £9.00 B81-10952

302 — Man. Psychological problems. Social aspects

Psychological problems : the social context / edtied by Philip Feldman and Jim Orford. — Chichester : Wiley, c1980. — xi,405p : ill ; 24cm
Includes bibliographies and index
ISBN 0-471-27741-x : £16.50 : CIP rev. B80-21404

302 — Man. Psychosocial development. Teaching aids: Games — *Collections*

Eight games for group leaders : a handbook of games and simulations for use with sixteen plus and adult training groups, with notes on the principles of gaming / ... compiled by ... Martin R. Goodlad and Eric Whitton ... — London : Methodist Church Division of Education and Youth, 1981. — 48p : ill,1map ; 30cm
ISBN 0-7192-0141-1 (pbk) : £2.00 B81-36796

302 — Man. Social behaviour. Effects of attitudes. Research

Message-attitude-behavior relationship : theory, methodology and application / edited by Donald P. Cushman, Robert D. McPhee. — New York ; London : Academic Press, 1980. — xii,339p : ill ; 24cm. — (Human communication research series)
Includes bibliographies and index
ISBN 0-12-199760-x : £17.40 B81-14605

302 — Man. Social behaviour. Explanation. Psychological aspects

The **Psychology** of ordinary explanations of social behaviour / edited by Charles Antaki. — London : Published in association with European Association of Experimental Social Psychology by Academic Press, 1981. — xv,335p : ill ; 24cm. — (European monographs in social psychology ; 23)
Bibliography: p310-326. — Includes index
ISBN 0-12-058960-5 : £15.00 B81-23413

302 — Man. Social behaviour. Influence of man's perception of society

The **Structure** of folk models / edited by Ladislav Holy and Milan Stuchlik. — London : Academic Press, 1981. — x,369p : ill ; 24cm. — (ASA monograph ; 20)
Conference papers. — Includes bibliographies and index
ISBN 0-12-353750-9 : £12.50 : CIP rev. B80-26510

302 — Man. Social development — *Anthroposophical viewpoints*

Large, Martin. Social ecology : exploring post-industrial society / Martin Large. — Gloucester (25 Reservoir Rd., Gloucester) : M. Large, c1981. — 162p : ill ; 21cm
ISBN 0-9507062-2-1 (pbk) : Unpriced B81-27893

302 — Man. Social relations

Hirst, Paul. Social relations and human attributes. — London : Tavistock, Dec.1981. — [300]p. — (Social science paperbacks ; 229)
ISBN 0-422-77220-8 (pbk) : £10.50 : CIP entry
ISBN 0-422-77230-5 (pbk) : £4.95 B81-31704

302 — Social exchange. Theories

Roloff, Michael E.. Interpersonal communication : the social exchange approach / Michael E. Roloff. — Beverly Hills ; London : Sage, c1981. — 151p : 1ill ; 23cm. — (The Sage CommText series ; v.6)
Bibliography: p137-149
ISBN 0-8039-1604-3 (cased) : Unpriced
ISBN 0-8039-1605-1 (pbk) : £4.95 B81-36732

302 — Social interactions

Baron, Robert A.. Social psychology : understanding human interaction / Robert A. Baron, Donn Byrne. — 3rd ed. — Boston [Mass.] ; London : Allyn and Bacon, c1981. — xviii,633p : ill(some col.),1map,ports ; 25cm
Previous ed.: 1977. — Ports on lining papers. — Bibliography: p577-620. — Includes index
ISBN 0-205-07238-0 : Unpriced B81-12098

Heiss, Jerold. The social psychology of interaction / Jerold Heiss. — Englewood Cliffs : Prentice-Hall, c1981. — ix,358p : ill ; 24cm. — (Prentice-Hall series in sociology)
Bibliography: p314-347. — Includes index
ISBN 0-13-817718-x (pbk) : £9.70 B81-22701

Interaction in everyday life : social strategies / edited by John Lofland. — Beverly Hills ; London : Sage, 1978. — 156p ; 22cm. — (Sage contemporary social science anthologies ; 1)
"The material in this publication originally appeared in 'Urban life and culture', July 1972 (Volume 1, Number 2), October 1972 (Volume 1, November 3), January 1974 (Volume 2, Number 4), and retitled 'Urban life', July 1976 (Volume 5, Number 2); also in 'Sociology of work and occupations', August 1976 (Volume 3, Number 3)" — T.p. verso. — Includes bibliographies
ISBN 0-8039-1035-5 (pbk) : Unpriced B81-26973

Layder, Derek. Structure, interaction and social theory / Derek Layder. — London : Routledge & Kegan Paul, 1981. — vii,155p : 1ill ; 23cm
Bibliography: p149-153. - Includes index
ISBN 0-7100-0762-0 : £9.50 : CIP rev. B81-14945

302 — Social psychology

Argyle, Michael. Social situations / Michael Argyle, Adrian Furnham, Jean Ann Graham. — Cambridge : Cambridge University Press, 1981. — ix,453p : ill ; 24cm
Bibliography: p403-440. - Includes index
ISBN 0-521-23260-0 (cased) : £30.00
ISBN 0-521-29881-4 (pbk) : £9.95 B81-17928

Confronting social issues. — London : Academic Press, Feb.1982. — [220]p. — (European monographs in social psychology ; v.28)
ISBN 0-12-673801-7 : CIP entry B81-35912

The **Development** of social psychology / edited by Robin Gilmour and Steve Duck. — London : Academic Press, 1980. — xii,355p ; 24cm
Bibliography: p319-346. - Includes index
ISBN 0-12-284080-1 (cased) : £19.60 : CIP rev.
(pbk) : £8.40 B80-09985

Freedman, Jonathan L.. Social psychology / Jonathan L. Freedman, David O. Sears, J. Merrill Carlsmith. — 4th ed. — Englewood Cliffs ; London : Prentice-Hall, c1981. — xiv,686p : ill ; 25cm
Previous ed.: 1978. — Bibliography: p646-674. — Includes index
ISBN 0-13-817783-x : £12.95 B81-25059

Lindgren, Henry Clay. An introduction to social psychology. — 3rd ed. / Henry Clay Lindgren, John H. Harvey. — St. Louis ; London : Mosby, 1981. — xvi,583p : ill,facsims ; 25cm
Previous ed.: New York ; Chichester : Wiley, 1973. — Bibliography: p543-571. — Includes index
ISBN 0-8016-3038-x : £12.50 B81-32998

Social cognition. — London : Academic Press, Oct.1981. — [350]p
ISBN 0-12-263560-4 (cased) : CIP entry
ISBN 0-12-263562-0 (pbk) : Unpriced B81-27352

Social psychology and behavioral medicine. — Chichester : Wiley, Sept.1981. — [576]p
ISBN 0-471-27994-3 : £17.50 : CIP entry B81-23739

Tajfel, Henri. Human groups and social categories : studies in social psychology / Henri Tajfel. — Cambridge : Cambridge University Press, 1981. — xiii,369p : ill ; 24cm
Bibliography: p344-361. - Includes index
ISBN 0-521-22839-5 (cased) : £25.00
ISBN 0-521-28073-7 (pbk) : £7.95 B81-19752

302 — Social skills — *Manuals*

Handbook of social skills. — London : Methuen
Vol.1: Social skills and health. — Nov.1981. — [745]p
ISBN 0-416-72980-0 (cased) : £8.50 : CIP entry
ISBN 0-416-72990-8 (pbk) : £3.95 B81-30568

Handbook of social skills. — London : Methuen
Vol.2: Social skills and work. — Nov.1981. — [250]p
ISBN 0-416-73000-0 (cased) : £8.50 : CIP entry
ISBN 0-416-73010-8 (pbk) : £3.95 B81-30567

302 — Social skills. Teaching — *Manuals*

Eisler, Richard M.. Perfecting social skills : a guide to interpersonal behaviour development / Richard M. Eisler and Lee W. Frederiksen. — New York ; London : Plenum, c1980. — ix,226p ; 24cm. — (Applied clinical psychology)
Bibliography: p215-221. — Includes index
ISBN 0-306-40592-x : Unpriced B81-13351

302'.01'8 — Social psychology. Methodology

Rosnow, Ralph L.. Paradigms in transition : the methodology of social inquiry / Ralph L. Rosnow. — New York ; Oxford : Oxford University Press, 1981. — x,170p ; 22cm
Includes index
ISBN 0-19-502876-7 : £10.50 B81-32551

302'.024372 — Social interactions — *For teaching*

Smith, Gene F.. Instructors manual to accompany Social psychology : understanding human interaction third edition, Robert A. Baron, Donn Byrne / prepared by Gene F. Smith, Bem P. Allen. — Boston, Mass. ; London : Allyn and Bacon, c1981. — viii,289p : ill ; 24cm
ISBN 0-205-07239-9 (pbk) : Unpriced B81-11239

302'.05 — Interpersonal relationships — *Serials*

Alternative lifestyles : changing patterns in marriage, family & intimacy. — Vol.1, no.1 (Feb.1978)-. — Beverly Hills ; London : Sage, 1978-. — v. : ill ; 22cm
Quarterly
ISSN 0161-570x = Alternative lifestyles : Unpriced B81-04191

302'.05 — Social psychology — *Serials*

The **British** journal of social psychology. — Vol.20, pt.1 (Feb.1981)-. — Leicester (48 Princess Rd East, Leicester LE1 7DR) : British Psychological Society, 1981-. — v. ; 25cm
Quarterly. — Continues in part: British journal of social and clinical psychology
ISSN 0144-6665 = British journal of social psychology : £45.00 per year B81-20452

Progress in applied social psychology. — Vol.1. — Chichester : Wiley, Sept.1981. — [400]p. — (Wiley series a progress in applied social psychology)
ISBN 0-471-27954-4 : £16.80 : CIP entry B81-27973

302'.07 — Social skills. Teaching — *Manuals*

Ellis, Roger. A guide to social skill training / Roger Ellis and Dorothy Whittington. — London : Croom Helm, c1981. — 240p : 1ill ; 23cm
Bibliography: p209-229. — Includes index
ISBN 0-7099-0295-6 : £12.95 : CIP rev. B81-08828

302'.072 — Social psychology. Research. Methodology

Social method and social life / edited by Michael Brenner. — London : Academic Press, 1981. — ix,249p ; 24cm
Includes bibliographies and index
ISBN 0-12-131550-9 : £12.00 : CIP rev. B80-26511

302'.0724 — Experimental social psychology — *Serials*

Advances in experimental social psychology. — Vol.13 (1980). — New York ; London : Academic Press, c1980. — vii,292p
ISBN 0-12-015213-4 : £12.60
ISSN 0065-2601 B81-16839

302'.0724 — Social activities. Participation of public. Simulations

Smith, David Horton. Participation in social and political activities / David Horton Smith, Jacqueline Macaulay and associates. — San Francisco ; London : Jossey-Bass, 1980. — xxv,682p : ill ; 24cm. — (The Jossey-Bass social and behavioral science series)
Bibliography: p545-647. — Includes index
ISBN 0-87589-463-1 : Unpriced B81-05379

302'.076 — Social psychology — *Questions & answers*

Lindgren, Henry Clay. An introduction to social psychology : a student study guide / prepared by Henry Clay Lindgren to accompany the third edition of An introduction to social psychology. — St. Louis ; London : Mosby, 1981. — vii,239p ; 24cm
ISBN 0-8016-3027-4 (pbk) : £5.00 B81-33042

302'.09 — Social psychology, *to 1980* — *Interviews*

Evans, Richard I.. The making of social psychology : discussions with creative contributors / by Richard I. Evans. — New York : Gardner Press ; London : Wiley, c1980. — xix,230p ; 24cm
Included bibliographies and index
ISBN 0-470-26811-5 (cased) : £13.55
ISBN 0-470-26812-3 (pbk) : £5.95 B81-10268

302.2 — Communication systems. Technological development. Social aspects

Pelton, Joseph N.. Global talk : the marriage of the computer, world communications and man / by Joseph N. Pelton. — Brighton : Harvester, 1981. — xiv,336p : ill,1map ; 25cm
Includes bibliographies and index
ISBN 0-7108-0371-0 : £16.95
ISBN 0-7108-0347-8 (pbk) : Unpriced B81-35366

302.2 — Interpersonal relationships. Communication

Adler, Ronald B.. Looking at / looking in : interpersonal communication / Ronald B. Adler, Neil Towne. — 3rd ed. — New York ; London : Holt, Rinehart and Winston, c1981. — vii,374p : ill ; 27cm
Previous ed.: 1978. — Includes bibliographies and index
ISBN 0-03-053836-x : Unpriced B81-08621

Argyle, Michael. Person to person : ways of communicating / Michael Argyle and Peter Trower. — London : Harper & Row, c1979. — 128p : ill(some col.) ; 24cm. — (The Cycle series)
Originally published: Holland : Multimedia, 1979. — Text, ports on inside cover. — Bibliography: p125. — Includes index
ISBN 0-06-318097-9 (cased) : Unpriced
ISBN 0-06-318098-7 (pbk) : £1.95 B81-13620

Patton, Bobby R.. Interpersonal communication in action : basic text and readings / Bobby R. Patton and Kim Giffin. — 3rd ed. — New York ; London : Harper & Row, 1981. — xi,499p : ill ; 23cm
Previous ed.: 1977. — Includes index
ISBN 0-06-045062-2 (pbk) : £8.50 B81-12602

Penman, Robyn. Communication processes and relationships / Robyn Penman. — London : Academic Press, 1980. — viii,155p : ill ; 24cm
Bibliography: p128-135. — Includes index
ISBN 0-12-550380-6 : £9.80 : CIP rev.
B80-19603

Ruffner, Michael. Interpersonal communication / Michael Ruffner, Michael Burgoon. — New York ; London : Holt, Rinehart and Winston, c1981. — vii,264p : ill ; 24cm
Includes bibliographies and index
ISBN 0-03-053521-2 (pbk) : £7.50 B81-11369

302.2 — Interpersonal relationships. Communication — *For professional personnel*

Hargie, Owen. Social skills in interpersonal communication / Owen Hargie, Christine Saunders and David Dickson. — London : Croom Helm, c1981. — 198p : ill ; 23cm
Bibliography: p184-194. — Includes index
ISBN 0-7099-0279-4 (cased) : £11.95
ISBN 0-7099-0280-8 (pbk) : £5.95 B81-13354

302.2 — Interpersonal relationships. Communication. Measurement. Theories

Woelfel, Joseph. The measurement of communication processes : Galileo theory and method / Joseph Woelfel, Edward L. Fink. — New York ; London : Academic Press, 1980. — 278p : ill ; 24cm. — (Human communication research series)
Bibliography: p269-274. — Includes index
ISBN 0-12-761240-8 : £16.00 B81-15129

302.2 — Interpersonal relationships. Communication networks. Analysis

Rogers, Everett M.. Communication networks : toward a new paradigm for research / Everett M. Rogers and D. Lawrence Kincaid. — New York : Free Press ; London : Collier Macmillan, c1981. — xiv,386p : ill ; 25cm
Bibliography: p349-373. — Includes index
ISBN 0-02-926740-4 : £11.95 B81-36122

302.2 — Symbolism

Symbol as sense : new approaches to the analysis of meaning / edited by Mary LeCron Foster, Stanley H. Brandes. — New York ; London : Academic Press, 1980. — xvi,416p : ill,maps ; 24cm. — (Language, thought, and culture)
Conference papers. — Includes bibliographies and index
ISBN 0-12-262680-x : £19.60 B81-06225

302.2'024658 — Man. Communication — *For business studies*

Udall, Rita. People and communication / Rita and Sheila Udall ; advisory editor Patricia Callender. — Amersham : Hulton Educational, 1979. — 172p : ill ; 24cm. — (Hulton BEC books)
ISBN 0-7175-0832-3 (pbk) : £2.40 B81-08291

302.2'09 — Communication, *to 1980 — Sociological perspectives*

Stevens, John D.. Communication history / John D. Stevens, Hazel Dicken Garcia. — Beverly Hills ; London : Sage, 1980. — 157p : ill ; 22cm. — (The Sage CommText series ; v.2)
Bibliography: p147-153. — Includes index
ISBN 0-8039-1258-7 (cased) : £7.85 B81-01917

302.2'2 — Cross-cultural communication. Role of English language — *Conference proceedings*

English for cross-cultural communication / edited by Larry E. Smith. — [London] : Macmillan, 1981. — xxiii,248p : ill ; 23cm
Conference papers. — Bibliography: p225-244. — Includes index
ISBN 0-333-26660-9 : £20.00 : CIP rev.
B80-03492

302.2'2 — Society. Role of literacy

Oxenham, John. Literacy : writing, reading and social organisation / John Oxenham. — London : Routledge & Kegan Paul, 1980. — x,141p : ill ; 20cm. — (Language and society series)
Bibliography: p139-141
ISBN 0-7100-0584-9 (cased) : £6.95 : CIP rev.
ISBN 0-7100-0619-5 (pbk) : £3.95 B80-10467

302.2'3 — Advertising. Social aspects — *Illustrations — For schools*

Smith, Gillian Crampton. Seeing's believing / [Gillian Crampton Smith and Sarah Curtis]. — [London] : [Longman], c1981. — 1portfolio (10parts) : ill ; 30cm + Teachers'notes (foldedsheet:[6]p:ill;30cm). — (Longman thinkstrips)
ISBN 0-582-22300-8 : Unpriced B81-09442

302.2'3 — California. Mass media

Tunstall, Jeremy. Media made in California : Hollywood, politics and the news / Jeremy Tunstall, David Walker. — New York ; Oxford : Oxford University Press, 1981. — vi,204p : 2maps ; 22cm
Bibliography: p199-204
ISBN 0-19-502922-4 : £12.00 B81-40378

302.2'3 — Cinema films, *to 1980 — Sociological perspectives*

Jowett, Garth. Movies as mass communication / Garth Jowett, James M. Linton. — Beverly Hills ; London : Sage, c1980. — 149p ; 23cm. — (The Sage CommText series ; v.4)
Bibliography: p133-142. - Includes index
ISBN 0-8039-1090-8 (cased) : £7.85
ISBN 0-8039-1091-6 (pbk) : £3.75 B81-00746

Reader, Keith. Cultures on celluloid. — London : Quartet, Oct.1981. — [224]p
ISBN 0-7043-2272-2 : £9.95 : CIP entry
B81-25707

302.2'3 — Developing countries. Television services. Cultural domination by developed countries. Theories

Lee, Chin-Chuan. Media imperialism reconsidered : the homogenizing of television culture / Chin-Chuan Lee ; foreword by Elihu Katz. — Beverley Hills ; London : Sage, c1980. — 276p : ill ; 23cm. — (People and communication ; v.10)
Bibliography: p251-264. — Includes index
ISBN 0-8039-1495-4 (cased) : £12.50
ISBN 0-8039-1496-2 (pbk) : £6.25 B81-14652

302.2'3 — Eastern Europe & Soviet Union. Mass media

Lendvai, Paul. The bureaucracy of truth : how Communist governments manage the news / Paul Lendvai. — London : Burnett, 1981. — 285p ; 23cm
Includes index
ISBN 0-233-97290-0 : £6.95 : CIP rev.
B80-18169

302.2'3 — England. Newspaper publishing industries: Northcliffe Newspapers Group. Publications: Provincial newspapers. Readership — *Serials*

Scanning the provinces. — 1980. — [London] ([Carmelite House, EC4Y 0JA]) : [Northcliffe Newspapers Group], [1980]. — 72p
Unpriced B81-09037

302.2'3 — English popular literature, *1578-1700.* **Readership**

Spufford, Margaret. Small books and pleasant histories. — London : Methuen, Apr.1981. — [280]p
ISBN 0-416-74150-9 : £12.50 : CIP entry
B81-03145

302.2'3 — Great Britain. Broadcasting, *to 1939.* **Social aspects**

Briggs, Susan. Those Radio times / Susan Briggs. — London : Weidenfeld and Nicolson, c1981. — 232p : ill(some col.),facsims,ports ; 26cm
Ill on lining papers
ISBN 0-297-77929-x : £8.95 B81-34739

302.2'3 — Great Britain. Families. Influence of television programmes — *Conference proceedings*

Television and the family / [edited by Rick Rogers]. — London : UK Association for the International Year of the Child and the University of London Department of Extra-Mural Studies, 1980. — 104p : ill,ports ; 21cm
Conference papers
ISBN 0-7187-0567-x (pbk) : Unpriced
B81-32363

302.2'3 — Great Britain. Information services — *Sociological perspectives*

Information and society : a collection of papers presented at meetings of the B.S.A. Libraries and Information Study Group, 1978-1980 / edited by Marian Barnes ... [et al.]. — [Leeds] ([28 Park Place, Leeds LS1 2SY]) : School of Librarianship, Leeds Polytechic, 1981. — 154p ; 30cm
ISBN 0-900738-21-9 (pbk) : £4.00 B81-17143

302.2'3 — Great Britain. Mass media

Curran, James. Power without responsibility : the press and broadcasting in Britain / James Curran and Jean Seaton. — [London] : Fontana, 1981. — 395p ; 18cm
Bibliography: p353-382. — Includes index
ISBN 0-00-634638-3 (pbk) : £2.95 B81-10895

302.2'3 — Great Britain. Press, *1918-1979 — Sociological perspectives*

The **Sociology** of journalism and the press / issue editor Harry Christian. — Keele : University of Keele, 1980. — 395p : ill,facsims ; 22cm. — (Sociological review monograph, ISSN 0081-1769 ; 29)
ISBN 0-904425-09-6 (cased) : Unpriced : CIP rev
ISBN 0-904425-10-x (pbk) : Unpriced
B80-12249

302.2'3 — Great Britain. Society. Role of broadcasting

Trethowan, *Sir* **Ian**. Broadcasting and society : a speech given by Sir Ian Trethowan at the University of East Anglia, Thursday 12 March 1981. — London : British Broadcasting Corporation, [1981]. — 16p ; 21cm
ISBN 0-563-17975-9 (pbk) : Unpriced
B81-26177

302.2'3 — Great Britain. Television programmes. Sociopolitical aspects

Hunt, Albert. The language of television : uses and abuses / Albert Hunt ; with a foreword by Raymond Williams. — London : Eyre Methuen, 1981. — 128p ; 21cm
ISBN 0-413-33730-8 (cased) : £5.95
ISBN 0-413-33740-5 (pbk) : Unpriced
B81-20915

302.2'3 — Mass communication. Research

McQuail, Denis. Communication models for the study of mass communications. — London : Longman, Oct.1981. — [196]p
ISBN 0-582-29572-6 (pbk) : £3.95 : CIP entry
B81-28084

302.2'3 — Mass communication. Research. Methodology

Research methods in mass communication / edited by Guido H. Stempel III & Bruce H. Westley. — Englewood Cliffs ; London : Prentice-Hall, c1981. — viii,405p : ill ; 24cm
Includes index
ISBN 0-13-774240-1 : £14.65 B81-33124

302.2'3 — Mass communication — *Serials*

Mass communication review yearbook. — Vol.1 (1980)-. — Beverly Hills ; London : Sasge, 1980-. — v. : ill ; 24cm
Unpriced B81-03844

302.2'3 — Mass communication — *Sociological perspectives*

The **Future** of the printed word. — Milton Keynes : Open University Press, Sept.1981. — 1v.
Originally published: 1980
ISBN 0-335-10048-1 (pbk) : £4.95 : CIP entry B81-23952

302.2'3 — Mass media. International political aspects

McPhail, Thomas L.. Electronic colonialism : the future of international broadcasting and communication / Thomas L. McPhail ; foreword by Everett M. Rogers. — Beverly Hills ; London : Sage, c1981. — 260p ; 23cm. — (Sage library of social research ; v.126)
Includes bibliographies and index
ISBN 0-8039-1602-7 (cased) : Unpriced
ISBN 0-8039-1603-5 (pbk) : £6.50 B81-37152

302.2'3 — Printed media. Effects of technological innovation

The **Future** of the printed word : the impact and the implications of the new communications technology / edited by Philip Hills. — London : Pinter, 1980. — 172p : ill,facsims ; 23cm
Includes bibliographies
ISBN 0-903804-70-0 : £10.00 B81-40286

302.2'3 — Printed media. Readership — *Conference proceedings*

Readership research. — London (27 Lexington St., W1R 3HQ) : Sigmatext, Jan.1982. — [400]p
Conference papers
ISBN 0-907338-02-x : £50.00 : CIP entry B81-38850

302.2'3 — Serials with British imprints. Readership — *Serials*

National readership survey / JICNARS. — 1980. — London (44 Belgrave Sq., SW1X 8QS) : JICNARS, [1981?]. — [273]p
£300.00 B81-21350

302.2'3 — Society. Role of mass media — *Conference proceedings*

Mass media and social change / edited by Elihu Katz and Tamás Szecskö. — London : Sage, c1981. — 271p : ill ; 22cm. — (Sage studies in international sociology ; 22)
Conference papers. — Includes bibliographies
ISBN 0-8039-9806-6 (cased) : Unpriced
ISBN 0-8039-9807-4 (pbk) : £6.50 B81-36267

302.2'3 — Television services — *Sociological perspectives*

Silverstone, Roger. The message of television : myth and narrative in contemporary culture / Roger Silverstone. — London : Heinemann Educational, 1981. — viii,248p : ill ; 23cm
Bibliography: p218-239. — Includes index
ISBN 0-435-82825-8 : £14.50 B81-10819

302.2'3 — United States. Children. Influence of television programmes

Children and the faces of televison : teaching, violence, selling / edited by Edward L. Palmer, Aimée Dorr. — New York ; London : Academic Press, c1980. — xvii,360p : ill ; 24cm
Includes bibliographies and index
ISBN 0-12-544480-x : £13.80 B81-17591

302.2'3 — United States. Mass media. Political aspects

Paletz, David L.. Media, power, politics / David L. Paletz and Robert M. Entman. — New York : Free Press ; London : Collier Macmillan, c1981. — xii,308p ; 25cm
Bibliography: p273-299. — Includes index
ISBN 0-02-923650-9 : £10.50 B81-36121

302.2'3 — United States. Newspapers, *to 1939.* **Social aspects**

Hughes, Helen MacGill. News and the human interest story / Helen MacGill Hughes ; with a new introduction by Arlene Kaplan Daniels. — New Brunswick ; London : Transaction, c1981. — xvi,313p ; 24cm. — ([Social science classics series])
Originally published: Chicago : University of Chicago Press, 1940. — Bibliography: p292-303. - Includes index
ISBN 0-87855-326-6 : £12.00
ISBN 0-87855-729-6 (pbk) : Unpriced B81-16470

302.2'3 — United States. Society. Effect of television programmes — *Sociological perspectives*

Comstock, George. Television in America / George Comstock. — Beverly Hills ; London : Sage, c1980. — 155p ; 23cm. — (The Sage CommText series ; v.1)
Bibliography: p149-154
ISBN 0-8039-1244-7 (cased) : £7.85
ISBN 0-8039-1245-5 (pbk£3.75) B81-01942

302.2'3 — United States. Television programmes. Audiences. Viewing behaviour

Frank, Ronald E.. The public's use of television : who watches and why / Ronald E. Frank, Marshall G. Greenberg ; foreword by Lloyd N. Morrisett. — Beverly Hills ; London : Sage, c1980. — 368p : forms ; 23cm. — (People and communication ; v.9)
Includes bibliographies
ISBN 0-8039-1389-3 : £14.00 B81-02307

302.2'3 — United States. Television programmmes. Control — *Sociological perspectives*

Cantor, Muriel G.. Prime-time television : content and control / Muriel G. Cantor. — Beverly Hills ; London : Sage, c1980. — 143p ; 23cm. — (The Sage commtext series ; v.3)
Bibliography: p127-134. — Includes index
ISBN 0-8039-1316-8 (cased) : £7.85
ISBN 0-8039-1317-6 (pbk) : £3.75 B81-10826

302.2'4 — Great Britain. Politics. Reporting by television. Bias. Social aspects

Francis, Richard, *1934-*. Television - the evil eye? / a speech given by Richard Francis to the Royal Television Society in London Tuesday 14 July 1981. — London : BBC, [1981]. — 14p ; 21cm
Unpriced (pbk) B81-38878

302.2'4 — Great Britain. Television programmes: News programmes. Subjectivity — *Case studies*

Bad news / Glasgow University Media Group. — London : Routledge & Kegan Paul
Vol.1. — 1976 (1981 [printing]). — xvi,310p : ill ; 22cm
Includes index
ISBN 0-7100-0792-2 (pbk) : £5.95 B81-14590

302.3 — Group discussions. Leadership — *Manuals*

Sampa, R. C.. Pocket book for discussion group leaders / by R.C. Sampa. — Wembley : Selecteditions, 1980. — 35p : ill ; 21cm
Cover title
ISBN 0-86237-004-3 (pbk) : £0.85 B81-23119

302.3 — Group dynamics

Groups at work / edited by Roy Payne and Cary L. Cooper. — Chichester : Wiley, c1981. — ix,268p : ill ; 24cm. — (Wiley series on individuals, groups and organizations)
Includes bibliographies and index
ISBN 0-471-27934-x : £12.70 : CIP rev. B81-22695

302.3 — Group dynamics. Psychological aspects

Group cohesion : theoretical and clinical perspectives / edited by Henry Kellerman. — New York ; London : Grune & Stratton, c1981. — xxviii,465p : ill ; 24cm
Includes bibliographies and index
ISBN 0-8089-1330-1 : £26.20 B81-40805

302.3 — Man. Collective action — *Sociological perspectives*

Class conflict and collective action / Louise A. Tilly, Charles Tilly, editors. — Beverly Hills ; London : Published in cooperation with the Social Science History Association [by] Sage, c1981. — 260p : ill ; 23cm. — (New approaches to social science history)
Bibliography: p2450-257
ISBN 0-8039-1587-x (cased) : Unpriced
ISBN 0-8039-1588-8 (pbk) : £6.50 B81-36730

302.3 — Social groups. Interpersonal relationships. Social psychology

Intergroup behaviour. — Oxford : Basil Blackwell, July 1981. — [256]p
ISBN 0-631-11711-3 (cased) : £12.50 : CIP entry
ISBN 0-631-12718-6 (pbk) : £5.50 B81-14970

302.3'3 — France. Crowds. Behaviour. Theories, *1880-1900*

Barrows, Susanna. Distorting mirrors : visions of the crowd in late nineteenth century France. — London : Yale University Press, Nov.1981. — [224]p. — (Yale historical publications. Miscellany ; 127)
ISBN 0-300-02588-2 : £14.00 : CIP entry B81-34718

302.3'3 — Man. Crowds. Behaviour — *Sociological perspectives*

Wright, Sam. Crowds and riots : a study in social organization / Sam Wright. — Beverly Hills ; London : Sage, c1978. — 207p : ill ; 23cm. — (Sociological observations ; 4)
Bibliography: p181-198. - Includes index
ISBN 0-8039-0995-0 (cased) : £11.85
ISBN 0-8039-0996-9 (pbk) : Unpriced B81-16614

302.3'4 — Group dynamics

Shaw, Marvin E.. Group dynamics : the psychology of small group behaviour / Marvin E. Shaw. — 3rd ed. — New York ; London : McGraw-Hill, c1981. — xvii,531p : ill ; 24cm. — (McGraw-Hill series in psychology)
Previous ed.: 1976. — Bibliography: p458-508. - Includes index
ISBN 0-07-056504-x : £15.75 B81-19473

302.3'4 — Small groups. Communication

Kell, Carl L.. Fundamentals of effective group communication / Carl L. Kell, Paul R. Corts. — New York : Macmillan ; London : Collier Macmillan, c1980. — ix,198p : ill,forms ; 23cm
Includes bibliographies and index
ISBN 0-02-362280-6 (pbk) : £5.95 B81-00747

302.3'4 — Small groups. Interaction

Palazzolo, Charles S.. Small groups : an introduction / Charles S. Palazzolo. — New York ; London : Van Nostrand, c1981. — xiii,352p : ill,ports ; 24cm
Bibliography: p325-337. - Includes index
ISBN 0-442-25868-2 : £11.95 B81-10185

302.3'4 — Task oriented small groups. Interactions

Seaman, Don F.. Working effectively with task-oriented groups / Don F. Seaman. — New York ; London : McGraw-Hill, c1981. — x,118p : ill ; 24cm. — (The Adult Education Association professional development series)
Bibliography: p111-113. - Includes index
ISBN 0-07-000554-0 : £8.95 B81-17106

302.3'4 — United States. Group dynamics — *For health services*

Sampson, Edward E.. Group process for the health professions / Edwards E. Sampson, Marya Marthas. — 2nd ed. — New York ; Chichester : Wiley, c1981. — viii,320p : ill ; 23cm. — (A Wiley medical publication)
Previous ed.: 1977. — Bibliography: p305-313. - Includes index
ISBN 0-471-08279-1 (pbk) : £7.95 B81-18677

302.3'5 — Man. Organisational behaviour — *Sociological perspectives*

Herbert, Theodore T.. Dimensions of organizational behavior / Theodore T. Herbert. — 2nd ed. — New York : Macmillan ; London : Collier Macmillan, c1981. — x,513p : ill ; 24cm. — (Collier Macmillan international editions)
Previous ed.: 1976. — Includes index
ISBN 0-02-353670-5 (cased) : Unpriced
ISBN 0-02-978560-x (pbk) : £12.50 B81-29323

302.3′5 — Man. Organisational behaviour — *Sociological perspectives* *continuation*

Organizational behavior : readings and exercises. — 6th ed. / [compiled by] Keith Davis, John W. Newstrom. — New York ; London : McGraw-Hill, c1981. — xvi,448p : ill,forms ; 24cm. — (McGraw-Hill series in management)
Previous ed.: 1977. — Includes index
ISBN 0-07-015500-3 (pbk) : £8.50 B81-19485

302.3′5 — Organisational behaviour

Contemporary perspectives in organizational behaviour / [edited by] Donald D. White. — Boston, Mass. ; London : Allyn and Bacon, c1982. — viii,412p : ill ; 24cm
Includes bibliographies
ISBN 0-205-07350-6 (pbk) : £12.50 B81-40102

Hutton, Geoffrey, *1928-*. Thinking about systems, ideas and action / Geoffrey Hutton. — Bath : University of Bath
1: Developments & repetitions in organization theory. — c1978. — 15leaves : ill ; 30cm. — (Working paper / Centre for the Study of Organizational Change and Development ; 78/10)
Bibliography: leaf 15
ISBN 0-900843-93-4 (pbk) : £0.75 B81-20376

Hutton, Geoffrey, *1928-*. Thinking about systems, ideas and action / Geoffrey Hutton. — Bath : University of Bath
2: In defence of systems ideas. — c1978. — 19,2leaves : ill ; 30cm. — (Working paper / Centre for the Study of Organizational Change and Development ; 78/11)
Bibliography: leaves 1-2
ISBN 0-900843-94-2 (pbk) : £0.90 B81-20375

Hutton, Geoffrey, *1928-*. Thinking about systems, ideas and action / Geoffrey Hutton. — Bath : University of Bath
3: Awareness, theory and reality. — c1978. — 39leaves : ill ; 30cm. — (Working paper / Centre for the Study of Organizational Change and Development ; 78/12)
Bibliography: leaves 38-39
ISBN 0-900843-95-0 (pbk) : £2.00 B81-20374

Hutton, Geoffrey, *1928-*. Thinking about systems, ideas and action / Geoffrey Hutton. — Bath : University of Bath
4: On the conduct of professional roles. — c1978. — 31leaves : ill ; 30cm. — (Working paper / Centre for the Study of Organizational Change and Development ; 78/13)
Bibliography: leaf 31
ISBN 0-900843-96-9 (pbk) : £1.50 B81-20373

Hutton, Geoffrey, *1928-*. Thinking about systems, ideas and action / Geoffrey Hutton. — Bath : University of Bath
5: Tasks, purposes and confusions. — c1979. — 15leaves : ill ; 30cm. — (Working paper / Centre for the Study of Organizational Change and Development ; 79/01)
Bibliography: leaf 15
ISBN 0-900843-97-7 (pbk) : £0.75 B81-20372

White, Donald D.. Instructor′s manual to accompany Contemporary perspectives in organizational behavior / Donald D. White. — Boston, Mass. ; London : Allyn and Bacon, c1982. — vi,106p ; 22cm
ISBN 0-205-07351-4 (pbk) : £1.00 B81-40101

302.3′5 — Organisations

Handy, Charles B.. Understanding organizations / Charles B. Handy. — 2nd ed. — Harmondsworth : Penguin, 1981. — 473p : ill ; 20cm. — (Organizational behaviour) (Penguin education) (Penguin modern management texts)
Previous ed.: 1976. — Bibliography: p408-460. — Includes index
ISBN 0-14-080960-0 (pbk) : £3.50 B81-25448

The **Organisation** in its environment / editor Norbert L. Paulus. — Stockport : Polytech. — (Business Education Council national award courses)
Vol.1 / contributors David M. Lee, Anthony P. Nisbett, Gerald G. Paulus. — 1979. — 326p : ill ; 22cm
Includes index
ISBN 0-85505-032-2 (pbk) : £4.20 B81-22912

The **Organisation** in its environment / editor Norbert L. Paulus. — Stockport : Polytech. — (Business Education Council national award courses)
Vol.2 / contributors Michael G. Butler, Gerald G. Paulus, Peter Short. — 1980. — 342p : ill ; 22cm
Includes index
ISBN 0-85505-050-0 (pbk) : £4.20 B81-22911

Organizations : structure and behavior / [edited by] Joseph A. Litterer. — 3rd ed. — New York ; Chichester : Wiley, c1980. — xi,625p : ill ; 24cm. — (Wiley series in management)
Previous ed.: 1969. — Bibliography: p610-613. — Includes index
ISBN 0-471-07786-0 (pbk) : £7.35 B81-00748

Scott, W. Richard. Organizations : rational, natural and open systems / W. Richard Scott. — Englewood Cliffs ; London : Prentice-Hall, c1981. — xviii,381p : ill ; 24cm
Bibliography: p337-368. — Includes index
ISBN 0-13-641977-1 : £12.30 B81-22723

302.3′5 — Organisations. Bureaucracy — *Sociological perspectives*

Jaques, Elliott. A general theory of bureaucracy / Elliott Jaques. — London : Heinemann, 1976 (1981 [printing]). — xi,412p : ill ; 22cm
Bibliography: p378-393. — Includes index
ISBN 0-435-82478-3 (pbk) : £6.50 B81-36788

302.3′5 — Organisations. Decision making — *Sociological perspectives*

Inbar, Michael. Routine decision-making : the future of bureaucracy / Michael Inbar. — Beverly Hills ; London : Sage, c1979. — 239p : ill ; 22cm. — (Sage library of social research ; v.74)
Bibliography: p229-239
ISBN 0-8039-1152-1 (cased) : Unpriced
ISBN 0-8039-1153-x (pbk) : £5.50 B81-18737

302.3′5 — Organisations. Design

Handbook of organizational design / edited by Paul C. Nystrom and William H. Starbuck. — Oxford : Oxford University Press
Vol.1: Adapting organizations to their environments. — 1981. — xxii,560p : ill ; 24cm
Includes bibliographies and index
ISBN 0-19-827241-3 : Unpriced : CIP rev. B80-22905

Handbook of organizational design / edited by Paul C. Nystrom and William H. Starbuck. — Oxford : Oxford University Press
Vol.2: Remodeling organizations and their environments. — 1981. — vi,552p ; 25cm
Includes bibliographies and index
ISBN 0-19-827242-1 : £24.00 : CIP rev. B80-22906

302.3′5 — Organisations. Design. Use of mathematical programming

Obel, Børge. Issues of organizational design : a mathematical programming view of organizations / by Børge Obel. — Oxford : Pergamon, 1981. — xi,273p : ill ; 22cm
Bibliography: p253-264. — Includes index
ISBN 0-08-025837-9 : £12.50 : CIP rev. B81-16845

302.3′5 — Organisations. Personnel. Behaviour — *For management*

Knowles, Michael C.. Organisational functioning : a behavioural analysis / Michael C. Knowles. — Farnborough, Hants. : Gower, c1980. — viii,142p : ill ; 23cm
Bibliography: p122-134. — Includes index
ISBN 0-566-00329-5 : £10.00 : CIP rev. B80-05793

302.3′5 — Organisations. Power — *Sociological perspectives*

Pfeffer, Jeffrey. Power in organizations / Jeffrey Pfeffer. — Marshfield, Mass. ; London : Pitman, 1981. — xiv,391p : ill ; 25cm
Bibliography: p371-386. — Includes index
ISBN 0-273-01638-5 (cased) : Unpriced
ISBN 0-273-01639-3 (pbk) : Unpriced B81-38439

302.3′5 — Organisations. Power. Theories

Crozier, Michel. Actors and systems : the politics of collective action / Michel Crozier and Erhard Friedberg ; translated by Arthur Goldhammer. — Chicago ; London : University of Chicago Press, 1980. — vii,333p ; 24cm
Translation of: L′acteur et le système. — Bibliography: p319-327. — Includes index
ISBN 0-226-12183-6 : £15.00 B81-12681

302.3′5 — Organisations — *Sociological perspectives*

Control and ideology in organizations / edited by Graeme Salaman and Kenneth Thompson. — Milton Keynes : Open University Press, 1980. — xii,330p : ill ; 22cm
Bibliography: p297-320. — Includes index
ISBN 0-335-00258-7 (pbk) : £5.95 : CIP rev. B79-34680

The **Sociology** of organizations : basic studies / edited by Oscar Grusky, George A. Miller. — 2nd ed. — New York : Free Press ; London : Collier Macmillan, c1981. — x,565p ; 24cm
Previous ed.: 1970. — Includes bibliographies and index
ISBN 0-02-913060-3 (cased) : Unpriced
ISBN 0-02-912930-3 (pbk) : £7.95 B81-21452

302.3′5 — Organisations. Sociopolitical aspects

Environments and organizations / Marshall W. Meyer ... [et al.]. — San Francisco ; London : Jossey-Bass, 1978 (1980 printing). — xiv,407p : ill ; 24cm. — (The Jossey-Bass social and behavioral science series)
Bibliography: p369-393. — Includes index
ISBN 0-87589-374-0 : £15.50 B81-40322

302.3′5 — Organisations. Structure

Hesseling, Pjotr. Effective organization research for development. — Oxford : Pergamon, Jan.1982. — [220]p
ISBN 0-08-024082-8 : £9.95 : CIP entry B81-34571

Organization and nation : the Aston Programme IV / edited by David J. Hickson, Charles J. McMillan. — Farnborough, Hants. : Gower, c1980. — xviii,227p : 1ill ; 23cm
Bibliography: p205-218. - Includes index
ISBN 0-566-00324-4 : £23.50 B81-11618

302.3′5 — Organisations. Theories — *For management*

International perspectives on management and organization / edited by Roger Mansfield and Michael Poole. — Aldershot : Gower, c1981. — vii,155p : ill ; 23cm
Bibliography: p138-147. — Includes index
ISBN 0-566-00469-0 : Unpriced : CIP rev. B81-19180

302.3′5′024658 — Organisations - *For business studies*

Gallant, Cyril. The world of work. — London : McGraw-Hill, June 1981. — [280]p. — (McGraw-Hill business education courses)
ISBN 0-07-084246-9 (pbk) : £4.50 : CIP entry B81-11967

302.3′5′024658 — Organisations — *For business studies*

Livesey, Frank. The organisation in its environment / F. Livesey, G.K. Pople and P.J. Davies. — London : Longman. — (Longman business education series)
Vol.2: Lecturers′ manual. — 1981. — 51p ; 30cm
ISBN 0-582-41248-x (spiral) : £4.95 B81-27054

302.3′5′024658 — Organisations — *For business studies — Questions & answers*

Paisley, Brenda. People at work / Brenda Paisley & Judith Parker. — London : Pitman, 1980. — iv,236p : ill,facsims,forms,1map,1plan ; 30cm. — (Pitman business education)
ISBN 0-273-01316-5 (pbk) : £4.95 B81-02899

302.3′5′05 — Organisations — *Sociological perspectives — Serials*

The **International** yearbook of organization studies. — 1981. — London : Routledge & Kegan Paul, Dec.1981. — [306]p
ISBN 0-7100-0996-8 : £18.00 : CIP entry B81-36993

302.3′5′071073 — United States. Educational institutions. Curriculum subjects: Organisational behaviour. Teaching methods. Experiential techniques
Experiential organizational behavior / [edited by] Theodore T. Herbert, Peter Lorenzi. — New York : Macmillan ; London : Collier Macmillan, c1981. — x,241p : ill ; 24cm
ISBN 0-02-353620-9 (pbk) : £4.95 B81-36168

302.4 — Aggression — *Sociological perspectives*
Aggression and violence. — Oxford : Blackwell, Sept.1981. — [288]p
ISBN 0-631-12742-9 : £15.00 : CIP entry B81-22627

302.5 — Alienation
Lachs, John. Intermediate man. — Brighton : Harvester Press, Sept.1981. — [144]p
ISBN 0-7108-0368-0 : £18.95 : CIP entry B81-20520

302.5 — Alienation. Theories
Schaff, Adam. Alienation as a social phenomenon / by Adam Schaff. — Oxford : Pergamon, 1980. — v,311p ; 22cm
Bibliography: p292-306. - Includes index
ISBN 0-08-021807-5 : £20.00 B81-00749

302.5 — Australia. Deviance — *Sociological perspectives*
Two faces of deviance : crimes of the powerless and the powerful / edited by Paul R. Wilson and John Braithwaite. — St. Lucia : University of Queensland ; Hemel Hempstead : Distributed by Prentice-Hall, c1978. — vi,309p ; 22cm
Includes index
ISBN 0-7022-1325-x (cased) : £13.50
ISBN 0-7022-1326-8 (pbk) : Unpriced B81-25163

302.5 — Deviance
Box, Steven. Deviance, reality and society / Steven Box. — 2nd ed. — London : Holt, Rinehart and Winston, c1981. — vii,248p : ill ; 22cm
Previous ed.: 1971. — Includes bibliographies and index
ISBN 0-03-910294-7 (pbk) : £4.95 B81-26336

302.5 — Deviance. Labelling. Theories
The **Labelling** of deviance : evaluating a perspective / edited by Walter R. Gove. — 2nd ed. — Beverly Hills ; London : Sage, c1980. — 428p ; 22cm
Previous ed.: 1975. — Includes bibliographies and index
ISBN 0-8039-1470-9 (cased) : £12.50
ISBN 0-8039-1473-3 (pbk) : £6.25 B81-01919

302.5 — England. Deviance. Social control. Role of Justices of Peace & constables, *1580-1625* — *Study regions: Wiltshire*
Wall, Alison D.. Riot, bastardy and other social problems : the role of constables and J.P.s 1580-1625 / by Alison D. Wall. — Trowbridge (Bythesea Rd., Trowbridge, Wilts.) : Wiltshire Library & Museum Service, 1980. — 21leaves ; 30cm. — (Wiltshire monographs ; no.1)
ISBN 0-86080-069-5 (pbk) : Unpriced B81-05662

302.5 — Loneliness — *Personal observations*
McCallion, Paul. The chains of eventuality : or ten years pass / Paul McCallion. — Bognor Regis : New Horizon, c1981. — 94p ; 21cm
ISBN 0-86116-267-6 : £3.75 B81-27254

302.5 — Man. Self-presentation
Impression management theory and social psychological research / edited by James T. Tedeschi. — New York ; London : Academic Press, c1981. — xix,369p : ill ; 24cm
Includes bibliographies and index
ISBN 0-12-685180-8 : £16.60 B81-35356

302.5 — United States. Deviance. Effects of mass media
Deviance and mass media / edited by Charles Winick. — Beverly Hills ; London : Sage, c1978. — 309p : ill ; 22cm. — (Sage annual reviews of studies in deviance ; v.2)
Includes bibliographies
ISBN 0-8039-1040-1 (cased) : £12.50 (pbk) : £6.25 B81-05467

302.5 — United States. Deviance — *Interviews*
Lowney, Jeremiah. Deviant reality : alternative world views. — 2nd ed. / Jeremiah Lowney, Robert W. Winslow, Virginia Winslow. — Boston, Mass. ; London : Allyn and Bacon, c1981. — xiv,406p ; 24cm
Previous ed.: by Robert W. Winslow and Virginia Winslow. 1974. — Includes bibliographies
ISBN 0-205-07243-7 (pbk) : £6.95 B81-11238

302.5 — United States. Deviance. Political aspects
Schur, Edwin M.. The politics of deviance : stigma contests and the uses of power / Edwin M. Schur. — Englewood Cliffs ; London : Prentice-Hall, c1980. — xi,241p ; 21cm. — (A Spectrum book)
Include bibliographies and index
ISBN 0-13-684753-6 (cased) : £7.75
ISBN 0-13-684746-3 (pbk) : £3.85 B81-08313

302.5 — United States. Deviance — *Sociological perspectives*
Liska, Allen E.. Perspectives on deviance / Allen E. Liska. — Englewood [Cliffs] ; London : Prentice-Hall, c1981. — xi,228p : ill,ports ; 24cm
Includes bibliographies and index
ISBN 0-13-660373-4 : Unpriced B81-36491

303 — SOCIAL PROCESSES

303.3′2 — Children. Socialisation
Blunder, Ruth. Social development. — Lancaster : MTP Press, Feb.1982. — [170]p. — (Studies in developmental paediatrics ; v.4)
ISBN 0-85200-304-8 : £8.95 : CIP entry B81-35857

Marion, Marian. Guidance of young children / Marian Marion. — St. Louis ; London : Mosby, 1981. — x,237p : ill ; 24cm
Includes bibliographies and index
ISBN 0-8016-3108-4 (pbk) : £7.75 B81-25048

303.3′2 — Children. Socialisation — *For schools*
Beecham, Yvonne. Childhood : a study in socialisation / Y. Beecham, J. Fiehn, J. Gates ; cartoons by Jo Nesbitt, Lesley Ruda. — London : Harrap, 1980. — 64p : ill,facsims ; 28cm. — (Themes in sociology)
ISBN 0-245-53253-6 (pbk) : £2.25 B81-02681

303.3′2 — Socialisation. Theories
Wentworth, William M.. Context and understanding : an inquiry into socialization theory / William M. Wentworth. — New York ; Oxford : Elsevier, c1980. — xii,183p : ill ; 24cm
Bibliography: p155-175. — Includes index
ISBN 0-444-99073-9 : £8.89 B81-05607

303.3′4 — Leadership. Charisma — *Sociological perspectives*
Theobald, Robin. Charisma : a critical review / by Robin Theobald. — London ([32-38 Wells St., WIP 3FG]) : Polytechnic of Central London, School of Social Sciences and Business Studies, [1979?]. — 36p ; 30cm. — (Research paper / Polytechnic of Central London. School of Social Sciences and Business Studies ; no.5)
Cover title. — Bibliography: p32-36
Unpriced (pbk) B81-33573

303.3′4 — Organisations. Leadership
Yukl, Gary A.. Leadership in organization / Gary A. Yukl. — Englewood Cliffs ; London : Prentice-Hall, c1981. — xii,340p : ill ; 24cm
Bibliography: p291-324. — Includes index
ISBN 0-13-527176-2 : £14.20 B81-40172

303.3′4 — Persuasion
Reardon, Kathleen Kelley. Persuasion : theory and context / Kathleen Kelley Reardon ; foreword by Gerald R. Miller ; Gail Theus Fairhurst, contributing author, chapter 10. — Beverly Hills ; London : Sage, c1981. — 283p ; 22cm. — (Sage library of social research ; v.122)
Bibliography: p263-282
ISBN 0-8039-1615-9 (cased) : Unpriced
ISBN 0-8039-1616-7 (pbk) : £6.50 B81-34189

303.3′6 — Europe. Authority & power, *ca 800-1500* — *Festschriften*
Authority and power : studies on medieval law and government presented to Walter Ullmann on his seventieth birthday / edited by Brian Tierney and Peter Linehan. — Cambridge : Cambridge University Press, 1980. — x,274p,[1]leaf of plates : 1port ; 24cm
Bibliography: p255-274
ISBN 0-521-22275-3 : £25.00
Primary classification 340.5′5 B81-03396

303.3′6 — Great Britain. Power. Misuse
Denning, Alfred Denning, *Baron*. Misuse of power : the Richard Dimbleby lecture, November 1980 / Lord Denning. — London : British Broadcasting Corporation, 1980. — 19p ; 21cm. — (The Richard Dimbleby lectures)
ISBN 0-563-17894-9 (pbk) : £1.50 B81-07758

303.3′6 — Power. Psychosocial aspects
Ng, Sik Hung. The social psychology of power / Sik Hung Ng. — London : Published in cooperation with European Association of Experimental Social Psychology by Academic Press, 1980. — xi,280p : 1ill ; 24cm. — (European monographs in social psychology ; 21)
Bibliography: p258-273. - Includes index
ISBN 0-12-518180-9 : £12.80 : CIP rev. B80-20218

303.3′72 — Society. Role of tradition
Shils, Edward. Tradition / Edward Shils. — London : Faber, 1981. — viii,334p ; 25cm
Includes index
ISBN 0-571-11756-2 : £15.00 : CIP rev. B81-23759

303.3′72′0947 — Soviet Union. Rituals — *Sociological perspectives*
Lane, Christel. The rites of rulers : ritual in industrial society : the Soviet case / Christel Lane. — Cambridge : Cambridge University Press, 1981. — ix,308p : ill ; 24cm
Bibliography: p291-301. — Includes index
ISBN 0-521-22608-2 (cased) : £20.00
ISBN 0-521-28347-7 (pbk) : £6.95 B81-27108

303.3′75′0941 — British propaganda, *1919-1939*
Taylor, Philip M.. The projection of Britain : British overseas publicity and propaganda 1919-1939 / Philip M. Taylor. — Cambridge : Cambridge University Press, 1981. — xv,363p ; 23cm
Bibliography: p339-351. — Includes index
ISBN 0-521-23843-9 : £25.00 : CIP rev. B81-21574

303.3′8 — Man. Attitudes to man. Assessment. Eysenck′s Inventory of Social Attitudes
Giorgi, Bruno. Eysenck′s inventory of social attitudes / Bruno Giorgi, Jr. — Belfast ([Psychology Dept., University of Ulster, Coleraine-Londonderry]) : B. Giorgi, 1979. — 37p : 1ill ; 21cm
Bibliography: p37
ISBN 0-9506855-0-x (pbk) : Unpriced B81-32710

303.3′8′05 — Public opinion — *Serials*
Index to international public opinion / prepared by Survey Research Consultants International, Inc.. — 1978-1979. — London : Macmillan, 1980-. — v. ; 29cm
Annual
ISSN 0193-905x : Unpriced B81-00750

Index to international public opinion / prepared by Survey Research Consultants International, Inc.. — 1979-1980. — Oxford : Clio Press, c1981. — xxvii,484p
ISBN 0-903450-48-8 : Unpriced B81-29048

303.3′8′0723 — Great Britain. Public opinion. Surveys. Methodology. Teaching
Slater, Robert, *1945-*. Teaching survey research methods and data analysis : a block course format / Robert Slater and Charles Jackson. — Cardiff (Llwyn-y-Grant, Penylan, Cardiff CF3 7UX Wales) : Department of Applied Psychology, University of Wales Institute of Science and Technology, [1981?]. — 30leaves ; 30cm. — (Occasional paper / Department of Applied Psychology. University of Wales Institute of Science and Technology ; no.11)
Bibliography: leaves 24—25
Unpriced (spiral) B81-29798

303.3'8'0941 — Great Britain. Public opinion, *1980*
The **Gallup** report / edited by Norman L. Webb and Robert J. Wybrow. — London : Sphere, 1981. — 188p : ill ; 20cm
Includes index
ISBN 0-7221-9022-0 (pbk) : £1.95 B81-26613

303.3'8'0973 — United States. Public opinion. Influence of mass media
Reader in public opinion and mass communication. — 3rd. ed. / edited by Morris Janowitz and Paul M. Hirsch. — New York : Free Press ; London : Collier Macmillan, c1981. — xv,440p : ill ; 24cm
Previous ed.: published as Reader in public opinion and communication / Bernard Berelson, Morris Janowitz. 1966. — Includes bibliographies and index
ISBN 0-02-916020-0 (pbk) : £7.95 B81-39024

303.3'85 — Discrimination & prejudice — *For schools*
Thom, Vivien. Prejudice / Vivien Thom. — London : Edward Arnold, 1981. — 16p : ill ; 30cm. — (Checkpoint ; 18)
Bibliography: p16
ISBN 0-7131-0531-3 (pbk) : £0.98 B81-34991

303.3'85 — Prejudice
Allport, Gordon W.. The nature of prejudice / Gordon W. Allport ; introduction by Kenneth Clark ; foreword by Thomas Pettigrew. — 25th anniversary ed. — Reading, Mass. ; London : Addison-Wesley, c1979. — xxxii,537p ; 22cm
Originally published: 1954. — Includes index
ISBN 0-201-00178-0 : £6.60
ISBN 0-201-00179-9 (pbk) : Unpriced B81-16181

303.4 — Genetic engineering. Social aspects
Genetic consequences of man made change. — London : Academic Press, Aug.1981. — [300]p
ISBN 0-12-101620-x : CIP entry B81-17522

303.4 — Industrial society
Kumar, Krishan. Prophecy and progress : the sociology of industrial and post-industrial society / Krishan Kumar. — Harmondsworth : Penguin, 1978 (1981 [printing]). — 416p ; 20cm. — (Pelican sociology)
Bibliography: p386-405. — Includes index
ISBN 0-14-022039-9 (pbk) : £2.95 B81-40095

303.4 — Industrialised societies. Development — *Forecasts*
Harman, Willis W.. An incomplete guide to the future / Willis W. Harman. — New York ; London : Norton, c1979. — xiii,160p : ill,1facsim ; 21cm
Originally published: Stanford, Calif.: Stanford Alumni Association, 1976. — Includes index
ISBN 0-393-95006-9 (pbk) : £2.50 B81-06302

303.4 — Industrialised societies. Social change
Etzioni-Halevy, Eva. Social change : the advent and maturation of modern society / Eva Etzioni-Halevy. — London : Routledge & Kegan Paul, 1981. — xiv,304p ; 23cm
Bibliography: p273-284. - Includes index
ISBN 0-7100-0767-1 (cased) : £10.95
ISBN 0-7100-0768-x (pbk) : £5.95 B81-18404

303.4 — Industrialised societies. Social change — *Conference proceedings*
The **Poverty** of progress. — Oxford : Pergamon, Feb.1982. — [275]p
Conference papers
ISBN 0-08-028906-1 : £17.00 : CIP entry B81-35946

303.4 — Progress. Theories, *to 1979*
Nisbet, Robert, *1913-*. History of the idea of progress / Robert Nisbet. — London : Heinemann, 1980. — xi,370p ; 24cm
Includes index
ISBN 0-435-82657-3 : £8.50 : CIP rev. B80-13707

303.4 — Social change
The **Social** ecology of change : from equilibrium to development / edited by Zdravko Mlinar and Henry Teune. — London : Sage, c1978. — 296p : ill,maps ; 23cm. — (Sage studies in international sociology ; 15)
Conference papers
ISBN 0-8039-9886-4 (cased) : £11.25
ISBN 0-8039-9887-2 (pbk) : £5.50 B81-02075

Toffler, Alvin. The third wave / Alvin Toffler. — London : Pan in association with Collins, 1981, c1980. — 543p ; 18cm
Originally published: London : Collins, 1980. — Bibliography: p492-522. — Includes index
ISBN 0-330-26337-4 (pbk) : £1.95 B81-22895

303.4 — Social change — *Early works*
The **Victorian** prophets : a reader from Carlyle to Wells / edited and with an introduction by Peter Keating. — [London] : Fontana, 1981. — 265p ; 18cm
Bibliography: p265
ISBN 0-00-635698-2 (pbk) : £2.95 B81-17815

303.4 — World — *Forecasts*
Wallechinsky, David. The People's almanac presents the book of predictions / by David Wallechinsky, Amy Wallace, Irving Wallace. — London : Elm Tree Books, 1981. — xviii,513p : ill,1map,ports ; 25cm
Includes index
ISBN 0-241-10607-9 : £7.50 B81-18000

303.4 — World, *to ca 2000* — *Forecasts*
Readings from Futures : a collection of articles from the journal Futures, 1974-80 / edited by Ralph Jones. — Guildford : Westbury House, c1981. — x,386p : ill ; 25cm
ISBN 0-86103-040-0 : Unpriced : CIP rev. B81-11968

303.4'01 — Social change. Theories
Strasser, Hermann. An introduction to theories of social change / Hermann Strasser and Susan C. Randall with special contributions by Karl Gabriel, Hans Jürgen Krysmanski and Karl Hermann Tjaden. — London : Routledge & Kegan Paul, 1981. — xi,340p : ill ; 22cm. — (International library of sociology)
Bibliography: p308-330. — Includes index
ISBN 0-7100-0789-2 (cased) : £11.95 : CIP rev.
ISBN 0-7100-0790-6 (pbk) : £5.95 B81-16377

303.4'0941 — Great Britain. Social change, *1900-1980*
Halsey, A. H.. Change in British society. — 2nd ed. — Oxford : Oxford University Press, Sept.1981. — [198]p
Previous ed.: 1978
ISBN 0-19-289156-1 (pbk) : £2.95 : CIP entry B81-22563

303.4'0941 — Great Britain. Social conditions — *Forecasts*
Bellini, James. Rule Britannia : a progress report for domesday 1986 / James Bellini. — London : Cape, 1981. — xv,280p : ill,2geneal.tables ; 23cm
Bibliography: p273-274. — Includes index
ISBN 0-224-01898-1 : £6.95 B81-20773

303.4'09438 — Poland. Social conditions — *Forecasts — Polish texts*
Sawulak, Mikołaj. Polskie zmartwienia / Mikołaj Sawulak. — London (27 Hamilton Rd., Bedford Park, W4 1AL) : Odnowa, 1980. — 23p ; 21cm
ISBN 0-903705-34-6 (pbk) : Unpriced B81-21030

Szczepański, Jan. Pozapolityczne wyznaczniki przyszłości narodu / Jan Szczepański. — London (27 Hamilton Rd., Bedford Park, W4 1AL) : Odnowa, 1979. — 32p ; 21cm. — (Polska w świecie współczesnym ; zesz.6)
ISBN 0-903705-30-3 (pbk) : Unpriced B81-21031

303.4'4 — Social systems. Evolution
Hawrylyshyn, Bohdan. Road maps to the future / by Bohdan Hawrylyshyn ; [a report to the Club of Rome]. — Oxford : Pergamon, 1980. — xv,193p : ill ; 22cm. — (Pergamon international library)
ISBN 0-08-026115-9 (cased) : £12.75 : CIP rev.
ISBN 0-08-026114-0 (pbk) : £4.50 B80-12728

303.4'4'0724 — Culture. Evolution. Mathematical models
Cavalli-Sforza, L. L.. Cultural transmission and evolution : a quantitative approach / L.L. Cavalli-Sforza and M.W. Feldman. — Princeton ; Guildford : Princeton University Press, 1981. — xiv,388p ; 23cm. — (Monographs in population biology ; 16)
Bibliography: p397-382. — Includes index
ISBN 0-691-08280-4 (cased) : £14.00
ISBN 0-691-08283-9 (pbk) : £5.90 B81-26231

303.4'8 — Western world. Social change. Role of creative thought — *Proposals*
De Bono, Edward. Future positive / Edward de Bono. — Harmondsworth : Penguin, 1980, c1979. — 234p ; 19cm. — (Pelican Books)
Originally published: London : Temple Smith, 1979
ISBN 0-14-022293-6 (pbk) : £1.50 B81-02398

303.4'82 — Cultural conflict, *to 1980*
Catchpole, Brian. The clash of cultures : aspects of culture conflict from Roman times to the present day / Brian Catchpole. — London : Heinemann Educational, 1981. — viii,184p : ill,maps,ports ; 25cm
Includes bibliographies and index
ISBN 0-435-31097-6 (pbk) : £3.95 : CIP rev. B80-13708

303.4'82 — International relations
Bandyopadhyaya, J.. North over south. — Brighton : Harvester Press, Jan.1982. — [352]p
ISBN 0-7108-0344-3 : £22.50 : CIP entry B81-33888

303.4'82'093 — Mediterranean Region. Cultural relations with Central Europe, *B.C.600-B.C.400*
Wells, Peter S.. Culture contact and culture change : Early Iron Age central Europe and the Mediterranean world / Peter S. Wells. — Cambridge : Cambridge University Press, 1980. — xi,171p : ill,maps ; 24cm. — (New series in archaeology)
Bibliography: p146-166. — Includes index
ISBN 0-521-22808-5 : £12.50 : CIP rev.
Primary classification 303.4'82'0936 B81-00016

303.4'82'0936 — Central Europe. Cultural relations with Mediterranean region, *B.C.600-B.C.400*
Wells, Peter S.. Culture contact and culture change : Early Iron Age central Europe and the Mediterranean world / Peter S. Wells. — Cambridge : Cambridge University Press, 1980. — xi,171p : ill,maps ; 24cm. — (New series in archaeology)
Bibliography: p146-166. — Includes index
ISBN 0-521-22808-5 : £12.50 : CIP rev.
Also classified at 303.4'82'093 B81-00016

303.4'82'0936 — North-western Europe. Cultural relations with Great Britain, *ca B.C.1500-ca B.C.700*
O'Connor, Brendan. Cross-channel relations in the Later Bronze Age : relations between Britain, North-Eastern France and the Low Countries during the Later Bronze Age and the Early Iron Age, with particular reference to the metalwork / Brendan O'Connor. — Oxford : B.A.R., 1980. — 2v.(858p) : ill,82maps ; 30cm. — (BAR. International series ; 91)
Bibliography: p611-681. — Includes index
ISBN 0-86054-105-3 (pbk) : £26.00
Primary classification 303.4'82'09361 B81-36611

303.4'82'09361 — Great Britain. Cultural relations with North-western Europe, *ca B.C.1500-ca B.C.700*
O'Connor, Brendan. Cross-channel relations in the Later Bronze Age : relations between Britain, North-Eastern France and the Low Countries during the Later Bronze Age and the Early Iron Age, with particular reference to the metalwork / Brendan O'Connor. — Oxford : B.A.R., 1980. — 2v.(858p) : ill,82maps ; 30cm. — (BAR. International series ; 91)
Bibliography: p611-681. — Includes index
ISBN 0-86054-105-3 (pbk) : £26.00
Also classified at 303.4'82'0936 B81-36611

303.4'82'094 — European Community. International relations — *Forecasts*

Brandt, Willy. The future of Europe in a world of change / by Willy Brandt. — [Southampton] : University of Southampton, 1980. — 15p ; 21cm. — (Lectures / University of Southampton, Fawley Foundation Lectures ; 26)
ISBN 0-85432-210-8 (pbk) : Unpriced B81-17223

303.4'82'09411 — Scotland. Relations with United States, ***1700-1800.*** **Historical sources**

Brock, William R.. Scotus Americanus : a survey of the sources for links between Scotland and America in the eighteenth century. — Edinburgh : Edinburgh University Press, Jan.1982. — [320]p
ISBN 0-85224-420-7 : £15.00 : CIP entry
Also classified at 303.4'82'0973 B81-37529

303.4'82'09416 — Northern Ireland. Relations with United States, ***to 1945***

The **Ulster** American Connection / edited by J.W. Blake. — [Coleraine] : [New University of Ulster], c1981. — iileaves,45p ; 30cm
ISBN 0-901229-31-8 (pbk) : Unpriced
Also classified at 303.4'82'0973 B81-37260

303.4'82'094235 — Devon. Relations with United States, ***to 1980***

The **Devon-American** story / edited by Charles Owen ; researched by Bridget Kloos and Hilary Fagg. — Exeter (Guildhall Shopping Centre, Exeter EX4 3HG) : Published for Devon International Festival by Exeter Rare Books, 1980. — 36p : ill,1map,1facsim ; 22cm
Bibliography: p32-33
ISBN 0-9507155-0-6 (pbk) : £1.00
Also classified at 303.4'82'0973 B81-21252

303.4'82'0943 — West Germany. Cultural relations

Arnold, Hans. Foreign cultural policy : a survey from a German point of view / Hans Arnold ; [translated by Keith Hamnett]. — Tübingen : Horst Erdmann Verlag ; London : Wolff, c1979. — 211p ; 21cm
ISBN 3-7711-0324-x (pbk) : Unpriced B81-09894

303.4'82'0947 — Eastern Europe. Relations with Soviet Union, ***1968-1980***

Soviet-East European dilemmas : coercion, competition and consent / edited by Karen Dawisha and Philip Hanson. — London : Heinemann for the Royal Institute of International Affairs, 1981. — xiii,226p ; 23cm
Includes index
ISBN 0-435-83220-4 (cased) : £14.95 : CIP rev.
ISBN 0-435-83221-2 (pbk) : £5.95
Also classified at 327.47 B81-03824

303.4'82'09485 — Sweden. International relations — *Forecasts*

Sweden in world society : thought about the future / a report prepared for the Swedish Secretariat for Futures Studies by Bo Huldt... [et al.] ; translated from the Swedish by M.F. Metcalf. — Oxford : Pergamon, 1980. — ix,227p : ill,1map ; 25cm. — (Pergamon international library)
Bibliography: p200-207. — Includes index
ISBN 0-08-025456-x (cased) : £13.50 : CIP rev. B80-09092

303.4'82'0973 — United States. International relations, ***1938-1950***

Ninkovich, Frank A.. The diplomacy of ideas : U.S. foreign policy and cultural relations, 1938-1950 / Frank A. Ninkovich. — Cambridge : Cambridge University Press, 1981. — x,253p ; 24cm
Bibliography: p222-246. - Includes index
ISBN 0-521-23241-4 : £15.00 B81-17933

303.4'82'0973 — United States. Relations with Devon, ***to 1980***

The **Devon-American** story / edited by Charles Owen ; researched by Bridget Kloos and Hilary Fagg. — Exeter (Guildhall Shopping Centre, Exeter EX4 3HG) : Published for Devon International Festival by Exeter Rare Books, 1980. — 36p : ill,1map,1facsim ; 22cm
Bibliography: p32-33
ISBN 0-9507155-0-6 (pbk) : £1.00
Primary classification 303.4'82'094235 B81-21252

303.4'82'0973 — United States. Relations with Northern Ireland, ***to 1945***

The **Ulster** American Connection / edited by J.W. Blake. — [Coleraine] : [New University of Ulster], c1981. — iileaves,45p ; 30cm
ISBN 0-901229-31-8 (pbk) : Unpriced
Primary classification 303.4'82'09416 B81-37260

303.4'82'0973 — United States. Relations with Scotland, ***1700-1800.*** **Historical sources**

Brock, William R.. Scotus Americanus : a survey of the sources for links between Scotland and America in the eighteenth century. — Edinburgh : Edinburgh University Press, Jan.1982. — [320]p
ISBN 0-85224-420-7 : £15.00 : CIP entry
Primary classification 303.4'82'09411 B81-37529

303.4'83 — Computer systems. Social aspects — *Forecasts*

Evans, Christopher. The mighty micro : the impact of the computer revolution. — New ed. — London : Gollancz, Jan.1982. — [272]p
Previous ed.: 1979
ISBN 0-575-03122-0 : £6.95 : CIP entry B81-40245

303.4'83 — Great Britain. Society. Effects of microelectronic devices

Harriman, Guy. The chips are down / Guy Harriman & Mike Bradford. — London (1 Hampstead Sq., N.W.3) : Holystone, 1980. — 12p ; 21cm. — (Go pamphlet ; no.3)
Cover title
£0.50 (pbk) B81-23300

303.4'83 — Scientists. Social responsibility

Wessel, Milton R.. Science and conscience / Milton R. Wessel. — New York ; Guildford : Columbia University Press, 1980. — xxv,293p ; 24cm
Includes index
ISBN 0-231-04746-0 : £8.80 B81-00751

303.4'83 — Social change. Role of computer systems

Laver, Murray. Computers and social change / Murray Laver. — Cambridge : Cambridge University Press, 1980. — vii,125p ; 24cm. — (Cambridge computer science texts ; 10)
Includes index
ISBN 0-521-23027-6 (cased) : £8.00
ISBN 0-521-29771-0 (pbk) : £2.95 B81-24489

303.4'83 — Social change. Role of technological innovation

Gosling, William. The kingdom of sand. — London : Council for Educational Technology, Nov.1981. — [96]p. — (Occasional paper / Council for Educational Technology, ISSN 0307-952x ; 9)
ISBN 0-86184-053-4 (pbk) : £4.00 : CIP entry B81-33633

303.4'83 — Society. Effects of microelectronic devices

Microelectronics and society / edited by Trevor Jones. — Milton Keynes : Open University Press, 1980. — vi,174p : ill ; 22cm
Bibliography: p171-174
ISBN 0-335-09002-8 (pbk) : £4.95 : CIP rev. B80-04073

303.4'83 — Society. Effects of microelectronic devices — *Conference proceedings*

The **Socio-economic** impact of microelectronics : this book is based on an international conference held in Zandvoort, The Netherlands, which was supported by The Netherlands Ministry of Science Policy / edited by J. Berting, S.C. Mills and H. Wintersberger. — Oxford : Pergamon, 1980. — vii,267p : ill ; 26cm
Includes bibliographies
ISBN 0-08-026776-9 : £22.25 : CIP rev. B80-21415

303.4'83 — Society. Effects of microprocessors

Burns, Alan, *1953-*. The microchip : appropriate or inappropriate technology? / Alan Burns. — Chichester : Horwood, 1981. — 180p : ill ; 24cm. — (The Ellis Horwood series in computers and their applications ; 11)
Bibliography: p173-178. — Includes index
ISBN 0-85312-261-x (cased) : £12.50 : CIP rev.
ISBN 0-85312-353-5 (Student ed.) : Unpriced B81-12900

Marsh, Peter, *1952-*. The silicon chip book / Peter Marsh. — London : Abacus, 1981. — 211p : ill ; 20cm
Includes index
ISBN 0-349-12286-5 (pbk) : £2.50 B81-09896

303.4'83 — Society. Role of chemical engineering

Turner, J. C. R.. A chemical engineer in society : an inaugural lecture delivered in the University of Exeter on 25 April 1980 / J.C.R. Turner. — [Exeter] : University of Exeter, 1980. — 17p,4p of plates : ill ; 21cm
ISBN 0-85989-107-0 (pbk) : £0.60 B81-14334

303.4'83 — Society. Role of computer systems

Sanders, Donald H.. Computers in society / Donald H. Sanders. — 3rd ed. — New York ; London : McGraw-Hill, c1981. — xxxi,622p,[8]p of plates : ill(some col.) ; 25cm
Previous ed.: 1977. — Includes index
ISBN 0-07-054672-x : £11.95 B81-10594

303.4'83 — Society. Role of science

Science in society. — London : Heinemann Educational, 1981. — 12v : ill,maps ; 22cm
ISBN 0-435-54042-4 (pbk) : £8.50 B81-09530

Science in society / project director John L. Lewis. — London : Heinemann Educational Teacher's guide. — 1981. — viii,256 : ill,maps ; 24cm
ISBN 0-435-54043-2 (pbk) : Unpriced B81-16428

303.4'83 — Society. Role of science & technology — *Soviet viewpoints*

Science, technology and the future : Soviet scientists' analysis of the problems of and prospects for the development of science and technology and their role in society / editors E.P. Velikhov, J.M. Gvishiani and S.R. Mikulinsky ; compilers N.I. Makeshin, L.E. Murtazina, A.L. Chernjak. — Oxford : Pergamon, 1980. — viii,480p : ill,maps,ports ; 26cm
Includes index
ISBN 0-08-024743-1 : £15.00 : CIP rev. B79-30518

303.4'83 — Technological change. Demographic aspects

Boserup, Ester. Population and technology / Ester Boserup. — Oxford : Blackwell, 1981. — xi,255p ; 24cm
Bibliography: p235-245. — Includes index
ISBN 0-631-12817-4 : £9.95 : CIP rev. B81-04322

303.4'83 — Technological change — *French texts*

Salomon, J. J.. Prométhée empêtré : la résistance au changement technique. — Oxford : Pergamon, Dec.1981. — [160]p. — (Collection futuribles)
ISBN 0-08-027064-6 (pbk) : £3.45 : CIP entry B81-36984

303.4'83 — Technological development. Socioeconomic aspects

Binswanger, Hans P.. Induced innovation : technology, institutions, and development / Hans P. Binswanger and Vernon W. Ruttan with Uri Ben-Zion ... [et al.]. — Baltimore ; London : Johns Hopkins University Press, c1978. — xiv,423p : ill ; 24cm
Includes index
ISBN 0-8018-2027-8 : Unpriced B81-08454

303.4'83 — Technology. Cultural aspects

The **Myths** of information : technology and postindustrial culture / edited by Kathleen Woodward. — London : Routledge & Kegan Paul, 1980. — xxvi,250p ; 24cm
ISBN 0-7100-0710-8 : £8.95 : CIP rev. B80-34509

303.4′83 — Western world. Society. Effects of technological development

Mishan, E. J.. Pornography, psychedelics and technology : essays on the limits to freedom / E.J. Mishan. — London : Allen & Unwin, 1980. — 182p ; 23cm
Includes index
ISBN 0-04-300081-9 : £12.50 : CIP rev.
B80-22910

303.4′83′0941 — Great Britain. Technological innovation. Social aspects — *Forecasts* — *For children*

Radnor, Alan. Living in the future / Alan Radnor. — London : ITV, 1981. — 61p : ill (some col.),1map ; 29cm
ISBN 0-900727-82-9 : £3.50
ISBN 0-356-07542-7 (Macdonald Phoebus)
B81-21230

303.4′83′0942 — England. Industrialisation, *1850-1980.* **Social aspects**

Wiener, Martin J.. English culture and the decline of the industrial spirit, 1850-1980 / Martin J. Wiener. — Cambridge : Cambridge University Press, 1981. — xi,217p ; 24cm
Includes index
ISBN 0-521-23418-2 : £9.95 B81-16417

303.4′83′0942781 — Cumbria. Furness & Barrow-in-Furness. Industrial development, *1700-1900.* **Social aspects**

Marshall, J. D.. Furness and the Industrial Revolution : an economic history of Furness (1711-1900) and the town of Barrow (1757-1897) with an epilogue / by J.D. Marshall. — Beckermet : Michael Moon, 1958, c1981 (1981 [printing]). — xxii,439p : ill,maps,plans,ports ; 23cm
Includes index
ISBN 0-904131-26-2 : £12.00 B81-28245

303.4′84 — England. Social reform, *1800-1900*

Taylor, Clare. Essays on Anglo-American reform / Clare Taylor. — Aberystwyth : [Department of History, The University College of Wales], 1981. — 3leaves ; 30cm
Unpriced (unbound)
Also classified at 303.4′84 B81-34256

303.4′84 — Islamic countries. Social reform — *Islamic viewpoints*

as-Sufi, ′Abd al-Qadir. Future Islam : a manifesto / ′Abd al-Qadir as-Sufi. — [S.l.] : [s.n.], [1981]. — 9p ; 21cm
Cover title
Unpriced (pbk) B81-10387

303.4′84 — Social movements. Analysis

Touraine, Alain. The voice and the eye : an analysis of social movements / Alain Touraine ; translated by Alan Duff ; with a foreword by Richard Sennett. — Cambridge : Cambridge University Press, 1981. — xiii,225p : ill ; 24cm
Translation of: La voix et le regard. — Bibliography: p223-225
ISBN 0-521-23874-9 (cased) : £15.50
ISBN 0-521-28271-3 (pbk) : £5.95 B81-17931

303.4′84 — United S†ates. Social reform, *1800-1900*

Taylor, Clare. Essays on Anglo-American reform / Clare Taylor. — Aberystwyth : [Department of History, The University College of Wales], 1981. — 3leaves ; 30cm
Unpriced (unbound)
Primary classification 303.4′84 B81-34256

303.6 — Ancient world. Civil disturbance, *B.C.750-B.C.330*

Lintott, Andrew. Violence, civil strife and revolution in the classical city 750-330 BC. — London : Croom Helm, Dec.1981. — [320]p
ISBN 0-7099-1605-1 : £13.95 : CIP entry
B81-31428

303.6 — Negotiation. Social aspects

Strauss, Anselm L.. Negotiations : varieties, contexts, processes, and social order / Anselm Strauss. — San Francisco ; London : Jossey-Bass, 1978. — xviii,275p ; 24cm. — (The Jossey-Bass social and behavioral science series)
Bibliography: p263-268. — Includes index
ISBN 0-87589-369-4 : £11.20 B81-15107

303.6 — Negotiation. Sociological perspectives

The **Negotiation** process : theories and applications / editor I. William Zartman. — Beverly Hills ; London : Sage, c1978. — 240p : ill ; 23cm
Bibliography: p225-236. — Includes index
ISBN 0-8039-1034-7 : £12.50 B81-15110

303.6 — Social conflict

Rummel, R. J.. Understanding conflict and war / R.J. Rummel. — Beverly Hills ; London : Sage Vol.5: The just peace. — c1981. — 317p : ill ; 24cm
Bibliography: p285-295. — Includes index
£17.00 B81-36735

303.6 — Social conflict. Political aspects

Handbook of political conflict : theory and research / edited by Ted Robert Gurr. — New York : Free Press ; London : Collier Macmillan, c1980. — ix,566p : ill ; 27cm. — (The Free Press series on political behavior)
Bibliography: p501-553. - Includes index
ISBN 0-02-912760-2 : £25.00 B81-15616

303.6′01 — Social conflict. Theories

Rex, John. Social conflict : a conceptual and theoretical analysis / John Rex. — London : Longman, 1981. — 136p ; 20cm. — (Aspects of modern sociology. Social process)
Includes index
ISBN 0-582-48123-6 (pbk) : £3.50 : CIP rev.
B81-30275

303.6′0941 — Great Britain. Social protest. Role of women, *1800-1850*

Thomis, Malcolm I.. Women in protest 1800-1850. — London : Croom Helm, Feb.1982. — [192]p
ISBN 0-7099-2407-0 : £12.95 : CIP entry
B81-37559

303.6′2 — Violence. Prediction

Monahan, John. Predicting violent behavior : an assessment of clinical techniques / John Monahan ; introduction by Stanley L. Brodsky ; foreword by Saleem A. Shah. — Beverly Hills ; London : Sage, c1981. — 183p : 2ill ; 23cm. — (Sage library of social research ; v.114)
Bibliography: p171-181
ISBN 0-8039-1313-3 (cased) : Unpriced
ISBN 0-8039-1314-1 (pbk) : Unpriced
B81-27169

303.6′2′019 — Violence. Psychological aspects — *Conference proceedings*

Texas Research Institute of Mental Sciences. *Symposium (12th : 1979 : Houston).* Violence and the violent individual : proceedings of the Twelfth Annual Symposium, Texas Research Institute of Mental Sciences, Houston, Thomm Kevin Roberts and Kenneth S. Solway / Lore Feldman technical editor. — Lancaster : MTP, c1981. — 446p : ill ; 24cm
Includes bibliographies and index
ISBN 0-85200-561-x : £17.95 B81-27088

303.6′4 — Permanent revolution

Löwy, Michael. The politics of combined and uneven development. — London : New Left Books, Nov.1981. — [256]p
ISBN 0-86091-023-7 (cased) : £10.00 : CIP entry
ISBN 0-86091-740-1 (pbk) : £4.00 B81-33637

303.6′4′0924 — Revolution. Theories of Lenin, V. I.

Lane, David. Leninism : a sociological interpretation / David Lane. — Cambridge : Cambridge University Press, 1981. — x,150p ; 24cm. — (Themes in the social sciences)
Bibliography: p139-147. - Includes index
ISBN 0-521-23855-2 (cased) : £13.50
B81-17025

303.6′4′0924 — Revolutions. Theories of Sorel, Georges

Vernon, Richard. Commitment and change : Georges Sores and the idea of revolution / essays and translations by Richard Vernon. — Toronto ; London : University of Toronto Press, c1978. — viii,148p ; 24cm
Bibliography: p141-145. — Includes index
ISBN 0-8020-5400-5 : £10.50 B81-21319

303.6′6′0973 — United States. Social life. Effects of participation of United States in wars, *1900-1980*

Stein, Arthur A.. The nation at war / Arthur A. Stein. — Baltimore ; London : Johns Hopkins University Press, c1980. — xii,151p : ill ; 24cm
Bibliography: p121-141. — Includes index
ISBN 0-8018-2441-9 : £7.75 B81-21091

303.6′6′0973 — United States. Warfare. Social aspects, *1600-1783*

Ferling, John E.. A wilderness of miseries : war and warriors in early America / John E. Ferling. — Westport, Conn. ; London : Greenwood Press, 1980. — xiv,227p,[4]p of plates : ports ; 25cm. — (Contributions in military history, ISSN 0084-9251 ; no.22)
Bibliography: p203-221. — Includes index
ISBN 0-313-22093-x : £15.95 B81-23478

304 — HUMAN ECOLOGY, GENETIC FACTORS, POPULATION, ETC

304 — Great Britain. Census data — *For local history*

Boreham, John M.. Census returns. — Brentwood (c/o Miss M. Baker, 4 Pennyfields, Brentwood, Essex CM14 5JP) : Essex Society for Family History, Nov.1981. — [16]p
ISBN 0-9504327-1-7 (pbk) : £0.50 : CIP entry
B81-32018

304.2 — Environment. Effects of ionising radiation

Nuclear radiation in warfare. — London : Taylor & Francis, Aug.1981. — [150]p
ISBN 0-85066-217-6 : £10.00 : CIP entry
B81-18056

304.2 — Environment. Effects of man

Fedorov, E. K.. Man and nature : the ecological crisis and social progress / E. Fedorov. — Moscow : Progress, 1980 ; [London] : Distributed by Central Books. — 176p ; 20cm
Translation of: Chelovek i priroda
ISBN 0-7147-1609-x (pbk) : £1.95 B81-23483

304.2 — Environment. Effects of man — *For schools*

Fawcett, Richard. Environment. — London : Edward Arnold, Apr.1981. — [64]p. — (Systematic secondary series)
ISBN 0-7131-0485-6 (pbk) : £2.00 : CIP entry
B81-03168

304.2 — Environment. Management. Ecological aspects

Park, Chris C.. Ecology and environmental management : a geographical perspective / Chris C. Park. — London : Butterworths, 1981, c1980. — 272p : ill,maps ; 26cm. — (Studies in physical geography, ISSN 0142-6389)
Originally published: Folkestone : Dawson, 1980. — Bibliography: p250-269. - Includes index
ISBN 0-408-10738-3 : £12.50 B81-11447

304.2 — Environment. Socioeconomic aspects

Cooper, Charles. Economic evaluation and the environment. — London : Hodder and Stoughton, July 1981. — [176]p
ISBN 0-340-26555-8 : £8.00 : CIP entry
B81-13492

304.2 — Environmental impact analysis - *Conference proceedings*

United Nations. *Economic Commission for Europe.* Environmental impact assessment. — Oxford : Pergamon, June 1981. — [368]p. — (ECE seminars and symposia)
ISBN 0-08-024445-9 : £25.00 : CIP entry
B81-10001

304.2 — Environmental studies

Education and environment. — Northwood : Science Reviews, Sept.1981. — [300]p
ISBN 0-905927-75-3 (pbk) : £9.50 : CIP entry
B81-25136

304.2 — Great Britain. Environment. Effects of disasters, *to 1980*

Perry, A. H.. Environmental hazards in the British Isles / A. H. Perry. — London : Allen & Unwin, 1981. — 191p : ill,maps ; 25cm
Includes bibliographies and index
ISBN 0-04-910069-6 (cased) : Unpriced
ISBN 0-04-910070-x (pbk) : Unpriced B81-24562

304.2 — Human geography

Behavioral problems in geography revisited. — London : Methuen, Dec.1981. — [320]p
ISBN 0-416-72430-2 (pbk) : £12.50 : CIP entry B81-31537

Fundamentals of human geography. — 2nd ed. — Milton Keynes : Open University Press. — (Social sciences : a second level course)
Previous ed.: 1977
Use of libraries and the literature of human geography / Paul Smith. — 1980. — 35p ; 30cm. — (D 204 LG)
ISBN 0-335-07208-9 (pbk) : Unpriced B81-26879

304.2 — Human geography - *Humanistic perspectives*

Relph, Edward. Rational landscapes and humanistic geography. — London : Croom Helm, Aug.1981. — [240]p
ISBN 0-7099-0016-3 : £17.95 : CIP entry B81-16373

304.2 — Man. Ecology

Clapham, W. B.. Human ecosystems / W.B. Clapham, Jr. — New York : Macmillan ; London : Collier Macmillan, c1981. — xii,419p : ill,maps ; 26cm
Includes bibliographies and index
ISBN 0-02-322510-6 (pbk) : £7.95 B81-29329

Roszak, Theodore. Person-planet : the creative disintegration of industrial society / Theodore Roszak. — London : Granada, 1981, c1978. — 350p ; 20cm. — (A Paladin book)
Originally published: Garden City, N.Y. : Anchor Press/Doubleday, 1978 ; London : Gollancz, 1979
ISBN 0-586-08366-9 (pbk) : £2.50 B81-18947

Sale, Kirkpatrick. Human scale / Kirkpatrick Sale. — London : Secker & Warburg, c1980. — 558p : ill ; 24cm
Includes index
ISBN 0-436-44090-3 (cased) : £10.00
ISBN 0-436-44091-1 (pbk) : £5.95 B81-00752

Schneider, Stephen H.. The primordial bond : exploring connections between man and nature through the humanities and sciences / Stephen H. Schneider and Lynne Morton. — New York ; London : Plenum, c1981. — xii,324p : ill,1map ; 22cm
Bibliography: p313-315. - Includes index
ISBN 0-306-40519-9 : Unpriced B81-08491

304.2 — Man. Ecology. Biosocial aspects

Birch, Charles. The liberation of life. — Cambridge : Cambridge University Press, Oct.1981. — [358]p
ISBN 0-521-23787-4 : £17.50 : CIP entry B81-31283

304.2 — Man. Relationships with alsatian dogs — *Case studies*

Richardson, Anthony, *b.1899*. One man and his dog / by Anthony Richardson. — London : Harrap, 1960 (1980 [printing]). — 251p,15p of plates : ill,ports ; 23cm
ISBN 0-245-52292-1 : £6.95
Primary classification 636.7′3 B81-09777

304.2 — Man. Relationships with animals — *For children*

Briquebec, John. Animals & man / author John Briquebec ; design Louise Burston. — Maidenhead : Purnell, 1981. — 57p : ill(some col.) ; 30cm
Ill on lining papers. — Includes index
ISBN 0-361-04654-5 : £3.99
Also classified at 591.6 B81-27769

304.2′0722 — Romania. Carpathian Mountains. Human geographical features — *Case studies*

Turnock, David. The human geography of the Romanian Carpathians with fieldwork case studies, 1977 / David Turnock and members of the Geographical Field Group. — Nottingham (c/o Department of Geography, University of Nottingham, University Park, Nottingham NG7 2RD) : The Group, c1980. — 131p : ill,maps,plans,1port ; 31cm. — (Regional studies / Geographical Field Group, ISSN 0078-2084 ; no.22)
£5.00 (£4.00 to members) (pbk) B81-32438

304.2′09181′2 — Western world. Human geographical features

Dicken, Peter. Modern western society : a geographical perspective on work, home and well-being / Peter Dicken and Peter E. Lloyd. — London : Harper & Row, 1981. — viii,396p : ill,maps ; 25cm
Bibliography: p368-381. — Includes index
ISBN 0-06-318030-8 (cased) : Unpriced : CIP rev.
ISBN 0-06-318048-0 (pbk) : Unpriced B81-13849

304.2′09361 — Great Britain. Environment. Effects of man, *B.C.1000-A.D.1000*

The Environment of man : the Iron Age to the Anglo-Saxon period / edited by Martin Jones and Geoffrey Dimbleby. — Oxford : B.A.R., 1981. — 336p : ill ; 30cm. — (BAR. British series ; 87)
Includes bibliographies
ISBN 0-86054-128-2 (pbk) : £12.00 B81-36633

304.2′09361 — Great Britain. Prehistoric man. Effects of environment

The Environment in British prehistory / edited by I.G. Simmons, M.J. Tooley. — London : Duckworth, 1981. — x,334p,[12]p of plates : ill,maps ; 23cm
Bibliography: p292-324. — Includes index
ISBN 0-7156-1362-6 (cased) : Unpriced : CIP rev.
ISBN 0-7156-1441-x (pbk) : unpriced B80-04076

304.2′09361′9 — South-west Ireland. Environment. Effects of man, *B.C.4000-A.D.800*

Lynch, Ann. Man and environment in South-West Ireland, 4000 B.C.-A.D. 800 : a study of man′s impact on the development of soil and vegetation / Ann Lynch. — Oxford : B.A.R., 1981. — vi,175p : ill,maps ; 30cm. — (BAR. British series ; 85)
Bibliography: p161-175
ISBN 0-86054-112-6 (pbk) : £6.50 B81-36629

304.2′09362′9 — Prehistoric Welsh civilization. Influence of environment

Culture and environment in prehistoric Wales : selected essays / edited by J.A. Taylor. — Oxford : B.A.R., 1980. — 397p : ill,plans ; 29cm. — (BAR. British series, ISSN 0143-3032 ; 76)
Includes bibliographies
ISBN 0-86054-079-0 (pbk) : £10.00 B81-16554

304.2′094 — Western Europe. Human geographical features

Ilbery, Brian W.. Western Europe : a systematic human geography / Brian W. Ilbery. — Oxford : Oxford University Press, 1981. — xii,180p : ill,maps ; 25cm
Includes bibliographies and index
ISBN 0-19-874089-1 (cased) : £12.50 : CIP rev.
ISBN 0-19-874090-5 (pbk) : £5.95 B81-11941

304.2′0942 — England. Social conditions, *ca 1650-1979.* **Geographical aspects**

Dennis, Richard, *1949-*. A social geography of England and Wales / by Richard Dennis and Hugh Clout. — Oxford : Pergamon, 1980. — viii,208p : ill,maps,plans ; 26cm. — (Pergamon international library) (Pergamon Oxford geographies)
Includes bibliographies and index
ISBN 0-08-021802-4 (cased) : £14.00 : CIP rev.
ISBN 0-08-021801-6 (pbk) : £5.95 B80-10951

304.2′0943 — West Germany. Human geographical features

Wild, M. Trevor. West Germany : a geography of its people / M.T. Wild. — London : Longman, c1981. — 255p : ill,maps ; 22cm
Previous ed.: Folkestone : Dawson, 1979. — Bibliography: p230-243. - Includes index
ISBN 0-582-30078-9 (pbk) : £7.50 B81-17755

304.2′095694 — Israel. Social conditions — *Anthropological perspectives — Case studies*

A Composite portrait of Israel / edited by Emanuel Marx. — London : Academic Press, 1980. — vii,290p ; 24cm
Includes bibliographies and index
ISBN 0-12-476450-9 : £12.80 : CIP rev. B80-20266

304.2′09669′5 — Nigeria. Lake Chad Basin. Man. Ecology, *to 1977 — Sources of data: Archaeological investigation*

Connah, Graham. Three thousand years in Africa : man and his environment in the Lake Chad region of Nigeria / Graham Connah. — Cambridge : Cambridge University Press, 1981. — xx,268p : ill,maps ; 26cm. — (New Studies in archaeology)
Bibliography: p255-263. — Includes index
ISBN 0-521-22848-4 : £25.00 : CIP rev. B81-03695

304.2′0967 — Africa. Tropical regions. Human geography — *For African students*

Udo, Reuben K.. The human geography of tropical Africa. — London : Heinemann Educational, Jan.1982. — [256]p
ISBN 0-435-95919-0 (pbk) : £5.95 : CIP entry B81-34565

304.2′3 — Civilization. Development. Implications of soil degradation, *to 1977*

Hudson, N. W.. Soil degradation and civilization : inaugural professorial address presented at the National College of Agricultural Engineering on 17th May, 1978 / N.W. Hudson. — [Bedford] ([Cranfield, Bedford, MK43 0AL]) : National College of Agricultural Engineering, 1980. — ii,13p : 1map ; 30cm. — (Occasional paper / National College of Agricultural Engineering ; no.9)
Bibliography: p12-13
£1.00 (pbk) B81-11325

304.2′5 — Climate. Changes. Socioeconomic aspects — *Conference proceedings*

Climatic constraints and human activities : Task Force on the nature of climate and society research February 4-6, 1980 / Jasse Ausubel and Asit K. Biswas editors. — Oxford : Pergamon, 1980. — xi,205p : ill,maps ; 26cm. — (IIASA proceedings series ; v.10)
Conference papers. — Includes bibliographies
ISBN 0-08-026721-1 : £13.00 : CIP rev. B80-18601

304.2′8 — Environment. Influence of man

Goudie, Andrew. The human impact : man′s role in environmental change / Andrew Goudie. — Oxford : Blackwell, 1981. — x,316p : ill,maps,ports ; 26cm
Bibliography: p285-311. — Includes index
ISBN 0-631-11121-2 (cased) : £15.00
ISBN 0-631-12554-x (pbk) : £6.50 B81-24202

304.5 — Human sociobiology

Rosenberg, Alexander. Sociobiology and the preemption of social science / Alexander Rosenberg. — Oxford : Blackwell, 1981, c1980. — xi,227p ; 24cm
Originally published: Baltimore : Johns Hopkins University Press, 1980. — Bibliography: p219-221. - Includes index
ISBN 0-631-12625-2 : £9.90 B81-17658

Sociobiology examined / edited by Ashley Montagu ; [contributors Jerome H. Barkow et al.]. — New York ; Oxford : Oxford University Press, 1980. — x,355p ; 22cm
Includes bibliographies
ISBN 0-19-502711-6 (cased) : £12.50 B81-00745

304.5 — Man. Social behaviour. Sociobiological aspects

Barash, David P.. Sociobiology : the whisperings within / David Barash. — [London] : Fontana, 1981, c1979. — 274p ; 18cm
Originally published: New York : Harper and Row, 1979 ; London : Souvenir, 1980. — Bibliography: p255—262. - Includes index
ISBN 0-00-636009-2 (pbk) : £2.50 B81-12016

304.6 — Demography. Techniques — *Manuals*

Pollard, A. H.. Demographic techniques / A.H. Pollard, Farhat Yusuf, G.N. Pollard. — 2nd ed. — Oxford : Pergamon, 1981. — ix,182p : ill ; 24cm
Previous ed.: 1974. — Includes bibliographies and index
ISBN 0-08-024817-9 (pbk) : £9.45 B81-34629

304.6 — Great Britain. Population. Censuses, *1981.* **Functional regions** — *Proposals*

Functional regions for the 1981 Census of Britain : a user's guide to the CURDS definitions / by M.G. Coombes ... [et al.]. — [Newcastle upon Tyne] : University of Newcastle upon Tyne, Centre for Urban and Regional Development Studies, 1980. — 25 leaves : ill,1map ; 30cm. — (Discussion paper / University of Newcastle upon Tyne Centre for Urban and Regional Development Studies, ISSN 0140-6515)
£1.00 (pbk) B81-04816

304.6 — Population. Distribution. Genealogical aspects — *Anthropological perspectives — Conference proceedings*

Genealogical demography : [proceedings of a symposium held at the forty-eighth annual meeting of the American Association of Physical Anthropologists, San Francisco, April 5, 1979] / edited by Bennett Dyke, Warren T. Morrill. — New York ; London : Academic Press, 1980. — xii,255p : ill ; 24cm. — (Population and social structure)
Includes bibliographies and index
ISBN 0-12-226380-4 : £11.00 B81-02892

304.6 — Population — *For schools*

Gibson, Charles, *1934-*. Population / Charles Gibson. — [Oxford] : Blackwell, c1980. — 64p : ill,maps,1facsim,plans ; 31cm. — (Geography applied)
Bibliography: p63. — Includes index
ISBN 0-631-10421-6 (cased) : Unpriced
ISBN 0-631-12673-2 (pbk£3.95) B81-02623

304.6 — Population. Geographical aspects

Jones, Huw R.. A population geography / Huw R. Jones. — London : Harper & Row, 1981. — 330p : ill,maps ; 24cm
Bibliography: p286-319. — Includes index
ISBN 0-06-318188-6 (cased) : Unpriced : CIP rev.
ISBN 0-06-318189-4 (pbk) : Unpriced
B81-06595

304.6'01 — Population. Theories, *to 1976 — Marxist-Leninist viewpoints*

An Outline theory of population / edited by D.I. Valentey ; [translated from the Russian by Katherine Judelson]. — Moscow : Progress Publishers ; [London] : Distributed by Central Books, 1980. — 307p ; 21cm
Translation of: Osnovy teorii narodonaseleniia
£3.25 B81-04862

304.6'0723 — Census data. Collection. Statistical methods: Sampling

Yates, Frank. Sampling methods for censuses and surveys / Frank Yates. — 4th ed., rev. and enl. — London : Griffin, 1981. — xvi,458p : ill ; 25cm
Previous ed.: 1960. — Bibliography: p416-450. — Includes index
ISBN 0-85264-253-9 : £21.00
Primary classification 001.4'222 B81-05944

304.6'0723 — Great Britain. Population. Census data. Analysis — *For schools*

People in Britain / [compiled by Daphne Turner] ; [prepared by the Office of Population Censuses and Surveys and the Central Office of Information]. — [London] : [H.M.S.O.], [1981]. — 4portfolios : ill(some col.),maps,facsims,ports ; 30cm
Unpriced B81-21042

304.6'0723 — Great Britain. Population. Census data. Indexing

Census indexes : and indexing / edited by Jeremy Gibson and Colin Chapman. — Plymouth (96 Beaumont St., Milehouse, Plymouth, Devon PL2 3AQ) : Federation of Family History Societies, 1981. — 36p ; 21cm
Text on inside covers
ISBN 0-907099-09-2 (pbk) : £1.00 B81-39997

304.6'09'01 — Prehistoric man. Demographic aspects

Hassan, Fekri A.. Demographic archaeology / Fekri A. Hassan. — New York ; London : Academic Press, c1981. — xiii,298p : ill,maps ; 24cm. — (Studies in archaeology)
Bibliography: p263-289. — Includes index
ISBN 0-12-331350-3 : £18.00 B81-35361

304.6'094 — Europe. Population, *1500-1820.* **Demographic aspects**

Flinn, M. W.. The European demographic system 1500-1820 / Michael W. Flinn. — Brighton : Harvester, 1981. — 175p ; 23cm. — (Pre-industrial Europe 1350-1850 ; no.5)
Bibliography: p138-170. — Includes index
ISBN 0-7108-0058-4 : £15.95 : CIP rev.
B81-16357

304.6'0941 — Great Britain. Population. Census data

Dewdney, John C.. The British Census / by J.C. Dewdney. — Norwich : Geo Abstracts, c1981. — 54p : maps,1form ; 21cm. — (Concepts and techniques in modern geography, ISSN 0306-6142 ; no.29)
Text on inside covers. — Bibliography: p22-28
ISBN 0-86094-070-5 (pbk) : Unpriced
B81-35347

304.6'0941 — Great Britain. Population. Density, *1951, 1961 & 1971*

Craig, John, *1935-*. Population density and concentration in Great Britain 1951, 1961 and 1971 / John Craig. — London : H.M.S.O., 1980. — v,45p : ill ; 30cm. — (Studies on medical and population subjects : no.42)
At head of title: Office of Population Censuses and Surveys
ISBN 0-11-690734-7 (pbk) : £6.80 B81-04070

304.6'09411 — Scotland. Population. Forecasting — *Conference proceedings*

Population projections and employment forecasts : report of a Planning Exchange Forum held in Glenrothes on 4 October 1978. — Glasgow : The Planning Exchange, 1978. — 40leaves : ill ; 30cm. — (Forum report / Planning Exchange ; 13)
Unpriced (pbk)
Also classified at 331.12'5'09411 B81-34611

304.6'09411 — Scotland. Rural regions. Population — *Conference proceedings*

Population and employment in rural areas : report of a seminar held on 1 and 2 May 1979, at the Station Hotel, Inverness. — Glasgow : The Planning Exchange, [1979]. — 68leaves : 3maps ; 30cm. — (Forum report / Planning Exchange ; 15)
Unpriced (pbk)
Also classified at 331.12'5'09411 B81-34609

304.6'09416 — Northern Ireland. Population, *1971-1980 — Conference proceedings*

The Contemporary population of Northern Ireland and population-related issues / edited by Paul A. Compton. — Belfast : Institute of Irish Studies, The Queen's University of Belfast, 1981. — 142p : ill,maps ; 25cm
Conference papers. — Includes bibliographies
ISBN 0-85389-195-8 (pbk) : Unpriced
B81-31482

304.6'0942 — England. Local authorities. Areas. Population. Estimates, *1961 compared with* **estimates,** *1971*

The revised mid-1971 population estimates for local authorities compared with the original estimates / Population Statistics Division, OPCS. — [London] ([10 Kingsway, WC2B 6JP]) : Office of Population Censuses and Surveys, 1981. — 32p : ill ; 30cm. — (Occasional paper / Office of Population Censuses and Surveys ; no.22)
ISBN 0-906197-23-6 (pbk) : £1.25 B81-30055

304.6'0942 — England. Population. Historical sources: Parish registers

Finlay, Roger. Parish registers : an introduction / by Roger Finlay. — Norwich : Geo Abstracts, 1981. — 49p : ill,2forms ; 22cm. — (Historical geography research series, ISSN 0143-638x ; no.7)
Bibliography: p45-49
ISBN 0-86094-067-5 (pbk) : £1.75 B81-29622

304.6'09421 — London. Population, *1580-1650.* **Social aspects**

Finlay, Roger. Population and metropolis : the demography of London 1580-1650 / Roger Finlay. — Cambridge : Cambridge University Press, 1981. — xii,188p : ill,maps ; 24cm. — (Cambridge geographical studies ; 12)
Bibliography: p175-183. — Includes index
ISBN 0-521-22535-3 : £22.50 B81-36684

304.6'09424'93 — West Midlands *(Metropolitan County).* **Halesowen. Population,** *1270-1400 — Sources of data: Manorial courts. Court rolls*

Razi, Zvi. Life, marriage and death in a medieval parish : economy and demography in Halesowen 1270-1400 / Zvi Razi. — Cambridge : Cambridge University Press, 1980. — xi,162p : ill,1map,geneal.tables ; 23cm. — (Past and present publications)
Bibliography: p154-160. — Includes index
ISBN 0-521-23252-x : £12.00 : CIP rev.
B80-19612

304.6'09429 — Wales. Population — *Forecasts — Serials*

Home population projections for the counties of Wales / Welsh Office. — 1978 based. — Cardiff (New Crown Buildings, Cathays Park, Cardiff) : Welsh Office, 1980. — 32p
Unpriced B81-04546

304.6'09946 — Population. Geographical aspects — *Study regions: Tasmania*

Dinkele, Geoff. Population geography / Geoff Dinkele. — London : Harrap, 1980. — 32p : ill,1chart,maps ; 30cm. — (Harrap's advanced geography topics)
Bibliography: p32
ISBN 0-245-53519-5 (pbk) : £1.00 B81-01742

304.6'2 — Population. Economic aspects

Schultz, Theodore W.. Investing in people : the economics of population quality / Theodore W. Schultz. — Berkeley ; London : University of California Press, c1981. — xii,173p : ill ; 23cm. — (The Royer lectures ; 1980)
Bibliography: p149-166. — Includes index
ISBN 0-520-04437-1 (pbk) : £7.75 B81-36413

304.6'2 — Population. Growth. Economic aspects

Simon, Julian L.. The ultimate resource. — Oxford : Martin Robertson, Oct.1981. — [336]p
ISBN 0-85520-440-0 : £7.95 : CIP entry
B81-30339

304.6'2 — Population. Growth. Geographical aspects

Robinson, H.. Population and resources / H. Robinson. — London : Macmillan, 1981. — 277p : ill,maps ; 23cm. — (Focal problems in geography)
Bibliography: p254-261. — Includes index
ISBN 0-333-18010-0 (cased) : Unpriced
ISBN 0-333-19127-7 (pbk) : Unpriced
B81-31136

Thomas, Ian, *1937-*. Population growth / Ian Thomas. — Basingstoke : Macmillan Education, 1980. — iv,60p : ill,maps ; 22cm. — (Aspects of geography)
Bibliography: p55-56
ISBN 0-333-28664-2 (pbk) : £1.30 : CIP rev.
B80-18172

304.6'2'09045 — Population. Growth, *1950-1970.* **Socioeconomic aspects**

Steinberg, Ira. The new lost generation. — Oxford : Martin Robertson, May 1981. — [150]p
ISBN 0-85520-293-9 (cased) : £8.50 : CIP entry
ISBN 0-85520-402-8 (pbk) : £3.95 B81-08805

304.6'2'094 — Europe. Population. Change. Social aspects — *Forecasts*
Demographic and social change in Europe, 1975-2000. — Liverpool : Published in association with the Council of Europe [by] Liverpool University Press, c1981. — xvii,167p ; 24cm
Bibliography: p161-163. — Includes index
ISBN 0-85323-114-1 (pbk) : £9.50 B81-23991

304.6'2'094 — Europe. Population. Growth *related to* **economic development of agricultural industries,** *1300-1911*
Grigg, David, *1934-*. Population growth and agrarian change : an historical perspective / David Grigg. — Cambridge : Cambridge University Press, 1980. — xi,340p : ill,maps ; 24cm. — (Cambridge geographical studies ; 13)
Includes index
ISBN 0-521-22760-7 (cased) : £20.00
ISBN 0-521-29635-8 (pbk) : £7.95
Also classified at 338.1'094 B81-08326

304.6'2'0941 — Great Britain & West Germany. Population. Decline. Socioeconomic aspects — *Comparative studies*
Population change and social planning. — London : Edward Arnold, Feb.1982. — [608]p
ISBN 0-7131-6345-3 : £35.00 : CIP entry B81-37562

304.6'2'0942276 — Hampshire. Southampton. Population. Growth. Socioeconomic aspects
Dimensions of change in a growth area : Southampton since 1960. — Aldershot : Gower, Jan.1982. — [250]p
ISBN 0-566-00426-7 : £12.50 : CIP entry B81-34279

304.6'3 — Great Britain. Families. Size. Decline, *ca 1850-ca 1900* — *Sociological perspectives*
Banks, J. A.. Victorian values : secularism and the size of families / J.A. Banks. — London : Routledge & Kegan Paul, 1981. — 203p ; 22cm
Includes index
ISBN 0-7100-0807-4 : £9.50 B81-40037

304.6'3 — Population. Fertility. Forecasting
Predicting fertility : demographic studies of birth expectations / edited by Gerry E. Hendershot, Paul J. Placek. — Lexington, Mass. : Lexington Books ; [Aldershot] : Gower [distributor], 1981. — viii,335p : ill,3maps ; 24cm
Includes bibliographies and index
ISBN 0-669-03618-8 : £15.00 B81-38601

304.6'3 — Population. Fertility. Homeostatic regulation — *Anthropological perspectives*
Abernethy, Virginia. Population pressure and cultural adjustment / Virginia Abernethy. — New York ; London : Human Sciences Press, c1979. — 189p ; 21cm
Includes index
ISBN 0-87705-329-4 : £17.50 B81-39455

304.6'3 — Population. Fertility - *Sociological perspectives - Conference proceedings*
Changing patterns of conception and fertility. — London : Academic Press, June 1981. — [200]p
Conference papers
ISBN 0-12-171350-4 : CIP entry B81-08913

304.6'3'091722 — Developed countries. Population. Fertility
Andorka, Rudolf. Determinants of fertility in advanced societies. — London : Methuen, Feb.1982. — [444]p
Originally published: 1978
ISBN 0-416-67350-3 (pbk) : £5.95 : CIP entry B81-35714

304.6'3'095692 — Lebanon. Population. Fertility. Influence of religion
Chamie, Joseph. Religion and fertility : Arab Christian-Muslim differentials / Joseph Chamie. — Cambridge : Cambridge University Press, 1981. — xvi,150p : ill ; 24cm. — (The Arnold and Caroline Rose monograph series of the American Sociological Association)
English text, Arabic summary. — Bibliography: p132-140. — Includes index
ISBN 0-521-23677-0 (cased) : £12.00
ISBN 0-521-28147-4 (pbk) : £3.95 B81-34528

304.6'3'095995 — Philippines. Cebu. Population. Fertility. Social factors
Yu, Elena. Fertility and kinship in the Philippines / Elena Yu and William T. Liu. — Notre Dame ; London : University of Notre Dame Press, c1980. — xvi,286p,[8]p of plates : ill,maps ; 24cm
Bibliography: p275-286
ISBN 0-268-00949-x : £13.00 B81-29545

304.6'3'0967 — Africa south of the Sahara. Tropical regions. Population. Fertility
Child-spacing in tropical Africa : traditions and change / edited by Hilary J. Page, Ron Lesthaeghe. — London : Academic Press, 1981. — xxiii,332p : ill,maps ; 24cm. — (Studies in population)
Includes bibliographies and index
ISBN 0-12-543620-3 : £15.00 B81-19326

304.6'4 — Death. Attitudes of society, *to 1980*
Mirrors of mortality. — London : Europa, Oct.1981. — [380]p. — (Europa social history of human experience ; 3)
ISBN 0-905118-67-7 : £19.50 : CIP entry B81-28036

304.6'4'0941428 — Scotland. Strathclyde Region. Greenock. Man. Mortality rate, *1857* — *Early works* — *Facsimiles*
Wallace, James, *fl.1860*. Observations on the causes of the great mortality in Greenock / by James Wallace. — [Glasgow] ([Southbrae Drive, Glasgow, G13 1PP]) : Jordanhill College, Local History Archives Group, 1977. — 32p ; 21cm
Cover title. — Facsimile of: 1st ed. S.l. : s.n., 1860
£0.40 (spiral) B81-38777

304.6'4'0973 — United States. Man. Mortality rate. Effects of air pollution control. Economic aspects. Methods development for assessing air pollution control benefits — *Critical studies*
Air pollution control and mortality - a critical commentary on the mortality study in 'Methods development for assessing air pollution control benefits, vol.1' by T.D. Crocker et al. / R.L. Akehurst ... [et al.]. — [Aberdeen] : University of Aberdeen Department of Political Economy, 1981. — 27leaves ; 30cm. — (Discussion paper / University of Aberdeen. Department of Political Economy ; 81-07)
Unpriced (pbk) B81-28290

304.6'6 — Family planning
Fertility control : biologic and behavioral aspects / edited by Rochelle N. Shain and Carl J. Pauerstein ; 18 contributors. — Hagerstown ; London : Harper & Row, c1980. — xvi,443p : ill,forms ; 26cm
Includes bibliographies and index
ISBN 0-06-142376-9 : £22.75 B81-03623

304.6'6 — Family planning. Attitudes of adolescents. Effects of social environment
Adolescents and fertility planning : a research review and bibliography / International Planned Parenthood Federation ; adapted from research undertaken by Philip Kreager for IPPF. — London : The Federation, 1979. — 41,xlip ; 30cm. — (Research for action ; no.5)
Bibliography: piii-xli
£1.75 (spiral) B81-05485

304.6'6 — United Nations Fund for Population Activities, *to 1979* — *Spanish texts*
Salas, Rafael M.. Ayuda internacional en población. — Oxford : Pergamon, Aug.1981. — [537]p
ISBN 0-08-026099-3 (cased) : £9.50 : CIP entry
ISBN 0-08-026098-5 (pbk) : £8.75 B81-19213

304.6'6'095957 — Singapore. Population. Control, *1946-1977*
Saw Swee-Hock. Population control for zero growth in Singapore / Saw Swee-Hock. — Singapore ; Oxford : Oxford University Press, 1980. — xviii,231p : ill ; 23cm
Bibliography: p213-224. — Includes index
ISBN 0-19-580430-9 : £13.50
ISBN 0-19-580487-2 (pbk) : Unpriced B81-17062

304.8'09 — Migration. Geographical aspects
Lewis, G. J.. Human migration. — London : Croom Helm, Jan.1982. — [240]p
ISBN 0-7099-0007-4 : £13.95 : CIP entry B81-34304

304.8'094111 — Scotland. Highlands & Islands. Migration — *Anthropological perspectives*
Lumb, Rosemary. Migration in the Highlands and Island of Scotland / by Rosemary Lumb. — Aberdeen (Edward Wright Building, Dunbar St., Aberdeen AB9 2TY) : Institute for the Study of Sparsely Populated Areas, University of Aberdeen, 1980. — ii,159p : ill ; 30cm. — (ISSPA research report ; no.3)
Bibliography: p157-159
ISBN 0-905933-02-8 (pbk) : £5.50 B81-09833

304.8'09412'95 — Scotland. Fife Region. Glenrothes. Migration, *1971-1979*
Migration study 1971-79 : Glenrothes new town : planning reaearch. — [Glenrothes] ([New Glenrothes House, North Street, Glenrothes]) : [Glenrothes Development Corporation], 1979. — 11leaves ; 30cm
Unpriced (unbound) B81-38622

304.8'09422'6 — West Sussex emigrants, *1817-1874* — *Lists*
Emigrants and transportees from West Sussex : 1778-c.1874 / edited by Alison McCann. — [Chichester] ([County Hall, Chichester, W. Sussex]) : [West Sussex County Council], 1980. — [20]leaves ; 30cm. — (Lists and indexes ; no.9)
Unpriced (unbound)
Also classified at 365'.34 B81-39692

304.8'096 — Africa. Internal migration
Redistribution of population in Africa. — London : Heinemann Educational, Sept.1981. — [256]p
ISBN 0-435-95030-4 : £15.50 : CIP entry B81-21630

304.8'0966 — West Africa. Migration, *1960-1975*. **Demographic aspects**
Zachariah, K. C.. Migration in West Africa : demographic aspects / [a joint World Bank - OECD study] ; K.C. Zachariah and Julien Condé. — New York ; Oxford : Published for the World Bank [by] Oxford University Press, c1981. — xiv,130p,22leaves of plates : ill,maps (some col.) ; 29cm
Bibliography: p124-126. — Includes index
ISBN 0-19-520186-8 (cased) : Unpriced
ISBN 0-19-520187-6 (pbk) : £4.50 B81-32544

304.8'2'0947 — Russia. Internal migration, *ca 1885-1910*. **Social aspects**
Anderson, Barbara A.. Internal migration during modernization in late nineteenth-century Russia / Barbara A. Anderson. — Princeton ; Guildford : Princeton University Press, c1980. — xxv,222p : ill,maps ; 23cm
Bibliography: p207-216. - Includes index
ISBN 0-691-09386-5 : Unpriced B81-13232

304.8'2'0973 — United States. Internal migration, *ca 1890-1977*
Oosterbaan, John. Population dispersal : a national imperative / John Oosterbaam. — Lexington : Lexington Books ; [Farnborough, Hants] : Gower [distributor], 1981, c1980. — xix,136p ; 24cm
Includes index
ISBN 0-669-03615-3 : Unpriced B81-13910

304.8'2'0973 — United States. Internal migration. Economic aspects
Greenwood, Michael J.. Migration and economic growth in the United States : national, regional, and metropolitan perspectives / Michael J. Greenwood. — New York ; London : Academic Press, c1981. — xiii,233p ; 24cm. — (Studies in urban economics)
Bibliography: p223-230. — Includes index
ISBN 0-12-300650-3 : £13.60 B81-33031

304.8'94 — Australia. Immigrants, *1788-1978*
Sherington, Geoffrey. Australia's immigrants 1788-1978 / Geoffrey Sherington. — Sydney ; London : Allen & Unwin, 1980. — 189p : ill,maps ; 22cm. — (The Australian experience ; no.1)
Bibliography: p178-183. — Includes index
ISBN 0-86861-010-0 (cased) : £11.95
ISBN 0-86861-018-6 (pbk) : £5.50 B81-11698

305 — SOCIAL STRATIFICATION

305 — Cultural pluralism

Three faces of pluralism : political, ethnic and religious / edited by Stanislaw Ehrlich and Graham Wootton. — Farnborough, Hants. : Gower, c1980. — ix,219p : ill ; 23cm
Conference papers
ISBN 0-566-00313-9 : £10.50 : CIP rev. B80-04080

305 — Social minorities. Protection by international organisations

Fawcett, J. E. S.. The international protection of minorities / by James Fawcett. — London (36 Craven St., WC2N 5NG) : Minority Rights Group, 1979. — 19p : ill ; 30cm. — (Report / Minority Rights Group, ISSN 0305-6252 ; no.41)
Bibliography: p19
£0.75 (pbk) B81-05354

305 — Social structure

Continuities in structural inquiry / Peter M. Blau and Robert K. Merton, editors. — London : Sage, c1981. — viii,396p : ill ; 23cm
Includes bibliographies and index
ISBN 0-8039-9808-2 : £15.00 : CIP rev. B80-32954

Heusch, Luc de. Why marry her?. — Cambridge : Cambridge University Press, Oct.1981. — [224]p. — (Cambridge studies in social anthropology ; 33)
Translation and revision of: Pourquoi l'épouser?
ISBN 0-521-22460-8 : £19.50 : CIP entry B81-30495

305'.07'12 — Secondary schools. Curriculum subjects: Social minorities. Teaching

Hicks, David W.. Minorities : a teacher's resource book for the multi-ethnic curriculum / David W. Hicks. — London : Heinemann Educatioanal, 1981. — 124p : ill ; 25cm
Bibliography: p113-122. — Includes index
ISBN 0-435-80416-2 (pbk) : £8.50 B81-09596

305'.09181'2 — Western world. Social structure

Mannheim, Karl. Man and society : in an age of reconstruction : studies in modern social structure : with a bibliographical guide to the study of modern society / by Karl Mannheim ; [translated from the German by Edward Shils] ; [revised and considerably enlarged by the author]. — London : Routledge & Kegan Paul, 1940 (1980 [printing]). — xxii,469p ; 23cm
Translation of: Mensch und Gesellschaft im Zeitalter des Umbaus. — Bibliography: p383-455. — Includes index
ISBN 0-7100-1788-x : £14.50 B81-04949

305'.09362'81 — Yorkshire. Social structure, *B.C.3500-B.C.750 — Sources of data: Antiquities*

Pierpoint, Stephen. Social patterns in Yorkshire prehistory 3500-750 B.C. / Stephen Pierpoint. — Oxford : B.A.R., 1980. — ix,311p,[16]p of plates : ill,maps ; 30cm. — (BAR. British series, ISSN 0143-3032 ; 74)
Bibliography: p280-300
ISBN 0-86054-078-2 (pbk) : £10.00 B81-16553

305'.0937 — Ancient Rome. Social structure

Hopkins, Keith. Conquerors and slaves / Keith Hopkins. — Cambridge : Cambridge University Press, 1978 ([1980] printing). — xiv,268p,[4]p of plates : ill,1map,ports ; 23cm. — (Sociologcal studies in Roman history ; v.1)
Bibliography: p243-253. — Includes index
ISBN 0-521-28181-4 (pbk) : £5.50 B81-14647

305'.0938'5 — Ancient Greece. Social structure

Finley, M. I.. Economy and society in Ancient Greece. — London : Chatto & Windus, May 1981. — [288]p
ISBN 0-7011-2549-7 : £12.00 : CIP entry B81-07617

305'.0943'55 — Social minorities. Attitudes of society. Influence of education — *Study regions: West Germany. Ruhr*

Schönbach, Peter. Education and intergroup attitudes / Peter Schönbach and Peter Gollwitzer, Gerd Stiepel, Ulrich Wagner. — London : Published in cooperation with European Association of Experimental Social Psychology by Academic Press, c1981. — viii,199p : ill ; 24cm. — (European monographs in social psychology ; 22)
Bibliography: p187-194. — Includes index
ISBN 0-12-632380-1 : £10.20 B81-26355

305'.0946'7 — Spain. Catalonia. Social structure

Giner, Salvador. The social structure of Catalonia / by Salvador Giner. — Sheffield (c/o Dr Alan Yates, Department of Hispanic Studies, The University, Sheffield S10 2TN) : Anglo-Catalan Society, 1980. — viii,78p : maps ; 21cm. — (The Anglo-Catalan Society occasional publications, ISSN 0144-5863; ; no.1)
Bibliography: p77-78
ISBN 0-9507137-0-8 (pbk) : Unpriced B81-14519

305'.0947 — Eastern Europe. Social structure, *1945-1980*

Tarniewski, Marek. The new regime. — London : Allison & Busby, Dec.1981. — [192]p
ISBN 0-85031-417-8 (cased) : £9.95 : CIP entry
ISBN 0-85031-418-6 (pbk) : £4.95 B81-31628

305'.0964'2 — Morocco. Rif region. Social structure — *French texts*

Jamous, Raymond. Honneur et baraka : les structures sociales traditionnelles dans le Rif / Raymond Jamous. — Cambridge : Publié avec le concours du Centre National de la Recherche Scientifique [by] Cambridge University Press, 1981. — x,303p : ill,maps ; 24cm. — (Atelier d'anthropologie sociale)
Bibliography: p285-288. — Includes index
ISBN 0-521-22318-0 : £22.50 B81-16421

305'.0964'3 — Morocco. Rabat. Social structure. Effects of French colonial policies on social planning in Rabat, *1912-1956*

Abu-Lughod, Janet L.. Rabat : urban apartheid in Morocco / by Janet L. Abu-Lughod. — Princeton ; Guildford : Princeton University Press, c1980. — xxii,374p,[8]p of plates : ill,maps ; 25cm. — (Princeton studies on the Near East)
Bibliography: p341-356. - Includes index
ISBN 0-691-05315-4 (cased) : £16.70
ISBN 0-691-10098-5 (pbk) : £7.00 B81-16576

305'.096894 — Zambia. Gwembe District. Social stratification. Effects of secondary education

Scudder, Thayer. Secondary education and the formation of an elite : the impact of education on Gwembe District, Zambia / Thayer Scudder, Elizabeth Colson. — New York ; London : Academic Press, c1980. — xiv,190p : 1map ; 24cm. — (A University of Zambia research enterprise) (Studies in anthropology)
Bibliography: p177-181. - Includes index
ISBN 0-12-634280-6 : £13.80 B81-17375

305'.0973 — United States. Social minorities. Attitudes of society, *1954-1978*

Nunn, Clyde Z.. Tolerance for nonconformity / Clyde Z. Nunn, Harry J. Crockett, Jr., J. Allen Williams, Jr. — San Francisco ; London : Jossey-Bass, 1978. — xvi,212p ; 24cm. — (The Jossey-Bass social and behavioral science series)
Bibliography: p192-203. — Includes index
ISBN 0-87589-362-7 : £10.40 B81-16431

305'.098 — America. Spanish colonies. Social structure, *1521-1610*

Bacigalupo, Marvyn Helen. A changing perspective : attitudes toward Creole society in New Spain (1521-1610) / Marvyn Helen Bacigalupo. — London : Tamesis, c1981. — 159p : ill ; 25cm
Bibliography: p149-159
ISBN 0-7293-0072-2 : Unpriced B81-31760

305'.0994 — Australia. Social stratification

Wild, R. A.. Social stratification in Australia / R.A. Wild. — Sydney ; London : Allen & Unwin, 1978. — 202p : 2ill ; 23cm. — (Studies in society ; 3)
Bibliography: p181-194. — Includes index
ISBN 0-86861-304-5 (cased) : £8.95
ISBN 0-86861-312-x (pbk) : £4.50 B81-02932

305.2'3 — Adolescence

Coleman, John C.. The nature of adolescence / John C. Coleman. — London : Methuen, 1980. — ix,214p : ill ; 23cm
Bibliography: p191-206. - Includes index
ISBN 0-416-72620-8 : £8.00 : CIP rev.
ISBN 0-416-72630-5 (pbk) : £4.25 B80-04682

Rogers, Dorothy, *1914-*. Adolescents and youth / Dorothy Rogers. — 4th ed. — Englewood Cliffs ; London : Prentice-Hall, c1981. — xvii,476p : ill ; 25cm
Previous ed.: published as The psychology of adolescence. 1977. — Bibliography: p449-470. — Includes index
ISBN 0-13-008748-3 : £12.30 B81-22356

305.2'3 — Adolescents

Crabtree, Tom. [Tom Crabtree on teenagers]. Living with teenagers / Tom Crabtree. — London : Macdonald Futura, 1981, c1980. — 254p ; 18cm
Originally published: London : Elm Tree, 1980
ISBN 0-7088-2083-2 (pbk) : £1.75 B81-29213

305.2'3 — Adolescents. Deviance

Kaplan, Howard B.. Deviant behaviour in defense of self / Howard B. Kaplan. — New York ; London : Academic Press, 1980. — xi,255p ; 24cm
Bibliography: p231-241. — Includes index
ISBN 0-12-396850-x : £12.40 B81-03931

305.2'3 — Adolescents. Separation from parents. Psychological aspects

Bloom, Michael W.. Adolescent-parental separation / Michael V. Bloom. — New York : Gardner ; New York ; London : Distributed by Halsted, c1980. — 177p ; 24cm
Bibliography: p169-173. — Includes index
ISBN 0-470-26739-9 : Unpriced B81-09256

305.2'3 — Babies — *Quotations — Collections*

What is a baby? : parents and grandparents describe the fun and frustrations of bringing up baby / selected by Richard and Helen Exley from the responses of over 10,000 people — mostly mothers ; edited by Richard & Helen Exley. — Watford : Exley, 1980. — 63p : ill (some col.) ; 22cm
ISBN 0-905521-29-3 : £2.95 : CIP rev. B80-17746

305.2'3 — Childhood — *Sociological perspectives*

The **Sociology** of childhood. — London : Batsford, Jan.1982. — [288]p
ISBN 0-7134-3695-6 (cased) : £12.50 : CIP entry
ISBN 0-7134-3696-4 (pbk) : £5.95 B81-33838

305.2'3 — Children — *Records of achievement — For children*

Cleaver, Pamela. The sparrow book of record-breakers / Pamela Cleaver ; cover illustration by John Miller ; text illustrations by Ross. — London : Sparrow, 1981. — 94p : ill ; 18cm
ISBN 0-09-926010-7 (pbk) : £0.85 B81-13163

305.2'3 — Children. Sex roles. Development

Brooks-Gunn, Jeanne. He & she : how children develop their sex-role identity / Jeanne Brooks-Gunn and Wendy Schempp Matthews. — Englewood Cliffs ; London : Prentice-Hall, c1979. — xiv,338p : ill ; 21cm. — (A Spectrum book)
Bibliography: p300-331. - Includes index
ISBN 0-13-384388-2 (cased) : £8.40
ISBN 0-13-384370-x (pbk) : £4.50 B81-03776

305.2'3 — Children. Social development. Effects of interpersonal relationships

Youniss, James. Parents and peers in social development : a Sullivan-Piaget perspective / James Youniss. — Chicago ; London : University of Chicago Press, 1980. — xviii,301p ; 24cm
Bibliography: p293-295. — Includes index
ISBN 0-226-96484-1 : £10.50 B81-00017

305.2'3 — Children. Social development. Role of play
Sluckin, Andy. Growing up in the playground : the social development of children / Andy Sluckin. — London : Routledge & Kegan Paul, 1981. — viii,131p ; 23cm
Bibliography: p126-128. — Includes index
ISBN 0-7100-0788-4 : £9.50 : CIP rev. B81-28086

305.2'3 — Children. Social perception
Selman, Robert L.. The growth of interpersonal understanding : developmental and clinical analyses / Robert L. Selman. — New York ; London : Academic Press, 1980. — 343p : ill ; 24cm. — (Developmental psychology series)
Bibliography: p325-331. — Includes index
ISBN 0-12-636450-8 : £14.00 B81-22394

305.2'3 — High risk children. Interpersonal relationships
High-risk infants and children : adult and peer interactions / editor Tiffany Martini Field ; co-editors Susan Goldberg, Daniel Stern, Anita Millar Sostek. — New York ; London : Academic Press, 1980. — xviii,387p : ill ; 24cm. — (Developmental psychology series)
Includes bibliographies and index
ISBN 0-12-255550-3 : £15.20 B81-03192

305.2'3 — Young persons. Social skills. Teaching — *Manuals*
McGuire, James. Life after school. — Oxford : Pergamon, Sept.1981. — [230]p
ISBN 0-08-025192-7 (cased) : £12.00 : CIP entry
ISBN 0-08-025193-5 (pbk) : £5.00 B81-21554

305.2'3'05 — Children, to 8 years — *Serials*
Early childhood. — Issue no.1 (Oct.1980)-. — Weybridge (270 Station Rd, Addlestone, Weybridge, Surrey) : Early Childhood, 1980-. — v. : ill,ports ; 28cm
Monthly
ISSN 0260-7808 = Early childhood : £10.00 per year B81-15153

305.2'3'0941 — Great Britain. Adolescents. Attitudes
Fisher, Susie. Too much too young? / Susie Fisher and Susan Holder. — London : Pan, 1981. — 216p ; 18cm
ISBN 0-330-26480-x (pbk) : £1.25 B81-22896

305.2'3'09411 — Scotland. Adolescents, 16 years — *Practical information*
Young Scot. — Edinburgh (4 Queensferry St., Edinburgh EH2 4PA) : Scottish Community Education Centre, [1981]. — 88p : ill ; 21x10cm
Includes index
Unpriced (pbk) B81-40020

305.2'3'094238 — Somerset. Society. Participation of young persons
Give us a say in things : a practical guide to youth participation / [prepared by] GUST. — Leicester : National Youth Bureau, 1981. — 12p : ill ; 30cm
Cover title. — Bibliography: p11
ISBN 0-86155-042-0 (pbk) : £0.85 B81-28734

305.2'3'0942498 — West Midlands *(Metropolitan County)*. Coventry. Young persons
Frith, Simon. Downtown : young people in a city centre / Simon Frith. — Leicester : National Youth Bureau, 1981. — 19p ; 30cm. — (National Youth Bureau research report ; no.1)
ISBN 0-86155-041-2 (pbk) : £1.10 B81-40640

305.2'3'0943 — Germany. Youth movements, *1900-1945*
Stachura, Peter D.. The German Youth movement 1900-1945 : an interpretative and documentary history / Peter D. Stachura. — London : Macmillan, 1981. — x,246p ; 23cm
Bibliography: p217-232. — Includes index
ISBN 0-333-27572-1 : £20.00 : CIP rev. B80-24328

305.2'3'0944 — France. Young persons, *1940-1944*
Halls, W. D.. The youth of Vichy France / by W.D. Halls. — Oxford : Clarendon, 1981. — xi,492p : 1map ; 22cm
Includes index
ISBN 0-19-822577-6 : £20.00 B81-22121

305.2'3'0971 — Canada. Children. Social aspects, *1870-1920*
Sutherland, Neil. Children in English-Canadian society : framing the twentieth-century consensus / Neil Sutherland. — Toronto ; London : University of Toronto Press, c1976 (1978 [printing]). — xii,336p,[11]p of plates : ill ; 23cm
Bibliography: p315-322. — Includes index
ISBN 0-8020-6345-4 (pbk) : £13.95 B81-05060

305.2'3'0973 — United States. Adolescents
Cohen, Stewart. Instructor's manual to accompany The adolescent : development, relationships, and culture, third edition F. Philip Rice / prepared by Stewart Cohen. — Boston ; London : Allyn and Bacon, c1981. — 180p : ill ; 24cm
ISBN 0-205-07304-2 (pbk) : £1.00 B81-20963

Rice, F. Philip. The adolescent : development, relationships, and culture / F. Philip Rice. — 3rd ed. — Boston [Mass.] ; London : Allyn and Bacon, c1981. — xii,596p : ill ; 25cm
Previous ed.: 1978. — Includes bibliographies and index
ISBN 0-205-07303-4 . £11.95 B81-12100

305.2'3'0994 — Australia. Children
Children Australia / edited by R.G. Brown. — Sydney ; London : Allen & Unwin in association with the Morialta Trust of South Australia, 1980. — 282p ; 23cm
Includes index
ISBN 0-86861-186-7 (cased) : £13.95
ISBN 0-86861-194-8 (pbk) : £6.50 B81-11368

305.2'4 — Man. Ageing. Social aspects
The **Social** challenge of ageing / edited by David Hobman. — London : Croom Helm, 1979, c1978. — 288p ; 22cm
Includes index
ISBN 0-7099-0147-x (pbk) : £4.50 B81-17957

305.2'4 — Man. Ageing. Social aspects. Research
International handbook on ageing : contemporary developments and research / edited by Erdman Palmore. — London : Macmillan, 1980. — xviii,529p ; 24cm
Includes bibliographies and index
ISBN 0-333-27828-3 : £30.00 B81-04149

305.2'4 — Middle age. Personal adjustment
Pitt, Brice. Mid-life crisis / Brice Pitt. — London : Sheldon, 1980. — x,101p ; 20cm. — (Overcoming common problems)
Includes index
ISBN 0-85969-299-x (pbk) : £1.95 B81-05754

305.2'6 — Australia. Old age — *Sociological perspectives*
Russell, Cherry. The aging experience. — London : Allen & Unwin, Jan.1982. — [350]p
ISBN 0-86861-267-7 : £15.00 : CIP entry B81-34071

305.2'6 — Great Britain. Retirement
Long, Phil. Retirement : planned liberation? / Phil Long. — London : Institute of Personnel Management, 1981. — 153p ; 29cm. — (IPM information report ; 33)
Bibliography: p152-153
ISBN 0-85292-294-9 (pbk) : Unpriced B81-38363

305.2'6 — Man. Ageing. Social aspects — *Conference proceedings*
Transitions of aging / edited by Nancy Datan, Nancy Lohmann. — New York ; London : Academic Press, 1980. — xv,221p : ill ; 24cm
Conference papers. — Includes bibliographies and index
ISBN 0-12-203580-1 : £10.40 B81-02676

305.2'6 — Old age
George, James. Text items to accompany The realities of aging : Cary S. Kart / prepared by James George. — Boston, Mass. ; London : Allyn and Bacon, c1981. — 78p ; 22cm
ISBN 0-205-07335-2 (pbk) : £3.50 B81-40103

Kart, Cary S.. The realities of aging : an introduction to gerontology / Cary S. Kart. — Boston [Mass.] ; London : Allyn and Bacon, c1981. — viii,376p : ill ; 25cm
Includes bibliographies and index
ISBN 0-205-07334-4 : £16.95 B81-18896

Skeet, Muriel. The third age. — London : Darton Longman & Todd, June 1981. — [156]p
ISBN 0-232-51484-4 (pbk) : £3.95 : CIP entry B81-16390

305.2'6 — Old age. Personal adjustment — *Manuals*
Stott, Mary. Ageing for beginners / Mary Stott. — Oxford : Basil Blackwell, 1981. — 214p ; 19cm. — (Understanding everyday experience)
Bibliography: p207-208. — Includes index
ISBN 0-631-11591-9 (cased) : £7.95
ISBN 0-631-12777-1 (pbk) : £2.25 B81-31930

305.2'6 — Old age — *Sociological perspectives*
Pincus, Lily. The challenge of a long life. — London : Faber, Oct.1981. — [160]p
ISBN 0-571-11775-9 : £5.95 : CIP entry B81 25305

305.2'6 — Old persons — *Conference proceedings*
Geographical perspectives on the elderly. — Chichester : Wiley, Feb.1982. — [480]p
Conference papers
ISBN 0-471-09976-7 : £18.50 : CIP entry B81-35731

305.2'6 — Retirement — *Humour*
Kellehar, Cecil. The cautionary tale of Samuel Berk and the encouraging example of Albert Bright : a light-hearted look at planning for retirement / by Cecil Kellehar ; illustrations by Bob Manning. — Norwich (21, The Green, North Burlingham Norwich NR13 4SY) : Strategy for Retirement, 1981. — ill ; 21cm
Cover title: Knees up Samuel Berk!
ISBN 0-9507500-0-x (pbk) : Unpriced B81-21797

305.2'6 — United States. Retirement, *to 1978*
Graebner, William. A history of retirement : the meaning and function of an American institution, 1885-1978 / William Graebner. — New Haven ; London : Yale University Press, c1980. — x,293p ; 25cm
Includes index
ISBN 0-300-02356-1 : £14.20 : CIP rev. B80-27866

305.2'6'05 — Old age — *Serials*
Research on aging : a quarterly of social gerontology. — Vol.1, no.1 (Mar.1979)-. — Beverly Hills ; London : Sage, 1979-. — v. ; 22cm
ISSN 0164-0275 = Research on aging : Unpriced B81-04907

305.2'6'05 — Old persons. Social aspects — *Serials*
Ageing and society. — Vol.1, pt.1 (Mar. 1981)-. — Cambridge : Cambridge University Press, 1981-. — v. ; 24cm
Three issues yearly. — Journal of: The Centre for Policy on Ageing and the British Society of Gerontology
ISSN 0144-686x = Ageing and society : £24.00 per year B81-38199

305.2'6'0922 — England. Old age — *Personal observations — Collections*
Blythe, Ronald. The view in winter : reflections on old age / Ronald Blythe. — Harmondsworth : Penguin, 1981, c1979. — 321p ; 18cm
Originally published: London : Allen Lane, 1979. — Bibliography: p320-321
ISBN 0-14-005743-9 (pbk) : £1.95 B81-25204

305.2'6'0941 — Great Britain. Old persons
Gray, Muir. Our elders / Muir Gray and Gordon Wilcock. — Oxford : Oxford University Press, 1981. — 256p : ill ; 21cm
Bibliography: p249-251. — Includes index
ISBN 0-19-217698-6 (cased) : £8.50 : CIP rev.
ISBN 0-19-286012-7 (pbk) : Unpriced B80-23130

305.2'6'0941 — Great Britain. Old persons *continuation*

Profiles of the elderly. — Mitcham (60 Pitcairn Rd., Mitcham, Surrey CR4 3LL) : Published for the Research Unit by Age Concern
Text on inside covers
Vol.6 ; 8: Their use of the Social Services. — c1981. — 36p ; 30cm
ISBN 0-904502-96-1 (pbk) : Unpriced B81-38037

305.2'6'0941 — Great Britain. Old persons. Social aspects

An **Ageing** population. — Milton Keynes : Open University Press
At head of title: The Open University
Block 5: Long term perspectives. — 1979. — 67p : ill,ports ; 30cm. — (P252 ; block 5, units 15 and 16)
Bibliography: p67. — Contents: Unit 15: The allocation of resources - Unit 16: An eye to the future
ISBN 0-335-00284-6 (pbk) : Unpriced B81-14721

305.2'6'0942 — England. Old persons. Great Britain. *Department of Health and Social Security.* **'Happier old age'** — *Critical studies*

MIND. Mental health of elderly people : MIND's response to the DHSS discussion paper A happier old age. — [London] : MIND, 1979 (1980 [printing]). — 74p ; 30cm
£1.70 (pbk) B81-29346

305.2'6'0973 — United States. Old persons. Socioeconomic aspects

Aging and income : programs and prospects for the elderly / edited by Barbara Rieman Herzog. — New York ; London : Human Sciences Press, c1978. — 352p : ill ; 22cm. — (Special publication sponsored by the Gerontological Society ; no.4) (Aging series)
Includes bibliographies and index
ISBN 0-87705-369-3 : £25.50 B81-39456

Pampel, Fred C.. Social change and the aged : recent trends in the United States / Fred C. Pampel. — Lexington, Mass. : Lexington Books ; [Aldershot] : Gower [distribution], 1981. — xix,212p : ill ; 24cm
Bibliography: p199-206. — Includes index
ISBN 0-669-02928-9 : £13.50 B81-39697

305.3 — Men. Interpersonal relationships with women — *Feminist viewpoints*

Lazarre, Jane. On loving men. — London : Virago, Nov.1981. — [208]p
ISBN 0-86068-206-4 (pbk) : £3.50 : CIP entry B81-30401

305.3 — Men. Interpersonal relationships with women. Psychosocial aspects

Psychosexual imperatives : their role in identity formation / edited by Marie Coleman Nelson and Jean Ikenberry ; with a foreword by the editors. — New York ; London : Human Sciences Press, c1979. — 397p : ill ; 22cm. — (Self-in-process series ; v.2)
Bibliography: p349-388. — Includes index
ISBN 0-87705-302-2 : £25.50 B81-39452

305.3 — Sex differences

Seward, John P.. Sex differences : mental and temperamental / John P. Seward, Georgene H. Seward. — Lexington : Lexington Books ; [Farnborough, Hants.] : Gower [distributor], 1981, c1980. — xi,215p : ill ; 24cm
Includes bibliographies and index
ISBN 0-669-03629-3 : £13.50 B81-09597

305'.3 — Women. Economic conditions

Leghorn, Lisa. Women's worth. — London : Routledge & Kegan Paul, Sept.1981. — [344]p
ISBN 0-7100-0836-8 (cased) : £9.95 : CIP entry
ISBN 0-7100-0855-4 (pbk) : £4.95 B81-21498

305'.3 — Work. Attitudes of society. Evaluation. Methodology

The **Experience** of work. — London : Academic Press, Nov.1981. — [270]p
ISBN 0-12-187050-2 : CIP entry B81-28791

305.4 — Women's studies

Women in futures research. — Oxford : Pergamon, Aug.1981. — [124]p
ISBN 0-08-028100-1 : £6.25 : CIP entry B81-23791

305.4'05 — Women's studies — *Serials*

[Women's studies newsletter *(London)***]**. Women's studies newsletter : Workers Educational Association. — No.1 (1977)-. — London : The Association, 1977-. — v. : ill ; 21cm
Quarterly. — Description based on: No.13 (Summer 1980)
ISSN 0260-6127 = Women's studies newsletter (London) : £6.50 per year B81-06288

305.4'06'041 — Great Britain. Women's organisations: National Federation of Women's Institutes. Annual general meetings. Resolutions, *to 1980*

National Federation of Women's Institutes. Keeping ourselves informed : our concern, our resolutions, our action. — 2nd revision. — London : WI Books, c1981. — iv,172p ; 21cm
Resolutions passed by Women's Institutes at the Annual General Meetings. — Previous ed.: i.e. 1st revision : 1974. — Includes index
ISBN 0-900556-65-x (pbk) : Unpriced B81-27813

305.4'09172'4 — Developing countries. Women — *Conference proceedings*

Women and national development : the complexities of change / [based on a conference on women and development held June 2-6, 1976 sponsored by the Center for Research on Women in Higher Education and the Professions, Wellesley College ... [et al.] ; [edited by] Wellesley Editorial Committee, Ximena Bunster B. ... [et al.]. — Chicago ; London : University of Chicago Press, 1977. — xiv,346p : ill ; 23cm
Includes index
ISBN 0-226-89314-6 (cased) : Unpriced
ISBN 0-226-89315-4 (pbk) : £3.50 B81-38561

305.4'0941 — Great Britain. Working class women. Social conditions, *1930-1939*

Spring Rice, Margery. Working-class wives : their health and conditions / Margery Spring Rice ; photographs by Edith Tudor-Hart. — 2nd ed. / foreword by Cecil Robertson ; introduction by Barbara Wootton. — London : Virago, 1981. — xviii,212p,[8]p of plates : ill ; 20cm
Previous ed.: Harmondsworth : Penguin, 1939
ISBN 0-86068-153-x (pbk) : £2.95 B81-07137

305.4'2 — Communist countries. Women. Social discrimination by society — *Communist Party of Great Britain viewpoints*

Women, oppression & liberation / Communist Party Education Dept.. — [London] : [Communist Party of Great Britain], 1980
Cover title. — Bibliography: p17
Part 3: Women, liberation and socialism. — 17p : ill ; 21x27cm
ISBN 0-86224-002-6 (pbk) : £0.60
Also classified at 305.4'2 B81-07322

305.4'2 — Developing countries. Women. Discrimination by society

Rogers, Barbara. The domestication of women : discrimination in developing societies / Barbara Rogers. — London : Tavistock Publications, 1981, c1980. — 200p ; 22cm. — (Social science paperback ; 213)
Originally published: New York, N.Y. : St. Martin's Press, 1979. — Includes index
ISBN 0-422-77630-0 (pbk) : £3.95 B81-19665

305.4'2 — Feminism

Building feminist theory : essays from Quest : a feminist quarterly / Charlotte Bunch ... [et al.]. — New York ; London : Longman, 1981. — xxiii,280p : ill ; 23cm
Bibliography: p268-274. — Includes index
ISBN 0-582-28210-1 (pbk) : £6.50 B81-38260

Eisenstein, Zillah R.. The radical future of liberal feminism / Zillah R. Eisenstein. — New York ; London : Longman, c1981. — xi,260p : ill ; 24cm. — (London series in feminist theory)
Includes index
ISBN 0-582-28205-5 (cased) : £11.95
ISBN 0-582-28206-3 (pbk) : Unpriced B81-12763

Richards, Janet Radcliffe. The sceptical feminist : a philosophical enquiry / Janet Radcliffe Richards. — London : Routledge & Kegan Paul, 1980. — x,306p ; 23cm
Bibliography: p300-301. — Includes index
ISBN 0-7100-0673-x : £12.00 : CIP rev. B80-26538

305.4'2 — Feminism *related to* **Marxism**

Barrett, Michèle. Women's oppression today : problems in Marxist feminist analysis / Michèle Barrett. — London : NBL, c1980. — 269p ; 21cm
Bibliography: p261-264. — Includes index
ISBN 0-86091-033-4 (cased) : £10.00 : CIP rev.
ISBN 0-86091-730-4 (pbk) : £3.95
Also classified at 335.4 B80-19044

305.4'2 — Feminism, *to 1978*

Banks, Olive. Faces of feminism. — Oxford : Robertson, July 1981. — [250]p
ISBN 0-85520-261-0 (cased) : £12.50 : CIP entry
ISBN 0-85520-260-2 (pbk) : £4.95 B81-13752

305.4'2 — Great Britain. Women. Social control

Controlling women. — London : Croom Helm, July 1981. — [192]p. — (The Oxford women's series)
ISBN 0-7099-0469-x (cased) : £10.95 : CIP entry
ISBN 0-7099-1218-8 (pbk) : £6.50 B81-14893

305.4'2 — Great Britain. Women's liberation movements — *Communist Party of Great Britain viewpoints*

Women, oppression & liberation / Communist Party Education Dept.. — [London] : [Communist Party of Great Britain], 1980
Cover title. — Bibliography: p17
Part 3: Women, liberation and socialism. — 17p : ill ; 21x27cm
ISBN 0-86224-002-6 (pbk) : £0.60
Primary classification 305.4'2 B81-07322

305.4'2 — Great Britain. Women's liberation movements. Effects of social class

Tension, Evelyn. You don't need a degree to read the writing on the wall / Evelyn Tension. — [London?] : No Press ; [London] (27 Clerkenwell Close, E.C.2) : People's Distribution Cooperative [distributor], 1980?. — 23p ; 21cm
ISBN 0-9506353-0-8 (pbk) : £0.45 B81-03668

305.4'2 — Middle-aged women. Social adjustment

Rubin, Lillian B.. Women of a certain age : the midlife search for self / by Lillian B. Rubin. — New York ; London : Harper & Row [1981, c1979]. — x,309p ; 21cm
Originally published: 1979. — Bibliography: p262-302. — Includes index
ISBN 0-06-090833-5 (pbk) : £2.95 B81-29774

305.4'2 — Primitive societies. Role of women — *Anthropological perspectives*

Woman the gatherer / edited by Frances Dahlberg. — New Haven ; London : Yale University Press, c1981. — xi,250p : ill,1map ; 22cm
Includes bibliographies and index
ISBN 0-300-02572-6 : £9.45 B81-28224

305.4'2 — Society. Role of women

Newland, Kathleen. The sisterhood of man / Kathleen Newland. — New York ; London : Norton, c1979. — xi,242p : ill ; 22cm. — (A Worldwatch Institute book)
Bibliography: p225-229. — Includes index
ISBN 0-393-01235-2 (cased) : £7.25
ISBN 0-393-00935-1 (pbk) : £2.25 B81-02741

Women, power and political systems. — London : Croom Helm, July 1981. — [240]p
ISBN 0-7099-2204-3 : £12.50 : CIP entry B81-14904

305.4′2 — Society. Role of women — *Anthropological perspectives*

Leacock, Eleanor Burke. Myths of male dominance : collected articles on women cross-culturally / Eleanor Burke Leacock. — New York ; London : Monthly Review, c1981. — viii,344p : ill ; 21cm
Bibliography: p317-333. — Includes index
ISBN 0-85345-537-6 (cased) : £9.45
ISBN 0-85345-538-4 (pbk) : Unpriced B81-34925

305.4′2 — Society. Role of women. Biological factors — *Feminist viewpoints*

Sayers, Janet. Biological politics. — London : Tavistock, Feb.1982. — [200]p
ISBN 0-422-77870-2 (cased) : £10.50 : CIP entry
ISBN 0-422-77880-x (pbk) : £4.95 B81-35727

305.4′2 — Society. Role of women — *Feminist viewpoints*

Bernard, Jessie. The female world / Jessie Bernard. — New York : Free Press ; London : Collier Macmillan, c1981. — x,614p ; 25cm
Dibliography: p557-594. — Includes index
ISBN 0-02-903000-5 : £11.95 B81-39022

The **Body** politic : women′s liberation in Britain / compiled by Michelene Wandor. — London : Stage 1, 1972 (1978 [printing]). — [4],260p : ill ; 20cm
Bibliography: p[4]
ISBN 0-85035-029-8 (pbk) : £2.50 B81-38485

Greer, Germaine. The female eunuch / Germaine Greer. — London : Granada, 1981, c1970. — 415p ; 18cm. — (A Panther book)
Originally published: London : MacGibbon & Kee, 1970
ISBN 0-586-05406-5 (pbk) : £1.50 B81-11463

No turning back : writings from the Women′s Liberation Movement 1975-80 / edited by Feminist Anthology Collective. — London : Women′s Press, 1981. — 266p ; 20cm
ISBN 0-7043-3873-4 (pbk) : £4.95 : CIP rev. B81-13460

Women in society : interdisciplinary essays / the Cambridge Women′s Studies Group. — London : Virago, 1981. — 313p ; 20cm
Bibliography: p276-305. — Includes index
ISBN 0-86068-083-5 (pbk) : £4.95 : CIP rev. B81-16911

305.4′2 — Society. Role of women — *Socialist feminist viewpoints*

Walking a tightrope. — 2nd ed. — Liverpool (43a Hardman St., Liverpool 1) : Big Flame, 1980. — 36p : ill,ports ; 30cm. — (Big Flame women′s pamphlet)
Cover title. — Previous ed.: 1980. — Text on inside covers
ISBN 0-906082-05-6 (pbk) : £0.60 B81-25954

305.4′2 — Society. Role of women — *Socialist viewpoints*

Of marriage and the market. — London : C.S.E. Books, Oct.1981. — [224]p
ISBN 0-906336-24-4 (cased) : £12.00 : CIP entry
ISBN 0-906336-25-2 (pbk) : £4.95 B81-28116

305.4′2 — Society. Role of women — *Sociological perspectives*

Oakley, Ann. Subject women / Ann Oakley. — Oxford : Robertson, 1981. — x,406p : ill ; 23cm
Bibliography: p342-392. — Includes index
ISBN 0-85520-347-1 : £9.50 B81-35297

305.4′2 — Women. Interpersonal relationships with women — *Feminist viewpoints*

Rich, Adrienne. Women and honor : notes on lying / by Adrienne Rich. — [London] ([38 Mount Pleasant, W.C.1]) : [Only women], [1979]. — [11]p : 1ill,1port ; 21cm
Cover title
ISBN 0-906500-02-8 (pbk) : £0.35 B81-07731

305.4′2 — Women. Social status — *Feminist viewpoints*

Women and space : ground rules and social maps / edited by Shirley Ardener. — London : Croom Helm in association with the Oxford University Women′s Studies Committee, 1981. — 239p : ill ; 23cm. — (Oxford women′s series)
Bibliography: p229-236. — Includes index
ISBN 0-7099-0371-5 (cased) : £12.95 : CIP rev.
ISBN 0-7099-0372-3 (pbk) : Unpriced B81-16849

305.4′2′05 — Society. Role of women — *Campaign for the Feminine Woman viewpoints — Serials*

Vive la difference : the voice of the Campaign for the Feminine Woman (CFW) : Britain′s new & only organization to counter women′s lib. — No.1 (Apr.1979)-. — Swindon (P.O. Box 69, Swindon, Wilts.) : The Campaign, 1979-. — v. : ports,ill ; 32cm
Quarterly. — Description based on: No.4 (Spring 1980)
ISSN 0260-3993 = Vive la difference : £1.25 per year (free to members) B81-04629

305.4′2′05 — Society. Role of women — *Feminist viewpoints — Serials*

Insist : Birmingham women′s paper. — Issue 1 (Feb. & Mar.)-. — Birmingham (c/o Peace Centre, Moor St., Birmingham 4) : [Insist Collective], 1980-. — v. : ill ; 30cm
Six issues yearly. — Description based on: Issue 5 (Dec.-Jan.)
ISSN 0261-0884 = Insist : £0.30 per issue B81-17488

305.4′2′0604241 — Gloucestershire. Women′s organisations: Gloucestershire Federation of Women′s Institutes — *Serials*

Gloucestershire Federation of Women′s Institutes. County year book / Gloucestershire Federation of Women′s Institutes. — 1981. — Derby (20 Webster St., Derby) : Aces, [1981]. — 84p
Unpriced B81-32277

305.4′2′0604259 — Buckinghamshire. Women′s organisations: Buckinghamshire Federation of Women′s Institutes — *Serials*

Buckinghamshire Federation of Women′s Institutes. Year book and panel of speakers and judges / Buckinghamshire Federation of Women′s Institutes. — 1981. — Derby (20 Webster St., Derby) : Aces Publicity, [1981]. — 116p
ISSN 0306-1590 : Unpriced B81-29995

305.4′2′07041 — Great Britain. Society. Role of women, *1870-1928*. Information sources

Barrow, Margaret. Women 1870-1928 : a select guide to printed and archival sources in the United Kingdom / Margaret Barrow. — London : Mansell, 1981. — xv,249p ; 24cm
Includes index
ISBN 0-7201-0923-x : £25.00 : CIP rev. B80-22926

305.4′2′072 — Society. Role of women. Research projects

Doing feminist research / edited by Helen Roberts. — London : Routledge & Kegan Paul, 1981. — xi,207p ; 22cm
Includes bibliographies and index
ISBN 0-7100-0772-8 (pbk) : £4.95 : CIP rev. B81-04374

305.4′2′09 — Feminism, *to 1980*

Charvet, John. Feminism. — London : Dent, Feb.1982. — [164]p. — (Everyman′s university library)
ISBN 0-460-10255-9 (cased) : £7.95 : CIP entry
ISBN 0-460-11255-4 (pbk) : £3.95 B81-36232

305.4′2′091724 — Developing countries. Society. Role of women. Demographic aspects

Women′s roles and population trends in the Third World. — London : Croom Helm, Oct.1981. — [288]p
ISBN 0-7099-0508-4 : £15.95 : CIP entry B81-25711

305.4′2′091724 — Developing countries. Women. Sex discrimination by society. Effects of socialism

Molyneux, Maxine D.. Women′s emancipation under socialism : a model for the Third World? / by Maxine D. Molyneux. — Brighton : Institute of Development Studies, 1981. — 41p ; 21cm. — (Discussion paper / IDS, ISSN 0308-5864 ; 157)
Bibliography: p40-41
Unpriced (pbk) B81-24390

305.4′2′091724 — Developing countries. Women. Social conditions. Measurement. Social indicators. Information sources: Census data

Baster, Nancy. The measurement of women′s participation in development : the use of census data / by Nancy Baster. — Brighton : Institute of Development Studies, 1981. — 54p ; 21cm. — (Discussion paper / IDS, ISSN 0308-5864 ; 159)
Bibliography: p51-54
Unpriced (pbk) B81-24073

305.4′2′0917671 — Islamic countries. Society. Role of women, *ca 600-1979*

Waddy, Charis. Women in Muslim history / Charis Waddy ; artist′s impressions by Lynda Saltmarsh. — London : Longman, 1980. — vii,223p,[3]p of plates : ill(some col.) ; 23cm
Includes index
ISBN 0-582-78084-5 : £9.95 : CIP rev. B80-13713

305.4′2′0924 — Feminism. Wilson, Elizabeth — *Biographies*

Wilson, Elizabeth. Mirror writing. — London : Virago, Jan.1982. — [176]p
ISBN 0-86068-241-2 (pbk) : £3.50 : CIP entry B81-33763

305.4′2′0937 — Ancient Rome. Women. Social conditions — *Readings from contemporary sources*

Women′s life in Greece and Rome. — London : Duckworth, Nov.1981. — [272]p
ISBN 0-7156-1434-7 : £24.00 : CIP entry
Primary classification 305.4′2′0938 B81-28805

305.4′2′0938 — Ancient Greece. Women. Social conditions — *Readings from contemporary sources*

Women′s life in Greece and Rome. — London : Duckworth, Nov.1981. — [272]p
ISBN 0-7156-1434-7 : £24.00 : CIP entry
Also classified at 305.4′2′0937 B81-28805

305.4′2′0941 — Great Britain. Society. Role of women, *1800-1914*

A **Widening** sphere : changing roles of Victorian women / edited by Martha Vicinus. — London : Methuen, 1980, c1977. — xix,326p : ill,1facsim ; 24cm
Originally published: Bloomington : Indiana University Press, 1977. — Bibliography: p199-270. - Includes index
ISBN 0-416-74350-1 (pbk) : £4.95 : CIP rev. B80-20245

305.4′2′0941 — Great Britain. Society. Role of women, *1815-1914*

Suffer and be still : women in the Victorian age / edited by Martha Vicinus. — London : Methuen, 1980, c1972. — xv,239p : ill ; 24cm
Originally published: Bloomington : Indiana University Press, 1972. — Bibliography: p173-206. - Includes index
ISBN 0-416-74340-4 (pbk) : £4.95 : CIP rev. B80-20246

305.4′2′0941 — Great Britain. Society. Role of women — *Campaign for the Feminine Woman viewpoints*

Stayt, David W.. The campaign for the feminine woman. — Swindon (P.O. Box 69, Swindon SN6 8HS) : Campaign for the Feminine Woman, [1981?]. — [4]p ; 21cm
Author: David W. Stayt
Unpriced (unbound) B81-22123

305.4′2′0941 — Great Britain. Society. Role of women — *Labour Party (Great Britain) viewpoints*

Labour Party *(Great Britain)*. Women, sexism and socialism / The Labour Party. — London : The Party, [1981]. — 31p ; 21cm
Cover title. — Bibliography: p29-30
ISBN 0-86117-062-8 (pbk) : £0.40 B81-22985

305.4'2'0941 — Great Britain. Society. Role of women — *Sociological perspectives*

Delamont, Sara. The sociology of women : an introduction / Sara Delamont. — London : Allen & Unwin, 1980. — 244p ; 22cm. — (Studies in sociology ; 11)
Bibliography: p226-238. - Includes index
ISBN 0-04-301119-5 (cased) : £8.95 : CIP rev.
ISBN 0-04-301120-9 (pbk) : £3.95 B80-22928

305.4'2'0941 — Great Britain. Women. Social conditions, *1907-1980*

Ingham, Mary. Now we are thirty. — London : Eyre Methuen, Oct.1981. — [256]p
ISBN 0-413-47750-9 (cased) : £8.95 : CIP entry
ISBN 0-413-49300-8 (pbk) : £4.50 B81-25311

305.4'2'0944 — France. Society. Role of women, *1870-1940*

McMillan, James F.. Housewife or harlot : the place of women in French society 1870-1940 / James F. McMillan. — Brighton : Harvester, 1981. — 229p ; 23cm
Bibliography: p222-226. — Includes index
ISBN 0-85527-647-9 : £18.95 B81-26174

305.4'2'0947 — Soviet Union. Society. Role of women

McAndrew, Maggie. The new Soviet woman - model or myth / by Maggie McAndrew and Jo Peers. — London : 25 Wilton Rd., SW1 1JS : Change International Reports, 1981. — 28p : 1map ; 25cm. — (Change international reports)
ISBN 0-907236-02-2 (corrected : pbk) : £1.25 B81-22230

305.4'2'095 — Asia. Rural regions. Society. Role of women — *Case studies*

The **endless** day : some case material on Asian rural women. — Oxford : Pergamon, Dec.1981. — [181]p. — (Women in development ; v.3) (Pergamon international library)
ISBN 0-08-028106-0 : £12.50 : CIP entry B81-31356

305.4'2'095 — Asia. Society. Role of women

Women in Asia / edited by Rounaq Jahan ; contributors Hyoung Cho ... [et al.]. — London (36 Craven St., WC2N 5NG) : Minority Rights Group, 1980. — 24p : 1ill ; 30cm. — (Report / Minority Rights Group, ISSN 0305-6252 ; no.45)
£0.75 (pbk) B81-05032

305.4'2'0951 — China. Women's movements, *1900-1949*

Siu, Bobby. Women of China. — London : Zed, Sept.1981. — [240]p
ISBN 0-905762-58-4 : £14.95 : CIP entry B81-20524

305.4'2'0954 — India *(Republic)*. **Society. Role of women**

Gaur, Albertine. Women in India / Albertine Gaur. — London : British Library, c1980. — 29p : ill(some.col.) ; 27cm. — (British Library booklets)
Bibliography: p29
ISBN 0-904654-52-4 (pbk) : £1.50 : CIP rev. B80-32958

305.4'2'0954 — North-western India *(Republic)*. **Society. Role of women**

Sharma, Ursula. Women, work, and property in North-West India / Ursula Sharma. — London : Tavistock, 1980. — ix,226p : ill,2maps ; 23cm
Bibliography: p214-218. — Includes index
ISBN 0-422-77120-1 : £10.50 : CIP rev. B80-18604

305.4'2'095492 — Bangladesh. Rural regions. Women. Social conditions

Abdullah, Tahrunnessa A.. Village women of Bangladesh. — Oxford : Pergamon, Dec.1981. — [256]p. — (Women in development) (Pergamon international library)
ISBN 0-08-026795-5 : £13.50 : CIP entry B81-34725

305.4'2'09593 — Thailand. Society. Role of women

Thista, Khin. Providence and prostitution : image and reality for women in Buddhist Thailand. — London (62 Chandos Place, W.C.2) : Change, 1980. — 27p : 1map ; 23cm. — (Change international reports : women and society ; no.2)
Written by Khin Thista
£1.25 (pbk) B81-13027

305.4'2'095957 — Singapore. Society. Role of women

Wong, Aline K.. Economic development and women's place : women in Singapore / by Aline K. Wong. — London (62 Chandos Place, W.C.2.) : Change, 1980. — [20]p : 2maps ; 23cm. — (Change international reports : women and society ; no.1)
ISBN 0-907236-00-6 (pbk) : £1.25 B81-10099

305.4'2'096 — Africa. Women. Social conditions

African women in the development process. — London : Frank Cass, July 1981. — [144]p
ISBN 0-7146-3175-2 : £12.50 : CIP entry B81-14460

305.4'2'096 — Africa. Women. Social conditions, *ca 1900-1975*

Njoku, John E. Eberegbulam. The world of the African woman / John E. Eberegbulam Njoku. — Metuchen ; London : Scarecrow, 1980. — v,124p ; 23cm
ISBN 0-8108-1350-5 : £5.60 B81-05042

305.4'2'096216 — Egypt. Cairo. Poor women. Social conditons

Wikan, Unni. Life among the poor in Cairo / Unni Wikan ; translated by Ann Henning. — London : Tavistock Publications, 1980. — ix,173p,[4]p of plates : ill,1plan ; 23cm
Translation of: Fattigfolk i Cairo. —
Bibliography: p169-170 — Includes index
ISBN 0-422-76970-3 (cased) : £9.50 : CIP rev.
ISBN 0-422-76980-0 (pbk) : £4.95 B80-11318

305.4'2'09624 — Sudan. Society. Role of women

Hall, Marjorie. Sisters under the sun. — London : Longman, Sept.1981. — [288]p
ISBN 0-582-78017-9 : £12.00 : CIP entry B81-23842

305.4'2'09669 — Nigeria. Rural regions. Society. Role of women

Spiro, Heather M.. The fifth world : women's rural activities and time budgets in Nigeria / Heather M. Spiro. — London (Mile End Rd., E1 4NS) : Department of Geography, Queen Mary College, 1981. — 59p : ill ; 30cm. — (Occasional paper / Queen Mary College. Department of Geography, ISSN 0306-2740 ; no.19)
Bibliography: p53-59
ISBN 0-904791-19-x (pbk) : Unpriced B81-33331

305.4'2'0973 — United States. Feminism, *1850-1880.* **Sociopolitical aspects**

Leach, William. True love and perfect union : the feminist reform of sex and society / William Leach. — London : Routledge and Kegan Paul, 1981, c1980. — xii,449p ; 25cm
Originally pubulished: New York : Basic Books, 1980. — Includes index
ISBN 0-7100-0766-3 : £9.75 B81-05669

305.4'2'0973 — United States. Feminism, *1869-1921*

Hayden, Dolores. The grand domestic revolution : a history of feminist designs for American homes, neighborhoods, and cities / Dolores Hayden. — Cambridge (Mass.) ; London : M.I.T., c1981. — 367p : ill,facsim,plans,ports ; 24cm
Includes index
ISBN 0-262-08108-3 : £12.40 B81-38144

305.4'2'0973 — United States. Feminism, *1880-1914*

Tax, Meredith. The rising of the women : feminist solidarity and class conflict, 1880-1917 / by Meredith Tax. — New York ; London : Monthly Review, c1980. — 332p ; 21cm
Includes index
ISBN 0-85345-548-1 (cased) : £9.45
ISBN 0-85345-549-x (pbk) : Unpriced B81-14294

305.4'2'0973 — United States. Feminism, *to 1979*

Lerner, Gerda. The majority finds its past : placing women in history / Gerda Lerner. — Oxford : Oxford University Press, 1981, c1979. — xxxii,217p ; 21cm
Originally published: New York : Oxford University Press, 1979. — Includes index
ISBN 0-19-502899-6 (pbk) : £3.50 B81-36074

305.4'2'0973 — United States. Society. Role of women. Ossoli, Margaret Fuller. 'Women in the nineteenth century' — *Critical studies*

Urbanski, Marie Mitchell Olesen. Margaret Fuller's Woman in the nineteenth century : a literary study of form and content, of sources and influence / Marie Mitchell Olesen Urbanski. — Westport, Conn. ; London : Greenwood Press, 1980. — x,189p ; 22cm. — (Contributions in women's studies, ISSN 0147-104x ; no.13)
Bibliography: p175-182. - Includes index
ISBN 0-313-21475-1 : Unpriced B81-05015

305.4'2'0973 — United States. Urban regions. Society. Role of women

Women and the American city / edited by Catharine R. Stimpson ... [et al.]. — Chicago ; London : University of Chicago Press, c1981. — x,277p : ill,plans ; 24cm
Originally published: in Signs, supplement to vol.5, no.3 (Spring 1980). — Includes index
ISBN 0-226-77478-3 (cased) : £11.20
ISBN 0-226-77479-1 (pbk) : Unpriced B81-39642

305.4'2'09931 — New Zealand. Society. Role of women, *to 1979*

Women in New Zealand society / [edited by] Phillida Bunkle and Beryl Hughes. — Auckland ; London : Allen & Unwin, 1980. — 265p : ill ; 23cm
Includes bibliographies and index
ISBN 0-86861-026-7 (cased) : Unpriced
ISBN 0-86861-034-8 (pbk) : Unpriced B81-15709

305.4'2'19 — Society. Role of women. Political aspects — *Feminist viewpoints*

Elshtain, Jean Bethke. Public man, private woman. — Oxford : Robertson, Oct.1981. — [376]p
ISBN 0-85520-470-2 (cased) : £15.00 : CIP entry
ISBN 0-85520-471-0 (pbk) : £4.95 B81-26697

305.4'3 — United States. Displaced homemakers

Shields, Laurie. Displaced homemakers : organizing for a new life / by Laurie Shields ; epilogue by Tish Sommers. — New York ; London : McGraw-Hill, 1981. — xiv,272p ; 21cm
Bibliography: p261-264. - Includes index
ISBN 0-07-056802-2 (pbk) : £4.50 B81-19481

305.4'3 — United States. Women. Housework. Social aspects

André, Rae. Homemakers : the forgotten workers / Rae André. — Chicago ; London : University of Chicago Press, 1981. — xi,299p ; 24cm
Bibliography: p285-292. — Includes index
ISBN 0-226-01993-4 : £9.00 B81-29777

305.4'8 — Great Britain. Women, 30 years- — *Practical information*

Conran, Shirley. Futurewoman : how to survive life / Shirley Conran and Elizabeth Sidney. — Rev. ed. — Harmondsworth : Penguin, 1981. — 368p ; 20cm
Previous ed.: published as Futures. London : Sidgwick and Jackson, 1979. — Includes index
ISBN 0-14-005759-5 (pbk) : £1.95 B81-40336

305.4'8 — Israel. Subcultures. Women. Middle age. Personal adjustment — *Case studies*

Datan, Nancy. A time to reap : the middle age of women in five Israeli subcultures / Nancy Datan, Aaron Antonovsky, Benjamin Maoz. — Baltimore ; London : Johns Hopkins University Press, c1980. — ix,194p ; 24cm
Bibliography: p185-188. — Includes index
ISBN 0-8018-2516-4 : £8.50 B81-34465

305.4'8 — South Africa. Negro women. Social conditions, *1913-1980*
Women under apartheid : in photographs and text / [prepared by IDAF Research, Information and Publicity Department]. — London : International Defence and Aid Fund for Southern Africa in cooperation with the United Nations Centre Against Apartheid, 1981. — 119p : ill,ports ; 21cm
ISBN 0-904759-45-8 (pbk) : £3.00 B81-39971

305.4'8 — United States. Chicano women. Social conditions
Twice a minority : Mexican American women / edited by Margarita B. Melville. — St. Louis ; London : Mosby, 1980. — xi,270p : ill,1map ; 24cm
Includes bibliographies and index
ISBN 0-8016-3386-9 (pbk) : Unpriced B81-08564

305.4'8 — United States. Negro women — *Sociological perspectives*
The **Black** woman / edited by La Frances Rodgers-Rose. — Beverly Hills ; London : Sage, c1980. — 316p : ill ; 22cm. — (Sage focus editions)
Includes bibliographies
ISBN 0-8039-1311-7 (cased) : £11.85
ISBN 0-8039-1312-5 (pbk) : £6.25 B81-01918

305.4'8 — Women, 35-55 years
Franks, Helen. Prime time : the mid-life woman in focus / Helen Franks. — London : Pan, 1981. — 222p ; 18cm
Bibliography: p213-216. — Includes index
ISBN 0-330-26459-1 (pbk) : £1.50 B81-38162

305.5 — Equality
De Havilland, Raymond. Equality or inequality? / by Raymond de Havilland. — Birmingham (Room 113, Daimler House, 34 Paradise St., Birmingham B1 2BJ) : Traditional Press, 1981. — 94p ; 22cm. — (The Great debate series ; v.1)
ISBN 0-9507638-0-2 : 6.50 B81-37658

305.5 — France, Great Britain & United States. Social class, *1930-1979 — Comparative studies*
Marwick, Arthur. Class : image and reality in Britain, France and the USA since 1930 / Arthur Marwick. — [London] : Fontana, 1981, c1980. — 416p ; 18cm
Originally published: London : Collins, 1980. — Bibliography: p377-400. — Includes index
ISBN 0-00-636310-5 (pbk) : £2.95 B81-21110

305.5 — Social equality — *Conference proceedings*
Equality and social policy / edited by Walter Feinberg. — Urbana ; London : University of Illinois Press, c1978. — 190p : ill ; 24cm
Conference papers
ISBN 0-252-00215-6 : £6.00 B81-05614

305.5 — Social inequality — *Anthropological perspectives — Conference proceedings*
Social inequality : comparative and developmental approaches / [Burg Wartenstein symposium no.80 sponsored by the Wenner-Gren Foundation for Anthropological Research, August 25-September 3, 1978] ; edited by Gerald D. Berreman with the assistance of Kathleen M. Zaretsky. — New York ; London : Academic Press, c1981. — xvii,361p : ill ; 24cm. — (Studies in anthropology)
Includes bibliographies and index
ISBN 0-12-093160-5 : £18.20 B81-29818

305.5 — Sri Lanka. Karāva caste groups, *1500-1931*
Roberts, Michael. Caste conflict and elite formation. — Cambridge : Cambridge University Press, Jan.1982. — [382]p. — (Cambridge South Asian studies ; 24)
ISBN 0-521-23210-4 : £30.00 : CIP entry B81-34655

305.5'01 — Social class. Theories of Marxists
Parkin, Frank. Marxism and class theory : a bourgeois critique / Frank Parkin. — London : Tavistock Publications, 1981, c1979. — xi,217p ; 22cm. — (Social science paperback ; 217)
Originally published: 1979. — Bibliography: p205-211. — Includes index
ISBN 0-422-77810-9 (pbk) : £4.95 : CIP rev. B81-13470

305.5'07201812 — Western world. Social mobility, *1800-1976.* **Research**
Kaelble, Hartmut. Historical research on social mobility : Western Europe and the USA in the nineteenth and twentieth centuries / Hartmut Kaelble ; translated by Ingrid Noakes. — London : Croom Helm, c1981. — 160p : ill ; 23cm
Translation of: Historische Mobilitätsforschung. — Bibliography: p137-158. - Includes index
ISBN 0-7099-1505-5 : £8.50 B81-20784

305.5'072042 — England. Social class, *1680-1850.* **Historiography**
Neale, R. S.. Class in English history 1680-1850 / R.S. Neale. — Oxford : Blackwell, 1981. — vi,250p : ill,facsims,1port ; 22cm
Includes index
ISBN 0-631-12851-4 : £12.00 : CIP rev. B80-13716

305.5'09172'2 — Developed countries. Social class. Theories
Giddens, Anthony. The class structure of the advanced societies / Anthony Giddens. — 2nd ed. — London : Hutchinson, 1981. — 366p ; 22cm. — (Hutchinson University Library)
Previous ed.: 1973. — Bibliography: p347-354 — Includes index
ISBN 0-09-141891-7 (pbk) : £4.95 : CIP rev. B80-06300

305.5'0941 — England. Poor persons. Social conditions, *1849-1852 — Early works*
Labour and the poor in England and Wales, 1849-1852. — London : Cass, Sept.1981
Vol.1: Lancashire, Cheshire, Yorkshire. — [288]p
ISBN 0-7146-2907-3 : £12.50 : CIP entry B81-21486

305.5'0941 — Great Britain. Man. Social behaviour. Effects of social mobility — *Sociological perspectives*
Hopper, Earl. Social mobility : a study of social control and insatiability / Earl Hopper. — Oxford : Blackwell, 1981. — viii,335p : ill ; 24cm
Includes index
ISBN 0-631-11031-3 : £24.50 : CIP rev. B80-07235

305.5'0941 — Great Britain. Occupations *related to* **social stratification**
Stewart, A.. Social stratification and occupations / A. Stewart, K. Prandy and R.M. Blackburn. — London : Macmillan, 1980. — xiii,302p : ill ; 23cm. — (Cambridge studies in sociology)
Bibliography: p284-292. — Includes index
ISBN 0-333-24329-3 (cased) : £15.00 : CIP rev.
ISBN 0-333-24330-7 (pbk) : £5.95 B80-02330

305.5'0941 — Great Britain. Social class
Reid, Ivan. Social class differences in Britain / Ivan Reid. — 2nd ed. — London : Grant McIntyre, 1981. — xvi,328p : ill ; 21cm
Previous ed.: 1977. — Bibliography: p302-320. — Includes index
ISBN 0-86216-058-8 (cased) : £12.95 : CIP rev.
ISBN 0-86216-059-6 (pbk) : £5.95 B81-04274

305.5'0941 — Great Britain. Social class *related to* **social mobility**
Heath, Anthony. Social mobility / Anthony Heath. — [London] : Fontana, 1981. — 303p : ill ; 18cm. — (Fontana new sociology)
Bibliography: p286-298. - Includes index
ISBN 0-00-635601-x (pbk) : £2.50 B81-10332

305.5'0941 — Great Britain. Social equality. Effects of distribution of expenditure on public welfare services
Le Grand, Julian. The strategy of equality : redistribution and the social services. — London : Allen & Unwin, Jan.1982. — [208]p
ISBN 0-04-336074-2 (cased) : £12.50 : CIP entry
ISBN 0-04-336075-0 (pbk) : £4.50 B81-33918

305.5'0942 — England. Social class — *Humour*
Cooper, Jilly. Class : a view from middle England / Jilly Cooper ; with drawings by Timothy Jacques. — Rev. ed. — London : Corgi, 1980. — 366p : ill ; 18cm
Previous ed.: London : Eyre Methuen, 1979
ISBN 0-552-11525-8 (pbk) : £1.25 B81-00018

305.5'09429 — Wales. Social inequality
Poverty and social inequality in Wales / edited by Gareth Rees and Teresa L. Rees. — London : Croom Helm, c1980. — 279p : maps ; 23cm
Bibliography: p252-271. - Includes index
ISBN 0-7099-2200-0 (cased) : £11.95 : CIP rev.
ISBN 0-7099-2205-1 (pbk) : £5.50 B80-11319

305.5'09495 — Greece. Social classes. Conflict, *to 1453*
De Ste. Croix, G. E. M.. The class struggle in the Ancient Greek world. — London : Duckworth, Aug.1981. — [672]p
ISBN 0-7156-0738-3 : £28.00 : CIP entry B81-17500

305.5'0954 — India *(Republic).* **Caste system** — *Sociological perspectives*
Kolenda, Pauline. Caste in contemporary India : beyond organic solidarity / Pauline Kolenda. — Menlo Park ; London : Benjamin/Cummings, c1978. — 181p : ill,2maps ; 21cm. — (Benjamin/Cummings modular program in anthropology)
Bibliography: p152-170. - Includes index
ISBN 0-8053-5602-9 (pbk) : £4.10 B81-02972

305.5'0973 — United States. Social classes
The **New** class? / edited by B. Bruce-Briggs ; [contributions by] Robert L. Bartley ... [et al.]. — New York ; London : McGraw-Hill, 1981, c1979. — xvii,229p ; 21cm
Originally published: New Brunswick, N.J. : Transaction Books, 1979. — Includes index
ISBN 0-07-008573-0 (pbk) : £4.50 B81-38011

305.5'2 — England. Nobility, *1290-1536.* **Social aspects**
McFarlane, K. B.. The nobility of Later Medieval England : the Ford lectures for 1953 and related studies / by K.B. McFarlane. — Oxford : Clarendon, 1980, c1973. — xlii,315p,[1]leaf of plates : 1port ; 22cm
Originally published: 1973. — Bibliography: pxli-xlii. — Includes index
ISBN 0-19-822657-8 (pbk) : £6.95 : CIP rev. B80-10468

305.5'2 — Gloucestershire. Gentry, *1300-1400*
Saul, Nigel. Knights and esquires : the Gloucestershire gentry in the fourteenth century / by Nigel Saul. — Oxford : Clarendon, 1981. — xiii,316p : 1map,geneal.tables ; 23cm. — (Oxford historical monographs)
Bibliography: p293-301. — Includes index
ISBN 0-19-821883-4 : £17.50 B81-38465

305.5'2 — Great Britain. Hereditary peers
Winchester, Simon. Their noble lordships. — London : Faber, Sept.1981. — [328]p
ISBN 0-571-11069-x : £7.95 : CIP entry B81-20558

305.5'2 — Great Britain. Rich persons, *1809-1980*
Rubinstein, W. D.. Men of property : the very wealthy in Britain since the Industrial Revolution / W.D. Rubinstein. — London : Croom Helm, c1981. — 261p ; 23cm
Includes index
ISBN 0-85664-674-1 : £12.50 : CIP rev. B81-08824

305.5'2 — Power elites — *Sociological perspectives*
Marger, Martin N.. Elites and masses : an introduction to political sociology / Martin N. Marger. — New York ; London : Van Nostrand Reinhold, c1981. — xi,391p : ill ; 25cm
Includes bibliographies and index
ISBN 0-442-25410-5 : £11.95 B81-00753

305.5'2 — Welsh Marches. Barons. Social conditions, *1066-1272*
Meisel, Janet. Barons of the Welsh frontier : the Corbet, Pantulf, & Fitz Warin families 1066-1272 / Janet Meisel. — Lincoln [Neb.] ; London : University of Nebraska Press, c1980. — xix,231p : maps,geneal.tables ; 23cm
Bibliography: p211-218. - Includes index
ISBN 0-8032-3064-8 : £12.00 B81-12724

305.5′2 — Western world. Power elites. Members: Women — *Comparative studies*
Access to power : cross-national studies of women and elites / edited by Cynthia Fuchs Epstein and Rose Laub Coser. — London : Allen & Unwin, 1981. — x,259p : ill ; 25cm
Includes bibliographies and index
ISBN 0-04-301118-7 : £18.00 : CIP rev.
B80-22933

305.5′2′0941 — Great Britain. Power elites — *Interviews*
Griffin, Brian. Power : British management in focus. — London : Travelling Light, Oct.1981. — [128]p
ISBN 0-906333-13-x : £8.95 : CIP entry
B81-26700

305.5′2′0944 — France. Nobility, *1789-1799*
Higonnet, Patrice. Class, ideology and the rights of nobles during the French Revolution. — Oxford : Clarendon, Oct.1981. — [400]p
ISBN 0-19-822583-0 : £22.50 : CIP entry
B81-28186

305.5′5 — Arab countries. Executives — *Sociological perspectives*
Muna, Farid A.. The Arab executive / Farid A. Muna ; foreword by Kenneth Simmonds. — London : Macmillan, 1980. — xv,155p : ill,1form ; 23cm
Bibliography: p142-147. - Includes index
ISBN 0-333-29119-0 : £10.00 B81-01747

305.5′5 — England. Middle classes, *1837-1980*
Bradley, Ian, *1950-*. The English middle classes. — London : Collins, Jan.1982. — [250]p
ISBN 0-00-216276-8 (pbk) : £5.95 : CIP entry
B81-33975

305.5′5 — France. Society. Role of intellectuals, *1880-1980*
Debray, Régis. Teachers, writers, celebrities : the intellectuals of modern France / Régis Debray ; introduction by Francis Mulhern ; translated by David Macey. — London : New Left Books, 1981. — xxvi,251p ; 21cm
Translation of: Le pouvoir intellectuel en France. — Includes index
ISBN 0-86091-039-3 (cased) : £11.00 : CIP rev.
ISBN 0-86091-736-3 (pbk) : Unpriced
B81-05133

305.5′5 — Great Britain. Lower middle classes. Social conditions, *1870-1914*
The Lower middle class in Britain 1870-1914 / edited by Geoffrey Crossick. — London : Croom Helm, c1977 (1978 [printing]). — 213p ; 23cm
Includes index
ISBN 0-85664-348-3 : £11.95 B81-17376

305.5′5 — Intellectuals, *1900-1980* — *Personal observations*
Berlin, Isaiah. Personal impressions / Isaiah Berlin ; edited by Henry Hardy ; with an introduction by Noel Annan. — London : Hogarth, 1980. — xxx,219p,[8]p of plates : ports ; 23cm. — (Selected writings / Isaiah Berlin ; 4)
Includes index
ISBN 0-7012-0510-5 : £9.50
Also classified at 909.82′092′2 B81-10334

305.5′5 — Intellectuals — *Directories*
The International who′s who of intellectuals. — Cambridge : International Biographical Centre
Vol.1. — c1978. — 950p ; 25cm
Unpriced B81-21664

305.5′5 — Russia *(RSFSR)*. **Moscow. Merchants. Social conditions,** *1855-1905*
Owen, Thomas C.. Capitalism and politics in Russia : a social history of the Moscow merchants, 1855-1905 / Thomas C. Owen. — Cambridge : Cambridge University Press, 1981. — xi,295p ; 24cm
Bibliography: p277-284. — Includes index
ISBN 0-521-23173-6 : £20.00 B81-25925

305.5′5 — Society. Role of intellectuals
Béteille, André. Ideologies and intellectuals / André Béteille. — Delhi ; Oxford : Oxford University Press, 1980. — iii,51p ; 22cm
ISBN 0-19-561306-6 (pbk) : £1.25
Primary classification 145 B81-38591

305.5′5 — United States. Middle class negroes. Social aspects — *Study examples: Freemasons: Freemasons. Prince Hall Freemasons, to 1974*
Williams, Loretta J.. Black Freemasonary and middle-class realities / Loretta J. Williams. — Columbia ; London : University of Missouri Press, 1980. — 165p : ill ; 24cm. — (University of Missouri studies ; 69)
Bibliography: p139-156. — Includes index
ISBN 0-8262-0308-6 : £9.00 B81-07327

305.5′5 — United States. White-collar personnel, *1890-1940*. **Sociopolitical aspects**
Kocka, Jürgen. White collar workers in America 1890-1940 : a social-political history in international perspective / Jürgen Kocka ; translated [and edited] by Maura Kealey. — London : Sage, c1980. — v,403p ; 23cm. — (Sage studies in 20th century history ; v.10)
Translation of: Angestellte zwischen Faschismus und Demokratie. — Bibliography: p369-394. - Includes index
ISBN 0-8039-9844-9 (cased) : Unpriced
ISBN 0-8039-9845-7 (pbk) : Unpriced
B80-17565

305.5′5 — West Midlands *(Metropolitan County)*. *Coventry. Executives* — *Sociological perspectives*
Lee, Gloria L.. Who gets to the top? : a sociological study of business executives. — Aldershot : Gower, Nov.1981. — [168]p
ISBN 0-566-00497-6 : £10.50 : CIP entry
B81-30283

305.5′5′0904 — Middle classes, *1900-1980*. **Economic aspects**
The Petite bourgeoisie : comparative studies of the uneasy stratum / edited by Frank Bechhofer and Brian Elliott. — London : Macmillan, 1981. — xiii,206p : 2ill ; 23cm. — (Edinburgh studies in sociology)
Includes index
ISBN 0-333-23737-4 : £20.00 B81-21788

305.5′5′0941 — Great Britain. Middle classes — *Sociological perspectives*
King, Roger. The middle class. — 2nd ed. / Roger King and John Raynor with Dallas Cliff, Geoffrey Sparks. — London : Longman, c1981. — 267p ; 20cm. — (Aspects of modern sociology. The social structure of modern Britain)
Previous ed.: 1969. — Bibliography: p245-261. — Includes index
ISBN 0-582-29525-4 (pbk) : £5.50 B81-40147

305.5′6 — Africa. Urban regions. Poverty. Political aspects
Sandbrook, Richard. The politics of basic needs. — London : Heinemann Educational, Nov.1981. — [320]p. — (Studies in the economics of Africa)
ISBN 0-435-96536-0 (cased) : £13.50 : CIP entry
ISBN 0-435-96537-9 (pbk) : £4.95 B81-30164

305.5′6 — California. Agricultural industries. Personnel. Social conditions, *1870-1941*
Daniel, Cletus E.. Bitter harvest : a history of California farmworkers, 1870-1941 / Cletus E. Daniel. — Ithaca ; London : Cornell University Press, c1981. — 348p : ill,ports ; 24cm
Includes index
ISBN 0-8014-1284-6 : £11.75 B81-36416

305.5′6 — Capitalist countries. Social change. Role of working classes — *Marxist viewpoints*
Moskvin, L. B.. The working class and its allies / L. Moskvin ; [translated from the Russian by Nicholas Babrov]. — Moscow : Progress ; [London] : Central Books [distributor], 1980. — 283p ; 21cm
Translation of: Rabochiĭ klass i ego soiūzniki
ISBN 0-7147-1619-7 : £2.95 B81-29309

305.5′6 — Costa Rica. Peasants, *ca 1600-1979*. **Economic change,** *ca 1600-1979*
Seligson, Mitchell A.. Peasants of Costa Rica and the development of agrarian capitalism / Mitchell A. Seligson. — Madison ; London : University of Wisconsin Press, c1980. — xxxii,220p : ill,maps ; 24cm
Bibliography: p182-212. - Includes index
ISBN 0-299-07760-8 : £12.90 B81-02948

305.5′6 — Developing countries. Poverty
Galbraith, John Kenneth. The nature of mass poverty / John Kenneth Galbraith. — Harmondsworth : Penguin, 1980, c1979. — 120p ; 19cm. — (Pelican books)
Originally published: Cambridge, Mass : Harvard University Press, 1979. — Includes index
ISBN 0-14-022289-8 (pbk) : £1.25 B81-00019

Harrison, Paul, *1948-*. Inside the Third World : the anatomy of poverty / Paul Harrison. — 2nd ed. — Harmondsworth : Penguin, 1981. — 502p : maps ; 18cm. — (Pelican books)
Previous ed.: published Brighton : Harvester ; Harmondsworth : Penguin, 1979. — Bibliography: p461-475. — Includes index
ISBN 0-14-022057-7 (pbk) : £2.95 B81-20379

Murdoch, William W.. The poverty of nations : the political economy of hunger and population / William W. Murdoch. — Baltimore ; London : Johns Hopkins University Press, c1980. — xv,382p : ill ; 24cm
Bibliography: p367-368. — Includes index
ISBN 0-8018-2313-7 (cased) : £13.50
ISBN 0-8018-2462-1 (pbk) : £4.50 B81-21078

305.5′6 — Developing countries. Poverty. Influence of developed countries
Hayter, Teresa. The creation of world poverty / Teresa Hayter. — London : Pluto in association with Third World First, c1981. — 128p ; 20cm
Bibliography: p124-128
ISBN 0-86104-339-1 (pbk) : £2.50 B81-27556

305.5′6 — Developing countries. Urban regions. Poverty
Lloyd, Peter. A Third World proletariat?. — London : Allen & Unwin, Feb.1982. — [144]p. — (Controversies in sociology ; 11)
ISBN 0-04-301140-3 (cased) : £8.95 : CIP entry
ISBN 0-04-301141-1 (pbk) : £3.95 B81-35941

305.5′6 — Developing countries. Urban regions. Poverty — *Study regions: Costa Rica*
Herrick, Bruce. Urban poverty and economic development : a case study of Costa Rica / Bruce Herrick and Barclay Hudson. — London : Macmillan, 1981. — xiii,188p : ill,maps ; 23cm
Includes index
ISBN 0-333-28446-1 : £15.00 B81-25351

305.5′6 — England. Agricultural industries. Personnel: Harvesters. Social conditions, *1840-1900*
Morgan, David Hoseason. Harvesters and harvesting, 1840-1900. — London : Croom Helm, Dec.1981. — [240]p
ISBN 0-7099-1735-x : £12.95 : CIP entry
B81-31429

305.5′6 — England. Serfdom, *1100-1300*
Hyams, Paul R.. Kings, lords and peasants in Medieval England : the Common Law of villeinage in the twelfth and thirteenth centuries / by Paul R. Hyams. — Oxford : Clarendon Press, 1980. — xxii,295p ; 23cm. — (Oxford historical monographs)
Bibliography: p273-286. — Includes index
ISBN 0-19-821880-x : £17.50 : CIP rev.
B80-05797

305.5′6 — England. Working classes. Social conditions, *ca 1700-1780*
Malcolmson, Robert W.. Life and labour in England 1700-1780 / Robert W. Malcolmson. — London : Hutchinson, 1981. — 208p : 2maps ; 24cm. — (Hutchinson social history of England)
Includes index
ISBN 0-09-144380-6 (cased) : £12.00
ISBN 0-09-144381-4 (pbk) : £4.95 B81-26804

305.5′6 — France. Marlhes. Peasants. Family life. Effects of economic development, *ca 1800-1900*
Lehning, James R.. The peasants of Marlhes : economic development and family organization in nineteenth-century France / by James R. Lehning. — London : Macmillan, 1980. — xiv,218p : ill,maps ; 24cm
Originally published: Chapel Hill : University of North Carolina Press, 1980. — Bibliography: p203-214. — Includes index
ISBN 0-333-30708-9 : £15.00 B81-04888

305.5′6 — Germany. Working classes. Social conditions, *1888-1933*

The **German** working class 1888-1933. — London : Croom Helm, Dec.1981. — [256]p
ISBN 0-7099-0431-2 : £13.95 : CIP entry
B81-31442

305.5′6 — Great Britain. Deviance. Attitudes of society — *Study examples: Mods & rockers*

Cohen, Stanley, *1942-*. Folk devils and moral panics : the creation of the Mods and Rockers. — [New ed.]. — Oxford : Martin Robertson, 1980. — xxxiv,235p ; 23cm
Previous ed.: London : McGibbon and Kee. 1972. — Includes index
ISBN 0-85520-323-4 (cased) : £12.50 : CIP rev.
ISBN 0-85520-344-7 (pbk) : £5.95 B80-11753

305.5′6 — Great Britain. Poverty

Donnison, David. The politics of poverty. — Oxford : Martin Robertson, Nov.1981. — [224]p
ISBN 0-85520-480-x (cased) : £6.95 : CIP entry
ISBN 0-85520-481-8 (pbk) : £2.95 B81-31000

305.5′6 — Great Britain. Poverty, *1945-1980*

Berthoud, Richard. Poverty and the development of anti-poverty policy in the United Kingdom. — London : Heinemann Educational, Sept.1981. — [320]p. — (Policy Studies Institute series)
ISBN 0-435-83102-x (cased) : £13.50 : CIP entry
ISBN 0-435-83103-8 (pbk) : £6.50 B81-30260

305.5′6 — Great Britain. Poverty — *Cartoons*

Brick. Poverty : for near beginners / [by Brick]. — Nottingham (10, Heathcote St., Nottingham NG1 3AA) : Mushroom, [1981?]. — 25p : ill ; 15cm
ISBN 0-907123-00-7 (pbk) : £0.35 B81-37104

305.5′6 — Great Britain. Railway services. Personnel. Social conditions, *1840-1970*

McKenna, Frank. The railway workers 1840-1970 / Frank McKenna. — London : Faber, 1980. — 280p,[16]p of plates : ill,facsims,ports ; 23cm
Bibliography: p270. — Includes index
ISBN 0-571-11563-2 : £10.00 : CIP rev.
B80-07676

305.5′6 — Great Britain. Urban regions. Poverty — *Study regions: Nottinghamshire. Nottingham. St Ann′s*

Coates, Ken. Poverty : the forgotten Englishmen / Ken Coates and Richard Silburn. — Repr. with new introduction and epilogue. — Harmondsworth : Penguin, 1981. — 282p ; 18cm. — (Pelican books)
Previous ed.: 1970. — Includes index
(pbk) B81-07372

305.5′6 — Great Britain. Working classes, *1815-1914*

Hunt, E. H.. British labour history 1815-1914 / E.H. Hunt. — London : Weidenfeld and Nicolson, c1981. — xii,428p ; 24cm
Bibliography: p399-405. — Includes index
ISBN 0-297-77785-8 (cased) : £18.50
ISBN 0-297-77786-6 (pbk) : £8.95 B81-04741

305.5′6 — Great Britain. Working classes. Attitudes, *1800-1900 — Sources of data: Working classes. Autobiographies*

Vincent, David. Bread, knowledge and freedom : a study of nineteenth-century working class autobiography / David Vincent. — London : Europa, 1981. — 221p ; 25cm
Bibliography: p204-214. - Includes index
ISBN 0-905118-55-3 : £18.00 B81-18786

305.5′6 — Humberside. East Yorkshire *(District).* **Wolds. Itinerants: Wold rangers,** *to 1977*

Antrim, Angela. The Yorkshire Wold Rangers / by Angela Antrim. — Driffield (16 Howl La., Hutton, Driffield YO25 9QA) : Hutton Press, 1981. — 119p : ill,1map,ports ; 21cm
ISBN 0-907033-06-7 (pbk) : Unpriced
B81-37608

305.5′6 — India *(Republic).* **Orissa** *(State).* **Untouchables. Cultural processes,** *ca 1930-ca 1970 — Case studies*

Muli. Untouchable : an Indian life history / James M. Freeman. — London : Allen & Unwin, 1979. — vii,421p : ill ; 24cm
Autobiography of Muli as told to James M. Freeman. — Bibliography: p408-411. - Includes index
ISBN 0-04-920060-7 : £19.50 : CIP rev.
B79-34687

305.5′6 — India *(Republic).* **Varanasi. Women road sweepers. Socioeconomic status**

Searle-Chatterjee, Mary. Reversible sex roles : the special case of Benares sweepers / by Mary Searle-Chatterjee. — Oxford : Pergamon, 1981. — 112p,[14]p of plates : ill,maps,1plan ; 26cm. — (Women in development ; v.2)
Bibliography: p108-112
ISBN 0-08-025780-1 : £11.95 : CIP rev.
B80-05223

305.5′6 — Ireland (Republic). Poverty

Joyce, L.. Irish national report on poverty and policies to combat poverty. — Dublin (59 Lansdowne Road, Dublin 4) : Institute of Public Administration, Sept.1981. — 2v.[300]p
ISBN 0-906980-04-6 (pbk) : £14.00 : CIP entry
B81-30276

305.5′6 — Italy. Florence. Working classes, *1421-1737*

Cohn, Samuel Kline. The laboring classes in Renaissance Florence / Samuel Kline Cohn, Jr. — New York ; London : Academic Press, c1980. — xii,296p : ill ; 25cm. — (Studies in social discontinuity)
Bibliography: p281-289. — Includes index
ISBN 0-12-179180-7 : £16.60 B81-17422

305.5′6 — London. Destitute homeless persons — *Personal observations*

Wilkinson, Tony. Down and out / Tony Wilkinson. — London : Quartet, 1981. — 188p,[8]p of plates : ill ; 20cm
ISBN 0-7043-3366-x (pbk) : £2.50 B81-09329

305.5′6 — Mexico. Morelos *(State).* **Peasants. Social conditions,** *to 1980*

Warman, Arturo. "We come to object" : the peasants of Morelos and the national state / Arturo Warman ; translated by Stephen K. Ault. — Baltimore ; London : Johns Hopkins University Press, c1980. — viii,319p : maps ; 24cm. — (Johns Hopkins studies in Atlantic history and culture)
Translation of: Y venimos a contradecir. — Bibliography: p315-319
ISBN 0-8018-2170-3 : £12.00 B81-21093

305.5′6 — Migrant personnel. Social conditions

Living in two cultures. — Farnborough : Gower, Aug.1981. — [344]p
ISBN 0-566-00459-3 : £15.00 : CIP entry
B81-15907

305.5′6 — Morocco. Rif region. Peasants. Social conditions, *1870-1970*

Seddon, David. Moroccan peasants : a century of change in the eastern Rif 1870-1970 / David Seddon. — Folkestone : Dawson, 1981. — xvii,337p : maps ; 23cm
Includes index
ISBN 0-7129-0930-3 : Unpriced : CIP rev.
B80-18605

305.5′6 — Peasants, *to 1979.* **Socioeconomic aspects** — *Festschriften*

Peasants in history : essays in honour of Daniel Thorner / edited by E.J. Hobsbawm ... [et al.]. — Calcutta ; Oxford : Published for Sameeksha Trust by Oxford University Press, 1980. — xiii,319p,[1]p leaf of plates : 2ill,1port ; 23cm
Bibliography: p307-312. - Includes index
ISBN 0-19-561215-9 : £7.95 B81-14280

305.5′6 — Poverty. Political aspects

MacGregor, Susanne. The politics of poverty. — London : Longman, Nov.1981. — [176]p. — (Politics today)
ISBN 0-582-29524-6 (pbk) : £2.95 : CIP entry
B81-30184

305.5′6 — Scotland. Destitute homeless persons — *Personal observations*

McKay, Elizabeth. A discarded brat / Elizabeth McKay. — Inverness (Diriebught Rd., Inverness) : Highland Printers, 1980, c1979 (1981 printing). — 132p ; 19cm
£1.85 (pbk) B81-19720

305.5′6 — Scotland. Poor persons. Health — *Sociological perspectives*

Hubley, John, *1948-*. Poverty and health in Scotland : a review / John Hubley. — Paisley (High St., Paisley PA1 2BE) : Local Government Research Unit, Paisley College of Technology, 1980. — 31p ; 30cm. — (Working paper / Paisley College of Technology Local Government Research Unit ; no.10)
£1.00 (spiral) B81-04090

305.5′6 — Soviet Union. Personnel. Social conditions

The **Soviet** worker : illusions and realities / edited by Leonard Schapiro and Joseph Godson. — London : Macmillan, 1981. — xii,291p ; 23cm
Includes index
ISBN 0-333-28846-7 : £15.00 B81-24029

305.5′6 — United States. Southern states. Free negroes. Social conditions, *1775-1860*

Berlin, Ira. Slaves without masters : the free Negro in the antebellum South / Ira Berlin. — Oxford : Oxford University Press, 1981, c1974. — xxi,423p ; 21cm
Originally published: New York : Pantheon, 1974. — Includes index
ISBN 0-19-502905-4 (pbk) : £4.50 B81-36073

305.5′6 — United States. Southern states. Negro slaves. Social conditions, *1820-1860 — Readings from contemporary sources*

Advice among masters : the ideal in slave management in the Old South / edited by James O. Breeden. — Westport, Conn. ; London : Greenwood Press, 1980. — xxvi,350p : 1plan ; 22cm. — (Contributions in Afro-American and African studies, ISSN 0069-9624 ; no.51)
Bibliography: p339-343. - Includes index
ISBN 0-313-20658-9 : Unpriced B81-04155

305.5′6 — United States. Southern states. Working classes. Social conditions, *1800-1899*

The **Southern** common people : studies in nineteenth-century social history / edited by Edward Magdol and Jon L. Wakelyn. — Westport ; London : Greenwood Press, 1980. — xii,386p ; 25cm. — (Contributions in American history ; no.86)
Includes bibliographies and index
ISBN 0-313-21403-4 : Unpriced B81-05196

305.5′6′0941 — Great Britain. Working classes. Skilled personnel, *ca 1850-1914*

Gray, Robert, *19---*. The aristocracy of labour in nineteenth-century Britain, c.1850-1900 / prepared for the Economic History Society by Robert Gray. — London : Macmillan, 1981. — 79p ; 22cm. — (Studies in economic and social history)
Bibliography: p69-96. — Includes index
ISBN 0-333-25330-2 (pbk) : £2.40 B81-27885

305.6 — Cork *(County).* **Protestants. Social conditions,** *1812-1844*

D′Alton, Ian. Protestant society and politics in Cork 1812-1844 / Ian d′Alton. — [Cork] : Cork University Press, 1980. — xiv,264p : ill,maps,geneal.tables ; 22cm
Bibliography: p237-246. — Includes index
ISBN 0-902561-17-0 : Unpriced B81-40063

305.6′971′051 — China. Muslims. Social conditions, *to ca 1880*

Israeli, Raphael. Muslims in China : a study in cultural confrontation / Raphael Israeli ; preface by C.E. Bosworth. — London : Curzon, 1980, c1978. — x,272p : 1ill ; 23cm. — (Scandinavian Institute of Asian Studies monograph series, ISSN 0069-1712 ; no.29)
Bibliography: p251-265. - Includes index
ISBN 0-7007-0100-1 (pbk) : £5.50 : CIP rev.
B80-18606

305.6'996 — England. Rastafarians — *Sociological perspectives*
Cashmore, Ernest. Rastaman : the Rastafarian movement in England / Ernest Cashmore. — London : Allen & Unwin, 1979. — xi,263p ; 23cm
Bibliography: p249-257. — Includes index
ISBN 0-04-301108-x (cased) : £10.00 : CIP rev.
ISBN 0-04-301116-0 (pbk) : £3.95 B79-30523

305.8 — Ethnic groups. Social interactions
Van den Berghe, Pierre L.. The ethnic phenomenon / Pierre L. van den Berghe. — New York ; London : Elsevier, c1981. — xiv,301p : ill ; 24cm
Bibliography: p263-288. — Includes index
ISBN 0-444-01550-7 : Unpriced B81-28924

305.8'005 — Race - *Serials*
Folk and race : illustrated quarterly of racial awareness. — No.1 (Summer 1980)-. — London (BCM-Thule, WC1V 6XX) : [s.n.], 1980-. — v. : ill ; 21cm
£2.50 per year B81-06454

305.8'006'041 — Great Britain. Race relations. Organisations — *Directories*
Who's doing what : a directory of projects & groups involved in race relations / [Commission for Racial Equality]. — 2nd ed. — London : The Commission, 1980. — 54p ; 30cm
Previous ed.: 1979
£1.00 (pbk) B81-09881

305.8'006'04215 — London. East End. Race relations. Organisations: East London Workers Against Racism
Our flag stays red / East London Workers Against Racism. — London : Box 22, 136 Kingsland High St., E.8 : ELWAR. — [16]p : ill,facsims ; 22cm. — (Revolutionary Communist pamphlets, ISSN 0141-8874 ; no.9)
Cover title
£0.30 (pbk) B81-21046

305.8'006'042496 — West Midlands *(Metropolitan County).* **Birmingham. Race relations. Organisations: AFFOR** — *Serials*
AFFOR news. — No.1 (Spring 1978)-. — Birmingham (1 Finch Rd, Lozells, Birmingham B19) : AFFOR, 1978-. — v. : ill,facsims ; 31cm
Irregular. — Description based on: Spring 1981
ISSN 0261-6041 = AFFOR news : Unpriced B81-33291

305.8'0072 — Interethnic relations. Cross-cultural research. Methodology
Schermerhorn, R. A.. Comparative ethnic relations : a framework for theory and research / R.A. Schermerhorn. — Phoenix ed. / with a new preface. — Chicago ; London : University of Chicago Press, 1978. — xxvi,325p : ill ; 22cm
Previous ed.: 1970. — Bibliography: p302-315. - Includes index
ISBN 0-226-73757-8 (pbk) : £3.50 B81-13668

305.8'009182'1 — Caribbean region. Race relations, *to 1980 — Encyclopaedias*
Levine, Robert M.. Race and ethnic relations in Latin America and the Caribbean : an historical dictionary and bibliography / by Robert M. Levine. — Metuchen ; London : Scarecrow, 1980. — viii,252p ; 23cm
Includes index
ISBN 0-8108-1324-6 : £9.45
Primary classification 305.8'0098 B81-05017

305.8'0092'4 — Germany. Racism. Chamberlain, Houston Stewart — *Biographies*
Field, Geoffrey G.. Evangelist of race : the Germanic vision of Houston Stewart Chamberlain / Geoffrey G. Field. — New York ; Guildford : Columbia University Press, 1981. — x,565p : ill,ports ; 24cm
Bibliography: p519-543. - Includes index
ISBN 0-231-04860-2 : £14.45 B81-19366

305.8'0092'4 — Race. Attitudes of Roosevelt, Theodore
Dyer, Thomas G.. Theodore Roosevelt and the idea of race / Thomas G. Dyer. — Baton Rouge ; London : Louisiana State University Press, c1980. — xiii,182p ; 24cm
Bibliography: p171-176. — Includes index
ISBN 0-8071-0658-5 : £9.00 B81-02308

305.8'0094 — Western Europe. Ethnic minorities. Social conditions — *Anthropological perspectives — Conference proceedings*
'Nation' and 'State' in Europe : anthropological perspectives / edited by R.D. Grillo. — London : Academic Press, 1980. — x,201p : ill ; 24cm
Conference papers. — Includes bibliographies and index
ISBN 0-12-303060-9 : £9.80 : CIP rev.
Also classified at 306'.2 B80-22936

305.8'00941 — Great Britain. Coloured persons. Social conditions
Britain's black population / the Runnymede Trust and the Radical Statistics Race Group. — London : Heinemann Educational, 1980. — xiii,160p : ill ; 23cm
Bibliography: p142-153. — Includes index
ISBN 0-435-82781-2 (cased) : £13.70 : CIP rev.
ISBN 0-435-82782-0 (pbk) : Unpriced B80-20254

305.8'00941 — Great Britain. Race relations
Chase, Louis A.. Let the little flowers bloom / Louis A. Chase. — London : Methodist Church Division of Education and Youth, 1980. — 28p ; 21cm. — (MAYC King George VI memorial lectures ; 1980)
ISBN 0-7192-0143-8 (pbk) : £0.75 B81-20882

Husband, Charles. 'Race in Britain'. — London : Hutchinson Education, Feb.1982. — [320]p
ISBN 0-09-146911-2 (pbk) : £6.95 : CIP entry B81-35904

305.8'00941 — Great Britain. Race relations, *1953-1980*
Kapo, Remi. A savage culture. — London : Quartet, Sept.1981. — 1v.
ISBN 0-7043-2302-8 (pbk) : £2.95 : CIP entry B81-28464

305.8'00941 — Great Britain. Racial discrimination — *Inquiry reports*
Great Britain. *Parliament. House of Commons. Home Affairs Committee.* Fifth report from the Home Affairs Committee, session 1980-81 : racial disadvantage. — London : H.M.S.O., [1981]
Vol.1: Report with minutes of proceedings. — cxviip ; 25cm. — (HC ; 424-I)
ISBN 0-10-008481-8 (pbk) : £5.85 B81-38933

Great Britain. *Parliament. House of Commons. Home Affairs Committee.* Fifth report from the Home Affairs Committee, session 1980-81 : racial disadvantage. — London : H.M.S.O., [1981]
Vol.2: Evidence. — vi,621p : 3ill ; 25cm. — (HC ; 424-II)
ISBN 0-10-008241-6 (pbk) : £15.00 B81-38934

Great Britain. *Parliament. House of Commons. Home Affairs Committee.* Fifth report from the Home Affairs Committee, session 1980-81 : racial disadvantage. — London : H.M.S.O., [1981]
Vol.3: Evidence. — vi,1118p : ill,form ; 25cm. — (HC ; 424-III)
ISBN 0-10-008251-3 (pbk) : £15.00 B81-38935

Great Britain. *Parliament. House of Commons. Home Affairs Committee.* Fifth report from the Home Affairs Committee, session 1980-81 : racial disadvantage. — London : H.M.S.O., [1981]
Vol.4: Appendices. — iv,172p ; 25cm. — (HC ; 424-iv)
ISBN 0-10-008261-0 (corrected : pbk) : £7.00 B81-40716

305.8'009421'84 — London. Ealing *(London Borough).* **Southall. Race relations. Implications of unemployment**
Cameron, Jeremy. Unemployment in Southall : a report / Jeremy Cameron. — Southall (46 High St., Southall, Middx. UB1 3DB) : Published for National Association for Asian Youth by Scope Communication, [1981]. — 37p ; 30cm
ISBN 0-9505709-8-2 (unbound) : Unpriced B81-18314

305.8'009424'96 — West Midlands *(Metropolitan County).* **Birmingham. Handsworth. Race relations,** *1974-1978*
Ratcliffe, Peter. Racism and reaction : a profile of Handsworth / Peter Ratcliffe. — London : Routledge & Kegan Paul, 1981. — xvi,388p : ill ; 23cm. — (International library of sociology)
Bibliography: p373. — Includes index
ISBN 0-7100-0696-9 : £12.50 : CIP rev. B81-12812

305.8'009428'21 — South Yorkshire *(Metropolitan County).* **Sheffield. Ethnic minorities. Social conditions**
Mackillop, Jane. Ethnic minorities in Sheffield / Jane Mackillop [for the] Sheffield Metropolitan District Education Committee. — Sheffield (P.O. Box 67, Leopold St., Sheffield 1) : City of Sheffield Adult Education Department, c1981. — 85p ; 30cm
Cover title. — Bibliography: p14
ISBN 0-900660-65-1 (pbk) : Unpriced B81-29135

305.8'00947 — Eastern Europe. Ethnic groups — *Conference proceedings*
Ethnic diversity and conflict in Eastern Europe / Peter F. Sugar, editor. — Santa Barbara ; Oxford : ABC-Clio, c1980. — xii,553p ; 24cm. — (The Joint Committee on Eastern Europe publication series ; no.8)
Conference papers. — Includes index
ISBN 0-87436-297-0 : £12.25 B81-15095

305.8'009494 — Switzerland. Ethnic groups. Social interactions
Schmid, Carol L.. Conflict and consensus in Switzerland / Carol L. Schmid. — Berkeley ; London : University of California Press, c1981. — x,198p : ill,maps,facsims ; 25cm
Bibliography: p183-193. — Includes index
ISBN 0-520-04079-1 : £15.00 B81-39836

305.8'00968 — South Africa. Race relations, *1929-1979*
[Conflict and progress]. Race relations in South Africa, 1929-1979 / edited by Ellen Hellmann and Henry Lever. — London : Macmillan, 1980, c1979. — x,278p : ill ; 23cm
Originally published: Johannesburg : Macmillan South Africa, 1979. — Includes index
ISBN 0-333-29483-1 : £12.00 B81-01641

305.8'00968 — South Africa. Racial discrimination, *1950-1980*
Race discrimination in South Africa : a review / edited by Sheila T. van der Horst ; assistant editor Jane Reid. — Cape Town : David Philip ; London : Collings in association with the Centre for Inter-group Studies, Cape Town, 1981. — xvi,247p : 3maps ; 22cm
Includes index
ISBN 0-908396-39-2 (pbk) : £6.50 B81-29356

305.8'00968 — South Africa. Sports. Racial aspects
Woods, Donald. Black and white / Donald Woods ; with a foreword by Conor Cruise O'Brien. — Dublin (Knocksedan House, Swords, Co. Dublin) : Ward River Press, 1981. — 142p ; 18cm
ISBN 0-907085-12-1 (pbk) : £2.75 B81-19459

305.8'00973 — United States. Ethnic minorities — *Encyclopaedias*
Harvard encyclopedia of American ethnic groups / Stephen Thernstrom, editor ; Ann Orlov, managing editor ; Oscar Handlin, consulting editor. — Cambridge, Mass. ; London : Belknap Press of Harvard University Press, 1980. — xxv,1076p : maps ; 29cm
Includes bibliographies
ISBN 0-674-37512-2 : £30.00 B81-05199

305.8'00973 — United States. European immigrants. Social conditions, *1880-ca 1950 compared with* **social conditions of American negroes,** *1880-ca 1950*
Lieberson, Stanley. A piece of the pie : blacks and white immigrants since 1880 / Stanley Lieberson. — Berkeley ; London : University of California Press, c1980. — xiii,419p : ill ; 24cm
Folded sheet in pocket. — Bibliography: p395-406. — Includes index
ISBN 0-520-04123-2 : £20.75
Also classified at 305.8'96073 B81-27514

305.8'00973 — United States. Racial discrimination. Politico-economic aspects

Reich, Michael. Racial inequality : a political-economic analysis / Michael Reich. — Princeton ; Guildford : Princeton University Press, c1981. — xii,345p : ill ; 23cm
Bibliography: p315-339. — Includes index
ISBN 0-691-04227-6 : £12.50
ISBN 0-691-00365-3 (pbk) : £3.90 B81-24527

305.8'00973 — United States. Racism, *1776-1900*. Socioeconomic aspects

Takaki, Ronald T.. Iron cages : race and culture in nineteenth-century America / Ronald T. Takaki. — London : Athlone, 1980, c1979. — xviii,361p : ill ; 24cm
Originally published: New York : Knopf, 1979. — Bibliography: p333-349. - Includes index
ISBN 0-485-11213-2 : £12.50 B81-07276

305.8'0098 — Latin America. Race relations, *to 1980 — Encyclopaedias*

Levine, Robert M.. Race and ethnic relations in Latin America and the Caribbean : an historical dictionary and bibliography / by Robert M. Levine. — Metuchen ; London : Scarecrow, 1980. — viii,252p ; 23cm
Includes index
ISBN 0-8108-1324-6 : £9.45
Also classified at 305.8'009182'1 B81-05017

305.8'00994 — Australia. Ethnic minorities

Martin, Jean. The ethnic dimension. — London : Allen and Unwin, Jan.1982. — [185]p. — (Studies in society ; 9)
ISBN 0-86861-235-9 : £12.00 : CIP entry B81-33896

305.8'3932'0493 — Belgium. Flemings. Relations with Walloons, *to 1979*

Irving, R. E. M.. The Flemings and Walloons of Belgium / by R.E.M. Irving. — London (36 Craven St., WC2N 5NG) : Minority Rights Group, 1980. — 16p : 1ill,2maps ; 30cm. — (Report / Minority Rights Group, ISSN 0305-6252 ; no.46)
£0.75 (pbk) B81-05349

305.8'68'073 — United States. Spanish Americans. Demographic aspects

Jaffe, A. J.. The changing demography of Spanish Americans / A.J. Jaffe, ; with a foreword by Joseph P. Fitzpatrick. — New York ; London : Academic Press, c1980. — xiii,426p : ill,maps ; 24cm. — (Studies in population)
Bibliography: p327-333. — Includes index
ISBN 0-12-379580-x : £17.40 B81-17419

305.8'91412'0489 — Denmark. Pakistani immigrants. Children. Social adjustment

Siddiqi, Najma. The alien : the Pakistani child in Denmark / Najma Siddiqi, Farooq-i-Azam. — London : MIND, 1980, c1977. — 64p ; 21cm
Originally published: Odense : K. Jensen, 1977. — Bibliography: p63
ISBN 0-900557-41-9 (pbk) : £1.50 B81-29214

305.8'9147'0421 — London. Patidar immigrant communities

Tambs-Lyche, Harald. London Patidars : a case study in urban ethnicity / Harald Tambs-Lyche. — London : Routledge & Kegan Paul, 1980. — xiv,151p : ill ; 23cm. — (International library of sociology)
Bibliography: p144-148. - Includes index
ISBN 0-7100-8471-4 : £12.50 : CIP rev. B80-11754

305.8'91497'041 — Great Britain. Urban regions. Social minorities. Social structure — *Study examples: Gypsies*

Sibley, David. Outsiders in urban societies / David Sibley. — Oxford : Basil Blackwell, 1981. — x,212p : ill,maps ; 24cm
Bibliography: p200-207. — Includes index
ISBN 0-631-10731-2 (cased) : £12.50 : CIP rev. B81-14875

305.8'9159 — Pakistan. Swat. Pathans — *Anthropological perspectives*

Barth, Fredrik. Features of person and society in Swat : collected essays on Pathans. — London : Routledge & Kegan Paul, 1981. — 190,14p : ill,maps ; 23cm. — (Selected essays of Fredrik Barth ; v.2) (International library of anthropology)
Bibliography: p182-185. - Includes index
ISBN 0-7100-0620-9 : £12.95 B81-10103

305.8'924'043 — Germany. Society. Role of Jews, *1919-1933*

Niewyk, Donald L.. The Jews in Weimar Germany / Donald L. Niewyk. — [Manchester] : Manchester University Press, [1980?]. — viii,229p ; 24cm
Originally published: Baton Rouge : Louisiana State University Press, 1980. — Bibliography: p201-219. — Includes index
ISBN 0-7190-0828-x : £12.50 B81-04664

305.8'924'044 — France. Jews. Social integration, *ca 1855-1907*

Marrus, Michael R.. The politics of assimilation : the French Jewish community at the time of the Dreyfus Affair / by Michael R. Marrus. — Oxford : Clarendon, 1980, c1971. — viii,300p,ivp of plates : ill,ports ; 22cm
Bibliography: p286-289. — Includes index
ISBN 0-19-822591-1 (pbk) : £6.95 : CIP rev. B80-12730

305.8'924'05694 — Israel. Moshavs. Jewish settlers. Social conditions. Political aspects

Mars, Leonard. The village and the state : administration ethnicity and politics in an Israeli co-operative village / Leonard Mars. — Farnborough, Hants. : Gower, c1980. — x,216p : ill ; 23cm
Bibliography: p208-211. — Includes index
ISBN 0-566-00337-6 : £12.50 : CIP rev. B80-09990

305.8'9275694'05695 — Jordan. Palestinian Arab refugees, *1948-1957*

Plascov, Avi. The Palestinian refugees in Jordan 1948-1957 / Avi Plascov. — London : Cass, 1981. — xviii,268p,[8]p of plates : ill,facsims,plans ; 24cm
8 maps (some col.) on folded leaves in pocket. — Bibliography: p229-256. - Includes index
ISBN 0-7146-3120-5 : £28.00 : CIP rev. B80-12731

305.8'943 — Russia *(RSFSR)*. Tuva ASSR. Nomadic pastoral communities — *Anthropological perspectives*

Vaĭnshteĭn, S. I.. Nomads of South Siberia : the pastoral economies of Tuva / Sevyan Vainshtein ; edited and with an introduction by Caroline Humphrey ; translated by Michael Colenso. — Cambridge : Cambridge University Press, 1980. — x,289p : ill,1map ; 24cm. — (Cambridge studies in social anthropology ; 25)
Translation of: Istoricheskaīa etnografiīa tuvintsev. — Bibliography: p258-279. — Includes index
ISBN 0-521-22089-0 : £20.00 B81-07217

305.8'9435'04971 — Yugoslavia. Turkish communities

Bartlett, C. N. O.. The Turkish minority in Yugoslavia / C.N.O. Bartlett. — Bradford (Bradford BD7 1Dp) : Postgraduate School of Yugoslav Studies, University of Bradford, 1980. — 17p ; 30cm. — (Bradford studies on Yugoslavia, ISSN 0143-5043 ; no.3)
£1.00 (pbk) B81-14573

305.8'951'059 — South-east Asia. Chinese, *to 1980*. Sociopolitical aspects

Wang, Gungwu. Community and nation. — London : Allen & Unwin, Jan.1982. — [290]p. — (Southeast Asia publications series / Asian Studies Association of Australia ; no.6)
ISBN 0-86861-347-9 : £15.00 : CIP entry B81-35873

305.8'954'051 — China. Ethnic minorities — *Study examples: Tibetans*

Mullin, Chris. The Tibetans / by Chris Mullin. — London (36 Craven St., WC2N 5NG) : Minority Rights Group, 1981. — 16p : 1ill,2maps ; 30cm. — (Report / Minority Rights Group, ISSN 0305-6252 ; no.49)
Bibliography: p12
£1.20 (pbk) B81-27060

305.8'96 — Negroes. Racial segregation. Measurement. Quantitative methods

Morgan, Barrie S.. The measurement of residential segregation / Barrie S. Morgan. — [London] ([Strand, WC2R 2LS]) : University of London King's College, Department of Geography, 1980. — 26p : ill ; 30cm. — (Occasional paper / University of London King's College Department of Geography, ISSN 0309-2178 ; no.2)
Unpriced (spiral) B81-15678

305.8'96'0728 — Central America. Black Carib communities. Social structure. Effects of migration of Black Carib personnel

Gonzalez, Nancie L. Solien. Black Carib household structure : a study of migration and modernization / Nancie L. Solien Gonzalez. — Seattle ; London : University of Washington Press, c1969 (1980 [printing]). — xxiii,163p,[2] of plates : ill,maps ; 22cm. — (Monograph / American Ethnological Society ; 48)
Bibliography: p143-155. - Includes index
ISBN 0-295-95733-6 (pbk) : £4.50 B81-05441

305.8'96073 — United States. Negroes. Social conditions, *1880-ca 1950 compared with* social conditions of European immigrants, *1880-ca 1950*

Lieberson, Stanley. A piece of the pie : blacks and white immigrants since 1880 / Stanley Lieberson. — Berkeley ; London : University of California Press, c1980. — xiii,419p : ill ; 24cm
Folded sheet in pocket. — Bibliography: p395-406. — Includes index
ISBN 0-520-04123-2 : £20.75
Primary classification 305.8'00973 B81-27514

305.8'96073'074886 — Pennsylvania. Pittsburgh. Belmar. Negroes, *1973-1976 - Anthropological perspectives*

Williams, Melvin D.. On the street where I lived / by Melvin D. Williams. — New York ; London : Holt, Rinehart and Winston, c1981. — x,147p : ill,1map ; 24cm. — (Case studies in cultural anthropology)
Bibliography: p143-147
ISBN 0-03-056132-9 (pbk) : £3.25 B81-11475

305.8'961'06811 — Botswana. Kalahari Desert. G/wi. Cultural processes

Silberbauer, George B.. Hunter and habitat in the central Kalahari Desert / George B. Silberbauer. — Cambridge : Cambridge University Press, 1981. — xx,330p : ill,maps ; 24cm
Bibliography: p305-317. — Includes index
ISBN 0-521-23578-2 (cased) : £22.50
ISBN 0-521-28135-0 (pbk) : £7.50 B81-26192

305.8'963 — Southern Africa. Bantu. Cultural processes

The **Bantu-speaking** peoples of Southern Africa / edited by W.D. Hammond-Tooke. — 2nd ed. — London : Routledge & Kegan Paul, 1974 (1980 [printing]). — xxii,525p,[24]p of plates : ill ; 23cm
Previous ed.: 1937. — Bibliography: p473-510. - Includes index
ISBN 0-7100-0708-6 (cased) : Unpriced
ISBN 0-7100-7748-3 B81-11214

305.8'969729'0424 — England. Midlands. West Indians — *Sociological perspectives*

Pearson, David, *1945-*. Race, class and political activism : a study of West Indians in Britain / David Pearson. — Farnborough, Hants. : Gower, c1981. — vii,207p ; 23cm
Bibliography: p193-201. - Includes index
ISBN 0-566-00353-8 : £15.00 B81-05846

305.8'97 — North American Indians. Social change — *Anthropological perspectives*

Eggan, Fred. The American Indian : perspectives for the study of social change / Fred Eggan. — Cambridge : Cambridge University Press, 1980, c1966. — xi,193p ; 22cm. — (The Lewis Henry Morgan lectures ; 1964)
Originally published: New York : Aldine Publishing, 1966. — Bibliography: p179-190. — Includes index
ISBN 0-521-23752-1 (cased) : £12.50
ISBN 0-521-28210-1 (pbk) : £4.95 B81-23695

305.8′97′078 — Plains Indians. Anthropological perspectives — *Conference proceedings*

Anthropology on the Great Plains / edited by W. Raymond Wood and Margot Liberty. — Lincoln [Neb.] ; London : Unviersity of Nebraska Press, c1980. — vii,306p : ill,maps ; 27cm
Conference papers. — Includes bibliographies and index
ISBN 0-8032-4708-7 : £13.50 B81-11998

305.8′9915 — Australian aborigines. Ecological aspects

Kirk, R. L.. Aboriginal man adapting : the human biology of Australian Aboriginies / R. L. Kirk. — Oxford : Clarendon, 1981. — vii,229p : ill,maps ; 24cm. — ([Research monographs on human population biology])
Maps on lining papers. — Includes index
ISBN 0-19-857532-7 : £20.00 B81-25157

305.8′9992′04479 — France. Sainte-Engrâce. Basques. Cultural processes — *Anthropological perspectives*

Ott, Sandra. The circle of mountains : a Basque shepherding community / Sandra Ott. — Oxford : Clarendon Press, 1981. — xv,238p,[9]p of plates : ill,maps,1plan ; 23cm
Bibliography: p222-226. — Includes index
ISBN 0-19-823199-7 : £17.50 B81-26020

306 — CULTURE AND INSTITUTIONS

306 — Civilization. Sociopolitical aspects

Abdel-Malek, Anouar. Civilisation and social theory / Anouar Abdel-Malek. — London : Macmillan, 1981. — xiv,214p ; 23cm. — (Social dialectics ; v.1)
Translated from the French. — Includes index
ISBN 0-333-23812-5 : Unpriced : CIP rev. B80-20211

306 — Cultural processes

Anthropological realities : readings in the science of culture / edited by Jeanne Guillemin. — New Brunswick ; London : Transaction Books, c1981. — xx,509p ; 23cm. — (Transaction/society texts)
Includes bibliographies
ISBN 0-87855-783-0 (pbk) : £3.00 B81-16451

Keesing, Roger M.. Cultural anthropology : a contemporary perspective / Roger M. Keesing. — 2nd ed. — New York ; London : Holt, Rinehart and Winston, c1981. — xiii,560p : ill ; 25cm
Previous ed.: 1976. — Bibliography: p520-548. — Includes index
ISBN 0-03-046296-7 : £12.00 B81-22994

306 — Culture

Culture, media, language : working papers in cultural studies, 1972-79 / [edited by Stuart Hall et al.]. — London : Hutchinson in association with the Centre for Contemporary Cultural Studies, University of Birmingham, 1980. — 311p ; 25cm
Bibliography: p269-275. Includes index
ISBN 0-09-142070-9 (cased) : £10.95 : CIP rev.
ISBN 0-09-142071-7 (pbk) : £4.95 B80-13212

Popular culture. — London : Croom Helm, Oct.1981. — [320]p
ISBN 0-7099-1909-3 (pbk) : £5.25 : CIP entry B81-25714

Williams, Raymond. Problems in materialism and culture : selected essays / Raymond Williams. — London : Verso, c1980. — viii,277p ; 21cm
Includes index
ISBN 0-86091-028-8 (cased) : £10.00
ISBN 0-86091-729-0 (pbk) : £3.95 B81-02438

306 — Culture — *Anthropological perspectives*

Beyond the myths of culture : essays in cultural materialism / edited by Eric B. Ross. — New York ; London : Academic Press, c1980. — xxxix,422p : ill,maps ; 24cm. — (Studies in anthropology)
Includes bibliographies and index
ISBN 0-12-598180-5 : £17 40 B81-21845

Friedl, John. The human portrait : introduction to cultural anthropology / John Friedl. — [2nd ed.]. — Englewood Cliffs ; London : Prentice-Hall, c1981. — xv,268p : ill(some col.),col.maps,ports ; 24cm
Previous ed.: published as: Cultural anthropology. London : Harpers′ College Press, 1976. — Includes bibliographies and index
ISBN 0-13-445353-0 (pbk) : £9.05 B81-16593

306 — Culture. Origins

Thompson, William Irwin. The time falling bodies take to light : mythology, sexuality, and the origins of culture / William Irwin Thompson. — London : Rider/Hutchinson, c1981. — 280p : ill,plans ; 24cm
Includes index
ISBN 0-09-145241-4 (pbk) : £5.50 : CIP rev. B81-12318

306 — Culture. Political aspects — *Interviews*

Williams, Raymond. Politics and letters : interviews with New Left review / Raymond Williams. — London : Verso, 1981. — 444p ; 21cm
Originally published: London : NLB, 1979. — Includes index
ISBN 0-86091-735-5 : £4.50 : CIP rev. B81-03837

306 — Culture *related to* nature. Sexual aspects

Nature, culture and gender / edited by Carol P. MacCormack and Marilyn Strathern. — Cambridge : Cambridge Unviersity Press, 1980. — ix,227p : ill ; 22cm
Includes bibliographies and index
ISBN 0-521-23491-3 (cased) : £12.00
ISBN 0-521-28001-x (pbk) : £3.95
Also classified at 500 B81-09919

306 — Culture - *Reviews*

Scruton, Roger. The politics of culture and other essays. — Manchester : Carcanet Press, Aug.1981. — [288]p
ISBN 0-85635-362-0 : £7.95 : CIP entry B81-16898

306 — Culture — *Sociological perspectives*

Williams, Raymond. Culture / Raymond Williams. — [London] : Fontana, 1981. — 248p ; 18cm. — (Fontana new sociology)
Bibliography: p235-241. - Includes index
ISBN 0-00-635627-3 (pbk) : £2.50 B81-13048

306 — England. Literacy, *1500-1700*. Social aspects

Cressy, David. Literacy and the social order : reading and writing in Tudor and Stuart England / David Cressy. — Cambridge : Cambridge University Press, 1980. — x,246p : ill,maps ; 24cm
Bibliography: p231-243. — Includes index
ISBN 0-521-22514-0 : £12.50 : CIP rev. B80-25168

306 — Human sociobiology — *Sociological perspectives*

Bock, Kenneth. Human nature and history : a response to sociobiology / Kenneth Bock. — New York ; Guildford : Columbia University Press, 1980. — x,241p ; 22cm
Includes index
ISBN 0-231-05078-x : £10.50 B81-03778

306 — International relations

Change and the study of international relations. — London : Pinter, May 1981. — [225]p
ISBN 0-903804-83-2 : £13.50 : CIP entry B81-10431

306 — Primitive peoples — *Anthropological perspectives*

Pitt Rivers Museum. World on a glass plate : early anthropological photographs from the Pitt Rivers Museum, Oxford / Elizabeth Edwards, Lynne Williamson. — Oxford (Pitt Rivers Museum, Publications Department, Oxford) : Pitt Rivers Museum, c1981. — vi,41p : ill,1map,ports ; 21cm
Bibliography: p40-41
ISBN 0-902793-15-2 (pbk) : Unpriced B81-28297

306 — Social anthropology

Augé, Marc. The anthropological circle. — Cambridge : Cambridge University Press, Jan.1982. — [137]p. — (Cambridge studies in social anthropology)
Translation of: Symbole, fonction, histoire
ISBN 0-521-23236-8 (cased) : £12.50 : CIP entry
ISBN 0-521-28548-8 (pbk) : £4.95 B81-33801

Barth, Fredrik. Process and form in social life. — London : Routledge & Kegan Paul, 1981. — 243,14p : ill ; 23cm. — (Selected essays of Fredrik Barth ; v.1) (International library of anthropology)
Bibliography: p232-238. - Includes index
ISBN 0-7100-0720-5 : £13.95 B81-10102

Ember, Carol R.. Anthropology / Carol R. Ember, Melvin Ember. — 3rd ed. — Englewood Cliffs ; London : Prentice-Hall, c1981. — xxiii,582p : ill(some col.),maps(some col.),ports ; 24cm
Previous ed.: published as Cultural anthropology. 1977. — Bibliography: p539-565. — Includes index
ISBN 0-13-037002-9 : £11.65 B81-21013

Ember, Carol R.. Cultural anthropology / Carol R. Ember, Melvin Ember. — 3rd ed. — Englewood Cliffs ; London : Prentice-Hall, c1981. — xciii,397p : ill(some col.),col.maps,ports ; 24cm
Previous ed.: 1977. — Bibliography: p371-388. — Includes index
ISBN 0-13-195230-7 (pbk) : £9.05 B81-17213

306 — Social institutions. Economic aspects

Schotter, Andrew. The economic theory of social institutions / Andrew Schotter. — Cambridge : Cambridge University Press, 1981. — xiii,177p : ill ; 24cm
Bibliography: p170-173. — Includes index
ISBN 0-521-23044-6 : £15.00 B81-25187

306 — Social organization. Comparison. Methodology

Goodenough, Ward H.. Description and comparison in cultural anthropology / Ward H. Goodenough. — Cambridge : Cambridge University Press, 1980, c1970. — xi,173p ; 22cm. — (The Lewis Henry Morgan Lectures ; 1968)
Originally published: Chicago : Aldine, 1969. — Bibliography: p143-159. — Includes index
ISBN 0-521-23740-8 (cased) : £12.50
ISBN 0-521-28196-2 (pbk) : £4.95 B81-32623

306′.02493 — Social anthropology — *For archaeology*

Orme, Bryony. Anthropology for archaeologists : an introduction / Bryony Orme. — London : Duckworth, 1981. — x,300p : ill,maps,plans ; 23cm
Bibliography: p285-296. - Includes index
ISBN 0-7156-1442-8 (cased) : £22.50 : CIP rev.
ISBN 0-7156-1481-9 (pbk) : £7.95 B80-09090

306′.072 — Social anthropology. Fieldwork. Methodology

Agar, Michael H.. The professional stranger : an informal introduction to ethnography / Michael H. Agar. — New York ; London : Academic Press, c1980. — xi,227p ; 23cm. — (Studies in anthropology)
Bibliography: p205-213. - Includes index
ISBN 0-12-043850-x (pbk) : £7.00 B81-00754

The **Craft** of social anthropology / edited by A.L. Epstein ; introduction by Max Gluckman. — Oxford : Pergamon, c1979. — xxiv,274p,[1] leaf of plates : ill,form,1geneal.table ; 23cm
Originally published: London : Tavistock, 1967. — Bibliography: p149-463. - Includes index
ISBN 0-08-023693-6 : £10.00 : CIP rev. B78-31941

306′.1 — Great Britain. Subcultures. Style, *1960-1980*

York, Peter. Style wars / Peter York. — London : Sidgwick & Jackson, 1980. — 253p,[16]p of plates : ill,ports ; 23cm
ISBN 0-283-98673-5 : £7.95 B81-01540

306′.1′0941 — Great Britain. Informal social institutions

Can I have it in cash? : a study of informal institutions and unorthodox ways of doing things / edited by Stuart Henry. — London : Astragal, 1981. — xii,224p ; 23cm
Bibliography: p199-216. — Includes index
ISBN 0-906525-23-3 : £12.95 B81-17891

306′.1′094225 — East & West Sussex. Alternative society — *Serials*

[Link up *(Old Shoreham)***]**. Link up. — No.1 (Jan.-Mar.1980)-. — [Old Shoreham] ([The Old Schoolhouse, St. Nicholas La., Old Shoreham, W. Sussex BN4 5NH]) : Link Up ; [Upper Beeding] ([Link-Up Mailing List, Little Sele, New Rd, Upper Beeding, W. Sussex]) : [D. Welmans] [distributor], 1980. — v. : ill ; 21cm
Quarterly. — Description based on: No.5 (Jan.-Mar.1981)
ISSN 0261-5029 = Link up (Old Shoreham) : £1.00 per year B81-29079

306′.2 — Asia. Military forces. Personnel. Ethnicity — *Social perspectives*

Ethnicity and the military in Asia / edited by DeWitt C. Ellinwood, Cynthia H. Enloe. — New Brunswick ; London : Transaction, c1981. — 295p ; 24cm
Includes bibliographies
ISBN 0-87855-387-8 : £11.75 B81-12649

306′.2 — Authoritarianism — *Sociological perspectives*

Perlmutter, Amos. Modern authoritarianism. — London : Yale University Press, Nov.1981. — [192]p
ISBN 0-300-02640-4 : £12.25 : CIP entry B81-35025

306′.2 — Belfast. Protestant working classes. Political socialisation, *1868-1920*

Patterson, Henry. Class conflict and sectarianism : the Protestant working class and the Belfast labour movement 1868-1920 / Henry Patterson. — Belfast : Blackstaff, c1980. — xviii,172p ; 22cm. — (An Ulster Polytechnic book)
Bibliography: p160-166. — Includes index
ISBN 0-85640-226-5 : £8.95 : CIP rev. B80-22952

306′.2 — China. Political institutions — *Anthropological perspectives*

Ahern, Emily Martin. Chinese ritual and politics. — Cambridge : Cambridge University Press, Jan.1982. — [142]p. — (Cambridge studies in social anthropology ; 34)
ISBN 0-521-23690-8 : £14.50 : CIP entry B81-34587

306′.2 — Eastern Europe. Public administration. Bureaucracy — *Sociological perspectives*

Hirszowicz, Maria. The bureaucratic Leviathan : a study in the sociology of communism / Maria Hirszowicz. — Oxford : Martin Robertson, 1980. — x,208p ; 23cm
Includes bibliographies and index
ISBN 0-85520-309-9 : £12.50 B81-03032

306′.2 — England & France. Crowds. Political behaviour, *1730-1848*

Rudé, George. The crowd in history : a study of popular disturbances in France and England, 1730-1848 / George Rudé. — Rev. ed. — London : Lawrence and Wishart, 1981. — 279p : ill,maps ; 22cm
Previous ed.: Chichester : Wiley, 1964. — Bibliography: p270-272. — Includes index
ISBN 0-85315-552-6 (pbk) : £4.50 B81-29127

306′.2 — Europe. States. Development, *1550-1650.* **Social aspects** — *Marxist viewpoints*

Kiernan, V. G.. State and society in Europe 1550-1650 / V.G. Kiernan. — Oxford : Blackwell, 1980. — x,309p : maps ; 24cm
Bibliography: p277-295. - Includes index
ISBN 0-631-10681-2 : £12.00 : CIP rev. B80-13722

306′.2 — European countries. Governments — *Sociological perspectives*

Challenge to governance : studies in overload polities / edited by Richard Rose. — Beverly Hills ; London : Sage, c1980. — 238p ; 22cm
Includes bibliographies
ISBN 0-8039-9816-3 (pbk) : £6.25 : CIP rev. B80-04082

306′.2 — Great Britain. Community action — *Sociological perspectives*

Hoggart, Keith. Local decision-making autonomy : a review of conceptual and methodological issues / Keith Hoggart. — [London] : University of London King's College, Dept. of Geography, 1981. — 65p ; 30cm. — (Occasional paper / University of London King's College. Department of Geography, ISSN 0309-2178 ; no.13)
Bibliography: p51-65
Unpriced (spiral) B81-40827

306′.2 — Great Britain. Politics. Attitudes of old persons, *1964-1979*

Abrams, Mark. Political attitudes and ageing in Britain / Mark Abrams, John O'Brien. — Mitcham (60 Pitcairn Rd., Mitcham, Surrey CR4 3LL) : Age Concern England, c1981. — 19p ; 22cm. — (Age Concern Research Unit publications)
ISBN 0-86242-003-2 (pbk) : Unpriced B81-17762

306′.2 — Great Britain. Small communities. Politics. Participation of public — *Study regions: London. Covent Garden*

Hain, Peter. Neighbourhood participation / Peter Hain. — London : Temple Smith, 1980. — 237p : 2ill ; 23cm
Bibliography: p216-232. — Includes index
ISBN 0-85117-197-4 (cased) : £9.95
ISBN 0-85117-198-2 (£4.95) B81-09170

306′.2 — Italy. Venice. Government, *742-1797.* **Ritual aspects**

Muir, Edward. Civil ritual in Renaissance Venice / Edward Muir. — Princeton ; Guildford : Princeton University Press, c1981. — xiv,356p : ill,1map ; 23cm
Bibliography: p310-342. — Includes index
ISBN 0-691-05325-1 : £10.80 B81-33204

306′.2 — Japan. Politics. Role of women — *Sociological perspectives*

Pharr, Susan J.. Political women in Japan : the search for a place in political life / Susan J. Pharr. — Berkeley ; London : University of California Press, c1981. — xiv,239p ; 22cm
Bibliography: p213-233. — Includes index
ISBN 0-520-04071-6 : £15.00 B81-36452

306′.2 — Language. Political aspects

Shapiro, Michael J.. Language and political understanding. — London : Yale University Press, Nov.1981. — [272]p
ISBN 0-300-02590-4 : £18.20 : CIP entry B81-34719

306′.2 — Latin America. Urban regions. Politics. Participation of poor persons — *Study regions: Peru. Lima*

Dietz, Henry A.. Poverty and problem-solving under military rule : the urban poor in Lima, Peru / by Henry A. Dietz. — Austin ; London : University of Texas Press, c1980. — xiv,286p : ill,1map ; 24cm. — (Latin American monographs ; no.51)
Bibliography: p249-277. - Includes index
ISBN 0-292-76460-x : £12.00 B81-03947

306′.2 — Military forces. Reserves & reinforcements — *Sociological perspectives*

Supplementary military forces : reserves, militias, auxiliaries / edited by Louis A. Zurcher and Gwyn Harries-Jenkins. — Beverly Hills ; London : Sage, 1980. — 278p : 1map ; 23cm. — (Sage research progress series on war, revolution, and peacekeeping ; v.8)
Includes bibliographies
ISBN 0-8039-1109-2 (cased) : £12.50
ISBN 0-8039-1110-6 (pbk) : £6.25 B81-05325

306′.2 — Military operations. Strategy — *Sociological perspectives*

Strategy and the social sciences : issues in defence policy / edited by Amos Perlmutter and John Gooch. — London : Cass, c1981. — 102p : ill ; 23cm
ISBN 0-7146-3157-4 : £12.50 B81-26132

306′.2 — North Carolina. Congressional constituencies: Second Congressional District. Politics. Participation of negroes, *1872-1901*

Anderson, Eric. Race and politics in North Carolina 1872-1901 : the Black second / Eric Anderson. — Baton Rouge ; London : Louisiana State University Press, c1981. — xiv,372p ; 24cm
Bibliography: p351-362. — Includes index
ISBN 0-8071-0685-2 (cased) : £18.00
ISBN 0-8071-0784-0 (pbk) : Unpriced B81-25430

306′.2 — Norway. Politics. Participation of public. Equality of opportunity — *Sociological perspectives*

Lafferty, William M.. Participation and democracy in Norway : the Distant democracy revisited / William M. Lafferty. — Oslo : Universitetsforlaget ; London : Global Book [distributor], c1981. — 193p ; 22cm
Bibliography: p186-193
ISBN 82-00-05606-6 (pbk) : £8.55 B81-40150

306′.2 — Political authority — *Philosophical perspectives*

Flathman, Richard E.. The practice of political authority : authority and the authoritative / Richard E. Flathman. — Chicago ; London : University of Chicago Press, 1980. — xii,274p ; 24cm
Includes index
ISBN 0-226-25319-8 : £12.00 B81-00755

Schaar, John H.. Legitimacy in the modern state / John H. Schaar. — New Brunswick ; London : Transaction, c1981. — viii,359p ; 24cm
ISBN 0-87855-337-1 : £9.75 B81-16466

306.2 — Political beliefs. Subjectivity. Analysis. Q methodology

Brown, Steven R.. Political subjectivity : applications of Q methodology in political science / Steven R. Brown ; foreword by William Stephenson. — New Haven ; London : Yale University Press, c1980. — xiv,355p : ill ; 24cm
Bibliography: p335-350. - Includes index
ISBN 0-300-02363-4 (cased) : £22.00 CIP rev.
ISBN 0-300-02579-3 (pbk) : £6.30 B80-21445

306′.2 — Political groups — *Sociological perspectives*

Political clientism, patronage and development. — London : Sage, July 1981. — [320]p. — (Contemporary political sociology ; v.2)
ISBN 0-8039-9794-9 (cased) : £12.50 : CIP entry
ISBN 0-8039-9795-7 (pbk) : £6.25 B81-19169

306′.2 — Political identity. Psychological aspects — *Study regions: South Africa*

Du Preez, Peter. The politics of identity : ideology and the human image / Peter du Preez. — Oxford : Blackwell, 1980. — 178p : ill ; 23cm
Bibliography: p166-112. - Includes index
ISBN 0-631-12331-8 : £9.95 : CIP rev. B80-11321

306′.2 — Political stability

Sanders, David, *1950-*. Patterns of political instability / David Sanders. — London : Macmillan, 1981. — xvii,244p : ill ; 23cm
Includes index
ISBN 0-333-27313-3 : £20.00 B81-40726

306′.2 — Politics. Role of ethnic groups — *Sociological perspectives*

Rothschild, Joseph. Ethnopolitics : a conceptual framework / Joseph Rothschild. — New York ; Guildford : Columbia University Press, 1981. — x,290p ; 22cm
Bibliography: p259-281. — Includes index
ISBN 0-231-05236-7 : £15.80 B81-36250

306′.2 — Scotland. Politics — *Sociological perspectives*

. Capitalism, class and politics in Scotland / [edited by] Ron Parsler. — Farnborough, Hants. : Gower, c1980. — vii,166p ; 23cm
Includes bibliographies
ISBN 0-566-00390-2 : £11.50 : CIP rev. B80-19630

306′.2 — South-western United States. States. Legislatures. Members. Legislative behaviour. Influence of attitudes of electorate

Ingram, Helen M.. A policy approach to political representation : lessons from the Four Corners states / Helen M. Ingram, Nancy K. Laney, John R. McCain. — Baltimore ; London : Published for Resources for the Future by Johns Hopkins University Press, c1980. — xviii,270p : ill,map,forms ; 24cm
Maps on lining papers. — Includes index
ISBN 0-8018-2369-2 : £13.25 B81-05010

306′.2 — Soviet Union. Society. Role of communist ideology *compared with* **role of Christian church in society in United States**

Henry, Maureen. The intoxication of power : an analysis of civil religion in relation to ideology / Maureen Henry. — Dordrecht ; London : Reidel, c1979. — xiii,231p ; 23cm. — (Sovietica ; v.43)
Includes index
ISBN 90-277-1027-9 : Unpriced
Primary classification 261.1′0973 B81-06237

306′.2 — State — *Sociological perspectives*

Elias, Norbert. The civilizing process. — Oxford : Blackwell, June 1981
Translation of: Uber den Prozess der Zivilisation
Vol.2: State formation and civilization. — [352]p
ISBN 0-631-19680-3 : £15.00 : CIP entry B81-10486

306.2 — United States. *Army.* **New personnel. Attitudes** — *Interviews*

Gottlieb, David. Babes in arms : youth in the army / David Gottlieb. — Beverly Hills ; London : Sage, c1980. — 173p ; 23cm
ISBN 0-8039-1499-7 : £9.35 B81-07728

306′.2 — United States. Electorate. Voting behaviour. Influence of mass media — *Sociological perspectives*

MacKuen, Michael Bruce. More than news : media power in public affairs / Michael Bruce MacKuen, Steven Lane Coombs ; foreword by Warren E. Miller. — Beverly Hills ; London : Sage, c1981. — 231p : ill ; 22cm. — (People and communication ; v.12)
Bibliography: p227-230
ISBN 0-8039-1575-6 (cased) : Unpriced
ISBN 0-8039-1576-4 (pbk) : Unpriced B81-29178

306′.2 — United States. Local government. Role of women — *Sociological perspectives*

Women in local politics / edited by Debra W. Stewart. — Metuchen ; London : Scarecrow, 1980. — 232p : ill ; 23cm
Includes index
ISBN 0-8108-1312-2 : £8.75 B81-04102

306′.2 — United States. Young persons. Political beliefs & behaviour. Influence of parents′ political beliefs & behaviour

Jennings, M. Kent. Generations and politics : a panel study of young adults and their parents / M. Kent Jennings and Richard G. Niemi. — Princeton ; Guildford : Princeton University Press, c1981. — xii,427p : ill ; 25cm
Includes index
ISBN 0-691-07626-x (cased) : £14.60
ISBN 0-691-02201-1 (pbk) : £4.10 B81-26320

306′.2 — Western Europe. Governments. Relations with local communities — *Anthropological perspectives — Conference proceedings*

′Nation′ and ′State′ in Europe : anthropological perspectives / edited by R.D. Grillo. — London : Academic Press, 1980. — x,201p : ill ; 24cm
Conference papers. — Includes bibliographies and index
ISBN 0-12-303060-9 : £9.80 : CIP rev.
Primary classification 305.8′0094 B80-22936

306′.2 — Western world. Political socialisation

Political education in flux. — London : Sage Publications, Aug.1981. — [302]p. — (Sage annual review of social and educational change, ISSN 0140-2196 ; v.3)
ISBN 0-8039-9822-8 : £12.50 : CIP entry B81-20612

306′.2 — Women. Political power — *Sociological perspectives*

Stacey, Margaret. Women, power, and politics / Margaret Stacey and Marion Price. — London : Tavistock Publications, 1981. — ix,214p ; 21cm. — (Tavistock women′s studies)
Bibliography: p194-206. — Includes index
ISBN 0-422-76140-0 (cased) : Unpriced
ISBN 0-422-76150-8 (pbk) : Unpriced B81-28990

306′.2′05 — Political behaviour — *Serials*

The **Handbook** of political behavior. — Vol.2. — New York ; London ([88 Middlesex St., E1 7EX]) : Plenum Press, c1981. — xxix,351p
ISBN 0-306-40602-0 : Unpriced B81-35104

The **Handbook** of political behavior. — Vol.1-. — New York ; London ([88 Middlesex St., E1 7EX]) : Plenum Press, 1981-. — v. ; 24cm
Annual
Unpriced B81-35103

306′.2′05 — Politics — *Anthropological perspectives — Serials*

Political anthropology yearbook. — 1-. — New Brunswick, N.J. ; London : Transactions Books, 1980-. — v. ; 24cm
Unpriced B81-10248

306′.2′0942753 — Merseyside *(Metropolitan County).* **Liverpool. Politics,** *1868-1939.* **Social aspects**

Waller, P. J.. Democracy and sectarianism : a political and social history of Liverpool 1868-1939 / P.J. Waller. — [Liverpool] : Liverpool University Press, 1981. — xix,556p : maps ; 24cm
Bibliography: p519-532. — Includes index
ISBN 0-85323-074-9 : £24.50 B81-23067

306′.2′0954 — India *(Republic).* **Politics,** *ca 1800-ca 1980.* **Psychosocial aspects**

Nandy, Ashis. At the edge of psychology : essays in politics and culture / Ashis Nandy. — Delhi ; Oxford : Oxford University Press, 1980. — ix,133p ; 23cm
Includes index
ISBN 0-19-561205-1 : £4.75 B81-14282

306′.2′09595 — Malaysia. Chinese villages. Politics — *Sociological perspectives*

Strauch, Judith. Chinese village politics in the Malaysian state / Judith Strauch. — Cambridge, Mass. ; London : Harvard University Press, 1981. — xi,187p : ill,1map ; 24cm
Bibliography: p175-180. — Includes index
ISBN 0-674-12570-3 : £15.75 B81-39828

306′.3 — Africa. Society. Effects of slave trade

Forced migration. — London : Hutchinson Education, Jan.1982. — [336]p
ISBN 0-09-145900-1 (cased) : £12.00 : CIP entry
ISBN 0-09-145901-x (pbk) : £5.95 B81-34588

306′.3 — Australia. Work — *Sociological perspectives*

The **Future** of work. — London : Allen & Unwin, Jan.1982. — [200]p
ISBN 0-86861-283-9 : £12.00 : CIP entry B81-34076

306′.3 — Business enterprise — *Sociological perspectives*

Weeks, David. Business organization, work and society / David Weeks, Colin Inns. — London : Holt, Rinehart and Winston, c1981. — vi,216p : ill ; 25cm. — (Holt business texts)
Includes bibliographies and index
ISBN 0-03-910321-8 (pbk) : £3.95 : CIP rev.
Also classified at 306′.3 B81-06900

306′.3 — Careers. Personal adjustment of executives

Evans, Paul. Must success cost so much? / Paul Evans, Fernando Bartolomé. — London : Grant McIntyre, 1980. — viii,249p : forms ; 23cm
Bibliography: p241-245. - Includes index
ISBN 0-86216-034-0 : £7.95 : CIP rev. B80-21440

306′.3 — Classical antiquity. Slavery — *Readings from contemporary sources*

Wiedemann, Thomas. Greek and Roman slavery / Thomas Wiedemann. — London : Croom Helm, c1981. — 284p : 2maps ; 22cm
Includes index
ISBN 0-7099-0388-x (cased) : £10.95 : CIP rev.
ISBN 0-7099-0389-8 (pbk) : £6.95 B80-21436

306′.3 — Crafts. Social aspects, *to 1980*

Lucie-Smith, Edward. The story of craft : the craftsman′s role in society / Edward Lucie-Smith. — Oxford : Phaidon, 1981. — 288p : ill(some col.),facsims(some col.),ports ; 26cm
Bibliography: p282-284. — Includes index
ISBN 0-7148-2037-7 : £12.50 B81-39889

306′.3 — Developing countries. Agricultural industries. Farms. Management. Decision making — *Anthropological perspectives*

Agricultural decision making : anthropological contributions to rural development / edited by Peggy F. Barlett. — New York ; London : Academic Press, c1980. — xv,378p : ill ; 24cm. — (Studies in anthropology)
Includes bibliographies and index
ISBN 0-12-078880-2 : £14.60 B81-05326

306′.3 — Employment. Social aspects

Whitehead, A. K.. People and employment. — London : Butterworth, Sept.1981. — [288]p
ISBN 0-408-10691-3 (cased) : £9.00 : CIP entry
ISBN 0-408-10692-1 (pbk) : £4.95 B81-23950

306′.3 — England. Comprehensive schools. Teachers. Careers

Lyons, Geoffrey. Teacher careers and career perceptions : teacher careers and career perceptions in the secondary comprehensive school / Geoffrey Lyons. — Windsor : NFER Nelson, 1981, c1980. — 139p : ill,forms ; 22cm
Includes index
ISBN 0-85633-219-4 (pbk) : £6.95 B81-17771

306′.3 — England. Midlands. Catering establishments. Kitchen porters. Social stigma

Saunders, Conrad. Social stigma of occupations : the lower grade worker in service organisations / Conrad Saunders. — Farnborough, Hants. : Gower, c1981. — x,233p : ill,1map,facsims ; 23cm
Includes index
ISBN 0-566-00334-1 : £11.50 B81-12996

306′.3 — European Community countries. Shiftwork. Social aspects — *Case studies*

The **Effects** of shiftwork on health, social and family life. — [Dublin] ([Loughlinstown House, Shankill, Co. Dublin]) : European Foundation for the Improvement of Living and Working Conditions, [1980]. — 451p in various pagings : ill ; 29cm
Conference papers. — Includes bibliographies
Unpriced (pbk)
Also classified at 613.6′2 B81-09832

306′.3 — European Community countries. Shiftwork. Social aspects — *Case studies — French texts*

Effets du travail posté sur la santé, la vie sociale et la vie familiale / [Fondation européenne pour l′amélioration des conditions de vie et de travail]. — [Shankill] ([Loughlinstown House, Shankill, Co. Dublin]) : [European Foundation for the Improvement of Living and Working Conditions], [1980]. — [507]p : ill ; 30cm
Conference papers. — Includes bibliographies
£5.00 (pbk)
Also classified at 613.6′2 B81-05314

306′.3 — European Community countries. Shiftwork. Social aspects — *Case studies — Italian texts*

Gli **Effetti** del lavoro a turni sulla salute e sulla vita sociale e familiare / [Fondazione europea per il miglioramento delle condizioni di vita e di lavoro]. — [Shankill] ([Loughlinstown House, Shankill, Co. Dublin]) : [European Foundation for the Improvement of Living and Working Conditions], [1980]. — [501]p : ill ; 30cm
Conference papers. — Includes bibliographies
£5.00 (pbk)
Also classified at 613.6′2 B81-05785

306′.3 — European Community countries. Work. Organisation — *Case studies — Italian texts*

Formazione e organizzazione del lavoro / [Fondazione europea per il miglioramento delle condizioni di vita e di lavoro]. — [Shankill] ([Loughlinstown House, Shankill, Co. Dublin]) : [European Foundation for the Improvement of Living and Working Conditions], [1979]. — [580]p : ill ; 30cm
Conference papers. — Includes bibliographies
Unpriced (pbk) B81-05313

306′.3 — European Community countries. Work. Organisational change. Analysis — *Case studies*

The **Analysis** of change in work organisation / [European Foundation for the Improvement of Living and Working Conditions]. — [Shankill] ([Loughlinstown House, Shankill, Co. Dublin]) : [European Foundation for the Improvement of Living and Working Conditions], [1980]. — [630]p : ill ; 30cm
Conference papers. — Includes bibliographies
£5.00 (pbk) B81-05833

306′.3 — European Community countries. Work. Organisational change. Analysis — *Case studies — Danish texts*

Analyse af aendringer inden for arbejdsorganisation / [Europæuske institut til forbedring af leve- of arbejdvilkårene]. — [Shankill] ([Loughlinstown House, Shankill, Co. Dublin]) : [European Foundation for the Improvement of Living and Working Conditions], [1980]. — [472]p : ill ; 30cm
Conference papers. — Includes bibliographies
£5.00 (pbk) B81-05782

306′.3 — European Community countries. Work. Organisational change. Analysis — *Case studies — Dutch texts*

De Analyse van veranderingen in werkorganisatie / [Europese stichting tot verbetering van de levens- en arbeidsomstandigheden]. — [Shankill] ([Loughlinstown House, Shankill, Co. Dublin]) : [European Foundation for the Improvement of Living and Working Conditions], [1980]. — [524]p : ill ; ; 30cm
Conference papers. — Includes bibliographies
£5.00 (pbk) B81-05786

306′.3 — European Community countries. Work. Organisational change. Analysis — *Case studies — French texts*

L′**Analyse** des changements dans l′organisation du travail / [Fondation européenne pour l′amélioration des conditions de vie et de travail]. — [Shankill] ([Loughlinstown House, Shankill, Co. Dublin]) : [European Foundation for the Improvement of Living and Working Conditions], [1980]. — [422]p : ill ; 30cm
Conference papers. — Includes bibliographies
£5.00 (pbk) B81-05834

306′.3 — European Community countries. Work. Organisational change. Analysis — *Case studies — German texts*

Analyse von Änderungen in der Arbeitsorganisation / [Europäische Stiftung zur Verbesserung der Lebens-und Arbeitsbedingungen]. — [Shankill] ([Loughlinstown House, Shankill, Co. Dublin]) : [European Foundation for the Improvement of Living and Working Conditions], [1980]. — [505]p : ill ; 30cm
Conference papers. — Includes bibliographies
£5.00 (pbk) B81-05783

306′.3 — European Community countries. Work. Organisational change. Role of training of personnel — *Case studies — Danish texts*

Uddanelse of arbejdsorganisation / [Europæiske institut fil forbedring af leve- of arbejdsvilkårene]. — [Shankill] ([Loughlinstown House, Shankill, Co. Dublin]) : [European Foundation for the Improvement of Living and Working Conditions], [1979]. — [490]p ; 30cm
Conference papers. — Includes bibliographies
Unpriced (pbk) B81-05784

306′.3 — European Community countries. Work. Organisational change. Role of training of personnel — *Case studies — Dutch texts*

Opleiding en arbeidsorganisatie. — [Dublin] ([Loughlinstown House, Shankill, Co. Dublin]) : Europese stichting tot verbetering van de levens- en arbeidsomstandigheden, 1980. — 543p in various pagings ; 30cm
Conference papers
Unpriced (pbk) B81-11591

306′.3 — European Community countries. Work. Organisational change. Role of training of personnel — *Case studies — German texts*

Berufsbildung und Arbeitsorganisation / [Europäische Stiftung zur Verbesserung der Lebens-und Arbeitsbedingungen]. — [Shankill] ([Loughlinstown House, Shankill, Co. Dublin]) : [European Foundation for the Improvement of Living and Working Conditions], [1979]. — [565]p : ill ; 30cm
Conference papers. — Includes bibliographies
Unpriced (pbk) B81-05780

306′.3 — France. Civil service. Work. Organisational change — *Case studies — French Texts*

Les **Nouvelles** formes d′organisation du travail dans les services publics, France / [Fondation européenne pour l′amélioration des conditions de vie et de travail]. — [Shankill] ([Loughlinstown House, Shankill, Co. Dublin]) : [European Foundation for the Improvement of Living and Working Conditions], [1980]. — 301p ; 30
Conference papers. — Includes bibliographies
£5.00 (pbk) B81-05310

306′.3 — France. Work. Organisational change — *Case studies — French texts*

Expériences de réorganisation du travail dans la communauté européenne, France / [Fondation européenne pour l′amélioration des conditions de vie et de travail]. — [Shankill] ([Loughlinstown House, Shankill, Co. Dublin]) : [European Foundation for the Improvement of Living and Working Conditions], [1980]. — 217p : ill,forms ; 30cm
Conference papers. — Includes bibliographies
£5.00 (pbk) B81-05835

306′.3 — Great Britain. Business elites — *Sociological perspectives*

Fidler, John, *1949-*. The British business elite : its attitudes to class, status and power / John Fidler. — London : Routledge & Kegan Paul, 1981. — xvi,315,14p : ill ; 23cm. — (International library of sociology) (Routledge social science series)
Bibliography: p293-304. — Includes index
ISBN 0-7100-0770-1 : £15.95 : CIP rev.
B81-12814

306′.3 — Great Britain. Civil service. Industrial relations — *Sociological perspectives*

Kelly, Michael P.. White-collar proletariat : the industrial behaviour of British civil servants / Michael P. Kelly. — London : Routledge & Kegan Paul, 1980. — x,198p : ill ; 24cm
Bibliography: p180.194. - Includes index
ISBN 0-7100-0623-3 (pbk) : £6.95 : CIP rev.
B80-34536

306′.3 — Great Britain. Companies. Organisation structure — *Sociological perspectives*

Salaman, Graeme. Class and the corporation / Graeme Salaman. — [London] : Fontana, 1981. — 284p ; 18cm. — (Fontana new sociology)
Bibliography: p265-273. - Includes index
ISBN 0-00-635518-8 (pbk) : £2.50 B81-10330

306′.3 — Great Britain. Industries. Skilled personnel. Skills. Acquisition, *1870-1914*. **Social aspects**

More, Charles. Skill and the English working class, 1870-1914 / Charles More. — London : Croom Helm, c1980. — 252p ; 23cm. — (Croom Helm social history series)
Bibliography: p240-247. — Includes index
ISBN 0-7099-0327-8 : £12.95 : CIP rev.
B80-17581

306′.3 — Great Britain. Industries. Social aspects — *For business studies*

Callender, Patricia. The organisation in its environment : the business and social environment / Patricia Callender, Terence Jones. — Amersham : Hulton Educational, 1981. — 191p : ill,maps ; 24cm
Includes index
ISBN 0-7175-0836-6 (pbk) : £3.00 B81-17679

306′.3 — Great Britain. Professions. Role. Social aspects — *Fabian viewpoints*

Wilding, Paul. Socialism and professionalism / Paul Wilding. — London : Fabian Society, 1981. — 24p ; 22cm. — (Fabian tract, ISSN 0307-7535 ; 473)
Cover title
ISBN 0-7163-0473-2 (pbk) : £0.75 B81-17260

306′.3 — Great Britain. Society. Role of business firms

Donnelly, Graham. The firm in society. — London : Longman, Apr.1981. — [320]p
ISBN 0-582-41592-6 (pbk) : £8.50 : CIP entry
B81-03158

306′.3 — Great Britain. Strikes, *ca 1800-ca 1975* — *Sociological perspectives*

McCord, Norman. Strikes / Norman McCord. — Oxford : Blackwell, 1980. — 136p ; 23cm. — (Comparative studies in social and economic history ; no.2)
Includes index
ISBN 0-631-12622-8 (cased) : £10.00 : CIP rev.
ISBN 0-631-12632-5 (pbk) : £3.95 B80-09992

306.3 — Great Britain. Work patterns. Economic aspects

Bosworth, Derek L.. Work patterns. — Farnborough, Hants. : Gower, May 1981. — [270]p
ISBN 0-566-00310-4 : £12.50 : CIP entry
B81-06603

306′.3 — Great Britain. Work — *Personal observations*

Leighton, Martin. Men at work. — London : Jill Norman, Sept.1981. — [192]p
ISBN 0-906908-38-8 : £6.95 : CIP entry
B81-21579

306′.3 — Great Britain. Work — *Personal observations — For young people*

Coronas, Joe. I wanted to be a mechanic / Joe Coronas ; [illustrations by Peter Burclaff]. — Cambridge (18 Brooklands Ave., Cambridge CB2 2HN) : Basic Skills Unit, [1980]. — 28p : ill ; 21cm
ISBN 0-86082-199-4 (pbk) : Unpriced
B81-05008

306′.3 — Housing — *Sociological perspectives*

Housing and identity : cross-cultural perspectives / edited by James S. Duncan. — London : Croom Helm, c1981. — 250p : ill ; 23cm
Includes index
ISBN 0-7099-0322-7 : £13.95 : CIP rev.
B81-16371

306′.3 — Housing — *Sociological perspectives — Conference proceedings*

The **Consumer** experience of housing : cross-national perspectives / edited by Clare Ungerson and Valerie Karn ; with a foreword by Elizabeth Huttman and Sylvia F. Fava. — Farnborough, Hants, : Gower, c1980. — xxi,209p : ill,maps ; 23cm
Conference papers. — Includes bibliographies
ISBN 0-566-00359-7 : £15.00 : CIP rev.
B80-17566

306′.3 — Industrial sociology

The **Degradation** of work?. — London : Hutchinson, Nov.1981. — [256]p
ISBN 0-09-145400-x : £10.00 : CIP entry
B81-28841

306'.3 — Industrial sociology *continuation*
Hill, Stephen, *1946-*. Competition and control at work : the new industrial sociology / Stephen Hill. — London : Heinemann Educational, 1981. — viii,280p ; 23cm
Bibliography: p262-273. — Includes index
ISBN 0-435-82414-7 (cased) : £12.50 : CIP rev.
ISBN 0-435-82415-5 (pbk) : Unpriced
B81-03692

Hirszowicz, Maria. An introduction to industrial sociology. — Oxford : Martin Robertson, June 1981. — [256]p
ISBN 0-85520-425-7 (cased) : £12.50 : CIP entry
ISBN 0-85520-426-5 (pbk) : £4.95 B81-16861

306'.3 — Industries — *Sociological perspectives*
The **Sociology** of industry / S.R. Parker ... [et al.]. — 4th ed. — London : Allen & Unwin, 1981. — 208p ; 22cm. — (Studies in sociology ; 1)
Previous ed.: 1977. — Includes bibliographies and index
ISBN 0-04-301129-2 (pbk) : Unpriced : CIP rev. B81-12786

306'.3 — Japan. Houses. Cultural aspects
Fawcett, Chris. The new Japanese house : ritual and anti-ritual patterns of dwelling / Chris Fawcett. — London : Granada, 1980. — 192p : ill,plans ; 29cm
Ill on lining papers. — Bibliography: p187-189. - Includes index
ISBN 0-246-11267-0 : £15.00 : CIP rev.
B80-12259

306'.3 — Men. Sexual fantasies — *Collections*
Friday, Nancy. Men in love : men's sexual fantasies : the triumph of love over rage / Nancy Friday. — London : Hutchinson, 1980. — xii,527p ; 24cm
ISBN 0-09-143930-2 : £7.95 : CIP rev.
B80-24047

306'.3 — Mid Wales. Employment. Social aspects
Wenger, G. Clare. Mid-Wales : deprivation or development : a study of patterns of employment in selected communities / by G. Clare Wenger. — Cardiff : University of Wales Press, 1980. — vii,202p : 1,ap ; 25cm. — (Social science monographs ; no.5)
Bibliography: p197-202
ISBN 0-7083-0730-2 (pbk) : Unpriced : CIP rev. B80-02669

306'.3 — North America. Construction industry. Personnel — *Anthropological perspectives*
Applebaum, Herbert A.. Royal blue : the culture of construction workers / by Herbert A. Applebaum. — New York ; London : Holt, Rinehart and Winston, c1981. — xi,144p : ill ; 24cm. — (Case studies in cultural anthropology)
Bibliography: p137-144
ISBN 0-03-057309-2 (pbk) : £3.25 B81-13367

306'.3 — Papua New Guinea. Highlands. Food. Production — *Anthropological perspectives*
Steensberg, Axel. New Guinea gardens : a study of husbandry with parallels in prehistoric Europe / Axel Steensberg. — London : Academic Press, 1980. — xxiii,222p : ill,1map,plans ; 24cm
Bibliography: p210-218. — Includes index
ISBN 0-12-664940-5 : £10.80 : CIP rev.
Also classified at 306'.3 B80-11756

306'.3 — Papua New Guinea. Highlands. Traditional houses. Construction — *Anthropological perspectives*
Steensberg, Axel. New Guinea gardens : a study of husbandry with parallels in prehistoric Europe / Axel Steensberg. — London : Academic Press, 1980. — xxiii,222p : ill,1map,plans ; 24cm
Bibliography: p210-218. — Includes index
ISBN 0-12-664940-5 : £10.80 : CIP rev.
Primary classification 306'.3 B80-11756

306'.3 — Pennsylvania. Coal industries. Slav immigrant personnel, *1740-1902 — Sociological perspectives*
Barendse, Michael A.. Social expectations and perception : the case of the Slavic anthracite workers / Michael A. Barendse. — University Park, [Pa.] ; London : Pennsylvania State University Press, c1981. — 79p : 1map ; 23cm. — (Pennsylvania State University studies ; no.47)
Bibliography: p71-79
ISBN 0-271-00277-8 (pbk) : £2.15 B81-34538

306'.3 — Peru. Migrant personnel — *Sociological perspectives*
Laite, Julian. Industrial development and migrant labour / Julian Laite. — Manchester : Manchester University Press, c1981. — vi,229p : ill,1map ; 24cm. — (Manchester Latin American studies)
Bibliography: p214-220. — Includes index
ISBN 0-7190-0815-8 : £14.50 B81-38948

306'.3 — Property — *Sociological perspectives*
Property and social relations. — London : Heinemann Educational, Feb.1982. — [288]p
ISBN 0-435-82435-x (pbk) : £8.50 : CIP entry
B81-35694

306'.3 — Scotland. Capitalism. Development. Role of Calvinism, *1560-1707 — Sociological perspectives*
Marshall, Gordon. Presbyteries and profits : Calvinism and the development of capitalism in Scotland, 1560-1707 / Gordon Marshall. — Oxford : Clarendon Press, 1980. — x,406p ; 23cm
Bibliography: p373-401. - Includes index
ISBN 0-19-827246-4 : £18.00 : CIP rev.
B80-18174

306'.3 — Scotland. First employment & unemployment. Personal adjustment of school leavers — *Personal observations — Collections*
Tell them from me : Scottish school leavers write about school and life afterwards / edited and introduced by Lesley Gow and Andrew McPherson. — [Aberdeen] : Aberdeen University Press, 1980. — x,125p : ill ; 26cm
Bibliography: p123-125
ISBN 0-08-025738-0 (cased) : Unpriced : CIP rev.
ISBN 0-08-025739-9 (pbk) : Unpriced
Primary classification 373.18'092'2 B80-20489

306'.3 — Slavery — *Serials*
Slavery & abolition : [a journal of comparative studies]. — Vol.1, no.1 (May 1980)-. — London : Frank Cass, 1980-. — v. ; 22cm
Three issues yearly
ISSN 0144-039x = Slavery & abolition : £28.00 per year B81-01993

306'.3 — South Africa. Capitalism, *1890-1933 — Sociological perspectives*
Bozzoli, Belinda. The political nature of a ruling class : capital and ideology in South Affica 1890-1933 / Belinda Bozzoli. — London : Routledge & Kegan Paul, 1981. — xi,384,14p ; 23cm. — (International library of sociology)
Bibliography: p350-361. - Includes index
ISBN 0-7100-0722-1 : £4.00 : CIP rev.
B81-08820

306'.3 — South Africa. Negro migrant personnel — *Anthropological perspectives*
Black villagers in an industrial society : anthropological perspectives on labour migration in South Africa / edited by Philip Mayer. — Cape Town ; Oxford : Oxford University Press, 1980. — xiii,369p ; 23cm
Bibliography: p341-353. — Includes index
ISBN 0-19-570191-7 : £13.95 B81-26818

306'.3 — Southern Iran. Agricultural industries, *1962-1979.* **Social aspects**
Salmanzadeh, Cyrus. Agricultural change and rural society in Southern Iran / Cyrus Salmanzadeh ; introduction by Gwyn Jones ; postscript by Keith McLachlan. — Wisbech (Gallipoli House, The Cottons, Outwell, Wisbech, Cambridge, PE14 8TN) : Middle East & North African Studies Press, 1980. — xvi,275p : ill,maps ; 22cm
Includes index
ISBN 0-906559-02-2 (cased) : Unpriced
ISBN 0-906559-03-0 (pbk) : Unpriced
B81-09950

306'.3 — United States. Stock markets — *Sociological perspectives*
Smith, Charles W.. The mind of the market : a study of stock market philosophies, their uses, and their implications / Charles W. Smith. — London : Croom Helm, c1981. — 218p ; 22cm
Includes index
ISBN 0-7099-2327-9 : £11.95 B81-41022

306'.3 — United States. Working mothers. Psychosocial aspects
Roland, Alan, *1930-*. Career and motherhood : struggles for a new identity / Alan Roland and Barbara Harris with contributors. — New York ; London : Human Sciences Press, 1979. — 212p ; 22cm
Includes index
ISBN 0-87705-372-3 : £17.50 B81-39450

306'.3 — United States. Workplaces. Hazards, *1890-1980 — Sociological perspectives*
Gersuny, Carl. Work hazards and industrial conflict / Carl Gersuny. — Hanover, N.H. ; London : Published for University of Rhode Island by University Press of New England, 1981. — xiii,162p ; 22cm
Includes index
ISBN 0-87451-189-5 : £9.75 B81-39835

306'.3 — West Africa. Economic conditions — *Anthropological perspectives*
Meillassoux, Claude. Maidens, meal and money : capitalism and the domestic community / by Claude Meillassoux. — Cambridge : Cambridge University Press, 1981. — xiv,196p ; 24cm. — (Themes in the social sciences)
Translation of: Femmes, greniers et capitaux. — Bibliography: p162-188. — Includes index
ISBN 0-521-22902-2 (cased) : £14.50
ISBN 0-521-29708-7 (pbk) : £4.95 B81-14659

306'.3 — Western Scotland. Ring-net sea fishing, *to ca 1970.* **Social aspects**
Martin, Angus, *1952-*. The ring-net fisherman / Angus Martin ; with drawings by Will Maclean. — Edinburgh : Donald, c1981. — xi,263p : ill,maps,ports ; 25cm
Includes index
ISBN 0-85976-064-2 : £12.00 B81-09298

306'.3 — Wool fabrics. Harris tweed. Manufacture. Social aspects
Gladstone, Mary. 'The big cloth' : the history and making of Harris Tweed / [editor David B. Pirnie ; text Mary Gladstone ; illustrations James Proudfoot]. — Beauly (Beauly, Inverness-shire IV4 7EH) : Highland Craftpoint, [c1981]. — 36p : ill,1port ; 30x11cm
Text on cover
Unpriced (pbk) B81-40284

306'.3 — Work
Clutterbuck, David. The re-making of work. — London : Grant McIntyre, Nov.1981. — [250]p
ISBN 0-86216-044-8 : £8.95 : CIP entry
B81-31077

306'.3 — Work. Documents on work — *Reviews — Serials*
Work Research Unit book review. — No.1 [(197-)]-. — London (26 King St., SW1Y 6RB) : The Unit, [197-]-. — v. ; 30cm
Irregular. — Description based on: No.16 (June 1980)
ISSN 0260-793x = Work Research Unit book review : Unpriced B81-09182

306'.3 — Work — *Marxist viewpoints*
Hales, Mike — Living thinkwork : where do labour processes come from? / Mike Hales. — London (55 Mount Pleasant, WC1X 0AE) : CSE, 1980. — 185p : ill,facsims ; 21cm
Bibliography: p182-185
ISBN 0-906336-14-7 (cased) : £10.00 : CIP rev.
ISBN 0-906336-15-5 (pbk) : £3.50 B80-08612

306'.3 — Work. Psychosocial aspects
Argyle, Michael. The social psychology of work / Michael Argyle. — Harmondsworth : Penguin, 1974, c1972 ([1981 printing]). — xi,291p : ill ; 20cm. — (A Pelican book)
Originally published: London ; Allen Lane, 1972. — Bibliography: p264-281. — Includes index
ISBN 0-14-021419-4 (pbk) : £2.25 B81-40098

306'.3 — Work *related to sports — Marxist viewpoints*

Rigauer, Bero. Sport and work / Bero Rigauer ; translated by Allen Guttmann. — New York ; Guilford : Columbia Unviversity Press, 1981. — xxxiv,127p 22cm. — (European perspectives)
Translation of: Sport und Arbeit. — Includes index
ISBN 0-231-05200-6 : £9.75
Primary classification 796 B81-29270

306'.3 — Work. Social aspects

Schumacher, E. F.. Good work / E.F. Schumacher. — London : Abacus, 1980, c1979. — xi,147p ; 21cm
Originally published: London : Cape, 1979. — Includes index
ISBN 0-349-13133-3 (pbk) : £1.95 B81-03386

Working life : a social science contribution to work reform / edited by Bertil Gardell and Gunn Johansson. — Chichester : Wiley, c1981. — xiv,347p : ill ; 24cm
Includes bibliographies and index
ISBN 0-471-27801-7 : £16.00 B81-19000

306'.3 — Work — *Sociological perspectives*

The **Politics** of work and occupations / edited by Geoff Esland and Graeme Salaman. — Milton Keynes : Open University Press, 1980. — xiii,408p : ill ; 22cm
Bibliography: p374-395. - Includes index
ISBN 0-335-00264-1 (pbk) : £6.95 : CIP rev. B80-00580

306'.3 — Work - *Sociological perspectives*

Weeks, David. Business organization, work and society / David Weeks, Colin Inns. — London : Holt, Rinehart and Winston, c1981. — vi,216p : ill ; 25cm. — (Holt business texts)
Includes bibliographies and index
ISBN 0-03-910321-8 (pbk) : £3.95 : CIP rev.
Primary classification 306'.3 B81-06900

306'.3 — Working conditions — *Sociological perspectives — Conference proceedings*

International Conference on Changes in the Nature and Quality of Working Life *(1979 : Thessaloniki)*. Changes in working life : proceedings of an International Conference on Changes in the Nature and Quality of Working Life / sponsored by the Human Factors Panel of NATO Scientific Affairs Division ; edited by K.D. Duncan, M.M. Gruneberg, D. Wallis. — Chichester : Wiley, c1980. — xiv,568p : ill ; 24cm
Includes bibliographies and index
ISBN 0-471-27777-0 : Unpriced B81-10038

306'.3'095981 — Indonesia. West Sumatra *(Province)*. **Minangkabaus. Economic conditions** — *Anthropological perspectives — Study regions: Sungai Puar*

Kahn, Joel S.. Minangkabau social formations : Indonesian peasants and the world-economy / Joel S. Kahn. — Cambridge : Cambridge University Press, 1980. — xvi,228p : ill,3maps ; 24cm. — (Cambridge studies in social anthropology ; 30)
Bibliography: p215-221. — Includes index
ISBN 0-521-22993-6 : £15.00 : CIP rev. B81-03153

306'.4 — Alcoholic drinks. Consumption. Social aspects. Discussion groups. Organisation

Alcohol education : community core course : presenters handbook. — [Belfast] ([36/40 Victoria Sq., Belfast, BT1 4QB]) : NICA, 1980. — 74p ; 31cm. — (Decisions and drinking)
Unpriced (pbk) B81-13598

306'.4 — Alternative science — *Sociological perspectives*

Counter-movements in the sciences : the sociology of the alternatives to big science / edited by Helga Nowotny and Hilary Rose. — Dordrecht ; London : Reidel, c1981. — xv,293p ; 23cm. — (Sociology of the sciences ; v.3 - 1979)
ISBN 90-277-0971-8 (cased) : Unpriced
ISBN 90-277-0972-6 (pbk) : Unpriced B81-16599

306'.4 — Arts — *Sociological perspectives*

Wolff, Janet. The social production of art / Janet Wolff. — London : Macmillan, 1981. — 196p ; 23cm. — (Communications and culture)
Bibliography: p166-186. — Includes index
ISBN 0-333-27146-7 (cased) : £12.95
ISBN 0-333-27147-5 (pbk) : Unpriced B81-21765

306'.4 — Association football — *Anthropological perspectives*

Morris, Desmond. The soccer tribe / Desmond Morris. — London : Cape, 1981. — 320p : ill (some col.),col.coats of arms,music,facsims,ports(some col.) ; 29cm
Bibliography: p318. — Includes index
ISBN 0-224-01935-x : £12.50 : CIP rev. B81-20625

306'.4 — Cigarette smoking — *Illustrations — For schools*

Smith, Gillian Crampton. It's my life! / [Gillian Crampton Smith and Sarah Curtis]. — [London] : [Longman], c1981. — 1portfolio(10 parts) : ill ; 30cm + Teachers' notes(folded sheet:[6]p:ill;3cm). — (Longman)
ISBN 0-582-22301-6 : Unpriced B81-09440

306'.4 — Culture. Symbols: Cities

Dougherty, James. The fivesquare city : the city in the religious imagination / James Dougherty. — Notre Dame ; London : University of Notre Dame Press, c1980. — xiii,167p ; 24cm
Includes index
ISBN 0-268-00946-5 : £7.80 B81-01885

306'.4 — Dancing. Social aspects

Hanna, Judith Lynne. To dance is human : a theory of nonverbal communication / by Judith Lynne Hanna. — Austin ; London : University of Texas Press, 1979 (1980 printing). — xvi,327p : ill,ports ; 23cm
Bibliography: p271-312. — Includes index
ISBN 0-292-78042-7 (pbk) : £5.55 B81-40170

306'.4 — England. Buildings of historical importance. Use by public — *Serials*

English heritage monitor / Planning and Research Services, English Tourist Board. — 1978. — London (4, Grosvenor Gardens, SW1W 0DU) : The Board, 1978. — 49p
ISSN 0260-0420 : £3.00
Primary classification 720'.28'8 B81-04872

English heritage monitor / Planning and Research Services, English Tourist Board. — 1980. — London (4 Grosvenor Gardens, SW1W 0DU) : The Board, 1980. — 51p
ISSN 0260-0420 : £3.50
Primary classification 720'.28'8 B81-04871

306'.4 — England. Leisure facilities. Provision by local authorities — *Statistics — Serials*

Leisure and recreation statistics. estimates / Chartered Institute of Public Finance and Accountancy, Statistical Information Service. — 1979-80. — London : The Institute, 1979. — 112p
ISSN 0141-187x : £7.50 B81-12429

Leisure and recreation statistics. Estimates / CIPFA Statistical Information Service. — 1980-81. — London : Chartered Institute of Public Finance and Accountancy, 1980. — 107p
ISSN 0141-187x : £10.00
Also classified at 333.78'0942 B81-06788

306'.4 — England. Leisure facilities. Provision — *Inquiry reports*

Leisure provision and people's needs : being the main report on Stage II of the study of leisure provision and human need undertaken for the Department of the Environment by the Institute of Family and Environmental Research and Dartington Amenity Research Trust / Michael Dower ... [et al.]. — London : H.M.S.O., 1981. — viii,152p : ill,2plans ; 30cm
Bibliography: p149-152. — Includes index
ISBN 0-11-751490-x (pbk) : £9.95 B81-37390

306'.4 — England. Science, *1660-1688*. **Social aspects**

Hunter, Michael. Science and society in Restoration England / Michael Hunter. — Cambridge : Cambridge University Press, 1981. — xii,233p ; 23cm
Includes index
ISBN 0-521-22866-2 (cased) : £18.50 : CIP rev.
ISBN 0-521-29685-4 (pbk) : £5.95 B81-07945

306'.4 — England. Social values. Surveys. Methodology — *Study regions: London & Home Counties*

Phillips, David R.. Values and social problem indicators in contemporary Europe : the British pilot survey / David R. Phillips. — [London] ([162 Highbury Grove, N5 2AD]) : Polytechnic of North London, Department of Applied Social Studies and Sociology, Survey Research Unit, 1981, c1980. — 62p ; 30cm. — (Research report / Polytechnic of North London. Survey Research Unit ; no.11)
Bibliography: p43
ISBN 0-906970-09-1 (pbk) : £2.50 B81-36657

306'.4 — England. Thames River. Leisure activities, *1870-1914*

Burstall, Patricia. The golden age of the Thames / Patricia Burstall. — Newton Abbot : David & Charles, c1981. — 222p,[16]p of plates : ill,1maps,ports ; 23cm
Bibliography: p215-219. — Includes index
ISBN 0-7153-8171-7 : £8.95 : CIP rev. B81-09483

306'.4 — England. Tourist attractions. Visits — *Statistics — Serials*

Sightseeing in ... / prepared by: English Tourist Board Socio-economic Research Unit. — 1978-. — London (4 Grosvenor Gardens, SW1W 0DU) : The Board, 1979-. — v. ; 31cm
Annual
ISSN 0260-1583 = Sightseeing : £2.00 B81-04760

306'.4 — English folk songs: Suffolk folk songs: Blaxhall folk songs & Snape folk songs. Singing — *Sociological perspectives*

Dunn, Ginette. The fellowship of song : popular singing traditions in East Suffolk / Ginette Dunn. — London : Croom Helm, c1980. — 254p,[8]p of plates : ill,1map,music,plans,ports,2geneal.tables ; 23cm. — (Croom Helm social history series)
Bibliography: p245-248. - Includes index
ISBN 0-7099-0044-9 : £12.50 : CIP rev. B79-35694

306'.4 — Europe. Social values. Surveys. Methodology

Phillips, David R.. Values and social problem indicators in contemporary Europe : the British pilot survey / David R. Phillips. — [London] ([62 Highbury Grove, N5 2AD]) : Polytechnic of North London, Department of Applied Social Studies, Survey Research Unit, 1980. — 62p ; 30cm
Bibliography: p43
Unpriced (pbk) B81-12549

306'.4 — France. Science, *1774-1789*. **Social aspects**

Gillispie, Charles Coulston. Science and polity in France at the end of the old regime / Charles Coulston Gillispie. — Princeton ; Guildford : Princeton University Press, c1980. — xii,601p ; 25cm
Bibliography: p553-578. — Includes index
ISBN 0-691-08233-2 : £22.30 B81-18557

306'.4 — France. Sports. Social aspects, *ca 1870-ca 1940*

Holt, Richard, *1948-*. Sport and society in modern France / Richard Holt. — London : Macmillan in association with St Antony's College, Oxford, 1981. — xiii,256p,[8]p of plates : ill,ports ; 23cm. — (St Antony's/Macmillan series)
Bibliography: p237-250. — Includes index
ISBN 0-333-25951-3 : £20.00 B81-31901

306'.4 — Great Britain. Alcoholic drinks. Consumption, *1900-1979*. **Social aspects**

Williams, G. Prys. Drink in Great Britain 1900 to 1979 / by Gwylmor Prys Williams and George Thompson Brake ; indexed by Elizabeth Wallis. — London : Edsall, c1980. — vi,645p : ill ; 26cm
Bibliography: p625-627. — Includes index
ISBN 0-902623-26-5 : £25.00 B81-07064

306'.4 — Great Britain. Cannabis smoking, *1970-1975 — Sociological perspectives*

Auld, John. Marijuana use and social control / John Auld. — London : Academic Press, 1981. — xviii,238p ; 24cm
Includes index
ISBN 0-12-068280-x : £11.80 : CIP rev. B81-11937

306'.4 — Great Britain. Education. Curriculum subjects: Social aspects of science

Ziman, John. Teaching and learning about science and society / John Ziman. — Cambridge : Cambridge University Press, 1980. — ix,181p : ill ; 24cm
Includes index
ISBN 0-521-23221-x : £9.50 B81-04721

306'.4 — Great Britain. Leisure activities — *For schools*

Lines, C. J.. Using our leisure / authors Clifford Lines, Laurie Bolwell. — London : Macdonald Educational, 1981. — 48p : ill(some col.),col.maps,ports(some col.) ; 22cm. — (Town and around. social studies ; band 2)
Cover title
ISBN 0-356-07194-4 (pbk) : Unpriced B81-26338

306'.4 — Great Britain. Prehistoric man. Rituals

Burl, Aubrey. Rites of the gods / Aubrey Burl. — London : Dent, 1981. — xiii,258p,[8]p of plates : ill,maps ; 25cm
Bibliography: p242-243. — Includes index
ISBN 0-460-04313-7 : £12.00 : CIP rev. B80-18599

306'.4 — Great Britain. Single-parent families. Recreations

Give us a break : a survey of leisure and holiday opportunities for lone parents and their children / [One Parent Families]. — London (255 Kentish Town Rd., NW5 2LX) : One Parent Families, 1981. — 10p ; 30cm
Cover title. — Based on a dissertation Lone parents in pursuit of leisure by Anthony Lenton
Unpriced (pbk) B81-32713

306'.4 — Great Britain. Society. Effects of microelectronic devices — *Labour Party (Great Britain) viewpoints*

Microelectronics : a Labour Party discussion document. — [London] : The Party, [1980]. — 49p ; 21cm. — (Socialism in the 80s)
Cover title
ISBN 0-86117-061-x (pbk) : £0.80 B81-02931

306'.4 — Great Britain. Society. Role of information

Butler, David. Britain and the information society. — London : Heyden, July 1981. — [36]p. — (British Computer Society lecture series ; 3)
ISBN 0-85501-699-x (pbk) : CIP entry B81-20468

306'.4 — Great Britain. Tourist attractions

Smith, Celia. New to Britain : a study of some new developments in tourist attractions / Celia Smith. — London ([c/o British Tourist Authority]) : C. Smith, 1980. — 99 leaves ; 30cm
Bibliography : Leaf 95
Unpriced (pbk) B81-37514

306'.4 — Hallucinogenic drugs. Use by primitive peoples — *Anthropological perspectives*

Schultes, Richard Evans. Plants of the gods : origins of halucinogenic use / Richard Evans Schultes, Albert Hofmann. — London : Hutchinson, 1980, c1979. — 191p : ill(some col.),maps,ports ; 27cm
Originally published: New York : McGraw-Hill, 1979. — Bibliography: p186. — Includes index
ISBN 0-09-141600-0 : £12.95 B81-25155

306'.4 — Information science. Social aspects

McGarry, K. J.. The changing context of information. — London : Bingley, Oct.1981. — [190]p
ISBN 0-85157-325-8 : £10.00 : CIP entry B81-27403

306'.4 — Information systems. Social aspects — *Serials*

Information technology and people. — Vol.1, issue 1 (1981)-. — Uxbridge (PO Box 5, Ickenham, Uxbridge, Middlesex UB10 8AF) : CITECH, 1981-. — v. ; 22cm
Monthly
ISSN 0261-1732 = Information technology and people : Unpriced B81-38192

306'.4 — Ireland *(Republic).* **Young Catholics. Leisure activities** — *Serials*

Good news for youth : quarterly youth magazine : a youth educational service-forum for the activities, interests, and the good that young people do. — Vol.1 [(197-)]-. — Maynooth (Maynooth, Co. Kildare, Ireland) : Salesians of Don Bosco, [197-]-. — v. : ill,ports ; 26cm
Quarterly. — Description based on: Vol.3, no.2 (Spring 1981)
Unpriced B81-38184

306'.4 — Italy. Recreation & leisure. Policies of government, *1926-1939*

De Grazia, Victoria. The culture of consent : mass organization of leisure in fascist Italy / Victoria de Grazia. — Cambridge : Cambridge University Press, 1981. — x,310p : ill ; 24cm
Bibliography: p293-300. — Includes index
ISBN 0-521-23705-x : £30.00 B81-38000

306'.4 — Japan. Sakhalin Ainu. Medicine — *Anthropological perspectives*

Ohnuki-Tierney, Emiko. Illness and healing among the Sakhalin Ainu : a symbolic interpretation / Emiko Ohnuki-Tierney. — Cambridge : Cambridge University Press, 1981. — xvi,245p : ill,maps,ports ; 24cm
Bibliography: p226-238. — Includes index
ISBN 0-521-23636-3 : £20.00 B81-38914

306'.4 — Leisure. Social aspects

Neulinger, John. To leisure : an introduction / John Neulinger. — Boston [Mass.] ; London : Allyn and Bacon, c1981. — xvi,266p : 1ill,forms ; 25cm
Bibliography: p239-258. — Includes index
ISBN 0-205-06936-3 : Unpriced B81-00020

306'.4 — Leisure. Social aspects — *Study regions: United States*

Godbey, Geoffrey. Leisure in your life : an exploration / Geoffrey Godbey. — Philadelphia ; London : Saunders College, c1981. — viii,316p : ill ; 24cm
Bibliography: p308-309. — Includes index
ISBN 0-03-057673-3 (pbk) : £8.75 B81-25278

306'.4 — Leisure — *Sociological perspectives*

Jenkins, Clive. The leisure shock. — London : Eyre Methuen, Sept.1981. — [182]p
ISBN 0-413-48200-6 (cased) : £8.95 : CIP entry
ISBN 0-413-48210-3 (pbk) : £4.25 B81-23911

Roberts, Kenneth, *1940-*. Leisure. — 2nd ed. — London : Longman, Dec.1981. — [160]p. — (Aspects of modern sociology : the social structure of modern Britain)
Previous ed.: 1970
ISBN 0-582-29556-4 (pbk) : £3.50 : CIP entry B81-31371

306'.4 — Literacy

Simon, John, *19---*. Paradigms lost : reflections on literacy and its decline / John Simon ; illustrated by Michele Chessare. — London : Chatto & Windus, 1981, c1980. — xviii,222p : ill ; 23cm
Includes index
ISBN 0-7011-2601-9 : £9.95 : CIP rev. B81-27980

306'.4 — Literacy. Political aspects. Theories of Freire, Paulo

Literacy and revolution : the pedagogy of Paulo Freire / edited by Robert Mackie. — London : Pluto, 1980. — ix,166p ; 20cm. — (Pluto indeas in progress)
Bibliography: p160-166
ISBN 0-86104-330-8 (pbk) : £3.50 B81-06500

306'.4 — London. Winter visitors. Attitudes

Omand, Elizabeth. London in winter : some overseas visitors' views : report of joint survey conducted by BTA and GLC, Jan-March 1980 / [author Elizabeth Omand]. — [London] : GLC, 1981. — 47p ; 30cm
Cover title
ISBN 0-7168-1183-9 (spiral) : £5.00 B81-14324

306'.4 — Man. Perception *related to* **language** — *Anthropological perspectives*

Language, culture, and cognition : anthropological perspectives / [edited by] Ronald W. Casson. — New York : Macmillan ; London : Collier Macmillan, c1981. — ix,489p : ill,1map ; 25cm
Includes bibliographies
ISBN 0-02-320050-2 : £14.50 B81-36167

306'.4 — Medicine — *Sociological perspectives*

Medical work : realities and routines / edited by Paul Atkinson and Christian Heath. — Farnborough, Hants. : Gower, c1981. — xiv,187p ; 23cm
ISBN 0-566-00319-8 : £11.50 B81-12993

Social contexts of health, illness, and patient care / Elliot G. Mishler ... [et al.]. — Cambridge : Cambridge University Press, 1981. — x,277p ; 24cm
Bibliography: p254-272. — Includes index
ISBN 0-521-23559-6 (cased) : £20.00
ISBN 0-521-28034-6 (pbk) : £5.95 B81-27903

306'.4 — Mexico. Maya. Beliefs, *to 1980*

Luxton, Richard. Mayan dream walk : literate Shamanism in the Yucatan / Richard Luxton with Pablo Balam. — London : Rider, 1981. — 247p,[4]p of plates : ill,1map,1facsim ; 22cm
Bibliography: p245-246. — Includes index
ISBN 0-09-144821-2 (pbk) : £4.95 : CIP rev. B81-02087

306'.4 — New York *(City).* **SoHo. Artists. Social conditions**

Simpson, Charles R.. SoHo : the artist in the city / Charles R. Simpson. — Chicago ; London : University of Chicago Press, 1981. — ix,276p,[8]p of plates : ill,2maps ; 24cm
Includes index
ISBN 0-226-75937-7 : £12.00 B81-38146

306'.4 — North-west Zambia. Ndembu. Rituals — *Anthropological perspectives*

Turner, Victor. The drums of affliction : a study of religious processes among the Ndembu of Zambia / V.W. Turner. — London : International African Institute in association with Hutchinson University Library for Africa, 1981. — xi,326p,12p of plates : ill,2maps ; 22cm. — (Hutchinson university library for Africa)
Originally published: London : Clarendon Press, 1968. — Bibliography: p313-314. — Includes index
ISBN 0-09-143721-0 (pbk) : £4.95 : CIP rev. B81-12869

306'.4 — North-western France. Bocage regions. Witchcraft — *Anthropological perspectives*

Favret-Saada, Jeanne. Deadly words : witchcraft in the Bocage / Jeanne Favret-Saada ; translated by Catherine Cullen. — Cambridge : Cambridge University Press, 1980. — vii,273p : ill ; 24cm
Translation of: Les mots, la mort, les sorts. — Bibliography: p272-273
ISBN 0-521-22317-2 : £17.50 : CIP rev.
ISBN 0-521-29787-7 (pbk) : £5.95 B80-25091

306'.4 — Nuclear power. Social aspects

Addinall, Eric. Nuclear power in perspective. — London : Kogan Page, Jan.1982. — [240]p
ISBN 0-85038-510-5 : £9.95 : CIP entry B81-40253

Cottrell, *Sir* **Alan.** How safe is nuclear energy? / Sir Alan Cottrell. — London : Heinemann, 1981. — 123p ; 22cm
Includes index
ISBN 0-435-54175-7 (pbk) : £2.50 : CIP rev. B81-10439

306'.4 — Nuclear power. Social aspects — *Conference proceedings — French texts*
Energie nucléaire et société. — Oxford : Pergamon, Oct.1981. — [310]p
Conference papers
ISBN 0-08-027077-8 (pbk) : £12.90 : CIP entry B81-31945

306'.4 — Polywater. Research — *Sociological perspectives*
Franks, Felix. Polywater / Felix Franks. — Cambridge, Mass. ; London : M.I.T. Press, c1981. — ix,208p : ill ; 21cm
Bibliography: p197-203. — Includes index
ISBN 0-262-06073-6 : £10.50 B81-39648

306'.4 — Primitive visual arts — *Anthropological perspectives*
Layton, Robert, *1944-*. The anthropology of art / Robert Layton. — London : Elek : Granada, 1981. — x,227p : ill ; 24cm. — (Elek archaeology and anthropology)
Bibliography: p213-219. — Includes index
ISBN 0-246-11511-4 : £15.00 B81-32721

306'.4 — Science & technology. Social aspects
Wesson, Anthony J.. Technology, philosophy and the person : the Charles Coulson lecture delivered on Monday, October 27, 1980 at the Luton Industrial College / by Anthony J. Wesson. — London : Chester House, 1980. — 24p ; 19cm
Bibliography: inside cover
ISBN 0-7150-0079-9 (pbk) : £1.00 B81-20846

306'.4 — Science & technology. Social aspects — *Marxist viewpoints*
Outlines of a critique of technology / edited by Phil Slater. — London (271 Kentish Town Rd, NW5 2JS) : Ink Links, 1980. — 141p ; 21cm
Includes index
ISBN 0-906133-31-9 : £5.50 : CIP rev. B80-17557

306'.4 — Science & technology. Social aspects — *Serials*
Bulletin of science, technology & society. — Vol.1, no.1/2 (1981)-. — New York ; Oxford : Pergamon, 1981-. — v. : ill ; 23cm
Six issues yearly
ISSN 0270-4676 = Bulletin of science, technology & society : Unpriced B81-34031

306'.4 — Science. Social aspects
Brannigan, Augustine. The social basis of scientific discoveries. — Cambridge : Cambridge University Press, Oct.1981. — [213]p
ISBN 0-521-23695-9 (cased) : £12.50 : CIP entry
ISBN 0-521-28163-6 (pbk) : Unpriced B81-25817

Hepburn, H. R.. Milk and honey : being a collection of numerous and diverse essays, observations, expositions, telling comments etc. etc. that reveals the true nature and import of the oldest and most noble science, to wit, agriculture / by H.R. Hepburn and G. Mitchell ; illustrated by Colin Richards ; and prefaced by more or less irrelevant remarks from G. Baker. — Amsterdam ; Oxford : Elsevier/North-Holland Biomedical Press, 1981. — x,108p : ill ; 21x30cm
Bibliography: p103-104
ISBN 0-444-80272-x (pbk) : Unpriced B81-12542

Ziman, John. Puzzles, problems and enigmas. — Cambridge : Cambridge University Press, Oct.1981. — [371]p
ISBN 0-521-23659-2 : £12.50 : CIP entry B81-31278

306'.4 — Science. Social aspects, *to 1972*
Easlea, Brian. Liberation and the aims of science : an essay on obstacles to the building of a beautiful world. — Edinburgh : Published by Scottish Academic Press for Sussex University Press, 1980. — xiv,370p : ill ; 24cm
Originally published: London : Chatto and Windus for Sussex University Press, 1973. — Includes index
ISBN 0-7073-0282-x (pbk) : £6.75 B81-06665

306'.4 — Science, *to 1979.* **Social aspects —** *Philosophical perspectives*
Lamb, D.. The philosophy of scientific development. — Amersham : Avebury, Dec.1981. — [240]p
ISBN 0-86127-104-1 (cased) : £12.00 : CIP entry
ISBN 0-86127-115-7 (pbk) : £6.95 B81-33882

306'.4 — Science, *to 1979.* **Social aspects —** *Philosophical perspectives — Conference proceedings*
Science, pseudo-science and society / essays by Paul Thagard ... [et al.] ; edited by Marsha P. Hanan, Margaret J. Osler, and Robert G. Weyant. — Waterloo, Ont. : Published for the Calgary Institute for the Humanities by Wilfrid Laurier University Press ; Gerrards Cross : Distributed by Smythe, c1980. — x,303p ; 23cm
Conference papers
ISBN 0-88920-100-5 (pbk) : Unpriced B81-03129

306'.4 — Scotland. Fife Region. Lomond Hills. Recreation sites. Use
Visitor survey of Lomonds Regional Park recreation sites, Summer 1978 / [Fife Regional Council, Regional Planning Department]. — Glenrothes (Fife House, North St., Glenrothes, Fife) : The Council, 1979. — 32p : ill,maps,forms ; 30cm
Unpriced (pbk) B81-12048

306'.4 — Scotland. Petroleum industries. Industrial development. Social aspects
Varwell, Adrian. Way of life : in search of meaning / by Adrian Varwell. — London : Social Science Research Council, c1981. — 153p ; 21cm. — (North Sea Oil Panel occasional paper ; no.5)
Bibliography: p138-153
ISBN 0-86226-046-9 (pbk) : £2.80 B81-19021

306'.4 — Society. Role of ideologies
Walford, George. Ideologies : and their functions : a study in systematic ideology / George Walford. — London (186 Upper St., N1 1RH) : G. Walford, 1979. — 163p ; 23cm
ISBN 0-9505445-1-5 (cased) : £3.95
ISBN 0-9505445-2-3 (pbk) : £1.95 B81-10184

306'.4 — Society. Role of ideology — *Marxist viewpoints*
Abercrombie, Nicholas. The dominant ideology thesis / Nicholas Abercrombie, Stephen Hill, Bryan S. Turner. — London : Allen & Unwin, 1980. — x,212p ; 23cm
Bibliography: p192-203. — Includes index
ISBN 0-04-301117-9 : £12.50 : CIP rev. B80-19040

306'.4 — Sociology. Structuralism
Schwartz, Barry. Vertical classification : a study in structuralism and the sociology of knowledge / Barry Schwartz. — Chicago ; London : University of Chicago Press, 1981. — ix,243p : ill ; 23cm
Bibliography: p219-235. — Includes index
ISBN 0-226-74208-3 (pbk) : £12.60 B81-39824

306'.4 — Sri Lanka. Kataragama. Rituals — *Anthropological perspectives*
Obeyesekere, Gananath. Medusa's hair : an essay on personal symbols and religious experience / Gananath Obeyesekere. — Chicago ; London : University of Chicago Press, c1981. — xiii,217p,[4]p of plates : ill ; 23cm
Bibliography: p207-211. — Includes index
ISBN 0-226-61600-2 : £15.75 B81-38909

306'.4 — Surrey. Recreation centres. Use. Effects of proximity
Atkinson, J.. The impact of neighbouring sports and leisure centres : a study of usage at Guildford, Leatherhead, Woking, Farnborough and Elmbridge sports and leisure centres 1975-77 / by J. Atkinson and M.F. Collins. — London (70 Brompton Rd., SW3 1EX) : Sports Council, c1980. — 12p : ill,2maps,2forms ; 30cm. — (Sports Council research working papers, ISSN 0308-9754 ; 18)
ISBN 0-900979-99-2 (unbound) : £0.80 B81-05995

306'.4 — Technology, *1500-1980.* **Social aspects**
Alvares, Claude Alphonso. Homo faber : technology and culture in India, China and the West from 1500 to the present day / by Claude Alphonso Alvares. — The Hague ; London : Nijhoff, 1980. — xxi,275p ; 24cm
Includes index
ISBN 90-247-2283-7 : Unpriced B81-04481

306'.4 — Technology. Social aspects
Technology and human affairs / edited by Larry Hickman Azizah al-Hibri. — St. Louis ; London : Mosby, 1981. — ix,617p : ill ; 26cm
Bibliography: p609-617
ISBN 0-8016-2164-x (pbk) : £12.00 B81-18966

306'.4 — Technology. Social control
Collingridge, David. The social control of technology / David Collingridge. — Milton Keynes : Open University Press, 1981,, 1980. — 200p : ill ; 22cm
Originally published: New York : St. Martin's Press ; London : Pinter, 1980. — Includes bibliographies and index
ISBN 0-335-10031-7 (pbk) : £4.95 B81-23038

306'.4 — United States. Baseball, *1900-1920* **—** *Sociological perspectives*
Riess, Steven A.. Touching base : professional baseball and American culture in the progressive era / Steven A. Riess. — Westport, Conn. ; London : Greenwood Press, 1980. — xiv,268p : maps ; 22cm. — (Contributions in American studies ; no.48)
Bibliography: p239-255. — Includes index
ISBN 0-313-20671-6 : £14.75 B81-23465

306'.4 — United States. Cars. Driving by persons under the influence of alcoholic drinks — *Sociological perspectives*
Gusfield, Joseph R.. The culture of public problems : drinking-driving and the symbolic order / Joseph R. Gusfield. — Chicago ; London : University of Chicago Press, 1981. — xiv,263p : ill,facsims ; 24cm
Bibliography: p215-256. — Includes index
ISBN 0-226-31093-0 : £12.00 B81-21087

306'.4 — United States. Cinema films — *Sociological perspectives*
Politics, society and cinema in America. — Manchester : Manchester University Press, Oct.1981. — [192]p
ISBN 0-7190-0832-8 : £12.50 : CIP entry B81-27989

306'.4 — United States. Leisure activities — *Sociological perspectives*
Kando, Thomas M.. Leisure and popular culture in transition / Thomas M. Kando. — 2nd ed. — St Louis ; London : Mosby, 1980. — xx,343p : ill,1map,1facsim ; 25cm
Previous ed.: 1975. — Includes bibliographies and index
ISBN 0-8016-2618-8 : £10.50 B81-00021

306'.4 — United States. Sports & games — *Sociological perspectives*
Figler, Stephen K.. Sport and play in American life : a textbook in the sociology of sport / Stephen K. Figler. — Philadelphia ; London : Saunders College Publishing, c1981. — xii,356p : ill,ports ; 25cm
Includes bibliographies and index
ISBN 0-03-057672-5 : £10.95 B81-29298

306'.4 — United States. Witchcraft. Organisations — *Sociological perspectives — Case studies*
Scott, Gini Graham. Cult and countercult : a study of a spiritual growth group and a witchcraft order / Gini Graham Scott. — Westport, Conn. ; London : Greenwood Press, 1980. — xi,213p : ill ; 22cm. — (Contributions in sociology ; no.38)
Bibliography: p203-209. - Includes index
ISBN 0-313-22074-3 : Unpriced
Primary classification 306'.6 B81-07123

306'.4 — Western world. Entertainments. Celebrities. Cults, *1900-1978*
Sinclair, Marianne. Those who died young : cult heroes of the twentieth century / Marianne Sinclair. — London : Plexus, c1979. — 192p : ill,ports ; 31cm
Bibliography: p192
ISBN 0-85965-029-4 (cased) : £6.95 : CIP rev.
ISBN 0-85965-023-5 (pbk) : £3.95 B79-15832

306′.4 — Western world. Mathematics. Social aspects — *Anthropological perspectives*
Wilder, Raymond L.. Mathematics as a cultural system / by Raymond L. Wilder. — Oxford : Pergamon, 1981. — xii,182p : ill ; 22cm. — (Foundations and philosophy of science and technology series)
Bibliography: p167-171. — Includes index
ISBN 0-08-025796-8 : £9.50 : CIP rev. B81-00756

306′.4 — Women. Body. Psychosocial aspects
Kupfermann, Jeannette. The MsTaken body / Jeannette Kupfermann. — London : Granada, 1981, c1979. — 155p ; 20cm. — (A Paladin book)
Originally published: London : Robson, 1979. — Bibliography: p145-148
ISBN 0-586-08377-4 (pbk) : £1.95 B81-24932

306′.4 — Women. Cigarette smoking — *Feminist viewpoints*
Jacobson, Bobbie. The ladykillers : why smoking is a feminist issue / Bobbie Jacobson. — London : Pluto, 1981. — viii,135p ; 20cm. — (The Politics of health)
ISBN 0-86104-341-3 (pbk) : £1.95 B81-27488

306′.6 — France. Normandy. Society. Role of Abbaye du Bec, *1034-1136*
Vaughn, Sally N.. The Abbey of Bec and the Anglo-Norman state, 1034-1136 / Sally N. Vaughn. — Woodbridge : Boydell Press, c1981. — 168p ; 24cm
Includes index
ISBN 0-85115-140-x : £17.50 : CIP rev. B81-06585

306′.6 — Great Britain. Christian church. Public worship. Surveys. Methodology
Church and neighbourhood survey mk III : a do-it-yourself kit. — London (146 Queen Victoria St., EC4V 4BX) : Nationwide Initiative in Evangelism, [1980?]. — [25]p : forms ; 30cm
Cover title
£0.75 (pbk) B81-20975

306′.6 — Great Britain. Secularisation, *to 1979* — *Sociological perspectives*
Gilbert, Alan D.. The making of post-Christian Britain : a history of the secularization of modern society / Alan D. Gilbert. — London : Longman, c1980. — xv,173p ; 22cm
Bibliography: p159-168. — Includes index
ISBN 0-582-48563-0 (cased) : £8.95 : CIP rev.
ISBN 0-582-48564-9 (pbk) : £4.50 B80-25204

306′.6 — India. Hinduism. Worship, *to 1980* — *Anthropological perspectives — Study examples: Srī Pārtasārati Svāmi Temple*
Appadurai, Arjun. Worship and conflict under colonial rule : a South Indian case / Arjun Appadurai. — Cambridge : Cambridge University Press, 1981. — x,266p : ill,maps,1plan ; 23cm. — (Cambridge South Asian studies ; 27)
Bibliography: p247-255. — Includes index
ISBN 0-521-23122-1 : £19.50 B81-37652

306′.6 — Lay apostolate. Control by papacy — *Sociological aspects*
Vaillancourt, Jean-Guy. Papal power : a study of Vatican control over lay Catholic elites / Jean-Guy Vaillancourt. — Berkeley ; London : University of California Press, c1980. — xiv,361p ; 25cm
Bibliography: p325-336. - Includes index
ISBN 0-520-03733-2 : £10.25 B81-04146

306′.6 — Papua New Guinea. East Sepik *District.* **Ilahita. Arapesh. Religious cults** - *Anthropological perspectives*
Tuzin, Donald F.. The voice of the Tambaran : truth and illusion in Ilahita Arapesh religion / Donald F. Tuzin. — Berkeley ; London : University of California Press, c1980. — xxi,355p : ill,maps,1plan ; 24cm
Bibliography: p341-346. — Includes index
ISBN 0-520-03964-5 : £12.00 B81-11249

306′.6 — Religion — *Sociological perspectives*
Wilson, Bryan. Religion in sociological perspective. — Oxford : Oxford University Press, Jan.1982. — [192]p
ISBN 0-19-826663-4 (cased) : £8.00 : CIP entry
ISBN 0-19-826664-2 (pbk) : £3.95 B81-34380

306′.6 — United States. Anti-cult movements
Shupe, Anson D.. The new vigilantes : deprogrammers, anti-cultists, and the new religions / Anson D. Shupe, Jr. and David G. Bromley ; foreword by Joseph R. Gusfield. — Beverly Hills ; London : Sage, c1980. — 267p ; 22cm. — (Sage library of social research ; v.113)
Bibliography: p249-259. — Includes index
ISBN 0-8039-1542-x (pbk) : Unpriced B81-12211

306′.6 — United States. Religious cults: Inner Peace Movement — *Sociological perspectives*
Scott, Gini Graham. Cult and countercult : a study of a spiritual growth group and a witchcraft order / Gini Graham Scott. — Westport, Conn. ; London : Greenwood Press, 1980. — xi,213p : ill ; 22cm. — (Contributions in sociology ; no.38)
Bibliography: p203-209. - Includes index
ISBN 0-313-22074-3 : Unpriced
Also classified at 306′.4 B81-07123

306′.6 — United States. Religious cults — *Sociological perspectives — Case studies*
Damrell, Joseph. Search for identity : youth, religion and culture / Joseph Damrell ; introduction by John M. Johnson. — Beverly Hills ; London : Sage, c1978. — 232p ; 23cm. — (Sage library of social research ; v.64)
Bibliography: p229-231
ISBN 0-8039-0987-x (cased) : £11.25
ISBN 0-8039-0988-8 (pbk) : Unpriced B81-18842

306′.6 — Wales. Churches. Attendance, *1851* — *Statistics*
The religious census of 1851 : a calendar of the returns relating to Wales / edited by Ieuan Gwynedd Jones. — Cardiff : University of Wales Press on behalf of the Board of Celtic Studies, 1981. — (History and law series ; no.31)
Vol.2: North Wales. — 438p : facsims ; 26cm
ISBN 0-7083-0779-5 : £12.95 : CIP rev. B80-13718

306′.6 — Zambia. Religions, *to 1980* — *Sociological perspectives*
Binsbergen, Wim M. J. van. Religious change in Zambia : exploratory studies / Wim M.J. van Binsbergen. — London : Kegan Paul International, 1981. — xiii,423p,9p of plates : ill,maps ; 23cm. — (Monographs from the African Studies Centre, Leiden)
Bibliography: p370-398. — Includes index
ISBN 0-7103-0000-x (cased) : £18.00 : CIP rev.
ISBN 0-7103-0012-3 (pbk) : Unpriced B81-13577

306′.6 — Zimbabwe. Shona. Religious beliefs — *Anthropological perspectives*
Bucher, Hubert. Spirits and power : an analysis of Shona cosmology / Hubert Bucher. — Cape Town ; Oxford : Oxford University Press, 1980. — 231p : 3maps ; 22cm
Bibliography: p207-217. — Includes index
ISBN 0-19-570176-3 : £8.75 B81-38441

306.7 — Celebrities. Sex relations
Elson, Howard. The superstuds / by Howard Elson. — London : Proteus, 1980. — 91p : ill,ports ; 27cm
ISBN 0-906071-25-9 (pbk) : £3.95 B81-02269

306.7 — England. Paedophilia
Perspectives on paedophilia / edited by Brian Taylor. — London : Batsford Academic and Educational, 1981. — xxii,148p ; 22cm
Bibliography: p133-142. - Includes index
ISBN 0-7134-3718-9 (cased) : £14.95
ISBN 0-7134-3719-7 (pbk) : £5.95 B81-12563

306.7 — Flagellomania — *Serials*
The **New** derriere. — Vol.1, no.1-. — London (22 Charlton Kings Rd., N.W.5.) : Stop Press Press, c1981. — v. : ill (some col.)
Monthly. — Continues: Derriere
£2.50 per issue B81-31034

306.7 — Great Britain. Sexual problems, *1918-1928 — Correspondence, diaries, etc*
Dear Dr Stopes : sex in the 1920s / edited by Ruth Hall. — Harmondsworth : Penguin, 1981, c1978. — 222p ; 19cm
Originally published: London : Deutsch, 1978
ISBN 0-14-005536-3 (pbk) : £1.75 B81-27657

306.7 — Handicapped children. Sex relations — *For parents*
Greengross, Wendy. Sex and the handicapped child / by Wendy Greengross. — Rugby : National Marriage Guidance Council, c1980. — 23p ; 21cm
Bibliography: p23
ISBN 0-85351-051-2 (pbk) : £1.00 B81-09365

306.7 — Illegitimacy — *Sociological perspectives*
Teichman, Jenny. Illegitimacy. — Oxford : Blackwell, Jan.1982. — [192]p
ISBN 0-631-12807-7 : £8.50 : CIP entry B81-34295

306.7 — Men. Interpersonal relationships with women. Love. Secret communication
McCormick, Donald, *1911-*. Love in code : or, how to keep your secrets / Donald McCormick. — London : Eyre Methuen, 1980. — 216p,[8]p of plates : ill,facsims,ports ; 21cm
Bibliography: p208-211. — Includes index
ISBN 0-413-39410-7 : £6.50 : CIP rev. B80-18173

306.7 — Men. Sex relations
Botwin, Carol. The love crisis : hit-and-run lovers, jugglers, sexual stingies, unreliables, kinkies and other typical men today / Carol Botwin with Jerome L. Fine. — Toronto ; London : Bantam, 1980, c1979. — 239p ; 18cm
Originally published: New York : Doubleday, 1979
ISBN 0-553-13814-6 (pbk) : £1.25 B81-27830

306.7 — Paedophilia
Adult sexual interest in children / edited by Mark Cook and Kevin Howells. — London : Academic Press, 1981. — 275& : ill ; 24cm. — (Personality and psychopathology ; 22)
Includes bibliographies and index
ISBN 0-12-187250-5 : £16.40 B81-21988

306.7 — Sex relations. Communication
Andresen, Gail L.. Connective bargaining : communicating about sex / Gail L. Andresen, Barry K. Weinhold. — Englewood Cliffs ; London : Prentice-Hall, c1981. — viii,188p ; 21cm. — (A Spectum book)
Bibliography: p183-184. — Includes index
ISBN 0-13-167791-8 (cased) : Unpriced
ISBN 0-13-167783-7 (pbk) : £4.15 B81-28418

306.7 — Sex relations — *Interviews*
Leigh, Wendy. What makes a man good in bed? / Wendy Leigh. — London : Granada, 1981, c1980. — 208p ; 18cm. — (A Mayflower book)
Originally published: London : Muller, 1980. — Ill and text on inside covers
ISBN 0-583-13411-4 (pbk) : £1.25 B81-37122

306.7 — Sexual deviance. Bondage
Young, Pamela M.. Pamela′s book of discipline / by, Pamela M. Young. — [Bristol] ([SMG Leather Products, 154 Bedminster Down Rd., Bristol, BS13 7AF]) : People′s Press, 1981. — 41p : ill ; 22cm
Text on inside cover
Unpriced (pbk) B81-19450

306.7′01 — Sex roles. Theories, *to 1980* — *Feminist viewpoints*
Easlea, Brian. Science and sexual oppression : patriarchy′s confrontation with woman and nature / Brian Easlea. — London : Weidenfeld and Nicolson, c1981. — xiv,314p ; 24cm
Includes index
ISBN 0-297-77893-5 (cased) : £15.00
ISBN 0-297-77894-3 (pbk) : £7.50 B81-15627

306.7′0207 — Sex relations — *Humour*
Macdonald, Gerard. Once a week is ample. — London : Hutchinson, Oct.1981. — [64]p
ISBN 0-09-146500-1 : £2.50 : CIP entry B81-26797

Rushton, William. The filth amendment : Rushton versus sextremes / William Rushton. — London : Queen Anne Press, 1981. — 96p : ill ; 26cm
ISBN 0-362-00555-9 : £4.95 B81-39409

306.7'05 — Sex relations — *Serials*

Experience swingers. — No.1-. — [London] ([3 Valentine Place, S.E.1]) : [Tabor Publications], [1979]-. — v. : ill ; 21cm
Quarterly. — Description based on: No.4 (Feb./Mar.)
£1.00 per issue B81-39729

Listen with - Whitehouse. — No.1-. — London (Mail Order Division, 34 Upton La., E.7) : Bill Edwards, [1980?]. — v. : ill (chiefly col.) ; 30cm + sound disc
Monthly
£16.80 per year B81-31035

Louise London's Whitehouse all colour digest. — Issue 2-. — [London] ([34 Upton La., E.7]) : [Bill Edwards], [1980]-. — v. : chiefly col.ill ; 30cm
Monthly. — Continues: Whitehouse all colour digest. — Description based on: Issue 3
£1.50 per issue B81-39731

Lovebirds talks. — Issue 1-. — London (34 Upton La., E7) : Bill Edwards, [198-]-. — v. : ill ; 30cm
Monthly. — Description based on: Issue 3
ISSN 0260-8268 = Lovebirds talks : £16.80 per issue B81-09198

Playbirds erotic film guide. — Issue 1-. — [London] ([34 Upton La., E.7]) : [Bill Edwards], [197-?]-. — v. : ill(some col.) ; 30cm
Description based on: Issue 13
£1.20 per issue B81-39730

306.7'088041 — Men. Sex relations

Hite, Shere. The Hite report on male sexuality / Shere Hite. — London : Macdonald, 1981. — xxxiii,1129p ; 24cm
Originally published: New York : Knopf, 1981
ISBN 0-354-04634-9 (cased) : Unpriced
ISBN 0-354-04790-6 (pbk) : £9.95 B81-39406

306.7'0880565 — United States. Persons, 60 years-. Sex relations

Starr, Bernard D.. The Starr-Weiner report on sex and sexuality in the mature years / Bernard D. Starr & Marcella Bakur Weiner. — London : W.H. Allen, 1981. — ix,302p ; 22cm
Bibliography: p293-296. — Includes index
ISBN 0-491-02684-6 : £6.95 B81-35740

306.7'09 — Love affairs, *ca 1950*

Dorin, Walter. Great lovers / paintings by Walter Dorin ; text by George Melly. — London : Cape, 1981. — col.ill,col.ports ; 26cm
ISBN 0-224-01942-2 : £5.50 : CIP rev.
B81-20605

306.7'09 — Man. Sex relations, *to 1979.* **Social aspects**

Tannahill, Reay. Sex in history / Reay Tannahill. — [London] : Abacus, 1981, c1979. — x,463p,[24]p of plates : ill,2ports ; 20cm
Originally published: London : Hamilton, 1980. — Bibliography: p411-427. — Includes index
ISBN 0-349-13363-8 (pbk) : £2.95 B81-26682

306.7'09181'2 — Western world. Man. Sex relations, *1600-1977*

Foucault, Michel. The history of sexuality / Michel Foucault ; translated from the French by Robert Hurley. — Harmondsworth : Penguin. — (Pelican books)
Translation of: Histoire de la sexualité
Vol.1: An introduction. — 1981, c1978. — 168p ; 20cm
Originally published: New York : Pantheon, 1978 ; London : Allen Lane, 1979. — Includes index
ISBN 0-14-022299-5 (pbk) : £2.25 B81-25076

306.7'092'2 — Celebrities. Sex relations, *to 1980*

The **Intimate** sex lives of famous people / Irving Wallace ... [et al.]. — London : Hutchinson, 1981. — xx,491p,[16]p of plates : ports ; 23cm
ISBN 0-09-145700-9 : £7.95 : CIP rev.
B81-22614

306.7'092'2 — Women. Sex relations — *Personal observations — Collections*

Barbach, Lonnie. Shared intimacies : women's sexual experiences / Lonnie Barbach and Linda Levine. — London : Corgi, 1981, c1980. — 432p ; 18cm
Bibliography: p412-415. — Includes index
ISBN 0-552-11790-0 (pbk) : £1.75 B81-39664

306.7'092'4 — Sexology. Ellis, Havelock — *Biographies*

Grosskurth, Phyllis. Havelock Ellis : a biography / Phyllis Grosskurth. — London : Quartet, 1981, c1980. — xvi,492p,[87]p of plates : ports ; 20cm
Originally published: London : Allen Lane, 1980. — Bibliography: p471-480. — Includes index
ISBN 0-7043-3364-3 (pbk) : £4.95 B81-33657

306.7'0941 — Great Britain. Sex relations, *1837-1901*

Pearl, Cyril. The girl with the swansdown seat : an informal report on some aspects of mid-Victorian morality / Cyril Pearl. — London (27/29 Goodge St, London, W1P 1FD) : Robin Clark, 1980, c1955. — 277p,[4]p of plates : ill,ports ; 20cm
Originally published: London : Muller, 1955. — Includes index
ISBN 0-86072-043-8 (pbk) : £3.50 B81-11641

306.7'0947 — Soviet Union. Sex relations

Shtern, Mikhail. Sex in the Soviet Union / Mikhail Stern and August Stern ; translated from the French by Marc E. Heine. — London : W.H. Allen, 1981. — 221p : ill ; 23cm
Translation of: La vie sexuelle en U.R.S.S.
ISBN 0-491-02743-5 : £6.95 B81-14063

306.7'0973 — United States. Sex relations, *1953-1979*

Talese, Gay. Thy neighbour's wife / Gay Talese. — London : Pan in association with Collins, 1981, c1980. — 511p ; 18cm
Originally published: London : Collins, 1980. — Includes index
ISBN 0-330-26404-4 (pbk) : £1.75 B81-39008

306.7'4'0941 — Great Britain. Suburbs, *1920-1939*

Oliver, Paul. Dunroamin. — London : Barrie & Jenkins, Oct.1981. — [224]p
ISBN 0-09-145930-3 : £15.000 : CIP entry
B81-26782

306.7'4'0942132 — London. Covent Garden. Courtesans, *1793 — Lists — Early works — Facsimiles*

Harris's list of Covent-Garden ladies, or, Man of pleasure's kalender for the year 1793. — Edinburgh : P. Harris, Jan.1982. — [120]p. — (Gems of British social history ; 5)
Facsim. of ed.: London : Printed for H. Ranger, 1793
ISBN 0-86228-040-0 : £3.95 : CIP entry
B81-39214

306.7'4'0954792 — India *(Republic).* **Bombay. Prostitutes** — *Illustrations*

Mark, Mary Ellen. Falkland Road / photographs and text by Mary Ellen Mark. — London : Thames and Hudson, 1981. — 17p,[65]p of plates : col.ill ; 28cm
ISBN 0-500-27230-1 (pbk) : £5.95 B81-25342

306.7'6 — Homosexuality

Dannecker, Martin. Theories of homosexuality. — London (27 Priory Ave., N8 7RN) : Gay Men's Press, Oct.1981. — [128]p
Translation of: Der Homosexuelle und die Homosexualität
ISBN 0-907040-05-5 (pbk) : £1.95 : CIP entry
B81-26701

Hart, John, *1942-*. The theory and practice of homosexuality / John Hart, Diane Richardson with contributions from Kenneth Plummer ... [et al.]. — London : Routledge & Kegan Paul, 1981. — 206p : ill ; 22cm
Bibliography: p190-202. — Includes index
ISBN 0-7100-0838-4 (pbk) : £4.95 : CIP rev.
B81-15930

306.7'6 — Homosexuality — *Socialist viewpoints*

Homosexuality : power & politics / edited by Gay Left Collective. — London : Allison and Busby, 1980. — 223p ; 22cm
Includes index
ISBN 0-85031-374-0 (cased) : £9.95 : CIP rev.
ISBN 0-85031-375-9 (pbk) : £3.95 B80-17559

306.7'6 — Homosexuality — *Sociological perspectives*

The **Making** of the modern homosexual / Kenneth Plummer. — London : Hutchinson, 1981. — 280p ; 23cm
Bibliography: p253-274. - Includes index
ISBN 0-09-143150-6 (cased) : £12.00 : CIP rev.
ISBN 0-09-143151-4 (pbk) : £4.95 B80-22930

306.7'6 — Lesbian mothers

Hanscombe, Gillian E.. Rocking the cradle : lesbian mothers : a challenge in family living / Gillian E. Hanscombe and Jackie Forster. — London : Owen, 1981. — 172p ; 23cm. — (Contemporary issues series ; 13)
Bibliography: p168-170. — Includes index
ISBN 0-7206-0572-5 : £8.50 B81-05294

306.7'6 — Urban regions — *Sociological perspectives*

City, class and capital. — London : Edward Arnold, Oct.1981. — [224]p
ISBN 0-7131-6346-1 (pbk) : £6.50 : CIP entry
B81-25733

306.7'6'05 — Serials for male homosexuals: Serials with British imprints — *Texts*

Mister, incorporating quorum. — Vol.2, no.5. — London (283 Camden High St., NW1 7BX) : Millivres, [1979?]. — v. : ill (some col.),ports ; 29cm
Ten issues yearly. — Continues: Mister quorum. — Continued by: Mister magazine. — Only one issue published under this title
£13.00 per year B81-31036

Mister international. — No.1-No.8. — London (281 Camden High St., N.W.1.) : Mister international, [1976?-1977]. — v. : ill (some col.),ports ; 30cm
Monthly. — Merged with: part of Man to man quorum, to become Mister quorum. — Description based on: No.4
£1.50 per issue B81-31039

Mister magazine. — Vol.2, no.6-. — London (283 Camden High St., NW1) : Millivres ; London (174 Culford Rd., N1 4DS) : Walton Press [distributor], 1979-. — v. : ill (some col.),ports ; 30cm
Six issues yearly. — Continues: Mister, incorporating quorum. — Description based on: Vol.2, no.7
£15.00 per year B81-31037

Mister quorum. — No.9-Vol.2, no.4. — London (281 Camden High St., N.W.1.) : [Millivres], [1977-1978?]. — v. : ill (some col.),ports ; 30cm
Frequency varies. — Merger of: Mister international; and, in part Man to man quorum. — Continued by: Mister, incorporating quorum
£15.00 per year B81-31038

306.7'6'088355 — Generals. Homosexuality

Richardson, Frank. Mars without Venus : a study of some homosexual generals / Frank M. Richardson. — Edinburgh : W. Blackwood, 1981. — 188p,[8]p of plates : ports ; 23cm
Includes index
ISBN 0-85158-148-x : £5.95 B81-39059

306.7'6'0924 — Great Britain. Male homosexuality. Crisp, Quentin — *Biographies*

Crisp, Quentin. How to become a virgin / Quentin Crisp. — [London] : Fontana, c1981. — 191p ; 18cm
ISBN 0-00-635799-7 (pbk) : £1.50 B81-21118

Crisp, Quentin. How to become a virgin / Quentin Crisp. — London : Duckworth, 1981. — 192p ; 23cm
ISBN 0-7156-1577-7 : £6.95 B81-19092

306.7'6'094 — Europe. Urban regions. Growth, *1950-1975*
Urban Europe. — Oxford : Pergamon. — (Cross national comparative series)
Vol.1: A study of growth and decline. — Dec.1981. — [156]p
ISBN 0-08-023156-x : £18.75 : CIP entry B81-31806

306.7'6'094 — Western Europe. Homosexuality, *to 1300*
Boswell, John, *1947*. Christianity, social tolerance, and homosexuality : gay people in Western Europe from the beginning of the Christian era to the fourteenth century / John Boswell. — Chicago ; London : University of Chicago Press, c1980. — xviii,424p,12p of plates : ill,facsims ; 25cm
Bibliography: p403-409. — Includes indexes
ISBN 0-226-06710-6 : £16.50 B81-03528

306.7'6'0941 — Great Britain. Homosexual movements, *to 1973*
Come together : the years of gay liberation (1970-73) / edited and introduced by Aubrey Walter. — London (27 Priory Ave., N8 7RN) : Gay Men's Press, 1980. — 218p : ill,1facsim ; 20cm
ISBN 0-907040-04-7 (pbk) : £3.95 : CIP rev. B80-19616

306.7'6'0941 — Great Britain. Homosexuality — *Serials*
Gay noise. — No.1 (Thursday 14th Aug.1980)-. — London (149 Railton Rd, SE24) : Gay Noise Collective, 1980-. — v. ; 30cm
Fortnightly
ISSN 0260-6089 = Gay noise : £6.00 per year B81-02837

306.7'6'09417 — Ireland *(Republic).* **Homosexuality** *— Serials*
[In touch *(Dublin)***]**. In touch : journal of the National Gay Federation. — Vol.1, no.1 (1979)-. — Dublin ([10 Fownes St., Dublin 2]) : The Federation, 1979-. — v. : ill ; 31cm
Description based on: Vol.2, no.7 (Aug./Sept.[1980])
ISSN 0332-1312 = In touch : Free to Federation members B81-20441

306.7'6'0973 — United States. Homosexuals
White, Edmund. States of desire : travels in gay America / Edmund White. — Toronto ; London : Bantam, 1981. — 309p ; 18cm
Originally published: New York : Dutton, c1980
ISBN 0-553-14544-4 (pbk) : £3.50 B81-24306

306.8 — Capitalist countries. Professional personnel. Family life. Effects of careers *compared with* **effects of careers on family life of professional personnel in communist countries**
Rueschemeyer, Marilyn. Professional work and marriage : an East-West comparison / Marilyn Rueschemeyer. — London : Macmillan, 1981. — ix,197p ; 23cm. — (St Antony's/Macmillan series)
Bibliography: p184-190. — Includes index
ISBN 0-333-30080-7 : £20.00 B81-40730

306.8 — Families. Effects of social change — *Comparative studies*
Hutter, Mark. The changing family : comparative perspectives / Mark Hutter. — New York ; Chichester : Wiley, c1981. — xix,551p : ill,2maps ; 24cm
Bibliography: p518-536. — Includes index
ISBN 0-471-08394-1 : £8.90 B81-18994

306.8 — Families - *Sociological perspectives*
Rediscovery of the family and other lectures. — Aberdeen : Aberdeen University Press, Aug.1981. — [112]p. — (Sister Marie Hilda memorial lectures 1954-1973)
ISBN 0-08-025754-2 (pbk) : £5.00 : CIP entry B81-15807

306.8 — Great Britain. Family life. Effects of work *— Sociological perspectives*
Work and the family / edited by Peter Moss & Nickie Fonda. — London : Temple Smith, 1980. — 224p : ill ; 23cm
Bibliography: p211-220. - Includes index
ISBN 0-85117-199-0 : £11.95 B81-00757

306.8 — Marriage
Getting married / [authors Elizabeth Penrose ... et al.] ; [executive editor Evelyn Brown]. — [London] : British Medical Association, [c1981]. — 109p : ill(some col.) ; 20cm. — (A Family doctor special)
Previous ed.: 1979
£0.50 (unbound) B81-33130

Mackay, Dougal. Marriage does matter. — Loughton : Piatkus, Jan.1982. — [256]p
ISBN 0-86188-123-0 : £6.95 : CIP entry B81-33759

Scanzoni, Letha. Men, women and change : a sociology of marriage and family / Letha Dawson Scanzoni, John Scanzoni. — 2nd ed. — New York ; London : McGraw-Hill, c1981. — xvi,680,R26,[13]p : ill ; 25cm
Previous ed.: 1976. — Bibliography: pR1-R26. — Includes index
ISBN 0-07-055054-9 : £12.50 B81-23959

Thatcher, Floyd. Long-term marriage. — London : Hodder & Stoughton, Jan.1982. — [224]p
ISBN 0-340-27597-9 (pbk) : £1.95 : CIP entry B81-33923

306.8 — Marriage & divorce
Dominian, Jack. Marriage-making or breaking? / by J. Dominian. — London : British Medical Association, [1981]. — 31p ; 19cm. — (A Family doctor booklet)
Cover title
£0.40 (pbk) B81-09424

306.8 — Marriage & kinship — *Anthropological perspectives*
Fox, Robin. Kinship and marriage : an anthropological perspective / Robin Fox. — Harmondsworth : Penguin, 1967 (1981 [printing]). — 271p : ill ; 20cm
Bibliography: p263-266. — Includes index
ISBN 0-14-020884-4 (pbk) : £2.95 B81-40471

306.8 — Marriage. Role of women — *Feminist viewpoints*
Hamilton, Cicely. Marriage as a trade / Cicely Hamilton ; introduced by Jane Lewis. — London : Women's Press, 1981. — 149p ; 20cm
Originally published: London : Chapman and Hall, 1909
ISBN 0-7043-3870-x (pbk) : £2.95 : CIP rev. B81-10420

306.8 — Marriage, *to 1980.* **Social aspects**
Marriage and society. — London : Europa, Oct.1981. — [380]p. — (Europa social history of human experience ; 2)
ISBN 0-905118-62-6 : CIP entry B81-27389

306.8 — United States. Middle-class families. Life cycle. Psychosocial aspects
The **Family** life cycle : a framework for family therapy / edited by Elizabeth A. Carter, Monica Mc Goldrick [i.e. McGoldrick]. — New York : Gardner ; New York ; London : Wiley [distributor], c1980. — xxiii,468p : ill ; 24cm
Includes bibliographies and index
ISBN 0-470-26782-8 : £13.50 B81-01595

306.8'07201812 — Westewrn world. families, *1500-1714.* **Historiology**
Anderson, Michael, *1942-*. Approaches to the history of the western family, 1500-1914 / prepared for the Economic History Society by Michael Anderson. — London : Macmillan, 1980. — 96p ; 22cm. — (Studies in economic and social history)
Bibliography: p85-94. — Includes index
ISBN 0-333-24065-0 (pbk) : £2.25 : CIP rev. B80-24055

306.8'0882945 — Hindu families. Family life — *For schools*
Ewan, John. A Hindu home / [written and illustrated by John Ewan and N.V. Pancholi]. — London : Christian Education Movement, [c1981]. — [12]p : ill ; 22cm. — (Ask about religion)
Cover title. — Text on inside covers. — Bibliography: p[1]
ISBN 0-905022-74-2 (pbk) : Unpriced B81-27040

306.8'094 — Europe. Families, *1400-1980*
Mitterauer, Michael. The European family. — Oxford : Blackwell, Nov.1981. — [256]p
Translation of: Vom Patriarchat zur Partnerschaft
ISBN 0-631-12913-8 (cased) : £11.00 : CIP entry
ISBN 0-631-12923-5 (pbk) : £5.50 B81-30168

306.8'0941 — Great Britain. Families, *1900-1939 — Sociological perspectives*
Gittins, Diana. Social change and the family structure. — London : Hutchinson Education, Feb.1982. — [256]p
ISBN 0-09-145490-5 (cased) : £12.00 : CIP entry
ISBN 0-09-145491-3 (pbk) : £5.95 B81-35948

306.8'09426'57 — Great Britain. Marriage — *Sociological perspectives — Study regions: Cambridgeshire. Melbourn, 1780-1851*
Mills, Dennis R.. Aspects of marriage : an example of applied historical studies / D.R. Mills. — Milton Keynes : Faculty of Social Sciences, Open University, 1980. — ii,38p ; 30cm. — (Social science publications / Open University Faculty of Social Sciences)
Bibliography: p31-38
£1.10 (pbk) B81-17628

306.8'0943 — Germany. Families, *1800-1939 — Sociological perspectives*
The **German** family : essays on the social history of the family in nineteenth- and twentieth-century Germany / edited by Richard J. Evans and W.R. Lee. — London : Croom Helm, 1981. — 302p : ill ; 23cm
Includes index
ISBN 0-7099-0067-8 : £13.95 B81-17854

306.8'09481 — Norway. Marriage, *1841-1850*
Sundt, Eilert. On marriage in Norway / Eilert Sundt ; translated and introduced by Michael Drake. — Cambridge : Cambridge University Press, 1980. — xxi,168p : 2ill,1map ; 24cm
Translation of: Om giftermaal i Norge
ISBN 0-521-23199-x : £12.50 : CIP rev. B80-19617

306.8'0951 — China. Marriage, *1950-1977*
Croll, Elisabeth. The politics of marriage in contemporary China / Elisabeth Croll. — Cambridge : Cambridge University Press, 1981. — xiv,210p : plans ; 23cm. — (Contemporary China Institute publications)
Bibliography: p190-207. - Includes index
ISBN 0-521-23345-3 : £16.00 B81-11191

306.8'0951'25 — Hong Kong. Chinese families. Family life. Effects of employment of daughters *— Case studies*
Salaff, Janet W.. Working daughters of HongKong : filial piety or power in the family? / Janet W. Salaff ; with a foreword by Kingsley Davis. — Cambridge : Cambridge University Press, 1981. — xix,317p : ill,1map ; 24cm. — (The Arnold and Caroline Rose monograph series of the American Sociological Association)
Bibliography: p297-307. — Includes index
ISBN 0-521-23679-7 (cased) : £20.00
ISBN 0-521-28148-2 (pbk) : £6.50 B81-25184

306.8'095694 — Israel. Kibbutzim. Family life. Psychosocial aspects
Irvine, Elizabeth E.. The family in the Kibbutz / Elizabeth Irvine. — London (231 Baker St., NW1 6XL) : Study Commission on the Family, c1980. — 34p ; 21cm. — (Occasional paper / Study Commission on the Family)
ISBN 0-907051-03-0 (pbk) : £1.50 B81-10105

306.8'09681'6 — Lesotho. Rural regions. Family life. Effects of migration of personnel to South Africa
Murray, Colin. Families divided : the impact of migrant labour in Lesotho / Colin Murray. — Cambridge : Cambridge University Press, 1981. — xvi,219p : ill,maps ; 23cm. — (African studies series)
Bibliography: p204-215. — Includes index
ISBN 0-521-23501-4 : £18.50 : CIP rev. B81-25885

306.8'0973 — United States. Families. Decision making — *Sociological perspectives*

Scanzoni, John. Family decision-making : a developmental sex role model / John Scanzoni, Maximiliane Szinovacz. — Beverly Hills ; London : Sage, c1980. — 309p ; 22cm. — (Sage library of social research ; v.111)
Bibliography: p287-302. — Includes index
ISBN 0-8039-1533-0 (cased) : Unpriced
ISBN 0-8039-1534-9 (pbk) : £5.50 B81-18734

306.8'0973 — United States. Families. Economic aspects — *Conference proceedings*

Economics and the family / edited by Stephen J. Bahr. — Lexington : Lexington ; [Farnborough, Hants.] : [Gower] [distributor], 1980. — xv,183p : ill ; 24cm
Includes index
ISBN 0-669-03623-4 : £11.50 B81-10900

306.8'0973 — United States. Families. Psychological aspects

Eshleman, J. Ross. The family : an introduction / J. Ross Eshleman. — 3rd ed.. — Boston [Mass.] ; London : Allyn and Bacon, c1981. — xx,634p : ill ; 24cm
Previous ed.: 1934. — Includes bibliographies and index
ISBN 0-205-07241-0 : £19.90 B81-12102

306.8'0973 — United States. Families — *Sociological perspectives*

Young, Rosalie F.. Instructor's resource manual to accompany Eshleman's The family, third edition / prepared by Rosalie F. Young. — Boston ; London : Allyn and Bacon, c1981. — 207p : ill ; 24cm
Includes bibliographies
ISBN 0-205-07242-9 (pbk) : £1.00 B81-16163

306.8'0973 — United States. Families. Structure, *ca 1690-1970* — *Sociological perspectives*

Seward, Rudy Ray. The American family : a demographic history / Rudy Ray Seward ; foreword by Herman R. Lantz. — Beverly Hills ; London : Sage, c1978. — 223p ; 23cm. — (Sage library of social research ; v.70)
Bibliography: p203-210
ISBN 0-8039-1112-2 (cased) : £11.25
ISBN 0-8039-1113-0 (pbk) : £5.50 B81-03028

306.8'0973 — United States. Marriage & divorce. Influence of social change, *ca 1870-1930*

May, Elaine Tyler. Great expectations : marriage and divorce in post-Victorian America / Elaine Tyler May. — Chicago ; London : University of Chicago Press, 1980. — viii,200p ; 23cm
Includes index
ISBN 0-226-51166-9 : £9.00 B81-05388

306.8'09747'63 — New York *(State)*. **Utica. Family life,** *1790-1865*

Ryan, Mary P.. Cradle of the middle class : the family in Oneida County, New York, 1790-1865 / Mary P. Ryan. — Cambridge : Cambridge University Press, 1981. — xiv,321p ; 24cm. — (Interdisciplinary perspectives on modern history)
Bibliography: p293-307. — Includes index
ISBN 0-521-23200-7 : £19.50 B81-26157

306.8'09755'18 — United States. Chesapeake region. Planters. Family life, *1700-1799*

Smith, Daniel Blake. Inside the great house : planter family life in eighteenth-century Chesapeake society / Daniel Blake Smith. — Ithaca ; London : Cornell University Press, 1980. — 305p,[11]p of plates : ill,ports ; 23cm
Includes index
ISBN 0-8014-1313-3 : £10.50 B81-05572

306.8'3 — Kinship

Starcke, Carl Nicolai. The primitive family in its origin and development / Carl Nicolai Starcke ; edited and with an introduction by Rodney Needham. — Chicago ; London : University of Chicago Press, 1976. — xxxi,303p : 1port ; 21cm. — (Classics in anthropology)
Originally published: London : s.n., 1889. — Bibliography: p289-298. — Includes index
ISBN 0-226-77132-6 : £10.50 B81-38148

306.8'3 — Kinship — *Festschriften*

The **Versatility** of kinship / edited by Linda S. Cordell, Stephen Beckerman. — New York ; London : Academic Press, c1980. — xvii,379p : ill,1map,1ports ; 24cm
"Essays presented to Harry W. Basehart". — Includes bibliographies and index
ISBN 0-12-188250-0 : £25.80 B81-16724

306.8'3'096894 — Zambia. Luapula. Lunda. Matrilineal kinship — *Anthropological perspectives*

Poewe, Karla O.. Matrilineal ideology : male-female dynamics in Luapula, Zambia / Karla O. Poewe. — London : Published for the International African Institute [by] Academic Press, 1981. — ix,140p ; 24cm. — (Studies in anthropology)
Bibliography: p126-134. — Includes index
ISBN 0-12-558850-x : £8.00 B81-17713

306.8'3'097247 — Mexico. Tlaxcala. Rural regions. Compadrazgo, *to 1970*

Nutini, Hugo G.. Ritual kinship : the structure and historical development of the compadrazgo system in rural Tlaxcala / Hugo G. Nutini and Betty Bell. — New Jersey ; Guildford : Princeton University Press
Vol.1. — c1980. — xvi,494p : 1ill,maps ; 24cm
Bibliography: p473-482. - Includes index
ISBN 0-691-09382-2 (cased) : £15.80
ISBN 0-691-09383-0 (pbk) : Unpriced B81-11577

306.8'3'0979173 — United States. Kinship — *Study regions: Arizona. Phoenix*

Farber, Bernard. Conceptions of kinship / Bernard Farber. — New York ; Oxford : Elsevier, c1981. — x,250p ; 24cm
Bibliography: p233-243. - Includes index
ISBN 0-444-99076-3 : £12.18 B81-15481

306.8'4 — Remarriage — *Humour* — *For women*

Drummond, Maggie. How to survive as a second wife / Maggie Drummond ; illustrated by Peter Maddocks. — London : Robson, 1981. — 127p : ill ; 23cm
ISBN 0-86051-139-1 : £5.60 : CIP rev. B81-04345

306.8'4 — United States. Mixed marriage. Mathematical models

Johnson, Robert Alan. Religious assortative marriage in the United States / Robert Alan Johnson. — New York ; London : Academic Press, c1980. — xxvii,235p ; 24cm. — (Studies in population)
Bibliography: p219-229. - Includes index
ISBN 0-12-386580-8 : £14.00 B81-21219

306.8'5 — England. Local authority multi-storey flats. Families with children. Social conditions

Littlewood, Judith. Families in flats / Judith Littlewood and Anthea Tinker. — London : H.M.S.O., 1981. — 56p : ill ; 30cm
At head of title: Department of the Environment
ISBN 0-11-751548-5 (pbk) : £4.80 B81-37391

306.8'7 — Children, 2-3 years. Interpersonal relationships with parents

Lytton, Hugh. Parent-child interaction : the socialization process observed in twin and singleton families / Hugh Lytton. — New York ; London : Plenum, c1980. — xx,364p : ill,forms ; 24cm
Bibliography: p345-357. - Includes index
ISBN 0-306-40521-0 : Unpriced B81-08591

306.8'7 — Children. Interpersonal relationships with parents

Parent-child interaction : theory, research, and prospects / edited by Ronald W. Henderson. — New York ; London : Academic Press, 1981. — xii,335p : ill ; 24cm. — (Educational psychology)
Includes bibliographies and index
ISBN 0-12-340620-x : £19.60 B81-38869

306.8'7 — Children. Interpersonal relationships with parents. Conflict

Sheleff, Leon Shaskolsky. Generations apart : adult hostility to youth / by Leon Shaskolsky Sheleff. — New York ; London : McGraw-Hill, c1981. — xii,351p ; 24cm
Includes index
ISBN 0-07-056540-6 : £15.50 B81-26657

306.8'7 — Children of divorced parents. Interpersonal relationships with parents living apart from their children — *For parents*

Rowlands, Peter. Saturday parent / Peter Rowlands. — London : Unwin Paperbacks, 1981. — 121p ; 18cm
ISBN 0-04-649013-2 (pbk) : £1.95 : CIP rev. B81-15872

306.8'7 — Children. Socialisation. Role of families

Maccoby, Eleanor E.. Social development : psychological growth and the parent-child relationship / Eleanor E. Maccoby. — New York ; London : Harcourt Brace Jovanovich, c1980. — xii,436p : ill ; 24cm
Bibliography: p411-424. — Includes index
ISBN 0-15-581422-2 (pbk) : £7.10 B81-02399

306.8'7 — Daughters. Interpersonal relationships with mothers

Arcana, Judith. Our mothers' daughters / Judith Arcana ; introduced by Phyllis Chesler. — London : Women's Press, 1981, c1979. — 235p ; 20cm
Originally published: Berkeley : Shameless Hussy, 1979. — Bibliography: p227-235
ISBN 0-7043-3864-5 (pbk) : £2.95 B81-09926

Caplan, Paula J.. Barriers between women / Paula J. Caplan. — Lancaster : MTP, c1981. — 14p ; 24cm
Bibliography: p141-144. — Includes index
ISBN 0-85200-539-3 : £7.95 B81-24043

306.8'7 — Families. Conflict

Conflict in the family : a continuing education course. — Milton Keynes : Open University Press, 1980
Block 6: Wider perspectives. — 66p : ill ; 30cm. — (P253 : block 6, unit 15 and 16)
At head of title: The Open University. — Includes bibliographies. — Content: Unit 15: Self help - Unit 16: Continuing education
ISBN 0-335-10007-4 (pbk) : Unpriced B81-12770

306.8'7 — Families. Interpersonal relationships

Smart, Laura S.. Families : developing relationships / Laura S. Smart, Mollie S. Smart. — 2nd ed. — New York : Macmillan ; London : Collier Macmillan, c1980. — xi,532p : ill ; 24cm
Previous ed.: / Mollie S. Smart, Laura S. Smart. New York : Macmillan, c1976. — Includes bibliographies and index
ISBN 0-02-411930-x : £11.25 B81-00022

306.8'7 — Families. Interpersonal relationships. Conflict

Conflict in the family : a continuing education course. — Milton Keynes : Open University Press. — (p253 ; MB)
At head of title: The Open University Media booklet. — 1981. — 97p : 1ill,ports ; 30cm
Includes bibliographies
Unpriced (unbound) B81-27585

306.8'7 — Great Britain. Children. Interpersonal relationships with parents *related to* **interpersonal relationships between school teachers & students**

David, Miriam E.. The State, the family and education / Miriam E. David. — London : Routledge & Kegan Paul, 1980. — vii,280p ; 22cm. — (Radical social policy)
Bibliography: p249-267. - Includes index
ISBN 0-7100-0601-2 (pbk) : £5.95 : CIP rev.
Primary classification 371.1'02 B80-17623

306.8'7 — Great Britain. Universities: Open University. Curriculum subjects: Parenthood. Courses: First Years of Life & Preschool Child

Perkins, Elizabeth R.. Networks and dissemination : the case of the Open University parenthood courses / Elizabeth R. Perkins. — [Nottingham] : University of Nottingham, 1978. — 26,[7]leaves ; 30cm. — (Occasional paper / Leverhulme Health Education Project ; no.12)
Unpriced (pbk) B81-22734

306.8'7 — Marriage. Compatibility

Klein, Mavis. How to choose a mate / Mavis Klein. — London : Boyars, 1981. — 160p : ill ; 23cm
ISBN 0-7145-2727-0 : £5.95
Also classified at 155.2'8 B81-08398

306.8′7 — Mentally ill persons. Families. Interpersonal relationships. Communication

Studies of familial communication and psychopathology : a social-developmental approach to deviant behavior / [edited by] Rolv Mikkel Blakar. — Oslo : Universitetsforlaget ; Henley-on-Thames : Global [distributor], c1980. — 182p : ill ; 22cm
Bibliography: p166-178
ISBN 82-00-01999-3 (pbk) : £9.35 B81-04086

306.8′7 — Motherhood — *Interviews*

Oakley, Ann. [Becoming a mother]. From here to maternity : becoming a mother / Ann Oakley. — Harmondsworth : Penguin, 1981, c1979. — 328p ; 20cm
Originally published: Oxford : Martin Robertson, 1979
ISBN 0-14-022256-1 (pbk) : £2.25 B81-37419

306.8′7 — Mothers

Smith, Liz. The mother book / Liz Smith. — London : Granada, 1981, c1978. — 244p : ill ; 23cm
ISBN 0-246-11299-9 : £5.95 B81-21684

306.8′7 — Parenthood

Perkins, Elizabeth R.. Preparation for parenthood : a critique of the concept / Elizabeth R. Perkins, Beverley Morris. — [Nottingham] : University of Nottingham, 1979. — 27leaves ; 30cm. — (Occasional paper / Leverhulme Health Education Project ; no.17)
Unpriced (pbk) B81-22739

306.8′7 — Parenthood — *Serials*

[Parents *(London)*]. Parents. — No.1 (Apr.1976)-. — London (98 Baylis Rd, SE1) : Gemini Corporate and Marketing Services on behalf of Gemini Publishing, 1976-. — v. : ill ; 29cm
Monthly. — Description based on: No.44 (Nov.1979)
ISSN 0260-7514 = Parents (London) : £8.40 per year B81-05405

306.8′7 — Remarriage — *History* — *Conference proceedings*

International Colloquium on Historical Demography *(1979 : Kristiansand).* Marriage and remarriage in populations of the past / proceedings of the International Colloquium on Historical Demography Nuptiality and fertility : plural marriage and illegitimate fertility, Kristiansand, Norway, 7-9th September 1979 ; organized by the International Committee of Historical Sciences and the International Union for the Scientific Study of Population ; edited by J. Dupâquier ... [et al.]. — London : Academic Press, 1981. — xix,663p : ill,maps ; 24cm. — (Population and social structure)
English and French text. — Includes bibliographies and index
ISBN 0-12-224660-8 : £30.00 B81-29817

306.8′7 — Step-children. Interpersonal relationships with step-parents

Maddox, Brenda. [The half-parent]. Step-parenting : how to live with other people′s children / Brenda Maddox. — London : Unwin, 1980, c1975. — 219p ; 18cm
Originally published: London : Deutsch, 1975. — Includes index
ISBN 0-04-649004-3 (pbk) : £2.25 : CIP rev. B79-34686

306.8′7 — United States. Dual career families — *Sociological perspectives*

Dual-career couples / edited by Fran Pepitone-Rockwell. — Beverly Hills ; London : Sage, c1980. — 294p : ill ; 22cm. — (A Sage focus edition ; 24)
ISBN 0-8039-1436-9 (cased) : Unpriced
ISBN 0-8039-1437-7 (pbk) : £6.25 B81-18735

306.8′7 — United States. Fatherhood. Role of single fathers — *Case studies*

Rosenthal, Kristine M.. Fathers without partners : a study of fathers and the family after marital separation / Kristine M. Rosenthal, Harry F. Keshet. — Totowa : Rowman and Littlefield ; London : Distributed by Prior, 1981. — xxiii,187p ; 25cm
Bibliography: p171-179. — Includes index
ISBN 0-8476-6281-0 : £8.95 B81-11587

306.8′7 — United States. Firstborn babies. Attitudes of parents

Entwisle, Doris R.. The first birth : a family turning point / Doris R. Entwisle, Susan G. Doering. — Baltimore ; London : Johns Hopkins University Press, c1981. — xvi,331p : ill ; 24cm
Bibliography: p309-326. — Includes index
ISBN 0-8018-2408-7 : £15.00 B81-37174

306.8′7 — United States. Married couples. Interpersonal relationships. Effects of parenthood — *Sociological perspectives*

LaRossa, Ralph. Transition to parenthood : how infants change families / Ralph LaRossa and Maureen Mulligan LaRossa. — Berverly Hills ; London : Sage, c1981. — 262p ; 23cm. — (Sage library of social research ; v119)
Includes index
ISBN 0-8039-1566-7 (cased) : Unpriced
ISBN 0-8039-1567-5 (pbk) : £5.50 B81-18733

306.8′7 — United States. Parents. Interpersonal relationships with newborn babies. Effects of perinatal care services

Parent-infant relationships / edited by Paul M. Taylor. — New York ; London : Grune & Stratton, c1980. — xiv,371p : ill ; 24cm. — (Monographs in neonatology)
Includes index
ISBN 0-8089-1289-5 : £13.80 B81-15014

306.8′7 — United States. Urban regions. Children. Home care. Effects of interpersonal relationships between their mothers & grandmothers — *Study examples: Italian families*

Cohler, Bertram J.. Mothers, grandmothers, and daughters : personality and childcare in three-generation families / Bertram J. Cohler, Henry U. Grunebaum with the assistance of Donna Moran Robbins. — New York ; Chichester : Wiley, c1981. — xv,456p : ill ; 24cm. — (Wiley series on personality processes)
Bibliography: p365-402. - Includes index
ISBN 0-471-05900-5 : £12.00 B81-09827

306.8′7′0207 — Families. Interpersonal relationships — *Humour* — *For children*

Hawkesworth, Jenny. A handbook of family monsters / Jenny Hawkesworth ; illustrated by Colin McNaughton. — London : Dent, 1980. — 56p : ill ; 21cm
ISBN 0-460-06060-0 : £3.50 B81-04534

306.8′7′09667 — West Africa. Family life — *Study examples: Akan civil servants* — *Study regions: Ghana*

Oppong, Christine. Middle class African marriage. — London : Allen & Unwin, Nov.1981. — [208]p
Previously published as: Marriage among a matrilineal elite. Cambridge : Cambridge University Press, 1974
ISBN 0-04-301138-1 (pbk) : £4.95 : CIP entry B81-28147

306.8′7′0973 — United States. Families. Interpersonal relationships

Family strengths : positive models for family life / edited by Nick Stinnett ... [et al.]. — Lincoln [Neb.] ; London : University of Nebraska Press, c1980. — x,518p : ill ; 24cm
Includes bibliographies
ISBN 0-8032-4125-9 (cased) : £12.00
ISBN 0-8032-9122-1 (pbk) : £6.00 B81-03794

306.8′8 — Bereavement

Bereavement : what to expect and how to be helpful / MIND. — London : MIND, [1981?]. — 4p ; 21cm
Unpriced (unbound) B81-30109

306.8′8 — Bereavement — *Conference proceedings*

Bereavement papers / FWA. — London (501 Kingsland Rd., E. 8) : Family Welfare Association, c1978. — 63p ; 21cm
Conference papers
ISBN 0-900954-08-6 (pbk) : £1.25 B81-08077

306.8′8 — Bereavement. Personal adjustment of fathers — *Personal observations*

Leach, Christopher, *1925-*. Letter to a younger son / Christopher Leach. — London : Dent, 1981. — 155p ; 23cm
ISBN 0-460-04496-6 : £5.95 B81-08125

306.8′8 — Death

Shneidman, Edwin S.. Voices of death / Edwin Shneidman. — New York ; London : Harper & Row, c1980. — xii,206p ; 22cm
Includes index
ISBN 0-06-014023-2 : £5.95 B81-33753

306.8′8 — Death — *For schools*

Mullen, Peter. Death / Peter Mullen. — London : [Edward Arnold], 1981. — 16p : ill ; 30cm. — (Checkpoint ; 15)
Bibliography: p16
ISBN 0-7131-0528-3 (pbk) : £0.98 B81-34990

306.8′8 — France. Death. Attitudes of society, *1700-1800*

McManners, John. Death and the Enlightenment. — Oxford : Clarendon, Jan.1982. — [320]p
ISBN 0-19-826440-2 : £15.00 : CIP entry B81-34416

306.8′8 — Idaho. Kellogg. Silver mining industries: Sunshine Mine. Personnel. Fire victims, *1972.* **Wives. Widowhood. Personal adjustments**

Harvey, Carol D. H.. The Sunshine widows : adapting to sudden bereavement / Carol D.H. Harvey, Howard M. Bahr. — Lexington, Mass. : Lexington ; [Farnborough, Hants.] : Gower [distributor], 1980. — xiv,151p : ill ; 24cm
Includes bibliographies and index
ISBN 0-669-03375-8 : £12.00 B81-05323

306.8′8 — Man. Dying — *Sociological perspectives*

Lofland, Lyn H.. The craft of dying : the modern face of death / Lyn H. Lofland. — Beverly Hills ; London : Sage, c1978. — 119p ; 23cm
Bibliography: p109-118
ISBN 0-8039-1099-1 : £5.50 B81-15109

306.8′9 — Children. Effects of divorce

Inglis, Ruth. Must divorce hurt the children?. — London : Maurice Temple Smith, Jan.1982. — [240]p
ISBN 0-85117-220-2 : £8.00 : CIP entry B81-33832

306.8′9 — Great Britain. Wives. Sale, *1550-1928*

Menefee, Samuel Pyeatt. Wives for sale. — Oxford : Blackwell, June 1981. — [320]p
ISBN 0-631-11871-3 : £12.00 : CIP entry B81-10489

306.8′9′0942 — England. Divorce — *Manuals* — *For parents*

Hooper, Anne. Divorce and your children / by Anne Hooper. — London : Allen & Unwin, 1981. — 145p ; 23cm
Bibliography: p145
ISBN 0-04-649011-6 : Unpriced : CIP rev. B81-02352

307 — COMMUNITIES

307 — Community studies — *Study regions: Australia, Great Britain & United States*

Wild, R. A.. Australian community studies and beyond. — London : Allen & Unwin, Dec.1981. — [241]p. — (Studies in society ; 7)
ISBN 0-86861-219-7 : £18.00 : CIP entry B81-31540

307 — Human settlements

Wallis, Elizabeth B.. Settlement. — London : Edward Arnold, Apr.1981. — [64]p. — (Systematic secondary series)
ISBN 0-7131-0499-6 (pbk) : £2.00 : CIP entry B81-00023

307 — Human settlements. Social planning — *Conference proceedings*

Human settlements in the eighties : implications of the ″new international development strategy″ : papers and proceedings of the Habitat Forum U.K. debriefing conference, 10th July 1980, the Polytechnic of Central London / edited by Thomas L. Blair. — [London] : [The Polytechnic], [1980]. — vii, 93 leaves ; 30cm
Unpriced (pbk) B81-31381

307′.0914′2 — Islands. Prehistoric settlements. Environmental aspects — *Conference proceedings*

Environmental aspects of coasts and islands / edited by Don Brothwell and Geoffrey Dimbleby. — Oxford : B.A.R., 1981. — 206p : ill,maps ; 30cm. — (Symposia of the Association for Environmental Archaeology ; no.1) (BAR. International series ; 94)
Conference papers. — Includes bibliographies
ISBN 0-86054-110-x (pbk) : £8.00
Primary classification 307′.0914′6 B81-36587

307′.0914′6 — Coastal regions. Prehistoric settlements. Environmental aspects — *Conference proceedings*

Environmental aspects of coasts and islands / edited by Don Brothwell and Geoffrey Dimbleby. — Oxford : B.A.R., 1981. — 206p : ill,maps ; 30cm. — (Symposia of the Association for Environmental Archaeology ; no.1) (BAR. International series ; 94)
Conference papers. — Includes bibliographies
ISBN 0-86054-110-x (pbk) : £8.00
Also classified at 307′.0914′2 B81-36587

307′.09172′4 — Developing countries. Community development projects — *Case studies*

Community development : comparative case studies in India, the Republic of Korea, Mexico and Tanzania / edited by Ronald Dore and Zoë Mars ; contributions from Vincent S.R. Brandt ... [et al.]. — London : Croom Helm, c1981. — 446p : ill,maps ; 23cm
Includes index
ISBN 0-7099-0806-7 : £14.95 : CIP rev.
B81-08834

307′.0935 — Ancient Mesopotamia. Human settlements, *B.C. 6000-A.D. 1000*

Adams, Robert McC.. Heartland of cities : surveys of ancient settlement and land use on the central floodplain of the Euphrates / Robert McC. Adams. — Chicago ; London : University of Chicago Press, 1981. — xx,247p + map : col. ; on fold.sheet 72x42cm : ill,maps ; 29cm
Bibliography: p353-360. — Includes index
ISBN 0-226-00544-5 : £21.00 B81-28354

307′.09361 — Great Britain. Late Bronze Age settlements — *Conference proceedings*

Settlement and society in the British Later Bronze Age / edited by John Barrett and Richard Bradley. — Oxford : B.A.R., 1980. — 2v.(500p) : ill,maps ; 30cm. — (BAR. British series ; 83)
Conference papers. — Includes bibliographies
ISBN 0-86054-108-8 (pbk) : £16.00 B81-36637

307′.0941 — Great Britain. Human settlements. Social planning — *Conference proceedings*

Aspects of British planning experience : a presentation to overseas colleagues / edited by Thomas L. Blair. — [London] : Polytechnic of Central London. School of Environment, c1978. — 201p : ill ; 30cm
Conference papers. — Includes bibliographies
Unpriced (pbk) B81-31380

307′.2 — Developing countries. Internal migration *related to* **provision of health services**

Beenstock, Michael. Health, migration and development / Michael Beenstock. — Farnborough, Hants. : Gower, c1980. — vi,183p : ill ; 23cm
Includes bibliographies and index
ISBN 0-566-00369-4 : £9.50 : CIP rev.
Primary classification 362.1′09172′4 B80-10028

307′.2′0942184 — London. Ealing *(London Borough).* **Population** — *Forecasts*

Ealing in the future : a report on projected population change 1976-1991. — [London] (Town Clerk and Chief Executive's Office, [Town Hall, New Broadway, W5 2BY]) : London Borough of Ealing, 1980. — iii,24,[12] leaves : ill,maps ; 30cm
ISBN 0-86192-007-4 (pbk) : Unpriced
B81-10624

307′.2′0973 — United States. Rural regions. Migration from urban regions

New directions in urban-rural migration : the population turnaround in rural America / edited by David L. Brown, John M. Wardwell. — New York ; London : Academic Press, c1980. — xix,412p : ill,maps ; 24cm. — (Studies in population)
Includes bibliographies and index
ISBN 0-12-136380-5 : £16.60 B81-17590

307′.3 — Urban regions. Ethnic minorities. Housing. Segregation

Ethnic segregation in cities. — London : Croom Helm, Oct.1981. — [256]p
ISBN 0-7099-2012-1 : £12.95 : CIP entry
B81-25715

307.7 — Small communities — *Serials*

Fourth World news : for small nations, small communities & the human spirit. — Vol.1, no.1 (May 1981)-. — London (24 Abercorn Place, NW8) : Fourth World News, 1981-. — v. ; 30cm
Ten issues yearly
ISSN 0261-877x = Fourth World news : £2.50 per year B81-33934

307.7′2 — Developed countries. Rural regions — *Sociological perspectives*

Rural sociology of the advance societies : critical perspectives / edited by Frederick H. Buttel and Howard Newby. — Montclair : Allanheld, Osmun ; London : Croom Helm, 1980. — ix,529p : ill,maps ; 25cm
Includes index
ISBN 0-7099-0408-8 : £14.95 B81-05806

307.7′2 — Rural regions. Settlements

Bunce, Michael. Rural settlement in an urban world. — London : Croom Helm, Nov.1981. — [224]p
ISBN 0-7099-0651-x : £12.95 : CIP entry
B81-31080

307.7′2 — Scotland. Orkney. Rousay. Crofting communities. Conflict, *1840-1890*

Thomson, William P. L.. The little general and the Rousay crofters : crisis and conflict on an Orkney crofting estate / William P.L. Thomson. — Edinburgh : Donald, c1981. — x,234p,8p of plates : ill,maps,ports ; 24cm
Includes index
ISBN 0-85976-062-6 : £15.00 B81-23572

307.7′2′07204 — Europe. Rural communities. Research

Rural community studies in Europe : trends, selected and annotated bibliographies, analyses Vol.1 / edited by Jean-Louis Durand-Drouhin and Lili-Maria Szwengrub in collaboration with Ioan Mihailescu for the European Coordination Center for Research and Documentation in Social Sciences. — Oxford : Pergamon, 1981. — xi,332p : maps ; 26cm
ISBN 0-08-021384-7 : £30.00 : CIP rev.
B80-02664

307.7′2′09154 — Arid regions. Settlement

Settling the desert / edited by L. Berkofsky, D. Faiman, J. Gale. — Sede Boqer : Jacob Blaustein Institute for Desert Research ; London : Gordon and Breach Science, c1981. — xvi,274p : ill,maps ; 24cm
Includes index
ISBN 0-677-16280-4 : Unpriced
Primary classification 630′.915′4 B81-35182

307.7′2′0942 — England. Villages. Redevelopment

What future for villages? / edited and designed by Charles McKean. — London (66 Portland Pl., W1N 4AF) : ERA Publications Board, Eastern Region Royal Institute of British Architects in association with Land Decade Educational Council, Darlington Hall Trust, 1980. — 37p : ill ; 15x21cm. — (ERA broadsheet ; 3)
Text on inside cover
Unpriced (pbk) B81-15687

307.7′2′094248 — Warwickshire. Rural regions. Human settlements, *to 1900.* **Geographical aspects**

Slater, T. R.. Rural settlements in Warwickshire / by T.R. Slater and G. Bartley. — [Birmingham] : Birmingham Branch of the Geographical Association, c1981. — 44p : ill,maps ; 30cm
Ill on inside cover
ISBN 0-7044-0435-4 (pbk) : Unpriced
B81-19666

307.7′2′09426712 — Essex. Elmdon, *1964-1977* — *Sociological perspectives*

Strathern, Marilyn. Kinship at the core : an anthropology of Elmdon, a village in north-west Essex in the nineteen sixties / Marilyn Strathern ; with a foreword by Audrey Richards ; and an epilogue by Frances Oxford. — Cambridge : Cambridge University Press, 1981. — xxxiv,301p : ill,geneal.tables,1map,ports ; 24cm
Bibliography: p296-297. — Includes index
ISBN 0-521-23360-7 : £18.50 : CIP rev.
B81-13800

307.7′4 — Scotland. Peri-urban regions — *Conference proceedings*

Where town meets country. — Aberdeen : Aberdeen University Press, Jan.1982. — [150]p
Conference papers
ISBN 0-08-028442-6 (cased) : £9.50 : CIP entry
ISBN 0-08-028443-4 (pbk) : £6.50 B81-34635

307.7′4′0941 — Great Britain. Suburbs, *1837-1900*

Reeder, David A.. Suburbanity and the Victorian city / by David A. Reeder. — [Leicester] : Victorian Studies Centre, University of Leicester, 1980. — 24p ; 21cm. — (The H.J. Dyos memorial lecture)
Unpriced (pbk) B81-40213

307.7′4′0941 — Great Britain. Suburbs, *to 1980*

Edwards, Arthur M.. The design of suburbia : a critical study in environmental history / Arthur M. Edwards ; with new photographs by Graham & Miranda Jaggers and drawings by T. Affleck Greeves. — London : Pembridge, 1981. — viii,281p : ill ; 24cm
Bibliography: p262. — Includes index
ISBN 0-86206-002-8 : £16.50 B81-29381

307.7′4′0973 — United States. Suburbs. Social aspects

Muller, Peter O.. Contemporary suburban America / Peter O. Muller. — Englewood Cliffs ; London : Prentice-Hall, c1981. — xii,218p : ill,maps ; 23cm
Bibliography: p183-209. - Includes index
ISBN 0-13-170647-0 (pbk) : £6.45 B81-17304

307.7′6 — Capitalist countries. Urbanisation

Urbanization and urban planning in capitalist society / edited by Michael Dear and Allen J. Scott. — London : Methuen, 1981. — xxvii,619p : ill,maps ; 24cm
Includes bibliographies and index
ISBN 0-416-74640-3 (cased) : Unpriced : CIP rev.
ISBN 0-416-74650-0 (pbk) : Unpriced
B80-25179

307.7′6 — Cities. Inner areas

The Inner city in context. — London : Heinemann Educational, Nov.1981. — [224]p
ISBN 0-435-35717-4 (cased) : £12.50 : CIP entry
ISBN 0-435-35718-2 (pbk) : £5.50 B81-30162

307.7′6 — Cities. Social planning — *Comparative studies*

City, economy and society. — London : Harper and Row, Jan.1982. — [236]p
ISBN 0-06-318205-x (cased) : £12.50 : CIP entry
ISBN 0-06-318206-8 (pbk) : £6.95 B81-33969

307.7′6 — Great Britain. Residential areas — *For schools*

Lines, C. J.. Where we live / authors Clifford Lines, Laurie Bolwell. — London : Macdonald Educational, 1981. — 48p : ill(some col.),maps (some col.) ; 22cm. — (Town and around. Geography)
Cover title. — Text, ill on covers
ISBN 0-356-07189-8 : Unpriced B81-29911

307.7′6 — Scotland. New towns — *For schools*

Williams, Michael, *1938 June 4-*. New towns / by Michael Williams. — 3rd ed. — London : Heinemann Educational, 1981. — 57p : ill,maps,plans ; 20x22cm. — (Contemporary Scotland ; 2)
Previous ed.: 1975. — Bibliography: p57
ISBN 0-435-34203-7 (pbk) : £1.95 B81-09415

307.7′6 — United States. Conurbations

The **American** metropolitan system present and future / edited by Stanley D. Brunn and James O. Wheeler. — [Washington, D.C.] : Winston ; London : Edward Arnold, 1980. — viii,216p : ill,maps ; 24cm. — (Scripta series in geography)
Includes index
ISBN 0-7131-6297-x : £12.50 : CIP rev. B80-13712

307.7′6 — United States. Conurbations. Social aspects

Bollens, John C.. The metropolis : its people, politics, and economic life John C. Bollens, Henry J. Schmandt. — 4th ed. — New York ; London : Harper & Row, c1982. — xi,461p : ill,maps ; 25cm
Previous ed.: 1975. — Bibliography: p421-446. — Includes index
ISBN 0-06-040794-8 : Unpriced B81-40669

307.7′6 — Urban development — *Conference proceedings*

Dynamics of urban development : proceedings of an international conference held on the occasion of the 50th anniversary of the Netherlands Economic Institute in Rotterdam, September 4, 1979 / edited by L.H. Klaassen, W.T.M. Molle, J.H.P. Paelinck. — Farnborough : Gower, c1981. — xi,267p : ill,maps ; 23cm. — (Studies in spatial analysis)
Includes bibliographies
ISBN 0-566-00378-3 : £15.00 : CIP rev. B81-10476

307.76 — Urban development — *Conference proceedings*

World Congress of Engineers and Architects in Israel *(5th : 1979 : Israel)*. Urban development and urban renewal. — London : George Godwin, Sept.1981. — [296]p. — (International forum series)
ISBN 0-7114-5728-x : £16.00 : CIP entry B81-23853

307.7′6 — Urban regions

Palen, J. John. The urban world / J. John Palen. — 2nd ed. — New York ; London : McGraw-Hill, c1981. — xvii,477p : ill,1map ; 24cm
Previous ed.: 1975. — Bibliography: p443-468. — Includes index
ISBN 0-07-048107-5 : £13.25 B81-17042

307.7′6 — Urban regions. Social conditions. Influence of economic conditions — *Marxist viewpoints*

Mingione, Enzo. Social conflict and the city / Enzo Mingione. — Oxford : Blackwell, 1981. — 207p ; 24cm
Includes index
ISBN 0-631-10441-0 (cased) : £16.00
ISBN 0-631-12716-x (pbk) : £7.95 B81-24180

307.7′6 — Urban regions. Structure

Gordon, George, *1939-*. Urban morphology : structure and process / George Gordon. — [Glasgow] ([Royal College, 204 George St., Glasgow G1 1XW]) : [University of Strathclyde, Department of Geography], [1980?]. — 14,2 leaves : 2maps ; 30cm. — (Research seminar series / University of Strathclyde Department of Geography ; no.10)
Cover title. — Two leaves printed on both sides. — Bibliography: leaves 1-2
Unpriced (pbk) B81-03281

307.7′6 — Urban sociology

Saunders, Peter, *1950-*. Social theory and the urban question / Peter Saunders. — London : Hutchinson, 1981. — 310p ; 23cm. — (Hutchinson university library)
Bibliography: p293-302. — Includes index
ISBN 0-09-143600-1 (cased) : £12.00
ISBN 0-09-143601-x (pbk) : £4.95 B81-32516

307.7′6 — Urban studies

Urban change and conflict. — London : Harper and Row, Jan.1982. — [288]p
ISBN 0-06-318203-3 (cased) : £12.50 : CIP entry
ISBN 0-06-318204-1 (pbk £6.95) B81-34487

307.7′6′0151472 — Urban sociology. Applications of catastrophe theory

Wilson, A. G.. Catastrophe theory and bifurcation : applications to urban and regional systems / A.G. Wilson. — London : Croom Helm, c1981. — 331p : ill ; 23cm. — (Croom Helm series in geography and environment)
Bibliography: p310-313. - Includes index
ISBN 0-7099-2702-9 : £16.95 : CIP rev.
Also classified at 307.7′6′0151535 B80-34522

307.7′6′0151535 — Urban sociology. Applications of bifurcation theory

Wilson, A. G.. Catastrophe theory and bifurcation : applications to urban and regional systems / A.G. Wilson. — London : Croom Helm, c1981. — 331p : ill ; 23cm. — (Croom Helm series in geography and environment)
Bibliography: p310-313. - Includes index
ISBN 0-7099-2702-9 : £16.95 : CIP rev.
Primary classification 307.7′6′0151472 B80-34522

307.7′6′0715 — Scotland. Strathclyde Region. Glasgow. Adult education. Curriculum subjects: Urban studies. Courses — *Proposals*

Harvey, Colin. The cultures of affluence and poverty : a course in urban education / by Colin Harvey. — Milngavie (163 Mugdock Rd., Milngavie, Dunbartonshire G62 6BR) : Heatherbank Press for the Museum of Social Work, 1980. — 22leaves : 1facsim ; 31cm. — (Occasional paper / Museum of Social Work ; no.4)
Cover title. — Text on inside cover
ISBN 0-905192-25-7 (spiral) : £1.50 B81-29259

307.7′6′0722 — Developed countries. Urban regions. Planning — *Case studies*

Urban problems and planning in the developed world / edited by Michael Pacione. — London : Croom Helm, c1981. — 324p : ill,maps ; 23cm
Includes bibliographies and index
ISBN 0-7099-0191-7 : £13.50 B81-27576

307.7′6′0724 — Great Britain. Urban regions. Spatial analysis. Zoning systems. Broadbent′s rule — *Study regions: Merseyside (Metropolitan County)*

Brown, Peter J. B.. An empirical investigation of the application of Broadbent′s rule to spatial system design / by Peter J.B. Brown, Ian Masser. — Liverpool (P.O. Box 147, Liverpool L69 3BX) : Department of Civic Design, University of Liverpool, 1977. — 24 leaves : ill,1map ; 30cm. — (Working paper / University of Liverpool Department of Civic Design ; 4)
Bibliography: leaves 23-24
£1.00 (pbk) B81-06200

307.7′6′0724 — Urban regions. Mathematical models

Foot, David, *1939-*. Operational urban models. — London : Methuen, Nov.1981. — [250]p
ISBN 0-416-73320-4 (cased) : £10.00 : CIP entry
ISBN 0-416-73330-1 (pbk) : £5.00 B81-30396

307.7′6′09 — Cities, *to 1975*

Benevolo, Leonardo. The history of the city / Leonardo Benevolo ; translated by Geoffrey Culverwell. — London : Scolar, 1980. — 1011p : ill,maps,plans ; 25cm
Translation of: Storia della città. — Includes index
ISBN 0-85967-534-3 : £45.00 : CIP rev. B80-03046

307.7′6′091724 — Developing countries. Cities — *For schools*

Massingham, Bryan. Cities and industry in the developing world. — London : Edward Arnold, Sept.1981. — [64]p. — (Patterns of development)
ISBN 0-7131-0455-4 (pbk) : £2.25 : CIP entry
Also classified at 338′.091724 B81-23832

307.7′6′091724 — Developing countries. Urban regions. Social planning

Problems and planning in Third World cities. — London : Croom Helm, Sept.1981. — [304]p
ISBN 0-7099-0192-5 : £13.95 : CIP entry B81-21502

Urban planning practice in developing countries. — Oxford : Pergamon, Dec.1981. — [365]p. — (Urban and regional planning series ; v.25)
ISBN 0-08-022225-0 : £25.00 : CIP entry B81-31805

307.7′6′091812 — Western world. Urban regions. Human geographical features

Knox, Paul. Urban social geography. — London : Longman, Aug.1981. — [352]p
ISBN 0-582-30044-4 (pbk) : £9.95 : CIP entry B81-22551

307.7′6′094 — Western Europe. Urban development, *1950-1975*

Hall, Peter, *1932-*. Growth centres in the European urban system / Peter Hall, Dennis Hay. — London : Heinemann Educational, 1980. — xxii,278p : ill,maps ; 25cm
Bibliography: p264-270. — Includes index
ISBN 0-435-35380-2 : £13.50 : CIP rev. B80-01051

307.7′6′094 — Western Europe. Urbanisation, *1500-1970* — *Conference proceedings*

Patterns of European urbanisation since 1500 / edited by H. Schmal. — London : Croom Helm, c1981. — 309p : ill,maps ; 23cm
Conference papers. — Includes bibliographies
ISBN 0-7099-0365-0 : £12.95 B81-17876

307.7′6′0941 — Great Britain. Cities. Inner areas. Social planning

Lawless, Paul. Britain′s inner cities. — London : Harper and Row, May 1981. — [224]p
ISBN 0-06-318184-3 (cased) : £8.95 : CIP entry
ISBN 0-06-318185-1 (pbk) : £4.95 B81-06605

307.7′6′0941 — Great Britain. Town planning, *1945-1975* — *Sociological perspectives*

Ravetz, Alison. Remaking cities : contradictions of the recent urban environment / Alison Ravetz. — London : Croom Helm, c1980. — 375p ; 23cm
Bibliography: p349-370. - Includes index
ISBN 0-85664-293-2 : £14.95 : CIP rev. B80-13232

307.7′60941 — Great Britain. Urban development. Sociopolitical aspects — *Conference proceedings*

New perspectives in urban change and conflict. — London : Heinemann Educational, Sept.1981. — [256]p
ISBN 0-435-82404-x : £13.50 : CIP entry B81-23767

307.7′6′0941 — Great Britain. Urban sociology — *Conference proceedings*

Social interaction and ethnic segregation. — London : Academic Press, Dec.1981. — [250]p
Conference papers
ISBN 0-12-379080-8 : CIP entry B81-31340

307.7′6′09411 — Scotland. New towns — *Serials*

Reports of the Cumbernauld, East Kilbride, Glenrothes, Irvine and Livingston Development Corporations for the year ended 31st March .... — 1980. — Edinburgh : H.M.S.O., 1980. — 200p
ISBN 0-10-269280-7 : £7.25 B81-04406

307.7′6′0942574 — Environment planning. Sociopolitical aspects — *Study regins: Oxfordshire. Oxford*

Simmie, J. M.. Power, property and corporatism : the political sociology of planning / James Simmie. — London : Macmillan, 1981. — ix,351p : ill,maps ; 22cm
Bibliography: p321-345. — Includes index
ISBN 0-333-24345-5 (cased) : £15.00
ISBN 0-333-32359-9 (pbk) : Unpriced B81-38630

307.7′6′09426795 — Essex. Southend-on-Sea. Social planning

Planning handbook / Southend-on-Sea Borough Council. — [New ed.]. — London (Publicity House, Streatham Hill, SW2J) : Pyramid, 1980. — 48p : ill,1map ; 21cm
Previous ed.: 1978
Unpriced (pbk) B81-09904

307.7′6′0944 — France. Urbanisation, *1800-1900*

Merriman, John. French cities in the nineteenth century. — London : Hutchinson Education, Jan.1982. — [264]p
ISBN 0-09-145200-7 : £15.00 : CIP entry B81-34507

307.7′6′0947 — Eastern Europe & Soviet Union. Urbanisation

Musil, Jiří. Urbanization in socialist countries / Jiří Musil ; with a foreword by Simona Ganassi Agger. — White Plains, N.Y. : Sharpe ; London : Croom Helm, 1981, c1980. — xi,185p : maps ; 24cm
Originally published: White Plains, N.Y. : Sharpe, c1980. — Published simultaneously as International journal of sociology, v.10, no.2-3. 1980 (Summer-Fall). — Bibliography: p167-177. - Includes index
ISBN 0-7099-1719-8 : £10.50 B81-17875

307.7′6′0951 — China. Urban development, *1949-1980*

Murphey, Rhoads. The fading of the Maoist vision : city and country in China′s development / Rhoads Murphey. — New York ; London : Methuen, c1980. — xiii,169p : ill,maps ; 22cm
Bibliography: p161-166. - Includes index
ISBN 0-416-60201-0 : £11.00 B81-01757

307.7′6′097 — North America. Urban regions. Growth

Yeates, Maurice. North American urban patterns / Maurice Yeates. — [Washington, D.C.] : Winston ; London : Edward Arnold, 1980. — vii,168p : ill,maps ; 24cm. — (Scripta series in geography)
Bibliography: p149-154.. — Includes index
ISBN 0-7131-6299-6 : £10.95 : CIP rev.
ISBN 0-470-27017-9 B80-13711

307.7′6′0973 — United States. Cities. Development. Socioeconomic aspects

Clay, Grady. Close-up : how to read the American city / Grady Clay. — Phoenix ed. — Chicago ; London : University of Chicago Press, c1980. — 192p : ill,maps,facsims ; 25cm
Previous ed.: 1973. — Includes index
ISBN 0-226-10945-3 (pbk) : £4.20 B81-01535

307.7′6′0973 — United States. Cities. Inner areas. Social planning — *Comparative studies*

Personality, politics and planning : how city planners work / edited by Anthony James Catanese and W. Paul Farmer. — Beverly Hills ; London : Sage, c1978. — 227p ; 23cm
Includes index
ISBN 0-8039-0961-6 : £11.00 B81-04777

307.7′6′0973 — United States. Urban regions. Social aspects — *Conference proceedings*

Urban professionals and the future of the metropolis / edited by Paula Dubeck and Zane L. Miller. — Port Washington ; London : National University Publications : Kennikat, 1980. — ix,122p : ill ; 23cm. — (Interdisciplinary urban series)
Conference papers
ISBN 0-8046-9261-0 : £10.60 B81-05097

307.7′6′0973 — United States. Urbanisation, *1840-1860*

Pred, Allan. Urban growth and city-systems in the United States, 1840-1860 / Allan Pred. — Cambridge, Mass. ; London : Harvard University Press, 1980. — xv,282p : ill,maps ; 24cm. — (Harvard studies in urban history)
Includes index
ISBN 0-674-93091-6 : £16.80 B81-16566

307.7′6′0973 — United States. Urbanisation, *to 1980*

Chudacoff, Howard P.. The evolution of American urban society / Howard P. Chudacoff. — 2nd ed. — Englewood Cliffs ; London : Prentice-Hall, c1981. — viii,312p : ill,facsims,ports ; 23cm
Previous ed.: 1975. — Includes bibliographies and index
ISBN 0-13-293605-4 (pbk) : £7.75 B81-19647

307.7′6′098 — Latin America. Urbanisation

Butterworth, Douglas. Latin American urbanization / Douglas Butterworth, John K. Chance. — Cambridge : Cambridge University Press, 1981. — xi,243p : 1map ; 24cm. — (Urbanization in developing countries)
Bibliography: p216-237. - Includes index
ISBN 0-521-23713-0 (cased) : £15.00
ISBN 0-521-28175-x (pbk) : £5.50 B81-11193

307.7′6′09943 — Queensland. Open Cut. Working class communities. Social conditions

Williams, Claire. Open Cut. — London : Allen & Unwin, Jan.1982. — [218]p. — (Studies in society ; 8)
ISBN 0-86861-299-5 : £12.00 : CIP entry B81-33932

308.7′088042 — Women. Sex relations — *Feminist viewpoints*

Rich, Adrienne. Compulsory heterosexuality and lesbian existence / Adrienne Rich. — London (38 Mount Pleasant, WC1X 0AP) : Onlywomen Press, 1981. — 32p ; 21cm
This article originally published in Signs, vol.5, no.4, 1980
ISBN 0-906500-07-9 (pbk) : £0.90 B81-17734

310 — STATISTICS

310 — Social conditions — *Statistics*

The **world** in figures / editorial information compiled by The Economist. — 2nd ed. — London : Macmillan, 1980. — 294p : ill(some col.),maps(some col.) ; 27cm
Previous ed. i.e. 2nd ed.: 1978. — Includes index
ISBN 0-333-30464-0 (cased) : £15.00
ISBN 0-333-30468-3 (pbk) : £8.95 B81-02950

310 — Social sciences. Statistics

Powell, F. C.. Statistical tables for the social, biological and physical sciences. — Cambridge : Cambridge University Press, Feb.1982. — [96]p
ISBN 0-521-24141-3 (cased) : £7.50 : CIP entry
ISBN 0-521-28473-2 (pbk) : £2.95
Also classified at 574′.01028 B81-40268

310′.5 — World — *Statistics — For marketing — Serials*

Concise guide to international markets. Vol.1, Europe. — 1980/81-. — Kingston-upon-Thames (39a London Rd, Kingston-upon-Thames, Surrey KT2 6ND) : Leslie Stinton & Partners by arrangement with the International Advertising Association U.K. Chapter, 1980-. — v. ; 30cm
Irregular. — Continues in part: Concise guide to international markets
ISSN 0260-177x = Concise guide to international markets. Vol.1. Europe : Unpriced B81-15544

312 — POPULATION STATISTICS

312′.028′5 — Great Britain. Population. Census data, *1981*. Data processing. Confidentiality — *Inquiry reports*

1981 census of population : confidentiality and computing. — London : H.M.S.O., [1981]. — iii,16p ; 25cm. — (Cmnd. ; 8201)
Contents: Report of the British Computer Society - Government replies to the Society′s recommendations
ISBN 0-10-182010-0 (unbound) : £2.10 B81-18307

312′.0941 — Great Britain. Population. Census data. Small area statistics — *Statistics*

Craig, John, *1935-*. Variations between small areas in some 1971 Census Variables / John Craig. — [London] ([10 Kingsway, WC2B 6JP]) : Office of Population Censuses and Surveys, 1981. — 60p ; 30cm. — (Occasional paper / Office of Population Censuses and Surveys ; 17)
ISBN 0-906197-22-8 (pbk) : £1.00 B81-30054

312′.09414′1 — Scotland. Strathclyde Region. Population — *Statistics — Serials*

Strathclyde. *Strategic Issues Division*. Base projections : population, households, housing / Strathclyde Regional Council, Strategic Issues Division, Chief Executive′s Department. — 1978 to 1985-. — [Glasgow] ([19 Cadogan St., Glasgow G2]) : The Council, 1979-. — v. ; 30cm
Annual. — Description based on: 1979 to 1986 issue
ISSN 0261-2887 = Base projections — Strathclyde Regional Council. Strategic Issues Division. Chief Executive′s Department : £2.50 B81-25041

312′.09416 — Northern Ireland. Population — *Statistics — Serials*

[Annual report of the Registrar General *(Northern Ireland General Register Office)*]. Annual report of the Registrar General. — 57th (1978). — Belfast : H.M.S.O., 1981. — vi,259p
ISBN 0-337-11051-4 : £10.70 B81-27327

312′.0942 — England. Population — *Estimates — Tables*

Population estimates / Office of Population Censuses and Surveys. — 1979. — London : H.M.S.O., 1980. — 20p. — (Series PP1 ; no.4)
ISBN 0-11-690747-9 : £3.20 B81-11759

312′.0942 — England. Population. Official statistics

Great Britain. *Office of Population Censuses and Surveys*. Population and health statistics in England and Wales / [Office of Population Censuses and Surveys]. — [London] ([St. Catherines House, 10 Kingsway, WC2B 6JP]) : The Office, c1980. — 51p : forms ; 30cm
Cover title
Unpriced (pbk) B81-04814

312′.0942 — England. Population — *Statistics — Serials*

Local authority vital statistics / Office of Population Censuses and Surveys. — 1979. — London : H.M.S.O., 1981. — 31p. — (Series VS ; no.6)
ISBN 0-11-690752-5 : £3.60 B81-23510

312′.09425′3 — Lincolnshire. Population — *Statistics — Serials*

Lincolnshire, population : a digest of population characteristics and trends in Lincolnshire / County Planning Officer, Lincolnshire County Council. — No.1, 1979-. — Lincoln (County Offices, Newland, Lincoln LN1 1YJ) : The Council, 1979-. — v. : ill,maps ; 21cm
Annual
ISSN 0260-8405 = Lincolnshire. Population : £0.30 B81-09046

312′.2′072 — Survival data. Statistical models

Elandt-Johnson, Regina C.. Survival models and data analysis / Regina C. Elandt-Johnson, Norman L. Johnson. — New York ; Chichester : Wiley, c1980. — xvi,457p : ill ; 24cm. — (Wiley series in probability and mathematical statistics)
Includes bibliographies and index
ISBN 0-471-03174-7 : £18.70 B81-04110

312′.2′0883875 — Sailors. Deaths. Causes — *Statistics*

Barry, Michael, *19---*. Occupational health and safety of seafarers : survey of statistics : preliminary report / Michael Barry. — Rev. — London (17 Bury St., EC3A 5AH) : Sealife Programme, 1979. — 59p : ill,1form ; 30cm
Unpriced (spiral) B81-19882

312'.2'0904 — Man. Mortality rate, ***1901-1975*** **—** ***Statistics***

International mortality statistics / [compiled by] Michael Alderson. — London : Macmillan, 1981. — ix,524p ; 29cm. — (Macmillan reference books)
Includes bibliographies and index
ISBN 0-333-23969-5 : £45.00 B81-38804

312'.2'0942 — England. Deaths — ***Statistics — Serials***

Mortality statistics : review of the Registrar General on deaths in England and Wales / Office of Population Censuses and Surveys. — 1978. — London : H.M.S.O., 1980. — xvii,102p. — (Series DH1 ; no.6)
ISBN 0-11-690743-6 : £7.10 B81-07348

312'.3994'00942 — England. Man. Cancer — ***Statistics — Serials***

Cancer statistics, registrations / Office of Population Censuses and Surveys. — 1974. — London : H.M.S.O., 1980. — xii,112p. — (Series MB1 ; no.4)
ISBN 0-11-690738-x : £7.70
ISSN 0143-4829 B81-07815

Cancer statistics, registrations / Office of Population Censuses and Surveys. — 1975. — London : H.M.S.O., 1981. — xii,105p. — (Series MB1 ; no.5)
ISBN 0-11-690753-3 : £7.70
ISSN 0143-4829 B81-23512

312'.5'0942 — England. Marriage & divorce — ***Statistics — Serials***

Marriage and divorce statistics / Office of Population Censuses and Surveys. — 1978. — London : H.M.S.O., 1980. — xvi,100p. — (Series FM2 ; no.5)
ISBN 0-11-690748-7 : £7.70
ISSN 0140-8992 B81-09173

312'.8 — Great Britain. International migration — ***Statistics — Serials***

International migration / Office of Population Censuses and Surveys. — 1979. — London : H.M.S.O., 1981. — 42p. — (Series MN ; no. 6)
ISBN 0-11-690759-2 : £4.70 B81-29107

314 — GENERAL STATISTICS OF EUROPE

314.1 — Great Britain. Statistics. Information sources

Reviews of United Kingdom statistical sources. — Oxford : Pergamon
Vol.14: Rail transport; and, Sea transport. — Oct.1981. — [280]p
ISBN 0-08-026105-1 : £14.50 : CIP entry B81-25849

314.1'05 — Great Britain. Social conditions — ***Statistics — Serials***

Annual abstract of statistics / Central Statistical Office. — No.117 (1981 ed.). — London : H.M.S.O., 1981. — xiii,521p
ISBN 0-11-630775-7 : £14.00 B81-20035

Social trends / Central Statistical Office. — No.11 (1981 ed.). — London : H.M.S.O., 1980. — 253p
ISBN 0-11-630773-0 : £16.50
ISSN 0306-7742 B81-09231

314.1'07 — Great Britain. Social conditions. Statistics. Information sources

Statistical sources / [the Statistical Sources Course Team]. — Milton Keynes : Open University Press. — (Social sciences : a second level course)
At head of title: The Open University
Audiovision handbook 1. — 1981. — 51p : ill,forms ; 30cm. — (D291 ; AVH1)
ISBN 0-335-04636-3 (unbound) : Unpriced B81-27791

Statistical sources. — Milton Keynes : Open University Press. — (Social sciences : a second level course)
At head of title: The Open University
Population statistics / prepared for the course team by Bob Peacock. — 1981. — 96p ; 30cm. — (D291)
Bibliography: p94-96
ISBN 0-335-04631-2 (pbk) : Unpriced B81-18015

Statistical sources / [the Statistical Sources Course Team]. — Milton Keynes : Open Universty Press. — (Social sciences : a second level course)
Bibliography: p29-30
Surveying sexual behaviour / prepared for the Course Team by R. Stainton Rogers. — 1980. — 31p : ill ; 30cm. — (D291)
ISBN 0-335-04627-4 (pbk) : Unpriced B81-40713

314.11'05 — Scotland. Social conditions — ***Statistics — Serials***

Scottish abstract of statistics / Scottish Office. — No.10 (1981). — Edinburgh : H.M.S.O, 1981. — viii,174p
ISBN 0-11-491726-4 : £16.00 B81-34053

314.11'35'05 — Scotland. Shetland — ***Statistics — Serials***

Shetland in statistics. — No.10 (1981). — Lerwick (93 St Olaf St., Lerwick, Shetland) : Research and Development Department, Shetland Islands Council, [1981]. — 40p
ISBN 0-904562-13-1 : £0.75
ISSN 0142-2022 B81-30867

314.12'95 — Scotland. Fife Region. Glenrothes. Social conditions — ***Statistics***

Glenrothes Development Corporation statistical summary / compiled by Planning Section (Policy & Research). — Glenrothes (New Glenrothes House, Glenrothes, Fife) : Glenrothes Development Corporation, 1979. — 72p : ill,maps,plans ; 21x30cm
£1.00 (spiral) B81-38493

314.16 — Northern Ireland. Social conditions — ***Statistics — Serials***

Social and economic trends in Northern Ireland / Department of Finance, Northern Ireland. — No.6 (1980). — Belfast : H.M.S.O., 1980. — 80p
ISBN 0-337-23331-4 : £5.50 B81-03997

314.24'56 — Shropshire. Telford. Social conditions — ***Statistics — Serials***

Telford social trends / [Telford Development Corporation] Department of Social Development ; compiled by the Social Research Group. — No.1 (1980 ed.)-. — Telford (Malinslee House, Telford, Shropshire TF2 9NT) : The Department, [1980?]-. — v. : ill,maps ; 30cm
ISSN 0261-8672 = Telford social trends : Unpriced B81-34048

314.27'612 — Lancashire. Skelmersdale. Social conditions — ***Statistics — Serials***

[Population & social survey ***(Skelmersdale Development Corporation)*****]**. Population & social survey. — 1976. — [Skelmersdale] ([Main Office, High St., Skelmersdale, Lancashire]) : Skelmersdale Development Corporation, [1976]. — 87p
Unpriced B81-29977

[Population & social survey ***(Skelmersdale Development Corporation)*****]**. Population & social survey. — 1977. — [Skelmersdale] ([Main Office, High St., Skelmersdale, Lancashire]) : Skelmersdale Development Corporation, [1977]. — 96p
Unpriced B81-29978

[Population & social survey ***(Skelmersdale Development Corporation)*****]**. Population & social survey. — 1978. — [Skelmersdale] ([Main Office, High St., Skelmersdale, Lancashire]) : Skelmersdale Development Corporation, [1978]. — 94p
Unpriced B81-29979

[Population & social survey ***(Skelmersdale Development Corporation)*****]**. Population & social survey. — 1979. — [Skelmersdale] ([Main Office, High St., Skelmersdale, Lancashire]) : Skelmersdale Development Corporation, [1979]. — 108p
Unpriced B81-29980

[Population & social survey ***(Skelmersdale Development Corporation)*****]**. Population & social survey. — 1980. — [Skelmersdale] ([Main Office, High St., Skelmersdale, Lancashire]) : Skelmersdale Development Corporation, [1980]. — 108p
£3.50 B81-25037

314.28'46 — North Yorkshire. Malton. Social conditions, ***1841*** **—** ***Statistics***

Malton in the early nineteenth century / edited by D.J. Salmon ; introduced by A. Harris ; with illustrations and maps drawn by K. Ashcroft & M.H. Balshaw. — [Northallerton] (North Yorkshire County Record Office, County Hall, Northallerton, N. Yorkshire DL7 8AD) : North Yorkshire County Council, 1981. — 136p,(8fold.),[2]fold.leaves of plates : ill,maps ; 31cm. — (North Yorkshire County Record Office publications ; no.26)
Includes Statistics of the town and parishes of Malton, by William Charles Copperthwaite
ISBN 0-906035-15-5 (pbk) : £2.50 B81-24384

314.29'05 — Wales. Social conditions — ***Statistics — Serials***

Digest of Welsh statistics / Welsh Office. — No.26 (1980). — Cardiff : H.M.S.O., 1980. — ix,195p
ISBN 0-11-790143-1 : £16.50 B81-09176

315 — GENERAL STATISTICS OF ASIA

315.1'249 — Taiwan — ***Statistics — For marketing***

Taiwan market data. — Farnborough : Gower, Oct.1981. — [150]p
ISBN 0-566-02307-5 (pbk) : £25.00 : CIP entry B81-27950

315.1'25 — Hong Kong — ***Statistics — For marketing***

Hong Kong and Macau market data. — Farnborough, Hants. : Gower, Nov.1981. — [150]p
ISBN 0-566-02310-5 (pbk) : £25.00 : CIP entry B81-31257

315.19'5 — South Korea — ***Statistics — For marketing***

South Korea market data. — Farnborough : Gower, Nov.1981. — [150]p
ISBN 0-566-02309-1 (pbk) : £25.00 : CIP entry B81-31256

315.93 — Thailand - ***Statistics - For marketing***

Thailand market data. — Farnborough : Gower, July 1981. — [150]p
ISBN 0-566-02305-9 (pbk) : £25.00 : CIP entry B81-14931

315.951 — Malaysia - ***Statistics - For marketing***

Malaysia market data. — Farnborough : Gower, July 1981. — [150]p
ISBN 0-566-02304-0 (pbk) : £25.00 : CIP entry B81-14933

315.95'7 — Singapore - ***Statistics - For marketing***

Singapore market data. — Farnborough : Gower, July 1981. — [150]p
ISBN 0-566-02303-2 (pbk) : £25.00 : CIP entry B81-14934

315.98 — Indonesia - ***Statistics - For marketing***

Indonesia market data. — Farnborough : Gower, July 1981. — [150]p
ISBN 0-566-02306-7 (pbk) : £25.00 : CIP entry B81-14932

315.99 — Philippines — ***Statistics — For marketing***

Philippines market data. — Farnborough : Gower, Oct.1981. — [150]p
ISBN 0-566-02308-3 (pbk) : £25.00 : CIP entry B81-28047

316 — GENERAL STATISTICS OF AFRICA

316 — Africa. Social conditions. Statistics

Kpedekpo, G. M. K.. Social and economic statistics for Africa : their sources, collection, uses and reliability / G.M.K. Kpedekpo, P.L. Arya. — London : Allen & Unwin, 1981. — x,259p ; 22cm
Includes bibliographies and index
ISBN 0-04-310011-2 (pbk) : Unpriced : CIP rev. B81-15889

320 — POLITICAL SCIENCE

320 — Political power

Slack, Walter H.. The grim science : the struggle for power / Walter H. Slack. — Port Washington ; London : National University Publications : Kennikat, 1981. — 217p ; 24cm. — (Series in political science)
Bibliography: p215-217
ISBN 0-8046-9260-2 : £17.00 B81-10326

320 — Political science

Policy and action. — London : Methuen, Nov.1981. — [350]p
ISBN 0-416-30670-5 (cased) : £11.00 : CIP entry
ISBN 0-416-30680-2 (pbk) : £5.95 B81-30159

320 — Politics

Barry, Norman P.. An introduction to modern political theory / Norman P. Barry. — London : Macmillan, 1981. — xvi,250p ; 23cm
Bibliography: p236-242. — Includes index
ISBN 0-333-26890-3 (cased) : £12.50 : CIP rev.
ISBN 0-333-26891-1 (pbk) : Unpriced B80-09606

Blondel, Jean. The discipline of politics. — London : Butterworths, Aug.1981. — [240]p
ISBN 0-408-10681-6 (cased) : £12.00 : CIP entry
ISBN 0-408-10785-5 (pbk) : £6.95 B81-16928

Brown, A. Lee. Rules and conflict : an introduction to political life and its study / A. Lee Brown, Jr. — Englewood Cliffs ; London : Prentice-Hall, c1981. — xiv,368p : ill,facsims ; 23cm
Includes index
ISBN 0-13-783738-0 (pbk) : £6.45 B81-22756

Leeds, Christopher A.. Political studies / C.A. Leeds. — 3rd ed. — Plymouth : Macdonald and Evans, 1981. — ix,389p : ill ; 18cm. — (The M & E handbook series)
Previous ed.: 1975. — Bibliography: p358-361. - Includes index
ISBN 0-7121-1694-x (pbk) : £3.95 B81-09364

Lipson, Leslie. The great issues of politics : an introduction to political science / Leslie Lipson. — 6th ed. — Englewood Cliffs ; London : Prentice-Hall, c1981. — xix,407p : ill ; 24cm
Previous ed.: 1976. — Text on lining paper. — Bibliography: p393. - Includes index
ISBN 0-13-363903-7 : £11.00 B81-21248

Ponton, Geoffrey. Introduction to politics. — Oxford : Martin Robertson, Feb.1982. — [288]p
ISBN 0-85520-466-4 (cased) : £12.50 : CIP entry
ISBN 0-85520-467-2 (pbk) : £4.95 B81-35703

Winter, Herbert R.. People and politics : an introduction to political science / Herbert R. Winter, Thomas J. Bellows in collaboration with Conrad Waligorski and Stanley Erikson. — 2nd ed. — New York ; Chichester : Wiley, c1981. — xii,534p : ill,facsims,ports ; 24cm
Previous ed.: 1977. — Includes index
ISBN 0-471-08153-1 : £10.25 B81-17244

World politics / [the D233 'World Politics' Course Team]. — Milton Keynes : Open University Press. — (Social sciences : a second level course)
At head of title: The Open University
[Block 2]: A first perspective : power and security / prepared by the course team. — 1981. — 160p : ill,maps,facsims,ports ; 30cm. — (D233 ; II (2-5))
Includes bibliographies. — Contents: Paper 2: The Potsdam conference — Paper 3: State, nation and the international political system — Paper 4: Power and state behaviour — Paper 5: The state and the international system
ISBN 0-335-12026-1 (pbk) : Unpriced B81-27788

320 — Politics — *Early works*

Aristotle. [Politica. English]. The politics / Aristotle ; translated by T.A. Sinclair. — Rev. ed. / revised and re-presented by Trevor J. Saunders. — Harmondsworth : Penguin, 1981. — 506p ; 18cm. — (Penguin classics)
Translation of: Politica. — Previous ed.: 1962. — Bibliography: p477-488. — Includes index
ISBN 0-14-044421-1 (pbk) : £2.50 B81-38356

Burke, Edmund, *1729-1797*. The writings and speeches of Edmund Burke / general editor Paul Langford. — Oxford : Clarendon Press
Vol.2: Party, Parliament and the American crisis 1766-1774 / edited by Paul Langford ; textual editor for the writings William B. Todd. — 1981. — xviii,508p ; 24cm
Bibliography: pxv-xviii. — Includes index
ISBN 0-19-822416-8 : £40.00 : CIP rev. B80-22965

Machiavelli, Niccolò. The Prince and other political writings / Niccolò Machiavelli ; selected and translated with introduction and notes by Bruce Penman. — London : Dent, 1981. — xiii,354p ; 18cm. — (Everyman's library)
Includes index
ISBN 0-460-11280-5 (pbk) : £3.50 B81-27013

320 — Politics — *Festschriften*

From national development to global community : essays in honor of Karl W. Deutsch / edited by Richard L. Merritt and Bruce M. Russett. — London : Allen & Unwin, 1981. — 480p : ill,maps ; 24cm
Bibliography: p447-463. — Includes index
ISBN 0-04-327060-3 (cased) : £18.00 : CIP rev.
ISBN 0-04-327061-1 (pbk) : Unpriced B81-00025

320 — Politics — *For schools*

Renwick, Alan. Basic political concepts / Alan Renwick and Ian Swinburn. — London : Hutchinson, 1980. — 160p : ill ; 22cm
Bibliography: p155-156. — Includes index
ISBN 0-09-143291-x (pbk) : £2.50 : CIP rev. B80-13721

320'.01 — Politics. Concepts — *Philosophical perspectives*

Oppenheim, Felix E.. Political concepts : a reconstruction / Felix E. Oppenheim. — Oxford : Basil Blackwell, 1981. — x,227p ; 22cm
Originally published: Chicago : University of Chicago Press, 1981. — Bibliography: p211-219. — Includes index
ISBN 0-631-12758-5 (cased) : £9.95 : CIP rev.
ISBN 0-631-12759-3 (pbk) : £4.50 B81-02660

320'.01 — Politics — *Philosphical perspectives*

Reading Nozick : essays on anarchy, state and utopia. — Oxford : Blackwell, Jan.1982. — [400]p
ISBN 0-631-12977-4 (cased) : £20.00 : CIP entry
ISBN 0-631-12978-2 (pbk) B81-34296

320'.01 — Politics. Plato. Statesman — *Commentaries*

Miller, Mitchell H.. The philosopher in Plato's Statesman / by Mitchell H. Miller, Jr. — The Hague ; London : Nijhoff, 1980. — xix,144p : ill ; 25cm. — (Martinus Nijhoff classical philosophy library ; v.2)
Includes index
ISBN 90-247-2210-1 : Unpriced B81-06807

320'.01 — Politics. Realism — *Philosophical perspectives*

Berki, R. N.. On political realism / R.N. Berki. — London : Dent, 1981. — vi,282p ; 25cm
Includes index
ISBN 0-460-04367-6 : £15.00 : CIP rev. B81-13517

320'.01 — Politics. Theories

The Frontiers of political theory : essays in a revitalised discipline / edited by Michael Freeman and David Robertson. — Brighton : Harvester, 1980. — 308p ; 23cm
ISBN 0-85527-313-5 : £20.00 : CIP rev. B80-08113

Gamble, Andrew. An introduction to modern social and political thought / Andrew Gamble. — London : Macmillan, 1981. — vii,264p ; 23cm
Bibliography: p232-237. — Includes index
ISBN 0-333-27028-2 (cased) : Unpriced (pbk) : Unpriced
Also classified at 301 B81-40661

Leibniz, Gottfried Wilhelm. The political writings of Leibniz / translated and edited with an introduction and notes by Patrick Riley. — Cambridge : Cambridge University Press, 1972 (1981 [printing]). — viii,206p ; 22cm. — (Cambridge studies in the history and theory of politics)
Translation from the German. — Originally published: 1972. — Bibliography: p199-203. — Includes index
ISBN 0-521-28585-2 (pbk) : £5.95 : CIP rev. B81-31287

Politics as rational action : essays in public choice and policy analysis / edited by Leif Lewin and Evert Vedung. — Dordrecht ; London : Reidel, c1980. — xii,274p : ill ; 23cm. — (Theory and decision library ; v.23)
Includes bibliographies and index
ISBN 90-277-1040-6 : Unpriced B81-03419

Rousseau, Jean-Jacques. The social contract ; and Discourses / Jean-Jacques Rousseau ; translation and introduction by G.D.H. Cole. — New ed. / revised and augmented by J.H. Brumfitt and John C. Hall. — London : Dent, 1973 (1979 [printing]). — lii,330p ; 19cm. — (Everyman's library ; no.1660)
Translation of: Du contrat social. — Previous ed.: 1913. — Includes index
ISBN 0-460-01660-1 (pbk) : £1.40 B81-11410

Talmor, Ezra. Mind and polictical concepts / by Ezra Talmor. — Oxford : Pergamon, 1979. — xiii,132p ; 26cm. — (Pergamon international library)
Bibliography: p127-129. — Includes index
ISBN 0-08-023737-1 (cased) : £11.50 : CIP rev. (pbk) : £5.25 B79-07790

320'.01 — Politics. Theories — *Russian texts*

Fedoseev, Anatoliĭ. O novoĭ Rossii : al'ternativa / Anatoliĭ Fedoseev. — London : Overseas Publications, 1980. — 335p ; 19cm
Title on added t.p.: On new Russia
ISBN 0-903868-26-1 (pbk) : £7.50 B81-02317

320'.01'1 — Justice. Economic aspects

Posner, Richard A.. The economics of justice / Richard A. Posner. — Cambridge, Mass. ; London : Harvard University Press, 1981. — xiii,415p ; 25cm
Includes index
ISBN 0-674-23525-8 : £17.50 B81-38901

320'.01'1 — Politics. Theories - *Feminist viewpoints*

O'Brien, Mary. The politics of reproduction. — London : Routledge & Kegan Paul, July 1981. — [233]p
ISBN 0-7100-0810-4 : £13.50 : CIP entry B81-13724

320'.01'1 — Western world. Social values. Political aspects

Gordon, Scott. Welfare, justice, and freedom / Scott Gordon. — New York ; Guildford : Columbia University Press, 1980. — viii,234p ; 22cm
Includes index
ISBN 0-231-04976-5 : £9.60 B81-05497

320'.01'9 — Politics — *Psychoanalytical perspectives*

Davies, A. F.. Skills, outlooks and passions : a psychoanalytic contribution to the study of politics / A. F. Davies. — Cambridge : Cambridge University Press, 1980. — xiii,522p : ill ; 24cm
Includes index
ISBN 0-521-22081-5 (cased) : £27.50
ISBN 0-521-29349-9 (pbk) : £10.50 B81-05759

320'.01'9 — Politics. Rational choice

Laver, Michael. The politics of private desires / Michael Laver. — Harmondsworth : Penguin, 1981. — 186p : ill ; 20cm
Bibliography: p180-182. - Includes index
ISBN 0-14-022316-9 (pbk) : £1.75 B81-16169

320'.023'41 — Great Britain. Political science as a profession

Lovenduski, Joni. The profession of political science in Britain / by Joni Lovenduski. — [London] : Political Studies Association of the United Kingdom, 1981. — iv,37p ; 30cm. — (Studies in public policy, ISSN 0140-8240 ; no.84)
£1.50 (pbk) B81-31493

320'.07'1041 — Great Britain. Educational institutions. Curriculum subjects: Politics. Teaching — *Critical studies*

Brennan, Tom. Political education and democracy. — Cambridge : Cambridge University Press, Oct.1981. — [160]p
ISBN 0-521-28267-5 (pbk) : £3.95 : CIP entry B81-28845

320'.07'1141 — Great Britain. Higher education institutions. Curriculum subjects: Political science. Resources & facilities

Newton, Kenneth. Facilities and resources for political scientists / by K. Newton. — [Glasgow] : Political Studies Association of the United Kingdom, 1981. — iii,23,2[i.e.3]p ; 30cm. — (Studies in public policy, ISSN 0140-8240 ; no.79) (PSA/CSPP papers on the political science profession)
£1.50 (pbk) B81-19020

320'.072 — Political science. Research. Methodology

Kweit, Mary Grisez. Concepts and methods for political analysis / Mary Grisez Kweit, Robert W. Kweit. — Englewood Cliffs ; London : Prentice-Hall, c1981. — vii,374p : ill,1form ; 23cm
Bibliography: p340-349. — Includes index
ISBN 0-13-166520-0 (pbk) : £8.40 B81-17211

Manheim, Jarol B.. Empirical political analysis : research methods in political science / Jarol B. Manheim and Richard C. Rich, with contributions by Donna L. Bahry, Michael K. Brown, Doreen K. Ellis. — Englwood Cliffs ; London : Prentice-Hall, c1981. — xvii,359p : ill,1map,forms ; 25cm
Includes bibliographies and index
ISBN 0-13-274605-0 : £11.55 B81-18319

320'.072 — Political science. Research. Statistical methods. Implications of ideology

Beardsley, Philip L.. Redefining rigor : ideology and statistics in political inquiry / Philip L. Beardsley. — Beverly Hills ; London : Sage, c1980. — xii,199p : ill ; 23cm. — (Sage library of social research ; v.104)
Includes bibliographies
ISBN 0-8039-1472-5 (cased) : £11.25
ISBN 0-8039-1473-3 (pbk) : £5.50 B81-06817

320'.076 — Politics — *Questions & answers — For West African students*

Government. — London : Macmillan, 1981. — 92p ; 22cm. — (Macmillan certificate model answers)
ISBN 0-333-30493-4 (pbk) : £0.70 B81-23122

320'.09'04 — Politics — *Philosophical perspectives, 1900-1980*

Parekh, B. C.. Contemporary political thinkers. — Oxford : Martin Robertson, Feb.1982. — [224]p
ISBN 0-85520-337-4 (cased) : £10.00 : CIP entry
ISBN 0-85520-336-6 (pbk) : £3.95 B81-35705

320'.0917'671 — Islamic countries. Political science

Siddiqui, Kalim. Beyond the Muslim nation-states / Kalim Siddiqui. — London : Open Press in association with the Muslim Institute, 1980. — 16p ; 20cm
ISBN 0-905081-05-6 (pbk) : £1.00 B81-09003

320'.092'2 — Great Britain. Women political scientists

Lovenduski, Joni. Women in British political studies / by Joni Lovenduski. — [Glasgow] : Political Studies Association of the United Kingdom, 1981. — iv,38,2[i.e.3]p ; 30cm. — (Studies in public policy, ISSN 0140-8240 ; no.78) (PSA/CSPP papers on the political science profession)
£1.50 (pbk) B81-19019

320.1 — POLITICS. THE STATE

320.1'01 — State. Theories of Marxists

Wells, David, *1949-*. Marxism and the modern state : an analysis of fetishism in capitalist society / David Wells. — Brighton : Harvester, 1981. — x,214p ; 23cm. — (Marxist theory and contemporary capitalism ; 29)
Bibliography: p203-211. — Includes index
ISBN 0-85527-213-9 : £18.95 : CIP rev. B81-23846

320.1'092'4 — State. Theories of Bentham, Jeremy

Hume, L. J.. Bentham and bureaucracy / L.J. Hume. — Cambridge : Cambridge University Press, 1981. — xii,320p ; 23cm. — (Cambridge studies in the history and theory of politics)
Bibliography: p303-309. — Includes index
ISBN 0-521-23542-1 : £22.50 : CIP rev. B81-19164

320.1'094 — State. Theories of Western European writers

Dyson, Kenneth H. F.. The state tradition in Western Europe : a study of an idea and institution / Kenneth H.F. Dyson. — Oxford : Robertson, 1980. — vii,310p ; 25cm
Bibliography: p288-300. - Includes index
ISBN 0-85520-324-2 : £15.00 : CIP rev. B80-08618

320.1'2 — Politics. Geographical aspects

De Blij, Harm J.. Systematic political geography. — 3rd ed. / Martin Ira Glassner, Harm J. de Blij ; cartography by Leon Yacher. — New York ; Chichester : Wiley, c1980. — xvi,537p : ill,maps,plans,ports ; 25cm
Previous ed.: 1973. — Maps on lining papers. — Includes bibliographies and index
ISBN 0-471-05228-0 : £13.20 B81-09754

320.1'2 — Politics. Geographical factors

Political studies from spatial perspectives / Anglo-American essays on political geography ; edited by Alan D. Burnett and Peter J. Taylor. — Chichester : Wiley, c1981. — xv,519p : maps ; 25cm
Includes bibliographies and index
ISBN 0-471-27909-9 (cased) : £20.60 : CIP rev.
ISBN 0-471-27910-2 (pbk) : Unpriced B81-00759

320.1'2'09162 — Oceans. International political aspects

The **Maritime** dimension / edited by R.P. Barston and Patricia Birnie. — London : Allen & Unwin, 1980. — 194p : ill,maps ; 23cm
Includes index
ISBN 0-04-341015-4 (cased) : £11.95 : CIP rev.
ISBN 0-04-341016-2 (pbk) : £5.50 B80-22966

320.1'57'0924 — Sovereignty. Theories of Locke, John

Franklin, Julian H.. John Locke and the theory of sovereignty : mixed monarchy and the right of resistance in the political thought of the English Revolution / Julian H. Franklin. — Cambridge : Cambridge University Press, 1981 (1981 [printing]). — xi,146p ; 22cm. — (Cambridge studies in the history and theory of politics)
Bibliography: p136-142. — Includes index
ISBN 0-521-28547-x (pbk) : £3.95 B81-36896

320.3 — COMPARATIVE POLITICS

320.3 — Political systems — *Comparative studies*

Coulter, Edwin M.. Principles of politics and government / Edwin M. Coulter. — Boston [Mass.] ; London : Allyn and Bacon, c1981. — xii,312p : ill ; 24cm
Bibliography: p300-304. — Includes index
ISBN 0-205-07177-5 (pbk) : £6.25 B81-02046

320.3 — Politics — *Comparative studies*

Hitchner, Dell Gillette. Comparative government and politics / Dell Gillette Hitchner, Carol Levine. — 2nd ed. — Cambridge [Mass.] ; London : Harper & Row, c1981. — viii,344p ; 24cm
Previous ed.: New York : Dodd, Mead, 1967. — Bibliography: p291-326. — Includes index
ISBN 0-06-042828-7 (pbk) : Unpriced B81-19836

Wesson, Robert G.. Modern governments : three worlds of politics / Robert Wesson. — Englewood Cliffs ; London : Prentice-Hall, c1981. — xvi,414p : ill,maps ; 25cm
Includes index
ISBN 0-13-594945-9 : £11.65 B81-16597

320.4 — GOVERNMENT. STRUCTURE, FUNCTIONS, ACTIVITIES

320.441 — Great Britain. Civics

Padfield, Colin F.. British Constitution made simple / Colin F. Padfield. — 5th ed. / revised by A. Byrne. — London : Heinemann, 1981. — xi,355p : ill,1map ; 22cm. — (Made simple books)
Previous ed.: London : W.H. Allen, 1977. — Includes index
ISBN 0-434-98456-6 (pbk) : £2.50 B81-23209

320.441 — Great Britain. Civics — *For schools*

Keeley, R. D.. Civics and citizenship : for first examinations / R.D. Keeley and P.G. Smith. — Exeter : Wheaton, 1981. — 92p : ill,facsims,plans,ports ; 20cm
ISBN 0-08-025004-1 (pbk) : £1.75 B81-29679

320.441'05 — Great Britain. Civics — *Serials*

British government and politics. — 1981. — [Poole] ([51 Austin Ave., Lilliput, Poole BH14 8HD]) : [R.K. Mosley], [1981]. — 46p
Compiled by: R.K. Mosley
£0.80 B81-21939

320.473 — United States. Civics

Potter, Allen M.. American government and politics / Allen M. Potter, Peter Fotheringham, James G. Kellas. — New rev. ed. — London : Faber, 1981. — 363p ; 20cm
Previous ed.: 1978. — Includes bibliographies and index
ISBN 0-571-18044-2 (cased) : 9.50 : CIP rev.
ISBN 0-571-18049-3 (pbk) : Unpriced B81-21469

Press, Charles. American policy studies / Charles Press, Kenneth VerBurg. — New York ; Chichester : Wiley, c1981. — xiii,234p ; 28cm
ISBN 0-471-07866-2 (pbk) : £4.70 B81-18679

Watson, Richard A. (Richard Abernethy). Promise and performance of American democracy : with an in-depth analysis of the 1980 Presidential contest / Richard A. Watson. — 4th ed. / with Michael R. Fitzgerald. — New York ; Chichester : Wiley, c1981. — x,727,A55,I25p : ill(some col.),maps(some col.),facsims,ports ; 26cm
Previous ed.: 1978. — Index
ISBN 0-471-08381-x (cased) : £10.95 (National, state and local ed.)
ISBN 0-471-08380-1 (pbk. national ed.) : £10.50
ISBN 0-471-07964-2 (pbk. brief ed.) : £9.55 B81-24890

Weissberg, Robert. Understanding American government / Robert Weissberg. — Alternate ed. — New York ; London : Holt, Rinehart and Winston, c1981. — xiv,755p : ill(some col.),2facsims,ports ; 25cm
Previous ed.: 1980. — Text on lining papers. — Includes bibliographies and index
ISBN 0-03-058038-2 : £11.50 B81-22995

320.473 — United States. Civics — *For schools*

Sutton, J. S.. American government / by J.S. Sutton. — 2nd ed. — London : Harrap, c1980. — 222p(2fold.) : ill,maps,1facsim,1port ; 22cm
Previous ed.: 1974. — Includes index
ISBN 0-245-53562-4 (pbk) : Unpriced B81-10186

320.5 — POLITICAL THEORIES AND IDEOLOGIES

320.5 — Politics. Theories: Kalkism — *Critical studies*

Rajarishi. 'Kalkism' / Rajarishi. — Bognor Regis : New Horizon, c1980. — 168p : ill ; 22cm
ISBN 0-86116-200-5 : £4.75 B81-21780

320.5'0882971 — Politics. Theories of Muslims, *ca 700- ca 1600*

Lambton, Ann K. S.. State and government in medieval Islam : an introduction to the study of Islamic political theory : the jurists / by Ann K.S. Lambton. — Oxford : Oxford University Press, 1981. — xviii,364p ; 23cm. — (London oriental series ; v.36)
Bibliography: p338-354. — Includes index
ISBN 0-19-713600-1 : £19.50 B81-36144

320.5'092'4 — Politics. Theories of Burke, Edmund, *1729-1797*

Macpherson, C. B.. Burke / C.B. Macpherson. — Oxford : Oxford University Press, 1980. — 83p ; 19cm. — (Past masters)
Bibliography: p77. - Includes index
ISBN 0-19-287519-1 (cased) : £4.50 : CIP rev.
ISBN 0-19-287518-3 (pbk) : £0.95 B80-13235

320.5'092'4 — Politics. Theories of Hume, David, *1711-1776*

Miller, David. Philosophy and ideology in Hume's political thought. — Oxford : Clarendon Press, Feb.1982. — [234]p
ISBN 0-19-824658-7 : £15.00 : CIP entry B81-36967

320.5'092'4 — Politics. Theories of Machiavelli, Niccolò

Skinner, Quentin. Machiavelli / Quentin Skinner. — Oxford : Oxford University Press, 1981. — vii,102p ; 19cm. — (Past masters)
Bibliography: p93-97. — Includes index
ISBN 0-19-287517-5 (cased) : £4.50
ISBN 0-19-287516-7 (pbk) : £1.25 B81-24039

320.5'092'4 — Politics. Theories of Merleau-Ponty, Maurice

Kruks, Sonia. The political philosophy of Merleau-Ponty / Sonia Kruks. — Brighton : Harvester, 1981. — xiv,152p ; 23cm. — (Philosophy now ; 13)
Bibliography: p143-149. - Includes index
ISBN 0-85527-846-3 (cased) : £16.50 : CIP rev.
ISBN 0-85527-428-x (pbk) : Unpriced B80-34554

320.5'092'4 — Politics. Theories of Plato

Hall, Robert W.. Plato. — London : Allen & Unwin, Nov.1981. — [208]p. — (Political thinkers ; 9)
ISBN 0-04-320145-8 (cased) : £10.95 : CIP entry
ISBN 0-04-320146-6 (pbk) : £4.95 B81-28776

320.5'0973 — Politics. American theories, *1970-1979*

Abbott, Philip. Furious fancies- : American political thought in the post-liberal era / Philip Abbott. — Westport, Conn. ; London : Greenwood Press, 1980. — x,265p ; 22cm. — (Contributions in political science, ISSN 0147-1066 ; no.35)
Bibliography: p253-260. — Includes index
ISBN 0-313-20945-6 : Unpriced B81-06170

320.5'1 — Equality. Liberalist theories

Gutmann, Amy. Liberal equality / Amy Gutmann. — Cambridge : Cambridge University Press, 1980. — xi,318p ; 24cm
Bibliography: p289-306. Includes index
ISBN 0-521-22828-x (cased) : £20.00
ISBN 0-521-29665-x (pbk) : £6.50 B81-00763

320.5'1'0924 — Political ideologies: Liberalism. Theories of Green, Thomas Hill

Greengarten, I. M.. Thomas Hill Green and the development of liberal-democratic thought / I.M. Greengarten. — Toronto ; London : University of Toronto Press, c1981. — x,151p ; 24cm
Includes index
ISBN 0-8020-5503-6 : £12.00 B81-36562

320.5'1'0924 — Politics. Paine, Thomas — *Serials*

[Contact *(Nottingham)***]**. Contact / Thomas Paine Society. — (1) (Autumn 1980)-. — Nottingham (43 Eugene Gardens, Nottingham NG2 3LF) : The Society, 1980-. — v. ; 30cm
ISSN 0260-7646 = Contact (Nottingham) : Free to Society members only B81-06908

320.5'12 — Political ideologies: Individualism. Theories of Marxists, *to 1979*

Tucker, D. F. B.. Marxism and individualism / D.F.B. Tucker. — Oxford : Blackwell, 1980. — 255p ; 23cm
Includes index
ISBN 0-631-11531-5 : £12.00 : CIP rev. B80-05227

320.5'2'0941 — Great Britain. Political ideologies: Conservatism

Harris of High Cross, Ralph Harris, *Baron*. The challenge of a radical reactionary / Lord Harris of High Cross. — [London] ([8 Wilfred St., S.W.1]) : Centre for Policy Studies, 1980. — 11p ; 21cm
Cover title
ISBN 0-905880-36-6 (pbk) : £1.00 B81-30801

320.5'3'09421 — London. Radical movements, *1796-1821*

Hone, J. Ann. For the cause of truth. — Oxford : Clarendon Press, Feb.1982. — [350]p. — (Oxford historical monographs)
ISBN 0-19-821887-7 : £17.50 : CIP entry B81-35763

320.5'3'0973 — United States. Left-wing radical movements, *1946-1979*

Lader, Lawrence. Power on the left : American radical movements since 1946 / Lawrence Lader. — New York ; London : Norton, c1979. — xiv,410p,[12]p of plates : ill,ports ; 24cm
Includes index
ISBN 0-393-01258-1 : £9.25 B81-03965

320.5'315'0924 — Politics. Theories of Gramsci, Antonio

Adamson, Walter L.. Hegemony and revolution : a study of Antonio Gramsci's political and cultural theory / Walter L. Adamson. — Berkeley ; London : University of California Press, c1980. — x,304p ; 23cm
Bibliography: p285-296. - Includes index
ISBN 0-520-03924-6 : £12.00 B81-06120

Femia, Joseph V.. Gramsci's political thought. — Oxford : Clarendon Press, Nov.1981. — [300]p
ISBN 0-19-827251-0 : £17.50 : CIP entry B81-30336

320.5'315'0924 — Politics. Theories of Marx, Karl

Gilbert, Alan, *1944 Apr.24-*. Marx's politics : communists and citizens / Alan Gilbert. — Oxford : Robertson, 1981. — xv,326p : ill ; 24cm
Bibliography: p295-306. — Includes index
ISBN 0-85520-441-9 : £16.50 B81-39966

320.5'322'0924 — Politics. Theories of Lenin, V. I.

Harding, Neil. Lenin's political thought / Neil Harding. — London : Macmillan
Vol.2: Theory and practice in the Socialist revolution. — 1981. — 387p ; 23cm
Bibliography: p349-370. — Includes index
ISBN 0-333-21289-4 : £15.00 : CIP rev. B80-18176

320.5'4 — Nationalism

National separatism. — Cardiff : University of Wales Press, Jan.1982. — [300]p
ISBN 0-7083-0798-1 : £9.95 : CIP entry B81-34301

320.5'4 — Nationalism. Ethnic factors

Smith, Anthony D.. The ethnic revival. — Cambridge : Cambridge University Press, Oct.1981. — [244]p. — (Themes in the social sciences)
ISBN 0-521-23267-8 (cased) : £15.00 : CIP entry
ISBN 0-521-29885-7 (pbk) : £4.95 B81-27943

320.5'4'09174927 — Arab countries. Nationalism, *to 1970*

Tibi, Bassam. Arab nationalism : a critical enquiry / Bassam Tibi ; edited and translated by Marion Farouk-Sluglett and Peter Sluglett. — London : Macmillan, 1981. — xvi,286p ; 23cm
Translation of: Nationalismus in der Dritten Welt am arabishcen Beispiel. — Bibliography: p246-278. — Includes index
ISBN 0-333-23714-5 : £20.00 : CIP rev. B80-35687

320.5'4'0941 — Great Britain. Nationalism, *1640-1975 — Marxist viewpoints*

Nairn, Tom. The break-up of Britain. — London : NLB, Sept.1981. — [380]p
Originally published: 1977
ISBN 0-86091-706-1 (pbk) : £4.50 : CIP entry B81-30224

320.5'4'09415 — Ireland. Nationalism, *1842-1930*

Boyce, D. George. Nationalism in Ireland. — London : Croom Helm, Dec.1981. — [480]p
ISBN 0-85664-705-5 : £15.95 : CIP entry B81-31652

320.5'4'094384 — Poland. Poznań region. Poles. Nationalism, *1772-1914*

Hagen, William W.. Germans, Poles, and Jews : the nationality conflict in the Prussian East, 1772-1914 / William W. Hagen. — Chicago ; London : University of Chicago Press, c1980. — ix,406p,[8]p of plates : ill,1map,ports ; 24cm
Bibliography: p385-397. - Includes index
ISBN 0-226-31242-9 : £10.50 B81-06492

320.5'4'094771 — Ukraine. Nationalism, *1957-1972*

Farmer, Kenneth C.. Ukranian nationalism in the post-Stalin era : myth, symbols and ideology in Soviet nationalities policy / Kenneth C. Farmer. — The Hague ; London : Hijhoff, 1980. — x,241p : 1map ; 25cm. — (Studies in contemporary history ; v.4)
Bibliography: p217-233. - Includes index
ISBN 90-247-2401-5 : Unpriced B81-03807

320.5'4'0954 — India. Nationalism, *1885-1947 — Conference proceedings*

Essays in modern history / edited by B.R. Nanda. — Delhi ; Oxford : Oxford University Press, 1980. — 252p ; 23cm
Conference papers. — Includes index
ISBN 0-19-561147-0 : £6.50 B81-03194

320.5'4'09561 — Turkey. Pan-Turkism

Landau, Jacob M.. Pan-Turkism in Turkey. — London : Hurst, Oct.1981. — [222]p
ISBN 0-905838-57-2 : £11.50 : CIP entry B81-30624

320.5'4'0968 — South Africa. Nationalism. Role of workers' organisations, *1970-1979 — Marxist viewpoints*

Du Toit, D.. Capital and labour in South Afrca : class struggle in the 1970's / D. du Toit. — London : Kegan Paul International, 1981. — xii,495p ; 23cm. — (Monographs from the African Studies Centre, Leiden)
Bibliography: p469-478. — Includes index
ISBN 0-7103-0001-8 : £18.00 B81-09804

320.9 — POLITICS. HISTORICAL AND GEOGRAPHICAL TREATMENT

320.9'04 — Politics, *1945-1980*

Calvocoressi, Peter. World politics since 1945. — 4th ed. — London : Longman, Jan.1982. — [576]p
Previous ed.: 1977
ISBN 0-582-29586-6 (pbk) : £5.95 : CIP entry B81-37554

320.9172′4 — Developing countries. Politics — *Marxist viewpoints*

Politics and state in the Third World / edited by Harry Goulbourne. — London : Macmillan, 1979. — xvi,303p ; 23cm
Bibliography: p295-297. — Includes index
ISBN 0-333-26422-3 (cased) : £10.00 : CIP rev.
ISBN 0-333-26423-1 (pbk) : £4.50 B79-23695

320.917′4927 — Arab countries. Politics

Hudson, Michael C.. Arab politics : the search for legitimacy / Michael C. Hudson. — New Haven ; London : Yale University Press, c1977 (1979 printing). — xi,434p : ill,1map ; 24cm
Includes index
ISBN 0-300-02411-8 (pbk) : £5.65 B81-16158

320.917′4927 — Arab countries. Politics, *1967-1980*

Ajami, Fouad. The Arab predicament : Arab political thought and practice since 1967 / Fouad Ajami. — Cambridge : Cambridge University Press, 1981. — xvi,220p ; 25cm
Includes index
ISBN 0-521-23914-1 : £12.50 B81-34525

320.917′671 — Islamic countries. Politics. Attitudes of Western world

Hussain, Asaf. Western theoretical approaches to the political order of Muslim states : a critique / Asaf Hussain. — Leicester : Islamic Foundation, c1981. — 35p ; 30cm. — (Seminar papers / Islamic Foundation ; 11)
Bibliography: p28-35
ISBN 0-86037-087-9 (pbk) : Unpriced
B81-35080

320.9181′2 — Western world. Politics

Connolly, William E.. Appearance and reality in politics / William E. Connolly. — Cambridge : Cambridge University Press, 1981. — vii,218p ; 23cm
Bibliography: p211-214. - Includes index
ISBN 0-521-23026-8 : £15.00 B81-17027

320.9182′1 — Caribbean region. Commonwealth countries. Politics, *ca 1950-1980*

Payne, Anthony, *1952-*. Change in the Commonwealth Caribbean / Anthony Payne. — [London] : Royal Institute of International Affairs, c1981. — vi,58p : 1map ; 30cm. — (Chatham House papers, ISSN 0143-5795)
ISBN 0-905031-24-5 (pbk) : £5.00 B81-37826

320.94 — Western Europe. Anti-fascist movements. Role of intellectuals, *1930-1950*

Wilkinson, James D. 1943-. The intellectual resistance in Europe / James D. Wilkinson. — Cambridge, Mass ; London : Harvard University Press, 1981. — x,358p : ill ; 25cm
Bibliography: p331-347. — Includes index
ISBN 0-674-45775-7 : £14.00 B81-39777

320.94 — Western Europe. Politics

Fry, Earl H.. The other Western Europe : a political analysis of the smaller democracies / Earl H. Fry and Gregory A. Raymond in collaboration with David Bohn and James L. Waite. — Santa Barbara ; Oxford : ABC-Clio, c1980. — ix,251p ; 24cm. — (Studies in international and comparative politics ; 14)
Includes bibliographies and index
ISBN 0-87436-267-9 : £12.95 B81-04599

320.941 — Great Britain. Politics

Hanson, A. H.. Governing Britain : a guide-book to political institutions / A.H. Hanson, Malcolm Walles. — 3rd ed. — [London] : Fontana, 1980. — 353p : maps ; 18cm
Previous ed.: 1975. — Bibliography: p324-338. — Includes index
ISBN 0-00-636190-0 (pbk) : £2.50 B81-02727

Howell, David. Freedom and capital : prospects for the property-owning democracy / David Howell. — Oxford : Blackwell, 1981. — 127p ; 23cm. — (Mainstream series)
Includes index
ISBN 0-631-12552-3 : £6.95 B81-17663

Mackintosh, John P.. The government and politics of Britain. — 5th ed. — London : Hutchinson Education, Sept.1981. — [224]p
Previous ed.: 1977
ISBN 0-09-145531-6 (pbk) : £4.25 : CIP entry
B81-20181

Punnett, R. M.. British government and politics / R.M. Punnett. — 4th ed. — London : Heinemann, 1980. — xiv,558p ; 23cm
Previous ed.: 1976. — Bibliography: p444-534. - Includes index
ISBN 0-435-83739-7 : £10.50
ISBN 0-435-83738-9 (pbk) : £4.95 B81-05253

320.941 — Great Britain. Politics, *1680-1830*

The Whig ascendancy : colloquies on Hanoverian England / edited by John Cannon. — London : Edward Arnold, 1981. — xii,226p ; 24cm
Includes index
ISBN 0-7131-6277-5 : £12.50 B81-15603

320.941 — Great Britain. Politics, *1760-1770*

Brewer, John. Party ideology and popular politics at the accession of George III. — Cambridge : Cambridge University Press, Dec.1981. — [382]p
Originally published: 1976
ISBN 0-521-28701-4 (pbk) : £9.95 : CIP entry
B81-31607

320.941 — Great Britain. Politics, *1765-1795 — Early works*

Burke, Edmund, *1729-1797*. The writings and speeches of Edmund Burke / general editor Paul Langford. — Oxford : Clarendon
Vol.V: India : Madras and Bengal 1774-1785 / edited by P.J. Marshall ; textual editor for the writings William B. Todd. — 1981. — xv,667p ; 25cm
Bibliography: p28-31. — Includes index
ISBN 0-19-822417-6 : £55.00 : CIP rev.
B80-22972

320.941 — Great Britain. Politics, *1818-1860 — Correspondence, diaries, etc.*

Greville, Charles C. F.. [The Greville memoirs. Selections]. Greville's England : selections from the diaries of Charles Greville 1818-1860 / edited, introduced and annotated by Christopher Hibbert. — London : Folio Society, 1981. — 303p,[11]leaves of plates : ill,ports ; 26cm
In slip case. — Includes index
£10.75 B81-17697

320.941 — Great Britain. Politics, *1945-1975*

Johnson, Nevil. In search of the constitution : reflections on state and society in Britain / by Nevil Johnson. — London : Methuen, 1980, c1977. — xi,239p ; 22cm
Originally published: Oxford : Pergamon, 1977. — Includes index
ISBN 0-416-74120-7 (pbk) : £3.75 : CIP rev.
B80-17568

320.941 — Great Britain. Politics, *1945-1980*

Smith, Geoffrey, *1930 Feb.21-*. British government and its discontents / Geoffrey Smith & Nelson W. Polsby. — New York : Basic Books ; London : Harper & Row, c1981. — xvi,202p ; 22cm
Includes index
ISBN 0-06-337016-6 : £7.95 B81-11800

320.941 — Great Britain. Politics, *1974-1976*

Wymer, Ivor Keith. Labour in office 1974-76 and the quest for socialism / Ivor Keith Wymer. — Bognor Regis : New Horizon, c1980. — 169p ; 22cm
ISBN 0-86116-591-8 : £5.25 B81-21707

320.941 — Great Britain. Politics, *1974-1979*

Johnson, Paul. The recovery of freedom / Paul Johnson. — Oxford : Basil Blackwell, 1980. — 232p ; 24cm. — (Mainstream series)
Includes index
ISBN 0-631-12562-0 : £8.50 : CIP rev.
B80-09994

320.941 — Great Britain. Politics, *1980 — Marxist viewpoints*

Silver linings : some strategies for the eighties : contributions to the Communist University of London / edited by George Bridges and Rosalind Brunt. — London : Lawrence and Wishart, 1981. — 189p ; 22cm
ISBN 0-85315-546-1 (pbk) : £3.50 B81-27734

320.941 — Great Britain. Politics — *For schools*

Gabriel, Philip. British Government : an introduction to politics / Philip Gabriel. — 2nd ed. — London : Longman, 1981. — 108p : ill(some col.),1col.map,facsim,ports ; 24cm. — (Longman social science studies. Series 1)
Previous ed.: 1974. — Bibliography: p106. - Includes index
ISBN 0-582-23020-9 (pbk) : £2.05 B81-15244

320.941 — Great Britain. Politics — *Proposals*

Williams, Shirley. Politics is for people / Shirley Williams. — Harmondsworth : Penguin, 1981. — 230p ; 20cm
Includes index
ISBN 0-14-005888-5 (pbk) : £2.50 B81-17741

Williams, Shirley. Politics is for people / Shirley Williams. — London : Allen Lane, 1981. — 230p ; 23cm
Includes index
ISBN 0-7139-1423-8 : £8.50 B81-23347

320.941 — Great Britain. Politics. Reform — *Proposals*

Manifesto : a radical strategy for Britain's future / Francis Cripps ... [et al.]. — London : Pan, 1981. — 224p ; 18cm
Includes index
ISBN 0-330-26402-8 (pbk) : £1.95 B81-38167

320.941 — Great Britain. Politics. Role of press, *ca 1850-1945*

Koss, Stephen. The rise and fall of the political press in Britain / Stephen Koss. — London : Hamilton
Vol.1: The nineteenth century. — 1981. — viii,455p,[8]p of plates : ill,facsims ; 25cm
Includes index
ISBN 0-241-10561-7 : £20.00 : CIP rev.
B81-10414

320.941 — Great Britain. Radical movements, *1638-1657*

Brockway, Fenner. Britain's first socialists : the Levellers, Agitators and Diggers of the English Revolution / Fenner Brockway. — London : Quartet, 1980. — 168p,[16]p of plates : ill,facsims,ports ; 23cm
Bibliography: p1253-160. — Includes index
ISBN 0-7043-2207-2 : £5.95 B81-26663

320.941′05 — Great Britain. Politics — *Right-wing political viewpoints — Serials*

Nationalism today : the radical voice of British nationalism. — Issue no.1 (Mar.1980)-. — Halesworth (Hill House, Huntingfield, Halesworth, Suffolk) : N.T. Press, 1980-. — v. : ill ; 28cm
Monthly
ISSN 0260-2407 = Nationalism today : £5.00 per year B81-00760

320.941′072 — Great Britain. Politics. Research organisations: British Politics Group — *Directories*

British Politics Group. British Politics Group research register, 1981 / [compiled] by William D. Muller. — Glasgow (University of Strathclyde, Glasgow G1 1XO) : Published for the British Politics Group by Centre for the Study of Public Policy, c1981. — 68p ; 30cm. — (Studies in public policy, ISSN 0140-8240 ; no.77)
Includes index
Unpriced (pbk) B81-15757

320.941′072041 — Great Britain. Politics, *ca 1850-ca 1980.* **Research in higher education institutions —** *Directories*

Jones, J. Barry. A research register of territorial politics in the United Kingdom / by J. Barry Jones. — [2nd ed.]. — Glasgow (16 Richmond St., Glasgow G1 1XQ) : Centre for the Study of Public Policy, University of Strathclyde, 1980. — 50p ; 30cm. — (Studies in public policy, ISSN 0140-8240 ; no.70)
Previous ed.: published as A register of research into United Kingdom politics. 1978
£1.50 (pbk) B81-02344

320.941′092′2 — Great Britain. Radicalism, *1603-1691 — Biographies*

The **Biographical** dictionary of British radicals in the seventeenth century. — Brighton : Harvester Press
Vol.1. — Nov.1981. — [336]p
ISBN 0-85527-133-7 : £40.00 : CIP entry B81-30368

320.941′092′4 — Great Britain. Politics, *1866-1892 — Personal observations — Correspondence, diaries, etc*

Cranbrook, Gathorne Gathorne-Hardy, *Earl of.* The diary of Gathorne Hardy, later Lord Cranbrook, 1866-1892 : political selections / edited by Nancy E. Johnson. — Oxford : Clarendon Press, 1981. — xxxviii,908p,[1]leaf of plates : 1geneal.table,1port ; 24cm
Includes index
ISBN 0-19-822622-5 : £48.00 B81-35519

320.9411 — Scotland. Politics, *1945-1979*

Miller, William L.. The end of British politics? : Scots and English political behaviour in the seventies / by William L. Miller. — Oxford : Clarendon Press, 1981. — xi,281p : ill ; 21cm
Bibliography: p271-273. — Includes index
ISBN 0-19-827422-x : £17.50 B81-25403

320.9411 — Scotland. Politics. Effects of exploitation of petroleum deposits in North Sea, *1974-1979*

Miller, William L.. Oil and the Scottish voter 1974-1979 / by William L. Miller, Jack Brand, Maggie Jordan. — [London] : [Social Science Research Council], c1980. — 111p : ill ; 21cm. — (North Sea Oil Panel occasional paper ; no.2)
Bibliography: p108-111
ISBN 0-86226-031-0 (pbk) : £2.80 B81-09956

320.9411 — Scotland. Politics — *Liberal Party viewpoints*

Johnston, Russell. Scottish Liberal Party Conference speeches 1971-1978 / Russell Johnston. — [Inverness] ([Glendruidh, Inverness IV1 2AA]) : [R. Johnston], 1979. — 83p,[8]p of plates : ports ; 22cm
Cover title
£1.00 (pbk) B81-34678

320.9411 — Scotland. Self government — *Proposals*

Scotland′s claim of right to self-determination / Scotland - U.N. Committee. — [Kilmarnock] ([c/o John McGill, 66 Irvine Rd., Kilmarnock]) : [Scotland - U.N. Committee], [1979]. — viii,99,9 leaves ; 33cm
Cover title
Unpriced (pbk) B81-09516

320.9411′05 — Scotland. Politics — *Serials*

The **Bulletin** of Scottish politics. — No.1 = Vol.1, no.1 (Autumn 1980)-. — Edinburgh (58, Queen St., Edinburgh EH2 3NS) : Scottish International Institute, 1980-. — v. ; 21cm
Two issues yearly
ISSN 0260-6208 = Bulletin of Scottish politics : £2.25 per year B81-13102

Nor′-easter : the paper for the independent-minded Scot. — Issue 1-. — Aberdeen (c/o Student Union, Aberdeen University, Upper Kirkgate, Aberdeen) : Aberdeen Area, Federation of Student Nationalists, [1979?]. — v. : ill,map ; 32cm
ISSN 0260-2563 = Nor′-easter : Unpriced B81-00761

The **Scottish** government yearbook. — 1981. — Edinburgh : Paul Harris, 1980. — 330p
ISBN 0-904505-70-7 : £10.00 B81-11213

320.9412′25 — Scotland. Grampian Region. Peterhead. Politics

Bealey, Frank. The politics of independence. — Aberdeen : Aberdeen University Press, Apr.1981. — [272]p
ISBN 0-08-025736-4 : £15.00 : CIP entry B81-00762

320.9415 — Ireland. Politics, *ca 1790-1979 — Readings from contemporary sources*

The **Conflict** of nationality in modern Ireland / [compiled by] A.C. Hepburn. — London : Edward Arnold, 1980. — xvi,221p : ill,1map ; 20cm. — (Documents of modern history)
Bibliography: p219-221
ISBN 0-7131-6260-0 (cased) : £9.95 : CIP rev.
ISBN 0-7131-6261-9 (pbk) : £5.95 B80-08619

320.9415 — Ireland. Politics — *Labour Committee on Ireland viewpoints — Serials*

Labour & Ireland : bulletin of the Labour Committee on Ireland. — No.1 (May 1980)-. — London (5 Stamford Hill, N16) : The Committee, 1980-. — v. : ill ; 31cm
ISSN 0260-6615 = Labour & Ireland : £0.10 per issue B81-05319

320.9416 — Northern Ireland. Politics

The **Constitution** of Northern Ireland. — London : Heinemann Educational, Dec.1981. — [256]p. — (Joint studies in public policy ; 4)
ISBN 0-435-83807-5 (cased) : £15.00 : CIP entry
ISBN 0-435-83808-3 (pbk) : £6.50 B81-34726

320.9416 — Northern Ireland. Politics, *1921-1979*

Arthur, Paul, *1945-*. Government and politics of Northern Ireland / Paul Arthur. — Harlow : Longman, 1980. — viii,160p : maps ; 21cm. — (Political realities)
Bibliography: p152-155. - Includes index
ISBN 0-582-35300-9 (cased) : £4.25 : CIP rev.
ISBN 0-582-35301-7 (pbk) : £2.50 B80-25220

320.9417 — Ireland *(Republic).* **Politics,** *1973-1977*

Harvey, Brian, *1953-*. Cosgrave′s coalition / by Brian Harvey. — 2nd ed. — [Wembley] : Selecteditions, 1980. — 215p : ports ; 19cm
Previous ed.: Harrow : Eureditions, 1978
ISBN 0-86237-011-6 (pbk) : £1.50 B81-23120

320.942 — England. Politics, *1640-1642*

Fletcher, Anthony J.. The outbreak of the English Civil War / Anthony Fletcher. — London : Edward Arnold, 1981. — xxx,446p : 9maps ; 24cm
Includes index
ISBN 0-7131-6320-8 : £24.00 : CIP rev. B81-09974

320.9425′73 — Oxfordshire. Banbury region. Radical movements, *1832-1945*

Hodgkins, J. R.. Over the hills to glory : radicalism in Banburyshire 1832-1945 / J.R Hodgkins. — Southend (130 Alexandra Rd., Southend, Essex) : Clifton Press, [1981?]. — 217p,[8]p of plates : ill,1facsim,ports ; 22cm
ISBN 0-906516-01-3 : £5.99 B81-26303

320.9428′13 — West Yorkshire *(Metropolitan County).* **Colne Valley. Politics,** *1890-1910*

Clark, David, *1939-*. Colne Valley : radicalism to socialism : the portrait of a northern constituency in the formative years of the Labour Party 1890-1910 / David Clark. — London : Longman, 1981. — xiii,225p,[8]p of plates : ill,2maps,ports ; 24cm
Bibliography: p206-214. - Includes index
ISBN 0-582-50293-4 : £12.00 : CIP rev. B80-34555

320.943 — Germany. Politics, *1923-1945*

Broszat, Martin. The Hitler state : the foundation and development of the internal structure of the Third Reich / Martin Broszat ; translated by John W. Hiden. — London : Longman, 1981. — xvii,378p : 1ill,1map ; 22cm
Translation of: Der Staat Hitlers. — Bibliography: p362-369. — Includes index
ISBN 0-582-49200-9 (cased) : Unpriced
ISBN 0-582-48997-0 (pbk) : £6.50 B81-23675

320.943 — West Germany. Politics

Smith, Gordon, *1927-*. Democracy in Western Germany. — 2nd ed. — London : Heinemann Educational, Dec.1981. — [240]p
Previous ed.: 1979
ISBN 0-435-83792-3 (cased) : £9.50 : CIP entry
ISBN 0-435-83793-1 (pbk) : £5.50 B81-31702

320.943 — West Germany. Politics, *1950-1976*

Baker, Kendall L.. Germany transformed : political culture and the new politics / Kendall L. Baker, Russell J. Dalton, Kai Hildebrandt. — Cambridge, Mass. ; London : Harvard University Press, 1981. — xvii,381p : ill ; 24cm
Includes index
ISBN 0-674-35315-3 : £17.50 B81-39829

320.9436 — Austria. Politics, *1945-1980*

Sully, Melanie A.. Political parties and elections in Austria / by Melanie A. Sully. — London : C. Hurst, 1981. — xiii,194p : ill,maps,1form ; 23cm
Bibliography: p181-184. — Includes index
ISBN 0-905838-44-0 : £9.50 : CIP rev. B81-09469

320.9436′13 — Austria. Vienna. Politics. Role of Christian social movements, *1848-1897*

Boyer, John W.. Political radicalism in late imperial Vienna : origins of the Christian Social Movement 1848-1897 / John W. Boyer. — Chicago ; London : University of Chicago Press, 1981. — xvi,577p : 1map,1port ; 24cm
Bibliography: p531-561. — Includes index
ISBN 0-226-06957-5 : £21.00 B81-29781

320.9438 — Poland. Politics, *1918-1979 — Polish texts*

Nowak, Jan. Polska pozostata sob a / Jan Nowak (Zdzisław Jeziorański). — London ([10 Queen Anne′s Gardens, W4 1TU]) : Polonia, 1980. — 150p : 1facsims,7ports ; 22cm
ISBN 0-902352-16-4 (pbk) : Unpriced B81-01620

320.9438 — Poland. Politics, *1945-1980 — Polish texts*

Tarniewski, Marek. Neizalezność i demokracja / Marek Tarniewski. — London (27 Hamilton Rd., Bedford Park, W.4 1AL) : Odnowa, [1980?]. — 30p ; 21cm
ISBN 0-903705-32-x (pbk) : Unpriced B81-21022

320.9438 — Poland. Politics, *1980 — Trotskyist viewpoints*

Posadas, J.. Poland / J. Posadas. — [London] ([BCM Box 6220, WC1V 6XX]) : Scientific, Cultural and Political Editions, 1981. — 110p ; 21cm
£0.50 (pbk) B81-21440

320.944 — France. Politics, *1785-1795 — Readings from contemporary sources*

The **French** Revolution. — London : Edward Arnold, Nov.1981. — [256]p. — (Documents of modern history)
ISBN 0-7131-6327-5 (pbk) : £5.95 : CIP entry B81-30346

320.945 — Italy. Politics

Marengo, Franco Damaso. Rules of the Italian political game. — Aldershot : Gower, Oct.1981. — [144]p
ISBN 0-566-00301-5 : £8.50 : CIP entry B81-30194

320.947 — Soviet Union. Politics, *1916-1979 — Festschriften*

Authority, power and policy in the USSR : essays dedicated to Leonard Schapiro / edited by T.H. Rigby, Archie Brown and Peter Reddaway. — London : Macmillan, 1980. — xi,207p : ill,1port ; 23cm
Includes index
ISBN 0-333-25702-2 : £15.00 : CIP rev. B80-09995

320.947 — Soviet Union. Politics, *1920-1935*

Rakovskiĭ, Kh.. Selected writings on opposition in the USSR 1923-30 / Christian Rakovsky ; edited and with an introduction by Gus Fagan. — London : Allison and Busby, 1980. — 189p ; 23cm
Bibliography: p180-185. - Includes index
ISBN 0-85031-378-3 (corrected : cased) : £13.95 : CIP rev.
ISBN 0-85031-379-1 (pbk) : £4.95 B80-21461

320.947 — Soviet Union. Politics, *1953-1980*
Bialer, Seweryn. Stalin's successors : leadership, stability, and change in the Soviet Union / Seweryn Bialer. — Cambridge : Cambridge University Press, 1980. — v,312p ; 24cm
Includes index
ISBN 0-521-23518-9 : £12.50 B81-03994

320.947 — Soviet Union. Politics — *Soviet viewpoints*
Brezhnev, L. I.. Socialism, democracy and human rights / by L.I. Brezhnev. — Oxford : Pergamon, 1980. — xi,247p : ill ; 22cm
Translation from the Russian. — Includes index
ISBN 0-08-023605-7 : £12.00 : CIP rev. B80-08617

320.9489 — Denmark. Politics
Fitzmaurice, John. Politics in Denmark / by John Fitzmaurice. — London : Hurst, c1981. — xiv,173p ; 23cm
Includes index
ISBN 0-905838-54-8 : £8.50 : CIP rev. B81-09468

320.9497'2 — Yugoslavia. Croatia. Politics, *1918-1980 — Croatian texts*
Supek, Ivan. Krivovjernik na ljevici : političke uspomene, humanistička poruka / Ivan Supek. — Bristol : BC Review Publications, 1980. — 228p ; 21cm
£4.90 (pbk) B81-22212

320.951 — China. Politics
Waller, Derek J.. The government and politics of the People's Republic of China. — 2nd ed. — London : Hutchinson, July 1981. — [200]p
Previous ed. published as: The government & politics of Communist China. 1970
ISBN 0-09-144300-8 (cased) : £12.00 : CIP entry
ISBN 0-09-144301-6 (pbk) : £4.95 B81-16394

320.951 — China. Politics, *1965-1981 — Trotskyist viewpoints*
Posadas, J.. China / J. Posadas. — London (BCM Box 6220, WC1V 6XX) : Scientific, Cultural and Political Editions, 1981. — 128p ; 21cm
£1.35 (pbk) B81-28233

320.9'52 — Japan. Politics, *1941-1945*
Shillony, Ben-Ami. Politics and culture in wartime Japan. — Oxford : Clarendon, Oct.1981. — [272]p
ISBN 0-19-821573-8 : £17.50 : CIP entry B81-25846

320.952 — Japan. Politics, *1947-1979*
Political opposition and local politics in Japan / edited by Kurt Steiner, Ellis S. Krauss, and Scott C. Flanagan. — Princeton ; Guildford : Princeton University Press, c1980. — ix,486p : ill ; 24cm
Conference papers. — Includes index
ISBN 0-691-07625-1 (cased) : £16.70
ISBN 0-691-10109-4 (pbk) : £5.55 B81-19520

320.953'8 — Saudi Arabia. Politics, *1925-1980 — Conference proceedings*
State, society and economy in Saudi Arabia. — London : Croom Helm, Nov.1981. — [300]p
Conference papers
ISBN 0-7099-1806-2 : £13.95 : CIP entry
Also classified at 330.953'8 B81-31170

320.954 — South & South-east Asia. Politics, *1945-1979*
Pandey, B. N.. South and South-east Asia, 1945-1979 : problems and policies / B.N. Pandey. — London : Macmillan, 1980. — viii,236p : 1map ; 23cm. — (The Making of the 20th century)
Bibliography: p216-221. - Includes index
ISBN 0-333-01259-3 (cased) : £12.50 : CIP rev.
ISBN 0-333-04978-0 (pbk) : £4.95 B80-10952

320.9549'1 — Pakistan. Political development, *to 1979*
Ziring, Lawrence. Pakistan : the enigma of political development / Lawrence Ziring. — Folkestone : Dawson, 1980. — 294p : 2maps ; 23cm
Bibliography: p274-283. - Includes index
ISBN 0-7129-0954-0 : £12.00 : CIP rev. B80-10476

320.956 — Middle East. Politics, *1900-1979*
Kedourie, Elie. Islam in the modern world and other studies / Elie Kedourie. — London : Mansell, 1980. — 332p ; 24cm
Includes index
ISBN 0-7201-1570-1 : £10.00 : CIP rev. B80-08114

320.9561 — Turkey. Politics. Role of Atatürk, Kamâl, *1923-1938*
Atatürk. — London : Hurst, Nov.1981. — [228]p
ISBN 0-905838-67-x : £8.50 : CIP entry B81-33630

320.958'1 — Afghanistan. Politics, *1965-1981*
Male, Beverley. Revolutionary Afghanistan. — London : Croom Helm, Jan.1982. — [240]p
ISBN 0-7099-1716-3 : £13.95 : CIP entry B81-33894

320.96 — Africa. Politics — *Marxist viewpoints*
Gonidec, Pierre François. African politics / by Pierre François Gonidec ; [English translation by Mostyn Mowbray]. — The Hague ; London : Nijhoff, 1981. — 367p ; 25cm
Translation of: Les systèmes politiques africains. — Includes index
ISBN 90-247-2391-4 : Unpriced B81-08588

320.9667 — Ghana. Politics, *1957-1966*
Amonoo, Ben. Ghana 1957-1966. — London : Allen & Unwin, Jan.1982. — [288]p
ISBN 0-04-320147-4 (cased) : £12.50 : CIP entry
ISBN 0-04-320148-2 (pbk) : £4.50 B81-33921

320.9669 — Nigeria. Politics
Shagari, Shehu. My vision of Nigeria / Shehu Shagari ; selected speeches edited by Aminu Tijjani and David Williams. — London : Cass, 1981. — xxi,424p,[8]p of plates : ports ; 23cm
ISBN 0-7146-3181-7 : £15.00 B81-19596

320.967'7 — Horn of Africa. Politics
Legum, Colin. The Horn of Africa in continuing crisis / Colin Legum and Bill Lee. With Cuba : the new communist power in Africa / Zdenek Cervenka and Colin Legum. — New York ; London : Africana, 1979. — xvii,166p : 2maps ; 22cm. — (Current affairs series)
ISBN 0-8419-0491-x (pbk) : Unpriced B81-28444

320.968 — South Africa. Christian right-wing political movements
Knight, Derrick. Beyond the pale : the Christian political fringe / Derrick Knight. — London : Kogan Page, 1981. — 191p : ill,ports ; 22cm
Bibliography: p178-179. — Includes index
ISBN 0-85038-388-9 (pbk) : £2.95 : CIP rev. B80-24114

320.968 — Southern Africa. Politics
Legum, Colin. The western crisis over southern Africa : South Africa, Rhodesia, Namibia / Colin Legum. — New York ; London : Africana, 1979. — xi,260p : ill,maps ; 23cm. — (Current affairs series)
ISBN 0-8419-0492-8 (cased) : Unpriced
ISBN 0-8419-0496-0 (pbk) : Unpriced B81-28443

320.97295 — Puerto Rico. Politics, *1850-1979 — Readings from contemporary sources*
The **Intellectual** roots of independence : an anthology of Puerto Rican political essays / edited by Iris M. Zavala and Rafael Rodríguez ; with an introduction by Iris M. Zavala. — New York ; London : Monthly Review Press, c1980. — 376p ; 21cm
Translation of: Libertad y crítica en el ensayo político puertorriqueño. — Bibliography: p372-376
ISBN 0-85345-520-1 : £8.95 B81-07541

320.973 — United States. Politics
American politics, policies, and priorities / [compiled by] Alan Shank. — 3rd ed. — Boston [Mass.] ; London : Allyn and Bacon, c1981. — viii,410p : ill ; 24cm
Previous ed.: 1977. — Includes index
ISBN 0-205-07165-1 (pbk) : £8.95 B81-01878

DeLespinasse, Paul F.. Thinking about politics : American government in associational perspective / Paul F. deLespinasse. — New York ; London : D. Van Nostrand, c1981. — xix,517p : ill ; 24cm
Includes index
ISBN 0-442-25409-1 : £11.20 B81-09022

320.973 — United States. Politics, *1601-1776*
Lockridge, Kenneth A.. Settlement and unsettlement in early America : the crisis of political legitimacy before the Revolution / Kenneth A. Lockridge. — Cambridge : Cambridge University Press, 1981. — ix,134p,[2]leaves of plates : 1facsim,2ports ; 23cm. — (The Joanne Goodman lecture series)
Bibliography: p123-128. — Includes index
ISBN 0-521-23707-6 : £9.50 B81-36682

320.973 — United States. Politics, *1933-1938*
The **New** deal : analysis & interpretation / edited by Alonzo L. Hamby. — 2nd ed. — New York ; London : Longman, c1981. — ix,257p ; 23cm
Previous ed.: New York : Weybright and Talley, 1969. — Bibliography: p249-257
ISBN 0-582-28204-7 (pbk) : £5.50 B81-11484

320.973 — United States. Politics, *1960-1980*
Pynn, Ronald E.. American politics : changing expectations / Ronald E. Pynn. — New York ; London : Van Nostrand, c1981. — xix,619p : ill(some col.),maps(some col.),1facsim,ports ; 24cm
Includes bibliographies and index
ISBN 0-442-25865-8 : £13.45 B81-26008

320.973 — United States. Politics, *1977-1981*
McCarthy, Eugene J.. The ultimate tyranny : the majority over the majority / Eugene J. McCarthy. — New York ; London : Harcourt Brace Jovanovich, c1980. — 229p ; 22cm
Includes index
ISBN 0-15-192581-x : £7.95 B81-19591

320.973 — United States. Radical movements, *1890-1917*
Kraditor, Aileen S.. The radical persuasion 1890-1917 : aspects of the intellectual history and the historiography of three American radical organizations / Aileen S. Kraditor. — Baton Rouge ; London : Louisiana State University Press, c1981. — viii,381p ; 24cm
Includes index
ISBN 0-8071-0767-0 (cased) : £29.70
ISBN 0-8071-0864-2 (pbk) : Unpriced B81-39641

320.973'03'21 — United States. Politics — *Encyclopaedias*
Whisker, James B.. A dictionary of concepts on American politics / James B. Whisker. — New York ; Chichester : Wiley, c1980. — xi,285p ; 23cm
Includes index
ISBN 0-471-07716-x (pbk) : £4.00 B81-00026

320.9'73'0927 — United States. Politics
The **Clash** of issues : readings and problems in American government / [edited by] James A. Burkhart, Samuel Krislov, Raymond L. Lee. — 7th ed. — Englewood Cliffs ; London : Prentice-Hall, c1981. — ix,341p ; 24cm
Previous ed.: 1978
ISBN 0-13-135087-0 (pbk) : £6.95 B81-34950

320.9747 — New York *(State)*. **Politics,** *1893-1910*
McCormick, Richard L.. From realignment to reform : political change in New York State, 1893-1910 / Richard L. McCormick. — Ithaca ; London : Cornell University Press, c1981. — 352p : ill,ports ; 24cm
Bibliography: p279-290. — Includes index
ISBN 0-8014-1326-5 : £15.00 B81-36407

320.9797'77 — Washington *(State)*. **Seattle. Radical movements,** *1900-1920 — Personal observations*
O'Connor, Harvey. Revolution in Seattle : a memoir / Harvey O'Connor. — Seattle : Left Bank ; Orkney [distributor], 1981, c1964. — xv,300p,[10]p of plates : ill,1facsim,ports ; 21cm
Originally published: New York : Monthly Review, 1964. — Bibliography: p283-286. — Includes index
ISBN 0-939306-01-8 (pbk) : £5.00 B81-37151

320.98 — Latin America. Political development, *1800-1980*

Fitzgibbon, Russell H.. Latin America : political culture and development. — 2nd ed. / [Russell H. Fitzgibbon, Julio A. Fernandez]. — Englewood Cliffs ; London : Prentice-Hall, c1981. — vi,374p : ill,2maps ; 23cm
Previous ed.: New York : Appleton-Century-Crofts, 1971. — Bibliography: p363-369. — Includes index
ISBN 0-13-524348-3 (pbk) : £8.40 B81-12514

320.98'05 — Latin America. Politics — *Serials*

[Latin America *(Oxford)***]**. Latin America. — 1-. — Oxford ([The Centre, P.O. Box 20, Oxford OX1 1AA]) : [S.n.], 1980-. — v. : ill,maps,ports ; 30cm
Six issues yearly
ISSN 0260-7342 = Latin America (Oxford) : £3.50 per year B81-32799

320.983 — Chile. Politics, *ca 1930-1980*

Mobilization and socialist politics in Chile / edited by Benny Pollack. — Liverpool (P.O. Box 147, Liverpool L69 3BX) : Centre for Latin-American Studies, University of Liverpool, [1980?]. — v,72p ; 30cm. — (Monograph series / University of Liverpool. Centre for Latin-American Studies ; no.9)
Cover title
Unpriced (pbk) B81-37824

321 — POLITICS. FORMS OF STATES

321 — States

Abdel-Malek, Anouar. Nation and revolution / Anouar Abdel-Malek. — London : Macmillan, 1981. — 222p ; 23cm. — (Social dialectics ; v.2)
Translated from the French. — Includes index
ISBN 0-333-23876-1 : Unpriced : CIP rev. B80-20212

321.02'09 — Federalism, *to 1980*

Forsyth, Murray. Union of states. — Leicester : Leicester University Press, Sept.1981. — [256]p
ISBN 0-7185-1188-3 (cased) : £13.00 : CIP entry
ISBN 0-7185-1221-9 (pbk) : £6.00 B81-20638

321.02'094 — Western European countries. Integration, *1945-1950*

Lipgens, Walter. A history of European integration. — Oxford : Oxford University Press
Translation of: Die Anfänge der europäischen Einigungspolitik 1945-1950
Vol.1: 1945-1947. — Dec.1981. — [740]p
ISBN 0-19-822587-3 : £40.00 : CIP entry B81-31450

321.02'0941 — Great Britain. Federalism

Burrows, Bernard. Devolution or federalism? : options for a united kingdom / Bernard Burrows and Geoffrey Denton. — London : Macmillan, 1980. — xii,94p ; 23cm
Includes index
ISBN 0-333-28176-4 (cased) : £12.00
ISBN 0-333-28677-4 (pbk) : £4.95 B81-00764

321.02'0973 — United States. States. Politics — *Comparative studies*

Dye, Thomas R.. Politics in states and communities / Thomas R. Dye. — 4th ed. — Englewood Cliffs ; London : Prentice-Hall, c1981. — xvi,492p : ill,maps ; 25cm
Previous ed.: 1977. — Includes index
ISBN 0-13-685131-2 : £11.00 B81-12524

321'.04 — Europe. Political integration, *1945-1979*

Blacksell, Mark. Post-war Europe : a political geography / Mark Blacksell. — 2nd ed. — London : Hutchinson, 1981. — 220p : ill,maps ; 22cm
Previous ed.: Dawson, 1977. — Bibliography: p206-208. - Includes index
ISBN 0-09-143711-3 (pbk) : £4.50 : CIP rev. B80-20283

321'.04 — World. Government

Macfarlane, E. G.. Truth : opinions of a truth-seeker / E.G. Macfarlane. — Ilfracombe : Stockwell, 1981. — 45p ; 19cm
ISBN 0-7223-1473-6 (pbk) : £1.26 B81-36336

321'.05 — Nation states

The **Nation** state : the formation of modern politics / edited by Leonard Tivey. — Oxford : Robertson, 1981. — x,214p ; 23cm
Bibliography: p207-208. — Includes index
ISBN 0-85520-378-1 : £15.00 : CIP rev. B80-24115

321'.07 — Utopianism. Theories of English writers, *1516-1700*

Davis, J. C. (James Colin). Utopia and the ideal society : a study of English utopian writing 1516-1700 / J.C. Davis. — Cambridge : Cambridge University Press, 1981. — ix,427p ; 24cm
Bibliography: p389-417. — Includes index
ISBN 0-521-23396-8 : £25.00 : CIP rev. B81-07578

321'.07 — Utopias — *Early works*

Campanella, Tommaso. La Città del sole : dialogo poetico = The city of the sun : a poetical dialogue / Tommaso Campanella ; translated with introduction and notes by Daniel J. Donno. — Berkeley ; London : University of California Press, c1981. — 144p ; 21cm. — (Biblioteca italiana)
Text in English and Italian, introduction and notes in English. Bibliography: p143144
ISBN 0-520-04034-1 : £8.75 B81-27572

Plato. [Republic. English]. The Republic / Plato ; translated by G.M.A. Grube. — London : Pan, 1981, c1974. — xii,319p ; 20cm. — (Pan classics)
Originally published: Indianapolis : Hackett, 1974. — Bibliography: p301-304. - Includes index
ISBN 0-330-26260-2 (pbk) : £1.75 B81-09725

321'.07 — Utopias. Plato. Republic — *Critical studies*

Annas, Julia. An introduction to Plato's Republic / by Julia Annas. — Oxford : Clarendon Press, 1981. — viii,362p ; 22cm
Bibliography: p355-359. — Includes index
ISBN 0-19-827428-9 (cased) : £15.00 : CIP rev.
ISBN 0-19-827429-7 (pbk) : £5.95 B81-11910

321'.07 — Utopias. Theories

Taylor, Keith. The political ideas of the utopian socialists. — London : Cass, Oct.1981. — [240]p
ISBN 0-7146-3089-6 : £13.50 : CIP entry B81-31286

321.1'4 — North-western Europe. Kingship, *to ca 900*

Wallace-Hadrill, J. M.. Early Germanic Kingship in England and on the Continent : the Ford lectures delivered in the University of Oxford in Hilary term 1970 / by J.M. Wallace-Hadrill. — Oxford : Clarendon, 1971 (1980 [printing]). — viii,160p ; 22cm
Includes index
ISBN 0-19-873011-x (pbk) : £5.95 B81-06296

321.1'4 — Scotland. Kingship, *ca 500-ca 850 — Sources of data: Irish annals & regnal lists*

Anderson, Marjorie O.. Kings and kingship in early Scotland / Marjorie O. Anderson. — Rev. ed. — Edinburgh : Scottish Academic, 1980. — xviii,310p : 2geneal.tables ; 24cm
Previous ed.: 1973. — Bibliography: pxi-xviii. - Includes index
ISBN 0-7011-1930-6 : £6.50 B81-08752

321.3'0944 — France. Feudalism

Duby, Georges. The three orders : feudal society imagined / Georges Duby ; translated by Arthur Goldhammer ; with a foreword by Thomas N. Bisson. — Chicago ; London : University of Chicago Press, 1980. — x,382p ; 24cm
Translation of: Les trois ordres ou l'imaginaire du féodalisme. — Includes index
ISBN 0-226-16771-2 : £15.00 B81-12683

321.6'0942 — England. Monarchy. Theories, *1642-1689*

Weston, Corinne Comstock. Subjects and sovereigns : the grand controversy over legal sovereignty in Stuart England / Corinne Comstock Weston, Janelle Renfrow Greenberg. — Cambridge : Cambridge University Press, 1981. — viii,430p ; 23cm
Bibliography: p379-410. — Includes index
ISBN 0-521-23272-4 : £24.00 B81-08128

321.6'0944 — France. Monarchy. Theories, *ca 1500 — Early works*

Seyssel, Claude de. The Monarchy of France / Claude de Seyssel ; translated by J.H. Hexter ; edited, annotated, and introduced by Donald R. Kelley ; additional translations by Michael Sherman. — New Haven ; London : Yale University Press, c1981. — viii,191p ; 22cm
Translation of: La monarchie de France et deux autres fragments politiques. — Includes index
ISBN 0-300-02516-5 : £10.60 : CIP rev. B81-07486

321.8'01 — Democracy — *Philosophical perspectives*

Nelson, William N.. On justifying democracy / William N. Nelson. — London : Routledge & Kegan Paul, 1980. ix,176p ; 23cm. (International library of philosophy)
Bibliography: p171-174. — Includes index
ISBN 0-7100-0653-5 : £9.75 : CIP rev. B80-26586

321.8'01 — Democracy. Theories

Lively, Jack. Democracy / Jack Lively. — Oxford : Blackwell, c1975 (1980 [printing]). — vi,154p ; 22cm
Originally published: 1975. — Includes index
ISBN 0-631-11431-9 (pbk) : £4.25 B81-25610

321.8'0941 — Great Britain. Democracy — *Socialist viewpoints*

Benn, Tony. Arguments for democracy / Tony Benn ; edited by Chris Mullin. — London : Cape, 1981. — xiv,257p ; 23cm
Bibliography: p238. — Includes index
ISBN 0-224-01878-7 : £6.95 : CIP rev. B81-21652

321.8'09416 — Northern Ireland. Democracy

Bradbury, Farel. Northern Ireland and the voice of the people : a 10-minute dissertation for busy politicians / Farel Bradbury. — 2nd ed. — Ross-on-Wye (P.O.Box 4, Ross-on-Wye HR9 6EB) : Hydatum, 1981. — 4,vip ; 21cm
Previous ed.: 1980
ISBN 0-905682-25-4 (pbk) : £0.85 B81-37792

321.8'7'0944 — France. Representative government, *1484-1728*

Major, J. Russell. Representative government in early modern France / J. Russell Major. — New Haven ; London : Yale University Press, c1980. — xiv,731p : 1map ; 24cm. — (Studies presented to the International Commission for the History of Representative and Parliamentary Institutions = Études présentées à la Commission internationale pour l'histoire des assemblées d'états ; 63)
Bibliography: p673-713. - Includes index
ISBN 0-300-02300-6 : £28.40 B81-07050

321.9 — Great Britain. Corporatism

Newman, Otto. The challenge of corporatism / Otto Newman. — London : Macmillan, 1981. — xi,285p ; 22cm. — (New studies in sociology)
Bibliography: p261-275. — Includes index
ISBN 0-333-29173-5 (cased) : Unpriced
ISBN 0-333-29174-3 (pbk) : Unpriced B81-34197

321.9 — Totalitarianism

Totalitarianism reconsidered / edited by Ernest A. Menze. — Port Washington ; London : National University Publications : Kennikat, 1981. — viii,272p ; 23cm. — (Series in political science)
Includes index
ISBN 0-8046-9268-8 : £17.00 B81-10333

321.9'2 — Marxist-Leninist governments — *Comparative studies*

Marxist governments : a world survey / edited by Bogdan Szajkowski. — London : Macmillan, 1981. — 3v. : ill,maps ; 23cm
Includes bibliographies and index
ISBN 0-333-28669-3 : £50.00
ISBN 0-333-25703-0 (v.1) : £20.00
ISBN 0-333-25704-9 (v.2) : £20.00
ISBN 0-333-25705-7 (v.3) : £20.00 B81-38722

321.9′2 — Proletarian dictatorship - *Trotskyist viewpoints*

The **Withering** away of the state?. — London : Sage, June 1981. — [288]p. — (Sage modern politics series ; v.6)
ISBN 0-8039-9796-5 (cased) : £11.25 : CIP entry
ISBN 0-8039-9797-3 (pbk) : £5.50 B81-13569

322 — POLITICS. RELATION OF STATE TO ORGANISED GROUPS

322′.1′0924 — England. Christian church. Relations with state. Role of Winchelsey, Robert, *1294-1313*

Denton, Jeffrey H.. Robert Winchester and the Crown 1294-1313 : a study in the defence of ecclesiastical liberty / Jeffrey H. Denton. — Cambridge : Cambridge University Press, 1980. — x,341p ; 23cm. — (Cambridge studies in mediaeval life and thought. 3rd series ; v.14)
Bibliography: p303-317. — Includes index
ISBN 0-521-22963-4 : £17.50 B81-07224

322′.1′0941 — Great Britain. Politics. Role of Nonconformists, *1870-1914*

Bebbington, D. W.. The Nonconformist conscience. — London : Allen & Unwin, Jan.1982. — [192]p
ISBN 0-04-942173-5 : £10.00 : CIP entry
B81-33897

322′.1′09438 — Poland. Political parties. Relations with Catholic Church, *1936-1976 — Russian texts*

Mikhnik, Adam. Polskiĭ dialog : t͡serkov′ - levye / Adam Mikhnik ; perevod s pol′skogo N. Gorbanevskoĭ. — London : Overseas Publications, 1980. — 250p ; 19cm
Translation of: Kościół — lewica — dialog. — Title on added t.p.: The Church and the left
ISBN 0-903868-25-3 (pbk) : £6.50 B81-02765

322′.1′0947 — Soviet Union. Religions. Policies of government, *1917-1978*

Boiter, Albert. Religion in the Soviet Union / Albert Boiter ; foreword by David M. Abshire. — Beverly Hills ; London : Center for Strategic and International Studies [by] Sage, c1980. — 88p ; 22cm. — (The Washington papers ; vol.viii 78) (A Sage policy paper)
Bibliography: p85-88
ISBN 0-8039-1546-2 (pbk) : Unpriced
B81-09414

322′.2 — London. Craftsmen. Political movements, *1800-1840*

Prothero, I. J.. Artisans and politics in early nineteenth-century London : John Gast and his times / I.J. Prothero. — London : Methuen, 1981, c1979. — xi,418p ; 22cm
Originally published: Folkestone : Dawson, 1979. — Bibliography: p398-404. — Includes index
ISBN 0-416-74890-2 (pbk) : £5.95
Also classified at 331.88′092′4 B81-21325

322′.2 — Politics. Role of trade unions

Posadas, J.. The function of the trade unions : in the workers states and in the capitalist system / J. Posadas. — London (BCM Box 6220, London WCIV 6XX) : Scientific, Cultural and Political Editions, 1980. — 60p ; 20cm
£0.50 (pbk) B81-29295

322′.2′0941 — Great Britain. Coloured working class movements — *Feminist viewpoints*

James, Selma. Sex, race and class / Selma James with contributions from Barbara Beese ... [et al.]. — Bristol : Falling Wall Press, 1975. — 34p : 1map ; 21cm
ISBN 0-9502702-7-x (pbk) : £0.35 B81-32471

322′.2′094216 — South Inner London. Working class movements, *1848-1897 — Readings from contemporary sources*

Class struggles in South London 1850-1900 : selections from original sources / Dave Russell & Mike Tichelar. — London (58 Fearnley House, Vestry Rd., S.E.6) : Southwark-Lambeth History Workshop, 1980. — 35p ; 21cm
ISBN 0-9507360-0-7 (pbk) : £1.00 B81-14766

322′.2′0985 — Peru. Government. Relations with labour movements, *1968-1978 — Conference proceedings*

Angell, Alan. Peruvian labour and the military government since 1968 / by Alan Angell. — London (31 Tavistock Sq., WC1H 9HA) : University of London Institute of Latin American Studies, [1980?]. — 38,xiii p ; 25cm. — (Working papers / University of London Institute of Latin American Studies, ISSN 3142-1875 ; 3)
ISBN 0-901145-38-6 (pbk) : Unpriced
B81-06274

322.4′2 — Fascist revolutionary movements

Wilkinson, Paul. The new fascists. — London : Grant McIntyre, Oct.1981. — [224]p
ISBN 0-86216-060-x : £7.95 : CIP entry
B81-30309

322.4′2 — France. Provinces. Politics. Repression. Role of police, *1840-1852*

Forstenzer, Thomas R.. French provincial police and the fall of the Second Republic : social fear and counterrevolution / by Thomas R. Forstenzer. — Princeton ; Guildford : Princeton University Press, c1981. — xxi,336p ; 24cm
Bibliography: p319-329. — Includes index
ISBN 0-691-05318-9 : £14.60 B81-28431

322.4′2 — International terrorism. Organisation. Role of Soviet Union

Sterling, Claire. The terror network : the secret war of international terrorism / Claire Sterling. — London : Weidenfeld and Nicolson, 1981. — ix,357p : ill,ports ; 24cm
Bibliography: p343-347. — Includes index
ISBN 0-297-77968-0 : £7.95 B81-24277

322.4′2 — Marxist revolution

Revolutionary thought in the 20th century / edited by Ben Turok. — London : Zed, 1980. — vi,313p ; 23cm. — (Imperialism series)
Includes bibliographies and index
ISBN 0-905762-42-8 (cased) : £12.95 : CIP rev.
ISBN 0-905762-43-6 (pbk) : £4.50 B80-19058

322.4′2 — Nationalist movements

National and ethnic movements / edited by Jacques Dofny and Akinsola Akiwowo. — Beverly Hills ; London : Sage, c1980. — 277p : 1ill,1map ; 22cm. — (Sage studies in international sociology ; 19)
English and French text. — Includes bibliographies
ISBN 0-8039-9820-1 (cased) : £11.25 : CIP rev.
ISBN 0-8039-9821-x (pbk) : £5.50 B80-08115

322.4′2 — Politics. Violence. Influence of mass media

Clutterbuck, Richard. The media and political violence / Richard Clutterbuck ; foreword by Sir Robin Day. — London : Macmillan, 1981. — xx,191p ; 23cm
Bibliography: p176-184. — Includes index
ISBN 0-333-31484-0 : £15.00 B81-31978

322.4′2 — Socialist revolution. Role of working classes — *Early works*

Lenin, V. I.. The tasks of the proletariat in our revolution : (draft programme for the Proletarian Party) / Lenin. — Moscow : Progress Publishers ; [London] : Central Books [distributor], 1980. — 55p ; 21cm
Translation of: Zadachi proletariata v nasheĭ revoli͡ut͡sii. — Includes index
ISBN 0-7147-1634-0 (pbk) : £0.40 B81-32946

322.4′2 — Socialist revolution. Social factors — *Marxist viewpoints*

Zarodov, K. I.. The political economy of revolution : contemporary issues as seen from the historical standpoint / K. Zarodov ; [translated from the Russian by Laura Beraha]. — Moscow : Progress ; [London] : Central Books [distributor], 1981. — 231p ; 21cm
Translation of: Politicheskai͡a ėkonomii͡a revoli͡ut͡sii
ISBN 0-7147-1620-0 : £2.95 B81-29310

322.4′2 — Terrorism

British perspectives on terrorism / edited by Paul Wilkinson. — London : Allen & Unwin, c1981. — 193p ; 23cm
Originally published: in Terrorism, v.5, no.1 and 2. — Includes index
ISBN 0-04-327064-6 (cased) : Unpriced : CIP rev.
ISBN 0-04-327065-4 (pbk) : Unpriced
B81-20142

Clutterbuck, Richard. Guerrillas and terrorists / Richard Clutterbuck. — Chicago ; London : Ohio University Press, 1980, c1977. — 125p ; 23cm
Originally published: London : Faber, 1977. — Bibliography: p117-119. — Includes index
ISBN 0-8214-0590-x (cased) : £7.20
ISBN 0-8214-0592-6 (pbk) : £3.60
Also classified at 355′.02184 B81-22350

322.4′2 — Terrorism — *For schools*

Freeman, Charles. Terrorism / Charles Freeman. — London : Batsford Academic and Educational, 1981. — 72p : ill,ports ; 26cm. — (Today′s world)
Bibliography: p68-69. — Includes index
ISBN 0-7134-1230-5 : £5.50 B81-29481

322.4′2 — Terrorism. Influence of reporting of terrorism by news media

Schmid, Alex P.. Violence as communication : insurgent terrorism and the Western news media. — London : Sage Publications, Feb.1982. — [284]p
ISBN 0-8039-9789-2 : £17.00 : CIP entry
B81-37586

322.4′2′019 — Revolutionary movements. Psychological aspects

Le Bon, Gustave. The French Revolution and the psychology of revolution / Gustave LeBon ; with a new introduction by Robert A. Nye. — New Brunswick ; London : Transaction, c1980. — l,337p ; 24cm. — ([Social science classics series])
Translation of: La révolution française et la psychologie des révolutions. — Originally published: as The psychology of revolution. London : T.F. Unwin, 1913. — Includes index
ISBN 0-87855-310-x : £11.75
ISBN 0-87855-697-4 (pbk) : £4.25
Primary classification 944.04′01′9 B81-04122

322.4′2′0882971 — Islamic revolutionary movements — *Islamic viewpoints*

Siddiqui, Kalim. The state of the Muslim world today / Kalim Siddiqui. — London : Open Press in association with the Muslim Institute, 1980. — 20p ; 22cm
ISBN 0-905081-08-0 (pbk) : £1.00 B81-09005

322.4′2′089924 — Jewish anti-fascist revenge movements: DIN, *to 1960*

Elkins, Michael. Forged in fury / Michael Elkins. — Loughton : Piatkus, 1981, c1971. — 274p ; 23cm
Originally published: New York : Ballantine, 1971
ISBN 0-86188-098-6 : £6.95 : CIP rev.
B81-04378

322.4′2′089924 — New Left movement. Role of Jews

Cohen, Percy S.. Jewish radicals and radical Jews / Percy S. Cohen. — London : Published for the Institute of Jewish Affairs by Academic Press, 1980. — xviii,224p ; 24cm
Includes index
ISBN 0-12-178780-x : £10.80 B81-03191

322.4′2′0922 — Namibia & South Africa. Nationalist movements. Women — *Biographies*

To honour Women′s Day : profiles of leading women in the South African and Namibian liberation struggles / [prepared by IDAF Research, Information and Publications Department]. — London : International Defence and Aid Fund for Southern Africa in cooperation with United Nations Centre Against Apartheid, 1981. — 56p : ill,ports ; 22cm
Text on inside covers
ISBN 0-904759-46-6 (pbk) : £1.00 B81-39972

322.4′2′0922 — Revolutionary movements. Leaders, *1640-1968*

Rejai, Mostafa. Leaders of revolution / Mostafa Rejai with Kay Phillips. — Beverly Hills ; London : Sage, c1979. — 245p ; 23cm. — (Sage library of social research ; vol.73)
Bibliography: p223-239. — Includes index
ISBN 0-8039-1139-4 (cased) : Unpriced
ISBN 0-8039-1140-8 (pbk) : Unpriced
B81-10761

322.4′2′0924 — Ireland. Revolutionary movements: Fenian Brotherhood. Davitt, Michael, *1846-1882 - Biographies*

Moody, T. W.. Davitt and Irish revolution, 1846-1882. — Oxford : Clarendon Press, Aug.1981. — [628]p
ISBN 0-19-822382-x : £25.00 : CIP entry
B81-15840

322.4′2′0924 — Ireland. Revolutionary movements: Irish Republican Brotherhood. Kickham, Charles J. *— Biographies*

Comerford, R. V.. Charles J. Kickham : a study in Irish nationalism and literature / R.V. Comerford. — Portmarnock (98 Ardilaun, Portmarnock, Co. Dublin) : Wolfhound, c1979. — 255p : ill,facsims,map,ports ; 22cm
Bibliography: p241-249. — Includes index
ISBN 0-905473-14-0 : £8.50 B81-00765

322.4′2′0924 — Ukraine. Nationalist movements. Shukhevych, Roman *— Biographies*

Thirty years 1950-1980 : the martyrology of a Ukrainian father and son, Roman and Yuriy Shukhevych. — Toronto ; London : Ukrainian Central Information Service, 1980. — 32p : ill,ports ; 23cm
Unpriced (pbk)
Also classified at 365′.45′0924 B81-19802

322.4′2′094 — European Community countries. Terrorism

Terrorism : a challenge to the state / edited by Juliet Lodge. — Oxford : Robertson, 1981. — xi,247p ; 24cm
Bibliography: p231-236. — Includes index
ISBN 0-85520-297-1 : £12.50 : CIP rev.
B80-13726

322.4′2′0941 — Great Britain. Extremist political movements

Tomlinson, John. Left-right : the march of political extremism in Britain / by John Tomlinson. — London : J. Calder, 1981. — vi,152p : ill ; 22cm. — (A Platform book)
Bibliography: p143-144. — Includes index
ISBN 0-7145-3855-8 (pbk) : £4.95 B81-15654

322.4′2′0941 — Great Britain. Left-wing political movements *— Forecasts*

The **Crisis** and the future of the Left : the debate of the decade / contributions by Tony Benn .. [et al.] ; edited by Peter Hain. — London : Pluto, 1980. — 80p ; 20cm
ISBN 0-86104-313-8 (pbk) : £1.50 B81-05339

322.4′2′0941 — Great Britain. Revolutionary left-wing political movements

Baker, Blake. The far left : an exposé of the extreme left in Britain / Blake Baker. — London : Weidenfeld and Nicolson, 1981. — ix,182p ; 22cm
Includes index
ISBN 0-297-78033-6 (cased) : £6.95 B81-40203

322.4′2′09415 — Ireland. Revolutionary movements: Irish Republican Army, *to 1979*

Bell, J. Bowyer. The secret army : the IRA 1916-1979 / J. Bowyer Bell. — Rev. and updated ed. — Dublin : Academy Press, 1979. — xiv,481p,[16]p of plates : ill,maps,ports ; 24cm
Previous ed.: London : Blond, 1970. — Bibliography: p451-463. - Includes index
ISBN 0-906187-27-3 : Unpriced B81-03037

322.4′2′09438 — Poland. Revolutionary labour movements, *1980 — Labour Party (Great Britain). Young Socialists viewpoints*
Labour Party *(Great Britain). Young Socialists. National Committee.* Poland and workers′ democracy : Labour Party Young Socialists′ Conference document 1981 / by the Labour Party Young Socialists′ National Committee. — London : The Committee, 1981. — 15p : ill,ports ; 30cm
Cover title
£0.60 (pbk) B81-11559

322.4′2′0947 — Soviet Union. Revolutionary movements. Role of intellectuals, *1598-1908 — Russian texts*
Struve, Petr. Intelligentsiia i revoliutsiia = Intelligentsia & revolution / P. Struve. — Letchworth : Prideaux, 1980. — 21p ; 20cm. — (Russian titles for the specialist, ISSN 0305-3741 ; no.223)
Originally published: Moscow : s.n., 1909
£0.90 (pbk) B81-14759

322.4′2′094972 — Yugoslavia. Croatia. Separatist movements, *ca 1945-1980 — Interviews*
Veselica, Marko. Interview with Dr Marko Veselica / translated by M.M. Meštrović. — London (60 Brightwell Cres. S.W.17) : United Publishers, [1981?]. — 39p : 1port ; 21cm
Translation of: Razgovor s dr. Markom Veselicom. — Cover title: The Croatian national question
Unpriced (pbk) B81-20040

322.4′2′094972 — Yugoslavia. Croatia. Separatist movements, *ca 1945-1980 — Interviews — Croatian texts*
Veselica, Marko. Razgovor s dr. Markom Veselicom. — London (60 Brightwell Cres. S.W.17) : United Publishers, [1981?]. — 36p : 1port ; 21cm
Cover title: Zašto smo protiv
Unpriced (pbk) B81-23039

322.4′2′095 — Asia. Nationalist movements, *to 1977.* **Socioeconomic aspects** *— Marxist viewpoints*
Ul′ianovskiĭ, R. A.. Present-day problems in Asia and Africa : theory, politics, personalities / Rostislav Ulyanovsky ; [translated from the Russian by Barry Costello-Jones and Angus Roxburgh]. — Moscow : Progress Publishers ; [London] : Distributed by Central Books, c1980. — 239p ; 21cm
Translation of: Sovremennye problemy Azii i Afriki
ISBN 0-7147-1627-8 : £2.50
Also classified at 322.4′2′096 B81-32962

322.4′2′0956 — Middle East. Kurdish separatist movements, *1920-1979*
Sim, Richard. Kurdistan : the search for recognition / Richard Sim. — London (12 Golden Sq., W1R 3AF) : Institute for the Study of Conflict, 1980. — 21p : 1map ; 30cm. — (Conflict studies, ISSN 0069-8792 ; n.124)
Bibliography: p21
£2.00 (pbk) B81-07960

322.4′2′095694 — Palestinian Arab resistance movements: Palestine Liberation Organisation *— Israeli viewpoints*
Yodfat, Aryeh Y.. PLO strategy and politics / Aryeh Y. Yodfat and Yuval Arnon-Ohanna. — London : Croom Helm, c1981. — 225p ; 23cm
Bibliography: p207-218. — Includes index
ISBN 0-7099-2901-3 : £11.50 B81-18828

322.4′2′095694 — Palestinian Arab resistance movements: Palestine Liberation Organisation *— Palestine Liberation Organisation viewpoints*
Hamid, Rashid. What is the PLO? / [by Rashid Hamid]. — London ([52 Green St., W1]) : PLO, [1981]. — [22]p ; 21cm
Unpriced (unbound) B81-18648

322.4′2′095694 — Palestinian Arab resistance movements: Palestine Liberation Organisation *— Serials*
The **Palestine** report : a monthly newsletter / issued by the London Office of the Palestine Liberation Organisation. — No.1 (Nov.1979)-. — London (52 Green St., W.1.) : The Organisation, 1979-. — v. : ill,ports
Monthly. — Description based on: No.7 (July 1980)
ISSN 0260-2350 = Palestine report : Unpriced B81-04823

322.4′2′09598 — Indonesia. Revolutionary labour movements, *ca 1900-ca 1970*
Tichelman, Fritjof. The social evolution of Indonesia : the Asiatic mode of production and its legacy / by Fritjof Tichelman ; translated from the Dutch by Jean Sanders. — The Hague ; London : Nijhoff, c1980. — xiv,301p ; 25cm. — (Studies in social history ; 5)
Bibliography: p251-289. - Includes index
ISBN 90-247-2389-2 : Unpriced B81-16019

322.4′2′096 — Africa. Nationalist movements, *to 1977.* **Socioeconomic aspects** *— Marxist viewpoints*
Ul′ianovskiĭ, R. A.. Present-day problems in Asia and Africa : theory, politics, personalities / Rostislav Ulyanovsky ; [translated from the Russian by Barry Costello-Jones and Angus Roxburgh]. — Moscow : Progress Publishers ; [London] : Distributed by Central Books, c1980. — 239p ; 21cm
Translation of: Sovremennye problemy Azii i Afriki
ISBN 0-7147-1627-8 : £2.50
Primary classification 322.4′2′095 B81-32962

322.4′2′0968 — South Africa. Nationalist movements *— Serials*
Azania contact. — Vol.1, no.1. — [London] (1st Floor, 212 Church Rd, Willesden, NW10) : Pan Africanist Congress of Azania, Mission to the UK and Continental Europe, [197-]-. — v. : maps, ports ; 30cm
Description based on: Vol.1, no.3
ISSN 0260-0307 = Azania contact : Unpriced
B81-04639

322.4′2′0973 — United States. Black power movements: Student Nonviolent Coordinating Committee, *1960-1970*
Carson, Clayborne. In struggle : SNCC and the black awakening of the 1960s / Clayborne Carson. — Cambridge, Mass. ; London : Harvard University Press, 1981. — viii,359p,[8]p of plates : ill,ports ; 24cm
Includes index
ISBN 0-674-44725-5 : £13.20 B81-28447

322.4′2′098 — Latin America. Spanish colonies. Revolutionary movements, *1806-1830*
Domínguez, Jorge I.. Insurrection or loyalty : the breakdown of the Spanish American Empire / Jorge I. Domínguez. — Cambridge, Mass. ; London : Harvard University Press, 1980. — ix,306p ; 24cm
Includes index
ISBN 0-674-45635-1 : £18.00 B81-16564

322.4′3′094 — Western European countries. Politics. Influence of pressure groups
Organizing interests in Western Europe : pluralism, corporatism and the transformation of politics / edited by Suzanne Berger. — Cambridge : Cambridge University Press, 1981. — x,426p : 2ill ; 24cm. — (Cambridge studies in modern political economics)
Includes bibliographies and index
ISBN 0-521-23174-4 : £25.00 B81-38001

322.4′3′0941 — Great Britain. Politics. Influence of pressure groups
Coxall, W. N.. Parties and pressure groups / W.N. Coxall. — Harlow : Longman, 1981, c1980. — ix,150p ; 21cm. — (Political realities)
Bibliography: p143-146. - Includes index
ISBN 0-582-36610-0 (cased) : Unpriced
ISBN 0-582-36621-6 (pbk) : £2.25 B81-11337

322.4′3′0941 — Great Britain. Politics. Influence of pressure groups. Role of women, *1825-1860*
Tyrrell, Alex. 'Woman′s mission' and pressure group politics in Britain (1825-60) / by Alex Tyrrell. — Manchester : John Rylands University Library of Manchester, 1980. — p194-230,[1]leaf of plates : 1ill ; 25cm
£1.90 (pbk) B81-35547

322.4′3′0941 — Great Britain. Politics. Role of pressure groups
Buller, Henry. Pressure groups and the pluralist model of society : the example of local amenity societies / Henry Buller. — [London] : University of London King′s College, Dept. of Geography, 1981. — 55p ; 30cm. — (Occasional paper / University of London King′s College. Department of Geography, ISSN 0309-2178 ; no.14)
Bibliography: p42-55
Unpriced (spiral) B81-40832

322.4'3'0973 — United States. Interest groups. Political aspects

Wilson, Graham K.. Interest groups in the United States. — Oxford : Oxford University Press, Oct.1981. — [220]p
ISBN 0-19-827425-4 (cased) : £12.50 : CIP entry
ISBN 0-19-876095-7 (pbk) : £4.95 B81-26743

322.4'3'0973 — United States. Politics. Role of pressure groups

Garson, G. David. Group theories of politics / G. David Garson. — Beverly Hills ; London : Sage, c1978. — 215p ; 23cm. — (Sage library of social research ; v.61)
Includes bibliographies and index
ISBN 0-8039-0518-1 (cased) : £11.25
ISBN 0-8039-0519-x (pbk) : £5.50 B81-14026

322.4'3'0973 — United States. Pressure groups, ***to 1979***

Barbrook, Alec. Power and protest in American life / Alec Barbrook, Christine Bolt. — Oxford : Robertson, 1980. — xiv,375p : 1ill ; 22cm
Includes index
ISBN 0-85520-132-0 : £15.00 B81-17618

322.4'4 — Mexico. Oaxaca ***(State).*** **Liberal movements,** ***1856-1876***

Berry, Charles R.. The reform in Oaxaca, 1856-76 : a microhistory of the liberal revolution / Charles R. Berry. — Lincoln [Neb.] ; London : University of Nebraska Press, c1981. — xviii,282p : ill,1map ; 24cm
Bibliography: p253-267. — Includes index
ISBN 0-8032-1158-9 : Unpriced B81-22351

322.4'4'0922 — Massachusetts. Boston. Women reformers, ***1830-1865***

Taylor, Clare. Romantic reform and Anglo-American women, the great examples of Boston and Norwich / Clare Taylor. — Aberystwyth : [Department of History, The University College of Wales], 1981. — 21leaves ; 30cm
Unpriced (unbound)
Primary classification 322.4'4'0922 B81-34250

322.4'4'0922 — Norfolk. Norwich. Women reformers, ***1830-1865***

Taylor, Clare. Romantic reform and Anglo-American women, the great examples of Boston and Norwich / Clare Taylor. — Aberystwyth : [Department of History, The University College of Wales], 1981. — 21leaves ; 30cm
Unpriced (unbound)
Also classified at 322.4'4'0922 B81-34250

322.4'4'0924 — Chartism. McAdam, John — ***Biographies***

McAdam, John. Autobiography of John McAdam (1806-1883) : with selected letters / edited by Janet Fyfe. — Edinburgh : Printed for the Scottish History Society by Clark Constable, 1980. — xxi,225,[40]p ; 23cm. — (Scottish History Society. 4th series ; v.16)
Includes index
ISBN 0-906245-10-9 : Unpriced B81-40554

322.4'4'0924 — Chartism. O'Connor, Feargus, ***1832-1842 — Biographies***

Epstein, James. The lion of freedom : Feargus O'Connor and the Chartist movement, 1832-1842. — London : Croom Helm, Jan.1982. — [320]p
ISBN 0-85664-922-8 : £14.95 : CIP entry B81-33774

322.4'4'0924 — East Africa. Slavery. British abolitionist movements. Sulivan, George Lydiard — ***Biographies***

Collister, Peter. The Sulivans and the slave trade / Peter Collister. — London : Collins, 1980, c1979. — 197p,[5]p of plates : ill,1map,ports,1geneal.table ; 23cm
Bibliography: p184-186. - Includes index
ISBN 0-86036-121-7 : £8.00 B81-06869

322.4'4'0924 — Slavery. American abolitionist movement. Garrison, William Lloyd — ***Correspondence, diaries, etc.***

Garrison, William Lloyd. The letters of William Lloyd Garrison / edited by Walter M. Merrill and Louis Ruchames. — Cambridge, Mass. ; London : Belknap Press of Harvard University Press
Vol.6: To rouse the slumbering land 1868-1879. — 1981. — xx,637p : 1port ; 25cm
Includes index
ISBN 0-674-52666-x : £31.50 B81-38898

322.4'4'0924 — Slavery. American abolitionist movements. Channing, William Ellery — ***Biographies***

Delbanco, Andrew. William Ellery Channing : an essay on the liberal spirit in America / Andrew Delbanco. — Cambridge, Mass. ; London : Harvard University Press, 1981. — xviii,203p ; 22cm
Includes index
ISBN 0-674-95335-5 : £9.00 B81-29154

322.4'4'0924 — Slavery. British abolitionist movements. Wilberforce, William

Lean, Garth. God's politician : William Wilberforce's struggle / Garth Lean. — London : Darton, Longman & Todd, 1980. — xii,180p ; 21cm
Bibliography: p175-176. — Includes index
ISBN 0-232-51505-0 (pbk) : £2.50 B81-08253

322.4'4'0924 — Soviet Union. Society. Dissent, ***1968-1979 — Personal observations — Russian texts***

Plîûshch, Leonid. Na karnavale istorii / Leonid Plîûshch. — London (40 Elsham Rd., W14 8HB) : Overseas Publications Interchange, c1979. — 711p ; 19cm
Russian title transliterated. — Title on added t.p.: History's carnival
ISBN 0-903868-17-2 (pbk) : £10.00 B81-22214

322.4'4'0924 — United States. Negro slavery. American abolitionist movements. Douglas, Frederick — ***Biographies***

Preston, Dickson J.. Young Frederick Douglas : the Maryland years / Dickson J. Preston. — Baltimore ; London : Johns Hopkins University Press, c1980. — xvii,242p : ill,1map,1facsim,ports ; 24cm
Includes index
ISBN 0-8018-2439-7 : £9.00 B81-12660

322.4'4'0941 — Slavery. British abolitionist movements. Members: Women. Role, ***1830-1850***

Taylor, Clare. Romantic reform and Anglo-American women, London, the 1840 Convention and its aftermath / Clare Taylor. — Aberystwyth : [Department of History, The University College of Wales], 1981. — 24leaves ; 30cm
Unpriced (unbound)
Also classified at 322.4'4'0973 B81-34254

322.4'4'0942991 — Gwent. Newport. Chartism, ***1838-1848***

James, Leslie, *1944-*. The struggle for the Charter / [written by Leslie James] ; [and designed by Keith Phelpstead]. — Newport [Gwent] (John Frost Sq., Newport [Gwent NPT 1PA]) : Newport Museum and Art Gallery, 1973. — [6]p : ill,1map,1facsim,ports ; 30cm
Unpriced (unbound) B81-34701

322.4'4'0947 — Soviet Union. Society. Dissent, ***1825-1980.*** **Political aspects**

Ulam, Adam B.. Russia's failed revolution : from the Decembrists to the dissidents / Adam B. Ulam. — London : Weidenfeld and Nicolson, c1981. — vii,453p ; 24cm
Includes index
ISBN 0-297-77940-0 : £10.00 B81-19546

322.4'4'0947 — Soviet Union. Society. Dissent, ***to 1979.*** **Political aspects**

Medvedev, Roĭ A.. On Soviet dissent / Roy Medvedev ; interviews with Piero Ostellino ; translated from the Italian by William A. Packer ; edited by George Saunders. — London : Constable, 1980. — 158p ; 24cm
Translation of: Intervista sul dissenso in URSS. — Includes index
ISBN 0-09-463870-5 : £5.95 B81-05262

Shatz, Marshall S.. Soviet dissent in historical perpective / Marshall S. Shatz. — Cambridge : Cambridge University Press, 1980. — x,214p ; 24cm
Bibliography: p200-208. — Includes index
ISBN 0-521-23172-8 : £12.50 B81-16419

322.4'4'0947312 — Soviet Union. Moscow. Dissidents. Social life

Rubenstein, Joshua. Soviet dissidents. — London : Wildwood House, Aug.1981. — [320]p
ISBN 0-7045-3062-7 : £8.50 : CIP entry B81-23804

322.4'4'0973 — Slavery. American abolitionist movements. Members: Women. Role, ***1830-1850***

Taylor, Clare. Romantic reform and Anglo-American women, London, the 1840 Convention and its aftermath / Clare Taylor. — Aberystwyth : [Department of History, The University College of Wales], 1981. — 24leaves ; 30cm
Unpriced (unbound)
Primary classification 322.4'4'0941 B81-34254

322.4'4'0973 — Slavery. American abolitionist movements. Role of Lane Seminary, ***1828-1860***

Lesick, Lawrence Thomas. The Lane rebels : evangelicalism and antislavery in antebellum America / by Lawrence Thomas Lesick. — Metuchen ; London : Scarecrow, 1980. — ix,278p ; 23cm. — (Studies in evangelicalism ; no.2)
Bibliography: p239-262. — Includes index
ISBN 0-8108-1372-6 : £10.50 B81-17248

322.4'4'0973 — United States. Progressivism, ***1930-1945***

Feinman, Ronald L.. Twilight of progressivism : the western Republican senators and the New Deal / Ronald L. Feinman. — Baltimore ; London : Johns Hopkins University Press, c1980. — xiv,262p : ports ; 24cm. — (The Johns Hopkins University studies in historical and political science. 99th series ; 1)
Bibliography: p239-246. — Includes index
ISBN 0-8018-2373-0 : £11.00 B81-34466

322'.5 — Socialist countries. Government & society. Role of military forces. Political aspects

Soldiers, peasants and bureaucrats. — London : Allen and Unwin, Feb.1982. — [352]p
ISBN 0-04-322007-x : £18.00 : CIP entry B81-35924

322'.5'095493 — Sri Lanka. Attempted military coups d'état, ***1962.*** **Causes**

Horowitz, Donald L.. Coup theories and officers' motives : Sri Lanka in comparative perspective / Donald L. Horowitz. — Princeton ; Guildford : Princeton University Press, c1980. — xiv,239p ; 23cm
Includes index
ISBN 0-691-07622-7 (cased) : £8.90
ISBN 0-691-02199-6 (pbk) : £5.90 B81-05718

322'.5'0956 — Middle East. Military governments

Perlmutter, Amos. Political roles and military rulers / Amos Perlmutter. — London : Cass, 1981. — 313p : ill ; 23cm
Includes index
ISBN 0-7146-3122-1 : £13.50 : CIP rev. B79-03419

322'.5'09669 — Nigeria. Politics. Role of military forces, ***1970-1980***

Adekson, J. Bayo. Nigeria in search of a stable civil-military system. — Farnborough : Gower, July 1981. — [162]p
ISBN 0-566-00431-3 : £11.50 : CIP entry B81-14972

322'.5'0967 — Africa south of the Sahara. Military governments, ***1958-1978***

Kirk-Greene, A. H. M.. 'Stay by your radios' : documentation for a study of military government in tropical Africa / by A.H.M. Kirk-Greene. — Leiden : Afrika-Studiecentrum ; Cambridge (University of Cambridge, Free School La., Cambridge) : African Studies Centre, 1981. — 156p ; 25cm. — (African social research documents ; v.12)
ISBN 90-7011-029-6 (pbk) : Unpriced B81-24475

323 — POLITICS. RELATION OF STATE TO INDIVIDUALS AND SOCIAL CLASSES

323.1'06'01 — Social minorities. Civil rights. Organisations: Minority Rights Group — *Serials*

[Newsletter *(Minority Rights Group)*]. Newsletter / Minority Right[s] Group. — No.1 (Sept.1978)-. — London (36 Craven St., WC2N 5NG) : The Group, 1978-. — v. ; 30cm
Five issues yearly
ISSN 0260-6402 = Newsletter — Minority Rights Group : Unpriced B81-05029

323.1'13936'068 — South Africa. Afrikaners. Nationalism. Organisations: Broederbond, *to 1978*

Wilkins, Ivor. Broederbond : the super-Afrikaners / Ivor Wilkins and Hans Strydom. — London : Corgi, 1980, c1979. — 450,A299p : ill ; 18cm
Originally published: South Africa : Jonathan Ball Publishers, 1978 ; New York : London : Paddington, 1979. — Bibliography: p449-450
ISBN 0-552-11512-6 (pbk 350 £2.50) B81-07735

323.1'19159 — Iraq. Kurds. Nationalist movements, *1958-1970*

Jawad, Sa'ad. Iraq & the Kurdish question 1958-1970 / by Sa'ad Jawad. — London : Ithaca, 1981. — 377p : 1map ; 23cm
Bibliography: p350-370. — Includes index
ISBN 0-903729-77-6 : £11.50 B81-33272

323.1'1924'062 — Egypt. Nagids. Origins, *1065-1126*

Cohen, Mark R.. Jewish self-government in medieval Egypt : the origins of the Office of the Head of the Jews / Mark R. Cohen. — Princeton ; Guildford : Princeton University Press, c1980. — xxi,385p : facsims,1geneal.table ; 23cm. — (Princeton studies on the Near East)
Bibliography: p339-360. - Includes index
ISBN 0-691-05307-3 : £15.30 B81-14684

323.1'19275694 — Israel. Palestinian Arabs. Social control by government

Lustick, Ian. Arabs in the Jewish state : Israel's control of a national minority / by Ian Lustick. — Austin ; London : University of Texas Press, c1980. — xii,385p ; 24cm. — (Modern Middle East series ; no.6)
Bibliography: p343-362. - Includes index
ISBN 0-292-70347-3 (cased) : £12.00
ISBN 0-292-70348-1 (pbk) : £6.60 B81-01687

323.1'196073'006 — United States. Negroes. Civil rights. Organisations: National Association for the Advancement of Colored People, *to 1980*

Finch, Minnie. The NAACP : its fight for justice / by Minnie Finch. — Metuchen ; London : Scarecrow, 1981. — viii,275p ; 23cm
Bibliography: p262-264. — Includes index
ISBN 0-8108-1436-6 : £12.00 B81-38413

323.1'196073'024 — United States. Negroes. Civil rights movements. X, Malcolm — *Biographies*

Wolfenstein, Eugene Victor. The victims of democracy : Malcolm X and the black revolution / by Eugene Victor Wolfenstein. — Berkeley ; London : University of California Press, c1981. — xi,422p ; 24cm
Bibliography: p399-407. — Includes index
ISBN 0-520-03903-3 : £10.25 B81-28244

323.1'1968'00222 — South Africa. Negroes. Nationalism, *to 1980* — *Illustrations*

Gouwenius, Peder. Power to the people : South Africa in struggle : a pictorial history / Peder Gouwenius. — London : Zed, 1981. — 139p : ill ; 30cm. — (Africa series)
ISBN 0-905762-66-5 (pbk) : £4.50 B81-18501

323.1'197'073 — United States. Santees. Policies of government, *to 1970*

Meyer, Roy W.. History of the Santee Sioux : United States Indian policy on trial / by Roy W. Meyer. — Lincoln [Neb.] ; London : University of Nebraska Press, 1980, c1967. — xiv,434p,[32]p of plates : ill,maps, ports ; 21cm. — (A Bison book)
Originally published: 1967. — Bibliography: p403-416. - Includes index
ISBN 0-8032-8109-9 (pbk) : £4.80 B81-07540

323.1'68 — South Africa. Apartheid

Hick, John. Apartheid observed / written by John Hick ; cover drawing by Martin Lealan. — Birmingham (1 Finch Rd., Lozells, Birmingham B19 1HS) : AFFOR, 1980. — 16p ; 23x16cm
ISBN 0-907127-04-5 (pbk) : £0.60 B81-22246

323.1'68 — South Africa. Apartheid. Policies of government, *1976-1980*

Seidman, Judy. Face-lift apartheid : South Africa after Soweto / by Judy Seidman. — London (104 Newgate St., EC1A 7AP) : International Defence and Aid Fund for Southern Africa, 1980. — 87p ; 21cm
ISBN 0-904759-39-3 (pbk) : £1.20 B81-29030

323.1'68 — South Africa. Apartheid, *to 1980*

Addison, John. Apartheid / John Addison. — London : Batsford Academic and Educational, 1981. — 72p : ill,maps,2facsims,1form,ports ; 26cm. — (Today's world)
Bibliography: p70. - Includes index
ISBN 0-7134-2485-0 : £5.50 B81-12560

Dreyer, Peter. Martyrs and fanatics : South Africa and human destiny / by Peter Dreyer. — London : Secker & Warburg, 1980. — 255p,[8]p of plates : ill,1map,ports ; 23cm
Originally published: New York : Simon & Schuster, 1980. — Includes index
ISBN 0-436-13721-6 : £7.95 B81-04799

323.1'68'019 — South Africa. Apartheid. Psychological aspects

Lambley, Peter. The psychology of apartheid / Peter Lambley. — London : Secker & Warburg, 1980. — xxv,291p ; 23cm
Bibliography: p275-284. - Includes index
£9.75 B81-06248

323.1'68'05 — Southern Africa. Apartheid — *Serials*

Bulletin of the Continuation Committee of the World Conference against Apartheid, Racism and Colonialism in Southern Africa. — No.1 (Aug.1978)- No.2 (Nov.[1978]). — London ([30A Danbury St., N1 8JV]) : The Committee, 1978-1978. — 2v. : ill ; 30cm
Continued by: ICSA bulletin
Unpriced B81-05680

ICSA bulletin. — [No.1]-. — London (30A Danbury St., N1 8JV) : International Committee against Apartheid, Racism and Colonialism in Southern Africa, 1979-. — v. : ill ; 29cm
Irregular. — Continues: Bulletin of the Continuation Committee of the World Conference against Apartheid, Racism and Colonialism in Southern Africa. — Description based on Issue no.9 (Oct. 1980)
Unpriced B81-05683

323.1'687 — South Africa. Cape Town. Apartheid, *1950-1981*

Western, John. Outcast Cape Town. — London : Allen & Unwin, Feb.1982. — [361]p
ISBN 0-04-301139-x : £13.95 : CIP entry B81-35940

323.3 — Eastern Europe. Politics. Role of working classes — *Conference proceedings*

Blue-collar workers in Eastern Europe. — London : Allen & Unwin, Nov.1981. — [320]p
Conference papers
ISBN 0-04-321027-9 (cased) : £14.00 : CIP entry
ISBN 0-04-321028-7 (pbk) : £6.95 B81-28786

323.3 — England. Working classes. Radicalism, *1790-1830*

Calhoun, Craig Jackson. Before the working class. — Oxford : Blackwell, Sept.1981. — [272]p
ISBN 0-631-12905-7 : £12.50 : CIP entry B81-22645

323.3'2 — Southern India. Peasants. Relations with state, *ca 900-1500*

Stein, Burton. Peasant state and society in medieval South India / Burton Stein. — Delhi ; Oxford : Oxford University Press, 1980. — xvi,533p,[4]leaves of plates : 2ill,4maps ; 23cm
Bibliography: p489-518. — Includes index
ISBN 0-19-561065-2 : £12.50 B81-08258

323.3'4 — Politics. Role of women

The **Politics** of the second electorate : women and public participation : Britain, USA, Canada, Australia, France, Spain, West Germany, Italy, Sweden, Finland, Eastern Europe, USSR, Japan / edited by Joni Lovenduski and Jill Hills. — London : Routledge & Kegan Paul, 1981. — xviii,332p : ill ; 22cm
Includes bibliographies and index
ISBN 0-7100-0806-6 (pbk) : £6.95 : CIP rev. B81-16376

323.4 — CIVIL RIGHTS

323.4 — Amnesty International

Power, Jonathan. Amnesty International, the human rights story. — Oxford : Pergamon, Aug.1981. — [200]p
ISBN 0-08-028902-9 : £10.00 : CIP entry B81-22578

323.4 — Children. Civil rights — *Philosophical perspectives*

Wringe, C. A.. Children's rights. — London : Routledge & Kegan Paul, Nov.1981. — [176]p. — (International library of the philosophy of education)
ISBN 0-7100-0852-x : £12.50 : CIP entry B81-30598

323.4 — Great Britain. Children. Rights — *Conference proceedings*

Rights of children : papers presented at a conference organised by ABAFA (now BAAF) Legal Group to mark the International Year of the Child / edited by Diana Rawstron. — London (11 Southwark St., SE1 1RQ) : British Agencies for Adoption and Fostering, 1981. — 40p ; 21cm. — (Discussion series / British Agencies for Adoption and Fostering, ISSN 0260-082x ; 3)
Papers by Michael Freeman, Margaret Adcock, Hugh Bevan
ISBN 0-903534-35-5 (pbk) : £1.50 B81-37413

323.4 — Human rights

Alston, Philip. Human rights and the basic needs strategy for development / Philip Alston. — London (180 Brixton Rd., SW9 6AT) : Anti-Slavery Society, 1979. — 72leaves ; 30cm. — (Human rights and development working papers ; no.2)
Unpriced B81-16584

Hayes, David, *1955-*. Human rights / David Hayes. — Hove : Wayland, 1980. — 96p : ill,1facsim,ports ; 24cm. — (People, politics and powers)
Bibliography: p93-94. — Includes index
ISBN 0-85340-653-7 : £4.50 B81-00027

323.4 — Human rights — *Conference proceedings*

Rights and responsibilities : international, social and individual dimensions : proceedings of a conference sponsored by the Center for Study of the American Experience Annenberg School of Communications University of Southern California, November 1978. — Los Angeles : University of Southern California Press ; New Brunswick ; London : Distributed by Transaction, 1980. — 298p ; 24cm
ISBN 0-88474-095-1 : £11.00 B81-16469

323.4 — Human rights. Declarations: International Covenant on Economic, Social and Cultural Rights. Drafting & implementation. Role of United Nations. Specialised agencies

Alston, Philip. Making and breaking human rights : the UN's specialised agencies and implementation of the International Covenant on Economic, Social and Cultural Rights / Philip Alston. — London (180 Brixton Rd. SW9 6AT) : Anti-Slavery Society, 1979. — 44leaves ; 30cm. — (Human rights and development working papers ; no.1)
Unpriced (pbk) B81-16586

323.4 — Human rights — *For children*

Snyder, Gerald S.. Human rights / by Gerald S. Snyder. — New York ; London : Watts, 1980. — 63p : ill,1map,ports ; 23cm. — (A First book)
Includes index
ISBN 0-531-04103-4 : £2.99 B81-04416

323.4 — Human rights — *For schools*

Cunningham, Jeremy. Human rights & wrongs : an introduction to human rights / by Jeremy Cunningham. — [London] : Writers & Scholars Educational Trust ; London (21 Russell St., WC2B 5HP) : Distributed by Index on Censorship, 1981. — 20p : ill ; 30cm
Text on inside covers. — Bibliography: p20
ISBN 0-904286-25-8 (pbk) : Unpriced
B81-26122

323.4 — Human rights. Promotion. Role of policies of governments on foreign relations

Luard, Evan. Human rights and foreign policy / by Evan Luard. — Oxford : Published on behalf of the United Nations Association of Great Britain and Northern Ireland by Pergamon. — vii,38p ; 21cm
ISBN 0-08-027405-6 (pbk) : £2.75 B81-17361

323.4 — Human rights. Socioeconomic aspects

Human rights : cultural and ideological perspectives / edited by Adamantia Pollis and Peter Schwab. — New York ; London : Praeger, 1980. — xvi,165p ; 24cm. — (Praeger special studies)
Bibliography: p145-149. - Includes index
ISBN 0-03-057717-9 (pbk) : £6.50 B81-00766

323.4 — Social justice

Ackerman, Bruce A.. Social justice in the liberal state / Bruce A. Ackerman. — New Haven ; London : Yale University Press, 1980. — xii,392p : 1ill ; 24cm
Includes index
ISBN 0-300-02439-8 : £11.00 : CIP rev.
B80-21467

Ackerman, Bruce A.. Social justice in the liberal state. — London : Yale University Press, Nov.1981. — [408]p
ISBN 0-300-02757-5 (pbk) : £6.25 : CIP entry
B81-34716

323.4′01 — Human rights — *Philosophical perspectives*

Feinberg, Joel. Rights, justice and the bounds of liberty : essays in social philosophy / by Joel Feinberg. — Princeton ; Guildford : Princeton University Press, c1980. — xvi,318p ; 25cm. — (Princeton series of collected essays)
Includes index
ISBN 0-691-07254-x : £10.90
ISBN 0-691-02012-4 (pbkUnpriced) B81-06819

323.4′01 — Natural rights. Theories, *to 1700*

Tuck, Richard. Natural rights theories : their origin and development / Richard Tuck. — Cambridge : Cambridge University Press, 1981, c1979. — viii,185p ; 23cm
Includes index
ISBN 0-521-28509-7 (pbk) : £4.50 : CIP rev.
B81-14880

323.4′01′9 — Social justice. Psychological aspects — *Conference proceedings*

The **Justice** motive in social behavior : adapting to times of scarcity and change / edited by Melvin J. Lerner and Sally C. Lerner. — New York ; London : Plenum, 1981. — xxii,494p ; 23cm. — (Critical issues in social justice)
Conference papers. — Includes bibliographies and index
ISBN 0-306-40675-6 : Unpriced B81-40064

323.4′09172′4 — Developing countries. Human rights. Implications of economic development

The **Right** to development and its implications for development strategy : report of a seminar / rapporteur Sanjib Kumar Baruah. — London (180 Brixton Rd. SW9 6AT) : Anti-Slavery Society, 1979. — 98leaves ; 30cm. — (Human rights and development working papers ; no.3)
Unpriced (pbk) B81-16587

323.4′09172′4 — Developing countries. Social justice

Schaffer, Bernard. Can equity be organized? : equity, development analysis and planning / Bernard Schaffer, Geoff Lamb. — Farnborough, Hants. : Gower, 1981. — vi,166p ; 23cm
Bibliography: p151-156 — Includes index
ISBN 0-566-00432-1 : Unpriced B81-37127

323.4′0941 — Great Britain. Civil rights

Hewitt, Patricia. The abuse of power. — Oxford : Martin Robertson, Nov.1981. — [220]p
ISBN 0-85520-379-x (cased) : £10.00 : CIP entry
ISBN 0-85520-380-3 (pbk) : £3.75 B81-33645

323.4′0941 — Great Britain. Human rights. Promotion. Role of democracy

Benn, Tony. Democracy and human rights / Tony Benn. — [London] ([14 Parkfield Rd., N.W.10]) : Haldane Society of Socialist Lawyers, [1980]. — 15p ; 21cm. — (The Pritt memorial lecture ; 1979)
Cover title
£0.50 (pbk) B81-18815

323.4′09437 — Czechoslovakia. Human rights movements: Charta 77 *(Movement)*

Skilling, H. Gordon. Charter 77 and human rights in Czechoslovakia / H. Gordon Skilling. — London : Allen & Unwin, 1981. — xv,363p ; 24cm
Bibliography: p345-351. — Includes index
ISBN 0-04-321026-0 : Unpriced : CIP rev.
B81-15888

323.44 — Freedom

Sharp, James, *1923-*. Freedom. — Bognor Regis : New Horizon, c1979. — 120p ; 21cm
ISBN 0-86116-122-x : £2.50 B81-21801

323.44 — Liberty

Bay, Christian. Strategies of political emancipation / Christian Bay. — Notre Dame, Ind. ; London : University of Notre Dame Press, c1981. — xii,247p ; 21cm. — (Loyola lecture series in political analysis)
Includes index
ISBN 0-268-01702-6 : £2.30 B81-39822

323.44 — Liberty. Implications of theories of justice

Raphael, D. D.. Justice and liberty / D.D. Raphael. — London : Athlone, 1980. — 192p ; 23cm
Includes index
ISBN 0-485-11195-0 : £13.00 B81-00767

323.44′01 — Liberty — *Philosophical perspectives*

Crocker, Lawrence. Positive liberty : an essay in normative political philosophy / by Lawrence Crocker. — The Hague ; London : Nijhoff, 1980. — viii,146p ; 25cm. — (Melbourne international philosophy series ; v.7)
ISBN 90-247-2291-8 : Unpriced B81-04585

323.44′2′0947 — Soviet Union. Religious freedom

May one believe - in Russia? : violations of religious liberty in the Soviet Union. — [2nd ed.]. — London : Darton, Longman & Todd, 1980. — xiii,113p ; 22cm. — (Keston book ; no.19)
Previous ed.: published as White book on restrictions of religion in the USSR by Michael Bourdeaux. Brussels : International Committee for the Defence of Human Rights in the U.S.S.R., 1975
ISBN 0-232-51507-7 (pbk) : £3.45 B81-08301

323.44′5 — Foreign news. Censorship. Political aspects

Kelly, Sean. Access denied : the politics of press censorship / Sean Kelly. — Beverly Hills ; London : Sage [for] the Center for Strategic and International Studies, Georgetown University, c1978. — 80p ; 22cm. — (The Washington papers ; vol.VI, 55) (A Sage policy paper)
Bibliography: p77-80
ISBN 0-8039-1080-0 (pbk) : Unpriced
B81-17630

323.44′5 — Great Britain. Freedom of information

Secrecy, or the right to know? : a study of the feasibility of freedom of information for the United Kingdom. — London : published by the Library Association, for the Freedom of Information Campaign, c1980. — 110p ; 21cm
ISBN 0-85365-943-5 (pbk) : Unpriced
B81-12143

323.44′5 — Great Britain. Local authorities. Publications. Access by public

Access to local-government documentation / Capital Planning Information. — [London] : British Library ; London : Distributed by Publications, The British Library, Research and Development Department, 1981. — vii,73p : 2forms ; 30cm. — (British Library research & development reports, ISSN 0308-2385 ; no.5619)
ISBN 0-905984-68-4 (pbk) : Unpriced
B81-29260

323.44′5 — Great Britain. Public records. Access. Rights of public — *Inquiry reports*

Modern public records : selection and access : report of a committee appointed by the Lord Chancellor / Chairman Sir Duncan Wilson ; presented to Parliament by the Lord High Chancellor. — London : H.M.S.O., 1981. — xiii,256p,[1]leaf of plates : 1ill ; 25cm. — (Cmnd. ; 8204)
ISBN 0-10-182040-2 (pbk) : £8.10
Primary classification 025.17 B81-21676

323.44′5 — Mass media. Freedom of communication

International news : freedom under attack / edited by Dante B. Fascell ; with essays by David M. Abshire ... [et al.]. — Beverly Hills ; London : Sage [for] The Center for Strategic and International Studies, Georgetown University, c1979. — 319p : 1ill ; 23cm
Includes bibliographies
ISBN 0-8039-1229-3 : £9.50 B81-12974

323.44′83 — Privacy. Encroachment by machine-readable files of multinational companies

Katzan, Harry. Multinational computer systems : an introduction to transnational data flow and data regulation / Harry Katzan, Jr. — New York ; London : Van Nostrand Reinhold, 1980. — xiii,198p : ill ; 27cm. — (International series on data communications and networks)
Includes bibliographies and index
ISBN 0-442-21573-8 : £12.70 B81-07895

323.4′9 — United Nations. Petitions: Petitions concerning deprivation of human rights

Zuijdwijk, Ton J. M.. Petitions to the United Nations about violations of human rights. — Aldershot : Gower, Jan.1982. — [416]p
ISBN 0-566-00463-1 : £15.00 : CIP entry
B81-34281

323.4′9′09437 — Czechoslovakia. Human rights. Deprivation, *1968-1980*

On freedom and power. — London : Allison & Busby, Dec.1981. — 1v.
ISBN 0-85031-415-1 (cased) : £9.95 : CIP entry
ISBN 0-85031-416-x (pbk) : £4.95 B81-31627

323.4′9′095195 — South Korea. Human rights. Deprivation, *1960-1980*

Republic of Korea : violations of human rights : an Amnesty International report. — [London] : [Amnesty International Publications], [1981]. — 43p : ill,1map,ports ; 30cm
ISBN 0-86210-031-3 (unbound) : Unpriced
B81-24005

323.6 — CITIZENSHIP

323.6′5 — Citizenship. Obligation

Dunn, John, *1940-*. Political obligation in its historical context : essays in political theory / John Dunn. — Cambridge : Cambridge University Press, 1980. — x,355p : 1map ; 24cm
Includes index
ISBN 0-521-22890-5 : £14.50 : CIP rev.
B80-25229

324 — THE POLITICAL PROCESS. POLITICAL PARTIES, ELECTIONS

324′.1 — Third International, *1919-*. Organisation — *Russian texts*
Zinov′ev, G.. Kommunisticheskiĭ internat͡sional / G. Zinov′ev = The Communist International / G. Zinoviev. — Letchworth : Prideaux, 1980. — 38p ; 20cm. — (Russian titles for the specialist, ISSN 0305-3741 ; no.219)
Russian text. — Russian title transliterated. — Added t.p. in Russian. — Originally published: Petrograd : Izdatel′stvo kommunisticheskogo internat͡sionala, 192-
£1.20 (pbk) B81-06480

324.2 — Political parties
Janda, Kenneth. Political parties : a cross-national survey / Kenneth Janda. — New York : Free Press ; London : Collier Macmillan, c1980. — xviii,1019p : ill ; 29cm
Includes bibliographies
ISBN 0-02-916120-7 : £60.00 B81-06655

324.2 — Political parties *related to* electoral systems
Katz, Richard S.. A theory of parties and electoral systems / Richard S. Katz. — Baltimore ; London : Johns Hopkins University Press, c1980. — xii,151p : ill ; 24cm
Includes index
ISBN 0-8018-2435-4 : £7.75
Also classified at 324.6′3 B81-11318

324.2 — Revolutionary parties — *Marxist viewpoints*
Harman, Chris. Party and class / Chris Harman. — London (265 Seven Sisters Rd., N4 2DE) : Socialists Unlimited, 1980. — 20p ; 21cm. — (International socialism reprint ; no.4)
Cover title
ISBN 0-905998-17-0 (pbk) : £0.35 B81-08589

324.2′025 — Political parties — *Directories*
Political parties of the world : a Kessing′s reference publication / compiled and edited by Alan J. Day and Henry W. Degenhardt. — Harlow : Longman, 1980. — x,432p ; 26cm
Includes index
ISBN 0-582-90300-9 : £30.00 : CIP rev. B80-24140

324.2′04 — Politics. Linkage. Role of political parties — *Comparative studies*
Political parties and linkage : a comparative perspective / edited by Kay Lawson. — New Haven ; London : Yale University Press, c1980. — vi,410p : ill ; 25cm
Includes index
ISBN 0-300-02331-6 (cased) : £22.00
ISBN 0-300-02610-2 (pbk) : £5.65 B81-06738

324.2′09′04 — Communist parties, *1919-1980*
Narkiewicz, Olga A.. Marxism and the reality of power 1919-1980. — London : Croom Helm, Oct.1981. — [320]p
ISBN 0-85664-806-x : £14.95 : CIP entry B81-27965

324.2′09′04 — Communist parties, *ca 1945-1977*
The **Many** faces of communism / edited by Morton A. Kaplan. — New York : Free Press ; London : Collier Macmillan, c1978. — x,366p ; 25cm
Includes index
ISBN 0-02-917230-6 : £10.95 B81-05758

324.2′09′04 — Political parties, *1945-1977*
Political parties : development and decay / edited by Louis Maisel and Joseph Cooper. — Beverly Hills ; London : Sage, c1978. — 344p : ill ; 23cm. — (Sage electoral studies yearbook ; v.4)
Includes bibliographies
ISBN 0-8039-0738-9 (cased) : Unpriced
ISBN 0-8039-0739-7 (pbk) : Unpriced B81-13301

324.2′3 — Great Britain. Political parties. General election manifestos, *1974-1979* — *Digests*
Manifesto of manifestos : UK general elections 10th October ′74, 3rd May ′79 : an analysis by Bradbury Controls Ltd. based on published party manifestos and setting out the rules of analysis / with an introductory essay "The harmony of people" by Farel Bradbury. — 2nd ed. — Ross-on-Wye (P.O. Box 4, Ross-on-Wye HR9 6EB) : Hydatum, c1981. — iv,30p ; 21cm
Previous ed.: 1979
ISBN 0-905682-23-8 (pbk) : £2.50 B81-21401

324.24 — European Community countries. Political parties. Grouping
Pridham, Geoffrey. Transnational party co-operation and European integration : the process towards direct elections / Geoffrey Pridham and Pippa Pridham. — London : Allen & Unwin, 1981. — xii,307p ; 23cm
Bibliography: p292-301. - Includes index
ISBN 0-04-329032-9 : Unpriced B81-16341

324.24′03 — European Parliament. Political parties: European Democratic Group
European Democratic Group. A guide to the European Democratic Group in the European Parliament and the role of the Parliament in the European Community / edited by Maurice Trowbridge. — [London] ([2 Queen Anne′s Gate, SW1H 9AA]) : The Group, 1980. — 47p : ill,1map,1plan,ports ; 21cm
Unpriced (pbk) B81-06451

324.24′075′09 — Western Europe. Communist parties, *1945-1979*
The **Communist** parties of Italy, France and Spain : postwar change and continuity : a casebook / edited by Peter Lange, Maurizio Vannicelli ; with a foreword by Stanley Hoffmann. — London : Allen & Unwin, 1981. — xii,385p ; 26cm. — (Casebook series on European politics and society ; no.1)
Bibliography: p362-368
ISBN 0-04-329033-7 (cased) : Unpriced : CIP rev.
ISBN 0-04-329034-5 (pbk) : Unpriced B81-02350

324.24104 — Great Britain. Political parties: Conservative Party. Policies — *Communist Party of Great Britain viewpoints*
McLennan, Gordon. Oppose Tory policies : take Britain on a different course : a Communist Party pamphlet / by George McLennan. — [London] : [The Party], [1981]. — 36p : ill ; 21cm
Cover title. — Text and port. on inside cover
ISBN 0-86224-011-5 (pbk) : £0.30 B81-24087

324.24104 — Great Britain. Political parties: Conservative Party. Policies. Formulation. Role of Conservative Political Centre
Aughey, Arthur. Constituency attitudes and policy formulation : the role of the Conservative Political Centre / by Arthur Aughey. — [Hull] : Department of Politics, University of Hull, 1981. — 28leaves ; 30cm. — (Hull papers in politics, ISSN 0142-7377 ; no.7)
Unpriced (pbk) B81-13333

324.24104′09 — Great Britain. Political parties: Conservative Party, *to 1979*
Moore, Sheila. The Conservative Party : the first 150 years / Sheila Moore ; foreword by Margaret Thatcher. — Richmond-upon-Thames : Country Life Books, 1980. — 175p : ill(some col.),facsims,ports (some col.) ; 31cm
Includes index
ISBN 0-600-36777-0 : £10.00 B81-02298

324.24104′09412′35 — Scotland. Grampian Region. Aberdeen. Political parties: South Aberdeen Conservative Association — *Serials*
Aberdeen record. — Issue no.1 (Mar./May 1981)-. — Aberdeen (6 Albyn La., Aberdeen AB1 6SZ) : [South Aberdeen Conservative Association], 1981-. — v. ; 30cm
Quarterly. — Continues: South Aberdeen record
ISSN 0262-012x = Aberdeen record : Unpriced B81-38525

324.24104′09428′37 — Humberside. Hull. Political parties. Conservative Party
Tether, Philip. Kingston-upon-Hull conservative party : a case study of an urban Tory party in decline / by Philip Tether. — Hull : Department of Politics, University of Hull, 1980. — 51p : ill ; 30cm. — (Hull papers in politics, ISSN 0142-7377 ; no.19)
Unpriced (pbk) B81-13221

324.24106 — Great Britain. Political parties: Liberal Party. Cooperation with Social Democratic Party
Marquand, David. Liberalism and social democracy / David Marquand, Michael Meadowcroft. — London : Liberal Publication Department, [1981]. — 10p ; 21cm
Report of a dialogue held on Tuesday September 9th 1980 during the Liberal Assembly at Blackpool. — Cover title
£0.35 (pbk)
Also classified at 324.241′0972 B81-32875

324.24106 — Great Britain. Political parties: Liberal Party. Values
Meadowcroft, Michael. Liberal values for a new decade / Michael Meadowcroft. — London : Liberal Publication Department, [1980]. — 23p ; 22cm
Bibliography: p21-22
£0.50 (pbk) B81-04087

324.24106′09 — Great Britain. Political parties: Liberal Party, *1910-1931*
Adelman, Paul. The decline of the Liberal Party, 1910-1931. — London : Longman, Nov.1981. — [104]p. — (Seminar studies in history)
ISBN 0-582-35327-0 (pbk) : £1.85 : CIP entry B81-30294

324.24107 — Great Britain. Political parties: Labour Party *(Great Britain)*. Policies
Hodgson, Geoffrey. Labour at the crossroads. — Oxford : Martin Robertson, Sept.1981. — [256]p
ISBN 0-85520-462-1 (cased) : £12.50 : CIP entry
ISBN 0-85520-463-x (pbk) : £4.95 B81-20567

Kinnock, Neil. Why vote Labour? / Neil Kinnock, Nick Butler Toby Harris. — London : NCLC Publishing Society, 1979. — 21p ; 22cm
ISBN 0-7163-5012-2 (pbk) : £0.25 B81-38888

324.24107 — Great Britain. Political parties: Labour Party *(Great Britain)*. Policies, *1979-1990* — *Proposals*
Labour into the eighties / edited by David S. Bell. — London : Croom Helm, c1980. — 168p ; 23cm
Includes index
ISBN 0-7099-0443-6 (cased) : £9.95 : CIP rev.
ISBN 0-7099-0607-2 (pbk) : £5.50 B80-17574

324.24107 — Great Britain. Political parties: Labour Party *(Great Britain)*. Policies. Formulation. Role of annual conferences
Minkin, Lewis. The Labour Party Conference : a study in the politics of intra-party democracy / Lewis Minkin. — [New ed.] with minor corrections and new material. — Manchester : Manchester University Press, 1980. — xv,448p ; 24cm
Previous ed.: London : Allen Lane, 1978. — Includes index
ISBN 0-7190-0800-x (pbk) : £6.75 : CIP rev. B80-11767

324.24107′088042 — Great Britain. Political parties: Labour Party *(Great Britain)*. Role of women — *Serials*
[Focus *(London : 1981)*]. Focus : Labour women′s bulletin / the Labour Party. — No.1 (Mar.1981)-. — London : The Party, 1981-. — v. : ill,ports ; 30cm
Six issues yearly
ISSN 0260-9681 = Focus (London. 1981) : £0.50 per issue B81-33951

324.24107′09 — Great Britain. Political parties: Labour Party *(Great Britain)*, *1945-1977*
Warde, Alan. Consensus and beyond. — Manchester : Manchester University Press, Jan.1982. — [224]p
ISBN 0-7190-0849-2 : £13.50 : CIP entry B81-33829

324.24107′09 — Great Britain. Political parties: Labour Party *(Great Britain)*, *to 1980* — *Socialist Workers′ Party viewpoints*
Hallas, Duncan. The Labour Party : myth & reality / by Duncan Hallas. — London (265 Seven Sisters Rd., N4 2DE) : Socialists Unlimited, 1981. — 32p : ill,ports ; 21cm. — (A Socialist Workers Party pamphlet)
ISBN 0-905998-20-0 (pbk) : £0.35 B81-19579

324.24107'09428'17 — West Yorkshire *(Metropolitan County)*. Bradford. Political parties: Independent Labour Party, *1890-1914*

Bradford 1980-1914 : the cradle of the Independent Labour Party / edited by J.A. Jowitt & R.K.S. Taylor. — Bradford (10 Mornington Villas, Bradford BD87 7HB) : University of Leeds Centre for Adult Education, 1980. — 88p ; 21cm. — (Bradford Centre occasional papers ; no.2)
Unpriced (pbk) B81-10549

324.241'0938 — Great Britain. Political parties: National Front

Fielding, Nigel. The National Front / Nigel Fielding. — London : Routledge & Kegan Paul, 1981. — vii,252p ; 22cm. — (International library of sociology)
Includes index
ISBN 0-7100-0559-8 : £12.50 : CIP rev. B80-11326

324.241'0972 — Great Britain. Political parties: Social Democratic Party. Cooperation with Liberal Party

Marquand, David. Liberalism and social democracy / David Marquand, Michael Meadowcroft. — London : Liberal Publication Department, [1981]. — 10p ; 21cm
Report of a dialogue held on Tuesday September 9th 1980 during the Liberal Assembly at Blackpool. — Cover title
£0.35 (pbk)
Primary classification 324.24106 B81-32875

324.241'0972 — Great Britain. Political parties: Social Democratic Party — *Labour Party (Great Britain) viewpoints*

The Gang show. — London : Labour Party, 1981. — 33p ; 30cm. — (Information paper / Labour Party Research Department ; no.19)
At head of title: The Labour Party
£0.40 (unbound) B81-28416

324.2410972 — Great Britain. Political parties: Social Democratic Party, *to 1981*

Bradley, Ian, *1950-*. Breaking the mould?. — Oxford : Robertson, Sept.1981. — [176]p
ISBN 0-85520-468-0 (cased) : £7.95 : CIP entry
ISBN 0-85520-469-9 (pbk) : £2.95 B81-21549

324.241'0974 — Great Britain. Political parties: Socialist Workers' Party, *to 1980*

Birchall, Ian H.. The smallest mass party in the world : building the Socialist Workers Party, 1951-1979 / by Ian Birchall. — London (265 Seven Sisters Rd., N4 2DE) : Produced and distributed for the Socialist Workers Party by Socialists Unlimited, 1981. — 31p : ill ; 30cm. — (A Socialist Workers Party pamphlet)
ISBN 0-905998-21-9 (unbound) : £0.60 B81-32711

324.2417'072 — Ireland *(Republic)*. Political parties: Irish Democratic Youth Movement — *Serials*

[Challenge *(Dublin)*]. Challenge : newspaper of the Irish Democratic Youth Movement. — Vol.1, no.1 (1979)-. — Dublin (30 Gardiner Place, Dublin 1) : The Movement, 1979-. — v. : ill ; 27cm
Six issues yearly. — Description based on: Vol.2, no.1 (Jan. 1980)
£0.10 per issue B81-03573

324.243'038 — Germany. Political parties: Nationalsozialistische Deutsche Arbeiter-Partei, *1933-1945*

Government, party and people in Nazi Germany / edited by Jeremy Noakes. — Exeter : University of Exeter, 1980. — 103p ; 21cm. — (Exeter studies in history ; no.2)
Bibliography: p98-102
ISBN 0-85989-112-7 (pbk) : Unpriced B81-10037

324.243'038 — Germany. Political parties: Nationalsozialistische Deutsche Arbeiter-Partei. Women's organisations, *1919-1945*

Stephenson, Jill. The Nazi organisation of women / Jill Stephenson. — London : Croom Helm, 1981. — 246p ; 23cm
Bibliography: p231-237. — Includes index
ISBN 0-85664-673-3 : £11.95 : CIP rev. B80-21479

324.243'072 — Germany. Political parties: Sozialdemokratische Partei Deutschlands, *to 1933*

Guttsman, W. L.. The German Social Democratic Party, 1875-1933 : from ghetto to government / W.L. Guttsman. — London : Allen & Unwin, c1981. — xii,362p : ill ; 23cm
Bibliography: p338-356. - Includes index
ISBN 0-04-943024-6 : £18.50 B81-11514

324.2438 — Poland. Political parties: Komunistyczna Partia Polski. Opposition — *Polish texts*

Drewnowski, Jan. Problematyka opozycji w Polsce / Jan Drewnowski. — Londyn (2 Vista Way, Harrow, Middx HA3 0SW) : Jutro Polski, 1981. — 18p ; 20cm
Unpriced (pbk) B81-26280

324.2438'074'0922 — Poland. Political parties: Polska Partia Socjalistyczna, *to 1980* — *Biographies — Polish texts*

Ciołkosz, Adam. Ludzie P.P.S. / Adam Ciołkosz. — 2 wyd. — Londyn : Centralny Komitet Polskiej Partii Socjalistycznej, 1981. — 163p : 1col.ill,ports ; 22cm
Previous ed.: 1967. — Includes Wspomnienie o Adamie Ciołkoszu / Feliks Gross
Unpriced (pbk) B81-27076

324.244 — France. Political parties

Bell, David S.. Contemporary French political parties. — London : Croom Helm, Feb.1982. — [240]p
ISBN 0-7099-0633-1 : £14.95 : CIP entry B81-37555

324.244'07'09 — France. Left-wing political parties, *1968-1980*

Johnson, R. W. (Richard William). The long march of the French Left / R.W. Johnson. — London : Macmillan, 1981. — xv,345p ; 25cm
Includes index
ISBN 0-333-27417-2 (cased) : £20.00
ISBN 0-333-27418-0 (pbk) : Unpriced B81-21793

324.244'075 — France. Political parties: Parti communiste français. Factions. Formation

Hayward, J. E. S.. Surreptitious factionalism in the French Communist Party / by J.E.S. Hayward. — Hull : University of Hull, Department of Politics, 1981. — 20 leaves ; 30cm. — (Hull papers in politics ; no.20)
Unpriced (pbk) B81-17779

324.245'075'09 — Italy. Political parties: Partito comunista italiano, *to 1979*

Amyst, Grant. The Italian Communist Party : the crisis of the popular front strategy / Grant Amyst. — London : Croom Helm, c1981. — 252p ; 23cm
Bibliography: p232-241. - Includes index
ISBN 0-7099-0190-9 : £12.95 B81-18922

324.245'5 — Italy. Tuscany. Political parties, *1945-1980*

Pridham, Geoffrey. The nature of the Italian party system : a regional case study / Geoffrey Pridham. — London : Croom Helm, c1981. — 283p : 1map ; 23cm
Bibliography: p272-278. — Includes index
ISBN 0-85664-811-6 : £12.95 B81-18830

324.247'075 — Soviet Union. Political parties: Kommunisticheskaîa partiîa Sovetskogo Soîuza

Hill, Ronald J.. The Soviet Communist Party / Ronald J. Hill and Peter Frank. — London : Allen & Unwin, 1981. — 167p : ill ; 23cm
Bibliography: p154-164. — Includes index
ISBN 0-04-329035-3 (cased) : Unpriced : CIP rev.
ISBN 0-04-329036-1 (pbk) : Unpriced B81-13766

324.2495'075 — Greece. Political parties: Kommounistikon Komma tēs Hellados, *1941-1944*

Loulis, John C.. The Greek Communist Party, 1940-1944. — London : Croom Helm, Jan.1982. — [256]p
ISBN 0-7099-1612-4 : £12.50 : CIP entry B81-34781

324.251'075 — China. Political parties: Zhongguo gong chan dang, *1949-1981*

Resolution on CPC history (1949-81). — Oxford : Pergamon, Nov.1981. — [126]p
ISBN 0-08-028958-4 (pbk) : £2.00 : CIP entry B81-32091

324.259'075 — South-east Asia. Communist parties, *to 1979*

Van der Kroef, Justus M.. Communism in South-East Asia / Justus M. van der Kroef. — London : Macmillan, 1981. — ix,342p ; 23cm
Bibliography: p283-293. — Includes index
ISBN 0-333-24812-0 (cased) : Unpriced : CIP rev.
ISBN 0-333-24813-9 (pbk) : Unpriced B80-07246

324.266'5803 — Cape Verde Islands. Political parties: PAICV — *Conference proceedings*

PAICV. *Congress (1st : 1981 : Praia).* PAICV First Congress : Praia 16-20 January 1981. — Praia : PAICV ; London (34 Percy St., W1P 9FG) : Mozambique, Angola and Guine Information Centre, 1891. — 35p ; 30cm. — (State papers and party proceedings series III, no.1)
Unpriced (pbk) B81-35667

324.268'0975'09 — South Africa. Political parties: South African Communist Party, *1921-1971*

Lerumo, A.. Fifty fighting years : the Communist Party of South Africa 1921-1971 / A. Lerumo. — 2nd rev. ed. — London : Inkululeko, 1980. — 191p,[12]p of plates : maps,facsims,ports ; 22cm
Previous ed.: 1971. — Includes index
ISBN 0-9504225-1-7 : Unpriced B81-18766

324.273 — United States. Political parties

Clem, Alan L.. American electoral politics : strategies for renewal / Alan L. Clem. — New York ; London : Van Nostrand Reinhold, c1981. — viii,246p : ill ; 23cm
Bibliography: p235-240. — Includes index
ISBN 0-442-24475-4 (pbk) : £7.45
Primary classification 324.973 B81-17188

324.273'09 — United States. Political parties, *ca 1950-1979*

Paths to political reform / edited by William J. Crotty. — Lexington : Lexington, c1980 ; Farnborough, Hants. : Gower [distributor], 1981. — xxix,366p : ill ; 24cm. — (Policy Studies Organization series)
Includes bibliographies and index
ISBN 0-669-02395-7 : £16.00 B81-14059

324.273'.09 — United States. Political parties. Influence, *1850-1979*

Clubb, Jerome M.. Partisan realignment : voters, parties and government in American history / Jerome M. Clubb, William H. Flanigan, Nancy H. Zingale. — Beverly Hills ; London : Sage, c1980. — 311p : ill ; 23cm. — (Sage library of social research ; v.108)
Includes index
ISBN 0-8039-1445-8 (cased) : £11.85
ISBN 0-8039-1446-6 (pbk) : £5.50 B81-07341

324.273'09 — United States. Political parties, *to 1980*

Polakoff, Keith Ian. Political parties in American history / Keith Ian Polakoff. — New York ; Chichester : Wiley, c1981. — xiii,480p ; 23cm
Bibliography: p443-460. - Includes index
ISBN 0-471-07747-x (pbk) : £7.35 B81-13078

324.273'7 — South-western United States. Political parties: Socialist Party *(U.S.)*, *to 1943*

Green, James R.. Grass-roots socialism : radical movements in the Southwest 1895-1943 / James R. Green. — Baton Rouge ; London : Louisiana State University Press, c1978. — xxiv,450p : ill,maps,ports ; 24cm
Includes index
ISBN 0-8071-0773-5 (cased) : £12.00
ISBN 0-8071-0367-5 (pbk) : £5.40 B81-10843

324.294 — Australia. Political parties, *1966-1981*

Jupp, James. Party politics : Australia 1966-81. — London : Allen & Unwin, Jan.1982. — [309]p
ISBN 0-86861-315-0 : £18.00 : CIP entry B81-36041

324′.3 — London *(City).* **Whig clubs. Proceedings,** *1714-1717 — Minutes*

London politics 1713-1717. — London (Miss H. Creaton, c/o Institute of Historical Research, Senate House, WC1E 7HU) : London Record Society, 1981. — v,131p ; 26cm. — (Publications / London Record Society ; v.17)
Includes index. — Contents: Minutes of a Whig Club 1714-1717 / edited by H. Horwitz - London pollbooks 1713 / edited by W.A. Speck and W.A. Gray
ISBN 0-900952-17-2 : Unpriced
Also classified at 324.6′2 B81-26242

324′.3 — Peninsular Malaysia. Political parties. Women's organisations: Pergerakan Kaum Ibi UMNO, *1945-1972*

Manderson, Leonore. Women, politics, and change : the Kaum Ibu UMNO, Malaysia 1945-1972 / Leonore Manderson. — Kuala Lumpur ; Oxford : Oxford University Press, 1980. — xi,294p : ill,maps ; 25cm. — (East Asian social science monographs)
Bibliography: p262-283. — Includes index
ISBN 0-19-580437-6 (corrected cased) : £17.50
ISBN 0-19-580443-0 (pbk) : Unpriced
B81-40175

324′.4 — Politics. Role of interest groups

McCormick, Robert E.. Politicians, legislation, and the economy : an inquiry into the interest-group theory of government / Robert E. McCormick, Robert D. Tollison. — Boston, Mass. ; London : Nijhoff in cooperation with the Center for Research in Government Policy & Business, c1981. — x,134p : ill ; 24cm. — (Rochester studies in economics and policy issues)
Includes index
ISBN 0-89838-058-8 : Unpriced B81-33340

324.5′0973 — United States. Presidents. Elections, *1976.* **Candidates. Selection**

Aldrich, John H.. Before the convention : strategies and choices in presidential nomination campaigns / John H. Aldrich. — Chicago ; London : University of Chicago Press, 1980. — xiv,257p : ill ; 24cm
Bibliography: p237. - Includes index
ISBN 0-226-01269-7 (cased) : £15.00
ISBN 0-226-01270-0 (pbk) : £4.80 B81-04925

324.5′4′0973 — United States. Presidents. Primary elections

Davis, James W.. Presidential primaries : road to the White House / James W. Davis. — Westport ; London : Greenwood Press, 1980. — xv,395p : ill ; 25cm. — (Contributions in political science, ISSN 0147-1066 ; no.41)
Bibliography: p375-377. — Includes index
ISBN 0-313-22057-3 : Unpriced B81-05296

324.6 — Democracies. Electorate. Voting behaviour

Electoral participation : a comparative analysis / edited by Richard Rose. — Beverly Hills ; London : Sage, c1980. — 358p : ill ; 23cm. — (Sage studies in contemporary political sociology)
Conference papers. — Includes bibliographies and index
ISBN 0-8039-9811-2 : £15.00 : CIP rev.
B80-12737

324.6′2 — Great Britain. Electorate — *Statistics — Serials*

Electoral statistics / Office of Population Censuses and Surveys. — 1980. — London : H.M.S.O., 1981. — iv,24p
ISBN 0-11-690750-9 : £3.60 B81-15172

324.6′2 — London *(City).* **General elections,** *1713.* **Voters** — *Lists*

London politics 1713-1717. — London (Miss H. Creaton, c/o Institute of Historical Research, Senate House, WC1E 7HU) : London Record Society, 1981. — v,131p ; 26cm. — (Publications / London Record Society ; v.17)
Includes index. — Contents: Minutes of a Whig Club 1714-1717 / edited by H. Horwitz - London pollbooks 1713 / edited by W.A. Speck and W.A. Gray
ISBN 0-900952-17-2 : Unpriced
Primary classification 324′.3 B81-26242

324.6′3 — Electoral systems *related to* **political parties**

Katz, Richard S.. A theory of parties and electoral systems / Richard S. Katz. — Baltimore ; London : Johns Hopkins University Press, c1980. — xii,151p : ill ; 24cm
Includes index
ISBN 0-8018-2435-4 : £7.75
Primary classification 324.2 B81-11318

324.6′3 — European Parliament. British members. Elections, *1979*

Butler, David, *1924-*. European elections and British politics / David Butler and David Marquand. — London : Longman, 1981. — vi,193p : 1map,1facsim ; 23cm
Includes index
ISBN 0-582-29528-9 (cased) : £9.95
ISBN 0-582-29529-7 (pbk) : £4.95 B81-10219

324.6′3 — European Parliament. Northern Irish members. Direct election, *1979*

Elliott, Sydney. Northern Ireland : the first election to the European parliament / Sydney Elliott. — [Belfast] : Queen's University of Belfast, c1980. — 64p ; 21cm
ISBN 0-85389-189-3 (pbk) : Unpriced
B81-08498

324.6′3′094 — Western Europe. Electoral systems, *to 1979*

Carstairs, Andrew McLaren. A short history of electoral systems in Western Europe / Andrew McLaren Carstairs. — London : Allen & Unwin, 1980. — 236p ; 23cm
Bibliography: p225-231. — Includes index
ISBN 0-04-324006-2 : £12.50 : CIP rev.
B80-18177

324.7′0973 — United States. Elections. Campaigns — *Manuals*

Costikyan, Edward N.. How to win votes : the politics of 1980 / Edward N. Costikyan. — New York ; London : Harcourt Brace Jovanovich, c1980. — xix,200p ; 24cm
ISBN 0-15-142221-4 : £7.95 B81-15658

324.7′3′0973 — United States. Presidents. Elections. Influence of mass media, *1900-1968*

Barber, James David, *1930-*. The pulse of politics : electing presidents in the media age / James David Barber. — New York ; London : Norton, 1980. — 342p ; 24cm
Bibliography: p325-332. — Includes index
ISBN 0-393-01341-3 : £8.95 B81-05508

324.73′3 — United States. Television programmes. Special subjects: United States. Presidents. Elections, *1976.* **Candidates. Debates**

The **Presidential** debates : media, electoral, and policy perspectives / George F. Bishop, Robert G. Meadow, Marilyn Jackson-Beeck editors. — New York ; London : Praeger, 1980, c1978. — xxii,324p : 1ill ; 24cm. — (Praeger special studies)
Bibliography: p306-315. - Includes index
ISBN 0-03-057707-1 (pbk) : £7.50 B81-01737

324.941 — Great Britain. Electoral processes

McLean, Iain. Elections / Iain McLean. — 2nd ed. — London : Longman, 1980. — ix,102p ; 20cm. — (Political realities)
Previous ed.: 1976. — Bibliography: p98-100. — Includes index
ISBN 0-582-35323-8 (pbk) : £2.25 B81-00028

324.941 — Great Britain. Electorate. Voting behaviour, *1959-1974.* **Models**

How voters decide. — London : Academic Press, Dec.1981. — [250]p
ISBN 0-12-348950-4 : CIP entry B81-31336

324.941′081 — Great Britain. *Parliament. House of Commons.* **Members. Elections,** *1832-1980 — Statistics*

British electoral facts 1832-1980 / compiled and edited by F.W.S. Craig. — 4th ed. — Chichester : Parliamentary Research Services, 1981. — xix,203p ; 25cm
Previous ed.: 1976. — Bibliography: p193-198. — Includes index
ISBN 0-900178-20-5 (pbk) : £8.50 B81-37383

324.941′083 — Great Britain. *Parliament. House of Commons.* **Members. General elections,** *1935*

Stannage, Tom. Baldwin thwarts the opposition : the British general election of 1935 / Tom Stannage. — London : Croom Helm, c1980. — 320p : ill ; 23cm
Bibliography: p293-305. — Includes index
ISBN 0-7099-0341-3 : £19.95 : CIP rev.
B80-05233

324.941′085 — Great Britain. *Parliament. House of Commons.* **Members. General elections. Voting behaviour of Jews,** *1945-1979*

Alderman, Geoffrey. The Jewish vote in Great Britain since 1945 / by Geoffrey Alderman. — Glasgow ([16 Richmond St.] Glasgow, G1 1XQ) : Centre for the Study of Public Policy, University of Strathclyde, 1980. — 38p ; 30cm. — (Studies in public policy, ISSN 0140-8240 ; no.72)
£1.50 (pbk) B81-07961

324.941′0857′0722 — Great Britain. Electorate. Voting behaviour. Influence of policies of political parties, *1970-1974 — Case studies*

Miller, William L.. What was the profit in following the crowd? : the effectiveness of party strategies on immigration and devolution / by W.L. Miller. — Glasgow (McCance Building, 16 Richmond St., Glasgow G1 1XQ) : Centre for the Study of Public Policy, University of Strathclyde, 1979. — 35p : ill ; 30cm. — (Studies in public policy, ISSN 0140-8240 ; no.25)
Unpriced (pbk) B81-36901

324.9411′0857 — Scotland. Community councils. Members. Elections, *1976-1980*

Masterson, Michael P.. Electing the first community councils : the formation and election of councils throughout Scotland : a revised version of a report prepared for the Central Research Unit, Scottish Office / by M.P. Masterson and E.M. Masterman. — Edinburgh (New St Andrew's House, [St. James Centre], Edinburgh EH1 3SZ) : [Central Research Unit], c1981. — 12p ; 21cm
Cover title
Unpriced (pbk) B81-29536

324.9421′860855 — Harrow. *Borough Council.* **Members. Elections,** *1954-1963 — Statistics*

Gray, Colin J.. Harrow votes : the municipal borough of Harrow, 1954-1965 : a handbook of borough election results, covering the years 1954-1963 / compiled and edited by Colin J. Gray and Stephen Giles-Medhurst. — South Harrow (11, Lulworth Gardens, South Harrow, Middlesex) : C.J. Gray, 1981. — 63p : 1map ; 30cm
Cover title. — Originally published: 1980. — Includes index
£1.80 (pbk) B81-16224

324.9421′860856 — Harrow. *Borough Council.* **Members. Elections,** *1964-1978 — Statistics*

Gray, Colin J.. Harrow votes : the London borough of Harrow, 1964-1978 : a handbook of borough election results, covering the years 1964-1977 / compiled and edited by Colin J. Gray. — Rev. ed. — South Harrow (11, Lulworth Gardens, South Harrow, Middlesex) : C.J. Gray, [1981]. — 63p ; 30cm
Cover title. — Previous ed.: 1980. — Includes index
£1.80 (pbk) B81-16225

324.9427′9082 — Isle of Man. *Tynwald. House of Keys.* **Members. Elections,** *1919-1979.* **Results** — *Lists*

Isle of Man parliamentary election results 1919-1979 / compiled by Tom Sherratt. — [Warrington] ([10 Thornbury Ave., Lowton, Warrington WA3 2PG]) : [T. Sherratt], [1979?]. — 39p : 1map ; 30cm
Map on inside cover
Unpriced (pbk) B81-21907

324.9428′17 — Great Britain. *Parliament. House of Commons.* **Members. Elections in Bradford,** *1832-1906*

Nineteenth century Bradford elections / edited by J.A. Jowitt & R.K.S. Taylor. — Bradford (10 Mornington Villas, Bradford BD8 7HB) : University of Leeds Centre for Adult Education, 1979. — 87p ; 21cm. — (Bradford Centre occasional papers ; no.1)
Unpriced (pbk) B81-09958

324.943'0877 — West Germany. Federal elections, *1976*
Elections & parties / editors Max Kaase and Klaus von Beyme. — London : Sage, c1978. — 322p : ill ; 24cm. — (German political studies, ISSN 0307-7233 ; v.3)
Bibliography: p261-320
ISBN 0-8039-9888-0 (cased) : Unpriced
ISBN 0-8039-9889-9 (pbk) : Unpriced
B81-10093

324.943'0878 — West Germany. Federal elections, *1980*
Lodge, Juliet. The West German federal election of 1980 : "Security for the '80s" versus "With optimism against socialism" / by Juliet Lodge. — [Hull] : University of Hull, Department of Politics, 1981. — 71p : ill ; 30cm. — (Hull papers in politics, ISSN 0142-7377 ; no.21)
Unpriced (unbound) B81-23287

324.956'04 — Middle East. Elections, *ca 1940-1977 — Comparative studies*
Electoral politics in the Middle East : issues, voters and elites / edited by Jacob M. Landau, Ergun Özbudun, Frank Tachau. — London : Croom Helm, c1980. — 335p : ill ; 23cm
Includes index
ISBN 0-7099-0454-1 : £19.95 : CIP rev.
B80-10482

324.973 — United States. Electoral processes
Clem, Alan L.. American electoral politics : strategies for renewal / Alan L. Clem. — New York ; London : Van Nostrand Reinhold, c1981. — viii,246p : ill ; 23cm
Bibliography: p235-240. — Includes index
ISBN 0-442-24475-4 (pbk) : £7.45
Also classified at 324.273 B81-17188

324.973 — United States. Electorate. Voting behaviour. Changes. Effects, *to 1979*
Realignment in American politics : toward a theory / edited by Bruce A. Campbell and Richard J. Trilling. — Austin ; London : University of Texas Press, c1980. — xi,352p : ill ; 24cm
Bibliography: p329-352
ISBN 0-292-77019-7 : £13.50 B81-03780

324.973 — United States. Presidents. Elections, *to 1980*
Peirce, Neal R.. The people's President : the electoral college in American history and the direct vote alternative. — Rev. ed. / Neal R. Peirce and Lawrence D. Longley. — New Haven ; London : Yale University Press, c1981. — x,342p : facsims ; 24cm
Previous ed.: New York : Simon and Schuster, 1968. — Bibliography: p301-307. — Includes index
ISBN 0-300-02612-9 (cased) : £28.00 : CIP rev.
ISBN 0-300-02704-4 (pbk) : £6.95 B81-22693

324.973 — United States. Presidents. Elections. Voting behaviour of electorate
Fiorina, Morris P.. Retrospective voting in American national elections / Morris P. Fiorina. — New Haven ; London : Yale University Press, c1981. — xi,249p : ill ; 25cm
Includes index
ISBN 0-300-02557-2 (cased) : £24.50 : CIP rev.
ISBN 0-300-02703-6 (pbk) : £6.95 B81-22684

324.973 — United States. Presidents. Elections. Voting behaviour of electorate, *to 1980.* **Geographical aspects**
Archer, J. Clark. Section and party : a political geography of American presidential elections from Andrew Jackson to Ronald Reagan / J. Clark Archer, Peter J. Taylor. — Chichester : Research Studios Press, c1981. — xiv,271p : ill,maps ; 24cm. — (Geographical research studies series ; 4)
Bibliography: p239-265. — Includes index
ISBN 0-471-10014-5 : £16.50 : CIP rev.
B81-18122

324.973'092 — United States. Elections, *1944-1978*
Pomper, Gerald M.. Elections in America : control and influence in democratic politics / Gerald M. Pomper with Susan S. Lederman. — 2nd ed. — New York ; London : Longman, c1980. — xvi,256p : ill ; 23cm
Previous ed.: New York : Dodd, Mead, 1968. — Includes index
ISBN 0-582-28095-8 (pbk) : £5.95 B81-06992

324.973'092 — United States. Electoral processes, *1948-1976*
Bone, Hugh A.. Politics and voters / Hugh A. Bone, Austin Ranney. — 5th ed. — New York ; London : McGraw-Hill, c1981. — vii,136p : ill ; 21cm. — (Foundations of American government and political science)
Previous ed.: 1977. — Bibliography: p124-127. — Includes index
ISBN 0-07-006492-x (pbk) : £6.95 B81-26659

324.973'092 — United States. Electorate. Voting behaviour, *1956-1976.* **Theories**
The **electorate** reconsidered / edited by John C. Pierce and John L. Sullivan. — Beverly Hills ; London : Sage, c1980. — 293p : ill ; 22cm. — (Sage focus editions ; 20)
Bibliography: p279-293
ISBN 0-8039-1342-7 (cased) : £11.85
ISBN 0-8039-1343-5 (pbk) : £6.25 B81-00768

324.973'092 — United States. Presidents. Elections, *1964-1976.* **Campaigns. Candidates: Wallace, George C.**
Carlson, Jody. George C. Wallace and the politics of powerlessness : the Wallace campaigns for the presidency, 1964-1976 / Jody Carlson. — New Brunswick ; London : Transaction, c1981. — xv,331p ; 24cm
Bibliography: p287-318. — Includes index
ISBN 0-87855-344-4 : £14.00 B81-16524

324.973'0925 — United States. Presidents. Elections. Televised debates between candidates, *1976*
Bitzer, Lloyd. Carter vs Ford : the counterfeit debates of 1976 / Lloyd Bitzer and Theodore Rueter. — Madison ; London : University of Wisconsin Press, 1980. — xii,428p ; 22cm
Includes index
ISBN 0-299-08280-6 (cased) : £16.50
ISBN 0-299-08284-9 (pbk) : £5.95 B81-03781

324.9748'043 — United States. *Congress. Senate.* **Members. Elections. Campaigns: Campaigns in Pennsylvania,** *1964*
Falco, Maria J.. 'Bigotry!' : ethnic, machine and sexual politics in a senatorial election / Maria J. Falco. — Westport, Conn. ; London : Greenwood Press, 1980. — xvi,200p ; 22cm. — (Contributions in political science, ISSN 0147-1066 ; no.34)
Bibliography: p179-195. - Includes index
ISBN 0-313-20726-7 : Unpriced B81-08298

325.2 — POLITICS. EMIGRATION

325'.21'09 — Refugees, *to 1979*
D'Souza, Frances. The refugee dilemma : international recognition and acceptance / by Frances D'Souza. — London (36 Craven St., WC2N 5NG) : Minority Rights Group, 1980. — 19p : 1ill,1map ; 30cm. — (Report / Minority Rights Group, ISSN 0305-6252 ; no.43)
Bibliography: p19
£0.75 (pbk) B81-05184

325'.21'0924 — Europe. Romanian refugees, *1944-1945 — Personal observations*
Hilgarth, Anne-Marie. Anika / Anne-Marie Hilgarth. — Ilfracombe : Stockwell, 1980. — 54p ; 19cm
ISBN 0-7223-1391-8 : £3.30 B81-05596

325'.272'0973 — United States. Mexican illegal immigrant personnel. Repatriation, *1954*
Garciá, Juan Ramon. Operation Wetback : the mass deportation of Mexican undocumented workers in 1954 / Juan Ramon García. — Westport, Conn. ; London : Greenwood Press, 1980. — xviii,268p : ill ; 24cm. — (Contributions in ethnic studies, ISSN 0196-7088 ; no.2)
Bibliography: p251-262. — Includes index
ISBN 0-313-21353-4 : £15.95 B81-23476

325.3 — COLONIAL ADMINISTRATION

325'.3 — Colonialism
Naipaul, V. S.. The return of Eva Perón ; with, The killings in Trinidad / V.S. Naipaul. — Harmondsworth : Penguin, 1981, c1980. — 217p ; 18cm
Originally published: London : Deutsch, 1980
ISBN 0-14-005259-3 (pbk) : £1.50 B81-40470

325'.3'09034 — Colonies, *ca 1800-1979*
Lemon, Anthony. Studies in overseas settlement and population / Anthony Lemon, Norman Pollock. — London : Longman, 1980. — 337p : ill,maps,1port ; 24cm
Includes bibliographies
ISBN 0-582-48567-3 : £19.95 : CIP rev.
B80-13239

325'.3'0904 — Colonialism, *1870-1945*
Fieldhouse, D. K.. Colonialism 1870-1945 : an introduction / D.K. Fieldhouse. — London : Weidenfeld and Nicolson, c1981. — 151p ; 23cm
Bibliography: p124-137. - Includes index
ISBN 0-297-77873-0 : £8.95 B81-04469

325'.32 — Imperialism
Mommsen, Wolfgang J.. Theories of imperialism / Wolfgang J. Mommsen ; translated by P.S. Falla. — London : Weidenfeld and Nicolson, 1981, c1980. — x,180p ; 23cm
Translation of: Imperialismustheorien. — Originally published: New York : Random House, 1980. — Bibliography: p161-169. — Includes index
ISBN 0-297-77794-7 : £8.50 B81-07185

Reynolds, Charles. Modes of imperialism. — Oxford : Martin Robertson, May 1981. — [250]p
ISBN 0-85520-339-0 : £12.50 : CIP entry
B81-05137

325'.32'01 — Imperialism. Theories of Marxists, *to 1979*
Brewer, Anthony. Marxist theories of imperialism : a critical survey / Anthony Brewer. — London : Routledge & Kegan Paul, 1980. — xi,308p ; 22cm
Bibliography: p295-301. - Includes index
ISBN 0-7100-0531-8 : £12.50 : CIP rev.
ISBN 0-7100-0621-7 (pbk) : £6.95 B80-26583

325'.32'0904 — Imperialism, *1900-1976*
Thornton, A. P.. Imperialism in the twentieth century / by A.P. Thornton. — London : Macmillan, 1978, c1977 (1980 [printing]). — xii,363p ; 23cm
Originally published: Minneapolis : University of Minnesota Press, c1977. — Bibliography: p331-343. - Includes index
ISBN 0-333-30712-7 (pbk) : £8.95 B81-13402

325'.32'094 — European imperialism. Role of technological innovation
Headrick, Daniel R.. The tools of empire : technology and European imperialism in the nineteenth century / Daniel R. Headrick. — New York ; Oxford : Oxford University Press, 1981. — x,221p ; 22cm
Bibliography: p211-213. — Includes index
ISBN 0-19-502831-7 (cased) : Unpriced
ISBN 0-19-502832-5 (pbk) : £4.95 B81-36316

325'.32'0944 — French imperialism, *1912-1925*
Andrew, Christopher M.. France overseas : the Great War and the climax of French imperial expansion / Christopher M. Andrew and A.S. Kanya-Forstner. — London : Thames and Hudson, c1981. — 302p : maps ; 25cm
Bibliography: p255-261. - Includes index
ISBN 0-500-25075-8 : £12.00 B81-25066

325'.341'096 — Africa. British colonies. Colonial administration, *1938-1948*
Pearce, R. D.. The turning point in Africa. — London : Cass, Oct.1981. — [236]p
ISBN 0-7146-3160-4 : £14.00 : CIP entry
B81-24672

325'.3469'096 — Africa. Portuguese colonies. Colonial administration, *to 1974*
Newitt, Malyn. Portugal in Africa : the last hundred years / by Malyn Newitt. — Harlow : Longman, 1981. — viii,278p : maps ; 23cm
Bibliography: p250-263. — Includes index
ISBN 0-582-64379-1 (cased) : Unpriced
ISBN 0-582-64377-5 (pbk) : £4.50 B81-32860

325'.3469'096 — Africa. Portuguese colonies. Colonial administration, *to 1975*
Newitt, Malyn. Portugal in Africa. — London : Hurst, June 1981
ISBN 0-905838-37-8 (cased) : £8.50 : CIP entry
ISBN 0-905838-49-1 (pbk) : £3.95 B81-09470

325'.373'09599 — Philippines. Colonial administration by United States, *1900-1913*

May, Glenn Anthony. Social engineering in the Philippines : the aims, execution, and impact of American colonial policy, 1900-1913 / Glenn Anthony May. — Westport, Conn. ; London : Greenwood Press, 1980. — xxvii,268p : ill,1 map,ports ; 22cm. — (Contributions in comparative colonial studies ; no.2)
Bibliography: p247-254. — Includes index
ISBN 0-313-20978-2 : Unpriced B81-05621

325.4/9 — POLITICS. MIGRATION. GEOGRAPHICAL TREATMENT

325.41 — Great Britain. Immigration. Policies of government — *Proposals*

Dummett, Michael. Immigration : where the debate goes wrong / Michael Dummett. — London (c/o JCWI, 44 Theobald's Rd, London, WC1X 8SP) : Action Group on Immigration and Nationality, 1978 (1979 [printing]). — 15p ; 21cm
Cover title. — Text on inside covers
£0.40 (pbk) B81-37748

325.41'0212 — Great Britain. Immigration — *Statistics — Serials*

Control of immigration statistics United Kingdom / Home Office. — 1980. — London : H.M.S.O., 1981. — 55p. — (Cmnd. ; 8199)
ISBN 0-10-181990-0 : £4.80 B81-25001

325.6 — Africa. Colonial administration, *1870-1960*

Colonialism in Africa, 1870-1960. — Cambridge : Cambridge University Press. — (Hoover Institution publications)
Vol.1: The history and politics of colonialism, 1870-1914. — Feb.1982. — [532]p
Originally published: 1969
ISBN 0-521-28648-4 (pbk) : £12.50 : CIP entry B81-36239

Colonialism in Africa, 1870-1960. — Cambridge : Cambridge University Press. — (Hoover Institution publications)
Vol.2: The history and politics of colonialism, 1914-1960. — Feb.1982. — [563]p
Originally published: 1970
ISBN 0-521-28649-2 (pbk) : £12.50 : CIP entry B81-36238

326 — POLITICS. SLAVERY AND EMANCIPATION

326'.0975 — United States. Southern states. Negro slavery. Political aspects, *1828-1856*

Cooper, William J.. The South and the politics of slavery 1828-1856 / William J. Cooper, Jr. — Baton Rouge ; London : Louisiana State University Press, c1978 (1980 printing). — xv,401p ; 23cm
Bibliography: p381-394. — Includes index
ISBN 0-8071-0775-1 (pbk) : £4.80 B81-01920

327 — FOREIGN RELATIONS

327 — Foreign relations

Cohen, Raymond. International politics. — London : Longman, Sept.1981. — [192]p
ISBN 0-582-29558-0 (pbk) : £4.95 : CIP entry B81-25875

Issues in global politics / edited by Gavin Boyd and Charles Pentland. — New York : Free Press ; London : Collier Macmillan, c1981. — x,399p ; 24cm
Includes index
ISBN 0-02-904470-7 (pbk) : £7.95 B81-33399

Miller, J. D. B.. The world of states : connected essays / J.D.B. Miller. — London : Croom Helm, c1981. — 179p ; 23cm
Includes index
ISBN 0-7099-0442-8 : £12.50 B81-13000

Perspectives on world politics : a reader / edited by Michael Smith, Richard Little and Michael Shackleton at the Open University. — London : Croom Helm in association with the Open University Press, c1981. — 431p : ill ; 23cm. — (Open University set book)
Includes index
ISBN 0-7099-2302-3 (cased) : £12.95 : CIP rev.
ISBN 0-7099-2303-1 (pbk) : £5.25 B80-17572

Spanier, John. Games nations play : analyzing international politics / John Spanier. — 4th ed. — New York ; London : Holt, Rinehart and Winston, c1981. — xv,614p ; 24cm
Previous ed.: 1978. — Bibliography: p578-591. — Includes index
ISBN 0-03-058172-9 (pbk) : £8.25 B81-25280

Wendzel, Robert L.. International politics : policymakers and policymaking / Robert L. Wendzel. — New York ; Chichester : Wiley, c1981. — xviii,476p : ill,1map ; 24cm
Bibliography: p450-461. - Includes index
ISBN 0-471-05046-6 : Unpriced B81-13051

327 — Foreign relations. Crises

Lebow, Richard Ned. Between peace and war : the nature of international crisis / Richard Ned Lebow. — Baltimore ; London : Johns Hopkins University Press, c1981. — xi,350p ; 24cm
Includes index
ISBN 0-8018-2311-0 : £14.75 B81-34336

327 — Foreign relations. Role of international organisations

Convocation lectures [given at] the New University of Ulster / by Ralf Dahrendorf, Sir Edward Britton, Lord Justice Megaw. — [Coleraine] : New University of Ulster, 1979. — 51p ; 22cm
Unpriced (pbk)
Also classified at 379.41 ; 340'.11 B81-14141

327 — Weak states. Foreign relations

Handel, Michael. Weak states in the international system / Michael Handel. — London : Cass, 1981. — viii,318p : ill ; 23cm
Bibliography: p287-312. - Includes index
ISBN 0-7146-3117-5 : £15.00 : CIP rev. B79-20689

327'.05 — Foreign relations — *Serials*

The **Year** book of world affairs / published under the auspices of the London Institute of World Affairs. — 1981. — London : Stevens & Sons, 1981. — 399p in various pagings
ISBN 0-420-45980-4 : £13.50 B81-09064

327'.0724 — Foreign relations. Mathematical models

Foreign policy behavior : the interstate behavior analysis model / Jonathan Wilkenfeld ... [et al.]. — Beverly Hills ; London : Sage, c1980. — 288p : ill ; 23cm
Bibliography: p263-286
ISBN 0-8039-1476-8 : £14.00 B81-05627

327'.09'04 — Foreign relations, *1944-1980 — Soviet viewpoints*

Gromyko, A. A.. Lenin and the Soviet peace policy : articles and speeches 1944-1980 / Andrei Gromyko ; [compiled by G. Isakovsky]. — Moscow : Progress Publishers, c1980 ; [London] : Distributed by Central Books. — 495p,[1]leaf of plates : 1col.port ; 23cm
Translation of: V.I. Lenin i miroliubivai͡a vneshni͡ai͡a politika Sovetskogo Souiza. — Includes index
£4.50 B81-29318

327'.09'04 — Foreign relations, *1945-1980*

Bown, Colin. Cold war to détente 1945-80 / Colin Brown, Peter J. Mooney. — 2nd ed. — London : Heinemann Educational, 1981. — viii,214p : maps ; 22cm
Previous ed.: 1976. — Bibliography: p204-211. - Includes index
ISBN 0-435-32132-3 (pbk) : £3.95 B81-09527

Servan-Schreiber, Jean-Jacques. The world challenge / Jean-Jacques Servan-Schreiber. — London : Collins, 1981. — 302p ; 22cm
Translation of: Le défi mondial. — Originally published: New York : Simon and Schuster, c1981. — Bibliography: p281-289. — Includes index
ISBN 0-00-216878-2 (cased) : £9.95
ISBN 0-00-216883-9 (pbk) : Unpriced B81-37703

327'.09'04 — Great powers. Foreign relations, *1945-1980 - For schools*

Sayer, John. Super power rivalry. — London : Edward Arnold, July 1981. — [48]p. — (Links : twentieth century world history books)
ISBN 0-7131-0538-0 (pbk) : £1.75 : CIP entry B81-13736

327'.09171'3 — Western bloc countries. Détente with Soviet Union, *1971-1980 — Soviet viewpoints*

Brezhnev, L. I.. Peace, detente, cooperation / Leonid I. Brezhnev. — New York ; London : Consultants Bureau, c1981. — xiii,197p ; 22cm
Translations from the Russian. — Includes index
ISBN 0-306-10971-9 : Unpriced
Primary classification 327.470171'3 B81-18235

327'.09171'3 — Western bloc countries. Foreign relations with Soviet Union

Nixon, Richard. The real war / Richard Nixon. — London : Sidgwick & Jackson, 1980 (1981 [printing]). — xvi,366p : 2maps ; 18cm
Originally published: New York : Warner Books, 1980. — Includes index
ISBN 0-283-98776-6 (pbk) : £1.75
Also classified at 327.470171'3 B81-29539

327'.09172'4 — Developing countries. Foreign relations with Soviet Union, *1954-1980*

The **Soviet** Union in the third world : successes and failures / edited by Robert H. Donaldson. — Boulder : Westview ; London : Croom Helm, 1981. — xiv,458p ; 24cm
ISBN 0-7099-0801-6 : £14.95
Primary classification 327.470172'4 B81-33444

327'.0917'4927 — Arab countries. Foreign relations with Israel — *Conservative viewpoints*

Grayson, David. Europe & the Middle East / David Grayson & David Irwin. — Newcastle upon Tyne (86 Ovington Grove, Newcastle upon Tyne) : The Churchill Group, c1980. — 11p : 2maps ; 21cm
Cover title
Unpriced (pbk)
Primary classification 327.5694017'4927 B81-10849

327'.094 — Europe. Foreign relations, *1919-1939*

Wolfson, Robert. From peace to war : European relations 1919-39 / Robert Wolfson. — London : Edward Arnold, 1981. — 32p : ill,maps,ports ; 24cm. — (Links)
Bibliography: p31. — Includes index
ISBN 0-7131-0521-6 (corrected : pbk) : £1.50 B81-26954

327'.094 — Europe. Foreign relations, *1945-1980*

Jarvis, Margaret. Europe : conflicts and co-operation / Margaret Jarvis. — London : Harrap, 1981. — 48p : ill(some col.),col.maps,ports ; 30cm. — (Harrap's European studies course ; pt.3)
Map on inside cover
ISBN 0-245-53478-4 (pbk) : £1.65 B81-35618

327'.094 — European Community countries. Foreign relations with Africa

Europe & Africa : issues in post-colonial relations : texts of the Noel Buxton lectures, 1980 / edited by Margaret Cornell. — London : Overseas Development Institute, c1981. — vi,106p : ill ; 21cm
ISBN 0-85003-075-7 (pbk) : £2.50
Also classified at 327'.096 B81-26941

327'.094 — European Community countries. Foreign relations with Middle East. Policies of European Community

Moonman, Eric. EEC policy in relation to the Middle East, Israel and matters concerning Jews / by Eric Moonman. — [Leeds] : Leeds University Press, 1980. — 16p ; 21cm. — (The twenty-first Selig Brodetsky memorial lecture)
£0.75 (pbk)
Also classified at 327'.0956 B81-13960

327'.094 — European Community. Foreign relations

Heath, Edward. A British approach to European foreign policy / by Edward Heath. — Leeds : Leeds University Press, 1976. — 13p ; 22cm. — (The thirty-third Montague Burton lecture on international relations)
£0.45 (pbk) B81-10737

327'.094 — European countries. Foreign relations with other European countries, *1815-1914*

Bridge, F. R.. The great powers and the European states system 1815-1914 / F.R. Bridge and Roger Bullen. — London : Longman, 1980. — 208p : ill,maps ; 22cm
Bibliography: p180-189. - Includes index
ISBN 0-582-49134-7 (cased) : £9.95 : CIP rev.
ISBN 0-582-49135-5 (pbk) : £4.95 B80-25231

327'.094 — European countries. Foreign relations with other European countries, *1918-1939 — Readings from contemporary sources*
The **Lost** peace : international relations in Europe, 1918-1939 / [compiled by] Anthony Adamthwaite. — London : Edward Arnold, 1980. — 236p : maps ; 20cm. — (Documents of modern history)
Biliography: p227-231
ISBN 0-7131-6322-4 (pbk) : £4.95 : CIP rev.
B80-24133

327'.094 — Western Europe. Foreign relations, *1960-1980.* **Eastern Europe**
Windsor, Philip. Change in Eastern Europe / Philip Windsor. — London : Royal Institute of International Affairs, c1980. — vi,49p : 1map ; 30cm. — (Chatham House papers, ISSN 0143-5795 ; no.9)
ISBN 0-905031-19-9 (pbk) : £5.00
Also classified at 327'.0947 B81-02318

327'.094 — Western Europe. Foreign relations with Eastern Europe
East-West relations and the future of Eastern Europe. — London : Allen & Unwin, Aug.1981. — [288]p
ISBN 0-04-330317-x : £15.00 : CIP entry
Primary classification 327'.0947 B81-15887

327'.094 — Western Europe. Foreign relations with United States. Implications of Western European left-wing political parties, *1945-1979*
Political change in Europe : the left and the future of the Atlantic Alliance / edited by Douglas Eden and F.E. Short. — Oxford : Blackwell, 1980. — xii,163p ; 23cm
Includes index
ISBN 0-631-12525-6 : £8.95
Also classified at 327.7304 B81-12615

327'.0947 — Eastern Europe. Foreign relations, *1960-1980.* **Western Europe**
Windsor, Philip. Change in Eastern Europe / Philip Windsor. — London : Royal Institute of International Affairs, c1980. — vi,49p : 1map ; 30cm. — (Chatham House papers, ISSN 0143-5795 ; no.9)
ISBN 0-905031-19-9 (pbk) : £5.00
Primary classification 327'.094 B81-02318

327'.0947 — Eastern Europe. Foreign relations with Western Europe
East-West relations and the future of Eastern Europe. — London : Allen & Unwin, Aug.1981. — [288]p
ISBN 0-04-330317-x : £15.00 : CIP entry
Also classified at 327'.094 B81-15887

327'.0948 — Scandinavia. Foreign relations with United States, *1945-1949*
Lundestad, Geir. America, Scandinavia and the Cold War, 1945-1949 / Geir Lundestad. — New York ; Guildford : Columbia University Press, 1980. — vi,434p ; 24cm
Includes index
ISBN 0-231-04974-9 : £14.40
Primary classification 327.73048 B81-03727

327'.09496 — Balkan countries. Foreign relations with Russia, *1908-1914*
Rossos, Andrew. Russia and the Balkans : inter-Balkan rivalries and Russian foreign policy, 1908-1914 / Andrew Rossos. — Toronto ; London : University of Toronto Press, c1981. — xiii,313p : maps ; 24cm
Bibliography: p279-297. — Includes index
ISBN 0-8020-5516-8 : £21.00
Primary classification 327.470496 B81-34332

327'.095 — Asia. Foreign relations with Great Britain, *1795-1800*
Ingram, Edward. Commitment to Empire. — Oxford : Clarendon, Aug.1981. — [400]p
ISBN 0-19-822662-4 : £22.50 : CIP entry
Primary classification 327.4105 B81-15801

327'.095 — East Asia. Foreign relations with United States, *to 1980*
Thomson, James C.. Sentimental imperialists : the American experience in East Asia / James C. Thomson Jr., Peter W. Stanley, John Curtis Perry ; foreword by John King Fairbank. — New York ; London : Harper & Row, c1981. — xiv,323p : 3maps ; 24cm
Map on lining papers. — Includes index
ISBN 0-06-014282-0 : £9.50
Primary classification 327.7305 B81-40879

327'.095 — Far East. Foreign relations with Germany, *1933-1939*
Fox, John P.. Germany and the Far Eastern crisis 1931-1938. — Oxford : Clarendon Press, Jan.1982. — [400]p
ISBN 0-19-822573-3 : £22.50 : CIP entry
Primary classification 327.43'05 B81-34389

327'.095 — Far East. Foreign relations with Great Britain, *1819-1980*
Lowe, Peter. Britain in the far East : a survey from 1819 to the present / Peter Lowe. — London : Longman, 1981. — 264p : 6maps ; 23cm
Bibliography: p250-251. — Includes index
ISBN 0-582-48730-7 (cased) : Unpriced : CIP rev.
ISBN 0-582-48731-5 (pbk) : £5.75
Primary classification 327.4105 B80-26348

327'.0953'6 — Persian Gulf countries. Foreign relations
The **Security** of the Persian Gulf / edited by Hossein Amirsadeghi. — London : Croom Helm, c1981. — 287p : 2maps ; 23cm
Bibliography: p281-287. — Includes index
ISBN 0-7099-0505-x : £12.95 B81-18831

327'.0953'6 — Persian Gulf countries. Foreign relations. Implications of international security of Persian Gulf countries
Oil and security in the Arabian Gulf / edited by Abdel Majid Farid. — London : Croom Helm in association with the Arab Research Centre, c1981. — 162p ; 23cm
Conference papers. — Includes index
ISBN 0-7099-0507-6 : £10.95 : CIP rev.
B81-16874

327'.0954 — South Asia. Foreign relations with China, *1947-1980*
China South Asian relations 1947-1980. — Brighton : Harvester, 1981. — 2v. ; 23cm
Includes index
ISBN 0-7108-0356-7 : £60.00
ISBN 0-7108-0332-x (v.2) : Unpriced
Primary classification 327.51054 B81-33263

327'.0956 — Middle East. Foreign relations, *1941-1947*
Rubin, Barry. The great powers in the Middle East 1941-1947 : the road to the Cold War / Barry Rubin. — London : Cass, 1980. — xiv,254p : 1map ; 23cm
Bibliography: p239-244. - Includes index
ISBN 0-7146-3141-8 : £14.50 : CIP rev.
B80-06307

327'.0956 — Middle East. Foreign relations with European Community countries. Policies of European Community
Moonman, Eric. EEC policy in relation to the Middle East, Israel and matters concerning Jews / by Eric Moonman. — [Leeds] : Leeds University Press, 1980. — 16p ; 21cm. — (The twenty-first Selig Brodetsky memorial lecture)
£0.75 (pbk)
Primary classification 327'.094 B81-13960

327'.0956 — Middle East. Foreign relations with Great Britain. Policies of British government, *1914-1971*
Monroe, Elizabeth. Britain's moment in the Middle East 1914-1971 / Elizabeth Monroe. — New and rev. ed. / with a foreword by Peter Mansfield. — London : Chatto & Windus, 1981. — 254p : maps ; 23cm
Previous ed.: 1963. — Bibliography: p227-242. — Includes index
ISBN 0-7011-2555-1 : £9.50 : CIP rev.
Primary classification 327.41056 B81-03163

327'.0956 — Middle East. Foreign relations with Great Britain. Policies of British government, *1918-1922*
Darwin, John. Britain, Egypt and the Middle East : Imperial policy in the aftermath of war 1918-1922 / John Darwin. — London : Macmillan, 1981. — xvii,333p ; 23cm. — (Cambridge Commonwealth series)
Bibliography: p315-324. — Includes index
ISBN 0-333-27073-8 : £20.00 : CIP rev.
Primary classification 327.41056 B80-12738

327'.0956 — Middle East. Foreign relations with Soviet Union, *1945-1980*
Pryer, Melvyn. A view from the rimland : an appraisal of Soviet interests and involvement in the Gulf / by Melvyn Pryer. — Durham (Elvet Hill, Durham DH1 3TR) : Centre for Middle Eastern & Islamic Studies, University of Durham, c1981. — viii,98p : ill,maps ; 21cm. — (Occasional papers series / University of Durham, Centre for Middle Eastern and Islamic Studies, ISSN 0307-0654 ; no.8, 1981)
Bibliography: p88-98
Unpriced (pbk)
Primary classification 327.47056 B81-31321

327'.0956 — Middle East. Foreign relations with United States, *ca 1950-1978 — Conference proceedings*
The **Middle** East and the United States : perceptions and policies / edited by Hain Shaked, Itamar Rabinovich. — New Brunswick ; London : Transaction, c1980. — xx,419p : ill ; 24cm. — (Collected papers series / Shiloah Center for Middle Eastern and African Studies)
Conference papers. — Includes index
ISBN 0-87855-329-0 : £14.50
ISBN 0-87855-752-0 (pbk) : £4.25
Also classified at 327.73056 B81-09160

327'.0956 — Middle East. Foreign relations with United States. Diplomacy, *1939-1945*
Bryson, Thomas A.. Seeds of Mideast crisis : the United States diplomatic role in the Middle East during World War II / Thomas A. Bryson. — Jefferson, N.C. : McFarland (Folkestone) : Distributed by Bailey & Swinfen, 1981. — viii,216p ; 24cm
Bibliography: p202-206. — Includes index
ISBN 0-89950-019-6 : £12.75
Primary classification 327.73056 B81-37664

327'.0959 — South-east Asia. Foreign relations
Leifer, Michael. Conflict and regional order in South-east Asia / by Michael Leifer. — London : International Institute for Strategic Studies, 1980. — 39p ; 25cm. — (Adelphi papers, ISSN 0567-932x ; no.162)
Cover title
ISBN 0-86079-043-6 (pbk) : £1.50 B81-32340

327'.096 — Africa. Foreign relations with European Community countries
Europe & Africa : issues in post-colonial relations : texts of the Noel Buxton lectures, 1980 / edited by Margaret Cornell. — London : Overseas Development Institute, c1981. — vi,106p : ill ; 21cm
ISBN 0-85003-075-7 (pbk) : £2.50
Primary classification 327'.094 B81-26941

327.1 — Foreign relations. Effects of nuclear weapons, *to 1980*
Mandelbaum, Michael. The nuclear revolution : international politics before and after Hiroshima / Michael Mandelbaum. — Cambridge : Cambridge University Press, 1981. — xi,283p ; 24cm
Includes index
ISBN 0-521-23819-6 (cased) : £17.50
ISBN 0-521-28239-x (pbk) : £5.95 B81-32626

327.1 — War & peace
Beer, Francis A.. Peace against war : the ecology of international violence / Francis A. Beer. — Oxford : W.H. Freeman, c1981. — xxvi,447p : ill,2maps ; 24cm. — (A Series of books in international relations)
Bibliography: p361-421. — Includes index
ISBN 0-7167-1250-4 (cased) : £13.40
ISBN 0-7167-1251-2 (pbk) : £6.10 B81-36489

Foundations of peace and freedom : the ecology of a peaceful world / edited by Ted Dunn. — 2nd ed. — Swansea : Chistopher Davies, 1978. — 240p ; 22cm
Previous ed.: 1975. — Includes bibliographies and index
ISBN 0-7154-0443-1 (pbk) : £4.50 B81-32743

327.1'01 — Foreign relations. Theories, *1900-1979*
Thompson, Kenneth W.. Masters of international thought : major twentieth-century theorists and the world crisis / Kenneth W. Thompson. — Baton Rouge ; London : Louisiana State University Press, c1980. — xi,249p ; 24cm
Includes bibliographies
ISBN 0-8071-0580-5 (cased) : £12.00
ISBN 0-8071-0581-3 (pbk) : £4.20 B81-07027

327.1'01 — Foreign relations. Theories, *to 1980*
Mansbach, Richard W.. In search of theory : a new paradigm for global politics / Richard W. Mansbach and John A. Vasquez. — New York ; Guildford : Columbia University Press, 1981. — xvii,559p : ill ; 24cm
Includes index
ISBN 0-231-05060-7 : £14.45 B81-18923

327.1'01'9 — Foreign relations. Adaptative behaviour
Smith, Steven M.. Foreign policy adaptation. — Farnborough, Hants. : Gower, Sept.1981. — [160]p
ISBN 0-566-00370-8 : £10.00 : CIP entry B81-21562

327.1'12'09 — Balance of power, *1945-1980*
Millar, T. B.. The East-West strategic balance. — London : Allen & Unwin, Oct.1981. — [250]p
ISBN 0-04-355015-0 (cased) : £15.00 : CIP entry
ISBN 0-04-355017-7 (pbk) : £4.95 B81-25104

327.1'16 — Capitalist countries. Anti-communist strategy — *Proposals* — *Conference proceedings*
Towards a grand strategy for global freedom. — Richmond : Foreign Affairs Publishing, 1981. — xi,130p ; 23cm
Conference papers. — Editor: Geoffrey Stewart-Smith. — Includes index
ISBN 0-900380-28-4 : £5.00 B81-23537

327.1'16 — European Community countries. International security. Role of Norway
Norway's security and European foreign policy in the 1980s : report by the European Movement in Norway June 1980. — [Oslo] : [Universitetsforlaget] ; London : Global Book [distributor], c1981. — 80p ; 24cm
ISBN 82-00-05710-0 (pbk) : £7.55 B81-40148

327.1'16 — Indian Ocean. International security
Cottrell, Alvin J.. Sea power and strategy in the Indian Ocean / Alvin J. Cottrell and associates. — Beverly Hills ; London : Sage in cooperation with the Center for Strategic and International Studies, c1981. — 148p : ill ; 23cm
Bibliography: p139. — Includes index
ISBN 0-8039-1577-2 : Unpriced B81-29382

327.1'16 — National security *related to* **policies of government on energy resources**
Energy and security / edited by Gregory Treverton. — Farnborough, Hants. : Gower for The International Institute for Strategic Studies, c1980. — vii,165p : ill ; 23cm. — (The Adelphi library ; 1)
Includes index
ISBN 0-566-00343-0 : £8.50 : CIP rev.
Primary classification 333.79 B80-07256

327.1'16 — Persian Gulf countries. International security
Security in the Persian Gulf. — Farnborough, Hants. : Published for the International Institute for Strategic Studies by Gower
1: Domestic political factors / edited by Shahram Chubin. — c1981. — xiv,90p : 1map ; 22cm
Includes index
ISBN 0-566-00438-0 (pbk) : Unpriced B81-37499

327.1'16 — Western world. International security
Western security : what has changed? : what should be done? / Karl Kaiser ... [et al.]. — London : Royal Institute of International Affairs, c1981. — 48p ; 23cm
£1.00 (pbk) B81-17170

327.1'16'094 — Western Europe. International security
Crisis in Western security. — London : Croom Helm, Feb.1982. — [240]p
ISBN 0-7099-1214-5 : £12.95 : CIP entry B81-37557

327'.116'09536 — Persian Gulf countries. International security
Litwak, Robert. Sources of inter-state conflict. — Farnborough, Hants. : Gower, July 1981. — [118]p. — (Security in the Persian Gulf ; 2)
ISBN 0-566-00451-8 : £4.95 : CIP entry B81-14975

327.1'17 — International relations. War. Mathematical models
Bueno de Mesquita, Bruce. The war trap. — London : Yale University Press, Oct.1981. — [224]p
ISBN 0-300-02558-0 : £16.80 : CIP entry B81-31944

327.1'174927 — Arab countries. Economic integration
Ghantus, Elias T.. Arab industrial integration. — London : Croom Helm, Jan.1982. — [208]p
ISBN 0-7099-1117-3 : £12.95 : CIP entry B81-34316

327.1'2 — Espionage — *Amateurs' manuals* — *For children*
Andersen, Max. Spy school / Max Andersen ; illustrated by David Mostyn. — London : Beaver, 1981. — 95p : ill ; 18cm
ISBN 0-600-20386-7 (pbk) : £0.80 B81-34691

Healey, Tim. How to be a spy / by Tim Healey ; illustrated by Jeff Burn, George Fryer & Dave F. Smith. — London : Macdonald, 1981. — 64p : ill(some col.) ; 21cm. — (Whizz kids ; 22)
Includes index
ISBN 0-356-06382-8 (cased) : £2.95
ISBN 0-356-06342-9 (pbk) : £1.25 B81-38536

327.1'2'09 — Espionage, *to 1963* — *For children*
Garrett, Richard. A young person's file on spies / Richard Garrett ; illustrated by Bert Hill. — London : Granada, 1981. — 160p : ill ; 18cm. — (A Dragon book)
ISBN 0-583-30479-6 (pbk) : £0.95 B81-32915

327.1'2'09 — Espionage, *to 1980* — *For children*
Hindley, Geoffrey, *1935-*. Secret agents / Geoffrey Hindley ; line drawings by Paul Wright. — London : Angus & Robertson, 1980. — 124p : ill,ports ; 26cm
ISBN 0-207-95901-3 : £4.50 B81-00769

327.1'2'0922 — Soviet anti-American espionage. Boyce, Christopher John & Lee, Daulton — *Biographies*
Lindsey, Robert. The falcon and the snowman / Robert Lindsey. — Harmondsworth : Penguin, 1981, c1980. — 416p ; 19cm
Originally published: New York : Simon and Schuster, 1979 ; London : Cape, 1980
ISBN 0-14-005574-6 (pbk) : £1.75 B81-37495

327.1'2'0924 — British espionage. Reilly, Sidney — *Biographies*
Bruce Lockhart, Robin. Ace of spies / Robin Bruce Lockhart. — London : Macdonald Futura, 1981. — 252p ; 21cm
Originally published: London : Hodder and Stoughton, 1967
ISBN 0-354-04658-6 : £4.95 B81-10948

327.1'2'0924 — Soviet intelligence services. Sakharov, Vladimir — *Biographies*
Sakharov, Vladimir. High treason / by Vladimir Sakharov with Umberto Tosi. — London : Hale, 1981, c1980. — 318p ; 24cm
Originally published: New York : Putnam, 1980
ISBN 0-7091-8982-6 : £8.95 B81-22106

327.1'2'0941 — British intelligence services, *ca 1940-1980*
Lindsay, Kennedy. The British intelligence services in action : (includes Ambush at Tully-West) / Kennedy Lindsay. — Newtownabbey : Durod, 1980. — 288p,[24]p of plates : ill,ports ; 21cm
ISBN 0-86202-111-1 (cased) : Unpriced
ISBN 0-86202-112-x (pbk) : £5.50 B81-08435

327.1'2'0941 — British intelligence services: MI5, *to 1945*
West, Nigel. MI5 : British Security Service operations 1909-1945 / Nigel West. — London : Bodley Head, 1981. — 365p,[16]p of plates : ill,facsims,ports ; 23cm
Includes index
ISBN 0-370-30324-5 : £7.95 : CIP rev. B81-25762

327.1'2'0941 — British secret services. Infiltration by Soviet secret services, *ca 1940-1980*
Pincher, Chapman. Their trade is treachery / Chapman Pincher. — London : Sidgwick & Jackson, 1981. — xi,240p,[8]p of plates : ports ; 24cm
Includes index
ISBN 0-283-98781-2 : £7.95 B81-17857

327.1'2'0947 — Russia. *Vserossiĭskaīā chrezvychaĭnaīā komissiīā po borbe s kontrrevolīūtsieĭ i sabotazhem, to 1922*
Leggett, George. The Cheka : Lenin's political police : the All-Russian Extraordinary Commission for Combating Counter-revolution and Sabotage (December 1917 to February 1922) / by George Leggett. — Oxford : Clarendon, 1981. — xxxv,514p ; 23cm
Bibliography: p469-490. — Includes index
ISBN 0-19-822552-0 : £22.50 : CIP rev. B81-14833

327.1'2'0952 — Japanese secret services, *to 1980*
Deacon, Richard. A history of the Japanese secret service. — London : Muller, Feb.1982. — [336]p
ISBN 0-584-10383-2 : £12.50 : CIP entry B81-39248

327.1'2'095694 — Intelligence operations by Israeli secret services, *to 1979*
Steven, Stewart. The spymasters of Israel / Stewart Steven. — London : Hodder and Stoughton, 1981, c1980. — xxi,329p,[8]p of plates : ports ; 25cm
Bibliography: p319-321. - Includes index
ISBN 0-340-26248-6 : £8.95 B81-10522

327.1'2'0973 — American intelligence services, *1930-1979*
Rees, David, *1928-*. The crisis in United States intelligence / by David Rees. — London (12 Golden Sq., W1R 3AF) : Institute for the Study of Conflict, 1979. — 17p ; 30cm. — (Conflict studies, ISSN 0069-8792 ; no.114)
Cover title
£2.00 (pbk) B81-02335

327.1'6 — Foreign relations. Conflict
Mitchell, C. R.. The structure of international conflict / C.R. Mitchell. — London : Macmillan, 1981. — 355p : ill ; 23cm
Bibliography: p331-340. — Includes index
ISBN 0-333-27221-8 : £20.00 B81-40727

327.1'6'091724 — Developing countries. Conflict. International security aspects — *Conference proceedings*
International Institute for Strategic Studies. *Conference (22nd : 1980 : Stresa)*. Third-World conflict and international security / [papers presented at ... the Twenty-second Annual Conference of the IISS at Stresa, Italy, in September 1980]. — London : International Institute for Strategic Studies, 1981
Cover title
Pt.1. — 58p ; 25cm. — (Adelphi papers, ISSN 0567-932x ; no.166)
ISBN 0-86079-047-9 (pbk) : Unpriced B81-34886

International Institute for Strategic Studies. *Conference (22nd : 1980 : Stresa)*. Third-World conflict and international security / [papers presented at ... the Twenty-second Annual Conference of the IISS at Stresa, Italy, in September 1980]. — London : International Institute for Strategic Studies, 1981
Cover title
Pt.2. — 59p ; 25cm. — (Adelphi papers, ISSN 0567-932x ; no.167)
ISBN 0-86079-048-7 (pbk) : Unpriced B81-34887

327.1'7'094 — Europe. International cooperation
European co-operation today / edited by Kenneth J. Twitchett. — London : Europa, c1980. — xvi,285p ; 25cm
Bibliography: p260-272. — Includes index
ISBN 0-905118-57-x : £12.95 : CIP rev. B80-08623

327.1'72 — Pacifism
War : we say no. — London (6 Endsleigh St., W.C.1) : Peace Pledge Union, [1981?]. — [4]p : ill ; 30cm
£0.10 (unbound) B81-35266

327.1'72 — Peace. Crucé, Eméric. Nouveau Cynée. Copies
Van den Dungen, Peter. The hidden history of a peace 'classic' : Emeric Crucé's Le Nouveau Cynée / Peter van den Dungen. — London : Housmans, 1980. — 52p ; 22cm
Unpriced (pbk) B81-39768

327.1'72 — Peacemaking
Mitchell, C. R.. Peacemaking and the consultant's role / C.R. Mitchell. — Farnborough : Gower, c1981. — xvii,169p : ill ; 23cm
Bibliography: p163-167. — Includes index
ISBN 0-566-00389-9 : £12.50 B81-37911

327.1'72'01 — Peace — *Philosophical perspectives*
Francis, Chris. Love and peace / Chris Francis. — Bognor Regis : New Horizon, c1979. — 132,[16]p ; 22cm
ISBN 0-86116-171-8 : £3.25
Primary classification 128'.3 B81-21775

327.1'72'05 — Peace — *Soviet viewpoints — Serials*
Peace and disarmament. — 1980-. — Moscow : Progress Publishers ; [London] : Distributed by Central Books, 1980-. — v. ; 21cm
Issued by: Peace and Disarmament Research Council. — English edition of: Mir i razoruzhenie
£3.25 B81-32412

327.1'72'0601 — Women's International League for Peace and Freedom, *to 1965*
Bussey, Gertrude. [Women's International League for Peace and Freedom 1915-1965]. Pioneers for peace : Women's International League for Peace and Freedom 1915-1965 / Gertrude Bussey, Margaret Tims. — London (29 Great James St., WC1N 3ES) : WILPF British Section, c1980. — 255p ; 22cm
Originally published: London : Allen & Unwin, 1965. — Includes index
ISBN 0-9506968-0-3 (pbk) : £3.50 B81-04729

327.1'72'06041 — Great Britain. Pacifism. Organisations: Friends of Peace, *1793-1815*
Cookson, J.E.. The Friends of Peace. — Cambridge : Cambridge University Press, Jan.1982. — [328]p
ISBN 0-521-23928-1 : £24.00 : CIP entry B81-37551

327.1'72'09 — Pacifism, *to 1980*
Richards, Eleanor. Pacifism : a brief history / by Eleanor Richard. — London (6 Endsleigh St., W.C.1) : Peace Pledge Union, [1981?]. — [12]p : ill ; 30cm
Bibliography: p11
£0.30 (unbound) B81-35267

327.1'72'0924 — Northern Ireland. Peace. Peace movements. Patterson, Saidie — *Biographies*
Bleakley, David. Saidie Patterson : Irish peacemaker / David Bleakley. — Belfast : Blackstaff, c1980. — ix,118p : ill,facsims,ports ; 21cm
Includes index
£3.95 (pbk) B81-40770

327.1'72'0924 — Pacifism. Partridge, Frances — *Biographies*
Partridge, Frances. Memories / by Frances Partridge. — London : Gollancz, 1981. — 244p,[16]p of plates : 2ill,ports ; 23cm
Includes index
ISBN 0-575-02912-9 : £9.95 B81-05064

327.1'72'093 — Ancient world. Peace
Melko, Matthew. Peace in the ancient world / Matthew Melko and Richard D. Weigel with the collaboration of Sally L.D. Katary and Michael McKenny ; maps by Richard Ward. — Jefferson, N.C. : McFarland ; Folkestone : Distributed by Bailey Bros. & Swinfen, 1981. — v,223p : ill,maps ; 24cm
Bibliography: p198-203. — Includes index
ISBN 0-89950-020-x : £15.15 B81-38764

327.1'72'0941 — Great Britain. Peace movements: League of Nations Union, *to 1945*
Birn, Donald S.. The League of Nations Union 1918-1945 / by Donald S. Birn. — Oxford : Clarendon Press, 1981. — 269p ; 22cm
Bibliography: p256-263. — Includes index
ISBN 0-19-822650-0 : £18.50 : CIP rev. B81-06028

327.1'74 — Arms control
Arms control and military force / edited by Christoph Bertram. — Farnborough, Hants. : Published for the International Institute for Strategic Studies by Gower, c1980. — vii,258p ; 23cm. — (The Adelphi library ; 3)
Includes index
ISBN 0-566-00344-9 : £9.50 : CIP rev. B80-07244

327.1'74 — Arms control. International cooperation
The future of arms control. — London : International Institute for Strategic Studies, 1981. — (Adelphi papers, ISSN 0567-032x ; no.165)
Pt.4: The impact of weapons test restrictions / by Farooq Hussain. — 55p : ill ; 25cm
Cover title. — Text on inside covers
ISBN 0-86079-039-8 (pbk) : Unpriced B81-21272

327.1'74 — Disarmament
Ramphal, Shridath S.. Rationality without reason / by Shridath S. Ramphal. — London (Suite 54, 3 Whitehall Court, SW1A 2EF) : World Goodwill, 1981. — 7p ; 30cm. — (World Goodwill occasional paper ; Jan./Feb./Mar.1981)
Unpriced (pbk) B81-19402

327.1'74 — Nuclear disarmament. Political aspects
Protest and survive / edited by E.P. Thompson and Dan Smith. — Harmondsworth : Penguin, 1980. — 264p : 1map ; 18cm. — (A Penguin special)
Bibliography: p257-263
ISBN 0-14-052341-3 (pbk) : £1.50 B81-01534

327.1'74 — Nuclear weapons. Arms control
Joyce, James Avery. The war machine : the case against the arms race / James Avery Joyce. — London : Quartet, 1980. — 210p : ill,maps ; 25cm
Bibliography: p201-204. — Includes index
ISBN 0-7043-2254-4 : £6.95 B81-00029

Joyce, James Avery. The war machine / James Avery Joyce. — Updated. — London : Hamlyn Paperbacks, 1981, c1980. — 244p : ill,maps ; 18cm
Previous ed.: London : Quartet, 1980. — Bibliography: p235-237. — Includes index
ISBN 0-600-20435-9 (pbk) : £1.50 B81-29239

327.1'74 — Nuclear weapons. Disarmament — *Campaign for Nuclear Disarmament viewpoints*
Allaun, Frank. Questions and answers about nuclear weapons / by Frank Allaun. — London (11 Goodwin St., N4 3HQ) : Campaign for Nuclear Disarmament, [1981]. — 32p : ill ; 21cm
Cover title
£0.40 (pbk) B81-26648

327.1'74 — Peace. Implications of proliferation of nuclear weapons
Barnaby, Frank. Prospects for peace / by Frank Barnaby. — Oxford : Pergamon, 1980. — v,88p ; 22cm. — (Pergamon international library)
ISBN 0-08-027399-8 (cased) : Unpriced
ISBN 0-08-027398-x (pbk) : £4.75 B81-06970

327.1'74'07 — Educational institutions. Curriculum subjects: Disarmament. Teaching — *Proposals*
Approaching disarmament education / edited by Magnus Haavelsrud. — Guildford : Westbury House in association with the Peace Education Commission of the International Peace Research Association, c1981. — viii,280p : ill ; 22cm
ISBN 0-86103-043-5 : Unpriced : CIP rev. B81-12392

327.1'74'09 — Disarmament, *ca 1945-1975*
Myrdal, Alva. The game of disarmament : how the United States and Russia run the arms race / Alva Myrdal. — Nottingham : Spokesman, 1980, c1978. — xxx,397p ; 24cm
Originally published: New York : Pantheon, 1976. — Includes index
ISBN 0-85124-306-1 (pbk) : £4.25 B81-03030

327.1'74'094 — Europe. Arms control
Freedman, Lawrence. Arms control in Europe / Lawrence Freedman. — London : Royal Institute of International Affairs, c1981. — viii,59p ; 30cm. — (Chatham House papers, ISSN 0143-5795 ; no.11)
ISBN 0-905031-23-7 (pbk) : £5.00 B81-31319

327.1'74'094 — Europe. Nuclear disarmament
Eleventh hour for Europe : papers / by Ken Coates ... [et al.] ; edited by Ken Coates. — Nottingham : Spokesman, 1981. — 108p ; 22cm
ISBN 0-85124-308-8 (cased) : Unpriced
ISBN 0-85124-309-6 (pbk) : £2.75 B81-19938

327.1'74'0941 — Great Britain. Nuclear disarmament — *Ecology Party viewpoints*
Ecology Party. Nuclear disarmament and beyond / [Ecology Party]. — London (36 Clapham Rd., SW9 0JQ) : The Party, [1981]. — [8]p ; 21cm. — (Ecology Party defence policy paper ; 1)
Cover title
£0.20 (pbk) B81-26866

327.1'74'0941 — Great Britain. Nuclear disarmament movements, *to 1965*
Taylor, Richard, *1945-*. The protest makers : the British nuclear disarmament movement of 1958-1965, twenty years on / by Richard Taylor and Colin Pritchard. — Oxford : Pergamon, 1980. — ix,190p 8p of plates : ill ; 26cm
Bibliography: p182-186. — Includes index
ISBN 0-08-025211-7 : £10.00 : CIP rev. B80-22975

327.1'74'0942659 — Cambridgeshire. Cambridge. Nuclear disarmament movements — *Serials*
[Nucleus *(Cambridge)*]. Nucleus : anti-nuclear activity in Cambridge. — No.1 (Jan./Feb. '81)-. — [Cambridge] ([c/o Elizabeth Cary, 102 Hertford St., Cambridge]) : [Cambridge A.N.C.], 1981-. — v. : ill ; 28cm
Monthly
ISSN 0261-0604 = Nucleus (Cambridge) : £0.20 per issue B81-16232

327.1'74'0947 — Soviet Union. Strategic nuclear weapons. Arms control. Policies of government, *1968-1980*
Payne, Samuel B.. The Soviet Union and SALT / Samuel B. Payne, Jr.. — Cambridge, Mass. ; London : MIT, c1980. — 155p : ill ; 24cm
Bibliography: p139/152. — Includes index
ISBN 0-262-16077-3 : £15.50 B81-09652

327.1'74'0956 — Middle East. Arms control
Jabber, Paul. Not by war alone : security and arms control in the Middle East : Paul Jabber. — Berkeley ; London : University of California Press, c1981. — xii,212p ; 24cm
Bibliography: p193-205. — Includes index
ISBN 0-520-04050-3 : £11.00 B81-27510

327.2 — Foreign relations. Diplomacy
Alexandroff, Alan S.. The logic of diplomacy / Alan S. Alexandroff ; foreword by Richard N. Rosecrance. — Beverly Hills ; London : Sage, c1981. — 199p ; 22cm. — (Sage library of social research ; v.120)
Bibliography: p191—198
ISBN 0-8039-1572-1 (cased) : Unpriced
ISBN 0-8039-1573-x (pbk) : £5.50 B81-27713

327.2'09'047 — Foreign relations. Diplomacy, *1968-1975 — Readings from contemporary sources*
The End of the post-war era : documents on great-power relations 1968-1975 / edited by James Mayall and Cornelia Navari. — Cambridge : Cambridge University Press, 1980. — xix,642p ; 24cm. — (International studies)
ISBN 0-521-22698-8 : £25.00 B81-01936

327.2'092'4 — Foreign relations. Diplomacy — *Personal observations*
Jackson, *Sir* Geoffrey. Concorde diplomacy : the ambassador's role in the world today / by Sir Geoffrey Jackson. — London : Hamilton, 1981. — 254p ; 23cm
Bibliography: p243-245. — Includes index
ISBN 0-241-10524-2 : £9.95 B81-12287

327.2′092′4 — German diplomatic service. Herwarth, Johnnie von, *1930-1945 — Biographies*

Herwarth, Johnnie von. Against two evils : memoirs of a diplomat-soldier during the Third Reich / Johnnie von Herwarth with S. Frederick Starr. — London : Collins, 1981. — 318p ; 24cm
Includes index
ISBN 0-00-216279-2 : £10.95 B81-24523

327.3/9 — FOREIGN RELATIONS OF SPECIFIC COUNTRIES

327.41 — Great Britain. Foreign relations, *1649-1815*

Jones, J. R. (James Rees). Britain and the world 1649-1815 / J.R. Jones. — [London] : Fontana, 1980. — 349p : maps ; 18cm. — (Fontana history of England)
Bibliography: p331-336. — Includes index
ISBN 0-00-633758-9 (pbk) : £2.95 B81-02594

Jones, J. R. (James Rees). Britain and the world 1649-1815 / J.R. Jones. — Brighton : Harvester in association with Fontana, 1980. — 349p : maps ; 23cm
Bibliography: p331-336. — Includes index
ISBN 0-85527-225-2 : £16.50 : CIP rev.
B80-04094

327.41 — Great Britain. Foreign relations, *1906-1980*

Retreat from power : studies in Britain′s foreign policy of the twentieth century / edited by David Dilks. — London : Macmillan, 1981
Vol.1: 1906-1939. — vii,213p ; 22cm
Includes index
ISBN 0-333-29909-4 (cased) : £10.00 : CIP rev.
B80-38890

Retreat from power : studies in Britain′s foreign policy of the twentieth century / edited by David Dilks. — London : Macmillan, 1981
Vol.2: After 1939. — vii,189p ; 22cm
Includes index
ISBN 0-333-29319-3 (cased) : £10.00 : CIP rev.
ISBN 0-333-29320-7 (pbk) : £4.25 B80-35695

327.41 — Great Britain. Foreign relations. Policies of government, *1865-1980*

Kennedy, Paul M.. The realities behind diplomacy : background influences on British external policy, 1865-1980 / Paul Kennedy. — [London] : Fontana, 1981. — 416p ; 18cm
Bibliography: p401-403. — Includes index
ISBN 0-00-634681-2 (pbk) : £3.50 B81-15133

Kennedy, Paul M.. The realities behind diplomacy : background influences on British external policy, 1865-1980 / Paul Kennedy. — London : Allen & Unwin, 1981. — 416p ; 23cm
Bibliography: p401-403. - Includes index
ISBN 0-04-902005-6 : £12.50 B81-19860

327.41 — Great Britain. Foreign relations. Policies of government. Implications of Soviet invasion of Afghanistan — *Inquiry reports*

Great Britain. *Parliament. House of Commons. Foreign Affairs Committee.* Fifth report from the Foreign Affairs Committee, session 1979-80 : Afghanistan, the Soviet invasion and its consequences for British policy : together with two appendices, part of the proceedings of the Committee ... and part of the minutes of evidence ... — London : H.M.S.O., [1980]. — lvi,267p : 2ill ; 25cm. — ([HC] ; 745) ([HC] ; 362 v(part), viii, ix(part) to xii, xiv to xvii and xix)
ISBN 0-10-027459-5 (pbk) : £9.40 B81-20360

327.41′0092′4 — Great Britain. Foreign relations. Policies of government. Role of Morel, E. D., *1893-1924*

Cline, Catherine Ann. E.D. Morel 1873-1924 : the strategies of protest / Catherine Ann Cline. — Belfast : Blackstaff, c1980. — 180p ; 22cm
Bibliography: p158-164. - Includes index
ISBN 0-85640-213-3 : £9.95 : CIP rev.
B80-22976

327.410417 — Great Britain. Foreign relations with Ireland *(Republic)*

O′Brien, Conor Cruise. Neighbours : four lectures / delivered by Conor Cruise O′Brien in memory of Christopher Ewart-Biggs ; introduction by Jane Ewart-Biggs ; edited by Thomas Pakenham. — London : Faber, 1980. — 96p ; 20cm. — (The Ewart-Biggs memorial lectures ; 1978-1979)
ISBN 0-571-11645-0 (pbk) : £2.95 : CIP rev.
Also classified at 327.417041 B80-25233

327.41043 — Great Britain. Foreign relations with Germany, *1860-1914*

Kennedy, Paul M.. The rise of the Anglo-German antagonism 1860-1914 / Paul M. Kennedy. — London : Allen & Unwin, 1980. — xiv,604p ; 24cm
Bibliography: p550-586. — Includes index
ISBN 0-04-940060-6 : £27.50 : CIP rev.
Also classified at 327.43041 B80-18183

327.41044 — Great Britain. Foreign relations with France, *1200-1500*

Chaplais, Pierre. Essays in medieval diplomacy and administration. — London (35 Gloucester Ave., NW1 7AX) : Hambledon Press, May 1981. — [428]p
ISBN 0-9506882-2-3 : £30.00 : CIP entry
Also classified at 327.44041 B81-07466

327.41′047 — Great Britain. Foreign relations with Soviet Union, *1941-1947*

Rothwell, Victor. Britain and the cold war, 1941-1947. — London : Cape, Jan.1982. — [550]p
ISBN 0-224-01478-1 : £16.00 : CIP entry
Also classified at 327.47′041 B81-33977

327.41047 — Soviet anti-British espionage, *1930-1965 — Personal observations*

Mann, Wilfred B.. Was there a fifth man?. — Oxford : Pergamon, Dec.1981. — [128]p
ISBN 0-08-027445-5 : £12.00 : CIP entry
B81-32601

327.410485 — Great Britain. Foreign relations with Sweden, *1758-1773*

Roberts, Michael, *1908-*. British diplomacy and Swedish politics, 1758-1773 / Michael Roberts. — London : Macmillan, 1980. — xxv,528p ; 24cm
Bibliography: p497-512. — Includes index
ISBN 0-333-30034-3 : £20.00
Also classified at 327.485041 B81-22377

327.410492 — Great Britain. Foreign relations with Netherlands, *1940-1948*

Eisen, Janet. Anglo-Dutch relations and European unity 1940-1978 / Janet Eisen. — [Hull] : [University of Hull], 1980. — 60p ; 22cm. — (Occasional papers in modern Dutch studies, ISSN 0144-3070 ; no.1) (University of Hull publications)
Bibliography: p57-60
ISBN 0-85958-429-1 (pbk) : £3.50
Also classified at 327.492041 B81-26813

327.4105 — Great Britain. Foreign relations with Asia, *1795-1800*

Ingram, Edward. Commitment to Empire. — Oxford : Clarendon, Aug.1981. — [400]p
ISBN 0-19-822662-4 : £22.50 : CIP entry
Also classified at 327′.095 B81-15801

327.4105 — Great Britain. Foreign relations with Far East, *1819-1980*

Lowe, Peter. Britain in the far East : a survey from 1819 to the present / Peter Lowe. — London : Longman, 1981. — 264p : 6maps ; 23cm
Bibliography: p250-251. — Includes index
ISBN 0-582-48730-7 (cased) : Unpriced : CIP rev.
ISBN 0-582-48731-5 (pbk) : £5.75
Also classified at 327′.095 B80-26348

327.41056 — Great Britain. Foreign relations with Middle East. Policies of British government, *1914-1971*

Monroe, Elizabeth. Britain′s moment in the Middle East 1914-1971 / Elizabeth Monroe. — New and rev. ed. / with a foreword by Peter Mansfield. — London : Chatto & Windus, 1981. — 254p : maps ; 23cm
Previous ed.: 1963. — Bibliography: p227-242. — Includes index
ISBN 0-7011-2555-1 : £9.50 : CIP rev.
Also classified at 327′.0956 B81-03163

327.41056 — Great Britain. Foreign relations with Middle East. Policies of government, *1918-1922*

Darwin, John. Britain, Egypt and the Middle East : Imperial policy in the aftermath of war 1918-1922 / John Darwin. — London : Macmillan, 1981. — xvii,333p ; 23cm. — (Cambridge Commonwealth series)
Bibliography: p315-324. — Includes index
ISBN 0-333-27073-8 : £20.00 : CIP rev.
Also classified at 327′.0956 B80-12738

327.4105694 — Great Britain. Foreign relations with Israel, *1936-1980*

Wilson, Harold, *1916-*. The chariot of Israel : Britain, America and the State of Israel / Harold Wilson. — London : Weidenfeld and Nicolson : Joseph, c1981. — 406p,[8]p of plates : ill,maps,ports ; 24cm
Includes index
ISBN 0-7181-2002-7 : £14.95
Also classified at 327.5694041 B81-21425

327.41073 — Great Britain. *Embassy (U.S.).* **Dispatches,** *1941-1945 — Collections*

Washington despatches 1941-1945 : weekly political reports from the British Embassy / edited by H.G. Nicholas ; with an introduction by Isaiah Berlin. — London : Weidenfeld and Nicolson, c1981. — xviii,700p ; 24cm
Includes indexl
ISBN 0-297-77920-6 : £20.00 B81-36524

327.41073 — Great Britain. Foreign relations with United States, *1936-1939*

MacDonald, C. A.. The United States, Britain and appeasement, 1936-1939 / C.A. Macdonald. — London : Macmillan in association with St Antony′s College, Oxford, 1981. — xi,220p ; 23cm. — (St Antony′s/Macmillan series)
Bibliography: p205-214. — Includes index
ISBN 0-333-26169-0 : £15.00 : CIP rev.
Primary classification 327.73041 B80-10955

327.41073 — Great Britain. Foreign relations with United States, *1937-1941*

Reynolds, David. The creation of the Anglo-American alliance 1937-1941. — London : Europa, Oct.1981. — [416]p
ISBN 0-905118-68-5 : £20.00 : CIP entry
Also classified at 327.73041 B81-27466

327.41073 — Great Britain. Foreign relations with United States, *1944-1947*

Anderson, Terry H.. The United States, Great Britain and the Cold War 1944-1947 / Terry H. Anderson. — Columbia ; London : University of Missouri Press, 1981. — xi,256p ; 22cm
Includes index
ISBN 0-8262-0328-0 : £12.60
Also classified at 327.73041 B81-38212

327.411 — Scotland. Foreign relations — *Scottish nationalist viewpoints — Early works*

Lamont, Archie. Scottish neutrality : disarmament means prosperity / by Archie Lamont. — New ed. — Penicuik (Jess Cottage, Carlops, Penicuik, Midlothian, EH26 9NF) : Scots Secretariat, [1980]. — 46p : ill,ports ; 21cm. — (Scots Secretariat publications, ISSN 0141-4216 ; no.38)
Previous ed.: 1952
£0.50 (unbound) B81-32146

327.4110415 — Scotland. Foreign relations with Ireland, *ca 1630-1645*

Stevenson, David, *1942-*. Scottish covenanters and Irish confederates : Scottish-Irish relations in the mid-seventeenth century / David Stevenson. — Belfast : Ulster Historical Foundation, 1981. — xii,364p : ill,maps,ports ; 23cm. — (The U.H.F. historical series)
Bibliography: p340-348. — Includes index
ISBN 0-901905-24-0 : £15.00
Also classified at 327.4150411 B81-29723

327.4150411 — Ireland. Foreign relations with Scotland, *ca 1630-1645*

Stevenson, David, *1942-*. Scottish covenanters and Irish confederates : Scottish-Irish relations in the mid-seventeenth century / David Stevenson. — Belfast : Ulster Historical Foundation, 1981. — xii,364p : ill,maps,ports ; 23cm. — (The U.H.F. historical series)
Bibliography: p340-348. — Includes index
ISBN 0-901905-24-0 : £15.00
Primary classification 327.4110415 B81-29723

327.417041 — Ireland *(Republic).* **Foreign relations with Great Britain**

O'Brien, Conor Cruise. Neighbours : four lectures / delivered by Conor Cruise O'Brien in memory of Christopher Ewart-Biggs ; introduction by Jane Ewart-Biggs ; edited by Thomas Pakenham. — London : Faber, 1980. — 96p ; 20cm. — (The Ewart-Biggs memorial lectures ; 1978-1979)
ISBN 0-571-11645-0 (pbk) : £2.95 : CIP rev.
Primary classification 327.410417 B80-25233

327.42046 — England. Foreign relations with Spain, *1558-1603*

Wernham, R. B.. The making of Elizabethan foreign policy, 1558-1603 / R.B. Wernham. — Berkeley ; London : University of California Press, c1980. — vii,109p : 3maps ; 22cm. — (Una's lectures ; 3)
Bibliography: p97-99. — Includes index
ISBN 0-520-03966-1 (cased) : £9.25
ISBN 0-520-03974-2 (pbk) : Unpriced
Also classified at 327.46042 B81-11826

327.43 — Germany. Foreign relations. Policies of government, *1937-1939*

Weinberg, Gerhard L.. The foreign policy of Hitler's Germany : starting World War II, 1937-1939 / Gerhard L. Weinberg. — Chicago ; London : University of Chicago Press, 1980. — xii,728p : maps ; 24cm
Maps on lining papers. — Bibliography: p678-708. — Includes index
ISBN 0-226-88511-9 : £26.40 B81-14740

327.43041 — Germany. Foreign relations with Great Britain, *1860-1914*

Kennedy, Paul M.. The rise of the Anglo-German antagonism 1860-1914 / Paul M. Kennedy. — London : Allen & Unwin, 1980. — xiv,604p ; 24cm
Bibliography: p550-586. — Includes index
ISBN 0-04-940060-6 : £27.50 : CIP rev.
Primary classification 327.41043 B80-18183

327.43'05 — Germany. Foreign relations with Far East, *1933-1939*

Fox, John P.. Germany and the Far Eastern crisis 1931-1938. — Oxford : Clarendon Press, Jan.1982. — [400]p
ISBN 0-19-822573-3 : £22.50 : CIP entry
Also classified at 327'.095 B81-34389

327.44041 — France. Foreign relations with Great Britain, *1200-1500*

Chaplais, Pierre. Essays in medieval diplomacy and administration. — London (35 Gloucester Ave., NW1 7AX) : Hambledon Press, May 1981. — [428]p
ISBN 0-9506882-2-3 : £30.00 : CIP entry
Primary classification 327.41044 B81-07466

327.44073 — Foreign relations. Negotiations between France & United States, *1798*

Stinchcombe, William. The XYZ affair / William Stinchcombe. — Westport, Conn. ; London : Greenwood Press, 1980. — 167p : ports ; 22cm. — (Contributions in American history ; no.89)
Bibliography: p141-157. — Includes index
ISBN 0-313-22234-7 : £15.50 B81-23468

327.46042 — Spain. Foreign relations with England, *1558-1603*

Wernham, R. B.. The making of Elizabethan foreign policy, 1558-1603 / R.B. Wernham. — Berkeley ; London : University of California Press, c1980. — vii,109p : 3maps ; 22cm. — (Una's lectures ; 3)
Bibliography: p97-99. — Includes index
ISBN 0-520-03966-1 (cased) : £9.25
ISBN 0-520-03974-2 (pbk) : Unpriced
Primary classification 327.42046 B81-11826

327.47 — Soviet Union. Foreign relations, *1917-1980*

Lebedev, N. I.. Great October and today's world. — Oxford : Pergamon, Feb.1982. — [350]p
Translation of: Velikiĭ oktīabr'i perestroĭka mezhdunarodnykh otnosheniĭ
ISBN 0-08-023607-3 : £20.00 : CIP entry B81-40259

327.47 — Soviet Union. Foreign relations, *1980-1990 — Forecasts — Conference proceedings*

Prospects of Soviet power in the 1980s / edited by Christoph Bertram. — London : Macmillan in association with the International Institute for Strategic Studies, 1980. — 126p ; 26cm
Conference papers. — Originally published: in 2 vols London : International Institute for Strategic Studies, 1979. — Includes index
ISBN 0-333-28258-2 : £15.00 : CIP rev. B80-09139

327.47 — Soviet Union. Foreign relations — *Forecasts*

Walker, *Sir* **Walter.** The next domino? / Sir Walter Walker. — London : Covenant, 1980. — xvi,371p,[12]p of plates : ill,maps,plans,ports ; 25cm
Includes index
ISBN 0-85205-005-4 (cased) : £9.75
ISBN 0-85205-006-2 (pbk) : £7.50 B81-04516

327.47 — Soviet Union. Foreign relations. Policies of government, *1917-1980*

The Soviet Union in world politics / edited by Kurt London. — Boulder : Westview ; London : Croom Helm, 1980. — xiii,380p ; 24cm
Includes index
ISBN 0-7099-0415-0 : £14.95 B81-07105

327.47 — Soviet Union. Foreign relations. Policies of government, *1930-1979 — Readings from contemporary sources*

They mean what they say : a compilation of Soviet statements on ideology, foreign policy and the use of military force / [compiled by] Ian Greig. — London (27 Whitehall, SW1A 2BX) : Foreign Affairs Research Institute, [1981]. — 118p ; 25cm
Translation from the Russian. — Includes index
ISBN 0-900380-27-6 (pbk) : £5.00 B81-34972

327.47 — Soviet Union. Foreign relations. Policies of government. Influence of social conditions in Soviet Union

The Domestic context of Soviet foreign policy / edited by Seweryn Bialer. — Boulder : Westview ; London : Croom Helm, 1981. — xviii,441p : ill,1map ; 24cm. — (Studies of the Research Institute on International Change, Columbia University)
ISBN 0-7099-0623-4 : £14.95 B81-17873

327.47 — Soviet Union. Foreign relations with Eastern Europe, *1945-*

Soviet-East European dilemmas : coercion, competition and consent / edited by Karen Dawisha and Philip Hanson. — London : Heinemann for the Royal Institute of International Affairs, 1981. — xiii,226p ; 23cm
Includes index
ISBN 0-435-83220-4 (cased) : £14.95 : CIP rev.
ISBN 0-435-83221-2 (pbk) : £5.95
Primary classification 303.4'82'0947 B81-03824

327.470171'3 — Soviet Union. Détente with Western bloc countries, *1971-1980 — Soviet viewpoints*

Brezhnev, L. I.. Peace, detente, cooperation / Leonid I. Brezhnev. — New York ; London : Consultants Bureau, c1981. — xiii,197p ; 22cm
Translations from the Russian. — Includes index
ISBN 0-306-10971-9 : Unpriced
Also classified at 327'.09171'3 B81-18235

327.470171'3 — Soviet Union. Foreign relations with Western bloc countries

Nixon, Richard. The real war / Richard Nixon. — London : Sidgwick & Jackson, 1980 (1981 [printing]). — xvi,366p : 2maps ; 18cm
Originally published: New York : Warner Books, 1980. — Includes index
ISBN 0-283-98776-6 (pbk) : £1.75
Primary classification 327'.09171'3 B81-29539

327.470172'4 — Soviet Union. Foreign relations with developing countries, *1954-1980*

The Soviet Union in the third world : successes and failures / edited by Robert H. Donaldson. — Boulder : Westview ; London : Croom Helm, 1981. — xiv,458p ; 24cm
ISBN 0-7099-0801-6 : £14.95
Also classified at 327'.09172'4 B81-33444

327.47041 — Soviet anti-British espionage, *1930-1965*

Sutherland, Douglas, *1919-*. The fourth man : the story of Blunt, Philby, Burgess and Maclean / Douglas Sutherland. — London : Arrow, 1980. — 174p ; 18cm
Bibliography: p7. — Includes index
ISBN 0-09-923420-3 (pbk) : £1.25 B81-07523

327.47'041 — Soviet Union. Foreign relations with Great Britain, *1941-1947*

Rothwell, Victor. Britain and the cold war, 1941-1947. — London : Cape, Jan.1982. — [550]p
ISBN 0-224-01478-1 : £16.00 : CIP entry
Primary classification 327.41'047 B81-33977

327.47047'4 — Russia. Foreign relations with Baltic States, *1855-1914*

Russification in the Baltic Provinces and Finland, 1855-1914 / editor Edward C. Thaden ; coauthors Michael H. Haltzel ... [et al.]. — Princeton ; Guildford : Princeton University Press, c1981. — xiii,497p : maps ; 25cm
Bibliography: p471-482. — Includes index
ISBN 0-691-05314-6 (cased) : £22.30
ISBN 0-691-10103-5 (pbk) : Unpriced
Also classified at 327.4704897 ; 327.47'4047 ; 327.4897047 B81-25263

327.4704897 — Russia. Foreign relations with Finland, *1855-1914*

Russification in the Baltic Provinces and Finland, 1855-1914 / editor Edward C. Thaden ; coauthors Michael H. Haltzel ... [et al.]. — Princeton ; Guildford : Princeton University Press, c1981. — xiii,497p : maps ; 25cm
Bibliography: p471-482. — Includes index
ISBN 0-691-05314-6 (cased) : £22.30
ISBN 0-691-10103-5 (pbk) : Unpriced
Primary classification 327.47047'4 B81-25263

327.470495 — Russia. Foreign relations with Byzantine Empire, *1300-1400*

Meyendorff, John. Byzantium and the rise of Russia : a study of Byzantino-Russian relations in the fourteenth century / John Meyendorff. — Cambridge : Cambridge University Press, 1981. — xix,326p : 1map ; 24cm
Bibliography: pix-xvi. — Includes index
ISBN 0-521-23183-3 : £30.00
Also classified at 327.495047 B81-02862

327.470496 — Russia. Foreign relations with Balkan countries, *1908-1914*

Rossos, Andrew. Russia and the Balkans : inter-Balkan rivalries and Russian foreign policy, 1908-1914 / Andrew Rossos. — Toronto ; London : University of Toronto Press, c1981. — xiii,313p : maps ; 24cm
Bibliography: p279-297. — Includes index
ISBN 0-8020-5516-8 : £21.00
Also classified at 327'.09496 B81-34332

327.47051 — Soviet Union. Foreign relations with China & United States

The China factor. — London : Croom Helm, Nov.1981. — [208]p
ISBN 0-7099-2308-2 : £11.95 : CIP entry
Primary classification 327.51047 B81-30538

327.47051 — Soviet Union. Foreign relations with China, *1945-1970*

Wich, Richard. Sino-Soviet crisis politics : a study of political change and communication / Richard Wich. — [Cambridge, Mass.] : Council on East Asian Studies, Harvard University ; Cambridge, Mass. ; London : Distributed by Harvard University Press, 1980. — viii,313p ; 24cm. — (Harvard East Asian monographs ; 96)
Bibliography: 307-308. - Includes index
ISBN 0-674-80935-1 : £9.00
Also classified at 327.51047 B81-05653

327.47052 — Soviet Union. Foreign relations with Japan, *1945-1980*

Jain, R. K. (Rajendra Kumar). The USSR and Japan 1945-1980 / by Rajendra Kumar Jain. — Brighton : Harvester, 1981. — xx,397p ; 23cm
Bibliography: p380-390. — Includes index
ISBN 0-7108-0395-8 : £20.00 : CIP rev.
Also classified at 327.52047 B81-23841

327.47056 — Soviet Union. Foreign relations with Middle East, *1945-1980*

Pryer, Melvyn. A view from the rimland : an appraisal of Soviet interests and involvement in the Gulf / by Melvyn Pryer. — Durham (Elvet Hill, Durham DH1 3TR) : Centre for Middle Eastern & Islamic Studies, University of Durham, c1981. — viii,98p : ill,maps ; 21cm. — (Occasional papers series / University of Durham, Centre for Middle Eastern and Islamic Studies, ISSN 0307-0654 ; no.8, 1981)
Bibliography: p88-98
Unpriced (pbk)
Also classified at 327'.0956 B81-31321

327.47073 — Soviet Union. Foreign relations. Perception by American diplomats, *1933-1947*

De Santis, Hugh. The diplomacy of silence : the American Foreign Service, the Soviet Union, and the Cold War, 1933-1947 / Hugh De Santis. — Chicago ; London : University of Chicago Press, 1980. — x,270p ; 24cm
Bibliography: p246-261. — Includes index
ISBN 0-226-14337-6 : £13.80 B81-21092

327.47073 — Soviet Union. Foreign relations with United States, *1945-1950*

Paterson, Thomas G.. On every front : the making of the Cold War / Thomas G Paterson. — New York ; London : Norton, c1979. — xii,210p ; 20cm. — (The Norton essays in American history)
Bibliography: p178-201. — Includes index
ISBN 0-393-95014-x (pbk) : £2.50
Primary classification 327.73047 B81-05290

327.47073 — Soviet Union. Foreign relations with United States, *1945-1980*

LaFeber, Walter. America, Russia and the cold war 1945-1980 / Walter Lafeber. — 4th ed. — New York ; Chichester : Wiley, c1980. — xiii,334p : maps ; 22cm. — (America in crisis, ISSN 0195-4881)
Previous ed.: published as America, Russia and the cold war 1945-1975. 1976. — Bibliography: p306-315. — Includes index
ISBN 0-471-06226-x (pbk) : Unpriced
Also classified at 327.73047 B81-11053

327.47073 — Soviet Union. Foreign relations with United States, *1980*

Steele, Jonathan. A critical phase-East-West relations in the 1980s / an address by Jonathan Steele at the seminar on the subject of East-West relations, organised by Quaker Peace & Service in October 1980. — London : Quaker Peace & Service, [1981]. — [4]p ; 30cm
Unpriced (unbound)
Also classified at 327.73047 B81-09515

327.47073 — Soviet Union. Foreign relations with United States, *1980-1989*

Caldwell, Lawrence T.. Soviet-American relations in the 1980s : superpower politics and East-West trade / Lawrence T. Caldwell, William Diebold, Jr. ; introduction by John C. Campbell. — New York ; London : McGraw Hill, c1981. — xvi,314p : ill ; 24cm. — (1980s Project studies)
Bibliography: p217-230. - Includes index
ISBN 0-07-009615-5 (cased) : £6.55
ISBN 0-07-009616-3 (pbk) : £4.75
Also classified at 327.73047 B81-05085

327.47'4047 — Baltic States. Foreign relations with Russia, *1855-1914*

Russification in the Baltic Provinces and Finland, 1855-1914 / editor Edward C. Thaden ; coauthors Michael H. Haltzel ... [et al.]. — Princeton ; Guildford : Princeton University Press, c1981. — xiii,497p : maps ; 25cm
Bibliography: p471-482. — Includes index
ISBN 0-691-05314-6 (cased) : £22.30
ISBN 0-691-10103-5 (pbk) : Unpriced
Primary classification 327.47047'4 B81-25263

327.485041 — Sweden. Foreign relations with Great Britain, *1758-1773*

Roberts, Michael, *1908-*. British diplomacy and Swedish politics, 1758-1773 / Michael Roberts. — London : Macmillan, 1980. — xxv,528p ; 24cm
Bibliography: p497-512. — Includes index
ISBN 0-333-30034-3 : £20.00
Primary classification 327.410485 B81-22377

327.4897047 — Finland. Foreign relations with Russia, *1855-1914*

Russification in the Baltic Provinces and Finland, 1855-1914 / editor Edward C. Thaden ; coauthors Michael H. Haltzel ... [et al.]. — Princeton ; Guildford : Princeton University Press, c1981. — xiii,497p : maps ; 25cm
Bibliography: p471-482. — Includes index
ISBN 0-691-05314-6 (cased) : £22.30
ISBN 0-691-10103-5 (pbk) : Unpriced
Primary classification 327.47047'4 B81-25263

327.492 — Netherlands. Foreign relations. Policies of government, *1568-1977*

Voorhoeve, J. J. C.. Peace, profits and principles : a study of Dutch foreign policy / by J.J.C. Voorhoeve. — Hague ; London : Nijhoff, 1979. — xvi,378p : 1map ; 24cm
Bibliography: p326-360. — Includes index
ISBN 90-247-2237-3 : Unpriced B81-03232

327.492 — Netherlands. Foreign relations. Policies of government, *1648-1978*

Voorhoeve, J. J. C.. Peace, profits and principles : a study of Dutch foreign policy / by J.J.C. Voorhoeve. — The Hague ; London : Nijhoff, 1979. — xvi,378p : ill,1map,ports ; 25cm
Bibliography: p326-360. - Includes index
ISBN 90-247-2203-9 (pbk) : Unpriced
B81-07025

327.492041 — Netherlands. Foreign relations with Great Britain, *1940-1948*

Eisen, Janet. Anglo-Dutch relations and European unity 1940-1978 / Janet Eisen. — [Hull] : [University of Hull], 1980. — 60p ; 22cm. — (Occasional papers in modern Dutch studies, ISSN 0144-3070 ; no.1) (University of Hull publications)
Bibliography: p57-60
ISBN 0-85958-429-1 (pbk) : £3.50
Primary classification 327.410492 B81-26813

327.495047 — Byzantine Empire. Foreign relations with Russia, *1300-1400*

Meyendorff, John. Byzantium and the rise of Russia : a study of Byzantino-Russian relations in the fourteenth century / John Meyendorff. — Cambridge : Cambridge University Press, 1981. — xix,326p : 1map ; 24cm
Bibliography: pix-xvi. — Includes index
ISBN 0-521-23183-3 : £30.00
Primary classification 327.470495 B81-02862

327.51 — China. Foreign relations, *1949-1979*

Camilleri, Joseph. Chinese foreign policy : the Maoist Era and its aftermath / Joseph Camilleri. — Oxford : Robertson, 1980. — xiii,311p : 1map ; 25cm
Bibliography: p287-300. — Includes index
ISBN 0-85520-330-7 : £25.00 : CIP rev.
B80-08626

327.51 — China. Foreign relations. Policies of government, *1950-1969*

Gurtov, Melvin. China under threat : the politics of strategy and diplomacy / Melvin Gurtov and Byong-Moo Hwang. — Baltimore ; London : Johns Hopkins University Press, c1980. — xi,336p : maps ; 24cm
Bibliography: p314-326. — Includes index
ISBN 0-8018-2397-8 : £13.75 B81-21089

327.51047 — China. Foreign relations with Soviet Union & United States

The China factor. — London : Croom Helm, Nov.1981. — [208]p
ISBN 0-7099-2308-2 : £11.95 : CIP entry
Also classified at 327.47051 ; 327.73051
B81-30538

327.51047 — China. Foreign relations with Soviet Union, *1945-1970*

Wich, Richard. Sino-Soviet crisis politics : a study of political change and communication / Richard Wich. — [Cambridge, Mass.] : Council on East Asian Studies, Harvard University ; Cambridge, Mass. ; London : Distributed by Harvard University Press, 1980. — viii,313p ; 24cm. — (Harvard East Asian monographs ; 96)
Bibliography: 307-308. - Includes index
ISBN 0-674-80935-1 : £9.00
Primary classification 327.47051 B81-05653

327.51052 — China. Foreign relations with Japan. Policies of Chinese government, *1949-1980*

Jain, R. K. (Ravinder Kumar). China and Japan 1949-1980. — Rev.ed. — Oxford : Martin Robertson, July 1981. — [390]p
Previous ed.: 1977
ISBN 0-85520-415-x : £15.00 : CIP entry
Also classified at 327.52051 B81-20577

327.51054 — China. Foreign relations with South Asia, *1947-1980*

China South Asian relations 1947-1980. — Brighton : Harvester, 1981. — 2v. ; 23cm
Includes index
ISBN 0-7108-0356-7 : £60.00
ISBN 0-7108-0332-x (v.2) : Unpriced
Also classified at 327'.0954 B81-33263

327.51054 — China. Foreign relations with South Asia. Policies of Chinese government, *1947-1980*

China-South Asian relations 1947-1980. — Brighton : Harvester Press, Sept.1981. — 2v.[(640;728p)]
ISBN 0-7108-0356-7 : £60.00 : CIP entry
Also classified at 327.54051 B81-21471

327.51056 — China. Foreign relations with Middle East, *1955-1975*

Behbehani, Hashim S. H.. China's foreign policy in the Arab world 1955-75. — London : Kegan Paul International, Sept.1981. — [414]p
ISBN 0-7103-0008-5 : £20.00 : CIP entry
Primary classification 327.56051 B81-21479

327.51073 — China. Foreign relations with United States. Role of Stilwell, Joseph W., *1911-1945*

Tuchman, Barbara W.. [Stilwell and the American experience in China, 1911-45]. Sand against the wind : Stilwell and the American experience in China, 1911-45 / Barbara W. Tuchman. — London : Macdonald Futura, 1981, c1971. — xxii,794p,[16]p of plates : ill,maps,1facsim,ports ; 18cm. — (A Futura/Jade book)
Originally published: as Stilwell and the American experience in China, 1911-45. New York : Macmillan, 1970 ; as Sand against the wind. London : Macmillan, 1971. — Bibliography: p689-703. — Includes index
ISBN 0-7088-1990-7 (pbk) : £2.95
Primary classification 327.73051 B81-27156

327.52047 — Japan. Foreign relations with Soviet Union, *1945-1980*

Jain, R. K. (Rajendra Kumar). The USSR and Japan 1945-1980 / by Rajendra Kumar Jain. — Brighton : Harvester, 1981. — xx,397p ; 23cm
Bibliography: p380-390. — Includes index
ISBN 0-7108-0395-8 : £20.00 : CIP rev.
Primary classification 327.47052 B81-23841

327.52051 — Japan. Foreign relations with China. Policies of Chinese government, *1949-1980*

Jain, R. K. (Ravinder Kumar). China and Japan 1949-1980. — Rev.ed. — Oxford : Martin Robertson, July 1981. — [390]p
Previous ed.: 1977
ISBN 0-85520-415-x : £15.00 : CIP entry
Primary classification 327.51052 B81-20577

327.52073 — Japan. Foreign relations with United States, *1940-1980*

Shiels, Frederick L.. Tokyo and Washington : dilemmas of a mature alliance / Frederick L. Shiels. — Lexington, Mass. : Lexington Books ; [Aldershot] : Gower [distributor], 1981, c1980. — xiii,202p : ill,maps ; 24cm
Bibliography: p193-196. — Includes index
ISBN 0-669-03378-2 : £12.00
Primary classification 327.73052 B81-29592

327.54 — India. National security. Policies of British government, *1798-1850*
Yapp, Malcolm. Strategies of British India : Britain, Iran and Afghanistan 1798-1850 / M.E. Yapp. — Oxford : Clarendon Press, 1980. — vii,682p : maps ; 25cm
Bibliography: p631-645. - Includes index
ISBN 0-19-822481-8 : £40.00 : CIP rev.
B80-01971

327.54051 — South Asia. Foreign relations with China. Policies of Chinese government, *1947-1980*
China-South Asian relations 1947-1980. — Brighton : Harvester Press, Sept.1981. — 2v.[(640;728p)]
ISBN 0-7108-0356-7 : £60.00 : CIP entry
Primary classification 327.51054 B81-21471

327.54071 — India. Foreign relations with Canada, *1952-1957 — Personal observations*
Reid, Escott. Envoy to Nehru / Escott Reid. — Delhi ; Oxford : Oxford University Press, 1981. — x,301p,[5]p of plates : ports ; 23cm
Includes index
ISBN 0-19-561258-2 : Unpriced
Also classified at 327.71054 B81-34934

327.56051 — Middle East. Foreign relations with China, *1955-1975*
Behbehani, Hashim S. H.. China's foreign policy in the Arab world 1955-75. — London : Kegan Paul International, Sept.1981. — [414]p
ISBN 0-7103-0008-5 : £20.00 : CIP entry
Also classified at 327.51056 B81-21479

327.569105692 — Syria. Foreign relations with Lebanon. Policies of Syrian government. Decision making, *1975-1976*
Dawisha, Adeed I.. Syria and the Lebanese crisis / Adeed I. Dawisha. — London : Macmillan, 1980. — xii,208p ; 23cm
Bibliography: p195-200. — Includes index
ISBN 0-333-28598-0 : £15.00 : CIP rev.
Also classified at 327.569205691 B80-10479

327.569205691 — Lebanon. Foreign relations with Syria. Policies of Syrian government. Decision making, *1975-1976*
Dawisha, Adeed I.. Syria and the Lebanese crisis / Adeed I. Dawisha. — London : Macmillan, 1980. — xii,208p ; 23cm
Bibliography: p195-200. — Includes index
ISBN 0-333-28598-0 : £15.00 : CIP rev.
Primary classification 327.569105692
B80-10479

327.5694'0092'4 — Israel. Foreign relations, *to 1978 — Personal observations*
Rafael, Gideon. Destination peace : three decades of Israeli foreign policy : a personal memoir / Gideon Rafael. — London : Weidenfeld and Nicolson, c1981. — xi,403p ; 25cm
Includes index
ISBN 0-297-77862-5 : £14.95 B81-19370

327.5694017'4927 — Israel. Foreign relations with Arab countries — *Conservative viewpoints*
Grayson, David. Europe & the Middle East / David Grayson & David Irwin. — Newcastle upon Tyne (86 Ovington Grove, Newcastle upon Tyne) : The Churchill Group, c1980. — 11p : 2maps ; 21cm
Cover title
Unpriced (pbk)
Also classified at 327'.0917'4927 B81-10849

327.5694041 — Israel. Foreign relations with Great Britain, *1936-1980*
Wilson, Harold, *1916-*. The chariot of Israel : Britain, America and the State of Israel / Harold Wilson. — London : Weidenfeld and Nicolson : Joseph, c1981. — 406p,[8]p of plates : ill,maps,ports ; 24cm
Includes index
ISBN 0-7181-2002-7 : £14.95
Primary classification 327.4105694 B81-21425

327.598073 — Indonesia. Foreign relations with United States
Pringle, Robert. Indonesia and the Philippines : American interests in island Southeast Asia / Robert Pringle. — New York ; Guildford : Columbia University Press, c1980. — xiii,290p : maps ; 24cm
Includes index
ISBN 0-231-05008-9 (cased) : £16.60
ISBN 0-231-05009-7 (pbk) : £5.00
Primary classification 327.730598 B81-04665

327.599073 — Philippines. Foreign relations with United States
Pringle, Robert. Indonesia and the Philippines : American interests in island Southeast Asia / Robert Pringle. — New York ; Guildford : Columbia University Press, c1980. — xiii,290p : maps ; 24cm
Includes index
ISBN 0-231-05008-9 (cased) : £16.60
ISBN 0-231-05009-7 (pbk) : £5.00
Primary classification 327.730598 B81-04665

327.669 — Nigeria. Foreign relations, *1960-1980*
Aluko, Olajide. Essays on Nigerian foreign policy / Olajide Aluko. — London : Allen & Unwin, 1981. — 288p ; 23cm
Includes index
ISBN 0-04-327062-x (cased) : Unpriced : CIP rev.
ISBN 0-04-327063-8 (pbk) : Unpriced
B81-20093

327.71054 — Canada. Foreign relations with India, *1952-1957 — Personal observations*
Reid, Escott. Envoy to Nehru / Escott Reid. — Delhi ; Oxford : Oxford University Press, 1981. — x,301p,[5]p of plates : ports ; 23cm
Includes index
ISBN 0-19-561258-2 : Unpriced
Primary classification 327.54071 B81-34934

327.73 — United States. Foreign relations, *1914-1979*
Stoessinger, John G.. Crusaders and pragmatists : movers of modern American foreign policy / John G. Stoessinger. — New York ; London : Norton, c1979. — xvii,334 ; 21cm
Bibliography: p291-322. - Includes index
ISBN 0-393-95063-8 (pbk) : £3.25 B81-05980

327.73 — United States. Foreign relations, *1938-1980*
Ambrose, Stephen E.. Rise to globalism : American foreign policy, 1938-1980 / Stephen E. Ambrose. — 2nd rev. ed. — Harmondsworth : Penguin, 1980. — 428p : maps ; 18cm. — (Pelican history of the United States ; v.8)
Previous ed.: i.e. Rev ed., 1976. — Bibliography: p398-404. - Includes index
ISBN 0-14-021247-7 (pbk) : £2.50 B81-20662

327.73 — United States. Foreign relations. Policies of government, *1980*
President Reagan and American foreign policy. — London : Royal Institute of International Affairs, 1981. — iv,38p ; 25cm
ISBN 0-905031-21-0 (pbk) : £3.50 B81-12453

327.73 — United States. Foreign relations. Policies of government, *1981*
Eaks, Louis. From El Salvador to the Libyan Jamahiriya : a radical review of American foreign policy under the Reagan administration / researched and edited by Louis Eaks ; associate researchers Alan George, Phil Kelly. — London (13a Hillgate St., W8 7SP) : Third World Reports, [1981?]. — 86p : ill,ports ; 22cm
£1.00 (pbk) B81-35672

327.73 — United States. Foreign relations. Policies of government. Formulation. Role of United States. *Congress*
The Growing power of Congress / David M. Abshire, Ralph D. Nurnberger, editors ; with contributions by David M. Abshire ... [et al.] ; introduction by Clement J. Zablocki. — Beverly Hills ; London : Sage [for] The Center for Strategic and International Studies, c1981. — 328p ; 23cm
Includes bibliographies
ISBN 0-8039-1586-1 : £12.50 B81-36729

327.73 — United States. Foreign relations. Policies of government. Influence of Roosevelt, Franklin D, *1932-1945*
Dallek, Robert. Franklin D. Roosevelt and American foreign policy 1932-1945 / Robert Dallek. — Oxford : Oxford University Press, c1979 (1981 [printing]). — xii,657p : maps ; 21cm. — (A Galaxy book)
Bibliography: p619-628. — Includes index
ISBN 0-19-502894-5 (pbk) : Unpriced
B81-37940

327.73 — United States. Foreign relations. Policies of government. Role of policies on human rights
Shue, Henry. Basic rights : subsistence, affluence, and U.S. foreign policy / Henry Shue. — Princeton ; Guildford : Princeton University Press, c1980. — xiii,231p ; 23cm
Bibliography: p225-226. - Includes index
ISBN 0-691-07259-0 : £9.80
ISBN 0-691-02015-9 (pbk) : £2.75 B81-19879

Vogelgesang, Sandy. American dream, global nightmare : the dilemma of U.S. human rights policy / Sandy Vogelgesang. — New York ; London : Norton, [1980]. — 303p ; 22cm. — (A Council on Foreign Relations book)
Bibliography: p273-286. — Includes index
ISBN 0-393-01363-4 : Unpriced B81-20392

327.73 — United States. Foreign relations. Role of Eisenhower, Dwight D., *1953-1961*
Divine, Robert A.. Eisenhower and the Cold War / Robert A. Divine. — New York ; Oxford : Oxford University Press, 1981. — ix,181p ; 22cm
Includes index
ISBN 0-19-502823-6 : £7.50
ISBN 0-19-502824-4 (pbk) : Unpriced
B81-23545

327.73 — United States. Foreign relations, *to 1980 — 'Liberation' viewpoints*
Gilbert, Tony. Global interference : the consistent pattern of American foreign policy / [by Tony Gilbert and Pierre Joris]. — London (313/315 Caledonian Rd., London, N1) : Liberation, [1981]. — 64p ; 20cm
£0.75 (pbk) B81-34260

327.73 — United States. National security. Policies of government, *to 1980*
American security policy and policy-making : the dilemmas of using and controlling military force / edited by Robert Harkavy, Edward A. Kolodziej. — Lexington, Mass. : Lexington ; [Farnborough, Hants.] : Gower (distributor), 1980. — xii,268p : ill ; 24cm. — (Policy Studies Organization series)
Includes index
ISBN 0-669-01998-4 : £15.50 B81-08555

327.73 — United States. National security. Policies of United States. *Congress. Senate, 1979-1980*
Muravchik, Joshua. The Senate and national security : a new mood / Joshua Muravchik ; foreword by David M. Abshire. — Beverly Hills ; London : Sage, c1980. — 88p ; 22cm. — (The Washington papers ; vol.viii, 80) (A Sage policy paper)
Bibliography: p87-88
ISBN 0-8039-1547-0 (pbk) : Unpriced
B81-18716

327.73'003'21 — United States. Foreign relations. Diplomacy, *to 1980 — Encyclopaedias*
Findling, John E.. Dictionary of American diplomatic history / John E. Findling. — Westport, Conn. ; London : Greenwood Press, 1980. — xviii,622p ; 25cm
Includes index
ISBN 0-313-22039-5 : Unpriced B81-05411

327.7304 — United States. Foreign relations with Western Europe. Implications of Western European left-wing political parties, *1945-1979*
Political change in Europe : the left and the future of the Atlantic Alliance / edited by Douglas Eden and F.E. Short. — Oxford : Blackwell, 1980. — xii,163p ; 23cm
Includes index
ISBN 0-631-12525-6 : £8.95
Primary classification 327'.094 B81-12615

327.73041 — United States. Foreign relations with Great Britain, *1936-1939*
MacDonald, C. A.. The United States, Britain and appeasement, 1936-1939 / C.A. Macdonald. — London : Macmillan in association with St Antony's College, Oxford, 1981. — xi,220p ; 23cm. — (St Antony's/Macmillan series)
Bibliography: p205-214. — Includes index
ISBN 0-333-26169-0 : £15.00 : CIP rev.
Also classified at 327.41073 B80-10955

327.73041 — United States. Foreign relations with Great Britain, *1937-1941*
Reynolds, David. The creation of the Anglo-American alliance 1937-1941. — London : Europa, Oct.1981. — [416]p
ISBN 0-905118-68-5 : £20.00 : CIP entry
Primary classification 327.41073 B81-27466

327.73041 — United States. Foreign relations with Great Britain, *1944-1947*
Anderson, Terry H.. The United States, Great Britain and the Cold War 1944-1947 / Terry H. Anderson. — Columbia ; London : University of Missouri Press, 1981. — xi,256p ; 22cm
Includes index
ISBN 0-8262-0328-0 : £12.60
Primary classification 327.41073 B81-38212

327.73047 — United States. Foreign relations with Soviet Union, *1945-1950*
Paterson, Thomas G.. On every front : the making of the Cold War / Thomas G Paterson. — New York ; London : Norton, c1979. — xii,210p ; 20cm. — (The Norton essays in American history)
Bibliography. p178-201. — Includes index
ISBN 0-393-95014-x (pbk) : £2.50
Also classified at 327.47073 B81-05290

327.73047 — United States. Foreign relations with Soviet Union, *1945-1980*
LaFeber, Walter. America, Russia and the cold war 1945-1980 / Walter Lafeber. — 4th ed. — New York ; Chichester : Wiley, c1980. — xiii,334p : maps ; 22cm. — (America in crisis, ISSN 0195-4881)
Previous ed.: published as America, Russia and the cold war 1945-1975. 1976. — Bibliography: p306-315. — Includes index
ISBN 0-471-06226-x (pbk) : Unpriced
Primary classification 327.47073 B81-11053

327.73047 — United States. Foreign relations with Soviet Union, *1980*
Steele, Jonathan. A critical phase-East-West relations in the 1980s / an address by Jonathan Steele at the seminar on the subject of East-West relations, organised by Quaker Peace & Service in October 1980. — London : Quaker Peace & Service, [1981]. — [4]p ; 30cm
Unpriced (unbound)
Primary classification 327.47073 B81-09515

327.73047 — United States. Foreign relations with Soviet Union, *1980-1989*
Caldwell, Lawrence T.. Soviet-American relations in the 1980s : superpower politics and East-West trade / Lawrence T. Caldwell, William Diebold, Jr. ; introduction by John C. Campbell. — New York ; London : McGraw Hill, c1981. — xvi,314p : ill ; 24cm. — (1980s Project studies)
Bibliography: p217-230. - Includes index
ISBN 0-07-009615-5 (cased) : £6.55
ISBN 0-07-009616-3 (pbk) : £4.75
Primary classification 327.47073 B81-05085

327.73048 — United States. Foreign relations with Scandinavia, *1945-1949*
Lundestad, Geir. America, Scandinavia and the Cold War, 1945-1949 / Geir Lundestad. — New York ; Guildford : Columbia University Press, 1980. — vi,434p ; 24cm
Includes index
ISBN 0-231-04974-9 : £14.40
Also classified at 327'.0948 B81-03727

327.7305 — United States. Foreign relations with East Asia, *to 1980*
Thomson, James C.. Sentimental imperialists : the American experience in East Asia / James C. Thomson Jr., Peter W. Stanley, John Curtis Perry ; foreword by John King Fairbank. — New York ; London : Harper & Row, c1981. — xiv,323p : 3maps ; 24cm
Map on lining papers. — Includes index
ISBN 0-06-014282-0 : £9.50
Also classified at 327'.095 B81-40879

327.73051 — United States. Foreign relations with China & Soviet Union
The **China** factor. — London : Croom Helm, Nov.1981. — [208]p
ISBN 0-7099-2308-2 : £11.95 : CIP entry
Primary classification 327.51047 B81-30538

327.73051 — United States. Foreign relations with China. Role of Stilwell, Joseph W., *1911-1945*
Tuchman, Barbara W.. [Stilwell and the American experience in China, 1911-45]. Sand against the wind : Stilwell and the American experience in China, 1911-45 / Barbara W. Tuchman. — London : Macdonald Futura, 1981, c1971. — xxii,794p,[16]p of plates : ill,maps,1facsim,ports ; 18cm. — (A Futura/Jade book)
Originally published: as Stilwell and the American experience in China, 1911-45. New York : Macmillan, 1970 ; as Sand against the wind. London : Macmillan, 1971. — Bibliography: p689-703. — Includes index
ISBN 0-7088-1990-7 (pbk) : £2.95
Also classified at 327.51073 B81-27156

327.73052 — United States. Foreign relations with Japan, *1940-1980*
Shiels, Frederick L.. Tokyo and Washington : dilemmas of a mature alliance / Frederick L. Shiels. — Lexington, Mass. : Lexington Books ; [Aldershot] : Gower [distributor], 1981, c1980. — xiii,202p : ill,maps ; 24cm
Bibliography: p193-196. — Includes index
ISBN 0-669-03378-2 : £12.00
Also classified at 327.52073 B81-29592

327.73056 — United States. Foreign relations with Middle East, *ca 1950-1978 — Conference proceedings*
The **Middle** East and the United States : perceptions and policies / edited by Haim Shaked, Itamar Rabinovich. — New Brunswick ; London : Transaction, c1980. — xx,419p : ill ; 24cm. — (Collected papers series / Shiloah Center for Middle Eastern and African Studies)
Conference papers. — Includes index
ISBN 0-87855-329-0 : £14.50
ISBN 0-87855-752-0 (pbk) : £4.25
Primary classification 327'.0956 B81-09160

327.73056 — United States. Foreign relations with Middle East. Diplomacy, *1939-1945*
Bryson, Thomas A.. Seeds of Mideast crisis : the United States diplomatic role in the Middle East during World War II / Thomas A. Bryson. — Jefferson, N.C. : McFarland (Folkestone) : Distributed by Bailey & Swinfen, 1981. — viii,216p ; 24cm
Bibliography: p202-206. — Includes index
ISBN 0-89950-019-6 : £12.75
Also classified at 327'.0956 B81-37664

327.730598 — United States. Foreign relations with Indonesia
Pringle, Robert. Indonesia and the Philippines : American interests in island Southeast Asia / Robert Pringle. — New York ; Guildford : Columbia University Press, c1980. — xiii,290p : maps ; 24cm
Includes index
ISBN 0-231-05008-9 (cased) : £16.60
ISBN 0-231-05009-7 (pbk) : £5.00
Also classified at 327.730599 ; 327.598073 ; 327.599073 B81-04665

327.730599 — United States. Foreign relations with Philippines
Pringle, Robert. Indonesia and the Philippines : American interests in island Southeast Asia / Robert Pringle. — New York ; Guildford : Columbia University Press, c1980. — xiii,290p : maps ; 24cm
Includes index
ISBN 0-231-05008-9 (cased) : £16.60
ISBN 0-231-05009-7 (pbk) : £5.00
Primary classification 327.730598 B81-04665

327.94 — Australia. Foreign relations. Policies of government, *1971-1975*
Australia in world affairs 1971-75 / edited by W.J. Hudson. — Sydney ; London : Allen & Unwin, 1980. — 440p ; 24cm
Includes index
ISBN 0-86861-369-x : Unpriced B81-19936

328 — LEGISLATURES, PARLIAMENTS

328'.2 — Canada. Proposed secession of Quebec *(Province).* **Referendums,** *1980*
Fitzmaurice, John. Quebec and Canada : the Referendum of 20th May 1980 and its wider context / by John Fitzmaurice. — [Hull] : University of Hull, Department of Politics, 1981. — 31p ; 30cm. — (Hull papers in politics, ISSN 0142-7377 ; no.22)
Unpriced (unbound) B81-23289

328'.2 — Great Britain. Referendums. Political aspects, *1800-1980*
Bogdanor, Vernon. The people and the party system : the referendum and electoral reform in British politics / Vernon Bogdanor. — Cambridge : Cambridge University Press, 1981. — ix,285p : ill,forms ; 24cm
Bibliography: p274-279. — Includes index
ISBN 0-521-24207-x (cased) : £20.00
B81-36894

328'.2 — Scotland. Elected assemblies. Devolution of powers of British government. Referendums
The **Referendum** experience, Scotland 1979. — Aberdeen : Aberdeen University Press, Oct.1981. — [224]p
ISBN 0-08-025734-8 : £11.00 : CIP entry
B81-24601

328'.37 — European Parliament. Members. Direct election. Legislation in European Community countries
The **Legislation** of direct elections to the European Parliament / edited by Valentine Herman and Mark Hagger. — Farnborough, Hants : Gower, c1980 — ix,320p : ill ; 23cm
Bibliography: p303-311. — Includes index
ISBN 0-566-00247-7 : £12.50 : CIP rev.
B80-09999

328.41 — Great Britain. *Parliament compared with* **United States.** *Congress*
Bradshaw, Kenneth. Parliament and Congress / Kenneth Bradshaw & David Pring. — Rev. and updated. — London : Quartet, 1981. — 500p ; 21cm
Previous ed.: London : Constable, 1972. — Includes index
ISBN 0-7043-3353-8 (pbk) : £4.95
Also classified at 328.73 B81-23034

328.41'071 — Great Britain. *Parliament. House of Lords.* **Abolition** *— Fabian viewpoints*
Bell, Stuart, *19---*. How to abolish the Lords / Stuart Bell. — London : Fabian Society, 1981. — 25p ; 21cm. — (Fabian tract, ISSN 0307-7535 ; 476)
Cover title. — Bibliography: p25
ISBN 0-7163-0476-7 (pbk) : £0.80 B81-40519

328.41'07'109 — Great Britain. *Parliament. House of Lords, 1547-1558*
Graves, Michael A. R.. The House of Lords in the Parliaments of Edward VI and Mary I. — Cambridge : Cambridge University Press, Nov.1981. — [321]p
ISBN 0-521-23678-9 : £22.50 : CIP entry
B81-34007

328.41'072 — Great Britain. *Parliament. House of Commons*
Norton, Philip. The Commons in perspective / Philip Norton. — Oxford : Robertson, 1981. — vi,265p ; 24cm
Bibliography: p250-253. — Includes index
ISBN 0-85520-335-8 (cased) : £15.00
ISBN 0-85520-334-x (pbk) : £4.95 B81-35299

328.41'072 — Great Britain. *Parliament. House of Commons — For schools*
The **House** of Commons : general information. — [London] : [Public Information Office, House of Commons], [1980]. — 15p : ill,1map,facsims,ports ; 30cm. — (Education sheets ; 4)
Unpriced (unbound) B81-36716

328.41'072'09 — Great Britain. *Parliament. House of Commons, 1977-1980*
The **Commons** today / edited by S.A. Walkland and Michael Ryle for the Study of Parliament Group. — Rev. ed. — [London] : Fontana, 1981. — 333p : ill ; 18cm
Previous ed.: published as The Commons in the seventies. 1977. — Includes index
ISBN 0-00-636187-0 (pbk) : £2.95 B81-10898

328.41'073'0922 — Great Britain. *Parliament.* *House of Commons.* **Members,** *1932-1979 — Biographies*

Who's who of British members of Parliament : a biographical dictionary of the House of Commons based on annual volumes of 'Dod's parliamentary companion' and other sources. — Brighton : Harvester Press
Vol.IV: 1945-1979 / Michael Stenton and Stephen Lees. — 1981. — xv,424p ; 24cm
Includes index
ISBN 0-85527-335-6 : £40.00 : CIP rev.
B80-33029

328.41'0731 — Great Britain. Government. Social policies. Interests of Scottish Members of Parliament — *Lists — For Scottish voluntary organisations*

Speaking for Scotland : a guide to the social policy priorities of Scottish MPs. — Edinburgh (18 Claremont Cres., Edinburgh EH7 4QD) : Scottish Council of Social Service, 1981. — 45p
Cover title
ISBN 0-903589-51-6 (pbk) : £1.50 B81-08722

328.41'0731 — Great Britain. *Parliament. House of Commons.* **Private members. Specialisation**

Judge, David. Backbench specialisation in the House of Commons. — London : Heinemann Educational, Oct.1981. — [288]p
ISBN 0-435-83450-9 : £15.50 : CIP entry
B81-27958

328.41'0733 — Great Britain. *Parliament. House of Commons.* **Members. Superannuation schemes: Parliamentary Contributory Pension Fund** — *Accounts — Serials*

Parliamentary Contributory Pension Fund accounts. — 1979-80. — London : H.M.S.O., [1981]. — 7p
ISBN 0-10-230181-6 : £1.40 B81-30746

328.41'0733 — Great Britain. *Parliament.* **Members. Expense allowances & remuneration** — *Proposals*

Review Body on Top Salaries. Ministers of the Crown and Members of Parliament and the Peer's expenses allowance / Review Body on Top Salaries. — London : H.M.S.O., [1981]. — iii,10p ; 25cm. — (Cmnd. ; 8244) (Report / Review Body on Top Salaries ; no.17)
ISBN 0-10-182440-8 (unbound) : £1.70
Also classified at 354.41001'232 B81-27553

328.41'075 — Great Britain. Parliament. House of Commons. Debates — *Humour*

Hoggart, Simon. On the House. — London : Robson, Oct.1981. — [144]p
ISBN 0-86051-158-8 : £5.95 : CIP entry
B81-27452

328.41'07657 — Great Britain. *Parliament. House of Commons. Committee of Public Accounts, 1965-1978*

Flegmann, Vilma. Called to account : the Public Accounts Committee of the House of Commons 1965-66 - 1977-7, / Vilma Flegmann. — Farnborough, Hants. : Gower, c1980. — ix,318p : ill ; 23cm
Bibliography: p312. - Includes index
ISBN 0-566-00371-6 : CIP rev. B80-05231

328.41'07657 — Great Britain. *Parliament. House of Commons.* **Select committees** — *Lists — Serials*

Select committees : return to an order of the Honourable the House of Commons ... for session ... — 1979-80. — London : H.M.S.O., 1981. — 42p
ISBN 0-10-221781-5 : £4.70 B81-29405

328.41'077 — Great Britain. *Parliament.* **Public bills. Enactment,** *1970-1974*

Burton, Ivor. Legislation and public policy : public bills in the 1970-74 Parliament / by Ivor Burton and Gavin Drewry. — London : Macmillan, 1981. — xii,322p ; 23cm
Bibliography: p280-283. — Includes index
ISBN 0-333-15204-2 : £25.00 : CIP rev.
B80-12739

328.416'073 — Northern Ireland. Local authorities. Councillors. Role, *1970-1980*

Birrell, Derek. Local government councillors in Northern Ireland / by Derek Birrell. — Glasgow (McCance Building, 16 Richmond St., Glasgow G1 1XQ) : Centre for the Study of Public Policy, University of Strathclyde, 1981. — 66p ; 30cm. — (Studies in public policy, ISSN 0140-8240 ; no.83)
£2.25 (pbk) B81-38573

328.416'0733 — Northern Ireland. *Assembly.* **Members. Superannuation schemes: Assembly Contributory Pension Fund** — *Accounts — Serials*

[Accounts *(Assembly Contributory Pension Fund)*]. Accounts. — 1979-80. — Belfast : H.M.S.O., 1981. — 5p
ISBN 0-337-02326-3 : £1.30 B81-30713

328.416'0733 — Northern Ireland. *Parliament.* **Members. Superannuation schemes: Members' Contributory Pension (Northern Ireland) Fund** — *Accounts — Serials*

[Accounts *(Members' Contributory Pension (Northern Ireland) Fund)*]. Accounts. — 1979-80. — Belfast : H.M.S.O., 1981. — 6p
ISBN 0-337-02327-1 : £1.30 B81-30717

328.42'05 — England and Wales. *Parliament.* **Proceedings,** *1559-1603 — Parliamentary papers*

Proceedings in the parliaments of Elizabeth I / edited by T.E. Hartley. — [Leicester] : Leicester University Press
Vol.1: 1558-1581. — 1981. — xxxviii,564p ; 26cm
Ill on lining papers. — Includes index
ISBN 0-7185-1181-6 : £38.00 B81-36126

328.42'073 — England. Local authorities. Councillors. Role

Fudge, Colin. First steps to a career? : the problems of being a newly elected member in an English local authority / Colin Fudge, Alan Murie and Eugene Ring. — [Bristol] ([Bristol BS8 1TH]) : University of Bristol, [1980?]. — 140p : 1ill ; 21cm. — (Occasional paper / School for Advanced Urban Studies, ISSN 0141-4380 ; no.4)
Bibliography: p124-129
ISBN 0-906515-26-2 (pbk) : Unpriced
B81-13248

328.42'09 — England. *Parliament, to 1509*

The English parliament in the Middle Ages / R.G. Davis, J.H. Denton editors ; [a tribute to J.S. Roskill]. — Manchester : Manchester University Press, c1981. — x,214p : 1ports ; 24cm
Bibliography: p201-205. — Includes index
ISBN 0-7190-0833-6 : £13.95 : CIP rev.
B81-04359

328.42'09 — England. Parliaments, *ca 1377-ca 1465*

Roskell, J. S.. Parliament and politics in late medieval England. — London (35 Gloucester Ave., NW1 7AX) : Hambledon Press, Dec.1981. — (History series ; 7)
Vol.1. — 1v.
ISBN 0-9506882-8-2 : £18.00 : CIP entry
ISBN 0-9506882-7-4 (set) : £40.00 B81-31523

Roskell, J. S.. Parliament and politics in late medieval England. — London (35 Gloucester Ave., NW1 7AX) : Hambledon Press, Dec.1981. — (History series ; 8)
Vol.2. — [370]p
ISBN 0-9506882-9-0 : £22.00 : CIP entry
ISBN 0-9506882-7-4 (set) : £40.00 B81-31522

328.423'5073'0222 — Devon. *County Council.* **Councillors** — *Illustrations*

Devon. *County Council.* The faces of Devon County Council / [prepared by the Press and Publicity Office, County Hall, Exeter]. — Exeter (c/o Press and Publicity Office, County Hall, Exeter) : [Devon County Council], [1981]. — 45p,1folded leaf of plates : 1map ; 11x15cm
Cover title
ISBN 0-86114-332-9 (pbk) : Unpriced
B81-29038

328.73 — United States. *Congress*

Vogler, David J.. The politics of Congress / David J. Vogler. — 2nd ed. — Boston, Mass. ; London : Allyn and Bacon, 1977 (1978 printing). — x,338p ; 22cm
Previous ed.: 1974. — Includes index
ISBN 0-205-05792-6 (pbk) : £5.55 B81-11335

328.73 — United States. *Congress compared with* **Great Britain.** *Parliament*

Bradshaw, Kenneth. Parliament and Congress / Kenneth Bradshaw & David Pring. — Rev. and updated. — London : Quartet, 1981. — 500p ; 21cm
Previous ed.: London : Constable, 1972. — Includes index
ISBN 0-7043-3353-8 (pbk) : £4.95
Primary classification 328.41 B81-23034

328.73 — United States. Legislatures

Keefe, William J.. The American legislative process : Congress and the States / William J. Keefe, Morris S. Ogul. — 5th ed. — Englewood Cliffs ; London : Prentice-Hall, c1981. — xiii,495p : ill ; 24cm
Previous ed.: 1977. — Includes index
ISBN 0-13-028043-7 : £11.65 B81-12722

328.73'073 — United States. Cities. Local authorities. Negro councillors

Karnig, Albert K.. Black representation and urban policy / Albert K. Karnig and Susan Welch. — Chicago ; London : University of Chicago Press, 1980. — xiii,179p ; 24cm
Bibliography: p163-172. — Includes index
ISBN 0-226-42534-7 : £12.00 B81-21065

328.73'073 — United States. *Congress. Senate.* **Members: Liberals. Influence,** *1959-1972*

Foley, Michael, *1948-*. The new senate : liberal influence on a conservative institution 1959-1972 / Michael Foley. — New Haven ; London : Yale University Press, c1980. — x,342p : 1ill ; 25cm
Includes index
ISBN 0-300-02440-1 : £11.30 : CIP rev.
B80-21475

328.73'073454 — United States. Electoral divisions. Boundaries. Reform. Political aspects

Reapportionment politics : the history of redistricting in the 50 states / Leroy Hardy, Alan Heslop, and Stuart Anderson, editors. — Beverly Hills ; London : Sage, c1981. — 357p : maps ; 28cm
ISBN 0-8039-1663-9 (pbk) : £18.75 B81-40005

328.73'0762 — United States. *Congress.* **Leaders. Influence,** *to 1979*

Cohen, Richard E.. Congressional leadership : seeking a new role / Richard E. Cohen, Ralph D. Nurnberger ; foreword by David M. Abshire. — Beverly Hills ; London : [Published for] the Center for Strategic and International Studies [by] Sage, c1980. — 88p ; 22cm. — (The Washington papers ; vol.viii, 79)
Bibliography: p87-88
ISBN 0-8039-1548-9 (pbk) : Unpriced
B81-18821

328.73'078 — United States. *Congress.* **Lobbying** — *For businessmen*

Fox, Harrison W.. Doing business in Washington : how to win friends and influence government / Harrison W. Fox, Jr., Martin Schnitzer. — New York : Free Press ; London : Collier Macmillan, c1981. — x,240p : ill ; 25cm
Bibliography: p223-231. — Includes index
ISBN 0-02-910460-2 : £9.50 B81-39023

328.77'077'09 — United States. Mid-west region. States. Legislatures. Policies. Decision making, *1886-1895*

Campbell, Ballard C.. Representative democracy : public policy and Midwestern legislatures in the late nineteenth century / Ballard C. Campbell. — Cambridge, Mass. ; London : Harvard University Press, 1980. — xi,260p : 1ill ; 25cm
Includes index
ISBN 0-674-76275-4 : £12.00 B81-06118

328.797'0733 — Washington (*State*). Elected officials. Remuneration. Proposed increases. Protest by taxpayers, *1973*

Sheldon, Charles H.. Politicians, judges, and the people : a study in citizens' participation / Charles H. Sheldo and Frank P. Weaver. — Westport, Conn. ; London : Greenwood Press, 1980. — xii,206p ; 22cm. — (Contributions in political science, ISSN 0147-1066 ; no.36)
Bibliography: p191-200. - Includes index
ISBN 0-313-21492-1 : Unpriced
Primary classification 331.2'81347970714
B81-05997

330 — ECONOMICS

330 — Applied economics

Hanson, J. L.. Hanson's introduction to applied economics / J.L. Hanson. — 3rd ed. / revised by John Beardshaw. — Plymouth : Macdonald and Evans, 1981. — x,565p : ill ; 22cm
Previous ed.: published as An introduction to applied economics. London : Macdonald and Evans, 1975. — Includes index
ISBN 0-7121-0963-3 (pbk) : £6.95 B81-09595

330 — Capitalist societies

Urry, John. The anatomy of capitalist societies : the economy, civil society and the state / John Urry. — London : Macmillan, 1981. — 178p ; 23cm. — (Contemporary social theory)
Bibliography: p167-174. — Includes index
ISBN 0-333-29430-0 (cased) : £12.50
ISBN 0-333-29131-9 (pbk) : Unpriced
B81-21771

330 — Economics

Cairncross, *Sir* Alec. Introduction to economics. — 6th ed. — London : Butterworths, Dec.1981. — [512]p
Previous ed.: 1973
ISBN 0-408-71056-x (cased) : £12.00 : CIP entry
ISBN 0-408-71055-1 (pbk) : £6.50 B81-31717

Elkan, Peter G.. The new model economy. — Oxford : Pergamon, Feb.1982. — [130]p
ISBN 0-08-028112-5 : £9.75 : CIP entry
B81-35944

Growth, profits and property : essays in the revival of political economy / edited by Edward J. Nell. — Cambridge : Cambridge University Press, 1980. — xiv,304p : ill ; 27cm
Includes bibliographies
ISBN 0-521-22396-2 : £19.50 B81-37618

Harbury, C. D.. Economic behaviour : an introduction. — London : Allen & Unwin, 1980. — 265p : ill ; 23cm. — (Economics and society series)
Includes index
ISBN 0-04-330305-6 (cased) : £12.00 : CIP rev.
ISBN 0-04-330306-4 (pbk) : £4.95 B80-19065

Hardwick, Philip. An introduction to modern economics. — London : Longman, May 1981. — [560]p
ISBN 0-582-44051-3 (pbk) : £6.95 : CIP entry
B81-08846

Harvey, J.. Basic economics / J. Harvey. — Basingstoke : Macmillan Education, 1981. — 352p : ill ; 22cm
Includes index
ISBN 0-333-27985-9 (pbk) : £1.95 B81-22248

Harvey, J.. Mastering economics. — London : Macmillan, Oct.1981. — [352]p
ISBN 0-333-31287-2 (cased) : £6.50 : CIP entry
ISBN 0-333-30477-2 (pbk) : £2.95 B81-26722

Heilbroner, Robert L.. The economic problem / Robert L. Heilbroner, Lester C. Thurow. — 6th ed. — Englewood Cliffs ; London : Prentice-Hall, c1981. — 670p : ill(some col.) ; 25cm
Previous ed.: 1978. — Includes index
ISBN 0-13-233304-x : £12.95 B81-17179

Hunt, E. K.. Economics : an introduction to traditional and radical views / E.K. Hunt, Howard J. Sherman. — 4th ed. — New York ; London : Harper & Row, c1981. — xxx,736p : ill ; 24cm
Previous ed.: 1978. — Includes bibliographies and index
ISBN 0-06-043008-7 (pbk) : £5.95 B81-22981

Illich, Ivan. Shadow work / by Ivan Illich. — Boston, Mass. ; London : Boyars, 1981. — 152p ; 22cm. — (Open forum)
Bibliography: p118-152
ISBN 0-7145-2710-6 (cased) : £6.95
ISBN 0-7145-2711-4 (pbk) : £2.95 B81-23542

Kempner, Thomas. The economic environment / by Thomas Kempner. — Major revision. — [Henley-on-Thames] : [Administrative Staff College Henley], [1981]. — 93p : ill ; 30cm
Cover title. — Previous ed.: 1979
Unpriced (pbk) B81-16730

Lawal, O. A.. Success in economics / O.A. Lawal and Derek Lobley. — West African ed. — London : African Universities Press in association with Murray, 1981. — xiv,354p : ill ; 22cm. — (Success studybooks)
Bibliography: p347-349. — Includes index
ISBN 0-7195-3825-4 (pbk) : £3.00 : CIP rev.
B81-02665

Livesey, Frank. Economics / by Frank Livesey. — 2nd ed. — Stockport : Polytech, 1981. — 301p in various pagings : ill ; 23cm
Previous ed.: 1977. — Includes index
ISBN 0-85505-054-3 (pbk) : £5.00 B81-39047

Long, Kenneth E.. Introduction to economics / Kenneth E. Long ; foreword by Jeff R. Clark. — New York ; London : Van Nostrand, c1981. — xxi,505p : ill,ports ; 23cm
Includes index
ISBN 0-442-23894-0 (pbk) : £11.95 B81-26042

McConnell, Campbell R.. Economics : principles, problems and policies / Campbell R. McConnell. — 8th ed. — New York ; London : McGraw-Hill, c1981. — xxxii,911p : ill(some col.) ; 25cm
Previous ed.: 1978. — Text on lining paers. — Includes bibliographies and index
ISBN 0-07-044930-9 : £16.25 B81-36479

Mansfield, Edwin. Economics : principles, problems, decisions / Edwin Mansfield. — 3rd ed. — New York ; London : Norton, c1980. — xxvii,866p : ill ; 25cm
Previous ed.: 1977. — Includes index
ISBN 0-393-95118-9 : £8.95 B81-02188

Marschak, Jacob. Economic information, decision, and prediction : selected essays / Jacob Marschak. — Dordrecht ; London : Reidel. — (Theory and decision library ; v.7)
Vol.2. — c1974. — xii,362p : ill ; 23cm
Includes bibliographies and index. — Contents: Part II, Economics of information and organization
ISBN 90-277-0545-3 (cased) : Unpriced
ISBN 90-277-1196-8 (pbk) : Unpriced
B81-13655

Marschak, Jacob. Economic information, decision, and prediction : selected essays / Jacob Marschak. — Dordrecht ; London : Reidel. — (Theory and decision library ; v.7)
Vol.3. — c1974. — x,399p : ill ; 23cm
Includes bibliographies and index. — Contents: Part III, Money and other assets - Part IV, Economic measurements - Part V, Contributions to the logic of economics
ISBN 90-277-0546-1 (cased) : Unpriced
ISBN 90-277-1197-6 (pbk) : Unpriced
B81-13656

Robinson, Joan. Further contributions to modern economics / Joan Robinson. — Oxford : Blackwell, 1980. — xiv,202p : ill ; 22cm
ISBN 0-631-12624-4 (cased) : £12.00 : CIP rev.
ISBN 0-631-12634-1 (pbk) : £4.95 B80-22982

Understanding economics : an introduction for students / Paul Bennett ... [et al.] ; edited by David Burningham. — Sevenoaks : Hodder and Stoughton, 1978 (1980 [printing]). — 388p : ill ; 20cm. — (Teach yourself books)
Includes index
ISBN 0-340-22952-7 (pbk) : £3.50 : CIP rev.
B78-24945

Veseth, Michael. Coursebook to accompany Introductory economics and Introductory macroeconomics, Introductory microeconomics / by Michael Veseth. — New York ; London : Academic Press, c1981. — x,358p : ill ; 24cm
ISBN 0-12-719569-6 (pbk) : £5.20 B81-39786

Veseth, Michael. Introductory economics / Michael Veseth. — New York ; London : Academic Press, c1981. — xv,773p : ill(some col.) ; 25cm
Also published: in paperback in 2 vols. as Introductory macroeconomics and Introductory microeconomics. 1981. — Includes index
ISBN 0-12-719565-3 : £11.20 B81-29764

Weiss, Leonard W.. Economics and society / Leonard W. Weiss. — 2nd ed. — New York ; Chichester : Wiley, c1981. — xxiii,600p : ill (some col.) ; 24cm
Previous ed.: 1975. — Includes bibliographies and index
ISBN 0-471-03160-7 : £12.10 B81-17245

330 — Economics — *Festschriften*

Changing perceptions of economic policy. — London : Methuen, Oct.1981. — [256]p
ISBN 0-416-31550-x : £12.50 : CIP entry
B81-27374

Studies in economic theory and practice : essays in honor of Edward Lipiński / edited by N. Assorodobraj-Kula ... [et al.]. — Amsterdam ; Oxford : North-Holland, c1981. — xii,251p : ill ; 25cm
Includes bibliographies
ISBN 0-444-86010-x : £21.90 B81-36763

330 — Economics — *For schools*

Economic studies. — Christchurch, N.Z. ; London : Whitcoulls, 1981
3: The consumer in the economic system / W.M. Smyth and Phoebe Macdiarmid. — 189p : ill,facsims ; 22cm
Includes index
ISBN 0-7233-0649-4 : Unpriced B81-17880

Thomas, D. J. (Derek John). A first course in economics / D.J. Thomas. — London : Bell & Hyman, 1980, c1979. — x,298p : ill,2maps ; 21cm
Includes index
ISBN 0-7135-1093-5 (pbk) : Unpriced
B81-16574

330 — Economics — *For West African students*

Anderson, David J.. Intermediate economics for West Africa / David J. Anderson. — London : Macmillan, 1980. — 442p : ill ; 22cm
Includes index
ISBN 0-333-26193-3 (pbk) : £3.00 B81-12777

Teriba, O.. Certificate economics for West Africa / O. Teriba. — New ed.. — London : Longman, 1980. — 250p : ill,maps ; 24cm
Previous ed.: 1976. — Includes index
ISBN 0-582-60649-7 (pbk) : £2.35 B81-04717

330 — Economics — *Interviews*

Galbraith, John Kenneth. Almost everyone's guide to economics / John Kenneth Galbraith and Nicole Salinger. — Harmondsworth : Penguin, 1981, c1978. — 176p ; 18cm. — (Pelican books)
Originally published: London : Deutsch, 1979. — Includes index
ISBN 0-14-022238-3 (pbk) : £1.50 B81-06963

330 — Economics — *Islamic viewpoints*
Ṣiddīqī, Muḥammad Nejātullāh. Muslim economic thinking : a survey of contemporary literature / by Muhammad Nejatullah Siddiqi. — Jeddah : International Centre for Research in Islamic Ecnomics, King Abdul Azziz University ; Leicester : Islamic Foundations, 1401H, 1981. — vi,130p ; 22cm. — (Islamic economic series ; 1)
Bibliography: p83-125. — Includes index
ISBN 0-86037-082-8 (cased) : Unpriced
ISBN 0-86037-081-x (pbk) : Unpriced
B81-26097

330 — Economics — *Marxist viewpoints*
Fine, Ben. Theories of the capitalist economy. — London : Edward Arnold, Jan.1982. — [208]p
ISBN 0-7131-6357-7 (pbk) : £6.95 : CIP entry
B81-33839

Horvat, Branko. The political economy of socialism. — Oxford : Martin Robertson, Jan.1982. — [660]p
ISBN 0-85520-477-x : £20.00 : CIP entry
B81-33827

Shemīatenkov, V. G.. The enigma of capital : a Marxist viewpoint / V. Shemyatenkov ; [translated from the Russian by Yuri Sviridov]. — Moscow : Progress ; [London] : Distributed by Central Books, c1981. — 328p ; 21cm
Translation of: Zagadka kapitala. — Includes index
ISBN 0-7147-1614-6 : £3.50 B81-27753

330 — Economics — *Quotations* — *Collections*
A **Dictionary** of economic quotations / compiled by Simon James. — London : Croom Helm, c1981. — 244p ; 23cm
Includes index
ISBN 0-85664-617-2 : £9.95 : CIP rev.
B81-13801

330 — Economics. Role of altruism
Collard, David. Altruism and economy. — Oxford : Martin Robertson, Apr.1981. — [220]p
Originally published: 1978
ISBN 0-85520-381-1 (pbk) : £4.95 : CIP entry
B81-07418

330 — Economics. Social aspects
Drucker, Peter F.. Toward the next economics : and other essays / Peter F. Drucker. — London : Heinemann, 1981. — 212p ; 22cm
Originally published: New York : Harper and Row, 1981. — Includes index
ISBN 0-434-90404-x : £7.95 B81-32304

330 — Resources. Shortages. Economic aspects
Kornai, János. Economics of shortage / János Kornai. — Amsterdam ; Oxford : North Holland, 1980. — 2v.(xx,631p) : ill ; 23cm. — (Contributions to economic analysis ; 131)
Bibliography: p607-619. — Includes index
ISBN 0-444-86059-2 : £33.60 B81-32346

330'.01 — Economics. Disequilibria
Hey, John D.. Economics in disequilibrium. — Oxford : Martin Robertson, Aug.1981. — [250]p
ISBN 0-85520-399-4 : £15.00 : CIP entry
B81-16894

330'.01 — Economics — *Philosophical perspectives*
Dyke, C.. Philosophy of economics / C. Dyke. — Englewood Cliffs ; London : Prentice-Hall, c1981. — viii,184p : ill ; 23cm. — (Prentice-Hall foundations of philosophy series)
Bibliography: p179-182. — Includes index
ISBN 0-13-663336-6 (corrected : pbk) : £5.15
B81-27093

330'.01 — Economics — *Philosophical perspectives* — *Conference proceedings*
Philosophy in economics : papers deriving from and related to a workshop on testability and explanation in economics held at Virginia Polytechnic Institute and State University, 1979 / edited by Joseph C. Pitt. — Dordrecht ; London : Reidel, c1981. — 210p ; 23cm. — (The University of Western Ontario series in philosophy of science ; v.16)
Includes bibliographies and index
ISBN 90-277-1210-7 (cased) : Unpriced
ISBN 90-277-1242-5 (pbk) : Unpriced
B81-20833

330'.01 — Man. Rational economic expectations. Econometric models
Begg, David K. H.. The rational expectations revolution in macroeconomics. — Deddington : Philip Allan, Feb.1982. — [240]p
ISBN 0-86003-044-x (cased) : £12.00 : CIP entry
ISBN 0-86003-130-6 (pbk) : £5.95 B81-39246

330'.01'51 — Economics. Applications of optimal control theory
Kamien, Morton I.. Dynamic optimization : the calculus of variations and optimal control in economics and management / Morton I. Kamien and Nancy L. Schwartz. — Westport, Conn. ; London : Greenwood Press, c1981. — xi,331p : ill ; 24cm. — (Dynamic economics ; v.4)
Bibliography: p315-324. - Includes index
ISBN 0-444-00424-6 : £17.04
Also classified at 330'.01'51564 B81-23646

330'.01'51564 — Economics. Applications of calculus of variations
Kamien, Morton I.. Dynamic optimization : the calculus of variations and optimal control in economics and management / Morton I. Kamien and Nancy L. Schwartz. — Westport, Conn. ; London : Greenwood Press, c1981. — xi,331p : ill ; 24cm. — (Dynamic economics ; v.4)
Bibliography: p315-324. - Includes index
ISBN 0-444-00424-6 : £17.04
Primary classification 330'.01'51 B81-23646

330'.01'5192 — Economics. Applications of stochastic control theory
Applied stochastic control in econometrics and management science / edited by Alain Bensoussan, Paul Kleindorfer, Charles S. Tapiero. — Amsterdam ; Oxford : North-Holland, 1980. — xv,304p : ill ; 23cm. — (Contributors to economic analysis ; 130)
Includes bibliographies
ISBN 0-444-85408-8 : £21.73
Also classified at 658'.001'5192 B81-05826

Chow, Gregory C.. Econometric analysis by control methods / Gregory C. Chow. — New York ; Chichester : Wiley, c1981. — xv,320p : ill ; 24cm. — (A Wiley publication in applied statistics) (Wiley series in probability and mathematical statistics, ISSN 0271-6356)
Bibliography: p302-307. — Includes index
ISBN 0-471-08706-8 : £20.50 B81-23331

330'.01'51955 — Economics. Time series. Analysis. Econometric models
Harvey, A. C.. The econometric analysis of time series / A.C. Harvey. — Oxford : Philip Allan, 1981. — xi,384p : ill ; 24cm
Bibliography: p368-375. - Includes index
ISBN 0-86003-025-3 : £17.50 B81-05466

Harvey, A. C.. Time series models / A.C. Harvey. — Deddington : Philip Allan, 1981. — x,229p : ill ; 24cm
Bibliography: p218-222. — Includes index
ISBN 0-86003-032-6 : £13.95 : CIP rev.
B81-20473

330'.01'8 — Economics. Methodology
Blaug, Mark. The methodology of economics, or, How economists explain / Mark Blaug. — Cambridge : Cambridge University Press, 1980. — xiv,296p ; 22cm. — (Cambridge surveys of economic literature)
Bibliography: p270-285. - Includes index
ISBN 0-521-22288-5 (cased) : £15.00
ISBN 0-521-29437-1 (pbk) : £4.95 B81-09824

330'.024631 — Economics — *For agriculture*
Hill, Berkeley. An introduction to economics for students of agriculture / by Berkeley Hill. — Oxford : Pergamon, 1980. — ix,346p : ill ; 22cm. — (Pergamon international library)
Bibliography: p300-301. — Includes index
ISBN 0-08-020510-0 (cased) : £12.50 : CIP rev.
ISBN 0-08-020509-7 (pbk) : £5.90 B79-20700

330'.024658 — Economics — *For management*
Pappas, James L.. Fundamentals of managerial economics / James L. Pappas, Eugene F. Brigham. — Chicago ; London : Dryden, c1981. — 460p : ill ; 24cm
Includes index
ISBN 0-03-040841-5 : £14.50 B81-22973

330'.02469 — Economics — *For construction industries*
Seddon, V. J.. Economics for the construction industry checkbook. — London : Butterworth, Dec.1981. — [144]p
ISBN 0-408-00666-8 (cased) : £6.95 : CIP entry
ISBN 0-408-00655-2 (pbk) : £3.75 B81-31424

330'.02'724658 — Economics. Mathematical models — *For management*
Randall, Ken. Managerial economics. — London : Heinemann Educational, Oct.1981. — [192]p
ISBN 0-435-84540-3 (pbk) : £4.95 : CIP entry
B81-27435

330'.028 — Discrete-choice econometric models
Hensher, David A.. Applied discrete-choice modelling / David A. Hensher, Lester W. Johnson with contributions by J.J. Louviere and J. Horowitz. — London : Croom Helm, c1981. — 468p : ill ; 23cm
Bibliography: p437-461. - Includes index
ISBN 0-7099-0330-8 (cased) : £19.95
ISBN 0-7099-1203-7 (pbk) : £12.50 B81-04000

330'.028 — Econometric models
Evaluation of econometric models / edited by Jan Kmenta, James B. Ramsey. — New York ; London : Academic Press, c1980. — xiv,410p : ill ; 24cm
Includes bibliographies
ISBN 0-12-416550-8 : £22.20 B81-14609

330'.028 — Econometric models. Evaluation
The **Usefulness** of macroeconomic models. — London (EC2R 8AH) : Economics Division, Bank of England, c1981. — 89p : ill ; 30cm. — (Papers presented to the Panel of Academic Consultants, ISSN 0143-4691 ; no.14)
Includes bibliographies
ISBN 0-903312-37-9 (pbk) : Unpriced
B81-37823

330'.028 — Econometrics
Kelejian, Harry H.. Introduction to econometrics : principles and applications / H. Kelejian, Wallace E. Oates. — 2nd ed. — New York ; London : Harper & Row, c1981. — xv,347p : ill ; 24cm
Previous ed.: 1974. — Includes index
ISBN 0-06-043618-2 (cased) : Unpriced
ISBN 0-06-350387-5 (pbk) : £6.95 B81-22750

Maddala, G. S.. Econometrics / G.S. Maddala. — Tokyo ; London : McGraw-Hill Kogakusha, c1977. — xii,516p : ill ; 21cm. — (Economics handbooks series)
Includes index
ISBN 0-07-085464-5 (pbk) : £5.95 B81-12958

Mayes, David G.. Applications of econometrics. — Hemel Hempstead : Prentice-Hall, May 1981. — [350]p
ISBN 0-13-039180-8 (pbk) : £7.50 : CIP entry
B81-12912

Raj, Baldev. Econometrics : a varying coefficients approach / Baldev Raj and Aman Ullah. — London : Croom Helm, c1981. — xii,372p ; 23cm
Bibliography: p345-367. - Includes index
ISBN 0-7099-0313-8 : £11.95 B81-20786

Stewart, Mark B.. Introducing econometrics / Mark B. Stewart and Kenneth F. Wallis. — 2nd ed. — Oxford : Blackwell, 1981. — 337p : ill ; 22cm
Previous ed.: / Kenneth F. Wallis. London : Gray-Mills, 1972. — Includes index
ISBN 0-631-12568-x (cased) : £15.00 : CIP rev.
ISBN 0-631-12569-8 (pbk) : £6.50 B80-34576

330'.028 — Econometrics. Distributed lag models
Dhrymes, Phoebus J.. Distributed lags : problems of estimation and formulation / Phoebus J. Dhrymes. — 2nd rev.ed. — Amsterdam ; Oxford : North-Holland, 1981. — x,470p ; 23cm. — (Advanced textbooks in economics ; v.14)
Previous ed.: San Francisco : Holden-Day ; Edinburgh : Oliver and Boyd, 1971. —
Bibliography: p458-466. — Includes index
ISBN 0-444-86013-4 : Unpriced B81-29007

330′.028 — Econometrics. Statistical methods
Malinvaud, Edmond. Statistical methods of econometrics / E. Malinvaud ; translation by A. Silvey. — 3rd rev. ed. — Amsterdam ; Oxford : North-Holland, 1980. — xvi,769p : ill ; 23cm. — (Studies in mathematical and managerial economics ; v.6)
Translation of: Méthodes statistiques de l'économétrie. — Previous ed.: 1970. — Bibliography: p741-761. - Includes index
ISBN 0-444-85473-8 : £21.41 B81-07271

330′.028 — Econometrics. Use of fixed point estimation
The **Fix-point** approach to interdependent systems / Herman Wold, editor. — Amsterdam ; Oxford : North-Holland, c1981. — xiv,336p : ill ; 23cm. — (Contributions to economic analysis)
Bibliography: p323. - Includes index
ISBN 0-444-85451-7 : £20.11 B81-22202

330′.028 — Economics. Disequilibria
Casson, Mark. Unemployment : a disequilibrium approach / Mark Casson. — Oxford : Robertson, 1981. — xv,263p : ill ; 23cm
Bibliography: p245-258. — Includes index
ISBN 0-85520-438-9 (cased) : £15.00
B81-39968

330′.028 — General equilibrium theory. Equilibria. Computation. Applications of activity analysis
Ginsburgh, Victor A.. Activity analysis and general equilibrium modelling / Victor A. Ginsburgh and Jean L. Waelbroeck. — Amsterdam ; Oxford : North-Holland, c1981. — xvi,373p : ill ; 23cm. — (Contributions to economic analysis ; 125)
Bibliography: p357-364. — Includes index
ISBN 0-444-86011-8 : £26.63 B81-36754

330′.028 — Stochastic econometric models
Kendrick, *David A.*. Stochastic control for economic models / David Kendrick. — New York ; London : McGraw-Hill, c1981. — xiii,242p : ill ; 25cm. — (Economics handbook series)
Bibliography: p228-237. — Includes index
ISBN 0-07-033962-7 : £27.50 B81-31328

330′.03 — Economics — *Polyglot dictionaries*
Jong, Frits J. de. Quadrilingual economics dictionary : English/American, French, German, Dutch / by Frits J. de Jong. — The Hague ; London : Nijhoff ; [Brentford] : Kluwer [distributor], 1980. — viii,685p ; 25cm
Unpriced B81-33271

Jong, Frits J. de. Quadrilingual economics dictionary : English-American, French, German, Dutch / by Frits J. de Jong. — The Hague ; London : Nijhoff, 1980. — viii,685p ; 25cm
ISBN 90-247-2243-8 : Unpriced B81-25516

330′.03′21 — Economics — *Encyclopaedias*
Horner, C. F.. The Hamlyn pocket dictionary of business terms / C.F. Horner, L.M. Liebster. — London : Hamlyn, 1980. — 317p ; 15cm
ISBN 0-600-31599-1 (pbk) : £1.25 B81-00031

The **Macmillan** dictionary of modern economics / [edited by] David W. Pearce. — London : Macmillan, 1981. — 473p : ill ; 25cm
ISBN 0-333-26962-4 : £14.95 B81-38735

330′.07′1041 — Great Britain. Educational institutions. Curriculum subjects: Economics. Teaching, *1969-1975*
Lumsden, Keith. Economics education in the United Kingdom / Keith Lumsden, Richard Attiyeh and Alex Scott. — London : Heinemann, 1980. — 278p : ill ; 23cm
ISBN 0-435-84790-2 : £12.50 : CIP rev.
B80-13729

330′.07′1142132 — London. Westminster *(London Borough).* **Universities. Colleges: London School of Economics and Political Science** — *Serials*
London School of Economics and Political Science. Calendar / the London School of Economics and Political Science. — 1980-81. — London : The School, c1980. — 540p
ISBN 0-85328-069-x : £5.50
ISSN 0308-9681 B81-03799

330′.0724 — Continuous time dynamic econometric models
Gandolfo, Giancarlo. Qualitative analysis and econometric estimation of continuous time dynamic models / Giancarlo Gandolfo with contributions by Giancarlo Martinengo and Pietro Carlo Padoan. — Amsterdam ; Oxford : North-Holland, c1981. — xiv,253p : ill ; 23cm. — (Contributions to economic analysis ; 136)
Includes bibliographies and index
ISBN 0-444-86025-8 : £15.78 B81-36746

330′.0724 — Dynamic econometric models
Burmeister, Edwin. Capital theory and dynamics / Edwin Burmeister. — Cambridge : Cambridge University Press, 1980. — xii,330p : ill ; 22cm. — (Cambridge surveys of economic literature)
Bibliography: p310-321. — Includes index
ISBN 0-521-22889-1 (cased) : £15.00
ISBN 0-521-29703-6 (pbk) : £6.95 B81-05966

330′.0724 — Economic conditions. Mathematical models
Davies, Stephen, *1948 Dec.14-*. The Treasury World economic prospects model / by Stephen Davies. — London (Parliament St., SW1P 3AG) : HM Treasury, 1979. — 68p ; 30cm. — (Government Economic Service working paper, ISSN 0141-5158 ; no.25) (Treasury working paper ; no.10)
Unpriced (pbk) B81-05541

330′.0724 — Economics. Disequilibria
Iwai, Katsuhito. Disequilibrium dynamics. — London : Yale University Press, Oct.1981. — [352]p. — (Monograph / Cowles Foundation for Research in Economics at Yale University ; 27)
ISBN 0-300-02556-4 : £26.25 : CIP entry
B81-32083

330′.0724 — Economics. Disequilibria. Econometric models
Siebrand, Jan C.. Towards operational disequilibrium macro economics / Jan C. Siebrand. — London : Nijhoff, 1979. — xv,169p ; 24cm
Bibliography: p158-161. - Includes index
ISBN 90-247-2153-9 : Unpriced B81-16501

330′.0724 — Economics. Mathematical models — *Conference proceedings*
Dynamic modelling and control of national economies : proceedings of the 3rd IFAC-IFORS Conference Warsaw, Poland, 16-19 June 1980 / edited by J.M.L. Janssen, L.F. Pau, A.J. Straszak. — Oxford : Published for the International Federation of Automatic Control by Pergamon, 1981. — xiv,417p : ill,maps ; 31cm. — (IFAC proceedings series)
Includes bibliographies
ISBN 0-08-024485-8 : £37.50 : CIP rev.
B81-05153

330′.076 — Economics — *Questions & answers — For schools*
Harvey, J.. Basic economics workbook / J. Harvey. — Basingstoke : Macmillan Educational, 1981. — 59p : ill ; 25cm
ISBN 0-333-28656-1 (pbk) : Unpriced : CIP rev. B81-00030

Thomas, D. J.. Economics. — London : Bell & Hyman, Sept.1981. — [96]p
ISBN 0-7135-1286-5 (pbk) : £1.50 : CIP entry
B81-22523

330′.07′7 — Economics — *Programmed instructions*
Bingham, Robert C.. Economic concepts : a programmed approach / Robert C. Bingham. — 5th ed. — New York ; London : McGraw-Hill, c1978. — xii,316p : ill ; 26cm
Previous ed.: New York : McGraw-Hill, 1975
ISBN 0-07-044919-8 (pbk) : £6.50 B81-06934

330′.09 — Economics, *to 1980*
Hunt, E. K.. Property and prophets : the evolution of economic institutions and ideologies / E.K. Hunt. — 4th ed. — New York ; London : Harper & Row, 1981. — xiv,217p ; 24cm
Previous ed.: i.e. rev. 2nd ed., 1978. — Includes index
ISBN 0-06-043033-8 (pbk) : £4.95 B81-22979

330′.09′04 — Economics, *1945-1980*
Bauer, P. T.. Equality, the third world and economic delusion / P.T. Bauer. — London : Weidenfeld and Nicolson, c1981. — x,293p ; 24cm
Includes index
ISBN 0-297-77645-2 : £15.00 B81-21872

330′.092′4 — Economics. Galbraith, John Kenneth — *Biographies*
Galbraith, John Kenneth. A life in our times : memoirs / John Kenneth Galbraith. — London : Deutsch, 1981. — x,563p ; 24cm
Includes index
ISBN 0-233-97383-4 : £7.50 B81-26241

330′.092′4 — Economics. Tucker, Josiah — *Biographies*
Shelton, George. Dean Tucker and eighteenth-century economic and political thought / George Shelton. — London : Macmillan, 1981. — 289p ; 23cm
Includes index
ISBN 0-333-28521-2 : £15.00 : CIP rev.
B80-20302

330.1 — ECONOMICS. SYSTEMS AND THEORIES

330.1 — Economics. Applications of information theory
Galatin, Malcolm. Economics of information / Malcolm Galatin, Robert D. Leiter. — Boston, Mass. ; London : Nijhoff, c1981. — 257p : ill ; 24cm. — (Social dimensions of economics)
Includes bibliographies
ISBN 0-89838-067-7 : Unpriced B81-25513

330.1 — Economics *related to* **philosophy,** *ca 1750-ca 1850*
Fischer, Norman. Economy and self : philosophy and economics from the mercantilists to Marx / Norman Fischer. — Westport ; London : Greenwood Press, 1979. — x,264p ; 22cm. — (Contributions in economics and economic history ; no.24)
Bibliography: p251-259. — Includes index
ISBN 0-313-20888-3 : £14.75
Also classified at 109′.033 B81-11081

330.1 — Economics. Theories
Hicks, John, *1904-*. Wealth and welfare / John Hicks. — Oxford : Blackwell, 1981. — xviii,302p : ill ; 24cm. — (Collected essays on economic theory ; v.1)
Includes index
ISBN 0-631-12536-1 : £15.00 : CIP rev.
B81-14969

McConnell, John W.. Ideas of the great economists / John W. McConnell. — 2nd ed. — New York ; London : Barnes & Noble, 1980. — vii,241p ; 21cm
Previous ed.: published as Basic teachings of the great economists. New York : New Home Library, 1943. — Includes index
ISBN 0-06-463511-2 (pbk) : £2.50 B81-02443

Nevin, Edward. Textbook of economic analysis. — 5th ed. — London : Macmillan, June 1981. — [544]p
Previous ed.: London : Macmillan, 1976
ISBN 0-333-31318-6 (pbk) : £2.95 : CIP entry
B81-13789

Pasinetti, Luigi L.. Structural change and economic growth : a theoretical essay on the dynamics of the wealth of nations / Luigi L. Pasinetti. — Cambridge : Cambridge University Press, 1981. — xv,281p : ill ; 24cm
Includes index
ISBN 0-521-23607-x : £25.00 B81-18930

330.1 — Economics. Theories, *1860-1980*
Hutchinson, T. W.. The politics and philosophy of economics. — Oxford : Blackwell, July 1981. — [350]p
ISBN 0-631-12517-5 : £15.00 : CIP entry
B81-14876

330.1 — Economics. Theories of Marshall, Alfred — *Critical studies*
Alfred Marshall : critical assessments. — London : Croom Helm, Dec.1981. — 4v.([1456]p)
ISBN 0-7099-2705-3 : £200.00 : CIP entry
B81-31432

330.1 — Economics. Theories, *to 1979*

Gray, ***Sir*** **Alexander**. The development of economic doctrine : an introductory survey / Sir Alexander Gray. — 2nd ed. / revised by Alan Thompson. — London : Longman, 1980. — xvi,474p ; 19cm
Previous ed.: London : Longmans, Green & Co., 1931. — Bibliography: p450-459. - Includes index
ISBN 0-582-44871-9 (pbk) : £7.50 : CIP rev. B80-25242

330.1 — Great Britain. Economics. Theories, *ca 1870-1940*

Pioneers of modern economics in Britain / edited by D.P. O'Brien and John R. Presley. — London : Macmillan, 1981. — xix,272p : ill ; 23cm
Includes index
ISBN 0-333-23175-9 : £20.00 B81-40577

330.1 — Soviet Union. Economics. Theories, *ca 1920-1979*

Katsenelinboigen, Aron. Soviet economic thought and political power in the USSR / Aron Katsenelinboigen. — New York ; Oxford : Pergamon, c1980. — xiv,213p : ill ; 24cm. — (Pergamon policy studies on the Soviet Union and Eastern Europe)
Includes index
ISBN 0-08-022467-9 : £12.50 B81-22978

330.12′2 — Capitalism

Lestrade, Star Sebastian. Questions and answers - capitalist doctrine / Star Sebastian Lestrade. — Bognor Regis : New Horizon, c1981. — 73p ; 21cm
Bibliography: p73
ISBN 0-86116-442-3 : £2.95 B81-32571

330.12′2 — Capitalism — *Marxist viewpoints*

Hilferding, Rudolf. Finance capital : a study of the latest phase of capitalist development / Rudolf Hilferding ; edited with an introduction by Tom Bottomore ; from translations by Morris Watnick and Sam Gordon. — London : Routledge & Kegan Paul, 1981. — vi,466p ; 25cm
Translation of: Das Finanzkapital. — Bibliography: p438-444. — Includes index
ISBN 0-7100-0618-7 : £22.50 : CIP rev. B80-34580

Jessop, Bob. Theories of the capitalist state. — Oxford : Martin Robertson, Feb.1982. — [230]p
ISBN 0-85520-269-6 (cased) : £12.50 : CIP entry
ISBN 0-85520-268-8 (pbk) : £4.95 B81-35853

330.12′2 — Capitalism. Socioeconomic aspects — *Marxist viewpoints*

Beyond welfare capitalism : issues, actors and forces in societal change / Ulf Himmelstrand ... [et al.]. — London : Heinemann, 1981. — xviii,370p : ill ; 23cm
Bibliography: p346-357. — Includes index
ISBN 0-435-82405-8 : £19.50 B81-36791

330.12′2 — Capitalism. Theories of Marxists

Weeks, John. Capital and exploitation. — London : Edward Arnold, Nov.1981. — [224]p
ISBN 0-7131-6350-x (cased) : £11.50 : CIP entry
ISBN 0-7131-6351-8 (pbk) : £4.95 B81-30385

330.12′2′09 — Capitalism, *to 1980*

Schumpeter's vision. — Eastbourne : Praeger, Sept.1981. — [224]p
ISBN 0-03-060276-9 : £5.95 : CIP entry B81-25128

330.12′2′091812 — Western world. Capitalism, *to 1979*

Vaizey, John. Capitalism and socialism : a history of industrial growth / John Vaizey. — London : Weidenfeld and Nicolson, c1980. — vii,283p ; 23cm
Bibliography: p272-275. — Includes index
ISBN 0-297-77848-x : £12.50
Also classified at 335′.009181′2 B81-13191

330.12′2′0941 — Great Britain. Capitalism — *Marxist viewpoints*

Campbell, Mike. Capitalism in the UK : a perspective from Marxist political economy / Mike Campbell. — London : Croom Helm, c1981. — 204p ; 23cm
Bibliography: p193-200. - Includes index
ISBN 0-7099-0089-9 (cased) : £11.95
ISBN 0-7099-0090-2 (pbk) : £5.95 B81-13349

330.12′2′0942 — England. Capitalism, *1700-1900.* **Historiology**

Tribe, Keith. Genealogies of capitalism / Keith Tribe. — London : Macmillan, 1981. — xvi,175p : ill,1facsim ; 23cm
Bibliography: p155-170. — Includes index
ISBN 0-333-26832-6 : £15.00 B81-38640

330.12′2′0952 — Japan. Capitalism, *1853-1974 — Marxist viewpoints*

Halliday, Jon. A political history of Japanese capitalism / Jon Halliday. — New York ; London : Monthly Review, c1975. — xliii,466p : ill,map ; 21cm
Originally published: New York : Pantheon, 1975. — Includes index
ISBN 0-85345-471-x (pbk) : £5.25 B81-05018

330.12′2′09597 — Indo-China. Capitalism, *1870-1940*

Murray, Martin J.. The development of capitalism in colonial Indochina (1870-1940) / Martin J. Murray. — Berkley ; London : University of California Press, c1980. — xii,685p : 1map ; 24cm
Bibliography: p631-681. — Includes index
ISBN 0-520-04000-7 : £20.75 B81-34423

330.12′2′0962 — Egypt. Capitalism, *1760-1840.* **Socioeconomic aspects**

Gran, Peter. Islamic roots of capitalism : Egypt, 1760-1840 / by Peter Gran ; foreword by Afaf Lutfi Al-Sayyid Marsot. — Austin ; London : University of Texas Press, c1979. — xvii,278p ; 24cm. — (Modern Middle East series ; no.4)
Bibliography: p257-270. — Includes index
ISBN 0-292-70333-3 : Unpriced B81-11477

330.15′13 — Mercantilism

Tame, Chris R.. Against the new mercantilism : the relevance of Adam Smith / Chris R. Tame. — London (c/o 40 Floral St., WC2) : Libertarian Alliance, [1981?]. — 9p ; 23cm
Unpriced (unbound) B81-17939

330.15′2′0944 — France. Physiocracy, *ca 1770 — Humour — French texts — Early works*

Galiani, Ferdinando. La bagarre : Galiani's lost parody / edited with an introduction by Steven Laurence Kaplan. — The Hague ; London : Nijhoff, 1979. — 122p,6p of plates : ill,ports ; 24cm. — (Archives internationales d'histoire des idées = International archives of the history of ideas ; 92)
French text, English introduction. — Includes index
ISBN 90-247-2125-3 : Unpriced B81-16206

330.15′3 — Economics. Theories of Ricardo, David *— Critical studies*

Caravale, Giovanni A.. Ricardo and the theory of value distribution and growth / Giovanni A. Caravale and Domenico A. Tosato. — London : Routledge & Kegan Paul, 1980. — xii,238p : ill ; 23cm
Translation of: Un modello ricardiano di sviluppo economico. New rev. ed. — Bibliography: p203-234. - Includes index
ISBN 0-7100-0508-3 : £11.95 : CIP rev. B80-17575

330.15′3 — Economics. Theories of Ricardo, David *— Texts*

Ricardo, David. The works and correspondence of David Ricardo / edited by Piero Sraffa with the collaboration of M.H. Dobb. — Cambridge : Published for the Royal Economic Society [by] Cambridge University Press
Vol.1: On the principles of political economy and taxation. — 1951 (1981 [printing]). — lxii,447p : facsims ; 23cm
Text of 3rd ed., published 1821. — Includes index
ISBN 0-521-28505-4 (pbk) : £5.95 B81-38981

330.15′43 — General equilibrium theory

Baldry, J. C.. General equilibrium analysis : an introduction to the two-sector model / J.C. Baldry. — London : Croom Helm, c1980. — 228p : ill ; 23cm. — (A Halsted Press book)
Includes index
ISBN 0-7099-0143-7 (cased) : £12.95 : CIP rev.
ISBN 0-7099-0447-9 (pbk) : Unpriced B80-08629

330.15′5 — Welfare economics

Mishan, E. J.. Economic efficiency and social welfare : selected essays on fundamental aspects of the economic theory of social welfare / E.J. Mishan. — London : Allen & Unwin, 1981. — 280p : ill ; 26cm
Includes bibliographies and index
ISBN 0-04-330314-5 (cased) : Unpriced : CIP rev.
ISBN 0-04-330315-3 (pbk) : Unpriced B81-12837

Mishan, E. J.. Introduction to normative economics / E.J. Mishan. — New York ; Oxford : Oxford University Press, 1981. — xxi,548p : ill ; 23cm
Bibliography: p533-537. — Includes index
ISBN 0-19-502791-4 (pbk) : £9.95 B81-22788

Mishan, Ezra. Introduction to welfare economics. — London : Hutchinson, Sept.1981. — [224]p
ISBN 0-09-145390-9 (cased) : £12.00 : CIP entry
ISBN 0-09-145391-7 (pbk) : £4.95 B81-22552

Sugden, Robert. The political economy of public choice : an introduction to welfare economics / Robert Sugden. — Oxford : Robertson, 1981. — xiii,217p : ill ; 24cm
Bibliography: p204-211. — Includes index
ISBN 0-85520-277-7 (cased) : £15.00 : CIP rev.
ISBN 0-85520-276-9 (pbk) : £5.95 B81-08816

330.15′5 — Welfare economics. Econometric models

Measurement in public choice / edited by Steinar Strøm. — London : Macmillan, 1981. — xi,212p : ill ; 25cm
Includes bibliographies
ISBN 0-333-27767-8 : £15.00 B81-31311

330.15′6 — Economics. Keynes, John Maynard. General theory of employment, interest and money — *Critical studies*

Chakrabarti, Santi K.. The two-sector general theory model / Santi K. Chakrabarti. — London : Macmillan, 1979. — viii,56p : ill ; 22cm
Bibliography: p53-54. — Includes index
ISBN 0-333-27328-1 : £8.95 : CIP rev. B79-29921

Fender, John. Understanding Keynes : an analysis of The general theory / John Fender. — Brighton : Wheatsheaf, 1981. — ix,160p : ill ; 23cm
Bibliography: p152-157. — Includes index
ISBN 0-7108-0110-6 : £15.95 : CIP rev. B81-12808

330.15′7 — Economics. Theories of Walras, Leon

Morishima, Michio. Walras' economics : a pure theory of capital and money / Michio Morishima. — Cambridge : Cambridge University Press, 1977 (1981 [printing]). — viii,212p : ill ; 22cm
Includes index
ISBN 0-521-28522-4 (pbk) : £6.95 B81-37144

330.9 — ECONOMIC CONDITIONS

330.9 — Capitalist countries. Economic conditions. Effects of international capital

Murray, Robin, *1940-*. Multinational companies and nation states : two essays / by Robin Murray. — Nottingham : Spokesman, 1975. — 108p ; 19cm
ISBN 0-85124-139-5 (pbk) : £1.75 B81-33256

330.9 — Democracies. Economic policies. Political aspects

Usher, Dan. The economic prerequisite to democracy / Dan Usher. — Oxford : Blackwell, 1981. — xv,160p : ill ; 24cm
Includes index
ISBN 0-631-12512-4 : £9.50 B81-24178

330.9 — Economic conditions — *Forecasts*

Gribbin, John. Future worlds / John Gribbin for the Science Policy Research Unit, University of Sussex, Brighton, England. — New York ; London : Plenum, 1981, c1979. — 224p : ill ; 22cm
Originally published: London : Abacus, 1979. — Bibliography: p216-218. — Includes index
ISBN 0-306-40780-9 : Unpriced B81-31777

330.9 — Economic conditions. Geographical aspects

De Souza, Anthony R.. World space-economy / Anthony R. de Souza, J. Brady Foust. — Columbus ; London : Merrill, c1979. — xvi,615,[23]p : ill,maps,ports ; 26cm
Bibliography: p[1-15]. - Includes index
ISBN 0-675-08292-7 : £13.95 B81-02253

330.9 — Economic development

Dynamics of world development / edited by Richard Rubinson. — Beverly Hills ; London : Sage, c1981. — 264p ; 22cm. — (Political economy of the world-system annuals ; v.4)
Includes bibliographies
ISBN 0-8039-1591-8 (cased) : Unpriced : CIP rev.
ISBN 0-8039-1592-6 (pbk) : £6.50 B81-34188

Streeten, Paul. Development perspectives / Paul Streeten. — London : Macmillan, 1981. — vi,449p ; 23cm
Includes bibliographies and index
ISBN 0-333-28567-0 : £25.00 B81-38737

Streeten, Paul. The frontiers of development studies / Paul Streeten. — London : Macmillan, 1979, c1972. — x,498p : ill ; 22cm
Originally published: 1972. — Includes index
ISBN 0-333-13195-9 (cased) : £15.00 : CIP rev.
ISBN 0-333-27553-5 (pbk) : £5.95 B79-21609

330.9 — Economic development — *Case studies*

Roemer, Michael. Cases in economic development : projects, policies and strategies / Michael Roemer and Joseph J. Stern. — London : Butterworths, 1981. — xvi,287p : ill,1map ; 24cm. — (Butterworths advanced economic texts)
Includes bibliographies and index
ISBN 0-408-10729-4 (cased) : Unpriced : CIP rev.
ISBN 0-408-10730-8 (pbk) : Unpriced B81-07928

330.9 — Economic development. Inequalities

Disparities in economic development since the Industrial Revolution / edited by Paul Bairoch and Maurice Lévy-Leboyer. — London : Macmillan, 1981. — xviii,428p : ill,maps ; 23cm
Includes bibliographies and index
ISBN 0-333-26801-6 : £25.00 : CIP rev. B80-13731

Laidlaw, Kenneth. Fractured world. — London : Ash & Grant, Oct.1981. — [176]p
ISBN 0-904069-47-8 : £6.95 : CIP entry B81-28005

330.9 — Economic development. Inequalities. Alleviation. Independent Commission on International Development Issues. North-South, a programme for survival — *Critical studies*

Bowe, Paul. The Brandt report : commentary and summary / by Paul Bowe. — Dublin (St. Saviour's, Dublin 1) : Dominican Publications, 1981. — 36p ; 21cm
ISBN 0-907271-06-5 (pbk) : Unpriced B81-29238

Handbook of world development : the guide to the Brandt Report / compiled by GJW Government Relations with Peter Stephenson ; foreword by Willy Brandt. — Harlow : Longman, 1981. — x,177p ; 19cm
Bibliography: p175-176
ISBN 0-582-64386-4 (pbk) : £1.95 B81-40138

Towards one world. — London : Maurice Temple Smith, Oct.1981. — [352]p
ISBN 0-85117-218-0 (pbk) : £5.95 : CIP entry B81-31188

330.9 — Economic development. Inequalities. Alleviation — *Proposals*

Riddell, Robert, *1934-*. Ecodevelopment : economics, ecology and development : an alternative to growth imperative models / Robert Riddell. — Farnborough : Gower, c1981. — xxii,218p : ill,maps ; 23cm
Bibliography: p203-212. — Includes index
ISBN 0-566-00411-9 (cased) : £12.50 B81-36292

330.9 — Economic development. Inequalities. Spatial aspects

Cole, J. P.. The development gap : a spatial analysis of world poverty and inequality / J.P. Cole. — Chichester : Wiley, c1981. — x,454p : ill,maps ; 25cm
Bibliography: p447-450. - Includes index
ISBN 0-471-27796-7 : £16.90 B81-09752

330.9 — Economic development. Influence of economic theories — *Conference proceedings*

The Relevance of economic theories : proceedings of a conference held by the International Economic Association in collaboration with the Polish Economic Association at Warsaw, Poland / edited by Jozef Pajestka and C.H. Feinstein. — London : Macmillan, 1980. — xv,311p : ill ; 23cm
Includes index
ISBN 0-333-28601-4 : £20.00 : CIP rev. B80-18613

330.9 — Economic development. Political aspects

Hirschman, Albert O.. Essays in trespassing : economics to politics and beyond / Albert O. Hirschman. — Cambridge : Cambridge University Press, 1981. — viii,310p ; 25cm
Includes index
ISBN 0-521-23826-9 (cased) : £20.00
ISBN 0-521-28243-8 (pbk) : £6.95 B81-38912

330.9 — Economic development. Research projects: Research projects in British institutions — *Lists — Serials*

[Development studies *(Institute of Development Studies)*]. Development studies / the Institute of Development Studies at the University of Sussex, Brighton, England. — 1979-80. — Brighton : The Institute, 1980. — iv,329p
ISSN 0141-5476 : Unpriced B81-03586

330.9 — Economic development. Role of technology

Davies, Duncan. Technologists as national policymakers / by D.S. Davies. — Egham (Park House, Wick Rd., Egham, Surrey TW20 0HW) : Maurice Lubbock Memorial Fund, c1981. — 18p : ill ; 21cm. — (The fourteenth Maurice Lubbock memorial lecture)
£0.50 (pbk) B81-22415

330.9 — Economic policies

Political economy and taxation. — Milton Keynes : Open University Press. — (Social sciences : a third level course)
At head of title: The Open University
[Block 5]: [The control of public expenditure]
Unit 15: Planning and control of public expenditure in the UK / prepared for the course team by Peter Jackson. — 1979. — 54p : ill ; 30cm. — (D323 ; block 5, unit 15)
Bibliography: p53
ISBN 0-335-08513-x (pbk) : Unpriced B81-20370

Political economy and taxation. — Milton Keynes : Open University Press. — (Social sciences : a third level course)
At head of title: The Open University
[Block 5]: [The control of public expenditure]
Unit 16: The budgetary process / prepared for the course team by Peter Jackson. — 1979. — 44p : ill ; 30cm. — (D323 ; block 5, unit 16)
Bibliography: p41
ISBN 0-335-08514-8 (pbk) : Unpriced B81-20371

330.9 — Economics. Geographical aspects

O'Sullivan, Patrick. Geographical economics / Patrick O'Sullivan. — London : Macmillan, 1981. — 199p : ill ; 23cm
Includes index
ISBN 0-333-31854-4 : £15.00 B81-22380

330.9 — Ethnic minorities. Economic conditions

Sowell, Thomas. Markets and minorities / Thomas Sowell. — Oxford : Blackwell for the International Center for Economic Policy Studies, 1981. — xi,141p : ill ; 23cm
Includes index
ISBN 0-631-12674-0 (cased) : £7.95 : CIP rev.
ISBN 0-631-12607-4 (pbk) : Unpriced B81-06578

330.9 — Industrialised countries. Economic policies — *Conference proceedings*

The political economy of new and old industrial countries. — London : Butterworth, Apr.1981. — [296]p
Conference papers
ISBN 0-408-10774-x : £16.00 : CIP entry B81-04202

330.9 — World. Economic conditions, *1450-1980*

Wallerstein, Immanuel. The modern world-system / Immanuel Wallerstein. — New York ; London : Academic Press. — (Studies in social discontinuity)
1: Capitalist agriculture and the origins of the European world-economy in the sixteenth century. — c1974. — xiv,410p : ill ; 24cm
Bibliography: p359-386. — Includes index
ISBN 0-12-785919-5 (pbk) : £5.40 B81-22397

330.9 — World. Economic conditions. Models

Groping in the dark. — Chichester : Wiley, Feb.1982. — [308]p
ISBN 0-471-10027-7 : £10.15 : CIP entry B81-36236

330.9'001 — Economic development. Inequalities. Theories

Kubálková, V.. International inequality / V. Kubálková and A.A. Cruickshank. — London : Croom Helm, c1981. — 293p : ill ; 23cm
Includes index
ISBN 0-7099-0221-2 : £13.95 B81-27575

330.9'005 — Economic conditions — *History — Serials*

[Review *(Fernand Braudel Center for the Study of Economies, Historical Systems, and Civilizations)*]. Review : a journal of the Fernand Braudel Center for the Study of Economies, Historical Systems, and Civilizations. — Vol.1 (Summer 1977)-. — Beverly Hills, Cal. : Sage ; London : Sage [Distributor], 1977-. — v. ; 22cm
Quarterly. — Description based on: Vol.3, no.2 (Fall 1979)
ISSN 0147-9032 = Review — Fernand Braudel Center for the Study of Economies, Historical Systems, and Civilizations : Unpriced B81-08766

330.9'04 — Economic development, *1947-1967*

. Essays in modern economic development / edited by R.L. Smyth ; with an introduction by G.L.S. Shackle. — London : Duckworth, 1969 (1980 [printing]). — 327p : ill ; 23cm
Conference papers. — Includes index
ISBN 0-7156-1521-1 : £24.00 B81-08372

330.9'047 — Economic conditions, *1970-1980*

Frank, André Gunder. Crisis : in the world economy / André Gunder Frank. — London : Heinemann, 1980. — xvi,366p : ill ; 24cm
Bibliography: p329-355. - Includes index
ISBN 0-435-84357-5 (cased) : £13.50 : CIP rev.
ISBN 0-435-84358-3 (pbk) : £4.95 B80-20304

330.9'047 — Economic conditions, *ca 1970-1980 — Marxist viewpoints*

Mandel, Ernest. The second slump : a Marxist analysis of recession in the seventies / Ernest Mandel ; translated by Jon Rothschild. — London : Verso, 1980, c1978. — 226p : ill ; 21cm
Translation of: Ende der Krise oder Krise ohne Ende?. — Originally published: London : NLB, 1978. — Includes index
ISBN 0-86091-012-1 (cased) : £6.50
ISBN 0-86091-728-2 (pbk) : £2.95 B81-08753

330.9'048 — Economic conditions — *Forecasts — Serials*

[World outlook *(London : 1969)*]. World outlook / the Economist Intelligence Unit. — 1981. — London : The Unit, 1981. — 155p
ISSN 0424-3331 : Unpriced B81-17483

330.9′048 — Economic conditions. Political aspects

Contemporary political economy : studies on the interdependance of politics and economics / edited by Douglas A. Hibbs Jr. and Heino Fassbender with the assistance of R. Douglas Rivers. — Amsterdam ; Oxford : North-Holland, c1981. — x,282p : ill ; 23cm. — (Contributions to economic analysis ; 135)
Includes bibliographies
ISBN 0-444-86014-2 : £15.38 B81-19273

Frank, Andre Gunder. Reflections on the world economic crisis / Andre Gunder Frank. — London : Hutchinson, 1981. — 164p ; 21cm
ISBN 0-09-144990-1 (cased) : £6.95 : CIP rev.
ISBN 0-09-144991-x (pbk) : £3.50 B81-12817

330.9′048 — Economic conditions — *Serials*

The **World** economy : a quarterly journal on international economic affairs. — Vol.1, no.1 (Oct.1977)-. — Oxford : Blackwell for the Trade Policy Research Centre, 1977-. — v. ; 25cm
Published: Amsterdam : Elsevier, 1977-1980. — Description based on: Vol.4, no.1 (Mar.1981)
ISSN 0378-5920 = World economy : £14.00 per year (£26.00 to institutions) B81-33712

330.9′048 — Economic development. Econometric models

Hughes, Barry B.. World modeling : the Mesarovic-Pestel world model in the context of its contemporaries / Barry B. Hughes. — Lexington : Lexington Books ; [Farnborough, Hants.] : Gower [distributor], 1980. — xi,227p : ill ; 24cm
Bibliography: p207-218. - Includes index
ISBN 0-669-03401-0 : £15.00 B81-04422

330.9′048 — Economic development — *Serials*

World development report. — 1980. — New York ; Oxford : Published for the World Bank [by] Oxford University Press, c1980. — viii,166p
ISBN 0-19-502833-3 : £3.50
ISSN 0163-5085 B81-01976

330.9172′4 — Communist developing countries. Politico-economic systems

The **New** communist Third World. — London : Croom Helm, Nov.1981. — [352]p
ISBN 0-7099-2709-6 : £14.95 : CIP entry B81-31167

330.9′172′4 — Developing countries. Economic conditions — *Case studies*

Case studies in development economics. — London : Heinemann Educational, Sept.1981. — [160]p. — (Case studies in economic analysis ; 8)
ISBN 0-435-33937-0 : £4.50 : CIP entry B81-22593

330.9172′4 — Developing countries. Economic conditions. Effects of imperialism. Theories of Marxists

Warren, Bill. Imperialism : pioneer of capitalism / Bill Warren ; edited by John Sender. — London : Verso, 1980. — xvii,274p ; 21cm
Bibliography: p257-270. - Includes index
ISBN 0-86091-035-0 (cased) : £11.00 : CIP rev.
ISBN 0-86091-732-0 (pbk) : £3.95 B80-17576

330.9172′4 — Developing countries. Economic conditions. Effects of increases in prices of petroleum

Hallwood, Paul. Oil, debt and development : OPEC in the Third World / Paul Hallwood and Stuart W. Sinclair. — London : Allen & Unwin, 1981. — x,206p : ill ; 23cm
Bibliography: p192-198. - Includes index
ISBN 0-04-382027-1 : £15.00 B81-10622

330.9172′4 — Developing countries. Economic conditions — *Forecasts*

Yeats, Alexander J.. Trade and development policies : leading issues for the 1980s / Alexander J. Yeats. — London : Macmillan, 1981. — xiii,208p : ill ; 23cm
Bibliography: p200-205. — Includes index
ISBN 0-333-27598-5 : £15.00 B81-38734

330.9′1724 — Developing countries. Economic conditions. Implications of economic conditions of developed countries

Wionczek, Miguel S.. Some key issues for the world periphery. — Oxford : Pergamon, Dec.1981. — [480]p
ISBN 0-08-025783-6 : £37.00 : CIP entry B81-31726

330.9172′4 — Developing countries. Economic conditions. Political aspects

Frank, André Gunder. Crisis : in the Third World / Andre Gunder Frank. — London : Heinemann, 1981. — xvii,375p : ill ; 24cm
Bibliography: p339-366. — Includes index
ISBN 0-435-84362-1 (cased) : £13.50 : CIP rev.
ISBN 0-435-84363-x (pbk) : Unpriced B81-10417

330.9172′4 — Developing countries. Economic development

Development economics and policy : readings / edited by Ian Livingstone. — London : Allen & Unwin, 1981. — 353p : ill ; 26cm
Includes bibliographies and index
ISBN 0-04-382025-5 (cased) : £17.50 : CIP rev.
ISBN 0-04-382026-3 (pbk) : £7.95 B80-22984

The **Economics** of underdevelopment : a series of articles and papers / selected and edited by A.N. Agarwala and S.P. Singh. — Delhi ; London : Oxford University Press, 1958 (1979 [printing]). — 510p : ill ; 21cm
Includes index
ISBN 0-19-560674-4 (pbk) : £3.00 B81-39495

Guernier, Maurice. Third world, three quarters of the world. — Oxford : Pergamon, Oct.1981. — [192]p
Translation of: Tiers-monde, trois quarts du monde
ISBN 0-08-027065-4 (cased) : £8.70 : CIP entry
ISBN 0-08-027066-2 (pbk) : £4.40 B81-31946

Recent issues in World development : a collection of survey articles / edited by Paul P. Streeten and Richard Jolly. — Oxford : Pergamon, 1981. — vii,441p : ill ; 26cm
Includes bibliographies and index
ISBN 0-08-026812-9 : £20.00 B81-27691

Third world poverty : new strategies for measuring development progress / edited by William Paul McGreevey. — Lexington, Mass. : Lexington Books, c1980 ; [Farnborough, Hants.] : Gower [distributor], 1981. — xx,215p : ill ; 24cm. — (The Battelle Human Affairs Research Centers series)
Bibliography: p175-209. — Includes index
ISBN 0-669-02839-8 : £11.50 B81-12467

Todaro, Michael P.. Economic development in the Third World / Michael P. Todaro. — 2nd ed. — New York ; London : Longman, 1981. — xxxiii,588p : ill ; 24cm
Previous ed.: 1977. — Bibliography: p555-580. — Includes index
ISBN 0-582-29533-5 (pbk) : £7.95 B81-23679

330.9172′4 — Developing countries. Economic development, *1914-1939*

Latham, A. J. H.. The Depression and the developing world, 1914-1939 / A.J.H. Latham. — London : Croom Helm, c1981. — 230p ; 23cm
Bibliography: p205-216. — Includes index
ISBN 0-85664-920-1 : £12.95 B81-24201

330.9172′4 — Developing countries. Economic development *compared with* economic development of China, *1950-1979*

China's development experience in comparative perspective / edited by Robert F. Dernberger. — Cambridge, Mass. ; London : Harvard University Press, 1980. — vi,347p ; 1map ; 25cm. — (Harvard East Asian series ; 93)
Includes index
ISBN 0-674-11890-1 : £15.00
Primary classification 330.951′05 B81-09355

330.9172′4 — Developing countries. Economic development. Effects of imperialism

Kiernan, V. G.. Development, imperialism, and some misconceptions / Victor Kiernan. — Norwich : Geo Books, 1981. — 34p ; 21cm. — (Occasional paper / University College of Swansea. Centre for Development Studies, ISSN 0114-9494 ; no.13)
ISBN 0-86094-074-8 (pbk) : Unpriced B81-17568

330.9172′4 — Developing countries. Economic development — *Proposals*

Anell, Lars. The developing countries and the world economic order / Lars Anell and Birgitta Nygren. — London : Methuen, 1980. — 217p ; 22cm
Bibliography: p175-186. - Includes index
ISBN 0-416-74630-6 (pbk) : £3.25 B81-06294

330.9172′4 — Developing countries. Economic development. Role of professional education of accountants in developing countries

Enthoven, Adolf J. H.. Accounting education in economic development management / by Adolf J.H. Enthoven ; with a foreword by Jan Tinbergen. — Amsterdam ; Oxford : North-Holland, c1981. — ix,448p : ill ; 25cm
Bibliography: p433. — Includes index
ISBN 0-444-86195-5 : Unpriced B81-25512

330.9172′4 — Developing countries. Economic development. Speakers in Northern England — *Directories*

Speakers and contact book for the North of England on world development. — [Oxford] ([232 Cowley Rd., Oxford]) : [Third World First], [1980?]. — 36p : ill ; 21cm
Cover title. — Includes index
£0.55 (pbk) B81-07744

330.9172′4 — Developing countries. Economic policies

Killick, Tony. Policy economics : a textbook of applied economics on developing countries / Tony Killick. — London : Heinemann, 1980. — vi,312p : ill ; 25cm
Bibliography: p302-307. - Includes index
ISBN 0-435-97373-8 (pbk) : £5.95 : CIP rev. B80-30898

330.9172′4 — Developing countries. Tropical regions. Economic development

Hodder, B. W.. Economic development in the tropics / B.W. Hodder. — 3rd ed. — London : Methuen, 1980. — xiii,255p : 2ill ; 21cm
Previous ed.: 1973. — Bibliography: p246-252. — Includes index
ISBN 0-416-74250-5 (cased) : £7.50 : CIP rev.
ISBN 0-416-74260-2 (pbk) : £3.95 B80-12740

330.9173′2 — Urban regions. Politico-economic aspects

Anderson, James, *1941-*. The political economy of urbanism : an introduction and bibliography / James Anderson. — London (36 Bedford Sq., W.C.1.) : Department of Urban and Regional Planning, Architectural Association School of Architecture, 1975. — 29,38p ; 30cm
Unpriced (unbound) B81-11521

330.917′4927 — Arab countries. Economic conditions

Amin, Samir. The Arab economy today. — London : Zed Press, Oct.1981. — [96]p
Translation of: L'économie arabe contemporaine
ISBN 0-86232-081-x : £9.95 : CIP entry B81-27467

330.9′17′4927 — Arab countries. Economic conditions — *Comparative studies*

Sayigh, Yusif A.. The Arab economy. — Oxford : Oxford University Press, Jan.1982. — [160]p
ISBN 0-19-877188-6 : £7.95 : CIP entry B81-35902

330.917′7 — Organisation for Economic Co-operation and Development countries. Economic conditions

Anell, Lars. Recession, the Western economics and the changing world order. — London : Pinter, June 1981. — [230]p
ISBN 0-903804-94-8 : £12.50 : CIP entry B81-11951

330.917'7 — Organisation for Economic Co-operation and Development countries. Economic conditions, *1969-1979 — Conference proceedings*

Outlook and Policy for Industrial Structural Change in OECD Countries *(Conference : 1979).*
Western economies in transition : structural change and adjustment policies in industrial countries / [papers and proceedings of 'Outlook and Policy for Industrial Structural Change in OECD Countries', a conference conducted by the Hudson Institute, January 25-26, 1979] ; edited by Irving Leveson and Jimmy W. Wheeler with the editorial assistance of Ernest Schneider. — Boulder : Westview ; London : Croom Helm, c1980. — xvi,438p : ill ; 24cm. — (Hudson Institute studies on the prospects for mankind)
Includes index
ISBN 0-7099-0213-1 : Unpriced : CIP rev.
B79-36200

330.9181'2 — Western world. Economic conditions, *1917-1939.* **Theories of Soviet writers**

Day, Richard B.. The 'Crisis' and the 'Crash' : soviet studies of the West (1917-1939) / Richard B. Day. — London : NLB, c1981. — x,300p : ill ; 22cm
Bibliography: p289-297. - Includes index
ISBN 0-86091-038-5 : £9.50 : CIP rev.
B81-08833

330.9181'2 — Western world. Economic conditions, *1945-1980.* **Psychological aspects**

Katona, George. A new economic era / George Katona, Burkhard Strumpel. — New York ; Oxford : Elsevier, c1978. — vii,176p : ill ; 24cm
Bibliography: p169-172. - Includes index
ISBN 0-444-00258-8 : Unpriced B81-10386

330.9181'2 — Western world. Economic conditions, *1970-1980 — Conference proceedings*

Inflation, depression and economic policy in the West / edited by Anthony S. Courakis. — London : Mansell, 1981. — 376p : ill ; 25cm
Conference papers. — Includes index
ISBN 0-7201-0915-9 : £15.00 : CIP rev.
B79-18142

330.9181'2 — Western world. Economic policies. Formulation. Influence of international financial institutions, *to 1980*

MacBean, Alasdair I.. International institutions in trade and finance / A.I. MacBean and P.N. Snowden. — London : Allen & Unwin, 1981. — xiv,255p ; 23cm. — (Studies in economics ; 18)
Bibliography: p249-252. - Includes index
ISBN 0-04-382032-8 (cased) : Unpriced : CIP rev.
ISBN 0-04-382033-6 (pbk) : Unpriced
B81-15878

330.9182'1 — Caribbean region. Economic conditions *— Serials*

Latin America regional reports. Caribbean. — RC-79-01 (23 Nov.1979)-. — London (90 Cowcross St., EC1M 6BL) : Latin American Newletters, c1979-. — v. : ill ; 30cm
Ten issues yearly. — Description based on RC-80-03 (28 Mar.1980)
ISSN 0143-523x = Latin America regional reports. Caribbean : £45.00 per year
B81-04867

330.9182'3 — Western Pacific region. Economic conditions

Whitlam, E. Gough. A Pacific community / E. Gough Whitlam. — Cambridge, Mass. : Australian Studies Endowment in collaboration with Council of East Asian Studies, Harvard University ; London : distributed by Harvard University Press, 1981. — xii,122p ; 24cm
Bibliography: p103-117. — Includes index
ISBN 0-674-65070-0 : £7.50 B81-38273

330.9182'3'025 — Pacific region. Economic conditions. Information sources *— Directories*

Sources of Asian/Pacific economic information / edited by Euan Blauvelt and Jennifer Durlacher. — Farnborough : Gower
Vol.1. — 1981. — viii,387p ; 31cm
Includes index
ISBN 0-566-02233-8 : £30.00 : CIP rev.
Primary classification 330.95'0428'025
B80-25247

Sources of Asian/Pacific economic information / edited by Euan Blauvelt and Jennifer Durlacher. — Farnborough : Gower
Vol.2. — c1981. — 365p ; 31cm
Includes index
ISBN 0-566-02234-6 : £30.00 : CIP rev.
Primary classification 330.95'0428'025
B80-25249

330.94 — European Community countries. Economic conditions

Economic divergence in the European Community / edited by Michael Hodges and William Wallace. — London : Published for the Royal Institute of International Affairs by Allen & Unwin, 1981. — vii,227p ; 23cm
Includes index
ISBN 0-04-382029-8 : £15.00 : CIP rev.
B81-13764

330.94 — European Community countries. Economic conditions. Geographical aspects

Parker, Geoffrey, *1933-*. The logic of unity : a geography of the European Economic Community / Geoffrey Parker. — 3rd ed. — London : Longman, 1981. — 208p : ill,maps ; 24cm
Previous ed.: 1975. — Bibliography: p187-192. — Includes index
ISBN 0-582-30031-2 (pbk) : £4.95 B81-12271

330.94 — European Economic Community countries. Economic policies

Hu, Yao-su. Europe under stress. — London : Butterworths, Sept.1981. — [160]p. — (Butterworths European studies)
ISBN 0-408-10808-8 : £12.00 : CIP entry
B81-20474

330.94 — North-western Europe. Remote rural regions. Economic development *— Conference proceedings*

Development in remote rural areas : a note of the proceedings of a three-day conference, 23-25 September 1980, Stornoway. — Glasgow (186 Bath St., Glasgow G2 4HG) : Planning Exchange, [1980]. — 19leaves ; 30cm. — (Forum report ; 23)
Unpriced (pbk) B81-38624

330.94'01 — Western Europe. Economic conditions, *400-1100*

Latouche, Robert. The birth of western economy. — London : Methuen, Oct.1981. — [368]p. — (Methuen library reprints)
Translation of: Les origines de l'économie occidentale. — Originally published: 1961
ISBN 0-416-32090-2 : £18.00 : CIP entry
B81-27959

330.94'02 — Europe. Economic development, *1400-1800 compared with* **economic development of Asia,** *1400-1800*

Jones, E. L. (Eric Lionel). The European miracle : environments, economies, and geopolitics in the history of Europe and Asia / E.L. Jones. — Cambridge : Cambridge University Press, 1981. — ix,276p : 1map ; 22cm
Bibliography: p252-271. — Includes index
ISBN 0-521-23588-x (cased) : £15.00
ISBN 0-521-28055-9 (pbk) : Unpriced
Also classified at 330.95'03 B81-32079

330.94'055 — Western Europe. Economic policies. Formulation. Role of parliaments, *1945-1980 — Comparative studies*

Parliaments and economic affairs : in Britain, France, Italy and the Netherlands : the results of a survey / by the Committee of Cooperation for European Parliamentary Studies ; edited by David Coombes and S.A. Walkland. — London : Heinemann for the European Centre for Political Studies of the Policy Studies Institute, 1980. — x,238p ; 23cm
Bibliography: p229-231. - Includes index
ISBN 0-435-83804-0 : £13.00 : CIP rev.
B80-20306

330.941 — Great Britain. Economic development. Implications of government monetary policies, *to 1980*

Gould, Bryan. Monetarism or prosperity? / Bryan Gould, John Mills and Shaun Stewart ; foreword by Peter Shore. — London : Macmillan, 1981. — x,222p : ill ; 23cm
Bibliography: p211-212. — Includes index
ISBN 0-333-30782-8 (cased) : £15.00
ISBN 0-333-31973-7 (pbk) : Unpriced
B81-21769

330.9'41'058 — Great Britain. Economic conditions

Cairncross, Frances. The Guardian guide to the economy. — London : Methuen, Oct.1981. — [160]p
ISBN 0-416-32560-2 (cased) : £6.00 : CIP entry
ISBN 0-416-32570-x (pbk) : £2.50 B81-28000

330.941'07 — Great Britain. Economic conditions, *1700-1850*

Speed, P. F.. The growth of the British economy 1700-1850 / P.F. Speed. — Exeter : Wheaton, 1980. — vii,200p : ill,maps,ports ; 25cm
Bibliography: p195-196. - Includes index
ISBN 0-08-024158-1 (pbk) : £3.75 B81-02941

330.941'07 — Great Britain. Economic conditions, *1700-1977*

The **Economic** history of Britain since 1700. — Cambridge : Cambridge University Press, Aug.1981
Vol.1: 1700-1860. — 1v.
ISBN 0-521-23166-3 : CIP entry
ISBN 0-521-29842-3 (pbk) : Unpriced
B81-22550

330.941'081 — Great Britain. Economic conditions, *1800-1900*

McCloskey, Donald N.. Enterprise and trade in Victorian Britain : essays in historical economics / Donald N. McCloskey. — London : Allen & Unwin, 1981. — xix,211p : ill ; 23cm
Includes index
ISBN 0-04-942170-0 (cased) : £15.00 : CIP rev.
ISBN 0-04-942171-9 (pbk) : Unpriced
B81-00770

330.941'081 — Great Britain. Economic policies, *1870-1945*

Tomlinson, Jim. Problems of British economic policy, 1870-1945. — London : Methuen, June 1981. — [155]p
ISBN 0-416-30430-3 : £8.50 : CIP entry
ISBN 0-416-30440-0 (pbk) : £4.25 B81-10458

330.941'082 — Great Britain. Economic conditions, *1870-1980*

Kirby, M. W.. The decline of British economic power since 1870 / M.W. Kirby. — London : Allen & Unwin, 1981. — 205p ; 23cm
Bibliography: p185-200. - Includes index
ISBN 0-04-942169-7 : Unpriced : CIP rev.
B81-02549

330.941'082 — Great Britain. Regional economic development, *1919-1979*

Law, Christopher M.. British regional development since World War 1. — London : Methuen, Nov.1981. — [272]p
Originally published: 1980
ISBN 0-416-32310-3 (pbk) : £4.95 : CIP entry
B81-30554

330.941'085 — Great Britain. Economic conditions, *1945-1980*

Pollard, Sidney. The wasting of the British economy. — London : Croom Helm, Jan.1982. — [192]p
ISBN 0-7099-2019-9 : £10.95 : CIP entry
B81-33891

Stafford, G. B.. The end of economic growth? : growth and decline in the UK since 1945 / G.B. Stafford. — Oxford : Robertson, 1981. — iv,124p : ill ; 22cm
Bibliography: p118-122. — Includes index
ISBN 0-85520-390-0 (cased) : £9.95 : CIP rev.
ISBN 0-85520-396-x (pbk) : £3.95 B81-13738

330.941'085'06041 — Great Britain. Economic conditions. Organisations: Institute of Economic Affairs, *to 1981*

The **Emerging** consensus ... ? : essays on the interplay between ideas, interests and circumstances in the first 25 years of the IEA / Ralph Harris ... [et al.] ; edited by Arthur Seldon. — London : Institute of Economic Affairs, 1981. — xxxv,284p ; 19cm
Includes index
ISBN 0-255-36142-4 (pbk) : £3.60 B81-24316

330.941'0857 — Great Britain. Economic conditions, *1967-1980*

Black, John, *1931-*. The economics of modern Britain : an introduction to macroeconomics / John Black. — 2nd ed. — Oxford : Robertson, 1980. — xviii,282p : ill ; 22cm
Previous ed.: 1979. — Bibliography: p278. — Includes index
ISBN 0-85520-372-2 (cased) : £12.50 : CIP rev.
ISBN 0-85520-371-4 (pbk) : £4.95 B80-12268

330.941'0857 — Great Britain. Economic conditions, *1970-1980*

Hughes, John, *1927-*. Britain in crisis : de-industrialisation and how to fight it / by John Hughes ; with a foreword by Michael Foot. — Nottingham : Spokesman, 1981. — 106p ; 22cm. — (Spokesman university paperback ; no.30)
ISBN 0-85124-317-7 (cased) : Unpriced : CIP rev.
ISBN 0-85124-312-6 (pbk) : £2.25 B81-09982

330.941'0857 — Great Britain. Economic policies

Sartorius, Michael. The simple man's guide to national prosperity. — Porthmadoc (28f South Snowdon Quay, Porthmadoc, Gwynedd LL49 9ND) : Andreas, Sept.1981. — 1v.
ISBN 0-905539-01-x (pbk) : £3.00 : CIP entry B81-22585

330.941'0857 — Great Britain. Economic policies, *1970-1979*

National income and economic policy / [the D284 Course Team]. — Rev. and reset. — Milton Keynes : Open University Press. — (Social sciences : a second level course)
At head of title: The Open University. — Previous ed.: 1972
Unit 13: Money and national income (II) / by F.S. Brooman. Unit 14: Inflation : analysis / by Rosalind Levačić. — 1979. — 56p : ill ; 30cm. — (D284 ; 13 + 14)
Includes bibliographies
ISBN 0-335-07381-6 (pbk) : Unpriced B81-19465

National income and economic policy / [the D284 Course Team]. — Milton Keynes : Open University Press. — (Social sciences : a second level course)
At head of title: The Open University. — Previous ed.: 1972. — Bibliography: p37
Unit 16: Conclusion : the problem of economic policy / by Laurence Harris. — 1980. — 37p : ill ; 30cm. — (D284 ; 16)
ISBN 0-335-07383-2 (pbk) : Unpriced B81-19464

330.941'0858 — Great Britain. Economic conditions — *For retail trades — Serials*

[**Economic review** *(Co-operative Union. Economic & Research Department)*]. Economic review. — 1980-81. — London : Economic & Research Dept., Co-operative Union ([1980]). — 105p
Unpriced B81-02332

330.941'0858 — Great Britain. Economic conditions — *For schools*

Nobbs, Jack. Social economics / Jack Nobbs. — 3rd ed. — London : McGraw-Hill, 1981. — x,264p : ill,maps,forms ; 25cm
Previous ed.: 1975. — Includes index
ISBN 0-07-084643-x (pbk) : £3.95 B81-19466

Sendall, Wilfrid. The economic facts of life / [by Wilfrid Sendall]. — London : Macdonald Educational, 1979. — 13p : col.ill ; 28cm
Unpriced (unbound) B81-16223

330.941'0858 — Great Britain. Economic conditions. Geographical aspects

O'Sullivan, Patrick. Geographical economics / Patrick O'Sullivan. — Harmondsworth : Penguin, 1981. — 199 : ill,maps ; 20cm. — (Geography and environmental studies) (Penguin education)
Includes bibliographies and index
ISBN 0-14-080372-6 (pbk) : £3.95 B81-17035

Pounds, Norman. Success in economic geography / Norman Pounds ; consultant editor Jonathan Edwards. — London : Murray, 1981. — ix,374p : ill,maps ; 22cm. — (Success studybooks)
Bibliography: p362-366. — Includes index
ISBN 0-7195-3791-6 (pbk) : £3.95 B81-16627

330.941'0858 — Great Britain. Economic conditions — *Marxist viewpoints*

Aaronovitch, Sam. The political economy of British capitalism : a Marxist analysis / Sam Aaronovitch and Ron Smith with Jean Gardiner and Roger Moore. — London : McGraw-Hill, c1981. — ix,397p : ill ; 23cm
Bibliography: p382-388. — Includes index
ISBN 0-07-084121-7 (pbk) : £7.95 B81-20771

330.941'0858 — Great Britain. Economic conditions — *Social Democratic Party viewpoints*

Owen, David, *1938-*. Fourth Hoover Address : delivered at the University of Strathclyde, Glasgow / David Owen. — [Glasgow] ([George St., Glasgow G1 1XW]) : University of Strathclyde, 1981. — 19p ; 22cm
Unpriced (pbk) B81-32810

330.941'0858 — Great Britain. Economic conditions — *Trades Union Congress viewpoints — Serials*

Plan for growth : the economic alternative : TUC economic review 1981. — London : Trades Union Congress, 1981. — 40p : ill(some col.) ; 30cm. — (TUC campaign for social and economic advance)
Cover title
£1.00 (pbk) B81-22809

330.941'0858 — Great Britain. Economic development. Local projects

Local initiatives in Great Britain (1981) / edited by Stan Windass. — Banbury (The Rookery, Adderbury, Banbury, Oxon.) : Foundation for Alternatives, 1981. — 126p ; 22cm
ISBN 0-9505081-9-5 (pbk) : Unpriced B81-12474

330.941'0858 — Great Britain. Economic policies

Big government in hard times / edited by Christopher Hood, Maurice Wright. — Oxford : Robertson, 1981. — x,230p : 1ill ; 23cm
Includes bibliographies and index
ISBN 0-85520-416-8 (cased) : £15.00 : CIP rev.
ISBN 0-85520-417-6 (pbk) : £4.95 B81-23823

330.941'0858 — Great Britain. Economic policies — *Confederation of British Industry viewpoints*

The **Will** to win : summary. — London : Confederation of British Industry, 1981. — 35p : ill ; 21x20cm
£1.50 (pbk) B81-21919

330.941'0858 — Great Britain. Economic policies — *Convention of Scottish Local Authorities viewpoints*

Convention of Scottish Local Authorities. The COSLA critique : government economic strategy. — Edinburgh (3 Forres St., Edinburgh EH3 6BL) : The Convention, 1981. — 52p : ill ; 21cm
£0.95 (pbk) B81-29235

330.941'0858 — Great Britain. Economic policies. Decision making — *For schools*

Donaldson, Peter. The economy and decision making / Peter Donaldson and Jim Clifford. — 2nd ed. — London : Longman, 1980. — x,187p : ill ; 24cm + 1 teachers guide(55p : ill ; spiral). — (Understanding business)
Previous ed.: 1977. — Includes index
ISBN 0-582-35546-x (pbk) : £3.25
ISBN 0-582-35553-2 (Teacher's guide) : Unpriced B81-13013

330.941'0858 — Great Britain. Economic policies — *Inquiry reports*

Great Britain. *Parliament. House of Commons. Treasury and Civil Service Committee.* Second report from the Treasury and Civil Service Committee, session 1980/81 : the Government's economic policy, autumn review : together with the proceedings of the Committe, the minutes of evidence and appendices. — London : H.M.S.O.
Vol.1: Report. — [1980]. — xv p ; 25cm. — ([HC] ; 79-I)
ISBN 0-10-271081-3 (pbk) : £1.90 B81-20666

330.941'0858 — Great Britain. Economic policies — *Proposals*

Aaronovitch, Sam. The road from Thatcherism : the alternative economic strategy / by Sam Aaronovitch. — London : Lawrence and Wishart, 1981. — 138p ; 22cm
Bibliography: p131-132. — Includes index
ISBN 0-85315-534-8 (pbk) : £2.95 B81-20010

330.941'0858 — Great Britain. Economic policies - *Socialist viewpoints*

Holland, Stuart. Strategy for socialism. — 2nd ed. — Nottingham : Spokesman, May 1981. — [100]p
Previous ed.: 1975
ISBN 0-85124-313-4 (cased) : £6.00 : CIP entry
ISBN 0-85124-314-2 (pbk) : £2.00 B81-07474

330.941'0858 — Great Britain. Rural regions. Economic conditions

Future of the rural economy. — [London] : [Royal Institution of Chartered Surveyors], 1981. — 35p : ill ; 30cm
Bibliography: p32-34
£2.40 (£2.00 to members) (pbk) B81-22240

330.941'0858 — Great Britain. Rural regions. Economic development — *Developing countries viewpoints*

Rural decline in the United Kindom : a Third World view - / by B.S. Baviskar ... [et al.] ; edited by E.J. Woods. — Langholm (Langholm, Dumfriesshire DG13 0HL) : Arkleton Trust, c1980. — 27p ; 21cm
£2.00 (pbk) B81-09552

330.941'0858'0212 — Great Britain. Economic conditions — *Statistics — Serials*

Economic trends. Annual supplement / Central Statistical Office. — 1981 ed.. — London : H.M.S.O., 1980. — 235p
ISBN 0-11-726031-2 : £6.45
ISSN 0308-1133 B81-09175

330.941'0858'024381 — Great Britain. Economic conditions — *For grocery trades — Serials*

[**Economic bulletin** *(Institute of Grocery Distribution. Research Services)*]. Economic bulletin / Institute of Grocery Distribution Research Services. — 24 Mar.1981-. — [Watford] : The Institute, 1981-. — v. ; 30cm
Monthly. — Continues: Review of economic forecasts of the UK. Update ; and also a section in, Grocery bulletin
ISSN 0261-8648 = Economic bulletin - Institute of Grocery Distribution. Research Services : £36.00 per year B81-33710

330.941'0858'024381 — Great Britain. Economic conditions — *For retail trades — Serials*

[**Economic prospects** *(Manchester)*]. Economic prospects. — 1981/82-. — [Manchester] : The Department, 1981-. — v. : charts ; 30cm
Annual. — Continues: Economic review (Co-operative Union. Economic & Research Department)
ISSN 0262-1096 = Economic prospects (Manchester) : £10.00 B81-39735

330.941'0858'05 — Great Britain. Economic conditions — *Serials*

Barclays UK economic survey. — 1st May 1981-. — London (54 Lombard St., EC3P 3AH) : Barclays Bank Group Economics Department, 1981-. — v. : ill ; 30cm
Quarterly
ISSN 0261-2305 = Barclays UK economic survey : Unpriced B81-35123

The **Journal** of economic affairs. — Vol.1, no.1 (Oct. 1980)-. — Oxford : Blackwell in association with the Institute of Economic Affairs, 1980-. — v. : ill ; 25cm
Quarterly
ISSN 0260-8359 = Journal of economic affairs : £15.00 per year B81-20298

330.9411'0856 — Scotland. Economic development, *1960-1978*. Cyclical indicators

Cuthbert, M.. Cyclical indicators of the Scottish economy 1960-1978 / by M. Cuthbert. — Glasgow (100 Montrose St., Glasgow G4 0LZ) : Fraser of Allander Institute, 1980. — 35p : ill ; 21cm. — (Research monograph / Fraser of Allander Institute ; no.7)
Bibliography: p36
ISBN 0-904865-24-x (pbk) : £2.00 B81-19491

330.9411'106 — Scotland. Orkney, Shetland & Hebrides. Economic conditions, *1600-1700*

Shaw, Frances J.. The northern and western islands of Scotland : their economy and society in the seventeenth century / Frances J. Shaw. — Edinburgh (138 St Stephen St., Edinburgh [EH3 5AA]) : Donald, c1980. — ix,270p : ill,5maps ; 25cm
Bibliography: p243-247. - Includes index
ISBN 0-85976-059-6 : £15.00 B81-10822

330.9411'4 — Scotland. Western Isles. Isle of Lewis & Isle of Harris. Rural regions. Economic development

Abercrombie, Keith. Rural development in Lewis and Harris : the Western Isles of Scotland / by Keith Abercrombie. — Arkleton (Arkleton, Langholm, Dumfriesshire) : Arkleton Trust, c1981. — 28p : ill ; 21cm
£2.00 (pbk) B81-30668

330.9411'50858 — Scotland. Highland Region. Economic development — *Forecasts*

The **Highland** Region of Scotland : a preliminary study of economic resources and employment potential / prepared [by the Economist Intelligence Unit Ltd] in association with the Clydesdale Bank Ltd for the Highland Regional Council. — London : Economist Intelligence Unit, 1980. — xviii,211p ; 30cm
Unpriced (spiral) B81-34752

330.9412'350858 — Scotland. Grampian Region. Aberdeen. Economic conditions. Effects of exploitation of petroleum deposits in North Sea

Mackay, G. A.. North Sea oil and the Aberdeen economy / by G.A. Mackay and Ann C. Moir. — London : Social Science Research Council, c1980. — 105p : ill,2maps ; 21cm. — (Occasional paper / North Sea Oil Panel ; no.3)
Bibliography: p104-105
ISBN 0-86226-036-1 (pbk) : £2.80 B81-16172

330.9412'92 — Scotland. Fife Region. St Andrews region. Economic conditions. Effects of Open Championship *(1978 : St. Andrews)*

Blake, Christopher. The 1978 Open Championship at St. Andrews : an economic impact study / Christopher Blake, Stuart McDowall, Jennifer Devlen. — Edinburgh : Scottish Academic Press, 1979. — 47p in various pagings : forms ; 22cm
ISBN 0-7073-0254-4 (pbk) : £1.00 B81-24398

330.9414'54 — Scotland. Strathclyde Region. East Kilbride. Economic conditions, *to 1979*

Cameron, Gordon C.An economic study / conducted for the East Kilbride Development Corporation by G.C. Cameron ... [et al.]. — [East Kilbride] ([Atholl House, East Kilbride G74 1LU]) : [The Corporation], 1979. — vii,153p,[12]p of plates : ill ; 30cm
£5.00 (pbk) B81-07316

330.942 — England. Economic conditions, *1066-1979*

Chappell, D. J.. An economic history of England : from 1066 to the present day / D.J. Chappell. — Plymouth : Macdonald and Evans, 1980. — vii,286p ; 18cm. — (The M & E handbook series)
Includes index
ISBN 0-7121-0587-5 (pbk) : £2.25 B81-01554

330.942'0858 — England. Urban regions. Economic activity. Relationship to land use. Data. Canonical correlation analysis

Doling, J. F.. An analysis of function and form in fifty three British towns / J. Doling and E.M. Davies. — [Birmingham] : [Department of Geography, University of Birmingham], 1980. — 46p : maps ; 30cm. — (Occasional publication / Department of Geography, University of Birmingham ; no.11)
Bibliography: p42
ISBN 0-7044-0399-4 (pbk) : £1.00
Primary classification 333.77'13'0942
B81-39715

330.9425'085 — England. East Midlands. Economic conditions, *1953-1979*

Aldcroft, Derek H.. The East Midlands economy : an economic and business review of the East Midlands region, including a register of businesses / by Derek H. Aldcroft ; a survey commissioned by Pointon York Limited ... — London ([25 Bedford Row, WC1R 4HE]) : Pointon York, 1979. — 85p : 1map ; 30cm
Bibliography: p65-67
ISBN 0-906840-15-5 (spiral) : Unpriced
B81-08334

330.9427'0858 — Northern England. Regional economic development

Goddard, J. B.. Problems and prospects of economic development in the northern region of England / J.B. Goddard. — [Newcastle upon Tyne] : University of Newcastle upon Tyne, Centre for Urban and Regional Development Studies, 1981. — 12leaves ; 30cm. — (Discussion paper / University of Newcastle upon Tyne, Centre for Urban and Regional Development Studies, ISSN 0140-6515 ; no.33)
Unpriced (pbk) B81-13922

330.9428'70857 — Tyne and Wear *(Metropolitan County)*. **Economic development. Role of local authorities,** *1974-1979*

Dabinett, Gordon. The declaration of industrial improvement areas, and the provision of advance factories, loans and grants by local authorities in Tyne and Wear 1974-1979 / by Gordon Dabinett, Pamela Whisker. — Newcastle upon Tyne : Dept. of Town & Country Planning, University of Newcastle upon Tyne, 1981. — 63p,[3]leaves of plates : 3maps ; 30cm. — (Working paper / Inner City Employment Project ; no.2)
Bibliography: p60-61
£1.00 (spiral) B81-19391

330.9429'0858'05 — Wales. Economic conditions — *Statistics* — *Serials*

Welsh economic trends / Welsh Office. — No.7 (1980). — Cardiff : H.M.S.O., 1981. — viii,106p
ISBN 0-11-790142-3 : £11.00 B81-29439

330.943'08 — Germany. Economic conditions, *1910-1970*

Hardach, Karl. The political economy of Germany in the twentieth century / Karl Hardach. — Berkeley ; London : Univeristy of California Press, c1980. — xii,235p : maps ; 25cm
Translation of: Wirtschaftsgeschichte Deutschlands im 20. Jahrhundert. — Includes bibliographies and index
ISBN 0-520-03809-6 : £13.50 B81-11250

330.9438'05 — Poland. Economic conditions, *1945-1980.* **Political aspects** — *Polish texts*

Fallenbuchl, Zbigniew Marian. Polityka gospodarcza prl / Zbigniew Marian Fallenbuchl. — London (27 Hamilton Rd., Bedford Park, W4 1AL) : Odnowa, 1980. — 58p ; 21cm. — (Polska w świecie wspolczesnym ; zesz 7)
ISBN 0-903705-33-8 (pbk) : Unpriced
B81-21021

330.9438'055 — Poland. Economic conditions

Portes, Richard. The Polish crisis : Western economic policy options / Richard Portes. — London : Royal Institute of International Affairs, c1981. — vii,58p ; 25cm. — (Chatham House special)
ISBN 0-905031-22-9 (pbk) : £3.50 B81-12263

330.9439'053 — Hungary. Economic policies, *1968-1978*

Hungary : a decade of economic reform / edited by P.G. Hare, H.K. Radice and N. Swain. — London : Allen & Unwin, 1981. — xiv,257p ; 23cm
Includes bibliographies and index
ISBN 0-04-339021-8 : Unpriced : CIP rev.
B81-06577

330.944 — France. Economic development, *1730-1914*

Price, Roger, *1944-*. An economic history of modern France, 1730-1914 / Roger Price. — Rev. ed. — London : Macmillan, 1981. — xii,252p : maps ; 23cm
Previous ed.: published as The economic modernisation of France. London : Croom Helm, 1975. — Includes bibliographies and index
ISBN 0-333-30545-0 (cased) : Unpriced : CIP rev.
ISBN 0-333-29321-5 (pbk) : Unpriced
B80-24150

330.944'081 — France. Economic policies, *1900-1950*

Kuisel, Richard F.. Capitalism and the state in modern France : renovation and economic management in the twentieth century / Richard F. Kuisel. — Cambridge : Cambridge University Press, 1981. — xiv,344p ; 24cm
Bibliography: p332-334. — Includes index
ISBN 0-521-23474-3 : £20.00 B81-36656

330.944'38305 — France. Alsace. Economic conditions. Effects of Continental blockade, *1803-1813*

Ellis, Geoffrey. Napoleon's continental blockade : the case of Alsace / by Geoffrey Ellis. — Oxford : Clarendon, 1981. — xvi,355p : ill,maps ; 23cm. — (Oxford historical monographs)
Bibliography: p296-332. — Includes index
ISBN 0-19-821881-8 : £17.50 B81-18975

330.9'46'08 — Spain. Economic conditions. Political aspects, *1939-1980*

Lieberman, Sima. The contemporary Spanish economy. — London : Allen and Unwin, Feb.1982. — [384]p
ISBN 0-04-339026-9 : £20.00 : CIP entry
B81-35927

330.946'083 — Spain. Economic conditions — *For businessmen*

Box, Ben. Spain : business opportunities in the 1980s / by Metra Consulting and International Joint Ventures ; [written by Ben Box and Michael Wooller]. — London (42 Vicarage Cres., SW11 3LD) : Metra, c1980. — iv,292p : ill,3maps ; 30cm
ISBN 0-902231-23-5 (spiral) : £125.00
B81-11743

330.947 — Eastern Europe. Economic conditions — *For businessmen* — *Serials*

East European markets : the East European business and financial briefing, published alternate weeks. — Issue no.1 (1 June 1981)-. — London : Financial Times Business Information Ltd., 1981-. — v. : ill ; 30cm
ISSN 0262-0456 = East European markets : Unpriced B81-36544

330.947 — Eastern Europe. Economic policies, *1970-1980*

The **East** European economies in the 1970s. — London : Butterworths, Nov.1981. — [336]p. — (Butterworths studies in international political economy)
ISBN 0-408-10762-6 : £19.50 : CIP entry
B81-31181

330.947 — South-eastern Europe. Economic conditions, *1600-1800*

McGowan, Bruce. Economic life in Ottoman Europe. — Cambridge : Cambridge University Press, Jan.1982. — [226]p. — (Studies in modern capitalism = Etudes sur le capitalisme moderne, ISSN 0144-2333)
ISBN 0-521-24208-8 : £20.00 : CIP entry
B81-39255

330.947'0842 — Soviet Union. Economic policies, *1945-1953*

Dunmore, Timothy. The Stalinist command economy : the Soviet state apparatus and economic policy 1945-53 / Timothy Dunmore. — London : Macmillan, 1980. — xi,176p : 2ill,1map ; 23cm
Bibliography: p168-174. - Includes index
ISBN 0-333-27570-5 : £20.00 : CIP rev.
B80-12741

330.947'0853 — Soviet Union. Economic policies, *1966-1980*

Bland, W. B.. The restoration of capitalism in the Soviet Union / by W.B. Bland. — Wembley : Selecteditions, 1980. — xv,356p ; 19cm
ISBN 0-86237-000-0 (pbk) : £2.00 B81-23121

330.95'03 — Asia. Economic development, *1400-1800 compared with* **economic development of Europe,** *1400-1800*

Jones, E. L. (Eric Lionel). The European miracle : environments, economies, and geopolitics in the history of Europe and Asia / E.L. Jones. — Cambridge : Cambridge University Press, 1981. — ix,276p : 1map ; 22cm
Bibliography: p252-271. — Includes index
ISBN 0-521-23588-x (cased) : £15.00
ISBN 0-521-28055-9 (pbk) : Unpriced
Primary classification 330.94'02 B81-32079

330.95'0428'025 — Asia. Economic conditions. Information sources — *Directories*

Sources of Asian/Pacific economic information / edited by Euan Blauvelt and Jennifer Durlacher. — Farnborough : Gower
Vol.1. — 1981. — viii,387p ; 31cm
Includes index
ISBN 0-566-02233-8 : £30.00 : CIP rev.
Also classified at 330.9182'3'025 B80-25247

Sources of Asian/Pacific economic information / edited by Euan Blauvelt and Jennifer Durlacher. — Farnborough : Gower
Vol.2. — c1981. — 365p ; 31cm
Includes index
ISBN 0-566-02234-6 : £30.00 : CIP rev.
Also classified at 330.9182'3'025 B80-25249

330.95'0428'05 — East, South & South-east Asia. Economic conditions — *Serials*

Asia & Pacific annual review. — 1980. — Saffron Walden (21 Gold St., Saffron Walden, Essex CB10 1EJ) : World of Information, c1979. — 278p
ISBN 0-904439-14-3 : Unpriced
Also classified at 330.99'005 B81-10261

330.951'05 — China. Economic development, *1950-1979 compared with* **economic development of developing countries**

China's development experience in comparative perspective / edited by Robert F. Dernberger. — Cambridge, Mass. ; London : Harvard University Press, 1980. — vi,347p ; 1map ; 25cm. — (Harvard East Asian series ; 93)
Includes index
ISBN 0-674-11890-1 : £15.00
Also classified at 330.9172'4 B81-09355

330.951'05 — China. Economic development — *Conference proceedings*

China's new development strategy. — London : Academic Press, Feb.1982. — [320]p
Conference papers
ISBN 0-12-296840-9 : CIP entry B81-36067

330.9519'5043 — South Korea. Economic conditions — *For businessmen*

South Korea : business opportunities / by Metra Consulting. — London : 42 Vicarage Cres., SW11 3LD : Metra, c1980. — iv,216p : ill,2maps ; 30cm
ISBN 0-902231-26-x (corrected : spiral) : £125.00 B81-13674

330.952'03 — Japan. Economic conditions, *1867-1979*

Allen, G. C.. A short economic history of modern Japan / G.C. Allen. — 4th ed. — London : Macmillan, 1981. — x,305p ; 23cm
Previous ed.: London : Allen and Unwin, 1972. — Bibliography: p286-298. - Includes index
ISBN 0-333-26166-6 : £20.00 : CIP rev. B80-20308

330.952'03 — Japan. Economic development, *1897-1973*

Allen, G. C.. Japan's economic policy / G.C. Allen. — London : Macmillan, 1980. — x,215p : ill ; 23cm
ISBN 0-333-26165-8 : £15.00 : CIP rev. B79-27043

330.952'04 — Japan. Economic conditions, *1945-1980*

Allen, G. C.. The Japanese economy / G.C. Allen. — London : Weidenfeld and Nicolson, c1981. — ix,226p ; 23cm. — (The International economics series)
Bibliography: p216-219. — Includes index
ISBN 0-297-77950-8 (cased) : £10.00
ISBN 92-977795-1-6 (pbk) : £4.50 B81-36688

330.953'57053 — United Arab Emirates. Economic development, *1960-1980*

El Mallakh, Ragaei. The economic development of the United Arab Emirates / Ragaei El Mallakh. — London : Croom Helm, c1981. — 215p : 1map ; 23cm
Bibliography: p203-205. — Includes index
ISBN 0-7099-0209-3 : £13.95 : CIP rev. B81-13441

330.953'6053 — Arabia. Gulf States. Economic conditions — *For businessmen*

Hayman, Andrew. Business opportunities in the Gulf States : Bahrain, Kuwait, Oman, Qatar, U.A.E. / by Metra Consulting ; [prepared by Andrew Hayman]. — London : Metra, c1981. — ii,246p : ill,maps ; 30cm
ISBN 0-902231-24-3 (spiral) : £140.00 B81-16213

330.953'63053 — Qatar. Economic conditions — *Conference proceedings*

Focus on Qatar : proceedings of a one-day conference held on 5 November 1980 by th Arab-British Chamber of Commerce. — London (42 Berkeley Sq., W1æ 4BL) : Arab-British Chamber of Commerce, [c1980]. — 36p : 1map ; 30cm. — (Focus reports)
Cover title
Unpriced (pbk) B81-09514

330.953'65053 — Bahrain. Economic conditions — *Conference proceedings*

Focus on Bahrain : proceedings of a one-day conference held on 17 June 1981 by the Arab-British Chamber of Commerce. — London (PO Box 4BL, 42 Berkeley Square, London W1A 4BL) : Arab-British Chamber of Commerce, c1981. — 33p : ill ; 30cm. — (Focus reports, ISSN 0260-700x)
Cover title
Unpriced (pbk) B81-33084

330.953'67 — Kuwait. Economic development. Role of science & technology — *Conference proceedings*

National Symposium on Science and Technology *(1978 : Kuwait Institute for Scientific Research)*. Proceedings of Kuwait's National Symposium on Science and Technology. — London : Longman, Oct.1981. — [288]p
ISBN 0-582-78325-9 : £29.00 : CIP entry B81-28085

330.953'8 — Saudi Arabia. Economic conditions — *Conference proceedings*

State, society and economy in Saudi Arabia. — London : Croom Helm, Nov.1981. — [300]p
Conference papers
ISBN 0-7099-1806-2 : £13.95 : CIP entry
Primary classification 320.953'8 B81-31170

330.953'8 — Saudi Arabia. Economic conditions, *to 1980*

Johany, Ali D.. The myth of the OPEC cartel : the role of Saudi Arabia / Ali D. Johany. — Dhahran : University of Petroleum and Minerals ; Chichester : Wiley, c1980. — xi,107p : ill ; 24cm
Bibliography: p100-105. - Includes index
ISBN 0-471-27864-5 : £14.00
Primary classification 338.2'3 B81-04095

330.953'8 — Saudi Arabia. Economic development

El Mallakh, Ragaei. Saudi Arabia. — London : Croom Helm, Nov.1981. — [384]p
ISBN 0-7099-0905-5 : £14.95 : CIP entry B81-30534

330.953'8053 — Saudi Arabia. Economic conditions — *For businessmen*

Deane, Colin. Saudi Arabia : business opportunities II / by Metra Consulting ; [written by] Colin Deane. — London ([42 Vicarage Cres., SW11 3LD]) : Metra, c1978. — 223p : ill,maps ; 30cm
ISBN 0-902231-12-x (spiral) : £95.00 B81-11746

Saudi Arabia : keys to business success. — London : McGraw-Hill, Oct.1981. — [240]p
ISBN 0-07-084567-0 : £15.00 : CIP entry B81-24603

330.953'8053 — Saudi Arabia. Medina. Economic conditions

Makki, M. S.. Medina, Saudi Arabia. — Amersham : Avebury, Dec.1981. — [240]p
ISBN 0-86127-301-x (cased) : £15.95 : CIP entry
ISBN 0-86127-304-4 (pbk) : £7.95 B81-31642

330.954'052 — India *(Republic)*. **Economic conditions —** *For businessmen*

India : business opportunities in the 1980s / by Metra Consulting and McAlpine, Thorpe & Warrier. — London (42 Vicarage Cres., SW11 3LD) : Metra, c1980. — iv,330p : ill,3maps ; 31cm
Includes index
ISBN 0-902231-22-7 (spiral) : £125.00 B81-11744

330.954'82 — India *(Republic)*. **Tamil Nadu** *(State)*. **Rural regions. Economic conditions,** *1880-1955*

Baker, Christopher John. An Indian rural economy 1880-1955. — Oxford : Oxford University Press, Jan.1982. — [550]p
ISBN 0-19-821572-x : £30.00 : CIP entry B81-34378

330.9549'205 — Bangladesh. Rural regions. Economic development — *Conference proceedings*

Integrated rural development in Bangladesh : report of a seminar sponsored by the Commonwealth Foundation and the government of Bangladesh, held in Comilla, Bangladesh on 17-22 November 1980. — London (12 Great George St., SW1p 3AD) : CASLE on behalf of the Foundation and participating Commonwealth professional associations, 1981. — iii,303p : ill ; 30cm + summary(16p ; 21cm)
£7.50 (pbk) B81-16508

330.9549'3 — Sri Lanka. Economic conditions, *to 1980*

Johnson, B. L. C.. Sri Lanka : land, people and economy / B.L.C. Johnson and M.Le M. Scrivenor. — London : Heinemann, 1981. — x,154p : ill,maps ; 25cm
Bibliography: p146-147. — Includes index
ISBN 0-435-35489-2 : £9.50 : CIP rev. B80-14080

330.9549'303 — Sri Lanka. Economic conditions, *1948-1980*

Ponnambalam, Satchi. Dependent capitalism in crisis : the Sri Lankan economy 1948-1980 / Satchi Ponnambalam. — London : Zed, 1981, c1980. — xiii,233p : 1map ; 23cm. — (Asia series)
Bibliography: p219-225. — Includes index
ISBN 0-905762-85-1 : £14.95 : CIP rev. B80-33047

330.9549'6 — West central Nepal. Economic conditions

Blaikie, Piers M.. Nepal in crisis : growth and stagnation at the periphery / Piers Blaikie, John Cameron, David Seddon. — Oxford : Clarendon, 1980. — xii,311p : ill,maps ; 23cm
Bibliography: p285-294. - Includes index
ISBN 0-19-828414-4 : £17.50 : CIP rev. B80-06789

330.955'05 — Iran. Economic conditions, *1900-1970 — Socialist viewpoints*

Jazani, Bizhan. Capitalism and revolution in Iran / selected writings of Bizhan Jazani ; translated by the Iran Committee. — London : Zed, 1980. — xvi,151p : ill ; 23cm. — (Middle East series)
Translation from the Farsi
ISBN 0-905762-82-7 (cased) : £12.95
ISBN 0-905762-57-6 (pbk) : £4.50 B81-18187

330.955'052 — Iran. Economic conditions, *1926-1979*. **Political aspects**

Katouzian, Homa. The political economy of modern Iran : despotism and pseudo-modernism, 1926-1979 / Homa Katouzian. — London : Macmillan, 1981. — x,389p ; 25cm
Includes index
ISBN 0-333-26961-6 : £20.00 B81-22159

330.956 — Middle East. Economic conditions, *1800-1914*

Owen, Roger, *1935-*. The Middle East in the world economy 1800-1914 / Roger Owen. — London : Methuen, 1981. — xix,378p : maps ; 25cm
Bibliography: p246-370. - Includes index
ISBN 0-416-14270-2 : £18.00 : CIP rev.
B81-02654

330.956'04 — Middle East. Economic conditions. Information sources — *Directories*

Sources of African and Middle-Eastern economic information. — Farnborough, Hants. : Gower Press, Aug.1981
Vol.1. — [350]p
ISBN 0-566-02278-8 : £45.00 : CIP entry
Primary classification 330.96'0328 B81-18148

Sources of African and Middle-Eastern economic information. — Farnborough, Hants. : Gower Press, Aug.1981
Vol.2. — [350]p
ISBN 0-566-02279-6 : £45.00 : CIP entry
Primary classification 330.96'0328 B81-18149

330.9561'01 — Turkey. Economic conditions, *1800-1914*

The **Economic** history of Turkey 1800-1914 / [compiled by] Charles Issawi. — Chicago ; London : University of Chicago Press, 1980. — xvi,390p ; 25cm. — (Publications of the Center for Middle Eastern Studies ; no.13)
Includes translations of French, Turkish, German, Russian, Italian, Dutch, Hebrew and Armenian texts. — Bibliography: p377-386. — Includes index
ISBN 0-226-38603-1 : £10.00 B81-16970

330.9561'02 — Turkey. Economic development, *1923-1980*

Hale, William M.. The political and economic development of modern Turkey / William Hale. — London : Croom Helm, c1981. — 279p ; 23cm
Bibliography: p264-274. — Includes index
ISBN 0-7099-0014-7 : £13.50 : CIP rev.
B81-11909

330.9561'024 — Turkey. Economic conditions, *1923-1929*

Keyder, Caglar. The definition of a peripheral economy : Turkey 1923-1929 / Caglar Keyder. — Cambridge : Cambridge University Press, 1981. — viii,158p : ill ; 24cm. — (Studies in modern capitalism)
Bibliography: p150-155. — Includes index
ISBN 0-521-23699-1 : £16.00 : CIP rev.
B81-28125

330.9567'043 — Iraq. Economic conditions

Iraq : economic analysis. — London (Victoria St, SW1H 0ET) : Commercial Relations & Exports 5, Department of Trade, [1980?]. — 14p : 1map ; 30cm
Unpriced (unbound) B81-38494

330.95695 — Jordan. Jordan Valley region. Economic development

Khouri, Rami G.. The Jordan Valley. — London : Longman, Sept.1981. — [256]p
ISBN 0-582-78318-6 : £12.50 : CIP entry
B81-21491

330.959'053 — South-east Asia. Economic development, *1960-1969*

Fryer, Donald W.. Emerging Southeast Asia : a study in growth and stagnation / Donald W. Fryer. — 2nd ed. rev., enl. and re-set. — London : George Philip, c1979. — 540p : ill,maps ; 24cm
Previous ed.: 1970. — Maps on lining papers. — Bibliography: p497-526. — Includes index
ISBN 0-540-01037-5 : £9.95 : CIP rev.
B79-04148

330.9595'053 — Malaysia. Economic development. Inequalities

Snodgrass, Donald R.. Inequality and economic development in Malaysia : a study sponsored by the Harvard Institute for International Development / Donald R. Snodgrass. — Kuala Lumpur ; Oxford : Oxford University Press, 1980. — xx,326p ; 26cm. — (East Asian social science monographs)
Bibliography: p291-315. — Includes index
ISBN 0-19-580431-7 (cased) : £14.50
ISBN 0-19-580442-2 (pbk) : Unpriced
B81-17064

330.96'032 — Africa. Economic conditions, *1950-1980*

Political economy of Africa : selected readings / edited and introduced by Dennis L. Cohen and John Daniel. — London : Longman, 1981. — vi,289p ; 24cm
Includes bibliographies
ISBN 0-582-64284-1 (cased) : Unpriced
ISBN 0-582-64285-x (pbk) : £4.95 B81-40304

330.96'0328 — Africa. Economic conditions. Information sources — *Directories*

Sources of African and Middle-Eastern economic information. — Farnborough, Hants. : Gower Press, Aug.1981
Vol.1. — [350]p
ISBN 0-566-02278-8 : £45.00 : CIP entry
Also classified at 330.956'04 B81-18148

Sources of African and Middle-Eastern economic information. — Farnborough, Hants. : Gower Press, Aug.1981
Vol.2. — [350]p
ISBN 0-566-02279-6 : £45.00 : CIP entry
Also classified at 330.956'04 B81-18149

330.96'0328 — Africa. Economic development — *Case studies*

Indigenization of African economics / edited by Adelbayo Adedeji. — London : Hutchinson University Library for Africa in association with the African Association for Public Administration and Management, 1981. — 413p ; 23cm. — (Hutchinson university library for Africa)
Bibliography: p395-396. — Includes index
ISBN 0-09-143730-x (cased) : £12.00 : CIP rev.
ISBN 0-09-143731-8 (pbk) : £5.95 B81-02353

330.96'0328 — Africa. Economic development. Environmental aspects

Environment and development in Africa : a study / prepared by the Environmental Development Action (ENDA) for the United Nations Environment Programme. — Oxford : Published for the United Nations Environment Programme by Pergamon, 1981. — x,76p : ill,maps ; 22cm. — (UNEP studies ; v.2)
Bibliography: p64-75
ISBN 0-08-025667-8 : £6.25 : CIP rev.
B79-35193

330.96'0328 — Africa. Economic development. Political aspects

Ake, Claude. A political economy of Africa / Claude Ake. — Harlow : Longman, 1981. — viii,196p ; 24cm
Includes bibliographies and index
ISBN 0-582-64374-0 (cased) : Unpriced
ISBN 0-582-64370-8 (pbk) : £3.95 B81-32861

330.96'0328 — Africa. Economic development. Role of experts — *Conference proceedings*

Experts in Africa : proceedings of a colloquium at the University of Aberdeen, March 1980 / edited by J.C. Stone. — Aberdeen ([Taylor Building, King's College, Old Aberdeen, AB9 2UB]) : Aberdeen University African Studies Group, 1980. — 190,[3]p of plates : maps ; 30cm
Includes 1 paper in French. — Includes bibliographies
Unpriced (pbk) B81-16513

330.961'105 — Tunisia. Economic conditions — *Conference proceedings*

Focus on Tunisia : proceedings of a one-day conference held on 24 September 1980 by the Arab-British Chamber of Commerce 42 Berkeley Square, London. — [London] ([42 Berkeley Sq., W1A 4LB]) : [The Chamber of Commerce], [c1980]. — 32p ; 30cm. — (An Arab-British Chamber of Commerce publication) (Focus reports / Arab-British Chamber of Commerce)
Cover title
Unpriced (pbk) B81-27162

330.962'053 — Egypt. Economic conditions, *1952-1979*

Ikram, Khalid. Egypt : economic management in a period of transition : the report of a mission sent to the Arab Republic of Egypt by the World Bank / Khalid Ikram co-ordinating author. — Baltimore ; London : Published for the World Bank, Johns Hopkins University Press, c1980. — xx,444p : ill ; 1map ; 24cm
Includes index
ISBN 0-8018-2418-4 (cased) : £19.50
ISBN 0-8018-2419-2 (pbk) : £6.25 B81-21077

330.962'054 — Egypt. Economic conditions

Egypt : economic survey / a survey specially prepared by African business. — London (63 Long Acre, WC2E 9JH) : IC Magazines Ltd., [1981?]. — [24]p : ill,1map,ports ; 27cm
Cover title
Unpriced (unbound) B81-22958

330.962'054 — Egypt. Economic conditions — *For businessmen*

Mission report : Egypt 23rd-29th January 1981. — Birmingham (PO Box 360, 75 Harborne Rd., Birmingham B15 3DH) : Birmingham Chamber of Industry and Commerce, [1981]. — i,8p ; 30cm
Unpriced (unbound) B81-29621

330.964'05 — Morocco. Economic conditions — *Conference proceedings*

Focus on Morocco : proceedings of a one-day Conference held on 17 September 1980 by the Arab-British Chamber of Commerce 42 Berkeley Square, London. — [London] ([42 Berkeley Sq. W1A 4BL]) : [The Chamber of Commerce], [c1980]. — 32p : 1map ; 30cm. — (An Arab-British Chamber of Commerce publication)
Cover title
Unpriced (pbk) B81-27161

330.965'05 — Algeria. Economic conditions — *Conference proceedings*

Focus on Algeria : proceedings of a one-day conference held on 7 October 1980 by the Arab-British Chamber of Commerce 42 Berkeley Square, London. — [London] ([42 Berkeley Sq., W1A 4BL]) : [The Chamber of Commerce], [c1980]. — 32p : 1map ; 30cm. — (An Arab-British Chamber of Commerce publication) (Focus report / Arab-British Chamber of Commerce)
Cover title. — Map on inside cover
Unpriced (pbk) B81-27160

330.966 — Sahara Desert. Economic development, *to 500* — *Conference proceedings*

The **Sahara** : ecological change and early economic history / edited by J.A. Allan ; with contributions by G. Barker ... [et al.] ; the proceedings of a conference convened by the Centre of African Studies in association with the Centre of Middle Eastern Studies, the School of Oriental & African Studies, University of London. — Outwell : Middle East and North African Studies, 1981. — xii,146p : ill,maps ; 21cm. — (Menas monograph ; no.1)
Includes bibliographies
ISBN 0-906559-04-9 (pbk) : £4.50
Primary classification 574.5'2652'0966
B81-31132

330.966 — West Africa. Economic conditions — *For West African students*

Ekundare, R. Olufemi. An introduction to economics for West African students / R. Olufemi Ekundare. — London : Allen & Unwin, 1980. — 203p : ill ; 22cm
Includes index
ISBN 0-04-330301-3 (pbk) : £3.95 : CIP rev.
B80-08634

330.966′26 — Central Niger. Economic conditions, *1850-1960*
Baier, Stephen. An economic history of Central Niger / by Stephen Baier. — Oxford : Clarendon, 1980. — 325p : maps ; 23cm. — (Oxford studies in African affairs)
Bibliography: p290-315. - Includes index
ISBN 0-19-822717-5 : £15.00 : CIP rev. B80-01974

330.9669′05 — Nigeria, *1970-1980.* **Politico-economic aspects**
Kirk-Greene, A. H. M.. Nigeria since 1970 : a political and economic outline / Anthony Kirk-Greene and Douglas Rimmer. — London : Hodder and Stoughton, 1981. — xii,161p : 1map ; 24cm
ISBN 0-340-26207-9 (pbk) : £3.50 : CIP rev. B81-13885

330.9669′05 — Nigeria. Economic conditions, *ca 1955-1975*
Olaloku, F. A.. Structure of the Nigerian economy / F.A. Olaloku with A. Adejugbe ... [et al.]. — London : Macmillan, 1979. — ix,270p : ill ; 23cm
Includes index
ISBN 0-333-23316-6 : £10.95 : CIP rev.
ISBN 0-333-23317-4 (pbk) : £3.95 B79-05557

330.9676′204 — Kenya. Economic conditions — *For British businessmen*
Kenya and Zimbabwe, 24th October to 8th November 1980. — Birmingham (75 Harborne Rd., Birmingham B15 3DH) : Birmingham Chamber of Industry and Commerce, [1980]. — i,13p ; 30cm. — (Mission report)
Unpriced (pbk)
Also classified at 330.96891′04 B81-10732

330.9678 — Tanzania. Economic conditions, *1875-1961.* **Political aspects**
Tanzania under colonial rule / edited by M.H.Y. Kaniki for the Historical Associaton of Tanzania. — London : Longman, 1980, c1979. — vii,391p ; 22cm
Includes index
ISBN 0-582-64649-9 (pbk) : £3.95 : CIP rev. B79-36201

330.967′905 — Mozambique. Economic conditions *— For British businessmen*
Trade mission to Mozambique, 15-29 October 1980 / Tropical Africa Advisory Group. — [London] : British Overseas Trade Board, [1980]. — 54,xlviiip : 2maps ; 30cm
£6.00 (pbk) B81-15237

330.968′062 — Southern Africa. Economic development *— Conference proceedings*
SADCC2 *(Conference : 1980 : Maputo).*
SADCC2-Maputo : the proceedings of the Second Southern African Development Co-ordination Conference, held in Maputo, People′s Republic of Mozambique on 27-28 November 1980 / edited by Aloysius Kgarebe. — London (1 Cambridge Terrace, NW1 4JL) : SADCC Liaison Committee, 1981. — 287p : ill,maps ; 22cm
ISBN 0-9507150-2-6 (pbk) : £5.00 B81-37988

330.968′062 — Southern Africa. Economic policies *— Conference proceedings*
Southern Africa : toward economic liberation / edited by Amon J. Nsekela. — London : Collings, 1981. — xix,274p : 1map ; 24cm
Conference papers
ISBN 0-86036-154-3 : £14.00 B81-32500

330.9681′103 — Botswana. Economic conditions
Papers in the economy of Botswana / edited by Charles Harvey. — London : Heinemann, 1981. — xii,276p : ill,maps ; 23cm. — (Studies in the economics of Africa)
Includes bibliographies and index
ISBN 0-435-97199-9 (cased) : £12.50
ISBN 0-435-97200-6 (pbk) : £4.50 B81-40379

330.96891′04 — Zimbabwe. Economic conditions — *For British businessmen*
Kenya and Zimbabwe, 24th October to 8th November 1980. — Birmingham (75 Harborne Rd., Birmingham B15 3DH) : Birmingham Chamber of Industry and Commerce, [1980]. — i,13p ; 30cm. — (Mission report)
Unpriced (pbk)
Primary classification 330.9676′204 B81-10732

330.972′0833 — Mexico. Economic conditions — *For businessmen*
Mexico : business opportunites in the 1980s / by Metra Consulting and International Joint Ventures. — London : Metra Consulting, [1981]. — 361p : maps ; 30cm
ISBN 0-902231-28-6 (spiral) : Unpriced B81-25337

330.972′0833 — Mexico. Economic conditions — *Serials*
Latin America regional reports. Mexico & Central America. — RM-79-01 (16 Nov.1979)-. — London (90 Cowcross St. EC1M 6BL) : Latin American Newsletters, c1979-. — v. : ill ; 30cm
Ten issues yearly. — Description based on: RM-80-03 (21 Mar.1980)
ISSN 0143-5264 = Latin America regional reports. Mexico & Central America : £45.00 per year
Also classified at 330.9728′052 B81-02813

330.972′0833′05 — Mexico. Economic conditions — *For businessmen — Serials*
Business yearbook of Brazil, Mexico & Venezuela . — 1981-. — London : Graham & Trotman, 1980-. — v. ; 24cm
Annual
ISSN 0144-2767 = Business yearbook of Brazil, Mexico & Venezuela : Unpriced
Also classified at 330.981′063′05 ; 330.987′0633′05 B81-33306

330.9728′052 — Central America. Economic conditions *— Serials*
Latin America regional reports. Mexico & Central America. — RM-79-01 (16 Nov.1979)-. — London (90 Cowcross St. EC1M 6BL) : Latin American Newsletters, c1979-. — v. : ill ; 30cm
Ten issues yearly. — Description based on: RM-80-03 (21 Mar.1980)
ISSN 0143-5264 = Latin America regional reports. Mexico & Central America : £45.00 per year
Primary classification 330.972′0833 B81-02813

330.97298′3 — Trinidad. Economic conditions — *For British businessmen*
Trinidad : 22nd to 29th November, 1980. — Birmingham (PO Box 360, 75 Narborne Rd., Birmingham B15 3DH) : Birmingham Chamber of Industry and Commerce, [1981]. — 15p : 1map ; 30cm. — (Mission report / Birmingham Chamber of Industry and Commerce)
Unpriced (unbound) B81-17693

330.973 — United States. Economic conditions, *1776-1980*
Ransom, Roger L.. Coping with capitalism : the economic transformation of the United States, 1776-1980 / Roger L. Ransom. — Englewood Cliffs ; London : Prentice-Hall, c1981. — vi,186p ; 23cm
Bibliography: p176-182. — Includes index
ISBN 0-13-172288-3 (pbk) : £5.15 B81-22758

330.973 — United States. Economic conditions, *to 1940*
Lee, Susan Previant. A new economic view of American history / Susan Previant Lee and Peter Passell. — New York ; London : Norton, c1979. — 410p : ill,maps ; 24cm
Includes bibliographies and index
ISBN 0-393-95067-0 (pbk) : £11.25 B81-02954

330.973 — United States. Economic conditions, *to ca 1980*
Poulson, Barry W.. Economic history of the United States / Barry W. Poulson. — New York : Macmillan ; London : Collier Macmillan, c1981. — x,672p : ill,maps ; 24cm
Includes bibliographies and index
ISBN 0-02-396220-8 : £12.50 B81-36120

330.973′02 — United States. Economic conditions, *1600-1776*
Perkins, Edwin J.. The economy of colonial America / Edwin J. Perkins. — New York ; Guildford University Press, 1980. — xii,177p : 1map ; 22cm
Includes bibliographies and index
ISBN 0-231-04958-7 (cased) : £9.70
ISBN 0-231-04959-5 (pbk) : £3.30 B81-05291

330.973′092 — United States. Economic conditions, *1940-1980 — Conference proceedings*
The **American** economy in transition / edited by Martin Feldstein ; [National Bureau of Economic Research]. — Chicago ; London : University of Chicago Press, 1980. — viii,696p : ill ; 24cm
Conference papers. — Includes bibliographies and index
ISBN 0-226-24081-9 : £12.00 B81-16630

330.973′092 — United States. Economic conditions. Regional variations, *1945-1975 — Conference proceedings*
Alternatives to confrontation : a national policy toward regional change / edited by Victor L. Arnold. — Lexington : Lexington Books, c1980 ; [Farnborough, Hants] : Gower [distributor], 1981. — xv,381p : ill,maps ; 24cm
Conference papers
ISBN 0-669-03165-8 : £18.50 B81-05505

330.973′092 — United States. Economic policies. Decision making by presidents, *1980-1990*
The **Economy** and the President : 1980 and beyond / [edited by Walter E. Hoadley]. — Englewood Cliffs ; London : Prentice-Hall, c1980. — 180p : ill ; 21cm. — (A Spectrum book)
At head of title: The American Assembly, Columbia University. — Includes index
ISBN 0-13-234823-3 (cased) : £7.75
ISBN 0-13-234815-2 (pbk) : £3.20 B81-07898

330.973′0924 — United States. Economic policies, *1971-1976*
Blinder, Alan S.. Economic policy and the great stagflation / Alan S. Blinder. — Student ed. — New York ; London : Academic, c1981. — xiii,229p : ill ; 23cm
Previous ed.: 1979. — Bibliography: p219-223. — Includes index
ISBN 0-12-106162-0 (pbk) : £6.40 B81-38697

330.973′0926 — United States. Economic conditions, *1977-1981*
Kupferman, Martin. Slowth : the changing economy and how you can successfully cope / Martin Kupferman, Maurice D. Levi. — New York ; Chichester : Wiley, c1980. — xiv,250p ; 22cm
Bibliography: p235-236. — Includes index
ISBN 0-471-08090-x : £7.50 B81-04723

330.973′0926 — United States. Economic policies, *1977-1980*
Schwartz, Gail Garfield. Being number one : rebuilding the U.S. economy / Gail Garfield Schwartz, Pat Choate. — Lexington, Mass. : Lexington Books ; [Aldershot] : Gower [distributor], 1981, c1980. — xiii,132p : ill ; 24cm
Bibliography: p115-126. — Includes index
ISBN 0-669-04308-7 : £10.00 B81-32984

330.973′0926 — United States. Urban regions. Economic conditions, *ca 1980*
Watkins, Alfred J.. The practice of urban economics / Alfred J. Watkins ; foreword by Wilbur R. Thompson. — Beverly Hills ; London : Sage, c1980. — 248p : ill ; 22cm. — (Sage library of social research ; v.107)
Bibliography: p237-247
ISBN 0-8039-1380-x (cased) : Unpriced (pbk) : £5.50 B81-16611

330.973′0927 — United States. Economic conditions
Reynolds, Lloyd G.. The American economy in perspective / Lloyd G. Reynolds. — New York ; London : McGraw-Hill, c1981. — xxi,452p : ill(some col.),ports ; 24cm
Ports. on lining papers. — Includes index
ISBN 0-07-052028-3 (pbk) : £12.25 B81-17038

Thurow, Lester C.. The zero-sum society : distribution and the possibilities for economic change / Lester C. Thurow. — Harmondsworth : Penguin, 1981, c1980. — 230p ; 20cm
Originally published: New York : Basic Books, 1980. — Includes index
ISBN 0-14-005807-9 (pbk) : £2.50 B81-40437

330.973′0927 — United States. Economic conditions. Econometric models

Polenske, Karen R.. The U.S. multiregional input-output accounts and model / Karen R. Polenske. — Lexington, Mass. : Lexington Books ; [Farnborough, Hants.] : Gower [distributor], 1981, c1980. — xx,358p : ill ; 24cm. — (Multiregional input-output analysis ; vol.6)
Bibliography: p339-358
ISBN 0-669-02173-3 : £22.50 B81-23668

330.973′0927 — United States. Economic conditions — *For British businessmen*

U.S.A. : (based on Los Angeles), 21st to 28th March, 1981. — Birmingham (P.O. Box 360, 75 Harborne Rd., Birmingham B15 3DH) : Birmingham Chamber of Industry and Commerce, [1981]. — 9p : 1map ; 30cm. — (Mission report / Birmingham Chamber of Industry and Commerce)
Unpriced (pbk) B81-33591

330.973′0927 — United States. Economic conditions. Implications of technology transfer

Gee, Sherman. Technology transfer, innovation, and international competitiveness / Sherman Gee. — New York ; Chichester : Wiley, c1981. — x,228p : ill ; 24cm
Includes index
ISBN 0-471-08468-9 : £14.75 B81-24053

330.973′0927 — United States. Japanese. Economic conditions

Bonacich, Edna. The economic basis of ethnic solidarity : small businesses in the Japanese American community / Edna Bonacich and John Modell. — Berkeley ; London : University of California Press, c1980. — vii,290p ; 25cm
Bibliography: p273-283. — Includes index
ISBN 0-520-04155-0 : £11.50 B81-27502

330.973′0927 — United States. Regional economic conditions. Mathematical models — *Conference proceedings*

Modeling the multiregional economic system : perspectives for the eighties / edited by F. Gerard Adams,. Norman J. Glickman. — Lexington : Lexington Books, c1980 ; [Farnborough, Hants.] : Gower [distributor], 1981. — ix,310p : ill,1map,1form ; 24cm. — (The Wharton econometric studies series)
Conference papers. — Bibliography: p285-300. — Includes index
ISBN 0-669-03627-7 : £15.00 B81-23266

330.9747′043 — New York *(State).* **Economic conditions,** *1945-1980.* **Political aspects**

McClelland, Peter D.. Crisis in the making : the political economy of New York State since 1945 / Peter D. McClelland, Alan L. Magdovitz. — Cambridge : Cambridge University Press, 1981. — xvi,522p : ill,maps ; 24cm. — (Studies in economic history : the United States in the twentieth century)
Bibliography: p492-511. — Includes index
ISBN 0-521-23807-2 : £25.00 B81-32628

330.978′02 — United States. Western states. Economic conditions, *1800-1900*

Walsh, Margaret, *19---*. The American frontier revisited / prepared for the Economic History Society by Margaret Walsh. — London : Macmillan, 1981. — 88p : maps ; 22cm. — (Studies in economic and social history)
Bibliography: p73-85. — Includes index
ISBN 0-333-27967-0 (pbk) : £2.25 : CIP rev. B80-21491

330.98 — Andean Group countries. Economic conditions — *Serials*

Latin America regional reports. Andean Group. — RA-79-01 (30 Nov.1979)-. — London (90 Cowcross St. EC1M 6BL) : Latin American Newsletters, c1979-. — v. : ill ; 30cm
Ten issues yearly. — Description based on: RA-80-03 (4 Apr.1980)
£45.00 per year B81-06150

330.98 — Latin America. Economic development, *to 1980*

Morris, Arthur S.. Latin America : economic developments and regional differentiation / Arthur Morris. — London : Hutchinson, 1981. — 256p : ill,maps ; 23cm. — (Hutchinson university library)
Bibliography: p232-244. — Includes index
ISBN 0-09-143640-0 (cased) : £9.95
ISBN 0-09-143641-9 (pbk) : Unpriced B81-26817

330.98 — Southern South America. Economic conditions — *Serials*

Latin America regional reports. Southern Cone. — RS-79-01 (7 Dec. 1979)-. — London (90 Cowcross St., EC1M 6BL) : Latin American Newsletters, c1979-. — v. : ill ; 30cm
Ten issues yearly. — Description based on: RS-80-03 (18 Apr. 1980)
ISSN 0143-5256 = Latin America regional reports. Southern Cone : £45.00 per year B81-02004

330.98′0038′05 — Latin America. Economic conditions — *For businessmen* — *Serials*

Latin American markets : the Latin American business and financial briefing, published alternate weeks. — Issue no.1 (2 Mar.1981)-. — London : Financial Times Business Information Ltd., 1981-. — v. ; 30cm
ISSN 0261-7382 = Latin American markets : £210.00 per year B81-32685

330.981 — Brazil. Economic development, *to 1914*

Versiani, Flávio Rabelo. Industrial investment in an ′export′ economy : the Brazilian experience before 1914 / by Flávio Rabelo Versiani. — London : University of London, Institute of Latin American Studies, [1980]. — 25,xv p : ill ; 25cm. — (Working papers / University of London Institute of Latin American Studies, ISSN 0142-1875 ; 2)
Bibliography: px-xv
ISBN 0-901145-35-1 (pbk) : Unpriced B81-08300

330.981′063 — Brazil. Economic conditions — *For businessmen*

Coulson-Thomas, Colin. Brazil : business opportunities in the 1980s / by Metra Consulting and International Joint Ventures ; [written by Colin Coulson-Thomas]. — London (42 Vicarage Cres., SW11 3LD) : Metra, [1980]. — iv,268p : ill,maps ; 30cm
Bibliography: p237-245
ISBN 0-902231-18-9 (corrected : spiral) : £125.00 B81-13684

330.981′063 — Brazil. Economic conditions — *Serials*

Brazil land of the present. — 7. — London (Bucklersbury House, Walbrook, EC4N 8HP) : European Brazilian Bank, [1980?]. — 76p,[8]p of plates
Unpriced B81-12427

Latin America regional reports. Brazil. — RB-79-01 (9 Nov.1979)-. — London (90 Cowcross St., EC1M 6BL) : Latin American Newsletters, 1979-. — v. : ill ; 30cm
Ten issues yearly. — Description based on: RB-80-03 (14 Mar.1980)
£45.00 per year B81-04866

330.981′063′05 — Brazil. Economic conditions — *For businessmen* — *Serials*

Business yearbook of Brazil, Mexico & Venezuela . — 1981-. — London : Graham & Trotman, 1980-. — v. ; 24cm
Annual
ISSN 0144-2767 = Business yearbook of Brazil, Mexico & Venezuela : Unpriced
Primary classification 330.972′0833′05 B81-33306

330.982′064 — Argentina. Economic conditions — *For businessmen*

French, Michael. Argentina : business opportunities in the 1980s / by Metra Consulting and International Joint Ventures ; [prepared and written by Michael Frenchman]. — London ([42 Vicarage Cres., SW11 3LD]) : Metra, [1979]. — ii,340p : maps ; 30cm
ISBN 0-902231-16-2 (spiral) : £110.00 B81-11745

330.983′0646 — Chile. Economic policies, *1970-1973*

Chile 1970-73 : economic development and its international setting : self-criticism of the Unidad Popular Government′s policies / edited by S. Sideri in collaboration with B. Evers. — The Hague ; London : Nijhoff, 1979. — xxvi,400p : ill ; 25cm. — (Series on the development of societies ; v.4)
Conference papers. — Includes index
ISBN 90-247-2198-9 : Unpriced B81-16289

Gwynne, R. N.. Economic development and structural change : the Chilean case, 1970-1973 / R.N. Gwynne. — [Birmingham] : [Department of Geography, University of Birmingham], 1976. — 42p ; 30cm. — (Occasional publication / Department of Geography, University of Birmingham ; no.2)
Bibliography: p41-42
ISBN 0-7044-0353-6 (pbk) : £0.50 B81-39714

330.983′0647 — Chile. Economic policies. Influence of international financial institutions, *1973-1978*

Griffith-Jones, Stephany. The evolution of external finance, economic policy and development in Chile, 1973-78 / Stephany Griffith-Jones. — Brighton : Institute of Development Studies, 1981. — 61p ; 21cm. — (Discussion paper / IDS, ISSN 0308-5864 ; 160)
Bibliography: p60-61
Unpriced (pbk) B81-24072

330.987′0633′05 — Venezuela. Economic conditions — *For businessmen* — *Serials*

Business yearbook of Brazil, Mexico & Venezuela . — 1981-. — London : Graham & Trotman, 1980-. — v. ; 24cm
Annual
ISSN 0144-2767 = Business yearbook of Brazil, Mexico & Venezuela : Unpriced
Primary classification 330.972′0833′05 B81-33306

330.99′005 — Australasia & Pacific islands. Economic conditions — *Serials*

Asia & Pacific annual review. — 1980. — Saffron Walden (21 Gold St., Saffron Walden, Essex CB10 1EJ) : World of Information, c1979. — 278p
ISBN 0-904439-14-3 : Unpriced
Primary classification 330.95′0428′05 B81-10261

330.994′05 — Economic policies, *1945-1980.* **Social aspects** — *Study regions: Australia*

The Crime and the cure : a social credit secretariat analysis from The Social Crediter. — Sudbury : Bloomfield, 1980. — 20p ; 18cm
Originally published: Sydney : Tidal Publications, 1980
ISBN 0-85855-007-5 (pbk) : £0.55 B81-07823

330.994′063 — Australia. Economic conditions

Kahn, Herman. Will she be right? : the future of Australia / Herman Kahn and Thomas Pepper. — St. Lucia : University of Queensland Press ; Hemel Hempstead : Prentice-Hall [distributor], 1980. — xvii,199p : ill ; 23cm
Bibliography: p187-190. — Includes index
ISBN 0-7022-1568-6 (cased) : Unpriced
ISBN 0-7022-1569-4 (pbk) : £4.25 B81-16531

330.994′063 — Australia. Economic conditions — *For British businessmen*

Australia : 5-20 March 1981 / Birmingham Chamber of Industry and Commerce. — Birmingham (P.O. Box 360, 75 Harborne Rd., Birmingham B15 3DH) : The Chamber, [1981]. — 12,11p : 1map. — (Mission report / Birmingham Chamber of Industry and Commerce)
Unpriced (unbound) B81-29014

330.995′3 — Developing countries. Economic development. Role of law — *Marxist viewpoints* — *Study regions: Papua New Guinea*

Fitzpatrick, Peter, *1941-*. Law and state in Papua New Guinea / Peter Fitzpatrick. — London : Academic Press, 1980. — xi,290p ; 24cm. — (Law, state and society series ; 4)
Bibliography: p256-284. - Includes index
ISBN 0-12-257880-5 : £12.60 : CIP rev. B80-12271

331 — LABOUR ECONOMICS

331 — Industrial relations
Industrial relations in practice. — Dublin : O'Brien Press, Aug.1981. — [128]p. — (Issues in industrial relations, ISSN 0332-1991 ; 1)
ISBN 0-86278-008-x (cased) : £7.00 : CIP entry
ISBN 0-86278-009-8 (pbk) : £3.50 B81-21600

331 — Industrial relations - *Conference proceedings*
The **Behavioural** sciences and industrial relations. — Farnborough, Hants. : Gower, July 1981. — [208]p
Conference papers
ISBN 0-566-00383-x : £10.00 : CIP entry
Primary classification 300 B81-14874

331 — Industries. Personnel. Effects of automation
Automation and industrial workers : a fifteen nation study / edited by Jan Forslin, Adam Sarapata and Arthur M. Whitehill in collaboration with Frank Adler and Stephen Mills. — Oxford : Pergamon
Produced for the European Coordination Centre for Research and Documentation in Social Sciences
Vol.1, Pt.1. — 1979. — xx,249p : ill,forms ; 26cm
ISBN 0-08-023339-2 : Unpriced : CIP rev. B79-23098

Automation and industrial workers : a fifteen nation study / edited by Jan Forslin, Adam Sarapata and Arthur M. Whitehill in collaboration with Frank Adler and Stephen Mills. — Oxford : Pergamon
Produced for the European Coordination Centre for Research and Documentation in Social Sciences
Vol.1, Pt.2. — 1981. — xvii,303p : ill ; 26cm
ISBN 0-08-024310-x : Unpriced : CIP rev. B81-10000

331′.01 — Employment. Labour. Theories, *to 1979*
McNulty, Paul J.. The origins and development of labour economics : a chapter in the history of social thought / Paul J. McNulty. — Cambridge, Mass. ; London : MIT Press, c1980. — viii,248p ; 24cm
Includes index
ISBN 0-262-13162-5 : £10.85 B81-05265

331′.01′1207204 — Western Europe. Industrial democracy. Research
Industrial democracy in Europe / by Industrial Democracy in Europe (IDE) International Research Group. — Oxford : Clarendon, 1981. — viii,449p : ill ; 24cm
Bibliography: p421-435. - Includes index
ISBN 0-19-827258-8 : £20.00 B81-16494

331′.01′120941 — Great Britain. Industrial democracy
Archer, Keith. Industrial Democracy : ways forward in Britain and West Germany : a report on an Anglo-German study project conducted by the Greater Manchester Industrial Mission, Ev. Industrie- und Sozialpfarramt Stuttgart and Kath. Betriebsseelsorge Böblingen / by Keith Archer, Rainer B. Matschke, Paul Schobel. — London (St. Stephen's House, Victoria Embankment, London SW1A 2LA) : Anglo-German Foundation for the Study of Industrial Society, c1978. — 101p ; 30cm. — (Monograph series / Anglo-German Foundation for the Study of Industrial Society)
ISBN 0-905492-15-3 (pbk) : £2.00
Also classified at 331′.01′120943 B81-38070

331′.01′120941 — Great Britain. Industrial democracy — *Fabian viewpoints*
Carroll, Roger. The two wage worker : common ownership and economic democracy / Roger Carroll. — London : Fabian Society, 1980. — 16p ; 22cm. — (Fabian tract, ISSN 0307-7535 ; 470)
Cover title
ISBN 0-7163-0470-8 : £0.65
Also classified at 331.25′5 B81-04994

331′.01′120941 — Great Britain. Industrial democracy — *For trade unionism*
Burns, Patrick. Democracy at work / Patrick Burns and Mel Doyle. — London : Pan, 1981. — 164p : ill,1map,forms ; 20cm. — (Pan trade union studies)
Includes index
ISBN 0-330-26478-8 (pbk) : £1.75 B81-38233

331′.01′120941 — Great Britain. Industrial democracy. Role of trade unions
Radice, Giles. The industrial democrats : trade unions in an uncertain world / Giles Radice. — London : Allen & Unwin, 1978. — 241p ; 22cm
Includes index
ISBN 0-04-331075-3 (pbk) : £4.95 : CIP rev.
ISBN 0-04-331073-7 B78-30451

331′.01′120943 — West Germany. Industrial democracy
Archer, Keith. Industrial Democracy : ways forward in Britain and West Germany : a report on an Anglo-German study project conducted by the Greater Manchester Industrial Mission, Ev. Industrie- und Sozialpfarramt Stuttgart and Kath. Betriebsseelsorge Böblingen / by Keith Archer, Rainer B. Matschke, Paul Schobel. — London (St. Stephen's House, Victoria Embankment, London SW1A 2LA) : Anglo-German Foundation for the Study of Industrial Society, c1978. — 101p ; 30cm. — (Monograph series / Anglo-German Foundation for the Study of Industrial Society)
ISBN 0-905492-15-3 (pbk) : £2.00
Primary classification 331′.01′120941 B81-38070

331′.041072 — Great Britain. National newspaper publishing industries. Industrial relations, *1975-1980*
Martin, Roderick. New technology and industrial relations in Fleet Street. — Oxford : Clarendon Press, Dec.1981. — [300]p
ISBN 0-19-827243-x : £17.50 : CIP entry B81-31454

331′.0413388884 — Western Europe. Multinational companies. Industrial relations
Liebhaberg, Bruno. Industrial relations and multinational corporations in Europe / Bruno Liebhaberg. — Farnborough, Hants. : Gower in association with the European Centre for Study and Information on Multinational Corporations (ECSM), c1980. — xiv,107p : 1ill ; 23cm
ISBN 0-566-00363-5 : £9.50 : CIP rev. B80-25257

331′.0413621 — Health services. Industrial relations
Industrial relations and health services. — London : Croom Helm, Nov.1981. — [336]p
ISBN 0-7099-0379-0 : £14.95 : CIP entry B81-31168

331′.042′000941 — Great Britain. Engineering industries. Industrial relations *compared with* **industrial relations in engineering industries in West Germany**
Marsh, Arthur. Workplace relations in the engineering industry in the UK and the Federal Republic of Germany / by Arthur Marsh, Maria Hackmann, Douglas Miller. — London : [Anglo-German Foundation for the Study of Industrial Society], c1981. — 195p : 1map ; 23cm
ISBN 0-905492-30-7 : £10.00
Also classified at 331′.042′000943 B81-28226

331′.042′000943 — West Germany. Engineering industries. Industrial relations *compared with* **industrial relations in engineering industries in Great Britain**
Marsh, Arthur. Workplace relations in the engineering industry in the UK and the Federal Republic of Germany / by Arthur Marsh, Maria Hackmann, Douglas Miller. — London : [Anglo-German Foundation for the Study of Industrial Society], c1981. — 195p : 1map ; 23cm
ISBN 0-905492-30-7 : £10.00
Primary classification 331′.042′000941 B81-28226

331′.0422354′094291 — North Wales. Slate quarrying industries. Industrial relations, *1874-1922*
Jones, R. Merfyn. The North Wales quarrymen, 1874-1922 / R. Merfyn Jones. — Cardiff : University of Wales Press on behalf of the History and Law Committee of the Board of Celtic Studies, 1981. — x,359p,[1]leaf of plates : ill,1map ; 23cm. — (Studies in Welsh history, ISSN 0141-030x ; 4)
Map on lining papers. — Bibliography: p344-349. — Includes index
ISBN 0-7083-0776-0 : Unpriced B81-35749

331′.047′0941 — Great Britain. Manufacturing industries. Industrial relations
The **Changing** contours of British industrial relations : a survey of manufacturing industry / edited by William Brown ; with contributions by Eric Batstone ... [et al.]. — Oxford : Basil Blackwell, 1981. — xi,160p ; 23cm. — (Warwick studies in industrial relations)
Bibliography: p149-153. — Includes index
ISBN 0-631-12775-5 (cased) : £10.00 : CIP rev.
ISBN 0-631-12825-5 (pbk) : £4.50 B81-10451

331′.047′0941 — Great Britain. Manufacturing industries. Industrial relations — *Case studies*
Armstrong, P. J.. Ideology and shop-floor industrial relations / P.J. Armstrong, J.F.B. Goodman and J.D. Hyman. — London : Croom Helm, c1981. — 217p ; 23cm
Includes index
ISBN 0-7099-0465-7 : £12.95 : CIP rev. B80-24157

331′.07′041 — Great Britain. Industrial relations. Information sources
Smart, Carol R.. Industrial relations in Britain : a guide to sources of information / compiled by Carol Smart. — London (6 Castle St., Edinburgh EH2 3AT) : Capital Planning Information, 1980. — 63p ; 30cm. — (CPI information reviews ; no.5)
Includes index
ISBN 0-906011-09-4 (pbk) : £9.00 B81-27744

331′.07201812 — Western world. Industrial relations. Research, *1960-1975*
Industrial relations in international perspective : essays on research and policy / edited by Peter B. Doeringer with Peter Gourevitch, Peter Lange, Andrew Martin. — London : Macmillan, 1981. — ix,425p ; 23cm
Includes bibliographies and index
ISBN 0-333-25944-0 : £25.00 : CIP rev. B80-10959

331′.0722 — Industrial relations — *Case studies*
Kelly, Al. Strike! / Al Kelly. — Bognor Regis : New Horizon, c1981. — 204p : ill ; 21cm
ISBN 0-86116-694-9 : £5.75 B81-21798

331′.094 — Europe. Industrial relations
European industrial relations / by Industrial Democracy in Europe (IDE) International Research Group. — Oxford : Clarendon Press, 1981. — ix,277p : ill ; 24cm
Includes bibliographies and index
ISBN 0-19-827254-5 : £15.00 B81-17165

331′.094 — Western Europe. Industrial relations — *Case studies*
Kennedy, Thomas. European labor relations : text and cases / Thomas Kennedy. — Lexington : Lexington Books ; [Farnborough, Hants.] : Gower [distributor], 1980. — xv,427p : ill ; 24cm
Includes index
ISBN 0-669-02663-8 : £16.00 B81-04837

331′.0941 — Great Britain. Industrial relations
Appleton, J. D. S.. Labour economics / J.D.S. Appleton. — 2nd ed. — Plymouth : Macdonald and Evans, 1979. — ix,222p : ill ; 19cm. — (The M & E handbook series)
Previous ed.: 1975. — Bibliography: p205-207. — Includes index
ISBN 0-7121-1246-4 (pbk) : £3.50 B81-26084

331′.0941 — Great Britain. Industrial relations — *Big Flame Industrial Commission viewpoints*
Organising to win : a political manual about how to stop losing struggles at work / by the Big Flame Industrial Commission. — Liverpool (217 Wavertree Rd., Liverpool 7) : Big Flame, [1981]?. — 33p : ill,ports ; 30cm
Cover title
ISBN 0-906082-04-8 (pbk) : £0.60 B81-36690

331'.0941 — Great Britain. Industrial relations. Effects of manpower planning — *Case studies*
The **Approach** to industrial change : a comparative study of workplace industrial relations and manpower policies in British and West German enterprises / a report prepared for the Anglo-German Foundation for the Study of Industrial Society. — London : The Foundation. — (Research papers / Anglo-German Foundaton for the Study of Industrial Society ; B0179/1E)
1: The British experience. — c1978. — 100p ; 30cm
ISBN 0-905492-13-7 (pbk) : £4.00
Also classified at 331'.0943 B81-15052

331'.0941 — Great Britain. Industrial relations — *For business studies*
Johnston, T. L.. An introduction to industrial relations / T.L. Johnston. — Plymouth : Macdonald and Evans, 1981. — x, 243p ; 22cm. — (The M&E BECbook series)
Bibliography: p239. — Includes index
ISBN 0-7121-0960-9 (pbk) : £5.25 B81-31410

331'.0941 — Great Britain. Industrial relations — *Haldane Society of Socialist Lawyers viewpoints*
Gill, Tess. Fightback / [written for the Haldane Society by Tess Gill, Jeremy McMullen and Jeremy Smith]. — London (14 Parkfield Rd., N.W.10) : Haldane Society of Socialist Lawyers, [1980?]. — [4]p : ill ; 43cm
£0.10 (unbound) B81-19095

331'.0941 — Great Britain. Industrial relations. Policies of government, *1979-1981* — *Labour Party (Great Britain) viewpoints*
Employment and industrial relations : the Tory record. — London : Labour Party, 1981. — 40p ; 30cm. — (Information paper / Labour Party Research Department ; no.21)
At head of title: The Labour Party
£0.60 (unbound)
Primary classification 331.12'5'0941 B81-28279

331'.0943 — West Germany. Industrial relations. Effects of innovation
Weltz, Friedrich. Introduction of new technologies, employment policies, and industrial relations : a survey carried out for the Anglo-German Foundation for the Study of Industrial Society / by Friedrich Weltz with assistance from Gerd Schmidt. — [London] : [The Foundation], c1978. — 159p ; 30cm + Case studies(106p ; 30cm). — (Research papers / Anglo-German Foundation for the Study of Industrial Society ; B0179/2E & 3E)
ISBN 0-905492-07-2 (pbk) : £4.00
ISBN 0-905492-10-2 (Case studies) : £4.00
B81-14733

331'.0943 — West Germany. Industrial relations. Effects of manpower planning — *Case studies*
The **Approach** to industrial change : a comparative study of workplace industrial relations and manpower policies in British and West German enterprises / a report prepared for the Anglo-German Foundation for the Study of Industrial Society. — London : The Foundation. — (Research papers / Anglo-German Foundaton for the Study of Industrial Society ; B0179/1E)
1: The British experience. — c1978. — 100p ; 30cm
ISBN 0-905492-13-7 (pbk) : £4.00
Primary classification 331'.0941 B81-15052

331'.09669 — Nigeria. Industrial relations
Fashoyin, Tayo. Industrial relations in Nigeria : (development and practice) / Tayo Fashoyin. — London : Longman, 1980. — x,166p : ill ; 25cm
Bibliography: p155-160. - Includes index
ISBN 0-582-64250-7 (pbk) : £3.95 B81-08402

331'.0973 — United States. Industrial relations
Sloane, Arthur A.. Labor relations / Arthur A. Sloane, Fred Witney. — 4th ed. — Englewood Cliffs ; London : Prentice-Hall, c1981. — xiv,525p ; 25cm
Previous ed.: 1977. — Includes bibliographies and index
ISBN 0-13-519587-x : £12.95 B81-14678

331'.0994 — Australia. Industrial relations
Niland, John. Industrial relations in Australia. — London : Allen & Unwin, Jan.1982. — [340]p
ISBN 0-86861-330-4 : £18.00 : CIP entry
B81-33709

331.1 — LABOUR FORCE AND MARKET

331.1'0917'7 — Organisation for Economic Co-operation and Development countries. Employment, *1950-1979*
Shutt, Harry. The jobs crisis : increasing unemployment in the developed world / by Harry Shutt. — London : Economist Intelligence Unit, 1980. — 78p : ill ; 30cm. — (EIU special report ; no.85)
£40.00 (pbk) B81-02037

331.1'0942 — England. Community land scheme — *Accounts — Serials*
Community Land Act 1975, account. — 1979-1980. — London : H.M.S.O., 1981. — 18p
ISBN 0-10-223581-3 : £2.60 B81-25486

331.11'05 — Manpower — *Serials*
HRD international journal. — Vol.1, no.1 (Oct.1981)-. — Paisley (5 Sandyford Rd, Paisley, PA3 4HW) : HRA Publications, 1980-. — v. : ill ; 30cm
Quaterly
ISSN 0260-1524 = HRD international journal (corrected) : £8.00 per year B81-09048

International journal of manpower. — Vol.1, no.1 (1980)-. — Bradford (198 Keighley Rd, Bradford, West Yorkshire BD9 4JQ) : MCB Publications, 1980-. — v. : ill ; 30cm
Quarterly
ISSN 0143-7720 = International journal of manpower : £19.85 per year B81-00772

331.11'072041 — Research by Great Britain. *Manpower Services Commission — Serials*
[Research *(Great Britain. Manpower Services Commission)*]. Research / Department of Employment, Manpower Services Commission. — 1979-80. — London : H.M.S.O., 1980. — 101p
ISBN 0-11-361194-3 : £4.50
ISSN 0144-2112 B81-01924

331.11'0724 — Manpower planning. Mathematical models — *Conference proceedings*
Manpower planning : proceedings of a symposium organised by the Institute of Mathematics and its Applications held in London in October 1974. — Southend-on-Sea (Maitland House, Warrior Sq., Southend-on-Sea, Essex SS1 2JY) : The Institute, c1976. — v,82p : ill ; 20cm. — (Symposium proceedings series / Institute of Mathematics and its Applications ; no.8)
Unpriced (spiral) B81-13266

331.11'0953'67 — Kuwait. Manpower
Alessa, Shamlan Y.. The manpower problem in Kuwait / Shamlan Y. Alessa. — London : Kegan Paul International, 1981. — xv,140p ; 23cm. — (Arab world studies)
Bibliography: p128-133. — Includes index
ISBN 0-7103-0009-3 : £15.00 : CIP rev.
B81-22562

331.11'1'0941 — Great Britain. Manufacturing industries. Employment. Geographical aspects
Fothergill, Stephen. Unequal growth. — London : Heinemann Educational, Sept.1981. — [256]p
ISBN 0-435-84370-2 (cased) : £13.50 : CIP entry
ISBN 0-435-84371-0 (pbk) : £7.50 B81-23781

331.11'42 — Great Britain. Polytechnic leavers. First employment — *Statistics*
First destinations of polytechnic students qualifying in 1979 : a statistical report on those obtaining first degree and higher diplomas by full-time and sandwich course study / Polytechnic Careers Advisers Statistics Working Party. — London (309 Regent St., WIR 7PE) : Committee of Directors of Polytechnics, [1980]. — ix,103p ; 30cm
£6.50 (spiral) B81-03271

331.11'422 — Great Britain. Graduates. Mathematical skills. Requirements of industries — *Conference proceedings*
The **Mathematical** skills and qualities needed in graduate entrants to industry and commerce : proceedings of a symposium organised by the Institute of Mathematics and its Applications held in London on May 3rd, 1977. — Southend-on-Sea (Maitland House, Warrior Sq., Southend-on-Sea, Essex SS1 2JY) : The Institute, c1977. — v,97p : ill ; 20cm. — (Symposium proceedings series / Institute of Mathematics and its Applications ; no.17)
Unpriced (spiral) B81-13270

331.11'422 — Great Britain. Plastics injection moulding industries. Personnel. Technical skills
Kaufmann, M.. Implications of the SPRU study of the use of skills within the injection moulding sector of the plastics industry / M. Kaufmann, A.A.L. Challis, G. Christopher Karas. — [London] ([State House, High Holborn, London WC1R 4JA) : Polymer Engineering Directorate, [1980?]. — 29p : ill ; 30cm
ISBN 0-901660-44-2 (spiral) : Unpriced
B81-14632

331.11'422 — Great Britain. Plastics processing industries. Personnel. Technical skills
Karas, G. Christopher. Advanced technical education and training in plastics / G. Christopher Karas. — [London] : [Science Research Council], [1980?]. — 35p ; 30cm
'An edited version of A Study of the skills used in the plastics processing industry, carried out for the National Economic Development Office, 1973'
Unpriced (spiral) B81-14331

331.11'422 — Great Britain. School leavers. Mathematical skills. Requirements of industries — *Conference proceedings*
The **Mathematical** needs of industry and commerce from its entrants at the school level : proceedings of a symposium organised by the Institute of Mathematics and its Applications held in London on April 5th, 1977. — Southend-on-Sea (Maitland House, Warrior Sq., Southend-on-Sea, Essex SS1 2JY) : The Institute, c1979. — v,54p : ill ; 20cm. — (Symposium proceedings series / Institute of Mathematics and its Applications ; no.16)
Unpriced (spiral) B81-13274

331.11'423 — Great Britain. Hotel & catering industries. City and Guilds of London Institute qualified personnel. Employment — *Case studies*
Lobstein, Tim. The craft career : a report on the first two years of the careers of qualified City and Guilds craftworkers, 1975-1977 / [Tim Lobstein]. — [Wembley] ([Ramsey House, Central Sq., Wembley, Middx HA9 7AP]) : [Hotel and Catering Industry Training Board], [1981?]. — 76p : ill,forms ; 30cm
Unpriced (spiral) B81-33181

331.11'423 — Great Britain. Hotel & catering industries. Management. Ordinary National Diploma courses & Higher National Diploma courses. Graduates. Employment
Kelly, T. K.. Employment patterns of graduates from OND & HND courses in hotel, catering & institutional management subjects, stage two : a report of the first continuation study based on a survey of graduates / T.K. Kelly. — Wembley (Ramsey House, Central Sq., Wembley, Middx HA9 7AP) : Hotel & Catering Industry Training Board, 1975. — vii,39,[9]p : ill,forms ; 30cm
£1.50 (spiral) B81-33186

331.11'423 — Ireland *(Republic)*. Arts graduates. Careers. Development
Scholefield, Derek Arthur. Arts graduates : five years on : career development and personal satisfaction / report prepared by Derek Arthur Scholefield. — Dublin (21 Fitzwilliam Sq., Dublin 2) : Higher Education Authority, 1980. — 22p : 1form ; 24cm
ISBN 0-904556-12-3 (pbk) : £0.50
Also classified at 658.3'1422 B81-19620

331.11'423 — Ireland *(Republic)*. Graduates. Employment — *Statistics — Serials*

The **Pattern** of graduate employment : a review of the further study or training or employment taken up by men and women who qualified for full-time first degrees, higher degrees and the higher diploma in education in the academic year ... / Association of Irish University Careers and Appointments Services. — 1974-75-. — [Galway] ([c/o Careers Information Service, University College, Galway]) : The Association, 1976-. — v. ; 21cm
Annual. — Description based on: 1976-77
Unpriced B81-09205

331.11'423 — Scotland. Strathclyde Region. Glasgow. Colleges of education: Jordanhill College of Education. *Youth and Community Department*. Graduates, *to 1980*. Employment

Fagan, G. R.. Career patterns of youth and community workers 1964-1979 inclusive : research paper : interim report / G.R. Fagan, M. Hough, C.J. Rowlands. — [Glasgow] ([Southbrae Drive, Jordanhill, Glasgow G13 1PP]) : Jordanhill College of Education Youth and Community Department, 1981. — ill,1form ; 30cm
Cover title
Unpriced (pbk) B81-15235

331.11'9042 — Great Britain. Civil service. Manpower. Reduction — *Inquiry reports*

Great Britain. *Parliament. House of Commons. Treasury and Civil Service Committee*. Seventh report from the Treasury and Civil Service Committee, session 1980-81 : Civil Service manpower reductions : together with the proceedings of the Committee and an appendix. — London : H.M.S.O., [1981]. — vi,17p ; 25cm. — ([HC] ; 423)
ISBN 0-10-242381-4 (pbk) : £2.30 B81-40613

331.11'9042 — Great Britain. Nationalised industries. Boards of directors — *Lists — Serials*

Public boards. — 1980. — London : H.M.S.O., [1980]. — 29p. — (Cmnd. ; 8114)
ISBN 0-10-181140-3 : £3.60 B81-10574

331.11'913616'09429 — Wales. Local authorities. Social service departments. Personnel — *Statistics — Serials*

Staff of social services departments, year ended 30th September ... / Welsh Office. — 1978. — [Cardiff] (Economic Statistical Services, Welsh Office, Crown Building,) : [Welsh Office], [1979?]. — 63p
Unpriced B81-06633

331.11'913619411 — Scotland. Welfare services. Personnel — *Statistics — Serials*

Staff of Scottish social work departments. — 1978-. — Edinburgh (Room 422, 43 Jeffrey St., Edinburgh EH1 1DN) : Social Work Services Group, 1979-. — v. ; 21cm. — (Statistical bulletin / Social Work Services Group)
Annual. — Continues in part: Scottish social work statistics. — Description based on: 1979
ISSN 0260-5457 = Staff of Scottish social work departments : Unpriced B81-04828

331.11'913621'0942 — England. National health services. Manpower planning

Manpower planning in the National Health Service / edited by A.F. Long and G. Mercer. — Farnborough, Hants. : Gower, c1981. — vii,174p : ill ; 23cm
Bibliography: p164-169. - Includes index
ISBN 0-566-00425-9 : £12.50 B81-12994

331.11'91647944101'0212 — Great Britain. Hotel industries. Manpower, *1977* — *Statistics*

Manpower : in the hotel and catering industry. — Wembley (Ramsey House, Central Sq., Wembley [Middx] HA9 7AP) : Hotel & Catering Industry Training Board, [1981?]. — 47p ; 30cm
Cover title
Unpriced (pbk)
Also classified at 331.11'916479541'0212
B81-33189

331.11'916479541'0212 — Great Britain. Catering industries. Manpower, *1977* — *Statistics*

Manpower : in the hotel and catering industry. — Wembley (Ramsey House, Central Sq., Wembley [Middx] HA9 7AP) : Hotel & Catering Industry Training Board, [1981?]. — 47p ; 30cm
Cover title
Unpriced (pbk)
Primary classification 331.11'91647944101'0212
B81-33189

331.11'93'0941 — Great Britain. Agricultural industries. Manpower — *Serials*

Agricultural nampower. — No.1 (Autumn 1980)-. — Haslemere (Graham Ward, Estate and Growing Dept., ICI Plant Protection Division, Fernhurst, Haslemere, Surrey GU27 3JE) : Agricultural Manpower Society, 1980-. — v. : ill,ports ; 30cm
Two issues yearly. — Continues: Journal of agricultural labour science
£2.00 per year B81-13215

331.12 — Canada. Skilled personnel. Supply & demand, *1970-1977*

Dodge, William. Skilled labour supply imbalances : the Canadian experience / by William Dodge. — [London] : British-North American Committee, 1977. — viii,55p : 1ill ; 23cm. — (BN ; 21)
ISBN 0-902594-31-1 (pbk) : £1.50 B81-09951

331.12 — Capitalist countries. Labour market — *Marxist viewpoints*

Capital and labour : studies in the capitalist labour process / edited by Theo Nichols. — London : Athlone in association with Fontana, 1980. — 476p ; 23cm
Includes bibliographies and index
ISBN 0-485-11206-x : £9.95 : CIP rev.
B80-03066

331.12 — Industrialised societies. Labour market. Segmentation. Political aspects

Berger, Suzanne. Dualism and discontinuity in industrial societies / Suzanne Berger, Michael J. Piore. — Cambridge : Cambridge University Press, 1980. — xi,159p : ill ; 24cm
Bibliography: p150-151. — Includes index
ISBN 0-521-23134-5 : £10.50 B81-03208

331.12 — Labour market. Socioeconomic aspects

Essays in the dynamics of labour market segmentation. — London : Academic Press, July 1981. — [300]p
ISBN 0-12-752080-5 : CIP entry B81-14872

331.12 — United States. Socially disadvantaged persons. Work experience. Projects

Solow, Robert M.. The story of a social experiment and some reflections / Robert M. Solow. — Dublin : Economic and Social Research Institute, c1980. — 20p ; 21cm. — (Thirteenth Geary lecture ; 1980)
ISBN 0-7070-0039-4 (pbk) : £1.50 B81-16589

331.12'042 — Great Britain. Job creation programmes — *Case studies*

Making work : some examples of job creation schemes / edited by Nicholas Hinton. — London : Bedford Square Press, NCV0, 1980. — 23p : ill ; 21x30cm
ISBN 0-7199-1051-x (pbk) : £1.50 B81-29196

331.12'042 — Great Britain. Job creation. Role of projects in environment conservation

Barbier, Edward B.. Earthworks : environmental approaches to employment creation / by Edward B. Barbier. — London : Friends of the Earth, c1981. — i,26p ; 30cm
ISBN 0-905966-26-0 (pbk) : £0.75 B81-24293

331.12'042 — United States. Community based employment programmes

Hallman, Howard W.. Community-based employment programs / Howard W. Hallman. — Baltimore ; London : Johns Hopkins University Press, c1980. — viii,117p ; 21cm. — (Policy studies in employment and welfare ; no.36)
Includes index
ISBN 0-8018-2391-9 : £5.50 B81-03756

331.12'07'041 — Great Britain. Labour market. Information sources

Walsh, Kenneth. The UK labour market : the IMS guide to information / Kenneth Walsh, Ann Izatt and Richard Pearson. — London : Kogan Page, 1980. — 261p : ill ; 23cm
Includes index
ISBN 0-85038-372-2 : £15.00 B81-03223

331.12'0724 — Labour market. Effects of consumer goods demand. Econometric models

Barnett, William A.. Consumer demand and labor supply : goods, monetary assets, and time / William A. Barnett. — Amsterdam ; Oxford : North-Holland, 1981. — xviii,378p : ill ; 23cm. — (Studies in mathematical and managerial economics ; v.29)
Bibliography: p355-363. — Includes index
ISBN 0-444-86097-5 : Unpriced B81-39201

331.12'0724 — Labour market. Influence of uncertainty. Econometric models

Ellis, Christopher J.. Uncertainty, adjustment costs and expected Keynesian unemployment / Christopher J. Ellis. — Coventry ([Coventry CV4 7AL]) : Department of Economics, University of Warwick, 1981. — 29p : ill ; 31cm. — (Warwick economic research papers ; no.189)
Bibliography: p29
Unpriced (pbk) B81-30923

331.12'09181'2 — Western world. Labour market

Abbott, Lewis F.. Theories of the labour market and industrial employment : a review of the social science literature / by Lewis F. Abbott. — Manchester ([26 Brown St., Manchester M2 1DN]) : Industrial Systems Research, 1980. — 106p ; 28cm
Includes index
ISBN 0-906321-06-9 (pbk) : £14.95 B81-03804

331.12'092'4 — Labour market. Theories of Quijano, Aníbal

Middleton, Alan. The marginalised labour force, the reserve army and the relative surplus population revisited : a comment on Aníbal Quijano / by Alan Middleton. — [Glasgow] : [Institute of Latin American Studies], University of Glasgow, 1980. — 17p ; 30cm. — (Occasional papers / Institute of Latin American Studies, University of Glasgow, ISSN 0305-8647 ; no.31)
Cover title
Unpriced (pbk) B81-15493

331.12'0941 — Great Britain. Labour market

Hunter, L. C.. Economics of wages and labour. — 2nd ed. / L.C. Hunter and C. Mulvey. — London : Macmillan, 1981. — xii,418p ; 25cm
Previous ed.: 1969. — Bibliography: p405-412. - Includes index
ISBN 0-333-30061-0 : £20.00 : CIP rev.
ISBN 0-333-30062-9 (pbk) : Unpriced
B80-24152

Sapsford, David. Labour market economics / David Sapsford. — London : Allen & Unwin, 1981. — xi,251p : ill ; 23cm. — (Economics and society series ; no.9)
Bibliography: p233-251. — Includes index
ISBN 0-04-331082-6 (cased) : £12.00
ISBN 0-04-331083-4 (pbk) : £5.95 B81-10759

331.12'0941 — Great Britain. Labour market — *Conference proceedings*

The **Economics** of the labour marker : proceedings of a conference on the labour market sponsored by Her Majesty's Treasury, the Department of Employment and the Manpower Services Commission, 10-12th September, 1979 at Magdalen College Oxford / [edited by Zmira Hornstein, Joseph Grice and Alfred Webb]. — London : H.M.S.O., 1981. — 328p : ill ; 24cm
Includes bibliographies and index
ISBN 0-11-630291-7 (pbk) : £8.95 B81-37393

331.12'0941 — Great Britain. Labour market. Effects of taxation

Taxation and labour supply. — London : Allen & Unwin, Sept.1981. — [304]p
ISBN 0-04-336073-4 : £18.50 : CIP entry
B81-20139

331.12′09411′85 — Scotland. Highland Region. Lochaber *(District).* **Manpower. Supply & demand** — *Forecasts*

Labour supply & demand in Lochaber 1978-1988 / [Commissioned by the Lochaber District Council] ; [Scottish Council Research Institute]. — Fort Williams ([Tweeddale], Fort Williams) : The Council, 1978. — 59,viip : ill ; 30cm
Unpriced (pbk) B81-11854

331.12′09595 — Malaysia. Urban regions. Labour market *related to* **distribution of income**

Mazumdar, Dipak. The urban labor market and income distribution : a study of Malaysia / Dipak Mazumdar. — New York ; Oxford : Published for the World Bank [by] Oxford University Press, c1981. — xvi,375p : ill ; 24cm. — (A World Bank research publication)
Includes index
ISBN 0-19-520213-9 (cased) : £10.75
ISBN 0-19-520214-7 (pbk) : £4.75
Also classified at 339.2′09595 B81-25980

331.12′0973 — United States. Labour market. Effects of government policies

Keeley, Michael C.. Labor supply and public policy : a critical review / Michael C. Keeley. — New York ; London : Academic Press, c1981. — xi,196p : ill ; 24cm. — (Studies in labor economics)
Bibliography: p175-186. — Includes index
ISBN 0-12-403920-0 : £15.00 B81-40773

331.12′5 — Overseas employment — *Practical information — For British personnel*

Golzen, Godfrey. Working abroad : the Daily telegraph guide to working and living overseas / Godfrey Golzen & Margaret Stewart. — 4th ed. — London : Kogan Page, 1981. — 320p : ill ; 22cm
Previous ed.: 1980
ISBN 0-85038-406-0 (cased) : Unpriced
ISBN 0-85038-407-9 (pbk) : £4.50 B81-18509

Mitchell, Jacqueline. Work & travel / [by Jacqueline Mitchell]. — [St. Albans] ([132 Trowley Hill Rd., Flamstead, St. Albans, Herts. AL3 8DZ]) : Prospects Unlimited, c1980. — 39p : ill ; 21cm
Cover title
£1.35 (pbk) B81-10743

Tideswell, M.. Accepting a job abroad : a practical guide / M. Tideswell. — [London] : British Institute of Management Foundation, Research and Publications Division, 1980. — 46p ; 30cm. — (Managers guides ; no.1)
Bibliography: p43-44. — Includes index
ISBN 0-85946-105-x (spiral) : £7.50
B81-03511

331.12′5′072041 — Great Britain. Employment. Statistics. Compilation by Great Britain. *Department of Employment* **& Great Britain.** *Manpower Services Commission*

Review of statistical services in Department of Employment and Manpower Services Commission . — [London] : The Department, 1981. — [305]p in various pagings ; 30cm
'Action report' (27p) also available separately
£12.50 (pbk) B81-22215

331.12′5′0724 — Employment. Effects of technological change. Econometric models

Stoneman, Paul. Technology, diffusion, wages and employment / Paul Stoneman. — Coventry ([Coventry CV4 7AL]) : Department of Economics, University of Warwick, 1981. — 28p ; 31cm. — (Warwick economic research papers ; no.190)
Bibliography: p28
Unpriced (pbk) B81-30921

331.12′5′091724 — Developing countries. Employment. Effects of foreign trade

Trade and employment in developing countries. — Chicago ; London : University of Chicago Press
1: Individual studies / edited by Anne O. Krueger ... [et al.]. — 1981. — x,548p : ill ; 24cm
Includes bibliographies and index
ISBN 0-226-45492-4 : £23.40 B81-21179

331.12′5′091724 — Developing countries. Employment. Effects of underutilisation of industrial capital

Industrial capacity and employment : case studies of Sri Lanka, Nigeria, Morocco and over-all survey of other developing countries : a study prepared for the International Labour Office within the framework of the World Employment Programme / by N. Phan-Thuy ... [et al.]. — Farnborough, Hants. : Published on behalf of the International Labour Office by Gower, c1981. — vi,394p : ill ; 23cm
ISBN 0-566-00433-x : £15.00 B81-11603

331.12′5′091734 — Rural regions. Employment

Hodge, Ian. Rural employment. — London : Methuen, Dec.1981. — [300]p
ISBN 0-416-73080-9 : £17.00 : CIP entry
B81-31709

331.12′5′0941 — Great Britain. Employment. Effects of import controls — *Socialist Workers' Party viewpoints*

Harris, Nigel. Why import controls won't save jobs — / Nigel Harris & Duncan Hallas. — London (265 Seven Sisters Rd, N4 2DE) : Socialists Unlimited for the SWP, 1981. — 15p : ill ; 21cm. — (A Socialist Workers Party pamphlet)
ISBN 0-905998-19-7 (pbk) : £0.25 B81-14097

331.12′5′0941 — Great Britain. Employment. Effects of technological innovation — *Conference proceedings*

Technological change and the future of work : University of Sussex, 26 June 1979 : conference proceedings / edited by Derek Washington ; the conference was arranged and presented by South Standing Conference on Schools' Science and Technology. — Redhill (c/o Philip Research Laboratories, Cross Oak La., Redhill, Surrey RH1 5HA) : D. Washington, [1979]. — 80p ; 21cm
Bibliography: p80
Unpriced (pbk) B81-12026

331.12′5′0941 — Great Britain. Employment — *For employers — Serials*

The **Employer's** watchdog. — Apr.1979 ed.-. — Leicester (7 Castle St., Hinckley, Leicester LE10 1DA) : Industrial Relations & Personnel Consultants, 1979-. — v. : ill ; 30cm
Irregular. — Description based on: Nov.1980 ed.
ISSN 0260-8987 = Employer's watchdog : Free to the Consultatnts' clients only
B81-09051

331.12′5′0941 — Great Britain. Employment — *Forecasts — Serials*

[Survey of employment prospects, Manpower]. Survey of employment prospects / Manpower. — 2nd quarter 1979-. — Slough (National Westminster House, The Grove, Slough, SL1 1QD, Berks.) : Manpower Ltd., 1979-. — v. ; 30cm
Quarterly. — Continues: Index of work trends. — Description based on: 1st quarter 1981
ISSN 0260-8146 = Survey of employment prospects (1979) : Unpriced B81-09141

331.12′5′0941 — Great Britain. Employment. Policies of government, *1979-1981 — Labour Party (Great Britain) viewpoints*

Employment and industrial relations : the Tory record. — London : Labour Party, 1981. — 40p ; 30cm. — (Information paper / Labour Party Research Department ; no.21)
At head of title: The Labour Party
£0.60 (unbound)
Also classified at 331′.0941 B81-28279

331.12′5′0941 — Great Britain. Employment — *Practical information*

The **A-Z** world of work / [editor P.T. Holland]. — [Chelmsford] ([42 Lime Walk, Chelmsford, Essex CM2 9NG]) : [Myka Trading], [1979]. — [72]p : ill ; 30cm
Cover title. — Includes index
ISBN 0-9507244-0-8 (spiral) : Unpriced
B81-04910

331.12′5′09411 — Scotland. Employment. Forecasting — *Conference proceedings*

Population projections and employment forecasts : report of a Planning Exchange Forum held in Glenrothes on 4 October 1978. — Glasgow : The Planning Exchange, 1978. — 40leaves : ill ; 30cm. — (Forum report / Planning Exchange ; 13)
Unpriced (pbk)
Primary classification 304.6′09411 B81-34611

331.12′5′09411 — Scotland. Rural regions. Employment — *Conference proceedings*

Population and employment in rural areas : report of a seminar held on 1 and 2 May 1979, at the Station Hotel, Inverness. — Glasgow : The Planning Exchange, [1979]. — 68leaves : 3maps ; 30cm. — (Forum report / Planning Exchange ; 15)
Unpriced (pbk)
Primary classification 304.6′09411 B81-34609

331.12′5′094237 — Cornwall. Employment — *Proposals*

Action plan for Cornwall, phase IV / Cornwall County Council. — Truro (c/o H. Calder, County Planning Officer, County Hall, Truro) : Cornwall County Council, 1981. — 119p : ill,maps ; 30cm
ISBN 0-902319-36-1 (pbk) : £3.00 B81-36438

331.12′5′094253 — Lincolnshire. Employment — *For structure planning*

Employment and industry : a background paper to the Lincolnshire structure plan. — [Lincoln] ([County Offices, Lincoln LN1 1YL]) : Lincolnshire County Council, 1976. — 52p : ill,maps,1form ; 30cm
Unpriced (pbk) B81-32736

331.12′5′0942735 — Greater Manchester *(Metropolitan County).* **Tameside** *(District).* **Employment. Effects of use of microelectronic devices in industries**

Green, Kenneth. The effects of microelectronic technologies on employment prospects : a case study of Tameside : a report commissioned by Tameside Metropolitan Borough Council / by Kenneth Green, Rod Coombs, Keith Holroyd. — Farnborough, Hants. : Gower, c1980. — xx,197p. in various pagings ; 23cm
Bibliography: 25p
ISBN 0-566-00418-6 : £12.30 B81-03399

331.12′5′095125 — Hong Kong. Employment. Labour

Turner, H. A.. The last colony, but whose? : a study of the labour movement, labour market and labour relations in Hong Kong / H.A. Turner with Patricia Fosh...[et al.]. — Cambridge : Cambridge University Press, 1980. — xv,215p ; 24cm. — (Paper in industrial relations and labour)
Includes index
ISBN 0-521-23701-7 : £11.50 B81-02615

331.12′5′0965 — Algeria. Employment. Effects of economic development, *1962-1977*

Bennamane, Aissa. The Algerian development strategy and employment policy / Aissa Bennamane. — Norwich : Published for the Centre for Development Studies by Geo Abstracts, 1980. — 111p ; 21cm. — (Monograph / Centre for Development Studies University College of Swansea ; 9)
ISBN 0-86094-052-7 (pbk) : £4.00 B81-04993

331.12′5′0973 — United States. Employment. Policies of government

Employment and labor-relations policy / edited by Charles Bulmer, John L. Carmichael, Jr. — Lexington : Lexington ; [Farnborough, Hants.] : [Gower] [distributor], 1980. — x,276p : ill ; 24cm
Includes index
ISBN 0-669-03388-x : £14.50 B81-10897

331.12'577'00943 — Employment. Effects of industrialisation — *Study examples: Textile industries & trades — Study regions: West Germany*

Fröbel, Folker. The new international division of labour : Structural unemployment in industrial countries and industrialisation in developing countries / Folker Fröbel, Jürgen Heinrichs and Otto Kreye ; translated by Pete Burgess. — Cambridge : Cambridge University Press, 1980. — xiv,407p : ill ; 24cm. — (Studies in modern capitalism = Etudes sur le capitilisme moderne)
Translation of: Die neue internationale Arbeitsteilung
ISBN 0-521-22319-9 : £30.00 B81-25938

331.12'7 — Great Britain. Hotel & catering industries. Personnel. Mobility

Knight, I. B.. Patterns of labour mobility in the hotel and catering industry : report on the findings of a survey of hotel and catering staff for the H.C.I.T.B. / I.B. Knight. — [Wembley] : [Hotel & Catering Industry Training Board], [197-]. — xi,236p : ill,forms ; 30cm
Cover title
£3.00 (spiral) B81-33197

331.12'7 — United States. Doctors. Immigration

Mejía, Alfonso. Foreign medical graduates : the case of the United States / Alfonso Mejia, Helena Pizurki, Erica Royston. — Lexington, Mass. : Published for Sandoz Institute for Health and Socio-Economic Studies by Lexington Books ; [Aldershot] : Gower [distributor], 1981, c1980. — xxv,209p : ill ; 24cm
Includes index
ISBN 0-669-03760-5 : £13.50 B81-29597

331.12'791 — Arab countries. Skilled personnel. Migration — *Conference proceedings*

The **Arab** brain drain : proceedings of a seminar organised by the Natural Resources, Science and Technology Division of the United Nations Economic Commission for Western Asia Beirut 4-8 February 1980 / edited by A.B. Zahlan. — London : Published for the United Nations by Ithaca, 1981. — 309p ; 23cm
Includes index
ISBN 0-903729-62-8 : £12.50 B81-16107

331.12'8 — Great Britain. State employment services — *Proposals*

The **Employment** service in the 1980's : report of a steering group on the aims and objectives of the employment service / Employment Service Division, Manpower Services Commission. — [London] ([166 High Holborn, WC1V 6PB]) : The Commission, 1979. — 44p : col.ill,1map ; 30cm + summary(10p : ill ; 21cm)
Ill, map on inside covers
Unpriced (pbk) B81-19398

331.12'8 — United States. Companies. Cooperation with employment services for disadvantaged persons

Ferman, Louis A.. Agency and company : partners in human resource development / Louis A. Ferman, Roger Manela, David Rogers. — Beverly Hills ; London : Sage published in cooperation with the Continuing Education Program in the Human Services of the University of Michigan School of Social Work, c1980. — 135p : 1form ; 22cm. — (Sage human services guide ; vol.18)
ISBN 0-8039-1558-6 (pbk) : £4.70 B81-14613

331.12'8'0941 — Great Britain. Services for unemployed persons — *Proposals*

Review of services for the unemployed / MSC. — London (166 High Holborn, WC1V 6PF) : Manpower Services Commission, 1981. — 36p : col.ill,1port ; 30cm
ISBN 0-905932-26-9 (pbk) : Unpriced B81-20815

331.12'91027041 — Great Britain. Libraries. Personnel. Supply & demand

Slater, Margaret. Ratios of staff to users : implications for library-information work and the potential for automation / Margaret Slater. — London : Aslib, c1981. — iv,123p : 1facsim,1form ; 21cm. — (Aslib occasional publications ; no.24) (British Library research and development report ; no.5629)
ISBN 0-85142-144-x (pbk) : £17.00 B81-36092

331.12'913711'009416 — Northern Ireland. Schools. Teachers. Supply & demand — *Serials*

Northern Ireland Council for Educational Research. *Research Unit*. The staffing needs of schools : report of the ... survey of teacher deployment in schools, conducted at the request of the Northern Ireland Advisory Committee on the Supply and Training of Teachers / NICER Research Unit. — 1978-1979. — [Belfast] ([52 Malone Rd, Belfast BT9 5DS]) : Northern Ireland Council for Educational Research, 1978-1979. — 2v. ; 30cm
Annual. — Continued in part by: Northern Ireland Council for Educational Research. Research Unit. Staffing needs of post-primary schools
£0.50 B81-29971

331.12'913711'00942 — England. Schools. Teachers. Supply & demand, *1945-1980*. **Political aspects**

Dimmock, Clive A. J.. Policy making in the teacher labour markets of England and Wales and the United States since 1945 : state intervention or laissez faire? / Clive A.J. Dimmock. — [London] : London Association of Comparative Educationists, 1981. — 49p : ill ; 21cm. — (Occasional paper / London Association of Comparative Educationists ; 3)
ISBN 0-85473-104-0 (pbk) : Unpriced
Also classified at 331.12'913711'00973
B81-18429

331.12'913711'00973 — United States. Schools. Teachers. Supply & demand, *1945-1980*. **Political aspects**

Dimmock, Clive A. J.. Policy making in the teacher labour markets of England and Wales and the United States since 1945 : state intervention or laissez faire? / Clive A.J. Dimmock. — [London] : London Association of Comparative Educationists, 1981. — 49p : ill ; 21cm. — (Occasional paper / London Association of Comparative Educationists ; 3)
ISBN 0-85473-104-0 (pbk) : Unpriced
Primary classification 331.12'913711'00942
B81-18429

331.12'9137311'009416 — Northern Ireland. Secondary schools. Teachers. Supply & demand — *Serials*

Northern Ireland Council for Educational Research. *Research Unit*. The staffing needs of post-primary schools : report of the ... survey of teacher deployment in post-primary schools, conducted at the request of the Northern Ireland Advisory Committee on the Supply and Training of Teachers. — 1980-. — [Belfast] ([52 Malone Rd, Belfast BT9 5DS]) : [Northern Ireland Council for Educational Research], 1980-. — v. ; 30cm
Annual. — Report prepared by: NICER Research Unit. — Continues in part: Northern Ireland Council for Educational Research. Research Unit. Staffing needs of schools
ISSN 0261-2631 = Staffing needs of post-primary schools : £0.50 B81-29973

Northern Ireland Council for Educational Research. *Research Unit*. The staffing needs of schools : report of the ... survey of teacher deployment in post-primary schools, conducted at the request of the Northern Ireland Advisory Committee on the Supply and Training of Teachers / NICER Research Unit. — 1979. — [Belfast] ([52 Malone Rd, Belfast BT9 5DS]) : Northern Ireland Council for Educational Research, c1979. — 30p
£0.50 B81-29972

331.13'3 — Great Britain. Sikhs. Employment. Implications of Sikh religious customs — *For employers*

Great Britain. *Commission for Racial Equality*. Guidance note on Sikh men and women & employment / Commission for Racial Equality. — London : The Commission, 1980. — 5p ; 30cm
Unpriced (pbk) B81-06528

331.13'3 — Sweden. Equality of opportunity

Scott, Hilda. Sweden's 'right to be human'. — London : Allison & Busby, Feb.1982. — [168]p
ISBN 0-85031-452-6 (cased) : £7.95 : CIP entry
ISBN 0-85031-453-4 (pbk) : £3.95 B81-35839

331.13'7 — Unemployment

Price, Victoria Curzon. Unemployment and other non-work issues / by Victoria Curzon Price. — London : Trade Policy Research Centre, 1980. — viii,42p : 1ill ; 19cm. — (Thames essay, ISSN 0306-6991 ; no.25)
ISBN 0-900842-51-2 (pbk) : £3.00 B81-20395

331.13'7 — Unemployment *related to* **inflation**

Meade, James E.. Stagflation. — London : Allen & Unwin
Vol.1: Wage-fixing. — Jan.1982. — [224]p
ISBN 0-04-339023-4 (cased) : £15.00 : CIP entry
ISBN 0-04-339024-2 (pbk) : £5.95 B81-33917

331.13'7 — Unemployment. Self-help — *Manuals*

Nathan, Robert. How to survive unemployment. — London : Institute of Personnel Management, Oct.1981. — [240]p
ISBN 0-85292-303-1 (pbk) : £1.95 : CIP entry
B81-31108

331.13'7'019 — Unemployed persons. Psychological aspects

Hayes, John. Understanding the unemployed. — London : Tavistock, July 1981. — [192]p
ISBN 0-422-77820-6 (cased) : £7.95 : CIP entry
ISBN 0-422-77830-3 (pbk) : £3.50 B81-14865

331.13'74'09427 — Great Britain. National unemployment rates *compared with* **local unemployment rates** — *Study regions: Northern England*

Gillespie, Andrew. The relationship between national and local unemployment rates : a case study of the northern region, 1979-80 : paper presented at the Social Science Research Council Urban and Regional Seminar Group meeting, University of Glasgow, September 1980. — [Newcastle upon Tyne] : University of Newcastle upon Tyne, Centre for Urban and Regional Development Studies, 1981. — 34leaves : ill ; 30cm. — (Discussion paper / Centre for Urban and Regional Development Studies University of Newcastle upon Tyne, ISSN 0140-6515 ; no.34)
Authors: Andrew Gillespie and David Owen. — Bibliography: p32-34
Unpriced (pbk) B81-13920

331.13'787832'0722 — Great Britain. Tyre manufacturing industries. Personnel. Redundancy — *Case studies*

Carmichael, C. L.. Redundancy, re-employment and the tyre industry / C.L. Carmichael, L.M. Cook. — London : Manpower Services Commission, 1981. — viii,[74]p in various pagings : ill,maps,facsims ; 30cm
Bibliography: p74
Unpriced (pbk) B81-39285

331.13'791812 — Western world. Unemployment — *Conference proceedings*

Unemployment in western countries : proceedings of a conference held by the International Economic Association at Bischenberg, France / edited by Edmond Malinvaud and Jean-Paul Fitoussi. — London : Macmillan, 1980. — xiv,551p : ill ; 23cm
Includes bibliographies and index
ISBN 0-333-28415-1 : £20.00 : CIP rev.
B80-13249

331.13'7941 — Great Britain. Executives. Redundancy

Institute of Personnel Management. *Information Services*. Executive redundancy / [IPM Information Services]. — London : Institute of Personnel Management, 1980. — viii,133p : ill ; 30cm. — (IPM information report ; no.30)
Bibliography: p131-133
ISBN 0-85292-263-9 (pbk) : £15.00 B81-08097

331.13'7941 — Great Britain. Unemployed persons — *Case studies*

Marsden, Dennis. Workless. — Rev. and enlarged ed.. — London : Croom Helm, Nov.1981. — [288]p
Previous ed.: London : Penguin, 1975
ISBN 0-7099-1723-6 (pbk) : £6.95 : CIP entry
B81-31169

331.13'7941 — Great Britain. Unemployment

Crick, Bernard. Unemployment. — London : Methuen, July 1981. — [150]p
ISBN 0-416-32470-3 (pbk) : £2.50 : CIP entry
B81-14976

Sinfield, Adrian. What unemployment means / Adrian Sinfield. — Oxford : Robertson, 1981. — vii,167p : ill,1map ; 22cm
Bibliography: p158-164. — Includes index
ISBN 0-85520-406-0 (pbk) : £2.75 B81-17617

The **Workless** state : studies in unemployment / edited by Brian Showler and Adrian Sinfield. — Oxford : Robertson, 1981. — xvii,267p : 1ill ; 22cm
Bibliography: p243-259. — Includes index
ISBN 0-85520-327-7 (cased) : £15.00 : CIP rev.
ISBN 0-85520-340-4 (pbk) : £4.95 B80-29185

331.13'7941 — Great Britain. Unemployment. Economic aspects

The **Economics** of unemployment in Britain / edited by John Creedy. — London : Butterworths, 1981. — xv,263p : ill ; 22cm
Includes bibliographies and index
ISBN 0-408-10703-0 (pbk) : Unpriced : CIP rev. B81-06892

331.13'7941 — Great Britain. Unemployment — *Forecasts*

Allen, Rod. The shattered dream : employment in the eighties : an Arrow/LWT / Rod Allen, Anwer Bati, Jean-Claude Bragard. — London : Arrow, 1981. — 278p : ill ; 18cm
Bibliography: p277-278
ISBN 0-09-927100-1 (pbk) : £1.95 B81-29879

331.13'7941 — Great Britain. Unemployment. Policies of Liberal Party — *Proposals*

Titley, Simon. Fighting unemployment - the Liberal alternative / Simon Titley. — London : Liberal Publication Department, [1981]. — 23p ; 21cm
Cover title
£0.50 (pbk) B81-32872

331.13'7941 — Great Britain. Unemployment. Political aspects

Friend, Andrew. Slump city : the politics of mass unemployment / Andrew Friend & Andy Metcalf. — London : Pluto, 1981. — 194p ; 20cm
Includes index
ISBN 0-86104-342-1 (pbk) : £3.95 B81-27561

331.13'7941 — Great Britain. Unemployment — *Practical information*

Melville, Joy. The survivors guide to unemployment and redundancy / Joy Melville. — London : Corgi, 1981. — 199p ; 18cm
Bibliography: p198-199
ISBN 0-552-11739-0 (pbk) : £1.25 B81-33101

331.13'7941 — Great Britain. Unemployment — *Trades Union Congress viewpoints*

Unemployment : the fight for TUC alternatives. — London : Trades Union Congress, 1981. — 40p : ill,1port ; 30cm. — (TUC education)
Cover title. — Text, ill, port on inside covers
£0.50 (pbk) B81-22813

331.13'7941'0212 — Great Britain. Unemployment, *1850-1979*. Statistics

Garside, W. R.. The measurement of unemployment : methods and sources in Great Britain 1850-1979 / W.R. Garside. — Oxford : Blackwell, 1980. — xiii,274p : ill ; 23cm. — (Warwick studies in industrial relations)
Bibliography: p251-270. — Includes index
ISBN 0-631-12643-0 : £19.50 : CIP rev.
B80-24161

331.13'7942817 — West Yorkshire *(Metropolitan County)*. Keighley. Unemployment

Keighley's shrinking manufacturing base : a report by Keighley Information Centre for Keighley Trades Council on the crises of growing unemployment in the town. — Keighley (29 South St., Keighley, West Yorks.) : The Centre, 1981. — 15p : ill ; 30cm
Cover title
£0.30 (£0.50 to organisations) (pbk)
B81-22430

331.13'7994231 — South Australia. Adelaide. Unemployed persons. Effects of economic depressions, *1929-1938*

Broomhill, Ray. Unemployed workers : a social history of the Great Depression in Adelaide / Ray Broomhill. — St. Lucia : University of Queensland Press ; Hemel Hempstead : Distributed by Prentice-Hall, c1978. — xiv,220p : ill,1facsim,port ; 22cm
Bibliography: p201-213. — Includes index
ISBN 0-7022-1235-0 : £11.50 B81-25160

331.2 — WORKERS. CONDITIONS OF EMPLOYMENT

331.2 — Workplaces. Reorganisation. Participation of personnel

Lyons, Tom. Workplace reorganisation : an opportunity to participate / Tom Lyons. — Dublin (IPC House, 35 Shelbourne Rd, Dublin 4) : Labour/Management Service, Irish Productivity Centre, 1981. — 17p : col.ill ; 22cm
Text on inside cover
ISBN 0-902939-09-2 (pbk) : £1.50 B81-31289

331.2'04135441006 — Great Britain. Civil service. Personnel. Conditions of service

Beaumont, P. B.. Government as employer : setting an example? / P.B. Beaumont. — London : Royal Institute of Public Administration, 1981. — 79p ; 22cm. — (RIPA Studies)
ISBN 0-900628-20-0 (pbk) : £4.40 B81-26548

331.2'0413627'0941 — Great Britain. Youth workers. Working conditions — *Serials*

Joint Negotiating Committee for Youth Workers and Community Centre Wardens. Report of the Joint Negotiating Committee for Youth Workers and Community Centre Wardens. — 12th (1978) ; [no.1]. — London (c/o Secretary, Employers Panel, 41 Belgrave Sq., SW1X 8NZ) : The Committee, 1978-. — v. ; 21cm
Irregular. — Continues: Joint Negotiating Committee for Youth Leaders and Community Centre Wardens. Report of the Joint Negotiating Committee for Youth Leaders and Community Centre Wardens. — Description based on: [No.1]
ISSN 0260-9304 = Report of the Joint Negotiating Committee for Youth Workers and Community Centre Wardens : £1.25
Also classified at 331.2'04137428'0941
B81-12414

331.2'04137428'0941 — Great Britain. Community centres. Wardens. Working conditions — *Serials*

Joint Negotiating Committee for Youth Workers and Community Centre Wardens. Report of the Joint Negotiating Committee for Youth Workers and Community Centre Wardens. — 12th (1978) ; [no.1]. — London (c/o Secretary, Employers Panel, 41 Belgrave Sq., SW1X 8NZ) : The Committee, 1978-. — v. ; 21cm
Irregular. — Continues: Joint Negotiating Committee for Youth Leaders and Community Centre Wardens. Report of the Joint Negotiating Committee for Youth Leaders and Community Centre Wardens. — Description based on: [No.1]
ISSN 0260-9304 = Report of the Joint Negotiating Committee for Youth Workers and Community Centre Wardens : £1.25
Primary classification 331.2'0413627'0941
B81-12414

331.2'0416169803'0941 — Great Britain. Industrial medical services. Doctors. Conditions of service

The **Occupational** physician / developed by the Occupational Health Committee of the British Medical Association from the original pamphlet The doctor in industry. — London : BMA, c1980. — 23p : 1form ; 30cm
ISBN 0-7279-0066-8 (pbk) : Unpriced
Also classified at 616.9'803'02341 B81-19330

331.2'041651'09416 — Northern Ireland. Offices. Working conditions — *Serials*

Great Britain. *Department of Manpower Services (Northern Ireland)*. Office and Shop Premises Act (Northern Ireland) 1966 : report by the Department of Manpower Services for the year ended 31 December .... — 1979. — Belfast : H.M.S.O., 1980. — v. ; 25cm
Annual. — Continues: Great Britain. Department of Manpower Services (Northern Ireland). Office and Shop Premises Act (N.I.) 1966
ISSN 0261-5592 = Office and Shop Premises Act. Northern Ireland. 1966. Report by the Department of Manpower Services : £2.70
Also classified at 331.2'04165887'009416
B81-31886

331.2'04165887'009416 — Northern Ireland. Shops. Working conditions — *Serials*

Great Britain. *Department of Manpower Services (Northern Ireland)*. Office and Shop Premises Act (Northern Ireland) 1966 : report by the Department of Manpower Services for the year ended 31 December .... — 1979. — Belfast : H.M.S.O., 1980. — v. ; 25cm
Annual. — Continues: Great Britain. Department of Manpower Services (Northern Ireland). Office and Shop Premises Act (N.I.) 1966
ISSN 0261-5592 = Office and Shop Premises Act. Northern Ireland. 1966. Report by the Department of Manpower Services : £2.70
Primary classification 331.2'041651'09416
B81-31886

331.2'04292'0924 — Hungary. Budapest. Motor vehicle industries: Vörös Csillag Traktorgyár. Working conditions, *1970-1972 — Personal observations*

Haraszti, Miklós. A worker in a worker's state : piece-rates in Hungary / Miklós Haraszti ; translated by Michael Wright ; with a foreword by Heinrich Böll, a note about the author and a transcript of the author's trial. — Harmondsworth : Penguin in association with New Left Review, 1977 (1981 [printing]). — 175p ; 20
Translation of: Stücklohn
ISBN 0-14-021988-9 (pbk) : £2.25 B81-39688

331.2'04292222'0924 — France. Choisy. Citröen cars. Manufacture. Factories. Assembly lines. Working conditions — *Personal observations*

Linhart, Robert. The assembly line / by Robert Linhart ; translated by Margaret Crosland. — London : Calder, 1981. — 160p ; 22cm. — (A Platform book ; PB17)
Translation of: L'Etabli
ISBN 0-7145-3742-x (pbk) : £3.95 : CIP rev.
B81-09485

331.2'043'0942 — England. Agricultural industries. Working conditions, *1500-1900*

Fussell, G. E.. The English countryman : his life and work from Tudor times to the Victorian age / G.E. & K.R. Fussell. — London : Orbis Publishing, 1981. — 172p,[64]p of plates : ill,1facsim,ports ; 24cm
Originally published: London : Melrose, 1955. — Bibliography: p157-163. — Includes index
ISBN 0-85613-335-3 : £10.00 B81-26670

331.2'046'00941 — Great Britain. Chemical industries. Personnel. Working conditions — *Regulations*

Chemical and Allied Industries Joint Industrial Council. Constitution and schedule of wage rates and working conditions / Chemical and Allied Industries Joint Industrial Council. — [London] ([93 Albert Embankment, SE1 7TU]) : [Chemical Industries Association], 1980. — 47p ; 15cm
Unpriced (pbk) B81-12450

331.2'07204 — European Community countries. Working conditions. Research projects — *Directories*

Directory of research projects on working conditions in the European Community : feasibility study 1979-1980 / European Foundation Research Information System. — Shankill (Loughlinstown House, Shankill, Co. Dublin) : European Foundation for the Improvement of Living and Working Conditions, [1980]. — xiv,315p ; 30cm
English, French and Italian text. — Includes index
Unpriced (pbk) B81-08397

331.2'092'2 — London. Barnet *(London Borough).* **Working conditions,** *1919-1939 — Personal observations — Collections*

Reboul, P.. Those were the days / by P. Reboul ; with illustrations by Mary Spiegelhalter. — London (88 Temple Fortune Lane, NW11 7TX) : Hendon and District Archaeological Society, c1980. — 48p,[4]p of plates : ill ; 22cm. — (Occasional paper / Hendon and District Archaeological Society ; no.5)
ISBN 0-9503050-4-9 (pbk) : £0.95 B81-29795

331.2'0941 — Great Britain. Industries. Working conditions, *1700-1800*

Rule, John. The experience of labour in eighteenth-century industry / John Rule. — London : Croom Helm, c1981. — 227p ; 23cm
Bibliography: p217-223. - Includes index
ISBN 0-85664-524-9 : £13.95 : CIP rev.
B80-33057

331.2'1 — Great Britain. Wage bargaining

The **Future** of pay bargaining / edited by F.T. Blackaby. — London : Heinemann, 1980. — 238p : ill ; 23cm. — (Joint studies in public policy ; 2)
Conference papers. — Includes bibliographies and index
ISBN 0-435-83921-7 : £13.50
ISBN 0-435-83922-5 (pbk£6.50) B81-04666

331.2'1 — Great Britain. Wage bargaining *— For personnel management*

Bargaining strategy : the personnel manager's checklist for reviewing collective bargaining arrangements / [prepared by the IPM's National Committee on Employee Relations]. — London : Institute of Personnel Management, 1980. — 15leaves ; 30cm
ISBN 0-85292-296-5 (spiral) : Unpriced
B81-05348

331.2'15 — Great Britain. Coal industries. Personnel. Remuneration. Determination

Handy, L. J.. Wages policy in the British coalmining industry : a study of national wage bargaining / L.J. Handy. — Cambridge : Cambridge University Press, 1981. — xvii,313p : ill ; 24cm. — (Monographs / University of Cambridge, Department of Applied Economics ; 27)
Bibliography: p304-307. — Includes index
ISBN 0-521-23535-9 : £22.50 B81-24488

331.2'15 — Great Britain. Jute industries. Personnel. Remuneration. Determination, *1960-1978*

Abolition and after : the Jute Wages Council / [by Christine Craig ... et al.]. — [London] : [H.M.S.O.], 1980. — 54p : ill ; 30cm. — (Research paper / Department of Employment ; no.15)
Bibliography: p54
Unpriced (pbk) B81-13150

331.2'15 — Great Britain. Universities. Clerical personnel. Remuneration. Determination *— Inquiry reports*

Great Britain. *Standing Commission on Pay Comparability.* University clerical staff / Standing Commission on Pay Comparability. — London : H.M.S.O., [1981]. — v,21p ; 25cm. — (Cmnd. ; 8144) (Report ; no.13)
ISBN 0-10-181440-2 (unbound) : £2.40
B81-13643

331.2'15 — Great Britain. Universities. Personnel: Computer operators. Renumeration. Determination *— Inquiry reports*

Great Britain. *Standing Commission on Pay Comparability.* University computer operating staff / Standing Commission on Pay Comparability. — London : H.M.S.O., [1981]. — iv,23p ; 25cm. — (Cmnd. ; 8203) (Report ; no.15)
ISBN 0-10-182030-5 (unbound) : £2.40
B81-19014

331.2'15 — Remuneration. Determination. Influence of trade unions

Burkitt, Brian. Trade unions and wages : implications for economic theory / Brian Burkitt. — 2nd ed. — [Bradford] : Bradford University Press, 1980. — ix,240p : ill ; 22cm
Previous ed.: 1975. — Includes bibliographies and index
ISBN 0-901945-39-0 (pbk) : £6.95 B81-03350

331.2'15 — Remuneration. Determination. Influence of trade unions & industrial concentration

Cowling, Keith. Wage share, concentration and unionism / Keith Cowling and Ian Molho. — Coventry : Department of Economics, University of Warwick, 1981. — 23p ; 31cm. — (Warwick economic research papers ; no.188)
Bibliography: p22-23
Unpriced (pbk) B81-22956

331.2'15 — Scotland. Local authorities. Chief executives. Renumeration. Determination *— Inquiry reports*

Great Britain. *Standing Commission on Pay Comparability.* Chief officials of local authorities in Scotland / Standing Commission on Pay Comparability. — London : H.M.S.O., [1981]. — iv,23p ; 25cm. — (Cmnd. ; 8202) (Report ; no.14)
ISBN 0-10-182020-8 (unbound) : £2.40
B81-19015

331.2'15'0941 — Great Britain. Personnel. Remuneration. Determination

Genders, Peter. Wages and salaries. — London : Institute of Personnel Management, Oct.1981. — 1v.
ISBN 0-85292-275-2 (pbk) : £5.95 : CIP entry
B81-31107

331.2'15'0941 — Great Britain. Personnel. Remuneration. Determination. Economic aspects

The **1979-80** pay round / Confederation of British Industry. — London : Confederation of British Industry, 1979. — 14p : ill ; 30cm
£0.50 (pbk) B81-40372

331.2'15'0941 — Great Britain. Remuneration. Determination *— Liberal Party viewpoints*

Jones, Aubrey, *1911-*. The reform of pay determination / by Aubrey Jones. — London : Liberal Party Publication Department for the Unservile State Group, [1980?]. — 11p ; 21cm. — (Unservile state papers ; no.27)
£0.50 B81-06239

331.2'15'0973 — United States. Personnel. Remuneration. Determination. Role of manpower supply & demand, *to 1979*

Douty, H. M.. The wage bargain and the labor market / H.M. Douty. — Baltimore ; London : Johns Hopkins University Press, c1980. — viii,150p : ill ; 21cm. — (Policy studies in employment and welfare ; no.37)
Includes bibliographies and index
ISBN 0-8018-2393-5 : £7.25 B81-05340

331.2'15'0994 — Australia. Remuneration. Indexation, *1975-1981*

Plowman, David. Wage indexation. — London : Allen and Unwin, Jan.1982. — [192]p
ISBN 0-86861-363-0 : £10.00 : CIP entry
B81-34785

331.2'16 — Great Britain. Manual personnel. Remuneration *— Case studies*

White, Michael. Payment systems in Britain. — Farnborough : Gower, Oct.1981. — [120]p
ISBN 0-566-02294-x : £12.50 : CIP entry
B81-25826

331.2'162'0941 — Great Britain. Personnel. Remuneration. Time rates *— Serials*

Time rates of wages and hours of work / Department of Employment. — Apr.1980. — London : H.M.S.O., [1980]. — ix,290p : ill
ISBN 0-11-361192-7 : £12.00 B81-00032

331.2'164 — Great Britain. Profit sharing - *Conference proceedings*

Planning employee share schemes. — Farnborough : Gower, 1981. — [60]p. — (Gower executive report)
Conference papers
ISBN 0-566-03024-1 : £18.50 : CIP entry
B81-11945

331.2'166 — Great Britain. Sick personnel. Remuneration. Great Britain. *Department of Health and Social Security.* **Income during initial sickness** *— Critical studies*

Disability Alliance. The wrong strategy : the Disability Alliance's response to the government's Green Paper on income during initial sickness. — London (1 Cambridge Terrace, NW1 4JL) : The Alliance, 1980. — 11p ; 30cm
£0.50 (pbk) B81-08315

331.25'2 — Great Britain. Public bodies. Index-linked occupational superannuation schemes. Value. Inquiry into the value of pensions *— Aims of Industry viewpoints*

Sherman, Alfred. Pension time-bomb / the Scott report : by Alfred Sherman. — London : AIMS, 1981. — 15p ; 21cm
ISBN 0-7281-0094-0 (pbk) : £0.60 B81-26811

331.25'2 — Great Britain. Public bodies. Index-linked occupational superannuation schemes. Value *— Inquiry reports*

Inquiry into the value of pensions : report of an inquiry into the value of differences in the inflation protection of occupational pensions and the value of relative job security for the purposes of determining public sector pay and other conditions of service / chairman Sir Bernard Scott. — London : HMSO, [1981]. — v,55p ; 25cm. — (Cmnd. ; 8147)
ISBN 0-10-181470-4 (pbk) : £3.90 B81-13219

331.25'2'025 — Superannuation schemes *— Directories — Serials*

Pension funds and their advisers. — 1981. — London (9 Courtleigh Gardens, NW11 9JX) : A.P. Financial Registers, 1981. — 727p
ISBN 0-906247-05-5 (cased) : Unpriced
ISSN 0140-6647 B81-30754

331.25'2'0941 — Great Britain. Companies. Superannuation schemes *— For personnel*

Ward, Sue. Pensions : what to look for in company pension schemes and how to improve them / Sue Ward. — London : Pluto, 1981. — 267p ; 20cm. — (Workers' handbooks)
Bibliography: p260-261. — Includes index
ISBN 0-86104-333-2 (pbk) : £3.95 B81-27560

331.25'22 — Great Britain. Occupational superannuation benefits. Protection on change of occupations *— Inquiry reports*

Occupational Pensions Board. Improved protection for the occupational pension rights and expectations of early leavers : a report of the Occupational Pensions Board in accordance with section 66 of the Social Security Act 1973. — London : H.M.S.O., [1981]. — viii,146p : ill ; 25cm. — (Cmnd. ; 8271)
ISBN 0-10-182710-5 (pbk) : £6.30 B81-31490

331.25'5 — Great Britain. Companies. Shareholding by personnel

Wilken, Folkert. Liberation of capital. — London : Allen and Unwin, Apr.1981. — [300]p
ISBN 0-04-334005-9 : £12.00 : CIP entry
B81-01845

331.25'5 — Great Britain. Offices. Personnel. Fringe benefits *— Serials*

The **Survey** of fringe benefits for office staff / conducted by Alfred Marks Bureau Ltd. — 1975. — London : Careers Intelligence in association with Alfred Marks Buriau, 1975. — 32p
ISSN 0260-2555 : Unpriced B81-09146

The **Survey** of fringe benefits for office staff / conducted by Alfred Marks Bureau Ltd. — 1976. — London : Careers Intelligence in association with Alfred Marks Bureau, 1976. — 42p
ISSN 0260-2555 : Unpriced B81-13036

The **Survey** of fringe benefits for office staff / conducted by Alfred Marks Bureau. — 1977. — London : Careers Intelligence in association with Alfred Marks Bureau, 1977. — 54p
ISSN 0260-2555 : Unpriced B81-13037

331.25'5 — Great Britain. Offices. Personnel. Fringe benefits — *Serials* *continuation*

The **Survey** of fringe benefits for office staff / conducted by Alfred Marks Bureau Ltd. — 1978. — London : Careers Intelligence in association with Alfred Marks Bureau, 1978. — 51p
Unpriced B81-09143

The **Survey** of fringe benefits for office staff / conducted by Alfred Marks Bureau Ltd. — 1979. — London : Careers Intelligence in association with Alfred Marks Bureau, 1979. — 56p
ISSN 0260-2555 : Unpriced B81-09142

The **survey** of fringe benefits for office staff / conducted by Alfred Marks Bureau. — 1980. — London : Adia House, 84-86 Regent Street W1R 5PA : Careers Intelligence in association with Alfred Marks Bureau, c1980. — 66p
ISSN 0260-2555 : Unpriced B81-08696

331.25'5 — Great Britain. Personnel. Relocation allowances

Jago, Alison. Employee relocation expenses / Alison Jago. — London : Institute of Personnel Management, 1980. — 51p ; 30cm. — (IPM information report ; no.29)
Bibliography: p49-51
ISBN 0-85292-251-5 (pbk) : £5.00 B81-08098

331.25'5 — Great Britain. Redundancy payments. Rebates. Redundancy Fund — *Accounts — Serials*

Redundancy fund account. — 1979-80. — London : H.M.S.O., 1981. — 9p
ISBN 0-10-213681-5 : £1.40 B81-16820

331.25'5 — Great Britain. Shareholding by personnel — *Fabian viewpoints*

Carroll, Roger. The two wage worker : common ownership and economic democracy / Roger Carroll. — London : Fabian Society, 1980. — 16p ; 22cm. — (Fabian tract, ISSN 0307-7535 ; 470)
Cover title
ISBN 0-7163-0470-8 : £0.65
Primary classification 331'.01'120941
B81-04994

331.25'5'0941 — Great Britain. Companies. Personnel. Fringe benefits — *For personnel*

Cunningham, Michael, *1940-*. Non-wage benefits : 'fringe benefits' : what they are and how to win them / Michael Cunningham. — London : Pluto, 1981. — 296p ; 20cm. — (Worker's handbooks)
Includes index
ISBN 0-86104-334-0 (pbk) : £3.50 B81-27555

331.25'7 — European Community countries. Shiftwork. Economic aspects — *Case studies*

Economic aspects of shiftwork / [European Foundation for the Improvement of Living and Working Conditions]. — [Shankill] ([Loughlinstown House, Shankill, Co. Dublin]) : [European Foundation for the Improvement of Living and Working Conditions], [1980]. — [461]p : ill ; 30cm
Conference papers. — Includes bibliographies
£5.00 (pbk) B81-05317

331.25'7 — European Community countries. Shiftwork. Economic aspects — *Case studies — Danish texts*

Økonomiske aspekter ved skifteholdsarbejde / [Europæiske institut til forbedring af leve-og arbejdsvilkårene]. — [Shankill] ([Loughlinstown House, Shankill, Co. Dublin]) : [European Foundation for the Improvement of Living and Working Conditions], [1980]. — [434]p : ill ; 30cm
Conference papers. — Includes bibliographies
£5.00 (pbk) B81-05789

331.25'7 — European Community countries. Shiftwork. Economic aspects — *Case studies — French texts*

Aspects économiques du travail poste / [Fondation européenne pour l'amélioration des conditions de vie et de travail]. — [Shankill] ([Loughlinstown House, Shankill, Co. Dublin]) : [European Foundation for the Improvement of Living and Working Conditions], [1980]. — [480]p : ill ; 30cm
Conference papers. — Includes bibliographies
£5.00 (pbk) B81-05781

331.25'7 — European Community countries. Shiftwork. Economic aspects — *Case studies — German texts*

Wirtschaftliche Aspekte der Schichtarbeit / [Europäische Stiftung zur Verbesserung der Lebens und Arbeitsbedingungen]. — [Shankill] ([Loughlinstown House, Shankill, Co. Dublin]) : [European Foundation for the Improvement of Living and Working Conditions], [1980]. — [448]p : ill ; 30cm
Conference papers. — Includes bibliographies
£5.00 (pbk) B81-05788

331.25'7 — European Community countries. Shiftwork. Economic aspects — *Case studies — Italian texts*

Aspetti economici del lavoro a turni / [Fondazione europea per il miglioramento delle condizioni di vita e di lavoro]. — [Shankill] ([Loughlinstown House, Shankill, Co. Dublin]) : [European Foundation for the Improvement of Living and Working Conditions], 1980. — [469]p : ill ; 30cm
Conference papers. — Includes bibliographies
£5.00 (pbk) B81-05316

331.25'7 — European Community countries. Shiftwork. Innovations — *Case studies*

Cases of innovations in shiftwork / [European Foundation for the Improvement of Living and Working Conditions]. — [Shankill] ([Loughlinstown House, Shankill, Co. Dublin]) : [European Foundation for the Improvement of Living and Working Conditions], [1980]. — [595]p : ill ; 30cm
Conference papers. — Includes bibliographies
£5.00 (pbk) B81-05315

331.25'7 — European Community countries. Shiftwork. Innovations — *Case studies — Dutch texts*

Innovaties in de ploegenarbeid. — [Shankill] ([Loughlinstown House, Shankill, Co. Dublin]) : European Foundation for the Improvement of Living and Working Conditions, [1980]. — 638p in various pagings : ill ; 30cm
Conference papers
Unpriced (pbk) B81-14217

331.25'7 — European Community countries. Shiftwork. Innovations — *Case studies — French texts*

Innovations en matière de travail posté. — [Shankill] ([Loughlinstown House, Shankill, Co. Dublin]) : [European Foundation for the Improvement of Living and Working Conditions], [1980?]. — 642p in various pagings : ill ; 30cm
£5.00 (pbk) B81-10791

331.25'7 — European Community countries. Shiftwork. Innovations — *Case studies — German texts*

Innovationen in der Schichtarbeit / [Europäische Stiftung zur Verbesserung der Lebens- und Arbeitsbedingungen]. — [Shankill] ([Loughlinstown House, Shankill, Co. Dublin]) : [European Foundation for the Improvement of Living and Working Conditions], [1980]. — [617]p ; 30cm
Conference papers. — Includes bibliographies
£5.00 (pbk) B81-05787

331.25'7 — European Community countries. Shiftwork. Innovations — *Case studies — Italian texts*

Innovazioni nel lavoro a turni. — [Shankill] (Loughlinstown House, Shankill, Co. Dublin) : Fondazione europea per il miglioramento delle condizioni di vita e di lavoro, [1980?]. — 650p in various pagings ; 29cm
Unpriced (pbk) B81-12207

331.25'7 — Persons. Time. Allocation

Sharp, Clifford. The economics of time. — Oxford : Martin Robertson, July, 1981. — [224]p
ISBN 0-85520-162-2 : £12.50 : CIP entry
B81-13750

331.25'7 — Shiftwork

Studies of shiftwork / edited by W.P. Colquhoun and J. Rutenfranz. — London : Taylor & Francis, 1980. — xi,468p : ill ; 26cm
Includes bibliographies
ISBN 0-85066-210-9 : £16.50 : CIP rev.
B80-21442

331.25'7'094 — European Community countries. Working hours *compared with* **working hours in Great Britain**

Long suffering British workers : working time in Europe. — London (78 Blackfriars Rd., SE1 8HF) : LRD Publications, 1981. — 24p ; 21cm
Cover title
ISBN 0-900508-43-4 (pbk) : £0.60
Primary classification 331.25'7'0941 B81-34797

331.25'7'0941 — Great Britain. Reduced working hours

White, Michael, *1938-*. Shorter working time / Michael White. — London : Policy Studies Institute, c1980. — v,90p ; 21cm
ISBN 0-85374-184-0 (pbk) : £3.95 B81-05023

331.25'7'0941 — Great Britain. Working hours *compared with* **working hours in European Community countries**

Long suffering British workers : working time in Europe. — London (78 Blackfriars Rd., SE1 8HF) : LRD Publications, 1981. — 24p ; 21cm
Cover title
ISBN 0-900508-43-4 (pbk) : £0.60
Also classified at 331.25'7'094 B81-34797

331.25'7'0941 — Great Britain. Working hours — *For management*

Working time-guidelines for managers : an approach to the planning of changes in hours, holidays and working time generally / [Confederation of British Industry]. — London : CBI Publications, 1981. — 16p ; 20x22cm
£2.00 (pbk) B81-26439

331.25'72 — Flexible working hours

Ronen, Simcha. Flexible working hours : an innovation in the quality of work life / by Simcha Ronen. — New York ; London : McGraw-Hill, c1981. — xiv,353p : ill,forms ; 24cm
Bibliography: p333-335. — Includes index
ISBN 0-07-053607-4 : £13.95 B81-27187

331.25'72 — Great Britain. Overtime

Carby, Keith. The overtime dilemma / Keith Carby, Fiona Edwards-Stuart. — London : Institute of Personnel Management, 1981. — viii,107p ; 30cm. — (IPM information report ; 31)
Bibliography: p107
ISBN 0-85292-280-9 (pbk) : Unpriced
B81-24196

331.25'76 — Scotland. Shops. Closing days — *Calendars — Serials*

Scottish trades and shop holidays. — 1981. — Coupar Angus : Culross, [1981]. — 62p
ISBN 0-900323-46-9 : £0.70 B81-13193

331.25'763 — England. Personnel. Adult education. Provision of paid leave, *1976-1977*

Killeen, John, *1947-*. Education and work : a study of paid educational leave in England and Wales (1976/77) / by John Killeen and Margaret Bird. — Leicester : National Institute of Adult Education, 1981. — 147p : ill ; 21cm
Bibliography: p146-147
ISBN 0-900559-43-8 (pbk) : Unpriced
B81-11801

331.25'92 — Great Britain. Air services, travel agencies & tour operators. Industrial training. Organisations: Air Transport and Travel Industry Training Board — *Serials*

Air Transport and Travel Industry Training Board. Report and statement of accounts for the year ended 31st March ... / Air Transport and Travel Industry Training Board. — 1980. — Staines : The Board, [1980]. — 62p
Unpriced B81-03299

331.25'92 — Great Britain. Carpet industries. Industrial training. Organisations: Carpet Industry Training Board — *Serials*

Carpet Industry Training Board. Report and statement of accounts, year ended 31st March ... / Carpet Industry Training Board. — 1981. — [Wilmslow] ([32 Alderley Rd, Wilmslow, Cheshire SK9 1NX]) : [The Board], 1981. — [32]p
ISSN 0308-7204 : Unpriced B81-35805

331.25'92 — Great Britain. Clothing industries. Industrial training. Organisations: Clothing and Allied Products Industry Training Board — *Serials*

Clothing and Allied Products Industry Training Board. Report and statement of accounts for the year ended 31 March ... / Clothing and Allied Products Industry Training Board. — 1980. — Leeds (Tower House, Merrion Way, Leeds LS2 8NY) : The Board, 1980. — 40p
ISSN 0142-0259 : Unpriced B81-04756

331.25'92 — Great Britain. Construction industries. Industrial training. Organisations: Construction Industry Training Board — *Serials*

2 Construction Industry Training Board. Annual report / Construction Industry Training Board. — 1979/80. — [London] ([1272 London Rd, SW16 4EL]) : The Board, [1980]. — 36p
Unpriced B81-23496

Construction Industry Training Board. Annual report / Construction Industry Training Board. — 1975/76. — [London] ([1272 Radnor Rd, SW16 4EL]) : The Board, [1976]. — 48p
Unpriced B81-33299

Construction Industry Training Board. Annual report / Construction Industry Training Board. — 1976/77. — [London] ([1272 Radnor Rd, SW16 4EL]) : The Board, [1977]. — 36p
Unpriced B81-33300

Construction Industry Training Board. Annual report / Construction Industry Training Board. — 1977/78. — [London] ([1272 Radnor Rd, SW16 4EL]) : The Board, [1978]. — 36p
Unpriced B81-33298

Construction Industry Training Board. Annual report / Construction Industry Training Board. — 1978/79. — [London] ([1272 Radnor Rd, SW16 4EL]) : The Board, [1979]. — 36p
Unpriced B81-33301

331.25'92 — Great Britain. Distributive trades. Industrial training. Organisations: Distributive Industry Training Board — *Serials*

Distributive Industry Training Board. Report and statement of accounts for the year ended 31st March ... / Distributive Industry Training Board. — 1980. — Manchester (Maclaren House, Talbot Rd, Manchester M32 0FP) : The Board, 1980. — 82p
Unpriced B81-21354

331.25'92 — Great Britain. Engineering industries. Industrial training. Organisations: Engineering Industry Training Board — *Serials*

Engineering Industry Training Board. Annual report and accounts / Engineering Industry Training Board. — 1980/81. — Watford : The Board, c1981. — 110p
ISSN 0309-2879 : Unpriced B81-36534

331.25'92 — Great Britain. Flax, jute & wool industries. Industrial training. Organisations: Wool, Jute and Flax Industry Training Board — *Serials*

Wool, Jute and Flax Industry Training Board. Report and statement of accounts for the year ended 31st Marc ... / Wool, Jute and Flax Industry Training Board. — 1980. — Shipley (Butterfield House, Otley Rd., Baildon, Shipley, W.Yorks BD17 7HE) : The Board, [1980]-. — 42p
ISSN 0306-901x : Unpriced B81-05589

331.25'92 — Great Britain. Food, drinks & tobacco industries. Industrial training. Organisations: Food, Drink and Tobacco Industry Training Board — *Serials*

Food, Drink and Tobacco Industry Training Board. Report : annual report and accounts for the year ending 31 March ... / Food, Drink and Tobacco Industry Training Board. — 79/80. — Gloucester (Barton House, Barton St., Gloucester GL1 1QQ) : The Board, 1980. — 36p
Also entitled: Annual report and accounts for the year ended 31 March ...
£2.00 B81-04874

331.25'92 — Great Britain. Footwear, leather working & fur skin working industries. Industrial training. Organisations: Footwear, Leather and Fur Skin Industry Training Board — *Serials*

Footwear, Leather and Fur Skin Industry Training Board. Annual report : report and statement of accounts for the year ended 31st March ... / [Footwear, Leather and Fur Skin Industry Training Board]. — 1979/80-. — Sutton Coldfield (29 Birmingham Rd, Sutton Coldfield, West Midlands B72 1QE) : The Board, 1980-. — v. : ill,ports ; 20cm
Continues: Footwear, Leather and Fur Skin Industry Training Board. Report and statement of accounts for the year ended 31 March ...
ISSN 0260-5406 = Annual report - FLFSITB : Unpriced B81-04440

331.25'92 — Great Britain. Foundry industries. Industrial training. Organisations: Foundry Industry Training Committee — *Serials*

Foundry Industry Training Committee. Annual report / Foundry Industry Training Committee. — Apr.1979 to Mar.1980. — [London] ([50, Charlotte St., W1P 2EL]) : The Committee, [1980]. — 48p
ISSN 0140-3400 : Unpriced B81-05222

Foundry Industry Training Committee. Annual report / Foundry Industry Training Committee. — 1980/81. — London (50 Charlotte St., W1P 2EL) : The Committee, [1981]. — 12p
ISSN 0140-3400 : Unpriced B81-36009

331.25'92 — Great Britain. Furniture industries & timber industries. Industrial training. Grants from Furniture and Timber Training Board — *Serials*

Furniture and Timber Training Board. Guide to grants and levy abatement, 1 April ... 31 March ... / Furniture and Timber Training Board. — 1979-1980. — High Wycombe (31 Octagon Parade, High Wycombe, Bucks) : The Board, [1979?]. — 21p
Unpriced B81-20070

331.25'92 — Great Britain. Furniture industries & timber industries. Industrial training. Organisations: Furniture and Timber Industry Training Board — *Serials*

Furniture and Timber Industry Training Board. Report and statement of accounts for the year ended 31 March ... / Furniture and Timber Training Board. — 1980. — High Wycombe (31 Octagon Parade, High Wycombe, Bucks HP11 2JA) : The Board, [1980]. — 33p
Unpriced B81-20033

Furniture and Timber Training Board. Report and statement of accounts for the year ended 31st March ... / Furniture and Timber Training Board. — 1979. — High Wycombe (31, Octagon Parade, High Wycombe, Bucks HP11 2JA) : The Board, [1979?]. — 31p
Unpriced B81-20038

Furniture and Timber Training Board. Report and statement of accounts for the year ended 31st March ... / Furniture and Timber Training Board. — 1975. — High Wycombe (31, Octagon Parade, High Wycombe, Bucks HP11 2JA) : The Board, [1975?]. — 45p
Unpriced B81-20039

Furniture and Timber Training Board. Report and statement of accounts for the year ended 31st March ... / Furniture and Timber Training Board. — 1974. — High Wycombe (31, Octagon Parade, High Wycombe, Bucks HP11 2JA) : The Board, [1974?]. — 42p
Unpriced B81-20040

Furniture and Timber Training Board. Report and statement of accounts for the year ended 31st March ... / Furniture and Timber Training Board. — 1977. — High Wycombe (31, Octagon Parade, High Wycombe, Bucks HP11 2JA) : The Board, [1977?]. — 49p
Unpriced B81-20041

Furniture and Timber Training Board. Report and statement of accounts for the year ended 31st March ... / Furniture and Timber Training Board. — 1976. — High Wycombe (31, Octagon Parade, High Wycombe, Bucks HP11 2JA) : The Board, [1976?]. — 45p
Unpriced B81-20042

331.25'92 — Great Britain. Knitting, lace & net industries. Industrial training — *Serials*

Knitting, Lace and Net Industry Training Board. Report & statement of accounts for year ended 31 March ... / Knitting, Lace and Net Industry Training Board. — 1980. — Nottingham (4 Hamilton Rd, Nottingham NG5 1AU) : The Board, 1980. — 24p
ISSN 0307-7837 : Unpriced B81-20299

331.25'92 — Great Britain. Paper manufacturing industries & paper products industries. Industrial training — *Serials*

Paper and Paper Products Industry Training Board. Training for ... / Paper and Paper Products Industry Training Board. — 1981. — Potters Bar (Star House, Potters Bar, Herts EN6 2PG) : The Board, 1981. — 19p
Unpriced B81-24128

331.25'92 — Great Britain. Petroleum industries. Industrial training. Organisations: Petroleum Industry Training Board — *Serials*

Petroleum Industry Training Board. Annual report / Petroleum Industry Training Board. — 1979-1980. — Aylesbury (Kingfisher House, Walton St., Aylesbury, Buckinghamshire) : The Board, c1980. — iv,58p
£1.50 B81-03843

331.25'92 — Great Britain. Plastics & rubber industries. Industrial training. Organisations: Rubber and Plastics Processing Industry Training Board — *Serials*

Rubber and Plastics Processing Industry Training Board. Report and statement of accounts for the year ended 31 March ... / Rubber and Plastics Processing Industry Training Board. — 1978. — Brentford (Brent Houe, 950 Great West Rd., Brentford, Middlesex) : The Board, [1978?]. — 44p
Unpriced B81-06680

Rubber and Plastics Processing Industry Training Board. Report and statement of accounts for the year ended 31 March ... / Rubber and Plastics Processing Industry Training Board. — 1979. — Brentford (Brent House, 950 Great West Rd., Brentford, Middlesex) : The Board, [1979?]. — 48p
Unpriced B81-06681

Rubber and Plastics Processing Industry Training Board. Report and statement of accounts for the year ended 31 March ... / Rubber and Plastics Processing Industry Training Board. — 1980. — Brentford : The Board, [1980]. — 35p
Unpriced B81-12443

331.25'92 — Great Britain. Road transport services. Industrial training. Organisations: Road Transport Industry Training Board — *Serials*

Road Transport Industry Training Board. Report and statement of accounts for the year ended 31 March ... / Road Transport Industry Training Board. — 1977. — [Wembley] ([Capitol House, Empire Way, Wembley, Middlesex HA9 0NG]) : The Board, [1977]. — 127p
ISSN 0308-8707 : Unpriced B81-29449

Road Transport Industry Training Board. Report and statement of accounts for the year ended 31 March ... / Road Transport Industry Training Board. — 1978. — [Wembley] ([Capitol House, Empire Way, Wembley, Middlesex HA9 0NG]) : The Board, [1978]. — 147p
ISSN 0308-8707 : Unpriced B81-24689

Road Transport Industry Training Board. Report and statement of accounts for the year ended 31 March ... / Road Transport Industry Training Board. — 1979. — [Wembley] ([Capitol House, Empire Way, Wembley, Middlesex HA9 0NG]) : The Board, [1979]. — 188p
ISSN 0308-8707 : Unpriced B81-24690

Road Transport Industry Training Board. Report and statement of accounts for the year ended 31 March ... / Road Transport Industry Training Board. — 1980. — [Wembley] ([Capitol House, Empire Way, Wembley, Middlesex HA9 0NG]) : The Board, [1980]. — 159p
ISSN 0308-8707 : Unpriced B81-24691

331.25'92 — Great Britain. Shipbuilding industries. Industrial training. Levies. Exemption & rebates — *Serials*

Shipbuilding Industry Training Board. Levy exemption scheme and levy credits scheme / Shipbuilding Industry Training Board. — 17th levy period (1981/82). — South Harrow (Raebarn House, Northolt Rd, South Harrow, Middlesex) : The Board, [1981]. — 32p
Unpriced B81-26388

331.25'92 — Great Britain. Synthetic fibre industries. Industrial training. Organisations: Man-made Fibres Producing Industry Training Board — *Serials*

Man-made Fibres Producing Industry Training Board. Report and statement of accounts for the year ended 31 March ... / Man-Made Fibres Producing Industry Training Board. — 1980. — Rickmansworth (Langwood House, 63 High St., Rickmansworth, Herts. WD3 1EQ) : [The Board], [1980]. — 32p
Unpriced B81-10412

331.25'92 — North Humberside. Agricultural industries. Industrial training

Stevenson, Ann. Agricultural education and training in North Humberside : a survey of experience and attitudes / Ann Stevenson and David Symes. — [Hull] : Department of Geography, University of Hull, 1979. — iii,144p : ill,maps ; 30cm. — (Miscellaneous series / Department of Geography, University of Hull ; no.23)
ISBN 0-85958-108-x (spiral) : Unpriced
Primary classification 630'.7'114283 B81-02311

331.25'92 — Northern Ireland. Catering industries. Industrial training. Organisations: Northern Ireland Catering Industry Training Board — *Serials*

Northern Ireland Catering Industry Training Board. Report and statement of accounts for the period 1 April ... to 31 March ... / Northern Ireland Catering Industry Training Board. — 1979-1980. — Belfast : H.M.S.O., 1981. — 18p
ISBN 0-337-09135-8 : £2.20 B81-31572

331.25'92 — Northern Ireland. Clothing industries. Industrial training. Organisations: Northern Ireland Clothing and Footwear Industry Training Board — *Serials*

Northern Ireland Clothing and Footwear Industry Training Board. Report and statement of accounts for the period 1 April ... to 31 March ... / Northern Ireland Clothing and Footwear Industry Training Board. — 1979-1980. — Belfast, H.M.S.O., 1981. — 22p
ISBN 0-337-09127-7 : £2.30 B81-27326

331.25'92 — Northern Ireland. Construction industries. Industrial training. Organisations: Northern Ireland Construction Industry Training Board — *Serials*

Northern Ireland Construction Industry Training Board. Report and statement of accounts for the period 1 April ... to 31 March ... / Northern Ireland Construction Industry Training Board. — 1978/1979. — Belfast : H.M.S.O., 1980. — 30p
ISBN 0-337-09109-9 : £2.50 B81-04410

Northern Ireland Construction Industry Training Board. Report and statement of accounts for the period 1 April ... to 31 March ... / Northern Ireland Construction Industry Training Board. — 1979-1980. — Belfast : H.M.S.O., 1981. — 25p
ISBN 0-337-09139-0 : £2.50 B81-31571

331.25'92 — Northern Ireland. Distributive trades. Industrial training. Organisations: Northern Ireland Distributive Industry Training Board — *Serials*

Northern Ireland Distributive Industry Training Board. Report and statement of accounts for the period 1 April ... to 31 March ... / Northern Ireland Distributive Industry Training Board. — 1979-1980. — Belfast : H.M.S.O., 1981. — 19p
ISBN 0-337-09131-5 : £2.10 B81-31578

331.25'92 — Northern Ireland. Engineering industries. Industrial training. Organisations: Northern Ireland Engineering Industry Training Board — *Serials*

Northern Ireland Engineering Industry Training Board. Report and statement of accounts for the period 1 April ... to 31 March ... / Northern Ireland Engineering Industry Training Board. — 1979-1980. — Belfast : H.M.S.O., 1981. — 24p
ISBN 0-337-09132-3 : £2.50 B81-31577

331.25'92 — Northern Ireland. Food & drinks industries. Industrial training. Organisations: Northern Ireland Food and Drink Industry Training Board — *Serials*

Northern Ireland Food and Drink Industry Training Board. Report and statement of accounts for the period 1 April ... to 31 March ... / Northern Ireland Food and Drink Industry Training Board. — 1979-1980. — Belfast : H.M.S.O., 1981. — 26p
ISBN 0-337-09133-1 : £2.50 B81-31573

331.25'92 — Northern Ireland. Road transport services. Industrial training. Organisations: Northern Ireland Road Transport Industry Training Board — *Serials*

Northern Ireland Road Transport Industry Training Board. Report and statement of accounts for the period 1 April ... to 31 March ... / Northern Ireland Road Transport Industry Training Board. — 1979-1980. — Belfast : H.M.S.O., 1981. — 24p
ISBN 0-337-09138-2 : £2.50 B81-31574

331.25'92 — Northern Ireland. Synthetic fibre industries. Industrial training. Organisations: Northern Ireland Man-made Fibres Producing Industry Training Board — *Serials*

Northern Ireland Man-made Fibres Producing Industry Training Board. Report and statement of accounts for the period 1 April ... to 31 March ... / Northern Ireland Man-made Fibres Producing Industry Training Board. — 1979-1980. — Belfast : H.M.S.O., 1981. — 14p
ISBN 0-337-09134-x : £1.90 B81-31576

331.25'92 — Northern Ireland. Textile industries. Industrial training. Organisations: Northern Ireland Textiles Industry Training Board — *Serials*

Northern Ireland Textiles Industry Training Board. Report and statement of accounts for the period 1 April ... to 31 March ... / Northern Ireland Textiles Industry Training Board. — 1979-1980. — Belfast : H.M.S.O., 1981. — 24p
ISBN 0-337-09136-6 : £2.50 B81-31575

331.25'92'06041 — Great Britain. Industrial training boards. Abolition — *Proposals*

Elliot, Clive. Industrial training boards : why they should be dismantled / by Clive Elliot and Stanley Mendham. — London (8 Wilfred St., SW2E 6PL) : Centre for Policy Studies, 1981. — 27leaves ; 31cm
ISBN 0-905880-35-8 (spiral) : £3.00
B81-17646

331.25'92'0941 — Great Britain. Personnel. Training — *Proposals*

Colvin, Michael. An Open Tech : a proposal for tackling Britain's skill shortages / Michael Colvin. — London : Bow, [1980]. — [8]p : 1ill ; 30cm. — (A Bow paper)
£2.50 (unbound) B81-06096

331.25'92'09416 — Northern Ireland. Industrial training. Organisations: Northern Ireland Training Executive — *Serials*

Northern Ireland Training ExecutiveReport and statement of accounts / Northern Ireland Training Executive. — 1978-1979. — Belfast : H.M.S.O., 1980. — 30p
£2.50 B81-20334

Northern Ireland Training Executive. Report and statement of accounts for the period 1 April ... to 31 March ... / Northern Ireland Training Executive. — 1979-1980. — Belfast : H.M.S.O., 1981. — 30p
ISBN 0-337-09130-7 : £2.60 B81-27328

331.25'92'0973 — United States. Personnel. In-service training — *Conference proceedings*

Workplace perspectives on education and training / edited by Peter B. Doeringer. — Boston ; London : Nijhoff, c1981. — vii,172p ; 24cm. — (Boston studies in applied economics. Series on labor and employment ; v.1)
Conference papers
ISBN 0-89838-054-5 : Unpriced B81-22128

331.2'81347970714 — Washington (State). Judges. Remuneration. Proposed increases. Protest by taxpayers, *1973*

Sheldon, Charles H.. Politicians, judges, and the people : a study in citizens' participation / Charles H. Sheldo and Frank P. Weaver. — Westport, Conn. ; London : Greenwood Press, 1980. — xii,206p ; 22cm. — (Contributions in political science, ISSN 0147-1066 ; no.36)
Bibliography: p191-200. - Includes index
ISBN 0-313-21492-1 : Unpriced
Also classified at 328.797'0733 B81-05997

331.2'813516'096 — Africa. Civil service. Professional personnel & executives. Remuneration. Effects of remuneration of British professional personnel & executives

Bennell, Paul. African pay structures in a transnational context : the British connection / Paul Bennell and Martin Godfrey. — Brighton : Institute of Development Studies, 1980. — xvi,309columns : ill ; 21x31cm. — (IDS research reports, ISSN 0141-1314)
ISBN 0-903354-70-5 (spiral) : Unpriced
B81-24387

331.2'81355'00941 — British military forces. Personnel. Remuneration — *Proposals* — *Serials*

Review Body on Armed Forces Pay. Report / Review Body on Armed Forces Pay. — 10th (1981). — London : H.M.S.O., 1981. — v,105p. — (Cmnd. ; 8241)
ISBN 0-10-182410-6 : £5.80 B81-30833

331.2'81355345 — British military forces. Dentists. Remuneration — *Proposals*

Review Body on Armed Forces Pay. Service medical and dental officers : supplement to the tenth report, 1981 / Review Body on Armed Forces. — London : H.M.S.O., [1981]. — iii,28p ; 25cm. — (Cmnd. ; 8322)
ISBN 0-10-183220-6 (unbound) : £2.70
Also classified at 331.2'81355345 B81-40610

331.2'81355345 — British military forces. Doctors. Remuneration — *Proposals*

Review Body on Armed Forces Pay. Service medical and dental officers : supplement to the tenth report, 1981 / Review Body on Armed Forces. — London : H.M.S.O., [1981]. — iii,28p ; 25cm. — (Cmnd. ; 8322)
ISBN 0-10-183220-6 (unbound) : £2.70
Primary classification 331.2'81355345
B81-40610

331.2'81362712 — Great Britain. Childminders. Low pay

Coulter, Angela, *1948-*. Who minds about the minders? / Angela Coulter. — London (3 Poland St, WIV 3DG) : Low Pay Unit, 1981. — 43p ; 22cm. — (Pamphlet / Low Pay Unit, ISSN 0307-8116 ; no.17)
£1.00 (pbk) B81-34551

331.2'813711'009411 — Scotland. Teachers. Remuneration — *Proposals* — *Serials*

Scottish teachers salaries memorandum / Scottish Education Department. — 1980. — Edinburgh : H.M.S.O., 1980. — 67p
ISBN 0-11-491699-3 : £3.90
ISSN 0308-406x B81-10576

331.2'81374 — England. Further education institutions. Teachers. Remuneration. Burnham Scale — *Proposals* — *Serials*

Scales of salaries for teachers in establishments for further education, England and Wales ... / Department of Education and Science. — 1979. — London : H.M.S.O., 1980. — v,48p
ISBN 0-11-270465-4 : £2.75
ISSN 0260-1494 B81-00033

331.2′81379153′0941 — Great Britain. Local education authorities. Personnel: Advisers, inspectors & organisers. Remuneration — *Serials*

Committee on Salary Scales and Service Conditions of Inspectors, Organisers and Advisory Officers of Local Education Authorities. The Report of the Committee on Salary Scales and Service Conditions of Inspectors, Organisers and Advisory Officers of Local Education Authorities. — [16th (1980)]. — London (c/o Authorities Panel Secretary, 41 Belgrave) : [The Committee], 1980. — 27p
Unpriced B81-12418

331.2′8161′0941 — Great Britain. Doctors. Remunderation — *Proposals* — *Serials*

Review Body on Doctors′ and Dentists′ Remuneration. Report / Review Body on Doctors′ and Dentists′ Remuneration. — 11th (1981). — London : H.M.S.O., 1981. — v,89p. — (Cmnd. ; 8239)
ISBN 0-10-182390-8 : £4.60
Also classified at 331.2′816176′00941
B81-30837

331.2′816176′00941 — Great Britain. Dentists. Remuneration — *Proposals* — *Serials*

Review Body on Doctors′ and Dentists′ Remuneration. Report / Review Body on Doctors′ and Dentists′ Remuneration. — 11th (1981). — London : H.M.S.O., 1981. — v,89p. — (Cmnd. ; 8239)
ISBN 0-10-182390-8 : £4.60
Primary classification 331.2′8161′0941
B81-30837

331.2′8165842′0941 — Great Britain. Companies. Directors & chief executives. Remuneration — *Serials*

Vernon-Harcourt, Tony. Rewarding top management : a practical guide to remuneration, benefits and conditions for directors and senior executives / Tony Vernon-Harcourt. — Vol.1 (1980)-. — Farnborough : Gower, c1980. — v. ; 22cm
Two issues yearly
ISSN 0144-4956 = Rewarding top management : £10.00 per issue B81-04770

331.2′81658422′0941 — Great Britain. Companies. Directors & chief executives. Remuneration — *Serials*

The **Charterhouse** Group guide to directors′ remuneration. — Mar.1981-. — Saffron Walden (Debden Green, Saffron Walden, Essex CB11 3LX) : Monks Publications for the Charterhouse Group, 1981-. — v. ; 30cm
Two issues yearly. — Cover title: Charterhouse guide to director′s remuneration
ISSN 0261-2585 = Charterhouse Group guide to directors′ remuneration : £28.00 B81-24684

Rewarding management. — 1982. — Aldershot : Gower, Oct.1981. — [100]p
ISBN 0-566-02327-x : £15.00 : CIP entry
B81-31104

331.2′816671′0941 — Great Britain. Dry cleaning & laundry services. Low-income personnel

Crine, Simon. Dirty linen : low pay in laundries, dry cleaners and launderettes / Simon Crine. — London (9 Poland St., W2V 3DG) : Low Pay Unit, 1981. — 15p ; 21cm. — (Low pay report ; 7)
£0.75 (unbound) B81-25580

331.2′817452′0941 — Great Britain. Industrial design firms. Personnel. Remuneration — *Serials*

SIAD ... salary survey / Society of Industrial Artists and Designers. — 1979. — London (12 Carlton House Terrace, SW1Y 5AH) : The Society, 1979. — 28p
Unpriced B81-09191

331.2′817452′0941 — Great Britain. Industrial design services. Personnel. Remuneration

SIAD survey of salaried designers pay and conditions 1980. — [London] (12 Carlton House Terrace, SW1Y 5AH) : Society of Industrial Artists and Designers, c1981. — vi,139p : ill ; 30cm
Unpriced (pbk) B81-24291

Supplementary report to the Siad 1980 survey on salaried designers pay and conditions. — [London] ([12 Carlton House Terrace, SW1Y 5AH]) : Society of Industrial Artists and Designers, [1981?]. — 18p ; 30cm
Unpriced (pbk) B81-24292

331.2′941 — Great Britain. Economic conditions. Effects of increases in remuneration of personnel, *1981-1982*

Pay 1981/82 / CBI. — [London] : Confederation of British Industry, 1981. — 51p : ill ; 30cm
£2.00 (unbound) B81-34802

331.2′941 — Great Britain. Personnel. Low pay

Duncan, Colin. Low pay — its causes, and the post-war trade union response. — Chichester : Wiley, Nov.1981. — [176]p. — (Social policy research monographs ; 3)
ISBN 0-471-10052-8 : £17.50 : CIP entry
B81-30555

Routh, Guy. The roots of pay inequalities / Guy Routh, Dorothy Wedderburn, Barbara Wootton. — London (9 Poland St., W1W 3DG) : Low Pay Unit, [1980]. — 27p ; 21cm. — (Discussion series / Low Pay Unit ; no.1)
Unpriced (pbk) B81-13246

331.2′941 — Great Britain. Personnel. Remuneration

Cappelli, Peter. What people earn : the book of wages and salaries 1981 / Peter Cappelli. — London : MacDonald, 1981. — 238p ; 23cm
Includes index
ISBN 0-354-04710-8 (cased) : £7.95
ISBN 0-7088-2121-9 (pbk) : Unpriced
B81-38464

Greenhill, Richard. Employee remuneration and profit sharing / Richard Greeenhill. — Cambridge : Woodhead-Faulkner, 1980. — 210p : ill ; 24cm
Bibliography: p203-205. — Includes index
ISBN 0-85941-123-0 : £15.00 B81-38081

331.2′941 — Great Britain. Personnel. Remuneration. National agreements

Elliott, Robert F.. Are national agreements dead? and if so what are the implications for wage inflation? / R.F. Elliott. — [Old Aberdeen] ([Edward Wright Building, Dunbar St., Old Aberdeen AB9 2TY]) : [Department of Political Economy, University of Aberdeen], [1980?]. — 27leaves ; 30cm. — (Discussion paper / University of Aberdeen. Department of Political Economy, ISSN 0143-4543 ; 80-13)
Bibliography : leaves 26-27
Unpriced (pbk) B81-28996

331.2′941 — Great Britain. Personnel. Remuneration. National agreements. Effects

Elliott, Robert F.. Some further observations on the importance of national wage agreements / R.F. Elliott. — Old Aberdeen (Edward Wright Building, Dunbar St., Old Aberdeen AB9 2TY) : University of Aberdeen, Department of Political Economy, [1981]. — 10leaves ; 31cm. — (Discussion paper / University of Aberdeen Department of Political Economy ; no.81-01)
Bibliography: leaf 10
Unpriced (pbk) B81-09960

331.2′941 — Great Britain. Personnel. Remuneration *related to* **occupations,** *1906-1979*

Routh, Guy. Occupation and pay in Great Britain 1906-79 / Guy Routh. — 2nd ed. — London : Macmillan, 1980. — xvii,269p : ill ; 23cm
Previous ed. published as: Occupation and pay in Great Britain 1906-60. London : Cambridge University Press, 1965. — Includes index
ISBN 0-333-28417-8 : £15.00 : CIP rev.
ISBN 0-333-28653-7 (pbk) : £7.95 B80-03523

331.2′941′019 — Great Britain. Personnel. Remuneration. Psychological aspects

White, Michael, *1938-*. The hidden meaning of pay conflict / Michael White. — London : Macmillan, 1981. — vii,151p ; 23cm
Includes index
ISBN 0-333-26833-4 : £20.00 B81-40578

331.2′941′0212 — Great Britain. Personnel. Remuneration — *Statistics* — *Serials*

New earnings survey .... Part D, Analyses by occupation / Department of Employment. — 1980. — London : H.M.S.O., 1981. — 56p
ISBN 0-11-725502-5 : £7.90 B81-12403

New earnings survey .... Part A, Report: general and selected key results / Department of Employment. — 1980. — London : H.M.S.O., 1980-. — 72p
ISBN 0-11-725500-9 : £7.90 B81-06214

New earnings survey .... Part B, Analyses by agreement / Department of Employment. — 1980. — 52p. — £7.90
ISBN 0-11-725499-1 : 2351692 B81-06215

331.2′941′05 — Great Britain. Personnel. Low pay — *Serials*

Low pay review. — 1 (June 1980)-. — London (9 Poland St., W1V 3DG) : Low Pay Unit, 1980-. — v. ; 21cm
Six issues yearly. — Continues: Low pay bulletin
ISSN 0144-9834 = Low pay review : £0.50 per issue B81-08570

331.2′973 — United States. Personnel. Remuneration

Harrop, David. America′s paychecks : who makes what / by David Harrop. — New York : Facts on File ; Oxford : Distributed by Clio, c1980. — vi,254p ; 25cm
Includes index
ISBN 0-87196-311-6 : £9.10 B81-01966

331.3 — WORKERS. SPECIAL AGE GROUPS

331.3′1′0941 — Great Britain. Children. Employment

MacLennan, Emma. Working children / [Emma MacLennan]. — London (9 Poland St., W1V 3DG) : Low Pay Unit, 1980. — 30p ; 21cm. — (Pamphlet / Low Pay Unit ; no.15)
£1.00 (pbk) B81-06449

331.3′1′0941 — Great Britain. Children. Employment, *to 1980* — *For schools*

Tann, Jennifer. Children at work / Jennifer Tann. — London : Batsford Academic and Educational, 1981. — 72p : ill,1facsim ; 26cm. — (History in focus)
Bibliography: p70. — Includes index
ISBN 0-7134-3553-4 : £5.50 B81-27212

331.3′1′0941 — Great Britain. Industries. Personnel: Children. Working conditions, *1760-1881* — *For schools*

Cameron, A. D. (Alexander Durand). Young workers in the Industrial Revolution / A.D. Cameron. — Edinburgh : Oliver & Boyd, 1981. — 40p : ill,1map,facsims,ports ; 19x25cm. — (Exploring history)
Bibliography: p39. — Includes index
ISBN 0-05-003255-0 (pbk) : £1.40 B81-34933

331.3′1′0941 — Great Britain. Industries. Personnel: Children. Working conditions, *1830-1885* — *For schools*

Longmate, Elizabeth. Children at work 1830-1885 / Elizabeth Longmate ; illustrated from contemporary sources. — Harlow : Longman, 1981. — 96p : ill,2maps,facsims,ports ; 20cm. — (Then and there series)
Bibliography: p90. — Includes index
ISBN 0-582-22294-x (pbk) : £0.75 B81-16205

331.3′1′0945 — Italy. Children. Employment

Valcarenghi, Marina. Child labour in Italy : a general review / Marina Valcarenghi. — London (180 Brixton Rd., SW9 6AT) : Anti-Slavery Society, c1981. — 93p : ill ; 21cm. — (Child labour series ; report no.5)
English text, Italian and French appendices
ISBN 0-900918-12-8 (pbk) : £1.00 B81-31675

331.3′1′09593 — Thailand. Children. Employment

Banerjee, Sumanta. Child labour in Thailand : a general review / Sumanta Banerjee. — London (180 Brixton Rd., SW9 6AT) : Anti-Slavery Society, 1980. — 61p : ill ; 21cm. — (Child labour series ; report no.4)
ISBN 0-900918-13-6 (pbk) : £1.00 B81-13336

331.3′4′0941 — Great Britain. Young persons. Employment

O′Brien, *Sir* **Richard**. Young people, fitness and work : the seventeenth Basil Henriques memorial lecture delivered at the South Glamorgan Institute of Higher Education Cyncoed, Cardiff during the National Association of Boys′ Clubs Annual Conference, 6th July 1980 / Sir Richard O′Brien. — [London] (24 Highbury Grove, N5 2EA) : National Association of Boys′ Clubs, [1980]. — 12p : 1port ; 21cm. — (The ... Basil Henriques memorial lecture ; 1980) (The 1980 Basil Henriques memorial lecture)
£0.25 (pbk) B81-18940

331.3′4′0941 — Great Britain. Young persons. Employment. Effects of social policies of government — *Marxist viewpoints*

Blind alley : youth in a crisis of capital / edited by Mike Cole and Bob Skelton. — Ormskirk : Hesketh, 1980. — vii,97p ; 21cm
ISBN 0-905777-12-3 (pbk) : £3.80
Primary classification 379.41 B81-09805

331.3′4′09411 — Scotland. School leavers. First employment

Pollock, G. J.. Just the job : the employment and training of young school leavers : a summary report / G.J. Pollock and V.M. Nicholson. — [London] : Hodder and Stoughton for the Scottish Council for Research in Education, c1981. — v,54p ; 23cm. — (SCRE publication ; 74)
ISBN 0-340-26713-5 (cased) : Unpriced B81-32302

331.3′4′096813 — Swaziland. School leavers. First employment. Projects: School Leaver Tracer Project

Sullivan, Gerard. From school — to work : report on the School Leaver Tracer Project / Gerard Sullivan. — Oxford : Cotswold, c1981. — xvi,190p : 1map,forms ; 27cm
At head of title: Swaziland Government, Ministry of Education, Mbabane, March 1981
Unpriced (pbk) B81-33551

331.3′4′0973 — United States. Young persons. Employment

Osterman, Paul. Getting started : the youth labor market / Paul Osterman. — Cambridge, Mass. ; London : MIT, c1980. — 197p : ill,forms ; 24cm
Includes index
ISBN 0-262-15021-2 : £15.50 B81-09647

331.3′412042 — Great Britain. Unemployed young persons. Employment. Programmes: Youth Opportunities Programme, *to 1981*

Short, Clare. The Youth Opportunities Programme — short term palliative or long term gain? / by Clare Short ; summer meeting Thursday and Friday, 11 and 12 June 1981, Scarborough. — Sheffield : The Association of Colleges for Further and Higher Education, [1981]. — 7p ; 21cm
£0.75 (unbound) B81-31208

331.3′412042 — Northern Ireland. Unemployed young persons. Employment. Programmes: Employer Based Work Experience Programme

Harvey, Stephen. An evaluation of the Employer Based Work Experience Programme : report to the Department of Manpower Services of Northern Ireland / Stephen Harvey and Desmond Rea. — Newtownabbey (Shore Rd., Newtownabbey, Co. Antrim BT37 0QB) : Polytechnic Innovation and Resource Centre, Ulster Polytechnic, 1979. — iii,163,xxxixp : 2ill,2maps ; 30cm
Cover title. — At head of title: Youth Opportunities Programme
ISBN 0-9506475-1-9 (spiral) : Unpriced B81-12530

331.3′41377′0941 — Great Britain. Young persons. Unemployment. Alleviation. Use of local radio services

Local broad-casting for the young unemployed. — Leicester (17 Albion St., Leicester LE1 6GD) : National Youth Bureau, 1980. — 24p : 1map ; 30cm
Bibliography: p24
ISBN 0-86155-023-4 (pbk) : £0.95 B81-06554

331.3′4137941 — Great Britain. Young persons. Unemployment. Socioeconomic aspects — *Conference proceedings*

Youth unemployment in Great Britain and the Federal Republic of Germany : proceedings of a conference held by the International Institute of Social Economics, the Goethe Institute and the Anglo-German Foundation for the Study of Industrial Society / edited by Barrie O. Pettman and John Fyfe. — Bradford (198 Keighley Rd., Bradford, W. Yorks.) : M.C.B. Publications in association with International Institute of Social Economics, c1977. — ii,136p : ill ; 30cm
ISBN 0-905440-46-3 (pbk) : Unpriced
Also classified at 331.3′4137943 B81-37736

331.3′4137943 — West Germany. Young persons. Unemployment. Socioeconomic aspects — *Conference proceedings*

Youth unemployment in Great Britain and the Federal Republic of Germany : proceedings of a conference held by the International Institute of Social Economics, the Goethe Institute and the Anglo-German Foundation for the Study of Industrial Society / edited by Barrie O. Pettman and John Fyfe. — Bradford (198 Keighley Rd., Bradford, W. Yorks.) : M.C.B. Publications in association with International Institute of Social Economics, c1977. — ii,136p : ill ; 30cm
ISBN 0-905440-46-3 (pbk) : Unpriced
Primary classification 331.3′4137941
B81-37736

331.3′46 — Great Britain. Ethnic minorities. Young persons. Unemployment — *Inquiry reports*

Great Britain. *Commission for Racial Equality*. Ethnic minority youth unemployment : a paper presented to Government July 1980. — London (10 Allington St., SW1E 5EH) : Commission for Racial Equality, 1980. — 9p ; 30cm
Unpriced (pbk) B81-04628

331.3′46′0942527 — Nottinghamshire. Nottingham. Young coloured persons. Employment. Racial discrimination

Great Britain. *Commission for Racial Equality*. Half a chance? : a report on job discrimination against young blacks in Nottingham / Jim Hubbuck and Simon Carter. — London : Commission for Racial Equality in association with Nottingham and District Community Relations Council, 1980. — 50p ; 21cm
ISBN 0-902355-91-0 (pbk) : £1.00 B81-03131

331.3′822334′094246 — North Staffordshire. Coal mines. Personnel: Children. Working conditions, *1841 — Readings from contemporary sources — For schools*

Children in the mines. — [Stafford] ([P.O. Box 11, County Buildings, Martin St., Stafford ST16 2LH]) : Staffordshire County Council, [1981]. — 52p : ill ; 30cm. — (Staffordshire study book, ISSN 0306-5855 ; 10)
Unpriced (pbk) B81-14567

331.3′94 — Great Britain. Job release schemes, *to 1980*

Makeham, Peter. Evaluation of the Job Release Scheme / by Peter Makeham and Phillip Morgan. — [London] : Department of Employment, 1980. — 56p ; 30cm. — (Research paper / Department of Employment ; no.13)
Cover title
Unpriced (pbk) B81-06151

331.3′94 — Persons, 40 years-. Employment

Cooper, Cary L.. After forty. — Chichester : Wiley, Dec.1981. — [208]p
ISBN 0-471-28043-7 : £9.75 : CIP entry
B81-31827

331.3′98′0941 — Great Britain. Persons, 60 years-. Employment

Makeham, Peter. Economic aspects of the employment of older workers / by Peter Makeham. — [London] : Department of Employment, 1980. — 87p : ill ; 30cm. — (Research paper / Department of Employment ; no.14)
Cover title. — Bibliography: p83-87
Unpriced (pbk) B81-06152

331.4 — WOMEN WORKERS

331.4′0941 — England. Women personnel. Social conditions, *1750-1850*

Pinchbeck, Ivy. Women workers and the industrial revolution 1750-1850 / by Ivy Pinchbeck. — [3rd ed.] / with a new introduction by Kerry Hamilton. — London : Virago, 1981. — 342p ; 20cm
Previous ed.: i.e. 1st ed. reprinted London : Cass, 1969. — Bibliography: p322-331. - Includes index
ISBN 0-86068-170-x (pbk) : £3.50 B81-15647

331.4′0941 — Great Britain. Women. Employment, *ca 1740-1980 — For schools*

Harris, Sarah. Women at work / Sarah Harris. — London : Batsford Academic and Educational, 1981. — 72p : ill,facsims,ports ; 26cm. — (History in focus)
Bibliography: p70. — Includes index
ISBN 0-7134-3551-8 : £5.50 B81-27213

331.4′0941 — Great Britain. Women. Employment — *For trade unionism*

Aldred, Chris. Women at work / Chris Aldred. — London : Pan, 1981. — 173 : ill ; 20cm. — (Pan trade union studies)
Includes index
ISBN 0-330-26479-6 (pbk) : £1.75 B81-38229

331.4′0941 — Great Britain. Working class women. Employment, *1914-1918.* **Social aspects**

Braybon, Gail. Women workers in the First World War : the British experience / Gail Braybon. — London : Croom Helm, 1981. — 244p ; 23cm
Bibliography: p233-238. - Includes index
ISBN 0-7099-0603-x : £11.95 B81-07546

331.4′0973 — United States. Women. Employment. Effects of World War 1

Greenwald, Maurine Weiner. Women, war, and work : the impact of World War I on women workers in the United States / Maurine Weiner Greenwald. — Westport, Conn. ; London : Greenwood Press, 1980. — xxvii,309p : ill,ports ; 22cm. — (Contributions in women′s studies, ISSN 0147-104x ; no.12)
Bibliography: p285-300. — Includes index
ISBN 0-313-21355-0 : £17.95 B81-23467

331.4′0973 — United States. Women personnel. Effects of economic conditions, *1890-1940*

Scharf, Lois. To work and to wed : female employment, feminism and the Great Depression / Lois Scharf. — Westport, Conn. ; London : Greenwood Press, 1980. — xiii,240p ; 22cm. — (Contributions in women′s studies, ISSN 0147-104x ; no.15)
Includes index
ISBN 0-313-21445-x : Unpriced B81-05612

331.4′133′0941 — Great Britain. Women. Employment. Equality of opportunity — *Proposals*

Robarts, Sadie. Positive action for women : the next step in education, training and employment / Sadie Robarts with Anna Coote and Elizabeth Ball ; cartoons by Cath Jackson. — London : Rights for Women, National Council for Civil Liberties, 1981. — 107p : ill ; 20cm
Bibliography: p106-108
ISBN 0-901108-93-6 (pbk) : £2.00 B81-33249

331.4′133′0947 — Soviet Union. Women. Employment. Equality of opportunity. Economic aspects

McAuley, Alastair. Women′s work and wages in the Soviet Union / Alastair McAuley. — London : Allen & Unwin, 1981. — viii,228p : ill ; 24cm
Bibliography: p215-223. - Includes index
ISBN 0-04-339020-x : £18.00 B81-16340

331.4′21 — Women personnel. Low pay

Women and low pay / edited by Peter J. Sloane. — London : Macmillan, 1980. — ix,260p : ill ; 23cm
Prepared for the Royal Commission on the Distribution of Income and Wealth. — Includes bibliographies and index
ISBN 0-333-26817-2 : £15.00 : CIP rev.
B80-08123

331.4′21 — Women personnel. Renumeration. Increases. Negotiation — *Manuals — For women personnel*

Chastain, Sherry. Winning the salary game : salary negotiation for women / by Sherry Chastain. — New York ; Chichester : Wiley, c1980. — xiv,170p : 1ill,2forms ; 24cm
Bibliography: p164-165. - Includes index
ISBN 0-471-08433-6 (cased) : £6.50
ISBN 0-471-08023-3 (pbk) : £3.50 B81-05014

331.4′21′0941 — Great Britain. Personnel. Remuneration. Sex differentials

Sloane, Peter J.. The earnings gap between men and women in Britain : the current state of research knowledge / P.J. Sloane. — London : Social Science Research Council, 1981. — 53p ; 30cm
At head of title: Equal Opportunities Commission/Social Science Research Council Joint Panel on Equal Opportunities Research. — Bibliography: p48-53
ISBN 0-86226-090-6 (pbk) : £3.00 B81-20818

331.4′257 — Great Britain. Part-time women personnel. Working conditions — *Proposals*

National Council for Civil Liberties. Part-time workers need full-time rights / [National Council for Civil Liberties] ; Ann Sedley ; cartoons by Cath Jackson. — London : NCCL, Rights for Women Unit, 1980. — 31p : ill ; 21cm
ISBN 0-901108-86-3 (pbk) : £0.75 B81-08232

331.4′3′0973 — United States. Married women. Employment, ***1920-1940.*** **Socioeconomic aspects**

Wandersee, Winifred D.. Women's work and family values : 1920-1940 / Winifred D. Wandersee. — Cambridge, Mass. ; London : Harvard University Press, 1981. — 165p ; 24cm
Bibliography: p133-140. — Includes index
ISBN 0-674-95535-8 : £12.95 B81-39781

331.4′81 — Great Britain. Professions. Women personnel, ***1968-1979***

Fogarty, Michael P.. Women in top jobs 1968-1979 / Michael P. Fogarty, Isobel Allen and Patricia Walters. — London : Heinemann Educational, 1981. — vi,273p ; 23cm
At head of title: Policy Studies Institute. — Includes index
ISBN 0-435-83806-7 : £14.00 : CIP rev.
Also classified at 658.4′2′088042 B81-27935

331.4′8100164′0941 — Great Britain. Computer industries & services. Women personnel

Simons, G. L.. Women in computing / G.L. Simons. — Manchester : NCC Publications, 1981. — 210p : ill,ports ; 21cm
Bibliography: p169-179. — Includes index
ISBN 0-85012-296-1 (pbk) : £6.50 : CIP rev. B81-12849

331.4′8161′0941 — Great Britain. Women doctors. Careers

Ward, Audrey. Careers of medical women / Audrey Ward, project leader. — Sheffield (Beach Hill Rd., Sheffield S10 2RX) : Medical Care Research Unit, Department of Community Medicine, University of Sheffield Medical School, [1981]. — 158p : ill,1form ; 30cm
Unpriced (pbk) B81-33123

331.4′877′00974 — New England. Textile industries. Women personnel, ***1830-1860 — Correspondence, diaries etc***

Farm to factory : women's letters 1830-1860 / edited by Thomas Dublin. — New York ; Guildford, Surrey : Columbia University Press, 1981. — x,191p : ill,2facsims,1port ; 24cm
ISBN 0-231-05118-2 : £12.50 B81-37686

331.5 — WORKERS. CATEGORIES BY SOCIAL AND ECONOMIC STATUS

331.5′44 — Great Britain. Negro migrant personnel. Political aspects

Phizacklea, Annie. Labour and racism / Annie Phizacklea and Robert Miles. — London : Routledge & Kegan Paul, 1980. — viii,248p ; 23cm
Bibliography: p237-245. - Includes index
ISBN 0-7100-0678-0 (cased) : £9.75 : CIP rev.
ISBN 0-7100-0679-9 (pbk) : £5.95 B80-26622

331.5′44′0942 — England. Itinerant workers, ***to 1914***

Leeson, R. A.. Travelling brothers : the six centuries' road from craft fellowship to trade unionism / R.A. Leeson. — London : Granada, 1980, c1979. — 348p,[8]p of plates : ill,facsims ; 20cm
Originally published: London : Allen & Unwin, 1979. — Bibliography: p284-296. — Includes index
ISBN 0-586-08302-2 (pbk) : £2.50 B81-40329

Leeson, Robert. Travelling brothers : the six centuries' road from craft fellowship to trade unionism / R.A. Leeson. — London : Allen & Unwin, 1979. — 348p,[8]p of plates : ill,coats of arms,facsims ; 23cm
Ill on lining papers. — Bibliography: p284-296. - Includes index
ISBN 0-04-309011-7 : £9.50 : CIP rev. B78-30447

331.5′5 — Chimney sweeping services. Apprentices, ***to ca 1875***

Strange, Kathleen. The climbing boys. — London : Allison & Busby, Sept.1981. — [160]p
ISBN 0-85031-431-3 : £6.95 : CIP entry B81-25113

331.5′5 — Great Britain. Industries. Youth Opportunities Programme trainees. Literacy & numeracy — *For supervisors*

Literacy, numeracy and the young trainee : a handbook for supervisors of youth opportunities schemes / ALBSU, Adult Literacy & Basic Skills Unit. — London (229 High Holborn, WC1V 7DA) : The Unit, 1981. — 31p : ill ; 30cm
ISBN 0-906509-04-1 (pbk) : £1.00 B81-16148

331.5′9 — Great Britain. Down's Syndrome adults. Employment

Lane, David. The work needs of mentally handicapped adults / David Lane. — London (1 Cambridge Terrace, NW1 4JL) : Disability Alliance published in conjunction with The Down's Children Association, 1980. — 47p ; 21cm
Cover title
£1.00 (pbk) B81-07835

331.5′9 — Great Britain. Physically handicapped persons. Employment

The **Caboose** and the uncounted : a new look from an old motor caravan at disabled workseekers. — Great Malvern (Victoria Rd., Great Malvern WR14 2TD) : Guild of the Disabled, [1981]. — 13p ; 21cm
Cover title
£1.00 (pbk) B81-11549

331.5′9 — Great Britain. Physically handicapped persons. Employment. Policies of government — *Proposals*

Lonsdale, Susan. Job protection for the disabled / Susan Lonsdale. — London (9 Poland St., W1V 3DG) : Low Pay Unit, 1981. — 20p ; 21cm. — (Low pay report ; 6)
£0.75 (unbound) B81-25581

331.5′9′0941 — Great Britain. Handicapped persons. Employment

Occupational disability. — Lancaster : MTP Press, Dec.1981. — [310]p
ISBN 0-85200-433-8 : £12.00 : CIP entry B81-36997

331.5′9′0941 — Great Britain. Handicapped persons. Employment. Policies of government

Disability Alliance. Payment of benefits to unemployed people / comments by the Disability Alliance. — London (1 Cambridge Terrace, NW1 4JL) : The Alliance, 1981. — 10p ; 30cm
£0.50 (pbk)
Also classified at 368.4′2 B81-26440

331.6 — WORKERS. CATEGORIES BY RACIAL, ETHNIC, NATIONAL ORIGIN

331.6 — Ethnic minorities. Employment

Discrimination and disadvantage. — London : Harper and Row, Jan.1982. — [336]p
ISBN 0-06-318193-2 (cased) : £9.95 : CIP entry
ISBN 0-06-318194-0 (pbk) : £5.95 B81-33972

331.6′2′607292 — Jamaica. African immigrant indentured personnel, ***1841-1865***

Schuler, Monica. 'Alas, alas, Kongo' : a social history of indentured African immigration into Jamaica, 1841-1865 / Monica Schuler. — Baltimore ; London : Johns Hopkins University Press, c1980. — x,186p : 1ill,3maps ; 24cm. — (Johns Hopkins studies in Atlantic history and culture)
Bibliography: p165-177. — Includes index
ISBN 0-8018-2308-0 : £10.00 B81-03221

331.6′3′924042173 — London. Redbridge ***(London Borough).*** **Jews. Employment,** ***1978***

Kosmin, Barry A.. The work and employment of surburban Jews : the socio-economic findings of the 1978 Redbridge Jewish survey / Barry A. Kosmin and Caren Levy. — London (Woburn House, Upper Woburn Place, WC1H 0EP) : Research Unit, Board of Deputies of British Jews, 1981. — 39p : ill,maps ; 30cm
Unpriced (pbk) B81-38954

331.6′9′968 — South Africa. Negro personnel. Trade unions, ***to 1980 — Labour Party (Great Britain) viewpoints***

Non-racial trade unionism in South Africa. — London : Labour Party, 1981. — 8p ; 30cm. — (Information paper / Labour Party International Department ; no.16)
£0.20 (unbound) B81-38936

331.7 — LABOUR ECONOMICS OF SPECIAL OCCUPATIONS

331.7′0012 — Great Britain. Occupations — *Classification schedules*

Classification of occupations and coding index / Office of Population Censuses and Surveys. — London : H.M.S.O., 1980. — cxxxvi,113p ; 30cm
Includes index
ISBN 0-11-690728-2 (pbk) : Unpriced B81-12154

331.7′0022′2 — Occupations — *Illustrations — For children*

Daniels, Meg. What people do. — London : Blackie, Feb.1982. — [12]p. — (Blackie concertina books)
ISBN 0-216-91128-1 : £0.95 : CIP entry B81-36027

331.7′00942 — England. Occupations, ***ca 1890-1975***

Hudson, Kenneth. Where we used to work / Kenneth Hudson. — London : John Baker, 1980. — viii,162p : ill,5maps,facsims,ports ; 26cm
Includes index
ISBN 0-212-97025-9 : £7.95 : CIP rev. B80-04700

331.7′02 — Careers. Choice by young persons

Information sources in education and work / editors, Kenneth Dibden, James Tomlinson. — London : Butterworth, 1981. — xiii,166p ; 22cm. — (Butterworths guides to information sources)
Bibliography: p150-166. — Includes index
ISBN 0-408-70923-5 : Unpriced B81-10858

331.7′02′02854 — Great Britain. Careers guidance services. Applications of digital computer systems — *Inquiry reports*

Ballantine, Malcolm. The application of computers in the Careers Service : a report / by Malcoln Ballantine. — [London] : Department of Employment, Careers Service Branch, 1980. — 90p : forms ; 30cm
Bibliography: p61-63
Unpriced (spiral) B81-22219

331.7′02′0941 — Great Britain. Careers. Choice — *For school leavers*

Barber, Thelma. Careers and jobs without O-Levels : where to look and what's available / by Thelma Barber. — Cambridge : Hobsons, c1981. — 127p : ill ; 18cm. — (A CRAC publication)
ISBN 0-86021-414-1 (pbk) : £1.95 B81-36436

331.7'02'0941 — Great Britain. Careers. Choice — *For school leavers* *continuation*

March, Peter. Your choice at 17+ : a guide to choices after A-level / Peter March and Michael Smith. — 2nd ed. — Cambridge : Hobsons [for] CRAC, 1981. — 160p : ill ; 18cm
Previous ed.: 1976. — Bibliography: p154-156. — Includes index
ISBN 0-86021-395-1 (pbk) : £1.85 B81-33572

Segal, Audrey. Career choice / Audrey Segal. — London : Pan, 1981. — liii,426p ; 20cm. — (Pan information)
Includes index
ISBN 0-330-26152-5 (pbk) : £2.95 B81-22885

331.7'02'0941 — Great Britain. Careers. Choice — *For schools*

Longman, Ken. Learning for life : a programme for young people / Ken Longman. — Basingstoke : Macmillan Education, 1981. — vii,94p : ill 25cm + Tutor's guide(xxiv, 94p : ill ; 25cm)
ISBN 0-333-27656-6 (pbk) : £2.95 : CIP rev.
ISBN 0-333-27657-4 (Tutor's guide) : £4.95 B80-05807

Whitehead, Geoffrey. Choosing options for your future in the world of work / by Geoffrey Whitehead. — Huddersfield : Vyner, 1980. — 24p : ill,maps,ports ; 30cm. — (The Simplex careers series ; c.2)
ISBN 0-906628-02-4 (pbk) : £0.80 B81-38491

331.7'02'0941 — Great Britain. Careers — *For physically handicapped persons*

Fallon, Bernadette. Able to work / Bernadette Fallon ; designed and illustrated by Liz McQuiston. — London (126 Albert St., NW1 7NF) : Spinal Injuries Association, 1979. — 107p : ill ; 15x22cm
Includes index
ISBN 0-9504474-2-0 (spiral) : £2.50 B81-04705

331.7'02'0941 — Great Britain. Occupations — *Career guides*

Daily telegraph careers A-Z / Careers Information Service. — New rev. ed. — London : Collins, 1981. — 181p ; 20cm
Previous ed.: 1975
ISBN 0-00-434183-x (pbk) : £1.75 B81-17039

Miller, Ruth, *19---*. Equal opportunities : a careers guide for women and men. — 6th ed. / Ruth Miller assisted by Anna Alston. — Harmondsworth : Penguin, 1981. — xliii,516p ; 20cm. — (Penguin handbooks)
Previous ed.: i.e. Rev. ed., 1978. — Bibliography: pxlii-xliii. — Includes index
ISBN 0-14-046270-8 (pbk) : £2.95 B81-21038

331.7'02'0941 — Great Britain. Occupations — *Career guides — Serials*

Annual careers guide / Careers & Occupational Information Centre. — Autumn 1980 ed.. — London : H.M.S.O., 1980. — x,289p
ISBN 0-11-885323-6 : £4.95 B81-00773

331.7'02'09417 — Ireland *(Republic)*. **Careers. Choice —** *For students*

Jeffers, Gerry. Career choice : thinking it through / text Gerry Jeffers ; layout Lorna Johnston ; illustrations John Lucas, Alice Campbell, Frank O'Sullivan. — Dublin : Institute of Public Administration, c1981. — 21p : ill ; 21cm. — (Young citizen special)
ISBN 0-906980-05-4 (pbk) : £0.30 B81-35287

331.7'02'09417 — Ireland *(Republic)*. **Careers. Choice —** *For students — Serials*

School and college : the exam and career guide for students. — No.1-. — Dublin (Taney Rd, Dundrum, Dublin 14) : School and College Services, [1980]-. — v. : ill,maps,ports ; 30cm
Eight issues yearly
£0.40
Also classified at 373.13'02812 B81-07963

331.7'020942 — England. Residential institutions for children. School leavers. Career guides

Burgess, Charles. In care and into work. — London : Tavistock Publications, July 1981. — [192]p. — (Residential social work ; P216)
ISBN 0-422-77640-8 (cased) : £8.00 : CIP entry
ISBN 0-422-77650-5 (pbk) : £3.50 B81-13472

331.7'02'0973 — United States. Careers. Choice — *Manuals*

Carney, Clarke G.. Career planning : skills to build your future / Clarke G. Carney, Cindy Field Wells, Don Streufert. — New York ; London : Van Nostrand, c1981. — ix,246p : ill,forms ; 23cm
Includes index
ISBN 0-442-23350-7 (pbk) : £6.70 B81-06165

331.7'023 — France. School leavers. Careers. Influence of family life & school life, *1852-1870 — Sources of data: Duruy, Victor. Enquete sur l'enseignement professionel, 1864*

Harrigan, Patrick J.. Mobility, elites, and education in French society of the Second Empire / by Patrick J. Harrigan ; with a statistical appendix by James B. Whitney. — Waterloo, Ont. : Wilfred Laurier University Press ; Gerrards Cross : Smythe [distributor], c1980. — xv,203p ; 24cm
Bibliography: p189-198. - Includes index
£7.95 B81-04988

331.7'023'0941 — Great Britain. Careers — *For arts graduates*

National Advisory Centre on Careers for Women. Training and employment for the arts graduate : an introduction / National Advisory Centre on Careers for Women. — 3rd ed. — London (30 Gordon St., WC1H 0AX) : The Centre, 1980. — 100p ; 22cm
Previous ed.: 197-. — Includes index
ISBN 0-902323-13-x (pbk) : £2.25 B81-01967

331.7'023'0941 — Great Britain. Careers — *For graduates — Serials*

[Future *(London)*]. Future : the magazine for graduates and their employers. — Vol.1, no.1 (Jan.1979)-. — London (Yeoman House, 76 St. James's Lane, N10 3RD) : New Opportunity Press, 1979-. — v. : ill,chart,ports ; 28cm
Monthly. — Description based on: Vol.2, no.6 (Feb.1980)
ISSN 0144-9559 = Future (London) : £5.00 per year B81-04485

331.7'023'0941 — Great Britain. Occupations — *Career guides — For graduates — Serials*

Directory of opportunities for graduates. — 81. — London : 76 Dean St., W1A 1BU : Business and Career Publications, c1980. — 940p
ISBN 0-86024-126-2 : £11.50 B81-01772

331.7'023'0941 — Great Britain. Occupations — *Career guides — For school leavers in East Anglia & East Midlands — Serials*

Careers for school and college leavers. [East Midlands and East Anglia]. — '81. — London : VNU Business Publications, c1981. — 234p
ISBN 0-86271-004-9 : Unpriced B81-36003

331.7'023'0941 — Great Britain. Occupations — *Career guides — For school leavers in Home Counties & South-east England — Serials*

Careers for school and college leavers. [Home Counties and South East]. — '81. — London : VNU Business Publications, c1981. — 234p
ISBN 0-86271-001-4 : Unpriced B81-36001

331.7'023'0941 — Great Britain. Occupations — *Career guides — For school leavers in London — Serials*

Careers for school and college leavers. [Greater London]. — '81. — London : VNU Business Publications, c1981. — 234p
ISBN 0-86271-000-6 : Unpriced B81-35997

331.7'023'0941 — Great Britain. Occupations — *Career guides — For school leavers in North-east England — Serials*

Careers for school and college leavers. [North East]. — '81. — London : VNU Business Publications, c1981. — 234p
ISBN 0-86271-005-7 : Unpriced B81-35996

331.7'023'0941 — Great Britain. Occupations — *Career guides — For school leavers in North-west England & Northern Ireland — Serials*

Careers for school and college leavers. [North West and Northern Ireland]. — '81. — London : VNU Business Publications, c1981. — 234p
ISBN 0-86271-006-5 : Unpriced B81-36002

331.7'023'0941 — Great Britain. Occupations — *Career guides — For school leavers in Scotland — Serials*

Careers for school and college leavers. [Scotland]. — '81. — London : VNU Business Publications, c1981. — 234p
ISBN 0-86271-007-3 : Unpriced B81-36000

[Opportunities *(Scotland ed.)*]. Opportunities. — Scotland ed.. — 1979. — London (76 St James's Lane, N10 3RD) : The New Opportunity Press, c1978. — 272p
ISBN 0-903578-44-1 : Unpriced B81-09227

331.7'023'0941 — Great Britain. Occupations — *Career guides — For school leavers in South-west England — Serials*

Careers for school and college leavers. [Bristol and South West]. — '81. — London : VNU Business Publications, c1981. — 234p
ISBN 0-86271-002-2 : Unpriced B81-35998

331.7'023'0941 — Great Britain. Occupations — *Career guides — For school leavers in West Midlands — Serials*

Careers for school and college leavers. [Birmingham and West Midlands]. — '81. — London : VNU Business Publications, c1981. — 234p
ISBN 0-86271-003-0 : Unpriced B81-35999

331.7'023'0941 — Great Britain. Occupations — *Career guides — For school leavers — Serials*

Careers for school and college leavers. — '81. — London : VNU Business Publications, c1981. — 234p
ISBN 0-86271-008-1 : £11.50 B81-35995

331.7'12'0971 — Canada. Professions. Regulation *— Conference proceedings*

The **Professions** and public policy / edited by Philip Slayton and Michael J. Trebilcock. — Toronto ; London : University of Toronto Press, c1978. — x,346p : ill ; 24cm
Conference papers
ISBN 0-8020-5416-1 : £10.50 B81-25472

331.7'12'0973 — United States. Professions — *For graduates*

Nilsson, W. Daniel. Orientation to professional practice : for engineers, analysts, programmers, technicians, and scientists / W. Daniel Nilsson, Philip E. Hicks. — New York ; London : McGraw-Hill, c1981. — x,372p : ill,facsims,forms ; 25cm
Includes index
ISBN 0-07-046571-1 : £17.25 B81-10201

331.7'613442'00942753 — Merseyside *(Metropolitan County)*. **Liverpool. Solicitors,** *to 1979*

Williams, Peter Howell. A gentleman's calling : the Liverpool attorney-at-law / by Peter Howell Williams. — [Liverpool] ([c/o Bell & Joynson, 6 Castle St., Liverpool 2]) : Incorporated Law Society of Liverpool, 1980. — 398p,[31]p of plates : ill,facsims,1plan,ports ; 23cm
Published in a limited edition of 500 copies
£12.50 B81-13352

331.7'61352042 — England. Local authorities. Personnel — *For councillors*

Fowler, Alan. Local authority manpower : a guide for elected members / [Alan Fowler]. — London (11 Bury St, EC3A 5AP) : BKT Publications, [1981?]. — 75p : ill ; 21cm
ISBN 0-904677-16-8 (pbk) : £4.80 B81-26272

331.7'62'000941 — Great Britain. Engineering industries. Personnel: Young technologists

Connor, Helen. The young technologists : a study of their attitudes towards their jobs in the engineering industry and their education and training / Helen Connor. — Watford : Engineering Industry Training Board, c1980. — 68p ; 30cm. — (EITB research paper ; RP/3)
ISBN 0-85083-507-0 (spiral) : Unpriced B81-12768

331.7'62'000941 — Great Britain. Engineering industries. Skilled personnel

Venning, Muriel. The craftsman in engineering / Muriel Venning, Owen Frith, Chris Grimbley. — Watford : Engineering Industry Training Board, c1980. — 107p : ill ; 31cm
Bibliography: p103. - Includes index
ISBN 0-85083-506-2 : Unpriced B81-17633

331.7'62'00941 — Great Britain. Manufacturing industries. Personnel: Engineers. Role

Kennaway, A.. Engineers in industry : a management guide for engineers who wish to perform creatively in industry / by A. Kennaway. — London : Pergamon, 1981. — x,148p : ill,forms ; 22cm
Bibliography: p147-148
ISBN 0-08-026175-2 (cased) : Unpriced : CIP rev.
ISBN 0-08-026174-4 (pbk) : Unpriced B81-10470

331.7'6251'00941 — Great Britain. Railway construction industries. Navvies, *to 1900*

Coleman, Terry. The railway navvies : a history of the men who made the railways / Terry Coleman. — Harmondsworth : Penguin by arrangement with Hutchinson, 1968 (1981 [printing]). — 256p,[16]p of plates : ill,ports ; 18cm
Originally published: London : Hutchinson, 1965. — Bibliography: p244-246. — Includes index
ISBN 0-14-005542-8 (pbk) : £1.95 B81-21026

331.7'63'0967623 — Kenya. Coastal regions. Plantations. Employment. Labour, *1890-1925*

Cooper, Frederick. From slaves to squatters : plantation labor and agriculture in Zanzibar and coastal Kenya 1890-1925 / Frederick Cooper. — New Haven ; London : Yale University Press, c1980. — xv,328p : ill,maps ; 25cm
Bibliography: p303-317. - Includes index
ISBN 0-300-02454-1 : £15.75
Also classified at 331.7'63'096781 B81-17287

331.7'63'096781 — Tanzania. Zanzibar. Plantations. Employment. Labour, *1890-1925*

Cooper, Frederick. From slaves to squatters : plantation labor and agriculture in Zanzibar and coastal Kenya 1890-1925 / Frederick Cooper. — New Haven ; London : Yale University Press, c1980. — xv,328p : ill,maps ; 25cm
Bibliography: p303-317. - Includes index
ISBN 0-300-02454-1 : £15.75
Primary classification 331.7'63'0967623 B81-17287

331.7'6862'0973 — United States. Printing industries. Personnel. Effects of technological change

Rogers, Theresa F.. Printers face automation : the impact of technology on work and retirement among skilled craftsmen / Theresa F. Rogers, Nathalie S. Friedman. — Lexington : Lexington Books ; [Farnborough, Hants.] : Gower [distributor], 1980. — xviii,184p ; 24cm
Bibliography: p177-181. — Includes index
ISBN 0-669-03310-3 : £13.00 B81-03552

331.7'95'0941 — Great Britain. Public bodies. Socialist personnel. Role — *Socialist viewpoints*

. In and against the State / the London Edinburgh Weekend Return Group, a working group of the Conference of Socialist Economists. — Rev. and expanded ed. — London : Pluto, 1980. — 147p : 1ill ; 20cm
Previous ed.: London : London Edinburgh Weekend Return Group, 1979
ISBN 0-86104-327-8 (pbk) : £2.95 B81-06816

331.8 — TRADE UNIONS AND COLLECTIVE BARGAINING

331.87 — Great Britain. Industrial relations. Role of multi-union shop stewards committees — *Trade union viewpoints*

Trade union strategy in the face of corporate power : the case for multi-union combine shop stewards committees / British Aerospace Joint Shop Stewards' Committee (Dynamics Group) ... [et al.]. — [England] ([c/o Ron Mills, liaison officer for Lucas Aerospace Combine Committee, 163 Ulverley Green Rd., Olton, Solihull, W. Midlands]) : The Committee, [1981]. — [17]p ; 21cm
Cover title
£0.25 (pbk) B81-14625

331.87'0941 — Great Britain. Trade unions. Organisation structure

Campbell, Alan. Getting organized / Alan Campbell and John McIlroy. — London : Pan, 1981. — 208p : ill,forms ; 20cm. — (Pan trade union studies)
Bibliography: p200-201. — Includes index
ISBN 0-330-26476-1 (pbk) : £1.75 B81-38232

331.87'09485 — Sweden. Trade unions. Organisation structure

Lewin, Leif. Governing trade unions in Sweden / Leif Lewin. — Cambridge, Mass. ; London : Harvard University Press, 1980. — vi,180p : ill ; 25cm
Translation of: Hur styrs facket?. — Includes index
ISBN 0-674-35875-9 : £12.00 B81-04510

331.87'2 — Great Britain. Trade unions. Branches. Activities. Participation of members

Fosh, Patricia. The active trade unionist : a study of motivation and participation at branch level / Patricia Fosh. — Cambridge : Cambridge University Press, 1981. — ix,155p : ill ; 24cm. — (Paper in industrial relations and labour ; 6)
Bibliography: p148-151. — Includes index
ISBN 0-521-23700-9 : £10.50 : CIP rev. B81-13804

331.87'33 — Great Britain. Public bodies. Manual personnel. Trade unions: National Union of Public Employees. Branches. Secretaries. Duties — *Manuals*

National Union of Public Employees. Branch secretary's handbook / NUPE. — London : National Union of Public Employees, 1980. — 142p : ill,facsims,forms,ports ; 22cm
ISBN 0-907334-04-0 (pbk) : £1.00 to members B81-06808

331.87'33 — West Germany. Shop stewards

Koch, Karl. Trade union workshop representatives (Gewerkschaftliche Vertrauensleute) in the Federal Republic of Germany : an empirical study and a comparison with shop stewards in Great Britain : a report prepared for the Anglo-German Foundation for the Study of Industrial society / by Karl Koch. — London (St Stephens House, Victoria Embankment, London SW1A 2LA) : Anglo-German Foundation for the Study of Industrial Society, c1978. — 111p ; 30cm. — (Monograph series / Anglo-German Foundation for the Study of Industrial Society)
Includes appendix in German
ISBN 0-905492-14-5 (pbk) : £2.50 B81-38071

331.88 — TRADE UNIONS

331.88 — Trade unionism — *For children*

Althea. What is a union / by Althea ; illustrated by Chris Evans. — Over : Dinosaur, c1981. — [24]p : ill ; 16x19cm. — (Dinosaur's Althea books)
ISBN 0-85122-269-2 (cased) : £1.85
ISBN 0-85122-256-0 (pbk) : £0.70 B81-19478

331.88 — Trade unions

Jackson, Michael P.. Trade unions. — London : Longman, Dec.1981. — [192]p
ISBN 0-582-29580-7 : £3.95 : CIP entry B81-31370

331.88'01 — Trade unionism. Theories, *to 1980*

Poole, Michael, *1943-*. Theories of trade unionism : a sociology of industrial relations / Michael Poole. — London : Routledge and Kegan Paul, 1981. — xi,265p : ill ; 23cm
Bibliography: p221-242. - Includes index
ISBN 0-7100-0695-0 : £12.50 : CIP rev. B81-02380

331.88'01 — United States. Trade unions. Theories

Martin, Donald L.. An ownership theory of the trade union / Donald L. Martin. — Berkeley ; London : University of California Press, c1980. — xi,155p : ill ; 24cm
Bibliography: p147-151. - Includes index
ISBN 0-520-03884-3 : £10.00 B81-27267

331.88'025'41 — Great Britain. Trade unions — *Directories*

Marsh, Arthur. Trade union handbook : a guide and directory to the structure, membership, policy and personnel of the British trade unions / Arthur Marsh. — 2nd ed. — Farnborough : Gower, 1980. — x,396p : ill,facsims ; 23cm
Previous ed.: 1979. — Includes bibliographies
ISBN 0-566-02208-7 : £17.00 : CIP rev. B80-06311

331.88'06'041 — Great Britain. Trade unions. Organisations: Trades Union Congress. Organisation structure

Trades Union Congress. The organisation, structure and services of the TUC : a TUC consultative document. — London : Trades Union Congress, 1980. — 27p ; 30cm
Cover title
£2.00 (pbk) B81-22814

331.88'091 — Trade unions. International organisations

Windmuller, J. P.. The international trade union movement / by J.P. Windmuller. — Deventer ; London : Kluwer, 1980. — 174p ; 25cm
Bibliography: p167-168. — Includes index
ISBN 90-312-0121-9 : Unpriced B81-31419

331.88'0917'7 — Organisation for Economic Co-operation and Development countries. Trade unions

Trade unions in the developed economies. — London : Croom Helm, Aug.1981. — [240]p
ISBN 0-7099-1907-7 : £14.95 : CIP entry B81-16370

331.88'092'4 — Great Britain. Trade unionism. Gast, John — *Biographies*

Prothero, I. J.. Artisans and politics in early nineteenth-century London : John Gast and his times / I.J. Prothero. — London : Methuen, 1981, c1979. — xi,418p ; 22cm
Originally published: Folkestone : Dawson, 1979. — Bibliography: p398-404. — Includes index
ISBN 0-416-74890-2 (pbk) : £5.95
Primary classification 322'.2 B81-21325

331.88'092'4 — New Zealand. Trade unionism. Skinner, Tom — *Biographies*

Skinner, Tom, *1909-*. Man to man / Tom Skinner with John Berry. — Christchurch [N.Z.] ; London : Whitcoulls, 1980. — 204p,[24]p of plates : ill,ports ; 22cm
ISBN 0-7233-0639-7 : £9.95 B81-01174

331.88'092'4 — Poland. Trade unions: Solidarność, *1980 (August-December) — Personal observations*

Taylor, John. Five months with Solidarity. — London : Wildwood House, Dec.1981. — [128] p. — (Wildwood special)
ISBN 0-7045-0463-4 (pbk) : £2.95 : CIP entry B81-36987

331.88'0941 — Great Britain. Trade unions

Hawkins, Kevin. Trade unions / Kevin Hawkins. — London : Hutchinson, 1981. — 259p : ill ; 23cm
Bibliography: p255-256. — Includes index
ISBN 0-09-144310-5 (cased) : £12.00 : CIP rev.
ISBN 0-09-144311-3 (pbk) : £4.95 B81-14832

Williamson, Hugh. The trade unions. — 6th ed. — London : Heinemann Educational, Sept.1981. — [160]p. — (Studies in the British economy)
Previous ed.: 1979
ISBN 0-435-84584-5 (pbk) : £2.50 : CIP entry B81-28814

331.88'0941 — Great Britain. Trade unions, *1945-1980 — For trade unionism*
Baker, Chris. Unions and change since 1945 / Chris Baker and Peter Caldwell. — London : Pan, 1981. — 192p : ill,1map,forms ; 20cm. — (Pan trade union studies)
Includes index
ISBN 0-330-26475-3 (pbk) : £1.75 B81-38231

331.88'0941 — Great Britain. Trade unions, *1960-1980*
Change in trade unions : the development of UK unions since the 1960s / R. Undy ... [et al.]. — London : Hutchinson, 1981. — 399p : ill ; 25cm
Bibliography: p383-388. — Includes index
ISBN 0-09-143880-2 : £20.00 B81-23068

331.88'0941 — Great Britain. Trade unions *— For schools*
Armstrong, Paul, *1949-*. Trade unions and industrial relations / Paul Armstrong, Maurice Knights. — Exeter : Wheaton, 1979. — 54p : ill,facsims,forms,ports ; 21cm. — (Government, economics and commerce series)
ISBN 0-08-022570-5 (pbk) : £0.90 B81-11423

Freeman, Marian. Trade unions / Marian Freeman. — London : Evans, 1981. — 48p : ill,facsims,ports ; 25cm. — (Knowing British history topics)
ISBN 0-237-29260-2 (pbk) : Unpriced
B81-19857

331.88'0941 — Great Britain. Trade unions. Power
Arnold, Guy. The unions / by Guy Arnold. — London : Hamilton, 1981. — 240p ; 23cm
ISBN 0-241-10107-7 : £9.95 : CIP rev.
B81-19130

331.88'0941 — Great Britain. Trade unions. Relations with government, *1970-1974*
Dorfman, Gerald A.. Trade union influence in the Heath years : some reflections / by Gerald A. Dorfman. — Glasgow (McCance Building, 16 Richmond St., Glasgow G1 1XQ) : Centre for the Study of Public Policy, University of Strathclyde, c1979. — 13p ; 30cm. — (Studies in public policy, ISSN 0140-8240 ; no.35)
Unpriced (pbk) B81-36899

331.88'0941 — Great Britain. Trade unions — *Serials*
[Union fact sheet *(GFTU Research Service)***].** Union fact sheet / by the GFTU Research Service. — Issue no.1 (May 1979)-. — London (Central House, Upper Woburn Place, WC1H 0HY) : General Federation of Trade Unions, 1979-. — v. ; 30cm
Irregular. — Description based on: Issue no.11 (Oct.1980)
ISSN 0260-7891 = Union fact sheet - General Federation of Trade Unions : Free to Federation members only B81-06907

331.88'0941 — Great Britain. Trade unions, *to 1979*
Marsh, Arthur. Historical directory of trade unions / Arthur Marsh and Victoria Ryan ; foreword by Lord Briggs. — Farnborough : Gower
Vol.1: Non-manual unions. — c1980. — xxvi,228p ; 23cm
Bibliography: pxxiv-xxvi
ISBN 0-566-02160-9 : £17.50 : CIP rev.
B80-05810

331.88'0943 — Germany. Trade unions, *1869-1933*
Moses, John A.. Trade unionism in Germany from Bismarck to Hitler, 1869-1933. — London : George Prior
Vol.1. — Oct.1981. — [375]p
ISBN 0-86043-450-8 : £9.95 : CIP entry
B81-27441

Moses, John A.. Trade unionism in Germany from Bismarck to Hitler, 1869-1933. — London : George Prior
Vol.2. — Oct.1981. — [390]p
ISBN 0-86043-483-4 : £9.95 : CIP entry
B81-27444

331.88'09438 — Poland. Trade unions. NSZZ "Solidarność" *— Personal observations*
Dobbs, Michael. Poland, Solidarity, Walesa. — Oxford : Pergamon, Aug.1981. — [128]p
ISBN 0-08-028147-8 : £7.50 : CIP entry
B81-23893

331.88'09438 — Poland. Trade unions: Solidarity, *to 1981*
MacShane, Denis. Solidarity. — Nottingham : Spokesman, Aug.1981. — [150]p
ISBN 0-85124-319-3 (cased) : CIP entry
ISBN 0-85124-318-5 (pbk) B81-20649

331.88'09438 — Poland. Trade unions: Solidarność *— Russian texts*
Poland 1980 : 'Solidarity's' first year = Pol'sha 1980 : 'Solidarnosti' god pervyi / compiled and edited by Vladimir Malyshev. — London (40 Elsham Rd., W14 8HB) : Overseas Publications Interchange, 1981. — 239p : ill,ports ; 19cm
ISBN 0-903868-35-0 (pbk) : £4.50 B81-35401

331.88'0973 — United States. Manufacturing industries. Trade unions *— Conference proceedings*
The Shrinking perimeter : unionism and labor relations in the manufacturing sector / edited by Harvey A. Juris, Myron Roomkin. — Lexington : Lexington Books ; [Farnborough, Hants.] : Gower [distributor], 1980. — xi,226p ; 24cm
Includes bibliographies and index
ISBN 0-669-02939-4 : £13.50 B81-02624

331.88'0994 — Australia. Trade unionism
Rawson, D. W.. Unions and unionists in Australia / D.W. Rawson. — Sydney ; London : Allen & Unwin, 1980. — 166p ; 23cm
Bibliography: p162-164. - Includes index
ISBN 0-86861-176-x (cased) : £8.95
ISBN 0-86861-184-0 (pbk) : £4.50 B81-03761

331.88'11 — Great Britain. White-collar personnel. Trade unionism *— Study examples: National and Local Government Officers Association. Sheffield Branch*
Nicholson, N.. The dynamics of white collar unionism. — London : Academic Press, Nov.1981. — [220]p
ISBN 0-12-518020-9 : CIP entry B81-30296

331.88'11027041 — Great Britain. Libraries. Trade unions *— Serials*
LA trade union news. — Issue no.1 (1978)-. — London : General Services Division of the Library Association, 1978-. — v. ; 30cm
Three issues yearly. — Description based on: Issue no.8 (Oct.1980)
ISSN 0144-6827 = LA trade union news : Unpriced B81-06927

331.88'1135441006 — Great Britain. Civil service. Trade unions: Civil and Public Services Association, *1903-1978*
Civil and Public Services Association. From humble petition to militant action : a history of the Civil and Public Services Association 1903-1978 / by Eric Wigham. — [London] (215 Balham High Rd., SW17 7BN) : C.P.S.A., c1980. — 239p : ill,ports ; 26cm
Includes index
ISBN 0-901411-06-x (cased) : Unpriced
ISBN 0-901411-05-1 (pbk) : Unpriced
ISBN 0-901411-07-8 (limited ed) : Unpriced
B81-14049

331.88'1135441006 — Great Britain. Civil service. Trade unions: Institution of Professional Civil Servants, *to 1979*
Mortimer, J. E.. A professional union : the evolution of the Institution of Professional Civil Servants / James E. Mortimer, Valerie A. Ellis. — London : Allen & Unwin, 1980. — 450p,[12]p of plates : ill,ports ; 24cm
Bibliography: p430. - Includes index
ISBN 0-04-331076-1 : £15.00 : CIP rev.
B80-09612

331.88'1135441006 — Great Britain. Civil service. Trade unions. Organisations: Council of Civil Service Unions *— Serials*
The Bulletin of the Council of Civil Service Unions. — Vol.1, no.1 (Jan.1981)-. — London (19 Rochester Row, SW1) : The Council : 1981-. — v. : ill,ports ; 30cm
Monthly. — Continues: Whitley bulletin
ISSN 0261-3824 = Bulletin of the Council of Civil Service Unions : Unpriced B81-27136

331.88'1135494006 — Australia. Civil service. Trade unions: Administrative and Clerical Officers Association, *to 1979*
Juddery, Bruce. White collar power : a history of the ACOA / Bruce Juddery. — Sydney ; London : Allen & Unwin, 1980. — x,319p ; 23cm
Includes index
ISBN 0-86861-138-7 (cased) : £13.95
ISBN 0-86861-146-8 (pbk) : Unpriced
B81-16081

331.88'11'3850941 — Great Britain. Railway services. Trade unions: National Union of Railwaymen, *to 1980*
Bagwell, Philip S.. The railwaymen. — London : George Allen and Unwin
Vol.2: The Beeching era and after. — Jan.1982. — [456]p
ISBN 0-04-331084-2 : £15.00 : CIP entry
B81-33920

331.88'113871'094294 — South Wales. Dockers. Trade unions, *1889-1921*
Leng, Philip J.. The Welsh dockers / Philip J. Leng. — Ormskirk : Hesketh, 1981. — xii,117p,[12]p pf plates : ill,1map,1facsim,ports ; 21cm
Bibliography: p115-117. — Includes index
ISBN 0-905777-08-5 (pbk) : £1.50 B81-26299

331.88'1161'0941 — Great Britain. Doctors. Trade unions: British Medical Association
Jones, Philip R.. Doctors and the BMA : a case study in collective action / Philip R. Jones. — Farnborough : Gower, c1981. — 178p : ill ; 23cm
Bibliography: p163-174. — Includes index
ISBN 0-566-00338-4 : £11.50 B81-37912

331.88'116479541 — Great Britain. Licensed premises. Managers. Trade unions: National Association of Licensed House Managers *— Serials*
NALHM official reference book / the National Association of Licensed House Managers. — 1979. — London (86 Edgware Rd, W2 2YW) : Sterling Professional Publications, [1979]. — 344p
ISSN 0142-5250 : Unpriced B81-30842

NALHM official reference book / the National Association of Licensed House Managers. — 1981. — London (86 Edgware Rd., W2 2YV) : Sterling Publications, [1981]. — 324p
ISSN 0142-5250 : Unpriced B81-29055

331.88'11792028'0941 — Great Britain. Actors & actresses. Trade unions, *1800-1951*
Macleod, Joseph. The actor's right to act / Joseph Macleod. — London : Lawrence & Wishart for the friends of Equity, 1981. — 205p,[8]p of plates : ports ; 22cm
Includes index
ISBN 0-85315-538-0 : £5.95 B81-12534

331.88'1691'0941 — Great Britain. Iron & steel industries. Trade unions: Iron and Steel Trades Confederation *— Serials*
ISTC banner. — July 1980-. — London (Swinton House, 324 Gray's Inn Rd, WC1BX 8DD) : Iron and Steel Trades Confederation, 1980-. — v. : ill ; 44cm
Monthly. — Continues: Steelworkers' banner
ISSN 0260-0625 = ISTC banner : Free
B81-05303

331.88'3 — New York *(City).* **Women personnel. Trade unions: Women's Trade Union League of New York,** *to 1955*
Dye, Nancy Schrom. As equals and as sisters : feminism, the Labor Movement and the Women's Trade Union League of New York / Nancy Schrom Dye. — Columbia, Mo. ; London : University of Missouri Press, 1980. — 200p ; 24cm
Bibliography: p185-194. — Includes index
ISBN 0-8262-0318-3 : £11.35 B81-29554

331.88'92 — Great Britain. Closed shops — *Regulations*
Closed shop agreements and arrangements / [Department of Employment]. — [London] : The Department, 1980. — 18p ; 21x10cm. — (Code of practice / Department of Employment)
Cover title
Unpriced (pbk) B81-10363

331.88′92 — Great Britain, United States & West Germany. Industries. Closed shops — *Comparative studies*

Hanson, Charles. The closed shop. — Aldershot : Gower, Jan.1982. — [270]p
ISBN 0-566-00414-3 : £12.50 : CIP entry
B81-34284

331.88′92′0941 — Great Britain. Closed shops. Codes of practice. Drafts — *Inquiry reports*

Great Britain. *Parliament. House of Commons. Employment Committee.* The legal immunities of trade unions and other related matters : draft codes of practice on picketing and the closed shop : record report from the Employment Committee, Session 1979-80. — London : H.M.S.O., 1980. — viiip ; 25cm
ISBN 0-10-028229-6 (unbound) : £1.10
Also classified at 331.89′27′0941 B81-07323

331.89 — COLLECTIVE BARGAINING AND DISPUTES

331.89 — Poland. Lub region. Workers′ organisations: Chłopski Komitet Samoobrony Ziemi Lubelskiej, *to 1979 — Polish texts*

Rożek, Janusz. Powstanie Chłopskiego Komitetu Samoobrony Społecznej Ziemi Lubelskiej / Janusz Rożek ; słowo wstępne Wanda Ferens. — Warszawa : [Biblioteka Ruchu Chłopskiej Samoobrony Społecznej] ; Harrow : Pelski [distributor], 1979. — 22p ; 21cm. — (Biblioteka Ruchu Chłopskiej Samoobrony Społecznej ; zesz.1)
Unpriced (pbk) B81-40781

331.89′04135′0000973 — United States. Public sector. Collective bargaining

Lieberman, Myron. Public-sector bargaining : a policy reappraisal / Myron Lieberman. — Lexington, Mass. : Lexington Books ; [Aldershot] : Gower [distributor], 1981, c1980. — xx,180p ; 24cm
Bibliography: p165-169. — Includes index
ISBN 0-669-04110-6 : £13.00 B81-29594

331.89′0422334′09769154 — Kentucky. Harlan County. Coal industries. Industrial relations. Disputes, *1931-1939*

Hevener, John W.. Which side are you on? : the Harlan County Coal miners 1931-39 / John W. Hevener. — Urbana ; London : University of Illinois Press, c1978. — xiv,216p,[10]p of plates : ill,1map,ports ; 24cm
Bibliography: p187-198. - Includes index
ISBN 0-252-00270-9 : Unpriced B81-10183

331.89′0724 — Collective bargaining. Econometric models

Ellis, Christopher J.. A model of bilateral bargaining in the labour market / Christopher J. Ellis. — Coventry : Department of Economics, University of Warwick, 1980. — 31p : ill ; 31cm. — (Warwick economic research papers ; no.186)
Bibliography: p31
Unpriced (pbk) B81-15978

331.89′0973 — United States. Industrial relations. Role of collective bargaining

Herman, E. Edward. Collective bargaining and labor relations / E. Edward Herman, Alfred Kuhn. — Englewood Cliffs ; London : Prentice-Hall, c1981. — xix,572p ; 24cm
Bibliography: p543-560. - Includes index
ISBN 0-13-140558-6 : £12.95 B81-23108

331.89′0994 — Australia. Industrial relations. Disputes — *Case studies*

Industrial action : patterns of labour conflict / edited by Stephen J. Frenkel. — Sydney ; London : Allen & Unwin, 1980. — 176p : ill ; 22cm. — (Australian studies in industrial relations)
Bibliography: p163-167. - Includes index
ISBN 0-86861-122-0 (cased) : £12.95
B81-10618

331.89′1′0941 — Great Britain. Industrial relations. Procedure. Agreements — *For management*

Muir, John, *1927-*. Industrial relations procedures and agreements / John Muir. — Aldershot : Gower, c1981. — xv,184p ; 23cm
Includes index
ISBN 0-566-02275-3 : Unpriced : CIP rev.
B81-09503

331.89′143 — United States. Schools. Industrial relations. Disputes. Arbitration

Ostrander, Kenneth H.. A grievance arbitration guide for educators / Kenneth H. Ostrander. — Boston, [Mass.] ; London : Allyn and Bacon, c1981. — ix,194p : ill ; 25cm
Includes index
ISBN 0-205-07280-1 : £14.95 B81-24253

331.89′2 — Industrial relations. Strikes. Causes

Siebert, W. Stanley. Are strikes accidental? / by W. Stanley Siebert and John T. Addison. — [Aberdeen] : University of Aberdeen, Department of Political Economy, [1980]. — 24,ii,[3]leaves : 1ill ; 30cm. — (Occasional paper / University of Aberdeen Department of Political Economy, ISSN 0143-4543 ; 80-04)
Bibliography: leaves [2-3]
Unpriced (pbk) B81-00775

331.89′2′01 — England. Industrial relations. Strikes. Ethical aspects

Macfarlane, L. J.. The right to strike / L.J. Macfarlane. — Harmondsworth : Penguin, 1981. — 200p : ill ; 20cm. — (Pelican books)
Includes index
ISBN 0-14-022072-0 (pbk) : £2.25 B81-17033

331.89′25′0941 — Great Britain. Political strikes: General Strike, *1926.* **Causes**

Florey, R. A.. The General Strike of 1926 : the economic, political and social causes of the class war / R.A. Florey. — London : Calder, 1980. — 222p : ill,facsims,ports ; 23cm. — (Historical perspectives)
Bibliography: p209-211. - Includes index
ISBN 0-7145-3698-9 : £11.95 : CIP rev.
B80-17582

331.89′26 — Great Britain. Industries. Redundancy. Protest by personnel: Sit-ins & work-ins

Coates, Ken. Work-ins, sit-ins and industrial democracy. — Nottingham : Spokesman, May 1981. — [160]p
ISBN 0-85124-277-4 (cased) : £6.25 : CIP entry
ISBN 0-85124-278-2 (pbk) : £2.50 B81-08837

331.89′27′0941 — Great Britain. Industrial relations. Picketing — *Regulations*

Picketing / [Department of Employment]. — [London] : The Department, 1980. — 16p ; 21x10cm. — (Code of practice / Department of Employment)
Cover title
Unpriced (pbk) B81-10362

331.89′27′0941 — Great Britain. Picketing. Codes of practice. Drafts — *Inquiry reports*

Great Britain. *Parliament. House of Commons. Employment Committee.* The legal immunities of trade unions and other related matters : draft codes of practice on picketing and the closed shop : record report from the Employment Committee, Session 1979-80. — London : H.M.S.O., 1980. — viiip ; 25cm
ISBN 0-10-028229-6 (unbound) : £1.10
Primary classification 331.88′92′0941
B81-07323

331.89′281072142 — London. Camden *(London Borough).* **Newspaper publishing industries: Times Newspapers. Industrial relations. Strikes,** *1978-1979*

Jacobs, Eric. Stop press : the inside story of The Times dispute / Eric Jacobs. — London : Deutsch, 1980. — 166p,[4]p of plates : ill,ports ; 23cm
Includes index
ISBN 0-233-97286-2 : £6.95 : CIP rev.
B80-23002

331.89′282383′094382 — Poland. Gdansk. Dockyards: Stocznia Gdańska im. Lenina. Political strikes, *1980 — Polish texts*

Gdańsk 1980 : oczyma świadków / wybór i tłumaczenie Barbara Toruńczyk. — Londyn : Polonia Book Fund, 1980. — 135p : ill,ports ; 22cm
ISBN 0-902352-17-2 (pbk) : £4.50 B81-29775

331.89′2869142′0941 — Great Britain. Steel industries. Industrial reactions. Strikes, *1980 — Socialists workers′ party viewpoints*

Steel workers′ power : the steel strike and how we could have won it. — [London] ([265 Seven Sisters Rd., N.4]) : [Produced and distributed for the SWP by Socialists Unlimited], [1980]. — 32p : ill,ports ; 21cm
Cover title
ISBN 0-905998-12-x (pbk) : £0.30 B81-37872

331.89′287721′09427665 — Lancashire. Preston. Cotton manufacturing industries. Industrial relations. Strikes, *1853-1854*

Dutton, H. I.. 'Ten per cent and no surrender' : the Preston Strike, 1853-1854 / H.I. Dutton, J.E. King. — Cambridge : Cambridge University Press, 1981. — viii,274p : ill,1map ; 24cm
Bibliography: p251-261. — Includes index
ISBN 0-521-23620-7 : £18.50 B81-33219

331.89′2944581 — France. Loire *(Département).* **Industrial relations. Strikes,** *1871-1914.* **Socioeconomic aspects**

Hanagan, Michael P.. The logic of solidarity : artisans and industrial workers in three French towns 1871-1914 / Michael P. Hanagan. — Urbana ; London : University of Illinois Press, c1980. — xv,261p : ill,maps,1plan ; 24cm. — (The Working class in European history)
Bibliography: p222-252. - Includes index
ISBN 0-252-00758-1 : £9.00 B81-08773

331.89′2973 — United States. Industrial relations. Strikes, *1881-1974*

Edwards, P. K.. Strikes in the United States 1881-1974 / P.K. Edwards. — Oxford : Blackwell, 1981. — xvi,336p : ill ; 23cm. — (Warwick studies in industrial relations)
Includes index
ISBN 0-631-12518-3 : £19.50 : CIP rev.
B81-02574

332 — FINANCE

332 — Euro-currency markets. Borrowers, *1976-1979 — Directories*

The **Directory** of Euromarket borrowers. — London : Euromoney in association with Commerzbank, c1980. — xxx,301p ; 21cm
ISBN 0-903121-16-6 (pbk) : Unpriced
B81-11018

332 — Finance

Chandler, Lester V.. The economics of money and banking. — 8th ed. / Stephen M. Goldfeld, Lester V. Chandler. — New York ; London : Harper & Row, c1981. — xii,628p : col.ill,1col.map ; 24cm
Previous ed.: 1977. — Includes bibliographies and index
ISBN 0-06-041236-4 (pbk) : £6.95 B81-22977

Lomax, David F.. The euromarkets and international financial policies / David F. Lomax and P.T.G. Gutmann ; foreword by Samuel Brittan. — London : Macmillan, Oct. 1980. — xxxi,259p ; 23cm
Includes bibliographies and index
ISBN 0-333-23998-9 : £20.00 : CIP rev.
B80-20316

332 — International capital markets & international money markets

Kemp, L. J.. A guide to world money and capital markets. — London : McGraw-Hill, Sept.1981. — [648]p
ISBN 0-07-084566-2 : £40.00 : CIP entry
B81-20192

332 — International capital markets — *For investors*

International capital markets : an investors′ guide / prepared by Orion Bank. — London : Euromoney, c1979. — 99p : ill ; 30cm
ISBN 0-903121-11-5 (pbk) : Unpriced
B81-09874

332′.023′41 — Great Britain. Finance — *Career guides — For graduates — Serials*

Graduate careers in accountancy business & finance : for graduates and postgraduates. — 2nd ed. (1979)-. — London : New Opportunity Press, 1979-. — v. : ill ; 22cm
Irregular. — Continues: Graduate careers in accountancy, finance & law. — Description based on: 3rd ed. (1981)
ISSN 0260-0722 = Graduate careers in accountancy, business & finance for graduates and postgraduates : £2.50 B81-09104

332.024 — Personal finance

Wolf, Harold A.. Personal finance / Harold A. Wolf. — Boston, Mass. ; London : Allyn and Bacon, c1981. — xiii,560p : ill(some col.),facsims,forms ; 25cm
Previous ed.: c1978. — Includes index
ISBN 0-205-07298-4 : £19.95 B81-16300

332.024 — Personal finance — *For schools*

Butler, David, *19---*. Moneywise / David Butler. — London : Harrap, 1981. — 39p : ill ; 28cm
ISBN 0-245-53517-9 (pbk) : £1.75 B81-26562

332.024 — Personal finance — *Manuals*

Fingleton, Eamonn. The Penguin money book / Eamonn Fingleton and Tom Tickell. — Harmondsworth : Penguin, 1981. — 222p ; 19cm. — (Penguin handbooks)
ISBN 0-14-046384-4 (pbk) : £1.50 B81-11529

Wyn, Mary. A year of saving / Mary Wyn. — Bognor Regis : New Horizon, c1980. — 83p ; 22cm
ISBN 0-86116-433-4 : £3.25 B81-21705

332.024′0076 — Personal finance — *Questions & answers*

Morley, Jennifer. Managing your money / Jennifer Morley. — London : Edward Arnold, 1981. — iv,44p : ill,forms ; 25cm
ISBN 0-7131-0519-4 (pbk) : £1.60 B81-24952

332.024′00941 — Great Britain. Personal finance — *For expatriate British personnel*

Brown, Harry, *1933-*. Working abroad? : personal money management for the UK expatriate / by Harry Brown. — 4th ed. — London : Financial Times Business Publishing, 1981. — 122p : ill,1port ; 24cm
Previous ed.: 1979. — Includes index
ISBN 0-901369-59-4 (pbk) : Unpriced B81-28928

332.024′00941 — Great Britain. Personal finance — *Manuals*

Gibbs, Julian. Living with inflation / [Julian Gibbs]. — 4th ed. — Havant : Mason [for] Julian Gibbs Associates Limited
ISBN 0-85937-272-3 (pbk) : £1.25 B81-27017

Living with inflation. — Havant : Mason
2: A simple guide to saving money : profitably and tax efficiently / [Julian Gibbs, Diana Wright]. — Summer ed., 1981. — c1981. — 48p : ill ; 22cm
Previous ed.: 1981. — Includes index
ISBN 0-85937-273-1 (pbk) : £1.25 : CIP rev. B81-19214

Simpson, Desmond. Your money and your life / Desmond Simpson. — Bideford (Old Ford House, New Rd., Bideford, Devon, EX39 5JG) : Two Rivers, 1981. — 128p : ill ; 18cm
Includes index
ISBN 0-907639-00-3 (pbk) : £2.50 B81-38671

332′.024′00941 — Great Britain. Personal finance — *Manuals*

Wilson, Harriet. Money matters : the Money-go-round guide to personal finance / Harriet Wilson ; illustrated by Jim Friell. — London : Pan, 1981. — 223p : ill,2forms ; 18cm. — (Pan information)
ISBN 0-330-26180-0 (pbk) : £1.25 B81-05449

332.024′00941 — Great Britain. Personal finance — *Practical information*

Head, Robert. You and your cash : a lifetime′s guide to managing your money / by Robert Head and John Husband. — London : Mirror Books, 1981. — 28p : ill(some col.) ; 27cm
At head of title: Money Mirror
ISBN 0-85939-264-3 (unbound) : £0.50 B81-23241

The **Which?** book of money. — London : Consumers′ Association, 1980. — 240p : ill (some col.),col.facsims,col.map ; 26cm
Includes index
ISBN 0-340-25049-6 : £8.95 (£7.95 to members) B81-02050

332.024′00973 — United States. Personal finance

Schiller, Margery Kabot. Personal and family finance : principles and applications / Margery Kabot Schiller. — Boston [Mass.] ; London : Allyn and Bacon, c1981. — viii,300p : ill,forms ; 25cm
Includes index
ISBN 0-205-07095-7 : £12.75 B81-03473

332.024′00973 — United States. Personal finance — *For schools*

Poe, Roy W.. Getting involved with business / Roy W. Poe, Herbert G. Hicks, Olive D. Church. — New York ; London : McGraw-Hill, 1981. — x,566p : ill,forms ; 24cm
Includes index
ISBN 0-07-050335-4 : £9.95
Primary classification 658′.00722 B81-17037

332.024′00973 — United States. Personal finance — *Manuals*

Swaton, J. Norman. Personal finance : getting along and getting ahead / J. Norman Swaton. — New York ; London : D. Van Nostrand, 1981. — x,453p : ill,facsims,forms ; 23cm
Includes bibliographies and index
ISBN 0-442-28116-1 (pbk) : £11.95 B81-11441

332.024′01 — Great Britain. Early retirement. Financial provision — *Practical information*

Guide to early retirement / [IDS]. — London (140 Great Portland St., W.1) : Incomes Data Services Ltd, 1981. — 114p : 2ill,2forms ; 25cm
Bibliography: p111-112. — Includes index
Unpriced (pbk) B81-22192

332.024′01 — Great Britain. Retirement. Financial provision — *Practical information*

Assersohn, Roy. Express money book of prosperous retirement. — London : Quartet Books, Jan.1982. — [128]p
ISBN 0-7043-3397-x (pbk) : £2.50 : CIP entry B81-40249

Jackson, Stanley, *1945-*. Planning your pension / Stanley Jackson. — London : Oyez, 1980. — 152p : 1ill ; 22cm
Includes index
ISBN 0-85120-505-4 (pbk) : £8.50 B81-14490

332.024′01 — Great Britain. Retirement. Financial provision — *Practical information — For self-employed persons*

Self-employed pensions handbook 1981 / editor Janet Walford ; editorial assistant Coos Verweij. — London : Financial Times Business Publishing, c1981. — 230p ; 24cm
ISBN 0-901369-55-1 (pbk) : Unpriced B81-28927

332.024′01 — Great Britain. Retirement. Policies of government. Financial aspects

Fogarty, Michael P.. Retirement age and retirement costs / Michael P. Fogarty. — London : Policy Studies Institute, c1980. — iii,93p : 2ill ; 21cm. — (PSI report ; no.592)
ISBN 0-85374-187-5 (pbk) : £3.95 B81-05341

332.024′042′0941 — Great Britain. Women. Personal finance — *Serials*

YF : yours financially : managing your money, maximising your wealth. — No.1 (May 1980)-. — London (13 Golden Sq., W1R 4AG) : Stonehart & Chantry, 1980-. — v. ; 27x13cm
Monthly. — Continues: WFL
ISSN 0144-7165 = YF. Yours financially : £16.80 per year B81-02347

332′.03′21 — Finance — *Encyclopaedias*

Perry, F. E.. A selected vocabulary of financial terms / F.E. Perry. — London : Waterlow, 1981. — 127p ; 21cm
ISBN 0-900791-70-5 (pbk) : Unpriced B81-38658

Robinson, David F.. Key definitions in finance and accounting / David Robinson. — London : Muller, 1980. — 125p : ill ; 21cm. — (A language of its own)
ISBN 0-584-10546-0 (cased) : £5.95 : CIP rev.
ISBN 0-584-10556-8 (pbk) : £3.95
Also classified at 657′.03′21 B80-27258

332′.041 — Capital. Measurement

The **Measurement** of capital / edited by Dan Usher. — Chicago ; London : University of Chicago Press, 1980. — ix,557p : ill ; 24cm. — (Studies in income and wealth ; v.45)
Conference papers. — Includes bibliographies and index
ISBN 0-226-84300-9 : £24.00 B81-00776

332′.0415 — Capital formation

Giarini, Orio. Dialogue on wealth and welfare : an alternative view of world capital formation : a report to the Club of Rome / by Orio Giarini. — Oxford : Pergamon, 1980. — xxv,386p, 1 folded leaf of plates : ill,1map,2facsims ; 21cm. — (Pergamon international library)
Includes index
ISBN 0-08-026088-8 (cased) : £20.00
ISBN 0-08-026087-x (pbk) : £10.00 B81-03522

332′.0415 — Industries. Capital. Utilisation

Betancourt, Roger R.. Capital utilization : a theoretical and empirical analysis / Roger R. Betancourt, Christopher K. Clague. — Cambridge : Cambridge University Press, 1981. — xx,245p : ill ; 24cm
Bibliography: p234-240. — Includes index
ISBN 0-521-23583-9 : £25.00 B81-34524

332′.04154 — Industrial projects. Financing

Nevitt, *Peter K.*. Project financing / by Peter K. Nevitt. — London : Euromoney, c1980. — 175p : ill ; 30cm
Includes index
ISBN 0-903121-10-7 (pbk) : Unpriced B81-11016

332′.04154′094285 — Great Britain. New small firms. Financing, *1971-1979 — Study regions: Cleveland*

Storey, D. J.. Finance for the new firm / by D.J. Storey. — [Newcastle upon Tyne] ([Newcastle upon Tyne NE1 7RU]) : University of Newcastle upon Tyne Centre for Urban and Regional Development Studies, 1981. — 37leaves ; 30cm. — (Discussion paper / University of Newcastle upon Tyne Centre for Urban and Regional Development Studies, ISSN 0140-6515 ; no.36)
Bibliography: leaf 37
Unpriced (pbk) B81-30926

332′.042 — International finance

Feiger, George. Instructor′s manual and notes to cases to accompany International finance : text and cases / George Feiger, Bertrand Jacquillat. — Boston, Mass. ; London : Allyn and Bacon, c1981. — 81p : 1ill ; 22cm
Cover title
ISBN 0-205-07138-4 (pbk) : £1.00 B81-40104

Feiger, George. International finance : text and cases / George Feiger, Bertrand Jacquillat. — Boston ; London : Allyn and Bacon, c1982. — xxii,453p : ill ; 24cm
Includes index
ISBN 0-205-07137-6 (cased) : Unpriced
ISBN 0-205-07602-5 (international student ed) : £17.95 B81-29212

332′.042 — International finance — *For banking*

Cox, D. B.. Finance of international trade / by D.B. Cox. — Northwick (15 Constance Rd., Northwick, Worcester WR3 7NF) : Northwick, c1980. — 268p : ill,forms ; 30cm. — (Personal course for bankers)
ISBN 0-907135-03-x (pbk) : Unpriced B81-27706

332'.042'0904 — International finance, *1945-1979*
Argy, Victor. The postwar international money crisis : an analysis / Victor Argy. — London : Allen & Unwin, 1981. — x,438p : ill ; 23cm
Bibliography: p411-433. — Includes index
ISBN 0-04-332075-9 (cased) : Unpriced
ISBN 0-04-332076-7 (pbk) : Unpriced
B81-34277

332'.042'0959 — ASEAN countries. Finance. Regional cooperation
Skully, Michael T.. ASEAN regional financial co-operation developments in banking and finance / by Michael T. Skully. — [Singapore] : Institute of Southeast Asian Studies ; Caterham (26 Manor Ave., Caterham, Surrey) : Australiana, 1979. — 78 leaves ; 30cm
ISBN 0-909162-13-1 (spiral) : £5.50
B81-08345

332'.05 — Finance — *Serials*
Finance director's review. — Vol.1, no.1 (19 Nov.1980)-. — Croydon : Tolley, 1980-. — v. ; 30cm
Fortnightly
ISSN 0260-1176 = Finance director's review : £50.00 per year B81-09211

332'.072 — Finance. Research. Factor analysis & principal components analysis. Methodology
Johnson, K. J.. Pitfalls in applying principal components and factor analysis in finance / by K.J. Johnson. — Manchester ([P.O. Box 88], Manchester M60 1QD) : Department of Management Sciences, University of Manchester Institute of Science and Technology, [1980?]. — 26p ; 31cm. — (Occasional paper / Department of Management Sciences, University of Manchester Institute of Science and Technology ; no.8008)
Bibliography: p25-26
Unpriced (pbk) B81-09626

332'.09172'4 — Developing countries. Finance
Drake, P. J.. Money, finance and development / P.J. Drake. — Oxford : Robertson, 1980. — xi,244p : ill ; 23cm
Bibliography: p230-239. - Includes index
ISBN 0-85520-185-1 : £15.00 : CIP rev.
B80-08630

332'.092'4 — United States. Finance. Morgan, J. Pierpont — *Biographies*
Sinclair, Andrew. Corsair : the life of J. Pierpoint Morgan / Andrew Sinclair. — London : Weidenfeld and Nicolson, 1981. — xiv,269p,[16]p of plates : ill,ports ; 24cm
Bibliography: p251-255. — Includes index
ISBN 0-297-77864-1 : £10.00 B81-26076

332'.092'4 — Wales. Finance. Hodge, *Sir* Julian — *Biographies*
O'Sullivan, Timothy. Julian Hodge : a biography / Timothy O'Sullivan ; foreword by George Thomas. — London : Routledge & Kegan Paul, 1981. — xi,210p,[16]p of plates : ill,1facsim,port ; 24cm
Includes index
ISBN 0-7100-0592-x : £8.95 : CIP rev.
B81-21506

332'.0941 — Great Britain. Finance
Bain, Andrew D.. The economics of the financial system. — Oxford : Robertson, Oct.1981. — [288]p
ISBN 0-85520-451-6 (cased) : £15.00 : CIP entry
ISBN 0-85520-452-4 (pbk) : £5.95 B81-30179

Carter, H.. Applied economics in banking and finance. — 2nd ed. — Oxford : Oxford University Press, Sept.1981. — [416]p
Previous ed.: 1979
ISBN 0-19-877171-1 (cased) : £12.50 : CIP entry
ISBN 0-19-877172-x (pbk) : £5.95 B81-26690

332'.0941 — Great Britain. Finance — *For banking*
Heydon, Roy. Monetary economics 'B' : study guide / by Roy Heydon. — [Edinburgh] ([20 Rutland Square, Edinburgh]) : Institute of Bankers in Scotland, [1980?]. — 89p : ill ; 26cm
£2.50 (pbk) B81-07689

MacDougall, M. S.. Monetary economics 'A' : study guide / by M.S. MacDougall and D. Jenkins. — [Edinburgh] ([20 Rutland Square, Edinburgh]) : Institute of Bankers in Scotland, [1979?]. — 20p ; 25cm
£2.00 (pbk) B81-07688

332'.09669 — Nigeria. Finance
The **Foundations** of Nigeria's financial infrastructure / edited by J.K. Onoh. — London : Croom Helm, 1980. — 318p ; 23cm
Includes index
ISBN 0-7099-0448-7 (pbk) : £19.95 : CIP rev.
B80-09613

332'.097 — North America. Finance
Guenther, Harry. Banking and finance in North America / Harry Guenther. — London : Financial Times Business, c1981. — xi,269p ; 21cm. — (A Banker Research Unit survey)
ISBN 0-902998-43-9 (pbk) : Unpriced
B81-37726

332'.0973 — United States. Finance
Henning, Chales N.. Financial markets and the economy / Charles N. Henning, William Pigott, Robert Haney Scott. — 3rd ed. — Englewood Cliffs ; London : Prentice-Hall, c1981. — xii,602p : ill ; 25cm
Previous ed.: 1978. — Includes bibliographies and index
ISBN 0-13-316067-x : £13.65 B81-18318

Makinen, Gail E.. Money, banking, and economic activity / by Gail E. Makinen. — New York ; London : Academic Press, c1981. — xiv,561p : ill ; 25cm
Includes bibliographies and index
ISBN 0-12-468950-7 : £10.20 B81-35437

332.1 — BANKS AND BANKING

332.1 — Banking — *Islamic viewpoints*
Rahman, Afzalur. Banking and insurance / Afzalur Rahman. — London (78 Gillespie Rd, N5 1LN) : Muslim Schools Trust, 1979. — 424p ; 22cm. — (Economic doctrines of Islam ; v.4)
ISBN 0-907052-03-7 (cased) : £7.80
ISBN 0-907052-02-9 (pbk) : £3.80
Also classified at 368 B81-30091

332.1 — Banking. Role of capital, *to 1978*
Wilcox, Malcolm G.. Capital in banking : an historical survey / Malcolm G. Wilcox. — London : Institute of Bankers, [1979]. — 39p : 1ill,1port ; 22cm
Cover title
Unpriced (pbk) B81-22747

332.1 — Banks. Capital. Management
Gardener, Edward P. M.. Capital adequacy and banking supervision / Edward P.M. Gardener. — Bangor : University of Wales Press, 1981. — 189p : ill ; 26cm. — (Bangor occasional papers in economics, ISSN 0306-9338 ; no.19)
Bibliography: p177-189
ISBN 0-7083-0785-x (pbk) : Unpriced
B81-36094

332.1 — Financial institutions. Effects of inflation
Revell, Jack. Inflation & financial institutions / by Jock Revell assisted by members of the Institute of European Finance. — London : Financial Times Ltd., c1979. — 187p : ill ; 30cm
Includes index
ISBN 0-903199-30-0 (spiral) : Unpriced
B81-09280

332.1 — United States. Futures money markets
Powers, Mark. Inside the financial futures markets / Mark Powers, David Vogel. — New York ; Chichester : Wiley, c1981. — xvii,320p : ill ; 24cm
Includes index
ISBN 0-471-08136-1 : £12.50 B81-17246

332.1'023 — Banking — *Career guides*
Moss, Stephen. Careers in banking. — London : Kogan Page, Oct.1981. — [100]p
ISBN 0-85038-482-6 (cased) : £5.95 : CIP entry
ISBN 0-85038-483-4 (pbk) : £2.50 B81-30199

332.1'025 — Banks — *Directories* — *Serials*
The **Bankers'** almanac and year book. — 136th year (1980-81). — London : Thomas Skinner Directories, c1981. — 2596p in various pagings
ISBN 0-611-00647-2 : Unpriced B81-09126

332.1'025'5 — Asia. Financial institutions — *Directories* — *Serials*
Guide to banks & other financial institutions in Asia (including Iran & the Arab Region). — [19--]-. — Manchester (84 Liverpool Rd, Cadishead, Manchester M30 5AN) : Middle East Economic Publications, [19--]-. — v. ; 22cm
Description based on 1980 issue
ISSN 0260-6186 = Guide to banks & other financial institutions in Asia, including Iran & the Arab region : Unpriced B81-04827

332.1'025'56 — Middle East. Financial institutions — *Directories* — *Serials*
Middle East financial directory. — 1981. — London (21 John St., WC1N 2BP) : Middle East Economic Digest Ltd., 1981. — x,314p
ISBN 0-9505211-4-0 : Unpriced B81-32271

332.1'068'1 — Banks. Assets. Management. Mathematical models
Szegö, G. P.. Portfolio theory : with application to bank asset management / Giorgio P. Szegö. — New York ; London : Academic Press, 1980. — xiv,215p : ill ; 24cm. — (Economic theory, econometrics and mathematical economics)
Bibliography: p207-210. — Includes index
ISBN 0-12-680780-9 : £16.00 B81-21835

332.1'068'3 — Banking. Personal management — *Manuals*
Management and people in banking / editor Bryan L. Livy. — London : Institute of Bankers, 1980. — xi,262p : ill ; 21cm
ISBN 0-85297-058-7 (pbk) : £7.95 B81-04054

332.1'068'3 — Banks. Personnel management
Summers, Donald B.. Personnel management in banking / Donald B. Summers. — New York ; London : McGraw-Hill, c1981. — vi,698p : ill,forms ; 25cm
Bibliography: p687-690. — Includes index
ISBN 0-07-062558-1 : £29.95 B81-31874

332.1'068'8 — Banks. Services. Marketing. Techniques — *Manuals*
Richardson, Linda. Bankers in the selling role : a consultative guide to cross selling financial services / Linda Richardson. — New York ; Chichester : Wiley, c1981. — xiv,168p : forms ; 24cm
Includes index
ISBN 0-471-09010-7 : £13.35 B81-28310

332.1'068'8 — Great Britain. Marketing by banks
McIver, Colin. Marketing financial services / Colin McIver and Geoffrey Naylor ; with a foreword by Deryk Vander Weyer. — London : Institute of Bankers, 1980. — 291p : ill ; 22cm
Bibliography: p285-288. — Includes index
ISBN 0-85297-054-4 (cased) : £9.95
ISBN 0-85297-055-2 (pbk) : £7.95 B81-01811

332.1'09172'4 — Developing countries. Rural regions. Money markets
Borrowers & lenders : rural financial markets and institutions in developing countries / edited by John Howell. — London : Overseas Development Institute, c1980. — v,290p : ill ; 21cm
Includes index
ISBN 0-85003-072-2 (pbk) : £2.95 B81-05210

332.1'0917'4927 — Arab banking — *Serials*
Arab banker : journal of the Arab Bankers Association. — Vol.1, no.1 (Apr.1981)-. — London (1 Hanover St., W1R 9WB) : The Association. — v. ; 28cm
Six issues yearly
ISSN 0261-2925 = Arab banker : Unpriced
B81-33283

332.1'094 — European Community countries. Banking

Banking structures and sources of finance in the European Community / [edited by Anne Hendrie]. — 4th ed. — London : Financial Times Business Publishing, c1981. — 327p ; 21cm. — (A Banker Research Unit survey)
Previous ed.: 1979
ISBN 0-902998-40-4 (pbk) : Unpriced
B81-28929

332.1'094 — European Community countries. Banking. Regulation

The **Regulation** of banks in the member states of the EEC / edited by IBRO (Inter-Bank Research Organisation) ; foreword by Lord O'Brien of Lothbury. — Alphen aan den Rijn : Sijthoff & Noordhoff ; London : Graham & Trotman, 1978. — xi,323p ; 25cm
Summary table in pocket. — Includes bibliographies and index
ISBN 90-286-0738-2 : £40.00 B81-30930

332.1'0941 — Great Britain. Banking

Battrick, David. Using bank services in the United Kingdom / [written by David Battrick]. — [London] ([1 Little New St., EC4A 3TR]) : Touche Ross International, 1980. — v,46p ; 21cm
Text on inside covers
Unpriced (pbk) B81-12570

Holden, J. Milnes. The law and practice of banking. — 3rd ed. — London : Pitman
Vol.1: Banker and customer. — Dec.1981. — [544]p
Previous ed.: 1974
ISBN 0-273-01761-6 : £12.95 : CIP entry
B81-31462

Perry, F. E.. The elements of banking. — 3rd ed. — London : Methuen, Sept.1981. — [400]p
Previous ed.: 1977
ISBN 0-416-32080-5 (pbk) : £5.50 : CIP entry
B81-23785

Valentine, S. P.. Banking / Stuart Valentine and Stan Mason. — 2nd ed. — Sevenoaks : Teach Yourself Books, 1981. — viii,310p : forms ; 18cm. — (Business & management studies) (Teach yourself books)
Previous ed.: published as Basics of banking. 1976. — Bibliography: p303. — Includes index
ISBN 0-340-25979-5 (pbk) : £2.95 : CIP rev.
B81-13799

332.1'0941 — Great Britain. Banking *compared with* **banking in West Germany**

The **British** and German banking system : a comparative study / prepared by Economists Advisory Group Ltd. for the Anglo-German Foundation. — [London] : [The Foundation], c1981. — xx,419p ; 21cm
Bibliography: p409-418
ISBN 0-905492-35-8 (pbk) : £9.50
Also classified at 332.1'0943 B81-29872

332.1'0941 — Great Britain. Banking — *Questions & answers*

Ryder, F. R.. Banking problems and their solutions / compiled and edited by F.R. Ryder. — 2nd (rev.) ed. — London : Waterlow, 1980. — 198p ; 22cm
Previous ed.: 1970
ISBN 0-900791-61-6 : £8.50 B81-20006

332.1'0941 — Great Britain. Banks — *For consumers*

Elkington, Wendy. Beat your bank manager / Wendy Elkington. — London : Oyez, 1981. — 95p ; 21cm. — (Owl books)
Includes index
ISBN 0-7063-6018-4 (cased) : £4.95
ISBN 0-7063-6019-2 (pbk) : Unpriced
B81-27122

332.1'0941 — Great Britain. Financial institutions

Craig, Malcolm. Invisible Britain : handling money? - discover how to get the best deal / Malcolm Craig. — Newbury (3 Sandford House, Kingsclere, Newbury, Berks, RG15 8PA) : Scope, 1981. — iv,124p : ill,1map ; 23cm
ISBN 0-906619-08-4 : Unpriced : CIP rev.
B81-06615

332.1'09421'2 — London *(City).* **Financial institutions**

Irving, Joe, *1920-*. The City at work : a guide to the institutions that make up the City of London and their roles / Joe Irving ; introduction by Nicholas Goodison. — London : Deutsch, 1981. — 188p ; 23cm
Includes index
ISBN 0-233-97328-1 : £5.95 B81-22198

332.1'0943 — West Germany. Banking *compared with* **banking in Great Britain**

The **British** and German banking system : a comparative study / prepared by Economists Advisory Group Ltd. for the Anglo-German Foundation. — [London] : [The Foundation], c1981. — xx,419p ; 21cm
Bibliography: p409-418
ISBN 0-905492-35-8 (pbk) : £9.50
Primary classification 332.1'0941 B81-29872

332.1'0952 — Japan. Banking

Prindl, Andreas R.. Japanese finance. — London : Wiley, Dec.1981. — [144]p
ISBN 0-471-09982-1 : £8.50 : CIP entry
B81-31831

332.1'09669 — Nigeria. Banking

Ajayi, Simeon Ibi.. Money and banking : analysis and policy in the Nigerian context / Simeon Ibi. Ajayi and Oladeji O. Ojo. — London : Allen & Unwin, 1981. — x,274p : ill ; 22cm
Includes bibliographies and index
ISBN 0-04-330318-8 (pbk) : Unpriced : CIP rev.
Also classified at 332.4'9669 B81-15886

332.1'09669 — Nigeria. Financial institutions

Nwankwo, G. O.. The Nigerian financial system / G.O. Nwankwo. — London : Macmillan, 1980. — 184p : ill ; 26cm
Bibliography: p178-180. - Includes index
ISBN 0-333-25684-0 (cased) : £15.00 : CIP rev.
ISBN 0-333-25685-9 (pbk) : £6.95 B79-19004

332.1'0973 — United States. Financial institutions

Simpson, Thomas D.. Money, banking, and economic analysis / Thomas D. Simpson. — 2nd ed. — Englewood Cliffs ; London : Prentice-Hall, c1981. — xii,435p : ill,1map ; 25cm
Previous ed.: 1976. — Includes bibliographies and index
ISBN 0-13-600205-6 : £12.30 B81-17221

332.1'2'05 — Commercial banking — *Serials*

Retail banker international : a bi-weekly bulletin on consumer financial services worldwide. — Issue No.1 (18 May 1981)-. — London (392 Goldhawk Rd, W6 0SB) : Michael Lafferty Publications, 1981-. — v. : ports ; 30cm
ISSN 0261-1740 = Retail banker international : £198.00 per year B81-32662

332.1'2'0941 — Great Britain. Commercial banks: Yorkshire Bank Limited, *to 1980*

Broomhead, Leslie James. The great oak : a story of the Yorkshire Bank / Leslie James Broomhead. — Leeds (20 Merrion Way, Leeds LS2 8NZ) : Yorkshire Bank, 1981. — 100p,[10]leaves of plates : ill,ports ; 22cm
Unpriced (pbk) B81-27278

332.1'2'09411 — Scotland. Provincial banks, *1747-1864*

Munn, C. W.. The Scottish provincial banking companies 1747-1864 / Charles W. Munn. — Edinburgh : Donald, c1981. — 306p ; 25cm
Bibliography: p289-298. - Includes index
ISBN 0-85976-071-5 : £15.00 B81-17120

332.1'2'094279 — Isle of Man. Commercial banks: Dumbell's Banking Company, *to 1900*

Chappell, Connery. The Dumbell affair / Connery Chappell ; photographs by W.S. Basnett. — Prescot (Prescot, Merseyside [L34 5SD]) : Stephenson, 1981. — xii,126p : ill,facsims,ports(some col.) ; 26cm
ISBN 0-901314-21-8 : £8.95 B81-05855

332.1'2'09429 — Wales. Commercial banks: Commercial Bank of Wales, *to 1980*

A **Banking** enterprise / Commercial Bank of Wales Limited. — [Cardiff] ([114 St. Mary St., Cardiff CF1 1XJ]) : Commercial Bank of Wales Limited, 1981. — [8]p + 2leaves of text : col.ill ; 30cm
Cover title. — Ill on inside covers. — Two leaves of text as inserts
Unpriced (pbk) B81-19421

332.1'2'0973 — United States. Commercial banking

Compton, Eric N.. Inside commercial banking / Eric N. Compton. — New York ; Chichester : Wiley, c1980. — xiii,191p ; 24cm
Bibliography: p184-185. — Includes index
ISBN 0-471-07974-x : £10.95 B81-00034

332.1'2'0994 — Australia. Commercial banks. Diversification

Skully, Michael T.. The diversification of Australia's trading banks / M.T. Skully. — Caterham (26 Manor Ave., Catherham, Surrey) : Australiana Publications, c1980. — 61p ; 30cm
Cover title
ISBN 0-909162-15-8 (spiral) : £2.50
B81-05994

332.1'5 — International banking

Sampson, Anthony. The money masters. — London : Hodder & Stoughton, Sept.1981. — [320]p
ISBN 0-340-25719-9 : £8.50 : CIP entry
B81-20594

332.1'5 — International liquidity. Role of banks

Cohen, Benjamin J.. Banks and the balance of payments : private lending in the international adjustment process / Benjamin J. Cohen in collaboration with Fabio Basagni. — Montclair : Allanheld, Osmun ; London : Croom Helm, 1981. — xi,243p ; 24cm. — (An Atlantic Institute for International Affairs research volume)
Includes index
ISBN 0-7099-0711-7 : £15.95 B81-33443

332.1'5 — Lending by banks. Country risks. Assessment

Nagy, Pancras J.. Country risk : how to assess, quantify and monitor it / by Pancras J. Nagy. — London : Euromoney, c1979. — 111p : ill ; 30cm + flow chart(1sheet : 1ill ; 41x59cm)
ISBN 0-903121-07-7 (pbk) : Unpriced
B81-11014

332.1'5 — Offshore banking

Chown, John F.. Offshore financial centres. — 4th ed. / rev. by Mary Cook. — London : Financial Times Business, 1981. — xv,285p ; 21cm. — (A Banker Research Unit survey)
Written by John Chown. — Previous ed.: 1979
ISBN 0-902998-41-2 (pbk) : Unpriced
B81-36848

332.1'5 — Syndicated medium-term Euro-credit markets

Johnston, R. B.. Banks' international lending decisions and the determination of spreads on syndicated medium-term euro-credits / by R.B. Johnston. — London ([Threadneedle St., EC2R 8AH]) : Economics Division, Bank of England, c1980. — 47p ; 30cm. — (Discussion paper / Bank of England, ISSN 0142-6753 ; no.12)
Bibliography: p47
ISBN 0-903312-31-x (pbk) : Unpriced
B81-07994

332.1'5'02854404 — International banks. Computer systems. Networks

Veith, Richard H.. Multinational computer nets : the case of international banking / Richard H. Veith. — Lexington, Mass. : Lexington Books ; [Aldershot] : Gower [distributor], 1981. — xvii,133p : ill ; 24cm
Bibliography: p115-126. — Includes index
ISBN 0-669-04092-4 : £12.50 B81-38599

332.1′5′0941 — British international banks: Standard Chartered Bank, *to 1980*

A **History** of the Standard Chartered Bank. — [London] ([10 Clements La., E.C.4]) : Standard Chartered Bank, [1980]. — 4v. : ill,maps,facsims,ports ; 27cm
In slipcase. — Includes index. — Contents: Realms of silver / Compton Mackenzie. Originally published: London : Routledge & Kegan Paul, 1954 - The first hundred years of the Standard Bank / compiled by J.A. Henry and edited by H.A. Siepmann. Originally published: London : Oxford University Press, 1963 - Bankers in West Africa / Richard Fry. Originally published: London : Hutchinson, 1976 - A story brought up to date
Private circulation B81-22416

332.1′53 — International Development Association. Finance — *Proposals*

International Development Association. Sixth replenishment of IDA resources : advance contributions : resolution of the executive directors dated 8 August 1980. — London : H.M.S.O., [1981]. — [5]p ; 25cm. — (Cmnd. ; 8156)
ISBN 0-10-181560-3 (unbound) : £1.10 B81-13954

332.1′7 — United States. Finance. Exchange media. Applications of digital computer systems. Social aspects

Bequai, August. The cashless society : EFTS at the crossroads / August Bequai. — New York ; Chichester : Wiley, c1981. — xi,298p ; 24cm
Bibliography: p288-292. - Includes index
ISBN 0-471-05654-5 : £12.50 B81-17084

332.1′753′0941 — Great Britain. Banks. Lending. Control. Competition and Credit Control System, *to 1980*

Zawadzki, K. K. F.. Competition and credit control / K.K.F. Zawadzki. — Oxford : Basil Blackwell, 1981. — viii,184p : ill ; 22cm
Bibliography: p179-181. — Includes index
ISBN 0-631-12724-0 (cased) : £15.00
ISBN 0-631-12545-0 (pbk) : £5.95 B81-31928

332.1′753′0941 — Great Britain. Lending by banks. Implications of variation in trade cycles

Dyer, L. S.. Lending in booms and slumps / by L.S. Dyer ; delivered under the auspices of King′s College London. — [London] : King′s College London (London : Walter Bargery, [1981]). — 35p ; 25cm. — (Gilbart lectures on banking ; 1981)
Text on inside Cover
£2.00 (pbk) B81-15375

332.1′753′0941 — Great Britain. Lending by banks — *Manuals*

Dyer, L. S.. A practical approach to bank lending / L.S. Dyer. — 2nd ed. — London : Institute of Bankers, 1980. — viii,237p ; 21cm
Previous ed.: 1974. — Includes index
ISBN 0-85297-056-0 (pbk) : £4.50 B81-07705

332.2 — SPECIALISED BANKING INSTITUTIONS

332.2′1 — Great Britain. Trustee savings banks. Deposits — *Accounts* — *Serials*

Fund for the banks for savings accounts. — 1979-80. — London : H.M.S.O., 1981. — 6p
ISBN 0-10-237381-7 : £1.10 B81-35970

332.2′1′0941 — Great Britain. *Department for National Savings.* **Securities. Investment** — *Practical information*

Investing in national savings. — 1980 ed.. — [London] ([4th Floor, Charles House, 375, Kensington High St., W14 8SB]) : Department of National Savings, [1980?]. — 58p
B81-06481

332.3 — CREDIT AND LOAN INSTITUTIONS

332.3′2′0724 — Great Britain. Building societies. Econometric models

Pratt, M. J.. Building societies : an econometric model / by M.J. Pratt. — London ([Threadneedle St.,] EC2R 8AH) : Economics Division, Bank of England, c1980. — 53p ; 30cm. — (Discussion paper / Bank of England, ISSN 0142-6753 ; no.11)
Bibliography: p53
ISBN 0-903312-26-3 (pbk) : Unpriced
B81-02934

332.3′2′0941 — Great Britain. Building societies

Building societies and the consumer : a report / by Marianne Rigge and Michael Young of the Mutual Aid Centre. — London : National Consumer Council, c1981. — 77p ; 30cm
ISBN 0-905653-30-0 (spiral) : Unpriced
B81-17051

332.3′2′0941 — Great Britain. Building societies, *to 1979*

Ashworth, Herbert. The building society story / Herbert Ashworth. — London : Franey, 1980. — 252p,[8]p of plates : ports ; 22cm
Includes index
ISBN 0-900382-38-4 : Unpriced B81-38125

332.3′4 — Great Britain. Pawnbroking, *to 1981*

Hudson, Kenneth. Pawnbroking — an aspect of British social history. — London : Bodley Head, Feb.1982. — [168]p
ISBN 0-370-30447-0 : £6.95 : CIP entry
B81-36372

332.4 — MONEY

332.4 — Monetarism

Brittan, Samuel. How to end the ′Monetarist′ controversy : a journalist′s reflections on output, jobs, prices and money / Samuel Brittan. — London : Institute of Economic Affairs, 1981. — 132p : ill ; 22cm. — (Hobart papers, ISSN 0073-2818 ; 90)
Bibliography: p127-130
ISBN 0-255-36144-0 (pbk) : £2.50 B81-32752

Desai, Meghnad. Testing monetarism. — London : Frances Pinter, Dec.1981. — [288]p
ISBN 0-903804-77-8 : £15.00 : CIP entry
B81-40256

Is monetarism enough? : essays in refining and reinforcing the monetary cure for inflation / Patrick Minford ... [et al.] with contributions by Michael Beenstock ... [et al.] ; chairman, Arthur Seldon. — London : Institute of Economic Affairs, 1980. — x,117p : ill ; 21cm. — (IEA readings, ISSN 0305-814x ; 24)
Conference papers. — Includes bibliographies
ISBN 0-255-36131-9 (pbk) : £3.00 B81-00035

332.4 — Monetary systems

Hawthorne, Jennie. Theory and practice of money / Jennie Hawthorne. — London : Heinemann, 1981. — xiii,257p : ill ; 22cm. — (The Heinemann accountancy and administration series)
Includes index
ISBN 0-434-90715-4 (pbk) : £6.95 B81-35538

332.4 — Money

Crump, Thomas. The phenomenon of money. — London : Routledge & Kegan Paul, Oct.1981. — [356]p
ISBN 0-7100-0856-2 : £10.00 : CIP entry
B81-28080

Riboud, Jacques. The mechanics of money / Jacques Riboud ; translated by Stephen Harrison ; foreword by Fritz Machlup. — London : Macmillan, 1980. — 319p : ill ; 23cm
Translation of: Mécanique des monnaies, d′aujourd′hui et de demain. — Includes index
ISBN 0-333-27808-9 : £20.00 : CIP rev.
B80-09614

332.4′01 — Monetary system. Theories

Harris, Laurence. Monetary theory / Laurence Harris. — New York ; London : McGraw-Hill, c1981. — xi,481p : ill ; 25cm. — (Economics handbook series)
Bibliography: p465-476. — Includes index
ISBN 0-07-026840-1 : £16.95 B81-10767

332.4′028 — English gold folding coin balances, *ca 1700-ca 1900*

Crawforth, Michael A.. Weighing coins : English folding gold balances of the 18th and 19th centuries / by Michael A. Crawforth. — London (12 New Row, WC2N 4LF) : Cape Horn Trading, 1979. — viii,194p : ill,facsims ; 22cm
Bibliography: p181-184. — Includes index
ISBN 0-9506578-0-8 : £16.00 B81-02770

332.4′042′0942356 — Devon. Exeter. Coinage, *890-1872*

Andrews, John, *1934- Sept. 3-*. Exeter coinage / John Andrews William Elston, Norman Shiel. — [Exeter] (Department of Economic History, University of Exeter) : Exeter Industrial Archaeology Group, c1980. — 84p : ill,1map ; 21cm
Bibliography: p81-84
ISBN 0-906231-02-7 (pbk) : £2.40 B81-36731

332.4′042′0947717 — Ukraine. Crimea. Coinage, *B.C.400-A.D.1200*

Anokhin, V. A.. The coinage of Chersonesus : IV century B.C. -XII century A.D. / V.A. Anokhin ; translated from the Russian by H. Bartlett Wells. — Oxford : B.A.R., 1980. — 182p,[16]p of plates : ill ; 30cm. — (BAR. International series, ISSN 0143-3067 ; 69)
Bibliography: p175-181
ISBN 0-86054-074-x (pbk) : £8.50 B81-16551

332.4′042′0956 — Middle East. Coinage, *1100-1300* — *Conference proceedings*

Oxford Symposium on Coinage and Monetary History *(4th : 1979 Sept. 6-8)*. Coinage in the Latin East / the Fourth Oxford Symposium on Coinage and Monetary History ; edited by P.W. Edbury and D.M. Metcalf. — Oxford : B.A.R., 1980. — iv,148p : ill ; 30cm. — (BAR. International series ; 77)
ISBN 0-86054-086-3 (pbk) : £6.00 B81-16545

332.4′05 — Money — *Forecasts* — *Serials*

Currency forecasting service. — Issue 79-1 (Feb.12, 1979)-. — London (70 Warren St., W1P 5PA) : Institute for International Research, 1979-. — v. ; 28cm
Weekly. — Description based on: Issue 79-12 (July 16, 1979)
Unpriced B81-05180

332.4′1 — Finance. Inflation

Friedman, Irving S.. Inflation : a world-wide disaster / Irving S. Friedman. — London : Hamilton, 1980. — xxii,327p ; 21cm
Previous ed.: Boston, Mass : Houghton Mifflin ; London : Hamilton, 1973. — Includes index
ISBN 0-241-10554-4 (pbk) : £4.95 B81-08999

Hahn, Frank. Money and inflation. — Oxford : Basil Blackwell, Nov.1981. — [112]p. — (Mitsui lecture series)
ISBN 0-631-12917-0 : £6.95 : CIP entry
B81-30173

Hudson, John. Inflation. — London : Allen and Unwin, Feb.1982. — [176]p
ISBN 0-04-339025-0 : £13.95 : CIP entry
B81-35926

Tylecote, Andrew. The causes of the present inflation : an interdisciplinary explanation of inflation in Britain, Germany and the United States / Andrew Tylecote. — London : Macmillan, 1981. — xvi,236p : ill ; 23cm
Bibliography: p221-227. — Includes index
ISBN 0-333-19600-7 : £20.00 B81-22379

332.4′1 — Finance. Inflation. Theories

Jackman, Richard. The economics of inflation. — Oxford : Robertson, Sept.1981. — [220]p
Previous ed.: / by James Anthony Trevithick and Charles Mulvey. 1975
ISBN 0-85520-410-9 (cased) : £12.50 : CIP entry
ISBN 0-85520-411-7 (pbk) : £5.50 B81-23821

332.4'1'0941 — Great Britain. Finance. Inflation. Role of wage drift

Elliott, Robert F.. The diminishing importance of wage drift / by R.F. Elliott. — [Aberdeen] : [University of Aberdeen, Department of Political Economy], [1980]. — 30 leaves ; 30cm. — (Discussion paper / University of Aberdeen Department of Political Economy ; 80-10)
Bibliography: leaves 29-30
£1.00 (pbk) B81-06147

332.4'5 — Europe. Euro-dollar market, *1963-1979*

Fisher, Frederick G.. The Eurodollar bond market / by Frederick G. Fisher, III. — London : Nestor House, Playhous Yard, EC4 : Euromoney, c1979. — 200p : ill ; 30cm
Bibliography: p198. - Includes index
ISBN 0-903121-09-3 (pbk) : £30.00 B81-07152

332.4'5 — Foreign exchange

Walker, Townsend. A guide for using the foreign exchange market / Townsend Walker. — New York ; Chichester : Wiley, c1981. — ix,372p : ill ; 25cm
Bibliography: p363-365. — Includes index
ISBN 0-471-06254-5 : £16.75 B81-33155

332.4'5 — Foreign exchange. Risks. Management

Kenyon, Alfred. Currency risk management / Alfred Kenyon. — Chichester : Wiley, c1981. — vii,191p : ill ; 24cm
Includes bibliographies and index
ISBN 0-471-10003-x : £9.75 : CIP rev.
B81-27942

The **Management** of foreign exchange risk / edited by Richard Ensor and Boris Antl. — London : Euromoney, [1979?]. — 200p : ill ; 30cm
ISBN 0-903121-06-9 (pbk) : Unpriced
B81-11013

332.4'5 — International monetary system

Kindleberger, Charles P.. International money : a collection of essays / Charles P. Kindleberger. — London : Allen & Unwin, 1981. — viii,341p : 2ill ; 23cm
Includes index
ISBN 0-04-332077-5 (cased) : Unpriced : CIP rev.
ISBN 0-04-332078-3 (pbk) : Unpriced
B81-01841

332.4'5 — International monetary system, *1944-1980*

Gilbert, Milton. Quest for world monetary order : the gold-dollar system and its aftermath / Milton Gilbert ; with posthumous editing by Peter Oppenheimer and Michael Dealtry. — New York ; Chichester : Wiley, c1980. — xx,255p ; 24cm. — (A Twentieth Century Fund study)
Includes index
ISBN 0-471-07998-7 : £9.95 B81-03912

332.4'5 — International monetary system, *1945-1980 — Marxist viewpoints*

Parboni, Riccardo. Finance and international crisis. — London : New Left Books, Sept.1981. — [224]p
Translation of: Finanza e crisi internazionale
ISBN 0-86091-046-6 (cased) : £9.50 : CIP entry
ISBN 0-86091-744-4 (pbk) : £3.50 B81-30148

332.4'5 — International monetary system, *1945-1981*

Tew, Brian. The evolution of the international monetary system, 1945-1981. — 2nd ed. — London : Hutchinson Education, Jan.1982. — [272]p
Previous ed.: 1977
ISBN 0-09-145910-9 (cased) : £12.50 : CIP entry
ISBN 0-09-145911-7 (pbk) : £5.50 B81-34474

332.4'5 — International monetary system. Influence of commercial banks of United States

Aronson, Jonathan David. Money and power : banks and the world monetary system / Jonathan David Aronson ; preface by Susan Strange ; written under the auspices of the Center for International Affairs. — Beverly Hills ; London : Sage, c1977. — 224p ; 23cm. — (Sage library of social research ; v.66)
Bibliography: p199-211. — Includes index
ISBN 0-8039-0998-5 (cased) : £11.25
ISBN 0-8039-1046-0 (pbk) : Unpriced
B81-18846

332.4'5 — International monetary system. Reform. Role of stockpiling of commodities

Hallwood, Paul. Commodity stockpiling externalities and monetary reform / by Paul Hallwood. — [Aberdeen] : University of Aberdeen, Dept. of Political Economy, 1981. — 20p : ill. — (Discussion paper / University of Aberdeen. Department of Political Economy ; no.81-11)
Unpriced (pbk) B81-40834

332.4'5'02465 — Foreign exchange — *For companies*

Heywood, John, *1940-*. Foreign exchange and the corporate treasurer. — 3rd ed., rev. and extended. — London : Black, Nov.1981. — [208]p
Previous ed.: 1979
ISBN 0-7136-2185-0 : £9.95 : CIP entry
B81-30360

332.4'5'02854404 — Foreign exchange. Applications of real time computer systems

Hulle, Eddy van. Design of an integrated real-time foreign exchange application / Eddy Van Hulle. — Bognor Regis : New Horizon, c1980. — 181p : ill ; 22cm
Bibliography: p177-181
ISBN 0-86116-521-7 : £5.25 B81-21817

332.4'52 — Reserve currencies: American dollars

Morrell, James. The future of the dollar and the world reserve system / James Morrell. — London : Butterworths, 1981. — ix,145p : ill ; 24cm
Bibliography: p135-138. — Includes index
ISBN 0-408-10674-3 (cased) : Unpriced
ISBN 0-408-10675-1 (pbk) : Unpriced
B81-26064

332.4'54 — Euro-currency systems

Versluysen, Eugène L.. The political economy of international finance / Eugène L. Versluysen. — Farnborough, Hants. : Gower, c1981. — x,266p ; 23cm
Includes index
ISBN 0-566-00448-8 : Unpriced : CIP rev.
B81-09487

332.4'56 — Foreign exchange. Flexible rates — *Festschriften*

Flexible exchange rates and the balance of payments : essays in memory of Egon Sohmen / edited by John S. Chipman, Charles P. Kindleberger. — Amsterdam ; Oxford : North-Holland, 1980. — ix,368p : ill,1port ; 25cm. — (Studies in international econonmics ; v.7)
Bibliography: p355-358. — Includes index
ISBN 0-444-86045-2 : £23.17 B81-09431

332.4'56'0212 — Foreign exchange. Rates — *Tables — Serials*

Charles Fulton's foreign exchange yearbook : a listing of daily foreign exchange rates, Euro-currency deposit rates and sterling money market rates ... with a commentary on international developments. — 1981 ed.-. — Cambridge : Woodhead-Faulkner in association with Charles Fulton & Co., 1981-. — v. ; 30cm
Annual. — Continues: Foreign exchange yearbook
ISSN 0262-0979 = Charles Fulton's foreign exchange yearbook : Unpriced B81-37969

332.4'560941 — Sterling area, *1931-1939*

Drummond, Ian M.. The floating pound and the sterling area 1931-1939 / Ian M. Drummond. — Cambridge : Cambridge University Press, 1981. — vii,308p ; 24cm
Includes index
ISBN 0-521-23165-5 : £19.50 B81-17934

332.4'56'0945 — Italy. Foreign exchange. Rates. Adjustment. Effects of monetary policies, *1945-1978*

Tullio, Giuseppe. The monetary approach to external adjustment : a case study of Italy / Giuseppe Tullio ; foreword by Paolo Baffi. — London : Macmillan, 1981. — xx,127p : ill ; 22cm
Bibliography: p114-123. — Includes index
ISBN 0-333-27651-5 : £15.00
Primary classification 382.1'7'0945 B81-38726

332.4'56'0973 — United States. Foreign exchange. Rates. Effects of decisions of multinational companies on foreign exchange

Rodriguez, Rita M.. Foreign-exchange management in U.S. multinationals / Rita M. Rodriguez. — Lexington, Mass. : Lexington ; [Farnborough, Hants.] : Gower [distributor], 1980. — xii,128p : ill ; 24cm
Bibliography: p121-125. - Includes index
ISBN 0-669-02330-2 : £11.00 B81-05321

332.4'566'091722 — Developed countries. Monetary systems. Integration

Llewellyn, David J.. International financial integration : the limits of sovereignty / David T. Llewellyn. — London : Macmillan, 1980. — xii,215p : ill ; 24cm. — (Problems in economic integration)
Includes bibliographies and index
ISBN 0-333-16715-5 (pbk) : £12.00 : CIP rev.
ISBN 0-333-21130-3 (pbk) : £4.95 B80-18185

332.4'566'09174927 — Arab countries. Monetary systems. Integration — *Conference proceedings*

Arab monetary integration. — London : Croom Helm, Nov.1981. — [384]p
Conference papers
ISBN 0-7099-0712-5 : £14.95 : CIP entry
B81-31063

332.4'566'094 — European Community countries. Monetary systems. Integration

Kruse, D. C.. Monetary integration in Western Europe : EMU, EMS and beyond / D.C. Kruse. — London : Butterworths, 1980. — 274p ; 25cm. — (Butterworths European studies)
Includes index
ISBN 0-408-10666-2 : £16.00 : CIP rev.
B80-18614

332.4'6'942496 — West Midlands *(Metropolitan County).* Birmingham. Mints: Birmingham Mint, *1850-1980*

Sweeny, James O.. A numismatic history of the Birmingham Mint. — Birmingham (Icknield St., Birmingham B18 6RX) : Birmingham Mint, Oct.1981. — [256]p
ISBN 0-9507594-0-6 : £10.95 : CIP entry
B81-25744

332.4'91724 — Developing countries. Monetary policies

Money and monetary policy in less developed countries : a survey of issues and evidence / edited by Warren L. Coats, Jr and Deena R. Khatkhate. — Oxford : Pergamon, 1980. — xiv,827p : ill ; 26cm
Bibliography: p763-810. — Includes index
ISBN 0-08-024041-0 (cased) : £40.00 : CIP rev.
ISBN 0-08-024042-9 (pbk) : £8.50 B80-00079

332.4'91724 — Developing countries. Money

Ghatak, Subrata. Monetary economics in developing countries / by Subrata Ghatak. — London : Macmillan, 1981. — xi,174p : ill ; 25cm
Bibliography: p161-170. — Includes index
ISBN 0-333-26140-2 (cased) : Unpriced : CIP rev.
ISBN 0-333-26141-0 (pbk) : Unpriced
B80-20320

332.4'91812 — Western world. Monetary policies — *Conference proceedings*

Monetary targets / edited by Brian Griffiths and Geoffrey E. Wood. — London : Macmillan : Centre for Banking and International Finance at the City University, 1981. — x,238p : ill ; 23cm
Conference papers. — Includes bibliographies
ISBN 0-333-28746-0 : £20.00 B81-25332

332.4′937 — Ancient Rome. Monetary system, *300-400 — Conference proceedings*

Oxford Symposium on Coinage and Monetary History *(5th : 1979 Sept. 28-30).* Imperial revenue, expenditure and monetary policy in the fourth century A.D. / the Fifth Oxford Symposium on Coinage and Monetary History ; edited by C.E. King. — Oxford : B.A.R., 1980. — viii,280p : ill,maps ; 30cm. — (BAR. International series ; 76)
Includes 2 papers in French
ISBN 0-86054-084-7 (pbk) : £10.00 B81-16547

332.4′941 — Great Britain. Economic conditions. Effects of government monetary policies

Brennan, H. Geoffrey. Monopoly in money and inflation : the case for a constitution to discipline government / H. Geoffrey Brennan and James M. Buchanan. — London : Institute of Economic Affairs, 1981. — 68p : ill ; 22cm. — (Hobart paper, ISSN 0073-2818 ; 88)
Bibliography: p67-68
ISBN 0-255-36138-6 (pbk) : £1.50 B81-11046

332.4′941 — Great Britain. Foreign exchange. Rates *Related to* **money supply**

The **Money** supply and the exchange rate / edited by W.A. Eltis and P.J.N. Sinclair. — Oxford : Clarendon, 1981. — 364p : ill ; 24cm
Includes bibliographies and index
ISBN 0-19-877168-1 (pbk) : £7.95 : CIP rev. B81-23890

332.4′941 — Great Britain. Monetary policies

Artis, M. J.. Monetary control in the United Kingdom / M.J. Artis & M.K. Lewis. — Deddington : Philip Allan, 1981. — 156p : ill ; 23cm
Bibliography: p146-152. — Includes index
ISBN 0-86003-040-7 (cased) : £10.00 : CIP rev. B81-23901

332.4′941 — Great Britain. Monetary system

Dennis, Geoffrey E. J.. Monetary economics / Geoffrey E.J. Dennis. — London : Longman, 1981. — ix,312p : ill ; 24cm. — (Modern economics)
Bibliography: p286-300. — Includes index
ISBN 0-582-45573-1 (pbk) : £6.95 B81-03497

332.4′941 — Great Britain. Money supply. Control, *1970-1980*

Gowland, David. Controlling the money supply. — London : Croom Helm, Feb.1982. — [208]p
ISBN 0-7099-1105-x (cased) : £12.95 : CIP entry
ISBN 0-7099-1116-5 (pbk) : £7.95 B81-37556

332.4′941 — Great Britain. Money supply. Econometric models

Coghlan, Richard, *1944-.* Money, credit and the economy / Richard Coghlan. — London : Allen & Unwin, 1981. — x,208p : ill ; 23cm
Bibliography: p191-202. - Includes index
ISBN 0-04-332079-1 : Unpriced : CIP rev. B81-02544

Hilliard, B. C.. The Bank of England small monetary model : recent developments and simulation properties / by B.C. Hilliard. — London ([Threadneedle St.,] EC2R 8AH) : Economics Division, Bank of England, c1980. — 43p : ill ; 30cm. — (Discussion paper / Bank of England, ISSN 0142-6753 ; no.13)
Bibliography: p43
ISBN 0-903312-32-8 (pbk) : Unpriced B81-02882

332.4′941′0724 — Great Britain. Monetary system, *1964-1980.* **Dynamic econometric models**

Hoffman, J. M.. A quarterly small monetary model of the UK economy : preliminary estimation and simulation results / by J.M. Hoffman. — London (EC2R 8AH) : Economics Division, Bank of England, c1980. — 64p : ill ; 30cm. — (Discussion paper / Bank of England, ISSN 0142-6753 ; no.14)
Bibliography: p63-64
ISBN 0-903312-33-6 (pbk) : Unpriced B81-05489

332.4′94234 — Channel Islands. Money — *Early works — Facsimiles*

Ansted, D. T.. The Channel Islands : money, weights, and measures / D.T. Ansted. — St. Peter Port : Toucan Press, 1981. — [8]p ; 21cm
Facsim of: edition published 1862
ISBN 0-85694-238-3 (pbk) : Unpriced
Also classified at 389′.15′094234 B81-17680

332.4′942342 — Guernsey. Monetary policies, *1815-1836*

Holloway, Edward. How Guernsey beat the bankers : the story of how the Island of Guernsey created its own money, without cost to the taxpayer, and established a prosperous community free of debt / by Edward Holloway. — St. Peter Port : Toucan Press, 1981. — [12]p : 2ill ; 21cm. — (Guernsey historical monograph ; no.23)
ISBN 0-85694-239-1 (pbk) : Unpriced B81-25244

332.4′9669 — Nigeria. Monetary system

Ajayi, Simeon Ibi.. Money and banking : analysis and policy in the Nigerian context / Simeon Ibi. Ajayi and Oladeji O. Ojo. — London : Allen & Unwin, 1981. — x,274p : ill ; 22cm
Includes bibliographies and index
ISBN 0-04-330318-8 (pbk) : Unpriced : CIP rev.
Primary classification 332.1′09669 B81-15886

332.4′973 — United States. Economic conditions. Effects of rational expectations of monetary policies — *Conference proceedings*

Rational expectations and economic policy / edited by Stanley Fischer. — Chicago ; London : University of Chicago Press, 1980. — ix,293p : ill ; 24cm. — (A Conference report / National Bureau of Economic Research)
Includes bibliographies and index
ISBN 0-226-25136-5 : £13.20 B81-05798

332.4′994 — Australia. Monetary policies, *1950-1975*

Rowan, D. C.. Australian monetary policy 1950-1975 / D.C. Rowan. — Sydney ; London : Allen & Unwin, 1980, c1979. — 313p : ill ; 24cm
Bibliography: p302-309. - Includes index
ISBN 0-86861-360-6 (cased) : £15.95
ISBN 0-86861-368-1 (pbk) : £15.95 B81-11365

332.6 — INVESTMENT

332.6 — European Community countries. Investments. Protection — *Conference proceedings*

Fédération internationale pour le droit européen. *Congress (9th : 1980).* Reports of the ninth Congress, 25-27 September 1980 / Fédération Internationale pour le Droit Eruopéen. — [S.l.] : FIDE ; London : Sweet & Maxwell, 1980. — 2v. ; 21cm
Includes papers in French and German
ISBN 0-421-27850-1 (pbk) : £25.00
Primary classification 341.7′8 B81-07814

332.6 — Investment. Implications of inflation

Hill, G. P.. The feasibility of financing investments using borrowed money during a period of inflation and high interest rates / G.P. Hill. — [Ashford] (Wye College, Ashford, Kent TN25 5AH) : Farm Business Unit, School of Rural Economics, 1981. — 30p : ill ; 30cm. — (F.B.U. occasional paper ; no.6)
Bibliography: p29
ISBN 0-901859-93-1 (pbk) : £2.50 B81-33329

332.6 — Investment. Portfolio analysis

Elton, Edwin J.. Modern portfolio theory and investment analysis / Edwin J. Elton, Martin J. Gruber. — New York ; Chichester : Wiley, c1981. — xvii,553p : ill ; 24cm
Includes index
ISBN 0-471-04690-6 : Unpriced B81-08517

332.6 — Investment. Risks. Measurement — *Serials*

Risk measurement service / London Business School. — Vol.1, no.1 (Jan.1979)-. — London (Sussex Place, Regent′s Park, NW1 4SA) : LBS Financial Services, 1979-. — v. : ill ; 30cm
Quarterly. — Description based on: Vol.3, no.2 (Apr.1981)
ISSN 0261-3344 = Risk measurement service : £145.00 per year (£58.00 to academic libraries) B81-32274

332.6 — Investments

Sharpe, William F.. Investments / William F. Sharpe. — 2nd ed. — Englewood Cliffs ; London : Prentice-Hall, c1981. — xviii,654p : ill ; 24cm
Previous ed.: 1978. — Includes index
ISBN 0-13-504613-0 : £12.95 B81-22712

332.6′03′21 — Investment — *Encyclopaedias*

Brownstone, David M.. The VNR investor′s dictionary / David M. Brownstone, Irene M. Franck. — New York ; London : Van Nostrand Reinhold, c1981. — vi,326p ; 24cm
ISBN 0-442-21578-9 : £12.70 B81-02288

332.6′0724 — United States. Investment. Portfolios. Management. Simulations

Gitman, Lawrence J.. Portstrat : a portfolio strategy simulation / Lawrence J. Gitman, Abderrahman Robana, William D. Biggs. — New York ; Chichester : Wiley, c1981. — 132p : ill,forms ; 28cm
Bibliography: p79-81
ISBN 0-471-08416-6 (pbk) : £6.75 B81-09661

332.6′0941 — Great Britain. Investment

Davies, J. R. (Jeffrey Rowe). Investment in the British economy / J.R. Davies and S. Hughes. — London : Heinemann Educational, 1980. — 63p : ill ; 20cm. — (Studies in the British economy)
Includes index
ISBN 0-435-84352-4 (pbk) : £1.80 : CIP rev. B80-03526

Winfield, R. G.. Success in investment. — 2nd ed. — London : J. Murray, Oct.1981. — [384]p
Previous ed.: / by Peter Roots. 1974
ISBN 0-7195-3839-4 : £3.95 : CIP entry B81-28113

332.6′0941 — Great Britain. Investment — *For banking*

Lothian, Alexander. Theory and practice of investment : study guide / by Alexander Lothian. — 4th ed. — [Edinburgh] ([20 Rutland Sq., Edinburgh]) : Institute of Bankers in Scotland, [1980]. — 70p ; 30cm + specimen documents(21p : 33cm)
Cover title. — Bibliography: p57
£3.00 (pbk) B81-06632

332.6′0941 — Great Britain. Investment — *Serials*

Allied Hambro investment guide. — 1981. — London : Oyez Publishing, c1981. — x,267p
ISBN 0-85120-566-6 : Unpriced B81-28711

The **Fund** manager′s letter. — Issue no.1 (Nov.1980)-. — London (Bracken House, 10 Cannon St., EC4P 4BY) : Financial Times Business Information, 1980-. — v. ; 30cm
Monthly
ISSN 0261-0434 = Fund manager′s letter : Unpriced B81-15081

332.6′0973 — United States. Investment. Implications of inflation — *For investors*

Croom, George E.. How you can profit from inflation / George E. Croom, Jr., John Van Der Wal. — New York ; London : Van Nostrand Reinhold, c1981. — ix,245p : ill ; 24cm
Includes index
ISBN 0-442-25397-4 : £11.20 B81-21236

332.6′2′0942 — England. Commodity brokers — *Statistics — Serials*

Commodity brokers England & Wales. — 1st ed.-. — London : Inter Company Comparisons, 1978-. — v. ; 21x30cm. — (ICC financial survey)
Annual. — Description based on: 3rd ed.
ISSN 0261-5819 = ICC financial surveys. Commodity brokers England & Wales : £65.80 per year B81-33695

332.63 — Capital investment. Analysis

Steiner, Henry Malcolm. Public and private investments : socioeconomic analysis / Henry Malcolm Steiner. — New York ; Chichester : Wiley, c1980. — x,414p : ill ; 25cm
Includes bibliographies and index
ISBN 0-471-01625-x : £16.30 B81-00778

332.6'3 — Strategic metals. Investment

Robbins, Peter. Investing in strategic metals. — London : Kogan Page, Dec.1981. — [224]p
ISBN 0-85038-522-9 (cased) : £15.00 : CIP entry
ISBN 0-85038-522-9 (pbk) : £5.95 B81-30887

332.6'32 — Great Britain. Companies. Dividends — *Statistics — Serials*

Extel dividend record. — 1979/1980. — London (37, Paul St., EC2A 4PB) : Extel Statistical Services, c1980. — iii,286p
ISSN 0141-8327 : Unpriced B81-05639

332.63'2'0973 — United States. Investments: Securities. Investment

Tiniç, Seha M.. Investing in securities : an efficient markets approach / Seha M. Tiniç, Richard R. West. — Reading, Mass. ; London : Addison-Wesley, c1979. — xi,612p : ill ; 25cm
Includes bibliographies and index
ISBN 0-201-07631-4 : Unpriced B81-37977

332.63'22 — Great Britain. Companies. Shares. Marketing

Fanning, David. Marketing company shares. — Farnborough : Gower, Dec.1981. — [250]p
ISBN 0-566-02174-9 : £15.00 : CIP entry B81-31654

332.63'22 — Great Britain. Organisations issuing stocks & shares — *Directories — Serials*

The **Register** of registrars. — 1981. — London (37 Paul St., EC2A 4PB) : Extel Statistical Services, 1981. — iv,207p
ISSN 0482-1319 : Unpriced B81-22399

332.63'221 — India *(Republic)*. **Equity shares. Rate of return**

Gupta, L. C.. Rates of return on equities : the Indian experience / L.C. Gupta. — Delhi ; Oxford : Oxford University Press, 1981. — xv,148p ; 22cm
Bibliography: p143-144. — Includes index
ISBN 0-19-561312-0 : £5.95 B81-38506

332.63'222'0724 — Stocks & shares. Prices. Adjustment. Econometric models

Fung, W. K. H.. The empirical properties of alternative procedures for estimating betas with nonsynchronous data / W.K.H. Fung. — Manchester (P.O. Box 88, Manchester M60 1QD) : Department of Management Sciences, University of Manchester Institute of Science and Technology, 1981. — 11,8p ; 31cm. — (Occasional paper / Department of Management Sciences, University of Manchester Institute of Science and Technology ; no.8101)
Bibliography: p11
Unpriced (pbk) B81-18010

332.63'222'0941 — Great Britain. Stocks & shares. Prices adjusted for capital gains tax — *Statistics — Serials*

Extel capital gains tax service / compiled ... by Extel Statistical Services Limited. — 1965/66-1980/81. — London (37 Paul St., EC2A 4PB) : Extel Statistical Services, c1981. — 2v.
ISSN 0141-8335 : Unpriced B81-36561

Extel capital record / compiled ... by Extel Statistical Services Limited. — 1974/75-1980/81. — London (37 Paul St., EC2A 4PB) : Extel Statistical Services, c1981. — xxvi, 1364p
ISSN 0140-3214 : Unpriced B81-31025

332.63'24'0941 — Great Britain. Investments: Real property. Valuation

Baum, Andrew. The income approach to property valuation / Andrew Baum and David Mackmin. — 2nd ed. — London : Routledge & Kegan Paul, 1981. — xii,216p : ill ; 22cm
Previous ed.: 1979. — Bibliography: p206-210. — Includes index
ISBN 0-7100-0833-3 (pbk) : £4.95 B81-23075

332.63'24'0973 — United States. Real property. Investment

Greer, Gaylon E.. The real estate investment decision / Gaylon E. Grear. — Lexington : Lexington Books, c1979 ; [Farnborough, Hants.] : Gower [distributor], 1980. — xix,308p : ill ; 24cm. — (Lexington Books special series in real estate and urban land economics)
Includes index
ISBN 0-669-01951-8 : £14.75 B81-11080

McMullen, Charles W.. Real estate investments : a step by step guide / Charles W. McMullen. — New York ; Chichester : Wiley, c1981. — 174p : ill,forms ; 24cm. — (Real estate for professional practitioners)
Includes index
ISBN 0-471-08365-8 : £9.60 B81-16318

332.63'24'0973 — United States. Real property. Investment — *Manuals*

Walters, David W.. The intelligent investors guide to real estate / David W. Walters. — New York ; Chichester : Wiley, c1980. — xvii,367p ; 24cm. — (Real estate for professional practitioners, ISSN 0190-1087)
Includes index
ISBN 0-471-07874-3 : £9.60 B81-09788

332.63'244 — United States. Investments: Real property. Valuation. Mortgage-equity analysis

Johnson, Irvin E.. Instant mortgage-equity : extended tables of overall rates / Irvin E. Johnson. — Lexington : Published in conjunction with the National Association of Independent Fee Appraisers [by] Lexington, c1980 ; [Farnborough, Hants.] : Gower [distributor], 1981. — viii,454p : ill ; 24cm. — (Lexington Books special series in real estate and urban land economics)
Includes index
ISBN 0-669-03808-3 : £18.50 B81-17761

332.63'27 — Great Britain. Investment trusts — *Serials*

Investment trust year book. — 78-. — London : [Financial Times Business Publ. Ltd.] in Co-operation with the Association of Investment Trust Companies, 1978-. — v. : ports ; 26cm
Annual. — Official year book of: the Association of Investment Trust Companies. — Description based on: 79 issue
ISSN 0261-3891 = Investment trust year book : £8.45 per issue B81-33048

Investment trust year book. — 1980. — London : Financial Times Business Pub. Ltd. in co-operation with the Association of Investment Trust Companies, c1980. — 190p
ISBN 0-901369-48-9 : Unpriced
ISSN 0261-3891 B81-33054

Investment trust year book. — 81. — London : Financial Times Business Pub. Ltd. in co-operation with the Association of Investment Trust Companies, c1981. — 196p
ISBN 0-901369-57-8 : Unpriced
ISSN 0261-3891 B81-33055

332.63'27 — Great Britain. Unit trusts. Accounts — *Inquiry reports*

Unit Trust Association. Unit trust accounts : joint working party report / by the Unit Trust Association and Companies Division, Department of Trade. — London : Department of Trade, 1981. — 28p ; 30cm
At head of title: Department of Trade
Unpriced (pbk) B81-28723

332.63'27 — Great Britain. Unit trusts — *Serials*

The **Unit** trust year book. — 1981. — London : Financial Times Business Pub. Ltd. in co-operation with the Unit Trust Association, c1981. — 219p
ISBN 0-901369-58-6 : Unpriced B81-33718

332.63'27'0941 — Great Britain. Investment companies: Scotia Investments Limited — *Inquiry reports*

Bromley, Leonard. Scotia Investments Limited : investigations under section 165(b) of the Companies Act 1948 : report / by Leonard Bromley and John Selby Hillyer. — London : H.M.S.O., 1980. — 487,[111]p : ill,facsims ; 30cm
At head of title: Department of Trade
ISBN 0-11-513248-1 (pbk) : £21.00 B81-11346

332.63'28 — England & United States. Silver. Prices, *1273-1979*

Jastram, Roy W.. Silver : the restless metal / Roy W. Jastram. — New York ; Chichester : Wiley, c1981. — xvii,224p[3]folded leaves of plates : ill ; 24cm
Includes index
ISBN 0-471-03912-8 : £17.50 B81-33370

332.63'28 — Gold & silver. Prices — *Serials*

Gold & silver survey : world gold & silver market prices / prepared by the International Currency Review Research Unit. — Vol.1, no.1 (25 Feb.1980)-. — New York ; London (11 Regency Place, SW1P 2EA) : World Reports Ltd, 1980-. — v. : ill ; 30cm
Monthly
Unpriced B81-04831

332.64'241 — Great Britain. Securities. Prices. Determination by securities markets. Efficiency — *For accounting*

Keane, Simon M.. The efficient market hypothesis : and the implications for financial reporting / by Simon M. Keane. — London : Published for the Institute of Chartered Accountants of Scotland by Gee, 1980. — 37p ; 21cm
Bibliography. p35. - Includes index
ISBN 0-85258-198-x (pbk) : £2.95 B81-06141

332.64'4 — Commodity markets

Guide to world commodity markets / consultants John Edwards and Brian Reidy ; editor Ethel de Keyser ; assisted by Sue Brinkhurst, Anita Kogan and David Young. — [2nd ed.]. — London : Kogan Page, 1979. — 383p : ill,1map ; 24cm
Includes index
ISBN 0-85038-193-2 : £14.00 B81-10793

332.64'4 — London *(City)*. **Metal markets: London Metal Exchange —** *Serials*

Wolff's guide to the London Metal Exchange / by Rudolph Wolff & Co. Limited. — 2nd ed. (1980). — Worcester Park : Metal Bulletin, [1980]. — 320p
ISBN 0-900542-43-8 : £28.00
ISSN 0144-5960 B81-07048

332.64'4 — Metal markets — *Serials*

Economic review of the metal markets : aluminium, copper, gold, lead, nickel, platinum, silver, tin, zinc, cadmium, cobalt, molybdenum, minors / Rayner-Harwill Ltd. — 1977-1978-. — London (50 Mark La., EC3 7RJ) : Rayner-Harwill Ltd., 1978-. — v. ; 30cm
Annual. — 1979-1980 ed. issued in 2 parts. — Description based on: 1979-1980 issue
ISSN 0260-8901 = Economic review of the metal markets : £44.00 B81-09074

332.64'4'05 — Commodity markets — *Serials*

The **Public** ledger commodity year book. — 1981. — London (11 Tokenhouse Yard, EC2R 7AP) : UK Publications, c1981. — 196p
ISSN 0144-8307 : Unpriced B81-32195

332.64'52 — Stock market. Traded options — *Technical data — For investors — Serials*

Traded option service / Investment Research. — 23rd Sept.1980-. — Cambridge (28 Panton St., Cambridge CB2 1DH) : Investment Research, 1980-. — v. ; 21cm
Weekly
ISSN 0260-2296 = Traded option service : Unpriced B81-25494

332.64'52 — United States. Stock markets. Options — *For investors*

Stewart, Joseph T.. Dynamic stock option trading / Joseph T. Stewart, Jr. — New York ; Chichester : Wiley, c1981. — xvi,193p : ill,facsims,1form ; 25cm
Bibliography: p181. — Includes index
ISBN 0-471-08670-3 : £20.00 B81-24222

332.6'7254 — Great Britain. Superannuation schemes. Funds. Investment. Control by financial institutions

Minns, Richard. Pension funds and British capitalism : the ownership and control of shareholdings / Richard Minns. — London : Heinemann, 1980. — viii,176p : ill ; 23cm
Includes index
ISBN 0-435-84510-1 : £13.00 : CIP rev. B80-34622

332.6'7254 — Great Britain. Superannuation schemes. Funds. Investment. Control by financial institutions *continuation*

Plender, John. That's the way the money goes. — London : Andre Deutsch, Nov.1981. — [224]p
ISBN 0-233-97398-2 : £6.95 : CIP entry
B81-31075

332.6'73'0973 — United States. Capital investment by foreign investors

Starchild, Adam. Investing in the US : resolving the legal, financing, regulatory and tax issues / by Adam Starchild. — London : Euromoney, [1980?]. — 119p ; 30cm
ISBN 0-903121-12-3 (pbk) : Unpriced
B81-19765

332.6'73'0973 — United States. Investment by foreign investors

Khoury, Sarkis J.. Transnational mergers and acquisitions in the United States / Sarkis J. Khoury. — Lexington : Lexington Books ; [Farnborough, Hants.] : Gower [distributor], 1981, c1980. — xix,293p : ill ; 24cm
Includes index
ISBN 0-669-03960-8 : £17.50 B81-22950

332.6'7341'00212 — Foreign capital investment by British companies — *Statistics — Serials*

Census of overseas assets. Supplement / Business Statistics Office. — 1974-. — London : H.M.S.O., 1981. — v. ; 30cm. — (Business monitor ; MA4)
Issued every three years. — Supplement to: Overseas transactions. — Description based on: 1978 issue
ISSN 0261-8923 = Census of overseas assets. Supplement : £4.70 B81-35972

332.6'7341'0595 — Malaysia. Industries. Foreign capital investment by British companies, *1963-1972*

Saham, Junid. British industrial investment in Malaysia 1963-1971 / Junid Saham. — Kuala Lumpur ; Oxford : Oxford University Press, 1980. — xxi,353p : ill ; 26cm. — (East Asian social science monographs)
Bibliography: p328-346. — Includes index
ISBN 0-19-580418-x (cased) : £17.50
ISBN 0-19-580489-9 (pbk) : Unpriced
B81-25973

332.6'7341'081 — Brazil. Foreign capital investment by British investors

Schliemann, Peter Uwe. The strategy of British and German direct investors in Brazil / Peter Uwe Schliemann. — Farnborough, Hants. : Gower, c1981. — 193p : ill,1map,facsim,forms ; 23cm
Bibliography: p182-193
ISBN 0-566-00435-6 : £16.50
Also classified at 332.6'7343'081 B81-11604

332.6'7343'081 — Brazil. Foreign capital investment by German investors

Schliemann, Peter Uwe. The strategy of British and German direct investors in Brazil / Peter Uwe Schliemann. — Farnborough, Hants. : Gower, c1981. — 193p : ill,1map,facsim,forms ; 23cm
Bibliography: p182-193
ISBN 0-566-00435-6 : £16.50
Primary classification 332.6'7341'081
B81-11604

332.6'7373 — Foreign investment by American investors — *Manuals*

Pring, Martin J.. International investing made easy : proven money-making strategies with as little as 5000 [dollars] / Martin J. Pring. — New York ; London : McGraw-Hill, c1981. — xiv,236p : ill ; 24cm
Bibliography: p225-226. - Includes index
ISBN 0-07-050872-0 : £9.95 B81-05328

332.6'78 — Investment — *Manuals*

Craig, Malcolm. Investing to survive the '80s : inside information for businessmen and investors / Malcolm Craig. — Kingsclere (3 Sandford House, Kingsclere, Newbury, Berks. RG15 8PA) : Scope, 1980. — vii,162p : 1ill ; 23cm
Includes index
ISBN 0-906619-06-8 : £5.95 : CIP rev.
B80-04704

332.6'78'0941 — Great Britain. Private investment — *Manuals*

Craig, Malcolm. Successful investment / Malcolm Craig. — London : Allen & Unwin, 1979. — xii,188p : 2ill ; 23cm
Includes index
ISBN 0-04-332069-4 : £5.95 : CIP rev.
B78-34361

Living with inflation. — Havant : Mason
1: A simple guide to lump sum investment / [Julian Gibbs]. — Winter ed. — 1981. — 62p : ill ; 21cm
Previous ed.: 1980. — Includes index
ISBN 0-85937-262-6 (pbk) : £1.25 B81-22435

Living with inflation. — Havant : Mason
2: A simple guide to saving money : profitably and tax efficiently / [Julian Gibbs and Diana Wright]. — c1981. — 48p : ill ; 21cm
Includes index
ISBN 0-85937-269-3 (pbk) : £1.25 B81-22434

332.6'78'0973 — United States. Investment — *Manuals*

Bernstein, Jacob. The investor's quotient : the psychology of successful investing in commodities and stocks / Jacob Bernstein. — New York ; Chichester : Wiley, c1980. — x,275p : ill ; 22cm
Bibliography: p269-271. - Includes index
ISBN 0-471-07849-2 : £9.00 B81-01751

332.7 — CREDIT

332.7'2'0941 — Great Britain. Mortgages — *Practical information*

Raising the money to buy your home / [edited by Edith Rudinger]. — London : Consumers' Association, c1981. — 159p : ill ; 22cm
Includes index
ISBN 0-85202-190-9 (pbk) : Unpriced
B81-09948

332.7'43 — Great Britain. Consumer credit

Consumers and credit / National Consumer Council. — [London] : [The Council], 1980. — viii,324p ; 21cm
ISBN 0-905653-29-7 (pbk) : £14.50 B81-03415

332.7'5'0941 — Great Britain. Bankruptcy — *Statistics — Serials*

Great Britain. *Department of Trade.* Bankruptcy / Department of Trade. — 1980. — London : H.M.S.O., 1981. — 22p
ISBN 0-11-513484-0 : Unpriced B81-35809

332.7'6 — Great Britain. Banks. Branches. Sorting code numbers — *Lists — Serials*

Sorting code numbers directory. — 1981. — East Grinstead : Thomas Skinner Directories, c1981. — 314p
ISBN 0-611-00650-2 : Unpriced B81-09712

332.8 — INTEREST AND DISCOUNT

332.8'2'05 — Interest rates — *Serials*

Interest rate service : running commentary, rate tables, charts / prepared by the International Currency Review Research Unit. — Vol.1, no.1 (1977)-. — New York ; London (11 Regency Place, SW1P 2EA) : Advisory Information Services, 1977-. — v. : ill ; 30cm
20 issues per year. — Description based on: Vol.2, no.7 (Oct.1978)
ISSN 0308-9002 : Unpriced B81-04545

332.8'2'0973 — United States. Interest rates. Forecasting

Pring, Martin J.. How to forecast interest rates : a guide to profits for consumers, managers, and investors / Martin J. Pring. — New York ; London : McGraw-Hill, c1981. — x,196p : ill ; 24cm
Bibliography: p191. — Includes index
ISBN 0-07-050865-8 : £10.50 B81-39258

333.1 — PUBLIC LAND

333.1'0942 — England. Community land scheme. Transactions by local authorities — *Statistics — Serials*

Community Land Act statistics. Actuals / CIPFA Statistical Information Service. — 1977-78. — London : Chartered Institute of Public Finance and Accounting, 1979. — v. ; 30cm
Absorbed by: Planning and development statistics. Actuals, 1980
ISSN 0143-2281 = Community Land Act statistics. Actuals : £4.00 B81-06774

333.1'1 — England. Local authority housing. Sale. Implications — *Inquiry reports*

Great Britain. *Parliament. House of Commons. Environment Committee.* Second report from the Environment Committee, session 1980-81 : council house sales. — London : H.M.S.O.
Vol.1: Report : together with the proceedings of the Committee relating to the report. — [1981]. — cxxxixp ; 25cm. — (HC ; 366-I) (HC ; 535 i-x (1979-80))
ISBN 0-10-299781-0 (pbk) : £5.70 B81-39640

Great Britain. *Parliament. House of Commons. Environment Committee.* Second report from the Environment Committee, session 1980-81 : council house sales. — London : H.M.S.O.. — (HC ; 366-II) (HC ; 535 i-xi (1979-80))
Vol.2: Minutes of evidence. — [1981]. — viii,408p : ill ; 25cm
ISBN 0-10-008221-1 (pbk) : £10.80 B81-40910

333.1'1 — Great Britain. Rural regions. Local authority houses. Sale — *Study regions: Oxfordshire. South Oxfordshire (District)*

The **Sale** of council houses in a rural area : a case study of south Oxfordshire / by M. Beazley ... [et al.]. — [Oxford] ([Oxford OX3 0BP]) : [Department of Town Planning, Oxford Polytechnic], [1980]. — vi leaves,66p : maps ; 30cm. — (Working paper / Oxford Polytechnic Department of Town Planning ; no.44)
Bibliography: p65-66
Unpriced (pbk) B81-07695

333.1'3 — Ireland. Land. Purchase. Funds: Irish Land Purchase Fund — *Accounts — Serials*

Irish Land Purchase Fund account. — 1979-80. — London : H.M.S.O., 1980. — 4p
ISBN 0-10-028159-1 : £1.10 B81-06228

333.1'3 — Northern Ireland. Land. Purchase — *Accounts — Serials*

Great Britain. *Supreme Court of Judicature (Northern Ireland).* Land purchase account / Supreme Court of Judicature, Northern Ireland ; [for the Treasury]. — 1979-80. — Belfast : H.M.S.O., 1981. — [3]p
ISBN 0-10-212981-9 : £0.90 B81-26579

333.2 — COMMON LAND

333.2 — England. Open field systems, *to ca 1300 — Conference proceedings*

The **Origins** of open-field agriculture / edited by Trevor Rowley. — London : Croom Helm, c1981. — 258p : ill,maps ; 23cm. — (Croom Helm historical geography series)
Conference papers. — Bibliography: p226-242. - Includes index
ISBN 0-7099-0170-4 : £14.95 B81-20787

333.2 — London. Barnet *(London Borough).* **Common land: Finchley Common,** *to ca 1840*

Davis, Fred, *1929-.* Finchley Common : a notorious place / Fred Davis. — [London] ([c/o Borough Librarian, Hendon Catholic Social Centre, Church Walk, Egerton Gardens, NW4]) : Barnet Libraries Local History, [1981]. — [16]p : ill,maps ; 20x21cm
ISBN 0-903431-07-6 (unbound) : £0.50
B81-19341

333.2 — Meath *(County).* **Duleek. Common land,** *to 1979*

Synnott, Donal M.. A Common Green : Duleek : the botany and history of a Meath Commonage / by Donal Synnott ; illustrations by Simon Coleman ; historical account by Michael Ward. — [Duleek] (["Endevere", Duleek, Co. Meath]) : Duleek Historical Society, 1980. — 28p : ill ; 22x29cm
£1.00 (pbk)
Also classified at 581.9418'22 B81-21734

333.2 — North-east England. Enclosures, *1765-1820*

Russell, Rex C.. The enclosures of Alkborough 1765-1768, West Halton 1772-1773, Whitton 1773-1775, Scotter and Scotterthorpe, 1808-1820 / by Rex C. Russell. — [Scunthorpe] : Scunthorpe Museum & Art Gallery, 1981. — 24p,[12]folded p of plates : plans ; 30cm
Cover title. — Bibliography: inside back cover
ISBN 0-9501569-2-2 (pbk) : £1.50 B81-39687

333.2 — Suffolk. Sudbury. Freeman's land, *to 1979*

Berry, Allan W.. The freemen's lands of Sudbury, Suffolk / Allan W. Berry. — Colchester (10 Blackheath, Colchester, [Essex]) : A.W. Berry, 1980. — 13p ; 21cm
£0.65 (pbk) B81-09128

333.2 — Zimbabwe. Tribal trust lands, *to 1978*

Sibanda, Concern J.. The tribal trust lands of Rhodesia : problems of development / Concern J. Sibanda. — Norwich : Geo Books for the Centre for Development Studies, University College of Swansea, 1979 (1981 [printing]). — 60p : 1ill,maps ; 22cm. — (Monograph / Centre for Development Studies, University College of Swansea, ISSN 0114-9486 ; 6)
Bibliography: p58-60. — Includes index
ISBN 0-86094-094-2 (pbk) : £2.75 B81-39867

333.3 — PRIVATE LAND

333.3'092'4 — Great Britain. Real property. Ownership — *Personal observations*

Embury, Josh. How to become a property tycoon and possibly a millionaire / Josh Embury. — Bognor Regis : New Horizon, c1981. — 53p ; 21cm
ISBN 0-86116-747-3 : £3.25 B81-32570

333.3'0941 — Great Britain. Real property. Ownership — *Conference proceedings*

Land, property and finance / edited by Martin Boddy. — Bristol : University of Bristol, School for Advanced Urban Studies, c1979. — iv,75p ; 30cm. — (Working paper / University of Bristol School for Advanced Urban Studies, ISSN 0141-464x ; 2)
Conference papers. — Includes bibliographies
£1.00 (pbk) B81-05306

333.3'0942 — England. Estates, *to 1980*

Clemenson, Heather A.. The English landed estate. — London : Croom Helm, Oct.1981. — [256]p. — (Croom Helm historical geography series)
ISBN 0-85664-987-2 : £16.95 : CIP entry
 B81-27966

333.3'1'41165 — Scotland. Highland Region. Sutherland *(District).* **Estates: Sutherland Estate. Clearances,** *1806-1820*

Forbes, David. The Sutherland clearances 1806-1820 : an introduction / by David Forbes. — Golspie (Main St., Golspie, Sutherland) : Northern Times Limited, c1977. — 44p : 1ill,maps ; 22cm
Bibliography: p44
Unpriced (pbk) B81-14211

333.3'2'0942 — England. Real property. Ownership, *1870-1914.* **Political aspects**

Offer, Avner. Property and politics, 1870-1914. — Cambridge : Cambridge University Press, Sept.1981. — [448]p
ISBN 0-521-22414-4 : £27.50 : CIP entry
 B81-25884

333.3'22'0942 — England. Land tenure, *1086.* **Domesday book** — *Critical studies*

Nicol, Alexandra. Domesday book : facsimiles with introduction / by Alexandra Nicol. — London : H.M.S.O., 1981. — 6,[9]p : facsims ; 21x30cm. — (Public Record Office Museum pamphlets ; no.10)
ISBN 0-11-440106-3 (pbk) : £1.75 B81-38179

333.3'22'0942276 — Hampshire. Southampton. Priories: St. Denys *(Priory : Southampton).* **Ecclesiastical estates** — *Cartularies — Latin texts*

St. Denys *(Priory : Southampton).* The Cartulary of the Priory of St. Denys near Southampton / edited by E.O. Blake. — Southampton : Southampton University Press, 1981. — 2v.(cxiii,357p,[4]p of plates) : ill,maps,facsims,plans ; 25cm. — (The Southampton records series ; v.24-25)
English and Latin text. — Michofiche supplements I and 2 (6 microfiches ; 11x15cm) in pocket. — Bibliography: pxi-xv. — Includes index
ISBN 0-85432-203-5 : Unpriced B81-29603

333.3'22'0942641 — Suffolk. Blythburgh. Priories: Blythburgh Priory. Ecclesiastical estates — *Cartularies*

Blythburgh Priory. Blythburgh Priory cartulary / edited by Christopher Harper-Bill. — Woodbridge : Published for the Suffolk Records Society by Boydell & Brewer. — (Suffolk charters)
ISBN 0-85115-152-3 : Unpriced B81-27014

333.3'23 — Great Britain. Second homes. **Ownership & use** — *Study regions: Powys. Brecknock (District)*

Sarre, Philip. Second homes : a case study in Brecknock / Philip Sarre. — Milton Keynes (Walton Hall, Milton Keynes, MK7 6AA) : Faculty of Social Sciences, The Open University, 1981. — 22p : ill ; 30cm. — (Social science publications / Open University, ISSN 0260-8421)
Bibliography: p22
Unpriced (pbk) B81-38261

333.3'23'0942987 — Cardiff. Bute *(Family)* **estates. Management,** *1766-1947*

Davies, John, *1938-.* Cardiff and the Marquesses of Bute / by John Davies. — Cardiff : University of Wales Press on behalf of the History and Law Committee of the Board of Celtic Studies, 1981. — x,335p,[1]p of plates : 2maps,1port,1geneal.table ; 23cm. — (Studies in Welsh history, ISSN 0141-030x ; 3)
Bibliography: p301-316. — Includes index
ISBN 0-7083-0761-2 : £12.95 : CIP rev.
 B80-05730

333.33 — REAL PROPERTY

333.33 — Real property

Harvey, J.. The economics of real property / J. Harvey. — London : Macmillan, 1981. — xii,292p : ill ; 24cm
Includes bibliographies and index
ISBN 0-333-31828-5 (cased) : £20.00
ISBN 0-333-31829-3 (pbk) : Unpriced
 B81-39953

333.33'025'41 — Great Britain. Estate agents — *Directories — Serials*

Kemps property industry year book. — 1981. — London : Kemps, c1981. — 466p
ISBN 0-905255-98-4 : Unpriced
ISSN 0260-0048 B81-19412

333.33'068'1 — Great Britain. Estates. Financial management

Miles, C. W. N.. Estate finance and business management / by C.W.N. Miles. — 4th ed. — London : Estates Gazette, c1981. — xi,244p ; 22cm
Previous ed.: 1972. — Bibliography: p35. — Includes index
£7.75 (pbk) B81-25572

333.33'0941 — Great Britain. Estate agency

Stephens, Nigel. The practice of estate agency / by Nigel Stephens ; with a foreword by P.N. Brook. — London : Estates Gazette, 1981. — ix,411p : ill,1map,forms ; 22cm
Includes index
£10.00 (pbk) B81-19751

333.33'0941 — Great Britain. Real property. Management

Business property manual. — Farnborough : Gower, Aug.1981. — [300]p
ISBN 0-566-02157-9 : £65.00 : CIP entry
 B81-16881

333.33'0942 — England. Real property. Management

Stapleton, Tim. Estate management practice / by Tim Stapleton ; with a foreword by J.N.C. James. — London : Estates Gazette, 1981. — xv,287p : ill,1form ; 22cm
Includes bibliographies and index
£9.00 (pbk) B81-15199

333.33'09794 — California. Real property

California real estate principles / Dennis J. McKenzie ... [et al.]. — New York ; Chichester : Wiley, c1981. — viii,339p : ill,1map,forms ; 29cm. — (John Wiley series in California real estate)
Includes index
ISBN 0-471-01729-9 : £11.00 B81-23242

333.33'2 — Real property. Value

Howes, Christopher K.. Value maps : aspects of land and property values / Christopher K. Howes. — Norwich : Geo Books, 1980. — 146p : maps ; 24cm
Bibliography: p138-145
ISBN 0-86094-060-8 : £6.75 B81-30774

333.33'2'09411 — Scotland. Real property. Surveying, *1749-1793* — *Correspondence, diaries, etc.*

Papers on Peter May, land surveyor 1749-1793 / edited by Ian H. Adams. — Edinburgh : Printed for the Scottish History Society by T. and A. Constable, 1979. — xlii,314p,[10]p,[2] folded p of plates : 2geneal.tables ; 23cm. — (Scottish History Society. 4th series ; v.15)
Includes index
ISBN 0-906245-05-2 : Unpriced B81-40553

333.33'2'0942 — England. Real property. Surveying — *Manuals*

Pringle, J. W. H.. Points to remember in sale and purchase of property. — Rev. ed. / by J.W.H. Pringle. — [London] : Royal Institution of Chartered Surveyors, 1981. — 9p ; 21cm. — (Practice leaflet / Royal Institution of Chartered Surveyors Land Agency and Agriculture Division, ISSN 0305-4713 ; no.2)
Previous ed.: / by Sir Donald Hawley. 1974
ISBN 0-85406-129-0 (unbound) : £0.70 (£0.60 to members) B81-40967

333.33'2'0942 — England. Real property. Valuation — *Manuals*

Thomas, John R. (John Richard). Valuations for loan purposes / by John R. Thomas. — Reading (Whiteknights, Reading RG6 2AW) : Centre for Advanced Land Use Studies, College of Estate Management, 1981. — 35p ; 25cm. — (Property valuation handbook ; B3)
Includes index
ISBN 0-902132-55-5 (pbk) : Unpriced
 B81-30910

333.33'3'0942 — England. Real property. Sale. Standard conditions: Law Society. General Conditions of Sale — *Commentaries*

Aldridge, Trevor M.. Guide to the Law Society's conditions of sale, (1980 edition) / Trevor M. Aldridge. — London : Oyez, c1981. — 14p ; 26x11cm
ISBN 0-85120-554-2 (pbk) : £2.75 B81-13610

333.33'5 — Agricultural land. Land tenure. Economic aspects

Currie, J. M.. The economic theory of agricultural land tenure / J.M. Currie. — Cambridge : Cambridge University Press, 1981. — vii,194p : ill ; 24cm
Bibliography: p188-191. — Includes index
ISBN 0-521-23634-7 : £15.00 : CIP rev.
 B81-19116

333.33'5 — England. Agricultural land. Prices — *Statistics — Serials*

Agricultural land prices in England and Wales / Ministry of Agriculture, Fisheries and Food ; Welsh Office, Agriculture Department. — 1979/80. — Pinner (Tolcarne Drive, Pinner, Middx HA5 2DT) : The Ministry ; Aberystwyth (Plas Crug, Aberystwyth, Dyfed SY23 1NG) : The Department, c1981. — 29p
Unpriced B81-32665

333.33'5 — Scotland. Highlands. Crofters. Eviction, *1746-1886*
Richards, Eric. A history of the Highland clearances. — London : Croom Helm
Vol.1. — Jan.1982. — [352]p
ISBN 0-85664-496-x : £12.95 : CIP entry
B81-33775

333.33'5'091724 — Developing countries. Land tenure *related to* **poverty in agricultural communities**
Whittemore, Claire. Land for people : land tenure and the very poor / by Claire Whittemore. — Oxford : Oxfam Public Affairs Unit, 1981. — 55p,[8]p of ill ; 21cm
ISBN 0-85598-046-x (pbk) : £1.30
Primary classification 339.4'6'091724
B81-27735

333.33'5'0942 — England. Agricultural holdings. Tenancies. Agreements — *For chartered surveyors*
Stone, R. V.. Agricultural tenancy agreements / by R.V. Stone. — [London] : Royal Institution of Chartered Surveyors, 1981. — 6p ; 21cm. — (Practice leaflet / Royal Institution of Chartered Surveyors Land Agency and Agriculture Division, ISSN 0305-4713 ; no.14)
Bibliography: p5-6
ISBN 0-85406-130-4 (unbound) : Unpriced
B81-40968

333.33'5'097217 — Mexico. Agricultural land. Land tenure. Reform, *1917-1976 — Study regions: Sonora*
Sanderson, Steven E.. Agrarian populism and the Mexican state : the struggle for land in Sonora / Steven E. Sanderson. — Berkeley ; London : University of California Press, c1981. — xx,290p : 1ill,1map ; 25cm
Bibliography: p263-277. — Includes index
ISBN 0-520-04056-2 : £13.65 B81-27500

333.33'5'097291 — Cuba. Agricultural land. Land tenure. Reform, *1958-1966*
Pollitt, Brian H.. Agrarian reform and the agricultural proletariat in Cuba, 1958-66 : further notes and some second thoughts / by Brian H. Pollitt. — [Glasgow] : [Institute of Latin American Studies], University of Glasgow, 1980. — 33p ; 30cm. — (Occasional papers / Institute of Latin American Studies University of Glasgow, ISSN 0305-8647 ; no.30)
Cover title. — Bibliography: p32-33
Unpriced (pbk) B81-13341

333.33'5'0985 — Peru. Agricultural land. Land tenure. Reform, *1968-1977*
Cleaves, Peter S.. Agriculture, bureaucracy, and military government in Peru / Peter S. Cleaves, Martin J. Scurrah. — Ithaca ; London : Cornell University Press, 1980. — 329p : ill ; 23cm
Bibliography: p299-321. — Includes index
ISBN 0-8014-1300-1 : £13.50 B81-10953

333.33'6 — Surrey. Wisley. Aerodromes: Wisley Airfield. Sale. Complaints by public — *Inquiry reports*
Great Britain. *Parliamentary Commissioner for Administration*. The sale of Wisley Airfield / Parliamentary Commissioner for Administration. — London : H.M.S.O., [1981]. — 15p ; 25cm. — ([HC] ; 322)
'Fourth Report for Session 1980-1981' - cover
ISBN 0-10-232281-3 (pbk) : £1.90 B81-36262

333.33'7 — Great Britain. Residences. Purchase & sale — *Practical information*
Lewis, David B.. Buying and selling your home / David Lewis. — London : Teach Yourself Books, 1980. — vii,164p ; 18cm. — (Teach yourself books)
Includes index
ISBN 0-340-25114-x (pbk) : £1.25 : CIP rev.
B80-10495

333.33'7'0941 — Great Britain. Urban regions. Real property. Economic aspects
Balchin, Paul N.. Urban land economics / Paul N. Balchin and Jeffrey L. Kieve. — London : Macmillan, 1977 (1979 [printing]). — xviii,278p : ill ; 22cm. — (Macmillan building and surveying series)
Bibliography: p262-263. — Includes index
ISBN 0-333-26552-1 (pbk) : £4.95 B81-02903

333.33'8 — Australia, Great Britain & Sweden. Residences. Ownership by occupiers — *Comparative studies*
Kemeny, J.. The myth of home-ownership : private versus public choices in housing tenure / J. Kemeny. — London : Routledge & Kegan Paul, 1981. — xvi,179p : ill ; 24cm
Bibliography: p160-173. — Includes index
ISBN 0-7100-0634-9 (pbk) : £6.95 : CIP rev.
B81-12831

333.33'8 — Buildings. Daylight. Valuation — *Manuals*
Anstey, John. The valuation of rights of light / by John Anstey. — Reading (Whiteknights Reading RG6 2AW) : Centre for Advanced Land Use Studies, College of Estate Management, 1981. — 14p : ill ; 25cm. — (Property valuation handbook ; B4)
ISBN 0-902132-56-3 (pbk) : Unpriced
B81-30912

333.33'8 — England. Flats. Services — *For purchasers of flats*
Buying a flat? : don't buy a lifetime of problems as well. — [London] : [Royal Institution of Chartered Surveyors], [1981?]. — 20p : ill ; 21cm
Cover title
Unpriced (pbk) B81-23245

333.33'8 — England. Houses. Purchase & sale — *Practical information*
Bradshaw, Joseph. Bradshaw's guide to D.I.Y. house buying, selling and conveyancing / by Joseph Bradshaw. — Leamington Spa (Freepost, Blackdown, Leamington Spa, CV32 6BR) : Castle Books, c1980. — xii,163p,[3] folded leaves of plates : ill,forms ; 22cm
Includes index
ISBN 0-9507170-0-2 (pbk) : £4.95
Also classified at 344.2064'38 B81-04678

333.33'8 — England. Local authority housing. Rents — *Statistics — Serials*
Housing rents statistics at April ... / CIPFA Statistical Information Service. — 1980. — London : Chartered Institute of Public Finance and Accountancy, 1980. — 40p
ISSN 0260-406x : £10.00 B81-10254

Housing rents statistics at April ... / CIPFA Statistical Information Service. — 1979-. — London : The Chartered Institute of Public Finance and Accountancy, 1980-. — v. ; 30cm
Annual. — Continues: Housing statistics (England and Wales). Part 1, Rents, rebates and allowances as at April ...
ISSN 0260-406x = Housing rents statistics : £5.50 B81-08226

333.33'8 — Great Britain. Houses. Prices. Regional variations
McAvinchey, Ian D.. Reduced form and functional form : the case of house prices in the regions of the U.K. / Ian D. McAvinchey and Duncan Maclennan. — [Aberdeen] : University of Aberdeen, Department of Political Economy, [1981]. — 21,7p ; 31cm. — (Discussion paper / University of Aberdeen Department of Political Economy ; 81-02)
Bibliography: p21
Unpriced (pbk) B81-15099

333.33'8 — Great Britain. Houses. Purchase & sale — *Practical information*
Bowers, Arthur. Daily telegraph home ownership A-Z / Arthur Bowers. — Rev. ed. / revised by Bruce Kinloch. — London : Collins, 1981. — 179p ; 20cm
Previous ed.: 1977
ISBN 0-00-434186-4 (pbk) : £1.75 B81-26907

333.33'8 — Great Britain. Offices. Rents
Office rent contours / Hillier Parker Research. — London (77 Grosvenor St., W1A 2BT) : Research Department, Hillier Parker May & Rowden, 1981. — [8]p : ill,2col.maps ; 30cm
Unpriced (unbound) B81-34276

333.33'8 — Great Britain. Residences. Sale — *Amateurs' manuals*
O'Callaghan, John J.. How to sell your house without an estate agent / by John J. O'Callaghan. — Castletown (P.O. Box 3, Castletown, Isle of man) : Sales Dynamics Lts., c1980. — 68p ; 19cm
ISBN 0-907386-00-8 (pbk) : £0.99 B81-06441

333.33'8 — Great Britain. Shops. Rents — *Forecasts — Serials*
A **Forecast** of shop rents. — No.1 (July 1977)-. — London (77 Grosvenor St., W1A 2BT) : Research Department, Hillier Parker May & Rowden, 1977-. — v. ; 30cm
Annual. — Description based on: No.4 (Sept.1980)
ISSN 0260-8812 = Forecast of shop rents : Unpriced B81-09027

333.33'8 — Scotland. Residences. Valuation surveying by building societies
Building societies : valuations and surveys / prepared by the Scottish Consumer Council's Legal Advisory Group. — Glasgow (4 Somerset Place, Glasgow G3 7JT) : Scottish Consumer Council, [1981]. — 13p ; 30cm. — (A Scottish Consumer Council report)
ISBN 0-907067-03-4 (pbk) : £1.00 B81-40836

333.33'8'0924 — London. Rented accommodation. Landlords: Rachman, Peter — *Biographies*
Green, Shirley. Rachman / Shirley Green. — Feltham : Hamlyn Paperbacks, 1981, c1979. — 240p ; 18cm
Originally published: London : Joseph, 1979. — Bibliography: p235. - Includes index
ISBN 0-600-20378-6 (pbk) : £1.50 B81-22296

333.33'8'0942 — England. Residences. Purchase — *Manuals*
Hammond, David S.. The home ownership game : and how to win it / David S. Hammond. — Newton Abbot : David & Charles, c1981. — 111p : ill ; 23cm
Bibliography: p107-108. — Includes index
ISBN 0-7153-7710-8 : £4.95 : CIP rev.
B81-00036

Vickers, L. E.. Buying a house or flat / L.E. Vickers. — 2nd ed. — Harmondsworth : Penguin, 1981. — 176p : ill ; 18cm. — (A Penguin handbook)
Previous ed. i.e. rev. ed: 1977. — Includes index
ISBN 0-14-046279-1 (pbk) : £1.75 B81-29159

333.33'8'094221 — Surrey. Residences — *Buyers' guides — Serials*
Property guide. Homes in Surrey & Hampshire. — Vol.1, no.1 (Dec.1980)-. — London (150 Caledonian Rd, N1 9RD) : Wootten, 1980-. — v. : ill ; 30cm
Monthly. — Description based on: Vol.1, no.2 (Jan.1981)
£8.00 per year
Also classified at 333.33'8'094227 B81-16240

333.33'8'094223 — Kent. Residences — *Buyers' guides — Serials*
Property guide. Homes in Sussex & Kent. — Vol.1, no.1 (Dec.1980)-. — London (150 Caledonian Rd, N1 9RD) : Wootten, 1980-. — v. : ill ; 30cm
Monthly
ISSN 0261-0647 = Property guide. Homes in Sussex & Kent : £8.00 per year
Also classified at 333.33'8'094225 B81-16242

333.33'8'094225 — East & West Sussex. Residences — *Buyers' guides — Serials*
Property guide. Homes in Sussex & Kent. — Vol.1, no.1 (Dec.1980)-. — London (150 Caledonian Rd, N1 9RD) : Wootten, 1980-. — v. : ill ; 30cm
Monthly
ISSN 0261-0647 = Property guide. Homes in Sussex & Kent : £8.00 per year
Primary classification 333.33'8'094223
B81-16242

333.33′8′094227 — Hampshire. Residences — *Buyers′ guides — Serials*

Property guide. Homes in Surrey & Hampshire. — Vol.1, no.1 (Dec.1980)-. — London (150 Caledonian Rd, N1 9RD) : Wootten, 1980-. — v. : ill ; 30cm
Monthly. — Description based on: Vol.1, no.2 (Jan.1981)
£8.00 per year
Primary classification 333.33′8′094221
B81-16240

333.33′8′09425 — England. Southern East Midlands. Residences — *Buyers′ guides — Serials*

Property guide. Homes in Beds/Bucks/Berks & Oxon. — Vol.1, no.1 (Dec.1980)-. — London (150 Caledonian Rd, N1 9RD) : Wootten, 1980-. — v. : ill ; 30cm
Monthly
ISSN 0261-0655 = Property guide. Homes in Beds, Bucks, Berks & Oxon : £8.00 per year
B81-16241

333.33′8′094258 — Hertfordshire. Residences — *Buyers′ guides — Serials*

Property guide. Homes in Essex & Hertfordshire : incorporating Essex homes. — Vol.1, no.1 (Dec.1980). — London (150 Caledonian Rd, N1 9RD) : Wootten, 1980-. — v. : ill ; 30cm
Monthly. — Absorbed: Essex homes, 1980
ISSN 0261-0620 = Property guide. Homes in Essex & Hertfordshire : £8.00 per year
Also classified at 333.33′8′094267 B81-16243

333.33′8′094267 — Essex. Residences — *Buyers′ guides — Serials*

Essex homes. — Vol.1, no.1 (July 1980)-v.1, no.5 (Nov.1980). — London (150 Caledonian Rd, N1 9RD) : Wootten Publications, 1980-1980. — v. : ill ; 30cm
Monthly. — Absorbed by: Property guide. Homes in Essex & Hertfordshire. 1980
ISSN 0260-8928 = Essex homes : £6.00 per year B81-09075

Property guide. Homes in Essex & Hertfordshire : incorporating Essex homes. — Vol.1, no.1 (Dec.1980). — London (150 Caledonian Rd, N1 9RD) : Wootten, 1980-. — v. : ill ; 30cm
Monthly. — Absorbed: Essex homes, 1980
ISSN 0261-0620 = Property guide. Homes in Essex & Hertfordshire : £8.00 per year
Primary classification 333.33′8′094258
B81-16243

333.3′8 — England. Areas of outstanding natural beauty. Real property. Development. Control — *Study regions: Cotswolds*

Preece, R. A.. Patterns of development control in the Cotswold Area of Outstanding Natural Beauty / R. A. Preece. — Oxford (Mansfield Rd., Oxford OX1 3TB) : School of Geography [University of Oxford], 1981. — 36p : ill,maps ; 22cm. — (Research paper / School of Geography, University of Oxford, ISSN 0305-8190 ; 27)
Bibliography: p32-36
Unpriced (pbk) B81-31320

333.3′8 — England. Real property. Development

Green, Ernest H.. Building, planning and development / Ernest H. Green. — London : Macmillan, 1981. — ix,173p : ill,maps,plans ; 25cm. — (Macmillan building and surveying series)
Includes index
ISBN 0-333-19788-7 : £12.95 : CIP rev.
B80-10960

333.3′8 — Great Britain. Country estates. Development — *Conference proceedings*

Elson, Martin J.. Country estate development : the report of a seminar organised by the Royal Town Planning Institute at 26 Portland Place, London on 22nd February, 1980 / Martin J. Elson. — [Oxford] ([Gypsy La., Headington, Oxford OX3 0BP]) : Oxford Polytechnic, [1980]. — 24p ; 30cm. — (Working paper / Oxford Polytechnic Department of Town Planning ; no.48)
Unpriced (pbk) B81-07054

333.3′8 — Great Britain. Land. Development. Political aspects

Denman, D. R.. Land in a free society / Donald Denman. — London : Centre for Policy Studies, 1980. — xi,56p ; 22cm
Bibliography: p55-56
ISBN 0-905880-29-3 (pbk) : £2.75 B81-07250

333.3′8 — Great Britain. Real property development industries — *Directories*

United Kingdom property development companies / [Data Research Group]. — [1980]. — Great Missenden : The Group, 1980. — 73p
ISBN 0-86099-282-9 : Unpriced B81-06713

333.3′8 — Turks and Caicos Islands. Hotels. Development — *Inquiry reports*

Great Britain. *Parliament. House of Commons. Foreign Affairs Committee.* Third report from the Foreign Affairs Committee, session 1980-81 : Turks and Caicos Islands : hotel development : together with part of the proceedings of the committee relating to the report ; and the minutes of evidence taken before the Overseas Development Sub-Committee on 25 November and 16 December 1980, and 13 January 1981, with appendices. — London : H.M.S.O.. — ([HC] ; 26-II)
Vol.2: Minutes of evidence and appendices. — [1981]. — vi,145p ; 25cm
ISBN 0-10-008761-2 (pbk) B81-39635

333.5 — LAND. TENANCY

333.5′0941 — Great Britain. Leasing — *Serials*

The **Leasing** report : an independent guide to the leasing industry. — [Issue 1 (Jan. 1979)?]-. — London (42 New Broad St., EC2M 1QY) : The Leasing Report, [1979?]-. — v. ; 30cm
Monthly. — Description based on: Issue 8 (Aug.1979)
ISSN 0260-6992 = Leasing report : £18.00 per year B81-05638

333.7 — NATURAL RESOURCES

333.7 — Developed countries. Natural resources. Exploitation. Management

Butts, Peter. Resources and industry in the developed world. — London : Edward Arnold, Sept.1981. — [64]p. — (Patterns of development)
ISBN 0-7131-0453-8 (pbk) : £2.25 : CIP entry
B81-23831

333.7 — Energy resources. Models — *Conference proceedings*

Energy modelling studies and conservation. — Oxford : Pergamon, Sept.1981. — [600]p
Conference papers
ISBN 0-08-027416-1 : £40.00 : CIP entry
Also classified at 333.7′2 B81-22566

333.7 — Energy resources. Policies of governments — *Comparative studies — Conference proceedings*

Oil or industry?. — London : Academic Press, Oct.1981. — [350]p
Conference papers
ISBN 0-12-078620-6 : CIP entry B81-26789

333.7 — Environment

Maclean, Kenneth. Problems of our planet / an atlas of earth and man : by Kenneth Maclean and Norman Thomson. — 2nd ed. — Edinburgh : Bartholomew, 1977 (1980 [printing]). — 67p : ill(some col.),maps(some col.),ports ; 30cm
Previous ed.: 1975
ISBN 0-85152-969-0 (pbk) : £3.00 B81-03345

Man and his environment / edited by O.C. Nwankiti. — Harlow : Longman, 1981. — vi,178p : ill,maps ; 24cm
Includes bibliographies and index
ISBN 0-582-78527-8 (pbk) : £3.50 B81-29747

ReVelle, Penelope. The environment : issues and choices for society / Penelope ReVelle, Charles ReVelle. — New York ; London : Van Nostrand Reinhold, c1981. — xix,762p : ill,maps ; 24cm
Includes bibliographies and index
ISBN 0-442-22069-3 : £14.20 B81-17186

333.7 — Environment - *American & Chinese viewpoints - Conference proceedings*

The **Environment**. — London : Methuen, June 1981. — [397]p
Conference papers
ISBN 0-416-32050-3 : £10.00 : CIP entry
B81-13755

333.7 — Environment — *Conference proceedings*

Planet Earth Conference *(1980 : Aix-en-Provence)*. Man, earth and the challenges : the book of the 1980 Planet Earth Conference held at the Institute of Ecotechnics, Les Marronniers, Aix-en-Provence, France, December 12th-December 15th, 1980. — Santa Fe ; London (24 Old Gloucester St, W.C.1) : Synergetic Press, c1981. — 283p : ill,ports ; 21cm
Ill, ports on inside covers
£2.75 (pbk) B81-36088

333.7 — Environment. Policies. Economic aspects

Economics and resources policy / edited by J.A. Butlin. — London : Longman, 1981. — 206p : ill ; 24cm
Includes bibliographies and index
ISBN 0-582-45074-8 (pbk) : £5.50 : CIP rev.
B80-34516

333.7 — Environmental studies

Environmental science methods. — London : Chapman & Hall, Dec.1981. — [400]p
ISBN 0-412-23280-4 (cased) : £25.00 : CIP entry
ISBN 0-412-23290-1 (pbk) : £9.50 B81-31731

333.7 — Great Britain. Waste materials. Environmental aspects

Sondheimer, Julian. Waste, resources and the environment / Julian Sondheimer. — [Birmingham] ([102 Edmunds St., Birmingham B3 3DS]) : National Association for Environmental Education, [c1978]. — 7p ; 30cm. — (Occasional paper / NAEE ; 4)
Conference papers. — Cover title
£0.35 (pbk) B81-07191

333.7 — Land use. Planning. Implications of ecology

Selman, Paul H.. Ecology and planning. — London : George Godwin, Apr.1981. — [160]p
ISBN 0-7114-5555-4 : £9.50 : CIP entry
B81-07476

333.7 — Natural resources

Simmons, I. G.. The ecology of natural resources / I.G. Simmons. — 2nd ed. — London : Edward Arnold, 1981. — viii,438p : ill,maps ; 24cm
Previous ed.: 1974. — Bibliography: p377-416. - Includes index
ISBN 0-7131-6328-3 (pbk) : £8.50 B81-18480

333.7 — Natural resources. Exploitation. Policies of governments. International economic aspects — *Conference proceedings*

Wisconsin Seminar on Natural Resource Policies in Relation to Economic Development and International Cooperation *(1977-78)*. Resources and development : natural resource policies and economic development in an interdependent world : the Wisconsin Seminar on Natural Resource Policies in Relation to Economic Development and International Cooperation 1977-1978 / edited by Peter Dorner, Mahmond A. El-Shafie ; co-sponsored by University of Wisconsin-Madison ... et al.. — Madison : University of Wisconsin Press ; London : Croom Helm, 1980. — xv,500p : ill ; 24cm
Includes index and bibliographies
ISBN 0-7099-0382-0 : £11.95
ISBN 0-229-08250-4 (U.S.) B81-06933

333.7 — Natural resources — *For schools*

A Wasting world? : natural resources and energy : with a case study / Curriculum Development Unit. — Dublin : O'Brien, [1981]. — 80p : ill,maps ; 26cm
ISBN 0-905140-95-8 (cased) : £8.00
ISBN 0-905170-96-6 (pbk) : Unpriced
B81-15329

333.7 — Natural resources. International political aspects

Szuprowicz, Bohdan O.. How to avoid strategic materials shortages : dealing with cartels, embargoes, and supply disruptions / Bohdan O. Szuprowicz. — New York ; Chichester : Wiley, c1981. — xvii,312p : ill,maps ; 24cm
Includes bibliographies and index
ISBN 0-471-07843-3 : £12.50 B81-23327

333.7 — Renewable resources — *Conference proceedings*

CIQA International Conference *(1979 : Saltillo, Coahuila).* Renewable resources : a systematic approach / [papers presented at the CIQA International Conference in Saltillo, Coahuila, Mexico, August 1979] ; edited by Enrique Campos-López. — New York ; London : Academic Press, 1980. — x,410p : ill,1map ; 24cm
Includes index
ISBN 0-12-158350-3 (corrected) : £16.60 B81-30770

333.7'05 — Environment — *For industries — Serials*

[Report *(Environmental Data Services)*]. Report / Environmental Data Services. — 1(May 1978)-. — London (14 Great Smith St., SW1) : ENDS, 1978-. — v. ; 30cm
Fortnightly
ISSN 0260-1249 = Report - Environmental Data Services : Unpriced B81-32687

333.7'06'04 — Environment. European organisations — *Directories*

ENEX directory : environmental expertise in the European Communities. — Hitchin : Published for the Commission of the European Communities by Peregrinus, c1981. — 954p ; 30cm. — (EUR 7271)
ISBN 0-906048-58-3 (pbk) : Unpriced B81-40699

333.7'06'041 — Environment. British organisations: Institution of Environmental Sciences — *Serials*

[News sheet *(Institution of Environmental Sciences)*]. News sheet / Institution of Environmental Sciences. — Vol.1, no.1 (Oct.1976)-. — London (14 Princes Gate, Hyde Park, SW7) : The Institution, 1976-. — v. : ill,ports ; 30cm
Six issues yearly. — Description based on: Vol.5, no.2 & 3 (July 1980)
ISSN 0260-4825 = News sheet - Institution of Environmental Sciences : Unpriced B81-06911

333.7'07 — Education. Curriculum subjects: Environmental studies

Environmental education : a review / Department of Education and Science. — London : H.M.S.O., 1981. — 37p ; 30cm
Bibliography: p37
ISBN 0-11-270544-8 (pbk) : £1.95 B81-28724

333.7'07 — Environmental education — *Serials*

Environmental education and information. — Vol.1, no.1 (Jan.-Mar.1981)-. — London : Taylor & Francis in collaboration with the Institution of Evironmental Sciences, 1981-. — v. : maps ; 25cm
Quarterly
ISSN 0144-9281 = Evironmental education and information : £30.00 per year B81-33315

333.7'07'041 — Great Britain. Education. Curriculum subjects: Environmental studies — *Serials*

IES proceedings. — Vol.1 (1980)-. — London (14 Princes Gate, SW7 1PU) : Institution of Environmental Sciences, 1980-. — v. ; 20cm
ISSN 0260-4833 = IES proceedings : £1.50 per issue B81-16810

333.7'07'041 — Great Britain. Environmental education. Role of government

Gazzard, Roy. The role of the government in creating environmental awareness / Roy Gazzard. — [Birmingham] ([102 Edmunds St., Birmingham B3 3DS]) : National Association for Environmental Education, [c1978]. — 11p ; 30cm. — (Occasional paper / NAEE ; 5)
Conference papers. — Cover title
£0.35 (pbk) B81-07190

333.7'07'1041 — Great Britain. Schools. Curriculum subjects: Environmental studies. Information sources — *Lists*

Environmental education : sources of information 1981 / [prepared by the Department of Education and Science and the Central Office of Information]. — [2nd ed.]. — London : H.M.S.O., 1981. — 84p ; 30cm
Previous ed.: published as The environment. 1979. — Includes index
ISBN 0-11-270545-6 (pbk) : £2.95 B81-28725

333.7'072 — Environment. Policies. Econometric models

Nijkamp, Peter. Environmental policy analysis : operational methods and models / Peter Nijkamp in association with Wim Hafkamp ... [et al.]. — Chichester : Wiley, c1980. — xvi,283p : ill,maps ; 24cm
Includes bibliographies and index
ISBN 0-471-27763-0 : £15.00 : CIP rev. B80-25173

333.7'072041 — Great Britain. Field studies — *Serials*

[The Journal *(National Association of Field Studies Officers)*]. The Journal / the National Association of Field Studies Officers. — No.6 (1981). — Everdon (c/o R.W. Wilson, Everdon Field Centre, Everdon, Daventry, Northants. NN11 6BL) : The Association, 1981. — 72p
Cover title: NAFSO journal
ISSN 0141-674x : Unpriced B81-23508

333.7'072041 — Great Britain. *Science Research Council. Environment Committee — Serials*

Great Britain. *Science Research Council. Environment Committee.* Annual report / Science Research Council, Engineering Board, Environment Committee. — 1979/80-. — Swindon : The Council, 1980-. — v. ; 30cm
ISSN 0260-2237 = Annual report — Science Research Council. Engineering Board. Environment Committee : Unpriced B81-33459

333.7'072042 — England. Field study centres — *Directories*

Cocke, Carolyn. Directory of centres for outdoor studies in England and Wales / [compiled by Carolyn Cocke]. — Reading (School of Education, University of Reading, London Rd., Reading RG1 5AQ) : Council for Environmental Education, c1981. — 48p : 1map ; 22cm
Cover title. — Previous ed.: 197-?
ISBN 0-906711-01-0 (pbk) : Unpriced B81-23556

333.7'0932 — Egypt. Western Desert. Prehistoric environment

Wendorf, Fred. Prehistory of the eastern Sahara / Fred Wendorf, Romuald Schild. — New York ; London : Academic Press, c1980. — xviii,414p : ill,maps ; 19cm. — (Studies in archaeology)
Bibliography: p401-409. — Includes index
ISBN 0-12-743960-9 : £36.40
Primary classification 932 B81-07525

333.7'094 — Europe. Environment. Policies

Füllenbach, Josef. European environmental policy : East and West / Josef Füllenbach ; translated by Frank Carter and John Manton. — London : Butterworths, 1981. — ix,255p : ill ; 24cm. — (Butterworths European studies)
Translation of: Umweltschutz in Ost und West. — Bibliography: p231-244. — Includes index
ISBN 0-408-10689-1 : Unpriced : CIP rev. B81-13575

333.7'094 — European Community countries. Environment. Policies of European Economic Community

Ellington, Athleen. Europe : environment : the European Communities environmental policy / Athleen Ellington and Tom Burke. — London (16 Strutton Ground, S.W.1) : Ecobooks, c1981. — 23p ; 21cm
Unpriced (pbk) B81-12116

333.7'0941 — Great Britain. Environment — *For teaching*

Lines, C. J.. Teachers' book / authors Clifford Lines, Laurie Bolwell. — London : Macdonald Educational, 1981. — 24p : ill ; 21cm. — (Town and around)
Includes bibliographies and index
ISBN 0-356-07196-0 (pbk) : Unpriced B81-29913

333.7'0957 — Russian *(RSFSR).* **Siberia. Natural resources. Exploitation**

Sansone, Vito. Siberia : epic of the century / Vito Sansone ; [translated by Keith Hammond]. — Moscow : Progress Press ; [London] : Central Books [distributor], 1980. — 223p,[60]p of plates : ill(some col.),col.2maps,ports ; 21cm. — (Impressions of the USSR)
Translation of: Sibir'. — Map on lining papers. — Bibliography: p223
ISBN 0-7147-1629-4 : £1.95 B81-32948

333.7'097298'3 — Trinidad and Tobago. Natural resources

The Natural resources of Trinidad and Tobago / edited by St G.C. Cooper and P.R. Bacon. — London : Edward Arnold, 1981. — viii,223p : ill,maps ; 25cm
Includes bibliographies and index
ISBN 0-7131-8012-9 (pbk) : £18.00 B81-38432

333.7'0973 — United States. Environment. Policies of government

Marcus, Alfred A.. Promise and performance : choosing and implementing an environmental policy / Alfred A. Marcus. — Westport ; London : Greenwood Press, 1980. — xix,204p : ill ; 22cm. — (Contributions in political science, ISSN 0147-1066 ; no.39)
Bibliography: p185-198. — Includes index
ISBN 0-313-20707-0 : Unpriced B81-03534

333.7'0973 — United States. Environmental movements, *1970-1980*

Pilat, J. F.. Ecological politics : the rise of the green movement / J.F. Pilat ; foreword by Francis X. Murray. — Beverly Hills ; London : Center for Strategic and International Studies [by] Sage, c1980. — 96p ; 23cm. — (The Washington) (A Sage policy paper)
Bibliography: p95-96
Unpriced (pbk) B81-09413

333.7'09797'75 — Washington *(State).* **Puget Sound. Island County. Environment,** *to 1940*

White, Richard, *1947-*. Land use, environment, and social change : the shaping of Island County, Washington / Richard White. — Seattle ; London : University of Washington Press, c1980. — xi,234p.[8]p of plates : ill,maps ; 24cm
Bibliography: p205-227. — Includes index
ISBN 0-295-95691-7 : £7.80 B81-05515

333.7'0998'9 — Antarctic. Natural resources

Mitchell, Barbara. Antarctica and its resources / by Barbara Mitchell and Jon Tinker. — London (10 Percy St., W1P 0DR) : Earthscan, [c1980]. — 98p : ill,maps ; 21cm
Cover title
ISBN 0-905347-13-7 (pbk) : £2.50 B81-38455

333.7'1 — Environment. Management. Applications of environmental impact analysis — *Case studies*

Project appraisal and policy review / edited by Timothy O'Riordan and W.R. Derrick Sewell. — Chichester : Wiley, c1981. — xi,304p : ill,maps ; 24cm. — (Wiley series on studies in environmental management and resource development)
Includes bibliographies and index
ISBN 0-471-27853-x : £13.00 B81-34531

333.7'1 — Environmental impact analysis

Jain, R. K. (Ravinder Kumar). Environmental impact analysis : a new dimension on decision making / R.K. Jain, L.V. Urban, G.S. Stacey. — 2nd ed. — New York ; London : Van Nostrand Reinhold, c1981. — xv,393p : ill,forms ; 24cm. — (Van Nostrand Reinhold environmental engineering series)
Previous ed.: 1977. — Includes index
ISBN 0-442-23134-2 : £20.65 B81-03005

333.7'1'028 — Environmental impact analysis. Techniques

Lee, Norman, *1936-*. Methods of environmental impact assessment for use in project appraisal and physical planning / Norman Lee and Christopher Wood. — Manchester (Manchester M13 9PL) : Department of Town and Country Planning, University of Manchester, 1980. — 78p ; 30cm. — (Occasional paper / Department of Town and Country Planning University of Manchester ; no.7)
Unpriced (pbk) B81-04817

333.7'1'094 — European Community countries. Environment planning. Environmental impact analysis — *Conference proceedings*

Environmental impact assessment : from theory to practice : from a conference sponsored by the South East Branch of the Royal Town Planning Institute / editors Michael Breakell and John Glasson. — [Oxford] : Oxford Polytechnic. Department of Town Planning, 1981. — 181p : ill,maps,forms ; 30cm. — (Working paper / Oxford Polytechnic. Department of Town Planning ; no.50)
£5.00 (spiral) B81-25062

333.7'1'0941 — Great Britain. Environmental impact analysis — *For industries*

Environmental impact assessment / [general editor John Elkington] ; [contributors Brian Clark ... et al.]. — London : Oyez, c1981. — 96leaves : ill,1map ; 30cm. — (Oyez intelligence reports)
ISBN 0-85120-548-8 (spiral) : Unpriced B81-28529

333.7'17 — Natural resources. Allocation. International political aspects — *Forecasts*

Barnet, Richard J.. The lean years : politics in the age of scarcity / Richard J. Barnet. — [London] : Abacus, 1981, c1980. — 349p ; 20cm
Originally published: New York : Simon and Schuster, 1980. — Bibliography: p319-336. — Includes index
ISBN 0-349-10238-4 (pbk) : £2.50 B81-20768

333.7'2 — Energy resources. Conservation — *Conference proceedings*

Energy modelling studies and conservation. — Oxford : Pergamon, Sept.1981. — [600]p
Conference papers
ISBN 0-08-027416-1 : £40.00 : CIP entry
Primary classification 333.7 B81-22566

333.7'2 — Environment. Conservation

Conservation. — Leicester (Mill La., Leicester) : South Fields College, School of printing, c1981. — ix,66p : ill(some col.) ; 23cm
Ill on lining papers
Unpriced B81-29192

Moss, Rowland. The earth in our hands. — Leicester : Inter-Varsity Press, Sept.1981. — [96]p
ISBN 0-85110-427-4 (pbk) : £1.25 : CIP entry B81-25655

333.7'2 — Environment. Conservation — *Amateurs' manuals*

Up your street : an environmental action guide for young people / Youth Environmental Action. — London (173 Archway Rd., N6 5BL) : Youth Environmental Action, c1981. — 108p : ill ; 22cm
Text on inside covers
ISBN 0-905565-01-0 (pbk) : £1.20 : CIP rev. B78-32731

333.7'2'06041 — Great Britain. Environment. Conservation. Organisations — *Directories*

Civic Trust. Environmental directory : national and regional organisations of interest to those concerned with amenity and the environment / Civic Trust. — London : The Trust, 1981. — 56p ; 21cm
Includes index
ISBN 0-900849-99-1 (pbk) : Unpriced B81-24771

333.7'2'09177 — Organisation for Economic Co-operation and Development countries. Environment. Conservation. Role of policies of industries in Organisation for Economic Co-operation and Development countries, *ca 1960-1980*

Elkington, John. The ecology of tomorrow's world : industry's environment / John Elkington. — London : Associated Business Press, 1980. — xii,311p,[4]p of plates : ill,1map ; 23cm
Includes index
ISBN 0-85227-260-x (corrected) : £12.00 B81-05655

333.7'2'0941 — Great Britain. Environment. Conservation. Policies of Conservative Party — *Proposals*

Johnson, Stanley, *1940-*. Caring for the environment : a policy for Conservatives / Stanley Johnson ; with a foreword by Michael Heseltine. — London : Conservature Political Centre, 1981. — 26p ; 21cm
ISBN 0-85070-666-1 (pbk) : £1.00 B81-32369

333.7'2'0941 — Great Britain. Environment. Conservation. Role of volunteers

Gundrey, Elizabeth. Helping hands : a guide to conservation / Elizabeth Gundrey. — London : Unwin Paperbacks in association with the Observer, 1981. — 198p ; 18cm
ISBN 0-04-361048-x (pbk) : £2.25 : CIP rev. B81-20137

333.7'2'0941 — Great Britain. Environment. Conservation — *Serials*

Heritage outlook : the journal of the Civic Trusts. — Vol.1, no.1 (Jan./Feb.1981)-. — v. : ill ; 30cm
Six issues yearly. — Continues: Civic Trust news
ISSN 0261-1988 = Heritage outlook : £4.50 per year B81-20091

333.7'2'094235 — Devon. Environment. Conservation. Policies of Devon. *County Council.* **Implementation** — *Serials*

Devon. *Planning Department*. Conservation and primary industries / County Planning Department. — 1981-. — Exeter (County Hall, Topsham Rd, Exeter EX2 4QH) : Devon County Council Planning Department, 1981-. — v. : ill ; 30cm. — (Topic report / County Planning Department)
Annual
ISSN 0261-2453 = Conservation and primary industries topic report : £0.40 B81-33728

333.7'2'09423592 — Devon. Slapton region. Environment. Conservation — *Proposals*

Slapton study : opportunities for enhancing the landscape and wildlife qaulity of the Slapton area / [prepared on behalf of the Amenities and Countryside Committee by Devon County Planning Department]. — Exeter (County Hall, Exeter EX2 4QH) : Devon County Council, Planning Department, 1980. — 12p : ill,1map ; 30cm
ISBN 0-86114-299-3 (unbound) : £0.25 B81-09860

333.7'2'094257 — Oxfordshire. Environment. Conservation — *Serials*

Greenfly : Oxfordshire ecology newspaper. — No.1 (Mar./Apr.1980-). — Oxford (34 Cowley Road, Oxford OX4 1HZ) : Greenfly Press, 1980-. — v. : ill ; 30cm
Ten issues yearly. — Description based on: No.6 (Oct.1980)
£3.00 per year B81-05936

333.7'2'094267 — Essex. Coastal regions. Environment. Conservation — *Proposals*

Essex coast protection subject plan : draft / [Essex County Council]. — [Chelmsford] ([Planning Dept., County Hall, Chelmsford CM1 1LF]) : [The Council], 1981. — 8p,[40] leaves of plates(some folded) : ill,maps ; 30cm
£2.00 (pbk) B81-23035

333.7'2'094267 — Essex. Environment. Conservation

Conservation in Essex. — [Chelmsford] ([County Hall, Chelmsford, CM1 1LF]) : Essex County Council
No.5: Shopfronts. — 1981. — 17p : ill ; 31cm
ISBN 0-901355-75-5 (pbk) : £1.50 B81-35351

333.7'2'0942673 — Essex. Harlow. Environment. Conservation

Bardsley, Andrew T.. New town conservation : Harlow / by Andrew T. Bardsley. — London : Institution of Municipal Engineers, 1976. — 20p : ill,plans ; 21cm. — (Protection of the environment ; monograph no.29)
£1.00 (pbk) B81-09180

333.7'2'0952 — Japan. Environment. Conservation. Participation of public. Political aspects

McKean, Margaret A.. Environmental protest and citizen politics in Japan / Margaret A. McKean. — Berkeley ; London : University of California Press, c1981. — xv,291p : ill ; 25cm
Bibliography: p275-278. — Includes index
ISBN 0-520-04115-1 (pbk) : £17.00 B81-36415

333.7'2'0973 — North America. Environment. Conservation. Implications of organisational behaviour of electricity generation industries — *Case studies*

Roberts, Marc J.. The choices of power : utilities face the environmental challenge / Marc J. Roberts and Jeremy S. Bluhm with the assistance of Margaret Gerteis. — Cambridge [Mass.] ; London : Harvard University Press, 1981. — x,458p : ill,maps ; 24cm
Includes index
ISBN 0-674-12780-3 : £17.50 B81-40027

333.7'2'0973 — United States. Environment. Conservation, *1800-1900*

Mitchell, Lee Clark. Witnesses to a vanishing America : the nineteenth-century response / Lee Clark Mitchell. — Princeton ; Guildford, Surrey : Princeton University Press, c1981. — xvii,320p : ill,ports ; 24cm
Bibliography: p281-312. — Includes index
ISBN 0-691-06461-x : £10.70 B81-31669

333.73 — Arid regions. Natural resources. Management

Settling the desert / edited by L. Berkofsky, D. Faiman, J. Gale. — Sede Boqer : Jacob Blaustein Institute for Desert Research ; London : Gordon and Breach Science, c1981. — xvi,274p : ill,maps ; 24cm
Includes index
ISBN 0-677-16280-4 : Unpriced
Primary classification 630'.915'4 B81-35182

333.73 — Eastern Pennsylvania. Coal tips. Removal. Role of environment planning

Larkin, Robert P.. Land use planning and coal refuse disposal / Robert P. Larkin and Gary L. Peters. — [Oxford] ([Oxford OX3 0BP]) : [Geography Section, Faculty of Modern Studies, Oxford Polytechnic], 1980. — 41p : ill,maps ; 30cm. — (Discussion paper in geography / Oxford Polytechnic, ISSN 0309-1910 ; no.9)
Bibliography: p41
£1.00 (pbk) B81-06951

333.73 — Land use

Best, Robin H.. Land use and living space. — London : Methuen, Dec.1981. — [250]p
ISBN 0-416-73760-9 (cased) : £10.00 : CIP entry
ISBN 0-416-73770-6 (pbk) : £5.00 B81-31746

McRae, S. G.. Land evaluation. — Oxford : Clarendon, Dec.1981. — [200]p. — (Monographs on soil survey)
ISBN 0-19-854518-5 : £16.00 : CIP entry B81-31456

333.73 — Land use. Policies of governments — *Conference proceedings*

A Review of land policies / edited and compiled by D.H. Koenigsberger and S. Groák ; editorial consultant Nathaniel Lichfield. — Oxford : Pergamon, 1981, c1980. — vi,p373-701 : ill ; 29cm
Includes index
ISBN 0-08-026078-0 : £22.00 B81-11450

333.73 — West Glamorgan. Lower Swansea Valley. Derelict land. Reclamation

Lavender, Stephen J.. New land for old : the environmental renaissance of the Lower Swansea Valley / Stephen J. Lavender. — Bristol : Hilger, c1981. — xiv,137p : ill,maps,ports ; 26cm
Bibliography: p127-129. — Includes index
ISBN 0-85274-386-6 (cased) : £11.50 : CIP rev.
ISBN 0-85274-453-6 (pbk) : £6.95 B81-13732

333.73'0941 — Great Britain. Land use. Mapping — *Manuals*

Coleman, Alice. Field mapping manual / Alice Coleman, Janet E. Shaw. — London (Second Land Utilisation Survey of Britain, King's College, Strand, WC2R 2LS) : A. Coleman, 1980. — 73p : ill(some col.) ; 21cm. — (Land utilisation survey)
Unpriced (pbk) B81-11420

333.73'0941 — Great Britain. Land use. Planning. Geographical aspects

Hall, John M.. The geography of planning decisions. — Oxford : Oxford University Press, Jan.1982. — [64]p. — (Theory and practice in geography)
ISBN 0-19-874034-4 (pbk) : £2.50 : CIP entry B81-33902

333.73'0941 — Great Britain. Land use. Policies of government, *1945-1979*

Lichfield, Nathaniel. Land policy in planning / Nathaniel Lichfield and Haim Darin-Drabkin. — London : Allen & Unwin, 1980. — viii,321p ; 24cm. — (Urban and regional studies ; no.8)
Bibliography: p304-313. — Includes index
ISBN 0-04-333017-7 : £18.00 : CIP rev. B80-23014

333.73'09421'6 — North London. Land use. Management

Countryside management in the urban fringe : a report on experiments sponsored jointly by the Countryside Commission ... [et al.]. — Cheltenham (John Dower House, Crescent Place, Cheltenham, Glos. GL50 3RA) : The Commission, c1981. — viii,135p : ill,col.maps ; 30cm
ISBN 0-86170-022-8 (pbk) : £10.30 B81-33355

333.73'09422'5 — East Sussex. Land for non-residential development

Industrial, office and retail land commitment at 1st April 1981. — [Lewes] ([Southover House, Southover Rd., Lewes BN7 1YA]) : East Sussex County Planning Department, Monitoring Service, [1981]. — 36p,[20]leaves : maps ; 30cm. — (Information paper / East Sussex ; no. 39)
Cover title
Unpriced (pbk) B81-40520

333.73'0973 — United States. Land use. Planning

Bjork, Gordon C.. Life, liberty, and property : the economics and politics of land-use planning and environmental controls / Gordon C. Bjork. — Lexington : Lexington ; Farnborough, Hants. : Gower [distributor], c1980. — xii,137p ; 24cm
Includes index
ISBN 0-669-03952-7 : £10.50 B81-17832

333.73'13 — Man-made desertification. Control — *Case studies — Conference proceedings*

Desertification : associated case studies prepared for the United Nations Conference on Desertification / edited by Margaret R. Biswas and Asit K. Biwas [i.e. Biswas]. — Oxford : Pergamon, 1980. — ix,523p : ill,charts,maps ; 26cm + 14maps. — (Environmental sciences and applications ; v.12)
In slip case. — Ten maps (10 folded sheets in pocket) as insert. - 4 maps (4 folded sheets) in pocket on inside back cover. — Includes bibliographies
ISBN 0-08-023581-6 : £33.50 : CIP rev. B80-05127

333.73'13'0941 — Great Britain. Land use — *Ecology Party viewpoints*

Hardy, Shirley-Anne. The land question : 'which not to solve-' / by Shirley-Anne Hardy. — [Edinburgh] ([c/o Mrs Hardy, The Rocks, Pitlochry, Perthshire]) : [Ecology Party], 1981. — 27p ; 22cm
Cover title
£0.40 (pbk) B81-38596

333.73'13'0941 — Great Britain. Land use. Effects of social change

Moss, Graham. Britain's wasting areas : land use in a changing society / Graham Moss. — London : Architectural Press, 1981. — ix,230p : ill ; 24cm
Bibliography: p218-227. — Includes index
ISBN 0-85139-078-1 : £13.50 B81-07990

333.73'13'0942445 — Herefordshire. Marden. Land use, *ca 75-ca 1720*

Sheppard, June A.. The origins and evolution of field and settlement patterns in the Hertfordshire Manor of Marden / June A. Sheppard. — London : Department of Geography, Queen Mary College, University of London, 1979. — 44p : maps,plans ; 30cm. — (Occasional paper / Department of Geography, Queen Mary College, ISSN 0306-2740 ; no.15)
ISBN 0-904791-15-7 (pbk) : Unpriced B81-03666

333.73'13'09794 — California. Land use, *1978-1980.* **Effects of Proposition 13**

Chapman, Jeffrey I.. Proposition 13 and land use : a case study of fiscal limits in California / Jeffrey I. Chapman. — Lexington, Mass. : Lexington Books ; [Aldershot] : Gower [distributor], 1981. — xiii,190p : ill ; 24cm
Bibliography: p171-181. — Includes index
ISBN 0-669-03471-1 : £15.00 B81-39698

333.73'17'09171241 — South Pacific region. Commonwealth countries. Rural regions. Land use. Planning. Role of Commonwealth Association of Surveying and Land Economy — *Conference proceedings*

The **Role** of the CASLE professions in rural developments programes in the South Pacific : report of the proceedings of a CASLE Pacific regional seminar held in Papua New Guinea on 1-4 September 1980 / Commonwealth Association of Surveying and Land Economy. — London (12 Great George St., SW1P 3AD) : CASLE, 1980. — 265p ; 30cm
£6.00 (pbk) B81-10328

333.73'17'0973 — United States. Land use. Regulation, *1960-1980*

Popper, Frank J.. The politics of land-use reform / Frank J. Popper. — Madison ; London : University of Wisconsin Press, 1981. — xii,321p ; 22cm
Bibliography: p303-309. — Includes index
ISBN 0-299-08530-9 (cased) : £13.00
ISBN 0-299-08534-1 (pbk) : £4.85 B81-29380

333.73'17'0973 — United States. Land use. Regulation, *to 1979*

Jackson, Richard H.. Land use in America / Richard H. Jackson. — [Washington, D.C.] : Winston ; London : Edward Arnold, 1981. — v,226p : ill,maps ; 24cm. — (Scripta series in geography)
Includes index
ISBN 0-7131-6301-1 : £12.95 : CIP rev. B80-23015

333.75'09182'2 — Mediterranean region. Deforestation, *to 1980*

Thirgood, J. V.. Man and the Mediterranean forest. — London : Academic Press, July 1981. — [180]p
ISBN 0-12-687250-3 : CIP entry B81-13485

333.75'0941 — Great Britain. Woodlands. Conservation & management

Peterken, G. F.. Woodland conservation and management. — London : Chapman & Hall, Nov.1981. — [400]p
ISBN 0-412-12820-9 : £25.00 : CIP entry B81-31265

333.75'0941 — Great Britain. Woodlands. Management. Decision making

Williams, M. R. W.. Decision-making in forest management. — Chichester : Wiley, Nov.1981. — [160]p. — (Forestry research studies series ; 1)
ISBN 0-471-10097-8 : £15.00 : CIP entry B81-30285

333.75'0941 — Great Britain. Woodlands. Management — *For volunteers — Manuals*

Brooks, Alan, *19---*. Woodlands / compiled by Alan Brooks, with editorial assistance from Andy Follis ; illustrations by Andy Follis and Gay Voller, cover illustration by Peter Reynolds. — Reading (10 Duke St., Reading, Berks., RG1 4RU) : British Trust for Conservation Volunteers, 1980. — 187p : ill,1map ; 30cm. — (A Practical conservation handbook)
Bibliography: p179-183
ISBN 0-9501643-7-2 (spiral) : Unpriced B81-07528

333.76 — Rural regions. Land. Evaluation — *For rural land use planning*

Moss, R. P.. Concept and theory in land evaluation for rural land use planning / R.P. Moss. — [Birmingham] : [Department of Geography, University of Birmingham], 1978. — 35p : ill ; 30cm. — (Occasional publication / Department of Geography, University of Birmingham ; no.6)
Bibliography: p34-35
ISBN 0-7044-0357-9 (pbk) : £0.50 B81-39713

333.76'0913 — Tropical regions. Agricultural land. Land use. Effects of management of water resources — *Conference proceedings*

Tropical agricultural hydrology : watershed management and land use / edited by R. Lal and E.W. Russell. — Chichester : Wiley, c1981. — xiv,482p,[22]p of plates : ill,maps ; 24cm
Papers presented at a conference organized by the International Institute of Tropical Agriculture, Ibadan, Nigeria, in November 1979. — Includes bibliographies and index
ISBN 0-471-27931-5 : £26.50 B81-40205

333.76'13'07201724 — Developing countries. Rural regions. Land use. British research organisations: Land Resources Development Centre

Land evaluation and rural development : the work of the Land Resources Development Centre / [prepared for the Land Resources Development Centre and the Overseas Development Administration by the Central Office of Information]. — [London] : H.M.S.O., 1980. — 24p : ill(some col.),maps (some col.),plans ; 23cm
Maps on inside covers
Unpriced (pbk) B81-15215

333.76'15 — Eastern England. Fields. Hedgerows. Removal. Implications of conservation of environment

Sturrock, F. G.. Farm modernisation and the countryside : the impact of increasing field size and hedge removal on arable farms / Ford Sturrock and John Cathie. — [Cambridge] : University of Cambridge, Department of Land Economy, 1980. — 69p : ill ; 22cm. — (Occasional paper / Department of Land Economy Cambridge ; no.12)
Bibliography: p68-69
Unpriced B81-16309

333.76'16'0941 — Great Britain. Rural regions. Conservation

Green, Bryn. Countryside conservation : the protection and management of amenity ecosystems / Bryn Green. — London : Allen & Unwin, 1981. — xii,249p : ill ; 24cm. — (The Resource management series ; 3)
Bibliography: p232-243. — Includes index
ISBN 0-04-719001-9 (cased) : Unpriced : CIP rev.
ISBN 0-04-719002-7 (pbk) : Unpriced B81-10511

333.76'16'094267 — Essex. Rural regions. Environment. Conservation — *Proposals*

Countryside conservation plan : consultation draft / [prepared by A. Geoffrey Booth], County Planner. — [Chelmsford] ([County Hall, Chelmsford, CM1 1LF]) : Essex County Council, [1981]. — 86p : 1map ; 30cm
£3.50 (unbound) B81-35354

333.77 — Dorset. Land for residential development — *Serials*

[Land for residential development *(Dorchester)***]**. Land for residential development / Dorset Planning Officers' Panel. — Mar. 1979-. — [Dorchester] ([c/o Planning Department, County Hall, Dorchester DT1 1XJ]) : The Panel, 1980-. — v. : maps ; 30cm
Annual. — Description based on: Mar. 1981 issue
ISSN 0262-1541 = Land for residential development (Dorchester) : £5.00 B81-38988

333.77 — East Sussex. Land for residential development, *1980*

Housing land commitment at 1st April 1980 : summary tables and details of large sites. — [Lewes] ([Southover House, Southover Rd., Lewes BN7 1YA]) : East Sussex County Planning Department, [1980]. — [32]p,49leaves of plates : maps ; 30cm. — (Information paper / East Sussex County Planning Department ; no.37)
Cover title
Unpriced (spiral) B81-20228

333.77 — Great Britain. Commercial property — *Statistics — Serials*

Commercial and industrial property statistics / Department of the Environment. — 1979. — London : H.M.S.O., 1980. — vii,53p
ISBN 0-11-751497-7 : £5.50
ISSN 0143-5736 B81-09174

333.77 — Humberside. Cleethorpes *(District)* **& Great Grimsby** *(District).* **Land for residential development. Policies of local authorities**

Policies for housing land in Grimsby and Cleethorpes. — [Beverley] ([Manor Rd, Beverley HU17 7BX]) : [Humberside County Council], 1980. — 16p,4leaves of plates : col.maps ; 30cm
Cover title
£1.00 (spiral) B81-20003

333.77 — Norfolk. Norwich region. Housing land *— Proposals*

Norwich area housing land : analysis of potential growth locations / [Norfolk County Council]. — [Norwich] ([County Hall, Martineau La., Norwich NR1 2DH]) : The Council
Consultative summary report. — 1981. — [13] p,[4]leaves of plates : 4maps ; 30cm
Cover title
£0.20 (pbk) B81-28326

Norwich area housing land : analysis of potential growth locations / [Norfolk County Council]. — [Norwich] ([County Hall, Martineau La., Norwich NR1 2DH]) : The Council
Consultative technical report. — 1981. — 75p in various pagings, [4] leaves of plates : maps ; 30cm
Cover title
£0.75 (pbk) B81-28327

333.77 — Tyne and Wear *(Metropolitan County).* **Industrial regions** *— For environment planning*

Tyne and Wear. *County Council.* Older industrial areas survey (1976) / [Tyne and Wear County Council]. — [Newcastle upon Tyne] ([Planning Dept., Sandyford House, Newcatle upon Tyne NE2 1ED]) : [The Council]
Appendix 3: Sub-area sketches. — [1980]. — [95]p,[4] folded leaves of plates : ill,maps ; 30cm
£2.00 (pbk) B81-18937

333.77 — West Sussex. Land for residential development *— Statistics — Serials*

West Sussex *(County Council).* Land available for residential development in West Sussex at 1st July ... : joint report prepared by the County Council and the House-Builders Federation. — 1980-. — Chichester : County Planning Department, [West Sussex County Council], 1980-. — v. : maps ; 30cm
Annual
ISSN 0261-975x = Land available for residential development in West Sussex : £5.50
B81-35450

333.77′13′0942 — England. Urban regions. Land use. Relationship to economic activity. Data. Canonical correlation analysis

Doling, J. F.. An analysis of function and form in fifty three British towns / J. Doling and E.M. Davies. — [Birmingham] : [Department of Geography, University of Birmingham], 1980. — 46p : maps ; 30cm. — (Occasional publication / Department of Geography, University of Birmingham ; no.11)
Bibliography: p42
ISBN 0-7044-0399-4 (pbk) : £1.00
Also classified at 330.942′0858 B81-39715

333.78′092′4 — Landscape. Evaluation. Theories of Linton, D. L.

Appleton, Jay. David Linton′s contribution to landscape evaluation : a critical appraisal / Jay Appleton. — [Birmingham] : [Department of Geography, University of Birmingham], [1980]. — 21p ; 30cm. — (Occasional publication / Department of Geography, University of Birmingham ; no.13)
ISBN 0-7044-0401-x (pbk) : Unpriced
B81-39705

333.78′0941 — Great Britain. Outdoor recreation facilities *— For handicapped persons*

Croucher, Norman. Outdoor pursuits for disabled people / Norman Croucher ; foreword by John Disley. — Cambridge : Woodhead-Faulkner for the Disabled Living Foundation, 1981. — xii,180p ; 22cm
Includes bibliographies and index
ISBN 0-85941-185-0 (cased) : Unpriced
ISBN 0-85941-186-9 (pbk) : £4.75 B81-38082

333.78′0941 — Great Britain. Recreation facilities. Provision *— Trades Union Congress viewpoints*

Trades Union Congress. Sport and recreation : a TUC consultative paper. — London : Trades Union Congress, 1980. — 7p ; 21cm
Cover title
£0.15 (pbk) B81-06283

333.78′09413′7 — Scotland. Borders Region. Recreation facilities

Borders Region, *Regional Council.* Scottish tourism and recreation planning studies : Borders Region, 1980. — [Newtown St Boswells] ([Regional Headquarters, Newtown St Boswells, Roxburghshire TD6 0SA]) : Borders Regional Council, 1980. — v leaves,99p : ill,maps ; 30cm + factsheets([22]p : ill,maps ; 21x30cm)
£5.00 (pbk)
Primary classification 338.4′7914137
B81-27747

333.78′0942 — England. Recreation facilities. Provision by local authorities *— Statistics — Serials*

Leisure and recreation statistics. Estimates / CIPFA Statistical Information Service. — 1980-81. — London : Chartered Institute of Public Finance and Accountancy, 1980. — 107p
ISSN 0141-187x : £10.00
Primary classification 306′.4 B81-06788

333.78′09422′162 — Surrey. Guildford *(District).* **Recreation facilities** *— Serials*

Guildford. *Public Relations Unit.* Leisure for pleasure : a guide to Guildford Borough Council′s leisure and recreational facilities / ... produced by Guildford Borough Council′s Public Relations Unit in conjunction with the Leisure and Recreation Department. — [1976]-. — London : Borrow, 1976-. — v. : ill ; 21cm
Irregular. — Description based on: [1981]
ISSN 0261-3522 = Leisure for pleasure : Unpriced
Also classified at 790′.09422′162 B81-24702

333.78′09423′5 — Devon. Recreation facilities. Policies of Devon. *County Council.* **Implementation** *— Serials*

Devon. *Planning Department.* Tourism and recreation / County Planning Department. — 1981-. — Exeter (County Hall, Topsham Rd, Exeter EX2 4QH) : Devon County Council Planning Department, 1981-. — v. : ill,maps ; 30cm. — (Topic report / County Planning Department)
Annual
ISSN 0261-2445 = Tourism and recreation topic report : £0.40
Primary classification 338.4′7914235′005
B81-33729

333.78′09425 — England. East Midlands. Recreation facilities *— Proposals*

Regional Council for Sport and Recreation, East Midlands. Towards a regional strategy / The Regional Council for Sport and Recreation, East Midlands. — Nottingham (26 Musters Road, West Bridgford, Nottingham NG2 7PL) : [Regional Council for Sport & Recreation, East Midlands]
Issues report 1: Built facilities. — 1981. — 40,[18]p ; 30cm
Cover title
£2.00 (spiral) B81-37360

Regional Council for Sport and Recreation, East Midlands. Towards a regional strategy / The Regional Council for Sport and Recreation, East Midlands. — Nottingham (26 Musters Road, West Bridgford, Nottingham NG2 7PL) : [Regional Council for Sport and Recreation, East Midlands]
Issues report 2: Countryside recreation. — 1981. — 37p ; 30cm
Cover title
£2.00 (spiral) B81-37361

Regional Council for Sport and Recreation, East Midlands. Towards a regional strategy / The Regional Council for Sport and Recreation, East Midlands. — Nottingham (216 Musters Road, West Bridgford, Nottingham NG2 7PL) : [Regional Council for Sport and Recreation, East Midlands]
Issues report 4: Participation and opportunity. — 1981. — 33p ; 30cm
Cover title
£2.00 (spiral) B81-37362

Towards a regional strategy / the Regional Council for Sport and Recreation East Midlands. — Nottingham (26 Musters Rd., West Bridgford, Nottingham NG2 7PL) : The Sports Council
Issues report 1: Built facilities. — 1981. — 40p ; 30cm
Cover title
£2.00 (spiral) B81-23655

Towards a regional strategy / the Regional Council for Sport and Recreation East Midlands. — Nottingham (26 Musters Rd., West Bridgford, Nottingham NG2 7PL) : The Sports Council
Issues report 2: Countryside recreation. — 1981. — 37p ; 30cm
Cover title
£2.00 (spiral) B81-23656

333.78′09425′86 — Hertfordshire. Welwyn Hatfield *(District).* **Recreation facilities. Provision** *— Proposals*

Welwyn Hatfield. *District Council.* Recreation plan 1976-1991. — [Hatfield] ([16 St. Albans Road East, Hatfield, Herts.]) : Welwyn Hatfield District Council, [1976?]. — 73p : maps(some col.),col.plans,1form ; 30cm
Cover title
£1.00 (spiral) B81-40290

333.78′0973 — United States. Recreation facilities

Chubb, Michael. One third of our time? : an introduction to recreation behaviour and resources / Michael Chubb, Holly R. Chubb ; cartography by Sherman Hollander. — New York ; Chichester : Wiley, c1981. — xxiv,742p : ill(some col.),col.maps,facsims,col.maps,ports ; 24cm
Bibliography: p713-722. — Includes index
ISBN 0-471-15637-x : £13.50 B81-18443

333.78′3′0942353 — Devon. Dartmoor. National parks: Dartmoor National Park. Conservation *— Proposals*

The Crisis on Dartmoor and Exmoor. — [Plymouth] ([4 Oxford Gardens, Mannamead, Plymouth, Devon PL3 4SF]) : Dartmoor Preservation Association : Exmoor Society, 1980. — 8p : ill,maps ; 21cm
Unpriced (unbound)
Also classified at 333.78′3′0942385 B81-32486

333.78′3′0942385 — England. Exmoor. National parks: Exmoor National Park. Conservation *— Proposals*

The Crisis on Dartmoor and Exmoor. — [Plymouth] ([4 Oxford Gardens, Mannamead, Plymouth, Devon PL3 4SF]) : Dartmoor Preservation Association : Exmoor Society, 1980. — 8p : ill,maps ; 21cm
Unpriced (unbound)
Primary classification 333.78′3′0942353
B81-32486

333.78′3′094278 — Cumbria. Lake District. National parks: Lake District National Park *— Serials*

Lake District Special Planning Board. Lake District National Park report / [Lake District Special Planning Board]. — 1979/80. — [Kendal] ([County Offices, Kendal, Cumbria]) : [The Board], [1980]. — 44p
Unpriced B81-05447

333.78'3'094288 — Northumberland. National parks: Northumberland National Park. Recreation facilities — *For environment planning*

Recreation in the Northumberland National Park . — Newcastle upon Tyne ([c/o] National Park Officer, Bede House, All Saints Centre, Newcastle upon Tyne) : [Northumberland National Park and Countryside Committee], 1976. — 35p : ill,maps,forms ; 30cm. — (Working paper / Northumberland National Park ; 5)
Unpriced (spiral) B81-29613

333.78'313'0942511 — Great Britain. Heathland. Land use. Planning — *Study regions: Peak District National Park*

Parry, M. L.. A framework for land use planning in moorland areas : pilot survey in the Peak District National Park / M.L. Parry. — [Birmingham] : [Department of Geography, University of Birmingham], 1977. — 23p,[17]p of plates : ill,maps ; 30cm. — (Occasional publication / Department of Geography, University of Birmingham ; no.4)
Bibliography: p23
ISBN 0-7044-0355-2 (pbk) : £0.50 B81-39708

333.78'4 — Great Britain. Coastal regions. Environment. Conservation — *Manuals*

Coastlands : a practical conservation handbook / illustrations by Roy Allitt. — London : British Trust for Conservation Volunteers, 1979. — 120p : ill ; 30cm
Bibliography: p115-119
ISBN 0-9501643-6-4 (spiral) : £4.00 B81-40334

333.78'4 — Great Britain. Forests. Recreation facilities

Kassioumis, Costas. Recreationists response to forest and the implications for forestry & recreation management / Costas Kassioumis. — Reading (Whiteknights, Reading, RG6 2AB) : Department of Geography, University of Reading, 1981. — vi,64p : ill ; 1map ; 21cm. — (Geographical papers / Department of Geography, University of Reading, ISSN 0305-5914 ; no.74)
Tables (3 folded leaves) in pocket. — Bibliography: p61-63
ISBN 0-7049-0662-7 (pbk) : £1.50 B81-22226

333.78'4'0941 — Great Britain. Water recreation facilities

Parker, R. L.. The use of water for recreational purposes / by R.L. Parker. — London : Institution of Municipal Engineers, 1976. — 12p : 2ill,1map ; 21cm. — (Protection of the environment ; monograph no.28)
Bibliography: p.12
£0.50 (pbk) B81-08317

333.78'4'094267 — Essex. Coastal waters. Water recreation facilities — *Proposals*

Coastal water recreation in Essex : draft : strategic guidance on the future of moorings and marinas : public consultation / Essex County Council. — [Chelmsford] ([Planning Dept., County Hall, Chelmsford CM1 1LF]) : [The Council], 1981. — 116p,[28]leaves of plates(some folded) : maps ; 30cm
Bibliography: p116
£3.00 (pbk) B81-23036

333.78'4'09429 — Wales. Water recreation facilities — *Proposals*

Welsh Water Authority. *Directorate of Resource Planning*. A strategic plan for water-space recreation and amenity. — [Brecon] ([Cambrian Way, Brecon, Powys LD3 7HP]) : Welsh Water Authority, Directorate of Resource Planning, 1980. — iv,194p : ill,maps ; 24cm
Includes index
ISBN 0-86097-068-x (pbk) : £2.00 B81-19622

333.78'44'09411 — Scotland. Freshwater lochs. Effects of recreation

Tivy, Joy. The effect of recreation on freshwater lochs and reservoirs in Scotland / Joy Tivy ; commissioned by the Countryside Commission for Scotland. — Perth (Battleby, Redgorton, Perth [PH1 3EW]) : The Commission, c1980. — 202p,[6]p of plates(2folded) : ill,maps ; 30cm
Bibliography: p189-193. — Includes index
ISBN 0-902226-47-9 (pbk) : Unpriced B81-04067

333.79 — Alternative energy resources — *Conference proceedings*

International School of Energetics *(3rd : 1979 : Ettore Majorana Center for Scientific Culture)*. Energy for the year 2000 / [proceedings of the Third International School of Energetics, held at the Ettore Majorana Center for Scientific Culture, Erice, Sicily, Italy, September 1-11, 1979] ; edited by Richard Wilson. — New York ; London : Plenum, c1980. — viii,401p : ill,1map,ports ; 26cm. — (Ettore Majorana international science series. Physical sciences ; v.6)
Includes bibliographies and index
ISBN 0-306-40540-7 : Unpriced B81-05221

333.79 — Energy resources

Dorf, Richard C.. The energy factbook / Richard C. Dorf. — New York ; London : McGraw-Hill, c1981. — vii,227p : ill ; 24cm
Includes index
ISBN 0-07-017623-x (cased) : Unpriced
ISBN 0-07-017629-9 (pbk) : £5.50 B81-29515

Energy options - present and future options. — Wiley : Chichester, Aug.1981
Vol.1. — [384]p
ISBN 0-471-27922-6 : £24.00 : CIP entry B81-19177

Foley, Gerald, *1936-*. The energy question / Gerald Foley with Charlotte Nassim. — 2nd ed. — Harmondsworth : Penguin, 1981. — 327p : ill ; 20cm
Previous ed.: 1976. — Includes index
ISBN 0-14-021924-2 (pbk) : £1.95 B81-29160

Harker, J. H.. Fuel and energy / J.H. Harker and J.R. Backhurst. — London : Academic Press, 1981. — xi,362p : ill,maps ; 24cm. — (Energy science and engineering)
Includes bibliographies and index
ISBN 0-12-325250-4 (cased) : £21.00 : CIP rev.
ISBN 0-12-325252-0 (pbk) : Unpriced B81-08911

Ion, D. C.. Availability of world energy resources / D.C. Ion. — 2nd ed.. — London : Graham & Trotman, 1980. — 345p : ill,maps ; 25cm
Previous ed.: 1975. — Includes index
ISBN 0-86010-193-2 : £15.00 B81-02482

Odum, Howard T.. Energy basis for man and nature / Howard T. Odum, Elisabeth C. Odum. — 2nd ed. — New York ; London : McGraw-Hill, 1981. — xii,337p : ill,maps ; 24cm
Previous ed.: 1976. — Bibliography: p313-325. — Includes index
ISBN 0-07-047511-3 (cased) : Unpriced
ISBN 0-07-047510-5 (pbk) : £9.50 B81-36478

333.79 — Energy resources — *Conference proceedings*

International Conference on Energy Use Management *(3rd : 1981 : West Berlin)*. Beyond the energy crisis. — Oxford : Pergamon, Nov.1981. — 3v.[(2500p.)]
Conference papers
ISBN 0-08-027589-3 : £175.00 : CIP entry B81-30287

333.79 — Energy resources. Economic aspects

Energy economics : growth, resources and policies / Richard Eden ... [et al.]. — Cambridge : Cambridge University Press, 1981. — xiii,442p : ill ; 24cm
Bibliography: p423-432. — Includes index
ISBN 0-521-23685-1 : £19.50 B81-25933

Gordon, Richard L.. An economic analysis of world energy problems / Richard L. Gordon. — Cambridge, Mass. ; London : M.I.T., c1981. — xvii,282p : ill ; 24cm
Bibliography: p249-272. — Includes index
ISBN 0-262-07080-4 : £18.60 B81-38138

333.79 — Energy resources — *For children*

Satchwell, John. Future sources / John Satchwell. — London : Watts, 1981. — 38p : ill(some col.),col.maps,1col.port ; 30cm. — (Energy)
Text, and ill on lining papers. — Includes index
ISBN 0-85166-917-4 : £3.99 B81-34684

333.79 — Energy resources — *Forecasts*

Energy in the 80's / compiled by Mike Wild (general editor) ... [et al.] ; cover design Barry Perks. — York : Longman, 1980. — 297p : ill,facsims,maps,plans,port ; 30cm
ISBN 0-582-39606-9 : £8.95 B81-03110

333.79 — Energy resources. International political aspects

International energy policy / edited by Robert M. Lawrence, Martin O. Heisler. — Lexington : Lexington Books ; [Farnborough, Hants.] : Gower [distributor], c1980. — xii,218p : ill ; 24cm. — (Policy Studies Organization series)
Includes index
ISBN 0-669-02929-7 : £13.50 B81-01656

333.79 — Energy resources. Policies of governments *related to* **national security**

Energy and security / edited by Gregory Treverton. — Farnborough, Hants. : Gower for The International Institute for Strategic Studies, c1980. — vii,165p : ill ; 23cm. — (The Adelphi library ; 1)
Includes index
ISBN 0-566-00343-0 : £8.50 : CIP rev.
Also classified at 327.1'16 B80-07256

333.79 — Energy resources. Social aspects

Starr, Chauncey. Current issues in energy : a selection of papers / by Chauncey Starr. — Oxford : Pergamon, 1979. — xvi,202p,[1]leaf of plates : ill,1port ; 26cm. — (Pergamon international library)
ISBN 0-08-023243-4 (cased) : £10.50 : CIP rev.
ISBN 0-08-023244-2 (pbk) : £5.25 B79-01761

333.79 — Energy resources. Social aspects — *Conference proceedings*

Mankind and energy. — Oxford : Elsevier Scientific, Dec.1981. — [700]p. — (Studies in environmental science ; 16)
Conference papers
ISBN 0-444-99715-6 : £60.00 : CIP entry B81-33861

333.79 — Renewable energy resources

Hyde, Margaret O.. Energy : the new look / by Margaret O. Hyde. — New York ; London : McGraw-Hill, c1981. — 138p ; 21cm
Bibliography: p4. — Includes index
ISBN 0-07-031552-3 : £5.75 B81-32855

333.79'03'21 — Energy resources — *Encyclopaedias*

McGraw-Hill encyclopedia of energy / editor in chief Sybil P. Parker. — 2nd ed. — New York ; London : McGraw-Hill, c1981. — viii,838p : ill,maps ; 29cm
Previous ed.: 1976. — Bibliography: p815-820. - Includes index
ISBN 0-07-045268-7 : £24.50 B81-10342

333.79'07 — Energy resources. Information sources — *Lists*

World directory of energy information / compiled by Cambridge Information and Research Services Limited. — Farnborough, Hants. : Gower
Vol.1: Western Europe / [editors Christopher Swain, Andrew Buckley]. — c1981. — x,326p : ill,maps ; 31cm
Bibliography: p193-273
ISBN 0-566-02198-6 : Unpriced B81-36795

333.79'07041 — Great Britain. Renewable energy resources. Information sources — *Directories*

New and renewable sources of energy : a directory of UK expertise / compiled for the United Nations Conference on New and Renewable Sources of Energy, Kenya, 1981 by the Information Office, Energy Technology Support Unit, Atomic Energy Research Establishment. — London : Department of Energy, [1981]. — 32p ; 21cm
Includes index
Unpriced (pbk) B81-40650

333.79'07204 — European Community countries. Energy resources. Research projects: First Energy R & D Programme

McMullan, J. T.. Achievements of the European Community First Energy R & D Programme / by J.T. McMullan and A.S. Strub. — The Hague ; London : Nijhoff for the Commission of the European Communities, 1981. — 48p : ill(some col.),2col.maps ; 30cm
ISBN 90-247-2511-9 (pbk) : Unpriced B81-34670

333.79′0724 — Energy resources. Models — *Conference proceedings*

IIASA/IFAC Symposium on Modeling of Large-Scale Energy Systems *(1980)*. Modeling of large-scale energy systems : proceedings of the IIASA/IFAC Symposium on Modeling of Large-Scale Energy Systems, February 25-29, 1980 / W. Häfele, editor ; L.K. Kirchmayer, associate editor. — Oxford : Pergamon, 1981. — x,461p : ill,maps ; 26cm. — (IIASA proceedings series ; v.12)
Includes bibliographies
ISBN 0-08-025696-1 : £30.00 : CIP rev. B80-27952

333.79′0724 — Western world. Energy resources. Policies of governments. Mathematical models — *Conference proceedings*

NATO Advanced Research Institute on the Applications of Systems Science to Energy Policy Planning *(1979 : New York)*. Energy policy planning / [proceedings of the NATO Advanced Research Institute on the Applications of Systems Science to Energy Policy Planning, held November 12-16, 1979 in Upton, New York, sponsored by the NATO Special Program Panel on Systems Science] ; edited by B.A. Bayraktar ... [et al.]. — New York ; London : Published in cooperation with NATO Scientific Affairs Division by Plenum, c1981. — ix,467p : ill ; 26cm. — (NATO conference series. II, Systems science ; v.9)
Includes index
ISBN 0-306-40631-4 : Unpriced B81-10760

333.79′09172′4 — Developing countries. Energy resources. Environmental & socioeconomic factors — *Conference proceedings*

Energy and environment in the developing countries. — Chichester : Wiley, Jan.1982. — [352]p
Conference papers
ISBN 0-471-27993-5 : £18.00 : CIP entry B81-33803

333.79′09172′4 — Developing countries. Energy resources. Policies of governments

Energy strategies for developing nations / Joy Dunkerley ... [et al.]. — Baltimore ; London : Published for Resources for the Future by the Johns Hopkins University Press, c1981. — xvii,265p : ill,maps ; 24cm
Includes index
ISBN 0-8018-2596-2 (cased) : £14.50
ISBN 0-8018-2597-0 (pbk) : Unpriced B81-37177

333.79′09182′1 — Caribbean region. Energy resources — *Serials*

Quarterly energy review. Latin America & the Caribbean. — 1st quarter 1981-. — London : Economist Intelligence Unit, 1981-. — v. ; 30cm
Continues: Quarterly economic review of oil in Latin America and the Caribbean
ISSN 0144-9214 = Quarterly energy review. Latin America & the Caribbean : £65.00 per year
Primary classification 333.79′098 B81-29400

333.79′094 — Energy resources. Policies. Cooperation between Eastern & Western Europe — *Conference proceedings*

East and West in the energy squeeze : prospects for cooperation / edited by Christopher T. Saunders. — London : Macmillan in association with the Vienna Institute for Comparative Economic Studies, 1980. — 468p : ill ; 22cm. — (East-West European economic interaction ; 5)
Conference papers. — Includes index
ISBN 0-333-30515-9 : £20.00 : CIP rev. B80-10961

333.79′094 — Energy resources. Policies of European Community. Formulation. Mathematical models

Energy models for the European Community / edited by A. Strub. — Guildford : IPC Science and Technology for the Commission of the European Communities, 1979. — 154p : ill ; 28cm. — (An Energy policy special)
Includes bibliographies
ISBN 0-86103-011-7 (pbk) : Unpriced B81-39488

333.79′094 — European countries. Energy resources. Policies of governments

The **European** transition from oil. — London : Academic Press, Aug.1981. — [350]p
ISBN 0-12-290420-6 : CIP entry B81-18039

333.79′094 — Western Europe. Energy resources — *Serials*

Quarterly energy review. Western Europe. — 1st quarter 1981-. — London : Economist Intelligence Unit, 1981-. — v. ; 30cm
Continues: Quarterly economic review of oil in Western Europe
ISSN 0144-9222 = Quarterly energy review. Western Europe : £65.00 per year B81-29398

333.79′0941 — Energy resources — *Study regions: Great Britain — Conference proceedings*

British Association for the Advancement of Science. *Meeting (1979 : Heriot-Watt University)*. Energy in the balance : some papers from BA79 : papers given at the Annual Meeting of the British Association for the Advancement of Science, Heriot-Watt University, Edinburgh, 1979. — Guildford : Westbury House, c1980. — v,234p : ill,maps ; 21cm
Includes bibliographies
ISBN 0-86103-031-1 (pbk) : Unpriced : CIP rev. B80-21522

333.79′0941 — Great Britain. Energy resources

Energy : a key resource / [prepared by the Department of Energy and the Central Office of Information]. — London (Thames House South, Millbank, SW1P 4QJ) : Department of Energy, [Information Division], 1980. — 20p : ill(some col.) ; 30cm
Cover title
Unpriced (pbk) B81-09427

333.79′0941 — Great Britain. Energy resources — *For schools*

Energy resources / James Sage ... [et al.]. — Edinburgh : Oliver & Boyd in association with the National Centre for School Technology, 1980. — 92p : ill,maps ; 24cm. — (Schools Council modular courses in technology)
ISBN 0-05-003380-8 (pbk) : Unpriced B81-32468

333.79′0941 — Great Britain. Energy resources — *Serials*

Energy matters. — Issue 1 (Michaelmas 1980)-. — Cambridge (c/o Mr A. Bud, Christ′s College, Cambridge) : [s.n.], 1980-. — v. : ill ; 21cm
Three issues yearly
ISSN 0260-809x = Energy matters : Unpriced B81-10286

333.79′0947 — Eastern Europe & Soviet Union. Energy resources — *Serials*

Quarterly energy review. USSR & Eastern Europe. — 1st quarter 1981-. — London : Economist Intelligence Unit, 1981-. — v. ; 30cm
Supplement: Quarterly energy review. USSR & Eastern Europe. Annual supplement
ISSN 0144-9230 = Quarterly energy review. USSR & Eastern Europe : £65.00 per year B81-26387

333.79′0956 — Middle East. Energy resources — *Serials*

Quarterly energy review. Middle East. — 1st quarter 1981-. — London : Economist Intelligence Unit, 1981-. — v. ; 30cm
Continues: Quarterly economic review of oil in the Middle East. — Supplement: Quarterly energy review. Middle East. Annual supplement
ISSN 0144-8994 = Quarterly energy review. Middle East : £65.00 per year B81-29401

333.79′096 — Africa. Energy resources — *Serials*

Quarterly energy review. Africa. — Ist quarter 1981-. — London : Economist Intelligence Unit, 1981-. — v. ; 30cm
Description based on: 2nd quarter (1981)
ISSN 0144-9249 = Quarterly energy review. Africa : £65.00 per issue B81-32798

333.79′097 — North America. Energy resources — *Serials*

Quarterly energy review. North America. — 1st quarter 1981-. — London : Economist Intelligence Unit, 1981-. — v. ; 30cm
Continues: Quarterly economic review of oil in North America
ISSN 0144-9206 = Quarterly energy review. North America : £65.00 per year B81-32891

333.79′0973 — United States. Energy resources. Policies

Energy policy and public administration / edited by Gregory A. Daneke, George K. Lagassa. — Lexington, Mass : Lexington Books ; [Farnborough, Hants] : Gower [distributor], c1980. — vii,322p : ill ; 24cm
Includes index
ISBN 0-669-03395-2 : £17.50 B81-03643

333.79′0973 — United States. Energy resources. Policies of government

Prast, William G.. Securing U.S. energy supplies : the private sector as an instrument of public policy / William G. Prast. — Lexington, Mass. : Lexington Books ; [Aldershot] : Gower [distributor], 1981. — ix,111p : ill ; 24cm
Bibliography: p101-104. — Includes index
ISBN 0-669-03305-7 : £10.50 B81-38606

333.79′098 — Latin America. Energy resources — *Serials*

Quarterly energy review. Latin America & the Caribbean. — 1st quarter 1981-. — London : Economist Intelligence Unit, 1981-. — v. ; 30cm
Continues: Quarterly economic review of oil in Latin America and the Caribbean
ISSN 0144-9214 = Quarterly energy review. Latin America & the Caribbean : £65.00 per year
Also classified at 333.79′09182′1 B81-29400

333.79′0994 — Australia. Energy resources

Saddler, Hugh. Energy in Australia : politics and economics / Hugh Saddler. — Sydney ; London : Allen & Unwin, 1981. — x,205p : ill,maps ; 23cm
Bibliography: p193-199. — Includes index
ISBN 0-86861-298-7 (cased) : Unpriced
ISBN 0-86861-306-1 (pbk) : Unpriced B81-33169

333.79′11′091734 — Rural regions. Energy supply — *Conference proceedings*

Energy for rural and island communities : proceedings of the conference, held in Inverness, Scotland 22-24 September 1980 / edited by John Twidell. — Oxford : Pergamon, 1981. — ix,253p : ill ; 26cm
Includes bibliographies and index
ISBN 0-08-027290-8 : £18.50 : CIP rev. B81-06576

333.79′12 — Energy resources — *Forecasts*

Grenon, Michel. The nuclear apple and the solar orange : alternatives in world energy / Michael Grenon ; translated from the French by R. Peniston-Bird. — Oxford : Pergamon, c1981. — xxix,155p : ill ; 24cm. — (Pergamon international library)
Translation of: La pomme nucléaire et l′orange solaire
ISBN 0-08-026157-4 (cased) : Unpriced
ISBN 0-08-026156-6 (pbk) : £6.50 B81-12022

333.79′12 — Energy. Supply & demand

Gardel, André. Energy : economy and prospective : a handbook for engineers and economists / by André Gardel ; translated from the French by John Spreadborough. — Oxford : Pergamon, 1981. — xxi,561p : ill ; 26cm
Translation of: Energie. — Bibliography: p541-551. - Includes index
ISBN 0-08-025427-6 : £34.00 : CIP rev. B80-02700

333.79′12 — Energy. Supply & demand — *Forecasts*

Energy in a finite world : report / by the Energy Systems Program Group of the International Institute for Applied Systems Analysis ; Wolf Häfele, program leader. — Cambridge, Mass. : Ballinger ; [London] : Harper & Row
[Vol.2]: A global systems analysis. — c1981. — xli,837p : ill,maps ; 26cm
Text, ill on lining papers. — Includes bibliographies and index
ISBN 0-06-660695-0 (correced) : £29.50 B81-32176

333.79′12 — Energy. Supply & demand. Role of Organization of the Petroleum Exporting Countries — *Forecasts — Conference proceedings*

OPEC and future engery markets : the proceedings of the OPEC seminar held in Vienna, Austria, in October 1979 / prepared by the Public Information Department of OPEC. — London : Macmillan, 1980. — xi,290p : ill ; 24cm
ISBN 0-333-31126-4 : £20.00 B81-05840

333.79′12′091724 — Developing countries. Energy resources. Supply & demand

Fritz, Markus. Future energy consumption of the Third World : with special reference to nuclear power : an individual and comprehensive evaluation of 156 countries / by Markus Fritz. — Oxford : Pergamon, 1981. — xv,206,A62,B80,C54p : ill,maps ; 26cm
Includes index
ISBN 0-08-026168-x : £20.00 : CIP rev. B81-13445

Parikh, Jyoti K.. Energy systems and development : constraints, demand and supply of energy for developing regions / Jyoti K. Parikh. — Delhi ; Oxford : Oxford University Press, 1980. — xviii,152p : ill ; 23cm
Bibliography: p145-147. — Includes index
ISBN 0-19-561193-4 : £7.75 B81-34092

333.79′12′094 — Europe. Energy. Supply & demand — *Serials*

European energy profile. — Issue no.1 (21 Apr.1981)-. — London : Financial Times Business Information Ltd., 1981-. — v. ; 30cm
Irregular
ISSN 0261-7374 = European energy profile : Unpriced B81-32686

333.79′12′094 — Western Europe. Energy. Supply & demand — *Forecasts*

Energy in Europe : looking forward to the year 2000 / [prepared by Esso Europe Inc.]. — [London] ([Victoria St., SW1]) : Esso, [1981]. — 12p : ill ; 28cm
Cover title
Unpriced (pbk) B81-16512

333.79′12′0941 — Great Britain. Energy. Supply & demand. Elasticity. Effects of prices. Econometric models

Westoby, Richard. Interfuel substitution in the UK industrial and domestic sectors / by Richard Westoby. — [Aberdeen] : University of Aberdeen, Department of Political Economy, [1981]. — 13leaves ; 31cm. — (Discussion paper / University of Aberdeen Department of Political Economy ; no.81-10)
Unpriced (pbk) B81-38610

Westoby, Richard. Long run price elasticities for energy : an overview of existing energy models / by Richard Westoby. — [Aberdeen] : [University of Aberdeen. Department of Political Economy], [1981]. — 29p ; 30cm. — (Discussion paper ; 81-05)
Bibliography: p28-29
Unpriced (pbk) B81-17261

333.79′12′095 — Far East. Energy. Supply & demand

Far East oil and energy survey / editor Bryan Cooper ; associate editor Jeffrey Segal ; contributors K.J. Bradley ... [et al.] ; maps specially drawn by Martin J. Lubikowsky, based on original data provided by Petroconsultants. — London (107 Charterhouse St., EC1M 6AA) : Petroleum Economics ; Dublin : Petroconsultants, 1981. — 1v (looseleaf) : ill(some col.),maps(some col.) ; 32cm
ISBN 0-906618-03-7 : £160.00 B81-33132

333.79′12′174927 — Arab countries. Energy resources - *Forecasts*

Arab energy. — Oxford : Pergamon, Apr.1981. — [250]p
ISBN 0-08-027581-8 : £21.00 : CIP entry B81-04200

333.79′13 — Energy resources. Use — *Conference proceedings*

International School on Energetics *(4th : 1980 : Erice)*. Energy demand and efficient use / [proceedings of the fourth International School on Energetics, held July 15-24, 1980 in Erice, Sicily] ; edited by Fernando Amman and Richard Wilson. — New York ; London : Plenum, c1981. — vii,462p : ill ; 26cm. — (Ettore Majorana international science series. Physical sciences ; v.9)
Includes index
ISBN 0-306-40732-9 : Unpriced B81-33433

333.79′16 — Energy resources. Conservation

Gibbons, John H.. Energy : the conservation revolution / John H. Gibbons and William V. Chandler. — New York ; London : Plenum, c1981. — xv,258p : ill,1map ; 24cm
Includes index
ISBN 0-306-40670-5 : Unpriced B81-18558

Schumacher, E. F.. Schumacher on energy. — London : Cape, Feb.1982. — [240]p
ISBN 0-224-01965-1 : £7.95 : CIP entry B81-40273

333.79′16 — Great Britain. Passenger transport. Energy. Conservation — *Proposals*

Banister, David. Transport policy and energy : perspectives, options and scope for conservation in the passenger transport sector / by David Banister. — London (Gower St., WC1E 6BT) : University College London, 1981. — 48p ; 30cm. — (Town planning discussion paper ; no.36)
Bibliography: p45-48
£1.00 (pbk) B81-11553

333.79′16′02541 — Great Britain. Energy resources. Conservation. Projects — *Directories*

Energy conservation — TEAM Awards 1981 : details of entries. — London : LAMSAC, 1981. — 45p ; 30cm
ISBN 0-85497-123-8 (pbk) : Unpriced B81-40830

333.79′16′0941 — Great Britain. Cities. Inner areas. Energy resources. Conservation — *Proposals*

Green, David, *1954 Oct.30-*. Energy : a programme for the inner city / by David Green. — London : National Council for Voluntary Organisations, [1980]. — 24p : 1ill ; 30cm
Cover title. — Written for the NCVO Inner Cities Unit. — Bibliography: p24
£1.00 (pbk) B81-28986

333.79′16′0941 — Great Britain. Energy. Conservation. Projects - *Regulations*

European Community Scheme for energy saving projects : third round, January-April 1981 : notes for applicants / Department of Energy. — [London] ([Thames House South, Millbank, SW1P 4QJ]) : [The Department], [1980]. — [63]p : 1form ; 30cm
Cover title
Unpriced (pbk) B81-18219

333.79′16′0941 — Great Britain. Energy resources. Conservation. Organisations

Facing the energy future : does Britain need new energy institutions? : proceedings of an RIPA conference. — London : Royal Institute of Public Administration. — 80p ; 22cm
ISBN 0-900628-23-5 (pbk) : £3.00 B81-34365

333.79′16′0973 — United States. Energy resources. Conservation

Notes from the energy underground / collected by Malcolm Wells. — New York ; London : Van Nostrand Reinhold, c1980. — ix,162p ; 24cm
Includes index
ISBN 0-442-25697-3 : £8.20 B81-01546

333.79′17 — Great Britain. Industries. Energy supply. Pricing. Policies of government — *Inquiry reports*

Great Britain. *Parliament. House of Commons. Select Committee on Energy*. Second report from the Select Committee on Energy : together with minutes of evidence, appendices, and minutes of proceedings : session 1980-81 : industrial energy pricing policy. — London : H.M.S.O.
Vol.1: Report and minutes of proceedings. — [1981]. — xxxip ; 25cm. — (HC ; 422-I)
ISBN 0-10-008311-0 (pbk) : £2.60 B81-39929

Great Britain. *Parliament. House of Commons. Select Committee on Energy*. Second report from the Select Committee on Energy : together with minutes of evidence, appendices, and minutes of proceedings : session 1980-81 : industrial energy pricing policy. — London : H.M.S.O.. — (HC ; 422-II)
Vol.2: Minutes of evidence and appendices. — [1981]. — vi,437p : ill ; 25cm
ISBN 0-10-008581-4 (pbk) : £13.45 B81-39930

333.79′23 — Solar energy. Conversion. Environmental aspects

Yokell, Michael D.. Environmental benefits and costs of solar energy / Michael D. Yokell. — Lexington, Mass. : Lexington Books ; [Aldershot] : Gower [distributor], 1981, c1980. — xv,141p : ill,1map ; 24cm
Bibliography: p131-137. — Includes index
ISBN 0-669-03468-1 : £11.50 B81-29596

333.79′24 — Nuclear power. Environmental aspects

The **Environmental** impact of nuclear power : proceedings of a conference organized by the British Nuclear Energy Society, and supported by the UK Atomic Energy Authority, held in London on 1-2 April, 1981. — London : Telford for BNES, 1981. — 294p : ill,2maps ; 21cm
Includes bibliographies
£16.00 (pbk) B81-35405

333.79′24 — Nuclear power. Opposition

Atom′s eve : ending the nuclear age : an anthology / compiled and edited by Mark Reader with Ronald A. Hardert and Gerald L. Moulton. — New York ; London : McGraw-Hill, 1980. — xi,285p ; 21cm
Includes bibliographies, list of films and index
ISBN 0-07-051287-6 (pbk) : £3.55 B81-08392

333.79′24′0941 — Great Britain. Nuclear power. Policies of government, *1939-1945*. **Gowing, Margaret. Britain and atomic energy 1939-1945. Citations: Public records —** *Lists*

Britain and atomic energy 1939-1945 by Margaret Gowing (Macmillan, London, 1964) : references to official papers. — Didcot (Building 328, AERE, Harwell, Didcot, Oxon) : Authority Historian′s Office, 1980. — 32p ; 21cm
Unpriced (pbk)
Primary classification 355′.0335′41 B81-16103

333.79′24′0941 — Great Britain. Nuclear power. Policies of government, *1945-1952*. **Gowing, Margaret. Independence and deterrence. Citations: Public records —** *Lists*

Independence and deterrence Britain and atomic energy, 1945-1952 by Margaret Gowing (2 vols. Macmillan, London, 1974) : references to official papers. — Rev. ed. — Didcot (Building 328, AERE, Harwell, Didcot, Oxon) : Authority Historian′s Office, 1970. — 48p ; 21cm
Previous ed.: 1977
Unpriced (pbk)
Primary classification 355′.0335′41 B81-16104

333.79′24′0941 — Great Britain. Nuclear power. Policies of government — *Friends of the Earth viewpoints*

Flood, Michael. The pressurised water reactor : a critique of the Government′s nuclear power programme / by Michael Flood, Renée Chudleigh, Czech Conroy. — London (9 Poland St., W1V 3DG) : Friends of the Earth, c1981. — ii,71p : ill,1map ; 30cm. — (Friends of the Earth energy paper ; no.4)
Text on inside cover. — Bibliography: p71
ISBN 0-905966-25-2 (pbk) : £1.50 B81-28237

333.79′24′0943 — Nuclear power. Opposition — *Study regions: West Germany*

Nelkin, Dorothy. The atom besieged : extraparliamentary dissent in France and Germany / Dorothy Nelkin, Michael Pollak. — Cambridge, Mass. ; London : MIT, c1981. — x,235p : ill,2maps,facsims ; 24cm
Includes index
ISBN 0-262-14034-9 : £10.85
Also classified at 333.79′24′0944 B81-28253

333.79′24′0944 — Nuclear power. Opposition — *Study regions: France*

Nelkin, Dorothy. The atom besieged : extraparliamentary dissent in France and Germany / Dorothy Nelkin, Michael Pollak. — Cambridge, Mass. ; London : MIT, c1981. — x,235p : ill,2maps,facsims ; 24cm
Includes index
ISBN 0-262-14034-9 : £10.85
Primary classification 333.79′24′0943 B81-28253

333.79′24′0973 — United States. Nuclear power. Use. Social aspects, ***1950-1979***

Curtis, Richard. Nuclear lessons : an examination of nuclear power's safety, economic and political record / by Richard Curtis and Elizabeth Hogan with Shel Horowitz. — Wellingborough : Turnstone, 1980. — 285p ; 22cm
Includes index
ISBN 0-85500-147-x (pbk) : £3.95 : CIP rev. B80-21523

333.8 — SUBSURFACE RESOURCES

333.8′2 — Fuel resources: Coal

Grainger, L.. Coal utilisation. — London : Graham & Trotman, Sept.1981. — [400]p
ISBN 0-86010-266-1 : £18.00 : CIP entry B81-28143

333.8′2 — Fuel resources: Hydrocarbons

Rider, Don K.. Energy : hydrocarbon fuels and chemical resources / Don K. Rider. — New York ; Chichester : Wiley, c1981. — x,493p : ill,maps ; 24cm
Includes index
ISBN 0-471-05915-3 : £23.40 B81-28307

333.8′22′0941 — Great Britain. Fuel resources: Coal

Manners, Gerald. Coal in Britain / Gerald Manners. — London : Allen & Unwin, 1981. — 108p : ill,maps ; 24cm. — (The Resource management series ; 4)
Bibliography: p103-105. — Includes index
ISBN 0-04-333018-5 (cased) : Unpriced : CIP rev. B81-20141

333.8′23′0916336 — North Sea. British sector. Natural gas deposits & petroleum deposits. Exploitation. Political aspects

Dafter, Ray. North Sea oil and gas and British foreign policy / Ray Dafter and Ian Davidson. — London : Royal Institute of International Affairs, c1980. — vii,44p : ill,1map ; 30cm. — (Chatham House papers, ISSN 0143-5795)
ISBN 0-905031-18-0 (pbk) : £5.00 B81-06382

333.8′23′0916336 — North Sea. Natural gas deposits & petroleum deposits. Exploitation. Economic aspects

Davis, Jerome D.. High-cost oil and gas resources / Jerome D. Davis. — London : Croom Helm, c1981. — 266p : ill,maps ; 23cm
Includes index
ISBN 0-85664-588-5 : £16.95 B81-17848

333.8′23′0916336 — North Sea. Natural gas deposits & petroleum deposits. Exploitation. Policies of British government

Jenkin, Michael. British industry and the North Sea : state intervention in a developing industrial sector / Michael Jenkin. — London : Macmillan, 1981. — xiii,251p : ill ; 23cm
Includes index
ISBN 0-333-25606-9 : £20.00 : CIP rev. B80-24191

333.8′23′09575 — Russia ***(RSFSR).*** **Eastern Siberia. Natural gas deposits & petroleum deposits**

Meyerhoff, A. A.. The oil and gas potential of the Soviet Far East / A.A. Meyerhoff. — Beaconsfield : Scientific Press, c1981. — 176p : ill,maps ; 28cm
Bibliography: p135-159
ISBN 0-901360-13-9 (pbk) : Unpriced B81-40893

333.8′232′0916336 — North Sea. British petroleum deposits. Exploitation. Facilities. Planning — *Proposals*

Klitz, J. Kenneth. North sea oil : resource requirements for development of the U.K. sector / J. Kenneth Klitz. — Oxford : Pergamon, 1980. — xiv,260p : ill,2charts,2maps ; 24cm
Bibliography: p249-255. - Includes index
ISBN 0-08-024442-4 : £15.00 : CIP rev. B80-00083

333.8′232′0916336 — North Sea. Petroleum deposits. Exploitation. Environmental aspects - *Conference proceedings*

International Conference on Oil and the Environment *(1980 : University of Edinburgh).* Onshore impacts of offshore oil. — London : Applied Science, Sept.1981. — [288]p
ISBN 0-85334-974-6 : £24.00 : CIP entry B81-20161

333.8′232′094233 — Dorset. Petroleum deposits. Exploitation. Planning

Onshore oil in Dorset : a consultative document / [Dorset County Planning Department]. — Dorchester, [Dorset] (County Hall, Dorchester, [Dorset D.T.A. 1X5]) : The Planning Department, 1980. — 22[i.e.35]p : ill(some col.),maps(some col.) ; 30cm
ISBN 0-85216-274-x (pbk) : £1.00 B81-37050

333.8′232′0959 — South-east Asia. Offshore petroleum deposits. Politico-economic aspects

Siddayao, Corazón Morales. The off shore petroleum resources of South-East Asia : potential conflict situations and related economic considerations / Corazón Morales Siddayao. — Kuala Lumpur ; Oxford : Oxford University Press, 1978 (1980 [printing]). — xx,205p : ill,maps ; 23cm. — (Natural resources of South-East Asia)
Maps on lining papers. — Bibliography: p184-198. — Includes index
Unpriced (cased) B81-34738

333.8′232′0959 — South-east Asia. Petroleum deposits. Exploitation. Implications of property rights

Siddayao, Corazón Morales. The supply of petroleum reserves in South-East Asia : economic implications of evolving property rights arrangements / Corazón Morales Siddayao ; issued under the auspices of the Institute of Southeast Asian Studies, Singapore, and the East-West Resource Systems Institute, the East-West Center, U.S.A.. — Kuala Lumpur ; Oxford : Oxford University Press, 1980. — xix,240p : ill ; 23cm. — (Natural resources of South-East Asia)
Bibliography: p212-229. - Includes index
ISBN 0-19-580466-x : £12.50 B81-25972

333.8′232′09729 — West Indies. Petroleum deposits. Exploitation

Latin America and Caribbean oil report / general editor Bryan Cooper ; associate editor: Frank Niering Jr ; American editor: Edward Symonds ; contributors: Frank Niering Jr ... [et al.] ; maps specially drawn by Robin Whitworth. — London (5 Pemberton Row, Fleet St., EC4A 3DP) : Petroleum Economist, 1979. — 328p,[19]folded leaves of plates : ill,maps(some col.) ; 30cm
Maps on inside covers
ISBN 0-906618-00-2 (spiral) : £44.00
Primary classification 333.8′232′098 B81-10114

333.8′232′098 — South America. Petroleum deposits. Exploitation

Latin America and Caribbean oil report / general editor Bryan Cooper ; associate editor: Frank Niering Jr ; American editor: Edward Symonds ; contributors: Frank Niering Jr ... [et al.] ; maps specially drawn by Robin Whitworth. — London (5 Pemberton Row, Fleet St., EC4A 3DP) : Petroleum Economist, 1979. — 328p,[19]folded leaves of plates : ill,maps(some col.) ; 30cm
Maps on inside covers
ISBN 0-906618-00-2 (spiral) : £44.00
Also classified at 333.8′232′09729 B81-10114

333.8′2321′095357 — United Arab Emirates. Petroleum deposits. Exploitation. Concessions, ***1939-1981***

Al-Otaiba, Mana Saeed. The petroleum concession agreements of the United Arab Emirates 1939-1981. — London : Croom Helm
Vol.1: 1939-1971. — Jan.1982. — [176]p
ISBN 0-7099-1915-8 : CIP entry B81-38840

333.8′23217 — Industrialised countries. Petroleum. Emergency reserve storage. Policies of governments, ***ca 1970-1979***

Krapels, Edwards N.. Oil crisis management : strategic stockpiling for international security / Edward N. Krapels. — Baltimore ; London : Johns Hopkins University Press, c1980. — xii,173p : ill,1map ; 24cm
Includes index
ISBN 0-8018-2374-9 : £9.00 B81-05322

333.8′5 — Mineral resources. International political aspects

Tanzer, Michael. The race for resources : continuing struggles over minerals and fuels / Michael Tanzer. — New York ; London : Monthly Review, c1980. — 285p ; 21cm
Bibliography: p275-276. — Includes index
ISBN 0-435-84800-3 (pbk) : £4.50 : CIP rev. B80-20327

333.8′5 — Natural resources: Uranium. Supply & demand — *Forecasts*

The **Uranium** equation : balance of supply and demand 1980-95 / the Supply and Demand Committee. — [London] : Published for the Uranium Institute by Mining Journal Books, 1981. — vi,57p : ill ; 23cm
ISBN 0-900117-27-3 (pbk) : Unpriced B81-40080

333.8′5 — Oceans. Bed. Manganese nodules. Exploitation — *Conference proceedings*

Manganese nodules : dimensions and perspectives / prepared by the United Nations Ocean Economics and Technology Office. — Dordrecht ; London : Reidel, c1979. — ix,194p : ill ; 25cm. — (Natural resources forum library ; v.2)
Includes index
ISBN 90-277-0500-3 (cased) : Unpriced
ISBN 90-277-0902-5 (pbk) : Unpriced B81-15249

333.8′5′09162 — Oceans. Bed. Mineral deposits. Exploitation

Kent, *Sir* **Peter,** *1913-.* Minerals from the marine environment / Sir Peter Kent ; with contributions from N.C. Fleming. — London : Edward Arnold, 1980. — vii,88p : ill,maps ; 22cm. — (Resource and environmental science series)
Bibliography: p84-85. - Includes index
ISBN 0-7131-2813-5 (pbk) : £3.95 : CIP rev. B80-33090

333.8′8 — Energy resources: Geothermal energy

Geothermal systems : principles and case histories / edited by L. Rybach and L.J.P. Muffler. — Chichester : Wiley, c1981. — xiv,359p : ill,maps ; 27cm
Includes bibliographies and index
ISBN 0-471-27811-4 : £22.00 B81-18674

Gupta, Harsh K.. Geothermal resources : an energy alternative / by Harsh K. Gupta. — Amsterdam ; Oxford : Elsevier Scientific, 1980. — xiii,227p : ill,maps ; 25cm. — (Developments in economic geology ; 12)
Bibliography: p195-211. - Includes index
ISBN 0-444-41865-2 : £23.58 : CIP rev. B80-17585

333.9 — WATER, AIR, SPACE RESOURCES

333.91 — Agricultural industries. Natural resources: Water. Salinity. Management — *Conference proceedings*

Land and stream salinity. — Oxford : Elsevier Scientific, Aug.1981. — [390]p
Conference papers
ISBN 0-444-41999-3 : CIP entry B81-24632

333.91 — Natural resources: Water — *Conference proceedings*

Water resources : changing strategy? : proceedings of the conference held in London 2-5 October 1979 / [conference sponsored by the Institution of Civil Engineers ... et al.]. — London : The Institution, 1980. — 214p : ill,maps,plans ; 21cm
ISBN 0-7277-0097-9 : £18.00 B81-10117

333.91 — Natural resources: Water. Management — *Conference proceedings*

Water and related land resource systems : IFAC Symposium, Cleveland, Ohio, U.S.A. 28-31 May 1980 / [organized by American Geophysical Union] ; [sponsored by International Federation of Automatic Control Committee on Systems Engineering] ; [co-sponsored by American Geophysical Union ... et al.] ; editors Y. Haimes and J. Kindler. — Oxford : Published for the International Federation of Automatic Control by Pergamon, 1981, c1980. — xii,524p,[1]folded leaf of plates : ill,maps ; 31cm. — (IFAC proceedings series)
ISBN 0-08-027307-6 : £50.00 B81-18928

333.91'0028'51 — Natural resources: Water. Management. Applications of systems analysis

The **Application** of systems analysis to problems of irrigation, drainage and flood control : a manual for water and agricultural engineers / prepared by the Permanent Committee of the International Commission on Irrigation and Drainage (ICID) on the Application of Systems Analysis to Irrigation, Drainage and Flood Control. — Oxford : Published for the International Commission on Irrigation and Drainage by Pergamon, 1980. — viii,203p : ill ; 26cm. — (Water development, supply and management ; v.11)
Bibliography: p185-194. — Includes index
ISBN 0-08-023425-9 (cased) : £20.00
ISBN 0-08-023431-3 (pbk) : £7.50 B81-07164

333.91'005 — Natural resources: Water — *Serials*

Water research topics. — Vol.1-. — Chichester : Ellis Horwood for the Water Research Centre, 1981-. — v. : ill ; 24cm
£19.50 B81-31569

333.91'00724 — Natural resources: Water. Quality control. Models

Models for water quality management / edited by Asit K. Biswas. — New York ; London : McGraw-Hill, c1981. — xiv,348p : ill,maps ; 24cm. — (McGraw-Hill series in water resources and environmental engineering)
Includes index
ISBN 0-07-005481-9 : £19.95 : CIP rev. B80-18188

333.91'00724 — Water resource systems. Planning. Mathematical models

Loucks, Daniel P.. Water resource systems planning and analysis / Daniel P. Loucks, Jery R. Stedinger, Douglas A. Haith. — Englewood Cliffs ; London : Prentice-Hall, c1981. — xv,559p : ill,maps ; 24cm
Includes bibliographies and index
ISBN 0-13-945923-5 : £19.45 B81-12515

333.91'00915'4 — Arid regions. Natural resources: Water. Management — *Conference proceedings*

Training Workshop on Water Management for Arid Regions *(1978 : Cairo)*. Water management for arid lands in developing countries : papers from the Training Workshop on Water Management for Arid Regions / organized by the Ministry of Irrigation, Government of Egypt in cooperation with the United Nations Environment Programme, Egypt 2-14 December 1978 ; editors Asit K. Biswas ... [et al.]. — Oxford : Pergamon, 1980. — viii,252p,1leaf of plates : ill,3maps,ports ; 26cm. — (Water development, supply and management ; v.13)
Includes bibliographies
ISBN 0-08-022431-8 : £34.00 : CIP rev. B79-31589

333.91'00941 — Great Britain. Natural resources: Water. Planning

Parker, Dennis J.. Water planning in Britain / Dennis J. Parker and Edmund C. Penning-Rowsell. — London : Allen & Unwin, 1980. — xviii,277p : ill,maps ; 24cm. — (The Resource management series ; 1)
Bibliography: p254-266. — Includes index
ISBN 0-04-711006-6 (cased) : £15.00 : CIP rev.
ISBN 0-04-711007-4 (pbk) : £7.95 B80-26641

333.91'00942 — England. Natural resources: Water. Management

Water and effluent management to reduce costs / [consultant editor Philip E. Millington] ; [contributors R. Bidwell ... et al.]. — London : Oyez, 1981, c1980. — ix,78leaves : ill,1map ; 30cm. — (Oyez intelligence reports)
ISBN 0-85120-550-x (spiral) : Unpriced B81-28530

333.91'00973 — United States. Natural resources: Water. Quality control

Krenkel, Peter A.. Water quality management / Peter A. Krenkel, Vladimir Novotny. — New York ; London : Academic Press, 1980. — xii,671p : ill,maps ; 24cm
Includes bibliographies and index
ISBN 0-12-426150-7 : £36.40 B81-19050

333.91'04 — Natural resources: Ground water. Evaluation — *Case studies*

Case-studies in groundwater resources evaluation / edited by J.W. Lloyd. — Oxford : Clarendon, 1981. — 206p : ill,maps ; 26cm
Includes bibliographies and index
ISBN 0-19-854530-4 : £27.50 B81-18974

333.91'16 — Natural resources: Water. Conservation

Troeh, Frederick R.. Soil and water conservation : for productivity and environmental protection / Frederick R. Troeh, J. Arthur Hobbs, Roy L. Donahue ; editorial assistance Miriam R. Troeh. — Englewood Cliffs ; London : Prentice-Hall, c1980. — xv,718p : ill,maps ; 24cm
Includes bibliographies and index
ISBN 0-13-822155-3 : £16.20
Primary classification 631.4 B81-04426

333.91'4 — Oceans. Energy resources

Brin, André. Energy and the oceans / André Brin ; preface by Jean-Claude Colli. — Guildford : Westbury House, 1981. — ix,133p : ill,charts,maps ; 25cm
Translation of: Océan et énergie. —
Bibliography: p133
ISBN 0-86103-024-9 : Unpriced : CIP rev. B81-06048

333.91'4 — Oceans. Energy resources. Exploitation

Goldin, Augusta. Oceans of energy : reservoir of power for the future / Augusta Goldin. — New York ; London : Harcourt Brace Jovanovich, c1980. — xiii,144p : ill,1chart,maps,1facsim,1port ; 24cm
Bibliography: p135-139. - Includes index
ISBN 0-15-257688-6 : £4.75 B81-17268

333.91'4 — United States. Yellowstone Valley. Synthetic fuels. Conversion of coal. Use of water. Social aspects

Boris, Constance M.. Water rights and energy development in the Yellowstone River basin : an integrated analysis / Constance M. Boris and John V. Krutilla. — Baltimore ; London : Published for Resources for the Future by The Johns Hopkins University Press, c1980. — xvi,278p : ill,maps ; 24cm
Includes index
ISBN 0-8018-2368-4 : £15.00 B81-07903

333.91'62 — Drainage basins. Environment planning

River basin planning : theory and practice / edited by Suranjit K. Saha and Christopher J. Barrow. — Chichester : Wiley, c1981. — xiii,357p : ill,maps ; 24cm
Includes bibliographies and index
ISBN 0-471-09977-5 : £19.00 : CIP rev. B81-15927

333.91'64'0916336 — North Sea. Natural resources. Management. International cooperation — *Conference proceedings*

Greenwich Forum *(5th : 1979)*. The North Sea : a new international regime? : records of an international conference at the Royal Naval College, Greenwich 2, 3 & 4 May 1979 / Greenwich Forum V ; edited by Donald Cameron Watt. — Guildford : Westbury, c1980. — xv,263p : ill,maps ; 25cm
ISBN 0-86103-039-7 : Unpriced B81-24037

333.95 — BIOLOGICAL RESOURCES

333.95'16'0604238 — Somerset. Ecology action groups — *Serials*

Smoke & whispers. — No.1 (Apr./May 80)-. — Somerset (c/o Natural Foods, 18 Station Rd, Taunton) : [s.n.], 1980-. — v. : ill ; 30cm
Six issues yearly
ISSN 0260-3918 = Smoke & whispers : £0.15 B81-03297

333.95'6 — Oceans. Fisheries. Ecological aspects

Pitcher, T. G.. Fisheries ecology. — London : Croom Helm, Dec.1981. — [352]p
ISBN 0-85664-894-9 : £16.95 : CIP entry B81-31653

333.95'6 — United States. Columbia River. Salmon & steelheads. Effects of dam construction, *to 1979*

Netboy, Anthony. The Columbia River salmon and steelhead trout : their fight for survival / Anthony Netboy. — Seattle ; London : University of Washington Press, c1980. — xii,180p,[8]p of plates : ill,maps ; 23cm
Bibliography: p165-170. — Includes index
ISBN 0-295-95768-9 : £8.75 B81-22362

333.95'6'0973 — United States. Fisheries. Resources. Management — *Conference proceedings*

Limited entry as a fishery management tool : proceedings of a national conference to consider limited entry as a tool in fishery management, Denver, July 17-19, 1978 / R. Bruce Rettig and Jay J.C. Ginter, editors. — [Seattle] : A Washington Sea Grant publication in cooperation with the Institute for Marine Studies, University of Washington and National Marine Fisheries Service ; Seattle ; London : Distributed by University of Washington Press, [1980?]. — xix,463p : ill,1map ; 23cm
Bibliography: p451-455
ISBN 0-295-95741-7 (pbk) : £9.00 B81-17299

333.95'6'17 — Oceans. Fisheries. Resources. Exploitation. Optimisation. Mathematical models

Laevastu, Taivo. Marine fisheries ecosystem. — Farnham : Fishing News Books, Sept.1981. — [176]p
ISBN 0-85238-116-6 : £15.50 : CIP entry B81-21547

334 — COOPERATIVES

334 — Cooperatives

Local employment initiatives : a co-operative approach / [Political Ecology Research Group]. — [Oxford] : [The Group], 1981. — 18p ; 30cm. — (Special paper / Political Ecology Research Group, ISSN 0142-7989 ; SP-6)
£1.95 (pbk) B81-40801

334 — Cooperatives — *Conference proceedings*
Co-operative Seminar *(5th : 1980 : Hertford College).* Fifth Co-operative seminar, Hertford College, Oxford, April 9-11, 1980 : papers. — Oxford ([31 St. Giles, Oxford OX1 3LF]) : Plunkett Foundation for Co-operative Studies, [1980]. — 122p ; 30cm
ISBN 0-85042-034-2 (spiral) : Unpriced
B81-39460

334 — Cooperatives — *Forecasts*
Co-operatives in the year 2000 / foreword by the ICA director. — London (11 Upper Grosvenor St., W1X 9PA) : International Co-operative Alliance, c1980. — 76,21p ; 21cm. — (Studies and reports / ICA ; 15)
Contents: Resolution / adopted by the 27th Congress of the International Co-operative Alliance — Co-operatives in the year 2000 / a paper prepared for the 27th Congress of the International Co-operative Alliance, Moscow, October 1980 by A.F. Laidlaw - Co-operation of the Socialist Countries in the Year 2000 / joint document of Central Co-operative Unions and Societies of Bulgaria, Hungary, GDR, Poland, Czechoslovakia and the Soviet Union
ISBN 0-904380-48-3 (pbk) : £2.50 B81-29029

334′.09172′4 — Developing countries. Cooperatives. Organisation — *Manuals*
Verhagen, Koenraad. Guidelines for co-operative development programmes and projects / by Koenraad Verhagen. — Oxford : Plunkett Foundation for Co-operative Studies, c1981. — 25p : 1ill ; 21cm. — (Plunkett development series, ISSN 0143-8484 ; 2)
ISBN 0-85042-039-3 (pbk) : Unpriced
B81-17627

334′.0941 — Great Britain. Cooperative movements. Organisation structure — *Proposals*
″Winning support″ : a discussion document for consideration at the National Co-operative Education Association′s Annual Education Convention at Harrogate, Easter 1981 / Co-operative Union Ltd., Education Dept. — Loughborough (Stanford Hall, Loughborough, Leics., LE12 5QR) : Co-operative Union Ltd, Education Dept., [1981?]. — 34p : ill ; 20cm
Cover title
Unpriced (pbk) B81-17942

334′.0941 — Great Britain. Cooperatives — *Conference proceedings*
Co-operative Conference *(2nd : 1980 : New University of Ulster. Institute of Continuing Education).* Co-operative innovations in the United Kingdom and Ireland : papers presented to the Second Annual Co-operative Conference held at the New University of Ulster Institute of Continuing Education, May 1980. — Londonderry (Londonderry BT48 7JL) : The Institute, [c1981]. — 41leaves ; 29cm
ISBN 0-901229-27-x (pbk) : Unpriced
B81-25196

334′.0947 — Eastern Europe. Cooperative movements — *Conference proceedings*
Cooperative movements in Eastern Europe / edited by Aloysius Balawyder. — London : Macmillan, 1980. — x,211p : 1map ; 22cm
Conference papers. — Includes index
ISBN 0-333-30854-9 : £15.00 B81-23013

334′.0973 — Cooperatives — *Study regions: United States*
Heflebower, Richard B.. Cooperatives and mutuals in the market system / Richard B. Heflebower. — Madison ; London : University of Wisconsin Press, 1980. — x,245p ; 24cm
Includes index
ISBN 0-299-07850-7 : £13.50 B81-06304

334.1 — BUILDING AND HOUSING COOPERATIVES

334′.1 — Great Britain. Homeless single persons. Accommodation. Provision by housing associations — *Case studies*
Currie, Hector. Single initiatives : a study of single person and special needs housing by housing associations / by Hector Currie. — Edinburgh (4 Old Assembly Close, Edinburgh EH1 1QX) : Scottish Council for Single Homeless, 1980. — 44p : ill,plans ; 30cm
ISBN 0-907050-01-8 (pbk) : £1.25(£1.00 to members) B81-12240

334′.1′071142 — England. Housing associations. Personnel. In-service training — *Case studies*
Training in three housing organisations 1978-1979 . — London (Housing Research Group, The City University, St. John St., EC1V 4PB) : Housing Training Project, c1980. — 212p ; 30cm
ISBN 0-907255-09-4 (spiral) : £7.50
Primary classification 352.7′5′071142
B81-10195

334′.1′071142 — England. Housing associations. Personnel. Professional education
Basic training / Housing Training Project. — London ([City University, St John St., EC1V 4PB]) : Housing Research Group, c1980. — 44p ; 21cm. — (Guide to housing training ; no.2)
Cover title. — Bibliography: p42
ISBN 0-907255-01-9 (pbk) : Unpriced
Primary classification 352.7′5′071142
B81-06323

Getting started / Housing Training Project. — London ([City University, St John St., EC1V 4 PB]) : Housing Research Group, c1980. — 35p ; 21cm. — (Guide to housing training ; no.1)
Cover title. — Bibliography: p33-34
ISBN 0-907255-00-0 (pbk) : Unpriced
Primary classification 352.7′5′071142
B81-06324

334′.1′071142 — England. Housing associations. Personnel. Professional education. Assessment
Assessing the effects of training / Housing Training Project. — London ([City University, St John St., EC1V 4PB]) : Housing Research Group, c1980. — 43p : forms ; 21cm. — (Guide to housing training ; no.7)
Cover title. — Bibliography: 41-43
ISBN 0-907255-06-x (pbk) : Unpriced
Primary classification 352.7′5′071142
B81-06326

334′.1′091724 — Developing countries. Housing cooperatives. Organisation — *Manuals*
Lewin, A. C.. Housing co-operatives in developing countries : a manual for self-help in low-cost housing schemes / A.C. Lewin. — Chichester : Published in association with Intermediate Technology Publications Ltd by Wiley, c1981. — xv,170p : ill ; 24cm
Bibliography: p170
ISBN 0-471-27820-3 (cased) : £11.75
B81-14764

334′.1′0941 — Great Britain. Housing associations. Organisations: Housing Corporation — *Serials*
Housing Corporation. Report of the Housing Corporation for the year ended 31st March .... — 16th (1980). — London (149 Tottenham Court Rd, W1P 0BN) : The Corporation, [1980?]. — 44p
ISBN 0-901454-27-3 : Unpriced
ISSN 0306-5960 B81-25025

334′.1′0942 — England. Housing associations. Role of chartered surveyors
Chartered surveyors in the voluntary housing movement : the report of the Housing Association Working Party. — London : General Practice Division, Royal Institution of Chartered Surveyors, 1980. — 51p : ill ; 30cm
Bibliography: p50
£2.70 (£2.25 to members) (pbk) B81-22242

334′.1′09421 — Inner London. Housing associations. Role, *1974-1980*
Fasey, Antonia. Housing associations in Inner London / Antonia Fasey and Glynn Llewellyn. — London (32-8 Wells St., W1P 3FG) : Polytechnic of Central London, School of Social Sciences and Business Studies, 1981. — 46p ; 30cm. — (Research working paper / Polytechnic of Central London. School of Social Sciences and Business Studies ; no.13)
Cover title
Unpriced (spiral) B81-35077

334′.1′094249 — West Midlands *(Metropolitan County).* **Housing associations. Implications of availability of housing land**
Wilkinson, C. Milton. Land and housing associations / by C. Milton Wilkinson and Ian J. Thurman. — Bournville ([Estate Office, Oak Tree Lane] Bournville, Birmingham [B30 1UB]) : Bournville Village Trust, 1981. — x,196p,[1]folded leaf of plates : ill,col.maps,forms ; 30cm
Bibliography: p184-189. — Includes index
ISBN 0-905458-01-x (pbk) : Unpriced
B81-38660

334.5 — CONSUMERS′ COOPERATIVES

334′.5 — European Community countries. Agricultural products. Cooperative marketing
Foxall, Gordon. Co-operative marketing in European agriculture. — Aldershot : Gower, Feb.1982. — [114]p
ISBN 0-566-00512-3 : £13.50 : CIP entry
B81-36216

334′.5′09411 — Scotland. Cooperative societies: Scottish Co-operative Wholesale Society, *to 1978*
Kinloch, James. History of the Scottish Co-operative Wholesale Society Limited / by James Kinloch and John Butt. — [Manchester] ([New Century House, Manchester M60 4ES]) : Co-operative Wholesale Society, c1981. — xv,416p : ill(some col.),maps,ports ; 23cm
Bibliography: p405-409. — Includes index
ISBN 0-85195-130-9 : £10.00 B81-33581

334.6 — PRODUCTION COOPERATIVES

334′.6′02541 — Great Britain. Industrial cooperatives — *Directories*
Co-ops : a directory of industrial and service co-operatives. — London (20, Albert Embankment, SE1 7TJ) : The Agency, 1980. — 193p ; 22cm
ISBN 0-906737-03-6 (spiral) : £5.40
B81-29022

334′.6′0941 — Great Britain. Workers′ cooperatives. Development. Role of local authorities — *Socialist Environment and Resources Association viewpoints*
Taylor, Allan, *1946-.* Co-op development : how councils can help / by Alan Taylor. — London (9 Poland St., W1V 3DG) : Socialist Environment & Resources Association, [1981?]. — 32p ; 21cm
Cover title
£0.50 (pbk) B81-33555

334′.6′0941 — Great Britain. Workers′ cooperatives. Development. Role of local development agencies — *Socialist Environment and Resources Association viewpoints*
Taylor, Alan, *1946-.* Making the most of workers′ co-ops : the local agency approach / by Alan Taylor. — London (9 Poland St., W1V 3DG) : Socialist Environment & Resources Association, [1980]. — 48p ; 21cm
£0.50 (unbound) B81-33554

334′.6′0941 — Great Britain. Workers′ cooperatives — *Manuals*
Workers′ co-operatives : a handbook. — [Rev. and extended ed.] / Peter Cockerton ... [et al.]. — Aberdeen : Aberdeen People′s Press in association with the authors, c1981. — 123p ; 21cm
Previous ed.: Edinburgh : Scottish Council of Social Service, 1977
ISBN 0-906074-07-x (cased) : £5.50
ISBN 0-906074-06-1 (pbk) : £2.25 B81-31879

334′.6′0941 — Great Britain. Workers′ cooperatives — *Proposals*
Workers co-operatives : a Labour Party discussion document. — [London] : The Party, [1980]. — 34p ; 21cm. — (Socialism in the 80s)
Cover title
ISBN 0-86117-060-1 (pbk) : £0.60 B81-04996

334′.6′0941 — Great Britain. Workers′ cooperatives, *to 1980*
Thornley, Jenny. Workers′ co-operatives : jobs and dreams / Jenny Thornley. — London : Heinemann Educational, 1981. — vii,216p ; 23cm
Includes index
ISBN 0-435-83890-3 : £14.50 B81-10810

334'.6'09466 — Spain. Basque Provinces. Mondragon. Industrial cooperatives

Thomas, Henk. Mondragon. — London : Allen & Unwin, Jan.1982. — [200]p
ISBN 0-04-334007-5 (cased) : £15.00 : CIP entry
ISBN 0-04-334006-7 (pbk) : £7.95 B81-33919

334'.683 — Great Britain. Agricultural cooperatives. Finance — *For directors of agricultural cooperatives*

Absalom, W. L. G.. A directors' guide to financing marketing co-operatives. — London : Central Council for Agricultural and Horticultural Co-operation, [1981]. — 48p : ill ; 21cm
Cover title. — Author: W.L.G. Absalom
Unpriced (pbk) B81-37344

334'.683'02541 — Great Britain. Agricultural cooperatives — *Directories — Serials*

Directory of agricultural co-operatives in the United Kingdom / the Plunkett Foundation for Co-operative Studies. — 1981. — Oxford : The Foundation, 1981. — 161,xvip
ISBN 0-85042-040-7 : £5.00
ISSN 0307-689x B81-36299

334'.683'0683 — Peru. Agricultural cooperatives. Management. Participation of peasants, *1968-1975.* **Political aspects**

McClintock, Cynthia. Peasant cooperatives and political change in Peru / Cynthia McClintock. — Princeton ; Guildford : Princeton University Press, c1981. — xvii,418p ; 24cm
Bibliography: p381-410. — Includes index
ISBN 0-691-07627-8 (cased) : £15.30
ISBN 0-691-02202-x (pbk) : £3.85 B81-24173

334'.683'0947 — Soviet Union. Agricultural industries. Collectivisation — *Soviet viewpoints*

Agrarian relations in the USSR / [by P.A. Ignatovsky et al.] ; [translated from the Russian by Galina Sdobnikova]. — Moscow : Progress ; [London] : Distributed by Central Books, 1980. — 199p ; 21cm. — (Progress socialism today)
Translation of: Agrarnye otnosheniia v SSSR
£2.95 B81-05586

334'.683'0951 — China. Agricultural industries. Collectivisation, *1949-1956*

Shue, Vivienne. Peasant China in transition : the dynamics of development towards socialism, 1949-1956 / Vivienne Shue. — Berkeley ; London : University of California Press, c1980. — xvi,394p : ill ; 24cm
Bibliography: p347-385. - Includes index
ISBN 0-520-03734-0 : £15.50 B81-04123

334'.683'096695 — North-west Nigeria. Group farms — *Case studies*

Dickie, Anthea. Group farming in North West Nigeria : a report / by Anthea Dickie. — [Reading] : University of Reading, 1981. — 159p : maps(some col.) ; 30cm. — (Development study / University of Reading Department of Agricultural Economics & Management ; no.18)
Bibliography: p141-146
ISBN 0-7049-0694-5 (pbk) : £1.50 B81-38609

334'.6837'094292 — Gwynedd. Dairy cooperatives: South Caernarfon Creameries

Brooks-Jones, Iwan. Agricultural co-operation — principles and practice : a study of South Caernarfon Creameries Ltd / Iwan Brooks-Jones and Clare LeVay. — Aberystwyth : Department of Agricultural Economics, University College of Wales, [1981]. — 192p : ill,maps,1facsim ; 21cm
Bibliography: p189-192
£3.50 (pbk) B81-12276

Brooks-Jones, Iwan. Cydweithrediad amaethyddól : astudiaeth o Hufenfa De Arfon Cyf. / Iwan Brooks-Jones ; cyllidiwyd yr astudiaeth hon gan y Cyngor Canolog ar Gydweithrediad Amaethyddol a Garddwriaethol 1979-80. — Aberystwyth : Adran Economeg Amaethyddol, Coleg Prifysgol Cymru, 1981. — 92p : ill ; 21cm
Cover title. — Bibliography: p90-92
Unpriced (pbk) B81-37910

334'.6837'0944 — France. Dairy cooperative. Financing

Haines, Michael. The financing of French dairy co-operatives : an empirical investigation / by Michael Haines. — Aberystwyth : Department of Agricultural Economics, [University College of Wales], 1980. — 101p : ill,1map ; 29cm
£3.50 (pbk) B81-21761

334'.6864122'0954792 — India *(Republic).* **Maharashtra. Cane sugar processing cooperatives: Kisan Co-operative Sugar Factory**

Baviskar, B. S.. The politics of development : sugar co-operatives in rural Maharashtra / B.S. Baviskar. — Delhi ; Oxford : Oxford University Press, 1980. — viii,241p ; 22cm
Bibliography: p233-236. — Includes index
ISBN 0-19-561206-x : Unpriced B81-39048

334.7 — BENEFIT SOCIETIES

334'.7'0941 — Great Britain. Friendly societies: Independent Order of Odd Fellows

What the papers say about the Odd Fellows. — [Manchester] ([Oddfellows House, 40 Fountain St., Manchester N2 2AB]) : [Independent Order of Oddfellows], [1980]. — [4]p : chiefly facsims,ports ; 34cm
Unpriced (unbound) B81-11422

334'.7'09416 — Northern Ireland. Friendly societies — *Serials*

Great Britain. *Registrar of Friendly Societies.* Report of the Registrar of Friendly Societies for the year .... — 1979. — Belfast : H.M.S.O., 1981. — 26p
ISBN 0-337-06126-2 : £2.50 B81-26582

335 — SOCIALISM AND RELATED SYSTEMS

335 — Socialism

Vajda, Mihaly. The state and socialism : political essays / by Mihaly Vajda. — London : Allison & Busby, 1981. — 150p ; 23cm
Includes index
ISBN 0-85031-390-2 (cased) : £9.95 : CIP rev.
(pbk) : £4.50 B80-19079

335 — Socialism — *Soviet viewpoints*

Ponomarev, B. N.. Invincibility of the liberation movement / Boris Ponomarev. — Moscow : Novosti Press Agency ; [London] : Central Books [distributor], 1980. — 27p ; 17cm
Translated from the Russian
ISBN 0-7147-1571-9 (pbk) : £0.25 B81-14007

335 — Socialist movements. Role of women's movements — *Feminist viewpoints*

Rowbotham, Sheila. Beyond the fragments : feminism and the making of socialism / Sheila Rowbotham, Lynne Segal and Hilary Wainwright. — London : Merlin, 1980, c1979. — 253p ; 20cm
Originally published: Newcastle upon Tyne : Newcastle Socialist Centre, 1979
ISBN 0-85036-254-7 (pbk) : £2.25 B81-04157

335'.00171'3 — Western bloc countries. Socialism. Implications of development of communism in Soviet Union

Medvedev, Roĭ A.. Leninism and western socialism. — London : NLB, Sept.1981. — [304]p
Translated from the Russian
ISBN 0-86091-042-3 (cased) : £12.00 : CIP entry
ISBN 0-86091-739-8 (pbk) : £4.50 B81-27900

335'.005 — Socialism — *Serials*

The Socialist register. — 1980. — London : Merlin Press, 1980. — 338p
ISBN 0-85036-266-0 : £7.50 B81-16227

335'.0088042 — Socialist movements. Role of women's movements. Rowbotham, Sheila. Women's movement and organising for socialism — *Critical studies*

Brewer, Gordon. The politics of organisation / Gordon Brewer and Richard Gunn. — Edinburgh (43 Candlemaker Row, Edinburgh EH1 2QB) : First of May, 1980. — i,60p ; 21cm
Text on inside front cover. — Includes bibliographies
£1.00 (pbk) B81-09245

335'.0089924 — Russia. Jews. Socialist movements, *1862-1917*

Frankel, Jonathan. Prophecy and politics : socialism, nationalism and the Russian Jews, 1862-1917 / Jonathan Frankel. — Cambridge : Cambridge University Press, 1981. — xxii,686p : ill,ports ; 24cm
Bibliography: p630-655. — Includes index
ISBN 0-521-23028-4 : £30.00 B81-32625

335'.009 — Socialism, *to 1974*

Shafarevich, I. R.. The socialist phenomenon / Igor Shafarevich ; translated from the Russian by William Tjalsma ; foreword by Aleksandr I. Solzhenitsyn. — New York ; London : Harper & Row, c1980. — xvi,319p ; 25cm
Translation of: Sotsializm kak iavlenie mirovoi istorii. — Includes index
ISBN 0-06-337014-x : £9.95 B81-07044

335'.009 — Socialism, *to 1979 — Soviet viewpoints*

Ponomarev, B. N.. Selected speeches and writings / by P.N. Ponomarev. — Oxford : Pergamon, 1981. — xv,372p ; 22cm
Includes index
ISBN 0-08-023606-5 : £19.75 : CIP rev.
Primary classification 947.084 B80-18949

335'.009171'7 — Communist countries. Socialism — *Marxist viewpoints*

Sweezy, Paul M.. Post-revolutionary society : essays / by Paul M. Sweezy. — New York ; London : Monthly Review Press, c1980. — 156p ; 21cm
ISBN 0-85345-550-3 : £6.75 B81-04031

335'.009181'2 — Western world. Socialism, *to 1979*

Vaizey, John. Capitalism and socialism : a history of industrial growth / John Vaizey. — London : Weidenfeld and Nicolson, c1980. — vii,283p ; 23cm
Bibliography: p272-275. — Includes index
ISBN 0-297-77848-x : £12.50
Primary classification 330.12'2'091812
B81-13191

335'.0092'4 — Great Britain. Socialism. Carpenter, Edward, *b.1844 — Biographies*

Tsuzuki, Chushichi. Edward Carpenter 1844-1929 : prophet of human fellowship / Chushichi Tsuzuki. — Cambridge : Cambridge University Press, 1980. — x,237p,[9]p of plates : ports ; 24cm
Includes index
ISBN 0-521-23371-2 : £15.00 : CIP rev.
B80-27957

335'.0094 — Europe. Labour movements, *1848-1939*

Geary, Dick. European labour protest 1848-1939 / Dick Geary. — London : Croom Helm, c1981. — 195p ; 23cm. — (Croom Helm analysis in social history series)
Bibliography: p182-187. — Includes index
ISBN 0-85664-621-0 : £11.95 : CIP rev.
B81-05132

335'.009415 — Ireland. Socialism — *Serials*

Ireland socialist review : self-determination for the Irish people. — No.1 (Winter 1977/78)-. — London (60 Loughborough Rd, S.W.9) : [s.n.], 1977-. — v. : ill,maps,ports ; 30cm
Quarterly. — Description based on: No.5 (Summer 1979)
ISSN 0143-2729 = Ireland socialist review : £2.00 for 4 issues B81-03283

335'.00944 — France. Women's socialist movements, *1876-1980*

Sowerwine, Charles. Sisters or citizens?. — Cambridge : Cambridge University Press, Jan.1982. — [248]p
Translation and revision of: Les femmes et le socialisme
ISBN 0-521-23484-0 : £15.00 : CIP entry
B81-39253

335'.00947 — Eastern Europe. Socialism — *National Organisation of Labour Students viewpoints*

Pelikán, Jiří. New paths in Eastern Europe : neither reform nor revolution / Jiří Pelikan ; preface Eric Heffer. — London : 144 Walworth Rd, SE17 1JT : NOLS, [1980]. — 13p ; 22cm
Cover title
£0.20 (pbk) B81-00779

335′.00952 — Japan. Labour movements, *1919-1940*

Large, Stephen S.. Organized workers and socialist politics in interwar Japan / Stephen S. Large. — Cambridge : Cambridge University Press, 1981. — vii,326p ; 24cm
Bibliography: p302-312. — Includes index
ISBN 0-521-23675-4 : £25.00 : CIP rev.
B81-21568

335′.0096 — Africa. Socialism

Babu, Mohamed. African socialism or socialist Africa?. — London : Zed, July 1981. — [224]p
ISBN 0-905762-19-3 (pbk) : £4.50 : CIP entry
B81-18059

335′.009669 — Nigeria. Socialism

Madunagu, Edwin. Problems of socialism. — London : Zed Press, Oct.1981. — [144]p
ISBN 0-86232-027-5 (pbk) : £4.95 : CIP entry
B81-28806

335′.009678 — Tanzania. Socialism

Mittelman, James H.. Underdevelopment and the transition to socialism : Mozambique and Tanzania / James H. Mittelman. — New York ; London : Academic Press, c1981. — xxi,277p : ill,maps(some col.),ports ; 24cm. — (Studies in social discontinuity)
Maps on lining papers. — Bibliography: p257-267. — Includes index
ISBN 0-12-500660-8 : £18.20
Also classified at 335′.00967′9 B81-40803

335′.00967′9 — Mozambique. Socialism

Mittelman, James H.. Underdevelopment and the transition to socialism : Mozambique and Tanzania / James H. Mittelman. — New York ; London : Academic Press, c1981. — xxi,277p : ill,maps(some col.),ports ; 24cm. — (Studies in social discontinuity)
Maps on lining papers. — Bibliography: p257-267. — Includes index
ISBN 0-12-500660-8 : £18.20
Primary classification 335′.009678 B81-40803

335′.1092′4 — Great Britain. Labour movements. Spence, Thomas — *Critical studies*

Thomas Spence. — Nottingham : Spokesman, Oct.1981. — [150]p. — (Socialist classics ; no.2)
ISBN 0-85124-315-0 : £35.00 : CIP entry
B81-28045

335′.1′0941 — Great Britain. Labour movements - *Socialist viewpoints*

Hobsbawm, E. J.. The forward march of Labour halted?. — London (15 Greek St., W1V 5LF) : Verso, May 1981. — [160]p
ISBN 0-86091-041-5 (cased) : £8.50 : CIP entry
ISBN 0-86091-737-1 (pbk) : £2.95 B81-10430

335.1′3323 — Great Britain. *Army. Provost Service, to 1902*

Tyler, R. A. J.. Bloody Provost : an account of the Provost Service of the British Army, and the early years of the Corps of Royal Military Police / R.A.J. Tyler. — London : Phillimore, 1980. — 245p,[8]p of plates : ill,ports ; 23cm
Bibliography: p223-229. — Includes index
ISBN 0-85033-359-8 : £7.95 B81-02801

335′.14′09034 — Fabian socialism, *to 1914*

MacKenzie, Norman, *1921-*. The first Fabians / Norman and Jeanne MacKenzie. — London : Quartet, 1979, c1977. — 446p,[8]p of plates : ill,ports ; 21cm
Originally published: London : Weidenfeld and Nicolson, 1977. — Includes index
ISBN 0-7043-3251-5 (pbk) : £4.95 B81-17698

335′.2 — France. Socialism. Proudhon, P.-J.. Interpersonal relationships with Courbet, Gustave

Rubin, James Henry. Realism and social vision in Courbet & Proudhon / by James Henry Rubin. — Princeton ; Guildford : Princeton University Press, c1980. — xvii,177p,[27]p of plates (1folded) : ill(some col.),facsim,ports ; 25cm. — (Princeton essays on the arts ; 10)
Bibliography: p167-169. - Includes index
ISBN 0-691-03960-7 (cased) : £9.80
ISBN 0-691-00327-9 (pbk) : Unpriced
Primary classification 759.4 B81-17117

335′.2′0944 — France. Labour movements, *1789-1848*

Sewell, William H.. Work and revolution in France : the language of labor from the old regime to 1848 / William H. Sewell, Jr. — Cambridge : Cambridge University Press, 1980. — x,340p : 2ill ; 24cm
Bibliography: p318-328. - Includes index
ISBN 0-521-23442-5 (cased) : £20.00
ISBN 0-521-29951-9 (pbk) : £6.95 B81-09218

335.4 — MARXISM

335.4 — Marxism

Guerin, Daniel. Anarchism and Marxism : from a paper given in New York on 6 Nov. 1973 / Daniel Guerin ; with an introduction by the author. —- Orkney (Over the Water, Sanday, Orkney KW17 2BL) : Cienfuegos, 1981. — v,17p ; 21cm
ISBN 0-904564-43-6 (pbk) : £0.70 : CIP rev.
Primary classification 335′.83 B80-27960

Heilbroner, Robert L.. Marxism : for and against / Robert L. Heilbroner. — New York ; London : Norton, c1980. — 186p ; 22cm
Includes index
ISBN 0-393-01307-3 : £3.95 B81-05751

Lindsay, Jack. The crisis in Marxism / Jack Lindsay. — Bradford-on-Avon : Moonraker, 1981. — 183p ; 22cm
Bibliography: p171-178. — Includes index
ISBN 0-239-00200-8 : £7.95 B81-14037

Marxism and the good society / edited by John P. Burke, Lawrence Crocker, Lyman H. Legters. — Cambridge : Cambridge University Press, 1981. — ix,225p ; 24cm
ISBN 0-521-23392-5 : £16.00 B81-32078

Ollman, Bertell. Social and sexual revolution : essays on Marx and Reich / Bertell Ollman. — London : Pluto, 1979. — x,228p ; 21cm
ISBN 0-86104-082-1 (pbk) : £3.95 B81-13625

Worsley, Peter. Marx and Marxism. — Chichester : Ellis Horwood, Dec.1981. — [128] p. — (Key sociologists series)
ISBN 0-85312-348-9 : £6.50 : CIP entry
B81-31377

335.4 — Marxism — *Anarchist viewpoints*

The **poverty** of Statism : Bukharin, Fabbri, Rocker / [translated from the Spanish by Paul Sharkey]. — Sanday (Over-the-Water, Sanday, Orkney KW17 28L) : Cienfuegos Press, 1981. — 93p : ports ; 22cm
Contents: Anarchy and scientific communism / Nikolai Bukharin — Anarchy and scientific communism / Luigi Fabbri — Anarchy and Sovietism / Rudolf Rocker — Marx and anarchism / Rudolf Rocker
ISBN 0-904564-29-0 (cased) : Unpriced : CIP rev.
ISBN 0-904564-28-2 (pbk) : £2.00 B79-23106

335.4 — Marxism — *Early works*

Lenin, V. I.. Marxism and revisionism / Lenin. — Moscow : Progress Publishers ; [London] : Central Books [distributor], 1980. — 20p ; 21cm
Translation of: Marksizm i revizionizm. — Includes index
ISBN 0-7147-1636-7 (pbk) : £0.15 B81-32945

335.4 — Marxism *related to* **feminism**

Barrett, Michèle. Women's oppression today : problems in Marxist feminist analysis / Michèle Barrett. — London : NBL, c1980. — 269p ; 21cm
Bibliography: p261-264. — Includes index
ISBN 0-86091-033-4 (cased) : £10.00 : CIP rev.
ISBN 0-86091-730-4 (pbk) : £3.95
Primary classification 305.4′2 B80-19044

335.4 — Marxism *related to* **role of Christian church in society**

Bockmühl, Klaus. The challenge of Marxism : a Christian response / Klaus Bockmüehl. — Leicester : Inter-Varsity Press, 1980. — 187p ; 18cm
Translation of: Herausforderungen des Marxismus. — Includes index
ISBN 0-85110-417-7 (pbk) : £1.95 : CIP rev.
Primary classification 261.1 B80-21370

335.4 — Marxism — *Reviews — Anthologies — Serials*

Head and hand : newsletter of the CSE Bookclub. — No.1-. — London (55 Mount Pleasant, WC1) : The Bookclub, [1978]-. — v. : ill ; 21cm
Three issues yearly. — Size varies
ISSN 0260-8685 = Head and hand : £2.50 per year B81-09207

335.4′024658 — Marxism — *For management*

Watkins, K. W.. Marxism and managers / K.W. Watkins. — London : Aims of Industry, [1981]. — 12p ; 22cm
Bibliography: p11-12
ISBN 0-7281-0095-9 (pbk) : Unpriced
B81-35181

335.4′05 — Marxism — *Serials*

Marxist humanism. — Winter 1980/81-. — [London] ([Box NL, Rising Free, 182 Upper St., Islington, N1]) : [News and Letters Publications], 1980-. — v. : ill ; 43cm
Continues: News and letters (British edition)
ISSN 0260-7212 = Marxist humanism : £0.20 per issue B81-05593

Praxis international : a philosophical journal. — Vol.1, no.1 (Apr.1981)-. — Oxford : Blackwell, 1981-. — v. ; 25cm
Quarterly. — Text in English, French and German
ISSN 0260-8448 = Praxis international : £26.00 per year B81-29994

335.4′09 — Marxism, *to 1976*

Kolakowski, Leszek. Main currents of Marxism : its origins, growth and dissolution / Leszek Kolakowski ; translated from the Polish by P.S. Falla. — Oxford : Oxford University Press
Translation of: Glówne nurty marksizmu
1: The founders. — 1978 (1981 [printing]). — xiii,434p ; 21cm
Bibliography: p421-427. — Includes index
ISBN 0-19-285107-1 (pbk) : £3.95 B81-35314

Kolakowski, Leszek. Main currents of Marxism : its origins, growth and dissolution / Leszek Kolakowski ; translated from the Polish by P.S. Falla. — Oxford : Oxford University Press
2: The golden age. — 1978 (1981 [printing]). — viii,542p ; 21cm
Originally published: 1978. — Bibliography: p529-536. — Includes index
ISBN 0-19-285108-x (pbk) : £3.95 B81-29361

Kolakowski, Leszek. Main currents of Marxism : its origins, growth and dissolution / Leszek Kolakowski ; translated from the Polish by P.S. Falla. — Oxford : Oxford University Press
Translation of: Glówne nurty marksizmu
3: The breakdown. — 1978 (1981 [printing]). — xii,548p ; 21cm
Bibliography: p531-541. — Includes index
ISBN 0-19-285109-8 (pbk) : £3.95 B81-35313

335.4′09′04 — Marxism. Theories, *to 1980*

The **History** of Marxism. — Brighton : Harvester Press, Oct.1981
Vol.1: Marxism in Marx's day. — [500]p
ISBN 0-7108-0054-1 : CIP entry B81-24616

335.4′092′4 — Economics. Engels, Friedrich — *Critical studies*

Carver, Terrell. Engels / Terrell Carver. — Oxford : Oxford University Press, 1981. — 85p ; 19cm. — (Past masters)
Bibliography: p79-81. — Includes index
ISBN 0-19-287549-3 (cased) : £4.50 : CIP rev.
ISBN 0-19-287548-5 (pbk) : £1.25 B81-06610

335.4′092′4 — Economics. Marx, Karl — *Biographies*

Mehring, Franz. Karl Marx : the story of his life / by Franz Mehring ; translated by Edward Fitzgerald. — [Brighton] : Harvester Press, 1981. — xxi,575p ; 22cm
Originally published: London : John Lane, 1936. — Bibliography: p557. — Includes index
ISBN 0-7108-0073-8 (pbk) : £8.95 B81-29466

335.4'092'4 — Economics. Marx, Karl — *Biographies* *continuation*

Rubel, Maximilien. Marx : life and works / Maximilien Rubel ; translated by Mary Bottomore. — London : Macmillan, 1980. — 140p ; 23cm. — (Macmillan chronology series)
Translation from the French. — Bibliography: p125. - Includes index
ISBN 0-333-28048-2 (cased) : £10.00
ISBN 0-333-28049-0 (pbk) : £3.95 B81-13658

335.4'092'4 — Economics. Marx, Karl — *Correspondence, diaries, etc.*

Marx, Karl. The letters of Karl Marx / selected and translated with explanatory notes and an introduction by Saul K. Padover. — Englewood Cliffs ; London : Prentice-Hall, c1979. — xxvii,576p,[24]p of plates : ill,facsims,ports ; 24cm
Bibliography: p532-534. — Includes index
ISBN 0-13-531533-6 : £12.95 B81-05695

335.4'092'4 — Economics. Marx, Karl — *Critical studies*

Rubel, Maximilien. Rubel on Karl Marx : five essays / edited by Joseph O'Malley and Keith Algozin. — Cambridge : Cambridge University Press, 1981. — ix,309p ; 24cm
Translation from the French and German. — Bibliography: p290-296. — Includes index
ISBN 0-521-23839-0 : £15.00 B81-38283

335.4'092'4 — Economics. Marx, Karl — *Personal observations — Collections*

Karl Marx : interviews and recollections / edited by David McLellan. — London : Macmillan, 1981. — xxi,186p ; 23cm
Bibliography: p168-169. — Includes index
ISBN 0-333-28362-7 : £15.00 B81-38721

335.4'092'4 — Ireland. Marxism. Connolly, James — *Biographies*

Edwards, Ruth Dudley. James Connolly / Ruth Dudley Edwards. — Dublin : Gill and Macmillan, 1981. — 151p ; 19cm. — (Gill's Irish lives)
Bibliography: p147. — Includes index
ISBN 0-7171-1112-1 (cased) : £8.50
ISBN 0-7171-1111-3 (pbk) : £2.60 B81-40898

335.4'092'4 — Marxism. Theories of Althusser, Louis

One-dimensional Marxism : Althusser and the politics of culture / Simon Clarke ... [et al.]. — London : Allison & Busby, 1980. — 256p ; 23cm
ISBN 0-85031-367-8 (cased) : £9.95 : CIP rev.
ISBN 0-85031-368-6 (pbk) : £3.95 B80-09117

335.4'092'4 — Marxism. Theories of Habermas, Jürgen

Sensat, Julius. Habermas and Marxism : an appraisal / Julius Sensat, Jr. — Beverly Hills ; London : Sage, c1979. — 176p ; 23cm. — (Sage library of social research ; v.77)
Bibliography: p169-173. - Includes index
ISBN 0-8039-1044-4 (cased) : £11.25
ISBN 0-8039-1045-2 (pbk) : Unpriced
B81-10331

335.4'0952 — Japan. Marxist economics

Itoh, Makoto. Value and crisis : essays on Marxian economics in Japan / Makoto Itoh. — London : Pluto, 1980. — 192p ; 21cm
Includes index
ISBN 0-86104-326-x (cased) : £6.95
ISBN 0-86104-325-1 (pbk) : Unpriced
B81-33597

335.4'11 — Marxist philosophy

Issues in Marxist philosophy / edited by John Mepham and David-Hillel Ruben. — Brighton : Harvester. — (Marxist theory and contemporary capitalism ; 32)
Vol.4: Social and political philosophy. — 1981. — viii,242p ; 23cm
Includes bibliographies
ISBN 0-7108-0091-6 : £16.95 : CIP rev.
B81-16891

Labica, Georges. Marxism and the status of philosophy / Georges Labica ; translated from the French by Kate Soper & Martin Ryle. — Brighton : Harvester, 1980. — 397p ; 23cm. — (Marxist theory and contemporary capitalism ; 31)
Translation of: Le statut marxiste de la philosophie. — Bibliography: p391-397
ISBN 0-85527-955-9 : £26.50 : CIP rev.
B80-08130

335.4'119'0924 — Marxism. Historical materialism. Theories of Weber, Max

Loewenstein, Julius I.. Marx against Marxism / Julius I. Loewenstein ; translated from the German by Harry Drost. — London : Routledge & Kegan Paul, 1980. — xiii,222p ; 23cm
Translation of: Marx contra Marxismus. 2. Aufl.. — Bibliography: p205-121. - Includes index
ISBN 0-7100-0562-8 : £8.25 : CIP rev.
B80-17588

335.4'12 — Economics. Theories. Concepts: Need. Theories of Marx, Karl

Soper, Kate. On human needs : open and closed theories in a Marxist perspective / Kate Soper. — Brighton : Harvester, 1981. — 221p ; 23cm
Includes bibliographies and index
ISBN 0-7108-0092-4 : £13.95 : CIP rev.
B81-18120

335.4'12 — Economics. Theories of Marx, Karl & Engels, Friedrich — *Texts*

Collected works / Karl Marx, Frederick Engels. — London : Lawrence & Wishart
Vol.16: Marx and Engels : 1958-60. — 1980. — xxxii,768,[3]leaves of plates(some folded) : col.maps,facsims ; 23cm
Includes index
ISBN 0-85315-437-6 : £5.00 B81-27872

335.4'12 — Economics. Value. Theories

Hodgson, Geoff. Capitalism, value and exploitation. — Oxford : Martin Robertson, Sept.1981. — [220]p
ISBN 0-85520-414-1 : £12.50 : CIP entry
B81-23822

335.4'12 — Economics. Value. Theories — *Marxist viewpoints*

The **Value** controversy / Ian Steedman ... [et al.]. — London : NLB, c1981. — 300p : ill ; 23cm
ISBN 0-86091-040-7 : £13.50 : CIP rev.
ISBN 0-86091-738-x (pbk) : Unpriced
B81-30151

335.4'12 — Economics. Value. Theories of Marx, Karl

Lippi, Marco. Value and naturalism in Marx / Marco Lippi ; translated by Hilary Steedman. — London : NLB, 1979. — ix,136p ; 22cm
Translation of: Marx : il valore come costo sociale reale. — Includes index
ISBN 0-86091-018-0 : £7.50 B81-08389

335.4'12 — Marxist economics. Implications of theories of economics of Sraffa, Piero

Steedman, Ian. Marx after Sraffa. — London : New Left Books, Sept.1981. — [218]p
Originally published: 1977
ISBN 0-86091-747-9 (pbk) : £3.50 : CIP entry
B81-30149

335.4'12'0924 — Economics. Theories of Marx, Karl — *Critical studies*

Roemer, John E.. Analytical foundations of Marxian economic theory / John E. Roemer. — Cambridge : Cambridge University Press, 1981. — xi,220p : ill ; 24cm
Bibliography: p215-217. — Includes index
ISBN 0-521-23047-0 : £19.50 B81-36893

335.43 — Communism — *Correspondence, diaries, etc*

Lenin, V. I.. Letters to the workers of Europe and America / Lenin. — Moscow : Progress Publishers ; [London] : Central Books [distributor], 1980. — 63p ; 21cm
Translation of: Pis'ma k rabochim Evropy i Ameriki. — Includes index
ISBN 0-7147-1633-2 (pbk) : £0.25 B81-32943

335.43 — Communism — *Early works*

Lenin, V. I.. Collected works / V.I. Lenin. — London : Lawrence & Wishart
Vol.46: Index. Part 1: Index of works, name index. — 1978. — 334p ; 21cm
ISBN 0-85315-500-3 : £3.00 B81-09449

Lenin, V. I.. Collected works / V.I. Lenin. — London : Lawrence & Wishart
Vol.47: Index. Part 2 : Index subject. — c1980. — 664p ; 21cm
ISBN 0-85315-526-7 : £3.00 B81-09448

335.43 — Communism - *Homosexual viewpoints*

Fernbach, David. The spiral path. — London (27 Priory Avenue, N8 7RN) : Gay Men's Press, June 1981. — [216]p
ISBN 0-907040-07-1 (pbk) : £3.75 : CIP entry
B81-09465

335.43 — Leninism

Besançon, Alain. The intellectual origins of Leninism / Alain Besançon ; translated by Sarah Matthews. — Oxford : Blackwell, 1981. — 329p ; 24cm
Translation of: Les origines intellectuelles du Léninisme. — Bibliography: p309-317. — Includes index
ISBN 0-631-11401-7 : £12.00 B81-08464

335.43'01 — Communism. Theories

Mattick, Paul. Anti-bolshevik communism / by Paul Mattick. — London : Merlin, 1978. — xiii,231p ; 22cm
ISBN 0-85036-222-9 (cased) : £6.00
ISBN 0-85036-223-7 (pbk) : £2.50 B81-06365

335.43'09'04 — Communism, *1943-1980*

Westoby, Adam. Communism since World War II / Adam Westoby. — Brighton : Harvester, 1981. — xii,514p ; 25cm
Bibliography: p478-507. — Includes index
ISBN 0-85527-995-8 : £35.00 B81-38884

335.43'09'042 — Communism, *1920-1921* **—** *Early works*

Lenin, V. I.. The second congress of the communist international : July 19-August 7, 1920 : speeches and reports / Lenin. — Moscow : Progress Publishers ; [London] : Central Books [distributor], 1980. — 65p ; 21cm
Translation of: II Kongress kommunisticheskogo internatsionala. — Includes index
ISBN 0-7147-1632-4 (pbk) : £0.40 B81-32942

335.43'094 — Eurocommunism

In search of Eurocommunism / edited by Richard Kindersley. — London : Macmillan in association with St. Antony's College, Oxford, 1981. — xi,218p ; 23cm. — (St Antony's/Macmillan series)
Includes index
ISBN 0-333-27376-1 (cased) : £15.00
ISBN 0-333-27594-2 (pbk) : unpriced
B81-38874

The **Politics** of Eurocommunism : socialism in transition / edited by Carl Boggs and David Plotke. — London : Macmillan, 1980. — 479p ; 22cm
ISBN 0-333-29546-3 (cased) : £12.50 : CIP rev.
ISBN 0-333-29547-1 (pbk) : £4.95 B80-09119

335.5 — STATE SOCIALISM AND SOCIAL DEMOCRACY

335.5'0941 — Great Britain. Social democratic movements. Policies — *Proposals*

Owen, David, *1938-*. Face the future / David Owen. — Abridged ... with revisions and new preface. — Oxford : Oxford University Press, 1981. — xxi,279p ; 20cm
Previous ed.: London : Cape, 1981. — Includes index
ISBN 0-19-285117-9 (pbk) : £2.95 : CIP rev.
B81-22607

Owen, David, *1938-*. Face the future / David Owen. — London : Cape, 1981. — viii,552p ; 23cm
Includes index
ISBN 0-224-01956-2 : £12.50 B81-09301

335.5′0941 — Great Britain. Socialism

Crosland, Anthony. The future of socialism / C.A.R. Crosland. — Rev.ed. — London : Cape, 1964, c1963 (1980 [printing]). — 368p ; 21cm
Includes index
ISBN 0-224-01888-4 : £8.95 B81-04676

The **Popular** and the political : essays on socialism in the 1980s / edited by Mike Prior. — London : Routledge & Kegan Paul, 1981. — xii,239p ; 24cm
Includes index
ISBN 0-7100-0627-6 (pbk) : £6.95 B81-10687

335.5′0941 — Great Britain. Socialism — *Festschriften*

The **Socialist** agenda : Crosland's legacy / edited by David Lipsey and Dick Leonard. — London : Cape ; 1981. — vi,242p ; 23cm
Includes index
ISBN 0-224-01886-8 : £7.95 B81-04677

335.6 — NATIONAL SOCIALISM

335.6 — Fascism

Payne, Stanley G.. Fascism : comparison and definition / Stanley G. Payne. — Madison ; London : University of Wisconsin Press, 1980. — viii,234p ; 23cm
Bibliography: p215-217. - Includes index
ISBN 0-299-08060-9 : £10.00 B81-00037

335.6 — Spain. Anti-fascism, *1936-1939 — Personal observations — Collections*

The **Road** to Spain : anti-fascists at war 1936-1939 / introduced and edited by David Corkill and Stuart J. Rawnsley. — Dunfermline : Borderline, 1981. — xix,164p ; 21cm
ISBN 0-906135-03-6 (pbk) : £4.95
Primary classification 946.081 B81-40413

335.6′094 — Europe. Fascism, *ca 1920-1945*

Hills, C. A. R.. The fascist dictatorships / C.A.R. Hills. — London : Batsford, 1979. — 96p : ill,ports ; 26cm. — (Twentieth century world history)
Bibliography: p94. — Includes index
ISBN 0-7134-0979-7 : £5.95 B81-19537

335.6′094 — Europe. Fascism, *to 1980*

Fascism in Europe. — London : Methuen, Oct.1981. — [350]p
ISBN 0-416-30230-0 (cased) : £11.50 : CIP entry
ISBN 0-416-30240-8 (pbk) : £5.95 B81-25839

335.6′0943 — Germany. National socialism, *1922-1975*

Ayçoberry, Pierre. The Nazi question : an essay on the interpretations of national socialism (1922-1975) / by Pierre Ayçoberry ; translated from the French by Robert Hurley. — London : Routledge & Kegan Paul, 1981. — xiii,257p ; 22cm
Translation of: La question nazie. — Originally published: Paris : Editions du Seuil, 1979. — Bibliography: p242-247. — Includes index
ISBN 0-7100-0866-x : £12.50 : CIP rev. B81-21477

335.6′0943 — Germany. National socialism. Support by Britons, *1933-1939*

Griffiths, Richard, *1935-*. Fellow travellers of the right : British enthusiasts for Nazi Germany : 1933-39 / Richard Griffiths. — London : Constable, 1980. — 406p,[12]p of plates : ill,ports ; 23cm
Bibliography: p379-391. - Includes index
ISBN 0-09-463460-2 : £12.50 : CIP rev. B80-06797

335.6′09436 — Austria. National socialism, *1880-1938*

Pauley, Bruce F.. Hitler and the forgotten Nazis : a history of Austrian National Socialism / Bruce F. Pauley. — London : Macmillan, 1981. — xxi,292p : ill,facsims,ports ; 24cm
Bibliography: p267-282. — Includes index
ISBN 0-333-30709-7 : £20.00 B81-40729

335.7 — CHRISTIAN SOCIALISM

335′.7′0924 — Great Britain. Christian Socialist Movement. Ludlow, John — *Biographies*

Ludlow, John. John Ludlow : the autobiography of a Christian socialist / edited and introduced by A.D. Murray. — London : Cass, 1981. — xxxii,334p : ill,ports ; 23cm
Includes index
ISBN 0-7146-3085-3 : £16.00 : CIP rev. B79-14500

335.8 — SYNDICALISM, ANARCHISM, ETC

335′.83 — Anarchism

Guerin, Daniel. Anarchism and Marxism : from a paper given in New York on 6 Nov. 1973 / Daniel Guerin ; with an introduction by the author. — Orkney (Over the Water, Sanday, Orkney KW17 2BL) : Cienfuegos, 1981. — v,17p ; 21cm
ISBN 0-904564-43-6 (pbk) : £0.70 : CIP rev.
Also classified at 335.4 B80-27960

Meltzer, Albert. Anarchism : arguments for and against / Albert Meltzer. — Sanday : Cienfuegos, 1981. — vii,41p : ill ; 15cm. — (New anarchist library)
Ill on inside cover
ISBN 0-904564-44-4 (pbk) : £0.50 B81-36852

White, J. R.. The meaning of anarchism / J.R. White. — Orkney (Over the Water, Sanday, Orkney KW17 2BL) : Cienfuegos, [1980]. — ix,11p : ill,ports
Includes introducing essay: From loyalism to anarchism / by Albert Meltzer
ISBN 0-904564-42-8 (pbk) : £0.70 B81-08975

335′.83′01 — Anarchism. Theories

Ritter, Alan. Anarchism : a theoretical analysis / Alan Ritter. — Cambridge : Cambridge University Press, 1980. — vii,187p ; 23cm
Includes index
ISBN 0-521-23324-0 : £12.00 B81-02462

335′.83′0924 — Anarchism. Most, Johann — *Biographies*

Trautmann, Frederic. The voice of terror : a biography of Johann Most / Frederic Trautmann. — Westport, Conn. ; London : Greenwood Press, 1980. — xxv,288p : 3ports ; 22cm. — (Contributions in political science, ISSN 0147-1066 ; no.42)
Bibliography: p259-270. - Includes index
ISBN 0-313-22053-0 : Unpriced B81-06666

335′.83′0924 — Scotland. Anarchism. Christie, Stuart — *Biographies*

Christie, Stuart. The Christie file / Stuart Christie. — Seattle : Partisan ; Sanday (Box A, Over the Water, Sanday, Orkney Islands) : Cienfuegos, 1980. — 370p : ill,1facsim,ports ; 21cm
ISBN 0-904564-37-1 (pbk) : £6.00 : CIP rev. B80-03533

335.9 — SOCIALIST AND ANARCHIST COMMUNITIES

335′.941693′0924 — Donegal *(County)*. **Burtonport. Alternative communities: Atlantis** *(Alternative community) — Personal observations*

James, Jenny. Atlantis alive : love letters from a primal commune / by Jenny James. — Firle : Caliban, c1980. — 173p ; 23cm
ISBN 0-904573-30-3 : £7.00 B81-16156

James, Jenny. Atlantis is - / by Jenny James. — Firle : Caliban, 1980. — 132p ; 20cm
ISBN 0-904573-26-5 : £5.00 B81-03802

336 — PUBLIC FINANCE

336′.014′4 — Western Europe. Local government. Finance

The **Local** fiscal crisis in Western Europe : myths and realities / edited by L.J. Sharpe. — London : Sage, c1981. — 272p : ill ; 23cm
ISBN 0-8039-9813-9 : £12.50 B81-18729

336′.014′4 — Western European countries. Local government. Finance

Newton, Kenneth. Balancing the books : financial problems of local government in West Europe / Kenneth Newton. — London : Sage, c1980. — vii,218p : 1ill ; 22cm
Includes index
ISBN 0-8039-9802-3 (cased) : £12.50 : CIP rev.
ISBN 0-8039-9803-1 (pbk) : £6.25 B80-19647

336′.014′41 — Great Britain. Local government. Finance

Foster, C. D.. Local government finance in a unitary state / by C.D. Foster, R.A. Jackman, M. Perlman with the assistance of B. Lynch. — London : Allen & Unwin, 1980. — viii,634p : ill ; 25cm
Bibliography: p616-629. — Includes index
ISBN 0-04-336066-1 : £27.50 : CIP rev. B80-10964

Hepworth, N. P.. The finance of local government / by N.P. Hepworth. — 6th ed. — London : Allen & Unwin, 1980. — 344p ; 22cm. — (The New local government series ; no.6)
Previous ed.: 1979. — Bibliography: p335-337. - Includes index
ISBN 0-04-352087-1 (pbk) : £8.95 : CIP rev. B80-10503

336′.014′41605 — Northern Ireland. District councils — *Accounts — Serials*

District Councils summary of statements of accounts, year ended 31 March ... / Department of the Environment for Northern Ireland. — 1979. — Belfast : H.M.S.O., 1980. — 3p
ISBN 0-337-08158-1 : £1.50
ISSN 0141-0504 B81-02951

336′.014′42 — England. Local government. Finance *— Statistics — Serials*

Financial, general & rating statistics / CIPFA Statistical Information Service. — 1981-82. — London : Chartered Institute of Public Finance and Accountancy, 1981. — 100p in various pagings
ISSN 0141-5468 : £12.00 B81-35096

Local government financial statistics, England and Wales / Department of the Environment [and the] Welsh Office. — 1978/79. — London : H.M.S.O., 1981. — 58p
ISBN 0-11-751527-2 : £4.70
ISSN 0308-1745 B81-24116

336′.014′4290212 — Wales. Local government. Finance *— Statistics — Serials*

Welsh local government financial statistics / [Welsh Office]. — no.4 (1980). — Cardiff : H.M.S.O., 1980. — 92p
ISBN 0-11-790141-5 : £11.00 B81-09059

336′.014′73 — United States. Cities. Local government. Finance

Urban government finance : emerging trends / edited by Roy Bahl. — Beverly Hills ; London : Sage, c1981. — 287p : ill ; 22cm. — (Urban affairs annual reviews ; v.20)
Includes bibliographies
ISBN 0-8039-1564-0 (cased) : Unpriced
ISBN 0-8039-1565-9 (pbk) : Unpriced B81-18824

336′.09168 — European Community. Finance

Strasser, Daniel. The finances of Europe / Daniel Strasser. — New York ; London : Praeger, 1977. — xxvi,299p ; 25cm. — (Praeger special studies in international business, finance, and trade)
Translation of: Les finances de l'Europe. — Includes index
ISBN 0-03-022386-5 : £19.50 B81-02224

336.1 — PUBLIC FINANCE. NON-TAX REVENUES

336′.185′0973 — United States. Federal government. Fiscal aspects

Reagan, Michael D.. The new federalism. — 2nd ed. / Michael D. Reagan, John G. Sanzone. — New York ; Oxford : Oxford University Press, 1981. — 196p ; 21cm
Previous ed.: 1972. — Bibliography: p189-191. - Includes index
ISBN 0-19-502772-8 (pbk) : £2.95 B81-18941

336.2 — PUBLIC FINANCE. TAXATION

336.2 — Great Britain. Capital. Taxation

Bracewell-Milnes, Barry. Is capital taxation fair? : the tradition and the truth / by Barry Bracewell-Milnes. — London : Institute of Directors, 1974. — 144p ; 19cm
£2.00 (pbk) B81-38378

336.2 — Great Britain. Immigration & emigration. Implications of taxation

Migration : United Kingdom : a handbook on the taxation, exchange control and legal implications of coming to, investing in and leaving the United Kingdom / edited by J.R. Poole and P.G.D. Kiers. — Deventer ; London : Kluwer, 1978. — 197p ; 25cm
Bibliography: p194. — Includes index
ISBN 0-903393-36-0 (pbk) : £12.50 B81-06794

336.2 — Taxation — *Conference proceedings*

The **Political** economy of taxation / edited by Alan Peacock and Francesco Forte. — Oxford : Blackwell, 1981. — xi,211p : ill ; 24cm
Includes bibliographies and index
ISBN 0-631-12912-x : £14.00 : CIP rev.
B81-07942

336.2'005 — Taxation — *For tax avoidance — Serials*

The **Westgate** tax planner's letter. — Oct.1980-. — London (9 Holborn, EC1 2LL) : Fleet Financial Publishing, 1980-. — v. ; 30cm
Monthly
ISSN 0261-1635 = Westgate tax planner's letter : Unpriced B81-18803

336.2'0094 — Western Europe. Taxation

Taxation in Europe 1980 / Deloitte Haskins & Sells. — [London] : Oyez, 1980. — lx,221p (some folded) : ill ; 21cm
Previous ed.: London : Farringdon, 1978
ISBN 0-906052-06-8 (pbk) : £9.00 B81-14489

336.2'00941 — Great Britain. Regions. Taxation. Distribution, *1974-1978*

Short, John, *1948-*. Public expenditure and taxation in the UK regions / John Short. — Farnborough, Hants. : Gower, c1981. — viii,111p : 1map ; 23cm
Bibliography: p111
ISBN 0-566-00403-8 : £11.50
Also classified at 336.3'9'0941 B81-12995

336.2'00941 — Great Britain. Taxation

Kay, J. A.. The British tax system / by J.A. Kay, M.A. King. — 2nd ed. — Oxford : Oxford University Press, 1980. — xiii,266p : ill,1form ; 23cm
Previous ed.: 1978. — Bibliography: p248-255. - Includes index
ISBN 0-19-877159-2 (cased) : £10.00 : CIP rev.
ISBN 0-19-877160-6 (pbk) : £4.95 B80-08646

Williams, R. Glynne. Comprehensive aspects of taxation / R. Glynne Williams. — 33rd ed. / by A.D.W. Bertram and S.G. Edwards ; 1980 Finance Act by Henry Toch. — London : Cassell in association with Metropolitan College, 1980. — xiii,623p : forms ; 22cm. — (A Cassell professional handbook)
Previous ed.: Reading : Donnington Press, 1975. — Includes index
ISBN 0-304-30599-5 (pbk) : £12.95 B81-11799

336.2'00941 — Great Britain. Taxation. Forms. Filling — *Manuals*

Tax forms manual / edited by K.J.M. Ritchie. — London : Oyez, 1981. — xix,348p : forms ; 25cm
ISBN 0-85120-560-7 (pbk) : Unpriced
B81-21659

336'.2'00941 — Great Britain. Taxation. Policies of government, *1909-1910.* **Political aspects**

Murray, Bruce K.. The People's Budget 1909/10 : Lloyd George and Liberal politics / by Bruce K. Murray. — Oxford : Clarendon Press, 1980. — ix,352p ; 23cm
Bibliography: p336-342. — Includes index
ISBN 0-19-822626-8 : £17.50 : CIP rev.
B80-18618

336.2'00941 — Great Britain. Taxation — *Proposals — Serials*

The **Budget**. — 1980. — London : Confederation of British Industry, 1980. — 32p
Unpriced B81-13308

336.2'00941 — Great Britain. Taxation — *Serials*

Tax digest. — No.1 (Autumn 1980)-. — London : Institute of Chartered Accountants in England and Wales, 1980-. — v. ; 30cm
Irregular
ISSN 0260-6496 = Tax digest : Unpriced
B81-06708

Tax newsletter / Touche Ross & Co. — Mar. 1981-. — London (1 Little New St., EC4A 3TR) : Touche Ross & Co., 1981. — v. ; 30cm
Quarterly
ISSN 0261-8664 = Tax newsletter : Unpriced
B81-34046

336.2'00941 — Great Britain. Taxation — *Tables — Serials*

Butterworths budget tax tables. — 17th ed. (1981). — London : Butterworths, c1981. — [10]p
ISBN 0-406-50816-x : £2.10 B81-21937

Tolley's tax tables. — 1981-82. — Croydon : Tolly Publishing, [1981]. — 16p
ISBN 0-85459-032-3 : £1.95
ISSN 0307-6687 B81-25017

336.2'00941 — Great Britain. Taxation, *to 1980*

Sabine, B. E. V.. A short history of taxation / B.E.V. Sabine. — London : Butterworths, 1980. — 147p ; 23cm
ISBN 0-406-53520-5 : £7.95 B81-06231

336.2'00973 — United States. Taxation

Bernard, Michael M.. Constitutions, taxation, and land policy / Michael M. Bernard. — Lexington, Mass. : Lexington Books ; [Farnborough, Hants.] : Gower [distributor], 1980
Vol.2: Discussion and analysis of federal and state constitutional constraints on the use of taxation as an instrument of land-planning policy. — xi,128p ; 24cm
Bibliography: p103-104
ISBN 0-669-03462-2 : £11.50 B81-20367

Reese, Thomas J.. The politics of taxation / Thomas J. Reese. — Westport ; London : Quorum, 1980. — xxv,237p : ill ; 25cm
Bibliography: p223-229. — Includes index
ISBN 0-89930-003-0 : £15.95 B81-23460

336.2'00973 — United States. Taxation. Effects of War of American Independence, *1763-1783*

Becker, Robert A.. Revolution, reform, and the politics of American taxation, 1763-1783 / Robert A. Becker. — Baton Rouge ; London : Louisiana State University Press, c1980. — xi,323p ; 24cm
Bibliography: p293-313. - Includes index
ISBN 0-8071-0654-2 : £15.00 B81-07296

336.2'00973 — United States. Taxation. International aspects

McDaniel, Paul R.. Introduction to United States international taxation / by Paul R. McDaniel, Hugh J. Ault. — 2nd rev. ed. — Deventer ; London : Kluwer, 1981. — 209p ; 25cm. — (Series on international taxation ; no.3)
Previous ed.: 1977. — Includes index
ISBN 90-654-4004-6 : Unpriced B81-30652

336.2'00973 — United States. Taxation. Policies of government. Political aspects

Brennan, Geoffrey. The power to tax : analytical foundations of the fiscal constitution / Geoffrey Brennan, James M. Buchanan. — Cambridge : Cambridge University Press, 1980. — xiv,231p : ill ; 24cm
Bibliography: p221-225. - Includes index
ISBN 0-521-23329-1 : £10.50 B81-06306

336.2'013'73 — United States. States. Taxation

Hale, Lloyd S.. State tax liability and compliance manual / Lloyd S. Hale, Ruth Kramer. — New York ; Chichester : Wiley, c1981. — xx,347p ; 24cm
Bibliography: p250-252. - Includes index
ISBN 0-471-08488-3 : £21.50 B81-11301

336.2'05'0941 — Great Britain. Taxation. Abolition

MacMurchie, David A.. For God's sake set the people free and end legalised theft! a blue-print for full employment and national prosperity / David A. MacMurchie. — Dundee (30 Auchrannie Terrace, Dundee DD4 7QH) : [D.A. MacMurchie], [1980]. — [7]p ; 18cm
£0.10 (pbk) B81-06453

336.2'07 — Great Britain. Agricultural industries. Farms. Taxation

Camamile, G. H.. Taxation of farms and woodlands / G.H. Camamile, J.A. Davison, M.B. Sarson. — London : Institute of Chartered Accountants in England and Wales, 1981. — xxii,170p ; 21cm. — (Chartac taxation guides)
Includes index
ISBN 0-85291-290-0 (pbk) : Unpriced
B81-19518

336.2'07 — Great Britain. Business firms. Stock. Taxation

The **Reform** of stock relief / [report by CBI Taxation Committee]. — London : Confederation of British Industry, 1981. — 14p : 1ill ; 30cm
£2.00 (pbk) B81-21231

336.2'07 — Great Britain. Self-employed persons. Taxation — *For self-employed persons*

Edwards, Richard, *1946-*. Tax for the self-employed / Richard Edwards. — London : Oyez, 1980. — 95p : forms ; 21cm. — (Owl books)
Includes bibliographies and index
ISBN 0-7063-6014-1 (cased) : £3.95 : CIP rev.
ISBN 0-7063-6015-x (pbk£2.50) B80-17591

336.2'07'0941 — Great Britain. Business firms. Taxation — *For management*

Tax and VAT. — London : Hamlyn, c1980. — 207p : forms ; 22cm. — (Managing your business guides)
Includes index
ISBN 0-600-35368-0 : £5.00
Also classified at 368 B81-05451

336.2'07'09417 — Ireland *(Republic).* **Business firms. Tax incentives**

Tax incentives and industrial grants in Ireland. — [Dublin] (10 Fitzwilliam Square, Dublin 2) : Binder Dijker Otte, 1981. — 22p ; 25cm
Unpriced (pbk)
Also classified at 338.9417'02 B81-22967

336.22 — Cornwall. Hearth tax & poll tax, *1660-1664.* **Taxpayers** — *Lists*

Cornwall hearth and poll taxes 1660-1664 : direct taxation in Cornwall in the reign of Charles II / edited by T.L. Stoate. — Bristol (Lower Court, Almondsbury, Bristol) : T.L. Stoate, c1981. — xxiv,309p : 1map ; 30cm
Bibliography: pxxiii. — Includes index
£7.60 B81-15724

336.22 — Great Britain. Development land tax

Maas, Robert W.. Development land tax / by Robert W. Maas. — 3rd ed. — Croydon : Tolley, 1981. — xvii,234p ; 23cm
Previous ed.: 1979. — Includes index
ISBN 0-85459-010-2 (pbk) : £8.95 B81-32980

336.2'2 — Great Britain. Urban regions. Land. Value. Taxation, *1880-1980*

Prest, Alan Richmond. The taxation of urban land. — Manchester : Manchester University Press, Sept.1981. — [190]p
ISBN 0-7190-0817-4 : £10.00 : CIP entry
B81-23752

336.22'0942 — England. Rates — *Statistics — Serials*

Rate collection statistics. Actuals / CIPFA Statistical Information Service. — 1979-80. — London : Chartered Institute of Public Finance and Accountancy, 1981. — 68p
ISSN 0260-5546 : £10.00 B81-29086

336.2'3'0942545 — Leicestershire. Rutland *(District)*. Personal property. Taxation. Lary subsidy rolls, *1524-1525 — Texts*

The County community under Henry VIII : the military survey, 1522, and lay subsidy, 1524-5, for Rutland / edited for the Rutland Record Society by Julian Cornwall. — Oakham (Rutland County Museum, Catmos St., Oakham, Rutland, LE15 6HW) : The Society, 1980. — 134p : 1map ; 26cm. — (Rutland record series ; v.1)
Includes index
ISBN 0-907464-00-9 : £7.95
Also classified at 355.3'7'0942545 B81-11409

336.24 — Great Britain. Charities. Donations by deeds of covenant. Taxation

Norton, Michael. Covenants : a guide to the tax advantages of giving for charities / by Michael Norton. — London : Directory of Social Change, [c1980]. — 95p : forms ; 21cm
ISBN 0-907164-02-1 (pbk) : £1.95 B81-26810

336'.24'0212 — Great Britain. Income tax — *Tables — Serials*

Whillan's tax tables. — 3rd ed. (1980-81). — London : Butterworths, c1980. — 39p
ISBN 0-406-54315-1 : Unpriced
ISSN 2260-3926 B81-03537

336.24'0941 — Great Britain. Income tax

Chapman, A. L.. Taxation income tax manual. — 14th ed. / by A.L. Chapman. — London : Taxation Publishing
Previous ed.: 1977
Supplement / by F.G. Sandison. — 1980. — 32p ; 22cm
£1.00 (pbk) B81-32350

Thornton, Richard. The Daily telegraph guide to income tax. — Completely updated ed. / prepared by Richard Thornton. — London : Collins, 1981. — 111p ; 20cm
Previous ed.: 1980
ISBN 0-00-434188-0 (pbk) : £1.75 B81-18623

336.24'0941 — Great Britain. Income tax — *Serials*

Check your tax. — 1981/82. — London : Foulsham, 1981. — 80p
ISBN 0-572-01134-2 : £1.25 B81-25033

Daily mail income tax guide. — 1981-1982. — London ([Carmelite House, Carmelite St., EC4Y 0JA]) : Harmsworth Publications for Associated Newspapers Group, c1981. — 128p
£0.75 B81-30844

Income tax simplified. — 62nd ed. (1980 budget ed.). — Huddersfield : Arthur Fieldhouse, 1980. — 112p
£1.25 B81-02833

Income tax simplified. — 63rd ed. (1980 Finance Act ed.). — Huddersfield : Fieldhouse, 1980. — 112p
£1.25 B81-16230

Income tax simplified. — 64th ed.(1981 budget ed.). — Huddersfield : Fieldhouse, 1981. — 111p
£1.50 B81-32194

336.24'2 — Great Britain. Professional personnel. Taxation

Laventure, Brian. The taxation of specialised occupations and professions / by Brian Laventure. — London : Institute of Chartered Accountants in England and Wales, 1980. — xxiv,159p ; 22cm. — (Chartac taxation guides)
Includes index
ISBN 0-85291-280-3 (pbk) : £6.95 B81-03654

336.24'2 — Great Britain. Single-parent families. Taxation. Great Britain. *Treasury*. Taxation of husband and wife — *Critical studies*

One Parent Families. Lone parents and family taxation : a response to the Government's Green Paper The Taxation of Husband and Wife. — London (255 Kentish Town Road, NW5 2LX) : One Parent Families, [1981]. — 39p ; 30cm
Cover title
£1.00 (unbound) B81-40217

336.24'2'0880624 — Great Britain. Income tax. Liability of low-income families

Pond, Chris. Carried across the threshold : taxation and the low paid / Chris Pond, Clive Playford. — London (9 Poland St., WIV 3DG) : Low Pay Unit, 1981. — 16p ; 21cm. — (Low pay report ; 5)
£0.75 (unbound) B81-25578

336.24'22 — Great Britain. Dependent persons. Maintenance allowances. Taxation

Williams, Donald B.. Tax on maintenance payments 1981/82 / Donald B. Williams and Joel Newman. — 5th ed. — London : Oyez, 1981. — vii,49p : facsims ; 22cm. — (The Oyez practical tax series)
Previous ed.: 1980
ISBN 0-85120-605-0 (pbk) : Unpriced B81-37483

336.24'24 — United States. Investments: Real property. Transfer. Deferred taxation

McMullen, Charles W.. Tax deferred exchanges of real estate investments / Charles W. McMullen. — New York ; Chichester : Wiley, c1981. — xii,86p : ill ; 23cm. — (Real estate for professional practitioners)
Includes index
ISBN 0-471-08526-x (pbk) : £11.25 B81-38579

336.24'26 — United States. Investment income. Taxation — *For foreign investors*

Chown, John F.. The taxation of direct investment in the United States / by John Chown and Lionel Halpern. — London : Butterworths, 1980. — 158p : ill ; 30
Includes index
ISBN 0-406-53958-8 (pbk) : £17.00 B81-05190

336.24'3 — Great Britain. Capital gains tax

Cooper, J. M. (John Macneill). Capital gains tax / John M. Cooper. — London : Gee, 1980. — 96p ; 25cm. — (A Gee's study book)
Text on inside covers
ISBN 0-85258-206-4 (pbk) : £3.95 B81-12597

Cretton, C. P.. Capital gains tax / by Colin Cretton. — St Helier (P.O. Box 318, St Helier, Jersey) : Guild Press, c1980. — 389p ; 21cm. — (Standard works series)
Includes index
ISBN 0-9505174-9-6 (pbk) : £15.00 B81-03417

336.24'3'094 — Western Europe. Companies. Taxation

Company taxation in Europe / Binder Dijker Otte & Co.. — [London] ([10 Friar St., E.C.4]) : [Binder Hamlyn Fry & Co.], [1981]. — 112p ; 25cm
Unpriced (pbk) B81-27861

336.2'6'0941 — Great Britain. Customs duties — *Serials*

Great Britain. *Customs and Excise*. Report of the Commissioners of Her Majesty's Customs and Excise for the year ended 31 March .... — 1980. — London : H.M.S.O., 1980. — 141p. — (Cmnd ; 8099)
ISBN 0-10-180990-5 : £7.10
Also classified at 336.2'71'0941 B81-03306

336.2'64 — United States. Imports: Dumped goods. Import duties

Bryan, Greyson. Taxing unfair international trade practices : a study of U.S. antidumping and countervailing duty laws / Greyson Bryan. — Lexington : Lexington Books ; [Farnborough, Hants.] : Gower [distributor], 1981, c1980. — xxii,370p ; 24cm
Includes index
ISBN 0-669-03752-4 : £20.00 B81-22944

336.2'71'0941 — Great Britain. Excise — *Serials*

Great Britain. *Customs and Excise*. Report of the Commissioners of Her Majesty's Customs and Excise for the year ended 31 March .... — 1980. — London : H.M.S.O., 1980. — 141p. — (Cmnd ; 8099)
ISBN 0-10-180990-5 : £7.10
Primary classification 336.2'6'0941 B81-03306

336.2'714 — European Community countries. Value-added tax. International reclaiming

Reclaiming VAT across frontiers in the EEC : Value Added Tax in the EEC. — London (8 St. Bride St., EC4A 4DA) : Binder Dijker Otte & Co, [1981]. — 28p ; 25cm
Unpriced (pbk) B81-16962

336.2'714 — Great Britain. Value-added tax. Compliance. Costs

Costs and benefits of VAT / C.T. Sandford ... [et al.]. — London : Heinemann Educational, 1981. — xvi,248p : ill,1form ; 24cm
Bibliography: p242-244. — Includes index
ISBN 0-435-84782-1 : £18.75 B81-20023

336.2'714'094 — European Community countries. Value-added tax — *For businessmen*

Parkinson, Dennis. Value Added Tax in the EEC / Dennis Parkinson. — London : Graham & Trotman, 1981. — 227p ; 23cm
Includes index
ISBN 0-86010-190-8 : £16.00 B81-20916

336.2'714'0941 — Great Britain. Value-added tax

Relf, David G.. VAT guide / David G. Relf, Christopher A.L. Preston. — London : Oyez, c1981. — xxii,381p ; 24cm
Includes index
ISBN 0-85120-521-6 (pbk) : £15.00 B81-14488

336.2'714'0973 — United States. Value-added tax

Lindholm, Richard W.. The economics of vat : preserving efficiency, capitalism, and social progress / Richard W. Lindholm. — Lexington, Mass. : Lexington Books ; [Aldershot] : Gower [distributor], 1981, c1980. — xi,189p : ill ; 24cm
Includes index
ISBN 0-669-04111-4 : £12.50 B81-26970

336.2'76 — Great Britain. Capital transfer tax

McCutcheon, Barry D.. Understanding and planning for capital transfer tax : a new approach / Barry D. McCutcheon. — London : McGraw-Hill, c1980. — 1v.(loose-leaf) ; 30cm
Includes index
ISBN 0-07-084541-7 : Unpriced : CIP rev. B80-19084

336.2'78553282'0916336 — North Sea. Petroleum industries. Taxation by British government

Kemp, Alexander G.. The impact of the system of petroleum taxation in the UK on oil operations and government revenue / by Alexander G. Kemp & David Cohen. — Glasgow (100 Montrose St., Glasgow G4 0LZ) : Fraser of Allander Institute, University of Strathclyde, 1980. — 42p : ill ; 21cm. — (Research monograph / Fraser of Allander Institute ; no.8)
ISBN 0-904865-26-6 (pbk) : £2.50 B81-19496

336.2'78622'0973 — United States. Mining industries. Taxation

Conrad, Robert F.. Taxation of mineral resources / Robert F. Conrad, R. Bryce Hool. — Lexington, Mass. : Lexington Books, c1980 ; [Aldershot] : Gower [distributor], 1981. — xv,109p ; 24cm
Bibliography: p95-101. — Includes index
ISBN 0-669-04104-1 : £10.00 B81-33201

336.2'78636132 — Great Britain. Thoroughbred horses. Breeding. Taxation

Hunn, Richard George. Tax planning and the ownership of thoroughbred racehorses / by Richard George Hunn. — London (50 Tufton St., SW1P 3RA) : Company Communications Centre, 1980. — xi,84p ; 23cm
ISBN 0-906609-03-8 : £20.00
Also classified at 336.2'787984 B81-05069

336.2'787984 — Great Britain. Racehorses. Racing. Taxation

Hunn, Richard George. Tax planning and the ownership of thoroughbred racehorses / by Richard George Hunn. — London (50 Tufton St., SW1P 3RA) : Company Communications Centre, 1980. — xi,84p ; 23cm
ISBN 0-906609-03-8 : £20.00
Primary classification 336.2'78636132 B81-05069

336.2'94 — Great Britain. Direct taxation. Concessions

Inland Revenue practices and concessions / David S. Tallon ... [et al.]. — London : Oyez, c1981. — 1v.(loose-leaf) ; 26cm
Includes index
ISBN 0-85120-498-8 : £40.00 B81-14487

336.2'94 — Great Britain. Direct taxation — *Statistics — Serials*

Inland Revenue statistics / Board of Inland Revenue. — 1980. — London : H.M.S.O., 1980. — v,202p
ISBN 0-11-641030-2 : £10.50 B81-04397

336.2'94 — Western Europe. Direct taxation

Platt, C. J.. Tax systems of Western Europe : a guide for business and the professions / C.J. Platt. — Farnborough, Hants. : Gower, c1980. — xxi,166p ; 22cm
ISBN 0-566-02183-8 (pbk) : £12.50 : CIP rev. B80-17592

336.2'94'072 — Industrialised countries. Tax incidence. Mathematical models

Keller, Wouter J.. Tax incidence : a general equilibrium approach / Wouter J. Keller. — Amsterdam ; Oxford : North-Holland, 1980. — xv,348p : ill ; 23cm. — (Contributions to economic analysis ; 134)
Bibliography: p337-342. — Includes index
ISBN 0-444-86057-6 : £21.44 B81-04048

336.3 — PUBLIC FINANCE. PUBLIC DEBT AND EXPENDITURE

336.3'1'0941 — Great Britain. Financial assistance by government. Funds: National Loans Fund — *Accounts — Serials*

Accounts relating to issues from the National Loans Fund. — 1979-80. — London : H.M.S.O., 1981. — viii,142p
ISBN 0-10-216281-6 : £6.30 B81-26393

Consolidated Fund and National Loans Fund accounts. supplementary statements. — 1979-80. — London : H.M.S.O., 1980. — 67p
ISBN 0-10-204581-x : £3.90
Primary classification 336.3'1'0941 B81-10262

336.3'1'0941 — Great Britain. Government. Finance. Contingencies Fund — *Accounts — Serials*

Contingencies Fund accounts. — 1979-80. — London : H.M.S.O., [1981]. — 9p
ISBN 0-10-230081-x : £1.40 B81-30747

336.3'1'0941 — Great Britain. Government. Finance. Funds: Consolidated Fund — *Accounts — Serials*

Consolidated Fund and National Loans Fund accounts. supplementary statements. — 1979-80. — London : H.M.S.O., 1980. — 67p
ISBN 0-10-204581-x : £3.90
Also classified at 336.3'1'0941 B81-10262

336.3'1'09416 — Northern Ireland. Financial assistance by government. Government Loans Fund (Northern Ireland) — *Accounts — Serials*

[Accounts of the Government Loans Fund ... for the financial year ended 31st March ... *(Great Britain. Department of Finance for Northern Ireland)*]. Accounts of the Government Loans Fund ... for the financial year ended 31st March ... / Department of Finance for Northern Ireland. — 1979-80. — Belfast : H.M.S.O., 1980. — 19p
ISBN 0-337-23338-1 : £2.60 B81-30714

336.3'1'09416 — Northern Ireland. Government. Finance. Capital accounts — *Accounts — Serials*

Great Britain. *Department of Finance for Northern Ireland.* Accounts of capital receipts and payments, and of earnings on capital advances or investments, together with the various subsidiary accounts including Civil Contingencies Fund Account and the Ulster Land Fund Account for the year ended 31st March ... / Department of Finance for Northern Ireland. — 1979-80. — Belfast : H.M.S.O., 1980. — 21p
ISBN 0-337-23335-7 : £2.70 B81-26580

336.3'4'091724 — Developing countries: Non-petroleum exporting countries. Governments. Debts

Vaughan, G. Douglas. The debt burden of developing countries / by G. Douglas Vaughan. — London (Gresham College, Basinghall St., EC2V 5AH) : City University Business School, 1980. — 36 leaves : ill ; 30cm. — (Working paper series / City University Business School, ISSN 0140-1041 ; no.17)
Unpriced (pbk) B81-08314

336.3'431'410212 — Great Britain. Local authorities. Debts — *Statistics — Serials*

Return of outstanding debt as at 31st March ... / CIPFA Statistical Information Service. — 1980. — London : Chartered Institute of Public Finance and Accountancy, 1981. — 61p
ISSN 0143-103x : £10.00 B81-30742

336.3'431'4105 — Great Britain. Local authorities. Capital expenditure. Financial assistance. Loans from government. Organisations: Public Works Loan Board — *Serials*

Public Works Loan Board. Annual report / Public Works Loan Board. — 105th (1979-80). — London : H.M.S.O., 1981. — 17p
ISBN 0-11-630687-4 : £2.50 B81-10241

336.3'431'41605 — Northern Ireland. Local authorities. Loan pools — *Accounts — Serials*

Great Britain. *Department of Finance for Northern Ireland.* Accounts of the Department of Finance loans pool ... for the year ended 31st March ... / Department of Finance for Northern Ireland. — 1980. — Belfast : H.M.S.O., 1981. — 9p
ISBN 0-337-23336-5 : £1.40 B81-30716

336.3'9 — England. County council. Capital expenditure — *Statistics — Serials*

Capital expenditure of county councils / the Society of County Treasurers. — 1979-1980. — Reading : The Society, 1980. — [4]p
ISSN 0587-0305 : Unpriced B81-16828

336.3'9'0941 — Great Britain. *Department of Education and Science.* **Expenditure —** *Inquiry reports*

Great Britain. *Parliament. House of Commons. Committee of Public Accounts.* Department of Education and Science, University Grants Committee, Science Research Council, Office of Arts and Libraries, British Museum : matters relating to the Department of Education and Science : tenth report from the Committee of Public Accounts, together with the proceedings of the Committee, minutes of evidence and appendices, session 1980-81. — London : H.M.S.O., [1981]. — xviii,46p ; 25cm. — ([H.C.] ; 233)
ISBN 0-10-223381-0 (pbk) : £4.70 B81-32952

336.3'9'0941 — Great Britain. *Foreign and Commonwealth Office.* **Expenditure —** *Inquiry reports*

Great Britain. *Parliament. House of Commons. Foreign Affairs Committee.* Fourth report from the Foreign Affairs Committee, session 1980-81 : supply estimates 1981-82 (class II, votes 1,2,3,5, and 6) : together with part of the proceedings of the Committee relating to the report ; and the minutes of evidence taken before the Committee on 3 and 10 June with appendices. — London : H.M.S.O., [1981]
Vol.2: Minutes of evidence and appendices. — vi,119p ; 25cm. — ([HC] ; 343 II)
ISBN 0-10-008551-2 (pbk) : £5.85 B81-38928

336.3'9'0941 — Great Britain. Government. Capital expenditure — *Proposals*

Leslie, Shaun. Investing in the future : a British Road Federation paper / [written by Shaun Leslie]. — London (388 Oxford St., W1N 9HE) : the Federation, [1981]. — [4]p ; 30cm
Unpriced (unbound) B81-14018

336.3'9'0941 — Great Britain. Government. Excess expenditure — *Inquiry reports*

Great Britain. *Parliament. House of Commons. Committee of Public Accounts.* Excess votes : first report from the Committee of Public Accounts, together with appendices, session 1980-81. — London : H.M.S.O., [1981]. — vi,2p ; 25cm. — ([H.C.] ; 175)
ISBN 0-10-217581-0 (unbound) : £1.10 B81-22067

336.3'9'0941 — Great Britain. Government. Expenditure — *Accounts — Serials*

Great Britain. *Exchequer and Audit Department*
Appropriation accounts. Volume 3, Classes x-xv and xvii. — 1979-80. — London : H.M.S.O., 1981. — xlix,364p
ISBN 0-10-209881-6 : £13.80 B81-15088

336.3'9'0941 — Great Britain. Government. Expenditure. Decision making by Great Britain. *Cabinet Office, 1976-1977 — Case studies*

Burch, Martin. British Cabinet politics : public expenditure and the IMF / Martin Burch and Michael Clarke. — Ormskirk : Hesketh, 1980. — 69p : forms ; 22cm. — (Merlin series ; 1)
Bibliography: p69
ISBN 0-905777-11-5 (pbk) : Unpriced B81-10107

336.3'9'0941 — Great Britain. Government. Expenditure — *Forecasts — Serials*

The **Government's** expenditure plans : presented to Parliament by the Chancellor of the Exchequer by command of Her Majesty. — [1975-76 to 1978-79]-. — London : H.M.S.O., 1977-. — v. ; 25cm
Irregular. — Continues: Public expenditure to .... — Description based on: 1981-82 to 1983-4 issue
ISSN 0261-2119 : £9.30 B81-23155

Statement of excesses, supply estimates / [Treasury]. — 1979-80. — London : H.M.S.O., 1981. — 7p
ISBN 0-10-213781-1 : £1.10 B81-15071

336.3'9'0941 — Great Britain. Local authorities. Expenditure. Effects of government grants *compared with* **effects of government grants on expenditure by local authorities in United States**

Page, Edward. Grant dependence and changes in inter-governmental finance : a comparison of the United States and the United Kingdom / by Edward Page. — Glasgow : University of Strathclyde, 1981. — 30p : ill ; 30cm. — (Studies in public policy, ISSN 0140-8240 ; no.80)
£1.50 (pbk)
Also classified at 336.3'9'0973 B81-24386

336.3'9'0941 — Great Britain. Regions. Public expenditure. Distribution, *1974-1978*

Short, John, *1948-*. Public expenditure and taxation in the UK regions / John Short. — Farnborough, Hants. : Gower, c1981. — viii,111p : 1map ; 23cm
Bibliography: p111
ISBN 0-566-00403-8 : £11.50
Primary classification 336.2'00941 B81-12995

336.3'9'094141 — Strathclyde. *Regional Council.* **Expenditure —** *Serials*

Strathclyde. *Regional Council.* Strathclyde's budget / Strathclyde Regional Council. — 1980-81-. — [Glasgow] ([20 India St., Glasgow G2 4PF]) : The Council's Public Relations Department, 1980-. — v. ; 21x10cm
Annual
ISSN 0260-8065 = Strathclyde's budget : Unpriced B81-09190

336.3'9'09416 — Northern Ireland. Excess expenditure by British government — *Inquiry reports*

Great Britain. *Parliament. House of Commons. Committee of Public Accounts.* Excess votes - Northern Ireland : second report from the Committee of Public Accounts, session 1980-81. — London : H.M.S.O., [1981]. — viip ; 25cm. — ([H.C.] ; 176)
ISBN 0-10-217681-7 (unbound) : £1.10 B81-22068

336.3'9'09416 — Northern Ireland. Government. Expenditure — *Forecasts — Serials*

Great Britain. *Department of Finance for Northern Ireland.* Statement of sums required on account / Department of Finance for Northern Ireland. — 1981-82. — Belfast : H.M.S.O., 1981. — [4]p
ISBN 0-337-23339-x : £0.80 B81-27331

Spring supplementary estimate for services under the Government of Northern Ireland / Department of Finance, Stormont, Belfast. — 1980-81. — Belfast : H.M.S.O., 1981. — v,32p
ISBN 0-337-23337-3 : £2.90 B81-30712

336.3'9'09429 — Great Britain. *Welsh Office*. Expenditure. Supplementary estimates — *Inquiry reports*

Great Britain. *Parliament. House of Commons. Committee on Welsh Affairs*. First report from the Committee on Welsh Affairs, session 1980-81 : supplementary estimates. — London : H.M.S.O., [1980]. — ivp ; 25cm
ISBN 0-10-206181-5 (unbound) : £0.70 B81-20345

336.3'9'0973 — United States. Expenditure by government. Geographical aspects

Johnston, R. J.. The geography of federal spending in the United States of America / Ronald J. Johnston. — Chichester : Studies Press, c1980. — x,179p : maps ; 29cm. — (Geographical research studies series ; 2)
Bibliography: p173-179
ISBN 0-471-27865-3 (pbk) : £16.50 : CIP rev. B80-34640

336.3'9'0973 — United States. Local authorities. Expenditure. Effects of government grants *compared with* **effects of government grants on expenditure by local authorities in Great Britain**

Page, Edward. Grant dependence and changes in inter-governmental finance : a comparison of the United States and the United Kingdom / by Edward Page. — Glasgow : University of Strathclyde, 1981. — 30p : ill ; 30cm. — (Studies in public policy, ISSN 0140-8240 ; no.80)
£1.50 (pbk)
Primary classification 336.3'9'0941 B81-24386

336.4/9 — PUBLIC FINANCE. GEOGRAPHICAL TREATMENT

336.41 — Great Britain. Public finance - *Case studies*

Case studies in public sector economics. — London : Heinemann Educational, July 1981. — [160]p. — (Case studies in economic analysis)
ISBN 0-435-33939-7 (pbk) : £4.50 : CIP entry B81-13506

336.41'05 — Great Britain. Government. Finance — *Serials*

Great Britain. *Treasury*. Financial statement and budget report : ... as laid before the House by the Chancellor of the Exchequer when opening the budget. — 1981-82. — London : H.M.S.O., 1981. — 48p
ISBN 0-10-219781-4 : £4.40 B81-29988

336.416 — Northern Ireland. Government — *Accounts* — *Serials*

Finance accounts of Northern Ireland / Department of Finance for Northern Ireland. — 1978-79. — Belfast : H.M.S.O., 1980. — 34p
ISBN 0-337-23323-3 : £3.25 B81-20335

Great Britain. *Department of Finance for Northern Ireland*. Financial statement ... / Department of Finance for Northern Ireland. — 1980-81. — Belfast : H.M.S.O., 1980. — 10p
ISBN 0-337-23327-6 : £1.50 B81-20339

336.416'05 — Northern Ireland. Government — *Accounts* — *Serials*

Public income and expenditure for the year ended 31 March ... / Department of Finance for Northern Ireland. — 1980. — Belfast : H.M.S.O., 1980. — 5p
ISBN 0-337-23324-1 : £1.50 B81-16248

336.54 — Developing countries. Economic development. Role of public finance — *Study examples: India (Republic), 1960-1970*

Toye, John. Public expenditure and Indian development policy 1960-1970 / John Toye. — Cambridge : Cambridge University Press, 1981. — xviii,270p ; 23cm. — (Cambridge South Asian studies ; 25)
Bibliography: p257-268. — Includes index
ISBN 0-521-23081-0 : £20.00 B81-37134

336.73 — United States. Government. Finance. Policies of government

Fiscal stress and public policy / Charles H. Levine and Irene Rubin, editors. — Beverly Hills ; London : Sage, c1980. — 314p : ill ; 23cm. — (Sage yearbooks in politics and public policy ; v.9)
Includes bibliographies and index
ISBN 0-8039-1553-5 (cased) : Unpriced
ISBN 0-8039-1554-3 (pbk) : £7.50 B81-39372

Taxing and spending policy / edited by Warren J. Samuels, Larry L. Wade. — Lexington, Mass. : Lexington Books, c1980 ; [Farnborough, Hants] : Gower [distributor], 1981. — xvi,189p ; 24cm. — (Policy studies organization series)
Includes index
ISBN 0-669-03469-x : £13.50 B81-29607

336.94 — Australia. Public finance

Groenewegen, Peter. Public finance in Australia : theory and practice / Peter Groenewegen. — Sydney : Prentice-Hall of Australia Pty ; London : Prentice-Hall, c1979. — xiv,282p : ill ; 24cm
Bibliography: p264-271. - Includes index
ISBN 0-7248-1013-7 (pbk) : £7.75 B81-11370

337 — INTERNATIONAL ECONOMICS

337 — Economic relations

Chacholiades, Miltiades. Principles of international economics / Miltiades Chacholiades. — New York ; London : McGraw-Hill, c1981. — xvi,607p : ill ; 24cm
Includes bibliographies and index
ISBN 0-07-010345-3 : £13.75 B81-39415

Corden, W. M.. Inflation, exchange rates and the world economy. — 2nd ed. — Oxford : Oxford University Press, June 1981. — [176]p
Previous ed.: 1977
ISBN 0-19-877169-x (cased) : £10.00 : CIP entry
ISBN 0-19-877170-3 (pbk) : £3.95 B81-11940

Corea, Gamani. Need for change : towards the new international economic order : a selection from major speeches and reports with an introduction / by Gamani Corea. — Oxford : Pergamon, 1980. — xii,278p ; 26cm
Includes index
ISBN 0-08-026095-0 (cased) : £12.00 : CIP rev. B80-12791

Kenen, Peter B.. Essays in international economics / Peter B. Kenen. — Princeton ; Guildford : Princeton University Press, c1980. — xviii,422p ; 25cm. — (Princeton series of collected essays)
Includes index
ISBN 0-691-04225-x (cased) : £12.60
ISBN 0-691-00364-5 (pbk) : £3.25 B81-15219

Walter, Ingo. International economics. — 3rd ed. / Ingo Walter, Kaj Areskoug. — New York ; Chichester : Wiley, c1981. — xiv,510p : ill ; 24cm
Previous ed.: / by Ingo Walter. New York : Ronald Press, 1975. — Includes bibliographies and index
ISBN 0-471-04957-3 : £13.60 B81-16453

337 — Economic relations — *Conference proceedings*

Issues in international economics / edited by Peter Oppenheimer. — Stocksfield : Oriel, 1980, c1978. — xviii,335p : ill ; 23cm. — ([Oxford international symposia])
Conference papers. — Includes bibliographies and index
ISBN 0-85362-186-1 : £13.75 B81-03031

337'.09'04 — Economic relations, *1945-1979*

Scammell, W. M.. The international economy since 1945 / W.M. Scammell. — London : Macmillan, 1980. — x,226p ; 25cm
Includes index
ISBN 0-333-28267-1 (cased) : £12.00 : CIP rev.
ISBN 0-333-28269-8 (pbk) : £5.95 B80-09159

337'.09'04 — Economic relations, *1945-1980*. International political aspects

Spero, Joan Edelman. The politics of international economic relations. — 2nd ed. — London : Allen and Unwin, Jan.1982. — [356]p
Previous ed.: 1977
ISBN 0-04-382035-2 (pbk) : £6.95 : CIP entry B81-33913

337'.09172'2 — Developed countries. Economic relations with developing countries

Helleiner, G. K.. International economic disorder : essays in North-South relations / Gerald K. Helleiner. — London : Macmillan, 1980. — xii,245p ; 23cm
Includes bibliographies and index
ISBN 0-333-27738-4 : £15.00 : CIP rev.
Primary classification 337'.09172'4 B80-13770

Singer, Hans. Rich and poor countries. — 3rd ed. — London : Allen & Unwin, Nov.1981. — [272]p. — (Studies in economics ; no.12)
Previous ed.: 1978
ISBN 0-04-330321-8 (pbk) : £5.50 : CIP entry
Also classified at 337'.09172'4 B81-28764

337'.09172'2 — Developed countries. Economic relations with developing countries — *Conference proceedings*

The New international economic order : philosophical and socio-cultural implications / edited by Hans Köchler. — Guildford (53 Ridgemount, Guildford, Surrey GU2 5TH) : Guildford Educational Press, c1980. — xi,105p ; 24cm. — (Studies in international relations)
Conference papers. — Includes a preface and one chapter in French
ISBN 0-9506386-3-3 (pbk) : Unpriced
Also classified at 337'.09172'4 B81-17569

The World economic order : past and prospects / edited by Sven Grassman and Erik Lundberg. — London : Macmillan, 1981. — x,599p : ill ; 23cm
Conference papers. — Includes bibliographies and index
ISBN 0-333-26999-3 : £30.00 : CIP rev.
Also classified at 337'.09172'4 B80-13769

337'.09172'2 — Developed countries. Economic relations with developing countries — *Proposals*

The New international economic order : the north-south debate / Jagdish N. Bhagwati, editor. — Cambridge, Mass. ; London : MIT Press, 1977 (1978 printing). — xiv,390p : ill ; 24cm. — (MIT bicentennial studies)
Includes bibliographies and index
ISBN 0-262-02126-9 (cased) : £16.00
ISBN 0-262-52042-7 (pbk) : £7.00
Also classified at 337'.09172'4 B81-00780

337'.09172'4 — Developing countries. Economic relations

Lall, Sanjaya. Developing countries in the international economy : selected papers / Sanjaya Lall. — London : Macmillan, 1981. — xi,263p ; 23cm
Includes bibliographies and index
ISBN 0-333-28875-0 : £20.00 : CIP rev. B80-24370

337'.09172'4 — Developing countries. Economic relations with developed countries

Helleiner, G. K.. International economic disorder : essays in North-South relations / Gerald K. Helleiner. — London : Macmillan, 1980. — xii,245p ; 23cm
Includes bibliographies and index
ISBN 0-333-27738-4 : £15.00 : CIP rev.
Also classified at 337'.09172'2 B80-13770

Singer, Hans. Rich and poor countries. — 3rd ed. — London : Allen & Unwin, Nov.1981. — [272]p. — (Studies in economics ; no.12)
Previous ed.: 1978
ISBN 0-04-330321-8 (pbk) : £5.50 : CIP entry
Primary classification 337'.09172'2 B81-28764

337'.09172'4 — Developing countries. Economic relations with developed countries — *Conference proceedings*
The **New** international economic order : philosophical and socio-cultural implications / edited by Hans Köchler. — Guildford (53 Ridgemount, Guildford, Surrey GU2 5TH) : Guildford Educational Press, c1980. — xi,105p ; 24cm. — (Studies in international relations)
Conference papers. — Includes a preface and one chapter in French
ISBN 0-9506386-3-3 (pbk) : Unpriced
Primary classification 337'.09172'2 B81-17569

The **World** economic order : past and prospects / edited by Sven Grassman and Erik Lundberg. — London : Macmillan, 1981. — x,599p : ill ; 23cm
Conference papers. — Includes bibliographies and index
ISBN 0-333-26999-3 : £30.00 : CIP rev.
Primary classification 337'.09172'2 B80-13769

337'.09172'4 — Developing countries. Economic relations with developed countries — *Proposals*
The **New** international economic order : the north-south debate / Jagdish N. Bhagwati, editor. — Cambridge, Mass. ; London : MIT Press, 1977 (1978 printing). — xiv,390p : ill ; 24cm. — (MIT bicentennial studies)
Includes bibliographies and index
ISBN 0-262-02126-9 (cased) : £16.00
ISBN 0-262-52042-7 (pbk) : £7.00
Primary classification 337'.09172'2 B81-00780

337'.09172'4 — Developing countries. Economic relations with European Economic Community — *Serials*
EEC and the Third World : a survey. — 1-. — London : Hodder and Stoughton in association with the Overseas Development Institute and the Institute of Development Studies, 1981-. — v.
Annual
ISSN 0261-3484 = EEC and the Third World : £5.00
Primary classification 337.1'42 B81-23507

EEC and the Third World. — 2. — London : Hodder and Stoughton, Feb.1982. — [192]p
ISBN 0-340-27772-6 (pbk) : £5.95 : CIP entry
ISSN 0261-3484
Primary classification 337.1'42 B81-40247

337.1 — ACP countries. Economic relations with European Community countries
The **Political** economy of EEC relations with African, Caribbean and Pacific States : contributions to the understanding of the Lomé Convention on North-South relations / edited by Frank Long. — Oxford : Pergamon, 1980. — xii,193p ; 22cm. — (Pergamon international library)
Includes index
ISBN 0-08-024077-1 : £10.50 : CIP rev.
Primary classification 337.1'42 B80-08166

337.1 — ACP countries. Economic relations with European Community countries, ***1970-1979***
Twitchett, Carol Cosgrove. A framework for development : the EEC and the ACP / Carol Cosgrove Twitchett. — London : Allen & Unwin, 1981. — 160p : 1map ; 23cm
Bibliography: p149-153. — Includes index
ISBN 0-04-338094-8 : £12.00
Primary classification 337.1'42 B81-08450

337.1'0724 — International economic integration. Mathematical models
Allen, Polly Reynolds. Asset markets, exchange rates, and economic integration : a synthesis / Polly Reynolds Allen, Peter B. Kenen. — Cambridge : Cambridge University Press, 1980. — xiv,585p : ill ; 24cm
Includes index
ISBN 0-521-22982-0 : £27.50 B81-03068

337.1'1724 — Developing countries. Economic relations with Organization of the Petroleum Exporting Countries
Hallwood, Paul. OPEC's developing relationships with the Third World / Paul Hallwood, Stuart Sinclair. — Aberdeen : University of Aberdeen, Department of Political Economy, 1981. — 26p ; 30cm. — (Discussion paper / University of Aberdeen Department of Political Economy ; 81-04)
Unpriced (pbk)
Also classified at 337.1'177 B81-14514

337.1'174927 — Arab countries. Economic cooperation with Africa south of Sahara, ***ca 1975-1980***
Sylvester, Anthony. Arabs and Africans : co-operation for development / Anthony Sylvester ; with a preface by Chedly Ayari. — London : Bodley Head, 1981. — 251p,[8]p of plates : ill,1map,ports ; 23cm
Includes index
ISBN 0-370-30332-6 : £7.50 : CIP rev.
Also classified at 337.1'67 B81-08849

337.1'177 — Organization of the Petroleum Exporting Countries. Economic relations with developing countries
Hallwood, Paul. OPEC's developing relationships with the Third World / Paul Hallwood, Stuart Sinclair. — Aberdeen : University of Aberdeen, Department of Political Economy, 1981. — 26p ; 30cm. — (Discussion paper / University of Aberdeen Department of Political Economy ; 81-04)
Unpriced (pbk)
Primary classification 337.1'1724 B81-14514

337.1'4 — Europe. Economic integration, ***1815-1980***
Pollard, Sidney. The integration of the European economy since 1815 / Sidney Pollard. — London : University Association for Contemporary European Studies, 1981. — 109p ; 23cm. — (Studies on contemporary Europe ; 4)
Bibliography: p97-103. — Includes index
ISBN 0-04-336069-6 (cased) : £6.95
ISBN 0-04-336070-x (pbk) : £2.95 B81-22740

337.1'4 — Europe. Sovet ékonomicheeskoĭ vzaimopomoshchi countries. Economic integration, ***1950-1980***
Brabant, Josef M. van. Socialist economic integration : aspects of contemporary economic problems in Eastern Europe / Josef M. van Brabant. — Cambridge : Cambridge University Press, 1980. — xiv,362p : ill ; 23cm. — (Soviet and East European studies)
Bibliography: p335-351. - Includes index
ISBN 0-521-23046-2 : £15.00 B81-06311

337.1'42 — European Community countries. Economic development. Effects of economic integration
Integration and unequal development : the experience of the EEC / edited by Dudley Seers and Constantine Vaitsos with the assistance of Marja-Liisa Kiljunen. — London : Macmillan, 1980. — xxi,359p : ill,1map ; 23cm. — (Studies in the integration of Western Europe)
Includes index
ISBN 0-333-29188-3 : £25.00 B81-06761

337.1'42 — European Community countries. Economic relations with ACP countries
The **Political** economy of EEC relations with African, Caribbean and Pacific States : contributions to the understanding of the Lomé Convention on North-South relations / edited by Frank Long. — Oxford : Pergamon, 1980. — xii,193p ; 22cm. — (Pergamon international library)
Includes index
ISBN 0-08-024077-1 : £10.50 : CIP rev.
Also classified at 337.1 B80-08166

337.1'42 — European Community countries. Economic relations with ACP countries, ***1970-1979***
Twitchett, Carol Cosgrove. A framework for development : the EEC and the ACP / Carol Cosgrove Twitchett. — London : Allen & Unwin, 1981. — 160p : 1map ; 23cm
Bibliography: p149-153. — Includes index
ISBN 0-04-338094-8 : £12.00
Also classified at 337.1 B81-08450

337.1'42 — European Community countries. Integration
Building Europe. — London : Europa, May 1981. — [260]p
ISBN 0-905118-61-8 : CIP entry B81-13850

337.1'42 — European Community. Economic policies
Donges, Juergen B.. What is wrong with the European Communities? : eleventh Wincott Memorial Lecture delivered at Mary Sumner House, Westminster, on Thursday, 13 November 1980 / Juergen B. Donges. — London : Institute of Economic Affairs for the Wincott Foundation, 1981. — 31p ; 22cm. — (Occasional paper / IEA, ISSN 0073-909x ; 59)
Bibliography: p31
ISBN 0-255-36139-4 (pbk) : £1.00 B81-16171

337.1'42 — European Community. Socioeconomic advisory committees
Community advisory committees for the representation of socio-economic interests : the machinery for the consultation and participation of socio-economic interests in Community decision making / Economic and Social Committee of the European Communities, General Secretariat Directorate-General Studies and Documentation Division. — Farnborough, Hants. : Saxon House, c1980. — xvii,215p ; 23cm
Bibliography: pxii-xiv
ISBN 0-566-00328-7 : £8.50 : CIP rev.
B79-31680

337.1'42 — European Economic Community. Economic relations with developing countries — *Serials*
EEC and the Third World : a survey. — 1-. — London : Hodder and Stoughton in association with the Overseas Development Institute and the Institute of Development Studies, 1981-. — v.
Annual
ISSN 0261-3484 = EEC and the Third World : £5.00
Also classified at 337'.09172'4 B81-23507

EEC and the Third World. — 2. — London : Hodder and Stoughton, Feb.1982. — [192]p
ISBN 0-340-27772-6 (pbk) : £5.95 : CIP entry
ISSN 0261-3484
Also classified at 337'.09172'4 B81-40247

337.1'42 — European Economic Community. Enlargement
Seers, Dudley. The second enlargement of the EEC in historical perspective / by Dudley Seers. — Brighton : Institute of Development Studies, 1981. — 25p ; 21cm. — (Discussion paper / IDS, ISSN 0308-5864 ; 158)
Unpriced (pbk) B81-24075

337.1'42 — European Economic Community. Entry of Mediterranean region countries. Economic aspects
Tsoukalis, Loukas. The European Community and its Mediterranean enlargement / Loukas Tsoukalis. — London : Allen & Unwin, 1981. — 273p ; 23cm
Includes index
ISBN 0-04-382030-1 (cased) : £15.00 : CIP rev.
ISBN 0-04-382031-x (pbk) : £6.95 B81-13774

337.1'67 — Africa south of the Sahara. Economic cooperation with Arab countries, ***ca 1975-1980***
Sylvester, Anthony. Arabs and Africans : co-operation for development / Anthony Sylvester ; with a preface by Chedly Ayari. — London : Bodley Head, 1981. — 251p,[8]p of plates : ill,1map,ports ; 23cm
Includes index
ISBN 0-370-30332-6 : £7.50 : CIP rev.
Primary classification 337.1'174927 B81-08849

337.41068 — Great Britain. Economic relations with South Africa, ***1950-1970.*** **Political aspects**
Berridge, Geoff. Economic power in Anglo-South African diplomacy : Simonstown, Sharpeville and after / Geoff Berridge. — London : Macmillan, 1981. — xv,225p ; 23cm
Bibliography: p215-218. — Includes index
ISBN 0-333-26592-0 : £20.00
Also classified at 337.68041 B81-40728

337.41073 — Great Britain. Economic relations with United States, ***1942-1949***
Clarke, ***Sir*** **Richard**. Anglo-American economic collaboration in war and peace 1942-1949. — Oxford : Clarendon Press, Dec.1981. — [208]p
ISBN 0-19-828439-x : £10.00 : CIP entry
Also classified at 337.73041 B81-33859

337.43 — West Germany. Economic relations — *Conference proceedings*

West Germany : a European and global power / edited by Wilfrid L. Kohl, Giorgio Basevi. — Lexington : Lexington, c1980 ; [Farnborough, Hants] : Gower [distributor], 1981. — xv,224p : ill ; 24cm
Conference papers
ISBN 0-669-03162-3 : £10.50 B81-17603

337.67'9'068 — Southern Mozambique. Economic relations with South Africa, *1894-1981*

Katzenellenbogan, Simon E.. South Africa and Southern Mozambique. — Manchester : Manchester University Press, Jan.1982. — [237]p
ISBN 0-7190-0853-0 : £13.50 : CIP entry
Also classified at 337.68067'9 B81-33830

337.68041 — South Africa. Economic relations with Great Britain, *1950-1970.* **Political aspects**

Berridge, Geoff. Economic power in Anglo-South African diplomacy : Simonstown, Sharpeville and after / Geoff Berridge. — London : Macmillan, 1981. — xv,225p ; 23cm
Bibliography: p215-218. — Includes index
ISBN 0-333-26592-0 : £20.00
Primary classification 337.41068 B81-40728

337.68067'9 — South Africa. Economic relations with Southern Mozambique, *1894-1981*

Katzenellenbogan, Simon E.. South Africa and Southern Mozambique. — Manchester : Manchester University Press, Jan.1982. — [237]p
ISBN 0-7190-0853-0 : £13.50 : CIP entry
Primary classification 337.67'9'068 B81-33830

337.73 — United States. Economic relations, *1929-1976*

Pastor, Robert A.. Congress and the politics of U.S. foreign economic policy 1929-1976 / Robert A. Pastor. — Berkeley ; London : University of California Press, c1980. — xiii,366p : ill ; 25cm
Bibliography: p355-362. — Includes index
ISBN 0-520-03904-1 : £14.70 B81-04715

337.73 — United States. Economic relations, *1948* **—** *Inquiry reports*

United States. *Congress. Senate. Committee on Foreign Relations.* Foreign Relief Assistance Act of 1948 / with an introduction by Richard D. Challener. — New York ; London : Garland, 1979. — xiv,804p : 1ill,maps ; 24cm. — (The Legislative origins of American foreign policy ; 5) (The Senate Foreign Relations Committee's Historical series)
Proceedings of the Committee on Foreign Relations, United States Senate. — Originally published: Washington : U.S. Government Printing Office, 1973
ISBN 0-8240-3034-6 : £94.38 B81-26228

337.73 — United States. Economic relations, *1977-1979*

Bergsten, C. Fred. The international economic policy of the United States : selected papers of C. Fred Bergsten, 1977-1979 / C. Fred Bergsten. — Lexington : Lexington Books ; [Farnborough, Hants.] : Gower [distributor], 1980. — xiv,398p ; 24cm
Includes index
ISBN 0-669-03314-6 : £17.50 B81-04112

337.73041 — United States. Economic relations with Great Britain, *1942-1949*

Clarke, *Sir* **Richard**. Anglo-American economic collaboration in war and peace 1942-1949. — Oxford : Clarendon Press, Dec.1981. — [208]p
ISBN 0-19-828439-x : £10.00 : CIP entry
Primary classification 337.41073 B81-33859

338 — ECONOMICS. PRODUCTION, INDUSTRIES

338 — Industries. Economic aspects

Business economics / [The D324 Course Team]. — Milton Keynes : Open University Press, 1980. — (Social sciences : a third level course)
At head of title: The Open University
Unit 3: The determinants of market power / prepared for the Course Team by A.R. Pollard. — 43p : ill ; 30cm. — (D324 ; unit 3)
Bibliography: p43
ISBN 0-335-08567-9 (pbk) : Unpriced B81-12569

An **introduction** to industrial economics / by P.J. Devine ... [et al.]. — 3rd ed. — London : Allen & Unwin, 1979. — xi,502p : ill,1map ; 25cm. — (Minerva series of students' handbooks ; no.26)
Previous ed.: i.e. Rev. ed. 1976. — Includes index
ISBN 0-04-338086-7 (cased) : £20.00 : CIP rev.
ISBN 0-04-338087-5 (pbk) : £8.95 B79-30554

Sawyer, Malcolm C.. The economics of industries and firms : theories, evidence and policy / Malcolm C. Sawyer. — London : Croom Helm, c1981. — 287p : ill ; 23cm
Bibliography: p269-280. — Includes index
ISBN 0-7099-0094-5 : £14.95 : CIP rev.
ISBN 0-7099-0095-3 (pbk) : £6.95 B81-08826

338 — Mid Glamorgan. Services for industries — *Serials*

Mid Glamorgan directory of incentives and services to industry. — 1979. — Cardiff (Office of the County Clerk and Chief Executive, Mid Glamorgan County Hall, Cardiff CF1 3NE) : Mid Glamorgan County Council, 1979. — 51p
Unpriced B81-32425

Mid Glamorgan guide to incentives and services for industry. — 1980-. — Cardiff (Office of the County Clerk and Chief Executive, Mid Glamorgan County Hall, Cardiff, CF1 3NE) : Mid Glamorgan County Council, 1980-. — v. ; 21cm
Annual. — Continues: Mid Glamorgan directory of incentives and services to industry
ISSN 0261-2283 = Mid Glamorgan guide to incentives and services for industry : Unpriced B81-32426

338 — Production

Leake, Andrew. Consumption and production. — London : Macmillan, Feb.1982. — [48]p. — (Casebooks on economic theory)
ISBN 0-333-27988-3 (pbk) : £1.25 : CIP entry B81-35951

338'.001 — Asiatic production. Theories of Marxists, *to 1973*

The **Asiatic** mode of production : science and politics / edited by Anne M. Bailey and Josep R. Llobera. — London : Routledge & Kegan Paul, 1981. — xi,363p : ill ; 22cm
Bibliography: p336-353. — Includes index
ISBN 0-7100-0738-8 (pbk) : £7.95 : CIP rev. B81-16374

338'.0025'41 — Great Britain. Industries & wholesale trades — *Directories*

UK trade sources list. — London : Malcolm Stewart Books, c1981. — 58p ; 25cm. — (Kingfisher business guides)
ISBN 0-904132-55-2 (pbk) : £2.70 B81-11987

338'.0025'4297 — Mid Glamorgan. Industries — *Directories — Serials*

Mid Glamorgan industrial directory. — 1978-. — [Pontypridd] ([Room H001, Polytechnic of Wales, Treforest, Pontypridd, Mid Glamorgan CF37 1DL]) : [INDIS, Mid Glamorgan County Council], 1978-. — v. ; 21cm
Annual
ISSN 0261-2275 = Mid Glamorgan industrial directory : Unpriced B81-32431

Mid Glamorgan industrial directory. — 1979. — [Pontypridd] ([Room H001, Polytechnic of Wales, Treforest, Pontypridd, Mid Glamorgan CF37 1DL]) : [INDIS, Mid Glamorgan County Council], 1979. — ii,108p
ISSN 0261-2275 : Unpriced B81-32432

Mid Glamorgan industrial directory. — 1980. — [Pontypridd] ([Room H001, Polytechnic of Wales, Treforest, Pontypridd, Mid Glamorgan CF37 1DL]) : [INDIS, Mid Glamorgan County Council], 1980. — ii,115p
ISSN 0261-2275 : Unpriced B81-32433

338'.0025'51249 — Taiwan. Industries & wholesale trades — *Directories*

Hong Kong and Taiwan trade sources list : a selection of trade suppliers in Hong Kong and Taiwan. — 3rd ed. — London : Malcolm Stewart Books, 1979. — 30p ; 25cm. — (Kingfisher business guides)
Previous ed.: 1976
ISBN 0-904132-41-2 (pbk) : £0.85
Also classified at 338'.0025'5125 B81-11989

338'.0025'5125 — Hong Kong. Industries & wholesale trades — *Directories*

Hong Kong and Taiwan trade sources list : a selection of trade suppliers in Hong Kong and Taiwan. — 3rd ed. — London : Malcolm Stewart Books, 1979. — 30p ; 25cm. — (Kingfisher business guides)
Previous ed.: 1976
ISBN 0-904132-41-2 (pbk) : £0.85
Primary classification 338'.0025'51249 B81-11989

338'.0025'5195 — South Korea. Industries & wholesale trades — *Directories*

Japan and Korea trade sources list : a selection of trade suppliers in Japan and Korea. — 2nd ed. — London : Malcolm Stewart Books, 1978. — 30p ; 25cm. — (Kingfisher business guides)
Previous ed.: 1972. — Bibliography: p29
ISBN 0-904132-36-6 (pbk) : £0.85
Also classified at 338'.0025'52 B81-11988

338'.0025'52 — Japan. Industries & wholesale trades — *Directories*

Japan and Korea trade sources list : a selection of trade suppliers in Japan and Korea. — 2nd ed. — London : Malcolm Stewart Books, 1978. — 30p ; 25cm. — (Kingfisher business guides)
Previous ed.: 1972. — Bibliography: p29
ISBN 0-904132-36-6 (pbk) : £0.85
Primary classification 338'.0025'5195 B81-11988

338'.006'041 — Great Britain. Industries & trades. Organisations: Confederation of British Industry — *Serials*

Confederation of British Industry. CBI news / Confederation of British Industry. — No.1 (16 Jan.1981)-. — London : CBI, 1981-. — v. : ill,ports ; 30cm
Fortnightly. — Continues: Confederation of British Industry. CBI members bulletin
ISSN 0261-6661 = CBI news : Unpriced B81-32249

338'.0092'2 — West Cumbria. Industrial development, *1660-1760.* **Role of Lowther** *(Family)*

Beckett, J. V.. Coal and tobacco : the Lowthers and the economic development of West Cumberland, 1660-1760 / J.V. Beckett. — Cambridge : Cambridge University Press, 1981. — xiii,278p,[1]p of plates : ill,maps,geneal.table ; 24cm
Bibliography: p263-268. — Includes index
ISBN 0-521-23486-7 : £19.50 : CIP rev. B81-02110

338'.01 — Factors of production

Leake, Andrew. Factor markets. — London : Macmillan Education, Feb.1982. — [48]p. — (Casebooks on economic theory)
ISBN 0-333-27989-1 (pbk) : £1.25 : CIP entry B81-35949

338'.04 — Entrepreneurship

Casson, Mark. Unemployment. — Oxford : Martin Robertson, Oct.1981. — [250]p
ISBN 0-85520-306-4 (cased) : £12.50 : CIP entry
ISBN 0-85520-439-7 (pbk) : £3.75 B81-27400

Wealth. — s.l. : s.n., [1981?]. — [50]leaves : ill ; 21x33cm
ISBN 0-907066-10-0 (unbound) : Unpriced B81-38783

338'.04 — Middle classes. Entrepreneurship

Scase, Richard. The entrepreneurial middle class. — London : Croom Helm, Jan.1982. — [224]p
ISBN 0-7099-0450-9 : £12.95 : CIP entry B81-34308

338'.04'0722 — Great Britain. Entrepreneurship — *Case studies*
Hayward, George. Case studies of entrepreneurs in action : with specific reference to the small company / George Hayward. — London (Duncan House, High St., E15 2JB) : Anglian Regional Management Centre, c1981. — 159p : ill,plans ; 30cm. — (The Anglian Regional Management Centre case study series)
Unpriced (pbk) B81-26537

338'.04'0924 — India *(Republic)*. Entrepreneurship. Tandon, Prakash — *Biographies*
Tandon, Prakash. Return to Punjab / by Prakash Tandon. — Berkeley ; London : University of California Press, c1981. — 211p ; 23cm
ISBN 0-520-03990-4 : £11.00 B81-35756

338'.04'0941 — Great Britain. Entrepreneurship
Bartlett, Alan F. Profile of the entrepreneur : or machiavellian management / Alan F. Bartlett. — [South Croydon] ([Advertiser House, Brighton Rd., South Croydon, CR2 6UB, Surrey]) : [Jesse Ward Investments], c1981. — 114p ; 23cm
ISBN 0-9507646-0-4 : Unpriced B81-40078

338'.06 — Great Britain, Canada & United States. Industries. Innovation — *Inquiry reports*
Schott, Kerry. Industrial innovation in the United Kingdom, Canada and the United States / by Kerry Schott. — London (1 Gough Sq., EC4A 3DE) : British-North American Committee, 1981. — xvi,65p : ill ; 23cm. — (BN ; 29)
Text on inside cover
ISBN 0-902594-39-7 (pbk) : £2.25 B81-34677

338'.06 — Great Britain. Industries. Innovation — *Conference proceedings*
Industrial policy and innovation / edited by Charles Carter. — London : Heinemann Educational, 1981. — viii,241p ; 23cm. — (Joint studies in public policy ; 3)
Conference papers. — Includes bibliographies and index
ISBN 0-435-83115-1 : £14.50 : CIP rev.
ISBN 0-435-83116-x (pbk) : £6.50 B81-13562

338'.06 — Great Britain. Industries. Innovation. Effects of regional economic development
Goddard, J. B.. Industrial innovation and regional economic development in Britain / J.B. Goddard. — [Newcastle upon Tyne] : [University of Newcastle upon Tyne, Centre for Urban and Regional] Development Studies, 1980. — 59p : ill,maps ; 30cm. — (Discussion paper / University of Newcastle upon Tyne, Centre for Urban and Regional Development Studies University of Newcastle upon Tyne, ISSN 0140-6515 ; no.32)
Bibliography: p28-31
Unpriced (pbk) B81-13921

338'.06 — Great Britain. Regional economic development. Role of technological change
Thwaites, A. T.. Technological change, mobile plants and regional development / by A.T. Thwaites. — [Newcastle upon Tyne] ([Newcastle upon Tyne NE1 7RU]) : University of Newcastle upon Tyne Centre for Urban and Regional Development Studies, 1977. — 33leaves ; 30cm. — (Discussion paper series / University of Newcastle upon Tyne Centre for Urban and Regional Development Studies ; DP9)
Bibliography: leaves 29-33
Unpriced (pbk) B81-36902

338'.06 — Industries. Productivity. Measurement & analysis — *Conference proceedings*
New developments in productivity measurement and analysis / edited by John W. Kendrick and Beatrice N. Vaccara. — Chicago ; London : University of Chicago Press, 1980. — ix,717p : ill ; 24cm. — (Studies in income and wealth ; v.44)
Conference papers. — Includes bibliographies and index
ISBN 0-226-43080-4 : £31.20 B81-02947

338'.06 — Ireland *(Republic)*. Industries. Applications of microelectronic devices
Microelectronics : the implications for Ireland. — Dublin : National Board for Science and Technology, 1981
C: Bibliography. — 100p ; 30cm
ISBN 0-86282-008-1 (pbk) : IR£3.00 B81-40227

Microelectronics : the implications for Ireland : an assessment for the 1980s. — Dublin : National Board for Science and Technology, 1981
[A]. — xix,93p : ill ; 30cm
ISBN 0-86282-006-5 (pbk) : IR£7.00 B81-40225

Microelectronics : the implications for Ireland. — Dublin : National Board for Science and Technology, 1981
B: Sectoral profiles. — 198p : ill ; 30cm
ISBN 0-86282-007-3 (pbk) : IR£5.00 B81-40226

338'.06 — Technological innovation. Economic aspects — *Conference proceedings*
The **Economics** of technological progress : proceedings of a conference held by the European Production Study Group in Umeå, Sweden, 23-25 August 1978, including a bibliography on the subject / edited by Tönu Puu and Sören Wibe. — London : Macmillan, 1980. — xiii,336p : ill ; 23cm
Bibliography: p258.332. - Includes index
ISBN 0-333-28602-2 : £20.00 : CIP rev. B80-09618

338.'06 — United States. Industries. Technological innovation
Gold, Bela. Evaluating technological innovations : methods, expectations, and findings / Bela Gold, Gerhard Rosegger, Myles G. Boylan, Jr. — Lexington, Mass. : Lexington ; [Farnborough, Hants] : Gower [distributor], 1981, c1980. — xvii,358p : ill ; 24cm
Includes bibliographies and index
ISBN 0-669-03638-2 : £17.50 B81-05506

338'.06'0287 — Business firms. Productivity. Measurement — *Conference proceedings*
Productivity measurement : an international review of concepts, techniques, programmes and current issues / edited by David Bailey and Tony Hubert. — Farnborough, Hants. : Gower for the British Council of Productivity Associations, c1980. — xxxvi,247p : ill ; 23cm
Conference papers. — Bibliography: p244
ISBN 0-566-02230-3 : Unpriced B81-37492

338'.06'0287 — Industries. Productivity. Measurement
Adam, Everett E.. Productivity and quality : measurement as a basis for improvement / Everett E. Adam, Jr., James C. Hershauer, William A. Ruch. — Englewood Cliffs ; London : Prentice-Hall, c1981. — vi,218p : ill ; 24cm
Bibliography: p199-207. — Includes index
ISBN 0-13-725002-9 : £13.25 B81-33215

338'.06'094 — Europe. Industries. Innovation — *Serials*
[Bulletin *(European Innovation Network)*]. Bulletin / European Innovation Network. — No.1 (July 1980)-. — [Manchester] ([c/o Dr. B. Rawlings, Manchester Business School, Booth St. West, Manchester 15]) : The Network, 1980-. — v. : ill ; 30cm
Irregular
ISSN 0144-9532 = Bulletin - European Innovation Network : Free to members B81-06386

338'.06'094 — Western Europe. Industrialisation. Role of engineers, *1800-1930*
Ahlström, Göran. Engineers and industrial growth. — London : Croom Helm, Jan.1982. — [128]p
ISBN 0-7099-0506-8 : £11.95 : CIP entry B81-34310

338'.06'0973 — United States. Industries. Productivity
Aggregate and industry-level productivity analysis / edited by Ali Dogramaci, Nabil R. Adam. — Boston ; London : Nijhoff, c1981. — ix,195p : ill ; 24cm. — (Studies in productivity analysis ; v.2)
Includes bibliographies and index
ISBN 0-89838-037-5 : Unpriced B81-22130

Productivity : prospects for growth / edited by Jerome M. Rosow. — New York ; London : Van Nostrand Reinhold, c1981. — xxi,340p ; 24cm. — (Van Nostrand Reinhold/Work in America Institute series)
Includes index
ISBN 0-442-29326-7 : £14.95 B81-26565

338'.06'0973 — United States. Organisations. Productivity. Analysis
Productivity analysis at the organizational level / edited by Nabil R. Adam, Ali Dogramaci. — Boston, Mass ; London : Nijhoff, 1981. — ix,181p : ill ; 24cm. — (Studies in productivity analysis ; v.3)
Includes bibliographies and index
ISBN 0-89838-038-3 : Unpriced B81-30654

338.09 — Industries. Geographical aspects — *For schools*
Macleod, Peter. A place to work / Peter Macdonald. — London : Hutchinson, 1981. — 32p : ill,maps,1facsim ; 21x30cm. — (Down to earth)
ISBN 0-09-138641-1 : Unpriced : CIP rev. B79-14508

338'.091724 — Developing countries. Industries — *For schools*
Massingham, Bryan. Cities and industry in the developing world. — London : Edward Arnold, Sept.1981. — [64]p. — (Patterns of development)
ISBN 0-7131-0455-4 (pbk) : £2.25 : CIP entry
Primary classification 307.7'6'091724 B81-23832

338.09173'2 — Areas adjacent to ports. Industrial development — *Conference proceedings*
Cityport industrialization and regional development : spatial analysis and planning strategies / edited by B.S. Hoyle and D.A. Pinder. — Oxford : Pergamon, 1981. — xvii,348p : ill,maps,plans ; 26cm. — ([Urban and regional planning series], ISSN 0305-5582 ; [v.24]) (Pergamon international library)
Conference papers. — Includes bibliographies and index
ISBN 0-08-025815-8 : £25.00 B81-27712

338.09181'2 — Western world. Nationalised industries — *Conference proceedings*
State-owned enterprise in the Western economies / edited by Raymond Vernon and Yair Aharoni. — London : Croom Helm, c1981. — 203p ; 23cm
Conference papers. — Includes index
ISBN 0-7099-2600-6 : £11.95 : CIP rev. B80-21539

338.094 — Europe. Industrialisation, *1760-1970*
Pollard, Sidney. Peaceful conquest : the industrialization of Europe 1760-1970 / by Sidney Pollard. — Oxford : Oxford University Press, 1981. — xii,451p,2leaves of plates : 2maps ; 24cm
Bibliography: p385-434. — Includes index
ISBN 0-19-877093-6 : £17.50 B81-26022

338.0941 — Great Britain. Business enterprise
Thomas, R. E. (Raymond Elliott). The government of business / R.E. Thomas. — 2nd ed. — Oxford : P. Allan, 1981. — xi,268p ; 22cm
Previous ed.: 1976. — Bibliography: p262-263. — Includes index
ISBN 0-86003-513-1 (cased) : £14.00
ISBN 0-86003-613-8 (pbk) : £6.95 B81-40645

338.0941 — Great Britain. Business enterprise by government — *Accounts — Serials*
Trading accounts and balance sheets. — 1979-80. — London : H.M.S.O., 1980. — iv,59p
ISBN 0-10-202981-4 : £4.80 B81-06843

338.0941 — Great Britain. Cities. Inner areas. Industries
Lever, W. F.. Manufacturing and service industries in inner cities / W.F. Lever, M. Danson, J. Malcolm. — Glasgow ([Glasgow G12 8QQ]) : Department of Social and Economic Research, University of Glasgow for the Department of the Environment, 1980
Stage 3: Report. — 9 leaves ; 30cm
Unpriced (unbound) B81-10526

338.0941 — Great Britain. Industrialisation, *1760-1837 — For schools*

Farnworth, Warren. Industrial Britain. — London : Bell & Hyman, Oct.1981. — [80]p. — (History around us)
ISBN 0-7135-1289-x (pbk) : £3.95 : CIP entry
B81-25722

338.0941 — Great Britain. Industries & trades — *Conference proceedings — Serials*

Confederation of British Industry. National conference report ... / CBI. — 1977-. — London : CBI, [1977]-. — v. : ill ; 29cm
Annual
Unpriced B81-15079

338.0941 — Great Britain. Industries & trades — *Statistics — Serials — For marketing*

The **A-Z** of U.K. marketing data. — 1980-. — London : Euromonitor, 1980-. — v. ; 21cm. — (Euromonitor fact finder books)
Irregular
£15.00 B81-06679

338.0941 — Great Britain. Industries. Effects of European Economic Community law — *Confederation of British Industry viewpoints*

The **Impact** of EEC legislation on British business : a staff study made for the CBI Europe Committee. — London : Confederation of British Industry, 1981. — [39]p ; 30cm
£2.00 (pbk) B81-13294

338.0941 — Great Britain. Industries — *For schools*

Roberts, Frank, *1939-*. People at work / Frank and Bernie Roberts. — Basingstoke : Macmillan Education, 1981. — 31p : ill,maps ; 30cm. — (Looking at Britain ; 3)
ISBN 0-333-28410-0 (pbk) : £1.35 B81-21373

338.0941 — Great Britain. Industries — *Serials*

Industrial & business world. — Vol.2, no.4 (Jan. 31 1981)-. — [London] ([69, Fleet St., EC4]) : [S.n.], 1981-. — v. : ill ; 39cm
Weekly. — Continues: Industrial world
ISSN 0261-0825 = Industrial & business world : £0.20 B81-15448

338.0941 — Great Britain. Industries — *Statistics — Serials*

Report on the census of production. Introductory notes / Department of Industry, Business Statistics Office. — 1979. — London : H.M.S.O., c1981. — 34p
ISBN 0-11-513261-9 : £4.30 B81-14536

Report on the census of production. Miscellaneous manufacturing industries / Department of Industry, Business Statistics Office. — 1979. — London : H.M.S.O., c1981. — 13p. in various pagings. — (Business monitor ; PA499.2)
ISBN 0-11-513326-7 : £2.50 B81-32656

Report on the census of production. Provisional results. — 1979. — London : H.M.S.O., c1981. — 76p
ISBN 0-11-513262-7 : £6.10 B81-14535

Report on the census of production. Summary tables / Department of Industry, Business Statistics Office. — 1978. — London : H.M.S.O., c1981. — 336p. — (Business monitor ; PA1002)
ISBN 0-11-513166-3 : £12.50 B81-33308

338.0941 — Great Britain. Local industrial development

The **Mobilisation** of indigenous potential in the U.K. : a report to the regional policy directorate of the European Community / University of Newcastle upon Tyne, Centre for Urban and Regional Development Studies. — Newcastle upon Tyne : The Centre, 1979. — ii,149p : ill,maps ; 30cm
Bibliography: p139-149
£5.00 (pbk) B81-19883

338.'0941 — Great Britain. Nationalised industries

Tombs, *Sir* **Francis.** The role of nationalised industries : based on a lecture to the Bristol Centre of the Institute of Bankers on November 11 1980 / by Sir Francis Tombs. — [London] : [Electricity Council], [1980]. — 17p ; 30cm
Cover title
Unpriced (pbk) B81-03295

338.0941 — Great Britain. Nationalised industries, *1968-1980*

Pryke, Richard. The nationalised industries : policies and performance since 1968 / Richard Pryke. — Oxford : Robertson, 1981. — x,287p ; 23cm
Includes index
ISBN 0-85520-241-6 (cased) : £15.00
ISBN 0-85520-242-4 (pbk) : £5.50 B81-17615

338.0941 — Great Britain. Nationalised industries, *to 1979*

Redwood, John. Public enterprise in crisis : the future of the nationalised industries / John Redwood. — Oxford : Blackwell, 1980. — 211p ; 23cm. — (Mainstream series)
Includes index
ISBN 0-631-12582-5 : £8.50 : CIP rev.
B80-07693

338.09411 — Scotland. Industrialisation, *1700-1870 — For schools*

Patrick, John, *1931-*. The rise of Scottish industry / John Patrick. — London : Murray, c1980. — vi,90p : ill,maps,plans ; 25cm
Bibliography: p86. - Includes index
ISBN 0-7195-3773-8 (pbk) : £1.95 B81-04471

338.09412'7 — Scotland. Tayside Region. Dundee. Industries & trades — *Conference proceedings*

Dundee industry : one day conference 23 October 1980 : synopsis of principal speeches and seminar discussions. — [Dundee] (City Chambers, Dundee DD1 3BY) : City of Dundee District Council, [1981]. — 27p ; 30cm
Cover title
Unpriced (pbk) B81-27183

338.09416 — Northern Ireland. Industries, *1600-ca 1950*

McCutcheon, W. A.. The industrial archaeology of Northern Ireland / W.A. McCutcheon. — Belfast : H.M.S.O., 1980. — xiv,395p,156p of plates : ill,maps(some col.),facsims,plans,ports ; 29cm
At head of title: Department of the Environment for Northern Ireland. — Ill on lining papers. — Includes index
ISBN 0-337-08154-9 : £55.00
Also classified at 380.5'09416 B81-22222

338.09416 — Northern Ireland. Industries — *Statistics — Serials*

Report on the census of production of Northern Ireland. — 197?-. — Belfast : H.M.S.O., 197?. — v. ; 30cm
Annual. — Continues: Report on the censuses of production for Northern Ireland. — Description based on: 1976 issue
ISSN 0261-166x = Report on the census of production of Northern Ireland : £5.25
B81-24704

338.09417 — Ireland *(Republic).* **Industries & trades —** *Conference proceedings*

Industry report 1980. — Dublin (Confederation House, Kildare St., Dublin 2) : Confederation of Irish Industry, 1980. — 115p : ill,maps,ports ; 30cm. — (Business series ; no.4)
£4.00 (pbk) B81-07787

338.09417 — Ireland *(Republic).* **Industries & trades —** *Serials*

[Industry & commerce *(Dublin)*]. Industry & commerce / [Dublin Chamber of Commerce]. — Dec.1980-. — Dublin (1 Poolbeg St., Dublin 2) : Tara Publishing for the Chamber, 1980-. — v. : ill + ports ; 30cm
Monthly. — Official organ of: Association of Chambers of Commerce of Ireland. — Continues: Commerce (Dublin)
Unpriced B81-13690

338.09421'77 — London. Bexley *(London Borough).* **Crayford. Industries,** *to 1979*

Hamilton, J. E.. The industries of Crayford : a brief history / by J.E. Hamilton. — Bexley (Hall Place, Bexley) : Bexley London Borough Libraries and Museums Department, c1980. — 28p,[4]p of plates : ill ; 22cm
Bibliography: p27-28
ISBN 0-902541-12-9 (pbk) : Unpriced
B81-19582

338.09422'62 — West Sussex. Chichester. Industries & trades, *1700-1900*

Trade and industry in the 18th and 19th centuries / [researched and designed by members of the Chichester WEA local history workshop class]. — [Chichester] ([29 Little London, Chichester PO19 1PB]) : Chichester District Museum, [1979?]. — [8]p : ill,1map ; 21cm
£0.15 (unbound) B81-37223

338.09423 — South-west England. Business enterprise — *Serials*

Business West. — Vol.1, no.1 (Dec.1980)-. — Bristol (Golf Course La., Filton, Bristol BS12 7QS) : Business West Publishers, 1980-. — v. : ill,ports ; 27cm
Monthly. — Description based on: Vol.1, no.7 (June 1981)
ISSN 0262-0723 = Business West : £0.60 per issue B81-38198

338.09424'13 — Gloucestershire. Forest of Dean *(District).* **Industries,** *1750-1979*

Bick, David E.. The old industries of Dean / David E. Bick. — Newent : Pound House, c1980. — 80p : ill,maps,facsims,ports ; 23cm
Bibliography: p77. — Includes index
ISBN 0-906885-01-9 : £4.50 B81-08338

338.09424'65 — Staffordshire. Burton upon Trent region. Industries & trades — *Serials*

Business review of Burton upon Trent and district. — July 1980-. — [Derby] (Burton upon Trent and District Chamber of Commerce and Industry, 2 St. Paul's Sq., Burton upon Trent DE14 2EQ) : Published for the Burton upon Trent and District Chamber of Commerce and Industry by Prestige Publications, 1980-. — v. : ill,plans,ports ; 21cm
Monthly. — Cover title: Business review (Burton upon Trent and District Chamber of Commerce and Industry). — Continues: Journal of the Burton upon Trent and District Chamber of Commerce and Industry
ISSN 0260-096x = Business review of Burton upon Trent and district : Unpriced B81-38520

338.09425'31 — Lincolnshire. Gainsborough. Industries, *to 1900*

English, J. S.. Gainsborough's industrial history / J.S. English. — [Gainsborough] (1 Dorton Ave., Gainsborough, Lincs.) : [J.S. English], 1981. — 15p ; 22cm
£0.35 (unbound) B81-27817

338.09426'1 — Norfolk. Rural regions. Industrial estates. Industries, *1980*

Packman, John. Survey of activity on industrial estates in rural Norfolk 1980 / by John Packman. — [Norwich] ([County Hall, Martineau La., Norwich NR1 2DH]) : [Planning Department, Norfolk County Council], 1980. — x,69p : ill,1form ; 30cm
£1.00 (spiral) B81-19564

338.09426'4 — Suffolk. Industries — *For businessmen*

Suffolk / produced by Suffolk County Council, with the assistance of Suffolk District Councils. — Ipswich (c/o D. Ayre, Planning Dept., Suffolk County Council, St. Edmund Hse., Rope Walk, Ipswich IP4 1LZ) : The County Council, [1981?]. — 28p : ill(some col.),maps (some col.) ; 21x31cm
ISBN 0-86055-064-8 (spiral) : Unpriced
B81-10939

338.09427'32 — Greater Manchester *(Metropolitan County).* **Cadishead & Irlam. Industries,** *to 1977*

Wheaton, Cyril. Local industries / by Cyril Wheaton. — [Manchester] ([53, Sunningdale Drive, Irlam, Manchester M30 6NJ]) : Irlam, Cadishead & District Local History Society Part 2. — 1981. — 7leaves : ill ; 30cm
£0.15 (unbound) B81-40331

338.09427'33 — Greater Manchester *(Metropolitan County)*. **Manchester. Industries & trades,** *1892 — Early works*
'**Good** value and no humbug' : a discourse on some of the principal trades & manufactories of Manchester in 1892 / [edited by Neil Richardson]. — Manchester (375, Chorley Rd., Swinton, Manchester M27 2AY) : N. Richardson, [1981]. — 24p : ill ; 30cm
Cover title. — Facsim. of: The century's progress, 1892. — Ill and text on inside covers
£1.50 (pbk) B81-40569

338.09427'81 — Cumbria. Furness. Industries — *Practical information — For businessmen*
Industry in the Furness area / issued on authority of the Furness Area Development Committee of the North West Industrial Development Association. — Cheltenham : Burrow, 1981. — 56p : ill,1col.map ; 20cm
£1.25 (pbk) B81-39141

338.09428'5 — Cleveland. Teesside. Industries, *1820-1971*
Tomlin, David M.. Past industry along the Tees / David M. Tomlin. — [Eston] ([13 Albert Rd., Eston, Cleveland]) : [D.M. Tomlin], [c1980]. — [45]p : ill,1map ; 21cm
Bibliography: p[45]
ISBN 0-9506863-0-1 (unbound) : Unpriced B81-07821

338.09429'7 — Mid Glamorgan. Industries. Capacity — *Serials*
INDIS capacity register. — Autumn 1980-. — [Pontypridd] ([Room H001, Polytechnic of Wales, Treforest, Pontypridd, Mid Glamorgan CF37 1DL]) : [INDIS, Mid Glamorgan County Council], 1980-. — v. ; 22cm
Quarterly
ISSN 0261-1945 = INDIS capacity register : Unpriced B81-32434

338.0947 — Eastern Europe. Industries — *Conference proceedings*
The **industrial** enterprise in Eastern Europe / edited by Ian Jeffries. — Eastbourne : Praeger, 1981. — ix,165p : ill ; 24cm
Includes bibliographies and index
ISBN 0-03-059323-9 : £12.50 : CIP rev. B81-12835

338.0951'25 — Hong Kong. Industries — *For British businessmen*
Hong Kong, 6 to 14 March 1981. — Birmingham (75 Harborne Rd., Birmingham B15 3DH) : Birmingham Chamber of Industry and Commerce, [1981]. — i,21p ; 30cm. — (Mission report / Birmingham Chamber of Industry and Commerce)
Cover title
Unpriced (pbk) B81-28272

338.0952 — Japan. Business enterprise, *1600-1980*
Hirschmeier, Johannes. The development of Japanese business. — 2nd ed. — London : Allen & Unwin, Dec.1981. — [400]p
Previous ed.: 1975
ISBN 0-04-330322-6 (pbk) : £7.50 : CIP entry B81-31529

338.0956 — Middle East. Industries & trades — *Serials*
Middle East industry & transport. — Issue no.34 (Jan./Feb.1981)-. — London (PO Box 261, 63 Long Acre, WC2E 9JH) : IC Magazines, 1981-. — v. : ill
Six issues yearly. — Continues: Middle East transport
ISSN 0261-1473 = Middle East industry & transport (corrected) : £18.00 per year
Also classified at 380.5'0956 B81-16746

338.09561 — Turkey. Industrialisation. Role of nationalised industries, *1900-1976*
Wålstedt, Bertil. State manufacturing enterprise in a mixed economy : the Turkish case / Bertil Wålstedt. — Baltimore ; London : Published for the World Bank [by] Johns Hopkins University Press, c1980. — xxii,354p : ill,maps ; 24cm
Includes index
ISBN 0-8018-2226-2 : £15.00
ISBN 0-8018-2227-0 (pbk) : Unpriced B81-11319

338.095645 — Cyprus. Industries — *For British businessmen*
Cyprus and Lebanon 1st-8th December 1980. — Birmingham (PO Box 360, 75 Harborne Rd., Birmingham B15 3DH) : Birmingham Chamber of Industry and Commerce, [1981?]. — i,9p ; 30cm. — (Mission report / Birmingham Chamber of Industry and Commerce)
Cover title
Unpriced (pbk)
Also classified at 338.095692 B81-16590

338.09567 — Iraq. Industries — *For British businessmen*
Mission report : Iraq : 16th-23rd January 1981. — Birmingham (PO Box 360, 75 Harborne Rd., Birmingham B15 3DH) : Birmingham Chamber of Industry and Commerce, 1981. — i,9p ; 30cm
Unpriced (unbound) B81-22370

338.095692 — Lebanon. Industries — *For British businessmen*
Cyprus and Lebanon 1st-8th December 1980. — Birmingham (PO Box 360, 75 Harborne Rd., Birmingham B15 3DH) : Birmingham Chamber of Industry and Commerce, [1981?]. — i,9p ; 30cm. — (Mission report / Birmingham Chamber of Industry and Commerce)
Cover title
Unpriced (pbk)
Primary classification 338.095645 B81-16590

338.0959 — South-east Asia. Industrialisation *related to* **South-east Asian culture** — *Conference proceedings*
Culture and industrialization : an Asian dilemma / Rolf E. Vente, Peter S.J. Chen (eds.). — Singapore ; London : Published for the Institute of Asian Affairs [by] McGraw-Hill, c1980. — viii,295p ; 22cm
Conference papers. — Bibliography: p271-284. - Includes index
ISBN 0-07-099655-5 : £7.50
Also classified at 959'.053 B81-13662

338.09595 — Malaysia. Industries — *For British businessmen*
Malaysia and Indonesia, 10 to 24 October 1980. — Birmingham (75 Harborne Rd., Birmingham B15 3DH) : Birmingham Chamber of Industry and Commerce, [1981]. — i,27p ; 30cm. — (Mission report / Birmingham Chamber of Industry and Commerce)
Cover title
Unpriced (pbk)
Also classified at 338.09598 B81-10938

338.09598 — Indonesia. Industries — *For British businessmen*
Malaysia and Indonesia, 10 to 24 October 1980. — Birmingham (75 Harborne Rd., Birmingham B15 3DH) : Birmingham Chamber of Industry and Commerce, [1981]. — i,27p ; 30cm. — (Mission report / Birmingham Chamber of Industry and Commerce)
Cover title
Unpriced (pbk)
Primary classification 338.09595 B81-10938

338.096 — Africa. Industrialisation
Industry and accumulation in Africa. — London : Heinemann Educational, Jan.1982. — [416]p. — (Studies in the economics of Africa ; 11)
ISBN 0-435-97139-5 (cased) : £13.50 : CIP entry
ISBN 0-435-97140-9 (pbk) : £6.50 B81-34501

338.09669 — Nigeria. Industries — *For British businessmen*
Nigeria, 8th-21st March 1981. — Birmingham (P.O. Box 360, 75 Harborne Rd., Birmingham B15 3DH) : Birmingham Chamber of Industry and Commerce, [1981]. — i,12p ; 30cm. — (Mission report / Birmingham Chamber of Industry and Commerce)
Unpriced (unbound) B81-26841

338.0973 — United States. Industrialisation, *1750-1865*
Cochran, Thomas C.. Frontiers of change : early industrialism in America / Thomas C. Cochran. — New York ; Oxford : Oxford University Press, 1981. — 179p ; 22cm
Bibliography: p159-174. — Includes index
ISBN 0-19-502875-9 : £8.95 B81-25979

338.0973 — United States. Industries, *1850-1979 — Illustrations*
Industry and the photographic image : 153 great prints from 1850 to the present / edited by F. Jack Hurley. — Rochester [N.Y.] : George Eastman House in association with Dover ; London : Constable, 1980. — 150p : chiefly ill (some col.),ports ; 30cm
ISBN 0-486-23980-2 (pbk) : £4.45 B81-15626

338.0973 — United States. Industries — *For British businessmen*
Mission report : United States of America (take-off point New York) : 13th to 20th September, 1980 / Birmingham Chamber of Industry and Commerce. — Birmingham (PO Box 360, 75 Harborne Rd., Birmingham B15 3DH) : [The Chamber], [1980?]. — 8p ; 30cm
Cover title
Unpriced (pbk) B81-12702

338.098 — South America. Industrial development, *1750-1979*
Weaver, Frederick Stirton. Class, state, and industrial structure : the process of South American industrial growth / Frederick Stirton Weaver. — Westport, Conn. ; London : Greenwood Press, 1980. — xiv,247p : ill,1map ; 25cm. — (Contributions in economics and economic history ; no.32)
Bibliography: p199-241. - Includes index
ISBN 0-313-22114-6 : £17.95 B81-23645

338.0982 — Argentina. Industries — *For British businessmen*
Chile and Argentina : 25th October to 8th November, 1980 / Birmingham Chamber of Industry and Commerce. — Birmingham (P.O. Box 360, 75 Harborne Rd., Birmingham B15 3DH) : The Chamber, [1980]. — 19p : 1map ; 30cm. — (Mission report / Birmingham Chamber of Industry and Commerce)
Cover title
Unpriced
Also classified at 338.0983 B81-15681

338.0983 — Chile. Industries — *For British businessmen*
Chile and Argentina : 25th October to 8th November, 1980 / Birmingham Chamber of Industry and Commerce. — Birmingham (P.O. Box 360, 75 Harborne Rd., Birmingham B15 3DH) : The Chamber, [1980]. — 19p : 1map ; 30cm. — (Mission report / Birmingham Chamber of Industry and Commerce)
Cover title
Unpriced
Primary classification 338.0982 B81-15681

338'.0994 — Australia. Industries. Economic aspects
Industrial economics. — London : Allen and Unwin, Jan.1982. — [500]p
ISBN 0-86861-060-7 : £7.50 : CIP entry B81-34782

338.09945 — Australia. Victoria. Industries & trades — *Serials*
Business Victoria, Australia. — Sept./Oct.1980-. — London (Bush House, Strand, WC2B 4PA) : Victoria Promotion Committee, 1980-. — v. : ill,ports ; 29cm
Nine issues yearly. — Continues: News from Victoria, Australia. — Description based on: Nov.1980 issue
ISSN 0260-888x = Business Victoria, Australia : Unpriced B81-10570

338.1 — AGRICULTURAL INDUSTRIES

338.1 — Agricultural industries — *Conference proceedings*
International Conference of Agricultural Economists *(17th : 1979 : Banff, Alberta)*. Rural change : the challenge for agricultural economists : proceedings, Seventeenth International conference of Agricultural Economists, held at Banff, Canada, 3rd-12th September 1979 / edited by Glenn Johnson and Allen Maunder. — Oxford : International Association of Agricultural Economists, Institute of Agricultural Economics : Gower, 1981. — xv,738p : ill,maps ; 23cm
Includes index
ISBN 0-566-00401-1 : Unpriced B81-37123

338.1 — Agricultural industries — *Conference proceedings* continuation

International Conference of Agricultural Economists *(17th : 1979 : Banff, Canada).* The rural challenge. — Aldershot : Gower, Nov.1981. — [340]p. — (Occasional paper / International Association of Agricultural Economists ; no.2)
ISBN 0-566-00472-0 : £10.00 : CIP entry
B81-30969

338.1 — Capitalist countries. Economic development. Role of agricultural industries — *Marxist viewpoints*

Goodman, David, *1938-*. From peasant to proletarian : capitalist and agrarian transitions / David Goodman and Michael Redclift. — Oxford : Basil Blackwell, 1981. — 244p : ill ; 24cm
Bibliography: p218-238. — Includes index
ISBN 0-631-10361-9 : £15.00 : CIP rev.
B81-14949

338.1'06'04229 — Berkshire. Agricultural industries. Organisations: National Farmers' Union. *Oxford and Berkshire County Branch* — *Serials*

National Farmers' Union. *Oxford and Berkshire County Branch.* Oxford and Berkshire farmers' year book. — 1981. — Oxford (269 Banbury Rd, Oxford OX2 7JE) : Oxford and Berkshire Executive, National Farmers' Union, [1981]. — 62p
Unpriced
Also classified at 338.1'06'04257 B81-20420

338.1'06'04257 — Oxfordshire. Agricultural industries. Organisations: National Farmers' Union. *Oxford and Berkshire County Branch* — *Serials*

National Farmers' Union. *Oxford and Berkshire County Branch.* Oxford and Berkshire farmers' year book. — 1981. — Oxford (269 Banbury Rd, Oxford OX2 7JE) : Oxford and Berkshire Executive, National Farmers' Union, [1981]. — 62p
Unpriced
Primary classification 338.1'06'04229
B81-20420

338.1'09172'2 — Developed countries. Agricultural industries — *For schools*

Patterns of development. — London : Edward Arnold
Settlement and agriculture in the developed world / Richard Kemp. — 1981. — 64p : ill,maps,plans ; 24cm
ISBN 0-7131-0452-x (pbk) : £2.25 : CIP rev.
B80-13259

338.1'09172'4 — Developing countries. Agricultural industries. Economic development

Arnon, I.. Modernisation of agriculture in developing countries : resources, potentials and problems / I. Arnon. — Chichester : Wiley, c1981. — xxiii,565p : ill ; 24cm. — (Environmental monographs and symposia)
Includes bibliographies and index
ISBN 0-471-27928-5 : £29.50 B81-39798

McDonald, P. Benjamin. Investment projects in agriculture. — London : Longmans, Sept.1981. — [320]p
ISBN 0-582-64306-6 : £20.00 : CIP entry
B81-23757

338.1'0931 — China. Agricultural industries, *B.C.206-A.D.220*

Hsu, Cho-yun. Han agriculture : the formation of early Chinese agrarian economy (206 B.C.—A.D.220) / by Cho-yun Hsu ; edited by Jack L. Dull. — Seattle ; London : University of Washington Press, c1980. — xxv,377p : ill,maps,1geneal.table ; 25cm. — (Han Dynasty China ; v.2)
Maps on lining papers. — Bibliography: p337-357. — Includes index. — Includes documents of Han agriculture
ISBN 0-295-95676-3 : £12.00 B81-02684

338.1'094 — Europe. Agricultural industries, *1200-1978*

Abel, Wilhelm. Agricultural fluctuations in Europe : from the thirteenth to the twentieth centuries / Wilhelm Abel ; translated by Olive Ordish ; with a foreword and bibliography by Joan Thirsk. — London : Methuen, 1980. — xii,363p : ill,maps ; 24cm
Translation of: Agrarkrisen und Agrarkonjunktur. 3 Aufl. — Bibliography: p329-356. - Includes index
ISBN 0-416-72110-9 : £17.50 : CIP rev.
B80-07263

338.1'094 — Europe. Agricultural industries. Economic development *related to* **population growth,** *1300-1911*

Grigg, David, *1934-*. Population growth and agrarian change : an historical perspective / David Grigg. — Cambridge : Cambridge University Press, 1980. — xi,340p : ill,maps ; 24cm. — (Cambridge geographical studies ; 13)
Includes index
ISBN 0-521-22760-7 (cased) : £20.00
ISBN 0-521-29635-8 (pbk) : £7.95
Primary classification 304.6'2'094 B81-08326

338.1'094 — Europe. Agricultural industries, *to ca 1914.* **Historiography**

Fussell, G. E.. Agricultural history in Great Britain and Europe before 1914. — London (35 Palace Court, W2 4LS) : Pindar Press, Oct.1981. — [128]p
ISBN 0-907132-04-9 : £15.00 : CIP entry
B81-27995

338.1'0941 — Great Britain. Agricultural economics, *1900-1940*

Whetham, Edith H.. Agricultural economists in Britain 1900-1940 / by Edith H. Whetham. — [Oxford] : Institute of Agricultural Economics, University of Oxford, c1981. — vi,97p,[1]leaf of plates : ports ; 21cm
Includes index
ISBN 0-900034-11-4 (pbk) : Unpriced
B81-32881

338.1'0941 — Great Britain. Agricultural industries

Haines, Michael. Introduction to farming systems. — London : Longman, July 1981. — [180]p
ISBN 0-582-45081-0 (pbk) : £6.95 : CIP entry
B81-22680

Resilient, resourceful — and at risk. — London (Agriculture House, Knightsbridge, SW1X 7NJ) : National Farmers' Union, [1981?]. — [4]p : ill ; 30cm
Cover title
Unpriced (unbound) B81-13291

338.1'0941 — Great Britain. Agricultural industries, *1400-1979* — *For schools*

Burrell, R. E. C.. Food from the fields : (the story of farming) / R.E.C. Burrell. — Exeter : Wheaton, 1980. — 96p : ill,1map,plans,ports ; 21cm. — (The Making of the industrial revolution series ; bk 1)
ISBN 0-08-020545-3 (pbk) : £2.50 B81-05691

338.1'0941 — Great Britain. Agricultural industries — *For schools*

Roberts, Frank, *1939-*. The countryside / Frank and Bernie Roberts. — Basingstoke : Macmillan Education, 1981. — 30p : ill,maps ; 30cm. — (Looking at Britain ; 2)
ISBN 0-333-28411-9 (pbk) : £1.35 B81-21372

338.1'0941 — Great Britain. Agricultural industries — *Forecasts* — *Conference proceedings*

The **Outlook** for agriculture 1981 and beyond : proceedings of a conference held on 9 and 10 October 1980 at the Skean Dhu Hotel, Dyce, Aberdeen / edited by B.J. Revell. — Aberdeen (581 King St., Aberdeen, AB9 2UD) : School of Agriculture, Aberdeen, 1981. — v,126p : ill ; 30cm
£5.00 (spiral) B81-13599

338.1'0941 — Great Britain. Agricultural industries — *Serials*

Cardiganshire farmer : incorporating the Carmarthenshire farmer : report - news - information : the National Farmers' Union county journal. — Vol.1, no.1 (June 1980)-. — Dorchester (64a High West St., Dorchester, Dorset) : N.F.U. County Pubications, 1980-. — v. : ill ; 24cm
Monthly. — Publication of: the Cardiganshire County Branch of the National Farmers' Union. — Published concurrently and has majority of contents in common with: Carmarthenshire farmer
ISSN 0260-4949 = Cardiganshire farmer : £0.05 per issue B81-06757

338.1'0941 — Great Britain. Agricultural products — *Statistics*

Output and utilisation of farm produce in the United Kingdom / Ministry of Agriculture, Fisheries and Food. — 1973 to 1979. — Pinner (Tolcarne Drive, Pinner, Middlesex HA5 2DT) : The Ministry, 1980. — 35p
£6.00 B81-06676

338.1'09411 — Scotland. Agricultural industries

Thomson, J. K.. The structure of Scottish agriculture and food industries / ... by J.K. Thomson. — Edinburgh : Scottish Council Research Institute, 1978. — 5,[6]leaves ; 31cm
£2.00 (spiral)
Also classified at 338.4'7641'09411 B81-34342

338.1'09411 — Scotland. Agricultural industries — *Serials*

Agriculture in Scotland / Department of Agriculture and Fisheries for Scotland. — 1980. — Edinburgh : H.M.S.O., 1981. — vii,62p. — (Cmnd. ; 8234)
ISBN 0-10-182340-1 : £3.90 B81-33057

338.1'09416 — Northern Ireland. Agricultural industries — *Serials*

Northern Ireland agriculture. — 1980. — Belfast : H.M.S.O., 1980. — 152p
ISBN 0-337-05254-9 : £7.00 B81-20341

338.1'0942 — England. Agricultural industries — *Statistics* — *Serials*

Agricultural statistics, England / Ministry of Agriculture, Fisheries and Food. — 1978-1979. — London : H.M.S.O., 1981-. — v. ; 25cm
Continues in part: Agricultural statistics, England and Wales
ISSN 0262-2394 = Agricultural statistics. England : £16.50 B81-39727

Agricultural statistics, England and Wales / Ministry of Agriculture, Fisheries and Food. — 1976-1977. — London : H.M.S.O., 1980. — xiii,298p
ISBN 0-11-241169-x : £15.00 B81-12440

Farm incomes in England ... : (including a comparison with ... and some references to earlier years) : a report based on the Farm Management Survey / Ministry of Agriculture, Fisheries and Food. — 1978/79-. — London : H.M.S.O., 1980-. — v. : maps ; 30cm. — (Farm incomes series)
Annual. — Continues in part: Farm incomes in England and Wales
ISSN 0260-5015 = Farm incomes in England : £6.50 B81-04768

Farm incomes in England / Ministry of Agriculture, Fisheries and Food. — 1979/80. — London : H.M.S.O., 1981. — 69p. — (Farm incomes series ; no.33)
ISBN 0-11-241164-9 : £6.95
ISSN 0260-5015 B81-16826

338.1'0942 — England. Agricultural industries, *to 1939*

The **Agrarian** history of England and Wales / general editor Joan Thirsk. — Cambridge : Cambridge University Press
Vol.1. — 1981
Includes index
1: Prehistory / edited by Stuart Piggott. — xxi,51p,12p of plates : ill,maps,plans ; 24cm
ISBN 0-521-08741-4 : £27.50 B81-17069

338.1′0942 — England. Metropolitan counties. Agricultural industries

Thomson, Kenneth J.. Farming in the fringe : an analysis of agricultural census data drawn from parishes around the six metropolitan counties and London : a report to the Countryside Commission / by Kenneth J. Thomson. — Cheltenham (John Dower House, Crescent Place, Cheltenham, Glos. GL50 3RA) : Countryside Commission, c1981. — vi,105p : ill,maps ; 30cm
Bibliography: p102-105
ISBN 0-86170-034-1 (pbk) : £5.00 B81-29602

338.1′09422 — South-east England. Agricultural industries. Farms — *Statistics — Serials*

Farm business statistics for South East England. Supplement for ... / Farm Business Unit, School of Rural Economics and Related Studies. — 1980. — [Ashford] ([Wye College, Ashford, Kent TN25 5AH]), The School, [1980]. — 51p
ISBN 0-901859-87-7 : £1.60 B81-04407

338.1′09422 — Southern England. Agricultural industries. Farms — *Statistics — Serials*

Farm business data. — 1981. — Reading (Dept. of Agricultural Economics and Management, 4 Earley Gate, Whiteknights Road, Reading, R6L 2AR) : University of Reading, Department of Agricultural Economics and Management, 1981. — 63p
Unpriced B81-13098

338.1′09423 — South-west England. Agricultural industries. Farms — *Statistics — Serials*

Farm management handbook / University of Exeter Agricultural Economics Unit. — [1980]. — Exeter : The Unit, 1980. — vii,85p : ill ; 21cm
£2.00 (pbk) B81-12636

Farm management handbook / University of Exeter, Agricultural Economics Unit. — [1981]. — Exeter : The Unit, 1981. — vii,89p
ISSN 0524-4846 : £2.00 B81-31004

Farm management survey. — 1978/79. — Exeter : University of Exeter, Agricultural Economics Unit, 1979. — 53p. — (Report / University of Exeter, Agricultural Economics Unit, ISSN 0306-8277 ; no.207)
ISSN 0306-8277 : £1.75 B81-03583

Farm management survey. — 1979/80. — Exeter : University of Exeter, Agricultural Economics Unit, 1981. — 43p. — (Report / University of Exeter, Agricultural Economics Unit, ISSN 0306-8277 ; no.211)
£1.75 B81-30868

338.1′09425 — England. East Midlands. Agricultural industries — *Serials*

Farming in the East Midlands, financial results / University of Nottingham Department of Agriculture and Horticulture. — 1979-80. — Sutton Bonington : The Department, 1981. — 66p
£1.80 B81-15158

[Summary report *(University of Nottingham. Department of Agriculture and Horticulture)*]. Summary report / University of Nottingham, Department of Agriculture and Horticulture. — No.7 (Apr.1981). — [Loughborough] : The Department, 1981. — 14p
£0.50 B81-27126

338.1′09426 — East Anglia. Agricultural industries — *Statistics — Serials*

Report on farming in the Eastern counties of England. — 1979-80. — Cambridge (16-21, Silver St., Cambridge CB3 9EL) : Agricultural Economics Unit, Department of Land Economy, [1980]. — iii,134p
ISSN 0143-7194 : £2.50 B81-09082

338.1′09426′7 — Essex. Agricultural industries — *Serials*

Essex farmer′s journal handbook. — 1981. — Chelmsford (Agriculture House, New London Road, Chelmsford) : Essex Farmers′ Union, [1981]. — 72p
Unpriced B81-13093

338.1′09428′8 — Northumberland. National parks: Northumberland National Park. Agricultural industries — *For environment planning*

Agriculture in the Northumberland National Park. — Newcastle upon Tyne ([c/o] National Park Officer, Bede House, All Saints Centre, Newcastle upon Tyne) : [Northumberland National Park and Countryside Committee], 1975. — 24,xii,[4]p of plates : ill,maps ; 30cm. — (Working paper / Northumberland National Park ; 1)
£0.60 (spiral) B81-29619

338.1′09429 — Wales. Agricultural industries — *Statistics — Serials*

Welsh agricultural statistics / Welsh Office = Ystadegua amaethyddol Cymru / y Swyddfa Gymmig. — No.2 (1980). — Cardiff : H.M.S.O., 1980. — 100p
ISBN 0-11-790140-7 : £15.00 B81-02944

338.1′09429′2 — Gwynedd. Agricultural industries — *Serials*

Amaethwr Meirion : an edition of Gwynedd farmer, the official monthly journal of the National Farmers′ Union in Gwynedd. — Vol.1, no.1 (Oct.1980)-. — Dorchester (5 High St., Dorchester, Dorset) : N.F.U. Pubications, 1980-. — v. : ill ; 25cm
Monthly. — Continues: Chronicle Meirionnydd. — Description based on: Vol.1, no.3 = Cyfroll, Rhif3 (Dec./Rhag.1980)
Unpriced B81-13214

338.1′09429′89 — South Glamorgan. Llanblethian. Agricultural industries, *1660-1750*

Riden, Philip. Farming in Llanblethian, 1660-1750 / by Philip Riden. — [Cardiff] (38 Park Place, Cardiff) : University College Cardiff, Department of Extra-Mural Studies, 1980. — viii,62p,4p of plates : ill,maps ; 21cm. — (Park Place papers ; no.9)
£1.00 (pbk) B81-04900

338.1′09438 — Poland. Agricultural industries — *Polish texts*

Studziński, Bogumił. Wieś Polska w latach 1944-1978 / Bogumił Studziński. — Londyn : Polski, 1981. — 34p ; 20cm. — (Biblioteka Ruchu Chłopskiej Samoobrony Społecznej ; zesz. 2)
′Rzeszowska Umowa Społeczna w sprawie wsi i polityki rolnej′ (8p ; 20cm) as insert
Unpriced (pbk) B81-40388

338.1′0944 — France. Agricultural industries, *1800-1860*

Clout, Hugh. Agriculture in France on the eve of the railway age / Hugh Clout. — London : Croom Helm, c1980. — 239p : maps,2forms ; 25cm. — (Croom Helm historical geography series)
Bibliography: p231-233. — Includes index
ISBN 0-85664-919-8 : £19.95 : CIP rev. B79-29945

338.1′0954 — India *(Republic)*. Economic development. Role of agricultural industries

Rastiannikov, V. G.. Agrarian evolution in a multiform structure society : experience of independent India / V.G. Rastyannikov ; translated from the Russian by Konstantin A. Kostrov. — London : Routledge & Kegan Paul, 1981. — x,373p ; 23cm
Translation of: Agrarnaia ėvoliutsiia v mnogoukladnom obshchestve. — Bibliography: p347-363. — Includes index
ISBN 0-7100-0755-8 : £14.00 : CIP rev. B81-18155

338.1′09595′1 — Peninsular Malaysia. Agricultural industries, *to 1975*

Tan, Yee Kew. The land and the agricultural organisation of Peninsula Malaysia : a historical interpretation / Yee Kew Tan. — Norwich : Published for the Centre for Development Studies by Geo Books, 1981. — 58p : 1map ; 22cm. — (Monograph / University College of Swansea. Centre for Development Studies, ISSN 0114-9486 ; no.13)
Bibliography: p56-58
ISBN 0-86094-075-6 (pbk) : Unpriced B81-27171

338.1′0967 — Africa. Tropical regions. Agricultural industries

Livingstone, Ian. Agricultural economics for Tropical Africa / I. Livingstone, H.W. Ord. — London : Heinemann, 1981. — x,294p : ill,1map ; 25cm. — (Studies in the economics of Africa)
Includes index
ISBN 0-435-97431-9 (pbk) : £4.95 : CIP rev. B80-11782

338.1′0967 — Africa. Tropical regions. Agricultural industries. Development — *Case studies*

Rural development in tropical Africa / edited by Judith Heyer, Pepe Roberts and Gavin Williams ; preface by Keith Griffin. — London : Macmillan, 1981. — x,375p : ill,maps ; 22cm
Includes bibliographies and index
ISBN 0-333-28448-8 : £25.00 B81-38724

338.1′0973 — United States. Agricultural industries

Epp, Donald J.. Introduction to agricultural economics / Donald J. Epp, John W. Malone, Jr. — New York : Macmillan ; London : Collier Macmillan, c1981. — xi,354p : ill ; 24cm
Includes index
ISBN 0-02-333940-3 : £12.95 B81-36170

338.1′0981 — Brazil. Agricultural industries — *For British businessmen*

Frith, Dennis E.. The agriculture of Brazil and Venezuela : business opportunities / Dennis E. Frith. — London : Graham & Trotman, 1978. — 148p : maps ; 30cm
ISBN 0-86010-124-x (pbk) : £35.00
Also classified at 338.1′0987 B81-08341

338.1′0981 — Brazil. Agricultural industries — *Serials*

Brazilian agriculture & commodities / produced by the Centre for Technical & Economic Cooperation of the Institute of Brazilian Studies. — Vol.1, no.1 (July-Aug.1980)-. — Portsmouth (Charter House, Lord Montgomery Way, Portsmouth, Hampshire PO1 2SB) : Hambrook, 1980-. — v. : ill,maps ; 30cm
Ten issues yearly. — Text in English, introduction and summaries in English, French, German and Italian
ISSN 0260-2377 = Brazilian agriculture & commodities : £40.00 per year B81-06776

338.1′0987 — Venezuela. Agricultural industries — *For British businessmen*

Frith, Dennis E.. The agriculture of Brazil and Venezuela : business opportunities / Dennis E. Frith. — London : Graham & Trotman, 1978. — 148p : maps ; 30cm
ISBN 0-86010-124-x (pbk) : £35.00
Primary classification 338.1′0981 B81-08341

338.1′0994 — Australia. Agricultural industries, *to 1980*

Davidson, B. R.. European farming in Australia : an economic history of Australian farming / by Bruce R. Davidson. — Amsterdam ; Oxford : Elsevier Scientific, 1981. — x,437p : maps,plans ; 25cm
Includes bibliographies and index
ISBN 0-444-41993-4 : Unpriced : CIP rev. B81-13837

338.1′3 — Great Britain. Agricultural industries. Capital investment. Effects of inflation

Williams, N. T.. Appraising the profitability and feasibility of an agricultural investment under inflation / N.T. Williams. — Ashford, Kent : Publications, School of Rural Economics, Wye College, 1981. — 20p : 2ill ; 30cm. — (F.B.U. occasional paper ; no.5)
ISBN 0-901859-92-3 (pbk) : £2.00 B81-15101

338.1′3 — Great Britain. Sugar beet industries. Research. Finance. Home Grown Sugar Beet (Research and Education) Fund — *Accounts — Serials*

Home Grown Sugar Beet (Research and Education) Fund account. — 1979-80. — London : H.M.S.O., 1981. — 7p
ISBN 0-10-221381-x : £1.10 B81-26390

338.1'3 — Northern Ireland. Agricultural industries. Development. Financial assistance. Loans from funds: Agricultural Loans Fund (Northern Ireland) — *Accounts — Serials*

Accounts of the Agricultural Loans Fund (Northern Ireland) ... for the year ended 31 March ... / Department of Agriculture for Northern Ireland. — 1980. — Belfast : H.M.S.O., 1981. — 6p
ISBN 0-337-05256-5 : £1.50 B81-30719

338.1'3 — Pakistan. Farmers. Income. Effects of sugarcane industries. Evaluation. Applications of shadow prices — *Case studies*

Potts, David. The supply of sugarcane and the estimation of its shadow price : a case study from Pakistan / David Potts. — Bradford : University of Bradford Project Planning Centre for Developing Countries, [1980]. — 109p,[1] leaf of plates : ill,1map ; 30cm. — (Occasional paper / University of Bradford Project Planning Centre for Developing Countries, ISSN 0144-74535, ISSN no.6)
Cover title
ISBN 0-901945-40-4 (pbk) : £1.50 B81-17631

338.1'3 — Scotland. Feedingstuffs & fertilisers. Residual values — *Serials*

Scottish Standing Committee for the Calculation of Residual Values of Fertilizers and Feeding Stuffs. Residual values of fertilizers and feeding stuffs. — 32nd report (1980). — Edinburgh : H.M.S.O., 1980. — 14p
ISBN 0-11-491695-0 : £1.60 B81-06840

338.1'3 — Silage production machinery. Financing — *Case studies*

Sargent, E. D.. Financing new silage making machinery / E.D. Sargent, S.W. Ashworth, P.G. Smith. — Auchincruive (Auchincruive, Ayr) : West of Scotland Agricultural College, 1981. — iii,47p ; 30cm. — (Research and development publication / West of Scotland Agricultural College, ISSN 0140-7759 ; no.13)
Unpriced (pbk) B81-19017

338.1'3 — Wales. Agricultural industries. Farms. Income — *Serials*

Farm management survey. Farm incomes in Wales / Department of Agricultural Economics, the University College of Wales, Aberystwyth. — 1979-80. — [Aberystwyth] : The Department, 1981. — vi,100p
£2.00 B81-29082

338.1'3 — Western Scotland. Agricultural industries. Dairy farms. Profitability, *1976-1980*

Groves, C. R.. Trends in profitability of dairy farming / C.R. Groves, J.M. Tweddle. — [Auchincruive] ([Auchincruive, Ayr KA6 5HW]) : West of Scotland Agricultural College, Economics Division, 1980. — 59p : ill ; 30cm. — (FPI ; no.4)
Unpriced (pbk) B81-16692

338.1'3'094 — European Community countries. Agricultural industries. Finance — *Conference proceedings*

Farm financing and farm indebtedness in the Community : proceedings of a seminar held on March 20-21, 1980 at Wye / translated and edited by Claude Rosenfeld, Bridget Girling, Ian G. Reid. — Ashford, Kent : Wye College, c1980. — iv,169p : ill ; 30cm. — (Seminar paper / Centre for European Agricultural Studies (Agricultural Finance Study Group), ISSN 0307-1111 ; n.9)
ISBN 0-905378-35-0 (pbk) : £15.00 B81-07817

338.1'3'09429 — Wales. Agricultural industries. Farms. Finance — *Statistics — Serials*

Welsh agricultural statistics. Supplement / Welsh Office = Ystadegau amaethyddol Cymru. Atodiad / y Swyddfa Gymreig. — 1978/79-. — [Cardiff] ([Cathays Park, Cardiff CF1 3NQ]) : Welsh Office, [1981?]-. — v. ; 30cm
Annual. — Continues in part: Farm incomes in England and Wales. — Supplement to: Welsh agricultural statistics
ISSN 0262-2858 = Welsh agricultural statistics. Supplement : Unpriced B81-39726

338.1'3'095496 — Nepal. Agricultural industries. Finance

Jha, Kumar Kant. Agricultural finance in Nepal : an analytical study / Kumar Kant Jha. — New Delhi : Heritage ; London : Books from India [distributor], c1978. — xvi,241p ; 23cm
Bibliography: p225-238. - Includes index
£7.50 B81-09299

338.1'3'0973 — United States. Agricultural products. Prices

Tomek, William G.. Agricultural product prices / William G. Tomek, Kenneth L. Robinson. — 2nd ed. — Ithaca ; London : Cornell University Press, 1981. — 367p : ill ; 24cm
Previous ed.: 1972. — Includes bibliographies and index
ISBN 0-8014-1337-0 : £11.75 B81-10950

338.1'371'09425 — England. East Midlands. Milk. Production. Costs, *1976-1977*

Seabrook, M. F.. Milk production in the East Midlands : some observations on the economics of milk production (1976/77) on a sample of thirtyeight East Midland dairy herds / M.F. Seabrook, C.H. Tilston, R.M. Guilford. — [Nottingham] : University of Nottingham, Department of Agriculture and Horticulture, 1977. — [22]leaves : ill ; 30cm. — (Summary report / University of Nottingham Department of Agriculture and Horticulture ; no.4)
Cover title
£0.40 (pbk) B81-29925

338.1'6 — Developing countries. Agricultural industries. Projects. Appraisal — *Manuals*

Bridger, Gordon A.. Guidelines for the appraisal of agricultural projects / by Gordon A. Bridger. — London (10 Percy St., W1P 0JB) : Overseas Development Institute, 1980. — 43p ; 21cm. — (Agricultural administration network papers ; no.10)
Unpriced (unbound) B81-27055

338.1'6 — Western Scotland. Agricultural industries. Dairy farms. Productivity

Sargent, E. D.. Managing the dairy herd in difficult times : some lessons from the milk production systems investigation 1979/80 / E.D. Sargent, R.F. Munro. — [Auchincruive] ([Auchincruive, Ayr KA6 5HW]) : West of Scotland Agricultural College, Economics Division, 1980. — 33p ; 30cm. — (F.P.I. ; no.3)
Cover title
Unpriced (pbk) B81-27586

338.1'6'091724 — Developing countries. Agricultural development projects. Role of foreign multinational companies, *1920-1979 — Case studies*

Voll, Sarah Potts. A plough in field arable : western agribusiness in third world agriculture / Sarah Potts Voll. — Hanover, N.H. ; London : Published for University of New Hampshire by University Press of New England, 1980. — x,213p ; 24cm
Includes bibliographies and index
ISBN 0-87451-186-0 : £7.25 B81-11252

338.1'6'0941 — Great Britain. Agricultural industries. Productivity. Effects of multiple land use

Lukehurst, Clare T.. The effects of multiple land use policies upon the use and productivity of farmland : interim report / by Clare T. Lukehurst, Susan E. Thompson, Raja Jarrah ; [for the] Countryside Research Unit, Brighton Polytechnic. — Brighton : Brighton Polytechnic, 1981. — 42p : ill,1map ; 30cm
ISBN 0-907558-00-3 (spiral) : £1.75 B81-31883

338.1'62 — Agricultural land. Irrigation. Economic aspects

Clark, Colin, *1905-*. The economics of irrigation. — [revision and updating] / Ian Carruthers and Colin Clark ; with a foreword by G.H. Peters. — Liverpool : Liverpool University Press, 1981. — xviii,300p : ill ; 25cm
Previous ed.: / by Colin Clark. Oxford : Pergamon, 1970. — Bibliography: p269-283. - Includes index
ISBN 0-85323-254-7 : £20.00 : CIP rev. B80-17593

338.1'62 — Great Britain. Grassland. Use. Economic aspects — *Conference proceedings*

Grassland in the British economy : proceedings of a symposium held at the University of Reading, September 1980 / jointly organised by Department of Agriculture and Horticulture ... [et al.] ; edited by J. L. Jollans. — Reading (2 Earley Gate, Reading RG6 2AU) : Centre of Agricultural Strategy, University of Reading, 1981. — 592p,[1]folded leaf of plates : ill,maps (some col.) ; 21cm. — (CAS paper ; 10)
Includes bibliographies and index
ISBN 0-7049-0616-3 (pbk) : £20.00 B81-14564

338.1'7311'05 — Wheat industries & trades — *Serials*

Review of the world wheat situation / International Wheat Council. — 1979/80. — London (28, Haymarket, SW1Y 4SSD) : The Council, [1981]. — 121p
Unpriced B81-14531

338.1'7325421'09425 — England. East Midlands. Crops: Perennial ryegrass. Seeds. Production, *1978.* **Economic aspects**

Kerr, H. W. T.. Perennial ryegrass seed production : the 1978 crop / H.W.T. Kerr. — [Nottingham] : University of Nottingham, Department of Agriculture and Horticulture, 1979. — 7p ; 30cm. — (Summary report / University of Nottingham Department of Agriculture and Horticulture ; no.6)
Cover title. — Text on inside cover
£0.35 (pbk) B81-29928

338.1'73491'09411 — Scotland. Seed potatoes. Certified crops — *Lists — Serials*

[Register of basic seed potato crops *(Edinburgh)***].** Register of basic seed potato crops / Department of Agriculture and Fisheries for Scotland. — 1980. — Edinburgh : H.M.S.O., 1980. — vii,100p
ISBN 0-11-491697-7 : £5.40 B81-06944

338.1'73491'09416 — Northern Ireland. Seed potatoes. Certified crops — *Lists — Serials*

[Register of basic seed potato crops *(Belfast)***].** Register of basic seed potato crops / Department of Agriculture for Northern Ireland. — 1980-. — [Belfast] ([Dundonald House, Belfast BT4 3SB]) : [The Department], 1980-. — v. ; 24cm
Annual. — Continues: Register of growers of basic seed potatoes
ISSN 0260-6100 = Register of basic seed potato crops (Belfast) : Unpriced B81-04033

338.1'736'091724 — Commonwealth developing countries. Sugar industries. Implications of Common Agricultural Policy of European Economic Community

Sugar, the European Community and the developing Commonwealth : report of a conference held at the Royal Commonwealth Society on 13 April 1981 / rapporteur Carol Cosgrove Twitchett. — London : Public Affairs Department, Royal Commonwealth Society, [1981]. — [58]p ; 30cm
Bibliography: p[45]-[46]
ISBN 0-905067-95-9 (spiral) : Unpriced B81-37153

338.1'7411'0941 — Great Britain. Eating apple production industries — *Inquiry reports*

. Apples / [Apple Industry Committee, European Democratic Group]. — London (32 Smith Sq., SW1P 3HH) : European Democratic Group, [1980]. — 28p : ill ; 22cm
£0.50 (pbk) B81-07634

338.1'749'094288 — Northumberland. National parks: Northumberland National Park. Forestry industries — *For environment planning*

Forestry in the Northumberland National Park. — Newcastle upon Tyne ([c/o] National Park Officer, Bede House, All Saints Centre, Newcastle upon Tyne) : [Northumberland National Park and Countryside Committee], 1976. — 29,xiii,[9]p of plates : ill,maps ; 30cm. — (Working paper / Northumberland National Park ; 4)
Unpriced (spiral) B81-29616

338.1'75'0941 — Great Britain. Horticultural industries — *Statistics — Serials*
Financial results of horticultural holdings / [University of Reading Department of Agricultural Economics & Management]. — 1979 crop year. — [Reading] : The Department, 1981. — 18p
ISBN 0-7049-0692-9 : £1.00 B81-24699

338.1'7525'09425 — England. East Midlands. Dry bulb onions. Production, *1971-1977.* Economic aspects
Kerr, H. W. T.. Dry bulb onions : the 1977 crop / H.W.T. Kerr. — [Nottingham] : University of Nottingham, Department of Agriculture and Horticulture, 1979. — 7p ; 30cm. — (Summary report / University of Nottingham Department of Agriculture and Horticulture ; no.5)
Cover title. — Text on inside cover
£0.35 (pbk) B81-29923

338.1'75642'0941 — Great Britain. Tomato industries
Nicholson, J. A. H.. Outlook for the glasshouse tomato industry / J.A.H. Nicholson. — [Ashford, Kent] : Wye College, University of London, Farm Business Unit, 1980. — 125p ; 30cm. — (Agricultural enterprise studies in England and Wales. Report ; no.72)
Cover title
ISBN 0-901859-89-3 (pbk) : £6.00 B81-38648

338.1'76'0094 — Europe. Livestock production industries — *Conference proceedings*
Pointer, C. G.. Report on 31st Annual Meeting of the Study Commissions of the European Association of [i.e. for] Animal Production, Munich, West Germany, 1-4 September, 1980 / C.G. Pointer. — [London] ([Great Westminster House, Horseferry Rd, SW1P 2AE]) : ADAS, [1981]. — 13p ; 30cm
Cover title. — At head of title: Ministry of Agriculture, Fisheries and Food
Unpriced (pbk) B81-36271

338.1'76'0094 — European Community countries. Livestock industries. Effects of enlargement of European Economic Community
Greece, Spain, Portugal and the EEC : an evaluation of the implications of EEC enlargement for the meat and livestock industry / [MLC Economic Information Service]. — Bletchley (PO Box 44, Queensway House, Bletchley, MK2 2EF) : Meat and Livestock Commission, 1980. — iii,74p : ill,maps ; 30cm. — (European booklet ; 80/5)
£5.00 (pbk)
Also classified at 338.4'766490094 B81-08270

338.1'760883'0941 — Great Britain. Meat production industries & meat trades — *Statistics — Serials*
UK meat and livestock statistics. Volume 1, Livestock numbers, slaughterings, meat production, trade, supplies and prices / MLC Economic Information Service. — 1981-. — Bletchley (PO Box 44, Queensway House, Bletchley, MK2 2EF) : Meat and Livestock Commission, 1981-. — v. ; 30cm
Annual. — Continues: UK meat and livestock statistics. Volume 1, Trade, slaughterings, meat production and supplies, prices
ISSN 0261-3239 = UK meat and livestock statistics. Volume 1. Livestock numbers, slaughterings, meat production, trade, supplies and prices : £2.00 B81-25005

338.1'762'0091724 — Developing countries. Cattle industries
Crotty, Raymond. Cattle, economics and development / R. Crotty. — Slough : Commonwealth Agricultural Bureaux, c1980. — xv,253p : ill ; 26cm
Bibliography: p231-238. — Includes index
ISBN 0-85198-452-5 : £15.00 B81-08387

338.1'762'00941 — Great Britain. Cattle industries — *Statistics — Serials*
UK meat and livestock statistics. Volume 2, Cattle numbers and holdings / MLC Economic Information Services. — 1981-. — Bletchley (PO Box 44, Queensway House, Bletchley MK2 2EF) : Meat and Livestock Commission, 1981-. — v. : maps ; 30cm
Annual. — Continues: UK meat and livestock statistics. Volume 2. Section A, Cattle numbers and holdings
ISSN 0262-0138 = UK meat and livestock statistics. Volume 2. Cattle numbers and holdings : £2.00 B81-38507

338.1'762142 — England. Dairy farming industries — *Serials*
Breeding and Production Organisation. Report of the Breeding and Production Organisation / Milk Marketing Board. — No.30 (1979/80). — Thames Ditton : [The Board], 1980. — 114p
Unpriced B81-13088

338.1'763'0094 — European Community countries. Sheep production industries. Implications of Common Agricultural Policy
CAP - sheepmeat : an explanation of the EEC sheepmeat regime / MLC, Economic Information Service. — Milton Keynes (PO Box 44, Queensway House, Queensway, Bletchley, Milton MK2 2EF) : Meat and Livestock Commission, 1981. — 35p : 2ill,1map ; 30cm. — (European booklet ; 81/1)
Cover title
£3.00 (pbk) B81-07319

338.1'76313'09424 — England. Midlands. Livestock: Fat lambs. Production, *1976.* Economic aspects
Macaskill, R. A.. Lowland sheep : a study of fat lamb production in 40 eve flocks in 1976 / R.A. Macaskill. — [Nottingham] : University of Agriculture and Horticulture, 1977. — i,10p ; 30cm. — (Summary report / University of Nottingham Department of Agriculture and Horticulture ; no.3)
Cover title
£0.30 (pbk) B81-29924

338.1'764'009426 — Eastern England. Pig production industries — *Statistics — Serials*
Pig management scheme results. — 1980. — Cambridge (19 Silver St., Cambridge CB3 9EP) : Agricultural Economics Unit, Department of Land Economy, University of Cambridge, [1981]. — 32p. — (Agricultural enterprise studies in England and Wales. Economic report ; no.76)
£1.50 B81-20071

338.1'77'094 — European Community countries. Dairy industries & trades — *Statistics — Serials*
EEC dairy facts and figures. — 1980. — Thames Ditton : Economics Division, Milk Marketing Board, [1980]. — xvi,182p
£2.50 B81-06916

338.1'77'0941 — Great Britain. Dairy industries & trades — *Serials*
The **Dairyman's** yearbook / National Dairymen's Association. — 1978-. — London (19 Cornwall Terrace, NW1 4QP) : The Association, 1978-. — v. : ill,ports ; 30cm
Annual
ISSN 0144-5251 = Dairyman's yearbook : £7.50 B81-02011

National Dairymen's Association. The dairyman's yearbook / National Dairymen's Association. — 1979. — London (19 Cornwall Terrace, NW1 4QP) : The Association, [1979]. — 104p
ISSN 0144-5251 : £7.50 B81-06920

National Dairymen's Association. The dairyman's yearbook / National Dairymen's Association. — 1980/81. — London (19 Cornwall Terrace, NW1 4QP) : The Association, 1980. — 112p
ISSN 0144-5251 : £8.50 B81-15212

338.1'77'0941 — Great Britain. Dairy industries & trades — *Statistics — Serials*
United Kingdom dairy facts and figures / Federation of United Kingdom Milk Marketing Boards. — 1980. — Thames Ditton : The Federation, [1980]. — 230p
£3.00 B81-09713

338.1'77'0941 — Great Britain. Dairy products industries — *Statistics — Serials*
Report on the census of production. Milk and milk products / Department of Industry, Business Statistics Office. — 1978. — London : H.M.S.O., c1980. — 13p in various pagings. — (Business monitor ; PA215)
ISBN 0-11-513140-x : £2.00 B81-05374

338.1'771'060411 — Scotland. Milk industries. Organisations: Scottish Milk Marketing Board, *to 1979*
Urquhart, Robert. History of the Scottish Milk Marketing Board / Robert Urquhart. — Paisley ([Underwood Rd., Paisly PA3 1TJ]) : Scottish Milk Marketing Board, c1979. — 89p,[25]p of plates : ill,ports ; 22cm
ISBN 0-903438-03-8 : Unpriced B81-16168

338.1'771'06042 — England. Milk industries. Organisations: Milk Marketing Board — *Serials*
Milk Marketing Board. Annual report and accounts. Milk Marketing Board. — 1980. — [Thames Ditton] : The Board, [1980]. — 28p
Unpriced B81-03275

Milk Marketing Board. Annual report and accounts / Milk Marketing Board. — 1981. — Thames Ditton : The Board, 1981. — 28p
Unpriced B81-36008

338.1'771'094 — European Community countries. Milk industries & trades. Policies of European Economic Community. Effects — *Forecasts*
Koester, U.. Milk policy in the European community : some alternatives : an analysis of the costs and benefits of different milk policy options open to the Council of Agricultural Ministers / U. Koester, E. Ryll, P.M. Schmitz. — Ashford : Wye College, c1981. — 33leaves ; 30cm. — (Occasional paper / Centre for European Agricultural Studies, ISSN 0306-2902 ; no.12)
ISBN 0-905378-31-8 (pbk) : £5.00 B81-10735

338.1'8 — Agricultural industries. Policies of governments. Economic aspects
Hallett, Graham. The economics of agricultural policy / Graham Hallett. — 2nd ed. — Oxford : Blackwell, 1981. — xi,365p : ill ; 23cm
Previous ed.: 1968. — Includes bibliographies and index
ISBN 0-631-12493-4 (cased) : £15.00 : CIP rev.
ISBN 0-631-12503-5 (pbk) : £6.50 B80-13733

338.1'81 — European Community countries. Agricultural industries. Policies of European Economic Community: Common Agricultural Policy. Reform — *Forecasts*
Marsh, John S.. The CAP in the 1980s : two views on revision / by J.S. Marsh, L.P. Mahé, M. Roudet. — Ashford : Wye College, 1981. — ii,66p ; 30cm. — (Occasional paper / Centre for European Agricultural Studies, ISSN 0306-2902 ; no.13)
Contents: The response of the CAP to the needs of Europe in the 1980s / by J.S. Marsh - French agricultural policy and green Europe : deadlock or reform? / by L.P. Mahé, M. Roudet
ISBN 0-905378-32-6 (pbk) : £6.50 B81-17571

338.1'81 — Green pound. Devaluation. Effects — *Forecasts*
Dickinson, Sheila. Effects of a green pound devaluation : a discussion paper / by Sheila Dickinson. — Ashford : Wye College, c1980. — 23p : 3ill ; 30cm. — (Occasional paper / Centre for European Agricultural Studies, ISSN 0306-2902 ; no.14)
ISBN 0-905378-34-2 (pbk) : £2.00 B81-10731

338.1'8425'3 — Lincolnshire. Peasant communities. Agricultural industries, *ca 1500-1914*
Thirsk, Joan. English peasant farming. — London : Methuen, Oct.1981. — [368]p. — (Methuen library reprints)
Originally published: London : Routledge & Kegan Paul, 1957
ISBN 0-416-30530-x : £18.50 : CIP entry B81-25726

338.1'847 — Soviet Union. Agricultural industries. Policies of government. Implementation, *1973-1980.* **Political aspects**
Gustafson, Thane. Reform in Soviet politics : lessons of recent policies on land and water / Thane Gustafson. — Cambridge : Cambridge University Press, 1981. — xii,218p : 1ill,2maps ; 24cm
Includes index
ISBN 0-521-23377-1 : £17.50 B81-38002

338.1′86811 — Botswana. Agricultural industries. Policies of government

Wily, Liz. Land allocation and hunter-gatherer land rights in Botswana : the impact of tribal grazing land policy / Liz Wily. — London (180 Brixton Rd. SW9 6AT) : Anti-Slavery Society, 1980. — 117p,[7]leaves of plates : maps ; 30cm. — (Human rights and development working papers ; no.4)
Bibliography: p111-117
Unpriced (pbk) B81-16585

338.1′873 — United States. Agricultural industries. Policies of government. Influence of pressure groups, *1975-1979*

Guither, Harold D.. The food lobbyists : behind the scenes of food and agri-politics / Harold D. Guither. — Lexington : Lexington Books ; [Farnborough, Hants] : Gower [distributor], 1981, c1980. — xiv,358p : maps ; 24cm
Includes index
ISBN 0-669-03539-4 : £15.00 B81-05507

338.1′9 — Food. Production. Economic aspects

Yates, Geoffrey. Food : need, greed and myopia : a review of the world food situation and its present and future economic implications for the world and the United Kingdom / Geoffrey Yates. — Newcastle upon Tyne (7 Blayney Row, Newburn, Newcastle upon Tyne NE15 8QD) : Earthright Publications, c1980. — 56p : ill ; 21cm
Bibliography: p52-55
ISBN 0-907367-00-3 (pbk) : £1.60 B81-23571

338.1′9′678 — Tanzania. Food production industries

Lappé, Frances Moore. Mozambique and Tanzania : asking the questions / Frances Moore Lappé, Adele Beccar-Varela. — San Francisco : Institute for Food and Development Policy ; Birmingham (151 Stratford Rd., Birmingham B11 1RD) : Third World [distributor], c1980. — 126p : ill,maps ; 22cm
Bibliography: p125-126
ISBN 0-935028-05-6 (pbk) : £2.40
Also classified at 338.1′9′679 B81-05764

338.1′9′679 — Mozambique. Food production industries

Lappé, Frances Moore. Mozambique and Tanzania : asking the questions / Frances Moore Lappé, Adele Beccar-Varela. — San Francisco : Institute for Food and Development Policy ; Birmingham (151 Stratford Rd., Birmingham B11 1RD) : Third World [distributor], c1980. — 126p : ill,maps ; 22cm
Bibliography: p125-126
ISBN 0-935028-05-6 (pbk) : £2.40
Primary classification 338.1′9′678 B81-05764

338.2 — ECONOMICS OF MINERAL PRODUCTS

338.2′05 — Mining industries — *Serials*

Mining annual review. — 1981. — London : Mining Journal, 1981. — 632p
ISBN 0-900117-26-5 : £20.00 B81-34059

338.2′0941 — Great Britain. Minerals industries & trades — *Statistics* **—** *Serials*

United Kingdom mineral statistics / Natural Environment Research Council, Institute of Geological Sciences. — 1980. — London : H.M.S.O., 1981. — viii,143p
ISBN 0-11-884164-5 : £13.00
ISSN 0308-5090 B81-29424

338.2′09417 — Ireland *(Republic).* **Mining industries —** *Conference proceedings*

Irish mining and exploration conference : status and future prospects : Gresham Hotel, Dublin, 20 June 1979. — [Dublin] ([Confederation House, Kildare St., Dublin 2]) : Irish Mining and Exploration Group, [1979?]. — 126p : ill,ports ; 29cm
Unpriced (pbk) B81-26631

338.2′09423′75 — Cornwall. Gwinear region. Metals mining industries, *1750-1900*

Jenkin, A. K. Hamilton. Mines and miners of Cornwall / A.K. Hamilton Jenkin. — Bracknell : Forge
Originally published: Truro : Truro Bookshop, 1963
5: Hayle, Gwinear and Gwithin. — 1980. — 64p : ill ; 22cm
Includes index
£1.80 (pbk) B81-09949

338.2′09429′61 — Dyfed. Cwmystwyth. Metals mining industries, *to 1980*

Hughes, Simon J. S.. The Cwmystwyth mines / by Simon J.S. Hughes. — [Sheffield] (41 Windsor Walk, South Anston, Sheffield S31 7EL) : Northern Mine Research Society, 1981. — 78p : ill,maps,1port ; 30cm. — (British mining, ISSN 0308-2199 ; no.17)
Bibliography: p78
ISBN 0-901450-20-0 (pbk) : Unpriced B81-23735

338.2′3 — England. Midlands. Land disturbed by opencast iron mining. Reclamation. Financial assistance. Funds. Ironstone Restoration Fund — *Accounts* **—** *Serials*

[Account *(Ironstone Restoration Fund)*]. Account. — 1979-80. — London : H.M.S.O., [1981]. — 6p
ISBN 0-10-223781-6 : £1.10 B81-28377

338.2′3 — Great Britain. Petroleum industries. Pricing, *1970-1980*

Grant, R. M. (Robert Morris). Pricing behaviour in the UK wholesale market for petrol 1970-80 : a ′structure-conduct′ analysis / by R.M. Grant. — London : [The City University Business School], c1981. — 30leaves : ill ; 30cm. — (Working paper / The City University Business School, ISSN 0140-1041 ; no.24)
Bibliography: leaf 30
Unpriced (pbk) B81-35249

338.2′3 — Middle East. Petroleum industries. Financial aspects. Information sources — *Lists* **—** *For businessmen*

Nicholas, David, *1947-*. The Middle East : its oil, economies and investment policies : a guide to sources of financial information / David Nicholas. — London : Mansell, 1981. — xxiv,199p : 1maps ; 22cm
Map on lining paper. — Includes index
ISBN 0-7201-0907-8 : £16.00 : CIP rev. B80-23064

338.2′3 — Petroleum industries. Financing

White, Norman A.. Financing the international petroleum industry / Norman A. White with the collaboration of Albert W. Angulo ... [et al.]. — London : Graham & Trotman, 1978. — xvi,257p : ill ; 25cm
Includes bibliographies and index
ISBN 0-86010-076-6 : £20.00 B81-03961

338.2′3 — Petroleum. Prices. Effects of energy demand — *Forecasts*

Pearce, D. W.. World energy demand and crude oil prices to the year 2000 / by David Pearce. — [Aberdeen] : University of Aberdeen, Department of Political Economy, [1980]. — 26leaves : 1ill ; 30cm. — (Discussion paper / University of Aberdeen Department of Political Economy ; 80-12)
Bibliography: leaves 25-26
£1.00 (pbk) B81-05307

338.2′3 — Petroleum. Prices — *Serials*

Petroleum times price report. — Vol.1, no.1 (1 Apr.1981)-. — Sutton : IPC Industrial Press ; Sutton : Distributed by IPC Business Press, 1981-. — v. ; 28cm
Issued twice a month. — Supplement to: Petroleum times (1981)
ISSN 0261-3883 = Petroleum Times price report : £48.00 per year (with Petroleum times) B81-33050

338.2′3 — Petroleum. Pricing. Policies of Organization of the Petroleum Exporting Countries

The Challenge of energy. — London : Longman, Nov.1981. — [128]p. — (Energy resources and policies of the Middle East and North Africa)
ISBN 0-582-78335-6 : £5.00 : CIP entry B81-31180

338.2′3 — Petroleum. Pricing. Role of Organisation of Petroleum Exporting Countries, *1960-1980*

Johany, Ali D.. The myth of the OPEC cartel : the role of Saudi Arabia / Ali D. Johany. — Dhahran : University of Petroleum and Minerals ; Chichester : Wiley, c1980. — xi,107p : ill ; 24cm
Bibliography: p100-105. - Includes index
ISBN 0-471-27864-5 : £14.00
Also classified at 330.953′8 B81-04095

338.2′3 — Petroleum producing countries. Petroleum industries. Revenue. Investment. Policies of governments

Jones, Aubrey, *1911-*. Oil : the missed opportunity : or naft and shaft / Aubrey Jones. — London : Deutsch, 1981. — 238p : ill,1map ; 23cm
Map on lining papers. — Bibliography: p228-230. — Includes index
ISBN 0-233-97368-0 : £14.95 B81-13596

338.2′724 — Coal industries. Environmental aspects

Gibson, J.. Coal and the environment. — Northwood : Science Reviews, July 1981. — [60]p
ISBN 0-905927-60-5 (pbk) : £1.75 : CIP entry B81-20576

338.2′724′05 — Coal industries — *Serials*

International coal report / Financial Times. — Issue no.1 (12 Sept.1980)-. — London (Bracken House, 10 Cannon St., EC4P 4BY) : Financial Times Business Information, 1980-. — v. : ill,maps ; 30cm
Fortnightly
ISSN 0260-4299 = International coal report : Unpriced B81-08323

338.2′724′0941 — Great Britain. Coal industries, *1973-1980 — National Union of Mineworkers viewpoints*

The Miners and the battle for Britain. — London (222 Euston Rd, N.W.1) : National Union of Mineworkers, [1981]. — 60p : ill ; 21cm
Cover title
Unpriced (pbk) B81-19735

338.2′724′0941 — Great Britain. Coal industries. Effects of policies of government — *Trade union viewpoints*

Iron and Steel Trades Confederation. What is the future? : steel - rail - coal / [Iron & Steel Trades Confederation, National Union of Railwaymen, National Union of Mineworkers]. — [London] ([324 Grays Inn Rd, WC1BX 8DD]) : [The Confederation], [1981]. — 12p ; 21cm
Cover title
Unpriced (pbk)
Primary classification 338.4′7669142′0941 B81-1973[illegible]

338.2′724′0941 — Great Britain. Coal industries — *Forecasts*

Robinson, Colin, *1932-*. What future for British coal : optimism or realism on the prospect to the year 2000 / Colin Robinson and Eileen Marshall. — [London] : Institute of Economic Affairs, 1981. — 104p : ill ; 22cm. — (Hobart paper, ISSN 0073-2818 ; 89)
ISBN 0-255-36143-2 (pbk) : £2.00 B81-2438[illegible]

338.2′724′0941 — Great Britain. Coal industries — *Statistics* **—** *Serials*

Report on the census of production. Coal mining / Department of Industry, Business Statistics Office. — 1979. — London : H.M.S.O., c1981. — 8,vp. — (Business monitor ; PA101)
ISBN 0-11-513307-0 : £2.50 B81-2964[illegible]

338.2′724′094252 — Nottinghamshire. Coal industries, *1881-1981*

Griffin, A. R.. The Nottinghamshire coalfield 1881-1981. — Ashbourne : Moorland Publishing, Dec.1981. — [96]p
ISBN 0-86190-046-4 : £5.95 : CIP entry B81-3883[illegible]

338.2′724′0942845 — North Yorkshire. Selby *(District).* **Coal industries,** *to 1980*
Arnold, Peter, *19---.* The development of the Selby coalfield : a study in planning / by Peter Arnold, Ian Cole. — York (Heslington, York YO1 5DD) : Dept. of Social Administration and Social Work, University of York, c1981. — xiii,157p : ill,maps ; 30cm. — (Selby research paper ; 1) (Papers in community studies ; 25)
ISBN 0-906723-04-3 (pbk) : £4.75 B81-37986

338.2′724′094294 — South Wales. Coal industries, *to 1970*
Powell, Afan. Welsh Miners Museum at Afan Argoed County Park : an illustrated guide to the history of the industry, to the development of the communities and to life in the valleys of South Wales / written by Afan Powell. — Port Talbot (c/o 25 Dunraven St., Glycorrwg, Port Talbot, W. Glam.) : Welsh Miners′ Museum Committee, 1977. — 29p : ill,2maps,1facsim,2plans ; 15x21cm
Bibliography: p29
Unpriced (pbk) B81-18638

338.2′724′0994 — Australia. Coal industries
Cook, P. Lesley. The supply of Australian coal / by P. Lesley Cook. — Brighton (Mantell Building, Falmer, Brighton, Sussex BN1 9RF) : Science Policy Research Unit, University of Sussex, c1981. — 109p : 1map ; 30cm. — (SPRU occasional paper series ; no.14)
Bibliography: p107-109
ISBN 0-903622-15-7 (spiral) : Unpriced B81-18938

338.2′728 — Mobile offshore drilling rigs — *Lists — Serials*
Register of offshore units, submersibles & diving systems / Lloyd′s Register of Shipping. — 1980-81. — London : The Register, c1980. — 410p in various pagings
ISSN 0141-4143 : Unpriced
Also classified at 387.2′045′0216 B81-08757

338.2′728 — Natural gas deposits & petroleum deposits. Exploitation. Offshore drilling rigs — *Lists — Serials*
The **Offshore** drilling register / compiled ... by H. Clarkson & Company Limited. — 1981. — London : The Company, c1981. — 155p
£40.00 B81-29112

338.2′728′0941 — Great Britain. Natural gas & petroleum industries — *Statistics — Serials*
Report on the census of production. Petroleum and natural gas / Department of Industry,Business Statistics Office. — 1978. — London : H.M.S.O., c1980. — 9p in various pagings. — (Business monitor ; PA104)
ISBN 0-11-513151-5 : £1.75 B81-05372

Report on the census of production. Petroleum and natural gas / Department of Industry, Business Statistics Office. — 1979. — London : H.M.S.O., c1981. — 13p in various pagings. — (Business monitor ; PA104)
ISBN 0-11-513312-7 : £2.50 B81-31021

338.2′728′0941 — Great Britain. Offshore natural gas & petroleum industries — *Serials*
Offshore oil & gas yearbook : [UK & Continental Europe]. — 1978/79-. — London : Kogan Page, 1978-. — v. : ill,maps ; 29cm
Every two years. — Continues: European offshore oil & gas yearbook
ISSN 0260-6437 = Offshore oil & gas yearbook (corrected) : £25.00 B81-05408

Offshore oil & gas yearbook : UK & continental Europe. — 4th ed. (1981-82). — London : Kogan Page, Dec.1981. — [400]p
ISBN 0-85038-498-2 : £45.00 : CIP entry B81-33866

338.2′7282 — Petroleum industries & trades
Al-Chalabi, Fadhil J.. OPEC and the international oil industry : a changing structure / by Fadhil J. Al-Chalabi. — Oxford : Oxford University Press on behalf of the Organization of Arab Petroleum Exporting Countries, 1980. — viii,165p : ill ; 23cm
ISBN 0-19-877167-3 (cased) : Unpriced : CIP rev.
ISBN 0-19-877155-x (pbk) : Unpriced B80-00614

338.2′7282 — Petroleum industries & trades. International political aspects
Banks, Ferdinand E.. The political economy of oil / Ferdinand E. Banks. — Lexington, Mass. : Lexington Books ; [Farnborough, Hants.] : Gower Publishing [distributor], 1981. — xiv,241p : ill ; 24cm
Bibliography: p227-236. - Includes index
ISBN 0-669-03402-9 : £14.00 B81-20917

338.2′7282 — Petroleum industries. Environmental aspects — *Conference proceedings*
Institute of Petroleum. *Conference (1979 : London).* Petroleum development and the environment : proceedings of the Institute of Petroleum 1979 Annual Conference London, UK. — London : Heyden on behalf of the Institute of Petroleum, c1980. — ix,142p : ill,maps,1plan ; 25cm
ISBN 0-85501-654-x : Unpriced : CIP rev. B80-13734

338.2′7282 — Petroleum industries. International politico-economic aspects
Odell, Peter R.. Oil and world power / Peter R. Odell. — 6th ed. — Harmondsworth : Penguin, 1981. — 294p : ill,maps ; 20cm
Previous ed.: 1979. — Bibliography: p279-285. — Includes index
ISBN 0-14-021169-1 (pbk) : £2.25 B81-27662

338.2′7282 — Scotland. Strathclyde Region. Services for North Sea petroleum industries — *Directories — Serials*
Strathclyde oil register. — May 1980. — Glasgow (21 Bothwell St., Glasgow G2 6NJ) : Strathclyde Regional Council, 1980. — 56p
Unpriced B81-11875

338.2′7′28205 — Petroleum industries — *Serials*
Oil and gas international yearbook. — 1982. — London : Longman, Jan.1982. — [694]p
ISBN 0-582-90310-6 : £40.00 : CIP entry B81-34574

338.2′7282′094 — Western Europe. Nationalised industries: Petroleum industries & trades — *Case studies*
Grayson, Leslie E.. National oil companies / Leslie E. Grayson. — Chichester : Wiley, c1981. — vii,269p : ill,maps ; 24cm
Includes index
ISBN 0-471-27861-0 : £15.90 : CIP rev. B81-00781

338.2′7282′0941 — Great Britain. Petroleum industries. Development. Role of government, *1865-ca 1930*
Jones, Geoffrey, *1952-.* The state and the emergence of the British oil industry / Geoffrey Jones. — London : Macmillan in association with Business History Unit, University of London, 1981. — xi,264p : ill,maps ; 23cm. — (Studies in business history)
Bibliography: p254-258. — Includes index
ISBN 0-333-27595-0 : £20.00 : CIP rev.
Also classified at 338.2′7282′0941 B80-29260

338.2′7282′0941 — Great Britain. Petroleum industries. Policies of government, *1865-ca 1930*
Jones, Geoffrey, *1952-.* The state and the emergence of the British oil industry / Geoffrey Jones. — London : Macmillan in association with Business History Unit, University of London, 1981. — xi,264p : ill,maps ; 23cm. — (Studies in business history)
Bibliography: p254-258. — Includes index
ISBN 0-333-27595-0 : £20.00 : CIP rev.
Primary classification 338.2′7282′0941 B80-29260

338.2′7282′095367 — Kuwait. Petroleum industries
Al-Sabah, Y. S. F.. The oil economy of Kuwait / Y.S.F. Al-Sabah. — London : Kegan Paul, 1980. — ix,166p : ill ; 23cm
Includes index
ISBN 0-7103-0003-4 : £15.00 : CIP rev. B80-12278

338.2′7282′09567 — Iraq. Petroleum industries. Nationalisation, *1972*
Hussein, Adil. Iraq : the eternal fire : 1972 Iraqi oil nationalization in perspective / Adil Hussein ; translated from the Arabic by A-W. Lúlúa. — London (117 Piccadilly, W.1.) : Third World Centre for Research and Publishing, 1981. — 256p ; 23cm
ISBN 0-86199-004-8 : £9.50 B81-33200

338.2′7282′0973 — United States. Petroleum industries & trades. Policies of government, *to 1980*
Wildavsky, Aaron. The politics of mistrust : estimating American oil and gas resources / Aaron Wildavsky, Ellen Tenenbaum with Pat Albin and the assistance of Natale Cippolina, Ehud Levy-Pascal and David Vachon. — Beverly Hills ; London : Sage, c1981. — 363p : ill ; 22cm. — (Managing information ; v.1)
Includes bibliographies and index
ISBN 0-8039-1582-9 (cased) : Unpriced
ISBN 0-8039-1583-7 (pbk) : Unpriced B81-29176

338.2′73 — Iron ore industries & trades — *Conference proceedings*
International Iron Ore Symposium *(2nd : 1981 : Frankfurt).* Proceedings of Metal bulletin′s Second International Iron Ore Symposium held on March 23-24 1981 at the Hotel Intercontinental, Frankfurt / edited by Raymond Cordero assisted by Patricia Lloyd. — Worcester Park : Metal Bulletin PLC, c1981. — 324p in various pagings : ill,maps,plans ; 31cm
ISBN 0-900542-54-3 : £35.00 B81-40121

338.2′7421′0942355 — Devon. Teign Valley. Silver mining industries, *1806-1880*
Schmitz, Christopher J.. The Teign Valley silver-lead mines : 1806-1880 / Christopher J. Schmitz. — Rev. — South Anston (41 Windsor Walk, South Anston, Sheffield S31 7EL) : Northern Mine Research Society, 1980. — vi,121p,[5]p of plates(some folded) : ill,maps ; 30cm. — (British mining, ISSN 0308-2199 ; no.15) (A Monograph of the Northern Mine Research Society)
Previous ed.: published as Teign Valley lead mines, 1973. — Bibliography: p118-121
ISBN 0-901450-18-9 (pbk) : Unpriced
Also classified at 338.2′744′0942355 B81-25982

338.2′743′094237 — Cornwall. Copper mining industries, *1850-1960*
Mining in Cornwall 1850-1960. — Ashbourne : Moorland
Vol.2 / [compiled by] J.H. Trounson on behalf of the Trevithick Society. — [1981]. — 134p : chiefly ill,maps ; 25cm
ISBN 0-903485-95-8 (pbk) : £3.50
Primary classification 338.2′7453′094237 B81-23084

338.2′744′0942355 — Devon. Teign Valley. Lead mining industries, *1806-1880*
Schmitz, Christopher J.. The Teign Valley silver-lead mines : 1806-1880 / Christopher J. Schmitz. — Rev. — South Anston (41 Windsor Walk, South Anston, Sheffield S31 7EL) : Northern Mine Research Society, 1980. — vi,121p,[5]p of plates(some folded) : ill,maps ; 30cm. — (British mining, ISSN 0308-2199 ; no.15) (A Monograph of the Northern Mine Research Society)
Previous ed.: published as Teign Valley lead mines, 1973. — Bibliography: p118-121
ISBN 0-901450-18-9 (pbk) : Unpriced
Primary classification 338.2′7421′0942355 B81-25982

338.2′744′0942383 — Somerset. Mendip region. Lead mining industries, *1683-1749 — Regulations*
The **Ancient** laws, customs and orders of the miners in the King′s forrest of Mendipp in the county of Somerset. — St. Peter Port : Toucan Press, 1981. — 7p ; 15cm
Facsim. of: edition published: London : William Cooper, 1687
ISBN 0-85694-234-0 (pbk) : Unpriced B81-18628

338.2′744′094284 — North Yorkshire. Dales. Lead mining industries, *to 1905*
Raistrick, Arthur. Lead mining in the Yorkshire Dales / by Arthur Raistrick. — Lancaster : Dalesman, 1981. — 40p : ill ; 19cm
Originally published: 1972
ISBN 0-85206-641-4 (pbk) : £0.75 B81-23022

338.2′7453′094237 — Cornwall. Tin mining industries, *1850-1960*

Mining in Cornwall 1850-1960. — Ashbourne : Moorland
Vol.2 / [compiled by] J.H. Trounson on behalf of the Trevithick Society. — [1981]. — 134p : chiefly ill,maps ; 25cm
ISBN 0-903485-95-8 (pbk) : £3.50
Also classified at 338.2′743′094237 B81-23084

338.2′74926 — Aluminium & bauxite industries — *Conference proceedings*

International Aluminium Congress *(1st : Madrid : 1980).* Proceedings of Metal bulletin's First International Aluminium Congress September 29-October 1, 1980, Madrid / edited by Norman Connell assisted by Patricia Lloyd. — London : Metal Bulletin, c1981. — 324p in various pagings : ill ; 30cm
ISBN 0-900542-49-7 (pbk) : £35.00
ISBN 0-900542-48-9 B81-19479

338.2′74926′0947 — Eastern Europe. Aluminium industries

Stankovich, Ivan D.. The aluminium industry in Eastern Europe and communist Asia / by Ivan D. Stankovich. — London : Metal Bulletin Ltd., c1981. — 83p : ill ; 30cm
ISBN 0-900542-48-9 (spiral) : £70.00
Also classified at 338.2′74926′095 B81-12982

338.2′74926′095 — Asia. Communist countries. Aluminium industries

Stankovich, Ivan D.. The aluminium industry in Eastern Europe and communist Asia / by Ivan D. Stankovich. — London : Metal Bulletin Ltd., c1981. — 83p : ill ; 30cm
ISBN 0-900542-48-9 (spiral) : £70.00
Primary classification 338.2′74926′0947
B81-12982

338.2′75 — Great Britain. Aggregates industries — *Statistics — Serials*

Production of aggregates in Great Britain / Department of the Environment. — 1978 and 1979. — [London] : H.M.S.O., 1981. — 19p
ISBN 0-11-751445-4 : £2.80 B81-13086

338.2′75′06041 — Great Britain. Quarrying industries. Organisations: Institute of Quarrying *— Directories — Serials*

Institute of Quarrying. UK supplement to register of members / the Institute of Quarrying. — [No.1]-. — Nottingham (7 Regent St., Nottingham NG1 5BY) : The Institute, 1980-. — v. ; 21cm
Irregular. — Supplement to: Institute of Quarrying. Register of members
ISSN 0260-9193 = UK supplement to register of members - Institute of Quarrying : £5.00
B81-11871

338.2′75′0941 — Great Britain. Quarrying industries *— Statistics — Serials*

Report on the census of production. Miscellaneous mining and quarrying / Department of Industry, Business Statistics Office. — 1979. — London : H.M.S.O., c1981. — 8,vp. — (Business monitor ; PA109)
ISBN 0-11-513291-0 : £2.50 B81-29651

Report on the census of production. Stone and slate quarrying and mining / Department of Industry, Business Statistics Office. — 1978. — London : H.M.S.O., c1980. — 14p in various pagings. — (Business monitor ; PA102)
ISBN 0-11-513095-0 : £2.00 B81-08353

Report on the census of production. Stone and slate quarrying and mining / Department of Industry, Business Statistics Office. — 1979. — London : H.M.S.O., c1981. — 17p in various pagings. — (Business monitor ; PA102)
ISBN 0-11-513346-1 : £2.80 B81-32504

338.2′761′0941 — Great Britain. Clay mining industries *— Statistics — Serials*

Report on the census of production. Chalk, clay sand and gravel extraction / Department of Industry, Business Statistics Office. — 1978. — London : H.M.S.O., c1980. — 14p in various pagings. — (Business monitor ; PA103)
ISBN 0-11-513108-6 : £2.00
Also classified at 338.2′768 ; 338.2′762′0941
B81-05007

Report on the census of production. Chalk, clay sand and gravel extraction / Department of Industry, Business Statistics Office. — 1979. — London : H.M.S.O., c1981. — 13p in various pagings. — (Business monitor ; PA103)
ISBN 0-11-513303-8 : £2.80
Also classified at 338.2′768 ; 338.2′762′0941
B81-30732

338.2′762′0941 — Great Britain. Sand & gravel mining industries *— Statistics — Serials*

Report on the census of production. Chalk, clay sand and gravel extraction / Department of Industry, Business Statistics Office. — 1978. — London : H.M.S.O., c1980. — 14p in various pagings. — (Business monitor ; PA103)
ISBN 0-11-513108-6 : £2.00
Primary classification 338.2′761′0941
B81-05007

Report on the census of production. Chalk, clay, sand and gravel extraction / Department of Industry, Business Statistics Office. — 1979. — London : H.M.S.O., c1981. — 13p in various pagings. — (Business monitor ; PA103)
ISBN 0-11-513303 8 : £2.80
Primary classification 338.2′761′0941
B81-30732

338.2′768 — Great Britain. Chalk mining industries *— Statistics — Serials*

Report on the census of production. Chalk, clay sand and gravel extraction / Department of Industry, Business Statistics Office. — 1978. — London : H.M.S.O., c1980. — 14p in various pagings. — (Business monitor ; PA103)
ISBN 0-11-513108-6 : £2.00
Primary classification 338.2′761′0941
B81-05007

Report on the census of production. Chalk, clay, sand and gravel extraction / Department of Industry, Business Statistics Office. — 1979. — London : H.M.S.O., c1981. — 13p in various pagings. — (Business monitor ; PA103)
ISBN 0-11-513303-8 : £2.80
Primary classification 338.2′761′0941
B81-30732

338.3 — ECONOMICS OF PRIMARY INDUSTRIES(OTHER THAN AGRICULTURE AND MINERALS)

338.3′71 — Aquaculture industries

Shang, Yung C.. Aquaculture economics : basic concepts and methods of analysis / Yung C. Shang. — Boulder : Westview ; London : Croom Helm, 1981. — xvi,153p : ill,forms ; 24cm
Bibliography: p139-143. — Includes index
ISBN 0-7099-2318-x : £10.95 B81-33441

338.3′727 — Fish products

Windsor, Malcolm. Introduction to fishery by-products. — Farnham : Fishing News Books, Aug.1981. — [208]p
ISBN 0-85238-115-8 : £13.50 : CIP entry
B81-18082

338.3′727 — Great Britain. White fish fishing industries. Organisations: White Fish Authority *— Accounts — Serials*

Herring Marketing Fund, Herring Industry Board, White Fish Authority accounts. — 1979-80. — London : H.M.S.O, 1981. — 14p
ISBN 0-10-215081-8 : £1.70
Primary classification 338.3′72755 B81-16244

338.3′727092941 — Great Britain. Freshwater fisheries *— Conference proceedings*

Fishery Conference *(1980 : New University of Ulster).* Fishery Conference 1980 / [organized by] the New University of Ulster Institute of Continuing Education in association with the Institute of Fisheries Management. — [Londonderry] ([Londonderry, Northern Ireland]) : [Institute of Continuing Education], [1981?]. — 77p : ill ; 30cm
Unpriced (pbk) B81-29534

338.3′727′0941 — Great Britain. Fishing industries. Effects of North Sea petroleum industries, *1970-1981*

Steel, David I. A.. North Sea oil and British fishing : some lines of approach / David I.A. Steel. — Edinburgh (Sea Fisheries House, 10 Young St., Edinburgh, EH2 4JQ) : Fishery Economics Research Unit, 1981. — 21p,[3]p of plates : maps ; 30cm. — (F.E.R.U. occasional paper series, ISSN 0309-605x ; no.1, 1981)
Bibliography: p19-21
Unpriced (spiral) B81-11324

338.3′727′0941 — Great Britain. Sea fishing industries. Finance *— Statistics — Serials*

Fish trawling, processing & merchanting. — 7th ed. — London (81 City Rd, EC1Y 1BD) : Inter Company Comparisons, c1981. — 15p. — (ICC financial survey)
ISBN 0-86191-461-9 : Unpriced B81-32683

338.3′727′0941 — Great Britain. Sea fishing industries *— Forecasts — Serials*

Fishing prospects / Ministry of Agriculture, Fisheries and Food, Directorate of Fisheries Research. — 1978-1979. — Lowestoft ([Fisheries Laboratory, Pakefield Rd, Lowestoft, Suffolk]) : The Ministry, c1979. — i,39p
ISSN 0308-0935 : Unpriced B81-19413

Fishing prospects / Ministry of Agriculture, Fisheries and Food, Directorate of Fisheries Research. — 1980-1981. — Lowestoft ([Fisheries Laboratory, Pakefield Rd, Lowestoft, Suffolk]) : The Ministry, 1980. — [iii],43p
ISSN 0308-0935 : Unpriced B81-30761

338.3′727′0941 — Great Britain. Sea fishing industries *— Statistics — Serials*

Sea fisheries statistical tables / Ministry of Agriculture, Fisheries and Food. — 1979. — London : H.M.S.O., 1981. — vi,41p
ISBN 0-11-241201-7 : £5.60 B81-30832

338.3′727′09411 — Scotland. Fishing industries — *Serials*

Scottish Fishermen's Federation. Official year book and diary / Scottish Fishermen's Federation. — 1981. — Aberdeen (11 Albyn Terrace, Aberdeen AB9 1SE) : Northern Publishers (Aberdeen) Ltd., [1981?]. — 264p
Unpriced B81-1554

338.3′727′09411 — Scotland. Sea fishing industries *— Statistics — Serials*

Scottish sea fisheries statistical tables / Department of Agriculture and Fisheries for Scotland. — 1980. — Edinburgh : H.M.S.O, 1981. — 63p
ISBN 0-11-491744-2 : £5.40 B81-3405

338.3′727′0941423 — Scotland. Strathclyde Region. Kintyre. Tarbert. Fishing industries

Johnson, Ronnie. Tarbert Lochfyne : the story of the fishermen / by Ronnie Johnson ; and illustrated by Ann Thomas. — Argyll (Tarbert Argyll) : Ann Thomas Gallery, 1980. — 41p : ill,1map ; 21cm
Unpriced (pbk) B81-3469

338.3′727′09416 — Northern Ireland. Fishing industries — *Serials*

Report on the sea and inland fisheries of Northern Ireland / Department of Agriculture. — 1979. — Belfast : H.M.S.O., 1980. — 27p
ISBN 0-337-05253-0 : £2.00 B81-2033

338.3′727′09422323 — Kent. Medway River. Fishing industries, *to 1978*

Coombe, Derek. The Bawleymen : fishermen and dredgermen of the River Medway / Derek Coombe with chapters by Leslie H. Hill and Leonard J. Wadhams. — Rainham (33 Broadview Ave., Rainham, Kent, ME8 9DB) : Pennant, 1979. — 112p,[32]p of plates : ill,1map,ports ; 24cm
Bibliography: p103-104. - Includes index
ISBN 0-9506413-0-8 : £4.95
Also classified at 338.4′762773′09422323
B81-036

338.3′727′09426 — East Anglia. Trawling industries, ***1900-1979 — Interviews***

Butcher, David R.. The trawlermen / by David Butcher. — Reading (9 Queen Victoria St., Reading) : Tops'l Books, 1980. — 152p : ill,maps,ports ; 25cm
Bibliography: p152
ISBN 0-906397-06-5 : £3.95 : CIP rev.
ISBN 0-906397-05-7 (pbk) : £3.75 B80-21551

338.3′727′09427 — North-west England. Fisheries — *Statistics — Serials*

Summary of fisheries statistics / North West Water Rivers Division. — 1979. — [Warrington] ([Dawson House, Liverpool Rd, Great Sankey, Warrington WA5 3LW]) : The Division, [1979?]. — 69p
ISSN 0144-9141 : Unpriced B81-33281

338.3′727′0942834 — Humberside. Grimsby. Fishing industries

Grimsby fishing handbook. — London : Published for the Grimsby Fishing Vessel Owners' Association [by] Burrow, [1980?]. — 76p : ill,1map ; 21cm
£0.75 (pbk) B81-23627

338.3′72755 — Great Britain. Herring fishing industries. Organisations: Herring Industry Board — *Accounts — Serials*

Herring Marketing Fund, Herring Industry Board, White Fish Authority accounts. — 1979-80. — London : H.M.S.O, 1981. — 14p
ISBN 0-10-215081-8 : £1.70
Also classified at 338.3′727 B81-16244

338.3′72755 — Great Britain. Herring fishing industries. Organisations: Herring Industry Board — *Serials*

Herring Industry Board. Annual report for the year ended 31st December ... / Herring Industry Board. — 46th (1980). — Edinburgh ([10 Young St., Edinburgh EH2 4JQ]) : [The Board], 1981. — 16p
ISBN 0-903959-09-7 : £0.50 B81-35954

338.4 — ECONOMICS OF SECONDARY INDUSTRIES

338.4′0941 — Great Britain. Regional economic development. Policies of government. Implications of regional variations in demand by manufacturing industries for business services

Marshall, J. N.. Spatial variations in manufactering industry demand for business services : some implications for the government economic policies / by J.N. Marshall. — [Newcastle upon Tyne] : University of Newcastle upon Tyne, Centre for Urban and Regional Development Studies, 1980. — 43,[23] leaves ; 30cm. — (Discussion paper / Centre for Urban and Regional Development Studies University of Newcastle upon Tyne ; no.35)
Bibliography: leaves 41-43
Unpriced (pbk) B81-13919

338.4′09427′53 — Merseyside *(Metropolitan County).* **Liverpool. Service industries,** ***1800-1900***

Anderson, G.. The service occupations of nineteenth century Liverpool / G. Anderson. — [Salford] : Department of Economics, University of Salford, [1981]. — 283leaves ; 30cm. — (Salford papers in economics ; 81-1)
Unpriced (spiral) B81-16808

338.4′3′000942 — England. Manufacturing industries. Finance, ***1830-1914***

Cottrell, P. L.. Industrial finance 1830-1914 : the finance and organization of English manufacturing industry / P.L. Cottrell. — London : Methuen, 1980. — xii,298p ; 24cm
Bibliography: p274-284. - Includes index
ISBN 0-416-85680-2 : £15.00 : CIP rev.
B79-32346

338.4′3002 — Books. Auction prices — *Lists — Serials*

Book auction records. — Vol.77 (For the auction season August 1979-July 1980). — Folkestone : Dawson, c1981. — xxxi,521p
ISBN 0-7129-1017-4 : Unpriced B81-09116

338.4′3002 — Great Britain. Antiquarian books & second-hand books. Auction prices — *Lists — Serials*

The **Lyle** offical books review. — 1980-. — Galashiels : Lyle, 1979-. — v. : ill ; 23cm
Annual. — Description based on: 1981 issue
ISSN 0260-6348 = Lyle offical books review : £7.50 B81-04170

338.4′3002 — Non-fiction: Academic books: Books with British imprints. Prices — *Serials*

Average prices of British academic books. — 1980. — [Loughborough] ([Loughborough, Leics. LE11 3TD]) : Centre for Library and Information Management, Department of Library and Information Studies, Loughborough University, c1980. — 11p. — (Report / CLAIM, ISSN 0261-0302 ; no.7) (British Library research and development reports, ISSN 0308-2385 ; 5635)
ISBN 0-904924-26-2 : £3.00
ISSN 0142-4955 B81-31045

338.4′33′0072041 — Great Britain. Social sciences. Research. Financing

Terms and conditions of social research funding in Britain : report of the working group. — London (35 Northampton Sq., EC1V 0AX) : Social Research Association, 1980. — v,36p ; 30cm
ISBN 0-9506477-2-1 (pbk) : £2.00 B81-29687

338.4′33558′05 — Militaria. Auction prices — *Lists — Serials*

The **Lyle** official arms and armour review. — 1979. — Galashiels : Lyle Publications, c1978. — 382p
ISBN 0-902921-84-3 : £6.00
ISSN 0307-7748 B81-03035

The **Lyle** official arms and armour review. — 1981. — Galashiels : Lyle Publications, c1980. — 414p
ISBN 0-86248-003-5 : £7.50
ISSN 0307-7748 B81-03033

338.4′336137′0942142 — London. Camden *(London Borough).* **Social services. Voluntary personnel. Expenses**

Orwell, Patricia. The cost of volunteering : a pilot survey of volunteers' out-of-pocket expenses and insurance / Patricia Orwell & Angela Whitcher. — Berkhamsted (29 Lower King's Rd., Berkhamsted, Herts. HP4 2AB) : Volunteer Centre, 1981. — 29p : 1form ; 21cm
Bibliography: p12
£0.80 (pbk)
Also classified at 338.4′336137′094258
B81-11254

338.4′336137′094258 — Hertfordshire. Social services. Voluntary personnel. Expenses

Orwell, Patricia. The cost of volunteering : a pilot survey of volunteers' out-of-pocket expenses and insurance / Patricia Orwell & Angela Whitcher. — Berkhamsted (29 Lower King's Rd., Berkhamsted, Herts. HP4 2AB) : Volunteer Centre, 1981. — 29p : 1form ; 21cm
Bibliography: p12
£0.80 (pbk)
Primary classification 338.4′336137′0942142
B81-11254

338.4′3361941 — Great Britain. Personal welfare services. Charges

Judge, Ken. Charging for social care : a study of consumer charges and the personal social services / Ken Judge, James Matthews. — London : Allen & Unwin, 1980. — 150p : ill ; 22cm. — (National Institute social services library ; no.38)
Bibliography: p141-146 — Includes index
ISBN 0-04-361040-4 (cased) : £10.95 : CIP rev.
ISBN 0-04-361041-2 (pbk) : £4.95 B80-18192

338.4′3361941 — Great Britain. Social services. Expenditure — *Inquiry reports*

Great Britain. *Parliament. House of Commons. Social Services Committee.* Third report from the Social Services Committee, session 1980-81 : public expenditure on the social services : together with the proceedings of the Committee, the minutes of evidence and appendices. — London : H.M.S.O.. — ([HC] ; 324-II)
Vol.2: Minutes of evidence and appendices. — [1981]. — ill ; 25cm
ISBN 0-10-008341-2 (pbk) : £6.30 B81-40614

338.4′336196894 — Zambia. Lusaka. Social services. Financial resources

Pasteur, D.. Financial resources for urban services and development in Lusakaa case study and an exercise / by D. Pasteur. — Birmingham : University of Birmingham, Institute of Local Government Studies, Development Administration Group, 1978. — 45p : 1ill ; 30cm. — (Occasional papers in development administration ; no.3)
ISBN 0-7044-0314-5 (pbk) : £1.00 B81-08293

338.4′33621′0941 — Great Britain. Health services. Cost-benefit analysis

Drummond, M. F.. Principles of economic appraisal in health care / M.F. Drummond. — Oxford : Oxford University Press, 1980. — xvi,132p : ill ; 22cm. — (Oxford medical publications)
Includes bibliographies and index
ISBN 0-19-261273-5 (pbk) : £4.95 : CIP rev.
B80-13261

Drummond, M. F.. Studies in economic appraisal in health care / M.F. Drummond. — Oxford : Oxford University Press, 1981. — 216p ; 23cm. — (Oxford medical publications)
Bibliography: p208-212. — Includes index
ISBN 0-19-261274-3 : £10.00 : CIP rev.
B81-00038

338.4′33621′0942 — England. National health services. Costs — *Statistics — Serials*

Health services costing returns, year ended 31st March / Department of Health and Social Security [and] Welsh office. — 1978. — London : H.M.S.O., 1980. — 115p
ISBN 0-11-320726-3 : £8.50
ISSN 0144-3259 B81-02601

Health services costing returns, year ended 31st March ... / Department of Health and Social Security [and] Welsh Office. — 1979. — London : H.M.S.O., 1981. — 115p
ISBN 0-11-320763-8 : £9.00
ISSN 0144-3259 B81-31032

338.4′33621′09429 — Wales. National health services. Costs — *Statistics — Serials*

Costing returns for the year ended 31 March .... Part 1, Hospital services, community health services, ambulance services / Welsh Office. — 1980. — [Cardiff] ([Cathays Park, Cardiff CF1 3NQ]) : Welsh Office, [1980?]. — 169p
Unpriced B81-06905

Costing returns for the year ended 31 March .... Part 2, Hospital services, supplementary statements / Welsh Office. — 1980. — [Cardiff] ([Cathays Park CF 3NQ]) : Welsh Office, [1980?]. — 205p
Unpriced B81-06906

338.4′336211′0973 — United States. Hospital services. Costs. Inflation. Role of health insurance

Feldstein, Martin S.. Hospital costs and health insurance / Martin Feldstein. — Cambridge, Mass. ; London : Harvard University Press, 1981. — ix,327p : ill ; 25cm
Bibliography: p309-321. — Includes index
ISBN 0-674-40675-3 : £15.00 B81-28352

338.4′336219819′00941 — Great Britain. Women with mastectomies. Counselling. Costs

Allen, David, *1942-*. The costs of breast cancer treatment / David Allen and Ann Pentol. — Manchester : Health Services Management Unit, Department of Social Administration, University of Manchester, 1981. — 16leaves ; 30cm. — (Working papers series / University of Manchester. Health Services Management Unit, ISSN 0141-2647 ; no.42)
Bibliography: p16
Unpriced (pbk) B81-26093

338.4'336221'0942 — England. Hospitals. Mental handicap units. Costs *compared with* cost of mental handicap units in hospitals

Felce, D.. Evaluation of locally based hospital units for the mentally handicapped in Wessex : a comparison of the capital and operating costs of Wessex locally-based hospital units and villas on traditional hospital campuses author D. Felce, J. Mansell and A. Kushlick. — Winchester (Dawn House, Sleepers Hill, Winchester, Hants. SO22 4NG) : Health Care Evaluation Research Team, 1980. — 90,A14p ; 30cm. — (Research report / Health Care Evaluation Research Team ; no.146)
Cover title. — Bibliography: p88-90
(spiral) B81-07495

338.4'33635'0941 — Great Britain. Housing. Expenditure by government. Distribution — *Inquiry reports*

Great Britain. *Parliament. House of Commons. Environment Committee*. Third report from the Environment Committee : session 1980-81 : DOE's housing policies : enquiry into government's expenditure plans 1981/82 to 1983/84 : together with the proceedings of the Committee relating to the report, the minutes of evidence and appendices. — London : H.M.S.O., [1981]. — xx,70p ; 25cm. — (HC ; 383) (HC ; 383 i-ii)
ISBN 0-10-238381-2 (pbk) : £5.10 B81-39916

338.4'33635'0941 — Great Britain. Housing. Finance

Grey, Alexander. Housing rents, costs and subsidies : a discussion document / Alexander Grey, Noel P. Hepworth, John Odling-Smee. — 2nd rev. ed. — [London] : [Chartered Institute of Public Finance and Accountancy], [1981]. — xx,161p : ill ; 21cm
Previous ed.: 1978. — Includes index
ISBN 0-85299-215-7 (pbk) : £6.00 B81-23436

338.4'33635'0942 — England. Housing. Finance — *Practical information*

Aughton, Henry. Housing finance : a basic guide / Henry Aughton. — London (157 Waterloo Rd., SE1 8UU) : Shelter, 1981. — 62p ; 22cm
ISBN 0-901242-58-6 (pbk) : £2.00 B81-36850

338.4'33635'0942 — England. Housing. Finance — *Serials*

Housing revenue account statistics. Estimates / CIPFA Statistical Information Service. — 1980-81. — London (Chartered Institute of Public Finance and Accountancy), 1981. — 35p
£5.00 B81-29052

338.4'336358 — England. Local authority housing. Finance — *Statistics — Serials*

Housing revenue account statistics. Actuals / CIPFA Statistical Information Service. — 1978-79-. — London : Chartered Institute of Public Finance and Accountancy, 1980-. — v. ; 30cm
Annual. — Continues in part: Housing statistics (Egland and Wales). Part 2, Housing revenue account
ISSN 0260-4078 = Housing revenue account statistics. Actuals (corrected) : £5.00
B81-08265

338.4'337'0942 — England. Education. Costs. Payment by parents

Bull, David, *1939-*. What price 'free' education / David Bull. — London (1 Macklin St., WC2B 5NH) : Child Poverty Action Group, 1980. — 88p ; 21cm. — (Poverty pamphlet ; 48)
£1.20 (pbk) B81-11045

338.4'3371'00942 — Great Britain. Schools. Costs — *Study regions: England*

Hough, J. R.. A study of school costs / J.R. Hough. — Windsor : NFER Nelson, 1981. — 216p : ill ; 22cm
Bibliography: p202-211. — Includes index
ISBN 0-85633-163-5 (pbk) : £10.50 B81-16088

338.4'337133 — Teaching aids: Audiovisual equipment & audiovisual materials. Costs. Analysis

Jamison, Dean T.. The costs of educational media : guidelines for planning and evaluation / Dean T. Jamison, Steven J. Klees, Stuart J. Wells ; foreword by Wilbur Schramm. — Beverly Hills ; London : Sage, c1978. — 255p ; 23cm. — (People and communication ; v.3)
Bibliography: p247-253. — Includes index
ISBN 0-8039-0747-8 (cased) : Unpriced
ISBN 0-8039-0748-6 (pbk) : Unpriced
B81-17775

338.4'337402 — Further education. Educational technology. Cost-benefit analysis

Wagner, Leslie. Cost analysis and educational media decisions / Leslie Wagner. — London : School of Social Sciences and Business Studies Polytechnic of Central London, 1980. — 30p ; 30cm. — (Research working paper / School of Social Sciences and Business Studies, Polytechnic of Central London ; no.9)
Cover title. — Bibliography: p30
£1.00 (spiral)
Also classified at 338.4'337817'078 B81-05181

338.4'337817'078 — Higher education. Educational technology. Cost-benefit analysis

Wagner, Leslie. Cost analysis and educational media decisions / Leslie Wagner. — London : School of Social Sciences and Business Studies Polytechnic of Central London, 1980. — 30p ; 30cm. — (Research working paper / School of Social Sciences and Business Studies, Polytechnic of Central London ; no.9)
Cover title. — Bibliography: p30
£1.00 (spiral)
Primary classification 338.4'337402 B81-05181

338.4'361'0720411 — Scotland. Medicine. Research. Financial assistance. Organisations: Scottish Hospital Endowments Research Trust — *Accounts — Serials*

Scottish Hospital Endowments Research Trust. Annual report and accounts for the year ended 31st July ... / Scottish Hospital Endowments Research Trust. — 1979. — Edinburgh : H.M.S.O., 1980. — iv,15p
ISBN 0-10-201681-x : £2.30 B81-05624

338.4'362'00028 — United States. Industrial equipment. Prices — *Lists — Serials*

Land's industrial machinery & equipment pricing guide. — 1981. — New York ; London : Van Nostrand Reinhold, c1981. — vi,249p
ISBN 0-442-28820-4 : £22.45 B81-29440

338.4'362131'0941 — Great Britain. Electricity supply. Charges. Payment. Methods — *Proposals*

The **Code** of practice on the payment of domestic electricity and gas bills : comments on its operation and interim suggestions for improvements / Electricity Consumers' Council. — London (119 Marylebone Rd., NW1 5PY) : The Council, 1980. — 26p ; 30cm. — (Discussion paper / Electricity Consumers' Council ; 7)
Unpriced (pbk)
Also classified at 338.4'366574'0941
B81-34744

338.4'362138932 — Home tape recording equipment. Levies — *Proposals*

A **Levy** on blank video and audio tapes and associated hardware : a summary of the proponents' arguments. — [London] ([33 Thurloe Place, SW7 2HQ]) : British Phonographic Industry, 1981. — [11]p ; 21cm
Unpriced (unbound) B81-29201

338.4'36214 — Great Britain. Energy supply. Charges. Allowances — *Feasibility studies*

Fuel allowance / Electricity Consumers' Council. — London (119 Marylebone Rd., NW1 5PY) : The Council, 1979. — 21p ; 30cm. — (Discussion paper / Electricity Consumers' Council ; 1)
Unpriced (pbk) B81-34750

338.4'3623 — Military equipment. Expenditure by governments

World military expenditure up again. — London (6 Endsleigh St., W.C.1) : Peace Pledge Union, [1981?]. — [8]p : ill,maps ; 30cm
£0.15 (unbound) B81-35264

338.4'3623'0973 — Great Britain. American military equipment. Sale — *Accounts — Serials*

Disposal of surplus United States mutual defence programme equipment account. — 1979-1980. — London : H.M.S.O., [1980]. — 2p. — (Cmnd. ; 8110)
ISBN 0-10-181100-4 : £0.70 B81-09229

338.4'36234'0941 — Great Britain. Royal ordnance factories. Trading operations — *Accounts — Serials*

Royal Ordnance Factories Trading Fund accounts. — London : H.M.S.O., 1978. — 17p
ISBN 0-10-268878-8 : £0.40 B81-09055

338.4'36281'0942 — England. Water supply industries. Charges — *Statistics — Serials*

Water services charges statistics / Water Finance Executive. — 1980/81. — London : Chartered Institute of Public Finance and Accounting, 1980. — 35p
ISSN 0141-7835 : £3.00 B81-20403

338.4'3629287'0941 — Great Britain. Motor vehicles. Maintenance & repair. Costs — *Serials*

The **I.C.M.E.** manual. — 47th year (1979 ed.). — Chertsey : Palgrave, 1979. — 400p
£8.70 B81-03840

The **I.C.M.E.** manual. — 48th year (1980 ed.). — Chertsey : Palgrave, 1980. — 409p
£9.70 B81-03839

338.4'3636132'0941 — Great Britain. Thoroughbred horses. Prices — *Lists — Serials*

The **Bloodstock** sales review and stud register. — 16th ed. (1981). — Bacton (Walnut Tree Farm House, Bacton, Suffolk) : Bloodstock Sales Review, [1981]. — 264p
Unpriced B81-25478

338.4'3644 — Residences. Energy. Conservation. Investment

Helcké, George. The energy saving guide : tables for assessing the profitability of energy saving measures with explanatory notes and worked examples / by George Helcke. — Oxford : Published for the Commission of the European Communities by Pergamon, 1981. — xii,224p ; 26cm
ISBN 0-08-026738-6 (cased) : £20.00
ISBN 0-08-026739-4 (pbk) : £6.75 B81-19103

338.4'36441'0942143 — London. Islington *(London Borough)*. Local authority housing estates: Packington Estate. Heating. Costs

Griffiths, Stephen. The Packington report / Stephen Griffiths. — [London] ([62 Highbury Grove, N5 2AD]) : Polytechnic of North London, Department of Applied Social Studies, Survey Research Unit, 1980. — 25,[1]p- ; 30cm. — (Research report / Polytechnic of North London Department of Applied Social Studies Survey Research Unit ; no.7)
ISBN 0-906970-06-7 (pbk) : £2.50 B81-12546

338.4'365815242 — Great Britain. Industrial equipment. Leasing. Financial aspects

Wainman, David. Leasing : the accounting & taxation implications. — 2nd ed. by David Wainman & Howard Brown. — St. Helier (Park Place House, Tunnel St., St. Helier, Jersey) : Guild, 1980. — 266p ; 21cm
Previous ed.: 1978. — Includes index
ISBN 0-9505174-8-8 (pbk) : £12.00 B81-00782

338.4'366574'0941 — Great Britain. Gas supply. Charges. Payment. Methods — *Proposals*

The **Code** of practice on the payment of domestic electricity and gas bills : comments on its operation and interim suggestions for improvements / Electricity Consumers' Council. — London (119 Marylebone Rd., NW1 5PY) : The Council, 1980. — 26p ; 30cm. — (Discussion paper / Electricity Consumers' Council ; 7)
Unpriced (pbk)
Primary classification 338.4'362131'0941
B81-34744

338.4'367122'0941 — Great Britain. Foundry equipment industries. Finance — *Statistics* — *Serials*

Foundry plant & equipment. — 7th ed. — London (81 City Rd, EC1Y 1BD) : Inter Company Comparisons, c1981. — 16p. — (ICC financial survey)
ISBN 0-86191-466-x : Unpriced B81-32688

338.4'36797'0941 — Great Britain. Tobacco products. Recommended retail prices — *Lists* — *Serials*

The **Smokers'** handbook. — 1981. — London (21 John Adam St., WC2N 6JH) : Tobacco, 1981. — 72p
ISBN 0-86108-089-0 : £2.50 B81-32272

338.4'367973'0973 — United States. Cigarettes. Prices. Effects of taxation

Sumner, Michael T.. Tax changes and cigarette prices / Michael T. Sumner and Robert Ward. — [Salford] : Department of Economics, University of Salford, [1981]. — 9leaves ; 30cm. — (Salford papers in economics ; 81-2)
Bibliography: p8
Unpriced (spiral) B81-16807

338.4'369066'0942356 — Devon. Exeter. Cathedrals: Exeter Cathedral. Maintenance & repair, *1279-1353* — *Accounts*

[Exeter Cathedral. Manuscript. D & C. Exeter 2600-2704/11]. The accounts of the fabric of Exeter Cathedral, 1279-1353 / edited and translated with an introduction by Audrey M. Erskine. — Exeter (c/o Assistant Secretary, c/o Devon and Exeter Institution, 7 The Close, Exeter) : Devon & Cornwall Record Society. — (New series / Devon & Cornwall Record Society ; v.24)
Translation from the Latin
Pt.1: 1279-1326. — 1981. — xxi,212p ; 25cm
ISBN 0-901853-24-0 (pbk) : Unpriced
B81-17162

338.4'369083'0941 — Great Britain. Houses. Rebuilding. Costs — *Tables* — *Serials*

Guide to house rebuilding costs for insurance valuation / prepared on behalf of the British Insurance Association by the Building Cost Information Service of the Royal Institution of Chartered Surveyors. — 1980/81 ed.. — 54p
ISBN 0-906182-03-4 : £3.00
ISSN 0261-2054 B81-20317

Guide to house rebuilding costs for insurance valuation / prepared on behalf of the British Insurance Association by the Building Cost Information Service of the Royal Institution of Chartered Surveyors. — [1978-79 ed.]-. — Kingston Upon Thames (85 Clarence St., Kingston upon Thames, Surrey KT1 1RB) : The Service, 1978-. — v. ; 30cm
Annual
ISSN 0261-2054 = Guide to house rebuilding costs for insurance valuation : Unpriced
B81-20315

Guide to house rebuilding costs for insurance valuation / prepared on behalf of the British Insurance Association by the Building Cost Information Service of the Royal Institution of Chartered Surveyors. — 1979/80 ed.. — Kingston Upon Thames (85 Clarence St., Kingston Upon Thames, Surrey KT1 1RB) : The Service, 1979. — 43p
ISBN 0-906182-01-8 : £2.50
ISSN 0261-2054 B81-20316

338.4'37 — Art objects. Auction prices — *Lists* — *Serials*

Art at auction : the year at Sotheby Parke Bernet. — 244th season (1977-78). — London : Sotheby Parke Bernet, 1978. — 496p
ISBN 0-85667-049-9 : Unpriced
ISSN 0084-6783 B81-14542

Art at auction : the year at Sotheby Parke Bernet. — 245th season (1978-79). — London : Sotheby Parke Bernet, c1979. — 496p
ISBN 0-85667-063-4 : £14.95 B81-14543

338.4'3711'0942 — England. Environment planning. Expenditure by local authorities — *Statistics* — *Serials*

Planning and development statistics. Actuals / CIPFA Statistical Information Service. — 1979-80. — London : Chartered Institute of Public Finance and Accountancy, 1981. — 40p
ISSN 0260-8642 : £10.00 B81-26378

338.4'37111 — England. Planning permission. Fees

Bowhill, Anthony. Planning application fees : from 1 April 1981 / Anthony Bowhill. — London : Oyez, 1981. — 16p ; 26x11cm
ISBN 0-85120-600-x (pbk) : Unpriced
B81-28232

338.4'3712'0941 — Great Britain. Landscape design. Prices

Spon's landscape price book / edited by Derek Lovejoy and Partners. — 2nd ed. / pricing sections contributed by Gerald Horsefield and Partners, R.E. Neighbour and Widnell and Trollope. — London : Spon, 1981. — x,230p : 1ill ; 24cm
Previous ed.: 1978. — Includes index
ISBN 0-419-11640-0 : Unpriced : CIP rev.
ISSN 0144-8404 B81-03823

338.4'37451'0941 — Antiques. Auction prices — *Lists* — *Serials*

The **Lyle** official antiques review. — 1979. — Galashiels : Lyle Publications, c1978. — 638p
ISBN 0-902921-82-7 : £6.00 B81-12556

The **Lyle** official antiques review. — 1981. — Galashiels : Lyle Publications, c1980. — 670p
ISBN 0-86248-001-9 : £7.50 B81-02640

338.4'375 — Paintings. Auction prices — *Lists* — *Serials*

The **Annual** art sales index. Oil paintings, watercolours and drawings, artists. — 1979/80. — Weybridge (Pond House, Weybridge, Surrey) : Art Sales Index, c1980. — 2v
ISSN 0143-0688 : Unpriced B81-10265

The **Lyle** official arts review. — 1979. — Galashiels : Lyle Publications, c1978. — 479p
ISBN 0-902921-83-5 : £6.00 B81-12555

The **Lyle** official arts review. — 1981. — Galashiels : Lyle Publications, c1980. — 511p
ISBN 0-86248-002-7 : £7.50 B81-01721

338.4'376956'05 — Investment: Postage stamps. Prices — *Serials*

Stamp price movements. — 3rd ed. (1960-1981). — Egham (Park House, Egham, Surrey TW20 0HW) : P-E Consulting Group, 1981. — 20leaves
ISBN 0-907138-01-2 : £6.25 B81-35466

338.4'3769569417 — Investments: Ireland *(Republic)* **postage stamps. Prices** — *Lists*

Marles, R. J.. Stamp varieties of Ireland : compilation of averaged selling-prices drawn from dealers' lists, auctions, philatelic catalogues and magazines / by R.J. Marles. — 3rd ed. — Torquay : Rotographic, 1981. — 96p : ill ; 16cm. — (Collectors' stamps)
ISBN 0-901170-24-0 (pbk) : £1.00 B81-36673

338.4'379'00942 — England. Local authority leisure facilities. Charges — *Statistics* — *Serials*

Charges for leisure services : a sample survey / CIPFA Statistical Information Service. — 1978-79-. — London : Chartered Institute of Public Finance and Accountancy, 1978-. — v. ; 30cm
Annual. — Description based on: 1980-81 issue
ISSN 0142-1484 = Charges for leisure services : £5.00 B81-35111

338.4'5 — Soviet Union. Technology transfer from Western world — *Study examples: Technology transfer in chemical industries, 1958-1978*

Sobeslavsky, V.. The transfer of technology to socialist countries : the case of the Soviet chemical industry / V. Sobeslavsky, P. Beazley. — Farnborough, Hants. : Published for The Royal Institute of International Affairs by Gower, c1980. — xiv,155p : maps ; 24cm
Includes index
ISBN 0-566-00325-2 : £10.50 : CIP rev.
B80-05819

338.4'5613636'0973 — United States. Regulated industries. Productivity. Measurement & analysis

Productivity measurement in regulated industries / edited by Thomas G. Cowing, Rodney E. Stevenson. — New York ; London : Academic Press, 1981. — xv,417p ; 24cm
Bibliography: p395-407. — Includes index
ISBN 0-12-194080-2 : £22.20 B81-33026

338.4'5624 — Ireland *(Republic).* **Cement & concrete. Consumption by construction industries**

O'Rourke, C.. Study of cement and concrete product consumption in the construction industry / C. O'Rourke. — Dublin (St. Martin's House, Waterloo Rd., Dublin 4) : Foras Forbartha, 1980. — 26p : ill,1map,1form ; 30cm
ISBN 0-906120-37-3 (spiral) : £1.00
B81-20812

338.4'5624'0973 — United States. Construction industries. Economic efficiency. Effects of unionisation

Bourdon, Clinton C.. Union and open-shop construction : compensation, work practices, and labor markets / Clinton C. Bourdon, Raymond E. Levitt. — Lexington : Lexington Books ; [Farnborough, Hants.] ; Gower [distributor], 1980. — xi,161p : ill,1form ; 24cm
Bibliography: p151-155. — Includes index
ISBN 0-669-02918-1 : £13.50 B81-04655

338.4'566'0094 — Europe. Chemical industries. Innovation — *Conference proceedings*

European Chemical Marketing Research Association. *International Conference (16th : 1980 : Estoril).* Innovation : still the basis for growth : proceedings of the International Confernece of the European Chemical Marketing Research Association : Hotel Estoril Sol, Estoril, October 27-29, 1980 / compiled by Joachim Pump. — Leverkusen : Bayer AG ; London : EVAF Central Secretariat [[distributor]], [1980]. — 330p : ill ; 21cm
Unpriced (pbk) B81-40459

338.4'5664'00941 — Great Britain. Food industries. Performance *compared with* **performance of French food industries,** *1975-1978* — *French texts*

Industries françaises et britanniques des produits alimentaires : analyse comparative des principales entreprises / ICC Ratios Financiers. — Londres [i.e. London] : ICC Ratios Financiers, [1981]. — [98]p : ill ; 30cm
ISBN 0-904540-05-7 (pbk) : Unpriced
Also classified at 338.4'5664'00944 B81-22848

338.4'5664'00944 — France. Food industries. Performance *compared with* **performance of British food industries,** *1975-1978* — *French texts*

Industries françaises et britanniques des produits alimentaires : analyse comparative des principales entreprises / ICC Ratios Financiers. — Londres [i.e. London] : ICC Ratios Financiers, [1981]. — [98]p : ill ; 30cm
ISBN 0-904540-05-7 (pbk) : Unpriced
Primary classification 338.4'5664'00941
B81-22848

338.4'5677'00973 — United States. Textile industries. Development. Role of British technology, *1790-ca 1830*

Jeremy, David J.. Transatlantic industrial revolution : the diffusion of textile technologies between Britain and America, 1790-1830s / David J. Jeremy. — Oxford : Blackwell, 1981. — xvii,384p : ill,facsims,1port ; 21x26cm
Originally published: Cambridge, Mass. : MIT Press, 1981. — Bibliography: p340-356. — Includes index
ISBN 0-631-12785-2 : £16.00 : CIP rev.
B81-06604

338.4'5686'0941 — Great Britain. Book industries & trades. Applications of digital computer systems — *Conference proceedings*

Books on-line : proceedings of a conference organised by the Working Party of Libraries and the Book Trade at Book House on 12th May 1981. — [London] : [Working Party on Library and Book Trade Relations], 1981. — i,86p : 1ill,ports ; 30cm
Original title: Library book funds ; 1978-80
ISBN 0-904572-05-6 (pbk) : Unpriced : CIP rev.
Also classified at 025'.0028'54 B79-15775

338.4'569'006041 — Great Britain. Building industries. Performance. Improvement. Organisations: National Building Agency — *Serials*

National Building Agency. Report for the year ended 31 March ... / the National Building Agency. — 1978-. — London : NBA, c1978-. — v. : ill,facsims,plans ; 30cm
Annual. — Cover title: Annual report (National Building Agency)
ISSN 0261-8745 = Report for the year - National Building Agency : Unpriced
B81-37239

338.4'7 — Consumer goods & consumer services. Demand. Econometric models

Theil, Henri. The system-wide approach to microeconomics / Henri Theil. — Oxford : Blackwell, 1980. — xii,260p : ill ; 24cm
Bibliography: p232-254. — Includes Index
ISBN 0-631-12522-1 (cased) : £15.00 : CIP rev.
ISBN 0-631-12523-9 (pbk) : £6.95 B80-05821

338.4'700164'05 — Computer industries & trades — *Serials*

Infomatics : the systems management weekly. — Vol.1, no.1 (1 Sept.1980)-. — London (53 Frith St., W1A 2HG) : VNU Business Publications, 1980-. — v. : ill ; 29cm
Description based on: Vol.1, no.15 (8/15 Dec.1980)
ISSN 0260-7247 = Infomatics : £30.00 per year B81-05591

338.4'7027473 — United States. Public libraries. Economic aspects

Getz, Malcolm. Public libraries : an economic view / Malcolm Getz. — Baltimore ; London : Johns Hopkins University Press, c1980. — xii,214p ; 24cm
Bibliography: p207-210. — Includes index
ISBN 0-8018-2395-1 : £7.50 B81-02706

338.4'70705'0941 — Great Britain. Book publishing industries — *Serials*

Cover to cover. — Vol.1, no.1 (Feb.1981)-. — Haywards Heath (25 Sergison Rd, Haywards Heath, West Sussex RN16 1HX) : Cover Drive Distribution, 1981-. — v. : ill,ports ; 42cm
Six issues yearly
ISSN 0261-2186 = Cover to cover : £1.50 per year B81-20085

338.4'70705'0941 — Great Britain. Feminist printing & publishing industries

Cadman, Eileen. Rolling our own : women as printers, publishers and distributors / Eileen Cadman, Gail Chester, Agnes Pivot. — London : Minority Press, 1981. — 117p : ill ; 22cm. — (Minority Press Group series ; no.4)
ISBN 0-906890-06-3 (cased) : £7.50
ISBN 0-906890-07-1 (pbk) : £2.25 B81-36332

338.4'70705'0941 — Great Britain. Printing & publishing industries — *Statistics* **—** *Serials*

Report on the census of production. General printing and publishing / Department of Industry, Business Statistics Office. — 1978. — London : H.M.S.O., c1980. — 13p in various pagings. — (Business monitor ; PA489)
ISBN 0-11-513101-9 : £2.00 B81-08348

Report on the census of production. General printing and publishing / Department of Industry, Business Statistics Office. — 1979. — London : H.M.S.O., c1981. — 13p. in various pagings. — (Business monitor ; PA489)
ISBN 0-11-513348-8 : £2.50 B81-32674

338.4'70705'0941 — Great Britain. Publishing industries

Curwen, Peter J.. The UK publishing industry / by Peter J. Curwen. — Oxford : Pergammon, 1981. — xii,167p ; 26cm
Bibliography: p148-160. — Includes index
ISBN 0-08-024081-x : £7.50 : CIP rev.
B81-06879

338.4'70705'0941 — Great Britain. Publishing industries — *Serials*

Publishing news : fortnightly for people in publishing. — 1979-. — London (37/49 Brick St., W1A 1AN) : Gradegate, 1979-. — v. : ill,ports ; 32cm
ISSN 0261-5398 = Publishing news : £9.00 per year B81-32704

338.4'70705'0941 — Great Britain. Publishing industries — *Statistics* **—** *Serials*

[Quarterly statistical bulletin *(Publishers Association)***]Quarterly** statistical bulletin / the Publishers Association. — June 1980-. — London : The Association, 1980-. — v. : ill ; 30cm
Continues: Statistics collection scheme and business monitor (Publishers Association)
ISSN 0260-5198 = Quarterly statistical bulletin - Publishers Association : Unpriced
B81-04441

338.4'70705'0941 — Great Britain. Specialist publishing industries — *Serials*

ALPSP bulletin : bulletin of the Association of Learned and Professional Society Publishers. — Oct. 1977-. — Chalfont St. Peter (c/o R.J. Millson, 30 Austenwood Close, Chalfont St. Peter, Gerrards Cross, Bucks. SL9 9DE) : The Association, 1977-. — v. ; 21cm
Quarterly. — Description based on: Dec.1980 issue
ISSN 0260-9428 = ALPSP bulletin : Free to Association members B81-12395

338.4'7070572 — Science. Serials with British imprints. Economic aspects

Royal Society. *Scientific Information Committee*. A study of the scientific information system in the United Kingdom / the report of a study undertaken by the Scientific Information Committee of the Royal Society, with the aid of a grant from the British Library and with the full-time assistance of Mr J.F.B. Rowland. — London : The Society, 1981. — 44p : ill ; 30cm. — (British Library R & D report ; no.5626)
Bibliography: p42-44
ISBN 0-85403-166-9 (pbk) : Unpriced
B81-26116

338.4'7070572'02573 — United States. Periodical publishing industries — *Directories* **—** *Serials*

MIMP : magazine industry market place. — 1981. — New York : Bowker, c1980. — xiii,713p
ISBN 0-8352-1292-0 : Unpriced
ISSN 0000-0434 B81-02434

338.4'7070572'0941 — Great Britain. Serials publishing industries — *Statistics* **—** *Serials*

Report on the census of production. Printing, publishing of newspapers and periodicals / Department of Industry, Business Statistics Office. — 1979. — London : H.M.S.O., c1981. — 13p. in various pagings. — (Business monitor ; PA485)
ISBN 0-11-513328-3 : £2.50 B81-32679

338.4'70705794'0973 — United States. Music printing & publishing industries, *1787-1825*

Wolfe, Richard J.. Early American music engraving and printing : a history of music publishing in America from 1787 to 1825 with commentary on earlier and later practices / Richard J. Wolfe. — Urbana ; London : Published in cooperation with the Bibliographical Society of America by the University of Illinois Press, c1980. — xix,321p : ill,music,facsims ; 24cm. — (Music in American life)
Bibliography: p301-303. - Includes index
ISBN 0-252-00726-3 : £15.00 B81-05858

338.4'7070593'05 — Publishing industries. Little presses — *Serials*

Poetry and little press information. — No.1 (May 1980)-. — London (262 Randolph Ave, W9) : Association of Little Presses, 1980-. — v. ; 30cm
Quarterly. — Continues: Poetry information
ISSN 0260-9339 = Poetry and little press information : £2.00 per year B81-10553

338.4'734411 — Scotland. Legal services. Royal Commission on Legal Services in Scotland. Report — *Critical studies*

Scottish Consumer Council. The Scottish Consumer Council's response to the Hughes report : the report of the Royal Commission on Legal Services in Scotland (Volume one : Cmnd 7846). — Glasgow (4 Somerset Pl., Glasgow G3 7JT) : The Council, [1981]. — 28p ; 30cm
ISBN 0-907067-02-6 (pbk) : £1.00 B81-38365

338.4'73442 — England. Legal services

Legal services in the eighties. — Oxford : Martin Robertson, Oct.1981. — [256]p
ISBN 0-85520-444-3 : £12.00 : CIP entry
B81-30178

338.4'7361 — Social services. Policies. Economic aspects. Theories

Culyer, A. J.. The political economy of social policy / A.J. Culyer. — [New ed.]. — Oxford : Martin Robertson, 1980. — xii,340p : ill ; 24cm
Previous ed.: published as The economics of social policy. 1973. — Includes bibliographies and index
ISBN 0-85520-369-2 (cased) : £18.00 : CIP rev.
ISBN 0-85520-370-6 (pbk) : £7.50 B80-17595

338.4'73621 — Health services. Economic aspects — *Conference proceedings*

World Conference on Health Economics *(1980 : Leiden)*. Health, economics, and health economics : proceedings of the World Congress on Health Economics, Leiden, the Netherlands, September 1980 / edited by Jacques van der Gaag and Mark Perlman. — Amsterdam ; Oxford : North-Holland, 1981. — xvi,400p : ill ; 23cm. — (Contributions to economic analysis ; 137)
Bibliography: p369-392. — Includes index
ISBN 0-444-86210-2 : Unpriced B81-39206

338.4'736211'0973 — United States. Hospitals. Economic aspects

Sloan, Frank A.. Insurance, regulation, and hospital costs / Frank A. Sloan, Bruce Steinwald. — Lexington : Lexington ; [Farnborough, Hants.] : [Gower] [distributor], 1980. — xvii,266p : ill ; 24cm
Bibliography: p245-258. — Includes index
ISBN 0-669-03472-x : £16.50 B81-10893

338.4'736261'0941 — Great Britain. Residential homes for old persons. Economic aspects

Davies, Bleddyn. Old people's homes and the production of welfare / Bleddyn Davies, Martin Knapp. — London : Routledge & Kegan Paul, 1981. — viii,256p : ill ; 23cm. — (Library of social work, ISSN 0305-4381)
Bibliography: p218-242. — Includes index
ISBN 0-7100-0700-0 : £11.50 B81-09803

338.4'73635 — Housing. Economic aspects

Maclennan, Duncan. Housing economics. — London : Longman, Feb.1982. — [220]p
ISBN 0-582-44381-4 (pbk) : £6.95 : CIP entry
B81-36018

338.4'737'0941 — Great Britain. Education. Economic aspects

Simkins, Tim. Economics and the management of resources in education / Tim Simkins. — [Sheffield] ([Pond St., Sheffield, S1 1WB]) : Sheffield City Polytechnic, Department of Education Management, 1981. — ii,90p : ill ; 30cm. — (Sheffield papers in education management ; no.17)
Bibliography: p85-88
ISBN 0-903761-32-7 (pbk) : Unpriced
B81-35348

338.4'73781982 — Great Britain. Higher education institutions. Foreign students. Economic aspects

The **Overseas** student question : studies for a policy / edited by Peter Williams. — London : Heinemann for the Overseas Students Trust, 1981. — xviii,301p ; 22cm
Bibliography: p292-294. - Includes index
ISBN 0-435-83485-1 (pbk) : £6.50 B81-23374

338.4'737873 — United States. Universities. Administration. Economic aspects

Garvin, David A.. The economics of university behavior / David A. Garvin. — New York ; London : Academic Press, 1980. — xv,176p : ill ; 24cm
Bibliography: p162-168. — Includes index
ISBN 0-12-276550-8 : £9.80 B81-21844

338.4'755382 — Diamonds industries & trades

Green, Timothy. The world of diamonds / Timothy Green. — London : Weidenfeld and Nicolson, c1981. — vi,261p : 1map ; 23cm
Bibliography: p253. - Includes index
ISBN 0-297-77926-5 : £7.95 B81-22442

338.4'76'0973 — United States. Technological development. Economic aspects
Ramo, Simon. America's technology slip / Simon Ramo. — New York ; Chichester : Wiley, c1980. — vi,297p ; 24cm
Includes index
ISBN 0-471-05976-5 : £8.00 B81-02418

338.4'761231'0973 — United States. Rural regions. Electricity supply industries, *to 1944*
Brown, D. Clayton. Electricity for rural America : the fight for the REA / D. Clayton Brown. — Westport, Conn. ; London : Greenwood Press, 1980. — xvi,178p ; 22cm. — (Contributions in economics and economic history ; no.29)
Bibliography: p153-169. - Includes index
ISBN 0-313-21478-6 : Unpriced B81-05342

338.4'76151'0941 — Great Britain. Pharmaceutical industries, *1950-1979*
The **Pharmaceutical** industry and the nation's health : the lengthening lifeline. — 10th ed. — London (162 Regent St., W1R 6DD) : The Association of the British Pharmaceutical Industry, 1980. — 46p : col.ill ; 21x10cm
Cover title. — Previous ed.: 1978
Unpriced (pbk) B81-03597

338.4'76151'0941 — Great Britain. Pharmaceutical industries — *Statistics — Serials*
Report on the census of production. Pharmaceutical chemicals and preparations / Department of Industry, Business Statistics Office. — 1978. — London : H.M.S.O., c1980. — 13p in various pagings. — (Business monitor ; PA272)
ISBN 0-11-513067-5 : £2.00 B81-20406

338.4'76177'005 — Ophthalmic industries — *Serials*
International optical year book and diary. — 77th ed. (1981). — London : IPC Consumer Industries Press, c1980. — 352,[110]p
ISBN 0-617-00341-6 : £15.00 B81-03498

338.4'762'00028 — Great Britain. Industrial equipment industries — *Directories — Serials*
Kompass register industrial section. 39, Scientific and industrial instruments. — 1981/82. — East Grinstead : Kompass, c1981. — 243p in various pagings
Cover title: Euro Kompass United Kingdom. Scientific and industrial instruments
ISBN 0-900505-90-7 : Unpriced
ISSN 0260-7263 B81-32242

338.4'762'00028 — Great Britain. Industrial equipment industries — *Statistics — Serials*
Report on the census of production. Industrial (including process) plant and steelwork / Department of Industry, Business Statistics Office. — 1978. — London : H.M.S.O., c1980. — 13p in various paging. — (Business monitor ; PA 341)
ISBN 0-11-513094-2 : £2.00 B81-11767

Report on the census of production. Scientific and industrial instruments and systems / Department of Industry, Business Statistics Office. — 1978. — London : H.M.S.O., c1980. — 13p in various pagings. — (Business monitor ; PA354)
ISBN 0-11-513138-8 : £2.00
Primary classification 338.4'768175'0941
B81-05000

338.4'762'00028
Kompass register industrial section. 39. Scientific and industrial instruments : an extract from the Kompass register of British industry & commerce. — 1980/81-. — East Grinstead : Kompass, 1980-. — v. : ill ; 30cm
Annual. — Introduction in English, text also in French, German, Spanish and Italian
Unpriced
Primary classification 338.7'68175'0251
B81-05929

338.4'762'0005 — Engineering equipment industries — *Serials*
Plant & works engineering. — No.1 (Feb. 1981)-. — East Molesey (3 Spencer Rd, East Molesey, Surrey KT8 0SP) : Industrial Trade Journals, 1981-. — v. : ill,ports ; 42cm
Monthly
ISSN 0262-0227 = Plant & works engineering : £18.00 per year B81-38997

338.4'7620106'0941 — Great Britain. Fluid power equipment industries — *Statistics — Serials*
Report on the census of production. Compressors and fluid power equipment / Department of Industry, Business Statistics Office. — 1978. — London : H.M.S.O., c1980. — 15p. in various pagings. — (Business monitor ; PA333.3)
ISBN 0-11-513135-3 : £2.00
Also classified at 338.4'762151'0941
B81-05047

338.4'7621'0941 — Great Britain. Mechanical engineering industries — *Statistics — Serials*
Report on the census of production. Precision chains and other mechanical engineering / Department of Industry, Business Statistics Office. — 1978. — London : H.M.S.O., c1980. — 13p in various pagings. — (Business monitor ; PA349.2)
ISBN 0-11-513131-0 : £2.00 B81-08784

Report on the census of production. Precision chains and other mechanical engineering / Department of Industry, Business Statistics Office. — 1979. — London : H.M.S.O., c1981. — 13p in various pagings. — (Business monitor ; PA349.2)
ISBN 0-11-513365-8 : £2.50 B81-32234

338.4'76213'0941 — Great Britain. Electrical engineering industries. Effects of imports of electric equipment from developing countries
Cable, Vincent. British electronics and competition with newly industrialising countries / Vincent Cable and Jeremy Clarke. — London : Overseas Development Institute, c1981. — v,125p ; 21cm
ISBN 0-85003-076-5 (pbk) : £2.50 B81-30082

338.4'762131'04202541 — Great Britain. Electric equipment industries — *Directories — Serials*
Kompass register industrial section. 37, Electrical and electronic equipment. — 1980/81. — East Grinstead : Kompass, c1980. — 454p in various pagings
Unpriced
Also classified at 338.4'7621381'02541
B81-03587

338.4'762131042'06041 — Great Britain. Electric equipment industries. Organisations: British Electrical and Allied Manufacturers' Association — *Directories — Serials*
British Electrical and Allied Manufacturers' Association. BEAMA handbook. — 1980-1981. — London (8 Leicester St., WC2H 7BN) : British Electrical and Allied Manufacturers' Association, c1980. — 58p
ISSN 0404-5386 : £2.50 B81-20068

338.4'762131042'0941 — Great Britain. Electric machinery industries — *Statistics — Serials*
Report on the census of production. Electrical machinery / Department of Industry, Business Statistics Office. — 1979. — London : H.M.S.O., c1981. — 13p in various pagings. — (Business monitor ; PA361)
ISBN 0-11-513409-3 : £2.50 B81-36308

338.4'762131'0941 — Great Britain. Electricity supply industries. Efficiency. Evaluation — *Proposals*
Performance indicators in the electricity supply industry / Electricity Consumers' Council. — London (119 Marylebone Rd., NW1 5PY) : The Council, 1980. — 16p ; 30cm. — (Discussion paper / Electricity Consumers' Council ; 6)
Unpriced (pbk) B81-34745

338.4'762131'0941 — Great Britain. Electricity supply industries. Services for blind persons
Electricity Board services for blind consumers / Electricity Consumers' Council. — London (119 Marylebone Rd., NW1 5PY) : The Council, 1980. — 6p ; 30cm. — (Discussion paper / Electricity Consumers' Council ; 5)
Unpriced (pbk) B81-34749

338.4'762131'0941 — Great Britain. Electricity supply industries — *Statistics — Serials*
Report on the census of production. Electricity / Department of Industry, Business Statistics Office. — 1979. — London : H.M.S.O., c1981. — 7,vp. — (Business monitor ; PA602)
ISBN 0-11-513298-8 : £2.50 B81-29649

338.4'762131'0942 — England. Electricity supply industries. Consumer protection services: Electricity Consumers' Council — *Serials*
Electricity Consumers' Council. Annual report / Electricity Consumers' Council. — 1979-. — London (119 Marylebone Rd, NW1 5PY) : The Council, [1980]-. — v. ; 21cm
Description based on: 1980 issue
ISSN 0261-2127 = Annual report — Electricity Consumers' Council : Unpriced
B81-23495

338.4'762131'09428 — North-east England. Electricity supply industries. Consumer protection services: North Eastern Electricity Consultative Council — *Serials*
North Eastern Electricity Consultative Council. Report of the North Eastern Electricity Consultative Council for the year ended 31 March .... — 1980. — [Newcastle upon Tyne] ([Bamburgh House, Market St., Newcastle upon Tyne NE1 6JD]) : The Council, [1980]. — 26p
ISSN 0141-9439 : Unpriced B81-20025

North Eastern Electricity Consultative Council. Report of the North Eastern Electricity Consultative Council for the year ended 31st March .... — 1979. — [Newcastle upon Tyne] ([Bamburgh House, Market St., Newcastle upon Tyne NE1 6JD]) : The Council, [1979]. — 24p
ISSN 0141-9439 : Unpriced B81-20026

338.4'762131225'0973 — United States. Electricity generation industries. Use of nuclear power. Social aspects
Shrader-Frechette, K. S.. Nuclear power and public policy : the social and ethical problems of fission technology / by K.S. Shrader-Frechette. — Dordrecht ; London : Reidel, c1980. — xvi,176p ; 23cm
Includes index
ISBN 90-277-1054-6 (cased) : Unpriced
ISBN 90-277-1080-5 (pbk) : Unpriced
B81-08327

338.4'762131242'0941 — Great Britain. Battery industries — *Statistics — Serials*
Report on the census of production. Primary and secondary batteries / Department of Industry, Business Statistics Office. — 1978. — London : H.M.S.O., c1980. — 13p in various pagings. — (Business monitor ; PA369.2)
ISBN 0-11-513099-3 : £2.00 B81-01803

338.4'762131244 — Solar energy. Conversion. Use of hydrogen. Economic aspects
Bockris, J. O'M. Energy options : real economics and the solar-hydrogen system / J.O'M. Bockris. — London : Taylor & Francis, 1980. — xvii,441p : ill,2maps ; 25cm
Includes index
ISBN 0-85066-204-4 : £15.00 : CIP rev.
B80-25335

338.4'7621313'05 — Electricity generation equipment industries & trades — *Serials*
European power news. — No.1 (Jan./Feb.1981)-. — Redhill (Queensway House, Queensway, Redhill, Surrey RH1 1QS) : Fuel and Metallurgical Journals, 1981-. — v. : ill ; 40cm
Six issues yearly. — Continues: Power generation industrial
ISSN 0261-8214 = European power news : £14.00 per year B81-36302

338.4'7621322'0941 — Great Britain. Electric industries lighting — *Statistics — Serials*
Report on the census of production. Electric lamps, electric light fittings, wiring acces[s] ories, etc. / Department of Industry, Business Statistics Office. — 1978. — London : H.M.S.O., c1980. — 13p in various pagings. — (Business monitor ; PA369.4)
ISBN 0-11-513165-5 : £2.00 B81-08778

338.4'7621322'0941 — Great Britain. Electric lighting industries — *Statistics — Serials*
Report on the census of production. Electric lamps, electric light fittings, wiring accessories, etc. / Department of Industry, Business Statistics Office. — 1979. — London : H.M.S.O., c1981. — 13p. in various pagings. — (Business monitor ; PA369.4)
ISBN 0-11-513321-6 : £2.50 B81-32649

338.4′762138′0941 — Great Britain. Telecommunication equipment industries — *Statistics*

Lawson, Gary. Employment and training in the telecommunications equipment manufacturing industry / Gary Lawson. — Watford : Engineering Industry Training Board, c1980. — 53p : ill ; 30cm. — (EITB reference paper ; RP1/80)
ISBN 0-85083-508-9 (spiral) : Unpriced
B81-21128

338.4′7621381 — Electronics industries — *Conference proceedings*

World Electronic — Strategies for Success *(Conference : 1980 : Monte Carlo).* World Electronics — Strategies for Success : Monte Carlo, May 5-7, 1980 : Speakers′ papers / sponsors Financial Times, Mackintosh International. — London (Minster House, Arthur St., EC4R 9AX) : Financial Times Conference Organisation, [1980?]. — 176p : ill ; 30cm
Unpriced (unbound) B81-37968

338.4′7621381′02541 — Great Britain. Electronic equipment industries — *Directories* — *Serials*

Kompass register industrial section. 37, Electrical and electronic equipment. — 1980/81. — East Grinstead : Kompass, c1980. — 454p in various pagings
Unpriced
Primary classification 338.4′762131′04202541
B81-03587

338.4′7621381′094 — Europe. Electronic equipment industries — *Serials*

European electronics. — 1/81-. — München : Europa-Fachpresse ; London (109 Waterloo Rd, SE1 8UL) : Business Publications, 1981-. — v. : ill,ports ; 28cm
Six issues yearly
£12.00 per year B81-38994

338.4′7621381′0941 — Great Britain. Electronic equipment industries — *Statistics* — *Serials*

Report on the census of production. Radio, radar and electronic capital goods / Department of Industry, Business Statistics Office. — 1978. — London : H.M.S.O., c1980. — 13p in various pagings. — (Business monitor ; PA367)
ISBN 0-11-513161-2 : £2.00 B81-05360

Report on the census of production. Radio, radar and electronic capital goods / Department of Industry, Business Statistics Office. — 1979. — London : H.M.S.O., 1981. — 13p in various pagings. — (Business monitor ; PA367)
ISBN 0-11-513398-4 : £2.50 B81-35974

338.4′7621381′0941 — Great Britain. Household electronic equipment industries & trades — *Statistics* — *Serials* — *For marketing*

Home entertainment : U.K. consumer electronics markets. — 1980-. — London : Euromonitor, 1980-. — v. ; 30cm
Irregular
ISSN 0260-6534 = Home entertainment : £75.00 B81-06690

338.4′762138151′0941 — Great Britain. Electronic components industries — *Statistics* — *Serials*

Report on the census of production. Radio and electronic components / Department of Industry, Business Statistics Office. — 1978. — London : H.M.S.O., c1980. — 13p in various pagings. — (Business monitor ; PA364)
ISBN 0-11-513120-5 : £2.00 B81-01804

338.4′762138152′0973 — United States. Semiconductor industries

Watson, Robert W.. Innovation, competition, and government policy in the semiconductor industry / Robert W. Wilson, Peter K. Ashton, Thomas P. Egan. — Lexington, Mass. : Lexington Books, c1980 ; [Farnborough, Hants] : Gower [distributor], 1981. — xv,219p : ill ; 24cm. — (A Charles River Associates research study)
Bibliography: p199-206. — Includes index
ISBN 0-669-03995-0 : £14.00 B81-29606

338.4′76213817′094 — European Community countries. Microelectronic industries. Policies of European Economic Community — *European Democratic Group viewpoints*

Micro-electronics : can Europe switch on? / [European Democratic Group]. — London : The Group, c1981. — 47p ; 21cm
Unpriced (pbk) B81-29502

338.4′762138195′0941 — Great Britain. Computer industries — *Statistics* — *Serials*

Report on the census of production. Electronic computers / Department of Industry, Business Statistics Office. — 1978. — London : H.M.S.O., c1980. — 13p in various pagings. — (Business monitor ; PA366)
ISBN 0-11-513117-5 : £2.00 B81-04973

Report on the census of production. Electronic computers / Department of Industry, Business Statistics Office. — 1979. — London : H.M.S.O., c1981. — 13p. in various pagings. — (Business monitor ; PA366)
ISBN 0-11-513360-7 : £2.50 B81-32673

338.4′7621382′0941 — Great Britain. Telegraph equipment industries — *Statistics* — *Serials*

Report on the census of production. Telegraph and telephone apparatus and equipment / Department of Industry, Business Statistics Office. — 1978. — London : H.M.S.O., c1980. — 13p in various pagings. — (Business monitor ; PA363)
ISBN 0-11-513156-6 : £2.00
Also classified at 338.4′7621385′0941
B81-05364

338.4′7621385′0941 — Great Britain. Telephone equipment industries — *Statistics* — *Serials*

Report on the census of production. Telegraph and telephone apparatus and equipment / Department of Industry, Business Statistics Office. — 1978. — London : H.M.S.O., c1980. — 13p in various pagings. — (Business monitor ; PA363)
ISBN 0-11-513156-6 : £2.00
Primary classification 338.4′7621382′0941
B81-05364

338.4′7621388′0098312 — Developing countries. Industries. Decentralisation. Effects of import substitution — *Study regions: Chile. Arica* — *Study examples: Television equipment industries, 1962-1974*

Gwynne, R. N.. Import substitution and the decentralisation of industry in less developed countries : the television industry in Chile, 1962-1974 / R. N. Gwynne. — [Birmingham] : [Department of Geography, University of Birmingham], 1980. — 30p ; 30cm. — (Occasional publication / Department of Geography, University of Birmingham ; no.12)
Bibliography: p30
ISBN 0-7044-0400-1 (pbk) : £1.00 B81-39707

338.4′762138932 — Great Britain. Sound disc & pre-recorded tape recordings industries — *Statistics* — *Serials*

Report on the census of production. Gramophone records and tape recordings / Department of Industry, Business Statistics Office. — 1978. — London : H.M.S.O., c1980. — 13p. in various pagings. — (Business monitor ; PA363.1)
ISBN 0-11-513163-9 : £2.00 B81-05345

Report on the census of production. Gramophone records and tape recordings / Department of Industry, Business Statistics Office. — 1979. — London : H.M.S.O., c1981. — 13p in various pagings. — (Business monitor ; PA365.1)
ISBN 0-11-513371-2 : £2.50 B81-34030

338.4′76214′00941 — Great Britain. Industrial engines industries — *Statistics* — *Serials*

Report on the census of production. Industrial engines / Department of Industry, Business Statistics Office. — 1978. — London : H.M.S.O., c1980. — 13p in various pagings. — (Business monitor ; PA334)
ISBN 0-11-513084-5 : £2.00 B81-04408

Report on the census of production. Industrial engines / Department of Industry, Business Statistics Office. — 1979. — London : H.M.S.O., c1981. — 13p in various pagings. — (Business monitor ; PA334)
ISBN 0-11-513352-6 : £2.50 B81-32223

338.4′762147′0973 — United States. Solar energy. Economic aspects

Feldman, Stephen L.. On the economics of solar energy : the public-utility interface / Stephen L. Feldman, Robert M. Wirtshafter. — Lexington, Mass. : Lexington ; [Farnborough, Hants] : Gower [distributor], 1981, c1980. — xi,256p : ill ; 24cm
Bibliography: p239-256
ISBN 0-669-03449-5 : £16.50 B81-05504

338.4′76214834 — Fast breeder reactors. Socioeconomic aspects — *Conference proceedings*

The Fast breeder reactor : need? cost? risk? / edited by Colin Sweet. — London : Macmillan, 1980. — viii,232p : ill,1map ; 24cm
Conference papers. — Includes index
ISBN 0-333-27973-5 : £20.00 : CIP rev.
B80-09620

338.4′762151′0941 — Great Britain. Compressors industries — *Statistics* — *Serials*

Report on the census of production. Compressors and fluid power equipment / Department of Industry, Business Statistics Office. — 1978. — London : H.M.S.O., c1980. — 15p. in various pagings. — (Business monitor ; PA333.3)
ISBN 0-11-513135-3 : £2.00
Primary classification 338.4′7620106′0941
B81-05047

338.4′762156′0941 — Great Britain. Refrigeration equipment industries — *Statistics* — *Serials*

Report on the census of production. Refrigerating machinery, space-heating, ventilating and air-conditioning equipment / Department of Industry, Business Statistics Office. — 1978. — London : H.M.S.O., c1980. — 13p in various pagings. — (Business monitor ; PA339.3)
ISBN 0-11-513137-x : £2.00
Also classified at 338.4′7697′000941
B81-05373

338.4′762157 — Temperature controlled storage services — *Directories* — *Serials*

TCS & D directory : temperature controlled storage & distribution. — 1st ed.-. — Redhill (2 Queensway, Redhill, Surrey RH1 1QS) : Retail Journals, [1980]-. — v. : ill ; 30cm
Issued every two years
ISSN 0260-9932 = TCS & D directory : £35.00
Primary classification 380.5′24 B81-11227

338.4′762158 — Ice industries & trades — *Conference proceedings*

Ice carrying trade at sea : the proceedings of a symposium held at the National Maritime Museum on 8 September 1979 / edited by D.V. Proctor. — London : Trustees of the National Maritime Museum, 1981. — iv,55p : ill,maps,1facsim ; 30cm. — (Maritime monographs and reports, ISSN 0307-8590 ; no.49)
Bibliography: p50
ISBN 0-905555-48-1 (pbk) : £4.15 B81-17626

338.4′76216′0941 — Great Britain. Pumps industries — *Statistics* — *Serials*

Report on the census of production. Pumps / Department of Industry, Business Statistics Office. — 1978. — London : H.M.S.O., c1980. — 15p in various pagings. — (Business monitor ; PA333.1)
ISBN 0-11-513144-2 : £2.00 B81-05369

338.4′7621822′0941 — Great Britain. Bearings industries — *Statistics* — *Serials*

Report on the census of production. Ball, roller, plain and other bearings / Department of Industry, Business Statistics Office. — 1978. — London : H.M.S.O., c1980. — 13p in various pagings. — (Business monitor ; PA349.1)
ISBN 0-11-513143-4 : £2.00 B81-04998

Report on the census of production. Ball, roller, plain and other bearings / Department of Industry, Business Statistics Office. — 1979. — London : H.M.S.O., c1981. — 13p. in various pagings. — (Business monitor ; PA349.1)
ISBN 0-11-513344-5 : £2.50 B81-32677

338.4′762184 — Great Britain. Valves industries — *Statistics — Serials*
Report on the census of production. Valves / Department of Industry, Business Statistics Office. — 1978. — London : H.M.S.O., c1980. — 15p in various pagings. — (Business monitor ; PA333.2)
ISBN 0-11-513152-3 : £2.50 B81-05365

Report on the census of production. Valves / Department of Industry, Business Statistics Office. — 1979. — London : H.M.S.O., c1981. — 13p in various pagings. — (Business monitor ; PA333.2)
ISBN 0-11-513401-8 : £2.50 B81-36312

338.4′762186′0941 — Great Britain. Mechanical handling equipment industries — *Statistics — Serials*
Report on the census of production. Mechanical handling equipment / Department of Industry, Business Statistics Office. — 1978. — London : H.M.S.O., c1980. — 13p in various pagings. — (Business monitor ; PA337)
ISBN 0-11-513150-7 : £2.00 B81-04975

338.4′76219′00941 — Great Britain. Small manufacturing tools industries — *Statistics — Serials*
Report on the census of production. Engineers′ small tools and gauges / Department of Industry, Business Statistics Office. — 1978. — London : H.M.S.O., c1980. — 13p in various pagings. — (Business monitor ; PA390)
ISBN 0-11-513093-4 : £2.00 B81-07392

Report on the census of production. Engineers′ small tools and gauges / Department of Industry, Business Statistics Office. — 1979. — London : H.M.S.O., c1981. — 13p. in various pagings. — (Business monitor ; PA390)
ISBN 0-11-513340-2 : £2.50 B81-32906

338.4′7621902′0604 — Western Europe. Machine tools industries & trades. Organisations: Association of European Machine Tool Merchants — *Directories — Serials*
Association of European Machine Tool Merchants. Directory / Association of European Machine Tool Merchants. — 1981. — Watford (70 St Albans Rd, Watford, Herts. WD1 1DY) : The Association, [1981]. — 68p
Unpriced B81-28380

338.4′7621902′0941 — Great Britain. Portable power tools industries — *Statistics — Serials*
Report on the census of production. Scales and weighing machinery and portable power tools / Department of Industry, Business Statistics Office. — 1978. — London : H.M.S.O., c1980. — 13p in various pagings. — (Business monitor ; PA339.5)
ISBN 0-11-513110-8 : £2.00
Primary classification 338.4′76812 B81-05359

338.4′7621908′0941 — Great Britain. Hand tools industries — *Statistics — Serials*
Report on the census of production. Hand tools and implements / Department of Industry, Business Statistics Office. — 1978. — London : H.M.S.O., c1980. — 13p in various paging. — (Business monitor ; PA391)
ISBN 0-11-513087-x : £2.00 B81-11768

Report on the census of production. Hand tools and implements / Department of Industry, Business Statistics Office. — 1979. — London : H.M.S.O., c1981. — 13p in various pagings. — (Business monitor ; PA391)
ISBN 0-11-513329-1 : £2.50 B81-30733

338.4′762192 — Great Britain. Abrasive equipment industries — *Statistics — Serials*
Report on the census of production. Abrasives / Department of Industry, Business Statistics Office. — 1978. — London : H.M.S.O., c1980. — 13p in various pagings. — (Business monitor ; PA469.1)
ISBN 0-11-513157-4 : £2.00 B81-05370

Report on the census of production. Abrasives / Department of Industry, Business Statistics Office. — 1979. — London : H.M.S.O., c1981. — 13p. in various pagings. — (Business monitor ; PA469.1)
ISBN 0-11-513317-8 : £2.50 B81-32658

338.4′7622′028 — Great Britain. Mining machinery industries — *Statistics — Serials*
Report on the census of production. Mining machinery / Department of Industry, Business Statistics Office. — 1978. — London : H.M.S.O., c1980. — 13p in various pagings. — (Business monitor ; PA339.1)
ISBN 0-11-513160-4 : £2.00 B81-05368

Report on the census of production. Mining machinery / Department of Industry, Business Statistics Office. — 1979. — London : H.M.S.O., c1981. — 8,vp. — (Business monitor ; PA339.1)
ISBN 0-11-513295-3 : £2.50 B81-29646

338.4′7′623 — Military equipment industries
Tuomi, Helen. Transnational corporations, armaments and development. — Aldershot : Gower, Feb.1982. — [328]p
Originally published: Tampere : Tampere Peace Research Institute, 1980
ISBN 0-566-00506-9 : £12.50 : CIP entry B81-36217

338.4′76234′0941 — Great Britain. Armaments industries — *Statistics — Serials*
Report on the census of production. Ordnance and small arms / Department of Industry, Business Statistics Office. — 1978. — London : H.M.S.O., c1980. — 13p in various pagings. — (Business monitor ; PA342)
ISBN 0-11-513088-8 : £2.00 B81-01795

338.4′76234′0973 — United States. Armaments industries
Gansler, Jacques S.. The defense industry / Jacques S. Gansler. — Cambridge, Mass. ; London : MIT, c1980. — 346p : ill ; 24cm
Bibliography: p321-330. - Includes index
ISBN 0-262-07078-2 : £12.40 B81-04563

338.4′762382′00941 — Great Britain. Boatbuilding industries & boat trades — *Serials*
[Boating business *(London)***].** Boating business. — Jan.1981-. — London : Carlton Communications, 1981-. — v. : ill,ports ; 30cm
Monthly
ISSN 0260-9452 = Boating business (London) : £12.00 per year B81-14369

338.4′762382′00941 — Great Britain. Shipbuilding industries, *ca 1850-1980*
Walter, Fred M.. Steel ship building / Fred M. Walker. — Princes Risborough : Shire, 1981. — 32p : ill,1plan ; 21cm. — (Shire album ; 73)
Bibliography: p32
ISBN 0-85263-569-9 (pbk) : £0.95 B81-40864

338.4′762382′00941 — Great Britain. Shipbuilding industries — *Statistics — Serials*
Report on the census of production. Shipbuilding and marine engineering / Department of Industry, Business Statistics Office. — 1978. — London : H.M.S.O., c1980. — 13p in various pagings. — (Business monitor ; PA370)
ISBN 0-11-513127-2 : £2.00
Also classified at 338.4′762387′0941 B81-05001

Report on the census of production. Shipbuilding and marine engineering / Department of Industry, Business Statistics Office. — 1979. — London : H.M.S.O., c1981. — 13p. in various pagings. — (Business monitor ; PA370)
ISBN 0-11-513338-0 : £2.50
Also classified at 338.4′762387′0941 B81-32653

338.4′762382′00942276 — Hampshire. Southampton. Shipbuilding industries, *1837-1901*
Rance, Adrian B.. Shipbuilding in Victorian Southampton / by Adrian B. Rance. — Southampton : Southampton University Industrial Archaeology Group, 1981. — 68p : ill,maps,plans,ports ; 30cm
Text and map on inside covers
ISBN 0-905280-02-4 (pbk) : £1.80 B81-33595

338.4′762387′0941 — Great Britain. Marine engineering industries — *Statistics — Serials*
Report on the census of production. Shipbuilding and marine engineering / Department of Industry, Business Statistics Office. — 1978. — London : H.M.S.O., c1980. — 13p in various pagings. — (Business monitor ; PA370)
ISBN 0-11-513127-2 : £2.00
Primary classification 338.4′762382′00941 B81-05001

Report on the census of production. Shipbuilding and marine engineering / Department of Industry, Business Statistics Office. — 1979. — London : H.M.S.O., c1981. — 13p. in various pagings. — (Business monitor ; PA370)
ISBN 0-11-513338-0 : £2.50
Primary classification 338.4′762382′00941 B81-32653

338.4′7624 — Construction industries. Ergonomic aspects
Human factors/ergonomics for building and construction / edited by Martin Helander. — New York ; Chichester : Wiley, c1981. — xvi,361p : ill ; 24cm. — (Construction management and engineering)
Includes bibliographies and index
ISBN 0-471-05075-x : £24.10 B81-28306

338.4′7624′028 — Great Britain. Construction equipment industries — *Statistics — Serials*
Report on the census of production. Construction and earth-moving equipment / Department of Industry, Business Statistics Office. — 1979. — London : H.M.S.O., c1981. — 8,vp. — (Business monitor ; PA336)
ISBN 0-11-513296-1 : £2.50
Also classified at 338.4′7629225 B81-29652

338.4′7624′0941 — Great Britain. Construction industries
British construction companies / industry commentary by Andrew Melrose. — London : Jordan & Sons (Surveys) Ltd, 1980. — 75p ; 30cm. — (A Jordan Survey)
ISBN 0-85938-140-4 (pbk) : £70.00 B81-11762

338.4′7624′0941 — Great Britain. Construction industries — *Serials*
House′s guide to the regulations, recommendations, and statutory and advisory bodies of the construction industry. — 8th ed. (1981-82). — London (1 Cresswell Park SE3 9RG) : House Information Services, c1981. — 299,48p
ISBN 0-903716-17-8 : £25.00
ISSN 0142-7415 B81-20724

338.4′7624′0941 — Great Britain. Construction industries — *Statistics — Serials*
[Housing and construction statistics *(Annual volume)***].** Housing and construction statistics / Department of the Environment, Scottish Development Department, Welsh Office. — 1969-1979-. — London : H.M.S.O., 1980-. — v. ; 30cm
Complements: Housing and construction statistics (Quarterly)
ISSN 0260-7719 = Housing and construction statistics (Annual volume) : £14.00
Primary classification 363.5′0941 B81-11757

338.4′7624′09417 — Ireland *(Republic).* **Construction industries** — *Statistics — Serials*
Construction industry statistics. — 1980. — Dublin (St. Martins House, Waterloo Rd, Dublin 4) : An Foras Forbartha, 1980. — ix,76p
ISBN 0-906120-36-5 : Unpriced B81-24994

338.4′76252′0941 — Great Britain. Rolling stock manufacturing industries — *Statistics — Serials*
Report on the census of production. Locomotives, railway track equipment, railway carriages, wagons and trams / Department of Industry, Business Statistics Office. — 1978. — London : H.M.S.O., c1980. — 13p in various pagings. — (Business monitor ; PA384)
ISBN 0-11-513136-1 : £2.00 B81-08782

Report on the census of production. Locomotives, railway track equipment, railway carriages, wagons and trams / Department of Industry, Business Statistics Office. — 1979. — London : H.M.S.O., c1981. — 8,vp. — (Business monitor ; PA384)
ISBN 0-11-513300-3 : £2.50 B81-29647

338.4'762773'09422323 — Kent. Medway River. Dredging industries, *to 1978*

Coombe, Derek. The Bawleymen : fishermen and dredgermen of the River Medway / Derek Coombe with chapters by Leslie H. Hill and Leonard J. Wadhams. — Rainham (33 Broadview Ave., Rainham, Kent, ME8 9DB) : Pennant, 1979. — 112p,[32]p of plates : ill,1map,ports ; 24cm
Bibliography: p103-104. - Includes index
ISBN 0-9506413-0-8 : £4.95
Primary classification 338.3'727'09422323
B81-03669

338.4'7628 — Great Britain. Water industries

The **Structure** and management of the British water industry / editor Bernard Dangerfield. — London : The Institution of Water Engineers and Scientists, 1979. — xiii,255p : ill,maps ; 22cm. — (Water practice manuals ; 1)
Includes index
ISBN 0-901427-07-1 : Unpriced B81-37331

338.4'76281'02541 — Great Britain. Water supply industries — *Directories* — *Serials*

Water services yearbook. — 1981-. — Redhill (Queensway House, 2 Queensway, Redhill, Surrey RH1 1QS) : Fuel & Metallurgical Journals, [1980]-. — v. : ill ; 30cm
Continues: Water services yearbook
ISSN 0140-1742 = Water services yearbook : £14.50 B81-03293

338.4'76281'0941 — Great Britain. Water supply industries — *Statistics* — *Serials*

Report on the census of production. Water supply / Department of Industry, Business Statistics Office. — 1978. — London : H.M.S.O., c1980. — 13p in various pagings. — (Business monitor ; PA603)
ISBN 0-11-513111-6 : £2.00 B81-05363

Report on the census of production. Water supply / Department of Industry, Business Statistics Office. — 1979. — London : H.M.S.O., c1981. — 13p in various pagings. — (Business monitor ; PA603)
ISBN 0-11-513347-x : £2.50 B81-32228

338.4'76291'0941 — Great Britain. Aerospace engineering industries — *Statistics* — *Serials*

Report on the census of production. Aerospace equipment, manufacturing and repairing / Department of Industry, Business Statistics Office. — 1978. — London : H.M.S.O., c1980. — 13p in various pagings. — (Business monitor ; PA383)
ISBN 0-11-513082-9 : £2.00 B81-08349

Report on the census of production. Aerospace equipment, manufacturing and repairing / Department of Industry, Business Statistics Office. — 1979. — London : H.M.S.O., c1981. — 13p in various pagings. — (Business monitor ; PA383)
ISBN 0-11-513310-0 : £2.50 B81-31019

338.4'76291'3009422145 — Surrey. Weybridge. Brooklands. Aircraft industries, *1910-1980*

Johnson, Howard. Wings over Brooklands. — Weybridge (The Oil Mills, Weybridge, Surrey) : Whittet Books, Oct.1981. — [160]p
ISBN 0-905483-20-0 (cased) : £8.95 : CIP entry
ISBN 0-905483-21-9 (pbk) : £4.95
Also classified at 629.13'009422'145
B81-27990

338.4'76291343 — Great Britain. Aircraft accessories industries — *Statistics* — *Serials*

Report on the census of production. Equipment for motor vehicles, cycles and aircraft / Department of Industry, Business Statistics Office. — 1978-. — London : H.M.S.O., 1980-. — v. ; 30cm. — (Business monitor ; PA369.1)
Continues: Report on the census of production. Electrical equipment for motor vehicles, cycles and aircraft
ISSN 0260-7301 = Report on the census of production. Equipment for motor vehicles, cycles and aircraft : £2.00
Primary classification 338.4'76292 B81-05352

338.4'7629136'02541 — Great Britain. Civil airport equipment industries — *Directories* — *Serials*

British airport equipment catalogue. — 1st ed. (1980)-. — Farnborough (PO Box 4, Farnborough, Hampshire GU14 7LR) : Combined Service Publications, 1980-. — v. : ill ; 31cm
Annual. — English text with foreword and introduction in English, French, German, Spanish and Italian
ISSN 0260-4507 = British airport equipment catalogue : £35.00 B81-04592

338.4'76292 — Great Britain. Motor vehicle accessories & components industries & trades — *Serials*

Car parts & accessories : including the motorcycle aftermarket. — Vol.1, issue 1 (Oct. 1980)-. — Croydon (Faversham House, 111 St. James's Rd, Croydon, Surrey CR9 2TH) : Automedia, 1980-. — v. : ill ; 43cm
Monthly
ISSN 0144-8250 = Car parts & accessories : £14.00 per year B81-04547

338.4'76292 — Great Britain. Motor vehicle accessories industries — *Statistics* — *Serials*

Report on the census of production. Equipment for motor vehicles, cycles and aircraft / Department of Industry, Business Statistics Office. — 1978-. — London : H.M.S.O., 1980-. — v. ; 30cm. — (Business monitor ; PA369.1)
Continues: Report on the census of production. Electrical equipment for motor vehicles, cycles and aircraft
ISSN 0260-7301 = Report on the census of production. Equipment for motor vehicles, cycles and aircraft : £2.00
Also classified at 338.4'76291343 B81-05352

338.4'76292 — Great Britain. Motor vehicle components industries, *to 1980*

Ward, J. Scott. The changing face of the UK automotive components industry / by J. Scott Ward. — London : Economist Intelligence Unit, c1981. — 88p : ill(some col.) ; 30cm. — (EIU special report ; no.91)
Unpriced (pbk) B81-11326

338.4'76292'06041 — Great Britain. Motor vehicle industries & trades. Organisations — *Directories* — *Serials*

Society of Motor Manufacturers and Traders. List of members / the Society of Motor Manufacturers and Traders Limited. — 1980. — London : The Society, c1980. — vi,197p
Unpriced B81-06694

338.4'76292'0941 — Great Britain. Motor vehicle industries — *Statistics* — *Serials*

The **Motor** industry of Great Britain / the Society of Motor Manufacturers and Traders. — 1980. — London : The Society, [1980?]. — 276p
£22.00 (£12.00 to members) B81-04863

Report on the census of production. Motor vehicle manufacturing / Department of Industry, Business Statistics Office. — 1978. — London : H.M.S.O., c1980. — 13p in various pagings. — (Business monitor ; PA381.1)
ISBN 0-11-513090-x : £2.00 B81-12742

Report on the census of production. Motor vehicle manufacturing / Department of Industry, Business Statistics Office. — 1979. — London : H.M.S.O., c1981. — 13p. in various pagings. — (Business monitor ; PA381.1)
ISBN 0-11-513343-7 : £2.50 B81-32672

338.4'7629225 — Great Britain. Earth-moving machinery industries — *Statistics* — *Serials*

Report on the census of production. Construction and earth-moving equipment / Department of Industry, Business Statistics Office. — 1979. — London : H.M.S.O., c1981. — 8,vp. — (Business monitor ; PA336)
ISBN 0-11-513296-1 : £2.50
Primary classification 338.4'7624'028
B81-29652

338.4'7629226'0941 — Great Britain. Caravan & trailer industries — *Statistics* — *Serials*

Report on the census of production. Trailers, caravans and freight containers / Department of Industry, Business Statistics Office. — 1979. — London : H.M.S.O., c1981. — 13p in various pagings. — (Business monitor ; PA381.2)
ISBN 0-11-513319-4 : £2.50
Also classified at 338.4'76888 B81-31018

338.4'7629227'0941 — Great Britain. Motorcycle & bicycle industries — *Statistics* — *Serials*

Report on the census of production. Motor cycle, tricycle and pedal cycle manufacturing / Department of Industry, Business Statistics Office. — 1979. — London : H.M.S.O., c1981. — 13p in various pagings. — (Business monitor ; PA382)
ISBN 0-11-513316-x : £2.50 B81-31017

338.4'76292272'0941 — Great Britain. Bicycle industries & trades — *Statistics* — *For marketing*

U.K. bicycle market : market position report / G. Crow ... [et al.]. — Manchester (Booth St. West, Manchester M15 6PB) : Centre for Business Research in association with Manchester Business School, University of Manchester, [1981?]. — 55p : ill ; 30cm. — (Research report. Market position series / Centre for Business Research)
Unpriced (spiral) B81-27058

338.4'76292275'0941 — Great Britain. Motorcycle industries, *to 1980*

Hopwood, Bert. Whatever happened to the British motorcycle industry / Bert Hopwood. — Yeovil : Haynes, 1981. — 315p : ill,ports ; 24cm. — (A Foulis motorcycling book)
Includes index
ISBN 0-85429-241-1 : £8.95 B81-20914

338.4'7629282 — Great Britain. Private enterprise. Transfer of statutory testing of public service vehicles & heavy commercial vehicles. Proposals — *Inquiry reports*

Great Britain. *Parliament. House of Commons. Transport Committee*. Fourth report from the Transport Committee, session 1980-81 : the proposed transfer of HGV and PSV testing to the private sector : together with the proceedings of the Committee, minutes of evidence and appendices. — London : H.M.S.O., [1981]. — xxxiii,107p : 1map ; 25cm. — ([HC] ; 344)
Map on folded leaf on back cover
ISBN 0-10-234481-7 (pbk) : £5.70 B81-40609

338.4'762982 — Great Britain. Automatic vending industries & trades. Organisations: Automatic Vending Association of Britain — *Directories* — *Serials*

Automatic Vending Association of Britain. Handbook and list of members of the Automatic Vending Association of Britain. — January, 1980 ed. — Kingston-upon-Thames (50 Eden St., Kingston-upon-Thames, Surrey KT1 1EE) : The Association, [1980?]. — 114p
ISSN 0306-4204 : Unpriced B81-06696

Automatic Vending Association of Britain. Handbook and list of members of the Automatic Vending Association of Britain. — January, 1979 Golden Jubilee ed.. — Kingston-upon-Thames (50 Eden St., Kingston-upon-Thames, Surrey KT1 1EE) : The Association, [1979?]. — 129p
ISSN 0306-4204 : Unpriced B81-06697

Automatic Vending Association of Britain. Handbook and list of members of the Automatic Vending Association of Britain. — January, 1978 ed.. — Kingston-upon-Thames (50 Eden St., Kingston-upon-Thames, Surrey KT1 1EE) : The Association, [1978?]. — 114p
ISSN 0306-4204 : Unpriced B81-06698

Automatic Vending Association of Britain. Handbook and list of members of the Automatic Vending Association of Britain. — January, 1981 ed.. — Kingston-on-Thames (50 Eden St., Kingston-upon-Thames, Surrey KT1 1EE) : The Association, [1981]. — 112p
ISSN 0306-4204 : Unpriced B81-24153

338.4'7641'05 — Food & drinks industries & trades — *Forecasts — Serials*
World commodity outlook. Food, feedstuffs and beverages. — 1981. — London : Economist Intelligence Unit, 1980. — 110p
ISSN 0142-6117 : £30.00 B81-08761

338.4'7641'0941 — Great Britain. Food & drinks industries & trades — *Serials*
The **Food** and drink trade handbook. — 1981. — Farnborough (Federation House, 17 Farnborough St., Farnborough, Hants., GU14 8AG) : National Food and Drink Federation, [1980?]. — 88p
£7.50 B81-08760

338.4'7641'0941 — Great Britain. Food & drinks industries. Political aspects — *Serials*
Indigestion. — 1-5. — Oxford (35 Cowley Rd, Oxford) : Uhuru Collective, [197-]-1980. — 5v. : ill ; 33cm
Irregular. — Description based on: 5
Unpriced B81-17490

338.4'7641'09411 — Scotland. Food & drinks industries
Thomson, J. K.. The structure of Scottish agriculture and food industries / ... by J.K. Thomson. — Edinburgh : Scottish Council Research Institute, 1978. — 5,[6]leaves ; 31cm
£2.00 (spiral)
Primary classification 338.1'09411 B81-34342

338.4'76413'005 — Food industries & trades — *Serials*
Canadean world food report : incorporating Eurofood. — No.01 (9 Oct.1980)-. — London (60 Kingly St., W1R 5LH) : Agra-Canadean Publications, 1980-. — v. ; 30cm
Weekly. — Continues in part: Eurofood
£150.00 per year B81-05178

Food trades directory and food buyer's yearbook. — 1981-82. — London : Newman, [1981]. — viii,1051p
ISSN 0309-0264 : Unpriced B81-33326

338.4'76413'00941 — Great Britain. Food industries & trades
The **Food** distribution chain : an IGD Review : a report prepared by the Information Unit for the 1981 Annual Convention. — Watford (Letchmore Heath, Watford WD2 8DQ) : Institute of Grocery Distribution, c1981. — 52p : ill ; 30cm
Unpriced (pbk) B81-23170

338.4'76413'00941 — Great Britain. Food industries & trades — *Serials*
Good food : official journal of the Delicatessen and Fine Food Association. — Vol.3, no.2 (July/Aug.1980)-. — Staines (3 Fairfield Ave, Staines, Middlesex TW18 4AB) : DAFFA, 1980-. — v. : ill,ports ; 30cm
Six issues yearly. — Continues: Good foods. — Description based on: Vol.3, no.4 (Nov./Dec.1980)
ISSN 0261-2534 = Good food : £5.50 B81-21345

338.4'764672'05 — Beauty care industries & trades — *Serials*
Beauty salon : [the new quarterly for health and beauty therapists]. — Vol.1, no.1 (Autumn 1980)-. — London : IPC Consumer Industries Press, 1980-. — v. : ill ; 29cm
Description based on: Vol.1, no.3 (Spring 1981)
ISSN 0261-4146 = Beauty salon : £6.00 per year B81-34033

338.4'7647944101 — Great Britain. Hotel industries — *For careers guidance*
A **Guide** to careers information. — Wembley : HCITB, [1978?]. — 36p ; 21cm
Cover title. — Text on inside covers
Unpriced (pbk)
Also classified at 338.4'76479541 B81-33193

338.4'764794427801'05 — Cumbria. Lake District. Hotel industries — *Serials*
Lakeland catering and hotel year book. — 1981. — Carlisle (12, Lonsdale St., Carlisle) : Border Press Agency, [1980?]. — 24p
ISSN 0309-3999 : Unpriced
Also classified at 338.4'7647954278'05 B81-09024

338.4'764795'028 — Great Britain. Catering equipment industries & trades — *Statistics — Serials*
Catering equipment manufacturers & distributors. — 1st ed.-. — London : Inter Company Comparisons, 1979-. — v. ; 21x30cm. — (ICC financial survey)
Annual. — Description based on: 2nd ed.
ISSN 0261-5800 = ICC financial survey. Catering equipment manufacturers & distributors : £60.80 per year B81-33696

338.4'76479541 — Great Britain. Catering industries — *For careers guidance*
A **Guide** to careers information. — Wembley : HCITB, [1978?]. — 36p ; 21cm
Cover title. — Text on inside covers
Unpriced (pbk)
Primary classification 338.4'7647944101 B81-33193

338.4'76479541'0212 — Gret Britain. Catering industries — *Statistics — Serials*
Catering and allied trades / Business Statistics Office. — 1977. — London : H.M.S.O., c1981. — 64p. — (Business monitor ; SD029)
ISBN 0-11-512693-7 : £5.60 B81-20729

338.4'76479541'05 — Great Britain. Catering industries — *Serials*
Independent retailer and caterer. — Vol.15., no.1 (Jan. 1981)-. — London (5, Southwark St., SE1 1RQ) : William Reed, 1981-. — v. : ill ; 40cm
Monthly. — Continues: Cash & carry news
ISSN 0261-0833 = Independent retailer and caterer : £7.00 per year
Primary classification 381'.1'0941 B81-15446

338.4'7647954278'05 — Cumbria. Lake District. Catering industries — *Serials*
Lakeland catering and hotel year book. — 1981. — Carlisle (12, Lonsdale St., Carlisle) : Border Press Agency, [1980?]. — 24p
ISSN 0309-3999 : Unpriced
Primary classification 338.4'764794427801'05 B81-09024

338.4'76591 — Advertising. Economic aspects
Chiplin, Brian. Economics of advertising. — 2nd ed. — Eastbourne : Holt, Rinehart & Winston, Sept.1981. — [128]p
ISBN 0-03-910315-3 : £12.50 : CIP entry B81-22694

338.4'76591 — Advertising industries
Reekie, W. Duncan. The economics of advertising / W. Duncan Reekie. — London : Macmillan, 1981. — xii,194p : ill ; 23cm
Includes index
ISBN 0-333-27204-8 : £20.00 B81-40735

338.4'7659157'0941 — Great Britain. Point of sale advertising industries — *Serials*
Point of sale & screenprinting. — Vol.31, no.1 (Jan.1981)-. — London (Pembroke House, Campsbourne Rd, Hornsey, N8) : Batiste Publications, 1981-. — v. : ill ; 30cm
Monthly. — Continues: Point of sale news
£11.00 per year
Also classified at 338.4'76862316 B81-16735

338.4'76592'06041 — Great Britain. Public relations industries. Organisations: Institute of Public Relations — *Directories — Serials*
Institute of Public Relations. Register of members / the Institute of Public Relations. — 1981. — London (1 Great James St., WC1N 3DA) : The Institute, c1981. — 149p
Unpriced B81-29409

338.4'766 — Chemical industries, *1881-1981*
The **Chemical** industry. — Chichester : Ellis Horwood, Dec.1981. — [600]p
ISBN 0-85312-388-8 : £32.50 : CIP entry B81-35019

338.4'766'00941 — Great Britain. Chemical industries — *Serials*
Speciality chemicals : production, marketing and applications. — Vol.1, no.1 (Feb.1981)-. — Redhill (2 Queensway, Redhill, Surrey RH1 1QS) : Fuel & Metallurgical Journals, 1981-. — v. : ill ; 30cm
Quarterly. — Description based on: Vol.1, no.2 (May 1981)
ISSN 0262-2262 = Speciality chemicals : £18.00 per year B81-39531

UK chemical industry statistics handbook / Chemical Industries Association. — 12th rev. ed. (1980). — London : The Association, c1980. — 168p
ISSN 0309-2356 : Unpriced B81-09100

338.4'766'00941 — Great Britain. Chemical industries — *Statistics — Serials*
Report on the census of production. Miscellaneous chemicals / Department of Industry, Business Statistics Office. — 1979. — London : H.M.S.O., c1981. — 13p in various pagings. — (Business monitor ; PA271.3)
ISBN 0-11-513320-8 : £2.50 B81-31015

338.4'766'00948 — Scandinavia. Chemical industries — *Statistics*
Chemfacts, Scandinavia. — 2nd ed. — Sutton : Chemical Data Services, IPC Industrial Press, 1981. — vi,145p : maps ; 30cm
Previous ed.: 1977
ISBN 0-617-00427-7 (pbk) : Unpriced B81-38883

338.4'766'009493 — Belgium. Chemical industries — *Statistics*
Chemfacts : Belgium. — 2nd ed. — Sutton (IPC Industrial Press Ltd., Quadrant House, The Quadrant, Sutton, Surrey SM2 5AS) : Chemical Data Services, 1981. — 92p : maps ; 30cm
Previous ed.: 1977
ISBN 0-617-00432-3 (pbk) : £45.00 B81-32755

338.4'76602'098 — South America. Chemical engineering industries — *For businessmen*
Process equipment and plant opportunities in South America : Argentina, Brazil, Chile Colombia, Ecuador, Peru, Venezuela : a consultant's overview / by Metra Consulting. — London (42 Vicarage Cres., SW11 3LD) : Metra, c1981. — 208p : ill,maps ; 30cm
ISBN 0-902231-27-8 (spiral) : Unpriced B81-11742

338.4'766028 — Chemical engineering industries. Projects. Economic aspects. Evaluation
Allen, Derek H.. A guide to the economic evaluation of projects / by Derek H. Allen. — 2nd ed. — Rugby : Institution of Chemical Engineers, c1980. — vii,94p : ill ; 21cm
Previous ed.: 1972
ISBN 0-85295-131-0 (pbk) : £3.50 B81-06299

338.4'7661'00941 — Great Britain. Inorganic chemicals industries — *Statistics — Serials*
Report on the census of production. Inorganic chemicals / Department of Industry, Business Statistics Office. — 1978. — London : H.M.S.O., c1980. — 13p in various pagings. — (Business monitor ; PA271.1)
ISBN 0-11-513132-9 : £2.00 B81-08783

Report on the census of production. Inorganic chemicals / Department of Industry, Business Statistics Office. — 1979. — London : H.M.S.O., c1981. — 13p in various pagings. — (Business monitor ; PA271.1)
ISBN 0-11-513306-2 : £2.50 B81-30731

338.4'766122'0212 — Sulphuric acid industries — *Statistics*
World sulphuric acid atlas. — 3rd ed. / [editor B. Nielsen]. — London : 25 Wilton Rd. SW1V 1NH : British Sulphur Corporation, 1980. — 90p : ill,col.maps ; 31cm
Previous ed.: published as: World sulphur and sulphuric acid atlas / by British Sulphur Corporation. 1976. — Includes index
ISBN 0-902777-44-0 : Unpriced B81-16571

338.4'7661324 — Sodium carbonate industries & trades
The **Economics** of soda ash. — London (2 Clapham Rd., SW9 0JA) : Roskill Information Services, 1981. — iv,170,[92]p : ill ; 30cm
ISBN 0-86214-182-6 (pbk) : Unpriced B81-09621

338.4'76614 — North-east Yorkshire. Alum industries, *to 1870*
Morrison, Alan, *1915-*. Alum : North East Yorkshire's fascinating story of the first chemical industry / Alan Morrison. — Solihull (7 Broadfern Rd., Solihull, W. Midlands [B93 9DE]) : A. Morrison, [1981]. — 28p : 1map ; 21cm
Cover title. — Map on inside cover
£1.00 (pbk) B81-37343

338.4'766142 — Bromine industries & trades
The **Economics** of bromine. — 2nd ed. — London (2 Clapham Rd., SW9 0JA) : Roskill Information Services, 1980. — iv,71,[42]p : 1map ; 30cm
Previous ed.: 197-
ISBN 0-86214-179-6 (pbk) : Unpriced B81-09428

338.4'766143 — Bentonite industries & trades
The **Economics** of bentonite, Fuller's earth and allied clays / [Roskill Information Services Ltd]. — 3rd ed. — London (14 Great College St., SW1P 3RZ) : Roskill Information Services, 1978. — 211p in various pagings ; 30cm
Previous ed.: 1976
Unpriced (pbk) B81-26922

338.4'766143 — Diatomite industries & trades
The **Economics** of diatomite. — 2nd ed. — London (2 Clapham Rd., SW9 3JA) : Roskill Information Services, 1981. — ii,73,[71]p ; 30cm
Previous ed.: 197-
ISBN 0-86214-181-8 (pbk) : Unpriced B81-15983

338.4'766143 — Feldspars & nepheline syenite industries & trades
The **Economics** of feldspar. — 3rd ed. — London (2 Clapham Rd., SW9 0JA) : Roskill Information Services, c1981. — iv,109,[46]p ; 30cm
Previous ed.: 197-
ISBN 0-86214-921-5 (pbk) : Unpriced B81-15982

338.4'766143 — Great Britain. Asbestos industries — *Statistics — Serials*
Report on the census of production. Asbestos / Department of Industry, Business Statistics Office. — 1979. — London : H.M.S.O., c1981. — v,8p. — (Business monitor ; PA429.1)
ISBN 0-11-513292-9 : £2.50 B81-29438

338.4'766143 — Pyrophyllite & talc industries & trades
The **Economics** of talc and pyrophyllite / [Roskill Information Services Ltd]. — 3rd ed. — London (2 Clapham Rd., SW9 0JA) : Roskill Information Services, 1981. — 489p in various pagings ; 30cm
Previous ed.: 197-?. — Bibliography: pD1-D5
Unpriced (pbk) B81-26925

338.4'766163 — Anhydrite & gypsum industries & trades — *Statistics*
Statistical supplement, 1980 to The economics of gypsum (second edition 1978). — London : Roskill Information Services, c1980. — 156p in various pagings ; 30cm
ISBN 0-86214-180-x (pbk) : Unpriced B81-39691

338.4'76618'00941 — Great Britain. Organic compounds industries — *Statistics — Serials*
Report on the census of production. Organic chemicals / Department of Industry, Business Statistics Office. — 1979. — London : H.M.S.O., c1981. — 13p. in various pagings. — (Business monitor ; PA271.2)
ISBN 0-11-513322-4 : £2.50 B81-32659

338.4'7661804 — Petrochemicals industries. Forecasting
Manual of economic analysis of chemical processes : feasibility studies in refinery and petrochemical processes / Institut Français du Pétrole ; [written by] Alain Chauvel ... [et al.] ; translated from the French by Ryle Miller and Ethel B. Miller. — New York ; London : McGraw-Hill, c1981. — xiv,462p : ill ; 25cm
Translation of: Manuel d'évaluation économique des procédés. — Bibliography: p441-453. - Includes index
ISBN 0-07-031745-3 : £24.50 B81-10587

338.4'7661804'09411 — Scotland. Petrochemicals industries. Effects — *Conference proceedings*
The **Implications** of large-scale petrochemical development. — [Dundee] ([Perth Rd., Dundee DD1 4HT]) : Department of Town & Regional Planning, Duncan of Jordanstone College of Art/Dundee University, 1979. — 106p in various pagings : ill,charts,1map,1form ; 30cm. — (Occasional paper / Department of Town & Regional Planning, Duncan of Jordanstone College of Art/Dundee University ; no.1)
Conference papers. — Includes bibliographies
Unpriced (pbk) B81-13644

338.4'7661804'0973 — United States. Petrochemicals industries
Petrochemical technology assessment / Dale F. Rudd ... [et al.]. — New York ; Chichester : Wiley, c1981. — ix,370p : ill ; 24cm
Bibliography: p28-34. — Includes index
ISBN 0-471-08912-5 : £29.50 B81-33157

338.4'7661808'0941 — Great Britain. Photographic chemical industries — *Statistics — Serials*
Report on the census of production. Photographic chemical materials / Department of Industry, Business Statistics Office. — 1979. — London : H.M.S.O., c1981. — 13p in various pagings. — (Business monitor ; PA279.7)
ISBN 0-11-513301-1 : £2.50 B81-36311

338.4'76622'0941 — Great Britain. Explosives & fireworks industries — *Statistics — Serials*
Report on the census of production. Explosives and fireworks / Department of Industry, Business Statistics Office. — 1979. — London : H.M.S.O., c1981. — 13p in various pagings. — (Business monitor ; PA279.3)
ISBN 0-11-513294-5 : £2.50 B81-30729

338.4'766272'0941 — Great Britain. Coke manufacturing industries — *Statistics — Serials*
Report on the census of production. Coke ovens and manufactured fuels / Department of Industry, Business Statistics Office. — 1979. — London : H.M.S.O., c1981. — 13p in various pagings. — (Business monitor ; PA261)
ISBN 0-11-513305-4 : £2.50 B81-30725

338.4'76629 — Carbon industries & trades
Carbon and graphite / [Roskill Information Services Ltd]. — 2nd ed. — London (14 Great College St., SW1P 3RZ) : Roskill Information Services, 1978. — vi,189,187p ; 30cm
Previous ed.: 197-?
Unpriced (pbk) B81-26914

338.4'7663'05 — Drinks industries & trades — *Serials*
Canadean world drinks report. — No.01 (14 Oct.1980)-. — London (60 Kingly St., W1R 5LH) : Agra-Canadean Publications, 1980-. — v. ; 30cm
Fortnightly. — Continues in part: Eurofood
£125.00 per year B81-05179

338.4'7663'09422372 — Kent. Tonbridge region. Bottled drinks industries & trades, *ca 1850-ca 1920*
Tucker, Peter, *1946-*. Yesterdays bottles : a local guide for Tunbridge Wells, Tonbridge and district / by Peter Tucker & Keith Hetherington. — [Southborough] ([c/o Peter Tucker, 29 Meadow Rd., Southborough, Kent]) : Kent & Sussex Bottle Club, 1981. — 80p : ill,facsims,2ports ; 21cm
Unpriced (pbk) B81-29236

338.4'76631'0941 — Great Britain. Alcoholic drinks industries & trades — *Statistics*
Drink in the Uk : an analysis of the marketing and distribution of alcoholic beverages. — London : Economist Intelligence Unit, 1980. — 182p : ill ; 30cm. — (EIU special report ; no.87)
£40.00 (pbk) B81-03303

338.4'76631'0973 — United States. Alcoholic drinks industries, *to 1980 — Encyclopaedias*
Downard, William L.. Dictionary of the history of the American brewing and distilling industries / William L. Downard. — Westport, Conn. ; London : Greenwood Press, 1980. — xxv,268p ; 24cm
Bibliography: p245-254. — Includes index
ISBN 0-313-21330-5 : £21.95 B81-23598

338.4'766322'0941 — Great Britain. Sparkling & table wines industries & trades — *Statistics — For marketing*
The **U.K** market for table and sparkling wines / Haline Czajka ... [et al.]. — Manchester (Booth St. West, Manchester M15 6PB) : Centre for Business Research in association with Manchester Business School, University of Manchester, [1981?]. — 104p : ill ; 30cm. — (Research report. Market position series / Centre for Business Research)
Unpriced (spiral) B81-27059

338.4'76633'02541 — Great Britain. Brewing industries — *Directories — Serials*
Incorporated Brewers' Guild. The Incorporated Brewers' Guild directory. — 54 (1980). — London (8, Ely Place, EC1N 6SD) : Published by J.H. Griffiths for the Guild, c1980. — 303p
ISSN 0309-7625 : Unpriced B81-03852

338.4'76633'06041 — Great Britain. Brewing industries. Organisations: Institute of Brewing — *Directories — Serials*
Institute of Brewing. List of members / the Institute of Brewing. — 1979. — London (33, Clarges St., W1Y 8EE) : The Institute, [1980?]. — 110p
Unpriced B81-04699

338.4'76633'0941 — Great Britain. Brewing industries & malting industries — *Statistics — Serials*
Report on the census of production. Brewing and malting / Department of Industry, Business Statistics Office. — 1978. — London : H.M.S.O., c1980. — 13p in various pagings. — (Business monitor ; PA231)
ISBN 0-11-513159-0 : £2.00 B81-04979

Report on the census of production. Brewing and malting / Department of Industry, Business Statistics Office. — 1979. — London : H.M.S.O., 1981. — 13p in various pagings. — (Business monitor ; PA231)
ISBN 0-11-513381-x : £2.50 B81-35977

338.4'76633'0941 — Great Britain. Brewing industries — *Statistics*
The **British** brewing industry / industry commentary by A.V. Evans. — London : Jordan & Sons (Surveys), c1981. — xxiv,69p : ill ; 30cm. — (A Jordan survey)
ISBN 0-85938-144-7 (corrected : pbk) : Unpriced B81-22238

338.4'76633'0941 — Great Britain. Brewing industries, *to 1980*
Lovett, Maurice. Brewing and breweries / Maurice Lovett. — Princes Risborough : Shire, 1981. — 32p ; 21cm. — (Shire album ; 72)
Bibliography: p32
ISBN 0-85263-568-0 (pbk) : £0.95 B81-40862

338.4'76633'0942716 — Cheshire. Macclesfield. Brewing industries, *to 1950*
Wreglesworth, Paul. The pubs and breweries of Macclesfield / Paul Wreglesworth, Neil Richardson, Alan Gall. — Macclesfield (81 Thornton Ave., Macclesfield, Cheshire SK11 7XL) : P. Wreglesworth, N. Richardson, A. Gall. — 40p : ill,facsims,ports ; 30cm
ISBN 0-907511-00-7 (pbk) : £1.50
Also classified at 647'.9542716 B81-16733

338.4'76633'0942733 — Greater Manchester *(Metropolitan County).* **Manchester. Brewing industries,** *ca 1850-1940*
Gall, Alan. Manchester Breweries : of times gone / by Alan Gall. — Swinton (375 Chorley Rd., Swinton M27 2AY) : Neil Richardson, [1981?]. — 16p : ill,maps,facsims,plans,1port ; 30cm
Cover title. — Ill., text on inside covers
£1.00 (pbk) B81-37087

338.4'76635'00941 — Great Britain. Alcoholic drinks industries. Distilleries — *Statistics — Serials*
Report on the census of production. Spirit distilling and compounding / Department of Industry, Business Statistics Office. — 1978. — London : H.M.S.O., c1980. — 13p in various pagings. — (Business monitor ; PA239.1)
ISBN 0-11-513142-6 : £2.00 B81-05006

338.4′766352′09411 — Scotland. Whisky industries & trades, *to 1980*

Cooper, Derek. The whisky roads of Scotland. — London : Jill Norman, Oct.1981. — [196]p
ISBN 0-906908-21-3 : £7.95 : CIP entry
B81-27459

338.4′766352′09411 — Scotland. Whisky industries, *1780-1980*

Moss, Michael S.. The making of scotch whisky : a history of the scotch whisky distilling industry / Michael S. Moss, John R. Hume. — Edinburgh (Cockburnhill House, Balerno, Midlothian) : James & James, 1981. — 303p,[16]p of plates : ill(some col.),maps(some col.),facsims,ports ; 26cm
Published to commemorate the centenary of Bruichladdich Distillery, Islay, 1881-1981. — Maps on lining paper. — Bibliography: p197-198. — Includes index
ISBN 0-907383-00-9 : £18.00 : CIP rev.
B81-13573

338.4′76636′0941 — Great Britain. Soft drinks industries — *Statistics* — *Serials*

Report on the census of production. Soft drinks / Department of Industry, Business Statistics Office. — 1978. — London : H.M.S.O., c1980. — 13p in various pagings. — (Business monitor ; PA232)
ISBN 0-11-513116-7 : £2.00 B81-05362

338.4′766362′0941 — Great Britain. Mixer drinks industries & trades

Frost, Graham. The mixer drinks market / Graham Frost, Damien Hunt, Judith Mortimer. — Manchester (Booth Street West, Manchester M15 6PB) : Centre for Business Research in association with Manchester Business School, University of Manchester, [1980]. — v,54 leaves : ill ; 30cm. — (Research report. Market position series / Centre for Business Research)
Bibliography: leaf 54
Unpriced (spiral) B81-14286

338.4′7664′005 — New products: Food & drinks — *Serials*

Canadean world new products. — No.01 (23 Oct.1980)-. — London (Kingly St.,W1R 5LH) : Agra-Canadean Publications, 1980-. — v. ; 30cm
Eleven issue yearly. — Continues in part: Eurofood
£65.00 per year B81-05175

338.4′7664′00941 — Great Britain. Food processing industries — *Serials*

Annual Campden lecture / the Campden Food Preservation Research Association. — 1st-. — Chipping Campden (Chipping Campden, Gloucestershire GL55 6LD) : The Association, 1979-. — v. ; 30cm
Description based on: 3rd
ISSN 0262-0987 = Annual Campden lecture : Unpriced B81-38985

338.4′76641′0941 — Great Britain. Sugar refining industries — *Statistics* — *Serials*

Report on the census of production. Sugar / Department of Industry, Business Statistics Office. — 1978. — London : H.M.S.O., c1980. — 13p in various pagings. — (Business monitor ; PA216)
ISBN 0-11-513010-1 : £2.00 B81-04978

Report on the census of production. Sugar / Department of Industry, Business Statistics Office. — 1979. — London : H.M.S.O., c1981. — 13p in various pagings. — (Business monitor ; PA216)
ISBN 0-11-513269-4 : £2.50 B81-20448

338.4′7664153′0941 — Great Britain. Confectionery industries — *Statistics* — *Serials*

Report on the census of production. Cocoa, chocolate and sugar confectionery / Department of Industry, Business Statistics Office. — 1978. — London : H.M.S.O., c1980. — 13p. in various pagings. — (Business monitor ; PA217)
ISBN 0-11-513104-3 : £2.00 B81-05335

338.4′76642′0941 — Great Britain. Starch industries — *Statistics* — *Serials*

Report on the census of production. Starch and miscellaneous foods / Department of Industry, Business Statistics Office. — 1978. — London : H.M.S.O., c1980. — 13p in various pagings. — (Business monitor ; PA229.2)
ISBN 0-11-513091-8 : £2.00 B81-04394

Report on the census of production. Starch and miscellaneous foods / Department of Industry, Business Statistics Office. — 1979. — London : H.M.S.O., c1981. — 13p in various pagings. — (Business monitor ; PA229.2)
ISBN 0-11-513359-3 : £2.50 B81-32225

338.4′766432′0941 — Great Britain. Margarine manufacturing industries — *Statistics* — *Serials*

Report on the census of production. Margarine / Department of Industry, Business Statistics Office. — 1979. — London : H.M.S.O., c1981. — 13p in various pagings. — (Business monitor ; PA229.1)
ISBN 0-11-513268-6 : £2.50 B81-20442

338.4′766463′0941 — Great Britain. Low-calorie food & drinks industries & trades — *Statistics* — *For marketing*

Short, D.. U.K. market for low calorie foods : market position report / by D. Short, P. Greenshaw, M. Wissels. — Manchester (Booth Street West, Manchester M15 6PB) : Centre for Business Research in association with Manchester Business School, University of Manchester, [1981?]. — 104p : ill ; 30cm. — (Research report. Market position series)
Unpriced (spiral) B81-13226

338.4′766472′00941 — Great Britain. Cereals milling industries — *Statistics* — *Serials*

Report on the census of production. Grain milling / Department of Industry, Business Statistics Office. — 1979. — London : H.M.S.O., c1981. — 13p in various pagings. — (Business monitor ; PA211)
ISBN 0-11-513271-6 : £2.50 B81-20444

338.4′7664752′0941 — Great Britain. Baking industries — *Serials*

Baking today. — Vol.1, no.1 (May 1980)-. — Croydon : Maclaren, 1980-. — v. : ill ; 30cm
Ten issues yearly. — Continues : Baking industries journal
ISSN 0144-8374 = Baking today : £10.00 per year B81-02014

338.4′7664752′0941 — Great Britain. Baking industries — *Statistics* — *Serials*

Report on the census of production. Bread and flour confectionary / Department of Industry Business Statistics Office. — 1978. — London : H.M.S.O., c1980. — 13p in various pagings. — (Business monitor ; PA212)
ISBN 0-11-513134-5 : £2.00 B81-04972

338.4′766447525 — Great Britain. Biscuits industries — *Statistics* — *Serials*

Report on the census of production. Biscuits / Department of Industry, Business Statistics Office. — 1979. — London : H.M.S.O., c1981. — 13p. in various pagings. — (Business monitor ; PA213)
ISBN 0-11-513356-9 : £2.50 B81-32910

338.4′766476′0212 — Feedingstuffs industries & trades — *Statistics* — *Serials*

International grain & feed markets forecast and statistical digest. — 1978. — London (886, High Road, Finchley, N12 9SB) : Turret Press, c1978. — 42p
ISSN 0260-2687 : Unpriced B81-05318

International grain & feed markets forecast and statistical digest. — 1981. — London (886 High Rd., Finchley, N12 9SB) : Turret Press, c1981. — 48p
ISSN 0260-2687 : Unpriced B81-36301

338.4′766476′0941 — Great Britain. Feedingstuffs industries — *Statistics* — *Serials*

Report on the census of production. Animal and poultry foods / Department of Industry, Business Statistics Office. — 1978. — London : H.M.S.O., c1980. — 13p in various pagings. — (Business monitor ; PA219)
ISBN 0-11-513139-6 : £2.00 B81-05371

338.4′76648′00941 — Great Britain — *Fruit & vegetable processing industries* — *Statistics* — *Serials*

Report on the census of production. Fruit and vegetable products / Department of Industry, Business Statistics Office. — 1978. — London : H.M.S.O., c1980. — 13p. in various pagings. — (Business monitor ; PA218)
ISBN 0-11-513124-8 : £2.00 B81-05050

Report on the census of production. Fruit and vegetable products / Department of Industry, Business Statistics Office. — 1979. — London : H.M.S.O., c1981. — 13p. in various pagings. — (Business monitor ; PA218)
ISBN 0-11-513336-4 : £2.50 B81-32657

338.4′76649′0094 — European Community countries. Meat industries & trades — *Statistics*

EEC production, consumption and trade in meat and livestock / MLC Economic Information service. — Bletchley : Meat and Livestock Commission, 1980. — 31p : ill ; 30cm. — (European booklet ; 80/1)
Cover title
Unpriced (pbk) B81-08656

338.4′766490094 — European Community countries. Meat industries. Effects of enlargement of European Economic Community

Greece, Spain, Portugal and the EEC : an evaluation of the implications of EEC enlargement for the meat and livestock industry / [MLC Economic Information Service]. — Bletchley (PO Box 44, Queensway House, Bletchley, MK2 2EF) : Meat and Livestock Commission, 1980. — iii,74p : ill,maps ; 30cm. — (European booklet ; 80/5)
£5.00 (pbk)
Primary classification 338.1′76′0094 B81-08270

338.4′76649′00941 — Great Britain. Animal products industries — *Statistics* — *Serials*

Report on the census of production. Bacon curing, meat and fish products / Department of Industry, Business Statistics Office. — 1978. — London : H.M.S.O., c1980. — 13p in various pagings. — (Business monitor ; PA214)
ISBN 0-11-513115-9 : £2.00 B81-05376

338.4′766649453 — Small scale fish freezing industries

Economic aspects of small-scale fish freezing / P.R. Street ... [et al.]. — London : Tropical Products Institute, 1980. — iv,46p ; 30cm
English text, summaries in English, French and Spanish
ISBN 0-85954-128-2 (pbk) : £1.70 B81-04069

338.4′76654′09411 — Scotland. Gas supply industries. Consumer protection services: Scottish Gas Consumers′ Council — *Serials*

Scottish Gas Consumers′ Council. Report of the Scottish Gas Consumers′ Council for the year ended 31st March ... — 1981. — Edinburgh (86 George St., Edinburgh EH2 3BU) : The Council, 1981. — 24p
ISBN 0-904792-06-4 : Unpriced B81-36016

338.4′766553′0941 — Great Britain. Petroleum refining industries — *Statistics* — *Serials*

Report on the census of production. Mineral oil refining / Department of Industry, Business Statistics Office. — 1978. — London : H.M.S.O., c1980. — 13p in various pagings. — (Business monitor ; PA262)
ISBN 0-11-513149-3 : £2.00 B81-05367

Report on the census of production. Mineral oil refining / Department of Industry, Business Statistics Office. — 1979. — London : H.M.S.O., c1981. — 13p. in various pagings. — (Business monitor ; PA262)
ISBN 0-11-513327-5 : £2.50 B81-32675

338.4′766655385′0941 — Great Britain. Lubricating oils industries & lubricating greases industries — *Statistics* — *Serials*

Report on the census of production. Lubricating oils and greases / Department of Industry, Business Statistics Office. — 1979. — London : H.M.S.O., c1981. — 8,vp. — (Business monitor ; PA263)
ISBN 0-11-513293-7 : £2.50 B81-29650

338.4'76657'0941 — Great Britain. Gas industries — *Statistics — Serials*

Report on the census of production. Gas / Department of Industry, Business Statistics Office. — 1979. — London : H.M.S.O., c1981. — 13p in various pagings. — (Business monitor ; PA601)
ISBN 0-11-513265-1 : £2.50 B81-20447

338.4'76657'0941 — Great Britain. Gas industries, *to 1980*

Williams, Trevor I.. A history of the British gas industry / Trevor I. Williams. — Oxford : Oxford University Press, 1981. — xvii,304p,[17]p of plates : ill,maps,facsims ; 24cm
Includes bibliographies and index
ISBN 0-19-858157-2 : £18.50 : CIP rev. B81-26750

338.4'766574'0942534 — Lincolnshire. Lincoln. Gas supply industries, *1828-1949*

Roberts, D. E.. The Lincoln gas undertaking 1828-1949 / prepared for EMGAS by D.E. Roberts. — [Leicester] ([51 DeMontfort) : [East Midlands Gas], [1981]. — 46p : ill,1map,facsims,ports ; 21cm
Ill on inside covers. — Bibliography: p45-46
ISBN 0-9506339-4-1 (pbk) : Unpriced B81-24262

338.4'76661'0941 — Great Britain. Glass industries — *Statistics — Serials*

Report on the census of production. Glass / Department of Industry, Business Statistics Office. — 1978. — London : H.M.S.O., c1980. — 13p in various pagings. — (Business monitor ; PA463)
ISBN 0-11-513146-9 : £2.00 B81-05004

Report on the census of production. Glass / Department of Industry, Business Statistics Office. — 1979. — London : H.M.S.O., 1981. — 13p in various pagings. — (Business monitor ; PA463)
ISBN 0-11-513400-x : £2.50 B81-35979

338.4'766619 — South Yorkshire *(Metropolitan County)*. Rotherham. Glass container industries: Beatson, Clark & Company, *1925-1971 — Personal observations*

Clark, Alec W.. Through a glass clearly / Alec W. Clark. — London : Golden Eagle, 1980. — 159p,[24]p of plates : ill,1facsim,ports ; 22cm
Ill on lining papers
ISBN 0-901482-28-5 : £5.50 B81-01575

338.4'76663942463 — Staffordshire. Potteries, *The* . Pottery & porcelain industries, *to 1980*

Sekers, David. The Potteries / David Sekers. — Princes Risborough : Shire, 1981. — 32p ; 21cm. — (Shire album ; 62)
ISBN 0-85263-564-8 (pbk) : £0.95 B81-40863

338.4'76666'0941 — Great Britain. Pottery industries — *Statistics — Serials*

Report on the census of production. Pottery / Department of Industry, Business Statistics Office. — 1978. — London : H.M.S.O., c1980. — 13p in various pagings. — (Business monitor ; PA462)
ISBN 0-11-513078-0 : £2.00 B81-04395

Report on the census of production. Pottery / Department of Industry, Business Statistics Office. — 1979. — London : H.M.S.O., c1981. — 13p. in various pagings. — (Business monitor ; PA462)
ISBN 0-11-513337-2 : £2.50 B81-32676

338.4'76666'0942538 — Lincolnshire. Stamford. Pottery industries, *850-1250*

Kilmurry, Kathy. The pottery industry of Stamford, Lincolnshire c.A.D. 850-1250 : its manufacture, trade and relationship with continental wares, with a classification and chronology / Kathy Kilmurry. — Oxford : B.A.R., 1980. — 348p : ill,maps ; 30cm. — (BAR. British series ; 84)
Bibliography: p323-339. — Includes index
ISBN 0-86054-109-6 (pbk) : £12.00 B81-36627

338.4'76666'094257 — Oxfordshire. Pottery industries, *to ca 1900*

Stebbing, Nancy. Oxfordshire potters / Nancy Stebbing, John Rhodes, Maureen Mellor. — Woodstock (c/o Oxfordshire County Museum, Woodstock OX7 1SN) : Oxfordshire County Council, Department of Museum Services, c1980. — 36p : ill,maps,facsims ; 20x21cm. — (The Clay industries of Oxfordshire) (Oxfordshire Museums Service publication ; no.13)
Text, ill on inside covers. — Bibliography: [1]p
ISBN 0-901036-08-0 (pbk) : Unpriced B81-15224

338.4'7666737'0941 — Great Britain. Bricks industries, *to 1980*

Hammond, Martin. Bricks and brickmaking / Martin Hammond. — Princes Risborough : Shire, 1981. — 32p : ill,plans ; 21cm. — (Shire album ; 75)
Bibliography: p32
ISBN 0-85263-573-7 (pbk) : £0.95 B81-40861

338.4'7666737'094257 — Oxfordshire. Bricks industries, *1550-1954*

Bond, James, *1944-*. Oxfordshire brickmakers / James Bond, Sarah Gosling, John Rhodes. — Woodstock (c/o Oxfordshire County Museum, Woodstock OX7 1SN) : Oxfordshire County Council, Department of Museum Services, c1980. — 32p : ill,maps,facsims,1plan ; 20x21cm. — (The Clay industries of Oxfordshire) (Oxfordshire Museums Service publication no.14)
Text, ill on inside covers. — Bibliography: [1]p. - Includes index
ISBN 0-901036-07-2 (pbk) : Unpriced B81-15225

338.4'766694'0941 — Great Britain. Cement industries — *Statistics — Serials*

Report on the census of production. Cement / Department of Industry, Business Statistics Office. — 1979. — London : H.M.S.O., c1981. — 13p in various pagings. — (Business monitor ; PA464)
ISBN 0-11-513353-4 : £2.50 B81-32231

338.4'766738'094 — Europe. Textile printing industries, *1700-1800*

Chapman, S. D.. European textile printers in the eighteenth century : a study of Peel and Oberkampf / S.D. Chapman and S. Chassagne. — London : Heinemann Educational : The Pasold Fund, 1981. — xii,257p : ill,maps,facsims,2ports,2geneal.tables ; 23cm
Includes index
ISBN 0-435-32170-6 : £15.00 : CIP rev. B81-02572

338.4'76675'0941 — Great Britain. Printing ink industries — *Statistics — Serials*

Report on the census of production. Printing ink / Department of Industry, Business Statistics Office. — 1979. — London : H.M.S.O., c1981. — 13p in various pagings. — (Business monitor ; PA279.5)
ISBN 0-11-513299-6 : £2.50 B81-30727

338.4'766772'0941 — Great Britain. Polishes industries — *Statistics — Serials*

Report on the census of production. Polishes / Department of Industry, Business Statistics Office. — 1978. — London : H.M.S.O., c1980. — 13p in various pagings. — (Business monitor ; PA279.1)
ISBN 0-11-513086-1 : £2.00 B81-01791

Report on the census of production. Polishes / Department of Industry, Business Statistics Office. — 1979. — London : H.M.S.O., c1981. — 8,vp. — (Business monitor ; PA279.1)
ISBN 0-11-513297-x : £2.50 B81-29653

338.4'76679'0941 — Great Britain. Coatings industries — *Statistics — Serials*

Report on the census of production. Paint / Department of Industry, Business Statistics Office. — 1979. — London : H.M.S.O., c1981. — 13p. in various pagings. — (Business monitor ; PA274)
ISBN 0-11-513324-0 : £2.50 B81-32651

338.4'76681'0941 — Great Britain. Soap & detergents industries — *Statistics — Serials*

Report on the census of production. Soap and detergents / Department of Industry, Business Statistics Office. — 1979. — London : H.M.S.O., c1981. — 13p in various pagings. — (Business monitor ; PA275)
ISBN 0-11-513273-2 : £2.50 B81-20443

338.4'76683'02541 — Great Britain. Adhesives industries — *Directories — Serials*

Adhesives directory. — 1981. — Rickmansworth : Wheatland Journals, [1980?]. — 192p
ISSN 0305-3199 : £5.50 B81-03242

338.4'76683'0941 — Great Britain. Adhesives industries — *Statistics — Serials*

Report on the census of production. Formulated adhesives, gelatine, etc. / Department of Industry, Business Statistics Office. — 1978. — London : H.M.S.O., c1980. — 13p in various pagings. — (Business Monitor ; PA279.2)
ISBN 0-11-513089-6 : £2.00 B81-20405

Report on the census of production. Formulated adhesives, gelatine, etc. / Department of Industry, Business Statistics Office. — 1979. — London : H.M.S.O., c1981. — 13p in various pagings. — (Business monitor ; PA279.2)
ISBN 0-11-513313-5 : £2.50 B81-31022

338.4'76684'095957 — Singapore. Plastics industries — *For British businessmen*

Singapore : a compact review. — London : British Plastics Federation, 1980. — 37p : 1map ; 30cm
£10.00 (free to members) (spiral) B81-24070

338.4'766849'0941 — Great Britain. Plastics products industries — *Statistics — Serials*

Report on the census of production. Plastics products / Department of Industry, Business Statistics Office. — 1978. — London : H.M.S.O., c1980. — 13p in various pagings. — (Business monitor ; PA496)
ISBN 0-11-513126-4 : £2.00 B81-05366

338.4'7668497'0941 — Great Britain. Plastics packaging industries — *Statistics — Serials*

Packaging — plastics. — 6th ed. — London : Inter Company Comparisons, c1980. — 15leaves. — (ICC financial survey)
ISBN 0-86191-207-1 : Unpriced B81-35120

338.4'76685'09 — Cosmetics, perfumes & toiletries industries, *to 1980*

Allen, Margaret, *1933-*. Selling dreams : inside the beauty business / Margaret Allen. — London : Dent, 1981. — 286p,[8]p of plates : ill,1facsim,ports ; 23cm
Originally published: New York: Simon and Schuster, 1981. — Includes index
ISBN 0-460-04415-x : £7.95 B81-37757

338.4'76685'0941 — Great Britain. Cosmetics, perfumes & toiletries industries — *Statistics — Serials*

Report on the census of production. Toilet preparations / Department of Industry, Business Statistics Office. — 1979. — London : H.M.S.O., c1981. — 13p in various pagings. — (Business monitor ; PA273)
ISBN 0-11-513335-6 : £2.50 B81-30726

338.4'76686241 — Urea industries — *Forecasts*

Urea : world analysis and prospects 1970-1980 / the British Sulphur Corporation Limited. — London (25 Wilton Rd., SW1V 1NH) : The Corporation, 1975. — 44p : ill(some col.),1col.map ; 30cm
Unpriced (spiral) B81-22961

338.4'766865'0941 — Great Britain. Pesticides industries — *Statistics — Serials*

Report on the census of production. Formulated pesticides, etc. / Department of Industry, Business Statistics Office. — 1978. — London : H.M.S.O., c1980. — 13p in various pagings. — (Business monitor ; PA279.4)
ISBN 0-11-513103-5 : £2.00 B81-08352

338.4'766865'0941 — Great Britain. Pesticides industries — *Statistics — Serials*
continuation
Report on the census of production. Formulated pesticides, etc. / Department of Industry, Business Statistics Office. — 1979. — London : H.M.S.O., c1981. — 13p in various pagings. — (Business monitor ; PA279.4)
ISBN 0-11-513315-1 : £2.50 B81-31020

338.4'76689'0941 — Great Britain. Synthetic polymers industries — *Statistics — Serials*
Report on the census of production. Synthetic resins and plastics materials and synthetic rubber / Department of Industry, Business Statistics Office. — 1978. — London : H.M.S.O., c1980. — 13p. in various pagings. — (Business monitor ; PA276)
ISBN 0-11-513148-5 : £2.00 B81-05337

Report on the census of production. Synthetic resins and plastics materials and synthetic rubber / Department of Industry, Business Statistics Office. — 1979. — London : H.M.S.O., c1981. — 13p. in various pagings. — (Business monitor ; PA276)
ISBN 0-11-513308-9 : £2.50 B81-32650

338.4'7669 — Great Britain. Base metals industries — *Statistics — Serials*
Report on the census of production. Miscellaneous base metals / Department of Industry, Business Statistics Office. — 1978. — London : H.M.S.O., c1980. — 13p in various pagings. — (Business monitor ; PA323)
ISBN 0-11-513114-0 : £2.00 B81-01808

Report on the census of production. Miscellaneous base metals / Department of Industry, Business Statistics Office. — 1979. — London : H.M.S.O., c1981. — 13p in various pagings. — (Business monitor ; PA323)
ISBN 0-11-513354-2 : £2.50 B81-32224

338.4'7669 — Nonferrous metals industries & trades
Robbins, Peter. Guide to non-ferrous metals and their markets / Peter Robbins and John Edwards. — 2nd rev. ed. — London : Kogan Page, 1980. — 213p : ill,1map ; 24cm
Previous ed.: 1979
ISBN 0-85038-302-1 : £16.95 B81-02435

338.4'7669'0212 — Metals industries — *Statistics — Serials*
Metal bulletin handbook. — 13th ed. (1980). — Worcester Park : Metal Bulletin, c1980. — 916p
ISBN 0-900542-45-4 : £18.00
ISSN 0076-664x B81-15283

338.4'76690282 — United States. Rocky Mountains. Smelting industries, *to 1910*
Fell, James E.. Ores to metals : the rocky mountain smelting industry / James E. Fell, Jr. — Lincoln [Neb.] ; London : University of Nebraska Press, c1979. — xi,341p : ill,1map,ports ; 23cm
Bibliography: p311-323. — Includes index
ISBN 0-8032-1951-2 : £12.90 B81-06795

338.4'76691'0941 — Great Britain. Iron & steel industries. Nationalisation. Political aspects, *1945-1970*
McEachern, Doug. A class against itself : power and the nationalism of the British steel industry / Doug McEachern. — Cambridge : Cambridge University Press, 1980. — x,229p ; 24cm
Bibliography: p219-226. — Includes index
ISBN 0-521-22985-5 : £12.50 : CIP rev.
B80-25339

338.4'76691'0941 — Great Britain. Iron & steel industries — *Statistics — Serials*
Iron and steel industry annual statistics for the United Kingdom. — 1980. — Croydon (P.O. Box 230, 12 Addiscombe Rd, Croydon CR9 6BS) : Iron and Steel Statistics Bureau, [1981]. — 72p
£15.00 B81-29985

Report on the census of production. Iron and steel (general) / Department of Industry, Business Statistics Office. — 1978. — London : H.M.S.O., c1980. — 13p in various pagings. — (Business monitor ; PA311)
ISBN 0-11-513130-2 : £2.00 B81-04976

Report on the census of production. Iron and steel (general) / Department of Industry, Business Statistics Office. — 1979. — London : H.M.S.O., 1981. — 13p in various pagings. — (Business monitor ; PA311)
ISBN 0-11-513389-5 : £2.50 B81-35978

338.4'7669141'0941 — Great Britain. Iron industries, *to 1980*
Gale, W. K. V.. Ironworking / W.K.V. Gale. — Princes Risborough : Shire, 1981. — 32p ; 21cm. — (Shire album ; 64)
ISBN 0-85263-546-x (pbk) : £0.95 B81-40855

338.4'7669142'09048 — Steel industries, *1980-1990 — Conference proceedings*
The **steel** industry in the eighties : proceedings of an international conference organized by the Metals Society and held at the RAI Centre, Amsterdam, The Netherlands, 11-14 September 1979. — London : Metals Society, c1980. — 168p : ill ; 31cm
Includes index
ISBN 0-904357-31-7 : £30.00 B81-04857

338.4'7669142'0941 — Great Britain. Steel industries. Effects of policies of government — *Trade union viewpoints*
Iron and Steel Trades Confederation. What is the future? : steel - rail - coal / [Iron & Steel Trades Confederation, National Union of Railwaymen, National Union of Mineworkers]. — [London] ([324 Grays Inn Rd, WC1BX 8DD]) : [The Confederation], [1981]. — 12p ; 21cm
Cover title
Unpriced (pbk)
Also classified at 385'.0941 ; 338.2'724'0941
B81-19736

338.4'76692'0941 — Great Britain. Precious metals industries — *Statistics — Serials*
Report on the census of production. Jewellery and precious matals / Department of Industry, Business Statistics Office. — 1978. — London : H.M.S.O., c1980. — 13p in various pagings. — (Business monitor ; PA396)
ISBN 0-11-513164-7 : £2.00
Also classified at 338.4'773927'0941
B81-08779

338.4'766922 — Gold industries & trades
The **Economics** of gold / [Roskill Information Services Ltd]. — London (14 Great College St., SW1P 3RZ) : Roskill Information Services, c1978. — vi,257,A110p ; 30cm
Unpriced (pbk) B81-26923

338.4'766922 — Gold industries & trades — *Statistics*
Statistical supplement, 1981 to the economics of gold ... — London (2 Clapham Rd., SW9 0JA) : Roskill Information Services Ltd, c1981. — 98p,[221]p ; 30cm. — (Roskill reports on metals & minerals)
ISBN 0-86214-191-5 (pbk) : Unpriced
B81-38649

338.4'76692922 — Thorium industries & trades
The **Economics** of thorium / [Roskill Information Services Ltd]. — 3rd ed. — London (14 Great College St., SW1P 3RZ) : Roskill Information Services, 1978. — vi,86,A52p ; 30cm
Previous ed.: 197-?
Unpriced (pbk) B81-26915

338.4'76692931 — Uranium industries — *Conference proceedings*
Uranium and nuclear energy : proceedings of the Fourth International Symposium held by the Uranium Institute London, September 10-12, 1979 / edited ... by Mining Journal Books Limited in co-operation with the Uranium Institute. — London (15 Wilson St., EC2M 2TR) : Mining Journal Books, 1980. — xiii,313p : ill,maps ; 25cm
Includes bibliographies
ISBN 0-900117-20-6 : Unpriced B81-11754

338.4'76692931'091812 — Western world. Uranium industries & trades. Political aspects
Radetzki, Marian. Uranium : a strategic source of energy / Marian Radetzki. — London : Croom Helm, c1981. — 156p : ill ; 23cm. — (Croom Helm commodity series)
Bibliography: p148-154. - Includes index
ISBN 0-7099-0340-5 : £123.95 : CIP rev.
B80-34663

338.4'76693 — Copper industries & trades
The **Economics** of copper / [Roskill Information Services Ltd]. — 2nd ed. — London (2 Clapham Rd., SW9 0JA) : Roskill Information Services, 1981. — 436p in various pagings ; 30cm
Previous ed.: 197-?
Unpriced (pbk) B81-26926

338.4'76693'0941 — Great Britain. Copper & copper alloy industries — *Statistics — Serials*
Report on the census of production. Copper, brass and other copper alloys / Department of Industry, Business Statistics Office. — 1978. — London : H.M.S.O., c1980. — 13p in various pagings. — (Business monitor ; PA322)
ISBN 0-11-513092-6 : £2.00 B81-07391

338.4'76694 — Lead industries & trades
The **Economics** of lead / [Roskill Information Services Ltd]. — 2nd ed. — London (14 Great College St., SW1P 3RZ) : Roskill Information Services, 1979. — 826p in various pagings : 2ill ; 30cm
Previous ed.: 197-?
Unpriced (pbk) B81-26920

338.4'76696 — Tin industries & trades
The **Economics** of tin. — 3rd ed. — London (2 Clapham Rd., SW9 0JA) : Roskill Information Services, c1981. — viii,354,[142]p : ill ; 30cm
Previous ed.: 1977
ISBN 0-86214-924-x (pbk) : Unpriced
B81-36920

338.4'76696'0212 — Tin industries & trades — *Statistics — Serials*
Tin statistics / International Tin Council. — 1969-1979. — London (1, Oxendon St., SW1Y 4EQ) : The Council, [1980]. — 64p
£12.00 B81-20062

338.4'76697 — Platinum metals industries & trades
The **Economics** of the platinum group metals / [Roskill Information Services Ltd]. — 2nd ed. — London (14 Great College St., SW1P 3RZ) : Roskill Information Services, 1979. — vi,207,A160p ; 30cm
Previous ed.: 197-?
Unpriced (pbk) B81-26924

338.4'76697 — Rhenium industries & trades
The **Economics** of rhenium / [Roskill Information Services Ltd]. — 2nd ed. — London (14 Great College St., SW1P 3RZ) : Roskill Information Services, 1978. — vi,71,A6p ; 30cm
Previous ed.: 197-?
Unpriced (pbk) B81-26918

338.4'766971 — Mercury industries & trades
The **Economics** of mercury / [Roskill Information Services Ltd]. — 4th ed. — London (14 Great College St., SW1P 3RZ) : Roskill Information Services, 1978. — vi,139,A20p ; 30cm
Previous ed.: 197-?
Unpriced (pbk) B81-26913

338.4'7669723 — Magnesium industries & trades
The **Economics** of magnesite, dolomite and magnesium compound / [Roskill Information Services Ltd]. — 2nd ed. — London (14 Great College St., SW1P 3RZ) : Roskill Information Services, 1978. — 392p in various pagings ; 30cm
Previous ed.: 1973. — Includes index
Unpriced (pbk) B81-26917

338.4'7669723'0212 — Magnesium industries & trades — *Statistics*
Statistical supplement, 1981 to The Economics of magnesite, dolomite and magnesium compounds. 2nd ed. 1978. — London (2 Clapham Rd., SW9 0JA) : Roskill Information Services, c1981. — 55,[180]p ; 30cm. — (Roskill reports on metals & minerals)
Unpriced (pbk) B81-09836

Statistical supplement 1981 to The Economics of magnesium metal. Second edition. 1978 / [Roskill Information Services Ltd]. — London (2 Clapham Rd., SW9 0JA) : Roskill Information Services, [1981?]. — 65,A67,B11,C5p ; 30cm. — (Roskill reports on metals & minerals)
Unpriced (pbk) B81-19401

338.4'7669725 — Strontium industries & trades

The **Economics** of strontium / [Roskill Information Services Ltd]. — 2nd ed. — London (14 Great College St., SW1P 3RZ) : Roskill Information Services, 1978. — 110p in various pagings : 1ill ; 30cm
Previous ed.: 197-?
Unpriced (pbk) B81-26919

338.4'766973 — Ferro-alloys industries — *Conference proceedings*

International Ferro-alloys Conference *(2nd : 1979 : Copenhagen).* Proceedings of Metal bulletin's second International Ferro-alloys Conference held on October 15, 16 & 17, 1979 at the Hotel Scandinavia, Copenhagen / edited by T.J. Tarring, assisted by Marina Crussell. — Worcester Park : Metal Bulletin Ltd, 1980. — 94p : ill,maps ; 30cm
ISBN 0-900542-44-6 (pbk) : £35.00 B81-02979

338.4'7669732 — Manganese industries & trades

The **Economics** of manganese / [Roskill Information Services Ltd]. — 2nd ed. — London (14 Great College St., SW1P 3RZ) : Roskill Information Services, 1978. — ix,216,A119p ; 30cm
Unpriced (pbk) B81-26916

338.4'7669732 — Manganese industries & trades — *Statistics*

Statistical supplement 1981 to The economics of manganese (Second edition 1978). — London (2 Clapham Rd., SW9 0JA) : Roskill Information Services, c1981. — 65p,[135]p ; 30cm. — (Roskill reports on metals & minerals)
ISBN 0-86214-912-6 (pbk) : Unpriced
B81-15226

338.4'7669732 — Vanadium industries & trades

The **Economics** of vanadium. — 4th ed. — London : Roskill Information Services, 1981. — iii,151,[45]p ; 30cm
Previous ed.: published as Vanadium. 1977
ISBN 0-86214-188-5 (pbk) : Unpriced
B81-34094

338.4'76697332 — Nickel industries & trades

The **Economics** of nickel / [Roskill Information Services Ltd]. — 3rd ed. — London (2 Clapham Rd., SW9 0JA) : Roskill Information Services Ltd, c1981. — 505p in various pagings ; 30cm
Previous ed.: 197-?
ISBN 0-86214-185-0 (pbk) : Unpriced
B81-19441

338.4'7669734 — Chromium industries & trades — *Statistics*

Statistical supplement 1981 to The Economics of chromium. 3rd ed. 1978 / Roskill Information Services Ltd. — London (2 Clapham Rd., SW9 0JA) : Roskill Information Services Ltd, c1981. — 132,A145,B17p ; 30cm. — (Roskill reports on metals & minerals)
ISBN 0-86214-166-4 (pbk) : Unpriced
B81-19442

338.4'7669734 — Molybdenum industries & trades — *Statistics*

Statistical supplement, 1981 to The Economics of molybdenum. 2nd ed. 1978. — London (2 Clapham Rd., SW0 3JA) : Roskill Information Services, c1981. — 128,[108]p ; 30cm. — (Roskill reports on metals & minerals)
Unpriced (pbk) B81-18827

338.4'7669734 — Tungsten industries & trades

Tungsten / [Roskill Information Services Ltd]. — 3rd ed. — London (14 Great College St., SW1P 3RZ) : Roskill Information Services, 1977. — 380p in various pagings ; 30cm
Previous ed.: 1974
Unpriced (pbk) B81-26921

338.4'766979 — Boron industries & trades

The **Economics** of boron. — 3rd ed. — London (2 Clapham Rd., SW9 0JA) : Roskill Information Services, 1981. — 237p in various pagings ; 30cm
Previous ed.: 1977. — Includes index
ISBN 0-86214-184-2 (pbk) : Unpriced
B81-16186

338.4'766979 — Gallium industries & trades — *Statistics*

The **Economics** of gallium. — 3rd ed. — London (2 Clapham Rd., SW9 0JA) : Roskill Information Services, c1981. — v,102,[36]p ; 30cm
Previous ed.: 1977
ISBN 0-86214-189-3 (pbk) : Unpriced
B81-36921

338.4'766979 — Germanium industries & trades

The **Economics** of germanium. — 3rd ed. — London (2 Clapham Rd., SW9 0JA) : Roskill Information Services, c1981. — iv,79,A31,B6p ; 30cm
Previous ed.: 1977. — Includes index
ISBN 0-86214-190-7 (pbk) : Unpriced
B81-36919

338.4'767'0941 — Great Britain. Manufacturing equipment industries — *Statistics — Serials*

Report on the census of production. Miscellaneous (non-electrical) machinery / Department of Industry, Business Statistics Office. — 1978. — London : H.M.S.O., c1980. — 13p in various pagings. — (Business monitor ; PA339.9)
ISBN 0-11-513129-9 : £2.00 B81-05005

338.4'767'0941 — Great Britain. Manufacturing industries. Performance. Effects of motivation of managers — *Case studies*

Fiegehen, G. C.. Companies, incentives and senior managers / by G.C. Fiegehan in collaboration with W.B. Reddaway. — Oxford : Oxford University Press for the Institute for Fiscal Studies, 1981. — xiii,141p : 2ill ; 23cm
Includes index
ISBN 0-19-829002-0 : £12.00 : CIP rev.
B81-04357

338.4'767'0941 — Great Britain. Manufacturing industries — *Statistics — Serials*

Analyses of United Kingdom manufacturing (local) units by employment size / Department of Industry, Business Statistics Office. — 1978. — London : H.M.S.O., c1981. — 45p. — (Business monitor ; PA1003)
ISBN 0-11-512880-8 : £4.70 B81-36310

Analysis of United Kingdom manufacturing (local) units by employment size / Department of Industry, Business Statistics Office. — 1977. — London : H.M.S.O., c1980. — 44p. — (Business monitor. PA1003)
ISBN 0-11-513183-3 : £4.00 B81-08355

338.4'7671'0941 — Great Britain. Metal products industries — *Statistics — Serials*

Report on the census of production. Miscellaneous metal manufacture / Department of Industry, Business Statistics Office. — 1978. — London : H.M.S.O., c1980. — 13p in various pagings. — (Business monitor ; PA399.8)
ISBN 0-11-513125-6 : £2.00 B81-05003

Report on the census of production. Miscellaneous metal manufacture / Department of Industry, Business Statistics Office. — 1979. — London : H.M.S.O., c1981. — 13p. in various pagings. — (Business monitor ; PA399.8)
ISBN 0-11-513331-3 : £2.50 B81-32654

338.4'76718 — Great Britain. Metal hollow ware industries — *Statistics — Serials*

Report on the census of production. Metal hollow-ware / Department of Industry, Business Statistics Office. — 1979. — London : H.M.S.O., c1981. — 13p in various pagings. — (Business monitor ; PA339.6)
ISBN 0-11-513345-3 : £2.50 B81-32229

338.4'7671823 — Great Britain. Sheet metal industries — *Serials*

Sheet metal industries year book. — 1981. — Redhill (Queensway House, 2, Queensway, Redhill, Surrey) : Sheet Metal Industries, [1981]. — 299p
ISBN 0-86108-077-7 : £15.00
ISSN 0305-7798 B81-13317

338.4'767183 — Great Britain. Cans & metal boxes industries — *Statistics — Serials*

Report on the census of production. Cans and metal boxes / Department of Industry, Business Statistics Office. — 1979. — London : H.M.S.O., c1981. — 13p in various pagings. — (Business monitor ; PA395)
ISBN 0-11-513311-9 : £2.50 B81-31014

338.4'767184 — Great Britain. Chain manufacturing industries, *to ca 1950*

Fogg, Charles. Chains and chainmaking / Charles Fogg. — Princes Risborough : Shire, 1981. — 32p : 1facsim ; 21cm. — (Shire album ; 69)
Bibliography: p32
ISBN 0-85263-561-3 (pbk) : £0.95 B81-40852

338.4'7671842'0941 — Great Britain. Wire manufacturing industries — *Statistics — Serials*

Report on the census of production. Wire and wire manufactures / Department of Industry, Business Statistics Office. — 1979. — London : H.M.S.O., c1981. — 13p. in various pagings. — (Business monitor ; PA394)
ISBN 0-11-513309-7 : £2.50 B81-32682

338.4'76722'0941 — Great Britain. Iron castings industries — *Statistics — Serials*

Report on the census of production. Iron castings, etc. / Department of Industry, Business Statistics Office. — 1978. — London : H.M.S.O., c1980. — 13p in various pagings. — (Business monitor ; PA313)
ISBN 0-11-513154-x : £2.00 B81-08781

338.4'767283 — Great Britain. Steel tubes industries — *Statistics — Serials*

Report on the census of production. Steel tubes / Department of Industry, Business Statistics Office. — 1978. — London : H.M.S.O., c1980. — 13p in various pagings. — (Business monitor ; PA312)
ISBN 0-11-513155-8 : £2.00 B81-04980

338.4'7674'0941 — Great Britain. Timber industries — *Statistics — Serials*

Report on the census of production. Timber / Department of Industry, Business Statistics Office. — 1978. — London : H.M.S.O., c1980. — 13p in various pagings. — (Business monitor ; PA471)
ISBN 0-11-513098-5 : £2.00 B81-05002

338.4'76748'0941 — Great Britain. Timber products industries — *Statistics — Serials*

Report on the census of production. Miscellaneous wood and cork manufactures / Department of Industry, Business Statistics office. — 1978. — London : H.M.S.O., c1980. — 13p in various pagings. — (Business monitor ; PA479)
ISBN 0-11-513063-2 : £2.00
Also classified at 338.4'76749 B81-01802

338.4'767482'0941 — Great Britain. Basket making & wooden container industries — *Statistics — Serials*

Report on the census of production. Wooden containers and baskets / Department of Industry, Business Statistics Office. — 1978. — London : H.M.S.O., c1980. — 13p in various pagings. — (Business monitor ; PA475)
ISBN 0-11-513107-8 : £2.00 B81-07389

338.4'76749 — Great Britain. Cork products industries — *Statistics — Serials*

Report on the census of production. Miscellaneous wood and cork manufactures / Department of Industry, Business Statistics office. — 1978. — London : H.M.S.O., c1980. — 13p in various pagings. — (Business monitor ; PA479)
ISBN 0-11-513063-2 : £2.00
Primary classification 338.4'76748'0941
B81-01802

338.4'76752'0941 — Great Britain. Leather working industries — *Statistics — Serials*

Report on the census of production. Leather (tanning and dressing) and fellmongery / Department of Industry, Business Statistics Office. — 1978. — London : H.M.S.O., c1980. — 13p. in various pagings. — (Business monitor ; PA431)
ISBN 0-11-513118-3 : £2.00 B81-05048

338.4'76753'0941 — Great Britain. Fur industries — *Statistics — Serials*

Report on the census of production. Fur / Department of Industry, Business Statistics Office. — 1978. — London : H.M.S.O., c1980. — 13p in various pagings. — (Business monitor ; PA433)
ISBN 0-11-513112-4 : £2.00 B81-04981

Report on the census of production. Fur / Department of Industry, Business Statistics Office. — 1979. — London : H.M.S.O., c1981. — 13p. in various pagings. — (Business monitor ; PA433)
ISBN 0-11-513323-2 : £2.50 B81-33317

338.4'7676'0941 — Great Britain. Paper & boards industries — *Statistics — Serials*

Report on the census of production. Paper and board / Department of Industry, Business Statistics Office. — 1979. — London : H.M.S.O., c1981. — 13p in various pagings. — (Business monitor ; PA481)
ISBN 0-11-513263-5 : £2.50 B81-20445

338.4'767614 — Great Britain. Jute industries — *Statistics — Serials*

Report on the census of production. Jute / Department of Industry, Business Statistics Office. — 1978. — London : H.M.S.O., c1980. — 13p in various pagings. — (Business monitor ; PA415)
ISBN 0-11-513069-1 : £2.00 B81-04396

338.4'7676183'0941 — Great Britain. Board packaging industries — *Statistics — Serials*

Report on the census of production. Cardboard boxes, cartons and fibre-board packing cases / Department of Industry, Business Statistics Office. — 1979. — London : H.M.S.O., c1981. — 13p in various pagings. — (Business monitor ; PA482.1)
ISBN 0-11-513264-3 : £2.50 B81-20446

338.4'7677'005 — Textile industries — *Serials*

WP report. — Vol.1, no.1 [(Apr.-May 1980)]-. — Stockport (1 London Place, New Mills, Stockport SK12 4ER) : Technical Industrial Services, c1980-. — v. : ill ; 30cm
Six issues yearly. — Description based on: Vol.1 no.3 [(Aug.-Sept.1980)]
ISSN 0143-8670 = WP report : £25.00 per year B81-04829

338.4'7677'009 — Textile industries, *to ca 1850 — For schools*

Burrell, R. E. C.. What are you wearing? : the story of textiles / R.E.C. Burrell. — Exeter : Wheaton, 1980. — 101p : ill,maps,ports ; 21cm. — (The Making of the Industrial Revolution series ; bk.2)
ISBN 0-08-020577-1 (pbk) : £2.10 B81-01923

338.4'7677'0094 — Europe. Textile industries, *1400-1600 — Festschriften*

Cloth and clothing in medieval Europe. — London : Heinemann Educational, Feb.1982. — [448]p. — (Pasold studies in textile history ; 2)
ISBN 0-435-32382-2 : £15.00 : CIP entry B81-35691

338.4'7677'0094 — European Community countries. Textile industries

Textiles in the eighties : a policy for the textile industry / [the report of a working party of members of the European Democratic Group in the European Parliament]. — London : 32 Smith Sq., SW1P 3HH : EDG, [1980]. — vi,41p ; 21cm
Unpriced (pbk)
Also classified at 338.4'7687'094 B81-08133

338.4'7677'00941 — Great Britain. Textile industries — *Statistics — Serials*

Report on the census of production. Miscellaneous textile industries / Department of Industry, Business Statistics Office. — 1979. — London : H.M.S.O., c1981. — 13p in various pagings. — (Business monitor ; PA429.2)
ISBN 0-11-513304-6 : £2.50 B81-31016

338.4'7677'00941 — Great Britain. Textile industries, *to 1980 — For schools*

Hale, Don. Textiles. — London : Edward Arnold, Sept.1981. — [32]p. — (People and progress)
ISBN 0-7131-0587-9 (pbk) : £1.50 : CIP entry B81-22516

338.4'7677028242 — Great Britain. Warp knitting industries — *Statistics — Serials*

Report on the census of production. Warp knitting / Department of Industry, Business Statistics Office. — 1979. — London : H.M.S.O., c1981. — 13p. in various pagings. — (Business monitor ; PA417.2)
ISBN 0-11-513351-8 : £2.50 B81-32678

338.4'7677702825'0941 — Great Britain. Textile finishing industries — *Statistics — Serials*

Report on the census of production. Textile finishing / Department of Industry, Business Statistics Office. — 1978. — London : H.M.S.O., c1980. — 14p in various pagings. — (Business monitor ; PA423)
ISBN 0-11-513122-1 : £2.50 B81-10307

Report on the census of production. Textile finishing / Department of Industry, Business Statistics Office. — 1979. — London : H.M.S.O., c1981. — 14p. in various pagings. — (Business monitor ; PA423)
ISBN 0-11-513361-5 : £2.80 B81-32905

338.4'76770285'0941 — Great Britain. Textile machinery industries — *Statistics — Serials*

Report on the census of production. Textile machinery and accessories / Department of Industry, Business Statistics Office. — 1979. — London : H.M.S.O., 1981. — 13p in various pagings. — (Business monitor ; PA335)
ISBN 0-11-513392-5 : £2.50 B81-35973

338.4'767702864'0941 — Great Britain. Narrow fabrics industries — *Statistics — Serials*

Report on the census of production. Narrow fabrics / Department of Industry, Business Statistics Office. — 1979. — London : H.M.S.O., c1981. — 8,vp. — (Business monitor ; PA421)
ISBN 0-11-513302-x : £2.50 B81-29654

338.4'7677'0941 — Great Britain. Textile industries — *Trades Union Congress viewpoints*

Textiles, clothing & footwear : policies for the future / a statement prepared by the TUC Textile, Clothing and Footwear Industries Committee. — London : Trades Union Congress, 1980. — 23p : ill ; 21cm. — (TUC campaign for social and economic advance)
£0.35 (pbk)
Also classified at 338.4'7687'0941 B81-22812

338.4'76771122 — Great Britain. Flax spinning industries — *Statistics — Serials*

Report on the census of production. Spinning and doubling on the cotton and flax systems / Department of Industry, Business Statistics Office. — 1979. — London : H.M.S.O., c1981. — 13p in various pagings. — (Business monitor ; PA412)
ISBN 0-11-513334-8 : £2.50
Primary classification 338.4'76772122 B81-30724

338.4'767713'0941 — Great Britain. Jute industries — *Statistics — Serials*

Report on the census of production. Jute / Department of Industry, Business Statistics Office. — 1979. — London : H.M.S.O., c1981. — 13p in various pagings. — (Business monitor ; PA415)
ISBN 0-11-513270-8 : £2.50 B81-20449

338.4'767721'0941 — Great Britain. Cotton manufacturing industries, *to ca 1920*

Aspin, Chris. The cotton industry / Chris Aspin. — Aylesbury : Shire, 1981. — 32p : ill,1facsim ; 21cm. — (Shire album ; 63)
ISBN 0-85263-545-1 (pbk) : £0.95 B81-17555

338.4'767721'0945 — Northern Italy. Cotton manufacturing industries, *1100-1600*

Mazzaoui, Maureen Fennell. The Italian cotton industry in the later Middle Ages 1100-1600 / Maureen Fennell Mazzaoui. — Cambridge : Cambridge University Press, 1981. — xiv,250p : 2ill,1map ; 24cm
Bibliography: p227-243. — Includes index
ISBN 0-521-23095-0 : £24.00 : CIP rev. B81-19109

338.4'76772122 — Great Britain. Cotton spinning industries — *Statistics — Serials*

Report on the census of production. Spinning and doubling on the cotton and flax systems / Department of Industry, Business Statistics Office. — 1979. — London : H.M.S.O., c1981. — 13p in various pagings. — (Business monitor ; PA412)
ISBN 0-11-513334-8 : £2.50
Also classified at 338.4'76771122 B81-30724

338.4'767731'0941 — Great Britain. Wool industries — *Statistics — Serials*

Report on the census of production. Woollen and worsted / Department of Industry, Business Statistics Office. — 1979. — London : H.M.S.O., c1981. — 13p in various pagings. — (Business monitor ; PA414)
ISBN 0-11-513330-5 : £2.50 B81-31013

338.4'76774'0941 — Great Britain. Synthetic fibre industries — *Statistics — Serials*

Report on the census of production. Production of man-made fibres / Department of Industry, Business Statistics Office. — 1978. — London : H.M.S.O., c1980. — 13p in various pagings. — (Business monitor ; PA411)
ISBN 0-11-513097-7 : £2.00 B81-08785

Report on the census of production. Production of man-made fibres / Department of Industry, Business Statistics Office. — 1979. — London : H.M.S.O., c1981. — 13p. in various pagings. — (Business monitor ; PA411)
ISBN 0-11-513342-9 : £2.50 B81-32909

338.4'767754 — Bedfordshire. Basket making industries, *to 1949*

Bagshawe, Thomas Wyatt. Basket making in Bedfordshire / Thomas Wyatt Bagshawe. — [Luton] ([Wardown Park, Luton LU2 7HA]) : Luton Museum & Art Gallery, 1981. — 61p : ill,2maps,1port ; 21cm
Unpriced (pbk) B81-29959

338.4'7677643'0941 — Great Britain. Carpet industries — *Statistics — Serials*

Report on the census of production. Carpets / Department of Industry, Business Statistics Office. — 1979. — London : H.M.S.O., c1981. — 13p. in various pagings. — (Business monitor ; PA419)
ISBN 0-11-513339-9 : £2.50 B81-32681

338.4'7677653'0941 — Great Britain. Lace industries — *Statistics — Serials*

Report on the census of production. Lace / Department of Industry, Business Statistics Office. — 1979. — London : H.M.S.O., c1981. — 13p in various pagings. — (Business monitor ; PA418)
ISBN 0-11-513357-7 : £2.50 B81-32227

338.4'76777'0941 — Great Britain. Cordage industries — *Statistics — Serials*

Report on the census of production. Rope, twine and net / Department of Industry, Business Statistics Office. — 1979. — London : H.M.S.O., c1981. — 13p in various pagings. — (Business monitor ; PA416)
ISBN 0-11-513349-6 : £2.50 B81-32232

338.4'76778 — Great Britain. Sanitary tampons industries & trades — *Inquiry reports*

Great Britain. *Monopolies and Mergers Commission.* Tampons : a report on the supply in the United Kingdom of tampons / Monopolies and Mergers Commission. — London : H.M.S.O., [1980]. — vi,57p ; 25cm. — (Cmnd. ; 8049)
Includes index
ISBN 0-10-180490-3 (pbk) : £3.80 B81-04506

338.4'76778'0941 — Great Britain. Surgical dressings industries — *Statistics — Serials*

Report on the census of production. Surgical bandages, etc / Department of Industry, Business Statistics Office. — 1979. — London : H.M.S.O., c1981. — 13p in various pagings. — (Business monitor ; PA279.6)
ISBN 0-11-513318-6 : £2.50 B81-30728

338.4'76782 — Rubber industries & trades

Grilli, Enzo R.. The world rubber economy : structure, changes, and prospects / Enzo R. Grilli, Barbara Bennett Agostini, and Maria J.'t Hooft-Welvaars. — Baltimore ; London : Published for the World Bank [by] The Johns Hopkins University Press, c1980. — xviii,204p ; 23cm. — (World Bank staff occasional papers ; no.30)
Bibliography: p200-204
ISBN 0-8018-2421-4 (pbk) : £4.00 B81-11816

338.4'767862 — Natural rubber industries & trades. Treaties: International Natural Rubber Agreement. Economic aspects

Natural rubber : a detailed examination of aspects of the International natural rubber agreement and its wider implications. — London : Economist Intelligence Unit, c1980. — xxi,375p ; 30cm. — (An EIU commodity monograph)
Bibliography: p373-375
Unpriced (spiral) B81-15029

338.4'76797'091724 — Developing countries. Tobacco industries. Socioeconomic aspects

Leaf tobacco : its contribution to the economic and social development of the Third World. — London : Economist Intelligence Unit, c1980. — iii,366p : ill,maps ; 30cm. — (An EIU commodity monograph)
Unpriced (spiral) B81-15030

338.4'76797'0941 — Great Britain. Tobacco industries — *Statistics — Serials*

Report on the census of production. Tobacco / Department of Industry, Business Statistics Office. — 1979. — London : H.M.S.O., c1981. — 13p in various pagings. — (Business monitor ; PA240)
ISBN 0-11-513355-0 : £2.50 B81-32230

338.4'768 — Great Britain. Business equipment industries. Organisations: Business Equipment Trade Association — *Directories — Serials*

Business Equipment Trade Association. List of members / Business Equipment Trade Association. — 1981. — London (8 Southampton Place, WC1A 2EF) : The Association, [1981?]. — 54p
ISSN 0308-9479 : Unpriced B81-31029

338.4'7681 — Great Britain. Office machinery industries — *Statistics — Serials*

Report on the census of production. Office machinery / Department of Industry, Business Statistics Office. — 1979. — London : H.M.S.O., c1981. — 13p in various pagings. — (Business monitor ; PA338)
ISBN 0-11-513363-1 : £2.50 B81-32233

338.4'768111'0941 — Great Britain. Clockmaking & watchmaking industries — *Statistics — Serials*

Report on the census of production. Watches and clocks / Department of Industry, Business Statistics Office. — 1979. — London : H.M.S.O., c1981. — 13p in various pagings. — (Business monitor ; PA352)
ISBN 0-11-513325-9 : £2.50 B81-30730

338.4'76812 — Great Britain. Weighing equipment industries — *Statistics — Serials*

Report on the census of production. Scales and weighing machinery and portable power tools / Department of Industry, Business Statistics Office. — 1978. — London : H.M.S.O., c1980. — 13p in various pagings. — (Business monitor ; PA339.5)
ISBN 0-11-513110-8 : £2.00
Also classified at 338.4'7621902'0941
B81-05359

338.4'7681418'0941 — Great Britain. Photographic equipment industries — *Statistics — Serials*

Report on the census of production. Photographic and document copying equipment / Department of Industry, Business Statistics Office. — 1978. — London : H.M.S.O., c1980. — 13p in various pagings. — (Business monitor ; PA351)
ISBN 0-11-513141-8 : £2.00
Also classified at 338.4'768165'0941
B81-05375

338.4'76816'0941 — Great Britain. Printing equipment industries — *Statistics — Serials*

Report on the census of production. Printing, bookbinding and paper goods machinery / Department of Industry, Business Statistics Office. — 1978. — London : H.M.S.O., c1980. — 13p. in various pagings. — (Business monitor ; PA339.2)
ISBN 0-11-513106-x : £2.00 B81-05336

338.4'768165'0941 — Great Britain. Copying equipment industries — *Statistics — Serials*

Report on the census of production. Photographic and document copying equipment / Department of Industry, Business Statistics Office. — 1978. — London : H.M.S.O., c1980. — 13p in various pagings. — (Business monitor ; PA351)
ISBN 0-11-513141-8 : £2.00
Primary classification 338.4'7681418'0941
B81-05375

338.4'768175'0941 — Great Britain. Scientific equipment industries — *Statistics — Serials*

Report on the census of production. Scientific and industrial instruments and systems / Department of Industry, Business Statistics Office. — 1978. — London : H.M.S.O., c1980. — 13p in various pagings. — (Business monitor ; PA354)
ISBN 0-11-513138-8 : £2.00
Also classified at 338.4'762'00028 B81-05000

338.4'7681761 — Great Britain. Surgical applicances industries & surgical equipment industries — *Statistics — Serials*

Report on the census of production. Surgical instruments and appliances / Department of Industry, Business Statistics Office. — 1978. — London : H.M.S.O., c1980. — 13p in various pagings. — (Business monitor ; PA353)
ISBN 0-11-513145-0 : £2.00 B81-07386

338.4'7681763'0941 — Great Britain. Agricultural equipment industries — *Statistics*

Agricultural business manufacturers : an industry sector analysis / ICC Business Ratios. — 4th ed. — London (81 City Rd., EC1Y 1BD) : ICC Business Ratios, [1981]. — [72]p ; 30cm. — (ICC business ratio report)
ISBN 0-86261-076-1 (pbk) : Unpriced
B81-40837

338.4'76817664'0941 — Great Britain. Food & drinks industries equipment industries — *Statistics — Serials*

Report on the census of production. Food and drink processing machinery and packaging and bottling machinery / Department of Industry, Business Statistics Office. — 1978. — London : H.M.S.O., c1980. — 13p. in various pagings. — (Business monitor ; PA339.7)
ISBN 0-11-513128-0 : £2.00 B81-05054

Report on the census of production. Food and drink processing machinery and packaging and bottling machinery / Department of Industry, Business Statistics Office. — 1979. — London : H.M.S.O., c1981. — 13p in various pagings. — (Business monitor ; PA339.7)
ISBN 0-11-513367-4 : £2.50 B81-32226

338.4'76818'0941 — Great Britain. Musical instruments industries — *Statistics — Serials*

Report on the census of production. Musical instruments / Department of Industry, Business Statistics Office. — 1978. — London : H.M.S.O., c1980. — 13p in various pagings. — (Business monitor ; PA499.1)
ISBN 0-11-513102-7 : £2.00 B81-04982

Report on the census of production. Musical instruments / Department of Industry, Business Statistics Office. — 1979. — London : H.M.S.O., c1981. — 13p in various pagings. — (Business monitor ; PA499.1)
ISBN 0-11-513266-x : £2.50 B81-20450

338.4'76824 — Great Britain. Architectural ironmongery industries — *Statistics — Serials*

Architectural ironmongers. — 2nd ed. — London : ICC Business Ratios, c1981. — [72]p. — (ICC Business Ratio report)
ISBN 0-86261-102-4 : £80.00 B81-26600

338.4'768383'0941 — Great Britain. Household electric appliance industries — *Statistics — Serials*

Report on the census of production. Electrical appliances primarily for domestic use / Department of Industry, Business Statistics Office. — London : H.M.S.O., c1980. — 13p in various pagings. — (Business monitor ; PA368)
ISBN 0-11-513162-0 : £2.00 B81-08780

Report on the census of production. Electrical appliances primarily for domestic use / Department of Industry, Business Statistics Office. — 1979. — London : H.M.S.O., 1981. — 13p in various pagings. — (Business monitor ; PA368)
ISBN 0-11-513403-4 : £2.50 B81-35975

338.4'7'68408'0941 — Great Britain. Do-it-yourself industries & trades — *Statistics — Serials — For marketing*

D.I.Y. and home improvements : ... report. — 1978-. — London : Euromonitor, 1978-. — v. ; 30cm
Irregular
ISSN 0260-6542 = D.I.Y. and home improvements : £75.00 B81-06689

338.4'76841'00941 — Great Britain. Furniture industries & trades — *Statistics — Serials*

British furniture manufacturers & wholesalers. — [1980]. — London : Jordan & Sons (Surveys) Ltd., c1980. — xii,75p
ISBN 0-85938-131-5 : £85.00 B81-22405

338.4'76841'00941 — Great Britain. Furniture industries — *Statistics — Serials*

Report on the census of production. Furniture and upholstery / Department of Industry, Business Statistics Office. — 1978. — London : H.M.S.O., c1980. — 13p in various pagings. — (Business monitor ; PA472)
ISBN 0-11-513079-9 : £2.00 B81-01787

338.4'7684105'0941 — Great Britain. Metal furniture industries — *Statistics — Serials*

Report on the census of production. Metal furniture / Department of Industry, Business Statistics Office. — 1979. — London : H.M.S.O., c1981. — 13p. in various pagings. — (Business monitor ; PA399.1)
ISBN 0-11-513333-x : £2.50 B81-32652

338.4'76843 — Great Britain. Bedding industries — *Statistics — Serials*

Report on the census of production. Bedding, etc. / Department of Industry, Business Statistics Office. — 1979. — London : H.M.S.O., 1981. — 13p in various pagings. — (Business monitor ; PA473)
ISBN 0-11-513395-x : £2.50 B81-35980

338.4'76843'0941 — Great Britain. Soft furnishing industries — *Statistics — Serials*

Report on the census of production. Bedding, etc / Department of Industry, Business Statistics Office. — 1978. — London : H.M.S.O., c1980. — 13p in various pagings. — (Business monitor ; PA473)
ISBN 0-11-513113-2 : £2.00 B81-07390

338.4'7685'0941 — Great Britain. Leather products industries — *Statistics — Serials*

Report on the census of production. Leather goods / Department of Industry, Business Statistics Office. — 1978. — London : H.M.S.O., c1980. — 13p in various pagings. — (Business monitor ; PA432)
ISBN 0-11-513121-3 : £2.00 B81-04999

338.4'7685'0941 — Great Britain. Leather products industries — *Statistics — Serials*
continuation

Report on the census of production. Leather goods / Department of Industry, Business Statistics Office. — 1979. — London : H.M.S.O., c1981. — 13p in various pagings. — (Business monitor ; PA432)
ISBN 0-11-513402-6 : £2.50 B81-36309

338.4'76853'0941 — Great Britain. Footwear industries — *Statistics — Serials*

Report on the census of production. Footwear / Department of Industry, Business Statistics Office. — 1978. — London : H.M.S.O., c1980. — 13p in various pagings. — (Business monitor ; PA450)
ISBN 0-11-513119-1 : £2.00 B81-08347

Report on the census of production. Footwear / Department of Industry, Business Statistics Office. — 1979. — London : H.M.S.O., c1981. — 13p. in various pagings. — (Business monitor ; PA450)
ISBN 0-11-513362-3 : £2.50 B81-32908

338.4'76854'0941 — Great Britain. Glove industries — *Statistics — Serials*

Report on the census of production. Gloves / Department of Industry, Business Statistics Office. — 1979. — London : H.M.S.O., c1981. — 13p. in various pagings. — (Business monitor ; PA449.2)
ISBN 0-11-513314-3 : £2.50 B81-32680

338.4'7686'02573 — United States. Book industries & trades — *Directories*

American book trade directory / edited and compiled by the Jaques Cattell Press. — 26th ed (1980). — New York ; London : Bowker, c1980. — xiii,1133p
ISBN 0-8352-1252-1 : Unpriced B81-03459

338.4'7686'09424 — England. West Midlands. Book industries & trades, *to 1850 — Lists*

Working papers for an historical directory of the West Midlands book trade to 1850 / compiled by members of the Birmingham Bibliographical Society and edited by P.B. Freshwater. — Birmingham ([Main Library, University of Birmingham, PO Box 363, Birmingham B15 2TT]) : The Society
No.5: 1810-1819 / edited by Pamela C. Freck, Nesta Jenkins. — 1981, c1980. — iii,27p ; 30cm
Cover title. — Bibliography: pii-iii
ISBN 0-904474-05-4 (pbk) : £1.50 (£1.25 to members) B81-34447

338.4'7686'09428 — North-east England. Book industries & trades, *to 1860 — Lists*

Wallis, Peter John. The North-East book trade to 1860 : imprints and subscriptions / by Peter John Wallis. — 2nd enl. ed. — Newcastle upon Tyne ([School of Education, University of Newcastle upon Tyne, 6 Kensington Terrace, Newcastle upon Tyne NE1 7RU]) : Project for Historical Biobibliography, 1981. — 44p in various pagings ; 30cm. — (PHIBB ; 268)
Previous ed.: 1977
ISBN 0-7017-0026-2 (unbound) : £1.00 B81-34253

338.4'7686'0973 — United States. Book industries — *Serials*

The **Bowker** annual of library & book trade information. — 26th ed. (1981). — New York ; London : Bowker, c1981
ISBN 0-8352-1343-9 : Unpriced
Primary classification 020'.973 B81-33466

338.4'76862'06041 — Great Britain. Printing industries. Organisations: British Printing Industries Federation — *Serials*

Printing industries annual. — 1981. — London : British Printing Industries Federation, [1981]. — 784p
ISBN 0-85168-134-4 : Unpriced
ISSN 0308-1443 B81-29666

338.4'76862'09 — Printing industries — *History — Serials*

[**Bulletin** *(Printing Historical Society)*]. Bulletin / Printing Historical Society. — 1 (Sept. 1980)-. — London (St. Bride Institute, Bride La., Fleet St., EC4) : The Society, 1980-. — v. ; 25cm
Three issues yearly. — Continues: Newsletter (Printing Historical Society)
ISSN 0144-7505 = Bulletin — Printing Historical Society : £8.00 per year B81-02030

338.4'76862'0941 — Great Britain. Printing industries

Prospects for print : the difficulties and challenges facing the printing industry / TUC Printing Industries Committee. — [London] : NATSOPA, 1981. — 17p : col.ill,1col.map ; 21cm
Unpriced (unbound) B81-31856

338.4'76862'0941 — Great Britain. Private presses, *1891-1975*

Take a look at the book : the Allan collection. — [Glasgow] ([Richmond St., Glasgow G1 1XQ) : Collins Exhibition Hall, University of Strathclyde], c1981. — [19]p : facsims ; 18cm
ISBN 0-907114-03-2 (unbound) : £0.50 B81-35531

338.4'76862'0943 — West Germany. Printing industries. Innovation, *1869-1978*

Erd, Rainer. Innovation in the printing industry in the Federal Republic : a survey / carried out for the Anglo-German Foundation for the Study of Industrial Society by Rainer Erd and Walther Müller-Jentsch. — [London] : Anlo-German Foundation for the Study of Industrial Society, [1980]. — 77p ; 30cm. — (Research papers / Anglo-German Foundation for the Study of Industrial Society)
ISBN 0-905492-12-9 (pbk) : £4.00 B81-12261

338.4'76862'095414 — India *(Republic)*. **Calcutta. Printing industries,** *to 1800*

Shaw, Graham. Printing in Calcutta to 1800 : a description and checklist of printing in late 18th century Calcutta / by Graham Shaw. — London : Bibliographical Society, 1981. — xi,249p : 1map,facsims ; 25cm. — (Bibliographical Society publication for the year 1976)
Includes index
ISBN 0-19-721792-3 : Unpriced : CIP rev. B81-02359

338.4'76862316 — Great Britain. Screen printing industries — *Serials*

Point of sale & screenprinting. — Vol.31, no.1 (Jan.1981)-. — London (Pembroke House, Campsbourne Rd, Hornsey, N8) : Batiste Publications, 1981-. — v. : ill ; 30cm
Monthly. — Continues: Point of sale news
£11.00 per year
Primary classification 338.4'7659157'0941 B81-16735

338.4'7687 — Children's clothing industries & trades — *Serials*

Childrens clothing international. — Mar. 1981-. — London (149 Upper St., N1) : Childrens Clothing International Magazine Ltd., 1981-. — v. : ill,maps,plans,ports ; 29cm
Quarterly
ISSN 0261-6025 = Childrens clothing international : £10.00 for 2 years B81-33290

338.4'7687 — Great Britain. Babies' clothing industries & women's clothing industries — *Statistics — Serials*

Report on the census of production. Dresses, lingerie, infants' wear etc. / Department of Industry, Business Statistics Office. — 1978. — London : H.M.S.O., c1980. — 13p in various pagings. — (Business monitor ; PA445)
ISBN 0-11-513158-2 : £2.00 B81-07388

Report on the census of production. Dresses, lingerie, infants' wear, etc. / Department of Industry, Business Statistics Office. — 1979. — London : H.M.S.O., 1981. — 13p in various pagings. — (Business monitor ; PA445)
ISBN 0-11-513384-4 : £2.50 B81-35976

338.4'7687 — Great Britain. Men's clothing industries — *Statistics — Serials*

Report on the census of production. Overalls and men's shirts, underwear, etc, / Department of Industry, Business Statistics Office. — 1978. — London : H.M.S.O., c1980. — 13p in various pagings. — (Business monitor ; PA444)
ISBN 0-11-513153-1 : £2.00
Primary classification 338.4'768716 B81-05357

338.4'7687'094 — European Community countries. Clothing industries

Textiles in the eighties : a policy for the textile industry / [the report of a working party of members of the European Democratic Group in the European Parliament]. — London : 32 Smith Sq., SW1P 3HH : EDG, [1980]. — vi,41p ; 21cm
Unpriced (pbk)
Primary classification 338.4'7677'0094 B81-08133

338.4'7687'0941 — Great Britain. Clothing industries — *Trades Union Congress viewpoints*

Textiles, clothing & footwear : policies for the future / a statement prepared by the TUC Textile, Clothing and Footwear Industries Committee. — London : Trades Union Congress, 1980. — 23p : ill ; 21cm. — (TUC campaign for social and economic advance)
£0.35 (pbk)
Primary classification 338.4'7677'0941 B81-22812

338.4'7687'0973 — United States. Clothing industries

Jarnow, Jeannette A.. Inside the fashion business : text and readings. — 3rd ed. / Jeannette A. Jarnow, Beatrice Judelle, Miriam Guerreiro. — New York ; Chichester : Wiley, c1981. — xii,427p : ill,maps,facsims ; 25cm
Previous ed.: 1974. — Includes bibliographies and index
ISBN 0-471-06038-0 : £12.25 B81-24228

Solinger, Jacob. Apparel manufacturing handbook : analysis, principles and practice / Jacob Solinger. — New York ; London : Van Nostrand Reinhold, c1980. — xiii,795p : ill,forms ; 26cm
Bibliography: p671-681. — Includes index
ISBN 0-442-21904-0 : £45.00 B81-23256

338.4'76871 — Great Britain. Men's outerwear industries — *Statistics — Serials*

Report on the census of production. Men's and boys' tailored outerwear / Department of Industry, Business Statistics Office. — 1978. — London : H.M.S.O., c1980. — 13p in various pagings. — (Business monitor ; PA442)
ISBN 0-11-513109-4 : £2.00 B81-05358

338.4'76871 — Great Britain. Women's outerware industries — *Statistics — Serials*

Report on the census of production. Women's and girls' tailored outerwear / Department of Industry, Business Statistics Office. — 1978. — London : H.M.S.O., c1980. — 13p in various pagings. — (Business monitor ; PA443)
ISBN 0-11-513147-7 : £2.00 B81-07387

338.4'768714 — Great Britain. Weatherproof outerwear industries — *Statistics — Serials*

Report on the census of production. Weatherproof outerwear / Department of Industry, Business Statistics Office. — 1979. — London : H.M.S.O., c1981. — 13p in various pagings. — (Business monitor ; PA441)
ISBN 0-11-513372-0 : £2.50 B81-34029

338.4'768716 — Great Britain. Protective clothing industries — *Statistics — Serials*

Report on the census of production. Overalls and men's shirts, underwear, etc, / Department of Industry, Business Statistics Office. — 1978. — London : H.M.S.O., c1980. — 13p in various pagings. — (Business monitor ; PA444)
ISBN 0-11-513153-1 : £2.00
Also classified at 338.4'7687 B81-05357

338.4′76873′0941 — Great Britain. Hosiery & knitwear industries — *Statistics* — *Serials*

Knitstats : a half-yearly statistical bulletin for the Hosiery and Knitwear Industry / compiled from official and other sources by a Joint Industry Working Party representing Hatra ... [et al.]. — 1 (June 1976)-. — Nottingham (Information Department, Hatra, 7 Gregory Boulevard, Nottingham) : Hatra, 1976-. — v. ; 30cm
Description based on: 9 (Aug.1980)
ISSN 0260-8855 = Knitstats : £2.50 per issue
B81-09197

Report on the census of production. Hosiery and other knitted goods / Department of Industry, Business Statistics Office. — 1978. — London : H.M.S.O., c1980. — 13p in various pagings. — (Business monitor ; PA417.1)
ISBN 0-11-513105-1 : £2.00 B81-04977

Report on the census of production. Hosiery and other knitted goods / Department of Industry, Business Statistics Office. — 1979. — London : H.M.S.O., c1981. — 13p. in various pagings. — (Business monitor ; PA417.1)
ISBN 0-11-513350-x : £2.50 B81-32907

338.4′76887 — Great Britain. Coin slot recreational machinery industries & trades — *Serials*

Coin slot location. — Vol.1:1 (Autumn 1980)-. — Oldham (P.O. Box 57, Daltry St., Oldham, Lancs. OL14 4BB) : World's Fair, 1980-. — v. : ill(some col.),ports ; 30cm
Quarterly
ISSN 0261-6866 = Coin slot location : £10.20 per year B81-33460

338.4′76887′0941 — Great Britain. Toy industries & trades & games equipment industries & trades — *Serials*

Toys & games trader. — Vol.121, no.880 (Apr.1981)-. — Rickmansworth (4 Local Board Rd, Watford WD1 2JS) : Trade Papers, 1981-. — v. : ill,ports ; 30cm
Monthly. — Merger of: Toy trader ; and, Games and toys
ISSN 0262-2351 = Toys & games trader : Unpriced B81-39511

338.4′768872′0941 — Great Britain. Toy industries

Toys & games / industry commentary by John Stevens. — London : Jordan & Sons (Surveys) Ltd, c1980. — 68p ; 30cm. — (A Jordan survey)
ISBN 0-85938-142-0 (pbk) : £30.00 B81-10673

338.4′768872′0941 — Great Britain. Toy industries — *Statistics* — *Serials*

Report on the census of production. Toys, games and children's carriages / Department of Industry, Business Statistics Office. — 1978. — London : H.M.S.O., c1980. — 13p in various pagings. — (Business monitor ; PA494.1)
ISBN 0-11-513076-4 : £2.00 B81-01806

Report on the census of production. Toys, games and children's carriages / Department of Industry, Business Statistics Office. — 1979. — London : H.M.S.O., c1981. — 13p. in various pagings. — (Business monitor ; PA494.1)
ISBN 0-11-513332-1 : £2.50 B81-32655

338.4′768876′0941 — Great Britain. Sports equipment industries & trades — *Serials*

Sports trade news. — [No.1] 1978-1980. — [Sidcup] ([104 Station Rd, Sidcup, Kent]) : [Stone Industrial Publications, 1978-1980. — v. : ill,ports ; 41cm
Monthly. — Absorbed by: Leisure trade news, 1980. — Description based on: 6/80 issue
£6.00 per year B81-03580

338.4′768876′0941 — Great Britain. Sports equipment industries — *Statistics* — *Serials*

Report on the census of production. Sports equipment / Department of Industry, Business Statistics Office. — 1978. — London : H.M.S.O., c1980. — 13p in various pagings. — (Business monitor ; PA494.3)
ISBN 0-11-513096-9 : £2.00 B81-01799

Report on the census of production. Sports equipment / Department of Industry, Business Statistics Office. — 1979. — London : H.M.S.O., c1981. — 13p. in various pagings. — (Business monitor ; PA494.3)
ISBN 0-11-513341-0 : £2.50 B81-32671

338.4′76888 — Great Britain. Freight container industries — *Statistics* — *Serials*

Report on the census of production. Trailers, caravans and freight containers / Department of Industry, Business Statistics Office. — 1979. — London : H.M.S.O., c1981. — 13p in various pagings. — (Business monitor ; PA381.2)
ISBN 0-11-513319-4 : £2.50
Primary classification 338.4′7629226′0941
B81-31018

338.4′769′006041 — Great Britain. Building industries. Organisations. Chartered Institute of Building — *Serials*

Chartered Institute of Building. The Chartered Institute of Building year book. — 1980-1981-. — Ascot : The Institute, 1980-. — v. : ill,ports ; 24cm
Continues: Institute of Building year book and directory of members
ISSN 0260-7727 = Chartered Institute of Building year book : £3.00 B81-06677

338.4′769′006041 — Great Britain. Building industries. Organisations: Institute of Building — *Directories* — *Serials*

Institute of Building. Year book and directory of members / the Institute of Building. — 1979-1980. — Ascot : The Institute, [1979?]. — 401p in various pagings
ISBN 0-906600-16-2 : £15.00
ISSN 0073-9014 B81-04935

338.4′769′0060411 — Scotland. Building industries. Organisations: Federation of Master Builders. *Northern Counties & Scotland Region* — *Serials*

Federation of Master Builders. *Northern Counties & Scotland Region.* Year book / Federation of Master Builders, Northern Counties & Scotland Region. — 1981-82. — [Newcastle-upon-Tyne] ([4 Hutton Terrace, Newcastle-upon-Tyne NE2 1QT]) : [The Federation], [1981]. — 176p
Spine title: FMB year book ... Northern Counties & Scotland Region
ISBN 0-901724-44-0 : Unpriced
ISSN 0141-366x
Primary classification 338.4′769′0060427
B81-35988

338.4′769′0060421 — London. Building industries: National Federation of Building Trades Employers. *London Region* — *Directories* — *Serials*

National Federation of Building Trades Employers. *London Region.* National Federation of Building Trades Employers, London Region. — 1980/81. — London (18 Duchess Mews, W1N 3AD) : The Region, [1980?]. — 46p
£1.50 B81-08759

338.4′769′0060421 — London. Building industries. Organisations: Federation of Master Builders. *London Region* — *Serials*

Federation of Master Builders. *London Region.* Year book / Federation of Master Builders London Region. — 1981-82. — London (33 John St., WC1N 2BB) : The Federation, [1981]. — 260p
Spine title: FMB year book ... London Region
ISBN 0-901724-42-4 : Unpriced
ISSN 0141-3643 B81-35463

338.4′769′0060422 — Southern England. Building industries. Organisations: Federation of Master Builders. *Southern Counties Region* — *Serials*

Federation of Master Builders. *Southern Counties Region.* Year book / Federation of Master Builders, Southern Counties Region. — 1981-82. — [Sevenoaks] ([71 London Rd, Sevenoaks, Kent]) : [The Federation], [1981]. — 192p
Spine title: FMB year book ... Southern Counties Region
ISBN 0-901724-46-7 : Unpriced
ISSN 0261-8680 B81-35986

338.4′769′0060422 — Southern England. Building industries. Organisations: National Federation of Building Trades Employers. *Southern Region* — *Directories* — *Serials*

National Federation of Building Trades Employers. *Southern Region.* Year book and register of members / National Federation of Building Trades Employers, Southern Region. — 1981/82. — Horsham (Sterling Buildings, Carfax, Horsham) : The Federation, Southern Region, [1981]. — 204p
ISSN 0305-1153 : Unpriced B81-29668

338.4′769′0060423 — South-west England. Building industries. Organisations: Federation of Master Builders. *South West Region* — *Serials*

Federation of Master Builders. *South West Region.* Year book / Federation of Master Builders, South West Region. — 1981-82. — [Bristol] ([1 St. Paul's Rd, Clifton, Bristol BS8 1LZ]) : [The Federation], [1981]. — 196p
Spine title: FMB year book ... South West Region
ISBN 0-901724-48-3 : Unpriced
ISSN 0141-3708 B81-35989

338.4′769′0060424 — England. Midlands. Building industries. Organisations: Federation of Master Builders. *Midland Region* — *Directories* — *Serials*

Federation of Master Builders. *Midland Region.* Year book / Federation of Master Builders, Midland Region. — 1981-82. — [Warley] ([780 Hagley Rd West, Oldbury, Warley, West Midlands B68 0PJ]) : The Federation, [1981]. — 204p
ISBN 0-901724-43-2 : Unpriced
ISSN 0533-0378 B81-33304

338.4′769′0060426 — East Anglia. Building industries. Organisations: National Federation of Building Trades Employers. *Eastern Region* — *Directories* — *Serials*

National Federation of Building Trades Employers. *Eastern Region.* Directory & year book / Eastern Region, National Federation of Building Trades Employers. — 1981. — Cambridge (95 Tenison Rd, Cambridge CB1 2DL) : The Federation, Eastern Region, [1981]. — 140p
ISSN 0305-8115 : Unpriced B81-29669

338.4′769′0060426 — Eastern England. Building industries. Organisations: Federation of Master Builders. *Eastern Counties Region* — *Serials*

Federation of Master Builders. *Eastern Counties Region.* Year book / Federation of Master Builders, Eastern Counties Region. — 1981-82. — [Cambridge] ([4 Brooklands Ave., Cambridge CB2 2BB]) : [The Federation], [1981]. — 147p
Spine title: FMB year book ... Eastern Counties Region
ISBN 0-901724-41-6 : Unpriced
ISSN 0141-3686 B81-35985

338.4′769′0060427 — North-West England. Building industries. Organisations: Federation of Master Builders. *North West Region* — *Serials*

Federation of Master Builders. *North West Region.* Year book / Federation of Master Builders, North West Region. — 1981-82. — [Birkdale] ([William & Glyn's Bank Chambers, 3 Liverpool Rd, Birkdale, Lancs.]) : [The Federation], [1981]. — 248p
Spine title: FMB year book ... North West Region
ISBN 0-901724-45-9 : Unpriced
ISSN 0141-3651 B81-35984

338.4′769′0060427 — North-west England. Building industries. Organisations: National Federation of Building Trades Employers. *North Western Region* — *Directories* — *Serials*

National Federation of Building Trades Employers. *North Western Region.* Year book and directory / the National Federation of Building Trades Employers (North Western Region). — 1980-81. — [Manchester] ([2 Conyngham Rd, Victoria Park, Manchester M14 5SH]) : [The Federation], [1980?]. — 187p
Unpriced B81-10273

338.4'769'0060427 — Northern England. Building industries. Organisations: Federation of Master Builders. *Northern Counties & Scotland Region — Serials*

Federation of Master Builders. *Northern Counties & Scotland Region.* Year book / Federation of Master Builders, Northern Counties & Scotland Region. — 1981-82. — [Newcastle-upon-Tyne] ([4 Hutton Terrace, Newcastle-upon-Tyne NE2 1QT]) : [The Federation], [1981]. — 176p
Spine title: FMB year book ... Northern Counties & Scotland Region
ISBN 0-901724-44-0 : Unpriced
ISSN 0141-366x
Also classified at 338.4'769'0060411
B81-35988

338.4'769'0060428 — North-east England. Building industries. Organisations: National Federation of Building Trades Employers. *Northern Counties Region — Serials*

National Federation of Building Trades Employers. *Northern Counties Region.* Directory & year book / Northern Counties Region, National Federation of Building Trades Employers. — 1980/1981. — Durham City (Green Lane, Old Elret, Durham City, Co. Durham DH1 3JY) : The Federation, [1980?]. — 129p
Unpriced B81-03853

338.4'769'00604281 — Yorkshire. Building industries. Organisations: Federation of Master Builders. *Yorkshire Region — Serials*

Federation of Master Builders. *Yorkshire Region.* Year book / Federation of Master Builders Yorkshire Region. — 1981-82. — Leeds (29 Basinghall Buildings, Butts Court, Leeds LS1 5HX) : The Federation, [1981]. — 172p
Spine title: FMB year book ... Yorkshire Region
ISBN 0-901724-49-1 : Unpriced
ISSN 0141-3678 B81-35464

338.4'769'00604294 — South Wales. Building industries. Organisations: Federation of Master Builders. *South Wales Region — Serials*

Federation of Master Builders. *South Wales Region.* Year book / Federation of Master Builders, South Wales Region. — 1981-82. — [Cardiff] ([275 Cowbridge Road East, Cardiff CF5]) : [The Federation], [1981]. — 120p
Spine title: FMB year book ... South Wales Region
ISBN 0-901724-47-5 : Unpriced
ISSN 0141-3694 B81-35987

338.4'7690'0941 — Great Britain. Building industries, *1815-1979*

Powell, C. G. An economic history of the British building industry, 1815-1979. — London : Methuen, Jan.1982. — [224]p
ISBN 0-416-32010-4 (pbk) : £4.95 : CIP entry
B81-34400

338.4'7690521 — Great Britain. Shopfitting industries *— Statistics — Serials*

Report on the census of production. Shop and office fitting / Department of Industry, Business Statistics Office. — 1978. — London : H.M.S.O., c1980. — 13p in various pagings. — (Business monitor ; PA474)
ISBN 0-11-513100-0 : £2.00
Also classified at 338.4'7690523 B81-01807

Shopfitters. — 2nd ed. — London : ICC Business Ratios, c1981. — [72]p. — (ICC Business Ratio report)
ISBN 0-86261-084-2 : £80.00 B81-26603

338.4'7690523 — Great Britain. Office fitting industries *— Statistics — Serials*

Report on the census of production. Shop and office fitting / Department of Industry, Business Statistics Office. — 1978. — London : H.M.S.O., c1980. — 13p in various pagings. — (Business monitor ; PA474)
ISBN 0-11-513100-0 : £2.00
Primary classification 338.4'7690521
B81-01807

338.4'76908'0941 — Great Britain. Housing construction industries. Small firms *— Serials*

BJ : the builders journal : the business magazine for the small builder and home improvement contractor. — Vol.1, no.1 (Nov.1978)-. — Watford (32 Vale Rd, Bushey, Watford, Herts.) : Published by Hamerville for Shannon Business Press, 1980-. — v. : ill,ports ; 29cm
Ten issues yearly. — Continues: The builder and decorator. — Description based on: Vol.2, no.6
ISSN 0260-5120 = BJ. The builders journal : £15.00 B81-03279

338.4'7691 — Great Britain. Building materials supply industries *— Serials*

Building products. — Oct.1977-. — Stanford-le-Hope (One Grover Walk, Corringham Town Centre, Stanford-le-Hope, Essex SS17 7BR) : Patey Doyle (Pub.), 1977-. — v. : ill ; 31cm
Monthly. — Description based on: Jan.1981
ISSN 0261-8761 = Building products : £24.00 per year B81-33938

338.4'7691 — Great Britain. Building product industries *— Statistics*

Building material manufacturing & quarrying / industry commentary by Stephen Bloomfield. — London : Jordan, c1980. — xx,74p ; 30cm. — (A Jordan survey)
ISBN 0-85938-143-9 (pbk) : £30.00 B81-11761

338.4'7691'0941 — Great Britain. Building materials manufacturing industries *— Statistics — Serials*

Report on the census of production. Miscellaneous building materials and mineral products / Department of Industry, Business Statistics Office. — 1978. — London : H.M.S.O., c1980. — 13p in various pagings. — (Business monitor ; PA469.2)
ISBN 0-11-513133-7 : £2.00 B81-05361

338.4'7697'000941 — Great Britain. Air conditioning, heating & ventilation equipment industries *— Statistics — Serials*

Report on the census of production. Refrigerating machinery, space-heating, ventilating and air-conditioning equipment / Department of Industry, Business Statistics Office. — 1978. — London : H.M.S.O., c1980. — 13p in various pagings. — (Business monitor ; PA339.3)
ISBN 0-11-513137-x : £2.00
Primary classification 338.4'762156'0941
B81-05373

338.4'773927'0941 — Great Britain. Jewellery industries *— Statistics — Serials*

Report on the census of production. Jewellery and precious matals / Department of Industry, Business Statistics Office. — 1978. — London : H.M.S.O., c1980. — 13p in various pagings. — (Business monitor ; PA396)
ISBN 0-11-513164-7 : £2.00
Primary classification 338.4'76692'0941
B81-08779

338.4'776'0028 — Great Britain. Graphic design equipment & materials trades & services for graphic design industries *— Directories — Serials*

Graphics world. Services and supplies directory. — 1980/81-. — Maidstone (Miller House, 43 Lower Stone St., Maidstone, Kent ME15 6LQ) : Graphics World, [1980]-. — v. : ill ; 30cm
Annual. — Supplement to: Graphics world
ISSN 0260-4930 = Graphics World services and supplies directory : £7.50 (free to subscribers of Graphics world) B81-02003

338.4'77785992 — Great Britain. Videorecording industries *— Serials*

Music & video week : Europe's leading music business paper. — Jan. 17 1981-. — London (40 Long Acre, WC2E 9JT) : Music Week, 1981-. — ill ; 37cm
Weekly. — Continues: Music week
ISSN 0261-0817 = Music & video week : £0.90
Primary classification 338.4'778991'0941
B81-15441

338.4'778991'0941 — Great Britain. Music recording industries *— Serials*

Music & video week : Europe's leading music business paper. — Jan. 17 1981-. — London (40 Long Acre, WC2E 9JT) : Music Week, 1981-. — ill ; 37cm
Weekly. — Continues: Music week
ISSN 0261-0817 = Music & video week : £0.90
Also classified at 338.4'77785992 B81-15441

338.4'779'0094 — European Community countries. Leisure activities. Economic aspects *— Forecasts*

Edwards, Anthony. Leisure spending in the European Community : forecasts to 1990 / by Anthony Edwards. — London : Economist Intelligence Unit, c1981. — 158p ; 30cm. — (EIU special report ; no.93)
Unpriced (pbk) B81-14130

338.4'779'00941 — Great Britain. Leisure industries, *to 1979*

Ornstien, Edwin J. The marketing of leisure / Edwin Ornstien and Austin Nunn. — London : Associated Business Press, 1980. — xiv,238p : ill ; 23cm
Bibliography: p229-233. - Includes index
ISBN 0-85227-219-7 : £11.50 B81-04115

338.4'779823'09423 — South-west England. Riding establishments

Warren, Martyn F. Riding establishments in the South West : with special reference to Devon and Cornwall / Martyn F. Warren. — Newton Abbot (Newton Abbot, Devon [TQ12 6NQ]) : [Seale-Hayne College], 1981. — 68p : 2maps ; 30cm
Bibliography: p66-67
£2.50 (pbk) B81-28467

338.4'791 — Great Britain. Travel agencies & tour operators *— Statistics — Serials*

Travel agents & tour operators. — 3rd ed. — London : ICC Business Ratios, c1981. — [96]p. — (ICC Business Ratio report)
ISBN 0-86261-085-0 : £95.00 B81-26602

338.4'7'91 — Tourist industries. Planning. Geographical aspects

Pearce, Douglas. Tourist development. — London : Longman, Jan.1982. — [160]p. — (Topics in applied geography)
ISBN 0-582-30053-3 (pbk) : £4.95 : CIP entry
B81-34325

338.4'791'0212 — Great Britain. Travel agencies & tour operators *— Statistics — Serials*

British travel agents & tour operators. — [1981]. — London : Jordan & Sons (Surveys) Ltd., c1981. — xxviii,82p
£25.00 B81-30849

338.4'791'02854 — Great Britain & United States. Travel agencies. Applications of digital computer systems

A plain person's guide to existing technological systems that affect the marketing of travel services in Europe and the USA. — London : British Tourist Authority, [1981]. — 47p ; 30cm
£5.00 (pbk) B81-37498

338.4'79141 — Great Britain. Tourism. Role of transport services *— Conference proceedings*

Transport in Britain : a report of the conference organised by the British Tourist Authority at the Bowater Conference Centre, London on November 9, 1979. — London : British Tourist Authority, [1980]. — [59]p ; 30cm
ISBN 0-7095-0655-4 (pbk) : £5.00 B81-03647

338.4'79141'0025 — Great Britain. Tourist information centres *— Directories — Serials*

Directory of tourist information centres ... in England, Scotland, Wales, N. Ireland, Isle of Man & Channel Islands / English Tourist Board. — 1980-. — London ([4 Grosvenor Gardens, SW1W 0DU]) : The Board, 1980-. — v. : maps ; 21cm
Annual. — Text in English, contents list and introduction also in French and German. — Continues: Tourist information centres, in England, Scotland, Wales & N. Ireland
ISSN 0260-5686 = Directory of tourist information centres ... in England, Scotland, Wales, N. Ireland, Isle of Man & Channel Islands : Unpriced B81-04807

338.4'79141'007 — Great Britain. Tourism. Information sources

Tourism : a guide to sources of information / compiled by the Tourism and Recreation Research Unit, University of Edinburgh. — London (6 Castle St., Edinburgh EH2 3AT) : Capital Planning Information, 1981. — 73p ; 30cm. — (CPI information reviews ; no.4)
ISBN 0-906011-10-8 (pbk) : £11.50 B81-27746

338.4'791411 — Scotland. Tourism. Planning — *Proposals*

Scottish Council Research Institute. Increasing the benefits from tourism : a policy position paper / [Scottish Council Research Institute]. — Edinburgh : The Institute, 1980. — 14leaves : ill ; 31cm
£2.00 (spiral) B81-34341

338.4'7914137 — Scotland. Borders Region. Tourism

Borders Region, *Regional Council*. Scottish tourism and recreation planning studies : Borders Region, 1980. — [Newtown St Boswells] ([Regional Headquarters, Newtown St Boswells, Roxburghshire TD6 0SA]) : Borders Regional Council, 1980. — v leaves,99p : ill,maps ; 30cm + factsheets([22]p : ill,maps ; 21x30cm)
£5.00 (pbk)
Also classified at 333.78'09413'7 B81-27747

338.4'7914225'005 — East Sussex. Tourism — *Serials*

Focus on tourism : a regular look at tourism in East Sussex. — Spring 1980-. — [Lewes] ([Southover House, Southover Rd, Lewes, East Sussex BN7 1YA]) : East Sussex Country Planning Dept., 1980-. — v. : ill ; 22x30cm
Quarterly
ISSN 0260-1559 = Focus on tourism : £0.85 per issue B81-00783

338.4'791423 — South-West England. Tourists. Guides — *Directories — Serials*

[Registered guides *(West Country Tourist Board)***]** . Registered guides / West Germany Tourist Board. — 1978-1979. — [Exeter] ([Trinity Court, 37 Southernhay East, Exeter EX1 1Q5]) : West Country Tourist Board, 1978-1979. — 2v. ; 22cm
Annual. — Description based on: 1979 issue
Unpriced B81-03614

338.4'7914235'005 — Devon. Tourism. Policies of Devon. *County Council.* **Implementation —** *Serials*

Devon. *Planning Department*. Tourism and recreation / County Planning Department. — 1981-. — Exeter (County Hall, Topsham Rd, Exeter EX2 4QH) : Devon County Council Planning Department, 1981-. — v. : ill,maps ; 30cm. — (Topic report / County Planning Department)
Annual
ISSN 0261-2445 = Tourism and recreation topic report : £0.40
Also classified at 333.78'09423'5 B81-33729

338.5 — PRODUCTION ECONOMICS

338.5 — Economics. Markets. Analysis

Gifford, Elli. Money making matters : new insights into market analysis techniques / Elli Gifford. — Warwick (46, High St., Warwick CV34 4AX) : Exchange Buildings Commodity Syndicate, 1981. — 309p : ill,facsims ; 22cm
ISBN 0-9507357-0-1 (pbk) : Unpriced B81-39277

338.5 — Economics. Markets. Effects of government policies

Leake, Andrew. Government and markets. — London : Macmillan Education, Feb.1982. — [48]p. — (Casebooks in economic theory)
ISBN 0-333-27990-5 (pbk) : £1.25 : CIP entry B81-35950

338.5 — Microeconomics

Garb, Gerald. Microeconomics : theory, applications, innovations / Gerald Garb. — New York : Macmillan ; London : Collier Macmillan, c1981. — x,342p : ill ; 24cm
Includes bibliographies and index
ISBN 0-02-340400-0 : £7.95 B81-29322

Gisser, Micha. Intermediate price theory : analysis, issues and applications / Micha Gisser. — New York ; London : McGraw-Hill, c1981. — xviii,653p : ill ; 25cm
Includes index
ISBN 0-07-023312-8 : £13.50 B81-32940

Gravelle, Hugh. Microeconomics / Hugh Gravelle and Ray Rees. — London : Longman, 1981. — xiii,620p : ill ; 24cm. — (Modern economics)
Includes bibliographies and index
ISBN 0-582-44075-0 (pbk) : £9.95 : CIP rev. B79-24994

Hartley, K.. Microeconomic policy. — Chichester : Wiley, Jan.1982. — [408]p
ISBN 0-471-28026-7 : £19.50 : CIP entry
ISBN 0-471-28027-5 (pbk) : £5.95 B81-34645

Haveman, Robert H.. The market system : an introduction to microeconomics / Robert H. Haveman, Kenyon A. Knopf. — 4th ed. — New York ; Chichester : Wiley, c1981. — xviii,280p : ill ; 23cm. — (Introduction to economics series)
Previous ed.: 1978. — Includes index
ISBN 0-471-08530-8 (pbk) : £6.00 B81-10542

Heilbroner, Robert L.. Understanding microeconomics / Robert L. Heilbroner, Lester C. Thurow. — 5th ed. — Englewood Cliffs ; London : Prentice-Hall, c1981. — 313p : ill (some col.) ; 24cm
Previous ed.: 1978. — Includes index
ISBN 0-13-936567-2 (pbk) : £7.65 B81-34954

Laidler, David E. W.. Introduction to microeconomics / David Laidler. — 2nd ed. — Oxford : Philip Allan, 1981. — xii,312p : ill ; 23cm
Previous ed.: 1974. — Bibliography: p307-309. — Includes index
ISBN 0-86003-033-4 (corrected: cased) : £12.00
ISBN 0-86003-131-4 (pbk) : £5.95 B81-35177

McCann, Roger A.. Markets, decisions, and organizations : intermediate microeconomic theory / Roger A. McCain. — Englewood Cliffs ; London : Prentice-Hall, c1981. — xiv,555p : ill ; 25cm
Includes bibliography and index
ISBN 0-13-557884-1 : £14.25 B81-16518

Mansfield, Edwin. Microeconomics : theory and applications / Edwin Mansfield. — 3rd ed. — New York ; London : Norton, c1979. — xxii,548p : ill(some col.) ; 25cm
Previous ed.: 1975. — Includes bibliographies and index
ISBN 0-393-95002-6 : £7.25 B81-02511

Mansfield, Edwin. Principles of microeconomics / Edwin Mansfield. — 3rd ed. — New York ; London : Norton, c1980. — xvi,472p : ill(some col.),ports ; 24cm
Previous ed.: 1977. — Includes index
ISBN 0-393-95128-6 (pbk) : £4.50 B81-02512

Microeconomic analysis : essays in microeconomics and economic development / edited by D. Currie, D. Peel and W. Peters. — London : Croom Helm, c1981. — 495p : ill ; 23cm
Conference papers. — Includes bibliographies
ISBN 0-7099-0709-5 : £19.95 B81-22088

Readings in applied microeconomics / edited by Leslie Wagner. — 2nd ed. — Oxford : Oxford University Press in association with the Open University Press, 1981. — viii,403p : ill ; 24cm
Previous ed.: 1973. — Includes index
ISBN 0-19-877163-0 (cased) : £14.00 : CIP rev.
ISBN 0-19-877162-2 (pbk) : Unpriced B80-24228

Sher, William. Microeconomic theory : a synthesis of classical theory and the modern approach / William Sher, Rudy Pinola. — London : Edward Arnold, c1981. — xvi,752p : ill ; 26cm
Bibliography: p741-743. — Includes index
ISBN 0-7131-6338-0 : £15.00 B81-24955

Shone, R. (Ronald). Applications in intermediate microeconomics / Ronald Shone. — Oxford : Robertson, 1981. — xi,292p : ill ; 23cm
Includes bibliographies and index
ISBN 0-85520-387-0 (cased) : £16.00 : CIP rev.
ISBN 0-85520-388-9 (pbk) : £6.95 B81-06601

Thompson, Arthur A.. Economics of the firm : theory and practice / Arthur A. Thompson, Jr. — 3rd ed. — Englewood Cliffs ; London : Prentice-Hall, c1981. — xx,635p : ill ; 25cm
Previous ed.: 1977. — Includes bibliographies and index
ISBN 0-13-231423-1 : £12.95 B81-17209

Veseth, Michael. Introductory microeconomics / Michael Veseth. — New York ; London : Academic Press, c1981. — xiv,362p : ill(some col.) ; 24cm
Also published: in hardback with Introductory macroeconomics as Introductory economics. 1981. — Includes index
ISBN 0-12-719540-8 (pbk) : £7.40 B81-29766

Wilson, J. Holton. Microeconomics : concepts and applications / J. Holton Wilson. — New York ; London : Harper & Row, c1981. — xv,413p : ill ; 25cm
Includes bibliographies and index
ISBN 0-912212-13-6 : Unpriced B81-26198

338.5'076 — Microeconomics — *Questions & answers*

Mansfield, Edwin. Microeconomic problems : case studies and exercises for review / Edwin Mansfield. — 3rd ed. — New York ; London : Norton, c1979. — vii,241p : ill ; 26cm
Previous ed.: 1975
ISBN 0-393-95004-2 (pbk) : £2.95 B81-04800

338.5'12 — Great Britain. Personnel. Dismissal. Costs

The **Real** cost of dismissal / by Incomes Data Services ; ... prepared by Elizabeth Whitehead and Roger Bronkhurst, assisted by other members of the 'Brief' staff. — London : Financial Times, c1979. — 226p ; 30cm. — (An International management report)
ISBN 0-903199-21-1 (spiral) : Unpriced B81-38066

338.5'144 — Excess capacity. Political aspects

The **International** politics of surplus capacity : competition for market shares in the world recession / edited by Susan Strange, Roger Tooze. — London : Allen & Unwin, 1981. — viii,229p ; 23cm
Includes bibliographies and index
ISBN 0-04-382034-4 : Unpriced : CIP rev. B81-25142

338.5'144 — Industries. Capacity. Expansion. Mathematical models

Freidenfelds, John. Capacity expansion : analysis of simple models with applications / John Freidenfelds. — New York ; Oxford : North Holland, c1981. — xii,291p : ill ; 24cm
Includes bibliographies and index
ISBN 0-444-00562-5 : £23.67 B81-36747

338.5'16'0941 — Great Britain. Industries. Profitability, *1961-1977*

Williams, N. P. (Norman Philip). Influences on the profitability of twenty-two industrial sectors / by N.P. Williams. — London : Economics Division, Bank of England, 1981. — 80p : ill ; 30cm. — (Discussion paper / Bank of England, ISSN 0142-6753 ; no.15)
Bibliography: p80
ISBN 0-903312-34-4 (pbk) : Unpriced B81-19018

338.5'16'0941 — Great Britain. Industries. Profitability — *Conference proceedings*

The **Economics** of the profits crisis : papers and proceedings of the seminar on profits held in London 1 April 1980 / edited by W.E. Martin. — London : H.M.S.O., 1981. — xii,226p : ill ; 23cm
At head of title: Department of Industry. — Includes index
ISBN 0-11-513251-1 (cased) : £8.95
ISBN 0-11-512977-4 (pbk) : £4.95 B81-37388

338.5'2 — Great Britain. Imports: Manufactured goods. Prices. Determination
Bond, I. D.. The determination of UK manufactured import prices / by I.D. Bond. — London ([Threadneedle St.] EC2R 8AH) : Economics Division, Bank of England, 1981. — 41p : ill ; 30cm. — (Discussion paper / Bank of England, ISSN 0142-6753 ; no.16)
Bibliography: p40-41
ISBN 0-903312-35-2 (pbk) : Unpriced
B81-19495

338.5'2'01 — Prices. Theories
Kessel, Reuben A.. Essays in applied price theory / by Reuben A. Kessel ; edited by R.H. Coase & Merton H. Miller. — Chicago ; London : University of Chicago Press, 1980. — xii,370p : ill ; 25cm
Includes bibliographies and index
ISBN 0-226-43200-9 : £15.00 B81-12685

338.5'2'05 — Commodities. Wholesale prices — *Serials*
The **Westgate** commodities letter. — 22 Sept.1980-31 Mar.1981. — London (9 Holborn, EC1N 2LL) : Fleet Financial Publishing, 1980-1981. — 13v. ; 30cm
Fortnightly. — Description based on: 13 Oct.1980 issue
£90.00 per year B81-20087

338.5'2'05 — Primary commodities. Prices. Analysis — *Serials — For marketing*
Technical commodity yearbook. — 1981-. — New York ; London : Van Nostrand Reinhold, 1981-. — v. ; 29cm
Annual
£28.15 B81-20086

338.5'2'09411 — Scotland. Sparsely populated regions. Retail prices
Rural Scotland price survey : Spring 1981 : a report for the Scottish Consumer Council and Highlands and Islands Development Board / edited by G.A Mackay and Anne C. Moir of the Institute for the Study of Sparsely Populated Areas, University of Aberdeen. — [Glasgow] ([4 Somerset Place, Glasgow G3]) : [The Consumer Council], 1981. — 24p ; 30cm
£1.00 (pbk) B81-29140

338.5'2'09422 — South-east England. Retail prices. Effects of credit card services
Frazer, P. A. T.. Survey of retail prices : a survey to compare prices charged by retailers which accept credit cards with prices charged by retailers which do not / P.A.T. Frazer, P.G. Hirsch, J.E. Root. — London (Moor House, London Wall, EC2Y 5ET) : Inter-Bank Research Organisation, 1978, c1980. — 125leaves(some folded) : ill ; 30cm
ISBN 0-903689-01-4 (spiral) : £12.00
B81-05333

338.5'22 — Free markets. Legal aspects
Courts and free markets. — Oxford : Clarendon Press
Vol.1. — Feb.1982. — [350]p
ISBN 0-19-825366-4 : £25.00 : CIP entry
B81-36968

Courts and free markets. — Oxford : Clarendon Press
Vol.2. — Feb.1982. — [380]p
ISBN 0-19-825392-3 : £25.00 : CIP entry
B81-38328

338.5'22 — Transfer pricing by multinational companies
Multinationals beyond the market : intra-firm trade and the control of transfer pricing / edited by Robin Murray. — Brighton : Harvester, 1981. — 335p : 1ill ; 24cm. — (Harvester studies in development ; 3)
Includes bibliographies and index
ISBN 0-85527-203-1 : £22.50 : CIP rev.
B81-04193

338.5'23 — Oligopolies. Kinked demand curve theory
Reid, Gavin C.. The kinked demand curve analysis of oligopoly : theory and evidence / Gavin C. Reid. — Edinburgh : Edinburgh University Press, c1981. — ix,113p : ill ; 22cm
Bibliography: p105-110. — Includes index
ISBN 0-85224-390-1 : £6.00 B81-32480

338.5'26 — Western world. Retail prices. Discrimination. Control by governments
Grant, R. M.. Recent developments in the control of price discrimination in countries outside North America / by R.M. Grant. — London (Gresham College, Basinghall St., EC2V 5AH) : City University Business School, c1980. — 35leaves ; 30cm. — (Working paper / City University Business School, ISSN 0140-1041 ; no.19)
Unpriced (pbk) B81-07114

338.5'28 — Commodities. Prices. International indexation
Newbery, David M. G.. The theory of commodity price stabilization. — Oxford : Clarendon Press, July 1981. — [516]p
ISBN 0-19-828417-9 (cased) : £20.00 : CIP entry
ISBN 0-19-828438-1 (pbk) : £8.50 B81-16858

338.5'28 — Great Britain. Wholesale prices. Indices — *Serials*
Great Britain. *Central Statistical Office.* Wholesale price index : principles and procedures / Central Statistical Office. — London : H.M.S.O., 1980. — vi,49p : 1form ; 30cm. — (Studies in official statistics ; no.32)
ISBN 0-11-630162-7 (pbk) : £5.60 B81-07394

338.5'28 — Prices. Indices — *For schools*
Retail price index / [Schools Council Project on Statistical Education]. — Slough : Published for the Schools Council by Foulsham Educational, c1981. — 16p : ill ; 21cm + teachers' notes(16p : forms ; 21cm). — (Statistics in your world. [Level 4])
ISBN 0-572-01088-5 (pbk) : Unpriced
ISBN 0-572-01115-6 (teachers' notes) : Unpriced B81-16719

338.5'42 — Capitalist countries. Economic cycles, *1800-1979 — Marxist viewpoints*
Mandel, Ernest. Long waves of capitalist development : the Marxist interpretation / Ernest Mandel. — Cambridge : Cambridge University Press, 1980. — viii,151p : ill ; 21cm. — (Studies in modern capitalism = Etudes sur le capitalisme moderne)
Based on the Marshall lectures given at the University of Cambridge 1978. — Includes index
ISBN 0-521-23000-4 : £7.95 B81-09922

338.5'42 — Economic depressions. Social aspects — *Forecasts*
Toffler, Alvin. The eco-spasm report / by Alvin Toffler. — New York ; London : Bantam, 1975 (1980 [printing]). — 116p ; 18cm
Bibliography: p109-110. - Includes index
ISBN 0-553-14474-x (pbk) : £1.00 B81-21392

338.5'42 — Trade cycles
Lucas, Robert E. Studies in business-cycle theory / Robert E. Lucas Jr. — Oxford : Basil Blackwell, 1981. — 300p : ill ; 24cm
Includes bibliographies and index
ISBN 0-631-12848-4 : £9.95 : CIP rev.
B81-06620

338.5'42 — Trade cycles. Analysis — *Conference proceedings*
CIRET Conference *(14th : 1979 : Lisbon).* Business cycle analysis : papers presented at the 14th CIRET Conference : proceedings, Lisbon 1979 / edited by Werner H. Strigel. — Farnborough, Hants : Gower, c1980. — viii,446p : ill ; 23cm
Includes bibliographies
ISBN 0-566-00368-6 : £17.50 : CIP rev.
B80-07270

338.5'42 — United States. Economic depressions, *1929*
The **Great** Depression revisited / edited by Karl Brunner. — Boston ; London : Nijhoff, c1981. — vii,360p : ill ; 24cm. — (Rochester studies in economics and policy issues ; v.2)
Includes bibliographies
ISBN 0-89838-051-0 : Unpriced B81-17109

338.5'42 — United States. Stock markets. Economic depressions, *1929*
Thomas, Gordon. The day the bubble burst : a social history of the Wall Street crash / Gordon Thomas and Max Morgan-Witts. — London : Arrow, 1980, c1979. — 573p,[16]p of plates : ill,1plan,ports ; 18cm
Originally published: London : Hamilton, 1979. — Bibliography: p536-553. - Includes index
ISBN 0-09-923370-3 (pbk) : £1.95 B81-00039

338.5'44 — Business firms. Economic forecasting
Hanke, John E.. Business forecasting / John E. Hanke and Arthur G. Reitsch. — Boston, Mass. : Allyn and Bacon, c1981. — x,369p : ill ; 25cm
Text on lining papers. — Includes bibliographies and index
ISBN 0-205-07139-2 : £9.95 B81-16295

338.5'44'025 — Economic forecasting. Organisations - *Directories*
World index of economic forecasts. — 2nd ed. — Farnborough, Hants. : Gower, July 1981. — [500]p
Previous ed.: 1978
ISBN 0-566-02199-4 : £65.00 : CIP entry
B81-14882

338.5'44'076 — Business firms. Economic forecasting — *Questions & answers*
Hanke, John E.. Instructor's manual to accompany Business forecasting / John E. Hanke and Arthur G. Reitsch. — Boston [Mass.] ; London : Allyn and Bacon, c1981. — 78p : ill ; 22cm
ISBN 0-205-07140-6 (unbound) : £1.00
B81-26436

338.5'442 — Economic forecasting. Dynamic econometric models
Wallis, Kenneth F.. Dynamic models and expectations hypotheses / Kenneth F. Wallis. — Coventry : Department of Economics, University of Warwick, 1981. — 16p ; 31cm. — (Warwick economic research papers ; no.187)
Bibliography: p16
Unpriced (pbk) B81-22957

338.5'442 — Economic forecasting. Econometric models
Pindyck, Robert S.. Econometric models and economic forecasts / Robert S. Pindyck and Daniel L. Rubinfeld. — 2nd ed. — New York ; London : McGraw-Hill, c1981. — xxii,630p : ill ; 25cm
Previous ed.: 1976. — Includes index
ISBN 0-07-050096-7 : £15.95 B81-09775

Pindyck, Robert S.. Econometric models and economic forecasts / Robert S. Pindyck, Daniel L. Rubinfeld. — 2nd ed., International student ed. — Auckland ; London : McGraw-Hill International, c1981. — xxii,630p : ill ; 21cm
Previous ed.: 1976. — Includes index
ISBN 0-07-066481-1 (pbk) : £6.50 B81-32475

338.5'442 — Great Britain. Business firms. Failure. Economic forecasting. Use of discriminant analysis
Taffler, Richard J.. Forecasting company failure in the UK using discriminant analysis and financial ratio data / by R.J. Taffler. — Rev. version. — [London] : [City University Business School], c1981. — 31leaves : ill ; 30cm. — (Working paper / City University Business School, ISSN 0140-1041 ; no.23)
Previous ed.: published as Finding those firms in danger using discriminant analysis and financial ratio data, 1977. — Bibliography: leaves 22-24
Unpriced (pbk) B81-27516

338.5'442 — Regional planning. Economic forecasting. Econometric models
Madden, M.. A demographic-economic forecasting framework for regional strategic planning / by M. Madden & P.W.J. Batey and L. Worrall. — Liverpool (P.O. Box 147, Liverpool L69 3BX) : Department of Civic Design, University of Liverpool, 1981. — 42leaves,[4]leaves of plates : ill ; 30cm. — (Working paper / Department of Civic Design, University of Liverpool, ISSN 0309-8753 ; WP14)
Bibliography: leaves 40-42
ISBN 0-906109-07-8 (unbound) : £2.30
B81-23359

338.6 — ECONOMICS. ORGANISATION OF PRODUCTION

338.6 — Business enterprise — *Stories, anecdotes*

Winkworth, Stephen. Great commercial disasters / Stephen Winkworth ; illustrated by Michael ffolkes ; introduction by Sir Peter Parker. — London : Macmillan, 1980. — 123p : ill ; 23cm
Bibliography: p123
ISBN 0-333-29510-2 : £3.95 B81-03784

338.6 — Industries. Ownership. Rights of personnel

Abrahamson, Bengt. The rights of labor / Bengt Abrahamsson and Anders Broström ; [translated from the Swedish by David McCune]. — Beverly Hills ; London : Sage, c1980. — 301p : ill ; 23cm
Translation of: Om arbetets rätt. — Bibliography: p281-294. — Includes index
ISBN 0-8039-1477-6 : £15.75 B81-05795

338.6′041′0941 — Great Britain. Business firms. Finance — *For banking*

Walker, T. M.. Management accounting and business finance : study guide / by T.M. Walker. — 2nd ed. — [Edinburgh] ([20 Rutland Square, Edinburgh]) : Institute of Bankers in Scotland, [1979?]. — 149p ; 21cm
Previous ed.: 1974. — Includes index
£2.25 (pbk)
Also classified at 658.1′511′0941 B81-07690

338.6′041′0941 — Great Britain. Industries & trades. Finance, *1975-1978* — *Statistics*

Industrial performance analysis : a financial analysis of U.K. industry & commerce. — 5th ed. — London (81 City Rd., EC1Y 1BD) : Business Ratios Division of Inter Company Comparisons, c1979. — xvii,139p : ill ; 30cm
Previous ed.: 1978
ISBN 0-904540-22-7 (pbk) : £20.00 B81-25395

338.6′042 — Great Britain. Manufacturing industries. Efficiency. Effects of location

Townroe, P. M.. Local-external economies for British manufacturing industry / P.M. Townroe, N.J. Roberts. — Farnborough, Hants, : Gower, c1980. — x,177p : ill,maps ; 23cm
Bibliography: p170-174. - Includes index
ISBN 0-566-00391-0 : £11.50 : CIP rev. B80-20373

338.6′042 — Great Britain. Scientific instruments industries. Location. Effects of technological development — *Case studies*

Oakey, R. P.. High technology industry and industrial location / the instruments industry example ; R.P. Oakey. — Farnborough : Gower, c1981. — viii,134p : ill,maps ; 23cm
Bibliography: p130-134
ISBN 0-566-00419-4 : £12.50 : CIP rev. B81-16364

338.6′042 — Industries. Location. Spatial analysis

Spatial analysis, industry and the industrial environment : progress in research and applications. — Chichester : Wiley
Vol.2: International industrial systems / edited by F.E. Ian Hamilton and G.J.R. Linge. — c1981. — xix,652p : ill,maps ; 24cm
Bibliography: p581-613. — Includes index
ISBN 0-471-27918-8 : £26.00 : CIP rev. B81-00784

338.6′042′01 — Industries. Location. Theories

Industrial location and regional systems : spatial organization in the economic sector / John Rees, Geoffrey J.D. Hewings, Howard A. Stafford, editors. — New York : Bergin ; London : Croom Helm, 1981. — vi,260p : ill,maps ; 24cm
Includes bibliographies and index
ISBN 0-7099-0414-2 : £15.95 B81-33440

Smith, David M. (David Marshall). Industrial location : an economic geographical analysis / David M. Smith. — 2nd ed. — New York ; Chichester : Wiley, c1981. — xiv,492p : ill ; 24cm
Previous ed.: 1971. — Bibliography: p459-479. — Includes index
ISBN 0-471-06078-x : £15.10 B81-17247

338.6′042′05 — Industries. Location — *Serials*

The **Business** location file. The Annual investment file. — [Vol.4 (1980)?]-. — Richmond, Surrey (17 The Green, Richmond, Surrey TW9 1PX) : Urban Pub. Co., 1980-. — v. : ill,maps,ports ; 30cm
Cover title: The Annual investment file. — Continues in part: The Business location file. — Description based on: Vol.5 (Mar.1981)
ISSN 0261-5258 = Business location file. Annual investment file (corrected) : £6.00 B81-30876

The **Project** search file. — Vol.5 (July 1981)-. — Richmond, Surrey (17 The Green, Richmond, Surrey TW9 1PX) : Urban Pub. Co., 1981-. — v. : ill,maps,ports ; 30cm
Also entitled: The Business location file. The Project search file. — Continues in part: The Business location file
ISSN 0261-8931 = Project search file : £4.00 B81-36013

338.6′042′0941 — Great Britain. Industries. Relocation, *1966-1975*

Pounce, R. J.. Industrial movement in the United Kingdom 1966-75 / by R. J. Pounce. — London : H.M.S.O., 1981. — 112p : ill,maps ; 30cm
At head of title: Department of Industry. — Bibliography: p111-112
ISBN 0-11-513182-5 (pbk) : £5.20 B81-40003

338.6′042′0941 — Great Britain. Manufacturing industries. Location — *For schools*

Bale, John, *1940-*. The location of manufacturing industry : an introductory approach / John Bale ; maps and diagrams drawn by Tim Smith. — 2nd ed. — Edinburgh : Oliver & Boyd, 1981. — 224p : ill,maps,2facsims ; 24cm. — (Conceptual frameworks in geography)
Previous ed.: 1976. — Includes bibliographies and index
ISBN 0-05-003452-9 (pbk) : £4.00 B81-32954

338.6′042′0944 — France. Industries. Location

Tuppen, John N.. France / John N. Tuppen. — Folkestone : Dawson, 1980. — xii,243p : ill,maps ; 23cm. — (Studies in industrial geography, ISSN 0308-6615)
Bibliography: p232-236. - Includes index
ISBN 0-7129-0981-8 : £10.00 : CIP rev. B80-11355

338.6′042′0947 — Eastern Europe. Industries. Location

Turnock, David. Eastern Europe / David Turnock. — Folkestone : Dawson, 1980, c1978. — xi,273p : maps ; 22cm. — (Studies in industrial geography, ISSN 0308-6615)
Bibliography: p255-259. - Includes index
ISBN 0-7129-1015-8 (pbk) : £6.00 B81-10100

338.6′048 — Manufacturing industries. Competitiveness. Decline. Causes. Econometric models

Buiter, Willem H.. Oil, disinflation, and export competitiveness : a model of the ″Dutch disease″ / Willem H. Buiter and Douglas D. Puruis. — Coventry : Department of Economics, University of Warwick, 1980. — 40p : ill ; 31cm. — (Warwick economic research papers ; no.185)
Bibliography: p39-40
Unpriced (pbk) B81-15976

338.6′048′0941 — Great Britain. Industries. Competitiveness. Improvement — *Proposals*

The **Will** to win. — London : Confederation of British Industry, 1981. — 1portfolio(82p) ; 30cm + summary(35p ill ; 20x21cm)
£2.50 B81-18207

338.6′048′0973 — United States. Industries. Competition. Policies of government — *Proposals*

Sherman, Roger. Antitrust policies and issues / Roger Sherman. — Reading, Mass. ; London : Addison-Wesley, c1978. — xii,97p : ill ; 24cm. — (Perspectives on economics series) (Addison-Wesley series in economics)
Includes bibliographies and index
ISBN 0-201-08363-9 (pbk) : £4.90 B81-04743

338.6′0941 — Great Britain. Regional economic development. Effects of centralisation of ownership of industries

Watts, H. D.. The branch plant economy : a study of external control / H.D. Watts. — Harlow : Longman, 1981. — 104p : ill,maps ; 24cm. — (Topics in applied geography)
Bibliography: p97-100. — Includes index
ISBN 0-582-30028-2 (pbk) : £4.50 : CIP rev. B81-31824

338.6′1 — Private enterprise. Relations with public enterprise — *Conference proceedings*

Public and private enterprise in a mixed economy : proceedings of a conference held by the International Economic Association in Mexico City / edited by William J. Baumol. — London : Macmillan, 1980. — xi,308p ; 23cm. — (International Economic Association publication)
Includes bibliographies and index
ISBN 0-333-28319-8 : £20.00 : CIP rev.
Also classified at 338.6′2 B80-13736

338.6′1′0941 — Great Britain. Private enterprise. Promotion. Role of government — *Proposals*

Institute of Directors. Free enterprise - the only way : an Institute of Directors message to the Government. — London : Institute of Directors, 1981. — 20p ; 30cm
£3.00 (pbk) B81-38377

338.6′2 — Public enterprise. Relations with private enterprise — *Conference proceedings*

Public and private enterprise in a mixed economy : proceedings of a conference held by the International Economic Association in Mexico City / edited by William J. Baumol. — London : Macmillan, 1980. — xi,308p ; 23cm. — (International Economic Association publication)
Includes bibliographies and index
ISBN 0-333-28319-8 : £20.00 : CIP rev.
Primary classification 338.6′1 B80-13736

338.6′32 — London *(City)*. **Barbers. Guilds: Worshipful Company of Barbers,** *to 1978*

Dobson, Jessie. Barbers and barber-surgeons of London : a history of the barbers′ and barber-surgeons′ companies / by Jessie Dobson and R. Milnes Walker ; foreword by Sir Lionel Denny. — Oxford : Blackwell Scientific for The Worshipful Company of Barbers, 1979. — xix,171p,[10] leaves of plates : ill(some col.),col.coats of arms,col.facsims,plans,ports (some col.) ; 25cm
Ill on lining papers. — Bibliography: p149-152. — Includes index
ISBN 0-632-00263-8 : £9.50 : CIP rev. B78-35923

338.6′32′094212 — London *(City)*. **Guilds**

Melling, John Kennedy. Discovering London′s guilds and liveries / John Kennedy Melling. — 3rd ed. — Aylesbury : Shire, 1981. — 80p : 1map ; 18cm. — (Discovering series ; 180)
Previous ed.: 1978. — Bibliography: p77-78
ISBN 0-85263-553-2 (pbk) : £1.25 B81-17560

338.6′34 — Great Britain. *Crofters Commission* — *Serials*

Great Britain. *Crofters Commission*. Annual report for ... / The Crofters Commission. — 1978. — Edinburgh : H.M.S.O., 1979. — vi,43p
ISBN 0-11-491613-6 : £1.25 B81-06945

338.6′34 — Scotland. Highlands & Islands. Agricultural industries. Crofting, *to 1979*

Stewart, Katharine. Crofts and crofting / Katharine Stewart. — Edinburgh : William Blackwood, 1980. — [8],64p : ill,1map ; 21cm. — (Scottish connection)
Bibliography: p[6]
ISBN 0-85158-137-4 (pbk) : £1.85 B81-07203

338.6′34′094 — Western Europe. Rural industries, *1600-1850*

Kriedte, Peter. Industrialization before industrialization. — Cambridge : Cambridge University Press, Jan.1982. — [338]p. — (Studies in modern capitalism, ISSN 0144-2333)
Translation of: Industrialisierung vor der Industrialisierung
ISBN 0-521-23809-9 (cased) : £25.00 : CIP entry
ISBN 0-521-28228-4 (pbk) : £7.95 B81-38816

338.6'42 — England. Agricultural industries. Smallholdings — *Serials*

Annual report to Parliament on smallholdings in England / Ministry of Agriculture, Fisheries and Food. — 30th (1st Apr.1979 to 31st Mar.1980). — [Pinner] ([Tolcarne Drive, Pinner, Middx HA5 2DT]) : The Ministry, [1980?]. — 5,[7]p
ISSN 0144-6215 : Unpriced B81-30823

338.6'42 — England. Agricultural industries. Smallholdings — *Statistics* — *Serials*

Smallholdings statistics / Society of County Treasurers. — 1979-80. — Beverley : The Society, 1980. — 10p
ISSN 0307-8299 : Unpriced B81-13311

338.6'42 — Great Britain. Small firms. Finance. Sources

The **Director's** guide to sources of finance for the smaller company. — Completely rev. — London : Institute of Directors, 1980. — 112p ; 21cm
Previous ed.: 1978
£1.90 (pbk) B81-38381

338.6'42 — Great Britain. Small firms. Financial assistance by governments

Mortlock, P. John. Fiscal aid for small firms / by P. John Mortlock. — Henley-on-Thames (Enterprise House, Henley-on-Thames) : National Chamber of Trade, [1981]. — 9p ; 30cm
Cover title. — Text on inside cover
Unpriced (pbk) B81-16588

338.6'42 — Great Britain. Small scale agricultural industries — *Conference proceedings*

Small farming and the nation : proceedings of a conference organised by the Smallfarmers' Association of the UK and held at the Department of Agriculture and Horticulture, University of Reading in March 1980 / edited by R.B. Tranter. — Reading (2 Earley Gate, Reading RG6 2AU) : Centre for Agricultural Strategy, University of Reading, 1981. — 40p ; 21cm. — (CAS paper ; 9)
ISBN 0-7049-0615-5 (pbk) : £2.00 B81-14569

338.6'42 — Kent. Meopham. Agricultural industries. Smallholdings. Averill, Edward. Personal property. Probate, *1674* — *Accounts*

Carley, James. Edward Averill 1619-1674 / James Carley. — Meopham (Wrenbury, Wrotham Rd., Meopham, Kent, DA13 0HX) : Meopham Publications Committee, [1981?]. — 12p : facsims,1geneal.table ; 21cm. — (Meopham biographies ; 2)
£0.35 (unbound) B81-33684

338.6'42 — London. Small firms. Finance. Sources

Bloomfield, David C.. Sources of finance for small firms / written and compiled by David C. Bloomfield. — London (69 Cannon St., EC4N 5AB) : London Enterprise Agency, [1981?]. — 47p ; 27cm
Previous ed.: S.l. : s.n., 1978
Unpriced (pbk) B81-37802

338.6'42 — Wales. Agricultural industries. Smallholdings — *Serials*

Great Britain. *Welsh Office*. Adroddiad blynyddol i'r Senedd ar fanddaliadau yng Nghymru / Y Swyddfa Gymreig. — 1 Ebr. 1979 hyd 31 Mawr. 1980. — [Cardiff] ([Crown Building, Cathays park, Cardiff CF1 3NQ]) : [Swyddfa Gymreig], [1980?]. — 14,14p
Unpriced B81-30762

338.6'42'06042 — England. Rural regions. Small firms. Organisations: Council for Small Industries in Rural Areas — *Serials*

Council for Small Industries in Rural Areas. Report / Council for Small Industries in Rural Areas. — 1978-79. — Salisbury : CoSIRA, 1980. — 20p
£3.00 B81-16827

338.6'42'0941 — Great Britain. Regional development. Role of advance factories

Slowe, Peter M.. The advance factory in regional development. — Farnborough : Gower Publishing, Sept.1981. — [290]p
ISBN 0-566-00437-2 : £15.00 : CIP entry B81-23886

338.6'42'0941 — Great Britain. Regional development. Role of new small firms

Cross, Michael. New firm formation and regional development / Michael Cross. — Farnborough, Hants. : Gower, c1981. — vii,342p : ill,maps ; 23cm
Bibliography: p290-324. - Includes index
ISBN 0-566-00372-4 : £11.50 B81-12991

338.6'42'0941 — Great Britain. Small firms. Economic aspects

Bannock, Graham. The economics of small firms : return from the wilderness / Graham Bannock. — Oxford : Blackwell, 1981. — ix,130p : ill ; 23cm. — (Mainstream series)
Bibliography: p126-127. — Includes index
ISBN 0-631-11391-6 : £7.95 B81-12667

338.6'42'0941 — Great Britain. Small firms. Owners

Scase, Richard. The real world of the small business owner / Richard Scase and Robert Goffee. — London : Croom Helm, c1980. — 166p ; 23cm
ISBN 0-7099-0452-5 : £10.95 : CIP rev. B80-26708

338.6'44'0941 — Great Britain. Big business. Political aspects

Utton, M. A.. The political economy of big business. — Oxford : Martin Robertson, Feb.1982. — [220]p
ISBN 0-85520-409-5 : £12.50 : CIP entry B81-35704

338.6'44'0973 — United States. Big business

Herman, Edward S.. Corporate control, corporate power / Edward S. Herman. — Cambridge : Cambridge University Press, 1981. — xv,432p : 1ill ; 24cm. — (A Twentieth Century Fund study)
Includes index
ISBN 0-521-23996-6 : £25.00 B81-34530

338.6'44'0973 — United States. Large firms. Policies of government

Business and public policy / edited by John T. Dunlop. — Boston [Mass.] : Division of Research, Graduate School of Business Administration, Harvard University ; Cambridge, Mass. ; London : Harvard University Press [distributor], 1980. — xvii,118p : 2ill ; 24cm
ISBN 0-87584-119-8 : £4.20 B81-08234

338.6'5 — Great Britain. Large factories. Closure — *Conference proceedings*

Closure of major manufacturing plants : a note of the proceedings of a one day seminar, 13 May 1981, at the Ingram hotel, Glasgow. — Glasgow (186 Bath St, Glasgow G2 4HG) : Planning Exchange, [1981]. — 12,[4]leaves ; 30cm. — (Planning Exchange forum report ; 29)
Unpriced (unbound) B81-39636

338.7 — INDUSTRIAL ENTERPRISE. ORGANISATIONS AND THEIR STRUCTURE

338.7 — Business enterprise — *For Irish students*

O'Connor, John, *1949-*. Business organisation for the 1980s / John O'Connor. — Dublin : Folens, c1981. — 400p : ill ; 25cm
Includes index
Unpriced (pbk) B81-19586

338.7 — Business firms

Business economics / [the D324 Course Team]. — Milton Keynes : Open University Press. — (Social sciences : a third level course)
At head of title: The Open University. — Includes bibliographies
Unit 4: Business accounts and performance indicators / prepared for the Course Team by David Leece. — 1980. — 45p : 1ili ; 30cm. — (D324 ; unit 4)
ISBN 0-335-08568-7 (pbk) : Unpriced B81-19968

Business economics / [the D324 Course Team]. — Milton Keynes : Open University Press. — (Social sciences : a third level course)
At head of title: The Open University. — Includes bibliographies
Unit 6: Financial decisions / prepared for the Course Team by Rosalind Levačić. — 1980. — 48p : ill ; 30cm. — (D342 ; unit 6)
ISBN 0-335-08570-9 (pbk) : Unpriced B81-19967

Business economics / [The D324 Course Team]. — Milton Keynes : Open University Press. — (Social sciences : a third level course)
At head of title: The Open University. — Includes bibliographies
Units 7 & 8: The pricing decision and oligopoly conduct / prepared for the Course Team by Neil Costello. — 1980. — 45p ; 30cm. — (D324 ; units 7 & 8)
ISBN 0-335-08571-7 (pbk) : Unpriced B81-19969

Business economics / [the D324 Course Team]. — Milton Keynes : Open University Press. — (Social sciences : a third level course)
At head of title: The Open University
Unit 12: Business performance and industrial policy / prepared for the Course Team by Rosalind Levačić. — 1980. — 23p : ill,1facsim ; 30cm. — (D324 ; unit 12)
Bibliography: p23
ISBN 0-335-08576-8 (pbk) : Unpriced B81-19970

338.7 — Business firms. Social factors

Livesey, Frank. The organisation in its environment / F. Livesey, G.K. Pople and P.J. Davies. — London : Longman. — (Longman business education series)
Vol.2. — 1981. — 239p : ill ; 24cm
Includes index
ISBN 0-582-41186-6 (pbk) : £4.95 B81-22178

338.7 — Great Britain. Quakers. Family firms, *1700-*

Windsor, David Burns. The Quaker enterprise : Friends in business / David Burns Windsor. — London : Muller, 1980. — 16p,[10]p of plates : ill,ports ; 25cm
Includes index
ISBN 0-584-10257-7 : £10.95 : CIP rev. B80-13737

338.7'09 — Business firms — *History* — *Serials*

Business history newsletter. — Issue no.1 (Oct.1980)-. — London (The Editor, Lionel Robbins Building, 10 Portugal St., WC2A 2HD) : Business History Unit, 1980-. — v. ; 30cm
Two issues yearly
ISSN 0260-5171 = Business history newsletter : Unpriced B81-08322

338.7'09 — Great Britain & United States. Higher education institutions. Curriculum subjects: Business history

Hannah, Leslie. New horizons for business history? : a report to the Economic and Social History Committee of the Social Science Research Council / Leslie Hannah. — London : The Council, 1981. — 31p ; 30cm
ISBN 0-86226-080-9 (pbk) : £2.00 B81-22217

338.7'092'4 — Great Britain. Business enterprise. Lipman, M. J. — *Biographies*

Lipman, M. I.. Memoirs of a socialist business man / by M.I. Lipman ; with an introduction by John Saville. — London : Lipman Trust, c1980. — iii,407p ; 23cm
Unpriced B81-07261

338.7'094 — Western Europe. Industries. Organisation structure. Economic aspects

The **Structure** of European industry / editor H.W. de Jong. — The Hague ; London : Nijhoff, 1981. — xii,322p : ill ; 25cm. — (Studies in industrial organization ; v.1)
Includes bibliographies and index
ISBN 90-247-2416-3 (cased) : Unpriced
ISBN 90-247-2420-1 (pbk) : Unpriced B81-20836

338.7′0941 — Great Britain. Business firms
Frain, John. The organisation in its environment / John Frain. — London : Cassell
1. — 1981. — ix,274p : ill ; 22cm. — (Cassell′s BEC series. National level)
Bibliography: p266-268. - Includes index
ISBN 0-304-30334-8 (pbk) : £4.50 B81-21365

George, Kenneth D.. Industrial organisation : competition, growth and structural change / by Kenneth D. George and Caroline Joll. — 3rd ed. — London : Allen & Unwin, 1981. — x,336p : ill ; 23cm. — (Studies in economics ; 5)
Previous ed.: 1974. — Includes index
ISBN 0-04-338095-6 : Unpriced
ISBN 0-04-338096-4 (pbk) : unpriced B81-19389

Lawton, M. M.. The structure of business / M.M. Lawton, J. Maguire. — 2nd ed. / J.R.M. Aslett. — Amsterdam : Hulton Educational, c1980. — 255p ; 20cm
Previous ed.: 1972. — Bibliography: p254-255
ISBN 0-7175-0859-5 (pbk) : £2.70 B81-07183

338.7′09427 — Great Britain. Regional economic development. Role of new business firms — *Study regions: Northern England*
Johnson, P. S.. New firms and regional development : some issues and evidence / by P.S. Johnson. — [Newcastle upon Tyne] ([Newcastle upon Tyne NE1 7RU]) : Centre for Urban and Regional Development Studies, University of Newcastle upon Tyne, 1978. — 17leaves ; 30cm. — (Discussion paper / University of Newcastle upon Tyne Centre for Urban and Regional Development Studies ; no.11)
Bibliography: leaves 16-17
Unpriced (pbk) B81-36898

338.7′4 — Great Britain. Large manufacturing companies. Growth, *1909-1970*
Prais, S. J.. The evolution of giant firms in Britain : a study of the growth of concentration in manufacturing industry in Britain 1909-70 / by S.J. Prais. — 2nd impression / with a new preface on developments in 1970-6. — Cambridge : Cambridge University Press, 1981. — xxii,321p : ill ; 23cm. — (NIESR students′ edition ; 5)
Originally published: 1976. — Bibliography: p302-315. - Includes index
ISBN 0-521-28273-x (pbk) : £7.50 B81-11201

338.7′4 — Great Britain. Medium-sized manufacturing companies. Growth
Growth in manufacturing industry / Confederation of British Industry. — London : The Confederation, 1981. — 36p ; 30cm
Unpriced (pbk) B81-25091

338.7′4′02341 — Great Britain. Companies — *Career guides — For graduates — Serials*
Go : the annual guide to graduate opportunities. — 81. — London (Yeoman House, 76 St. James La., N10 3RD) : New Opportunity Press, 1980. — 1119p
ISSN 0144-9591 : Unpriced B81-00040

338.7′4′025174927 — Arab countries. Companies — *Directories — Serials*
Major companies of the Arab world. — 1982. — London : Graham & Trotman, Nov.1981. — [800]p
ISBN 0-86010-330-7 (cased) : £67.00 : CIP entry
ISBN 0-86010-329-3 (pbk) : £60.00 B81-33631

338.7′4′0254 — European Community countries. Companies — *Directories — Serials*
Principal companies of the European Economic Community. — 1980/81. — London : Graham & Trotman, 1980. — x,718p
ISBN 0-86010-207-6 : £52.00
ISSN 0144-2732 B81-13410

338.7′4′02541 — Great Britain. Industries. Companies with 500+ personnel — *Directories — Serials*
United Kingdom industrial companies with 500 or more employees / [Data Research Group]. — 1980. — Great Missenden : The Group, 1980. — 259p in various pagings
ISBN 0-86099-280-2 : £30.00 B81-09693

338.7′4′025669 — Nigeria. Companies — *Directories — Serials*
Major companies of Nigeria. — 1979/80-. — London : Graham & Trotman, 1979-. — v. : ill ; 30cm
Annual. — Text in English, list of index categories also in French and German. — Description based on: 1980/81 issue
ISSN 0144-2740 = Major companies of Nigeria : £30.00 B81-06710

Major companies of Nigeria. — 1982. — London : Graham & Trotman, Sept.1981. — [284]p
ISBN 0-86010-304-8 (cased) : £42.00 : CIP entry
ISBN 0-86010-305-6 (pbk) : £35.00 B81-28144

338.7′4′02572 — Mexico. Companies — *Directories — Serials*
Major companies of Argentina, Brazil, Mexico & Venezuela. — 1982. — London : Graham & Trotman, Oct.1981. — [470]p
ISBN 0-86010-328-5 (cased) : £67.00 : CIP entry
ISBN 0-86010-327-7 (pbk) : £60.00
Primary classification 338.7′4′02582 B81-31184

Major companies of Brazil, Mexico and Venezuela. — 1979/1980. — London : Graham & Trotman, 1979. — 405p
ISBN 0-86010-165-7 : Unpriced
ISSN 0144-2759
Primary classification 338.7′4′02581 B81-25024

Major companies of Brazil, Mexico and Venezuela. — 1979/80-. — London : Graham & Trotman, 1979-. — v. ; 30cm
Annual. — Text in English, list of index categories also in French, German, Spanish and Italian. — Description based on: 1980/81 issue
ISSN 0144-2759 = Major companies of Brazil, Mexico and Venezuela : Unpriced
Primary classification 338.7′4′02581 B81-06709

338.7′4′02573 — United States. Industries. Large companies — *Directories*
Everybody′s business : an almanac : the irreverent guide to corporate America / edited by Milton Moskowitz, Michael Katz, Robert Levering. — San Francisco ; London : Harper & Row, c1980. — 916p : ill,facsims,ports ; 24cm
Includes index
ISBN 0-06-250620-x (cased) : Unpriced
ISBN 0-06-250621-8 (pbk) : £4.95 B81-40878

338.7′4′02581 — Brazil. Companies — *Directories — Serials*
Major companies of Argentina, Brazil, Mexico & Venezuela. — 1982. — London : Graham & Trotman, Oct.1981. — [470]p
ISBN 0-86010-328-5 (cased) : £67.00 : CIP entry
ISBN 0-86010-327-7 (pbk) : £60.00
Primary classification 338.7′4′02582 B81-31184

Major companies of Brazil, Mexico and Venezuela. — 1979/1980. — London : Graham & Trotman, 1979. — 405p
ISBN 0-86010-165-7 : Unpriced
ISSN 0144-2759
Also classified at 338.7′4′02572 ; 338.7′4′02587 B81-25024

Major companies of Brazil, Mexico and Venezuela. — 1979/80-. — London : Graham & Trotman, 1979-. — v. ; 30cm
Annual. — Text in English, list of index categories also in French, German, Spanish and Italian. — Description based on: 1980/81 issue
ISSN 0144-2759 = Major companies of Brazil, Mexico and Venezuela : Unpriced
Also classified at 338.7′4′02572 ; 338.7′4′02587 B81-06709

338.7′4′02582 — Argentina. Companies — *Directories — Serials*
Major companies of Argentina, Brazil, Mexico & Venezuela. — 1982. — London : Graham & Trotman, Oct.1981. — [470]p
ISBN 0-86010-328-5 (cased) : £67.00 : CIP entry
ISBN 0-86010-327-7 (pbk) : £60.00
Also classified at 338.7′4′02581 ; 338.7′4′02572 ; 338.7′4′02587 B81-31184

338.7′4′02587 — Venezuela. Companies — *Directories — Serials*
Major companies of Argentina, Brazil, Mexico & Venezuela. — 1982. — London : Graham & Trotman, Oct.1981. — [470]p
ISBN 0-86010-328-5 (cased) : £67.00 : CIP entry
ISBN 0-86010-327-7 (pbk) : £60.00
Primary classification 338.7′4′02582 B81-31184

Major companies of Brazil, Mexico and Venezuela. — 1979/1980. — London : Graham & Trotman, 1979. — 405p
ISBN 0-86010-165-7 : Unpriced
ISSN 0144-2759
Primary classification 338.7′4′02581 B81-25024

Major companies of Brazil, Mexico and Venezuela. — 1979/80-. — London : Graham & Trotman, 1979-. — v. ; 30cm
Annual. — Text in English, list of index categories also in French, German, Spanish and Italian. — Description based on: 1980/81 issue
ISSN 0144-2759 = Major companies of Brazil, Mexico and Venezuela : Unpriced
Primary classification 338.7′4′02581 B81-06709

338.7′4′09046 — Large companies, *1962-1978 — Statistics*
Dunning, John H.. The world′s largest industrial enterprises / John H. Dunning, Robert D. Pearce. — Farnborough, Hants. : Gower, c1981. — v,164p ; 31cm
ISBN 0-566-00422-4 : £35.00 B81-14523

338.7′4′0941 — Great Britain. Companies. Inspection
Great Britain. *Department of Trade.* Handbook of the companies inspection system : inspections and departmental enquiries under the Companies Acts / Department of Trade. — London : H.M.S.O., 1980. — 71p ; 21cm
ISBN 0-11-512976-6 (pbk) : £3.00 B81-09219

338.7′4′0941 — Great Britain. Companies — *Statistics — Serials*
The **Hambro** company guide : a detailed guide to every company listed in the Financial times. — Vol.1 (1978/9)-. — London (6 Broad Street Place, EC2M 7JH) : Investment Evaluator (UK), 1979-. — v. : ill ; 25cm
Two issues yearly
ISSN 0144-2015 = Hambro company guide : £4.50 B81-00041

338.7′4′09411 — Scotland. Companies — *Statistics — Serials*
Scotland′s top 500 companies. — 1981. — London : Jordan & Sons Ltd., c1981. — xx,51p
ISBN 0-85938-147-1 : £15.00 B81-24127

338.7′4′09411 — Scotland. Limited companies, *1856-1895*
Payne, Peter L.. The early Scottish limited companies 1856-1895 : an historical and analytical survey / Peter L. Payne. — Edinburgh : Scottish Academic Press, 1980. — xii,140p : ill ; 24cm
Bibliography: p123-128. - Includes index
ISBN 0-7073-0277-3 : £12.50 B81-09382

338.7′4′09416 — Northern Ireland. Companies — *Statistics — Serials*
Companies general annual report / Department of commerce. — 1979. — Belfast : H.M.S.O., 1980. — 11p
ISBN 0-337-06125-4 : £1.50 B81-20333

338.7′4′09489 — Denmark. Companies — *Statistics — Serials*
Danmarks 2000 største virksomheder. — 13. udg. (1980). — København : Teknisk Forlag ; London : Dun & Bradstreet [distributor], 1980. — 193p
ISBN 87-571-0637-1 : Unpriced B81-35448

338.7′610705′025 — Publishing industries — *Directories — Serials*
5,001 hard to find publishers and their addresses. — 1981/82 ed.-. — Edinburgh (8 Queen Victoria St., Reading RG1 1TG) : Alan Armstrong & Associates, [1981]-. — v. ; 30cm
Irregular
ISSN 0262-0464 = 5,001 hard to find publishers and their addresses : £11.50 B81-36549

338.7′610705′025 — Publishing industries — *Directories — Serials* *continuation*

International literary market place. — 1978-79. — Epping : Bowker, c1978. — 525p
ISBN 0-85935-061-4 : Unpriced
ISSN 0074-6827 B78-22531

338.7′610705′02541 — Great Britain. Publishing industries — *Directories — Serials*

A directory of British publishers and their terms including agents for overseas publishers. — 1981. — London : Booksellers Association, 1981. — 469p
ISBN 0-901690-69-4 : Unpriced B81-23505

338.7′610705′02573 — United States. Publishing industries & trades — *Directories — Serials*

Publishers and distributors of the United States. — [2nd. ed.]. — New York ; London : Bowker, c1980. — 280p
ISBN 0-8352-1299-8 : Unpriced B81-10557

338.7′610705′02573 — United States. Publishing industries — *Directories — Serials*

Literary market place with names and numbers. — 1981 ed. — New York ; London : Bowker, 1981. — xii,849p
ISBN 0-8352-1324-2 : Unpriced
ISSN 0075-9899 B81-18810

338.7′610705′0924 — Great Britain. Publishing industries: Hodder and Stoughton Limited. Books on Christianity, *ca 1965-1981 — Personal observations*

England, Edward. An unfading vision : the adventure of books. — London : Hodder & Stoughton, Feb.1982. — [224]p
ISBN 0-340-27603-7 (pbk) : £1.95 : CIP entry
B81-36221

338.7′61′07050942 — Great Britain. Publishing industries: Nonesuch Press, *to 1980*

Dreyfus, John. A history of the Nonesuch Press. — London : Nonesuch Press, Nov.1981. — [320]p
ISBN 0-370-30397-0 : £95.00 : CIP entry
B81-30515

338.7′610705′09421 — Great Britain. Publishing industries: Butterworth & Co. (Publishers), *to 1979*

Jones, H. Kay. Butterworths : history of a publishing house / H. Kay Jones. — London : Butterworths, 1980. — x,285p : ill,facsims,ports ; 26cm
Includes index
ISBN 0-406-17606-x : £12.00 B81-01591

338.7′610705′0942132 — Great Britain. Publishing industries: Reader′s Digest Association, *to 1980*

The **Story** of Reader′s Digest : how the company began and flourished in the United States and how its London offshoot has developed into one of Britain′s largest publishing houses. — London : Reader′s Digest Association, c1981. — 24p : col.ill,col.map,col.facsims,col.ports ; 23cm
Unpriced (pbk) B81-22936

338.7′610705′0942355 — Great Britain. Publishing industries: David & Charles *(Firm), to 1980*

Good books come from Devon : the David & Charles twenty-first birthday book. — Newton Abbott : David & Charles, 1981. — 104p : ill,facsims,ports ; 26cm
Cover title
ISBN 0-7153-8139-3 (pbk) : £1.95 B81-23086

338.7′61070572′025 — Serials publishing industries — *Directories — Serials*

Benn′s press directory. Volume 2, Overseas. — 126th ed. (1978)-. — Tonbridge : Benn, 1978-. — v. ; 30cm
Annual. — Continues in part: Newspaper press directory. — Description based on: 127th ed. (1979)
ISSN 0140-6170 = Benn′s press directory. Volume 2. Overseas : £15.00 B81-29102

Benn′s press directory. Vol.2, Overseas. — 129th ed. (1981). — Tunbridge Wells : Benn, c1981. — 316p
ISBN 0-510-49026-3 : £25.00
ISSN 0141-6170 B81-30741

338.7′61070572′02541 — Great Britain. Serials publishing industries — *Directories — Serials*

Benn′s press directory. Volume 1, United Kingdom. — 127th ed. (1979). — Tonbridge : Benn, c1979. — viii,458p
ISBN 0-510-49017-4 : £20.00 B81-33309

Benn′s press directory. Volume 1, UK. — 129th ed. (1981). — Tunbridge Wells : Benn, c1981. — 532p
ISBN 0-510-49025-5 : £30.00
ISSN 0141-1772
Also classified at 072′.025 B81-30743

338.7′61070579 — Great Britain. Audiovisual materials publishing industries — *Directories*

Geddes, George T.. AVSCOT checklist of UK audio visual software producers / compiled by George Geddes and Jim Mackechnie. — Glasgow : The Scottish Branch of the Audiovisual Group of the Library Association, 1981. — 54p ; 30cm
ISBN 0-907510-00-0 (spiral) : £1.25
B81-18915

338.7′610705795′025 — Micropublishing industries — *Directories — Serials*

Microform market place. — 1980-1981. — Westport, Conn. : Microform Review Inc. ; London : Mansell Pub., c1980. — 212p
ISBN 0-7201-1605-8 : £12.50 B81-29044

338.7′610705795′02541 — Great Britain. Micropublishing industries — *Directories — Serials*

Micrographics year book. — 1981. — Guildford (54 Quarry St., Guildford, Surrey GU1 3UF) : G.G. Baker & Associates, 1981. — v. : ill ; 22cm
Annual
ISSN 0260-7069 = Micrographics year book : £7.50 B81-28383

338.7′6107′0922 — Newspaper publishing industries. Owners — *Biographies — For children*

Rickard, Graham. Great press barons / Graham Rickard. — Hove : Wayland, 1981. — 64p : ill (some col.),1col.coat of arms,facsims,ports(some col.) ; 23cm. — (In profile)
Bibliography: p62. — Includes index
ISBN 0-85340-881-5 : £3.95 B81-40617

338.7′610721 — Newspapers with London imprints: Observer, *The* . Purchase by George Outram & Company — *Inquiry reports*

Great Britain. *Monopolies and Mergers Commission*. The Observer and George Outram & Company Limited : a report on the proposed transfer of The Observer, a newspaper of which Atlantic Richfield Company is a proprietor, to George Outram & Company Limited, a subsidiary of Scottish and Universal Investments Limited, whose parent company is Lonrho Limited / Monopolies and Mergers Commission. — London : H.M.S.O., [1981]. — v,88p : 2maps ; 25cm. — (H.C. ; 378)
ISBN 0-10-237881-9 (pbk) : £4.40 B81-34825

338.7′61072876′0924 — Tyne and Wear *(Metropolitan County)*. Newcastle upon Tyne. Newspaper publishing industries: Newcastle Chronicle and Journal Limited — *Personal observations*

Clough, Robert. A public eye / by Robert Clough. — London : Hamilton, 1981. — 201,[8]p of plates : ill,ports ; 23cm
ISBN 0-241-10472-6 : £8.95 B81-14748

338.7′613442′0025 — England. Solicitors employing articled clerks — *Directories — Serials*

The **solicitors′** maxilist : an historical record of private firms of solicitors that have employed articled clerks between ... and .... — [No.1]-. — [Sheffield] ([c/o Careers Advisory Service, University of Sheffield, Sheffield S10 2TN]) : AGCAS Working Party on the Legal Profession in England and Wales, 1979-. — v. ; 30cm
Annual
ISSN 0260-7433 = Solicitor′s maxilist : Unpriced B81-11859

338.7′6136211′028 — Great Britain. Hospital equipment industries & trades — *Directories — Serials*

Health Service buyers guide. — 1981. — Epsom : Sell′s, 1981. — xiv,209p
ISBN 0-85499-688-5 : Unpriced
ISSN 0140-5748 B81-16239

338.7′6136344′0924 — Prostitution. Madams: Hollander, Xaviera — *Biographies*

Hollander, Xaviera. Xaviera′s magic mushrooms / Xaviera Hollander. — London : New English Library, 1981. — 221p ; 19cm
ISBN 0-450-05064-5 (pbk) : £1.50 B81-40626

338.7′616151′02541 — Great Britain. Pharmaceutical industries & trades — *Directories — Serials*

Chemist & druggist directory and tablet & capsule identification guide. — 1981. — London : Benn Publications, c1981. — 384p
ISBN 0-510-48760-2 : £24.00 B81-20438

338.7′616151′02541 — Great Britain. Pharmaceutical industries. Qualified chemists — *Directories*

Royal Society of Chemistry. Register of qualified persons : named under the provisions of Directive 75/319/EEC of the European Communities / Royal Society of Chemistry. — London : The Society, [1981]. — vi,55p ; 20cm
Cover title
£1.00 (free to members) (pbk) B81-37659

338.7′616151′0924 — Pharmaceutical industries. Wellcome, *Sir Henry* — *Biographies*

Turner, Helen. Henry Wellcome : the man, his collection and his legacy / Helen Turner. — London : The Wellcome Trust and Heinemann, 1980. — 96p : ill,ports ; 23cm
Includes index
ISBN 0-435-32860-3 : £7.95 : CIP rev.
B80-25345

338.7′6162′000941 — Great Britain. Consulting engineering. Partnerships: Preece Cardew & Rider *(Firm), to 1979*

Baker, E. C.. Preece and those who followed : consulting engineers in the twentieth century / E.C. Baker. — Brighton (8 Bond St., Brighton, Sussex) : Reprographic Centre, 1980. — xiv,288p,[17]p of plates : ill,maps,facsims,ports ; 25cm
Includes index
ISBN 0-9506928-0-8 : £7.50 B81-34428

338.7′61624′028 — Great Britain. Construction equipment hire services — *Directories — Serials*

UK plant hire guide. — 1981. — Sutton : IPC Building & Contract Journals, [1981]. — 108p
ISSN 0307-2630 : £2.00 B81-29426

United Kingdom plant hire companies / [Data Research Group]. — 1980/81. — Great Missenden : The Group, [1981]. — [vii],205p
ISBN 0-86099-293-4 : £27.00 B81-36012

338.7′61647944275401 — Merseyside *(Metropolitan County)*. Prescot & Whiston. Inns. Licensees, *1556-1981 — Lists*

Knowles, Jack. Inns of Prescot and Whiston : (including hotels, public houses, taverns and alehouses) / Jack Knowles. — Liverpool (Reference and Information Department, Central Library, Derby Rd., Huyton, Liverpool L36 9UJ) : Knowsley Library Service, c1981. — 32p ; 21cm
Cover title
£0.35 (pbk)
Primary classification 338.7′616479542754
B81-37789

338.7′616479542754 — Merseyside *(Metropolitan County)*. Prescot & Whiston. Public houses. Licensees, *1556-1981 — Lists*

Knowles, Jack. Inns of Prescot and Whiston : (including hotels, public houses, taverns and alehouses) / Jack Knowles. — Liverpool (Reference and Information Department, Central Library, Derby Rd., Huyton, Liverpool L36 9UJ) : Knowsley Library Service, c1981. — 32p ; 21cm
Cover title
£0.35 (pbk)
Also classified at 338.7′61647944275401
B81-37789

338.7′616591′025 — Advertising industries — *Directories — Serials*
Advertiser′s annual. — 56th ed. (1981). — East Grinstead (Windsor Court, East Grinstead House, East Grinstead, Sussex RH19 1XA) : IPC Media Publications, c1981. — xlviii,1128,F376p
Unpriced B81-35109

338.7′616592991416′005 — Northern Ireland. Tourism. Promotion. Organisations: Northern Ireland Tourist Board — *Serials*
Northern Ireland Tourist Board. Annual report for the year ended 31 December ... / Northern Ireland Tourist Board. — 1979. — [Belfast?] : The Board, [1980]. — 32p
Unpriced B81-07791

338.7′617 — London. Visual arts. Art dealing. Organisations: Thos. Agnew & Sons Ltd., *1967-1981 — Personal observations*
A dealer′s record : Agnew′s 1967-81. — London : Barrie & Jenkins, 1981. — 191p : ill(some col.),ports(some col.) ; 27cm
Includes index
ISBN 0-09-146200-2 : £25.00 : CIP rev.
B81-22591

338.7′6172′02541 — Great Britain. Architectural design. Partnerships — *Directories — Serials*
United Kingdom architectural partnerships / [Data Research Group]. — [1981]. — Great Missenden : The Group, 1981. — 155p
ISBN 0-86099-306-x : £27.00 B81-37227

338.7′617451′0288 — Great Britain. Antiques restoration services — *Directories*
The **First** guidebook of specialist in repair, restoration, renovation and conservation / Guild of Master Craftsmen. — Lewis (17 High St., Lewis, E. Sussex) : The Guild, [1981]. — 263p : ill ; 21cm
Includes index
£6.95 (pbk)
Primary classification 338.7′69024′02541
B81-36261

338.7′617785992 — Great Britain. Videorecording industries — *Directories — Serials*
[Production *(London : 1976)*]. Production : a comprehensive guide to Britain′s film and video production companies, with sections on production, film & video facilities, distribution and advertising agencies. — 76-. — London (111a Wardour St., W1V 3TD) : Broadcast, 1976-. — v. : ill ; 30cm
Annual. — Description based on: 81-82
ISSN 0262-0960 = Production (London. 1976) : £3.50
Primary classification 384′.8′02541 B81-38990

338.7′6178991′02541 — Great Britain. Music recording industries — *Directories*
British record company & music industry index. — Staverton (8 Nelson Close, Staverton, Totnes, Devon) : R.S. Productions, [1981]. — 18p in various pagings ; 30cm
ISBN 0-906888-09-3 (unbound) : £1.50
B81-38976

338.7′61′789910924 — Music recording industries. Culshaw, John — *Biographies*
Culshaw, John. Putting the record straight. — London : Secker & Warburg, Oct.1981. — [352]p
ISBN 0-436-11802-5 : £8.95 : CIP entry
B81-32087

338.7′61791′02541 — Great Britain. Entertainment industries — *Directories — Serials*
Showcall. — 1981. — London (Stage House, 47 Bermondsey St., SE1 3XT) : Carson & Comerford, c1980. — 2v.
Unpriced B81-06918

338.7′6179633463′0924 — England. Association football. Clubs. Management. Chapman, Herbert — *Biographies*
Studd, Stephen. Herbert Chapman : football emperor : a study in the origins of modern soccer / Stephen Studd ; foreword by Sir Stanley Rous. — London : Peter Owen, 1981. — 160p,[8]p of plates : ill,ports ; 23cm
Bibliography: p254-155. — Includes index
ISBN 0-7206-0581-4 : £8.50 B81-37667

338.7′6179633463′0924 — England. Association football. Clubs. Management — *Personal observations*
Taylor, Peter, *1928-*. With Clough / by Taylor (with Mike Langley). — [Rev. and updated ed.]. — [London] : New English Library, 1981, c1980. — 170p,[16]p of plates : ill,ports ; 18cm
Previous ed.: London : Sidgwick and Jackson, 1980. — Includes index
ISBN 0-283-98795-2 (pbk) : £1.50 B81-36137

338.7′6191′0924 — Great Britain. Travel agencies. Cook, Thomas, *1808-1892 — Biographies*
Heath, G. R.. Thomas Cook of Melbourne, 1808-1892 / [G.R. Heath]. — [Melbourne] (['Penn-gate′ Salisbury La., Melbourne, Derbyshire, DE7 1ER]) : [G.R. Heath], [1981?]. — 16p : ill,facsims ; 22cm
Cover title
£0.50 (pbk) B81-30102

338.7′6191411′005 — Scotland. Tourism. Promotion. Organisations: Scottish Tourist Board *— Serials*
Scottish Tourist Board. Annual report / Scottish Tourist Board. — 12th (1980-81)-. — Edinburgh : The Board, [1981]-. — v. ; 30cm
Continues: Scottish Tourist Board. Report
ISSN 0262-0731 · £2.50 B81-36550

338.7′619142′005 — England. Tourism. Promotion. Organisations: English Tourist Board — *Serials*
English horizon : marketing news from the ETB / English Tourist Board. — July 1980-. — London (4 Grosvenor Gardens, SW1W 0DU) : The Board, 1980. — v. : ill ; 42cm
Quarterly. — Continues: Network (London : 1976)
ISSN 0260-0439 = English horizon : Free
B81-03277

English Tourist Board. Annual report for the year ended 31 March ... / English Tourist Board. — 1981. — London : The Board, 1981. — 70p
£5.00 B81-34032

338.7′62′0002541 — Great Britain. Engineering industries & trades — *Directories — Serials*
Engineering Employers′ Federation. Engineering Employers′ Federation directory. — 1981 ed.. — Redhill : International Newspapers on behalf of the Federation, [1981]. — 368p
ISSN 0141-7592 : Unpriced B81-25477

338.7′62′00025417 — Ireland *(Republic)*. **Engineering industries & trades —** *Directories*
Irish engineering directory : companies, products & services. — Dublin (Ballymun Rd., Dublin 9) : Institute for Industrial Research and Standards, c1981. — xvi,388p : ill ; 30cm
Includes index
ISBN 0-900450-44-4 (pbk) : Unpriced
B81-37794

338.7′62′00025423 — South-west England. Engineering industries — *Directories — Serials*
Annual directory, buyers guide and classified index of plant and services / the Bristol & West of England Engineering Manufacturers′ Association Limited. — 41st ed (1980/81). — Bristol (B.E.M.A. House, 4, Broad Plain, Bristol BS2 0NG) : The Association, [1980]. — 290p
Unpriced B81-10580

338.7′62′00028 — Great Britain. Industrial equipment industries — *Directories — Serials*
Kompass register industrial section. 40, Industrial machinery and equipment : an extract from the Kompass register of British industry & commerce. — 1981/82-. — East Grinstead : Kompass, c1981-. — v. ; 30cm
Annual. — Introduction in English, text also in French, German, Spanish and Italian. — Cover title: Euro Kompass United Kingdom. Industrial machinery and equipment
ISSN 0261-3336 = Kompass register industrial section. 40. Industrial machinery and equipment : Unpriced B81-32280

338.7′62′000941 — Great Britain. Engineering industries: John Brown and Company, *to 1980*
Mensforth, Eric. Family engineers. — London : Ward Lock, Nov.1981. — [160]p
ISBN 0-7063-6170-9 (cased) : £9.95 : CIP entry
ISBN 0-7063-6171-7 (pbk) : £7.95 B81-30298

338.7′62′000941 — Great Britain. Engineering industries: Northern Engineering Industries — *Serials*
NEI news : the newspaper of Northern Engineering Industries Ltd. — No.1 (Dec.1977)-. — [Newcastle upon Tyne] ([NEI House, Regent Centre, Newcastle upon Tyne NE3 3SB]) : Northern Engineering Industries, 1977-. — v. : ill,ports ; 43cm
Quarterly. — Description based on: No.14 (Apr.1981)
ISSN 0262-0057 = NEI news : Unpriced
B81-37242

338.7′62086 — Great Britain. Emergency equipment industries: RFD Group, *to 1979*
Nockolds, Harold. Rescue from disaster : the history of the RFD Group / Harold Nockolds. — Newton Abbot : David & Charles, c1980. — 224p : ill,ports ; 24cm
Bibliography: p218. - Includes index
ISBN 0-7153-7969-0 : £10.50 : CIP rev.
B80-11796

338.7′62086 — Great Britain. Industrial safety equipment industries & trades — *Directories — Serials*
Health & safety marketguide. — 81-. — Aylesbury (Aydee Marketing Ltd., 2 Castle St., Aylesbury, Bucks. HP20 2RF) : Safety Workshops, 1981-. — v. : ill ; 30cm
Annual
ISSN 0261-8036 = Health & safety marketguide : £10.00 B81-33727

338.7′621′02541 — Great Britain. Mechanical engineering industries — *Directories — Serials*
Machinery buyers guide. — 1981. — Beckenham (1 Copers Cope Rd, Beckenham, Kent BR3 1NB) : Machinery Buyers Guide Ltd., [1981]. — [1,360]p in various pagings
ISSN 0142-0658 : £12.00 B81-25489

338.7′621042′0941 — Great Britain. Energy industries. Organisation structure
Pearson, Lynn F.. The organization of the energy industry / Lynn F. Pearson. — London : Macmillan, 1981. — xiv,252p : ill ; 23cm
Bibliography: p234-243. - Includes index
ISBN 0-333-27084-3 : £20.00 : CIP rev.
B80-04102

338.7′62131′02541 — Great Britain. Electricity supply industries — *Directories — Serials*
Electricity supply handbook. — 1981. — Sutton (Quadrant House, The Quadrant, Sutton, Surrey SM2 SAS) : IPC Electrical Electronic Press, c1981. — 305p
ISBN 0-617-00245-2 : £6.00 B81-20067

338.7′62131042′02541 — Great Britain. Electric equipment industries & trades — *Directories — Serials*
Electrical and electronics trades directory. — 99th ed. (1981). — Stevenage : Peter Peregrinus, c1981. — 736p
ISBN 0-906048-49-4 : Unpriced B81-18811

338.7′62131′04202541 — Great Britain. Electric equipment industries — *Directories — Serials*
Kompass register industrial section. 37, Electrical and electronic equipment. — 1981/82. — East Grinstead : Kompass, c1981. — 470p in various pagings
Cover title: Euro Kompass United Kingdom. Electrical and electronic equipment
ISBN 0-900505-89-3 : Unpriced
Also classified at 338.7′621381′02541
B81-32243

338.7′62131′094111 — Northern Scotland. Electricity supply industries: North of Scotland Hydro-Electric Board — *Serials*
North of Scotland Hydro-Electric Board. Report and accounts 1 April ... to 31 March .. / North of Scotland Hydro-Electric Board. — 1980/1981. — [Edinburgh] ([16 Rothesay Terrace, Edinburgh EH3 7SE]) : [The Board], [1981]. — vi,58p
Unpriced B81-33716

338.7′62131′09413 — Southern Scotland. Electricity supply industries: South of Scotland Electricity Board — *Serials*

South of Scotland Electricity Board. Annual report and accounts for the year ended 31 March ... / South of Scotland Electricity Board. — 1981. — Glasgow (Cathcart House, Glasgow G44 4BE) : [The Board], [1981]. — 66p
Cover title: Report and accounts (South of Scotland Electricity Board)
£1.00 B81-34049

338.7′62131′0942 — England. Electricity generation & transmission industries: Central Electricity Generating Board — *Inquiry reports*

Great Britain. *Monopolies and Mergers Commission*. Central Electricity Generating Board : a report on the operation by the Board of its system for the generation and supply of electricity in bulk / the Monopolies and Mergers Commission. — London : H.M.S.O., 1981. — vii,360p(some folded) : ill,1map ; 25cm. — (HC ; 315)
ISBN 0-10-231581-7 (pbk) : £9.30 B81-26112

338.7′621319′094275 — Merseyside *(Metropolitan County)*. **Electricity distribution industries: Merseyside and North Wales Electricity Board** — *Serials*

Merseyside and North Wales Electricity Board. Report and accounts for the year ended 31st March ... / Merseyside and North Wales Electricity Board. — 1980. — Chester (Sealand Rd, Chester CH1 4LR) : The Board, c1980. — 32p
Unpriced
Also classified at 338.7′621319′094291
B81-03294

338.7′621319′09428 — North-east England. Electricity distribution industries: North Eastern Electricity Board — *Serials*

North Eastern Electricity Board. Annual report and accounts for the year ended 31 March ... / the North Eastern Electricity Board. — 1977-. — [Newcastle upon Tyne] ([Carliol House, Newcastle upon Tyne NE99 1SE]) : NEEB, 1977-. — v. : ill(chiefly col.),col.maps ; 30cm
Annual. — Continues: North Eastern Electricity Board. Annual report and statement of accounts for the year ended 31 March ... — Description based on: 1981
ISSN 0262-0146 = Annual report and accounts - North Eastern Electricity Board : Unpriced B81-39545

338.7′621319′094291 — North Wales. Electricity distribution industries: Merseyside and North Wales Electricity Board — *Serials*

Merseyside and North Wales Electricity Board. Report and accounts for the year ended 31st March ... / Merseyside and North Wales Electricity Board. — 1980. — Chester (Sealand Rd, Chester CH1 4LR) : The Board, c1980. — 32p
Unpriced
Primary classification 338.7′621319′094275
B81-03294

338.7′62138044′02573 — United States. Audiovisual equipment industries & trades — *Directories* — *Serials*

Audiovisual market place. — 1981. — New York ; London : R.R. Bowker, c1981. — xii,468p
Spine title: AVMP
ISBN 0-8352-1333-1 : Unpriced
ISSN 0067-0553 B81-29983

338.7′621381′02541 — Great Britain. Electronic equipment industries & trades — *Directories* — *Serials*

The **Directory** of instruments, electronics, automation. — 15th ed. (1981). — London (30 Calderwood St., SE18 6QH) : Morgan-Grampian in association with Control & instrumentation and Electronic engineering, c1981. — 333p
ISBN 0-86213-020-4 : £15.00 B81-20706

338.7′621381′02541 — Great Britain. Electronic equipment industries — *Directories* — *Serials*

Kompass register industrial section. 37, Electrical and electronic equipment. — 1981/82. — East Grinstead : Kompass, c1981. — 470p in various pagings
Cover title: Euro Kompass United Kingdom. Electrical and electronic equipment
ISBN 0-900505-89-3 : Unpriced
Primary classification 338.7′62131′04202541
B81-32243

338.7′621381′0941 — Great Britain. Electronic equipment industries: Aveley Laboratories Limited — *Inquiry reports*

McCowan, Anthony James Denys. Aveley Laboratories Limited : investigation under section 165(b) of the Companies Act 1948 / report by Anthony James Denys McCowan and Alan Peter Humphries. — London : H.M.S.O., 1981. — iii,89p ; 30cm
At head of title : Department of Trade
ISBN 0-11-513470-0 (pbk) : £7.50 B81-37490

338.7′62138195′09425895 — Hertfordshire. Borehamwood. Computer industries: GEC Computers — *Serials*

[Datalink *(Borehamwood)*]. Datalink : GEC Computers′ internal newsletter. — Issue no.1 (Feb.1976)-. — Borehamwood (Publicity Department, Elstree Way, Borehamwood, Herts. WD6 1RX) : GEC Computers, 1976-. — v. : ill,ports ; 30cm
Quarterly. — Description based on: Issue no.20 (Spring 1981)
ISSN 0261-8869 = Datalink (Borehamwood) : Unpriced B81-35092

338.7′6213895′025424 — England. West Midlands. Minicomputer & microcomputer industries & services — *Directories*

West Midlands regional mini-micro computing directory. — Birmingham (6 Innage Rd., Northfield, Birmingham B31 2DX) : Chris Martin & Associates, [1981?]. — 42leaves ; 30cm
ISBN 0-907695-00-0 (spiral) : Unpriced
B81-32739

338.7′62156′02541 — Great Britain. Refrigeration equipment industries — *Directories* — *Serials*

United Kingdom heating, refrigeration & ventilating equipment manufacturers / [Data Research Group]. — [1981]. — Great Missenden : The Group, 1981. — 74leaves
Cover title: Heating, refrigeration & ventilation equipment manufacturers
ISBN 0-86099-316-7 : Unpriced
Primary classification 338.7′697′0002541
B81-29067

338.7′62159′025 — Cryogenics industries — *Directories*

Cryogenics handbook / edited by Beverly Law. — Guildford : Westbury House, c1981. — vii,423p : ill ; 22cm
ISBN 0-86103-021-4 : Unpriced B81-09892

338.7′621902′02541 — Great Britain. Machine tools industries — *Directories* — *Serials*

United Kingdom machine tool manufacturers / [Data Research Group]. — 1980. — Great Missenden : The Group, [1980]. — 61p
ISBN 0-86099-262-4 : £22.00 B81-09699

United Kingdom machine tool manufacturers / [Data Research Group]. — [1981]. — Great Missenden : The Group, 1981. — 36leaves
ISBN 0-86099-313-2 : Unpriced B81-29064

338.7′622′025 — Mining industries — *Directories* — *Serials*

Financial times mining international year book. — 1981. — London : Longman, c1980. — 714p
ISBN 0-582-90306-8 : Unpriced
ISSN 0141-3244 B81-16834

338.7′622′0924 — South Africa. Mining industries. Oppenheimer, *Sir Ernest* — *Biographies*

Jessup, Edward. Ernest Oppenheimer : a study in power / Edward Jessup. — London : Collings, 1979. — 357p,[16]p of plates : ill,3maps,facsims,ports,1geneal.table
Bibliography: p343-345. — Includes index
ISBN 0-86036-087-3 : £12.95 B81-02715

338.7′6222334′02541 — Great Britain. Coal industries — *Directories* — *Serials*

Guide to the coalfields. — 1981. — Redhill (2 Queensway, Redhill, Surrey RH1 1QS) : Colliery guardian, [1981]. — 629p
£13.50 B81-35126

338.7′622334′0942467 — Staffordshire. Cannock Chase *(District)*. **Coal industries: Cannock Chase Colliery Company,** *to 1947*

Francis, J. Roger. A history of Cannock Chase Colliery Company / by J. Roger Francis. — [Rugeley] ([Slitting Mill, Rugeley, Staffs.]) : Staffordshire Industrial Archaeology Society, c1980. — 73p : ill,maps,1facsim,plans ; 30cm
Cover title. — Bibliography: p72-73
£1.50 (pbk) B81-07118

338.7′6223382′025 — Petroleum industries — *Directories* — *For North Sea petroleum deposit exploitation* — *Serials*

North sea oil directory. — 1981. — Kingston-upon-Thames (Rowe House, Fife Rd., Kingston-upon-Thames, Surrey KT1 1TA) : Spearhead Publications, c1981. — lxxx,820p
ISSN 0307-0344 : £17.95 B81-29054

338.7′6223382′0941 — Great Britain. Petroleum industries: British National Oil Corporation. Finance. National Oil Account — *Accounts* — *Serials*

National Oil Account account .... — 1979-80. — London : H.M.S.O., [1981]. — 11p
ISBN 0-10-226881-9 : £1.40 B81-30752

338.7′6223382′0941 — Great Britain. Petroleum industries: British National Oil Corporation — *Serials*

Oil spot : the staff newspaper of the British National Oil Corporation. — Dec.1978-. — Glasgow (150 St. Vincent St., Glasgow G2 5LJ) : The Corporation, 1978-. — v. : ill,ports ; 39cm
Monthly. — Description based on: Feb.1981
ISSN 0261-3247 = Oil spot : Unpriced
B81-23152

338.7′62234′0924 — Africa. Metals mining industries. Prain, *Sir Ronald* — *Biographies*

Prain, *Sir* **Ronald**. Reflections on an era : fifty years of mining in changing Africa : the autobiography of Sir Ronald Prain. — [Worcester Park] : Metal Bulletin, c1981. — 262p : maps,ports ; 25cm
Bibliography: p246. — Includes index
ISBN 0-900542-52-7 : £10.00 B81-29151

338.7′622343′0942712 — Cheshire. Bickerton. Copper mining industries: Gallantry Bank Copper Mine, *to 1920*

Carlon, Chris J.. The Gallantry Bank Copper Mine, Bickerton, Cheshire : with a review of mining in the Triassic rocks of the Cheshire-Shropshire Basin / Chris J. Carlon. — South Anston (41 Windsor Walk, South Anston, Sheffield S31 7EL) : Northern Mine Research Society, 1981. — 50p,[8]p of plates : ill,1facsim,maps ; 30cm. — (British mining, ISSN 0308-2199 ; no.16) (A Monograph of the Northern Mine Research Society)
Bibliography: p50
ISBN 0-901450-19-7 (pbk) : Unpriced
B81-26183

338.7′62382 — Ships′ equipment industries — *Directories* — *Serials*

International shipping and shipbuilding directory. Volume 2, Buyers′ guide. — 1981. — London : Benn Publications, 1981. — 325p
Spine title: ISSD buyers′ guide
ISBN 0-510-49717-9 : £14.00 B81-25501

338.7′624′02541 — Great Britain. Civil engineering industries — *Directories* — *Serials*

United Kingdom civil engineering companies / [Data Research Group]. — 1980. — Great Missenden : The Group, [1980?]. — 170p
ISBN 0-86099-290-x : Unpriced B81-13408

338.7′6281′025 — Water supply industries — *Directories — Serials*

The **International** who's who in water supply = Annuaire international who's who de distribution d'eau = Das internationale wer ist wer in der Wasserversorgung. — 1st ed. — London (23 Ramillies Place, W1A 3BF) : Marlborough Publishing for the International Water Supply Association, 1979-. — v. : ill ; 21cm
Annual. — Text in English, French and German
ISSN 0260-4604 = International who's who in water supply : £10.00 B81-06194

338.7′6281′02541 — Great Britain. Water supply industries *— Directories — Serials*

Who's who in the water industry / National Water Council. — 1981. — Rickmansworth, Wheatland Journal, [1981?]. — 159p
Unpriced B81-15444

338.7′6281′094244 — Hereford and Worcester. East Worcestershire. Water supply industries: East Worcestershire Waterworks Company. Efficiency *— Inquiry reports*

Great Britain. *Monopolies and Mergers Commission*. Severn-Trent Water Authority, East Worcestershire Waterworks Company and the South Staffordshire Waterworks Company : a report on water services supplied by the Authority and the Companies / Monopolies and Mergers Commission. — London : H.M.S.O., 1981. — x,467p : ill,maps ; 25cm. — (HC ; 339)
ISBN 0-10-233981-3 (pbk) : £10.80
Primary classification 352.6′1′09424 B81-29625

338.7′6281′094246 — Staffordshire. Water supply industries: South Staffordshire Waterworks Company. Efficiency *— Inquiry reports*

Great Britain. *Monopolies and Mergers Commission*. Severn-Trent Water Authority, East Worcestershire Waterworks Company and the South Staffordshire Waterworks Company : a report on water services supplied by the Authority and the Companies / Monopolies and Mergers Commission. — London : H.M.S.O., 1981. — x,467p : ill,maps ; 25cm. — (HC ; 339)
ISBN 0-10-233981-3 (pbk) : £10.80
Primary classification 352.6′1′09424 B81-29625

338.7′628922′025 — Fire protection industries — *Directories — Serials*

Fire protection directory. — 1981. — Ewell (172 Kingston Rd, Ewell, Nr. Epsom, Surrey KT19 0SB) : A.E. Morgan Publications, [1981]. — 199p
£23.00
Also classified at 352.3′025 B81-29104

338.7′6291′0254 — Western Europe. Aerospace industries *— Directories — Serials*

Aviation Europe. — 1981/2. — Epsom : Sell's Publications, [1981]. — 201p
ISBN 0-85499-889-6 : £20.00
ISSN 0143-1145 B81-31602

338.7′6291′0941 — Great Britain. Aerospace engineering industries: British Aerospace — *Serials*

British Aerospace. Annual report and accounts / British Aerospace. — 1979. — Weybridge (Brooklands Rd, Weybridge, Surrey) : British Aerospace, [1980?]. — 56p
ISBN 0-906351-02-2 : £2.00
ISSN 0141-9102 B81-26590

British Aerospace. Annual report and accounts / British Aerospace. — 1980. — [London] ([100 Pall Mall, SW1Y 5HR]) : British Aerospace, [1981]. — 64p
ISSN 0141-9102 : Unpriced B81-30848

338.7′6291′0941 — Great Britain. Aerospace engineering industries: British Aircraft Corporation, *to 1977*

Gardner, Charles. British aircraft corporation : a history / by Charles Gardner. — London : Batsford, 1981. — 320p,[32]p of plates : ill (some col.),ports ; 24cm
Includes index
ISBN 0-7134-3815-0 : £12.50 B81-29576

338.7′6291′0941 — Great Britain. Aerospace engineering industries: Lucas Aerospace. Diversification. Proposals: Lucas Aerospace Combine Shop Stewards Committee. Lucas Aerospace alternative corporate plan, *to 1980*

Wainwright, Hilary. The Lucas struggle. — London : Allison & Busby, Oct.1981. — [192]p
ISBN 0-85031-429-1 (cased) : £7.95 : CIP entry
ISBN 0-85031-430-5 (pbk) : £2.95 B81-28002

338.7′62913′009 — Aircraft industries. Companies, *to 1979*

Gunston, Bill. The plane makers / Bill Gunston. — London : New English Library, 1980. — 253p : ill(some col.),ports ; 31cm
Ill on lining papers. — Includes index
ISBN 0-450-04754-7 : £12.95 B81-08380

338.7′62913435′0941 — Great Britain. Aircraft engines industries: Rolls-Royce — *Serials*

The **Rolls-Royce** magazine. — No.1 (June/Aug.1979)-. — London (65 Buckingham Gate, SW1E 6AT) : Rolls-Royce, 1979-. — v. : ill(some col) ; 30cm
Quarterly. — Continues: Rolls-Royce today
ISSN 0142-9469 = Rolls-Royce magazine : Unpriced B81-06391

338.7′62913435′0941 — Great Britain. Aircraft engines industries: Rolls-Royce, *to 1980*

Donne, Michael. Leader of the skies : Rolls-Royce : the first seventy-five years / by Michael Donne. — London : Muller, 1981. — 158p : ill(some col.),1facsim,ports ; 22x29cm
Bibliography: p158. — Includes index
ISBN 0-584-10476-6 : £10.00 B81-11575

338.7′6292′02541 — Great Britain. Motor vehicle industries & trades *— Directories — Serials*

Buyers' guide to the motor industry of Great Britain. — 1980-81. — London : Society of Motor Manufacturers and Traders, c1980-81. — 145p
£5.00 B81-08749

338.7′6292′0924 — United States. Motor vehicle industries: General Motors Corporation, *1956-1973 — Personal observations*

De Lorean, John Z.. On a clear day you can see General Motors : John Z. De Lorean's look inside the automotive giant / by J. Patrick Wright. — London : Sidgwick & Jackson, 1981, c1979. — xi,237p ; 24cm
Originally published: Grosse Pointe : Wright Enterprises, 1979 ; London : Sidgwick and Jackson, 1980
ISBN 0-283-98794-4 (pbk) : £2.95 B81-23205

338.7′6292′0941 — Great Britain. Motor vehicle industries: BL Limited. Financial assistance by government *— Inquiry reports*

Great Britain. *Parliament. House of Commons. Industry and Trade Committee*. Third report from the Industry and Trade Committee, session 1980-81 : finance for BL : together with the proceedings of the Committee relating to the report, the minutes of evidence and appendices. — London : H.M.S.O., [1981]. — viii,74p ; 25cm. — ([HC] ; 294)
ISBN 0-10-229481-x (pbk) : £5.00 B81-33037

338.7′6292′0941 — Great Britain. Motor vehicle industries: Jaguar Cars Ltd., *to 1980*

Whyte, Andrew. Jaguar : the history of a great British car / Andrew Whyte ; foreword by Sir William Lyons. — Cambridge : Stephens, 1980. — 249p : ill,ports ; 25cm
Ill on lining papers. — Includes index
ISBN 0-85059-470-7 : £9.95 B81-29272

338.7′6292′0943 — West Germany. Motor vehicle industries: Volkswagenwerk, *to 1979*

Sloniger, Jerrold E.. The VW story / Jerry Sloniger. — Cambridge : Stephens, 1980. — 216p : ill,maps,1facsim,ports ; 25cm
Ill on lining papers. — Includes index
ISBN 0-85059-441-3 : £9.50 B81-32723

338.7′62′92220941 — Great Britain. Car industries: Rover-British Leyland UK Limited, *to 1980*

Robson, Graham. The Rover story. — 2nd ed. — Cambridge : Stephens, Oct.1981. — [192]p
Previous ed.: 1977
ISBN 0-85059-543-6 : £9.95 : CIP entry B81-28018

338.7′6292222′0924 — United States. Car industries. Ford, Henry, *1863-1947 — Biographies — For children*

Stoney, Barbara. Henry Ford. — London : Hodder and Stoughton Children's Books, Oct.1981. — [128]p. — (Twentieth century people series)
For adolescents
ISBN 0-340-25913-2 : £4.95 : CIP entry B81-27985

338.7′6292222′0941 — Great Britain. Car industries: Austin Motor Company, *1905-1952*

Wyatt, R. J. (Robert John). The Austin 1905-1952 / R.J. Wyatt. — Newton Abbot : David & Charles, c1981. — 298p : ill,1facsim,1plan,ports ; 24cm
Ill on lining papers. — Includes index
ISBN 0-7153-7948-8 : £12.50 B81-21908

338.7′6292222′0941 — Great Britain. Car industries: Bentley Motors, *to 1979*

Frostick, Michael. Bentley : Cricklewood to Crewe / Michael Frostick. — London : Osprey, 1980. — 302 : ill(some col.),facsims,ports ; 26cm
Includes index
ISBN 0-85045-376-3 : £12.50 : CIP rev. B80-19104

338.7′62922233′0942184 — London. Ealing *(London Borough)***. Bus industries: Park Royal Vehicles Limited,** *to 1980*

Park Royal Coachworks Ltd. / [compiled] by Alan Townsin. — Glossop : Transport Publishing Company
Vol.1: 1924-1944. — c1979. — 183p : chiefly ill(some col.),plans ; 21x30cm
Ill, text on lining papers. — Includes index
ISBN 0-903839-17-2 : £7.95 B81-36083

338.7′629226′02541 — Great Britain. Caravan industries *— Directories — Serials*

Caravan industry supplies and services directory. — 1981. — Epsom (172 Kingston Rd., Ewell, Epsom, Surrey) : A.E. Morgan, c1980. — 104p
£3.70 B81-07310

338.7′6292275′0977595 — Wisconsin. Milwaukee. Motorcycle industries: Harley-Davidson Motor Company, Milwaukee, *to 1980*

Sucher, Harry V.. Harley-Davidson : the Milwaukee marvel / Harry V. Sucher. — Yeovil : Foulis : Haynes, 1981. — 283p : ill,facsims,ports ; 25cm. — (A Foulis motorcycling book)
Includes index
ISBN 0-85429-261-6 : Unpriced B81-39978

338.7′629228′0941 — Great Britain. Racing car industries: English Racing Automobiles Limited, *to 1980*

Weguelin, David. The history of English Racing Automobiles Limited : and the continuing story of the cars 1933-1980 / by David Weguelin ; editors Narisa Chakrabongse ... [et al.]. — London (50 Porchester Terrace, W2 3TP) : White Mouse, 1980. — 288p : ill(some col.),facsims,ports(some col.) ; 28x35cm
In a slip case. — Bibliography: p284. — Includes index
ISBN 0-904568-24-5 : Unpriced B81-05820

338.7′6292542′0942 — England. Motor vehicle battery industries: Chloride Automotive Batteries Ltd *— Serials*

Automotive news : the company newspaper of Chloride Automotive Batteries Ltd. — No.1 (1978)-. — Dagenham (Dagenham, Essex) : Chloride Automotive Batteries Ltd., 1978-. — v. : ill,ports ; 37cm
Three issues yearly. — Continues in part: EPS news. — Description based on: No.5 (Autumn 1979)
ISSN 0262-1800 = Automotive news : Unpriced B81-38987

338.7′62982 — Great Britain. Vending machine industries & trades *— Directories — Serials*

Vending International manual : the handbook of vending / compiled by the staff of Vending International. — 11th ed.-. — Tonbridge (47 High St., Tonbridge Kent) : Weald of Kent Publications, c1981-. — v. : ill ; 22
Annual. — Continues: Vending Times manual. — Description based on: 12th ed.
ISSN 0143-4381 = Vending International manual : £5.75 B81-22406

338.7′63′0924 — Warwickshire. Burton Dassett. Agriculture. Temple, Peter. Accounts, *1543-1555*

Temple, Peter. Warwickshire grazier and London skinner, 1532-1555. — Oxford : Oxford University Press for the British Academy, Dec.1981. — [240]p. — (Records of social and economic history. New series ; 5)
ISBN 0-19-726008-x : £24.00 : CIP entry
Also classified at 381′.4567731′0924
B81-31448

338.7′63′0941463 — Scotland. Strathclyde Region. Dunlop. Agricultural industries: Robert Howie & Sons, *to 1978*

Robert Howie & Sons. Things I remember : the story of Robert Howie & Sons 1850-1978 : the memoirs of James M. Howie. — [Kilmarnock] ([Parkhead, Dunlop, Kilmarnock, Ayrshire KA3 4AK]) : [Howie and Sons], [1978?]. — 52p : ill,ports,1geneal.table ; 22cm
Unpriced (pbk) B81-21045

338.7′633491′025416 — Northern Ireland. Certified seed potato industries — *Directories* — *Serials*

Register of growers of basic seed potatoes / Department of Agriculture for Northern Ireland. — 1979. — [Belfast] : H.M.S.O., [1979?]. — 63p
Unpriced B81-06675

338.7′63382 — Great Britain. Hop industries: Guinness Hop Farms Ltd., *to 1976*

Brown, J. F.. Guinness and hops / J.F. Brown. — London (Park Royal Brewery, N.W.10) : Arthur Guinness, c1980. — xv,264p ; 21cm
Includes index
ISBN 0-85112-222-1 : Unpriced B81-04404

338.7′63382 — Kent. Hop picking industries, *ca 1900* — *Childhood reminiscences* — *Collections*

Old days in the Kent hop gardens / [edited by Mary Lewis]. — Rev. ed. — Maidstone (64 College Rd., Maidstone, Kent) : West Kent Federation of Women′s Institutes, 1981. — 59p : ill ; 21cm
Previous ed.: 1962
Unpriced (pbk) B81-21904

338.7′63941′0924 — Eastern England. Coastal waters. Oyster fisheries, *ca 1945-ca 1980* — *Personal observations*

Frost, Michael. Half a gale. — Havant : K. Mason, Sept.1981. — [128]p
ISBN 0-85937-263-4 : £5.95 : CIP entry
B81-20637

338.7′6413′00941 — Great Britain. Food industries. Companies — *Statistics* — *Serials*

Companies in the food industry / Institute of Grocery Distribution, Research Services. — 1979/80. — [Watford] ([Letchmore Health, Watford WD2 8DQ]) : [The Institute], [1980]. — x,79 leaves
Unpriced B81-09148

338.7′66′002541 — Great Britain. Chemical industries — *Directories* — *Serials*

Chemical industry directory and who′s who. — 1981. — Tunbridge Wells : Benn, c1981. — 418p in various pagings
ISBN 0-510-48713-0 : £30.00 B81-30751

Kompass register industrial section. 30/31 & 40 (part), Rubber and plastics, chemicals and chemical products, machinery and equipment. — 1981/82. — East Grinstead : Kompass, c1981. — 488p in various pagings
Cover title: Euro Kompass United Kingdom. Chemicals, plastics and rubber
ISBN 0-900505-88-5 : Unpriced
Also classified at 338.7′6684′02541 B81-32241

United Kingdom chemical manufacturers / [Data Research Group]. — [1981]. — Great Missenden : The Group, 1981. — 69leaves
ISBN 0-86099-294-2 : £25.00 B81-37235

338.7′66028′002541 — Great Britain. Chemical engineering equipment industries — *Directories* — *Serials*

Process engineering directory. — 1981. — London (30 Calderwood St., SE18 6QH) : Morgan-Grampian in association with Process Engineering, c1981. — v,374p
ISBN 0-86213-021-2 : £15.00
ISSN 0143-1455 B81-24991

338.7′6606′02552 — Japan. Industrial biology industries — *Directories*

Biotechnology Japan : - a special report from IMSWORLD Publications. — London (37 Queen Sq., WC1N 3BL) : IMSWORLD, 1981. — [50]leaves ; 30cm + supplement([3]leaves ; 30cm)
Unpriced (spiral) B81-38175

338.7′66292 — Carbon fibres industries & trades — *Directories* — *Serials*

World-wide carbon fibre directory. — [No.1]-. — Slough (48 Wellington St., Slough SL1 1UB) : Pammac Directories Ltd., [1981]-. — v. : ill (some col.) ; 15x21cm
Irregular. — Spine title: Carbon fibre directory
ISSN 0260-4051 = Worldwide carbon fibre directory (corrected) : Unpriced B81-34044

338.7′663 — Great Britain. Drinks bottling industries — *Directories* — *Serials*

[Binsted′s bottling directory *(British Isles edition)*]. Binsted′s bottling directory. — British Isle ed. — 1981. — London (Binsted House, Devonshire Close, Devonshire St., W1N 2DL) : International bottler and packer, 1981. — 110p
£14.00
Also classified at 338.7′6888 B81-33053

338.7′6632′00254 — Europe. Wines industries & wines agents allowing visits — *Directories*

Hogg, Anthony. Guide to visiting vineyards / Anthony Hogg. — Rev. ed. — London : Joseph, 1981. — 229p : ill,maps ; 22cm
Previous ed.: 1976. — Includes index
ISBN 0-7181-1975-4 : £7.50 B81-19549

338.7′66402853′02541 — Great Britain. Frozen food industries & trades — *Directories* — *Serials*

Frozen foods year book. — 1981. — Redhill (2 Queensway, Redhill, Surrey RH1 1QS) : Retail Journals, 1981. — 224p
ISBN 0-86108-090-4 : £12.00 B81-35121

338.7′664752′02541 — Great Britain. Baking industries — *Directories* — *Serials*

United Kingdom bakers with three or more outlets / [Data Research Group]. — [1981]. — Great Missenden : The Group, 1981. — 53leaves
ISBN 0-86099-304-3 : £24.00 B81-37234

338.7′6657′025 — Gas industries — *Directories* — *Serials*

Gas directory and who′s who. — 1981. — London : Benn, c1981. — 284p
ISBN 0-510-49612-1 : £22.00
ISSN 0307-3084 B81-20713

338.7′6657′0941 — Great Britain. Gas industries: British Gas Corporation — *Serials*

British Gas Corporation. Report and accounts for the year ended 31st March ... / British Gas Corporation. — 1981. — London (152 Grosvenor Rd, SW1V 3JT) : The Corporation : H.M.S.O. [distributor], [1981]. — 76p
Cover title: Annual report and accounts (British Gas Corporation)
ISBN 0-903545-29-2 : £2.00
ISSN 0072-0216 B81-35990

338.7′6657′0941 — Great Britain. Gas industries: British Gas Corporation, *to 1980*

Gas chronology : the development of the British gas industry / [British Gas]. — London (152 Grosvenor Rd., SW1V 3JL) : British Gas, Public Relations Department, 1980. — [28]p : ill,1port ; 21cm
Unpriced (pbk) B81-18216

338.7′6657′0942557 — Northamptonshire. Northampton. Gas industries: Northampton Gas-Light Company, *to 1949*

East Midlands Gas. The Northampton gas undertaking 1823-1949 / prepared for Emgas by D.E. Roberts, J.H. Frisby. — Leicester (De Montfort St., Leicester) : East Midlands Gas, 1980. — 38p : ill,ports ; 21cm. — (Studies in East Midlands gas history)
Bibliography: p38
ISBN 0-9506339-3-3 (pbk) : £0.75 B81-01789

338.7′666 — Great Britain. Tableware industries & trades — *Directories* — *Serials*

The **Tableware** reference book. — 1981. — Redhill (Queensway House, 2 Queensway, Redhill, Surrey) : International Trade Publications, [1981]. — 80p
ISBN 0-86108-086-6 : £7.00 B81-11221

338.7′6663942463 — Staffordshire. Stoke-on-Trent. Pottery & porcelain industries: Shelley Potteries, *to 1966*

Watkins, Chris. Shelley Potteries : the history and production of a Staffordshire family of potters / Chris Watkins, William Harvey, Robert Senft. — London : Barrie & Jenkins, 1980. — 176p,xvip of plates : ill(some col.),facsims, ports ; 24cm
Bibliography: p172. - Includes index
ISBN 0-09-143270-7 : £15.00 B81-03985

338.7′66672 — Tyne and Wear *(Metropolitan County)*. **Wallsend. Vitreous silica industries: Thermal Syndicate,** *to 1981*

Hetherington, G.. Portrait of a company : Thermal Syndicate Limited, 1906-1981 / G. Hetherington. — Wallsend ([P.O. Box 6, Neptune Rd.], Wallsend, Tyne and Wear NE28 6DG) : TSL Thermal Syndicate, 1981. — xv,253p : ill(some col.),facsims(some col.),plans,forms,ports(some col.) ; 25cm
ISBN 0-9507630-0-4 : Unpriced B81-38240

338.7′666893′02541 — Great Britain. Concrete industries & trades — *Directories* — *Serials*

The **concrete** year book. — 57th ed. (1981). — Slough : Cement and Concrete Association, 1981. — 575p. — (Viewpoint publications)
ISBN 0-7210-1215-9 : Unpriced B81-10247

338.7′6684′02541 — Great Britain. Plastics industries — *Directories* — *Serials*

Kompass register industrial section. 30/31 & 40 (part), Rubber and plastics, chemicals and chemical products, machinery and equipment. — 1981/82. — East Grinstead : Kompass, c1981. — 488p in various pagings
Cover title: Euro Kompass United Kingdom. Chemicals, plastics and rubber
ISBN 0-900505-88-5 : Unpriced
Primary classification 338.7′66′002541
B81-32241

338.7′6691′0941 — Great Britain. Iron & steel industries: British Steel Corporation. Corporate planning, *1981-1982*. **Effects. Great Britain.** *Parliament. House of Commons. Industry and Trade Committee.* **Fourth report. Session 1980-81** — *Critical studies*

Great Britain. Third special report from the Industry and Trade Committee, session 1980-81 : effects of BSC′s corporate plan : observations by the Government on the fourth report of the Committee in session 1980-81. — London : H.M.S.O., [1981]. — viip ; 25cm. — ([HC] ; 444)
ISBN 0-10-244481-1 (unbound) : £1.30
B81-39926

338.7′6691′0941 — Great Britain. Iron & steel industries: British Steel Corporation. Corporate planning, *1981-1982*. **Effects** — *Inquiry reports*

Great Britain. *Parliament. House of Commons. Industry and Trade Committee.* Fourth report from the Industry and Trade Committee : session 1980-81 : effects of BSC′s corporate plan : together with the proceedings of the Committee relating to the report, the minutes of evidence and appendices. — London : H.M.S.O., [1981]. — xxxiiip ; 25cm. — ([HC] ; 336-1)
ISBN 0-10-294581-0 (pbk) : £2.90 B81-39927

338.7′669142′0922 — Steel industries & trades — *Biographies* — *Serials*

Who′s who in steel. — 3rd ed. (1981). — Worcester Park : Metal Bulletin Books, c1981. — viii,65p
ISBN 0-900542-51-9 : £5.00
ISSN 0143-6872 B81-32219

338.7′669142′0924 — United States. Steel industries. Holley, Alexander L. - *Biographies*

McHugh, Jeanne. Alexander Holley and the makers of steel / by Jeanne McHugh. — Baltimore ; London : Johns Hopkins University Press, c1980. — xiv,402p : ill,1plan,ports ; 24cm. — (Johns Hopkins studies in the history of technology. New series ; no.4)
Bibliography: p384-39. - Includes index
ISBN 0-8018-2329-3 : £16.50 B81-05668

338.7′6693′025 — Copper industries & trades — *Directories — Serials*

World copper survey. — 1980-. — Worcester Park : Metal Bulletin, 1980-. — ill ; 25cm
Irregular
ISSN 0260-3403 : £18.00 B81-15557

338.7′67 — Giftware industries & trades — *Directories — Serials*

Gifts international directory. — 1981-. — Tunbridge Wells : Benn, 1981-. — v. : ill ; 30cm
Annual. — Continues: Gifts annual buyers' guide
ISSN 0261-4006 = Gifts international directory : £18.00 B81-29093

338.7′671′028 — Great Britain. Metal products manufacturing equipment industries — *Directories — Serials*

Fab guide. — 81. — Guildford : IPC Science and Technology Press, 1981. — 132p
ISSN 0043-2245 : Unpriced B81-15555

338.7′6712′02541 — Great Britain. Foundry industries — *Directories — Serials*

The **Foundry** directory and register of forges. — 11th ed. (1981-1982). — Tonbridge : Standard Catalogue Information Services, [1981]. — [268]p in various pagings
£10.00 B81-31583

United Kingdom founders / [Data Research Group]. — [1981]. — Great Missenden : The Group, 1981. — 106p
ISBN 0-86099-300-0 : £27.00 B81-37231

338.7′67152′02541 — Great Britain. Welding industries — *Directories — Serials*

United Kingdom welders / [Data Research Group]. — [1981]. — Great Missenden : The Group, 1981. — 179p
ISBN 0-86099-303-5 : Unpriced B81-29068

338.7′672′0942494 — West Midlands *(Metropolitan County)*. **Oldbury. Steel products industries: T I Metsec,** *to 1981*

Ti Metsec : 1931-1981 : steel components for the world's industries. — London : Melland, c1981. — 56p,[4]p of plates : ill(some col.),ports ; 22cm
ISBN 0-9500730-7-5 (pbk) : £4.00 B81-27283

338.7′6748′02541 — Great Britain. Timber products industries — *Directories — Serials*

TTJ telephone address book. — 1981. — London : Benn in association with Timber trades journal & Wood processing, c1981. — 396p
ISBN 0-510-49837-x : £9.60
ISSN 0141-5735
Also classified at 380.1′45674′02541
B81-30866

338.7′6762′025 — Paper & paper products industries & trades — *Directories — Serials*

Phillips paper trade directory. — 1981. — London (25 New Street Sq., ED4A 3JA) : Paper, c1981. — xxi,1073p
ISBN 0-510-49027-1 : £36.00 B81-15075

338.7′6762′0941 — Great Britain. Paper manufacturing industries: Bowater Corporation, *1880-1980*

Reader, W. J.. Bowater. — Cambridge : Cambridge University Press, Nov.1981. — [426]p
ISBN 0-521-24165-0 : £25.00 : CIP entry
B81-31263

338.7′67632 — Folding carton industries — *Directories — Serials*

Folding carton manual and directory. — 1981. — London (Binsted House, Devonshire Close, Devonshire St., W1N 2DL) : Binsted, 1981. — 84p
£15.00 B81-19408

338.7′677′002541 — Great Britain. Textile industries — *Directories — Serials*

Kompass register industrial section. 23/24 & 40 (part), Textiles, clothing, machinery. — 1981/82. — East Grinstead : Kompass, c1981. — 365p in various pagings
Cover title: Euro Kompass United Kingdom. Textiles and clothing
ISBN 0-900505-91-5 : Unpriced
Also classified at 338.7′687′02541 B81-32244

338.7′677′00922 — United States. Textile industries — *Biographies*

Textile world's leaders in the textile industry / Laurence A. Christiansen, Jr. editor ; Theodor V. Shumeyko, Richard G. Mansfield associate editors. — New York ; London : McGraw-Hill, c1979. — viii,328p ; 24cm
ISBN 0-07-063721-0 : £25.00 B81-09379

338.7′6770285′09421 — London. Textile machinery industries & trades: Hai Tung Engineering Company, *to 1976*

Hamburger, Otto. Hai Tung / Otto Hamburger. — London ([9 Cheyne Gardens, S.W.3]) : O. Hamburger, 1980. — 80,8p,[28]p of plates : ill,facsims,ports ; 21cm
Unpriced (pbk)
Also classified at 338.7′6770285′0951132
B81-35533

338.7′6770285′0951132 — China. Shanghai. Textile machinery industries & trades: Hai Tung Engineering Company, *to 1950*

Hamburger, Otto. Hai Tung / Otto Hamburger. — London ([9 Cheyne Gardens, S.W.3]) : O. Hamburger, 1980. — 80,8p,[28]p of plates : ill,facsims,ports ; 21cm
Unpriced (pbk)
Primary classification 338.7′6770285′09421
B81-35533

338.7′679 — London. Camden *(London Borough)*. **Men's wigmakers: Ravenscroft** *(Firm)*, *1889 — Personal observations — Early works*

Sketches at a wig maker's. — St. Peter Port : Toucan Press, 1981. — [7]p : ill ; 21cm
First published in the Pall Mall budget, May 30, 1889
ISBN 0-85694-237-5 (pbk) : Unpriced
B81-13339

338.7′68 — Great Britain. Business equipment industries. Organisations: Business Equipment Trade Association — *Directories — Serials*

Business Equipment Trade Association. List of members / Business Equipment Trade Association. — 1979. — London (109, Kingsway, WC2B 6PU) : The Association, [1979?]. — 48p
Unpriced B81-03856

Business Equipment Trade Association. List of members / Business Equipment Trade Association. — 1980. — London (109, Kingsway, WC2 6PU) : The Association, [1980?]. — 52p
Unpriced B81-03857

338.7′68 — Great Britain. Shops equipment industries & trades — *Directories — Serials*

Shop equipment & materials guide. — 1981. — Morden (Crown House, Morden, Surrey SM4 5EB) : Westbourne Journals, [1981?]. — 85p
ISSN 0143-0971 : Unpriced B81-14533

338.7′68 — Great Britain. Sign manufacturing industries — *Directories — Serials*

Sign makers and suppliers directory. — 1978-. — Ewell (172 Kingston Rd, Ewell Epsom, Surrey) : A.E. Morgan Publications, [1978]-. — v. : ill ; 23cm
Annual. — Continues: Sign makers and suppliers year book and directory. — Description based on: 1981 issue
ISSN 0261-8974 = Sign makers and suppliers directory : £2.80 B81-36007

338.7′68′02541 — Great Britain. Craft equipment & materials industries & wholesale trades — *Directories*

Crafts and hobbies trade sources list : a selection of trade sources in the field of crafts and hobbies. — London : Malcolm Stewart Books, 1978. — 27p ; 25cm. — (Kingfisher business guides)
Bibliography: p27
ISBN 0-904132-37-4 (pbk) : £0.85 B81-11985

338.7′68′025427 — Northern England. Craft industries — *Directories*

Cowell, Margaret. Directory of northern craft / compiled by Margaret Cowell. — Ashington (Wansbeck House, Wansbeck Sq., Ashington, Northumberland) : Mid Northumberland Arts Group, 1978. — [38]p ; 30cm
Includes index
ISBN 0-904790-04-5 (pbk) : £1.00 (£0.05 to subscribers) B81-08340

338.7′681118′0922 — London. Chronometer manufacturing industries. Frodsham *(Family), to 1980*

Mercer, Vaudrey. The Frodshams : the story of a family of chronometer makers / Vaudrey Mercer ; with an introduction by Frank Leslie Thirkell. — [Ticehurst] ([New House, High St., Ticehurst, Wadhurst, Sussex TN5 7AL]) : Antiquarian Horological Society, 1981. — xvii,458p : ill,maps,facims,ports ; 25cm. — (Monograph / Antiquarian Horological Society ; no.21)
Bibliography: p334-339. — Includes index
ISBN 0-901180-22-x : Unpriced B81-29511

338.7′681118′0942585 — Hertfordshire. St. Albans. Chronometer manufacturing industries: Thomas Mercer Ltd., *to 1978*

Mercer, Tony. Mercer chronometers : radical Tom Mercer and the house he founded / by Tony Mercer. — 2nd ed. — Ashford, Kent : Brant Wright, c1978. — xxiv,251p,[24]p of plates : ill(some col.),facsims,ports ; 26cm
Previous ed.: 1978. — Bibliography: p251. — Includes index
ISBN 0-903512-19-x : £40.00 B81-40223

338.7′681418 — West Yorkshire *(Metropolitan County)*. **Bradford. Magic lantern slide industries: Riley Bros.,** *to 1900*

By gaslight in winter : a Victorian family history through the magic lantern / [compiled by] Colin Gordon ; designed by Craig Dodd. — London : Elm Tree, 1980. — 127p : ill(some col.),facsims,1port ; 24cm
ISBN 0-241-10474-2 : £9.95 B81-00042

338.7′681418′0941 — Great Britain. Photographic industries: Polaroid (UK) Ltd — *Serials*

Instant record : a newspaper published by Polaroid (UK) Limited for its business and professional customers. — [No.1]-. — [St. Albans] ([Ashley Rd, St. Albans, Hertfordshire AL1 5BR]) : Polaroid (UK), [1980]-. — v. : ill,ports ; 40cm
Three issues yearly
ISSN 0260-9363 = Instant record : Unpriced
B81-10565

338.7′6817 — Great Britain. Laboratory equipment industries & trades — *Directories — Serials*

Laboratory equipment directory. — 8th ed. (1981). — London (30 Calderwood St., SE18 6QH) : Published in association with Laboratory equipment digest by Morgan-Grampian Book Publishing Co., c1981 — v,260p
ISBN 0-86213-022-0 : £15.00
ISSN 0141-8963 B81-29051

338.7′68175′0251 — Great Britain. Industrial equipment industries — *Directories — Serials*

Kompass register industrial section. 39. Scientific and industrial instruments : an extract from the Kompass register of British industry & commerce. — 1980/81-. — East Grinstead : Kompass, 1980-. — v. : ill ; 30cm
Annual. — Introduction in English, text also in French, German, Spanish and Italian
Unpriced
Also classified at 338.4′762′00028 B81-0592

338.7′68176 — Industrial catering equipment industries — *Directories — Serials*

Industrial Catering Association. Buyers′ guide / the Industrial Catering Association. — 1981. — [Richmond] ([14, Victoria Parade, by 331 Sandycombe Road, Richmond, Surrey TW9 3NB]) : [The Association], [1981]. — [5]p
Unpriced B81-12420

338.7′681763′02541 — Europe. Agricultural machinery industries — *Directories — Serials*

Farm and garden equipment guide. — ′81. — Sutton (Surrey House, 1 Throwley Way, Sutton, Surrey SM1 4QQ) : Published by Agricultural Press for IPC Business Press, [1980?]. — 234p
ISBN 0-617-00213-4 : Unpriced B81-10666

338.7′6817671′025 — Metals manufacturing equipment industries — *Directories*

Metallurgical plantmakers of the world / edited by Richard Serjeantson ; compiled by Sylvia Danon. — 2nd ed. — Worcester Park : Metal Bulletin Books, 1981. — 751p ; 23cm
Previous ed.: 1973. — Includes index
ISBN 0-900542-47-0 : £33.00 B81-24260

338.7′683′02541 — Great Britain. Hardware industries & trades — *Directories — Serials*

Benn′s hardware & DIY directory. — 1980-. — Tunbridge Wells : Benn, 1980-. — v. : ill ; 30cm
Annual. — Continues: Benn′s hardware directory. — Description based on: 1981 issue
ISSN 0261-1465 = Benn′s hardware & DIY directory : £25.00
Also classified at 338.7′68408′02541
B81-15551

338.7′6838′02541 — Great Britain. Household equipment industries & wholesale trades — *Directories*

Household products trade sources list : a selection of trade sources of goods for the home. — London : Malcolm Stewart Books, 1978. — 29p ; 25cm. — (Kingfisher business guides)
ISBN 0-904132-38-2 (pbk) : £0.85 B81-11986

338.7′684′002541 — Great Britain. Furnishings industries & trades — *Directories — Serials*

Directory to the furnishing trade. — 23rd ed. (1981). — London : Benn [for] Cabinet Maker and Retail Furnisher, c1981. — [436]p in various pagings
ISBN 0-510-49212-6 : £34.00 B81-30862

338.7′68408′02541 — Great Britain. Do-it-yourself industries & trades — *Directories — Serials*

Benn′s hardware & DIY directory. — 1980-. — Tunbridge Wells : Benn, 1980-. — v. : ill ; 30cm
Annual. — Continues: Benn′s hardware directory. — Description based on: 1981 issue
ISSN 0261-1465 = Benn′s hardware & DIY directory : £25.00
Primary classification 338.7′683′02541
B81-15551

338.7′6841′002541 — Great Britain. Furniture industries & trades — *Directories*

Johnson, Lorraine. The decorator′s directory / Lorraine Johnson. — London : Joseph, 1981. — 318p : ill(some col.) ; 26cm
Includes index
ISBN 0-7181-2008-6 : £9.95
Primary classification 338.7′698′02541
B81-34539

338.7′6841′002541 — Great Britain. Furniture industries — *Directories — Serials*

United Kingdom furniture manufacturers and upholsterers / [Data Research Group]. — [1981]. — Great Missenden : The Group, 1981. — 153p
ISBN 0-86099-256-x : £27.00 B81-37237

338.7′686′025 — Book industries & trades — *Directories — Serials*

Who distributes what and where : an international directory of publishers, imprints, agents and distributors. — [No.1]-. — New York ; London : Bowker, 1980. — v. ; 28cm
Annual
Unpriced B81-04940

338.7′686′025174927 — Arab countries. Book industries & trades — *Directories*

Rudkin, Anthony. A book world directory of the Arab countries, Turkey and Iran / compiled by Anthony Rudkin and Irene Butcher. — London : Mansell, 1981. — xiv,143p ; 29cm
ISBN 0-7201-0830-6 : £27.50 B81-24900

338.7′6862′02541 — Great Britain. Printing industries — *Directories — Serials*

Printing trades directory. — 1981. — Tunbridge Wells : Benn Publications, c1981. — 332p
ISBN 0-510-49167-7 : £30.00 B81-29050

338.7′6862′025417 — Ireland *(Republic)*. **Printing industries** — *Directories — Serials*

Irish printer yearbook & diary. — 1980. — Blackrock (22 Brookfield Ave., Blackrock, Co. Dublin) : Jemma Publications, [1980?]. — [106]p
Unpriced B81-29997

Irish printer yearbook & diary. — 1981. — Blackrock ; London (153 Brondesbury Park, NW2 5JL) : Jemma Pulications, [1981?]. — [78]p
Unpriced B81-29996

338.7′687′02541 — Great Britain. Clothing industries & trades — *Directories — Serials*

The **British** clothing industry year book / sponsored by the Clothing Export Council of Great Britain. — 1981. — London : Kemps, c1981. — 345p
ISBN 0-905255-95-x : Unpriced
ISSN 0141-1470 B81-10246

338.7′687′02541 — Great Britain. Clothing industries & wholesale clothing trades — *Directories*

Clothing trade sources list : a selection of clothing manufacturers, wholesalers and other clothing trade suppliers in the UK. — 2nd ed. — London : Malcolm Stewart, 1979. — 29p ; 25cm. — (Kingfisher business guides)
Previous ed.: / by M. Knightley. London : Kingfisher Books, 1974. — Includes index
£0.85 (pbk) B81-12988

338.7′687′02541 — Great Britain. Clothing industries — *Directories — Serials*

Clothing and Footwear Institute. Yearbook and membership register / the Clothing and Footwear Institute. — 1980/81-. — London (86 Edgware Rd, W2 2YW) : Sterling Publications, 1980-. — v. : ill ; 30cm
Continues: Clothing Institute. Yearbook and membership register
ISSN 0261-2690 = Yearbook and membership register - Clothing and Footwear Institute :
Unpriced B81-20301

Kompass register industrial section. 23/24 & 40 (part), Textiles, clothing, machinery. — 1981/82. — East Grinstead : Kompass, c1981. — 365p in various pagings
Cover title: Euro Kompass United Kingdom. Textiles and clothing
ISBN 0-900505-91-5 : Unpriced
Primary classification 338.7′677′002541
B81-32244

338.7′68876′02541 — Great Britain. Sports equipment industries & trades — *Directories — Serials*

Harpers guide to the sports trade. — 1981. — London (Harling House, 47-51 Grt. Suffolk Street SE1 0BS) : Harper Trade Journals Limited, [1980?]. — 138p
Unpriced B81-12400

Sports trader. Annual buyers′ guide. — 1981. — London : Sports Trader, c1981. — 204p
ISBN 0-510-49836-1 : £10.00 B81-08790

338.7′6888 — Great Britain. Bottling equipment industries & trades — *Directories — Serials*

[Binsted′s bottling directory *(British Isles edition)*]. Binsted′s bottling directory. — British Isle ed. — 1981. — London (Binsted House, Devonshire Close, Devonshire St., W1N 2DL) : International bottler and packer, 1981. — 110p
£14.00
Primary classification 338.7′663 B81-33053

338.7′6888′02541 — Great Britain. Packaging industries — *Directories — Serials*

Packaging directory. — 23rd ed. (1981). — London (c/o Wheathead Journals, Penn House, Penn Place, Rickmansworth, Herts WD3 1SN) : Packaging, [1980?]. — 208p
£20.50 B81-05933

Packaging review directory & buyers guide. — 6th ed. (1981). — Sutton : IPC Business Press, c1981. — 241p
£15.00 B81-33700

United Kingdom packers / [Data Research Group]. — [1981]. — Great Missenden : The Group, 1981. — 61leaves
ISBN 0-86099-310-8 : £23.00 B81-37230

338.7′69′002541 — Great Britain. Building industries — *Directories — Serials*

United Kingdom builders / [Data Research Group]. — 1980. — Great Missenden : The Group, [1980]. — 347p
ISBN 0-86099-287-x : £35.00 B81-09692

338.7′69′0028 — Great Britain. Building equipment industries & trades — *Directories — Serials*

Sell′s building index. — 58th year (1981). — Epsom : Sell′s Publications, 1981. — 482p
ISBN 0-85499-588-9 : Unpriced
ISSN 0080-8717 B81-15556

338.7′69′00942143 — London. Islington *(London Borough)*. **Building industries: Dove Brothers,** *to 1981*

Braithwaite, David. Building in the blood : the story of Dove Brothers of Islington 1781-1981 / David Braithwaite. — London : Godfrey Cave Associates, 1981. — 160p : ill(some col.),facsims,plans(some col.),ports ; 28cm
Bibliography: p148. — Includes index
ISBN 0-906223-03-2 : £13.95 B81-14022

338.7′69′00942337 — Dorset. Poole. Building industries: Burt & Vick Ltd, *to 1979*

Hercock, Christine. A history of Burt & Vick Ltd Poole / by Christine Hercock. — Poole (The Guildhall, Market St., Poole BH15 1NP) : Borough of Poole Museums Service, c1980. — 24p : ill,facsims,1geneal.table,ports ; 21cm. — (Poole local history publication ; no.2)
Cover title. — Text, ill on covers. — Bibliography: p24
ISBN 0-86251-000-7 (pbk) : Unpriced
B81-30033

338.7′69018 — Great Britain. Fencing contracting industries — *Directories — Serials*

United Kingdom fencing contractors / [Data Research Group]. — [1981]. — Great Missenden : The Group, 1981. — 55leaves
ISBN 0-86099-301-9 : £23.00 B81-37229

338.7′69024′02541 — Great Britain. Building renovation services — *Directories*

The **First** guidebook of specialist in repair, restoration, renovation and conservation / Guild of Master Craftsmen. — Lewis (17 High St., Lewis, E. Sussex) : The Guild, [1981]. — 263p : ill ; 21cm
Includes index
£6.95 (pbk)
Also classified at 338.7′617451′0288
B81-36261

338.7′690521 — Great Britain. Shopfitting industries — *Directories*

United Kingdom shopfitters & exhibition stand contractors / [Data Research Group]. — [1980]. — Great Missenden : The Group, 1980. — 103p
ISBN 0-86099-279-9 : Unpriced B81-06711

338.7′697 — Great Britain. Heating engineering contracting industries — *Directories — Serials*

United Kingdom heating engineering contractors / [Data Research Group]. — 1980/81. — Great Missenden : The Group, [1981?]. — 185p
ISBN 0-86099-288-8 : Unpriced B81-13407

338.7′697′0002541 — Great Britain. Air conditioning, heating & ventilation equipment industries — *Directories — Serials*

United Kingdom heating, refrigeration & ventilating equipment manufacturers / [Data Research Group]. — [1981]. — Great Missenden : The Group, 1981. — 74leaves
Cover title: Heating, refrigeration & ventilation equipment manufacturers
ISBN 0-86099-316-7 : Unpriced
Also classified at 338.7′62156′02541
B81-29067

338.7′697′000942574 — Oxfordshire. Oxford. Heating & ventilation equipment installation services. Private companies: Fred. G. Alden (Heating) Ltd., *to 1978*

Mann, Cecil. The Alden Heating story : a history of Fred. G. Alden (Heating) Ltd, Oxford / by Cecil Mann. — Oxford : Alden Press, 1981. — 66p,[10]p of plates : ill,ports ; 23cm
Unpriced B81-13192

338.7′698′02541 — Great Britain. Decorating materials industries & trades — *Directories*

Johnson, Lorraine. The decorator's directory / Lorraine Johnson. — London : Joseph, 1981. — 318p : ill(some col.) ; 26cm
Includes index
ISBN 0-7181-2008-6 : £9.95
Also classified at 338.7′6841′002541
B81-34539

338.7′7615269′02541 — Great Britain. Surveying services — *Directories — Serials*

The **Directory** of land and hydrographic survey services in the United Kingdom / the Royal Institution of Chartered Surveyors. — 1979/80-. — London : The Institution, c1980-. — v. : maps ; 30cm
Annual
ISSN 0260-5007 = Directory of land and hydrographic survey services in the United Kingdom : Unpriced B81-08225

338.8 — INDUSTRIAL ENTERPRISE. COMBINATIONS, MONOPOLIES, MERGERS, MULTINATIONAL COMPANIES

338.8 — Market structure

Shubik, Martin. Market structure and behavior / Martin Shubik with Richard Levitan. — Cambridge, Mass. ; London : Harvard University Press, 1980. — xi,252p : ill ; 25cm
Bibliography: p235-243. - Includes index
ISBN 0-674-55026-9 : £11.10 B81-03013

338.8′042′01 — Great Britain. Diversified companies. Theories

Laitinen, Kenneth. A theory of the multiproduct firm / Kenneth Laitinen. — Amsterdam ; Oxford : North-Holland, 1980. — xiv,227p : ill ; 23cm. — (Studies in mathematical and managerial economics ; v.28)
Bibliography: p217-221. - Includes index
ISBN 0-444-85495-9 : £16.80 B81-07051

338.8′0941 — Great Britain. Manufacturing industries. Concentration, *1935-1975*

Hart, P. E.. Concentration in British industry 1935-75 : a study of the growth, causes and effects of concentration in British manufacturing industries / P.E. Hart and R. Clarke. — Cambridge : Cambridge University Press, 1980. — xiv,164p ; 24cm. — (Occasional papers / The National Institute of Economic and Social Research ; 32)
Includes index
ISBN 0-521-23393-3 : £10.00 : CIP rev.
B80-25351

338.8′2 — Developing countries. Economic conditions. Effects of monopolies by capitalist countries — *Marxist viewpoints*

Nukhovich, E.. International monopolies and developing countries / E. Nukhovich. — Moscow : Progress Publishers ; [London] : Distributed by Central Books, 1980. — 302p ; 21. — (Problems of the developing countries)
Translation of: Mezhdunarodnye monopolii i razvivaīushchiesīa strany
£3.25 B81-05311

338.8′2613636 — Public utilities. Monopolies. Regulation — *Conference proceedings*

Regulated industries and public enterprise : European and United States perspectives / edited by Bridger M. Mitchell, Paul R. Kleindorfer. — Lexington, Mass. : Lexington Books ; [Aldershot] : Gower [distributor], 1980. — ix,291p : ill,1map ; 24cm
Conference papers. — Includes bibliographies and index
ISBN 0-669-03474-6 : £17.50 B81-30768

338.8′26292272′0941 — Great Britain. Bicycle industries: TI Raleigh Industries & TI Raleigh. Fair trading practice — *Inquiry reports*

TI Raleigh Industries Limited, TI Raleigh Limited : a report by the Director General of Fair Trading on an investigation under section 3 of the Competition Act 1980. — London ([Field House Registry, Room 05, Field House, Breams Buildings, London EC4A 1PR]) : [Office of Fair Trading?], 1981. — 34p ; 30cm
Unpriced (spiral) B81-25215

338.8′3′0941 — Great Britain. Business firms. Economic efficiency. Effects of mergers

Mergers and economic performance / Keith Cowling ... [et al.]. — Cambridge : Cambridge University Press, 1980. — viii,379p : ill ; 24cm
Includes bibliographies and index
ISBN 0-521-22394-6 : £19.50 B81-01700

338.8′3′0941 — Great Britain. Companies. Mergers & take-overs. Codes of conduct. City Working Party. City code on take-overs and mergers, *to 1981*

The **City** code on take-overs and mergers. — Rev. / [Council for the Securities Industry]. — London (101 Cannon St., EC4N 5BA) : Issuing Houses Association, 1981. — 81p ; 22cm
Previous ed.: / City Working Party. 1976. — Pamphlets "Practice note no.17", "Principal amendments to the City code" in pocket
£1.50 (pbk) B81-18395

338.8′361072 — Great Britain. Newspaper publishing industries: Berrow's Organisation Ltd. Mergers with Reed International Ltd — *Inquiry reports*

Great Britain. *Monopolies and Mergers Commission.* The Berrow's Organisation Ltd and Reed International Ltd : a report on the proposed transfer of forty-five newspapers owned by The Berrow's Organisation Ltd (a wholly-owned subsidiary of News International Ltd) to Reed International Ltd / the Monopolies and Mergers Commission. — London : H.M.S.O., [1981]. — v,30p : 1map ; 25cm. — (Cmnd. ; 8337)
ISBN 0-10-183370-9 (pbk) : £3.20 B81-37806

338.8′366412′0941 — Great Britain. Sugar trades: S & W Berisford Limited. Mergers with British Sugar Corporation — *Proposals*

Great Britain. *Monopolies and Mergers Commission.* S & W Berisford Limited and British Sugar Corporation Limited : a report on the proposed merger / Monopolies and Mergers Commission. — London : H.M.S.O., [1981]. — v,122p ; 25cm. — ([H.C] ; 241)
ISBN 0-10-224181-3 (pbk) : £5.30 B81-21905

338.8′366694′0941 — Great Britain. Cement industries: Blue Circle Industries. Mergers with Armitage Shanks Group — *Inquiry reports*

Great Britain. *Monopolies and Mergers Commission.* Blue Circle Industries Limited and Armitage Shanks Group Limited : a report on the proposed merger / Monopolies and Mergers Commission. — London : H.M.S.O., [1980]. — v,55p ; 25cm. — (Cmnd. ; 8039)
ISBN 0-10-180390-7 (pbk) : £3.80
Also classified at 338.8′36961 B81-05203

338.8′36961 — Great Britain. Ceramic sanitary appliances industries: Armitage Shanks Group. Mergers with Blue Circle Industries — *Inquiry reports*

Great Britain. *Monopolies and Mergers Commission.* Blue Circle Industries Limited and Armitage Shanks Group Limited : a report on the proposed merger / Monopolies and Mergers Commission. — London : H.M.S.O., [1980]. — v,55p ; 25cm. — (Cmnd. ; 8039)
ISBN 0-10-180390-7 (pbk) : £3.80
Primary classification 338.8′366694′0941
B81-05203

338.8′6 — Great Britain. Holding companies: Dunlop Holdings Limited. Shares. Purchase by Lorient Nominees Pte Ltd, *1980 — Inquiry reports*

Ingram, Collingwood William Malcolm. Dunlop Holdings Limited : investigation under Section 172 of the Companies Act 1948 : interim report / by Collingwood William Malcolm Ingram and Francis Herbert Pulling [for] the Department of Trade. — London : H.M.S.O., 1981. — [50]p ; 30cm
ISBN 0-11-513181-7 (pbk) : £6.00 B81-16303

338.8′6′0941 — Great Britain. Holding companies: Kina Holdings Limited — *Inquiry reports*

Denny, William. Kina Holdings Limited : investigation under Section 165(b) of the Companies Act 1948 : report / by William Denny and Kenneth Webb. — London : H.M.S.O., 1981. — 276,[116]p ; 21cm
At head of title: Department of Trade
ISBN 0-11-513179-5 (pbk) : £16.20 B81-19624

338.8′6′0941 — Great Britain. Holding companies: Saint Piran Limited — *Inquiry reports*

Godfrey, G. M.. Saint Piran Limited : investigation under Section 165(b) and Section 172 of the Companies Act 1948 : final report / by G.M. Godfrey and A.J. Hardcastle. — London : H.M.S.O., 1981. — 228p : ill ; 30cm
At head of title: Department of Trade
ISBN 0-11-513473-5 (pbk) : £14.00 B81-29187

338.8′7 — United States. Companies. Interlocking directorates

Pennings, Johannes M.. Interlocking directorates / Johannes M. Pennings. — San Francisco ; London : Jossey-Bass, 1980. — xvi,220p : ill ; 24cm. — (The Jossey-Bass social and behavioral science series)
Bibliography: p199-209. - Includes index
ISBN 0-87589-469-0 : £11.95 B81-05862

338.8′8 — International business enterprise

Mason, R. Hal. International business / R. Hal Mason, Robert R. Miller, Dale R. Weigel. — 2nd ed. — New York ; Chichester : Wiley, c1981. — vii,428p : ill ; 24cm. — (Wiley series in management)
Previous ed.: published as The economics of international business. 1975. — Includes bibliographies and index
ISBN 0-471-06217-0 : £12.25 B81-16338

338.8′8 — Multinational companies

Dunning, John H.. International production and the multinational enterprise / John H. Dunning. — London : Allen & Unwin, 1981. — viii,439p : ill ; 23cm
Includes bibliographies and index
ISBN 0-04-330319-6 (cased) : Unpriced : CIP rev.
ISBN 0-04-330320-x (pbk) : Unpriced
B81-26717

Vernon, Raymond. Economic environment of international business / Raymond Vernon, Louis T. Wells, Jr. — Englewood Cliffs ; London : Prentice Hall, 1981. — x,246p : ill ; 23cm
Previous ed.: 1976. — Includes bibliographies and index
ISBN 0-13-224329-6 (pbk) : £9.05 B81-16527

338.8′8 — Multinational companies. Economic aspects

The **New** international economy. — London : Sage, Jan.1982. — [320]p
ISBN 0-8039-9792-2 : £12.50 : CIP entry
B81-33842

Rugman, Alan M.. Inside the multinationals : the economics of internal markets / Alan M. Rugman. — London : Croom Helm, c1981. — 179p ; 22cm
Bibliography: p165-174. — Includes index
ISBN 0-7099-2207-8 : £11.95 : CIP rev.
B81-14818

338.8′8 — Multinational companies — *Radical viewpoints*

Hymer, Stephen Herbert. The multinational corporation : a radical approach : papers / by Stephen Herbert Hymer ; edited by Robert B. Cohen ... [et al.]. — Cambridge : Cambridge University Press, 1979. — xii,323p ; 24cm
Includes index
ISBN 0-521-22695-3 : £21.00 B81-25188

338.8′8 — Multinational companies. Regulation. Codes of conduct — *Confederation of British Industry viewpoints — Conference proceedings*
International codes of conduct / CBI. — London : Confederation of British Industry, 1981. — 80p ; 30cm
Conference papers
£7.50 (pbk) B81-29138

338.8′8′0924 — International business enterprise, *ca1950-1979 — Personal observations*
Preston, Jack, *19---*. More funny business / Jack Preston. — London : Hale, 1981. — 190p ; 23cm
ISBN 0-7091-8750-5 : £6.95 B81-23565

338.8′83 — Developing countries. Economic development. Effects of restrictive practices of multinational companies
Long, Frank. Restrictive business practices, transnational corporation, and development : a survey / Frank Long. — Boston, Mass. ; London : Nijhoff, c1981. — xv,166p : ill ; 24cm. — (Dimensions of international business)
Includes index
ISBN 0-89838-057-x : Unpriced B81-36721

338.8′87 — America. Agricultural industries. Multinational companies
Burbach, Roger. Agribusiness in the Americas / by Roger Burbach and Patricia Flynn. — New York ; London : Monthly Review Press, c1980. — 314p : ill ; 21cm
Includes index
ISBN 0-85345-535-x (cased) : £8.00
ISBN 0-85345-536-8 (pbk) : £3.25 B81-08603

338.8′87 — Motor vehicle industries. Multinational companies
Maxcy, George. The multinational motor industry / George Maxcy. — London : Croom Helm, c1981. — 290p ; 23cm
Bibliography: p281-284. — Includes index
ISBN 0-7099-0312-x : £14.95 : CIP rev.
B81-05126

338.8′87 — Tin mining industries. Multinational companies
Thoburn, John T.. Multinationals, mining and development : a study of the tin industry / John Thoburn. — Farnborough : Gower, c1981. — viii,183p ; 23cm
Bibliography: p173-179. — Includes index
ISBN 0-566-00417-8 : £10.50 : CIP rev.
B81-14884

338.8′88′0254 — Western Europe. Companies. Subsidiaries — *Directories — Serials*
Who owns whom. Continental Europe. — 1981. — London : Dun & Bradstreet, 1981. — 2v.
ISSN 0140-6582 : Unpriced B81-23135

338.8′881724 — Developing countries. Economic development. Effects of multinational companies
Balasubramanyam, V. N.. Multinational enterprises and the Third World / by V.N. Balasubramanyam. — London : Trade Policy Research Centre, c1980. — x,79p ; 19cm. — (Thames essays, ISSN 0306-6991 ; no.26)
ISBN 0-900842-48-2 (pbk) : £3.00 B81-32349

338.8′8851 — China. Western companies. Joint ventures with public bodies — *Practical information*
Cohen, Jerome Alan. China′s needs today : foreign investment and joint ventures : an edited text based upon The Economist seminars given in London and Zürich by Professor Jerome Cohen in January and February 1981. — London : Economist Intelligence Unit, 1981. — 46p ; 30cm
Unpriced (pbk) B81-22431

338.8′8868 — Southern Africa. Economic conditions. Effects of multinational companies in South Africa, *ca 1960-1980*
Makgetla, Neva. Outposts of monopoly capitalism : southern Africa in the changing global economy / by Neva Makgetla and Ann Seidman. — Westport : Lawrence Hill ; London : Zed, c1980. — xiii,370p : ill,2maps ; 22cm
Includes index
ISBN 0-86232-020-8 (cased) : £15.95
ISBN 0-86232-015-1 (pbk) : £4.50 B81-03760

338.8′8973′08 — Latin America. American multinational companies. Nationalisation
Sigmund, Paul E.. Multinationals in Latin America : the politics of nationalization / Paul E. Sigmund. — Wisconsin ; London : University of Wisconsin Press, 1980. — xi,426p ; 22cm. — (A Twentieth Century Fund study)
Bibliography: p383-402. — Includes index
ISBN 0-299-08260-1 (cased) : £13.50
ISBN 0-299-08264-4 (pbk) : £3.90 B81-06793

338.9 — ECONOMIC PLANNING

338.9 — Economic planning
Bowles, Roger A.. Macroeconomic planning / Roger A. Bowles and David K. Whynes. — London : Allen & Unwin, 1979. — viii,202p : ill ; 23cm. — (Studies in economics ; 14)
Bibliography: p194-200. — Includes index
ISBN 0-04-330294-7 (cased) : £10.00 : CIP rev.
ISBN 0-04-330295-5 (pbk) : £3.95 B78-39527

338.9 — Economic planning — *Comparative studies*
Cave, Martin. Alternative approaches to economic planning / Martin Cave and Paul Hare. — London : Macmillan, 1981. — viii,226p : ill ; 25cm
Bibliography: p213-222. — Includes index
ISBN 0-333-26689-7 (cased) : £15.00 : CIP rev.
ISBN 0-333-26690-0 (pbk) : Unpriced
B80-29311

338.9 — State. Economic aspects
Whynes, David K.. The economic theory of the state / David K. Whynes, Roger A. Bowles. — Oxford : Robertson, 1981. — xv,236p : ill ; 23cm
Bibliography: p225-234. — Includes index
ISBN 0-85520-375-7 : £15.00 : CIP rev.
B80-21574

338.9′0028 — Economic planning. Role of econometrics
Frisch, Ragnar. Economic planning studies : a collection of essays / by Ragnar Frisch ; selected, introduced and edited by Frank Long. — Dordrecht ; London : Reidel, c1976. — xv,198p,[1] folded leaf : 1port ; 23cm. — (International studies in economics and econometrics ; v.8)
Includes index
ISBN 90-277-0245-4 (cased) : Unpriced
ISBN 90-277-1194-1 (pbk) : Unpriced
B81-03233

338.9′0072041 — Industrialised societies. Industries. Relations with governments. Research in British institutions — *Directories*
Wilks, S. R. M.. Register of research into relations between government and industry : for the SSRC Working Party on Government and Industry Relations / S.R.M. Wilks. — London : Social Science Research Council, c1981. — 38p ; 30cm
Includes index
ISBN 0-86226-021-3 (pbk) : £1.50 B81-38368

338.9′009 — Technology transfer, *to 1914*
Kenwood, A. G.. Technological diffusion and industrialization before 1914. — London : Croom Helm, Dec.1981. — [224]p
ISBN 0-7099-1508-x : £13.95 : CIP entry
B81-31427

338.9′009173′4 — Rural regions. Industrial development. Planning
Austin, Vincent. Rural industrial development : a practical handbook for planners, project managers and field staff / Vincent Austin. — London : Cassell, 1981. — xiii,257p : ill,forms ; 22cm
Bibliography: p211-221. — Includes index
ISBN 0-304-30731-9 (pbk) : £5.95 B81-32382

338.91′09172′4 — Developing countries. Technology transfer from developed countries. Role of industries — *Conference proceedings*
World Congress of Engineers and Architects in Israel *(5th : 1979 : Israel)*. Industrial development and technology transfer. — London : George Godwin, Sept.1981. — [152] p. — (International forum series)
ISBN 0-7114-5729-8 : £12.00 : CIP entry
B81-23854

338.91′0947 — Soviet Union. Economic development. Role of Western technology
Vander Elst, Philip. Capitalist technology for Soviet survival / Philip Vander Elst. — London : Institute of Econmomic Affairs, 1981. — 63p ; 22cm. — (Research monographs / Institute of Economic Affairs, ISSN 0073-9103 ; 35)
Summary (1sheet) as insert. — Bibliography: p59
ISBN 0-255-36140-8 (pbk) : £1.50 B81-19436

338.91′095 — Asia. Commonwealth countries. Foreign assistance. Organisations — *Directories*
Commonwealth Asian and South Pacific directory of aid agencies : charities, trusts, foundations and official bodies offering assistance in Commonwealth countries in Asia and the South Pacific / consultant editor Michael Collins. — London : Commonwealth Foundation, 1981. — 147p : maps ; 21cm
Bibliography: p137-138. — Includes index
ISBN 0-903850-18-4 (pbk) : £3.00
Also classified at 338.91′0996 B81-28235

338.91′0996 — South Pacific region. Commonwealth countries. Foreign assistance. Organisations — *Directories*
Commonwealth Asian and South Pacific directory of aid agencies : charities, trusts, foundations and official bodies offering assistance in Commonwealth countries in Asia and the South Pacific / consultant editor Michael Collins. — London : Commonwealth Foundation, 1981. — 147p : maps ; 21cm
Bibliography: p137-138. — Includes index
ISBN 0-903850-18-4 (pbk) : £3.00
Primary classification 338.91′095 B81-28235

338.91′1722′05492 — Developing countries. Economic development. Foreign assistance by developed countries. Policies of governments. Effectiveness — *Study regions: Bangladesh*
Aid and influence : the case of Bangladesh / edited by Just Faaland ; contributors Just Faaland, Nurul Islam, Jack Parkinson. — London : Macmillan, 1981. — xii, : ill ; 23cm
Includes index
ISBN 0-333-28985-4 : £15.00 : CIP rev.
B80-10973

338.91′172′401722 — Developing countries. Economic development. Foreign assistance by developed countries. Theories
Dependency theory. — London : Pinter, June 1981. — [220]p
ISBN 0-903804-84-0 : £13.50 : CIP entry
B81-10425

338.91′1812′047 — Soviet Union. Technology transfer from Western world, *1955-1980*
Hanson, Philip. Trade and technology in Soviet-Western relations / Philip Hanson. — London : Macmillan in association with the Centre for Russian and East European Studies, University of Birmingham, 1981. — xiv,271p ; 23cm. — (Studies in Soviet history and society)
Includes index
ISBN 0-333-28056-3 : £20.00 B81-31849

338.91′4 — European Community countries. Economic development. Grants & loans from European Community
Scott, Gay. A guide to European Community grants and loans : for commerce, industry, local authorities, academic and research institutions / compiled by Gay Scott. — Biggleswade (20 Caldecote Rd., Ickwell, Biggleswade, Bedfordshire SG18 9EH) : Euroinformation Ltd., 1980. — i,111p ; 30cm
ISBN 0-907304-00-1 (spiral) : £9.50
B81-04772

338.91′4′0411 — Scotland. Economic development. Promotion by local authorities. Financial assistance from European Economic Community, *1973-1980*
Waters, N.. Scottish local authorities, economic development and the E.E.C. : based on a report to the Anglo-German Foundation for the Study of Industrial Society / N. Waters and I. Watson. — Glasgow (186 Bath St., Glasgow G2 4HG) : The Planning Exchange, c1980. — 79p : 4maps ; 30cm. — (Research paper / Planning Exchange ; no.8)
£4.00 (pbk) B81-08320

338.91'41 — Great Britain. *Foreign Compensation Commission — Accounts — Serials*
Great Britain. *Foreign Compensation Commission.* Accounts / Foreign Compensation Commission. — 1979-80. — London : H.M.S.O., 1981. — 6p
ISBN 0-10-218781-9 : £1.10 B81-27915

338.91'41'0171241 — Commonwealth developing countries. Economic development. Financial assistance. British organisations: Commonwealth Development Corporation — *Serials*
Commonwealth Development Corporation. Annual report and statement of accounts / Commonwealth Development Corporation. — 1980. — London (33 Hill St., W1A 3AR) : The Corporation, [1981]. — 116p
Cover title: Report and accounts (Commonwealth Development Corporation)
ISBN 0-903799-13-8 : Unpriced B81-30864

Commonwealth Development Corporation. Partners in development / Commonwealth Development Corporation. — 1980. — London (33, Hill Street W1A 3AR) : The Corporation, [1980]. — 23p
Unpriced B81-08695

338.91'41'017240212 — Developing countries. Economic development. Financial assistance by Great Britain — *Statistics — Serials*
Great Britain. *Overseas Development Administration.* British aid statistics / Overseas Development Administration. — 1975-1979. — London : H.M.S.O., 1980. — xvi,111p
ISBN 0-11-580224-x : £9.50 B81-09684

338.91'41'0438 — Great Britain. Industries. International cooperation with Polish industries
Paliwoda, Stanley J.. Joint East-West marketing and production ventures / Stanley J. Paliwoda. — Aldershot : Gower, c1981. — ix,215p ; 23cm
ISBN 0-566-00473-9 : Unpriced : CIP rev.
Also classified at 338.91'438'041 B81-21563

338.91'417'01724 — Developing countries. Foreign assistance by Ireland *(Republic).* **Role of Irish Christian missionaries**
Quinn, Richard F.. The missionary factor in Irish aid overseas / by Richard F. Quinn with Robert Carroll. — Dublin (St Saviour's, Dublin 1, [Eire]) : Dominican Publications, c1980. — 92p ; 22cm
ISBN 0-9504797-8-0 (pbk) : Unpriced B81-21361

338.91'438'041 — Poland. Industries. International cooperation with British industries
Paliwoda, Stanley J.. Joint East-West marketing and production ventures / Stanley J. Paliwoda. — Aldershot : Gower, c1981. — ix,215p ; 23cm
ISBN 0-566-00473-9 : Unpriced : CIP rev.
Primary classification 338.91'41'0438 B81-21563

338.91'52'01724 — Developing countries. Foreign assistance by Japan. Policies of Japanese government, *ca 1950-1979*
Rix, Alan. Japan's economic aid : policy-making and politics / Alan Rix. — London : Croom Helm, c1980. — 286p : ill ; 23cm
Bibliography: p274-277. - Includes index
ISBN 0-7099-0433-9 : £14.95 : CIP rev. B80-10471

338.91'73'01717 — Communist countries. Technology transfer from United States
United States. *Congress. Office of Technology Assessment.* Technology and East-West trade / Office of Technology Assessment, Congress of the United States. — Montclair, N.J. : Allanheld, Osmun ; Farnborough, Hants. : Gower, 1981. — vi,303p : ill,1form ; 24cm
Includes the text of the Export Administration Act, 1979
ISBN 0-566-00436-4 : Unpriced B81-37124

338.94 — European Community countries. Industries. Policies of European Economic Community — *European Democratic Group viewpoints*
Report on industry policy / European Democratic Group. — London : The Group, [1981?]. — 32p : 1port ; 21cm
Cover title
Unpriced (pbk) B81-29500

338.94 — European Community. Economic policies
The Collaboration of nations. — Oxford : Robertson, Sept.1981. — [256]p
ISBN 0-85520-389-7 : £10.50 : CIP entry B81-22583

338.94'02 — European Community countries. Regional economic development. Financial incentives, *1980*
European regional incentives, 1980 : a survey of regional incentives in the countries of the European Community / edited by Douglas Yuill and Kevin Allen. — Glasgow : European Regional Policy Monitoring Unit, Centre for the Study of Public Policy, University of Strathclyde, 1980. — xiv,382p : maps ; 23cm
ISBN 0-907243-01-0 (cased) : £25.00 B81-09315

338.9'41 — Great Britain. Economic planning, *1905-1915*
French, David. British economic and strategic planning 1905-1915. — London : Allen & Unwin, Feb.1982. — [224]p
ISBN 0-04-942174-3 : £12.50 : CIP entry B81-35942

338.941 — Great Britain. Economic planning. Control by personnel — *Socialist Environment and Resources Association viewpoints*
Taylor, Alan, *1946-.* Democratic planning through workers' control / Alan Taylor. — London (9 Poland St., W1V 3DG) : Socialist Environment & Resources Association, [1981?]. — 28p ; 21cm
Cover title
£1.00 (pbk) B81-33556

338.941 — Great Britain. Enterprise zones
Lloyd, Greg. Enterprise zones : some economic and spatial implications / Greg Lloyd. — [Aberdeen] ([Edward Wright Building, Old Aberdeen, Aberdeen AB9 2TY]) : [University of Aberdeen, Dept. of Land Economy], 1980. — 12leaves ; 30cm. — (Discussion paper / University of Aberdeen Department of Land Economy)
£1.00 (unbound) B81-37323

338.941 — Great Britain. Industries. Intervention by government — *Trade union viewpoints*
State intervention in industry : a workers' inquiry / Coventry, Liverpool, Newcastle, N. Tyneside Trades Councils. — Newcastle-upon-Tyne (5 Queens St., Newcastle-upon-Tyne) : Coventry, Liverpool, Newcastle and North Tyneside Trades Councils, 1980. — 182p : ill ; 21cm
Bibliography: p181-182
ISBN 0-9507281-0-1 (pbk) : £2.00 B81-12297

338.941 — Great Britain. Industries. Policies of government, *1972-1979*
Grant, Wyn. The political economy of industrial policy. — London : Butterworths, Dec.1981. — [172]p
ISBN 0-408-10765-0 : £14.00 : CIP entry B81-33877

338.941 — Great Britain. Industries. Policies of government. Administration. Responsibility of government agencies & government departments — *Study examples: Administration of government policies on industries in Scotland & Wales*
Hogwood, Brian W.. In search of accountability : the territorial dimension of industrial policy / by Brian W. Hogwood. — Glasgow (Glasgow G1 1XQ) : Centre for the Study of Public Policy, University of Strathclyde, 1981. — 31p ; 30cm. — (Studies in public policy, ISSN 0140-8240 ; no.82)
Unpriced (pbk) B81-27743

338.941 — Great Britain. Industries. Policies of government — *Fabian viewpoints*
Sainsbury, David, *1940-.* Government and industry : a new partnership / David Sainsbury. — London : Fabian Society, 1981. — 29p ; 22cm. — (Fabian research series, ISSN 0305-3555 ; 347)
Cover title
ISBN 0-7163-1347-2 (pbk) : £0.80 B81-13155

338.941 — Great Britain. Nationalised industries. Finance — *Inquiry reports*
Great Britain. *Parliament. House of Commons. Committee of Public Accounts.* Fifteenth report from the Committee of Public Accounts : together with the proceedings of the Committee, minutes of evidence and appendices : session 1980-81 : H.M. Treasury : nationalised industries: capital structure and internal reserves, private finance for nationalised industries and publicly owned companies. — London : H.M.S.O., [1981]. — xiv,23p ; 25cm
ISBN 0-10-234981-9 (pbk) : £2.90 B81-40607

Great Britain. *Parliament. House of Commons. Treasury and Civil Service Committee.* Eighth report from the Treasury and Civil Service Committee, session 1980-81 : financing of the nationalised industries : together with the proceedings of the Committee, and the minutes of evidence and appendices. — London : H.M.S.O., [1981]
Vol.1: Report. — xlip ; 25cm. — ([HC] ; 348-I)
ISBN 0-10-008701-9 (pbk) : £3.55 B81-40912

Great Britain. *Parliament. House of Commons. Treasury and Civil Service Committee.* Eighth report from the Treasury and Civil Service Committee, session 1980-81 : financing of the nationalised industries : together with the proceedings of the committee, and the minutes of evidence and appendices. — London : H.M.S.O.. — ([HC] ; 348-II)
Vol.2: Minutes of evidence. — [1981]. — v,233p : 1ill ; 25cm
ISBN 0-10-008791-4 (pbk) : £9.15 B81-39630

Great Britain. *Parliament. House of Commons. Treasury and Civil Service Committee.* Eighth report from the Treasury and Civil Service Committee, session 1980-81 : financing of the nationalised industries : together with the proceedings of the Committee, and the minutes of evidence and appendices. — London : H.M.S.O., [1981]
Vol.3: Appendices. — iv,73p : ill ; 25cm. — ([HC] ; 348-III)
ISBN 0-10-008651-9 (pbk) : £4.75 B81-40911

338.941 — Great Britain. Regional economic planning
Hallett, Graham. Second thoughts on regional policy / Graham Hallett. — London : Centre for Policy Studies, 1981. — v,76p ; 21cm
ISBN 0-905880-19-6 (pbk) : £3.75 B81-40015

338.941'02 — Great Britain. Industries. Financial incentives of government
Financial incentives and assistance for industry : a comprehensive guide / ... written and produced by Arthur Young McClelland Moores & Co. .... — London (69 Cannon St., EC4N 5AB) : London Enterprise Agency, [1980]. — 72p : col.maps ; 30cm
Unpriced (pbk) B81-37801

338.941'02 — Great Britain. Industries. Regional financial assistance by government. Effectiveness. Measurement — *Inquiry reports*
Great Britain. *Parliament. House of Commons. Committee of Public Accounts.* Fifth report from the Committee of Public Accounts : together with the proceedings of the Committee, minutes of evidence and an appendix, session 1980-81 : Department of Industry, Scottish Economic Planning Department, Welsh Office: measuring the effectiveness of regional industrial policy. — London : H.M.S.O., [1981]. — xv,42p ; 25cm. — ([HC] ; 206)
ISBN 0-10-220681-3 (pbk) : £4.40 B81-35381

338.941'02 — Great Britain. Regional economic development. Financial incentives: Loans from government — *Accounts — Serials*
Local Employment Act 1972, accounts / [Department of Industry]. — 1979-80. — London : H.M.S.O., 1981. — 8p
ISBN 0-10-218681-2 : £1.40 B81-23140

338.941'02 — Great Britain. Regional economic development. Financial incentives of government — *Serials*

Industry Act 1972, annual report by the Secretaries of State for Industry, Scotland and Wales for the year ended 31 March. — London : H.M.S.O., 1980. — iv,119p
ISBN 0-10-027729-2 : £5.20 B81-03903

338.941'02 — Great Britain. Rural regions. Economic development. Financial assistance by government. Development Fund — *Accounts* — *Serials*

Development Fund accounts. — 1979-80. — London : H.M.S.O., 1981. — 8p
ISBN 0-10-211681-4 : £1.40 B81-18808

338.941'02'025 — Great Britain. Industries. Financial assistance by government — *Directories* — *For businessmen*

Walker, Gesa. Industrial aids in Britain : 1981 : a businessman's guide / Gesa Walker and Kevin Allen. — Glasgow (University of Strathclyde, 16 Richmond St., Glasgow) : Centre for the Study of Public Policy, 1981. — 310p : 2maps ; 24cm
Includes index
ISBN 0-907243-02-9 (cased) : Unpriced
ISBN 0-907243-03-7 (pbk) : Unpriced
B81-26159

338.941'02'05 — Great Britain. Industries. Financial assistance by government — *Serials*

Official sources of finance and aid for industry in the U.K. / National Westminster Bank Limited. — 1981-. — London (Market Intelligence Department, 41 Lothbury, EC2P 2BP) : The Bank, 1981-. — v. : maps ; 30cm
Annual. — Continues: Official sources of finance and aid for industry and agriculture in the U.K.
ISSN 0261-5533 = Official sources of finance and aid for industry in the U.K. : £4.95
B81-31024

338.9411'02 — Scotland. Regional economic development. Financial incentives of government. Withdrawal & reduction. Effects — *Forecasts* — *Conference proceedings*

Economic development prospects in areas affected by changes in regional policy : a note of the proceedings of a two day conference, 9-10 June 1980, Peebles. — Glasgow (186 Bath St., Glasgow G2 4HG) : Planning Exchange, 1980. — 8leaves,[3]leaves of plates : maps ; 30cm. — (Occasional paper / Planning Exchange ; no.7)
£0.75 (pbk) B81-07697

338.9416'02'05 — Northern Ireland. Industrial development. Finance. Industrial Enterprise Fund — *Accounts* — *Serials*

Industrial Enterprise Fund account / Department of Commerce. — 1979-1980. — Belfast : H.M.S.O., 1980. — 1p
ISBN 0-337-06122-x : £0.30 B81-20332

338.9417 — Ireland *(Republic)*. **Regional industrial development. Policies of government,** *1950-1979*

Ross, Miceal. Regional industrial policies in the Republic of Ireland : a review of economic studies / by Miceal Ross. — Glasgow (McCance Building, 16 Richmond St., Glasgow G1 1XQ) : Centre for the Study of Public Policy, University of Strathclyde, 1981. — vi,115p : 2ill ; 30cm. — (Studies in public policy, ISSN 0140-8240 ; no.85)
Bibliography: p104-110
£3.00 (pbk) B81-38572

338.9417'02 — Ireland *(Republic)*. **Industrial development. Grants from Industrial Development Authority**

Tax incentives and industrial grants in Ireland. — [Dublin] (10 Fitzwilliam Square, Dublin 2) : Binder Dijker Otte, 1981. — 22p ; 25cm
Unpriced (pbk)
Primary classification 336.2'07'09417
B81-22967

338.9427'006 — North-west England. Industrial development. Promotion. Organisations: North West Industrial Development Association, *to 1981*

North West Industrial Development Association. Norwida : 50 Years of Service, 1931/1981 / North West Industrial Development Association. — Manchester (Brazenose House, Brazehose St., Manchester) : The Association, [1981]. — 20p ; 21cm
Cover title
Unpriced (pbk) B81-30649

North West Industrial Development Association. Norwida : 50 years of service 1931/1981 / North West Industrial Development Association. — Manchester (Brazennose House, Brazennose St., Manchester M2 5AZ) : The Association, [1981]. — 20p : 1port ; 21cm
Cover title
Unpriced (pbk) B81-37511

338.944 — France. Industries. Policies of government, *1970-1980*

Green, Diana, *19---*. Managing industrial change? : French policies to promote industrial adjustment / Diana Green. — London : H.M.S.O., [1981]. — vi,81p : ill ; 30cm
At head of title: Department of Industry. — Bibliography: p77-78. - Includes index
ISBN 0-11-512997-9 (pbk) : £5.95 B81-22221

338.947 — Eastern Europe. Economic planning — *Conference proceedings*

Economic Reforms in Eastern Europe and Prospects for the 1980s *(Conference : 1980 : Brussels)*. Economic reforms in Eastern Europe and Prospects for the 1980s : colloquium 16-18 April 1980 Brussels = Réformes économiques en Europe de l'Est et pespectives pour les années 80 : colloque 16-18 avril 1980 Bruxelles / Economics Directorate, Information Directorate (eds.). — Oxford : Pergamon, 1980. — xiv,320p : ill,ports ; 24cm
Includes bibliographies
ISBN 0-08-026801-3 : £35.00
ISBN 0-08-026800-5 (pbk) : Unpriced
B81-10790

338.9492 — Regional economic planning. Applications of input-output analysis. Evaluation — *Study regions: Netherlands*

Oosterhaven, Jan. International input-output analysis and Dutch regional policy problems. — Aldershot : Gower, Jan.1982. — [230]p
ISBN 0-566-00521-2 : £12.50 : CIP entry
B81-34283

338.965 — Algeria. National economic planning. Five-year plans, *1980-1984*

The **1980-84** Algerian five year plan : an assessment of future development trends and of opportunities in Algeria for British firms : incorporating the results of a COMET survey of British films on patterns of trades between the UK and French-speaking African markets. — London (33 Bury St., SW1Y 6AX) : Committee for Middle East Trade, 1981. — 54p : 1map ; 30cm. — (A COMET report)
£5.00 (spiral) B81-26555

338.9676'2 — Kenya. Economic planning

Planning African development / edited by Glen Norcliffe and Tom Pinfold. — Boulder : Westview ; London : Croom Helm, c1981. — 201p : ill,maps ; 23cm
Includes index
ISBN 0-7099-1802-x : £11.95 B81-17849

338.973 — United States. Government. Relations with private enterprise

Private management and public policy : reciprocal impacts / edited by Lewis Benton. — Lexington : Lexington Books, c1980 ; [Farnborough, Hants.] : Gower [distributor], 1981. — xiv,239p : 2ill ; 24cm
Includes index
ISBN 0-669-03063-5 : £12.50 B81-03454

338.973 — United States. Industries. Regulation by government

Government, regulation, and the economy / edited by Bernard H. Siegan. — Lexington : Lexington Books, c1980 ; [Farnborough, Hants.] : Gower [distributor], 1981. — v,146p ; 24cm
Includes index
ISBN 0-669-02664-6 : £11.00 B81-05025

Weidenbaum, Murray L.. Business, government, and the public / Murray L. Weidenbaum. — 2nd ed. — Englewood Cliffs ; London : Prentice-Hall, c1981. — viii,407p : ill,facsim,forms ; 24cm
Previous ed.: 1977. — Includes index
ISBN 0-13-099325-5 : £11.00 B81-12723

White, Lawrence J.. Reforming regulation : processes and problems / Lawrence J. White. — Englewood Cliffs ; London : Prentice-Hall, c1981. — xii,244p : ill ; 24cm
Includes index
ISBN 0-13-770115-2 (cased) : Unpriced
ISBN 0-13-770107-1 (pbk) : £6.25 B81-34953

338.973'02 — United States. Public bodies. Financial assistance by government. Political aspects

Political benefits : empirical studies of American public programs / edited by Barry S. Rundquist. — Lexington : Lexington Books ; [Farnborough, Hants.] : Gower [distributor], 1980. — xxi,262p : ill ; 24cm
Includes bibliographies and index
ISBN 0-669-02509-7 : £16.50 B81-06279

339 — MACROECONOMICS, CONSUMPTION, ETC

339 — Applied macroeconomics

Okun, Arthur M.. Prices and quantities : a macroeconomic analysis / Arthur M. Okun. — Oxford : Blackwell, 1981. — xiii,367p : ill ; 24cm
Includes index
ISBN 0-631-12898-0 (cased) : £15.00 : CIP rev.
ISBN 0-631-12899-9 (pbk) : £5.95 B81-13855

339 — Macroeconomic policies

Beenstock, Michael. A neoclassical analysis of macroeconomic policy / Michael Beenstock. — Cambridge : Cambridge University Press, 1980. — xii,231p : ill ; 24cm
Bibliography: p224-228. - Includes index
ISBN 0-521-23077-2 : £18.50 : CIP rev.
B80-35846

Carrington, John C.. Reversing economic decline / John C. Carrington and George T. Edwards. — London : Macmillan, Aug. 1980. — xv,194p ; 23cm
Includes index
ISBN 0-333-26929-2 : £15.00 : CIP rev.
B80-10485

339 — Macroeconomics

Barro, Robert J.. Money, expectations, and business cycles : essays in macroeconomics / Robert J. Barro. — New York ; London : Academic Press, c1981. — xi,375p ; 24cm. — (Economic theory, econometrics, and mathematical economics)
Includes index
ISBN 0-12-079550-7 : £14.00 B81-29768

Branson, William H.. Macroeconomics / William H. Branson / James M. Litvack. — 2nd ed. — New York ; London : Harper & Row, c1981. — xviii,407p : ill ; 25cm
Previous ed.: 1976. — Includes bibliographies and index
ISBN 0-06-040937-1 : £13.50 B81-28452

Dornbusch, Rudiger. Macro-economics / Rudiger Dornbusch, Stanley Fischer. — 2nd ed. — New York ; London : McGraw-Hill, c1981. — xiii,737p : col.ill ; 24cm
Previous ed.: 1978. — Includes index
ISBN 0-07-017754-6 : £12.95 B81-23956

Dornbusch, Rudiger. Macro-economics / Rudiger Dornbusch, Stanley Fischer. — 2nd ed. — Auckland ; London : McGraw-Hill, c1981. — xiii,738p : ill ; 21cm
Previous ed.: 1978. — Includes index
ISBN 0-07-066257-6 (pbk) : £6.95 B81-24558

Dornbusch, Rudiger. Supplement to Instructor's manual to accompany Macro-economics / Rudiger Dornbusch, Stanley Fischer. — New York ; London : McGraw-Hill, c1978. — 83p : ill ; 26cm
Bibliography: p82-83
ISBN 0-07-017753-8 (pbk) : £4.25 B81-10236

339 — Macroeconomics *continuation*

DRI readings in macro-economics / [edited by] Allen R. Sanderson. — New York ; London : McGraw-Hill, c1981. — xii,419p : ill ; 24cm
ISBN 0-07-054659-2 (pbk) : £5.95 B81-37270

Essays in fiscal and monetary policy. — Oxford : Oxford University Press, Sept.1981. — [256]p
ISBN 0-19-829001-2 : £15.00 : CIP entry B81-21634

Gwartney, James D.. Macroeconomics : private and public choice / James D. Gwartney, Richard Stroup with the assistance of A.H. Studenmund. — 2nd ed. — New York ; London : Academic Press, c1980. — xix,526,[50]p : ill(some col.),ports ; 26cm
Previous ed.: 1977. — Bibliography: pR1-R6. - Includes index
ISBN 0-12-311070-x (pbk) : £5.60 B81-05868

Heilbroner, Robert L.. Understanding macroeconomics. — 7th ed. / Robert L. Heilbroner, Lester C. Thurow. — Englewood Cliffs ; London : Prentice-Hall, c1981. — vi,358p : ill(some col.),2ports ; 24cm
Previous ed.: 1978. — Includes index
ISBN 0-13-936559-1 (pbk) : £7.10 B81-25509

Kelly, William A.. Macroeconomics / William A. Kelly, Jr. — Englewood Cliffs ; London : Prentice-Hall, c1981. — xvii,478p : ill ; 24cm
Ill on lining papers. — Includes index
ISBN 0-13-542761-4 : £11.65 B81-26098

Kornai, János. Growth, shortage and efficiency. — Oxford : Blackwell, Oct.1981. — [128]p. — (Yrjö Jahnsson lectures)
ISBN 0-631-12787-9 : £7.95 : CIP entry B81-28068

Leake, Andrew. Macroeconomics. — London : Macmillan, July 1981. — [48]p
ISBN 0-333-27991-3 (pbk) : £1.25 : CIP entry B81-16351

MacMillan, Alexander, *1942-*. Macroeconomics : the Canadian context / Alexander MacMillan. — Scarborough, Ont. ; London : Prentice-Hall, c1980. — xii,356p : ill ; 24cm
Includes index
ISBN 0-13-542696-0 (pbk) : £7.75 B81-00043

Macroeconomic analysis : essays in macroeconomics and econometrics / edited by D. Currie, R. Nobay and D. Peel. — London : Croom Helm, c1981. — 491p : ill ; 23cm
Conference papers. — Includes bibliographies
ISBN 0-7099-0311-1 : £19.95 : CIP rev. B81-04271

Mansfield, Edwin. Principles of macroeconomics / Edwin Mansfield. — 3rd ed. — New York ; London : W.W. Norton, c1980. — xix,562p : ill(some col.),facsim,ports ; 24cm
Previous ed.: 1977. — Includes index
ISBN 0-393-95120-0 (pbk) : £4.50 B81-02742

Perlman, Morris. Macroeconomics / Morris Perlman. — 2nd ed. — London : Weidenfeld and Nicolson, 1981. — viii,168p : ill ; 23cm. — (London School of Economics handbooks in economic analysis)
Previous ed.: 1974. — Includes bibliographies and index
ISBN 0-297-77958-3 (cased) : £11.50
ISBN 0-297-77959-1 (pbk) : £5.95 B81-31965

Phelps, Edmund S.. Studies in macroeconomic theory / Edmund S. Phelps. — New York ; London : Academic Press. — (Economic theory, econometrics, and mathematical economics)
Vol.2: Redistribution and growth. — c1980. — xii,358p : ill ; 24cm
Includes bibliographies
ISBN 0-12-554002-7 : £11.80 B81-20368

Philpot, Gordon. The national economy : an introduction to macroeconomics / Gordon Philpot. — New York ; Chichester : Wiley, c1980. — xix,188p : ill ; 23cm. — (Introduction to economics series)
Includes index
ISBN 0-471-05591-3 (pbk) : £4.75 B81-09657

Poindexter, J. C.. Macroeconomics / J.C. Poindexter. — 2nd ed. — Chicago ; London (1 St Anne's Rd., Eastbourne, E. Sussex BN21 3UN) : Dryden, c1981. — xii,525p : ill ; 25cm
Previous ed.: 1976. — Includes bibliographies and index
ISBN 0-03-050271-3 : £11.95 B81-22999

Veseth, Michael. Introductory macroeconomics / Michael Veseth. — New York ; London : Academic Press, c1980. — xv,411p : ill ; 24cm
Bibliography: p393-396. - Includes index
ISBN 0-12-719550-5 (pbk) : £4.60 B81-00044

Veseth, Michael. Introductory macroeconomics / Michael Veseth. — New York ; London : Academic Press, c1981. — xv,415p : ill(some col.) ; 24cm
Also published: in hardback with Introductory microeconomics as Introductory economics. 1981. — Includes index
ISBN 0-12-719552-1 (pbk) : £7.40 B81-29765

Wykoff, Frank C.. Macroeconomics : theory, evidence, and policy / Frank C. Wykoff. — 2nd ed. — Englewood Cliffs ; London : Prentice-Hall, c1981. — x8518p : ill ; 24cm
Previous ed.: 1976. — Includes bibliographies and index
ISBN 0-13-543967-1 : £13.95 B81-29907

339′.01 — Macroeconomics. Theories

Leijonhufvud, Axel. Information and coordination : essay in macroeconomic theory / Axel Leijonhufvud. — New York ; Oxford : Oxford University Press, 1981. — x,388p ; 23cm
Bibliography: p361-369. — Includes index
ISBN 0-19-502814-7 (cased) : £14.95
ISBN 0-19-502815-5 (pbk) : £6.95 B81-38958

339′.024658 — Macroeconomics — *For management*

Hatten, Mary Louise. Macroeconomics for management / Mary Louise Hatten. — Englewood Cliffs ; London : Prentice-Hall, c1981. — xv,381p : ill ; 24cm
Bibliography: p366-375. — Includes index
ISBN 0-13-542498-4 : £12.95 B81-16646

339′.09172′4 — Developing countries. Macroeconomic policies. Formulation. Mathematical models

Taylor, Lance. Macro models for developing countries / Lance Taylor. — New York ; London : McGraw-Hill, c1979. — xii,271p : ill ; 25cm. — (Economics handbook series)
Includes bibliographies and index
ISBN 0-07-063135-2 : £20.75 B81-39414

339.2 — Income. Distribution — *Conference proceedings*

Colston Research Society. *Symposium (31st : 1979 : University of Bristol)*. Income distribution : the limits to redistribution : proceedings of the thirty-first Symposium of the Colston Research Society held in the University of Bristol, March 1979 / editors: David Collard, Richard Lecomber and Martin Slater. — Bristol : Scientechnica, 1980. — xi,267p : ill ; 25cm. — (Colston papers ; v.31)
Includes bibliographies and index
ISBN 0-85608-027-6 : £25.00 : CIP rev. B80-12759

339.2 — Income. Distribution. Demographic aspects

Kuznets, Simon. Growth, population, and income distribution : selected essays / Simon Kuznets. — New York ; London : Norton, c1979. — vii,308p ; 22cm
ISBN 0-393-95061-1 : £12.50
Primary classification 339.5 B81-05293

339.2′01 — National income. Distribution. Theories

Mitra, Ashok. The share of wages in national income / Ashok Mitra. — Calcutta ; Oxford : Oxford University Press, 1980. — vi,152p : ill ; 22cm
Includes index
ISBN 0-19-561301-5 : £7.50 B81-38505

339.2′09172′4 — Developing countries. Income. Distribution. Effects of inflation

Leibenstein, Harvey. Inflation, income distribution and X-efficiency theory : a study prepared for the International Labour Office within the framework of the World Employment Programme / Harvey Leibenstein. — London : Croom Helm, c1980. — 122p : ill ; 23cm
Includes index
ISBN 0-7099-0306-5 : £9.95 : CIP rev. B80-02360

339.2′09172′4 — Developing countries. Income. Distribution *related to* **economic growth**

Fields, Gary S.. Poverty, inequality and development / Gary S. Fields. — Cambridge : Cambridge University Press, 1980. — xi,281p : ill ; 22cm
Bibliography: p258-272. - Includes index
ISBN 0-521-22572-8 (cased) : £16.00
ISBN 0-521-29852-0 (pbk) : £5.50
Also classified at 339.5′09172′4 B81-09924

339.2′094 — European Community countries. Income. Distribution. Inequalities

Saunders, Christopher. Pay inequalities in the European Community. — London : Butterworth, Sept.1981. — [312]p. — (Butterworths European studies)
ISBN 0-408-10727-8 : £19.00 : CIP entry B81-23906

339.2′095 — Asia. Income. Distribution

Paukert, Felix. Income distribution, structure of economy and employment : the Philippines, Iran, the Republic of Korea and Malaysia : a study prepared for the International Labour Office within the framework of the World Employment Programme / Felix Paukert, Jiri Skolka and Jef Maton. — London : Croom Helm, c1981. — 169p : ill ; 23cm. — ([An ILO-WEP study])
Bibliography: p158-165. — Includes index
ISBN 0-7099-2006-7 : £12.95 B81-25152

339.2′095 — Asia. Income. Distribution *related to* **education**

Richards, P. J.. Education and income distribution in Asia : a study prepared for the International Labour Office within the framework of the World Employment Programme / P. Richards and M. Leonor. — London : Croom Helm, c1981. — 190p : 2ill ; 23cm
Includes index
ISBN 0-7099-2201-9 : £12.95 B81-07145

339.2′0951′249 — Taiwan. Income. Distribution. Effects of economic growth

Fei, John C. H.. Growth with equity : the Taiwan case / John C.H. Fei, Gustav Ranis, Shirley W.Y. Kuo with the assistance of Yu-Yuan Bian, Julia Chang Collins. — New York ; Oxford : Published for the World Bank [by] Oxford University Press, c1979. — xxii,422p : ill,forms ; 24cm. — (A World Bank research publication)
Includes index
ISBN 0-19-520115-9 (cased) : £9.50
ISBN 0-19-520116-7 (pbk) : Unpriced B81-26847

339.2′09595 — Malaysia. Urban regions. Income. Distribution *related to* **labour market**

Mazumdar, Dipak. The urban labor market and income distribution : a study of Malaysia / Dipak Mazumdar. — New York ; Oxford : Published for the World Bank [by] Oxford University Press, c1981. — xvi,375p : ill ; 24cm. — (A World Bank research publication)
Includes index
ISBN 0-19-520213-9 (cased) : £10.75
ISBN 0-19-520214-7 (pbk) : £4.75
Primary classification 331.12′09595 B81-25980

339.2′0973 — United States. Remuneration. Distribution. Inequalities. Effects of trade unions

Pettengill, John S.. Labor unions and the inequality of earned income / John S. Pettengill. — Amsterdam ; Oxford : North-Holland, 1980. — x,336p : ill ; 23cm. — (Contributions to economic analysis ; 129)
Bibliography: p321-330. — Includes index
ISBN 0-444-85409-6 : £21.00 B81-04883

339.2′0981 — Brazil. Income. Distribution. Econometric models

Models of growth and distribution for Brazil / Lance Taylor ... [et al.]. — New York ; Oxford : Published for the World Bank Oxford University Press, c1980. — xii,355p : ill ; 24cm. — (A World Bank research publication)
Includes bibliographies and index
ISBN 0-19-520206-6 : £10.95
ISBN 0-19-520207-4 (pbk) : £5.95
Primary classification 339.5′0981 B81-19755

339.2′2 — Great Britain. Families. Income — *Inquiry reports*

Study Commission on the Family. *Working Party on the Financial Circumstances of Families.* Family finances : the interim report of the Working Party on the Financial Circumstances of Families / prepared for the Working Party by Malcolm Wicks and Lesley Rimmer. — London : Study Commission on the Family, c1981. — 39p : 1ill ; 21cm
ISBN 0-907051-06-5 (pbk) : £1.80 B81-17726

339.2′2′01 — Personal income. Distribution. Theories

Hartog, Joop. Personal income distribution : a multicapability theory / Joop Hartog. — Boston ; London : Nijhoff, c1981. — xii,221p : 1ill ; 24cm
Bibliography: p203-208. - Includes index
ISBN 0-89838-047-2 : Unpriced B81-04790

339.2′2′0724 — United States. Personal wealth. Transmission. Mathematical models

Modeling the distribution and intergenerational transmission of wealth / edited by James D. Smith. — Chicago ; London : University of Chicago Press, 1980. — viii,336p : ill ; 24cm. — (Studies in income and wealth ; v.46)
Conference papers. — Includes bibliographies and index
ISBN 0-226-76454-0 : Unpriced B81-29954

339.2′2′0941 — Great Britain. Families. Income. Distribution. Effects of taxation & welfare benefits

Bradshaw, Jonathan. Equity and family incomes / Jonathan Bradshaw. — London : Study Commission on the Family, c1980. — 28p ; 21cm. — (Occasional paper / Study Commission on the Family ; no.5)
ISBN 0-907051-05-7 (pbk) : £1.50 B81-07862

339.2′2′0973 — United States. Personal wealth & income. Distribution. Inequalities, *1650-1979*

Williamson, Jeffrey. American inequality : a macroeconomic history / Jeffrey G. Williamson, Peter H. Lindert. — New York ; London : Academic Press, c1980. — xx,362p : ill ; 24cm. — (Institute for Research on Poverty monograph series)
Bibliography: p335-349. — Includes index
ISBN 0-12-757160-4 : £16.50 B81-16622

339.2′3′0941 — Great Britain. Industries. Input-output analysis — *Statistics — Serials*

Input-output tables for the United Kingdom / compiled by the Central Statistical Office. — 1974. — London : H.M.S.O., c1981. — 104p. — (Business monitor ; PA1004)
ISBN 0-11-512700-3 : £7.10 B81-20451

339.2′3′0947 — Soviet Union. Economic conditions. Input-output analysis

Studies in Soviet input-output analysis / edited by Vladimir G. Treml ; foreword by Wassily Leontief. — New York ; London : Praeger, 1977. — xx,446p : ill ; 25cm. — (Praeger special studies in international economics and development)
Includes bibliographies and index
ISBN 0-275-56550-5 : £24.50 B81-01586

339.2′6′0724 — Great Britain. Funds. Flow. Econometric models

Short, John, *1948-*. Money flows in the UK regions / John Short with David J. Nicholas. — Farnborough, Hants. : Gower, c1981. — xiv,217p : ill ; 23cm
Bibliography: p216-217
ISBN 0-566-00421-6 : Unpriced : CIP rev. B81-02659

339.3 — Income. Value. Measurement

Lee, T. A.. Income and value measurement : theory and practice / T.A. Lee. — 2nd ed. — Walton-on-Thames : Nelson, 1980. — x,205p : 1ill ; 22cm. — (Nelson series in accounting and finance) (Nelson series in accounting and finance)
Previous ed.: 1974. — Bibliography: p175-200. - Includes index
ISBN 0-17-761053-0 (cased) : £8.50 : CIP rev.
ISBN 0-17-771131-0 (pbk) : £4.50 B80-13276

339.3 — National accounts. Statistics

Allen, R. G. D.. An introduction to national accounts statistics / R.G.D. Allen. — London : Macmillan, 1980. — vii,126p : ill ; 23cm
Includes index
ISBN 0-333-28195-0 (cased) : £15.00 : CIP rev.
ISBN 0-333-30438-1 (pbk) : £5.95 B80-24234

339.341 — Great Britain. National accounts

Copeman, Harold. The national accounts : a short guide / Harold Copeman. — London : H.M.S.O., 1981. — v,[133]p : ill ; 30cm. — (Studies in official statistics ; no.36)
At head of title: Central Statistical Office. — Bibliography: 2p. — Includes index
ISBN 0-11-620000-6 (pbk) : £5.50 B81-38753

339.341′0212 — Great Britain. National income — *Statistics — Serials*

National income and expenditure / Central Statistical Office. — 1980 ed.. — London : H.M.S.O., 1980. — vi,139p
ISBN 0-11-630776-5 : £10.50
Also classified at 339.4′7′0941 B81-02943

339.343 — East Germany. National income. Compared with national income of West Germany

Wilkens, Herbert. The two German economies : a comparison between the national product of the German Democratic Republic and the Federal Republic of Germany / Herbert Wilkens ; translated from the German by Lux Furtmüller. — Farnborough, Hants. : Gower, 1981. — xiii,180p : ill ; 23cm
Translation and revision of: Das Sozialprodukt der Deutschen Demokratischen Republik im Vergleich mit dem der Bundesrepublik Deutschland. — Bibliography: p167-176. — Includes index
ISBN 0-566-00304-x : Unpriced B81-37128

339.4′2′0956 — Middle East. Cost of living — *Statistics — For British businessmen — Serials*

Middle East living costs / CBI. — 1981-. — London : Confederation of British Industry, 1981-. — v. ; 20cm
Irregular. — Continues: Middle East costs
ISSN 0261-2569 = Middle East living costs : £18.00 B81-21348

339.4′3′0922 — Great Britain. Private investment, *ca 1930-1980 — Personal observations — Collections*

Gleeson, Adrienne. People and their money : 50 years of private investment / Adrienne Gleeson. — [London] ([Three Quays, Tower Hill, E.C.3]) : M. & G. Group, 1981. — xii,163p : ill,ports ; 24cm
Bibliography: p157-158. — Includes index
ISBN 0-86021-392-7 (cased) : £9.50
ISBN 0-86021-393-5 (pbk) : Unpriced B81-25093

339.4′6′091724 — Developing countries. Agricultural communities. Poverty *related to* **land tenure**

Whittemore, Claire. Land for people : land tenure and the very poor / by Claire Whittemore. — Oxford : Oxfam Public Affairs Unit, 1981. — 55p,[8]p of ill ; 21cm
ISBN 0-85598-046-x (pbk) : £1.30
Also classified at 333.33′5′091724 B81-27735

339.4′7 — Conspicuous consumption

Mason, Roger S.. Conspicuous consumption : a study of exceptional consumer behaviour / Roger S. Mason. — Farnborough, Hants. : Gower, c1981. — x,156p ; 23cm
Includes index
ISBN 0-566-00404-6 : £11.50 B81-12992

339.4′7 — Consumer behaviour. Economic aspects - *Festschriften*

Essays in the theory and measurement of consumer behaviour. — Cambridge : Cambridge University Press, Aug.1981. — [374]p
ISBN 0-521-22565-5 : £25.00 : CIP entry B81-19168

339.4′7 — Demand. Management

Demand management, supply constraints and inflation. — Manchester : Manchester University Press, Nov.1981. — [238]p
ISBN 0-7190-0846-8 : £12.50 : CIP entry B81-30956

339.4′7 — Great Britain. Cities. Inner areas. Low-income families. Standard of living. Effects of low pay & unemployment

Playford, Clive. In the shadow of decline / Clive Playford. — London (9 Poland St., W1V 3DG) : Low Pay Unit, 1981. — 31p : ill ; 21cm. — (Pamphlet / Low Pay Unit, ISSN 0307-8116 ; no.16)
£1.00 (pbk) B81-24383

339.4′7 — Great Britain. Families. Expenditure. Social surveys. Methodology

Kemsley, W. F. F.. Family expenditure survey handbook : sampling, fieldwork, coding procedures and related methodological experiments : an account of the operations carried out by Social Survey Division of OPCS on behalf of the Department of Employment / W.F.F. Kemsley, R.U. Redpath and M. Holmes. — London : H.M.S.O., 1980. — viii,147p : ill,forms ; 30cm
Bibliography: p146-147
ISBN 0-11-690744-4 (pbk) : £11.60 B81-09839

339.4′7 — Great Britain. Families. Expenditure — *Statistics — Serials*

Family expenditure survey / Department of Employment. — 1979. — London : H.M.S.O., 1980. — vii,182p
ISBN 0-11-361195-1 : £10.50 B81-10582

339.4′7 — Great Britain. Low-income persons. Standard of living. Effects of rent stop

Allbeson, Janet. 'Rent-stop' / by Janet Allbeson. — London (1 Macklin St., WC2B 5NH) : Child Poverty Action Group, 1980. — 39p : 1facsim ; 21cm. — (Poverty pamphlet ; 46)
£0.80 (pbk) B81-08221

339.4′7 — Great Britain. Regional economic development. Implications of supply of & demand for business services

Marshall, J. N.. Business service activities in provincial conurbations : implications for regional economic development / by J.N. Marshall. — [Newcastle upon Tyne] ([Newcastle upon Tyne NE1 7RU]) : University of Newcastle upon Tyne Centre for Urban and Regional Development Studies, 1981. — 40p,[24]leaves ; 30cm. — (Discussion paper / University of Newcastle upon Tyne Centre for Urban and Regional Development Studies, ISSN 0140-6515 ; no.37)
Bibliography: leaves 38-40
Unpriced (pbk) B81-30924

339.4′7 — Northern Ireland. Families. Expenditure *— Statistics — Serials*

Northern Ireland family expenditure survey / [Northern Ireland Department of Finance, Central Economic Service]. — 1978. — Belfast : H.M.S.O., 1980. — 55p
ISBN 0-337-23325-x : £4.00
ISSN 0308-2008 B81-16251

339.4′7 — Western Europe. Consumer goods. Demand — *For exporting*

Jenner, Paul. Europe : an exporters handbook / Paul Jenner. — London : Euromonitor, 1981. — 403p : maps ; 23cm. — (Factfinders)
ISBN 0-903706-26-1 : £15.00 B81-37072

339.4′7 — Western Europe. Consumer goods. Demand — *Forecasts — For marketing*

The Book of forecasts / researched, compiled & published by Euromonitor Publications Ltd. — London : Euromonitor, 1981. — [170]leaves ; 21x32cm
ISBN 0-903706-57-1 (spiral) : Unpriced B81-37086

339.4'7'07 — Supply & demand. Information sources — *Lists* — *For marketing*

World sources of market information. — Farnborough, Hants. : Gower, Apr.1981
Vol.1: Asia/Pacific. — [300]p
ISBN 0-566-02179-x : £35.00 : CIP entry
B81-03157

339.4'7'094 — Western Europe. Cost of living — *Statistics* — *Serials* — *For British businessmen*

West European living costs / Confederation of British Industry. — 1980. — London : The Confederation, 1980. — 94p
ISSN 0142-646x : £18.00 B81-09200

339.4'7'0941 — Great Britain. National expenditure — *Statistics* — *Serials*

National income and expenditure / Central Statistical Office. — 1980 ed.. — London : H.M.S.O., 1980. — vi,139p
ISBN 0-11-630776-5 : £10.50
Primary classification 339.341'0212 B81-02943

339.4'7'0942 — England. Regions served by ATV Network Ltd.. Consumer behaviour — *Statistics* — *For marketing*

ATV marketing manual : marketing & research services. — London (17 Great Cumberland Pl., W1A 1AG) : ATV Network Ltd., 1979. — 95p : col.ill,col.maps ; 22x32cm
Cover title. — Text on inside cover
Unpriced (spiral) B81-30081

339.4'833276 — Great Britain. Credit card services. Supply — *Inquiry reports*

Great Britain. *Monopolies and Mergers Commission*. Credit card franchise services : a report on the supply of credit card franchise services in the United Kingdom / Monopolies and Mergers Commission. — London : H.M.S.O., 1980. — vi,262p : ill ; 25cm. — (Cmnd. ; 8034)
Includes index
ISBN 0-10-180340-0 (pbk) : £8.05 B81-04685

339.4'83621'0973 — United States. Health services. Supply & demand. Influence of physicians. Economic aspects

Pauly, Mark V.. Doctors and their workshops : economic models of physician behavior / Mark V. Pauly. — Chicago ; London : University of Chicago Press, 1980. — ix,132p ; 24cm. — (A National Bureau of Economic Research monograph)
Includes index
ISBN 0-226-65044-8 : £10.20 B81-13672

339.4'83635'0724 — Housing. Supply & demand. Mathematical models

Botman, J. J.. Dynamics of housing and planning : a regional simulation model / by J.J. Botman. — Delft : Delft University Press ; The Hague ; London : Nijhoff, 1981. — 270p : ill ; 24cm
ISBN 90-247-2499-6 (pbk) : Unpriced
B81-23165

339.4'83635'0942837 — Humberside. Hull region. Housing. Supply & demand

Hull area joint housing study : a first report / Humberside County Council ... [et al.]. — [Beverley] ([Manor Rd., Beverley, NU17 7BX]) : The Council, [1981]. — 10[i.e.29]p,[9]leaves of plates : ill ; 30cm
Cover title
£1.00 (spiral) B81-16511

339.4'83636 — Public utilities. Services. Demand. Forecasting — *Conference proceedings*

Forecasting public utilities : proceedings of the international conference held at Nottingham University, March 1980 / edited by O.D. Anderson. — Amsterdam ; Oxford : North-Holland, 1980. — v,209p : ill ; 23cm
ISBN 0-444-86046-0 : £17.13 B81-02860

339.4'85535 — North Wales. Naturally occurring aggregates. Supply & demand — *Forecasts*

Regional commentary / North Wales Working Party on Aggregates. — Mold (Shire Hall, Mold CH7 6NG) : Clwyd County Council on behalf of the Working Party
Part 1. — 1981. — ii,65p,[5]leaves of plates : maps ; 30cm
ISBN 0-904444-55-4 (pbk) : Unpriced
B81-38039

339.4'86151'0941 — Great Britain. Retail pharmaceutical trades. Consumer behaviour

McGoldrick, Peter J.. Retail pharmacy customers : their motivations and their decisions to make purchases / Peter J. McGoldrick. — Manchester (P.O. Box 88 Manchester M60 1QD) : Department of Management Sciences University of Manchester Institute of Science and Technology, 1981. — 33p : 1form ; 31cm. — (Occasional paper / Department of Management Sciences, University of Manchester Institute of Science and Technology ; no.8107)
Bibliography: p32-33
Unpriced (pbk) B81-30915

339.4'86331'05 — Cereals. Supply & demand — *Serials*

International grain & feed markets forecast and statistical digest. — 1976-. — London (886 High Rd, Finchley, N12 9SB) : Turret Press, c1976-. — v. : ill ; 30cm
Annual. — Continues in part: International milling & feed manual. — Description based on: 1979
ISSN 0260-2687 = International grain & feed markets forecast and statistical digest : £19.00
B81-02008

339.4'863475'0942 — England. Strawberries. Supply & demand

Hinton, Lynn. English strawberries : an economic study of the production and marketing of strawberries / by Lynn Hinton. — [Cambridge] ([Silver St., Cambridge CB3 9EL]) : Agricultural Economics Unit, Department of Land Economy, Cambridge University, 1981. — 35p : ill,map ; 30cm. — (Occasional papers / University of Cambridge Agricultural Economics Unit ; no.23)
Bibliography: p26
£2.50 (pbk) B81-15100

339.4'86373'094 — European Community countries. Cheeses. Demand. Econometric models

Keane, Michael. Factors affecting demand for cheese in the European Community / Michael Keane. — Dublin : Marketing Dept., Economics and Rural Welfare Research Centre, An Foras Taluntais, 1981. — iv,151p : ill ; 21cm
ISBN 0-905442-53-9 (pbk) : £3.00 B81-40327

339.4'8637541'0941 — Great Britain. Eggs. Demand & supply. Forecasting. Role of econometric models

Hallam, David. Econometric forecasting in the UK egg market / David Hallam. — Tunbridge Wells (Union House, Eridge Rd., Tunbridge Wells, Kent TN4 8HF) : Eggs Authority, 1981. — 125p : ill ; 30cm
Cover title. — Bibliography: p123-125
Unpriced (pbk) B81-18952

339.4'86413'00941 — Great Britain. Food. Consumption — *Serials*

Great Britain. *Ministry of Agriculture, Fisheries and Food*. Household food consumption and expenditure : annual report of the National Food Society Survey Committee. — 1979. — London : H.M.S.O., 1981. — xi,218p
ISBN 0-11-241167-3 : £12.50 B81-09689

339.4'8647944201'0216 — England. Hotels. Occupancy — *Statistics* — *Serials*

The **English** hotels occupancy survey. — 1977 to 1979. — London (4, Grosvenor Gardens, SW1W 0DU) : Planning and Research Services Branch, English Tourist Board, 1980. — 26p
ISSN 0260-2539 : Unpriced B81-08325

339.4'864794441 — Great Britain. Vacation accommodation industries. Consumer behaviour — *Forecasts*

Self, Diana. The UK accommodation and eating-out market : trends and prospects to 1985 / by Diana Self. — London (42, Colebrooke Row, N1 8AF) : Staniland Hall Associates Ltd., c1981. — x,86p : ill ; 22x30cm
£78.00 (spiral)
Also classified at 339.4'86479541 B81-27098

339.4'86479541 — Great Britain. Catering industries. Consumer behaviour — *Forecasts*

Self, Diana. The UK accommodation and eating-out market : trends and prospects to 1985 / by Diana Self. — London (42, Colebrooke Row, N1 8AF) : Staniland Hall Associates Ltd., c1981. — x,86p : ill ; 22x30cm
£78.00 (spiral)
Primary classification 339.4'864794441
B81-27098

339.4'86591342 — Great Britain. Roadside advertising posters. Supply — *Inquiry reports*

Great Britain. *Monopolies and Mergers Commission*. Roadside advertising services : a report on the supply in the United Kingdom of roadside advertising services / Monopolies and Mergers Commission. — London : H.M.S.O., [1981]. — v,130p ; 25cm. — ([H.C.] ; 365)
Includes index
ISBN 0-10-236581-4 (pbk) : £5.70 B81-33417

339.4'86631'0941 — Great Britain. Alcoholic drinks. Consumption. Policies of government. Implications of effects of prices & advertising on demand

Duffy, M.. Advertising, taxation and the demand for beer, spirits and wine in the United Kingdom, 1963-1978 / M. Duffy. — Manchester (P.O. Box 88, Manchester M60 1QD) : Department of Management Sciences, University of Manchester Institute of Science and Technology, 1980. — 60p : 2ill ; 31cm. — (Occasional paper / Department of Management Sciences, University of Manchester Institute of Science and Technology ; no.8009)
Bibliography: p58-59
Unpriced (pbk) B81-09627

339.4'86631'0941 — Great Britain. Alcoholic drinks. Demand — *Forecasts*

Duffy, M.. Forecasting the demand for alcoholic drink in the United Kingdom / M. Duffy.— Manchester (P.O. Box 88 Manchester M60 1QD) : Department of Management Sciences University of Manchester Institute of Science and Technology, 1981. — 32p : ill ; 31cm. — (Occasional paper / Department of Management Sciences. University of Manchester Institute of Science and Technology ; no.8108)
Conference paper. — Bibliography: p32
Unpriced (pbk) B81-30916

339.4'86631'0942 — England. Alcoholic drinks. Consumption

Brake, George Thompson. Alcohol : its consumption and control / by George Thompson Brake. — 3rd rev. ed. — London (36 Eccleston Sq., SW1 1PF) : Edsall, 1981. — 47p ; 22cm
Previous ed.: 197-. — Includes index
ISBN 0-902623-27-3 (pbk) : £2.70 B81-18592

Wilson, Paul, *1949 Feb. 10-*. Drinking in England and Wales : an enquiry carried out on behalf of the Department of Health and Social Security. — London : H.M.S.O., 1980. — ix,78p : ill,forms ; 30cm
At head of title: Office of Population Censuses and Surveys Social Survey Division
ISBN 0-11-690740-1 (pbk) : £8.00 B81-07393

339.4'866466 — Great Britain. Catfood & dogfood. Demand — *For marketing*

Report on the U.K. pet food market / Centre for Business Research. — Manchester (Booth Street West, Manchester M15 6PB) : Centre for Business Research in association with Manchester Business School, [1980?]. — ii,59 leaves ; 30cm. — (Research report. Market position series / Centre for Business Research, ISSN 0306-5227)
Unpriced (spiral) B81-10845

339.4'86655'0724 — Petroleum. Supply & demand. Forecasting. Mathematical models

Choucri, Nazli. International energy futures : petroleum prices, power and payments / Nazli Choucri with David Scott Ross and the collaboration of Brian Pollins. — Cambridge, Mass. ; London : M.I.T., c1981. — x,247p : ill ; 24cm
Bibliography: p228-231. — Includes index
ISBN 0-262-03075-6 : £17.00 B81-38131

339.4'8665773'0941 — Great Britain. Liquefied petroleum gas in storage containers. Supply — *Inquiry reports*

Liquefied petroleum gas : a report on the supply in the United Kingdom of liquefied petroleum gas in containers of not more than 50 kilograms capacity and not less than 150 grams capacity / the Monopolies and Mergers Commission. — London : H.M.S.O., [1981]. — v,85p ; 25cm. — (147)
ISBN 0-10-214781-7 (pbk) : £4.60 B81-15608

339.4'867'0941 — Great Britain. Manufactured goods. Supply & demand — *Serials*

Market assessment : home, office, leisure surveys / by BLA Research & Advisory Services. — Issue no.1 (Aug./Sept.1979)-. — London (2 Duncan Terrace, N1 8BZ) : BLA Publications, 1979-. — v. : ill ; 30cm
Six issues yearly. — Issue no.6 (June/July 1980) erroneously called Issue no.5 (Apr./May 1980) on contents page. — Description based on: Issue no.6 (June/July 1980)
ISSN 0260-5759 = Market assessment : £240.00 per year B81-04830

339.4'8674'0973 — United States. Natural resources: Timber. Supply & demand

Hyde, William F.. Timber supply, land allocation, and economic efficiency / William F. Hyde. — Baltimore ; London : Published for Resources for the Future by Johns Hopkins University Press, c1980. — xvii,224p : ill ; 24cm
Includes index
ISBN 0-8018-2489-3 : £11.50 B81-07799

339.4'8676142'0941 — Great Britain. Paper manufacturing industries & paperboard manufacturing industries. Raw materials: Waste paper. Supply — *Inquiry reports*

Great Britain. *Committee on Waste Paper Supply*. Report of the Committee on Waste Paper Supply. — London : Department of Industry, 1980. — ii,111p ; 30cm
£4.25 (pbk) B81-04632

339.4'8681418 — Great Britain. 35mm cameras. Consumer behaviour — *For marketing*

35mm camera survey : a report on a survey carried out by NOP Market Research Limited. — [London] ([Tower House, Southampton St., WC2E 7HN]) : NOP Market Research Limited, 1980. — 110,3leaves ; 30cm
Publisher's no.: NOP/5975
Unpriced (spiral) B81-38715

339.4'868876'0941 — Great Britain. Sports equipment. Demand

Martin, William H.. The UK sports market / by W.H. Martin & S.Mason. — Sudbury (Lint Growis, Foxearth, Sudbury, Suffolk) : Leisure Consultants, 1980. — 166p ; 30cm
Bibliography: p162-166
ISBN 0-9504627-1-3 (spiral) : £70.00
Also classified at 339.4'8796'0941 B81-04453

339.4'869'00941 — Great Britain. Building. Construction. Demand — *Forecasts — Serials*

[Forecasts *(BMP Forecasting Panel)*]. Forecasts : report of the BMP Forecasting Panel. — July 1979-. — London (33 Alfred Place, WC1E 7EN) : National Council of Building Material Producers, 1979-. — v. ; 30cm
Three issues yearly. — Description based on: July 1980 issue
ISSN 0144-9060 = Forecasts - National Council of Building Material Producers : £12.00 (free to members of the Council) B81-04821

339.4'8778599 — Video discs. Supply & demand — *Forecasts*

Consumer video discs. — Luton (Mackintosh House, Napier Rd., Luton, Bedfordshire LU1 1RG) : Mackintosh Publications, 1980. — x,145p : ill ; 30cm. — (A Mackintosh monitor report)
Report of Mackintosh International
ISBN 0-904705-29-3 (pbk) : £295.00 B81-08401

339.4'8778599 — Videocassette tape recording equipment. Supply & demand — *Forecasts*

VCRs, cameras and blank tapes. — Luton (Mackintosh House, Napier Rd., Luton LU1 1RG) : Mackintosh Publications, [1980]. — x,196p : ill ; 30cm. — (A Mackintosh monitor report)
Report of Mackintosh International
ISBN 0-904705-30-7 (pbk) : £295.00 B81-08400

339.4'8796'0941 — Great Britain. Sports facilities. Demand

Martin, William H.. The UK sports market / by W.H. Martin & S.Mason. — Sudbury (Lint Growis, Foxearth, Sudbury, Suffolk) : Leisure Consultants, 1980. — 166p ; 30cm
Bibliography: p162-166
ISBN 0-9504627-1-3 (spiral) : £70.00
Primary classification 339.4'868876'0941 B81-04453

339.5 — Capitalist countries. Economic growth. Role of large industrial companies

Odagiri, Hiroyuki1946-. The theory of growth in a corporate economy : management preference, research and development and economic growth / Hiroyuki Odagiri. — Cambridge : Cambridge University Press, 1981. — xiv,220p : ill ; 24cm
Bibliography: p211-217. — Includes index
ISBN 0-521-23132-9 : £20.00 B81-38003

339.5 — Economic growth

Guha, Ashok S.. An evolutionary view of economic growth. — Oxford : Clarendon Press, Jan.1982. — [128]p
ISBN 0-19-828431-4 : £8.50 : CIP entry B81-34385

Rostow, W. W.. Why the poor get richer and the rich slow down : essays in the Marshallian long period / W.W. Rostow. — London : Macmillan, 1980. — xvii,376p : ill ; 24cm
Includes index
ISBN 0-333-30002-5 : £15.00 : CIP rev. B80-10019

339.5 — Economic growth. Effects of differentials in remuneration. Mathematical models

Sgro, Pasquale M.. Wage differentials and economic growth / Pasquale M. Sgro. — London : Croom Helm, c1980. — 147p : ill ; 23cm
Bibliography: p138-143. - Includes index
ISBN 0-85664-612-1 : £13.50 : CIP rev. B80-00100

339.5 — Economic growth. Effects of population growth

Kuznets, Simon. Growth, population, and income distribution : selected essays / Simon Kuznets. — New York ; London : Norton, c1979. — vii,308p ; 22cm
ISBN 0-393-95061-1 : £12.50
Also classified at 339.2 B81-05293

339.5 — Economic growth. Theories of Stockholm School, *1927-1937 — Critical studies*

Hansson, Björn A.. The Stockholm School and the development of dynamic method. — London : Croom Helm, Oct.1981. — [304]p
ISBN 0-7099-1225-0 : £13.95 : CIP entry B81-31103

339.5 — Great Britain. Private enterprise. Employment. Subsidies by government: Temporary Employment Subsidy. Effectiveness

Deakin, B. M.. Effects of the temporary employment subsidy. — Cambridge : Cambridge University Press, Jan.1982. — [236] p. — (Occasional paper / University of Cambridge. Department of Applied Economics ; 53)
ISBN 0-521-24358-0 : £15.00 : CIP entry B81-39211

339.5 — Incomes policy

Incomes policy. — Oxford : Clarendon Press, Sept.1981. — [224]p
ISBN 0-19-877145-2 (cased) : £12.50 : CIP entry
ISBN 0-19-877146-0 (pbk) : £4.95 B81-23889

339.5'09172'4 — Developing countries. Economic growth *related to* **income distribution**

Fields, Gary S.. Poverty, inequality and development / Gary S. Fields. — Cambridge : Cambridge University Press, 1980. — xi,281p : ill ; 22cm
Bibliography: p258-272. - Includes index
ISBN 0-521-22572-8 (cased) : £16.00
ISBN 0-521-29852-0 (pbk) : £5.50
Primary classification 339.2'09172'4 B81-09924

339.5'09181'2 — Western world. Incomes policy, *1945-1980*

Incomes policies, inflation and relative pay / edited by J.L. Fallick and R.F. Elliott. — London : Allen & Unwin, 1980. — 284p : ill ; 23cm
Includes bibliographies and index
ISBN 0-04-331077-x (cased) : £14.00
ISBN 0-04-331078-8 (pbk) : £5.95 B81-11357

339.5094 — Europe. Economic growth, *1400-1955*

Phelps Brown, Henry. A perspective of wages and prices. — London : Methuen, Oct.1981. — [256]p
ISBN 0-416-31950-5 : £11.00 : CIP entry B81-27348

339.5'094897 — Finland. Incomes policy

Addison, John T.. Finnish incomes policy / by John T. Addison. — [Old Aberdeen] ([Edward Wright Building, Dunbar St., Old Aberdeen AB9 2TY]) : [Department of Political Economy, University of Aberdeen], [1980?]. — 26leaves ; 30cm. — (Discussion paper / University of Aberdeen. Department of Political Economy, ISSN 0143-4543 ; 80-14)
Bibliography: leaf 26
Unpriced (pbk) B81-28997

339.5'0981 — Brazil. Economic growth. Econometric models

Models of growth and distribution for Brazil / Lance Taylor ... [et al.]. — New York ; Oxford : Published for the World Bank Oxford University Press, c1980. — xii,355p : ill ; 24cm. — (A World Bank research publication)
Includes bibliographies and index
ISBN 0-19-520206-6 : £10.95
ISBN 0-19-520207-4 (pbk) : £5.95
Also classified at 339.2'0981 B81-19755

340 — LAW

340 — Capitalist societies. Law. Political aspects

Mathiesen, Thomas. Law, society and political action : towards a strategy under late capitalism / Thomas Mathiesen. — London : Academic Press, 1980. — ix,323p ; 24cm. — (Law, state and society series ; 5)
Includes index
ISBN 0-12-479940-x : £17.80 : CIP rev. B80-13739

340 — Law — *Marxist viewpoints*

Pashukanis, E. B.. Law and Marxism : a general theory / Evgeny B. Pashukanis ; translated by Barbara Einhorn ; edited and introduced by Chris Arthur. — London (271 Kentish Town Rd, NW5 2JS) : Ink Links, 1978. — 195p ; 23cm
Translation of: Allgemeine Rechtslehre und Marxismus
ISBN 0-906133-04-1 : £5.95 B81-02487

340'.023 — Legal profession. Professional conduct

Hazard, Geoffrey C.. Ethics in the practice of law / Geoffrey C. Hazard, Jr. — New Haven ; London : Yale University Press, c1978. — xviii,159p ; 21cm
Includes index
ISBN 0-300-02601-3 (pbk) : £4.40 : CIP rev. B80-21577

340'.023'4 — Western Europe. Legal profession, *1450-1750*

Lawyers in early modern Europe and America / edited by Wilfrid Prest. — London : Croom Helm, c1981. — 216p : ill ; 23cm
Includes index
ISBN 0-7099-0060-0 : £12.50 B81-07128

340'.023'411 — Scotland. Legal profession — *Directories — Serials*

The **Scottish** law directory. — 1981. — Glasgow : Hodge, c1981. — [646]p in various pagings
ISBN 0-85279-091-0 : Unpriced B81-23147

340′.023′411 — Scotland. Solicitors. Complaints by clients. Adjudication by Law Society of Scotland — *Inquiry reports — Serials*

Great Britain. *Scottish Lay Observer.* Annual report of the Scottish Lay Observer. — 4th (1980). — Edinburgh : H.M.S.O, 1981. — 9p
ISBN 0-10-234281-4 : £1.60
ISSN 0140-9476 B81-34054

340′.023′42 — England. Legal profession — *Career guides*

Hogan, Brian. A career in law / by Brian Hogan. — London : Sweet & Maxwell, 1981. — vii,98p ; 18cm
Bibliography: p92-95. — Includes index
ISBN 0-421-28050-6 (pbk) : £1.95 : CIP rev. B81-14863

340′.023′42 — England. Solicitors. Complaints by clients. Adjudication. Role of Law Society — *Serials*

Annual report of the Lay Observer : laid before Parliament by the Lord High Chancellor .... — 1980. — London : H.M.S.O., [1981]. — 11p
ISBN 0-10-229181-0 : £1.90 B81-30749

340′.028′54 — Great Britain. Solicitors. Professional education. Curriculum subjects: Applications of digital computer systems in legal services

Tomorrow′s lawyers : computers and legal training : a paper prepared by the Society′s Legal Education Committee to discuss the teaching of computer applications to intending lawyers and to qualified practitioners / Society for Computers and Law. — Milton, Oxon (11 High St., Milton, Nr. Abingdon, Oxon, OX14 4ER) : Society for Computers and Law, 1981. — 7p ; 22cm
ISBN 0-906122-08-2 (pbk) : Unpriced B81-25358

340′.028′5442 — Law. Machine-readable files — *Directories*

Law databases / Online Information Centre. — London (3 Belgrave Sq., SW1X 8PL) : [The Centre], c1981. — 13p ; 30cm
Unpriced (unbound) B81-30813

340′.05 — Law — *Serials*

Current legal problems. — Vol.33 (1980). — London : Stevens & Sons, 1980. — xvii,286p
ISBN 0-420-45970-7 : Unpriced B81-04004

[Legal studies *(London : 1981)*]. Legal studies : the journal of the Society of Public Teachers of Law. — Vol.1, no.1-. — [London] : Butterworths, c1981-. — v. ; 25cm
Three issues yearly. — Continues: Journal of the Society of Public Teachers of Law
ISSN 0261-3875 = Legal studies (London. 1981) : Unpriced B81-33049

Oxford journal of legal studies. — Vol.1, no.1 (Spring 1981)-. — London : Oxford University Press on behalf of the Faculty of Law, University of Oxford, 1981-. — v. ; 23cm
Three issues yearly
ISSN 0143-6503 = Oxford journal of legal studies : £18.00 per year B81-20429

340′.07′114134 — Edinburgh. Universities: University of Edinburgh. *Faculty of Law* — *Serials*

The **Old** college times. — [No.1]-. — [Edinburgh] ([c/o Edinburgh University Students Association, Student Centre House, Bristo Sq., Edinburgh]) : [Law Students′ Council], [1981]-. — v. : ill,ports ; 30cm
ISSN 0262-0065 = Old college times : Unpriced B81-37244

340′.09 — Law. Evolution. Theories, *to ca 1900*

Stein, Peter. Legal evolution : the story of an idea / Peter Stein. — Cambridge : Cambridge University Press, 1980. — xi,131p ; 23cm
ISBN 0-521-22783-6 : £9.50 B81-25535

340′.098 — Latin America. Legal services. Foreign assistance by United States

Gardner, James A.. Legal imperialism : American lawyers and foreign aid in Latin America / James A. Gardner. — Madison ; London : University of Wisconsin Press, 1980. — xii,401p ; 22cm
Includes index
ISBN 0-299-08130-3 : £12.00 B81-25913

340.1 — LAW. PHILOSOPHY AND THEORY

340′.1 — Jurisprudence

Christie, George C.. Law, norms and authority. — London : Duckworth, Feb.1982. — [192]p
ISBN 0-7156-1593-9 : £18.00 : CIP entry B81-36225

Duncanson, Ian. Jurisprudence in a nutshell / Ian Duncanson, Geoffrey Samuel. — London : Sweet & Maxwell, 1980. — vii,84p : 2 ill ; 18cm. — (New nutshells)
Includes bibliographies and index
ISBN 0-421-27310-0 (pbk) : £1.50 : CIP rev. B80-13277

Harris, J. W. (James William). Legal philosophies / by J.W. Harris. — London : Butterworths, 1980. — x,282p ; 22cm
Includes bibliographies and index
ISBN 0-406-59361-2 (pbk) : £5.95 B81-19788

340′.1 — Law — *Philosophical perspectives*

Lloyd of Hampstead, Dennis Lloyd, *Baron.* The idea of law / Dennis Lloyd. — Repr. with revisions. — Harmondsworth : Penguin, 1981. — 365p ; 20cm. — (Pelican books)
Originally published: 1964. — Bibliography: p360. — Includes index
ISBN 0-14-020688-4 (pbk) : £2.95 B81-40472

340′.109 — Jurisprudence. Theories of Hart, H. L. A.

MacCormick, Neil. H.L.A. Hart / Neil MacCormick. — London : Edward Arnold, 1981. — 184p ; 22cm. — (Jurists)
Includes index
ISBN 0-7131-6333-x (cased) : Unpriced : CIP rev.
ISBN 0-7131-6334-8 (pbk) : £4.95 B81-09973

340′.109 — Jurisprudence. Theories of Hume, David & Smith, Adam, *1723-1790*

Haakonssen, Knud. The science of a legislator : the natural jurisprudence of David Hume and Adam Smith / Knud Haakonssen. — Cambridge : Cambridge University Press, 1981. — vii,240p : ill ; 24cm
Bibliography: p227-229. — Includes index
ISBN 0-521-23891-9 : £17.50 : CIP rev. B81-22655

340′.109 — Law. Theories of Marx, Karl & Engels, Friedrich

Phillips, Paul. Marx and Engels on law and laws / Paul Phillips. — Oxford : Robertson, 1980. — xiii,238p ; 23cm. — (Law in society series)
Bibliography: p225-238
ISBN 0-85520-355-2 (cased) : £15.00 : CIP rev.
ISBN 0-85520-356-0 (pbk) : £5.25 B80-11798

340′.11 — Law. Role of justice

Convocation lectures [given at] the New University of Ulster / by Ralf Dahrendorf, Sir Edward Britton, Lord Justice Megaw. — [Coleraine] : New University of Ulster, 1979. — 51p ; 22cm
Unpriced (pbk)
Primary classification 327 B81-14141

340′.112 — Obligations: Duties. Law — *Festschriften*

Fundamental duties : a volume of essays by present and former members of the Law Faculty of the University of Exeter to commemorate the Silver Jubilee of the University / edited by D. Lasok ; with a foreword by Lord Denning of Whitchurch. — Oxford : Pergamon, 1980. — 269p : 1ill ; 26cm. — (Pergamon international library)
ISBN 0-08-024048-8 (cased) : £12.50 : CIP rev.
ISBN 0-08-024049-6 (pbk) : £4.95 B80-23092

340′.115 — Law. Economic aspects

The **Economic** approach to law. — London : Butterworths, Aug.1981. — [336]p
ISBN 0-408-10686-7 (cased) : £18.00 : CIP entry
ISBN 0-408-10685-9 (pbk) : £8.95 B81-16929

Oliver, J. M.. Law and economics : an introduction / J.M. Oliver. — London : Allen & Unwin, 1979. — 108p ; 23cm. — (Economics and society series ; no.7)
Includes index
ISBN 0-04-330297-1 (cased) : £7.95 : CIP rev.
ISBN 0-04-330298-x (pbk) : £3.50 B79-31624

340′.115 — Law. Economic aspects — *Serials*

International review of law and economics. — Vol.1, no.1 (June 1981)-. — Sevenoaks : Butterworths, 1981-. — v. ; 25cm
Two issues yearly
ISSN 0144-8188 = International review of law and economics : £25.00 per year B81-38193

340′.115 — Law. Social aspects

Law and social control / edited by Eugene Kamenka and Alice Erh-Soon Tay. — London : Edward Arnold, 1980. — ix,198p ; 23cm. — (Ideas and ideologies)
Includes index
ISBN 0-7131-6175-2 (cased) : £8.95 : CIP rev.
ISBN 0-7131-6176-0 (pbk) : £4.95 B80-18631

340′.115 — Law — *Sociological perspectives*

Black, Donald, *1941-.* The behaviour of Law / Donald Black. — New York ; London : Academic Press, [1980], c1976. — xi,175kp ; 23cm
Bibliography: p139-164. — Includes index
ISBN 0-12-102652-3 (pbk) : £3.80 B81-06186

Sociological approaches to law / edited by Adam Podgórecki and Christopher J. Whelan. — London : Croom Helm, c1981. — 251p ; 23cm
Includes bibliographies and index
ISBN 0-7099-2701-0 : £12.95 : CIP rev. B81-14814

Vago, Steven. Law and society / Steven Vago. — Englewood Cliffs ; London : Prentice-Hall, c1981. — xi,372p ; 24cm
Includes bibliographies and index
ISBN 0-13-526483-9 : £13.25 B81-27781

340′.115 — Law — *Sociological perspectives — Conference proceedings*

Law, state and society / edited by Bob Fryer ... [et al.]. — London : Croom Helm, c1981. — 234p ; 23cm. — (Explorations in sociology)
Conference papers. — Includes bibliographies and index
ISBN 0-7099-1004-5 : £14.95 B81-18829

340′.115 — United States. Law. Economic aspects — *Conference proceedings*

Lexeconics : the interaction of law and economics / Gerald Sirkin editor. — Boston ; London : Nijhoff, c1981. — 271p ; 24cm. — (Social dimensions of economics ; v.2)
Conference papers
ISBN 0-89838-053-7 : Unpriced B81-17108

340′.115′0942 — England. Law — *Sociological perspectives*

Essays in law and society / edited by Zenon Bankowski and Geoff Mungham. — London : Routledge & Kegan Paul, 1980. — vii,207p ; 24cm
Includes bibliographies and index
ISBN 0-7100-0489-3 (pbk) : £6.50 : CIP rev. B80-18632

Roshier, Bob. Law and society in England / Bob Roshier and Harvey Teff. — London : Tavistock Publications, 1980. — 258p ; 23cm
Bibliography: p226-242. - Includes index
ISBN 0-422-76720-4 (cased) : £1.00 : CIP rev.
ISBN 0-422-76730-1 (pbk) : £4.95 B80-11357

340′.1′9 — Law. Applications of psychology

Robinson, Daniel N.. Psychology and law : can justice survive the social sciences? / Daniel N. Robinson. — New York ; Oxford University Press, 1980. — viii,221p ; 22cm
Bibliography: p215-216. — Includes index
ISBN 0-19-502725-6 (cased) : £8.50 B81-17063

340.3 — LAW REFORM

340′.3′06042 — England. Law. Reform. Organisations: Haldane Society of Socialist Lawyers, *to 1980*

Haldane Society of Socialist Lawyers. Wigs and workers : a history of the Haldane Society of Socialist Lawyers 1930-1980 / Nick Blake and Harry Rajak. — London (17 Parkfield Rd., N.W.10) : The Society, 1980. — 79p : ill,facsims ; 21cm
£1.50 (pbk) B81-18816

340′.3′0941 — Great Britain. Law. Reform. Social aspects

McGregor, O. R.. Social history and law reform / by O.R. Mcgregor. — London : Stevens, 1981. — x,66p ; 19cm. — (The Hamlyn lectures ; 31st series)
Includes index
ISBN 0-420-45920-0 (cased) : £9.50
ISBN 0-420-45930-8 (pbk) : £4.25 B81-33081

340′.3′09411 — Scotland. Law. Reform — *Statutes*

Great Britain. [Law Reform (Miscellaneous Provisions) (Scotland) Act 1980]. Law Reform (Miscellaneous Provisions) (Scotland) Act 1980 : Chapter 55. — London : H.M.S.O., [1980]. — ii,27p ; 25cm
ISBN 0-10-545580-6 (unbound) : £2.40
B81-04418

340′.3′0942 — Great Britain. ***Law Commission*** — *Serials*

Great Britain. *Law Commission.* Annual report / Law Commission. — 15th (1979-1980). — London : H.M.S.O., 1981. — v,54p
ISBN 0-10-216181-x : £3.90 B81-20304

340′.3′0952 — Japan. Law. Reform, *1867-1881*

Ch′en, Paul Heng-chao. The formation of the early Meiji legal order. — Oxford : Oxford University Press, Dec.1981. — [240]p. — (London oriental series ; v.35)
ISBN 0-19-713601-x : £12.00 : CIP entry
B81-31742

340.5 — SYSTEMS OF LAW

340.5′5 — Europe. Law, *ca 800-1500* — *Festschriften*

Authority and power : studies on medieval law and government presented to Walter Ullmann on his seventieth birthday / edited by Brian Tierney and Peter Linehan. — Cambridge : Cambridge University Press, 1980. — x,274p,[1]leaf of plates : 1port ; 24cm
Bibliography: p255-274
ISBN 0-521-22275-3 : £25.00
Also classified at 303.3′6 B81-03396

340.5′9 — Islamic law

Murad, Khurram. Sharī'ah : the way to God. — Leicester (223 London Road, Leicester LE2 1ZE) : Islamic Foundation, Sept.1981. — [24]p
ISBN 0-86037-098-4 (pbk) : £0.50 : CIP entry
B81-28050

Murad, Khurram. Sharī'ah : the way of justice. — Leicester (223 London Road, Leicester LE2 1ZE) : Islamic Foundation, Sept.1981. — [24]p
ISBN 0-86037-099-2 (pbk) : £0.50 : CIP entry
B81-28368

340.9 — CONFLICT OF LAWS

340.9 — Conflict of laws — *Treaties*

Hague Conference on Private International Law *(14th : 1980).* Final act of the Fourteenth Session of the Hague Conference on Private International Law including draft conventions and decisions, The Hague, 25 October 1980. — London : H.M.S.O., [1981]. — 41p : forms ; 25cm. — (Cmnd. ; 8281) (Miscellaneous ; no.14 (1981))
ISBN 0-10-182810-1 (unbound) : £3.00
B81-33357

340.9′17 — Europe. Illegitimacy — *Treaties*

European Convention on the Legal Status of Children born out of Wedlock : Strasbourg, 15 October 1975. — London : H.M.S.O., [1981]. — 7p ; 25cm. — (Treaty series ; no.43 (1981)) (Cmnd. ; 8287)
'... Previously published as Miscellaneous no.2 (1976) Cmnd.6358'
ISBN 0-10-182870-5 (unbound) : £1.10
B81-34451

340.9′77 — Western Europe. Foreign debts. Payment. Location. Treaties: European convention on the place of payment of money liabilities — *Inquiry reports*

Great Britain. *Law Commission.* Private international law : Council of Europe conventions on foreign money liabilities (1967) and on the place of payment of money liabilities (1972) : report on a reference under section 3(1)(e) of the Law Commission Act 1965 / The Law Commission and the Scottish Law Commission. — London : H.M.S.O., [1981]. — iv,54p ; 25cm. — (Law Com. ; no.109) (Scot. Law Com. ; no.66) (Cmnd. ; 8318)
Includes the texts of the conventions
ISBN 0-10-183180-3 (pbk) : £3.60
Primary classification 340.9′77 B81-36471

340.9′77 — Western Europe. Foreign debts. Treaties: European convention on foreign money liabilities — *Inquiry reports*

Great Britain. *Law Commission.* Private international law : Council of Europe conventions on foreign money liabilities (1967) and on the place of payment of money liabilities (1972) : report on a reference under section 3(1)(e) of the Law Commission Act 1965 / The Law Commission and the Scottish Law Commission. — London : H.M.S.O., [1981]. — iv,54p ; 25cm. — (Law Com. ; no.109) (Scot. Law Com. ; no.66) (Cmnd. ; 8318)
Includes the texts of the conventions
ISBN 0-10-183180-3 (pbk) : £3.60
Also classified at 340.9′77 B81-36471

341 — INTERNATIONAL LAW

341 — International law

Merrills, J. G.. Anatomy of international law : a study of the role of international law in the contemporary world / by J.G. Merrills. — 2nd ed. — London : Sweet and Maxwell, 1981. — xv,146p ; 19cm. — (Modern legal studies)
Previous ed.: 1976. — Bibliography: p137-141. — Includes index
ISBN 0-421-28010-7 (cased) : £9.85 : CIP rev.
ISBN 0-421-28020-4 (pbk) : £6.00 B81-09506

Von Glahn, Gerhard. Law among nations : an introduction to public international law / Gerhard von Glahn. — 4th ed. — New York : Macmillan ; London : Collier Macmillan, c1981. — xv,810p ; 25cm
Previous ed.: 1976. — Includes bibliographies and index
ISBN 0-02-423160-6 : £15.95 B81-25987

341′.026 — Treaties, *1850-1980* — *Collections*

Degenhardt, Henry W.. Treaties and alliances of the world. — 3rd ed. — London : Longman, Oct.1981. — [450]p. — (Keesing′s reference publications)
Previous ed.: 1974
ISBN 0-582-90250-9 : £25.00 : CIP entry
B81-27998

341′.02644 — European Community — *Treaties* — *Collections*

Sweet & Maxwell′s European Community treaties : including the European Communities Act 1972 / edited by Sweet & Maxwell′s legal editorial staff ; advisory editor K.R. Simmonds. — 4th ed. — London : Sweet & Maxwell, 1980. — xvi,410p ; 25cm
Previous ed.: 1977
ISBN 0-421-27210-4 (cased) : £11.50 : CIP rev.
ISBN 0-421-27220-1 (pbk) : £8.50 B80-13278

341′.0268 — International law — *Cases*

International law reports. — Vol.58. — Cambridge (P.O. Box 15, Cambridge CB3 9BP) : Grotius. — xvi,738p ; 23cm
Includes index
ISBN 0-906496-07-1 : Unpriced
ISSN 0309-0671 B81-14317

341′.0268 — International law — *Cases* — *Serials*

International law reports. — Vol.59. — Cambridge (PO Box 115, Cambridge CB3 9BP) : Grotius Publications, 1980. — xxxiv,610p
ISBN 0-906496-08-x : Unpriced
ISSN 0309-0671 B81-32889

International law reports. — Vol.60. — Cambridge (P.O. Box 115, Cambridge CB3 9BP) : Grotius, c1981. — xxxv,698p
ISBN 0-906496-09-8 : Unpriced
ISSN 0309-0671 B81-36296

341′.03′31 — International law — *German & English dictionaries*

Gilbertson, Gerard. Harrap′s German and English glossary of terms in international law / Gerard Gilbertson. — London : Harrap, 1980. — xi,355p ; 24cm
ISBN 0-245-53524-1 : £25.00 B81-08113

341′.05 — International law — *Serials*

The British year book of international law. — 51st (1980). — Oxford : Clarendon, Dec.1981. — [420]p
ISBN 0-19-825386-9 : £35.00 : CIP entry
B81-31739

341′.094 — European Community. Law

Hartley, T. C.. The foundations of European Community law : an introduction to the constitutional and administrative law of the European Community / by T.C. Hartley. — Oxford : Clarendon, 1981. — xxxiv,551p : ill ; 23cm. — (Clarendon law series)
Includes bibliographies and index
ISBN 0-19-876081-7 (cased) : £20.00 : CIP rev.
ISBN 0-19-876082-5 (pbk) : Unpriced
B81-13792

Mathijsen, P. S. R. F.. A guide to European Community law / by P.S.R.F. Mathijsen ; preface by J.D.B. Mitchell. — 3rd ed. — London : Sweet & Maxwell, 1980. — xxxiii,256p ; 23cm
Previous ed.: 1975. — Includes index
ISBN 0-421-25900-0 (cased) : £12.95 : CIP rev.
ISBN 0-421-25910-8 (pbk) : £9.75 B80-13279

Plender, Richard. A practical introduction to European Community law / by Richard Plender. — London : Sweet & Maxwell, 1980. — xxiii,166p ; 22cm
Bibliography: p147-163. - Includes index
ISBN 0-421-25270-7 (pbk) : £6.25 : CIP rev.
B80-35855

Usher, J. A.. European Community law and national law : the irreversible transfer? / John Usher. — London : University Association for Contemporary European Studies, 1981. — 96p ; 23cm. — (Studies on contemporary Europe ; 3)
Bibliography: p85-91. - Includes index
ISBN 0-04-341017-0 : £6.95
ISBN 0-04-341018-9 (pbk) : Unpriced
B81-16030

341′.094 — European Community. Law — *Collections*

Cases and materials on the law of the European Communities / [compiled by] Richard Plender and John Usher ; with a foreword by Lord Mackenzie Stuart. — London : Macmillan, 1980. — xxxv,457p ; 25cm
Includes bibliographies and index
ISBN 0-333-23144-9 (cased) : £25.00 : CIP rev.
ISBN 0-333-23145-7 (pbk) : £15.00 B79-27131

341′.094 — European Community. Law. Secondary legislation — *Inquiry reports*

Great Britain. *Parliament. House of Commons. Select Committee on European Legislation, &c.* . Thirtieth report from the Select Committee on European Legislation, &c. : together with the proceedings of the Committee : session 1980-81 : documents considered by the Committee including: (Restructuring of the Community budget (Com(81)300) †, sheepmeat regime: variable premiums and ′claw back′ (7538/81). — London : H.M.S.O., [1981]. — 19p ; 25cm
ISBN 0-10-008491-5 (unbound) : £2.10
B81-40608

341'.094 — European Community. Law. Secondary legislation — *Inquiry reports* *continuation*

Great Britain. *Parliament. House of Commons. Select Committee on European Legislation, &c.* . Thirty-first report from the Select Committee on European Legislation, &c. : together with the proceedings of the Committee : session 1980-81 : documents considered by the Committee including : steel industry (7847/81), fishing agreement with Norway, 1981. — London, [1981]. — 13p ; 25cm. — (HC ; 32-xxxi)
ISBN 0-10-008661-6 (unbound) : £1.90 B81-40913

Great Britain. *Parliament. House of Commons. Select Committee on European Legislation, &c.* . Twenty-fifth report from the Select Committee on European Legislation, &c. : together with the proceedings of the Committee, session 1980-81 : documents considered by the Committee including - inter-regional air services (11859-80), asbetos (5682/80, 9953/80), new information technologies (9361/80), health problems affecting trade in fresh poultry meat (5704/81). — London : H.M.S.O., [1981]. — 21p ; 25cm. — (HC ; 32-xxv)
ISBN 0-10-298381-x (pbk) : £2.10 B81-39981

Great Britain. *Parliament. House of Commons. Select Committee on European Legislation, &c.* . Twenty-fourth report from the Select Committee on European Legislation, &c. : together with the proceedings of the Committee, session 1980-81 : documents considered by the Committee including : company law: interim reporting (4356/79, 8286/80). — London : H.M.S.O., [1981]. — 21p ; 25cm. — (HC ; 32-xxiv)
ISBN 0-10-296381-9 (pbk) : £2.10 B81-39920

Great Britain. *Parliament. House of Commons. Select Committee on European Legislation, etc.* . Eighteenth report from the Select Committee on European Legislation, etc., session 1980-81 : together with the proceedings of the committee : documents considered by the committee. — London : H.M.S.O., [1980]. — 20p ; 25cm. — (HC32 ; xviii)
ISBN 0-10-288281-9 (pbk) : £2.10 B81-35677

Great Britain.. *Parliament. House of Commons. Select Committee on European Legislation, etc.* . Fifteenth report from the Select Committee on European Legislation, etc., session 1980-81 : together with the minutes of the evidence taken on 11th March 1981 : agricultural proposals 1981/82 (5091/81) : agricultural markets 1980 (5191/81) : Special aid for Ireland in the livestock sector. — London : H.M.S.O., [1980]. — 23p ; 25cm. — (HC32 ; xv) (HC208 ; ii)
ISBN 0-10-284881-5 (pbk) : £3.00 B81-35394

Great Britain. *Parliament. House of Commons. Select Committee on European Legislation, etc.* . Fourteenth report from the Select Committee on European Legislation, etc. session 1980-81 : together with the minutes of the evidence taken on 4th March 1981 and the proceedings of the Committee : commission reflections on the Common Agricultural Policy (12271/80). — London : H.M.S.O., [1981]. — xvi,14p ; 25cm. — (HC 32 ; xiv) (HC 208 ; i)
ISBN 0-10-283081-9 (pbk) : £2.40 B81-36256

Great Britain. *Parliament. House of Commons. Select Committee on European Legislation, etc.* . Nineteenth report from the Select Committee on European Legislation, etc., session 1980-81 : together with the proceedings of the committee : documents considered by the committee. — London : H.M.S.O., [1980]. — 15p ; 25cm. — (HC32 ; xix)
ISBN 0-10-289281-4 (pbk) : £1.70 B81-34826

Great Britain. *Parliament. House of Commons. Select Committee on European Legislation, etc.* . Seventh report from the Select Committee on European Legislation, &c. : together with the proceedings of the Committee, session 1980-81. — London : H.M.S.O., [1981]. — 24p ; 25cm. — (HC ; 32-vii)
ISBN 0-10-274981-7 (unbound) : £2.40 B81-13638

Great Britain. *Parliament. House of Commons. Select Committee on European Legislation, etc.* . Sixteenth report from the Select Committee on European Legislation, etc., session 1980-81 : together with the proceedings of the committee : documents considered by the committee including : Proprietary medicinal products parallel importing (7583/80), insurance contracts (8144/79) (4124/81). — London : H.M.S.O., [1980]. — 22p ; 25cm. — (HC32 ; xvi)
ISBN 0-10-284781-9 (pbk) : £2.10 B81-36320

Great Britain. *Parliament. House of Commons. Select Committee on European Legislation, etc.* . Thirteenth report from the Select Committee on European Legislation, etc., session 1980-81 : together with the proceedings of the committee : documents considered by the committee. — London : H.M.S.O., [1980]. — 13p ; 25cm. — (HC32 ; xiii)
ISBN 0-10-282081-3 (pbk) : £1.70 B81-34923

Great Britain. *Parliament. House of Commons. Select Committee on European Legislation, etc.* . Twentieth report from the Select Committee on European Legislation, etc., session 1980-81 : together with the proceedings of the committee : documents considered by the committee. — London : H.M.S.O., [1980]. — 14p ; 25cm. — (HC. ; 52 -xx)
ISBN 0-10-289381-0 (pbk) : £1.70 B81-34975

Great Britain. *Parliament. House of Commons. Select Committee on European Legislation, etc.* . Twenty-first report from the Select Committee on European Legislation, etc., session 1980-81 : together with the proceedings of the Committee : documents considered by the Committee including : Swedish vessels fishing in member states' waters : Faroese vessels fishing in member states' waters. — London : H.M.S.O., [1980]. — 21p ; 25cm. — (HC32 ; xxi)
ISBN 0-10-292681-6 (pbk) : £2.10 B81-35395

Great Britain. *Parliament. House of Commons. Select Committee on European Legislation, etc.* . Twenty-second report from the Select Committee on European Legislation, &c. : together with the proceedings of the Committee, session 1980-81 : documents considered by the Committee including: Total allowable catches, 1981 (6021/81). — London : H.M.S.O., [1981]. — 21p ; 25cm. — (HC ; 32-xxii)
ISBN 0-10-294081-9 (pbk) : £2.10 B81-35397

Great Britain. *Parliament. House of Commons. Select Committee on European Legislation, etc.* . Twenty-third report from the Select Committee on European Legislaton, &c. : together with the proceedings of the Committee, session 1980-81 : documents considered by the Committee including: Motor vehicle insurance (9747/80), Standing Veterinary Committee (6497/80), Asbestos (5682/80). — London : H.M.S.O., [1981]. — 20p ; 25cm. — (HC ; 32-xxii)
ISBN 0-10-294881-x (pbk) : £2.10 B81-35396

341'.094 — European Economic Community. Law

Parry, Anthony. EEC law. — 2nd ed. — London : Sweet & Maxwell, Sept.1981. — [500]p
Previous ed.: 1973
ISBN 0-421-26090-4 (cased) : £21.00 : CIP entry
ISBN 0-421-26100-5 (pbk) : £14.00 B81-23772

341.2 — INTERNATIONAL LEGAL ORGANISATIONS

341.2 — Intergovernmental organisations. Constitutions — *Collections*

International governmental organizations : constitutional documents / [edited] by Amos J. Peaslee. — Rev. 3rd ed. / prepared by Dorothy Peaslee Xydis. — The Hague ; London : Nijhoff
Previous ed.: i.e. Rev. 2nd ed. in 2 v. / prepared by the editor and Dorothy Peaslee Xydis. 1961
Pt.3 and Pt.4: Education, Culture, Copyright, Science, Health. — 1979. — xl,616p ; 25cm
Includes index
ISBN 90-247-2087-7 : Unpriced B81-16612

341.23 — International law. Role of United Nations

Bokor-Szegő, Hanna. The role of the United Nations in international legislation / by Hanna Bokor-Szegő ; [translated by Sándor Simon]. — Amsterdam ; Oxford : North-Holland, 1978. — 191p ; 25cm
Translation of: Az ENSZ helye a nemzetközi jogalkotásban. — Bibliography: p183-187. — Includes index
ISBN 0-444-85041-4 : Unpriced B81-10113

341.23 — United Nations — *For children*

Schofield, Victoria. The United Nations : people, politics and powers / Victoria Schofield. — Hove : Wayland, 1979. — 95p : ill,maps,ports ; 23cm
Bibliography: p93. — Includes index
ISBN 0-85340-656-1 : £4.50 B81-12296

341.23'09 — United Nations, *to 1979*

Holmes, John W.. The changing pattern of international institutions / by J.W. Holmes. — [Leeds] : Leeds University Press, 1980. — 24p ; 21cm. — (The thirty-fifth Montague Burton lecture on international relations)
£1.00 (pbk) B81-13959

341.24'09171'7 — Sovet ékonomicheskoĭ vzaimopomoshchi. Organisation structure

Schiavone, Giuseppe. The institutions of Comecon / Giuseppe Schiavone. — London : Macmillan, 1981. — 260p ; 23cm
Bibliography: p187-246. — Includes index
ISBN 0-333-28302-3 : £20.00 : CIP rev. B80-18628

341.24'22 — European Community

Rutherford, Malcolm. Can we save the Common Market?. — Oxford : Blackwell, Nov.1981. — [120]p. — (Mainstream series)
ISBN 0-631-12933-2 : £6.50 : CIP entry B81-30172

. The state of the union of Europe : report of the CADMOS Group to the European people / edited by Denis De Rougemont ; translated by V. Ionescu. — Oxford : Pergamon, 1979. — viii,100p ; 22cm
ISBN 0-08-024483-1 (cased) : £6.25 : CIP rev.
ISBN 0-08-024476-9 (pbk) : Unpriced B81-12270

341.24'22 — European Community. Political institutions

Henig, Stanley. Power and decision in Europe : v the political institutions of the European Community / Stanley Henig. — London : Europotentials, 1980. — 156p ; 23cm
Bibliography: p126-128. - Includes index
ISBN 0-906039-01-0 : £8.95 : CIP rev. B80-19664

341.24'22 — European Community. Pressure groups

Kirchner, Emil. The role of interest groups in the European Community. — Farnborough, Hants. : Gower, Aug.1981. — [182]p
ISBN 0-566-00257-4 : £10.00 : CIP entry B81-16365

341.24'22 — European Economic Community

Swann, Dennis. The economics of the Common Market / Dennis Swann. — 4th ed., reprinted with revisions and addendum. — Harmondsworth : Penguin, 1981. — 352p : ill ; 18cm. — (Penguin modern economics texts) (Penguin education)
Previous ed.: 1976. — Bibliographies: p335-342 . — Includes index
ISBN 0-14-080189-8 (pbk) : £2.95 B81-25441

341.24'22 — European Parliament

Palmer, Michael, *1933 Feb.2-*. The European Parliament : what it is, what it does, how it works / by Michael Palmer. — Oxford : Pergamon, 1981. — viii,222p,[1]leaf of plates : ill ; 22cm. — (Pergamon international library)
ISBN 0-08-024536-6 (cased) : Unpriced : CIP rev.
ISBN 0-08-024535-8 (pbk) : £4.50 B81-07950

341.24'22 — European Parliament — *For personnel of Confederation of British Industry*

The European Parliament and the CBI : a brief guide for CBI regional offices and their EP linkmen. — London : Confederation of British Industry, 1980. — 28p ; 30cm
£1.50 (pbk) B81-15690

341.24′22′024657 — European Community — *For accounting*

Evans, Dennis, *1921-*. Accountants guide to the European Communities / Dennis Evans. — Plymouth : Macdonald and Evans, 1981. — xix,361p,[1]leaf of plates : ill,maps,1port ; 24cm
Includes index
ISBN 0-7121-0156-x : £15.00 B81-17358

341.24′22′0321 — European Community — *Encyclopaedias*

Parker, Geoffrey, *1933-*. A dictionary of the European Communities / Geoffrey Parker, Brenda Parker. — London : Butterworths, 1981. — 84p ; 23cm
Bibliography: p84
ISBN 0-408-10733-2 (cased) : Unpriced : CIP rev.
ISBN 0-408-10732-4 (pbk) : Unpriced B81-31733

341.24′22′05 — European Economic Community. Policies — *For British businessmen — Serials*

Directors guide to the EEC / Institute of Directors European Association. — 1980-. — [London] ([116 Pall Mall, SW1]) : The Association, 1980-. — v. ; 30cm
Irregular
ISSN 0260-8332 = Directors guide to the EEC : £3.50 (free to Association members) B81-09201

341.24′22′05 — European Economic Community — *Serials*

[European review *(London : 1981)*]. European review / Arthur Andersen & Co. — No.1 (Jan.1981)-. — [London] ([1 Surrey St., WC2R 2PS]) : Arthur Andersen & Co, 1981-. — v. ; 30cm
Quarterly
ISSN 0261-8249 = European review (London. 1981) : Unpriced B81-33708

341.24′22′09 — European Community, *to 1981*

Tatford, Frederick A.. Ten nations — what now? : the European Community and its future / by Fredk. A. Tatford. — Eastbourne (Upperton House, The Avenue, Eastbourne, E.Sussex BN21 3YB) : Upperton Press, c1980. — 30p : ill,1 map, 2 ports ; 19cm
£0.50 (pbk) B81-05483

341.24′22′09048 — European Community, *1980*

Developments in the European Community July-December 1980. — London : H.M.S.O., [1981]. — 43p ; 25cm. — (European Communities ; no.19 (1981)) (Cmnd. ; 8195)
ISBN 0-10-181950-1 (unbound) : £3.00 B81-20656

341.24′3 — Caribbean Community, *to 1979*

Payne, Anthony, *1952-*. The politics of the Caribbean Community 1961-79 : regional integration amongst new states / Anthony Payne. — Manchester : Manchester University Press, 1980. — xi,299p : 2ill,1map ; 23cm
Bibliography: p290-291. - Includes index
ISBN 0-7190-0793-3 : £17.50 : CIP rev. B80-05853

341.24′9 — Organization of African Unity, *to 1980*

Mbuyinga, Elenga. Pan-Africanism or neo-colonialism. — London : Zed Press, Jan.1982. — [240]p
ISBN 0-86232-076-3 (cased) : £16.95 : CIP entry
ISBN 0-86232-013-5 (pbk) : £4.95 B81-37538

341.3 — RELATIONS BETWEEN STATES. DIPLOMACY AND TREATIES

341.3′3 — Great Britain. Foreign diplomatic service — *Serials*

At the Court of St. James′s. — 1980. — London (58 Theobalds Rd, W.C.1) : Diplomatist Associates Limited, 1980. — 120p
£5.00 B81-32896

341.4 — JURISDICTION AND JURISDICTIONAL RELATIONS OF STATES

341.4′09 — Territorial claims. Disputes, *to 1979*

Downing, David. An atlas of territorial and border disputes / David Downing. — London : New English Library, c1980. — 121p : ill,col.maps ; 24cm
Col maps on lining papers. — Bibliography: p116. — Includes index
ISBN 0-450-04804-7 : £7.95 B81-03205

341.42 — Antarctic. International law. Political aspects

Auburn, F. M.. Antarctic law and politics. — London : C. Hurst, Dec.1981. — [384]p
ISBN 0-905838-39-4 : £16.50 : CIP entry B81-33875

341.4′2 — Egypt. Gaza Strip. Territorial claims by Palestinian Arabs

Hassan ibn Talal, *Crown Prince of Jordan*. Palestinian self-determination : a study of the West Bank and Gaza Strip / Hassan bin Talal, Crown Prince of Jordan. — London : Quartet, 1981. — 138p,[16]p of plates : ill,2facsims,maps,ports ; 24cm
ISBN 0-7043-2312-5 : £6.95
Also classified at 341.4′2 B81-28936

341.4′2 — Jordan. West Bank. Territorial claims by Palestinian Arabs

Hassan ibn Talal, *Crown Prince of Jordan*. Palestinian self-determination : a study of the West Bank and Gaza Strip / Hassan bin Talal, Crown Prince of Jordan. — London : Quartet, 1981. — 138p,[16]p of plates : ill,2facsims,maps,ports ; 24cm
ISBN 0-7043-2312-5 : £6.95
Primary classification 341.4′2 B81-28936

341.4′4′0916535 — Persian Gulf. International law

Amin, S. H.. International and legal problems of the Gulf / by S.H. Amin. — London (Gallipoli House, Ontwell, Wisbech, Cambridgeshire PE14 8TN) : Middle East and North African Studies Press, 1981. — 235p : maps ; 22cm
Bibliography: p225-228. — Includes index
ISBN 0-906559-05-7 : £16.50 B81-31672

341.4′48 — Persian Gulf. Coastal waters. Territorial claims by Iran & Saudi Arabia. International legal aspects

MacDonald, Charles G.. Iran, Saudi Arabia and the law of the sea : political interaction and legal development in the Persian Gulf / Charles G. MacDonald. — Westport, Conn. ; London : Greenwood Press, 1980. — xv,226p : maps ; 22cm. — (Contributions in political science, ISSN 0147-1066 ; no.48)
Bibliography: p207-218. — Includes index
ISBN 0-313-20768-2 : £18.50 B81-23474

341.4′5 — Oceans. International law. Policies of American government, *1945-1980*

Hollick, Ann L.. U.S. foreign policy and the law of the sea / Ann L. Hollick. — Princeton ; Guildford, Surrey : Princeton University Press, c1981. — xii,496p : 1ill ; 25cm
Bibliography: p483-488. — Includes index
ISBN 0-691-09387-3 (cased) : £18.80
ISBN 0-691-10114-0 (pbk) : Unpriced B81-29033

341.4′7 — Outer space. International law

Reijnen, Gijsbertha Cornelia Maria. Utilization of outer space and international law / Gijsbertha C.M. Reijnen. — Amsterdam ; Oxford : Elsevier Scientific, 1981. — xvi,179p : ill ; 25cm
Bibliography: p169-171. — Includes index
ISBN 0-444-41965-9 : Unpriced : CIP rev. B81-07449

341.4′81 — Human rights. International legal aspects — *Conference proceedings*

Development, human rights and the rule of law. — Oxford : Pergamon, Oct.1981. — [240]p
Conference papers
ISBN 0-08-028921-5 (cased) : £9.00 : CIP entry
ISBN 0-08-028951-7 (pbk) : £3.75 B81-31955

341.4′81 — Western Europe. Human rights. International law. Treaties: European Convention on Human Rights — *Critical studies*

Beddard, Ralph. Human rights and Europe : a study of the machinery of human rights protection of the Council of Europe / by Ralph Beddard. — 2nd ed. — London : Sweet & Maxwell, 1980. — vii,217p ; 20cm. — (Modern legal studies)
Previous ed.: 1973. — Bibliography: p212. - Includes index
ISBN 0-421-26440-3 (cased) : £12.00 : CIP rev.
ISBN 0-421-26450-0 (pbk) : £8.25 B80-13741

Nedjati, Zaim M.. Human rights under the European Convention / by Zaim M. Nedjati. — Amsterdam ; Oxford : North-Holland, c1978. — xviii,298p ; 23cm. — (European studies in law ; v.8)
Includes index
ISBN 0-444-85218-2 : Unpriced B81-02743

341.4′81 — Western Europe. Human rights. International law. Treaties: European Convention on Human Rights — *Serials*

Yearbook of the European Convention on Human Rights / Council of Europe. — 22 (1979). — The Hague ; London : Martinus Nijhoff, 1980. — xvii,664p
ISBN 90-247-2383-3 : Unpriced B81-06866

341.4′81 — Western Europe. Personal records. Machine-readable files. Control — *Treaties*

[Convention for the Protection of Individuals with regard to Automatic Processing of Personal Data; *1981*]. Convention for the Protection of Individuals with regard to Automatic Processing of Personal Data (with explanatory report), Strasbourg, 28 January 1981. — London : H.M.S.O., [1981]. — 33p ; 25cm. — (Cmnd. ; 8341) (Miscellaneous ; no.19 (1981))
ISBN 0-10-183410-1 (pbk) : £3.05 B81-39919

341.4′84 — Double taxation. Disputes. Arbitration

Lindencrona, Gustaf. Arbitration in taxation / Gustaf Lindencrona, Nils Mattsson. — Deventer ; London : Kluwer, c1981. — 92p ; 22cm
ISBN 90-654-4000-3 (pbk) : Unpriced B81-31422

341.4′84 — Double taxation — *Treaties between Great Britain & Canada*

Canada. [Treaties, etc. Great Britain 1978 Sept.8. Protocols, etc. 1980 Apr.15]. Convention between the Government of the United Kingdom of Great Britain and Northern Ireland and the Government of Canada for the avoidance of double taxation and the prevention of fiscal evasion with respect to taxes on income and capital gains, London, 8 September 1978 : with amending protocol, Ottawa 15 April 1980. — London : H.M.S.O., [1981]. — 54p ; 25cm. — (Treaty series ; no.36 (1981)) (Cmnd. ; 8261)
Text in English and French. — Convention previously published as: Canada No.1 (1979) Cmnd.7413 and the Protocol as: Canada No.1 (1980) Cmnd.8024
ISBN 0-10-182610-9 (unbound) : £3.40 B81-30053

341.4′84 — Double taxation — *Treaties between Great Britain & Cyprus*

Cyprus. [Treaties, etc. Great Britain, 1974 June 20. Protocols, etc., 1980 Apr.2]. Protocol between the government of the United Kingdom of Great Britain and Northern Ireland and the government of the Republic of Cyprus amending the Convention for the avoidance of double taxation and the prevention of fiscal evasion with respect to taxes on income, signed in Nicosia on 20 June 1974, Nicosia, 2 April 1980. — London : H.M.S.O., [1981]. — 3p ; 25cm. — (Treaty series ; no.18 (1981)) (Cmnd. ; 8198)
ISBN 0-10-181980-3 (unbound) : £0.70 B81-23186

341.4'84 — Double taxation — *Treaties between Great Britain & Denmark*
Denmark. [Treaties, etc. Great Britain, 1980 Nov.11]. Convention between the Government of the United Kingdom of Great Britain and Northern Ireland and the Government of the Kingdom of Denmark for the avoidance of double taxation and the prevention of fiscal evasion with respect to taxes on income and capital gains : Copenhagen, 11 November 1980. — London : H.M.S.O., [1981]. — 40p ; 25cm. — (Treaty series ; no.20 (1981)) (Cmnd. ; 8211)
Parallel English and Danish text
ISBN 0-10-182110-7 (unbound) : £3.00
B81-25239

341.4'84 — Double taxation — *Treaties between Great Britain & Finland*
Finland. [Treaties, etc. Great Britain, 1969 July 17. Protocols, etc. 1979 Nov.16]. Protocol between the Government of the United Kingdom of Great Britain and Northern Ireland and the Government of the Republic of Finland amending the Convention for the Avoidance of Double Taxation and the prevention of Fiscal Evasion with respect to Taxes on Income and Capital, signed at London on 17 July 1969 as modified by the Protocol signed at London on 17 May 1973, London, 16 November 1979. — London : H.M.S.O., [1981]. — 9p ; 25cm. — (Treaty series ; no.22 (1981)) (Cmnd. ; 8225)
Text in English and Finnish
ISBN 0-10-182250-2 (unbound) : £1.40
B81-27551

341.4'84 — Double taxation — *Treaties between Great Britain & Netherlands*
Great Britain. [Treaties, etc. Netherlands, 1980 Nov.7]. Convention between the Government of the United Kingdom of Great Britain and Northern Ireland and the Government of the Kingdom of the Netherlands for the avoidance of double taxation and the prevention of fiscal evasion with respect to taxes on income and capital gains : the Hague, 7 November 1980. — London : H.M.S.O., [1981]. — 44p ; 25cm. — (Treaty series ; no.38 (1981)) (Cmnd. ; 8268)
Parallel English and Dutch text
£3.00 (unbound) B81-33412

341.4'84 — Double taxation — *Treaties between Great Britain & Norway*
Great Britain. [Treaties, etc. Norway, 1969 Jan. 22. Protocols, etc. 1979 Oct. 16]. Protocol between the Government of the United Kingdom of Great Britain and Northern Ireland and the Government of the Kingdom of Norway, further amending the Convention for the Avoidance of Double Taxation and the Prevention of Fiscal Evasion with Respect to Taxes on Income and Capital signed at London on 22 January 1969, as amended by the protocol signed at Oslo on 29 March 1978, Oslo, 16 October 1979. — London : H.M.S.O., [1981]. — 7p ; 25cm. — (Treaty series ; no.9 (1981)) (Cmnd. ; 8153)
Text in English and Norwegian
ISBN 0-10-181530-1 (unbound) : £1.10
B81-14114

Great Britain. [Treaties, etc. Norway, 1969 Jan. 22. Protocols, etc. 1979 Oct. 16]. Protocol between the Government of the United Kingdom of Great Britain and Northern Ireland and the Government of the Kingdom of Norway, further amending the Convention for the Avoidance of Double Taxation and the Prevention of Fiscal Evasion with Respect to Taxes on Income and Capital, signed at London on 22 January 1969, as amended by the protocols signed at London on 23 June 1977, at Oslo on 19 March 1978, and at Oslo on 16 October 1979, Oslo, October 1979. — London : H.M.S.O, [1981]. — 5p ; 25cm. — (Treaty series ; no.10 (1981)) (Cmnd. ; 8154)
Text in English and Norwegian
ISBN 0-10-181540-9 (unbound) : £1.10
B81-14115

341.4'84 — Double taxation. Treaties between Great Britain & United States — *Commentaries*
Hamilton, Neil. US/UK double taxation : a comprehensive guide, including a complete analysis of the 1980 treaty / by Neil Hamilton. — London (50 Tufton St., SW1P 3RA) : Company Communications Centre, 1980. — xxiii,184p : forms ; 23cm
Includes index
ISBN 0-906609-01-1 : £15.00. B81-04662

341.4'84 — Double taxation. Treaties between Great Britain & United States — *Critical studies*
UK/US, tax planning under the treaty / edited by J.R. Dewhurst. — [London] : Oyez, [c1981]. — iv,48leaves ; 30cm
ISBN 0-85120-539-9 (spiral) : £35.00
B81-14482

341.5 — DISPUTES BETWEEN STATES

341.5'8 — Peace keeping. Role of United Nations
Verrier, Anthony. International peacekeeping : United Nations forces in a troubled world / Anthony Verrier. — Harmondsworth : Penguin, 1981. — xxxi,172p : maps ; 21cm. — (Penguin education)
Includes index
ISBN 0-14-080444-7 (pbk) : £5.95 B81-40483

341.6 — LAW OF WAR

341.6'09 — War. International law, ***1856-1981*** — *Treaties*
Documents on the laws of war. — Oxford : Clarendon Press, Dec.1981. — [432]p
ISBN 0-19-876117-1 (cased) : £18.50 : CIP entry
ISBN 0-19-876118-x (pbk) : £10.95 B81-33860

341.6'7 — Great Britain. German enemy property. Assets — *Accounts — Serials*
Great Britain. *Administrator of German Enemy Property*. Account : ... sums received and paid by the Administrator of German Enemy Property for the two years ended 31st March .... — 1978-80. — London : H.M.S.O., [1981]. — 3p
ISBN 0-10-223181-8 : £0.70 B81-28376

341.6'9 — German war criminals. Trials. Policies of Allied forces. Formulation, ***1944-1945***
Smith, Bradley F.. The road to Nuremberg / Bradley F. Smith. — London : Deutsch, 1981. — 303p ; 22cm
Bibliography: p287-290. — Includes index
ISBN 0-233-97412-1 (corrected) : £7.95
B81-38678

341.6'9 — West Germany. Nuremberg. German war criminals. Trials, ***1945-1946*** — *Personal observations*
Neave, Airey. Nuremberg : a personal record of the trial of the major Nazi war criminals in 1945-6 / Airey Neave. — London : Coronet, 1980, c1978. — 382p,[12]p of plates : ill,ports ; 18cm
Originally published: London : Hodder and Stoughton, 1978. — Includes index
ISBN 0-340-25450-5 (pbk) : £1.95 : CIP rev.
B80-07273

341.7 — INTERNATIONAL COOPERATION. LEGAL ASPECTS

341.7'28 — Trident I nuclear weapon system. Acquisition by Great Britain — *Treaties between Great Britain & United States*
Great Britain. [Treaties, etc. United States, 1980 Sept. 30]. Exchange of notes between the Government of the United Kingdom of Great Britain and Northern Ireland and the Government of the United States of America concerning the acquisition by the United Kingdom of the Trident I weapons system under the Polaris Sales Agreement, signed on 6 April 1963, Washington, 30 September 1980. — London : H.M.S.O., [1980]. — 3p ; 25cm. — (Treaty series ; no.86(1980)) (Cmnd. ; 8070)
ISBN 0-10-180700-7 (unbound) : £0.70
B81-04505

341.7'5 — European Community. Commercial law
Lasok, D.. The law of the economy in the European Communities / by D. Lasok with a chapter on agriculture by J.W. Bridge. — London : Butterworths, 1980. — xxxviii,455p ; 23cm
Bibliography: p431-442. — Includes index
ISBN 0-406-26896-7 (cased) : £18.95
ISBN 0-406-26897-5 (pbk) : £11.95 B81-05501

341.7'5 — European Community countries. Taxation. European Economic Community law
Easson, A. J.. Tax law and policy in the EEC / A. J. Easson. — London : Sweet & Maxwell, 1980. — xxi,284p ; 26cm
Bibliography: p270-276. — Includes index
ISBN 0-421-27020-9 : £20.00 B81-05264

341.7'5 — Iraq. Economic relations with Great Britain — *Treaties between Great Britain & Iraq*
Great Britain. [Treaties, etc. Iraq, 1981 June 24]. Agreement between the Government of the United Kingdom of Great Britain and Northern Ireland and the Government of the Republic of Iraq on economic and technical co-operation London, 24 June. — London : H.M.S.O., [1981]. — 5p ; 25cm. — (Cmnd. ; 8319) (Iraq ; no.1 (1981))
ISBN 0-10-183190-0 (unbound) : £1.10
B81-36713

341.7'5 — Morocco. Agricultural property of Britons. Expropriation. Compensation — *Treaties between Great Britain & Morocco*
Great Britain. [Treaties, etc. Morocco, 1981 Feb.12]. Agreement between the Government of the United Kingdom of Great Britain and Northern Ireland and the Government of the Kingdom of Morocco concerning compensation for properties transferred to the state under the Dahir of 2 March 1973. — London : H.M.S.O., 1981. — 3p ; 25cm. — (Cmnd. ; 8249) (Morocco ; no.1 (1981))
ISBN 0-10-182490-4 (unbound) : £0.70
B81-28287

341.7'5'0614 — European Economic Community. Entry of Greece — *Treatie between European Economic Community & Switzerland*
European Economic Community. [Treaties, etc. Switzerland, 1972 July 22. Protocols, etc. 1980 July 17]. Additional protocol to the Agreement between the European Economic Community and the Swiss Confederation consequent on the accession of the Hellenic Republic to the Community, Brussels, 17 July 1980. — London : H.M.S.O., [1981]. — 23p ; 23cm. — (European Communities ; no.8 (1981)) (Cmnd. ; 8146)
ISBN 0-10-181460-7 (unbound) : £2.10
B81-13645

341.7'5'0614 — European Economic Community. Entry of Greece — *Treaties between Austria & European Economic Community*
Austria. [Treaties, etc. European Economic Community, 1972 July 22. Protocols, etc. 1980 Nov.28]. Additional protocol to the agreement between the European Economic Community and the Republic of Austria consequent on the accession of the Hellenic Republic to the Community, Brussels, 28 November 1980. — London : H.M.S.O., [1981]. — 26p ; 25cm. — (European Communities ; no.22 (1981)) (Cmnd. ; 8190)
ISBN 0-10-181900-5 (unbound) : £2.40
B81-20777

341.7'5'0614 — European Economic Community. Entry of Greece — *Treaties between European Economic Community & Finland*
European Economic Community. [Treaties, etc. Finland, 1973 Oct. 5. Protocols, etc. 1980 Nov. 6]. Additional protocol to the agreement between the European Economic Community and the Republic of Finland consequent on the Accession of the Hellenic Republic to the Community, Brussels, 6 November 1980. — London : H.M.S.O., 1981. — 26p ; 25cm. — (European Communities ; no.13 (1981)) (Cmnd. ; 8159)
ISBN 0-10-181590-5 (unbound) : £2.40
B81-14318

341.7'5'0614 — European Economic Community. Entry of Greece — *Treaties between European Economic Community & Iceland*
European Economic Community. [Treaties etc. Iceland, 1972. Protocols, etc. 1980 Nov. 6]. Additional protocol to the Agreement between the European Economic Community and the Republic of Iceland consequent on the accession of the Hellenic Republic to the Community, Brussels 6 November 1980. — London : H.M.S.O., [1981]. — 23p ; 25cm. — (European Communities ; no.16 (1981)) (Cmnd. ; 8167)
ISBN 0-10-181670-7 (unbound) : £2.10
B81-13951

341.7′5′0614 — European Economic Community. Entry of Greece — *Treaties between European Economic Community & Norway*

European Economic Community. [Treaties, etc. Norway, 1973 May 14. Protocols, etc. 1980 Nov. 6]. Additional protocol to the Agreement between the European Economic Community and the Kingdom of Norway consequent on the accession of the Hellenic Republic to the Community, Brussels, 6 November 1980. — London : H.M.S.O., [1981]. — 23p ; 25cm. — (European Communities ; no.7(1981)) (Cmnd. ; 8145)
ISBN 0-10-181450-x (unbound) : £2.10
B81-14109

341.7′5′0614 — European Economic Community. Entry of Greece — *Treaties between European Economic Community & Sweden*

European Economic Community. [Treaties, etc. Sweden, 1972 Jul.22. Protocols, etc., 1980 Nov.6]. Additional protocol to the agreement between the European Economic Community and the Kingdom of Sweden consequent on the accession of the Hellenic Republic to the Community, Brussels, 6 November 1980. — London : H.M.S.O., 1981. — 25p ; 25cm. — (Cmnd. ; 8188) (European Communities ; no.21 (1981))
ISBN 0-10-181880-7 (unbound) : £2.40
B81-20994

341.7′5′0614 — Zimbabwe. Economic relations with European Economic Community — *Treaties between European Economic Community & Zimbabwe*

European Economic Community. [Treaties, ect. Zimbabwe, 1980 Nov.4]. Interim agreement between the European Economic Community and the Republic of Zimbabwe with final act, Luxembourg, 4 November 1980. — London : H.M.S.O., 1981. — 93p : forms ; 25cm. — (European Communities ; no. 26 (1981)) (Cmnd. ; 8218)
ISBN 0-10-182180-8 (pbk) : £4.60 B81-26870

341.7′51 — Finance. International law

International financial law : lending, capital transfers and institutions / edited by Robert S. Rendell. — London : Euromoney, c1980. — 319p ; 30cm
ISBN 0-903121-13-1 (pbk) : Unpriced
B81-11015

341.7′51 — International finance. International legal aspects

Wood, Philip. Law and practice of international finance / by Philip Wood. — London : Sweet & Maxwell, 1980. — xiii,462p ; 26cm
Includes index
ISBN 0-421-26410-1 : £35.00 : CIP rev.
B80-34707

341.7′51 — International giro services — *Treaties*

[Giro Agreement *(1979)*]. Giro Agreement : (together with detailed regulations), Rio de Janeiro, 26 October 1979 / Universal Postal Union. — London : H.M.S.O., [1981]. — iii,146p : forms ; 25cm. — (Cmnd. ; 8180)
French text with English translation
ISBN 0-10-181800-9 (pbk) : £6.30 B81-21886

341.7′51 — Taxation. International law

Knechtle, Arnold A.. Basic problems in international fiscal law / Arnold A. Knechtle ; translated from the German by W.E. Weisflog. — London : HFL, 1979. — xxi,264p : ill ; 23cm
Translation of: Grundfragen des Internationalen Steuerrechts erläutert an Beispielen des Internationalen Steuerrechts der Schwerz und der Bundesrepublik Deutschland. — Bibliography: p197-202. — Includes index
ISBN 0-372-30012-x : £13.50 B81-28971

341.7′52′02664105493 — Foreign investment — *Treaties between Great Britin & Sri Lanka*

Great Britain. [Treaties, etc. Sri Lanka, 1980 Feb.13]. Agreement between the Government of the United Kingdom of Great Britain and Northern Ireland and the Government of the Democratic Socialist Republic of Sri Lanka for the promotion and protection of investments, Colombo, 13 February 1980. — London : H.M.S.O., 1981. — 17p ; 25cm. — (Cmnd. ; 8186) (Treaty series ; no.14 (1981))
English and Singhalese text. — Originally published: as Sri Lanka no.1 (1980), Cmnd. 7984
ISBN 0-10-181860-2 (ubound) : Unpriced
B81-18420

341.7′52′02664105493 — Hong Kong. Extension of treaties on foreign investment between Great Britain & Sri Lanka — *Treaties between Great Britain & Sri Lanka*

Great Britain. [Treaties, etc. Sri Lanka, 1980 Feb.13. Protocols, etc. 1981 Jan.14]. Exchange of notes between the Government of the United Kingdom and Northern Ireland and the Government of the Democratic Socialist Republic of Sri Lanka concerning the extension to Hong Kong of the Agreement for the Protection and Promotion of Investments, signed at Colombo on 13 February, 1980, Colombo, 14 January 1981. — London : H.M.S.O., [1981]. — 3p ; 25cm. — (Treaty series ; no.35 (1981)) (Cmnd. ; 8253)
ISBN 0-10-182530-7 (unbound) : £0.70
B81-29009

341.7′52′0266410599 — Foreign investment — *Treaties between Great Britain & Philippines*

Great Britain. [Treaties, etc. Philippines, 1980 Dec. 3]. Agreement between the government of the United Kingdom of Great Britain and Northern Ireland and the Republic of the Philippines for the promotion and protection of investments, London, 3 December 1980. — London : H.M.S.O., 1981. — 14p ; 25cm. — (Cmnd. ; 8148) (Treaty series ; no.7 (1981))
English and Filipino text
ISBN 0-10-181480-1 (unbound) : £12.70
B81-14510

341.7′52′0266410663 — Foreign investment — *Treaties between Great Britain & Senegal*

Great Britain. [Treaties, etc. Senegal, 1980 May 7]. Agreement between the Government of the United Kingdom of Great Britain and Northern Ireland and the Government of the Republic of Senegal for the promotion and protection of investments London, 7 May 1980. — London : H.M.S.O., [1980]. — 7p ; 25cm. — (Senegal ; no.1 (1980)) (Cmnd. ; 8079)
ISBN 0-10-180790-2 (unbound) : £1.10
B81-05390

341.7′52′02664106816 — Foreign investment — *Treaties between Great Britain & Lesotho*

Great Britain. [Treaties, etc. Lesotho, 1981 Feb.18]. Agreement between the Government of the United Kingdom of Great Britain and Northern Ireland and the Government of the Kingdom of Lesotho for the promotion and protection of investments Maseru, 18 February 1981. — London : H.M.S.O., [1981]. — 7p ; 25cm. — (Treaty series ; no.31 (1981)) (Cmnd. ; 8246)
ISBN 0-10-182460-2 (unbound) : £1.10
B81-28269

341.7′52′0266410892 — Foreign investment — *Treaties between Great Britain & Paraguay*

Great Britain. [Treaties, etc. Paraguay, 1981 June 4]. Agreement between the Government of the United Kingdom of Great Britain and Northern Ireland and the Government of the Republic of Paraguay for the promotion and protection of investments, London, 4 June 1981. — 7p ; 25cm. — (Paraguay ; no.1 (1981)) (Cmnd. ; 8329)
ISBN 0-10-183290-7 (pbk) : £1.15 B81-39979

341.7′52′0266410953 — Foreign investment — *Treaties between Great Britain & Papua New Guinea*

Great Britain. [Treaties, etc. Papua New Guinea, 1981 May 14]. Agreement between the Government of the United Kingdom of Great Britain and Northern Ireland and the Government of the Independent State of Papua New Guinea for the promotion and protection of investments, London, 14 May 1981. — London : H.M.S.O., [1981]. — 7p ; 25cm. — (Papua New Guinea ; no.1 (1981)) (Cmnd. ; 8307)
ISBN 0-10-183070-x (unbound) : £1.10
B81-35386

341.7′53 — European Community countries. Industries. Competition. European Economic Community law

Kerse, C. S.. EEC antitrust procedure. — London (4 Bloomsbury Sq., WC1A 2RL) : European Law Centre, May 1981. — [320]p
ISBN 0-907451-03-9 : £34.00 : CIP entry
B81-14779

Korah, Valentine. An introductory guide to EEC competition law and practice. — 2nd ed. — Oxford (25 Beaumont St., Oxford OX1 2NP) : ESC Publishing, July 1981. — [162]p
Previous ed.: 1978
ISBN 0-906214-08-4 (pbk) : £8.75 : CIP entry
B81-21580

341.7′54 — British goods. Purchase by Honduras. Financial assistance. Loans from Great Britain — *Treaties between Great Britain & Honduras*

Great Britain. [Treaties, etc. Honduras, 1980 Sept.11]. Exchange of notes concerning an interest free loan by the Government of the United Kingdom of Great Britain and Northern Ireland to the Government of the Republic of Honduras (The United Kingdom-Honduras Loan 1980) Tegucigalpa, 11 September-24 December 1980. — London : H.M.S.O., [1980]. — 6p ; 25cm. — (Treaty series ; no.24 (1981)) (Cmnd. ; 8230)
Text in English and Spanish
ISBN 0-10-182300-2 (unbound) : £1.10
B81-27548

341.7′54 — Britons. Commercial transactions with Sierra Leoneans. Debts of Sierra Leoneans. Repayment — *Treaties between Great Britain & Sierra Leone*

Sierra Leone. [Treaties, etc. Great Britain, 1980 June 30]. Agreement between the government of the Republic of Sierra Leone and the government of the United Kingdom of Great Britain and Northern Ireland on certain commercial debts. — London : H.M.S.O., 1981. — 7p ; 25cm. — (Treaty series ; no.12 (1981)) (Cmnd. ; 8163)
ISBN 0-10-181630-8 (unbound) : £1.10
B81-14323

341.7′54 — Britons. Commercial transactions with Togolese. Debts of Togolese. Repayment — *Treaties between Britain & Togo*

Great Britain. [Treaties, etc. Togo, 1980 June 18]. Agreement between the Government of the United Kingdom of Great Britain and Northern Ireland and the Government of the Republic of Togo on certain commercial debts Lome, 18 June 1980. — London : H.M.S.O., [1980]. — 11p ; 25cm. — (Treaty series ; no.95 (1980)) (Cmnd. ; 8094)
English and French text
ISBN 0-10-180940-9 (unbound) : £1.40
B81-03897

341.7′54 — Britons. Commercial transactions with Turks. Debts of Turks. Repayment — *Treaties between Great Britain & Turkey*

Great Britain. [Treaties, etc. Turkey, 1979 Dec. 20]. Agreement between the Government of the United Kingdom of Great Britain and Northern Ireland and the Government of the Republic of Turkey on certain commercial debts Ankara, 20 December 1979. — London : H.M.S.O., [1980]. — 7p ; 25cm. — (Treaty series ; no.87 (1980)) (Cmnd. ; 8071)
Previously published: as Turkey no.1 (1980), Cmnd. 7867
ISBN 0-10-180710-4 (unbound) : £1.10
B81-02600

341.7′54 — Britons. Commercial transactions with Turks. Debts of Turks. Repayment — *Treaties between Great Britain & Turkey*

continuation

Great Britain. [Treaties, etc. Turkey, 1980, Dec.5]. Agreement between the Government of the United Kingdom of Great Britain and Northern Ireland and the Government of the Republic of Turkey on certain commercial debts, Ankara, 5 December 1980. — London : H.M.S.O., 1981. — 7p ; 25cm. — (Cmnd. ; 8189) (Turkey ; no.1 (1981))
ISBN 0-10-181890-4 (unbound) : £1.10
B81-20993

341.7′54 — European Community countries. Foreign trade with ACP countries. Treaties: ACP-EEC Convention of Lomé. Accession of Zimbabwe — *Treaties between Zimbabwe & European Economic Community*

Agreement on the accession of the Republic of Zimbabwe to the Second ACP-EEC Convention signed at Lomé on 31 October 1979 with final act, Luxembourg, 4 November 1980. — London : H.M.S.O., 1981. — 10p : ill ; 25cm. — (Cmnd. ; 8150) (European Communities ; no.9 (1981))
ISBN 0-10-181500-x (unbound) : £1.40
B81-14512

341.7′54 — Foreign trade. Dumping. Legal aspects

Dale, Richard. Anti-dumping law in a liberal trade order / Richard Dale. — London : Macmillan for the Trade Policy Research Centre, 1980. — xv,237p : ill ; 23cm
Bibliography: p225-231. — Includes index
ISBN 0-333-27650-7 : £20.00 B81-05499

341.7′54 — Foreign trade. International law

Day, D. M.. The law of international trade / by D.M. Day. — London : Butterworths, 1981. — xxii,254p,[2]p of plates : 1form ; 22cm
Includes index
ISBN 0-406-57202-x (cased) : Unpriced
ISBN 0-406-57201-1 (pbk) : Unpriced
B81-35285

341.7′54′0265 — European Economic Community. Foreign trade with Cyprus — *Treaties between Cyprus & European Economic Community*

Cyprus. [Treaties, etc. European Economic Community, 1972 Dec.19. Protocols, etc., 1980 Feb.7]. Transitional protocol to the agreement establishing an association between the European Economic Community and the Republic of Cyprus, Brussels, 7 February 1980. — London : H.M.S.O., 1981. — 3p ; 25cm. — (European Communities ; no.44 (1981)) (Cmnd. ; 8331)
ISBN 0-10-183310-5 (unbound) : £0.70
B81-38759

Cyprus. [Treaties, etc. European Economic Community, 1980 Feb.7. Protocols, etc., 1981 Mar.18]. Protocol concerning the arrangements to be applied during 1981, in the framework of the decision adopted by the Association Council on 24 November 1980 establishing the process into the second stage of the Association agreement between the European Economic Community and the Republic of Cyprus, Brussels, 18 March 1981. — London : H.M.S.O., 1981. — 3p ; 25cm. — (European Communities ; no.47 (1981)) (Cmnd. ; 8332)
ISBN 0-10-183320-2 (unbound) : £0.70
B81-38756

341.7′54′0265 — European Economic Community. Foreign trade with Israel — *Treaties between European Economic Community & Israel*

European Economic Community. [Treaties, etc. Israel, 1975 May 11. Protocols, etc., 1981 Mar.18]. Second additional protocol to the agreement between the European Economic Community and the State of Israel, Brussels, 18 March 1981. — London : H.M.S.O., 1981. — 3p ; 25cm. — (European Communities ; no.45 (1981)) (Cmnd. ; 8327)
ISBN 0-10-183270-2 (unbound) : £0.70
B81-38758

341.7′54′0265 — Romania. Foreign trade with European Economic Community — *Treaties between European Economic Community & Romania*

European Economic Community. [Treaties, etc. Romania, 1980 July 28]. Agreement between the European Economic Community and the Socialist Republic of Romania on trade in industrial products, Bucharest, 28 July 1980. — London : H.M.S.O., [1981]. — 27p ; 25cm. — (European Communities ; no.6 (1981)) (Cmnd. ; 8141)
ISBN 0-10-181410-0 (unbound) : £2.40
B81-13641

European Economic Community. [Treaties, etc. Romania, 1980 July 28]. Agreement between the European Economic Community and the Socialist Republic of Romania on the establishment of the Joint Committee, Bucharest, 28 July 1980. — London : H.M.S.O., 1981. — 3p ; 25cm. — (European Communities ; no.46 (1981)) (Cmnd. ; 8330)
ISBN 0-10-183300-8 (unbound) : £0.70
B81-38755

341.7′5471311′0265 — Foreign trade in wheat — *Treaties*

[International Wheat Agreement (1971). *Protocols, etc., 1981 Mar.24*]. Protocols for the sixth extension of the Wheat Convention, 1971 and the first extension of the Food Aid Convention, 1980, constituting the International Wheat Agreement, 1971, Washington, 24 March to 15 May 1981. — London : H.M.S.O., [1981]. — 10p ; 25cm. — (Cmnd. ; 8303) (Miscellaneous ; no.17 (1981))
ISBN 0-10-183030-0 (unbound) : £1.40
B81-35390

341.7′5471361′0265 — European Community countries. Imports from ACP countries: Cane sugar. Guaranteed prices — *Treaties between ACP countries & European Economic Community*

Agreement in the form of an exchange of letters between the European Economic Community and Barbados, the People′s Republic of the Congo, Fiji, the Co-operative Republic of Guyana, Jamaica, the Republic of Kenya, the Democratic Republic of Madagascar, the Republic of Malawi, Mauritius, the Republic of Suriname, the Kingdom of Swaziland, the United Republic of Tanzania, Trinidad and Tobago and the Republic of Uganda on the guaranteed prices for cane sugar for 1980/81, Brussels, 17 December 1980. — London : H.M.S.O., 1981. — 3p ; 25cm. — (European communities ; no.41(1981)) (Cmnd. ; 8306)
ISBN 0-10-183060-2 (unbound) : £0.70
B81-37017

341.7′5471361′0265 — European Community countries. Imports from India *(Republic)*: Cane sugar. Guaranteed prices — *Treaties between European Economic Community & India (Republic)*

European Economic Community. [Treaties, etc. India, 1980 Dec.22]. Agreement in the form of an exchange of letters between the European Economic Community and the Republic of India on the guaranteed prices for cane sugar for 1980/81, Brussels, 22 December 1980. — London : H.M.S.O., 1981. — 3p ; 25cm. — (European communities ; no.40(1981)) (Cmnd. ; 8310)
ISBN 0-10-183100-5 (unbound) : £0.70
B81-37018

341.7′5471374′0265 — Foreign trade in cocoa — *Treaties*

[International Cocoa Agreement, 1980 *(1981)*]. International Cocoa Agreement, 1980 : New York, 5 January-31 March 1981. — London : H.M.S.O., [1981]. — 42p ; 25cm. — (Cmnd. ; 8226) (Miscellaneous ; no.10 (1981))
ISBN 0-10-182260-x (unbound) : £3.00
B81-25234

341.7′54716313′0265 — European Community countries. Imports from Australia: Lamb & mutton — *Treaties between European Economic Community & Australia*

European Economic Community. [Treaties, etc. Australia, 1980 Nov.14]. Exchange of letters comprising an Agreement between the European Economic Community and Australia on trade in mutton, lamb and goatmeat, Brussels 14 November 1980. — London : H.M.S.O., 1981. — 6p ; 25cm. — (European communities ; no.25 (1981)) (Cmnd. ; 8208)
ISBN 0-10-182080-1 (unbound) : £1.10
Also classified at 341.7′547163913′0265
B81-26089

341.7′54716313′0265 — European Community countries. Imports from New Zealand: Lamb & mutton — *Treaties between European Economic Community & New Zealand*

European Economic Community. [Treaties, etc. New Zealand, 1980 Oct.17]. Exchange of letters comprising an Agreement between the European Economic Community and New Zealand on trade in mutton, lamb and goatmeat and exchange of letters comprising an Understanding relevant to clause 2 of the Agreement, Brussels, 17 October 1980. — London : H.M.S.O., 1981. — 7p ; 25cm. — (European communities ; no.24 (1981)) (Cmnd. ; no.8207)
ISBN 0-10-182070-4 (unbound) : £1.10
Also classified at 341.7′547163913′0265
B81-26088

341.7′547163913′0265 — European Community countries. Imports from Australia: Goatmeat — *Treaties between European Economic Community & Australia*

European Economic Community. [Treaties, etc. Australia, 1980 Nov.14]. Exchange of letters comprising an Agreement between the European Economic Community and Australia on trade in mutton, lamb and goatmeat, Brussels 14 November 1980. — London : H.M.S.O., 1981. — 6p ; 25cm. — (European communities ; no.25 (1981)) (Cmnd. ; 8208)
ISBN 0-10-182080-1 (unbound) : £1.10
Primary classification 341.7′54716313′0265
B81-26089

341.7′547163913′0265 — European Community countries. Imports from New Zealand: Goatmeat — *Treaties between European Economic Community & New Zealand*

European Economic Community. [Treaties, etc. New Zealand, 1980 Oct.17]. Exchange of letters comprising an Agreement between the European Economic Community and New Zealand on trade in mutton, lamb and goatmeat and exchange of letters comprising an Understanding relevant to clause 2 of the Agreement, Brussels, 17 October 1980. — London : H.M.S.O., 1981. — 7p ; 25cm. — (European communities ; no.24 (1981)) (Cmnd. ; no.8207)
ISBN 0-10-182070-4 (unbound) : £1.10
Primary classification 341.7′54716313′0265
B81-26088

341.7′547173′0265 — European Community countries. Imports from Austria: Cheeses — *Treaties between Austria & European Economic Community*

Austria. [Treaties, etc. European Economic Community, 1981 Apr.6]. Agreement in the form of an exchange of letters between Austria and the European Economic Community amending the agreement on price observance and the arrangements for the importation of certain types of cheese, Brussels, 6 April 1981. — London : H.M.S.O., [1981]. — 3p ; 25cm. — (European Communities ; no.48 (1981)) (Cmnd. ; 8340)
ISBN 0-10-183400-4 (unbound) : £0.70
B81-39921

341.7'547224'0265 — European Coal and Steel Community. Entry of Greece — *Treaties between members of European Coal and Steel Community & Austria*

Austria. [Treaties, etc. European Coal and Steel Community, 1980 Nov.28]. Additional Protocol to the agreement between the member states of the European Coal and Steel Community and the European Coal and Steel Community of the one part, and the Republic of Austria, of the other part, consequent on the accession of the Hellenic Republic to the Community with exchange of letters, Brussels, 28 November 1980. — London : H.M.S.O., 1981. — 6p ; 25cm. — (European Communities ; no.28 (1981)) (Cmnd. ; 8224)
ISBN 0-10-182240-5 (unbound) : £1.10
B81-25363

341.7'547224'0265 — European Coal and Steel Community. Entry of Greece — *Treaties between members of European Coal and Steel Community & Finland*

[Agreement between the member states of the European Coal and Steel Community and the European Coal and Steel Community, of the one part, and the Republic of Finland, of the other part (1973). *Protocols, etc. 1980 Nov. 6*]. Additional protocol to the Agreement between the member states of the European Coal and Steel Community and the European Coal and Steel community, of the one part and the Republic of Finland, of the other part, consequent on the accession of the Hellenic Republic to the Community, Brussels, 6 November 1980. — London : H.M.S.O., [1981]. — 5p ; 25cm. — (European Communities ; no.18 (1981)) (Cmnd. ; 8169)
ISBN 0-10-181690-1 (unbound) : £1.10
B81-13953

341.7'547224'0265 — European Coal and Steel Community. Entry of Greece — *Treaties between members of European Coal and Steel Community & Iceland*

[Agreement between the member states of the European Coal and Steel Community and the Republic of Iceland (1972). *Protocols, etc. 1980 Nov. 6*]. Additional protocol to the Agreement between the member states of the European Coal and Steel Community and the Republic of Iceland consequent on the accession of the Hellenic Republic to the Community, Brussels, 6 November 1980. — London : H.M.S.O., [1981]. — 3p ; 25cm. — (European Communities ; no.17 (1981)) (Cmnd. ; 8168)
ISBN 0-10-181680-4 (unbound) : £0.70
B81-13950

341.7'547224'0265 — European Coal and Steel Community. Entry of Greece — *Treaties between members of European Coal and Steel Community & Liechtenstein*

[Agreement between the member states of the European Coal and Steel Community and the Swiss Confederation (1972). *Protocols, etc. 1980 July 17*]. Supplementary protocol to the Additional agreement concerning the validity of the Principality of Liechtenstein, of the Agreement between the member states of the European Coal and Steel Community and the Swiss Confederation consequent on the accession of the Hellenic Republic to the Community, Brussels, 17 July 1980. — London : H.M.S.O., [1981]. — 3p ; 25cm. — (European Communities ; no.12 (1981)) (Cmnd. ; 8158)
ISBN 0-10-181580-8 (unbound) : £0.70
B81-13949

341.7'547224'0265 — European Coal and Steel Community. Entry of Greece — *Treaties between members of European Coal and Steel Community & Norway*

[Agreement between the member states of the European Coal and Steel Community and the European Coal and Steel Community, of the one part and the Kingdom of Norway, of the other part (1973). *Protocols, etc. 1980 Nov. 6*]. Additional protocol to the Agreement between the member states of the European Coal and Steel Community and the European Coal and Steel Community, of the one part, and the Kingdom of Norway, of the other part, consequent on the accession of the Hellenic Republic to the Community, Brussels, 6 November 1980. — London : H.M.S.O., [1981]. — 5p ; 25cm. — (European Communities ; no.14 (1981)) (Cmnd. ; 8164)
ISBN 0-10-181640-5 (unbound) : £1.10
B81-13952

341.7'547224'0265 — European Coal and Steel Community. Entry of Greece - *Treaties between members of European Coal and Steel Community & Sweden*

[Agreement between the member states of the European Coal and Steel Community and the European Coal and Steel Community, of the one part, and the Kingdom of Sweden of the other part (1972). *Protocols, etc. 1980 Nov.6*]. Additional protocol to the Agreement between the member states of the European Coal and Steel Community and the European Coal and Steel Community, of the one part, and the Kingdom of Sweden, of the other part, consequent on the accession of the Hellenic Republic to the Community, Brussels, 6 November 1980. — London : H.M.S.O., [1981]. — 5p ; 25cm. — (European Communities ; no.15 (1981)) (Cmnd. ; 8165)
ISBN 0-10-181650-2 (unbound) : £1.10
B81-13947

341.7'547224'0265 — European Coal and Steel Community. Entry of Greece — *Treaties between members of European Coal and Steel Community & Switzerland*

[Agreement between the member states of the European Coal and Steel Community and the Swiss Confederation (1972). *Protocols, etc. 1980 July 17*]. Additional protocol to the Agreement between the member states of the European Coal and Steel Community and the Swiss Confederation consequent on the accession of the Hellenic Republic to the Community, Brussels, 17 July 1980. — London : H.M.S.O., [1981]. — 5p ; 25cm. — (European Communities ; no.11 (1981)) (Cmnd. ; 8157)
ISBN 0-10-181570-0 (unbound) : £1.10
B81-13948

341.7'547224'0265 — European Community countries. Imports from Zimbabwe: Coal — *Treaties*

Agreement within the Province of the European Coal and Steel Community between the member States of the Community and the Republic of Zimbabwe, Luxembourg, 4 November 1980. — London : H.M.S.O., 1981. — 3p ; 25cm. — (Cmnd. ; 8151) (European Communities ; no.10 (1981))
ISBN 0-10-181510-7 (unbound) : £0.70
Also classified at 341.7'54756728'0265
B81-14511

341.7'5475664362'0265 — European Community countries. Imports from Algeria: Olive oil. Import duties — *Treaties between Algeria & European Economic Community*

Agreement in the form of an exchange of letters between the European Economic Community and the People's Democratic Republic of Algeria fixing the additional amount to be deducted from the levy on imports into the Community of untreated olive oil, originating in Algeria, for the period from 1 November 1980 to 31 October 1981. — London : H.M.S.O., 1981. — 3p ; 25cm. — (Cmnd. ; 8250) (European Communities ; no.29 (1981))
ISBN 0-10-182500-5 (unbound) : £0.70
B81-28286

341.7'5475664362'0265 — European Community countries. Imports from Morocco: Olive oil. Import duties — *Treaties between European Economic Community & Morocco*

Agreement in the form of an exchange of letters between the European Economic Community and the Kingdom of Morocco fixing the additional amount to be deducted from the levy on imports into the Community of untreated olive oil, originating in Morocco, for the period from 1 November 1980 to 31 October 1981. — London : H.M.S.O., 1981. — 3p ; 25cm. — (Cmnd. ; 8258) (European Communities ; no.33 (1981))
ISBN 0-10-182580-3 (unbound) : £0.70
B81-28288

341.7'5475664362'0265 — European Community countries. Imports from Tunisia: Olive oil. Import duties — *Treaties between European Community countries & Tunisia*

European Economic Community. [Treaties, etc. Tunisia, 1980 Dec.22]. Agreement in the form of an exchange of letters between the European Economic Community and the Republic of Tunisia fixing the additional amount to be deducted from the levy on imports into the Community of untreated olive oil originating in Tunisia, for the period from 1 November 1980 at 31 October 1981, Brussels, 22 December 1980. — London : H.M.S.O., [1981]. — 3p ; 25cm. — (European Communities ; no.35 (1981)) (Cmnd. ; 8260)
ISBN 0-10-182600-1 (unbound) : £0.70
B81-29793

341.7'5475664362'0265 — European Community countries. Imports from Turkey: Olive oil. Import duties — *Treaties between European Economic Community & Turkey*

European Economic Community. [Treaties, etc. Turkey, 1980 Dec.22]. Agreement in the form of an exchange of letters between the European Economic Community and Turkey fixing the additional amount to be deducted from the levy on imports into the Community of untreated olive oil, originating in Turkey, for the period from 1 November 1980 to 31 October 1981, Brussels, 22 December 1980. — London : H.M.S.O., [1981]. — 3p ; 25cm. — (European Communities ; no.34 (1981)) (Cmnd. ; 8259)
ISBN 0-10-182590-0 (unbound) : £0.70
B81-29800

341.7'54756648 — European Community countries. Imports from Algeria: Preserved fruit salads — *Treaties between European Economic Community & Algeria*

Algeria. [Treaties, etc. European Economic Community, 1980 Dec.22]. Agreement in the form of an exchange of letters between the European Economic Community and the People's Democratic Republic of Algeria concerning the import into the Community of preserved fruit salads originating in Algeria : Brussels, 22 December 1980. — London : H.M.S.O., [1981]. — 3p ; 25cm. — (European communities ; no.32 (1981)) (Cmnd. ; 8264)
ISBN 0-10-182640-0 (unbound) : £0.70
B81-31488

341.7'54756648 — European Community countries. Imports from Israel: Preserved fruit salads — *Treaties between European Economic Community & Israel*

European Economic Community. [Treaties, etc. Israel, 1975 May 11. Protocols, etc. 1980 Dec.22]. Agreement in the form of an exchange of letters relating to Article 9 of Protocol no.1 to the Agreement between the European Economic Community and the State of Israel and concerning the importation into the Community of preserved fruit salads originating in Israel (1981) : Brussels, 22 December 1980. — London : H.M.S.O., [1981]. — 3p ; 25cm. — (European communities ; no.37 (1981)) (Cmnd. ; 8262)
ISBN 0-10-182620-6 (unbound) : £0.70
B81-31487

341.7'54756648 — European Community countries. Imports from Morocco: Preserved fruit salads — *Treaties between European Economic Community & Morocco*

European Economic Community. [Treaties, etc. Morocco, 1980 Dec.22]. Agreement in the form of an exchange of letters between the European Economic Community and the Kingdom of Morocco concerning the import into the Community of preserved fruit salads originating in Morocco : Brussels, 22 December 1980. — London : H.M.S.O., [1981]. — 3p ; 25cm. — (European Communities ; no.39 (1981)) (Cmnd. ; 8286)
ISBN 0-10-182860-8 (unbound) : £0.70
B81-34450

341.7'54756648 — European Community countries. Imports from Tunisia: Preserved fruit salads — *Treaties between European Economic Community & Tunisia*

European Economic Community. [Treaties, etc. Tunisia, 1980 Dec.22]. Agreement in the form of an exchange of letters between the European Economic Community and the Republic of Tunisia concerning the import into the Community of preserved fruit salads originating in Tunisia, Brussels, 22 December 1980. — London : H.M.S.O., [1981]. — 3p ; 23cm. — (Cmnd. ; 8280) (European Communities ; no.38 (1981))
ISBN 0-10-182800-4 (unbound) : £0.70
B81-33349

341.7'5475664805642 — European Community countries. Imports from Algeria: Tomato concentrates. Import duties — *Treaties between Algeria & European Economic Community*

Algeria. Agreement in the form of an exchange of letters between the European Economic Community and the People's Democratic Republic of Algeria on the importation into the Community of tomato concentrates originating in Algeria : Brussels, 22 December 1980. — London : H.M.S.O., [1981]. — 3p ; 25cm. — (European communities ; no.36 (1981)) (Cmnd. ; 8263)
ISBN 0-10-182630-3 (unbound) : £0.70
B81-31489

341.7'547566494 — European Community countries. Imports from Portugal: Preserved sardines — *Treaties between European Economic Community & Portugal*

European Economic Community. [Treaties, etc. Portugal, 1980 Dec.22]. Agreement in the form of an exchange of letters relating to Article 8 of the Supplementary Protocol to the agreement between the European Economic Community and the Portuguese Republic : Brussels, 22 December 1980. — London : H.M.S.O., [1981]. — 3p ; 25cm. — (European Communities ; no.31 (1981)) (Cmnd. ; 8267)
ISBN 0-10-182670-2 (unbound) : £0.70
B81-33416

341.7'5475665538'0265 — Petroleum products. Foreign trade between Austria & European Community countries — *Treaties between Austria & European Economic Community*

Austria. [Treaties, etc. European Economic Community, 1972 July 22. Protocols, etc. 1981 Mar.6]. Agreement in the form of an exchange of letters derogating further from Article 1 of Protocol No.3 to the Agreement between the European Economic Community and the Republic of Austria : Brussels, 6 March 1981. — London : H.M.S.O., [1981]. — 3p ; 25cm. — (Cmnd. ; 8351) (European Communities ; no.54 (1981))
ISBN 0-10-183510-8 (unbound) : £0.70
B81-40795

341.7'5475665538'0265 — Petroleum products. Foreign trade between Finland & European Community countries — *Treaties between Finland & European Economic Community*

European Economic Community. [Treaties. etc. Finland, 1973 Oct.5. Protocols, etc. 1981 Mar.18]. Agreement in the form of an exchange of letters derogating further from Article 1 of Protocol no.3 to the Agreement between the European Economic Community and the Republic of Finland : Brussells, 18 March 1981. — London : H.M.S.O., [1981]. — 3p ; 25cm. — (Cmnd. ; 8352) (European Communities ; no.55 (1981))
ISBN 0-10-183520-5 (unbound) : £0.70
B81-40794

341.7'5475665538'0265 — Petroleum products. Foreign trade between Iceland & European Community countries — *Treaties between Iceland & European Economic Community*

European Economic Community. [Treaties, etc. Iceland, 1972 July 22. Protocols, etc. 1981 Mar.18]. Agreement in the form of an exchange of letters derogating further from Article 1 of Protocol No.3 to the agreement between the European Economic Community and the Republic of Iceland : Brussels, 18 March 1981. — London : H.M.S.O., [1981]. — 3p ; 25cm. — (European communities ; no.50 (1981)) (Cmnd. ; 8346)
ISBN 0-10-183460-8 (unbound) : £0.70
B81-40963

341.7'5475665538'0265 — Petroleum products. Foreign trade Switzerland & European Community countries — *Treaties between Switzerland & European Economic Community*

European Economic Community. [Treaties, etc. Switzerland, 1972 July 22. Protocols, etc. 1981 Mar.18]. Agreement in the form of an exchange of letters derogating further from Article 1 of Protocol No.3 to the agreement between the European Economic Community and the Swiss Confederation : Brussels, 18 March 1981. — London : H.M.S.O., [1981]. — 3p ; 25cm. — (European communities ; no.51 (1981)) (Cmnd. ; 8345)
ISBN 0-10-183450-0 (unbound) : £0.70
B81-40965

341.7'54756728'0265 — European Community countries. Imports from Zimbabwe: Steel products — *Treaties*

Agreement within the Province of the European Coal and Steel Community between the member States of the Community and the Republic of Zimbabwe, Luxembourg, 4 November 1980. — London : H.M.S.O., 1981. — 3p ; 25cm. — (Cmnd. ; 8151) (European Communities ; no.10 (1981))
ISBN 0-10-181510-7 (unbound) : £0.70
Primary classification 341.7'547224'0265
B81-14511

341.7'547567628 — European Community countries. Imports from Finland: Paper products. Import quotas — *Treaties between European Economic Community & Finland*

European Economic Community. [Treaties, etc. Finland, 1973 Oct. 5. Protocols, etc. 1980 Sept. 19]. Agreement in the form of an exchange of letters amending certain zero-duty tariff quotas opened by the United Kingdom for 1980 in accordance with Protocol no.1 of the Agreement between the European Economic Community and the Republic of Finland, Brussels, 19 September 1980. — London : H.M.S.O., [1981]. — 3p ; 25cm. — (European Communities ; no.5 (1981)) (Cmnd. ; 8135)
ISBN 0-10-181350-3 (unbound) : £0.70
B81-14108

341.7'54756770286'0265 — European Community countries. Imports from Philippines: Textile products — *Treaties between European Economic Community & Philippines*

European Economic Community. [Treaties, etc. Philippines, 1980 Oct.29]. Agreement between the European Economic Community and the Republic of the Philippines on trade in textile products including exchanges of letters, Brussels, 29 October 1980. — London : H.M.S.O., 1981. — 39p ; 25cm. — (Cmnd. ; 8174) (European Communities ; no.20 (1981))
ISBN 0-10-181740-1 (unbound) : £3.40
B81-18421

341.7'547567713'0265 — European Community countries. Imports from Bangladesh: Jute products — *Treaties between Bangladesh & European Economic Community*

Bangladesh. [Treaties, etc. European Economic Community 1980 Nov.20]. Agreement between the European Economic Community and the People's Republic of Bangladesh on trade in jute products, Brussels, 20 November 1980. — London : H.M.S.O., 1981. — 11p ; 25cm. — (European communities ; no.30 (1981)) (Cmnd. ; 8256)
ISBN 0-10-182560-9 (unbound) : £1.40
B81-30917

341.7'55 — British wood burning power stations. Equipment. Purchase by Philippines. Financial assistance. Loans from Great Britain — *Treaties between Great Britain & Philippines*

Great Britain. [Treaties, etc. Philippines, 1980 Sept.23]. Exchange of notes concerning a loan by the Government of the United Kingdom of Great Britain and North Ireland to the Government of the Republic of the Philippines (United Kingdom/Philippines Loan No.2 1980) Manila, 23 September 1980. — London : H.M.S.O., [1980]. — 9p ; 25cm. — (Treaty series ; no.94 (1980)) (Cmnd. ; 8096)
ISBN 0-10-180960-3 (unbound) : £1.40
B81-04608

341.7'55 — North Sea. Natural gas deposits. Murchison Field Reservoir. Exploitation — *Treaties between Great Britain & Norway*

Great Britain. [Treaties, etc. Norway, 1979 Oct.16]. Agreement between the Government of the United Kingdom of Great Britain and Northern Ireland and the Government of the Kingdom of Norway relating to the exploitation of the Murchison Field Reservoir and the offtake of petroleum therefrom : Oslo, 16 October 1979. — London : H.M.S.O., [1981]. — 30p : ill ; 25cm. — (Treaty series ; no.39 (1981)) (Cmnd. ; 8270)
Parallel English and Norwegian text
ISBN 0-10-182700-8 (unbound) : £2.40
B81-33414

341.7'56 — Europe. Perishable food. International freight transport — *Treaties*

Agreement on the international carriage of perishable foodstuffs and on the special equipment to be used for such carriage (ATP) : Geneva, 1 September 1970-31 May 1971. — London : H.M.S.O., [1981]. — 46p : forms ; 25cm. — (Treaty series ; no.42 (1981)) (Cmnd. ; 8272)
'... previously published as Miscellaneous ; no.11 (1976) Cmnd.6441'
ISBN 0-10-182720-2 (unbound) : £3.00
B81-33413

Great Britain. Proposed amendments to annex 1 to the Agreement on the International Carriage of Perishable Foodstuffs and on the Special Equipment to be used for such Carriage (ATP) 1970. — London : H.M.S.O., [1981]. — 6p : 1form ; 25cm. — (Cmnd. ; 8342) (Miscellaneous ; no.18 (1981))
"These amendments were proposed by the Government of the United Kingdom ..." - p3
ISBN 0-10-183420-9 : £1.15 B81-39918

341.7'566 — Shipping. Treaties. Status

Status of multilateral conventions and instruments in respect of which the Inter-Governmental Maritime Consultative Organization or its Secretary-General performs depositary or other functions : as at 31 December 1980 / IMCO. — London : Inter-Governmental Maritime Consultative Organization, [1981]. — 244p ; 30cm
Unpriced (unbound) B81-20817

341.7'5665 — British merchant ships. Tonnage. Certificates. Recognition by Lebanon — *Treaties between Great Britain & Lebanon*

Great Britain. [Treaties, etc. Lebanon, 1975 Aug.6]. Agreement between the Government of the United Kingdom of Great Britain and Northern Ireland and the Government of the Lebanese Republic concerning the mutual recognition of tonnage certificates of merchant ships : London, 6 August 1975. — London : H.M.S.O., [1981]. — [4]p ; 25cm. — (Treaty series ; no.41 (1981)) (Cmnd. ; 8278)
'... previously published as Lebanon ; no.1 (1975) Cmnd.6262'
ISBN 0-10-182780-6 (unbound) : £0.70
Also classified at 341.7'5665 B81-33415

341.7'5665 — Lebanese merchant ships. Tonnage. Certificates. Recognition by Great Britain — *Treaties between Great Britain & Lebanon*

Great Britain. [Treaties, etc. Lebanon, 1975 Aug.6]. Agreement between the Government of the United Kingdom of Great Britain and Northern Ireland and the Government of the Lebanese Republic concerning the mutual recognition of tonnage certificates of merchant ships : London, 6 August 1975. — London : H.M.S.O., [1981]. — [4]p ; 25cm. — (Treaty series ; no.41 (1981)) (Cmnd. ; 8278)
'... previously published as Lebanon ; no.1 (1975) Cmnd.6262'
ISBN 0-10-182780-6 (unbound) : £0.70
Primary classification 341.7'5665 B81-33415

341.7'5665 — Ships. Safety measures — *Treaties*

. [International Convention for the Safety of Life at Sea, 1974. Protocols, etc. 1978 1 June-1979 1 Mar]. Protocol of 1978 relating to the International Convention for the Safety of Life at Sea, 1974, London, 1 June 1978-1 March 1979. — London : H.M.S.O., [1981]. — 27p : forms ; 25cm. — (Cmnd. ; 8277) (Treaty series ; no.40 (1981))
Previously published: as Miscellaneous no.26 (1978), Cmnd.7346
ISBN 0-10-182770-9 (unbound) : £2.40
B81-33351

341.7'5678'026641047 — Air services — *Treaties between Great Britain & Soviet Union*

Great Britain. [Treaties, etc. Union of Soviet Socialist Republics, 1957 Dec.19. Protocols, etc., Feb.20]. Protocol supplementary to the Air Services Agreement between the Government of the United Kingdom of Great Britain and Northern Ireland and the Government of the Union of Soviet Socialist Republics signed at London on 19 December, 1957, Moscow, 20 February 1981. — London : H.M.S.O., [1981]. — 5p ; 25cm. — (Treaty series ; no.47(1981)) (Cmnd. ; 8305)
Parallel English and Russian text
ISBN 0-10-183050-5 (unbound) : £1.10
B81-35388

341.7'5678'026641062 — Air services — *Treaties between Great Britain & Egypt*

Egypt. [Treaties, etc. Great Britain, 1981 May 14]. Agreement between the Government of the United Kingdom of Great Britain and Northern Ireland and the Government of the Arab Republic of Egypt for air services between and beyond their respective territories : Cairo, 14 May 1981. — London : H.M.S.O., [1981]. — 10p ; 25cm. — (Egypt ; no.1 (1981)) (Cmnd. ; 8348)
ISBN 0-10-183480-2 (unbound) : £1.50
B81-40962

341.7'5678'0266410678 — Air services — *Treaties between Great Britain & Tanzania*

Great Britain. [Treaties, etc. Tanzania, 1980 July 1]. Agreement between the Government of the United Kingdom of Great Britain and Northern Ireland and the Government of the United Republic of Tanzania for air services between and beyond their respective territories, Dar-es-Salaam, 1 July 1980. — London : H.M.S.O., [1981]. — 10p ; 25cm. — (Tanzania ; no.1 (1981)) (Cmnd. ; 8229)
ISBN 0-10-182290-1 (unbound) : £1.40
B81-25197

341.7'5678'026641071 — Air services — *Treaties between Great Britain & Canada*

Great Britain. [Treaties, etc. Canada, 1949 Aug. 19. Protocols, etc. 1981 Apr. 14]. Exchange of notes between the Government of the United Kingdom of Great Britain and Northern Ireland and the Government of Canada amending the agreement for air services between and beyond their their respective territories signed on 19 August 1949 as amended by exchanges of notes dated 18 August 1958 and 6 September 1960, London, 14 April 1981. — London : H.M.S.O, 1981. — 6p ; 25cm. — (Treaty series ; no.50(1981)) (Cmnd. ; 8291)
ISBN 0-10-182910-8 (unbound) : £1.10
B81-35086

341.7'5678'026641073 — Air services — *Treaties between Great Britain & United States*

Great Britain. [Treaties, etc. United States, 1977 July 23. Protocols, etc. 1980 Dec.4]. Exchange of notes between the Government of the United Kingdom of Great Britain and Northern Ireland and the Government of the United States of America further amending the agreement concerning air services, signed at Bermuda on 23 July 1977, as amended on 25 April 1978 and 27 December 1979 (with exchange of letters), Washington, 4 December 1980. — London : H.M.S.O., 1981. — 23p ; 25cm. — (Treaty series ; no.21 (1981)) (Cmnd. ; 8222)
ISBN 0-10-182220-0 (unbound) : £2.10
B81-25364

341.7'5679 — European Space Agency. Organisation — *Treaties*

Convention on the Establishment of a European Space Agency, Paris, 30 May to 31 December 1975. — London : H.M.S.O., [1981]. — 34p ; 25cm. — (Treaty series ; no.30 (1981)) (Cmnd. ; 8200)
'... previously published as Miscellaneous no.24 (1975), Cmnd. 4854'
ISBN 0-10-182000-3 (unbound) : £2.70
B81-29797

341.7'5688'02664105645 — International road freight transport services — *Treaties between Cyprus & Great Britain*

Cyprus. [Treaties, etc. Great Britain, 1980 Sept.9]. Agreement between the Government of the United Kingdom of Great Britain and Northern Ireland and the Government of the Republic of Cyprus on the international carriage of goods by road, London, 9 September 1980. — London : H.M.S.O., 1980. — 6p ; 25cm. — (Cyprus ; no.2 (1980)) (Cmnd. ; 8076)
ISBN 0-10-180760-0 (unbound) : £1.10
B81-04457

341.7'56883 — Europe. Perishable food. International road freight transport — *Treaties*

[Agreement on the international carriage of perishable foodstuffs and on the special equipment to be used for such carriage (ATP) *(1970). Protocols, etc., 1981 Apr.28*]. Amendment to annex 3 to the Agreement on the International Carriage of Perishable Foodstuffs and on the Special Equipment to be used for such Carriage (ATP) 1970. — London : H.M.S.O., [1981]. — [3]p ; 25cm
ISBN 0-10-182200-6 (unbound) : £0.70
B81-25235

Amendments to Annex 1 to the Agreement on the International Carriage of Perishable Foodstuffs and on the Special Equipment to be used for such Carriage (ATP) 1970. — London : H.M.S.O., 1981. — 6p ; 25cm. — (Treaty series ; no.29 (1981)) (Cmnd. ; 8221)
ISBN 0-10-182210-3 (unbound) : £1.10
B81-26869

341.7'56883'0265 — International road freight transport services — *Treaties*

[Convention on the Contract for the International Carriage of Goods by Road (CMR) (1956). *Protocols, etc. 1978 Sept.1-1979 Aug.31*]. Protocol to the Convention on the Contract for the International Carriage of Goods by Road (CMR), Geneva, 1 September 1978-31 August 1979. — London : H.M.S.O., [1981]. — 6p ; 25cm. — (Treaty series ; no.6 (1981)) (Cmnd. ; 8138)
'Previously published as Miscellaneous ; no.2 (1979) Cmnd. 7480'
ISBN 0-10-181380-5 (unbound) : £1.10
B81-20235

341.7'56883'0265 — International road freight transport services. Treaties: Convention on the Contract for the International Carriage of Goods by Road (CMR) (1956) — *Critical studies*

Donald, Alan E.. The CMR : the Convention on the Contract for the International Carriage of Goods by Road / by Alan E. Donald. — London (P.O. Box 29, Twickenham TW1 3BN) : Derek Beattie, 1981. — xx,219p ; 23cm
English text, appendices in several languages. — Includes index
ISBN 0-907591-00-0 : Unpriced B81-27721

341.7'56883'0266410417 — International road freight transport services — *Treaties between Ireland (Republic) & Great Britain*

Great Britain. [Treaties, etc. Ireland, 1980 Apr. 9]. Agreement between the Government of the United Kingdom of Great Britain and Northern Ireland and the Government of the Republic of Ireland on the international carriage of goods by road, Dublin, 9 April 1980. — London : H.M.S.O., [1980]. — 7p ; 25cm. — (Treaty series ; no.74 (1980)) (Cmnd. ; 8015)
ISBN 0-10-180150-5 (unbound) : £1.10
B81-13642

341.7'573 — International parcel post — *Treaties*

[Postal Parcels Agreement *(1979)*]. Postal Parcels Agreement : (together with final protocol and detailed regulations), Rio de Janeiro, 26 October 1979 / Universal Postal Union. — London : H.S.M.O., [1981]. — 280p : forms ; 25cm. — (Cmnd. ; 8182)
French text with English translation
ISBN 0-10-181820-3 (pbk) : £8.10 B81-21885

341.7'573'0265 — International postal services — *Treaties*

[Universal Postal Convention *(1979)*]. Universal Postal Convention : (together with final protocol and detailed regulations), Rio de Janeiro, 26 October 1979 / Universal Postal Union. — London : H.M.S.O., [1981]. — iii,455p : ill,forms ; 25cm. — (Cmnd. ; 8183)
French text with English translation
ISBN 0-10-181830-0 (pbk) : £10.50 B81-21887

341.7'573'0265 — Universal Postal Union. Constitution — *Treaties*

Union postale universelle. Declarations, general regulations, final protocol and rules of procedure of congresses : Rio de Janeiro, 26 October 1979 / Universal Postal Union. — London : H.M.S.O., [1981]. — iii,113p ; 25cm. — (Cmnd. ; 8181)
French text with English translation
ISBN 0-10-181810-6 (pbk) : £5.30 B81-21888

341.7'577'0265 — European Community countries. Telecommunication systems. Research — *Treaties*

European Economic Community. [Treaties, etc. 1981 Jan.22]. Community-COST concertation agreement on a concerted action project in the field of teleinformatics (COST project 11 bis) : Brussels, 22 January 1981. — London : H.M.S.O., [1981]. — 11p ; 25cm. — (European communities ; no.43 (1981)) (Cmnd. ; 8356)
Agreement between the European Economic Community, Finland and Sweden
ISBN 0-10-183560-4 (unbound) : £1.50
B81-40876

341.7'58 — European Community countries. Intellectual property. European Community law

Guy, Diana. The EEC and intellectual property / Diana Guy and Guy I.F. Leigh. — London : Sweet & Maxwell, 1981. — xxiv,375p ; 25cm
Includes index
ISBN 0-421-23420-2 : £30.00 : CIP rev.
B81-09994

341.7'582 — European Community countries. Music. Sound recordings. Copyright. European Economic Community law

Davies, Gillian. The piracy of phonograms. — Oxford (25 Beaumont St., Oxford OX1 2NP) : ESC Publishing, July 1981. — [120]p
ISBN 0-906214-07-6 (pbk) : £15.00 : CIP entry
B81-21583

341.7'59 — African Development Bank. Establishment — *Treaties*

Agreement establishing the African Development Bank : Khartoum, 4 August 1963 as amended. — London : H.M.S.O., [1981]. — 51p ; 25cm. — (Cmnd. ; 8284) (Miscellaneous ; no.15)
ISBN 0-10-182840-3 (unbound) : £3.40
B81-35011

341.7'59 — British goods. Purchase by Turkey. Financial assistance. Loans from Great Britain — *Treaties between Great Britain & Turkey*

Great Britain. [Treaties, etc. Turkey, 1980 Dec.19]. Exchange of notes concerning a loan by the government of the United Kingdom of Great Britain and Northern Ireland to the government of the Republic of Turkey (The United Kingdom/Turkey (Ankara Water Project) Loan 1980), Ankara, 19 December 1980. — London : H.M.S.O., [1981]. — 6p ; 25cm. — (Treaty series ; no.15 (1981)) (Cmnd. ; 8194)
ISBN 0-10-181940-4 (unbound) : £1.10
B81-23185

341.7'59 — Common Fund for Commodities. Establishment — *Treaties*

Agreement establishing the common fund for commodities, New York, 1 October 1980 to 30 September 1981. — London : H.M.S.O., 1981. — 50p ; 25cm. — (Cmnd. ; 8192) (Miscellaneous ; no.7 (1981))
ISBN 0-10-181920-x (unbound) : £3.40
B81-22367

341.7′59 — European Development Fund. Finance — *Treaties*

[Internal Agreement on the Financing and Administration of Community Aid *(1979). Protocols, etc., 1980 Dec.16*]. Internal agreement amending the internal agreement on the financing and administration of community aid of 20 November 1979. — London : H.M.S.O., 1981. — 3p ; 25cm. — (Cmnd. ; 8219) (European Communities ; no.27 (1981))
ISBN 0-10-182190-5 (unbound) : £0.70
B81-22368

341.7′59 — Nepal. Economic development. Financial assistance. Loans from Great Britain. Repayment. Waiver — *Treaties between Great Britain & Nepal*

Great Britain. [Treaties, etc. Nepal, 1980 Feb.26]. Exchange of notes between the Government of the United Kingdom of Great Britain and Northern Ireland and His Majesty's Government of Nepal constituting the United Kingdom-Nepal Retrospective Terms Agreement 1980 : Kathmandu, 26 and 28 February 1980. — London : H.M.S.O., [1980]. — 6p : form ; 25cm. — (Treaty series ; no.78 (1980)) (Cmnd. ; 8023)
ISBN 0-10-180230-7 (unbound) : £1.10
B81-02274

341.7′59 — Turkey. Economic development. Financial assistance. Loans from Great Britain — *Treaties between Great Britain & Turkey*

Great Britain. [Treaties, etc. Turkey, 1980 Dec.5]. Exchange of notes between the government of the United Kingdom of Great Britain and Northern Ireland and the government of the Republic of Turkey concerning a refinancing loan (The United Kingdom Refinancing Agreement (No.1) 1980) Ankara, 5 December 1980. — London : H.M.S.O., 1981. — 7p ; 25cm. — (Treaty series ; no.16 (1981)) (Cmnd. ; 8209)
ISBN 0-10-182090-9 (unbound) : £1.10
B81-26085

Great Britain. [Treaties, etc. Turkey, 1980 Dec.5]. Exchange of notes between the government of the United Kingdom of Great Britain and Northern Ireland and the government of the Republic of Turkey concerning a refinancing loan (The United Kingdom/Turkey Refinancing Loan Agreement (No.3) 1980). — London : H.M.S.O., 1981. — 5p ; 25cm. — (Treaty series ; no.19 (1981)) (Cmnd. ; 8210)
ISBN 0-10-182100-x (unbound) : £1.10
B81-26086

Great Britain. [Treaties, etc. Turkey, 1980 Dec.5]. Exchange of notes between the Government of the United Kingdom of Great Britain and Northern Ireland and the Government of the Republic of Turkey concerning a refinancing loan (The United Kingdom-Turkey Refinancing Loan Agreement (No.2) 1980). — London : H.M.S.O., [1981]. — 14p ; 25cm. — (Treaty series ; no.23 (1981)) (Cmnd. ; 8213)
ISBN 0-10-182130-1 (unbound) : £1.70
B81-27549

341.7′6 — Social security benefits — *Treaties between Great Britain & Austria*

Austria. [Treaties, etc. Great Britain, 1980 July 22]. Convention on social security between the United Kingdom of Great Britain and Northern Ireland and the Republic of Austria Vienna, 22 July 1980 with protocol concerning benefits in kind. — London : H.M.S.O., [1980]. — 24p ; 25cm. — (Austria ; no.1 (1980)) (Cmnd. ; 8048)
ISBN 0-10-180480-6 (unbound) : £2.40
B81-02942

Austria. [Treaties, etc. Great Britain, 1980 July 22]. Convention on social security between the United Kingdom of Great Britain and Northern Ireland and the Republic of Austria, Vienna, 22 July 1980. — London : H.M.S.O., 1981. — 49p ; 25cm. — (Treaty series ; no.25 (1981)) (Cmnd. ; 8231)
English and German text. — '... previously published as Austria No.1 (1980), Cmnd. 8048'
ISBN 0-10-182310-x (unbound) : £3.40
B81-26110

341.7′62 — Natural resources. Allocation. International legal aspects

Fawcett, J. E. S.. Law and international resource conflicts / by J.E.S. Fawcett and Audrey Parry. — Oxford : Issued under the auspices of the Royal Institute of International Affairs [by] Clarendon Press, 1981. — xiv, 254p ; 23cm
Bibliography: p244-246. — Includes index
ISBN 0-19-825359-1 : £20.00 : CIP rev.
B81-14825

341.7′62 — North Sea. Oil fields: Statfjord Oil Field. Exploitation — *Treaties between Great Britain & Norway*

Great Britain. [Treaties, etc. Norway, 1979 Oct.16]. Agreement between the Government of the United Kingdom of Great Britain and Northern Ireland and the Government of the Kingdom of Norway relating to the exploitation of the Statfjord Field Reservoirs and the offtake of petroleum therefrom, Oslo, 16 October 1979. — London : H.M.S.O., [1981]. — 31p ; 25cm. — (Cmnd. ; 8282) (Treaty series ; no.44 (1981))
Text in English and Norwegian. — Previously published: as Norway No.1 (1980), Cmnd.7813
ISBN 0-10-182820-9 (unbound) : £2.40
B81-33350

341.7′622 — Antarctic. Coastal waters. Marine organisms of economic importance. Conservation — *Treaties*

Convention on the Conservation of Antarctic Marine Living Resources, Canberra, 1 August-31 December 1980 : with extracts from the final act of the conference held at Canberra 7-20 May 1980. — London : H.M.S.O., 1981. — 19p ; 25cm. — (Cmnd. ; 8217) (Miscellaneous ; no.9 (1981))
ISBN 0-10-182170-0 (unbound) : £2.10
B81-26087

341.7′622′0265 — Senegal. Coastal waters. Fishing by European Community ships. Regulation — *Treaties between European Economic Community & Senegal*

European Economic Community. [Treaties, etc. Senegal, 1979 June 15]. Agreement between the European Economic Community and the Government of the Republic of Senegal on fishing off the coast of Senegal with protocol and exchange of letters on provisional application Brussels, 15 June 1979. — London : H.M.S.O., [1980]. — 21p : forms ; 25cm. — (European Communities ; no.74 (1980)) (Cmnd. ; 8062)
ISBN 0-10-180620-5 (unbound) : £2.10
B81-03915

341.7′622′0265 — Sweden. Coastal waters. Fisheries. Management — *Treaties between Sweden & European Economic Community — Texts*

European Economic Community. [Treaties, etc. Sweden, 1977 Mar. 21]. Agreement on fisheries between the European Economic Community and the Government of Sweden, Brussels, 21 March 1977. — London : H.M.S.O., [1980]. — 6p ; 25cm. — (European Communities ; no.48 (1980)) (Cmnd. ; 8056)
ISBN 0-10-180560-8 (unbound) : £1.10
B81-03916

341.7′623 — European Community countries. Atmosphere. Pollutants. Chemical properties & physical properties. Research — *Treaties*

European Economic Community. [Treaties, etc., 1980 Mar.27]. Community-COST concertation agreement on a concerted action project in the field of physico-chemical behaviour of atmospheric pollutants (COST Project 61a bis) Brussels, 27 March 1980. — London : H.M.S.O., [1981]. — 7p ; 25cm. — (European communities ; no.23 (1981)) (Cmnd. ; 8196)
Signatories: European Economic Community, Austria and Sweden
ISBN 0-10-181960-9 (unbound) : £1.10
B81-23183

341.7′623 — Pollution by petroleum. Civil liability — *Treaties*

Protocol to the International Convention on Civil Liability for Oil Pollution Damage, 1969, London, 19 November 1976. — London : H.M.S.O., 1981. — 5p ; 25cm. — (Treaty series ; no.26 (1981)) (Cmnd. ; 8238)
ISBN 0-10-182380-0 (unbound) : £1.10
B81-26868

341.7′63 — Gambia. British personnel. Conditions of service — *Treaties between Great Britain & Gambia*

Great Britain. [Treaties, etc. Gambia, 1971 Mar.22. Protocols, etc., 1981 Mar.30]. Exchange of notes between the Government of the United Kingdom of Great Britain and Northern Ireland and the Government of the Republic of the Gambia amending and extending the Overseas Service (The Gambia) (continuance) Agreement 1971/76 (The Overseas Service (The Gambia) Agreement 1971/81) : Banjul, 30 March 1981. — London : H.M.S.O., [1981]. — 3p ; 25cm. — (Treaty series ; no.45 (1981)) (Cmnd. ; 8285)
ISBN 0-10-182850-0 (unbound) : £0.70
B81-34449

Great Britain. [Treaties, etc. Gambia, 1976 Mar.9. Protocols, etc. 1981 Mar.30]. Exchange of notes between the Government of the United Kingdom of Great Britain and Northern Ireland and the Government of the Republic of The Gambia amending and extending the British Expatriates Supplementation (The Gambia) Agreement 1976 (The British Expatriates Supplementation (The Gambia) Agreement 1976/81) Banjul, 30 March 1981. — London : H.M.S.O., 1981. — 3p ; 25cm. — (Treaty series ; no.53 (1981)) (Cmnd. ; 8295)
ISBN 0-10-182950-7 (unbound) : £0.70
B81-34889

341.7′63 — Industrial relations. Public administration — *Treaties*

International Labour Convention no.150 : Concerning labour administration : role, functions and organisation / adopted by the General Conference of the International Labour Organisation at its Sixty-fourth Session, Geneva 27 June 1978. — London : H.M.S.O., [1981]. — 7p ; 25cm. — (Treaty series ; no.32 (1981)) (Cmnd. ; 8251)
Previously published in Cmnd.7786
ISBN 0-10-182510-2 (unbound) : £1.10
B81-29010

341.7′63 — International Labour Organisation. Membership of United States

Galenson, Walter. The International Labor Organization : an American view / Walter Galenson. — Madison ; London : University of Wisconsin Press, 1981. — xi,351p : ill ; 23cm
Includes index
ISBN 0-299-08540-6 (cased) : £13.95
ISBN 0-299-08544-9 (pbk) : £5.05 B81-34452

341.7′63 — Kenya. British personnel. Conditions of service — *Treaties between Great Britain & Kenya*

Great Britain. [Treaties, etc. Kenya, 1971 Mar.12. Protocols, etc., 1981 Mar.25]. Exchange of notes between the Government of the United Kingdom of Great Britain and Northern Ireland and the Government of the Republic of Kenya amending and extending the British Expatriates Supplementation (Kenya) (Continuance) Agreement 1971/76 (the British Expatriates Supplementation (Kenya) Agreement 1971/81), Nairobi, 25 March 1981. — London : H.M.S.O., 1981. — 3p ; 25cm. — (Treaty series ; no.59 (1981)) (Cmnd. ; 8333)
ISBN 0-10-183330-x (unbound) : £0.70
B81-38757

Great Britain. [Treaties, etc. Kenya, 1971 Mar.29. Protocols, etc., 1981 Mar.25]. Exchange of notes between the Government of the United Kingdom of Great Britain and Northern Ireland and the Government of the Republic of Kenya amending the Overseas Service Aid (Kenya) (Continuance) Agreement 1971/76 (the Overseas Service Aid (Kenya) Agreement 1971/81), Nairobi, 25 March 1981. — London : H.M.S.O., 1981. — 3p ; 25cm. — (Treaty series ; no.60 (1981)) (Cmnd. ; 8335)
ISBN 0-10-183350-4 (unbound) : £0.70
B81-38754

341.7′63 — Lesotho. British personnel. Conditions of service — *Treaties between Great Britain & Lesotho*

Great Britain. [Treaties, etc. Lesotho, 1976 Aug.2. Protocols, etc. 1981 Mar.13]. Exchange of notes between the Government of the United Kingdom of Great Britain and Northern Ireland and the Government of the Kingdom of Lesotho amending and extending the British Expatriates Supplementation (Lesotho) Agreement 1976 as amended in 1978 (The British Expatriates Supplementation (Lesotho) Agreement 1976/81) Masaru, 13 March 1981. — London : H.M.S.O., 1981. — 3p ; 25cm. — (Treaty series ; no.51 (1981)) (Cmnd. ; 8292)
ISBN 0-10-182920-5 (unbound) : £0.70
B81-34890

341.7′63 — Public bodies. Personnel. Conditions of service. Determination. Role of workers' organisations — *Treaties*

International Labour Convention no.151 : Concerning the protection of the right to organise and procedures for determining conditions of employment in the public service / adopted by the General Conference of the International Labour Organisation at its Sixty-fourth Session, Geneva 27 June 1978. — London : H.M.S.O., [1981]. — 7p ; 25cm. — (Treaty series ; no.33 (1981)) (Cmnd. ; 8252)
Previously published in Cmnd.7786
ISBN 0-10-182520-x (unbound) : £1.10
B81-29011

341.7′632 — European Centre for Medium-Range Weather Forecasts. Personnel. Social security benefits — *Treaties between Great Britain & European Centre for Medium-Range Weather Forecasts*

European Centre for Medium-Range Weather Forecasts. [Treaties, etc. Great Britain, 1977 Apr.22. Protocols, etc. 1981 May 1]. Exchange of notes amending the agreement of 1977 between the Government of the United Kingdom of Great Britain and Northern Ireland and the European Centre for Medium-Range Weather Forecasts concerning social security arrangements for staff at the Centre, London, 1 May 1981. — London : H.M.S.O., [1981]. — 3p ; 25cm. — (Cmnd. ; 8255) (Miscellaneous ; no.12 (1981))
ISBN 0-10-182550-1 (unbound) : £0.70
B81-29792

341.7′632 — Ghana. Civil service. British personnel. Conditions of service — *Treaties between Great Britain & Ghana*

Ghana. [Treaties, etc. Great Britain, 1971 Mar.23. Protocols, etc. 1981 Mar.31]. Exchange of notes between the Government of the United Kingdom of Great Britain and Northern Ireland and the Government of Ghana amending and extending the Public Service (Ghana) (Continuance) Agreement 1971/76 (The Public Service (Ghana) Agreement 1971/81) : Accra, 31 March 1981. — London : H.M.S.O., [1981]. — 3p ; 25cm. — (Cmnd. ; 8353) (Treaty series ; no.65 (1981))
ISBN 0-10-183530-2 (unbound) : £0.70
B81-40796

341.7′632 — Kiribati. Civil service. British personnel. Conditions of service — *Treaties between Great Britain & Kiribati*

Great Britain. [Treaties, etc. Kiribati, 1980 Dec.18]. Exchange of notes between the Government of the United Kingdom of Great Britain and Northern Ireland and the Government of the Republic of Kiribati constituting the Overseas Service Aid (Kiribati) Agreement 1980. — London : H.M.S.O., [1981]. — 3p ; 25cm. — (Treaty series ; no.37 (1981)) (Cmnd. ; 8339)
ISBN 0-10-183390-3 (unbound) : £0.70
B81-39925

341.7′632 — Lesotho. Civil service. British personnel. Conditions of service — *Treaties between Great Britain & Lesotho*

Great Britain. [Treaties, etc. Lesotho, 1971 Jan.7. Protocols, etc. 1981 Mar.13]. Exchange of notes between the Government of the United Kingdom of Great Britain and Northern Ireland and the Government of the Kingdom of Lesotho amending and extending the Overseas Service (Lesotho) (Continuance) Agreement 1971/76 (The Overseas Service (Lesotho) (Continuance) Agreement 1971/81) Maseru, 13 March 1981. — London : H.M.S.O., 1981. — 3p ; 25cm. — (Treaty series ; no.52 (1981)) (Cmnd. ; 8294)
ISBN 0-10-182940-x (unbound) : £0.70
B81-34888

341.7′632 — Seychelles Islands. Civil service. British personnel. Conditions of service — *Treaties between Great Britain & Seychelles Islands*

Great Britain. [Treaties, etc. Seychelles, 1981 Mar.31]. Exchange of notes between the Government of the United Kingdom of Great Britain and Northern Ireland and the Government of the Republic of Seychelles constituting the Overseas Service Aid Scheme (Seychelles) Agreement 1981, Victoria, 31 March 1981. — London : H.M.S.O., [1981]. — 6p ; 25cm. — (Treaty series ; no.63 (1981)) (Cmnd. ; 8343)
ISBN 0-10-183430-6 (pbk) : £1.15 B81-39923

341.7′632 — Sierra Leone. British teachers. Conditions of service — *Treaties between Great Britain & Sierra Leone*

Great Britain. [Treaties, etc. Sierra Leone, 1971. Protocols, etc., 1981 Jan.13]. Exchange of notes between the Government of the United Kingdom of Great Britain and Northern Ireland and the Government of Sierra Leone amending and extending the Public Service and Teachers (Sierra Leone) (Continuance) Agreement 1971/76 (the Public Service and Teachers (Sierra Leone) Agreement 1971/81), Freetown, 13 January 1981. — London : H.M.S.O., [1981]. — 2p ; 25cm. — (Treaty series ; no.17 (1981)) (Cmnd. ; 8197)
ISBN 0-10-181970-6 (unbound) : £0.70
Primary classification 341.7′632 B81-20657

341.7′632 — Sierra Leone. Civil service. British personnel. Conditions of service — *Treaties between Great Britain & Sierra Leone*

Great Britain. [Treaties, etc. Sierra Leone, 1971. Protocols, etc., 1981 Jan.13]. Exchange of notes between the Government of the United Kingdom of Great Britain and Northern Ireland and the Government of Sierra Leone amending and extending the Public Service and Teachers (Sierra Leone) (Continuance) Agreement 1971/76 (the Public Service and Teachers (Sierra Leone) Agreement 1971/81), Freetown, 13 January 1981. — London : H.M.S.O., [1981]. — 2p ; 25cm. — (Treaty series ; no.17 (1981)) (Cmnd. ; 8197)
ISBN 0-10-181970-6 (unbound) : £0.70
Also classified at 341.7′632 B81-20657

341.7′632 — Vanuatu. Civil service. British personnel. Conditions of service — *Treaties between Great Britain & Vanuatu*

Great Britain. [Treaties, etc. Vanuatu, 1981 Feb.19]. Exchange of notes between the Government of the United Kingdom of Great Britain and Northern Ireland and the Government of the Republic of Vanuatu constituting the Overseas Service Aid (Vanuatu) Agreement 1981, Port Vila, 19 February/16 March 1981. — London : H.M.S.O., [1981]. — 5p ; 25cm. — (Treaty series ; no.62 (1981)) (Cmnd. ; 8338)
ISBN 0-10-183380-6 (pbk) : £1.15 B81-39922

341.7′632 — Zambia. Civil service. British personnel. Conditions of service — *Treaties between Great Britain & Zambia*

Great Britain. [Treaties, etc. Zambia, 1979 May 7]. Exchange of notes between the Government of the United Kingdim of Great Britain and Northern Ireland and the Government of the Republic of Zambia amending the British expatriates' supplementation (Zambia) (continuance) agreements 1971-1976 (The British expatriates' supplementation (Zambia) agreements 1971-1976) (Amendment 1979), Lusaka 7 May and 4 June 1979. — London : H.M.S.O., [1981]. — [2]p ; 25cm. — (Treaty series ; no. 11 (1981)) (Cmnd. ; 8162)
ISBN 0-10-181620-0 (unbound) : £0.70
B81-13955

341.7′636 — Kenya. Civil service. British personnel. Superannuation — *Treaties between Great Britain & Kenya*

Great Britain. [Treaties, etc. Kenya, 1977 Mar. 29. Protocols, etc. 1980 Sept. 9-19]. Exchange of notes between the Government of the United Kingdom of Great Britain and Northern Ireland and the Government of the Republic of Kenya amending the Public Officers' Pensions (Kenya) Agreement 1977, Nairobi, 9 and 19 September 1980. — London : H.M.S.O., [1981]. — 3p ; 25cm. — (Treaty series ; no.8 (1981)) (Cmnd. ; 8152)
ISBN 0-10-181520-4 (unbound) : £0.70
B81-14113

341.7′636 — Mauritius. Expatriate British personnel. Remuneration — *Treaties between Great Britain & Mauritius*

Great Britain. [Treaties, etc. Mauritius, 1981 Mar. 31]. Exchange of notes between the Government of the United Kingdom of Great Britain and Northern Ireland and the Government of Mauritius constituting the British Expatriates Supplementation (Mauritius) Agreement 1981, Port Louis, 31 March 1981. — London : H.M.S.O, 1981. — 6p ; 25cm. — (Treaty series ; no.46 (1981)) (Cmnd. ; 8289)
ISBN 0-10-182890-x (unbound) : £1.10
B81-35084

341.7′636 — Seychelles Islands. British personnel. Remuneration — *Treaties between Great Britain & Seychelles Islands*

Great Britain. [Treaties, etc. Seychelles, 1981 Mar.31]. Exchange of notes between the Government of the United Kingdom of Great Britain and Northern Ireland and the Government of the Republic of the Seychelles constituting the British Expatriates Supplementation (Seychelles) Agreement 1981, Victoria, 31 March 1981. — London : H.S.M.O., [1981]. — 7p ; 23cm. — (Cmnd. ; 8344) (Treaty series ; no.64 (1981))
ISBN 0-10-183440-3 (pbk) : £1.15 B81-39924

341.7′636 — Tuvalu. Civil service. British personnel. Remuneration — *Treaties between Great Britain & Tuvalu*

Great Britain. [Treaties, etc. Tuvalu, 1981 Mar. 3]. Exchange of notes between the Government of the United Kingdom of Great Britain and Northern Ireland and the Government of Tuvalu constituting the Overseas Service Aid (Tuvalu) Agreement 1981, Suva, 3 March/Funafuti, 6 March 1981. — London : H.M.S.O., 1981. — 3p ; 25cm. — (Treaty series ; no.49 (1981)) (Cmnd. ; 8290)
ISBN 0-10-182900-0 (unbound) : £0.70
B81-35085

341.7′636′02664109611 — Fiji. British personnel. Remuneration — *Treaties between Great Britain & Fiji*

Great Britain. [Treaties, etc. Fiji, 1971. Protocols, etc., 1981 Mar.26]. Exchange of notes between the Government of the United Kingdom of Great Britain and Northern Ireland and the Government of Fiji amending and extending the Overseas Service (Fiji) (continuance) Agreement 1971/76 (the Overseas Service (Fiji) Agreement 1971/81), Sava, 26th March 1981. — London : H.M.S.O., [1981]. — 3p ; 25cm. — (Treaty series ; no.55 (1981)) (Cmnd. ; 8298)
ISBN 0-10-182980-9 (unbound) : £0.70
B81-35387

341.7′636′02664109612 — Tonga. British personnel. Remuneration — *Treaties between Great Britain & Tonga*

Great Britain. [Treaties, etc, Tonga, 1971. Protocols, etc., 1976 Mar.15]. Exchange of notes between the Government of the United Kingdom of Great Britain and Northern Ireland and the Government of Tonga amending and extending the Overseas Service (Tonga) Agreement 1971, Nuku'alofa, 15 March 1976 and 31 March 1981. — London : H.M.S.O., [1981]. — 5p ; 25cm. — (Treaty series ; no.54 (1981)) (Cmnd. ; 8299)
ISBN 0-10-182990-6 (unbound) : £1.10
B81-35389

341.7′66 — Western Europe. Children. Custody — *Treaties*

European Convention on Recognition and Enforcement of Decisions Concerning Custody of Children and on Restoration of Custody of Children (with explanatory report), Luxembourg, 20 May 1980. — London : H.M.S.O., [1981]. — 27p ; 25cm. — (Cmnd. ; 8155) (Miscellaneous ; no.6 (1981))
ISBN 0-10-181550-6 (unbound) : £2.40
B81-14110

341.7′67 — Switzerland. Extension of EURONET — *Treaties between European Economic Community & Switzerland*

European Economic Community. [Treaties, etc. Switzerland, 1979 Sept.28]. Agreement in the form of an exchange of letters between the European Economic Community and the Swiss Confederation on the extension of the community network for data transmission (EURONET) to Switzerland, Brussels, 28 September 1979. — London : H.M.S.O., [1980]. — 11p ; 25cm. — (Cmnd. ; 8030) (European Communities ; no.41 (1980))
Text in French and English
ISBN 0-10-180300-1 (unbound) : £1.40
B81-04462

341.7′67 — Unesco. Constitution — *Treaties*

Unesco. Amendments to Article V of the Constitution of the United Nations Educational, Scientific and Cultural Organisation adopted by the General Conference of the Organisation at its twenty-first session on 4 October 1980. — London : H.M.S.O., [1981]. — 3p ; 25cm. — (Treaty series ; no.56(1981)) (Cmnd. ; 8304)
Parallel English and French text
ISBN 0-10-183040-8 (unbound) : £0.70
B81-35398

341.7′67′026641047 — Great Britain. Cultural & scientific relations with Soviet Union — *Treaties between Great Britain & Soviet Union*

Great Britain. [Treaties, etc. Union of Soviet Socialist Republics, 1981 Mar.23]. Agreement between the Government of the United Kingdom of Great Britain and Northern Ireland and the Government of the Union of Soviet Socialist Republics on relations in the scientific, educational and cultural fields for 1981-83 with agreed minute, Moscow, 23 March 1981. — London : H.M.S.O., [1981]. — 35p ; 25cm. — (Treaty series ; no.48 (1981)) (Cmnd. ; 8300)
Parallel English and Russian text
ISBN 0-10-183000-9 (unbound) : £2.70
B81-35391

341.7′67′026641051 — China. Cultural relations with Great Britain — *Treaties between Great Britain & China*

China. [Treaties, etc. Great Britain, 1979 Nov.1]. Agreement between the Government of the United Kingdom of Great Britain and Northern Ireland and the Government of the People′s Republic of China on co-operation in the fields of education and culture, London, 1 November 1979. — London : H.M.S.O., [1980]. — 9p ; 25cm. — (Treaty series ; no.68 (1980)) (Cmnd. ; 8000)
English and Chinese text. — Previously published: as China no.1 (1980), Cmnd. 7835
ISBN 0-10-180000-2 (unbound) : £1.25
B81-20047

341.7′67′026641064 — Morocco. Cutlural relations with Great Britain — *Treaties between Great Britain & Morocco*

Great Britain. [Treaties, etc. Morocco, 1980 Oct. 27]. Cultural agreement between the United Kingdom of Great Britain and Northern Ireland and the Kingdom of Morocco, Rabat, 27 October 1980. — London : H.M.S.O., [1981]. — 4p ; 25cm. — (Morocco ; no.1 (1981)) (Cmnd. ; 8140)
ISBN 0-10-181400-3 (unbound) : £0.70
B81-13640

341.7′67′026641065 — Great Britain. Cultural relations with Algeria — *Treaties between Great Britain & Algeria*

Algeria. [Treaties, etc. Great Britain, 1981 May 27]. Agreement on cultural cooperation between the Government of the United Kingdom of Great Britain and Northern Ireland and the Government of the Democratic and Popular Republic of Algeria, Algiers, 27 May 1981. — London : H.M.S.O., 1981. — 9p ; 25cm. — (Treaty series ; no.58 (1981)) (Cmnd. ; 8334)
English and Arabic text
ISBN 0-10-183340-7 (unbound) : £1.50
B81-38750

341.7′67′0266410861 — Colombia. Cultural relations with Great Britain — *Treaties between Great Britain & Colombia*

Colombia. [Treaties etc. Great Britain, 1979 July 3]. Cultural convention between the Government of the United Kingdom of Great Britain and Northern Ireland and the Government of the Republic of Colombia London, 3 July 1979. — London : H.M.S.O., [1980]. — 5p ; 25cm. — (Treaty series ; no.69 (1980)) (Cmnd. ; 8001)
English and Spanish text. — Previously published: as Columbia no.1 (1979), Cmnd. 7693
ISBN 0-10-180010-x (unbound) : £1.00
B81-02599

341.7′672 — Western Europe. International law. Information. Dissemination — *Treaties*

[European Convention on Information on Foreign Law *(1968). Protocols, etc., 1978 Mar. 15*]. Additional protocol to the European Convention on Information on Foreign Law, Strasbourg 15 March 1978. — London : H.M.S.O., 1981. — 6p ; 25cm. — (Cmnd. ; 8149) (Miscellaneous ; no.5 (1981))
ISBN 0-10-181490-9 (unbound) : £1.10
B81-14513

341.7′673 — Europe. Higher education institutions. Students. Qualifications. International recognition — *Treaties*

[Convention on the Recognition of Studies, Diplomas and Degrees concerning Higher Education in the States belonging to the Europe Region *(1979)*]. Convention on the Recognition of Studies, Diplomas and Degrees concerning Higher Education in the States belonging to the Europe Region, Paris, 21 December 1979. — London : H.M.S.O., [1981]. — 11p ; 25cm. — (Miscellaneous ; no.8 (1981)) (Cmnd. ; 8206)
ISBN 0-10-182060-7 (unbound) : £1.40
B81-23182

341.7′6752 — Ascension Island. American astronautical bases — *Treaties between Great Britain & United States*

Great Britain. [Treaties, etc. United States, 1965 July 7. Protocols, etc., 1980 Nov. 18-Dec.19]. Exchange of notes between the Government of the United Kingdom of Great Britain and Northern Ireland and the Government of the United States of America modifying the Agreement concerning the establishment on Ascension Island of an additional facility to be operated for the United States National Aeronautics and Space Administration of 7 July, 1965 , London 18 November-19 December 1980. — London : H.M.S.O., [1981]. — 3p ; 25cm. — (Treaty series ; no.13 (1981)) (Cmnd. ; 8166)
ISBN 0-10-181660-x (unbound) : £0.70
B81-13944

341.7′6754 — European Community countries. Food. Effects of preservative thermal processing. Research — *Treaties*

European Economic Community. [Treaties, etc. 1981 Jan.22]. Community-COST concertation agreement on a concerted action project on the effects of thermal processing and distribution on the quality and nutritive value of food (COST project 91) : Brussels, 22 January 1981. — London : H.M.S.O., [1981]. — 10p ; 25cm. — (European communities ; no.42 (1981)) (Cmnd. ; 8355)
Agreement between the European Economic Community, Sweden and Switzerland
ISBN 0-10-183550-7 (unbound) : £1.50
Also classified at 341.7′6754 B81-40875

341.7′6754 — European Community countries. Food. Physical distribution. Effects. Research — *Treaties*

European Economic Community. [Treaties, etc. 1981 Jan.22]. Community-COST concertation agreement on a concerted action project on the effects of thermal processing and distribution on the quality and nutritive value of food (COST project 91) : Brussels, 22 January 1981. — London : H.M.S.O., [1981]. — 10p ; 25cm. — (European communities ; no.42 (1981)) (Cmnd. ; 8355)
Agreement between the European Economic Community, Sweden and Switzerland
ISBN 0-10-183550-7 (unbound) : £1.50
Primary classification 341.7′6754 B81-40875

341.7′7 — High seas. Piracy. International law

Dubner, Barry Hart. The law of international sea piracy / by Barry Hart Dubner. — The Hague ; London : Nijhoff, 1980. — xiii,176p ; 25cm. — (Developments in international law ; v.2)
Bibliography: p167-173. — Includes index
ISBN 90-247-2191-1 : Unpriced B81-03906

341.7′8 — East Germany. Civil courts. Judgments. Recognition under civil law in Great Britain — *Treaties between Great Britain & East Germany*

Germany *(Democratic Republic)*. [Treaties, etc. Great Britain, 1980 Feb.28]. Convention between the United Kingdom of Great Britain and Northern Ireland and the German Democratic Republic regarding legal proceedings in civil matters Berlin, 28 February 1980. — London : H.M.S.O., [1980]. — 18p ; 25cm. — (Treaty series ; no.28 (1981)) (Cmnd. ; 8240)
English and German text. — Previously published: as German Democratic Republic no.1 (1980), Cmnd.7918
ISBN 0-10-182400-9 (unbound) : £2.10
Primary classification 341.7′8 B81-28268

341.7′8 — European Community. Law. Remedies — *Conference proceedings*

Fédération internationale pour le droit européen. *Congress (9th : 1980)*. Reports of the ninth Congress, 25-27 September 1980 / Fédération Internationale pour le Droit Eruopéen. — [S.l.] : FIDE ; London : Sweet & Maxwell, 1980. — 2v. ; 21cm
Includes papers in French and German
ISBN 0-421-27850-1 (pbk) : £25.00
Also classified at 332.6 B81-07814

341.7′8 — Great Britain & Tonga. Civil courts. Judgments. Mutual recognition — *Treaties between Great Britain & Tonga*

Great Britain. [Treaties, etc. Tonga, 1979 June 28]. Convention between the Government of the United Kingdom of Great Britain and Northern Ireland and the Government of Tonga providing for the reciprocal enforcement and recognition of judgements in civil matters London, 28 June 1979. — London : H.M.S.O., [1980]. — 10p ; 25cm. — (Treaty series ; no.89 (1980)) (Cmnd. ; 8075)
Previously published: as Tonga no.1 (1979) Cmnd.7716
ISBN 0-10-180750-3 (unbound) : £1.40
B81-20400

341.7′8 — Great Britain. Civil courts. Judgments. Recognition under civil law in East Germany — *Treaties between Great Britain & East Germany*

Germany *(Democratic Republic)*. [Treaties, etc. Great Britain, 1980 Feb.28]. Convention between the United Kingdom of Great Britain and Northern Ireland and the German Democratic Republic regarding legal proceedings in civil matters Berlin, 28 February 1980. — London : H.M.S.O., [1980]. — 18p ; 25cm. — (Treaty series ; no.28 (1981)) (Cmnd. ; 8240)
English and German text. — Previously published: as German Democratic Republic no.1 (1980), Cmnd.7918
ISBN 0-10-182400-9 (unbound) : £2.10
Also classified at 341.7′8 B81-28268

342 — COMPARATIVE LAW

342′.09 — Law, *to 1600* **—** *Comparative studies — Early works — Facsimiles*

Lloyd, Lodowick. A briefe conference of divers lawes / Lodowick Lloyd. — New York ; London : Garland, 1978. — 143p ; 23cm. — (Classics of English legal history in the modern era)
Facsim of: 1602 ed. printed by Thomas Creede, London. — Includes index
ISBN 0-8240-3051-6 : £45.00 B81-15044

342.2′2 — Constitutions. Drafting

McWhinney, Edward. Constitution-making : principles, process, practice / Edward McWhinney. — Toronto ; London : University of Toronto Press, c1981. — xiii,231p ; 24cm
Bibliography: p219-225. — Includes index
ISBN 0-8020-5553-2 : £12.00 B81-36563

342.2′29′094 — Europe. Constitutional law, *1150-1650*

Tierney, Brian. Religion, law, and the growth of constitutional thought 1150-1650. — Cambridge : Cambridge University Press, Feb.1982. — [114]p
ISBN 0-521-23495-6 : £12.50 : CIP entry B81-39208

342.2′85′094 — European Community countries. Human rights. Law — *Cases — Serials*

European human rights reports. — Pt.1 (Jan. 1979)-. — London ([4 Bloomsbury Sq., WC1A 2RL]) : [European Law Centre], 1979. — v. ; 25cm
Quarterly. — Description based on: Part 5 (Jan. 1900)
ISSN 0260-4868 = European human rights reports : Unpriced B81-10287

342.35′26 — Western Europe. Business firms. Foreign executives. Income tax. Tax avoidance

Phillips, David, *1929-*. Tax savings for the expatriate executive and manager in Western Europe : Belgium, France, Federal Republic of Germany, Italy, Netherlands / by David Phillips. — London : Economist Intelligence Unit, 1981. — 94p ; 30cm. — (EIU special report ; no.92)
Unpriced (pbk) B81-13345

342.3′71′094 — European Community countries. Consumer protection. Law — *Comparative studies — German texts*

Reich, Norbert. Verbraucherschutzrecht in den EG-Staaten : eine vergleichende Analyse : eine Studie im Auftrage der EG Kommission / Norbert Reich, Hans-W. Micklitz ; Ubersetzung aus den Englischen von Doris Schmitt. — New York ; London : Van Nostrand Reinhold, 1981. — xiv,235p ; 24cm
Translated from the English. — Includes index
ISBN 0-442-30413-7 : £15.00 B81-21175

342.3′772 — Petroleum. Production. Licences. Law — *Comparative studies*

The **Legal** character of petroleum licences : a comparative study / edited by Terence Daintith. — Dundee : University of Dundee, Centre for Petroleum and Mineral Law Studies, 1981. — xv,225p : 1map ; 21cm
Conference papers
ISBN 0-906343-08-9 (pbk) : £13.00 B81-19768

342.3′82′094 — European Community countries. Consumer goods. Advertising & labelling. Law

Lawson, R. G.. Advertising and labelling laws in the Common Market / R.G. Lawson. — 2nd ed. — Bristol : Jordans, 1981. — 1v.(loose-leaf) ; 31cm
Previous ed.: 1975. — Includes index
ISBN 0-85308-063-1 : £80.00 B81-23301

342.4′1 — European Community countries. Companies. Industrial democracy. Law. Commission of the European Communities. Proposal for a fifth directive on company structure — *Critical studies*

Institute of Directors. The EEC Vth Directive - a Trojan bullock? / prepared by Andrew Hutchinson. — London : Institute of Directors, 1980. — 48p ; 30cm
£5.00 (pbk) B81-38380

342.4′2′05 — Social security. Law — *Serials*

The **corporate** guide to international social security : the monthly international advisory service on statutory social security obligations, contributions and benefits, including health, accident, disability, unemployment, dependants′ and retirement pensions. — Vol.1, issue no.1. (May 1980)-. — Sudbury (Rectory Rd, Great Waldingfield, Sudbury, Suffolk CO10 0TL) : Monitor Press, 1980-. — v. ; 30cm
Description based on: Vol.1, issue no.6 (Oct.1980)
ISSN 0260-1028 = Corporate guide to international social security : Unpriced B81-04633

342.4′44′01 — Man. Mental illness. Law — *Philosophical perspectives*

Mental illness : law and public policy / edited by Baruch A. Brody and H. Tristram Engelhardt, Jr.. — Dordrecht ; London : Reidel, c1980. — xvii,254p ; 23cm. — (Philosophy and medicine ; v.5)
Includes index
ISBN 90-277-1057-0 : Unpriced B81-04611

342.5′77 — Criminal law. Post-conviction remedies — *Comparative studies*

Robbins, Ira P.. Comparative postconviction remedies / Ira P. Robbins. — Lexington : Lexington Books, c1980 ; [Farnborough, Hants.] : Gower [distributor], 1981. — x,105p ; 24cm
Includes index
ISBN 0-669-03023-6 : £10.50 B81-05794

342.61 — Islamic personal law — *Codes — Texts with commentaries*

Tanzilurraḥmān. A code of Muslim personal law / by Tanzil-ur-Rahman. — Karachi : Handard Academy ; [London] : Oxford University Press [distributor]
Vol.1: Containing laws of marriage, dower, maintenance, divorce, dissolution of marriage, khula′a mubarat, ′iddat, parentage, legitimacy and custody of children etc. codified and re-stated in the light of the Holy Qur′ān, Sunnah and authentic books of fiqh. — 1978. — xvi,775p ; 26cm
Includes index
£23.00 B81-39913

Tanzilurraḥmān. A code of Muslim personal law / by Tanzil-ur-Rahman. — Karachi : Islamic Publications ; [London] : Oxford University Press [distributor]
Vol.2: Containing laws of gift, waqf, will and inheritance codified and re-stated in the light of the Holy Qur′ a n, Sunnah and authentic book of fiqh. — 1980. — xvi,688p ; 25cm
Includes index
£27.50 B81-39912

342.6′2 — Contracts

Macneil, Ian R.. The new social contract : an inquiry into modern contractual relations / Ian R. Macneil. — New Haven ; London : Yale University Press, c1980. — xiii,164p ; 22cm. — (1979 Rosenthal lectures)
Bibliography: p149-158. - Includes index
ISBN 0-300-02542-4 : £8.20 B81-09612

342.6′2′01 — Contractual liability. Ethical aspects

Fried, Charles. Contract as promise : a theory of contractual obligation / Charles Fried. — Cambridge, Mass. ; London : Harvard University Press, 1981. — 162p ; 25cm
Includes index
ISBN 0-674-16925-5 : £8.40 B81-38274

342.63′2 — Medicine. Negligence. Law — *Comparative studies*

Medical malpractice / edited by J. Leahy Taylor ; with a foreword by Lord Richardson. — Bristol : John Wright, 1980. — xiv,326p : 2ill,2forms ; 23cm
Includes index
ISBN 0-7236-0550-5 : £15.00 : CIP rev. B80-12288

342.63′82 — Products. Defects. Liability of manufacturers & retailers. Law — *For design*

Abbott, Howard. Safe enough to sell? : design and product liability / Howard Abbott. — London : Design Council, 1980. — 192p : ill ; 24cm
Includes index
ISBN 0-85072-113-x : £7.95 : CIP rev. B80-17608

342.63′82 — Products. Defects. Liability of manufacturers — *Conference proceedings*

Product Liability and Reliability *(Conference : 1980 : University of Aston in Birmingham).* Proceedings of the British Society for Strain Measurement and Institution of Production Engineers International Conference "Product Liability and Reliability" held at University of Aston in Birmingham 1-5 September, 1980. — Newcastle upon Tyne (281 Heaton Rd, Newcastle upon Tyne NE6 5QB) : The Society
Vol.1. — 1980. — 396p in various pagings : ill ; 29cm
ISBN 0-9506351-5-4 : Unpriced
Primary classification 620.1′123′0287 B81-38156

342.64′32′089912 — Thought processes — *Anthropological perspectives — Study examples: Land tenure. Disputes. Study regions: Papua New Guinea. Trobriand Islands*

Hutchins, Edwin. Culture and inference : a Trobriand case study / Edwin Hutchins. — Cambridge, Mass. ; London : Harvard University Press, 1980. — x,143p : ill,2maps ; 25cm. — (Cognitive science series ; 2)
Bibliography: p135-137. - Includes index
ISBN 0-674-17970-6 : £8.40 B81-16615

342.64′32′08998 — South American Indians. Land tenure. Legal aspects — *Anthropological perspectives*

Grasmick, Joseph. Land tenure and the South American Indian : an anthropological and legal perspective / Joseph Grasmick. — London (180 Brixton Rd. SW9 6AT) : Anti-Slavery Society, 1980. — 138p : maps ; 30cm. — (Human rights and development working papers ; no.5)
Unpriced (pbk) B81-24021

342.64′5 — Environment planning. Law — *Conference proceedings*

Proceedings of the seminar on planning law for industry : March 29th-April 2nd 1981, Churchill College, Cambridge, England / organised by the Committee of Environmental Law (Committee F), Section on Business Law, International Bar Association ; edited with discussion summaries by John Salter and Patricia Thomas. — London (St. James′s St., SW1A 1EE) : International Bar Association in cooperation with Sweet and Maxwell, c1981. — 2v. : forms ; 21cm
Cover title: Planning law for industry
ISBN 0-9505876-2-1 (pbk) : Unpriced B81-26835

342.64′8′091717 — Communist countries. Industrial property. Law — *Serials*

I.P. reports from socialist countries : patents, trade marks, copyright and licensing. — Pt.1 (June 1979)-. — London (4 Bloomsbury Sq., WC1) : European Law Centre, 1979-. — v. ; 25cm
Two issues yearly
ISSN 0260-4876 = IP reports from socialist countries : Unpriced B81-08949

342.64′82 — Copyright

McFarlane, Gavin. A practical introduction to copyright. — London : McGraw-Hill, Oct.1981. — [256]p. — (Business law series)
ISBN 0-07-084569-7 : £14.00 : CIP entry B81-24602

Ploman, Edward W.. Copyright : intellectual property in the information age / Edward W. Ploman and L. Clark Hamilton. — London : Routledge & Kegan Paul, 1980. — viii,248p : ill ; 23cm
Bibliography: p230-235. - Includes index
ISBN 0-7100-0539-3 : £12.50 : CIP rev. B80-17609

342.64′82 — Digital computer systems. Programs. Copyright. Law

Niblett, Bryan. Legal protection of computer programs / Bryan Niblett. — London : Oyez, c1980. — xii,155p ; 22cm
Includes index
ISBN 0-85120-509-7 : £10.00 B81-13608

342.64'82'05 — Copyright. Law — *Serials*
Copywright law symposium / sponsored by the American Society of Composers Authors and Publishers. — no.25. — New York ; Guildford : Columbia University Press, 1980. — 247p
ISBN 0-231-04866-1 : Unpriced
ISSN 0069-9950 B81-09171

342.65'9'09171241 — Commonwealth countries. Trusts. Law — *Comparative studies*
Keeton, George W.. The comparative law of trusts in the Commonwealth and the Irish Republic / by George W. Keeton & L.A. Sheridan. — Chichester : Rose
1st supplement. — 1981. — xiii,27p ; 24cm
Includes index
ISBN 0-85992-175-1 (pbk) : £8.50 B81-21869

342.6'7 — Foreign investment. Agreements. Renegotiation
Stoever, William A.. Renegotiations in international business transactions : the process of dispute-resolution between multinational investors and host societies / William A. Stoever. — Lexington, Mass. : Lexington Books ; [Aldershot] : Gower [distributor], 1981. xiii,380p : ill ; 24cm
Bibliography: p351-365. — Includes index
ISBN 0-669-03057-0 : £18.50 B81-38602

342.6'7'096 — Africa. Common law countries. Commercial law — *Cases* — *Serials*
The **African** law reports. Commercial law series. — 1975, vol.1. — Oxford ([c/o Trinity College, Oxford OX1 3BH]) : African Law Reports, c1980. — xlix,394p
ISBN 0-903826-43-7 : Unpriced B81-18812

342.6'78'094 — European Community countries. Bankruptcy. Law — *Proposals*
Great Britain. *Department of Trade*. Text of the E.E.C. draft bankruptcy Convention with explanatory notes / Department of Trade. — [London] ([2 Bunhill Row, EC1Y 8LL]) : [The Department], 1980. — 182p : forms ; 30cm
Unpriced (pbk) B81-21043

342.7'12 — Law courts. Jurisdiction. Political aspects
Shapiro, Martin. Courts : a comparative and political analysis / Martin Shapiro. — Chicago ; London : University of Chicago Press, 1981. — ix,245p ; 24cm
Includes index
ISBN 0-226-75042-6 : £12.00 B81-28349

342.7'9'05 — Arbitration. Law — *Serials*
Yearbook commercial arbitration / International Council for Commercial Arbitration. — Vol.1 (1976)-. — Deventer ; London : Kluwer, 1976-. — v. ; 25cm
Description based on: Vol.6 (1981)
Unpriced B81-39529

343 — LAW. ANCIENT WORLD

343.7064'346 — Ancient Rome. Rented residences. Leases. Law
Frier, Bruce W.. Landlords and tenants in Imperial Rome / by Bruce W. Frier. — Princeton ; Guildford : Princeton University Press, c1980. — xxxii,251p,8p of plates : ill,1plan ; 23cm
Includes index
ISBN 0-691-05299-9 : £9.80 B81-09161

343.805'252 — Ancient Greece. Homicide. Law
Gagavin, Michael. Drakon and early Athenian homicide law. — London : Yale University Press, Nov.1981. — [208]p. — (Yale classical monographs ; 3)
ISBN 0-300-02627-7 : £14.00 : CIP entry B81-35027

344 — LAW. EUROPE

344.04 — European Community countries. Social policies. Harmonisation. Law
Holloway, John. Social policy harmonisation in the European Community / John Holloway. — Farnborough, Hants. : Gower, c1981. — vi,318p ; 23cm
Bibliography: p305-318
ISBN 0-566-00196-9 : £10.50 B81-12989

344.06'66 — Western Europe. Companies. Law
Meinhardt, P.. Company law in Europe / P. Meinhardt. — 3rd ed. — Farnborough, Hants. : Gower, 1981. — 1v.(loose-leaf) ; 26cm
Previous ed.: 1978. — Includes bibliographies and index
ISBN 0-566-02245-1 : £40.00 : CIP rev. B80-29366

344.1 — LAW. GREAT BRITAIN

344.1'001'9 — Great Britain. Law. Applications of psychology — *Conference proceedings*
Psychology in legal contexts : applications and limitations / edited by Sally M.A. Lloyd-Bostock. — London : Macmillan, 1981. — xix,246p ; 23cm. — (Oxford socio-legal studies)
Includes index
ISBN 0-333-27275-7 : £20.00 : CIP rev. B80-29319

344.1'0025 — Great Britain. Barristers — *Directories* — *Serials*
The **Bar** list of the United Kingdom. — 1981. — London : Stevens, 1981. — xxiv,610p
ISBN 0-420-46100-0 : £19.50 : CIP rev.
ISSN 0140-0746 B81-13552

344.1'009 — Great Britain. Law, *1166-1871* — *Conference proceedings*
Legal History Conference *(3rd : 1977 : Edinburgh)*. Law-making and law-makers in British history : papers presented to the Edinburgh Legal History Conference, 1977 / edited by Alan Harding. — London : Royal Historical Society, 1980. — viii,223p : ill ; 23cm. — (Royal Historical Society studies in history series ; no.22)
Includes index
ISBN 0-901050-77-6 : £15.25 B81-07288

344.102 — Great Britain. Constitutional law
De Smith, S. A.. Constitutional and administrative law / de Smith. — 4th ed. / by Harry Street, Rodney Brazier. — Harmondsworth : Penguin, 1981. — 728p ; 20cm. — (Foundations of law) (Penguin education)
Previous ed.: 1977. — Includes index
ISBN 0-14-080455-2 (pbk) : £6.95 B81-40476

Hartley, T. C.. Government and law : an introduction to the working of the constitution in Britain / T.C. Hartley, J.A.G. Griffith. — 2nd ed. — London : Weidenfeld and Nicholson, 1980. — xxxii,472p : ill ; 22cm. — (Law in context)
Previous ed.: 1975. — Bibliography: p464-468. — Includes index
ISBN 0-297-77974-5 (cased) : £15.00
ISBN 0-297-77973-7 (pbk) : £8.95 B81-36149

344.102'29 — Great Britain. Constitution, *1625-1660 — Readings from contemporary sources*
The **Constitutional** documents of the Puritan Revolution 1625-1660 / selected and edited by Samuel Rawson Gardiner. — 3rd ed., rev. — Oxford : Clarendon Press, 1906 (1979 [printing]). — lxiv,476p ; 19cm
Includes index
ISBN 0-19-822629-2 (pbk) : £4.95 : CIP rev. B79-25008

344.102'82 — Great Britain. Immigration. Law
Immigration law handbook. — 2nd ed. / Handsworth Law Centre. — Birmingham (Handsworth, Birmingham) : Handsworth Law Centre, 1980. — 58p : forms ; 21cm
Previous ed.: / by Clare Short. 197-?
£1.00 (pbk) B81-33094

344.102'83 — British nationality. Law. British Nationality Act 1981
Stanbrook, Ivor. British nationality : the new law. — London (34 Middleton Rd., E8 4BS) : Clement Publishers, Jan.1982. — [192]p
ISBN 0-907027-02-4 : £9.50 : CIP entry B81-38848

344.102'83 — British nationality. Law. Reform. Proposals. Great Britain. *Home Office*. British nationality law: outline of proposed legislation — *Critical studies*
Great Britain. *Commission for Racial Equality*. Proposed nationality law : Commission for Racial Equality's comments on the government's White Paper on British nationality law, submitted to the Home Office in October 1980. — London : The Commission, 1980. — 3p ; 30cm
Cover title
Unpriced (pbk) B81-06783

344.102'85 — Great Britain. Civil rights. Law
O'Higgins, Paul. Cases and materials on civil liberties / by Paul O'Higgins. — London : Sweet & Maxwell, 1980. — xxxv,482p ; 26cm
Bibliography: pxxxi-xxxiii. - Includes index
ISBN 0-421-25050-x (cased) : £17.25 : CIP rev.
ISBN 0-421-25060-7 (pbk) : £14.25 B80-18633

344.102'85 — Great Britain. Human rights. Law — *Proposals*
Scarman, *Sir* **Leslie**. The protection of human rights in the United Kingdom / Sir Leslie Scarman. — London : Cobden Trust, 1977. — 12p ; 21cm. — (The 1976 Cobden Trust Human Rights Day lecture)
ISBN 0-900137-11-8 (pbk) : £0.75 B81-36672

344.102'87 — Great Britain. Sex discrimination. Law: Sex Discrimination Act 1975 — *For advertising*
Great Britain. *Equal Opportunities Commission*. The Sex Discrimination Act and advertising : guidance notes / [Equal Opportunities Commission]. — Manchester (Overseas House, Quay St, Manchester M3 3HW) : The Commission, 1980. — 15p : ill ; 21cm
ISBN 0-905829-31-x (pbk) : Unpriced B81-15350

344.102'873 — Great Britain. Racial discrimination. Law
Lustgarten, Laurence. Legal control of racial discrimination / Laurence Lustgarten. — London : Macmillan, 1980. — xxv,263p ; 25cm
Includes index
ISBN 0-333-24387-0 (cased) : £25.00
ISBN 0-333-24388-9 (pbk) : £12.00 B81-06182

344.103'14'05 — British military forces. Discipline. Law — *Inquiry reports* — *Serials*
Great Britain. *Parliament. House of Commons. Select Committee on the Armed Forces Bill*. Special report from the Select Committee on the Armed Forces Bill. — Session 1980-81. — London : H.M.S.O., 1981. — xix,130p
ISBN 0-10-225381-1 : £7.00 B81-31044

344.1034 — Great Britain. Taxation. Law
Cowdrey, M. R.. The budget 1981 / by M.R. Cowdrey and R.E. Holloway. — Nottingham (145 Derby Rd., Nottingham NG7 1NE) : Holloway, Cowdrey & Co., [1981]. — 13p ; 30cm
£1.50 (spiral) B81-18378

Personal and business taxation (including the taxation of trusts and estates). — 2nd ed. — [Guildford] : College of Law, c1980. — 83p : ill ; 22cm. — (College of law lectures, ISSN 0309-3166)
Previous ed.: 1980
£4.00 (pbk) B81-05676

Pinson, Barry. Pinson on revenue law : comprising income tax, capital gains tax, development land tax, corporation tax, capital transfer tax, value added tax, stamp duties, tax planning / by Barry Pinson. — 13th ed. / sections on value added tax and development land tax by John Gardiner. — London : Sweet & Maxwell, 1980. — lxi,686p ; 26cm
Previous ed.: 1978. — Includes index
ISBN 0-421-26170-6 (cased) : £30.00
ISBN 0-421-26180-3 (pbk) : £17.75 B80-24251

344.103'4 — Great Britain. Taxation. Law
Pinson, Barry. Pinson on revenue law. — 14th ed. — London : Sweet & Maxwell, Nov.1981. — [700]p
Previous ed.: 1980
ISBN 0-421-29050-1 (cased) : £30.00 : CIP entry
ISBN 0-421-29060-9 (pbk) : £19.00 B81-31174

344.1034 — Great Britain. Taxation. Law

Simon, John Allsebrook Simon, *Viscount.*
Simon's Taxes. — London : Butterworths, 1981
Cover title
the provisions relating to income tax, corporation tax and capital gains tax. — 167p ; 24cm
ISBN 0-406-06846-1 (pbk) : Unpriced
B81-26878

344.1034 — Great Britain. Taxation. Law: Finance Act 1981 — *Critical studies*

The **Finance** Act 1981. — [London] ([1 Little New Street, EC4A 3TR]) : Touche Ross, 1981. — viii,83p ; 21cm. — (Touche Ross tax guide)
Unpriced (pbk) B81-39812

Maas, Robert W.. A guide to the Finance Act 1981 / by R.W. Maas with R.E. Newstone. — London : Dawn, c1981. — 126p ; 30cm + 1pamphlet([6]p : 30cm)
ISBN 0-9507762-0-3 (pbk) : Unpriced
B81-39055

344.1034 — Great Britain. Taxation. Law — *For tax avoidance*

Sumption, Anthony. Sumption and Lawton's tax and tax planning. — 9th ed. / Anthony Sumption. — London : Oyez, 1981. — xxii,198p ; 22cm
Previous ed.: published as : Tax and tax planning / by Philip Lawton and Anthony Sumption, 1979. — Includes index
ISBN 0-85120-525-9 (pbk) : £10.75 B81-13614

344.1034 — Great Britain. Taxation. Law. Great Britain. *Parliament. House of Commons.* **Finance Bill. Session 1980-81** — *Critical studies*

Dean, P. R.. The budget and Finance Bill 1981 / P.R. Dean. — [Guildford] ([Braboeuf Manor, Portsmouth Rd., St. Catherine's, Guildford, Surrey]) : [College of Law], c1981. — 26p ; 22cm. — (Crash course lecture / the College of Law, ISSN 0309-2771 ; 1981)
Cover title
£1.40 (pbk) B81-39984

344.1034'02632 — Great Britain. Direct taxation. Law — *Statutes — Collections*

Great Britain. [Laws, etc.]. The taxes acts : the income tax, corporation tax and capital gains tax enactments in force from 6 April 1975 up to and including the Finance Act 1980 / Inland Revenue. — London : H.M.S.O., 1981. — 5v. ; 25cm
Previous ed.: 1978. — Includes index
ISBN 0-11-641206-2 (pbk) : Unpriced
B81-15610

344.103'4'02632 — Great Britain. Direct taxation. Law — *Statutes — Collections — Serials*

Great Britain. [Laws, etc.]. Butterworths yellow tax handbook. — 19th ed. (1980-81). — London : Butterworths, 1980. — 1236p in various pagings
ISBN 0-406-50996-4 : £13.50 B81-01829

344.1034'02633 — Great Britain. Taxation. Law — *Statutes — Texts with commentaries*

Great Britain. [Finance Act 1980]. The Finance Act 1980 / edited by Butterworths legal editorial staff ; contributors J.F. Avery Jones ... [et al.]. — London : Butterworths, 1980. — iv,275p ; 25cm. — (Annotated legislation service ; v.269)
Includes index
ISBN 0-406-54797-1 : £14.50 B81-07642

344.1034'0264 — Great Britain. Taxation. Law — *Cases — Serials*

Simon's tax cases. — 1980. — London : Butterworths, c1980. — 742p
ISBN 0-406-06989-1 : Unpriced B81-15156

Simon's tax cases. Cumulative tables and index. — 1973-1980. — London : Butterworths, 12981. — 126p
ISBN 0-406-06991-3 : Unpriced B81-15157

344.1034'02648 — Great Britain. Direct taxation. Law. Cases — *Digests — Serials*

Tolley's tax cases. — 5th ed. (1981). — Croydon : Tolley Pub. Co., 1981. — xviii,435p
ISBN 0-85459-030-7 : £9.50 B81-30846

344.1034'05 — Great Britain. Direct taxation. Law. Statutes — *Commentaries — Serials*

Rowland's tax guide. — 4th ed. (1980-81). — London : Butterworths, 1980. — 783p in various pagings
ISBN 0-406-35915-6 : Unpriced
ISSN 0143-280x B81-04791

344.1034'05 — Great Britain. Taxation. Law — *For tax avoidance — Serials*

Tolley's tax planning. — 1980-81. — Oxford (P.O. Box 1, Watlington, Oxford) : Tax Lawyer Pub., c1980. — xxxvii,734p
£17.50 B81-24094

344.1034'092'2 — Great Britain. Vestey *(Family).* **Tax avoidance,** *1915-1980*

Knightley, Phillip. The Vestey affair / Phillip Knightley. — London : Macdonald, 1981. — 159p,[8]p of plates : ill,ports,1geneal.table ; 23cm
ISBN 0-354-04708-6 : £7.95 B81-29150

344.1035'2 — Great Britain. Income tax. Law

Andrews, John M. (John Malcolm). Taxation of directors and employees : the law under Schedule E / by John M. Andrews. — 2nd ed. — London : Institute of Chartered Accountants in England and Wales, 1980. — xxiv,299p ; 21cm. — (Chartac taxation guides)
Previous ed.: 1977. — Includes index
ISBN 0-85291-283-8 (pbk) : Unpriced
B81-20396

344.1035'2 — Great Britain. Personal income tax. Law — *Questions & answers — For accounting*

Homer, Arnold. Schedule E / [... prepared for the Trust by Arnold Homer and Rita Burrows]. — London : Certified Accountants Educational Trust, c1980. — 41p ; 21cm. — (Taxation) (Workbook ; no.T12)
Unpriced (pbk) B81-41025

344.1035'2'05 — Great Britain. Income tax. Law — *Serials*

Key to income tax. — 88th ed. (1980-81). — London : Taxation Pub., [1980?]. — 260p. — (Taxation master key series)
ISSN 0305-5655 : £6.00 B81-12435

Tolley's income tax. — 65th ed. (1980-81). — London : Tolley, c1980. — x,434p
ISBN 0-85459-018-8 : £8.50
ISBN 0-85459-018-8 B81-03510

344.1035'245 — Great Britain. Capital gains tax. Law

Caulfield, B. I.. Capital taxation now / B.I. Caulfield. — [Guildford] ([Braboeuf Manor, Portsmouth Rd., St. Catherine's, Guildford, Surrey]) : [College of Law], [1981]. — 19p ; 22cm. — (Crash course lecture / the College of Law, ISSN 0309-2771 ; 1981)
Cover title
£1.40 (pbk)
Also classified at 344.1035'3 B81-39986

Vine, L. F.. Capital gains tax : the provisions of the Capital Gains Tax Act 1979 (as amended by the Finance Act 1980). — Rev. ed / L.F. Vine. — London (29 Lincoln's Inn Fields, WG2A 3EE) : Certified Accountants Educational Trust, 1980. — 124p ; 24cm. — (Certified Accountants technical publication)
Previous ed.: 1976. — Includes index
£5.50 (pbk) B81-23975

344.1035'245'05 — Great Britain. Capital gains tax. Law — *Serials*

Key to capital gains tax. — 1980. — London : Taxation Publishing, [1980]. — 420p
Unpriced B81-09097

Tolley's capital gains tax. — 1980-81. — London : Tolley, c1980. — x,221p
ISSN 0143-1633 (corrected) : £6.95 B81-04163

344.1035'3 — Great Britain. Capital transfer tax. Law

Caulfield, B. I.. Capital taxation now / B.I. Caulfield. — [Guildford] ([Braboeuf Manor, Portsmouth Rd., St. Catherine's, Guildford, Surrey]) : [College of Law], [1981]. — 19p ; 22cm. — (Crash course lecture / the College of Law, ISSN 0309-2771 ; 1981)
Cover title
£1.40 (pbk)
Primary classification 344.1035'245 B81-39986

344.1035'3 — Great Britain. Capital transfer tax. Law — *Serials*

Tolley's capital transfer tax. — 1980-81. — London : Tolley, c1980. — viii,160p
ISBN 0-85459-020-x : £6.75
ISBN 0-85459-003-x
ISSN 0144-4042 B81-05232

344.1035'3 — Great Britain. Capital transfer tax. Law — *Statutes — Collections — Serials*

The **Taxes** Acts. The Capital Transfer tax enactments in force from 27 March 1974 to and including the Finance Act ... / Inland Revenue. — 1980 ed.. — London : H.M.S.O., 1981. — ix,296p
ISBN 0-11-641232-1 : £8.50 B81-24108

344.1035'3 — Great Britain. Capital transfer tax. Tax avoidance

Newman, Geoffrey, *1946-.* Revised planning for capital transfer tax / Geoffrey Newman & Raymond Godfrey. — 3rd ed. — St. Helier (P.O. Box 318, St. Helier, Jersey, C.I.) : Guild Press, 1980. — 178p ; 22cm
Previous ed.: 1977. — Includes index
ISBN 0-907342-00-0 (pbk) : £12.00 B81-10058

344.1035'46'02632 — Great Britain. Development land tax. Law — *Statutes — Collections — Serials*

The **Taxes** Acts. The Development land tax enactments in force from 22 July 1976 up to and including the Finance Act ... / Inland Revenue. — 1980 ed.. — London : H.M.S.O., 1981. — iv,376p
ISBN 0-11-641231-3 : £9.95 B81-24109

344.1035'5 — Great Britain. Value-added tax. Law — *Cases*

Relf, David G.. VAT casebook / David G. Relf and Christopher A. L. Preston. — London : Oyez, c1981. — xxiii,268p ; 24cm
Includes index
ISBN 0-85120-522-4 (pbk) : £12.50 B81-13613

344.1035'582282'02632 — Great Britain. Petroleum industries. Taxation. Law — *Statutes — Collections — Serials*

The oil taxation acts : the oil taxation enactments in force from 8 May 1975 up to and including the Finance Act ... with other legislation and statutory regulations affecting the application of the tax, and an index / Inland Revenue. — 1980 ed.-. — London (Somerset House [Strand WC2]) : Board of Inland Revenue, 1981-. — v. ; 25cm
Irregular
ISSN 0261-3670 = Oil taxation acts : £7.00
B81-24995

344.1035'582282'02633 — Great Britain. Petroleum revenue tax. Law — *Statutes — Texts with commentaries*

Great Britain. [Laws, etc.]. United Kingdom oil and gas tax legislation / edited and annotated by J. Gordon McClure, Anne G. Lavies. — Woking (73 Goldsworth Rd., Woking, Surrey GU21 1JY) : Tax & Financial Planning, 1980. — v,232p ; 23cm + Supplement(32p ; 21cm)
Four cards 23x15cm as insert
£20.00 (pbk) B81-34453

344.1035'7 — Great Britain. Capital duty & stamp duties. Law

Harper, A. C.. Stamp duty and capital duty / by A.C. Harper. — London : Institute of Chartered Accountants, 1979. — xxviii,345p : ill ; 22cm. — (Chartac taxation guides)
Includes index
ISBN 0-85291-226-9 (pbk) : Unpriced
B81-39054

344.1035'7 — Great Britain. Stamp duties. Law

Sergeant, E. G.. Sergeant and Sims on stamp duties. — London : Butterworths
2nd supplement to seventh ed. / by B.J. Sims ; assistant editor E.M.E. Sims ; consultant editor A.K. Tavaré. — 1980. — xi,B97p : forms ; 24cm
ISBN 0-406-37034-6 (pbk) : £6.95 B81-28998

344.1036'7 — Great Britain. Companies. Taxation. Implications of reorganisation. Legal aspects

Gammie, Malcolm. Tax on company reorganizations / Malcolm Gammie and Susan Ball. — London : Taxation Publishing, 1980. — xxiv,397p ; 22cm
Includes index
£12.00 (pbk) B81-03596

344.1036'7 — Great Britain. Corporation tax. Tax avoidance

Gammie, Malcolm. Tax strategy for companies. — 2nd ed. / by Malcolm Gammie. — London : Oyez, 1981. — xx,275p : ill ; 22cm
Previous ed.: / by Michael Z. Hepker. 1975. — Includes index
ISBN 0-85120-540-2 (pbk) : £10.50 B81-14491

344.1036'7'05 — Great Britain. Corporation tax. Law — *Serials*

Tolley's corporation tax. — 1980-81. — London : Tolley, c1980. — viii,260p
ISBN 0-85459-017-x : £6.00
ISBN 0-85459-000-5
ISSN 0305-8921 B81-03509

344.1036'8 — Great Britain. Capital allowances. Law

Shock, John W.. Capital allowances / by John W. Shock. — London : Oyez, c1981. — xxxviii,403p ; 24cm
Includes index
ISBN 0-85120-486-4 : £25.00 B81-19825

344.1036'8 — Great Britain. Capital allowances. Law — *Questions & answers — For accounting*

Homer, Arnold. Capital allowances / [... prepared for the Trust by Arnold Homer and Rita Burrows]. — London : Certified Accountants Educational Trust, c1980. — 53p ; 21cm. — (Taxation) (Workbook ; no.T13)
Unpriced (pbk) B81-41026

344.103'7 — Great Britain. Industries. Law

Smith, I. T.. Industrial law / I.T. Smith, Sir John C. Wood. — London : Butterworths, 1980. — 422p ; 26cm
Includes index
ISBN 0-406-38141-0 (cased) : £18.00
ISBN 0-406-38140-2 (pbk) : £11.95 B81-00787

344.103'71 — Great Britain. Consumer protection. Law

Borrie, Gordon J.. The consumer, society and the law / Gordon Borrie and Aubrey L. Diamond. — 4th ed. — Harmondsworth : Penguin, 1981. — 360p : 1facsim ; 20cm. — (Pelican books)
Previous ed.: 1973. — Bibliography: p340-343. — Includes index
ISBN 0-14-020647-7 (pbk) : £2.95 B81-21039

Harries, John V.. Consumers : know your rights / John V. Harries. — 2nd ed. — London : Oyez, 1981. — xii,234p ; 21cm. — (Its your law)
Previous ed.: 1978. — Includes index
ISBN 0-85120-499-6 (cased) : Unpriced
ISBN 0-85120-500-3 (pbk) : £4.95 B81-24419

344.103'71'024381 — Great Britain. Consumer protection. Law — *For motor vehicle trades*

Worsdall, Anthea. Consumer law for the motor trade / by Anthea Wordsall ; foreword by Anthony Frazer and Alan M. Dix. — London : Butterworths, 1981. — xi,219p : ill,forms ; 22cm
Includes index
ISBN 0-406-42590-6 (pbk) : £7.50 B81-23033

344.103'71'024658 — Great Britain. Consumer protection. Law — *For businessmen*

Snow, R. F.. Product liability and consumer protection : some problems for the business client / R.F. Snow. — [Guildford] ([Braboeuf Manor, Portsmouth Rd., St. Catherine's, Guildford, Surrey]) : [College of Law], 1981. — 21p ; 22cm. — (Crash course lecture / the College of Law, ISSN 0309-2771 ; 1981)
Cover title
£1.40 (pbk) B81-39985

344.103'72 — Great Britain. Industries. Competition. Law — *Statutes — Texts with commentaries*

Great Britain. [The Competition Act 1980]. The Competition Act 1980 / introductory commentary by James P. Cunningham ; the Act annotated by John Tinnion. — London : Sweet & Maxwell, 1980. — 57,[43]p ; 25cm
ISBN 0-421-27880-3 (pbk) : £8.00 : CIP rev. B80-13742

Miscellaneous Acts / annotated by Butterworths legal editorial staff with a contribution on the Employment Act 1980 by B.W. Napier. — London : Butterworths, 1980. — 178p ; 25cm. — (Annotated legislation service ; v.271)
Includes index
ISBN 0-406-54800-5 : Unpriced
Primary classification 344.104'7'02633 B81-13359

344.103'772'05 — Great Britain. Continental shelf. Offshore natural gas & petroleum industries. Law — *Serials*

. United Kingdom offshore legislation guide. — 1980-. — London : Kogan Page, 1980-. — v. ; 30cm
Annual
ISSN 0260-6135 = United Kingdom offshore legislation guide : £25.00 B81-04947

United Kingdom offshore legislation guide. — 2nd ed. (1981). — London : Kogan Page, Nov.1981. — [240]p
ISBN 0-85038-499-0 (pbk) : £30.00 : CIP entry B81-33640

344.103'78624 — Great Britain. Construction. Government contracts. Standard conditions. Great Britain. *Department of the Environment.* **General conditions of Government contracts for building and civil engineering work. Claims**

Wood, R. D. (Reginald Douglas). Contractors' claims under the GC/Works/1 — Edition 2 form of contract / by R.D. Wood. — Englemere : Institute of Building, 1980. — 68p : ill ; 30cm. — (Studies in contractual claims ; 7)
ISBN 0-906600-23-5 (pbk) : Unpriced : CIP rev. B79-32367

344.103'87'0264 — Great Britain. Foreign trade. Law — *Cases*

Cases & materials on the law of international trade / edited by Mark S.W. Hoyle. — London ([10 Wandon Rd., SW6 2JJ]) : Laureate, c1980. — viii,282p : forms ; 31cm
ISBN 0-907392-00-8 (cased) : Unpriced
ISBN 0-907392-01-6 (pbk) : Unpriced B81-17194

344.103'94'05 — Great Britain. Road traffic. Law — *Serials*

Kitchin's road transport law. — 22nd ed (1981). — London : Butterworth, 1981. — ix,331p
ISBN 0-406-26473-2 : £10.95
ISSN 0308-8987 B81-09120

344.103'944 — Great Britain. Heavy commercial vehicles. Law

Summers, Dennis. HGV law guide. — London : Butterworths, Sept.1981. — [96]p
ISBN 0-408-00569-6 : £5.95 : CIP entry B81-23951

344.103'944 — Great Britain. Motor vehicles. Engineering aspects. Standards. Law: Motor Vehicles (Construction and Use) Regulations 1973 — *Commentaries*

Toyne, C. C.. Motor vehicle technical regulations / C. C. Toyne. — 2nd ed. — Northwood (Evington House, The Avenue, Northwood, Middx.) : Lifton Engineering Services
Previous ed.: 1974
ISBN 0-9500679-6-2 (pbk) : Unpriced
Also classified at 344.103'944 B81-26609

344.103'944 — Great Britain. Motor vehicles. Lights. Standards. Law: Road Vehicles Lighting Regulations 1971 — *Commentaries*

Toyne, C. C.. Motor vehicle technical regulations / C. C. Toyne. — 2nd ed. — Northwood (Evington House, The Avenue, Northwood, Middx.) : Lifton Engineering Services
Previous ed.: 1974
ISBN 0-9500679-6-2 (pbk) : Unpriced
Primary classification 344.103'944 B81-26609

344.103'946 — Great Britain. Dangerous materials for transport by road. Safety aspects. Statutory regulations

Great Britain. *Health and Safety Executive*. A guide to the Dangerous Substances (Conveyance by Road in Road Tankers and Road Tank Containers) Regulations 1981. — London : H.M.S.O., Dec.1981. — [50]p. — (HS(R))
ISBN 0-11-883476-2 : CIP entry B81-38852

344.103'9483 — Great Britain. Road freight transport. Law — *Serials*

The **Transport** manager's handbook. — 11th ed. — 11th ed. (1981). — London : Kogan Page, 1980. — 372p
ISBN 0-85038-333-1 : £11.95 : CIP rev.
ISSN 0306-9435 B80-24253

The **Transport** manager's handbook. — 12th ed. (1982). — London : Kogan Page, Dec.1981. — [500]p
ISBN 0-85038-492-3 : £13.50 : CIP entry B81-33865

344.103'9483'05 — Great Britain. Road freight transport services. Law — *Serials*

[Yearbook *(Freight Transport Association)*]. Yearbook. — 1981. — Tunbridge Wells (Hermes House, St. Johns Rd, Tunbridge Wells, Kent TN4 9UZ) : Freight Transport Association, 1981. — 217p
ISSN 0306-1523 : £9.75 B81-21353

344.103'965 — Great Britain. Shipping. Law

Arnould, *Sir* **Joseph**. Arnould's law of marine insurance and average. — 16th ed. — London : Stevens, Oct.1981. — 2v. [(1360)p.]. — (British shipping laws)
Previous ed.: published as The law of marine insurance and average / by Lord Chorley of Kendal and C.T. Bailhache
ISBN 0-420-44500-5 : £120.00 : CIP entry B81-25313

344.103'975 — Great Britain. Aeroplanes. Flying. Statutory regulations — *For private pilots*

Aviation law for applicants for the Private Pilot's licence / Civil Aviation Authority. — 6th ed. — London : The Authority, 1981. — iv,62p : ill ; 22cm. — (CAP ; 85)
Previous ed.: 1979
ISBN 0-86039-134-5 (pbk) : £0.60 B81-39599

344.103'9945 — Great Britain. Broadcasting services: British Broadcasting Corporation — *Charters*

Great Britain. *Home Office*. Broadcasting : copy of the Royal Charter for the continuance of the British Broadcasting Corporation. — London : H.M.S.O., [1981]. — 18p ; 25cm. — (Cmnd. ; 8313)
At head of title: Home Office
ISBN 0-10-183130-7 (unbound) : £2.10 B81-35399

344.103'9945 — Great Britain. Broadcasting services: British Broadcasting Corporation — *Charters — Proposals*

Great Britain. *Home Office*. Broadcasting : draft of Royal Charter for the continuance of the British Broadcasting Corporation for which the Secretary of State for the Home Department proposes to apply. — London : H.M.S.O., 1981. — 18p ; 25cm. — (Cmnd. ; 8232)
ISBN 0-10-182320-7 (unbound) : £2.10 B81-26091

344.104'1 — Great Britain. Employment. Labour. Law
Pearl, David. Social welfare law / David Pearl and Kevin Gray. — London : Croom Helm, c1981. — 308p ; 23cm
Bibliography: p265. — Includes index
ISBN 0-85664-644-x (cased) : £14.95
ISBN 0-7099-2004-0 (pbk) : £8.95
Also classified at 344.2061'5 ; 344.104'2 ; 344.2064'344 B81-29850

344.104'1 — Great Britain. Industrial relations. Law
McMullen, Jeremy. Employment law under the Tories : a guide to the current attack on workers' rights / Jeremy McMullen. — London : Pluto, 1981. — viii,120p : ill ; 20cm. — (Workers' handbooks)
Includes index
ISBN 0-86104-314-6 (pbk) : £1.95 B81-16485

Riddall, J. G.. The law of industrial relations / by J.G. Riddall. — London : Butterworths, 1981. — xxiv,319p ; 25cm
Includes index
ISBN 0-406-64810-7 (pbk) : Unpriced B81-29710

344.104'1'02632 — Great Britain. Industrial relations. Law — *Statutes — Collections*
Sweet & Maxwell's labour relations statutes and materials 80/81 / edited by Sweet & Maxwell's Legal Editorial Staff ; advisory editors B.A. Hepple, Paul O'Higgins, Lord Wedderburn of Charlton. — London : Sweet & Maxwell, 1981. — vii,175p ; 25cm
Includes index
ISBN 0-421-28370-x (pbk) : £9.85 B81-26556

344.104'1125 — Great Britain. Employment. Law
Hepple, B. A.. Employment law. — 4th ed. — London : Sweet & Maxwell, Nov.1981. — [430]p
Previous ed.: 1979
ISBN 0-421-28830-2 (pbk) : £13.25 : CIP entry B81-31172

Marsh, G. Barrie. Employer and employee : a complete and practical guide to the modern law of employment / by G. Barrie Marsh. — 2nd ed. — London : Shaw & Sons, 1981. — lxi,616p ; 23cm
Previous ed.: 1977. — Includes index
ISBN 0-7219-0741-5 : Unpriced B81-40382

Selwyn, Norman M.. Law of employment / by Norman M. Selwyn. — 3rd ed. — London : Butterworths, 1980. — xxxi,407p : forms ; 22cm
Previous ed.: 1978. — Includes index
ISBN 0-406-65342-9 (pbk) : £8.95 B81-02452

Whincup, Michael. Modern employment law : a guide to job security and safety at work / Michael Whincup. — 3rd ed. — London : Heinemann, 1980. — xli,318p : ill ; 22cm
Previous ed.: 1978. — Includes index
ISBN 0-434-92244-7 (pbk) : £8.50 B81-12640

344.104'1125 — Great Britain. Employment. Law: Employment Act 1980 — *Critical studies*
Beat the Act : TUC workbook on the Employment Act. — London : Trades Union Congress, 1981. — 43p : ill(some col.),1port ; 30cm. — (TUC education)
Cover title. — Text, port on inside cover
£0.75 (pbk) B81-22810

Eccles, George. The Employment Act 1980 : a practical guide / George Eccles. — London : Oyez, 1980. — 225p in various pagings : 2ill ; 22cm
Includes index
ISBN 0-85120-506-2 (pbk) : £9.50 B81-05757

The **Employment** Act, 1980. — London (346 Harrow Rd., W9 2HP) : Industrial Relations Briefing, c1980. — 62p ; 21cm. — (IRB question & answer series ; no.9)
ISBN 0-86231-005-9 (pbk) : £5.95 B81-30066

Lewis, Roy. Striking a balance?. — Oxford : Martin Robertson, Oct.1981. — [224]p
ISBN 0-85520-442-7 (cased) : £12.50 : CIP entry
ISBN 0-85529-443-5 (pbk) : £4.50 B81-27426

TUC handbook on the Employment Act 1980. — London : Trades Unions Congress, 1981. — 53p ; 21cm
Originally published: 1980
£0.75 (pbk) B81-22811

344.104'1125 — Great Britain. Employment. Law: Employment Act 1980 — *For management*
Janner, Greville. Janner's practical guide to the Employment Act, 1980 : industrial relations and employment law / Greville Janner ; illustrations by Tobi. — London : Business Books, 1980. — xv,282p : ill ; 23cm
Includes index
ISBN 0-09-142990-0 : £15.00 : CIP rev. B80-18197

344.104'1125 — Great Britain. Employment. Law — *Encyclopaedias*
Chandler, Peter, *1936-*. An A-Z of employment and safety law / Peter Chandler. — London : Kogan Page, 1981. — xi,516p : 1facsim,forms ; 24cm
Includes index
ISBN 0-85038-446-x : £16.95 : CIP rev.
Also classified at 344.104'465 B81-08877

344.104'1125'024658 — Great Britain. Employment. Law — *For management — Serials*
Employment law for management. — Vol.1, issue 1 (Nov.1980)-. — Sudbury (Rectory Rd, Great Wallingfield, Sudbury, Suffolk CO10 0TL) : Monitor Press, 1980-. — v. ; 30cm
Monthly
ISSN 0261-2518 = Employment law for management : Unpriced B81-21346

344.104'1125'02632 — Great Britain. Employment. Law — *Statutes & statutory instruments — Collections*
Butterworths employment law handbook / edited by Peter Wallington. — 2nd ed. — London : Butterworths, 1981. — xlii,616p ; 25cm
Previous ed.: 1979. — Includes index
ISBN 0-406-14261-0 (pbk) : Unpriced B81-36510

344.104'1125'02632 — Great Britain. Employment. Law — *Statutes — Collections — Texts with commentaries*
Great Britain. [Laws, etc]. The employment acts 1974-1980 : with commentary / by Charles D. Drake and Brian Bercusson. — London : Sweet & Maxwell, 1981. — vii,43p ; 25cm
ISBN 0-421-28250-9 (pbk) : £9.50 B81-29208

344.104'1125'02633 — Great Britain. Employment. Law — *Statutes — Texts with commentaries*
Great Britain. [Employment Protection (Consolidation) Act 1978]. Employment Protection (Consolidation) Act 1978 / introduction by R.J. Harvey ; annotations by Andrew E.C. Thompson. — London : Butterworths, 1979. — xvi,357p ; 25cm. — (Annotated legislation service ; v.263)
Includes index
ISBN 0-406-54771-8 : £27.00 B81-07637

Miscellaneous Acts / annotated by Butterworths legal editorial staff with a contribution on the Employment Act 1980 by B.W. Napier. — London : Butterworths, 1980. — 178p ; 25cm. — (Annotated legislation service ; v.271)
Includes index
ISBN 0-406-54800-5 : Unpriced
Primary classification 344.104'7'02633 B81-13359

344.104'1133 — Great Britain. Homosexual personnel. Employment. Equality of opportunity. Law. Reform — *Proposals*
Beer, Chris. Gay workers : trade unions and the law / Chris Beer, Roland Jeffery and Terry Munyard ; introduction by Tony Benn ; cartoons by Dominic Poelsma. — [London] : National Council for Civil Liberties, 1981. — 53p ; 20cm
ISBN 0-901108-90-1 (pbk) : £1.20 B81-33252

344.104'12 — Great Britain. Workplaces. Improvement notices & prohibition notices. Law
Improvement notices & prohibition notices : what they are & how they work. — London (346 Harrow Rd., W9 2HP) : Industrial Relations Briefing, c1981. — 41p : forms ; 21cm. — (IRB question & answer series ; no.1)
ISBN 0-86231-000-8 (pbk) : £5.95 B81-30065

344.104'12'02632 — Great Britain. Factories. Working conditions. Law — *Statutes & statutory instruments — Texts with commentaries*
Redgrave, Alexander. Redgrave's health and safety in factories : (replacing Redgrave's factories acts 22nd edition). — London : Butterworth
Includes index
2nd cumulative supplement / by Ian Fife and E. Anthony Machin consulting editors and Shaun Thorpe and Peter Stickland. — 1981. — viii,B179p : forms ; 18cm
ISBN 0-406-35305-0 (pbk) : Unpriced B81-26615

344.104'125 — Great Britain. Employment. Labour. Law
Drake, Charles D.. Labour law. — 3rd ed. — London : Sweet and Maxwell, July 1981. — [285]p. — (Concise college texts)
Previous ed.: 1974
ISBN 0-421-28100-6 (cased) : £12.50 : CIP entry
ISBN 0-421-28110-3 (pbk) : £10.50 B81-13471

344.104'1252 — Great Britain. Occupational superannuation schemes. Law
Smith, Ian, *1949-*. Occupational pensions / Ian Smith. — London : Sweet & Maxwell, 1980. — vii,83p ; 18cm. — (Law at work)
Bibliography: p78. - Includes index
ISBN 0-421-27260-0 (pbk) : £1.95 : CIP rev. B80-20398

344.104'1252 — Great Britain. Occupational superannuation schemes. Trustees. Law — *For trade unionism*
Law of trusts and pension schemes : note of guidance. — London : Trades Union Congress, 1980. — 12p ; 21cm
£0.25 (pbk) B81-22815

344.104'12596 — Great Britain. Personnel. Dismissal & redundancy. Law
Waud, Christopher. Redundancy and unfair dismissal : a guide in plain language to the employment laws, including equal pay, sex discrimination, race relations and how to put your case at industrial tribunals 1981-82 / by Christopher Waud. — [London] ([8 Stratton St., W1X 6AT]) : Published by Harmsworth Publications for Associated Newspapers Group, c1981. — 79p ; 21
Includes index
ISBN 0-85144-179-3 (pbk) : £1.00 B81-27048

344.104'12596 — Great Britain. Personnel. Dismissal for misconduct. Legal aspects
Misconduct at the workplace. — London (346 Harrow Rd., W9 2HP) : Industrial Relations Briefing, c1981. — 51p : forms ; 21cm. — (IRB question & answer series ; no.3)
ISBN 0-86231-002-4 (pbk) : £5.95 B81-30064

344.104'12596 — Great Britain. Personnel. Dismissal. Law
Mead, Malcolm. Unfair dismissal / Malcolm Mead. — London : Oyez, c1981. — xxxv,287p ; 24cm
Includes index
£15.00 (pbk) B81-21286

Upex, Robert. Dismissal / Robert Upex. — London : Sweet & Maxwell, 1980. — vii,87p : 2forms ; 18cm. — (Law at work)
Includes index
ISBN 0-421-27270-8 (pbk) : £1.95 : CIP rev. B80-20399

344.104'12596 — Great Britain. Personnel. Lay-offs & short time working. Law
Lay-offs and short-time. — London (140 Gt. Portland St., W.1.) : Incomes Data Services, 1981. — 87p : 1form ; 21cm. — (IDS handbook series ; no.19)
Includes index
£5.00 (pbk) B81-30919

344.104'12596 — Great Britain. Personnel. Lay-offs, short time working & redundancy. Legal aspects
Lay-off, short time working & redundancy. — London (346 Harrow Rd., W9 2HP) : Industrial Relations Briefing, c1981. — 60p : forms ; 21cm. — (IRB question & answer series ; no.2)
ISBN 0-86231-001-6 (pbk) : £5.95 B81-30061

344.104'12596 — Great Britain. Redundancy. Law
Bourn, Colin. Job security / Colin Bourn. — London : Sweet & Maxwell, 1980. — 90p ; 18cm. — (Law at work)
Includes index
ISBN 0-421-27280-5 (pbk) : £1.95 : CIP rev. B80-20400

344.104'12596 — Great Britian. Personnel. Dismissal for absenteeism. Legal aspects
Sickness, absenteeism and dismissal. — London (346 Harrow Rd., W9 2HP) : Industrial Relations Briefing, c1981. — 54p : forms ; 21cm. — (IRB question & answer series ; no.5)
ISBN 0-86231-004-0 (pbk) : £5.95 B81-30063

344.104'12598 — Great Britain. Personnel. Discipline. Law
Napier, Brian. Discipline / Brian Napier. — London : Sweet & Maxwell, 1980. — vii,84p ; 18cm. — (Law at work)
Bibliography: p78. - Includes index
ISBN 0-421-27230-9 (pbk) : £1.95 : CIP rev. B80-20401

344.104'14 — Great Britain. Women personnel. Sex discrimination by employers. Law
Adams, Shelley. Sex discrimination / Shelley Adams. — London : Sweet & Maxwell, 1980. — vi,90p : ill ; 18cm. — (Law at work)
Includes index
ISBN 0-421-26710-0 (pbk) : £1.95 : CIP rev. B80-20402

344.104'1425763 — Great Britain. Women personnel. Maternity rights. Legal aspects
Coussins, Jean. Maternity rights for working women / Jean Coussins. — 2nd ed., completely rev. — London : NCCL Rights for Women Unit, 1980. — 38p : 1ill ; 20cm
Previous ed.: 1976
ISBN 0-901108-89-8 (pbk) : £0.75 B81-12985

344.104'17613875 — Merchant ships. Personnel. Employment. British law
Kitchen, Jonathan S.. The employment of merchant seamen / Jonathan S. Kitchen. — London : Croom Helm, c1980. — 658p ; 23cm
Includes index
ISBN 0-85664-527-3 : £60.00 : CIP rev. B79-07138

344.104'188 — Great Britain. Trade unions. Disclosure of information: Disclosure by employers. Law: Employment Protection Act 1975. Implementation
Marsh, Arthur. Disclosure to unions : how the law is working : a study of the implementation of ss.17-21 of the Employment Protection Act 1975 / by Arthur Marsh and Roger Hussey. — [London] ([3 London Wall Buildings EC2M 5PH]) : Touche Ross and St Edmunds Hall Industrial Relations Annexe, 1979 (1980 [printing]). — 94p : form ; 21cm
Unpriced (pbk) B81-10718

344.104'188 — Great Britain. Trade unions. Law — *For employers*
Employing union members / [Incomes Data Services Ltd]. — London (140 Great Portland St., W.1) : Incomes Data Services Ltd, 1980. — 191p ; 21cm. — (IDS handbook series ; no.18)
Unpriced (pbk) B81-11555

344.104'188 — Great Britain. Trade unions. Law. Reform. Great Britain. *Department of Employment*. Trade union immunities — *Critical studies*
Institute of Directors. [Trade union law and the pursuit of prosperity - the next step] : submission to the Secretary of State for Employment in response to the green paper on trade union immunities / [prepared by] Roderick Thomas. — London : Director Publications, 1981. — 66p ; 30cm
At head of title: Institute of Directors
£4.95 (pbk) B81-38376

344.104'188 — Great Britain. Trade unions. Members. Rights. Law
Campbell, Alan. Trade unions and the individual / by Alan Campbell and John Bowyer with assistance from Michael Soole ; foreword by Lord Wilberforce. — Oxford : ESC Publishing, 1980. — xliv,491p ; 23cm
Includes index
ISBN 0-906214-05-x : Unpriced B80-10022

344.104'189 — Great Britain. Industrial relations. Disputes. Law. Reform — *Proposals*
Whose 'law & order'? : the increasing use of law against strikes, picketing, occupations and demonstrations / Campaign Against a Criminal Trespass Law. — London (c/o 35 Wellington St., W.C.2) : CACTL, 1979. — 22p ; 21cm
£0.20 (unbound) B81-38018

344.104'18915 — Great Britain. Personnel. Dismissal. Appeals. Procedure of industrial tribunals
Sacked? Made redundant? : your rights if you lose your job : a handbook for applicants to industrial tribunals / by Chapeltown Citizens Advice Bureau Tribunal Assistance Unit ; cartoons by Harry Hamill. — [London] ([11, Drury Lane, WC2B 5SW]) : National Association of Citizens Advice Bureaux, c1981. — v,199p : ill ; 21cm
Includes index
ISBN 0-906072-02-6 (pbk) : £2.50 B81-39056

344.104'1892 — Great Britain. Industrial relations. Strikes. Law
Elias, Patrick. Trade disputes / Patrick Elias — London : Sweet & Maxwell, 1980. — vi,87p ; 18cm. — (Law at work)
Includes index
ISBN 0-421-27240-6 (pbk) : £19.95 : CIP rev. B80-20403

344.104'18927 — Great Britain. Industrial relations. Picketing. Law. Reform — *Proposals*
Centre for Policy Studies. *Trade Union Reform Committee*. Give the picketing code the sanction of law : submission by the Trade Union Reform Committee of the Centre for Policy Studies to the Rt Hon. James Prior MP, Secretary of State for Employment in response to his request for the pulic's views as part of a process of consultation. — [London] ([Wilfred St., SW1]) : The Centre, 1980. — 18,6p ; 32cm
ISBN 0-905880-31-5 (spiral) : Unpriced B81-07153

344.104'2 — Great Britain. Social security benefits. Increase. Law. Statutory instruments. Drafts. Financial aspects — *Inquiry reports*
Great Britain. *Government Actuary*. Report by the Government Actuary on the draft of the Social Security Benefits Up-rating order 1981. — London : H.M.S.O., [1981]. — 4p ; 25cm. — (Cmnd. ; 8296)
ISBN 0-10-182960-4 (unbound) : £1.40 B81-33359

344.104'2 — Great Britain. Social security benefits. Law
Fulbrook, Julian. Social security / Julian Fulbrook. — London : Sweet & Maxwell, 1980. — vii,88p ; 18cm. — (Law at work)
Bibliography: p84. - Includes index
ISBN 0-421-26720-8 (pbk) : £1.95 : CIP rev. B80-20405

Pearl, David. Social welfare law / David Pearl and Kevin Gray. — London : Croom Helm, c1981. — 308p ; 23cm
Bibliography: p265. — Includes index
ISBN 0-85664-644-x (cased) : £14.95
ISBN 0-7099-2004-0 (pbk) : £8.95
Primary classification 344.104'1 B81-29850

344.104'2 — Great Britain. Social security benefits. Law. Statutory instruments. Drafts — *Inquiry reports*
Great Britain. *National Insurance Advisory Committee*. Social Security (Determination of Claims and Questions) Miscellaneous Amendments Regulations 1980 (S.I. 1980 No.1622) : report of the National Insurance Advisory Committee in accordance with Section 139(3) of the Social Security Act 1975 preceded by a statement made by the Secretary of State for Social Services in accordance with Section 139(4) of that Act. — London : H.M.S.O., 1980. — 4p ; 25cm. — ([HC] ; 803)
ISBN 0-10-028039-0 (unbound) : £0.70 B81-19800

Great Britain. *National Insurance Advisory Committee*. Social Security (General Benefits, Claims, and Payments) Regulations 1980 (S.I. 1980 No.1621) : report of the National Insurance Advisory Committee in accordance with Section 139(3) of the Social Security Act 1975 preceded by a statement made by the Secretary of State for Social Services in accordance with Section 139(4) of that Act. — London : H.M.S.O., 1980. — 4p ; 25cm. — ([H.C.] ; 802)
ISBN 0-10-028029-3 (unbound) : £0.70 B81-19801

344.104'2 — Great Britain. Social security contributions. Exemption. Statutory instruments. Drafts — *Inquiry reports*
Great Britain. *National Insurance Advisory Committee*. Social Security (Categorisation of Earners) Amendment Regulations 1980 (S.I.1980 No.1713) : report of the National Insurance Advisory Committee in accordance with Section 139(3) of the Social Security Act 1975 preceded by a statement made by the Secretary of State for Social Services in accordance with Section 139(4) of that Act. — London : H.M.S.O., 1980. — 1folded sheet ([4])p ; 25cm. — (Cmnd. ; 8082)
ISBN 0-10-180820-8 : £0.70 B81-06159

344.104'2'02632 — Great Britain. Social security. Law — *Statutes — Codes — Serials*
Encyclopedia of social security law. — London : Sweet & Maxwell, 1980-. — v. ; 25cm
ISSN 0260-3829 = Encyclopedia of social security law : Unpriced B81-24124

344.104'2'0269 — Great Britain. Social security tribunals. Appellants. Representation. Role of advice centres — *Study regions: England: West Midlands*
Lawrence, Roger. Tribunal representation : the role of advice and advocacy services / Roger Lawrence. — London : Published in association with the National Association of Citizens Advice Bureaux by the Bedford Square Press of the National Council for Voluntary Organisations, 1980. — vii,98p : maps ; 30cm
ISBN 0-7199-1044-7 (pbk) : £3.95 B81-32722

344.104'224 — Great Britain. National insurance benefits: Maternity grants. Law. Statutory instruments. Drafts — *Inquiry reports*
Great Britain. *Social Security Advisory Committee*. The Social Security (Maternity Grant) Regulations 1981 (S.I.1981 No.1157) : report of the Social Security Advisory Committee in accordance with Section 10(3) of the Social Security Act 1980 preceded by a statement made by the Secretary of State for Social Services in accordance with Section 10 (4) of that Act. — London : H.M.S.O., [1981]. — 5p ; 25cm. — (Cmnd. ; 8336)
ISBN 0-10-183360-1 (unbound) : £1.15 B81-36917

344.104'23 — Great Britain. State superannuation schemes. Contracting-out. Law. Statutory instruments. Drafts — *Inquiry reports*
Occupational Pensions Board. The Contracting-out and Preservation (Further Provisions) Regulations 1981 (S.I. 1981 no.129) : report of the Occupational Pensions Board preceded by a statement by the Secretary of State for Social Services in accordance with section 68(2) of the Social Security Act 1973 and section 61(3) of the Social Security Pensions Act 1975. — London : H.M.S.O., 1981. — 7p ; 25cm. — (Cmnd. ; 8161)
ISBN 0-10-181610-3 (unbound) : £1.10 B81-14568

344.104'3216 — Great Britain. Local authorities. Welfare services for chronically sick persons. Law: Chronically Sick and Disabled Persons Act 1970. Enactment & operation
Topliss, Eda. A charter for the disabled / Eda Topliss and Bryan Gould. — Oxford : Blackwell, 1981. — 182p ; 23cm. — (Aspects of social policy)
Includes index
ISBN 0-631-12833-6 (cased) : £9.50
ISBN 0-631-12748-8 (pbk) : £3.95
Also classified at 344.104'324 B81-24181

344.104'324 — Great Britain. Local authorities. Welfare services for physically hanicapped persons. Law: Chronically Sick and Disabled Persons Act 1970. Enactment & operation

Topliss, Eda. A charter for the disabled / Eda Topliss and Bryan Gould. — Oxford : Blackwell, 1981. — 182p ; 23cm. — (Aspects of social policy)
Includes index
ISBN 0-631-12833-6 (cased) : £9.50
ISBN 0-631-12748-8 (pbk) : £3.95
Primary classification 344.104'3216 B81-24181

344.104'327 — Great Britain. Children. Care. Law — *For welfare work*

Leeding, A. E.. Child care legislation : a guide for social workers / [Alfred Leeding, Alastair Sinclair, Robert Moore]. — [London] : [IPC], [1980?]. — 44p ; 21cm. — (Community care)
Cover title
ISBN 0-617-00229-0 (pbk) : £1.50 B81-17597

344.104'4 — Great Britain. Statutory nuisances. Complaints by public. Procedure — *Manuals*

Statutory nuisance & section 99 Public Health Act 1936. — London (157 Waterloo Rd., SE1 8UU) : Shelter National Housing Aid Trust, 1980. — 33p : forms ; 21cm. — (Practice notes / Shelter National Housing Aid Trust ; 1)
ISBN 0-86265-002-x (pbk) : Unpriced B81-30909

344.104'41 — Great Britain. Medicine. Legal aspects

Legal issues in medicine. — Aldershot : Gower, Sept.1981. — [233]p
ISBN 0-566-00428-3 : £15.00 : CIP entry B81-22595

344.104'423 — Great Britain. Food & drugs. Law

Butterworths law of food and drugs / editor A.A. Painter ; co-ordinating editor Brian Harvey. — London : Butterworths, 1981. — 1v.(loose-leaf) : ill,forms ; 25cm
Five hundred and forty eight p in various pagings on publication
ISBN 0-406-11610-5 : Unpriced B81-27843

344.104'4232 — Great Britain. Food. Hygiene. Law

Quayle, V. J.. Food hygiene / by V.J. Quayle. — London : Shaw. — 47p ; 22cm. — (The Shaway guides ; no.6)
ISBN 0-7219-0874-8 (pbk) : Unpriced B81-21066

344.104'4232 — Great Britain. Food industries & trades. Hygiene. Law

Quayle, V. J.. Food hygiene / by V.J. Quayle. — London : Shaw. — (The Shaway guides ; no.5)
1: Markets, stalls and delivery vehicles : a guide to the Food Hygiene (Markets, Stalls and Delivery Vehicles) Regulations 1966 (as amended). — 1981. — 37p ; 22cm
ISBN 0-7219-0873-x (pbk) : Unpriced B81-12695

344.104'46342 — Great Britain. Workplaces. Air. Pollutants: Lead. Control. Standards. Law: Control of Lead at Work Regulations 1980 — *Critical studies*

Control of lead at work : report on proceedings of a series of seminars organized by LDA during March/May 1981 in the United Kingdom, designed to provide guidance for lead users on the requirements of the new regulations. — London (34, Berkeley Sq., W1X 6AJ) : Lead Development Association, [1981]. — 39p : ill ; 30cm
Unpriced (pbk) B81-40570

344.104'465 — Great Britain. *Health and Safety Executive*. Notification of accidents in workplaces. Law: Notification of Accidents and Dangerous Occurrences Regulations 1980 — *Critical studies*

The Notification of accidents and dangerous occurrences regulations, 1980. — London (346 Harrow Rd., W9 2HP) : Industrial Relations Briefing, c1981. — 56p ; 21cm. — (IRB question & answer series ; no.10)
ISBN 0-86231-006-7 (pbk) : £5.95 B81-30060

344.104'465 — Great Britain. Industrial health & industrial safety. Law

Croner's health and safety at work / edited by Shelagh Sweeney ; assistant editor Debra Holliman. — New Malden : Croner, [1981?]. — 1v.(loose-leaf) ; 23cm
Updated bi-monthly. — Includes index
Unpriced B81-10657

344.104'465 — Great Britain. Industrial health & industrial safety. Law — *For hotel & catering industries*

Notes for health, safety, hygiene and fire training. — Wembley : Hotel and Catering Industry Training Board, [197-]. — 12p ; 21cm
Unpriced (unbound) B81-33196

344.104'465 — Great Britain. Industrial health & safety. Law: Health and Safety at Work etc. Act 1974 — *Commentaries*

Wrigglesworth, Frank. A guide to the Health and Safety at Work Act / by Frank Wrigglesworth with Barry Earl. — Rev. — London : Industrial Society, 1978, c1974. — 50p ; 22cm
ISBN 0-85290-171-2 (pbk) : £1.75 B81-06357

344.104'465 — Great Britain. Industrial safety. Law — *Encyclopaedias*

Chandler, Peter, *1936-*. An A-Z of employment and safety law / Peter Chandler. — London : Kogan Page, 1981. — xi,516p : 1facsim,forms ; 24cm
Includes index
ISBN 0-85038-446-x : £16.95 : CIP rev.
Primary classification 344.104'1125 B81-08877

344.104'465 — Great Britain. Safety committees. Law

Hamilton, Margaret, *1912-*. Safety committees / by Margaret Hamilton. — Birmingham : Royal Society for the Prevention of Accidents, 1980. — vii,37p ; 21cm
Includes index. — Publication no.: IS185
ISBN 0-900635-32-0 (pbk) : £2.40 (£2.00 to RoSPA members) B81-06359

344.104'465'02462 — Great Britain. Industrial health & industrial safety. Law — *For engineering*

Health and safety legislation : professional brief / The Institution of Electrical Engineers. — [London] : [IEE], 1981. — 25p ; 21cm
Cover title
Unpriced (pbk) B81-37339

344.104'472 — Great Britain. Woodworking machines. Safety measures. Regulations: Woodworking Machines Regulations 1974 - *Critical studies*

Woodworking machines : guide to the 1974 regulations. — London : Health & Safety Excutive, July 1981. — [20]p. — (HS(R))
Originally published: / Department of Employment. 1974
ISBN 0-11-883437-1 (pbk) : CIP entry B81-15823

344.104'63635 — Great Britain. Housing. Law: Housing Act 1980 — *Critical studies*

The Housing Act 1980 : a guide for the practitioner. — [Guildford] : College of Law, c1981. — v,64p ; 22cm. — (College of Law lectures, ISSN 0309-3166)
£4.00 (pbk) B81-27229

McGurk, Peter. Housing Act 1980 : a reprint of eight articles from Local government chronicles / [author Peter McGurk, Bert Bucknall, David Hoath]. — London (Publications Division, 11 Bury St., EC3A 5AP) : Brown, Knight & Truscott (Holdings), [1981?]. — 35p ; 21cm
Text on inside cover
ISBN 0-904677-14-1 (pbk) : £3.00 B81-26270

Smith, Jerry, *1948-*. A guide to the Housing Act 1980 : for community workers and tenants / written by Jerry Smith. — [London] (60 Highbury Grove, N5 2AG) : Community Projects Foundation, 1981. — 35p ; 30cm
£0.50 (pbk) B81-31882

344.104'63635 — Great Britain. Housing. Laws: Housing Act 1980 — *Commentaries*

Macey, John P.. The Housing Act 1980 / by John P. Macey in collaboration with Keith Davies and Charles V. Baker. — London : Estates Gazette, 1981. — vi,99p ; 22cm
Includes index
£5.50 (pbk) B81-11597

344.104'63635'02633 — Great Britain. Housing. Law — *Statutes*

Great Britain. [Housing Act 1980]. Housing Act 1980 : Chapter 51. — London : H.M.S.O., [1980]. — vii,190p ; 25cm
Cover title
ISBN 0-10-545180-0 (pbk) : £6.90 B81-01739

344.104'63635'02633 — Great Britain. Housing. Law — *Statutes — Texts with commentaries*

Great Britain. [Housing Act 1980]. The Housing Act 1980 / with annotations by Andrew Arden. — London : Sweet and Maxwell, 1980. — 265p in various pagings ; 25cm. — (Current law statutes reprints)
ISBN 0-421-28140-5 (pbk) : £7.50 B81-01750

Smith, P. F.. Housing Act 1980 / by P.F. Smith. — London : Butterworths, c1981. — xx,379p ; 26cm
Includes index
ISBN 0-406-65790-4 : Unpriced B81-16093

344.104'636358 — Great Britain. Homeless persons. Housing. Provision. Powers of local authorities. Law: Housing (Homeless Persons) Act 1977. Implementation — *For homeless persons*

SHAC. Homeless? : know your rights. — London (189a Brompton Rd, SW5 0AR) : SHAC, 1979. — 8p ; 21cm
Unpriced (pbk) B81-35309

344.104'636358 — Great Britain. Local authority housing. Law: Housing Act 1980 — *Critical studies*

Liell, Peter. Council houses and the Housing Act 1980 / Peter Liell. — London : Butterworths, 1981. — xxxi,457p : ill,forms ; 23cm
Includes index
ISBN 0-406-27030-9 : £19.50 B81-23032

344.104'7'02633 — Great Britain. Education. Law — *Statutes — Texts with commentaries*

Miscellaneous Acts / annotated by Butterworths legal editorial staff with a contribution on the Employment Act 1980 by B.W. Napier. — London : Butterworths, 1980. — 178p ; 25cm. — (Annotated legislation service ; v.271)
Includes index
ISBN 0-406-54800-5 : Unpriced
Also classified at 344.103'72 ; 344.104'1125'02633 B81-13359

344.104'99 — Great Britain. Recreations: Hang gliding. Licensing — *For chartered surveyors*

Mackay, K. F.. Points to note in preparing a licence to authorise hang gliding / by K.F. Mackay. — [London] : Royal Institution of Chartered Surveyors, 1980. — 6p ; 21cm. — (Practice leaflet / Royal Institution of Chartered Surveyors Land Agency and Agriculture Division, ISSN 0305-4713 ; no.11)
Unpriced (unbound) B81-40966

344.105'231 — Great Britain. Terrorism. Prevention. Law: Prevention of Terrorism (Temporary Provisions) Act 1974. Operation, *1974-1980 — National Council for Civil Liberties viewpoints*

Scorer, Catherine. The Prevention of Terrorism Act : the case for repeal / Catherine Scorer and Patricia Hewitt. — London : National Council for Civil Liberties, 1981. — 68p ; 20cm
ISBN 0-901108-94-4 (pbk) : £1.75 B81-33250

344.105'234 — Great Britain. Contempt of court. Law. Reform — *Proposals*

Nicol, Andrew. Changing contempt of court / Andrew Nicol, Heather Rogers. — [London] : National Council for Civil Liberties, 1981. — 40p ; 20cm
ISBN 0-901108-92-8 (pbk) : £1.20 B81-33251

344.105′242 — Great Britain. Industrial safety offences. Liability of personnel

Safety prosecution of directors, managers & employers. — London (346 Harrow Rd., W9 2HP) : Industrial Relations Briefing, c1981. — 52p ; 21cm. — (IRB question & answer series ; no.4)
ISBN 0-86231-003-2 (pbk) : £5.95 B81-30062

344.105′247 — Great Britain. Traffic offences. Law

Wilkinson, G. S.. Wilkinson's road traffic offences. — 10th ed. / Patrick Halnan, John Spencer. — London : Oyez, 1980. — cii,1093p : ill,forms ; 24cm
Previous ed.: 1977. — Includes index
ISBN 0-85120-479-1 : £42.50 B81-13609

Wilkinson, G. S.. Wilkinson's road traffic offences. — London : Oyez
1st supplement to tenth ed / Patrick Halnan, John Spencer. — 1981. — viii,120p ; 24cm
ISBN 0-85120-596-8 (pbk) : Unpriced B81-28896

344.105′5 — Great Britain. Criminal courts. Procedure — *Sociological perspectives*

McBarnet, Doreen J.. Conviction : law, the state and the construction of justice / Doreen J. McBarnet. — London : Macmillan, 1981. — vii,182p ; 23cm. — (Oxford socio-legal studies)
Bibliography: p173-176. — Includes index
ISBN 0-333-25536-4 : £20.00 B81-31902

344.105′52 — Great Britain. Extradition. Law

Stanbrook, Ivor. The law and practice of extradition / by Ivor Stanbrook and Clive Stanbrook ; with a foreword by Lord Hailsham of St. Marylebone. — Chichester : Rose, 1980. — 202,xxvp : forms ; 26cm
Includes index
ISBN 0-85992-162-x : £30.00 B81-01960

344.105′7 — Great Britain. Criminal law. Cases

Dobson, A. P.. Cases and statutes on criminal law. — 2nd ed. — London : Sweet & Maxwell, Dec.1981. — [144]p. — (Concise college case notes)
Previous ed.: / by John C.N. Slater. 1973
ISBN 0-421-24810-6 (pbk) : £3.50 : CIP entry B81-31708

344.105′8 — Great Britain. Young offenders. Justice. Administration — *Conference proceedings*

Juvenile justice : proceedings of a day conference 23.3.80 / Allison Morris ... [et al.]. — [Lancaster] : Centre of Youth, Crime and Community. Department of Social Administration. University of Lancaster, [1980?]. — 49p ; 30cm
Cover title. — Bibliography: p48-49
£1.25 (pbk) B81-25945

344.106′0652 — Great Britain. Small firms. Law

Clayton, Pat. Law for the small business. — London : Kogan Page, Sept.1981. — [180]p
ISBN 0-85038-472-9 (cased) : £8.25 : CIP entry
ISBN 0-85038-486-9 (pbk) : £4.95 B81-21578

344.106′2 — Great Britain. Contracts. Bonds. Law

Contract bonds and guarantees / CBI Performance Bonds Group. — [Rev. ed.]. — London : CBI Publications, 1981. — 35p : ill ; 20x21cm
Previous ed.: published as Performance bonds and guarantees. 1978?
£5.00 (pbk) B81-40841

344.106′2′076 — Education. Curriculum subjects: Great Britain. Contracts. Law. Examinations. Techniques

Skinner, Michael, *1939-*. How to pass examinations in law of contract / Michael Skinner. — London : Cassell, 1981. — x,300p ; 22cm
Includes index
ISBN 0-304-30763-7 (pbk) : £5.95 B81-31664

344.106′3 — Great Britain. Torts. Law

Salmond, *Sir* **John William**. Salmond and Heuston on the law of torts. — 18th ed. — London : Sweet & Maxwell, Nov.1981. — [600]p
Previous ed.: 1977
ISBN 0-421-28700-4 (cased) : £19.00 : CIP entry
ISBN 0-421-28710-1 (pbk) : £14.50 B81-31171

344.1064′4 — Great Britain. Land use. Regulation by local authorities. Law. Enforcement

Enforcement of planning control : law and practice / discussion papers from a course held by the Department of Urban and Regional Planning, University of Strathclyde in June 1979 ; edited by Tony Ramsay and Eric Young. — Glasgow (16 Richmond St., Glasgow G1 1XQ) : The Continuing Education Office, University of Strathclyde, c1980. — ii,81 leaves ; 21x30cm
ISBN 0-9507279-0-3 (pbk) : Unpriced B81-10400

344.1064′4 — Great Britain. Real property. Development. Control. Law — *For councillors*

Heap, *Sir* **Desmond**. Town and country planning, or, How to control land development / by Sir Desmond Heap. — 2nd ed. — Chichester : Rose, 1981. — vii,55p ; 22cm
Previous ed.: 1973
ISBN 0-85992-212-x (pbk) : £3.30 B81-18901

344.1064′69164 — Great Britain. Coastal waters. Bed. Law

Marston, Geoffrey. The marginal seabed : United Kingdom legal practice / Geoffrey Marston. — Oxford : Clarendon Press, 1981. — xiii,316p ; 22cm
Bibliography: p299-302. — Includes index
ISBN 0-19-825369-9 : £18.50 : CIP rev. B81-08946

344.1064′8 — Great Britain. Industrial property. Use. International licensing. Law — *For businessmen*

Hearn, Patrick. The business of industrial licensing : a practical guide to patents, know-how trade marks and industrial design / Patrick Hearn. — Farnborough, Hants. : Gower, c1981. — ix,262p ; 23cm
Includes index
ISBN 0-566-02212-5 : £10.50 B81-20018

344.1064′8 — Great Britain. Intellectual property. Law

Cornish, W. R.. Intellectual property : patents, copyright, trade marks and allied rights / by W.R. Cornish. — London : Sweet & Maxwell, 1981. — lxi,630p ; 23cm
Includes index
ISBN 0-421-24310-4 (cased) : £26.50 : CIP rev.
ISBN 0-421-24330-9 (pbk) : £16.50 B81-02655

344.1064′8 — Great Britain. Inventions by personnel. Law: Patents Act 1977 — *Conference proceedings*

Proceedings of the CIA conference on the empoloyee inventors awards sections of the Patents Act 1977 : held at the Charing Cross Hotel, London on 31 December 1978 / editor L.S. Adler. — [London] : Chemical Industries Association, c1979. — 47p ; 30cm
Unpriced (spiral) B81-12448

344.1064′82 — Great Britain. Copyright. Law. Reform — *Proposals*

Great Britain. *Department of Trade*. Reform of the law relating to copyright, designs and performers' protection : a consultative document / [presented to Parliament by the Secretary of State for Trade]. — London : H.M.S.O, 1981. — iii,61p ; 25cm. — (Cmnd. ; 8302)
ISBN 0-10-183020-3 (pbk) : £3.90 B81-35083

344.1064′82′024092 — Great Britain. Copyright. Law — *For librarianship*

Taylor, L. J. (Laurence John). Copyright for librarians / by L.J. Taylor. — Hastings (West Hill Cottage, Exmouth Place, Hastings, E. Sussex) : Tamarisk, 1980. — viii,164p ; 21cm
Bibliography: p145-152. - Includes index
ISBN 0-907221-00-9 (pbk) : Unpriced : CIP rev. B80-21602

344.1064′82′024097 — Great Britain. Copyright. Law — *For publishing*

Scarles, Christopher. Copyright / Christopher Scarles. — Cambridge : Cambridge University Press, 1980. — iv,40p ; 22cm. — (Cambridge authors' and publishers' guides)
ISBN 0-521-29740-0 (pbk) : £1.80
Also classified at 347.3064′82′024097
B81-09826

344.1064′86 — Great Britain. Patents. Licensing — *Forms*

Standard clauses in a licensing agreement. — 2nd ed. — Havant : K. Mason, Oct.1981. — [47]p
Previous ed.: 1970
ISBN 0-85937-114-x (pbk) : £7.50 : CIP entry B81-31097

344.1064′88 — Great Britain. Trade marks. Law

Michaels, Amanda. A practical guide to trade marks. — Oxford (25 Beaumont St., Oxford OX1 2NP) : ESC Publishing, Oct.1981. — [160]p
ISBN 0-906214-09-2 (pbk) : £9.95 : CIP entry B81-31952

344.1065′9 — Great Britain. Trusts. Law — *For tax avoidance*

Thomas, Geraint W.. Taxation and trusts / by Geraint W. Thomas. — London : Sweet & Maxwell, 1981. — xxiv,205p ; 19cm. — (Modern legal studies)
Includes index
ISBN 0-421-27720-3 (cased) : Unpriced
ISBN 0-421-27730-0 (pbk) : £6.95 B81-33100

344.1065′9′024657 — Great Britain. Trusts. Law — *For accounting*

Griffiths, Michael, *1945 Sept. 27-*. The law of trusts / [... prepared for the Trust by Michael Griffiths]. — London : Certified Accountants Educational Trust, c1980. — 17p : ill ; 21cm. — (Company law) (Workbook ; no.L30)
Unpriced (pbk) B81-41024

344.106′6 — Great Britain. Organisations. Law — *For business studies*

Shears, Peter. The organisation in its environment : the legal environment / Peter Shears ; advisory editor Patricia Callender. — Amsterdam : Hulton, 1981. — 189p ; 24cm. — (Hulton BEC books)
Includes index
ISBN 0-7175-0837-4 (pbk) : Unpriced B81-40113

344.106′66 — Great Britain. Companies. Law

Butterworths company law handbook / edited by Keith Walmsley. — 2nd ed. — London : Butterworths, 1980. — ix,705p,22p : forms ; 25cm
Previous ed.: 1978. — Includes index
ISBN 0-406-14311-0 (pbk) : £11.95 B81-20057

Gower, L. C. B.. Gower's principles of modern company law. — 4th ed / by L.C.B. Gower et al. — London : Stevens
Supplement / by L.C.B. Gower. — 1981. — x,[80]p ; 24cm
ISBN 0-420-46060-8 (pbk) : £2.00 B81-12265

Jones, Frank H.. One thousand questions and answers on company law / by Frank H. Jones. — 4th ed. (rev. and reset). — St Albans (36 Lattimore Rd, St. Albans, Herts. AL1 3XP) : Barkeley, 1978. — xvi,[453p] ; 22cm
Previous ed.: 1975. — Includes index
Unpriced (pbk) B81-00788

Northey, J. F.. Northey & Leigh's introduction to company law. — 2nd ed. / by L.H. Leigh, V.H. Joffe, D. Goldberg. — London : Butterworths, 1981. — xli,419p ; 23cm
Previous ed.: published as Introduction to company law. 1971. — Includes index
ISBN 0-406-63102-6 : Unpriced
ISBN 0-406-63103-4 (pbk) : Unpriced B81-16708

Oliver, M. C.. Company law / M.C. Oliver. — 8th ed. — Plymouth : Macdonald & Evans, 1981. — xxx,386p ; 18cm. — (The M & E handbook series)
Previous ed.: 1979. — Includes index
ISBN 0-7121-0465-8 (pbk) : £3.95 B81-20765

344.106'66 — Great Britain. Companies. Law *continuation*

Ranking, D. F. de l'Hoste. Ranking & Spicer's company law. — 12th ed. / J.M. Gullick. — London : HFL in association with Chart Foulks Lynch, 1981. — xxvii,488p : 1facsim ; 22cm
Previous ed.: 1970. — Includes index
ISBN 0-372-30050-2 (pbk) : £9.00 B81-28534

Smith, Kenneth, *1910-1966*. Company law / Kenneth Smith and Denis Keenan. — 4th ed. / by Denis Keenan. — London : Pitman, 1981. — x,506p ; 22cm
Previous ed.: 1976. — Includes index
ISBN 0-273-01680-6 (pbk) : Unpriced B81-38442

Walker, D. (Dennis), *1933-*. Company law / by D. Walker. — Walton-on-Thames : Celtic Revision Aids, 1981. — 147p ; 19cm. — (Celtic revision notes. Law)
ISBN 0-17-751356-x (pbk) : £1.85 B81-16503

344.106'66 — Great Britain. Companies. Law: Companies Act 1980 — *Commentaries*

Guide to the Companies Act 1980 / Arthur Anderson & Co.. — London : Graham & Trotman, 1980. — 207p ; 21cm
Includes the text of the Companies Act 1980
ISBN 0-86010-256-4 (pbk) : £5.75 B81-30929

344.106'66 — Great Britain. Companies. Law: Companies Act 1980 — *Critical studies*

Savage, Nigel. The Companies Act 1980 : a new business code / Nigel Savage. — London : McGraw-Hill, c1980. — xi,192p ; 23cm
Includes index
ISBN 0-07-084551-4 (pbk) : £5.95 B81-19713

344.106'66 — Great Britain. Companies. Law: Companies Bill. Session 1980-81 — *Critical studies*

Companies Bill 1981. — [London] ([1 Surrey St., W.C.2.]) : [Arthur Anderson & Co.], c1981. — 20p ; 30cm
Cover title
Unpriced (pbk) B81-18403

344.106'66 — Great Britain. Companies. Law — *For company directors*

Franks, John A.. The company director and the law / John A. Franks. — 3rd ed. — Norwich : Oyez, 1981. — xiii,227p ; 21cm. — (It's your law series)
Previous ed.: 1977. — Includes index
ISBN 0-85120-507-0 : £5.95 B81-22796

344.106'66 — Great Britain. Companies. Law — *Texts with commentaries*

Palmer, *Sir* Francis Beaufort. Palmer's company law. — 23rd ed. — London : Stevens
Previous ed.: 1976
Vol.1: The treatise. — Nov.1981. — [1250]p
ISBN 0-420-45760-7 : CIP entry B81-31246

344.106'66'024657 — Great Britain. Companies. Law — *For accounting* — *Serials*

Binder Hamlyn briefing. — No.1 (Feb.1981)-. — London (8 St. Bride St, EC4A 4DA) : Binder Hamlyn, 1981-. — v. ; 21cm
Quarterly
ISSN 0262-009x = Binder Hamlyn briefing : Private circulation B81-38522

344'.106'6602632 — Great Britain. Companies. Law — *Statutes* — *Collections*

Great Britain. [Companies Acts 1948 to 1980]. Sweet & Maxwell's Companies acts / editor Maurice Kay. — London : Sweeet & Maxwell, 1980. — 561p ; 26cm
Includes index
ISBN 0-421-25930-2 (cased) : £14.25 : CIP rev.
ISBN 0-421-25940-x (pbk) : £10.50 B80-35871

344.106'66'02633 — Great Britain. Companies. Law — *Statutes* — *Texts with commentaries*

Prentice, Daniel D.. Companies Act 1980 / by Daniel D. Prentice. — London : Butterworths, 1980. — xvii,337p : 1ill ; 26cm
Includes index
ISBN 0-406-34160-5 : £23.00 B81-06162

344.106'66'02638 — Great Britain. Companies. Law — *Digests* — *Serials*

Company law digest : every development in company law. — No.1 (Oct.1979)-. — Newcastle upon Tyne (Exchange Buildings Quayside, Newcastle upon Tyne) : North of England Law Book Pub., 1979-. — v. ; 30cm
Two issues yearly
ISSN 0260-4620 = Company law digest : £2.00 per year B81-09153

344.106'66'0269 — Great Britain. Companies. Law. Procedure — *Manuals*

Nelson, Bertram. Nelson's tables : company procedure : with bankruptcy and deeds of arrangement. — 7th ed. / C.N. Gorman and A. Robertson. — London : Oyez, 1981. — ix,78p ; 24cm
Previous ed.: 1978
ISBN 0-85120-542-9 (pbk) : Unpriced B81-22800

344.106'6622 — Great Britain. Small firms. Incorporation. Law — *Proposals*

A **New** form of incorporation for small firms : a consultative document. — London : H.M.S.O., [1981]. — iii,44p ; 25cm. — (Cmnd. ; 8171)
ISBN 0-10-181710-x (pbk) : £3.20 B81-13946

344.106'664 — Great Britain. Company secretaryship — *Manuals*

Hall, L.. Company secretarial practice / L. Hall. — 5th ed. — Plymouth : Macdonald and Evans, 1981. — xii,304p : forms ; 18cm. — (The M & E handbook series)
Previous ed.: 1977. — Includes index
ISBN 0-7121-0381-3 (pbk) : £4.95 B81-26942

344.106'6642 — Great Britain. Companies. Directors & company secretaries. Legal status — *For accounting*

Griffiths, Michael, *1945 Sept.27-*. Directors and the secretary / [... prepared for the Trust by Michael Griffiths]. — London : Certified Accountants Educational Trust, c1981. — 21p ; 21cm. — (Company law) (Workbook ; no.L27)
Unpriced (pbk) B81-41027

344.106'6648 — Great Britain. Companies. Auditing. Law: Companies Act 1980 — *Critical studies*

The **Companies** Act 1980 and the auditor / Auditing Practices Committee of the Consultative Committee of Accountancy Bodies. — [London] ([PO Box 433, Chartered Accountants' Hall, Moorgate Place, EC2P 2BJ]) : APC, 1981. — 48p ; 21cm. — ('Audit briefs' series)
ISBN 0-85291-297-8 (pbk) : Unpriced B81-21255

344.106'666 — Great Britain. Companies. Shares. Law — *For accounting*

Griffiths, Michael, *1945 Sept.27-*. Shares and share capital / [... prepared for the Trust by Michael Griffiths]. — London : Certified Accountants Educational Trust, c1981. — 25p : ill ; 21cm. — (Company law) (Workbook ; no.L26)
Unpriced (pbk) B81-41028

344.106'668 — Great Britain. Private companies. Law: Companies Act 1980 — *Critical studies*

Godfrey, M.. Private companies after the Companies Act 1980 / M. Godfrey. — [Guildford] ([Braboeuf Manor, Portsmouth Rd., St. Catherine's, Guildford, Surrey]) : [College of Law], [1981]. — 20p ; 22cm. — (Crash course lecture / the College of Law, ISSN 0309-2771 ; 1981)
Cover title
£1.40 (pbk) B81-39982

344.106'668 — Great Britain. Private companies. Law — *Forms & precedents*

Company law materials 1 : private and limited companies : a selection of forms and documents indexed and annotated / [published and compiled by Jordan & Sons Ltd]. — 5th ed. — Bristol : Jordan, 1981. — 181p : facsims,forms ; 30cm
Cover title. — Previous ed.: 1980
ISBN 0-85308-066-6 (pbk) : Unpriced B81-39620

344.106'68 — Great Britain. Self-employed persons. Retirement. Financial provision. Law

Brindley, L. P. K.. Retirement planning for the self-employed / L.P.K. Brindley. — [Guildford] ([Braboeuf Manor, Portsmouth Rd., St. Catherine's, Guildford, Surrey]) : [College of Law], c1981. — 31p ; 22cm. — (Crash course lecture / the College of Law, ISSN 0309-2771 ; 1981)
Cover title
£1.40 (pbk) B81-39987

344.106'682 — Great Britain. Partnerships. Law

Burgess, Robert. Partnership law and practice : in England and Scotland / by Robert Burgess and Geoffrey Morse. — London : Sweet & Maxwell in association with the Institute of Chartered Secretaries and Administrators, 1980. — xxv,273p ; 22cm
Includes index
ISBN 0-421-26420-9 (cased) : £16.50 : CIP rev.
ISBN 0-421-26430-6 (pbk) : £12.50 B80-18634

344.106'7 — Great Britain. Commercial law

Cooper, Ian. The business world and the law / Ian Cooper. — London : Edward Arnold, 1980. — 138p : ill,facsims,forms ; 25cm
Includes index
ISBN 0-7131-0513-5 (pbk) : £4.25 : CIP rev. B80-33229

Schmitthoff, Clive M.. Commercial law in a changing economic climate / Clive M. Schmitthoff. — 2nd ed. — London : Sweet & Maxwell, 1981. — xii,78p ; 22cm
Previous ed.: 1977. — Includes index
ISBN 0-421-26830-1 (pbk) : £5.25 : CIP rev. B81-02656

344.106'72 — Great Britain. Goods. Sale. Law

Benjamin's sale of goods / [general editor A.G. Guest]. — 2nd ed. — London : Sweet & Maxwell, 1981. — cxl,1401p ; 26cm. — (The Common law library ; no.11)
Previous ed.: 1974. — Includes index
ISBN 0-421-26280-x : £65.00 : CIP rev. B81-22571

344.106'72'02633 — Great Britain. Goods. Sale. Law — *Statutes* — *Texts with commentaries*

Blair, Michael C.. Sale of Goods Act 1979 / by Michael C. Blair. — London : Butterworths, 1980. — xx,126p ; 25cm. — (Annotated legislation service ; v.266)
Includes index
ISBN 0-406-54790-4 : £15.00 B81-07640

344.106'72'0264 — Great Britain. Goods. Sale. Law — *Cases*

Adams, John. Cases and materials on sale of goods. — London : Croom Helm, Jan.1982. — [160]p. — (Croom Helm study guides to commercial law)
ISBN 0-7099-0509-2 : £5.95 : CIP entry B81-34312

344.106'73 — Great Britain. Consumer credit. Law: Consumer Credit Act 1974 — *Critical studies*

Bennion, F. A. R. The consumer credit act manual / Francis Bennion. — 2nd ed. — London : Oyez, c1981. — ix,208p ; 24cm
Previous ed. : 1978. — Includes index
ISBN 0-85120-565-8 (pbk) : Unpriced B81-28527

Lawson, R. G.. Consumer credit / R.G. Lawson. — Plymouth : Macdonald and Evans, 1981, c1980. — xiii,153p ; 18cm. — (The M & E handbook series)
Includes index
ISBN 0-7121-0399-6 : £3.95 B81-23995

344.106'8 — Great Britain. Insurance. Law

Birds, J.. Modern insurance law. — London : Sweet & Maxwell, Jan.1982. — [350]p
ISBN 0-421-27760-2 (cased) : £14.75 : CIP entry
ISBN 0-421-27770-x (pbk) : £11.00 B81-34394

344.106'82 — Great Britain. Banking. Law

Perry, F. E.. Law and practice relating to banking / F.E. Perry. — Rev. 3rd ed. — London : Methuen, 1981. — xi,549p : forms ; 20cm
Previous ed.: i.e. 3rd ed. 1977. — Includes index
ISBN 0-416-30840-6 (pbk) : £6.95 B81-08741

344.106'82'02633 — Great Britain. Banking. Law — *Statutes — Texts with commentaries*
Morison, Ian. Banking Act 1979 / by Ian Morison, Paul Tillett, Jane Welch. — London : Butterworths, 1979. — iv,205p ; 25cm. — (Annotated legislation service ; v.264)
Includes index
ISBN 0-406-54785-8 : £15.50 B81-07638

344.106'8226 — Great Britain. Trustee savings banks. Law. Reform — *Proposals*
Great Britain. *Law Commission.* Trustee Savings Banks Bill : report on the consolidation of the Trustee Savings Banks Acts 1969 to 1978 / the Law Commission and the Scottish Law Commission. — London : H.M.S.O., 1981. — 11p ; 25cm
ISBN 0-10-182570-6 (unbound) : £1.40 B81-30920

344.106'86'00321 — Great Britain. Insurance. Law — *Encyclopaedias*
Ivamy, E. R. Hardy. Dictionary of insurance law / by E.R. Hardy Ivamy. — London : Butterworths, 1981. — 166p ; 23cm. — (Butterworths professional dictionary series)
ISBN 0-406-60300-6 (cased) : Unpriced
ISBN 0-406-60301-4 (pbk) : Unpriced B81-39808

344.106'8622 — Shipping. Insurance. British law
Templeman, F.. Templeman on marine insurance : its principles and practice. — 5th ed / R.J. Lambeth. — Plymouth : Macdonald and Evans, 1981. — xxv,574p ; 25cm
Previous ed.: published as Marine insurance / F. Templeman and C.T. Greenacre. 1934. — Includes index
ISBN 0-7121-1395-9 : £18.50 B81-17357

344.106'92 — Great Britain. Companies. Shares. Insider trading. Law: Companies Act 1980. Part V — *Critical studies*
Ashe, T. Michael. Insider trading / by T. Michael Ashe. — London (50 Tufton St., SW1P 3RA) : Company Communications Centre, 1980. — xi,106p ; 23cm
Includes index
ISBN 0-906609-02-x : £12.50 B81-05763

344.106'926 — Great Britain. Companies. Shares. Insider trading. Law
Insider dealing : guidance for members following the Companies Act 1980. — London : Institute of Directors, 1981. — 21p ; 22cm
£3.95 (pbk) B81-38375

344.107'5 — Great Britain. Litigation. Procedure
Raymond, Brian. Introduction to criminal and civil litigation / Brian Raymond. — London : Oyez, 1981. — 170p : facsims,forms ; 24cm
ISBN 0-85120-556-9 (pbk) : Unpriced B81-29951

344.107'5 — Great Britain. Supreme Court of Judicature. Procedure — *Encyclopaedias*
Williams, Emlyn, *1946-*. ABC guide to the practice of the Supreme Court. — 40th ed. — London : Sweet & Maxwell, Sept.1981. — [250]p
Previous ed.: 1978
ISBN 0-421-27710-6 (pbk) : £10.00 : CIP entry B81-23784

344.108'22 — Great Britain. Law. Statutes
Bennion, F. A. R.. Statute law / F.A.R. Bennion. — London : Oyez, c1980. — xxii,276p : 1ill,2forms ; 22cm
Bibliography: p265-267. - Includes index
ISBN 0-85120-544-5 : £10.00 B81-14492

344.108'22 — Great Britain. Law — *Statutes — Texts with commentaries — Collections*
Great Britain. [Laws, etc.]. Miscellaneous acts / annotated by Butterworths legal editorial staff. — London : Butterworths, 1980. — xi,173p ; 25cm. — (Annotated legislation service ; v.268)
Includes index
ISBN 0-406-54794-7 : £14.00 B81-07639

Great Britain. [Laws, etc.]. Miscellaneous acts / annotated by Butterworths legal editorial staff. — London : Butterworths, 1981. — v,189p ; 25cm. — (Annotated legislation service ; v.273)
ISBN 0-406-54801-3 : Unpriced B81-18720

344.108'22'05 — Great Britain. Law — *Statutes — Collections — Serials*
The public general acts and General Synod measures. — 1980. — London : HMSO, 1980. — 2
ISBN 0-11-840194-7 : Unpriced B81-13097

344.108'22'05 — Great Britain. Law. Statutes — *Serials*
Statute law review. — Spring 1980-. — Andover : Sweet & Maxwell, 1980-. — v. ; 25cm
Three issues yearly. — Published in association with: the Statute Law Society
ISSN 0144-3593 = Statute law review : £25.00 per year B81-00789

344.108'22'05 — Great Britain. Law — *Statutes — Texts with commentaries — Collections — Serials*
Great Britain. [Laws, etc.]. Current law statutes annotated. — 1980. — London : Sweet & Maxwell, 1981. — 2v.
ISBN 0-421-28420-x : Unpriced
ISSN 0307-5184 B81-34047

344.108'25 — Great Britain. Law. Statutory instruments — *Inquiry reports*
Great Britain. *Parliament. House of Commons. Select Committee on Statutory Instruments.* Eighteenth report from the Select Committee on Statutory Instruments, session 1980-81. — London : H.M.S.O., [1981]. — [4]p ; 25cm. — ([HC] ; 19-xix)
ISBN 0-10-295281-7 (unbound) : £0.70 B81-35393

Great Britain. *Parliament. House of Commons. Select Committee on Statutory Instruments.* Eighth report from the Select Committee on Statutory Instruments : session 1980-81. — London : H.M.S.O., 1981. — 1folded sheet(3p) ; 25cm. — ([H.C.] ; 19-viii)
ISBN 0-10-276381-x : £0.70 B81-14036

Great Britain. *Parliament. House of Commons. Select Committee on Statutory Instruments.* Eleventh report from the Select Committee on Statutory Instruments : session 1980-81. — London : H.M.S.O., [1981]. — 3p ; 25cm. — ([HC] ; 19-xi)
ISBN 0-10-283681-7 (unbound) : £0.70 B81-27889

Great Britain. *Parliament. House of Commons. Select Committee on Statutory Instruments.* Fifteenth report from the Select Committee on Statutory Instruments, session 1980-81. — London : H.M.S.O., [1981]. — [4]p ; 25cm. — ([HC] ; 19-xvi)
ISBN 0-10-292381-7 (unbound) : £0.70 B81-33061

Great Britain. *Parliament. House of Commons. Select Committee on Statutory Instruments.* First report from the Select Committee on Statutory Instruments, session 1980-81. — London : H.M.S.O., 1980. — 6p ; 25cm. — ([HC] ; 19-i)
ISBN 0-10-270081-8 (unbound) : £1.10 B81-24969

Great Britain. *Parliament. House of Commons. Select Committee on Statutory Instruments.* Fourteenth report from the Select Committee on Statutory Instruments, session 1980-81. — London : H.M.S.O., [1981]. — [4]p ; 25cm. — ([HC] ; 19-xv)
ISBN 0-10-288781-0 (unbound) : £0.70 B81-33060

Great Britain. *Parliament. House of Commons. Select Committee on Statutory Instruments.* Nineteenth report from the Select Committee on Statutory Instruments, session 1979-80. — London : H.M.S.O., [1980]. — 3p ; 25cm. — ([HC] ; 147-xx)
ISBN 0-10-279380-8 (unbound) : £0.50 B81-20667

Great Britain. *Parliament. House of Commons. Select Committee on Statutory Instruments.* Second report from the Select Committee on Statutory Instruments, session 1980-81. — London : H.M.S.O., [1980]. — 3p ; 25cm. — ([HC] ; 19-ii)
ISBN 0-10-270181-4 (unbound) : £0.70 B81-20673

Great Britain. *Parliament. House of Commons. Select Committee on Statutory Instruments.* Seventeenth report from the Select Committee on Statutory Instruments, session 1980-81. — London : H.M.S.O., [1981]. — [4]p ; 25cm. — ([HC] ; 19-xviii)
ISBN 0-10-293781-8 (unbound) : £0.70 B81-35392

Great Britain. *Parliament. House of Commons. Select Committee on Statutory Instruments.* Sixteenth report from the Select Committee on Statutory Instruments, session 1980-81. — London : H.M.S.O., [1981]. — [4]p ; 25cm
ISBN 0-10-293181-x (unbound) : £0.70 B81-34366

Great Britain. *Parliament. House of Commons. Select Committee on Statutory Instruments.* Thirteenth report from the Select Committee on Statutory Instruments, session 1980-81. — London : H.M.S.O., [1981]. — [4]p ; 25cm. — ([HC] ; 19-xiii)
ISBN 0-10-288081-6 (unbound) : £0.70 B81-33059

Great Britain. *Parliament. House of Commons. Select Committee on Statutory Instruments.* Thirty-second report from the Select Committee on Statutory Instruments, session 1979-80. — London : H.M.S.O., [1980]. — 3p ; 25cm. — ([HC] ; 147-xxxiv)
ISBN 0-10-297280-x (unbound) : £0.50 B81-20671

Great Britain. *Parliament. House of Commons. Select Committee on Statutory Instruments.* Thirty-third report from the Select Committee on Statutory Instruments, session 1979-80. — London : H.M.S.O., [1980]. — 3p ; 25cm. — ([HC] ; 147-xxxv)
ISBN 0-10-298580-4 (unbound) : £0.50 B81-20672

Great Britain. *Parliament. House of Commons. Select Committee on Statutory Instruments.* Twelfth report from the Select Committee on Statutory Instruments : session 1980-81. — London : H.M.S.O., [1981]. — 3p ; 25cm. — ([HC] ; 19-xii)
ISBN 0-10-284381-3 (unbound) : £0.70 B81-27890

Great Britain. *Parliament. House of Commons. Select Committee on Statutory Instruments.* Twenty-eighth report from the Select Committee on Statutory Instruments, session 1979-80. — London : H.M.S.O., [1980]. — 3p ; 25cm. — ([HC] ; 147-xxx)
£0.50 (unbound) B81-20670

Great Britain. *Parliament. House of Commons. Select Committee on Statutory Instruments.* Twenty-second report from the Select Committee on Statutory Instruments, session 1979-80. — London : H.M.S.O., [1980]. — 3p ; 25cm. — ([HC] ; 147-xxiii)
ISBN 0-10-282580-7 (unbound) : £0.50 B81-20668

Great Britain. *Parliament. House of Commons. Select Committee on Statutory Instruments.* Twenty-sixth report from the Select Committee on Statutory Instruments, session 1979-80. — London : H.M.S.O., [1980]. — 3p ; 25cm. — ([HC] ; 147-xxviii)
ISBN 0-10-286080-7 (unbound) : £0.50 B81-20669

Great Britain. *Parliament. Joint Committee on Statutory Instruments.* Eighth report from the Joint Committee on Statutory Instruments : session 1980-1981. — London : H.M.S.O., 1981. — 12p ; 25cm. — (HL ; 80) (HC ; 18-xii)
ISBN 0-10-408081-7 (unbound) : £1.70 B81-14507

Great Britain. *Parliament. Joint Committee on Statutory Instruments.* First report from the Joint Committee on Statutory Instruments, session 1980-81. — London : H.M.S.O., [1980]. — 12p ; 25cm. — (HL ; 9) (HC ; 18-i)
ISBN 0-10-400981-0 (unbound) : £1.70 B81-20349

344.108′25 — Great Britain. Law. Statutory instruments — *Inquiry reports* *continuation*
Great Britain. *Parliament. Joint Committee on Statutory Instruments.* Forty-third report from the Joint Committee on Statutory Instruments, Session 1979-80. — London : H.M.S.O., [1980]. — 7p ; 25cm. — (HL ; 377) (HC ; 146-lxv)
ISBN 0-10-437780-1 (unbound) : £1.10
B81-20348

Great Britain. *Parliament. Joint Committee on Statutory Instruments.* Fourth report from the Joint Committee on Statutory Instruments, session 1980-81. — London : H.M.S.O., [1980]. — 6p ; 25cm. — (HL ; 45) (HC ; 18-vii)
ISBN 0-10-404581-7 (unbound) : £1.10
B81-20347

Great Britain. *Parliament. Joint Committee on Statutory Instruments.* Second report from the Joint Committee on Statutory Instruments, session 1980-81. — London : H.M.S.O., [1980]. — 14p ; 25cm. — (HL ; 27) (HC ; 18-iii)
ISBN 0-10-402781-9 (unbound) : £1.70
B81-20351

Great Britain. *Parliament. Joint Committee on Statutory Instruments.* Third report from the Joint Committee on Statutory Instruments, session 1980-81. — London : H.M.S.O., [1980]. — 6p ; 25cm. — (HL ; 33) (HC ; 18-v)
ISBN 0-10-403381-9 (unbound) : £1.10
B81-20350

Great Britain. *Parliament. Joint Committee on Statutory Instruments.* Thirty-fifth report from the Joint Committee on Statutory Instruments, session 1979-80. — London : H.M.S.O., [1980]. — 3p ; 25cm. — (HL ; 312) (HC ; 146-iii)
ISBN 0-10-431280-7 (unbound) : £0.50
B81-20354

Great Britain. *Parliament. Joint Committee on Statutory Instruments.* Thirty-first report from the Joint Committee on Statutory Instruments, session 1979-80. — London : H.M.S.O., [1980]. — 9p ; 25cm. — (HL ; 282) (HC ; 146-xli)
ISBN 0-10-428280-0 (unbound) : £1.25
B81-20353

Great Britain. *Parliament. Joint Committee on Statutory Instruments.* Thirty-second report from the Joint Committee on Statutory Instruments, session 1979-80. — London : H.M.S.O., [1980]. — 3p ; 25cm. — (HL ; 291) (HC ; 146-xlvii)
ISBN 0-10-429180-x (unbound) : £0.50
B81-20352

Great Britain. *Parliament. Joint Committee on Statutory Instruments.* Thirty-sixth report from the Joint Committee on Statutory Instruments, session 1979-80. — London : H.M.S.O., [1980]. — 4p ; 25cm. — (HL ; 315) (HC ; 146-iii)
ISBN 0-10-431580-6 (unbound) : £0.50
B81-20346

Great Britain. *Parliament. Joint Committee on Statutory Instruments.* Twenty-fifth report from the Joint Committee on Statutory Instruments, session 1980-81. — London : H.M.S.O., [1981]. — 5p ; 25cm. — (H.L. ; 229) (H.C. ; 18-xxxix)
ISBN 0-10-422981-0 (pbk) : £1.10 B81-39994

344.108′27′05 — Great Britain. Law. Statutes — *Citators — Serials*
Current law citator. — 1980. — London : Sweet & Maxwell, 1981. — 739p
ISSN 0526-4448 : Unpriced
Primary classification 344.208′47′05 B81-35454

Scottish current law citator. — 1980. — Edinburgh : W. Green, 1981. — 739p
ISBN 0-414-00673-9 : Unpriced
Primary classification 344.1108′47′05
B81-33467

344.108′28 — Great Britain. Law. Statutes — *Indexes — Serials*
Great Britain. [Laws, etc.]. The public and general acts and General Synod measures. Tables and index. — 1979. — London : H.M.S.O., 1980. — a-l,cdx p
ISBN 0-11-840195-5 : £10.00 B81-03472

The **public** general acts and General Synod measures. — 1980. — London : H.M.S.O., 1980. — A-L, CDXp
Unpriced B81-13106

344.11 — LAW. SCOTLAND

344.11 — Scotland. Law
Stair, James Dalrymple, *Viscount of.* The institutions of the law of Scotland : deduced from its originals, and collated with the civil, canon and feudal laws, and with the customs of neighbouring nations in iv books / by James, Viscount of Stair ; edited by David M. Walker. — Edinburgh : University Presses of Edinburgh and Glasgow. — xvii,1186p,[1]leaf of plates : 1port ; 24cm
Originally published: Edinburgh : s.n., 1693. — Includes index
ISBN 0-85224-397-9 : £40.00 B81-32133

344.11 — Scotland. Law. Stair, James Dalrymple, *Viscount.* **Institutions of the law of Scotland** — *Critical studies*
Sutherland, Robert. Lord Stair and the law of Scotland : the Institutions of the Law of Scotland 1681 / Robert Sutherland. — [Glasgow] ([The University, Glasgow G12 8QQ]) : [Hunterian Museum], c1981. — 35p ; 21cm
Bibliography: p34-35
ISBN 0-904254-03-8 (pbk) : £0.50 B81-26263

344.11′0028′54 — Scotland. Legal services. Applications of digital computer systems. Great Britain. *Royal Commission on Legal Services in Scotland.* **Final report** — *Critical studies*
Society of Computers and Law. Response by the Society for Computers and Law to the reports by the English and Scottish Royal Commissions on Legal Services which were published in October 1979 and May 1980 respectively. — Milton (11 High St., Milton, Oxon OX14 4ER) : The Society, 1981. — 19p ; 21cm
ISBN 0-906122-05-8 (pbk) : £1.00
Primary classification 344.2′0028′54 B81-12277

344.11′005 — Scotland. Law — *Serials*
The **Parliament** house book. — 1981. — Edinburgh : W. Green, 1981. — 1v. in 2
ISBN 0-414-00675-5 : Unpriced B81-30753

344.11′0092′4 — Edinburgh. Museums: Canongate Tolbooth Museum. Exhibits: Items associated with Stair, James Dalrymple, *Viscount of* — *Catalogues*
′**A Gentleman** of excellent parts′ : [catalogue of] an exhibition to celebrate Sir James Dalrymple of Stair′s The Institutions of the Law of Scotland 1681 : [held at] Hunterian Museum, University of Glasgow 30 March-16 May, Mon-Fri. 9-5, Sat 9-12, closed 17-20 April, 4 May ; Canongate Tolbooth, Royal Mile, Edinburgh 29 May-11 July, Mon-Sat 10-5. — [Glasgow] ([The University, Glasgow G12 8QQ]) : [Hunterian Museum], [1981?]. — 27p : ill,2facsims,ports ; 21cm
ISBN 0-85261-167-6 (pbk) : £0.50
Primary classification 344.11′0092′4 B81-26264

344.11′0092′4 — Scotland. Strathclyde Region. Glasgow. Museums: University of Glasgow. *Hunterian Museum.* **Exhibits: Items associated with Stair, James Dalrymple,** *Viscount of* — *Catalogues*
′**A Gentleman** of excellent parts′ : [catalogue of] an exhibition to celebrate Sir James Dalrymple of Stair′s The Institutions of the Law of Scotland 1681 : [held at] Hunterian Museum, University of Glasgow 30 March-16 May, Mon-Fri. 9-5, Sat 9-12, closed 17-20 April, 4 May ; Canongate Tolbooth, Royal Mile, Edinburgh 29 May-11 July, Mon-Sat 10-5. — [Glasgow] ([The University, Glasgow G12 8QQ]) : [Hunterian Museum], [1981?]. — 27p : ill,2facsims,ports ; 21cm
ISBN 0-85261-167-6 (pbk) : £0.50
Also classified at 344.11′0092′4 B81-26264

344.1104′1′0269 — Scotland. Industrial tribunals. Procedure
Leslie, William. Industrial tribunal practice in Scotland / by William Leslie. — Edinburgh : Green, 1981. — xxxxi,323p : forms ; 21cm
Includes index
ISBN 0-414-00680-1 (pbk) : Unpriced
B81-37607

344.1104′32732′0240431 — Scotland. Children in care. Law — *For parents*
Your rights if your child is in care / Scottish Council for Civil Liberties. — Glasgow (146 Holland St., Glasgow G2 4NG) : The Council, [1980]. — 1folded sheet([6]p). — (SCCL rights factsheet ; no.9)
£0.05 B81-13142

344.1104′7 — Scotland. Education. Law. Great Britain. *Parliament. House of Commons.* **Education (Scotland) Bill. Session 1980-81** — *Critical studies*
Scottish Parent Teacher Council. SPTC comments on the Education (Scotland) Bill, 1981. — Edinburgh (4 Queensferry St., Edinburgh EH2 4PA) : Scottish Parent Teacher Council, 1981. — 10leaves ; 30cm
Unpriced (pbk) B81-38592

344.1104′7 — Scotland. Education. Law. Reform — *Proposals*
Great Britain. *Scottish Law Commission.* Education (Scotland) Bill : report on the consolidation of certain enactments relating to education in Scotland / Scottish Law Commission. — Edinburgh : H.M.S.O., [1980]. — 6p ; 25cm. — (Cmnd. ; 7688) (Scot. Law Com. ; no.58)
ISBN 0-10-176880-x (unbound) : £1.00
B81-30944

344.1105′024362 — Scotland. Criminal law - *For welfare work*
Moore, George. Social work and criminal law in Scotland. — Aberdeen : Aberdeen University Press, Apr.1981. — [224]p
ISBN 0-08-025731-3 : £7.50 : CIP entry
B81-04354

344.1105′0264 — Scotland. Criminal law — *Cases*
Gane, Christopher H. W.. A casebook on Scottish criminal law / by Christopher H.W. Gane and Charles N. Stoddart. — Edinburgh : W. Green, 1980. — xxii,495p ; 22cm
Includes index
ISBN 0-414-00664-x (pbk) : £10.00 B81-03964

344.1105′5 — Scotland. Criminal law. Advocacy — *Manuals*
Harper, J. Ross. My client My Lord : a practical guide to advocacy for solicitors in the criminal court / J.Ross Harper. — Edinburgh (PO Box 75, 26 Drumsheugh Gardens, Edinburgh EH3 7YR) : Law Society of Scotland, 1981. — 61p ; 21cm
ISBN 0-902023-03-9 (pbk) : £3.50 B81-11093

344.1105′5 — Scotland. Criminal law. Procedure
Harper, J. Ross. A practitioner′s guide to criminal procedure / J. Ross Harper. — Edinburgh (PO Box 75, 26 Drumsheugh Gardens, Edinburgh EH3 7YR) : Law Society of Scotland, 1981. — 89p ; 21cm
ISBN 0-902023-02-0 (pbk) : £5.00 B81-11092

344.1105′5′02633 — Scotland. Criminal law. Justice. Administration. Procedure. Law — *Statutes — Texts with commentaries*
Great Britain. [Criminal Justice (Scotland) Act 1980]. The Criminal Justice (Scotland) Act 1980 / [annotated] by Gerald H. Gordon. — Edinburgh : W. Green, 1981. — xxvii,165p ; 25cm
Includes index
ISBN 0-414-00674-7 (pbk) : Unpriced
B81-24188

344.1105′8 — Scotland. Young offenders. Justice. Administration
Martin, F. M.. Children out of court / by F.M. Martin, Sanford J. Fox and Kathleen Murray in collaboration with Patricia and Michelle Myers. — Edinburgh : Scottish Academic, c1981. — xi,331p,4p of plates : ill ; 26cm
Bibliography: p322-324. — Includes index
ISBN 0-7073-0287-0 : £15.00 B81-22797

344.1106′15′02632 — Scotland. Families. Law — *Statutes — Collections*
Great Britain. [Laws, etc.]. Scots statutes : children, husband and wife, judicial factors, succession, trustees and executors. — Edinburgh : W. Green, 1980. — 330p ; 19cm
Cover title. — ′Reprinted from Parliament house book 1980′. — Includes index
ISBN 0-414-00655-0 (pbk) : £2.50 B81-09580

344.1106'15'02632 — Scotland. Families. Law — *Statutes — Collections — Serials*

Great Britain. [Laws, etc.]. Scots statutes. — 1981. — Edinburgh : W. Green, [1981]. — H334
ISBN 0-414-00678-x : £3.50 B81-30750

344.11063'23'02633 — Scotland. Death. Damages. Rights of dependants. Law: Damages (Scotland) Act 1976. Reform — *Proposals*

Great Britain. *Scottish Law Commission.* Report on section 5 of the Damages (Scotland) Act 1976 / Scottish Law Commission. — Edinburgh : H.M.S.O., [1981]. — iii,8p ; 25cm. — ([HC] ; 272)
ISBN 0-10-227281-6 (pbk) : £1.80 B81-25236

344.11064'3'0269 — Great Britain. *Scottish Land Court.* **Proceedings** — *Serials*

Great Britain. *Scottish Land Court.* Appendices to report by the Scottish Land Court as to their proceedings under the Small Landholders (Scotland) Acts 1886 to 1931 and other acts. — 1979. — Edinburgh (1 Grosvenor Cres. Edinburgh EH12 5ER) : Scottish Land Court, 1980. — vi,152p
Unpriced B81-09426

Great Britain. *Scottish Land Court.* Report as to proceedings under the Agriculture and the Agricultural Holdings (Scotland) Acts, the Small Landholders (Scotland) Acts 1886 to 1931, the Crofters (Scotland) Acts 1955 and 1961 and the Crofting Reform (Scotland) Act 1976, 1st January ... to 31st December ... / the Scottish Land Court. — 1979. — Edinburgh : H.M.S.O., 1980. — 17p. — (Cmnd. ; 8038)
ISBN 0-10-180380-x : £2.10 B81-01873

344.11064'32 — Scotland. Prescription. Law

Walker, David M. (David Maxwell). The law of prescription and limitation of actions in Scotland / by David M. Walker. — 3rd ed. — Edinburgh : W. Green, 1981. — xix,136p ; 25cm
Previous ed.: 1976. — Includes index
ISBN 0-414-00667-4 (pbk) : Unpriced
Also classified at 344.1107'52 B81-22828

344.11064'344'02633 — Scotland. Rented residences. Tenancies. Law — *Statutes*

Great Britain. [Tenants' Rights, etc. (Scotland) Act 1980]. Tenants' Rights, etc. (Scotland) Act 1980 : Chapter 52. — London : H.M.S.O., [1980]. — iv,70p ; 25cm
ISBN 0-10-545280-7 (pbk) : £4.15 B81-19809

Great Britain. [Tenants' Rights, etc. (Scotland) Amendment Act 1980]. Tenants' Rights, etc. (Scotland) Amendment Act 1980 : Elizabeth II, 1980, Chapter 61. — London : H.M.S.O., [1980]. — 3p ; 25cm
ISBN 0-10-546180-6 (unbound) : £0.70 B81-19808

344.11064'38 — Great Britain. *Department of the Registers of Scotland* — *Serials*

Great Britain. *Department of the Registers of Scotland.* Report by the Keeper of the Registers of Scotland. — 1981. — Edinburgh (Meadowbank House, [153 London Rd], Edinburgh [EH8 7AU]) : [Department of the Registers of Scotland], 1981. — 12p
Unpriced B81-32903

344.11064'38 — Scotland. Real property. Title. Registration. Law

Registration of title practice book / [editor W.D.C. Andrews]. — Edinburgh : H.M.S.O., 1981. — 1v.(loose-leaf) : 2plans,forms ; 27cm
Includes index
ISBN 0-11-491725-6 : £27.00 B81-14327

344.11064'38'02632 — Scotland. Real property. Conveyancing. Law — *Statutes — Collections*

Great Britain. [Conveyancing acts]. Scots conveyancing statutes. — Edinburgh : W. Green, 1980. — 318p ; 19cm
Cover title. — 'Reprinted from Parliament house book 1980'. — Includes index
ISBN 0-414-00653-4 (pbk) : £2.50 B81-08117

344.11064'5'05 — Scotland. Environment planning. Law — *Serials*

Scottish planning law & practice. — No.1 (Sept.1980)-. — Glasgow (186 Bath Street, Glasgow G2 4HG) : Planning Exchange in conjunction with the Law Society of Scotland, 1980-. — v. ; 30cm
Three issues yearly. — Supplement to: Journal of the Law Society of Scotland
£5.00 per year B81-26956

344.11064'691'002633 — Scotland. Natural resources: Water. Law — *Statutes*

Great Britain. [Water (Scotland) Act 1980]. Water (Scotland) Act 1980 : Chapter 45. — London : H.M.S.O., [1980]. — v,114p ; 25cm
Cover title
ISBN 0-10-544580-0 (pbk) : £5.30 B81-04686

344.11065'2 — Scotland. Succession. Law

Nichols, David Ian. In the event of death — : wills and inheritance in Scotland / David Ian Nichols. — Edinburgh (c/o R. McCreadie, Faculty of Law, Edinburgh University) : Scottish Legal Education Trust, c1980. — 70p : ill ; 21cm
ISBN 0-9507056-0-8 (pbk) : £1.50
ISBN 0-905831-02-0 (Scottish Association of Citizens Advice Bureaux) : £1.50 B81-01836

344.1106'7'02632 — Scotland. Commercial law — *Statutes — Collections — Serials*

Great Britain. [Laws, etc.]. Scots mercantile law statutes. — 1980. — Edinburgh : Green, [1980]. — I542,J80p
ISBN 0-414-00654-2 : £6.00
ISSN 0308-1176 B81-09063

Great Britain. [Laws, etc.]. Scots mercantile law statutes. — 1981. — Edinburgh : W. Green, [1981]. — I664,J80p
ISBN 0-414-00677-1 : £7.00
ISSN 0308-1176 B81-30744

344.1106'8632 — Scotland. Married women. Life assurance. Law — *Statutes*

Great Britain. [Married Women's Policies of Assurance (Scotland) (Amendment) Act 1980]. Married Women's Policies of Assurance (Scotland) (Amendment) Act 1980 : Elizabeth II 1980. Chapter 56. — London : H.M.S.O., [1980]. — 3p ; 25cm
ISBN 0-10-545680-2 (unbound) : £0.70 B81-19805

344.1107'1 — Scotland. Civil courts. Proceedings — *Statistics — Serials*

Civil judicial statistics, Scotland : statistics relating to the civil and business courts, licensing boards and legal and public departments for the year ... / Scottish Courts Administration. — 1979-. — Edinburgh : H.M.S.O., 1981-. — v. ; 25cm
Annual. — Cover title: Civil judicial statistics. — Continues: Civil judicial statistics (including licensing and bankruptcy)
ISSN 0261-0809 : £4.80 B81-15443

344.1107'17'02636 — Scotland. Legal aid. Law — *Statutory instruments — Collections*

Compendium of legal aid. — [Edinburgh] : W. Green, [1981]. — 180p,p301-334 ; 19cm
Cover title. — "Reprinted from the Parliament House Book, 1981"
ISBN 0-414-00676-3 (pbk) : £2.75 B81-32315

Great Britain. [Legal aid acts]. Compendium of legal aid. — [Edinburgh] : W. Green, [1980]. — 334p ; 19cm
Cover title. — 'Reprinted from the Parliament house book 1980'. — Includes index
ISBN 0-414-00652-6 (pbk) : £2.50 B81-08123

344.1107'212 — Scotland. Sheriff courts districts — *Gazetteers*

McCaffray, Charles. Index to sheriff court districts in Scotland / by Charles McCaffray. — Edinburgh : W. Green, 1980. — vii,66p : 1col.map ; 22cm
'Sheriffdoms & sheriff court districts' (1 folded sheet) as insert
ISBN 0-414-00666-6 (pbk) : Unpriced B81-09535

344.1107'23 — Great Britain. *Court of Session.* **Petitions. Procedure**

McBryde, William W.. Petition procedure in the Court of Session / by William W. McBryde and Norman J. Dowie. — Edinburgh : W. Green, 1980. — xvii,94p ; 22cm
Includes index
ISBN 0-414-00663-1 (pbk) : £7.00 B81-07252

344.1107'52 — Scotland. Limitation of actions. Law

Walker, David M. (David Maxwell). The law of prescription and limitation of actions in Scotland / by David M. Walker. — 3rd ed. — Edinburgh : W. Green, 1981. — xix,136p ; 25cm
Previous ed.: 1976. — Includes index
ISBN 0-414-00667-4 (pbk) : Unpriced
Primary classification 344.11064'32 B81-22828

344.1108'26'05 — Scotland. Law — *Digests — Serials*

Scottish current law year book. — 1980. — Edinburgh : W. Green, 1981. — 1200p in various pagings
ISBN 0-414-00672-0 (corrected) : Unpriced
ISSN 0308-7166 B81-35456

344.1108'47'05 — Scotland. Law. Cases — *Citators — Serials*

Scottish current law citator. — 1980. — Edinburgh : W. Green, 1981. — 739p
ISBN 0-414-00673-9 : Unpriced
Also classified at 344.108'27'05 B81-33467

344.15 — LAW. IRELAND

344.1508'4'09 — Ireland. Law. Cases, *1671-1976*

Comyn, James. Irish at law : a selection of famous and unusual cases / James Comyn. — London : Secker & Warburg, 1981. — ix,261p,[1]leaf of plates : 1port ; 23cm
ISBN 0-436-10580-2 : £8.50 : CIP rev. B81-13473

344.16 — LAW. NORTHERN IRELAND

344.16'005 — Northern Ireland. Law — *Serials*

Bulletin of Northern Ireland law. — No.1 (1981-)-. — Belfast (Faculty of Law, Queen's University [University Rd] Belfast [BT7 1NN]) : S.L.S., 1981-. — v. ; 30cm
Ten issues yearly
ISSN 0260-6550 = Bulletin of Northern Ireland law : £35.00 per year B81-33293

344.1604'1'0269 — Northern Ireland. Industrial tribunals

Bateson, Phyllis. Industrial tribunals in Northern Ireland : a practical guide / by Phyllis Bateson and John McKee. — Belfast : SLS Publications, Faculty of Law, Queen's University, Belfast, 1981. — xi,146p : forms ; 21cm. — (The Law in action series)
Includes index
ISBN 0-85389-191-5 (pbk) : Unpriced B81-18399

344.1606'64 — Northern Ireland. Charities. Law: Charities Act (Northern Ireland) 1964. Administration — *Serials*

Northern Ireland. *Department of Finance.* Charities. — 1978. — Belfast : H.M.S.O., 1980 — 15p
ISBN 0-337-23322-5 : £1.50 B81-04412

344.1607 — Northern Ireland. Justice. Administration. Social aspects

Boyle, Kevin. Ten years on in Northern Ireland : the legal control of political violence / Kevin Boyle, Tom Hadden, Paddy Hillyard. — London (186 Kings Cross Rd., WC1X 9DE) : Cobden Trust, 1980. — 119p ; 21cm
Includes bibliographies
ISBN 0-900137-16-9 (pbk) : £2.50 B81-12984

344.1608'22 — Northern Ireland. Law. Statutes. Repeal — *Statutes*

Great Britain. [Statute Law Revision (Northern Ireland) Act 1980]. Statute Law Revision (Northern Ireland) Act 1980 : Elizabeth II 1980 Chapter 59. — London : H.M.S.O., [1980]. — 21p ; 25cm
ISBN 0-10-545980-1 (unbound) : £2.10 B81-0239.

344.1608′25 — Northern Ireland. Law — *Statutory instruments — Collections — Serials*

Great Britain. [Laws, etc.]. Orders in council. — 1979. — Belfast : H.M.S.O., 1980. — viii,384p
Spine title: Northern Ireland statutes
ISBN 0-337-48000-1 : £17.50 B81-27325

344.17 — LAW. IRELAND(REPUBLIC)

344.17 — Ireland *(Republic).* **Law**

Doolan, Brian, *1945-*. Principles of Irish law / Brian Doolan. — Dublin : Gill and Macmillan, 1981. — xx,300p ; 22cm
Includes index
ISBN 0-7171-1124-5 (pbk) : £6.30 B81-25920

Grimes, Richard H.. Introduction to law in the Republic of Ireland : its history, principles, administration & substance / Richard H. Grimes and Patrick T. Horgan. — Portmarnock : Wolfhound, 1981. — 368p ; 22cm
Bibliography: p348-351. — Includes index
ISBN 0-905473-55-8 : £15.00
ISBN 0-905473-56-6 (pbk) : unpriced
B81-39288

344.17034′05 — Ireland *(Republic).* **Direct taxation. Law** — *Serials*

Tolley's taxation in the Republic of Ireland. — 1980-81. — Croydon : Tolley, c1980. — viii,164p
ISBN 0-85459-006-4 : £6.50 B81-06080

344.1705′1 — Dublin. District courts. Cases — *Stories, anecdotes*

McCafferty, Nell. In the eyes of the law / Nell McCafferty. — Dublin (Knocksedan House, Swords, Co. Dublin) : Ward River Press, 1981. — 185p ; 18cm
ISBN 0-907085-05-9 (pbk) : £2.50 B81-26000

344.17061′5 — Ireland *(Republic).* **Families. Law**

Shatter, Alan Joseph. Family law in the Republic of Ireland / Alan Joseph Shatter. — 2nd ed. — Portmarnock : Wolfhound, 1981. — 408p ; 26cm
Previous ed.: 1977. — Includes index
ISBN 0-905473-43-4 : £20.00 : CIP rev.
ISBN 0-905473-44-2 (pbk) : Unpriced
B80-28112

344.17065′2 — Leinster *(Dukes of).* **Succession. Claims**

Estorick, Michael. Heirs & graces : the claim to the Dukedom of Leinster / Michael Estorick. — London : Weidenfeld and Nicolson, c1981. — xi,164p,[8]p of plates : ill,ports,geneal.tables ; 25cm
Includes index
ISBN 0-297-77955-9 : £6.95 B81-23429

344.2 — LAW. ENGLAND

344.2 — England. Law

Barrister. Every man's own lawyer. — 71st ed. / by a barrister. — London : Macmillan, 1981. — 1v.(various pagings) : 1ill ; 25cm
Previous ed.: London : Every Man's Own Lawyer Publishing Co. Ltd, 1971. — Includes index
ISBN 0-333-21849-3 (cased) : £15.00
B81-23019

Dominic, Josephine. General principles of law in a nutshell / Josephine Dominic. — London : Sweet & Maxwell, 1981. — vii,82p ; 18cm. — (New nutshells)
Includes index
ISBN 0-421-27830-7 (pbk) : £1.75 B81-10805

Halsbury, Hardinge Stanley Giffard, *Earl of.* Halsbury's laws of England. — London : Butterworths
Previous ed.: 1952-1964
Vol.34 / [editor-in-chief] Lord Hailsham of St. Marylebone. — 1980. — 651p ; 26cm
Includes index
ISBN 0-406-03434-6 : Unpriced
ISBN 0-406-03554-7 (De Luxe ed.) : Unpriced
ISBN 0-406-03400-1 (Set. Standard ed.) : Unpriced
ISBN 0-406-03520-2 (Set. Deluxe ed.) : Unpriced B81-13244

Halsbury, Hardinge Stanley Giffard, *Earl of.* Halsbury's laws of England. — 4th ed. / [editor in chief] Lord Hailsham of St. Marylebone. — London : Butterworths
Vol.36. — 1981. — 134,678p ; 26cm
Includes index
ISBN 0-406-03436-2 : Unpriced
ISBN 0-406-03400-1 (set) : Unpriced
ISBN 0-406-03556-3 (de luxe binding) : Unpriced B81-23284

Halsbury's Laws of England, annual abridgement. — London : Butterworths
1980 / editor Kenneth Mugford, assistant editor Gillian Mather. — c1981. — 854p ; 26cm
Includes index
ISBN 0-406-03367-6 : Unpriced B81-39637

Walker, D. (Dennis), *1933-*. Principles of law / by D. Walker. — Walton-on-Thames : Celtic Revision Aids, 1981. — 154p ; 19cm. — (Celtic revision notes. Law)
ISBN 0-17-751352-7 (pbk) : £1.85 B81-16505

Your guide to the law / editor Michael Molyneux ; contributors Charles Blake ... [et al.]. — London : Pan, 1981. — 448p ; 20cm
Includes index
ISBN 0-330-26348-x (pbk) : £3.50 B81-38767

Your guide to the law / editor Michael Molyneux ; contributors Charles Blake ... [et al.]. — London : Secker & Warburg, c1981. — 448p ; 23cm
Includes index
ISBN 0-436-28457-x : £10.00 : CIP rev.
B81-19129

344.2 — England. Law, *ca 1100-ca 1490.* **Early works**

Plucknett, T. F. T.. Early English legal literature / by T.F.T. Plucknett. — London (6 Borneo St., S.W.15) : Seer, 1980, c1958. — viii,120p ; 22cm
Originally published: Cambridge : University Press, 1958. — Includes index
ISBN 0-907230-00-8 : £7.50 B81-03910

344.2 — England. Law — *Early works*

Bracton, Henry de. [Bracton de legibus et consuetudinibus Angliae. English]. Bracton on the laws and customs of England / translated, with revisions and notes, by Samuel E. Thorne. — Cambridge, Mass. ; London : Published in association with the Selden Society, The Belknap Press of Harvard University Press
Vol.3. — 1977. — lii,412,412p ; 27cm
Parallel Latin text and English translation. — Opposite pages bear duplicate numbering
ISBN 0-674-08038-6 : £59.00 B81-34948

344.2 — England. Law — *Early works — Facsimiles*

Enchiridion legum. Speculum juris anglicani / John Brydall. — New York ; London : Garland, 1978. — 140,150p ; 19cm. — (Classics of English legal history in the modern era ; 142)
Facsim. reprints: Enchiridion legum originally published : London : Printed by E. Flesher, J. Streater and H. Twyford, 1673. — Speculum juris anglicani originally published: London : Printed by J. Streater, E. Flesher and H. Twyford, 1673
ISBN 0-8240-3056-7 : Unpriced B81-27498

344.2 — England. Law. Making

Zander, Michael. The law-making process / Michael Zander. — London : Weidenfeld and Nicolson, c1980. — xxvi,309p ; 22cm. — (Law in context)
Bibliography: pxi-xxiii. — Includes index
ISBN 0-297-77750-5 (cased) : Unpriced
ISBN 0-297-77751-3 (pbk) : £6.95 B81-40695

344.2′00207 — England. Law — *Humour*

Williams, Donald B.. On the lighter side of the law / by Donald B. Williams ; illustrations by John Craig. — Chichester : Rose, 1981. — 92p ; 23cm
ISBN 0-85992-191-3 : £6.95 B81-18906

344.2′0023 — England. Solicitorship. Law

Cordery, Arthur. Cordery's law relating to solicitors. — 7th ed. / Graham J. Graham-Green assisted by Frederic T. Horne. — London : Butterworths, 1981. — xci,457p ; 26cm
Previous ed.: 1968. — Includes index
ISBN 0-406-16156-9 : Unpriced B81-26313

344.2′0023 — South-west England. Barristers, *ca 1400-1980*

Harwood, Antony. Circuit ghosts : a Western Circuit miscellany / by Antony Harwood. — Winchester (Jewry St., Winchester, Hants.) : Copying Centre, 1980. — 261p : 1ill ; 21cm
Includes index
Unpriced (pbk) B81-32492

344.2′0024333 — England. Law — *For land use management*

Card, Richard. Law for land management students / by Richard Card, John Murdoch and Peter Schofield. — London : Butterworths, 1981. — xli,649p,[1]leaf of plates : 1ill ; 25cm
Includes index
ISBN 0-406-56290-3 (pbk) : Unpriced
B81-33740

344.2′002436 — England. Law — *For welfare work*

Anderson-Ford, David. The social worker's law book : an introductory manual / David Anderson-Ford. — London : McGraw-Hill, c1980. — xxi,154p : ill,forms ; 25cm
Includes bibliographies and index
ISBN 0-07-084633-2 (pbk) : £3.95 : CIP rev.
B80-18630

344.2′0024362 — England. Law — *For welfare work*

Zander, Michael. Social workers, their clients and the law / Michael Zander. — 3rd ed. — London : Sweet & Maxwell, 1981. — xiv,180p ; 22cm. — (Social work and law)
Previous ed.: 1977. — Includes index
ISBN 0-421-27930-3 (pbk) : £5.75 : CIP rev.
B81-19185

344.2′00243632 — England. Law — *For police*

Moriarty, Cecil C. H.. Moriarty's police law : an arrangement of law and regulations for the use of police officers. — 24th ed. / by the late James Fryer and Sir Walter Stansfield. — London : Butterworths, 1981. — xviii,767p ; 19cm
Previous ed.: 1976. — Includes index
ISBN 0-406-84608-1 (pbk) : Unpriced
B81-27036

344.2′0028′54 — England. Legal services. Applications of digital computer systems. Great Britain. *Royal Commission on Legal Services.* **Final report** — *Critical studies*

Society of Computers and Law. Response by the Society for Computers and Law to the reports by the English and Scottish Royal Commissions on Legal Services which were published in October 1979 and May 1980 respectively. — Milton (11 High St., Milton, Oxon OX14 4ER) : The Society, 1981. — 19p ; 21cm
ISBN 0-906122-05-8 (pbk) : £1.00
Also classified at 344.11′0028′54 B81-12277

344.2′005 — England. Law — *Serials*

Current law year book. — 1980. — London : Sweet & Maxwell, 1981. — [1095]p in various pagings
ISBN 0-421-28410-2 : Unpriced
ISSN 0307-5141 B81-35455

The **Lawyer's** remembrancer. — 1981. — London : Butterworths, 1980. — 413,[138]p
ISBN 0-406-26913-0 : Unpriced
ISSN 0142-7490 B81-04798

344.2′0068 — England. Solicitorship. Private practice. Management — *Manuals*

Organization and management of a solicitor's practice / general editors Peter J. Purton, David Andrews ; taxation editor L. Peter K. Brindley. — London : Oyez, c1980. — 1v. (loose-leaf) : forms ; 26cm
Includes index
ISBN 0-85120-480-5 : £60.00 B81-17053

344.2′009 — England, *400-1485*. Law

Lyon, Bryce. A constitutional and legal history of medieval England / Bryce Lyon. — 2nd ed. — New York ; London : Norton, c1980. — xviii,669p : maps ; 24cm
Previous ed.: 1960. — Bibliography: p650-652. - Includes index
ISBN 0-393-95132-4 : £9.50
Also classified at 350′.000942 B81-03966

344.2′009 — England. Common law, *to ca 1700*

Milsom, S. F. C.. Historical foundations of the common law / S.F.C. Milsom. — 2nd ed. — London : Butterworths, 1981. — xiii,475p ; 22cm
Previous ed.: 1969. — Includes index
ISBN 0-406-62502-6 (cased) : Unpriced
ISBN 0-406-62503-4 (pbk) : Unpriced
B81-19352

344.2′0092′4 — England. Law. Dicey, A. V. — *Biographies*

Cosgrove, Richard A.. The rule of law : Albert Venn Dicey, Victorian jurist / by Richard A. Cosgrove. — London : Macmillan, 1980. — xv,319p : ill,ports ; 24cm
Bibliography: p301-314. - Includes index
ISBN 0-333-30707-0 : £15.00 B81-05665

344.2′0092′4 — England. Law. James, Edwin — *Biographies*

Lewis, J. R. (John Royston). Certain private incidents : the rise and fall of Edwin James QC, MP / J.R. Lewis. — Newcastle upon Tyne (207 Western Way, Ponteland, Newcastle upon Tyne) : Templar North Publications, c1980. — 166p : ill,1facsim,ports ; 27cm
Bibliography: p165-166
Unpriced B81-11135

344.202′29 — England. Constitution, *to 1702* — *Early works — Facsimiles*

De Lolme, Jean Louis. The rise and progress of the English constitution / Jean Louis de Lolme. — New York ; London : Garland, 1978. — 2v.(clxxxi,1139p,[5]folded leaves of plates, [2]p of plates) : geneal.tables ; 23cm. — (Classics of English legal history in the modern era)
Facsim of: edition published London : Parker, 1838. — Includes index
ISBN 0-8240-3069-9 : £90.00 B81-16467

344.202′85 — England. Citizens — *Practical information*

Leach, Robert, *1950-*. Coping with the system : a brief citizens' manual / by Robert Leach. — Cambridge (18 Brooklands Ave., Cambridge CB2 2HW) : National Extension College, 1980. — vi,111p : ill,maps,forms ; 22cm
Bibliography: p106-107
ISBN 0-904571-33-5 (pbk) : £1.95 B81-05796

344.202′85′0264 — England. Civil rights. Law — *Cases*

Bailey, S. H.. Civil liberties : cases and materials / S.H. Bailey, D.J. Harris, B.L. Jones. — London : Butterworths, 1980. — xxvii,447p ; 26cm
Includes index
ISBN 0-406-55481-1 (cased) : £18.00
ISBN 0-406-55480-3 (pbk) : £11.95 B81-01592

344.202′85′03 — England. Citizens. Rights — *Encyclopaedias*

Reader's Digest Association. You and your rights : an A to Z guide to the law / Reader's Digest. — 2nd ed. — London : Reader's Digest Association, c1980. — 751p : ill(some col.),facsims,forms ; 27cm
Previous ed.: 1980. — Facsim on lining papers. — Includes index
£12.95 B81-02834

344.202′85′0321 — England. Citizens. Rights — *Encyclopaedias*

You and your rights : an A to Z guide to the law / Reader's Digest. — 3rd ed. — London : Reader's Digest Association, 1981. — 751p : ill (some col.),facsims,forms ; 27cm
Previous ed.: 1980. — Facsim on lining papers. — Includes index
£12.95 B81-22942

344.202′858 — England. Privacy. Encroachment. Control. Law

Wacks, Raymond. The protection of privacy / by Raymond Wacks. — London : Sweet & Maxwell, 1980. — xx,185p ; 19cm. — (Modern legal studies)
Includes index
ISBN 0-421-26840-9 (cased) : £11.50 : CIP rev.
ISBN 0-421-26850-6 (pbk) : £6.50 B80-25361

344.202′87 — England. Children. Law

Children and the courts. — [Guildford] : College of Law, c1980. — viii,83p ; 22cm. — (College of Law lectures, ISSN 0309-3166)
£4.00 (pbk) B81-07192

Hall, *Sir* William Clarke. Law relating to children and young persons / Clarke Hall and Morrison. — 9th ed. / consulting editor Joseph Jackson ; editors Margaret Booth, Brian Harris ; foreword by Sir George Baker. — London : Butterworths
Previous ed.: 1972
2: Cumulative supplement. — 1981. — xxiv,B652p : forms ; 25cm
ISBN 0-406-15808-8 (pbk) : Unpriced
B81-28939

344.202′9 — England. Local government. Law: Local Government, Planning and Land Act 1980 — *Critical studies*

Local Government, Planning and Land Act 1980 : a reprint of eight articles from Local government chronicle / edited by Geoffrey Smith and Crispin Derby. — London (Publications Division, 11 Bury St., EC3A 5AP) : Brown, Knight & Truscott (Holdings), [1981?]. — 39p ; 21cm
ISBN 0-904677-15-x (pbk) : £3.00 B81-26269

344.202′9′02632 — England. Local government. Law — *Statutes — Codes — Serials*

Encyclopedia of local government law. — Vol.1-. — London : Sweet & Maxwell, 1980-. — v. ; 25cm. — (The Local government library)
ISSN 0261-3689 = Encyclopedia of local government law : Unpriced B81-24122

344.202′9′02633 — England. Local government. Law — *Statutes*

Great Britain. [The Local Government, Planning and Land Act 1980]. The Local Government, Planning and Land Act 1980 / with annotations by Victor Moore and Louise Catchpole. — London : Sweet & Maxwell, 1981. — [294]p ; 25cm. — (Current Law statutes reprints)
ISBN 0-421-28870-1 (pbk) : £10.00 B81-25904

344.202′9′02633 — England. Local government. Law — *Statutes — Texts with commentaries*

Arnold-Baker, Charles. Local Government, Planning and Land Act 1980 / by Charles Arnold-Baker. — London : Butterworths, 1981. — vii,322p ; 25cm. — (Annotated legislation service ; v.275)
Includes index
ISBN 0-406-54796-3 : Unpriced B81-33354

Great Britain. [The Local Government, Planning and Land Act 1980]. Local Government Planning and Land Act 1980 / [edited and annotated] by Charles Arnold-Baker. — London : Butterworths, 1981. — vii,322p ; 25cm
Includes index
ISBN 0-406-58430-3 : Unpriced B81-33032

344.203′12 — English Civil War. Royalist forces. Raising — *Prerogative instruments*

England and Wales. *Sovereign (1625-1649 : Charles I).* A copy of the Commission of Array : granted from His Majesty, to the Marquess of Hertford. — Mount Durand : Toucan, 1981. — [8]p ; 21cm
Facsim. of: ed. published London: For E. Husbands and I. Frank, 1642
ISBN 0-85694-244-8 (pbk) : Unpriced
B81-26842

344.2034 — England. Children. Financial provision. Implication of taxation

White, Peter, *1944 May 4-*. Children in tax planning / Peter White. — London : Oyez, 1980. — xviii,136p ; 21cm. — (The Oyez practical tax series)
Includes index
ISBN 0-85120-513-5 (pbk) : £8.50 B81-14495

344.203′4 — England. Defamation. Law

Gatley, J. C. C.. Gatley on libel and slander. — 8th ed. — London : Sweet & Maxwell, Dec.1981. — [700]p. — (The Common law library ; no.8)
Previous ed.: 1974
ISBN 0-421-24340-6 : CIP entry B81-31173

344.2034 — England. Taxation. Law

Monroe, H. H.. Intolerable inquisition? : reflections on the law of tax / by Hubert Monroe. — London : Stevens published under the auspices of Hamlyn Trust, 1981. — xiii,84p ; 19cm. — (The Hamlyn lectures ; 33 series)
ISBN 0-420-46190-6 (cased) : £11.25 : CIP rev.
ISBN 0-420-46200-7 (£4.60) B81-05162

344.2035′4 — England. Matrimonial causes. Financial settlements. Tax avoidance. Law

White, Peter, *1944 May 4-*. Tax planning on marriage breakdown / Peter White. — London : Oyez, 1980. — xix,187p : ill ; 21cm. — (The Oyez practical tax series)
Includes index
ISBN 0-85120-503-8 (pbk) : £9.95 B81-13607

344.2035′4 — England. Rates. Law

Ryde, Walter Cranley. Ryde on rating : the law and practice. — 13th ed. / by David Widdicombe, David Trustram Eve and Anthony Anderson. — London : Butterworth
2nd cumulative supplement / by Guy Roots. — 1981. — xvii,130p : ill ; 25cm
ISBN 0-406-36313-7 (pbk) : Unpriced
B81-26375

344.203′74 — England. Finance. Personal sureties. Law

Rowlatt, *Sir* Sidney Arthur Taylor. Rowlatt on the law of principal and surety. — 4th ed. — London : Sweet & Maxwell, Nov.1981. — [250]p
Previous ed.: 1936
ISBN 0-421-26240-0 : £16.00 : CIP entry
B81-31245

344.203′769 — England. Game animals, *1671-1831*. Law. Social aspects

Munsche, P. B.. Gentlemen and poachers. — Cambridge : Cambridge University Press, Dec.1981. — [255]p
ISBN 0-521-23284-8 : £18.50 : CIP entry
B81-31828

344.203′78 — England. Catering industries & hotel industries. Law

Richards, Margaret. Legal aspects of the hotel and catering industry. — 2nd ed. — London : Bell & Hyman, Nov.1981. — [266]p
Previous ed.: 1975
ISBN 0-7135-1176-1 (pbk) : £6.95 : CIP entry
B81-34723

344.203′78624 — England. Construction. Contracts. Law — *Encyclopaedias*

Fletcher, Leonard. Construction contract dictionary / Leonard Fletcher, Reginald Lee, John A. Tackaberry. — Reading : College of Estate Management, 1981. — 121p ; 22cm
Bibliography: p121
ISBN 0-902132-65-2 (cased) : Unpriced
ISBN 0-902132-63-6 (pbk) : Unpriced
B81-40698

344.203′7869 — England. Buildings. Construction. Legal aspects — *For architectural design*

Greenstreet, Bob. Architects' guide to legal and contractual procedures / Bob Greenstreet. — London : Architectural Press, 1981. — 96p : ill,forms ; 21x30cm
Bibliography: p93. — Includes index
ISBN 0-85139-370-5 (pbk) : £5.95 B81-26150

344.203′7869 — England. Buildings. Construction - *Statutory instruments - Texts with commentaries*

Whyte, W. S.. The Building Regulations explained and illustrated for residential buildings. — 5th ed. (metric). — London : Granada, July 1981. — 1v.
This ed. originally published: Crosby Lockwood Staples, 1978
ISBN 0-246-11611-0 (pbk) : £5.95 : CIP entry
B81-13906

344.203'7869 — England. Buildings. Construction. Statutory regulations — *Proposals*
The Future of building control in England and Wales. — London : H.M.S.O., [1981]. — 17p ; 25cm. — (Cmnd. ; 8179)
ISBN 0-10-181790-8 (unbound) : £2.10 B81-15609

344.203'7869 — England. Law — *For building industries*
Manson, Keith. Building law for students / Keith Manson. — 4th rev. ed. — London : Cassell, 1981. — xx,271p ; 22cm
Previous ed.: 1974. — Includes index
ISBN 0-304-30792-0 (pbk) : £5.95 B81-31667

344.203'78'690 — England. Construction industries. Law
Uff, John. Construction law. — 3rd ed. — London : Sweet & Maxwell, Sept.1981. — [250]p. — (Concise college texts)
Previous ed.: 1978
ISBN 0-421-28300-9 (cased) : £12.75 : CIP entry B81-21576

344.203'786928 — England. Buildings. Construction. Contracts. Conditions - *Manuals*
Audas, J. M.. A builder's guide to the agreement for minor building works. — Ascot : Chartered Institute of Building, May 1981. — [22]p. — (Surveying information service, ISSN 0140-649x ; no.3)
ISBN 0-906600-32-4 (pbk) : CIP entry B81-12363

344.203'94 — England. Road traffic. Law — *For motoring*
Spencer, John, *1936-*. Questions of motoring law / John Spencer. — Feltham : Hamlyn Paperbacks, 1981. — ix,179p ; 18cm. — (A Hamlyn original)
Includes index
ISBN 0-600-20319-0 (pbk) : £1.25 B81-23569

344.203'94 — England. Road traffic. Law — *Inquiry reports*
Report of the Inter-Departmental Working Party on Road Traffic Law. — London : H.M.S.O., 1981. — vii,66p ; 25cm
ISBN 0-11-550549-0 (pbk) : £4.20 B81-40140

344.203'942'02632 — England. Highways. Law — *Statutes — Texts with commentaries*
Great Britain. [Highways Act 1980]. The Highways Act 1980 / with annotations by Charles Cross and Stephen Sauvain. — London : Sweet & Maxwell, 1981. — xxix,[532]p ; 25cm. — (Current law statutes reprints)
Includes index
ISBN 0-421-28130-8 : £15.00 B81-36331

Hamilton, Susan. Highways Act 1980 / by Susan Hamilton. — London : Butterworths, 1981. — xxxi,774p ; 25cm. — (Annotated legislation service ; v.274)
Includes index
ISBN 0-406-54799-8 : Unpriced B81-28236

Hamilton, Susan. The modern law of highways / by Susan Hamilton. — London : Butterworths, 1981. — xxxi,774p ; 26cm
Includes index. — Includes the texts of the Highways Act 1980 and Public Utilities Street Works Act 1950
ISBN 0-406-22080-8 : Unpriced B81-28238

344.203'944 — England. Abandoned motor vehicles. Disposal. Law
Disposal of abandoned vehicles and other refuse : a guide to the relevant provisions of the Refuse Disposal (Amenity) Act 1978 and the Road Traffic Regulation Act 1967. — London : Shaw, 1981. — 29p ; 22cm. — (The Shaway guides ; no.4)
ISBN 0-7219-0875-6 (pbk) : Unpriced B81-40055

344.203'958 — England. Railway services. Law
James, Leslie, *1914-*. The law of the railway / Leslie James. — London : Barry Rose, c1980. — xlii,479p ; 25cm
Includes index
ISBN 0-85992-158-1 (pbk) : £12.00 B81-39312

344.204'1'0264 — England. Employment. Labour. Law — *Cases*
Elias, Patrick. Labour law : cases and materials / Patrick Elias, Brian Napier, Peter Wallington. — London : Butterworths, 1980. — xl,819p
Includes index
ISBN 0-406-57758-7 (cased) : £26.00
ISBN 0-406-57759-5 (pbk) : £15.95 B81-10637

344.204'1'0264 — England. Industrial relations. Law — *Cases — Serials*
Industrial cases reports. — 1980. — London : Incorporated Council of Law Reporting for England and Wales, 1980. — xiv,834p
ISSN 0306-2163 : Unpriced B81-13085

344.204'1'0269 — England. Industrial tribunals. Procedure
Angel, John. How to prepare yourself for an industrial tribunal / John Angel. — London : Institute of Personnel Management, 1980. — x,299p : ill,forms ; 22cm
Includes index
ISBN 0-85292-254-x (pbk) : £9.45 : CIP rev. B80-29358

344.204'3'02632 — England. Social services. Law — *Statutes — Codes — Serials*
Encyclopedia of social services law and practice. — Vol.1-. — London : Sweet & Maxwell, 1981-. — v. ; 25cm
ISSN 0261-3573 = Encyclopedia of social services law and practice : Unpriced B81-24123

344.204'31'02632 — England. Welfare work. Law — *Statutes — Collections*
Great Britain. [Laws etc.]. Sweet & Maxwell's social work statutes / edited by Richard M. Jones. — London : Sweet & Maxwell, 1980. — vii,168p ; 25cm
Includes index
ISBN 0-421-26160-9 (pbk) : £4.60 B81-03538

344.204'313 — England. Welfare work. Law
McClean, J. D.. The legal context of social work / by J. D. McClean. — London : Butterworths, 1980. — xxi,229p ; 23cm
Previous ed.: 1975. — Includes index
ISBN 0-406-62123-3 (cased) : £11.00
ISBN 0-406-62124-1 (pbk) : £6.95 B81-20390

Roberts, Gwyneth. Essential law for social workers / Gwyneth Roberts. — 2nd ed. — London : Oyez, 1981. — 242p ; 22cm
Previous ed.: 1978. — Includes index
ISBN 0-85120-514-3 (pbk) : Unpriced B81-37477

344.204'321 — England. Health services. Law
Finch, John D.. Health services law / by John D. Finch. — London : Sweet & Maxwell, 1981. — xix,338p ; 23cm
Includes index
ISBN 0-421-26460-8 (cased) : £11.30 : CIP rev.
ISBN 0-421-26470-5 (pbk) : £7.30 B81-09505

344.204'321'02633 — England. Health services. Law — *Statutes*
Great Britain. [Health Services Act 1980]. Health Services Act 1980 : Chapter 53. — London : H.M.S.O., [1980]. — iii,63p ; 25cm
ISBN 0-10-545380-3 (pbk) : £3.90 B81-19806

344.204'321'05 — England. Health services. Law — *Serials*
Digest and journal of hospital and health service law. — Vol.1-. — Beckenham : Ravenswood Publications, 1981-. — v. ; 21cm
Annual
ISSN 0143-5191 = Digest and journal of hospital and health service law : Unpriced B81-38991

344.204'3211 — England. Hospitals. Patients. Care. Law
Brennan, J. L.. Medico-legal problems in hospital practice / J.L. Brennan. — Beckenham : Ravenswood, 1980. — 106p ; 22cm. — (Studies in law and practice for health service management ; v.10)
Bibliography: p105-106
ISBN 0-901812-36-6 (cased) : £13.25
ISBN 0-901812-37-4 (pbk) : £10.25 B81-07342

344.204'32795 — England. Children. Care. Law
Hoggett, Brenda M.. Parents and children / Brenda M. Hoggett. — 2nd ed. — London : Sweet and Maxwell, 1981. — xxxvii,244p ; 22cm. — (Social work and law)
Previous ed.: 1977. — Bibliography: pxxv-xiv. — Includes index
ISBN 0-421-27910-9 (pbk) : £6.85 : CIP rev. B81-16350

344.204'414 — England. Law — *For nursing*
Young, Ann P.. Legal problems in nursing practice / Ann P. Young. — London : Harper & Row, c1981. — 183p : ill,forms ; 21cm. — (Lippincott nursing series)
Bibliography: p178-179. — Includes index
ISBN 0-06-318181-9 (cased) : Unpriced : CIP rev.
ISBN 0-06-318182-7 (pbk) : Unpriced B81-20550

344.204'44 — England. Mental health services. Law
Whitehead, Tony. Mental illness and the law. — Oxford : Blackwell, June 1981. — [192]p
ISBN 0-631-12721-6 (cased) : £10.00 : CIP entry (pbk) : £3.95 B81-09499

344.204'44'0269 — England. Mental health tribunals. Procedure — *For compulsorily detained patients in mental illness hospitals*
Mental health review tribunals : a step by step guide to leaving hospital. — London : MIND, [1981?]. — 1sheet ; 21x45cm folded to 21x15cm
Unpriced (unbound) B81-29216

344.204'446 — England. Alcoholism & drug abuse. Law
Farrier, David. Drugs and intoxication / by David Farrier. — London : Sweet & Maxwell, 1980. — xix,262p ; 19cm. — (Modern legal studies)
Includes index
ISBN 0-421-27100-0 (cased) : £11.30 : CIP rev.
ISBN 0-421-27090-x (pbk) : £8.00 B80-25368

344.204'46 — England. Environmental health. Law
Webster, Charles A. R.. Environmental health law / by Charles A.R. Webster. — London : Sweet & Maxwell, 1981. — xxiii,177p ; 22cm
Includes index
ISBN 0-421-26620-1 (cased) : £11.50 : CIP rev.
ISBN 0-421-26630-9 (pbk) : £1.50 B81-09965

344.204'462 — England. Buildings. Drainage. Law
Garner, J. F.. The law of sewers and drains under the Public Health Acts / by J.F. Garner. — 6th ed. — London : Shaw & Sons, 1981. — xxxviii,206p : ill ; 22cm
Previous ed.: 1975. — Includes index
ISBN 0-7219-0581-1 (pbk) : Unpriced B81-18614

344.204'63635 — England. Residences. Conversion & improvement. Law
Garner, J. F.. Alteration or conversion of houses / J.F. Garner. — 5th ed. — London : Oyez, 1981. — viii,112p ; 22cm. — (Oyez practice notes ; 47)
Previous ed.: 1975. — Includes index
ISBN 0-85120-555-0 (pbk) : Unpriced B81-29584

344.204'636358 — England. Public housing. Law
Hughes, D. J. (David John), *1945-*. Public sector housing law / by D.J. Hughes. — London : Butterworths, 1981. — xxxiv,359p ; 22cm
Includes bibliographies and index
ISBN 0-406-60061-9 (cased) : Unpriced
ISBN 0-406-60060-0 (pbk) : Unpriced B81-32964

344.205 — England. Criminal law
Seago, Peter. Criminal law / Peter Seago. — London : Sweet & Maxwell, 1981. — xvii,246p ; 23cm. — (Concise college texts)
Bibliography: p236-237. — Includes index
ISBN 0-421-23990-5 (cased) : £13.00 : CIP rev.
ISBN 0-421-24000-8 (pbk) : £8.50 B81-10485

Walker, D. (Dennis), *1933-*. Criminal law / by D. Walker. — Walton-on-Thames : Celtic Revision Aids, 1981. — 130p ; 19cm. — (Celtic revision notes. Law)
ISBN 0-17-751353-5 (pbk) : £1.85 B81-16504

344.205 — England. Criminal law. Great Britain. *Parliament. House of Commons.* **Criminal Law Bill. Session 1976-77** — *Haldane Society of Socialist Lawyers viewpoints*
Haldane Society of Socialist Lawyers. Criminal Law Bill : a criticism. — London (35 Wellington St., W.C.2) : Haldane Society of Socialist Lawyers, 1977. — 44p ; 30cm
Unpriced (unbound) B81-18950

344.205'02648 — England. Criminal law — *Cases — Digests*
Bingham, Richard. The modern cases and statutes on Crown Court crime / by Richard Bingham. — Chichester : Rose. — xlix,532p ; 26cm
Includes index
ISBN 0-85992-186-7 : £34.75 B81-07122

Bingham, Richard. The modern cases and statutes on Crown Court crime / by Richard Bingham. — Chichester : Rose
1st cumulative supplement. — 1981. — [88]p ; 24cm
ISBN 0-85992-221-9 (pbk) : £7.50 B81-27082

344.205'02648 — England. Criminal law. Cases in assize courts in Home Counties, *1558-1625* — *Digests*
Calendar of assize records / edited by J.S. Cockburn. — London : H.M.S.O.
Kent indictments : James I. — 1980. — vii,267p ; 26cm
Includes index
ISBN 0-11-440107-1 : £27.00 B81-15214

344.205'1 — England. Local authorities. Personnel: Prosecutors. Duties — *Manuals*
Stott, D.. To prosecute or not to prosecute / D. Stott. — Chichester : Rose, 1980. — 61p : ill ; 21cm
ISBN 0-85992-197-2 (pbk) : £5.00 B81-10347

344.205'12 — England. Criminal courts: Magistrates' courts. Justice. Administration
King, Michael, *1942-*. The framework of criminal justice / Michael King. — London : Croom Helm, c1981. — 159p ; 23cm
Bibliography: p153-156. - Includes index
ISBN 0-7099-0430-4 (cased) : £10.95 : CIP rev.
ISBN 0-7099-1500-4 (pbk) : £6.50 B80-21596

344.205'12 — England. Criminal courts: Magistrates' courts. Procedure
Conduct of criminal proceedings. — [Guildford] ([Braboeuf Manor, Portsmouth Rd, St Catherine's, Guildford, Surrey]) : College of Law, c1980. — vii,84p : 1form ; 22cm. — (College of Law lectures, ISSN 0309-3166)
£4.00 (pbk) B81-03851

344.205'12 — England. Magistrates' courts. Advocacy — *Manuals*
Chatelier, Trevor M.. Criminal advocacy in the magistrates' court / by Trevor M. Chatelier. — Chichester : Rose, c1981. — 53p ; 22cm
ISBN 0-85992-219-7 (pbk) : £3.35 B81-18765

344.205'12 — England. Magistrates' courts. Chairmanship — *Manuals*
Young, Agnes F.. Chairmanship in Magistrates' Courts / by Agnes F. Young and Keith C. Clarke. — 3rd ed. — Chichester : Rose, 1980. — 93p ; 22cm
Previous ed.: 1976. — Bibliography: p88-90. - Includes index
ISBN 0-85992-187-5 (pbk) : £4.00 B81-10348

344.205'12 — England. Magistrates' courts. Court orders. Procedure — *Manuals*
Harris, Brian, *1932-*. The magistrate's companion : a guide for magistrates in announcing sentence and other orders of the court / Brian Harris. — 2nd ed. — Chichester : Rose, 1981. — 86p ; 18cm
Previous ed.: 1977. — Text on inside cover
ISBN 0-85992-213-8 (pbk) : £2.50 B81-18763

344.205'12 — England. Magistrates' courts. Justice. Administration. Expenditure by local authorities — *Forecasts — Serials*
Administration of justice statistics, based on estimates / the Society of County Treasurers. — 1980/81. — Reading (c/o Shire Hall, Reading RG1 3EX) : The Society, 1980. — 8p
Unpriced
Also classified at 344.207'4 B81-08227

344.205'12 — England. Magistrates' courts — *Manuals*
A **Magistrate's** ABC : a Jutice of the Peace guide. — Chichester : Justice of the Peace, 1980. — iv,64p ; 26cm
Bibliography: p64
ISBN 0-85992-198-0 (corrected: pbk) : £3.30 B81-13049

344.205'12'02633 — England. Magistrates' courts. Law — *Statutes — Texts with commentaries*
Great Britain. [Magistrates' Courts Act 1980]. Magistrates' Courts Act 1980 / annotated by Butterworths Legal editiorial staff. — London : Butterworths, 1981. — xv,216p ; 24cm. — (Annotated Legislation service ; 276)
Includes index
ISBN 0-406-54802-1 : Unpriced B81-39001

344.205'12'05 — England. Magistrates' courts. Law — *Serials*
Stone's justices' manual. — 113th ed. (1981). — London : Butterworth, 1981. — 3v
ISBN 0-406-38652-8 : Unpriced B81-25488

344.205'12'05 — England. Magistrates' courts. Procedure — *Serials*
Anthony & Berryman's magistrates' court guide. — 1981. — London : Butterworth, 1981. — viii,379p
ISBN 0-406-10834-x : Unpriced B81-15161

344.205'12'0942132 — Great Britain. *Magistrates' Court (Marlborough Street), to 1979*
Lock, Joan. Marlborough Street : the story of a London court / by Joan Lock. — London : Hale, 1980. — 200p,[16]p of plates : ill,3facsims,ports ; 23cm
Bibliography: p196-197
ISBN 0-7091-8581-2 : £7.50 B81-04683

344.205'14'02643 — Great Britain. *Crown Court.* **Sentencing** — *Statistics*
The **Crown** Court pattern of sentencing : (offenders aged 14 and over) : being extracts from the criminal statistics for England and Wales 1971-1978 / [compiled] by Ian McLean. — Chichester : Rose, 1981. — 252p in various pagings ; 18cm
Includes index
ISBN 0-85992-209-x : £17.70 B81-21865

344.205'231 — England. Treason. Trials, *1945-1960*
West, Rebecca. The meaning of treason. — 3rd ed. — London : Virago, Feb.1982. — [448]p
Previous ed.: Harmondsworth : Penguin, 1965
ISBN 0-86068-256-0 (pbk) : £4.50 : CIP entry
Also classified at 347.305'231 B81-40235

344.205'247 — England. Motoring offences. Law — *For motoring*
Lawrence, R. H.. RAC driver's guide to the law / R.H. Lawrence. — Plymouth : Macdonald and Evans in association with the Royal Automobile Club, 1980 (1981 [printing]). — 174p : ill ; 22cm
Includes index
ISBN 0-7121-1285-5 (pbk) : £2.95 B81-23061

344.205'247 — England. Traffic offences. Law
Halnan, Patrick. Road traffic / Patrick Halnan. — Chichester : Rose for the Magistrates' Association, [c1981]. — 50p ; 21cm
ISBN 0-85992-207-3 (pbk) : £2.50 B81-10349

344.205'248 — England. Vagrancy. Law. Great Britain. *Parliament. House of Commons. Home Affairs Committee.* **'Vagrancy offences'** — *Critical studies*
Great Britain. *Home Office.* The Government's reply to the third report from the Home Affairs Committee, session 1980-1981 HC271, Vagrancy offences / presented to Parliament by the Secretary of State for the Home Department. — London : H.M.S.O., [1981]. — 3p ; 25cm. — (Cmnd. ; 8311)
ISBN 0-10-183110-2 (unbound) : £0.70 B81-35679

344.205'2523'0922 — Dorset. Poole. Greene, Alice & Beard, Agnes. Murder, *1598.* **Trial of suspects,** *1610*
Wilnecker, Pat. The High Street murders 1598 / by Pat Wilnecker. — Poole (The Guildhall, Market St., Poole BH15 1NP) : Borough of Poole Museums Service, c1980. — 16p : 1map,1facsim ; 21cm. — (Poole local history publicatons ; no.1)
Cover title. — Text on covers
ISBN 0-86251-001-5 (pbk) : Unpriced B81-29704

344.205'2523'0922 — Somerset. Buttersworth, Jane. Murder. Trial of Branch, Elizabeth & Branch, Mary
Branch, Elizabeth. [The cruel mistress]. The trial of Elizabeth Branch and her daughter for the murder of Jane Butterworth. — St Peter Port : Toucan, 1981. — p189-228 : ill ; 24cm. — (Ilchester and district occasional papers, ISSN 0306-6010 ; no.28)
Facsim. of: The Cruel mistress. London : C. Simpson, 1740
ISBN 0-85694-226-x (unbound) : Unpriced B81-39036

344.205'2523'0924 — West Midlands *(Metropolitan County).* **Birmingham. Infanticide. Trial of Watkins, William Arthur**
Pugh, John. Goodbye forever : the victim of a system / by John Pugh. — London : Rose, c1981. — 224p,[16]p of plates : ill,facisms,ports ; 21cm
Includes index
ISBN 0-85992-167-0 : £8.50 B81-23233

344.205'253 — England. Adolescents. Sexual intercourse. Age of consent. Law. Reform — *Inquiry reports*
Great Britain. *Policy Advisory Committee on Sexual Offences.* Report on the age of consent in relation to sexual offences / Policy Advisory Committee on Sexual Offences ; presented to Parliament by the Secretary of State for the Home Department. — London : H.M.S.O., 1981. — v,32p ; 25cm. — (Cmnd. ; 8216)
ISBN 0-10-182160-3 (unbound) : £2.70 B81-21677

344.205'2532 — England. Crimes: Rape. Law — *Sociological perspectives*
Edwards, Susan S. M.. Female sexuality and the law : a study of constructs of female sexuality as they inform statute and legal procedure / Susan S.M. Edwards. — Oxford : Robertson, 1981. — 195p ; 23cm. — (Law in society series)
Bibliography: p183-190. — Includes index
ISBN 0-85520-382-x (cased) : £12.50
ISBN 0-85520-385-4 (pbk) : £4.95 B81-35298

344.205'2534 — England. Prostitution. Law: Contagious Diseases Act 1866 & Contagious Diseases Act 1869. Repeal. Campaigns, *1870-1886.* **Social aspects**
Walkowitz, Judith R.. Prostitution and Victorian society : women, class and the state / Judith R. Walkowitz. — Cambridge : Cambridge University Press, 1980. — ix,347p ; 24cm
Bibliography: p323-335. — Includes index
ISBN 0-521-22334-2 : £15.00 B81-08254

344.205'2536 — London. Boys. Indecent assault. Trial of men — *Personal observations*
Moody, Roger. Indecent assault / by Roger Moody. — London (c/o Caledonian Rd., N.1) : Word is Out, 1980. — 64p : ill,facsims ; 22cm
£0.80 (pbk) B81-16222

344.205'262 — England. Theft. Law
Newman, Catherine. Bar finals guide / Catherine Newman. — London : Sweet & Maxwell, 1980. — xlvi,258p ; 20cm
Includes index
ISBN 0-421-27010-1 (pbk) : £7.50 : CIP rev.
Primary classification 344.206 B80-11359

344.205'274 — England. Obscenity. Law
Obscenity and film censorship. — Abridged ed. — Cambridge : Cambridge University Press, Oct.1981. — [176]p
Previous ed.: published as Report of the Committee on Obscenity and Film Censorship. London : H.M.S.O., 1979
ISBN 0-521-24267-3 (cased) : £12.50 : CIP entry
ISBN 0-521-28565-8 (pbk) : £4.95 B81-31240

344.205′274 — London. Obscene libel. Publication. Trial of Besant, Annie & Bradlaugh, Charles

Chandrasekhar, S. (Sripati). A dirty filthy book : the writings of Charles Knowlton and Annie Besant on reproductive physiology and birth control and an account of the Bradlaugh-Besant trial / by S. Chandrasekhar. — Berkeley ; London : University of California Press, c1981. — xi,217p,[3]p of plates : ill,facsims,ports ; 22cm
Bibliography: p79-83. — Includes index. — Includes: Fruits of philosophy / by Charles Knowlton. Originally published: London : Freethought Publishing, 1877 — The law of population / by Annie Besant. Originally published: London : Freethought Publishing, 1877 — Theosophy and the law of population / by Annie Besant. Originally published : London : Theosophical Publishing, 1904
ISBN 0-520-04168-2 : £10.25 B81-39755

344.205′288 — England. Blasphemy. Law

Blom-Cooper, Louis. Blasphemy : an ancient wrong or a modern right? / by Louis Blom-Cooper. — [London] ([1 Essex St., Strand, WC2R 3HY]) : [Essex Hall Bookshop], [1981]. — [15]p ; 21cm. — (The 1981 Essex Hall lecture)
Cover title
Unpriced (pbk) B81-23048

344.205′288 — England. Blasphemy. Law — *Buddhist viewpoints*

Sangharakshita, *Bikshu, Sthavira*. Buddhism and blasphemy : Buddhist reflections on the 1977 blasphemy trial / Sangharakshita (D.P.E. Lingwood). — London (51 Roman Rd. E2 3HU) : Windhorse, 1978 (1979 [printing]). — 24p ; 23cm
Unpriced (pbk) B81-37370

344.205′288 — England. Offences against religion. Law. Reform — *Proposals*

Great Britain. *Law Commission*. Offences against religion and public worship / the Law Commission. — London : H.M.S.O., 1981. — vi,166p ; 21cm. — (Working paper / Great Britain. Law Commission ; no.79)
ISBN 0-11-730159-0 (pbk) : £5.70 B81-27547

344.205′4 — England. Crimes. Responsibility. Theories, *1840-1870*

Smith, Roger, *1945-*. Trial by medicine : insanity and responsibility in Victorian trials / Roger Smith. — Edinburgh : Edinburgh University Press, c1981. — ix,238p ; 23cm
Bibliography: p230-231. - Includes index
ISBN 0-85224-407-x : £15.00 B81-23088

344.205′5 — England. Criminal law. Procedure

Chiswell, P. G.. Criminal law and practice up-to-date / P.G. Chiswell. — [Guildford] ([Braboeuf Manor, Portsmouth Rd., St. Catherine's, Guildford, Surrey]) : [College of Law], [1981]. — 19p ; 22cm. — (Crash course lecture / the College of Law, ISSN 0309-2771 ; 1981)
Cover title
£1.40 (pbk) B81-39988

344.205′5042 — England. Offenders. Prosecution. Procedure

Baldwin, John. Courts, prosecution and conviction. — Oxford : Clarendon, July 1981. — [240]p
ISBN 0-19-825355-9 : £12.00 : CIP entry B81-13871

344.205′5042 — England. Offenders. Prosecution. Procedure — *Manuals*

Bates, J. V.. The prosecutor's handbook / by J.V. Bates. — London : Oyez, c1980. — xxvi,121p ; 22cm
Includes index
ISBN 0-85120-510-0 (pbk) : £8.95 B81-13611

344.205′52 — England. Police. Powers. Legal aspects

Blake, Nick. The police, the law and the people / Nick Blake. — London (14 Parkfield Rd., N.W.10) : Haldane Society of Socialist Lawyers, [1981]. — 47p ; 21cm
£0.75 (pbk) B81-18813

344.205′6 — England. Criminal courts. Evidence. Law

Carter, P. B.. Cases and statutes on evidence. — London : Sweet & Maxwell, Oct.1981. — [852]p
ISBN 0-421-20320-x (cased) : £35.00 : CIP entry
ISBN 0-421-20330-7 (pbk) : £23.50 B81-28821

344.205′6 — England. Criminal courts. Evidence. Law — *Early works — Facsimiles*

Bentham, Jeremy. Rationale of judicial evidence / Jeremy Bentham. — New York ; London : Garland. — 1978. — (Classics of English legal history in the modern era)
Facsim. of: edition published London : Hunt and Clarke, 1827
Vol.2. — xii,700p ; 19cm
ISBN 0-8240-3085-0 : Unpriced B81-26935

Bentham, Jeremy. Rationale of judicial evidence / Jeremy Bentham. — New York ; London : Garland. — (Classics of English legal history in the modern era)
Facsim. of: edition published London : Hunt and Clarke, 1827
Vol.3. — 1978. — xii,658p ; 19cm
ISBN 0-8240-3085-0 : Unpriced B81-26936

Bentham, Jeremy. Rationale of judicial evidence / Jeremy Bentham. — New York ; London : Garland. — (Classics of English legal history in the modern era)
Facsim. of: edition published London : Hunt and Clarke, 1827
Vol.4. — 1978. — xii,645p ; 19cm
ISBN 0-8240-3085-0 : Unpriced B81-26937

Bentham, Jeremy. Rationale of judicial evidence / Jeremy Bentham. — New York ; London : Garland. — (Classics of English legal history in the modern era)
Facsim. of : edition published London : Hunt and Clarke, 1827
Vol.5. — 1978. — xii,787p ; 19cm
Includes index
ISBN 0-8240-3085-0 : Unpriced B81-26938

344.205′72 — England. Criminal law. Justice. Administration. Plea bargaining

Plea-bargaining / edited by William F. McDonald, James A. Cramer. — Lexington : Lexington Books ; [Farnborough, Hants.] : Gower [distributor], 1980. — xi,204p : ill ; 24cm
Includes bibliographies and index
ISBN 0-669-02363-9 : £13.00
Also classified at 347.305′72 B81-19877

344.205′72 — England. Criminal law. Summonses & charges — *Forms & precedents — For police*

Coase, Brian G.. Precedents for police use / by Brian G. Coase. — Chichester : Rose, c1980. — xxxvi,87p : forms ; 26cm
Includes index
ISBN 0-85992-153-0 : £12.00 B81-06012

344.205′772 — England. Criminal courts. Sentencing

Cross, *Sir* Rupert. The English sentencing system. — 3rd ed. / by Sir Rupert Cross and Andrew Ashworth. — London : Butterworths, 1981. — xvii,244p ; 23cm
Previous ed.: 1975. — Bibliography: p235-236. - Includes index
ISBN 0-406-57014-0 (cased) : Unpriced
ISBN 0-406-57015-9 (pbk) : Unpriced B81-29831

344.205′772 — England. Criminal courts. Sentencing. Role of mitigation pleas

Shapland, Joanna. Between conviction and sentence : the process of mitigation / Joanna Shapland. — London : Routledge & Kegan Paul, 1981. — vii,167p ; 23cm
Bibliography: p165-166. — Includes index
ISBN 0-7100-0945-3 : £10.50 B81-40825

344.205′8 — England. Juvenile courts. Procedure

Chatterton, Clifford E. M.. What when and how in the juvenile court : the orders of the court / by Clifford E.M. Chatterton. — Chichester : Rose, 1981. — iv,129p ; 29cm
ISBN 0-85992-203-0 (spiral) : £5.95 B81-15473

344.205′8 — England. Young offenders. Justice. Administration

Parker, Howard. Receiving juvenile justice : adolescents and state care and control / Howard Parker, Maggie Casburn, David Turnbull. — Oxford : Basil Blackwell, 1981. — 259p : 1ill ; 23cm
Bibliography: p253-256. — Includes index
ISBN 0-631-12727-5 (cased) : £12.00 : CIP rev.
ISBN 0-631-12745-3 (pbk) : £5.50 B81-09498

344.205′8 — England. Young offenders. Treatment. Law: Children and Young Persons Act 1969. Operation, *1970-1980*

Giller, Henri. Care and discretion : social workers' decisions with delinquents / Henri Giller, Allison Morris. — London : Burnett in association with Deutsch, 1981. — 127p ; 21cm
Bibliography: p120-123. — Includes index
ISBN 0-233-97294-3 (cased) : £5.95 : CIP rev.
ISBN 0-233-97373-7 (pbk) : £3.50 B81-07938

344.205′8 — England. Young offenders. Treatment. Law: Children and Young Persons Act 1969. Operation — *Case studies*

Thorpe, D. H.. Punishment and welfare : case studies of the workings of the 1969 Children and Young Persons Act / by David Thorpe, Christopher Green and David Smith. — [Lancaster] : Centre of Youth, Crime and Community. Centre of Social Administration. University of Lancaster, 1980. — 35p : ill ; 30cm
Cover title
£1.00 (pbk) B81-25946

344.205′81 — England. Juvenile courts. Chairmen. Interpersonal relationships with defendants. Communication — *Manuals*

Gray, Barbara, *19---*. Communication and chairmanship in the Juvenile Court / by Barbara Gray. — Chichester : Rose, c1980. — vi,47p ; 21
Bibliography: p45-47
ISBN 0-85992-183-2 (pbk) : £3.00 B81-10345

344.205′87 — Lancashire. Young offenders. Sentencing

Merriman, Phillipa. Sending young adults down / by Phillipa Merriman ; edited and with an introduction by David Smith. — [Lancaster] : Centre of Youth, Crime and Community, Department of Social Administration, University of Lancaster, [1981?]. — 23,iiip ; 30cm. — (CYCC occasional paper ; no.3)
Cover title
£1.00 (pbk) B81-29796

344.206 — England. Private law

Newman, Catherine. Bar finals guide / Catherine Newman. — London : Sweet & Maxwell, 1980. — xlvi,258p ; 20cm
Includes index
ISBN 0-421-27010-1 (pbk) : £7.50 : CIP rev.
Also classified at 344.205′262 B80-11359

344.206′04 — England. Law. Equity

Curzon, L. B.. Equity / L.B. Curzon. — 3rd ed. — Plymouth : Macdonald and Evans, 1979. — xxv,274p ; 18cm. — (The M. & E. handbooks series)
Previous ed.: 1974. — Includes index
ISBN 0-7121-0567-0 (pbk) : £3.50 B81-34974

Hanbury, Harold Greville. Modern equity. — 11th ed. — London : Stevens, Oct.1981. — [700]p
Previous ed.: 1976
ISBN 0-420-46130-2 (cased) : £27.50 : CIP entry
ISBN 0-420-46140-x (pbk) : £20.00 B81-25315

344.2061′35 — England. Children. Responsibility. Law — *For recreation services*

Madge, Nic. Out of school legal responsibility for children / Nic Madge and Jan Loxley. — London (7 Exton St., SE1 8UE) : Out of School Project, British Association of Settlements and Social Action Centres, 1981. — 10p : ill ; 30cm
ISBN 0-9503452-3-7 (pbk) : £1.00 B81-32712

344.2061'35 — England. Children, *to 1980*. Legal aspects

Childhood, welfare and justice : a critical examination of children in the legal and childcare systems / edited by Michael King ; with contributions from Michael King ... [et al.]. — London : Batsford Academic and Educational, 1981. — 145p ; 22cm
Bibliography: p137-142. — Includes index
ISBN 0-7134-3713-8 (pbk) : £5.95 B81-19643

344.2061'38 — England. Mentally disordered persons. Law — *For mentally disordered persons*

Gostin, Larry O.. Patients' rights handbook / Larry Gostin. — [London] : MIND, 1981. — 53p ; 21cm
Bibliography: p45-46
ISBN 0-900557-43-5 (pbk) : £1.95 B81-29215

344.2061'5 — England. Families. Law

Pace, P. J.. Family law / P.J. Pace. — Plymouth : Macdonald and Evans, 1981. — xxiv,283p ; 18cm. — (The M & E handbook series)
Includes index
ISBN 0-7121-0632-4 (pbk) : £4.95 B81-23996

Pearl, David. Social welfare law / David Pearl and Kevin Gray. — London : Croom Helm, c1981. — 308p ; 23cm
Bibliography: p265. — Includes index
ISBN 0-85664-644-x (cased) : £14.95
ISBN 0-7099-2004-0 (pbk) : £8.95
Primary classification 344.104'1 B81-29850

Richman, John. Practical family law / John Richman and F.S.T. Dealy. — Chichester : Rose, c1980. — 57p ; 21cm
ISBN 0-85992-208-1 (pbk) : £3.50 B81-10351

Walker, D.. Family law / by D. Walker. — Walton-on-Thames : Celtic Revision Aids, 1981. — 128p ; 19cm. — (Celtic revision notes. Law)
ISBN 0-17-751354-3 (pbk) : £1.85 B81-21249

344.206'15'02632 — England. Families. Law - *Statutes - Collections*

. Sweet & Maxwell's family law statutes. — 3rd ed. — London : Sweet & Maxwell, Aug.1981. — [535]p
Previous ed.: 1976
ISBN 0-421-28080-8 (pbk) : CIP entry
ISBN 0-421-28090-5 (pbk) B81-16405

344.2061'5'0264 — England. Families. Law — *Cases — Serials*

Family law reports. — Vol.1, no.1 (1980)-. — [Bristol] : [Rose/Jordan Ltd.], 1980-. — v. ; 24cm
Irregular. — Description based on: Vol.1, no.4 (1980)
ISSN 0261-4375 = Family law reports : Unpriced B81-36543

344.2061'5'0269 — England. Families. Law. Cases. Procedure of magistrates' courts

Domestic proceedings in the Magistrates' Court. — [Guildford] : The College of Law, c1979. — 91p : forms ; 22cm. — (College of Law lectures, ISSN 0309-3166)
£4.00 (pbk) B81-28271

Harris, Brian, *1932-*. A guide to the new law of family proceedings in magistrates courts including adoption / Brian Harris. — 2nd ed. — Chichester : Rose, 1981. — v,52p ; 21cm
Previous ed.: 1979. — Bibliography: p50. — Includes index
ISBN 0-85992-206-5 (pbk) : £3.50 B81-18908

344.206'15'0269 — England. Families. Law. Cases. Procedure of magistrates' courts. Law: Domestic Proceedings and Magistrates' Courts Act 1978 — *Critical studies*

Freeman, M. D. A.. The matrimonial jurisdiction of magistrates' courts / by M.D.A. Freeman and Christina M. Lyon. — Chichester : Rose, c1980. — xxv,222p ; 21cm
Includes index
ISBN 0-85992-199-9 (pbk) : £10.80 B81-10816

344.2061'5'0269 — Great Britain. *High Court of Justice. Family Division — Cases — Serials*

The **Law** reports. Family Division and on appeal therefrom in the Court of Appeal and decisions in the Ecclesiastical Courts. — 1980. — London : The Incorporated Council of Law Reporting for England and Wales, c1980. — xii,108p
Unpriced B81-28384

344.2061'6 — England. Cohabiting persons. Law

Parker, Stephen, *19---*. Cohabitees / Stephen Parker. — Chichester : Rose, 1981. — xxii,230p ; 21cm
Bibliography: p224-225. — Includes index
ISBN 0-85992-210-3 (cased) : £15.70
ISBN 0-85992-226-x (pbk) : £10.50 B81-34675

Parry, Martin L.. Cohabitation / by Martin L. Parry ; with a foreword by H.K. Bevan. — London : Sweet and Maxwell, 1981. — xxv,162p ; 22cm. — (Social work and law)
Includes bibliographies and index
ISBN 0-421-26730-5 (pbk) : £5.75 : CIP rev. B81-05164

344.2061'6'0269 — England. Marriage. Law. Procedure

Berkin, Martyn. Matrimonial suits and property proceedings : a practitioner's index of practice and procedure / by Martyn Berkin and Maurice Young. — Chichester : Rose
First supplement. — 1981. — 66p ; 21cm
ISBN 0-85992-222-7 (pbk) : £7.50 B81-26564

344.2061'66 — England. Divorce. Financial settlements & maintenance orders. Law

Griffiths, L. R. H.. Financial and property orders on divorce / L.R.H. Griffiths. — [Guildford] ([Braboeuf Manor, Portsmouth Rd., St. Catherine's, Guildford, Surrey]) : [College of Law], [1981]. — 21p ; 22cm. — (Crash course lecture / the College of Law, ISSN 0309-2771 ; 1981)
Cover title
£1.40 (pbk) B81-39983

344.2061'66 — England. Divorce. Financial settlements & maintenance orders. Law — *For prospective divorced persons*

Harper, W. M.. Divorce and your money / W.M. Harpe. — 2nd ed. — London : Unwin Paperbacks, 1981. — vii,196p ; 18cm
Previous ed.: London : Allen and Unwin, 1979. — Includes index
ISBN 0-04-347004-1 (pbk) : £1.95 : CIP rev.
Also classified at 344.2064 B81-04198

344.2061'66 — England. Divorce. Financial settlements & maintenance orders. Law. Reform. Great Britain. *Law Commission*. Financial consequences of divorce — *National Council for One Parent Families viewpoints*

Maintenance : putting children first : a response to the Law Commission's discussion paper on the financial consequences of divorce / [One Parent Families]. — London (255 Kennish Town Rd., NW5 2LX) : One Parent Families, 1981. — 8p ; 30cm
Cover title
£0.50 (pbk) B81-32714

344.2061'66 — England. Divorce. Law

On getting divorced / [edited by Edith Rudinger]. — Rev. repr. — London : Consumers' Association, 1979. — 155p ; 21cm
Previous ed.: 1978. — Includes index
ISBN 0-85202-151-8 (pbk) : Unpriced B81-39853

344.2061'66 — England. Divorce. Law. Reform. Proposals. Archbishop of Canterbury's Group on the Divorce Law. Putting asunder — *Critical studies*

Bullimore, John W.. Pushing asunder / by John W. Bullimore. — Bramcote : Grove, 1981. — 24p ; 22cm. — (Grove booklet on ethics, ISSN 0305-4241 ; no.41)
ISBN 0-907536-01-8 (pbk) : £0.60 B81-33035

344.2061'66 — England. Matrimonial causes. Financial settlements. Law

Jackson, Joseph. Jackson's matrimonial finance and taxation. — 3rd ed. / by Joseph Jackson and D.T.A. Davies. — London : Butterworth, 1980. — lxi,502p ; 26cm
Previous ed.: 1975
ISBN 0-406-25444-3 : £32.50 B81-00790

344.2061'66'0269 — England. Matrimonial causes. Law. Cases. Costs

Matrimonial finance and costs. — [Guildford] (Braboeuf Manor, St. Catherine's, Guildford GU3 1HA) : The College of Law, c1981. — 86p ; 22cm. — (College of Law lectures, ISSN 0309-3166)
£4.00 (pbk)
Primary classification 344.2064 B81-16969

344.2061'66'0269 — England. Matrimonial causes. Procedure of magistrates' courts

Brown, George G.. Brown on separation / by George G. Brown. — London : Shaw & Sons, 1981. — 301p in various pagings : forms ; 22cm
Includes index
ISBN 0-7219-0840-3 (pbk) : Unpriced B81-14095

Pugh, Leslie M.. Pugh's matrimonial proceedings before magistrates. — 4th ed. / J. Basil Horsman. — London : Butterworths, 1981. — xli,820p : forms ; 26cm
Previous ed.: 1974. — Includes index
ISBN 0-406-34602-x : Unpriced B81-37651

Strachan, W. A. W.. Matrimonial proceedings in magistrates' courts. — London : Sweet and Maxwell, Dec.1981. — [120]p
ISBN 0-421-28970-8 (pbk) : CIP entry B81-31539

344.2061'7 — England. Divorced fathers. Children. Custody

Maidment, Susan. Child custody : what chance for fathers? / by Susan Maidment. — London (255 Kentish Town Rd., NW5 2LX) : National Council for One Parent Families, 1981. — 23p ; 21cm. — (Forward from Finer ; no.7)
Text on inside cover
£0.80 (pbk) B81-33332

344.2061'78 — England. Children. Adoption. Law

Josling, J. F.. Adoption of children / J.F. Josling. — 9th ed. — London : Oyez, 1980, c1981. — xvi,256p : forms ; 22cm. — (Oyez practice notes ; 3)
Previous ed.: 1977. — Includes index
ISBN 0-85120-541-0 (pbk) : £9.95 B81-14112

344.2062 — England. Contracts. Law

Atiyah, P. S.. An introduction to the law of contract / by P.S. Atiyah. — 3rd ed. — Oxford : Clarendon, 1981. — x,335p ; 23cm. — (Clarendon law series)
Previous ed.: 1971. — Includes index
ISBN 0-19-876140-6 (cased) : Unpriced : CIP rev.
ISBN 0-19-876141-4 (pbk) : £5.95 B81-13857

344.206'2 — England. Contracts. Law

Davies, F. R.. Contract. — 4th ed. — London : Sweet & Maxwell, June 1981. — [206]p. — (Concise college texts)
Previous ed.: 1977
ISBN 0-421-27550-2 (cased) : CIP entry
ISBN 0-421-27560-x (pbk) B81-09964

344.2062 — England. Contracts. Law

Treitel, G. H.. Doctrine and discretion in the law of contract : an inaugural lecture delivered before the University of Oxford on 7 March 1980 / by G.H. Treitel. — Oxford : Clarenden, 1981. — 31p ; 22cm
ISBN 0-19-951527-1 (pbk) : £1.95 : CIP rev. B81-05123

344.206'2 — England. Contracts. Law — *Early works — Facsimiles*

Chitty, Joseph. A practical treatise on the law of contracts / Joseph Chitty, Jr. — New York ; London : Garland, 1978. — li,792p ; 23cm. — (Classics of English legal history in the modern era)
Facsim. of: 2nd ed. London : Sweet, 1834. — Includes index
ISBN 0-8240-3074-5 : Unpriced B81-26931

344.206′2 — England. Contracts. Law — *Early works — Facsimiles continuation*
Powell, John Joseph. Essay upon the law of contracts and agreements / John Joseph Powell. — New York ; London : Garland, 1978. — 2v(xv,452; 297,[131]p) ; 19cm. — (Classics of English legal history in the modern era)
Facsim. of: edition published London, 1790. — Includes index
ISBN 0-8240-3073-7 : Unpriced B81-27279

344.206′2 — England. Contracts. Law — *For business firms*
Tillotson, John. Contract law in perspective / by John Tillotson. — London : Butterworths, 1981. — xvii,179p : forms ; 23cm
Includes bibliographies and index
ISBN 0-406-66620-2 : Unpriced B81-33236

344.206′29 — England. Agency. Law
Kobrin, D. L.. Agency / David Kobrin. — London : Anderson Keenan, 1981. — viii,68p ; 24cm. — (Law unit)
Includes index
ISBN 0-906501-23-7 (pbk) : £1.95 B81-33438

344.206′29 — England. Powers of attorney. Law
Caplin, Charles. Powers of attorney / Charles Caplin assisted by Arnold Wexler. — 5th ed. / by Trevor M. Aldridge. — London : Oyez, 1981. — ix,132p : forms ; 22cm. — (Oyez practice notes ; OPN7)
Previous ed.: 1971. — Includes index
ISBN 0-85120-579-8 (pbk) : Unpriced B81-38392

344.2063 — England. Torts. Law
Baker, C. D. (Charles David). Tort / by C.D. Baker. — 3rd ed. — London : Sweet & Maxwell, 1981. — xxviii,347p ; 22cm. — (Concise college texts)
Previous ed.: 1976. — Includes index
ISBN 0-421-27030-6 (cased) : £11.00 : CIP rev.
ISBN 0-421-27040-3 (pbk) : £6.85 B81-14853

Butler, Michael, *1953-*. Torts / Michael Butler and Neil Lucas. — London : Anderson Keenan, 1981. — ix,109p ; 24cm. — (Law unit)
Includes index
ISBN 0-906501-24-5 (pbk) : £2.45 B81-33439

Clerk, John Frederic. Clerk & Lindsell on torts. — 15th ed. — London : Sweet and Maxwell, Feb.1982. — [2000]p. — (The Common law library ; no.3)
Previous ed.: 1975
ISBN 0-421-26250-8 : CIP entry B81-39252

Walker, D. (Dennis), *1933-*. Law of tort / by D. Walker. — Walton-on-Thames : Celtic Revision Aids, 1981. — 150p ; 19cm. — (Celtic revision notes. Law)
ISBN 0-17-751355-1 (pbk) : £1.85 B81-16502

344.2063′0264 — England. Torts. Law — *Cases*
Tort : cases and materials / [compiled by] B.A. Hepple, M.H. Matthews. — 2nd ed. — London : Butterworths, 1980. — xlii,757p ; 26cm
Previous ed.: 1974. — Includes index
ISBN 0-406-59482-1 (cased) : £19.50
ISBN 0-406-59483-x (pbk) : £12.95 B81-07139

344.2063′2 — England. Hospitals. Negligence. Law — *Cases*
Farndale, W. A. J.. Medical negligence / by W.A.J. Farndale. — Rev.. — Beckenham : Ravenswood, 1976. — 36p ; 19cm. — (Case studies on hospital management law and practice ; v.1)
Originally published: Beckenham : White′s, 1969
ISBN 0-901812-02-1 (pbk) : £2.50 B81-33118

344.2063′2 — England. Hospitals. Negligence. Liability. Law — *Cases*
Farndale, W. A. J.. Legal liability for claims arising from hospital treatment / by W.A.J. Farndale and E.C. Larman. — Rev. 2nd ed. — Beckenham : Ravenswood, 1976. — 54p ; 22cm. — (Case studies on hospital management law and practice ; v.4)
Previous ed.: 1973. — Includes index
ISBN 0-901812-13-7 (cased) : £6.50
ISBN 0-901812-14-5 (pbk) : £4.50 B81-33117

344.2063′2′0264 — England. Negligence. Law — *Cases*
Leading cases in the law of negligence for ′A′ level. — London : Butterworths, 1980. — 149p ; 25cm
ISBN 0-406-01680-1 (pbk) : £2.95 B81-05744

344.2063′2′0264 — England. Negligence. Law — *Cases — For schools*
Weir, Tony. Negligence for ′A′ level / Tony Weir. — London : Sweet & Maxwell, 1981. — 207p ; 24cm
ISBN 0-421-28980-5 (pbk) : £3.75 : CIP rev. B81-14973

344.2063′2′088344 — England. Solicitors. Negligence. Liability. Law
Woodhams, Brian. The professional negligence of solicitors (and how to avoid it) : a short guide for solicitors / by Barry Woodhams. — Chichester : Rose, 1981. — viii,56,64p ; 22cm
ISBN 0-85992-214-6 (pbk) : £4.25 B81-21873

344.2063′23′0269 — England. Accidents. Personal injuries. Damages. Claims. Law. Procedure
Pritchard, John M.. Personal injury litigation / John M. Pritchard. — 3rd ed. — London : Oyez, 1981. — xxi,274p : ill,forms ; 22cm. — (Oyez practitioner series)
Previous ed.: 1978. — Includes index
ISBN 0-85120-523-2 (pbk) : £11.00 B81-20008

344.2063′6 — England. Squatting. Law
Prichard, A. M.. Squatting / by A.M. Prichard. — London : Sweet & Maxwell, 1981. — xvi,177p ; 19cm. — (Modern legal studies)
Includes index
ISBN 0-421-26740-2 (cased) : £9.50
ISBN 0-421-26750-x (pbk) : £5.75 B81-26055

344.2064 — England. Matrimonial property. Apportionment on divorce. Law
Matrimonial finance and costs. — [Guildford] (Braboeuf Manor, St. Catherine′s, Guildford GU3 1HA) : The College of Law, c1981. — 86p ; 22cm. — (College of Law lectures, ISSN 0309-3166)
£4.00 (pbk)
Also classified at 344.2061′66′0269 B81-16969

344.2064 — England. Matrimonial property. Apportionment on divorce. Law — *For prospective divorced persons*
Harper, W. M.. Divorce and your money / W.M. Harpe. — 2nd ed. — London : Unwin Paperbacks, 1981. — vii,196p ; 18cm
Previous ed.: London : Allen and Unwin, 1979. — Includes index
ISBN 0-04-347004-1 (pbk) : £1.95 : CIP rev.
Primary classification 344.2061′66 B81-04198

344.2064 — England. Matrimonial property. Law
Duckworth, Peter. Matrimonial property and finance / Peter Duckworth. — London : Oyez, c1980. — xxvi,238p ; 23cm
Includes index
ISBN 0-85120-545-3 : £14.50 B81-13612

344.2064′2′0264 — England. Matrimonial property. Interests. Law. Cases: Williams & Glyn′s Bank Ltd v. Boland — *Conference proceedings*
Williams & Glyn′s Bank Ltd v. Boland : Report of a conference on problems of conflict of interest in the matrimonial home. — Farnborough, Hants. : Gower, c1981. — 64p ; 22cm
ISBN 0-566-03020-9 (pbk) : £10.00 B81-11608

344.2064′3 — England. Real property. Law
Gray, Kevin J.. Real property and real people : principles of land law / K.J. Gray, P.D. Symes. — London : Butterworths, 1981. — xxxi,655p : ill ; 26cm
Includes index
ISBN 0-406-59110-5 (cased) : Unpriced
ISBN 0-406-59111-3 (pbk) : Unpriced B81-37770

Green, E. Swinfen. Land law / by E. Swinfen Green. — 4th ed. / by N. Henderson. — London : Sweet & Maxwell, 1980. — xiv,188p ; 22cm. — (Concise college texts)
Previous ed.: 1975. — Includes index
ISBN 0-421-25460-2 (cased) : £9.00 : CIP rev.
ISBN 0-421-25470-x (pbk) : £7.25 B80-18635

344.2064′3′0264 — England. Real property. Law — *Cases*
Maudsley, R. H.. Land law : cases and materials / by R.H. Maudsley and E.H. Burn. — 4th ed. — London : Butterworths, 1980. — lxxx,881p : 3facsims,1form ; 26cm
Previous ed.: 1975
ISBN 0-406-62306-6 (cased) : £24.00
ISBN 0-406-62307-4 (pbk) : £15.95 B81-01644

344.2064′3′02648 — England. Real property. Law — *Cases — Serials*
The Estates Gazette digest of land and property cases. — 1979. — London : Estates Gazette, [1980?]. — xv,1063p
Unpriced B81-14529

344.2064′32 — England. Shooting rights. Tenancies. Law
Wilbraham, *Sir* **Randle Baker**. The letting and taking of shooting rights in England and Wales / by Sir Randle Baker Wilbraham. — Rev. ed. / revised by D.J. Yorke. — [London] : Royal Institution of Chartered Surveyors, 1980. — 7p ; 21cm. — (Practice leaflet / Royal Institution of Chartered Surveyors Land Agency and Agriculture Division ; no.4)
Previous ed.: 1974
Unpriced (unbound) B81-11557

344.206′434 — England. Local authorities. Complaints by tenants of sub-standard rented residences. Procedure — *Manuals*
Unfitness. — London (157 Waterloo Rd., SE1 8UU) : Shelter National Housing Aid Trust, 1981. — 32p ; 21cm. — (Practice notes / Shelter National Housing Aid Trust ; 2)
ISBN 0-86265-003-8 (pbk) : Unpriced B81-30908

344.2064′34 — England. Residences. Short-term tenancies. Law
Fitzmaurice, Jon. The Housing Act 1980 : its implications for the short-term use of vacant property / [written by Jon Fitzmaurice]. — London (157 Waterloo Rd., SE1 8UU) : HEO, c1981. — 50p : ill ; 21cm
Cover title
Unpriced (pbk) B81-24086

344.2064′34 — England. Tenancies. Law
Aldridge, Trevor M.. Rent control and leasehold enfranchisement / Trevor M. Aldridge. — 8th ed. — London : Oyez, 1980. — 205p ; 22cm
Previous ed.: 1977. — Includes index
ISBN 0-85120-546-1 (pbk) : £9.50 B81-13615

Donell, R. A.. Landlord and tenant up-to-date / R.A. Donell. — [Guildford] ([Braboeuf Manor, Portsmouth Rd., St. Catherine′s, Guildford, Surrey]) : [College of Law], [1981]. — 16p ; 22cm. — (Crash course lecture / the College of Law, ISSN 0309-2771 ; 1981)
Cover title
£1.40 (pbk) B81-39990

344.2064′344 — England. Rented residences. Tenancies. Law
Pearl, David. Social welfare law / David Pearl and Kevin Gray. — London : Croom Helm, c1981. — 308p ; 23cm
Bibliography: p265. — Includes index
ISBN 0-85664-644-x (cased) : £14.95
ISBN 0-7099-2004-0 (pbk) : £8.95
Primary classification 344.104′1 B81-29850

344.2064′344 — England. Rented residences. Tenancies. Law: Rent Act 1977 — *Critical studies*
Pettit, Philip H.. Private sector tenancies / Philip H. Pettit. — 2nd ed. — London : Butterworths, 1981. — li,327p ; 26cm
Previous ed.: published as Landlord and tenant under the Rent Act 1979. 1978. — Includes index
ISBN 0-406-33722-5 : Unpriced B81-19461

344.2064′344 — England. Rented residences. Tenancies. Law. Social aspects
Partington, Martin. Landlord and tenant : text and materials on housing and law / Martin Partington. — 2nd ed. — London : Weidenfeld and Nicolson, c1980. — xxxviii,554p : ill ; 23cm. — (Law in context)
Previous ed.: 1975. — Bibliography: p533-544. - Includes index
ISBN 0-297-77790-4 (cased) : £20.00
ISBN 0-297-77791-2 (pbk) : £10.50 B81-01870

344.2064′344 — England. Residences. Variable rents. Law

Clarke, D. N.. Rent reviews and variable rents / D.N. Clarke, J.E. Adams. — London : Oyez, c1981. — xxxiii,292p ; 24cm
Bibliography: pxi-xii. - Includes index
ISBN 0-85120-491-0 : Unpriced B81-22798

344.2064′346 — West Midlands *(Metropolitan County)*. Birmingham. Saltley. Leasehold houses. Leases. Enfranchisement. Rights of leaseholders. Enforcement

Stewart, Ann. Housing action in an industrial suburb / Ann Stewart. — London : Academic Press, 1981. — 226p : ill ; 24cm. — (Law, state and society series ; 6)
Bibliography: p217-222. — Includes index
ISBN 0-12-669250-5 : £12.50 B81-21152

344.2064′3462 — England. Business premises. Leases. Drafting — *Manuals*

Ross, Murray J.. Drafting and negotiating commercial leases / by Murray J. Ross ; foreword by John Stuart Colyer. — London : Butterworths, 1980. — xxxv,316p ; 23cm
Includes index
ISBN 0-406-35905-9 . £12.95 B81 05863

344.2064′3462 — England. Business premises. Leasing. Law — *For businessmen*

Aldridge, Trevor M.. Letting business premises / Trevor M. Aldridge. — 4th ed. — London : Oyez, 1981. — xxxi,178p ; 22cm
Previous ed.: 1978. — Includes index
ISBN 0-85120-561-5 (pbk) : Unpriced
B81-28231

344.2064′364 — England. Mortgages. Law

Fairest, Paul B.. Mortgages / by Paul B. Fairest. — 2nd ed. — London : Sweet & Maxwell, 1980. — xviii,157p ; 20cm. — (Modern legal studies)
Previous ed.: 1975
ISBN 0-421-24840-8 (cased) : £11.25 : CIP rev.
ISBN 0-421-24850-5 (pbk) : £6.50 B80-08662

344.2064′38 — England. Freehold real property. Conveyancing. Costs — *Tables*

Wilson, Michael, *19---*. Conveyancing : fees and duties on sale of freehold / [by Michael Wilson]. — 2nd ed. — London : Fourmat, c1981. — 1folded sheet ; 30x32cm folded to 30x11cm. — (Lawyers costs & fees series ; 5)
Previous ed.: 1979
ISBN 0-906840-37-6 : £1.60 B81-19497

344.2064′38 — England. Houses. Conveyancing — *Amateurs′ manuals*

Bradshaw, Joseph. Bradshaw′s guide to D.I.Y. house buying, selling and conveyancing / by Joseph Bradshaw. — Leamington Spa (Freepost, Blackdown, Leamington Spa, CV32 6BR) : Castle Books, c1980. — xii,163p,[3] folded leaves of plates : ill,forms ; 22cm
Includes index
ISBN 0-9507170-0-2 (pbk) : £4.95
Primary classification 333.33′8 B81-04678

344.2064′38 — England. Leasehold real property. Conveyancing. Costs — *Tables*

Wilson, Michael, *19---*. Conveyancing : fees and duties on dealings with leaseholds / [by Michael Wilson]. — 3rd ed. — London : Fourmat, c1981. — 1folded sheet ; 30x32cm folded to 30x11cm. — (Lawyers costs & fees series ; 6)
Previous ed.: 1980
ISBN 0-906840-38-4 : £1.60 B81-19498

344.2064′38 — England. Real property. Conveyancing. Costs — *Tables — Serials*

Conveyancing fees and charges. — 6th ed. (1981). — London : Oyez Publishing, 1981. — 57p
ISBN 0-85120-577-1 : Unpriced
ISBN 0-85120-570-4 (pbk) B81-28708

344.2064′38 — England. Real property. Conveyancing. Law

Conveyancing — some recent developments. — Guildford (Braboeuf Manor, St. Catherine′s Guildford, Surrey GU3 1HA) : College of Law, [1981]. — vi,61p ; 22cm. — (College of Law lectures, ISSN 0309-3166)
£4.00 (pbk) B81-31484

Emmet, Lewis Emanuel. Emmet′s notes on perusing titles and on practical conveyancing. — 17th ed. / by J.T. Farrand and J. Gilchrist Smith. — London : Oyez
2nd cumulative supplement / J.T. Farrand, J. Gilchrist Smith. — c1981. — 40,cxxxvp ; 24cm
Includes index
ISBN 0-85120-602-6 (pbk) : Unpriced
B81-40139

Holbrooke, R. G.. Conveyancing 1981 / R.G. Holbrook. — [Guildford] ([Braboeuf Manor, Portsmouth Rd., St. Catherine′s, Guildford, Surrey]) : [College of Law], [1981]. — 13p ; 22cm. — (Crash course lecture / the College of Law, ISSN 0309-2771 ; 1981)
Cover title
£1.40 (pbk) B81-39989

Kenny, P. H.. Conveyancing law / P.H. Kenny, C.M. Bevan. — Plymouth : Macdonald and Evans, 1980. — xx,284p : forms ; 19cm. — (The M. & E. handbook series)
Bibliography: p268. — Includes index
ISBN 0-7121-0357-0 (pbk) : £3.50 B81-00791

Tannett, Angela. Conveyancing in a nutshell / Angela Tannett. — London : Sweet & Maxwell, 1980. — 84p : 1ill,2forms ; 18cm. — (New nutshells)
Includes index
ISBN 0-421-27810-2 (pbk) : £1.50 : CIP rev.
B80-25377

344.2064′38 — England. Real property. Title. Registration. Organisations: Land Registry — *Serials*

Land Registry. Report to the Lord Chancellor on H.M. Land Registry for the year ... — 1979-1980. — London : H.M.S.O., 1980. — 13p
ISBN 0-11-390242-5 : £1.75 B81-12438

344.2064′38 — England. Registered land. Conveyancing. Law

Hayton, David J.. Registered land / by David J. Hayton. — 3rd ed. — London : Sweet & Maxwell, 1981. — xxiii,222p : ill ; 20cm. — (Modern legal studies)
Previous ed.: 1977. — Includes index
ISBN 0-421-28160-x (cased) : £10.00
ISBN 0-421-28170-7 (pbk) : £6.50 B81-22976

344.206′44′02633 — England. Rented residences. Tenancies. Law — *Statutes — Collections — Texts with commentaries*

Rent Acts and regulations as amended and annotated. — London : Sweet & Maxwell, Sept.1981. — [445]p
ISBN 0-421-28220-7 : £15.00 : CIP entry
B81-23769

344.2064′5 — England. Environment planning. Law

Garner, J. F.. Practical planning law : a handbook for planners, architects and surveyors / J.F. Garner. — London : Croom Helm, c1981. — 246p ; 23cm
Bibliography: p241-243. — Includes index
ISBN 0-7099-1106-8 (cased) : £14.95 : CIP rev.
ISBN 0-7099-1107-6 (pbk) : Unpriced
B81-15904

Hamilton, R. N. D.. A guide to development and planning / by R.N.D. Hamilton. — 7th ed. — London : Oyez, 1981. — lxiv,510p ; 23cm
Previous ed.: 1975. — Includes index
ISBN 0-85120-549-6 : Unpriced B81-26045

344.206′45 — England. Town planning. Law. Appeals

Blundell, Lionel Alleyne. Blundell and Dobry′s planning appeals and inquiries. — 3rd ed. — London : Sweet and Maxwell, Jan.1982. — [150]p
Previous ed.: 1970
ISBN 0-421-25350-9 (pbk) : £10.00 : CIP entry
B81-34393

344.2064′5 — England. Town planning. Law — *Manuals*

Grant, Malcolm. Planning law handbook. — London : Sweet and Maxwell, Oct.1981. — [330]p
ISBN 0-421-28570-2 (pbk) : £12.00 : CIP entry B81-25857

344.2064′5′0269 — England. Environment planning. Procedure. Legal aspects

Hamilton, R. N. D.. Planning procedure tables / R.N.D. Hamilton. — 4th ed. — London : Oyez, 1981. — xvii,142p ; 24cm
Previous ed.: 1976
ISBN 0-85120-558-5 (pbk) : Unpriced
B81-26124

344.2064′675 — England. Forests. Law, *ca 1600 — Early works — Facsimiles*

Manwood, John. A treatise and discourse of the lawes of the forrest / John Manwood. — New York ; London : Garland, 1978. — 167leaves ; 19cm. — (Classics of English legal history in the modern era)
Facsim. of: edition published: London : Thomas Wight and Bonham Norton, 1598. — Includes index
ISBN 0-8240-3087-7 : Unpriced B81-14703

344.2064′676 — England. Agricultural land. Law

Gregory, Michael, *1925-*. Essential law for landowners and farmers / Michael Gregory and Margaret Parrish. — London : Granada, 1980. — xxii,265 , 23cm
Includes index
ISBN 0-246-11213-1 : £7.95 : CIP rev.
B80-18200

344.2065′2 — England. Probate. Law

Tristram, Thomas Hutchinson. Tristram and Coote′s probate practice. — 25th ed. / editors R.B. Rowe, Edmund Heward and G.F. Dawe ; consulting editor D.H. Colgate. — London : Butterworth
Previous ed.: 1973
3rd cumulative supplement / by R.B. Rowe, Edmund Heward and B. Kay. — 1981. — ix,52p ; 24cm
ISBN 0-406-40315-5 (pbk) : Unpriced
B81-26197

344.2065′2 — England. Probate — *Manuals*

Best, Keith. The right way to prove a will : how to sort out probate, property and assets / by Keith Best. — Kingswood : Elliot Right Way, c1981. — 127p ; 18cm. — (Paperfronts)
Includes index
ISBN 0-7160-0666-9 (pbk) : £0.75 B81-24314

344.2065′2 — England. Succession. Law

Williams, *Sir* Edward Vaughan. Williams and Mortimer on executors, administrators and probate. — London : Stevens, Dec.1981. — [1200]p. — (Property and conveyancing library ; no.10)
Being the 16th edition of Williams on executors and the 4th edition of Mortimer on probate
ISBN 0-420-45500-0 : £78.00 : CIP entry
B81-31707

344.2065′2′02461 — England. Succession. Law — *Case studies — For medical personnel*

Virdi, P. K.. Law on wills and succession / by P.K. Virdi. — Beckenham : Ravenswood, c1981. — 174p ; 22cm. — (Studies in law & practice for health service management ; no.11)
ISBN 0-901812-41-2 (cased) : Unpriced
ISBN 0-901812-42-0 (pbk) : Unpriced
B81-28313

344.2065′6 — England. Inherited property: Estates. Administration — *Manuals*

Taylor, J. N. R.. Executorship law and accounts / J.N.R. Taylor. — 4th ed. — Plymouth : Macdonald and Evans, 1979. — xv,176p ; 19cm. — (The M. & E. handbook series)
Previous ed.: 1977. — Includes index
ISBN 0-7121-0562-x (pbk) : £3.25 B81-30835

344.2065′6′024657 — England. Inherited property: Estates. Administration. Law — *For accountancy*

Sherring, Tony. Law and accounts for executors and trustees : including capital transfer tax / Tony Sherring and Michael Sladen. — London : Gee, 1981. — xvi,257p : forms ; 24cm
Bibliography: p248. — Includes index
ISBN 0-85258-195-5 : £12.50 B81-25195

344.2065′6′0264 — England. Inherited property: Estates. Administration. Law. Cases: Swinfen V. Swinfen
Clayton, Howard. The great Swinfen case / by Howard Clayton. — London : Regency Press, c1980. — 211p,[4]p of plates : ill,1map,1facsim,ports,geneal.table ; 23cm
Includes index
ISBN 0-7212-0630-1 : £4.80 B81-06769

344.2065′9 — England. Trusts. Law
Curzon, L. B.. Law of trusts / L.B. Curzon. — 2nd ed. — Plymouth : Macdonald and Evans, 1980. — xxxi,316p ; 19cm. — (The M & E handbook series)
Previous ed.: 1974. — Bibliography: p.277. - Includes index
ISBN 0-7121-1255-3 (pbk) : £4.50 B81-00048

344.206′62 — England. Law — *For businessmen*
Field, David, *1945-*. Inside business law : a guide for managers / David Field. — London : Pan, 1981. — 281p ; 18cm
Includes index
ISBN 0-330-26349-8 (pbk) : £1.95 B81-22899

344.206′63 — England. Law — *For accountancy*
Leal, A. R.. Essential law for accountancy students. — London : Edward Arnold, Jan.1982. — [208]p
ISBN 0-7131-0605-0 (pbk) : £6.95 : CIP entry
B81-33905

344.206′64 — England. Charities. Law
Picarda, Hubert. The law and practice relating to charities / Hubert Picarda ; with a foreword by Lord Wilberforce. — London : Butterworths, 1977. — xcii,765p ; 26cm
Bibliography: pxci-xcii. — Includes index
ISBN 0-406-64276-1 : Unpriced B81-26010

344.206′65 — England. Business firms. Law
Bradley, K. R.. The legal environment : business law / K.R. Bradley, R.A. Clark. — London : Holt, Rinehart and Winston, 1981. — ix,404p : ill ; 22cm
Includes index
ISBN 0-03-910308-0 (pbk) : £4.50 : CIP rev.
B81-00049

344.206′662 — England. Companies. Voluntary liquidation. Procedure
Loose, Peter. Loose on liquidators : the role of a liquidator in a voluntary winding-up. — 2nd ed. / Michael Crystal and John Higham. — Bristol : Jordan, 1981. — xxviii,219p : forms ; 23cm
Previous ed.: 1972. — Includes index
ISBN 0-85308-064-x : £10.50 B81-29527

344.206′6626 — England. Private companies. Transfer. Law
Wine, Humphrey. Buying and selling private companies and businesses / Humphrey Wine. — London : Butterworths, 1980. — xvii,206p : forms ; 23cm
Includes index
ISBN 0-406-42416-0 : £10.50 B81-04929

344.206′682 — England. Partnerships. Law
Ivamy, E. R. Hardy. Principles of the law of partnership. — 11th ed. / by E.R. Hardy Ivamy with a chapter on partnership taxation by D.R. Jones. — London : Butterworths, 1981. — xx,241p : forms ; 22cm
Previous ed.: published as Underhill's principles of the law of partnership. 1975. — Includes index
ISBN 0-406-66906-6 : Unpriced
ISBN 0-406-66905-8 (pbk) : Unpriced
B81-38974

344.206′7 — England. Commercial law
Marsh, S. B.. Business law / S.B. Marsh and J. Soulsby. — 2nd ed. — London : McGraw-Hill, c1981. — xxiii,268p ; 25cm
Previous ed.: i.e. Rev. ed. 1978. — Bibliography: p259-260. — Includes index
ISBN 0-07-084631-6 (pbk) : £4.75 : CIP rev.
B81-10492

Ruff, Anne R.. Commercial and industrial law / Anne R. Ruff. — 2nd ed. — Plymouth : Macdonald and Evans, 1981. — xxvi,309p ; 18cm. — (The M & E handbook series)
Previous ed.: 1978. — Includes index
ISBN 0-7121-0464-x (pbk) : £4.95 B81-32750

Shears, Peter. Business law / Peter Shears ; advisory editor Patricia Callender. — Amersham : Hulton Educational, 1980. — 239p ; 24cm. — (Hulton BEC books)
Includes index
ISBN 0-7175-0839-0 (pbk) : £3.50 B81-03338

344.206′7 — England. Commercial law — *For marketing*
Livermore, John. Legal aspects of marketing / John Livermore. — 3rd ed. — London : Published on behalf of the Institute of Marketing and the CAM Foundation [by] Heinemann, 1981. — xvi,300p ; 24cm
Previous ed.: 1979. — Bibliography: p279-281. — Includes index
ISBN 0-434-91144-5 (pbk) : £8.95 B81-15726

344.206′7′076 — England. Commercial law — *Questions & answers*
Grewal, B. S. (Baghel Singh). General principles of business law : questions and answers / by B.S. Grewal, J.D. de Freitas. — London (3 Station Parade, Balham High Rd., S.W.12) : Castlevale Printers, c1980. — 192p ; 18cm
ISBN 0-907235-00-x (pbk) : Unpriced
B81-32716

344.206′72 — England. Goods. Sale. Law
Chalmers, *Sir* M. D.. Chalmers' Sale of Goods Act 1979 : including the Factors Acts 1889 & 1890. — 18th ed. / by Michael Mark with assistance from Jonathan Mance. — London : Butterworths, 1981. — xcv,405p ; 23cm
Previous ed.: published as Chalmers' Sale of Goods Act 1893. 1975. — Includes index
ISBN 0-406-56448-5 (cased) : Unpriced
ISBN 0-406-56449-3 (pbk) : Unpriced
B81-29906

344.206′73 — England. International banking. Documentary credits. Law
Gutteridge, H. C.. The law of bankers' commercial credits. — [6th ed.] / by the late H.C. Gutteridge and Maurice Megrah. — London : Europa, 1979. — xxxiii,318p : forms ; 25cm
Previous ed.: 1976. — Includes index
ISBN 0-905118-42-1 : £9.00 : CIP rev.
B79-18194

344.206′78 — England. Companies. Liquidation. Receivership. Procedure
Samwell, Stanley David. Corporate receiverships : a practical approach / by Stanley Samwell. — London : Institute of Chartered Accountants in England and Wales, 1981. — xv,190p : forms ; 22cm
Includes index
ISBN 0-85291-287-0 : Unpriced B81-14342

344.206′78 — England. Insolvency. Law
Insolvency : (bankruptcy, receivership and liquidation). — [Guildford] : The College of Law, c1981. — xi,152p : forms ; 22cm. — (College of Law lectures, ISSN 0309-3166)
£5.00 (pbk) B81-28270

344.206′82 — England. Banking. Law
Palfreman, David. The law of banking / David Palfreman. — Plymouth : Macdonald and Evans, 1980. — xvi,319p ; 18cm. — (The M & E handbook series)
Includes index
ISBN 0-7121-1234-0 (pbk) : £2.95 B81-00050

344.206′82′0264 — England. Banking. Law — *Cases*
Smart, P. E.. Cases in the law of banking 1977-1980 / by P.E. Smart. — London : Sweet & Maxwell, 1981. — xvi,61p ; 22cm
Includes index
ISBN 0-421-28290-8 (pbk) : £3.50 B81-12258

344.207 — England. Legal system. Law — *Collections*
Zander, Michael. Cases and materials on the English legal system / Michael Zander. — 3rd ed. — London : Weidenfeld and Nicolson, 1980. — xxvii,476p : ill ; 23cm. — (Law in context)
Previous ed.: 1976. — Includes index
ISBN 0-297-77822-6 (cased) : £17.50
ISBN 0-297-77823-4 (pbk) : £8.95 B81-06163

344.207′1 — England. Funds in court — *Accounts — Serials*
Funds in court in England and Wales, accounts. — 1979-80. — London : H.M.S.O., 1981. — 21p
ISBN 0-10-228381-8 : £2.10 B81-29084

344.207′1′025 — England. Law courts — *Directories*
The **Fourmat** legal directory / general editor Theodore Ruoff. — London : Fourmat, 1981. — 285p ; 22cm
Includes index
ISBN 0-906840-41-4 (spiral) : £11.50
Primary classification 062 B81-26310

344.207′1′025421 — London. Law courts — *Directories*
Goodman, Andrew, *1956-*. The court guide / by Andrew Goodman. — London : Sweet & Maxwell, 1980. — xiv,AI,91p ; 18cm
ISBN 0-421-27590-1 (pbk) : £4.20 : CIP rev.
B80-18638

344.207′14 — England. Judiciary. Role
Devlin, Patrick Devlin, *Baron*. The judge / Patrick Devlin. — Oxford : Oxford University Press, 1979 (1981 [printing]). — xi,207p ; 20cm
Includes index
ISBN 0-19-285105-5 (pbk) : £2.95 B81-24088

344.207′14 — England. Judiciary. Role. Political aspects
Griffiths, J. A. G.. The politics of the judiciary / J.A.G. Griffith. — 2nd ed. — [London] : Fontana, 1981. — 255p : ill ; 18cm. — (Political issues of modern Britain)
Previous ed.: 1977. — Includes index
ISBN 0-00-636451-9 (pbk) : £2.50 B81-40132

344.207′16 — England. Justices of the Peace. Jurisdiction
Maddox, Alan J.. The work of a magistrate / Alan J. Maddox. — 4th ed. — London : Shaw, 1980. — xiii,222p ; 19cm
Previous ed.: 1975. — Includes index
ISBN 0-7219-0561-7 (pbk) : Unpriced
B81-07279

344.207′21′02648 — Buckinghamshire. *Court of Quarter Sessions*. Cases, *1724-1730* — *Digests*
Buckinghamshire. Calendar to the Sessions records / County of Buckingham. — Aylesbury : The County Council
Includes index
Vol.7: 1724-1730 / edited by William Le Hardy. — 1980. — xvi,285p ; 33cm
ISBN 0-86059-117-4 (pbk) : Unpriced
B81-14055

344.207′21′05 — England. County courts. Procedure — *Serials*
The **County** court practice. — 1981. — London : Butterworths, 1981. — clxxiii,2120,183p
ISBN 0-406-16314-6 : Unpriced B81-31584

344.207′25 — England. Civil law. Cases. Procedure of Great Britain. *High Court of Justice*
Odgers, William Blake. Odgers' principles of pleading and practice. — 22nd ed. — London : Stevens, Oct.1981. — [600]p
Previous ed.: 1975
ISBN 0-420-45710-0 (pbk) : £13.00 : CIP entry
B81-25314

344.207′25 — England. Civil law. Cases. Procedure of Great Britain. *High Court of Justice — Conference proceedings*
Major changes in High Court practice and procedure : conference papers. — [London] : Sweet and Maxwell, 1981. — 1v.(loose leaf) ; 31cm. — (Sweet & Maxwell professional conferences)
ISBN 0-421-29130-3 : £30.00 B81-37971

344.207′252 — Great Britain. *High Court of Justice — Accounts — Serials*
Great Britain. *High Court of Justice*Account of receipts and expenditure of the High Court and Court of Appeal for the financial year ... ended 31st March ... 1979-80. — London : H.M.S.O., 1980. — 5p
ISBN 0-10-206881-x : £1.10
Also classified at 344.207′322 B81-10314

344.207′26′0264 — Great Britain. *High Court of Justice. Chancery Division — Cases — Serials*

The **Law** reports. Chancery Division and on appeal therefrom in the Court of Appeal and decisions in the Court of Protection. — 1980. — London : The Incorporated Council of Law Reporting for England and Wales, c1980. — xv,641p
Unpriced B81-29406

344.207′27′0264 — Great Britain. *High Court of Justice. Queen′s Bench Division — Cases — Serials*

The **Law** reports. Queen′s Bench Division and on appeal therefrom in the Court of Appeal and decisions in the Court of Appeal Criminal Division and Employment Appeal Tribunal. — 1980. — London : The Incorporated Council of Law Reporting for England and Wales, c1980. — xxiv,710p
Unpriced B81-29411

344.207′29′05 — Great Britain. *Supreme Court of Judicature.* **Procedure** — *Serials*

Great Britain. *Supreme Court of Judicature.* The Supreme Court practice. — 1982. — London : Sweet & Maxwell, Sept.1981. — 2v. [(1900;1600p.)]
ISBN 0-421-27200-7 : £110.00 : CIP entry
B81-28155

344.207′322 — Great Britain. *Court of Appeal — Accounts — Serials*

Great Britain. *High Court of Justice*Account of receipts and expenditure of the High Court and Court of Appeal for the financial year ... ended 31st March ... 1979-80. — London : H.M.S.O., 1980. — 5p
ISBN 0-10-206881-x : £1.10
Primary classification 344.207′252 B81-10314

344.207′39′0264 — Great Britain. Courts of appeal: Great Britain. *Parliament. House of Lords — Cases — Serials*

The **Law** reports. House of Lords and Judicial Committee of the Privy Council and Peerage cases. — 1980. — London : The Incorporated Council of Law Reporting for England and Wales, c1980. — xx,1205p
Spine title: Law reports. Appeal cases
Unpriced B81-29410

344.207′4 — England. Coroners′ courts. Justice. Administration. Expenditure by local authorities — *Forecasts — Serials*

Administration of justice statistics, based on estimates / the Society of County Treasurers. — 1980/81. — Reading (c/o Shire Hall, Reading RG1 3EX) : The Society, 1980. — 8p
Unpriced
Primary classification 344.205′12 B81-08227

344.207′4 — Great Britain. *Court of Protection.* **Procedure**

Heywood, Nathaniel Arthur. Court of protection practice / Heywood & Massey. — 10th ed. — London : Stevens
Supplement : up to date to February 1, 1981 / by Eric R. Taylor. — 1981. — 12p ; 25cm
ISBN 0-420-46270-8 (pbk) : Unpriced
B81-21735

344.207′4 — London. Ealing *(London Borough).* **Southall. Peach, Blair. Death. Inquests** — *Friends of Blair Peach Committee viewpoints*

Ransom, David. The Blair Peach case : licence to kill / by David Ransom for the Friends of Blair Peach Committee. — [London] ([P.O. Box 353, London NW5]) : [The Committee], [1980]. — 79p : ill,2maps,ports ; 21cm
ISBN 0-906224-04-7 (pbk) : £1.20 B81-33089

344.207′4 — Oxfordshire. Oxford. Universities. Law courts: University of Oxford. *Chancellor′s Court.* **Judgments,** *1498-1506 — Digests*

Registrum cancellarii 1498-1506 / edited by W.T. Mitchell. — Oxford : Clarendon for the Oxford Historical Society, 1980. — 346p ; 23cm. — (New series / Oxford Historical Society ; v.27)
English and Latin text. — Includes index
Unpriced B81-08046

344.207′5 — England. Civil law. Procedure

Harmer, C. G.. Civil litigation - some recent changes / C.G. Harmer. — [Guildford] ([Braboeuf Manor, Portsmouth Rd., St. Catherine′s, Guildford, Surrey]) : [College of Law], [1981]. — 27p ; 22cm. — (Crash course lecture / the College of Law, ISSN 0309-2771 ; 1981)
Cover title
£1.40 (pbk) B81-39991

344.207′5 — England. Civil law. Procedure — *Manuals — For solicitors*

O′Hare, John, *1949-.* Civil litigation / John O′Hare, Robert N. Hill. — London : Oyez, c1980. — xxvi,360p : forms ; 22cm. — (Oyez practitioner series)
Includes index
ISBN 0-85120-524-0 (pbk) : £11.50 B81-03412

344.207′5 — England. Law. Procedure

Stevens, Elizabeth. Civil and criminal procedure in a nutshell / Elizabeth Stevens. — London : Sweet & Maxwell, 1981. — vii,86p ; 18cm. — (New nutshells)
Includes index
ISBN 0-421-28040-9 (pbk) : £1.75 B81-17918

344.207′52 — England. Limitation of actions. Law — *Statutes*

Great Britain. [Limitation Act 1980]. Limitation Act 1980 : Chapter 58. — London : H.M.S.O., [1980]. — iii,34p ; 25cm
ISBN 0-10-545880-5 (pbk) : £2.70 B81-19803

344.207′55 — England. Civil law. Procedure — *Forms & precedents*

Atkin, James Richard Atkin, *Baron.* Atkin′s encyclopaedia of court forms in civil proceedings. — 2nd ed., 1980 issue. — London : Butterworths
Vol.6: Acknowledgment of service, arbitration, auction bailment, banking and bills of exchange. — 1980. — xxxii,471p : forms ; 26cm
Previous ed.: published as The encyclopaedia of court forms and precedents in civil proceedings, 1961. — Includes index
ISBN 0-406-01052-8 : Unpriced
ISBN 0-406-01020-x (set) : Unpriced
B81-18835

Atkin, James Richard Atkin, *Baron.* Atkin′s encyclopaedia of court forms in civil proceedings. — 2nd ed. / by the late Lord Evershed and other lawyers. — London : Butterworths
Previous ed.: published as Encycolpaedia of court forms and precedents in civil proceedings. 1961-1971
Vol.8: Bills of sale, bonds, building contracts, carriers, charities, civil aviation, commercial court commons
1981 issue / [edited by Ingrid Persadingh]. — 1981. — xxiii,511p : forms ; 26cm
Includes index
ISBN 0-406-01061-7 : Unpriced
ISBN 0-406-01020-x (set) : Unpriced
B81-29706

Atkin, James Richard Atkin, *Baron.* Atkin′s encyclopaedia of court forms in civil proceedings. — 2nd ed. / by the late Lord Evershed and other lawyers. — London : Butterworth
Previous ed.: published as The encyclopaedia of court forms and precedents in civil proceedings in 16 vols, 1937-50
Vol.33 : 1981 issue
Rating, receivers, references and inquiries by the court, rent charges and annuities / [editor Ingrid Persadsingh]. — 1981. — xxxix,405p ; 26cm
Includes index
ISBN 0-406-01186-9 : Unpriced
ISBN 0-406-01020-x (set of 42 vols) : £533.00
B81-27287

Atkin, James Richard Atkin, *Baron.* Atkin′s encyclopaedia of court forms in civil proceedings. — 2nd ed. / by the late Lord Evershed and other lawyers. — London : Butterworth
Previous ed.: published as The encyclopaedia of court forms and precedents in civil proceedings in 16 vols, 1937-50
Vol.37 : 1981 issue
Specific performance, stay of proceedings, stock exchange, theatres, third party procedure / [editor Ingrid Persadsingh]. — 1981. — xxxix,406p ; 26cm
Includes index
ISBN 0-406-01207-5 : Unpriced
ISBN 0-406-01020-x (Set of 42 vols) : £533.00
B81-24957

Atkin, James Richard Atkin, *Baron.* Atkin′s Encyclopaedia of court forms in civil proceedings. — 2nd ed. — London : Butterworths
Supplement 1981. — 1981. — 376p ; 26cm
ISBN 0-406-01577-5 : Unpriced (set) : unpriced
B81-40606

Atkins, James Richard Atkins, *Baron.* Atkin′s Encyclopaedia of court forms in civil proceedings. — 2nd ed. / by the late Lord Evershed and other lawyers. — London : Butterworths
Vol.24: Landlord and tenant. Lands Tribunal 1981 issue. — 1981. — xxxiv,491p ; 26cm
Includes index
ISBN 0-406-01142-7 : Unpriced
ISBN 0-406-01020-x (set) : Unpriced
B81-39647

344.207′6 — England. Law courts. Evidence. Law

Murphy, Peter. A practical approach to evidence / Peter Murphy. — London (136 Bramley Rd, W1O 6SR) : Financial Training, 1980. — xl,409p ; 23cm
Includes index
ISBN 0-906322-05-7 (pbk) : £9.95 B81-00792

Phipson, Sidney L.. Phipson and Elliott manual of the law of evidence. — 11th ed. / by D.W. Elliott. — London : Sweet & Maxwell, 1980. — xxxii,376p ; 23cm
Previous ed.: published as Phipson′s manual of the law of evidence. 1972. — Includes index
ISBN 0-421-23740-6 (cased) : £15.65 : CIP rev.
ISBN 0-421-23750-3 (pbk) : £12.00 B80-08666

Seabrooke, Stephen. Evidence in a nutshell / Stephen Seabrooke. — London : Sweet & Maxwell, 1981. — vii,84p ; 18cm. — (New nutshells)
Includes index
ISBN 0-421-27820-x (pbk) : £1.75 B81-10806

344.207′6 — England. Law courts. Evidence. Law — *Early works*

Bentham, Jeremy. Rationale of judicial evidence / Jeremy Bentham. — New York ; London : Garland. — (Classics of English legal history in the modern era)
Facsimile of: edition published London : Hunt and Clarke, 1827
Vol.1. — 1978. — xxii,606p ; 19cm
ISBN 0-8240-3085-0 : Unpriced B81-25527

344.207′67 — England. Law courts. Medical evidence — *Inquiry reports*

Medical evidence : the report of a Joint Committee of the British Medical Association, the Senate of the Inns of the Court and the Bar and the Law Society. — London : B.M.A., 1981. — iiileaves,37p ; 30cm
Unpriced (spiral) B81-34895

344.207′72 — England. Civil law. Cases. Documents. Discovery & inspection. Law. Compared with law of discovery in United States

Levine, Julius Byron. Discovery. — Oxford : Clarendon Press, Dec.1981. — [300]p
ISBN 0-19-825368-0 : £15.00 : CIP entry
Also classified at 347.307′72 B81-31740

344.207'77 — England. Civil courts. Judgments. Enforcement — *Manuals*

Civil litigation : the judgment and its enforcement. — [Guildford] ([Braboeuf Manor, Portsmouth Rd, St Catherine's, Guildford, Surrey]) : College of Law, c1980. — v,26p ; 22cm. — (College of Law lectures, ISSN 0309-3166)
£1.20 (pbk) B81-04987

344.207'77 — England. Equitable remedies

Spry, I. C. F.. The principles of equitable remedies : injunctions, specific performance and equitable damages / by I.C.F. Spry. — 2nd ed. — London : Sweet & Maxwell, 1980. — lii,616p ; 25cm
Previous ed.: published as Equitable remedies. Sydney: Law Book Co., 1971. — Includes index
ISBN 0-421-27320-8 : £27.50 B81-05525

344.207'77 — England. Law courts. Denning, Alfred Denning, *Baron.* **Judgments**

Justice, Lord Denning and the constitution / edited by Peter Robson and Paul Watchman. — Farnborough, Hants. : Gower, c1981. — xvi,253p ; 23cm
Bibliography: px-xi. — Includes index
ISBN 0-566-00399-6 (cased) : £10.50 : CIP rev.
ISBN 0-566-00454-2 (pbk) : £5.95 B81-14045

344.207'9 — England. Arbitration. Law: Arbitration Act 1979 — *Conference proceedings*

The **Arbitration** Act 1979 : and its effect on commercial disputes : a one-day conference organised by Lloyd's of London Press, the London Hilton, November 20, 1980. — [London] : Lloyd's of London Press, [1980]. — 79leaves in various pagings ; 31cm
ISBN 0-904093-92-1 : Unpriced B81-22146

344.207'9 — England. Law. Cases. Disputes. Compromise

Foskett, David. The law and practice of compromise / by David Foskett. — London : Sweet & Maxwell, 1980. — xxx,198p : forms ; 23cm
Includes index
ISBN 0-421-24220-5 : £18.50 : CIP rev. B80-09639

344.208'22 — England. Law — *Statutes — Texts with commentaries — Collections*

Great Britain. [Laws, etc.]. Miscellaneous acts / annotated by Butterworths legal editorial staff. — London : Butterworths, 1980. — iii,123p ; 25cm. — (Annotated legislation service ; v.265)
Includes index
ISBN 0-406-54788-2 : £7.00 B81-07641

344.208'25 — England. Law — *Statutory instruments — Collections*

Great Britain. Halsbury's statutory instruments : being a companion work to Halsbury's statutes of England / prepared by Butterworths legal editorial staff. — London : Butterworth, 1981
Vol.1: Insurance ... [to] Local government. — 4th re-issue / revised by F.G. Kearney and Caroline Millar. — vi,356p ; 26cm
Includes index
ISBN 0-406-04622-0 : Unpriced B81-16968

Great Britain. [Laws, etc.]. Halsbury's Statutory instruments : being a companion work to Halsbury's Statutes of England / prepared by Butterworths legal editorial staff. — 4th re-issue. — London : Butterworth
Vol.19: Registration concerning the individual. Revenue. Royal forces. Sale of goods and hire-purchase. Savings banks. — 1981. — vi,460p ; 26cm
Includes index
ISBN 0-406-04693-x : Unpriced
ISBN 0-406-04500-3 (set) : Unpriced B81-39645

344.208'46 — England. Law. Cases — *Digests*

The **English** and Empire digest with complete and exhaustive annotations. Replacement volumes . — London : Butterworth
1981 reissue. — 1981. — xlvii,603p ; 26cm
ISBN 0-406-02626-2 : Unpriced
ISBN 0-406-02500-2 (Set) : Unpriced B81-26639

344.208'47'05 — England. Law. Cases — *Citators — Serials*

Current law citator. — 1980. — London : Sweet & Maxwell, 1981. — 739p
ISSN 0526-4448 : Unpriced
Also classified at 344.108'27'05 B81-35454

344.208'6 — England. Law — *Encyclopaedias*

Jowitt, William Allen Jowitt, *Earl.* Jowitt's dictionary of English law / by the late Earl Jowitt and Clifford Walsh. — 2nd ed. / [edited] by John Burke. — London : Sweet & Maxwell
Previous ed.: published as The dictionary of English law. 1959
1st supplement / by Emlyn Williams. — 1981. — v,101p ; 26cm
ISBN 0-421-26970-7 : £11.00 : CIP rev. B81-06893

344.23'40352'05 — Channel Islands. Income tax. Law — *Serials*

Tolley's taxation in the Channel Islands and Isle of Man. — 1981. — Croydon : Tolley Pub. Co., c1981. — vi,163p
ISBN 0-85459-026-9 : £6.25
Also classified at 344.27'90352'05 B81-31889

344.23'4067 — Channel Islands. Commercial law — *For businessmen*

The **Channel** Islands : basic business information / Deloitte Haskins & Sells. — 2nd ed. — [London] : Oyez, 1980. — 40p ; 21cm
Previous ed.: 1978
ISBN 0-85120-517-8 (pbk) : £4.95 B81-14494

344.2703'92'02632 — North-west England. Water supply — *By-laws — Texts with commentaries*

North West Water Authority. A guide to the Authority's water byelaws / North West Water. — Warrington (Dawson House, Great Sankey, Warrington, Cheshire) : North West Water Authority, 1980. — 1v.(loose-leaf) : ill,facsims ; 24cm
Includes index
£4.50 B81-40283

344.27'90352'05 — Isle of Man. Income tax. Law — *Serials*

Tolley's taxation in the Channel Islands and Isle of Man. — 1981. — Croydon : Tolley Pub. Co., c1981. — vi,163p
ISBN 0-85459-026-9 : £6.25
Primary classification 344.23'40352'05 B81-31889

344.27'9067 — Isle of Man. Commercial law — *For businessmen*

The **Isle** of Man : basic business information / Pannell Kerr Forster. — [London] : Oyez, 1980. — 36p : 1form ; 21cm
ISBN 0-85120-518-6 (pbk) : £4.95 B81-14493

344.28'10392 — Yorkshire. Water supply — *By-laws — Texts with commentaries*

Yorkshire Water Authority. A guide to the Authority's water supply byelaws / Yorkshire Water Authority. — [Leeds] ([West Riding House, 67 Albion St., Leeds, LS1 5AA]) : Yorkshire Water Authority, 1980. — 210p : ill ; 22cm
Includes index
£3.50 (pbk) B81-33235

344.2902'878'09 — Wales. Society. Role of women, *to 1536.* **Legal aspects** — *Festschriften*

The **Welsh** law of women : studies presented to Professor Daniel A. Binchy on his eightieth birthday, 3 June 1980 / edited by Dafydd Jenkins and Morfydd E. Owen. — Cardiff : Published on behalf of the Board of Celtic Studies [by] University of Wales Press, c1980. — x,253P : 1port ; 22cm
Includes index
ISBN 0-7083-0771-x : £12.95 : CIP rev. B80-08658

344.3/9 — LAW. EUROPEAN COUNTRIES(OTHER THAN GREAT BRITAIN AND IRELAND)

344.304'1'09 — Germany. Industrial relations. Law, *1868-1933*

Kahn-Freund, *Sir* **Otto**. Labour law and politics in the Weimar Republic / Otto Kahn-Freund ; edited, with an introduction and appendices, by Roy Lewis, Jon Clark ; translated by Jon Clark. — Oxford : Blackwell, 1981. — 260p ; 23cm. — (Warwick studies in industrial relations)
Translation of the German. — Bibliography: p246-251. — Includes index
ISBN 0-631-12825-5 : £15.00 : CIP rev. B81-16931

344.306 — West Germany. Private law

Horn, Norbert. German private and commercial law. — Oxford : Clarendon Press, Jan.1982. — [400]p
Translated from the German
ISBN 0-19-825382-6 (cased) : £14.95 : CIP entry
ISBN 0-19-825383-4 (pbk) : £7.95 B81-33901

344.403'71 — France. Consumer protection. Law — *French texts*

Le **droit** de la consommation en France : une étude préparée pour la Commission de la Communauté Européenne / dirigée par J. Calais-Auloy avec la collaboration de H. Bricks ... [et al.]. — New York ; London : Van Nostrand Reinhold, c1981. — xi,198p : ill ; 24cm. — (Le Droit de la consommation dans les pays-membres de la CEE)
Includes index
ISBN 0-442-30414-5 : £15.00 B81-12149

344.405'2'31 — France. Treason. Law, *1328-1494*

Cuttler, S. H.. The law of treason and treason trials in later medieval France. — Cambridge : Cambridge University Press, Feb.1982. — [278] p. — (Cambridge studies in medieval life and thought ; 16)
ISBN 0-521-23968-0 : £25.00 : CIP entry B81-36949

344.4061'5'09 — France. Families. Law, *1700-1804*

Traer, James F.. Marriage and the family in eighteenth-century France / James F. Traer. — Ithaca ; London : Cornell University Press, 1980. — 208p ; 23cm
Bibliography: p199-203. — Includes index
ISBN 0-8014-1298-6 : £9.00 B81-01610

344.41'0413 — Great Britain. Dental profession. Law

Seear, John. Law and ethics in dentistry. — 2nd ed. — Bristol : Wright, Sept.1981. — [272]p. — (A Dental practitioner handbook ; no.19)
Previous ed.: 1975
ISBN 0-7236-0588-2 (pbk) : £6.50 : CIP entry B81-26692

344.5036'7 — Italy. Transfer pricing by foreign companies. Taxation. Law

Transfer pricing : the Italian experience / translation of the circular letter no. 9.2267 issued by the Italian Ministry of Finance on September 22, 1980, denominated: 'The transfer prices in the computation of taxable income of enterprises subject to foreign control' ; edited by Studio Trivoli. — Deventer ; London : Kluwer, 1981. — 102p ; 25cm
English and Italian text
ISBN 90-654-4010-0 : Unpriced B81-31139

344.505'288 — Italy. Friuli. Heresy. Trials of Menocchio

Ginzburg, Carlo. The cheese and the worms : the cosmos of a sixteenth-century miller / Carlo Ginzburg ; translated by John and Anne Tedeschi. — London : Routledge & Kegan Paul, 1980. — xxxvii,177p : ill ; 24cm
Translation of: Il formaggio e i vermi. — Includes index
ISBN 0-7100-0591-1 : £7.95 : CIP rev. B80-11803

344.7'009 — Russia. Law, *1100-1500*

Kaiser, Daniel H.. The growth of the law in medieval Russia / Daniel H. Kaiser. — Princeton ; Guildford : Princeton University Press, c1980. — xii,308p ; 24cm
Bibliography: p275-308. — Includes index
ISBN 0-691-05311-1 : £14.00 B81-26186

344.702'29 — Soviet Union. Constitutions, *1918-1977*

Unger, Aryeh L.. Constitutional development in the USSR. — London : Methuen, Aug.1981. — [320]p
ISBN 0-416-71680-6 (cased) : £15.00 : CIP entry
ISBN 0-416-71690-3 (pbk) : £7.50 B81-16403

344.8505'5042 — Sweden. Offenders. Prosecution. Procedure

Leigh, L. H.. The management of the prosecution process in Denmark, Sweden and the Netherlands. — Leamington Spa (2a Upper Grove St., Leamington Spa, CV23 5AN) : James Hall, Oct.1981. — [96]p
ISBN 0-907471-01-3 (pbk) : £5.50 : CIP entry
Primary classification 344.8905'5042
B81-31239

344.8903'71 — Denmark. Consumer protection. Law

Dahl, Børge. Consumer legislation in Denmark : a study prepared for the EC Commission / Børge Dahl. — New York ; London : Van Nostrand Reinhold, c1981. — x,149p ; 24cm. — (Consumer legislation in the EC countries)
Bibliography: p138-142. — Includes index
ISBN 0-442-30425-0 : £15.00 B81-31863

344.8905'5042 — Denmark. Offenders. Prosecution. Procedure

Leigh, L. H.. The management of the prosecution process in Denmark, Sweden and the Netherlands. — Leamington Spa (2a Upper Grove St., Leamington Spa, CV23 5AN) : James Hall, Oct.1981. — [96]p
ISBN 0-907471-01-3 (pbk) : £5.50 : CIP entry
Also classified at 344.8505'5042 ; 344.9205'5042 B81-31239

344.9205'5042 — Netherlands. Offenders. Prosecution. Procedure

Leigh, L. H.. The management of the prosecution process in Denmark, Sweden and the Netherlands. — Leamington Spa (2a Upper Grove St., Leamington Spa, CV23 5AN) : James Hall, Oct.1981. — [96]p
ISBN 0-907471-01-3 (pbk) : £5.50 : CIP entry
Primary classification 344.8905'5042
B81-31239

344.9303'71 — Belgium & Luxembourg. Consumer protection. Law — *French texts*

Fontaine, M.. Le droit de la consommation en Belgique et au Luxembourg : une étude préparée pour la Commission des Communautés Européennes / M. Fontaine, Th. Bourgoignie. — New York ; London : Van Nostrand Reinhold, c1981. — xvii,257p ; 24cm
Includes index
ISBN 0-442-30416-1 : £15.00 B81-25382

344.9705'231'0924 — Yugoslavia. Crimes against the state. Trial of Tuđman, Franjo

Tuđman, Franjo. Croatia on trial : the case of the Croatian historian Dr. F. Tudjman / translated by Zdenka Palić-Kušan. — London (60 Brightwell Cresc., S.W.17) : United Publishers, [1981?]. — 47p : 1port ; 21cm
Translated from the Serbo-Croatian
Unpriced (pbk) B81-41021

344.9705'231'0924 — Yugoslavia. Crimes against the state. Trial of Tudman, Franjo — *Serbo-Croatian texts*

Tuđman, Franjo. Na suđenju dr. Tuđmanu sudilo se Hrvatskoj. — London (60 Brightwell Cres., S.W.17) : United Publishers, 1981. — 39p : port ; 21cm
Unpriced (pbk) B81-27145

345 — LAW. ASIA

345.1 — China. Jurisprudence

Kim, Hyung I.. Fundamental legal concepts of China and the West : a comparative study / Hyung I. Kim. — Port Washington ; London : National University Publications : Kennikat, 1981. — xiii,175p ; 23cm. — (Multi-disciplinary studies in the law)
Bibliography: p165-175
ISBN 0-8046-9275-0 : £14.85 B81-29475

345.1'009 — China. Law, *B.C.1122-A.D.1912*

Essays on China's legal tradition / edited by Jerome Alan Cohen, R. Randle Edwards and Fu-mei Chang Chen. — Princeton ; Guildford : Princeton University Press, c1980. — 438p ; 25cm. — (Studies in East Asian law, Harvard University)
Bibliography: p359-394. - Includes index
ISBN 0-691-09238-9 : £16.50 B81-17582

345.1'24905231 — Taiwan. Political offenders. Trials, *1979*

Ming, Anne. Taiwanese voice : the Kaohsiung incident / by Anne Ming. — London : Division of International Affairs of the British Council of Churches, c1981. — 27p ; 21cm
ISBN 0-85169-087-4 (pbk) : £0.50 B81-27604

345.202'2 — Japan. Constitution — *Inquiry reports*

Japan. *Kempō Chōsakai*. Japan's Commission on the Constitution : the final report / translated and edited by John M. Maki. — Seattle ; London : University of Washington Press, c1980. — x,413p ; 24cm. — (Asian law series ; 7)
Selected translation of: Kempō Chōsakai hōkokusho. — Bibliography: p405-408. — Includes index
ISBN 0-295-95767-0 : £15.00 B81-22348

345.3'32067 — Yemen *(Arab Republic)*. **Commercial law**

Business laws and practices of the Yemen Arab Republic / Shair Management Services. — London (401 Bond Street House, 14 Clifford St., W1X 1RD) : Arabian Information, 1979. — 210p ; 30cm. — (Arabian business laws and practices series)
ISBN 0-86010-902-x (pbk) : £125.00
B81-16759

345.3'53067 — Oman. Commercial law

Business laws and practices of Oman / Shair Management Services. — London (401 Bond Street House, 14 Clifford St., W1X 1RD) : Arabian Information, 1979. — 163p ; 30cm. — (Arabian business laws and practices series)
ISBN 0-86010-907-0 (pbk) : £125.00
B81-16763

345.3'6'009 — Arabia. Gulf States. Law, *to 1957-1979*

Ballantyne, W. M.. Legal development in Arabia : a selection of articles and addresses on the Arabian Gulf / W.M. Ballantyne. — London : Graham & Trotman, 1980. — x,125p ; 24cm
Includes index
ISBN 0-86010-167-3 : £18.00 B81-07275

345.3'6071'0924 — Arabia. Gulf States. Law courts — *Personal observations — Humour*

Overton, Robert. Palm court / Robert Overton ; illustrations by John Lawrence. — London (27 George St., W1P 1FD) : Robin Clark, 1980, c1979. — 153p : ill ; 20cm
Originally published: London : O. Hamilton, 1979
ISBN 0-86072-038-1 (pbk) : £1.95
Also classified at 349.07'1'0924 B81-03565

345.3'63067 — Qatar. Commercial law

Business laws and practices of Qatar / Shair Management Services. — London (401 Bond Street House, 14 Clifford St., W1X 1RD) : Arabian Information, 1979. — 106p ; 30cm. — (Arabian business laws and practices series)
ISBN 0-86010-905-4 (pbk) : £125.00
B81-16762

345.3'65067 — Bahrain. Commercial law

Business laws and practices of Bahrain / Shair Management Services. — London (401 Bond Street House, 14 Clifford St., W1X 1RD) : Arabian Information, 1979. — 160p ; 30cm. — (Arabian business laws and practices series)
ISBN 0-86010-903-8 (pbk) : £125.00
B81-16766

345.3'8067 — Saudi Arabia. Commercial law

Business laws and practices of Saudi Arabia / Shair Management Services. — London (401 Bond Street House, 14 Clifford St., W1X 1RD) : Arabian Information, 1979. — 159p ; 30cm. — (Arabian business laws and practices series)
ISBN 0-86010-901-1 (pbk) : £125.00
B81-16761

Kay, Ernest, *1929-*. Legal aspects of business in Saudi Arabia / Ernest Kay. — London : Graham & Trottman, 1979. — 162p : forms ; 23cm
Includes index
ISBN 0-86010-131-2 : £18.00 B81-05522

345.402'42 — India. Personal law. Conflict of laws

Pearl, David. Interpersonal conflict of laws in India, Pakistan and Bangladesh / David Pearl ; foreword by M. Hidayafullah. — London : Stevens, 1981. — xxviii,176p ; 25cm
Bibliography: p165-169. — Includes index
ISBN 0-420-45770-4 : £19.50 B81-37119

345.49'1052523 — Pakistan. Murder. Conspiracy. Trial of Bhutto, Zulfikar Ali

Schofield, Victoria. Bhutto : trial and execution / Victoria Schofield. — London : Cassell, 1979. — xii,250p,[8]p of plates : 2ill,ports ; 23cm
Includes index
ISBN 0-304-30539-1 : £7.95 B81-04055

345.49'3022 — Sri Lanka. Constitution, *1978*

Wilson, A. Jeyaratnam. The Gaullist system in Asia : the constitution of Sri Lanka (1978) / A. Jeyaratnam Wilson. — London : Macmillan, 1980. — xvii,218p ; 23cm
Bibliography: p158-162. - Includes index
ISBN 0-333-27276-5 : £20.00 : CIP rev.
B80-09630

345.645034 — Cyprus. Taxation. Law — *For businessmen*

Demetriades, Chrysses. Cyprus in international tax planning : a practical guide for foreign firms and individuals / Chrysses Demetriades. — London : Kluwer, 1980. — xvi,447p : ill,maps ; 24cm
Includes index
ISBN 0-903393-51-4 : Unpriced B81-31140

345.6706'7'02632 — Iraq. Commercial law — *Statutes — Collections*

Iraq. Business laws of Iraq / translated from Arabic into English by Nicola H. Karam. — London : Graham & Trotman, c1980. — lv,(loose-leaf) ; 25cm. — (Middle East business law series)
Includes index
ISBN 0-86010-252-1 : £120.00 B81-34082

345.69506'7 — Jordan. Commercial law

Business laws and practices of Jordan / Shair Management Services. — London (401 Bond Street House, 14 Clifford St., W1X 1RD) : Arabian Information, 1979. — 159p ; 30cm. — (Arabian business laws and practices series)
ISBN 0-86010-906-2 (pbk) : £125.00
B81-16764

346 — LAW. AFRICA

346.06'7'0264 — Africa. Common law countries. Commercial law — *Cases — Serials*

. The African law reports. Commercial law series. — 1974, vol.2. — Oxford (c/o Trinity College, Oxford OX1 3BH) : African Law Reports, c1979. — xlix,403p
ISBN 0-903826-40-2 : Unpriced B81-01775

346.206'7 — Egypt. Commercial law

Business laws and practices of Egypt / Shair Management Services. — London (401 Bond Street House, 14 Clifford St., W1X 1RD) : Arabian Information, 1979. — 198p ; 30cm. — (Arabian business laws and practices series)
ISBN 0-86010-904-6 (pbk) : £125.00
B81-16765

346.207'1 — Egypt. Mixed courts, *to 1949*

Maakad, Adib. General principles of the Egyptian mixed courts. — London : Laureate Press, Nov.1981. — [500]p
Translation of: Notions générales sur les juridictions mixtes d'Egypte
ISBN 0-907612-00-8 : £30.00 : CIP entry
B81-33632

346.2406'7 — Sudan. Commercial law

Business laws and practices of Sudan / Shair Management Services. — London (401 Bond Street House, 14 Clifford St., W1X 1RD) : Arabian Information, 1979. — 294p : forms ; 30cm. — (Arabian business laws and practices series)
ISBN 0-86010-900-3 (pbk) : £125.00
B81-16760

346.2407'6 — Sudan. Law courts. Evidence. Law

Vasdev, Krishna. The law of evidence in the Sudan / by Krishna Vasdev. — London : Butterworths, 1981. — xlviii,486p ; 22cm
Includes index
ISBN 0-406-40610-3 (pbk) : Unpriced
B81-32963

346.6905 — Nigeria. Criminal law

Okonkwo, C. O.. Okonkwo and Naish on criminal law in Nigeria. — 2nd ed. / by C.O. Okonkwo. — London : Sweet & Maxwell, 1980. — xxxiii,389p ; 23cm
Previous ed.: published as Criminal law in Nigeria (excluding the North) / by C.O. Okonkwo and Michael E. Naish. 1964. — Includes index
ISBN 0-421-26600-7 (cased) : £24.00 : CIP rev.
ISBN 0-421-26610-4 (pbk) : £18.00 B80-04720

346.69'05 — Nigeria. Southern States. Criminal law

Aguda, T. Akinola. The criminal law and procedure of the southern states of Nigeria. — 3rd ed. — London : Sweet & Maxwell, Dec.1981. — [1000]p. — (Nigerian practice library)
Previous ed.: published as Brett and McLean's The criminal law and procedure of the six southern states of Nigeria / by C.O. Madarikan and T. Akinola Aguda. 1974
ISBN 0-421-24920-x : £75.00 : CIP entry
B81-31745

346.6906'7'0264 — Nigeria. Commercial law — *Cases — Serials*

The **Nigerian** commercial law reports. — 1966. — Oxford : The African Law Reports, 1981. — xliv,451p
ISBN 0-903826-17-8 : Unpriced B81-24132

346.805'231 — South Africa. Political offenders. Trials. Statements, *1960-1978 — Collections*

The **Sun** will rise : statements from the dock by Southern African political prisoners / edited by Mary Benson. — Rev. and enl. ed. — London (104 Newgate St., EC1) : International Defence and Aid Fund, 1981. — 80p : ports ; 21cm
Previous ed.: 1974
ISBN 0-904759-43-1 (pbk) : £1.20 B81-35412

347 — LAW. NORTH AMERICA

347.1'0024613 — Canada. Law — *For nursing*

Creighton, Helen, *1914-*. Law every nurse should know / Helen Creighton. — 4th ed. — Philadelphia ; London : Saunders, 1981. — xv,422p ; 26cm
Previous ed.: 1975. — Includes index
ISBN 0-7216-2753-6 (pbk) : £7.50
Primary classification 347.3'0024613
B81-11374

347.102'3 — Canada. Constitution. Law: British North America Acts. Reform. Role of Great Britain. *Parliament — Inquiry reports*

Great Britain. *Parliament. House of Commons. Foreign Affairs Committee.* Second report from the Foreign Affairs Committee, session 1980-81 : supplementary report on the British North America Acts : the role of Parliament : together with part of the proceedings of the Committee relating to the report. — London : H.M.S.O., [1981]. — xxiii ; 25cm. — ([HC] ; 295)
ISBN 0-10-229581-6 (pbk) : £2.30 B81-33038

347.104'1 — Canada. Industrial relations. Law

Arthurs, H. W.. Labour law and industrial relations in Canada / by H.W. Arthurs, D.D. Carter, H.J. Glasbeek. — Deventer ; London : Kluwer, 1981. — 291p : ill ; 25cm
" ... originally published as a monograph in the 'International Encyclopaedia for Labour Law and Industrial Relations'". — Includes index
ISBN 90-312-0139-1 : Unpriced
ISBN 0-409-81184-x (Butterworths) B81-31144

347.28202'2 — Belize. Constitution — *Conference proceedings*

Great Britain. *Belize Constitutional Conference (1981)*. Report of the Belize Constitutional Conference, London, April 1981. — London : H.M.S.O., 1981. — 29p ; 25cm. — (Miscellaneous ; no.11 (1981)) (Cmnd. ; 8245)
ISBN 0-10-182450-5 (unbound) : £2.40
B81-26111

347.3'0024613 — United States. Law — *For nursing*

Creighton, Helen, *1914-*. Law every nurse should know / Helen Creighton. — 4th ed. — Philadelphia ; London : Saunders, 1981. — xv,422p ; 26cm
Previous ed.: 1975. — Includes index
ISBN 0-7216-2753-6 (pbk) : £7.50
Also classified at 347.1'0024613 B81-11374

347.3'0092'4 — United States. Law. Landis, James M. *- Biographies*

Ritchie, Donald A.. James M. Landis : dean of the regulators / Donald A. Ritchie. — Cambridge, Mass. ; London : Harvard University Press, 1980. — ix,267p : 1port ; 25cm
Includes index
ISBN 0-674-47171-7 : £10.50 B81-06667

347.3'0092'4 — United States. Law. White, Edward Douglass — *Biographies*

Highsaw, Robert B.. Edward Douglass White : defender of the conservative faith / Robert B. Highsaw. — Baton Rouge ; London : Louisiana State University Press, c1981. — xiv,212p,[6]p of plates : ill,ports ; 24cm. — (Southern biography series)
Bibliography: p201-205. — Includes index
ISBN 0-8071-0753-0 : £12.00 B81-25941

347.302 — United States. Constitutional law

Corwin, Edward S.. Edward S. Corwin's the Constitution and what it means today. — 14th ed. / revised by Harold W. Chase and Craig R. Ducat. — Princeton ; Guildford : Princeton University Press
Previous ed.: 1974. — Includes index
1980 supplement : Supreme Court decisions of 1977 through 1980 / by Harold W. Chase and Craig R. Ducat. — c1980. — 214p ; 24cm
ISBN 0-691-02761-7 (pbk) : £1.60 B81-12446

347.302'2 — United States. Constitution. Influence of theories of politics of Hume, David & Federalist, *The*

Wills, Garry. Explaining America : The Federalist / Garry Wills. — London : Athlone, 1981. — xxii,286p ; 23cm
Bibliography: p271-272. — Includes index
ISBN 0-485-30003-6 : £14.50 : CIP rev.
B81-14924

347.302'52 — United States. Constitutional law. Implications of political aspects of decisions of United States. *Supreme Court*

Grossman, Joel B.. Constitutional law and judicial policy making / edited and written by Joel B. Grossman, Richard S. Wells. — 2nd ed. — New York ; Chichester : Wiley, c1980. — xxviii,1379p : ill ; 27cm
Previous ed.: 1972. — Includes index
ISBN 0-471-32849-9 : £12.70 B81-02746

347.302'85'01 — United States. Human rights. Law *— Philosophical perspectives*

Values in conflict : life, liberty, and the rule of law / [compiled by] Burton M. Leiser. — London : Collier Macmillan, c1981. — xii,478p ; 24cm
ISBN 0-02-369520-x (pbk) : £7.50 B81-33407

347.302'87 — United States. Negro slaves. Law, *1820-1828 — Cases*

Noonan, John T.. The antelope : the ordeal of the recaptured Africans in the administrations of James Monroe and John Quincy Adams / John T. Noonan, Jr. — Berkeley ; London : University of California Press, c1977. — vii,198p ; 23cm
Includes index
ISBN 0-520-03319-1 : £7.70 B81-22069

347.302'872 — United States. North American Indians. Law

Medcalf, Linda. Law and identity : lawyers, native Americans and legal practice / Linda Medcalf ; preface by Stuart A. Scheingold. — Beverly Hills ; London : Sage, c1978. — 147p ; 23cm. — (Sage library of social research ; v.62)
Bibliography: p141-145
ISBN 0-8039-0980-2 (cased) : £11.25
B81-21960

347.302'878 — United States. Women. Rights. Litigation by women's liberation movements

O'Connor, Karen. Women's organizations' use of the courts / Karen O'Connor. — Lexington, Mass. : Lexington ; [Farnborough, Hants.] : Gower [distributor], 1980. — xi,157p : ill ; 24cm
Includes index
ISBN 0-669-03093-7 : £12.00 B81-06976

347.303'143 — United States. Embezzlement. Court-martial of Flipper, Henry O.

Johnson, Barry C.. Flipper's dismissal : the ruin of Lt. Henry O. Flipper, U.S.A., first coloured graduate of West Point / by Barry C. Johnson. — London (39a Kildare Terrace W.2) : [B.C. Johnson], [1980?]. — 132p : 1port ; 22cm
Limited ed. of 150 numbered copies
£5.00 B81-23634

347.3036'6 — United States. Taxation. Liability of organisations. Exemption. Law

Hopkins, Bruce R.. The law of tax-exempt organizations / Bruce R. Hopkins. — 3rd ed. — New York ; Chichester : Wiley
1981 supplement. — c1981. — v,119p ; 23cm
Includes index
ISBN 0-471-09351-3 (pbk) : £12.50 B81-24225

347.303'7 — United States. Economic development. Law: National Industrial Recovery Act of 1933. Operation, *to 1935*

Weinstein, Michael M.. Recovery and redistribution under the NIRA / Michael M. Weinstein. — Amsterdam ; Oxford : North-Holland, 1980. — xv,171p : ill ; 25cm. — (Studies in monetary economics ; v.6)
Bibliography: p151-161. — Includes index
ISBN 0-444-86007-x : £14.82 B81-09577

347.303'7 — United States. Economic policies. Legal aspects

Law and economics : an institutional perspective / edited by Warren J. Samuels, A. Allan Schmid. — Boston [Mass.] ; London : Nijhoff, c1981. — vii,268p : 2ill ; 24cm
Includes bibliographies and index
ISBN 0-89838-049-9 : Unpriced B81-06977

347.303'7 — United States. Industries. Regulation. Judicial review

Siegan, Bernard H.. Economic liberties and the constitution / Bernard H. Siegan. — Chicago ; London : University of Chicago Press, 1980. — 383p ; 24cm
Includes index
ISBN 0-226-75663-7 : £11.70 B81-21063

347.303'72 — United States. Industries. Competition. Law

Neale, A. D.. The antitrust laws of the United States of America : a study of competition enforced by law. — 3rd ed. / A.D. Neale and D.G. Goyder ; with a foreword by Abe Fortas. — Cambridge : Cambridge University Press, 1980. — xvi,526p ; 24cm. — (Economic and social studies ; 19)
Previous ed.: / by A.D. Neale, 1970. — Bibliography: p498-501. - Includes index
ISBN 0-521-23569-3 (cased) : £24.50
ISBN 0-521-28044-3 (pbk) : £7.95 B81-11203

The **Political** economy of antitrust / principal paper by William Baxter ; edited by Robert D. Tollison. — Lexington : Lexington Books ; [Farnborough, Hants.] : Gower [distributor], 1981, c1980. — ix,147p ; 24cm
Conference papers
ISBN 0-669-03876-8 : £11.00 B81-22945

347.303'877 — United States. Imports. Law — *For businessmen*

Rossides, Eugene T.. U.S. customs tariffs and trade / Eugene T. Rossides. — Washington, D.C. : Bureau of National Affairs ; London : Graham and Trotman, c1977. — xv,826p : forms ; 24cm
Includes index
ISBN 0-87179-241-9 : £30.00 B81-19621

347.304 — United States. Government. Social policies. Implementation. Legal aspects

Policy implementation : penalties or incentives? / edited by John Brigham and Don W. Brown. — Beverley Hills ; London : Sage, c1980. — 271p : ill ; 23cm. — (Sage focus editions ; 25)
Includes bibliographies
ISBN 0-8039-1350-8 (cased) : £11.85
ISBN 0-8039-1351-6 (pbk) : £6.25 B81-14653

347.304'321 — United States. Health services. Law

Legal aspects of health policy : issues and trends / edited by Ruth Roemer and George McKray. — Westport ; London : Greenwood Press, 1980. — x,473p ; 25cm
Bibliography: p451-459. — Includes index
ISBN 0-313-21430-1 : £27.90 B81-23458

347.304'41 — United States. Medicine. Emergency treatment. Law

George, James E.. Law and emergency care / James E. George. — St. Louis ; London : Mosby, 1980. — ix,283p : forms ; 25cm
Includes index
ISBN 0-8016-1834-7 : £16.75 B81-04912

347.304'41'05 — United States. Medical personnel. Law — *Serials*

Legal medicine. — 1980-. — Philadelphia ; London : Saunders, c1980-. — v. : ill ; 24cm
Annual. — Continues: Legal medicine annual
£15.75
Primary classification 614'.1'0973 B81-00911

347.304'419 — United States. Abortion. Legal aspects

The Law and politics of abortion / edited by Carl E. Schneider, Maris A. Vinovskis. — Lexington : Lexington, c1980 ; [Farnborough, Hants.] : Gower [distributor], 1981. — xlvii,268p : ill ; 24cm
Includes index
ISBN 0-669-03386-3 : £11.50 B81-17763

347.304'44 — United States. Man. Mental illness. Law

Wexler, David B.. Mental health law : major issues / David B. Wexler. — New York ; London : Plenum, c1981. — x,270p ; 24cm. — (Perspectives in law & psychology ; v.4)
Includes index
ISBN 0-306-40538-5 : Unpriced B81-16194

347.304'46342 — United States. Atmosphere. Pollution by coal industries. Law

Ackerman, Bruce A.. Clean coal - dirty air : or how the Clean Air Act became a multibillion-dollar bail-out for high-sulfur coal producers and what should be done about it / Bruce A. Ackerman and William T. Hassler. — New Haven ; London : Yale University Press, c1981. — x,193p ; 22cm. — (A Yale fastback)
Includes index
ISBN 0-300-02628-5 (cased) : Unpriced : CIP rev.
ISBN 0-300-02643-9 (pbk) : £3.50 B81-12367

347.304'541 — United States. Alcoholic drinks. Consumption by young persons. Law

Minimum-drinking-age laws : an evaluation / edited by Henry Wechsler. — Lexington : Lexington Books ([Farnborough, Hants.]) : Gower [distributor], 1981, c1980. — iii,187p : ill ; 24cm
Originally published: 1980. — Includes index
ISBN 0-669-03380-4 : £11.50 B81-09386

347.304'7 — United States. Schools. Law

McCarthy, Martha M.. Public school law : teachers' and students' rights / Martha M. McCarthy, Nelda H. Cambron. — Boston [Mass.] ; London : Allyn and Bacon, c1981. — xii,336p ; 25cm
Includes index
ISBN 0-205-07278-x : Unpriced B81-28981

347.305 — United States. Criminal law. Reform. Projects: BASICS Program

Conner, Ross F.. Attorneys as activists : evaluating the American Bar Association's BASICS program / Ross F. Conner, C. Ronald Huff. — Beverly Hills ; London : Sage, c1979. — 263p : ill,forms ; 22cm. — (Contemporary evaluation research ; 1)
Bibliography: p259-261
ISBN 0-8039-1363-x (cased) : Unpriced
ISBN 0-8039-1364-8 (pbk) : £6.25 B81-21665

347.305'06 — United States. Criminal courts. Evidence. Presentation & evaluation

Bennett, W. Lance. Reconstructing reality in the courtroom. — London : Tavistock, Sept.1981. — [180]p
ISBN 0-422-77840-0 : £8.25 : CIP entry B81-22474

347.305'231 — United States. Treason. Trials, *1945-1960*

West, Rebecca. The meaning of treason. — 3rd ed. — London : Virago, Feb.1982. — [448]p
Previous ed.: Harmondsworth : Penguin, 1965
ISBN 0-86068-256-0 (pbk) : £4.50 : CIP entry
Primary classification 344.205'231 B81-40235

347.305'2532 — United States. Crimes: Rape. Trials. Juries. Decision making

Feild, Hubert S.. Jurors and rape : a study in psychology and law / Hubert S. Feild, Leigh B. Bienen. — Lexington : Lexington Books ; [Farnborough, Hants.] : Gower [distributor], 1981, c1980. — xiv,473p : ill,2ports ; 24cm
Includes bibliographies and index
ISBN 0-669-01148-7 : £21.00 B81-22947

347.305'5042 — United States. Offenders. Prosecution. Procedure

Weimer, David Leo. Improving prosecution? : the inducement and implementation of innovations for prosecution management / David Leo Weimer. — Westport, Conn. ; London : Greenwood Press, 1980. — xiv,237p : ill ; 22cm. — (Contributions in political science, ISSN 0147-1066 ; no.49)
Bibliography: p227-231. — Includes index
ISBN 0-313-22247-9 : £15.95 B81-23470

347.305'72 — United States. Criminal law. Justice. Administration. Plea bargaining

Plea-bargaining / edited by William F. McDonald, James A. Cramer. — Lexington : Lexington Books ; [Farnborough, Hants.] : Gower [distributor], 1980. — xi,204p : ill ; 24cm
Includes bibliographies and index
ISBN 0-669-02363-9 : £13.00
Primary classification 344.205'72 B81-19877

347.305'772 — United States. Federal courts. Sentencing

Phillips, Charles David. Sentencing councils in the federal courts : a question of justice / Charles David Phillips. — Lexington, Mass. : Lexington Books, c1980 [Aldershot] : Gower [distributor], 1981. — xxiii,151p : ill ; 24cm
Bibliography: p143-147. — Includes index
ISBN 0-669-03514-9 : £13.50 B81-33209

347.305'772 — United States. Offenders. Sentencing

Sentencing / edited by Hyman Gross, Andrew von Hirsch. — New York ; Oxford : Oxford University Press, 1981. — ix,397p ; 25cm
ISBN 0-19-502763-9 : £12.75
ISBN 0-19-502764-7 (pbk) : £6.50 B81-18301

347.305'81 — United States. Juvenile courts. Law. Compliance by juvenile courts

Sprowls, James T.. Discretion and lawlessness : compliance in the juvenile court / James T. Sprowls. — Lexington : Lexington ; [Farnborough, Hants.] : [Gower] [distributor], 1980. — xiii,121p ; 24cm
Bibliography: p109-115. — Includes index
ISBN 0-669-03540-8 : £9.50 B81-10892

347.305'87 — United States. Juvenile courts. Defendants. Rights. Understanding by defendants. Assessment — *Psychological perspectives*

Grisso, Thomas. Juveniles' waiver of rights : legal and psychological competence / Thomas Grisso. — New York ; London : Plenum, c1981. — xiii,295p : ill ; 24cm. — (Perspectives in law & psychology ; v.3)
Bibliography: p279-286. — Includes index
ISBN 0-306-40526-1 : Unpriced B81-16193

347.3061'3 — United States. Slavery. Law. Cases involving Scott, Dred

Fehrenbacher, Don E.. Slavery, law, and politics : the Dred Scott case in historical perspective / Don E. Fehrenbacher. — Abridged ed. — Oxford : Oxford University Press, 1981. — viii,326p : 2ill ; 21cm. — (A Galaxy book)
Previous ed.: i.e. full ed. published as Dred Scott case. 1978. — Bibliography: p309-311. — Includes index
ISBN 0-19-502882-1 (cased) : Unpriced
ISBN 0-295-02883-x (pbk) : Unpriced B81-37941

347.3063'32 — United States. Psychotherapy. Malpractices. Law

Furrow, Barry R.. Malpractice in psychotherapy / Barry R. Furrow. — Lexington, Mass. : Lexington Books ; [Aldershot] : Gower [distributor], 1981, c1980. — xiv,157p ; 24cm
Includes index
ISBN 0-669-03399-5 : £12.50 B81-32986

347.3063'82 — United States. Products. Defects. Liability of manufacturers & retailers. Law

Smith, Charles O.. Products liability : are you vulnerable / Charles O. Smith. — Englewood Cliffs ; London : Prentice-Hall, c1981. — xi,340p : ill ; 25cm
Includes index
ISBN 0-13-725036-3 : £16.20 B81-14675

347.3064'82 — United States. Copyright. Law

Strong, William S.. The copyright book : a practical guide / William S. Strong. — Cambridge, Mass. ; London : MIT Press, c1981. — x,211p ; 21cm
Includes index
ISBN 0-262-19194-6 : £8.75 B81-39638

347.3064'82 — United States. Copyright. Law — *For authors*

Patton, Warren L.. An author's guide to the copyright law / Warren L. Patton. — Lexington, Mass. : Lexington Books ; [Aldershot] : Gower [distributor], 1980. — x,192p ; 24cm
Includes index
ISBN 0-669-00740-4 : £13.00 B81-30641

347.3064'82'024097 — United States. Copyright. Law — *For publishing*

Scarles, Christopher. Copyright / Christopher Scarles. — Cambridge : Cambridge University Press, 1980. — iv,40p ; 22cm. — (Cambridge authors' and publishers' guides)
ISBN 0-521-29740-0 (pbk) : £1.80
Primary classification 344.1064'82'024097 B81-09826

347.3065'4 — United States. Wills. Law — *For testators*

Ashley, Paul P.. You and your will : the planning and management of your estate / Paul P. Ashley. — Rev. ed. — New York ; London : McGraw-Hill, c1977. — xiii,274p ; 22cm
Previous ed.: 1975. — Includes index
ISBN 0-07-002415-4 : £8.65 B81-05107

347.306'66 — United States. Public companies. Company information. Disclosure. Law. Social aspects

Stevenson, Russell B.. Corporations and information : secrecy, access and disclosure / Russell B. Stevenson, Jr. — Baltimore ; London : Johns Hopkins University Press, c1980. — xii,226p ; 24cm
Includes index
ISBN 0-8018-2344-7 : £10.75 B81-04931

347.306′6642 — United States. Companies. Managers. Responsibility. Legal aspects

Groening, William A.. The modern corporate manager : responsibility and regulation / William A. Groening. — New York ; London : McGraw-Hill, c1981. — xii,274p ; 25cm. — (Regulation of American business and industry series)
Includes index
ISBN 0-07-024940-7 : £17.50 B81-32453

347.306′666 — United States. ***Securities and Exchange Commission, to 1980***

Phillips, Susan M.. The SEC and the public interest / Susan M. Phillips and J. Richard Zecher. — Cambridge, Mass ; London : MIT, c1981. — 177p : ill ; 23cm. — (MIT Press series on the regulation of economic activity ; 2)
Bibliography: p167-174. — Includes index
ISBN 0-262-16080-3 : £12.25 B81-39759

347.306′7 — United States. Commercial law

Harron, Thomas J.. Business law / Thomas J. Harron. — Boston, Mass. ; London : Allyn and Bacon, c1981. — 1038p in various pagings : col.ill ; 25cm
Includes index
ISBN 0-205-07259-3 : Unpriced B81-26215

Harron, Thomas J.. Instructor's manual to accompany Business law / Thomas J. Harron. — Boston ; London : Allyn and Bacon, c1981. — iv,208p ; 22cm
ISBN 0-205-07260-7 (pbk) : Unpriced B81-27705

347.306′7′076 — United States. Commercial law — *Questions & answers*

Harron, Thomas J.. Test manual to accompany Business law / Thomas J. Harron. — Boston [Mass.] ; London : Allyn and Bacon, c1981. — 366p ; 22cm
ISBN 0-205-07552-5 (pbk) : £1.00 B81-26398

347.3071 — United States. Judiciary. Political aspects

Neely, Richard. How courts govern America. — London : Yale University Press, Sept.1981. — [256]p
ISBN 0-300-02589-0 : £9.45 : CIP entry B81-30242

347.307′24′09 — United States. Federal courts of appeal, *1960-1979 — Case studies*

Howard, J. Woodford. Courts of appeals in the federal judicial systems : a study of the Second, Fifth, and District of Columbia Circuits / J. Woodford Howard, Jr. — Princeton ; Guildford : Princeton University Press, c1981. — xxvi,415p : ill ; 25cm
Includes index
ISBN 0-691-07623-5 (cased) : £18.10
ISBN 0-691-10100-0 (pbk) : £7.00 B81-26119

347.307′26′09 — United States. ***Supreme Court, 1969-1975***

Woodward, Bob. The brethren : inside the Supreme Court. — London : Hodder & Stoughton, Nov.1981. — [576]p. — (Coronet books)
Originally published: London : Secker & Warburg, 1980
ISBN 0-340-26781-x (pbk) : £1.95 : CIP entry B81-30137

347.307′262 — United States. Constitutional law. Interpretation. Role of United States. ***Supreme Court***

Choper, Jesse H.. Judicial review and the national political process : a functional reconsideration of the role of the Supreme Court / Jesse H. Choper. — Chicago ; London : University of Chicago Press, 1980. — xviii,494p ; 24cm
Includes index
ISBN 0-226-10443-5 : £17.10 B81-08333

347.307′5 — United States. Law courts. Procedure. Psychosocial aspects

The **Trial** process / edited by Bruce Dennis Sales. — New York ; London : Plenum, c1981. — xvi,506p : ill,2forms ; 24cm. — (Perspectives in law & psychology ; v.2)
Includes bibliographies and index
ISBN 0-306-40491-5 : Unpriced B81-18206

347.307′72 — United States. Civil law. Cases. Documents. Discovery & inspection. Law. Compared with law of discovery in England

Levine, Julius Byron. Discovery. — Oxford : Clarendon Press, Dec.1981. — [300]p
ISBN 0-19-825368-0 : £15.00 : CIP entry
Primary classification 344.207′72 B81-31740

347.4407′1′0264 — Massachusetts. Boston. Civil courts. Cases, ***1880-1900.*** **Social aspects**

Silverman, Robert A.. Law and urban growth : civil litigation in the Boston trial courts, 1880-1900 / Robert A. Silverman. — Princeton ; Guildford : Princeton University Press, c1981. — xiv,217p : maps ; 23cm
Bibliography: p199-211. — Includes index
ISBN 0-691-04677-8 : £9.20 B81-18560

347.47061′8 — New York ***(City).*** **Vanderbilt, Gloria,** ***1924-.*** **Custody. Petition by Vanderbilt, Gloria,** ***1904-1965, 1934***

Goldsmith, Barbara. Little Gloria — happy at last / Barbara Goldsmith. — London : Macmillan, 1980. — xvii,650p : ill,facsims,geneal.tables,ports ; 24cm
Originally published: New York : Knopf, 1980. — Geneal.tables on lining papers. — Bibliography: p622-632. — Includes index
ISBN 0-333-29508-0 : £9.95 B81-02851

347.47064′09 — New York ***(State).*** **Married women. Property. Law,** ***1837-1902***

Rabkin, Peggy A.. Fathers to daughters : the legal foundations of female emancipation / Peggy A. Rabkin. — Westport, Conn. ; London : Greenwood Press, 1980. — viii,214p ; 25cm. — (Contributions in legal studies, ISSN 0147-1074 ; no.11)
Bibliography: p191-205. — Includes index
ISBN 0-313-20670-8 : £15.95 B81-23464

347.502′873 — United States. Southern states. Negro slavery. Law

Tushnet, Mark. The American law of slavery 1810-1860 : considerations of humanity and interest. — Princeton ; Guildford : Princeton University Press, 1981. — viii,262p ; 23cm
Bibliography: p248-250. — Includes index
ISBN 0-691-04681-6 (cased) : £12.30
ISBN 0-691-10104-3 (pbk) : £5.85 B81-39260

347.94035′4 — California. Real property. Taxation. Law. Reform. Proposals: Proposition 13

Kemp, Roger L.. Coping with Proposition 13 / Roger L. Kemp. — Lexington : Lexington Books ; [Farnborough, Hants.] : Gower [distributor], 1981, c1980. — xv,222p : ill ; 24cm
Bibliography: p205-215. — Includes index
ISBN 0-669-03974-8 : £13.50 B81-22949

347.9505′4 — United States. Criminal law. Defences: Insanity *— Study regions: Oregon*

Nissman, David M.. Beating the insanity defense : denying the license to kill / David M. Nissman, Brian R. Barnes, Geoffrey P. Alpert. — Lexington, Mass : Lexington Books ; [Aldershot] : Gower [distributor], 1981, c1980. — vii,179p ; 24cm
Bibliography: p171-175. — Includes index
ISBN 0-669-03943-8 : £12.00 B81-26971

349 — LAW. OCEANIA, ATLANTIC OCEAN ISLANDS, POLAR REGIONS, ETC

349.07′1′0924 — South Pacific islands. Law courts *— Personal observations — Humour*

Overton, Robert. Palm court / Robert Overton ; illustrations by John Lawrence. — London (27 George St., W1P 1FD) : Robin Clark, 1980, c1979. — 153p : ill ; 20cm
Originally published: London : O. Hamilton, 1979
ISBN 0-86072-038-1 (pbk) : £1.95
Primary classification 345.3′6071′0924 B81-03565

349.31063′23 — New Zealand. Accidents. Personal injuries. Compensation. Law

Ison, Terence G.. Accident compensation : a commentary on the New Zealand scheme / Terence G. Ison. — London : Croom Helm, c1980. — 201p ; 23cm
Includes index
ISBN 0-7099-0249-2 : £14.95 : CIP rev. B80-18636

349.31063′23 — New Zealand. Accidents. Personal injuries. Compensation. Law. Reform, ***1967-1979***

Palmer, Geoffrey, *19---*. Compensation for incapacity : a study of law and social change in New Zealand and Australia / Geoffrey Palmer. — Wellington [N.Z.] ; Oxford : Oxford University Press, c1979. — 460p ; 25cm
Includes index
ISBN 0-19-558045-1 : £17.25
Also classified at 349.4063′23 B81-04578

349.4061′3 — Queensland. Australian aborigines. Legal status

Nettheim, Garth. Victims of the law. — London : Allen & Unwin, Jan.1982. — [216]p
ISBN 0-86861-395-9 : £17.95 : CIP entry B81-34636

349.4063′23 — Australia. Accidents. Personal injuries. Compensation. Law. Reform, ***1973-1979***

Palmer, Geoffrey, *19---*. Compensation for incapacity : a study of law and social change in New Zealand and Australia / Geoffrey Palmer. — Wellington [N.Z.] ; Oxford : Oxford University Press, c1979. — 460p ; 25cm
Includes index
ISBN 0-19-558045-1 : £17.25
Primary classification 349.31063′23 B81-04578

350 — PUBLIC ADMINISTRATION

350′.0001 — Public administration. Theories

Steiss, Alan Walter. Performance administration : improved responsiveness and effectiveness in public service / Alan Walter Steiss, Gregory A. Daneke. — Lexington : Lexington Books ; [Farnborough, Hants.] : Gower [distributor], 1981, c1980. — xi,267p : ill ; 24cm
Includes index
ISBN 0-669-03637-4 : £13.50 B81-09607

350′.0007′1141 — Great Britain. Further education institutions & higher education institutions. Curriculum subjects: Public administration. Teaching *— Serials*

Teaching public administration. — Vol.1, no.4 (May 1979)-. — London : [Public Administration Committee], Joint University Council for Social and Public Administration ; Manchester (Department of Administrative Studies, University of Manchester, Precinct Centre, Oxford Rd, Manchester M13 9QS) : The Editor [Distributor], 1979-. — v. ; 21cm
Two issues yearly. — Issued in collaboration with: The Politics Association. — Continues: Public administration teacher. — Description based on: Vol.1, no.5 (Jan.1980)
ISSN 0144-7394 = Teaching public administration : Unpriced B81-00793

350′.0009172′4 — Developing countries. Public administration *— Serials*

Public administration and development : an international journal of training, research and practice. — Vol.1, no.1 (Jan.-Mar.1981)-. — Chichester : Wiley, 1981-. — v. ; 25cm
Quarterly. — Journal of: Royal Institute of Public Administration. — Continues: Journal of administration overseas
ISSN 0271-2075 : £25.00 per year B81-20427

350′.000941 — Great Britain. Public administration, ***1780-1870***

Chester, ***Sir*** **Norman**. The English administrative system 1780-1870 / Sir Norman Chester. — Oxford : Clarendon Press, 1981. — 398p ; 23cm
Bibliography: p385-389. — Includes index
ISBN 0-19-822643-8 : £22.50 : CIP rev. B81-00794

350′.000941 — Great Britain. Public administration *— For business studies*

Sallis, E. J.. The machinery of government : an introduction to public administration / E.J. Sallis. — London : Holt, Rinehart and Winston, c1981. — 70p : ill,maps ; 30cm. — (Holt business texts)
ISBN 0-03-910303-x (pbk) : £1.50 B81-23099

350′.000942 — England. Public administration, *400-1485*

Lyon, Bryce. A constitutional and legal history of medieval England / Bryce Lyon. — 2nd ed. — New York ; London : Norton, c1980. — xviii,669p : maps ; 24cm
Previous ed.: 1960. — Bibliography: p650-652. - Includes index
ISBN 0-393-95132-4 : £9.50
Primary classification 344.2′009 B81-03966

350′.0009669 — Nigeria. Public administration

Adebayo, Augustus. Principles and practice of public administration in Nigeria / Augustus Adebayo. — Chichester : Published in association with Spectrum by Wiley, c1981. — xiv,193p ; 24cm
Includes index
ISBN 0-471-27897-1 (cased) : £10.00 : CIP rev.
ISBN 0-471-27898-x (pbk) : Unpriced
B81-02108

350′.00096894 — Zambia. Public administration, *1964-1978*

Administration in Zambia / edited by William Tordoff. — Manchester : Manchester University Press, 1980. — xi,306p : 1map ; 23cm
Bibliography: p278-294. — Includes index
ISBN 0-7190-0785-2 : £22.50 : CIP rev.
B80-11807

350′.000973 — United States. Public administration

Gortner, Harold F.. Administration in the public sector / Harold F. Gortner. — 2nd ed. — New York ; Chichester : Wiley, c1981. — xiii,413p : ill ; 24cm
Previous ed.: 1977. — Includes bibliographies and index
ISBN 0-471-06320-7 : £9.35 B81-11309

350′.001 — Bureaucracy

Jackson, Peter McLeod. The political economy of bureaucracy. — Oxford : Philip Allan, Oct.1981. — [296]p
ISBN 0-86003-024-5 : £12.50 : CIP entry
B81-31949

350′.001′0947 — Soviet Union. Public administration. Bureaucracy, *1600-1930*

Russian officialdom : the bureaucratization of Russian society from the seventeenth to the twentieth century / edited by Walter McKenzie Pintner and Don Karl Rowney ; contributors Helju Aulik Bennett ... [et al.]. — London : Macmillan, 1980. — xvii,396p ; 24cm
Originally published: Chapel Hill : University of North Carolina Press, 1980. — Bibliography: p381-286. - Includes index
ISBN 0-333-28748-7 : £20.00 : CIP rev.
B80-04116

351 — CENTRAL GOVERNMENT ADMINISTRATION

351 — Governments. Efficiency. Effects of size

Rose, Richard, *1933-*. What if anything is wrong with big government / by Richard Rose. — Glasgow (16 Richmond St., Glasgow G1 1XQ) : University of Strathclyde, Centre for the Study of Public Policy, 1981. — 47p : 1ill ; 30cm. — (Studies in public policy, ISSN 0140-8240 ; no.76)
Bibliography: p42-47
Unpriced (pbk) B81-11340

351′.000966 — West Africa. Government, *to 1980* *— For West African students*

Ward, W. E. F.. Government in West Africa / by W.E.F. Ward. — 6th rev. ed.. — London : Allen & Unwin, 1981. — 383p ; 22cm
Previous ed.: 1976. — Bibliography: p10. — Includes index
ISBN 0-04-351059-0 (pbk) : Unpriced : CIP rev. B81-12838

351.003′73′096 — Government. Role of law courts *— Study regions: Africa. English speaking countries*

Amissah, A. N. E.. The contribution of the courts to government. — Oxford : Clarendon Press, July 1981. — [385]p
ISBN 0-19-825356-7 : £22.50 : CIP entry
B81-19197

351.007′2 — Governments. Policies. Formulation. Role of law *— Serials*

Law & policy quarterly : an interdisciplinary journal. — Vol.1, no.1 (Jan.1979)-. — Beverly Hills ; London : Sage, 1979-. — v. ; 22cm
Description based on: Vol.2, no.1 (Jan.1980)
ISSN 0164-0267 = Law & policy quarterly : Unpriced B81-29091

351.007′25′091713 — Western bloc countries. Governments. Policies. Change. Decision making

Peters, B. Guy. Policy succession : the dynamics of policy change / B. Guy Peters & Brian W. Hogwood. — Glasgow (University of Strathclyde, McCance Building, 16 Richmond St., Glasgow G1 1XQ) : Centre for the Study of Public Policy, 1980. — 41,3p : 1ill ; 30cm. — (Studies in public policy, ISSN 0140-8240 ; no.69)
£1.50 (pbk) B81-07959

351.007′3 — Government. Centralisation

Waller, Michael. Democratic centralism. — Manchester : Manchester University Press, Aug.1981. — [140]p
ISBN 0-7190-0802-6 : £10.00 : CIP entry
B81-17502

351.009 — Governments. Agents in Great Britain: Crown Agents for Overseas Governments and Administrations. *Holdings and Realisation Board — Accounts — Serials*

Crown Agents for Overseas Governments and Administrations. *Holdings and Realisation Board.* Accounts / Crown Agents Holdings and Realisation Board. — 1980-. — London : H.M.S.O, 1981-. — v. ; 25cm
Annual
ISSN 0262-0901 = Accounts - Crown Agents Holdings and Realisation Board : £3.00
B81-37247

351.72′2′091724 — Developing countries. Economic planning. Budgeting. Techniques

Beenhakker, Arie. A system for development planning and budgeting / Arie Beenhakker. — Farnborough, Hants. : Gower, c1980. — xii,187p : forms ; 23cm
Bibliography: p181-183. - Includes index
ISBN 0-566-00326-0 : £12.50 : CIP rev.
B80-01103

351.72′32 — Governments. Auditing

State audit : developments in public accountability / edited by B. Geist. — London : Macmillan, 1981. — xxvii,396p : ill ; 25cm
Includes index
ISBN 0-333-26569-6 : £25.00 B81-30679

351.82′33′091724 — Developing countries. Agricultural industries. Administration. Role of ministries of agriculture

Howell, John, *19---*. Ministries of agriculture and the administration of agricultural development / by John Howell. — London (10 Percy St., W1P 0JB) : Overseas Development Institute, 1980. — 14p : ; 21cm. — (Agricultural administration network discussion paper ; 4)
Unpriced (unbound) B81-27056

352 — LOCAL GOVERNMENT

352′.00023′41 — Great Britain. Local government *— Career guides*

Taylor, Felicity. Careers in local government. — London : Kogan Page, Oct.1981. — [100]p. — (Kogan Page careers series)
ISBN 0-85038-437-0 (cased) : £5.95 : CIP entry
ISBN 0-85038-438-9 (pbk) : £2.50 B81-30638

352′.00028′54 — United States. Local authorities. Digital computer systems. Management

Kraemer, Kenneth L.. The management of information systems / Kenneth L. Kraemer, William H. Dutton, Alana Northrop. — New York ; Guildford : Columbia University Press, 1981. — xvii,416p : ill ; 24cm
Includes bibliographies and index
ISBN 0-231-04886-6 : £13.80 B81-11372

352′.00028′5404 — Great Britain. Local government. Applications of microcomputer systems

′Potential demand, impact and implications of microcomputer applications′ / [LAMSAC]. — London (3 Buckingham Gate, SW1E 6JH) : [LAMSAC], 1981. — 128p : 1form ; 30cm. — (Micro computing in local government ; 3)
£3.00 (spiral) B81-38067

352′.00047 — England. Local authorities. Meetings. Law & procedure

Knowles, Raymond S. B.. The law and practice relating to local authority meetings / by Raymond S.B. Knowles. — Chichester : Rose Supplement to the first edition. — 1981. — viii,36p ; 22cm
Includes index
ISBN 0-85992-216-2 (pbk) : £5.75 B81-21870

352′.00047 — London. Waltham Forest *(London Borough).* **Local government. Corporate management**

Rowlands, David, *19---*. The impact of the introduction of corporate management on the London Borough of Waltham Forest / David Rowlands. — London (Wandsworth Rd, SW8 2JZ) : Polytechnic of South Bank, Faculty of the Built Environment, c1981. — 29leaves : ill ; 30cm. — (Occasional paper / Polytechnic of the South Bank. Department of Town Planning, ISSN 0143-4888 ; OP 1/81)
ISBN 0-905267-18-4 (spiral) : £2.00
B81-34751

352′.0004725′0941 — Great Britain. Local authorities. Decision making. Participation of public

Deprivation, participation and community action / edited by Leo Smith and David Jones. — London : Routledge & Kegan Paul, 1981. — xv,224p ; 24cm. — (Community work series ; 6)
ISBN 0-7100-0827-9 (pbk) : £5.95 : CIP rev.
B81-16379

352′.000473 — England. Local government. Reorganisation

Richards, Peter G.. The reformed local government system / by Peter G. Richards. — 4th ed. — London : Allen & Unwin, 1980. — 188p : ill ; 22cm. — (The New local government series ; no.5)
Previous ed.: 1978. — Bibliography: p180-181. — Includes index
ISBN 0-04-352090-1 (pbk) : £3.95 : CIP rev.
B80-13292

352′.000473 — France. Local government. Reform, *1940-1978.* **Political aspects**

Gourevitch, Peter Alexis. Paris and the provinces : the politics of local government reform in France / Peter Alexis Gourevitch. — London : Allen & Unwin, 1980. — xiii,251p ; 23cm
Bibliography: p239-242. — Includes index
ISBN 0-04-352095-2 : £18.00 : CIP rev.
B80-20425

352′.000473 — Great Britain. Local authorities. Management. Operations research

Pinkus, Charles E.. Solving local government problems : practical applications of operations research in cities and regions / Charles E. Pinkus, Anne Dixson. — London : Allen & Unwin, 1981. — xi,310p : ill,maps ; 24cm
Bibliography: p306-310. — Includes index
ISBN 0-04-658232-0 (cased) : Unpriced : CIP rev.
ISBN 0-04-658233-9 (pbk) : Unpriced
B81-25144

352′.000473 — Local government. Reorganisation *— Comparative studies*

Local government reform and reorganization : an international perspective / edited by Arthur B. Gunlicks. — Port Washington, N.Y. ; London : National University Publications : Kennikat, 1981. — viii,243p : ill,maps ; 23cm. — (Series in political science)
Includes index
ISBN 0-8046-9272-6 : Unpriced B81-40552

352'.000473'0942 — England. Local authorities. Organisational change. Management aspects

Haynes, Robert J.. Organisation theory and local government / Robert J. Haynes. — London : Allen & Unwin, 1980. — xii,219p : ill ; 23cm. — (The New local government series ; no.19)
Bibliography: p210-213. - Includes index
ISBN 0-04-352088-x (cased) : £12.00 : CIP rev.
ISBN 0-04-352089-8 (pbk) : £4.95 B80-13291

352'.002 — England. Local government. Complaints by public — *Serials*

Commission for Local Administration in England
Report for the year ended 31 March ... / Commission for Local Administration in England. — 1975. — [London] ([21, Queen Anne's Gate, S.W.1.]) : The Commission, 1975. — [13]p
Unpriced B81-06389

Commission for Local Administration in England. Your local ombudsman : report of the Commission for Local Administration in England for the year ended 31 March .... — 1976-. — London (21 Queen Anne's Gate, SW1H 9BU) : The Commission, 1976-. — v. ; 21cm
Continues: Commission for Local Administration in England. Report for the year ended 31 March ... (1975). — Description based on: 1979
Unpriced B81-16750

Commission for Local Administration in England. Your local ombudsman / Commission for Local Administration in England. — 1980. — London (21 Queen Anne's Gate, SW1H 9BU) : The Commission, [1980?]. — 64p
Unpriced B81-16749

352'.002 — Great Britain. Local government. Corruption, *ca 1955-1972:* **Poulson case**

Gillard, Michael. Nothing to declare : the political corruptions of John Poulson / by Michael Gillard and Martin Tomkinson. — London : John Calder, 1980. — xii,340p ; 23cm. — (A Platform book)
Includes index
ISBN 0-7145-3625-3 (cased) : £12.95 : CIP rev.
ISBN 0-7145-3629-6 (pbk) : £6.95 B80-10541

352'.002 — Northern Ireland. Local government. Complaints by public — *Serials*

Great Britain. *Northern Ireland Commissioner for Complaints***Annual** report of the Northern Ireland Commissioner for Complaints. — 1980. — London : H.M.S.O., 1981. — 134p
ISBN 0-10-235181-3 : £5.70 B81-33311

352'.002 — Scotland. Local government. Complaints by public — *Serials*

Great Britain. *Commissioner for Local Administration in Scotland.* Report of the Commissioner for Local Administration in Scotland for the year ended 31 March ... — 1981. — Edinburgh : Commission for Local Authority Accounts in Scotland : [Distributed by H.M.S.O.], 1981. — 25p
ISBN 0-11-887418-7 : £2.50
ISSN 0140-4407 B81-36552

352'.0072 — Cities. Local government. Geographical aspects

Barlow, I. M.. Spatial dimensions of urban government / I.M. Barlow. — Chichester : Research Studies Press, c1981. — x,199p : ill,maps ; 24cm. — (Geographical research studies series)
Bibliography: p185-194. — Includes index
ISBN 0-471-27978-1 : £17.50 : CIP rev.
B81-01843

352'.0072'072073 — United States. Urban regions. Local authorities. Services. Operations research

Larson, Richard C.. Urban operations research / Richard C. Larson and Amadeo R. Odoni. — Englewood Cliffs ; London : Prentice-Hall, c1981. — xviii,573p : ill ; 24cm
Bibliography: 559-560. — Includes index
ISBN 0-13-939447-8 : £20.80 B81-17204

352'.0072'09411 — Scotland. Community councils

Martin, Tony, *1942 Apr.22-.* Some aspects of the political geography of community councils in Scotland / Tony Martin. — [Glasgow] : University of Strathclyde, Department of Geography, 1981. — 17leaves : ill,maps ; 30cm. — (Research seminar series / University of Strathclyde Department of Geography ; no.11)
Some leaves printed on both sides
Unpriced (pbk) B81-29255

352'.0072'09411 — Scotland. Community councils — *Inquiry reports*

Developing democracy : the first report of the Community Councils Working Party. — Edinburgh : Scottish Council of Social Service, 1980. — 21p ; 30cm
Cover title
ISBN 0-903589-43-5 (pbk) : £0.50 B81-32342

352'.0072'094125 — Scotland. Tayside Region. Community councils, *1976-1979*

Masterson, Michael P.. Community councils in Tayside and Fife Regions : the first three years (October 1976-1979) : final report of research project / undertaken by M.P. Masterson ; for the Scottish Development Department. — Edinburgh (Central Research Unit, Room 5/72, New St. Andrew's House, Edinburgh EH1 3SZ) : Scottish Office, 1980. — vi,87p ; 30cm
Text on cover. — Bibliography: p86-87
Unpriced (pbk)
Also classified at 352'.0072'094129 B81-29930

352'.0072'094129 — Scotland. Fife Region. Community councils, *1976-1979*

Masterson, Michael P.. Community councils in Tayside and Fife Regions : the first three years (October 1976-1979) : final report of research project / undertaken by M.P. Masterson ; for the Scottish Development Department. — Edinburgh (Central Research Unit, Room 5/72, New St. Andrew's House, Edinburgh EH1 3SZ) : Scottish Office, 1980. — vi,87p ; 30cm
Text on cover. — Bibliography: p86-87
Unpriced (pbk)
Primary classification 352'.0072'094125
B81-29930

352'.0072'094141 — Scotland. Strathclyde Region. Community councils, *1976-1979*

Cosgrove, D. F.. Community councils in Strathclyde Region : the first three years (October 1976-1979) : final report of research project / undertaken by D.F. Cosgrove and H.N. Sheldon ; for the Scottish Development Department. — Edinburgh (Central Research Unit, Room 5/72, New St. Andrew House, Edinburgh EH1 3SZ) : Scottish Office, 1980. — ix,61p : ill ; 30cm
Text on cover
Unpriced (pbk) B81-29929

352'.0072'09429 — Wales. Community councils. Boundaries — *Proposals*

Local Government Boundary Commission for Wales. Special community review / Local Government Boundary Commission for Wales = Arolwg cymdeithas arbennig / Comisiwn Ffiniau Llywodraeth Leol i Gymru. — [Cardiff] ([Queens Court, Plymouth St., Cardiff CF1 4DA]) : [The Commission]
Parallel Welsh and English text
Draft proposals Aberconwy = Cynigion drafft Aberconwy. — [1981]. — 16p : 1col.map ; 30cm
Col.map (1 folded sheet) as insert
Unpriced (spiral) B81-14111

Local Government Boundary Commission for Wales. Special community review / Local Government Boundary Commission for Wales = Arolwg cymdeithas arbennig / Comisiwn Ffiniau Llywodraeth Leol i Gymru. — [Cardiff] ([Queens Court, Plymouth St., Cardiff CF1 4DA]) : [The Commission]
Report and proposals for Borough of Delyn = Adroddiad a chynigion ar gyfer Bwrdeistref Delyn. — [1981?]. — 177p : 1col.map ; 30cm
Parallel Welsh and English text. — Map on folded sheet in pocket
Unpriced (spiral) B81-37875

Local Government Boundary Commission for Wales. Special community review / Local Government Boundary Commission for Wales = Arolwg cymdeithas arbennig / Comisiwn Ffiniau Llywodraeth Leol i Gymru. — [Cardiff] ([Queens Court, Plymouth St., Cardiff CFI 4DA]) : [The Commission]
Parallel Welsh and English text
Report and proposals for Borough of Ogwr = Adroddiad a chynigion ar gyfer Bwrdeistref Ogwr. — [1980]. — 209p : 1col.map ; 30cm
Map on folded sheet in pocket
Unpriced (spiral) B81-07536

Local Government Boundary Commission for Wales. Special community review / Local Government Boundary Commission for Wales = Arolwg cymdeithas arbennig / Comisiwn Ffiniau Llywodraeth Leol i Gymru. — [Cardiff] ([Queens Court, Plymouth St., Cardiff CF1 4DA]) : [The Commission]
Report and proposals for District of Alyn and Deeside = Adroddiad a chynigion ar gyfer Dosbarth Alun A Glannau Dyfrdwy. — [1981?]. — 123p,[1]leaf of plates : 2col.maps ; 30cm
Parallel Welsh and English text. — Map on folded sheet in pocket
Unpriced (spiral) B81-37874

Local Government Boundary Commission for Wales. Special community review / Local Government Boundary Commission for Wales = Arolwg cymdeithas arbennig / Comisiwn Ffiniau Llywodaeth Leol i Gymru. — [Cardiff] ([Queens Court, Plymouth St., Cardiff CF1 4DA]) : [The Commission]
Parallel Welsh and English text
Report and proposals for District of Meirionnydd = Adroddiad a chynigion ar gyfer Dosbarth Meirionnydd. — [1979]. — 173p : 1col.map ; 30cm
Map on folded sheet in pocket
Unpriced B81-07535

Local Government Boundary Commission for Wales. Special community review / Local Government Boundary Commission for Wales = Arolwg cymdeithas arbennig / Comisiwn Ffiniau Llywodraeth Leol i Gymru. — [Cardiff] ([Queens Court, Plymonth St., Cardiff CF1 4DA]) : [The Commission]
Report and proposals for District of South Pembrokeshire = Adroddiad a chynigion ar gyfer Dosbarth de Penfro. — [1981]. — 127p : 1map ; 30cm
Unpriced (spiral) B81-33353

352'.00722 — England. Parish councils. Role — *Proposals*

Future of English local government from the view point of the parishes. — London (108 Great Russell St., WC1B 3LD) : National Association of Local Councils, [1981]. — [16]p ; 21cm
Unpriced (unbound)
Also classified at 352'.00723'0942 B81-18636

352'.00723'0942 — England. Town councils. Role — *Proposals*

Future of English local government from the view point of the parishes. — London (108 Great Russell St., WC1B 3LD) : National Association of Local Councils, [1981]. — [16]p ; 21cm
Unpriced (unbound)
Primary classification 352'.00722 B81-18636

352'.00724 — Cities. Local government. Political aspects

Goldsmith, Michael. Politics, planning and the city / Michael Goldsmith. — London : Hutchinson, 1980. — 216p : ill,1map ; 23cm. — (The Built environment series)
Bibliography: p198-209. — Includes index
ISBN 0-09-141370-2 (cased) : £9.50 : CIP rev.
ISBN 0-09-141371-0 (pbk) : £4.95 B80-23102

352'.0073'06042 — England. County councils. Organisations: Association of County Councils — *Serials*

Association of County Councils. Year book / Association of County Councils. — 1980-81. — London (Eaton House, 66A, Eaton Square, SW1 9BH) : The Association, 1980. — 157p
ISSN 0305-2044 : £1.00 B81-10267

352′.0073′09411 — Scotland. Counties. Government, *1700-1900*
Whetstone, Ann E.. Scottish county government : in the eighteenth and nineteenth centuries / Ann E. Whetstone. — Edinburgh (138 St. Stephen St., Edinburgh) : John Donald Publishing Ltd., c1981. — xiv,165p ; 24cm
Bibliography: p151-159. — Includes index
ISBN 0-85976-061-8 : £12.50 B81-12268

352′.0073′0942 — England. Local authorities. Wards. Establishment, *1973-1980*
Local Government Boundary Commission for England. Local Government Boundary Commission for England report no.413. — London : H.M.S.O., 1981. — iii,18p ; 25cm
ISBN 0-11-751558-2 (pbk) : £3.00 B81-39993

352′.0073′094233 — Dorset. Boundaries. Reform, *to 1974*
Wood, R. L. C.. Dorset : the county's boundary / R.L.C. Wood. — [Sherborne] ([27 Richmond Road, Sherborne, Dorset DT9 3HL]) : R.L.C. Wood, [1981]. — 15p : 1map ; 30cm
Unpriced (pbk) B81-40216

352′.0094′0973 — United States. Conurbations. Local government. Political aspects
Lewis, Eugene. Urban America : politics and policy. — 2nd ed. / Eugene Lewis, Frank Anechiarico. — New York ; London : Holt, Rinehart and Winston, c1981. — xiii,295p : ill,maps ; 24cm
Previous ed.: published as The urban political system / by Eugene Lewis. Hinsdale : Dryden Press, 1973. — Includes bibliographies and index
ISBN 0-03-050391-4 (pbk) : £8.50 B81-22883

352.041 — Great Britain. Local authorities — *Directories*
The **Oyez** directory of local authorities : in England, Wales and Scotland. — 1980 ed. — London : Oyez, 1981. — viii,159p ; 25cm
Previous ed.: London : Solicitors' Law Stationery Society, 1961
ISBN 0-85120-557-7 (pbk) : Unpriced B81-29952

352.041 — Great Britain. Local government
Byrne, A.. Local government in Britain : everyone's guide to how it all works / Tony Byrne. — Harmondsworth : Penguin, 1981. — 347p : ill ; 20cm. — (Pelican books)
Bibliography: p299-307. — Includes index
ISBN 0-14-022225-1 (pbk) : £2.95 B81-37254

352.041 — Great Britain. Local government — *For health services administration*
Wood, Bruce. The organisation of local government for Health Service administrators / B. Wood. — Manchester ([c/o Mrs. W. Bennett, Booth Street West, Manchester M15 6PB]) : Health Services Management Unit Department of Social Administration, University of Manchester, 1981. — 14,3leaves ; 30cm. — (Working paper series / University of Manchester. Health Services Management Unit, ISSN 0141-2647 : no.39)
£2.00 (pbk) B81-16696

352.041′025 — Great Britain. Local authorities — *Directories — Serials*
Public authorities directory. — 1981. — London (11 Bury St., EC34 5AP) : Brown Knight & Truscott (Holdings) Ltd, [1981]. — 462p
ISBN 0-904677-13-3 : £16.00
ISSN 0306-0470 B81-30737

352.0411 — Scotland. Local authorities — *Directories — Serials*
Scotlands regions. — 49th ed. (1980-81). — Coupar Angus : Culross & Son in association with the Scottish Council (Development and Industry), [1980?]. — xi,360p
ISBN 0-900323-44-2 : Unpriced
ISSN 0305-6562 B81-05217

352.0413′1′05 — Central Region. *Regional Council.* **Policies —** *Serials*
Central Region. *Regional Council.* Central Region regional report. — 1976-. — [Stirling] ([Viewforth, Stirling FK8 2ET]) : Central Regional Council, 1976-. — v. ; 30cm
Issued every two years. — Description based on: 1978 issue
ISSN 0260-8529 = Central Region regional report : £2.50 B81-10253

352.0413′18 — Scotland. Central Region. Falkirk. Community councils: Falkirk Central Community Council — *Serials*
[News letter *(Falkirk Central Community Council)*]. News letter / Falkirk Central Community Council. — No.1 (Jan.1981)-. — Falkirk (c/o Mrs. A. Kay, 6a Weir St., Falkirk FK1 1RA) : The Council, 1981-. — v. : ill ; 21cm
Six issues yearly
ISSN 0261-8877 = News letter - Falkirk Central Community Council : Unpriced B81-36293

352.0415 — Ireland. Local government
Roche, D.. Local government in Ireland. — Dublin : Institute of Public Administration, Oct.1981. — [300]p
ISBN 0-906980-06-2 : £12.00 : CIP entry B81-30637

352.042 — England. Local authorities. Organisation structure
Patterns of management in local government / Royston Greenwood ... [et al.]. — Oxford : Robertson, 1980. — 185p : ill ; 23cm. — (Government and administration series)
Bibliography: p173-197. - Includes index
ISBN 0-85520-244-0 : £12.50 : CIP rev. B80-11806

352.042 — England. Local authorities. Powers — *For Labour Party (Great Britain) councillors*
Local government hand book : England & Wales. — 7th ed. — [London] : Labour Party, 1981. — 1v.(loose-leaf) ; 23cm
Previous ed.: 1977. — Includes index
ISBN 0-86117-064-4 : £7.50 B81-15981

352.042 — England. Local government. Reform, *1888-1974*
Pearce, Clifford. The machinery of change in local government 1888-1974 : a study of central involvement / Clifford Pearce. — London : Allen & Unwin for the Institute of Local Government Studies, University of Birmingham, 1980. — 263p ; 23cm
Bibliography: p252-254. — Includes index
ISBN 0-04-352091-x : £15.00 : CIP rev. B80-18201

352.0422′91 — Newbury. *District Council.* **Management —** *Proposals*
Newbury. *Performance Review Committee.* Review of establishment : a new management structure for the 80's : first report of the Performance Review Committee, Newbury District Council. — [Newbury] ([Council Offices, Cheap St., Newbury RG14 5BJ]) : [The Council], 1981. — 1v(various pagings) : 2ill ; 30cm
Unpriced (spiral) B81-24773

352.0423′38 — Winton. *Urban District Council*
Young, J. A. (John Anthony). Winton and Moordown, 1894 to 1901 / J.A. Young. — Bournemouth (The Teachers' Centre, 40 Lowther Rd., Bournemouth) : Bournemouth Local Studies Publications, 1981. — 38p : 2maps ; 21cm
ISBN 0-906287-32-4 (pbk) : £0.50 B81-33021

352.0425′2 — Nottinghamshire. Community councils: Community Council for Nottinghamshire — *Serials*
Nottinghamshire link : the newsletter of the Community Council for Nottinghamshire. — Vol.1, no.1 (Spring 1978)-. — Nottingham (110 Mansfield Rd, Nottingham NG1 3HL) : The Council, 1978-. — v. : ill ; 30cm
Quarterly
ISSN 0144-0683 = Nottinghamshire link : Unpriced B81-09215

352.0428′43′0922 — North Yorkshire. York. Lord mayors, *to 1980*
Kightly, Charles. Lords of the city : the lord mayors of York and their mansion house / Charles Kightly and Rachel Semlyen ; with illustrations by Ingrid Johnson. — [York] ([Dr Grey House, Exhibition Sq., York YO1 2HB]) : York City Council, c1981. — 96p : ill,facsims,ports(some col.) ; 25cm
Unpriced (pbk) B81-25194

352.0428′76 — England. Local government. Political aspects — *Study regions: Tyne and Wear (Metropolitan County). Newcastle upon Tyne*
Green, David G.. Power and party in an English city : an account of single-party rule / David G. Green. — London : Allen & Unwin, 1981. — 230p ; 23cm. — (The new local government series ; no.20)
Bibliography: p220-227. — Includes index
ISBN 0-04-352094-4 : £15.00 : CIP rev. B80-23103

352.044′28 — France. Mons-en-Baroeul. Local government. Role of Union de la gauche, *ca 1975-1978*
Loew, Sebastian. An experiment in local democracy in France / Sebastian Loew. — London (Wandsworth Rd., SW8 2JZ) : Polytechnic of the South Bank Faculty of the Built Environment, c1980. — 25p ; 30cm. — (Occasional paper / Polytechnic of South Bank Department of Town Planning, ISSN 0143-4888 ; 1/80)
ISBN 0-905267-15-x (spiral) : Unpriced B81-16514

352.0563 — Turkey. Istanbul. Galata. Local government, *ca 1850-1870*
Rosenthal, Steven T.. The politics of dependency : urban reform in Istanbul / Steven T. Rosenthal. — Westport, Conn. ; London : Greenwood Press, 1980. — xxix,220p : ill,2maps,1port ; 22cm. — (Contributions in comparative colonial studies, ISSN 0163-3813 ; no.3)
Bibliography: p207-213. — Includes index
ISBN 0-313-20927-8 : Unpriced B81-04656

352.0595′1 — Peninsular Malaysia. Local government, *ca 1900-1979*
Norris, M. W.. Local goverment in peninsular Malaysia / M.W. Norris. — Farnborough, Hants. : Gower, c1980. — viii,121p : ill,maps ; 23cm
Bibliography: p115-117. - Includes index
ISBN 0-566-00283-3 : £9.50 : CIP rev. B80-02711

352.073 — United States. Local government
Berman, David R.. State and local politics / David R. Berman ; John C. Bollens, Consulting editor. — 3rd ed. — Boston [Mass.] ; London : Allyn and Bacon, c1981. — xiv395p : ill,maps ; 25cm
Previous ed: Boston, Mass. : Holbrook Press, 1978. — Bibliography: p259-380. - Includes index
ISBN 0-205-07219-4 : £16.95
Also classified at 353.9 B81-00795

Maddox, Russell W.. State and local government / Russell W. Maddox, Robert F. Fuquay. — 4th ed. — New York ; London : Van Nostrand, c1981. — ix,454p : 1ill ; 25cm
Previous ed.: 1975. — Includes index
ISBN 0-442-24454-1 : £15.25
Primary classification 353.9 B81-37025

352.0773′11′0924 — Illinois. Chicago. Mayors: Daley, Richard J. — *Irish texts*
Ó Gadhra, Nollaig. Rịchard J. Daley : meạra Chicago / Nollaig Ó Gadhra. — Baile Átha Ċliath [i.e. Dublin] ([29 Sraid Ui Chonaill Ioch] Baile Átha Cliath 1) : Foilseacháin Náisiúnta. — 246p,[4]p of plates : ill,ports ; 23cm
Includes index
£3.00 B81-21890

352.0778′411 — Missouri. Kansas City. Local government. Corruption. Role of Pendergast, Jim & Pendergast, Tom
Dorsett, Lyle W.. The Pendergast machine / Lyle W. Dorsett. — Lincoln, Neb. ; London : University of Nebraska Press, 1980, c1968. — xiv,163p : maps ; 22cm
Originally published: New York : Oxford University Press, 1968. — Bibliography: p151-152. - Includes index
ISBN 0-8032-1655-6 (cased) : £8.00
ISBN 0-8032-6554-9 (pbk) : £2.40 B81-06462

352.0931 — New Zealand. Local government

Bush, Graham W. A.. Local government and politics in New Zealand / Graham W.A. Bush. — Auckland ; London : Allen & Unwin, 1980. — 256p : ill ; 23cm
Bibliography: p247. — Includes index
ISBN 0-86861-074-7 (cased) : £12.95
ISBN 0-86861-082-8 (pbk) : £5.95 B81-04881

Scott, Claudia D.. Local and regional government in New Zealand, : function and finance / Claudia D. Scott. — Sydney ; London : Allen & Unwin, 1979. — 154p ; 23cm
Bibliography: p150-154
ISBN 0-86861-041-0 (cased) : £15.00
ISBN 0-86861-049-6 (pbk) : £7.95 B81-18451

352.1′2′018 — Wales. Local authorities. Expenditure. Calculation. Methodology

Welsh rate support grant : a methodology for the assessment on standard expenditure : report of the Distribution Sub-Group to the Welsh Consultative Council on Local Government Finance. — [Cardiff] ([Crown Building, Cathays park, Cardiff CF1 3NO]) : Welsh Office, 1980. — 70p : ill,1form ; 30cm
Cover title
Unpriced (spiral) B81-06448

352.1′2′0722 — England. County boroughs. Budgeting, *1959-1969* — *Case studies*

Danziger, James N.. Making budgets : public resource allocation / James N. Danziger ; preface by Robert T. Golembiewski. — Beverly Hills ; London : Sage, c1978. — 255p ; 23cm. — (Sage library of social research ; v.63)
Bibliography: p243-249. — Includes index
ISBN 0-8039-0999-3 (cased) : Unpriced
ISBN 0-8039-1010-x (pbk) : Unpriced B81-10758

352.1′2′094239 — Avon. *County Council.* Budgeting — *Proposals — Serials*

Avon. *County Council.* Policy budget / County of Avon [Council]. — 1981-1982 to 1983-1984. — [Bristol] ([P.O. Box 11, Avon House, Haymarket, Bristol BS 99 7DE]) : [The Council], [1981]. — xviii,117p
ISBN 0-86063-111-7 : £5.00 B81-23506

352.1′2′09482 — Urban regions. Local authorities. Budgeting — *Study regions: Norway. Oslo*

Cowart, Andrew T.. Decisions, politics, and change : a study of Norwegian urban budgeting / Andrew T. Cowart and Karl Eric Brofoss. — Oslo : Universitetsforlaget, c1979 ; London : Global [distributor], [1981]. — 149p : ill ; 22cm
ISBN 82-00-01882-2 (pbk) : £7.30 B81-37861

352.1′22′0941 — Great Britain. Local authorities. Economic policies. Formulation *compared with* formulation of economic policies of local authorities in West Germany

Johnson, Nevil. Economic policy making by local authorities in Britain and West Germany / Nevil Johnson, Allan Cochrane. — London : Allen & Unwin, 1981. — x,182p ; 23cm. — (The New local government series ; no.21)
Includes index
ISBN 0-04-352097-9 : Unpriced : CIP rev.
Also classified at 352.1′22′0943 B81-15885

352.1′22′0943 — West Germany. Local authorities. Economic policies. Formulation *compared with* formulation of economic policies of local authorities in Great Britain

Johnson, Nevil. Economic policy making by local authorities in Britain and West Germany / Nevil Johnson, Allan Cochrane. — London : Allen & Unwin, 1981. — x,182p ; 23cm. — (The New local government series ; no.21)
Includes index
ISBN 0-04-352097-9 : Unpriced : CIP rev.
Primary classification 352.1′22′0941 B81-15885

352.1′232′0941 — Great Britain. Local authorities. Expenditure. Reduction — *Conference proceedings*

Economy and local government / edited by Eamonn Butler and Madsen Pirie ; with papers by Madson Pirie ... [et al.]. — London : 50 Westminster Mansions, SW1P 3DQ : Adam Smith Institute, 1981. — 88p ; 21cm
ISBN 0-906517-10-9 (pbk) : £3.45 B81-17969

352.1′232′09421 — London. Local authorities. Expenditure. Reduction. Decision making. Political aspects *compared with* political aspects of decision making on expenditure cuts by local authorities in New York *(City)*

Glassberg, Andrew D.. Responses to fiscal crisis : big city government in Britain and America / by Andrew D. Glassberg. — Glasgow (13 Richmond St., Glasgow G1 1XQ) : Centre for the Study of Public Policy, University of Strathclyde, 1980. — 23p ; 30cm. — (Studies in public policy, ISSN 0140-8240 ; no.55)
Unpriced (pbk)
Also classified at 352.1′232′097471 B81-07964

352.1′232′097471 — New York *(City).* Local authorities. Expenditure. Reduction. Decision making. Political aspects *compared with* political aspects of decision making on expenditure cuts by local authorities in London

Glassberg, Andrew D.. Responses to fiscal crisis : big city government in Britain and America / by Andrew D. Glassberg. — Glasgow (13 Richmond St., Glasgow G1 1XQ) : Centre for the Study of Public Policy, University of Strathclyde, 1980. — 23p ; 30cm. — (Studies in public policy, ISSN 0140-8240 ; no.55)
Unpriced (pbk)
Primary classification 352.1′232′09421
B81-07964

352.1′71′0942 — England. Local authorities. Accounting. Standards. Institute of Chartered Accountants in England and Wales. Statements of standard accounting practice — *Critical studies*

Draft guidance notes on the application of statements of standard accounting practice to local authorities in England and Wales : published for discussion purposes : these draft notes, covering SSAP′s 5, 6, 8, 10, 13 and 15, have been prepared by the Chartered Institute of Public Finance and Accountancy. — London (P.O. Box 443, Chartered Accountants′ Hall, Moorgate Place, EC2P 2BJ) : Accounting Standards Committee, c1981. — 18p ; 21cm. — (Guidance notes / Accounting Standards Committee)
£1.00 (pbk) B81-29016

352.1′72′09411 — Scotland. Local authorities. Auditing. Organisations: Commission for Local Authority Accounts in Scotland — *Accounts — Serials*

Commission for Local Authority Accounts in Scotland. Account / Commission for Local Authority Accounts in Scotland. — 1979-80. — London : H.M.S.O., 1981. — 5p
ISBN 0-10-214681-0 : £1.10 B81-20306

352.1′72′0942 — Great Britain. *Advisory Committee on Local Government Audit — Serials*

Great Britain. *Advisory Committee on Local Government Audit.* Report : presented to the Consultative Council on Local Government Finance / Advisory Committee on Local Government Audit. — 1st-. — London : H.M.S.O., 1980. — v. ; 30cm
Annual
ISSN 0260-566x = Report — Advisory Committee on Local Government Audit : £3.80 B81-06777

352.3′025 — Fire brigades — *Directories — Serials*

Fire protection directory. — 1981. — Ewell (172 Kingston Rd, Ewell, Nr. Epsom, Surrey KT19 0SB) : A.E. Morgan Publications, [1981]. — 199p
£23.00
Primary classification 338.7′628922′025
B81-29104

352.3′09411 — Scotland. Fire brigades — *Serials*

Great Britain. *Fire Services Inspectorate.* Report for ... / Her Majesty′s Inspector of Fire Services for Scotland. — 1979. — Edinburgh : H.M.S.O., 1980. -- vi,26p
ISBN 0-10-180220-x : £2.90 B81-00796

352.3′0942 — England. Fire brigades — *Statistics — Serials*

Fire service statistics. Estimates / CIPFA Statistical Information Service. — 1981-82. — London : Chartered Institute of Public Finance and Accountancy, [1981]. — 15p
ISSN 0307-0573 : £6.00 B81-35097

352.3′09421 — London. Fire brigades: London Fire Brigade — *Proposals*

Greater London Council. The future development of the London fire brigade : a statement of policies. — London : Greater London Council, [1981]. — 55p : ill,maps ; 15x21cm
Cover title
ISBN 0-7168-1187-1 (pbk) : Unpriced
B81-39716

352.3′09425′9 — Buckinghamshire. Fire brigades: Buckinghamshire Fire Brigade — *Serials*

Talk through / Buckinghamshire Fire Brigade. — [No.1]-. — Croydon (31 George St., Croydon, Surrey CR0 1LB) : M. & W. Publications, [1980]-. — v. : ill,ports ; 25cm
Two issues yearly. — Description based on: [No.2]
ISSN 0261-894x = Talk through : Unpriced
B81-36011

352.4′09411 — Scotland. Health authorities. Policies — *Proposals*

′Scottish Health Authorities priorities for the eighties′ and its implementation : presentations made at a study day, arranged by the Planning Unit, Scottish Home and Health Department and the Management Education and Training Division, held in the Scottish Health Service Centre 12 May 1981 / [edited and produced by G.H. France]. — Edinburgh (Crewe Road South, Edinburgh EH4 2LF) : Scottish Health Service Centre, [1981]. — 88p : ill ; 30cm
Unpriced (pbk) B81-40294

352.4′0941′15 — Scotland. Highland Region. Health boards: Highland Health Board — *Serials*

Highland Health Board. Year book / Highland Health Board. — 1980-81. — Inverness (17 Old Edinburgh Rd, Inverness, IV2 3HG) : The Board, 1980. — 47p
Unpriced B81-09139

352.4′09413′2 — Scotland. Lothian Region. Health boards: Lothian Health Board, *1974-1979*

Lothian Health Board. Quinquennial report of the Lothian Health Board 1974-1979. — Edinburgh (11 Drumsheugh Gardens, Edinburgh) : Lothian Health Board, 1980. — 130p : maps ; 29cm
Unpriced (pbk) B81-23303

352.4′09414′43 — Scotland. Strathclyde Region. Glasgow region. Health boards: Greater Glasgow Health Board — *Serials*

Greater Glasgow Health Board. Year book / Greater Glasgow Health Board. — 1981-82. — Glasgow (351 Sauchiehall St., Glasgow G2 3HT) : [The Board], [1981]. — 35p
Unpriced B81-35095

352.4′09422 — Central Southern England. Regional health authorities: Wessex Regional Health Authority — *Directories — Serials*

Wessex Regional Health Authority. . — 1981. — Winchester (Highcroft, Romsey Road) : The Authority, [1980]. — 39p
Unpriced B81-09688

352.4′09429 — Wales. Health authorities. Resources. Allocation — *Inquiry reports*

Great Britain. *Steering Committee on Resource Allocations.* The distribution of resources to health authorities in Wales : fifth report of the Steering Committee [on Resource Allocations]. — [Cardiff] : Welsh Office, 1981. — 33p ; 30cm
Cover title
(spiral) B81-39980

352.6′1 — Scotland. Borders Region. Tweed River region. River purification boards: Tweed River Purification Board — *Serials*

Tweed River Purification Board. Annual report for the year ended 31st December ... / River Tweed Purification Board. — 1980. — [Galashiels] ([District Council Chambers, Paton St., Galashiels TD1 3AS]) : [The Board], [1981]. — 39p
Unpriced B81-32697

352.6'1 — Scotland. Forth River Basin. River purification boards: Forth River Purification Board — *Serials*

Forth River Purification Board. Annual report for year ended 31 December ... / Forth River Purification Board. — 1979. — [Edinburgh] ([Colinton Dell House, West Mill Rd, Colinton, Edinburgh EH13 0PH]) : The Board, [1980]. — 95p
Unpriced B81-09186

352.6'1'09422 — Southern England. Regional water authorities: Southern Water Authority — *Serials*

Southern Water Authority. Annual report and accounts / Southern Water Authority. — 1979-80. — Worthing (Guildbourne House, Worthing, West Sussex) : The Authority, [1980]. — 28p
Pocket contains: Accounts for the year ended 31st March 1980 (26p) ; and, Appendices for the year ended 31st March 1980 (24p)
ISSN 0309-8664 : £3.00 B81-04834

352.6'1'09423 — South-west England. Regional water authorities: South West Water Authority — *Serials*

South West Water Authority. Annual report and accounts for the year ended 31 March ... / South West Water Authority. — 1980. — Exeter (3 Barnfield Rd, Exeter) : The Authority, [1980]. — 49p
ISSN 0141-2957 : £2.50 B81-03302

352.6'1'09423 — South-west England. Regional water authorities: Wessex Water Authority — *Serials*

Wessex Water Authority. Wessex Water Authority report & accounts for the year ended 31 March ... — 1980. — Bristol (Wessex House, Passage St., Bristol BS2 0JQ) : The Authority, [1980]. — 63p
ISSN 0141-2809 : £2.00 B81-04825

352.6'1'09424 — England. Severn River Basin & Trent River Basin. Regional water authorities: Severn-Trent Water Authority. Efficiency — *Inquiry reports*

Great Britain. *Monopolies and Mergers Commission*. Severn-Trent Water Authority, East Worcestershire Waterworks Company and the South Staffordshire Waterworks Company : a report on water services supplied by the Authority and the Companies / Monopolies and Mergers Commission. — London : H.M.S.O., 1981. — x,467p : ill,maps ; 25cm. — (HC ; 339)
ISBN 0-10-233981-3 (pbk) : £10.80
Also classified at 338.7'6281'094244 ; 338.7'6281'094246 B81-29625

352.6'1'09427 — North-West England. Regional water authorities: North West Water Authority — *Serials*

North West Water Authority. Annual report / North West Water. — 6th (1979-1980). — Warrington (Dawson House, Liverpool Rd, Great Sankey, Warrington WA5 3LW) : The Authority, [1980]. — 37,21p
ISSN 0308-1141 : £2.00 B81-04824

352.6'1'09428 — North-east England. Regional water authorities: Northumbrian Water Authority — *Serials*

Northumbrian Water Authority. Annual report and accounts / Northumbrian Water Authority. — 1977-1978. — [Gosforth] ([Northumbria House, Regent Centre, Gosforth, Northumbria]) : The Authority, [1978?]. — 69p
ISSN 0141-2892 : Unpriced B81-09150

Northumbrian Water Authority. Annual report and accounts / Northumbrian Water. — 78/79. — [Gosforth] ([Northumbria House, Regent Centre, Gosforth, Northumbria]) : [The Authority], [1979?]. — 75p
ISSN 0141-2892 : Unpriced B81-13035

352.6'1'094281 — Yorkshire. Regional water authorities: Yorkshire Water Authority — *Serials*

Yorkshire Water Authority. Annual report and accounts for the year ended 31 March ... / Yorkshire Water Authority. — 1980. — Leeds (West Riding House, 67 Albion St., Leeds LS1 4AA) : The Authority, [1980]. — 27p
ISBN 0-905057-10-4 : £1.50 B81-06722

352.7'5 — Great Britain. Local authority housing. Maintenance. Administration. Applications of digital computer systems

Pettitt, Raymond. Computer aids to housing maintenance management / Raymond Pettitt. — London : H.M.S.O., 1981. — 68p : ill ; 20x21cm
At head of title: Department of the Environment
ISBN 0-11-751547-7 (pbk) : £3.95 B81-39999

352.7'5'071142 — England. Local authorities. Housing departments. Personnel. In-service training — *Case studies*

Training in three housing organisations 1978-1979 . — London (Housing Research Group, The City University, St. John St., EC1V 4PB) : Housing Training Project, c1980. — 212p ; 30cm
ISBN 0-907255-09-4 (spiral) : £7.50
Also classified at 334'.1'071142 B81-10195

352.7'5'071142 — England. Local authorities. Housing departments. Personnel. Professional education

Basic training / Housing Training Project. — London ([City University, St John St., EC1V 4PB]) : Housing Research Group, c1980. — 44p ; 21cm. — (Guide to housing training ; no.2)
Cover title. — Bibliography: p42
ISBN 0-907255-01-9 (pbk) : Unpriced
Also classified at 334'.1'071142 B81-06323

Getting started / Housing Training Project. — London ([City University, St John St., EC1V 4 PB]) : Housing Research Group, c1980. — 35p ; 21cm. — (Guide to housing training ; no.1)
Cover title. — Bibliography: p33-34
ISBN 0-907255-00-0 (pbk) : Unpriced
Also classified at 334'.1'071142 B81-06324

352.7'5'071142 — England. Local authorities. Housing departments. Personnel. Professional education. Assessment

Assessing the effects of training / Housing Training Project. — London ([City University, St John St., EC1V 4PB]) : Housing Research Group, c1980. — 43p : forms ; 21cm. — (Guide to housing training ; no.7)
Cover title. — Bibliography: 41-43
ISBN 0-907255-06-x (pbk) : Unpriced
Also classified at 334'.1'071142 B81-06326

352.94'2'0942 — England. Local authorities. Consumer protection services — *Statistics* — *Serials*

Trading standards and consumer protection statistics. Actuals / The Society of County Trading Standards Officers, The Society of County Treasurers. — 1978-9-. — Northampton : Society of County Trading Standards Officers ; [Northallerton] ([Honorary Treasurer, Society of County Treasurers, County Hall, Northallerton DL7 8AL]) : Society of County Treasurers [Distributor], 1979-
Annual. — Continues: Trading standards statistics. Actuals
ISSN 0260-6372 = Trading standards and consumer protection statistics. Actuals (corrected) : £2.50 B81-06195

Trading standards and consumer protection statistics. estimates / The Society of County Trading Standards Officers, The Society of County Treasurers. — 1980-81. — Northampton : Society of County Trading Standards Officers ; [Northallerton] ([Honorary Treasurer, Society of County Treasurers, County Hall, Northallerton Dl7 8AL]) : Society of County Treasurers [Distributor], 1980-. — 31p
ISSN 0140-4881 : Unpriced B81-12428

352.94'4'0941 — Great Britain. Local authorities. Social service departments. Organisation structure

Kakabadse, Andrew. Culture of the social services. — Aldershot : Gower, Jan.1982. — [200]p
ISBN 0-566-00366-x : £12.50 : CIP entry B81-34285

352.94'4'0942 — England. Local authorities. Social services departments. Organisation

Organizing social services departments : further studies by the Brunel Social Services Unit / David Billis ... [et al.]. — London : Heinemann, 1980. — xix,226p : ill ; 23cm
Bibliography: p215-221. — Includes index
ISBN 0-435-82085-0 (cased) : £13.00 : CIP rev. B80-13295

352.94'41'0942819 — England. Regional hospital boards. Role, *to 1974* — *Study examples: Leeds Regional Hospital Board*

Ham, Christopher. Policy-making in the National Health Service : a case study of the Leeds Regional Hospital Board / Christopher Ham. — London : Macmillan, 1981. — xiv,224p : 2ill,1map ; 23cm. — (Studies in social policy)
Includes index
ISBN 0-333-29137-9 : £18.00 : CIP rev. B80-21469

352.9'61'0973 — United States. Urban regions. Central business districts. Development. Control. Use of zoning

Cook, Robert S.. Zoning for downtown urban design : how cities control development / Robert S. Cook, Jr. — Lexington : Lexington Books, c1980 ; [Farnborough, Hants.] : Gower [distributor], 1980. — xi,178p : ill ; 24cm
Bibliography: p165-174. — Includes index
ISBN 0-669-03642-0 : £12.50 B81-15040

353 — FEDERAL AND STATE ADMINISTRATIVE STRUCTURE. UNITED STATES

353 — United States. Government. Relations with press

Grossman, Michael Baruch. Portraying the president : the White House and the news media / Michael Baruch Grossman and Martha Joynt Kumar. — Baltimore ; London : Johns Hopkins University Press, c1981. — x,358p : ill ; 24cm
Includes index
ISBN 0-8018-2375-7 (cased) : £16.00
ISBN 0-8018-2537-7 (pbk) : Unpriced B81-34464

353.001'3242 — United States. Government. Loyalty-security program, *1947-1952*

Thompson, Francis H.. The frustration of politics : Truman, Congress, and the loyalty issue 1945-1953 / Franics H. Thompson. — Rutherford : Fairleigh Dickinson University Press ; London : Associated University Presses, c1979. — 246p ; 22cm
Bibliography: p232-237. — Includes index
ISBN 0-8386-2132-5 : £8.50 B81-37484

353.004 — United States. Civil service. Senior women personnel. Role, *1933-1945*

Ware, Susan. Beyond suffrage : women in the New Deal / Susan Ware. — Cambridge [Mass.] ; London : Harvard University Press, 1981. — 204p ; 24cm
Includes index
ISBN 0-674-06921-8 : £12.95 B81-40030

353.0071'2 — United States. Purchasing by public bodies. Management

Page, Harry Robert. Public purchasing and materials management / Harry Robert Page. — Lexington : Lexington, c1980 ; [Farnborough, Hants.] : Gower [distributor], 1981. — xiv,510p : ill,facsim,forms ; 24cm
Bibliography: p491-495. - Includes index
ISBN 0-669-03059-7 : £18.00 B81-17757

353.0071'2 — United States. Purchasing by public bodies — *Practical information* — *For marketing*

Holtz, Herman. Directory of federal purchasing offices : where, what, how to sell to the U.S. Government / Herman Holtz. — New York : Chichester, c1981. — ix,415p : ill,maps ; 26cm
Includes index
ISBN 0-471-08227-9 : £33.30 B81-39800

353.0072'2 — United States. Government. Budgeting
LeLoup, Lance T.. The fiscal congress : legislative control of the budget / Lance T. LeLoup. — Westport, Conn. ; London : Greenwood Press, 1980. — xii,227p : 1ill,facisms ; 25cm. — (Contributions in political science, ISSN 0147-1066 ; no.47)
Bibliography: p215-219. — Includes index
ISBN 0-313-22009-3 : £15.95 B81-23590

353.0072'2 — United States. Government. Expenditure. Cost-benefit analysis
Gramlich, Edward M.. Benefit-cost analysis of government programs / Edward M. Gramlich. — Englewood Cliffs ; London : Prentice-Hall, c1981. — xiii,273p : ill ; 24cm
Includes index
ISBN 0-13-074757-2 : Unpriced B81-36595

353.0072'22043 — United States. Government. Zero-based budgeting
Hammond, Thomas H.. A zero-based look at zero-base budgeting : why its failures in State government are being duplicated in Washington / Thomas H. Hammond and Jack H. Knott. — New Brunswick ; London : Transaction, c1980. — xii,135p : ill ; 24cm
Originally published: 117-124. — Bibliography: p117-124. — Includes index
ISBN 0-87855-365-7 : £8.75 B81-12651

353.0072'232 — United States. Government. Expenditure. Restrictions
Wildavsky, Aaron. How to limit government spending : or how a constitutional amendment tying public spending to economic growth will decrease taxes and lessen inflation ... / Aaron Wildavsky. — Berkeley ; London : University of California Press, c1980. — lx,197p ; 23cm
Includes index
ISBN 0-520-04227-1 : £5.50 B81-05274

353.0074 — United States. Coastal waters. Coastal police: United States Coast Guard. Management
Bragaw, Louis K.. Managing a Federal agency : the hidden stimulus / Louis K. Bragaw. — Baltimore ; London : Johns Hopkins University Press, c1980. — xx,300p : ill,1chart,maps ; 24cm
Bibliography: p285-291. - Includes index
ISBN 0-8018-2265-3 : £12.00 B81-03755

353.0082 — United States. Government. Bureaucracy — *Study examples: Experimental Technology Incentives Program*
Britan, Gerald M.. Bureaucracy and innovation : an ethnography of policy change / Gerald M. Britan. — Beverly Hills ; London : Sage, 1981. — 167p ; 23cm. — (Sage library of social research ; v.115)
Bibliography: p163-166
ISBN 0-8039-1506-3 (corrected : cased) : Unpriced B81-22237

353.0082 — United States. Government. Policies. Formulation. Role of economic advisers, *1946-1979*
Sobel, Robert. The worldly economists / by Robert Sobel. — New York : Free Press ; London : Collier Macmillan, c1980. — xi,260p,[8]p of plates : ports ; 25cm
Bibliography: p247-253. - Includes index
ISBN 0-02-929780-x : £9.50 B81-03771

353.0082'32 — United States. Natural resources. Conservation & exploitation. Planning. Organisations: Nationaal Resources Planning Board
Clawson, Marion. New Deal planning : the National Resources Planning Board / Marion Clawson. — Baltimore ; London : Published for Resources for the Future by Johns Hopkins University Press, c1981. — xxii,356p ; 24cm
Includes index
ISBN 0-8018-2595-4 : £22.75 B81-40026

353.0082'43 — United States. Counsellors & psychologists. Licensing
Fretz, Bruce R.. Licensing and certification of psychologists and counselors : a guide to current policies, procedures, and legislation / Bruce R. Fretz, David H. Mills. — San Francisco ; London : Jossey-Bass, 1980. — xii,194p ; 24cm. — (The Jossey-Bass social and behavioral science series)
Bibliography: p181-189. — Includes index
ISBN 0-87589-470-4 : £11.20 B81-05964

353.0082'6 — United States. *Federal Trade Commission, 1970-1979*
The **Federal** Trade Commission since 1970 : economic regulation and bureaucratic behavior / edited by Kenneth W. Clarkson and Timothy J. Muris. — Cambridge : Cambridge University Press, 1981. — x,379p ; 24cm
Bibliography: p369-371. — Includes index
ISBN 0-521-23378-x : £25.00 B81-27905

353.0085'5 — United States. Presidents. Scientific advice from scientific advisers, *1970-1976*
Burger, Edward J.. Science at the White House : a political liability / Edward J. Burger, Jr.. — Baltimore ; London : Johns Hopkins University Press, c1980. — xx,180p : ill ; 24cm
Includes index
ISBN 0-8018-2433-8 : £9.00 B81-11474

353.0089 — United States. *Foreign Service, to 1980*
Etzold, Thomas H.. The conduct of American foreign relations : the other side of diplomacy / Thomas H. Etzald. — New York ; London : New Viewpoints, 1977. — x,159p ; 22cm
Bibliography: p133-154. — Includes index
ISBN 0-531-05390-3 (cased) : £9.00
ISBN 0-531-05597-3 (pbk) : Unpriced
Also classified at 353.1'09 B81-02617

353'.01 — United States. Government. Bureaucracy
Browne, William P.. Politics, programs, and bureaucrats / William P. Browne. — Port Washington ; London : National University Publications : Kennikat, 1980. — 180p : ill ; 23cm. — (Series in political science)
Includes index
ISBN 0-8046-9263-7 : £14.85 B81-05516

353.03'1 — United States. Presidency
Laski, Harold J.. The American presidency : an interpretation / Harold J. Laski ; with a new introduction by James MacGregor Burns. — New Brunswick ; London : Transaction Books, c1980. — ix,278p ; 24cm. — ([Social science classics series])
Originally published: New York : Harper ; London : Allen & Unwin, 1940
ISBN 0-87855-390-8 (cased) : £12.00
ISBN 0-87855-821-7 (pbk) : Unpriced
B81-19822

353.03'1 — United States. Presidency, *1933-1980*
Hodgson, Godfrey. All things to all men : the false promise of the modern American presidency / by Godfrey Hodgson. — London : Weidenfeld and Nicolson, c1980. — 296p ; 25cm
Originally published: New York : Simon and Schuster, 1980. — Bibliography: p277-283. — Includes index
ISBN 0-297-77809-9 : £8.95 B81-00797

353.03'1 — United States. Presidency — *Conference proceedings*
The **Presidency** in the constitutional order / edited by Joseph M. Bessette and Jeffrey Tulis. — Baton Rouge ; London : Louisiana State University Press, c1981. — xii,349p ; 24cm
Conference papers. — Includes index
ISBN 0-8071-0774-3 (cased) : £21.00
ISBN 0-8071-0781-6 (pbk) : Unpriced
B81-25429

353.03'2 — Political events. Secret role of United States presidents, *1960-1976*
Orman, John M.. Presidential secrecy and deception : beyond the power to persuade / John M. Orman. — Westport ; London : Greenwood Press, 1980. — xv,239p : ill ; 22cm. — (Contributions in political science, ISSN 0147-1066 ; no.43)
Bibliography: p219-229. — Includes index
ISBN 0-313-22036-0 : Unpriced B81-05631

353.03'2 — United States. Presidency. Progressivism, *1901-1969*
Blum, John Morton. The progressive presidents : Roosevelt, Wilson, Roosevelt, Johnson / John Morton Blum. — New York ; London : Norton, c1980. — 221p ; 22cm
Bibliography: p211-214. — Includes index
ISBN 0-393-01330-8 : £6.95 B81-05267

353'.072 — United States. Government. Policies. Evaluation — *Conference proceedings*
Educating policymakers for evaluation : legislation / edited by Franklin M. Zweig, Keith E. Marvin. — Beverly Hills ; London : Published in cooperation with the Evaluation Research Society [by] Sage, c1981. — 160p : ill ; 22cm. — (Sage research progress series in evaluation ; v.9)
Conference papers. — Includes bibliographies
ISBN 0-8039-1529-2 (cased) : Unpriced
ISBN 0-8039-1530-6 (pbk) : Unpriced
B81-26979

353'.072 — United States. Government. Policies. Formulation
The **Determinants** of public policy / edited by Thomas R. Dye, Virginia Gray. — Lexington : Lexington Books ; [Farnborough, Hants.] : Gower [distributor], 1980. — viii,227p : ill ; 24cm. — (Policy studies organization series)
Includes index
ISBN 0-669-02777-4 : £14.00 B81-05471

353'.072 — United States. Government. Policies. Implementation
Effective policy implementation / edited by Daniel A. Mazmanian, Paul A. Sabatier. — Lexington, Mass. : Lexington Books ; [Aldershot] : Gower [distributor], 1981. — xv,220p : ill,1map ; 24cm. — (Policy Studies Organization series)
Includes index
ISBN 0-669-03311-1 : £14.50 B81-38468

353'.0725 — United States. Government. Policies. Decision making — *Conference proceedings*
The **Policy** cycle / Judith V. May and Aaron B. Wildavsky editors. — Beverly Hills ; London : Sage, c1978. — 332p : ill ; 23cm. — (Sage yearbooks in politics and public policy ; v.5)
Conference papers. — Includes bibliographies
ISBN 0-8039-0825-3 (cased) : £12.50 (pbk) : £6.95 B81-16272

353.09'1 — United States. Government agencies. Influence of industries
Quirk, Paul J.. Industry influence in federal regulatory agencies / Paul J. Quirk. — Princeton ; Guildford : Princeton University Press, c1981. — xi,260p ; 23cm
Bibliography: p241-254. — Includes index
ISBN 0-691-09388-1 (cased) : £25.00
ISBN 0-691-02823-0 (pbk) : £11.30 B81-27884

353.09'2 — United States. Public enterprise. Management
Studies in the management of government enterprise / Richard J. Horn, editor. — Boston ; London : Nijhoff, c1981. — 179p : ill ; 24cm. — (Social dimensions of economics ; v.1)
ISBN 0-89838-052-9 : Unpriced B81-29762

353.1'09 — United States. *Department of State, to 1980*
Etzold, Thomas H.. The conduct of American foreign relations : the other side of diplomacy / Thomas H. Etzald. — New York ; London : New Viewpoints, 1977. — x,159p ; 22cm
Bibliography: p133-154. — Includes index
ISBN 0-531-05390-3 (cased) : £9.00
ISBN 0-531-05597-3 (pbk) : Unpriced
Primary classification 353.0089 B81-02617

353.9 — United States. State governments
Berman, David R.. State and local politics / David R. Berman ; John C. Bollens, Consulting editor. — 3rd ed. — Boston [Mass.] ; London : Allyn and Bacon, c1981. — xiv395p : ill,maps ; 25cm
Previous ed: Boston, Mass. : Holbrook Press, 1978. — Bibliography: p259-380. - Includes index
ISBN 0-205-07219-4 : £16.95
Primary classification 352.073 B81-00795

Maddox, Russell W.. State and local government / Russell W. Maddox, Robert F. Fuquay. — 4th ed. — New York ; London : Van Nostrand, c1981. — ix,454p : 1ill ; 25cm
Previous ed.: 1975. — Includes index
ISBN 0-442-24454-1 : £15.25
Also classified at 352.073 B81-37025

354 — CENTRAL ADMINISTRATIVE STRUCTURE(OTHER THAN UNITED STATES)

354.1'13 — International organisations. Personnel: British specialists. Recruitment & selection

Opportunities overseas in international organisations / Overseas Development Administration. — [London] : [ODA], [1979]. — 31p ; 21cm
Cover title
Unpriced (pbk) B81-04645

354.1'722 — European Community. Budgets. British contributions & receipts — *Forecasts — Serials*

Statement of the ... Community budget. — 1981-. — London : H.M.S.O., 1981-. — v. ; 25cm. — (Cmnd. ; 8187)
Annual
ISSN 0261-1619 : £1.10 B81-16259

354.3207'3 — Ancient Egypt. Government. Reform, *to ca B.C.2160*

Kanawati, Naguib. Governmental reforms in old kingdom Egyt / Naguib Kanawati. — Warminster : Aris & Phillips, c1980. — ix,163p : 2 maps,2plans ; 22cm. — (Modern Egyptology)
Bibliography: p148-153. — Includes index
ISBN 0-85668-168-7 (pbk) : £12.00 : CIP rev. B80-09137

354.41 — Great Britain. Government

Birch, Anthony H.. The British system of government. — 5th ed. — London : Allen and Unwin, Feb.1982. — [304]p. — (Minerva series of students' handbooks ; no.20)
Previous ed.: 1980
ISBN 0-04-320149-0 (pbk) : £4.95 : CIP entry B81-35925

Rush, Michael. Parliamentary government in Britain / Michael Rush. — London : Pitman, 1981. — vii,288p ; 23cm
Bibliography: p273-277. — Includes index
ISBN 0-273-01615-6 : Unpriced B81-40381

354.41 — Great Britain. Government departments

Pitt, Douglas C.. Government departments : an organizational perspective / D.C. Pitt and B.C. Smith. — London : Routledge & Kegan Paul, 1981. — ix,149p : ill ; 24cm. — (Routledge direct editions)
Bibliography: p140-143. — Includes index
ISBN 0-7100-0742-6 (pbk) : £6.50 : CIP rev. B81-02585

354.41 — Great Britain. Government — *For schools*

Parliament and government. — [London] : [Public Information Office, House of Commons], [1980]. — 9p : ill,1map,facsims,ports ; 30cm. — (Education sheets ; 1)
Unpriced (unbound) B81-36715

354.41'0009 — Great Britain. Government, *1951-1955*

Seldon, Anthony. Churchill's Indian summer. — London : Hodder & Stoughton, Oct.1981. — [640]p
ISBN 0-340-25456-4 : £14.95 : CIP entry B81-26736

354.41'00092'2 — Great Britain. Government, *1964-1970 & 1974-1979 — Personal observations — Collections*

Policy and practice : the experience of government. — London : Royal Institute of Public Administration, 1980. — 103p : 1 ill ; 22cm. — (RIPA studies)
ISBN 0-900628-21-9 (pbk) : £5.50 B81-03943

354.41'00092'2 — Great Britain. Government. Ministers, *to ca 1980 — Lists*

Pickrill, D. A.. Ministers of the Crown. — London : Routledge & Kegan Paul, Jan.1982. — [135]p. — (Routledge direct editions)
ISBN 0-7100-0916-x : £10.00 : CIP entry B81-33893

354.41001'01 — Great Britain. Police. Manpower planning. Management aspects. Applications of automated information processing systems — *Study regions: Scotland. Strathclyde Region*

Hough, J. M.. Uniformed police work and management technology / J.M. Hough. — London : Home Office, c1980. — v,51p : ill ; 30cm. — (Research Unit paper / Home Office)
Bibliography: p48-51
Unpriced (pbk) B81-10413

354.41001'232 — Great Britain. *Civil Service Pay Research Unit — Serials*

Great Britain. *Civil Service Pay Research Unit. Board.* Report of the Civil Service Pay Research Unit Board and the Civil Service Pay Research Unit. — 1980. — London : H.M.S.O., 1980. — ix,71p
ISBN 0-11-630431-6 : £3.75 B81-09061

Great Britain. *Civil Service Pay Research Unit. Board.* Report of the Civil Service Pay Research Unit Board and the Civil Service Pay Research Unit. — 1981. — London : H.M.S.O., 1981. — ix,34p
ISBN 0-11-630442-1 : £2.70 B81-34023

354.41001'232 — Great Britain. Government. Ministers. Expense allowances & remuneration — *Proposals*

Review Body on Top Salaries. Ministers of the Crown and Members of Parliament and the Peer's expenses allowance / Review Body on Top Salaries. — London : H.M.S.O., [1981]. — iii,10p ; 25cm. — (Cmnd. ; 8244) (Report / Review Body on Top Salaries ; no.17)
ISBN 0-10-182440-8 (unbound) : £1.70
Primary classification 328.41'0733 B81-27553

354.41001'232 — Great Britain. Public bodies. Personnel. Remuneration, *ca 1950-1975*

Elliott, Robert F.. Pay in the public sector / R.F. Elliott and J.L. Fallick. — London : Macmillan, 1981. — xv,178p : ill ; 23cm
Includes bibliographies and index
ISBN 0-333-23738-2 : £15.00 : CIP rev. B80-12768

354.41001'232 — Great Britain. Public bodies. Senior personnel. Remuneration — *Proposals*

Review Body on Top Salaries. Interim report on top salaries / Review Body on Top Salaries. — London : H.M.S.O., [1981]. — iv,67p ; 25cm. — (Cmnd. ; 8243) (Report / Review Body on Top Salaries ; no.16)
ISBN 0-10-182430-0 (pbk) : £4.80 B81-27550

354.41001'31'05 — Great Britain. Civil service. Personnel. Recruitment — *Serials*

Great Britain. *Civil Service Commission.* Annual report / Civil Service Commission. — 114th (1980). — Basingstoke ([Alencon Link, Basingstoke, Hants. RG21 1JB]) : The Commission, 1981. — 56p
ISBN 0-903741-61-x : Unpriced
ISSN 0141-0024 B81-31587

354.41'002 — Great Britain. Civil service — *Directories — Serials*

Great Britain. *Civil Service Department.* Civil service year book. Abridged and updated edition / Civil Service Department. — Mid 1980. — London : H.M.S.O., 1980. — vii p.,459columns
ISBN 0-11-630429-4 : £6.20 B81-06841

354.41'002 — Great Britain. Civil service. Personnel: Social scientists — *Directories — Serials*

Register of social scientists in government. — No.1 (1977)-. — [Watford] ([c/o Jean Henderson, Building Research Station, Bucknalls La., Garston, Watford, Hertfordshire]) : Social Scientists in Government, 1977-. — v. ; 30cm
Annual. — Description based on: No.3 (Nov. 1980)
ISSN 0260-8898 = Register of social scientists in government : Unpriced B81-11862

354.41005 — Great Britain. Civil service. Superannuation schemes: Principal Civil Service Pension Scheme. Allocation

Great Britain. *Civil Service Department.* Allocation of pension : Civil Service pension scheme / Civil Service Department ; explanatory memorandum, rules, and tables prepared by the Government Actuary. — 2nd ed. — London : H.M.S.O., 1981. — 34p ; 21cm
Previous ed.: 1974
ISBN 0-11-630436-7 (pbk) : £2.70 B81-22224

354.41005 — Great Britain. Civil service. Superannuation schemes: Principal Civil Service Pension Scheme — *Rules*

Great Britain. *Civil Service Department.* The Principal Civil Service Pension Scheme 1974 : rules / Civil Service Department. — 2nd ed. — London : H.M.S.O., 1979. — vii,147p ; 21cm
Previous ed.: 1974
ISBN 0-11-630420-0 (pbk) : £3.50 B81-37871

354.41006 — Great Britain. *Civil Service Commission, to 1975*

Great Britain. *Civil Service Commission.* The Civil Service Commission : 1855-1975 / K.M. Reader. — London : H.M.S.O., 1981. — vi,99p ; 25cm. — (Civil Service studies ; 5)
ISBN 0-11-630437-5 (pbk) : £7.50 B81-39631

354.41006 — Great Britain. *Civil Service Department.* **Great Britain.** *Parliament. House of Commons. Treasury and Civil Service Committee.* **Future of the Civil Service Department** — *Critical studies*

Great Britain. The future of the Civil Service Department : Government observations on the first report from the Treasury and Civil Service Committee, Session 1980-81, HC54. — London : H.M.S.O., 1981. — 8p ; 25cm. — (Cmnd. ; 8170)
Cover title
ISBN 0-10-181700-2 (pbk) : £1.40 B81-19937

354.41006 — Great Britain. *Civil Service Department.* **Statistical services**

Great Britain. *Civil Service Department.* Statistical services in the Civil Service Department : report by the Rayner Survey Officer and statement of decisions by ministers : Rayner review of government statistical services. — London ([Whitehall, SW1A 2AZ]) : The Department, 1981. — 38p ; 30cm
£1.00 (spiral) B81-23659

354.41006 — Great Britain. Civil service. Efficiency

Efficiency in the Civil Service. — London : H.M.S.O., [1981]. — 14p : ill ; 25cm. — (Cmnd. ; 8293)
ISBN 0-10-182930-2 (unbound) : £2.10 B81-33418

354.41006'0212 — Great Britain. Civil service — *Statistics — Serials*

Civil Service statistics / Civil Service Department. — 1980. — London : H.M.S.O., 1980. — 71p
ISBN 0-11-630353-0 : £7.50 B81-03722

354.41006'023 — Great Britain. Civil service — *Career guides*

Medina, Peter. Careers in the Civil Service / Peter Medina. — London : Kogan Page, 1981. — 112p : ill ; 19cm
ISBN 0-85038-464-8 (corrected,cased) : Unpriced : CIP rev.
ISBN 0-85038-465-6 (pbk) : £2.50 B81-20598

354.41006'09 — Great Britain. Civil service. Management, *1970-1980*

Garrett, John, *1931-*. Managing the civil service / John Garrett ; foreword by Denis Healey. — London : Heinemann, 1980. — 197p ; 22cm
Includes index
ISBN 0-434-90655-7 : £7.50 B81-04028

354.410061 — Great Britain. *Colonial Office.* **Policies,** *1945-1966.* **Effects of World War 2**

Lee, Martin. The Colonial Office, war and redevelopment policy. — London : Maurice Temple Smith, Jan.1982. — [320]p
ISBN 0-85117-221-0 : £15.00 : CIP entry B81-33831

354.410071′2′05 — Great Britain. Public bodies. Goods. Supply. Organisations: PSA supplies — *Accounts — Serials*
PSA supplies trading fund accounts .... — 1979-80. — London : H.M.S.O., 1981. — 14p
ISBN 0-10-215381-7 : £2.00 B81-16237

354.410071′3′05 — Great Britain. Government property. Maintenance. Organisations: Property Services Agency *— Serials*
Property Services Agency. Annual report / Property Services Agency. — 1979/80. — [Croydon] ([c/o PSA Library, Whitgift Centre, Wellesley Rd, Croydon]) : The Agency, [1980]. — [16]p
ISSN 0143-3997 : £1.00 B81-24693

354.410071′34 — Great Britain. Civil service. Typing pools. Word processing equipment. Use, *1979-1980*
A **Report** of trials of stand-alone word processors in UK government typing pools 1979-80 / Central Computer and Telecommunications Agency. — London (Civil Service Department, Riverwalk House, 157 Millbank, SW1P 4RT) : The Agency, 1980. — 34p,[22]leaves : ill ; 30cm
ISBN 0-7115-0028-2 (pbk) : Unpriced B81-14329

354.410071′45 — Great Britain. *Ministry of Defence.* **Magnetic tapes. Security** *— Inquiry reports*
Great Britain. *Security Commission.* Report of the Security Commission, May 1981. — London : H.M.S.O., 1981. — 9p ; 25cm. — (Cmnd. ; 8235)
ISBN 0-10-182350-9 (unbound) : £1.40 B81-26867

354.410072′32 — Great Britain. Government departments. Internal auditing *— Inquiry reports*
Great Britain. *Parliament. House of Commons. Committee of Public Accounts.* Internal audit in central government : ninth report from the Committee of Public Accounts, together with the proceedings of the Committee, minutes of evidence and appendices, session 1980-81. — London : H.M.S.O., [1981]. — xv,54p ; 25cm. — ([H.C.] ; 270)
ISBN 0-10-227081-3 (pbk) : £3.90 B81-32951

354.410072′4 — Great Britain. Taxpayers. Accounts. Investigation by Great Britain. *Board of Inland Revenue*
Reader, M.. Tax investigation handbook : the law and practice of Inland Revenue accounts investigation / by M. Reader. — London : Butterworth, 1981. — xvi,158p ; 22cm
ISBN 0-406-25410-9 (pbk) : Unpriced B81-26106

354.410072′46 — Great Britain. *Customs and Excise, to 1979*
Smith, Graham, *1934-.* Something to declare : 1000 years of Customs and Excise / Graham Smith. — London : Harrap, 1980. — vi,230p,[16]p of plates : ill,coats of arms,facsims,1port ; 25cm
Ill on lining papers. — Bibliography: p217-218. — Includes index
ISBN 0-245-53472-5 : £9.95 B81-03096

354.410074 — England. Police. Complaints by public. Administration. Procedure *— Inquiry reports*
Great Britain. *Home Office.* The establishment of an independent element in the investigation of complaints against the police : report of a working party appointed by the Home Secretary / Home Office. — London : H.M.S.O., [1981]. — ii,12p ; 25cm. — (Cmnd. ; 8193)
ISBN 0-10-181930-7 (unbound) : £1.70 B81-25238

354.410074 — Great Britain. Police. Complaints by public. Administration. Organisations: Police Complaints Board *— Serials*
Police Complaints Board. Account / Police Complaints Board. — 1979-80. — London : H.M.S.O., 1980. — 2p
ISBN 0-10-202581-9 : £0.70 B81-12439

Police Complaints Board. Report of the Police Complaints Board. — 1980. — London : H.M.S.O., 1981. — iv,18p
ISBN 0-10-223981-9 : £3.00 B81-29441

354.410075 — Great Britain. *Health and Safety Commission* **& Great Britain.** *Health and Safety Executive — Accounts — Serials*
Great Britain. *Health and Safety Commission.* Accounts / Health and Safety Commission [and] Health and Safety Executive. — 1979-80. — London : H.M.S.O., 1981. — 11p
ISBN 0-10-220181-1 : £1.70 B81-24112

354.410076 — Great Britain. Betting industries. Licences & permits *— Statistics*
Betting licensing statistics, Great Britain : for the period ended 31 May ... / [Home Office]. — June 1979-May 1980-. — London : H.M.S.O., 1980-. — v. ; 25cm
Annual. — Continues: Betting licensing statistics
£3.00 B81-06904

354.410076 — Great Britain. Gambling. Regulation. Organisations: Gaming Board for Great Britain *— Serials*
Gaming Board for Great Britain. Report of the Gaming Board for Great Britain. — 1980. — London : H.M.S.O., 1981. — 47p
ISBN 0-10-226281-0 : £3.50 B81-29422

354.410076 — Great Britain. Racehorses. Racing. Betting. Organisations: Horserace Betting Levy Board *— Serials*
Horserace Betting Levy Board. Report and statement of accounts of the Horserace Betting Levy Board and the Horserace Totalisator Board for the year 1st April ... to 31st March .... — 1979-1980. — London : 17, Southampton Row, WC1B 5HH : Horserace Betting Levy Board ; London : Horserace Totalisator Board, [1980?]. — vii,103p
Unpriced
Primary classification 354.410076 B81-13316

354.410076 — Great Britain. Racehorses. Racing. Totalisator betting. Organisations: Horserace Totalisator Board *— Serials*
Horserace Betting Levy Board. Report and statement of accounts of the Horserace Betting Levy Board and the Horserace Totalisator Board for the year 1st April ... to 31st March .... — 1979-1980. — London : 17, Southampton Row, WC1B 5HH : Horserace Betting Levy Board ; London : Horserace Totalisator Board, [1980?]. — vii,103p
Unpriced
Also classified at 354.410076 B81-13316

354.410081 — Great Britain. Government departments. Statistical services *— Inquiry reports*
Government statistical services. — London : H.M.S.O, [1981]. — 17p ; 25cm. — (Cmnd. ; 8236)
ISBN 0-10-182360-6 (unbound) : £2.10 B81-29389

354.410081′1′05 — Great Britain. *Standing Advisory Commission on Human Rights — Serials*
Great Britain. *Standing Advisory Commission on Human Rights.* Annual report for ... / [Standing Advisory Commission on Human Rights]. — 1979-80. — London : H.M.S.O., 1981. — 22p
ISBN 0-10-214381-1 : £2.10 B81-26594

354.410081′4 — Great Britain. *Commission for Racial Equality — Accounts — Serials*
Great Britain. *Commission for Racial Equality.* Account / Commission for Racial Equality. — 1979-80. — London : H.M.S.O., 1981. — [4]p
ISBN 0-10-218181-0 : £0.70 B81-27916

354.410081′4 — Great Britain. *Commission for Racial Equality — Serials*
Great Britain. *Commission for Racial Equality.* Annual report of the Commission for Racial Equality. — Jan.-Dec.1980. — London : H.M.S.O., 1981. — iv,93p
ISBN 0-10-239981-6 : £4.90
ISSN 0142-0879 B81-36298

354.410081′8′05 — Great Britain. *Development Commission — Serials*
Great Britain. *Development Commission.* Report of Her Majesty's Development Commissioners for the year ended 31st March .... — 38th (1980). — London : H.M.S.O., 1980. — vii,18p
ISBN 0-10-027989-9 : £2.80 B81-01861

354.410081′9 — Great Britain. Government. Statistical services
The **Review** of the government statistical services : initial study of the Office of Population Censuses and Surveys. — [London] ([10 Kingsway, WC2B 6JP]) : [The Office?], [1981?]. — [53]p ; 30cm
Cover title. — Bibliography: p[41-42]
Unpriced (pbk) B81-23652

354.410081′9 — Great Britain. *Home Office. Statistical Department.* **Statistical services** *— Inquiry reports*
Great Britain. *Home Office.* Review of Home Office statistical services / R.M. Morris. — London (Room 1617, Tolworth Tower, Surbiton, Surrey KT6 7DS) : Home Office, 1980. — 75p ; 30cm
Unpriced (pbk) B81-38020

354.410082 — Great Britain. *Co-operative Development Agency — Serials*
Great Britain. *Co-operative Development Agency.* Annual report and accounts for the year ended 31st March / Co-operative Development Agency. — 1980. — London : H.M.S.O., 1980. — iii,25p
ISBN 0-10-027629-6 : £2.40 B81-07820

354.410082 — Great Britain. Cooperatives. Promotion. Organisations: Co-operative Development Agency *— Accounts — Serials*
Co-operative Development Agency. Accounts / Co-operative Development Agency. — 1980-81. — London : H.M.S.O., 1981. — 10p
ISBN 0-10-237581-x : £1.40 B81-35971

354.410082 — Great Britain. *Price Commission — Accounts — Serials*
Great Britain. *Price Commission.* Statement of account for the period ... / Price Commission. — 1 Apr.1979 to 4 May 1980. — London : H.M.S.O., 1981. — [4]p. — (Cmnd. ; 8185)
ISBN 0-10-181850-5 : £0.70 B81-29085

354.410082′2 — Great Britain. Mints: Royal Mint. Trading operations *— Accounts — Serials*
Royal Mint Trading Fund accounts. — 1979-80. — London : H.M.S.O., 1980. — 13p
ISBN 0-10-027959-7 : £2.10 B81-06644

354.410082′326 — Great Britain. *Crown Estate Commissioners — Accounts — Serials*
Crown Estate abstract accounts : abstract accounts of the Crown Estate Commissioners for the year ended 31st March ... — 1979-80. — London : H.M.S.O, 1981. — 7p
ISBN 0-10-222581-8 : £1.10 B81-25031

354.410082′328′05 — Great Britain. Nature conservation. Organisations: Nature Conservancy Council *— Serials*
Nature Conservancy Council. Report covering the Period 1 April ... 31 March ... / Nature Conservancy Council. — 1979-1980. — London : H.M.S.O., 1981-. — vi,100p
ISBN 0-10-215981-5 : £4.90
ISSN 0309-3190 B81-24686

354.410082′33 — Great Britain. Agricultural products. Surplyses. Purchase. Organisations: Intervention Board for Agricultural Produce *— Serials*
Intervention Board for Agricultural Produce. Report for the calendar year / Intervention Board for Agricultural Produce. — 1980. — London : H.M.S.O., 1981. — 55p. — (Cmnd. ; 8283)
ISBN 0-10-182830-6 : £4.20 B81-34024

354.410082′338 — Great Britain. *Forestry Commission.* **Denationalisation** *— Proposals*
Miller, Robert. State forestry for the axe : a study of the Forestry Commission and de-nationalisation by the market / Robert Miller. — London : Institute of Economic Affairs, 1981. — 68p : ill ; 22cm. — (Hobart paper, ISSN 0073-2818 ; 91)
Bibliography: p68
ISBN 0-255-36145-9 (pbk) : £1.50 B81-38781

354.410082′338′05 — Great Britain. *Forestry Commission — Serials*
Great Britain. *Forestry Commission.* Annual report and accounts of the Forestry Commission for the year ended 31 March ... together with the Comptroller and Auditor General's report on the accounts. — 60th (1980). — London : H.M.S.O., 1980. — 106p
ISBN 0-10-201481-7 : £7.20 B81-06844

354.410082′388 — Great Britain. Continental shelf. Natural gas deposits & petroleum deposits. Prospecting & exploitation. Licences — *Serials*
Continental Shelf Act 1964, report for the year / [prepared by the Department of Energy]. — 1979-80. — London : H.M.S.O., 1980. — 35p
ISBN 0-10-027859-0 : £3.00 B81-01857

354.410082′4 — Great Britain. Patents. Registration — *Serials*
Great Britain. *Patent Office.* Patents, designs and trade marks : report of the Comptroller-General of Patents, Designs and Trade Marks. — 98th (1980). — London : H.M.S.O., 1981. — v,43p
ISBN 0-10-230381-9 : £4.20 B81-30865

354.410082′42 — Great Britain. Iron & steel products industries & textile industries. Levies by government — *Accounts — Serials*
Accounts, Wool Textile Industry (Export Promotion Levy) .... — London : H.M.S.O., 1981. — 6p
ISBN 0-10-213381-6 : £1.10 B81-20307

354.410082′43 — Great Britain. Doctors. Registration. Organisations: General Medical Council — *Serials*
General Medical Council. Annual report / General Medical Council. — 1979. — London (44 Hallam St., W1N 6AE) : The Council, 1980. — 32p
Unpriced B81-20422

354.410082′5 — Great Britain. *Department of Trade.* **Bankruptcy Estates Account & Companies Liquidation Account** — *Accounts — Serials*
Insolvency Services (Accounting and Investment) Act, 1970 accounts .... — 1979-80. — London : H.M.S.O., 1981. — 8p
ISBN 0-10-215481-3 : £1.40
Primary classification 354.410082′5 B81-16258

354.410082′5 — Great Britain. *National Debt Commission.* **Insolvency Services Investment Account** — *Accounts — Serials*
Insolvency Services (Accounting and Investment) Act, 1970 accounts .... — 1979-80. — London : H.M.S.O., 1981. — 8p
ISBN 0-10-215481-3 : £1.40
Also classified at 354.410082′5 B81-16258

354.410082′56 — Great Britain. *Social Security Advisory Committee.* **Role**
Dear SSAC / edited by Jean Coussins. — London (1 Macklin St., WC2B 5NH) : Child Poverty Action Group, 1980. — 70p ; 21cm. — (Poverty pamphlet ; 49)
Cover subtitle: An open letter to the Social Security Advisory Committee
£1.00 (pbk) B81-17705

354.410083′2 — Great Britain. *Central Arbitration Committee — Serials*
Great Britain. *Central Arbitration Committee.* Annual report / Central Arbitration Committee. — 1980. — London (1 The Abbey Garden, Great College St., SW1P 3SE) : [The Committee], 1981. — 49p
Unpriced B81-29412

354.410083′2 — Great Britain. Industrial relations. Disputes. Conciliation. Organisations: Advisory, Conciliation and Arbitration Service — *Serials*
Advisory, Conciliation and Arbitration Service. Accounts / Advisory, Conciliation and Arbitration Service, Certification Officer, Central Arbitration Committee. — 1979-80. — London : H.M.S.O., 1980. — 3p
ISBN 0-10-027979-1 : £0.70 B81-12437

Advisory, Conciliation and Arbitration Service. Annual report / Advisory, Conciliation and Arbitration Service. — 1979. — [London] ([Cleveland House, Page St., SW1P 4ND]) : [ACAS], 1980. — 128p
Unpriced B81-30757

Advisory, Conciliation and Arbitration Service. Annual report / Advisory, Conciliation and Arbitration Service. — 1980. — [London] ([Cleland House, Page St., SW1P 4ND]) : [ACAS], 1981. — 166p
Unpriced B81-29419

354.410083′3 — Great Britain. *Employment Service Division.* **Relations with employment services** — *Inquiry reports*
Great Britain. *Parliament. House of Commons. Employment Committee.* Third report from the Employment Committee, session 1980-81 : the work of the Department of Employment Group : the Employment Service Division of the Manpower Services Commission and the private employment agencies : together with the proceedings of the Committee. — London : H.M.S.O., [1981]. — vp ; 25cm. — ([HC] ; 51)
ISBN 0-10-205181-x (unbound) : £1.15
B81-38932

354.410083′3 — Great Britain. *Equal Opportunities Commission — Accounts — Serials*
Great Britain. *Equal Opportunities Commission.* Account / Equal Opportunities Commission. — 1979-80. — London : H.M.S.O., 1981. — 3p
ISBN 0-10-212881-2 : £0.70 B81-15543

354.410083′3 — Great Britain. *Manpower Services Commission — Accounts — Serials*
Great Britain. *Manpower Services Commission.* Accounts / Manpower Services Commission. — 1979-80. — London : H.M.S.O., 1981. — 24p
ISBN 0-10-221581-2 : £3.00 B81-24111

354.410083′3 — Great Britain. *Manpower Services Commission.* **Corporate planning,** *1981-1985 — Proposals*
Great Britain. *Manpower Services Commission.* MSC corporate plan 1981 1982 1983 1984 1985 / Manpower Services Commission. — London (166 High Holborn, WC1V 6PF) : The Commission, [1981]. — 31p : 2col.ill,1col.map,1port ; 30cm
Cover title. — Map on inside cover
ISBN 0-905932-27-7 (pbk) : Unpriced
B81-23664

354.410083′3 — Great Britain. *Manpower Services Commission — Serials*
Great Britain. *Manpower Services Commission.* Annual report / Manpower Services Commission. — 1979-80. — London (166 High Holborn, WC1V 6PB) : The Commission, [1980]. — 44p
Unpriced B81-35959

Manpower review. — 1980-. — London (Selkirk House, 166 High Holborn, WC1V 6PF) : Manpower Services Commission, 1980-. — v. : ill ; 30cm
Annual. — Description based on: 1981 issue
ISSN 0261-6831 = Manpower review : Unpriced B81-33461

354.410083′5 — Great Britain. Occupational superannuation schemes. Organisations: Occupational Pensions Board — *Serials*
Occupational Pensions Board. Annual report of the Occupational Pensions Board to the Secretary of State for Social Services in accordance with Section 66(6) of the Social Security Act 1973 for the period 1 January ... to 31 December .... — 7th (1980). — London : H.M.S.O., 1981. — iv,21p
ISBN 0-10-233881-7 : £2.40 B81-31599

354.410084′1 — Great Britain. Hospitals. National health services facilities. Use by private patients. Organisations: Health Services Board — *Accounts — Serials*
Health Services Board. Account ... and account for the period 1st April to 8th August ... / Health Services Board. — 1979-80. — London : H.M.S.O., 1981. — 3p. — (Cmnd. ; 8248)
ISBN 0-10-182480-7 : £0.70 B81-33945

354.410085 — Great Britain. *Department of Education and Science — Serials*
Great Britain. *Department of Education and Science.* Annual report / Department of Education and Science. — 1980. — London : H.M.S.O., 1981. — ix,81p
ISBN 0-11-270528-6 : £4.80
ISSN 0142-0887 B81-36297

354.410085′5 — Great Britain. Government. Scientific advice. Supply
Royal Society. *Council.* The provision and coordination of scientific advice to government : a submission to the House of Lords Select Committee on Science and Technology / by the Council of the Royal Society (submitted 12 March 1981). — London : The Society, 1981. — 17p ; 21cm
£0.80 (pbk) B81-22441

354.410085′5515′05 — Great Britain. *Meteorological Office — Serials*
Great Britain. *Meteorological Office.* Annual report on the Meteorological Office. — 1979. — London : H.M.S.O., 1980. — 166p
ISBN 0-11-400319-x : £7.80
ISSN 0072-6605 B81-09056

354.410085′6 — Great Britain. Inventions. Development. Organisations: National Research Development Corporation — *Serials*
National Research Development Corporation. Annual report and statement of accounts / NRDC. — 27th(1975-76). — London (66-74 Victoria St., SW1E 6SL) : The Corporation, [1976]. — 48p
Unpriced B81-32419

National Research Development Corporation. Annual report and statement of accounts / NRDC. — 28th(1976-77). — London (66-74 Victoria St., SW1E 6SL) : The Corporation, [1977]. — 48p
Unpriced B81-32420

National Research Development Corporation. Annual report and statement of accounts / NRDC. — 29th(1977-78). — London (66-74 Victoria St., SW1E 6SL) : The Corporation, [1978]. — 52p
Unpriced B81-32421

National Research Development Corporation. Annual report and statement of accounts / NRDC. — 30th(1978-79). — London (66-74 Victoria St., SW1E 6SL) : The Corporation, [1979]. — 56p
Unpriced B81-32422

National Research Development Corporation. Annual report and statement of accounts / NRDC. — 31st(1979-80). — London (66-74 Victoria St., SW1E 6SL) : The Corporation, [1980]. — 60p
Unpriced B81-32423

354.410087′45543 — Great Britain. Commercial television services. Companies. Levies. Administration. Great Britain. *Parliament. House of Commons. Committee of Public Accounts.* **Fifth report. Session 1979-80** — *Critical studies*
Great Britain. *Treasury.* Treasury minute on the fifth report from the Committee of Public Accounts : session 1979-80. — London : H.M.S.O., [1980]. — 2p ; 25cm. — (Cmnd. ; 7992)
ISBN 0-10-179920-9 (unbound) : £0.50
Primary classification 363.2 B81-39928

354.410087′5 — Great Britain. *Department of Transport.* **Statistical services** — *Inquiry reports*
The Review of statistical services by Sir Derek Rayner : the report of the study officer for the Departments of the Environment and Transport and the decision statement as approved by the Secretaries of State for Environment and Transport. — London ([2 Marsham St., SW1P 3EB]) : Departments of the Environment and Transport, c1981. — ii,161,[22]p : 2ill ; 30cm
Cover title. — Text on inside covers
£9.00 (pbk)
Primary classification 354.41068 B81-37516

354.410087′6′05 — Great Britain. Inland waterways. Organisations: British Waterways Board — *Serials*
British Waterways Board. Annual report and accounts for the year ended 31st December ... / British Waterways Board. — 1980. — London : Produced through H.M.S.O. for the Board, 1981. — x,77p
ISBN 0-903218-24-0 : £2.50
ISSN 0068-2683 B81-34066

354.410087'71 — Great Britain. Ports. Organisations: National Ports Council — *Serials*

National Ports Council. Annual report and statement of accounts for the year ended 31st December ... / National Ports Council. — 1979. — London : The Council, [1980]. — vii,49p
ISBN 0-86073-050-6 : £0.75
ISSN 0072-6974 B81-01768

National Ports Council. Annual report and statement of accounts for the year ended 31st December ... / National Ports Council. — 1980. — London : The Council, [1981]. — vi,30p
ISBN 0-86073-055-7 : £0.75
ISSN 0072-6974 B81-30824

354.410087'715 — Great Britain. Docks. Personnel. Employment. Organisations: National Dock Labour Board — *Serials*

National Dock Labour Board. Annual report and accounts / National Dock Labour Board. — 1980-. — London (22 Albert Embankment, SE1 7TE) : The Board, [1981]-. — v. : maps ; 25cm
Continues: National Dock Labour Board. Annual report with statement of accounts
ISSN 0261-8656 = Annual report and accounts — National Dock Labour Board : £1.00 B81-34019

354.410087'7155'0289 — Great Britain. Lighthouse services. Finance. General Lighthouse Fund — *Accounts — Serials*

General lighthouse fund / presented by the Department of Trade. — 1978-79. — London : H.M.S.O., 1980. — 7p
ISBN 0-10-027919-8 : £1.40 B81-04927

354.410087'77 — Great Britain. Air services. Organisations: Civil Aviation Authority

Civil Aviation Authority. Britain's Civil Aviation Authority / [Civil Aviation Authority]. — [London] : CAA, c1980. — 31p,[4]p of plates : col.ill,col.maps ; 20cm
Cover title. — List of films: p31
ISBN 0-86039-088-8 (pbk) : Unpriced B81-00051

Civil Aviation Authority. Britain's Civil Aviation Authority. — London (WC2LB 6TE) : CAA, 1981. — 31p : ill(some col.),1map,1plan ; 20x21cm. — (CAA documents ; no.225)
Cover title. — Text on inside covers. — Bibliography: p30. — List of films: p31
ISBN 0-86039-137-x (pbk) : Unpriced B81-39998

354.410087'834 — Great Britain. Motor vehicles. Registration. Index marks — *Lists — Serials*

Glass's index of suffix marks. — 1973-1981. — Weybridge (Elgin House, St. George's Ave., Weybridge, Surrey KT13 0BX) : Glass's Guide Service, c1981. — 32p
£3.25 B81-32402

354.410088 — Great Britain. *Public Trustee Office — Serials*

Great Britain. *Public Trustee Office*. Annual report of the Public Trustee. — 1979-1980. — London : H.M.S.O., 1980. — 6p
ISBN 0-11-701071-5 : £0.90 B81-03902

354.410089'2 — British diplomatic service — *Directories — Serials*

The **Diplomatic** Service list / Foreign and Commonwealth Office. — 16th ed. (1981). — London : H.M.S.O., 1981. — vi,350p
ISBN 0-11-591653-9 : £12.50 B81-26591

354.41009'1 — Great Britain. *Parliamentary Commissioner for Administration — Cases*

Great Britain. *Parliamentary Commissioner for Administration*. Selected cases 1981 Parliamentary Commissioner for Administration. — London : H.M.S.O., [1981]
Vol.2 : third report-session 1980-81. — 77p ; 25cm. — ([HC] ; 250)
ISBN 0-10-225081-2 (pbk) : £4.20 B81-35383

354.41009'1 — Great Britain. *Parliamentary Commissioner for Administration — Serials*

Great Britain. *Parliamentary Commissioner for Administration*. Annual report for ... / Parliamentary Commissioner for Administration. — 1980. — London : H.M.S.O., 1981. — 47p
ISBN 0-10-214881-3 : £3.60 B81-16816

354.4103 — Great Britain. Government agencies & government departments — *Directories — For offshore engineering industries*

Offshore operator's handbook : a guide to communications with government departments and agencies. — Aylesbury (Kingfisher House, Walton St., Aylesbury, Bucks) : Petroleum Industry Training Board, 1981. — 52p : 1map ; 30cm
Cover title. — Bibliography: p35-49. — Includes index
Unpriced (pbk) B81-18820

354.4103'12 — Great Britain. Monarchy — *Republican Party of England viewpoints*

Victory to the people of England!. — Accrington (44 Water St., Accrington, Lancs. BB5 6QZ) : The Republican Party of England, [1981?]. — [4]p ; 22cm
Unpriced (unbound) B81-37738

354.4104'09 — Great Britain. *Cabinet, to 1976*

Mackintosh, John P.. The British Cabinet / by John P. Mackintosh. — 3rd ed. — London : Stevens, 1977 ; London : Methuen [distributor], 1981. — xv,656p ; 22cm
Previous ed.: 1968. — Includes index
ISBN 0-416-31380-9 (pbk) : £5.95 B81-22124

354.41061 — Great Britain. *Overseas Development Administration.* **Expenditure** — *Inquiry reports*

Great Britain. *Parliament. House of Commons. Committee of Public Accounts*. Fourth report from the Committee of Public Accounts : together with the proceedings of the Committee, minutes of evidence and appendices, session 1980-81 : Overseas Development Administration : assessing the effectiveness of bilateral aid ; charges made by the Crown Agents for services carried out for the Overseas Development Administration ; advances to the Commonwealth Development Corporation. — London : H.M.S.O., [1981]. — xviii,40p ; 25cm. — ([HC] ; 183)
ISBN 0-10-218381-3 (pbk) : £4.40 B81-35382

354.41061 — Great Britain. *Overseas Development Administration.* **Overseas organisations** — *Inquiry reports*

Great Britain. *Parliament. House of Commons. Foreign Affairs Committee*. Fourth report from the Foreign Affairs Committee, session 1979-80 : development divisions : together with the proceedings of the Committee relating to the report and the minutes of evidence taken before the Sub-Committee on Overseas Development from 15 April to 1 July and appendices. — London : H.M.S.O., [1980]. — ([HC] ; 407-vi to xii)
Vol.1: Report and proceedings. — xli ; 25cm. — ([HC] ; 718-I)
ISBN 0-10-009069-9 (pbk) : £3.00 B81-20358

Great Britain. *Parliament. House of Commons. Foreign Affairs Committee*. Fourth report from the Foreign Affairs Committee, session 1979-80 : development divisions : together with the proceedings of the Committee relating to the report and the minutes of evidence taken before the Sub-Committee on Overseas Development from 15 April to 1 July and appendices. — London : H.M.S.O., [1980]. — ([HC] ; 407-vi to xii)
Vol.2: Minutes of evidence and appendices. — viii,289p ; 25cm. — ([HC] ; 718-II)
ISBN 0-10-009079-6 (pbk) : £8.75 B81-20359

354.41061 — Great Britain. *Overseas Development Administration.* **Statistical services**

Ireton, B. R.. Review of government statistical services : ODA departmental study / B.R. Ireton. — [Surbiton] ([Tolworth Tower, Surbiton, Surrey KT6 7DY]) : [Overseas Development Administration?], 1981. — 41p in various pagings ; 30cm
Cover title. — Bibliography: p41
Unpriced (pbk) B81-23660

354.41062 — Great Britain. *Exchequer and Audit Department.* **Role. Great Britain.** *Parliament. House of Commons. Committee of Public Accounts.* **First special report ... session 1980-81** — *Critical studies*

Great Britain. *Treasury*. The role of the Comptroller and Auditor General / presented to Parliament by the Chancellor of the Exchequer ... — London : H.M.S.O., [1981]. — 7p ; 25cm
ISBN 0-10-183230-3 (unbound) : £1.10 B81-36464

354.41062 — Great Britain. *Exchequer and Audit Department.* **Role** — *Inquiry reports*

Great Britain. *Parliament. House of Commons. Committee of Public Accounts*. First special report from the Committee on Public Accounts : together with the proceedings of the Committee, minutes of evidence and appendices, session 1980-81 : the role of the Comptroller and Auditor General. — London : H.M.S.O., [1981]
Vol.1: Report. — lxxixp ; 25cm. — ([HC] ; 115-1)
ISBN 0-10-277681-4 (pbk) : £4.20 B81-36257

354.41063 — Great Britain. *Scottish Office.* **Role**

Ross, J. M. (James Matthews). The Secretary of State for Scotland and the Scottish Office / J.M. Ross. — Glasgow : University of Strathclyde, Centre for the Study of Public Policy, 1981. — 35p ; 30cm. — (Studies in public policy, ISSN 0140-8240 ; no.87)
Unpriced (pbk) B81-39598

354.41068 — Great Britain. *Department of the Environment.* **Statistical services** — *Inquiry reports*

The **Review** of statistical services by Sir Derek Rayner : the report of the study officer for the Departments of the Environment and Transport and the decision statement as approved by the Secretaries of State for Environment and Transport. — London ([2 Marsham St., SW1P 3EB]) : Departments of the Environment and Transport, c1981. — ii,161,[22]p : 2ill ; 30cm
Cover title. — Text on inside covers
£9.00 (pbk)
Also classified at 354.410087'5 B81-37516

354.4107'2 — Great Britain. Government departments. Planning units — *Conference proceedings*

Departmental planning units : summary of the proceedings of a workshop for departmental planning units held on 7-9 May 1980 / Civil Service College. — Ascot (Sunningdale, Ascot, Berks SL5 0QE) : Civil Service College, 1980. — 12p : ill ; 30cm. — (C.S.C. working papers ; no.27)
Unpriced (unbound) B81-38496

354.4107'2 — Great Britain. Government. Policies. Formulation *compared with* **formulation of government policies in France**

Ashford, Douglas E.. British dogmatism and French pragmatism. — London : Allen & Unwin, Nov.1981. — [432]p. — (The New local government series ; no.22)
ISBN 0-04-352096-0 : £27.50 : CIP entry
Also classified at 354.4407'2 B81-28785

354.4107'2 — Great Britain. Government. Policies. Influence of political parties, *1957-1979*

Rose, Richard, *1933-*. Do parties make a difference? / Richard Rose. — London : Macmillan, 1980. — xii,176p : ill ; 23cm
Includes index
ISBN 0-333-28841-6 : £15.00 B81-05793

354.4107'2 — Great Britain. Government. Policies — *Proposals*

Harris of High Cross, Ralph Harris, *Baron*. The end of government —? / Ralph Harris. — London : Institute of Economic Affairs, 1980. — 79p ; 22cm. — (Occasional paper / IEA, ISSN 0073-909x ; 58)
Bibliography: p77-79
ISBN 0-255-36136-x (pbk) : £1.50 B81-04567

354.4107'2'0207 — Great Britain. Government. Policies, ***1979-1980 — Humour***

Beaton, Alistair. The Thatcher papers : an exposé of the secret face of the Conservative government / based on information received by Alistair Beaton & Andy Hamilton. — London : New English Library, 1980. — [128]p : ill,ports ; 19cm
ISBN 0-450-05129-3 (pbk) : £1.50 B81-03104

354.4107'2'09 — Great Britain. Government. Policies, ***1979-1980***

Government policy initiatives 1979-80 : some case studies in public administration : an interim report of an RIPA working group / edited by P.M. Jackson. — [London] : [Royal Institute of Public Administration], [1981]. — vii,235p ; 29cm
£3.80 (pbk) B81-26136

354.4107'2'09 — Great Britain. Government. Policies, ***1979-1981 — Labour Party (Great Britain) viewpoints***

Bad for Britain : a dictionary of disastrous government. — [London] : Labour Party, 1981. — 51p ; 15cm
Cover title
£0.25 (pbk) B81-21679

354.4107'22 — Great Britain. Government departments. Administration. Use of computer systems & telecommunication systems. Advisory services: Central Computer and Telecommunications Agency. ***Technical Services Organisation.*** **Role** ***— Inquiry reports***

The **Technical** Services Organisation of Central Computer and Telecommunications Agency : CSD Rayner review. — London ([Whitehall, SW1A 2AZ]) : Civil Service Department, 1981. — 106p ; 30cm
ISBN 0-7115-0033-9 (spiral) : £1.00 B81-37752

354.4107'22 — Great Britain. Management consultants. Use by government departments — ***Rules***

Code of practice for the use of management consultants by government departments / Civil Service Department Management Services. — 3rd ed. — London : H.M.S.O., 1980. — 15p ; 21cm
Previous ed.: 1975
ISBN 0-11-630434-0 (pbk) : £2.10 B81-14505

354.4107'25 — Great Britain. Government. Policies. Decision making

Policies, people and administration / [The D336 'Policies, People and Administration' Course Team]. — Milton Keynes : Open University Press. — (Social sciences : a third level course)
At head of title: The Open University
Block 2: Making policy / prepared for the Course Team. — 1980. — 151p : ill,1facsim,ports ; 30cm. — (D336 ; block 2 (papers 8-11))
Includes bibliographies. — Contents: Paper 8: Power and rationality - Paper 9: Making budgets - Paper 10: The administrative machine - Paper 11: Policy-making in crisis
ISBN 0-335-08531-8 (pbk) : Unpriced B81-10716

Policies, people and administration / [The D336 'Policies, People and Administration' Course Team]. — Milton Keynes : Open University Press. — (Social sciences : a third level course)
At head of title: The Open University
Block 4: Participation / prepared for the Course Team. — 1980. — 118p : ill ; 30cm. — (D336 ; block 4 (papers 16-18))
Includes bibliographies. — Contents: Paper 16: Open organization? - Paper 17: Administrative law and the redress of grievance - Paper 18: Citizens, clients, victims
ISBN 0-335-08533-4 (pbk) : Unpriced B81-10717

Policies, people and administration / [The D336 'Policies, People and Administration' Course Team]. — Milton Keynes : Open University Press. — (Social sciences : a third level course)
At head of title: The Open University
Block 6: Overview / prepared for the Course Team. — 1980. — 29p : 2ill ; 30cm. — (D336 ; block 6 (paper 19))
Bibliography: p29. — Contents: Paper 19 : Overview
ISBN 0-335-08534-2 (pbk) : Unpriced B81-10715

Wright, Maurice. The policy process in central government / Maurice Wright. — Manchester ([c/o Mrs. W. Bennett, Booth Street West, Manchester M15 6PB]) : Health Services Management Unit, Department of Social Admistration, University of Manchester, 1981. — 16,3leaves ; 30cm. — (Working paper series / University of Manchester. Health Services Management Unit, ISSN 0141-2647 ; no.37)
£2.00 (pbk) B81-16698

354'.4107'3 — Great Britain. Government. Organisational change, ***1950-1979***

Fry, Geoffrey K.. The administrative 'revolution' in Whitehall. — London : Croom Helm, Nov.1981. — [224]p
ISBN 0-7099-1010-x : £11.95 : CIP entry B81-30984

354.4107'3 — Great Britain. Public administration. Management. Systems analysis

Hood, Christopher, *1947-*. Bureaumetrics : the quantitative comparison of British central government agencies / Christopher Hood and Andrew Dunsire with assistance of K. Suky Thomson. — Farnborough : Gower, c1981. — xiv,312p : ill ; 23cm
Bibliography: p286-294. — Includes index
ISBN 0-566-00311-2 : £15.50 B81-36291

354.4108'2 — Scotland. Elected assemblies. Devolution of powers of British government — ***Labour Party (Great Britain) viewpoints***

Labour Party *(Great Britain). Scottish Executive.* Interim policy statement on devolution / presented by the Scottish Executive to the 66th Scottish Conference of the Labour Party, Perth, 1981. — Glasgow : Labour Party, Scottish Council, [1981]. — 22p ; 21cm
£0.40 (pbk) B81-16961

354.41'082 — Wales. Elected assemblies. Devolution of powers of British government. Referendums, ***1979***

Cledwyn of Penrhos, Cledwyn Hughes, *Baron.* The referendum = Y refferendwm. — Cardiff : Univ. of Wales Press, Jan.1982. — [32]p
English and Welsh text
ISBN 0-7083-0808-2 (pbk) : £1.00 : CIP entry B81-34302

354.4108'3 — Great Britain. Government. Relations with local authorities

Rhodes, R. A. W.. Control and power in central-local government relations / R.A.W. Rhodes. — Farnborough, Hants. : Gower, c1981. — viii,194p ; 23cm
Bibliography: p134-187. — Includes index
ISBN 0-566-00333-3 : Unpriced : CIP rev. B81-06078

354.4109'1 — Great Britain. Government inspectorates

Rhodes, Gerald. Inspectorates in British government : law enforcement and standards of efficiency / Gerald Rhodes. — London : Allen & Unwin for the Royal Institute of Public Administration, 1981. — xiii,281p : 1ill ; 23cm
Includes index
ISBN 0-04-351056-6 : £15.00 B81-10623

354.4110082 — Scotland. Economic development. Organisations: Scottish Development Agency. Organisation structure

Kirwan, F. X.. The Scottish Development Agency : structure and functions / by F.X. Kirwan. — Glasgow (c/o Publications Officer, Centre for the Study of Public Policy, University of Strathclyde, 16 Richmond St., Glasgow G1 1QX) : Centre for the Study of Public Policy, University of Strathclyde, 1981. — 33p : 1ill ; 30cm. — (Studies in public policy, ISSN 0140-8240 ; no.81)
£1.50 (pbk) B81-23285

354.4110082 — Scotland. Economic development. Organisations: Scottish Development Agency — ***Serials***

Scottish Development Agency. Report / Scottish Development Agency. — 79. — Glasgow (120, Bothwell St., Glasgow G2 7JP) : The Agency, [1979?]. — 86p
£1.00 B81-02027

Scottish Development Agency. Report / Scottish Development Agency. — 80. — Glasgow (120, Bothwell St., Glasgow G2 7JP) : The Agency, 1980. — 71p
ISSN 0140-5217 : £1.00 B81-02028

354.4110082 — Scotland. Economic development. Organisations: Scottish Development Agency — ***Accounts — Serials***

Scottish Development Agency. Accounts / Scottish Development Agency. — 1979-80. — London : H.M.S.O., 1981. — 33p
ISBN 0-10-219881-0 : £3.40 B81-23141

354.4110082'05 — Scotland. Highlands & Islands. Economic development. Organisations: Highlands and Islands Development Board — ***Accounts — Serials***

Highlands and Islands Development Board. Accounts / Highlands and Islands Development Board. — 1979-80. — London : H.M.S.O., 1981. — 23p
ISBN 0-10-220781-x : £2.60 B81-26389

354.4110082'05 — Scotland. Highlands & Islands. Economic development. Organisations: Highlands and Islands Development Board — ***Serials***

Highlands and Islands Development Board. Report / Highlands and Islands Development Board. — 14th (1979). — Inverness ([27 Bank St., Inverness IV1 1QR]) : The Board, 1980. — 130p
ISBN 0-902347-65-9 : £2.00 B81-33303

Highlands and Islands Development Board. Report / Highlands and Islands Development Board. — 15th (1980). — Inverness ([27 Bank St., Inverness IV1 1QR]) : The Board, 1981. — 130p
Cover title: Annual report (Highlands and Islands Development Board)
ISBN 0-902347-67-5 : £3.00 B81-31582

354.4110084'1 — Scotland. National health services. Organisations: Scottish Health Service Planning Council — ***Serials***

Scottish Health Service Planning Council. Report for ... / Scottish Health Service Planning Council. — 1979. — Edinburgh : H.M.S.O., 1980. — 29p
ISBN 0-11-491678-0 : £2.25 B81-00052

354.4110084'1'05 — Scotland. National health services — ***Accounts — Serials***

National Health Service (Scotland) Act 1978, accounts. — 1979-80. — London : H.M.S.O., 1981. — 25p
ISBN 0-10-231381-4 : £2.40 B81-30838

354.4110085'9 — Scotland. Antiquities. Organisations: Ancient Monuments Board for Scotland — ***Serials***

Ancient Monuments Board for Scotland. Annual report / Ancient Monuments Board for Scotland. — 27th (1980). — Edinburgh : H.M.S.O., 1981. — [13]p
ISBN 0-10-234181-8 : £2.10
ISSN 0306-591x B81-33468

354.4110086'3 — Scotland. Landscape conservation. Organisations: Countryside Commission for Scotland — ***Accounts — Serials***

Countryside Commission for Scotland. Account / Countryside Commission for Scotland. — 1979-80. — London : H.M.S.O., [1981]. — 9p
ISBN 0-10-226181-4 : £1.40 B81-30748

354.4110086'3 — Scotland. Landscape conservation. Organisations: Countryside Commission for Scotland — ***Serials***

Countryside Commission for Scotland. Report / Countryside Commission for Scotland. — 12th (1Jan.-31Dec.1979. — Redgorton (Battleby, Redgorton, Perth PH1 3EW) : The Commission, 1980. — [vii],48p
ISBN 0-902226-48-7 : £1.75 B81-36555

354.4110086'3'05 — Scotland. Landscape conservation. Organisations: Countryside Commission for Scotland — ***Serials***

Countryside Commission for Scotland. Report / Countryside Commission for Scotland. — 13th (1980). — [Perth] (The Commission) ; [London] : [H.M.S.O.] [distributor], [1981]. — 55p
ISBN 0-902226-54-1 : £2.25 B81-32695

354.416'0009 — Northern Ireland. Government, *1921-1979*

Birrell, Derek. Policy and government in Northern Ireland : lessons of devolution / Derek Birrell and Alan Murie. — Dublin : Gill and Macmillan, 1980. — 353p ; 23cm
Bibliography: p334-348. — Includes index
ISBN 0-7171-0890-2 : £20.00 B81-01608

354.416'0009 — Northern Ireland. Government, *1972-1981*

Wallace, Martin. British government in Northern Ireland. — Newton Abbot : David & Charles, Feb.1982. — [160]p
ISBN 0-7153-8153-9 : £6.50 : CIP entry B81-35821

354.4160077 — Northern Ireland. Industrial health & industrial safety. Organisations: Health and Safety Agency for Northern Ireland — *Serials*

Health and Safety Agency for Northern Ireland. Report and statement of accounts together with the report of the Comptroller and Auditor-General / Health and Safety Agency for Northern Ireland. — Belfast : H.M.S.O., 1980-. — v. ; 25cm
Annual
£1.25 B81-04877

354.4160078'2 — Northern Ireland. Fire protection & fire fighting. Organisations: Fire Authority for Northern Ireland — *Accounts* — *Serials*

Fire Authority for Northern Ireland. Statement of accounts / Fire Authority for Northern Ireland. — 1979. — Belfast : H.M.S.O., 1980. — 12p
ISBN 0-337-08159-x : £1.50 B81-20344

Fire Authority for Northern Ireland. Statement of accounts, year ended 31 March ... / Fire Authority for Northern Ireland. — 1980. — Belfast : H.M.S.O., 1981. — 10p
ISBN 0-337-08168-9 : £1.60 B81-27332

354.4160081'3'05 — Northern Ireland. Women. Equality of opportunity. Organisations: Equal Opportunities Commission for Northern Ireland — *Accounts* — *Serials*

Equal Opportunities Commission for Northern Ireland. Statement of accounts for the year ended 31 March ... together with the report of the Comptroller and Auditor-General / the Equal Opportunities Commission for Northern Ireland. — 1980. — Belfast : H.M.S.O., 1981. — iii,2p
ISBN 0-10-239381-8 : £1.20 B81-35461

354.4160081'3'05 — Northern Ireland. Women. Equality of opportunity. Organisations: Equal Opportunities Commission for Northern Ireland — *Serials*

Equal Opportunities Commission for Northern Ireland. Report of the Equal Opportunities Commission for Northern Ireland 1 April ... to 31 March .... — 4th (1979-1980). — Belfast : H.M.S.O., 1981. — 29p
ISBN 0-10-231681-3 : £2.40
ISSN 0140-9689 B81-31600

354.4160082 — Northern Ireland. Economic development. Organisations: Northern Ireland Development Agency — *Accounts* — *Serials*

Advances to the Northern Ireland Development Agency for year ended 31 March ... / Department of Commerce. — 1980. — Belfast : H.M.S.O., 1980. — [3]p
ISBN 0-337-02324-7 : £0.80 B81-27329

Development Agency. Accounts of the Northern Ireland Development Agency for the 12 months ended 31 March .... — 1979. — Belfast : H.M.S.O., 1981. — 23p. — (Cmnd. 8137)
ISBN 0-10-181370-8 : £2.70 B81-15437

Great Britain. *Department of Commerce (Northern Ireland)*. Advances to the Northern Ireland Development Agency for the year ended 31 March ... / Department of Commerce. — 1979. — Belfast : H.M.S.O., [1981?]. — [2]p
ISBN 0-337-02322-0 : £0.60 B81-26578

354.4160082'382046'05 — Northern Ireland. Mineral deposits. Prospecting & exploitation. Licences — *Serials*

Mineral Development Act (Northern Ireland) 1969 statement of the year ended 29 February ... / Department of Commerce, Northern Ireland. — 1980. — Belfast : H.M.S.O., 1980. — 5p
ISBN 0-337-06118-1 : £1.50 B81-10824

354.4160083'3 — Northern Ireland. Employment. Organisations: Fair Employment Agency for Northern Ireland — *Accounts* — *Serials*

Fair Employment Agency for Northern Ireland. Statement of accounts for the year ended 31 March ... together with the report of the Comptroller and Auditor-General / the Fair Employment Agency for Northern Ireland. — 1980. — Belfast : H.M.S.O., 1981. — ii,3p
ISBN 0-10-239281-1 : £1.20 B81-35462

354.4160083'3 — Northern Ireland. Employment. Organisations: Fair Employment Agency for Northern Ireland — *Serials*

Fair Employment Agency for Northern Ireland. Report of the Fair Employment Agency for Northern Ireland 1 April ... - 31 March ... — 4th (1979-1980). — Belfast : H.M.S.O., 1981. — 37p
ISBN 0-10-229081-4 : £2.70
ISSN 0140-9670 B81-29404

354.4160084'05 — Northern Ireland. Social services. Organisations: Eastern Health and Social Services Board, Northern Ireland — *Serials*

Eastern Health and Social Services Board, Northern Ireland. Annual report, year ended 31st December ... / Eastern Health and Social Services Board, Northern Ireland. — 1979. — [Belfast] (65 University St., Belfast BT7 1HN) : The Board, 1980. — viii,150p
ISSN 0144-7084 : £2.00 B81-04042

354.4160084'1'05 — Northern Ireland. Health services — *Accounts* — *Serials*

Great Britain. *Department of Health and Social Services, Northern Ireland*. Summary of health and personal social services accounts, together with the report of the Comptroller and Auditor-General / Department of Health and Social Services, Northern Ireland. — 1979-1980. — Belfast : H.M.S.O., [1981]. — 29p. — (Cmnd. ; 8178)
ISBN 0-10-181780-0 : £2.80 B81-26581

354.4160086'05 — Northern Ireland. Public works. Organisations: Enterprise Ulster — *Serials*

Enterprise Ulster. Annual report / Enterprise Ulster. — 1979-1980. — Belfast : H.M.S.O., 1980-. — v. ; 25cm
Continues in part: Enterprise Ulster. Annual report and statement of accounts
ISSN 0260-9940 = Annual report - Enterprise Ulster : £2.50 B81-16255

Enterprise Ulster. Annual report and statement of accounts / Enterprise Ulster. — 6th (1978-1979). — Belfast : H.M.S.O., 1980. — 59p
ISBN 0-337-09105-6 : £4.00
ISSN 0308-2008 B81-16253

354.416009'1 — Northern Ireland. Public administration. Complaints by public — *Serials*

Great Britain. *Northern Ireland Parliamentary Commissioner for Administration***Annual** report of the Northern Ireland Parliamentary Commissioner for Administration. — 1980. — London : H.M.S.O., 1981. — 68p
ISBN 0-10-235081-7 : £3.90 B81-33312

354.416068 — Northern Ireland. *Department of the Environment* — *Serials*

Northern Ireland. *Department of the Environment*. Annual report for the period ending 1 April ... to 31 March / Department of the Environment, Northern Ireland. — 1978/1979. — Belfast : H.M.S.O., 1980. — 73p
ISBN 0-337-08157-3 : £3.50
ISSN 0140-1602 B81-10825

354.420082'325'05 — England. Natural resources: Water. Organisations: National Water Council — *Serials*

National Water Council. Annual report and accounts / National Water Council. — 1979/80. — [London] ([1, Queen Anne's Gate, SW1H 9BT]) : The Council, c1980. — 74p
ISBN 0-904561-93-3 : £2.00 B81-01673

354.420084'1'05 — England. National health services — *Accounts* — *Serials*

National Health Service Reorganisation Act 1973 and National Health Service Act 1977, accounts. — 1979-80. — London : H.M.S.O., 1981. — 38p
ISBN 0-10-231281-8 : £2.70 B81-30839

354.420084'93'05 — England. Prisoners. Parole. Organisations: Parole Board — *Serials*

Parole Board. Report of the Parole Board for ... — 1980. — London : H.M.S.O., 1981. — x,44p
ISBN 0-10-234081-1 : £4.00 B81-33056

354.420086'35 — Great Britain. *Water Space Amenity Commission* — *Serials*

Great Britain. *Water Space Amenity Commission*. Annual report / Water Space Amenity Commission. — 1979-80. — London (1, Queen Anne's Gate, SW1H 9BT) : The Commission, [1980]. — 23p
ISSN 0309-1015 : £1.00 B81-03841

354.420087'22 — England. Electricy generation & transmission industries: Central Electricy Generating Board. Management. Effects of economic conditions in Great Britain

England, Glyn. Managing for low growth / by Glyn England. — London (Press and Publicity Office, Sudbury House, 15 Newgate St., EC1A 7AU) : Central Electricity Generating Board, 1981. — [11]p : 1port ; 21cm
Unpriced (pbk) B81-08050

354.42009'1 — England. Kings. Petitions of Irish persons, *1200-1400* — *Collections* — *Polyglot texts*

Documents on the affairs of Ireland before the King's council / edited by G.O. Sayles. — Dublin : Stationery Office for the Irish Manuscripts Commission, 1979. — xxv,336p ; 25cm
Old French and Latin text. — Includes index
Unpriced B81-15218

354.4208'3 — England. Monarchy. Relations with local communities, *1400-1500*

The **crown** and local communities in England and France in the fifteenth century. — Gloucester : Alan Sutton, Oct.1981. — [192]p
ISBN 0-904387-67-4 (cased) : £8.95 : CIP entry
ISBN 0-904387-79-8 (pbk) : £4.95
Also classified at 354.4408'3 B81-30175

354.4290081'8 — Wales. Rural regions. Social development. Organisations: Development Board for Rural Wales — *Accounts* — *Serials*

Development Board for Rural Wales. Accounts / Development Board for Rural Wales. — 1979-80. — London : H.M.S.O., 1981. — 15p
ISBN 0-10-214981-x : £2.10 B81-16250

354.4290082 — Wales. Economic development. Organisations: Welsh Development Agency — *Serials*

Welsh Development Agency. Report for the year 1 April ... to 31 March ... / Welsh Development Agency. — 1980-1981. — Pontypridd (Treforest Industrial Estate, Pontypridd, Mid Glamorgan CF37 5UT) : The Agency, [1981]. — 48p
ISSN 0144-3658 : Unpriced B81-36538

354.4290082 — Wales. Economic development. Organisations: Welsh Development Agency — *Serials* — *Welsh texts*

Welsh Development Agency. Adroddiad ar gyfer y flwyddyn 1 Ebrill ... hyd 31 Mawrth ... / Awdurdod Datblygu Cymru. — 1980-1981. — Pontypridd (Ystâd Ddiwydiannol Trefforest, Pontypridd, Morgannwg Ganol CF37 5UT) : Yr Awdurdod, [1981]. — 48p
ISSN 0144-3666 : Unpriced B81-36539

354.4290082'325'0212 — Wales. Water authorities: Welsh Water Authority — *Statistics — Serials*

Welsh Water Authority. Abstract of statistics / Welsh Water Authority = Crynodeb ystadegol / Awdurdod Dŵr Cymru. — 1979-. — Brecon (Directorate of Resource Planning, Planning Data Group, Cambrian Way, Brecon, Powys LD3 7HP) : The Authority, 1979-. — v. ; 21cm
Irregular
ISSN 0260-0331 = Abstract of statistics - Welsh Water Authority : Free B81-03256

354.4290082'325'05 — Wales. Water authorities: Welsh Water Authority — *Serials*

Welsh Water Authority. Annual report (including the annual accounts) for the year ending 31st March ... / Welsh Water Authority. — 6th (1980)-. — Brecon (Cambrian Way, Brecon, Powys LD3 7HP) : The Authority, 1980-. — v. : ill,maps
Continues: Welsh Water Authority. Annual report (including the annual accounts) and annual report of the Water Quality Committee for the year ending 31st March ...
ISSN 0260-7859 = Annual report, including the annual accounts — Welsh Water Authority : £2.00 B81-06673

354.4290082'326'05 — Wales. Community land scheme. Organisations: Land Authority for Wales — *Accounts — Serials*

Land Authority for Wales. Accounts / Land Authority for Wales. — 1979-80. — London : H.M.S.O., 1981. — 10p
ISBN 0-10-216581-5 : £1.80 B81-23142

354.4290082'326'05 — Wales. Community land scheme. Organisations: Land Authority for Wales — *Serials*

Land Authority for Wales. Annual report for year ending 31st March ... / Land Authority for Wales. — 1977. — [Cardiff] ([Brunel House, Cardiff CF2 1SQ]) : The Authority, [1977]. — [13]p
Unpriced B81-20295

354.4290085'1'05 — Wales. Education. Organisations: Welsh Joint Education Committee — *Serials*

Welsh Joint Education Committee. Annual report / Welsh Joint Education Committee = Adroddiad blynyddol / Cyd-Bwyllgor Addysg Cymru. — 1980-81. — [Cardiff] ([245 Western Ave., Cardiff]) : The Committee, [1981]. — 16p
Unpriced B81-33305

354.4303'73 — West Germany. Government. Role of judiciary

Blair, Philip M.. Federalism and judicial review in West Germany / by Philip M. Blair. — Oxford : Clarendon Press, 1981. — xvii, 332p ; 23cm
Bibliography: p314-322. — Includes index
ISBN 0-19-827427-0 : £22.50 : CIP rev. B81-06026

354.44'0009 — France. Government, *1770-1848*

Church, Clive H.. Revolution and red tape : the French ministerial bureaucracy 1770-1850 / by Clive H. Church. — Oxford : Clarendon, 1981. — xi,425p ; 23cm
Bibliography: p386-411. — Includes index
ISBN 0-19-855562-8 : £22.00 B81-25158

354.4407'2 — France. Government. Policies. Formulation *compared with* **formulation of government policies in Great Britain**

Ashford, Douglas E.. British dogmatism and French pragmatism. — London : Allen & Unwin, Nov.1981. — [432]p. — (The New local government series ; no.22)
ISBN 0-04-352096-0 : £27.50 : CIP entry
Primary classification 354.4107'2 B81-28785

354.4408'3 — France. Monarchy. Relations with local communities, *1400-1500*

The **crown** and local communities in England and France in the fifteenth century. — Gloucester : Alan Sutton, Oct.1981. — [192]p
ISBN 0-904387-67-4 (cased) : £8.95 : CIP entry
ISBN 0-904387-79-8 (pbk) : £4.95
Primary classification 354.4208'3 B81-30175

354.47'0009 — Soviet Union. Government, *ca 1940 — Polish texts*

Dmowski, Roman. Przyszłość Rosji zagadnienie rządu / Roman Dmowski. — London (66 Kenway Rd., S.W.5) : Księgarnia Polska Orbis, [1981]. — 75p ; 20cm
ISBN 0-901149-17-9 (pbk) : Unpriced B81-40386

354.47063'09 — Russia. *Ministerstvo vnutrennilch dĭel, 1802-1881*

Orlovsky, Daniel T.. The limits of reform : the Ministry of Internal Affairs in Imperial Russia, 1802-1881 / Daniel T. Orlovsky. — Cambridge, Mass. ; London : Harvard University Press, 1981. — viii,299p ; 24cm. — (Russian Research Center studies ; 81)
Bibliography: p259-285. — Includes index
ISBN 0-674-53435-2 : £15.00 B81-29207

354.4707'2'09 — Soviet Union. Government. Policies, *1918-*

Lenin, V. I.. Declaration of the rights of the working and exploited people : a collection / Lenin. — Moscow : Progress Publishers ; [London] : Central Books [distributor], c1980. — 28p ; 21cm
Translation of: Deklaratsii͡a prav trudi͡ashchikhsi͡a i ekspluatiruemogo naroda
ISBN 0-7147-1635-9 (pbk) : £0.20 B81-32944

354.4707'2'09 — Soviet Union. Government. Policies, *1938-1945*

Tolstoy, Nikolai. Stalin's secret war / Nikolai Tolstoy. — London : Cape, 1981. — xvi,463p : 1map ; 24cm
Map on lining papers. — Includes index
ISBN 0-224-01665-2 : £9.50 : CIP rev. B81-14918

354.51003'09 — China. Civil service. Examinations, *589-1911*

Miyazaki, Ichisada. China's examination hell : the Civil Service examinations of Imperial China / by Ichisada Miyazaki ; translated by Conrad Schirokauer. — New Haven ; London : Yale University Press, 1981. — 144p ; 24cm
Translation of: Kakyo. — Originally published: New York : Weatherhill, 1976. —
Bibliography: P131-135. — Includes index
ISBN 0-300-02639-0 (pbk) : £3.45 : CIP rev. B81-23790

354.95'300722 — Papua New Guinea. Government. Budgeting. Decision making

Allan, Bill. Planning policy analysis and public spending. — Aldershot : Gower, Feb.1982. — [160]p
ISBN 0-566-00496-8 : £11.50 : CIP entry B81-36218

355 — MILITARY FORCES

355 — Defence. Cooperation between Great Britain and United States, *1939-1980*

Baylis, John. Anglo-American defence relations 1939-1980 : the special relationship / John Baylis. — London : Macmillan, 1981. — xxii,259p ; 23cm
Bibliography: p234-247. — Includes index
ISBN 0-333-23646-7 : £20.00 B81-38638

355 — Defence — *Serials*

Seaford House papers. — 1979. — [London] ([37, Belgrave Sq., SW1X 8NS]) : [Royal College of Defence Studies], [1980]. — 170p
Unpriced B81-06700

355'.001 — Military forces. Soviet theories

Lider, Julian. Military force : an analysis of Marxist-Leninist concepts / Julian Lider. — Farnborough, Hants. : Gower, c1981. — xiii,345p ; 23cm. — (Swedish studies in international relations ; 11)
Bibliography: p312-336. - Includes index
ISBN 0-566-00296-5 : £12.50 B81-13637

355'.005 — Military forces — *Serials*

RUSI and Brassey's defence yearbook. — 1982. — London : Pergamon, Nov.1981. — [360]p
ISBN 0-08-027039-5 (cased) : £10.00 : CIP entry
ISBN 0-08-027040-9 (pbk) : £10.00 B81-28761

R.U.S.T. and Brassey's defence yearbook / edited by the Royal United Services Institute for Defence Studies. — 91st (1981). — Oxford : Brassey's, c1980. — xxxvi,357p
ISBN 0-08-027007-7 : Unpriced
ISSN 0097-4803 B81-09178

355'.0074'02164 — London. Southwark *(London Borough).* **Museums: Imperial War Museum** — *Visitors' guides*

Imperial War Museum. Imperial War Museum handbook. — [Rev. ed.]. — [London] : The Museum, 1976. — 48p : ill,facsims,ports ; 20x21cm
Previous ed.: London : H.M.S.O., 1972
£0.50 (pbk) B81-04486

355'.0074'02657 — Cambridgeshire. Duxford. Museums: Imperial War Museum — *Visitors' guides*

Imperial War Museum. Duxford handbook / Imperial War Museum. — [London] ([Lambeth Rd., SE1 6HZ]) : The Museum, 1977. — 67p : ill,1coat of arms,1map,1plan,ports ; 20x22cm
Cover title
£0.50 (pbk) B81-04487

355'.0092'2 — Military forces, *to 1976 — Biographies — For children*

Monham, Kathleen. Famous names in warfare / Kathleen Monham. — Hove : Wayland, 1980. — 48p : ill,ports ; 24cm
Bibliography: p47. - Includes index
ISBN 0-85340-791-6 : £2.95 B81-04007

355'.00937 — Romania. Dobruja. Ancient Roman armies. Literary sources

Aricescu, Andrei. The army in Roman Dobrudja / Andrei Aricescu ; translated from the Romanian by Nubar Hampartumian. — Oxford : B.A.R., 1980. — 225p : maps ; 30cm. — (BAR. International series ; 86)
Bibliography: p186-188
ISBN 0-86054-099-5 (pbk) : £10.00 B81-36589

355'.00939'4 — Middle Eastern armies, *B.C.3500-A.D.612*

Wise, Terence. Ancient armies of the Middle East / text by Terence Wise ; colour plates by Angus McBride. — London : Osprey, 1981. — 40p,A-Hp of plates : ill(some col.),1map ; 25cm. — (Men-at-arms series ; 109)
English text ; notes on col.plates in French and German. — Bibliography: p2
ISBN 0-85045-384-4 (pbk) : £2.95 B81-26223

355'.00941 — Great Britain. *Army*

Barker, Dennis. Soldiering on : an unofficial portrait of the British Army / Dennis Barker. — London : Deutsch, 1981. — 256p,[8]p of plates : ill,ports ; 24cm
ISBN 0-233-97391-5 : £8.50 : CIP rev. B81-26746

355'.00941 — Great Britain. *Army, 1485-1980*

Barthorp, Michael. The armies of Britain 1485-1980 / Michael Barthorp. — [London] : [National Army Museum], [1980]. — 296p : ill (some col.),maps,coats of arms,1facsim,ports (some col.) ; 31cm
Includes index
ISBN 0-905353-02-1 : £4.50 B81-05020

355'.00941 — Great Britain. *Army, 1945-1980*

Gander, Terry. Encyclopaedia of the modern British Army / Terry Gander. — Cambridge : Stephens, 1980 (1981 [printing]). — 280p : ill,maps ; 25cm
Ill on lining papers. — Includes index
ISBN 0-85059-435-9 : £14.95 : CIP rev. B80-17613

355'.00942 — England and Wales. *Army. New Model Army, to 1660*

Asquith, Stuart A.. New Model Army 1645-60 / text by Stuart Asquith ; colour plates by Chris Warner. — London : Osprey, 1981. — 40p,A-Hp of plates : ill(some col.),maps,ports ; 25cm. — (Men-at-arms series ; 110)
English text; notes on col. plates in French and German. — Bibliography: p2
ISBN 0-85045-385-2 (pbk) : £2.95 B81-26864

355'.00942 — Hundred Years' War. Battle of Crécy & Battle of Poitiers. Armies

Rothero, Christopher. The armies of Crecy and Poitiers / text and colour plates by Christopher Rothero. — London : Osprey, 1981. — 40p,A-Hp of plates : ill(some col.),coats of arms,2maps ; 25cm. — (Men-at-arms series ; 111)
English text ; notes on col. plates in French and German
ISBN 0-85045-393-3 (pbk) : £2.95 B81-26011

355'.009431 — Germany *(Democratic Republic). Nationale Volksarmee, to 1979*

Forster, Thomas M.. The East German army : the second power in the Warsaw Pact / Thomas M. Forster ; with an introduction by Sir Harry Tuzo ; translated by Deryck Viney. — London : Allen & Unwin, 1980. — 310p,[2]p of plates : ill(some col.),facsims,1plan,ports ; 24cm
Translation of: Die NVA - Kernstück der Landesverteidigung der DDR. 5 Aufl. — Includes index
ISBN 0-04-355012-6 : £12.00 B81-04458

355'.00947 — Soviet military forces, *to 1981*

Scott, Harriet Fast. The armed forces of the USSR / Harriet Fast Scott, William F. Scott. — 2nd ed. rev. and updated. — Boulder : Westview ; London : Arms & Armour, 1981. — xxiv,447p : ill,1map ; 24cm
Previous ed.: 1979. — Bibliography: p403-412. — Includes index
ISBN 0-85368-287-9 : £12.95 B81-33264

355'.00947 — Union of Soviet Socialist Republics. *Armiia, 1956-1980*

Suvorov, Viktor. The liberators. — London : H. Hamilton, Sept.1981. — [224]p
ISBN 0-241-10675-3 : £8.95 : CIP entry B81-20118

355'.0095 — Mongol armies, *1167-1280*

Turnbull, S. R.. The Mongols / text by S.R. Turnbull ; colour plates by Angus McBride. — London : Osprey, 1980. — 40p,A-Hp of plates : ill(some col.),plans,2ports ; 24cm. — (Men-at-arms series ; 105)
English text, English, French and German captions to plates
ISBN 0-85045-372-0 (pbk) : £2.95 B81-13931

355'.00954 — India *(Dominion).* **Army,** *to 1947*

Mollo, Boris. The Indian Army. — Poole : Blandford, Oct.1981. — [192]p
ISBN 0-7137-1074-8 : £10.50 : CIP entry B81-28017

355'.02 — Great powers. Wars, *ca 1860-1979.* **Theories**

Organski, A. F. K.. The war ledge / A.F.K. Organski, Jacek Kugler. — Chicago ; London : University of Chicago Press, 1980. — xi,292p : ill ; 23cm
Bibliography: p271-282. - Includes index
ISBN 0-226-63279-2 : £15.00 B81-07734

355'.02 — Tribal societies. Warfare

Feest, Christian. The art of war / Christian Feest. — London : Thames and Hudson, 1980. — 92,[4]p : ill(some col.),1map ; 25cm
Bibliography: p[2]. — Includes index
ISBN 0-500-06010-x (pbk) : £4.95 B81-03106

355'.02 — Warfare — *Early works*

Sun, Tzu. The art of war. — London : Hodder & Stoughton, Nov.1981. — [96]p
ISBN 0-340-27604-5 (pbk) : £3.50 : CIP entry B81-30548

355'.02 — Warfare — *Marxist viewpoints*

Marxism and the science of war / edited, with an introdction, by Bernard Semmel. — Oxford : Oxford University Press, 1981. — xvi,302p ; 22cm
Includes index
ISBN 0-19-876112-0 (cased) : £15.95 : CIP rev.
ISBN 0-19-876113-9 (pbk) : £5.95 B81-08841

355'.02 — Warfare. Technological innovation

The **Impact** of new military technology / edited by Jonathan Alford. — Farnborough, Hants. : Published for the International Institute for Strategic Studies by Gower, c1981. — vi,132p : ill ; 23cm. — (The Adelphi library ; 4)
Includes index
ISBN 0-566-00345-7 : £10.50 B81-11623

355'.02 — Western Europe. Warfare. Chivalry, *1400-1525*

Vale, M. G. A.. War and chivalry : warfare and aristocratic culture in England, France and Burgundy at the end of the Middle Ages / Malcolm Vale. — London : Duckworth, 1981. — 206p : ill,1map,coats of arms,facsims,ports ; 24cm
Ill. on lining papers. — Bibliography: p187-200. — Includes index
ISBN 0-7156-1042-2 : £18.00 : CIP rev. B81-09977

355'.02'05 — Warfare — *For children* — *Serials*

Battle picture weekly annual. — 1981. — London : IPC Magazines, c1980. — 127p
ISBN 0-85037-520-7 : £1.50 B81-06860

The **War** picture library annual. — 1981. — London : IPC Magazines, c1980. — 95p
ISBN 0-85037-591-6 : £1.50 B81-06859

355'.02'09 — Warfare, *to 1920*

Delbrück, Hans. History of the art of war : within the framework of political history / by Hans Delbrück ; translated from the German by Walter J. Renfroe, Jr.. — Westport, Conn. ; London : Greenwood Press. — (Contributions in military history, ISSN 0084-9251 ; no.20)
Translation of: Geschichte der Kriegskunst im Rahmen der politischen Geschichte. 3rd ed
Vol.2: The Germans. — 1980. — 505p ; 24cm
Includes index
ISBN 0-8371-8163-1 : £24.95 B81-23650

355'.02'09 — Warfare, *to 1980* — *For children*

Maynard, Christopher. Weapons and warfare / written and designed by Maynard & Jefferis. — London : Pan, 1981. — 91p : ill(some col.),col.maps ; 18cm. — (A Piccolo factbook)
Text on inside cover. — Includes index
ISBN 0-330-26361-7 (pbk) : £1.25 B81-38769

Maynard, Christopher. Weapons and warfare / written and designed by Maynard & Jefferis ; editor Jacqui Bailey. — London : Kingfisher, 1981. — 91pp : ill(some col.) ; 19cm. — (A Kingfisher factbook)
Includes index
ISBN 0-86272-011-7 : £2.50 : CIP rev. B81-14403

355'.02'0924 — War. Attitudes of Jefferson, Thomas

Stuart, Reginald C.. The half-way pacifist : Thomas Jefferson's view of war / Reginald C. Stuart. — Toronto ; London : University of Toronto Press, c1978. — x,93p ; 24cm
Bibliography: p85-90. - Includes index
ISBN 0-8020-5431-5 : £8.75 B81-05573

355'.02'093 — Ancient world. Warfare, *B.C.800-A.D.450*

Connolly, Peter. Greece and Rome at war / Peter Connolly. — London : Macdonald, 1981. — 320p : col.ill,col maps,plans(some col.) ; 29cm
Bibliography: p314-315. — Includes index
ISBN 0-356-06798-x : £12.95 B81-33261

355'.02'094 — Europe. Land warfare, *1939-1940*

Deighton, Len. Blitzkrieg : from the rise of Hitler to the fall of Dunkirk / Len Deighton ; with a foreword by W.K. Nehring. — [St Albans] : Triad, 1981, c1979. — 382p,[32]p of plates : ill,maps,ports ; 18cm
Originally published: London : Cape, 1979. — Bibliography: p365-374. — Includes index
ISBN 0-586-05207-0 (pbk) : £1.95 B81-36578

355'.02'094 — Europe. Warfare, *1792-1815*

Glover, Michael, *1922-*. Warfare in the age of Bonaparte / Michael Glover. — London : Cassell, 1980. — 255p : ill(some col.),maps,plans ; 26cm. — ([History of warfare])
Ill on lining papers. — Bibliography: p252. — Includes index
ISBN 0-304-30722-x : £8.95 B81-28915

355'.02'094 — Europe. Warfare. Effects of development of military weapons, *to 1977* — *For children* — *Welsh texts*

Williams, Brian, *1943-*. [Exploring war and weapons. Welsh]. Rhyfel ac arfau / Brian Williams ; ymgynghorwr D. Huw Owen ; cynlluniwyd gan David Nash ; arlunwyr John Berry ... [et al.]. — Caerdydd : Gwasg y Dref Wen, c1980. — [24]p : col.ill ; 23cm. — (Darganfod)
Translation of: Exploring war and weapons
£1.95 B81-04985

355'.0213 — Militarism, *1861-1979*

Berghahn, Volker R.. Militarism : the history of an international debate, 1861-1979. — Leamington Spa (24 Binswood Ave., Leamington Spa CV32 5SQ) : Berg Publishers, Nov.1981. — [144]p
ISBN 0-907582-01-x : £7.95 : CIP entry B81-31060

355'.0217 — Nuclear warfare

Levi, Werner. The coming end of war / Werner Levi. — Beverly Hills ; London : Sage, c1981. — 183p ; 23cm. — (Sage library of social research ; v.117)
Bibliography: p179-182
ISBN 0-8039-1523-3 (cased) : Unpriced
ISBN 0-8039-1524-1 (pbk) : Unpriced B81-27170

355'.0217 — Nuclear warfare. Causes & effects — *Forecasts*

Beres, Louis René. Apocalypse : nuclear catastrophe in world politics / Louis René Beres ; with a foreword by Paul C. Warnke. — Chicago ; London : University of Chicago press, 1980. — xvi,315p ; 24cm
Includes index
ISBN 0-226-04360-6 : £12.00 B81-05577

355'.0217 — Nuclear warfare. Deterrence

The **Future** of strategic deterrence / edited by Christoph Bertram. — London : Macmillan : IISS, 1981. — 108p ; 26cm. — (International Institute for Strategic Studies conference papers)
Conference proceedings. — Includes index
ISBN 0-333-32394-7 : £15.00 B81-38736

Strategic deterrence in a changing environment / edited by Christoph Bertram. — Farnborough, Hants. : Published for the International Institute for Strategic Studies by Gower, c1981. — vi,194p : ill,maps ; 23cm. — (Adelphi library ; 6)
Includes index
ISBN 0-566-00346-5 : £9.50 B81-11622

355'.0217 — Nuclear warfare. Effects — *Forecasts*

How to survive the nuclear age : what the government will not tell you!. — [London] ([42 Warriner Gardens, SW11 4DU]) : Ecology Party, [1980?]. — 21p : ill (some col.),ports ; 30cm
Cover title
£0.80 (pbk) B81-31383

Richardson, Frank. The public and the bomb / Frank M. Richardson. — Edinburgh : William Blackwood, 1981. — viii,104p ; 18cm
ISBN 0-85158-150-1 (pbk) : £1.50 B81-19282

Zuckerman, Solly Zuckerman, *Baron*. Nuclear illusion and reality. — London : Collins, Jan.1982. — [151]p
ISBN 0-00-216555-4 (cased) : £7.50 : CIP entry
ISBN 0-00-216554-6 (pbk) : £4.95 B81-34583

355'.0217 — Nuclear warfare. Effects — *Study regions: Great Britain*

Clarke, Magnus. The nuclear destruction of Britain. — London : Croom Helm, Oct.1981. — [224]p
ISBN 0-7099-0458-4 : £11.95 : CIP entry B81-24655

355'.0217 — Nuclear warfare — *Forecasts*

Calder, Nigel. Nuclear nightmares : an investigation into possible wars / Nigel Calder. — Harmondsworth : Penguin, 1981, c1979. — vi,168p ; 20cm
Originally published: London : British Broadcasting Corporation, 1979. — Bibliography: p163-164. — Includes index
ISBN 0-14-005867-2 (pbk) : £1.50 B81-40443

Lee, Christopher, *1941-*. The final decade : will we survive the 1980s / Christopher Lee. — London : Hamilton, 1981. — 190p,[8]p of plates : ill,1map ; 24cm
Bibliography: p182. — Includes index
ISBN 0-241-10424-6 : £8.95 : CIP rev. B81-02648

Ryle, *Sir* **Martin**. Towards the nuclear holocaust / Sir Martin Ryle. — 2nd print. (with glossary). — London : Menard, 1981, c1980. — 31p ; 22cm
ISBN 0-903400-61-8 (pbk) : £0.75 B81-26854

355'.0217 — Nuclear weapons. Proliferation — *Campaign for Nuclear Disarmament viewpoints*

Kennard, Peter. No nuclear weapons : the case for nuclear disarmament / photomontage by Peter Kennard ; text by Ric Sissons. — London : Pluto : Campaign for Nuclear Disarmament, 1981. — [44]p : ill,2maps ; 21cm
Text on inside cover
ISBN 0-86104-337-5 (pbk) : £1.00 B81-27558

355'.0217 — South Asia. Nuclear weapons. Proliferation, *1973-1980*

Jones, Rodney W.. Nuclear proliferation : Islam, the bomb and South Asia / Rodney W. Jones ; foreword by Amos A. Jordon, Jr. — Beverly Hills ; London : Sage [for] the Center for Strategic and International Studies, c1981. — 88p ; 22cm. — (The Washington papers ; vol.ix, 82) (A Sage policy paper)
Bibliography: p86-88
ISBN 0-8039-1609-4 (pbk) : £2.50 B81-29263

355'.02184 — Africa. Guerrilla warfare, *to 1979*

Davidson, Basil. The people's cause. — London : Longman, Jan.1982. — [256]p
ISBN 0-582-64680-4 (cased) : £9.95 : CIP entry
ISBN 0-582-64681-2 (pbk) : £4.95 B81-34557

355'.02184 — Guerrilla warfare

Clutterbuck, Richard. Guerrillas and terrorists / Richard Clutterbuck. — Chicago ; London : Ohio University Press, 1980, c1977. — 125p ; 23cm
Originally published: London : Faber, 1977. — Bibliography: p117-119. — Includes index
ISBN 0-8214-0590-x (cased) : £7.20
ISBN 0-8214-0592-6 (pbk) : £3.60
Primary classification 322.4'2 B81-22350

355'.02184 — Guerrilla warfare by Great Britain. Army, *1945-1970.* **Kitson, Frank. Low intensity operations** — *Critical studies*

Ronin. High intensity subversion / by 'Ronin'. — Over the Water (Over the Water, Sanday, Orkney KW17 2BL) : Cienfuegos, 1981. — x,70p : ill,facsims,ports ; 30cm
Ill on inside covers
ISBN 0-904564-32-0 (pbk) : £3.50
Also classified at 363.3'0941 B81-29191

355'.027 — Wars. Participation by United States, *1812-1950.* **Causes**

Small, Melvin. Was war necessary? : national security and U.S. entry into war / Melvin Small. — Beverly Hills ; London : Sage, c1980. — 311p ; 23cm. — (Sage library of social research ; vol.105)
Includes bibliographies
ISBN 0-8039-1486-5 (cased) : £11.25 B81-07825

355'.027'028 — War. Causes. Theories. Statistical methods

Wilkinson, David, *1939-*. Deadly quarrels : Lewis F. Richardson and the statistical study of war / David Wilkinson. — Berkeley ; London : University of California Press, c1980. — viii,206p ; 24cm
Bibliography: p187-194. — Includes index
ISBN 0-520-03829-0 : £11.00 B81-01550

355'.027'0903 — Wars. Causes. Theories of liberals, *1500-1975*

Howard, Michael. War and the liberal conscience : the George Macaulay Trevelyan lectures in the University of Cambridge, 1977 / Michael Howard. — Oxford : Oxford University Press, 1981, c1978. — 143p : ill ; 20cm
Originally published: London : Temple Smith, 1978. — Includes index
ISBN 0-19-285111-x (pbk) : £1.95 : CIP rev. B81-15802

355'.028 — Wars. Termination

On the endings of wars / edited by Stuart Albert and Edward C. Luck. — Port Washington ; London : National University Publications : Kennikat, 1980. — 174p ; 22cm. — (Series in political science)
Includes index
ISBN 0-8046-9240-8 : £14.85 B81-05494

355'.031'091821 — North Atlantic Treaty Organization. Role, *1980-1990*

NATO : the next thirty years : the changing political, economic and military setting / edited by Kenneth A. Myers. — Boulder : Westview ; London : Croom Helm, 1980. — xxiii,469p ; 24cm
Conference papers. — Includes index
ISBN 0-7099-1700-7 : £14.95 B81-07344

355'.031'091821 — North Atlantic Treaty Organization, *to 1980*

Britain and NATO : over thirty years of collective defence / [prepared by Ministry of Defence Public Relations and the Central Office of Information]. — [London] : [H.M.S.O.], [1981?]. — 26p : ill,maps,1facsim,1port ; 30cm
Cover title
Unpriced (pbk) B81-24790

355'.033 — Military power. International political aspects, *to 1980*

Estimating foreign military power. — London : Croom Helm, Nov.1981. — [288]p
ISBN 0-7099-0434-7 : £13.95 : CIP entry B81-30348

355'.033043 — Germany. Rearmament, *1928-1939*

Deist, Wilhelm. The Wehrmacht and German rearmament / by Wilhelm Deist ; [translated from the German ms.] ; foreword by A.J. Nicholls. — London : Macmillan, 1981. — xiii,151p ; 23cm. — (St Antony's/Macmillan series)
Bibliography: p129-145. — Includes index
ISBN 0-333-26462-2 : £20.00 B81-31904

355'.033047 — Soviet Union. Military relations — *Soviet viewpoints*

The lie of a Soviet war threat / [translated from the Russian]. — Moscow : Progress ; [London] : Central Books [distributor], c1980. — 102p ; 20cm
Translation of: Protiv mifa o <<sovetskoĭ voennoĭ ugroze>>
ISBN 0-7147-1622-7 (pbk) : £0.95 B81-29307

355'.0335 — Military policies

New directions in strategic thinking / edited by Robert O'Neill and D.M. Horner. — London : Allen & Unwin, 1981. — xiv,318p ; 23cm
Bibliography: p298-309. — Includes index
ISBN 0-04-355013-4 : Unpriced : CIP rev. B81-20138

355'.0335'05 — Military policies — *Serials*

Strategic survey / the International Institute for Strategic Studies. — 1980-1981. — London : The Institute, 1981. — [iii],138p
£4.00 B81-30756

355'.0335'1713 — Western bloc countries. Military policies

Churchill, Winston S. (Winston Spencer), *1940-*. Defending the West. — London : Maurice Temple Smith, Sept.1981. — [224]p
ISBN 0-85117-210-5 : £8.95 : CIP entry B81-28496

355'.0335'41 — Great Britain. Military policies

Smith, Dan, *1951-*. The defence of the realm in the 1980s / Dan Smith. — London : Croom Helm, c1980 (1981 [printing]). — 276p ; 22cm
Includes index
ISBN 0-7099-2332-5 (pbk) : £6.95 B81-33276

355'.0335'41 — Great Britain. Military policies, *1847-1942*

Gooch, John. The prospect of war : studies in British defence policy 1847-1942 / John Gooch. — London : Cass, 1981. — viii,163p ; 23cm
ISBN 0-7146-3128-0 : £11.00 : CIP rev. B80-21626

355'.0335'41 — Great Britain. Military policies — *Fabian viewpoints*

Brown, Neville. A British approach to peace / Neville Brown. — London : Fabian Society, 1981. — 24p ; 22cm. — (Fabian tract, ISSN 0307-7535 ; 474)
Cover title
ISBN 0-7163-0474-0 (pbk) : £0.75 B81-24792

355'.0335'41 — Great Britain. Military policies. Formulation, *1845-1970*

Politicians and defence : studies in the formulation of British defence policy 1845-1970 / edited by Ian Beckett and John Gooch. — Manchester : Manchester University Press, c1981. — xxii,202p : ports ; 25cm
Includes index
ISBN 0-7190-0818-2 : £16.50 B81-20770

355'.0335'41 — Great Britain. Military policies — *Proposals*

Great Britain. The United Kingdom defence programme : the way forward. — London : H.M.S.O., [1981]. — 14p ; 25cm. — (Cmnd. ; 8288)
ISBN 0-10-182880-2 (corrected : unbound) : £1.70 B81-33380

355'.0335'41 — Great Britain. Nuclear weapons. Policies of government

McMahan, Jeff. British nuclear weapons. — London : Junction Books, Nov.1981. — [224]p
ISBN 0-86245-047-0 (cased) : £9.95: CIP entry
ISBN 0-86245-049-7 (pbk) : £3.95 B81-30631

Neild, R. R.. How to make up your mind about the bomb / Robert Neild. — London : Deutsch, 1981. — 144p : 2maps ; 22cm
Includes index
ISBN 0-233-97382-6 (pbk) : £2.95 B81-22852

355'.0335'41 — Great Britain. Nuclear weapons. Policies of government, *1939-1945.* **Gowing, Margaret. Britain and atomic energy 1939-1945. Citations: Public records** — *Lists*

Britain and atomic energy 1939-1945 by Margaret Gowing (Macmillan, London, 1964) : references to official papers. — Didcot (Building 328, AERE, Harwell, Didcot, Oxon) : Authority Historian's Office, 1980. — 32p ; 21cm
Unpriced (pbk)
Also classified at 333.79'24'0941 B81-16103

355'.0335'41 — Great Britain. Nuclear weapons. Policies of government, *1945-1952.* **Gowing, Margaret. Independence and deterrence. Citations: Public records** — *Lists*

Independence and deterrence Britain and atomic energy, 1945-1952 by Margaret Gowing (2 vols. Macmillan, London, 1974) : references to official papers. — Rev. ed. — Didcot (Building 328, AERE, Harwell, Didcot, Oxon) : Authority Historian's Office, 1970. — 48p ; 21cm
Previous ed.: 1977
Unpriced (pbk)
Also classified at 333.79'24'0941 B81-16104

355′.0335′41 — Great Britain. Nuclear weapons. Policies of government, *1945-1979*

Freedman, Lawrence. Britain and nuclear weapons / Lawrence Freedman. — London : Macmillan for the Royal Institute of International Affairs, 1980. — xv,160p ; 23cm
Includes index
ISBN 0-333-30494-2 (cased) : £12.00 : CIP rev.
ISBN 0-333-30511-6 (pbk) : £3.25 B80-21627

355′.0335′41 — Great Britain. Nuclear weapons. Policies of government — *Communist Party of Great Britain viewpoints*

Chater, Tony. The case for peace and disarmament / Tony Chater. — [London] : [Communist Party], [1980]. — 30p : 1port ; 21cm. — (A Communist Party pamphlet)
ISBN 0-86224-008-5 (unbound) : £0.30
B81-06235

355′.0335′47 — Russia. Military policies, *1700-1800*

Duffy, Christopher. Russia's military way to the West : origins and nature of Russian military power 1700-1800 / Christopher Duffy. — London : Routledge & Kegan Paul, 1981. — xiii,256p : ill,maps,ports ; 25cm
Bibliography: p243-250. — Includes index
ISBN 0-7100-0797-3 : £15.00 : CIP rev.
B81-28115

355′.0335′47 — Soviet Union. Military policies

Soviet military thinking. — London : Allen & Unwin, Oct.1981. — [304]p
ISBN 0-04-355014-2 (cased) : £14.50 : CIP entry
ISBN 0-04-355016-9 (pbk) : £6.95 B81-25143

Soviet strategy / edited by John Baylis and Gerald Segal. — London : Croom Helm, c1981. — 263p ; 23cm
Includes index
ISBN 0-7099-0609-9 (cased) : £12.50 : CIP rev.
ISBN 0-7099-0629-3 (pbk) : £6.95 B81-08831

355′.0335′73 — United States. Military policies, *ca 1870-1920*

Abrahamson, James L.. America arms for a new century : the making of a great military power / James L. Abrahamson. — New York : Free Press ; London : Collier Macmillan, c1981. — xv,253p,[16]p of plates : ill,ports ; 25cm
Bibliography: p237-244. — Includes index
ISBN 0-02-900190-0 : £10.95 B81-39020

355.1 — MILITARY LIFE

355.1′092′4 — Austrailia. Great Britain. *Army.* **Soldiers. Army life,** *1941-1945 — Personal observations*

Bates, Tom H.. The general's mess : anecdotes from a general's mess, during a war which we never got to / Tom H. Bates. — Ilfracombe : Stockwell, 1980. — 64p,[8]p of plates : ill,ports ; 19cm
ISBN 0-7223-1396-9 : £3.40 B81-08264

355.1′0941 — Great Britain. *Army.* **Soldiers. Army life,** *ca 1800-1914*

Farwell, Byron. [Mr. Kipling's army]. For Queen and Country / Byron Farwell. — London : Allen Lane, 1981. — 256p : ill ; 22cm
Originally published: New York : Norton, 1980. — Includes index
ISBN 0-7139-1241-3 : £8.50 B81-25587

355.1′342 — British military forces. Awards of medals, *1885:* **Abu Klea Medal** — *Lists*

Webb, J. V.. The Abu Klea medal rolls : to which are added the rolls of the remaining Camel Corps Detachments, and many of the 'Odd Men' who served in the Nile Expedition 1884-5 and at Suakin in 1885 / J.V. Webb. — London ([22 Highbury Terrace], Highbury, N5) : J.V. Webb, 1981. — xviii,158p : 1map,1plan ; 25cm
£10.00 B81-37384

355.1′342′0937 — Ancient Roman armies. Decorations

Maxfield, Valerie. The military decorations of the Roman Army / Valerie A. Maxfield. — London : Batsford, 1981. — 304p,16p of plates : ill,maps ; 24cm
Bibliography: p295-297. — Includes index
ISBN 0-7134-2718-3 : £14.95 B81-33062

355.1′4 — Great Britain. *Army.* **Battledress,** *1937-1961*

Jewell, Brian, *1925-*. British battledress 1937-61 / text by Brian Jewell ; colour plates by Mike Chappell. — London : Osprey, 1981. — 40p,A-Hp of plates : ill(some col.),ports ; 25cm. — (Men-at-arms series ; 112)
English text ; notes on col. plates in French and German
ISBN 0-85045-387-9 (pbk) : £2.95 B81-26222

355.1′4′09 — Armies. Uniforms, *to 1980 — For children*

Kershaw, Andrew. Guide to military uniform / Andrew Kershaw ; illustrated by Pete Robinson. — London : Watts, 1981, c1980. — 24p : chiefly col.ill ; 23cm. — (Explorer guides)
Bibliography: p24. — Includes index
ISBN 0-85166-933-6 : £2.99 B81-26019

355.1′4′094 — Europe. Military forces. Uniforms, *700-1500*

Funcken, Liliane. The age of chivalry / Liliane and Fred Funchen. — London : Ward Lock. — (Arms and uniforms)
Translation of: Le costume, l'armure et les armes au temps de la chevalerie
Pt.2: Castles, forts and artillery, 8th to 15th century .... — 1981. — 109p : col.ill ; 25cm
Ill on lining papers. — Includes index
ISBN 0-7063-5936-4 : £7.95 : CIP rev.
Also classified at 623′.094 B81-03701

Funcken, Liliane. The age of chivalry. — London : Ward Lock
Part 3: The Renaissance. — Feb.1982. — [112]p
ISBN 0-7063-5937-2 : £6.95 : CIP entry
Also classified at 623′.094 B81-37566

355.1′4′0944 — France. *Armée.* **Uniforms,** *1789-1802*

Haythornthwaite, Philip J.. Uniforms of the French Revolutionary Wars 1789-1802 / Philip J. Haythornthwaite ; illustrated by Christopher Warner. — Poole : Blandford, 1981. — 147p : ill(some col.) ; 26cm
Bibliography: p145-147
ISBN 0-7137-0936-7 : £10.50 : CIP rev.
B81-00799

355.1′6 — Great Britain. *Commonwealth War Graves Commission — Serials*

Great Britain. *Commonwealth War Graves Commission*. Annual report / Commonwealth War Graves Commission. — 61st [(1979-1980)]. — [Maidenhead] ([2 Marlow Rd., Maidenhead, Berks SL6 7DX]) : [The Commission], [1980]. — 44p
Unpriced B81-03589

355.2 — MILITARY RESOURCES

355.2′05 — Military resources — *Serials*

The **Military** balance / the International Institute for Strategic Studies. — 1980-81. — London : The Institute, 1980. — 119p
ISBN 0-86079-040-1 : £5.00
ISSN 0459-7222 B81-03759

The **Military** balance. — 1980-1981. — London : Arms and Armour Press in association with the International Institute of Strategic Studies, c1980
1980-81. — [144]p
ISBN 0-85368-197-x : £6.95 : CIP entry
ISSN 0459-7222 B80-20429

355.2′0941 — Great Britain. Military resources — *Serials*

Great Britain. *Ministry of Defence*. Statement on the defence estimates : presented to Parliament by the Secretary of State for Defence .... 1. — 1980-. — London : H.M.S.O., 1980-. — v. ; 30cm
Annual. — Continues in part: Statement on the defence estimates. — Description based on: 1981 issue
ISSN 0261-3980 = Statement on the defence estimates. 1 : £5.00 B81-29428

355.2′0941 — Great Britain. Military resources — *Statistics — Serials*

Great Britain. *Ministry of Defence*. Statement on the defence estimates : presented to Parliament by the Secretary of State for Defence .... 2, Defence statistics. — 1980-. — London : H.M.S.O., 1980-. — v. ; 30cm
Annual. — Continues in part: Statement on the defence estimates. — Description based on: 1981 issue
ISSN 0261-3999 = Statement on the defence estimates. 2. Defence statistics : £5.00
B81-29427

355.2′1 — American military forces. Effectiveness. Assessment

Combat effectiveness : cohesion, stress, and the volunteer military / Sam C. Sarkesian, editor. — Beverly Hills ; London : Sage, c1980. — 305p : ill ; 23cm. — (Sage research progress series on war, revolution, and peacekeeping ; v.9)
Bibliography: p279-295. — Includes index
ISBN 0-8039-1440-7 (cased) : Unpriced
ISBN 0-8039-1441-5 (pbk) : Unpriced
B81-26980

355.2′2 — Islamic countries. Military slavery, *to 840*

Pipes, Daniel. Slave soldiers and Islam : the genesis of a military system / Daniel Pipes. — New Haven ; London : Yale University Press, c1980. — xxx,246p ; 22cm
Bibliography: p219-231. — Includes index
ISBN 0-300-02447-9 : £15.75 B81-21094

355.2′2′0941 — British military forces. Personnel — *Statistics — Serials*

Great Britain. *Ministry of Defence*. Ministry of Defence Votes A for the year ending 31st March .... — 1981-82. — London : H.M.S.O., 1981. — 6p
ISBN 0-10-212381-0 : £1.10 B81-16835

355.2′236 — Great Britain. *Army.* **Officers. Commissions. Purchase,** *1660-1871*

Bruce, A. P. C.. The purchase system in the British Army, 1660-1871 / Anthony Bruce. — London : Royal Historical Society, 1980. — viii,194p ; 23cm. — (Royal Historical Society studies in history series ; no.20)
Includes index
ISBN 0-901050-57-1 : £14.00 B81-04415

355.2′2363′0941 — Great Britain. National service, *to ca 1965*

Called up : a National Service scrapbook / [compiled by] George Forty. — London : Ian Allan, 1980. — 128p : ill,facsims,ports ; 30cm
Ill on lining papers
ISBN 0-7110-1050-1 : £8.95 B81-04071

355.3 — MILITARY ORGANISATION

355.3′1′0941 — Great Britain. *Army.* *Lovat Scouts, to 1980*

Melville, Michael Leslie. The story of the Lovat Scouts 1900-1980 / by Michael Leslie Melville. — Edinburgh : St. Andrew Press, 1981. — xii,118p,[26]p of plates : ill,maps,music,ports ; 22cm
ISBN 0-7152-0474-2 (corrected) : £6.75
B81-30937

355.3′1′0954016 — Great Britain *Foreign and Commonwealth Office* **Libraries: India Office Library and Records. Stock:Archives of India Office** *Military Department - Lists*

Farrington, Anthony. Guide to the records of the India Office Military Department. — London : India Office Library and Records, May 1981. — 1v.
ISBN 0-903359-30-8 : CIP entry B81-07462

355.3′31′0924 — Great Britain. *Army.* **Alanbrooke, Alan Francis Brooke,** *Viscount — Biographies*

Fraser, *Sir* **David,** *1920-*. Alanbrooke. — London : Collins, Jan.1982. — [591]p
ISBN 0-00-216360-8 : £12.50 : CIP entry
B81-34582

355.3'31'0924 — Great Britain. *Army*. Colville, *Sir* Charles — *Biographies*

Colville, John. The portrait of a general : a chronicle of the Napoleonic wars / John Colville. — Salisbury : Michael Russell, 1980. — ix,246p,[1] leaf of plates : maps,1col.port ; 24cm
Maps on lining papers
ISBN 0-85955-076-1 : £6.95 B81-10592

355.3'31'0924 — Great Britain. *Army*. French, *Sir* John — *Biographies*

Holmes, Richard. The little Field-Marshal. — London : Cape, Oct.1981. — [400]p
ISBN 0-224-01575-3 : £9.95 : CIP entry B81-27334

355.3'31'0924 — Great Britain. *Army*. Montgomery of Alamein, Bernard Law Montgomery, *Viscount* — *Biographies*

Hamilton, Nigel, *1944-*. Monty : the making of a general 1887-1942 / Nigel Hamilton. — London : Hamilton, 1981. — xix,871p,[32]p of plates : ill,maps,facsims,plans,ports ; 24cm
Bibliography: p849-854. - Includes index
ISBN 0-241-10583-8 : £12.00 : CIP rev. B81-11943

355.3'31'0924 — Great Britain. *Army*. Wavell, Archibald Percival, *Earl Wavell* — *Biographies*

Lewin, Ronald. The chief : Field Marshal Lord Wavell : commander-in-chief and viceroy 1939-1947 / Ronald Lewin. — London : Hutchinson, 1980. — 282p,[8]p of plates : ill,maps,facsims,ports ; 23cm
Bibliography: p257-260. — Includes index
ISBN 0-09-142500-x : £7.95 : CIP rev. B80-13298

355.3'32'0924 — Great Britain. *Army*. Lord, J. C. — *Personal observations — Collections*

Alford, Richard. To revel in God's sunshine : the story of the army career of the late academy Sergeant Major J.C. Lord as related by former recruits, cadets, comrades / compiled by Richard Alford. — [Oxford] ([52 New Inn Hall St., Oxford, OX1 2B5]) : [Medical Education Services], c1981. — 155p : ill,ports ; 22cm
Includes index
Unpriced B81-39675

355.3'32'0941 — Great Britain. *Army*. Officers — *Lists — Serials*

The **Army** list. Part 1. — 1980. — London : H.M.S.O., 1980. — ix,738p
ISBN 0-11-771943-9 : £15.00 B81-05939

355.3'41 — Paraguay. Chaco region. Military postal services, *1932-1935*

Shepherd, A.. Postal history of the Chaco War : (Paraguay) / by A. Shepherd. — Halifax (3 Willowfield Rd., Halifax HX2 7JN) : A. Shepherd, c1981. — 19p : maps,facsims ; 30cm
Bibliography: p2
Unpriced (pbk) B81-27823

355.3'46 — Great Britain. *Army*. Personnel. Skiing. Organisations: Army Ski Association — *Serials*

[Year book *(Army Ski Association)*]. Year book / the Army Ski Association. — 1979-80-. — [Aldershot] ([c/o Lt. Colonel P. Kemmis Betty, Ministry of Defence (ASGB), Clayton Barracks, Aldershot, Hants. GU11 2BG]) : The Association, 1979-. — v. : ill,ports ; 30cm
Continues: Yearbook (Army Ski Association). — Description based on: 1980-81 issue
ISSN 0260-6143 = Year book - Army Ski Association : Unpriced B81-03301

355.3'5 — France. *Armée. Légion Etrangère*. Uniforms, *to 1981*

Windrow, Martin. Uniforms of the French Foreign Legion 1831-1981 / by Martin Windrow ; colour illustrations by Michael Chappell. — Poole : Blandford Press, 1981. — 159p : ill(some col.),ports ; 26cm
Includes index
ISBN 0-7137-1010-1 : £10.50 B81-00800

355.3'56'0937 — Ancient Roman armies. Auxiliary units, *to 117*

Holder, Paul A.. Studies in the Auxilia of the Roman Army from Augustus to Trajan / Paul A. Holder. — Oxford : B.A.R., 1980. — 352p,11p of plates : ill ; 30cm. — (BAR. International series, ISSN 0143-3067 ; 70)
Bibliography: p335-345. — Includes index
ISBN 0-86054-075-8 (pbk) : £11.00 B81-25467

355.3'7'0942545 — Leicestershire. Rutland *(District)*. Militia. Muster rolls, *1522 — Texts*

The **County** community under Henry VIII : the military survey, 1522, and lay subsidy, 1524-5, for Rutland / edited for the Rutland Record Society by Julian Cornwall. — Oakham (Rutland County Museum, Catmos St., Oakham, Rutland, LE15 6HW) : The Society, 1980. — 134p : 1map ; 26cm. — (Rutland record series ; v.1)
Includes index
ISBN 0-907464-00-9 : £7.95
Primary classification 336.2'3'0942545 B81-11409

355.3'7'0942961 — Cardiganshire. *Royal Cardigan Artillery Militia, to 1957*

Parfitt, G. Archer. Some notes on the Royal Cardigan Militia and its heirs and successors being the auxiliary forces of Cardiganshire / by G. Archer Parfitt. — Shrewsbury (Delbury, 26 Priory Ridge, Shrewsbury) : G. Archer Parfitt, 1981. — viii,39,a-r leaves,[4]leaves of plates : ill ; 30cm
Limited ed. of 30 copies
Unpriced (pbk) B81-36103

355.4 — MILITARY OPERATIONS

355.4 — Military operations by Cheshire persons, *1345-1399*

Bostock, A. J.. The chivalry of Cheshire / by A.J. Bostock. — Didsbury : Morten, 1980. — 147p,[5]leaves of plates : ill,coats of arms ; 25cm
Bibliography: p141. - Includes index
ISBN 0-85972-039-x : £8.95 B81-06254

355.4'092'4 — Military operations. Role of Muhammad *(Prophet)*

Rahman, Afzalur. Muhammad as a military leader / Afzalur Rahman. — London (78 Gillespie Rd, N5 1LN) : Muslim Schools Trust, 1980. — xii,314p ; 22cm : 1map,plans
ISBN 0-907052-07-x (cased) : £8.50
ISBN 0-907052-06-1 (pbk) : £6.00 B81-30095

355.4'0941 — Army operations by Great Britain. *Army*. Role of Great Britain. *Royal Air Force, to 1977*

Robertson, Bruce. The army and aviation : a pictorial history / Bruce Robertson. — London : Hale, 1981. — 255p : ill,maps,ports ; 24cm
Includes index
ISBN 0-7091-8924-9 : £9.95 B81-24554

355.4'09931 — Military operations by New Zealand military forces, *1820-1975*

King, Michael, *1945-*. New Zealanders at war / Michael King. — Auckland ; Tadworth : Heinemann, 1981. — 308p : ill,map,facsims, ports ; 29cm
Ill on lining papers
ISBN 0-86863-399-2 : £18.00 B81-35364

355.4'2'09034 — Land welfare. Tactics, *1808-1973*

Griffith, Paddy. Forward into battle : fighting tactics from Waterloo to Vietnam / Paddy Griffith ; with an introduction by John Keegan. — Chichester (Strettington House, Strettington, Chichester, Sussex) : Antony Bird, 1981. — 156,[8]p of plates : ill,map ; 24cm
Bibliography: p149-151. — Includes index
ISBN 0-907319-01-7 : £9.95 B81-37749

355.4'5 — Nuclear power stations. War damage. Prevention

Ramberg, Bennett. Destruction of nuclear energy facilities in war : the problem and the implications / Bennett Ramberg ; [written under the auspices of the Center for International and Strategic Affairs, University of California, Los Angeles, and the Center of International Studies, Princeton University]. — Lexington [Mass.] : Lexington Books ; Farnborough, Hants. : Gower [distributor], 1981. — xvi,203p : ill,maps ; 24cm
Includes index
ISBN 0-669-03767-2 : £12.50 B81-15479

355.5 — MILITARY TRAINING AND MANOEUVRES

355.5'4'0941 — Great Britain. *Army*. Soldiers. Training, *1715-1795*

Houlding, J. A.. Fit for service : the training of the British Army, 1715-1795 / J.A. Houlding. — Oxford : Clarendon, 1981. — xxi,459p : maps ; 23cm
Bibliography: p423-440. — Includes index
ISBN 0-19-822647-0 : £25.00 : CIP rev. B81-05143

355.6 — MILITARY ADMINISTRATION

355.6'2 — Great Britain. *Army*. Regimental agents, *1715-1763*

Guy, Alan J.. Regimental agency in the British standing army, 1715-1763 : a study of Georgian military administration / by Alan J. Guy. — Manchester : John Rylands University Library of Manchester, 1980. — 58p ; 25cm
£2.30 (pbk) B81-35546

355.7 — MILITARY ESTABLISHMENTS

355.7'1 — Prisoners of war, *1337-1975*

Garrett, Richard. P.O.W. / Richard Garrett. — Newton Abbot : David & Charles, c1981. — 240p,[16]p of plates : ill,1map,1port ; 24cm
Bibliography: p233-235. — Includes index
ISBN 0-7153-7986-0 : £9.50 B81-25354

355.7'9'094288 — Northumberland. National parks: Northumberland National Park. Military training areas — *For environment planning*

The **Otterburn** military training area. — Newcastle upon Tyne ([c/o] National Park Officer, Bede House, All Saints Centre, Newcastle upon Tyne) : [Northumberland National Park and Countryside Committee], 1976. — i,10p,[2]p of plates : 3maps ; 30cm. — (Working paper / Northumberland National Park ; 7)
Unpriced (spiral) B81-29614

355.8 — MILITARY EQUIPMENT AND SUPPLIES

355.8'1 — Leather military equipment, *to 1945*

Waterer, John W.. Leather and the warrior. — London (9 St. Thomas St., SE1 9SA) : Museum of Leathercraft, Dec.1981. — [200]p
ISBN 0-9504182-1-8 : £20.00 : CIP entry B81-34727

355.8'2 — Military operations. Military equipment: Weapons - *Forecasts*

Baker, David. The shape of wars to come. — Cambridge : Patrick Stephens, Sept.1981. — [176]p
ISBN 0-85059-483-9 : £9.95 : CIP entry B81-20132

355.8'2 — Military operations. Military equipment: Weapons — *Forecasts*

Langford, David. War in 2080 : the future of military technology / David Langford. — London : Sphere, 1981, c 1979. — xiv,242p,[8]p of plates : ill ; 18cm
Originally published: Newton Abbot : Westbridge Books, 1979. — Bibliography: p235-238. — Includes index
ISBN 0-7221-5393-7 (pbk) : £1.50 B81-19691

355.8'3 — Military vehicles. Markings, *1939-1945*

Wise, Terence. World War 2 military vehicle markings / Terence Wise ; text illustrations by John Major. — Cambridge : Stephens, 1981. — 116p : ill ; 25cm
Bibliography: p115-116
ISBN 0-85059-439-1 : £6.95 B81-29718

356 — FOOT FORCES

356'.11'0941 — Great Britain. *Army. Black Watch. Battalion, 1st*. Kirk sessions: Kirk Session 1st Battalion the Black Watch Royal Highland Regiment, *to 1979*

The **Kirk** Session of the 1st Battalion the Black Watch Royal Highland regiment : the first twenty-five years, 1954-1979 / [compiled by Norman W. Drummond]. — [S.l.] : [s.n.], 1979? (Perth : Woods). — 28p ; 21cm
Cover title
Unpriced (pbk) B81-10647

356'.11'0941 — Great Britain. *Army. Gordon Highlanders — History*

The **Life** of a regiment. — London : Warne
Vol.5: The Gordon Highlanders 1919-1945 / Wilfrid Miles. — 1980. — xv,422p,[15]p of plates : ill,maps,ports ; 24cm
Originally published: Aberdeen : Aberdeen University Press, 1961. — Includes index
ISBN 0-7232-2785-3 : £4.95 B81-33352

356'.11'0941 — Great Britain. *Army. Royal Green Jackets — Serials*

Great Britain. *Army. Royal Green Jackets.* The Royal Green Jacket chronicle. — Vol.15 (Jan.-Dec.1980). — Winchester (Regimental Headquarters, The Royal Green Jackets, Peninsula Barracks, Winchester) : The Regiment, [1981?]. — 157p
Unpriced B81-35110

356'.11'0941 — Great Britain. *Army. Royal Northumberland Fusiliers, 1674-1980*

Pratt, R. M.. The Royal Northumberland Fusiliers : story of "The Fifth" and an account of the Regimental Museum housed in the Abbot's Tower, Alnwick Castle, Northumberland / [text compiled by R.M. Pratt] ; [photography by Sydney W. Newbery]. — Derby : English Life Publications, c1981. — 11p,[4]p of plates : ill,ports ; 14x21cm
ISBN 0-85101-177-2 : £0.35 B81-20792

356'.11'0941 — Great Britain. *Army. Welsh Guards, to 1976*

Retallack, John. The Welsh Guards / by John Retallack ; with a foreword by HRH The Prince of Wales. — [London] : Warne, 1981. — xii,177p,16p of plates : ill,facsims,ports ; 23cm. — (Famous regiments)
Includes index
ISBN 0-7232-2746-2 : £9.95 B81-08132

356'.167 — Ninja

Weiss, Al. Ninja : clan of death / Al Weiss and Tom Philbin. — London : W.H. Allen, 1981. — 208p,[24]p of plates : ill,ports ; 18cm. — (A Star book)
Bibliography: p205-206
ISBN 0-352-30946-6 (pbk) : £1.25 B81-35758

356'.167'0941 — Military operations by Great Britain. *Army. Special Air Service Regiment, 1950-1980*

Geraghty, Tony. Who dares wins : the story of the Special Air Service 1950-1980 / Tony Geraghty. — [London] : Fontana, 1981, c1980. — vii,339p,[4]p of plates : ill,maps,ports ; 18cm
Originally published: London : Arms and Armour Press, 1980. — Bibliography: p323-325. — Includes index
ISBN 0-00-636235-4 (pbk) : £1.75 B81-29548

356'.183'0941 — Military operations by Great Britain. *Army. Royal Lincolnshire Regiment, 1950-1960*

Moore, Geoffrey. The last decade : the Tenth Foot Royal Lincolnshire Regiment 1950-1960 : by Geoffrey Moore / with a foreword by Sir Christopher Welby-Everard. — Huntingdon (2 Ivelbury Close, Buckden, Huntingdon PE18 9XE) : G. Moore, c1981. — 68p ; 21cm
Text on inside covers
ISBN 0-9506360-8-8 (pbk) : £2.50 B81-37506

356'.186 — Great Britain. *Army. Indian Army.* **Infantry regiments. Uniforms,** *1860-1914*

Barthorp, Michael. Indian infantry regiments 1860-1914 / text by Michael Barthorp ; colour plates by Jeffrey Burn. — London : Osprey, 1979. — 40p : ill(some col.),ports ; 25cm. — (Men-at-arms series)
English text with English, French and German captions
ISBN 0-85045-307-0 (pbk) : £2.95 B81-26464

356'.186'0941 — Great Britain. *Army.* **Infantry. Military equipment,** *1808-1908*

Chappell, Mike. British infantry equipments 1808-1908 / text and colour plates by Mike Chappell. — London : Osprey, 1980. — 40p,A-Hp of plates : ill(some col.),1port ; 24cm. — (Men-at-arms series ; 107)
English text, English, French and German captions to plates
ISBN 0-85045-374-7 (pbk) : £2.95 B81-13927

356'.186'0941 — Great Britain. *Army.* **Infantry. Military equipment,** *1908-1980*

Chappell, Mike. British infantry equipments 1908-80 / text and colour plates by Mike Chappell. — London : Osprey, 1980. — 40p,A-Hp of plates : ill(some col.) ; 24cm. — (Men at arms series ; 108)
English text, English, French and German captions to plates
ISBN 0-85045-375-5 (pbk) : £2.95 B81-13926

357 — MOUNTED FORCES

357'.1'0924 — England and Wales. *Army. King's Life Guard.* **Turbeville,** *Sir Troilus — Biographies*

Foster, Michael. Sir Troilus Turberville, Captain-Lieutenant of the King's Life Guard (? 1597-1645) : by Michael Foster. — London (10 Uphill Grove, NW7 4NJ) : Royal Stuart Society, c1980. — 33p ; 21cm. — (Royal Stuart papers, ISSN 0307-997x ; 16)
£0.75 (pbk) B81-07113

357'.1'094 — Napoleonic Wars. Armies. Hussar regiments

Ulyatt, Kenneth. Hussars : of the Napoleonic wars / Kenneth Ulyatt ; illustrated by Gino D'Achille. — London : Macdonald, 1981. — 61p : ill(some col.),col.maps ; 29cm. — (Macdonald living history)
Translation from the French. — Ill on lining papers. — Includes index
ISBN 0-356-06755-6 : Unpriced B81-38538

357'.1'0941 — Great Britain. *Army. Life Guards — For children*

Lewthwaite, Margaret. Changing of the Queen's Life Guard : a story of 'The Tins' and 'Blues and Royals' / written and illustrated by Margaret Lewthwaite. — London (14 Edwardes Sq., W8 6HE) : M. Lewthwaite, c1980. — 72p : ill(some col.) ; 19cm
Unpriced (pbk) B81-29908

357'.188 — Great Britain. *Army. Yorkshire Hussars.* **Uniforms,** *to 1914*

Barlow, L.. The Yorkshire Hussars / by L. Barlow and R.J. Smith ; illustrations by R.J. Marrion. — [Aldershot] : Robert Ogilby Trust ; Speldhurst : Midas Books [distributor], [1981]. — 16p : ill,ports ; 25cm. — (The Uniforms of the British yeomanry force, 1794-1914 ; 3)
Cover title. — Ill on inside covers
ISBN 0-85936-250-7 (pbk) : £1.75 B81-38258

358.1 — ARTILLERY, MISSILE AND ARMOURED FORCES

358'.17'0941 — Great Britain. Strategic nuclear weapon systems. Policies of government — *Inquiry reports*

Great Britain. *Parliament. House of Commons.* Fourth report from the Defence Committee : session 1980-81 : strategic nuclear weapons policy : together with the minutes of proceedings of the Committee relating to the report, and part of th minutes of evidence taken on 25 June, 9 and 23 July, 29 October 4,6,15,25 and 21 November, 2,3 and 17 December 1980, 4 March and 7 April 1981. — London : H.M.S.O., [1981]. — ixx,325p ; 24cm. — ([HC] ; 36) ([HC] ; 64 (1979-80))
ISBN 0-10-203681-0 (pbk) : £10.60 B81-39915

358'.17'0973 — United States. Strategic nuclear weapon systems. Policies of government, *1961-1963*

Ball, Desmond. Politics and force levels : the strategic missile program of the Kennedy administration / Desmond Ball. — Berkeley ; London : University of California Press, c1980. — xxvi,322p ; 24cm
Bibliography: p279-297. — Includes index
ISBN 0-520-03698-0 : £16.50 B81-27499

358'.18 — Anti-tank warfare

Simpkin, Richard E.. Antitank. — Oxford : Pergamon, Nov.1981. — [320]p
ISBN 0-08-027036-0 : £20.00 : CIP entry B81-28810

358.2 — MILITARY FORCES. ENGINEERS

358'.2 — Northern Ireland. Bombs. Disposal by Great Britain. *Army. Royal Army Ordnance Corps — Personal observations*

Patrick, Derrick. Fetch Felix : the fight against the Ulster bombers 1976-1977 / Derrick Patrick. — London : Hamilton, 1980. — 184p,[8]p of plates : ill,1map,ports ; 23cm
Includes index
ISBN 0-241-10371-1 : £7.95 : CIP rev. B81-03683

358.3 — MILITARY TECHNICAL FORCES

358.3 — Biological & chemical warfare — *Campaign for Nuclear Disarmament viewpoints*

Bays, David. The silent killers : new developments in gas and germ weapons / by David Bays. — London : 11, Goodwin St., N4 3HQ : Campaign for Nuclear Disarmament, [1981]. — 24p : ill ; 21cm
Cover title. — Text on inside covers
£0.40 (pbk) B81-26647

358'.39 — Nuclear weapons

Sweatman, Mike. Atomic weapons : a discussion : draft / Mike Sweatman, Bob Lowe. — Milton Keynes (Spencer St., New Bradwell, Milton Keynes) : Sweatman and Lowe, c1981. — 83p : ill ; 21cm
Cover title. — Bibliography: p77-83
ISBN 0-9507711-0-4 (pbk) : Unpriced B81-34819

358'.39 — Nuclear weapons. Proliferation — *Conference proceedings*

The **Nuclear** arms race : control or catastrophe?. — London : Frances Pinter, Feb.1982. — [250]p
Conference papers
ISBN 0-86187-229-0 : £12.50 : CIP entry B81-40254

358'.39 — Nuclear weapons. Proliferation — *Socialist Workers' Party viewpoints*

Binns, Peter. Missile madness : the new weapons systems & how they threaten your life / by Peter Binns. — London (265 Seven Sisters Rd, N4 2DE) : Produced and distributed for the SWP by Socialists Unlimited, 1980. — 32p : ill,ports ; 21cm. — (A Socialist Workers Party pamphlet)
ISBN 0-905998-14-6 (pbk) : £0.40 B81-02981

358'.39'09 — Nuclear weapons, *to 1980*

Cox, John. Overkill / John Cox. — 3rd ed. / with prefaces by Joseph Rotblat and Michael Pentz. — Harmondsworth : Penguin, 1981. — 252p,[16]p of plates : ill,maps,ports ; 18cm. — (Pelican books)
Previous ed.: New York : Crowell, 1978. — Bibliography: p238-240. — Includes index
ISBN 0-14-022377-0 (pbk) : £1.75 B81-40436

358'.39'094 — Europe. Nuclear weapons

Treverton, Gregory. Nuclear weapons in Europe / by Gregory Treverton. — London : International Institute for Strategic Studies, 1981. — 34p ; 25cm. — (Adelphi papers, ISSN 0567-932x ; no.168)
ISBN 0-86079-049-5 (pbk) : Unpriced B81-36613

358.4 — AIR FORCES

358.4'009 — Naval aviation, *to 1980*

Johnson, Brian, *1925-.* Fly navy : the history of maritime aviation / Brian Johnson. — Newton Abbot : David & Charles, c1981. — 383p : ill,ports ; 24cm
Includes index
ISBN 0-7153-8025-7 : £12.50 B81-08701

358.4'00941 — Great Britain. *Royal Navy. Fleet Air Arm, to 1945 — Illustrations*

. Fleet air arm / [compiled by] Roderick Dymott. — London : Ian Allen, 1981. — 96p : chiefly ill ; 24cm. — (1939-1945 portfolio)
ISBN 0-7110-1053-6 (pbk) : £3.95 B81-07212

358.4′00943 — Germany. *Luftwaffe, 1933-1945 — Illustrations*
The **Luftwaffe** 1933-1945 / [compiled by] Alfred Price. — London : Arms and Armour. — (Warbirds illustrated ; no.1)
Vol.1. — 1981. — 67p : chiefly ill(some col.),ports ; 25cm
ISBN 0-85368-218-6 (pbk) : £3.50 : CIP rev. B81-20475

The **Luftwaffe** 1933-1945 / [compiled by] Alfred Price. — London : Arms and Armour. — (Warbirds illustrated ; no.2)
Vol.2. — 1981. — 68p : chiefly ill(some col.),ports ; 25cm
ISBN 0-85368-228-3 (pbk) : £3.50 : CIP rev. B81-22589

358.4′00973 — United States. *Air Force.* **Flying units** — *Lists*
Mercer, Paul S.. The flying units of the United States Air Force / [Paul S. Mercer]. — Loughborough (36 Moat Rd., Loughborough, Leics. LE11 3PN) : Jackson Publications, c1981. — 26p : ill,maps ; 22x30cm
ISBN 0-9507133-9-2 (pbk) : Unpriced B81-15023

358.4′00973 — United States. *Air Force, to 1980*
Anderton, David A.. The history of the U.S. Air Force / David A. Anderton. — London : Hamlyn, 1981. — 255p : ill(some col.),ports ; 30cm
Includes index
ISBN 0-600-34985-3 : £9.95 B81-25541

358.4′1115 — Great Britain. *Royal Air Force.* **Personnel. Benevolent funds: Royal Air Force Benevolent Fund,** *to 1979*
Bishop, Edward. The debt we owe : the Royal Air Force Benevolent Fund 1919-1979 / by Edward Bishop. — 2nd ed., rev. and enl. — London : Allen & Unwin, 1979. — xix,202p,16p of plates : ill,ports ; 23cm
Previous ed.: Harlow : Longmans, 1969. — Includes index
ISBN 0-04-361035-8 : £7.50 : CIP rev. B79-32386

358.4′131′0941 — Great Britain. *Royal Air Force.* **Squadrons,** *to 1979*
Halley, James J.. The squadrons of the Royal Air Force / James J. Halley. — Tonbridge : Air-Britain, c1980. — 379p : ill,coats of arms ; 25cm
Includes index
ISBN 0-85130-083-9 : £12.50 B81-05191

358.4′13′320924 — Great Britain. *Royal Air Force.* **Bader, Douglas** — *Biographies*
Lucas, Laddie. Flying colours. — London : Hutchinson, Nov.1981. — 1v.
ISBN 0-09-146470-6 : £7.95 : CIP entry B81-30304

358.4′1332′0924 — Great Britain. *Royal Air Force.* **Malan, Sailor** — *Biographies*
Franks, Norman L. R.. Sky Tiger : the story of Group Captain Sailor Malan, DSO DFC / Norman L.R. Franks. — London : Kimber, 1980. — 220p : ill,maps,facsims,ports ; 25cm
Bibliography: p213. - Includes index
ISBN 0-7183-0487-x : £8.50 B81-04423

358.4′1332′0924 — Great Britain. *Royal Air Force.* **Mannock, Edward** — *Biographies*
Dudgeon, James M.. Mick : the story of Major Edward Mannock, VC, D50, MC Royal Flying Corps and Royal Air Force / James M. Dudgeon ; (with forewords by) Keith L. Caldwell, H.G. Clements, Sir Douglas Bader. — London : Hale, 1981. — 208p,[16]p of plates : ill,maps,facsims,ports ; 23cm
Includes index
ISBN 0-7091-9143-x : £8.25 B81-37068

358.4′154′0941 — Great Britain. *Royal Air Force.* **Pilots. Training. Great Britain.** *Parliament. House of Commons. Defence Committee.* **RAF pilot training** — *Critical studies*
RAF pilot training : first report from the Defence Committee : observations / presented by the Secretary of State for Defence. — London : H.M.S.O., [1981]. — 3p ; 25cm. — (Cmnd. ; 8265) (House of Commons paper ; HCS3-649 i-iii)
ISBN 0-10-182650-8 (unbound) : £0.70 B81-29017

358.4′17′02541 — British military aerodromes — *Directories*
Mercer, Paul S.. British military airfields / by Paul Mercer. — Loughborough (36 Moat Rd., Loughborough, Leics. LE11 3PN) : Jackson, c1981. — 43p : ill,maps ; 15x21cm
ISBN 0-9507133-8-4 (pbk) : Unpriced B81-21973

358.4′17′0942759 — Merseyside *(Metropolitan County).* **Woodvale. Air bases: Woodvale RAF Station,** *to 1979*
Ferguson, Aldon P.. A history of Royal Air Force Woodvale / by Aldon P. Ferguson ; preface by F.C.R. Dicks. — 2nd ed. — Liverpool : Merseyside Aviation Society, 1980. — 67p : ill,maps,ports ; 22cm. — (Military airfield history ; no.3) (A Merseyside Aviation Society publication)
Previous ed.: 1974. — Text, ill on inside covers
ISBN 0-902420-36-4 (pbk) : Unpriced B81-06271

358.4′174′0924 — Military aeroplanes. Test flying by test pilots of Germany. *Luftwaffe. Beute, E2, 1939-1945 — Personal observations*
Lerche, Hans-Werner. Luftwaffe test pilot : flying captured allied aircraft of World War 2 / Hans-Werner Lerche. — London : Jane′s, 1980. — 158p,[48]p of plates : ill,facsims,ports ; 24cm
Translation of: Testpilot und Beuteflugzeugen
ISBN 0-531-03711-8 : £8.95 B81-06759

358.4′183 — Great Britain. Military aircraft. Serial numbers — *Lists*
March, Peter R.. Military aircraft markings / Peter R. March. — [New and rev. ed.]. — London : I. Allan, 1981. — 96p : ill ; 19cm
Previous ed.: 1980
ISBN 0-7110-1103-6 (pbk) : £1.50 B81-29635

358.4′183 — Military aircraft. Camouflage & markings, *1914-1980*
Flying colours / compiled by William Green and Gordon Swanborough. — London : Salamander, c1981. — 207p : chiefly col. ill ; 31cm
Ill on lining paper
ISBN 0-86101-079-5 : £9.95 B81-34788

358.4′183 — Sabre F-86 aeroplanes. Camouflage & markings, *1948-1980 — Illustrations*
Davis, Larry. F-86 Sabre in color / by Larry Davis ; illustrated by Don Greer & Rob Stern. — Carrollton : Squadron-Signal Publications ; London : Arms & Armour, c1981. — 32p of ill (some col.) ; 28cm. — (Fighting colors)
Ill on inside covers
ISBN 0-89747-110-5 (pbk) : £3.00 B81-23582

358.4′183 — United States. *Air Force.* **Military aircraft. Camouflage & markings,** *1926-*
US air force colours. — London : Arms and Armour
Vol.2: ETO & MTO 1942-45 / by Dana Bell ; illustrated by Don Greer. — c1980. — 94p : ill (some col.) ; 29cm
Vol.2 has title Air force colours
ISBN 0-85368-247-x : £6.95 B81-13683

358.4′2 — Dive bombing, *to 1970*
Smith, Peter C. (Peter Charles), *1940-*. Impact! : the dive bomber pilots speak / Peter C. Smith. — London : Kimber, 1981. — 253p,[16]p of plates : ill,ports ; 24cm
Bibliography: p242-243. — Includes index
ISBN 0-7183-0078-5 : £9.50 B81-25178

358.4′3 — Air operations by Chance Vought Crusader aeroplanes, *to 1979*
Tillman, Barrett. MiG master : the story of the F-8 Crusader / by Barrett Tillman. — Cambridge : Stephens, 1981, c1980. — xii,224p : ill,ports ; 23cm
Originally published: Annapolis : Nautical & Aviation Publishing, 1980. — Bibliography: p221-222. - Includes index
ISBN 0-85059-525-8 : £9.95 B81-15272

358.4′3′07 — Great Britain. *Royal Air Force.* **Fighter aeroplanes. Pilots. Recruitment & training**
Strong, Colin. Fighter pilot / Colin Strong and Duff Hart-Darvis. — London : Queen Anne Press, 1981. — 167p,[16]p of plates : ill(some col.),ports ; 25cm
Includes index
ISBN 0-362-00578-8 : £8.95
ISBN 0-563-17971-6 (BBC) B81-40935

358.4′3′09 — Air operations by fighter aeroplanes, *to 1964*
Johnson, J. E.. Full circle / J.E. Johnson. — New York ; London : Bantam, 1980. — 280p : ill ; 18cm. — (A Bantam war book)
Originally published: London : Chatto & Windus, 1964. — Includes index
ISBN 0-553-13568-6 (pbk) : £1.25 B81-12219

358.4′3′0924 — Air operations by Great Britain. *Royal Air Force, 1972-1978.* **McDonnel Douglas F4 Phantom aeroplanes** — *Personal observations*
Prest, Robert. F4 Phantom : a pilot′s story / Robert Prest. — London : Corgi, 1981, c1979. — 254p ; 18cm
Originally published: London : Cassell, 1979
ISBN 0-552-11615-7 (pbk) : £1.50 B81-37332

358.4′4′0941 — Great Britain. *Royal Air Force. Queen′s Flight, to 1980*
Cooksley, Peter G.. Flight royal : the Queen′s Flight & royal flying in five reigns / Peter G. Cooksley. — Cambridge : Stephens, 1981. — 112p : ill,ports ; 25cm
Ill on lining papers. — Bibliography: p110. — Includes index
ISBN 0-85059-490-1 : £6.95
Primary classification 629.13′092′2 B81-32843

358.4′6′0711422735 — Great Britain. *Royal Air Force. Electrical and Wireless School.* **Apprentices,** *1922-1929*
Burch, L. L. R.. The Flowerdown link : a story of telecommunications and radar throughout the Royal Flying Corps and Royal Air Force / by L.L.R. Burch. — [Weymouth] ([33a Commercial Rd, Weymouth, Dorset DT4 8PL]) : [Sherren], c1980. — 342p : ill,facsims,ports ; 25cm
£8.75 B81-04587

359 — NAVAL FORCES

359 — Sea-power
Sea power and influence : old issues and new challenges / edited by Jonathan Alford. — Farnborough, Hants. : Published for the International Institute for Strategic Studies by Gower, c1980. — vi,220p : ill,maps ; 23cm. — (The Adelphi library ; 2)
Includes index
ISBN 0-566-00342-2 : £9.50 : CIP rev. B80-07288

359′.009 — Naval warfare, *to 1980*
Willmott, H. P.. Sea warfare : weapons, tactics and strategy / H.P. Willmott ; with an epilogue by Lord Hill-Norton. — Chichester : Bird, 1981. — 165p,[8]leaves of plates : ill ; 24cm
Bibliography: p155. — Includes index
ISBN 0-907319-02-5 (corrected) : £9.95 B81-37720

359′.009′04 — Foreign relations. Role of navies, *1919-1979*
Cable, James, *1920-*. Gunboat diplomacy 1919-1979 : political applications of limited naval force / James Cable. — 2nd ed. — London : Macmillan, 1981. — 288p ; 23cm. — (Studies in international security)
Previous ed.: London : Chatto and Windus for the Institute of Strategic Studies, 1971. — Bibliography: p268-278. — Includes index
ISBN 0-333-30428-4 : £20.00 : CIP rev. B80-10980

359′.009163′84 — Eastern Mediterranean Sea. Naval warfare, *1559-1863*
Anderson, Roger Charles. Naval wars in the Levant 1559-1863. — Liverpool : Liverpool University Press, Apr.1981. — [640]p
Originally published: 1952
ISBN 0-85323-112-5 : £10.00 : CIP entry
Also classified at 359′.009163′89 B81-10494

359'.009163'89 — Black Sea. Naval warfare, *1559-1863*
Anderson, Roger Charles. Naval wars in the Levant 1559-1863. — Liverpool : Liverpool University Press, Apr.1981. — [640]p
Originally published: 1952
ISBN 0-85323-112-5 : £10.00 : CIP entry
Primary classification 359'.009163'84
B81-10494

359'.00941 — British sea-power, *to 1945*
Howarth, David, *1912-*. Sovereign of the seas : the story of British sea power / David Howarth. — London : Quartet, 1980, c1974. — 382p,[16]p of plates : ill,maps,ports ; 21cm
Originally published: London : Collins, 1974. — Includes index
ISBN 0-7043-3341-4 (pbk) : £4.95 B81-00054

359'.00941 — Great Britain. *Royal Navy, 1837-1910*
Padfield, Peter. Rule Britannia : the Victorian and Edwardian Navy / Peter Padfield. — London : Routledge & Kegan Paul, 1981. — 246p : ill,ports ; 25cm
Bibliography: p236. — Includes index
ISBN 0-7100-0774-4 : £8.95 : CIP rev.
B81-21507

359'.00941 — Great Britain. *Royal Navy, 1935-1945*
Marder, Arthur J.. Old friends, new enemies : the Royal Navy and the Imperial Japanese Navy : strategic illusions, 1934-1941 / by Arthur J. Marder. — Oxford : Clarendon, 1981. — xxxii,533p,[14]p of plates : ill,3maps,ports ; 23cm
Includes index
ISBN 0-19-822604-7 : 19.00 : CIP rev.
Also classified at 359'.00952 B81-21524

359'.00941 — Great Britain. *Royal Navy, ca 1850-1981*
Hill-Norton, Peter, *Baron Hill-Norton*. Sea power. — London : Faber, Feb.1982. — [200]p
ISBN 0-571-11890-9 : £8.50 : CIP entry
B81-36978

359'.00941'07402162 — London. Greenwich *(London Borough).* **Museums: National Maritime Museum** — *Visitors' guides*
National Maritime Museum. Twenty-five things to see at the National Maritime Museum. — Greenwich : National Maritime Museum, 1975. — 25p : ill,plans,ports ; 20x21cm
Ill, plans on inside covers
Unpriced (pbk) B81-00055

359'.00943 — Germany. *Kriegsmarine, 1888-1919*
Herwig, Holger H.. 'Luxury' fleet : the Imperial German Navy 1888-1918 / Holger H. Herwig. — London : Allen & Unwin, 1980. — 314,12p of plates : ill,2plans, ports ; 23cm
Bibliography: p292-300. - Includes index
ISBN 0-04-943023-8 : £9.95 : CIP rev.
B79-35282

359'.00952 — Japan. *Kaigun, 1935-1945*
Marder, Arthur J.. Old friends, new enemies : the Royal Navy and the Imperial Japanese Navy : strategic illusions, 1934-1941 / by Arthur J. Marder. — Oxford : Clarendon, 1981. — xxxii,533p,[14]p of plates : ill,3maps,ports ; 23cm
Includes index
ISBN 0-19-822604-7 : 19.00 : CIP rev.
Primary classification 359'.00941 B81-21524

359'.03'0973 — United States. Naval policies, *1865-1917*
Still, William N.. American sea power in the old world : the United States Navy in European and Near Eastern waters, 1865-1917 / William N. Still, Jr.. — Westport, Conn. ; London : Greenwood Press, 1980. — xi,291p : ill,ports ; 25cm. — (Contributions in military history, ISSN 0084-9251 ; no.24)
Bibliography: p265-282. — Includes index
ISBN 0-313-22120-0 : £19.50 B81-23462

359.1 — Great Britain. *Royal Navy.* **Ratings. Socioeconomic aspects,** *1900-1939*
Carew, Anthony. The lower deck of the Royal Navy. — Manchester : Manchester University Press, Sept.1981. — [256]p
ISBN 0-7190-0841-7 : £12.50 : CIP entry
B81-21508

359.1'09'034 — London. Greenwich *(London Borough).* **Museums: National Maritime Museum. Stock: Photographs. Special subjects: Merchant sailing ships. Naval life,** *ca 1870-1920 — Illustrations*
Seafaring under sail. — Cambridge : Stephens, Nov.1981. — [232]p
ISBN 0-85059-466-9 : £12.95 : CIP entry
B81-30573

359.1'0941 — Great Britain. *Royal Navy.* **Warships. Sailing ships: Victory** *(Ship).* **Naval life** — *For children*
Morrison, Ian. How they lived in a sailing ship of war / Ian Morrison. — Guildford : Lutterworth, 1981. — 31p : ill(some col.) ; 23cm. — (How they lived ; 13)
Ill on lining papers. — Includes index
ISBN 0-7188-2441-5 : £1.95 B81-39068

359.1'15 — Great Britain. *Royal Navy.* **Ex-servicemen. Financial assistance. Organisations: Greenwich Hospital** — *Accounts — Serials*
Greenwich Hospital. Accounts / Greenwich Hospital and Travers Foundation. — 1979-80. — London : H.M.S.O., 1981. — 11p
ISBN 0-10-212481-7 : £2.10 B81-20308

359.1'334 — Great Britain. *Royal Navy.* **Sailing vessels: Bounty** *(Ship).* **Mutiny** — *Early works*
Barrow, *Sir* **John**. The mutiny of the Bounty. — Horsham (9 Queen St., Horsham, West Sussex, RH13 5AA) : Russel Sharp, Oct.1981. — [216]p
ISBN 0-907722-00-8 : £8.95 : CIP entry
B81-28824

Bligh, William. A book of the Bounty / William Bligh and others ; edited by George Mackaness ; New Introduction by Gavin Kennedy. — London : Dent, 1938 (1981 [printing]). — xxv,321p : ill,1map ; 19cm. — (Everyman's library ; [950])
ISBN 0-460-00950-8 : £5.95 B81-09782

359.1'334 — Scotland. Highland Region. Invergordon. Great Britain. *Royal Navy.* **Mutiny,** *1931 — Personal observations*
Ereira, Alan. The Invergordon mutiny : a narrative history of the last great mutiny in the Royal Navy and how it forced Britain off the Gold Standard in 1931 / Alan Ereira. — London : Routledge & Kegan Paul, 1981. — x,182p : 1ill,2maps ; 25cm
Ill on lining papers. — Bibliography: p173-174. — Includes index
ISBN 0-7100-0930-5 : £6.95 B81-38436

359.1'4 — Navies. Personnel. Insignia, *1939-1945*
Rosignoli, Guido. Naval and Marine badges and insignia of World War 2 / Guido Rosignoli. — Poole : Blandford, 1980. — 167p : ill(some col.) ; 20cm
ISBN 0-7137-0919-7 : £4.95 : CIP rev.
B80-13752

359.2'23'0941 — Great Britain. *Royal Navy.* **Sailors. Recruitment,** *1755-1762*
Gradish, Stephen F.. The manning of the British Navy during the Seven Years' War / Stephen F. Gradish. — London : Royal Historical Society, 1980. — ix,235p : 1ill ; 23cm. — (Royal Historical Society studies in history series ; no.21)
Bibliography: p219-222. — Includes index
ISBN 0-901050-58-x : £15.25 B81-04895

359.3'252 — Devon. Lundy. Great Britain. *Royal Navy.* **Battleships: Montagu** *(Ship).* **Sinking,** *1906*
The Loss of HMS Montague Lundy 1906 / compiled by G.M. Davis. — Atworth (6 Chapel Rise, Atworth, near Melksham, Wilts) : G.M. and R.C. Davis, c1981. — 59p : ill,1map,ports ; 23cm
Bibliography: p59
ISBN 0-9507391-0-3 (pbk) : £3.95 B81-21747

359.3'253'0941 — Naval operations by Great Britain. *Royal Navy, 1908-1948.* **Battle cruisers**
Bassett, Ronald. Battle-cruisers : a history 1908-48 / Ronald Bassett. — London : Macmillan, 1981. — xii,296p,[16]p of plates : ill,maps,plans,ports ; 23cm
Bibliography: p282-284. - Includes index
ISBN 0-333-28164-0 : £9.95 B81-24090

359.3'257'09 — Naval operations by submarines, *1914-1980*
Humble, Richard. Undersea warfare / Richard Humble. — London : New English Library, 1981. — 192p : ill(some col.),1facsim,maps (some col.),ports ; 29cm
Ill on lining papers. — Includes index
ISBN 0-450-04866-7 : £9.95 B81-27007

359.3'31'0924 — Great Britain. *Royal Navy.* **Beatty, David Beatty,** *Earl — Biographies*
Beatty, Charles. Our Admiral : a biography of Admiral of the Fleet Earl Beatty / by Charles Beatty. — London : W.H. Allen, 1980. — xi,211p,[8]p of plates : ill,1facsim,ports ; 25cm
Bibliography: p200-201. — Includes index
ISBN 0-491-02388-x : £7.95 B81-27543

Roskill, S. W.. Admiral of the Fleet Earl Beatty : the last naval hero : an intimate biography / Stephen Roskill. — London : Collins, 1980. — 430p,[16]p of plates : ill,maps,plans,ports ; 24cm
Includes index
ISBN 0-00-216278-4 : £12.95 B81-02593

359.3'31'0924 — Great Britain. *Royal Navy.* **Jellicoe, John Jellicoe,** *Earl — Biographies*
Winton, John. Jellicoe / John Winton. — London : Joseph, 1981. — 320p,[8]p of plates : ill,1map,plans,ports ; 25cm
Bibliography: p299-309. — Includes index
ISBN 0-7181-1813-8 : £12.50 B81-34520

359.3'31'0924 — Great Britain. *Royal Navy.* **Keyes, Roger Keyes,** *Baron — Correspondence, diaries, etc*
Keyes, Roger Keyes, *Baron*. The Keyes papers : selections from the private and official correspondence of Admiral of the Fleet Baron Keyes of Zeebrugge / edited by Paul G. Halpern. — London : Allen & Unwin for the Navy Records Society. — (Publications of the Navy Records Society ; v.122)
Vol.3: 1939-1945. — 1981. — xiv,398p,[1]leaf of plate : maps ; 23cm
Bibliography: p375-379. — Includes index
ISBN 0-04-942172-7 : £15.00 : CIP rev.
B81-02643

359.3'31'0941 — Great Britain. *Royal Navy.* **Admirals. Leadership,** *1750-1945*
Horsfield, John. The art of leadership in war : the Royal Navy from the age of Nelson to the end of World War II / John Horsfield. — Westport, Conn. ; London : Greenwood Press, 1980. — xiv,240p : ill,ports ; 22cm. — (Contributions in military history, ISSN 0084-9251 ; no.21)
Bibliography: p207-231. — Includes index
ISBN 0-313-20919-7 : £15.95 B81-23473

359.3'32'0922 — Great Britain. *Royal Navy.* **Officers,** *1917 — Biographies — Early works*
Great Britain. *Royal Navy.* The naval who's who 1917. — Polstead (The old Rectory, Polstead, Suffolk) : Hayward, c1981. — 344p ; 26cm
Facsim. of: The Royal Navy list, or, Who's who in the navy. London, 1917
ISBN 0-903754-91-6 : Unpriced B81-22233

359.3'32'0924 — Germany. *Kriegsmarine.* **Kretschmer, Otto,** *1939-1947 — Biographies*
Robertson, Terence. [The golden horseshoe]. Night raider of the Atlantic / by Terence Robertson ; preface by Sir George Creasy. — London : Evans, 1955 (1981 [printing]). — 210p,[16]p of plates : ill,ports ; 21cm
Includes index
ISBN 0-237-45549-8 : £6.28 : CIP rev.
B80-25398

359.3'32'0941 — Great Britain. *Royal Navy.* **Officers** — *Lists — Serials*
Great Britain. *Royal Navy.* The Navy list. — 1981. — London : H.M.S.O., 1981. — 517p in various pagings
ISBN 0-11-772293-6 : £11.60
ISSN 0141-6081 B81-35810

359.3'38'0924 — Great Britain. *Royal Navy.* **Other ranks,** *1918-1927 — Personal observations — Correspondence, diaries, etc.*
Weekes, Teddie. Voyage down memory lane / Teddie Weekes. — Bognor Regis : New Horizon, c1980. — 76p,[20]p of plates : ill,2facsims,ports ; 21cm
ISBN 0-86116-579-9 : £5.50 B81-21725

359.3'45'0924 — Great Britain. *Royal Navy.* **Surgeons. Naval life,** *1837-1861 — Correspondence, diaries, etc.*

Cree, Edward. The Cree journals. — Exeter : Webb & Bower, Sept.1981. — [256]p
ISBN 0-906671-36-1 : £9.95 : CIP entry
B81-25887

359.4'09 — Naval operations, *to 1945*

Winton, John. Below the belt : novelty, subterfuge and surprise in naval warfare / John Winton. — London : Conway Maritime, 1981. — 192p : ill,facsims ; 23cm
ISBN 0-85177-236-6 : £5.95 B81-17717

359.4'09'033 — Naval operations, *1660-1805*

Mahan, A. T.. The influence of sea power upon history 1660-1805 / Alfred Thayer Mahan. — London : Hamlyn, 1980. — 256p : ill(some col.),maps(some col.),1coat of arms,facsims,plans(some col.),ports(some col.) ; 32cm. — (A Bison book)
Abridgement of: The influence of sea power upon history 1660-1783, together with extracts from The influence of sea power upon the French Revolution 1793-1812. Includes index
ISBN 0-600-34162-3 : £8.95 B81-04859

359.7 — Singapore. British naval bases: Singapore Naval Base, *to 1942*

Neidpath, James. The Singapore naval base and the defence of Britain's eastern empire, 1919-1941 / James Neidpath. — Oxford : Clarendon, 1981. — xvii,296p : 2maps ; 23cm
Bibliography: p274-284. — Includes index
ISBN 0-19-822474-5 : £22.50 B81-33436

359.9'6332'0924 — Great Britain. *Royal Marines.* **Warren, Alan** *— Biographies*

Skidmore, Ian. Marines don't hold their horses / Ian Skidmore. — London : W.H. Allen, 1981. — 128p ; 22cm
Includes index
ISBN 0-491-02694-3 : £5.95 B81-17768

361 — SOCIAL PROBLEMS AND SOCIAL WELFARE

361 — Great Britain. Community minibus services. Organisation *— Manuals*

Taylor, John, *1952-.* Starting up : how to run a community minibus : a comprehensive guide / written by John Taylor, Richard Armitage ; cartoons by John Nuttall. — 2nd ed. — Manchester (31 Portland St., Ancoats, Manchester) : Community Transport, 1980. — 38p : ill ; 30cm
Cover title. — Previous ed.: 1979. — Text and ill. on inside covers
ISBN 0-904890-01-5 (pbk) : £0.60 B81-38038

361 — Urban regions. Welfare work

Davis, Martin. The essential social worker. — London : Heinemann Educational, Apr.1981. — [256]p. — (Community care handbooks)
ISBN 0-435-82267-5 (cased) : £12.50 : CIP entry
ISBN 0-435-82268-3 (pbk) : £4.95 B81-04313

361 — Welfare services

Golding, Peter. Images of welfare. — Oxford : Robertson, Jan.1982. — [224]p. — (Aspects of social policy)
ISBN 0-85520-447-8 (cased) : £10.00 : CIP entry
ISBN 0-85520-448-6 (pbk) : £3.95 B81-33777

361 — Welfare work

Theories of practice in social work. — London : Academic Press, Feb.1982. — [300]p
ISBN 0-12-324780-2 : CIP entry B81-36065

361'.001 — Welfare work *— Philosophical perspectives*

Downie, R. S.. Caring and curing : a philosophy of medicine and social work / R.S. Downie and Elizabeth Telfer. — London : Methuen, 1980. — x,174p ; 22cm
Bibliography: p169-170. - Includes index
ISBN 0-416-71800-0 (cased) : £8.50 : CIP rev.
ISBN 0-416-71810-8 (pbk) : £3.95
Also classified at 610'.1 B80-18203

Social welfare : why and how? / edited by Noel Timms. — London : Routledge & Kegan Paul, 1980. — x,306p ; 22cm. — (The International library of welfare and philosophy)
Bibliography: p291-306
ISBN 0-7100-0615-2 : £9.25 B81-02426

Wilkes, Ruth. Social work with undervalued groups. — London : Tavistock Publications, Sept.1981. — [208]p. — (Tavistock library of social work practice ; SSP218)
ISBN 0-422-77100-7 (cased) : £9.50 : CIP entry
ISBN 0-422-77110-4 (pbk) : £4.50 B81-21557

361'.0023'41 — Great Britain. Part-time welfare workers

Hall, Anthony S.. Part-time social work / Tony Hall and Phoebe Hall. — London : Heinemann Educational, 1980. — xviii,214p : 1ill ; 23cm. — (Studies in social policy and welfare ; 11)
Includes index
ISBN 0-435-82401-5 : £12.50 : CIP rev.
B80-06328

361'.0025'41 — Great Britain. Welfare services *— Directories — Serials*

Social services year book. — 1981/82. — London : Councils and Education Press, c1981. — 979p
ISBN 0-900313-69-2 : £18.50
ISSN 0307-093x B81-29423

361'0025'417 — Ireland *(Republic).* **Social services** *— Directories*

Directory of social service organisations / National Social Service Council. — [4th ed.]. — [Dublin] : [The Council], [c1980]. — 229p ; 21cm
Previous ed.: 1978. — Includes index
£2.50 (pbk) B81-03265

361'.005 — Social services. Evaluation *— Serials*

Evaluation studies review annual. — Vol.3 (1978). — Beverly Hills ; London : Sage Publications, c1978. — 783p
ISBN 0-8039-1075-4 : Unpriced B81-13313

361'.0068 — United States. Welfare services. Administration

Abels, Paul. Administration in the human services : a normative systems approach / Paul Abels, Michael J. Murphy. — Englewood Cliffs ; London : Prentice-Hall, c1981. — xi,244p : ill ; 24cm
Includes index
ISBN 0-13-005850-5 : £12.55 B81-37178

361'.007 — Great Britain. Teachers. Professional education. Curriculum subjects: Community & youth work. Courses *— Directories*

Youth and community courses in teacher education. — Leicester : National Youth Bureau, 1979. — 16p ; 21cm
ISBN 0-86155-013-7 (unbound) : £0.45
B81-39061

361'.007'11 — Welfare workers. Professional education *— Sociological perspectives*

Heraud, Brian. Training for uncertainty : a sociological approach to social work education / Brian Heraud. — London : Routledge & Kegan Paul, 1981. — 153p ; 23cm. — (Library of social work) (Library of social work)
Bibliography: p141-149. — Includes index
ISBN 0-7100-0889-9 : £8.95 : CIP rev.
B81-21499

361'.007'1141 — Great Britain. Welfare workers. Professional education. Organisations: Central Council for Education and Training in Social Work *— Accounts — Serials*

Council for the Education and Training of Health Visitors. Accounts / Council for the Education and Training of Health Visitors [and] Central Council for Education and Training in Social Work. — 1979-80. — London : H.M.S.O., 1981. — 7p
ISBN 0-10-231481-0 : £1.10
Also classified at 362.1'4'071141 B81-31598

361'.0072 — Social services. Evaluation research *— Serials*

Evaluation quarterly : a journal of applied social research. — Vol.1, no.1 (Feb.1977)-. — Beverly Hills ; London : Sage, 1977-. — v. : ill ; 22cm
ISSN 0145-4692 = Evaluation quarterly : Unpriced B81-03846

361'.0072 — Welfare work. Research. Methodology

Tripodi, Tony. Research techniques for clinical social workers / Tony Tripodi and Irwin Epstein. — New York ; Guildford : Columbia University Press, 1980. — viii,255p : ill ; 22cm
Includes bibliographies and index
ISBN 0-231-04652-9 : £8.30 B81-02730

361'.0072041 — Great Britain. Welfare services. Research & development supported by Great Britain. *Department of Health and Social Security — Directories — Serials*

DHSS handbook of research and development / Department of Health and Social Security. — 1980. — London : H.M.S.O., 1980. — v,124p
ISBN 0-11-320730-1 : £6.00 B81-12421

361'.00723 — Developing countries. Social surveys. Sampling

Casley, D. J.. Data collection in developing countries / D.J. Casley and D.A. Lury. — Oxford : Clarendon, 1981. — xi,244p : ill ; 24cm
Includes index
ISBN 0-19-877123-1 : £15.00 : CIP rev.
B80-21447

361'.00723 — Great Britain. Social surveys, *1860-1960*

Kent, Raymond A.. A history of British empirical sociology. — Aldershot : Gower, Oct.1981. — [235]p
ISBN 0-566-00415-1 : £9.50 : CIP entry
B81-28071

361'.00723 — Social surveys. Methodology

Survey design and analysis : current issues / edited by Duane F. Alwin. — Beverly Hills ; London : Sage, 1978. — 156p : ill ; 22cm. — (Sage contemporary social science issues ; 46)
Includes bibliographies
ISBN 0-8039-1021-5 (pbk) : Unpriced
B81-17625

361'.05 — Great Britain. Residential care

Davis, Ann. The residential solution. — London : Tavistock Publications, Sept.1981. — [192]p. — (Tavistock library of social work practice)
ISBN 0-422-77320-4 (cased) : £9.50 : CIP entry
ISBN 0-422-77330-1 (pbk) : £4.50 B81-21629

361'.05 — Great Britain. Residential institutions. Inmates. Admission

Brearley, Paul. Admission to residential care / Paul Brearley, with Penny Gutridge ... [et al.]. — London : Tavistock Publications, 1980. — xi,225p ; 21cm. — (Residential social work)
Bibliography: p206-216. — Includes index
ISBN 0-422-76930-4 (cased) : £8.00 : CIP rev.
ISBN 0-422-76940-1 (pbk) : £3.50 B80-25402

361'.05 — Residential care *— For welfare work*

Davis, Leonard. Residential care. — London : Heinemann Educational, Feb.1982. — [192]p. — (Community care practice handbooks ; 8)
ISBN 0-435-82264-0 (pbk) : £2.95 : CIP entry
B81-35696

361'.06 — Great Britain. Community work. Resource centres. Organisation *— Manuals*

Thorne, Kaye. Community resource centres / Kaye Thorne. — [Great Britain] : Flat Publications, 1981. — 1v. : ill,1map,forms ; 23x32cm. — (BL RDR ; 5636)
Includes bibliographies
Unpriced B81-27738

361'.06 — London. Westminster *(London Borough).* **Law courts. Buildings: Royal Courts of Justice. Citizens' advice bureaux**

Kellaher, Leonie A.. The Citizens Advice Bureau at the Royal Courts of Justice : the evaluation of and experimental information and advice service / Leonie A. Kellaher. — [London] ([62 Highbury Grove, N5 2AD]) : Polytechnic of North London, Department of Applied Social Studies, Survey Research Unit, 1980. — iv,77p ; 30cm. — (Research report / Polytechnic of North London Department of Applied Social Studies Survey Research Unit ; no.5)
Bibliography: p77
ISBN 0-906970-04-0 (pbk) : £3.50 B81-12548

361′.06 — Tyne and Wear *(Metropolitan County)*. Newcastle. North Kenton. Community advice centres: North Kenton Advice Centre, *to 1979*

Phillips, Hilary. Two years on : a study of the tirst two years of operation at North Kenton Advice Centre / by Hilary Phillips. — [London] : Dr Barnardo′s, c1980. — 48p : ill ; 21cm. — (Barnardo social work paper ; no.10)
Unpriced (pbk) B81-16029

361′.06 — West Midlands *(Metropolitan County)*. Birmingham. Inner areas. Community advisory services & community information services. Provision

Local advice needs in the Birmingham inner city partnership area. — [Birmingham] ([Dr. Johnson House, Colmore Circus Subway, Birmingham B4 6AJ]) : [Birmingham Citizens′ Advice Bureau], 1981. — iv,70p : maps ; 30cm
Unpriced (spiral) B81-36912

361′.06 — West Yorkshire *(Metropolitan County)*. Leeds *(District)*. Community information services: TUCRIC, *to 1979*

Dee, Marianne. TUCRIC : the first year / Marianne Dee and John Allred with assistance from the other TUCRIC workers. — Leeds (28 Park Place, Leeds, LS1 2SY) : Leeds Polytechnic School of Librarianship, 1980. — 25p ; 21cm
Cover title
ISBN 0-900738-24-3 (pbk) : £1.50
Primary classification 026′.33188′0942819
B81-14094

361.1 — SOCIAL PROBLEMS

361′1.001 — Welfare services. Political aspects — *Philosophical perspectives*

Plant, Raymond. Political philosophy and social welfare : essays on the normative basis of welfare provision / Raymond Plant, Harry Lesser, Peter Taylor-Gooby. — London : Routledge & Kegan Paul, 1980. — xiii,262p ; 23cm ; cased. — (The international library of welfare and philosophy)
Bibliography: p247-257. — Includes index
ISBN 0-7100-0611-x : £8.95 : CIP rev.
ISBN 0-7100-0631-4 (pbk) : £4.95 B80-34786

361.1′0941 — Great Britain. Social problems. Committees of inquiry. Proposals. Implementation. Great Britain. *Parliament. House of Commons. Home Affairs Committee.* Home Office reports — *Critical studies*

Great Britain. *Home Office*. Home Office reports : the Government′s reply to the First report from the Home Affairs Committee, session 1980-81 H.C.23 / presented to Parliament by the Secretary of State for the Home Department ... — London : H.M.S.O., [1981]. — 4p ; 25cm. — (Cmnd. ; 8214)
ISBN 0-10-182140-9 (unbound) : £1.10
B81-28536

361.1′0973 — United States. Social problems

Rubington, Earl. The study of social problems : five perspectives. — 3rd ed. / Earl Rubington and Martin S. Weinberg. — New York ; Oxford : Oxford University Press, 1981. — ix,243p ; 23cm
Previous ed.: New York : Oxford University Press, 1977. — Includes bibliographies
ISBN 0-19-502825-2 (pbk) : £5.95 B81-32729

Smith, Ronald W.. Social problems : role, institutional and societal perspectives / Ronald W. Smith, Andrea Fontana with the assistance of Kathleen J. Ferraro ... [et al.]. — New York ; London : Holt, Rinehart and Winston, c1981. — xv,445p,[8]p of plates : ill(some col.),1map,ports ; 25cm
Includes bibliographies and index
ISBN 0-03-043696-6 : £10.95 B81-22877

361.2 — SOCIAL WELFARE

361.2 — Great Britain. Welfare benefits

Lister, Ruth. Welfare benefits. — London : Sweet & Maxwell, Oct.1981. — [250]p. — (Social work and law)
ISBN 0-421-24960-9 (pbk) : £7.50 : CIP entry
B81-25294

361.3 — SOCIAL WORK

361.3 — Great Britain. Local authorities. Welfare workers. Cooperation with general practitioners — *Proposals*

Medical Practitioners′ Union. *Manchester Branch*. The role of social workers - a medical viewpoint : evidence by the Manchester Branch of the Medical Practitioners′ Union (a section of ASTMS) to the enquiry into the role of social workers conducted by the National Institute for Social Work. — [Chorley] ([c/o The Secretary, 2 Keats Close, Langton Brow, Eccleston, Chorley, Lancs.]) : [The Branch], [1981]. — [8]p ; 30cm
Unpriced (unbound) B81-19337

361.3 — Welfare work. Evaluation - *Conference proceedings*

Evaluative research in social care. — London : Heinemann Educational, June 1981. — [320]p. — (Policy Studies Institute series)
Conference papers
ISBN 0-435-83352-9 (pbk) : £7.50 : CIP entry
B81-15900

361.3′01 — Welfare work. Theories

Radical social work and practice / edited by Mike Brake and Roy Bailey. — London : Edward Arnold, 1980. — 255p ; 20cm
Bibliography: p232-244. — Includes index
ISBN 0-7131-6280-5 (pbk) : £4.75 : CIP rev.
B80-08145

361.3′023′41 — Great Britain. Welfare work — *Career guides*

Page, Anne. Careers in social work / Anne Page. — London : Kogan Page, 1980. — 128p ; 19cm
ISBN 0-85038-404-4 (cased) : £4.95
ISBN 0-85038-405-2 (pbk) : £2.50 B81-08467

Summers, Barbara. Working with people : an introduction to the caring professions / Barbara Summers. — London : Cassell, 1981. — 136p : ill ; 22cm
Includes bibliographies and index
ISBN 0-304-30604-5 (pbk) : £3.95 B81-35417

361.3′09172′4 — Developing countries. Welfare work. Influence of welfare work in developed countries

Midgley, James. Professional imperialism : social work in the third world / James Midgley. — London : Heinemann, 1981. — xiv,191p ; 23cm. — (Studies in social policy and welfare ; 16)
Includes index
ISBN 0-435-82588-7 : £16.00 B81-23587

361.3′0941 — Great Britain. Welfare work

Olsen, M. Rolf. The question of social work / M. Rolf Olsen. — Birmingham : University of Birmingham, 1980. — 20p ; 21cm
Cover title
ISBN 0-7044-0428-1 (pbk) : Unpriced
B81-11096

Pinker, Robert. The enterprise of social work : an inaugural lecture / Robert Pinker. — London : London School of Economics and Political Science, 1981. — 20p ; 21cm
ISBN 0-85328-072-x (pbk) : Unpriced
B81-29163

361.3′0941 — Great Britain. Welfare work — *Serials*

Welfare & social services journal : official publication of the Institute of Welfare Officers. — Vol.1, no.1 (Oct.-Dec.1980)-. — Manchester (25 Cross St., Manchester M2 1WL) : Marylebone Press, 1980-. — v. : ill,ports ; 30cm
Quarterly. — Continues: The Welfare officer
ISSN 0261-4049 = Welfare & social services journal : £2.00 per issue B81-31050

361.3′0941 — Great Britain. Welfare work — *Socialist viewpoints*

Towards socialist welfare work : working in the state / Steve Bolger ... [et al.]. — London : Macmillan, 1981. — xiii,159p ; 23cm. — (Critical texts in social work and the welfare state)
Bibliography: p157-159
ISBN 0-333-28905-6 : £10.00 : CIP rev.
ISBN 0-333-28906-4 (pbk) : Unpriced
B80-35906

361.3′09411 — Scotland. Welfare work — *Serials*

[Research highlights *(Edinburgh)*]. Research highlights. — No.1-. — Edinburgh : Scottish Academic Press, 1981-. — v. : ill ; 21cm
Two issues yearly. — Produced by: Aberdeen University in association with Scottish Social Services Research Group
ISSN 0261-5568 = Research highlights (Edinburgh) : £8.00 per year B81-31046

361.3′0942 — England. Welfare work

Collins, John, *1929-*. Achieving change in social work / John and Mary Collins. — London : Heinemann Educational, 1981. — 106p : ill ; 22cm. — (Community care ; 6)
Bibliography: p103-104. — Includes index
ISBN 0-435-82186-5 (pbk) : £2.95 : CIP rev.
B81-12341

Goldberg, E. Mathilde. Ends and means in social work : the development and outcome of a case review system for social workers / E. Matilda [i.e. Mathilde] Goldberg and R. William Warburton. — London : Allen & Unwin, 1979. — 155p : ill,forms ; 23cm. — (National Institute social services library ; no.35)
Bibliography: p137-141. — Includes index
ISBN 0-04-360053-0 (cased) : £10.95 : CIP rev.
ISBN 0-04-360054-9 (pbk) : £4.95 B79-30581

361.3′2 — Welfare work. Casework. Task-centred treatment

Epstein, Laura. Helping people : the task-centered approach / Laura Epstein. — St. Louis ; London : Mosby, 1980. — xiii,265p : ill ; 24cm
Includes bibliographies and index
ISBN 0-8016-1509-7 (pbk) : Unpriced
B81-08565

361.3′2′019 — United States. Welfare workers. Stress

Cherniss, Cary. Staff burnout : job stress in the human services / Cary Cherniss. — Beverly Hills ; London : Sage, 1980. — 199p ; 23cm. — (Sage studies in community mental health ; 2)
Bibliography: p193-197
ISBN 0-8039-1338-9 (cased) : Unpriced
ISBN 0-8039-1339-7 (pbk) : Unpriced
B81-14616

361.3′2′0942 — England. Local authorities. Welfare workers — *Case studies*

Satyamurti, Carole. Occupational survival : the case of the local authority social worker / Carole Satyamurti. — Oxford : Basil Blackwell, 1981. — 216p ; 22cm. — (The Practice of social work)
Bibliography: p207-213. — Includes index
ISBN 0-631-12441-1 (cased) : £9-95
ISBN 0-631-12595-7 (Pbk) : £4.95 B81-24269

361.3′2′0973 — United States. Welfare work. Casework — *Manuals*

Pippin, James A.. Developing casework skills / James A. Pippin. — Beverly Hills ; London : Sage published in cooperation with the University of Georgia Office of Continuing Social Work Education, c1980. — 159p ; 22cm. — (Sage human services guides ; v.15)
Bibliography: p155
ISBN 0-8039-1503-9 (pbk) : Unpriced
B81-14614

361.3′7 — Great Britain. Secondary schools. Curriculum subjects: Community work

Scrimshaw, Peter. Community service, social education and the curriculum. — London : Hodder & Stoughton Educational, Oct.1981. — [96]p
ISBN 0-340-24450-x (pbk) : £3.95 : CIP entry
B81-26741

361.3′7′0683 — Great Britain. Social services. Voluntary personnel. Recruitment — *Manuals*

Hodgkinson, Mike. Organising volunteer recruitment programmes / [by Mike Hodgkinson]. — Berkhamsted (29 Lower King′s Rd, Berkhamsted, Herts. HP4 2AB) : The Volunteer Centre Media Project, 1981. — 12p ; 30cm
Bibliography: p12
Unpriced (unbound) B81-11749

361.3'7'0941 — Great Britain. Social services. Voluntary personnel. Role

The **voluntary** worker in the social services : report of a committee set up in 1966 by the National Council of Social Service (now the National Council for Voluntary Organisations) and the National Institute for Social Work Training (now the National Institute for Social Work) under the chairmanship of Geraldine M. Aves. — New impression / with additional foreword by Dame Geraldine M. Aves. — Berkhamsted (29 Lower King's Rd., Berkhamsted, Herts. HP4 2AB) : The Volunteer Centre, 1981. — 224p ; 22cm
Originally published: London : Allen & Unwin, 1969. — Bibliography: p216-219. — Includes index
ISBN 0-904647-13-7 (pbk) : £1.95 B81-28234

361.4 — SOCIAL GROUP WORK

361.4 — Welfare work: Group work

Garvin, Charles D.. Contemporary group work / Charles D. Garvin. — Englewood Cliffs ; London : Prentice-Hall, c1981. — xiii,306p : ill ; 24cm
Bibliography: p295-300. - Includes index
ISBN 0-13-170233-5 : £10.85 B81-16592

361.4'0941 — Great Britain. Welfare services. Intake teams

Buckle, Joanna. Intake teams. — London : Tavistock Publications, Sept.1981. — [240]p. — (Tavistock library of social work practice ; SSP 220)
ISBN 0-422-77300-x : £9.50 : CIP entry
ISBN 0-422-77310-7 (pbk) : £4.50 B81-21558

361.6 — PUBLIC SOCIAL WELFARE

361.6 — Great Britain. Local authorities. Social service departments. Area teams

Parsloe, Phyllida. Social services area teams / Phyllida Parsloe. — London : Allen & Unwin, 1981. — 189p : ill,forms ; 23cm. — (Studies in the personal social services ; no.4)
Bibliography: p163-167. — Includes index
ISBN 0-04-362039-6 (cased) : Unpriced CIP rev.
ISBN 0-04-362040-x (pbk) : Unpriced B81-15882

361.6 — Great Britain. Local authorities. Social service departments. Information sources. Use by personnel

Wilson, Thomas D.. You can observe a lot — : a study of information use in local authority social services departments conducted by Project INISS / T.D. Wilson and D.R. Streatfield. — [Sheffield] ([Sheffield S10 2TN]) : University of Sheffield, Postgraduate School of Librarianship and Information Science, 1980. — 157p : ill ; 30cm. — (Occasional publications series / University of Sheffield. Postgraduate School of Librarianship and Information Science ; no.12)
Bibliography: p155-157
ISBN 0-903522-11-x (pbk) : Unpriced B81-35346

361.6 — Great Britain. Local authorities. Social services departments. Information systems

Streatfield, David. The vital link : information in social services departments / David Streatfield and Tom Wilson. — Sheffield : Published by the Joint Unit for Social Services Research at Sheffield University in collaboration with Community Care, 1980. — vi,40p : ill ; 30cm. — (Social services monographs)
ISBN 0-617-00360-2 (pbk) : £1.95 B81-04068

361.6 — Great Britain. Local authorities. Social services departments. Teams. Specialisation

Stevenson, Olive. Specialisation in social service teams / Olive Stevenson. — London : Allen & Unwin, 1981. — 160p : 2ill ; 23cm. — (Studies in the personal social services ; no.5)
Bibliography: p152-156. — Includes index
ISBN 0-04-362045-0 (cased) : Unpriced : CIP rev.
ISBN 0-04-362046-9 (pbk) : Unpriced B81-20484

361.6 — Great Britain. Local authority social services. Participation of clients

Deakin, Rose. Participation in local social services : an exploratory study / [Rose Deakin, Phyllis Willmott]. — London (2 Torrington Place, WC1E 7HN) : Personal Social Services Council, 1979. — 39p : ill ; 30cm. — (Studies in participation ; 1)
Bibliography: p38-39
£2.00 (pbk) B81-38177

361.6 — Social development — *Conference proceedings*

European studies in development : new trends in European development studies / edited by Jacques De Bandt, Péter Mándi and Dudley Seers. — London : Macmillan in association with the European Association of Development, 1980. — xviii,302p : ill,maps ; 23cm
Conference papers. — Includes index
ISBN 0-333-27947-6 : £20.00 : CIP rev. B80-07681

361.6'05 — Social planning - *Serials*

Progress in planning. — Vol.13. — Oxford : Pergamon, July 1981. — [178]p
ISBN 0-08-028398-5 : £25.00 : CIP entry B81-15853

361.6'05 — Social planning — *Serials*

Progress in planning. — Vol.14. — Oxford : Pergamon, Nov.1981. — [310]p
ISBN 0-08-028432-9 : £24.00 : CIP entry B81-31084

Progress in planning. — Vol.15. — Oxford : Pergamon, Nov.1981. — [264]p
ISBN 0-08-028433-7 : £24.00 : CIP entry B81-31085

361.6'09171'241 — Commonwealth countries. Foreign assistance

Commonwealth Fund for Technical Co-operation. Commonwealth skills for Commonwealth needs : the work of the Commonwealth Fund for Technical Co-operation. — [New ed.]. — London : Commonwealth Secretariat, [1981]. — 24p : ill,ports ; 25cm
Previous ed.: 1977. — Text, ill on inside covers
Unpriced (pbk) B81-40655

361.6'09181'2 — Western world. Social development — *Proposals*

Meyer, Niels I.. Revolt from the center / Neils I. Meyer, K. Helveg Petersen and Villy Sørensen ; translated by Christine Hauch. — London : Boyars, 1981. — 190p ; 23cm. — ([Open forum])
Translation of: Oprør fra midten. — Bibliography: p187-188. — Includes index
ISBN 0-7145-2701-7 (cased) : £7.95 : CIP rev.
ISBN 0-7145-2702-5 (pbk) : £3.95 B81-02587

361.6'094 — Western Europe. Regional development

Regional development in Western Europe / editor Hugh D. Clout. — 2nd ed. — Chichester : Wiley, c1981. — xiv,417p : maps ; 26cm
Previous ed.: 1975. — Includes bibliographies and index
ISBN 0-471-27846-7 (cased) : £16.00 : CIP rev.
ISBN 0-471-27845-9 (pbk) : Unpriced B81-00056

361.6'0941 — Great Britain. Non-contributory welfare benefits — *For low-income persons — Serials*

National welfare benefits handbook. — 10th ed. (1980/81). — London (1 Macklin St., WC2B 5NH) : Child Poverty Action Group, [1980]. — 168p
ISSN 0308-5996 : £1.50 B81-35115

361.6'0941 — Great Britain. Public welfare services

Randall, F.. British social services. — 3rd ed. / F. Randall. — Plymouth : Macdonald and Evans, 1981. — xiii,265p ; 18cm. — (The M & E handbook series)
Previous ed.: by F.J. Wright. 1976. — Bibliography: p238-246. — Includes index
ISBN 0-7121-0286-8 (pbk) : £4.95 B81-23259

Taylor-Gooby, Peter. Social theory and social welfare / Peter Taylor-Gooby and Jennifer Dale. — London : Edward Arnold, 1981. — 294p : ill ; 20cm
Bibliography: p269-281. — Includes index
ISBN 0-7131-6332-1 (pbk) : £5.95 : CIP rev. B81-13787

361.6'0941 — Great Britain. Public welfare services — *For schools*

Valentine, Ruth. Talking about the welfare state / Ruth Valentine. — Hove : Wayland, 1980. — 96p : ill,1port ; 24cm. — (Wayland talking points)
Bibliography: p93. - Includes index
ISBN 0-85340-742-8 : £4.50 B81-07295

361.6'09428'13 — West Yorkshire *(Metropolitan County).* **Batley. Community development projects: Batley Community Development Project**

Butterworth, Eric, *1929-*. The challenge of community work : the final report of Batley CDP / Eric Butterworth, Ray Lees, Peter Arnold. — [York] : [Department of Social Administration and Social Work, University of York], 1981. — xiv,249p : ill,1map ; 30cm. — (Papers in community studies ; no.24)
Includes bibliographies and index
ISBN 0-906723-03-5 (pbk) : £5.75 B81-32512

361.6'09429 — Wales. Local authorities. Social service departments — *Statistics — Serials*

Activities of social services departments, year ended 31st March .... — 1979. — Cardiff (31, Cathedral Rd., Cardiff CF1 9UJ) : Economic Services Division, Welsh Office, [1980?]. — 49p
Unpriced B81-03842

361.6'0947 — Soviet Union. Regional planning

Pallot, Judith. Planning in the Soviet Union / Judith Pallot and Denis J.B. Shaw. — London : Croom Helm, 1981. — 303p : ill,maps ; 23cm
Bibliography: p275-296. — Includes index
ISBN 0-85664-571-0 : £16.95 B81-13353

361.6'09931 — New Zealand. Public welfare services

Easton, Brian. Social policy and the welfare state in New Zealand / Brian Easton. — Auckland ; London : Allen & Unwin, 1980, c1979. — 182p : ill ; 22cm
Includes bibliographies
ISBN 0-86861-393-2 (cased) : £12.95
ISBN 0-86861-002-x (pbk) : £5.95 B81-07704

361.6'1 — Governments. Social policies — *Comparative studies*

Rodgers, Barbara N.. The study of social policy : a comparative approach / by Barbara N. Rodgers with Abraham Doron and Michael Jones. — London : Allen & Unwin, 1979. — xiii,232p ; 23cm
Includes bibliographies and index
ISBN 0-04-360048-4 (cased) : £12.00 : CIP rev.
ISBN 0-04-360049-2 (pbk) : £4.95 B79-31531

361.6'1 — Policy studies

The **Analysis** of policy impact / edited by John G. Grumm, Stephen L. Wasby. — Lexington, Mass. : Lexington Books ; [Aldershot] : Gower [distributor], 1981. — xii,209p : ill ; 24cm
Includes bibliographies and index
ISBN 0-669-03951-9 : £14.50 B81-38605

Dunn, William N.. Public policy analysis : an introduction / William N. Dunn. — Englewood Cliffs ; London : Prentice-Hall, c1981. — xii,388p : ill ; 24cm
Includes bibliographies and index
ISBN 0-13-737957-9 : £12.30 B81-23114

Nagel, Stuart S.. The policy-studies handbook / Stuart S. Nagel. — Lexington : Lexington, c1980 ; [Farnborough, Hants] : Gower [distributor], 1981. — xiii,221p : ill,1form ; 24cm
Includes bibliographies and index
ISBN 0-669-03777-x : £11.00 B81-15200

Policy analysis and policy innovation : patterns, problems and potentials / editors Peter R. Baehr, Björn Wittrock. — London : Sage, 1981. — 238p : ill ; 22cm. — (Sage modern politics series ; v.5)
Conference papers. — Includes bibliographies
ISBN 0-8039-9809-0 (cased) : £12.50 : CIP rev.
ISBN 0-8039-9810-4 (pbk) : £5.50 B80-18596

361.6′1 — Regional planning. Problem solving. Applications of dynamic programming

Hopkins, Lewis D.. Generating alternative solutions to planning problems : a procedure for dynamic programming models / by Lewis D. Hopkins. — Liverpool (P.O Box 147, Liverpool L69 3BX) : Department of Civic Design, University of Liverpool, 1981. — 17leaves,[9]leaves of plates : ill,maps ; 30cm. — (Working paper / University of Liverpool. Department of Civic Design, ISSN 0309-8753 ; 16)
Bibliography: leaf 17
ISBN 0-906109-08-6 (pbk) : £1.20 B81-32753

361.6′1 — Social planning

Progress in resource management and environmental planning. — Chichester : Wiley
Vol.3. — Oct.1981. — [320]p
ISBN 0-471-27968-4 : £15.00 : CIP entry
B81-28846

361.6′1 — Social policies

Marshall, T. H.. The right to welfare : and other essays / by T.H. Marshall ; with an introduction by Robert Pinker. — London : Heinemann Educational, 1981. — 184p ; 23cm. — (Studies in social policy and welfare ; 14)
Includes index
ISBN 0-435-82587-9 : £13.50 : CIP rev.
B81-03693

361.6′1 — Social services. Policies. Comparative studies

Higgins, Joan. States of welfare : comparative analysis in social policy / Joan Higgins. — Oxford : Basil Blackwell, 1981. — vi,193p ; 23cm. — (Aspects of social policy)
Bibliography: p177-185. — Includes index
ISBN 0-631-12546-9 (cased) : £12.00
ISBN 0-631-12547-7 (pbk) : £4.50 B81-31929

361.6′1′01 — Social planning. Theories of Marxists *compared with* policies of Soviet Union government on social services, *1917-1979*

George, Vic. Socialism, social welfare and the Soviet Union / Vic George and Nick Manning. — London : Routledge & Kegan Paul, 1980. — viii,212p : ill ; 22cm. — (Radical social policy)
Bibliography: p199-205. - Includes index
ISBN 0-7100-0608-x (pbk) : £5.95 : CIP rev.
Primary classification 361.6′1′0947 B80-26800

361.6′1′018 — Policy analysis. Methodology

Carley, Michael. Rational techniques in policy analysis / Michael Carley. — London : Heinemann Educational, 1980. — x,212p : ill ; 23cm
At head of title: Policy Studies Institute. — Includes bibliographies and index
ISBN 0-435-83801-6 (cased) : £12.50 : CIP rev.
ISBN 0-435-83802-4 (pbk) : £5.50 B80-13705

361.6′1′05 — Social planning — *Serials*

Progress in planning. — Vol.16. — Oxford : Pergamon, Jan.1982. — [246]p
ISBN 0-08-029080-9 (pbk) : £24.00 : CIP entry
B81-38299

361.6′1′0681 — Social planning. Cost-benefit analysis

Thompson, Mark S.. Benefit-cost analysis for progam evaluation / Mark S. Thompson. — Beverly Hills ; London : Sage, c1980. — 310p : ill ; 23cm
Bibliography: p296-303. - Includes index
ISBN 0-8039-1483-0 (cased) : £12.50
ISBN 0-8039-1484-9 (pbk) : £6.25 B81-00801

361.6′1′071141443 — Scotland. Strathclyde Region. Glasgow. Universities: University of Strathclyde. Curriculum subjects: Policy analysis. Projects: PAT Project

Policy analysis teaching package. — Glasgow (16 Richmond St., Glasgow G11XQ) : Centre for the Study of Public Policy
Introductory guide / Lewis A. Gunn and Brian W. Hogwood. — [1981]. — ii,17p ; 21cm
Bibliography: p14
Unpriced (unbound) B81-36725

361.6′1′072041 — Great Britain. Social planning. Research organisations: Policy Studies Institute, *to 1981*

Fifty years of Political and Economic Planning : looking forward 1931-1981 / the authors Lord Roll ... [et al.] ; edited by John Pinder. — London : Heinemann, 1981. — 228p : 1ill ; 23cm
Includes index
ISBN 0-435-83690-0 : £9.50 : CIP rev.
B81-13563

361.6′1′0724 — United States. Government. Social policies. Microeconometric models — *Conference proceedings*

Microeconomic simulation models for public policy analysis : a 1978 conference sponsored by The Institute for Research on Poverty, Mathematica Policy Research, Inc., The National Science Foundation. — New York ; London : Academic Press. — (Institute for Research on Poverty monograph series)
Vol.1: Distributional impacts / edited by Robert H. Haveman, Kevin Hollenbeck. — c1980. — xxx,303p : ill ; 24cm
Bibliography: p283-298. - Includes index
ISBN 0-12-333201-x : £16.60 B81-22201

361.6′1′091724 — Developing countries. Governments. Social policies. Implementation — *Case studies*

Politics and policy implementation in the Third World / edited by Merilee S. Grindle. — Princeton ; Guildford : Princeton University Press, c1980. — xv,310p : 3ill ; 25cm
Includes index
ISBN 0-691-07617-0 (cased) : £11.00
ISBN 0-691-02195-3 (pbk) : £4.45 B81-01703

361.6′1′091724 — Developing countries. Regional planning. Spatial development — *Case studies*

Development from above or below? : the dialectics of regional planning in developing countries / edited by Walter B. Stöhr and D.R. Fraser Taylor. — Chichester : Wiley, c1981. — xii,488p : ill,maps ; 24cm
Includes bibliographies and index
ISBN 0-471-27823-8 : £17.50 : CIP rev.
B81-03148

361.6′1′091724 — Developing countries. Social development. Influence of Western civilization

Cultural collisions : the efficacy of western ideas and education for the development of Third World countries : a report on the symposium held at Oxford Polytechnic, March 1979 / edited by Anna Cronin and John Minett. — [Oxford] ([Gypsy La., Headington, Oxford, OX3 0BP]) : [Oxford Polytechnic, Faculty of Architecture, Planning & Estate Management], 1980. — iii,121p : ill,1map ; 30cm. — (Working paper / Oxford Polytechnic Faculty of Architecture, Planning & Estate Management ; no.49)
Unpriced (pbk) B81-08268

361.6′1′091734 — Rural regions. Social development. Role of agricultural extension services

Extension education and rural development / edited by Bruce R. Crouch, Shankariah Chamala. — Chichester : Wiley, c1981
Vol.1: International experience in communication & innovation. — xxvi,371p : ill ; 24cm
Bibliography: p331-361. — Includes index
ISBN 0-471-27829-7 : £20.00 : CIP rev.
B80-29147

Extension education and rural development / edited by Bruce R. Crouch, Shankariah Chamala. — Chichester : Wiley, c1981
Vol.2: Experience in strategies for planned change. — xxvi,325p : ill ; 24cm
Bibliography: p283-313. — Includes index
ISBN 0-471-27675-8 : £18.00 : CIP rev.
B80-30845

361.6′1′0941 — Great Britain. Government. Social policies

Agenda for Britain. — Oxford : P. Allan
Vol.1: Micro policy choices for the 1980s. — Feb.1982. — [236]p
ISBN 0-86003-034-2 (cased) : £11.00 : CIP entry
ISBN 0-86003-132-2 (pbk) : £5.50 B81-39224

361.6′1′0941 — Great Britain. Government. Social policies, *1900-1950 — For schools*

Wood, Sydney. The British welfare state, 1900-1950. — Cambridge : Cambridge University Press, Nov.1981. — [45]p. — (Cambridge introduction to the history of mankind)
ISBN 0-521-22843-3 (pbk) : £1.95 : CIP entry
B81-32529

361.6′1′0941 — Great Britain. Government. Social policies, *1960-1980.* Political aspects

Ashford, Douglas E.. Policy and politics in Britain : the limits of consensus / Douglas E. Ashford. — Oxford : Basil Blackwell, c1981. — xv,330p ; 21cm. — (Policy and politics in industrial states)
Bibliography: p301-317. — Includes index
ISBN 0-631-12722-4 (cased) : £12.00
ISBN 0-631-12519-1 (pbk) : £4.95 B81-24172

361.6′1′0941 — Great Britain. Government. Social policies, *1964-1979*

Jordan, Bill. Automatic poverty / Bill Jordan. — London : Routledge & Kegan Paul, 1981. — x,197p : ill ; 23cm
Includes index
ISBN 0-7100-0824-4 (cased) : £9.75 : CIP rev.
ISBN 0-7100-0825-2 (pbk) : £4.95 B81-04367

361.6′1′0941 — Great Britain. Government. Social policies. Role of taxation

Taxation and social policy / edited by Cedric Sandford, Chris Pond and Robert Walker. — London : Heinemann Educational, 1980. — xiii,242p : ill ; 23cm. — ([Studies in social policy and welfare])
Includes bibliographies and index
ISBN 0-435-82789-8 : £14.00 : CIP rev.
B80-25160

361.6′1′0941 — Great Britain. Policy studies — *Serials*

Policy studies : the journal of the Policy Studies Institute. — Vol.1, pt.1 (July 1980)-. — London : Policy Studies Institute, 1980-. — v. ; 21cm
Quarterly
ISSN 0144-2872 = Policy studies : £10.00 per year B81-01990

361.6′1′0941 — Great Britain. Rural regions. Social development — *Labour Party (Great Britain) viewpoints*

Labour Party *(Great Britain)*. Out of town out of mind. — [London] : Labour Party, 1981. — 39p ; 21cm
ISBN 0-86117-069-5 (pbk) : £0.80 B81-21678

361.6′1′0941 — Great Britain. Social policies. Decision making. Applications of social sciences research

Social policy research / edited by Martin Bulmer. — London : Macmillan, 1978. — xiv,373p ; 23cm
Bibliography: p313-326. — Includes index
ISBN 0-333-23142-2 (cased) : Unpriced : CIP rev.
ISBN 0-333-23143-0 (pbk) : £5.95 B78-08821

361.6′1′0947 — Soviet Union. Social services. Policies of government, *1917-1979 compared with* theories of social planning of Marxists

George, Vic. Socialism, social welfare and the Soviet Union / Vic George and Nick Manning. — London : Routledge & Kegan Paul, 1980. — viii,212p : ill ; 22cm. — (Radical social policy)
Bibliography: p199-205. - Includes index
ISBN 0-7100-0608-x (pbk) : £5.95 : CIP rev.
Also classified at 361.6′1′01 B80-26800

361.6′1′0948 — Scandinavia. Governments. Social policies

The Nordic model : studies in public policy innovation / edited by Clive Archer, Stephen Maxwell. — Farnborough, Hants. : Gower Publishing Co., c1980. — 161p : 2ill ; 23cm
ISBN 0-566-00341-4 : £9.50 : CIP rev.
B80-09089

361.6'1'0951 — China. Social development, *1949-1977*

China's road to development / edited by Neville Maxwell. — 2nd ed. — Oxford : Pergamon, 1979. — xii365p,[9] p of plates : ill,1map ; 26cm. — (Pergamon international library)
Previous ed.: published in World development. Vol.3, no.7&8, 1976
ISBN 0-08-023140-3 (cased) : £21.00
ISBN 0-08-023139-x (pbk) : £8.25 B81-14131

361.6'1'096891 — Zimbabwe. Social development — *Serials*

[News bulletin *(Zimbabwe Project)***]**. News bulletin / Zimbabwe Project. — No.1 (Dec. 1980)-. — London (1 Cambridge Terrace NW1 4JL) : The Project, 1980-. — v. ; 21cm
Monthly
ISSN 0261-3549 = News bulletin - Zimbabwe Project : Unpriced B81-24105

361.6'1'0973 — United States. Government. Social policies

Dye, Thomas R.. Understanding public policy / Thomas R. Dye. — 4th ed. — Englewood Cliffs ; London : Prentice Hall, c1981. — xiii,401p : ill ; 24cm
Previous ed.: 1978. — Includes bibliographies and index
ISBN 0-13-936260-6 : £11.00 B81-16528

361.6'1'0973 — United States. Government. Social policies. Unintended effects

Sieber, Sam D.. Fatal remedies : the ironies of social intervention / Sam D. Sieber. — New York ; London : Plenum, c1981. — xx,234p ; 22cm. — (Environment, development, and public policy. Public policy and social services)
Bibliography: p217-277. — Includes index
ISBN 0-306-40717-5 : Unpriced B81-40582

361.6'1'0973 — United States. Social planning by local authorities. Political aspects

Catanese, Anthony James. Planners and local politics : impossible dreams / Anthony James Catanese. — Beverly Hills ; London : Sage, c1974. — 188p : ill ; 23cm. — (Sage library of social research ; v.7)
Bibliography: p181-184. — Includes index
ISBN 0-8039-0397-9 (cased) : Unpriced
ISBN 0-8039-0378-2 (pbk) : Unpriced
B81-17236

361.6'1'0973 — United States. Social policies

Huttman, Elizabeth Dickerson. Introduction to social policy / Elizabeth Dickerson Huttman. — New York ; London : McGraw-Hill, c1981. — xvi,382p : ill ; 24cm
Bibliography: p349-365. - Includes index
ISBN 0-07-031548-5 : £10.50 B81-10369

361.6'1'0973 — United States. Social policies. Implementation by government agencies

Williams, Walter. Government by agency : lessons from the social program grant-in-aid experience / Walter Williams with the assistance of Betty Jane Narver. — New York ; London : Academic Press, c1980. — xvi,289p ; 24cm. — (Quantitative studies in social relations)
Includes index
ISBN 0-12-755950-7 : £12.60 B81-06013

361.6'1'0973 — United States. Social policies. Influence of social history

Social history and social policy / edited by David J. Rothman, Stanton Wheeler. — New York ; London : Academic Press, c1981. — xii,336p ; 24cm
Includes index
ISBN 0-12-598680-7 : £15.40 B81-33028

361.6'1'0994 — Australia. Social policies, *1972-1978*

Graycar, Adam. Welfare politics in Australia : a study in policy analysis / Adam Graycar. — London : Macmillan, 1979 (1981 [printing]). — viii,231p : ill ; 22cm
Bibliography: p210-228. — Includes index
ISBN 0-333-29880-2 (cased) : Unpriced
ISBN 0-333-29882-9 (pbk) : £6.95 B81-31848

361.6'12 — Social indicators

Carley, Michael. Social measurement and social indicators. — London : Allen and Unwin, Apr.1981. — [208]p. — (Contemporary social research series ; 1)
ISBN 0-04-310009-0 : £12.95 : CIP entry
Also classified at 300'.28'7 B81-00058

361.6'12 — Social planning. Role of assessment of values

Hardy, Jean. Values in social policy : nine contradictions / Jean Hardy. — London : Routledge & Kegan Paul, 1981. — iv,132p ; 22cm. — (Radical social policy)
Bibliography: p120-127. — Includes index
ISBN 0-7100-0782-5 (pbk) : £4.95 : CIP rev.
B81-07943

361.6'14'091732 — Urban regions. Social planning. Applications of welfare economics

Walker, Bruce. Welfare economics and urban problems / Bruce Walker. — London : Hutchinson, 1981. — 319p : ill ; 23cm. — (The Built environment series)
Bibliography: p295-311. — Includes index
ISBN 0-09-141360-5 (cased) : £12.00 : CIP rev.
ISBN 0-09-141361-3 (pbk) : £5.95 B80-13231

361.6'172'4 — Developing countries. Foreign assistance by developed countries

McNeill, Desmond. The contradictions of foreign aid. — London : Croom Helm, Sept.1981. — [128]p
ISBN 0-7099-1713-9 : £8.95 : CIP entry
B81-21504

361.7 — PRIVATE SOCIAL WELFARE

361.7 — Great Britain. Community work by young persons. Projects. Organisation — *Manuals*

Induction pack : for young volunteer organisers and new workers involved in community service schemes. — Rev. — Leicester (17-23 Albion St, Leicester) : NYB, 1979. — 1portfolio : ill ; 32cm. — (Social action special)
Title from container. — Previous ed.: 1978
ISBN 0-86155-010-2 (unbound) : £1.00
B81-38476

361.7 — United States. Community work. Self-help groups

Silverman, Phyllis R.. Mutual help groups : organizations and development / Phyllis R. Silverman. — Beverly Hills ; London : Published in cooperation with the Continuing Education Program in the Human Services of the Univeristy of Michigan School of Social Work [by] Sage, c1980. — 143p : ill ; 22cm. — (A Sage human services guide ; 16)
Includes bibliographies
ISBN 0-8039-1519-5 (pbk) : Unpriced
B81-12215

361.7 — Voluntary social services

Kramer, Ralph M.. Voluntary agencies in the welfare state / Ralph M. Kramer ; with a foreword by Harold L. Wilensky. — Berkeley ; London : University of California Press, c1981. — xxix,334p : ill ; 25cm
Bibliography: p305-330. — Includes index
ISBN 0-520-04290-5 : £17.50 B81-39840

361.7 — Wiltshire. Swindon. Community work by students of Park School *(Swindon), to 1980*

Coggin, Philip A.. Through learning to service : twenty years of community service at Park School, Swindon / an account compiled by Philip A. Coggin. — [Swindon] ([Marlowe Ave., Walcot, Swindon, Wilts. SN3 3HW]) : Park School, c1980. — 96p : ill,facsim,ports ; 21cm
£1.00 (pbk) B81-08525

361.7'06041 — Overseas voluntary work. British organisations: Returned Volunteer Action — *Serials*

RVA business news supplement. — [No.1]-. — [London] ([1a Cambridge Terrace, NW1]) : [Returned Volunteer Action], [1978]-. — v. ; 30cm
Irregular. — Supplement to: Comeback
ISSN 0260-7697 = RVA business news supplement : Unpriced(free to members)
B81-11868

361.7'06'042174 — London. Havering *(London Borough)***. Upminster, Cranham. Residents. Organisations: Upminster & Cranham Ratepayers' & Residents' Association,** *to 1980*

Upminster & Cranham Ratepayers & Residents' Association. The watchdog on local affairs : a history of the Ratepayers' Association in Upminster and Cranham. — [London] ([c/o 11-19 Vyner St., E2 9DG]) : The Association, 1981. — 11p ; 21cm
Unpriced (unbound) B81-09242

361.7'07'041 — Great Britain. Volunteer welfare workers. Training — *Serials*

Training action. — No.1 (Mar.1981)-. — London : Training Information and Development Service NCVO, 1981-. — v. ; 30cm
Six issues yearly
ISSN 0261-0337 = Training action : £6.00 per year (£3.00 to members) B81-25495

361.7'072041 — Great Britain. Voluntary welfare services. Provision. Research

Hadley, Roger. Research on the voluntary sector : some proposals for exploring alternative patterns of welfare provision : a report to the SSRC Sociology and Social Administration Committee / by Roger Hadley and Stephen Hatch. — London : Social Science Research Council, c1980. — 45p ; 30cm
Bibliography: p37-38
ISBN 0-86226-040-x (pbk) : Unpriced
B81-14326

361.7'072041 — Great Britain. Voluntary welfare work. Research projects, *1977-1980 — Lists*

Selwyn, Shirley. Research into voluntary action 1977-1980 : a directory / compiled by Shirley Selwyn ; edited by Stephen Humble. — Berkhamsted (29 Lower King's Rd., Berkhamsted, Herts HP4 2AB) : Volunteer Centre, c1981. — 72p ; 30cm
Bibliography: p72. — Includes index
ISBN 0-904647-12-9 (pbk) : £3.00 B81-24772

361.7'0941 — Great Britain. Charities. Fund raising *— Manuals*

Industrial sponsorship and joint promotions. — London (9 Mansfield Place, NW3 1HS) : Directory of Social Change, Nov.1981. — [128]p
ISBN 0-907164-07-2 (pbk) : £2.95 : CIP entry
B81-33623

Raising money from government. — London (9 Mansfield Place, NW3 1HS) : Directory of Social Change, Nov.1981. — [144]p
ISBN 0-907164-06-4 (pbk) : £2.95 : CIP entry
B81-33626

Raising money from industry. — London (9 Mansfield Place, NW3 1HS) : Directory of Social Change, Nov.1981. — [128]p
ISBN 0-907164-05-6 (pbk) : £2.95 : CIP entry
B81-33625

Raising money from trusts. — London (9 Mansfield Place, NW3 1HS) : Directory of Social Change, Nov.1981. — [128]p
ISBN 0-907164-04-8 (pbk) : £2.95 : CIP entry
B81-33624

361.7'0941 — Great Britain. Charities. Fund raising. Role of broadcasting

Leat, Diana. Charitable fundraising by means of radio and television : an exploratory study / Diana Leat. — Berkhamsted (29 Lower King's Rd., Berkhamsted, Herts. HP4 2AB) : The Volunteer Centre Media Project, 1981. — ii,40p ; 30cm
Cover title
£1.50 (pbk) B81-33679

361.7'0941 — Great Britain. Social services. Role of voluntary work

Leat, Diana. Voluntary and statutory collaboration : rhetoric or reality? / Diana Leat, Gerry Smolka, Judith Unell. — London : Bedford Square Press, NCVO, 1981. — 216p ; 22cm
Bibliography: p214-216
ISBN 0-7199-1054-4 (pbk) : £9.95 B81-31940

361.7'0941 — Great Britain. Society. Role of voluntary social services

Voluntary and State social services : what should the relationship be?. — Liverpool (14 Castle St., Liverpool L2 0NJ) : Liverpool Council for Voluntary Service on behalf of the Welfare Organisations Committee, 1981. — 16p ; 30cm
Cover title
£0-45 (pbk) B81-23027

361.7'0941 — Great Britain. Voluntary organisations. Fund raising — *Manuals*

Volunteer Centre. Fund raising for and by small groups of volunteers / [compiled by T.W. Cynog-Jones]. — Berkhamsted (29 Lower Kings Rd., Berkhamsted, Herts.) : Volunteer Centre, 1980. — 118p ; 21cm
£4.50 (spiral) B81-04989

361.7'0941 — Great Britain. Voluntary social services

Johnson, Norman. Voluntary social services / Norman Johnson. — Oxford : Basil Blackwell, 1981. — 184p ; 23cm. — (Aspects of social policy)
Bibliography: p168-179. — Includes index
ISBN 0-85520-403-6 (cased) : £12.50 : CIP rev.
ISBN 0-85520-404-4 (pbk) : £4.50 B81-13740

361.7'0941 — Great Britain. Voluntary welfare services. Policies of government. Government and the voluntary sector. Criticism

The **Government** and the voluntary sector : analysis of the response to the consultative document / the Voluntary Services Unit. — London : Home Office, 1981. — x,139p ; 21cm
ISBN 0-903727-98-6 (pbk) : £1.50 B81-37615

361.7'09411 — Scotland. Social planning by community action groups — *Manuals*

Thinking ahead : a guide to communities producing their own plans. — [Edinburgh] ([19 Claremont Cres., Edinburgh, EH7 4QD]) : [Scottish Council of Social Service], [1979?]. — 12p ; 22cm
Cover title
ISBN 0-903589-31-1 (pbk) : £0.15 B81-07757

361.7'09422'61 — West Sussex. Crawley. Tenants' associations: Wybourne Tenants Association — *Serials*

Wybourne Tenants Association. Wybourne news : the newsletter of the Wybourne Tenants Association. — Vol.1, no.1 (Oct.1980)-. — [Ifield] (c/o Mrs A. Todd, 20 Berrymeade Walk, [Ifield, West Sussex]) : The Association, 1980-. — v. ; 21cm
Monthly
ISSN 0260-9908 = Wybourne news : Free to Association members only B81-11907

361.7'09427'33 — Greater Manchester *(Metropolitan County).* **Manchester. Voluntary social services** — *Serials*

Voluntary action Manchester : journal of the Manchester Council for Voluntary Science. — Feb. 1981-. — Manchester (274 Deansgate, Manchester M3 4FT) : The Council, 1981-. — v. : ,ports ; 27cm
Monthly. — Continues: CVS news
ISSN 0261-1333 = Voluntary action Manchester : Unpriced B81-15288

361.7'09428'17 — West Yorkshire *(Metropolitan County).* **Wilsden. Amenity societies: Wilsden Village Society,** *to 1980*

Wilsden village society 1970 to 1980 : a study in the origins and development of a society / [edited by Astrid Hansen] ; illustrations by R. Fawcett and A. Saul. — [Wilsden] ([25 Birchlands Ave., Wilsden, Bradford, W. Yorkshire]) : Wilsden Village Society, c1980. — 55p : ill,1map ; 21cm
£1.75 (£1.25 to members of the Society) (pbk) B81-17925

361.7'0973 — United States. Charities. Fund raising. Regulation by government

Hopkins, Bruce R.. Charity under siege : government regulation of fund raising / Bruce R. Hopkins. — New York ; Chichester : Wiley, c1980. — xiv,274p : 1form ; 24cm
Bibliography: p247-250. — Includes index
ISBN 0-471-08170-1 : Unpriced B81-08723

361.7'0973 — United States. Fund raising — *Manuals*

Sladek, Frea E.. Grant budgeting and finance : getting the most out of your grant dollar / Frea E. Sladek and Eugene L. Stein. — New York ; London : Plenum, c1981. — xvii,328p : ill,forms ; 24cm
Includes index
ISBN 0-306-40607-1 : Unpriced B81-38262

361.7'4'088042 — England. Philanthropy. Role of women, *1800-1900*

Prochaska, F. K.. Women and philanthropy in nineteenth-century England / by F.K. Prochaska. — Oxford : Clarendon Press, 1980. — ix,301p,[9]p of plates : ill ; 23cm
Bibliograhy: p253-292 - Includes index
ISBN 0-19-822627-6 : £15.95 : CIP rev.
ISBN 0-19-822628-4 (pbk) : £6.95 B80-21636

361.7'4'0924 — Japan. Philanthropy. Sasakawa, Ryoichi — *Biographies*

Sasakawa : the warrior for peace, the global philanthropist / edited by Paula Daventry. — Oxford : Pergamon, 1981. — viii,111p,[24]p of plates : ill(some col.),ports(some col.) ; 21cm
ISBN 0-08-028126-5 (pbk) : £3.75 : CIP rev. B81-14780

361.7'5 — Kilkenny *(County).* **Catholic voluntary welfare services: Kilkenny Social Services,** *to 1980*

Kennedy, Stanislaus. Who should care? : the development of Kilkenny Social Services 1963-1980 / Stanislaus Kennedy. — Dublin : Turoe, c1981. — 228p : ill,1map ; 22cm
Bibliography: p220-228
ISBN 0-905223-26-8 (pbk) : Unpriced B81-26258

361.7'63'02541 — Great Britain. Charities — *Directories — Serials*

Charities digest / [Family Welfare Association]. — 87th ed. (1981). — London (501, Kingsland Rd., Dalston, E8 4AU) : Family Welfare Association, c1980. — 333p
ISBN 0-561-00311-4 : £5.50
ISSN 0590-9783 B81-06842

361.7'63'02541 — Great Britain. Grant making charities — *Directories — Serials*

Directory of grant-making trusts / [Charities Aid Foundation]. — 7th compilation. — Tonbridge (48, Pembury Rd, Tonbridge, Kent TN9 2JD) : CAF Publications, 1981. — xxv,1050p
ISBN 0-904757-11-0 : £32.50
ISSN 0070-5624 B81-26598

361.7'63'0681 — England. Charities. Honorary treasurers. Duties — *Manuals*

Fenton, Lawrence S.. The honorary treasurer : charities and voluntary organisations / Lawrence S. Fenton. — [London] : Institute of Chartered Accountants in England and Wales, 1980. — vi,50p ; 21cm
ISBN 0-85291-284-6 (pbk) : Unpriced B81-07746

361.7'63'0681 — Great Britain. Charities. Donations by deeds of covenant. Administration

Charitable deeds of covenant : their meaning, application and management. — 2nd ed. — Tonbridge (48 Pembury Rd., Tonbridge, Kent) : CAF Publications, 1981. — 39p : ill,forms ; 21cm
Previous ed.: 1979
ISBN 0-904757-10-2 : £4.00 B81-16441

361.7'63'0681 — Great Britain. Charities. Financial management

Blume, Hilary. Accounting and financial management for charities / [written by Hilary Blume and Michael Norton with the assistance of Bruce Galley] ; [illustrations by Ollie Duke]. — [London] : Directory of Social Change, [c1980]. — 112p : ill,forms ; 21cm
ISBN 0-907164-00-5 (pbk) : £2.25 B81-26815

361.7'63'0688 — Great Britain. Charities. Trading operations — *Manuals*

Blume, Hilary. The charity trading handbook / by Hilary Blume. — London : 9 Mansfield Place, NW3 1HS : Charity Trading Advisory Group, 1981. — 234p : ill,forms ; 22cm
Includes index
ISBN 0-907164-03-x (pbk) : £4.95 B81-26814

361.7'63'0942 — Great Britain. *Charity Commission — Serials*

Great Britain. *Charity Commission*. Report of the Charity Commission for England and Wales for the year ... — 1980. — London : H.M.S.O., 1981. — 52p
ISBN 0-10-233281-9 : £3.60 B81-32913

361.7'63'0942576 — Oxfordshire. Abingdon. Charities: Christ's Hospital *(Abingdon), to 1900*

Carter, John, *1931-*. Give & take : scenes from the history of Christ's Hospital, Abingdon 1553-1900 / by John Carter and Jacqueline Smith. — [Abingdon] ([55 The Motte, Oxon]) : [J. Carter and J. Smith], [c1981]. — 112p : ill,maps ; 21cm
Bibliography: p105-107. — Includes index
ISBN 0-9507680-0-6 (pbk) : Unpriced B81-37728

361.7'63'0942644 — Suffolk. Bury St Edmunds. Charities: Guildhall Feoffment Trust, *to 1981*

Statham, Margaret. Jankyn Smyth and the Guildhall Feoffees, 1481-1981 / by Margaret Statham. — [Ipswich] ([Central Library, Northgate St., Ipswich IP1 3DE]) : Published by the Guildhall Feoffment Trust in conjunction with the Suffolk Record Office, c1981. — 14p : ill ; 26cm
ISBN 0-86055-079-6 (pbk) : Unpriced B81-34261

361.7'65 — Communities. Involvement of business firms — *Conference proceedings*

Anglo-American Conference on Community Involvement *(1980 : Sunningdale Park).* Anglo-American Conference on Community Involvement : Sunningdale Park, England, 9-10 April 1980 : papers and proceedings. — London : Department of the Environment, 1980. — 102p ; 30cm
£2.15 (pbk) B81-40343

361.7'65 — Great Britain. Community work by business firms. Organisations: Action Resource Centre — *Serials*

[ARC news *(London : 1979)*]. ARC news : business skills in community action / Action Resource Centre. — No.14 (Oct.1979)-. — London (Henrietta House, 9 Henrietta Place, W1M 9AG) : The Centre, 1979-. — v. : ill ; 30cm
Quarterly. — Continues: Arclight
ISSN 0144-9745 = ARC news (London. 1979) : Unpriced B81-04865

Arclight : news from Action Resource Centre. — Apr.1976-July 1979. — London ([Henrietta House, 9 Henrietta Place, W1M 9AG]) : The Centre, 1976-1979. — [13?]v. : ill ; 30cm
Quarterly. — Continued by: ARC news (London : 1979). — Description based on: Apr.1977
ISSN 0260-4000 = Arclight : Unpriced B81-04864

361.8 — COMMUNITY SOCIAL WELFARE

361.8 — Community organisation — *Manuals*

Rothman, Jack. Changing organizations and community programs / Jack Rothman, John L. Erlich, Joseph G. Teresa. — Beverly Hills ; London : Published in cooperation with the Continuing Education Program in the Human Services of the University of Michigan School of Social Work [by] Sage, c1981. — 160p : forms ; 22cm. — (A Sage human services guide ; 20)
Abridged revision of the authors' Promoting innovation and change in organizations and communities. New York ; London : Wiley, 1976
ISBN 0-8039-1618-3 (pbk) : £5.00 B81-37804

361.8 — Community work

Social & community work in a multiracial society . — London : Harper and Row, Jan.1982. — [336]p
ISBN 0-06-318197-5 (cased) : £9.95 : CIP entry
ISBN 0-06-318198-3 (pbk) : £5.95 B81-33968

361.8 — Great Britain. Community action. Use of videorecording — *Case studies*
Wade, Graham, *1949-*. Street video / Graham Wade. — Leicester (74 Highcross St., Leicester) : Blackthorn Press, 1980. — 96p : ill,1facsim,ports ; 21cm
ISBN 0-907340-00-8 (pbk) : £1.80 B81-06175

361.8′0941 — Great Britain. Community work
Readings in community work / edited by Paul Henderson, David N. Thomas. — London : Allen & Unwin, 1981. — x,198p : ill ; 29cm
Facsim. reprints. — Bibliography: p185-198
ISBN 0-04-361045-5 (cased) : Unpriced : CIP rev.
ISBN 0-04-361046-3 (pbk) : Unpriced
B81-04197

361.8′0941 — Great Britain. Community work — *Manuals*
Henderson, Paul. Skills in neighbourhood work / Paul Henderson, David N. Thomas. — London : Allen & Unwin, 1980. — viii,294p ; 23cm. — (National Institute social services library ; no.39)
Bibliography: p279-289. — Includes index
ISBN 0 04-361042-0 (cased) : £10.95 : CIP rev.
ISBN 0-04-361043-9 (pbk) : £4.95 B80-23116

361.9 — SOCIAL SERVICES. HISTORICAL AND GEOGRAPHICAL TREATMENT

361′.91812 — Western world. Welfare services, *to 1975*
The **Development** of welfare states in Europe and America / edited by Peter Flora and Arnold J. Heidenheimer. — New Brunswick ; London : Transaction, 1981. — 417p ; 24cm
Includes bibliographies and index
ISBN 0-87855-357-6 : £10.00 B81-16492

361′.941 — Great Britain. Personal welfare services
A **New** look at the personal social services / edited by E. Matilda [i.e. Mathilde] Goldberg and Stephen Hatch. — London : Policy Studies Institute, 1981. — 86p ; 21cm. — (Discussion paper / Policy Studies Institute ; no.4)
ISBN 0-85374-189-1 (pbk) : £3.75 B81-17692

361′.941 — Great Britain. Public welfare services. Policies of government, *to 1980 compared with* **policies of West German government on public welfare services,** *to 1980*
The **Emergence** of the welfare state in Britain and Germany 1850-1950 / edited by W.J. Mommsen in collaboration with Wolfgang Mock. — London : Croom Helm on behalf of the German Historical Institute, c1981. — 443p : ill ; 23cm
Includes index
ISBN 0-7099-1710-4 : £12.95
Also classified at 361′.943 B81-19864

361′.941 — Great Britain. Social services. Administration. Discretion
Discretion and welfare / [edited by] Michael Adler and Stewart Asquith. — London : Heinemann Educational, 1981. — vii,296p ; 23cm. — ([Studies in social policy and welfare])
Conference papers. — Bibliography: p273-287. — Index
ISBN 0-435-82009-5 : £15.00 : CIP rev.
B81-23766

361′.941 — Great Britain. Social services. Policies of government, *1870-1945* — *Conference proceedings*
The **Origins** of British social policy / edited by Pat Thane. — London : Croom Helm, 1981, c1978. — 209p ; 22cm
Conference papers. — Originally published: Totowa, N.J. : Rowman and Littlefield, 1978. — Includes index
ISBN 0-7099-2400-3 (cased) : Unpriced
B81-17878

361′.941 — Great Britain. Social services — *Proposals*
Care in action : a handbook of policies and priorities for the health and personal social services in England / Department of Health and Social Security. — London : H.M.S.O., 1981. — 52p : ill ; 21cm
Includes bibliographies
ISBN 0-11-320755-7 (pbk) : £3.30
Also classified at 362.1′0941 B81-23661

361′.941 — Great Britain. Welfare services

Carter, *Sir* **Charles,** *1919-*. Discussing the welfare state / Charles Carter, Thomas Wilson. — London : Policy Studies Institute, c1980. — 48p : 1ill ; 21cm. — (Discussion paper / Policy Studies Institute ; no.1)
ISBN 0-85374-179-4 (pbk) : £2.75 B81-05844

Stevenson, Olive. The realities of a caring community : the twenty-sixth Eleanor Rathbone memorial lecture delivered at the University of Reading on 4 November 1980 / by Olive Stevenson. — [Liverpool] ([Editorial & Publishing Office, P.O. Box 147, Liverpool L69 3BX]) : [University of Liverpool], c1980. — 32p : 1ill ; 22cm. — (Eleanor Rathbone memorial lectures ; 26)
ISBN 0-906370-09-4 (pbk) : £1.00 B81-27714

361′.941 — Great Britain. Welfare services, *1945-1980*
Hadley, Roger. Social welfare and the failure of the state : centralised social services and participatory alternatives / Roger Hadley, Stephen Hatch. — London : Allen & Unwin, 1981. — 186p ; 23cm
Bibliography: p176-182. — Includes index
ISBN 0-04-361049-8 (cased) : Unpriced : CIP rev.
ISBN 0-04-361050-1 (pbk) : Unpriced
B81-20136

361′.941 — Great Britain. Welfare services. Decentralisation — *Conference proceedings*
The **Welfare** State : diversity & decentralisation / Muriel Nissel ... [et al.] ; with introduction by Sir Charles Carter. — London : Policy Studies Institute, 1980. — 55p ; 21cm. — (Discussion paper / Policy Studies Institute ; no.2)
Conference papers
ISBN 0-85374-181-6 (pbk) : £2.75 B81-04571

361′.941 — Great Britain. Welfare services, *to 1980* — *For schools*
Wright, Christopher, *1924-*. The welfare state / Christopher Wright. — London : Batsford Academic and Educational, 1981. — 75p : ill ; 26cm. — (Today′s world)
Bibliography: p70. - Includes index
ISBN 0-7134-2375-7 : £5.50 B81-15957

361′.941′024613 — Great Britain. Social services — *For nursing*
The **Nurse** and the welfare state / edited by Jean Gaffin ; contributors Judith Allsop ... [et al.]. — Aylesbury : HM+M, c1981. — viii,166p : ill ; 20cm. — (Topics in community health)
Includes bibliographies and index
ISBN 0-85602-089-3 (pbk) : £4.75 B81-19547

361′.941′0321 — Great Britain. Social services — *Encyclopaedias*
Clegg, Joan. Dictionary of social services : policy and practice / Joan Clegg. — 3rd ed. — London : Bedford Square Press, NCVO, 1980. — x,148p ; 21cm
Previous ed.: 1977. — Bibliography: p140-144
ISBN 0-7199-1039-0 (pbk) : £5.95 B81-00802

361′.941′05 — Great Britain. Social services — *Serials*
Guide to the social services / the Family Welfare Association. — 69th ed. (1981). — London : 501, Kingsland Rd., Dalston, E8 4AU : The Association, c1981. — 278p
£5.50 B81-09103

361′.941′05 — Great Britain. Welfare services — *Serials*
The **year** book of social policy in Britain. — 1979. — London : Routledge & Kegan Paul, 1980. — xiv,231p
ISBN 0-7100-0690-x : £9.95 : CIP rev.
ISSN 0307-0476 B80-26802

361′.941′05 — Great Britain. Welfare services — *Socialist viewpoints — Serials*
CSP : critical social policy : a journal of socialist theory and practice in social welfare. — Vol.1, no.1 (Summer 1981)-. — Leicester (c/o Mr G. Peters, School of Social Work, University of Leicester, 107 Princess Rd. East, Leicester LE1 7LA) : Critical Social Policy ; London : Pluto Press [trade distributor], 1981-. — v. : ill ; 21cm
Three issues yearly
ISSN 0261-0183 = CSP. Critical social policy : £6.00 per year (£12.00 to institutions)
B81-35814

361′.9′410924 — Great Britain. Social administration. Fitzpatrick, *Sir* **Jeremiah,** *1783-1802 - Biographies*
MacDonagh, Oliver. The Inspector General. — London : Croom Helm, June 1981. — [352]p
ISBN 0-85664-421-8 : £12.95 : CIP entry
B81-10010

361′.9411 — Scotland. Social services — *Conference proceedings*
Changing social goals : three talks given at a day conference held in Glasgow on 13 November 1980 and organised by the Scottish Council of Social Service. — Edinburgh : Scottish Council of Social Service, [1980]. — 31p ; 20cm
ISBN 0-903589-53-2 (pbk) : £1.50 (£1.00 to members of the SCSS) B81-26630

361′.9411′0212 — Scotland. Welfare services — *Statistics — Serials*
Social work case statistics. — 1976-1977-. — Edinburgh (Room 422, 43 Jeffrey St., Edinburgh EH1 1DN) : Social Work Services Group, 1979-. — v. ; 21cm. — (Statistical bulletin / Social Work Services Group)
Annual. — Continues in part: Scottish social work statistics. — Description based on: 1979
ISSN 0260-5465 = Social work case statistics : Unpriced B81-07696

361′.9411′05 — Scotland. Social services — *Serials*
[**NB** *(Edinburgh)*]. NB : the news bulletin of the Scottish Council of Social Service. — Vol.1, no.1 (Sept./Oct.1980)-. — Edinburgh (18 Claremount Cres., Edinburgh, EH7 4QD) : The Council, 1980-. — v. : ill ; 30cm
Six issues yearly. — Continues: Annual review (Scottish Council of Social Service)
ISSN 0260-0218 = NB (Edinburgh) : Unpriced
B81-06702

361′.9417 — Ireland *(Republic).* **Social services**
Curry, John, *1943-*. The Irish social services / John Curry. — Dublin : Institute of Public Administration, 1980. — 289p ; 22cm
Bibliography: p265-270. - Includes index
ISBN 0-902173-97-9 (pbk) : £9.90 B81-00060

361′.942′0212 — England. Personal welfare services — *Statistics — Serials*
Personal social services statistics. Actuals / CIPFA Statistical Information Service. — 1979-80. — London : Chartered Institute of Public Finance and Accountancy, 1981. — 27p
ISSN 0309-653x : £10.00 B81-26381

Personal social services statistics. Estimates / CIPFA Statistical Information Service. — 1980-81. — London : Chartered Institute of Public Finance and Accountancy, 1980. — 23p
ISSN 0144-610x : £10.00 B81-06787

361′.94216 — South-east London. Social services. Implications of closure of Camberwell Reception Centre
South East London Consortium. *Consortium Joint Planning Group.* The proposed closure of Camberwell Reception Centre and its implications for services in S.E. London : a report from the Consortium Joint Planning Group. — London (131 Camberwell Rd, SE5 0HB) : S.E. London Consortium, 1981. — [50] leaves ; 30cm
Unpriced (pbk) B81-21151

361′.942183 — London. Hillingdon *(London Borough).* Welfare services. Relations with comprehensive schools

Johnson, Daphne, *1927-*. Secondary schools and the welfare network / by Daphne Johnson and Elizabeth Ransom ... [et al.]. — London : Allen & Unwin, 1980. — xii,207p ; 23cm. — (Unwin education books)
Bibliography: p201-203. — Includes index
ISBN 0-04-371071-9 (cased) : £8.50 : CIP rev.
ISBN 0-04-271072-7 (pbk) : £3.95
Primary classification 373.2′5′0942182
B79-34064

361′.943 — West Germany. Public welfare services. Policies of government, *to 1980 compared with* policies of British government on public welfare services, *to 1980*

The **Emergence** of the welfare state in Britain and Germany 1850-1950 / edited by W.J. Mommsen in collaboration with Wolfgang Mock. — London : Croom Helm on behalf of the German Historical Institute, c1981. — 443p : ill ; 23cm
Includes index
ISBN 0-7099-1710-4 : £12.95
Primary classification 361′.941 B81-19864

361′.95694 — Palestine. Social services & welfare services — *Palestine Liberation Organisation viewpoints*

The **Other** face of Palestinian resistance. — London ([52 Green St., W1]) : Palestine Liberation Organisation, [1981]. — 11p : ill ; 21cm
Unpriced (unbound) B81-18644

361′.973 — United States. Social services

Handbook of the social services / edited by Neil Gilbert and Harry Specht. — Englewood Cliffs ; London : Prentice-Hall, c1981. — xvi,703p : ill ; 25cm
Includes bibliographies and index
ISBN 0-13-381806-3 : £27.95 B81-27779

361′.973 — United States. Social services. Evaluation

Toward reform of program evaluation / Lee J. Cronbach ... [et al.]. — San Francisco ; London : Jossey-Bass, 1980. — xxii,438p : ill ; 24cm. — (The Jossey-Bass series in social and behavioral science & in higher education)
Bibliography: p384-412. - Includes index
ISBN 0-87589-471-2 : £13.55 B81-05878

361′.973 — United States. Social services. Projects. Evaluation

Anderson, Scarvia B.. The profession and practice of program evaluation / Scarvia B. Anderson, Samuel Ball. — San Francisco ; London : Jossey-Bass, 1978. — xvii,252p : ill ; 24cm. — (The Jossey-Bass series in social and behavioural science) (The Jossey-Bass series in higher education)
Bibliography: p221-242. — Includes index
ISBN 0-87589-375-9 : £11.20 B81-34203

361′.973 — United States. Social services, *to 1920*

McClymer, John F.. War and welfare : social engineering in America, 1890-1925 / John F. McClymer. — Westport, Conn. ; London : Greenwood Press, 1980. — xiii,248p ; 22cm. — (Contributions in American history ; no.84)
Bibliography: p223-235. - Includes index
ISBN 0-313-21129-9 : £14.75 B81-23648

361′.973 — United States. Welfare services — *Conference proceedings*

National Conference on Social Welfare. *Forum (107th : 1980 : Cleveland).* The social welfare forum, 1980 : official proceedings 107th Annual Forum, National Conference on Social Welfare, Cleveland, Ohio, May 18-21, 1980. — New York ; Guildford : Published for the National Conference on Social Welfare by Columbia University Press, 1981. — xvi,239p : 1port ; 24cm
Includes index
ISBN 0-231-05290-1 (cased) : Unpriced
ISBN 0-231-05291-x (pbk) : Unpriced
B81-40766

361′.973 — United States. Welfare services. Evaluation research

Utilizing evaluation : concepts and measurement techniques / edited by James A. Ciarlo. — Beverly Hills ; London : Published in cooperation with the Evaluation Research Society [by] Sage, c1981. — 152p ; 22cm. — (Sage research progress series in evaluation ; v.6)
Conference papers. — Includes bibliographies
ISBN 0-8039-1521-7 (cased) : Unpriced
ISBN 0-8039-1522-5 (pbk) : £4.95 B81-18606

361′.973′0285404 — United States. Social services. Administration. Applications of microcomputer systems

Taylor, James B.. Using microcomputers in social agencies / James B. Taylor with Jacque Gibbons. — Beverly Hills ; London : Sage in cooperation with the Continuing Education Program in the Human Services of the University of Michigan School of Social Work, c1981. — 119p : ill,1form ; 22cm. — (A Sage human services guide ; 19)
Includes bibliographies
£4.70 (corrected pbk) B81-35657

362 — SOCIAL WELFARE. PROBLEMS AND SERVICES

362′.0424′0973 — United States. Social problems. Prevention

Bloom, Martin. Primary prevention : the possible science / Martin Bloom. — Englewood Cliffs ; London : Prentice-Hall, c1981. — xi,242p : ill ; 23cm
Bibliography: p215-232. — Includes index
ISBN 0-13-700062-6 (pbk) : £7.65
Also classified at 614.4′4′0973

362′.0425 — Scotland. Day care centres — *Statistics — Serials*

Home care services, day care establishments, day services ... Scotland. — 1976-1977-. — Edinburgh (Room 424, 43 Jeffrey St., Edinburgh EH1 1DN) : Statistics Branch, Social Work Services Group, 1979-. — v. ; 21cm. — (Statistical bulletin / Social Work Services Group)
Annual. — Description based on: 1978-79
Unpriced
Also classified at 362.1′4′09411 B81-04764

362′.0425′0973 — United States. Social problems. Alleviation

The **Solution** of social problems : five perspectives. — 2nd ed. / edited by Martin S. Weinberg, Earl Rubington, Sue Kiefer Hammersmith. — New York ; Oxford : Oxford University Press, 1981. — viii,226p ; 23cm
Previous ed.: 1973. — Includes index
ISBN 0-19-502787-6 (pbk) : £3.95 B81-32728

362.1 — WELFARE SERVICES FOR THE PHYSICALLY ILL

362.1 — Great Britain. General practice. Separation from hospital services, *1911-1968*

Honigsbaum, Frank. The division in British medicine : a history of the separation of general practice from hospital care 1911-1968 / Frank Honigsbaum. — London : Kogan Page, 1979. — xvi,445p ; 24cm
Bibliography: p419-423. — Includes index
ISBN 0-85038-133-9 (cased) : £12.50
ISBN 0-85038-219-x (pbk) : £6.95 B81-07058

362.1 — Great Britain. Private health services — *Directories — Serials*

Directory of private hospitals and health services. — 1980-. — Bishop′s Stortford (38 Hockerill St., Bishop′s Stortford, Herts. CM23 2DW) : MMI Medical Market Information, 1980-. — v. : ill ; 22cm
Annual
ISSN 0260-8820 = Directory of private hospitals and health services : £12.50
Also classified at 362.1′1 B81-09101

362.1 — Medicine. Implications of social sciences

The **Relevance** of social science for medicine / edited by Leon Eisenberg and Arthur Kleinman. — Dordrecht ; London : Reidel, c1981. — x,422p : ill ; 25cm. — (Culture, illness, and healing ; v.1)
Includes bibliographies and index
ISBN 90-277-1176-3 (cased) : Unpriced
ISBN 90-277-1185-2 (pbk) : Unpriced
B81-09286

362.1 — Medicine. Social aspects

Dubos, René. Quest : reflections on medicine, science and humanity / René Dubos & Jean-Paul Escande ; translated by Patricia Ranum. — New York ; London : Harcourt Brace Jovanovich, c1980. — xvi,128p ; 22cm
Translation of: Chercher
ISBN 0-15-175705-4 : £5.95 B81-19590

362.1 — Sick persons. Visiting

Autton, Norman. A handbook of sick visiting. — Oxford : Mowbray, Oct.1981. — [176]p
ISBN 0-264-66779-4 (pbk) : £3.50 : CIP entry
B81-30635

362.1′023 — Health services — *Career guides*

Humphries, Judith. Careers in medicine, dentistry and mental health. — London : Kogan Page, Dec.1981. — [112]p
ISBN 0-85038-514-8 (cased) : £5.95 : CIP entry
ISBN 0-85038-515-6 (pbk) : £2.50 B81-34216

362.1′025′41 — Great Britain. Health services — *Directories*

The **Hospitals** and health services year book and directory of hospital suppliers. — 1981. — London : Institute of Health Service Administrators, c1981. — 1101p
ISBN 0-901003-20-4 : Unpriced
Primary classification 362.1′1′02541 B81-16754

362.1′028′54 — Primary health services. Applications of computer systems — *Conference proceedings*

IFIP-IMIA(TC4) Working Conference on the Computer in the Doctor′s Office *(1980 : Hannover).* The computer in the doctor′s office : proceedings of the IFIP-IMIA(TC4) Working Conference on the Computer in the Doctor′s Office, Hannover, West Germany, 25-29 April 1980 / organised by IMIA, International Medical Informatics Association, special interest group of the International Federation for Information Processing (IFIP) ; edited by O. Rienhoff and M.E. Abrams. — Amsterdam ; Oxford : North-Holland, 1980. — xix,352p : ill,1map ; 23cm
Includes index
ISBN 0-444-86051-7 : £19.27 B81-06385

362.1′042 — Man. Diseases. Symptoms. Reactions of patients — *Sociological perspectives*

Locker, David. Symptoms and illness : the cognitive organization of disorder / David Locker. — London : Tavistock Publications, 1981. — xii,193p ; 25cm
Bibliography: p184-188. — Includes index
ISBN 0-422-77460-x : £12.00 : CIP rev.
B81-14834

362.1′042 — Man. Health. Social aspects

The **biocultural** basis of health : expanding views of medical anthropology / Lorna G. Moore ... [et al.]. — St. Louis ; London : Mosby, 1980. — x,278p : ill,4maps ; 24cm
Includes bibliographies and index
ISBN 0-8016-3481-4 (pbk) : £8.25 B81-00803

362.1′0422 — Medical services. Risks

Weitz, Martin. Health shock : a guide to ineffective and hazardous medical treatment / Martin Weitz. — Newton Abbot : David and Charles, c1980. — 303p : ill ; 24cm
Includes index
ISBN 0-7153-7946-1 : £7.95 : CIP rev.
B80-13300

362.1′0425 — Community health services

Kark, Sidney L.. The practice of community-oriented primary health care / Sidney L. Kark. — New York ; [London] : Appleton-Century-Crofts, c1981. — x,253p ; 23cm
Includes index
ISBN 0-8385-7865-9 (pbk) : £8.80 B81-22761

362.1′0425 — Community medicine — *Serials*

Recent advances in community medicine. — No.2. — Edinburgh : Churchill Livingstone, Oct.1981. — [212]p
ISBN 0-443-02357-3 : £15.00 : CIP entry
ISSN 0144-1256 B81-25317

362.1'0425 — England. Community health councils — *Co-operative Party viewpoints*

Co-operative Party. *National Executive Committee.* CHCs : Community Health Councils : a policy statement / by the National Executive Committee of the Co-operative Party. — London (158 Buckingham Palace Rd., SW1W 9UB) : Co-operative Party for the Co-operative Union, 1981. — 10p ; 21cm
Unpriced (unbound) B81-40192

362.1'0425 — General practice

Morrell, D. C.. An introduction to primary medical care. — 2nd ed. — Edinburgh : Churchill Livingstone, Nov.1981. — [168]p
Previous ed.: 1976
ISBN 0-443-02459-6 (pbk) : £5.95 : CIP entry B81-32014

362.1'0425 — General practice. Applications of digital computer systems — *Conference proceedings*

Computers and the general practitioner. — Oxford : Pergamon, Nov.1981. — [142]p
Conference papers
ISBN 0-08-026865-x : £10.00 : CIP entry B81-31067

362.1'0425 — General practice. Delegation

Bowling, Ann. Delegation in general practice. — London : Tavistock Publications, Sept.1981. — [256]p
ISBN 0-422-77490-1 : £10.50 : CIP entry B81-22473

362.1'0425 — General practice. Role of welfare workers — *Sociological perspectives*

Huntington, June. Social work and general medical practice : collaboration or conflict? / June Huntington ; foreword by Margot Jeffreys. — London : Allen & Unwin, 1981. — xii,196p ; 23cm
Bibliography: p183-193. — Includes index
ISBN 0-04-360059-x (cased) : Unpriced : CIP rev.
ISBN 0-04-360060-3 (pbk) : Unpriced B81-15884

362.1'0425 — Great Britain. Community health services — *Conference proceedings*

Community work and health / edited by John Hubley ; proceedings of a conference organised by the West and Central Scotland Branch of the Community Training Group, held at Glasgow on 21st and 22nd April 1980. — Paisley (High St., Paisley PA1 2BE) : Local Government Unit, Paisley College of Technology, 1980. — 89p ; 30cm. — (Working paper / Paisley College of Technology Local Government Unit ; no.11)
Bibliography: p84-86
£1.00 (spiral) B81-21127

362.1'0425 — Great Britain. Community health services — *Proposals*

Great Britain. *Department of Health and Social Security.* Care in the community : a consultative document on moving resources for care in England / Department of Health and Social Security. — [London] ([Alexander Fleming House, Elephant and Castle, SE1 6BY]) : Department of Health and Social Security, 1981. — 21p ; 30cm
Cover title
Unpriced (pbk) B81-36104

362.1'0425 — Great Britain. Community health services. Teams

Bruce, Nigel. Teamwork for preventive care / Nigel Bruce. — Chichester : Research Studies Press, c1980. — xix,241p ; 24cm. — (Social policy research monographs series ; 1)
Bibliography: p223-235. - Includes index
ISBN 0-471-27883-1 : £18.50 B81-06229

362.1'0425 — Great Britain. Community medicine

Elwood, J. Harold. Medicine and the community : an inaugural lecture delivered before the Queen's University of Belfast on 27 February 1980 / J.H. Elwood. — [Belfast] : Queen's University of Belfast, c1980. — 20p,[4]p of plates : 4ports ; 21cm. — (New lecture series / Queen's University of Belfast ; no.121)
ISBN 0-85389-180-x (pbk) : £0.40 B81-05872

Smith, Alwyn. The role of community medicine / Alwyn Smith. — Manchester ([c/o Mrs. W. Bennett, Booth Street West, Manchester M15 6PB]) : Health Services Management Unit, Department of Social Administration, University of Manchester, 1981. — 14,3leaves ; 30cm. — (Working paper series / University of Manchester. Health Services Management Unit, ISSN 0141-2647 ; no.38)
£2.00 (pbk) B81-16699

362.1'0425 — Great Britain. General practice. Attitudes of general practitioners & patients, *1977*

Cartwright, Ann. General practice revisited : a second study of patients and their doctors / Ann Cartwright and Robert Anderson. — London : Tavistock Publications, 1981. — xii,228p ; 22cm
Bibliography: p216-220. — Includes index
ISBN 0-422-77360-3 : Unpriced B81-11573

362.1'0425 — Great Britain. General practice. Management

Running a practice : a manual of practice management / R.V.H. Jones ... [et al.]. — 2nd ed. — London : Croom Helm, c1981. — 229p : ill ; 22cm
Previous ed.: 1978. — Includes index
£7.95 (pbk) B81-13030

362.1'0425 — Great Britain. General practice — *Manuals*

Marshall, S. G.. A primer of primary care / S.G. Marshall, A.P.R. Eckersley. — London : Lloyd-Luke, 1980. — 153p : 1ill ; 19cm
Includes index
ISBN 0-85324-147-3 (pbk) : £3.75 B81-01952

362.1'0425 — Great Britain. General practice, *to 1948*

Cule, John. A doctor for the people : 2000 years of general practice in Britian / John Cule. — London : 33 Alfred Place, WC1E 7DP : Update, 1980. — 145p,[16]p of plates : ill(some col.),1coat of arms,facsims(some col.), ports (some col.) ; 27cm
Ill. on lining papers. — Bibliography: p131-134. - Includes index
ISBN 0-906141-29-x : Unpriced : CIP rev. B80-13755

362.1'0425 — Great Britain. General practice, *to 1980*

Gibson, *Sir* **Ronald**. The family doctor : his life and history. — London : Allen & Unwin, Nov.1981. — [256]p
ISBN 0-04-610017-2 : £9.50 : CIP entry B81-28789

362.1'0425 — Great Britain. General practitioners. Lists. Size

Butler, John R.. How many patients? : a study of list sizes in general practice / J.R. Butler. — London : Bedford Square Press of the National Council for Voluntary Organisations, 1980. — 144p : 1ill ; 22cm. — (Occasional papers on social administration ; 64)
Bibliography: p136-144
ISBN 0-7199-1041-2 (pbk) : £4.50 B81-04774

362.1'0425 — Great Britain. Medicine. Nursing. Social aspects, *to 1979*

Baly, Monica E.. Nursing and social change / Monica E. Baly. — 2nd ed. — London : Heinemann Medical, 1980. — xii,516p,[4]p of plates : ill,facsims ; 22cm
Previous ed.: 1973. — Includes bibliographies and index
ISBN 0-433-01161-0 (pbk) : £12.00 B81-02783

362.1'0425 — Great Britain. Patients. Care by general practitioners. Quality. Assessment

Watkins, C. J.. The measurement of quality of general practitioner care / C.J. Watkins. — London : Royal College of General Practitioners, 1981. — 18p : 1ill ; 28cm. — (Occasional paper / Royal College of General Practitioners ; 15)
Bibliography: p16-18
ISBN 0-85084-078-3 (pbk) : £3.00 B81-17629

362.1'0425 — Great Britain. Universities. Curriculum subjects: General practice

Howie, J. G. R.. Academic general practice : paradox or priority? / J.G.R. Howie. — [Edinburgh] ([Edinburgh EHB 9YL]) : University of Edinburgh, 1981. — 24p : ill,1facsim ; 23cm. — (Inaugural lecture / University of Edinburgh ; no.67)
Cover title
Unpriced (pbk) B81-32436

362.1'0425 — Great Britrain. General practice — *Career guides*

Norell, J. S.. Entering general practice : an outline guide for doctors in training and others / compiled by J.S. Norell ; foreword by J.P. Horder. — Burgess Hill (The Brow, Burgess Hill, West Sussex RH15 9NE) : Schering Chemicals Limited, 1981. — 74p : form ; 21cm
The NHS (vocational training) regulations 1979, certification procedure (1 folded sheet) as insert. — Bibliography: p70-71
ISBN 0-9507443-0-1 (pbk) : Unpriced B81-17012

362.1'0425 — London. General practice — *Statistics*

A **Survey** of primary care in London : report prepared for the Royal Royal College of General Practitioners / [co-ordinator] Brian Jarman. — London : H.M.S.O., 1981. — 139p : maps,1coat of arms ; 28cm. — (Occasional paper / Royal College of General Practitioners ; no.16)
Bibliography: p136. — Includes index
ISBN 0-85084-080-5 (pbk) : Unpriced B81-25366

362.1'0425 — Nottinghamshire. Sutton-in-Ashfield. District nursing services

Perkins, Elizabeth R.. Community nursing and midwifery in the Sutton area : opportunities for health education / Elizabeth R. Perkins. — [Nottingham] : University of Nottingham, 1977. — 26,iileaves ; 30cm. — (Occasional paper / Leverhulme Health Education Project ; no.5)
Unpriced (pbk) B81-22817

362.1'0425 — Patients. Rehabilitation

Brechin, Ann. Look at it this way : new perspectives in rehabilitation. — London : Hodder & Stoughton, Nov.1981. — [328]p
ISBN 0-340-27632-0 : £5.95 : CIP entry B81-32008

Mattingly, Stephen. Rehabilitation today in Great Britain. — 2nd ed. — London : Update Publications, Sept.1981. — [182]p
Previous ed.: 1977
ISBN 0-906141-34-6 (pbk) : £7.00 : CIP entry B81-24626

362.1'0425 — United States. Community health services. Nursing

Clemen, Susan Ann. Comprehensive family and community health nursing / Susan Ann Clemen, Diane Gerber Eigsti, Sandra L. McGuire. — New York ; London : McGraw Hill, c1981. — xi,625p : ill,forms ; 25cm
Includes bibliographies and index
ISBN 0-07-011324-6 : £13.95 B81-36313

362.1'0425 — United States. Community health services. Nursing services

Family-centered community nursing : a sociocultural framework / edited by Adina M. Reinhardt, Mildred D. Quinn. — St. Louis ; London : Mosby
Vol.2. — 1981. — xxi,249p : ill,forms ; 24cm
Includes bibliographies and index
ISBN 0-8016-4121-7 (pbk) : £9.25 B81-19045

362.1'0425 — United States. Community health services. Nursing services. Coordination

Continuity of care : the hospital and the community / editor Sally R. Beatty. — New York ; London : Grune & Stratton, c1980. — xiii,253p : ill,forms ; 24cm
Includes index
ISBN 0-8089-1304-2 : £9.80 B81-18180

362.1′0425 — United States. Community medicine — *For nursing*

Primary care : a contemporary nursing perspective / edited by Ingeborg G. Mauksch. — New York ; London : Grune & Stratton ; London : Academic Press [distributor], c1981. — xi,172p : ill,forms ; 23cm
Conference papers. — Includes bibliographies and index
ISBN 0-8089-1392-1 (pbk) : £8.40 B81-40779

362.1′0425 — United States. Health maintenance organisations

Luft, Harold S.. Health maintenance organizations : dimensions of performance / Harold S. Luft. — New York ; Chichester : Wiley, c1981. — xxiv,468p : ill ; 24cm. — (Health, medicine, and society)
Bibliography: p407-450. — Includes index
ISBN 0-471-01695-0 : £21.00 B81-24227

362.1′04256 — Great Britain. General practice. Preventive medicine

Health and prevention in primary care : report of a Working Party appointed by the Council of the Royal College of General Practitioners. — London : The College, 1981. — vi,24p ; 28cm. — (Report from general practice ; 18)
Bibliography: p23-24
£3.00 (pbk) B81-13337

362.1′04256 — Great Britain. Hospitals. Chaplains. Professional education. Courses — *Serials*

Hospital Chaplaincies Council. Training courses / Hospital Chaplaincies Council of the General Synod. — 1981. — [London] ([Church House, Dean's Yard, Westminster SW1 3NZ]) : [The Synod], [1980?]. — 15p
Unpriced B81-09706

362.1′06′041 — Great Britain. Chronically sick persons. Organisations — *Directories* — *Serials*

Self-help and the patient. — 7th ed. 1980. — London (11 Dartmouth St., SW1H 9BN) : The Patients Association, 1980. — 59p
£1.20
Primary classification 362.4′06′041 B81-08767

362.1′068 — Developing countries. Health services. Management — *Study regions: Afghanistan*

Managing health systems in developing areas : experiences from Afghanistan / edited by Ronald W. O'Connor. — Lexington [Mass.] : Lexington Books ; Farnborough, Hants. : Gower [distributor], 1981, c1980. — xvii,314p : ill ; 24cm
Bibliography: p301-304. — Includes index
ISBN 0-669-03646-3 : £16.50 B81-14668

362.1′068 — Great Britain. National health services. Decision making

Hunter, David J.. Coping with uncertainty : policy and politics in the National Health Service / David J. Hunter. — Chichester : Research Studies Press, c1980. — xix,292p ; 24cm. — (Social policy research monographs series ; 2)
Bibliography: p249-286. - Includes index
ISBN 0-471-27906-4 : Unpriced B81-08486

362.1′068 — Great Britain. National health services. Management. Statistical methods

Goldstone, Leonard A.. Health service management statistics / L.A. Goldstone. — [Manchester] ([c/o Mrs. Wyn Bennett, Manchester Business School, Booth Street West, Manchester M15 6PB) : Health Services Management Unit, University of Manchester, 1981. — 31,[26]leaves : ill ; 30cm. — (Working paper series / University of Manchester. Health Services Management Unit, ISSN 0141-2647 ; no.44)
£2.00 (pbk) B81-35345

362.1′068 — United States. General practice. Organisation

The **Physician's** practice / edited by John M. Eisenberg, Sankey V. Williams with Ellen S. Smith. — New York ; Chichester : Wiley, c1980. — xiv,274p : ill,forms ; 27cm
Includes index
ISBN 0-471-05469-0 : £10.00 B81-04052

362.1′068 — West Germany. Health services. Administration

Stone, Deborah A.. The limits of professional power : national health care in the Federal Republic of Germany / Deborah A. Stone. — Chicago ; London (University of Chicago Press), 1980. — xi,212p : ill ; 24cm
Bibliography: p201-205. — Includes index
ISBN 0-226-77553-4 : £11.10 B81-21061

362.1′068′1 — Great Britain. National health services. Financial management

Macaulay, R.. Financial management in the National Health Service / R. Macaulay, R. Gore. — Manchester ([c/o Mrs. W. Bennett, Booth Street West, Manchester M15 6PB]) : Health Services Management Unit, Department of Social Administration, University of Manchester, 1981. — 25,3leaves : 1ill ; 30cm. — (Working paper series / University of Manchester. Health Services Management Unit, ISSN 0141-2647 ; no.40)
£2.00 (pbk) B81-16697

362.1′068′1 — Northern Ireland. National health services. Financial management

Report to the Royal Commission on the National Health Service on the management of financial resources in the National Health Service with particular reference to Northern Ireland. — Craigavon (30 Portmore St., Portadown, Craigavon BT62 3NG) : Decision Partnership, 1978. — 211p : ill ; 30cm
ISBN 0-9506475-0-0 (spiral) : Unpriced B81-12535

362.1′068′1 — United States. Public health services. Financial management. Budgeting — *Forecasts*

New directions in public health care : a prescription for the 1980s / Cotton M. Lindsay, editor. — 3rd ed. / Alain Enthoven ... [et al.], [contributors]. — New Brunswick ; London : Transaction Books, 1980. — xi,286p : ill ; 22cm
Previous ed.: San Francisco : Institute for Contemporary Studies, 1976. — Bibliography: p273-277. — Includes index
ISBN 0-87855-394-0 : £10.00 B81-04742

362.1′068′4 — Great Britain. National health services. Organisational change. Management aspects — *Conference proceedings*

Allen, David, *1942-*. Changes of management arrangements for medical staff following 'Patients First' / David Allen, Duncan Nichol. — [Manchester] ([c/o Mrs. Wyn Bennett, Manchester Business School, Booth Street West, Manchester M15 6PB]) : Health Services Management Unit, University of Manchester, 1981. — 6,3leaves ; 30cm. — (Working paper series / University of Manchester. Health Services Management Unit, ISSN 0141-2647 ; no.43)
Cover title: A report of a seminar on the changes of management arrangements for medical staff following 'Patients First'
£2.00 (pbk) B81-35342

362.1′068′7 — United States. Health services. Materials management

Reisman, Arnold, *1934-*. Materials management for health services / Arnold Reisman. — Lexington, Mass. : Lexington Books ; [Aldershot] : Gower [distributor], 1981. — xxi,488p : ill ; 24cm
Bibliography: p381-388. — Includes index
ISBN 0-669-03458-4 : £23.50 B81-40902

362.1′07′04227 — Hampshire. Health services. Organisations. Information sources

Gann, Robert. Help for health : the needs of health care practitioners for information about organisations in support of health care : final report for the period May 1979 to October 1980 on project number SI/G/306 / Robert Gann. — Southampton (Southampton General Hospital, Southampton SO9 4XY) : Wessex Regional Library & Information Service, 1981. — xiii,103p : 1map ; 30cm. — (BL R & D report ; no.5613)
At head of title: Hampshire Area Health Authority (Teaching). — Bibliography: p73-74
ISBN 0-906132-02-9 (pbk) : Unpriced B81-23731

362.1′072041 — Great Britain. Health services. Research

Matters of moment : management, inner cities, maternity, collaboration / essays by R.H.L. Cohen ... [et al.] ; edited by Gordon McLachlan. — Oxford : Oxford University Press for the Nuffield Provincial Hospitals Trust, c1981. — 152p : ill ; 22cm
ISBN 0-19-721226-3 (pbk) : £6.50 B81-32563

362.1′072042 — England. Health services. Research, *to 1980*

Health in England : a topic for debate : based on the proceedings of a symposium, chaired by Professor Sir John Butterfield at the Royal College of Obstetricians and Gynaecologoists on the 11th September 1980 / written by David Taylor. — London : Office of Health Economics, c1981. — 27p : col.ill ; 30cm
£2.00 (pbk) B81-09304

362.1′08991404273 — Great Britain. Health services. Requirements of south Asian immigrants — *Study regions: Greater Manchester (Metropolitan County)*

Health care provision for the Asian community / Jayne Murphy ... [et al.]. — [Manchester] ([c/o Mrs. Wyn Bennett, Manchester Business School, Booth Street West, Manchester M15 6PB]) : Health Services Management Unit, University of Manchester, 1981. — 36,[11] leaves : 2maps ; 30cm : 2forms. — (Working paper series / University of Manchester. Health Services Management Unit, ISSN 0141-2647 ; no.45)
Bibliography: leaves 35-36
£2.00 (pbk) B81-35343

362.1′09172′4 — Developing countries. Health services for families

Maternal and child health around the world / edited by Helen M. Wallace and G.J. Ebrahim. — London : Macmillan, 1981. — x,379p : ill,maps ; 26cm
Includes bibliographies and index
ISBN 0-333-28631-6 : £35.00 : CIP rev. B80-24300

362.1′09172′4 — Developing countries. Health services. Provision *related to* **internal migration**

Beenstock, Michael. Health, migration and development / Michael Beenstock. — Farnborough, Hants. : Gower, c1980. — vi,183p : ill ; 23cm
Includes bibliographies and index
ISBN 0-566-00369-4 : £9.50 : CIP rev.
Also classified at 307′.2 B80-10028

362.1′0941 — Great Britain. Health services

The **Litmus** papers : a National Health Dis-service / [edited by Arthur Seldon] ; [contributions Digby Anderson et al.]. — London (8 Wilfred St., SW1) : Centre for Policy Studies, 1980. — v,147p ; 26cm
ISBN 0-905880-28-5 (pbk) : £5.55 B81-06986

362.1′0941 — Great Britain. Health services. Political aspects — *Serials*

Politics of health. — 1 (Nov.1980)-. — [London] ([c/o BSSRS, 9 Poland St., W1]) : Politics of Health Group, 1980-. — v. : ill ; 31cm
Three issues yearly
ISSN 0260-7700 = Politics of health B81-06924

362.1′0941 — Great Britain. Health services — *Proposals*

Care in action : a handbook of policies and priorities for the health and personal social services in England / Department of Health and Social Security. — London : H.M.S.O., 1981. — 52p : ill ; 21cm
Includes bibliographies
ISBN 0-11-320755-7 (pbk) : £3.30
Primary classification 361′.941 B81-23661

362.1′0941 — Great Britain. National health services

Windass, Stan. Health / Stan Windass. — [Adderbury] ([The Rookery, Adderbury, Oxon.]) : [Alternative Society], 1979. — 28p : ill ; 21cm. — (Where do we go from here?)
Cover title. — Bibliography: p21
Unpriced (pbk) B81-16951

362.1′0941 — Great Britain. National health services, *1940-1950*

Pater, John E.. The making of the National Health Service / by John E. Pater ; foreword by Sir George Godber. — London : King Edward's Hospital Fund for London, c1981. — xii,210p,[8]p of plates : 9ports ; 24cm. — (King's Fund historical series ; 1)
Bibliography: p193-200. — Includes index
ISBN 0-900889-84-5 : Unpriced : CIP rev. B81-10426

362.1′0941 — Great Britain. National health services. Complaints by public

Health Service Commissioner : second report for session 1980-81 : selected investigations completed October 1980-March 1981. — London : H.M.S.O., 1981. — 273p ; 25cm. — ([HC] ; 306)
ISBN 0-10-230681-8 (pbk) : £8.10 B81-32994

362.1′0941 — Great Britain. National health services. Organisation — *For doctors*

Allen, David, *1942-*. In conclusion. The management of medicine : how the Health Service works - a guide for doctors / D. Allan and D. Grimes. — Manchester ([c/o Mrs. W. Bernett, Booth Street West, Manchester M15 6PB]) : Health Services Management Unit, Department of Social Administration University of Manchester, 1981. — 5,31leaves ; 30cm. — (Working paper series / University of Manchester. Health Services Management Unit, ISSN 0414-2647 ; no.41)
£2.00 (pbk) B81-16695

362.1′0941 — Great Britain. National health services. Policies of government. Formulation. Role of Great Britain. *Parliament, 1970-1975*

Ingle, Stephen. Parliament and health policy : the role of MPs 1970-75 / Stephen Ingle, Philip Tether. — Farnborough, Hants. : Gower, c1981. — vi,171p ; 23cm
Includes index
ISBN 0-566-00388-0 : £11.50 : CIP rev. B80-29413

362.1′0941 — Great Britain. Primary health services

Pritchard, Peter. Manual of primary health care. — 2nd ed. — Oxford : Oxford University Press, Nov.1981. — [200]p. — (Oxford medical publications)
Previous ed.: 1978
ISBN 0-19-261355-3 (pbk) : £4.95 : CIP entry B81-30530

362.1′09411 — Scotland. Health services — *Statistics — Serials*

Scottish health statistics / Information Services Division, Common Services Agency for the Scottish Health Service. — 1979. — Edinburgh : H.M.S.O., 1981. — viii,210p
ISBN 0-11-887411-x : £12.50 B81-24114

362.1′09421′43 — London. Islington *(London Borough).* **Health services. Attitudes of residents of Lewis Trust Estate**

Torrisi, Jean. Housing, health & the NHS in the Lewis Trust buildings / [Jean Torrisi for Islington Community Health Council]. — London (Liverpool Road Hospital, Liverpool Rd., Islington N1 0QE) : Islington Community Health Council, 1981. — 15p ; 30cm
Unpriced (unbound)
Also classified at 363.5′09421′43 B81-33099

362.1′09421′43 — London. Islington *(London Borough).* **Health services. Use**

Summary of surveys of Ashley Road Family Health Clinic, Barnsbury Health Clinic, Lewis Trust Estate and Loraine Estate carried out Oct—Dec 1980. — [London] ([Liverpool Road Hospital, Liverpool Rd., N1]) : Islington Community Health Council, 1981. — 1sheet ; 30cm
Unpriced B81-33097

362.1′09427′6 — Lancashire. Health services, *ca 1750-1950.* **Social aspects**

Health, disease and medicine in Lancashire 1750-1950 : four papers on sources problems and methods / edited by J.V. Pickstone ; prepared for a history workshop in Manchester, 8 November 1980 organised by the University of Manchester Extra-Mural Department. — Manchester (P.O. Box 88, Manchester M60 1QD) : Department of History of Science & Technology UMIST, c1980. — 103p ; 30cm. — (Occasional publications / Department of History of Science & Technology UMIST ; no.2)
Bibliography: p89-103
£2.00 (corrected : pbk) B81-14520

362.1′09428′79 — Tyne and Wear *(Metropolitan County).* **North Tyneside** *(District).* **Health services. Implications of unemployment**

Colledge, Malcolm M.. Unemployment and health : report / by Malcolm Colledge. — [North Shields] ([c/o Beryl Sloan, Secretary, Stephenson House, Stephenson St., North Shields, NE30 1ET]) : North Tyneside Community Health Council, 1981. — 85p : ill,maps ; 21x30cm
Bibliography: p82-85
Unpriced (pbk) B81-34687

362.1′09429 — Wales. Medical services — *Statistics — Serials*

Health and personal social services statistics for Wales. — No.7 (1980). — Cardiff : H.M.S.O., 1980. — vi,137p
ISBN 0-11-790144-x : £20.00
ISSN 0307-0840 B81-12407

362.1′09429′81 — England. Health services. Geographical aspects — *Study regions: West Glamorgan*

Phillips, David R.. Contemporary issues in the geography of health care / David R. Phillips. — Norwich : Geo Books, c1981. — xi,191p : ill,maps ; 24cm
Bibliography: p171-187. — Includes index
ISBN 0-86094-062-4 : £8.50
ISBN 0-86094-063-2 (international student ed.) : £4.25 B81-18667

362.1′09485 — Sweden. Health services

The **Shaping** of the Swedish health system / edited by Arnold J. Heidenheimer and Nils Elvander with the assistance of Charly Hultén. — London : Croom Helm, c1980. — 245p : ill ; 23cm
Includes index
ISBN 0-7099-0186-0 : £16.95 : CIP rev. B80-08147

362.1′096897 — Malawi. Rural regions. Health services

Msukwa, Louis A. H.. Meeting the basic health needs of rural Malawi : an alternative strategy / Louis A.H. Msukwa. — Norwich : Geo Books for the Centre for Development Studies, University College of Swansea, 1981. — 63p : maps ; 22cm. — (Monographs / Centre for Development Studies University College of Swansea, ISSN 0114-9486 ; 12)
Bibliography: p61-63
ISBN 0-86094-093-4 (pbk) : £2.55 B81-39864

362.1′0973 — United States. Health services

Federal health programs : problems and prospects / edited by Stuart H. Altman, Harvey M. Sapolsky. — Lexington, Mass. : Lexington Books ; [Aldershot] : Gower [distributor], 1981. — xxi,248p : ill ; 24cm. — (University Health Policy Consortium series)
Includes index
ISBN 0-669-03690-0 : £16.00 B81-38470

Miller, Alfred E.. Options for health and health care : the coming age of post-clinical medicine / Alfred E. Miller, Maria G. Miller ; foreword by Wilbur J. Cohen. — New York ; Chichester : Wiley, c1981. — xviii,478p : ill ; 24cm
Includes bibliographies and index
ISBN 0-471-60409-7 : £18.50 B81-23712

362.1′0973 — United States. Health services. Financial assistance by government

Marcus, Isabel. Dollars for reform : the OEO neighborhood health centers / Isabel Marcus. — Lexington, Mass. : Lexington Books ; [Aldershot] : Gower [distributor], 1981. — xxii,178p ; 24cm
Bibliography: p163-172. — Includes index
ISBN 0-669-03092-9 : £13.50 B81-38467

362.1′0973 — United States. Health services. Quality — *Sociological perspectives*

Spiegel, Allen D.. Curing and caring : a review of the factors affecting the quality and acceptability of health care / Allen D. Spiegel and Bernard H. Backhaut. — New York ; London : SP Medical & Scientific Books ; [Lancaster] : MTP Press [distributor], c1980. — xv,261p ; 24cm. — (Health systems management ; v.13)
Includes bibliographies and index
ISBN 0-89335-099-0 : £14.95 B81-03226

362.1′0973 — United States. Health services. Regulation — *Conference proceedings*

Issues in health care regulation / edited by Richard S. Gordon. — New York ; London : McGraw-Hill, c1980. — xv,375p : ill ; 25cm. — (Regulation of American business and industry series)
Includes index
ISBN 0-07-023780-8 : £30.50 B81-10204

362.1′0973 — United States. Medical services, *1720-1940*

Sickness and health in America : readings in the history of medicine and public health / edited by Judith Walzer Leavitt and Ronald L. Numbers. — Madison ; London : University of Wisconsin Press, 1978. — ix,454p,[11]p of plates : ill ; 24cm
Bibliography: p433-441. - Includes index
ISBN 0-299-07620-2 (cased) : Unpriced
ISBN 0-299-07624-5 (pbk) : Unpriced B81-09019

362.1′0973 — United States. Medicine. Social aspects

In sickness and in health : social dimensions of medical care / Ralph Hingson ... [et al.]. — St. Louis ; London : Mosby, 1981. — vii,289p : ill ; 24cm
Includes bibliographies and index
ISBN 0-8016-4411-9 (pbk) : £11.25 B81-33045

362.1′0973 — United States. Public health. Promotion

Strategies for public health : promoting health and preventing disease / edited by Lorenz K.Y. Ng and Devra Lee Davis. — New York ; London : Van Nostrand Reinhold, c1981. — 416p : ill,1map,forms ; 24cm
Includes index
ISBN 0-442-24428-2 : £16.45 B81-11435

362.1′0973 — United States. Urban regions. Medical services. Inequalities — *Sociological perspectives*

Milner, Murray. Unequal care : a case study of interorganizational relations in health care / Murray Milner, Jr.. — New York ; Guildford : Columbia University Press, 1980. — x,204p ; 24cm
Includes index
ISBN 0-231-05006-2 : £12.50 B81-03777

362.1′1 — Great Britain. Independent hospitals — *Directories — Serials*

Directory of private hospitals and health services. — 1980-. — Bishop's Stortford (38 Hockerill St., Bishop's Stortford, Herts. CM23 2DW) : MMI Medical Market Information, 1980-. — v. : ill ; 22cm
Annual
ISSN 0260-8820 = Directory of private hospitals and health services : £12.50
Primary classification 362.1 B81-09101

The **Register** of approved private hospitals and nursing homes. — 1980-81. — Exeter (Northernhay St., Exeter) : Joseph Banks and Son, 1980. — 80p
ISSN 0142-0445 : £1.40
Also classified at 362.1′6′02541 B81-13209

362.1'1 — Great Britain. Independent hospitals. Organisations: Association of Independent Hospitals and Kindred Organisations — *Serials*

Association of Independent Hospitals and Kindred Organisations. Yearbook and suppliers guide / the Association of Independent Hospitals and Kindred Organisations. — 1981. — London (14 Fitzroy Sq., WIP LAH) : The Association, 1981. — 123p
Cover title: Association of Independent Hospitals yearbook
ISSN 0260-0870 : Unpriced B81-32895

362.1'1 — Hospitals — *For children*

Wade, Barrie. Linda goes to hospital. — London : A. & C. Black, Oct.1981. — [32]p
ISBN 0-7136-2154-0 : £3.50 : CIP entry B81-24680

362.1'1'02541 — Great Britain. Hospitals — *Directories*

The **Hospitals** and health services year book and directory of hospital suppliers. — 1981. — London : Institute of Health Service Administrators, c1981. — 1101p
ISBN 0-901003-20-4 : Unpriced
Also classified at 362.1'025'41 B81-16754

362.1'1'02541 — Great Britain. Hospitals — *Directories — Serials*

United Kingdom nursing homes, hospitals / [Data Research Group]. — 1980/81. — Great Missenden : The Group, [1981]. — 252p in various pagings
ISBN 0-86099-295-0 : £29.00
Also classified at 362.1'6'02541 B81-36010

362.1'1'028 — Hospital equipment — *For Middle Eastern countries — Serials*

Middle East hospital : equipment, supplies, services. — Vol.1, no.1 (May 1981)-. — Ewell (172 Kingston Rd, Ewell, Epsom, Surrey) : A.E. Morgan Publications, 1981-. — v. : ill (some col.) ; 37cm
Monthly
ISSN 0262-0073 = Middle East hospital : Unpriced B81-35963

362.1'1'068 — Great Britain. Hospitals. Wards. Management. Role of ward sisters

Pembrey, Susan E. M.. The ward sister - key to nursing : a study of the organisation of individualised nursing / Susan E.M. Pembrey. — London (Henrietta Place, Cavendish Sq., W1M 0AB) : Royal College of Nursing, c1980. — [103]p : 1ill,forms ; 22cm
Bibliography: p101-103
ISBN 0-902606-61-1 (pbk) : £4.00 : CIP rev B80-22227

362.1'1'0681 — Great Britain. Hospitals. Financial management. Budgeting. Role of consultants — *Conference proceedings*

Financial budgets for hospital consultants : paper and comments presented at a seminar arranged by the Chief Scientist Office, Scottish Home and Health Department in association with the Management Education and Training Division held in the Scottish Health Service Centre 28 February 1979 / [edited and produced by G.H. France]. — Edinburgh : Scottish Health Service Centre, Common Services Agency, Management Education and Training Division, [1981]. — 29p : ill ; 30cm
Cover title. — Bibliography: p26-27
Unpriced (pbk) B81-21994

362.1'1'0681 — United States. Hospitals. Financial management

Furst, Richard W.. Financial management for health care institutions / Richard W. Furst. — Boston, Mass. ; London : Allyn and Bacon, c1981. — xii,232p ; 25cm
Includes bibliographies and index
ISBN 0-205-07214-3 : £19.95 B81-26187

362.1'1'0681 — United States. Hospitals. Financial management. Role of information systems

Malvey, Mari. Simple systems, complex environments : hospital financial information systems / Mari Malvey. — Beverly Hills ; London : Sage, c1981. — 188p : ill ; 23cm. — (Managing information ; v.2)
Bibliography: p177-178. — Includes index
ISBN 0-8039-1541-1 : £17.00 B81-36736

362.1'1'0683 — United States. Hospitals. Personnel management — *Case studies*

Hospital administrator-physician relationships / edited by James O. Hepner. — St. Louis ; London : Mosby, 1980. — xx,422p : ill,forms ; 24cm. — (Case studies in health administration ; v.2)
Includes index
ISBN 0-8016-2158-5 (pbk) : £15.75 B81-03991

362.1'1'0684 — Hospitals. Management. Operations research

Cope, David, *1948-*. Organisation development and action research in hospitals / David E. Cope. — Aldershot : Gower, c1981. — ix,163p : ill ; 23cm
Bibliography: p152-161. — Includes index
ISBN 0-566-00387-2 : Unpriced : CIP rev. B81-08817

Operational research applied to health services / edited by Duncan Boldy. — London : Croom Helm, c1981. — 266p : ill ; 23cm
Includes index
ISBN 0-7099-0380-4 : £15.95 : CIP rev. B80-35219

362.1'1'094128 — Scotland. Tayside Region. Perth. Hospitals: King James VI Hospital, *to 1979*

A **History** of King James VI Hospital on the site of the earlier Carthusian Monastery / ... by Primary VII Caledonian Road School under the supervision of Miss R. Fothergill. — [Perth?] : [Perth Civic Trust?], [1980?]. — 8p : ill ; 22cm
Unpriced (unbound) B81-13024

362.1'1'094128 — Scotland. Tayside Region. Perth. Hospitals: Murray Royal Hospital, *to 1927*

Murray Royal Hospital. The history of Murray Royal Hospital, 1827-1977. — [Perth] ([Muirhall Rd., Perth, PH2 7BH]) : [Murray Royal Hospital], [197-]. — 36p,[4]p of plates : ill,ports ; 21cm
Bibliography: p36. — Contents: Centenary history 1827-1927 / Walter Duncanson Chambers - The next fifty years 1927-1977 / Harry Stalker
Unpriced (pbk) B81-12137

362.1'1'0942 — England. Hospitals. In-patients — *Statistics — Serials*

Hospital in-patient enquiry, preliminary tables. — 1978. — London : H.M.S.O., 1980. — 24p. — (Series MB4 ; no.11)
ISBN 0-11-690741-x : £4.20
ISSN 0140-2595 B81-12410

362.1'1'0942133 — London. Kensington and Chelsea *(London Borough).* **Hospitals: St. Charles Hospital,** *to 1981*

St. Charles Hospital. St. Charles Hospital, 1881-1981 : a century of service / [written by B. Curle]. — [London] ([Sector Administrator, Exmoor St., W10 6DZ]) : [St. Charles Hospital], [1981]. — [20]p : ill ; 25cm
£1.00 (unbound) B81-37767

362.1'1'0942393 — Avon. Bristol. Hospitals: Bristol Royal Infirmary, *1904-1974*

Bristol Royal Infirmary. The Bristol Royal Infirmary 1904-1974 / C. Bruce Perry. — Bristol : Portishead Press in association with the University of Bristol and the Special Trustees of the United Bristol Hospitals, c1981. — 130p : ill ; 21cm
Includes index
ISBN 0-906515-88-2 (cased) : Unpriced
ISBN 0-906515-85-8 (pbk) : Unpriced B81-23169

362.1'1'0942753 — Merseyside *(Metropolitan County).* **Liverpool. Hospitals: Liverpool Royal Infirmary,** *1887-1978*

Brewer, Clifford. A brief history of the Liverpool Royal Infirmary 1887-1978 / Clifford Brewer. — Liverpool (Orleans House, Edmund St., Liverpool L3 9NG) : Liverpool Area Health Authority (Teaching), 1980. — 143p : ill ; 30cm : ports
Bibliography: p142-143
£2.00 (pbk) B81-16079

362.1'1'0942865 — Durham *(County).* **Sherburn. Hospitals: Sherburn Hospital,** *to 1981*

Sherburn Hospital. Sherburn Hospital / C.W. Gibby. — [Durham] : [The Hospital], [1981?]. — 32p : ill,2ports ; 21cm
Cover title
Unpriced (pbk) B81-34998

362.1'1'0974461 — Massachusetts. Boston. Hospitals, *1870-1930*

Vogel, Morris J.. The invention of the modern hospital : Boston 1870-1930 / Morris J. Vogel. — Chicago ; London : University of Chicago Press, 1980. — ix,171p ; 24cm
Includes index
ISBN 0-226-86240-2 : £9.30 B81-01882

362.1'2 — New York *(State).* **Rochester. Hospitals: Genesee Hospital. Outpatient departments. Services. Evaluation**

Stratmann, William C.. Evaluating hospital-based ambulatory care : a case study / William C. Stratmann, Ralph Ullman. — Lexington, Mass. : Lexington Books ; [Aldershot] : Gower [distributor], 1981, c1980. — xii,177p : ill,forms ; 24cm
Includes index
ISBN 0-669-02096-6 : £13.50 B81-30027

362.1'2'0941 — Great Britain. Day care centres for adults. Projects

Carter, Jan. Day services for adults : somewhere to go / Jan Carter. — London : Allen & Unwin, 1981. — xix,381p : ill ; 23cm. — (National Institute social services library ; no.40)
Includes bibliographies and index
ISBN 0-04-362035-3 : Unpriced B81-10869

362.1'2'0942143 — London. Islington *(London Borough).* **Health centres: Ashley Road Family Health Clinic**

DeAntonio, Luisa. Survey of the Ashley Road Family Health Clinic / [Luisa De Antonio]. — London (Liverpool Road Hospital, Liverpool Rd., N1) : Islington Community Health Council, 1981. — 5p ; 30cm
Unpriced (unbound) B81-33098

362.1'2'0942143 — London. Islington *(London Borough).* **Health centres: Barnsbury Health Clinic**

Survey of Barnsbury Health Clinic. — [London] ([Liverpool Road Hospital, Liverpool Rd., N1]) : Islington Community Health Council, 1981. — 4p ; 30cm
Unpriced (unbound) B81-33096

362.1'4 — Great Britain. Health visiting. Research, *1960-1980*

Clark, June. What do health visitors do? : a review of the research 1960-1980 / June Clark. — London (Henrietta Place, Cavendish Sq., W1M 0AB) : Royal College of Nursing of the United Kingdom, c1981. — 127p ; 22cm
Bibliography: p127
ISBN 0-902606-63-8 (pbk) : £4.00 : CIP rev. B81-08929

362.1'4 — Hospitals. Discharged patients. Aftercare services. Planning

Continuing care : a multidisciplinary approach to discharge planning / edited by Kathleen M. McKeehan ; instructional design by Barbara R. Pollack. — St. Louis ; London : Mosby, 1981. — xviii,254p : ill,forms ; 24cm
Bibliography: p213-227. — Includes index
ISBN 0-8016-3285-4 (pbk) : £8.50 B81-18965

362.1'4 — Sick persons. Community care — *For welfare work*

Halliburton, Primrose. Get help : a guide for social workers to the management of illness in the community. — London : Tavistock, Dec.1981. — [240]p. — (Social science paperbacks)
ISBN 0-422-77560-6 (cased) : £9.50 : CIP entry
ISBN 0-422-77570-3 (pbk) : £4.50 B81-31744

362.1′4 — Sick persons. Home care by medical personnel

Going home : a guide for helping the patient on leaving hospital / J.E. Peter Simpson, Ruth Levitt ; foreword by Sir Peter Medawar. — Edinburgh : Churchill Livingstone, 1981. — xiii,334p : ill ; 22cm
Includes bibliographies and index
ISBN 0-443-01839-1 (pbk) : £7.95 B81-27106

362.1′4′071141 — Great Britain. Health visitors. Professional education. Organisations: Council for the Education and Training of Health Visitors — *Accounts — Serials*

Council for the Education and Training of Health Visitors. Accounts / Council for the Education and Training of Health Visitors [and] Central Council for Education and Training in Social Work. — 1979-80. — London : H.M.S.O., 1981. — 7p
ISBN 0-10-231481-0 : £1.10
Primary classification 361′.007′1141 B81-31598

362.1′4′09411 — Scotland. Home help services — *Statistics — Serials*

Home care services, day care establishments, day services ... Scotland. — 1976-1977-. — Edinburgh (Room 424, 43 Jeffrey St., Edinburgh EH1 1DN) : Statistics Branch, Social Work Services Group, 1979-. — v. ; 21cm. — (Statistical bulletin / Social Work Services Group)
Annual. — Description based on: 1978-79
Unpriced
Primary classification 362′.0425 B81-04764

362.1′4′094271 — Cheshire. Home help services

The **Home** help service in Cheshire : a report / prepared by Research and Intelligence Section Central Policy Unit for the Social Services Department. — [Chester] ([County Hall, Chester CH1 1SF]) : [Cheshire County Council], 1980. — 2v. : ill,1form
Contents: Clients and their needs. - Consumer view
ISBN 0-906768-01-2 (pbk) : Unpriced
B81-10941

362.1′6 — Great Britain. Residential institutions for incurably sick persons: Leonard Cheshire Homes. Cheshire, Leonard, *1946-1980 — Biographies*

Cheshire, Leonard. The hidden world / Leonard Cheshire. — London : Collins, 1981. — 154p,[16]p of plates : ill,1map,ports ; 23cm
ISBN 0-00-211875-0 : £7.95 : CIP rev.
B81-07463

362.1′6 — Hospices — *Conference proceedings*

Hospice. — London : Edward Arnold, Nov.1981. — [192]p
Conference papers
ISBN 0-7131-4398-3 (pbk) : £5.00 : CIP entry
B81-30595

362.1′6 — Illinois. Nursing homes. Efficiency. Effects of ownership

Koetting, Michael. Nursing-home organization and efficiency : profit versus nonprofit / Michael Koetting. — Lexington, Mass. : Lexington Books ; Farnborough, Hants. : Gower [distributor], 1980. — lx,141p ; 24cm
Includes index
ISBN 0-669-03290-5 : £12.50 B81-01937

362.1′6′02541 — Great Britain. Nursing homes — *Directories — Serials*

The **Register** of approved private hospitals and nursing homes. — 1980-81. — Exeter (Northernhay St., Exeter) : Joseph Banks and Son, 1980. — 80p
ISSN 0142-0445 : £1.40
Primary classification 362.1′1 B81-13209

United Kingdom nursing homes, hospitals / [Data Research Group]. — 1980/81. — Great Missenden : The Group, [1981]. — 252p in various pagings
ISBN 0-86099-295-0 : £29.00
Primary classification 362.1′1′02541 B81-36010

362.1′6′02542 — England. Convalescent homes — *Directories — Serials*

Directory of convalescent and other homes serving Greater London / King Edward′s Hospital Fund for London. — 1981-. — London : The Fund, [1981]-. — v. ; 21cm
Annual. — Continues: Directory of convalescent homes serving Greater London
ISSN 0260-9487 = Directory of convalescent and other homes serving Greater London : £1.75 B81-14353

362.1′6′0973 — United States. Chronically sick persons. Long-term care. Reform — *Proposals*

Reforming the long-term-care system : financial and organizational options / edited by James J. Callahan, Jr., Stanley S. Wallack. — Lexington, Mass. : Lexington Books ; [Aldershot] : Gower [distributor], 1981. — ix,261p : ill ; 24cm
Includes bibliographies and index
ISBN 0-669-04040-1 : £16.00 B81-38604

362.1′7 — Blood banks

Greendyke, Robert M.. Introduction to blood banking. — 3rd ed. / Robert M. Greendyke. — Bern : Huber ; London : Kimpton, 1980. — 338p : ill ; 21cm
Previous ed.: / by Robert M. Greendyke with Jane Corner Banzhaf. Flushing, N.Y. : Medical Examination Pub. Co., 1974. — Includes bibliographies and index
ISBN 0-87488-975-8 (pbk) : £8.00 B81-00804

362.1′7 — Drugs. Provision. Policies

Pharmaceuticals and health policy : international perspectives on provision and control of medicines / editors Richard Blum ... [et al.]. — London : Croom Helm, c1981. — 272p ; 23cm
Includes bibliographies and index
ISBN 0-7099-0608-0 : £17.95 B81-13357

362.1′7 — Multiphasic health testing services — *Conference proceedings*

International Conference on Automated Multiphasic Health Testing and Services *(1980 : Tokyo)*. Progress in health monitoring (AMHTS) : proceedings of the International Conference on Automated Multiphasic Health Testing and Services, Tokyo, October 4-6, 1980 / editor T. Yasaka. — Amsterdam ; Oxford : Excerpta Medica, 1981. — xvi,545p : ill ; 24cm. — (International Congress series ; no.539)
Includes bibliographies and index
ISBN 90-219-0482-9 : Unpriced B81-38107

362.1′8 — United States. Urban regions. Ambulance services — *Case studies*

Mannon, James M.. Emergency encounters : a study of an urban ambulance service / James M. Mannon. — Port Washington, N.Y. ; London : National University Publications : Kennikat, 1981. — viii,193p ; 23cm. — (Series in the sociology of medicine)
Includes index
ISBN 0-8046-9281-5 : Unpriced B81-40555

362.1′8′097526 — Maryland. Baltimore. Emergency medical services

Franklin, Jon. Shocktrauma / Jon Franklin and Alan Doelp. — Feltham : Hamlyn, 1981, c1980. — 246p ; 18cm
Originally published: New York : St. Martin′s Press, 1980
ISBN 0-600-20306-9 (pbk) : £1.25 B81-14140

362.1′9 — Terminally ill children. Care. Psychosocial aspects — *Conference proceedings*

National Symposium on Coping with Crisis and Handicap *(1979 : Boston)*. Coping with crisis and handicap / edited by Aubrey Milunsky ; [proceedings of the National Symposium on Coping with Crisis and Handicap ... held September 10-11, 1979, at the Copley Plaza Hotel, Boston, Massachusetts]. — New York ; London : Plenum, c1981. — xv,358p : ill,ports ; 23cm
Includes bibliographies and index
ISBN 0-306-40660-8 : Unpriced
Also classified at 362.4′088054 B81-37714

362.1′9 — Terminally ill persons. Care

The **Dying** patient. — Lancaster : MTP Press, Aug.1981. — [375]p. — (Current status of modern therapy ; v.10)
ISBN 0-85200-339-0 : £19.95 : CIP entry
B81-21545

McKerrow, Margaret M.. A time to care : a study in terminal illness / by Margaret M. McKerrow. — [England] : [M.M. McKerrow], 1980 (Bodmin : Designed and printed at the Industrial Therapy Unit, St. Lawrence′s Hospital). — 28p ; 22cm
£0.60 (pbk) B81-04751

362.1′9 — United States. Terminally ill children — *Personal observations*

Herrmann, Nina. Go out in joy! / Nina Herrmann. — Eastbourne : Kingsway, 1981, c1977. — 214p ; 18cm
Originally published: Atlanta : John Knox Press, 1977
ISBN 0-86065-107-x (pbk) : £1.60 B81-19843

362.1′9 — Welfare work with terminally ill persons — *Case studies*

Poss, Sylvia. Towards death with dignity : caring for dying people / Sylvia Poss. — London : Allen & Unwin, 1981. — xv,144 ; 22cm. — (National Institute social services library ; no.41)
Bibliography: p132-138. — Includes index
ISBN 0-04-362041-8 (cased) : Unpriced : CIP rev.
ISBN 0-04-362042-6 (pbk) : Unpriced
B81-15881

362.1′9′088042 — United States. Health services. Patients: Women — *Feminist viewpoints*

Marieskind, Helen I.. Women in the health system : patients, providers, and programs / Helen I. Marieskind. — St. Louis ; London : Mosby, 1980. — xiii,329p : ill,facsims ; 25cm. — (Issues and problems in health care)
Bibliography: p323-325. - Includes index
ISBN 0-8016-3106-8 (pbk) : £11.00 B81-07043

362.1′96042 — Genetic counselling

Inheritance - a guide to genetic counselling. — London (1 South Audley St., W1Y 6JS) : National Association for Maternal and Child Welfare, c1980. — 4p ; 21cm
Unpriced (unbound) B81-18262

362.1′961 — Hospitals. Cardiovascular care units — *Conference proceedings*

Coronary care units : proceedings of a European seminar held in Pisa, Italy : sponsored by the European Economic Communities CMSI (ad hoc Committee for monitoring the seriously ill) / edited by Attilio Maseri ... [et al.]. — The Hague ; London : Nijhoff for The Commission of the European Communities, 1981. — xvi,292p : ill ; 25cm. — (Developments in cardiovascular medicine ; v.10)
ISBN 90-247-2456-2 : Unpriced B81-13647

362.1′961 — Patients with cardiovascular diseases. Rehabilitation — *Conference proceedings*

Course on Functional Evaluation and Rehabilitation in Cardiology *(1st : 1979 : Erice)*. Selected topics in exercise cardiology and rehabilitation / [proceedings of the first Course on Functional Education and Rehabilitation in Cardiology, held in Erice, Sicily, Italy, October 15-20, 1979] ; edited by A. Raineri, J.J. Kellermann and V. Rulli. — New York ; London : Plenum, c1980. — xi,279p : ill ; 26cm. — (Ettore Majorana international science series. Life sciences ; v.4)
Includes bibliographies and index
ISBN 0-306-40566-0 : Unpriced B81-14646

362.1′9612′00924 — United States. Terminally ill persons: Persons with heart diseases — *Personal observations*

Lear, Martha. Heartsounds / Martha Lear. — London : Arrow, 1981, c1980. — 395p ; 18cm
Originally published: New York : Simon and Schuster, 1980
ISBN 0-09-925520-0 (pbk) : £1.50 B81-18559

362.1′96123′00973 — United States. Man. Heart. Coronary diseases. Socioeconomic aspects

Social and economic impacts of coronary artery disease / edited by Edgar D. Charles, Jennie J. Kronenfeld. — Lexington, Mass. : Lexington Books ; Farnborough, Hants. : Gower [distributor], 1980. — xii,141p : ill,2maps ; 24cm
Includes bibliographies and index
ISBN 0-669-02912-2 : £11.50 B81-01903

362.1'965'00942496 — West Midlands *(Metropolitan County).* Birmingham. Hospitals: Skin Hospital *(Birmingham), to 1981*
Skin Hospital *(Birmingham).* A century of skin care 1881-1981 / the Skin Hospital, Birmingham ; [D.L. Hall]. — [Birmingham] ([George Rd, Edgbaston, Birmingham B15 2PR]) : [Skin Hospital], [1981]. — [16]p : ill,ports ; 21cm
Cover title
Unpriced (pbk) B81-23570

362.1'96722'00924 — Rheumatoid arthritics — *Personal observations*
La Fane, Pamela. It's a lovely day, outside : an autobiography / by Pamela La Fane. — London : Gollancz, 1981. — 159p : ill ; 22cm
ISBN 0-575-03014-3 : £5.95 B81-38121

362.1'9681 — Man. Brain. Strokes. Personal adjustment — *Personal observations*
Law, Diana. Living after a stroke / Diana Law and Barbara Paterson. — London : Souvenir, 1980. — 208p ; 23cm. — (Human horizons series)
Bibliography: p204
ISBN 0-285-64914-0 (cased) : £5.95
ISBN 0-285-64915-9 (pbk) : £3.95 B81-02408

Millican, Keith D.. A stroke of luck / Keith D. Millican. — Bognor Regis : New Horizon, c1980. — 224p ; 21cm
ISBN 0-86116-202-1 : £6.25 B81-21714

362.1'9681'00924 — Persons with strokes — *Personal observations*
Gibbs, Kristine. Only one way up / Kristine Gibbs ; foreword by A.S. Duncan. — London : Darton, Longman & Todd, 1981. — vii,168p ; 22cm
ISBN 0-232-51446-1 (pbk) : £3.95 : CIP rev. B80-20439

362.1'96835'00924 — Poliomyelitis victims — *Personal observations*
Giddings, Robert. You should see me in pyjamas / Robert Giddings. — London : Hamilton, 1981. — x,214p ; 23cm
ISBN 0-241-10534-x (corrected) : £8.95 B81-11763

362.1'96994 — Man. Cancer. Personal adjustment
Living and dying with cancer / Paul Ahmed, editor. — New York ; Oxford : Elsevier, c1981. — xxix,314p ; 24cm. — (Coping with medical issues)
Includes bibliographies and index
ISBN 0-444-00575-7 : £19.16 B81-35330

Simonton, O. Carl. Getting well again : a step-by-step, self-help guide to overcoming cancer for patients and their families / O. Carl Simonton, Stephanie Matthews-Simonton, James L. Creighton. — Toronto ; London : Bantam, 1980, c1978. — x,245p : ill ; 18cm
Originally published: Los Angeles : Tarcher, 1978. — Bibliography: p223-239. — Includes index
ISBN 0-553-12268-1 (pbk) : £1.50 B81-32918

362.1'96994 — Terminally ill cancer patients. Care — *Conference proceedings*
The **Continuing** care of terminal cancer patients : proceedings of an international seminar on continuing care of terminal cancer patients Milan, 19-20 October 1979 / editors Robert G. Twycross, Vittorio Ventafridda. — Oxford : Pergamon, 1980. — xix,280p : ill,ports ; 26cm
Includes bibliographies and index
ISBN 0-08-024943-4 : £18.00 : CIP rev. B80-12776

362.1'96994'00924 — Cancer victims. Kelly, Kay — *Biographies*
Kelly, Kay. With love from Kay / [Kay Kelly]. — Great Wakering : Mayhew-McCrimmon, 1981. — 108p : ill,ports ; 19cm
ISBN 0-85597-305-6 (pbk) : Unpriced B81-33126

362.1'96994'00924 — Hospices. Cancer patients. Death — *Personal observations*
Zorza, Rosemary. A way to die : living to the end / Rosemary and Victor Zorza. — London : Deutsch, 1980. — 254p ; 23cm
ISBN 0-233-97355-9 : £5.95 B81-05649

Zorza, Rosemary. A way to die : living to the end / Rosemary and Victor Zorza. — London : Sphere, 1981, c1980. — 254p ; 18cm
Originally published: London : Deutsch, 1980
ISBN 0-7221-9443-9 (pbk) : £1.50 B81-38569

362.1'96994'00924 — Persons with cancer — *Personal observations*
Gunn, Alec. The world belongs to Charlie / Alec Gunn. — Bognor Regis : New Horizon, c1980. — 184p ; 21cm
ISBN 0-86116-446-6 : £4.75 B81-21805

Hunt, Jessie. Forever tomorrow / by Jessie Hunt. — Durham City (36 Claypath, Durham City) : Casdec, 1981. — 101p : ill ; 22cm
ISBN 0-907595-01-4 (cased) : £4.95 B81-27818

362.1'96994'00924 — Terminally ill persons: Cancer victims — *Personal observations*
Ryan, Cornelius. A private battle / Cornelius Ryan and Kathryn Morgan Ryan. — London : New English Library, 1980, c1979 (1981 [printing]). — 448p ; 18cm
Originally published: New York : Simon & Schuster, 1979
ISBN 0-450-05206-0 (pbk) : £1.95 B81-29578

362.1'96994'00973 — United States. Cancer patients. Rehabilitation
Dietz, J. Herbert. Rehabilitation oncology / J. Herbert Dietz, Jr. — New York ; Chichester : Wiley, c1981. — xi,180p : ill,1form ; 27cm. — (A Wiley medical publication)
Includes bibliographies and index
ISBN 0-471-08414-x : £15.50 B81-23384

362.1'96998 — Man. Leprosy. Christian medical mission: Leprosy Mission — *Stories, anecdotes*
Bock, Valerie. The road to new life : a true story of Thailand today / by Val Bock ; photographs by Klaus Prinz and Rüdiger Anlauf. — London (50 Portland Place, W1N 3DG) : Leprosy Mission, [1981?]. — [20]p : ill ; 21x30cm
Cover title
Unpriced (pbk) B81-27842

362.1'96998'00924 — Man. Leprosy. Christian medical missions: Leprosy Mission — *Personal observations*
Bock, Valerie. Leprosy, leeches and love / Val Bock. — Eastbourne : Published for the Leprosy Mission by Kingsway Publications, 1981. — 187p ; 18cm
ISBN 0-86065-140-1 (pbk) : £1.35 B81-38076

362.1'971028'0924 — Road accident victims: Adolescents. Severe injuries. Recovery — *Personal observations*
Miller, Barbara. [Kathy]. All I need is time / Barbara Miller with Charles Paul Conn. — Eastbourne : Kingsway, 1981, c1980. — 126p ; 18cm
Originally published: Old Tappan, N.J. : F.H. Revell, 1980
ISBN 0-86065-106-1 (pbk) : £1.75 B81-19842

362.1'97151 — Fractured neck patients — *Personal observations — Collections*
Willis, Jack. - but there are always miracles / Jack and Mary Willis. — London : Macdonald Futura, 1980, c1974. — 181p ; 18cm
Originally published: New York : Viking Press, 1974
ISBN 0-7088-1948-6 (pbk) : £1.10 B81-08608

362.1'9'7554 — Colostomists & ileostomists. Self-help — *Manuals*
Schindler, Margaret. Living with a colostomy. — Wellingborough : Thorsons, Nov.1981. — [128]p
ISBN 0-7225-0680-5 (cased) : £6.50 : CIP entry
ISBN 0-7225-0681-3 (pbk) : £2.95 B81-30447

362.1'975541 — England. Midlands. Ileostomists. Organisations: Ileostomy Association of Great Britain and Ireland. ***Midlands Division, to 1981***
Ileostomy Association of Great Britain and Ireland. *Midlands Divisions.* 251A 1956-1981 : IA Midlands Divisions the first twenty five years. — [Halesowen] ([49 Windsor Rd, Halesowen, West Midlands]) : [Midlands Divisions of the Ileostomy Association of Gt. Britain & Ireland], [1981]. — [56]p : ill,ports ; 15x21cm
Cover title
Unpriced (pbk) B81-23363

362.1'976'0068 — United States. Dental services. Practices. Management
Domer, Larry R.. Dental practice management : concepts and applications / Larry R. Domer, Thomas L. Snyder, David W. Heid. — St. Louis ; London : Mosby, 1980. — xiv,381p : ill,facsims,forms ; 25cm
Includes index
ISBN 0-8016-1422-8 : £24.25 B81-04961

362.1'976'0091724 — Developing countries. Dental services. Foreign assistance — *Conference proceedings*
Assisting dental education and dental public health in developing countries : a symposium / [edited by Martin Hobdell]. — London : AHRTAG, c1981. — 136p : ill ; 30cm
ISBN 0-907320-01-5 (pbk) : Unpriced B81-39474

362.1'976'00941 — Great Britain. Dental health services
Dental public health / edited by Geoffrey L. Slack in collaboration with Brian A. Burt. — 2nd ed. — Bristol : John Wright, 1981. — ix,343p : ill ; 22cm
Previous ed.: 1974. — Includes bibliographies and index
ISBN 0-7236-0578-5 (pbk) : Unpriced B81-17653

362.1'976'00973 — United States. Dental health services
Cormier, Patricia P.. Community oral health : a systems approach for the dental health profession / Patricia P. Cormier, Joyce I. Levy ; Joanne L. Cohen, consulting editor ; foreword by I. Lawrence Kerr. — New York : Appleton-Century-Crofts ; London : Prentice-Hall, c1981. — xiii,237p : ill ; 24cm
Includes index
ISBN 0-8385-1184-8 (pbk) : £9.70 B81-17306

Dental public health and community dentistry / edited bvy Anthony Jong. — St. Louis ; London : Mosby, 1981. — xi,290p : ill ; 24cm
Includes bibliographies and index
ISBN 0-8016-2575-0 (pbk) : £12.75 B81-33047

362.1'976'00973 — United States. Hospitals. Dental services
Hospital dental practice / [edited by] James R. Hooley, Lewell G. Daun. — St. Louis ; London : Mosby, 1980. — x,380p : ill,plans,forms ; 27cm
Includes bibliographies and index
ISBN 0-8016-2226-3 : Unpriced B81-08660

362.1'97601 — Man. Dental health. Social aspects
Fredericks, Marcel A.. Dental care in society : the sociology of dental health / by Marcel A. Fredericks, Ralph R. Lobene and Paul Mundy. — Jefferson, N.C. : McFarland ; Folkestone : distributed by Bailey & Swinfen, 1980. — xii,180p : ill ; 25cm
Bibliography: p162-171. — Includes index
ISBN 0-89950-001-3 : £12.75 B81-37040

362.1'977'09417 — Ireland *(Republic).* Hospitals. Ophthalmology departments — *Proposals*
Development of hospital ophthalmic services : a discussion document. — Dublin (Corrigan House, Fenian St., Dublin 2) : Comhairle na n-Ospidéal, 1981. — 39p ; 21cm
Unpriced (pbk) B81-15310

362.1'98 — Health services for women — *Feminist viewpoints*
Women, health and reproduction / edited by Helen Roberts. — London : Routledge & Kegan Paul, 1981. — xi,196p ; 22cm
Bibliography: p187-190. — Includes index
ISBN 0-7100-0703-5 (pbk) : £5.50 B81-15043

362.1'982 — Developing countries. Traditional birth attendants. Training

Williams, Maureen, *1948-*. The training of traditional birth attendants : guidelines for midwives working in underdeveloped countries / Maureen Williams. — London (1 Cambridge Terrace, NW1 4JL) : Catholic Institute for International Relations, [1980]. — 34p : ill ; 21cm
Bibliography: p34
ISBN 0-904393-52-6 (pbk) : £0.75 B81-06938

362.1'982 — Scotland. Midwifery. Organisations: Central Midwives Board for Scotland — *Regulations*

Central Midwives Board for Scotland. Rules / Central Midwives Board for Scotland. — Edinburgh : Scottish Academic, [1981]. — 28p : forms ; 25cm
ISBN 0-7073-0107-6 (unbound) : Unpriced B81-28325

362.1'982'00942 — England. Maternity health services, *1900-1939*. **Political aspects**

Lewis, Jane. The politics of motherhood : child and maternal welfare in England, 1900-1939 / Jane Lewis. — London : Croom Helm, c1980. — 235p : ill ; 23cm
Includes index
ISBN 0-7099-0259-x : £10.95 : CIP rev.
Also classified at 362.1'9892'000942 B80-12777

362.1'9824'094252 — Nottinghamshire. Antenatal clinics. Attendance by pregnant women

Parsons, Wendy D.. Why don't women attend for antenatal care? / Wendy D. Parsons and Elizabeth R. Perkins. — [Nottingham] : University of Nottingham, 1980. — [44]leaves : forms ; 30cm. — (Occasional paper / Leverhulme Health Education Project ; no.23)
Unpriced (pbk) B81-22733

362.1'9824'094252 — Nottinghamshire. Central Nottinghamshire. Antenatal classes. Attendance by pregnant women

Perkins, Elizabeth R.. Attendance at antenatal classes : a district study / Elizabeth R. Perkins. — [Nottingham] : University of Nottingham, 1978. — 38leaves in various pagings ; 30cm. — (Occasional paper / Leverhulme Health Education Project ; no.13)
Unpriced (pbk) B81-22732

362.1'9824'0973 — United States. Hospitals. Obstetric departments. Childbirth. Preparation

Sumner, Philip E.. Birthing rooms : concept and reality / Philip E. Sumner, Celeste R. Phillips ; editorial consultants Samuel Smith, John Wheeler. — St. Louis ; London : Mosby, 1981. — xix,213p : ill,forms ; 24cm
Includes bibliographies and index
ISBN 0-8016-4873-4 (pbk) : £9.25 B81-32999

362.1'9892 — Chronically sick children. Nursing. Psychological aspects

McCollum, Audrey T.. The chronically ill child. — 2nd ed. — London : Yale University Press, Nov.1981. — [240]p
Previous ed. published as: Coping with prolonged health impairment in your child. Boston : Little, Brown, 1975
ISBN 0-300-02764-8 (cased) : £17.50 : CIP entry
ISBN 0-300-02782-6 (pbk) : £4.15 B81-35892

362.1'9892 — Great Britain. Health services. Paediatric outpatient clinics. Location. Economic aspects

Cullis, John G.. The economics of outpatient clinic location : the paediatrics case / John G. Cullis, Steve Heasell, Sam Weller. — Aldershot : Gower, c1981. — vii,207p : ill ; 23cm
Bibliography: p190-198. — Includes index
ISBN 0-566-00303-1 : £11.50 : CIP rev. B80-29428

362.1'9892 — Hospitals. Patients: Children. Care — *For children*

Children in hospital : perhaps it isn't going to be so bad after all - / Thomas Bergman ... [et al.] ; translated by Irène D. Morris. — Harmondsworth : Kestrel Books, 1981. — [47]p : ill,ports ; 25cm
Translation of: Barn på sjukhus
ISBN 0-7226-5678-5 : £4.25 B81-11805

Wilson, Pearl M.. Katie goes to hospital / Pearl M. Wilson ; photographs by James Barbone. — London : Angus & Robertson, 1981, c1979. — [32]p : col.ill ; 22cm
Originally published: West Melbourne : Nelson, 1979
ISBN 0-207-95967-6 : £2.95 B81-23064

362.1'9892 — Hospitals. Patients: Children. Care. Role of families — *Conference proceedings*

The **Family** in child health care / edited by Pat Azarnoff, Carol Hardgrove. — New York ; Chichester : Wiley, c1981. — xvii,247p ; 23cm. — (A Wiley medical publication)
Conference papers
ISBN 0-471-08663-0 (pbk) : £9.55 B81-24891

362.1'9892'000941 — Great Britain. Community health services for children

Child health in the community / edited by Ross G. Mitchell ; foreword by S.D.M. Court. — 2nd ed. — Edinburgh : Churchill Livingstone, 1980. — vi,348p ; 25cm
Previous ed.: 1977. — Includes bibliographies and index
ISBN 0-443-02195-3 : £16.00 B81-00061

362.1'9892'000942 — England. Health services for children, *1900-1939*. **Political aspects**

Lewis, Jane. The politics of motherhood : child and maternal welfare in England, 1900-1939 / Jane Lewis. — London : Croom Helm, c1980. — 235p : ill ; 23cm
Includes index
ISBN 0-7099-0259-x : £10.95 : CIP rev.
Primary classification 362.1'982'00942 B80-12777

362.1'9892'000942527 — Nottinghamshire. Nottingham. Paediatric clinics

Spencer, N. J.. Nottingham child health clinic survey / N.J. Spencer F.L. Power. — [Nottingham] : University of Nottingham, 1978. — 23,leaves : 1map,forms ; 30cm. — (Occasional paper / Leverhulme Health Education Project ; no.14)
Bibliography: p23
Unpriced (pbk) B81-22737

362.1'9892'000971 — Canada. Hospitals. Patients: Children. Care

Robinson, Geoffrey C.. The hospital care of children : a review of contemporary issues / Geoffrey C. Robinson, Heather F. Clarke. — New York ; Oxford : Oxford University Press, 1980. — viii,270p : ill,1map,1plan,forms ; 24cm
Includes bibliographies and index
ISBN 0-19-502673-x : £12.00 B81-08247

362.1'9897 — Great Britain. Hospitals. Welfare work with old persons. Group work — *Case studies*

Cooper, Joan D.. Social groupwork with elderly people in hospital / Joan D. Cooper ; with a foreword by Olive Stevenson. — Stoke-on-Trent (Parkfield House, Princes Rd., Hartshill, Stoke-on-Trent) : Beth Johnson Foundation, 1980. — 104p ; 22cm. — (Beth Johnson Foundation publications)
Text on inside covers
ISBN 0-9505771-7-0 (pbk) : £3.25 B81-15478

362.1'9897'00941 — Great Britain. Medical services for old people

Establishing a geriatric service. — London : Croom Helm, Jan.1982. — [240]p
ISBN 0-7099-0700-1 : £13.95 : CIP entry B81-34313

362.2 — WELFARE SERVICES FOR THE MENTALLY ILL

362.2 — Great Britain. Psychological services

Reconstructing psychological practice / edited by Ian McPherson and Andrew Sutton. — London : Croom Helm, c1981. — 202p ; 23cm
Bibliography: p173-194. - Includes index
ISBN 0-7099-0419-3 (cased) : £10.95
ISBN 0-7099-1709-0 (pbk) : Unpriced B81-17961

362.2 — Great Britain. Suicide

Wells, N. E. J.. Suicide and deliberate self-harm / [researched and written by Nicholas Wells]. — London : Office of Health Economics, c1981. — 56p : col.ill ; 21cm. — (Studies of current health problems, ISSN 0473-8837 ; no.69)
Bibliography: p53-55
£0.60 (pbk) B81-09423

362.2 — Great Britain. Voluntary welfare services for suicidal persons: Samaritans, *to 1980*

The **Samaritans** in the '80s : to befriend the suicidal and despairing / edited and with an introduction by Chad Varah. — London : Constable, 1980. — 279p ; 23cm
ISBN 0-09-463220-0 (cased) : £6.50
ISBN 0-09-463130-1 (pbk) : Unpriced B81-29316

362.2 — Mental health services for disaster victims

Cohen, Raquel E.. Handbook for mental health care of disaster victims / Raquel E. Cohen and Frederick L. Ahearn, Jr. — Baltimore ; London : Johns Hopkins University Press, c1980. — xvii,126p ; 24cm
Bibliography: p115-121. — Includes index
ISBN 0-8018-2427-3 : £7.75 B81-05630

362.2 — Suicidal schizophrenics — *Case studies*

Reynolds, David K.. The family shadow : sources of suicide and schizophrenia / David K. Reynolds and Norman L. Farberow. — Berkeley ; London : University of California Press, c1981. — xi,177p ; 24cm
Bibliography: p171-173. — Includes index
ISBN 0-520-04213-1 : £12.00 B81-36454

362.2 — United States. Negro offenders. Mental health

Owens, Charles E.. Mental health and black offenders / Charles E. Owens. — Lexington, Mass. : Lexington Books ; [Aldershot] : Gower [distributor], 1980. — xviii,187p ; 24cm
Bibliography: p161-177. — Includes index
ISBN 0-669-02645-x : £13.50 B81-30781

362.2'042 — Man. Mental disorders — *Sociological perspectives*

Cockerham, William C.. Sociology of mental disorder / William C. Cockerham. — Englewood Cliffs : Prentice-Hall, c1981. — viii,408p ; 24cm
Bibliography: p376-402. — Includes index
ISBN 0-13-820886-7 : £12.95 B81-22699

362.2'042'094 — North-western Europe. Mentally ill persons. Attitudes of society, *1600-1900*

Doerner, Klaus. Madmen and the bourgeoisie : a social history of insanity and psychiatry / Klaus Doerner ; translated by Joachim Neugroschel and Jean Steinberg. — Oxford : Blackwell, 1981. — vi,361p ; 24cm
Translation of: Bürger und Irre. — Includes index
ISBN 0-631-10181-0 : £15.00 : CIP rev.
Also classified at 616.89'0094 B81-20187

362.2'0422 — Man. Mental illness — *Sociological perspectives*

Miles, Agnes. The mentally ill in contemporary society : a sociological introduction / Agnes Miles. — Oxford : Robertson, 1981. — x,224p : ill ; 22cm
Bibliography: p208-220. — Includes index
ISBN 0-85520-376-5 (cased) : £13.00
ISBN 0-85520-377-3 (pbk) : £4.95 B81-17616

362.2'0425 — Communities. Mental health. Self-help groups — *Manuals*

Ernst, Sheila. In our own hands : a book of self-help therapy / Sheila Ernst & Lucy Goodison. — London : Women's Press, 1981. — 328p : 2ports ; 21cm
Includes bibliographies and index
ISBN 0-7043-3841-6 (pbk) : £3.95 B81-08721

362.2'0425 — Dyfed. Carmarthen. Mental illness hospitals: St. David's Hospital. Patients. Rehabilitation & resettlement

Off the waiting list : a report of a day seminar on the forging of links between housing authorities in Dyfed and the rehabilitation team at St. David's Hospital, Carmarthen ... — Cardiff : MIND Office in Wales, 1979. — 26p : 1map ; 30cm
£0.80 (pbk) B81-29543

362.2′0425 — Great Britain. Mental illness hospitals. Ex-patients. Accommodation. Provision. Role of housing associations — *Conference proceedings*

Allies on the touch line : a report on a day seminar on the potential for cooperation between housing associations, the responsible statutory authorities and voluntary organisations in the task of rehousing ex-psychiatric patients / jointly organised by the Housing Corporation (Office for Wales) and the MIND Office in Wales. — Cardiff : MIND Office in Wales, 1979. — 33p ; 30cm
Conference papers
£0.85 (pbk) B81-29342

362.2′0425 — Great Britain. Mentally disordered persons. Rehabilitation

Handbook of psychiatric rehabilitation practice / edited by John K. Wing and Brenda Morris. — Oxford : Oxford University Press, 1981. — x,188p ; 22cm. — (Oxford medical publications)
Bibliography: p179-186. — Includes index
ISBN 0-19-261276-x (pbk) : £5.95 : CIP rev.
B81-30449

362.2′0425 — Great Britain. Mentally ill persons. Community treatment

Butterworth, Charles Anthony. Caring for the mentally ill in the community / Charles Anthony Butterworth, David Skidmore. — London : Croom Helm, c1981. — 125p : ill ; 22cm
Includes bibliographies and index
ISBN 0-7099-0071-6 (cased) : £9.95 : CIP rev.
ISBN 0-7099-0072-4 (pbk) : Unpriced
B81-14889

362.2′0425 — London. Hackney *(London Borough)*. Restaurant clubs for psychiatric patients: Downs Park Club

Wilder, John. Setting up a restaurant club facility / John Wilder. — London (2 Downs Rd., Hackney E5) : Produced for Mental Health Foundation [by] the Downs Park Club, [1980?]. — 11p : ill ; 30cm
Unpriced (unbound) B81-40923

362.2′0425 — Man. Mental illness. Prevention. Environmental factors

Environmental variables and the prevention of mental illness / edited by Paul M. Insel. — Lexington, Mass. : Lexington Books ; [Aldershot] : Gower [distributor], 1981, c1980. — xi,226p ; 24cm
Includes bibliographies and index
ISBN 0-669-03457-6 : £16.00 B81-32987

362.2′04256 — Mentally handicapped persons. Families. Genetic counselling

Kirman, Brian H.. Genetic counselling in mental handicap / Brian Kirman. — London : National Society for Mentally Handicapped Children and Adults, c1981. — 10p ; 21cm
ISBN 0-85537-064-5 (pbk) : £0.50 B81-29585

362.2′06′041 — Great Britain. Mental health services. Organisations: MIND. Activities

MIND development papers / John Payne (editor). — London : MIND, [1978?]. — 50pieces ; 30cm
Unpriced (unbound) B81-41016

362.2′0880565 — Great Britain. Welfare sevices for mentally ill old persons

Plank, David. What next for elderly people? : an overview of service provision and research concerning elderly mentally infirm people / ... David Plank ... Sheila Peace. — [London] : MIND, 1979. — 37p ; 30cm
Bibliography: p28-30
£1.60 (pbk) B81-29343

362.2′092′4 — United States. Mentally ill persons — *Personal observations*

Gordon, Barbara. I′m dancing as fast as I can / Barbara Gordon. — Toronto ; London : Bantam, 1981, c1979. — 307p ; 18cm
Originally published: New York : Harper & Row, 1979
ISBN 0-553-17729-x (pbk) : £1.50 B81-12218

362.2′094 — Europe. Mentally ill persons. Care — *Conference proceedings*

Alternatives to mental hospitals : report of a European workshop. — [London] ([126 Albert St., NW1 7NX]) : International Hospital Federation, [1981?]. — 2v. ; 30cm
Unpriced (pbk) (Pt.1) : £0.75 (Pt.2) : £1.00
B81-33389

362.2′0942 — England. Man. Mental disorders, *1600-1700* — *Sociological perspectives*

MacDonald, Michael. Mystical bedlam : madness, anxiety and healing in seventeenth century England / Michael MacDonald. — Cambridge : Cambridge University Press, 1981. — xvi,323p : ill,maps,1port ; 24cm. — (Cambridge monographs on the history of medicine)
Includes index
ISBN 0-521-23170-1 : £27.50 B81-39907

362.2′0942 — England. Medicine. Psychiatry, *1800-1900*. Social aspects

Madhouses, mad-doctors and madmen : the social history of psychiatry in the Victorian era / Andrew Scull, editor. — London : Athlone, 1981. — xv,384p : ill ; 24cm
ISBN 0-485-30002-8 : £16.00 : CIP rev.
B81-23755

362.2′09421′34 — London. Kensington and Chelsea *(London borough)*. Community mental health services: Chelsea Mind Centre

Perry, Penny. Help yourself to care : an assessment of the Chelsea Mind Centre / by Penny Perry. — [Boston Spa] ([c/o British Library Lending Division, Boston Spa, Wetherby, W. Yorkshire LS23 7BQ]) : [P. Perry], [1980?]. — iv,95,5p : 1form ; 30cm
At head of title: Mental Health Foundation. — Limited ed. of 12 copies
Unpriced (spiral) B81-33683

362.2′09714′281 — Quebec *(Province)*. Montreal. Psychiatric patients. Home care *compared with* hospitalisation

Home and hospital psychiatric treatment. — London : Croom Helm, Nov.1981. — [240]p
ISBN 0-7099-0350-2 : £12.95 : CIP entry
B81-30349

362.2′0973 — United States. Population. Mental health. Sociopolitical aspects — *Conference proceedings*

Vermont Conference on the Primary Prevention of Psychopathology *(5th : 1980?)*. Prevention through political action and social change / Justin M. Joffe and George W. Albee, editors. — Hanover ; London : Published for the Vermont Conference on the Primary Prevention of Psychopathology by University Press of New England, 1981. — x,366p ; 23cm. — (Primary prevention of psychopathology)
Includes bibliographies and index
ISBN 0-87451-187-9 : £14.00 B81-39761

362.2′1 — Central Southern England. Hospitals. Mental handicap units. Patients. Behaviour. Improvement *compared with* improvement in behaviour of mental handicap hospital patients

Evaluation of locally-based hospital units for the mentally handicapped in Wessex : a comparison of the changes in behaviour of clients in five locally-based hospital units and comparable ′control′ clients in traditional units. — Winchester (Dawn House, Sleepers Hill, Winchester, Hants. SO22 4NG) : Health Care Evaluation Research Team
Part 1: Report / author John Smith ... [et al.]. — 1979. — 88p : ill ; 30cm. — (Research report / Health Care Evaluation Research Team ; no.144)
Cover title. — Bibliography: p81-85
(spiral) B81-07494

362.2′1 — England. Mental illness hospitals. Patients. Compulsory admission

Bean, Philip. Compulsory admissions to mental hospitals / Philip Bean. — Chichester : Wiley, c1980. — xii,278p : 1form ; 24cm
Bibliography: p267-273. — Includes index
ISBN 0-471-27758-4 : £16.70 : CIP rev.
B80-13303

362.2′1 — Great Britain. Psychiatric hospitals. Patients. Rehabilitation

Morgan, Roger, *1924-*. Psychiatric rehabilitation / by Roger Morgan and John Cheadle. — Surbiton (79 Victoria Rd, Surbiton, Surrey KT6 4NS) : National Schizophrenia Fellowship, c1981. — iv,122p : ill ; 21cm
Bibliography: p118-121. — Includes index
£4.95 (pbk) B81-31291

362.2′1′068 — Nottinghamshire. Rampton. Special hospitals: Rampton Hospital. Management: Great Britain. *Department of Health and Social Security*. **Report of the review of Rampton Hospital** — *Critical studies*

Campaign for Mentally Handicapped People. Leaving there : comments on the Report of the review of Rampton hospital / the Campaign for Mentally Handicapped People. — London (15 Fitzroy Sq., W1P 5HQ) : [CMH], [1981]. — 17p ; 30cm
Cover title
Unpriced (pbk) B81-17450

362.2′1′068 — Nottinghamshire. Rampton. Special hospitals: Rampton Hospital. Management — *Inquiry reports*

Great Britain. *Department of Health and Social Security*. Report of the review of Rampton Hospital / Department of Health and Social Security. — London : H.M.S.O., 1980. — vii,176p : ill ; 25cm. — (Cmnd. ; 8073)
ISBN 0-10-180730-9 (pbk) : £6.70 B81-04051

362.2′1′0941 — Great Britain. Mental illness hospitals. Patients. Care. Complaints by nurses

Beardshaw, Virginia. Conscientious objectors at work. — London (9 Poland St., W1V 3DG) : Social Audit, Sept.1981. — [90]p
ISBN 0-9503392-6-1 (pbk) : £3.50 : CIP entry
B81-28158

362.2′1′09415 — Ireland. Psychiatric hospitals, *1817-1914*

Finnane, Mark. Insanity and the insane in post-famine Ireland / Mark Finnane. — London : Croom Helm, c1981. — 241p : 1map ; 23cm
Includes index
ISBN 0-7099-0402-9 : £13.95 : CIP rev.
B81-04364

362.2′1′09417 — Ireland *(Republic)*. Psychiatric hospitals. Patients — *Statistics* — *Serials*

Activities of Irish psychiatric hospitals and units / the Medico-Social Research Board. — 1978. — Dublin (73 Lower Baggot St., Dublin 2) : The Board, 1980. — 64p
ISSN 0332-2602 : Unpriced B81-10245

362.2′1′0942356 — Devon. Exeter. Mental illness hospitals: Bowhill House, *1801-1869*

Hervey, Nicholas. Bowhill House : St. Thomas′s Hospital for Lunatics : asylum for the four western counties 1801-1869 / by Nicholas Hervey. — [Exeter] : University of Exeter, 1980. — xii,76p : ill,1map,1plan,ports ; 21cm
Plan on inside cover
ISBN 0-85989-106-2 (pbk) : £2.00 B81-14682

362.2′1′0942837 — Humberside. Hull. Mental illness hospitals: Hull Borough Asylum, *to 1883*

Bickford, J. A. R.. The old Hull Borough Asylum : (1849-1883) / by J.A.R. Bickford. — [Hull] (City Records Office, 79 Lowgate, Hull) : [J.A.R. Bickford], c1981. — 52p ; 22cm
ISBN 0-9507536-0-2 (pbk) : £2.00 B81-31976

362.2′1′09429 — Wales. Psychiatric hospitals — *Statistics* — *Serials*

Mental health statistics for Wales / Welsh Office. — 1977-1978-. — Cardiff (Economic Services Division 5c, Welsh Office, Crown Building, Cardiff) : The Office, [1980]-. — v. ; 30cm
Issued every two years. — Continues: Mental illness and mental handicap. Hospitals and units in Wales
ISSN 0260-5252 = Mental health statistics for Wales : Unpriced B81-02346

Mental health statistics for Wales / Welsh Office. — 1979. — Cardiff (Economic and Statistical Services Division 5c, Welsh Office, New Crown Building, Cardiff CF1 3NQ) : The Office, [1981]. — vi,104p
ISBN 0-904251-44-6 : Unpriced
ISSN 0260-5252 B81-23513

362.2′1′097443 — Massachusetts. Worcester. Mental illness hospitals: Worcester State Hospital. Patients. Care, *1830-1979*
Morrissey, Joseph P.. The enduring asylum : cycles of institutional reform at Worcester State Hospital / Joseph P. Morrissey, Howard H. Goldman, Lorraine V. Klerman and associates. — New York ; London : Grune & Stratton, c1980. — xi,356p : ill,ports ; 24cm
Bibliography: p315-341. - Includes index
ISBN 0-8089-1291-7 : £17.80 B81-15194

362.2′1′0974733 — New York *(State)*. **Wingdale. Mental illness hospitals: Harlem Valley Psychiatric Center. Organisational change,** *1974-1978*
Levine, Murray. From state hospital to psychiatric center : the implementation of planned organizational change / Murray Levine ; foreword by Yoosuf A. Haveliwala. — Lexington, Mass. : Lexington Books ; [Aldershot] : Gower [distributor], 1981, c1980. — xix,137p ; 24cm
Bibliography: p129-132. — Includes index
ISBN 0-669-03810-5 : £11.00 B81-30031

362.2′2 — United States. Community mental health services. Nursing
Community mental health nursing : an ecological perspective / [edited by] Jeanette Lancaster. — St. Louis ; London : Mosby, 1980. — x,278p : ill ; 24cm
Includes bibliographies and index
ISBN 0-8016-2816-4 (pbk) : £8.00 B81-08458

362.2′2′0880565 — England. Day hospitals for mentally ill old persons
Peace, Sheila M.. Caring from day to day : a report on the development of the day hospital within the service for elderly people who are mentally infirm / Sheila M. Peace. — [London] : MIND, c1980. — 61p : 1form ; 30cm
Bibliography: p60-61
£1.70 (pbk) B81-29347

362.2′2′0880565 — Great Britain. Mentally ill old persons. Day care
Approaches to day care : for elderly people who are mentally infirm. — [London] : MIND, 1979. — 17p ; 30cm
£0.80 (pbk) B81-29345

362.2′2′0942 — England. Day care centres for mentally ill persons — *Conference proceedings*
Day care for the mentally ill : report of a conference held by the Oxford Mental Health Association (MIND). — [Oxford] ([125 Walton St., Oxford]) : [Oxford Mental Health Association], [1981?]. — 25leaves ; 30cm
Cover title
Unpriced (pbk) B81-31656

362.2′3′025421 — London. Accommodation for mentally ill persons — *Directories*
Handbook of access to special housing for mentally ill and mentally handicapped adults in Greater London / co-producers Sharron Crook ... [et al.] ; [sponsored by NAVH and MIND]. — London (33 Long Acre, WC2E 9LA) : NAVH ; London : MIND, 1980. — 56p : 1map ; 21cm
£1.65 (pbk)
Also classified at 362.3′025′421 B81-29458

362.2′8′0973 — United States. Emergency psychiatric services
Matthews, Daryl B.. Disposable patients : situational factors in emergency psychiatric decisions / Daryl B. Matthews. — Lexington : Lexington Books, c1980 ; [Farnborough, Hants.] : Gower [distributor], 1981. — xii,107p ; 24cm
ISBN 0-669-02164-4 : £11.50 B81-23265

362.2′9 — Alcoholism & drug abuse
Jaffe, Jerome. Addictions : issues and answers / Jerome Jaffe, Robert Petersen, Ray Hodgson. — London : Harper & Row, 1980. — 128p : ill (some col.) ; 24cm. — (The life cycle series)
Includes index
ISBN 0-06-318106-1 (cased) : £4.95
ISBN 0-06-318105-3 (pbk) : £2.25 B81-02226

362.2′9′05 — Alcoholism & drug abuse — *Serials*
Sage annual reviews of drug and alcohol abuse. — Vol.5. — Beverly Hills ; London : Sage, c1981. — 272p
ISBN 0-8039-1634-5 : Unpriced B81-35967

362.2′92 — Alcoholic drinks. Consumption. Causes & effects
Community core course / [Northern Ireland Council on Alcohol]. — [Belfast] ([36 Victoria Sq., Belfast BT2 4QB]) : [The Council], [1981]. — 7v. : ill ; 30cm
Includes bibliographies
Unpriced (unbound) B81-16142

362.2′92 — Alcoholics. Treatment: Controlled drinking
Heather, Nick. Controlled drinking. — London : Methuen, Oct.1981. — [350]p
ISBN 0-416-71970-8 : £19.50 : CIP entry B81-28083

362.2′92 — Alcoholism
Dennison, Darwin. Alcohol and behaviour : an activated education approach / Darwin Dennison, Thomas Prevet, Michael Affleck. — St. Louis ; London : Mosby, 1980. — x,130p : ill ; 24cm
Includes index
ISBN 0-8016-1252-7 (pbk) : Unpriced B81-08567

Goodwin, Donald W.. Alcoholism : the facts / by Donald W. Goodwin. — Oxford : Oxford University Press, 1981. — vi,135p : ill ; 23cm. — (Oxford medical publications)
Includes index
ISBN 0-19-261297-2 : £4.95 : CIP rev. B81-04272

362.2′92 — Alcoholism — *Conference proceedings*
Alcoholism. — Lancaster : MTP Press, Oct.1981. — [750]p
Conference papers
ISBN 0-85200-409-5 : £24.95 : CIP entry B81-30903

362.2′92 — Family life. Effects of alcoholism
Alcohol and the family. — London : Croom Helm, Jan.1982. — [272]p
ISBN 0-7099-0473-8 : £14.95 : CIP entry B81-34309

362.2′92′05 — Alcoholism — *Serials*
[Combat *(Cleckheaton)*]. Combat : for problem drinkers and those who live and work with them. — No.1 (Jan.1981)-. — Cleckheaton (66 High St., Cleckheaton, West Yorkshire BD19 3PX) : P. Brearey, 1981-. — v. : ill ; 28cm
Monthly
ISSN 0260-7123 = Combat (Cleckheaton) : £0.20 per issue B81-20325

362.2′92′07073 — United States. Education. Curriculum subjects: Alcoholism. Teaching — *Manuals*
Finn, Peter. Teaching about alcohol : concepts, methods, and classroom activities / Peter Finn, Patricia A. O'Gorman. — Boston, Mass. ; London : Allyn and Bacon, c1981. — xvii,241p : ill ; 28cm
Includes bibliographies and index
ISBN 0-205-07195-3 (pbk) : Unpriced B81-13189

362.2′92′088042 — Women. Alcoholism
Women & alcohol / Camberwell Council on Alcoholism. — London : Tavistock Publications, 1980. — xiii,207p ; 21cm
Includes bibliographies and index
ISBN 0-422-76950-9 (cased) : £7.95 : CIP rev.
ISBN 0-422-76960-6 (pbk) : £3.95 B80-13304

362.2′92′0941 — Great Britain. Alcoholism
Taylor, David, *1946-*. Alcohol : reducing the harm / [by David Taylor]. — London : Office of Health Economics, c1981. — 60p : ill ; 21cm. — (Studies of current health problems, ISSN 0473-8837 ; no.70)
Bibliography: p54-58
£0.60 (pbk) B81-19023

362.2′923 — Alcoholism. Psychosocial aspects
Hunt, Linda. Alcohol related problems. — London : Heinemann Educational, Feb.1982. — [128]p. — (Community care practice handbooks ; 7)
ISBN 0-435-82450-3 (pbk) : £2.95 : CIP entry B81-35692

362.2′9256′0941 — Great Britain. Alcoholism. Policies of government
Tuck, Mary. Alcholism and social policy : are we on the right lines? / by Mary Tuck. — London : H.M.S.O., 1980. — 30p ; 25cm. — (A Home Office Research Unit report) (Home Office research study ; no.65)
Bibliography: p25-26
ISBN 0-11-340705-x (pbk) : £2.70 B81-12769

362.2′928′0973 — United States. Alcoholism. Treatment. Evaluation
Polich, J. Michael. The course of alcoholism : four years after treatment / J. Michael Polich, David J. Armor, Harriet B. Braiker. — New York ; Chichester : Wiley, c1981. — xiv,334p : ill,1form ; 24cm. — (Wiley series on personality processes, ISSN 0195-4008)
Bibliography: p312-324. — Includes index
ISBN 0-471-08682-7 : £17.00 B81-23345

362.2′9286′0941 — Great Britain. Alcoholism. Control — *Proposals*
Brake, George Thompson. Agenda for action on alcohol : what measures ought to be taken in a co-ordinated approach to the alcohol problem as it presents itself in the last quarter of the 20th century? / by George Thompson Brake. — London ([12 Caxton St., SW1H 0QS]) : Christian Economic and Social Research Foundation, [1981]. — 32p ; 25cm
ISBN 0-905651-07-3 (pbk) : £0.50 B81-11095

362.2′93 — Great Britain. Children. Solvent sniffing — *For teaching*
Peers, Ian S.. Solvent abuse : educational implications / Ian S. Peers. — Rev. ed. — [Manchester] ([2 Mount St., Manchester M2 5NG]) : [TACADE], [1981]. — 27leaves : 1ill ; 30cm
Previous ed.: 197-?
ISBN 0-9506350-5-7 (spiral) : Unpriced B81-26529

362.2′93 — Psychotropic drugs. Drug abuse
The **Misuse** of psychotropic drugs / editors Robin Murray ... [et al.]. — London (17 Belgrave Sq., S.W.1) : Gaskell, 1981. — 104p : ill ; 25cm. — (Special publication / The Royal College of Psychiatrists ; 1)
Includes bibliographies and index
ISBN 0-902241-06-0 (pbk) : Unpriced B81-17881

362.2′93′0724 — United States. Drug abuse. Mathematical models
Quantitative explorations in drug abuse policy / edited by Irving Leveson. — Lancaster : MTP, c1980. — 191p : ill ; 24cm
Includes bibliographies and index
ISBN 0-85200-550-4 : £17.95 B81-10329

362.2′93′0924 — West Germany. Adolescent girls. Heroin addiction — *Personal observations*
Christiane F.. 'H', autobiography of a child prostitute and heroin addict / Christiane F.. — [London] : Corgi, 1981, c1980. — 297p ; 18cm
Translation of: Wir Kinder vom Banhoff Zoo. — Originally published: London : Arlington, 1980
ISBN 0-552-11772-2 (pbk) : £1.50 B81-37272

362.2′93′0941 — Great Britain. Drug abuse, *1966-1976*
Drug problems in Britain : a review of ten years / edited by Griffith Edwards and Carol Busch. — London : Academic Press, 1981. — viii,333p ; 24cm
Includes bibliographies and index
ISBN 0-12-232780-2 : £14.80 : CIP rev. B81-13557

362.2′93′0941 — Great Britain. Drug abuse — *Statistics — Serials*
Statistics of the misuse of drugs, United Kingdom.. Supplementary tables / Home Office. — 1978-1979. — London (Statistical Dept., Room 1706, Tolworth Tower, Surbiton, Surrey KT6 7DS) : Home Office, [1980]-. — v. ; 30cm
Supplement to: Statistics of the misuse of drugs, United Kingdom
ISSN 0260-4590 = Statistics of the misuse of drugs, United Kingdom. Supplementary tables : £2.00 B81-04484

362.2'93'0973 — United States. Heroin addiction. Social control

Lidz, Charles W.. Heroin, deviance and morality / Charles W. Lidz and Andrew L. Walker with the assistance of Leroy C. Gould. — London : Sage, c1980. — 269p : ill ; 22cm. — (Sage library of social research ; v.112)
Bibliography: p255-262. — Includes index
ISBN 0-8039-1549-7 (cased) : Unpriced
ISBN 0-8039-1550-0 (pbk) : Unpriced
B81-13629

362.3 — WELFARE SERVICES FOR THE MENTALLY RETARDED

362.3 — Down's syndrome babies — *Personal observations*

Boston, Sarah. Will, my son : the life and death of a Mongol child / Sarah Boston. — London : Pluto, c1981. — 121p ; 20cm
ISBN 0-86104-346-4 (pbk) : £1.95 B81-27485

362.3 — Down's syndrome children. Care — *Personal observations*

Bondo, Ulla. Ida : life with my handicapped child / Ulla Bondo ; translated from the Danish by Elisabeth Mills. — London : Faber, 1980. — 128p : ports ; 21cm
Translation of: Ida. — Bibliography: p125-128
ISBN 0-571-11589-6 (cased) : £7.95 : CIP rev.
(pbk) : £3.50 B80-17620

362.3 — Mentally handicapped persons

Retardation : issues, assessment, and intervention / [edited by] John T. Neisworth, Robert M. Smith. — New York ; London : McGraw-Hill, c1978. — viii,566p : ill ; 25cm. — (McGraw-Hill series in special education)
Bibliography: p490-541. - Includes index
ISBN 0-07-046201-1 : £14.20 B81-00805

362.3 — Mentally handicapped persons. Care

Clarke, David. Mentally handicapped people. — London : Baillière Tindall, Jan.1982. — [352]p
ISBN 0-7020-0894-x (pbk) : £10.00 : CIP entry
B81-34300

362.3'025'421 — London. Accommodation for mentally handicapped persons — *Directories*

Handbook of access to special housing for mentally ill and mentally handicapped adults in Greater London / co-producers Sharron Crook ... [et al.] ; [sponsored by NAVH and MIND]. — London (33 Long Acre, WC2E 9LA) : NAVH ; London : MIND, 1980. — 56p : 1map ; 21cm
£1.65 (pbk)
Primary classification 362.2'3'025421
B81-29458

362.3'088054 — Great Britain. Mentally handicapped children. Care. Attitudes of parents

Hunter, Alisa B. J.. The family and their mentally handicapped child : the views of parents of mentally handicapped children on what they need to maintain a satisfactory quality of life / by Alisa B.J. Hunter. — Barkingside ([Tanners La., Barkingside, Ilford, Essex IG6 1QG]) : Dr. Barnardo's, c1980. — 74p : 1ill,maps,facsims ; 21cm. — (Barnardo social work paper ; no.12)
Bibliography: p72-74
Unpriced (pbk) B81-13286

362.3'088054 — Mentally handicapped children. Handicaps. Assessment

Assessing the handicaps and needs of mentally retarded children. — New York ; London : Academic Press, June 1981. — [350]p
ISBN 0-12-188020-6 : CIP entry B81-11930

362.3'088054 — Mid Glamorgan. Welfare services for severely educationally subnormal children

Reid, Ken, *19---*. Whose children? : the interface of the medical, social and educational facilities for E.S.N(S) children and their families in one county area in South Wales / by Ken Reid. — Porthcawl (c/o A. Thomas, 24 The Green Ave., Porthcawl, M. Glam. CF36 3AX) : Porthcawl Spastics Aid Group, [1980]. — 89p ; 22cm
£2.00 B81-00806

362.3'088054 — Scotland. Mentally handicapped children. Social aspects — *Study regions: Western Central Scotland*

Richardson, J. Neill. 'Julie? She's a love' : a study of 76 young mentally handicapped children and their families / J. Neill Richardson. — Glasgow : Scottish Society for the Mentally Handicapped, [1981?]. — xv,272p : ill,forms ; 21cm
Bibliography: p270-272
ISBN 0-9506697-1-7 (pbk) : £7.50 B81-40697

362.3'088054 — West Sussex. Mid Sussex *(District)*. **Welfare services for mentally handicapped children** — *For parents of mentally handicapped children*

Coping with mental handicap in Mid-Sussex / compiled by Maris Elfield ... [et al.]. — Chichester : West Sussex County Council, c1981. — v,50p : ill,1map ; 20x22cm
Bibliography: p47
ISBN 0-86260-013-8 (spiral) : £1.00
B81-31770

362.3'0941 — Great Britain. Services for mentally handicapped adults

Baranyay, Eileen. Towards a full life : provisions for mentally handicapped adults / Eileen Baranyay. — London : MENCAP, 1981. — v,137p ; 21cm
Bibliography: p136
ISBN 0-85537-063-7 (pbk) : £5.95 B81-29391

362.3'09411'1 — Rural regions. Mentally handicapped persons — *Study regions: Scotland. Highlands & Islands*

Seed, Philip. Mental handicap : who helps in rural and remote communities? / by Philip Seed. — Tunbridge Wells : Costello Educational, c1980. — 134p : ill,forms ; 23cm
Includes index
ISBN 0-7104-0038-1 : Unpriced B81-16152

362.3'0973 — United States. Mentally retarded adults

Schulman, Eveline D.. Focus on the retarded adult : programs and services / Eveline D. Schulman. — St. Louis ; London : Mosby, 1980. — xv,535p : ill,forms ; 26cm
Bibliography: p489-518. - Includes index
ISBN 0-8016-4367-8 (pbk) : £13.50 B81-08197

362.3'5'0942 — England. Services for mentally handicapped persons. Joint planning

Plank, Morag. An enquiry into joint planning of services for mentally handicapped people / Morag Plank. — London (96 Portland Place, W1N 4EX) : Campaign for the Mentally Handicapped, 1979. — 7p ; 30cm
Unpriced (unbound) B81-16310

362.3'53'0941 — Great Britain. Welfare work with mentally handicapped persons

Hanvey, Christopher P.. Social work with mentally handicapped people / Christopher P. Hanvey. — London : Heinemann Educational, 1981. — 104p ; 22cm. — (Community care practice handbooks ; 4)
Bibliography: p96-100. - Includes index
ISBN 0-435-82403-1 (pbk) : £2.95 B81-23373

362.3'53'0973 — United States. Welfare work with mentally handicapped persons

Dickerson, Martha Ufford. Social work practice with the mentally retarded / Martha Ufford Dickerson. — New York : Free Press ; London : Collier Macmillan, 1981. — xv,224p : 1ill ; 25cm. — ([Fields of practice series])
Bibliography: p207-218. — Includes index
ISBN 0-02-907430-4 : £9.50 B81-33409

362.3'56'0941 — Great Britain. Welfare services for mentally handicapped persons. Policies of government, *1971-1980* — *Campaign for Mentally Handicapped People viewpoints*

Campaign for Mentally Handicapped People. Even better services? : a critical review of mental handicap policies in the 1970'ss / by Alan Tyne and Alison Wertheimer. — London (16 Fitzroy Sq., W1P 5HQ) : Campaign for Mentally Handicapped People, [1980]. — 23p ; 32cm
Report written for the Campaign for Mentally Handicapped People
Unpriced (pbk) B81-08364

362.3'8 — Great Britain. Welfare services for mentally handicapped persons. Decision making. Role of families

Tyne, Alan. Participation by families of mentally handicapped people in policy making and planning : paper read to PSSC / by Alan Tyne. — London (2 Torrington Place, WC1E 7HN) : Personal Social Services Council, 1978. — [8]p ; 21cm
£0.50 (unbound) B81-38171

362.3'8'0941 — Great Britain. Services for mentally handicapped persons — *Practical information*

A-Z : your question answered. — New ed., no.16. — London (MENCAP National Centre, 123 Golden La., EC1Y 0RT) : National Society for Mentally Handicapped Children and Adults, c1981. — 51p ; 21cm. — (MENCAP information bulletin)
Previous ed.: 1979
ISBN 0-85537-061-0 (pbk) : £1.00
Also classified at 025 B81-09420

362.3'8'0941 — Great Britain. Welfare services for mentally handicapped persons

Malin, Nigel. Services for the mentally handicapped in Britain / Nigel Malin, David Race and Glenys Jones. — London : Croom Helm, c1980. — 266p : ill ; 23cm
Bibliography: p236-258. - Includes index
ISBN 0-85664-869-8 (cased) : £11.95
ISBN 0-85664-870-1 (pbk) : £6.95 B81-07544

362.3'86'094239 — Avon. Adult training centres. Clients: Mentally handicapped persons

Survey of adult training centre clients aged over 25 living at home / Avon County Council Social Services Department. — Bristol (PO Box 30, Avon House North, St James Barton, Bristol BS99 7NB) : Director of Social Services, [1980]. — 49p : 1ill ; 30cm
Cover title
ISBN 0-86063-086-2 (spiral) : £3.00
B81-19792

362.3'86'09429 — Wales. Adult training centres for mentally handicapped persons — *Conference proceedings*

The Role and function of adult training centres : report of the Special Interest Seminars held in Llandudno in November and December 1975 / Welsh Office, Social Work Service. — [Cardiff] : [Welsh Office], [1981]. — 74p ; 30cm
Cover title. — Bibliography: p58-74
Unpriced (spiral) B81-40342

362.4 — WELFARE SERVICES FOR THE PHYSICALLY HANDICAPPED

362.4 — Developing countries. Handicapped poor persons

Moyes, Adrian. One in ten : disability and the very poor / by Adrian Moyes. — Oxford : Oxfam Public Affairs Unit, 1981. — 33,vi p : ill ; 21cm
ISBN 0-85598-055-9 (pbk) : £1.10 B81-20974

362.4 — England. Rehabilitation centres. Acutely head injured patients. Rehabilitation — *Case studies*

Rehabilitation after severe head injury / edited by C.D. Evans. — Edinburgh : Churchill Livingstone, 1981. — vi,218p : ill ; 22cm
Includes bibliographies and index
ISBN 0-443-01693-3 (pbk) : £5.95 B81-40144

362.4 — Great Britain. Handicapped persons. Social discrimination by society

Getting around : the barriers to access for disabled people / [National Consumer Council]. — London : The Council, c1981. — vi,41p ; 30cm
ISBN 0-905653-31-9 (corrected : spiral) :
Unpriced B81-33387

362.4 — Great Britain. Shopping facilities. Access by physically handicapped persons

Centre on Environment for the Handicapped. Access in the High Street / advice on how to make shopping more manageable for disabled people ; [Centre on Environment for the Handicapped] ; by Stephen Thorpe ; profiles and research by Rosalind Purcell ; text and sketch drawings by Stephen Thorpe ; photography by George Goff with additional photographs by Anthea Sieveking, the Co-operative Union and Marks and Spencer Limited ; cartoons by Louis Hellman. — London (126 Albert St NW1 7NF) : The Centre, 1981. — 16p : ill,plans,ports ; 30cm
Bibliography: on inside cover
ISBN 0-903976-04-8 (pbk) : Unpriced
B81-34704

362.4 — Handicapped persons

The **Handicapped** person in the community. — Milton Keynes : Open University Press. — (A post experience and second level course)
At head of title: The Open University
Block 3 (pt.2): What about the neighbours?. — 1980. — 64p,[2]p of plates : ill(some col.) ; 30cm — (P251 ; block 3 pt.2, 9 and 10)
Bibliography: p60-63. — Contents : Units 9/10. Communication handicap
ISBN 0-335-00113-0 (pbk) : Unpriced
B81-39151

362.4 — Handicapped persons. Attitudes of society

Shearer, Ann. Disability : whose handicap? / Ann Shearer. — Oxford : Basil Blackwell, 1981. — 208p ; 20cm. — (Understanding everyday experience)
Bibliography: p198-203. — Includes index
ISBN 0-631-12671-6 (cased) : £8.50 : CIP rev.
B81-14878

362.4 — Physically handicapped persons. Rehabilitation. Policies of governments - *Sociological perspectives - Conference proceedings*

Cross-national rehabilitation policies. — London : Sage, Aug.1981. — [290]p. — (Sage studies in international sociology ; 25)
Conference papers
ISBN 0-8039-9793-0 : £12.50 : CIP entry
B81-18096

362.4 — Physically handicapped persons — *Sociological perspectives*

Handicap in a social world. — London : Hodder & Stoughton, Nov.1981. — [336]p
ISBN 0-340-27625-8 : £7.50 : CIP entry
B81-30130

362.4 — United States. Man. Physical handicaps. Personal adjustment

DeLoach, Charlene. Adjustment to severe physical disability : a metamorphosis / Charlene DeLoach, Bobby G. Greer. — New York ; London : McGraw-Hill, c1981. — xv,310p ; 25cm. — (McGraw-Hill series in special education)
Includes bibliographies and index
ISBN 0-07-016281-6 : £14.50 B81-17107

362.4′028 — Great Britain. Equipment for physically handicapped persons — *Buyers′ guides*

Equipment for the disabled
Hoists, walking aids. — 4th ed. / editors P.J.R. Nichols, E.R. Wilshere. — Oxford : Oxford Area Health Authority (Teaching), 1980 ; Portslade (2, Foredown Drive, Portslade, Sussex BN4 2BB) : Equipment for the Disabled [distributor]. — 64p : ill ; 30cm
Previous ed.: Horsham : National Fund for Research into Crippling Diseases, 1974. — Bibliography: p59. — Includes index
Unpriced (pbk) B81-25506

362.4′0457′0941 — Great Britain. Welfare services for handicapped persons. Participation of voluntary organisations

Low, Colin. Participation in services for the handicapped : two contrasting models / [Colin Low, Glenn Rose, Beverley Cranshaw]. — London (2 Torrington Place, WC1E 7HN) : Personal Social Services Council, 1979. — 32p ; 30cm. — (Studies in participation ; 2)
£1.50c (pbk) B81-38178

362.4′048 — Physically handicapped persons. Rehabilitation — *Manuals*

Nichols, Philip. Disabled : an illustrated manual of help and self-help / Philip Nichols with Ros Haworth and Joy Hopkins ; introduced by Earl of Snowdon. — Newton Abbot : David & Charles, c1981. — 191p : ill ; 26cm
Includes index
ISBN 0-7153-7999-2 : £7.95 : CIP rev.
Also classified at 362.4′048 B80-10552

362.4′048 — Physically handicapped persons. Self help — *Manuals*

Nichols, Philip. Disabled : an illustrated manual of help and self-help / Philip Nichols with Ros Haworth and Joy Hopkins ; introduced by Earl of Snowdon. — Newton Abbot : David & Charles, c1981. — 191p : ill ; 26cm
Includes index
ISBN 0-7153-7999-2 : £7.95 : CIP rev.
Primary classification 362.4′048 B80-10552

362.4′048′088054 — North Buckinghamshire. Services for handicapped children — *Directories*

Handicapped children : handbook for families in Milton Keynes and North Bucks. — [Milton Keynes] ([c/o Oliver Wells School, Netherfield, Milton Keynes]) : Milton Keynes & District Toy Library, 1980. — 42p ; 22cm
Cover title. — Includes index
£0.50 (pbk) B81-05448

362.4′0482′0941 — Great Britain. Handicapped children. Welfare benefits

Cooper, Alison. A guide to benefits for handicapped children and their families / by Alison Cooper ; cartoons by Sam Smith. — London (1, Cambridge Terrace, NW1 4JL) : Disability Alliance, [1981]. — 33p : ill ; 30cm. — (Check your rights ; 1)
Cover title. — Text on inside covers
Unpriced (pbk) B81-35250

362.4′0482′094284 — Great Britain. Welfare benefits. Application by physically handicapped persons — *Study regions: North Yorkshire*

Phillips, Helen. Who benefits? : report of a welfare rights project with people with disabilities in North Yorkshire / Helen Phillips and Caroline Glendinning. — London (1 Cambridge Terrace, NW1 4JL) : Disability Alliance, 1981. — 64p ; 21cm
Bibliography: p61-64
£1.00 (pbk) B81-21251

362.4′0483 — Northamptonshire. Corby. Day care centres for handicapped persons: Stone House

Tuckey, Bob. An ordinary place : the Stone House : a community work approach to disabled people / Bob and Linda Tuckey. — Windsor : NFER-Nelson, 1981. — 112p ; 22cm
Includes index
ISBN 0-85633-226-7 (pbk) : £5.50 B81-35602

362.4′0485′09411 — Scotland. Residential institutions for handicapped persons — *Statistics — Serials*

Residential accommodation for the elderly and certain other adults, Scotland. — 1978-. — Edinburgh (Room 424, 43 Jeffrey St., Edinburgh EH1 1DN) : Statistics Branch, Social Work Services Group, 1979-. — v. : ill ; 21cm. — (Statistical bulletin / Social Work Services Group)
Annual. — Continues in part: Scottish social work statistics. — Description based on: 1979
ISSN 0260-549x = Residential accommodation for the elderly and certain other adults, Scotland : Unpriced
Primary classification 362.6′1′09411 B81-04765

362.4′0485′09429 — Wales. Residential institutions for physically handicapped persons, to 65 years — *Statistics — Serials*

Residential accommodation for the elderly and younger physically handicapped, year ended 31st March ... / Welsh Office. — 1977. — Cardiff : Welsh Office, [1977?]. — 82p
Unpriced
Primary classification 362.6′1′09429 B81-06526

362.4′0486′0973 — United States. Handicapped persons. Rehabilitation counselling

Parker, Randall M.. Rehabilitation counseling : foundations, consumers, service delivery / Randall M. Parker, Carl E. Hansen. — Boston [Mass.] ; London : Allyn and Bacon, c1981. — viii,364p : ill ; 25cm
Includes bibliographies and index
ISBN 0-205-07094-9 : £16.95 B81-05276

362.4′06′041 — Great Britain. Handicapped persons. Organisations — *Directories — Serials*

Self-help and the patient. — 7th ed. 1980. — London (11 Dartmouth St., SW1H 9BN) : The Patients Association, 1980. — 59p
£1.20
Also classified at 362.1′06′041 B81-08767

362.4′06′041 — Great Britain. Physically handicapped persons. Organisations: Phab — *Serials*

Phab. — Vol.1, no.1 (Spring 1981)-. — London (38 Mount Pleasant, WC1X 0AP) : Meadowbank Publications, 1981-. — v. : ill,ports ; 31cm
Continues: Phab. Bulletin
Unpriced B81-32900

362.4′088054 — Buckinghamshire. Milton Keynes *(District).* **Services for handicapped children** — *Directories — Serials*

Handicapped children : a handbook for families in Milton Keynes and North Bucks / Milton Keynes Community Services Association. — No.1 (1977/1978)-. — Milton Keynes ([263 Queensway, Bletchley, Milton Keynes]) : The Association, 1977-. — v. ; 21cm
Annual
ISSN 0309-8079 = Handicapped children : £0.25 B81-04597

362.4′088054 — Great Britain. Handicapped children

Serfe, Lorna. Children with handicaps. — London : Hodder & Stoughton, Oct.1981. — [256]p. — (Teach yourself books)
ISBN 0-340-26819-0 (pbk) : £1.25 : CIP entry
B81-27390

362.4′088054 — Great Britain. Handicapped children. Care. Participation of parents

Pugh, Gillian. Parents as partners : intervention schemes and group work with parents of handicapped children / Gillian Pugh with contributions by John Hattersley, Laurence Tennant and Peter Wilcock. — London (8 Wakley St., EC1V 7QE) : National Children′s Bureau, 1981. — 111p : ill ; 22cm
Includes bibliographies
ISBN 0-902817-18-3 (pbk) : £3.50 (£2.50 to members) B81-06252

362.4′088054 — Handicapped children. Care. Psychosocial aspects — *Conference proceedings*

National Symposium on Coping with Crisis and Handicap *(1979 : Boston).* Coping with crisis and handicap / edited by Aubrey Milunsky ; [proceedings of the National Symposium on Coping with Crisis and Handicap ... held September 10-11, 1979, at the Copley Plaza Hotel, Boston, Massachusetts]. — New York ; London : Plenum, c1981. — xv,358p : ill,ports ; 23cm
Includes bibliographies and index
ISBN 0-306-40660-8 : Unpriced
Primary classification 362.1′9 B81-37714

362.4′088054 — Handicapped children — *For parents*

Deppe, Philip R.. The high-risk child : a guide for concerned parents / Philip R. Deppe and Judith L. Sherman with Sydelle Engel. — New York : Macmillan ; London : Collier Macmillan, c1981. — xiii,198p : ill ; 24cm
Bibliography: p187-189. — Includes index
ISBN 0-02-531010-0 : £7.95 B81-38652

362.4′092′2 — Humberside. Hull. Hospitals. Physically handicapped young persons′ units: Castle Hill Hospital. *Unit for Younger Disabled — Personal observations — Collections — Serials*
Castle Lodge news and views / the Unit for Younger Disabled, Castle Hill Hospital, near Hull. — No.1 (Summer 1980)-. — [Cottingham] ([c/o Mr. C.Bibby, Castle Lodge, Castle Hill Hospital, Cottingham, North Humberside]) : The Unit, 1980-. — v. ; 21cm
Quarterly
ISSN 0260-0544 = Castle Lodge news and views : Free B81-08362

362.4′092′2 — Physically handicapped women — *Personal observations — Collections*
Images of ourselves : women with disabilities talking / edited by Jo Campling. — London : Routledge & Kegan Paul, 1981. — viii,140p : ill ; 22cm
ISBN 0-7100-0822-8 (pbk) : £3.95 : CIP rev. B81-02661

362.4′092′2 — United States. Handicapped persons *— Personal observations — Collections — Interviews*
Roth, William. The handicapped speak / William Roth. — Jefferson, N.C. : McFarland ; Folkestone : distributed by Bailey & Swinfen, 1981. — xi,211p : ports ; 24cm
ISBN 0-89950-022-6 : £12.75 B81-37034

362.4′092′4 — Deaf-blind persons: Keller, Helen — *Biographies*
Lash, Joseph P.. Helen and teacher : the story of Helen Keller and Anne Sullivan Macy / Joseph P. Lash. — London : Allen Lane, 1980. — xiv,811p,[48]p of plates : ill,1facsim,ports ; 24cm
Originally published: New York : Delacorte / Seymour Lawrence, 1980. — Text on lining papers. — Bibliography: p787-789. - Includes index
ISBN 0-7139-1363-0 : £8.95 B81-06643

362.4′092′4 — England. Physically handicapped persons — *Personal observations*
Guest, Joyce. Nobody′s perfect : (an autobiography) / by Joyce Guest. — Birmingham (516 Coventry Rd., Small Heath, Birmingham 10) : Trinity Arts, c1981. — 68p : ports ; 22cm
£1.00 (pbk) B81-29531

362.4′0941 — Great Britain. Handicapped persons
Disability in Britain. — Oxford : Martin Robertson, Nov.1981. — [176]p. — (Aspects of social policy)
ISBN 0-85520-459-1 (cased) : £7.95 : CIP entry
ISBN 0-85520-460-5 (pbk) : £2.95 B81-31062

The **Handicapped** person in the community. — Milton Keynes : Open University Press
At head of title: The Open University
Using the literture / prepared by Sheila Dale for the course team. — 1981. — 39p ; 30cm. — (P251 ; UL)
ISBN 0-335-00114-9 (pbk) : Unpriced B81-37727

362.4′0941 — Great Britain. Physically handicapped persons. Attitudes of society
Dartington, T.. A life together : the distribution of attitudes around the disabled. — London : Tavistock, Dec.1981. — [148]p
ISBN 0-422-77900-8 (cased) : £6.50 : CIP entry
ISBN 0-422-77910-5 (pbk) : £3.50 B81-31630

362.4′0941 — Great Britain. Physically handicapped persons. Social adjustment
Integrating the disabled : a summary of the report of the Snowdon Working Party on Integration of the Disabled. — Horsham (Vincent House, Springfield Rd., Horsham, W. Sussex RH12 2PN) : Action Research, 1981. — [12]p : ill ; 15x22cm
£0.15 (pbk) B81-18394

362.4′0941 — Great Britain. Society. Role of physically handicapped persons
Sutherland, Allan T.. Disabled we stand / Allan T. Sutherland. — London : Souvenir, 1981. — 158p : 1ill ; 23cm. — (Human horizons series)
ISBN 0-285-64936-1 (cased) : £5.95
ISBN 0-285-64937-x (pbk) : £3.95 B81-39371

362.4′1′028 — Equipment for partially sighted persons
Holloway, Geraldine. Good news for the partially sighted / by Geraldine Holloway. — Hove (40 Wordsworth St., Hove, E. Sussex) : Partially Sighted Society, c1980. — 52p ; 30cm
£1.25 (spiral) B81-04489

362.4′1′0924 — England. Blind spastic persons: Berwick, Lin — *Biographies*
Berwick, Lin. Undefeated / Lin Berwick. — London : Epworth, 1980. — viii,151p ; 19cm
ISBN 0-7162-0354-5 (pbk) : £1.95 B81-06994

362.4′1′0924 — Man. Sight. Recovery. Personal adjustment of blind persons — *Personal observations*
Hocken, Sheila. Emma V.I.P. / by Sheila Hocken. — London : Gollancz, 1980. — 184p,[16]p of plates : ill,ports ; 23cm
ISBN 0-575-02914-5 : £5.50 B81-02693

362.4′1′0924 — Partially sighted persons: Monkhouse, June — *Biographies*
Monkhouse, June. Sight in the dark / June Monkhouse. — London : Hodder and Stoughton, 1981. — 176p,[3]p of plates : ill,ports ; 23cm
ISBN 0-340-26343-1 : £6.95 B81-25577

362.4′18 — Deaf-blind adults. Care — *Conference proceedings*
Work with adults who suffer from a combined hearing and sight impairment : report of the seminar held at the Hill Conference Centre, Abergavenny, 16-18 October 1978 / Welsh Office, Social Work Service. — [Cardiff] : [Welsh Office], [1981]. — iii,69p : ill ; 30cm
Cover title
Unpriced (spiral) B81-40341

362.4′2 — Deaf persons — *Conference proceedings*
Papers presented at the Triennial Congress Scarborough, June 1980 / the British Deaf Association. — Carlisle (38 Victoria Place, Carlisle, Cumbria) : British Deaf Association, [1980]. — 29p : ill,ports ; 25cm
Unpriced (unbound) B81-22807

362.4′2 — Man. Deafness. Personal adjustment
No need to shout! / [editorial : John Doyle, Julie Payne, Eric Smith]. — London : ITV Books in association with Tyne Tees Television, 1981. — 109p : ill ; 20cm
ISBN 0-900727-85-3 (pbk) : £1.50 B81-17911

362.4′2′019 — Deaf persons. Influence of environment. Psychological aspects
Levine, Edna S.. The ecology of early deafness : guides to fashioning environments and psychological assessments / Edna Simon Levine. — New York ; Guildford : Columbia University Press, 1981. — xv,422p : ill,forms ; 24cm
Includes bibliographies and index
ISBN 0-231-03886-0 : £19.30 B81-36249

362.4′2′060422 — South-east England. Hearing disordered persons. Organisations — *Serials*
South East England deaf news. — Vol.1, no.1 (Jan./Feb.1981)-. — Eastbourne (c/o 101 Bridgemere Rd, Eastbourne, East Sussex BN22 8TY) : S.E.E.D. News, 1981-. — v. : ill ; 21cm
Six issues yearly
ISSN 0260-5961 = South East England deaf news : £2.50 B81-21926

362.4′2′088054 — Deaf children — *For parents*
Freeman, Roger D.. Can′t your child hear?. — London : Croom Helm, Sept.1981. — [352]p
ISBN 0-7099-1018-5 (pbk) : £8.95 : CIP entry B81-25690

362.4′2′088054 — Hearing disordered children. Care — *For parents*
Nolan, Michael. The hearing impaired child and the family / by Michael Nolan and Ivan Tucker. — London : Souvenir, 1981. — 238p,[24]p of plates : ill ; 22cm. — (Human horizon series) (A Condor book)
Includes index
ISBN 0-285-64920-5 (cased) : £6.95
ISBN 0-285-64921-3 (pbk) : £4.95 B81-28728

Some of the problems encountered by parents of hearing-impaired children / Kim McArthur ... [et al.]. — London (45 Hereford Rd., W2 5AH) : National Deaf Children′s Society, c1981. — 28p ; 21cm
Includes index
£0.30 (pbk) B81-37773

362.4′2′0880565 — United States. Deaf old persons. Social adjustment
Becker, Gaylene. Growing old in silence / Gaylene Becker. — Berkeley ; London : University pf California Press, c1980. — xi,148p ; 22cm
Bibliography: p131-143. - Includes index
ISBN 0-520-03900-9 : £6.00 B81-03067

362.4′2′0941 — Great Britain. Deaf persons. Attitudes of public
Bunting, Claire. Public attitudes to deafness : a survey carried out on behalf of the Department of Health and Social Security / Claire Bunting. — London : H.M.S.O., 1981. — vi,43p : 1form ; 30cm
At head of title: Office of Population Censuses and Surveys Social Survey Division
ISBN 0-11-690751-7 (pbk) : £6.80 B81-23658

362.4′28′0880565 — United States. Hearing disordered old persons. Rehabilitation — *Conference proceedings*
Aural rehabilitation for the elderly / [the symposium was sponsored by the Division of Communication Disorders and the Center for Studies on Aging North Texas State University, and held in the University Union, October 12-14, 1978] ; [partial support was granted by the Department of Human Resources with the Moody Foundation and the Governor′s Committee on Aging] ; [symposium director Miriam A. Henoch] ; edited by Miriam A. Henoch. — New York ; London : Grune & Stratton, c1979. — ix,223p : ill,1port ; 24cm
Includes bibliographies and index
ISBN 0-8089-1186-4 : £11.40 B81-10933

362.4′3 — Leg amputees. Rehabilitation
Troup, I. M.. Total care of the lower limb amputee. — London : Pitman, Feb.1982. — [160]p
ISBN 0-272-79641-7 : £12.95 : CIP entry B81-35782

362.4′3′0924 — Cerebral palsied children — *Personal observations*
Collins, Patricia. Mary : a mother′s story / Patricia Collins. — London : Sphere, 1981, c1980. — 243p,[8]p of plates : ill,ports ; 18cm
Originally published as: ″Your daughter is brain damaged″: New York : Hawthorn/Dutton, 1981
ISBN 0-7221-2482-1 (pbk) : £1.50 B81-36145

362.4′3′0924 — England. Paralysed persons. Rehabilitation — *Personal observations*
Ellis, Bill. The long road back : the story of a triumph over sudden and total disablement / Bill Ellis ; [edited by Mary Kenny] ; [photography: Jane Hill]. — Great Wakering : Mayhew-McCrimmon, 1981. — 184p : ill,ports ; 22cm
ISBN 0-85597-309-9 (pbk) : £2.65 B81-26144

362.4′3′0924 — Oregon. Portland. Hydrocephalic children — *Personal observations*
Payton, Everett. I won′t be crippled when I see Jesus / Everett Payton. — Eastbourne : Kingsway, 1981, c1979. — 158p ; 18cm
Originally published: Minneapolis, Minn. : Hugsburg Pub. House, c1979
ISBN 0-86065-119-3 (pbk) : £1.50 B81-07377

362.5 — WELFARE SERVICES FOR THE POOR

362.5′56′0944 — France. Poor persons. Policies of government, *1789-1799*
Forrest, Alan, *1945-.* The French Revolution and the poor / Alan Forrest. — Oxford : Blackwell, 1981. — x,198p ; 23cm
Bibliography: p177-190. — Includes index
ISBN 0-631-10371-6 : £12.50 : CIP rev. B80-20444

362.5′8 — England. Legal aid — *Accounts — Serials*

Legal Aid Fund account. — 1979-80. — London : H.M.S.O., 1981. — 9p
ISBN 0-10-225681-0 : £1.40 B81-29992

362.5′8 — England. Legal aid — *Serials*

Law Society. Legal aid : annual reports of the Law Society and of the Lord Chancellor′s Advisory Committee. — 30th (1979-80). — London : H.M.S.O., 1981. — 133p
ISBN 0-10-216081-3 : £5.70 B81-16811

362.5′8 — Legal aid — *Comparative studies*

Perspectives on legal aid : an international survey / edited by Frederick H. Zemans. — London : Pinter, 1979. — 363p ; 23cm
Conference papers
ISBN 0-903804-41-7 : £15.00 B81-04840

362.5′8 — Northern Ireland. Legal aid. Finance. Legal Aid (Northern Ireland) Fund — *Accounts — Serials*

Legal Aid and Advice Act (Northern Ireland) 1965, statement of accounts. — 1979-80. — Belfast : H.M.S.O., 1981. — [3]p
ISBN 0-10-225781-7 : £0.90 B81-31888

362.5′8 — Northern Ireland. Legal aid — *Serials*

Report of the Incorporated Law Society of Northern Ireland on the Legal Aid Scheme. — 1978-79. — Belfast : H.M.S.O., 1980. — 43p
ISBN 0-337-03034-0 : £2.50 B81-20340

362.5′8 — Scotland. Legal aid — *Accounts — Serials*

Legal Aid (Scotland) Fund account. — 1979-80. — London : H.M.S.O., 1981. — 8p
ISBN 0-10-225881-3 : £1.40 B81-29991

362.5′8′091724 — Developing countries. Poverty relief. Policies of British government

Fight world poverty : Mass Lobby report / [edited and compiled by John Mitchell and Russell Price]. — London (Bedford Chambers, Covent Garden, WC2E 8HA) : World Development Movement, c1981. — 71p : ill,facsims,ports ; 22cm
ISBN 0-903272-21-0 (pbk) : £0.95 B81-31292

362.5′8′091724 — Developing countries. Poverty relief. Role of cooperatives — *Conference proceedings*

Report of an experts′ consultation on co-operatives and the poor / convened by the International Cooperative Alliance at the Co-operative College, Loughborough, UK 5-8 July 1977. — London : I.C.A., 1978. — 96p : ill ; 22cm. — (Studies and reports / International Co-operative Alliance ; 13)
Includes bibliographies
ISBN 0-904380-35-1 (pbk) : £2.00 B81-04928

362.5′8′0941 — Great Britain. Poverty relief. Reform — *Proposals*

Field, Frank, *1942-*. Inequality in Britain : freedom, welfare and the state / Frank Field. — [London] : Fontana, 1981. — 252p ; 19cm
Includes index
ISBN 0-00-635759-8 (pbk) : £2.50 B81-12018

362.5′8′0941 — Great Britain. Welfare services for homeless persons

Background papers for the day conference on social work and homelessness, 23rd June 1981, Manchester. — Lancaster (c/o Dept. of Social Administration, Fylde College, University of Lancaster, Lancaster LA1 4YF) : Social Work and Homelessness Group, c1981. — 12p ; 30cm
Unpriced (unbound) B81-28337

362.5′8′09411 — Scotland. Poverty relief, *1745-1845*

Cage, R. A.. The Scottish poor law 1745-1845 / R.A. Cage. — Edinburgh : Scottish Academic Press, 1981. — v,180p,5p of plates : maps ; 23cm
Bibliography: p158-175. — Includes index
ISBN 0-7073-0289-7 : £8.75 B81-30110

362.5′8′094167 — Belfast. Poverty relief services, *1920-1939*

Devlin, Paddy. Yes we have no bananas : outdoor relief in Belfast 1920-39 / Paddy Devlin. — Belfast : Blackstaff, c1981. — ix,195p ; 21cm
Includes index
ISBN 0-85640-246-x (pbk) : £3.95 : CIP rev. B81-20652

362.5′8′0942 — England. Poverty relief, *1800-1914*

Williams, Karel. From pauperism to poverty / Karel Williams. — London : Routledge & Kegan Paul, 1981. — 383p : ill,plans ; 23cm
Bibliography: p369375. — Includes index
ISBN 0-7100-0698-5 : £22.50 : CIP rev. B81-02382

362.5′82 — United States. Income maintenance programmes — *Conference proceedings*

A Guaranteed annual income : evidence from a social experiment / edited by Philip K. Robins ... [et al.]. — London : Academic Press, 1980. — xxiv,330p ; 24cm. — (Quantitative studies in social relations)
Includes bibliographies and index
ISBN 0-12-589880-0 : £15.80 B81-16781

362.5′85′094233 — Dorset. Workhouses

Dorset workhouses / Dorset Countryside Treasures. — [Dorchester] ([County Library, Colliton Park, Dorchester DT1 1XJ]) : Dorset County Council, 1980. — 38p : ill,1map,1plan ; 22x30cm
Cover title. — Bibliography: p37-38
ISBN 0-85216-236-7 (pbk) : £1.00 B81-19610

362.5′85′0942389 — Somerset. Ilchester. Almshouses: Ilchester Almshouse, *1819-1837 — Early works — Facsimiles*

Ilchester Almshouse : reports of the commissioners concerning charities 1819-1837. — St. Peter Port : Toucan, 1980. — p69-84 : 3ill,ports ; 25cm. — (Ilchester and district occasional papers, ISSN 0306-6010 ; no.24)
ISBN 0-85694-222-7 (unbound) : Unpriced B81-25214

362.6 — WELFARE SERVICES FOR OLD PEOPLE

362.6 — London. Islington *(London Borough)*. **Welfare services. Requirements of old persons in private households**

The Elderly at home in Islington : report of a survey carried out between October and December 1977 by Islington Community Health Council / [Islington Community Health Council, Working Party on Services for the Elderly]. — London (Liverpool Road Hospital, Liverpool Rd., N1), 1978. — 6p ; 30cm
Unpriced (unbound) B81-31207

362.6 — Old persons. Care

Health care of the elderly : essays in old age medicine, psychiatry and services / edited by Tom Arie. — London : Croom Helm, c1981. — 240p : ill ; 23cm
Includes index
ISBN 0-7099-0252-2 : £13.95 : CIP rev. B81-06580

Mortimer, Eunice. Working with the elderly. — London : Heinemann Educational, Feb.1982. — [128]p. — (Community care practice handbooks ; 9)
ISBN 0-435-82607-7 (pbk) : £2.95 : CIP entry B81-35693

362.6 — Old persons. Care — *Sociological perspectives*

The Impact of ageing : strategies for care / edited by David Hobman. — London : Croom Helm, c1981. — 258p ; 23cm
Includes index
ISBN 0-7099-0233-6 : £12.95 B81-17852

362.6′06′042 — England. Welfare services for old persons. Organisations: Age Concern

Dickson, Niall. Age Concern at work / [written by Niall Dickson] ; [edited by Lee Bennett]. — Mitcham (60 Pitcairn Rd., Mitcham, Surrey CR4 3LL) : Age Concern England, c1981. — 30p : ill,2ports ; 30cm
Cover title. — Text, port. on inside covers
ISBN 0-86242-001-6 (pbk) : Unpriced B81-21737

362.6′094 — Europe. Old persons. Care

Open care for the elderly in seven European countries : a pilot study in the possibilities and limits of care / edited by Anton Amann. — Oxford : Pergamon, 1980. — xii,225p ; 26cm
ISBN 0-08-025215-x : £15.00 : CIP rev. B80-18647

362.6′0941 — Great Britain. Old persons. Care

In defence of the old : the need for a co-ordinated approach to the care of Britain′s elderly : a report from COHSE′s Research Department. — Banstead (Glen House, High St., Banstead, Surrey SM7 2LH) : Confederation of Health Service Employees, 1981. — 27leaves ; 30cm
Bibliography: leaves 26-27
Unpriced (pbk) B81-18596

Whitehead, Tony. A ripe old age / by Tony Whitehead. — London (22 Harley St., W1N 2ED) : MIND National Association for Mental Health, 1979. — 24p : ill,1port ; 21cm
£0.85 (pbk) B81-29459

362.6′0941 — Great Britain. Old persons. Care — *Conference proceedings*

Old age : today & tomorrow : 1-day symposium at Scientific Societies Lecture Theatre, 23 Savile Row, London W.1. — London (23 Savile Row, W1X 1AB) : British Association for the Advancement of Science, [1977]. — 63,vp : ill ; 30cm
£2.50 (spiral) B81-02814

362.6′0941 — Great Britain. Welfare services for old persons

Growing older / presented to Parliament by the Secretary of State for Social Services ... [et al.]. — London : H.M.S.O., [1981]. — v,69p : ill,maps ; 25cm. — (Cmnd. ; 8173)
ISBN 0-10-181730-4 (pbk) : £4.20 B81-16306

The **Provision** of care for the elderly / edited by John Kinnaird, Sir John Brotherston, James Williamson ; foreword by Leo A. Kaprio. — Edinburgh : Churchill Livingstone, 1981. — 224p : ill ; 23cm
Includes bibliographies and index
ISBN 0-443-02347-6 : £10.00 : CIP rev. B81-00062

Tinker, Anthea. The elderly in modern society / Anthea Tinker. — London : Longman, 1981. — xii,298p : ill ; 20cm. — (Social policy in modern Britain)
Bibliography: p287-290. - Includes index
ISBN 0-582-29513-0 (pbk) : £5.95 B81-03326

362.6′0941 — Great Britain. Welfare services for old persons — *Conference proceedings*

Appropriate Care for the Elderly : Some Problems *(Conference : 1980 : Royal College of Physicians of Edinburgh)*. Conference, Appropriate Care for the Elderly : Some Problems : held on 22nd October 1980 in the Hall of the Royal College of Physicians of Edinburgh / edited by J.M.G. Wilson. — Edinburgh : The College, 1981. — 104p,[1] folded leaf of plates : ill ; 22cm. — (Publication / Royal College of Physicians of Edinburgh ; no.54)
ISBN 0-85405-037-x (pbk) : Unpriced B81-27716

Health and welfare services for the elderly : initiatives in the 80′s / John Brocklehurst ... [et al.]. — [Lancaster] : [Department of Social Administration, University of Lancaster], 1981. — 38p : ill ; 30cm. — (Occasional paper / Department of Social Administration, University of Lancaster ; no.1)
Cover title
Unpriced (pbk) B81-36248

362.6′0941 — Great Britain. Welfare services for old persons. Policies — *Conference proceedings*

Policies for the elderly : report of a seminar, 10-12 July 1978 / edited by Chris Ham and Randall Smith. — [Bristol] ([Rodney Lodge, Grange Rd., Clifton, Bristol BS8 4EA]) : University of Bristol, School of Advanced Urban Studies, c1979. — 59p : ill ; 30cm. — (Working paper / University of Bristol School for Advanced Urban Studies, ISSN 0141-464x : 4)
ISBN 0-906515-27-0 (pbk) : £1.25 B81-10631

362.6′0941 — Great Britain. Welfare work with old persons

Rowlings, Cherry. Social work with elderly people / Cherry Rowlings. — London : Allen & Unwin, 1981. — 146p ; 23cm. — (Studies in the personal social services ; no.3)
Bibliography: p134-141. — Includes index
ISBN 0-04-362036-1 : £7.95
ISBN 0-04-362037-x (pbk) : £3.50 B81-20234

362.6′09422′56 — East Sussex. Brighton. Welfare services for old persons

Growing old in Brighton : a Development Group exercise in Brighton 1977-79 / Department of Health and Social Security, Social Work Service Development Group/Southern Region, East Sussex Social Services Department. — London : H.M.S.O., 1980. — 119p : ill,forms ; 21cm
Bibliography: p116-117
ISBN 0-11-320731-x (pbk) : £4.50 B81-09841

362.6′09423′9 — Avon. Welfare services for old persons

Towards a happier old age : a guide to services for the elderly in Avon / [prepared by the Director of Social Services]. — Bristol (P.O. Box 11, Avon House, The Haymarket, Bristol, BS99 7DE) : County Public Relations and Publicity Department, [1981]. — 29p : col.ill ; 15x21cm
Includes index
ISBN 0-86063-107-9 (pbk) : Free B81-28901

362.6′09424′96 — West Midlands *(Metropolitan County).* Birmingham. Inner areas. Ethnic minorities. Old persons. Social problems

Bhalla, Anir. Elders of the minority ethnic groups. — Birmingham (1 Finch Road, Lozells, Birmingham B19 1HS) : AFFOR, Sept.1981. — [50]p
ISBN 0-907127-06-1 (pbk) : £1.00 : CIP entry B81-28321

362.6′0973 — United States. Old persons. Care — *For auxiliary personnel in health services*

Mummah, Hazel R.. The geriatric assistant / Hazel R. Mummah, E. Marsella Smith. — New York ; London : McGraw-Hill, c1981. — xiii,306p : ill ; 24cm
Includes bibliographies and index
ISBN 0-07-044015-8 (pbk) : £10.50 B81-10064

362.6′0973 — United States. Old persons. Care. Policies of government

Public policies for an aging population / edited by Elizabeth W. Markson, Gretchen R. Batra. — Lexington : Lexington ; Farnborough, Hants. : Gower [distributor], c1980. — viii,141p ; 24cm. — (The Boston University series in gerontology)
Includes index
ISBN 0-669-03398-7 : £10.50 B81-17826

362.6′0973 — United States. Old persons. Policies of government

Lowy, Louis. Social policies and programs on aging : what is and what should be in the later years / Louis Lowy. — Lexington : Lexington Books ; [Farnborough, Hants.] : Gower [distributor], 1981, c1980. — xv,267p : ill ; 24cm
Bibliography: p249-259. — Includes index
ISBN 0-669-02342-6 : £13.50 B81-22943

362.6′1 — Residential homes for old persons. Inmates. Depression — *For personnel*

Macdonald, Alastair, *1947-*. Depression and elderly people in residential homes : some notes for care staff / Alastair Macdonald. — [London] : MIND, 1980. — 14p : 1ill ; 30cm
£0.70 (pbk) B81-29348

362.6′1′0722 — England. Residential homes for old persons — *Sociological perspectives — Case studies*

Clough, Roger. Old age homes / Roger Clough. — London : Allen & Unwin, 1981. — 221p : ill,2plans,1form ; 23cm. — (National Institute social services library ; no.42)
Bibliography: p215-218. — Includes index
ISBN 0-04-362043-4 (cased) : Unpriced : CIP rev.
ISBN 0-04-362044-2 (pbk) : Unpriced B81-20485

362.6′1′0723 — Great Britain. Residential homes for old persons. Inmates. Social conditions. Surveys. Methodology

Peace, Sheila M.. The quality of life of the elderly in residential care : a feasibility study of the development of survey methods / Sheila M. Peace, John F. Hall, Graham Hamblin ; with foreword by Mark Abrams. — London (62 Highbury Grove, N5 2AD) : Polytechnic of North London, Department of Applied Social Studies, Survey Research Unit, 1979. — iv,176p ; 30cm. — (Research report / Polytechnic of North London, Department of Applied Social Studies, Survey Research Unit ; no.1)
Bibliography: p157-176
ISBN 0-906970-00-8 (pbk) : £5.00 B81-12551

PSS : consumer study in old people′s homes : pilot report / Dianne M. Willcocks ... [et al.]. — London (62 Highbury Grove, N5 2AD) : Polytechnic of North London, Department of Applied Social Studies, Survey Research Unit, 1980. — ii,145p ; 30cm. — (Research report / Polytechnic of North London Survey Research Unit Department of Applied Social Studies Survey Research Unit ; no.6)
Cover title. — Bibliography: p142-145
£5.00 (pbk) B81-12547

362.6′1′0941 — Great Britain. Old persons. Residential care

Gupta, Himu. Choosing how to live : alternative lifestyles in residential care for elderly people / foreword Sheila Peace ; [by] Himu Gupta, Rose Dunphy and Brian Lodge. — [London] : MIND, 1979 (1980 [printing]). — 14p ; 30cm
£0.80 (pbk) B81-29314

362.6′1′09411 — Scotland. Old persons. Residential care *compared with* residential care of old persons in United States — *Case studies*

Kayser-Jones, Jeanie Schmit. Old, alone and neglected : care of the aged in Scotland and the United States / Jeanie Schmit Kayser-Jones. — Berkeley ; London : University of California Press, c1981. — xx,151p ; 23cm. — (Comparative studies of health systems and medical care)
Bibliography: p135-146. — Includes index
ISBN 0-520-04153-4 : £9.00
Also classified at 362.6′1′0973 B81-39756

362.6′1′09411 — Scotland. Residential institutions for old persons — *Statistics — Serials*

Residential accommodation for the elderly and certain other adults, Scotland. — 1978-. — Edinburgh (Room 424, 43 Jeffrey St., Edinburgh EH1 1DN) : Statistics Branch, Social Work Services Group, 1979-. — v. : ill ; 21cm. — (Statistical bulletin / Social Work Services Group)
Annual. — Continues in part: Scottish social work statistics. — Description based on: 1979
ISSN 0260-549x = Residential accommodation for the elderly and certain other adults, Scotland : Unpriced
Also classified at 362.4′0485′09411 B81-04765

362.6′1′0942188 — London. Haringey *(London Borough).* Local authority residential homes for old persons. Small group units

Peace, Sheila M.. The Haringey Group Living Evaluation Project : an experiment in residential care of the elderly / Sheila M. Peace, Stephen S. Harding. — London (62 Highbury Grove, N5 2AD) : Polytechnic of North London, Department of Applied Social Studies, Survey Research Unit, 1980. — iv,140p : plans ; 30cm. — (Research report / Polytechnic of North London, Department of Applied Social Studies, Survey Research Unit ; no.2)
Bibliography: p140
ISBN 0-906970-01-6 (pbk) : £5.00 B81-12552

362.6′1′09429 — Wales. Residential institutions for old persons — *Statistics — Serials*

Residential accommodation for the elderly and younger physically handicapped, year ended 31st March ... / Welsh Office. — 1977. — Cardiff : Welsh Office, [1977?]. — 82p
Unpriced
Also classified at 362.4′0485′09429 B81-06526

362.6′1′0973 — United States. Old persons. Residential care *compared with* residential care of old persons in Scotland — *Case studies*

Kayser-Jones, Jeanie Schmit. Old, alone and neglected : care of the aged in Scotland and the United States / Jeanie Schmit Kayser-Jones. — Berkeley ; London : University of California Press, c1981. — xx,151p ; 23cm. — (Comparative studies of health systems and medical care)
Bibliography: p135-146. — Includes index
ISBN 0-520-04153-4 : £9.00
Primary classification 362.6′1′09411 B81-39756

362.6′3 — Ireland *(Republic).* Old persons. Welfare benefits — *For old persons*

Entitlements for the elderly, April 1981 / NSSC. — Dublin (71 Lower Leeson St., Dublin 2) : National Social Service Council, 1981. — 64p ; 15x21cm
Unpriced (pbk) B81-32817

362.7 — WELFARE SERVICES FOR YOUNG PERSONS

362.7 — Great Britain. Community youth work. Use of videorecording

Dowmunt, Tony. Video with young people / Tony Dowmunt ; foreword by Ed Berman. — London : Inter-Action Inprint in association with the Institute for Social Enterprise, 1980. — 88p : ill ; 21cm. — (The Inter-Action community arts series)
ISBN 0-904571-27-0 (cased) : £6.95 : CIP rev.
ISBN 0-904571-28-9 (pbk) : £2.95 B80-19691

362.7 — Great Britain. Short term child care services

Cunningham, John, *1944-*. The babysitter book : how to solve all your childminding problems / John Cunningham and Jennifer Curry. — Feltham : Hamlyn, 1981. — 128p : 1ill ; 18cm
Bibliography: p126-128
ISBN 0-600-20341-7 (pbk) : £1.25 B81-10173

362.7′023′41 — Great Britain. Occupations involving children — *Career guides*

Lawson, Joan, *1925-*. Working with children / Joan Lawson. — London : Watts, c1980. — 64p : ill ; 26cm. — (Choosing a career)
Includes index
ISBN 0-85166-849-6 : £3.95 B81-03465

362.7′025′41 — Great Britain. Voluntary youth work — *Directories — Serials*

National Council for Voluntary Youth Services. Annual directory / National Council for Voluntary Youth Services. — 1978-9. — [Leicester] ([29 Albion St., LE1 6GD]) : The Council, [1978?]. — ii,18p
Unpriced B81-23511

362.7′044 — Battered children

O′Doherty, Neil. The battered child. — London : Baillière Tindall, July 1981. — [64]p
ISBN 0-7020-0734-x : £12.50 : CIP entry B81-13463

362.7′044 — Children. Sexual abuse by adults

Sexually abused children and their families / edited by Patricia Beezley Mrazek and C. Henry Kempe. — Oxford : Pergamon, 1981. — xii,271p : ill ; 26cm
Includes bibliographies and index
ISBN 0-08-026796-3 : £12.50 : CIP rev. B81-22564

362.7′044 — Physically abused children. Interpersonal relationships with parents

Kadushin, Alfred. Child abuse : an interactional event / Alfred Kadushin and Judith A. Martin with the assistance of James McGloin. — New York ; Guildford : Columbia University Press, 1981. — x,304p : 1form ; 24cm
Includes bibliographies and index
ISBN 0-231-04774-6 : £15.45 B81-24019

362.7′044 — United States. Children. Abuse & neglect

The Battered child / edited by C. Henry Kempe and Ray E. Helfer. — 3rd ed., rev. and expanded. — Chicago ; London : University of Chicago Press, 1980. — xvii,440p : ill ; 25cm
Previous ed.: 1974. — Includes index
ISBN 0-226-43038-3 : £12.00 B81-13673

362.7′044 — United States. Children. Abuse & neglect *continuation*

Damaged parents : an anatomy of child neglect / Norman A. Blansky ... [et al.]. — Chicago ; London : University of Chicago Press, 1981. — xii,271p ; 24cm
Bibliography: p255-264. — Includes index
ISBN 0-226-67221-2 : £9.00 B81-30028

362.7′044 — United States. Children. Abuse by parents

Gabarino, James. Understanding abusive families / James Garbarino, Gwen Gilliam. — [Lexington, Mass.] : Lexington Books ; [Farnborough, Hants.] : Gower [distributor], [1981], c1980. — xvi,263p : ill ; 24cm
Includes index
ISBN 0-669-03621-8 : £11.00 B81-21921

The **maltreatment** of the school-aged child / edited by Richard Volpe and Margot Breton, Judith Mitton. — Lexington : Lexington ; Farnborough, Hants. : Gower [distributor], c1980. — xiii,210p ; 24cm
Includes bibliographies and index
ISBN 0-669-03463-0 : £12.00
ISBN 0-669-04151-3 (pbk) : Unpriced
B81-17825

362.7′044 — United States. Children. Sexual abuse by adults — *Sociological perspectives*

Finkelhor, David. Sexually victimized children / David Finkelhor. — New York : Free Press ; London : Collier Macmillan, c1979 (1981 [printing]). — xii,228p ; 24cm
Bibliography: p215-221. — Includes index
ISBN 0-02-910400-9 (pbk) : £4.95 B81-36323

362.7′06′041 — Great Britain. Welfare services for children. Voluntary welfare work. Organisations: National Children′s Home. *Associations of Friends — Serials*

Sharecare / Associations of Friends of the National Children′s Home. — Issue no.1 (Summer 1979)-. — [London] : [National Children′s Home], 1979-. — v. : ill,ports ; 45cm
Quarterly
ISSN 0261-5797 = Sharecare : £0.10 per issue
B81-35108

362.7′06′07471 — New York *(City)*. **Manhattan. Welfare work with young persons. Organisations: Mobilization for Youth,** *1962-1972*

Helfgot, Joseph H.. Professional reforming : mobilization for youth and the failure of social science / Josph H. Helfgot. — Lexington, Mass. : Lexington Books ; [Aldershot] : Gower [distributor], 1981. — xiv,218p ; 24cm
Bibliography: p209-218. — Includes index
ISBN 0-669-04100-9 : £14.50 B81-38600

362.7′092′4 — England. Welfare work with children. Fry, Elizabeth

Taylor, Clare. Elizabeth Fry and the care of children / Clare Taylor. — Aberystwyth : [Department of History, The University College of Wales], 1981. — 11leaves ; 30cm
Unpriced (unbound) B81-34255

362.7′092′4 — England. Welfare work with children. O′Neill, Tom — *Biographies*

O′Neill, Tom. A place called hope : caring for children in distress / Tom O′Neill. — Oxford : Blackwell, 1981. — xiv,129p ; 22cm. — (The Practice of social work ; 7)
Includes index
ISBN 0-631-12963-4 (cased) : £9.90
ISBN 0-631-12654-6 (pbk) : £3.50 B81-17659

362.7′092′4 — England. Welfare work with children — *Personal observations*

Holman, Bob. Kids at the door : a preventive project on a council estate / Bob Holman with Dave Wiles and Sandie Lewis. — Oxford : Blackwell, 1981. — vii,211p : ill ; 22cm. — (The Practice of social work ; 8)
Includes index
ISBN 0-631-12586-8 (cased) : £9.95
ISBN 0-631-12587-6 (pbk) : £4.95 B81-17660

362.7′0941 — Great Britain. Children. Care. Inquiry reports, *1959-1976*

Rogers, Rick. Crowther to Warnock : how fourteen reports tried to change children′s lives / Rick Rogers. — London : Heinemann Educational in association with The International Year of the Child, 1980. — vl,296p : ill ; 23cm
Includes bibliographies and index
ISBN 0-435-80762-5 (cased) : £12.50 : CIP rev.
ISBN 0-453-80761-7 (pbk) : £4.95
Primary classification 370′.942 B80-13759

362.7′1 — Children. Abuse by parents. Prevention. Psychological aspects

Psychological approaches to child abuse / edited by Neil Frude. — London : Batsford Academic and Educational, 1980. — 240p : ill ; 22cm
Includes bibliographies and index
ISBN 0-7134-3714-6 (cased) : £15.00 : CIP rev.
ISBN 0-7134-3715-4 (pbk) : £6.50 B80-11809

362.7′1 — Ireland. Play facilities for children. Provision — *Proposals*

Andrews, Sean. Space for play / Sean Andrews, Ciaran O′Connor. — Dublin (23 Essex Quay, Dublin 2) : Comhchairdeas, c1980. — 139p : ill,plan ; 21cm
Bibliography: p134-137
ISBN 0-9507113-0-6 (pbk) : £2.75 B81-21909

362.7′12 — Great Britain. Childminding

Jackson, Brian, *1932-*. Childminder : a study in action research / Brian Jackson and Sonia Jackson. — Harmondsworth : Penguin, 1981, c1979. — xii,282p ; 20cm. — (Pelican books)
Originally published: London : Routledge & Kegan Paul, 1979. — Bibliography: p271-276. — Includes index
ISBN 0-14-022337-1 (pbk) : £2.95 B81-33612

362.7′12 — Pre-school children. Day care

Wood, David, *1944 Dec. 24-*. Working with under fives / David Wood, Linnet McMahon and Yvonne Cranstown. — London (39 Great Russell Street, London WC1B 3PH) : Grant McIntyre, 1980. — xviii,256p ; 20cm
Bibliography: p253-254. — Includes index
ISBN 0-86216-027-8 (cased) : £10.95 : CIP rev.
ISBN 0-86216-028-6 (pbk) : £4.95 B80-21649

362.7′12 — Pre-school children. Day care. Role of parents

Smith, Teresa. Parents and preschool / Teresa Smith. — London (39 Great Russell Street, London WC1B 3PH) : Grant McIntyre, 1980. — 185p ; 20cm
Bibliography: p177-181. — Includes index
ISBN 0-86216-029-4 (cased) : £9.95 : CIP rev.
(pbk) : £3.95 B80-21650

362.7′12′0941 — Great Britain. Combined day care centres & nursery schools

Combined nursery centres : a new approach to education and day care / Elsa Ferri ... [et al.]. — London : Macmillan, 1981. — 221p : plans ; 22cm. — (National Children′s Bureau series)
Bibliography: p312-217. - Includes index
ISBN 0-333-29485-8 (cased) : £12.95 : CIP rev.
ISBN 0-333-29486-6 (pbk) : £5.95 B80-24312

362.7′12′09415 — Ireland. Day care centres for pre-school children — *For working mothers*

Lentin, Ronit. Who′s minding the children? / Ronit Lintin & Geraldine Niland ; Northern Ireland section by Stella Mahon. — Dublin (2 Strand Rd., Baldoyle, Dublin 13) : Arlen House, c1980. — 137p : ill ; 19cm
Bibliography: p135-137
ISBN 0-905223-21-7 (pbk) : £2.25 B81-09790

362.7′32 — Great Britain. Welfare services for children: Dr Barnardo′s. Volunteers. Role

Working with volunteers / by Tony Churchill ... [et al.]. — Barkingside (Barkingside, Essex) : Dr Barnardo′s, c1980. — 53p : forms ; 21cm. — (Barnardo social work paper ; no.11)
Bibliography: p53
Unpriced (pbk) B81-06210

362.7′32 — Residential homes for children. Small group units

Group care for children. — London : Tavistock, Dec.1981. — [320]p. — (Social science paperbacks)
ISBN 0-422-77290-9 (cased) : £11.00 : CIP entry
ISBN 0-422-77850-8 (pbk) : £5.50 B81-31705

362.7′32′071141 — Great Britain. Residential institutions for young persons. Welfare workers. Training

Millham, Spencer. Learning to care : the training of staff for residential social work with young people / Spencer Millham, Roger Bullock, Kenneth Hosie. — Farnborough, Hants : Gower, c1980. — vi,131p : ill ; 23cm
Includes index
ISBN 0-566-00400-3 : £7.95 : CIP rev.
B80-25893

362.7′32′0924 — Avon. Bristol. Orphanages. Müller, George, *1805-1898 — Biographies*

Steer, Roger. George Muller : delighted in God : a biography / by Roger Steer. — [Rev. and abridged ed.]. — London : Hodder and Stoughton, 1981. — 320p ; 18cm
Previous ed.: 1975
ISBN 0-340-26709-7 (pbk) : £1.95 : CIP rev.
B81-11911

362.7′32′0924 — Berkshire. Reading. Residential homes for children: Tree Tops *(Hostel) — Personal observations*

Pick, Pamela. Children at Tree Tops : an example of creative residential care / Pamela Pick. — London (357 The Strand WC2R OHB) : Residential Care Association, c1981. — 144p ; 22cm
ISBN 0-901244-06-6 (pbk) : £4.50 : CIP rev.
B81-19136

362.7′32′0941 — Great Britain. Child care services. Policies of government, *1945-1980*

Packman, Jean. The child′s generation : child care policy in Britain / Jean Packman. — 2nd ed. — Oxford : Blackwell, 1981. — 202p ; 22cm. — (Aspects of social policy)
Previous ed.: 1975. — Includes index
ISBN 0-631-12664-3 (pbk) : £5.50 : CIP rev.
B80-24314

362.7′32′0941 — Scotland. Orphanages: Aberlour Trust — *Serials*

[Advance *(Stirling)*]. Advance. — Christmas 79. — Stirling (36, Park Terrace, Stirling FK8 2JR) : Aberlour Child Care Trust, [1980?]. — [17]p
Free to subscribers B81-13312

362.7′32′09411 — Scotland. Local authorities. Child care services — *Statistics — Serials*

Children in care or under supervision, Scotland. — 1976-77-. — Edinburgh (Room 422A, 43 Jeffrey St., Edinburgh EH1 1DN) : [Social Work Services Group], 1979-. — v. ; 21cm. — (Statistical bulletin / Social Work Services Group)
Annual. — Continues in part: Scottish social work statistics. — Description based on: 1979
ISSN 0260-5473 = Children in care or under supervision, Scotland : Unpriced B81-04041

362.7′32′09413 — South-east Scotland. Residential homes for children. Inmates. Visiting by volunteers

McCaw, Pat. Someone special / by Pat McCaw and Shelagh McGuire ; cover drawing by Nicholas. — Edinburgh (21 Castle St., Edinburgh EH2 3DW) : Family Care, c1980. — 24p ; 21cm
Unpriced (pbk) B81-18006

362.7′32′09415 — Ireland. Residential institutions for homeless children, *1700-1900*

Robins, Joseph. The lost children : a study of charity children in Ireland, 1700-1900 / Joseph Robins. — Dublin : Institute of Public Administration, 1980. — viii,366p,[44]p of plates : 2ill,2ports ; 22cm
Bibliography: p335-356. — Includes index
ISBN 0-902173-98-7 : £10.89 : CIP rev.
B80-13757

362.7′32′0942 — England. Welfare services for children. Organisations: Church of England. *Children′s Society.* **Residential institutions for children,** *to 1980*

Children first : a photo-history of England′s children in need / written and compiled by Bill Bowder for the Church of England Children′s Society 1881-1981. — London : Mowbray, c1980. — 78p : chiefly ill,facsims,ports ; 27cm
Facsims on inside covers
ISBN 0-264-66738-7 (pbk) : £2.95 B81-07853

362.7′32′0942142 — London. Camden *(London Borough).* **Orphanages: Foundling Hospital,** *1700-1800*

McClure, Ruth K.. Coram's children. — London : Yale University Press, Sept.1981. — [336]p
ISBN 0-300-02465-7 : £15.00 : CIP entry B81-30247

362.7′32′0973 — United States. Children. Residential care

Lewis, Dana K.. Working with children : effective communication through self-awareness / Dana K. Lewis. — Beverly Hills ; London : Sage in Cooperation with the Continuing Education Program the Human Services of the University of Michigan School of Social Work, c1981. — 160p ; 22cm. — (A Sage human service guide ; 22)
Bibliography: p142-159
ISBN 0-8039-1620-5 (pbk) : £5.30 B81-36159

362.7′33′06041 — Great Britain. Children. Foster care. Organisations: British Agencies for Adoption & Fostering — *Serials*

British Agencies for Adoption & Fostering. BAAF news / British Agencies for Adoption & Fostering. — No.1 (Jan.1981)-. — London (11 Southwark St., SE1 1RQ) : BAAF, 1981-. — v. ; 30cm
Irregular. — Continues: ABAFA news
ISSN 0260-3888 = BAAF news : Unpriced
Also classified at 362.7′34′06041 B81-32239

362.7′33′094223 — Kent. Children, 14-17 years. Foster care, *1975-1980*

Hazel, Nancy. A bridge to independence : the Kent family placement project / Nancy Hazel. — Oxford : Blackwell, 1981. — 173p : ill ; 23cm. — (The Practice of social work ; 9)
Bibliography: p170. - Includes index
ISBN 0-631-12943-x (cased) : £9.95
ISBN 0-631-12596-5 (pbk) : £4.95 B81-17661

362.7′33′0973 — United States. Children. Foster care

Lauffer, Armand. Resources : for child placement and other human services / by Armand Lauffer with contributions by Bonnie Carlson, Kayla Conrad, and Lynn Nybell. — Beverly Hills ; London : Published in cooperation with the North American Center on Adoption, Inc. and the Continuing Education Program in the Human Services of the University of Michigan School of Social Work [by] Sage, c1979. — 192p : ill,forms ; 22cm. — (A Project CRAFT publication) (Sage human services guides ; v.6)
Includes bibliographies
ISBN 0-8039-1218-8 (pbk) : Unpriced
Also classified at 362.7′34′0973 B81-37807

362.7′34 — Children, 2-12 years. Adoption. Personal adjustment of children — *For parents*

Aston, Elaine. Getting to know you : a picture book for new parents of older children-toddlers to twelves / words Elaine Aston ; drawings Jim Bray. — [London] : British Agencies for Adoption & Fostering, [1981]. — 44p : ill ; 15x21cm
Cover title. — Bibliography: p43-44
ISBN 0-903534-36-3 (pbk) : £2.50 B81-40706

362.7′34 — Children. Adoption — *For children*

Scott, Elaine. Adoption / Elaine Scott. — New York ; London : Watts, 1980. — 58p : ill,ports ; 23cm. — (A First book)
Bibliography: p55. - Includes index
ISBN 0-531-02937-9 : £2.99 B81-03638

362.7′34 — United States. Socially disadvantaged children. Adoption

No child is unadoptable : a reader on adoption of children with special needs / a Project CRAFT publication ; edited by Sallie R. Churchill, Bonnie Carlson and Lynn Nybell. — Beverly Hills ; London : Sage, c1979. — 173p ; 22cm. — (Sage human services guides ; v.8)
Includes bibliographies
ISBN 0-8039-1215-3 (pbk) : £4.40 B81-16322

362.7′34′06041 — Great Britain. Children. Adoption. Organisations: British Agencies for Adoption & Fostering — *Serials*

British Agencies for Adoption & Fostering. BAAF news / British Agencies for Adoption & Fostering. — No.1 (Jan.1981)-. — London (11 Southwark St., SE1 1RQ) : BAAF, 1981-. — v. ; 30cm
Irregular. — Continues: ABAFA news
ISSN 0260-3888 = BAAF news : Unpriced
Primary classification 362.7′33′06041 B81-32239

362.7′34′0941 — Great Britain. Children. Adoption — *Practical information*

Adopting a child : a brief guide for prospective adopters. — 1981 ed. — London (11 Southwark St., SE1 1RQ) : British Agencies for Adoption & Fostering, 1981. — 26p : ill ; 21cm
Cover title. — Previous ed.: i.e. rev. ed. 1977. — Bibliography: p8. — Includes index
ISBN 0-903534-32-0 (pbk) : £0.50 B81-13168

Wagstaff, Sue. Wayne is adopted. — London : A. & C. Black, Oct.1981. — [24]p
ISBN 0-7136-2141-9 : £2.95 : CIP entry B81-26724

362.7′34′0973 — United States. Children. Adoption

Lauffer, Armand. Resources : for child placement and other human services / by Armand Lauffer with contributions by Bonnie Carlson, Kayla Conrad, and Lynn Nybell. — Beverly Hills ; London : Published in cooperation with the North American Center on Adoption, Inc. and the Continuing Education Program in the Human Services of the University of Michigan School of Social Work [by] Sage, c1979. — 192p : ill,forms ; 22cm. — (A Project CRAFT publication) (Sage human services guides ; v.6)
Includes bibliographies
ISBN 0-8039-1218-8 (pbk) : Unpriced
Primary classification 362.7′33′0973 B81-37807

362.7′4 — Maladjusted children

Stott, Denis H.. Helping the maladjusted child. — Milton Keynes : Open University Press, Nov.1981. — [128]p. — (Children with special needs)
ISBN 0-335-10044-9 (pbk) : £9.95 : CIP entry
ISBN 0-335-10039-2 (pbk) : £4.95 B81-31087

362.7′4 — Visually handicapped children — *For children*

Chapman, Elizabeth. Suzy. — London : Bodley Head, Oct.1981. — [32]p. — (Special situation picture books ; 7)
ISBN 0-370-30375-x : £3.25 : CIP entry B81-25770

362.7′4′05 — Maladjusted children — *Serials*

New growth : journal of the Association of Workers for Maladjusted Children and Therapeutic Education. — Vol.1, no.1 (Spring 1981)-. — Newport, Gwent (c/o Mr. A. Fox, Ty Bryn and Pollards Well, Lodge Rd, Caerleon, Newport, Gwent NP6 1XQ) : The Association, 1981-. — v. ; 24cm
Two issues yearly. — Merger of: Therapeutic education ; and, Journal of the Association of Workers for Maladjusted Children
ISSN 0261-0477 = New growth : £4.00 per year B81-32797

362.7′95 — Great Britain. Pre-school children. Day care

Under fives : a programme of research : a handbook published by the Under Fives Research Dissemination Group. — [S.l.] : [Under Fives Research Dissemination Group] ; Stanmore (Publications Despatch Centre, Honeypot La., Canons Park, Stanmore, Middlesex HA7 1AZ) : Department of Education and Science [distributor], 1981. — 25p ; 30cm
Includes bibliographies
Unpriced (pbk)
Primary classification 372′.21′0941 B81-28292

362.7′95′02341 — Great Britain. Welfare work with children — *Career guides*

Humphries, Judith. Careers working with children / Judith Humphries. — London : Kegan Page, 1981. — 155p ; 19cm
ISBN 0-85038-434-6 (cased) : Unpriced B81-33616

362.7′95′0973 — United States. Children. Social problems, *1974-1980*

America's troubled children / edited by Jeanne Burr & Melinda Maidens. — Oxford : Clio Press, 1980. — vii,184p : ill,facsims,ports ; 29cm
Originally published: New York : Facts on File, 1980. — Includes index
ISBN 0-87196-369-8 : £10.60 B81-15278

362.7′95′0973 — United States. Welfare work with children

Stein, Theodore J.. Social work practice in child welfare / Theodore J. Stein. — Englewood Cliffs ; London : Prentice-Hall, 1981. — viii,279p : ill ; 24cm
Includes index
ISBN 0-13-819524-2 : £10.35 B81-24045

362′.7′96 — Welfare work with adolescents

Social work with adolescents / edited by Ray Jones, Colin Pritchard. — London : Routledge & Kegan Paul, 1980. — ix,249p : ill ; 22cm. — (Library of social work)
Bibliography: p225-245. — Includes index
ISBN 0-7100-0633-0 (pbk) : £5.50 : CIP rev. B80-34797

362.7′96′0973 — United States. Welfare work with adolescents

Responding to adolescent needs / edited by Max Sugar. — Lancaster : MTP Press, c1980. — 254p : 1ill ; 24cm
Includes bibliographies and indexes
ISBN 0-85200-531-8 : £14.95 B81-04530

362.8 — WELFARE SERVICES FOR FAMILIES, UNMARRIED MOTHERS, MINORITY GROUPS, ETC

362.8 — England. Welfare services for deviants — *Directories — Serials*

Directory of projects (England & Wales) ... for adult offenders, alcoholics, drug takers, homeless single people and people with histories of mental illness / co-produced by FARE ... [et al.]. — 1980/81. — [Chichester] : Rose, 1980. — xiii,257p
ISBN 0-85992-188-3 : [Unpriced] B81-04576

362.8 — London. Voluntary welfare services for bereaved persons: St Christopher's Hospice. *Bereavement Service*

Bereavement visiting / edited by Geoffrey Dyne ; preface by Colin Murray Parkes. — London : King Edward's Hospital Fund for London, c1981. — 68p : forms ; 21cm
Bibliography: p53. — Includes index
ISBN 0-900889-86-1 (pbk) : Unpriced B81-25367

362.8 — Scotland. Services for itinerants. Provision — *Conference proceedings*

Scotland's travelling people : second report, Spring 1980. — Glasgow : The Planning Exchange, [1980]. — 33leaves : 1map ; 30cm. — (Forum report / Planning Exchange ; 19)
Conference papers
Unpriced (pbk) B81-34608

362.8′2 — England. Divorce. Role of court welfare services

Murch, Mervyn. Justice and welfare in divorce / Mervyn Murch. — London : Sweet & Maxwell, 1980. — viii,307p ; 22cm
Includes index
ISBN 0-421-26400-4 (pbk) : £10.75 : CIP rev. B80-07299

362.8′2 — Families with handicapped children

Featherstone, Helen. A difference in the family : life with a disabled child / Helen Featherstone. — New York : Basic Books ; London : Harper & Row, 1980. — viii,262p ; 24cm
Bibliography: p251-255. - Includes index
ISBN 0-06-337015-8 : £7.75 B81-13257

362.8′2 — Great Britain. Electricity supply & gas supply. Consumers: Low-income families. Debts. Payment

Fuel debts handbook / compiled by Phil Gagg ... [et al.]. — 2nd ed. — London (609 York Rd., SW18 2PU) : Wandsworth Rights Umbrella Group, c1981. — [76]p ; 21cm
Previous ed.: 1977. — Includes index
£1.50 (pbk) B81-18464

362.8'2 — Great Britain. Fuel supply. Consumers: Low-income families. Debts — *Child Poverty Action Group viewpoints*

Child Poverty Action Group. Poor and powerless : fuel problems and disconnections / by Jane Lorant. — London : Child Poverty Action Group, 1981. — 45p ; 21cm. — (Poverty pamphlet, ISSN 0306-1868 ; 52)
ISBN 0-903963-42-6 (pbk) : £1.00 B81-39634

362.8'2 — Parents of handicapped children

Understanding and working with parents of children with special needs / James L. Paul editor. — New York ; London : Holt, Rinehart and Winston, c1981. — xvi,299p : ill ; 24cm
Includes bibliographies and index
ISBN 0-03-054146-8 (pbk) : £6.50 B81-25558

362.8'2 — United States. Women prisoners. Children

Stanton, Ann M.. When mothers go to jail / Ann M. Stanton. — Lexington, Mass. : Lexington ; [Farnborough, Hants.] : Gower [distributor], 1980. — xiii,206p : ill,forms ; 24cm
Bibliography: p193-199. — Includes index
ISBN 0-669-03461-4 : £14.00 B81-05496

362.8'2 — Welfare work. Family therapy

Psychotherapy with families. — London : Routledge & Kegan Paul, Nov.1981. — [171]p
ISBN 0-7100-0854-6 : £6.95 : CIP entry
B81-30599

362.8'2 — Welfare work with families with handicapped children & welfare work with families with sick children

Lansdown, Richard. More than sympathy : the everyday needs of sick and handicapped children and their families / Richard Lansdown. — London : Tavistock Publications, 1980. — viii,226p : ill ; 21cm
Bibliography: p201-207. — Includes index
ISBN 0-422-76630-5 (cased) : £7.95 : CIP rev.
ISBN 0-422-76640-8 (pbk) : £3.50 B80-34805

362.8'2'06041 — Great Britain. Single-parent families. Organisations: National Council for One Parent Families, *to 1978*

Graham-Dixon, Sue. Never darken my door : working for single parents and their children 1918-1978 / [Sue Graham-Dixon]. — London (255 Kentish Town Rd., NW5 2LX) : National Council for One Parent Families, 1981. — 36p : ill,facsims,ports ; 30cm
Unpriced (pbk) B81-17380

362.8'2'0926 — Maryland. Columbia. Low-income families. Social problems — *Case studies*

Sandberg, Neil C.. Stairwell 7 : family life in the welfare state / Neil C. Sandberg. — Beverley Hills ; London : Sage, c1978. — 239p ; 23cm
Bibliography: p235-238
ISBN 0-8039-0969-1 (cased) : £11.25
ISBN 0-8039-0970-5 (pbk) : £5.50 B81-14654

362.8'2'0926 — New York *(City)*. **Welfare services for families with marital problems** — *Case studies*

Weissman, Harold H.. Integrating services for troubled families / Harold H. Weissman. — San Francisco ; London : Jossey-Bass, 1978. — xviii,148p ; 24cm. — (The Jossey-Bass social and behavioral science series)
Bibliography: p139-142. — Includes index
ISBN 0-87589-385-6 : £9.60 B81-16437

362.8'2'0941 — Great Britain. Families on supplementary benefits — *Case studies*

Burghes, Louie. Living from hand to mouth : a study of 65 families living on supplementary benefit / Louie Burghes. — London (207 Old Marylebone Rd., NW1) : Family Service Units, 1980. — 80p ; 21cm. — (Poverty pamphlet ; 50)
£1.20 (pbk) B81-11048

362.8'2'0941 — Great Britain. Mentally ill old persons. Families

Who cares about relatives? : support groups for relatives of elderly people who are mentally ill / MIND. — London : MIND, [1981?]. — [4]p ; 21cm
£0.15 (unbound) B81-30112

362.8'2'0941 — Great Britain. Single-parent families — *Manuals*

Forster, Jane. Take one parent / by Jane Forster and Chris Stenhouse ; drawings by Donna ... [et al.]. — Edinburgh (44 Albany St., Edinburgh EH1 3QR) : Scottish Council for Single Parents, c1980. — 32p : ill ; 22cm
£0.60 (pbk) B81-08055

362.8'2'09421 — London. Welfare services for socially disadvantaged families: Family groups — *Correspondence, diaries, etc*

A Funny thing happened to me on the way to becoming a group leader —. — London (68 Chalton St., NW1 1JR) : CoPE (UK), Oct.1981. — [96]p
ISBN 0-907760-00-7 (pbk) : £1.75 : CIP entry
B81-31094

362.8'2'097 — North America. Single-parent families

Schlesinger, Benjamin. The one-parent family : perspectives and annotated bibliography / Benjamin Schlesinger. — 4th ed. — Toronto ; London : University of Toronto Press, 1978 (1980 [printing]). — x,224p ; 24cm
Previous ed.: 1975. — Includes bibliographies and index
ISBN 0-8020-2335-5 : £7.50
Primary classification 016.3628'2 B81-25471

362.8'2'0973 — United States. Families with handicapped children. Personal problems

Heward, William L.. Working with parents of handicapped children / William L. Heward, Jill C. Dardig, Allison Rossett. — Columbus [Ohio] ; London : Merrill, c1979. — xiv,299p : ill,facsims,forms ; 26cm
Bibliography: p259-269. - Includes index
ISBN 0-675-08310-9 : £11.95 B81-05345

362.8'23 — Parents. Alcoholism. Social aspects — *For young persons*

Seixas, Judith S.. [Living with a parent who drinks too much]. How to cope with an alcoholic parent / Judith S. Seixas. — Edinburgh : Canongate, 1980, c1979. — ix,86p ; 19cm
Originally published: New York : Greenwillow, 1979
ISBN 0-903937-93-x (cased) : £3.95
ISBN 0-86241-003-7 (pbk) : £0.95 B81-05205

362.8'23 — Scotland. Low-income families. Standard of living. Effects of fuel prices — *Serials*

Fuel poverty news. — No.1 (Feb. 1979)-. — Glasgow ([c/o Scottish Council of Social Service, 342 Argyle St., Glasgow]) : Scottish Fuel Poverty Forum, 1979-. — v. : ill ; 32cm
Six issues yearly. — Description based on: No.6 (Jan. 1980)
ISSN 0260-3683 = Fuel poverty news :
Unpriced B81-09151

362.8'23'09424 — England. Midlands. Families. Deprivation — *Case studies*

Coffield, Frank. A cycle of deprivation? : a case study of four families / Frank Coffield, Philip Robinson, Jacquie Sarsby. — London : Heinemann Educational, 1980. — ix,226p : ill,geneal.tables ; 23cm. — (Studies in deprivation and disadvantage ; 2)
Bibliography: p215-221. - Includes index
ISBN 0-435-82145-8 : £11.50 : CIP rev.
B80-31260

362.8'253 — England. Welfare work with families with divorced parents

Wilkinson, Martin. Children and divorce / Martin Wilkinson. — Oxford : Basil Blackwell, 1981. — 200p ; 22cm. — (The Practice of social work)
Bibliography: p195. — Includes index
ISBN 0-631-12514-0 : £9.95
ISBN 0-631-12524-8 (pbk) : £4.95 B81-24272

362.8'253'09411 — Scotland. Welfare work with problem families — *Inquiry reports*

Child Health Programme Planning Group. Vulnerable families : a report / by the Child Health Programme Planning Group of the Scottish Health Service Planning Council. — Edinburgh : H.M.S.O., 1980. — 69p : 1ill ; 21cm
At head of title: Scottish Home and Health Department, Scottish Education Department
ISBN 0-11-491643-8 (pbk) : £3.00 B81-04533

362.8'253'094252 — Nottinghamshire. Welfare work with mothers

Spencer, N. J.. Group work with mothers in general practice : some preliminary observations / N.J. Spencer. — [Nottingham] : University of Nottingham, 1980. — 15leaves ; 30cm. — (Occasional paper / Leverhulme Health Education Project ; no.21)
Unpriced (pbk) B81-22730

362.8'253'0942527 — Nottinghamshire. Nottingham. Welfare work with families of prisoners

Monger, Mark. Throughcare with prisoners' families / by Mark Monger and John Pendleton with Jenny Roberts. — Nottingham : University of Nottingham, Department of Social Administration and Social Work, [1980]. — 205p ; 30cm. — (Social work studies, ISSN 0307-8574 ; no.3)
£3.50 (spiral) B81-06197

362.8'254'0941 — Great Britain. Family service units. Team-work — *Case studies*

Holder, Dave. Teamwork and the development of a unitary approach / Dave Holder and Mike Wardle. — London : Routledge & Kegan Paul, 1981. — xvi,195p : ill ; 22cm. — (Library of social work)
Bibliography: p193-195
ISBN 0-7100-0776-0 (pbk) : £5.50 B81-13729

362.8'256 — Families. Policies of governments — *Comparative studies*

Kamerman, Sheila B.. Child care, family benefits, and working parents : a study in comparative policy / Sheila B. Kamerman, Alfred J. Kahn. — New York ; Guildford : Columbia University Press, 1981. — xii,327p ; 24cm
Includes index
ISBN 0-231-05170-0 : £15.45 B81-27079

362.8'256'0941 — Great Britain. Families. Effects of British government policies

Coussins, Jean. The family in the firing line : a discussion document on family policy / by Jean Coussins and Anna Coote. — London (1 Macklin St., WC2B 5NH) : Child Poverty Action Group : National Council for Civil Liberties, 1981. — 42p : ill ; 21cm. — (Poverty pamphlet, ISSN 0306-1868 ; 51)
ISBN 0-903963-41-8 (pbk) : £1.20 B81-20655

362.8'256'0941 — Great Britain. Families. Effects of British government policies — *Proposals*

Field, Frank, *1942-*. Fair shares for families : the need for a family impact statement / Frank Field. — London (231 Baker St., NW1 6WL) : Study Commission on the Family, c1980. — 22p ; 21cm. — (Occasional paper / Study Commission on the Family ; no.3)
Bibliography: p22
ISBN 0-907051-02-2 (pbk) : £1.00 B81-04887

362.8'256'0941 — Great Britain. Families. Policies of government

Bottomley, Peter. Options for family policy / by Peter Bottomley. — London (501 Kingsland Rd., E8 4AU) : Family Welfare Association, [1979]. — 12leaves ; 31cm. — (The Loch memorial lecture ; 1979)
Unpriced (pbk) B81-08996

362.8'256'0973 — United States. Families. Policies of government

Giraldo, Z. I.. Public policy and the family : wives and mothers in the labor force / Z.I Giraldo. — Lexington : Lexington ; Farnborough, Hants. : Gower [distributor], c1980. — xxii,217p : ill ; 24cm
Includes bibliographies and index
ISBN 0-669-03762-1 : £13.50 B81-17829

362.8'2561'0941 — Great Britain. Families. Policies of government — *Proposals*

Brayshaw, A. J.. Public policy and family life / A.J. Brayshaw. — London : Policy Studies Institute, c1980. — v,73p ; 21cm. — (Discussion paper / Policy Studies Institute ; no.3)
ISBN 0-85374-182-4 (pbk) : £2.75 B81-00807

362.8′28 — London. Haringey *(London Borough)*. Domiciliary family planning services, *1968-1975*

Christopher, Elphis. A survey of the Haringey Domiciliary Family Planning Service 1968-1975 / Elphis Christopher, Leonie A. Kellaher, Andrée von Koch. — London (62 Highbury Grove, N5 2AD) : Polytechnic of North London, Department of Applied Social Studies, Survey Research Unit, 1980. — vii,155p ; 30cm. — (Research report / Polytechnic of North London, Department of Applied Social Studies, Survey Research Unit ; no.3)
Bibliography: p155
ISBN 0-906970-02-4 (pbk) : £5.00 B81-12550

362.8′28′0941 — Great Britain. Welfare work with problem families

Lahiff, Maureen Evelyn. Hard-to-help families / Maureen Evelyn Lahiff. — Aylesbury : HM+M, c1981. — viii,134p : ill ; 20cm. — (Topics in community health)
Includes bibliographies and index
ISBN 0-85602-043-5 (pbk) : £3.95 B81-19544

362.8′28′094227 — Hampshire. Services for families with young children

Poulton, Geoff. Families with young children : a Hampshire-based study project : report, May 1979 / Geoff Poulton, George Campbell. — Southampton ([The University, Southampton SO9 5NH]) : Hampshire Area Health Authority in association with University of Southampton, Department of Education, 1979. — ii,51p ; 30cm
ISBN 0-85432-192-6 (pbk) : Unpriced B81-18631

362.8′282′06041 — Great Britain. Low-income families. Poverty relief. Organisations: Child Poverty Action Group — *Serials*

CPAG newsletter / Child Poverty Action Group. — Nov.1979-. — London (1 Macklin St., WC2B 5NH) : The Group, 1979-. — v. ; 30cm
Quarterly. — Continues: Branches newsletter (Child Poverty Action Group). — Description based on: July 1980 issue
ISSN 0260-6410 = CPAG newsletter : Unpriced B81-05034

362.8′282′094 — European Community countries. Child benefits

Bradshaw, Jonathan. Child support in the European Community / Jonathan Bradshaw, David Piachaud. — London : Bedford Square Press, 1980. — 144p : ill ; 22cm. — (Occasional papers on social administration ; no.66)
ISBN 0-7199-1045-5 (pbk) : £6.95 B81-04660

362.8′282′0941 — Great Britain. Family allowances. Policies of government, *to 1945*

Macnicol, John. The movement for family allowances, 1918-45 : a study in social policy development / John Macnicol. — London : Heinemann, 1980. — xiii,243p ; 23cm. — (Studies in social policy and welfare ; 12)
Bibliography: p221-234. - Includes index
ISBN 0-435-82555-0 : £15.00 : CIP rev. B80-12301

362.8′286 — England. Marriage counselling. Griffith, Edward F. — *Biographies*

Griffith, Edward F.. The pioneer spirit / Edward F. Griffith. — Upton Grey (The Road House, Upton Grey, Basingstoke, Hants, RG25 2RH) : Green Leaves Press, 1981. — 134p,[1]leaf of plates : facsims,1port ; 24cm
Includes index
ISBN 0-907557-01-5 (cased) : £6.95
ISBN 0-907557-00-7 (pbk) : £3.95 B81-25356

362.8′286 — Family planning services

Cowper, Ann. Family planning : fundamentals for health professionals. — London : Croom Helm, 1981. — 160p : ill ; 22cm
Bibliography: p155-157. — Includes index
ISBN 0-85664-907-4 (cased) : £11.95 : CIP rev.
ISBN 0-85664-908-2 (pbk) : Unpriced
Primary classification 613.9′4 B81-13747

362.8′286 — Parents of handicapped children. Counselling

Murphy, Albert T.. Special children, special parents : personal issues with handicapped children / Albert T. Murphy. — Englewood Cliffs ; London : Prentice-Hall, c1981. — ix,198p ; 21cm. — (A Spectrum book)
Includes index
ISBN 0-13-826412-0 (cased) : Unpriced B81-22759

362.8′286′0973 — United States. Family violence victims. Counselling

Conflict intervention in social and domestic violence / [edited by] Carmen Germaine Warner. — London : Prentice-Hall, c1981. — xiii,283p : ill ; 23cm
Includes index
ISBN 0-87619-855-8 (cased) : Unpriced
ISBN 0-87619-854-x (pbk) : £7.75 B81-24908

362.8′3 — Greater Manchester *(Metropolitan County)*. Manchester. Battered wives — *Case studies*

Clout / written and illustrated by Ann ... [et al.]. — Manchester (61 Bloom St., Manchester) : Commonword, [1981?]. — 68p : ill ; 21cm
ISBN 0-9505997-3-5 (pbk) : £0.50 B81-33547

362.8′3 — Scotland. Battered women. Care & protection — *Practical information*

Information kit for agencies / Scottish Women′s Aid. — [Edinburgh] ([11 St. Colme Street, Edinburgh EH3 6AA]) : [Scottish Women′s Aid], [1981?]. — 1portfolio ; 23cm
Bibliography: 1 sheet
Unpriced (unbound) B81-35507

362.8′3 — United States. Women. Physical abuse

Hirsch, Miriam F.. Women and violence / Miriam F. Hirsch. — New York ; London : Van Nostrand Reinhold, c1981. — xxv,385p ; 24cm
Includes bibliographies and index
ISBN 0-442-26148-9 : £13.45 B81-17147

362.8′3′0973 — United States. Women. Community organisation — *Case studies*

Masi, Dale A.. Organizing for women : issues, strategies and services / Dale A. Masi. — Lexington, Mass. : Lexington Books ; [Aldershot] : Gower [distributor], 1981. — xv,221p : ill ; 24cm
Includes index
ISBN 0-669-02577-1 : £13.50 B81-39702

362.8′4 — United States. Ethnic minorities. Counselling

Sue, Derald Wing. Counseling the culturally different : theory and practice / Derald Wing Sue with chapter contributions by Edwin H. Richardson, Rene A. Ruiz, Elsie J. Smith. — New York ; Chichester : Wiley, c1981. — xvi,303p : ill,2forms ; 24cm. — (Wiley series in counseling and human development)
Includes bibliographies and index
ISBN 0-471-04218-8 : £14.00 B81-23328

362.8′4′00973 — United States. Welfare work with ethnic minorities

Devore, Wynetta. Ethnic-sensitive social work practice / Wynetta Devore, Elfriede G. Schlesinger. — St. Louis ; London : Mosby, 1981. — xi,285p : ill ; 23cm
Includes bibliographies and index
ISBN 0-8016-1268-3 (pbk) : £8.50 B81-30123

362.8′5 — Great Britain. Welfare services for fishermen: Royal National Mission to Deep Sea Fishermen, *1881-1981*

Pritchard, Stanley. Fish and ships : Royal National Mission to Deep Sea Fishermen 1881-1981 / by Stanley Pritchard ; foreword by Hammond Innes. — London : Mowbray, 1980. — 176p,[16]p of plates : ill,ports ; 18cm. — (Mowbray′s popular Christian paperbacks)
Bibliography: p176
ISBN 0-264-66558-9 (pbk) : £1.50 B81-03045

362.8′7 — Great Britain. Refugees. Resettlement

Levin, Michal. What welcome? reception and resettlement of refugees in Britain / Michal Levin. — London : Acton Society Trust, [1981]. — vi,118p ; 21cm
Bibliography: p118
ISBN 0-85000-017-3 (pbk) : £3.95 B81-39060

362.8′8 — Business firms. Executives. Abduction by terrorists. Prevention

Cole, Richard B.. Executive security : a corporate guide to effective response to abduction and terrorism / Richard B. Cole. — New York ; Chichester : Wiley, c1980. — x,323p : ill ; 24cm
Bibliography: p307-313. - Includes index
ISBN 0-471-07736-4 : £13.35 B81-04623

362.8′8 — Edinburgh. Welfare services for rape victims. Organisations: Edinburgh Rape Crisis Group — *Serials*

[Report *(Edinburgh Rape Crisis Centre)*]. Report / Edinburgh Rape Crisis Centre. — Jan.1981-. — Edinburgh (P.O. Box 120, Head Post Office, Edinburgh) : Edinburgh Rape Crisis Group, 1981-. — v. ; 30cm
ISSN 0261-3808 = Report — Edinburgh Rape Crisis Centre : Unpriced B81-25013

362.8′8 — Great Britain. Criminal injuries. Compensation. Organisations: Criminal Injuries Compensation Board — *Serials*

Criminal Injuries Compensation Board. Report, accounts for the year ended 31st March ... / Criminal Injuries Compensation Board. — 1980. — London : H.M.S.O., 1980. — 67p. — (Cmnd. ; 8081)
ISBN 0-10-180810-0 : £3.70 B81-06138

362.8′8′0973 — United States. Services for victims of crimes. Evaluation — *Conference proceedings*

Evaluating victim services / edited by Susan E. Salisin ; foreword by Bertram S. Brown. — Beverly Hills ; London : Published in cooperation with the Evaluation Research Society [by] Sage, 1981. — 168p ; 22cm. — (Sage research progress series in evaluation ; v.7)
Conference papers. — Includes bibliographies
ISBN 0-8039-1525-x (cased) : Unpriced
ISBN 0-8039-1526-8 : Unpriced B81-26976

362.9 — SPECIALISED WELFARE SERVICES. HISTORICAL AND GEOGRAPHICAL TREATMENT

362′.924 — Ireland. Social reform. Cusack, M. F. — *Biographies*

Eagar, Irene ffrench. Margaret Anna Cusack : one woman′s campaign for women′s rights : a biography / Irene ffrench Eagar. — Rev. ed. — Dublin : Arlen House, The Women′s Press, 1979. — xvi,250p ; 22cm
Previous ed. published as: The Nun of Kenmare. Cork : Mercier Press, 1970. — Includes index
ISBN 0-905223-11-x (pbk) : £3.58 B81-16634

363 — PUBLIC SAFETY, POLICE, HOUSING AND OTHER PUBLIC SERVICES

363 — Emergency services. Planning. Information sources

Farmer, Penny. Emergency planning : a state of the art review and a guide to sources of information / compiled by Penny Farmer. — London (6 Castle St., Edinburgh EH2 3AT) : Capital Planning Information, 1980. — 36p ; 30cm. — (CPI topicguide, ISSN 0142-1859 ; no.4)
Bibliography: p31-36
ISBN 0-906011-08-6 (pbk) : £4.50 B81-27745

363 — Rural regions. Amenities. Accessibility. Measurement — *Study regions: Wales*

Nutley, S. D.. The evaluation of accessibility levels in rural areas : an example from rural Wales / S.D. Nutley. — [Cardiff] : Welsh Office, c1981. — ii,43p : ill,maps ; 30cm
Bibliography: p28-30
ISBN 0-904251-47-0 (spiral) : Unpriced B81-40339

363′.025′426795 — Essex. Southend-on-Sea. Public services — *Directories*

Southend-on-Sea. *Borough Council.*
Southend-on-sea services information handbook / issued by the authority of the Southend Borough Council in co-operation with the Publicity Department. — Wallington : Home Publishing, [1981]. — 36p : ill ; 21cm
£0.28 (pbk) B81-39017

363'.025'4297 — Mid Glamorgan. Public services — *Directories — For consumers*

What's where in Mid Glamorgan / [compiled by Helen Buswell]. — Cardiff (8 St. Andrews Place, Cardiff CF1 3BE) : Welsh Consumer Council, 1980. — iii,49p : maps ; 30cm
Unpriced (pbk) B81-28733

363'.0941 — Great Britain. Local authorities. Public services — *Proposals*

Forsyth, Michael. Re-servicing Britain / Michael Forsyth. — 2nd ed. — London : Adam Smith Institute, 1981. — [16]p : ill ; 21cm
Previous ed.: 1980
ISBN 0-906517-12-5 (pbk) : £1.00 B81-35258

363'.0941 — Great Britain. Public health — *Serials*

[Handbook *(Royal Institute of Public Health and Hygiene)*]. Handbook / the Royal Institute of Public Health and Hygiene. — 1980/12981-. — London : 75 Little Britain, EC1A 7EY : Myddleton Pub. on behalf of the Institute [1980-]. — v. : ill,ports ; 22cm
Annual
ISSN 0260-5309 = Handbook - Royal Institute of Public Health and Hygiene : Unpriced
B81-09085

363'.0941 — Great Britain. Public services — *For schools*

Harrex, Joan. Public services and the council / Joan Harrex. — Glasgow : Blackie, 1981. — 36p : ill,facsims,1form ; 22cm. — (Home economics topic books)
Cover title
ISBN 0-216-90872-8 (pbk) : Unpriced
B81-08496

363'.0941 — Great Britain. Public works — *Conference proceedings*

Public Works Congress *(1981 : Birmingham?)*. Papers / Public Works Congress 1981. — Birmingham (Monaco House, Bristol St., Birmingham B5 7AS) : Public Works and Municipal Services Congress & Exhibition Council, [1981]. — 680p in various pagings : ill,maps,ports ; 22cm
Unpriced B81-16573

363'.0942 — England. Rural regions. Public services. Innovation — *Proposals*

Woollett, Stephen. Alternative rural services : a community initiatives manual / Stephen Woollett. — London : Bedford Square Press, NCV0, 1981. — x,103p ; 30cm
ISBN 0-7199-1055-2 (pbk) : £3.50 B81-29199

363'.0942 — England. Urban regions. Public health

Sugden, F. G.. Health protection in the urban environment / F.G. Sugden. — London : Associated Business Press, 1980. — 206p : ill ; 23cm
Includes index
ISBN 0-85227-261-8 : £11.00 B81-06540

363'.0973 — United States. Public works. Social impact assessment

Finsterbusch, Kurt. Understanding social impacts : assessing the effects of public projects / Kurt Finsterbusch. — Beverley Hills ; London : Sage, c1980. — 309p : ill ; 22cm. — (Sage library of social research ; v.110)
Bibliography: p289-309
ISBN 0-8039-1015-0 (cased) : Unpriced
ISBN 0-8039-1016-9 (pbk) : Unpriced
B81-17794

363.1 — PUBLIC SAFETY SERVICES

363.1 — Risks

Risk : a second level course. — Milton Keynes : Open University Press
At head of title: The Open University
Block 3: The world of physical risk / prepared for the course team. — 1980. — 169p : ill ; 30cm. — (U201 ; block 3, units 11-13)
Includes bibliographies. — Contents: Unit 11. Risk to life and limb — Unit 12. Safety systems — Unit 13. Megarisks
ISBN 0-335-00272-2 (pbk) : Unpriced
B81-39479

Risk : a second level course. — Milton Keynes : Open University Press
At head of title: The Open University
Reflections / prepared for the course team. — 1980. — 81p : ill ; 30cm. — (U201 ; units 31-32)
Includes bibliographies. — Contents: Unit 31. On risk and religion — Unit 32. On uncertain things
ISBN 0-335-00276-5 (pbk) : Unpriced
B81-39484

363.1 — Risks. Assessment. Implications of social aspects of science & technology — *Conference proceedings*

Society, Technology and Risk Assessment *(Conference : 1979 : Wölfersheim)*. Society, technology and risk assessment : based on the proceedings of an international workshop, 'Society, Technology and Risk Assessment', held at Wölfersheim, Germany, from June 5-8, 1979 / edited by J. Conrad. — London : Academic Press, 1980. — xxvii,303p : ill ; 24cm
Includes bibliographies and index
ISBN 0-12-186450-2 : £15.20 : CIP rev.
B80-10082

363.1'00941 — Great Britain. Accidents — *Serials*

The facts about accidents / RoSPA. — [1980 ed.]. — [Birminghm] : RoSPA, 1980. — 56p
Unpriced B81-29660

363.1'07'088054 — Children. Accidents. Prevention — *Serials*

The Tufty times. — Spring 1979-. — Birmingham : The Royal Society for the Prevention of Accidents, 1979-. — v. : ill ; 30cm
Three issues yearly. — Continues: The Tufty Club newsletter. — Description based on: Summer 1981
ISSN 1261-8893 = Tufty times : Unpriced
B81-39739

363.1'1 — Great Britain. Laboratories. Safety aspects — *For technicians*

Hawkins, M. D.. Technician safety and laboratory practice / M.D. Hawkins. — London : Cassell, 1980. — 239p : ill,facsims ; 22cm. — (Cassell's TEC series)
Includes index
ISBN 0-304-30550-2 (pbk) : £3.95 B81-02608

363.1'1 — Great Britain. Workplaces. Biological hazards

Price. Biological hazards : the hidden threat / Price, Le Serve and Parker. — Walton-on-Thames : Nelson, 1981. — vi,89p : ill ; 22cm. — (Health & safety in the workplace)
ISBN 0-17-771111-6 (pbk) : £1.40 B81-15315

363.1'1 — Industrial health

Occupational health practice / edited by R.S.F. Schilling. — 2nd ed. — London : Butterworths, 1981. — xviii,630p : ill,maps,forms,ports ; 24cm
Previous ed.: 1973. — Includes bibliographies and index
ISBN 0-407-33701-6 : £18.00 : CIP rev.
B80-18318

363.1'1 — Industrial safety — *For children*

Moore, C. J.. Industrial safety : safety and health at work / C.J. Moore and R.V. Allott. — London : Heinemann Educatiooonal, 1981. — 32p : ill ; 19cm. — (Heinemann science and technical readers. Elementary level)
ISBN 0-435-29004-5 (pbk) : £0.85 : CIP rev.
B80-13350

363.1'1 — Industries. Explosions. Safety aspects

Bodurtha, Frank T.. Industrial explosion prevention and protection / Frank T. Bodurtha. — New York ; London : McGraw-Hill, c1980. — xix,167p : ill ; 24cm
Includes bibliographies and index
ISBN 0-07-006359-1 : £13.50 B81-02939

363.1'1'07 — Great Britain. Hotel & catering industries. Personnel. Training. Curriculum subjects: Industrial health & industrial safety — *Manuals*

Training for health and safety : in the hotel & catering industry. — [Wembley] ([Ramsey House, Central Sq., Wembley, Middx HA9 7AP]) : Hotel and Catering Industry Training Board, [c1981]. — 61p : ill,forms ; 30cm
Cover title. — Text on inside cover
Unpriced (pbk) B81-33185

363.1'1'07041 — Great Britain. Industrial health. Information sources — *Serials*

[Resources *(Isleworth)*]. Resources : [for occupational health practice, research and education]. — Vol.1 (Spring 1981)-. — Isleworth (465 Twickenham Rd, Isleworth. Middx TW7 7DZ) : Resources, 1981-. — v. ; 21cm
Quarterly
ISSN 0261-0760 = Resources (Isleworth) : Unpriced B81-32898

363.1'1'072041 — Great Britain. *Health and Safety Executive.* **Research projects** — *Serials*

Health and safety research / Health and Safety Executive. — 1979. — London : H.M.S.O., 1980. — 40p
ISBN 0-11-883268-9 : £3.80
ISSN 0309-684x B81-06433

363.1'1'078 — Great Britain. Hotel & catering industries. Personnel. Training. Curriculum subjects: Industrial health & industrial safety. Teaching aids — *Catalogues*

Health, safety and hygiene source list / compiled by the Training Development Unit of the H.C.I.T.B.. — [Wembley] ([Ramsey House, Central Sq., Wembley, Middx HA9 7AP]) : [Hotel and Catering Industry Training Board], [1979]. — 118p ; 30cm
Unpriced (spiral) B81-33184

363.1'1'0941 — Great Britain. Industrial health

Jones, Alan L.. Occupational hygiene : an introductory guide / Alan L. Jones, David M.W. Hutcheson and Sarah M. Dymott. — London : Croom Helm, c1981. — 182p : ill ; 23cm
Includes bibliographies and index
ISBN 0-7099-1404-0 : £9.95 : CIP rev.
B81-14891

363.1'1'0941 — Great Britain. Industrial health & industrial safety — *For business firms*

Employees, health and safety. — London : Hamlyn, c1980. — 207p : ill,1map,1facsim,forms ; 22cm. — (Managing your business guides)
Includes index
ISBN 0-600-35367-2 : £5.00
Also classified at 658.3'0941 B81-05454

363.1'1'0941 — Great Britain. Industrial health & industrial safety — *For trade unionism*

Eva, Dave. Health and safety at work / Dave Eva and Ron Oswald. — London : Pan, 1981. — 188p : ill,2facsims,1form ; 20cm. — (Pan trade union studies)
Includes index
ISBN 0-330-26477-x (pbk) : £1.75 B81-38230

363.1'1'0941 — Great Britain. Industrial health & industrial safety — *Serials*

Manufacturing and service industries. — 1980. — London : H.M.S.O., Jan.1982. — [100]p
ISBN 0-11-883457-6 (pbk) : CIP entry
B81-34115

On guard : newsletter of safety hints and events. — Vol.1, no.1 (Jan. 1976)-. — Dublin ([Davitt House], Mespil Rd, Dublin 4) : National Industrial Safety Organisation, 1976-. — v. : ill,ports ; 30cm
Six issues yearly
Unpriced B81-04630

363.1'1'0941 — Great Britain. Industrial health & industrial safety - *Statistics*

Health and safety statistics. — 1978-79. — London : Health & Safety Executive, June 1981. — [60]p
ISBN 0-11-883438-x (pbk) : CIP entry
B81-14822

363.1'1'0941 — Great Britain. Industrial safety. Rules. Enforcement
Enforcement of workplace safety rules. — London (346 Harrow Rd., W9 2HP) : Industrial Relations Briefing, c1980. — 54p ; 21cm. — (IRB question & answer series ; no.6)
£5.95 (pbk) B81-33268

363.1'1'0973 — United States. Industrial health
Patty, Frank Arthur. Patty's industrial hygiene and toxicology. — 3rd rev. ed. / George D. Clayton, Florence E. Clayton editors. — New York ; Chichester : Wiley
Vol.2A: Toxicology / contributors R.R. Beard ... [et al.]. — c1981. — xviiip,p1467-2878 : ill ; 24cm
Includes index
ISBN 0-471-16042-3 : £62.00
Also classified at 615.9'02 B81-23243

363.1'1'0973 — United States. Industrial safety
Hammer, Willie. Occupational safety management and engineering / Willie Hammer. — 2nd ed. — Englewood Cliffs : Prentice-Hall, c1981. — xvi,494p : ill,forms ; 25cm
Previous ed.: 1975. — Includes index
ISBN 0-13-629410-3 : £12.95 B81-22705

363.1'11 — Factories. Accidents. Role of alcohol
Argyropoulos-Grisanos, M. A.. Alcohol and industrial accidents / M.A. Argyropoulos-Grisanos, P.J.L. Hawkins. — London (12 Caxton Street, SW1H OQS) : Christian Economic Research Foundation, [1980?]. — 52p : ill ; 22cm
Bibliography: p51-52
£2.50 (pbk) B81-31116

363.1'156'09485 — Sweden. Industrial health & industrial safety. Regulation by government *compared with* regulation by government of industrial health & industrial safety in United States
Kelman, Steven. Regulating America, regulating Sweden : a comparative study of occupational safety and health policy / Steven Kelman. — Cambridge, Mass. ; London : M.I.T., c1981. — x,270p ; 24cm
Includes index
ISBN 0-262-11076-8 : £12.40
Primary classification 363.1'156'0973 B81-38133

363.1'156'0973 — United States. Industrial health & industrial safety. Regulation by government *compared with* regulation by government of industrial health & industrial safety in Sweden
Kelman, Steven. Regulating America, regulating Sweden : a comparative study of occupational safety and health policy / Steven Kelman. — Cambridge, Mass. ; London : M.I.T., c1981. — x,270p ; 24cm
Includes index
ISBN 0-262-11076-8 : £12.40
Also classified at 363.1'156'09485 B81-38133

363.1'165 — Factories. Accidents. Investigation. Methods
Ferry, Ted S.. Modern accident investigation and analysis : an executive guide / Ted S. Ferry. — New York ; Chichester : Wiley, c1981. — xxiv,273p : ill ; 25cm + 3sheets
Sheets in pocket. — Includes index
ISBN 0-471-07776-3 : £17.40 B81-23321

363.1'195 — United States. Industrial health & safety. Role of collective bargaining
Bacow, Lawrence S.. Bargaining for job safety and health / Lawrence S. Bacow. — Cambridge, Mass. ; London : MIT Press, c1980. — x,159p ; 24cm
Bibliography: p150-154. - Includes index
ISBN 0-262-02152-8 : £9.90 B81-04918

363.1'1962131'0942 — England. Electricity supply industries. Industrial safety — *Serials*
[Safety review *(Electricity Council. Safety Branch)*]. Safety review / issued by the Safety Branch of the Electricity Council. — 30. — London : The Council, 1981. — 58p
Unpriced B81-36015

363.1'19622'09416 — Northern Ireland. Mining & quarrying. Industrial safety — *Serials*
Mines and quarries report / Department of Commerce, Northern Ireland. — 1979. — Belfast : H.M.S.O., 1980. — 10p
ISBN 0-337-06124-6 : £1.50 B81-20331

363.1'19622334'0941 — Great Britain. Coal mines. Industrial health — *Serials*
National Coal Board. *Medical Service.* Annual report / National Coal Board Medical Service. — 1979-80. — [London] ([Hobart House, Grosvenor Place, SW1X 7AE]) : The Service, [1981]. — 32p
ISSN 0307-9899 : £2.00 B81-35953

363.1'19622334'0941298 — Scotland. Fife Region. Cowdenbeath. Mine rescue services: Cowdenbeath Mines Rescue Station, *to 1980*
Cowdenbeath Mines Rescue Station. 70 years / Cowdenbeath Mines Rescue Station. — [Cowdenbeath?] : [The Station?], [1980]. — 12p : ports ; 21cm
Unpriced (pbk) B81-17647

363.1'19622334'094223 — Kent. Coal mines. Industrial health & safety — *Serials*
Coal mines. Southern District. — 1979. — [London] ([259, Marylebone Rd., NW1 5RR]) : Health and Safety Executive, 1980. — 9p
ISBN 0-7176-0051-3 : £0.60 B81-06733

363.1'19622334'09424 — England. South Midlands. Coal mines. Industrial health & safety — *Serials*
Coal mines. South Midlands district. — 1979. — [London] ([259, Marylebone Rd., NW1 5RR]) : Health and Safety Executive, 1980. — 11p
ISBN 0-7176-0056-4 : £1.00 B81-06731

363.1'19622334'09424 — England. West Midlands. Coal mines. Industrial health & safety - *Serials*
Coal mines. West Midlands and North Western District. — 1979. — [London] ([259, Marylebone Rd., NW1 5RR]) : Health and Safety Executive, 1980. — 18p
ISBN 0-7176-0054-8 : £1.00
Also classified at 363.1'19622334'09427 B81-06732

363.1'19622334'09427 — North-west England. Coal mines. Industrial health & safety — *Serials*
Coal mines. West Midlands and North Western District. — 1979. — [London] ([259, Marylebone Rd., NW1 5RR]) : Health and Safety Executive, 1980. — 18p
ISBN 0-7176-0054-8 : £1.00
Primary classification 363.1'19622334'09424 B81-06732

363.1'19624'0941 — Great Britain. Construction industries. Industrial safety — *Conference proceedings*
Safe construction for the future : proceedings of a conference / organized by the Institution of Civil Engineers and held in London on 29 January 1980. — London : Institution of Civil Engineers, 1980. — vi,114p : forms ; 22cm
ISBN 0-7277-0105-3 : £8.50 B81-10084

363.1'19641 — Great Britain. Food & drinks industries & trades. Safety measures, *1975-1980*
The **Drinks** industry 1975-1980. — London : H.M.S.O., Dec.1981. — [60]p
ISBN 0-11-883458-4 (pbk) : CIP entry B81-31376

363.1'19658875 — Great Britain. Warehouses. Accidents: Explosions — *Inquiry reports*
The **Fire** and explosions at Permaflex Ltd, Trubshaw Cross, Longport, Stoke on Trent, 11 February 1980 / Health and Safety Executive. — Newcastle-under-Lyme (c/o Area Director, Marches Area, The Marches House, Midway, Newcastle-under-Lyme, Staffs ST5 1DT) : The Executive 1981. — [8]p : 1map,1plan ; 30cm
Ill on inside cover
ISBN 0-7176-0073-4 (pbk) : £1.00 B81-17382

363.1'22'0941 — Great Britain. Railways. Accidents, *1906-1960*
Hamilton, J. A. B.. Trains to nowhere : British Steam train accidents 1906-1960 / J.A.B. Hamilton. — 2nd ed. / rev. by Malcolm Gerard. — London : Allen & Unwin, 1981. — 96p : ill,ports ; 23cm. — (Steam past)
Previous ed.: published as British railway accidents of the twentieth century. 1967. — Includes index
ISBN 0-04-385084-7 : £6.95 : CIP rev. B81-04252

363.1'2265'0941 — Great Britain. Railways. Accidents — *Inquiry reports*
Great Britain. *Department of Transport.* Railway accident : report on the derailment that occurred on 13th August 1979 at Bushbury Junction, in the London Midland Region, British Railways / Department of Transport. — London : H.M.S.O., 1980. — 7p,[1] leaf of plates : ill,1map ; 30cm
Map, ill on 2 folded leaves attached to inside cover
ISBN 0-11-550525-3 (pbk) : £2.20 B81-00808

Great Britain. *Department of Transport.* Railway accident : report on the accident that occurred on 22nd December 1978 at Milford Level Crossing in the Southern Region British Railways / Department of Transport. — London : H.M.S.O., 1980. — 4p : maps ; 30cm
ISBN 0-11-550526-1 (unbound) : £1.20 B81-02129

Great Britain. *Department of Transport.* Railway accident : report on the derailment that occurred on 16th February 1980 at Bushey in the London Midland Region British Railways. — London : H.M.S.O., 1981. — 13p,[4]p of plates : ill ; 31cm
At head of title: Department of Transport. — General site plan (folded leaf) attached to inside back cover
ISBN 0-11-550537-7 (pbk) : £4.70 B81-25583

Great Britain. *Department of Transport.* Railway accident : report on the collision that occurred on 5th June 1980 at Hyndland Junction, near Glasgow in the Scottish Region British Railways / Department of Transport. — London : H.M.S.O, 1981. — 9p : 1ill,2maps ; 30cm
ISBN 0-11-550546-6 (unbound) : £2.20 B81-33592

Great Britain. *Department of Transport.* Railway accident : report on the collision that occurred on 1st March 1979 at Naas Public Level Crossing in the Western Region British Railways / Department of Transport. — London : H.M.S.O., 1981. — 12p,[1]leaf of plates : 1ill,1map ; 30cm
Map on folded sheet tipped in
ISBN 0-11-550551-2 (pbk) : £3.50 B81-38752

Great Britain. *Department of Transport.* Railway accident, report on the collision that occurred on 8th November 1977 at Napsbury in the London Midland Region, British Railways / Department of Transport. — London : H.M.S.O., 1981. — 11p : ill ; 30cm
ISBN 0-11-550535-0 (unbound) : £2.20 B81-23184

Great Britain. *Railway Inspectorate.* Railway accident, report on the accident that occurred on 15th November 1980 at Riccall Turnhead AHB Level Crossing in the Eastern Region British Railways / Department of Transport [Railway Inspectorate]. — London : H.M.S.O., 1981. — 2p : 1ill,1map ; 30cm
ISBN 0-11-550544-x (unbound) : £1.90 B81-30051

Great Britain. *Railway Inspectorate.* Railway accident, report on the collision that occurred on 6th February 1978 at Hertford North Station in the Eastern Region of British Railways / Department of Transport [Railway Inspectorate]. — London : H.M.S.O., 1981. — 13p : 2ill,1map ; 30cm
ISBN 0-11-550542-3 (unbound) : £2.20 B81-30049

Great Britain. *Railway Inspectorate.* Railway accident, report on the collision that occurred on 16th April 1979 near Paisley (Gilmour Street) in the Scottish Region British Railways / Department of Transport [Railway Inspectorate]. — London : H.M.S.O., 1981. — 11p,[3]p of plates : ill ; 30cm
Folded leaf attached to back cover
ISBN 0-11-550545-8 (pbk) : £3.20 B81-38575

363.1'2265'0941 — Great Britain. Railways. Accidents — *Inquiry reports* *continuation*
Great Britain. *Railway Inspectorate.* Railway accident, report on the collision that occurred on 17th January 1979 between Leyton and Stratford on the Central Line of London Transport Railways / Department of Transport [Railway Inspectorate]. — London : H.M.S.O., 1981. — 5p,[1]folded leaf of plates : 1ill,1map ; 30cm
ISBN 0-11-550541-5 (pbk) : £2.70 B81-30050

Great Britain. *Railway Inspectorate.* Railway accident, report on the collision that occurred on 22nd October 1979 at Invergowrie in the Scottish Region British Railways / Department of Transport [Railway Inspectorate]. — London : H.M.S.O., 1981. — 22p : ill,1 map,1plan ; 30cm
ISBN 0-11-550543-1 (unbound) : £2.50 B81-38574

363.1'23 — Freight transport. Shipping. Ships. Bulk cargoes. Safety — *Standards*
Inter-Governmental Maritime Consultative Organization. Code of safe practice for solid bulk cargoes : including cargoes which may liquefy and those possessing chemical hazards / [Inter-Governmental Maritime Consultative organization]. — [4th ed.]. — London : The Organization, 1980. — 91p : ill ; 21cm
Previous ed.: published as Code of safe practice for bulk cargoes. 1977. — Includes index
ISBN 92-8011-105-1 (pbk) : Unpriced B81-06295

363.1'23'091631 — North Atlantic Ocean. Liners: Andrea Doria *(Ship).* **Sinking,** *1956*
Hoffer, William. Saved! : the story of the Andrea Doria - the greatest sea rescue in history / William Hoffer. — London : Macmillan, 1980. — 249p,[16]p of plates : ill(some col.),1map,ports ; 23cm
Ill on lining papers. — Includes index
ISBN 0-333-27877-1 : £6.95 B81-12164

363.1'23'091631 — North Atlantic Ocean. Passenger transport. Shipping. Steam liners: Andrea Doria *(Ship).* **Sinking,** *1956*
Hoffer, William. Saved! : the story of the Andrea Doria — the greatest sea rescue in history / William Hoffer. — London : Pan in association with Macmillan, 1981, c1979. — 224p,[8]p of plates : ill,1map ; 18cm
Originally published: New York : Summit, 1979 ; London : Macmillan, 1980. — Includes index
ISBN 0-330-26232-7 (pbk) : £1.50 B81-08552

363.1'23'094237 — Cornwall. Coastal waters. Shipwrecks, *1872-1967* — *Illustrations*
Shipwreck / text by John Fowles ; photography by the Gibsons of Scilly. — London : Sphere, 1981, c1974. — [48]p : chiefly ill,2maps ; 21x25cm
Originally published: London : Cape, 1974. — Bibliography: p[16]
ISBN 0-7221-3635-8 (pbk) : Unpriced B81-28918

363.1'23'0942381 — Somerset. Berrow. Coastal waters. Shipwrecks: Nornen *(Ship),* *1897*
Jordan, Christopher. The Berrow wreck / by Christopher Jordan. — Bristol (17 Russet Close, Olveston, Bristol, BS12 3EE) : C. Jordan, 1978 (1979 [printing]). — [4]p,[5]p of plates : ill ; 21cm
Cover title
£0.35 (pbk) B81-09319

363.1'2365 — British merchant ships. Sinking — *Inquiry reports*
The **Merchant** Shipping Act 1894, report of Court no.8068, m.v. Pool Fisher, formal investigation. — London : H.M.S.O., 1981. — 9p ; 30cm
ISBN 0-11-511663-x (pbk) : £2.50 B81-14571

363.1'2381 — Sea rescue services. Organisation — *Manuals*
IMCO search and rescue manual / Inter-Governmental Maritime Consultative Organization. — London ([101 Piccadilly, W1V 0AE]) : The Organization, 1980. — vi,151p : ill,forms ; 25cm
ISBN 92-8011-107-8 (pbk) : Unpriced B81-40680

363.1'2381'06041 — Great Britain. Lifeboat services. Organisations: Royal National Life-boat Institution, *to 1980*
Howarth, Patrick. Lifeboat : in danger's hour / Patrick Howarth ; foreword by Clare Francis. — London : Hamlyn, 1981. — 144p : ill(some col.),1map,1facsim,ports(some col.) ; 31cm
Includes index
ISBN 0-600-34959-4 : £6.95 B81-24464

363.1'2381'0922 — England. Coastal waters. Rescues by lifeboat services, *1939-1979* — *Personal observations* — *Collections*
Beattie, John, *1941-.* Lifeboats to the rescue / John Beattie. — Newton Abbot : David & Charles, c1980. — 172p,[16]p of plates : ill,ports ; 23cm
ISBN 0-7153-8103-2 : £5.95 : CIP rev. B81-07491

363.1'2381'094253 — Lincolnshire. Lifeboat services, *1827-1864*
Farr, Grahame. The Lincolnshire Coast Shipwreck Association 1827-1864 / Grahame Farr. — Bristol (98 Combe Ave., Portishead, Bristol BS20 9JX) : G. Farr, 1981. — 16p : ill,1map ; 21cm. — (Papers on life-boat history ; no.6)
Cover title. — Text, map on covers
ISBN 0-905033-07-8 (pbk) : £0.60 B81-37834

363.1'2381'0942612 — Norfolk. Cromer. Lifeboat services, *to 1979*
Malster, Robert. The Cromer lifeboats 1804-1979 / [R.W. Malster and P.J.R. Stibbons]. — Cromer ([4A Chesterfield Villas, West St., Cromer, Norfolk NR27 9ED]) : Poppyland, 1979. — 24p : ill(some col.),1facsim,ports ; 21cm
Text and ill on inside covers
ISBN 0-9504300-2-1 (pbk) : £0.60 B81-21861

363.1'2381'0942612 — Norfolk. Cromer. Lifeboat services, *to 1981*
Malster, Robert. The Cromer lifeboats 1804-1981 / R.W. Malster and P.J.R. Stibbons. — 2nd (rev.) ed. — Norfolk : Poppyland Publishing, 1981. — 24p : ill,1facsim,ports ; 21cm
Cover title. — Previous ed.: 1979. — Text on inside covers
ISBN 0-9504300-9-9 (pbk) : £0.90 B81-41032

363.1'2381'0942612 — Norfolk. Sheringham. Lifeboat services, *to 1981*
Malster, Robert. The Sheringham lifeboats 1838-1981 / R.W. Malster. — Norfolk : Poppyland Publishing, 1981. — 24p : ill ; 21cm
Cover title. — Text on inside covers
ISBN 0-9504300-8-0 (pbk) : £0.90 B81-41031

363.1'2381'0942854 — Cleveland. Redcar. Lifeboat services, *to 1980*
Phillipson, David, *1944-.* Come along brave boys, come along! : a history of Redcar's lifeboats / by David Phillipson. — Redcar : Sotheran, c1981. — 64p : ill,port ; 21x22cm
ISBN 0-905032-10-1 (cased) : Unpriced
ISBN 0-905032-11-x (pbk) : £1.95 B81-29896

363.1'24 — Air passenger transport services. Safety aspects
Norris, William, *1933-.* The unsafe sky / William Norris. — London : Arrow, 1981. — 223p ; 18cm
ISBN 0-09-926600-8 (pbk) : £1.50 B81-29878

363.1'24'05 — British registered aircraft. Accidents — *Serials*
Accidents to aircraft on the British register / Civil Aviation Authority. — 1979. — Cheltenham (Greville House, 37 Gratton Rd., Cheltenham) : The Authority, 1980. — viii,72p. — (CAP 433)
ISBN 0-86039-121-3 : Unpriced
ISSN 0306-3550 B81-06551

363.1'24'05 — Great Britain. Civil aircraft. Accidents — *Serials*
Civil Aviation Authority. Follow-up action on accident reports / Civil Aviation Authority. — F1/79. — Redhill (Brabazon House, Redhill, Surrey RH1 1SQ) : Accident Analysis Branch, 1979-. — v. ; 30cm
Irregular. — Description based on: F1/81
ISSN 0261-9792 = Follow-up action on accident reports - Civil Aviation Authority : Unpriced B81-36531

363.1'2465 — Aircraft. Accidents — *Inquiry reports*
Great Britain. *Accidents Investigation Branch.* Cessna 421 G-AYMM : report on the accident near Stansted Airport, Essex, on 4th September 1978 / Accidents Investigation Branch. — London : H.M.S.O., c1979. — 19p ; 30cm. — (Aircraft accident report ; 6/80)
ISBN 0-11-513174-4 (pbk) : £2.80 B81-15756

Great Britain. *Accidents Investigation Branch.* Cessna F150L G-BAZP, Socata Rallye 150ST G-BEVX : report on the collision at Biggin Hill Aerodrome, Kent on 25 November 1978 / Accidents Investigation Branch. — London : H.M.S.O., 1980. — 16p : ill,2maps ; 30cm. — (Aircraft accident report ; 4/80)
ISBN 0-11-512982-0 (pbk) : £2.80 B81-02500

Great Britain. *Accidents Investigation Branch.* Piper PA-34 (Seneca II) G-BFKO : report on the accident at Beaulieu Heath, Hampshire, on 17 November 1979 / Department of Trade, Accidents Investigation Branch. — London : H.M.S.O., c1979. — 29p,3leaves of plates (1folded) : ill,charts ; 29cm. — (Aircraft accident report ; 7/80)
Bibliography: p29
ISBN 0-11-513175-2 (pbk) : £3.80 B81-26982

Great Britain. *Accidents Investigation Branch.* Report on the accident to BAe HS 748 G-BEKF at Sumburgh Airport, Shetland Islands, on 31 July 1979 / Department of Trade, [Accidents Investigation Branch]. — London : H.M.S.O., 1981. — 44,[8]p,[11]p of plates : ill,1maps ; 30cm. — (Aircraft accident report ; 1/81)
ISBN 0-11-513177-9 (pbk) : £5.40 B81-33593

Great Britain. *Accidents Investigation Branch.* Report on the accident to Cessna 414 G-BAOZ near Leeds/Bradford Airport on 23 March 1980 / Department of Trade [Accidents Investigation Branch]. — London : H.M.S.O., 1981. — iii,14p ; 30cm. — (Aircraft accident report ; 2/81)
ISBN 0-11-513495-6 (pbk) : £2.80 B81-36186

Great Britain. *Accidents Investigation Branch.* Report on the accident to Vickers Viscount 735 G-BFYZ at Kirkwall Airport, Orkney Islands on 25 October 1979 / Department of Trade [Accidents Investigation Branch]. — London : H.M.S.O., 1981. — 22p,[5]leaves of plates(one folded) : ill,1map,1plan ; 30cm. — (Aircraft accident report ; 4/81)
ISBN 0-11-513497-2 (pbk) : £4.15 B81-38751

Report on the accident to Boeing 747-121 N771PA at London Heathrow Airport, on 27 December 1979 / Department of Trade [Accidents Investigation Branch]. — London : H.M.S.O., c1981. — 28p : ill ; 30cm. — (Aircraft accident report ; 5/81)
ISBN 0-11-513498-0 (pbk) : £4.15 B81-40394

Report on the accident to Canadair CL44G-ATZH near Waglan Island, Hong Kong, on 2nd September 1977 / Civil Aviation Department, Accident Investigation Division. — London : H.M.S.O., 1980. — 20,[11]p : ill,1map ; 30cm. — (Aircraft accident report ; 8/80)
ISBN 0-11-512984-7 (pbk) : £3.10 B81-14620

United States. *National Transportation Safety Board.* Report on the accident to Redcoat Air Cargo Ltd. Bristol Britannia 253F G-BRAC at Billerica, Massachusetts, U.S.A., on 16 February 1980 / ... by the United States National Transportation Safety Board. — London : H.M.S.O., 1981. — ii,43p(1fold.) : ill,1map ; 30cm. — (Aircraft accident report ; 3/81)
At head of title: Department of Trade
ISBN 0-11-513178-7 (pbk) : £4.50 B81-36105

363.1'2492 — Great Britain. Aircraft. Airmisses — *Case studies* — *Serials*
General aviation airmisses : [a review of selected incidents] / Joint Airmiss Working Group. — May 1980-. — London : Civil Aviation Authority, 1980-. — v. ; 30cm
Quarterly
ISSN 0144-2481 = General aviation airmisses : Free to General Aviation operators only B81-02010

363.1'25 — Great Britain. Motorways & trunk roads. Road works. Implications of Health and Safety at Work etc. Act 1974

Notes for guidance in relation to the implementation of the requirements of the Health and Safety at Work etc. Act 1974 so far as they affect personnel who are required to undertake work on motorways and trunk roads : joint report, providing / Department of Transport/County Surveyors' Society. — London (2 Marsham St., SW1P 3EB) : Department of Transport, 1980. — 94p : 1form ; 30cm
£2.50 (pbk) B81-40448

363.1'25'0941 — Great Britain. Road traffic. Accidents — *Statistics* — *Serials*

Road accidents, Great Britain / Department of Transport, Scottish Development Department [and] Welsh Office. — 1979. — London : H.M.S.O., 1981. — xx,52p
ISBN 0-11-550421-4 : £5.00
ISSN 0307-6822 B81-34045

363.1'2564 — Great Britain. Motorists. Blood & urine. Alcohol. Measurement. Analytical chemists — *Directories*

Royal Society of Chemistry. Road Traffic Act 1972 : alcohol content of blood and urine. — Revised. — London (30 Russell Sq., WC18 5DT) : Royal Society of Chemistry, 1981. — [15]p : 1map ; 15cm
Unpriced (unbound) B81-11550

363.1'2565 — Great Britain. Road traffic. Accidents. Investigation — *Manuals*

Byatt, R.. Manual of road accident investigation / R. Byatt, R. Watts. — London : Pitman
Vol.2. — 1981. — vi,167p : ill ; 23cm
Includes index
ISBN 0-273-01600-8 : Unpriced B81-11583

363.1'257 — Hertfordshire. Road traffic. Accidents. Effects of improvement of blacksites, ***1971-1980***

Before and after study : traffic accidents : black sites : up dated to 1st January 1981. — [Hertford] ([Goldings, Hertford SG14 2PY]) : Hertfordshire County Council, Highways Dept., [1981]. — [22]leaves ; 30cm. — (H.C.C. T/287/1)
Unpriced (spiral) B81-38043

363.1'2572 — Road traffic. Fatal accidents. Reduction. Effects of compulsory wearing of motor vehicle seat belts

Adams, John, *1938 Aug. 13-*. The efficacy of seat belt legislation : a comparative study of road accident fatality statistics from 18 countries / John Adams. — London (26 Bedford Way, WC1H 0AP) : Department of Geography, University College London, 1981. — 20p : ill ; 30cm. — (Occasional papers / University College, London. Department of Geography ; no.38)
Unpriced (pbk) B81-39039

363.1'2575 — Motor vehicles. Seat belts. Safety aspects

Seatbelt sense / RoSPA. — Birmingham : Royal Society for the Prevention of Accidents, [1981?]. — 6p ; 30cm
Unpriced (unbound) B81-24794

363.1'2575 — Road safety

Foot, Hugh C.. Road safety. — Eastbourne : Praeger, Aug.1981. — [196]p
ISBN 0-03-060054-5 : £12.50 : CIP entry B81-18172

363.1'2575 — Road safety — *For children*

Wise, Rachel. Let's go across the road / by Rachel Wise. — London : Watts, c1980. — 32p : col.ill ; 22cm. — (Let's go series)
ISBN 0-85166-785-6 : £2.99 B81-00063

363.1'2575'0941 — Great Britain. Road safety — *For road safety officers*

Handbook for road safety officers / written and compiled by road safety officers in conjunction with the Royal Society for the Prevention of Accidents. — Birmingham : The Society, 1980. — 112p : ill ; 24cm
Includes bibliographies and index
£12.50 (spiral) B81-22073

363.1'2575'09417 — Ireland ***(Republic).*** **Motor vehicles. Driving. Road safety** — *For motorists*

Eccles, Jim. Questions and answers to help for the Eire driving test / [Jim Eccles & Des Murphy]. — [Dundalk] ([8, Boyle O'Reilly Terrace, Dundalk, Eire]) : J. Eccles and D. Murphy, c1981. — 15p ; 16cm
Unpriced (pbk) B81-40364

363.1'3'0941 — Great Britain. Residences. Accidents

Home safety facts & figures : the basic facts and figures about home safety ... a valuable quick reference guidc for the professional. — Birmingham : Royal Society for the Prevention of Accidents, 1981. — 9p ; 30cm
Cover title
Unpriced (pbk) B81-09430

363.1'3'0973 — United States. Domestic emergencies — *Amateurs' manuals*

Home emergency repair book / by Xyzyx Information Corporation. — New York ; London : McGraw-Hill, c1978. — 191p : ill ; 28cm
Originally published: in 2 vols. H.E.L.P., home emergency ladies pal ; and, More H.E.L.P. for home care. 1972
ISBN 0-07-072229-3 (pbk) : £5.95
Also classified at 643'.7'0973 B81-16444

363.1'37 — Residences. Accidents. Prevention — *Manuals*

Ewart, Neil. Unsafe as houses : a guide to home safety / Neil Ewart. — Poole : Blandford, 1981. — 157p : ill ; 23cm
ISBN 0-7137-1090-x : £4.95 B81-10777

363.1'4 — Mountain rescue, ***1935-1979*** — *Case studies*

High drama : mountain rescue stories from four continents / [edited by] Hamish MacInnes. — London : Hodder and Stoughton, 1980. — 208p,[16]p of plates : ill,maps,ports ; 23cm
Includes index
ISBN 0-340-24559-x : £7.95 : CIP rev. B80-18323

363.1'4 — Mountain rescue — *Manuals*

Setnicka, Tim J.. Wilderness search and rescue / Tim J. Setnicka ; edited by Kenneth Andrasko ; illustrations by Valerie Cohen and Judith DuBois. — Leicester : Cordee, c1980. — xi,640p : ill,maps,ports ; 22cm
Includes bibliographies and index
ISBN 0-904405-21-4 (pbk) : £8.50 B81-25392

363.1'775 — Dangerous materials for transport by road. Safety measures — *Proposals*

Great Britain. *Health and Safety Commission*. Proposals for dangerous substances (conveyance by road in road tankers and tank containers) regulations 1980 : second consultative document / Health and Safety Commission. — London : H.M.S.O., 1980. — 64p : ill ; 30cm
ISBN 0-11-883270-0 (pbk) : £3.00 B81-20052

363.1'79 — Chemistry laboratories. Safety measures — *Manuals*

Hazards in the chemical laboratory. — 3rd ed / edited by L. Bretherick. — London : Royal Society of Chemistry, 1981. — xxi,567p : ill ; 22cm
Previous ed.: Chemical Society, 1977. — Includes bibliographies and index
ISBN 0-85186-419-8 (pbk) : Unpriced : CIP rev. B81-05141

363.1'79 — Great Britain. Compressed gases. Accidents. Emergency action — *Manuals*

British Compressed Gases Association. Guidance notes on the preparation of major procedures / [British Compressed Gases Association]. — London (c/o Chemical Industries Association Ltd, 93 Albert Embankment, SE1 7TU) : British Compressed Gases Association, 1977. — 16p ; 21cm
Unpriced (pbk) B81-25950

363.1'79 — Great Britain. Dangerous industrial chemicals. Exposure of personnel. Safety aspects. Information sources — *For safety representative*

Chemical information - a guide for safety reps. — London : LRD, 1981. — 30p : 1form ; 21cm
ISBN 0-900508-42-6 (pbk) : £0.70 B81-29709

363.1'79 — Great Britain. Electricity. Generation. Fuels. Health aspects

Ferguson, R. A. D.. Comparative risks of electricity generating fuel systems in the UK. — Stevenage : Peregrinus, Nov.1981. — [216]p
ISBN 0-906048-66-4 : £30.00 : CIP entry B81-34212

363.1'79 — Great Britain. Ionising radiation. Safety measures. Organisations: National Radiological Protection Board — *Accounts* — *Serials*

National Radiological Protection Board. Account / National Radiological Protection Board. — 1979-80. — London : H.M.S.O., 1981. — 4p
ISBN 0-10-212781-6 : £0.70 B81-16821

363.1'79 — Great Britain. Nuclear power. Safety measures, ***1939-1980***

Chicken, John C.. Nuclear power hazard control policy. — Oxford : Pergamon, Dec.1981. — [280]p
ISBN 0-08-023254-x (cased) : £20.00 : CIP entry
ISBN 0-08-023255-8 (pbk) : £7.50 B81-32603

363.1'79 — Great Britain. Radioactive waste materials. Disposal — *Serials*

Annual survey of radioactive discharges in Great Britain / prepared by the Department of the Environment for the Secretaries of State for the Environment, Scotland and Wales. — 1979. — London (Beckett House, Room 419, Lambeth Palace Rd, SE1 7ER) : Department of the Environment, Radioactive Waste Administrative Division, 1980. — v,65p
ISSN 0144-834x : Unpriced B81-03889

363.1'79 — Great Britain. Testing laboratories. Specimens: Salmonella typhi. Safety measures — *Standards*

British Association for Chemical Specialities. Code of practice for the handling of Salmonella typhi NCTC 786 / [British Association for Chemical Specialities]. — London (93 Albert Embankment SE1 7TU) : [The Association], [1981]. — 7leaves : 2facsims ; 32cm
Unpriced (pbk) B81-37365

363.1'79 — Ionising radiation. Public health aspects

Living with radiation / National Radiological Protection Board. — 2nd ed. — [London] : [H.M.S.O.], 1981. — 48p : ill,1map ; 20x21cm
Cover title. — Previous ed.: 1973. — Bibliography: p44
ISBN 0-85951-145-6 (pbk) : £0.50 B81-22225

363.1'79 — Ionising radiation. Safety measures — *Conference proceedings*

European Scientific Seminar *(1979 : Luxembourg)*. Radiation protection optimization : present experience and methods : proceedings of the European Scientific Seminar held in Luxembourg, October 3-5, 1979 / editors A. Oudiz ... [et al.]. — Oxford : Pergamon, 1981. — xi,322p : ill,maps ; 26cm
At head of title: Commission of the European Communities, Commissariat à l'énergie atomique
ISBN 0-08-027291-6 : £20.00 B81-17362

363.1'79 — Italy. Seveso. Chemical engineering plants. Accidents: Explosions, ***1976.*** **Effects**

Margerison, Tom. The superpoison 1976-1978 / Tom Margerison, Marjorie Wallace, Dalbert Hallenstein. — London : Macmillan, 1981. — 236p ; 23cm
Originally published: 1979. — Bibliography: p227-229. — Includes index
ISBN 0-333-22797-2 : £7.95 B81-23262

363.1'79 — Liquefied petroleum gas. Hazards

Jones, Clive, *1939-*. Great balls of fire / Clive Jones, Richard L. Sands. — Coventry (26 Exhall Green, Exhall, Coventry) : C. Jones, R.L. Sands, 1981. — 103p : ill ; 30cm
Includes index
Unpriced (pbk) B81-07502

363.1'79 — Microbiology laboratories. Safety measures — *Manuals*

Laboratory safety : theory and practice / edited by Anthony A. Fuscaldo, Barry J. Erlick, Barbara Hindman. — New York ; London : Academic Press, 1980. — xiv,357p : ill ; 24cm
Includes bibliographies and index
ISBN 0-12-269980-7 : £22.20 B81-17592

363.1′79 — N-nitroso compounds. Public health aspects — *Conference proceedings*
Safety evaluation of nitrosatable drugs and chemicals / edited by G.G. Gibson and C. Ioannides. — London : Taylor & Francis, 1981. — ix,285p : ill ; 24cm
Conference papers. — Includes bibliographies and index
ISBN 0-85066-212-5 : £15.00 : CIP rev. B81-04199

363.1′79 — Nuclear power. Hazards
Caldicott, Helen. Nuclear madness : what you can do! : with a new chapter on Three Mile Island / Helen Caldicott with the assistance of Nancy Herrington & Nahum Stiskin. — New York ; London : Bantam, 1980. — 116p : 1map ; 18cm
Originally published: Sydney : Methuen of Australia, 1979. — Bibliography: p106-116
ISBN 0-553-14606-8 (pbk) : £1.25 B81-17168

Garrison, Jim, *1951-*. From Hiroshima to Harrisburg / Jim Garrison. — London : SCM Press, 1980. — x,275p : ill,1map ; 22cm
Ill on inside covers. — Includes index
ISBN 0-334-00504-3 (pbk) : £5.50 B81-37094

Murphy, Dervla. Race to the finish?. — London : J. Murray, Oct.1981. — [288]p
ISBN 0-7195-3884-x (cased) : £9.50 : CIP entry
ISBN 0-7195-3890-4 (pbk) : £4.95 B81-28106

363.1′79 — Radioisotopes. Ionising radiation. Safety aspects
Hughes, Donald. Notes on ionising radiations. — Northwood : Science Reviews, Dec.1981. — [120]p. — (Occupational hygiene monographs, ISSN 0141-7568 ; 5)
ISBN 0-905927-80-x (pbk) : £5.00 : CIP entry B81-36996

363.1′79 — Tritium. Safety aspects
Martin, E. B. M.. Health physics aspects of tritium. — Northwood : Science Reviews, Dec.1981. — [120]p. — (Occupational hygiene monographs, ISSN 0141-7568 ; 6)
ISBN 0-905927-85-0 (pbk) : £5.00 : CIP entry B81-36994

363.1′79 — United States. Dangerous chemicals. Spillage. Control measures. Management
Smith, Al J.. Managing hazardous substances accidents / Al J. Smith, Jr.. — New York ; London : McGraw-Hill, c1981. — xiv,188p : ill ; 24cm
Includes index
ISBN 0-07-058467-2 : £13.95 B81-23446

363.1′79 — Western Scotland. Coastal waters. Solutions of plutonium nitrate. Freight transport by ships. Safety aspects
Taylor, Peter, *1948-*. A critical review of safety assessments for the transport of plutonium nitrate solution between Dounreay and Windscale : a report / prepared for Greenpeace Ltd. by P. Taylor. — [London] ([c/o Greenpeace, 22 Colombo St., S.E.1]) : Political Ecology Research Group, c1980. — 14leaves ; 30cm. — (Special paper / Political Ecology Research Group, ISSN 0142-7989 ; SP-5)
Unpriced (pbk) B81-29252

363.1′89 — Computer systems. Visual display terminals. Health aspects
Guidance for safe working with visual display units. — London (93 Albert Embankment, SE1 7TU) : Chemical Industry Safety and Health Council of the Chemical Industries Association, 1980. — 12p ; 21cm
Unpriced (pbk) B81-14047

363.1′89 — Hospitals. Electric equipment. Safety measures
Ward, C. S.. Electrical safety in hospitals / C.S. Ward. — London : Kimpton, 1981. — viii,197p : ill ; 22cm
Includes index
ISBN 0-85313-807-9 (pbk) : £10.25 B81-24898

363.1′89 — Medicine. Radiology. Safety measures
Mould, R. F.. Radiation protection for nurses / by R.F. Mould. — [London] : [IPC Business], c1978. — [12]p : ill ; 30cm
ISBN 0-617-00225-8 (unbound) : £0.50 B81-36505

363.1′89 — Welders. Effects of fumes
Newhouse, Muriel L.. The present position concerning the biological effects of exposure to fume in welders / by Muriel L. Newhouse and Robert Murray. — Cambridge : Welding Institute, c1981. — 13p : 1ill ; 30cm
ISBN 0-85300-150-2 (pbk) : £5.20 B81-18503

363.1′9 — Great Britain. Toys. Safety aspects. Statutory regulations. Operation — *Personal observations*
Marcus, Stuart. Point five : an adventure story in politics / by Stuart Marcus with Roberta Routledge. — Swaffham ([Castleacre Rd., Swaffham, Norfolk]) : Trailworth, c1981. — 79p ; 22cm
Unpriced (pbk) B81-12210

363.1′92 — Food. Additives. Toxic effects
Handbook of international food regulatory toxicology. — Lancaster : MTP
Vol.2: Profiles / [edited by] Gaston Vettorazzi. — c1981. — 191p ; 24cm
Bibliography: p132-185. - Includes index
ISBN 0-85200-552-0 : £14.95 B81-19502

363.1′92 — Food. Contaminants — *Conference proceedings*
Group of European Nutritionists. *Symposium (16th : 1978 : Budapest)*. Foreign substances and nutrition : 16th Symposium of the Group of European Nutritionists, Budapest, November 8-10, 1978 / editors J.C. Somogyi, R. Tarjan. — Basel ; London : Karger, 1980. — 130p : ill ; 24cm. — (Bibliotheca nutritio et dieta ; no.29)
Includes one paper in German
ISBN 3-8055-0621-x (pbk) : £21.80 B81-03911

363.1′92 — Food. Contaminants: Fungi: Moulds. Growth. Determination. Use of quantitative analysis of chitin content
Smith, P. R.. The determination of chitin : a short literature review in relation to quantification of mould growth / P.R. Smith. — Leatherhead (Randalls Rd., Leatherhead, Surrey) : British Food Manufacturing Industries Research Accociation, 1980. — 11p : ill ; 30cm. — (Scientific and technical surveys / Leatherhead Food R.A., ISSN 0144-2074 ; no.124)
English text, English, French and German summaries. — Bibliography: p9-11
Unpriced (pbk) B81-16315

363.1′92 — Food. Contaminants: Pesticides — *Conference proceedings*
International Congress of Pesticide Chemistry *(4th : 1978 : Zurich)*. Pesticide residues : a contribution to their interpretation, relevance and legislation / editors H. Frehse, H. Geissbühler. — Oxford : Pergamon, c1979. — v,100p : ill ; 28cm
Includes index
ISBN 0-08-023931-5 : £14.50 : CIP rev. B79-10374

363.1′92 — Food. Contamination
Food safety / edited by Howard R. Roberts. — New York ; Chichester : Wiley, c1981. — xiii,339p ; 25cm
Includes index
ISBN 0-471-06458-0 : £24.50
Also classified at 613.2 B81-23425

363.1′92 — Food. Contamination by metal compounds
Reilly, Conor. Metal contamination of food / Conor Reilly. — London : Applied Science, c1980. — xvi,235p ; 23cm
Includes bibliographies and index
ISBN 0-85334-905-3 : £17.00 : CIP rev. B80-11896

363.1′92 — Food. Contamination by packaging materials: Plastics
Crosby, N. T.. Food packaging materials : aspects of analysis and migration of contaminants / N.T. Crosby. — London : Applied Science, c1981. — xiii,190p : ill ; 23cm
Includes index
ISBN 0-85334-926-6 : £14.00 B81-16779

363.1′9262 — Great Britain. Pre-cooked chilled food — *Standards*
Great Britain. *Department of Health and Social Security*. Guidelines on pre-cooked chilled food / Department of Health and Social Security. — London : H.M.S.O., 1980. — 16p ; 21cm
ISBN 0-11-320733-6 (unbound) : £1.90 B81-06127

363.1′927 — Food. Hygiene — *Manuals*
Alcock, P. A.. Food hygiene manual / by P.A. Alcock. — London : H.K. Lewis, 1980. — x,339p : 2ill,1plan ; 23cm
Bibliography: p335-336. — Includes index
ISBN 0-7186-0448-2 : £14.00 B81-00809

363.1′929 — Meat. Production. Public health aspects
Thornton, Horace. Thornton′s meat hygiene. — 7th ed. / J.F. Gracey. — London : Baillière Tindall, 1981. — viii,436p,4p of plates : ill (some col.) ; 26cm
Previous ed.: published as Textbook of meat hygiene / Horace Thornton and J.F. Gracey. 1974. — Includes index
ISBN 0-7020-0831-1 : £18.00
Also classified at 636.089′6 B81-22407

363.1′946′0973 — United States. Drugs. Regulation
Temin, Peter. Taking your medicine : drug regulation in the United States / Peter Temin. — Cambridge, Mass. ; London : Harvard University Press, 1980. — vii,274p : ill ; 25cm
Bibliography: p249-267. - Includes index
ISBN 0-674-86725-4 : £11.10 B81-05208

363.1′9475 — Drugs. Safety. Risk-benefit analysis — *Conference proceedings*
Risk-benefit analysis in drug research : proceedings of an international symposium held at the University of Kent at Canterbury, England 27 March 1980 / edited by J.F. Cavalla. — Lancaster : MTP, 1981. — x,197p : ill ; 25cm
Includes index
ISBN 0-85200-364-1 : £14.95 B81-19587

363.2 — POLICE

363.2 — England. Equipment. Purchase by police. Monitoring by Great Britain. *Home Office*. Great Britain. *Parliament. House of Commons. Committee of Public Accounts*. Fifth report. Session 1979-80 — *Critical studies*
Great Britain. *Treasury*. Treasury minute on the fifth report from the Committee of Public Accounts : session 1979-80. — London : H.M.S.O., [1980]. — 2p ; 25cm. — (Cmnd. ; 7992)
ISBN 0-10-179920-9 (unbound) : £0.50
Also classified at 354.410087′45543 B81-39928

363.2 — Great Britain. Security services
Aubrey, Crispin. Who′s watching you? / Crispin Aubrey. — Harmondsworth : Penguin, 1981. — 204p,[8]p of plates : ill,ports ; 18cm. — (Pelican books)
Bibliography: p197-199. - Includes index
ISBN 0-14-022283-9 (pbk) : £1.50 B81-07242

363.2 — Society. Role of police — *Case studies*
Shane, Paul G.. Police and people : a comparison of five countries / Paul G. Shane. — St. Louis ; London : Mosby, 1980. — ix,219p : ill,maps ; 24cm
Includes bibliographies and index
ISBN 0-8016-4556-5 (pbk) : £8.25 B81-08124

363.2 — West Midlands *(Metropolitan County)*. Birmingham. Handsworth. West Indian young persons. Relations with police — *Interviews*
Talking blues / [edited by Derek Bishton and Brian Homer] ; [patois edited by Phil Nanton] ; [additional material by Danzie Stewart] ; [interviews compiled by Carlton Green] ; [transcribed by Marcia Stewart and Cina Corcoran] ; [cover drawing by Martin Lealan] [photos by John Reardon, Derek Bishton and Brian Homer]. — Birmingham (1 Finch Rd., Lozells, Birmingham B21 9HE) : AFFOR, 1978 (1980 [printing]). — 47p : ill,1facsim ; 22cm
ISBN 0-907127-05-3 (pbk) : £0.80 B81-2224.

363.2′025′41 — Great Britain. Police — *Directories — Serials*

Police and constabulary almanac. — 1981. — Henley-on-Thames (P.O. Box 39, Henley-on-Thames, Oxon. RG9 SUA) : R. Hazell, 1981. — 292p
ISBN 0-901718-22-x : Unpriced
ISBN 0-901718-23-8 (pbk)
ISSN 0477-2008 B81-18797

363.2′092′2 — Merseyside *(Metropolitan County).* **Liverpool. Police: Merseyside Police.** *′A′ Division — Personal observations — Collections*

McClure, James. Spike Island : portrait of a police division / James McClure ; with a preface by K.G. Oxford. — London : Pan in association with Macmiillan, 1981, c1980. — 532p ; 18cm
Originally published: London : Macmillan, 1980
ISBN 0-330-26278-5 (pbk) : £1.95 B81-14117

363.2′092′4 — London. Police: Metropolitan Police. Slipper, Jack — *Biographies*

Slipper, Jack. Slipper of the Yard / Jack Slipper. — London : Sidgwick & Jackson, 1981. — xi,179p,[11]p of plates : ill,facsims,ports ; 24cm
Includes index
ISBN 0-283-98702-2 (cased) : £5.95
ISBN 0-283-98819-3 (pbk £1.50) B81-15400

363.2′092′4 — London. Southwark *(London Borough).* **Police: Metropolitan Police,** *1952-1979 — Personal observations*

Cole, Harry. Policeman′s lot / Harry Cole. — London : Fontana, 1981. — 219p ; 18cm
ISBN 0-00-636317-2 (pbk) : £1.50 B81-32925

363.2′0941 — Great Britain. Police

Modern policing / edited by David Watts Pope and Norman L. Weiner. — London : Croom Helm, c1981. — 271p : ill,1map ; 22cm
Includes bibliographies and index
ISBN 0-7099-2002-4 (cased) : £13.95 : CIP rev.
ISBN 0-7099-2008-3 (pbk) : Unpriced
B81-08823

363.2′0941 — Great Britain. Police — *For children*

Haddrell, Allan. A day with a policeman / Allan & Christine Haddrell. — Hove : Wayland, 1980. — 55p : ill ; 24cm. — (A day in the life)
Bibliography: p55
ISBN 0-85340-780-0 : £3.25 B81-02877

363.2′0941 — Great Britain. Police — *Illustrations — For children*

Gray, David T.. The police / illustrated by David T. Gray ; [text by] Constance Milburn. — Glasgow : Blackie, 1981. — 32p : chiefly col.ill ; 21cm. — (Inside story)
Includes index
ISBN 0-216-91034-x (pbk) : £0.95 B81-29244

363.2′09411 — Scotland. Police, *to 1979*

Gordon, Paul, *1954-.* Policing Scotland / Paul Gordon. — Glasgow (146 Holland St., Glasgow G2 4NG) : Scottish Council for Civil Liberties, c1980. — 133p : 1map ; 20cm
Bibliography: p130-133
ISBN 0-906502-03-9 (cased) : £5.95
ISBN 0-906502-02-0 (pbk) : £2.25 B81-00810

363.2′0942 — England. Police — *Statistics — Serials*

Police statistics. Actuals / CIPFA Statistical Information Service. — 1979-80. — London : Chartered Institute of Public Finance and Accountancy, 1980. — 23p
ISSN 0144-9915 (corrected) : £5.00 B81-04494

Police statistics. Estimates / CIPFA Statistical Information Service. — 1981-82. — London : Chartered Institute of Public Finance and Accountancy, 1981. — 47p in various pagings
ISSN 0144-9885 : £12.00 B81-35098

363.2′0942 — England. Society. Role of police, *1744-1913*

Policing and punishment in nineteenth-century Britain / edited by Victor Bailey. — London : Croom Helm, c1981. — 248p ; 23cm
Includes index
ISBN 0-7099-0626-9 : £11.95 : CIP rev.
Also classified at 364′.942 B81-12828

363.2′09421 — London. Police: Metropolitan Police — *Serials*

Metropolitan Police. *Commissioner.* Report of the Commissioner of Police of the Metropolis for the year ... : presented to Parliament by the Secretary of State for the Home Department ... — 1980. — London : H.M.S.O., 1981. — vi,112p. — (Cmnd. ; 8254)
ISBN 0-10-182540-4 : £6.40 B81-32912

363.2′09422′7 — Hampshire. Police: Hampshire Constabulary — *Serials*

Copperplate : the magazine of the Hampshire Constabulary. — Vol.1, no.1 (1978)-. — Liverpool (42 Stanley St., Liverpool L1 6AL) : M. W. Publications (Liverpool), 1978-. — v. : ill,ports ; 25cm
Two issues yearly. — Description based on: Vol.1, no.6 (Spring 1981)
ISSN 0261-5894 = Copperplate : £0.10 per issue B81-31590

363.2′09423′3 — Great Britain. Police — *Study regions: Dorset*

Sturman, Clive. Police / [Clive Sturman] ; editor Wendy Hobson ; designer Roger Perry. — Maidenhead : Purnell, 1981. — 123p : ill,ports ; 30cm
Ill on lining papers
ISBN 0-361-05082-8 : £4.50 B81-36891

363.2′0944′59 — France. Auvergne. Criminal law. Enforcement, *1720-1790*

Cameron, Iain A.. Crime and repression in the Auvergne and the Guyenne, 1720-1790. — Cambridge : Cambridge University Press, Dec.1981. — [283]p
ISBN 0-521-23882-x : £18.50 : CIP entry
Also classified at 363.2′0944′7 B81-32597

363.2′0944′7 — France. Guienne. Criminal law. Enforcement, *1720-1790*

Cameron, Iain A.. Crime and repression in the Auvergne and the Guyenne, 1720-1790. — Cambridge : Cambridge University Press, Dec.1981. — [283]p
ISBN 0-521-23882-x : £18.50 : CIP entry
Primary classification 363.2′0944′59 B81-32597

363.2′0973 — United States. Ghettos. Police. Role

Cooper, John L.. The police and the ghetto / John L. Cooper. — Port Washington, N.Y. ; London : National University Publications : Kennikat Press, 1980. — 158p ; 23cm. — (Multi-disciplinary studies in the law)
ISBN 0-8046-9250-5 : £11.45 B81-06016

363.2′0973 — United States. Police

Black, Donald, *1941-.* The manners and customs of the police / Donald Black. — New York ; London : Academic Press, c1980. — xiii,274p : forms ; 24cm
Bibliography: p247-264. — Includes index
ISBN 0-12-102880-1 (cased) : £15.80
ISBN 0-12-102882-8 (pbk) : £5.40 B81-17425

363.2′0973 — United States. Urban regions. Police, *1860-1920*

Monkkonen, Eric H.. Police in urban America 1860-1920 / Eric H. Monkkonen. — Cambridge : Cambridge University Press, 1981. — xv,220p : ill ; 24cm. — (Interdisciplinary perspectives on modern history)
Includes index
ISBN 0-521-23454-9 : £16.00 B81-17935

363.2′09778′66 — United States. Urban regions. Police. Cooperation — *Study regions: Missouri. St Louis region*

McDavid, James C.. Police cooperation and performance : the Greater St. Louis interlocal experience / by James C. McDavid. — University Park ; London : Pennsylvania State University Press, c1979. — 92p ; 23cm. — (The Pennsylvania State University studies ; no.46)
Bibliography: p87-92
ISBN 0-271-00221-2 (pbk) : Unpriced
B81-11714

363.2′2′0941 — Great Britain. Police. Duties — *Manuals*

English, J.. Police training manual / J. English, R. Houghton. — 3rd ed. — London : McGraw-Hill, c1981. — x,412p ; 24cm
Previous ed.: 1978. — Includes index
ISBN 0-07-084554-9 (pbk) : £4.95 B81-14588

363.2′2′0941 — Great Britain. Police. Front-line personnel. Organisational behaviour — *Sociological perspectives*

Jones, J. Mervyn. Organisational aspects of police behaviour / J. Mervyn Jones. — Farnborough, Hants. : Gower, c1980. — vi,182p : ill ; 23cm
Bibliography: p170-178. — Includes index
ISBN 0-566-00402-x : £11.50 : CIP rev.
B80-20455

363.2′32 — Washington, D.C.. Patrols by policewomen

Martin, Susan Ehrlich. Breaking and entering : policewomen on patrol / Susan Ehrlich Martin. — Berkeley ; London : University of California Press, c1980. — xvi,265p,[8]p of plates : ill,2ports ; 23cm
Bibliography: p235-248. - Includes index
ISBN 0-520-03908-4 : £9.00 B81-04527

363.2′32′0973 — United States. Police. Patrols

Hale, Charles D.. Police patrol : operations and management / Charles D. Hale ; editorial consultant Samuel. — New York ; Chichester : Wiley, c1981. — xiv,328p : ill,forms ; 25cm
Bibliography: p313-322. - Includes index
ISBN 0-471-03291-3 : Unpriced B81-08515

363.2′5 — England. Suspects. Interrogation by police. Tape recording — *Feasibility studies*

Barnes, J. A. (John Anthony). Police interrogation : tape recording / J.A. Barnes and N. Webster [for the] Royal Commission on Criminal Procedure. — London : H.M.S.O., 1980. — x,106p ; 25cm. — (Research study / Royal Commission on Criminal Procedure ; no.8)
Bibliography: p49
ISBN 0-11-730127-2 (pbk) : £4.75 B81-08331

363.2′5 — Forensic science

. Introduction to forensic sciences / edited by William G. Eckert. — St. Louis ; London : Mosby, 1980. — xiii,242p : ill ; 24cm
Bibliography: p213-222. — Includes index
ISBN 0-8016-1489-9 (pbk) : Unpriced
B81-08569

363.2′5 — Scenes of crimes. Criminal investigation

Svensson, Arne, *1914-.* Techniques of crime scene investigation. — 3rd ed. / Arne Svensson, Otto Wendel, Barry A.J. Fisher. — New York ; Oxford : Elsevier, c1981. — xvi,498p : ill,1plan ; 24cm. — (Elsevier series in forensic and police science)
Previous ed.: 1965. — Bibliography: p475-484. - Includes index
ISBN 0-444-00427-0 : £13.16 B81-23604

363.2′5 — United States. Arson. Investigation — *Manuals*

Roblee, Charles L.. The investigation of fires / Charles L. Roblee, Allen J. McKechnie. — Englewood Cliffs ; London : Prentice-Hall, c1981. — xiii,201p : ill ; 24cm
Bibliography: p189-191. — Includes index
ISBN 0-13-503169-9 : £9.70 B81-12676

363.2′5′072042 — England. Forensic science. Research organisations: Central Research Establishment — *Serials*

Central Research Establishment. Annual report / Home Office Central Research Establishment. — 1975. — [Aldermaston] ([Aldermaston, Reading, Berks. RG7 4PN]) : The Establishment, [1976]. — 103p
Unpriced B81-04037

Central Research Establishment. Annual report of the Director of the Central Research Establishment. — 1976. — Aldermaston (Aldermaston, Reading, Berks. RG7 4PN) : The Establishment, [1977]. — 90p
ISSN 0144-7246 : Unpriced B81-04038

Central Research Establishment. Annual report of the Director of the Central Research Establishment. — 1977. — Aldermaston (Aldermaston, Reading, Berks. RG7 4PN) : The Establishment, [1978]. — 123p
ISSN 0144-7246 : Unpriced B81-04039

363.2′5′072042 — England. Forensic science. Research organisations: Central Research Establishment — *Serials* *continuation*

Central Research Establishment. Annual report of the Director of the Central Research Establishment. — 1979. — Aldermaston (Aldermaston, Reading, Berks. RG7 4PN) : The Establishment, 1980. — 60p
ISSN 0144-7246 : Unpriced B81-04040

Central Research Establishment. Annual report of the Director of the Central Research Establishment. — 1980. — Aldermaston (Aldermaston, Reading, Berks. RG7 4PN) : [The Establishment], c1981. — [vi],85p
ISSN 0144-7246 : Unpriced B81-31030

363.2′5′0924 — Zimbabwe. Forensic science, *1963-1977* — *Personal observations*

Thompson, John, *1913 Feb.2-*. Crime scientist / John Thompson. — London : Harrap, 1980. — xi,184p,[16]p of plates : ill,2ports ; 23cm
Includes index
ISBN 0-245-53609-4 : £6.95 B81-04613

363.2′5′0941 — Great Britain. Criminal investigation, *1876-1941*

McConnell, Jean. The detectives : turning points in criminal investigation / Jean McConnell. — Large print ed. — Bath : Chivers, 1981, c1976. — 247p ; 23cm. — (A New Portway large print book)
Originally published: Newton Abbot : David & Charles, 1976
ISBN 0-85119-117-7 : £4.95 B81-23254

363.2′5′0942 — England. Crime. Investigation by police

Steer, David, *1944-*. Undercovering crime : the police role / David Steer. — London : H.M.S.O., 1980. — vii,136p ; 25cm. — (Research study / Royal Commission on Criminal Procedure ; no.7)
At head of title: Royal Commission on Criminal Procedure. — Bibliography: p127-129
ISBN 0-11-730126-4 (pbk) : £5.00 B81-08308

363.2′52′0924 — Great Britain. Informers: O′Mahoney, Maurice — *Biographies*

O′Mahoney, Maurice. King squealer / Maurice O′Mahoney with Dan Wooding. — London : Sphere, 1981, c1978. — 216p ; 18cm
Originally published: London : W.H. Allen, 1978
ISBN 0-7221-6555-2 (pbk) : £1.10 B81-14594

363.2′54 — United States. Lie dectectors. Use

Lykken, David Thoreson. A tremor in the blood : uses and abuses of the lie detector / David Thoreson Lykken. — New York ; London : McGraw-Hill, c1981. — xiii,317p ; 24cm
Includes index
ISBN 0-07-039210-2 : £8.95 B81-02940

363.2′89′025 — Private detectives — *Directories* — *Serials*

The **Regency** international directory of private investigators, private detectives, debt collecting agencies : covering also certificated bailiffs, status enquiry agents and trade protection societies. — 14th ed. (1981/81)-. — Folkestone : Regency International, c1980-. — v. ; 21cm
Annual. — Text in English, introduction and contents list also in French, German, Italian and Spanish. — Continues: The Regency international directory of enquiry agents, private detectives, debt collecting agencies
ISSN 0260-7778 = Regency international directory of private investigators, private detectives, debt collecting agencies : Unpriced B81-09041

363.3 — PUBLIC ORDER, DISASTER, FIRE SERVICES, ETC

363.3′0941 — Public order services. Role of Great Britain. *Army, 1945-1970.* **Kitson, Frank. Low intensity operations** — *Critical studies*

Ronin. High intensity subversion / by ′Ronin′. — Over the Water (Over the Water, Sanday, Orkney KW17 2BL) : Cienfuegos, 1981. — x,70p : ill,facsims,ports ; 30cm
Ill on inside covers
ISBN 0-904564-32-0 (pbk) : £3.50
Primary classification 355′.02184 B81-29191

363.3′1′0944 — France. Censorship, *1530-1607*

Grendler, Paul F.. Culture and censorship in late Renaissance Italy and France / Paul F. Grendler. — London : Variorum Reprints, 1981. — 318p in various pagings : facsims,1port ; 24cm
Includes index
ISBN 0-86078-084-8 : £24.00 : CIP rev.
Also classified at 363.3′1′0945 ; 944′.028 ; 945′.06 B81-22670

363.3′1′0945 — Italy. Censorship, *1530-1607*

Grendler, Paul F.. Culture and censorship in late Renaissance Italy and France / Paul F. Grendler. — London : Variorum Reprints, 1981. — 318p in various pagings : facsims,1port ; 24cm
Includes index
ISBN 0-86078-084-8 : £24.00 : CIP rev.
Primary classification 363.3′1′0944 B81-22670

363.3′48 — Great Britain. Helicopter rescue services, *to 1979*

Chartres, John. Helicopter rescue / John Chartres. — London : Ian Allan, 1980. — 160p : ill,maps,facsims,ports ; 30cm
Bibliography: p160
ISBN 0-7110-1062-5 : £9.95 B81-01760

363.3′483 — Disaster relief. Emergency housing — *Conference proceedings*

Disasters and the small dwelling / editor Ian Davis. — Oxford : Pergamon, 1981. — ix,220p : ill ; 29cm
Conference papers. — Includes index
ISBN 0-08-024753-9 : £12.50 B81-36482

363.3′492 — Famines caused by drought, *1972.* **Social aspects**

Drought and man. — Oxford : Pergamon, Sept.1981
Vol.2: The constant catastrophe. — [304]p
ISBN 0-08-025824-7 : £23.25 : CIP entry B81-23883

363.3′492 — Nigeria. Famines caused by drought, *1972-1974*

Apeldoorn, G. Jan van. Perspectives on drought and famine in Nigeria / G. Jan van Apeldoorn. — London : Allen & Unwin, 1981. — xii,184p : maps ; 23cm
Bibliography: p170-178. — Includes index
ISBN 0-04-301135-7 : Unpriced : CIP rev. B81-25141

363.3′497 — Russia *(RSFSR).* **Kyshtym. Nuclear explosions,** *ca 1957*

Medvedev, Zhores A.. Nuclear disaster in the Urals / Zhores A. Medvedev ; translated by George Saunders. — London : Angus & Robertson, 1979. — vii,214p : ill,facsims ; 22cm
Translation from the Russian. — Bibliography: p201-208. - Includes index
ISBN 0-207-95896-3 : £5.95 B81-19385

363.3′49875 — Nuclear warfare. Safety measures — *Manuals*

Goodwin, Peter. Nuclear war. — London (9 Henrietta St., W.C.2) : Ash and Grant, May 1981. — [128]p
ISBN 0-904069-43-5 : £4.95 : CIP entry B81-07589

363.3′5 — Nuclear warfare. Safety measures — *Manuals* — *For households*

Popkess, Barry. The nuclear survival handbook : living through and after a nuclear attack / Barry Popkess. — London : Arrow, 1980. — xiv,375p : ill,1map,1plan ; 18cm
Bibliography: p363-373. - Includes index
ISBN 0-09-924510-8 (pbk) : £1.75 B81-00064

363.3′5′05 — Civil defence — *Serials*

Protect & survive monthly & British civil defence news. — No.1 (Jan.1981)-. — London (80 Fleet St., EC4Y 1EL) : [Protect & Survive Ltd], 1981-. — v. : ill(some col.),plans,ports ; 30cm
Description based on: No.3 (Mar.1981)
ISSN 0261-2607 = Protect & survive monthly & British civil defence news : £11.00 per year B81-30002

363.3′5′0941 — Great Britain. Civil defence. Policies of government — *Peace Pledge Union viewpoints*

Civil defence. — London (6 Endsleigh St., W.C.1) : Peace Pledge Union, [1981?]. — 7-10p : ill ; 30cm
£0.10 (unbound) B81-35265

363.3′7′0941 — Great Britain. Fires — *Statistics* — *Serials*

Fire statistics United Kingdom / Home Office. Supplement for fire brigades. — 1978-. — London (50 Queen Anne′s Gate, SW1H 9AT) : Home Office, 1980-. — v. ; 30cm
Annual. — Continues in part: United Kingdom fire statistics
£1.00 B81-05935

Five statistics : United Kingdom 1979 : supplement for fire brigades. — London : Home Office, 1981. — [21]p ; 30cm
ISBN 0-903727-83-8 (spiral) : £1.50 B81-12540

363.3′765 — Fires. Investigation — *Manuals*

Richards, N. F.. How did it start? : a practical guide to tracing the cause of a fire / by N.F. Richards. — Leicester (148 New Walk, Leicester LE1 7QB) : Institution of Fire Engineers, c1980. — vi,58p : ill,1port ; 21cm
Unpriced (corrected : pbk) B81-06086

363.3′77′0941 — Great Britain. Fire protection services. Use of helicopters & light aircraft — *Proposals*

Joint Committee on Fire Brigade Operations. Report on the role of the helicopter and light aeroplane in the fire service / Joint Committee on Fire Brigade Operations. — London (Horseferry House, Dean Ryle St., S.W.1.) : Home Office, Fire Department, 1980. — 45p : 2ill ; 30cm
At head of title : Central Fire Brigades Advisory Councils for England, Wales and for Scotland
Unpriced (pbk) B81-37513

363.3′77′094261 — Norfolk. Fire prevention — *Manuals*

Norfolk fire prevention handbook / Norfolk Fire Service. — London (Publicity House, Streatham Hill, SW2 4TR) : Malcolm Page, [1981]. — 40p ; 21cm
Unpriced (pbk) B81-24083

363.3′78′0941 — Great Britain. Fire brigades — *For children*

Healey, Tim. Let′s go to a fire station / Tim Healey ; general editor Henry Pluckrose ; photography by Peter Acty. — London : Watts, 1981. — 32p : col.ill ; 22cm. — (Let′s go series)
ISBN 0-85166-938-7 : £2.99 B81-29193

363.4 — SERVICES FOR CONTROL OF PUBLIC MORALS

363.4′1′0973 — United States. Alcoholic drinks. Prohibition, *1920-1933*

Cashman, Sean Dennis. Prohibition : the lie of the land / Sean Dennis Cashman. — New York : Free Press ; London : Collier Macmillan, c1981. — xiv,290p,[16]p of plates : ill,maps,facsims,ports ; 25cm
Maps on lining papers. — Bibliography: p269-279. — Includes index
ISBN 0-02-905730-2 : £10.95 B81-36325

363.4′4′0924 — France. Courtesans: Otero, Caroline — *Biographies*

Castle, Charles, *1939-*. La Belle Otero : the last great courtesan / Charles Castle. — London : Joseph, 1981. — 192p,[16]p of plates : ill,ports ; 23cm
Includes index
ISBN 0-7181-1935-5 : £8.95 B81-34517

363.4′4′0924 — United States. Prostitution. Kimball, Nell — *Biographies*

Kimball, Nell. Nell Kimball : her life as an American madam / by herself ; edited and with an introduction by Stephen Longstreet. — London : Granada, 1981, c1970. — 336p ; 18cm. — (A Mayflower book)
Originally published: New York : Macmillan, 1970
ISBN 0-583-13347-9 (pbk) : £1.50 B81-27053

363.4'4'097471 — New York *(City)*. Prostitution

Cohen, Bernard, *1937-*. Deviant street networks : prostitution in New York City / Bernard Cohen. — Lexington : Lexington Books ; [Farnborough, Hants.] : Gower [distributor], c1980. — xvii,200p : ill ; 24cm
Bibliography: p183-187. — Includes index
ISBN 0-669-03949-7 : £12.50 B81-27617

363.4'6 — Abortion — *For schools*

Finnis, J. M.. What do you know about abortion? / by J.M. Finnis and C.W.A. Flynn ; drawings by Cherry Denman. — Rev. ed. — Witney (Bridge House, Witney, Oxon.) : Oxford School Publications, 1980. — iii,37p : ill,facsims ; 21x30cm
Previous ed.: 1976
ISBN 0-905697-02-2 (pbk) : £2.10 B81-14479

363.4'6 — Abortion. Social aspects

Abortion and sterilization : medical and social aspects / edited by Jane E. Hodgson. — London : Academic Press, 1981. — x,594p : ill ; 24cm
Includes bibliographies and index
ISBN 0-12-792030-7 : £20.20 B81-26322

363.4'6'0942496 — West Midlands *(Metropolitan County)*. Birmingham. Abortion, *1967-1977*

Abortion in Birmingham - ten years on : 1967 to 1977. — [Birmingham] ([135 Trafalgar Rd., Moseley, Birmingham 13]) : [Birmingham National Abortion Campaign], [1977]. — 16p : ill ; 27cm
Cover title
£0.25 (pbk) B81-10682

363.4'6'0973 — United States. Abortion

Jaffe, Frederick S.. Abortion politics : private morality and public policy / by Frederick S. Jaffe, Barbara L. Lindheim, Philip R. Lee. — New York ; London : McGraw-Hill, c1981. — viii,216p ; 24cm
Includes index
ISBN 0-07-032189-2 : £10.45 B81-10590

363.4'7 — Pornography — *Sociological perspectives*

Dworkin, Andrea. Pornography. — London : Women's Press, Oct.1981. — [304]p
ISBN 0-7043-3876-9 (pbk) : £4.75 : CIP entry B81-28064

Griffin, Susan. Pornography and silence. — London : Women's Press, Oct.1981. — [288]p
Originally published: New York : Harper & Row, 1981
ISBN 0-7043-3877-7 (pbk) : £4.75 : CIP entry B81-27968

363.4'9 — Homosexuals. Counselling

Woodman, Natalie Jane. Counseling with gay men and women : a guide for facilitating positive life-styles / Natalie Jane Woodman, Harry R. Lenna. — San Francisco ; London : Jossey-Bass, c1980. — xiv,144p ; 24cm. — (Jossey-Bass social and behavioral science series)
Bibliography: p130-139. — Includes index
ISBN 0-87589-468-2 : £10.35 B81-05600

363.5 — HOUSING

363.5 — Democracies. Housing. Policies of governments

Pugh, Cedric. Housing in capitalist societies / Cedric Pugh. — Farnborough : Gower, c1980. — xvii,300p ; 23cm
Includes bibliographies and index
ISBN 0-566-00336-8 : £15.00 : CIP rev. B80-19626

363.5 — England. Local authority housing. Coloured tenants. Harassment

Racial harassment on local authority housing estates : a report / prepared by the London Race and Housing Forum. — London : Commission for Racial Equality, 1981. — 25p : ill ; 30cm
Unpriced (pbk) B81-20658

363.5 — Scotland. Local authority housing. Tenants. Rent arrears. Recovery

Wilkinson, Diana. Rent arrears in public authority housing in Scotland / Diana Wilkinson [for the] Scottish Office, Central Research Unit. — Edinburgh : H.M.S.O., 1980. — vii,115p ; 25cm. — (A Scottish Office social research study)
ISBN 0-11-491691-8 (pbk) : £5.10 B81-09840

363.5 — Scotland. Northern Scotland. Mobile homes. Sites

Shelter. *Shelter (Scotland)*. Neglected too long : a report on the plight of mobile home residents in North and North-East Scotland / by Isla Laing and Nigel Lindsay. — Edinburgh (6 Castle St., Edinburgh EH2 3AT) : SHELTER (Scotland), [1980]. — 20p : ill ; 30cm
Cover title. — Ill on inside cover
£1.00 (pbk) B81-19449

363.5'068 — Great Britain. Housing. Management. Organisations: Institute of Housing — *Serials*

[Year book *(Institute of Housing)*]. Year book / the Institute of Housing. — 1980-. — London (12 Upper Belgrave St., SW1X 8BA) : The Institute, 1980-. — v. : ill ; 30cm
Continues: Year book with list of members and buyers' guide (Institute of Housing)
ISSN 0260-7239 = Year book - Institute of Housing : Unpriced B81-03887

[Year book with list of members and buyers' guide *(Institute of Housing)*]. Year book with list of members and buyers' guide / the Institute of Housing. — 1979. — London ([12 Upper Belgrave St., SW1X 8BA]) : The Institute, 1979. — 1v. : ill ; 30cm
Continues: Year book and list of members (Institute of Housing). — Continued by: Year book (Institute of Housing)
ISSN 0141-8769 = Year book with list of members and buyers' guide - Institute of Housing : £15.00 B81-03888

363.5'09172'4 — Developing countries. Housing. Provision

Hardoy, Jorge E.. Shelter : need and response : housing, land and settlement policies in seventeen Third World nations / Jorge E. Hardoy and David Satterthwaite. — Chichester : Wiley, c1981. — viii,288p : maps ; 26cm
Includes index
ISBN 0-471-27919-6 : £16.95 B81-21080

363.5'09172'4 — Developing countries. Urban regions. Low-income families. Housing

Drakakis-Smith, D. W.. Urbanisation, housing and the development process / David Drakakis-Smith. — London : Croom Helm, c1981. — 234p,[8]p of plates : ill,maps,plans ; 23cm. — (Croom Helm series in geography and environment)
Bibliography: p213-230. - Includes index
ISBN 0-7099-0464-9 : £15.95 : CIP rev. B80-19627

Shankland Cox Partnership. Third World urban housing : aspirations, resources, programmes, projects : a report prepared for the Overseas Division, Building Research Establishment, UK, from a study finance by Ministry of Overseas Development / by Shankland Cox Partnership. — Watford : Building Research Establishment, c1977. — 249p(2fold.) : ill,maps,plans,forms ; 30cm
Text on inside cover
Unpriced (pbk) B81-12543

363.5'09173'2 — Urban regions. Housing. Geographical aspects

Bourne, Larry S.. The geography of housing / Larry S. Bourne. — London : Edward Arnold, 1981. — viii,288p : ill,maps ; 24cm. — (Scripta series in geography)
Bibliography: p265-280. - Includes index
ISBN 0-7131-6300-3 (cased) : Unpriced : CIP rev.
ISBN 0-7131-6340-2 (pbk) : £6.50 B80-22943

363.5'0941 — Great Britain. Housing — *Statistics*

Housing facts and figures / Shelter. — 3rd ed. / [compiled by Steve Schifferes]. — London (157 Waterloo Rd., SE1 8UU) : Shelter, c1980. — 16p : ill ; 21x10cm
Previous ed.: 1978
ISBN 0-901242-53-5 (pbk) : £0.85 B81-18843

363.5'0941 — Great Britain. Housing — *Statistics — Serials*

[Housing and construction statistics *(Annual volume)*]. Housing and construction statistics / Department of the Environment, Scottish Development Department, Welsh Office. — 1969-1979-. — London : H.M.S.O., 1980-. — v. ; 30cm
Complements: Housing and construction statistics (Quarterly)
ISSN 0260-7719 = Housing and construction statistics (Annual volume) : £14.00
Also classified at 338.4'7624'0941 B81-11757

363.5'0941 — Great Britain. Urban regions. Central areas. Residences — *Conference proceedings*

Living over the shop : the report of a conference studying the factors preventing the increase of residential accommodation in town and city centres / arranged and edited by Charles McKean. — [London] ([66 Portland Place W1N 4AF]) : ERA Publications Board of the Eastern Region RIBA, 1976. — 24p : ill,plans ; 24cm
Text, ill on inside covers
£0.75 (pbk) B81-37052

363.5'09411 — Scotland. Rural regions. Housing — *Conference proceedings*

Issues in rural housing : report of a seminar held on 1 and 2 November 1979 at the Salutation Hotel, Perth. — Glasgow : The Planning Exchange, [1980]. — 66p : ill ; 30cm. — (Forum report / Planning Exchange ; 18)
Unpriced (pbk) B81-34610

363.5'09412'32 — Scotland. Grampian Region. Gordon *(District)*. Housing — *Proposals*

Gordon. *District Council*. Gordon District Council housing plan 1980. — [Inverurie] ([Council Offices, 3 High St., Inverurie, Aberdeenshire AB5 9QA]) : [The Council], [1980]. — [23]p ; 30cm
Unpriced (pbk) B81-23041

363.5'09412'6 — Scotland. Tayside Region. Angus *(District)*. Housing. Planning — *Proposals — Serials*

Angus. *District Council*. Housing plans and programmes / Angus District Council. — 1979/80 to 1983/84-. — [Forfar] ([Planning Department, County Buildings, Forfar DD8 3LG]) : The Council, 1978-. — v. ; 30cm
Annual. — Continues: Angus. District Council. Housing needs study. — Description based on: 1980/81 to 1984/85 issue
ISSN 0261-5932 = Housing plans and programmes - Angus District Council : Unpriced B81-31562

363.5'09412'95 — Scotland. Fife Region. Kirkcaldy *(District)*. Housing. Planning — *Proposals*

Kirkcaldy. *District Council*. Kirkcaldy District Council housing plans 1979. — [Kirkcaldy] ([Town House, Kirkcaldy, Fife KY1 1XW]) : [The Council], [1979?]. — 39p ; 30cm
Cover title
Unpriced (pbk) B81-20225

363.5'09414'1 — Scotland. Strathclyde Region. Housing. Planning

Coon, Anthony. An appraisal of the housing aspects of the Strathclyde structure plan / Anthony Coon. — [Glasgow] ([177 Renfrew St., Glasgow G3 6RQ]) : Department of Planning, Glasgow School of Art, 1979. — 40leaves ; 30cm
Cover title
£1.20 (spiral) B81-12713

363.5'09414'63 — Scotland. Strathclyde Region. Kilmarnock and Loudoun *(District)*. Housing. Planning — *Proposals*

Kilmarnock and Loudoun. *District Council*. Third interim planning policy statement on housing development 1981 / Kilmarnock and Loudoun District Council. — Kilmarnock (Civic Centre, Kilmarnock) : The Council, 1981. — 87p in various pagings : plans ; 30cm
Unpriced (pbk) B81-28902

363.5′09414′63 — Scotland. Strathclyde Region. Kilmarnock and Loudoun *(District)*. Housing — *Proposals — Serials*
Kilmarnock and Loudoun. *District Council.* Housing plan / Kilmarnock and Loudoun District Council. — 1981/86. — [Kilmarnock] ([Civic Centre, Kilmarnock KA1 1BY]) : The Council, [1981?]. — 54p
£0.50 B81-24697

363.5′0942 — England. Rural regions. Housing. Policies
Dunn, Michael, *1948-*. Rural housing : competition and choice / Michael Dunn, Marilyn Rawson, Alan Rogers. — London : Allen & Unwin, 1981. — x,277p : ill,maps ; 23cm. — (Urban and regional studies ; no. 9)
Bibliography: p256-264. — Includes index
ISBN 0-04-309105-9 : £18.00 : CIP rev. B81-04204

Shucksmith, Mark. No homes for locals? / Mark Shucksmith. — Farnborough, Hants. : Gower, 1981. — ix,143p : ill ; 23cm
Includes index
ISBN 0-566-00465-8 : Unpriced : CIP rev. B81-14936

363.5′09421 — London. Housing — *Forecasts*
Lansley, Stewart. The London report : prospects and policies for housing re [Stewart Lansley, Geoffrey Randall, Nick Raynsford]. — London : 189a Old Brompton Rd., SW5 0AR : SHAC, 1981. — 47p : ill ; 30cm. — (Research report / SHAC ; 3)
£3.75 (pbk) B81-31786

363.5′09421′43 — London. Islington *(London Borough)*. Housing. Attitudes of residents of Lewis Trust Estate
Torrisi, Jean. Housing, health & the NHS in the Lewis Trust buildings / [Jean Torrisi for Islington Community Health Council]. — London (Liverpool Road Hospital, Liverpool Rd., Islington N1 0QE) : Islington Community Health Council, 1981. — 15p ; 30cm
Unpriced (unbound)
Primary classification 362.1′09421′43 B81-33099

363.5′09422′6 — West Sussex. Housing. Planning — *Proposals*
Housing policies : West Sussex Structure Plan Review. — Chichester : West Sussex County Council, 1981. — 18p : ill ; 30cm. — (Discussion paper / West Sussex County Council ; no.1)
ISBN 0-86260-011-1 (spiral) : Unpriced B81-37983

363.5′09425′3 — Lincolnshire. Housing — *Serials*
Lincolnshire, housing / County Planning Officer, Lincolnshire County Council. — Vol.1 (1980). — [Lincoln] ([County Offices, Newland, Lincoln LN1 1YL]) : [The Council], 1980-. — v. : ill,maps ; 21cm
Annual
ISSN 0261-0752 = Lincolnshire. Housing : Unpriced B81-29078

363.5′09426′18 — Norfolk. Great Yarmouth. Housing. Planning — *Proposals*
Additional housing allocations : Great Yarmouth area : Belton? Hopton? Fritton? St. Olaves? Bradwell? Burgh Castle? : an opportunity for discussion. — [Norwich] ([County Hall, Martineau La., Norwich, Norfolk NR1 2DH]) : [Norfolk County Council], [1981]. — 10p,[3] leaves of plates : maps ; 30cm
Cover title
£0.20 (pbk) B81-19561

363.5′09427′53 — Merseyside *(Metropolitan County)*. Liverpool. Housing — *Statistics*
Cormack, Margaret. Liverpool housing : facts and figures / edited by Deirdre Morley. — Liverpool (14 Castle St., Liverpool L2 0NJ) : Liverpool Council for Voluntary Service, 1981. — iv,120p : ill,1map ; 30cm
ISBN 0-906878-02-0 (spiral) : £4.95 B81-23024

363.5′0964′6 — Morocco. Marrakesh. Housing
Schwerdtfeger, Friedrich W.. Traditional housing in African cities. — Chichester : Wiley, Nov.1981. — [350]p
ISBN 0-471-27953-6 : £20.00 : CIP entry
Primary classification 363.5′09669 B81-30978

363.5′09669 — Nigeria. Ibadan & Zaria. Housing
Schwerdtfeger, Friedrich W.. Traditional housing in African cities. — Chichester : Wiley, Nov.1981. — [350]p
ISBN 0-471-27953-6 : £20.00 : CIP entry
Also classified at 363.5′0964′6 B81-30978

363.5′0971 — Canada. Urban regions. Housing market — *Conference proceedings*
Urban housing markets : recent directions in research and policy : proceedings of a conference held at the University of Toronto October 27-29, 1977 / edited by Larry S. Bourne, John R. Hitchcock with the assistance of Judith M. Kjellberg. — Toronto ; London : University of Toronto Press, c1978. — 334p : ill ; 23cm
Includes bibliographies
ISBN 0-8020-2339-8 (pbk) : £8.75 B81-17909

363.5′1 — Great Britain. Housing. Shortages
And I'll blow your house down : housing need in Britain : present & future : a report from SHELTER national campaign for the homeless with CHAR Campaign for Single Homeless People. — London (157 Waterloo Rd., SE1 8UU) : SHELTER, 1980. — 30p : ill ; 29cm
ISBN 0-901242-54-3 (pbk) : £1.50 B81-11548

363.5′1 — London. Homelessness — *Conference proceedings*
Homelessness : prospects for the 1980s : a one day conference organised by SHAC, the London Housing Aid Centre, and held at the Independent Broadcasting Authority, 70 Brompton Road, London SW3. — London (189a Old Brompton Rd., SW5 0AR) : SHAC, 1981. — 28p ; 30cm. — (Policy paper / SHAC ; 5)
£2.75 (pbk) B81-31318

363.5′1′09421 — London. Housing conditions — *Labour Party (Great Britain) viewpoints*
Mills, John, *1938-*. Capital crisis : London's housing needs / [John Mills, Tony McBrearty and Matthew Warburton]. — [London] ([72 Albert St., NW1 7NR]) : Labour Group on the London Boroughs Association, [1980]. — 31p ; 22cm
£0.90 (pbk) B81-05932

363.5′56′0941 — Great Britain. Housing. Policies of government
Burke, Gill. Housing and social justice : the role of policy in British housing / Gill Burke. — London : Longman, 1981. — x,227p ; 20cm. — (Social policy in modern Britain)
Bibliography: p218-221. - Includes index
ISBN 0-582-29514-9 (pbk) : £4.50 : CIP rev. B80-19050

363.5′56′0941 — Great Britain. Housing. Policies of government, *1914-1923*
Swenarton, Mark. Homes fit for heroes : the politics and architecture of early state housing in Britain / Mark Swenarton. — London : Heinemann Educational, 1981. — viii,216p : ill,plans ; 23cm
Includes index
ISBN 0-435-32994-4 : £14.50 B81-12743

363.5′56′0941 — Great Britain. Housing. Policies of government, *1915-1978*
Butler, Stuart M.. More effective than bombing : government intervention in the housing market / Stuart M. Butler. — London : Adam Smith Institute, [1981]. — 23p ; 21cm
ISBN 0-906517-03-6 (pbk) : £1.00 B81-15115

363.5′56′0973 — United States. Housing. Policies of government
Housing policy for the 1980s / edited by Roger Montgomery, Dale Rogers Marshall. — Lexington : Lexington ; [Farnborough, Hants.] : [Gower] [distributor], 1980. — xxiii,243p : ill ; 24cm
Includes index
ISBN 0-669-03443-6 : £13.50 B81-10896

363.5′56′0973 — United States. Housing. Policies of government. Implications of research on movement of households — *Conference proceedings*
Residential mobility and public policy / edited by W.A.V. Clark and Eric G. Moore. — Beverly Hills ; London : Sage, c1980. — 320p : ill ; 23cm. — (Urban affairs reviews ; v.19)
Conference papers. — Includes bibliographies
ISBN 0-8039-1447-4 (cased) : Unpriced
ISBN 0-8039-1448-2 (pbk) : Unpriced B81-16317

363.5′8 — England. Local authority housing. Subsidies. Delayed financial claims — *Inquiry reports*
Great Britain. *Parliament. House of Commons. Committee of Public Accounts.* Department of the Environment : delays in the receipt of final claims for housing subsidies and other associated grants, fraud at the East Anglian Area Office of the Directorate of Ancient Monuments and Historic Buildings : eighth report from the Committee of Public Accounts, together with the proceedings of the Committee and minutes of evidence, session 1980-81. — London : H.M.S.O., [1981]. — xiii,16p ; 25cm. — ([H.C.] ; 247)
ISBN 0-10-224781-1 (pbk) : £2.60
Also classified at 364.1′63 B81-33238

363.5′8 — Great Britain. Houses. Conversion, improvement & purchase. Grants from government — *Practical information*
Hawkins, Nigel. Housing grants : a guide to improvement and other grants and subsidies / Nigel Hawkins. — London : Kogan Page, 1981. — 240p : forms ; 23cm
ISBN 0-85038-487-7 : £8.95 : CIP rev. B81-19133

363.5′8 — Great Britain. Houses. Renovation. Policies of government, *1950-1980*
Good housekeeping : an examination of housing repair improvement policy. — London (189a Old Brompton Rd, SW5 0AR) : SHAC, 1981. — 30p : ill ; 30cm. — (Policy paper / SHAC ; 4)
£2.75 (pbk) B81-17229

363.5′8 — Great Britain. Local authority housing
The Future of council housing. — London : Croom Helm, Jan.1982. — [208]p
ISBN 0-7099-0900-4 : £11.95 : CIP entry B81-34658

363.5′8 — Great Britain. Local authority housing. Tenants. Re-housing. Management. Applications of digital computer systems
LAMSAC. *Computer Panel.* The use of computers in the rehousing process : report of the Computer Panel of LAMSAC. — London : Local Authorities Management Services and Computer Committee, 1981. — 25p : ill ; 30cm
ISBN 0-85497-121-1 (pbk) : £3.00 B81-25258

363.5′8 — Great Britain. Local authority housing, *to 1981 — Socialist viewpoints*
Homes for the people : the story of council housing. — Sowerby Bridge (c/o A. Graham, 4 Upper Gaukroger, Sowerby New Rd., Sowerby Bridge, W. Yorkshire) : Calder Voice, 1981. — 12p ; 22cm. — (A Calder Voice pamphlet)
£0.10 (unbound) B81-3261

363.5′8 — Great Britain. Physically handicapped persons' housing benefits. Great Britain. *Department of the Environment.* **'Assistance with housing costs'** *— Disability Alliance viewpoints*
Disability Alliance. Assistance with housing costs : the Disability Alliance's response to a Department of the Environment consultative document. — London (1 Cambridge Terrace, NW1 4JL) : The Alliance, 1981. — 35p ; 30cm
£0.80 (pbk) B81-3325

363.5′8 — London. Homeless persons. Housing. Advice. Provision. Role of SHAC, *1975-1977*
Richardson, Paul, *19---*. The homeless in London : a comparative study of voluntary and local authority experience / Paul Richardson. — London (189a Old Brompton Rd, SW5 0AR) : SHAC (the London Housing Aid Centre), 1980. — 60p : 1form ; 30cm. — (Research report / SHAC ; 2)
£2.50 (pbk) B81-1072

363.5'8 — London. Housing advice centres: SHAC, *to 1980*

SHAC. A decade of housing aid : SHAC 1970/80 / [report written by Jane Morton] ; [photographs by Edith Dorsey-Raff and Richard Platt]. — London (189a Old Brompton Rd., SW5 3AR) : SHAC (The London Housing Aid Centre), [1980]. — 33p : ill ; 30cm
£2.50 (pbk) B81-16308

363.5'8 — Scotland. Local authority housing. Improvement & maintenance. Participation of tenants — *Serials*

TPAS notes / Tenant Participation Advisory Service. — No.1 (Oct.1980)-. — Glasgow (266 Clyde St., Glasgow G1 4JH) : The Advisory Service, 1980-. — v. : ill ; 30cm
Quarterly
ISSN 0261-197x = TPAS notes : £0.25 per issue B81-17469

363.5'8'094134 — Edinburgh. Housing. Improvement — *Proposals*

Edinburgh. *District Council*. Rehabilitation in the 1980's : policy report / [City of Edinburgh District Council]. — Edinburgh (c/o Director of Housing, 23 Waterloo Place, Edinburgh) : [The Council], [1981]. — 84leaves in various foliations : maps ; 30cm
Unpriced (pbk) B81-23536

363.5'9 — England. Residences for old persons. Provision by local authorities & housing associations — *Inquiry reports*

Report of a survey of housing for old people provided by local authorities and housing associations in England and Wales. — London (2 Marsham St., SW1) : Department of the Environment, [1981?]. — [83]p : 1ill,2maps ; 30cm
£2.00 (unbound) B81-37392

363.5'9 — England. Women. Housing

Brion, Marion. Women in housing : access and influence / by Marion Brion and Anthea Tinker. — London : Housing Centre Trust, 1980. — x,150p : ill ; 21cm
Bibliography: p149-150
ISBN 0-9502005-7-3 (pbk) : £4.90 B81-02724

363.5'9 — Great Britain. Ethnic minorities. Housing. Segregation — *Study regions: Lancashire. Blackburn*

Robinson, Vaughan. The dynamics of ethnic succession : a British case study / Vaughan Robinson. — Oxford (Mansfield Rd., Oxford. OX1 3TB) : School of Geography, 1981. — 28p : ill ; 30cm. — (Working papers / School of Geography University of Oxford ; no.2)
Bibliography: p25-28
Unpriced (pbk) B81-13970

363.5'9 — Great Britain. Physically handicapped persons. Housing — *For design*

Penton, John. A handbook of housing for disabled people / by John Penton in association with Anthony Barlow for the London Housing Consortium West Group. — 2nd ed. (with additional chapters). — Hayes (1122 Uxbridge Rd., Hayes, Middx UB4 8JX) : London Housing Consortium West Group, 1980. — 73p : ill ; 30cm
Previous ed.: 1976
ISBN 0-9505495-1-7 (pbk) : Unpriced B81-37766

363.5'9 — Scotland. Battered women. Housing

The **Housing** needs of battered women in Scotland / Scottish Women's Aid. — [Edinburgh] ([11 St. Colme St., Edinburgh EH3 6AA]) : [Scottish Women's Aid], [1980]. — 16p ; 30cm
Cover title
Unpriced (pbk) B81-11853

363.5'9 — Scotland. Sheltered housing units for old persons

Clark, David, *1946-*. Sheltered housing for the elderly in Scotland / David Clark. — [Glasgow] ([42 York Place, Edinburgh EH1 3HE]) : [Scottish Federation of Housing Associations], [1981?]. — [46]leaves,[2]leaves of plates ; 30cm
Unpriced (unbound) B81-35263

363.5'9 — Scotland. Single persons. Housing. Requirements

Buchanan, Glen. Think single : an assessment of the accommodation experiences, needs and preferences of single people / by Glen Buchanan. — Edinburgh (4 Old Assembly Close, Edinburgh EH1 1QX) : Scottish Council for Single Homeless, [1981]. — xii,80p : ill,1map ; 30cm
ISBN 0-907050-02-6 (pbk) : £2.50 (£2.00 for members) B81-26135

363.6 — PUBLIC UTILITY SERVICES

363.6'0973 — United States. Public utilities. Regulation — *Conference proceedings*

Issues in public-utility pricing and regulation / edited by Michael A. Crew. — Lexington, Mass. : Lexington Books ; [Aldershot] : Gower [distributor], 1981, c1980. — x,225p : ill ; 24cm
Conference papers. — Bibliography: p209-222
ISBN 0-669-03606-4 : £14.00 B81-29595

363.6'2 — Scotland. Electricity supply. Consumers: Low-income families. Debts. Non-payment. Sanctions: Disconnection of supply

Edwards, Rob. 'Living in the dark ages' / by Rob Edwards and Alistair Grimes. — Glasgow (266 Clyde St., Glasgow G1 4JH) : Scottish Fuel Poverty Action Group, 1981. — 33p : ill ; 21cm
Cover title
ISBN 0-903589-52-4 (pbk) : £1.50 B81-14335

363.6'2 — Scotland. Electricity supply systems. Capacity. Planning. Influence of forecasts of demand

McGuire, Alistair. Excess capacity and the demand for electricity in Scotland / by Alistair McGuire. — Aberdeen : University of Aberdeen. Department of Political Economy, [1981?]. — 28p ; 30cm. — (Discussion paper / University of Aberdeen Department of Political Economy ; 81-03)
Bibliography: p28
Unpriced (pbk) B81-14515

363.6'9 — Buildings of historical importance. Recording — *Manuals*

McDowall, R. W.. Recording old houses : a guide / R. W. McDowall. — London : Council for British Archaeology, 1980. — 33p : ill,plans ; 21cm
Bibliography: p20
ISBN 0-906780-03-9 (pbk) : £1.95 B81-05569

363.6'9 — Great Britain. Listed buildings — *Serials*

The **Period** home : for those who own and enjoy listed buildings. — Vol.1, no.1-. — Tenterden (Caston House, High St., Tenterden, Kent TN30 6BD) : Period Home Publications, 1980-. — v. : ill ; 30cm
Six issues yearly
ISSN 0261-3204 = Period home : £7.50 per year B81-23145

363.6'9 — Gwent. Usk region. Listed buildings — *Lists*

Buildings of special architectural or historic interest, former rural district of Pontypool, Monmouth district (part). Gwent / Welsh Office. — [London] ([Gwydyr House, Whitehall SW1A 2ER]) : [The Office], [1980]. — v,43p ; 30cm
Unpriced (spiral) B81-15353

363.6'9 — Scotland. Listed buildings

Scotland's listed buildings : a guide to their protection. — [Edinburgh] ([25 Drumsheugh Gdns., Edinburgh EH3 7RN]) : [Scottish Development Department], [1981]. — 8p ; 21cm
Cover title. — Bibliography: On inside cover
Unpriced (pbk) B81-37799

363.6'9'060411 — Scotland. Buildings of historical importance. Organisations: National Trust for Scotland, *to 1980*

Skinner, Basil C.. A place in trust / Basil Skinner. — Edinburgh (11 Buccleuch Place, Edinburgh 8) : University of Edinburgh Department of Extra-Mural Studies, 1981. — 48p ; 21cm
Bibliography: p48
Unpriced (pbk)
Primary classification 719'.06'042 B81-23164

363.6'9'06042 — England. Buildings of historical importance. Organisations: National Trust, *to 1980*

Skinner, Basil C.. A place in trust / Basil Skinner. — Edinburgh (11 Buccleuch Place, Edinburgh 8) : University of Edinburgh Department of Extra-Mural Studies, 1981. — 48p ; 21cm
Bibliography: p48
Unpriced (pbk)
Primary classification 719'.06'042 B81-23164

363.6'9'09416 — Northern Ireland. Buildings of historical importance. Conservation — *Serials*

Historic Buildings Council for Northern Ireland. Annual report / Historic Buildings Council Northern Ireland. — 5th (1978-79). — Belfast : H.M.S.O., 1980. — 15p
ISBN 0-337-08161-1 : £1.00 B81-16247

363.6'9'0942 — England. Buildings of historical importance. Conservation — *Serials*

Historic Buildings Council for England. Annual report / Historic Buildings Council for England. — 1979-80. — London : H.M.S.O., [1981]. — 65p
ISBN 0-10-228981-6 : £4.50 B81-30745

363.6'9'09429 — Wales. Buildings of historical importance. Conservation — *Serials*

Historic Buildings Council for Wales. Annual report / Historic Buildings Council for Wales. — 27th (1979-1980). — London : H.M.S.O., 1981. — 23p
ISBN 0-10-228181-5 : £2.90 B81-29987

363.6'9'094297 — Glamorgan. Houses of historical importance. Preservation — *Proposals*

Royal Commission on Ancient and Historical Monuments in Wales. The greater houses of Glamorgan from the Reformation to the Industrial Revolution : fifteenth interim report / The Royal Commission on Ancient and Historical Monuments in Wales. — London : H.M.S.O., [1981]. — 3p ; 25cm. — (Cmnd. ; 8266)
ISBN 0-10-182660-5 (unbound) : £0.70 B81-36710

363.7 — ENVIRONMENTAL PROBLEMS AND SERVICES

363.7 — Environment. Pollutants. Chromatography

Fishbein, Lawrence. Chromatography of environmental hazards. — Oxford : Elsevier Scientific
Vol.4: Drugs of abuse. — Oct.1981. — [500]p
ISBN 0-444-42024-x : CIP entry B81-28176

363.7 — Environmental health. Risks. Assessment

Kates, Robert W.. Risk assessment of environmental hazard / Robert W. Kates. — Chichester : Published on behalf of the Scientific Committee on Problems of the Environment (SCOPE) of the International Council of Scientific Unions (ICSU) by Wiley, c1978 (1981 [printing]). — xvii,112p : ill ; 24cm. — (SCOPE ; 8)
Bibliography: p101-107. — Includes index
ISBN 0-471-09983-x : £6.95 B81-23312

363.7'28 — Oceans. Industrial waste materials. Dumping — *Conference proceedings*

International Ocean Dumping Symposium *(1st : 1978 : University of Rhode Island)*. Ocean dumping of industrial wastes / edited by Bostwick H. Ketchum, Dana R. Kester and P. Kilho Park ; based on the proceedings of the first International Ocean Dumping Symposium held October 10-13 1978 at the University of Rhode Island, West Greenwich, Rhode Island. — New York ; London : Plenum, c1981. — ix525p : ill,charts,maps ; 26cm. — (Marine science ; v.12)
Includes bibliographies and index
ISBN 0-306-40653-5 : Unpriced B81-23410

363.7'295750941 — Great Britain. Cordage industries. Industrial safety

Great Britain. *Factory Inspectorate. Wire, Rope, Cable National Industry Group*. Wire, rope, cable. — London : Health & Safety Executive, May 1981. — [503]p. — (NIG reports)
ISBN 0-11-883424-x (pbk) : CIP entry B81-06059

363.7'3 — Environment. Non-point pollution
Novotny, Vladimir, *1938-*. Handbook of nonpoint pollution : sources and management / Vladimir Novotny and Gordon Chesters. — New York ; London : Van Nostrand Reinhold, c1981. — xiii,555p : ill,maps ; 24cm. — (Van Nostrand Reinhold environmental engineering series)
Includes index
ISBN 0-442-22563-6 : £20.85 B81-36816

363.7'3 — Environment. Pollution
Dix, H. M.. Environmental pollution : atmosphere, land, water, and noise / H.M. Dix. — Chichester : Wiley, c1981. — x,286p : ill ; 24cm. — (The Institution of Environmental Sciences series)
Bibliography: p277-278. - Includes index
ISBN 0-471-27797-5 : £14.95
ISBN 0-471-27905-6 (pbk) : Unpriced
B81-07235

Holdgate, M. W.. A perspective of environmental pollution / M. W. Holdgate. — Cambridge : Cambridge University Press, 1979 (1980 [printing]). — x,278p : ill,maps ; 23cm
Bibliography: p258-270. — Includes index
ISBN 0-521-29972-1 (pbk) : £5.95
ISBN 0-521-22197-8 B81-02490

363.7'303 — Atmosphere. Pollution. Control measures - *English-Russian dictionaries*
Milovanov, E. L.. English-Russian dictionary of environmental control. — Oxford : Pergamon, Apr.1981. — [368]p
Originally published: Moscow : Russkiĭ Ĩazyk, 1980
ISBN 0-08-023576-x : £20.00 : CIP entry
B81-09981

363.7'3'05 — Environment. Pollution. Public health aspects — *Serials*
Developments in environmental control and public health. — 2. — London : Applied Science, c1981. — x,314p. — (Developments series)
ISBN 0-85334-941-x : £25.00
ISSN 0260-0862 B81-24101

363.7'3'0941 — Great Britain. Environment. Pollution — *Statistics* — *Serials*
Digest of environmental pollution and water statistics / Department of the Environment. — No.3 (1980)-. — London : H.M.S.O., 1980-. — v. : ill,maps ; 30cm
Annual. — Merger of: Digest of environmental pollution statistics; and, Water data (London)
ISSN 0260-7298 = Digest of environmental pollution and water statistics : £9.80
B81-06923

363.7'3'0947 — Soviet Union. Environment. Pollution
Komarov, Boris. The destruction of nature in the Soviet Union / Boris Komarov ; [translated by Michel Vale and Joe Hollander]. — London : Pluto, [1980]. — 150p ; 20cm
Translation of: Unichtozhenie prirody. — Includes index
ISBN 0-86104-323-5 (pbk) : £2.95 B81-07745

363.7'31 — Man. Effects of radioactive environmental pollutants from nuclear power stations
Pentreath, R. J.. Nuclear power, man and the environment / R.J. Pentreath. — London : Taylor & Francis, 1980. — 255p : ill,maps ; 22cm. — (Wykeham science series)
Includes index
ISBN 0-85109-840-1 (pbk) : £6.00 : CIP rev.
B80-23308

363.7'32 — Environment. Pollution. Hazards
Hildyard, Nicholas. Cover up : the facts they don't want you to know / Nicholas Hildyard. — London : New English Library, 1981. — 221p ; 23cm
Includes index
ISBN 0-450-04845-4 : £5.95 B81-34792

363.7'36'0941 — Great Britain. Government. Policies. Implementation — *Study examples: Policies of government on control of pollution of environment*
Levitt, Ruth, *1950-*. Implementing public policy / Ruth Levitt. — London : Croom Helm, c1980. — 213p : ill ; 23cm
Includes index
ISBN 0-7099-0068-6 : £19.95 : CIP rev.
B80-12402

363.7'363 — Environment. Pollution. Biological monitoring — *Conference proceedings*
Biological monitoring for environmental effects / edited by Douglas L. Worf. — Lexington, Mass. : Lexington Books ; [Aldershot] : Gower [distributor], 1980. — xii,227p : ill,forms,2maps,1plan ; 24cm
Includes bibliographies and index
ISBN 0-669-03306-5 : £15.50 B81-31223

363.7'363 — Environment. Pollution. Monitoring. Use of biological specimens
Monitoring environmental materials and specimen banking : proceedings of the international workshop, Berlin (West), 23-28 October 1978 / edited by N.-P. Luepke. — The Hague ; London : Nijhoff, 1979. — xiii,591p : ill,maps ; 25cm
ISBN 90-247-2303-5 : Unpriced B81-05288

363.7'364 — Man. Health. Effects of environmental pollutants. Assessment. Use of biological specimens — *Conference proceedings*
The **Use** of biological specimens for the assessment of human exposure to environmental pollutants : proceedings of the International Workshop at Luxembourg, 18-22 April 1977 / organized jointly by Commission of the European Communities, Directorate General for Employment and Social Affairs Health and Safety Directorate, United States Environmental Protection Agency, and World Health Organisation ; editors A. Berlin, A.H. Wolff and Y. Hasegawa. — The Hague ; London : Nijhoff for the Commission of the European Communities, 1979. — viii,368p : ill ; 24cm
ISBN 90-247-2168-7 : Unpriced B81-16433

363.7'38 — Environment. Pollutants: Nickel
Nickel in the environment / edited by Jerome O. Nriagu. — New York ; Chichester : Wiley, c1980. — xi,833p : ill,maps ; 24cm. — (Environmental science and technology, ISSN 0194-0287)
Text on lining papers. — Includes bibliographies and index
ISBN 0-471-05885-8 : Unpriced B81-08448

363.7'38 — Man. Health. Effects of lead pollutants
Ratcliffe, J. M.. Lead in man and the environment / J.M. Ratcliffe. — Chichester : Horwood, 1981. — 240p : ill ; 24cm. — (Ellis Horwood series in environmental science)
Bibliography: p211-235. — Includes index
ISBN 0-85312-257-1 : £23.50 : CIP rev.
ISBN 0-470-27184-1 (Wiley) : £23.50
B81-08921

363.7'384 — Environment. Effects of copper in sewage sludge fertilisers & pig slurry — *Conference proceedings*
Copper in animal wastes and sewage sludge : proceedings of the EEC Workshop organised by the Institut national de la recherche agronomique (INRA), Station d'agronomie, Bordeaux, France, and held at Bordeaux, October 8-10, 1980 / sponsored by the Commission of the European Communities Directorate-General for Agriculture and Directorate-General for Research, Science and Education ; edited by P. L'Hermite and J. Dehandt. — Dordrecht ; London : Reidel, c1981. — xiv,378p : ill,1map ; 24cm
Includes bibliographies
ISBN 90-277-1293-x : Unpriced
Primary classification 636.4'0855 B81-28462

363.7'384 — Environment. Pollutants: Toxic chemicals. Detection & measurement. Paper chromatography & thin-layer chromatography
Getz, M. E.. Paper and thin layer chromatographic analysis of environmental toxicants / M.E. Getz. — London : Heyden, c1980. — x,164p : ill ; 25cm. — (Heyden international topics in science)
Includes index
ISBN 0-85501-451-2 : Unpriced B81-08432

363.7'384 — Environment. Pollution by lead
Harrison, R. M.. Lead pollution : causes and control / R.M. Harrison, D.P.H. Laxen. — London : Chapman and Hall, 1981. — 168p : ill,maps ; 24cm
Includes index
ISBN 0-412-16360-8 : Unpriced B81-28965

363.7'384 — United States. DDT. Use. Opposition, *to 1979*
Dunlap, Thomas R.. DDT : scientists, citizens and public policy / Thomas R. Dunlap. — Princeton ; Guildford : Princeton University Press, c1981. — 318p ; 23cm
Bibliography: p289-309. — Includes index
ISBN 0-691-04680-8 : £10.80 B81-2841

363.7'387 — Environment. Pollution by combustion
Chigier, N. A.. Energy, combustion, and environment / Norman Chigier. — New York ; London : McGraw-Hill, c1981. — xi,496p : il ; 25cm. — (McGraw-Hill series in energy, combustion and environment)
Bibliography: p469-482. — Includes index
ISBN 0-07-010766-1 : £19.25 B81-2753

363.7'392 — Air. Pollution. Causes & control measures
Wark, Kenneth. Air pollution : its origin and control / Kenneth Wark, Cecil F. Warner. — 2nd ed. — New York ; London : Harper & Row, c1981. — xv,526p : ill ; 24cm
Previous ed.: New York : IEP, 1976. — Includes index
ISBN 0-7002-2534-x : £19.95 B81-2845

363.7'392 — Atmosphere. Pollution
Atmospheric pollution : its history, origins and prevention / by A.R. Meetham ... [et al.]. — 4th (rev.) ed. in S.I. units. — Oxford : Pergamon, 1981. — xi,232p : ill,maps ; 26cm. — (Pergamon international library)
Previous ed.: 1964. — Bibliography: p223-226. — Includes index
ISBN 0-08-024003-8 (cased) : Unpriced : CIP rev.
ISBN 0-08-024002-x (pbk) : £6.75 B80-1145

363.7'392 — Great Britain. Workplaces. Air. Pollutants: Lead. Control — *Standards*
Great Britain. *Health and Safety Commission*. Control of lead at work : approved code of practice / Health and Safety Commission. — London : H.M.S.O., 1980. — vi,27p : forms ; 30cm
ISBN 0-11-883411-8 (pbk) : £2.00 B81-3122

363.7'392'06041 — Great Britain. Atmosphere. Pollution. Organisations: National Society for Clean Air — *Serials*
National Society for Clean Air. NSCA members handbook. — 1981. — Brighton (136 North St., Brighton, BN1 1RG) : National Society fo Clean Air, [1981]. — 142p
ISSN 0140-6787 : Unpriced B81-3155

363.7'392'0941 — Great Britain. Atmosphere. Pollution, *1820-1975*
Ashby, Eric. The politics of clean air. — Oxford : Clarendon Press, Oct.1981. — [200]p. — (Monographs on science, technology, and society)
ISBN 0-19-858330-3 : £9.50 : CIP entry
B81-2674

363.7'392'0941 — Great Britain. Atmosphere. Pollution — *Serials*
Health and safety. Industrial air pollution. — 1979. — London : H.M.S.O., 1981. — iii,42p
ISBN 0-11-883425-8 : £3.00 B81-2499

363.7'3926'09416 — Northern Ireland. Atmosphere. Pollution by gases from chemical engineering plants. Control — *Serials*
Great Britain. *Chief Alkali Inspector*. Report of the Chief Alkali Inspector. — 1979. — Belfast : H.M.S.O., 1980. — 14p
ISBN 0-337-08160-3 : £1.25 B81-2033

363.7'39263 — Air quality monitoring stations. Networks. Design & siting
Munn, R. E.. The design of air quality monitoring networks / R.E. Munn. — London : Macmillan, 1981. — xiii,109p : ill,maps ; 25cm. — (Air pollution problems ; 2)
Bibliography: p101-107. — Includes index
ISBN 0-333-30460-8 : £20.00 B81-3995

363.7′3927 — Atmosphere. Pollution. Control. Role of planning of location of industries

Guldmann, Jean-Michel. Industrial location and air quality control : a planning approach / Jean-Michel Guldmann, Daniel Shefer. — New York ; Chichester : Wiley, c1980. — xii,237p : ill,maps ; 24cm. — (Environmental science and technology, ISSN 0194-0287)
Includes index
ISBN 0-471-05377-5 : £17.00 B81-09732

363.7′394 — North Sea. Pollution by petroleum. Monitoring

Monitoring oil pollution 1977-78 / Napier College of Commerce and Technology. — [Edinburgh] ([Colinton Rd, Edinburgh]) : [The College], [1978]. — 143p in various pagings : ill,maps ; 30cm
Cover title. — Includes bibliographies
Unpriced (spiral) B81-02036

363.7′394 — Oceans. Pollution

Marine environmental pollution / edited by Richard A. Geyer. — Amsterdam ; Oxford : Elsevier Scientific. — (Elsevier oceanography series ; 27a)
1: Hydrocarbons. — 1980. — xxii,591p : ill,maps ; 25cm
Bibliography : p531-568. — Includes index
ISBN 0-444-41847-4 : Unpriced : CIP rev. B80-19276

363.7′394 — Oceans. Pollution by discharges from oil tankers, ***1967-1979***

Dawson, James. Superspill : the future of ocean pollution / James Dawson. — London : Jane′s, 1980. — 128p : ill ; 23cm
Bibliography: p128
ISBN 0-7106-0064-x : £7.50 B81-04889

363.7′394 — Oceans. Pollution by petroleum. Control. International organisations

Action against oil pollution : a guide to the main intergovernmental and industry organisations concerned with oil pollution in the marine environment. — London : Witherby, 1981. — 20p ; 21cm
Cover title
ISBN 0-900886-60-9 (pbk) : £1.25 B81-38885

363.7′394 — Oceans. Pollution — ***Conference proceedings***

Marine environmental pollution / edited by Richard A. Geyer. — Amsterdam ; Oxford : Elsevier Scientific
2: Dumping and mining. — 1981. — xxi,574p (16 folded) : ill,maps ; 25cm. — (Elsevier oceanography series ; 27B)
Includes bibliographies and index
ISBN 0-444-41855-5 : Unpriced B81-31125

363.7′394 — Water. Pollution

Laws, Edward A.. Aquatic pollution / Edward A. Laws. — New York ; Chichester : Wiley, c1981. — xii,482p : ill,maps ; 24cm. — (Environmental science and technology)
Includes bibliographies and index
ISBN 0-471-05797-5 : £18.60 B81-23314

363.7′394 — Water. Pollution - ***Conference proceedings***

Water pollution research and development. — Oxford : Pergamon, June 1981. — [1073]p
Conference papers
ISBN 0-08-026025-x : £85.00 : CIP entry B81-16860

363.7′394 — Water supply. Health aspects — ***Conference proceedings***

Water supply and health : proceedings of an International Symposium, Noordwijkerhout, The Netherlands, 27-29 August 1980 / edited by H. van Lelyveld and B. C. J. Zoeteman. — Amsterdam ; Oxford : Elsevier Scientific, 1981. — xxii,397p : ill,maps ; 25cm. — (Studies in environmental science ; 12)
Cover title. — ″These papers have been published as a special issue of The Science of the Total Environment, Vol.18, 1981″. — Includes index
ISBN 0-444-41960-8 : £30.65 B81-22204

363.7′3945′095694 — Israel. Natural resources: Water. Quality. Management

Water quality management under conditions of scarcity : Israel as a case study / edited by Hillel I. Shuval. — New York ; London : Academic Press, 1980. — xii,352p : ill,maps ; 24cm. — (Water pollution)
Includes bibliographies and index
ISBN 0-12-641280-4 : £24.00 B81-14757

363.7′39463 — United States. Water. Pollution. Biological monitoring. Use of fish — ***Conference proceedings***

Biological monitoring of fish / edited by Charles H. Hocutt, Jay R. Stauffer, Jr. — Lexington : Lexington, c1980 ; [Farnborough, Hants.] : Gower [distributor], 1981. — xi,416p : ill,maps,forms ; 24cm
Conference papers. — Includes bibliographies and index
ISBN 0-669-03309-x : £20.00 B81-17760

363.7′43 — Industries. Personnel. Hearing disorders. Prevention

Hearing protection in industry. — London : Croom Helm, Apr.1981. — [400]p
ISBN 0-7099-0501-7 : £19.95 : CIP entry B81-07445

363.7′43 — Occupational noise

TUC handbook on noise at work. — London : TUC Publications, 1981. — 73p : ill ; 21cm
Bibliography: p65-66
£0.80 (pbk) B81-23021

363.7′456 — Great Britain. Buildings. Sound insulation. Policies of government — ***Inquiry reports***

A **Study** of Government noise insulation policies : report by a working group of the Council / the Noise Advisory Council. — London : H.M.S.O., 1980. — iv,18p ; 25cm
ISBN 0-11-751488-8 (pbk) : £2.10 B81-21000

363.7′46′0941 — Great Britain. Aircraft. Noise. Control

Action against aircraft noise / [prepared by the Department of Trade and the Central Office of Information]. — [London] ([1 Victoria St., SW1H 0ET]) : The Department, 1979. — 16p : ill(some col.),col.maps ; 30cm
Unpriced (pbk) B81-05897

363.7′5 — Great Britain. Local authority crematoria — ***Statistics — Serials***

Crematoria statistics / CIPFA Statistical Information Service. — 1979-80. — London : Chartered Institute of Public Finance and Accountancy, 1981. — 15p
ISSN 0534-2104 : £5.00 B81-31560

363.7′8 — Pests: Insects

Busvine, James R.. Insects and hygiene : the biology and control of insect pests of medical and domestic importance / James R. Busvine. — 3rd ed. — London : Chapman and Hall, 1980. — vii,568p : ill ; 25cm
Previous ed.: London : Methuen, 1966. — Bibliography: p546-560. — Includes index
ISBN 0-412-15910-4 : £22.50 : CIP rev. B79-34941

363.8 — FOOD SUPPLY

363.8 — Developing countries. Famines. Causes — ***Case studies***

Sen, Amartya. Poverty and famines : an essay on entitlement and deprivation / Amartya Sen. — Oxford : Clarendon, 1981. — ix,257p : ill,maps ; 23cm
Bibliography: p217-249. — Includes index
ISBN 0-19-828426-8 : £9.85 : CIP rev. B81-04361

363.8 — Famines

Famine : its causes, effects and management / edited by John R.K. Robson. — New York ; London : Gordon and Breach, c1981. — x,170p : ill,maps ; 24cm. — (Food and nutrition in history and anthropology, ISSN 0275-5769 ; v.2)
Includes bibliographies and index
ISBN 0-677-16180-8 : Unpriced B81-29288

363.8 — Food. Political aspects — ***Serials***

Food and politics / [written and produced by the London Agricapital Group]. — Issue 1 (1981)-. — London (9 Poland St., W1V 3DG) : BSSRS Publications, 1981-. — v. : ill ; 22cm
Quarterly
ISSN 0261-8907 = Food and politics : £0.40 per issue B81-35093

363.8′1 — Food supply. Effects of increases in population

The **Rising** tide : population food and famine : with a case study / Curriculum Development Unit. — Dublin : O′Brien, 1981. — 63p : ill,map,facsim ; 26cm
ISBN 0-905140-93-1 (cased) : £7.00
ISBN 0-905140-94-x (pbk) : Unpriced B81-15330

363.8′2 — Food supply. Shortages. Geographical aspects — ***For schools***

Elliott, G.. Geography of hunger / Gordon Elliott. — [Glasgow] : Collins for the Schools Council, c1980. — 4v. : ill,maps ; 26cm. — (Place, time and society 8-13)
ISBN 0-00-380095-4 (unbound) : £9.95
ISBN 0-00-380096-2
ISBN 0-00-380097-0
ISBN 0-00-380098-9
ISBN 0-00-380099-7 B81-20980

363.8′56′0973 — United States. Nutrition. Policies of government

Schmandt, Jurgen. Nutrition policy in transition / Jurgen Schmandt, RoseAnn Shorey, Lilas Kinch and members of the Nutrition Policy Research Project, the University of Texas. — Lexington, Mass. : Lexington Books, c1980 ; [Farnborough, Hants.] : Gower [distributor], 1981. — xxv,289p : ill ; 24cm
Includes index
ISBN 0-669-03596-3 : £13.50 B81-09372

363.8′8 — Developing countries. Food supply. Foreign assistance by United States

Wallerstein, Mitchel B.. Food for war - food for peace : United States food aid in a global context / Mitchel B. Wallerstein. — Cambrdige, Mass. ; London : MIT Press, c1980. — xxii,312p : ill ; 24cm
Bibliography: p283-299. - Includes index
ISBN 0-262-23106-9 : £18.60 B81-05343

363.9 — POPULATION PROBLEMS

363.9 — Commonwealth countries. Migration. Policies of governments, ***1945-1979***

Smith, T. E. (Thomas Edward). Commonwealth migration : flows and policies / by T.E. Smith with contributions from Charles Price ... [et al.]. — London : Macmillan, 1981. — viii,216p ; 23cm. — (Cambridge Commonwealth series)
Includes index
ISBN 0-333-27898-4 : £20.00 : CIP rev. B80-21420

363.9′6 — Man. Artificial insemination. Social aspects

Snowden, Robert. The artificial family : a consideration of artificial insemination by donor / R. Snowden and G.D. Mitchell. — London : Allen & Unwin, 1981. — 138p ; 23cm
Bibliography: p128-136. - Includes index
ISBN 0-04-176001-8 : Unpriced : CIP rev. B81-07587

363.9′6′05 — Family planning — ***Serials***

The **British** journal of family planning : the journal of the National Association of Family Planning Doctors. — Vol.3, no.1 (Apr.1977). — London (BMA House, Tavistock Sq., WC1H 9JR) : Published by Professional and Scientific Publications for The Association, 1977-. — v. : ill ; 25cm
Quarterly. — Continues: Journal of family planning doctors. — Description based on: Vol.6, no.2 (July 1980)
ISSN 0144-8625 = British journal of family planning : £12.00 per year B81-04754

IPPF open file. — Nov.26, 1976-. — London (18 Lower Regent St., SW1Y 4PW) : IPPF Central Office, 1976-. — v. ; 30cm
Fortnightly. — Absorbed: IPPF law file ; IPPF medical file ; and, IPPF youthline, 1981. — Description based on: Mar.27, 1981
ISSN 0261-6998 = IPPF open file : Unpriced B81-32247

364 — CRIMINOLOGY

364 — Crime & punishment — *Sociological perspectives*

Christie, Nils. Limits to pain. — Oxford : Martin Robertson, Oct.1981. — [144]p
ISBN 0-85520-476-1 (cased) : £8.95 : CIP entry
ISBN 0-85520-475-3 (pbk) : £3.95 B81-31100

364 — Criminology

Conklin, John E.. Criminology / John E. Conklin. — New York : Macmillan ; London : Collier Macmillan, c1981. — xii,500p : ill ; 27cm
Includes index
ISBN 0-02-324180-2 : £11.50 B81-33386

364 — United States. Victims of crimes — *Sociological perspectives*

Perspectives on crime victims / edited by Burt Galaway, Joe Hudson. — St. Louis ; London : Mosby, 1981. — xiii,435p : ill ; 24cm
Includes bibliographies and index
ISBN 0-8016-1733-2 (pbk) : £12.00 B81-14990

Ziegenhagen, Eduard A.. Victims, crime, and social control / Eduard A. Ziegenhagen. — New York ; London : Praeger, 1977. — xii,156p ; 24cm. — (Praeger special studies in U.S. economic, social, and political issues)
Includes index
ISBN 0-275-56560-2 : £12.50 B81-02284

364'.01 — Criminology. Theories

Radical criminology : the coming crises / edited by James A. Inciardy. — London : Sage, c1980. — 320p ; 23cm. — (Sage focus editions)
Includes bibliographies
ISBN 0-8039-1489-x (cased) : £11.85
ISBN 0-8039-1490-3 (pbk) : £6.95 B81-13627

364'.01 — Criminology. Theories — *Conference proceedings*

Understanding crime : current theory and research / edited by Travis Hirschi and Michael Gottfredson. — Beverly Hills ; London : Published in cooperation with the American Society of Criminology [by] Sage, c1980. — 144p : ill ; 23cm. — (Sage research progress series in criminology ; v.18)
Conference papers. — Includes bibliographies
ISBN 0-8039-1517-9 (corrected cased) : Unpriced
ISBN 0-8039-1518-7 (pbk) : Unpriced
B81-26977

364'.042 — Crime. Spatial aspects

Crime : a spatial perspective / Daniel E. Georges-Abeyie and Keith D. Harries, editors. — New York ; Guildford : Columbia University Press, 1980. — xii,301p : ill,maps ; 24cm
Includes index
ISBN 0-231-04734-7 : £13.80 B81-08604

Davidson, R. N.. Crime and environment. — London : Croom Helm, Oct.1981. — [208]p. — (Croom Helm series in geography and environment)
ISBN 0-7099-0803-2 : £12.95 : CIP entry
B81-25712

364'.05 — Criminology — *Serials*

Crime and justice. — Vol.2. — Chicago ; London : University of Chicago Press, c1980. — ix,470p
ISBN 0-226-53957-1 : Unpriced
ISSN 0192-3234 B81-25022

Criminology review yearbook. — Vol.1-. — Beverly Hills ; London : Sage, c1979-. — v. ; 24cm
Unpriced B81-02343

Criminology review yearbook. — Vol.2. — Beverly Hills ; London : Sage, c1980. — 733p
ISBN 0-8039-1309-5 : Unpriced B81-02430

364'.072 — Criminology. Controversial research — *Conference proceedings*

Taboos in criminology / edited by Edward Sagarin. — Beverly Hills ; London : Published in cooperation with the American Society of Criminology [by] Sage, c1980. — 152p ; 23cm. — (Sage research progress series in criminology ; v.15)
Conference papers. — Includes bibliographies
ISBN 0-8039-1513-6 (cased) : Unpriced
ISBN 0-8039-1514-4 (pbk) : Unpriced
B81-26975

364'.072073 — United States. Crime & punishment. Historiology — *Conference proceedings*

History and crime : implications for criminal justice policy / edited by James A. Inciardi, Charles E. Faupel ; preface by Richard M. Rau. — Beverly Hills ; London : Sage, c1980. — 288p ; 23cm. — (Sage focus editions ; 27)
Conference papers
ISBN 0-8039-1410-5 (cased) : Unpriced
ISBN 0-8039-1411-3 (pbk) : £6.25 B81-18732

364'.072073 — United States. Criminology. Research. Statistical methods

Johnson, Edwin S.. Research methods in criminology and criminal justice / Edwin S. Johnson. — Englewood Cliffs ; London : Prentice-Hall, c1981. — xii,418p : ill ; 24cm
Includes bibliographies and index
ISBN 0-13-774349-1 : £11.65 B81-12669

364'.0941 — Great Britain. Criminology

Crime and society. — London : Routledge & Kegan Paul, Dec.1981. — [498]p
ISBN 0-7100-0944-5 : £6.95 : CIP entry
B81-31640

364'.0973 — United States. Criminology, *1930-1979*

Gibbons, Don C.. The criminological enterprise : theories and perspectives / Don C. Gibbons. — Englewood Cliffs ; London : Prentice-Hall, 1979. — xiii,226p ; 23cm. — (Prentice-Hall series in sociology)
Includes index
ISBN 0-13-193615-8 (pbk) : £5.80 B81-01925

364.1 — CRIMES

364.1'05 — Crimes — *Serials*

True crime monthly : incorporating Official detective. — Apr.1981-. — London (12 Paul St., EC2A) : Illustrated Publications Co. Ltd., 1981-. — v. : ill,ports ; 29cm
ISSN 0261-264x = True crime monthly : £0.60 per issue B81-29970

364.1'06 — Chinese secret societies: Triads

Bresler, Fenton. The trail of the Triads : an investigation into international crime / Fenton Bresler. — London : Weidenfeld and Nicolson, c1980. — xiii,226p,[8]p of plates : ill,ports ; 23cm
Bibliography: p219. - Includes index
ISBN 0-297-77771-8 : £7.50 B81-00811

364.1'06'073 — United States. Organised crimes

Block, Alan A.. Organizing crime / Alan A. Block, William J. Chambliss. — New York ; Oxford : Elsevier, c1981. — 238p ; 24cm
Includes index
ISBN 0-444-99079-8 : Unpriced B81-28925

364.1'06'073 — United States. Organised crimes. Control

Abadinsky, Howard. Organized crime / Howard Abadinsky. — Boston [Mass.] ; London : Allyn and Bacon, c1981. — ix,324p : ill,1map,forms ; 25cm. — (The Allyn and Bacon criminal justice series)
Bibliography: p294-316. - Includes index
ISBN 0-205-07097-3 : £13.95 B81-06305

364.1'09'04 — Crimes, *1916-1972* — *Case studies*

Grex, Leo. These crimes made headlines / by Leo Grex. — London : Hale, 1980. — 176p ; 23cm
ISBN 0-7091-8602-9 : £5.95 B81-01605

364.1'09181'2 — Western world. Crimes, *1901-1952*

Gribble, Leonard. Crime stranger than fiction / by Leonard Gribble. — London : Hale, 1981. — 160p ; 23cm
ISBN 0-7091-9042-5 : £6.95 B81-22105

364.1'092'2 — Criminals, *to 1979* — *Encyclopaedias*

Green, Jonathon. The directory of infamy : the best of the worst : an illustrated compendium of over 600 of the all-time great crooks / Jonathon Green. — London : Mills & Boon, 1980. — 288p : ill,facsims,ports ; 26cm
Bibliography: p284-285. - Includes index
ISBN 0-263-06453-0 : £8.95 B81-04461

364.1'092'4 — London. East End. Gangsters: Harding, Arthur, *1886-* — *Biographies*

Harding, Arthur, *1886-*. East End underworld : chapters in the life of Arthur Harding / [edited by] Raphael Samuel. — London : Routlege & Kegan Paul, 1981. — viii,355p,[8]p of plates : ill,ports ; 23cm. — (History Workshop series)
Includes index
ISBN 0-7100-0725-6 (cased) : £11.50
ISBN 0-7100-0726-4 (pbk) : £6.95 B81-18702

364.1'0941 — Great Britain. Crimes, *1700-1835* — *Readings from contemporary sources*

Tales from the Newgate calendar / [compiled by] Rayner Heppenstall. — London : Constable, 1981. — 254p : ill,ports ; 23cm
Includes index
ISBN 0-09-464130-7 : £8.50 B81-25265

364.1'0942 — England. Crime — *Statistics* — *Serials*

Criminal statistics, England and Wales / Home Office. — 1979. — London : H.M.S.O., 1980. — 548p. — (Cmnd. ; 8098)
ISBN 0-10-180980-8 : £16.80 B81-09060

364.1'31 — France. Treason. Guilt of Dreyfus, Alfred. Exoneration

Hoffman, Robert L.. More than a trial : the struggle over Captain Dreyfus / Robert L. Hoffman. — New York : Free Press ; London : Collier Macmillan, c1980. — viii,247p,[12]p of plates : ill,ports ; 25cm
Bibliography: p229-236. - Includes index
ISBN 0-02-914770-0 : £9.50 B81-05648

364.1'31 — Jerusalem. Hotels: King David Hotel. Bombing by Jewish terrorists, *1966*

Clarke, Thurston. By blood and fire : the attack on the King David Hotel / Thurston Clarke. — London : Hutchinson, 1981. — 346p,[8]p of plates : ill,1map,plans,ports ; 23cm
Bibliography: p331-336. — Includes index
ISBN 0-09-145290-2 : £8.95 : CIP rev.
B81-03678

364.1'323'0968 — South Africa. Politics. Muldergate affair

Rees, Mervyn. Muldergate : the story of the Info scandal / Mervyn Rees, Chris Day. — [Johannesburg] ; [London] : Macmillan, [1980]. — xvi,222p,[8]p of plates : ill,ports ; 25cm
ISBN 0-86954-089-0 : £7.50 B81-32499

364.1'323'0973 — United States. Politics. Watergate affair

Woodward, Bob. All the president's men. — London : Hodder & Stoughton, Nov.1981. — [352]p. — (Coronet books)
Originally published: London : Quartet, 1974
ISBN 0-340-26780-1 (pbk) : £1.75 : CIP entry
B81-30126

364.1'323'0973 — United States. Politics. Watergate affair — *Personal observations*

Sirica, John J.. To set the record straight : the break-in, the tapes, the conspirators, the pardon / John J. Sirica. — New York ; London : Norton, c1979. — 394p : ports ; 25cm
Includes index
ISBN 0-393-01234-4 : £9.25 B81-05523

364.1'323'0973 — United States. Politics. Watergate affair. Psychological aspects

Rangell, Leo. The mind of Watergate : an exploration of the compromise of integrity / Leo Rangell. — New York ; London : Norton, c1980. — 318p ; 24cm
Bibliography: p305-308. - Includes index
ISBN 0-393-01308-1 : £7.75 B81-02953

364.1′5′0973 — United States. Crimes of violence — *Conference proceedings*

Violent crime : historical and contemporary issues / edited by James A. Inciardi and Anne E. Pottieger. — Beverly Hills ; London : Sage in cooperation with the American Society of Criminology, c1978. — 160p ; 23cm. — (Sage research progress series in criminology ; v.5)
Conference papers. — Includes bibliographies
ISBN 0-8039-1107-6 (cased) : £8.00
ISBN 0-8039-1108-4 (pbk£4.00) B81-03505

364.1′51′0904 — Genocide, *ca 1900-1980*

Kuper, Leo. Genocide / Leo Kuper. — Harmondsworth : Penguin, 1981. — 255p ; 20cm
Bibliography: p221-236. — Includes index
ISBN 0-14-022242-1 (pbk) : £2.95 B81-37916

364.1′522′019 — Suicide. Psychosocial aspects

Maris, Ronald W.. Pathways to suicide : a survey of self-destructive behaviors / Ronald W. Maris in association with Bernard Lazerwitz. — Baltimore : Johns Hopkins University Press, c1981. — xxii,375p : ill ; 24cm
Bibliography: p351-368. — Includes index
ISBN 0-8018-2437-0 : £16.00 B81-36455

364.1′523′09 — Murder, *to 1980 — Stories, anecdotes*

Weekend book of ghosts and horror / edited by Richard Whittington-Egan. — London : Published by Harmsworth Publications for Associated Newspapers Ltd, c1981. — 128p : ill,ports ; 22cm
ISBN 0-85144-178-5 (pbk) : £1.00
Primary classification 133 B81-24182

364.1′523′0903 — Murder, *1788-1977 — Readings from contemporary sources*

Murder most foul : and other great crime stories from the world press / edited by Rob Warden and Martha Groves. — Chicago ; London : Swallow, c1980. — ix,348p : 2facsims,ports ; 24cm
Includes index
ISBN 0-8040-0796-9 : £9.00 B81-12610

364.1′523′09034 — Murder, *1827-1978 — Encyclopaedias*

Gaute, J. H. H.. The murderer′s who′s who : outstanding international cases from the literature of murder in the last 150 years / J.H.H. Gaute and Robin Odell ; with a foreword by Colin Wilson. — London : Pan, 1980, c1979. — 382p,[8]p of plates : ill,ports ; 18cm
Originally published: London : Harrap, 1979. — Bibliography: p354-371. — Includes index
ISBN 0-330-26206-8 (pbk) : £1.95 B81-00812

364.1′523′0922 — California. San Francisco. White persons. Murder by Black Muslims, *1975*

Howard, Clark. [Zebra]. The zebra killings / Clark Howard. — London : New English Library, 1981, c1979. — 414p ; 18cm
Originally published: New York : Marek, 1979 ; London : New English Library, 1980
ISBN 0-450-04951-5 (pbk) : £1.95 B81-29549

364.1′523′0924 — Europe. Wilson, Norman. Murder

Taylor, Lawrence. Trail of the Fox : the true story of a perfect murder / Lawrence Taylor. — London : Harrap, 1981, c1980. — 302p,[16]p of plates : ill,facsims,ports ; 24cm
Originally published: New York : Simon and Schuster, 1980
ISBN 0-245-53765-1 : £6.95 B81-29730

364.1′523′0924 — Great Britain. Murderers: Fontaine, Roy — *Biographies*

Copeland, James, *1937-*. The butler / James Copeland. — London : Granada, 1981. — 204p,[8]p of plates : ill,ports ; 18cm. — (A Panther book)
Includes index
ISBN 0-586-04906-1 (pbk) : £1.50 B81-29281

364.1′523′0924 — Northern England. Women. Murder by Sutcliffe, Peter, *1946-*

Yallop, David A.. Deliver us from evil / David A. Yallop. — London : Macdonald Futura, 1981. — 374p,[32]p of plates : ill,1map,facims,ports ; 19cm
Includes index
ISBN 0-354-04565-2 (cased) : £6.95
ISBN 0-354-04565-2 (pbk) : Unpriced B81-27815

364.1′523′0924 — Staffordshire. Rugeley. Canals: Trent and Mersey Canal. Collins, Christina. Murder

Godwin, John, *1922-*. The murder of Christina Collins on the Trent and Mersey Canal at Rugeley in 1839 / written by John Godwin. — Stafford (Friars Terrace, Stafford [St19 4AY]) : Staffordshire Country Library, 1981. — 18p : 1map ; 21cm
ISBN 0-903363-08-9 (pbk) : £0.20 B81-09317

364.1′523′0942 — England. Murder. Criminal investigation by Metropolitan Police. *Murder Squad, to 1978 — Case studies*

Tullett, Tom. [Strictly murder]. Murder Squad : famous cases of Scotland Yard′s Murder Squad / Tom Tullett. — London : Granada, 1981, c1979. — 318p,[16]p of plates : ill,ports ; 18cm. — (A Triad Panther book)
Originally published: London : Bodley Head, 1979. — Includes index
ISBN 0-586-05218-6 (pbk) : £1.50 B81-32839

364.1′524′0922 — United States. Kennedy, John F. & Lincoln, Abraham. Assassination. Ballistic aspects

Lattimer, John K.. Kennedy and Lincoln : medical and ballistic comparisions of their assassinations / by John K. Lattimer. — New York ; London : Harcourt Brace Jovanovich, c1980. — xxi,378p : ill,facsims, ports ; 27cm
Bibliography: p367-369. - Includes index
ISBN 0-15-152281-2 : £11.80 B81-20279

364.1′524′0924 — England. William III, *King of England.* **Attempted assassination by Jacobites,** *1696*

Garrett, Jane. The triumphs of providence : the assassination plot, 1696 / Jane Garrett. — Cambridge : Cambridge University Press, 1980. — xi,289p,[8]p of plates : ill,facsims,1map,ports ; 24cm
Facsim on lining papers. — Bibliography: p281-283. — Includes index
ISBN 0-521-23346-1 : £10.50 : CIP rev. B80-28149

364.1′524′0924 — Switzerland. Lausanne. Vorovskiĭ, V. V.. Assassination

Senn, Alfred Erich. Assassination in Switzerland : the murder of Vatslav Vorovsky / Alfred Erich Senn. — Madison ; London : University of Wisconsin Press, 1981. — xi,219p : ill,facsims,1plan,ports ; 22cm
Includes index
ISBN 0-299-08550-3 : £15.00 B81-40320

364.1′532′0973 — United States. Rape victims — *Sociological perspectives*

Sanders, William B.. Rape and woman′s identity / William B. Sanders ; foreword by Gilbert Geis. — Beverly Hills ; London : Sage, c1980. — 184p : 1form ; 23cm. — (Sage library of social research ; v.106)
Bibliography: p179-183
ISBN 0-8039-1449-0 (cased) : £11.25
ISBN 0-8039-1450-4 (pbk) : £5.50 B81-04605

364.1′552 — Great Britain. Mugging — *Sociological perspectives*

Pratt, Michael, *1937-*. Mugging as a social problem / Michael Pratt. — London : Routledge and Kegan Paul, 1980. — x,236p : ill,maps ; 23cm
Bibliography: p224-232. — Includes index
ISBN 0-7100-0564-4 : £11.95 : CIP rev. B80-26832

364.1′552′0924 — Buckinghamshire. Aylesbury Vale *(District).* **Trains. Robbery. Great Train Robbery. Biggs, Ronald,** *to 1980 — Biographies*

Biggs, Ronald. Ronnie Biggs : his own story. — London : Joseph, 1981. — 237p,[8]p of plates : ill,ports ; 23cm
ISBN 0-7181-1972-x : £7.95 B81-16665

364.1′552′0924 — New Hampshire. Armed robbery. Hart, Warren — *Biographies*

Greenberg, Norman. The man with a steel guitar : a portrait of ambition, desperation, and crime / Norman Greenberg ; foreword by Stuart Palmer. — Hanover, N.H. ; London : University Press of New England, 1980. — xiii,165p ; 23cm
ISBN 0-87451-175-5 : £6.50 B81-12009

364.1′555 — Northern Ireland. Suspected terrorists. Alleged brutality by Royal Ulster Constabulary, *1976-1979*

Taylor, Peter, *1942-*. Beating the terrorists? : interrogation at Omagh, Gough and Castlereagh / Peter Taylor. — Harmondsworth : Penguin, 1980. — 347p : 1ill ; 18cm. — (A Penguin special)
ISBN 0-14-052337-5 (pbk) : £1.50 B81-02728

364.1′62 — Europe. Museums. Stock: Art objects. Theft, *1911-1962*

The **Connoisseur** crimes : great art thefts of the century / AA. — London : Drive Pubications for the Automobile Association, 1981. — 48p : ill(some col.),maps(some col.),facsims,ports (some col.) ; 16cm
Bibliography: p48
Unpriced (pbk) B81-30012

364.1′62 — Great Britain. Residences. Burglary

Walsh, Dermot. Break-ins : burglary from private houses / Dermot Walsh. — London : Constable, 1980. — 207p : 1ill ; 23cm
Bibliography: p195-203. - Includes index
ISBN 0-09-463700-8 : £8.00 B81-00065

364.1′62 — Italian painting. Leonardo, *da Vinci.* **Mona Lisa. Theft,** *1911*

Reit, Seymour. The day they stole the Mona Lisa / Seymour V. Reit. — London : Hale, 1981. — 254p,[8]p of plates : ill,ports ; 23cm
Includes index
ISBN 0-7091-9197-9 : £7.25 B81-27083

364.1′62 — Ontario. Toronto. Residences. Burglary

Waller, Irvin. Burglary : the victim and the public / Irvin Waller & Norman Okihiro. — Toronto ; London : Published in association with the Centre of Criminology, University of Toronto by University of Toronto Press, c1978. — xii,190p : 2facsims,1form,1map ; 25cm
Bibliography: p175-186. — Includes index
ISBN 0-8020-5421-8 : £10.50 B81-05628

364.1′63 — England. Commercial fraud

Leigh, Leonard H.. The control of commercial fraud. — London : Heinemann Educational, Apr.1981. — [352]p. — (Cambridge studies in criminology ; 45)
ISBN 0-435-82519-4 : £17.50 : CIP entry B81-07483

364.1′63 — Great Britain. Banknotes. Forgery. Criminal investigation, *1972-1975*

Whittemore, Hank. [Find the magician]. Fiver! : the counterfeiting crime of the century / Hank Whittemore & Mark Yarry. — London : Weidenfeld and Nicolson, 1981. — 228p ; 23cm
Originally published: New York : Viking, 1980
ISBN 0-297-77891-9 : £6.50 B81-11796

364.1′63 — Great Britain. *Directorate of Ancient Monuments and Historic buildings. East Anglian Area Office.* **Fraud** — *Inquiry reports*

Great Britain. *Parliament. House of Commons. Committee of Public Accounts.* Department of the Environment : delays in the receipt of final claims for housing subsidies and other associated grants, fraud at the East Anglian Area Office of the Directorate of Ancient Monuments and Historic Buildings : eighth report from the Committee of Public Accounts, together with the proceedings of the Committee and minutes of evidence, session 1980-81. — London : H.M.S.O., [1981]. — xiii,16p ; 25cm. — ([H.C.] ; 247)
ISBN 0-10-224781-1 (pbk) : £2.60
Primary classification 363.5′8 B81-33238

364.1′63 — International maritime fraud

Conway, Barbara. The piracy business / Barbara Conway. — Feltham : Hamlyn, 1981. — 160p ; 18cm
Includes index
ISBN 0-600-20428-6 (pbk) : £1.50 B81-34689

364.1′63 — International maritime fraud *continuation*

Ellen, Eric. International maritime fraud. — London : Sweet & Maxwell, Oct.1981. — [170]p
ISBN 0-421-27150-7 (pbk) : CIP entry B81-25858

364.1′63 — Organisations. Fraud — *Serials*

Corporate crime. — Vol.1, no.1 (Jan.1981)-. — Lausanne ; Oxford : Elsevier Sequoia, 1981-. — v. ; 30cm. — (Elsevier international bulletins)
Monthly
ISSN 0144-9893 = Corporate crime : £95.00 per year B81-27137

364.1′63′0942 — England. Long-firm fraud. Organisation & control

Levi, Michael. The phantom capitalists. — London : Heinemann Educational, Aug.1981. — [384]p. — (Cambridge studies in criminology ; 44)
ISBN 0-435-82520-8 : £15.50 : CIP entry B81-16414

364.1′64 — English pirates — *Biographies* — *For children*

Pascall, Jeremy. Pirates and privateers / Jeremy Pascall. — Hove : Wayland, 1981. — 64p : ill (some col.),maps(some col.),1facsim,ports(some col.) ; 23cm. — (In profile)
Bibliography: p62. — Includes index
ISBN 0-85340-880-7 : £3.95
Primary classification 910.4′5′0922 B81-40616

364.1′64 — Maghreb. Coastal waters. English piracy, *ca 1520-ca 1830*

Lloyd, Christopher, *1906-*. English corsairs on the Barbary coast / Christopher Lloyd. — London : Collins, 1981. — 178p,[12]p of plates : ill,maps,ports ; 22cm
Bibliography: p167-169. — Includes index
ISBN 0-00-216289-x : £7.50 B81-05941

364.1′64 — Piracy, *to ca 1850*

Thrower, Rayner. The pirate picture / by Rayner Thrower. — London : Phillimore, 1980. — x,177p,[8]p of plates : ill,2maps ; 23cm
Bibliography: p164-165. — Includes index
ISBN 0-85033-357-1 : £5.95 B81-01568

364.1′68 — United States. White-collar crimes. Prevention

A **National** strategy for containing white-collar crime / edited by Herbert Edelhertz, Charles Rogovin. — Lexington : Lexington ; Farnborough, Hants. : Gower [distributor], c1980. — xii,138p ; 24cm. — (The Battelle Human Affairs Research Centers series)
Conference papers
ISBN 0-669-03166-6 : £10.50 B81-17824

364.1′68′094 — Europe. White-collar crimes — *Conference proceedings*

Economic crime in Europe / edited by L.H. Leigh. — London : Macmillan [for] the London School of Economics and Political Science, 1980. — xii,211p : 1ill ; 23cm
Conference papers. — Includes bibliographies and index
ISBN 0-333-24840-6 : £20.00 : CIP rev. B80-08681

364.1′68′0973 — United States. White-collar crime

Horoszowski, Pawel. Economic special-opportunity conduct and crime / Pawel Horoszowski. — Lexington, Mass. : Lexington Books, c1980 ; [Farnborough, Hants.] : Gower [distributor], 1981. — x,207p ; 24cm
Includes index
ISBN 0-669-02849-5 : £14.00 B81-17858

364.1′73′0942 — England. Crimes: Drunkenness — *Statistics* — *Serials*

Chief Constables′ reports : England and Wales ; and Scotland. Part 1, Drink offences. — 28th (1980). — London (12 Caxton St., SW1H 0QS) : Christian Economic and Social Research Foundation, 1981. — 12p
£0.20 B81-33701

364.1′77′0924 — South-east Asia. Heroin. Drug traffic by Chinese secret societies: Triads — *Personal observations*

Bresler, Fenton. [The Trail of the Triads]. The Chinese Mafia / Fenton Bresler. — London : Hamlyn Paperbacks, 1981, c1980. — 268p,[8]p of plates : ill,1map,ports ; 18cm
Originally published: London : Weidenfeld and Nicolson, c1980. — Bibliography: p259. — Includes index
ISBN 0-600-20392-1 (pbk) : £1.50 B81-37863

364.2 — CAUSES OF CRIME AND DELINQUENCY

364.2′4 — Crime. Role of consumption of alcoholic drinks

Drinking and crime. — London : Tavistock Publications, Oct.1981. — [350]p. — (The Guilford alcohol studies series)
ISBN 0-422-78080-4 : £18.00 : CIP entry B81-26698

364.2′56 — Guyana. Crime *related to* **race**

Jones, Howard, *1918-*. Crime, race and culture. — Chichester : Wiley, Jan.1982. — [192]p
ISBN 0-471-27996-x : £12.95 : CIP entry B81-34560

364.3 — CRIMINALS

364.3′6 — Delinquent girls

Campbell, Anne, *19---*. Girl delinquents / Anne Campbell. — Oxford : Blackwell, 1981. — 266p ; 23cm
Bibliography: p242-255. — Includes index
ISBN 0-631-12741-0 (cased) : £12.00
ISBN 0-631-12575-2 (pbk) : £4.50 B81-39945

364.3′6 — Juvenile delinquency. Psychosocial aspects

Berry, Jim. Permission to live / Jim Berry. — Bognor Regis : New Horizon, c1981. — v,252p : ill ; 21cm
Bibliography: p250-252
ISBN 0-86116-457-1 : £6.75 B81-40117

364.3′6′0924 — Great Britain. Juvenile delinquency — *Personal observations* — *For young persons*

Ruddock, Patrick. Deaf out / Patrick Ruddock. — [Cambridge] ([18 Brooklands Ave., Cambridge CB2 2HN]) : Basic Skills Unit, c1980. — 29p : ill ; 22cm
ISBN 0-86082-197-8 (pbk) : Unpriced B81-04967

364.3′6′0942 — England. Juvenile delinquency — *For parents*

Gillespie, Veronica. Children and young people in trouble / by Veronica Gillespie ; with a section on Juvenile Courts by Barbara Bullivant ; illustrated by Ruth Bartlett ; general editor, John Allard. — [Billericay] ([17 Jacksons Lane, Billericay, CM11 1AH]) : Home and School Council, c1981. — 24p : ill ; 21cm. — (A Home and School Council publication)
Text and ill. on inside covers
ISBN 0-901181-37-4 (pbk) : Unpriced B81-38553

364.3′6′0942987 — Juvenile delinquency. Geographical aspects — *Study regions: Cardiff*

Evans, David J.. Geographical perspectives on juvenile delinquency / David J. Evans. — Farnborough, Hants. : Gower, c1980. — x,132p : maps,form ; 23cm
Bibliography: p82-88
ISBN 0-566-00351-1 : £9.50 : CIP rev. B80-08682

364.3′6′0973 — United States. Juvenile delinquency

Gibbons, Don C.. Delinquent behavior / Don C. Gibbons. — 3rd ed. — Englewood Cliffs ; London : Prentice-Hall, c1981. — xii,386p : ill ; 24cm
Previous ed.: 1976. — Includes index
ISBN 0-13-197962-0 : £11.65 B81-12672

364.3′6′0973 — United States. Juvenile delinquency — *Sociological perspectives*

Sanders, William B.. Juvenile delinquency : causes, patterns, and reactions / William B. Sanders. — New York ; London : Holt, Rinehart and Winston, c1981. — x,307p : ill ; 25cm
Includes index
ISBN 0-03-040776-1 : £9.50 B81-05690

364.3′6′0973 — United States. Juvenile delinquency. Measurement & analysis

Hindelang, Michael J.. Measuring delinquency / Michael J. Hindelang, Travis Hirschi, Joseph G. Weis. — Beverly Hills ; London : Sage, c1981. — 248p : ill ; 22cm. — (Sage library of social research ; v.123)
Bibliography: p239-245. — Includes index
ISBN 0-8039-1598-5 (cased) : Unpriced
ISBN 0-8039-1599-3 (pbk) : £6.50 B81-36160

364.3′7′0973 — United States. Condemned prisoners — *Interviews*

Magee, Doug. Slow coming dark. — London : Quartet, Jan.1982. — [192]p
Originally published: New York : Pilgrim Press, 1980
ISBN 0-7043-2318-4 : CIP entry B81-34643

364.4 — CRIME PREVENTION

364.4 — Crime. Prevention. Effects of imprisonment of dangerous criminals

Floud, Jean. Dangerousness and criminal justice. — London : Heinemann Educational, Dec.1981. — [256]p. — (Cambridge studies in criminology ; no.47)
ISBN 0-435-82307-8 : £13.50 : CIP entry B81-31843

364.4′094 — Western Europe. Crime. Prevention — *Conference proceedings*

The **Cranfield** papers : the proceedings of the 1978 Cranfield conference on the prevention of crime in Europe. — London (14 St. Cross St., EC1N 8FE) : Peel Press, [1979?]. — 235p : ill ; 22cm
Cover title. — Includes bibliographies
ISBN 0-85164-977-7 (pbk) : Unpriced B81-14266

364.4′0941 — Great Britain. Terrorism. Protection

Yallop, H. J.. Protection against terrorism / by H.J. Yallop. — Chichester : Rose, 1980. — 92p : ill ; 22cm
ISBN 0-85992-202-2 (pbk) : £8.75 B81-10812

364.4′0973 — United States. Crimes. Prevention

O′Block, Robert L.. Security and crime prevention / Robert L. O′Block. — St. Louis ; London : Mosby, 1981. — xi,452p : ill ; 25cm
Includes index
ISBN 0-8016-3738-4 : £10.50 B81-33034

364.4′6 — Great Britain. Crime. Prevention — *Study examples: Schools. Vandalism* — *Study regions: Greater Manchester (Metropolitan County). Manchester*

Gladstone, F. J.. Co-ordinating crime prevention efforts : a Home Office Crime Policy Planning Unit report / by F.J. Gladstone. — London : H.M.S.O., 1980. — v,73p : ill,1form ; 25cm. — (Home Office research study ; no.62)
Bibliography: p69-70
ISBN 0-11-340702-5 (pbk) : £3.95 B81-04992

364.6 — PUNISHMENT OF CRIME

364.6 — England. Juvenile delinquents. Treatment

Out of care : the community support of juvenile offenders / D.H. Thorpe ... [et al.]. — London : Allen & Unwin for the Centre of Youth, Crime and Community, University of Lancaster, 1980. — vii,183p ; 23cm
Includes index
ISBN 0-04-364018-4 (cased) : £10.95 : CIP rev.
ISBN 0-04-364019-2 (pbk) : £3.95 B80-23138

364.6 — England. Juvenile delinquents. Treatment — *Fabian viewpoints*

May, John, *1947-*. Justice, welfare and juvenile delinquents / John May. — London : Fabian Society, 1980. — 19p ; 22cm. — (Fabian tract, ISSN 0307-7535 ; 472)
Cover title
ISBN 0-7163-0472-4 (pbk) : £0.80 B81-07343

364.6 — Great Britain. Juvenile delinquency. Intermediate treatment — *Case studies*

A **Measure** of diversion? : case studies in intermediate treatment / edited by Robert Adams ... [et al.]. — Leicester (17 Albion St., Leicester LE1 6GD) : National Youth Bureau, 1981. — 347p : ill ; 21cm
Includes index
ISBN 0-86155-040-4 (pbk) : £6.95 B81-23992

364.6 — Great Britain. Juvenile delinquency. Intermediate treatment. Group work

One night a week? : aspects of groupwork in Intermediate Treatment / contributions by Mike Anderson ... [et al.] ; edited by Trevor Locke. — Leicester (17 Albion St., Leicester LE1 6GD) : National Youth Bureau, 1981. — 20p : ill,forms ; 30cm. — (IT papers / National Youth Bureau)
Bibliography: p20
ISBN 0-86155-029-3 (pbk) : £1.65 B81-11258

364.6 — Great Britain. Young offenders. Treatment — *Inquiry reports*

Parliamentary All-Party Penal Affairs Group. Young offenders : a strategy for the future / Parliamentary All-Party Penal Affairs Group. — Chichester : Rose, 1981. — 100p ; 21cm
ISBN 0-85992-225-1 (pbk) : £6.85 B81-32735

364.6 — Ireland *(Republic).* **Young offenders. Treatment**

Youth and justice : young offenders in Ireland / by a staff-student working party Dept. of Social Administration UCD ; edited by Helen Burke, Claire Carney and Geoffrey Cook ; research by Maeve McMahon. — Dublin : Turoe, c1981. — xi,222p ; 22cm
Bibliography: p209-215. - Includes index
ISBN 0-905223-24-1 (pbk) : £7.97 (Irish) B81-21811

364.6 — Quebec *(Province).* **Montreal. Juvenile delinquency. Treatment. Role of parents**

Parizeau, Alice. Parenting and delinquent youth / Alice Parizeau ; translated by Dorothy R. Crelinsten. — Lexington : Lexington Books, c1980 ; [Farnborough, Hants.] : Gower [distributor], 1981. — xxii,179p : ill ; 24cm
Translation from the French. — Bibliography: p173-176. — Includes index
ISBN 0-669-03620-x : £14.00 B81-05500

364.6 — United States. Offenders. Corrective treatment

Corrections at the crossroads : designing policy / edited by Sherwood E. Zimmerman and Harold D. Miller. — Beverly Hills ; London : Sage, c1981. — 176p : ill ; 22cm. — (Perspectives in criminal justice ; 1)
ISBN 0-8039-1579-9 (cased) : Unpriced
ISBN 0-8039-1580-2 (pbk) : Unpriced B81-29941

Keve, Paul W.. Corrections / Paul W. Keve. — New York ; Chichester : Wiley, c1981. — xix,506p : ill,1map,1plan,1port ; 24cm
Includes bibliographies and index
ISBN 0-471-03004-x : £9.30 B81-11303

364.6 — Wales. Juvenile delinquents. Treatment — *Conference proceedings*

Social Work Service, Welsh Office, an integrated approach to children in trouble : a report of two workshops held at the Hill Residential College, Abergavenny during February and April 1980. — [Cardiff] : [Welsh Office], [1981]. — 79p : ill ; 30cm
Cover title
Unpriced (spiral) B81-40340

364.6 — Young offenders. Treatment. Role of psychiatry

Abnormal offenders, delinquency and the criminal justice system. — Chichester : Wiley, Feb.1982. — [352]p. — (Wiley series on current research in forensic psychiatry and psychology ; v.1)
ISBN 0-471-28047-x : £17.50 : CIP entry B81-36200

364.6′01 — Punishment — *Philosophical perspectives*

Bean, Philip. Punishment : a philosophical and criminological inquiry / Philip Bean. — Oxford : Robertson, 1981. — viii,215p ; 23cm
Bibliography: p202-210. — Includes index
ISBN 0-85520-391-9 : £12.50 : CIP rev. B81-06582

364.6′092′4 — Punishment. Theories of Plato

Mackenzie, Mary Margaret. Plato on punishment / Mary Margaret Mackenzie. — Berkeley [Calif.] ; London : University of California Press, c1981. — vii,278p ; 25cm
Bibliography: p251-259. — Includes index
ISBN 0-520-04169-0 : £17.25 B81-39775

364.6′0941 — Great Britain. Penal system

Society against crime : penal practise [i.e. practice] in modern Britain / edited by Howard Jones. — Harmondsworth : Penguin, 1981. — 284p ; 20cm. — (Penguin education)
Includes bibliographies
ISBN 0-14-080437-4 (pbk) : £3.95 B81-40473

Watson, David, *1913-*. Criminals and the man in the street / David Watson. — Bognor Regis : New Horizon, c1980. — 255p ; 21cm
ISBN 0-86116-277-3 : £5.25 B81-21729

364.6′0973 — United States. Offenders. Punishment

Reid, Sue Titus. The correctional system : an introduction / Sue Titus Reid. — New York ; London : Holt, Rinehart and Winston, c1981. — 506p : ill ; 25cm
Bibliography: p485-489. — Includes index
ISBN 0-03-042331-7 : £10.95 B81-13964

364.6′2′0942 — England. Prisoners. Parole — *Inquiry reports*

Review of parole in England and Wales / [Home Office]. — London (50 Queen Anne's Gate, SW1H 9AT) : Home Office, 1981. — 22,[44]p : ill ; 30cm
ISBN 0-86252-002-9 (pbk) : Unpriced B81-38021

364.6′3′06041 — Great Britain. Probation officers. Organisations: National Association of Probation Officers — *Directories* — *Serials*

NAPO probation directory / National Association of Probation Officers. — 1974. — London (73, Willifield Way, NW11) : Published for the Association by Owen Wells, c1974. — 96p
ISBN 0-904553-00-0 : £1.60
ISSN 0142-1328 B81-00066

NAPO probation directory / National Association of Probation Officers. — 1976. — London (73, Willifield Way, NW11) : Published for the Association by Owen Wells, c1976. — 125p
ISSN 0142-1328 (corrected) : £1.75 B81-12502

NAPO probation directory / National Association of Probation Officers. — 1979. — Ilkley (66, The Grove, Ilkley, West Yorkshire) : Published for the Association by Owen Wells, 1979. — 143p
ISBN 0-904553-04-3 : £2.50 B81-00067

NAPO probation directory / National Association of Probation Officers. — 1981. — Ilkley (30 St James Rd, Ilkley, West Yorkshire) : Owen Wells for the Association, c1981. — 154p
ISBN 0-904553-11-6 : £3.25
ISSN 0142-1328 B81-24120

364.6′3′0941 — Great Britain. Probation services — *Socialist viewpoints*

Walker, Hilary. Probation work : critical theory and socialist practice / Hilary Walker and Bill Beaumont. — Oxford : Basil Blackwell, 1981. — 218p ; 22cm
Includes index
ISBN 0-631-12729-1 (pbk) : £5.50 : CIP rev. B81-22626

364.6′3′0941 — Great Britain. Welfare work with probationers

Day, Peter R. Social work and social control / Peter R. Day. — London : Tavistock Publications, 1981. — 243p : 1ill ; 23cm
Bibliography: p224-234. — Includes index
ISBN 0-422-77520-7 (cased) : £9.00
ISBN 0-422-77530-4 (pbk) : Unpriced B81-30689

364.6′3′0942 — England. Probation services — *Statistics* — *Serials*

Probation and after-care statistics, England and Wales. — 1979. — London : Home Office, 1980. — 57p
ISBN 0-903727-93-5 : £2.50
ISSN 0142-1093
Also classified at 364.8′0942 B81-09172

Probation service statistics. Actuals / the Conference of Chief Probation Officers [and] the Society of County Treasurers. — 1979-80. — Leicester (30 Millstone La., Leicester) : The Conference, 1980. — 9p
ISSN 0140-8291 (corrected) : Unpriced B81-15164

364.6′3′094249 — Multiracial communities. Role of probation services — *Study regions: West Midlands (Metropolitan County)*

West Midlands County Probation and After-Care Service. Probation and after-care in a multi-racial society / compiled by Wendy Taylor [for the West Midlands County Probation and After-Care Service]. — London : Commission for Racial Equality, 1981. — 135p : maps ; 21cm
ISBN 0-902355-93-7 (pbk) : £2.00 B81-26549

364.6′3′0973 — United States. Probation & parole

Trester, Harold B.. Supervision of the offender / Harold B. Trester. — Englewood Cliffs ; London : Prentice-Hall, c1981. — xii,336p : 2forms ; 24cm. — (Prentice-Hall series in criminal justice)
Includes bibliographies and index
ISBN 0-13-876938-9 : £10.35 B81-16596

364.6′6′0973 — United States. Capital punishment — *Amnesty International viewpoints*

Amnesty International. Proposal for a Presidential Commission on the death penalty in the United States of America / Amnesty International. — [London] : Amnesty International Publications, 1980. — 4p ; 30cm
Cover title
ISBN 0-86210-011-9 (pbk) : Unpriced B81-11084

364.6′8 — Exile. Psychological aspects

Mental health and exile : papers arising from a seminar on mental health and Latin American exile. — [London] ([20 Compton Terrace, N1 2UN]) : World University Service, [1981]. — 40p ; 30cm
Cover title
ISBN 0-9505721-8-7 (pbk) : £2.00 B81-26301

364.6′8 — Scotland. Strathclyde Region. Juvenile delinquency. Intermediate treatment

Downie, Janet. Intermediate treatment research / Janet Downie, Janet Ames. — [Sheffield] : [University of Sheffield Joint Unit for Social Services Research], [c1981]. — ii,45p ; 21cm. — (Social services monographs)
Bibliography: p33-45
ISBN 0-907484-00-x (pbk) : Unpriced B81-16040

364.6′8 — United States. Reparation by offenders — *Conference proceedings*

Victims, offenders, and alternative sanctions / edited by Joe Hudson, Burt Galaway. — Lexington : Lexington Books, c1980 ; [Farnborough, Hants.] : Gower [distributor], 1981. — x,204p : ill ; 24cm
Conference papers. — Includes index
ISBN 0-669-03758-3 : £12.50 B81-23267

364.8 — DISCHARGED PRISONERS

364.8 — Georgia & Texas. Discharged prisoners. Rehabilitation. Financial assistance by United States. *Department of Labor*

Rossi, Peter H.. Money, work, and crime : experimental evidence / Peter H. Rossi, Richard A. Berk, Kenneth J. Lenihan. — New York ; London : Academic Press, c1980. — xxiii,334p : forms ; 24cm. — (Quantitative studies in social relations)
ISBN 0-12-598240-2 : £16.40 B81-05768

364.8′088042 — United States. Women offenders. Rehabilitation

Chapman, Jane Roberts. Economic realities and the female offender / Jane Roberts Chapman. — Lexington, Mass. : Lexington Books, c1980 ; [Farnborough, Hants.] : Gower [[distributor]], 1981. — xiv,234p ; 24cm
Bibliography: p199-222. - Includes index
ISBN 0-669-03515-7 : £13.50 B81-17745

364.8′0942 — England. Discharged prisoners. Aftercare services — *Statistics — Serials*

Probation and after-care statistics, England and Wales. — 1979. — London : Home Office, 1980. — 57p
ISBN 0-903727-93-5 : £2.50
ISSN 0142-1093
Primary classification 364.6′3′0942 B81-09172

364.8′0973 — United States. Offenders. Rehabilitation

Allen, Francis A.. The decline of the rehabilitative ideal : penal policy and social purpose / Francis A. Allen. — New Haven ; London : Yale University Press, c1981. — xii,132p ; 22cm. — (Storrs lectures on jurisprudence)
Includes index
ISBN 0-300-02565-3 : £9.45 : CIP rev.
B81-12368

364.9 — CRIMINOLOGY. HISTORICAL AND GEOGRAPHICAL TREATMENT

364.9172′4 — Developing countries. Crime & punishment — *Marxist viewpoints — Conference proceedings*

Crime, justice and underdevelopment. — London : Heinemann Educational, Sept.1981. — [272]p. — (Cambridge studies in criminology ; v.46)
Conference papers
ISBN 0-435-82888-6 : £17.50 : CIP entry
B81-23768

364′.91732 — Urban regions. Crime. Geographical aspects

Herbert, David, *1935-*. The geography of urban crime. — London : Longman, Jan.1982. — [160]p. — (Topics in applied geography)
ISBN 0-582-30046-0 (pbk) : £4.95 : CIP entry
B81-34558

364′.94 — Western Europe. Crime, *1500-1900.* **Social aspects**

Crime and the law : the social history of crime in Western Europe since 1500 / edited by V.A.C. Gatrell, Bruce Lenman and Geoffrey Parker. — London : Europa, c1980. — xii,381p ; 25cm. — (The Europa social history of human experience)
Includes index
ISBN 0-905118-54-5 : Unpriced : CIP rev.
B80-08683

364′.941 — Great Britain. Crime & punishment, *1939-1945 — Sociological perspectives*

Smithies, Edward. Crime in wartime. — London : Allen & Unwin, Jan.1982. — [224]p
ISBN 0-04-364020-6 : £9.50 : CIP entry
B81-33916

364′.941 — Great Britain. Crime, *1800-1830*

Low, Donald A.. Thieves′ kitchen. — London : Dent, Jan.1982. — [204]p
ISBN 0-460-04438-9 : £8.95 : CIP entry
B81-34511

364′.941′0212 — Great Britain. Crime. Statistics

Bottomley, A. Keith. Understanding crime rates : police and public roles in the production of official statistics / Keith Bottomley, Clive Coleman. — Farnborough : Gower, c1981. — ix,170p ; 23cm
Bibliography: p155-160. — Includes index
ISBN 0-566-00309-0 : £11.50 B81-37913

364′.941′0212 — Great Britain. Crime. Statistics. Information sources

Walker, Monica A.. Crime / by Monica A. Walker. — Oxford : Published for the Royal Statistical Society and the Social Science Research Council by Pergamon, 1981. — xii,406p : forms ; 26cm. — (Reviews of United Kingdom statistical sources ; v.15)
Bibliography: p281-284. — Includes index
ISBN 0-08-026104-3 : £18.25 : CIP rev.
B81-15925

364′.9417′0723 — (Republic) Ireland. Crime. Data. Statistical analysis

Rottman, David B.. Crime in the Republic of Ireland : statistical trends and their interpretation / David B. Rottman. — Dublin : Economic and Social Research Institute, 1980. — 154p : ill,1map ; 25cm. — (Paper / Economic and Social Research Institute ; no.102)
Bibliography: p150-154
ISBN 0-7070-0036-x (pbk) : Unpriced
B81-05421

364′.942 — England. Crime & punishment, *1744-1913*

Policing and punishment in nineteenth-century Britain / edited by Victor Bailey. — London : Croom Helm, c1981. — 248p ; 23cm
Includes index
ISBN 0-7099-0626-9 : £11.95 : CIP rev.
Primary classification 363.2′0942 B81-12828

364′.942 — England. Crime & punishment — *Sociological perspectives*

Wootton, Barbara. Crime and the criminal law : reflections of a magistrate and social scientist / by Barbara Wootton. — 2nd ed. — London : Stevens, 1981. — xii,119p ; 19cm. — (The Hamlyn lectures ; 15th series)
Previous ed.: 1963
ISBN 0-420-46170-1 (cased) : Unpriced : CIP rev.
ISBN 0-420-46180-9 (pbk) : £5.00 B81-15928

364′.942′0212 — England. Criminal law. Justice. Administration — *Statistics — Serials*

Statistics of the criminal justice system England and Wales / Home Office. — 1969-79. — London : H.M.S.O., 1980. — x,104p
ISBN 0-11-340735-1 : £5.80 B81-20027

364′.942542 — Leicester. Crime, *1837-1901*

Tanner, Michael. Crime and murder in Victorian Leicestershire : 1837-1901 / by Michael Tanner. — Leicester ([29 The Fairway, Blaby, Leicester]) : Anderson, c1981. — 50p : ill,facsims,ports ; 21cm
ISBN 0-9504777-9-6 (pbk) : £1.60 B81-29453

364′.973 — Crime & punishment. Attitudes in United States

Crime and punishment : changing attitudes in America / Arthur L. Stinchcombe ... [et al.]. — San Francisco ; London : Jossey-Bass, 1980. — xviii,171p : ill ; 24cm. — (The NORC series in social research)
Bibliography: p162-166. - Includes index
ISBN 0-87589-472-0 : £12.75 B81-10829

Skogan, Wesley G.. Coping with crime : individual and neighborhood reactions / Wesley G. Skogan, Michael G. Maxfield. — Beverly Hills ; London : Sage, c1981. — 280p : ill ; 23cm. — (Sage library of social research ; v.124)
Bibliography: p269-278. — Includes index
ISBN 0-8039-1632-9 (cased) : Unpriced
ISBN 0-8039-1633-7 (pbk) : £6.50 B81-36733

364′.973 — United States. Criminal law. Justice. Administration

Gray, Virginia. The organizational politics of criminal justice : policy in context / Virginia Gray, Bruce Williams. — Lexington : Lexington Books ; [Farnborough, Hants.] : Gower [distributor], 1981, c1980. — xiv,175p : ill ; 24cm
Includes index
ISBN 0-669-02108-3 : £12.00 B81-22948

364′.973 — United States. Criminal law. Justice. Administration — *Conference proceedings*

Improving management in criminal justice / edited by Alvin W. Cohn and Benjamin Ward. — Beverly Hills ; London : Published in cooperation with the American Society of Criminology [by] Sage, c1980. — 159p ; 23cm. — (Sage research progress series in criminology ; v.17)
Conference papers. — Includes bibliographies
ISBN 0-8039-1515-2 (cased) : Unpriced
ISBN 0-8039-1516-0 (pbk) : Unpriced
B81-26978

364′.973 — United States. Criminal law. Justice. Administration. Evaluation

Handbook of criminal justices evaluation / edited by Malcolm W. Klein and Katherine S. Teilmann. — Beverly Hills ; London : Sage, c1980. — 693p ; 24cm
Includes bibliographies and index
ISBN 0-8039-1052-5 : £25.00 B81-15111

364′.973 — United States. Criminal law. Justice. Administration. Participation of community action groups

Alper, Benedict S.. Beyond the courtroom : programs in community justice and conflict resolution / Benedict S. Alper, Lawrence T. Nichols. — Lexington, Mass. : Lexington Books ; [Aldershot] : Gower [distributor], 1981. — xx,299p : ill ; 24cm
Bibliography: p273-288. — Includes index
ISBN 0-669-02724-3 : £14.50 B81-39700

364′.973 — United States. Criminal law. Justice. Administration. Racial factors

Race, crime, and criminal justice / edited by R.L. McNeely and Carl E. Pope. — Beverly Hills ; London : Sage, c1981. — 176p : 1ill ; 23cm. — (Perspectives in criminal justice ; 2)
Includes bibliographies
ISBN 0-8039-1584-5 (cased) : Unpriced
ISBN 0-8039-1585-3 (pbk) : Unpriced
B81-29942

365 — DETENTION INSTITUTIONS

365 — Imprisonment — *Sociological perspectives*

Incarceration : the sociology of imprisonment / edited by Donal E.J. McNamara and Fred Montanino. — Beverly Hills ; London : Sage, 1978. — 156p ; 22cm. — (Sage contemporary social science issues ; 45)
Reprinted from Criminology. Vol.14, no.4, Feb.1977. — Includes bibliographies
ISBN 0-8039-1024-x (pbk) : Unpriced
B81-18825

365′.023′74768 — New York *(State).* **Auburn. Prisons: Auburn Correctional Facility. Prison officers**

Lombardo, Lucien X.. Guards imprisoned : correctional officers at work / by Lucien X. Lombardo ; with a foreword by Hans Toch. — New York ; Oxford : Elsevier, c1981. — xiv,207p : forms ; 24cm
Bibliography: p195-202. — Includes index
ISBN 0-444-99080-1 : Unpriced B81-30088

365′.068 — England. Prisons. Administration, *1750-*

McConville, Seán. A history of English prison administration / Seán McConville. — London : Routledge & Kegan Paul
Vol.1: 1750-1877. — 1981. — xvii,534p ; 23cm
Bibliography: p483-505. — Includes index
ISBN 0-7100-0694-2 : £25.00 : CIP rev.
B81-06575

365′.34 — Australia. British criminals. Transportation. Voyages by sailing ships, *1831-1835 — Correspondence, diaries, etc.*

Mason, George, *fl.1826-1938*. The journal of Captain Mason : of the 4th (King′s Own) Regiment of Foot, his voyage to Australia, his service there and his return journey 1831-1835 / transcribed by Edith Tyson from the original document in the collection of the Museum of The King′s Own Royal Regiment (Lancaster). — [Lancaster] ([Old Town Hall, Market Sq., Lancaster LA1 1HT]) : [Lancaster Museum], c1981. — [63]p : ill ; 30cm. — (A Lancaster Museum publication)
Unpriced (pbk) B81-39894

365′.34 — West Sussex criminals. Transportation, *1778-1853 — Lists*

Emigrants and transportees from West Sussex : 1778-c.1874 / edited by Alison McCann. — [Chichester] ([County Hall, Chichester, W. Sussex]) : [West Sussex County Council], 1980. — [20]leaves ; 30cm. — (Lists and indexes ; no.9)
Unpriced (unbound)
Primary classification 304.8′09422′6 B81-39692

365'.44'0924 — Germany. Concentration camps. Prisoners: Male homosexuals, *1939-1945 — Personal observations*

Heger, Heinz. The men with the pink triangle / Heinz Heger ; translated by David Fernbach. — London (27 Priory Ave., N8 7RN) : Gay Men's Press, 1980. — 117p ; 20cm
Translation of: Die Männer mit dem rosa Winkel
ISBN 0-907040-03-9 (pbk) : £2.25 : CIP rev.
B80-13309

365'.44'0924 — United States. Male prisoners — *Personal observations*

Abbott, Jack Henry. In the belly of the beast. — London : Hutchinson, Jan.1982. — [192]p
Originally published: New York : Random House, 1981
ISBN 0-09-147330-6 : £6.95 : CIP entry
B81-39221

365'.45 — Guatemala. Political prisoners. Torture & execution, *1978-1980*

Guatemala : a government program of political murder. — London : Amnesty International, 1981. — 32p : ill,ports ; 30cm. — (An Amnesty International report)
Cover title
ISBN 0-86210-026-7 (pbk) : Unpriced
B81-14098

365'.45 — Soviet Union. Psychiatric hospitals. Patients: Political dissidents. Detention — *Russian texts*

Bloch, Sidney, *1941-*. [Russia's political hospitals]. Diagnosis : political dissent : an abridged version of Russia's political hospitals, the abuse of psychiatry in the Soviet Union / Sidney Bloch and Peter Reddaway ; foreword by Vladimir Bukovsky = Diagnoz : inakomyslie : kak sovetskie psikhiatry lechat ot politicheskogo inakomyslīia / Sidneĭ Bloch i Piter Reddaueĭ ; predislovie Vladimira Bukovskogo ; sokrashchennyĭ perevod s angliĭskogo. — London : Overseas Publications Interchange, 1981. — 418p ; 19cm
Russian text. — Added t.p. in Russian. — Includes index
ISBN 0-903868-33-4 (pbk) : £7.00 B81-39016

365'.45'0601 — Amnesty International

Power, Jonathan. Against oblivion : Amnesty International's fight for human rights / Jonathan Power. — [London] : Fontana, 1981. — 254p ; 18cm
Includes index
ISBN 0-00-636426-8 (pbk) : £1.95 B81-40131

365'.45'0601 — Amnesty International — *Serials — Spanish texts*

Amnesty International. Amnistía Internacional informe. — 1979. — Londres [London] : Publicaciones Amnistía Internacional, 1980. — vii,222p
ISBN 0-86210-003-8 : Unpriced B81-20410

365'.45'0601 — Amnesty International, *to 1981 — Illustrations*

Photo file 1961-1981 / Amnesty International. — London : Amnesty International Publications, 1981. — 1portfolio : ill,1facsim, ports ; 30cm
Unpriced B81-37338

365'.45'0922 — Israel. Political prisoners: Palestinian Arabs, *1974-1979 — Personal observations — Collections*

Langer, Felicia. These are my brothers : Israel & the occupied territories, Part II / Felicia Langer. — London : Ithaca, 1979. — ix,145p : 1map ; 23cm
ISBN 0-903729-50-4 (cased) : £6.50 B81-33213

365'.45'0924 — Argentina. Political prisoners, *1977-1979 — Personal observations*

Timerman, Jacobo. Prisoner without a name, cell without a number / Jacobo Timerman ; translated from the Spanish by Toby Talbot. — London : Weidenfeld and Nicolson, 1981. — viii,164p ; 22cm
Translation of: Preso sin nombre, celda sin numero
ISBN 0-297-77995-8 : £7.95 B81-29888

365'.45'0924 — Kenya. Political prisoners. Prison life, *1977-1978 — Personal observations*

Ngũgĩ wa Thiong'o. Detained : a writer's prison diary / Ngũgĩ wa Thiong'o. — London : Heinemann, 1981. — xxiii,232p : ill,1facsim ; 20cm
ISBN 0-435-90650-x (cased) : £7.50
ISBN 0-435-90240-7 (pbk) : Unpriced
B81-27029

365'.45'0924 — Ukraine. Political prisoners. Shukhevych, Ĭuriĭ — *Biographies*

Thirty years 1950-1980 : the martyrology of a Ukrainian father and son, Roman and Yuriy Shukhevych. — Toronto ; London : Ukrainian Central Information Service, 1980. — 32p : ill,ports ; 23cm
Unpriced (pbk)
Primary classification 322.4'2'0924 B81-19802

365'.45'09567 — Iraq. Political prisoners. Torture

Iraq : evidence of torture : an Amnesty International report. — [London] : [Amnesty International Publications], 1981. — 44p : maps,1port ; 30cm
ISBN 0-86210-032-1 (unbound) : Unpriced
B81-24004

365'.64 — Michigan. Jackson. Prisons: State Prison Southern Michigan. Contraband

Kalinich, David B.. The inmate economy / David B. Kalinich. — Lexington : Lexington ; Farnborough, Hants. : Gower [distributor], c1980. — vii,119p : ill,1form ; 24cm
Bibliography: p111-115. — Includes index
ISBN 0-669-03595-5 : £10.50 B81-17887

365'.64 — Political prisoners. Torture — *Society of Friends viewpoints*

Baker, Eric, *1920-*. Public policy and the use of torture / Eric Baker. — London : Quaker Peace & Service in association with Amnesty International, 1980. — 32p ; 21cm
ISBN 0-901689-11-4 (pbk) : £0.50
ISBN 0-86210-023-4 (Amnesty International)
B81-12020

365'.64 — United States. Detention institutions. Inmates. Victimisation

Bowker, Lee H.. Prison victimization / Lee H. Bowker. — New York ; Oxford : Elsevier, c1980. — x,231p ; 24cm
Bibliography: p211-225. — Includes index
ISBN 0-444-99077-1 (cased) : £9.58
ISBN 0-444-00551-x (pbk) : Unpriced
B81-05605

365'.641 — Northern Ireland. Prisoners. Protests, *1971-1980*

Berry, Steve. To the bitter climax of death if necessary : the H-block hunger strike and the struggle for political status / by Steve Berry. — London (265 Seven Sisters Rd, N4 2DE) : Produced and distributed for the SWP by Socialists Unlimited, 1980. — 21p : ill ; 30cm. — (A Socialist Workers Party pamphlet)
ISBN 0-905998-15-4 (unbound) : £0.50
B81-06216

365'.641 — Soviet Union. German prisoners of war. Escapes, *1945-1952 — Personal observations*

Bauer, Josef Martin. As far as my feet will carry me / J.M. Bauer ; translated from the German by Lawrence Wilson. — London : Granada, 1966 (1980 printing). — 222p ; 18cm. — (A Mayflower book)
Translation of: So weit die Füsse tragen. — Originally published: New York : Random House ; London : Deutsch, 1957
ISBN 0-583-12506-9 (pbk) : £1.25 B81-00814

365'.66 — China. Political offenders. Rehabilitation, *1949-1980 — Personal observations*

Fyfield, J. A.. Re-educating Chinese class enemies. — London : Croom Helm, Nov.1981. — [144]p
ISBN 0-7099-1017-7 : £9.95 : CIP entry
B81-30535

365'.66 — Christian church. Fellowships for prisoners: Prison Fellowship

Colson, Charles W.. Life sentence / Charles W. Colson. — London : Hodder and Stoughton, 1981, c1979. — 306p ; 18cm
Originally published: Lincoln, Va : Chosen Books, 1979
ISBN 0-340-26934-0 (pbk) : £1.75 : CIP rev.
B81-23931

365'.7'0924 — England. Prisons. Reform. Fry, Elizabeth — *Biographies*

Rose, June. Elizabeth Fry / June Rose. — London : Macmillan, 1980 (1981 [printing]). — 218p,[4]p of plates : ill,1geneal.table.ports ; 22cm
Bibliography: p208-210. — Includes index
ISBN 0-333-31921-4 (pbk) : £3.95 B81-30644

365'.91812 — Western world. Prisons, *1550-1979 — Marxist viewpoints*

Melossi, Dario. The prison and the factory : origins of the penitentiary system / Dario Melossi and Massimo Pavarini ; translated by Glynis Cousin. — London : Macmillan, 1981. — xii,243p ; 23cm. — (Critical criminology series)
Translation of: Carcere e fabbrica. — Includes index
ISBN 0-333-26667-6 (cased) : Unpriced : CIP rev.
ISBN 0-333-26668-4 (pbk) : Unpriced
B80-20466

365'.941 — Great Britain. Prisons

Evans, Peter, *1932-*. Prison crisis / by Peter Evans ; foreword by Sir Robert Mark. — London : Allen & Unwin, 1980. — xviii,165p ; 23cm
ISBN 0-04-365003-1 (cased) : £7.50 : CIP rev.
ISBN 0-04-365004-x (pbk) : £3.95 B80-18205

Fitzgerald, Mike. British prisons. — 2nd ed. — Oxford : Blackwell, Sept.1981. — [176]p
Previous ed.: 1979
ISBN 0-631-12606-6 (pbk) : £3.95 : CIP entry
B81-22625

365'.9411'05 — Scotland. Prisons — *Serials*

Great Britain. *Scottish Home and Health Department*. Prisons in Scotland / Scottish Home and Health Department. — 1979. — Edinburgh : H.M.S.O., [1980]. — iv,66p. — (Cmnd. ; 8037)
ISBN 0-10-180370-2 : £5.00
ISSN 0308-9835 B81-02392

365'.9416 — Northern Ireland. Prisons — *Serials*

Great Britain. *Northern Ireland Office*. Report on the administration of the prison service / Northern Ireland Office. — 1979. — Belfast : H.M.S.O., [1980]. — 57p
ISBN 0-10-028009-9 : £3.80 B81-01865

365'.942 — England. Prisons

King, Roy D.. The future of the prison system / Roy D. King, Rod Morgan with J.P. Martin, J.E. Thomas. — Farnborough, Hants. : Gower, c1980. — x,229p ; 23cm
Bibliography: p211-217. - Includes index
ISBN 0-566-00348-1 : £11.50 : CIP rev.
B80-19701

365'.942'05 — England. Prisons — *Serials*

Great Britain. *Prison Department*. Report on the work of the Prison Department. — 1980. — London : H.M.S.O., 1981. — iv,113p. — (Cmnd. ; 8228)
ISBN 0-10-182280-4 : £6.50 B81-30736

365'.942389 — Somerset. Ilchester. Prisons: Ilchester Gaol. Administration, *1821 — Regulations — Facsimiles*

Ilchester gaol : rules and orders for the government of the common gaol and house of correction, 1821. — St. Peter Port : Toucan, 1980. — 46p : 2ill,1map ; 25cm. — (Ilchester and district occasional papers, ISSN 0306-6010 ; no.26)
Facsim. reprint: Taunton : Printed by J.W. Marriott, 1821?
ISBN 0-85694-224-3 (unbound) : Unpriced
B81-25213

365′.9426752 — Essex. Chelmsford. Prisons: Chelmsford Prison, *to 1980*

Torry, Gilbert. Chelmsford Prison / by J.G. Torry. — Ipswich : East Anglian Magazine Ltd., c1980. — 101p : ill,facsims,ports ; 23cm
Bibliography: p101. - Includes index
ISBN 0-900227-51-6 (pbk) : £3.50 B81-03659

366 — ASSOCIATIONS

366′.0097 — North America. Fraternities — *Encyclopaedias*

Schmidt, Alvin J.. Fraternal organizations / Alvin J. Schmidt ; advisory editor Nicholas Babchuk. — Westport ; London : Greenwood Press, 1980. — xxxiii,410p ; 25cm. — (Greenwood encyclopedia of American institutions)
Includes index
ISBN 0-313-21436-0 : £21.95 B81-23459

366′.1 — Freemasonary

Carr, Harry. The Freemason at work. — 6th revised ed. — Shepperton : A. Lewis, May 1981. — 1v.
Previous ed.: London : The author, 1976
ISBN 0-85318-126-8 : £6.95 : CIP entry B81-06053

366′.1 — Freemasonry

Bailey, Foster. The spirit of masonry / by Foster Bailey. — London : Lucis, 1957 (1979 [printing]). — 153p ; 19cm
£1.50 (pbk) B81-07002

366′.1 — Freemasonry — *Correspondence, diaries, etc.*

Locke, John. A letter of the famous Mr John Locke, relating to Free-masonry : found in the desk or scritoir of a deceased brother. — [St. Peter Port] : Toucan, 1981. — [4]p ; 21cm
Facsim of: ed. published in The Gents magazine, v.23, 1753
ISBN 0-85694-246-4 (pbk) : Unpriced B81-32740

366′.1 — Freemasonry — *Early works*

The **Grand** mystery : being a reprint of two tracts of the eighteenth century on the secrets of Free-Mansonry / with an introduction by Nigel Pennick. — Bar Hill ([142 Pheasant Rise, Bar Hill, Cambridge CB3 8SD]) : Fenris-Wolf, 1980. — 5p ; 30cm. — (Megalithic vision antiquarian papers ; no.16)
Unpriced (unbound) B81-38621

366′.1′02542 — England. Freemasons: Ancient and Accepted Rite for England and Wales — *Directories — Serials*

Ancient and Accepted Rite for England and Wales. Rules and regulations for the government of the degrees from the 4° to 33° inclusive under the Supreme Council 33° of the Ancient and Accepted Rite for England and Wales and its districts and chapters overseas together with list of subscribing members. — 1981. — London (10 Duke St., St. James′, SW1Y 6BS) : The Supreme Council, [1981?]. — 573p
£3.00 B81-20081

366′.1′02542 — England. Freemasons: United Grand Lodge of England — *Directories — Serials*

Masonic year book for .... — 1980-81. — London (Freemasons′ Hall, Great Queen St., WC2 B5AZ) : United Grand Lodge of England, c1980. — 797p
Unpriced B81-09091

366′.1′0254233 — Dorset. Freemasons: Freemasons. *Provincial Grand Lodge of Dorset — Directories — Serials*

Freemasons. *Provincial Grand Lodge of Dorset.* Dorset masonic calendar / compiled under the authority of Provincial Grand Lodge. — 1980. — [Weymouth] ([c/o N. Byles, 21 Marina Gardens, Weymouth DT4 9QZ]) : [Provincial Grand Lodge of Dorset], [1980]. — 271,xiip
£0.50 B81-31009

366′.1′09411 — Scotland. Freemasons: Antient Free and Accepted Masons of Scotland — *Serials*

Antient Free and Accepted Masons of Scotland. Year Book of the Grand Lodge of Antient Free and Accepted Masons of Scotland. — 30th ed. (1981). — Edinburgh (96 George St, Edinburgh EH2 3DH) : The Grand Lodge, 1981. — 191p
ISBN 0-902324-19-5 : £2.00 to members of a regular lodge B81-16756

366′.1′0942 — England. Freemasonry. Orders & degrees

Jackson, Keith B.. Beyond the craft / Keith B. Jackson. — London : Lewis Masonic, c1980. — 90p : ill ; 19cm
ISBN 0-85318-118-7 (pbk) : £3.95 B81-07826

366′.1′0942 — England. Freemasons: Ancient and Accepted Rite for England and Wales, *to 1979*

Jackson, A. C. F.. Rose Croix : the history of the Ancient and Accepted Rite for England and Wales / A.C.F. Jackson. — London : Lewis Masonic, c1980. — xiv,298p : ill,facsims,ports ; 22cm
Bibliography: p280-283. - Includes index
ISBN 0-85318-119-5 : £7.85 : CIP rev. B80-07722

366′.1′094235 — Devon. Freemasons: Mark Master Masons. *Province of Devonshire, to 1980*

Chudley, Ron. A history of the Mark Master Masons in the Province of Devonshire / Ron Chudley. — Exmouth (3 Hartley Rd., Exmouth EX8 2SG) : [R. Chudley], 1980. — 203p : facsims,ports ; 25cm
Unpriced (pbk) B81-16676

366.3′9′0941 — Great Britain. Government. Expenditure. Reduction — *Confederation of British Industry viewpoints*

Report of the CBI Working Party on Government Expenditure. — London : Confederation of British Industry, 1981. — 49p : ill ; 30cm. — (CBI publications)
£5.00 (pbk) B81-40689

367 — SOCIAL CLUBS

367′.068 — Great Britain. Social clubs. Management — *Manuals*

A **Handbook** of social club management. — Manchester (St. James′s House, Charlotte St., Manchester M1 4DZ) : PA Management Consultants, Oct.1981. — [240]p
ISBN 0-902453-09-2 (pbk) : £11.95 : CIP entry B81-32089

368 — INSURANCE

368 — Business firms. Insurance — *Conference proceedings*

Choosing and using an insurance market. — Aldershot : Gower, July 1981. — [100]p
Conference papers
ISBN 0-566-03025-x : £19.50 : CIP entry B81-22678

368 — Developing countries. Agricultural industries. Insurance

Ray, P. K.. Agricultural insurance : theory and practice and application to developing countries / by P.K. Ray. — 2nd ed. — Oxford : Pergamon, 1981. — xxviii,419p,[1]folded leaf of plates : ill,maps,forms ; 26cm
Previous ed.: 1967. — Bibliography: p407-411. — Includes index
ISBN 0-08-025787-9 : £37.50 : CIP rev. B80-11373

368 — Great Britain. Business firms. Insurance — *For management*

Tax and VAT. — London : Hamlyn, c1980. — 207p : forms ; 22cm. — (Managing your business guides)
Includes index
ISBN 0-600-35368-0 : £5.00
Primary classification 336.2′07′0941 B81-05451

368 — Great Britain. Construction industries. Insurance

Eaglestone, F. N.. Insurance for the construction industry / F.N. Eaglestone ; foreword by Robert Porter. — London : Godwin, 1979. — 252p : forms ; 24cm
Includes index
ISBN 0-7114-5507-4 : £13.50 : CIP rev. B79-32411

368 — Insurance

Cockerell, H. A. L.. Insurance / H.A.L. Cockerell. — 4th ed.. — London : Teach Yourself Books, 1980. — 237p ; 18cm. — (Business and management studies) (Teach yourself books)
Previous ed.: 1977. — Bibliography: p228-230. — Includes index
ISBN 0-340-26019-x (corrected : pbk) : £1.95 B81-13364

Dickson, G. C. A.. Elements of insurance / G.C.A. Dickson, J.T. Steele. — Plymouth : Macdonald and Evans, 1981. — xii,206p : ill ; 22cm. — (The M & E BECbook series)
Includes index
ISBN 0-7121-0584-0 (pbk) : £4.75 B81-26257

International insurance industry guide. — [London] ([Abacus House, Gutter La., Cheapside EC2V 8AH]) : Coopers & Lybrand Associates Ltd., c1981. — 202p : ill ; 23cm
Unpriced (pbk) B81-25943

368 — Insurance — *Islamic viewpoints*

Rahman, Afzalur. Banking and insurance / Afzalur Rahman. — London (78 Gillespie Rd, N5 1LN) : Muslim Schools Trust, 1979. — 424p ; 22cm. — (Economic doctrines of Islam ; v.4)
ISBN 0-907052-03-7 (cased) : £7.80
ISBN 0-907052-02-9 (pbk) : £3.80
Primary classification 332.1 B81-30091

368 — London. Insurance companies. Foreign shareholders. Influence

Neave, J. A. S.. Changing world insurance markets : London at risk : overseas influences : a paper read by J.A.S. Neave on Thursday 5th March 1981 at a seminar, London At Risk given by City Financial Conference Services Limited in London. — [S.l.] : [Mercantile and General Reinsurance Company], c1981. — 8p ; 21cm
Text on inside cover
Unpriced (pbk) B81-21758

368′.001′5192 — Insurance. Applications of probabilities & statistical mathematics. Applications of digital computer systems — *Conference proceedings*

Actuarial Research Conference on Computational Probability *(1975 : Brown University, Providence).* Computational probability : the proceedings of the Actuarial Research Conference on Computational Probability, held at Brown University, Providence, Rhode Island on August 28-30, 1975 / sponsored by the Committee on Research of the Society of Actuaries and the Department of Applied Mathematics of Brown University ; edited by P.M. Kahn. — New York ; London : Academic Press, 1980. — xi,340p : ill,1port ; 24cm
ISBN 0-12-394680-8 : £11.80 B81-06219

368′.0025 — Insurance companies — *Directories — Serials*

Financial times world insurance year book. — 1981. — London : Longman, c1980. — 467p
ISBN 0-582-90305-x : Unpriced
ISSN 0309-751x B81-13696

368′.0025′41 — Great Britain. Insurance — *Directories — Serials*

The **Insurance** directory & year book (Post magazine almanack). — 139th year of publication (1980/81). — Brentford : Buckley Press, [1980]. — xv,440p
ISSN 0074-0691 : £17.50 B81-09033

368′.006′041 — Great Britain. Insurance. Organisations: Chartered Insurance Institute — *Directories — Serials*

Chartered Insurance Institute. List of fellows & aasociates / the Chartered Insurance Institute. — 1980. — London (20 Aldermanbury, EC2V 7HY) : The Institute, [1981]. — 93p
£1.00 B81-24140

368′.007′114 — Europe. Universities. Curriculum subjects: Insurance

Stark, P.. A survey of risk and insurance teaching in Europe 1979-1980 / P. Stark ; funded by L′Association internationale pour l′étude de l′economie de l′assurance (Geneva Association), Geneva. — Nottingham (University Park, Nottingham NG7 2RD) : University of Nottingham, Department of Industrial Economics, 1981. — iv,255,ivp : ill,maps,forms ; 30cm
Includes bibliographies and index
Unpriced (pbk) B81-38391

368′.00941 — Great Britain. Insurance companies: Baptist Insurance Company, *to 1980*

Colvin, C. J. L.. The Baptist Insurance Company Limited : a short history of seventy-five years 1905-1980 / C.J.L. Colvin. — [London] ([4 Southampton Row, W.C.1]) : [Baptist Insurance Co. Ltd.], [1980]. — 24p ; 21cm
Cover title
Unpriced (pbk) B81-10289

368′.01′060411 — Scotland. Actuaries. Organisations: Faculty of Actuaries — *Serials*

Faculty of Actuaries. Year book / the Faculty of Actuaries. — 1980-81. — Edinburgh ([23 St. Andrew Square, Edinburgh, EH2 1AQ]) : [The Faculty], 1980. — 224p
Unpriced B81-08756

368′.012 — Internatational reinsurance. Effects of interdepenence of economic relations

Neave, J. A. S.. The effect on international reinsurance of changing patterns in economic interrelationships : a paper read by J.A.S. Neave at the International Insurance Seminar of the Israel Insurance Institute, March 1975. — [London] ([Moorfields House, Moorfields, EC2T 9AL]) : [Mercantile and General Reinsurance Co.], 1977. — 17p ; 21cm
Unpriced B81-06204

368′.012 — International insurance. Role of insurance companies in London, *ca 1970-1977*

Neave, J. A. S.. London as an international insurance and reinsurance centre : a paper read by J.A.S. Neave at conferences organized by the Committee on Invisible Exports in Manila, 21st to 23rd February, 1977 and Mexico, 15th to 17th June 1977. — [London] ([Moorfields House, Moorfields, EC2T 9AL]) : [Mercantile and General Reinsurance Co.], [1977]. — 11p ; 21cm
Unpriced (pbk) B81-06207

368′.012 — International reinsurance

Neave, J. A. S.. The financial service of international reinsurance : a paper read by J.A.S Neave at the International Press Symposium held on Toward new world trade and investment policies, by the Sperry Rand Corporation at St Paul de Vence, 25th-27th October, 1978. — [London] ([Moorfields House, Moorfields, EC2T 9AL]) : [Mercantile and General Reinsurance Co.], c1978. — 12p ; 21cm
Unpriced (pbk) B81-06205

Neave, J. A. S.. Some observations on the contemporary reinsurance scene / J.A.S. Neave. — [London] ([Moorfields House, Moorfields, EC2Y 9AL]) : Mercantile and General Reinsurance Co., c1980. — 12p ; 21cm
Cover title
Unpriced (pbk) B81-32470

368′.012 — International reinsurance. Role of reinsurance brokers & reinsurance underwriters

Neave, J. A. S.. The impact of market problems on the reinsurer : a paper read by J.A.S. Neave to the Insurance Institute of Dublin at the Royal Hibernian Hotel on 6 February 1978. — [London] ([Moorfields House, Moorfields, EC2T 9AL]) : [Mercantile and General Reinsurance Co.], [1978]. — 15p ; 21cm
Unpriced (pbk) B81-06201

368′.012 — Reinsurance

Bellerose, R. Philippe. Reinsurance for the beginner / by R. Philippe Bellerose. — 2nd ed. — London : Witherby, 1980. — 82p : ill,forms ; 21cm. — (Monument series)
Previous ed.: 1978
ISBN 0-900886-48-x (pbk) : Unpriced B81-14518

Carter, Robert L.. Reinsurance / R.L. Carter. — Brentford : Kluwer in association with the Mercantile and General Reinsurance Co. Ltd., 1979. — xi,590p : ill ; 24cm
Bibliography: p577-582. - Includes index
ISBN 0-903393-38-7 : £44.50 B81-01875

A **Selection** of papers on reinsurance topics 1978-1980 / Insurance Institute of London. — London : [The Institute], 1980. — 66p ; 21cm
Cover title
Unpriced (pbk) B81-06954

368′.012 — Reinsurance companies. Attitudes of governments

Neave, J. A. S.. The attitudes of supervisory authorities towards reinsurance : a paper read by J.A.S. Neave at a conference jointly promoted by the C.I.I. and M.A.L.I.C. on How government legislation affects reinsurance, at the Cumberland Hotel, London on 22nd February, 1978. — [London] ([Moorfields House, Moorfields, EC2T 9AL]) : Mercantile and General Reinsurance Company, 1978. — 12p ; 21cm
Unpriced (pbk) B81-06202

368′.012 — Reinsurance companies. Effects of policies of governments

Neave, J. A. S.. Financial problems of reinsurers : paper read by J.A.S. Neave to the Insurance Institute of South Africa seminar on financial problems in the changing economy, Johannesburg 5th May 1975. — [London] ([Moorfields House, Moorfields, EC2T 9AL]) : [Mercantile and General Reinsurance Co.], [1976?]. — 12p ; 21cm
Unpriced (pbk) B81-06203

368′.012 — Reinsurance — *Serials*

The **Re** report / Institute for International Research. — Issue 80-1 (Apr.14 1980)-. — London (70 Warren St., W1P 5PA) : The Institute, 1980-. — v. ; 28cm
Twenty-five issues yearly
ISSN 0143-9669 = Re report : £95.00 per year B81-04591

368′.012 — Reinsurance. Underwriting. Role of governments, *to 1977*

Neave, J. A. S.. The development of government involvement in reinsurance underwriting : a paper presented by J.A.S. Neave to the XIII International Insurance Seminar in Oslo, 7th-11th August, 1977. — [London] ([Moorfields House, Moorfields, EC2T 9AL]) : [Mercantile and General Reinsurance Co.], [1977]. — 19p ; 21cm
Appendix, Government participation in reinsurance underwriting, (21p) in pocket
Unpriced (pbk) B81-06206

368′.023 — Insurance — *Career guides*

Verner, Jordan. Careers in insurance. — London : Kogan Page, Jan.1982. — [100]p
ISBN 0-85038-474-5 (cased) : £5.95 : CIP entry
ISBN 0-85038-475-3 (pbk) : £2.50 B81-40252

368′.092′0331 — Motor vehicles. Insurance — *German & English dictionaries*

Motor insurance : German and English. — Berlin : Langenscheidt ; London : Sweet & Maxwell, c1980. — 152p ; 21cm. — (European glossary of legal and administrative terminology ; v.27)
Parallel German text and English translation. — Added t.p. in German. — Bibliography: p12-13. — Includes index
ISBN 0-421-28790-x (pbk) : £6.00 B81-35271

368.1 — PROPERTY INSURANCE

368.1 — Great Britain. Churches. Insurance

It won′t happen to us. — Rev. ed. — London (Dean′s Yard, SW1P 3NZ) : CIO Publishing [for] the Council for the Care of Churches, 1981. — 11p : 2ill ; 21cm
Previous ed.: 1970
ISBN 0-7151-7539-4 (pbk) : £0.80 B81-34806

368.1 — Underinsured property. Implications of inflation

Dickinson, Gerald M.. Underinsurance on a portfolio of property exposures in an inflationary environment / by G.M. Dickinson and L.A. Roberts. — London (Gresham College, Basinghall St., EC2V 5AH) : City University Business School, c1981. — 27leaves : ill ; 30cm. — (Working paper series / City University Business School, ISSN 0140-1041 ; no.21)
Bibliography: leaf 27
Unpriced (pbk) B81-14570

368.2 — TRANSPORT INSURANCE

368.2′2 — Freight transport. Shipping. Ships. Cargoes. Insurance — *Conference proceedings*

Marine insurance ′81 (cargo conference) : the London Press Centre, June 4/5, 1981. — [London] : [Lloyd′s of London], [1981]. — 152leaves in various foliations : ill ; 31cm
ISBN 0-907432-20-4 : Unpriced B81-37623

368.2′2 — Shipping. Insurance — *Conference proceedings*

Marine insurance ′81 (hull conference) : the London Press Centre, June 2/3, 1981. — [London] : [Lloyd′s of London Press], [1981]. — 149leaves in various foliations ; 31cm
ISBN 0-907432-15-8 : Unpriced B81-37622

368.3 — INSURANCE AGAINST DEATH, OLD AGE, ILLNESS, INJURY

368.3′2′0060411 — Scotland. Life assurance. Organisations: Associated Scottish Life Offices. Role

Life Offices′ Association. Organisation and role / The Life Offices′ Assocation, Associated Scottish Life Offices. — London (Aldermary House, Queen St., EC4N 1TP) : The Association, [1981]. — 8p ; 21cm
Cover title
Unpriced (pbk)
Primary classification 368.3′2′006042
B81-17804

368.3′2′006042 — England. Life assurance. Organisations: Life Offices′ Association. Role

Life Offices′ Association. Organisation and role / The Life Offices′ Assocation, Associated Scottish Life Offices. — London (Aldermary House, Queen St., EC4N 1TP) : The Association, [1981]. — 8p ; 21cm
Cover title
Unpriced (pbk)
Also classified at 368.3′2′0060411 B81-17804

368.3′2′00941 — Great Britain. Life assurance companies: National Mutual Life Assurance Society, *to 1980*

Street, Eric. The history of the National Mutual Life Assurance Society 1830-1980 / compiled by Eric Street ; edited by Richard Glenn. — London (5 Bow Churchyard, EC4M 9DH) : The Society, 1980. — v,122p folded leaf : ill,ports ; 27cm
Spine title: The National Mutual Life Assurance Society 1930-1980
Unpriced B81-03267

368.3′2′00941 — Great Britain. Life assurance companies: Pearl Assurance Co. — *Serials*

Field operations. — Vol.1, no.1 (Mar.1981)-. — [London] (252 High Holborn, [WC1]) : Information Unit, Pearl Assurance Co., 1981-. — v. : ill,ports ; 33cm
Monthly. — Continues: Marketplace. — Description based on: Vol.1, no.4 (June 1981)
ISSN 0261-8990 = Field operations : Unpriced B81-38508

368.3′2′00941 — Great Britain. Life assurance. Policies — *Serials*

Life policy market. — Vol.79, no.3293 (Jan. 1980)-. — London : Stone & Cox, 1980-. — ill,port ; 30cm
Cover title: Policy market. — Continues on part: Policy. — With: General policy market. — Description based on: Jan.1981 issue
ISSN 0261-085x = Life policy market : £12.00 per year B81-15436

368.3′2011 — Great Britain. Annuitants. Mortality rate — *Forecasts — Tables — For life assurance*

a (90) tables for annuitants. — [London] ([Staple Inn Hall, High Holborn, WC1V 7QJ]) : Institute of Actuaries : Faculty of Actuaries, 1979
Vol.1: Single-life functions at rates of interest from 0% to 73/4% - Functions for two lives at rates of interest from 0% to 71/2%. — xv,341p ; 26cm
Unpriced B81-16128

a (90) tables for annuitants. — [London] ([Staple Inn Hall, High Holborn, WC1V 7QJ]) : Institute of Actuaries : Faculty of Actuaries, 1979
Vol.2: Single-life functions and functions for two lives at rates of interest from 8% to 16%. — xv,355p ; 26cm
Unpriced B81-16129

368.3′2011 — Great Britain. Old age pensioners. Mortality rate — *Forecasts — Tables — For life assurance*

PA (90) tables for pensioners. — [London] ([Staple Inn Hall, High Holborn, WC1V 7QJ]) : Institute of Actuaries : Faculty of Actuaries, 1979
Vol.1: Single-life functions and functions for two lives at rates of interest from - 5% to 51/4%. — xiv,355p ; 26cm
Unpriced B81-16130

PA (90) tables for pensioners. — [London] ([Staple Inn Hall, High Holborn, WC1V 7QJ]) : Institute of Actuaries : Faculty of Actuaries, 1979
Vol.2: Single-life functions and functions for two lives at rates of interest from 51/2% to 16%. — xiv,363p ; 26cm
Unpriced B81-16127

368.3′62′009416 — Northern Ireland. Industrial assurance — *Serials*

Industrial assurance : report of the Industrial Assurance Commissioner for the year ended 31st December .... — 1979. — Belfast : H.M.S.O., 1981. — 10p
ISBN 0-337-06127-0 : £1.50 B81-27330

368.3′82′00941 — Great Britain. Private health insurance — *Statistics — For marketing*

Jakeways, I.. The U.K. private health insurance market : market position report / I. Jakeways, T. O'Brien, C. Richardson. — Manchester (Booth Street West, Manchester M15 6PB) : Centre for Business Research in association with Manchester Business School, University of Manchester, [1981?]. — 60 leaves : ill ; 30cm. — (Research report. Market position series / Centre for Business Research)
Unpriced (spiral) B81-13220

368.4 — NATIONAL INSURANCE

368.4 — Great Britain. National insurance contribution records. Validation. Procedure. Cost-effectiveness — *Inquiry reports*

Brought to account : report of the Rayner scrutiny team on the validation of national insurance contribution records / [prepared by] Nick Montagu, Trevor Millar, Julie Partridge. — London ([10 John Adam St., WC2N 6HD]) : Department of Health and Social Security, 1981. — 93p : 1form ; 30cm
ISBN 0-902650-29-7 (pbk) : £2.10 B81-37496

368.4′00880624 — Great Britain. Low-income personnel. National insurance contributions

Pond, Chris. Insuring poverty at work / Chris Pond, Emma MacLennan. — London (9 Poland St., W1V 3DG) : Low Pay Unit, 1981. — 19p ; 21cm
£0.75 (unbound) B81-25579

368.4′00941 — Great Britain. Low-income families. Social security benefits. Policies — *Child Poverty Action Group viewpoints*

Child Poverty Action Group. Moving back to the means test : a memorandum to the Chancellor of the Exchequer from the Child Poverty Action Group / by Ruth Lister. — London (1 Macklin St., WC2B 5NH) : The Group, 1980. — 32p ; 21cm. — (Poverty pamphlet ; 47)
£0.70 (pbk) B81-06953

368.4′00941 — Great Britain. Social security benefits, *1981 — For trade unionism*

State benefits : a guide for trade unionists / Labour Research Department. — London : LRD, 1981. — 32p ; 21cm
Cover title
£0.60 (pbk) B81-11261

368.4′00941 — Great Britain. Social security benefits — *For welfare work*

Cohen, Ruth. Welfare rights. — London : Heinemann Educational, Feb.1982. — [128]p. — (Community care practice handbooks ; 10)
ISBN 0-435-82175-x (pbk) : £2.95 : CIP entry B81-35695

368.4′00941 — Great Britain. Social security — *Statistics — Serials*

Social security statistics. — 1978. — London : H.M.S.O., 1980. — 239p
ISBN 0-11-760676-6 : £11.50 B81-04734

368.4′00941 — Great Britain. Supplementary benefits — *For claimants*

Great Britain. *Department of Health and Social Security*. Supplementary benefits handbook : a guide to claimants' rights / Department of Health and Social Security. — Rev. — London : H.M.S.O., 1981, c1980. — 143p ; 21cm
Previous ed.: / Supplementary Benefit Commission. 1980. — Text on inside cover. — Includes index
ISBN 0-11-760698-7 (pbk) : £2.40 B81-05942

Lynes, Tony. The Penguin guide to supplementary benefits : supplementary benefits, the new regulations, the family income supplement and the appeals tribunal / Tony Lynes. — 4th ed. / with a foreword by Lord Scarman. — Harmondsworth : Penguin, 1981. — 319p ; 18cm
Previous ed.: 1975. — Includes index
ISBN 0-14-046423-9 (pbk) : £2.50 B81-33615

368.4′00941 — Great Britain. Supplementary benefits — *Serials*

Great Britain. *Department of Health and Social Security Commission*. Report of the Supplementary Benefits Commission for the year ended 31 December .... — 1979. — London : H.M.S.O., 1980. — xi,183p. — (Cmnd ; 8033)
Cover title: Supplementary Benefits Commission annual report
ISBN 0-10-180330-3 : £6.70 B81-08282

368.4′009416 — Northern Ireland. Supplementary benefits

Great Britain. *Department of Health and Social Services, Northern Ireland. Supplementary Benefits Commission*. Final report of the Supplementary Benefits Commission. — Belfast : H.M.S.O., 1980. — xi,82p ; 25cm
ISBN 0-337-07208-6 (pbk) : £4.20 B81-15752

368.4′015′0941 — Great Britain. National insurance — *Accounts — Serials*

National Insurance Fund account. — 1979-80. — London : H.M.S.O., 1981. — 15p
ISBN 0-10-219581-1 : £1.70 B81-26592

368.4′015′09416 — Northern Ireland. National insurance — *Accounts — Serials*

Northern Ireland Insurance Fund account. — 1979-80. — Belfast : H.M.S.O., 1981. — 10p
ISBN 0-337-02328-x : £1.40 B81-35113

Northern Ireland National Fund account. — 1978-79. — Belfast : H.M.S.O., 1980. — 7p
ISBN 0-337-02321-2 : £1.25 B81-07818

368.4′1 — Great Britain. Industrial injuries. Compensation — *Proposals*

Walker, Alan, *1949-*. The case for reforming the industrial injuries scheme : the response of the Disability Alliance to the DHSS discussion document Industrial injuries compensation / Alan Walker. — London (1 Cambridge Terr., N.W.1) : The Alliance, 1980. — 34p : facsims ; 30cm
Unpriced (pbk) B81-11466

368.4′2 — Great Britain. Mental handicap hospitals. Long-stay patients. Social security benefits. Expenditure

Disability Alliance. Patients' money in long-stay hospitals : the Disability Alliance' response to a DHSS consultative paper. — London (1 Cambridge Terrace, NW1 4JL) : The Alliance, 1981. — 9p ; 30cm
£0.50 (pbk) B81-26437

368.4′2 — Great Britain. Non-contributory invalidity pensions. Eligibility of handicapped housewives. Household Duties Test

Glendinning, Caroline. "After working all these years" : a response to the report of the National Insurance Advisory Committee on the "household duties" test for non-contributory invalidity pension for married women / Caroline Glendinning. — London (1 Cambridge Terrace, NW1 4JL) : Disability Alliance, 1980. — 64p ; 21cm
£0.80 (£1.00 by post) (pbk) B81-05484

368.4′2 — Great Britain. Unemployed handicapped persons. Social security benefits

Disability Alliance. Payment of benefits to unemployed people / comments by the Disability Alliance. — London (1 Cambridge Terrace, NW1 4JL) : The Alliance, 1981. — 10p ; 30cm
£0.50 (pbk)
Primary classification 331.5′9′0941 B81-26440

368.4′2 — United States. State prescription drug insurance

Silverman, Milton. Pills & the public purse : the routes to national drug insurance / Milton Silverman, Philip R. Lee, Mia Lydecker. — Berkeley ; London : University of California Press, c1981. — xviii,232p ; 24cm
Bibliography: p201-202. — Includes index
ISBN 0-520-04381-2 : £9.50 B81-36568

368.4′24015′0941 — Great Britain. Women personnel. Maternity pay. Maternity Pay Fund — *Accounts — Serials*

Maternity Pay Fund account. — 1979-80. — London : H.M.S.O., 1981. — 6p
ISBN 0-10-213581-9 : £1.10 B81-16246

368.4′3 — Great Britain. Death grants. Reform — *Proposals*

Kendall, Ian. Beyond our means : the rise and fall of the death grant / Ian Kendall. — Mitcham (60 Pitcairn Rd., Mitcham, Surrey CR4 3LL) : Age Concern England, 1980. — 28p ; 21cm. — (Age Concern policy discussion paper)
ISBN 0-86242-002-4 (pbk) : £1.00 B81-09579

368.4′4′00941 — Great Britain. Unemployed persons. Social security benefits. Payment. Methods — *Inquiry reports*

Payment of benefits to unemployed people / Department of Employment, Department of Health and Social Security. — London : H.M.S.O., 1981. — 101p : ill ; 30cm
ISBN 0-11-361198-6 (pbk) : £2.35 B81-22220

368.5 — ACCIDENT INSURANCE

368.5 — Professional liability insurance — *Conference proceedings*

Professional liability insurance : a one-day conference organised by Lloyd's of London Press Ltd., the London Press Centre, October 3, 1980. — [London] ([Lloyd's of London Press]), [1981]. — [58] leaves in various pagings : ill,forms ; 31cm
ISBN 0-904093-93-x : £20.00 B81-09510

368.5′7 — Great Britain. Road freight transport services. Liability insurance — *Conference proceedings*

Goods in transit : UK liability and insurance : report of a conference held in September 1980 / contributors A.E. Donald ... [et al.] ; series editor George Cyriax. — Aldershot : Gower, c1981. — 101p ; 30cm. — (Gower executive report)
ISBN 0-566-03021-7 (pbk) : Unpriced B81-37130

368.5'76 — Great Britain. Airports. Security measures. Aviation Security Fund - *Accounts* - *Serials*

Aviation Security Fund accounts. — 1979-80. — London : H.M.S.O., 1981. — 8p
ISBN 0-10-212681-x : £1.10 B81-15542

368.8 — INSURANCE. MISCELLANEOUS TYPES

368.8'15'00941 — Great Britain. Business firms. Consequential losses. Insurance

Riley, Denis. Consequential loss and business interruption insurances and claims. — 5th ed. — London : Sweet & Maxwell, Jan.1982. — [475]p
Previous ed. published as: Consequential loss insurances and claims. 1977
ISBN 0-421-28780-2 : £30.00 : CIP entry
B81-34968

368.9 — INSURANCE. HISTORICAL AND GEOGRAPHICAL TREATMENT

368'.941 — Great Britain. Insurance companies. Regulation by government

Wiltshire, J. A.. The official supervision of the insurance industry in the UK / by J.A. Wiltshire. — London (20 Aldermanbury, EC2V 7HY) : Chartered Insurance Institute, c1980. — 63p ; 26cm
£1.00 (pbk) B81-23065

368'941 — Great Britain. Insurance — *Manuals*

Knox, Patricia. Insurance: are you covered? / Patricia Knox. — London : Owl Books, 1980. — 95p ; 21cm
Includes index
ISBN 0-7063-6012-5 (cased) : £3.95
ISBN 0-7063-6013-3 (pbk) : £2.50 B81-01938

368'.941'0212 — Great Britain. Insurance companies — *Statistics* — *Serials*

Insurance business statistics / Business Statistics Office. — 1977. — London : H.M.S.O., c1980. — 74p. — (Business monitor ; MA16)
ISBN 0-11-512875-1 : £5.00 B81-20728

368'.941'0212 — Great Britain. Insurance — *Statistics* — *Serials*

Insurance facts and figures. — 1979. — London (Aldermary House, Queen St., EC4N 1TU) : British Insurance Association, 1980. — 22p
ISSN 0308-8308 : Unpriced B81-04753

368'.941'0321 — Great Britain. Insurance — *Encyclopaedias*

Cockerell, H. A. L.. Witherby's dictionary of insurance / by Hugh Cockerell. — London : Witherby, 1980. — vii,235p ; 23cm
ISBN 0-900886-50-1 : £12.50 B81-10797

368'.941'05 — Great Britain. Insurance. Policies — *Serials*

General policy market. — Vol.79, no.3293 (Jan. 1980). — London : Stone & Cox, 1980-. — ill ; 30cm
Cover title: Policy market. — Continues in part: Policy. — With insert: Life policy market. — Description based on: Vol.80, no.3305 (Jan. 1981)
ISSN 0261-0841 = General policy market : £12.00 per year B81-15435

368'.9416'05 — Northern Ireland. Insurance companies — *Serials*

Insurance companies general report for the year ended 31 December ... and the period ended 31 May ... / Department of Commerce [Northern Ireland]. — 1979-1980. — Belfast : H.M.S.O., 1980. — 12p
ISBN 0-337-06120-3 : £1.20 B81-16252

369.4 — YOUTH ORGANISATIONS

369.4 — Youth groups for homosexuals. Organisation — *Manuals*

Gay Youth groups. — [Liverpool] ([Link, 14 Colquitt St., Liverpool L1 4DE]) : Joint Council for Gay Teenagers, 1980. — 7p : 1ill ; 22cm
Unpriced (unbound) B81-19580

369.4'025'41 — Great Britain. Young persons' voluntary organisations — *Directories* — *Serials*

National Council for Voluntary Youth Services. NCVYS annual directory. — 1980/81. — Leicester (29 Albion St., Leicester LE1 6GD) : National Council for Voluntary Youth Services, [1980?]. — 22p
Unpriced B81-20292

369.4'0941 — Great Britain. Youth clubs, *to 1980*

Bunt, Sidney. The policies of youth clubs / Sidney Bunt and Ron Gargrave. — Leicester : National Youth Bureau, c1980. — 183p ; 21cm
ISBN 0-86155-034-x (pbk) : £3.45 B81-09163

369.4'09411 — Scotland. Youth movements. Organisations: BYC (Scotland) — *Serials*

BYC (Scotland) news. — March 1980-. — Edinburgh (1 Queensferry Street, Edinburgh EH2 4PA) : BYC Scotland, 1980-. — v. : ill
Irregular
Unpriced B81-13212

369.4'09414'34 — Scotland. Strathclyde Region. Bearsden and Milngavie *(District).* **Young persons' voluntary organisations** — *Proposals*

Harvey, Colin. A Fourth World youth club and Volunteering (a newsheet for young people) / by Colin Harvey. — Milngavie (163 Mugdock Rd., Milngavie, Dunbartonshire G62 6BR) : Heatherbank Press for the Museum of Social Work, 1980. — 12,10leaves ; 31cm. — (Occasional paper / Museum of Social Work ; no.5)
Cover title. — Text on inside covers
ISBN 0-905192-26-5 (spiral) : £1.50
B81-29258

369.42'0941 — Great Britain. Boys' clubs

National Association of Boys' Clubs. Principles and aims of Boys' Clubs / by Kenneth Kirk. — London (24 Highbury Grove, N5 2EA) : National Association of Boys' Clubs, 1980. — 28p ; 21cm
Unpriced (pbk) B81-10866

369.43 — Cub scouting — *Manuals*

The **Cub** scout programme booklet / [Scout Association]. — 3rd ed. — London : The Association, 1981. — 64p : col.ill ; 11x15cm
Cover title. — Previous ed.: published as part of The Cub scout membership kit. 2nd ed. 1979
ISBN 0-85165-166-6 (pbk) : Unpriced
B81-36576

369.43 — Poland. Venture scouting — *Polish texts*

Pancewicz, B. M.. Jak pracują wędrownicy : Polish Venture Scouts in the world : a handbook for leader / Bronislaw Pancewicz. — Londyn : Główna Kwatera Harcerzy, 1980. — ii,106p : ill,1map ; 21cm
Unpriced (pbk) B81-32620

369.43'0941 — Great Britain. Boys' organisations: Scout Association — *Regulations*

Scout Association. The policy, organisation and rules of the Scout Association. — London : Scout Association
Pt.1: Organisation. — c1977 (1981 [printing]). — 168p ; 18cm
ISBN 0-85165-128-3 (pbk) : Unpriced
B81-30946

369.43'09427'623 — Lancashire. Darwen. Scouting, *to 1979*

Darwen District Scout Council. The history of scouting in Darwen, 1909-1979 / written by Howard Peters ; layout Bill Watson. — [Darwen] ([c/o W. Watson, 146 Higher Avondale Rd, Darwen, Lancs.]) : Darwen District Scout Council, [1979]. — iii,92p : ill,1facsim,ports ; 21cm
Unpriced (pbk) B81-22177

369.46'3 — Brownie Guides. Activities — *Manuals*

The **Brownie** gift book. — Maidenhead : Purnell, 1981. — 61p : ill(some col.) ; 27cm
ISBN 0-361-05074-7 : £2.75 B81-29675

369.46'3'0941 — Great Britain. Girl Guides

Scott, Nancy. Girl guides / by Nancy Scott ; photographed by John Moyes. — Loughborough : Ladybird, c1980. — 51p : col.ill,ports ; 18cm. — (Hobbies)
Ill, text on lining papers. — Includes index
ISBN 0-7214-0643-2 : £0.40 B81-06989

369.5 — SERVICE CLUBS

369.5 — Leicestershire. Leicester. Rotary clubs: Rotary Club of Leicester, *to 1980*

Rotary Club of Leicester. Rotary in Leicester 1916-1980 : a history of the Rotary Club of Leicester / by Brian Thompson. — [Leicester] ([6 The Fairway, Oadby, Leicester LE2 2HH]) : The Club, 1980. — 43p : ill,ports ; 21cm
£2.00 (pbk) B81-01988

369.5 — Round Tables: Association of Ex-Tablers' Clubs — *Directories* — *Serials*

Association of Ex-Tablers' Clubs. Directory / the Association of ex-Tablers' Clubs. — 1974-1975. — Bramhall (Maple House, Maple Rd., Bramhall SK7 2DL) : The Association, [1975?]. — 23p
Unpriced B81-14357

Association of Ex-Tablers' Clubs. Directory / the Association of Ex-Tablers' Clubs. — 1975-1976. — Bournemouth (1, Poole Rd., Bournemouth BH2 5QQ) : The Association, [1976?]. — 23p
Unpriced B81-14358

Association of Ex-Tablers' Clubs. Directory / the Association of Ex-Tablers' Clubs. — 1976-1977. — Bournemouth (1, Poole Rd., Bournemouth BH2 5QQ) : The Association, [1977?]. — 28p
Unpriced B81-14359

Association of Ex-Tablers' Clubs. Directory / Association of Ex-Tablers' Clubs. — 1977-1978. — Bournemouth (1, Poole Rd., Bournemouth BH2 5QQ) : The Association, [1978?]. — 31p
Unpriced B81-14360

Association of Ex-Tablers' Clubs. Directory / the Association of Ex-Tablers' Clubs. — 1978-1979. — Bournemouth (1, Poole Rd., Bournemouth BH2 5QQ) : The Association, [1979?]. — 35p
Unpriced B81-14361

Association of Ex-Tablers' Clubs. Directory / the Association of Ex-Tablers' Clubs'. — 1979-1980. — Bournemouth (1, Poole Rd., Bournemouth BH2 5QQ) : The Association, [1980?]. — 39p
Unpriced B81-14362

Association of Ex-Tablers' Clubs. Directory / the Association of Ex-Tablers' Clubs. — 1980. — Harpenden (78, Station Rd., Harpenden, Herts. AL5 4TZ) : The Association, [1980?]. — 23p
Unpriced B81-14363

370 — EDUCATION

370 — Education

Lawton, Denis. An introduction to teaching and learning / Denis Lawton. — London : Hodder and Stoughton, 1981. — 142p ; 22cm. — (Studies in teaching and learning)
Bibliography: p137-140. — Includes index
ISBN 0-340-26077-7 (pbk) : £2.95 : CIP rev.
B81-07447

Standards, schooling and education : a reader / edited by Alex Finch and Peter Scrimshaw for the Contemporary Issues in Education Course at the Open University. — Sevenoaks : Hodder and Stoughton in association with the Open University Press, c1980. — 406p : ill ; 22cm. — (Contemporary issues in education) (Open University set books)
Includes bibliographies and index
ISBN 0-340-25757-1 (pbk) : £5.60 : CIP rev.
B80-24332

370 — Education — *For primary school teaching in Africa*

Farrant, J. S.. Principles and practice of education / J.S. Farrant. — New ed. — [London] : Longman, 1980. — xii,386p : ill,forms ; 25cm
Previous ed.: published as : Principles and practice of education for use in African training colleges. 1964. — Includes index
ISBN 0-582-60772-8 (pbk) : £4.00 B81-16260

370 — Education. Innovation

Adams, Raymond S.. The process of educational innovation. — London : Kogan Page, Nov.1981. — [286]p
ISBN 0-85038-511-3 (pbk) : £10.50 : CIP entry
B81-31086

370 — Multicultural societies. Education

The **School** in the multicultural society. — London : Harper and Row, Jan.1982. — [330]p
ISBN 0-06-318195-9 (cased) : £9.95 : CIP entry
ISBN 0-06-318196-7 (pbk) : £5.95 B81-33970

370′.1 — Children. Education. Theories, ***1861-1862***

Tolstoĭ, L. N.. Tolstoy on education. — London : Athlone Press, Nov.1981. — [328]p
ISBN 0-485-11198-5 : £18.00 : CIP entry
B81-30559

370′.1 — Education. Applications of theories of liberty

Strike, Kenneth. Liberty and learning. — Oxford : Robertson, Dec.1981. — [224]p. (Issues and ideas in education series)
ISBN 0-85520-431-1 (cased) : £10.00 : CIP entry
ISBN 0-85520-432-x (pbk) : £3.95 B81-31649

370′.1 — Education — *Philosophical perspectives*

Matthews, Michael R.. The Marxist theory of schooling : a study of epistemology and education / Michael R. Matthews. — Brighton : Harvester, 1980. — x,214p ; 23cm. — ([Studies in philosophy] ; [no.24])
Bibliography: p203-210. — Includes index
ISBN 0-85527-443-3 : £18.95 : CIP rev.
B80-19703

O′Hear, Anthony. Education, society and human nature : an introduction to the philosophy of education / Anthony O′Hear. — London : Routledge & Kegan Paul, 1981. — xi,173p ; 23cm
Bibliography: p165-167. — Includes index
ISBN 0-7100-0747-7 : £7.95 : CIP rev.
ISBN 0-7100-0748-5 (pbk) : £3.95 B81-14836

370′.1 — Education — *Philosophical perspectives — For teaching*

Barrow, Robin. The philosophy of schooling / Robin Barrow. — Brighton : Wheatsheaf, c1981. — 211p ; 23cm
Bibliography: p206-208. - Includes index
ISBN 0-7108-0105-x : £15.95 (pbk) : Unpriced
B81-19600

370′.1 — Education. Theories

Dancy, John C.. Wisdom and education : an inaugural lecture delivered in the University of Exeter on 19 October 1979 / John C. Dancy. — [Exeter] : University of Exeter, 1980. — 20p ; 22cm
ISBN 0-85989-181-x (pbk) : £0.60 B81-10640

Peters, R. S.. Essays on educators / R.S. Peters. — London : Allen & Unwin, 1981. — 149p ; 23cm. — (Unwin education books)
Includes index
ISBN 0-04-370103-5 : £10.00
ISBN 0-04-370104-3 (pbk) : £3.95 B81-16046

370′.1 — Education. Theories of Steiner, Rudolf

Spock, Marjorie. Teaching as a lively art / by Marjorie Spock. — Spring Valley, N.Y. : Anthroposophic Press ; London : Steiner [distributor], c1978. — iii,138p : ill ; 21cm
Bibliography: p138
ISBN 0-910142-81-5 (pbk) : £2.50 B81-02984

370.11 — Islamic education. Objectives — *Conference proceedings*

Aims and objectives of Islamic education / edited by Syed Muhammad al-Naguib al-Attas. — Sevenoaks : Hodder and Stoughton [for] King Abdulaziz University, Jeddah, 1979. — xvi,169p : ill ; 24cm. — (Islamic education series)
Conference papers. — Bibliography: p137-156
ISBN 0-340-23607-8 : Unpriced : CIP rev.
B79-25056

370.11′14 — Children. Moral education — *For parents*

Peters, R. S.. Moral development and moral education. — London : Allen & Unwin, Oct.1981. — [192]p. — (Unwin education books)
ISBN 0-04-370107-8 (pbk) : £4.50 : CIP entry
B81-26787

370.11′3 — Vocational education. Curriculum. Development

Bortz, Richard F.. Handbook for developing occupational curricula / Richard F. Bortz. — Boston [Mass.] ; London : Allyn and Bacon, c1981. — xiv,366p : ill,facsims,forms ; 24cm
Bibliography: p355-360. — Includes index
ISBN 0-205-07118-x (pbk) : £11.95 B81-06990

370.11′3′0941 — Great Britain. Vocational education — *Conference proceedings*

Training for skills : a report of the BACIE/ITO national conference held on 28 and 29 November 1978. — London : British Association for Commercial and Industrial Education, c1979. — 32p : ill,ports ; 30cm
ISBN 0-85171-072-7 (pbk) : £2.00 B81-20844

370.11′4′0971 — Canada. Schools. Moral education

Gow, Kathleen M.. Yes Virginia, there is right and wrong! : values education survival kit / Kathleen M. Gow. — Toronto ; Chichester : Wiley, c1980. — 248p : ill ; 22cm
Includes index
ISBN 0-471-79953-x (pbk) : £3.75 B81-01695

370.11′5 — Adolescents. Social education — *Manuals*

Finnegan, Gerry. From school to work- : What next? / by Gerry Finnegan, Maggie Jardine, Denis Palmer ; illustrations by Blotski. — Belfast (50 University St., Belfast BT7 1HB) : Standing Conference of Youth Organisations in Northern Ireland, 1980. — 84p : ill ; 23cm
ISBN 0-906797-05-5 (spiral) : Unpriced
B81-07803

370.15 — Children. Education — *Psychoanalytical perspectives*

Hoffer, Willi. Early development and education of the child / by Willi Hoffer ; edited by Marjorie Brierley ; with a foreword by Anna Freud. — London : Hogarth, 1981. — xvi,220p ; 23cm. — (The international psycho-analytical library ; no.102)
Bibliography: p207-214. — Includes index
ISBN 0-7012-0404-4 : £12.00 : CIP rev.
Primary classification 155.4 B81-12844

370.15 — Education. Applications of behaviourism

Steinberg, Ira S.. Behaviorism and schooling / Ira S. Steinberg. — Oxford : Martin Robertson, 1980. — ix,126p ; 23cm. — (Issues and ideas in education series)
Bibliography: p121-123. — Includes index
ISBN 0-85520-295-5 (cased) : £8.50 : CIP rev.
ISBN 0-85520-294-7 (pbk) : Unpriced
B80-08684

370.15 — Education. Psychological aspects — *For teaching*

Child, Dennis. Psychology and the teacher / Dennis Child. — 3rd ed. — London : Holt, Rinehart and Winston, 1981. — xv,396p : ill ; 25cm
Previous ed.: 1977. — Includes bibliographies and index
ISBN 0-03-910293-9 (pbk) : £3.95 B81-22993

370.15 — Educational psychology

Entwistle, N. J.. Styles of learning and teaching : an integrated outline of educational psychology for students, teachers and lecturers / Noel Entwistle. — Chichester : Wiley, c1981. — xi,293p : ill ; 24cm
Bibliography: p278-287. — Includes index
ISBN 0-471-27901-3 (cased) : £19.00
ISBN 0-471-10013-7 (pbk) : Unpriced
B81-37106

370.15 — Educational psychology — *For teaching*

Gibson, Janice T.. Psychology for the classroom / Janice T. Gibson. — 2nd ed. — Englewood Cliffs ; London : Prentice-Hall, c1980. — xxiv,568p : ill ; 24cm
Previous ed.: 1976. — Bibliography: p529-551. — Includes index
ISBN 0-13-733352-8 (pbk) : £11.65 B81-22727

Tomlinson, Peter. Understanding teaching : interactive educational psychology / Peter Tomlinson. — London : McGraw-Hill, c1981. — 382p : ill ; 23cm
Bibliography: p340-368. - Includes index
ISBN 0-07-084125-x (pbk) : £5.95 : CIP rev.
B81-09970

370.15 — Schools. Students. Behaviour. Personal construct theory — *For educational psychology*

Pope, Maureen L.. Personal construct psychology and education / Maureen L. Pope, Terence R. Keen. — London : Academic Press, 1981. — xii,185p : ill ; 24cm. — (Educational psychology)
Bibliography: p168-178. — Includes index
ISBN 0-12-561520-5 : £9.80 : CIP rev.
B81-12334

370.15′05 — Educational psychology — *Serials*

[Educational psychology ***(Dorchester-on-Thames)*****]**. Educational psychology : an international journal of experimental educational psychology. — Vol.1, no.1 (1981)-. — Dorchester-on-Thames (Haddon House, Dorchester-on-Thames, Oxford OX9 9JZ) : Carfax, 1981-. — v. : ill ; 26cm
Quarterly
ISSN 0144-3410 = Educational psychology (Dorchester-on-Thames) : £30.00 per year
B81-33322

370.15′09172′4 — Developing countries. Children. Education. Psychological aspects

Siann, Gerda. Educational psychology in a changing world / Gerda Siann, Denis C.E. Ugwuegbu. — London : Allen & Unwin, 1980. — x,255p : ill ; 25cm
Bibliography: p241-248. — Includes index
ISBN 0-04-370099-3 (cased) : Unpriced : CIP rev.
ISBN 0-04-370100-0 (pbk) : unpriced
B80-26842

370.15′0973 — United States. Education. Psychological aspects

Contemporary issues in educational psychology / [edited by] Harvey F. Clarizio, Robert C. Craig, William A. Mehrens. — 4th ed. — Boston, Mass. : Allyn and Bacon, c1981. — xiv,319p : ill ; 24cm
Previous ed.: 1977. — Includes bibliographies and index
ISBN 0-205-07331-x (pbk) : £9.95 B81-16294

370.15′23 — Experiential learning by students

Walter, Gordon A.. Experiential learning and change : theory, design and practice / Gordon A. Walter, Stephen E. Marks. — New York ; Chichester : Wiley, c1981. — xii,333p : ill ; 24cm
Bibliography: p287-314. — Includes index
ISBN 0-471-08355-0 : £15.40 B81-30021

370.15′23 — Learning by school students. Psychosocial aspects

The **Social** psychology of school learning / edited by James H. McMillan. — New York ; London : Academic Press, 1980. — xii,262p : ill ; 24cm. — (Educational psychology)
Includes bibliographies and index
ISBN 0-12-485750-7 : £11.80 B81-04111

370.15′5 — Schols. Students. Visual perception. Teaching aids

Brennan, W. K.. Look : visual perception materials / Wilfred Brennan and Jean Jackson. — London : Macmillan Education
Teachers′ handbook. — Rev. ed. — 1981. — vi,81p : ill ; 23cm
Previous ed.: 1979?. — Bibliography: p80-81
ISBN 0-333-29533-1 (pbk) : Unpriced
B81-31981

370.15′6 — Mathematics. Academic achievement of women — *Conference proceedings*

Women and Mathematics *(Conference : 1976 : Boston)*. Women and the mathematical mystique : proceedings of the Eighth Annual Hyman Blumberg Symposium on Research in Early Childhood Education : expanded version of a symposium of the American Association for the Advancement of Science entitled Women and Mathematics / edited by Lynn H. Fox, Linda Brody, and Dianne Tobin. — Baltimore ; London : Johns Hopkins University Press, c1980. — viii,211p : ill ; 24cm
Includes bibliographies and index
ISBN 0-8018-2341-2 (cased) : £10.00
B81-03900

370.15′6 — Schools. Curriculum subjects: Mathematics & science. Learning of mathematics & science. Students. Role of cognitive development. Research — *Conference proceedings*

Cognitive development research in science and mathematics : proceedings of an international seminar held in the Centre for Studies in Science Education, School of Education, University of Leeds, 17-21 September, 1979 / edited by W.F. Archenhold ... [et al.]. — Leeds (School of Education, The University of Leeds, Leeds LS2 9JT) : Centre for Studies in Science Education, University of Leeds, c1980. — ix,484p : ill ; 21cm
Bibliography: p442-474
ISBN 0-904421-07-4 (pbk) : £8.00 B81-03995

370.15′7 — Creativity. Teaching

Shallcross, Doris J.. Teaching creative behavior : how to teach creativity to children of all ages / Doris J. Shallcross ; [illustrations by Terez Waldoch]. — Englewood Cliffs ; London : Prentice-Hall, c1981. — vi,168p : ill,forms ; 24cm
Bibliography: p163-166. — Includes index
ISBN 0-13-891945-3 (cased) : Unpriced
ISBN 0-13-891937-2 (pbk) : £3.20 B81-22753

370.19 — Education. Social aspects

Family, work and education : a reader / edited by Sarah Reedy and Martin Woodhead for the Contemporary Issues in Education course at the Open University. — Sevenoaks : Hodder and Stoughton in association with the Open University Press, c1980. — vii,456p : ill ; 22cm. — (Contemporary issues in education)
Includes bibliographies and index
ISBN 0-340-25759-8 (pbk) : £5.60 : CIP rev.
B80-20472

Silver, Harold. Education and the social condition / Harold Silver. — London : Methuen, 1980. — 213p ; 23cm
Includes index
ISBN 0-416-74020-0 (pbk) : £9.50 : CIP rev.
ISBN 0-416-74030-8 (pbk) : Unpriced
B80-17622

370.19 — Education — *Sociological perspectives*

Bantock, G. H.. The parochialism of the present : contemporary issues in education / G.H. Bantock. — London : Routledge & Kegan Paul, 1981. — viii,147p ; 23cm. — (Routledge education books)
Includes index
ISBN 0-7100-0746-9 : £8.95 : CIP rev.
B81-14817

Meighan, Roland. A sociology of educating / Roland Meighan with contributions by Len Barton and Stephen Walker. — London : Holt, Rinehart and Winston, 1981. — xi,404p : ill,plans ; 24cm
Bibliography: p374-395. - Includes index
ISBN 0-03-910289-0 (pbk) : £3.95 : CIP rev.
B81-01837

Schooling, ideology and the curriculum / edited and introduced by Len Barton, Roland Meighan and Stephen Walker. — Lewes (Falmer House, Barcombe, Lewes, Sussex BN8 5DL) : Falmer Press, 1980. — 207p ; 24cm
Conference papers
ISBN 0-905273-13-3 (cased) : Unpriced
B81-13059

Shaw, Beverley. Educational practice and sociology : an introduction / Beverley Shaw. — Oxford : Robertson, 1981. — xv,251p : ill ; 22cm. — (Issues and ideas in education series)
Bibliography: p232-241. — Includes index
ISBN 0-85520-433-8 (cased) : £15.00 : CIP rev.
ISBN 0-85520-434-6 (pbk) : £4.95 B81-27952

Society, education and the state. — Milton Keynes : Open University Press. — (Educational studies : a third level course)
At head of title: The Open University
Block 1: The state and the politics of education. — 1981. — 2v.(102;85p) : ill,facsims ; 30cm. — (E353 ; block 1)
Includes bibliographies. — Contents: Unit 1: Education and popular politics — Unit 2: Education and the corporate economy — Unit 3: The state and education, some theoretical approaches — Unit 4: Education for the labour market
ISBN 0-335-13055-0 (pbk) : Unpriced
ISBN 0-335-13056-9 (part 2) : Unpriced
B81-10753

Society, education and the state. — Milton Keynes : Open University Press. — (Educational studies : a third level course)
At head of title: The Open University
Introduction and guide to the course / prepared by Ross Fergusson for the Course Team. — 1981. — 25p ; 30cm. — (E353 ; IG)
ISBN 0-335-13063-1 (pbk) : Unpriced
B81-10752

370.19 — Education — *Sociological perspectives — For Nigerian students*

Uche, Ukaonu W.. Sociology of education for NCE students : a study in foundations of education / Ukaonu W. Uche. — London : Allen & Unwin, 1980. — x,116p : ill ; 20cm
Bibliography: p107-110. — Includes index
ISBN 0-04-370106-x (pbk) : Unpriced : CIP rev. B81-03670

370.19 — Education. Sociopolitical aspects

Education and the state / Roger Dale ... [et al.]. — Lewes : Falmer in association with The Open University Press
Vol.1: Schooling and the national interest / Roger Dale ... [et al.]. — 1981. — xii,402p ; 24cm
Bibliography: p387. - Includes index
ISBN 0-905273-16-8 (cased) : £14.25
ISBN 0-905273-15-x (pbk) : £7.95 B81-14691

Education and the state / edited by Roger Dale ... [et al.]. — Lewes : Falmer in association with the Open University Press. — (Politics and education series)
Vol.2: Politics, partriarchy and practice. — 1981. — ix,420p ; 24cm
Includes index
ISBN 0-905273-18-4 (cased) : Unpriced
ISBN 0-905273-17-6 (pbk) : Unpriced
B81-27189

370.19 — Schools. Psychosocial aspects

Clancy, Laurie. Essays in the psychology and sociology of education / Laurie Clancy. — Bognor Regis : New Horizon, c1981. — 247p ; 21cm
Includes bibliographies
ISBN 0-86116-228-5 : £5.25 B81-40116

370.19 — Sociology of education

Robinson, Philip, *1943-*. Perspectives on the sociology of education : an introduction / Philip Robinson. — London : Routledge & Kegan Paul, 1981. — vii,243p : 1ill ; 22cm. — (Routledge education books)
Bibliography: p204-233. — Includes index
ISBN 0-7100-0787-6 (pbk) : £4.95 : CIP rev.
B81-14961

Salter, Brian. Education, politics and the state. — London : Grant McIntyre, Nov.1981. — [256]p
ISBN 0-86216-075-8 (cased) : £12.95 : CIP entry
ISBN 0-86216-076-6 (pbk) : £5.95 B81-30512

370.19′01 — Education. Sociological perspectives. Theories

Demaine, Jack. Contemporary theories in the sociology of education / Jack Demaine. — London : Macmillan, 1981. — ix,173p ; 23cm
Bibliography: p161-168. — Includes index
ISBN 0-333-23448-0 (cased) : £15.00 : CIP rev.
B80-20259

370.19′05 — Education. Social aspects — *Serials*

Schooling & culture. — Issue 1 (Mar. 1978)-. — London (Gateforth St., NW8 8EH) : [The Cultural Studies Department], ILEA Cockpit Arts Workshop, 1978-. — v. : ill ; 26cm
Three issues yearly. — Published: Arts Department, 1978-1979
ISSN 0262-1045 = Schooling & culture : Unpriced B81-39736

370.19′0942 — England. Children. Education, *1800-1900*. **Social aspects**

Digby, Anne, *1942-*. Children, school and society in nineteenth century England / Anne Digby and Peter Searby. — London : Macmillan, 1981. — 258p : facsims ; 23cm
Includes index
ISBN 0-333-24678-0 (cased) : Unpriced : CIP rev.
ISBN 0-333-24679-9 (pbk) : Unpriced
B80-20473

370.19′0942 — England. Education — *Sociological perspectives*

Cohen, Louis. Perspectives on classrooms and schools / Louis Cohen, Lawrence Manion. — London : Holt, Rinehart and Winston, c1981. — xiv,452p : ill,maps,1plan ; 25cm
Bibliography: p420-436. — Includes index
ISBN 0-03-910290-4 (pbk) : £3.95 : CIP rev.
B81-02543

370.19′09669 — Nigeria. Education — *Sociological perspectives*

DuBey, D. L.. An introduction to the sociology of Nigerian education / D.L. DuBey, D.A. Eden, A.S. Thakur. — London : Macmillan, 1979. — viii,100p : 2ill ; 22cm. — (Studies in Nigerian education)
Spine title: The sociology of Nigerian education. — Bibliography: p93-96.. — Includes index
ISBN 0-333-25658-1 (pbk) : £2.95 : CIP rev.
B79-06262

370.19′0967 — Africa south of the Sahara. Education — *Sociological perspectives*

Blakemore, Kenneth, *1948-*. A sociology of education for Africa / Kenneth Blakemore and Brian Cooksey ; with a foreword by A. Babs Fafunwa. — London : Allen & Unwin, 1980 c1981. — 274p ; 22cm
Bibliography: p262-270. — Includes index
ISBN 0-04-370105-1 (pbk) : Unpriced
B81-16048

370.19′0968 — Southern Africa. Education. Socioeconomic aspects — *Conference proceedings*

Independence without freedom : the political economy of colonial education in southern Africa / edited and with an introduction by Agrippah T. Mugomba and Mougo Nyaggah. — Santa Barbara ; Oxford : ABC-Clio, c1980. — x,289p ; 24cm. — (Studies in international and comparative politics ; 13)
Conference papers. — Bibliography: p263-276. - Includes index
ISBN 0-87436-293-8 : £14.65 B81-13385

370.19′0973 — United States. Education. Policies — *Sociological perspectives*

The **Future** of education : policy issues and challenges / edited by Kathryn Cirincione-Coles. — Beverly Hills ; London : Sage, c1981. — 274p ; 22cm. — (Sage focus editions ; 28)
Includes bibliographies
ISBN 0-8039-1538-1 (cased) : Unpriced
ISBN 0-8039-1539-x (pbk) : £6.95 B81-34187

370.19′0973 — United States. Education — *Sociological perspectives*

Chesler, Mark A.. A sociology of education : access to power and privilege / Mark A. Chesler, William M. Cave. — New York : Macmillan ; London : Collier Macmillan, c1981. — xi,388p : ill ; 24cm
Includes index
ISBN 0-02-322150-x : £10.95 B81-15621

370.19′0973 — United States. Education — *Sociological perspectives* *continuation*

Reitman, Sandford W.. Education, society and change / Sandford W. Reitman. — Boston, Mass. ; London : Allyn and Bacon, c1981. — xi,491p : ill ; 24cm
Previous ed.: published as Foundations of education for prospective teachers. 1977. — Includes index
ISBN 0-205-07254-2 (pbk) : Unpriced B81-19601

370.19′0973 — United States. Education — *Sociological perspectives — Questions & answers*

Reitman, Sandford W.. Author's remarks and test items to accompany Education, society, and change / Sandford W. Reitman. — Boston, [Mass.] ; London : Allyn and Bacon, c 1981. — 88p ; 22cm
ISBN 0-205-07255-0 (pbk) : Unpriced B81-24252

370.19′0973 — United States. Education. Sociopolitical aspects

Giroux, Henry A.. Ideology culture & the process of schooling / Henry A. Giroux. — London : Falmer, 1981. — 168p ; 24cm
Includes index
ISBN 0-905273-19-2 : Unpriced B81-32614

370.19′3′0952 — Japan. Education. Equality of opportunity. Social aspects

Cummings, William K.. Education and equality in Japan / William K. Cummings. — Princeton ; Guildford : Princeton University Press, c1980. — xvi,305p : ill ; 24cm
Bibliography: p289-301. - Includes index
ISBN 0-691-09385-7 (cased) : £11.00
ISBN 0-691-10088-8 (pbk) : £5.35 B81-04477

370.19′31 — East & West Sussex. Education. Relations with industries. Organisations — *Directories*

The **Register** of links between education and industry/commerce. — [Brighton] ([c/o R.J. Tiffin, Brighton Polytechnic, Falmer, Brighton BN1 9PH]) : South East Forum, 1980. — 21p ; 21cm
Unpriced (pbk) B81-14554

370.19′31 — England. Education. Relations with industries — *Conference proceedings*

Industry and education - our needs for the future : Brighton Polytechnic, 25 April 1980 : conference proceedings / edited by Robert J. Tiffin ; the conference was arranged and presented by the South East Forum in association with Brighton Polytechnic. — Brighton (Brighton Polytechnic, Falmer, Brighton BN1 9PH) : R.J. Tiffin, [1980]. — 45p ; 21cm
Unpriced (pbk) B81-12025

370.19′31 — Great Britain. Education. Role of parents — *Conference proceedings*

March Education Conference *(1981 : Goldsmiths' College)*. Parents and Education : report of the proceedings of the March Education Conference 1981 / edited by Leslie A. Smith. — London : University of London, Goldsmiths' College, c1981. — 33p ; 21cm
Unpriced (pbk) B81-37324

370.19′31 — Scotland. Lothian Region. Educational home visiting services: Lothian Region Educational Home Visiting Scheme

McCail, Gail. Mother start : an account of an education home visiting scheme for pre-school children / by Gail McCail. — [Edinburgh] ([16 Moray Place, Edinburgh EH3 6DR]) : Scottish Council for Research in Education, c1981. — vii,104p ; 22cm
Bibliography: p99-101. — Includes index
ISBN 0-901116-29-7 (pbk) : £3.30 B81-33115

370.19′31 — United States. Education. Participation of parents

Berger, Eugenia Hepworth. Parents as partners in education : the school and home working together / Eugenia Hepworth Berger. — St. Louis ; London : Mosby, 1981. — xv,424p : ill,forms ; 24cm
Includes bibliographies and index
ISBN 0-8016-0637-3 (pbk) : £8.50 B81-33036

370.19′31′0973 — United States. Local communities. Relations with schools

Wallat, Cynthia. Home school community interaction : what we know and why we don't know more / Cynthia Wallat, Richard Goldman. — Columbus ; London : Merrill, c1979. — vii,232p : ill,forms ; 24cm
Bibliography: p223-232
ISBN 0-675-08281-1 : Unpriced B81-04731

370.19′31′0973 — United States. Schools. Role of communities

Communities and their schools / Don Davies, editor ; Miriam Clasby ... [et al.]. — New York ; London : McGraw-Hill, c1981. — xi,372p ; 24cm
Includes index
ISBN 0-07-015503-8 : £11.95 B81-24280

370.19′312′060411 — Scotland. Parent-teacher associations. Organisations: Scottish Parent Teacher Council. Role

Boyd, Hugh, *1926-*. What is the Scottish Parent Teacher Council? / by Hugh Boyd. — Edinburgh (67 York Place, Edinburgh) : Scottish Parent Teacher Council, [1981?]. — [4]p ; 21cm. — (Booklet / Scottish Parent Teacher Council ; 1)
Unpriced (unbound) B81-38202

370.19′312′09411 — Scotland. Parent-teacher associations

Why have a P.T.A.?. — Edinburgh (4 Queensferry St., Edinburgh EH2 4PA) : SPTC, [1981?]. — 7p ; 21cm. — (Booklet / Scottish Parent Teacher Council ; 2)
Unpriced (unbound) B81-38207

370.19′312′09411 — Scotland. Parent-teacher associations. Organisation

Setting up a P.T.A.. — Edinburgh (4 Queensferry St., Edinburgh EH2 4PA) : SPTC, [1981?]. — 8p ; 21cm. — (Booklet / Scottish Parent Teacher Council ; 3)
Unpriced (unbound) B81-38206

370.19′34′0941 — Great Britain. Education, *1960-1979.* **Sociocultural aspects**

Dennison, W. F. Education in jeopardy : problems and possibilities of contraction / W.F. Dennison. — Oxford : Basil Blackwell, 1981. — 168p : ill ; 23cm. — (Theory and practice in education ; 3)
Bibliography: p162-165. — Includes index
ISBN 0-631-12548-5 (cased) : £9.95 : CIP rev. B81-21476

370.19′342 — Arkansas. Little Rock. Secondary schools: Central High School *(Little Rock).* **Desegregation,** *1957-1958 — Personal observations*

Huckaby, Elizabeth. Crisis at Central High : Little Rock, 1957-58 / Elizabeth Huckaby ; foreword by Harry S. Ashmore. — Baton Rouge ; London : Louisiana University Press, c1980. — xvii,222p,[14]p of plates : ill,ports ; 24cm
ISBN 0-8071-0779-4 : £7.80 B81-07725

370.19′342 — Israel. Jerusalem. Schools. Integration — *Case studies*

Klein, Zev. Integrating Jerusalem schools / Zev Klein, Yohanan Eshel. — New York ; London : Academic Press, c1980. — xiii,175p : ill ; 24cm. — (Quantitative studies in social relations)
Bibliography: p165-172. — Includes index
ISBN 0-12-413250-2 : £11.00 B81-17710

370.19′342 — United States. Urban regions. Schools. Desegregation

Race and schooling in the city / edited by Adam Yarmolinsky, Lance Liebman and Corinne S. Schelling. — Cambridge, Mass. ; London : Harvard University Press, 1981. — ix,279p ; 25cm
Includes bibliographies and index
ISBN 0-674-74577-9 : £10.50 B81-28255

370.19′342′0941 — Great Britain. Educational institutions. Racial aspects

Mullard, Chris. Racism in society and schools : history, policy and practice / Chris Mullard. — [London] : University of London, Institute of Education, c1980. — 24p ; 21cm. — (Occasional paper / Centre for Multicultural Education, University of London Institute of Education ; no.1)
ISBN 0-85473-101-6 (pbk) : Unpriced B81-21125

370.19′345 — Great Britain. Education. Sex discrimination

Sutherland, Margaret B.. Sex bias in education / Margaret B. Sutherland. — Oxford : Basil Blackwell, 1981. — 242p ; 22cm. — (Theory and practice in education ; 2)
Bibliography: p224-235. — Includes index
ISBN 0-631-10851-3 (cased) : £10.00 B81-24270

370.19′346 — Rural regions. Education — *Conference proceedings*

Can education change rural fortunes? : report of a seminar on education, the farmer and rural change, held in Scotland from 7-14 June 1980. — Dumfriesshire (Langholm, Dumfriesshire DG13 0HL, Scotland) : Arkleton Trust, c1981. — 35p ; 21cm
£2.00 (pbk) B81-29871

370.19′346 — Rural regions. Primary & secondary education — *Sociological perspectives*

Nash, Roy. Schooling in rural societies / Roy Nash. — London : Methuen, 1980. — 160p ; 20cm. — (Contemporary sociology of the school)
Bibliography: p150-158. - Includes index
ISBN 0-416-73300-x (cased) : £6.50 : CIP rev.
ISBN 0-416-73310-7 (pbk) : £2.55 B80-08613

370.19′348′0941 — Great Britain. Urban regions. Inner areas. Education

Education for the inner city / compiled and edited by Michael Marland with papers by Tessa Blackstone ... [et al.]. — London : Heinemann Educational, 1980. — lx,230p : ill ; 23cm. — (Heinemann organisation in schools series)
Bibliography: p213-217. — Includes index
ISBN 0-435-80588-6 : £9.50 : CIP rev. B80-04137

370.19′4 — Community education

Poster, Cyril. Community education. — London : Heinemann Educational, Oct.1981. — [192]p. — (Organization in schools series)
ISBN 0-435-80641-6 : £9.50 : CIP entry B81-28167

370.19′4′0941 — Great Britain. Community education

Issues in community education / edited and introduced by Colin Fletcher & Neil Thompson. — Lewes (Falmer House, Barcombe, Lewes, Sussex BN8 5DL) : Falmer, c1980. — 214p : ill ; 22cm. — (Politics and education series)
Bibliography: p191-197. - Includes index
ISBN 0-905273-09-5 (cased) : £8.25
ISBN 0-905273-08-7 (pbk) : £3.95 B81-05011

Keeble, R. W. J.. Community & education : some relationships and some issues / R.W.J. Keeble. — Leicester (17 Albion St., Leicester LE1 6GD) : National Youth Bureau, 1981. — 141p ; 22cm
ISBN 0-86155-038-2 (pbk) : £3.15 B81-10350

370.19′4′09411 — Scotland. Community education — *Serials*

Scottish Council For Community Education. Information release / Scottish Council for Community Education. — No.1. — Edinburgh ([New St Andrews House, Edinburgh EH1 3SY]) : The Council, 1979-. — v. ; 21cm
ISSN 0261-2682 = Information release - Scottish Council for Community Education : Unpriced B81-20297

370.19'5'018 — Comparative education. Methodology
Holmes, Brian. Comparative education : some consideration of method / Brian Holmes. — London : Allen & Unwin, 1981. — 195p : ill ; 23cm. — (Unwin education books)
Bibliography: p176-190. — Includes index
ISBN 0-04-370101-9 : £10.00
ISBN 0-04-370102-7 (pbk) : £3.95 B81-16047

370.19'6 — Commonwealth countries. Universities. Administrators & librarians. Awards
Grants for study visits : by University administrators and librarians : for travel : (a) from one Commonwealth country to another and (b) either way, between Commonwealth and foreign countries. — London : Association of Commonwealth Universities, 1979. — 15p ; 23cm
Cover title. — Text on inside cover. — Includes index
ISBN 0-85143-059-7 (pbk) : £1.00 B81-32483

370.19'62 — Great Britain. Young persons. Exchange visits. Grants by British Council — *Serials*
Grants for youth exchanges. — 1981-1982. — London : British Council, c1980. — 16p
Unpriced B81-15442

370.19'62 — Scotland. Schools. Students. Foreign visits. Organisation. Role of parent-teacher associations
Aitchison, J. D.. P.T.A.s & foreign travel / J.D. Aitchison. — Edinburgh (4 Queensferry St., Edinburgh EH2 4PA) : Scottish Parent Teacher Council, [1981?]. — 8p ; 21cm. — (Booklet / Scottish Parent Teacher Council ; 7)
Unpriced (unbound) B81-38205

370.19'63 — Commonwealth countries. Universities. Teachers. Awards — *Serials*
Awards for Commonwealth university academic staff : fellowships, visiting professorships, grants etc open to university academic staff in a Commonwealth country who wish to carry out research, make study visits, or teach for a while at a university in another Commonwealth country. — 1981-83-. — London : Association of Commonwealth Universities, 1980-. — v. ; 23cm
Every two years. — Continues: Awards for Commonwealth university staff
ISSN 0144-4611 = Awards for Commonwealth University academic staff : £5.55 B81-09147

370'.3'21 — Education — *Encyclopaedias*
Rowntree, Derek. A dictionary of education. — London : Harper & Row, Sept.1981. — [320]p. — (Harper reference)
ISBN 0-06-318157-6 : £6.95 : CIP entry B81-28193

370'.5 — Education — *Serials*
Aspects of education. — 24. — [Hull] : University of Hull Institute of Education, 1980. — 59p
ISBN 0-85958-210-8 : Unpriced
ISSN 0066-8672 B81-13197

Educational analysis. — Vol.1 no.1 (summer 1979)-. — Lewes (Falmer House, Barcombe, Lewes, Sussex) : Falmer Press, 1979-. — v. ; 25cm
Two issues yearly
ISSN 0260-0994 = Educational analysis : £10.00 per year B81-03591

World yearbook of education. — 1981. — London : Kogan Page, July 1981. — [400]p
ISBN 0-85038-457-5 : £13.95 : CIP entry B81-19216

[World yearbook of education *(1979)*]. World yearbook of education. — 1979-. — London : Kogan Page, 1979-. — v. ; 24cm
Continues: World year book of education (1965). — Description based on: 1980 issue
ISSN 0084-2508 = World yearbook of education : £12.50 B81-10566

370'.6'041 — Great Britain. Education. Organisations — *Directories — Serials*
The **Education** authorities directory and annual. — 1981. — Redhill : School Government Pub. Co., c1981. — lxxx,1274p
ISBN 0-900640-13-8 : £18.00 B81-15286

370'.7'041 — Great Britain. Education. Information sources
Wallis, Elizabeth. Where to look things up : A-Z of sources on all major educational topics. — 2nd ed. / compiled by Elizabeth Wallis for the Advisory Centre for Education. — London : Advisory Centre for Education, 1980. — 109p ; 22cm. — (An ACE handbook)
Previous ed.: / compiled by Ann Duncan. 1974. — Bibliography: p3. - Includes index
ISBN 0-900029-56-0 (pbk) : £2.50 B81-07651

370'.7'105 — Teachers. Professional education — *Serials*
JET : journal of education for teaching. — Vol.7, no.1 (Jan.1981)-. — London : Methuen, 1981-. — v. ; 25cm
Three issues yearly. — Continues: British journal of teacher education
ISSN 0260-7476 = JET. Journal of education for teaching : £17.00 per year B81-29989

370'.7'1094 — European Community countries. Teachers. Professional education — *Conference proceedings*
Network of European Teacher Educators. *Inaugural Conference (1979 : Antwerp).* Proceedings of an inaugural conference, Antwerp 1979 / Network of European Teacher Educators ; edited by G.H. Bell, R.C. Pennington. — [Middlesbrough] ([Flatts Lane, Middlesbrough, Cleveland TS6 0QS]) : [Department of Educational Studies, Teesside Polytechic], 1980. — ix,105p : ill,1form ; 30cm
Includes bibliographies
Unpriced (pbk)
Primary classification 370'.94 B81-21996

370'.7'1094 — European Community countries. Teachers. Professional education. Development
Bell, Gordon H.. Developing teacher education in the European Community : a case study / Gordon H. Bell ; contributors: D.W. Gooderham, J. van Daele, E. Ricatti. — 2nd ed. — [Middlesbrough] ([Flatts La., Middlesbrough, Cleveland TS6 0QS]) : Department of Educational Studies, Teesside Polytechnic, 1980. — 123,xivp ; 30cm. — (Occasional studies in teacher applicable research)
Previous ed.: 1979. — Bibliography: 3p
Unpriced (pbk) B81-39690

370'.7'109411 — Scotland. Teachers. Professional education — *Proposals*
Teacher training for the eighties : a study by the Association of Educational Advisers in Scotland. — [s.l.] : The Association, 1980. — A8,B56p ; 30cm
Unpriced (spiral) B81-40725

370'.7'122088042 — Great Britain. Primary schools. Women teachers. Professional education, *1840-1914 — Feminist viewpoints*
Widdowson, Frances. Going up into the next class : women and elementary teacher training, 1840-1914 / Frances Widdowson. — London (190 Upper St, N.1) : Women's Research and Resources Centre, 1980. — 95p : ill,1facsim ; 21cm. — (Explorations in feminism ; no.70)
Bibliography: p89-92
ISBN 0-905969-06-5 (pbk) : £2.45 B81-17224

370'.7'124 — Adult education institutions. Teachers. Professional education. Applications of personal construct theory
Candy, Philip C.. Mirrors of the mind : personal construct theory in the training of adult educators / Philip C. Candy. — Manchester : Department of Adult and Higher Education University of Manchester, 1981. — ix,102p ; 21cm. — (Manchester monographs ; 16)
Bibliography: p91-102
ISBN 0-903717-25-5 (pbk) : Unpriced B81-40797

370'.7'3 — England. Church colleges. Role
Gay, John D.. The Christian campus? : the role of the English Churches in higher education / by John D. Gay. — 2nd ed. — Abingdon ([The Malthouse, 60 East St., Helen St., Abingdon, Oxon OX14 5EB]) : Culham College of Education, 1979. — ii,70p : ill ; 30cm. — (Working papers / Culham College of Education)
Previous ed.: 1978. — Includes bibliographies. — Includes Diversification into distinctiveness : a Church College route into the 1990's (Working paper no.2)
£2.00 (pbk) B81-07673

370'.7'309411 — Scotland. Colleges of education
The **Future** of the colleges of education in Scotland : an alternative solution : discussion paper. — Falkirk (Falkirk FK1 1YS) : Callendar Park College of Education, [1980 or 1981]. — 15p ; 30cm
Unpriced (pbk) B81-18001

370'.7'30941235 — Scotland. Grampian Region. Aberdeen. Special schools: Camphill Rudolf Steiner Schools. *Faculty of Curative Education.* **Courses in professional education of teachers in special schools**
Curative education : the course at the Camphill Rudolf Steiner Schools, Aberdeen. — [Aberdeen] : Published for the Faculty of Curative Education on behalf of the Association of Camphill Communities by Aberdeen University Press, 1981. — x,30p ; 21cm
Report of a working party
ISBN 0-08-028440-x (pbk) : £1.00 : CIP rev. B81-16870

370'.7'30942142 — London. Camden *(London Borough).* **Universities: University of London.** *Institute of Education — Serials*
University of London. *Institute of Education.* Calendar / University of London Institute of Education. — 1980-81. — London : The Institute, 1980. — 178p
ISBN 0-85473-093-1 : Unpriced
ISSN 0307-563x B81-20418

370'.7'30942262 — West Sussex. Chichester. Colleges of education: Bishop Otter College, *to 1980*
McGregor, G. P.. Bishop Otter College : and policy for teacher education 1839-1980 / by G.P. McGregor ; foreword by Lord Briggs of Lewes. — London (16 Pembridge Rd., W11) : Pembridge, 1981. — 285p,[8]p of plates : ill,ports ; 23cm
Includes index
£11.50 B81-27068

370'.7'30942356 — Devon. Exeter. Colleges of education: St. Luke's College, Exeter, *1839-1978*
Saint Luke's College 1839-1978. — [Exeter] ([St. Luke's College, Exeter University, Exeter]) : [c/o J.G. Priestley], 1978. — 55p : ill,1map,facsims, 1plan,ports ; 21x30cm
Ill and text on inside covers
Unpriced (pbk) B81-29875

370'.7'30942659 — Cambridgeshire. Cambridge. Colleges of education: Cambridge University Schoolmasters' Training College. Ex-students, *1891-1938 — Lists*
Barnwell, P. J.. The Cambridge University Schoolmasters' Training College, 1891-1938 : a nominal roll of 'Fox's Martyrs' and earlier students, with commentary and notes on sources / compiled by P.J. Barnwell. — [Cambridge] ([6, Almoners Ave., Cambridge]) : P.J. Barnwell, [1981]. — 73p ; 21cm
Unpriced (pbk) B81-39052

370'.7'30942659 — Cambridgeshire. Cambridge. Colleges of education: Homerton College, *to 1978*
Homerton College. Homerton College : 1695-1978 : from dissenting academy to Approved Society in the University of Cambridge / T.H. Simms. — [Cambridge] : Trustees of Homerton College, 1979. — 109p : ill,1coat of arms,1facsim,2plans,ports ; 22cm
Includes index
Unpriced B81-39937

370'.7'32'0942 — England. Teachers. Professional education. In-service B.Ed. courses
Evans, Norman. Preliminary evaluation of the in-service BEd degree : with particular reference to further professional training / Norman Evans. — Windsor : NFER : Nelson, 1981, c1980. — 168p : maps ; 25cm
ISBN 0-85633-221-6 (pbk) : £10.50 B81-14626

370'.7'320942 — England. Teachers. Professional education. Postgraduate Certificate of Education courses — *Conference proceedings*

Developments in PGCE courses / edited by Robin Alexander and Jean Whittaker. — Guildford (University of Surrey, Guildford, Surrey, GU2 5XH) : Teacher Education Group, Society for Research into Higher Education, 1980. — iv,177p : ill,1 facsim,forms ; 22cm
Conference papers. — Bibliography: p155-160
ISBN 0-9506737-1-4 (pbk) : £3.00 B81-05556

370'.7'330966 — West Africa. Teachers. Professional education. Teaching practice

Olaitan, Samson O.. Principles of practice teaching / Samson O. Olaitan and Obiora N. Agusiobo. — Chichester : Wiley, c1981. — 165p : ill,1form ; 24cm. — (Education in Africa)
Includes index
ISBN 0-471-27805-x (cased) : £9.75
ISBN 0-471-27804-1 (pbk) : Unpriced
B81-26323

370'.7'8 — Education. Research

Verma, Gajendra K.. What is educational research? : perspectives on techniques of research / Gajendra K. Verma, Ruth M. Beard. — Aldershot : Gower, c1981. — ix,209p : ill ; 23cm
Bibliography: p192-202. — Includes index
ISBN 0-566-00323-6 (cased) : Unpriced : CIP rev.
ISBN 0-566-00429-1 (pbk) : Unpriced
B81-09504

370'.7'8 — Education. Research — *Conference proceedings*

The **Meritocratic** intellect : studies in the history of educational research / edited by James V. Smith, David Hamilton. — [Aberdeen] : Aberdeen University Press, 1980. — 142p ; 26cm
Conference papers. — Includes index
ISBN 0-08-025720-8 : Unpriced : CIP rev.
B80-09150

370'.7'8073 — United States. Education. Research. Methodology — *Manuals*

Best, John W.. Research in education / John W. Best. — 4th ed. — Englewood Cliffs ; London : Prentice-Hall, c1981. — ix,431p : ill,1map ; 24cm
Previous ed.: 1977. — Includes bibliographies and index
ISBN 0-13-774026-3 : £12.30 B81-23116

370'.782 — Education. Research. Use of case studies

Towards a science of the singular : essays about case study in educational research and evaluation / edited by Helen Simons. — Norwich : Centre for Applied Research in Education University of East Anglia, 1980. — iii,262p ; 21cm. — (CARE occasional publications ; no.10)
Bibliography: p251-262
ISBN 0-904510-08-5 (pbk) : Unpriced
B81-14316

370.9 — EDUCATION. HISTORICAL AND GEOGRAPHICAL TREATMENT

370'.917'671 — Islamic countries. Education

Husain, Syed Sajjad. Crisis in Muslim education / Syed Sajjad Husain and Syed Ali Ashraf. — Sevenoaks : Hodder and Stoughton, 1979. — x,133p ; 25cm. — (Islamic education series)
ISBN 0-340-23608-6 : £4.50 : CIP rev.
B79-25058

370'.918'2 — Western world. Education, *ca 1530-*

Bowen, James. A history of Western education. — London : Methuen, June 1981
Vol.3: The modern West : Europe and the New World. — [560]p
ISBN 0-416-16130-8 (cased) : £17.50 : CIP entry
ISBN 0-416-85160-6 (pbk) : £7.95 B81-09993

370'.92'2 — England. Education, *1745-1915* — *Biographies*

Biography and education : some eighteenth and nineteenth century studies / edited by Roy Lowe. — Leicester (4 Marydene Drive, Evington, Leicester LE5 6HD) : History of Education Society, 1980. — 70p ; 21cm. — (Occasional publication / History of Education Society, ISSN 0141-2426 ; no.5)
Bibliography: p59-70
Unpriced (pbk) B81-04164

370'.92'4 — England. Education. Gilpin, William, *1757-1848* — *Correspondence, diaries, etc.*

Gilpin, William, *1757-1848*. My dearest Betsy : a self-portrait of William Gilpin 1757-1848, schoolmaster and parson, from his letters and notebooks / edited by Peter Benson. — London : Dobson, 1981. — 265p,[8]p of plates : ill,facsims,1port,1geneal.table ; 19cm
Geneal.table on lining papers. — Includes index
ISBN 0-234-72036-0 : £6.95 B81-17135

370'.938 — Classical antiquity. Education, *to 600*

Marrou, Henri. A history of education in antiquity / H.I. Marrou. — London : Sheed and Ward, 1956 (1981 [printing]). — xiv,466p,folded leaf of plates : 1map ; 22cm
Translation of: Histoire de l'éducation dans l'antiquité. 3e éd. — Bibliography: p453-460. — Includes index
ISBN 0-7220-4116-0 (pbk) : £11.00 B81-40907

370'.94 — European Community countries. Education — *Conference proceedings*

Network of European Teacher Educators. *Inaugural Conference (1979 : Antwerp)*. Proceedings of an inaugural conference, Antwerp 1979 / Network of European Teacher Educators ; edited by G.H. Bell, R.C. Pennington. — [Middlesbrough] ([Flatts Lane, Middlesbrough, Cleveland TS6 0QS]) : [Department of Educational Studies, Teesside Polytechic], 1980. — ix,105p : ill,1form ; 30cm
Includes bibliographies
Unpriced (pbk)
Also classified at 370'.7'1094 B81-21996

370'.941 — Great Britain. Education

Clegg, Alec. About our schools / Alec Clegg. — Oxford : Blackwell, 1980. — x,182p ; 23cm
Includes index
ISBN 0-631-12881-6 (cased) : £9.95 : CIP rev.
ISBN 0-631-12832-8 (pbk) : £3.95 B80-08155

Contemporary issues in education / [the E200 Course Team]. — Milton Keynes : Open University Press. — (Educational studies : a second level course)
At head of title: The Open University
Block 1: Introductions
1: Education through autobiography / prepared by Peter Barnes for the Course Team. — 1981. — 37p : ill,2plans,1port ; 30cm. — (E200 ; [block 1, unit 1])
Bibliography: p35-36
ISBN 0-335-13000-3 (pbk) : Unpriced
B81-11454

Contemporary issues in education / [the E200 Course Team]. — Milton Keynes : Open University Press. — (Educational studies : a second level course)
At head of title: The Open University
Block 2: The family as educator : the childhood years
3: Learning in the family / prepared by Peter Barnes, Martin Woodhead and Peter Woods for the Course Team. — 1981. — 66p : ill ; 30cm. — (E200 ; [block 2, unit 3])
Includes bibliographies
ISBN 0-335-13002-x (pbk) : Unpriced
B81-11456

Contemporary issues in education / [The E200 Course Team]. — Milton Keynes : Open University Press. — (Educational studies : a second level course)
At head of title: The Open University
Block 2: The family as educator : the childhood years
4: Mother-child interaction / prepared by Will Swann for the Course Team. — 1981. — 40p : ill ; 30cm. — (E200 ; [block 2, unit 4])
Bibliography: p38-39
ISBN 0-335-13003-8 (pbk) : Unpriced
B81-11455

Contemporary issues in education / [the E200 Course Team]. — Milton Keynes : Open University Press. — (Educational studies : a second level course)
At head of title: The Open University
Block 3: Control and choice in education
11: Responding to falling school rolls / prepared by Tim Horton for the Course Team. — 1981. — 26p : ill ; 30cm. — (E200 ; [block 3, unit 11])
Bibliography: p35
ISBN 0-335-13010-0 (pbk) : Unpriced
B81-27597

Contemporary issues in education / [the E200 Course Team]. — Milton Keynes : Open University Press. — (Educational studies : a second level course)
At head of title: The Open University
Block 3: Control and choice in education
14: William Tyndale : the system under stress / prepared by Peter Scrimshaw and Tim Horton for the Course Team. — 1981. — 24p : ill ; 30cm. — (E200 ; [block 3, unit 14])
Bibliography: p21
ISBN 0-335-13013-5 (pbk) : Unpriced
B81-27596

Contemporary issues in education / [the E200 Course Team]. — Milton Keynes : Open University Press. — (Educational studies : a second level course)
At head of title: The Open University
Block 4: Educational standards
16: Education and equality / prepared by Donald Mackinnon for the Course Team. — 1981. — 30p ; 30cm. — (E200 ; [block 4, unit 16])
Bibliography: p29
ISBN 0-335-13015-1 (pbk) : Unpriced
B81-27595

Contemporary issues in education / [the E200 Course Team]. — Milton Keynes : Open University Press. — (Educational studies : a second level course)
At head of title: The Open University
Block 4: Educational standards. — 1981. — (E200 ; [block 4; unit 18/19])
Bibliography: p54-56
18/19: Examinations and assessment / prepared by Desmond L. Nuttall and Peter Barnes for the Course Team. — 56p : ill,1form ; 30cm
ISBN 0-335-13017-8 (pbk) : Unpriced
B81-25373

Contemporary issues in education / [the E200 Course Team]. — Milton Keynes : Open University Press. — (Educational studies : a second level course)
At head of title: The Open University
Block 4: Educational standards. — 1981. — (E200 ; [block 4, unit 20])
Bibliography: p51-52
20: Certification, education and work / prepared by Ronald Dore for the Course Team, with contributions from Angela Little. — 55p : ill,facsims,form ; 30cm
ISBN 0-335-13019-4 (pbk) : Unpriced
B81-25374

Education in the eighties : the central issues / edited by Brian Simon and William Taylor. — London : Batsford, 1981. — 267p : ill ; 23cm
Bibliography: p251-264. - Includes index
ISBN 0-7134-3679-4 (cased) : £14.95 : CIP rev.
ISBN 0-7134-3680-8 (pbk) : £4.95 B81-04305

370'.941 — Great Britain. Education. Implications of decline of manufacturing industries

Smith, *Sir* **Alex,** *1922-*. A coherent set of decisions / by Sir Alex Smith. — Sheffield (Woodside, Sheffield S3 9PD) : Education Department, Stanley Tools Limited, c1980. — 12p : ill ; 30cm. — (The Stanley lecture ; [3])
Unpriced (pbk) B81-26129

370'.941 — Great Britain. Education — *Serials*

Westminster studies in education. — Vol.3 (1980). — Oxford (Haddon House, Dorchester-on-Thames, Oxford OX9 8JZ) : Carfax Publishing Company, c1980. — 103p
Unpriced B81-13700

370'.9411 — Scotland. Rural regions. Education

Off the beaten track : studies of education in rural areas of Scotland / Scottish Education Department. — Edinburgh : H.M.S.O., 1981. — 95p ; 22cm. — (Occasional papers / Scottish Education Department)
ISBN 0-11-491722-1 (pbk) : £4.20 B81-23663

370'.9415 — Ireland. Education, *to 1980*

Coolahan, John. Irish education. — Dublin : Institute of Public Administration, Sept.1981. — [250]p
ISBN 0-906980-03-8 : £10.00 : CIP entry B81-22579

370'.9416 — Northern Ireland. Education — *Serials*

Great Britain. *Department of Education for Northern Ireland*. Education in Northern Ireland in ... : a report of the Department of Education for Northern Ireland for the year ended 31 December .... — 1979. — Belfast : H.M.S.O., [1981]. — 31p
ISBN 0-337-04116-4 : £2.30 B81-26577

370'.9417 — Ireland *(Republic)*. **Education**

Murphy, Christina. School report : a guide for parents, teachers and students / Christina Murphy. — Dublin (Knocksedan House, Swords, Co. Dublin) : Ward River, 1980. — viii,248p : 1map ; 18cm
Bibliogrpahy: p212-214
ISBN 0-907085-00-8 (pbk) : £2.00 B81-01627

370'.9417 — Ireland *(Republic)*. **Education** — *Conference proceedings*

Educational Studies Association of Ireland. *Education Conference (5th : 1980 : Limerick)*. Proceedings of the Fifth Annual Education Conference of the Educational Studies Association of Ireland held in Mary Immaculate College of Education Limerick : 10th April-12th April, 1980 / compiled and edited by John Coolahan in association with the Editorial Board of the E.S.A.I.. — [Dublin] ([c/o J. Coolahan, University College, Dublin]) : [The Association], [1981?]. — ix,296p : ill ; 21cm
Includes: Papers read at E.S.A.I. Symposium on History of Education, Trinity College Dublin, November 1979
Unpriced (pbk) B81-40848

370'.942 — England. Education

Williams, Shirley. Education : the divisions widen / by Shirley Williams. — Swansea : University College of Swansea, 1981. — 12p ; 21cm. — (Charles Gittins memorial lecture)
'Delivered at the College on February 10, 1981'
ISBN 0-86076-023-5 (pbk) : Unpriced B81-27749

370'.942 — England. Education, *1816-1978 — Readings from contemporary sources*

Educational documents : England and Wales : 1816 to the present day / [compiled by] J. Stuart Maclure. — 4th ed. — London : Methuen, 1979. — ix,416p : ill ; 24cm. — (Education paperbacks)
Previous ed. :1973. — Includes index
ISBN 0-416-72810-3 (pbk) : £5.95 : CIP rev. B79-20005

370'.942 — England. Education, *1850-1900 — Readings from contemporary sources*

Educating our masters : addresses and essays / by G. Combe ... [et al.] ; edited with an introduction by David A. Reeder. — [Leicester] : Leicester University Press, 1980. — viii,240p ; 23cm. — (The Victorian library)
ISBN 0-7185-5036-6 : £11.50 : CIP rev. B80-06336

370'.942 — England. Education, *1911-1920 — Sociological perspectives*

Sherington, Geoffrey. English education, social change and war, 1911-20. — Manchester : Manchester University Press, Oct.1981. — [176]p
ISBN 0-7190-0840-9 : £12.50 : CIP entry B81-25831

370'.942 — England. Education — *Encyclopaedias*

A Glossary of educational terms and terminology / prepared by South East Forum. — [Brighton] ([c/o R.J. Tiffin, Brighton Polytechnic, Falmer, Brighton BN1 9PH) : South East Forum for Science and Technology [[1980]]. — 17p ; 21cm
Cover title
Unpriced (pbk) B81-12027

370'.942 — England. Education — *Statistics — Serials*

Education statistics. Estimates / CIPFA Statistical Information Service. — 1980-81. — London : Chartered Institute of Public Finance and Accountancy, 1980. — 83p
ISSN 0307-0514 : £10.00 B81-09130

370'.942 — England. Education, *to 1979*

Midwinter, Eric. Schools in society : the evolution of English education / Eric Midwinter. — London : Batsford, 1980. — 191p ; 23cm
Bibliography: p181-185. — Includes index
ISBN 0-7134-0658-5 (cased) : £12.50
ISBN 0-7134-0659-3 (pbk) : £4.95 B81-00815

370'.942 — England. Schools. Students. Education. Inquiry reports, *1959-1978*

Rogers, Rick. Crowther to Warnock : how fourteen reports tried to change children's lives / Rick Rogers. — London : Heinemann Educational in association with The International Year of the Child, 1980. — vl,296p : ill ; 23cm
Includes bibliographies and index
ISBN 0-435-80762-5 (cased) : £12.50 : CIP rev.
ISBN 0-453-80761-7 (pbk) : £4.95
Also classified at 362.7'0941 B80-13759

370'.9422'9 — Berkshire. Education — *Serials*

Education in the Royal County of Berkshire. — [No.1]-. — Reading (223 Southampton St., Reading RG1 2RB) : Coles & Sons [in conjunction with Berkshire Education Department], [1981]-. — v. : ill,ports ; 30cm
Irregular
ISSN 0261-8966 = Education in the Royal County of Berkshire : Unpriced B81-36294

370'.9429 — Wales. Education — *Serials*

Great Britain. *Welsh Office*. Education in Wales : a report to Parliament by the Secretary of State for Wales. — 1978-. — [Cardiff] ([Cathays Park, Cardiff CF1 3NQ]) : [The Office], [1979]-. — v. ; 30cm
Annual. — Continues: Great Britain. Welsh Office. Schools in Wales. — Description based on: 1980
ISSN 0261-8885 = Education in Wales : Unpriced B81-38986

370'.9429 — Wales. Education — *Statistics — Serials*

Statistics of education in Wales / Welsh Office. — No.5 (1980). — Cardiff : H.M.S.O., 1981. — xii,137p
ISBN 0-11-790145-8 : £8.00 B81-24099

370'.947 — Soviet Union. Education

Zajda, Joseph I.. Education in the USSR / by Joseph I. Zajda. — Oxford : Pergamon, 1980. — x,272p : ill ; 22cm. — (International studies in education and social change) (Pergamon international library)
Bibliography: p251-260. - Includes index
ISBN 0-08-025807-7 (cased) : £12.00 : CIP rev.
ISBN 0-08-025806-9 (pbk) : £5.00 B80-26850

370'.95645 — Cyprus. Turkish-occupied region. Education

Crellin, Clifford T.. Turkish education in Cyprus : an outline of current provision with particular reference to that in elementary schools / Clifford T. Crellin. — [London] ([c/o Middlesex Polytechnic, Bounds Green Rd., N.11]) : [C.T. Crellin], 1979. — 35p : 1map ; 30cm
Cover title
ISBN 0-904804-05-4 (pbk) : £1.00 B81-11366

370'.9669 — Nigeria. Education — *For trainee teachers*

Bello, Joseph Y.. Basic principles of teaching. — Chichester : Wiley, Oct.1981. — [176]p. — (Education in Africa)
ISBN 0-471-27979-x (cased) : £11.00 : CIP entry
ISBN 0-471-27981-1 (pbk) : £4.00 B81-28042

370'.9669'5 — Nigeria. Northern states. Education, *to 1981*

Ozigi, Albert. Education in northern Nigeria. — London : Allen & Unwin, Jan.1982. — [160]p
ISBN 0-04-372036-6 (pbk) : £4.50 : CIP entry B81-33914

370'.973 — United States. Education

Armstrong, David G.. Education : an introduction / David G. Armstrong, Kenneth T. Henson, Tom V. Savage. — New York : Macmillan ; London : Collier Macmillan, c1981. — xvi,524p : ill ; 25cm
Includes bibliographies and index
ISBN 0-02-304050-5 : £11.50 B81-33395

Crucial issues in education / [edited by] Henry Ehlers. — 7th ed. — New York ; London : Holt, Rinehart and Winston, c1981. — xiii,306p ; 24cm
Previous ed.: 1977. — Includes index
ISBN 0-03-058089-7 (pbk) : £8.50 B81-34429

Innovations in education : reformers and their critics / [compiled by] John Martin Rich. — 3rd ed. — Boston [Mass.] ; London : Allyn and Bacon, c1981. — xii,344p ; 24cm
Previous ed: 1978. — Includes bibliographies and index
ISBN 0-205-07141-4 (pbk) : £6.95 B81-00816

370'.973 — United States. Education — *For teaching*

Bloom, Benjamin S.. All our children learning : a primer for parents, teachers, and other educators / Benjamin S. Bloom. — New York ; London : McGraw-Hill, c1981. — xii,275p ; 24cm
Includes bibliographies and index
ISBN 0-07-006120-3 : £11.20 B81-02227

370'.973 — United States. Education. Role of consultation

Consultation in schools : theory, research, procedures / edited by Jane Close Conoley ; with a foreword by Seymour B. Sarason. — New York ; London : Academic Press, 1981. — xvii,315p ; 24cm. — (The Educational technology series)
Includes bibliographies and index
ISBN 0-12-186020-5 : £14.60 B81-29772

371 — SCHOOLS

371'.00941 — Great Britain. Schools, *1900 — For schools*

Purkis, Sallie. At school in 1900 / Sallie Purkins. — Harlow : Longman, 1981. — 24p : ill ; 21cm. — (Into the past ; 3)
Cover title. — Text and ill on inside covers
ISBN 0-582-18434-7 (pbk) : £0.65 B81-27232

371'.00941 — Great Britain. Schools. Choice by parents

Kemble, Bruce. How to choose a school / Bruce Kemble. — London : Express Books, 1981. — 127p ; 18cm
ISBN 0-85079-109-x (pbk) : £1.00 B81-16506

371'.009417 — Ireland *(Republic)*. **Schools**

McHugh, Stan. The school survival kit : a guide to primary and post-primary schooling in Ireland for parents, teachers and students / Stan McHugh ; cartoons by Jeanette Dunne. — Portmarnock (98 Ardilaun, Portmarnock, County Dublin) : Wolfhound, c1980. — 135p : ill ; 21cm
Bibliography: p131. — Includes index
ISBN 0-905473-53-1 (pbk) : £2.75 B81-03913

371'.009423'37 — Dorset. Poole. Schools, *to 1980*

Young, D. E. W.. Schools of old Poole : South Road and before 1628-1980 / [by D.E.W. Young]. — Poole (56 Broadwater Ave., Poole, Dorset BH14 8QH) : Polus, c1980. — 157p : ill,facsims,ports ; 22cm
Bibliography: p155. — Includes index
ISBN 0-907296-00-9 (pbk) : £2.95 B81-22141

371'.009425'79 — Oxfordshire. Brightwell-cum-Sotwell. Schools, *1726-1980*

Heyworth, Joy. Education in Brightwell-cum-Sotwell / by Joy Heyworth. — [Wallingford] ([Middle Farm, Church La., Brightwell-cum-Sotwell, Wallingford OX10 0SD]) : [K. Owen], 1981. — 16p ; 22cm
Unpriced (pbk) B81-35505

371'.009427'53 — Merseyside *(Metropolitan County).* **Liverpool. Schools,** *1880-1980*

Yesterday's schools / [editor D. Rice]. — [Liverpool] ([14 Sir Thomas St., Liverpool L1 6BJ]) : City of Liverpool Education Department, 1980. — 126p : ill,1map,facsims ; 30cm
Unpriced (pbk) B81-07970

371'.00943 — West Germany. Schools. Reform. Role of political parties, *1948-1973*

Betts, Robin S.. The CDU, the SPD and the West German school reform question 1948-73 / Robin S. Betts. — [London] : London Association of Comparative Educationists, 1981. — 29p ; 21cm. — (Occasional paper / London Association of Comparative Educationists ; 4)
ISBN 0-85473-107-5 (pbk) : Unpriced B81-18430

371'.00973 — United States. Schools. Social aspects

Jarolimek, John. The schools in contemporary society : an analysis of social currents, issues and forces / John Jarolimek. — New York : Macmillan ; London : Collier Macmillan, c1981. — xi,324p : ill ; 24cm
Includes bibliographies and index
ISBN 0-02-360430-1 : £11.50 B81-33398

371'.009773'11 — Illinois. Chicago. Schools

Wynne, Edward A.. Looking at schools : good, bad and indifferent / Edward A. Wynne. — Lexington, Mass. : Lexington Books ; [Farnborough, Hants.] [distributor], c1980. — xxiii,235p ; 24cm
Includes index
ISBN 0-669-03292-1 : £13.50 B81-08388

371'.02'02541 — Great Britain. Independent schools — *Directories — Serials*

Schools. — 57th ed. (1980/81). — London : Truman & Knightly Educational Trust, [1980]. — 741p
ISBN 0-900755-31-8 : £6.00
ISSN 0080-6897 B81-03227

The **Schools** of England, Wales, Scotland & Ireland with tutors, careers and continental sections. — 70th ed (1981). — London : Burrow, 1981. — 375p
£6.50 B81-12411

United Kingdom schools, private / [Data Research Group]. — 1980/81. — Great Missenden : The Group, [1981?]. — 183p
ISBN 0-86099-296-9 : Unpriced B81-13406

371'.02'025411 — Scotland. Independent schools — *Directories — Serials*

Which school? / ISIS Scotland. — 1980-81-. — Edinburgh (22 Hanover St., Edinburgh EH2 2EP) : ISIS (Scotland), 1980-. — v. ; 21cm
Annual. — Continues: Independent Schools Information Service (Scotland)
ISSN 0260-7255 = Which school? : Unpriced B81-06926

371'.02'025422 — South-east England. Independent schools — *Directories — Serials*

London and South East Independent Schools Information Service. — 1981. — London (3, Vandon St., SW1H 0AN) : ISIS London and South East, [1980]. — 76p
ISSN 0309-4162 : Unpriced B81-09098

London and South East Independent Schools Information Service. — 1980. — London : Murray House, 3 Vandon St., SW1 0AG : ISIS (London and South East), [1980]. — 68p
ISSN 0309-4162 : Unpriced B81-13310

371'.02'025423 — South-west England. Independent schools — *Directories — Serials*

ISIS : the Independent Schools Information Service, South and West. — 1981. — Exeter (7, Baring Crescent , Exeter, Devon) : ISIS, South & West, [1981]. — 26p
Unpriced B81-12423

371'.02'025426 — East Anglia. Independent schools — *Directories — Serials*

Schools in eastern England / Independent Schools Information Service - East. — 11th ed. (1981). — Cambridge (73 Grange Rd., Cambridge CB8 9AB) : ISIA (East) [1980?]. — 48p
ISSN 0309-6173 : Unpriced B81-06728

Schools in Eastern England / Independent Schools Information Service - East. — 10th ed. (1980). — Cambridge (73, Grange Rd., Cambridge CB3 9AB) : ISIS (East), [1979?]. — 48p
ISSN 0309-6173 : Unpriced B81-06727

371'.02'0941 — Great Britain. Independent schools

Freedom under fire / Independent Schools Information Service. — London (26 Caxton St., SW1H 0RG) : ISIS, [1980]. — [8]p ; 22cm
Cover title. — Text on inside cover. — One sheet ([2])p as insert
Unpriced (pbk) B81-11091

371'.02'0941 — Great Britain. Independent schools — *For parents — Serials*

The **Parents'** guide to independent schools / prepared by Hobsons Press (Cambridge) Ltd. — 2nd ed. (1981). — Maidenhead (10 Queen St., Maidenhead, Berks.) : SFIA Educational Trust, 1981. — 1096p
ISBN 0-906695-05-8 : £25.00 : CIP rev. B81-03719

371'.02'0942 — England. Independent schools

Independent education in England. — Rev. ed. — [London] ([6 Sackville St. Piccadilly, W1X 2BR]) : [Gabbitas-Thring Educational Trust], 1980. — 18p ; 14cm
Previous ed.: 1977
Unpriced (unbound) B81-32960

371'.02'0942676 — Essex. Brentwood. Boys' schools: Brentwood School, *to 1980*

Lewis, R. R.. The history of Brentwood School / R.R. Lewis. — Brentwood (Brentwood, Essex CM15 8HS) : Governors of Sir Antony Browne's School, 1981. — xxiv,401p,[45]p of plates : ill(some col.),facsims,port,geneal.tables ; 22cm
Ill on lining papers. — Includes index
Unpriced B81-29383

371'.03'0942876 — Tyne and Wear *(Metropolitan County).* **Newcastle upon Tyne. Community schools** — *Conference proceedings*

Community schools for Newcastle : a conference report. — Newcastle on Tyne (Mea House, Ellison Place, Newcastle on Tyne NE1 8XS) : Inner City Forum, [1981]. — 32p : ill ; 30cm
Cover title. — Bibliography: p32
£0.50 (pbk) B81-21331

371'.04 — Home-based education — *Personal observations*

Kiddle, Catherine. What shall we do with the children?. — Barnstaple : Spindlewood, Sept.1981. — [110]p
ISBN 0-907349-05-6 : £4.95 : CIP entry B81-28807

371.1 — TEACHING AND TEACHING PERSONNEL

371.1'0023 — Teaching — *Career guides*

Honeyford, R.. Starting teaching. — London : Croom Helm, Jan.1982. — [176]p
ISBN 0-7099-1226-9 (cased) : £10.95 : CIP entry
ISBN 0-7099-1227-7 (pbk) : £3.95 B81-33895

371.1'006'041 — Great Britain. Schools. Teachers. Organisations. Sociopolitical aspects

Ozga, Jennifer. Teachers, professionalism and class : a study of organized teachers / Jennifer Ozga and Martin Lawn. — Lewes (Falmer House, Barcombe, Lewes, Sussex) : Falmer Press, 1981. — x,153p ; 22cm. — (Politics and education series)
Includes index
ISBN 0-905273-20-6 : Unpriced B81-39413

371.1'0089969729 — London. Schools. West Indian teachers

Gibbes, Norma. West Indian teachers : speak out their experiences in some of London's schools / by Norma Gibbes in association with the Caribbean Teachers' Association and Lewisham Council for Community Relations. — London (8 Camberwell Green, S.E.5) : Caribbean Teachers' Association, [1980]. — 24p : 1port ; 21cm
Bibliography: p24
ISBN 0-9507335-0-4 (pbk) : £0.70 B81-12023

371.1'0092'4 — England. Teaching, *1919-1980 — Personal observations*

Campbell, P. J.. Refuge from fear. — London : Hamilton, Feb.1982. — [192]p
ISBN 0-241-10736-9 : £7.95 : CIP entry B81-36385

371.1'0092'4 — South Africa. Transkei. Christian mission schools. Teaching, *1922-1962 — Personal observations*

Elder, Joanna. Teacher on trek : times remembered / Joanna Elder ; designed, produced and illustrated by Nils Solberg Jnr. — [Forest Row] Walhatch, Forest Row, Sussex] : N. Solberg, Jnr, c1980. — 86p : ill,1map ; 21cm
Unpriced (pbk) B81-05975

371.1'00942 — England. Teachers — *Statistics — Serials*

Statistics of education. Vol.4 Teachers [England & Wales] / Department of Education and Science. — 1978. — London : H.M.S.O., 1980. — xiv,58p
ISBN 0-11-270507-3 : £7.50 B81-04451

371.1'02 — Great Britain. Schools. Teachers. Interpersonal relationships with students *related to* **interpersonal relationships between children & parents**

David, Miriam E.. The State, the family and education / Miriam E. David. — London : Routledge & Kegan Paul, 1980. — vii,280p ; 22cm. — (Radical social policy)
Bibliography: p249-267. - Includes index
ISBN 0-7100-0601-2 (pbk) : £5.95 : CIP rev.
Also classified at 306.8'7 B80-17623

371.1'02 — Schools. Teachers. Interpersonal relationships with students — *Sociological perspectives — Study regions: United States*

Thelen, Herbert A.. The classroom society : the construction of educational experience / Herbert A. Thelen. — London : Croom Helm, c1981. — 226p ; 23cm. — (A Halstead Press book)
Includes index
ISBN 0-7099-2402-x : £12.95 : CIP rev. B81-16369

371.1'02 — Schools. Teaching. Applications of research on cognitive development of children

Klausmeier, Herbert J.. Learning and teaching concepts : a strategy for testing applications of theory / Herbert J. Klausmeier, with the assistance of Thomas S. Sipple. — New York ; London : Academic Press, 1980. — xx,228p : ill ; 24cm. — (Educational psychology)
Includes bibliographies and index
ISBN 0-12-411450-4 : £14.60 B81-15130

371.1'02 — Schools. Teaching — *Manuals*

Cruickshank, Donald R.. Teaching is tough / Donald R. Cruickshank and associates. — Englewood Cliffs ; London : Prentice Hall, c1980. — x,342p : ill ; 21cm. — (Applied education) (A Spectrum book)
Includes bibliographies and index
ISBN 0-13-893495-9 (cased) : £9.70
ISBN 0-13-893487-8 (pbk) : £4.50 B81-01631

371.1′02 — Teaching — *Manuals*
Dawson, Colin. How to face a class : a practical guide to classroom teaching in schools and colleges / Colin Dawson. — London : Harrap, 1981. — 40p : ill ; 18cm
Bibliography: p40
ISBN 0-245-53713-9 (pbk) : £1.50 B81-19681

371.1′02 — Teaching. Objectives
Objectives for instruction and evaluation / Robert J. Kibler ... [et al.]. — 2nd ed. — Boston [Mass.] ; London : Allyn and Bacon, c1981. — viii,232p : ill ; 22cm
Previous ed.: 1974. — Includes bibliographies and index
ISBN 0-205-07154-6 (cased) : £11.95
ISBN 0-205-07174-0 (pbk) : £8.95 B81-06188

371.1′02 — United States. Schools. Students. Classroom behaviour. Influence of peer teaching
The **Utilization** of classroom peers as behavior change agents / edited by Phillip S. Strain. — New York ; London : Plenum, c1981. — xii,366p : 1form ; 24cm. — (Applied clinical psychology)
Includes bibliographies and index
ISBN 0-306-40618-7 : Unpriced B81-29133

371.1′02′01 — Teaching — *Philosophical perspectives*
Passmore, John. The philosophy of teaching / John Passmore. — London : Duckworth, 1980. — xi,259p ; 24cm
Includes index
ISBN 0-7156-1031-7 (cased) : Unpriced : CIP rev.
ISBN 0-7156-1465-7 (pbk) : £8.50 B80-00652

371.1′02′01 — Teaching. Theories
Ashton-Warner, Sylvia. Teacher / by Sylvia Ashton-Warner ; with a new introduction by Dora Russell. — London : Virago, 1980. — 224p : ill,facsims ; 20cm
Originally published: New York : Simon and Schuster ; London : Secker and Warburg, 1963
ISBN 0-86068-162-9 (pbk) : £2.95 B81-00817

371.1′02′02461 — Teaching — *For medicine*
The **medical** teacher. — Edinburgh : Churchill Livingstone, Jan.1982. — [320]p
ISBN 0-443-02446-4 (pbk) : £12.00 : CIP entry B81-34506

371.1′02′05 — Teaching — *Serials*
Staffroom news. — [No.1]-. — Wetherby (P.O. Box 10, Wetherby, West Yorkshire LS23 7EL) : [s.n.], [197-]-. — v. : ill,ports ; 42cm
Description based on: Autumn Term 1980 issue
ISSN 0261-0671 = Staffroom news : £0.12 per issue B81-17482

371.1′02′07 — United States. Nursery schools. Teachers. In-service training. Curriculum subjects: Teaching skills
Beaty, Janice J.. Skills for preschool teachers / Janice J. Beaty. — Columbus [Ohio] ; London : Merrill, c1979. — xi,225p : ill,1plan,forms ; 25cm
Includes bibliographies and index
ISBN 0-675-08283-8 (pbk) : £5.95 B81-13986

371.1′02′072 — Schools. Action research — *For teachers*
A **Teacher's** guide to action research : evaluation, enquiry and development in the classroom / edited by Jon Nixon. — London : Grant McIntyre, 1981. — 209p : ill ; 21cm
ISBN 0-86216-040-5 (cased) : Unpriced : CIP rev. B81-03718

371.1′02′072041 — Great Britain. Schools. Teaching. Research — *Conference proceedings*
Understanding classroom life / edited by Ray McAleese and David Hamilton. — Windsor : NFER, 1978. — 131p ; 22cm
Conference papers. — Includes bibliographies and index
ISBN 0-85633-158-9 (pbk) : £6.00 B81-01763

371.1′02′0973 — United States. Schools. Teaching
Duck, Lloyd. Teaching with charisma / Lloyd Duck. — Boston, Mass. ; London : Allyn and Bacon, c1981. — xii,312p : ill,facsims ; 24cm
Bibliography: p279-303. — Includes index
ISBN 0-205-07257-7 (pbk) : £8.95 B81-11243

371.1′02′0973 — United States. Teaching — *Manuals*
Davies, Ivor K.. Instructional technique / Ivor K. Davies. — New York ; London : McGraw-Hill, c1981. — x,369p : ill,forms ; 25cm
Bibliography: p347-355. — Includes index
ISBN 0-07-015502-x : £9.95 B81-05514

371.1′022 — Teaching. Role of encouragement
Martin, Robert J.. Teaching through encouragement : techniques to help students learn / Robert J. Martin. — Englewood Cliffs ; London : Prentice-Hall, c1980. — xv,188p ; 21cm. — (A Spectrum book)
Bibliography: p180-181. - Includes index
ISBN 0-13-896266-9 (cased) : Unpriced
ISBN 0-13-896258-6 (pbk) : £3.20 B81-12718

371.1′024 — Children. Classroom behaviour. Behaviour modification
Walker, James E.. Behavior modification : a practical approach for educators / James E. Walker, Thomas M. Shea. — 2nd ed. — St. Louis ; London : Mosby, 1980. — xii,185p,[45] leaves : ill,plans,forms ; 24cm
Previous ed.: 1976. — Includes bibliographies and index
ISBN 0-8016-5338-x (pbk) : £9.25 B81-00818

371.1′024 — Schools. Classrooms. Discipline — *For teaching*
Robertson, John, *1937-*. Effective classroom control / John Robertson. — London : Hodder and Stoughton, c1981. — 117p ; 22cm. — (Studies in teaching and learning)
Bibliography: p115-117
ISBN 0-340-26085-8 (pbk) : £2.95 : CIP rev. B81-10441

371.1′024 — Schools. Classrooms. Students. Discipline — *For teaching*
Madsen, Charles H.. Teaching/discipline : a positive approach for educational development / Charles H. Madsen Jr, Clifford K. Madsen. — 3rd ed. — Boston [Mass.] ; London : Allyn and Bacon, c1981. — iv,317p : ill,forms ; 25cm
Previous ed.: 1974. — Bibliography: p306-310. — Includes index
ISBN 0-205-07228-3 (cased) : £11.95 B81-12097

371.1′024 — United States. Schools. Classrooms. Discipline
Jones, Vernon F.. Responsible classroom discipline : creating positive learning environments and solving problems / Vernon F. Jones, Louise S. Jones. — Boston, Mass. ; London : Allyn and Bacon, c1981. — viii,350p : ill,forms ; 25cm
Bibliography: p329-343. — Includes index
ISBN 0-205-07270-4 : Unpriced B81-24234

371.1′024′0973 — United States. Schools. Classrooms. Discipline — *For teaching*
Gnagey, William J.. Motivating classroom discipline / William J. Gnagey. — New York : Macmillan ; London : Collier Macmillan, c1981. — xii,148p ; 21cm
Bibliography: p135-143. — Includes index
ISBN 0-02-344140-2 (pbk) : £3.75 B81-29317

371.1′44′0973 — United States. Teachers. Evaluation
Handbook of teacher evaluation / edited by Jason Millman. — Beverly Hills ; London : Sage in Cooperation with the National Council on Measurement in Education, c1981. — 356p : ill,1form ; 23cm
Includes bibliographies and index
ISBN 0-8039-1597-7 : £18.75 B81-36141

371.1′46 — Educational institutions. Teachers. In-service training. Courses. Topics
Stone, Michael M.. In-service education : a research vocabulary / Michael M. Stone with Anthony F. Sacco ... [et al.]. — Durham : University of Durham, School of Education, 1980. — ix,229p ; 21cm
Bibliography: p223-226. — Includes index
ISBN 0-903380-04-8 (pbk) : Unpriced B81-22928

371.1′46 — Schools. Teachers. In-service training
In-service : the teacher and the school. — London : Kogan Page, Nov.1981. — [220]p
ISBN 0-85038-497-4 (pbk) : £9.75 : CIP entry B81-30888

Morant, Roland W.. In-service education within the school. — London : Allen & Unwin, Jan.1982. — [128]p. — (Unwin education books)
ISBN 0-04-370111-6 (cased) : £10.00 : CIP entry
ISBN 0-04-370112-4 (pbk) : £3.50 B81-33915

Rudduck, Jean. Making the most of the short in-service course. — London : Methuen Educational, Dec.1981. — [160]p. — (Schools Council working paper, ISSN 0533-1668 ; 71)
ISBN 0-423-50850-4 (pbk) : £5.75 : CIP entry B81-31701

371.1′46 — Teachers. In-service training. Role of classroom observation
Day, Christopher. Classroom based in-service teacher education : the development and evaluation of a client-centred model / [Chris Day]. — [Brighton] ([Education Development Building, Falmer, Brighton. BN1 9RG]) : [University of Sussex Education Area], 1981. — 86p : ill ; 21cm. — (Occasional paper / University of Sussex. Education, Area ; 9)
Bibliography p82-86
ISBN 0-905414-08-x (pbk) : Unpriced B81-36465

371.1′46′0722 — England. Schools. Teachers. In-service training — *Case studies*
Henderson, Evan S.. Change and development in schools : case studies in the management of school-focused in-service education / Evan S. Henderson and George W. Perry. — London : McGraw-Hill, c1981. — 188p : ill ; 22cm
Bibliography: p186-188
ISBN 0-07-084117-9 (pbk) : £3.95 : CIP rev. B80-18651

371.1′46′0941 — Great Britain. Schools. Teachers. In-service training: B.Ed courses — *Case studies*
Evans, Norman. The in-service B.Ed. : six case studies / Norman Evans. — [Cambridge] : Cambridge Institute of Education, 1980. — 133p : 2maps ; 30cm
Cover title
Unpriced (pbk) B81-12028

371.1′46′0941 — Great Britain. Teachers. In-service training. Role of teachers' centres. Evaluation — *Conference proceedings*
National Conference of Teachers' Centre Leaders. *Conference (1980 : Grantham)*. Evaluation, inset and the teachers' centre : proceedings of the 1980 Conference of N.C.T.C.L. / edited by John Brand, John Hughes. — [Sheffield] ([Pond St., Sheffield S1 1WB]) : Sheffield City Polytechnic, Department of Education Management for the Wardens of the East Midlands, 1980. — 157p ; 22cm. — (Sheffield papers in education management ; no.13)
ISBN 0-903761-27-0 (pbk) : £1.75 B81-35318

371.2 — SCHOOL ADMINISTRATION

371.2 — Educational institutions. Administration. Applications of theories of organisational behaviour
Owens, Robert G.. Organizational behaviour in education / Robert G. Owens. — 2nd ed. — Englewood Cliffs ; London : Prentice-Hall, c1981. — xii,340p : ill ; 24cm
Previous ed.: 1970. — Includes bibliographies and index
ISBN 0-13-641050-2 : £12.30 B81-22718

371.2 — United States. Schools. Evaluation
DeRoche, Edward F.. An administrator's guide for evaluating programs and personnel / Edward F. DeRoche. — Boston, Mass. ; London : Allyn and Bacon, c1981. — xi,274p : ill,forms ; 25cm
Includes bibliographies and index
ISBN 0-205-07252-6 : Unpriced B81-26217

371.2 — United States. Schools. Supervision
Alfonso, Robert J.. Instructional supervision : a behavior system / Robert J. Alfonso, Gerald R. Firth, Richard F. Neville. — 2nd ed. — Boston, Mass. ; London : Allyn and Bacon, c1981. — xi,488p : ill,charts ; 25cm
Previous ed. 1975. — Includes index
ISBN 0-205-07142-2 : £12.95 B81-00819

371.2'009181'2 — Western world. Schools. Administration. Political aspects — *Comparative studies*

The **Politics** of school government / edited by George Baron. — Oxford : Pergamon, 1981. — viii,298p ; 22cm. — (International studies in education and social change)
Includes bibliographies and index
ISBN 0-08-025213-3 : £20.00 B81-27690

371.2'00941 — Great Britain. Schools. Administration

John, Denys. Leadership in schools / Denys John. — London : Heinemann Educational, 1980. — x,181p : ill ; 23cm. — (Heinemann organization in schools series)
Bibliography: p173. — Includes index
ISBN 0-435-80468-5 : £5.95 : CIP rev.
B80-05844

371.2'00941 — Great Britain. Schools due to be closed. Management

Whiting, Norman. Management within the closing school / by Norman Whiting. — [Sheffield] ([Pond St., Sheffield S1 1WB]) : Sheffield City Polytechnic, Department of Education Management, 1980. — 31leaves ; 22cm
ISBN 0-903761-25-4 (pbk) : £0.60 B81-35317

371.2'00941 — Great Britain. Schools. Management

Management and the school / [E323 Management and the School Course Team]. — Milton Keynes : Open University Press. — (Educational studies : a third level course)
At head of title: The Open University
Block 1: Management in action : an introduction to school management / prepared by Colin Riches for the Course Team. — 1981. — 76p : ill,ports ; 30cm. — (E323 ; block 1)
Bibliography: p75-76
ISBN 0-335-13070-4 (pbk) : Unpriced
B81-19400

Management and the school. — Milton Keynes : Open University Press. — (Educational studies : a third level course)
At head of title: The Open University
Block 3: Managerial processes in schools. — 1981. — 72p : ill ; 30cm. — (E323 ; block 3)
Includes bibliographies
ISBN 0-335-13072-0 (pbk) : Unpriced
B81-14597

Management and the school. — Milton Keynes : Open University Press. — (Educational studies : a third level course)
At head of title: The Open University
Block 4: Policy-making, organization and leadership in schools. — 1981. — 88p : ill ; 30cm. — (E323 ; 6)
Includes bibliographies
ISBN 0-335-13073-9 (pbk) : Unpriced
B81-14598

Paisey, Alan. Organization and management in schools : perspectives for practising teachers / Alan Paisey. — London : Longman, 1981. — 149p : ill ; 22cm
Bibliography: p135-145. — Includes index
ISBN 0-582-49709-4 (pbk) : £4.95 : CIP rev.
B81-13827

371.2'00973 — United States. Schools. Administration

Stoops, Emery. Handbook of educational administration : a guide for the practitioner / Emery Stoops, Max Rafferty, Russell E. Johnson. — 2nd ed. — Boston [Mass.] ; London : Allyn and Bacon, c1981. — xiv,499p : ill,forms ; 25cm
Previous ed.: 1975. — Includes bibliographies and index
ISBN 0-205-07133-3 : £21.95 B81-02447

371.2'00973 — United States. Schools. Administration. Political aspects

Wiles, David K.. Practical politics for school administrators / David K. Wiles, Jon Wiles, Joseph Bondi. — Boston [Mass.] ; London : Allyn and Bacon, c1981. — x,225p : ill ; 25cm
Includes index
ISBN 0-205-07132-5 : £15.95 B81-06965

371.2'01 — Great Britain. Educational institutions. Managers. Training & development

Crump, James. Management development and management performance / by James Crump. — [Sheffield] ([Pond St., Sheffield S1 1WB]) : Sheffield City Polytechnic, Department of Education Management, 1980. — 26leaves ; 21cm. — (Sheffield papers in education management ; no.15)
Bibliography: leaves 21-26
ISBN 0-903761-26-2 (pbk) : £1.00 B81-35319

371.2'07 — United States. Educational institutions. Management. Planning. Decision making

Tanner, C. Kenneth. Educational planning and decision making : a view through the organizational process / C. Kenneth Tanner, Earl J. Williams. — Lexington, Mass. : Lexington Books ; [Aldershot] : Gower [distributor], 1981. — xvi,238p : ill,forms ; 24cm
Includes index
ISBN 0-669-04330-3 : £15.00 B81-39694

371.2'52 — Great Britain. Schools. Mixed ability groups. Teaching

Mixed ability teaching. — London : Croom Helm, Oct.1981. — [128]p
ISBN 0-7099-2315-5 : £9.95 : CIP entry
B81-25716

371.2'6 — Schools. Students. Academic achievement. Assessment — *Conference proceedings*

Issues in evaluation and accountability. — London : Methuen, Nov.1981. — [200]p
Conference papers
ISBN 0-416-74740-x (cased) : £7.50 : CIP entry
ISBN 0-416-74750-7 (pbk) : £3.95 B81-30553

371.2'6 — Schools. Students. Assessment

Lidz, Carol Schneider. Improving assessment of schoolchildren / Carol Schneider Lidz. — San Francisco ; London : Jossey-Bass, 1981. — xiv,223p ; 24cm. — (The Jossey-Bass social and behavioral science series)
Bibliography: p176-214. — Includes index
ISBN 0-87589-488-7 : £11.95 B81-26100

Satterly, David. Assessment in schools / David Satterly. — Oxford : Basil Blackwell, 1981. — viii,365p : ill ; 22cm. — (Theory and practice in education ; 1)
Bibliography: p336-343. — Includes index
ISBN 0-631-11151-4 (cased) : £12.00
ISBN 0-631-12564-7 (pbk) : £4.95 B81-24273

371.2'64 — Schools. Students. Academic achievement. Assessment

Bloom, Benjamin S.. Evaluation to improve learning / Benjamin S. Bloom, George F. Madaus, J. Thomas Hastings. — New York ; London : McGraw-Hill, c1981. — ix,356p : ill,forms ; 24cm
Includes bibliographies and index
ISBN 0-07-006109-2 (pbk) : £11.25 B81-36516

371.2'64 — Schools. Students. Academic achievement. Testing

Hopkins, Kenneth D.. Educational and psychological measurement and evaluation / Kenneth D. Hopkins, Julian C. Stanley. — 6th ed. — Englewood Cliffs ; London : Prentice-Hall, c1981. — xxi,517p : ill,facsims,forms ; 25cm. — (Prentice-Hall series in educational measurement, research and statistics)
Previous ed.: Englewood Cliffs : Prentice-Hall, 1972. — In the previous ed. J.C. Stanley's name appeared first on the title page. — Bibliography: p472-505. — Includes index
ISBN 0-13-236273-2 : £14.65 B81-26911

371.2'64 — Schools. Students. Academic achievement. Testing — *For teaching*

Brown, Frederick. Measuring classroom achievement / Frederick G. Brown. — New York ; London : Holt, Rinehart and Winston, c1981. — x,224p : ill ; 24cm
Bibliography: p214-216. - Includes index
ISBN 0-03-052421-0 (pbk) : £5.50 B81-12750

371.2'64 — Students. Academic achievement. Assessment

Gronlund, Norman E.. Measurement and evaluation in teaching / Norman E. Gronlund. — 4th ed. — New York : Macmillan ; London : Collier Macmillan, c1981. — vii,597p : ill,forms ; 25cm
Previous ed.: 1976. — Includes bibliographies and index
ISBN 0-02-348020-3 (cased) : £12.50
ISBN 0-02-978700-5 (pbk) : Unpriced
B81-21449

Popham, W. James. Modern educational measurement / W. James Popham. — Englewood Cliffs : Prentice-Hall, c1981. — xiii,441p : ill,forms ; 25cm
Includes bibliographies and index
ISBN 0-13-591982-7 : £12.95 B81-22700

371.2'64 — Students. Academic achievement. Assessment — *Questions & answers*

Ahmann, J. Stanley. Test items based on Evaluating student progress : principles of tests and measurements. 6th ed. / J. Stanley Ahmann, Marvin D. Glock. — Boston, Mass. ; London : Allyn and Bacon, c1981. — 81p : 1ill ; 22cm
ISBN 0-205-06562-7 (pbk) : Unpriced
B81-10740

371.2'64 — United States. Schools. Students. Assessment

Anderson, Lorin W.. Assessing affective characteristics in the schools / Lorin W. Anderson. — Boston, Mass. ; London : Allyn and Bacon, c1981. — xiii,271p : ill ; 25cm
Bibliography: p261-266. — Includes index
ISBN 0-205-07277-1 : Unpriced B81-26218

371.2'95 — Children. School phobia

Kahn, Jack. Unwillingly to school : school phobia or school refusal : a psychosocial problem / foreword to first edition by Mildred Creak. — 3rd ed. / by Jack H. Kahn and Jean P. Nursten and Howard C.M. Carroll. — Oxford : Pergamon, 1981. — xxiv,229p ; 22cm. — (Pergamon international library)
Previous ed.: 1968. — Bibliography: p217-223. - Includes index
ISBN 0-08-025229-x (cased) : £12.00
ISBN 0-08-025230-3 (pbk) : £5.00 B81-11444

371.2'95 — Truancy

Out of school : modern perspectives in truancy and school refusal / edited by Lionel Hersov and Ian Berg. — Chichester : Wiley, c1980. — xii,377p : ill ; 24cm. — (Wiley series on studies in child psychiatry)
Includes bibliography and index
ISBN 0-471-27743-6 : £15.50 : CIP rev.
B80-25434

371.3 — TEACHING METHODS

371.3 — Developing countries. Distance study. Organisations: International Extension College, *to 1981*

International Extension College. Ten-year report 1971-1981 / International Extension College. — Cambridge (18 Brooklands Ave., Cambridge CB2 2HN) : International Extension College, 1981. — 27p ; 21cm
ISBN 0-903632-20-9 (pbk) : Unpriced
B81-31326

371.3 — Distance study

Holmberg, Börje. Status and trends of distance education / Börje Holmberg. — London : Kogan Page, 1981. — 200p : 1ill,forms ; 23cm
Bibliography: p141-194. — Includes index
ISBN 0-85038-414-1 : £11.95 B81-27892

371.3 — Education. Courses. Development

Rowntree, Derek. Developing courses for students. — London : McGraw-Hill, July 1981. — [304]p. — (McGraw-Hill series for teachers)
ISBN 0-07-084126-8 (pbk) : £4.95 : CIP entry
B81-15829

371.3 — Education. Problem-solving — *Serials*

Problem-solving news : the newsletter of the Bulmershe-Comino Problem-Solving Research Project. — Issue no.1 (Nov.1980)-. — Reading (Bulmershe College of Higher Education, Woodlands Ave., Earley, Reading, Berks. RG6 1HY) : The Project, 1980-. — v. ; 30cm
Three issues yearly
ISSN 0260-5554 = Problem-solving news : Unpriced B81-09213

371.3 — England. Distance study — *National Association of Teachers in Further and Higher Education viewpoints*

National Association of Teachers in Further and Higher Education. Open learning : a policy statement, 1981 / NATFHE. — [London] : NATFHE, [1981]. — 8p ; 15x21cm
Cover title
£0.35 (pbk) B81-29451

371.3 — Scotland. Distance study. Courses — *Directories*

A **Guide** to distance (open) learning opportunities for people in Scotland 1981 / S.C.E.T.. — Glasgow (74 Victoria Crescent Rd., Glasgow G12 9JN) : Scottish Council for Educational Technology, 1981. — 32p ; 15x21cm
Cover title. — Includes index
ISBN 0-86011-036-2 (pbk) : Unpriced B81-18637

371.3 — Student centred teaching methods — *Manuals*

Hoover, Kenneth H.. A sourcebook of student activities : techniques for improving instruction / Kenneth H. Hoover. — Boston, Mass. ; London : Allyn and Bacon, c1981. — xi,236p : ill,forms ; 28cm
Includes index
ISBN 0-205-07253-4 (pbk) : £10.50 B81-11241

371.3'028'12 — Multiple-choice questions. Answering — *Manuals* — *For Caribbean students*

Halcrow, Elizabeth M.. Students' guide to multiple choice tests / Elizabeth M. Halcrow. — London : Heinemann, 1981. — 49p ; 25cm. — (Heinemann CXC history)
ISBN 0-435-98420-9 (pbk) : £1.25 B81-29935

371.3'028'12 — Schools. Students. Study techniques. Teaching — *Manuals*

Devine, Thomas G.. Teaching study skills : a guide for teachers / Thomas G. Devine. — Boston [Mass.] ; London : Allyn and Bacon, c1981. — xxi,347p : 1ill ; 25cm
Includes bibliographies and index
ISBN 0-205-07269-0 : Unpriced B81-28985

371.3'028'12 — Study techniques — *Manuals*

Parsons, Chris. How to study effectively / Chris Parsons. — London : Arrow, 1979 (1980 printing). — 94p : forms ; 20cm
ISBN 0-09-912400-9 (pbk) : £1.00 B81-00068

371.3'028'14 — Schools. Students. Study techniques - *For teaching*

Hamblin, D.. Teaching study skills. — Oxford : Blackwell, May 1981. — [176]p
ISBN 0-631-12533-7 (pbk) : CIP entry B81-08931

371.3'028'2 — Residential homes for children. Children. Teaching methods. Social learning

Brown, Barrie. Social learning practice in residential child care. — Oxford : Pergamon, July 1981. — [150]p. — (Pergamon international library)
ISBN 0-08-026779-3 : £10.50 : CIP entry
ISBN 0-08-026778-5 (pbk) : £5.00 B81-13909

371.3'07'8 — Educational technology — *Conference proceedings*

Aspects of educational technology. — London : Kogan Page
Conference papers
Vol.15: Distance learning and evaluation. — Dec.1981. — [336]p
ISBN 0-85038-494-x : £14.95 : CIP entry
ISSN 0141-5956 B81-34224

371.3'07'8 — Great Britain. Teachers' centres — *Serials*

[Insight *(National Conference of Teachers' Centre Leaders)*]. Insight : journal of the National Conference of Teachers' Centre Leaders. — Vol.1, no.1 (Apr. 1977)-. — [Enfield] ((c/o D. Goddard, Enfield Teachers' Centre, Craddock Rd, Enfield]) : The Conference, 1977. — v. ; 30cm
Three issues yearly. — Description based on: Vol.3, no.3 (June 1980)
ISSN 0144-8471 = Insight (National Conference of Teachers' Centre Leaders) : £3.00 per year B81-02015

371.3'07'8 — Scotland. Schools. Educational resources. Attitudes of teachers

Hamilton, David D.. Teachers and resources : the views of 200 unpromoted teachers / David D. Hamilton. — Glasgow : SCET, 1981. — 65p : forms ; 30cm
ISBN 0-86011-037-0 (pbk) : Unpriced B81-26128

371.3'07'8 — Teaching aids. Selection — *For teachers*

Gall, Meredith Damien. Handbook for evaluating and selecting curriculum materials / Meredith Damien Gall. — Boston, Mass. ; London : Allyn and Bacon, c1981. — xvii,127p : ill,1form ; 24cm
Includes bibliographies and index
ISBN 0-205-07294-1 (spiral) : Unpriced
ISBN 0-205-07301-8 (pbk) : Unpriced B81-11480

371.3'07'8 — Teaching materials. Bias. Racial aspects

Hicks, Dave. Images of the world : an introduction to bias in teaching materials / Dave Hicks. — [London] : University of London Institute of Education, c1980. — 20p : ill ; 21cm. — (Occasional paper / Department for Education in Developing Countries and the Centre for Multicultural Education, University of London Institute of Education ; no.2)
ISBN 0-85473-102-4 (pbk) : Unpriced B81-21126

371.3'07'8 — United States. Schools. Curriculum. Development. Role of media units

The **Library** media specialist in curriculum development / edited by Nevada Wallis Thomason. — Metuchen ; London : Scarecrow, 1981. — x,278p : ill ; 23cm
Bibliography: p262-273. — Includes index
ISBN 0-8108-1406-4 : £10.50 B81-25966

371.3'2 — School texts. Readability. Assessment

Harrison, Colin, *1945-*. Readability in the classroom / Colin Harrison. — Cambridge : Cambridge University Press, 1980. — viii,189p : ill ; 23cm
Bibliography: p181-185. - Includes index
ISBN 0-521-22712-7 (cased) : £8.95
ISBN 0-521-29621-8 (pbk) : £3.50 B81-00820

371.3'3 — Teaching aids: Audiovisual equipment

Henderson, JohnAudio visual handbook / edited by John Henderson and Fay Humphries. — [2nd ed.]. — London : Kogan Page, 1981. — 141p : ill ; 30cm
Previous ed.: published as NAVAC audio visual handbook. 1980. — Bibliography: p132-139
ISBN 0-85038-454-0 (pbk) : £9.95 : CIP rev. B81-19215

371.3'32 — Great Britain. Secondary schools. Students. Study techniques — *For teaching*

Information skills in the secondary curriculum. — London : Methuen Educational, Sept.1981. — [60]p. — (Schools Council curriculum bulletin ; 9)
ISBN 0-423-50910-1 (pbk) : £4.00 : CIP entry B81-22643

371.3'358 — Education. Role of television

Television and education / edited by Chester M. Pierce. — Beverley Hills ; London : Sage, 1978. — 104p ; 22cm. — (Sage contemporary social science issues ; 44)
Includes bibliographies
ISBN 0-8039-1028-2 (pbk) : £3.10 B81-04667

371.3'7 — Educational institutions. Teaching methods: Group discussions

Hill, L. A.. Techniques of discussion / L.A. Hill. — London : Evans, 1980. — 58p ; 22cm
ISBN 0-237-50141-4 (pbk) : £1.25 B81-00821

371.3'94'0973 — United States. Schools. Students. Individualised instruction

Charles, C. M.. Individualizing instruction / C.M. Charles. — 2nd ed. — St. Louis ; London : Mosby, 1980. — xiii,284p : ill,facsims,forms ; 24cm
Previous ed.: 1976. — Includes bibliographies and index
ISBN 0-8016-0974-7 (pbk) : Unpriced B81-07885

371.3'94422 — Self-teaching courses. Teaching materials. Design & development — *For teaching*

Lewis, Roger. How to write self-study materials. — London : Council for Educational Technology, Oct.1981. — [64]p. — (Guidelines / Council for Educational Technology for the United Kingdom, ISSN 0308-0323 ; 10)
ISBN 0-86184-036-4 (pbk) : £5.00 : CIP entry B81-32001

371.3'9445 — Computer assisted learning

Computer-based instruction : a state-of-the-art assessment / edited by Harold F. O'Neil, Jr.. — New York ; London : Academic Press, 1981. — xii,260p : ill ; 24cm. — (Educational technology series)
Includes bibliographies and index
ISBN 0-12-526760-6 : £15.60 B81-38698

Selected readings in computer based learning. — London : Kogan Page, Sept.1981. — [220]p
ISBN 0-85038-473-7 : £10.95 : CIP entry B81-21542

371.3'9445 — Computer assisted learning — *Conference proceedings*

CAL 81 Symposium *(University of Leeds)*. Computer assisted learning. — Oxford : Pergamon, Nov.1981. — [150]p
ISBN 0-08-028111-7 : £12.00 : CIP entry B81-30288

IFIP TC3 Working Conference on Computer Assisted Learning — Scope, Progress and Limits *(1979 : Roehampton)*. Computer assisted learning : scope, progress and limits / proceedings of the IFIP TC3 Working Conference on Computer Assisted Learning — Scope, Progress and Limits, Roehampton, England, 3-7 September 1979 ; edited by R. Lewis and E.D. Tagg ; organized by Working Group 3.3 of IFIP Technical Committee 3, Education. — London : Heinemann Educational, 1981, c1980. — vii,223p : ill ; 24cm
Originally published: Amsterdam : London : North Holland, 1980. — Includes bibliographies
ISBN 0-435-77700-9 (pbk) : £4.95 B81-36787

371.3'9445 — Education. Teaching methods: Computer assisted learning. Programs: MACAID program

Ahmed, K.. Software for educational computing : a general-purpose Driver for computer-assisted instruction, interrogation and system simulation ('MACAID') / by K. Ahmed, D. Ingram and C.J. Dickinson. — Lancaster : MTP, c1980. — ix,182p : ill ; 24cm
Bibliography: p115-116. — Includes index
ISBN 0-85200-359-5 : £19.95 : CIP rev. B80-08688

371.3'9445 — Schools. Teaching methods. Applications of digital computer systems. Software

Payne, A.. Computer software for schools / A. Payne, B. Hutchings, P. Ayre. — London : Pitman, 1980. — 263p : ill,2maps,forms ; 25cm
Includes index
ISBN 0-273-01583-4 (pbk) : £11.95 B81-03629

371.3′9445 — Training. Applications of digital computer systems

Brooke, J. B.. Interactive instruction in solving fault finding problems / J.B. Brooke, K.D. Duncan and E.C. Marshall. — Cardiff (c/o R. Slater, Department of Applied Psychology, UWIST, Llwyn-y-Grant, Penylan, Cardiff CF3 7UX) : [UWIST Department of Applied Psychology], 1977. — 7,[13]leaves : ill ; 30cm. — (Occasional paper / UWIST Department of Applied Psychology ; no.6)
Bibliography: leaf 7
£0.50 (spiral) B81-24799

371.3′9445′09411 — Scotland. Teaching. Applications of computer systems — *Serials*

Phase two : a periodical reporting on educational computing in Scotland. — Vol.1, no.1 (1981)-. — Glasgow (74 Victoria Crescent Rd, Glasgow G12 9JN) : Scottish Microelectronics Development Programme, 1981-. — v. : ill,maps,ports ; 30cm
Quarterly
ISSN 0260-5562 = Phase two : Unpriced B81-30004

371.3′97 — Education. Simulations

Learning with simulations and games / edited by Richard L. Dukes, Constance J. Seidner. — Beverly Hills ; London : Sage, 1978. — 152p : 1ill ; 22cm. — (Sage contemporary social science anthologies ; 2)
"The material in this publication originally appeared in 'Simulation & games' June 1975 (Volume 7, Number 2), December 1975 (Volume 7, Number 4), and March 1976 (Volume 8, Number 1), and in 'The Psychology of Teaching Methods 1976' the Seventy-Fifth Yearbook, Part I (pp. 217-251), National Society for the Study of Education" — T.p. verso. — Includes bibliographies
ISBN 0-8039-1036-3 (pbk) : Unpriced B81-26974

371.4 — EDUCATION. GUIDANCE AND COUNSELLING

371.4′0941 — Great Britain. Schools. Students. Counselling

David, Kenneth. Pastoral care in schools and colleges : with specific references to health education and drugs, alcohol and smoking / Kenneth David, James Cowley. — London : Edward Arnold, 1980. — ix,139p ; 22cm
Bibliography: p105-111
ISBN 0-7131-0476-7 (pbk) : £3.25 : CIP rev. B80-13837

371.4′0941 — Great Britain. Schools. Students. Counselling — *Case studies*

Galloway, David M.. Teaching and counselling : pastoral care in primary and secondary schools / David Galloway. — London : Longman, 1981. — vii,168p ; 24cm
Bibliography: p160-164. — Includes index
ISBN 0-582-48987-3 (pbk) : £5.50 B81-08236

371.4′0973 — United States. Education. Counselling services

Gysbers, Norman C.. Improving guidance programs / Norman C. Gysbers, Earl J. Moore. — Englewood Cliffs ; London : Prentice-Hall, c1981. — x,212p ; 24cm
Includes bibliographies and index
ISBN 0-13-452656-2 : £8.40 B81-19649

371.4′0973 — United States. Schools. Students. Counselling

Baker, Stanley B.. School counselor's handbook : a guide for professional growth and development / Stanley B. Baker. — Boston, Mass. ; London : Allyn and Bacon, c1981. — xii,300p ; 25cm
Includes bibliographies and index
ISBN 0-205-07279-8 : Unpriced B81-26214

Gibson, Robert L.. Introduction to guidance / Robert L. Gibson, Marianne H. Mitchell. — New York : Macmillan ; London : Collier Macmillan, 1981. — xvii,469p : ill ; 24cm
Bibliography: p395-400. — Includes index
ISBN 0-02-341730-7 : £11.50 B81-33408

371.4′25′05 — Careers guidance — *Serials*

Careers journal : journal of the Institute of Careers Officers. — Vol.1, no.1-. — Stourbridge (2nd Floor, Old Board Chambers, 37a High St., Stourbridge, West Midlands, DY8 1TA) : The Institute, [1980]-. — v. : ill ; 21cm
Three issues yearly. — Continues: Careers quarterly
ISSN 0260-5694 = Careers journal : £0.75 B81-04167

371.4′25′06041 — Great Britain. Careers guidance. Organisations: Institute of Careers Officers — *Serials*

Institute of Careers Officers. Reference book and list of members / The Institute of Careers Officers. — 1980-. — London (25 Catherine St., WC2B 5JW) : Millbank Publications, 1980-. — v. : ill ; 21cm
Annual
Free to Institute members only B81-05675

371.4′25′09417 — Ireland *(Republic)*. Careers guidance — *Serials*

[Journal *(Institute of Guidance Counsellors)*]. Journal / Institute of Guidance Counsellors. — Vol.4(Spring 1981)-. — [Eire] ([c/o H. O'Brien, Curriculum Development Unit, Trinity College, Dublin]) : [The Institute], 1981-. — v. : ill,ports ; 31cm
Two issues yearly. — Continues: Career guidance and counselling
£1.50 per issue B81-32392

371.4′6 — Great Britain. Schools. Welfare work

Education and social services : a partnership / Josephine Dunn ... [et al.]. — [Lancaster] ([Bailrigg, Lancaster]) : [University of Lancaster], 1981. — 37p ; 30cm. — (Joint occasional publication / Centre of Youth, Crime and Community and Centre for Educational Research and Development. University of Lancaster ; no.1)
Cover title. — Bibliography: p37
Unpriced (pbk) B81-36605

371.5 — SCHOOL DISCIPLINE

371.5′8 — United States. Schools. Students. Criminal behaviour

Violence and crimes in the schools / edited by Keith Baker, Robert J. Rubel. — Lexington, Mass. : Lexington Books, c1980 ; [Aldershot] : Gower [distributors], 1981. — viii,295p : ill ; 24cm
Bibliography: p253-283. — Includes index
ISBN 0-669-03389-8 : £11.50 B81-33134

371.5′8 — United States. Schools. Vandalism

Casserly, Michael D.. School vandalism : strategies for prevention / Michael D. Casserly, Scott A. Bass, John R. Garrett. — Lexington : Lexington Books, c1980 ; [Farnborough, Hants.] : Gower [distributor], 1981. — x,166p : forms ; 24cm
Bibliography: p137-159. — Includes index
ISBN 0-669-03956-x : £11.50 B81-23268

371.7 — SCHOOL HEALTH AND SAFETY

371.7′1′09411 — Scotland. Schools. Health services — *Inquiry reports*

Child Health Programme Planning Group. Towards better health care for school children in Scotland : a report / by the Child Health Programme Planning Group of the Scottish Health Service Planning Council. — Edinburgh : H.M.S.O., 1980. — xv,146p : ill ; 21cm
At head of title: Scottish Home and Health Department, Scottish Education Department
ISBN 0-11-491648-9 (pbk) : £5.00 B81-03042

371.7′1′094252 — Nottinghamshire. Schools. Health visiting

Perkins, Elizabeth R.. Is your journey really necessary? : the role of the health visitor in schools / Elizabeth R. Perkins. — [Nottingham] : University of Nottingham, 1978. — 11,14,6leaves ; 30cm. — (Occasional paper / Leverhulme Health Education Project ; no.8)
Unpriced (pbk) B81-22822

371.7′1′0973 — United States. Schools. Health services

Schaller, Warren E.. The school health program. — 5th ed. / Warren E. Schaller. — Philadelphia ; London : Saunders, c1981. — xiii,574p : ill,forms ; 25cm
Previous ed.: / by the late Alma Nemir and Warren E. Schaller, 1975. — Includes bibliographies and index
ISBN 0-03-057702-0 : £12.75
Also classified at 613′.0432 B81-23092

371.7′12 — Great Britain. Schools. Nursing — *Serials*

[The School nurse *(School Nurses' Forum)*]. The School nurse : journal of the School Nurses' Forum, Royal College of Nursing. — Issue no.1 (1980)-. — London (c/o Ms J. Kendrick, 4 Dumbarton Rd, SW2 5LU) : The Forum, 1980-. — v. ; 20cm
Quarterly. — Description based on: Issue no.2 (Nov.1980)
ISSN 0260-5325 = School nurse (Royal College of Nursing. School Nurses' Forum) : £0.50 per issue B81-30830

371.7′12 — Scotland. Schools. Dental services — *Inquiry reports*

Child Health Programme Planning Group. Dental services for children at school : a report / by the Child Health Programme Planning Group of the Scottish Health Service Planning Council. — Edinburgh : H.M.S.O., 1980. — 48p ; 21cm
At head of cover title: Scottish Home and Health Department, Scottish Education Department. — Bibliography: p36-37
ISBN 0-11-491645-4 (pbk) : £2.50 B81-07822

371.7′12 — United States. Schools. Nursing services

Wold, Susan J.. School nursing : a framework for practice / Susasn J. Wold. — St. Louis ; London : Mosby, 1981. — xiv,571p : ill,forms,3ports ; 26cm
Includes bibliographies and index
ISBN 0-8016-5611-7 (pbk) : £14.00 B81-28922

371.7′16′0942 — England. School meals services — *Lancashire School Meals Campaign viewpoints*

Lang, Tim. Now you see them, now you don't : a report on the fate of school meals and the loss of 300,000 jobs / [written by Tim Lang]. — Accrington (c/o M. Jones, 17 Marlowe Ave., Baxenden, Accrington, Lancs.) : The Lancashire School Meals Campaign, 1981. — 48p : ill ; 21cm
Cover title
ISBN 0-9507475-0-5 (pbk) : £1.00 B81-26179

371.7′75 — Schools. Laboratories. Electrical equipment. Safety measures — *Manuals*

Electrical safety for the users for school laboratories / by the Development Group of the Provision of Science Equipment. — Hatfield (College La., Hatfield, Herts. AL10 9AA) : Association for Science Education, c1978. — 14p : ill ; 22cm
ISBN 0-902786-50-4 (pbk) : Unpriced B81-10678

371.8 — EDUCATION. STUDENTS

371.8′1′0973 — United States. Schools & universities. Students. Attitudes. Effects of environment

Moos, Rudolf H.. Evaluating educational environments / Rudolf H. Moos. — San Francisco ; London : Jossey-Bass, 1979. — xvi,334p : ill ; 24cm. — (The Jossey-Bass social and behavioral science series) (Jossey-Bass higher education series)
Bibliography: p299-324. — Includes index
ISBN 0-87589-401-1 : £11.20 B81-15102

371.8′2 — Great Britain. Educational institutions. Students: Refugees. Policies of government — *Proposals*

World University Service. Refugee students : - education policy is failing : - proposals for change. — London (20 Compton Terrace, N.1) : World University Service, 1981. — 25p : ill ; 30cm
Cover title. — Text on inside covers
ISBN 0-9505721-9-5 (pbk) : £1.00 B81-37803

371.9 — SPECIAL EDUCATION

371.9 — Children. Learning disorders

Reid, D. Kim. A cognitive approach to learning disabilities / D. Kim Reid, Wayne P. Hresko. — New York ; London : McGraw-Hill, c1981. — xiii,400p : ill ; 25cm. — (McGraw-Hill series in special education)
Bibliography: p329-377. — Includes index
ISBN 0-07-051768-1 : £11.75 B81-31751

Ross, Alan O.. Learning disability : the unrealized potential / Alan O. Ross. — New York ; London : McGraw-Hill, 1980, c1977. — xviii,202p ; 21cm
Bibliography: p192-197. - Includes index
ISBN 0-07-053878-6 (pbk) : £3.50 B81-19493

Tansley, Paula. Children with specific learning difficulties : a critical review of research / Paula Tansley, John Panckhurst. — Oxford : NFER-Nelson, 1981. — 339p ; 22cm
Bibliography: p273-324. — Includes index
ISBN 0-85633-216-x (pbk) : £9.75 B81-22196

Wallace, Gerald. Learning disabilities : concepts and charactistics / Gerald Wallace, James A. McLoughlin. — 2nd ed. — Columbus ; London : Merrill, c1979. — viii,518p : ill,facsims,forms ; 26cm
Previous ed.: 1975. — Includes bibliographies and index
ISBN 0-675-08263-3 : £11.95 B81-09328

371.9 — Children. Learning disorders. Diagnostic tests: Pupil Rating Scale

Myklebust, Helmer R.. The pupil rating scale revised : screening for learning disabilites / Helmer R. Myklebust. — New York ; London : Grune & Stratton, c1981. — x,84p ; 25cm
Previous ed.: published as The pupil rating scale. 1971. — Bibliography: p83-84. — Includes 1 specimen form
ISBN 0-8089-1329-8 (pbk) : £5.40
ISBN 0-8089-1358-1 (manual and 50 forms) B81-18026

371.9 — Children. Learning disorders — *Information processing perspectives*

Parrill-Burnstein, Melinda. Problem solving and learning disabilities : an information processing approach / Melinda Parrill-Bunstein. — New York ; London : Grune & Stratton ; London : Distributed by Academic Press, c1981. — x,212p : ill ; 24cm
Includes bibliographies and index
ISBN 0-8089-1340-9 : £13.00 B81-39790

371.9 — England. Schools. Handicapped students. Education — *For teaching*

Morgenstern, Franz. Teaching plans for handicapped children. — London : Methuen, Oct.1981. — [224]p
ISBN 0-416-73260-7 (cased) : £7.50 : CIP entry
ISBN 0-416-73270-4 (pbk) : £3.95 B81-25296

371.9 — Exceptional children. Education

Handbook of special education / edited by James M. Kauffman, Daniel P. Hallahan. — Englewood Cliffs ; London : Prentice-Hall, c1981. — xv,807p : ill ; 29cm
Includes bibliographies and index
ISBN 0-13-381756-3 : £38.95 B81-17217

371.9 — Great Britain. Handicapped young persons. Vocational preparation

Hutchinson, David. Work preparation for the handicapped. — London : Croom Helm, Dec.1981. — [112]p. — (Croom Helm special education series)
ISBN 0-7099-0283-2 (pbk) : £5.95 : CIP entry B81-31440

371.9 — Great Britain. Hospitals. Patients: Children. Teaching — *Personal observations*

Reavill, E. G.. Children of mischance / by E.G. Reavill. — Godalming : Ladywell Press, [1980]. — 92p : ill,ports ; 22cm
£5.00 (pbk) B81-06530

371.9 — Handicapped children. Education

Gearheart, Bill R.. Special education for the '80s / Bill R. Gearheart. — St. Louis ; London : Mosby, 1980. — xviii,498p : ill ; 25cm
Includes bibliographies and index
ISBN 0-8016-1759-6 : Unpriced B81-08677

371.9 — Handicapped children, to 5 years. Education

Lerner, Janet W.. Special education for the early childhood years / Janet Lerner, Carol Mardell-Czudnowski, Dorothea Goldenberg. — Englewood Cliffs ; London : Prentice-Hall, c1981. — xii,369p : ill ; 24cm
Includes bibliographies and index
ISBN 0-13-826461-9 : £11.65 B81-22720

371.9 — Handicapped students. Assessment — *For teaching*

Howell, K. W.. Evaluating exceptional children : a task analysis approach / K.W. Howell, J.S. Kaplan, C.Y. O'Connell. — Columbus ; London : Merrill, c1979. — xii,284p : ill,1facsim ; 26cm
Bibliography: p275-279. - Includes index
ISBN 0-675-08389-3 : £11.95 B81-05851

371.9 — Severely handicapped children. Education

Van Etten, Glen. The severely and profoundly handicapped : programs, methods, and materials / Glen Van Etten, Claudia Arkell, Carlene van Etten. — St. Louis ; London : Mosby, 1980. — ix,490p : ill,forms ; 25cm
Includes bibliographies and index
ISBN 0-8016-5215-4 : £14.00 B81-08044

371.9 — Special education

The **Fourth** review of special education / editors Lester Mann, David A. Sabatino. — New York ; London : Grune & Stratton, c1980. — xi,499p ; 24cm
Includes bibliographies and index
ISBN 0-8089-1263-1 : £25.00 B81-15015

The **Nature** of special education. — London : Croom Helm, Dec.1981. — [352]p
ISBN 0-7099-1910-7 : £4.50 : CIP entry B81-31430

The **Practice** of special education : a reader / edited by Will Swann for the Special Needs in Education Course Team at the Open University. — Oxford : Blackwell in association with the Open University Press, 1981. — xi,452p : ill ; 23cm
Includes bibliographies and index
ISBN 0-631-12879-4 (cased) : £16.00 : CIP rev.
ISBN 0-631-12885-9 (£4.95) B81-16932

Special education. — London : Harper and Row, Oct.1981. — [264]p
ISBN 0-06-318199-1 (cased) : £8.95 : CIP entry
ISBN 0-06-318200-9 (pbk) : £5.95 B81-24623

371.9'043 — Children with special educational needs. Assessment

Mahan, Thomas. Assessing children with special needs : a practical guide educational measures / Thomas Mahan and Aline Mahan. — New York ; London : Holt, Rinehart and Winston, c1981. — ix,229p : ill ; 24cm
Includes bibliographies and index
ISBN 0-03-052981-6 (pbk) : £7.50 B81-22874

371.9'043 — Learning disordered children. Remedial education. Teaching methods: Dance

The **Thunder** Tree : teaching material / Ludus Special Schools Project. — [Lancaster] ([Owen House, 6 Thurnham St., Lancaster, LA1 1YD]) : [Ludus], c1981. — 1v.(loose-leaf) : ill(some col.) ; 32x26cm
Comic and poster in plastic wallet. — Bibliography: 2p. — List of films: 1p
Unpriced (unbound) B81-31219

371.9'043 — Learning disordered children. Teaching

Smith, Deborah Deutsch. Teaching the learning disabled / Deborah Deutsch Smith. — Englewood Cliffs ; London : Prentice-Hall, c1981. — xii,356p : ill ; 25cm
Includes bibliographies and index
ISBN 0-13-893511-4 : £12.30 B81-22719

371.9'043 — United States. Schools. Learning disordered children & deviant children. Assessment. Techniques

Blankenship, Colleen. Mainstreaming students with learning and behavior problems : techniques for the classroom teacher / Colleen Blankenship, M. Stephen Lilly. — New York ; London : Holt, Rinehart and Winston, c1981. — xi,353p : ill ; 25cm
Includes index
ISBN 0-03-046051-4 : £12.00 B81-22968

371.9'043'0973 — United States. Handicapped children. Teaching

Charles, C. M.. The special student : practical help for the classroom teacher / C.M. Charles, Ida M. Malian. — St. Louis ; London : Mosby, 1980. — xvii,246p : ill,facsims,forms ; 24cm
Includes bibliographies and index
ISBN 0-8016-1132-6 (pbk) : £7.00 B81-08138

371.9'043'0973 — United States. Learning disordered children. Education. Teaching methods

Gearheart, Bill R.. Learning disabilities : educational strategies / Bill R. Gearheart. — 3rd ed. — St Louis ; London : Mosby, 1981. — xiv,302p : ill ; 25cm
Previous ed.: 1977. — Includes bibliographies and index
ISBN 0-8016-1768-5 : £12.75 B81-30115

371.9'044 — Handicapped children. Education. Curriculum subjects: Reading. Teaching

Gillespie-Silver, Patricia. Teaching reading to children with special needs : an ecological approach / Patricia Gillespie-Silver. — Columbus [Ohio] ; London : Merrill, c1979. — x,459p : ill,forms ; 25cm
One sound disc : 331/3 rpm, mono. as insert. — Includes bibliographies and index
ISBN 0-675-08274-9 : £11.95 B81-13989

371.9'044 — Handicapped children. Remedial teaching. Role of assessment of *their* language skills

Müller, David J.. Language assessment for remediation. — London : Croom Helm, Aug.1981. — [176]p
ISBN 0-7099-1706-6 (cased) : £9.95 : CIP entry
ISBN 0-7099-1707-4 (pbk) : £5.50 B81-16850

371.9'044 — Handicapped persons. Physical education

Crowe, Walter C.. Principles and methods of adapted physical education and recreation. — 4th ed. / Walter C. Crowe, David Auxter, Jean Pyfer. — St. Louis ; London : Mosby, 1981. — x,524p : ill,forms,plans ; 25cm
Previous ed.: / Daniel D. Arnheim, David Auxter, Walter C. Crowe. 1977. — Includes bibliographies and index
ISBN 0-8016-0327-7 : £15.50 B81-31156

371.9'044 — United States. Schools. Handicapped students. Curriculum subjects: Physical education. Individualised instruction

Geddes, Dolores. Psychomotor individualized educational programs : for intellectual, learning, and behavioral disabilities / Dolores Geddes. — Boston ; London : Allyn and Bacon, 1981. — x,253p : ill,forms ; 28cm
Includes bibliographies and index
ISBN 0-205-07274-7 (pbk) : Unpriced B81-16510

371.9'05 — Special education — *Serials*

Wessex studies in special education. — 1981-. — Winchester (Winchester [SO22 4NR]) : King Alfred's College, 1981-. — v. : ill ; 30cm
ISSN 0144-5359 = Wessex studies in special education : Unpriced B81-29968

371.9'0941 — Great Britain. Handicapped adolescents. Education

Rowan, Patricia. What sort of life? : a paper for the OECD project The Handicapped adolescent / Patricia Rowan. — Windsor : NFER, 1980. — 138p : 1ill ; 21cm
Includes index
ISBN 0-85633-200-3 (pbk) : £5.50 B81-04626

371.9'0941 — Great Britain. Handicapped young persons. Special education. Great Britain. *Committee of Enquiry into the Education of Handicapped Children and Young People.* 'Special educational needs' — *Critical studies*

Stratford, Brian. Children with special educational needs : an overview of the Warnock report / by Brian Stratford. — [Nottingham] : Nottingham University, School of Education, 1981. — 24p ; 30cm
Bibliography: p22-24
ISBN 0-85359-080-x (pbk) : Unpriced
B81-17950

371.9'0973 — United States. Adolescents. Special education

Special education for adolescents : issues and perspectives / [edited by] Douglas Cullinan, Michael H. Epstein. — Columbus ; London : Merrill, c1979. — vii,424p : ill,ports ; 24cm. — (The Merrill personal perspectives in special education series)
Bibliography: p355-389. - Includes index
ISBN 0-675-08407-5 : Unpriced B81-06753

371.9'0973 — United States. Handicapped children. Education

Gearheart, Bill R.. The handicapped student in the regular classroom / Bill R. Gearheart, Mel W. Weishahn. — 2nd ed. — St. Louis ; London : Mosby, 1980. — xv,303p : ill,forms ; 25cm
Previous ed.: published as The handicapped child in the regular classroom. 1976. — List of films: p265-267. - Includes bibliographies and index
ISBN 0-8016-1760-x : Unpriced B81-13062

Meeting the needs of the handicapped : a resource for teachers and librarians / edited with a preface and introduction by Carol H. Thomas and James L. Thomas. — Phoenix : Oryx ; London : Mansell [[distributor]], 1980. — xxiv,479p : ill ; 24cm
Bibliography: p373-384. — Includes index
ISBN 0-7201-1601-5 : £11.50 : CIP rev.
B80-10031

371.9'0973 — United States. Learning disordered students. Education

Mercer, Cecil D.. Children and adolescents with learning disabilities / Cecil D. Mercer with contributions by Rex E. Schmid ... [et al.]. — Columbus ; London : Merrill, c1979. — ix,485p : ill,facsims,forms,ports ; 26cm
Includes bibliographies and index
ISBN 0-675-08272-2 : £11.95 B81-05850

371.91 — Great Britain. Colleges of further education. Facilities for physically handicapped students. Provision

Panckhurst, John. Focus on physical handicap : provisions for young people with special needs in further education / John Panckhurst. — Windsor : NFER, 1980. — 158p : ill,forms ; 22cm
Bibliography: p148-153. - Includes index
ISBN 0-85633-217-8 (pbk) : £5.75 B81-02266

371.91'092'4 — Great Britain. Physically handicapped children. Teaching — *Personal observations*

Mann, Ann L.. Behind the door / Ann L. Mann. — Bognor Regis : New Horizon, c1981. — 117p ; 21cm
ISBN 0-86116-719-8 : £4.50 B81-40190

371.91'09417 — Ireland *(Republic).* Physically handicapped children. Education — *Conference proceedings*

Education for the physically handicapped : report of a seminar. — [Dublin] ([35 Parnell Square, Dublin 1]) : Irish National Teachers' Organisation, 1981. — 42p ; 20cm
Conference papers
Unpriced (pbk) B81-39811

371.91'1 — Visually handicapped children. Education

Chapman, Elizabeth K.. Visually handicapped children and young people / Elizabeth K. Chapman. — London : Routledge & Kegan Paul, 1978 (1980 [printing]). — xi,162p ; 22cm. — (Special needs in education)
Bibliography: p151-158. - Includes index
ISBN 0-7100-0699-3 : £3.25 B81-00822

371.91'14 — Visually handicapped children. Perceptuo-motor skills. Teaching

Tooze, Doris. Independence training for visually handicapped children / Doris Tooze. — London : Croom Helm, c1981. — 104p : ill ; 25cm. — (Croom Helm special education series)
Bibliography: p102. — Includes index
ISBN 0-7099-0290-5 (pbk) : £6.95 : CIP rev.
B81-14894

371.91'2 — Primary schools. Preparation of hearing disordered children — *For parents*

Preparing your child for school / Michael Nolan ... [et al.]. — London (45 Hereford Rd., W2 5AH) : National Deaf Children's Society, c1981. — 8p : ill ; 21cm
£0.15 (pbk) B81-37771

371.91'2'0722 — Great Britain. Hearing disordered children. Education — *Case studies*

Ways and means 3 : hearing impairment : a resource book of information, technical aids, teaching materials, and methods used in the education of hearing impaired children / co-ordinated by Anne Jackson. — Basingstoke (Houndmills, Basingstoke RG21 2XS) : Globe Education on behalf of Somerset Education Authority, 1981. — x,190p : ill,music ; 30cm
Includes bibliographies
ISBN 0-333-29668-0 (pbk) : £11.95 B81-31310

371.91'23 — Schools. Deaf children. Communication. Teaching

Savage, R. D.. Psychology and communication in deaf children / R.D. Savage, L. Evans, J.F. Savage. — Sydney ; London : Grune & Stratton, c1981. — x,307p : ill ; 24cm
Bibliography: p271-298. — Includes index
ISBN 0-8089-1339-5 : £16.60 B81-35430

371.91'24 — Hearing disordered children. Remedial education. Music therapy

Wisbey, Audrey S.. Music as the source of learning / Audrey S. Wisbey. — Lancaster : MTP, 1980. — 165p : ill,music ; 22cm
Bibliography: p145-165
ISBN 0-85200-256-4 : £5.95 B81-03653

371.91'27 — Deaf persons. Visual communication

O'Neill, John J. (John Joseph), *1920-*. Visual communication for the hard of hearing : history, research, methods / John J. O'Neill, Herbert J. Oyer. — Englewood Cliffs ; London : Prentice-Hall, c1981. — vii,211p : ill ; 24cm
Previous ed.: 1961. — Includes bibliographies and index
ISBN 0-13-942466-0 : £10.35 B81-22754

371.91'4 — Reading disordered children. Curriculum subjects: Reading. Remedial teaching. Role of tracing letters in words

Hulme, Charles. Reading retardation and multi-sensory teaching / Charles Hulme. — London : Routledge & Kegan Paul, 1981. — 200p : ill ; 23cm. — (International library of psychology)
Bibliography: p177-193. — Includes index
ISBN 0-7100-0761-2 : £12.50 : CIP rev.
B81-13731

371.91'4 — Reading disordered children. Remedial education

Spache, George D.. Diagnosing and correcting reading disabilities / George D. Spache. — 2nd ed. — Boston [Mass.] ; London : Allyn and Bacon, c1981. — viii,454p : ill,facsims,forms ; 25cm
Previous ed.: 1976. — Includes bibliographies and index
ISBN 0-205-07175-9 : £17.95 B81-03527

371.91'4 — Reading disordered children. Remedial education — *For teaching*

Jeffree, Dorothy M.. Let me read / Dorothy Jeffree and Margaret Skeffington. — London : Souvenir, 1980. — 170p : ill,forms ; 23cm. — (Human horizons series)
Includes bibliographies
ISBN 0-285-64909-4 (cased) : £5.95
ISBN 0-285-64908-6 (pbk) : £3.50 B81-00823

371.91'4 — Secondary schools. Reading disordered students. Remedial education — *For teaching*

Cassell, Christine. Teaching poor readers in the secondary school. — London : Croom Helm, Jan.1982. — [80]p. — (Croom Helm special education series)
ISBN 0-7099-0294-8 (pbk) : £4.95 : CIP entry
B81-34306

371.91'4 — Secondary schools. Reading disordered students. Remedial education. Use of phonics — *For teaching*

Gregory, Jill. Phonics. — London : J. Murray, Dec.1981. — [168]p
ISBN 0-7195-3851-3 (pbk) : £6.95 : CIP entry
B81-31532

371.91'6 — Cerebral palsy victims. Adult literacy education — *For teaching*

Widening horizons : a handbook for literacy tutors working with spastic adults. — London (229 High Holborn WC1V 7DA) : Adult Literacy and Basic Skills Unit, 1981. — 36p : ill ; 21cm
Text on inside Covers
ISBN 0-906509-10-6 (pbk) : £1.00 B81-37069

371.92'0942 — England. Educationally subnormal children. Education — *Sociological perspectives*

Tomlinson, Sally. Educational subnormality : a study in decision-making / Sally Tomlinson. — London : Routledge & Kegan Paul, 1981. — xiii,386p : ill ; 23cm. — (International library of sociology)
Bibliography: p356-372. — Includes index
ISBN 0-7100-0697-7 : £12.50 : CIP rev.
B81-02381

371.92'64 — Great Britain. Secondary schools. Slow learning students. Curriculum subjects: History. Teaching

Cowie, Evelyn E.. History and the slow-learning child : a practical approach / by Evelyn E. Cowie. — London : Historical Association, c1980. — 47p : ill ; 21cm. — (Teaching of history series ; no.41)
Bibliography: p46-47
ISBN 0-85278-222-5 (corrected : pbk) : £1.40
B81-31670

Hodgkinson, Keith. Designing a history syllabus for slow-learning children / by Keith Hodgkinson. — London : Historical Association, [1981?]. — 15p : ill ; 21cm. — (Information leaflet / Historical Association ; 7)
ISBN 0-85278-240-3 (unbound) : Unpriced
B81-24979

371.92'64 — United States. Slow learning children, to 8 years. Language skills. Assessment

Miller, Jon F.. Assessing language production in children : experimental procedures / by Jan F. Miller with chapter by Thomas M. Klee and Rhea Paul and Robin S. Chapman and contributions and procedures by Ursula Bellugi ... [et al.]. — London : Edward Arnold, c1981. — viii,186p : ill ; 29cm
Bibliography: p173-177. — Includes index
ISBN 0-7131-6339-9 : £12.50 B81-18556

371.92'8 — Mentally handicapped children. Education — *Conference proceedings*

NCSE Conference *(1975 : University of Bradford).* Proceedings of the 1975 N C S E Conference held at Bradford University, April 2nd-5th 1975 / edited by P.F. Simpson. — [Bradford] : Bradford & District Branch, National Council for Special Education, [1975?]. — 92p : ill ; 30cm
Includes bibliographies
Unpriced (pbk) B81-29034

371.92'8 — Mentally handicapped children. Teaching — *Manuals*

Kiernan, Chris. Analysis of programmes for teaching / Chris Kiernan. — Basingstoke : Globe Education, 1981. — 113p : ill,forms ; 30cm
ISBN 0-333-29604-4 (pbk) : £5.95 B81-13635

371.92′804 — Mentally handicapped persons. Education. Use of handicrafts — *For teaching*

Atack, Sally M.. Art activities for the handicapped / by Sally M. Atack. — London : Souvenir, 1980. — 135p,[8]p of plates : ill ; 23cm. — (Human horizons series)
ISBN 0-285-64905-1 (cased) : £5.95
ISBN 0-285-64904-3 (pbk) : £3.95 B81-04104

371.92′8′0941 — Great Britain. Mentally handicapped children. Education

Furneaux, Barbara. The special child : the education of mentally handicapped children / Barbara Furneaux. — 3rd ed. — Harmondsworth : Penguin, 1981. — 272p ; 20cm. — (Pelican Books)
Previous ed.: Harmondworth : Penguin Education, 1973
ISBN 0-14-022329-0 (pbk) : £2.25 B81-16988

371.92′8′0973 — United States. Mentally retarded children. Education

Klein, Nancy Krow. Curriculum analysis and design for retarded learners / Nancy Krow Klein, Marvin Pasch, Thomas W. Frew. — Columbus ; London : Merrill, c1979. — xi,372p : ill,plans ; 24cm
Includes bibliographies and index
ISBN 0-675-08273-0 : £11.25 B81-14500

371.93 — United States. Schools. Students. Behavioural disorders. Therapy — *Case studies — For teaching*

Millman, Howard L.. Therapies for school behaviour problems / Howard L. Millman, Charles E. Schaefer, Jeffrey J. Cohen. — San Francisco ; London : Jossey-Bass, 1980. — xxvii,530p ; 24cm. — (The Jossey-Bass social and behavioral science series)
Includes bibliographies and index
ISBN 0-87589-483-6 : £15.15 B81-29470

371.93′092′4 — Behaviourally disordered children. Teaching — *Personal observations*

Hayden, Torey L.. One child / by Torey L. Hayden. — London : Souvenir, 1981, c1980. — 251p ; 23cm
Originally published: New York : Putnam, 1980
ISBN 0-285-62474-1 : £6.95 B81-11516

371.93′09423′93 — Avon. Bristol. Experimental schools for habitual truants: Bayswater Centre

White, Roger, *1948-*. Absent with cause : lessons of truancy / Roger White. — London : Routledge & Kegan Paul, 1980. — xi,285p ; 22cm. — (Routledge education books)
Bibliography: p281-283
ISBN 0-7100-0665-9 (pbk) : £5.95 : CIP rev. B80-17625

371.94 — Behaviourally disordered children. Education

Stainback, Susan. Educating children with severe maladaptive behaviors / Susan Stainback, William Stainback. — New York ; London : Grune & Stratton, c1980. — xi,307p : ill,2ports ; 24cm
Includes bibliographies and index
ISBN 0-8089-1269-0 : £13.80 B81-05281

371.94 — Maladjusted adolescents. Education

Towns, Peyton. Educating disturbed adolescents : theory and practice / Peyton Towns. — New York ; London : Grune & Stratton, c1981. — xi,255p : ill ; 24cm. — (Current issues in behavioral psychology)
Bibliography: p201-214. — Includes index
ISBN 0-8089-1312-3 : £11.00 B81-20860

371.94 — Schools. Maladjusted students. Treatment

Help starts here. — London : Tavistock, Dec.1981. — [346]p
ISBN 0-422-77380-8 (cased) : £16.00 : CIP entry
ISBN 0-422-77390-5 (pbk) : £6.95 B81-31706

371.94 — United States. Maladjusted children. Remedial education — *Personal observations*

MacCracken, Mary. A circle of children / Mary MacCracken. — London : Sphere, 1981, c1974. — 221p ; 18cm
Originally published: Philadelphia : Lippincott ; London : Gollancz, 1974
ISBN 0-7221-5715-0 (pbk) : £1.25 B81-28983

371.94′0973 — United States. Maladjusted children. Education

Reinert, Henry R.. Children in conflict : educational strategies for the emotionally disturbed and behaviorally disordered / Henry R. Reinert. — 2nd ed. — St. Louis ; London : Mosby, 1980. — xii,254p : ill,forms ; 25cm
Previous ed.: 1976. — List of films and video tape recordings: p223-230. - Includes bibliographies and index
ISBN 0-8016-4109-8 : Unpriced B81-08664

371.95 — Gifted children. Education

Clark, Barbara. Growing up gifted : developing the potential of children at home and school / Barbara Clark. — Columbus, Ohio ; London : Merrill, c1979. — xviii,476p : ill,forms ; 26cm
Includes index
ISBN 0-675-08276-5 : £12.75 B81-00824

371.95′2 — Gifted children. Identification — *For parents & teaching*

Painter, Frieda. Who are the gifted? : definitions and identification / by Frieda Painter. — Knebworth (Caxtons, Knebworth, Herts.) : Pullen, c1980. — ii,52p : ill ; 21cm
£3.60 (pbk) B81-02836

371.96′7 — Belfast. Primary schools. Disadvantaged students: Boys. Language skills. Teaching. Intervention programmes — *Case studies*

Turner, Irené F.. The language dimension / by I.F. Turner and J. Whyte. — [Belfast] ([Research Unit, 52 Malone Rd., Belfast, BT9 5BS]) : Northern Ireland Council for Educational Research, c1979. — vii,132p ; 22cm. — (Publications of the Northern Ireland Council for Educational Research ; 17)
ISBN 0-903478-09-9 (pbk) : Unpriced B81-14214

371.96′7 — France. Working classes. Education. Attitudes of elites, *ca 1700-1800*

Chisick, Harvey. The limits of reform in the Enlightenment : attitudes towards the education of the lower classes in eighteenth-century France / Harvey Chisick. — Princeton ; Guildford : Princeton University Press, c1981. — xvi,324p ; 23cm
Bibliography: p291-311. — Includes index
ISBN 0-691-05305-7 : £13.90 B81-40722

371.96′7 — Great Britain. Working classes. Education, *1830-1850*. **Political aspects**

Paz, D. G.. The politics of working-class education in Britain, 1830-50 / D.G. Paz. — Manchester : Manchester University Press, c1980. — xi,203p ; 23cm
Bibliography: p183-198. - Includes index
ISBN 0-7190-0811-5 (corrected) : £14.50 B81-03996

371.96′7′0973 — United States. Nursery schools & primary schools. Socially disadvantaged students. Compensatory education. Projects: Project Follow Through

Making schools more effective : new directions from Follow Through / edited by W. Ray Rhine ; with a foreword by Edward F. Zigler. — New York ; London : Academic Press, 1981. — xxiv,360p : ill ; 24cm. — (Educational psychology)
Includes bibliographies and index
ISBN 0-12-587060-4 : £19.00 B81-39566

371.97 — Bilingual education

Lewis, E. Glyn. Bilingualism and bilingual education / E. Glyn Lewis. — Oxford : Pergamon, 1981. — xvi,455p : ill,maps ; 25cm. — (Bilingualism series)
Bibliography: p408-438. — Includes index
ISBN 0-08-025326-1 : £15.00 B81-17364

371.97 — Great Britain. Multiracial schools. Teaching — *Serials*

NAME : new approaches in multiracial education : the journal of the National Association of Multiracial Education. — Vol.6, no.3 (Summer 1978)-. — Derby (c/o Ms. M. Blakeley, 23 Doles La., Findern, Derby DE6 6AX) : The Association, 1978-. — v. : ill ; 30cm
Three issues yearly. — Continues: Multiracial school. — Description based on: Vol.7, no.1 (Autumn 1978)
ISSN 0144-719x = NAME. New approaches in multiracial education : £0.50 per issue (free to Association members) B81-00826

371.97 — Immigrant children. Education — *Comparative studies*

Educating immigrants / edited by Joti Bhatnagar. — London : Croom Helm, c1981. — 241p : ill ; 23cm
Includes index
ISBN 0-7099-0310-3 : £12.50 B81-17877

371.97′00973 — United States. Schools. Ethnic minority students. Education

Banks, James A.. Multiethnic education : theory and practice / James A. Banks. — Boston, Mass. ; London : Allyn and Bacon, c1981. — ix,326p : ill ; 25cm
Bibliography: p281-303. — Includes index
ISBN 0-205-07293-3 (cased) : £17.95
ISBN 0-205-07300-x (pbk) : £10.50 B81-16293

371.97′951′041 — Great Britain. Schools. Chinese students. Teaching

Teaching Chinese children : a teacher's guide. — London (Nuffield Lodge, Regents Park, NW1 4RZ) : Nuffield Foundation, 1981. — vii,135p : ill ; 25cm
ISBN 0-904956-22-9 (pbk) : Unpriced B81-34796

371.97′96′041 — Great Britain. Negro children. Education

Stone, Maureen. The education of the black child in Britain : the myth of multiracial education / Maureen Stone. — [London] : Fontana, 1981. — 286p : ill ; 18cm
Bibliography: p263-277. — Includes index
ISBN 0-00-635877-2 (pbk) : £1.95 B81-10899

371.97′96073′0755 — Virginia. Baptist secondary schools for negro students, *1887-1957*

Russell, Lester F.. Black Baptist Secondary schools in Virginia, 1887-1957 : a study in Black history / by Lester F. Russell. — Metuchen ; London : Scarecrow, 1981. — ix,200p,[8]p of plates : ill,1map,ports ; 23cm
Bibliography: p167-181. - Includes index
ISBN 0-8108-1373-4 : £8.75 B81-18269

371.97′969729′041 — Great Britain. Schools. West Indian students. Academic achievement — *Inquiry reports*

Great Britain. *Committee of Inquiry into the Education of Children from Ethnic Minority Groups*. West Indian children in our schools : interim report of the Committee of Inquiry into the Education of Children from Ethnic Minority Groups / chairman Anthony Rampton. — London : H.M.S.O., [1981]. — v,119p : ill ; 25cm. — (Cmnd. ; 8273)
ISBN 0-10-182730-x (pbk) : £5.30 B81-30056

372 — PRIMARY EDUCATION

372 — England. Primary schools. Closure. Prevention — *Manuals*

Rogers, Rick. Schools under threat : a handbook on closures / Rick Rogers. — London : Advisory Centre for Education, 1979. — 88p : ill ; 21cm
Bibliography: p67-69
ISBN 0-900029-47-1 (pbk) : £1.50 B81-03920

372 — Primary education — *For teaching*

Kirby, Norman. Personal values in primary education / Norman Kirby. — London : Harper & Row, 1981. — 150p ; 22cm. — (The Harper education series)
Bibliography: p137-141. — Includes index
ISBN 0-06-318130-4 (cased) : £6.95 : CIP rev.
ISBN 0-06-318131-2 (pbk) : £3.50 B81-11916

372.1 — PRIMARY SCHOOLS

372.11′02 — Nursery schools. Teaching

Hildebrand, Verna. Introduction to early childhood education / Verna Hildebrand. — 3rd ed. — New York : Macmillan ; London : Collier Macmillan, c1981. — x,518p : ill ; 24cm
Previous ed.: 1976. — Includes bibliographies and index
ISBN 0-02-354290-x : £11.50 B81-36166

372.11'02 — West Africa. Primary schools. Teachers. Interpersonal relationships with students

Asiedu-Akrofi, K.. A living classroom. — London : Allen & Unwin, Oct.1981. — [128]p
ISBN 0-04-370110-8 (pbk) : £3.50 : CIP entry
B81-25868

372.11'02'0941 — Great Britain. Primary schools. Teaching. Social aspects

Berlak, Ann. Dilemmas of schooling. — London : Methuen, June 1981. — [309]p
ISBN 0-416-74140-1 (cased) : £9.95 : CIP entry
ISBN 0-416-74110-x (pbk) : £4.95 B81-11965

372.11'02'09676 — East Africa. Primary schools. Teaching

Mary Jacinta, *Sister*. Primary methods handbook / Sister Mary Jacinta and Sister Mary Regina. — London : Hodder and Stoughton, 1981. — 128p ; 22cm
Bibliography: p128
ISBN 0-340-25952-3 (pbk) : £1.75 B81-10802

372.11'02'0973 — United States. Nursery schools. Teaching

Hendrick, Joanne. The whole child : new trends in early education / Joanne Hendrick. — 2nd ed. — St. Louis ; London : Mosby, 1980. — x,420p : ill ; 25cm
Previous ed.: 1975. — Bibliography: p349-370. - Includes index
ISBN 0-8016-2145-3 : Unpriced B81-08218

372.11'02'0973 — United States. Primary schools. Teaching

Jarolimek, John. Teaching and learning in the elementary school / John Jarolimek, Clifford D. Foster. — 2nd ed. — New York : Macmillan ; London : Collier Macmillan, c1981. — xiii,401p : ill ; 24cm
Previous ed.: 1976. — Includes bibliographies and index
ISBN 0-02-360400-x : £11.50 B81-33397

372.11'03 — England. Nursery & primary schools. School life. Involvement of parents — *For teaching*

Tizard, Barbara. Involving parents in nursery and infant schools : a source book for teachers / Barbara Tizard, Jo Mortimore and Bebb Burchell. — London : Grant McIntyre, 1981. — vii,247p ; 21cm
Bibliography: p241-243. — Includes index
ISBN 0-86216-062-6 (cased) : £11.95 : CIP rev.
ISBN 0-86216-063-4 (pbk) : £5.95 B81-08865

372.12'64 — England. Primary schools. Students. Academic achievement. Effects of teaching methods

Progress and performance in the primary classroom / edited by Maurice Galton and Brian Simon. — London : Routledge & Kegan Paul, 1980. — xiii,257p : ill ; 23cm
Bibliography: p246-250. — Includes index
ISBN 0-7100-0669-1 (cased) : £8.95 : CIP rev.
ISBN 0-7100-0670-5 (pbk) : £5.95 B80-26859

372.12'71 — Schools. Students, 10-11 years. Basic skills. Tests — *Texts*

Brandling, Redvers. Check up tests in workskills / Redvers Brandling. — London : Macmillan Education. — (Check up tests series)
Teacher's book. — 1981. — 55p : ill,maps ; 26cm
Text on inside covers
ISBN 0-333-31521-9 (spiral) : Unpriced
B81-31977

372.13 — England. Primary schools. Open plan education

Open plan schools : teaching, curriculum, design / Neville Bennett ... [et al.] ; [report of the Schools Council project Open Plan Schools : an Enquiry (5-11)]. — Windsor : NFER Publishing Company for the Schools Council, 1980. — 303p : ill,plans ; 25cm
Bibliography: p287-297. - Includes index
ISBN 0-85633-188-0 (pbk) : £9.75 B81-03973

372.13'2 — Great Britain. Books for primary school students, to 8 years. Selection & use — *For teaching*

Heeks, Peggy. Choosing and using books in the first school / Peggy Heeks. — London : Macmillan Education, 1981. — x,146p ; 22cm. — (Language guides)
Includes bibliographies
ISBN 0-333-27309-5 (cased) : £6.50
ISBN 0-333-32645-8 (pbk) : Unpriced
B81-38628

372.13'6 — Nursery schools. Projects — *For teaching*

Dowling, Marion. Early projects / Marion Dowling. — London : Longman, 1980. — 130p : ill ; 23cm. — (Longman early childhood education)
Bibliography: p129. — Includes index
ISBN 0-582-25022-6 (cased) : £4.95 : CIP rev.
B80-18207

372.13'92 — Pre-school children. Education. Montessori system

Hainstock, Elizabeth G. The essential Montessori / by Elizabeth G. Hainstock. — New York : New American Library ; London : New English Library, 1978. — 145p ; 18cm. — (A Mentor book)
Bibliography: p137-143
ISBN 0-451-61695-2 (pbk) : Unpriced
B81-29376

372.18'0941 — Great Britain. Infant schools. School life — *For children*

Althea. Starting school / by Althea ; illustrated by Maureen Galvani. — Cambridge : Dinosaur, 1975 (1979 [printing]). — [24]p : col.ill ; 15x18cm. — (Althea's Dinosaur books)
ISBN 0-85122-096-7 (pbk) : £0.50 B81-26808

Snell, Nigel. David's first day at school / Nigel Snell. — London : Hamilton, 1981. — [25]p : col.ill ; 16x17cm
ISBN 0-241-10641-9 : £2.50 : CIP rev.
B81-25759

372.18'1 — Pre-school educational institutions. Children. Creativity — *Case studies*

Paley, Vivian Gussin. Wally's stories / Vivian Gussin Paley. — Cambridge, Mass. ; London : Harvard University Press, 1981. — 223p ; 22cm
ISBN 0-674-94592-1 : £7.50 B81-28463

372.18'1 — Wales. Primary schools. Students. Achievement motivation. Effects of family life *compared with* **effects of family life on achievement motivation in primary school students in Malaysia**

Wan-Rafaei, A. R.. Achievement motivation in Malaysia and Great Britain : its determinants and its relationship in perceived child rearing behaviour / A.R. Wan-Rafaei & J.M. Smith. — Cardiff (c/o R. Slater, Department of Applied Psychology, UWIST, Llwyn-y-Grant, Penylan, Cardiff CF3 7UX) : [UWIST Department of Applied Psychology], 1979. — 17leaves : ill ; 30cm. — (Occasional paper / UWIST Department of Applied Psychology ; no.10)
Conference paper. — Bibliography: leaf 9
£0.50 (spiral) B81-24801

372.19 — Primary schools. Activities. Themes — *For group teaching* — *Welsh texts*

Tomos, Eirlys Wynn. Camau cywaith / Eirlys Wynn Tomos. — [Caerdydd] : Gwasg Prifysgol Cymru, 1981. — 94p : ill,col.maps ; 24cm
ISBN 0-7083-0804-x (pbk) : Unpriced
B81-36269

372.19 — Primary schools. Christmas activities — *For teaching*

Brandling, Redvers. Christmas in the primary school / Redvers Brandling. — London : Ward Lock Educational, 1980. — iv,188p : ill,music ; 22cm
Bibliography: p183-188
ISBN 0-7062-4068-5 (pbk) : £5.95 B81-07015

372.19'0941 — Great Britain. Primary schools. Curriculum

Blenkin, Geva M.. The primary curriculum / Geva M. Blenkin and A.V. Kelly. — London : Harper & Row, 1981. — 216p ; 22cm
Bibliography: p199-207. — Includes index
ISBN 0-06-318120-7 (cased) : £5.70 : CIP rev.
ISBN 0-06-318121-5 (pbk) : £3.95 B81-11947

372.19'09424'96 — West Midlands *(Metropolitan County)*. **Birmingham. Primary schools. Curriculum. Development** — *For teaching*

Further developments in the primary curriculum / City of Birmingham Education Department. — Birmingham (Margaret St., Birmingham B3 3BU) : The Department
Bibliography: p24
Drama. — 1980. — 24p : ill(some col.) ; 21cm
ISBN 0-7093-0043-3 (pbk) : Unpriced
B81-16996

Further developments in the primary curriculum / City of Birmingham Education Department. — Birmingham (Margaret St., Birmingham B3 3BU) : The Department
Bibliography: p20-21
French. — 1980. — 24p : col.ill ; 21cm
ISBN 0-7093-0045-x (pbk) : Unpriced
B81-16997

Further developments in the primary curriculum / City of Birmingham Education Department. — Birmingham (Margaret St., Birmingham B3 3BU) : The Department
Bibliography: p17
Religious education. — 1980. — 20p : ill(some col.) ; 21cm
ISBN 0-7093-0047-6 (pbk) : Unpriced
B81-16994

Further developments in the primary curriculum / City of Birmingham Education Department. — Birmingham (Margaret St., Birmingham B3 3BU) : The Department
Science. — 1980. — 19p : col.ill ; 21cm
ISBN 0-7093-0046-8 (pbk) : Unpriced
B81-16995

372.2 — LEVELS OF PRIMARY EDUCATION

372'.21 — Children, 3-5 years. Education

Warrell, Susan E.. Helping young children grow : a humanistic approach to parenting and teaching / Susan E. Warrell. — Englewood Cliffs ; London : Prentice-Hall, c1980. — xii,227p : ill ; 22cm. — (A Spectrum book)
Includes bibliographies and index
ISBN 0-13-386151-1 (cased) : Unpriced
ISBN 0-13-386144-9 (pbk) : £3.85 B81-12523

372'.21 — Children, to 5 years. Education

Hildebrand, Verna. Guiding young children / Verna Hildebrand. — 2nd ed. — New York : Macmillan ; London : Collier Macmillan, c1980. — xiv,418p : ill ; 24cm
Previous ed.: New York : Macmillan, 1975. — Includes bibliographies, lists of films and index
ISBN 0-02-354240-3 : £9.95 B81-01728

372'.21 — Pre-school children. Education — *Manuals*

Hatoff, Sydelle H.. Teacher's practical guide for educating young children : a growing program / Sydelle H. Hatoff, Claudia A. Byram, Marion C. Hyson [for] Research for Better Schools, Inc.. — Boston [Mass.] ; London : Allyn and Bacon, c1981. — x,278p : ill,2plans,forms ; 28cm
Includes bibliographies
ISBN 0-205-07126-0 (pbk) : £11.95 B81-05043

372'.21'0240431 — Pre-school children. Education — *For parents*

Thompson, Brenda. The pre-school book / Brenda Thompson. — London : Unwin Paperbacks, 1980, c1976. — 187p : ill ; 18cm
Originally published: London : Sidgwick and Jackson, 1976. — Bibliography: p183
ISBN 0-04-649003-5 (pbk) : £1.75 : CIP rev.
B79-34062

372'.21'0941 — Great Britain. Pre-school children. Education

Shinman, Sheila M.. A chance for every child? : access and response to pre-school provision / Sheila M. Shinman. — London : Tavistock Publications, 1981. — xii,226p : ill ; 23cm
Bibliography: p214-220. — Includes index
ISBN 0-422-77420-0 : Unpriced B81-08461

Under fives : a programme of research : a handbook published by the Under Fives Research Dissemination Group. — [S.l.] : [Under Fives Research Dissemination Group] ; Stanmore (Publications Despatch Centre, Honeypot La., Canons Park, Stanmore, Middlesex HA7 1AZ) : Department of Education and Science [distributor], 1981. — 25p ; 30cm
Includes bibliographies
Unpriced (pbk)
Also classified at 362.7'95 B81-28292

372'.21'09411 — Scotland. Pre-school educational institutions. Provision — *For parents*

Henderson, David, *1953-*. Providing for your under-fives / written by David Henderson and Christopher Gibson ; drawn Elizabeth Macdonald. — Edinburgh (4 Queensferry St., Edinburgh EH2 4PA) : Scottish Parent Teacher Council, [1978?]. — [11]p : ill ; 22cm
Unpriced (unbound) B81-38593

372'.21'0973 — United States. Children, to 8 years. Education — *For teaching*

Lundsteen, Sara Wynn. Guiding young children's learning : a comprehensive approach to early childhood education / Sara Wynn Lundsteen, Norma Bernstein Tarrow ; primary illustrator Sara Wynn Lundsteen. — New York ; London : McGraw-Hill, c1981. — xii,514p : ill,plans,forms ; 25cm
Includes bibliographies and index
ISBN 0-07-039105-x : £11.85 B81-23961

372'.21'0973 — United States. Pre-school children. Education

Hendrick, Joanne. Total learning for the whole child : holistic curriculum for children ages 2 to 5 / Joanne Hendrick. — St. Louis ; London : Mosby, 1980. — ix,405p : ill,music ; 25cm
Includes bibliographies and index
ISBN 0-8016-2150-x : Unpriced B81-08147

372'.216 — Cheshire. Crewe and Nantwich *(District)*. Playgroups. Organisations: Pre-school Playgroups Association. *Crewe and Nantwich Branch* — *Serials*

Pre-school Playgroups Association. *Crewe and Nantwich Branch*. Newsletter / Crewe and Nantwich Branch of Pre-school Playgroups Association. — [No.1]-. — [Crewe] ([c/o Mrs. A. Eckersley, 192 Ruskin Rd, Crewe, Cheshire]) : The Branch, [1979]-. — v. ; 30cm
Quarterly. — Description based on: No.8
ISSN 0261-5088 = Newsletter - Crewe and Nantwich Branch of Pre-school Playgroups Association : Unpriced B81-29643

372'.216 — Great Britain. Playgroups

Parents and playgroups. — London : Allen and Unwin, Apr.1981. — [288]p
ISBN 0-04-372030-7 : £8.95 : CIP entry B81-00069

372'.216 — Great Britain. Playgroups. Organisation — *Manuals*

Marsden, Diane. Starting a playgroup / [re-written by Diane Marsden] ; [illustrated by Joan Daunter]. — London (Alford House, Aveline St., SE11 5DH) : Pre-school Playgroups Association, c1981. — [4]p : ill ; 30cm. — (Publication / Pre-school Playgroups Association)
Previous ed.: / by Helen Smith. 1975
ISBN 0-901755-31-1 (unbound) : £0.35 B81-30085

372'.216 — Great Britain. Playgroups — *Statistics*

Facts and figures / [prepared by Bronwen Dorling ... et al.]. — London : Pre-school Playgroups Association, 1980. — 48p : ill ; 21cm
Cover title. — Text on inside covers
ISBN 0-901755-32-x (pbk) : £0.50 B81-33568

372'.216 — Mother & toddler groups. Organisation & management

Scottish Pre-School Playgroups Association. *Mother and Toddler Focus*. Mother & toddler groups, under fives groups : guidelines / [Mother and Toddler Focus, Scottish Pre-School Playgroups Association]. — [Glasgow] ([16 Sandyford Pl., Glasgow, G3 7NB]) : The Association, 1981. — 8p : ill ; 21cm
Cover title. — Text on inside cover
£0.20 (pbk) B81-21412

372'.216 — North-west England. Playgroups. Organisations: Pre-school Playgroups Association. *North West Region* — *Serials*

P.P.A. North West Region newsletter. — [Issue no.1 (197-)]-. — Manchester (Hotspur House, Gloucester St., Manchester M1 5QR) : North West Regional Centre, [197-]-. — v. ; 30cm
Description based on: Issue no.9 (May 1980)
ISSN 0260-7751 = P.P.A. North West Region newsletter : Unpriced B81-09216

372'.216 — Playgroups

Henderson, Ann. Pre-school playgroups. — London : Allen & Unwin. — [224]p
ISBN 0-04-372034-x (cased) : £12.50 : CIP entry
ISBN 0-04-372035-8 (pbk) : £4.50 B81-30216

372.3/8 — PRIMARY SCHOOL CURRICULUM

372.3'5 — Infant schools. Curriculum subjects: Science. Activities — *For teaching*

Harlan, Jean. Science experience for the early childhood years / Jean Harlan. — 2nd ed. — Columbus ; London : Merrill, c1980. — xi,237p : ill,music ; 25cm
Previous ed.: Columbus, Ohio : Merrill, 1976. — Includes bibliographies and index
ISBN 0-675-08155-6 (pbk) : Unpriced B81-14143

372.3'5 — Primary schools. Curriculum subjects: Floating objects — *For teaching*

Bryant, John, *1945-*. Floating and sinking / John Bryant. — Basingstoke (Houndsmill, Basingstoke RG21 2XS) : Globe Education for West Sussex County Council, 1981. — 31p : ill,1map,1form ; 30cm. — (Science horizons)
Bibliography: p9
ISBN 0-333-28536-0 (pbk) : Unpriced B81-22784

372.3'5 — Primary schools. Curriculum subjects: Man. Physiology — *For teaching*

Ensing, Jean. Finding out about ourselves / Jean Ensing. — Basingstoke (Houndsmill, Basingstoke RG21 2XS) : Globe Education for West Sussex County Council, 1981. — 45p : ill,1form ; 30cm. — (Science horizons. Level 1)
Bibliography: p13
ISBN 0-333-28532-8 (pbk) : Unpriced B81-22781

Matthews, Colin, *1931-*. Ourselves / Colin Matthews. — Basingstoke (Houndsmill, Basingstoke RG21 2XS) : Globe Education for West Sussex County Council, 1981. — 47 : ill,forms ; 30cm. — (Science horizons. Level 2a)
Bibliography: p10
ISBN 0-333-28537-9 (corrected: pbk) : Unpriced B81-22780

372.3'5 — Primary schools. Curriculum subjects: Science — *For teaching*

Teacher's handbook. — Basingstoke (Houndsmill, Basingstoke RG21 2XS) : Globe Education for West Sussex County Council, 1981. — 23p : ill ; 30cm. — (Science horizons)
ISBN 0-333-28571-9 (pbk) : Unpriced B81-22786

372.3'57 — Primary schools. Curriculum subjects: Air — *For teaching*

Hine, Pamela. What is air? / Pamela Hine. — Basingstoke (Houndsmill, Basingstoke RG21 2XS) : Globe Education for West Sussex County Council, 1981. — 39p : ill,1form ; 30cm. — (Science horizons. Level 2a)
Bibliography: p8
ISBN 0-333-28534-4 (pbk) : Unpriced B81-22783

372.3'57 — Primary schools. Curriculum subjects: Seeds, soils & trees — *For teaching*

Millyard, J.. Soil, seeds and trees / J. Millyard and C. Smithers. — Basingstoke (Houndsmill, Basingstoke RG21 2XS) : Globe Education for West Sussex County Council, 1981. — 32p : ill ; 30cm. — (Science horizons. Level 1)
Bibliography: p9
ISBN 0-333-28533-6 (pbk) : Unpriced B81-22785

372.3'57 — Primary schools. Curriculum subjects: Weather — *For teaching*

Barnes, Janet. Observing the weather / Janet Barnes. — Basingstoke (Houndsmill, Basingstoke RG21 2XS) : Globe Education for West Sussex County Council, 1981. — 31p : ill,forms ; 30cm. — (Science horizons. Level 1)
Bibliography: p11
ISBN 0-333-28529-8 (pbk) : Unpriced B81-22782

372.4 — Children, to 10 years. Reading skills. Development — *Personal observations*

Bissex, Glenda L.. Gnys at wrk : a child learns to write and read / Glenda L. Bissex. — Cambridge, Mass. ; London : Harvard University Press, 1980. — viii,223p : ill ; 25cm
Bibliography: p215-218. — Includes index
ISBN 0-674-35485-0 : £8.40
Also classified at 372.6'23 B81-13187

372.4 — Children, to 10 years. Reading skills. Teaching — *Manuals*

Aukerman, Robert C.. How do I teach reading? / Robert C. Aukerman, Louise R. Aukerman. — New York ; Chichester : Wiley, c1981. — x,543p : ill,facsims ; 25cm
Includes bibliographies and index
ISBN 0-471-03687-0 : £10.50 B81-23396

372.4 — Pre-school children. Reading skills. Teaching — *For parents*

McConnell, James, *1915 Oct.14-*. Early learning foundation / James McConnell. — Monxton (The Stables, Monxton, Near Andover, Hants. SP11 8AT) : Four Seasons, c1979. — 7pamphlets : ill(some col.) ; 30cm
ISBN 0-901131-17-2 (pbk) : Unpriced
Primary classification 372.6'23 B81-10788

372.4 — Primary schools. Curriculum subjects: Reading — *For teaching*

Southgate, Vera. Extending beginning reading / Vera Southgate, Helen Arnold and Sandra Johnson. — London : Published for the Schools Council by Heinemann Educational, 1981. — x,372p : ill,forms ; 23cm
Bibliography: p353-361. — Includes index
ISBN 0-435-10820-4 (cased) : £10.95
ISBN 0-435-10821-2 (pbk) : Unpriced B81-36253

372.4 — Primary schools. Curriculum subjects: Reading. Teaching

Thompson, Brenda. Reading success : a guide for teachers and parents / Brenda Thompson. — London : Arrow, 1981, c1979. — 252p ; 18cm
Originally published: London : Sidgwick and Jackson, 1979. — Bibliography: p242-245. — Includes index
ISBN 0-09-925970-2 (pbk) : £1.75 B81-35169

372.4'145 — United States. Primary schools. Curriculum subjects: Reading. Teaching. Use of phonics

Flesch, Rudolf. Why Johnny still can't read : a new look at the scandal of our schools / Rudolf Flesch ; foreword by Mary L. Burkhardt. — New York ; London : Harper & Row, c1981. — xxii,191p ; 22cm
Bibliography: p171-184. — Includes index
ISBN 0-06-014842-x : £10.95 B81-27783

372.5 — Primary schools. Curriculum subjects: Visual arts — *For teaching*

Hardiman, George W.. Art activities for children / George W. Hardiman, Theodore Zernich. — Englewood Cliffs ; London : Prentice-Hall, c1981. — ix,142p,[32]p of plates : ill(some col.) ; 28cm
Bibliography: p141-142
ISBN 0-13-046631-x : £11.00 B81-14106

372.5′044 — Children, 3-8 years: Visual arts. Teaching

Jenkins, Peggy Davison. [Art principles and practices]. Art for the fun of it : a guide for teaching young children / Peggy Davison Jenkins. — Englewood Cliffs ; London : Prentice-Hall, c1980. — viii,216p : ill ; 24cm. — (A Spectrum book)
Originally published: 1977. — Bibliography: p207-214. - Includes index
ISBN 0-13-047233-6 (pbk) : £4.50 B81-12716

372.5′044 — Primary schools. Curriculum subjects: Visual arts. Teaching — *Manuals*

Larkin, Diarmuid. Art learning and teaching : a seven-year manual for the primary/elementary teacher / Diarmuid Larkin. — Portmarnock : Wolfhound, c1981. — 255p : ill(some col.) ; 22cm
Bibliography: p255
ISBN 0-9503454-5-8 : Unpriced : CIP rev.
B80-28176

372.5′044′0973 — United States. Primary schools. Curriculum subjects: Visual arts. Teaching — *Manuals*

Lansing, Kenneth M.. The elementary teacher′s art handbook / Kenneth M. Lansing, Arlene E. Richards. — New York ; London : Holt, Rinehart and Winston, c1981. — xi,415p : ill ; 24cm
Includes bibliographies and index
ISBN 0-03-048211-9 : Unpriced B81-33135

372.5′0973 — United States. Primary schools. Curriculum subjects: Visual arts. Projects

Mattil, Edward L.. Meaning in children′s art : projects for teachers / Edward L. Mattil, Betty Marzan. — Englewood Cliffs ; London : Prentice-Hall, c1981. — x,324p : ill ; 28cm
Includes bibliographies and index
ISBN 0-13-567115-9 (cased) : Unpriced
ISBN 0-13-567107-8 (pbk) : £9.05 B81-22359

372.6 — England. Primary schools. Students, 11 years. Language skills. Assessment

Language performance in schools : report on the 1979 primary survey from the National Foundation for Educational Research in England and Wales to the Department of Education and Science, the Welsh Office and the Department of Education for Northern Ireland / by T.P. Gorman ... [et al.] with a statistical contribution by B. Sexton. — London : H.M.S.O., 1981. — 163p : ill ; 25cm + 2pamphlets(12p: ill ; 21cm). — (Primary survey report ; no.1)
At head of title: Assessment of Performance Unit. — Includes index
ISBN 0-11-270385-2 (pbk) : £6.40 B81-40398

372.6′044′0941 — Great Britain. Primary schools. Students. Language skills. Teaching

Hutchcroft, Diana M. R.. Making language work : a practical approach to literacy for teachers of 5- to 13-year-old children / Diana M.R. Hutchcroft [with the collaboration of] Iain G. Ball ... [et al.]. — London : McGraw-Hill, c1981. — 270p : ill ; 22cm. — (McGraw-Hill series for serving teachers)
Includes bibliographies and index
ISBN 0-07-084119-5 (pbk) : £4.95 B81-19675

372.6′1 — United States. Primary schools. Curriculum subjects: English language. Words. Meaning. Recognition. Teaching

Durkin, Dolores. Strategies for identifying words : a workbook for teachers and those preparing to teach / Dolores Durkin. — 2nd ed. — Boston [Mass.] ; London : Allyn and Bacon, c1981. — ix,146p : 2ill
Previous ed.: 1976. — Includes bibliographies and index
ISBN 0-205-07229-1 (spiral) : £9.50
B81-22236

372.6′22 — Children, to 10 years. Speech skills. Development — *For teaching — German texts*

Pretzell, Eva. Sprech- und Spracherziehung mit Kindern / Eva Pretzell. — Mainz ; London : Schott, c1980. — 188p ; 21cm. — (Bausteine für Musikerziehung, ISSN 0172-7222 ; B35)
Bibliography: p175-186
ISBN 3-7957-1035-9 (pbk) : £7.20 B81-15376

372.6′23 — Children, to 10 years. Writing skills. Development — *Personal observations*

Bissex, Glenda L.. Gnys at wrk : a child learns to write and read / Glenda L. Bissex. — Cambridge, Mass. ; London : Harvard University Press, 1980. — viii,223p : ill ; 25cm
Bibliography: p215-218. — Includes index
ISBN 0-674-35485-0 : £8.40
Primary classification 372.4 B81-13187

372.6′23 — Drawings — *Questions & answers — For acquisition of writing skills by children — For schools*

Aliprandi, Cecilia. Images / Cecilia Aliprandi, Rosanna Bissi ; illustrated by Attilio Cassinelli. — London : Good Reading, 1978, c1971. — 128p : all ill(some col.) ; 25cm
Originally published: Firenze: : Giunti, 1971
ISBN 0-904223-35-3 (pbk) : Unpriced
B81-18611

372.6′23 — Pre-school children. Curriculum subjects: Writing. Teaching — *For parents*

McConnell, James, *1915 Oct.14-*. Early learning foundation / James McConnell. — Monxton (The Stables, Monxton, Near Andover, Hants. SP11 8AT) : Four Seasons, c1979. — 7pamphlets : ill(some col.) ; 30cm
ISBN 0-901131-17-2 (pbk) : Unpriced
Also classified at 372.7′30442 ; 372.4
B81-10788

372.6′23′0941 — Great Britain. Primary schools. Curriculum subjects: Creative writing — *For teaching*

Maybury, Barry. Creative writing for juniors / Barry Maybury. — 2nd ed. — London : Batsford, 1981. — 240p ; 22cm
Previous ed.: 1967. — Includes index
ISBN 0-7134-3546-1 : £6.50 B81-37955

372.6′4 — Activities for children, 2-8 years: Activities connected with story-telling

Peterson, Carolyn Sue. Story programs : a source book of materials / Carolyn Sue Peterson and Brenny Hall. — Metuchen ; London : Scarecrow, 1980. — v,294p : ill,music ; 28cm
Bibliography: p264-266. - Includes index
ISBN 0-8108-1317-3 (pbk) : £8.75 B81-05346

372.6′6 — Multicultural societies. Primary schools. Activities: Drama — *For teaching*

Demmery, Sylvia. Drama in a multi-cultural society : the early years: 4 to 12 / [by Sylvia Demmery, Patricia Young]. — [Birmingham] ([102 Edmund St., Birmingham B3 3PN]) : Educational Drama Association, [1981?]. — 16p ; 21cm
Bibliography: p16
ISBN 0-904027-10-4 (pbk) : Unpriced
B81-19856

372.6′6 — Primary schools. Activities: Drama. Teaching

Heinig, Ruth Beall. Creative drama for the classroom teacher / Ruth Beall Heinig, Lyda Stillwell. — 2nd ed. — Englewood Cliffs ; London : Prentice-Hall, c1981. — xii,256p : ill ; 24cm
Previous ed.: published as Creative dramatics for the classroom teacher, 1974. — Includes bibliographies and index
ISBN 0-13-189415-3 : £9.05 B81-17280

372.7′3044 — Nursery schools & primary schools. Curriculum subjects: Mathematics. Teaching aids: Games — *Manuals — For teachers*

Baratta-Lorton, Mary. Workjobs II : number activities for early childhood / Mary Baratta-Lorton. — Menlo Park ; London : Addison-Wesley, c1979. — vi,153p : ill ; 28cm
ISBN 0-201-04302-5 (spiral) : £4.95
B81-11408

372.7′3044 — Primary schools. Curriculum subjects: Mathematics. Teaching aids: Games

Schminke, C. W.. Math activities for child involvement / C.W. Schminke, Enoch Dumas. — 3rd ed. — Boston, Mass. ; London : Allyn and Bacon, c1981. — xi,336p : ill ; 25cm
Previous ed.: 1977. — Includes index
ISBN 0-205-07295-x (cased) : Unpriced
ISBN 0-205-07302-6 (pbk) : Unpriced
B81-30086

372.7′3044 — Primary schools. Curriculum subjects: Mathematics. Teaching — *For West African students*

Ashworth, A. E.. The teaching of mathematics / A.E. Ashworth. — London : Hodder and Stoughton, 1981. — ix,118p : ill ; 22cm. — (Nigerian education series)
ISBN 0-340-25953-1 (pbk) : £1.75 B81-10801

372.7′3044 — Primary schools. Curriculum subjects: Mathematics. Teaching — *Manuals*

Barron, Linda. Mathematics experiences for the early childhood years / Linda Barron. — Columbus, Ohio ; London : Merrill, c1979. — viii,296p : ill ; 25cm
Includes bibliographies and index
ISBN 0-675-08284-6 (pbk) : £8.25 B81-03214

Copeland, Richard W.. Math activities for children : a diagnostic and developmental approach / Richard W. Copeland. — Columbus, Ohio ; London : Merrill, c1979. — x,214p : ill ; 23cm
Includes index
ISBN 0-675-08316-8 (pbk) : £5.60 B81-03215

Emery, W. J. Norman. Mathspan : a practical comprehensive guide to the what, why, how & when of teaching mathematics during the years 4-9 / by W.J. Norman Emery ; foreword by Peter Taylor. — Cardiff (67 Queen St., Cardiff CF1 4AY) : School Span
Bk.1: From the beginning with the fours & fives. — c1979. — ix,91p : ill,1form,1port ; 21cm
Port & text on inside cover
ISBN 0-906743-00-1 (pbk) : £2.50 B81-37864

Mathematics 5-11. — [Coventry] ([Elm Bank Teachers′ Centre, Mile La., Coventry CV1 2NN]) : Coventry L.E.A.
Measurement. — [1981]. — 80p : ill ; 30cm
Cover title
ISBN 0-901606-55-3 (pbk) : Unpriced
B81-19379

Mathematics 5-11. — [Coventry] ([Elm Bank Teachers′ Centre, Mile La., Coventry CV1 2NN]) : Coventry L.E.A.
Number. — [1981]. — 189p : ill ; 30cm
Cover title
ISBN 0-901606-45-6 (spiral) : Unpriced
B81-19377

Mathematics 5-11. — [Coventry] ([Elm Bank Teachers′ Centre, Mile La., Coventry CV1 2NN]) : Coventry L.E.A.
Towards graphs. — [1981]. — 17leaves : ill ; 30cm
Cover title
ISBN 0-901606-50-2 (pbk) : Unpriced
B81-19378

372.7′3044′0941 — Great Britain. Infant schools. Curriculum subjects: Mathematics. Teaching

Edwards, Suzanne. Numberland teacher′s guide / S. Edwards, C. Wild. — Glasgow : Collins Educational, c1981. — 45p : ill,forms ; 26cm
ISBN 0-00-315331-2 (pbk) : £1.95 B81-34245

Thyer, Dennis. Teaching mathematics to young children / Dennis Thyer, John Maggs. — 2nd ed. — London : Holt, Rinehart and Winston, c1981. — x,246p : ill ; 25cm
Previous ed.: 1971. — Includes index
ISBN 0-03-910292-0 (pbk) : £4.95 : CIP rev.
B81-00070

372.7′30442 — Pre-school children. Curriculum subjects: Mathematics. Teaching — *For parents*

McConnell, James, *1915 Oct.14-*. Early learning foundation / James McConnell. — Monxton (The Stables, Monxton, Near Andover, Hants. SP11 8AT) : Four Seasons, c1979. — 7pamphlets : ill(some col.) ; 30cm
ISBN 0-901131-17-2 (pbk) : Unpriced
Primary classification 372.6′23 B81-10788

372.8 — Primary schools. Christian religious education — *For teaching*

All God′s children : religious knowledge for primary schools / Northern Education Advisory Council. — London : Evans
Bk.5. — 1981. — 184p : ill,1map ; 22cm
ISBN 0-237-50599-1 (pbk) : Unpriced
B81-33455

372.8'3 — Primary schools. Curriculum subjects: Social studies — *For teaching*

Gunning, Stella. Topic teaching in the primary school. — London : Croom Helm, Sept.1981. — [224]p
ISBN 0-7099-0437-1 (cased) : £12.95 : CIP entry
ISBN 0-7099-1118-1 (pbk) : £5.95 B81-21503

372.8'3044 — Primary schools. Curriculum subjects: Social studies. Teaching — *Manuals*

Servey, Richard E.. Elementary social studies : a skills emphasis / Richard E. Servey. — Boston [Mass.] ; London : Allyn and Bacon, c1981. — viii,421p : ill,1map ; 25cm
Includes bibliographies and index
ISBN 0-205-07213-5 : £18.95 B81-25175

372.8'3044'0973 — United States. Primary schools. Curriculum subjects: Social studies. Teaching

Ellis, Arthur K.. Teaching and learning elementary social studies / Arthur K. Ellis. — 2nd ed. — Boston ; London : Allyn and Bacon, c1981. — x,534p : ill,maps,facsims,plans ; 25cm
Previous ed.: Boston : Allyn and Bacon, 1977. — Includes bibliographies and index
ISBN 0-205-07221-6 (corrected) : £17.50 B81-20661

Kenworthy, Leonard S.. Social studies for the eighties : in elementary and middle schools / Leonard S. Kenworthy. — 3rd ed. — New York ; Chichester : Wiley, c1981. — xiv,541p : ill ; 24cm
Previous ed.: published as Social studies for the seventies. Lexington, Mass. : Xerox College Pub., 1973. — Includes bibliographies and index
ISBN 0-471-05983-8 (pbk) : £8.90
Also classified at 300'.7'1273 B81-21167

Preston, Ralph C.. Teaching social studies in the elementary school / Ralph C. Preston, Wayne L. Herman, Jr. — 5th ed. — New York ; London : Holt, Rinehart and Winston, c1981. — xii,434p : ill,maps ; 24cm
Previous ed.: 1974. — Includes bibliographies and index
ISBN 0-03-043886-1 : £11.50 B81-22863

372.8'6 — Great Britain. Primary schools. Activities: Sports & games — *For teaching*

Mauldon, E.. Games teaching : an approach for the primary school / E. Mauldon, H.B. Redfern. — 2nd ed. — Plymouth : Macdonald and Evans, 1981. — ix,131p ; 22cm
Previous ed. 1969. — Includes index
ISBN 0-7121-0739-8 (pbk) : £3.75 B81-23104

372.8'6 — Infant schools. Curriculum subjects: Physical education — *For teaching*

Physical education for nursery and infant pupils / Cathy Clarke ... [et al.]. — [Coventry] ([Elm Bank Teachers' Centre, Mile La., Coventry CV1 2NN]) : Coventry L.E.A., [1981?]. — 203p : ill,plans ; 30cm
Includes bibliographies
ISBN 0-901606-11-1 (spiral) : Unpriced B81-38949

372.8'6044 — Primary schools. Curriculum subjects: Physical education. Teaching

Hoffman, Hubert A.. Meaningful movement for children : a developmental theme approach to physical education / Hubert A. Hoffman, Jane Young, Stephen E. Klesius. — Boston, Mass. ; London : Allyn and Bacon, c1981. — xii,420p : ill,forms ; 24cm
Bibliography: p405-411. - Includes index
ISBN 0-205-06952-5 : £13.55 B81-00827

372.8'7'0941 — Great Britain. Primary schools. Curriculum subjects: Music — *For parents*

Hope-Brown, Margaret. Children and music / by Margaret Hope-Brown ; illustrated by Ruth Bartlett ; general editor, John Allard. — [Billericay] ([17 Jacksons Lane, Billericay, CM11 1AH]) : Home and School Council, c1981. — 24p : ill ; 21cm. — (A Home and School Council publication)
Text and ill. on inside covers
ISBN 0-901181-36-6 (pbk) : Unpriced B81-38552

372.8'9 — Primary schools. Curriculum subjects: History — *For teaching*

Blyth, Joan E.. History in primary schools. — London : McGraw-Hill, Sept.1981. — [268]p. — (McGraw-Hill series for teachers)
ISBN 0-07-084128-4 : £4.95 : CIP entry B81-22672

372.8'91044'0941 — Great Britain. Primary schools. Curriculum subjects: Geography. Teaching

Geographical work in primary and middle schools / edited by David Mills. — Sheffield : Geographical Association, c1981. — viii,200p : ill,maps ; 25cm
Includes bibliographies and index
ISBN 0-900395-66-4 (pbk) : Unpriced
Also classified at 910'.7'1241 B81-25092

372.9 — PRIMARY EDUCATION. HISTORICAL AND GEOGRAPHICAL TREATMENT

372.92'4 — Essex. Little Baddow. Primary education, *1930-1960* — *Personal observations*

Turner, Constance L.. A country teacher looks back : being reflections of one Essex headmistress of this twentieth century / by Constance L. Turner. — [Chelmsford] ([County Library HQ Goldlay Gdns., Chelmsford, Essex CM2 0EW]) : Essex Libraries, c1980. — 81p,[7]p of plates : ill,ports ; 21cm
ISBN 0-903630-07-9 (pbk) : £1.20 B81-10308

372.9411'35 — Scotland. Shetland. Foula. Primary schools. Foula School, *to 1980*

Foula School centenary 1879-1979. — [Foula] : [The School], [1979]. — 29p ; 21cm
£0.75 (pbk) B81-17704

372.942 — England. Primary education — *For teaching*

Research and practice in the primary classroom / edited by Brian Simon and John Willcocks. — London : Routledge & Kegan Paul, 1981. — viii,198p ; 22cm
Bibliography: p190-194. — Includes index
ISBN 0-7100-0850-3 : £9.75 : CIP rev. B81-21482

372.9421'87 — London. Barnet *(London Borough).* **Primary schools: Deansbrook School,** *to 1981*

Pack, Mary B.. A history of Deansbrook School : Mill Hill : founded 25th August, 1931 / compiled, narrated and edited by Mary B. Pack. — [Stanmore] ([30 Brockley Ave., Stanmore, Middx HA7 4LX]) : [M.B. Pack], [1981]. — 84p : ill,1map,ports ; 22cm
Map on inside cover
Unpriced (pbk) B81-29190

372.9421'91 — London. Croydon *(London Borough).* **Thornton Heath. Primary schools: Gonville Primary School,** *to 1981*

Gonville Primary School. Gonville Primary School Golden Jubilee 1931-1981. — Thornton Heath (Gonville Rd, Thornton Heath, Surrey CR4 6DL) : The School, 1981. — 32p : ill,ports ; 25cm
Cover title
Unpriced (pbk) B81-34916

372.9424'12 — Gloucestershire. Gotherington. Primary schools: Gotherington School, *to 1981*

Stinchcombe, Owen. Lucky to survive : a centenary history of Gotherington School / by Owen Stinchcombe. — [Gotherington] ([c/o Gotherington School, Gotherington, Glos.]) : [O. Stinchcombe], [1981]. — 120p : ill,1map,ports ; 21cm
Map on inside cover
Unpriced (pbk) B81-29787

372.9425'31 — Lincolnshire. Dunholme. Primary schools: Dunholme School, *1860-1900*

Leach, Terence R.. Alas! poor Dunholme School : the story of education in Dunholme in the nineteenth century / Terence R. Leach. — Lincoln (3 Merleswen, Dunholme, Lincoln) : T.R. Leach, [c1981]. — 48p : 1facsim ; 30cm. — (Dunholme history pamphle ; no.2)
Cover title. — Facsim on cover. — Bibliography: p48
£1.75 (pbk) B81-28926

372.9425'7'0222 — Oxfordshire. Primary schools. School life, *1800-1914* — *Illustrations*

School days : elementary education in Oxfordshire 1800-1914 / [text by Malcolm Graham]. — Oxford (County Libraries' Headquarters, Holton, Oxford, OX9 1QQ) : Libraries' Department, Oxfordshire County Council, c1980. — [14]p : chiefly ill,facsims ; 21x30cm
Published in connection with an exhibition staged jointly by the County Libraries and the Department of Museum Services. — Cover title
Unpriced (pbk) B81-11758

372.972 — Mexico. Rural regions. Primary education

Brooke, Nigel. The quality of education in Mexican rural primary schools / Nigel Brooke with John Oxenham. — Brighton : Institute of Development Studies, 1980. — iv,101p ; 21cm. — (IDS research reports, ISSN 0141-1314) (Education report ; 5)
Bibliography: p101
ISBN 0-903354-67-5 (pbk) : Unpriced B81-28663

373 — SECONDARY EDUCATION

373'.01'15 — Adolescents. Social education. Teaching methods

Social education : methods and resources : a tutors' handbook. — Edinburgh (4 Queensferry St., Edinburgh EH2 4PA) : Scottish Community Education Centre, [1981]. — 58p : ill ; 29cm
Includes bibliographies
£2.00 (pbk) B81-40006

373'.01'15 — Scotland. Secondary schools. Social education. Projects: Scottish Social Education Project

Social education : the Scottish approach / John MacBeath ... [et al.]. — Glasgow (Room 565 Jordanhill College of Education, Southbrae Drive, Glasgow G13 1PP) : Scottish Social Education Project, 1981. — 65p : ill ; 30cm
Limited ed. of 1,000 copies
ISBN 0-903915-68-5 (pbk) : £1.50 B81-27534

373'.01'15 — Secondary schools. Curriculum subjects: Self-development. Teaching

Hopson, Barrie. Lifeskills teaching / Barrie Hopson and Mike Scally. — London : McGraw-Hill, 1981. — 256p : ill ; 22cm
Bibliography: p248-253. - Includes index
ISBN 0-07-084099-7 (pbk) : £4.95 : CIP rev. B80-13764

373.1 — SECONDARY SCHOOLS

373.11'02'0941 — Great Britain. Secondary schools. Teaching — *For trainee teachers*

Mills, Richard W.. On your marks : beginning secondary school teaching / Richard Mills. — London : Temple Smith, 1980. — 186p : 1ill,music,1facsim ; 22cm
Bibliography: p186
ISBN 0-85117-202-4 (cased) : £9.95
ISBN 0-85117-203-2 (pbk) : £3.95 B81-07901

373.11'02'0973 — United States. Middle schools. Teaching

Sale, Larry L.. Introduction to middle school teaching / Larry L. Sale. — Columbus ; London : Merrill, c1979. — xii,291p : ill,forms ; 24cm
Includes bibliographies and index
ISBN 0-675-08279-x : £10.50 B81-10060

373.11'024 — Secondary schools. Classrooms. Discipline

Problem behaviour in the secondary school : a systems approach / edited by Bill Gillham. — London : Croom Helm, c1981. — 195p ; 23cm
Bibliography: p184-191. — Includes index
ISBN 0-7099-0129-1 (cased) : £10.95
ISBN 0-7099-1102-5 (pbk) : Unpriced B81-18832

373.11'0942 — England. Secondary schools. Teaching methods

Button, Leslie. Group tutoring for the form teacher. — London : Hodder & Stoughton, Sept.1981
1: Lower secondary school : years one and two. — [128]p
ISBN 0-340-26691-0 (pbk) : £4.50 : CIP entry B81-22646

373.11′46′0942261 — West Sussex. Crawley. Middle schools: Desmond Anderson Middle School. Teachers. In-service training. Projects

Verrier, Ray L.. School-based in-service education : a case study of school consultancy relationships / Ray L. Verrier. — [Brighton] ([Falmer, Brighton, Sussex BN1 9RH]) : Education Area, University of Sussex, 1981. — 89p ; 21cm. — (University of Sussex Education Area occasional paper ; 8)
ISBN 0-905414-07-1 (pbk) : Unpriced
B81-12973

373.12′00973 — United States. Secondary schools. Administration

Hampton, Bill R.. Solving problems in secondary school administration : a human organization approach / Bill R. Hampton, Robert H. Lauer. — Boston [Mass.] ; London : Allyn and Bacon, c1981. — xii,312p : ill ; 25cm
Includes index
ISBN 0-205-06951-7 : £12.50 B81-02232

373.12′012′0924 — Hereford and Worcester. Great Malvern. Girls public schools: Malvern Girls′ College. Brooks, Iris M. — *Biographies*

Phillips, Grace W.. Smile, bow, & pass on : a biography of an avant-garde headmistress Miss Iris M. Brooks, MA (Cantab.) Malvern Girls′ College (1928-1954) / by Grace W. Philllips. — [s.l] : [s.n.], 1980 (Farnborough, Hants.) (Farnborough, Hampshire GU14 7NQ) (Saint Michael′s Abbey Press), 1980. — 236p : ill,plans,1port ; 22cm
ISBN 0-9507152-0-4 : £6.50 B81-05998

373.12′08 — Great Britain. Secondary schools. Departments. Management — *Manuals*

Departmental management / edited by Michael Marland and Sydney Hill ; with contributions by Colin Bayne-Jardine ... [et al.]. — London : Heinemann Educational, 1981. — x,177p ; 23cm. — (Heinemann organization in schools series)
Bibliography: p166-167. - Includes index
ISBN 0-435-80591-6 : £8.95 B81-23376

373.12′42′0941 — Great Britain. Secondary schools. Curriculum. Planning. Timetables. Compilation — *Bibliographies*

Watson, Leonard E.. Timetabling in the secondary school : an annotated bibliography / compiled by Leonard E. Watson. — [Sheffield] ([Pond St., Sheffield S1 1WB]) : Sheffield City Polytechnic, Department of Education Management, 1981. — 44p ; 21cm. — (Sheffield papers in education management ; 19)
ISBN 0-903761-34-3 (pbk) : £1.00 B81-35316

373.12′6′0942 — England. Educational institutions. Students, 16-19 years. Examinations — *Proposals*

Association of Colleges for Further and Higher Education. 16-19, examinations : a case for action / Association of Colleges for Further and Higher Education. — Sheffield : The Association, [1981]. — 8p ; 21cm
Cover title. — Text on inside cover
£1.00 (pbk) B81-17922

373.12′62 — Associated Examining Board G.C.E. examinations. Setting & marking

Associated Examining Board for the General Certificate of Education. How A.E.B. examinations are set and marked / the Associated Examining Board for the General Certificate of Education. — Aldershot (Wellington House, Aldershot, Hants. GU11 1BQ) : AEB, [1981?]. — 17p ; 21cm
Unpriced (pbk) B81-29748

373.12′62 — England. G.C.E. (A level) examining boards. Grading standards

Christie, T.. Defining public examination standards. — London : Macmillan, Sept.1981. — [80]p. — (Schools Council research studies)
ISBN 0-333-31496-4 (pbk) : £4.95 : CIP entry
B81-25694

373.12′62 — England. Secondary schools. G.C.E. (A level) examinations. Performance of students. Comparability

Christie, T.. Standards at GCE A-level : 1963 and 1973 : a pilot investigation of examination standards in three subjects / T. Christie, G.M. Forrest. — Basingstoke : Macmillan Education, 1980. — xii,272p : ill,forms ; 25cm. — (Schools Council research studies)
ISBN 0-333-24647-0 : £10.95 : CIP rev.
B80-05845

373.12′62 — Ireland *(Republic)*. Secondary schools. Public examinations. Design. Evaluation

Public Examination Evaluation Project. The Public Examinations Evaluation Project, final report / [written] by J. Heywood, S. Mc Guinness D. Murphy. — [Dublin] ([Dublin 2]) : [Department of Teacher Education, Trinity College, Dublin], c1980. — iv,249p : ill,forms ; 30cm
Unpriced (pbk) B81-21760

373.12′62′09416 — Northern Ireland. Secondary schools. Examinations. Organisations: Northern Ireland Schools Examinations Council — *Accounts — Serials*

Northern Ireland Schools Examinations Council. Accounts for the Northern Ireland Schools Examinations Council. — 1979-80. — Belfast : H.M.S.O., 1981. — [3]p
ISBN 0-337-04117-2 : £0.80 B81-30715

373.12′64 — Scotland. Secondary schools. Academic achievement. Diagnostic tests

Black, H. D.. Diagnostic assessment in secondary schools : a teacher′s handbook / by H.D. Black and W.B. Dockrell. — [Edinburgh] ([15 St John St., Edinburgh EH8 8JR]) : The Scottish Council for Research in Education, c1980. — ix,86p : ill,forms ; 22cm
Bibliography: p86
ISBN 0-901116-26-2 (pbk) : £2.20 B81-06513

373.13′02812 — Ireland *(Republic)*. Educational institutions. Leaving certificate examinations. Techniques — *For students — Serials*

School and college : the exam and career guide for students. — No.1-. — Dublin (Taney Rd, Dundrum, Dublin 14) : School and College Services, [1980]-. — v. : ill,maps,ports ; 30cm
Eight issues yearly
£0.40
Primary classification 331.7′02′09417
B81-07963

373.13′028′14 — Great Britain. Secondary schools. Curriculum subjects: Study techniques — *For teaching*

Hamblin, Douglas. Teaching study skills / Douglas Hamblin. — Oxford : Basil Blackwell, 1981. — 169p : ill,forms ; 24cm
Bibliography: p163-166. — Includes index
ISBN 0-631-12523-x (cased) : £9.95
ISBN 0-631-12533-7 (pbk) : £4.50 B81-31926

373.13′0973 — United States. Secondary schools. Teaching methods

Clark, Leonard H.. Secondary and middle school teaching methods / Leonard H. Clark, Irving S. Starr. — 4th ed. — New York : Macmillan ; London : Collier Macmillan, c1981. — viii,376p : ill,forms ; 25cm
Previous ed.: published as Secondary school teaching methods. New York : Macmillan, 1976. — Includes bibliographies and index
ISBN 0-02-322650-1 : £12.50 B81-35960

373.13′9445′0941 — Great Britain. Secondary schools. Teaching. Applications of microcomputer systems — *Conference proceedings*

Microcomputers in secondary education : issues and techniques / edited by J.A.M. Howe and P.M. Ross. — London : Kogan Page, 1981. — 159p : ill ; 22cm
Conference papers. — Includes bibliographies
ISBN 0-85038-479-6 (pbk) : £8.95 : CIP rev.
B81-18053

373.14 — Secondary schools. Students. Counselling. Techniques

Problems and practice of pastoral care / edited by Douglas Hamblin. — Oxford : Blackwell, 1981. — vii,306p : ill ; 23cm
Bibliography: p297-302. — Includes index
ISBN 0-631-12921-9 : £14.95 B81-08451

373.14′25 — Great Britain. Young persons, 16-18 years. Vocational preparation

Vocational preparation / Further Education Curriculum Review and Development Unit. — Stanmore (Publications Despatch Centre, Honeypot La., Canons Park, Stanmore, Middlesex, HA7 1AZ) : Department of Education and Science, 1981. — 45p : ill,forms ; 30cm
ISBN 0-85522-090-2 (pbk) : Unpriced
B81-17381

373.14′25′02854 — Great Britain. Secondary schools. Careers guidance. Applications of digital computer systems

Wallis, D.. Computer aids to guidance / D. Wallis. — Cardiff (c/o R. Slater, Department of Applied Psychology, UWIST, Llwyn-y-Grant, Penylan, Cardiff CF3 7UX) : [UWIST Department of Applied Psychology], 1977. — 12p ; 30cm. — (Occasional paper / UWIST Department of Applied Psychology ; no.3)
Bibliography: p12
£0.50 (spiral) B81-24800

373.14′25′0941 — Great Britain. Secondary schools. Careers guidance — *Serials*

NUT guide to careers work. — 1981. — London : New Opportunity Press for the National Union of Teachers, c1981. — 88p
ISSN 0309-9261 : Unpriced B81-16755

373.14′25′0942 — England. Secondary schools. Vocational preparation

Schools and working life : some initiatives / Department of Education and Science. — London : H.M.S.O., 1981. — iii,78p : ill ; 20x21cm
ISBN 0-11-270546-4 (pbk) : £2.50 B81-21044

373.14′6′0722 — Great Britain. Secondary schools. Education welfare work — *Case studies*

Bond, Catherine M.. Partnership in practice : a study of the pastoral care system and its interaction with a school social worker in a Haringey comprehensive school / Catherine M. Bond. — London (Ladbrok House, Highbury Grove, N5 2AD) : Polytechnic of North London, Department of Applied Social Studies, Survey Research Unit, 1981. — 154p ; 30cm. — (Research report / Polytechnic of North London. Survey Research Unit ; no.10)
Bibliography: p152-154
ISBN 0-906970-08-3 (pbk) : £3.00 B81-31134

373.14′6′0941 — Great Britain. Secondary schools. Education welfare work

Perspectives on pastoral care / edited by Ron Best, Colin Jarvis and Peter Ribbins. — London : Heinemann Educational, 1980. — xiii,292p : ill ; 23cm. — (Heinemann organization in schools series)
Bibliography: p283, - Includes index
ISBN 0-435-80066-3 : £8.50 : CIP rev.
B80-01135

373.16′8 — Essex. Secondary schools. Energy. Use. Management

Yannas, Simos. Energy strategies for secondary schools in Essex : report on phase 1 January 1978 / by Simos Yannas and George Wilkenfeld. — London (34 Bedford Sq., WC1B 3ES) : Architectural Association Graduate School, c1978. — 89p : ill ; 30cm. — (Energy programme research paper ; 1/78)
Unpriced (spiral) B81-18506

373.16′8 — Great Britain. Secondary schools. Energy. Use. Management. Participation of students & teachers — *Study regions: Essex*

Yannas, Simos. Education in energy management / Simos Yannas. — London (34 Bedford Sq., WC1B 3ES) : Architectural Association Graduate School, [1980?]. — 22p : ill,plans,forms ; 30cm. — (Energy studies programme)
Unpriced (unbound) B81-18504

373.16′8 — Great Britain. Secondary schools. Energy. Use. Management. Participation of students — *For teaching*

Energy education in schools : a teacher′s guide. — London (34 Bedford) : Architectural Association Graduate School, [1980?]. — ii,74,[57]p : ill,plans,forms ; 30cm. — (Energy studies programme)
Unpriced (unbound)
Primary classification 373.16′8 B81-18505

373.16′8 — Great Britain. Secondary schools. Energy. Use. Management. Participation of teachers

Energy education in schools : a teacher's guide. — London (34 Bedford) : Architectural Association Graduate School, [1980?]. — ii,74,[57]p : ill,plans,forms ; 30cm. — (Energy studies programme)
Unpriced (unbound)
Also classified at 373.16′8 B81-18505

373.16′8 — Great Britain. Secondary schools. Energy. Use. Management — *Study examples: St. Chad's School (Tilbury)*

Yannas, Simos. Energy management for schools / by Simos Yannas and George Wilkenfeld. — London (34 Bedford Sq., WC1B 3ES) : Architectural Association Graduate School, c1979. — 91p : ill,forms ; 30cm. — (Energy programme)
Unpriced (spiral) B81-18651

373.18′092′2 — Scotland. Secondary schools. School life — *Personal observations — Collections*

Tell them from me : Scottish school leavers write about school and life afterwards / edited and introduced by Lesley Gow and Andrew McPherson. — [Aberdeen] : Aberdeen University Press, 1980. — x,125p : ill ; 26cm
Bibliography: p123-125
ISBN 0-08-025738-0 (cased) : Unpriced : CIP rev.
ISBN 0-08-025739-9 (pbk) : Unpriced
Also classified at 306′.3 B80-20489

373.18′1 — Ireland *(Republic)*. **Secondary schools. First year students. Personal adjustment** — *For schools*

Gill, Albert. Plan your future, 1 : a programme for first year students / Albert Gill and Michael McCoy. — Dublin : Educational Company of Ireland, c1981. — 64p : ill ; 21cm
Unpriced (pbk) B81-34804

373.18′1 — Northern Ireland. Secondary schools. Adaptation of students

Spelman, B. J.. Pupil adaptation to secondary school : a study of transition from primary to secondary education and subsequent patterns of adjustment among 3050 pupils who first entered secondary schools in September 1975 / by B.J. Spelman. — [Belfast] ([Research Unit, 52 Malone Rd., Belfast, BT9 5BS]) : Northern Ireland Council for Educational Research, c1979. — x,370p : ill ; 30cm. — (Publications of the Northern Ireland Council for Educational Research ; 18)
Bibliography: p346-359
ISBN 0-903478-10-2 (pbk) : £4.00 B81-14210

373.18′1 — Outer London. Secondary schools. Disruptive students — *Case studies*

Lawrence, Jean. Dialogue on disruptive behavior : a study of a secondary school / Jean Lawrence, David Steed, Pamela Young with Gemma Hilton. — South Croydon (17 Winchelsey Rise South Croydon, Surrey) : P.J.D. Press, 1981. — 93p : 1form ; 21cm
ISBN 0-9507482-0-x (pbk) : Unpriced B81-23025

373.18′1 — Scotland. Secondary schools. Students. Return from List D schools — *Case studies*

Anderson, Rosemary R.. From 'List D' — to day school / Rosemary R. Anderson. — Dundee (Dundee College of Education, Gardyne Rd., Dundee DD5 1NY) : R. R. Anderson, c1980. — 149,[46]p,[17]leaves,[3]folded leaves of plates : ill,forms ; 30cm
Cover title. — Bibliography: 1 leaf
Unpriced (pbk) B81-33110

373.18′1′0968221 — South Africa. Soweto. Secondary schools. Negro students. Altitudes

Geber, Beryl A.. Soweto's children : the development of attitudes / Beryl A. Geber and Stanton P. Newman. — London : Published in cooperation with European Association of Experimental Social Psychology by Academic Press, 1980. — viii,215p ; 24cm. — (European monographs in social psychology ; 20)
Bibliography: p200-206. — Includes index
ISBN 0-12-278750-1 : £13.60 : CIP rev. B80-06854

373.19 — Great Britain. Secondary schools. Curriculum. Choice. Role of educational technology

Beckett, Leslie. Maintaining choice in the secondary curriculum : report of an investigation into the problems caused by falling rolls / Leslie Beckett. — London : Council for Educational Technology, 1981. — 113p : ill ; 21cm. — (Working paper / Council for Educational Technology, ISSN 0307-9511 ; 20)
ISBN 0-86184-034-8 (pbk) : £6.00 : CIP rev. B81-13836

373.19′09417 — Ireland *(Republic)*. **Secondary schools. Curriculum. Reform**

Mulcahy, D. G.. Curriculum and policy in Irish post-primary education / D.G. Mulcahy. — Dublin : Institute of Public Administration, 1981. — x,245p : ill,1form ; 23cm
Bibliography: p226-235. — Includes index
ISBN 0-906980-02-x : £9.90 : CIP rev. B81-14470

373.2 — SECONDARY SCHOOLS. SPECIAL TYPES AND LEVELS

373.2′22′02541 — Great Britain. Boys' public schools — *Directories — Serials*

Public & preparatory schools yearbook. — 1979. — London : A. & C. Black, 1979. — xxxvi,776p
ISBN 0-7136-1904-x : £4.75 B81-20294

Public & preparatory schools yearbook. — 1981. — London : A. & C. Black, 1981. — xxxviii,778p
ISBN 0-7136-2146-x : Unpriced : CIP rev. B81-03170

373.2′22′0941 — Great Britain. Public schools, *1964-1979*

Rae, John, *1931-*. The public school revolution : Britain's independent schools 1964-1979 / John Rae. — London : Faber, 1981. — 188p ; 23cm
Includes index
ISBN 0-571-11789-9 : £6.50 : CIP rev. B81-23761

373.2′36 — United States. Middle schools

Alexander, William M.. The exemplary middle school / William M. Alexander, Paul S. George. — New York ; London : Holt, Rinehart and Winston, c1981. — xii,356p : plans,forms ; 24cm
Includes bibliographies and index
ISBN 0-03-052301-x : £10.95 B81-25585

373.2′38′0941 — Great Britain. Tertiary colleges, *to 1979*

Tertiary : a radical approach to post-compulsory education / edited by A.B. Cotterell & E.W. Heley. — Cheltenham : Thornes, 1981, c1980. — 154p : ill,1plan,2forms ; 23cm
Includes index
ISBN 0-85950-402-6 : £6.25 : CIP rev. B80-21685

373.2′38′0941 — Great Britain. Young persons, 16-19 years. Education

16-19, education and training / Association of Colleges for Further and Higher Education. — Sheffield : ACGHE, 1981. — 28p ; 21cm
Cover title. — Bibliography: p27-28
£1.00 (pbk) B81-17810

373.2′38′0942 — England. Educational institutions. Students, 16-19 years. Education

16-19 : the tertiary college in practice / Association of Colleges for Further and Higher Education. — Sheffield (Sheffield City Polytechnic, Pond St., Sheffield S1 1WB) : ACFHE, 1981. — 28p ; 21cm
Cover title
Unpriced (pbk) B81-17869

373.2′38′0942 — England. Students, 16-19 years. Education

Education for 16-19 year olds : a review undertaken for the government and the local authority associations. — Stanmore : Department of Education and Science, [1981?]. — 52p : ill ; 30cm
Cover title
Unpriced (pbk) B81-09880

Macfarlane, Neil. Address to the annual general meeting / by Neil Macfarlane ; annual general meeting, Thursday and Friday 26 and 27 February 1981, the Institution of Electrical Engineers, Savoy Place, London WC2. — Sheffield : The Association of Colleges for Further and Higher Education, [1981]. — 11p ; 21cm
£0.75 (unbound) B81-31210

373.2′38′0942 — England. Young persons, 16-19 years. Education — *Proposals*

Association of Colleges for Further and Higher Education. 16-19, towards a tertiary system / Association of Colleges for Further and Higher Education. — Sheffield : The Association, [1980]. — 20p ; 21cm
Cover title. — Text on inside cover
£1.00 (pbk) B81-17923

373.2′5′0722 — England. Comprehensive schools — *Sociological perspectives — Case studies*

Ball, Stephen J.. Beachside Comprehensive : a case-study of secondary schooling / Stephen J. Ball. — Cambridge : Cambridge University Press, 1981. — xxi,328p : ill ; 24cm
Bibliography: p316-323
ISBN 0-521-23238-4 : £20.00 : CIP rev.
ISBN 0-521-29878-4 (pbk) : £6.95 B81-13531

373.2′5′0942 — England. Comprehensive schools. Sixth forms

Naylor, Fred. Crisis in the sixth form / by Fred Naylor. — London : Centre for Policy Studies, 1981. — iv,35leaves ; 32cm
ISBN 0-905880-38-2 (spiral) : £2.00 B81-30659

373.2′5′0942182 — London. Hounslow *(London Borough)*. **Comprehensive schools. Relations with welfare services**

Johnson, Daphne, *1927-*. Secondary schools and the welfare network / by Daphne Johnson and Elizabeth Ransom ... [et al.]. — London : Allen & Unwin, 1980. — xii,207p ; 23cm. — (Unwin education books)
Bibliography: p201-203. — Includes index
ISBN 0-04-371071-9 (cased) : £8.50 : CIP rev.
ISBN 0-04-271072-7 (pbk) : £3.95
Also classified at 373.2′5′0942183 ; 361′.942183 B79-34064

373.2′5′0942183 — London. Hillingdon *(London Borough)*. **Comprehensive schools. Relations with welfare services**

Johnson, Daphne, *1927-*. Secondary schools and the welfare network / by Daphne Johnson and Elizabeth Ransom ... [et al.]. — London : Allen & Unwin, 1980. — xii,207p ; 23cm. — (Unwin education books)
Bibliography: p201-203. — Includes index
ISBN 0-04-371071-9 (cased) : £8.50 : CIP rev.
ISBN 0-04-271072-7 (pbk) : £3.95
Primary classification 373.2′5′0942182 B79-34064

373.3/9 — SECONDARY EDUCATION. HISTORICAL AND GEOGRAPHICAL TREATMENT

373.41 — Great Britain. Secondary education — *Communist Party of Great Britain viewpoints*

Communist Party of Great Britain. Policy statement on secondary education / Communist Party. — [London] : [The Party], [1980]. — 23p ; 21cm
ISBN 0-86224-009-3 (unbound) : £0.40 B81-08976

373.415′09 — Ireland. Secondary education, *1870-1921*

McElligott, T. J.. Secondary education in Ireland : 1870-1921 / T.J. McElligott. — Blackrock : Irish Academic Press, c1981. — x,200p ; 22cm
Bibliography: p191-195. — Includes index
ISBN 0-7165-0074-4 : Unpriced B81-31880

373.418′35′09 — Dublin. Boys' public schools: St. Columba's College, *to 1974*

White, G. K.. A history of St. Columba's College 1843-1974 / G.K. White. — [Dublin] ([c/o Dublin University Press, Dublin 2]) : Old Columban Society, 1980. — 200p, [4]p of plates : ill,1 plan ports ; 25cm
Plans on lining papers. — Includes index
£11.00 B81-31404

373.42 — England. Secondary education, *1944-1980 — Sociological perspectives*

Unpopular education : schooling and social democracy in England since 1944 / Education Group, Centre for Contemporary Cultural Studies. — London : Hutchinson in association with the Centre for Contemporary Cultural Studies, University of Birmingham, 1981. — 307p : ill,2facsims ; 24cm
Includes index
ISBN 0-09-138960-7 (cased) : £12.00 : CIP rev.
ISBN 0-09-138961-5 (pbk) : £4.95 B81-03673

373.421'62 — London. Greenwich *(London Borough).* **Comprehensive schools: Eltham Green School,** *1970-1980*

Dawson, Peter, *1933-.* Making a comprehensive work : the road from Bomb Alley / Peter Dawson. — Oxford : Blackwell, 1981. — 188p ; 22cm
ISBN 0-631-12534-5 (cased) : £9.95
ISBN 0-631-12619-8 (pbk) : £3.95 B81-12257

373.421'64 — London. Southwark *(London Borough).* **Dulwich. Boys' public schools: Dulwich College,** *to 1980*

Hodges, Sheila. God's gift : a living history of Dulwich College / Sheila Hodges. — London : Heinemann, 1981. — xi,310p : ill,coat of arms,facsims,ports ; 23cm
Bibliography: p289-293. — Includes index
ISBN 0-435-32450-0 : £10.50 : CIP rev.
B81-03689

373.421'86 — London. Harrow *(London Borough).* **Boys' public schools: Harrow School** *— Visitors' guides*

Harrow School. Harrow School : guide book / [text by J.S. Golland]. — 2nd ed. — [Harrow-on-the-Hill] ([Harrow School Book Shop,7 High St., Harrow-on-the-Hill, Middx HA1 3HU]) : [The School], 1981. — 24p : ill,1facsim,1plan,ports ; 15x21cm
Cover title. — Previous ed.: 1978. — Text, ill on covers. — Bibliography: p24
Unpriced (pbk) B81-27847

373.421'95 — London. Richmond upon Thames *(London Borough).* **Girls' grammar schools: Twickenham County (Grammar) School for Girls,** *to 1980*

Hawkes, Kitty. The reward of success / by Kitty Hawkes. — [Twickenham] ([87 Cole Park Rd, Twickenham, Middlesex, TW1 1JA]) : [K. Hawkes], c1981. — 44p : ill,ports ; 21cm
Unpriced (pbk) B81-28537

373.422'162 — Surrey. Guildford. Boys' grammar schools: Royal Grammar School *(Guildford), to 1979*

Sturley, D. M.. The Royal Grammar School Guildford / D.M. Sturley. — [Guildford] : [Royal Grammar School], 1980. — xvi,173p,[17]p of plates : ill,maps,plans,ports ; 25cm
Plans, map on lining papers. — Bibliography: p164-167. - Includes index
£7.50 B81-04991

373.422'96 — Berkshire. Eton. Boys' public schools: Eton College, *1440-1880 — Personal observations — Collections*

The **Encouragement** of learning / edited by P.S.H. Lawrence. — Salisbury : Michael Russell, 1980. — xx,212p ; 24cm
Includes index
ISBN 0-85955-078-8 : £6.95 B81-10588

373.422'96 — Berkshire. Eton. Boys' public schools: Eton College, *1850-1919 — Illustrations*

An **Eton** camera 1850-1919 / [compiled by] P.S.H. Lawrence. — Salisbury : Michael Russell, 1980. — 96p : ill,col.plans,ports ; 31cm
Plans on lining papers
ISBN 0-85955-077-x : 6.95 B81-10584

373.424'48'0924 — Hereford and Worcester. Worcester. Boys' public schools: Abberley Hall, *to 1961 — Personal observations*

Ashton, Gilbert. Abberley Hall 1921-1961 : a personal record / by Gilbert Ashton. — Kidderminster : Tomkinson, 1980. — 244p,[9]p of plates : ill,1port ; 22cm
ISBN 0-907083-02-1 : Unpriced B81-07286

373.426'12 — Norfolk. North Walsham. Boys' grammar schools: Paston School, *to 1980*

Paston School. A history of the Paston School / by Charles Forder. — 2nd ed., rev. and enl. — [North Walsham] ([Paston Grammar School, School House, North Walsham, Norfolk]) : [The Governors of Paston School]
Supplementary notes. — 1980. — iv,47p : 1coat of arms ; 22cm
Unpriced (pbk) B81-25212

373.426'44 — Suffolk. Bury St Edmunds. Methodist public schools: Culford School, *to 1980*

Culford School. Culford School : the first hundred years 1881-1981 / F.E. Watson. — Edmunds ([Culford, Bury St. Edmunds, Suffolk IP28 6TX]) : Governors of Culford School, c1980. — 216p : ill,facsim,ports ; 24cm
Ill, map on lining papers. — Bibliography: p191-193. — Includes index
ISBN 0-9507185-0-5 : £5.00 B81-00828

373.426'59 — Cambridgeshire. Cambridge. Choir schools: King's College Choir School, *to 1980*

King's College Choir School. A history of King's College Choir School, Cambridge / R.J. Henderson. — Cambridge (West Rd., Cambridge CB3 9DN) : The School, 1981. — 132p : ill,1facsim,ports ; 21cm
Bibliography: p131-132
ISBN 0-9507528-0-0 : £7.65 B81-40574

373.426'712 — Essex. Felsted. Boys' public schools: Felsted School. Ex-students *— Lists*

Old Felstedian Society. Alumni Felstedienses : January 1908-September 1979 / issued by the Old Felstedian Society. — 10th ed. / edited by E.H. Lockwood. — Felsted ([Felsted School, Felsted, Essex]) : The Society, 1980. — xxx,268p ; 22cm
Previous ed.: 1971
Unpriced (pbk) B81-18719

373.427'31 — Greater Manchester *(Metropolitan County).* **Altrincham. Girls' grammar schools: Altrincham County Grammar School,** *to 1976*

Kendrick, Myra. A short history of Altrincham County Grammar School for Girls 1910 to 1974 / by Myra Kendrick. — [Altrincham] ([Altrincham Grammar School for Girls, Cavendish Road, Bowden, Altrincham, Cheshire WA1 2NL]) : The AGS Old Girls Society, [1976]. — 52p,[4]p of plates : ill,1coat of arms,ports ; 21cm
Unpriced (pbk) B81-37478

373.428'37 — Humberside. Hull. Boys' grammar schools: Hull Grammar School, *to 1979*

The **City** and the school : Hull Grammar School 500th anniversary of endowment 1479-1979. — [Hull] (c/o Fretwells Ltd, Scale La., Hull HU1 1LT]) : [The School], [1979]. — [67]p : ill,coats of arms(some col.),facsims,ports ; 21x30cm
Unpriced (pbk) B81-32375

373.428'63 — Durham *(County).* **Darlington. Girls' boarding schools: Polam Hall,** *to 1980*

Davies, Kathleen. Polam Hall : the story of a school / by Kathleen Davies. — Darlington : Prudhoe, c1981. — v,147p : ill,1facsim,2plans,ports ; 21cm
ISBN 0-9507796-0-1 (pbk) : Unpriced
B81-40880

373.54 — India *(Republic).* **Secondary education**

Verma, Gajendra K.. Illusion and reality in Indian secondary education / Gajendra K. Verma, Christopher Bagley, Kanka Mallick. — Farnborough, Hants. : Saxon House, c1980. — xvii,146p ; 23cm
Bibliography: p139-140. — Includes index
ISBN 0-566-00292-2 : £8.50 : CIP rev.
B79-31667

374 — ADULT AND FURTHER EDUCATION

374 — Adult education

Hostler, John. The aims of adult education / John Hostler. — Manchester : Department of Adult and Higher Education, The University, 1981. — v,77p ; 21cm. — (Manchester monographs ; 17)
Bibliography: p64-77
ISBN 0-903717-26-3 (pbk) : Unpriced
B81-40800

Kreitlow, Burton W.. Examining controversies in adult education / Burton W. Kreitlow and associates. — San Francisco ; London : Jossey-Bass, 1981. — xxiv,290p ; 24cm. — (The AEA handbook series in adult education) (The Jossey-Bass series in higher education)
Bibliography: p257-276. — Includes index
ISBN 0-87589-489-5 : £12.75 B81-26102

Turner, John D.. The meaning of adult education / by J.D. Turner. — Manchester : John Rylands University Library of Manchester, 1980. — p171-193 ; 25cm
£1.30 (pbk) B81-35542

374 — Adult education *— Comparative studies*

Harris, W. J. A.. Comparative adult education : practice, purpose and theory / W.J.A. Harris. — London : Longman, 1980. — ix,198p ; 22cm
Bibliography: p185-194. — Includes index
ISBN 0-582-29510-6 (pbk) : £5.95 : CIP rev.
B80-29458

374 — Adult education *— Sociological perspectives — Conference proceedings*

Ruddock, Ralph. Perspectives on adult education / Ralph Ruddock. — 2nd ed. — [Manchester] : [University of Manchester. Department of Adult and Higher Education], 1980. — ix,85p ; 21cm. — (Manchester monographs ; 2)
Conference papers. — Previous ed.: published as Sociological perspectives on adult education. 1972. — Includes bibliographies
Unpriced (pbk) B81-05079

374 — England. Further education institutions. Curriculum. Information. Dissemination

Loud and clear? : a study of curriculum dissemination in further and higher education / commissioned by F.E.U. from Michael Humphries ... [et al.]. — [London] ([39 York Rd., SE1 7PH]) : [Further Education Curriculum Review and Development Unit], 1980. — 153p : ill,forms ; 30cm. — (Project report / Further Education Curriculum Review and Development Unit ; P.R.3)
Unpriced (pbk)
Also classified at 378'.199 B81-08194

374 — Further education institutions. Examinations. Constructed-answer questions

Ward, Christine. Preparing and using constructed-answer questions / Christine Ward. — Cheltenham : Thornes, 1981. — vii,201p : ill ; 22cm. — (ST(P) handbooks for further education)
Bibliography: p197. — Includes index
ISBN 0-85950-433-6 : £4.95 : CIP rev.
B80-13319

374 — Further education institutions. Examinations. Multiple-choice tests

Ward, Christine. Preparing and using objective questions. — Cheltenham : Thomas, Aug.1981. — [240]p. — (Handbooks for further education series ; 3)
ISBN 0-85950-438-7 : £5.60 : CIP entry
B81-20536

374 — Great Britain. Adult educational guidance services *— Directories*

Directory of educational guidance services for adults / compiled by the Educational Advisory Services Project. — Leicester (19b De Montfort St., Leicester LE1 7GE) : Advisory Council for Adult and Continuing Education, 1981. — [8]p ; 21cm
Unpriced (unbound) B81-37371

374 — Great Britain. Further education institutions. Experimental learning & participatory learning. Projects *— Directories*

Active learning : a register of experimental and participatory learning / commissioned by the F.E.U. from: Institute for Research and Development in Post Compulsory Education, University of Lancaster. — [London] ([Room 5/81, Elizabeth House, 39 York Rd., SE1 7PH]) : [Further Education Curriculum Review and Development Unit]. — (Project report / Further Education Curriculum Review and Development Unit ; P.R.1)
Part 1. — 1979. — 166p ; 30cm
Unpriced (pbk) B81-13277

374 — Great Britain. Further education institutions. Industrial safety

Safety in colleges. — London : National Association of Teachers in Further and Higher Education, 1980. — 56p : 2facsims ; 22cm
Cover title. — Bibliography: p52-56
£0.50 (pbk)
Also classified at 378'.19775 B81-11102

374 — Great Britain. Further education institutions. Students. Academic achievement. Assessment — *For teaching*

Ward, Christine. Designing a scheme of assessment / Christine Ward. — Cheltenham : Thornes, 1980. — vii,159p : ill ; 23cm. — (ST (P) handbooks for further education)
Bibliography: p153. - Includes index
ISBN 0-85950-428-x : £4.95 : CIP rev. B80-13320

374 — Lifelong education

Towards a system of lifelong education : some practical considerations / edited by A.J. Cropley. — [Hamburg] : Unesco Institute for Education ; Oxford : Pergamon, 1980. — xvi,219p : ill ; 22cm. — (Advances in lifelong education ; v.7)
Includes bibliographies and index
ISBN 0-08-026068-3 (cased) : £8.75 : CIP rev.
ISBN 0-08-026067-5 (pbk) : £4.50 B80-12786

374'.0025'41 — Great Britain. Adult education — *Directories* — *Serials*

National Institute of Adult Education (England and Wales). Year book of adult education : the year book of the National Institute of Adult Education (Enland and Wales). — 1980-81. — Leicester : The Institute, 1980. — 128p
ISSN 0084-2601 : £2.75 B81-03572

374'.0025'41 — Great Britain. Further education. Courses — *Directories* — *Serials*

Directory of further education / CRAC. — 1981/82. — Cambridge : Hobsons Press, c1981. — 818p
ISBN 0-86021-413-3 : Unpriced B81-33463

374'.0025'4183 — Dublin *(County)*. **Adult education. Courses** — *Directories* — *Serials*

The **Guide** to evening classes and leisure learning in Dublin (City and County). — 1980-1981. — Dublin : Wolfhound Press, c1980. — 112p
Cover title: Guide to evening classes in Dublin
ISBN 0-905473-54-x : Unpriced B81-18801

374'.0025'421 — London. Further education institutions — *Directories* — *Serials*

Conspectus for ... of further education in the inner and outer London region. — 1978?-. — London (Standard House, 28 Northumberland Ave., WC2N 5AL) : [Civil Service Council for Further Education], 1978?-. — v. ; 30cm
Annual. — Description based on: 1980 issue
ISSN 0260-3853 = Conspectus for ... of further education in the inner and outer London region : Unpriced B81-04492

374'.0025'422 — South-east England. Further education institutions — *Directories* — *Serials*

Conspectus for ... of further education in the southern region. — 1978?-. — London (Standard House, 28 Northumberland Ave., WC2N 5AL) : [Civil Service Council for Further Education], 1978?-. — v. ; 30cm
Annual. — Description based on: 1980 issue
ISSN 0260-3845 = Conspectus for ... of further education in the southern region : Unpriced B81-03287

374'.0068'1 — England. Colleges of further education. Financial management. Regulations — *Proposals*

Financial regulations for institutions of higher and further education in the maintained sector. — London : Chartered Institute of Public Finance and Accountancy, c1981. — iv,17p ; 21cm
ISBN 0-85299-216-5 (pbk) : £4.00
Also classified at 378'.02'0942 B81-12665

374'.0068'3 — Further education institutions. Staff development

Tolley, George. Staff development in further education : retrospect and prospect / by George Tolley. — Sheffield : Association of Colleges for Further and Higher Education, [1981]. — 16p ; 21cm
Paper presented at the Association of Colleges for Further and Higher Education Annual General Meeting, 26-27 Feb. 1981, the Institution of Electrical Engineers, London. — Bibliography: p16
£0.75 (pbk) B81-17808

374'.012 — Adult literacy education — *Serials*

[Newsletter *(National Institute of Adult Education (England and Wales). Adult Literacy & Basic Skills Unit)*]. Newsletter / Adult Literacy & Basic Skills Unit. — No.1 (Apr./May 1980)-. — London ([Kingsbourne House, High Holborn, WC1V 7DA]) : The Unit, 1980-. — v. : ill,ports ; 30cm
Five issues yearly. — Continues: Newsletter (National Institute of Adult Education (England and Wales). Adult Literacy Unit). — Description based on: No.2, June/July 1980
ISSN 0260-5104 = Newsletter — Adult Literacy & Basic Skills Unit (corrected) : Unpriced B81-07694

374'.012 — Adult literacy education. Teaching methods

Working together : an approach to functional literacy / Adult Literacy & Basic Skills Unit. — [2nd ed.]. — London (229 High Holborn, WC1V 7DA) : ALBSU, 1981. — 75p ; 23cm
Previous ed.: published as An Approach to functional literacy. London : Adult Literacy Resource Agency, 1977
ISBN 0-906509-06-8 (pbk) : £0.65 B81-23221

374'.012 — England. Adult literacy education & adult numeracy education. Teaching aids: Worksheets

From wages to Windscale : worksheets and how we have used them / Friends Centre Brighton. — London (Kingsbourne House, 229-231 High Holborn, WC1) : Adult Literacy & Basic Skills Unit, [198]. — [20]p : ill,facsims,forms ; 30cm + 62 worksheets(124p : ill ; 30cm)
Unpriced (pbk) B81-07953

374'.012 — England. Adult literacy education. Organisations: National Institute of Adult Education. *Adult Literacy Unit* — *Serials*

National Institute of Adult Education (England and Wales). *Adult Literacy Unit.* Adult literacy. — 1978/79. — London : H.M.S.O., 1980. — v,69p
ISBN 0-11-270463-8 : £3.25
ISSN 0144-5723 B81-01798

374'.012 — England. Adult literacy education. Organisations: National Institute of Adult Education (England and Wales). *Adult Literacy and Basic Skills Unit.* **Development projects,** *1978-1980*

Adult Literacy Unit development projects 1978-1980 / Adult Literacy & Basic Skills Unit. — London (229 High Holborn WC1V 7DA) : Adult Literacy & Basic Skills Unit, 1981. — 68p : ill ; 30cm
ISBN 0-906509-05-x (pbk) : £1.75 B81-21411

374'.012 — Great Britain. Adult literacy education. Applications of adult educational broadcasting services of British Broadcasting Corporation

Hargreaves, David. Adult literacy and broadcasting : the BBC's experience : a report to the Ford Foundation / David Hargreaves. — London : Pinter, c1980. — 257p : ill,facsims,forms ; 23cm
Bibliography: p257
ISBN 0-903804-68-9 : £10.00 B81-07892

374'.012 — Illiterate adults. Remedial education

Helping adults to learn : common approaches to developing adults' basic skills / Adult Literacy Support Services Fund. — London (252 Western Ave., W3 6XJ) : The Fund, c1980. — 36p ; 30cm
Cover title
ISBN 0-906965-03-9 (pbk) : £1.50 B81-05808

374'.012'0941 — Great Britain. Adult basic education — *Conference proceedings*

Papers on adult basic education / editor: Monica Hayes. — [Southampton] : Adult Education Training and Research Unit, Department of Adult Education, University of Southampton, [1980]. — 94p ; 30cm
Conference papers
ISBN 0-85432-213-2 (spiral) : £2.00 B81-08554

374'.013'0941 — Great Britain. Personnel. Vocational courses. Provision — *Proposals*

Great Britain. *Department of Education and Science.* Continuing education : post-experience vocational provision for those in employment : a paper for discussion / Department of Education & Science. — [Stanmore] ([c/o Publications Despatch Centre, Honeypot La., Canons Park, Stanmore, Middx. HA7 1AZ]) : [The Department], 1980. — 15p ; 30cm
Cover title
Unpriced (spiral) B81-04640

374'.0143 — Great Britain. Youth Opportunities Programme trainees. Social education — *Case studies* — *For supervisors*

Oxford, Alec. Knowing's not enough : five case studies of a social education approach in the Youth Opportunities Programme / by Alec Oxford, Derrick Spragg and Graham Swain. — Leicester (17 Albion St., Leicester LE1 6GD) : National Youth Bureau, 1981. — 5v. ; 32cm
Cover title
ISBN 0-86155-039-0 (pbk) : £2.50 B81-27507

374'.0143'0941 — Great Britain. Further education institutions. Social education

Beyond coping : some approaches to social education / report of a survey commissioned by FEU from the National Institute for Careers Education and Counselling. — Stanmore (Publications Despatch Centre, Honeypot La., Canons Park, Stanmore, Middx) : Further Education Curriculum Review and Development Unit, 1980. — i,98p : ill ; 30cm. — (Project report / Further Education Curriculum Review and Development Unit ; P.R.4)
Bibliography: p93-98
Unpriced (pbk) B81-13279

374'.02 — Adult education. Distance study

Distance teaching for higher and adult education / edited by Anthony Kaye and Greville Rumble. — London : Croom Helm in association with the Open University Press, c1981. — 342p : ill ; 23cm
Includes bibliographies and index
ISBN 0-7099-0468-1 : £15.95 : CIP rev.
Primary classification 378'.17 B80-21690

374'.02 — Adult education. Distance study — *Conference proceedings*

Education of adults at a distance. — London : Kogan Page, Dec.1981. — [276]p
Conference papers
ISBN 0-85038-415-x (pbk) : £9.95 : CIP entry B81-38847

374'.02 — Adult education. Teaching. Theories

Mackie, Karl. The application of learning theory to adult teaching / by Karl Mackie. — Nottingham (14 Shakespeare St, Nottingham) : Department of Adult Education, University of Nottingham, c1981. — 18p ; 21cm. — (Adults : psychological and educational perspectives ; 2)
Bibliography: p17-18
ISBN 0-902031-47-3 (pbk) : £1.25 B81-25241

374'.02 — Further education. Self-teaching

Noble, Pat. Resource-based learning in post compulsory education / by Pat Noble. — London : Kogan Page, 1980. — 192p : ill,plans,1form ; 23cm
Bibliography: p174-184. — Includes index
ISBN 0-85038-335-8 : £10.50 : CIP rev.
Primary classification 378'.17944 B80-11817

374'.02 — Further education. Teaching methods

Yorke, D. M.. Patterns of teaching : a source book for teachers in further education / D.M. Yorke. — London : Council for Educational Technology, 1981. — 155p : ill ; 21cm
Bibliography: p132-148. - Includes index
ISBN 0-86184-030-5 (pbk) : £8.00 B81-17652

374'.02 — Great Britain. Further education institutions. Teaching
Curzon, L. B.. Teaching in further education : an outline of principles and practice / L.B. Curzon. — 2nd ed. — London : Cassell, 1980. — viii,245p : ill ; 22cm
Previous ed.: 1976. — Bibliography: p238-239. - Includes index
ISBN 0-304-30605-3 (pbk) : £4.95 B81-00071

374'.02 — Great Britain. Further education institutions. Teaching aids. Management
Donovan, K. G.. Learning resources in colleges : their organization and management / K.G. Donovan. — London : Council for Educational Technology, 1981. — 1portfolio : ill,forms ; 32cm
ISBN 0-86184-016-x : £22.50 : CIP rev. B81-07443

374'.02 — Great Britain. Rural regions. Adult education. Role of mass media — *Conference proceedings*
Rural adult education workshop report : a report of a workshop convened to discuss the contribution that mass media can make to rural adult education and to rural communities / [written by members of a workshop on rural adult education convened by the National Extension College and the Chelmer Institute of Higher Education]. — Cambridge (18 Brooklands Ave., Cambridge CB2 2HN) : National Extension College, [1980]. — iv,33p ; 30cm. — (National Extension College report. series 2 ; no.5)
ISBN 0-86082-145-5 (pbk) : £1.00 B81-08100

374'.4 — Further education. Distance study. Tutoring
Lewis, Roger. How to tutor in an open learning scheme : group study version. — London : Council for Educational Technology, Sept.1981. — [200]p
ISBN 0-86184-051-8 (unbound) : £10.00 : CIP entry B81-28969

Lewis, Roger. How to tutor in an open learning scheme : self study version. — London : Council for Educational Technology, Sept.1981. — [200]p
ISBN 0-86184-050-x (spiral) : £7.00 : CIP entry B81-28976

374'.842182 — London. Hounslow *(London Borough)*. **Colleges of further education: Maria Grey College,** *to 1976*
Lilley, Irene M.. Maria Grey College 1878-1976 / by Irene M. Lilley. — [Twickenham] : [West London Institute of Higher Education], c1981. — 91[i.e.93]p,[43]p of plates : ill,1facsim,ports ; 22cm
ISBN 0-9507243-0-0 : Unpriced B81-25343

374'.8422792 — Hampshire. Portsmouth. Adult education institutions: New Road Centre *(Portsmouth), to 1980*
Workers' Educational Association. *Southern District*. The first year : New Road Centre Portsmouth report, 1979/80 / WEA Southern District. — [Southampton] ([4 Carlton Cres., Southampton SO9 5UG]) : [W.E.A. Southern District], [1980]. — [22]p ; 21cm
Cover title
Unpriced (pbk) B81-08573

374'.842441 — Hereford and Worcester. Kidderminster. Colleges of further education: Kidderminster College, *to 1979*
Kidderminster College 1879-1979. — [Kidderminster] ([Hoo Rd., Kidderminster, Worcs. DY10 1LX]) : Kidderminster College, 1981. — 43p : ill,ports ; 22cm
Unpriced (pbk) B81-19420

374'.842549 — Leicestershire. Hinckley. Colleges of further education: Hinckley College of Further Education, *to 1980*
Henderson, Evelyn. Milestones of Hinckley 1640-1981 / Evelyn Henderson. — [Hinckley] ([6 West Close, Barbage, Hinckley, Leics.]) : [E. Henderson], [1981]. — 69p : ill,maps,facsims,plans,ports,1geneal.table ; 30cm
Unpriced (pbk) B81-08395

374.9 — ADULT AND FURTHER EDUCATION. HISTORICAL AND GEOGRAPHICAL TREATMENT

374'.94 — Western Europe. Adult education — *Case studies*
Titmus, Colin. Strategies for adult education : practices in Western Europe / Colin Titmus. — Milton Keynes : Open University Press, 1981. — vi,239p ; 22cm
Bibliography: p227-231. — Includes index
ISBN 0-335-10042-2 (cased) : Unpriced : CIP rev.
ISBN 0-335-10032-5 (pbk) : £5.95 B81-13812

374'.94 — Western Europe. Lifelong education
Recurrent education in Western Europe : progress, projections and trends in recurrent, lifelong and continuing education / edited by Manfred Jourdan ; with a foreword by Otto Peters. — Windsor : NFER-Nelson, 1981. — 386p : ill ; 30cm
Bibliography: p344-386
ISBN 0-85633-204-6 (pbk) : £12.50 B81-25402

374'.941 — Great Britain. Adult education
Legge, Derek. The education of adults in Britain. — Milton Keynes : Open University Press, Feb.1982. — [256]p
ISBN 0-335-00267-6 : £12.95 : CIP entry B81-36981

374'.941 — Great Britain. Adult education — *Proposals*
Mee, Graham. Organisation for adult education / Graham Mee. — London : Longman, 1980. — xiv,114p : ill ; 22cm
Bibliography: p110-111. — Includes index
ISBN 0-582-49701-9 (pbk) : £4.95 : CIP rev. B80-25443

374'.941 — Great Britain. Further education institutions. Flexible study courses. Design — *Manuals*
Barnet College of Further Education. FlexiStudy : a manual for local colleges / Barnet College of Further Education. — 2nd ed. — Cambridge ([18 Brooklands Ave., Cambridge]) : National Extension College, c1980. — 29p : ill,forms ; 30cm. — (National Extension College reports. Series 2 ; no.4)
Previous ed.: 1978
ISBN 0-86082-193-5 (pbk) : Unpriced B81-06226

374'.941'0216 — Great Britain. Further education. Courses — *Lists*
Grading of courses : list of courses 1980 / Burnham Further Education Committee. — London (41 Belgrave Sq., SW1 8NZ) : Local Authorities Conditions of Service Advisory Board, c1980. — 87p ; 30cm
Includes index
Unpriced (pbk) B81-12473

374'.9416 — Northern Ireland. Further education. Equality of opportunity — *Inquiry reports*
Formal investigation into further education in Northern Ireland. — [Belfast] ([Lindsay House, Callendar St., Belfast BT1 5DT]) : Equal Opportunities Commission for Northern Ireland, 1981. — 60p,[1]folded leaf ; 22cm
ISBN 0-906646-05-7 (pbk) : £1.00 B81-17864

374'.942 — England. Further education institutions. Students, 16 years. One-year courses
Post-16 one year courses in further education / by Jack Mansell ; annual general meeting, Thursday and Friday 21 and 22 February 1980 the Institution of Electrical Engineers, Savoy Place, London WC2. — Sheffield : The Association of Colleges for Further and Higher Education, [1980]. — 13p ; 21cm
Cover title
£0.75 (pbk) B81-04860

374'.942'0212 — England. Further education — *Statistics — Serials*
Statistics of education. Vol.3, Further education, [England & Wales] / Department of Education and Science. — 1977. — London : H.M.S.O., 1980. — xxii,65p
ISBN 0-11-270504-9 : £6.50 B81-08351

374'.942'05 — England. Adult education — *Serials*
Advisory Council for Adult and Continuing Education. . — 1979-. — London : H.M.S.O., 1980-. — v. ; 25cm
£2.50 B81-08274

Advisory Council for Adult and Continuing Education. Annual report of the Advisory Council for Adult and Continuing Education for the year ending 31st March ... presented to the Secretaries of State for Education and Science and for Wales. — 1980. — London : H.M.S.O., 1981. — 35p
ISBN 0-11-270514-6 : £2.65
ISSN 0260-3306 B81-27921

374'.9421 — Inner London. Further education. Courses — *Directories — Serials*
Signpost : a guide to further and higher education in inner London / ILEA. — 1980-81-. — [London] ([9 Carmelite St., EC4Y 0JE]) : [Careers Service, ILEA], 1980-. — v. ; 22cm
Annual. — Continues: Guide to further and higher education in inner London. — Description based on: 1981-82 issue
£0.50
Also classified at 378.421 B81-25490

374'.9421 — Inner London. Further education institutions. Courses — *Directories — Serials*
A Guide to Further and higher education in inner London. — 1977-1978. — London : ILEA, [1977]. — 216p
ISBN 0-7085-0017-x : £0.15
Also classified at 378.421 B81-29089

A guide to further and higher education in inner London. — 1978-79. — London : ILEA, [1978]. — 232p
ISBN 0-7085-0023-4 : £0.20
Also classified at 378.421 B81-29088

A Guide to further and higher education in inner London. — 1979-80. — London : ILEA, [1979]. — 236p
ISBN 0-7085-0035-8 : £0.25
Also classified at 378.421 B81-29087

374'.942162 — London. Greenwich *(London Borough)*. **Continuing education, Role of Royal Arsenal Co-operative Society,** *1877-1957*
Attfield, John. With light of knowledge. — London : Journeyman Press, May 1981. — [160]p
ISBN 0-904526-67-4 (pbk) : £3.25 : CIP entry B81-07915

374'.9422 — London & Home Counties. Further education institutions. Business Education Council courses, Ordinary National Diploma courses & Technician Education Council courses — *Directories — Serials*
Alternatives to 'A' level : guide to full time B.E.C./T.E.C./O.N.D. courses / London and Home Counties Regional Advisory Council for Technological Education. — 1979/80-. — London (Tavistock House South, Tavistock Sq., WC1H 9LR) : The Council, 1978-. — v. ; 30cm
Issued every two years. — Continues: Guide to O.N.D. courses. — Description based on: 1981/83 issue
ISSN 0261-0582 = Alternatives to 'A' level : £0.50 B81-16734

374'.9422 — Southern England. Further education institutions. Implications of 'Special educational needs'
Southern Regional Council for Further Education. Further to Warnock - : the report of a working party established to examine the implications for the region of the Warnock Report and to make recommendations on policy & action / Southern Regional Council for Further Education. — Reading (26 Bath Rd, Reading, RG1 6NT) : [The Council], 1980. — 34p ; 30cm
Cover title
£1.00 (spiral) B81-23614

374'.9422'05 — London & Home Counties. Further education. Courses — *Directories — Serials*
[Index of courses *(London and Home Counties Regional Advisory Council for Technological Education)*]. Index of courses / London and Home Counties Regional Advisory Council for Technological Education. — 1980/81. — London : The Council, [1980]. — 99p
ISBN 0-85394-079-7 : £1.00 B81-06553

374'.9422'05 — London & Home Counties. Further education. Courses — *Directories — Serials* *continuation*

[Index of courses *(London and Home Counties Regional Advisory Council for Technological Education)*]. Index of courses / London and Home Counties Regional Advisory Council for Technological Education. — 1981/82. — London : The Council, 1981. — [59]p
ISBN 0-85394-087-8 : £1.50 B81-36304

374'.942821 — South Yorkshire *(Metropolitan County)*. **Sheffield. Adult education**

Adult education in Sheffield : a survey of the provision, needs, access and information-giving methods for adult learners / edited by L.E. Watson from the work of Mary E. Jackman ... [et al.]. — [Sheffield] ([Pond St., Sheffield, S1 1WB]) : Sheffield City Polytechnic in association with the Sheffield Working Group on Mature Entry to Education, 1980. — 135p : maps ; 30cm. — (Sheffield papers in education management ; no.10)
ISBN 0-903761-13-0 (pbk) : Unpriced B81-35350

374'.954 — India *(Republic)*. **Adult education. Projects: National Adult Education Programme,** *to 1980*

Non-formal education and the NAEP / edited by A.B. Shah and Susheela Bhan. — Delhi ; Oxford : Oxford University Press, 1980. — viii,245p ; 23cm
Includes index
ISBN 0-19-561256-6 : £6.75 B81-27000

374'.973 — United States. Lifelong education. Programmes. Planning & promotion

Lenz, Elinor. Creating and marketing programs in continuing education / Elinor Lenz. — New York ; London : McGraw-Hill, c1980. — xii,240p : ill,forms ; 24cm. — (McGraw-Hill series in the management and administration of continuing education)
Bibliography: p186. - Includes index
ISBN 0-07-037190-3 : £7.75 B81-06006

375 — CURRICULUM

375 — Schools. Curriculum. Sociopolitical aspects — *Marxist viewpoints*

Apple, Michael W.. Ideology and curriculum / Michael W. Apple. — London : Routledge & Kegan Paul, 1979 (1980 printing). — viii,203p ; 22cm. — (Routledge education books)
Includes index
ISBN 0-7100-0686-1 (pbk) : £3.95 B81-04106

375'.0001 — Schools. Curriculum. Theories

New directions in curriculum studies / edited and introduced by Philip H. Taylor. — Lewes (Falmer House, Barcombe, Lewes, Sussex BN8 5DL) : Falmer Press, 1979. — xii,180p ; 23cm
ISBN 0-905273-07-9 : Unpriced B81-33347

375'.00072 — Educational institutions. Curriculum. Research

Rethinking curriculum studies : a radical approach / edited by Martin Lawn and Len Barton. — London : Croom Helm, c1981. — 253p ; 23cm
Includes bibliographies and index
ISBN 0-7099-0438-x (cased) : £10.95
ISBN 0-7099-1602-7 (pbk) : £6.95 B81-17850

375'.001 — Educational institutions. Curriculum. Design. Applications of systems theory

Romiszowski, A. J.. Designing instructional systems / decision making in course planning and curriculum design ; A.J. Romiszowski. — London : Kogan Page, 1981. — xiv,415p : ill ; 24cm
Bibliography: p399-405. — Includes index
ISBN 0-85038-223-8 : £13.95 B81-27891

375'.001'0941 — Great Britain. Schools. Curriculum. Development

Bantock, G. H.. Dilemmas of the curriculum / G.H. Bantock. — Oxford : Robertson, 1980. — viii,146p ; 23cm. — (Issues and ideas in education series)
Bibliography: p139-142. - Includes index
ISBN 0-85520-310-2 (cased) : £9.95 (pbk) : £3.95 B81-06661

Curriculum change : the lessons of a decade / edited by Maurice Galton ; with contributions by Pat D'Arcy ... [et al.]. — [Leicester] : Leicester University Press, 1980. — 112p ; 22cm
Includes index
ISBN 0-7185-1183-2 (pbk) : £3.95 : CIP rev. B80-05848

375'.001'0973 — United States. Schools. Curriculum. Development

Wiles, Jon. Curriculum development : a guide to practice / Jon Wiles, Joseph Bondi, Jr. — Columbus ; London : Merrill, c1979. — ix,422p : ill,2ports ; 26cm
Includes bibliographies and index
ISBN 0-675-08315-x : £11.25 B81-27764

375'.001'0973 — United States. Schools. Curriculum. Planning

Saylor, J. Galen. Curriculum planning for better teaching and learning. — 4th ed. / J. Galen Saylor, William M. Alexander, Arthur J. Lewis. — New York ; London : Holt, Rinehart and Winston, c1981. — xi,419p : ill ; 24cm
Previous ed.: published as Planning curriculum for schools. 1974. — Includes bibliographies and index
ISBN 0-03-048761-7 : £10.95 B81-13940

375'.006 — Educational institutions. Curriculum. Evaluation — *Manuals*

Harris, Duncan. Evaluation resource pack / Duncan Harris and John Bailey. — London : Council for Educational Technology, 1981. — 1v.(various pagings) : ill,facsims,forms ; 30cm
Includes bibliographies
ISBN 0-86184-032-1 (unbound) : £30.00 B81-16131

375'.006 — Educational institutions. Curriculum. Innovation. Proposals

Anderson, Digby C.. Evaluating curriculum proposals : a critical guide / Digby C. Anderson. — London : Croom Helm, c1981. — 178p : ill ; 23cm. — (Croom Helm curriculum policy and research series)
Bibliography: p175-177. - Includes index
ISBN 0-7099-0248-4 : £10.95 : CIP rev. B80-21687

375'.006 — Schools. Curriculum. Evaluation

Curriculum evaluation : an approach to evaluation. — Milton Keynes : Open University Press
At head of title: The Open University. - Course developed as a joint project of the Schools Council and the Open University
Curriculum evaluation : using the literature / prepared by Kathy Morris for the Course team. — 1981. — 33p : ill ; 30cm. — (P234 ; UL)
ISBN 0-335-10017-1 (pbk) : Unpriced B81-16276

Curriculum in action : an approach to evaluation. — Milton Keynes : Open University Press
At head of title: The Open University. - Course developed as a joint project of the Schools Council and the Open University
Block 1: An approach to evaluation / prepared by Patricia Ashton ... [et al.] for the Course team. — 1980. — 27p : ill ; 21x30cm. — (P234 ; 1)
ISBN 0-335-10010-4 (pbk) : Unpriced B81-16274

Curriculum in action : an approach to evaluation. — Milton Keynes : Open University Press
At head of title: The Open University. - Course developed as a joint project of the Schools Council and the Open University
Block 2: The pupils and the curriculum / prepared by Patricia Ashton ... [et al.] for the Course team. — 1980. — 32,35,36p : ill ; 21x30cm + 1folded sheet(4p ; 20x29cm). — (P234 ; 2)
Contents: Unit 2: What did the pupils actually do? - Unit 3: What were they learning? - Unit 4: How worthwhile was it?
ISBN 0-335-10011-2 (pbk) : Unpriced B81-16275

375'.006'0942 — England. Schools. Curriculum. Evaluation by teachers

Self evaluation and the teacher. — [Hull] (University of Hull [Institute of Education]) : G. Elliott
Pt.1: An annotated bibliography / Gordon Elliott ... [et al.]. — [1980]. — 65p ; 30cm
Includes index
ISBN 0-85958-225-6 (spiral) : Unpriced B81-11829

Self evaluation and the teacher. — [Hull] (University of Hull [Institute of Education]) : G.Elliott
Bibliography: p36-42
Pt.2: A report on current practice 1980 / Gordon Elliott. — [c1981]. — 103p : forms ; 30cm
ISBN 0-85958-226-4 (spiral) : Unpriced B81-11830

375'.006'0994 — Australia. Schools. Curriculum. Evaluation — *For teaching*

Davis, Ed. Teachers as curriculum evaluators / Ed Davis. — Sydney ; London : Allen & Unwin, 1981, c1980. — xiv,175p : ill,forms ; 23cm. — (Classroom and curriculum in Australia ; no.4)
Bibliography: p165-170. - Includes index
ISBN 0-86861-090-9 : Unpriced
ISBN 0-86861-098-4 (pbk) : Unpriced B81-16024

375'.0085'0941 — Great Britain. Educational institutions. Curriculum subjects: Consumer education — *For teaching*

Giordan, Marion. Consumer education : a handbook for teachers / Marion Giordan. — London : Methuen, 1980. — vii,81p ; 21cm
Includes bibliographies and index
ISBN 0-416-72450-7 (cased) : £6.50 : CIP rev.
ISBN 0-416-72460-4 (pbk) : £2.75 B80-25861

375'.00941 — Great Britain. Schools. Curriculum

The Study of the curriculum / edited by Peter Gordon. — London : Batsford Academic and Educational, 1981. — 175p : ill ; 22cm. — (Batsford studies in education)
Bibliography: p163-171. - Includes index
ISBN 0-7134-2109-6 (cased) : £8.95
ISBN 0-7134-2092-8 (pbk) : £4.50 B81-12564

375'.009411 — Scotland. Schools. Curriculum — *Serials*

Great Britain. *Consultative Committee on the Curriculum*. Report / Consultative Committee on the Curriculum. — 4th (1974/80). — Edinburgh : H.M.S.O., 1980. — 80p
ISBN 0-11-491686-1 : £4.10 B81-06140

376 — EDUCATION OF WOMEN

376'.63 — Adolescent girls. Education — *For teaching*

Chandler, E. M.. Educating adolescent girls / E.M. Chandler. — London : Allen & Unwin, 1980. — xv,217p ; 23cm. — (Unwin education books)
Bibliography: p205-211. - Includes index
ISBN 0-04-370096-9 (cased) : £12.00 : CIP rev.
ISBN 0-04-370097-7 (pbk) : £4.95 B80-18208

376'.63 — Great Britain. Girls' public schools — *Directories — Serials*

Girls school yearbook. — 1981. — London : A. & C. Black, 1981. — xxix,446p
ISBN 0-7136-2103-6 : £4.95 : CIP rev.
ISSN 0072-4564 B81-00829

376'.91812 — Western world. Women. Education, *B.C.400-A.D.1900*

Classics in the education of girls and women / [edited] by Shirley Nelson Kersey. — Metuchen ; London : Scarecrow, 1981. — xii,323p ; 23cm
ISBN 0-8108-1354-8 : £12.25 B81-17098

376'.941 — Great Britain. Girls. Education — *Feminist viewpoints*

Stanworth, M. D.. Gender and schooling : a study of sexual divisions in the classroom / by Michelle Stanworth. — London (190 Upper St, N.1) : Women's Research and Resources Centre, 1981. — 58p ; 21cm. — (Explorations in feminism ; no.8)
Bibliography: p58
ISBN 0-905969-07-3 (pbk) : £1.80 B81-17230

376′.941 — Great Britain. Women. Education, *1837-1901*
Burstyn, Joan N.. Victorian education and the ideal of womanhood / Joan N. Burstyn. — London : Croom Helm, c1980. — 185p,[8]p of plates : ill ; 23cm
Bibliography: p173-180. - Includes index
ISBN 0-7099-0139-9 : £11.95 : CIP rev. B80-11376

377 — SCHOOLS AND RELIGION

377′.1 — England. Schools. Morning assembly — *Rites*
Johnson, A. T.. Weekly service for schools : 40 weekly services for the school year / by A.T. Johnson. — [s.l] : [s.n.] ; Stoke-on-Trent (Raymond St., Shelton, Stoke-on-Trent) : Students Bookshops [distributor], [1981]. — 120p ; 22cm
£3.95 (pbk) B81-09550

377′.1 — Great Britain. Middle schools & secondary schools. Morning assembly. Themes — *For schools*
Castle, Tony. Assemble together : a book of assemblies for middle and secondary schools / by Tony Castle. — London : Chapman, 1981. — 244p ; 22cm
List of sound recordings: p238-242. — Includes index
ISBN 0-225-66296-5 (pbk) : Unpriced : CIP rev. B81-08869

377′.1 — Great Britain. Schools. Morning assembly. Activities — *For teaching*
Smith, Harry. Assemblies. — London : Heinemann Educational, Sept.1981. — [256]p
ISBN 0-435-01830-2 (pbk) : £4.95 : CIP entry B81-23783

377′.1 — Great Britain. Schools. Morning assembly. Themes — *For schools*
Bailey, John, *1940 Nov.4-*. Theme work : assembly material for junior, middle and lower secondary schools / John Bailey. — London : Stainer & Bell, 1981. — 229p ; 25cm
Includes index
ISBN 0-85249-465-3 (pbk) : £5.50 B81-23062

377′.1 — Junior schools. Morning assembly. Stories — *Anthologies*
True stories for the junior assembly / edited by V.B. Frampton and J.C. Pedley. — Poole : Blandford, 1980. — xi,116p ; 20cm. — (Blandford school assembly books)
Includes index
ISBN 0-7137-1075-6 : £2.95 B81-10831

377′.1 — Primary schools. Morning assembly. Poems & stories — *Anthologies*
A Second book of 101 school assembly stories / [compiled] by Frank Carr. — London : Foulsham, c1981. — 159p : ill ; 25cm
ISBN 0-572-01017-6 (pbk) : Unpriced B81-18259

377′.1 — Primary schools. Morning assembly — *Prayers & readings*
Purton, Rowland W.. First assemblies / Rowland Purton and Caroline Storey. — [Oxford] : Blackwell, 1981. — ix,383p : ill ; 23cm
Includes index
ISBN 0-631-12783-6 : £5.25 B81-11469

377′.1 — Schools. Morning assembly. Activities. Special themes: Special occasions
Taylor, Dorothy J.. Exploring red letter days / Dorothy J. Taylor. — Guildford : Lutterworth Educational, 1981. — x,150p ; 25cm
Bibliography: p139-147
ISBN 0-7188-2479-2 (pbk) : £3.95 B81-14300

377′.1 — Schools. Morning assembly — *Prayers & readings*
Jones, Glyn, *1915-*. Good morning, children! : assemblies for junior and middle schools / Glyn Jones with contributions by I.P. Jones. — Leeds : E.J. Arnold, c1980. — 288p ; 23cm
ISBN 0-560-00802-3 (pbk) : £5.95 B81-15418

Their words, my thoughts. — Oxford : Oxford University Press, 1981. — 192p : ill(some col.),music ; 21cm
Includes index
ISBN 0-19-917034-7 (pbk) : £2.25 B81-22794

377′.1 — Schools. Morning assembly. Themes
Fisher, Robert, *1943-*. Together today : themes and stories for assembly : Robert Fisher. — London : Evans Brothers, 1981. — 288p : ill ; 23cm
Bibliography: p274-276. — List of music: p277-279
ISBN 0-237-29285-8 : Unpriced B81-23670

377′.1 — Secondary schools. Morning assembly — *Prayers & readings*
More words for worship / compiled and edited by Michael Davis. — London : Edward Arnold, 1980. — vii,176p ; 22cm
Includes index
ISBN 0-7131-0479-1 (pbk) : £3.95 : CIP rev. B80-18209

377′.6′095 — Far East. Christian missions: Overseas Missionary Fellowship. Schools for missionary children, *to 1980*
Miller, Sheila. Pigtails, petticoats and the old school tie / Sheila Miller. — Sevenoaks : O.M.F., 1981. — 224p : ill,2maps,music,1plan,1form,ports ; 21cm
ISBN 0-85363-140-9 (pbk) : Unpriced B81-40444

377′.82 — England. Catholic Church. Public worship in Catholic schools — *Serials*
Schools of prayer. — Issue 1 (Autumn 80)-. — Bedford (St. Mary's RE Centre, 118 Bromham Rd., Bedford MK40 2QR) : Religious Education Service, Diocese of Northampton, 1980-. — v. : ill ; 30cm
Three issues yearly. — Description based on: Issue 2 (Spring 81)
ISSN 0261-5703 = Schools of prayer : £2.00 per year B81-31057

377′.8242 — England. Education. Role of Catholic Church
Signposts and homecomings : the educative task of the Catholic community : a report to the Bishops of England and Wales. — Slough : St. Paul Publications, 1981. — viii,181p ; 23cm
Report commissioned by the Bishops' Conference. — Bibliography: p171-175. — Includes index
ISBN 0-85439-192-4 (pbk) : £3.95 B81-30042

377′.8242′05 — England. Catholic schools — *Directories — Serials*
Catholic education / the Catholic Education Council for England and Wales. — 1980. — London (41, Cromwell Rd., SW7 2DJ) : The Council, 1980. — 201p
£3.40 B81-05225

377′.8242133 — London. Hammersmith and Fulham *(London Borough)*. **Catholic schools,** *ca 1650-1979*
Evinson, Denis. Pope's Corner : an historical survey of the Roman Catholic institutions in the London Borough of Hammersmith and Fulham / by Denis Evinson. — London (c/o Fulham Library, 598 Fulham Rd., SW6 5NX) : Fulham and Hammersmith Historical Society, 1980. — ii,75p,[8]p of plates : ill,ports ; 21cm
Includes index
Unpriced (pbk)
Primary classification 282′.42133 B81-05308

377′.97 — Iraq. Baghdad. Islamic colleges: Madrasas, *ca 1000-ca 1100*
Makdisi, George. The rise of colleges. — Edinburgh : Edinburgh University Press, Dec.1981. — [376]p
ISBN 0-85224-375-8 : £20.00 : CIP entry B81-35895

378 — HIGHER EDUCATION

378 — Great Britain. Higher education institutions. Conferences, open days & visits — *Directories — For sixth formers*
Taylor, Felicity. Going places : how to find out about further education and training / Felicity Taylor. — [5th ed]. — London : Kogan Page, c1981. — 155p ; 22cm
Previous ed.: published as View from the sixth. 1979
ISBN 0-85038-452-4 (cased) : £6.50 : CIP rev.
ISBN 0-85038-463-x (pbk) : £3.50 B81-16387

378 — Higher education
Evans, Norman. The knowledge revolution : making the link between learning and work / Norman Evans. — London : Grant McIntyre, 1981. — ix,182p ; 21cm
Includes index
ISBN 0-86216-055-3 (cased) : £10.95 : CIP rev.
ISBN 0-86216-056-1 (pbk) : £4.50 B81-21540

378 — Higher education — *Comparative studies*
World guide to higher education. — 2nd ed. — Epping : Bowker, Nov.1981. — [362]p
ISBN 0-85935-066-5 : CIP entry B81-30471

378′.0025′171241 — Commonwealth countries. Universities — *Directories — Serials*
Commonwealth universities yearbook. — 1981. — London : Association of Commonwealth Universities, 1981. — 4v.
ISBN 0-85143-066-x : Unpriced
ISSN 0069-7745 B81-29105

378′.006′01 — Commonwealth countries. Universities. Organisations: Association of Commonwealth Universities — *Serials*
Association of Commonwealth Universities.
Annual report of the council together with the accounts of the Association for the year 1 August ... to 31 July ... / the Association of Commonwealth Universities. — 1979-80. — London : The Association, [1980]. — 55p
ISSN 0307-2274 : Unpriced B81-13411

378′.006′041 — Developing countries. Higher education. Development. British organisations: Inter-University Council, *1946-1971*
Maxwell, I. C. M.. Universities in partnership : the Inter-University Council and the growth of higher education in developing countries 1946-70 / I.C.M. Maxwell. — Edinburgh : Scottish Academic, 1980. — xii,480p,[16]p of plates : ill,maps,ports ; 26cm
Bibliography: p473-474. — Includes index
ISBN 0-7073-0270-6 : £15.00 B81-02867

378′.009 — Universities — *History — Serials*
History of universities. — Vol.1-. — Amersham : Avebury Pub. Co., 1981-. — v. ; 23cm
Annual
ISSN 0144-5138 = History of universities : £20.00 B81-38185

378′.009171′241 — Commonwealth countries. Universities — *Serials*
Acumen / Association of Commonwealth Universities. — No.1 (Jan.1978)-. — London : The Association, 1978-. — v. ; 30cm
Irregular
ISSN 0262-0758 = Acumen : Unpriced B81-38509

378′.009172′4 — Developing countries. Universities. Role
Universities, national development and education : a report of a workshop organised by the Department of Education in Developing Countries, February 1980 / edited by Jon Lauglo. — London : University of London Institute of Education, 1981. — 66p ; 30cm
Bibliography: p63-66
ISBN 0-85473-114-8 (spiral) : Unpriced B81-28230

378′.01 — Great Britain. Higher education institutions. Effectiveness. Appraisal
Society for Research into High Education. *Conference (15th : 1979 : Brighton Polytechnic)*. Indicators of performance : papers presented at the fifteenth annual conference of the Society for Research into Higher Education 1979 / editor David Billing. — Guildford : S.R.H.E., 1980. — 195p : ill ; 21cm. — (SRHE proceedings)
Includes bibliographies
ISBN 0-900868-76-7 (pbk) : Unpriced B81-15096

378′.013′02541 — Great Britain. Professional education. Courses — *Directories — Serials*
A Compendium of advanced courses in colleges of further and higher education. — 1981/2. — London : Published on behalf of the Regional Advisory Councils [by the] London and Home Counties Regional Advisory Council for Technological Education, c1981. — 110p
ISBN 0-85394-082-7 : £2.00 B81-15145

378'.01'305 — British qualifications — *Serials*

British qualifications. — 12th ed. (1981). — London : Kogan Paul, Dec.1981. — [880]p
ISBN 0-85038-503-2 : £15.95 : CIP entry
B81-33867

378'.02'0942 — England. Colleges of higher education. Financial management. Regulations — *Proposals*

Financial regulations for institutions of higher and further education in the maintained sector. — London : Chartered Institute of Public Finance and Accountancy, c1981. — iv,17p ; 21cm
ISBN 0-85299-216-5 (pbk) : £4.00
Primary classification 374'.0068'1 B81-12665

378'.02'0973 — United States. Higher education institutions. Financial management

Carter, E. Eugene. College financial management : basics for administrators / E. Eugene Carter. — Lexington : Lexington Books, c1980 ; [Farnborough, Hants.] : Gower [distributor], 1981. — xiv,186p : ill,facsims ; 24cm
Bibliography: p179-184. — Includes index
ISBN 0-669-03700-1 : £12.50 B81-12463

378.1 — HIGHER EDUCATION. ORGANISATION AND ADMINISTRATION

378'.103 — Society. Role of universities

Kallen, Denis. The universities and permanent education : a lost opportunity / Denis Kallen. — [London] : London Association of Comparative Educationists, 1980. — 15p ; 21cm. — (Occasional paper / London Association of Comparative Educationists ; 2)
Unpriced (pbk) B81-18428

378'.103'0973 — United States. Cities. Inner areas. Universities. Role

The **University** and inner city : a redefinition of relationships / edited by W. Franklin Spikes. — Lexington, Mass. : Lexington Books ; Farnborough, Hants. : Gower [distributor], 1980. — ix,191p : ill ; : forms ; 24cm
Includes bibliographies and index
ISBN 0-669-03444-4 : £13.50 B81-06307

378'.1056'0941 — Great Britain. Universities. Students. Admission. Applications — *Manuals — Serials*

How to apply for admission to a university / UCCA. — 1982. — Cheltenham (PO Box 28, Cheltenham, Glos. GL50 1HY) : Universities Central Council on Admissions, c1981. — 261p
ISBN 0-900951-38-9 : Unpriced B81-32696

378'.1057'0941 — Great Britain. Higher education institutions. First degree courses. Entrance requirements for Kent students

Survey of degree course offers / Kent Careers Service. — 3rd ed. (Jan.1978). — Maidstone (Kent County Council, Springfield, Maidstone, Kent ME14 2LJ) : Careers Advisory Section, Kent Education Committee, 1978. — xii,163p
ISBN 0-905155-20-3 : £2.95 B81-06940

A **Survey** of the A-level examination results and the offers made to Kent students who commenced degree courses in the United Kingdom in October 1980 / Careers Service. — 4th ed. — Maidstone : Kent County Council Education Department, 1981. — x,138p ; 21cm
Cover title: 'Grade expectations. — Previous ed.: published as Survey of degree course offers. 1978
ISBN 0-905155-33-5 (pbk) : £4.95 B81-18581

378'.107 — Higher education institutions. Management. Techniques: Linking Elements Concept

Management in institutions of higher learning / edited by Erwin Rausch with Robert A. Laudicina ... [et al.]. — Lexington : Lexington, c1980 ; Farnborough, Hants. : Gower [distributor], 1981. — xiv,301p : ill ; 24cm
Bibliography: p289-290. — Includes index
ISBN 0-669-02856-8 : £16.00 B81-14058

378'.11 — Great Britain. Higher education institutions. Staff development
Eraut, Michael. Training in curriculum development and educational technology in higher education / Michael Eraut, Brendan Connors, Eric Hewton. — Guildford : Society for Research into Higher Education, 1980. — 91p : 1ill ; 21cm. — (Research into higher education monographs ; 41)
Bibliography: p87-91
ISBN 0-900868-77-5 (pbk) : £6.00 B81-13342

378'.154 — England. Polytechnics. Courses — *Directories — Serials*
Polytechnic courses handbook ... England and Wales. — 10th ed. (1981-82). — Bradford, W. Yorks (c/o Country Press, Bradford BD8 8DH) : [s.n.], 1980. — xiv,416p
Published for: the Committee of Directors of Polytechnics
ISBN 0-905564-02-2 : £4.80 B81-04707

Whittington, Eric. Survey of polytechnic courses in England, Wales and N. Ireland / by Eric Whittington ; general editor Brian Heap. — Richmond, Surrey : Careers Consultants, 1979. — 127p ; 22cm
Includes index
ISBN 0-85660-037-7 (pbk) : £2.50 B81-12998

378'.154'0942 — England. Colleges of higher education & polytechnics
Matterson, Alan. Polytechnics and colleges / Alan Matterson. — London : Longman, 1981. — 297p ; 23cm
Bibliography: p275-286. — Includes index
ISBN 0-582-49095-2 : £13.50 B81-08242

378'.155'0941 — Great Britain. Universities. Administration — *Serials*
Great Britain. *University Grants Committee.* University Grants Committee annual survey [for the] academic year. — 1978-79. — London : H.M.S.O., 1980. — 25p. — (Cmnd. ; 8031)
ISBN 0-10-180310-9 : £2.40 B81-01869

378'.1552 — Sandwich courses — *Conference proceedings*
World Conference on Cooperative Education *(1st : 1979 : Brunel University).* Cooperative education today : papers presented at the First World Conference on Cooperative Education, Brunel University, May 1979 / edited by James V. Reed, Keith B. Duncan, Peter J. Vallance. — Windsor : NFER Publishing, c1980. — 210p : ill,forms ; 30cm
ISBN 0-85633-203-8 (pbk) : £15.00 B81-06156

378'.1552'0973 — United States. Higher education institutions. First degree courses. Development
Dressel, Paul L.. Improving degree programs / Paul L. Dressel. — San Francisco ; London : Jossey-Bass, 1980. — xxii,319p : ill ; 24cm. — (The Jossey-Bass series in higher education)
Bibliography: p291-306. — Includes index
ISBN 0-87589-486-0 : £12.75 B81-20776

378'.1553'02541 — Great Britain. Postgraduate courses — *Directories — Serials*
[Graduate studies *(Careers Research and Advisory Centre)*]. Graduate studies / [CRAC]. — 1981/82. — Cambridge : Hobsons Press, c1981. — 1013p
ISBN 0-86021-342-0 : Unpriced
ISSN 0309-0949 B81-33058

378'.1554'0941 — Great Britain. Adult & lifelong education. Role of universities
Rogers, Alan, *1933-.* Knowledge and the people : the role of the university in adult and continuing education : inaugural lecture / given by Alan Rogers. — Londonderry (New University of Ulster, Londonderry) : Institute of Continuing Education, 1980. — 31p ; 21cm
Bibliography: p31
£0.80 (pbk) B81-18303

378'.1554'0942276 — Hampshire. Southampton. Universities: University of Southampton. *Department of Adult Education.* Women students. Courses: Second Chance for Women
Women, class and adult education. — [Southampton] : University of Southampton, Department of Adult Education, [1981?]. — 65p ; 30cm
ISBN 0-85432-219-1 (spiral) : £2.00
B81-25388

378'.166'091724 — Commonwealth developing countries. Professional education. Examinations
Examinations in technical and commercial subjects : problems and prospects for Commonwealth developing countries. — London : Commonwealth Secretariat, Education Division, c1980. — 75p ; 30cm
Bibliography: p75
ISBN 0-85092-185-6 (pbk) : £2.00
Also classified at 607'.36 B81-37497

378'.1664 — Great Britain. Undergraduates. Academic achievement *related to* motivation — *Study examples: University of Birmingham. Undergraduates*
Wa'nkowski, J. A.. Random sample analysis : motives and goals in academic achievment : an epilogue / J.A. Wa'nkowski. — 2nd ed. — Birmingham : University of Birmingham Educational Survey & Counselling Unit, 1978. — 24,40leaves ; 33cm
Previous ed.: 1970. — Bibliography: leaf 24
ISBN 0-7044-0327-7 (spiral) : £1.50
Primary classification 378'.198'019 B81-09447

378'.1664 — Great Britain. Universities: Open University. Students, 16-21 years. Admission. Projects: Younger Students Pilot Scheme. Evaluation
Woodley, Alan. The door stood open / Alan Woodley and Naomi McIntosh. — Lewes : Falmer, 1980. — vii,261p : ill ; 21cm
Subtitle on cover: An evaluation of the Open University Younger Sudents Pilot Scheme
ISBN 0-905273-14-1 (pbk) : Unpriced
B81-04098

378'.1664 — Higher education institutions. Students. Academic achievement. Assessment
Clift, John C.. Assessing students, appraising teaching / John C. Clift and Bradford W. Imrie. — London : Croom Helm, c1981. — 176p : ill,forms ; 23cm. — (New patterns of learning series)
Bibliography: p162-170. — Includes index
ISBN 0-7099-0230-1 : £11.95
Also classified at 378'.199 B81-07061

378'.17 — Great Britain. Higher education institutions. Teaching aids: Games & simulations - *Conference proceedings*
Perspectives on academic gaming. — 6. — London : Kogan Page, July 1981. — [250]p
Conference papers
ISBN 0-85038-422-2 : £12.50 : CIP entry
ISSN 0141-5965 B81-15849

378'.17 — Great Britain. Higher education institutions. Teaching. Explanation
Brown, George. Explaining : studies from the higher education context : final report to SSRC / George Brown. — [Nottingham] : [University of Nottingham], [1981?]. — 119p ; 30cm
Cover title. — Bibliography: p76-80
Unpriced (spiral) B81-20842

378'.17 — Higher education. Distance study
Distance teaching for higher and adult education / edited by Anthony Kaye and Greville Rumble. — London : Croom Helm in association with the Open University Press, c1981. — 342p : ill ; 23cm
Includes bibliographies and index
ISBN 0-7099-0468-1 : £15.95 : CIP rev.
Also classified at 374'.02 B80-21690

378'.17 — Universities. Teaching aids: Simulations. Applications of digital computer systems — *Conference proceedings*
Computer simulation in university teaching : proceedings of the FEoLL Workshop Paderborn, Germany, 28-30 January, 1980 / edited by Detlef Wildenberg. — Amsterdam ; Oxford : North-Holland, 1981. — x,263p : ill ; 23cm
Includes bibliographies
ISBN 0-444-86142-4 : £18.69 B81-15665

378.1'7'02812 — Study techniques — *Manuals — For students in higher education institutions in United States*
Norman, Maxwell H.. How to read and study for success in college / Maxwell H. Norman, Enid S. Kass Norman. — 3rd ed. — New York ; London : Holt, Rinehart and Winston, c1981. — xviii,318p : 1ill,facsims,forms ; 24cm
Previous ed.: 1976. — Form on inside cover
ISBN 0-03-049621-7 (pbk) : £5.50 B81-05112

378'.17'028120973 — Study techniques — *Manuals — For students in American higher education institutions*

Walter, Tim. Student success : how to do better in college and still have time for your friends / Tim Walter, Al Siebert. — 2nd ed. — New York ; London : Holt, Rinehart and Winston, c1981. — xii,165p : ill ; 24cm
Previous ed.: 1976
ISBN 0-03-058184-2 (pbk) : £3.95 B81-22971

378'.17028'120973 — United States. Study techniques — *Manuals — For students in American higher education institutions*

Rubin, Dorothy. Reading and learning power / Dorothy Rubin. — New York : Macmillan ; London : Collier Macmillan, c1980. — xiv,476p : ill,forms ; 26cm
Includes index
ISBN 0-02-404290-0 (pbk) : £5.95
Also classified at 428.4'3 B81-00830

378'.17'02814 — Great Britain. Higher education institutions. Students. Study techniques — *For teaching*

Gibbs, Graham. Teaching students to learn : a student-centred approach / Graham Gibbs. — Milton Keynes : Open University, 1981. — x,111p : ill ; 22cm
Bibliography: p103-106. — Includes index
ISBN 0-335-10043-0 (cased) : Unpriced : CIP rev.
ISBN 0-335-10033-3 (pbk) : £3.95 B81-09462

378'.17'0973 — United States. Higher education institutions. Teaching methods

Milton, Ohmer. On college teaching / Ohmer Milton and associates. — San Francisco ; London : Jossey-Bass, 1978 (1980 printing). — xvii,404p ; 24cm. — (The Jossey-Bass series in social and behavioral science & in higher education)
Bibliography: p383-397. — Includes index
ISBN 0-87589-377-5 : £12.00 B81-16185

378'.173 — Higher education. Teaching aids: Audiovisual equipment & materials

Page, Colin Flood. Technical aids to teaching in higher education. — 3rd ed. / Colin Flood Page & John Kitching. — Guildford : Society for Research into Higher Education, 1981. — 92p ; 22cm. — (Research into higher education monographs ; 15)
Previous ed.: 1976. — Bibliography: p70-92. — Includes index
ISBN 0-900868-49-x (pbk) : £7.40 B81-23435

378'.173'0254 — Europe. Higher education institutions. Audiovisual centres — *Directories*

Dyke, Richard. Audio-visual centres in institutions of higher education in Europe = Centres audio-visuels dans les institutions d'enseignement supérieur en Europe / compiled & edited by Richard Dyke. — [Coventry] ([Coventry CV4 7AL]) : University of Warwick, 1979. — xx,283p : ill,maps ; 27cm
Text in English and French
Unpriced (pbk) B81-27812

378'.17943 — Higher education. Independent learning

Developing student autonomy in learning / edited by David Boud. — London : Kogan Page, 1981. — 222p : ill,1form ; 23cm
Bibliography: p211-216. — Includes index
ISBN 0-85038-416-8 : £12.50 : CIP rev. B81-08852

378'.17944 — Higher education. Self-teaching

Clarke, John. Resource-based learning for higher and continuing education. — London : Croom Helm, Nov.1981. — [176]p
ISBN 0-7099-0705-2 : £11.95 : CIP entry B81-30347

Noble, Pat. Resource-based learning in post compulsory education / by Pat Noble. — London : Kogan Page, 1980. — 192p : ill,plans,1form ; 23cm
Bibliography: p174-184. — Includes index
ISBN 0-85038-335-8 : £10.50 : CIP rev.
Also classified at 374'.02 B80-11817

378'.1795 — Higher education institutions. Teaching methods: Group methods

Bramley, Wyn. Group tutoring : concepts and case studies / Wyn Bramley. — London : Kogan Page, 1979. — 221p : ill ; 22cm
Bibliography: p215-217. — Includes index
ISBN 0-85038-203-3 (cased) : Unpriced
ISBN 0-85038-238-6 (pbk) : £5.95 B81-33248

378'.1796'0941 — Great Britain. Higher education institutions. Lecturing

Brown, George. Learning from lectures : a guide for students and their lecturers / George Brown. — [Nottingham] : University of Nottingham, c1979. — 52leaves : ill ; 30cm
Bibliography: leaf 52
Unpriced (spiral) B81-20843

378'.194'0973 — United States. Universities. Students. Counselling

Hanfmann, Eugenia. Effective therapy for college students / Eugenia Hanfmann. — San Francisco ; London : Jossey-Bass, 1978. — xviii,347p ; 24cm. — (The Jossey-Bass social and behavioral science series)
Bibliography: p339-342. Includes index
ISBN 0-87589-371-6 : £12.00 B81-15108

378'.196 — United States. Universities. Security measures

Powell, John W.. Campus security and law enforcement / John W. Powell. — Boston [Mass.] ; London : Butterworth, c1981. — viii,324p : forms ; 24cm
Bibliography: p269-314. — Includes index
ISBN 0-409-95028-9 : Unpriced B81-33029

378'.19775 — Great Britain. Higher education institutions. Industrial safety

Safety in colleges. — London : National Association of Teachers in Further and Higher Education, 1980. — 56p : 2facsims ; 22cm
Cover title. — Bibliography: p52-56
£0.50 (pbk)
Primary classification 374 B81-11102

378'.19775 — Great Britain. Universities. Physical education & sports. Safety measures

Safety in universities : code of practice : physical education, physical recreation and sport. — [Edinburgh] ([c/o Department of Physical Education, University of Edinburgh, 46 Pleasance, Edinburgh EH8 9TJ]) : British Universities Physical Education Association, 1980. — 219p ; 30cm
Cover title
Unpriced (pbk) B81-12279

378'.198 — Great Britain. Higher education institutions. Students living away from home — *Practical information*

Jones, Graham, *1956-*. Guide to student life away from home / Graham Jones. — Newton Abbot : David & Charles, c1981. — 192p : ill,maps ; 23cm
Includes index
ISBN 0-7153-8211-x : £4.95 : CIP rev. B81-22508

378'.198 — Great Britain. Higher education institutions. Students living away from home. Social life - *Practical information*

Jones, Graham. The TSB guide to student life away from home. — Newton Abbot : David & Charles, Aug.1981. — [192]p
ISBN 0-7153-8234-9 (pbk) : £3.95 : CIP entry B81-17499

378'.198'019 — Great Britain. Undergraduates. Motivation *related to* **academic achievement** — *Study examples: University of Birmingham. Undergraduates*

Wa'nkowski, J. A.. Random sample analysis : motives and goals in academic achievment : an epilogue / J.A. Wa'nkowski. — 2nd ed. — Birmingham : University of Birmingham Educational Survey & Counselling Unit, 1978. — 24,40leaves ; 33cm
Previous ed.: 1970. — Bibliography: leaf 24
ISBN 0-7044-0327-7 (spiral) : £1.50
Also classified at 378'.1664 B81-09447

378'.198'0973 — United States. Higher education institutions. Students. Development — *For counselling*

Morrill, Weston H.. Dimensions of intervention for student development / Weston H. Morrill, James C. Hurst with E.R. Oetting and others. — New York ; Chichester : Wiley, c1980. — xviii,339p : ill,1form ; 24cm. — (Wiley series in counseling and human development)
Includes bibliographies and index
ISBN 0-471-05249-3 : £14.25 B81-09751

378'.1981 — Learning by students in higher education institutions

Wilson, John D.. Student learning in higher education / John D. Wilson. — London : Croom Helm, c1981. — 194p : ill ; 23cm. — (New patterns of learning series)
Bibliography: p173-189. — Includes index
ISBN 0-7099-0238-7 : £10.95 : CIP rev. B81-14895

378'.1981 — United States. Students. Protest movements, *1930-1941*

Brax, Ralph S.. The first student movement : student activism in the United States during the 1930s / Ralph S. Brax. — Port Washington ; London : National University Publications . Kennikat, 1981 — 121p ; 22cm. — (Series in political science)
Bibliography: p110-116. — Includes index
ISBN 0-8046-9266-1 : £14.85 B81-21848

378'.1981 — United States. Universities. Saudi-Arabian students. Social values. Effects of education

Al-Banyan, Abdullah Saleh. Saudi students in the United States : a study of cross cultural education and attitude change / by Abdullah Saleh Al-Banyan. — London : Ithaca Press, 1980. — vi,91p : 1form ; 23cm
Bibliography: p75-80
ISBN 0-903729-61-x : £9.50 B81-04886

378'.1981'0973 — United States. Higher education institutions. Students. Attitudes, *1970-1980*

Levine, Arthur. When dreams and heroes died : a portrait of today's college student / Arthur Levine ; [prepared for the Carnegie Council on Policy Studies in Higher Education]. — San Francisco ; Loddon : Jossey-Bass, 1980. — xix,157p : ill ; 24cm. -- (The Carnegie Council series)
Bibliography: p148-152. — Includes index
ISBN 0-87589-481-x : £11.20 B81-16182

378'.1982 — Great Britain. Higher education institutions. Foreign students — *Inquiry reports*

Overseas students : the dramatic decline : the WUS report. — London (20 Compton Terrace, N1 2UN) : WUS UK, 1981. — 20p : ill ; 30cm
Cover title
Unpriced (pbk) B81-22383

378'.1983'0941956 — Cork *(County).* **Cork** *(City).* **Universities. Colleges. Student unions: University College, Cork.** *Students' Union — Serials*

The Sage : a Students' Union publication. — [No.1]-. — [Cork] ([4 Carrigside, College Rd, Cork]) : Students' Union, [University College, Cork], 1980-. — v. : ill ; 32cm
Monthly
Unpriced B81-11863

378'.199 — England. Higher education institutions. Curriculum. Information. Dissemination

Loud and clear? : a study of curriculum dissemination in further and higher education / commissioned by F.E.U. from Michael Humphries ... [et al.]. — [London] ([39 York Rd., SE1 7PH]) : [Further Education Curriculum Review and Development Unit], 1980. — 153p : ill,forms ; 30cm. — (Project report / Further Education Curriculum Review and Development Unit ; P.R.3)
Unpriced (pbk)
Primary classification 374 B81-08194

378'.199 — Higher education institutions. Courses. Evaluation

Clift, John C.. Assessing students, appraising teaching / John C. Clift and Bradford W. Imrie. — London : Croom Helm, c1981. — 176p : ill,forms ; 23cm. — (New patterns of learning series)
Bibliography: p162-170. — Includes index
ISBN 0-7099-0230-1 : £11.95
Primary classification 378'.1664 B81-07061

378′.199 — Higher education institutions. Curriculum subjects. Influence of feminism

Men's studies modified : the impact of feminism on the academic disciplines / editor Dale Spender. — Oxford : Pergamon, 1981. — xiii,248p ; 26cm. — (The Athene series) (Pergamon international library)
Includes bibliographies
ISBN 0-08-026770-x (cased) : Unpriced : CIP rev.
ISBN 0-08-026117-5 (pbk) : £6.00 B81-07604

378.3 — HIGHER EDUCATION. STUDENT FINANCES

378′.3 — Commonwealth countries. Universities. First degree courses. Students. Financial assistance. Organisations — *Directories — Serials*

Financial aid for first degree study at Commonwealth universities. — 1981-83. — London : Association of Commonwealth Universities, 1981. — 32p
ISBN 0-85143-067-8 : £1.60
ISSN 0260-0749 B81-09072

378′.3 — Greater Manchester *(Metropolitan County)*. **Manchester. Universities: University of Manchester. Students. Grants & awards** — *Serials*

[Grants and awards *(University of Manchester)*]
Grants and awards : fellowships, scholarships, exhibitions and prizes, etc.. — 1977. — Manchester (Manchester M13 9PL) : University of Manchester, 1977. — v. ; 21cm
Issued every 4 years. — Continued by: University awards (University of Manchester). — Only one issue published
Unpriced B81-13694

378′.34 — Great Britain. *Marshall Aid Commemoration Commission — Accounts — Serials*

Great Britain. *Marshall Aid Commemoration Commission.* Marshall Aid Commemoration Commission account. — 1979-80. — London : H.M.S.O., 1981. — 3p
ISBN 0-10-213481-2 : £0.70 B81-16249

378′.34 — Great Britain. *Marshall Aid Commemoration Commission — Serials*

Great Britain. *Marshall Aid Commemoration Commission.* Annual report of the Marshall Aid Commemoration Commission for the year ending 30 September .... — 1980. — London : H.M.S.O., 1980. — 10p. — (Cmnd. ; 8102)
ISBN 0-10-181020-2 : £1.40 B81-06726

378.4/9 — HIGHER EDUCATION. HISTORICAL AND GEOGRAPHICAL TREATMENT

378.4 — Western Europe. Universities. Political aspects — *Conference proceedings*

Universities, politicians and bureaucrats. — Cambridge : Cambridge University Press, Feb.1982. — [510]p
Conference papers
ISBN 0-521-23673-8 : £37.50 : CIP entry B81-36243

378.41 — Great Britain. Higher education

Education beyond school : higher education for a changing context / edited by Norman Evans. — London (39 Great Russell St., WC1B 3PH) : McIntyre, 1980. — 257p ; 20cm
Includes index
ISBN 0-86216-022-7 (cased) : £11.95 : CIP rev.
ISBN 0-86216-023-5 (pbk) : £5.95 B80-19151

378.41 — Great Britain. Universities, *1980-1990*

Murray, Rosemary, *1913-*. Universities after the 70's / [lecture] given by Rosemary Murray on 18th October 1979. — [Coleraine] ([Coleraine, Co. Londonderry, Northern Ireland BT52 1SA]) : New University of Ulster, c1980. — 11p ; 21cm. — (The New University of Ulster Seventh Annual Convocation lecture)
Unpriced (pbk) B81-11825

378.41 — Great Britain. University education

Hinton of Bankside, Christopher Hinton, *Baron.* Some speeches of a chancellor : addresses given by Lord Hinton of Bankside at his installation as Chancellor of the University of Bath on 10th November 1966 and at Degree Congregations 1967-80. — Bath : Bath University Press, c1981. — 63p : 1port ; 30cm
ISBN 0-86197-030-6 (pbk) : Unpriced B81-27709

378.411′01 — Scotland. Universities, *1800-1900 — Philosophical perspectives*

Davie, George Elder. The democratic intellect : Scotland and her universities in the nineteenth century. — Edinburgh : Edinburgh University Press, Dec.1981. — [372]p
ISBN 0-85224-435-5 (pbk) : £15.00 : CIP entry B81-39216

378.412′35′05 — Scotland. Grampian Region. Aberdeen. Universities: University of Aberdeen — *Serials*

University of Aberdeen. Aberdeen University calendar. — 1980-81. — Aberdeen (c/o The Secretary, University Office, Regent Walk, Aberdeen AB9 1FX) : The University, [1980?]. — 618p
ISBN 0-902604-26-0 : £5.00
ISSN 0305-6295 B81-06871

378.412′7′05 — Scotland. Tayside Region. Dundee. Universities: University of Dundee — *Serials*

University of Dundee. Calendar / University of Dundee. — 1980-81. — Dundee (c/o The Secretary, University of Dundee, Dundee DD1 4HN) : The University, [1980?]. — 384p
ISSN 0305-456x : £5.50 B81-03859

378.412′92 — Scotland. Fife Region. St Andrews. Universities: University of St Andrews — *Serials*

University of St Andrews. St Andrews University calendar. — 1980-81. — [Edinburgh] : [Blackwood for] the Senatus Academicus, 1980. — 560p
ISSN 0308-972x : £5.00 B81-06829

378.413′12 — Scotland. Central Region. Stirling. Universities: University of Stirling — *Serials*

University of Stirling. Calendar / University of Stirling. — 1980-81. — Stirling (c/o The Registrar, University of Stirling, Stirling FK9 4LA) : The University, 1980. — vi,516p
Accompanied by a supplement on microfiche (11x15cm)
£4.00 B81-00072

378.413′4′05 — Edinburgh. Universities: University of Edinburgh — *Serials*

University of Edinburgh. Edinburgh University calendar. — 1980-81. — Edinburgh : Published for the University by James Thin, 1980. — 809p
ISSN 0305-6058 : £3.00 B81-03849

378.414′43′05 — Scotland. Strathclyde Region. Glasgow. Universities: University of Glasgow — *Serials*

University of Glasgow. University of Glasgow calendar. — 1980-81. — Glasgow (c/o The Registrar, The University, Glasgow G12 8QQ) : The University, 1980. — iv,693p
ISBN 0-85261-163-3 : £3.50
ISSN 0305-5434 B81-03798

378.414′43′05 — Scotland. Strathclyde Region. Glasgow. Universities: University of Strathclyde — *Serials*

University of Strathclyde. Calendar / University of Strathclyde. — 1980-81. — Glasgow (c/o Secretary to Court, University of Strathclyde, George St., Glasgow G1 1XW) : The University, [1980?]. — 629,xxxiii p
ISBN 0-902013-35-1 : £7.00
ISSN 0305-3180 B81-03801

378.416′27 — Coleraine *(District)*. **Coleraine. Universities: New University of Ulster** — *Serials*

New University of Ulster. Calendar / the New University of Ulster. — 1980-81. — Coleraine : The University, 1980. — 406p
Unpriced B81-03854

378.418′35′05 — Dublin. Universities. Colleges: University College Dublin — *Serials*

University College Dublin. Calendar / University College Dublin. — 1980-1981. — [Dublin] ([Administration Buildings, Belfield, Dublin 4]) : [The College], [1980?]. — 711p in various pagings
ISBN 0-901120-63-4 : £3.50 B81-06488

378.418′35′05 — Dublin. Universities: Trinity College, *Dublin — Serials*

Trinity College *(Dublin)*. Dublin University calendar. — 1980-81. — Dublin (St Stephen's Court, Dublin 2) : Hodges Figgis, 1980. — 934p
£4.00 B81-05224

378.42 — England. Higher education institutions — *Inquiry reports*

Great Britain. *Parliament. House of Commons. Education, Science and Arts Committee.* Fifth report from the Education, Science and Arts Committee, session 1979-80 : the funding and organisation of courses in higher education : together with part of the proceedings of the Committee, the minutes of evidence and appendices. — London : H.M.S.O.. — (HC ; 363-i-xiv)
Vol.1: Report. — [1980]. — cxvip ; 25cm. — (HC ; 787-I)
ISBN 0-10-009349-3 (pbk) : £5.20 B81-20362

Great Britain. *Parliament. House of Commons. Education, Science and Arts Committee.* Fifth report from the Education, Science and Arts Committee, session 1979-80 : the funding and organisation of courses in higher education : together with part of the proceedings of the Committee, the minutes of evidence and appendices. — London : H.M.S.O.. — (HC ; 363-i-xiv)
Vol.2: Minutes of evidence. — [1980]. — viii,533p ; 25cm. — (HC ; 787-II)
ISBN 0-10-009279-9 (pbk) : £12.60 B81-20363

Great Britain. *Parliament. House of Commons. Education, Science and Arts Committee.* Fifth report from the Education Science and Arts Committee, session 1979-80 : the funding and organisation of courses in higher education : together with part of the proceedings of the Committee, the minutes of evidence and appendices. — London : H.M.S.O.. — (HC ; 363-i-xiv)
Vol.3: Appendices. — [1980]. — viii,p234-681 ; 25cm. — (HC ; 787-III)
ISBN 0-10-009359-0 (pbk) : £6.20 B81-20364

378.421 — Inner London. Higher education. Courses — *Directories — Serials*

Signpost : a guide to further and higher education in inner London / ILEA. — 1980-81-. — [London] ([9 Carmelite St., EC4Y 0JE]) : [Careers Service, ILEA], 1980-. — v. ; 22cm
Annual. — Continues: Guide to further and higher education in inner London. — Description based on: 1981-82 issue
£0.50
Primary classification 374′.9421 B81-25490

378.421 — Inner London. Higher education institutions. Courses — *Directories — Serials*

A Guide to Further and higher education in inner London. — 1977-1978. — London : ILEA, [1977]. — 216p
ISBN 0-7085-0017-x : £0.15
Primary classification 374′.9421 B81-29089

A guide to further and higher education in inner London. — 1978-79. — London : ILEA, [1978]. — 232p
ISBN 0-7085-0023-4 : £0.20
Primary classification 374′.9421 B81-29088

A Guide to further and higher education in inner London. — 1979-80. — London : ILEA, [1979]. — 236p
ISBN 0-7085-0035-8 : £0.25
Primary classification 374′.9421 B81-29087

378.421′05 — London. Universities: University of London. External students — *Regulations — Serials*
University of London. Regulations for external students / University of London. — 1980-81. — London : The University (c1980). — 501p in various pagings
ISBN 0-7187-0548-3 : Unpriced B81-06725

378.421′05 — London. Universities: University of London — *Regulations — Serials*
University of London. Regulations for internal students / University of London. — 1980-81. — London : The University, c1980. — 971p in various pagings
ISBN 0-7187-0547-5 : Unpriced B81-06724

378.421′05 — London. Universities: University of London — *Serials*
University of London. Calendar / University of London. — 1980-81. — London : The University, c1980. — xi,504p
ISBN 0-7187-0546-7 : Unpriced
ISSN 0309-4103 B81-03792

378.421′42′05 — London. Camden (London Borough). Universities. Colleges: University College, London — *Serials*
University College, London. Annual report / University College London. — 1979-1980. — London ([Gower St., WC1]) : The College, [1980]. — 163p
Unpriced B81-13309

University College, London. Calendar / University College, London. — 1980-81. — London (Gower St., WC1E 6BT) : The College, [1980?]. — 257p
ISSN 0260-6631 (corrected) : Unpriced B81-04034

378.421′43′09 — London. Islington *(London Borough).* **Universities: City University**
Teague, S. John. The City University : a history / S. John Teague. — London : City University, 1980. — 270p,[17]p of plates : ill,ports ; 22cm
Includes index
ISBN 0-904683-05-2 (cased) : £5.25
ISBN 0-904683-06-0 (pbk) : £3.50 B81-03954

378.421′83 — London. Hillingdon *(London Borough).* **Universities: Brunel University,** *to 1977*
Topping, James. The beginnings of Brunel University : from technical college to university / James Topping. — Oxford : Oxford University Press, 1981. — xii,449p,[16]p of plates : ill,maps,plans ; 22cm
Bibliography: p437-438. — Includes index
ISBN 0-19-920116-1 : £20.00 B81-32381

378.422′56′05 — East Sussex. Brighton. Universities: University of Sussex — *Serials*
Falmer news. — [No.1]-. — Brighton ([c/o Ann Eyles, Falmer House, University of Sussex, Falmer, Brighton BN1 9RH]) : University of Sussex Association, 1976-. — v. : ill ; 30cm
Quarterly. — Description based on: Issue 16 (Mar. 1981)
ISSN 0141-4704 = Falmer news : Unpriced B81-38984

378.422′76′05 — Hampshire. Southampton. Universities: University of Southampton — *Serials*
University of Southampton. Calendar / University of Southampton. — 1980-81. — [Southampton] : Southampton University Press, [1980?]. — 263p
ISBN 0-85432-205-1 : Unpriced
ISSN 0561-0796 B81-04924

378.422′93′05 — Berkshire. Reading. Universities: University of Reading — *Serials*
University of Reading. Calendar / University of Reading. — 1980-81. — Reading : The University, 1980. — 673p in various pagings
ISBN 0-7049-0012-2 : Unpriced
ISSN 0305-473x B81-04668

378.423′56′05 — Devon. Exeter. Universities: University of Exeter — *Serials*
University of Exeter. Calendar / University of Exeter. — 1980-81. — Exeter : The University, c1980. — v,801p
ISBN 0-85989-161-5 : £6.00
ISSN 0305-5388 B81-03564

378.423′93′05 — Avon. Bristol. Universities: University of Bristol — *Serials*
University of BristolCalendar / University of Bristol. — 1980-1981. — Bristol (Senate House, Tyndall Ave., Bristol BS8 1TH) : The University, [1980]. — 427p in various pagings
ISSN 0305-3334 : Unpriced B81-09092

378.424′62 — Staffordshire. Keele. Universities: University of Keele — *Serials*
University of Keele. Calendar / University of Keele. — 1980-81. — Keele : [The University], [1980]. — 300p in various pagings
ISSN 0305-3792 : £0.50 B81-08316

378.424′96′05 — West Midlands *(Metropolitan County).* **Birmingham. Universities: University of Birmingham** — *Serials*
University of Birmingham. Calendar / the University of Birmingham. — 1980-81. — Birmingham : The University, 1980. — 228p
ISSN 0306-0098 : Unpriced B81-03861

378.424′98′05 — West Midlands *(Metropolitan County).* **Coventry. Universities: University of Warwick** — *Serials*
University of Warwick. Calendar / University of Warwick. — 1980-81. — Coventry (c/o Academic Registrar, University of Warwick, Coventry CV4 7AL) : The University, [1980]. — 302p
ISSN 0140-0614 : £4.00 B81-04806

378.425′27′05 — Nottinghamshire. Nottingham. Universities: University of Nottingham — *Serials*
University of Nottingham. The Calendar of the University of Nottingham. — Session 1980-81. — Nottingham : The University, 1980. — 458p
Unpriced B81-04703

378.425′42′05 — Leicestershire. Leicester. Universities: University of Leicester — *Serials*
University of Leicester. Calendar / University of Leicester. — 1980-81. — Leicester : Published for the University by Leicester University Press, [1980?]. — 164p
ISBN 0-7158-9008-5 : Unpriced B81-04838

378.425′47′05 — Leicestershire. Loughborough. Universities: Loughborough University of Technology — *Serials*
Loughborough University of Technology. Calendar / Loughborough University of Technology. — 1980-81. — Loughborough (Loughborough, Leicestershire LE11 3TU) : The University, [1980]. — 173p
Unpriced B81-04436

378.425′74 — Oxfordshire. Oxford. Adult education institutions: Ruskin College. Social life, *1919*
Hodgkinson, George. A shop steward at Oxford 1919-1920 : selected manuscripts from the correspondence of George Hodgkinson, OBE / with an introduction by Royden Harrison ; foreword by Jack (J.L.) Jones ; edited by Richard Storey. — Coventry : University of Warwick Library, 1980. — 29p : 1facsim ; 21cm. — (Occasional publications / University of Warwick Library)
ISBN 0-903220-08-3 (pbk) : £1.00 B81-16085

378.425′74 — Oxfordshire. Oxford. Universities. Colleges: Wolfson College, *to 1979*
Jessup, Frank W.. Wolfson College Oxford : the early years / Frank Jessup. — Oxford : Wolfson College, 1979. — 32p : ill ; 22cm
£0.25 (pbk) B81-05299

378.425′74′05 — Oxfordshire. Oxford. Universities: University of Oxford. Courses — *Regulations — Serials*
University of Oxford. Examination decrees and regulations / University of Oxford. — 1980. — Oxford : Oxford University Press, c1980. — xii,798p
ISBN 0-19-920123-4 : £5.00
ISBN 0-19-951076-8
ISSN 0302-3567 B81-04002

378.425′74′05 — Oxfordshire. Oxford. Universities: University of Oxford — *Regulations — Serials*
University of Oxford. Statutes, decrees and regulations of the University of Oxford. — 1980. — Oxford : Clarendon Press, c1980. — xii,715p
ISBN 0-19-951068-7 : Unpriced B81-11209

378.425′74′09 — Oxfordshire. Oxford. Universities: University of Oxford, *to 1980*
Thackrah, J. R.. The University and colleges of Oxford / by John Richard Thackrah. — Lavenham : Terence Dalton, 1981. — vii,152p : ill,maps ; 24cm
Maps on lining papers. — Bibliography: p148. — Includes index
ISBN 0-86138-002-9 : £7.95 B81-25267

378.426′15′05 — Norfolk. Norwich. Universities: University of East Anglia — *Serials*
University of East Anglia. Calendar / University of East Anglia. — 1980-81. — Norwich (Norwich NR4 7TJ) : The University, [1980?]. — 394p
ISSN 0305-3326 : Unpriced B81-04036

378.426′59 — Cambridgeshire. Cambridge. Universities. Colleges: Newnham College, *to 1971.* **Alumni** — *Biographies*
Newnham College. Newnham College Register 1871-1971. — [2nd ed.]. — [Cambridge] : [The College]
Previous ed.: published in 2 vols. as Register, 1871-1950. 1964
Vol.II: 1924-1950. — [1981]. — ii,399p ; 21cm
Includes index
Unpriced (pbk) B81-33577

378.426′59 — Cambridgeshire. Cambridge. Universities. Colleges: University of Cambridge. *St John's College.* **Buildings,** *to 1885*
Crook, Alec C.. From the Foundation to Gilbert Scott : a history of the buildings of St. John's College, Cambridge 1511 to 1885 / by Alec C. Crook. — Cambridge ([Cambridge, CB2 1TP]) : [The College], 1980. — viii,183p,[12]p of plates : ill(some col.),plans ; 26cm
Includes index
ISBN 0-9501085-3-7 : £12.00 B81-21740

378.426′59 — Cambridgeshire. Cambridge. Universities: University of Cambridge. Intellectual life, *ca 1800-1919*
Rothblatt, Sheldon. The revolution of the dons : Cambridge and society in Victorian England / Sheldon Rothblatt. — Cambridge : Cambridge University Press, 1981, c1968. — 319p ; 23cm
Originally published: London : Faber, 1968. — Bibliography: p286-304. — Includes index
ISBN 0-521-23958-3 (cased) : £22.50 : CIP rev.
ISBN 0-521-28370-1 (pbk) : £6.95 B81-20613

378.426′59′09 — Cambridgeshire. Cambridge. Universities. Colleges: King's College, Cambridge, *1873-1972*
Wilkinson, L. P.. A century of King's 1873-1972 / by L.P. Wilkinson. — Cambridge : King's College, 1980. — xiv,182p ; 24cm
Includes index
ISBN 0-9502450-5-4 : Unpriced B81-05704

378.426′59′09 — Cambridgeshire. Cambridge. Universities: University of Cambridge. Reform, *1800-1860*
Garland, Martha McMackin. Cambridge before Darwin : the ideal of a liberal education, 1800-1860 / Martha McMackin Garland. — Cambridge : Cambridge University Press, 1980. — viii,196p ; 24cm
Bibliography: p184-192. - Includes index
ISBN 0-521-23319-4 : £14.50 B81-03007

378.426′59′0922 — Cambridgeshire. Cambridge. Universities. Colleges: King's College, Cambridge. Graduates, *1873-1979*
Wilkinson, L. P.. Kingsmen of a century : 1873-1972 / by L.P. Wilkinson. — Cambridge : King's College, 1980. — xv,394p ; 24cm
Includes index
ISBN 0-9502450-4-6 : Unpriced B81-05703

378.426′723 — Essex. Colchester. Universities: University of Essex — *Serials*
University of Essex. Calendar / University of Essex. — 1980-81. — Colchester (Wivenhoe Park, Colchester CO4 3SQ) : The University, 1980. — 187p
ISSN 0305-5531 : Unpriced B81-03858

University of Essex. Report of the Vice-chancellor / University of Essex. — 1979-80. — [Colchester] ([Wivenhoe Park, Colchester, Essex]) : [The University], [1980]. — 2v.
Unpriced B81-13195

378.427′32 — Greater Manchester *(Metropolitan County).* Salford. Universities: University of Salford — *Serials*

University of Salford. The University of Salford calendar. — 1980-81. — [Salford] ([c/o The Registrar, Room 102, The University of Salford, Salford M5 4WT]) : [The University], [1980]. — 473p
Unpriced B81-03848

378.427′33′05 — Greater Manchester *(Metropolitan County).* Manchester. Universities: University of Manchester — *Serials*

University of Manchester. Calendar / University of Manchester. — 1980-1981. — Manchester (Oxford Rd., Manchester M13 9PL) : The University, 1980. — xvi,392p
ISBN 0-906107-15-6 : Unpriced
ISSN 0305-6066 B81-04839

378.427′53′05 — Merseyside *(Metropolitan County).* Liverpool. Universities: University of Liverpool — *Serials*

University of Liverpool. Calendar / The University of Liverpool. — 1980-81. — Liverpool (P.O. Box 147, Liverpool L69 3BX) : The University, 1980. — xii,719p
ISBN 0-906370-07-8 : Unpriced
ISSN 0305-9227 B81-09118

378.427′53′09 — Merseyside *(Metropolitan County).* Liverpool. Universities: University of Liverpool, *to 1981*

Kelly, Thomas, *1909-*. For advancement of learning : the University of Liverpool 1881-1981 / by Thomas Kelly ; with a postscript by R.F. Whelan. — Liverpool : Liverpool University Press, 1981. — xv,560p : ill,maps(some col.),1facsim,ports ; 24cm
Maps on lining papers. — Bibliography: p461-517. — Includes index
ISBN 0-85323-214-8 (cased) : £18.00 : CIP rev.
ISBN 0-85323-304-7 (pbk) : £12.50 B81-04363

378.427′53′09 — Merseyside *(Metropolitan County).* Liverpool. Unversities: University of Liverpool, *to 1981*

Redbrick university : a portrait of University College, Liverpool, and the University of Liverpool 1881-1981. — [Liverpool] ([P.O. Box 147, Liverpool L67 3BX]) : [University of Liverpool], [1981]. — [68]p : ill,ports ; 22cm
Accompanies an exhibition held at Senate House, University of Liverpool 11th May-3rd July 1981. — Cover title. — Includes index
Unpriced (pbk) B81-26653

378.428′17 — West Yorkshire *(Metropolitan County).* Bradford. Universities: University of Bradford — *Serials*

University of Bradford. Calendar / University of Bradford. — 1980-81. — Bradford (The Registrar and Secretary, University of Bradford, Bradford West Yorkshire, BD7 1DP) : The University, [1980]. — iv, 669p
ISSN 0306-7459 : £5.00 B81-07309

378.428′19 — West Yorkshire *(Metropolitan County).* Leeds. Universities: University of Leeds — *Serials*

University of Leeds. The Calendar / the University of Leeds. Part 1. — 1980-81. — Leeds : The University, 1980. — 307p
Unpriced B81-29432

378.428′21 — South Yorkshire *(Metropolitan County).* Sheffield. Universities: University of Sheffield — *Serials*

University of Sheffield. Calendar / the University of Sheffield. — 1980-1981. — Sheffield : The University, [1980]. — vi,519p
ISSN 0307-6202 : Unpriced B81-29408

378.428′37′05 — Humberside. Hull. Universities: University of Hull — *Serials*

University of Hull. Calendar / the University of Hull. — 1980-81. — [Hull] : [The University], [1980]. — 579p in various pagings
ISBN 0-85958-306-6 : Unpriced
ISSN 0307-6210 B81-09054

378.428′65 — Durham *(County).* Durham. Universities: University of Durham — *Serials*

University of Durham. Calendar / University of Durham. — 1980-81. — Durham : The University, [1980]. — 1136p
ISSN 0305-3903 : £5.00 B81-03855

378.428′76′05 — Tyne and Wear *(Metropolitan County).* Newcastle upon Tyne. Universities: University of Newcastle upon Tyne — *Serials*

University of Newcastle upon Tyne. Calendar / University of Newcastle upon Tyne. — 1980-81. — Newcastle upon Tyne : The University, [1980]. — vii,983p
ISBN 0-7017-0025-4 : £6.50
ISSN 0545-8005 B81-03751

378.429′05 — Wales. Universities: University of Wales — *Serials*

University of Wales[Calendar for the academic year *(University of Wales)*]. Calendar for the academic year / University of Wales. — 1980-81. — [Cardiff] ([University Registry, Cathays Park, Cardiff CF1 3NS]) : [The University], [1980?]. — xvi,594p
Unpriced B81-09199

378.52 — Japan. Higher education. Cultural aspects, *1880-1945*

Roden, Donald. Schooldays in Imperial Japan : a study in the culture of a student elite / Donald Roden. — Berkeley ; London : University of California Press, c1980. — xiii,300p : ill,ports ; 24cm
Bibliography: p270-287. - Includes index
ISBN 0-520-03910-6 : £14.75 B81-15975

378.73 — United States. Higher education

The **Carnegie** Council on Policy Studies in Higher Education : a summary of reports and recommendations. — San Francisco ; London : Jossey-Bass, 1980. — xv,489p : ill ; 26cm
Includes index
ISBN 0-87589-474-7 : £20.00 B81-23517

378.73 — United States. Higher education institutions

Chickering, Arthur W.. The modern American college / Arthur W. Chickering and associates ; foreword by Nevitt Sanford. — San Francisco ; London : Jossey-Bass, 1981. — li,810p : ill ; 26cm. — (The Jossey-Bass series in higher education)
Includes bibliographies and index
ISBN 0-87589-466-6 : £23.95 B81-23518

378.73 — United States. Higher education institutions, *1970-1979*

Stadtman, Verne A.. Academic adaptations : higher education prepares for the 1980s and 1990s / Verne A. Stadtman. — San Francisco ; London : Jossey-Bass, 1980. — xvi,214p : ill ; 24cm. — (The Carnegie Council series)
Bibliography: p204-207. — Includes index
ISBN 0-87589-480-1 : £12.75 B81-16432

378.73 — United States. Higher education institutions. Administration

Jedamus, Paul. Improving academic management / Paul Jedamus, Marvin W. Peterson and associates. — San Francisco ; London : Jossey-Bass, 1980. — xxii,679p : ill ; 26cm. — (The Jossey-Bass series in higher education)
Includes bibliographies and index
ISBN 0-87589-477-1 : Unpriced B81-16609

Karol, Nathaniel H.. Managing the higher education enterprise / Nathaniel H. Karol, Sigmund G. Ginsburg. — New York ; Chichester : Wiley, c1980. — xiv,269p ; 24cm
Bibliography: p247-263. - Includes index
ISBN 0-471-05022-9 : £12.30 B81-06280

378.749′67′0922 — New Jersey. Princeton. Universities: College of New Jersey. Graduates, *1769-1775 — Biographies*

Harrison, Richard A.. Princetonians 1769-1775 : a biographical dictionary / by Richard A. Harrison. — Princeton ; Guildford : Princeton University Press, 1980. — xxxvi,585p : ports ; 25cm
Includes index
ISBN 0-691-04675-1 : £22.30 B81-26315

379.1/2 — PUBLIC EDUCATION

379.1′1′09417 — Ireland *(Republic).* Education. Expenditure by government

Tussing, A. Dale. Irish educational expenditures - past, present and future / A. Dale Tussing. — Dublin : Economic and Social Research Institute, c1978. — 187p : ill ; 25cm. — (Paper / Economic and Social Research Institute ; no.92)
Bibliography: p186-187
ISBN 0-7070-0012-2 (pbk) : £4.50 (Special rate for students £2.25) B81-29126

379.1′14 — Great Britain. Further education institutions. Full-time courses. Costs *compared with* costs of distance-study courses

Birch, Derek W.. Costing open learning in further education / Derek W. Birch, Robert E. Cuthbert. — London : Council for Educational Technology, 1981. — 65p ; 21cm
Includes bibliographies
ISBN 0-86184-033-x (pbk) : £5.50 : CIP rev. B81-12311

379.1′18′0942 — England. Higher education. Finance

Springett, J. A.. The finance of higher education / by T.A. Springett. — Sheffield : Association of Colleges for Further and Higher Education, [1981]. — 13p ; 21cm
Paper presented at the Association of Colleges for Further and Higher Education Meeting, Bournemouth, June 12th and 13th, 1980
£0.75 (pbk) B81-17813

379.1′18′0973 — United States. Higher education. Costs

Bowen, Howard R.. The costs of higher education : how much do colleges and universities spend per student and how much should they spend? / Howard R. Bowen. — San Francisco ; London : Jossey-Bass, 1980. — xxiii,287p : ill ; 24cm. — (The Carnegie Council series)
Bibliography: p267-279. — Includes index
ISBN 0-87589-485-2 : £12.75 B81-23523

379.1′21′068 — Educational institutions. Resources. Management

Collier, Gerald. Teaching & learning support services. — London : Council for Educational Technology
1: Higher education. — Nov.1981. — [40]p
ISBN 0-86184-037-2 (pbk) : £4.50 : CIP entry B81-35872

Collier, Gerald. Teaching & learning support services. — London : Council for Educational Technology
2: Further education. — Nov.1981. — [40]p
ISBN 0-86184-038-0 (pbk) : £4.50 : CIP entry B81-35871

Collier, Gerald. Teaching & learning support services. — London : Council for Educational Technology
Secondary, comprehensive, middle and primary schools. — Nov.1981. — [48]p
ISBN 0-86184-039-9 (pbk) : £4.50 : CIP entry B81-35870

379.1′22′09416 — Northern Ireland. Education and library boards — *Accounts — Serials*

[Statements and summary of the Education and Library Boards′ accounts for period 1 April ... to 31 March ... *(Great Britain. Department of Education for Northern Ireland)*]. Statements and summary of the Education and Library Boards′ accounts for period 1 April ... to 31 March ... / Department of Education for Northern Ireland. — 1977 to 1978-. — Belfast : H.M.S.O., 1979-. — v. ; 25cm
Continues: Summary of Education and Library Boards′ accounts for period 1 April ... to 31 March ... (Great Britain. Department of Education for Northern Ireland). — From 1978 to 1979, includes: Report of the Comptroller and Auditor-General for Northern Ireland
ISSN 0260-5228 = Statements and summary of the Education and Library Boards′ accounts for period 1 April ... to 31 March ... - Department of Education for Northern Ireland : £1.50 B81-04813

379.1'22'09416 — Northern Ireland. Education and library boards — *Accounts — Serials*
continuation
[Statements and summary of the Education and Library Boards' accounts for period 1 April ... to 31 March ... *(Great Britain. Department of Education for Northern Ireland)*]. Statements and summary of the Education and Library Board's accounts for period 1 April .. to 31 March ... / Department of Education for Northern Ireland. — 1979 to 1980. — Belfast : H.M.S.O., 1981. — 95p. — (Cmnd. ; 8143)
ISBN 0-10-181430-5 : £6.10
ISSN 0260-5228 B81-31887

379.1'5 — Education. Evaluation
Holt, Maurice. Evaluating the evaluators. — London : Hodder and Stoughton, Nov.1981. — [160]p. — (Studies in teaching and learning)
ISBN 0-340-27245-7 (pbk) : £2.95 : CIP entry B81-30248

379.1'5 — England. Education. Accountability
Becker, Tony. Policies for educational accountability. — London : Heinemann Educational, Sept.1981. — [196]p. — (Organization in schools series)
ISBN 0-435-80060-4 : £8.50 : CIP entry B81-22636

379.1'5 — England. Secondary education. Administration. Political aspects, *1944-1970*
Fenwick, I. G. K.. The comprehensive school 1944-1970 : the politics of secondary school reorganisation / I.G.K. Fenwick. — London : Methuen, 1976 (1980 [printing]). — 187p ; 22cm. — (Education paperbacks)
Bibliography: p164-165. — Includes index
ISBN 0-416-73490-1 (pbk) : £4.95 : CIP rev. B79-34068

379.1'5 — Great Britain. Educational institutions. Art teachers. Accountability
The **Aesthetic** imperative. — Oxford : Pergamon, Sept.1981. — [187]p. — (Curriculum issues in arts education ; v.2)
ISBN 0-08-026766-1 : £8.71 : CIP entry B81-20566

379.1'5 — South-west England. Schools. Inspection. Arnold, Edward Penrose — *Biographies*
Hopkinson, David. Edward Penrose Arnold : a Victorian family portrait / by David Hopkinson ; with a foreword by A.L. Rowse. — Penzance (5 Chapel St., Penzance, Cornwall) : Alison Hodge, 1981. — 112p : ill,ports ; 22cm
Bibliography: p109-110. — Includes index
ISBN 0-906720-02-8 : £4.95 B81-33090

379.1'5'0941 — Great Britain. Education. Administration
Fenwick, Keith. The government of education in Britain / Keith Fenwick, Peter McBride. — Oxford : Robertson, 1981. — xii,260p : ill ; 23cm
Bibliography: p238-247. — Includes index
ISBN 0-85520-255-6 (cased) : £15.00
ISBN 0-85520-254-8 (pbk) : £5.50 B81-35300

379.1'5'0942 — England. Schools. Accountability. Research projects: Great Britain. *Social Science Research Council. Cambridge Accountability Project*
The **Self-accounting** school. — London : Grant McIntyre, Nov.1981. — [250]p
ISBN 0-86216-074-x (cased) : £12.95 : CIP entry
ISBN 0-86216-077-4 (pbk) : £5.95 B81-32588

379.1'5'0966 — West Africa. Education. Administration
Edem, D. A.. Introduction to educational administration in Nigeria. — Chichester : Wiley, Dec.1981. — [160]p. — (Education in Africa)
ISBN 0-471-27983-8 (cased) : £11.00 : CIP entry
ISBN 0-471-27984-6 (pbk) : £4.00 B81-31368

379.1'53 — England. Education. Innovation. Role of local education authority advisory services
Bolam, R.. Local education authority advisers and the mechanisms of innovation / by R. Bolam, G. Smith and H. Canter. — Windsor : NFER Publishing, 1978. — viii,247p ; 22cm
Bibliography: p241-247
ISBN 0-85633-175-9 (pbk) : £7.95 B81-40315

379.1'531'0941 — Great Britain. Schools. Governors. Role
Brooksbank, Kenneth. School governors : a handbook of guidance for governors of county and voluntary schools / written by Kenneth Brooksbank and James Revell on behalf of the Society of Education Officers. — Harlow : Councils and Education, 1981. — 112p : ill ; 22cm
Bibliography: p105-106. - Includes index
ISBN 0-900313-16-1 (pbk) : £2.95 B81-18788

Wragg, E. C.. A handbook for school governors / E.C. Wragg and J.A. Partington. — London : Methuen, 1980. — viii,220p : ill,facsims,forms ; 21cm
Bibliography: p211-215. — Includes index
ISBN 0-416-71590-7 (cased) : £6.00 : CIP rev.
ISBN 0-416-71600-8 (pbk) : £2.75 B80-04732

379.1'54 — Education. Evaluation - *Serials*
Evaluation in education. — Vol.4. — Oxford : Pergamon, June 1981. — [361]p
ISBN 0-08-028404-3 : £27.00 : CIP entry B81-16386

379.1'54 — Education. Planning & evaluation. Applications of social indicators
Johnstone, James N.. Indicators of education systems / James N. Johnstone. — London : Kogan Page, 1981. — xvii,317p : ill,1map ; 22cm
At head of title: International Institute for Educational Planning. — Bibliography: p302-310. — Includes index
ISBN 0-85038-447-8 (pbk) : £10.95 B81-26345

379.1'54 — Great Britain. Educational institutions. Accountability
Calling education to account. — London : Heinemann Educational, Dec.1981. — [384]p
ISBN 0-435-80629-7 (pbk) : £6.50 : CIP entry B81-38292

379.1'54 — United States. Education. Evaluation — *Manuals*
Educational evaluation methodology : the state of the art / edited by Ronald A. Berk. — Baltimore ; London : John Hopkins University Press, c1981. — x,168p : ill ; 24cm
Includes bibliographies
ISBN 0-8018-2518-0 : £10.50 B81-39841

379.1'54 — United States. Rural regions. Schools. Innovation. Projects. Evaluation — *Case studies*
Abt, Wendy Peter. Reforming schools problems in program implementation and evaluation / Wendy Peter Abt and Jay Magidson ; with the assistance of David Hoaglin and David Napior ; foreword by Lavnor F. Carter. — Beverly Hills ; London : Sage, c1980. — 230p : ill ; 22cm. — (Contemporary evaluation research ; no.4)
Bibliography: p223-228
ISBN 0-8039-1459-8 (cased) : Unpriced (pbk) : Unpriced B81-15751

379.1'54 — United States. Schools. Efficiency. Improvement
Neale, Daniel C.. Strategies for school improvement : cooperative planning and organization development / Daniel C. Neale, William J. Bailey, Billy E. Ross. — Boston [Mass.] ; London : Allyn and Bacon, c1981. — xii,288p : ill,forms ; 25cm
Bibliography: p273-279. - Includes index
ISBN 0-205-06950-9 : £12.75 B81-03725

379.1'54'09411 — Scotland. Education. Planning. Reform — *Proposals*
Reid, R. W. Kenneth. Scottish education : a way forward : a review of educational planning mechanisms in Scotland / by R.W. Ken Reid and Don Skinner. — [Scotland?] : Scottish Education Policy Review Association, [1980?]. — 54p ; 30cm
Cover title
Unpriced (pbk) B81-09947

379'24 — Literacy. Role of music
Wisbey, Audrey S.. Learning through music / Audrey S. Wisbey. — Lancaster : MTP, 1980. — vii,92p : ill,music ; 22cm
ISBN 0-85200-251-3 (pbk) : £2.95 : CIP rev. B80-00654

379.3 — PRIVATE EDUCATION AND THE STATE

379.3'42 — Scotland. Strathclyde Region. Eastwood Park. Catholic secondary schools. Planning. Participation of public
McKechin, W. J.. A school in Eastwood Park : a case study in local authority decision making and public participation / W.J. McKechin. — Paisley (High St., Paisley PA1 2BE) : Local Government Unit, Paisley College of Technology, 1979. — 103p ; 30cm. — (Working paper / Paisley College of Technology Local Government Unit ; no.9)
£1.25 (spiral) B81-05587

379.4/9 — EDUCATION AND THE STATE. HISTORICAL AND GEOGRAPHICAL TREATMENT

379.41 — Great Britain. Education. Policies of government
Convocation lectures [given at] the New University of Ulster / by Ralf Dahrendorf, Sir Edward Britton, Lord Justice Megaw. — [Coleraine] : New University of Ulster, 1979. — 51p ; 22cm
Unpriced (pbk)
Primary classification 327 B81-14141

379.41 — Great Britain. Young persons. Education. Effects of social policies of government — *Marxist viwpoints*
Blind alley : youth in a crisis of capital / edited by Mike Cole and Bob Skelton. — Ormskirk : Hesketh, 1980. — vii,97p ; 21cm
ISBN 0-905777-12-3 (pbk) : £3.80
Also classified at 331.3'4'0941 B81-09805

379.42 — England. Further education & higher education. Policies of local authorities
Stevenson, John, *1927-*. Education in a cold climate / by John Stevenson ; summer meeting, Thursday and Friday, 11 and 12 June 1981, Scarborough. — Sheffield : The Association of Colleges for Further and Higher Education, [1981]. — 6p ; 21cm
£0.75 (unbound) B81-31209

379.73 — United States. Education. Policies — *Forecasts*
Future trends in education policy / edited by Jane Newitt. — Lexington, Mass. : Lexington Books, 1979 (1980 [printing]) ; [Farnborough, Hants.] : Gower Publishing [Distributor]. — xiii,142p : ill ; 24cm
Includes bibliographies
ISBN 0-669-02713-8 : £11.75 B81-18387

380.1 — TRADE

380.1 — Commerce
Hall, L.. Secretarial and administrative practice / L. Hall. — 4th ed. — Plymouth : Macdonald and Evans, 1981. — viii,288p : ill ; 18cm. — (The M. & E. handbook series)
Previous ed.: 1978. — Includes index
ISBN 0-7121-1968-x (pbk) : £4.25 B81-17356

Swift, Moira K.. Commerce. — 5th ed. / Moira K. Swift, Thelma B. Holden, Ronald Warson. — London : Edward Arnold, 1980. — 308p : ill,1map,facsims,forms ; 22cm. — (Basic business studies)
Previous ed.: 1973. — Includes index
ISBN 0-7131-0491-0 (pbk) : Unpriced : CIP rev. B80-34836

380.1 — Commerce — *For schools*
Whitcomb, Alan. Comprehensive commerce / Alan Whitcomb. — Walton-on-Thames : Nelson, 1980. — 189p : ill(some col.),col.maps,facsims,forms ; 25cm. — (Nelson business studies series)
Includes index
ISBN 0-17-438176-x (pbk) : £2.95 B81-07362

380.1 — Commerce — *For West African students*
Anderson, David J.. Commerce / David J. Anderson. — London : Macmillan, 1981. — vii,96p : ill ; 22cm. — (School certificate revision course)
ISBN 0-333-29166-2 (pbk) : £0.86 B81-40572

380.1 — Marketing. Economic aspects

Leake, Andrew. Market analysis. — London : Macmillan, July 1981. — [48]p
ISBN 0-333-27987-5 (pbk) : £1.25 : CIP entry
B81-14941

Stone, Merlin, *1948-*. Marketing and economics / Merlin Stone. — London : Macmillan, 1980. — vii,181p : ill ; 23cm
Bibliography: p175-176. — Includes index
ISBN 0-333-22348-9 : £15.00 : CIP rev.
B80-18210

380.1'025 — Industries & trades — *Directories — Serials*

Kelly's manufacturers and merchants directory. — 1980-81. — East Grinstead : Kelly's Directories, c1980. — xx,2292p
ISBN 0-610-00527-8 : Unpriced B81-03748

380.1'025'41 — Great Britain. Industries & trades — *Directories — For European Community countries — Serials*

Kelly's British industry & services in the Common Market. — 1981. — East Grinstead : Kelly's Directories, c1980. — 1272p in various pagings
ISBN 0-610-00537-5 : Unpriced B81-09053

380.1'025'41 — Great Britain. Industries & trades — *Directories — Serials*

British commercial classified business guide. — 1979/80 ed. — London (Oxford Circus House, 245 Oxford St., W1R 1LF) : United Publications, [1979?]. — x,536p
£5.50 B81-00073

British commercial classified business guide. — 1980/81 ed. — London (245 Oxford St., W1R 1LF) : United Publications, [1980?]. — 308p
Unpriced B81-35447

Business mans guides. — 1978/79. — Nuneaton (Liverpool Victoria Offices, St. Clares 24A, Coton Rd., Nuneaton, Warwickshire) : Faystrete, [1979?]. — 409p in varous pagings
ISSN 0144-7351 : Unpriced B81-06826

Kemps directory. — 1980/81 ed. — London : Kemps Group, c1980. — 3v
ISBN 0-905255-86-0 : Unpriced B81-00074

Key British enterprises / compiled by Dun & Bradstreet Directories Division. — 1981. — London : Dun & Bradstreet, 1981. — 2v.
Spine title: KBE
ISSN 0142-5048 : Unpriced B81-27925

Kompass [United Kingdom]. — 19th ed. — East Grinstead : Kompass, c1981. — 2v
Also entitled: UK Kompass register
ISBN 0-900505-86-9 : Unpriced B81-30763

Sell's directory. — 1981-. — Epsom : Sell's Publications in association with the Institute of Purchasing Management, 1981-. — v. : ill ; 31cm
Annual. — Merger of: Sell's directory of products & services. Alphabetical ; and, Sell's directory of products & services. Classified
ISSN 0261-5584 = Sell's directory (corrected) : £20.00 B81-34027

Stubbs directory. — 1981. — London : Dun & Bradstreet, c1981. — [1940]p in various pagings
ISSN 0143-098x : Unpriced B81-29437

Telekompass : a section of U.K. Kompass. — 1981-. — East Grinstead : Kompass, 1981-. — v. ; 30cm
Annual. — Continues: Dial industry
ISSN 0261-4030 = Telekompass : £8.00
B81-30755

Town & country trades guide. — 1980/81 ed. — London : BMR United Publications, [1981?]. — xii,393p
£5.50 B81-29081

380.1'025'411 — Scotland. Industries & trades — *Directories — Serials*

County trades finder : incorporating Town & district advertiser. Section 1, Northern. — Ed. 1978-79-. — [Northampton] ([Carlyle House, 198 Kettering Rd, Northampton NN1 4BR]) : Phillodge, [1979]-. — v. : ill ; 28cm
Annual. — Continues in part: County trades finder. — Absorbed in part: Town & district advertiser, 1979
ISSN 0144-8390 = County trades finder. Section 1. Northern : £2.75
Primary classification 380.1'025'427 B81-04948

Kelly's directory of British industry & services in .... Vol.1, Scotland & N. Ireland. — 1st ed. (1980/81)-. — East Grinstead : Kelly's Directories Ltd., 1980-. — v. ; 30cm
Annual
ISSN 0260-633x = Kelly's directory of British industry & services in ... . Vol.1. Scotland & N. Ireland : £9.00
Also classified at 380.1'025'416 B81-12740

Scottish national register of classified trades. — 1981. — Epsom : Sell's Publications, [1981]. — xxi,330,24p
ISBN 0-85499-608-7 : Unpriced
ISSN 0080-8148 B81-19406

UK Kompass management register. 1, The regional section for Scotland, Wales and Northern Ireland. — 1981/82-. — East Grinstead : Kompass, c1981-. — v. ; 30cm
Annual. — Continues: Company information for Scotland, Wales and N. Ireland
ISSN 0261-5959 = UK Kompass management register. 1. The regional section for Scotland, Wales and Northern Ireland : £15.00 per issue (£12.00 per issue if 7 vols purchased)
Also classified at 380.1'025'411 ; 380.1'025'429
B81-32281

UK Kompass management register. 1, The regional section for Scotland, Wales and Northern Ireland. — 1981/82-. — East Grinstead : Kompass, c1981-. — v. ; 30cm
Annual. — Continues: Company information for Scotland, Wales and N. Ireland
ISSN 0261-5959 = UK Kompass management register. 1. The regional section for Scotland, Wales and Northern Ireland : £15.00 per issue (£12.00 per issue if 7 vols purchased)
Primary classification 380.1'025'411 B81-32281

380.1'025'4121 — Scotland. Grampian Region. Industries & trades — *Directories — Serials*

Grampian directory : offshore directory, manufacturers & processors directory / NESDA. — 1981-. — Aberdeen (57 Queens Rd, Aberdeen AB1 6YP) : North East Scotland Development Authority, [1981]-. — v. : ill ; 30cm
Annual. — Merger of: Offshore directory ; and, Manufacturers & processors directory (North East Scotland Development Authority)
ISSN 0261-572x = Grampian directory : £1.00
B81-31899

380.1'025'41443 — Scotland. Strathclyde Region. Glasgow. Industries & trades — *Directories — Serials*

Glasgow Chamber of Commerce and Manufactures regional directory. — 1981. — London : Published on behalf of the Chamber of Commerce by Kemps, c1981. — 465p in various pagings
ISBN 0-905255-94-1 : Unpriced
ISSN 0260-0641 B81-19407

380.1'025'416 — Northern Ireland. Industries & trades — *Directories — Serials*

Kelly's directory of British industry & services in .... Vol.1, Scotland & N. Ireland. — 1st ed. (1980/81)-. — East Grinstead : Kelly's Directories Ltd., 1980-. — v. ; 30cm
Annual
ISSN 0260-633x = Kelly's directory of British industry & services in ... . Vol.1. Scotland & N. Ireland : £9.00
Primary classification 380.1'025'411 B81-12740

Northern Ireland Chamber of Commerce and Industry. Year book / Northern Ireland Chamber of Commerce and Industry. — 1980. — Belfast (22, Great Victoria St., Belfast BT2 7BJ) : The Chamber, [1980?]. — 127p
Unpriced B81-06828

380.1'025'417 — Ireland *(Republic)*. **Industries & trades** — *Directories — Serials*

Marketing guide to Ireland / Dun & Bradstreet. — 1st ed. (1979)-. — [Dublin] ([Holbrook House, Holles St., Dublin 2]) : Dun & Bradstreet-Stubbs, 1979-. — v. ; 28cm
Description based on: 2nd ed. (1980/81)
Unpriced B81-35964

380.1'025'421 — London. Industries & trades — *Directories — Serials*

Kelly's directory of British industry & services in .... Vol.7, Greater London. — 1st ed. (1980/81)-. — v. ; 30cm
Annual
ISSN 0260-6070 = Kelly's directory of British industry & services in ... . Vol.7. Greater London : £9.00 B81-04812

UK Kompass management register. 7, The regional section for Greater London. — 1981/82-. — East Grinstead : Kompass, c1981-. — v. ; 30cm
Annual. — Continues: Company information for Greater London
ISSN 0261-6017 = UK Kompass management register. 7. The regional section for Greater London : £15.00 per issue (£12.00 per issue if 7 vols purchased) B81-32287

380.1'025'421 — London. Industries & trades. Greek firms — *Diretories — Serials*

Aspis : the classified Greek commercial directory. — 1980-. — London (89 Tottenham Lane, N8 9BE) : Aspis Publications, 1980-. — v. : ill ; 30cm
Annual. — Text in English and Greek
ISSN 0260-2474 = Aspis : Unpriced
B81-04946

380.1'025'42132 — London. Westminster *(London Borough)*. **Industries & trades** — *Directories — Serials*

City of Westminster Chamber of Commerce. City of Westminster Chamber of Commerce directory. — 1981 ed. — London : Published on behalf of the Chamber by Kemps, c1981. — 278p in various pagings
ISBN 0-86259-007-8 : Unpriced B81-31002

380.1'025'42144 — London. Hackney *(London Borough)*. **Industries & trades** — *Directories — Serials*

Hackney and District Chamber of Commerce. Members' handbook of trade directory / Hackney and District Chamber of Commerce. — 1981. — London (229, Balham High Rd, SW17) : Raymond West, [1981?]. — 68p
Cover title: Handbook & directory (Hackney and District Chamber of Commerce)
Unpriced
Also classified at 380.1'025'4215 B81-24687

380.1'025'4215 — London. Tower Hamlets *(London Borough)*. **Industries & trades** — *Directories — Serials*

Hackney and District Chamber of Commerce. Members' handbook of trade directory / Hackney and District Chamber of Commerce. — 1981. — London (229, Balham High Rd, SW17) : Raymond West, [1981?]. — 68p
Cover title: Handbook & directory (Hackney and District Chamber of Commerce)
Unpriced
Primary classification 380.1'025'42144
B81-24687

380.1'025'422 — Central Southern & South-east England. Industries & trades — *Directories — Serials*

Kelly's directory of British industry & services in .... Vol.6, Southern England. — 1st ed. (1980/81)-. — East Grinstead : Kelly's Directories Ltd., 1980-. — v. ; 30cm
Annual
ISSN 0260-6062 = Kelly's directory of British industry & services in ... Vol.6 Southern England : £9.00 B81-08319

380.1'025'422 — Central Southern England. Industries & trades — *Directories — Serials*

Dorset/Hants, incorporating Isle-of-Wight : [area trades directory]. — 1980/81. — Harrow : Artrad, [1980?]. — 461p in various pagings
£5.50 B81-04694

380.1'025'422 — Southern England. Industries & trades — *Directories — Serials*

County trades finder : incorporating Town & district advertiser ; Section 3, Southern. — Ed. 1978-79-. — [Northampton] ([Carlyle House, 198 Kettering Rd, Northampton NN1 4BR]) : Phillodge, [1979]-. — v. : ill ; 28cm
Annual. — Continues in part: County trades finder. — Absorbed in part: Town & district advertiser, 1979
£2.75 B81-05534

UK Kompass management register. 6, The regional section for Southern England : covering the counties of Avon, Berkshire, Channel Islands, Cornwall, Devon, Dorset, Gloucestershire, Hampshire, Isle of Wight, Kent, Somerset, Surrey, East Sussex, West Sussex, Wiltshire. — 1981/82-. — East Grinstead : Kompass, c1981-. — v. ; 30cm
Annual. — Continues: Company information for Southern England
ISSN 0261-6009 = UK Kompass management register. 6. The regional section for Southern England : £15.00 per issue (£12.00 per issue if 7 vols purchased) B81-32286

380.1'025'42212 — Surrey. Sunbury-on-Thames. Industries & trades — *Directories — Serials*

[Year Book *(Sunbury & District Chamber of Commerce)*]. Year book / Sunbury & District Chamber of Commerce. — Ashford Common (Rowlands Buildings, 373 Staines Rd West, Ashford Common, Middlesex) : The Chamber, 1981. — 28p
Unpriced B81-09707

380.1'025'4229 — East Berkshire. Industries & trades — *Directories — Serials*

South Bucks & East Berks Chamber of Commerce & Industry. South Bucks & East Berks Chamber of Commerce & Industry directory. — 1979-. — Birmingham : Kemps Group in association with the Chamber of Commerce, 1979-. — v. : ill ; 30cm
Annual. — Text in English, indexes also in French, German, Spanish and Arabic. — Continues: Slough & District Chamber of Commerce & Industry. Slough & District Chamber of Commerce & Industry directory. — Description based on: 1980
Unpriced
Also classified at 380.1'025'4259 B81-07193

South Bucks & East Berks Chamber of Commerce & Industry. South Bucks & East Berks Chamber of Commerce & Industry directory. — 1981. — London : Kemps Group in association with the Chamber of Commerce, c1981. — 232p in various pagings
ISBN 0-905255-96-8 : Unpriced
ISSN 0260-7220
Also classified at 380.1'025'42598 B81-19410

380.1'025'423 — South-west England. Industries & trades — *Directories — Serials*

Kelly's directory of British industry & services in .... Vol.8, The South West & Wales. — 1st ed. (1980/81). — East Grinstead : Kelly's Directories Ltd., 1980-. — v. ; 30cm
Annual
ISSN 0260-616x = Kelly's directory of British industry & services in ... Vol.8. The South West & Wales : £9.00
Also classified at 380.1'025'429 B81-19703

380.1'025'42313 — Wiltshire. Swindon. Industries & trades — *Directories — Serials*

Swindon Chamber of Commerce. Yearbook and list of members / Swindon Chamber of Commerce. — 1981/82-. — Swindon (1 Commercial Rd, Swindon SN1 5NE, [Wiltshire]) : The Chamber, [1981]-. — v. : ill ; 22cm
Annual
ISSN 0262-1088 = Yearbook and list of members - Swindon Chamber of Commerce : £2.00 (free to Chamber members) B81-39738

380.1'025'424 — England. Midlands. Industries & trades — *Directories — Serials*

County trades finder : incorporating Town & district advertiser. Section 2, Central. — Ed. 1978-1979-. — [Northampton] ([Carlyle House, 198 Kettering Rd Northampton NN1 4BR]) : Phillodge, [1979]-. — v. : ill ; 28cm
Annual. — Continues in part: County trades finder. — Absorbed in part: Town & district advertiser, 1979
ISSN 0260-079x = County trades finder. Section 2. Central : £2.75
Also classified at 380.1'025'429 B81-05536

Kelly's directory of British industry & services in .... Vol.4, The Midlands. — 1st ed. (1980/81)-. — East Grinstead : Kelly's Directories Ltd., 1980-. — v. ; 30cm
Annual
ISSN 0260-6194 = Kelly's directory of British industry & services in ... . Vol.4. The Midlands : £9.00 B81-12741

UK Kompass management register. 4, The regional section for the Midlands : covering the counties of Derbyshire, Hereford & Worcester, Leicestershire, Northamptonshire, Nottinghamshire, Salop, Staffordshire, Warwickshire, West Midlands. — 1981/82-. — East Grinstead : Kompass, c1981-. — v. ; 30cm
Annual. — Continues: Company information for the Midlands
ISSN 0261-5983 = UK Kompass management register. 4. The regional section for the Midlands : £15.00 per issue (£12.00 per issue if 7 vols purchased) B81-32284

380.1'025'424 — England. West Midlands. Industries & trades — *Directories — Serials*

Birmingham & West Midland chambers of commerce directory. — 1981. — Birmingham : Industrial Newspapers, [1981]. — 668p
ISBN 0-86108-022-x : Unpriced B81-16256

380.1'025'42498 — West Midlands *(Metropolitan County)*. **Coventry. Industries & trades** — *Directories — Serials*

Coventry Chamber of Commerce and Industry. Coventry Chamber of Commerce & Industry directory. — 1980-81. — Birmingham : Published on behalf of the Chamber by Kemps, c1980. — 124p
ISBN 0-905255-90-9 : Unpriced
ISSN 0140-8186 B81-07222

380.1'025'425 — England. East Midlands. Industries & trades — *Directories — Serials*

Kelly's directory of British industry & services in .... Vol.5, Eastern England. — 1st ed. (1980/81)-. — East Grinstead : Kelly's Directories Ltd., 1980-. — v. ; 30cm
Annual
ISSN 0260-6054 = Kelly's directory of British industry & services in ... Vol.5 . Eastern England : £9.00
Primary classification 380.1'025'426 B81-16953

UK Kompass management register. 5, The regional section for Eastern England : covering the counties of Bedfordshire, Buckinghamshire, Cambridgeshire, Essex, Hertfordshire, Norfolk, Oxfordshire, Suffolk. — 1981/82-. — East Grinstead : Kompass, c1981-. — v. ; 30cm
Annual. — Continues: Company information for Eastern England
ISSN 0261-5991 = UK Kompass management register. 5. The regional section for Eastern England : £15.00 per issue (£12.00 per issue if 7 vols purchased)
Also classified at 380.1'025'426 B81-32285

380.1'025'4259 — South Buckinghamshire. Industries & trades — *Directories — Serials*

South Bucks & East Berks Chamber of Commerce & Industry. South Bucks & East Berks Chamber of Commerce & Industry directory. — 1979-. — Birmingham : Kemps Group in association with the Chamber of Commerce, 1979-. — v. : ill ; 30cm
Annual. — Text in English, indexes also in French, German, Spanish and Arabic. — Continues: Slough & District Chamber of Commerce & Industry. Slough & District Chamber of Commerce & Industry directory. — Description based on: 1980
Unpriced
Primary classification 380.1'025'4229 B81-07193

380.1'025'42598 — South Buckinghamshire. Industries & trades — *Directories — Serials*

South Bucks & East Berks Chamber of Commerce & Industry. South Bucks & East Berks Chamber of Commerce & Industry directory. — 1981. — London : Kemps Group in association with the Chamber of Commerce, c1981. — 232p in various pagings
ISBN 0-905255-96-8 : Unpriced
ISSN 0260-7220
Primary classification 380.1'025'4229 B81-19410

380.1'025'426 — East Anglia. Industries & trades — *Directories — Serials*

Kelly's directory of British industry & services in .... Vol.5, Eastern England. — 1st ed. (1980/81)-. — East Grinstead : Kelly's Directories Ltd., 1980-. — v. ; 30cm
Annual
ISSN 0260-6054 = Kelly's directory of British industry & services in ... Vol.5 . Eastern England : £9.00
Also classified at 380.1'025'425 B81-16953

UK Kompass management register. 5, The regional section for Eastern England : covering the counties of Bedfordshire, Buckinghamshire, Cambridgeshire, Essex, Hertfordshire, Norfolk, Oxfordshire, Suffolk. — 1981/82-. — East Grinstead : Kompass, c1981-. — v. ; 30cm
Annual. — Continues: Company information for Eastern England
ISSN 0261-5991 = UK Kompass management register. 5. The regional section for Eastern England : £15.00 per issue (£12.00 per issue if 7 vols purchased)
Primary classification 380.1'025'425 B81-32285

380.1'025'4261 — Norfolk. Industries & trades — *Directories — Serials*

Norwich and Norfolk Chamber of Commerce and Industry. Norwich & Norfolk, Gt Yarmouth & Lowestoft Chambers of Commerce directory. — 1981/82-. — Norwich (112 Barrack St., Norwich, Norfolk NR3 1UB) : Norwich and Norfolk Chamber of Commerce and Industry, [1981]-. — v. : ill,maps ; 30cm
Annual. — Continues: Norwich Incorporated Chambers of Commerce. Norwich, Great Yarmouth & Lowestoft Chambers of Commerce directory
ISSN 0261-880x = Norwich & Norfolk, Gt Yarmouth & Lowestoft Chambers of Commerce directory : Unpriced
Also classified at 380.1'025'42641 B81-35119

380.1'025'42641 — Suffolk. Lowestoft. Industries & trades — *Directories — Serials*

Norwich and Norfolk Chamber of Commerce and Industry. Norwich & Norfolk, Gt Yarmouth & Lowestoft Chambers of Commerce directory. — 1981/82-. — Norwich (112 Barrack St., Norwich, Norfolk NR3 1UB) : Norwich and Norfolk Chamber of Commerce and Industry, [1981]-. — v. : ill,maps ; 30cm
Annual. — Continues: Norwich Incorporated Chambers of Commerce. Norwich, Great Yarmouth & Lowestoft Chambers of Commerce directory
ISSN 0261-880x = Norwich & Norfolk, Gt Yarmouth & Lowestoft Chambers of Commerce directory : Unpriced
Primary classification 380.1'025'4261 B81-35119

380.1'025'427 — North-west England. Industries & trades — *Directories — Serials*

Kelly's directory of British industry & services in .... Vol.3, The North West. — 1st ed. (1980/81)-. — East Grinstead : Kelly's Directories Ltd., 1980-. — v. ; 30cm
Annual
ISSN 0260-6178 = Kelly's directory of British industry & services in ... Vol.3. The North West : £9.00 B81-06525

North West England industrial classified directory. — 1981-82 ed.. — Birmingham : Published on behalf of the North West Industrial Development Association by Kemps, c1981. — 275p in various pagings
ISBN 0-86259-008-6 : Unpriced
ISSN 0260-0587 B81-33287

380.1'025'427 — North-west England. Industries & trades — *Directories — Serials* *continuation*

UK Kompass management register. 3, The regional section for North-West England : covering the counties of Cheshire, Greater Manchester, Isle of Man, Lancashire, Merseyside. — 1981/82-. — East Grinstead : Kompass, c1981-. — v. ; 30cm
Annual. — Continues: Company information for North-West England
ISSN 0261-5975 = UK Kompass management register. 3. The regional section for North-West England : £15.00 per issue (£12.00 per issue if 7 vols purchased) B81-32283

380.1'025'427 — Northern England. Industries & trades — *Directories — Serials*

County trades finder : incorporating Town & district advertiser. Section 1, Northern. — Ed. 1978-79-. — [Northampton] ([Carlyle House, 198 Kettering Rd, Northampton NN1 4BR]) : Phillodge, [1979]-. — v. : ill ; 28cm
Annual. — Continues in part: County trades finder. — Absorbed in part: Town & district advertiser, 1979
ISSN 0144-8390 = County trades finder. Section 1. Northern : £2.75
Also classified at 380.1'025'411 B81-04948

Kelly's directory of British industry & services in .... Vol.2, Northern England. — 1st ed. (1980/81)-. — East Grinstead : Kelly's Directories Ltd., 1980-. — v. ; 30cm
Annual
ISSN 0260-6151 = Kelly's directory of British industry & services in ... . Vol.2. Northern England : £9.00 B81-12739

380.1'025'4273 — Greater Manchester *(Metropolitan County).* **Industries & trades** — *Directories — Serials*

Manchester Chamber of Commerce and Industry. Manchester Chamber of Commerce and Industry regional directory. — 1981-82. — Birmingham : Published on behalf of the Chamber by Kemps, c1981. — 359p in various pagings
ISBN 0-86259-006-x : Unpriced
ISSN 0140-1068 B81-29403

380.1'025'4278 — Cumbria. Industries & trades — *Directories — Serials*

Cumbria guide, industry and commerce. — 8th ed. (1980/1981). — Stockport (Borough Chambers, St. Petersgate, Stockport SK1 1EB) : G.W. Foster Associates, [1981]. — 210p
ISSN 0309-8338 : Unpriced B81-10243

380.1'025'428 — North-east England. Industries & trades — *Directories — Serials*

UK Kompass management register. 2, The regional section for North and North-East England : covering the counties of Cleveland, Cumbria, Durham, Humberside, Lincolnshire, Northumberland, Tyne and Wear, North Yorkshire. — 1981/82-. — East Grinstead : Kompass, c1981-. — v. ; 30cm
Annual. — Continues: Company information for North and North-East England
ISSN 0261-5967 = UK Kompass management register. 2. The regional section for North and North-East England : £15.00 per issue (£12.00 per issue if 7 vols purchased) B81-32282

380.1'025'42819 — West Yorkshire *(Metropolitan County).* **Leeds. Industries & trades. Organisations: Leeds Chamber of Commerce and Industry** — *Directories — Serials*

Leeds Chamber of Commerce and Industry. Leeds Chamber of Commerce and Industry directory. — 1978-. — Macclesfield (Charles Roe House, Chestergate, Macclesfield, Cheshire SK11 7DZ) : Published on behalf of the Chamber by McMillan Martin Ltd., 1978-. — v. : ill ; 30cm
Annual. — Continues: Leeds Chamber of Commerce and Industry. Classified trade directory of members, with list of trade names and consular list. — Description based on: 1981 issue
ISSN 0261-3832 = Leeds Chamber of Commerce and Industry directory : Unpriced B81-32275

380.1'025'429 — Wales. Industries & trades — *Directories — Serials*

Available from Wales : the directory of the Federation of Welsh Chambers of Commerce (Incorporated) : incorporating lists of members of the Cardiff, Neath, Newport, Port Talbot and Swansea Chambers of Commerce. — 1979 ed.-. — Birmingham : Published on behalf of the Federation by Kemps, 1979-. — v. : ill ; 30cm
Annual. — Text in English, indexes in English, French, German and Arabic
ISSN 0260-5422 = Available from Wales : £9.00(£6.00 to members of Chambers of Commerce) B81-12735

Available from Wales : the directory of the Federation of Welsh Chambers of Commerce (Incorporated). — 1980 ed. — Birmingham : Published on behalf of the Federation by Kemps, c1980. — 265p in various pagings
ISBN 0-905255-80-1 : £9.00(£6.00 to members of Chambers of Commerce)
ISSN 0260-5422 B81-12734

Available from Wales : the directory of the Federation of Welsh Chambers of Commerce (Incorporated). — 1981 ed. — London : Published on behalf of the Federation by Kemps, c1981. — 278p in various pagings
ISBN 0-905255-97-6 : Unpriced
ISSN 0260-5422 B81-19409

County trades finder : incorporating Town & district advertiser. Section 2, Central. — Ed. 1978-1979-. — [Northampton] ([Carlyle House, 198 Kettering Rd Northampton NN1 4BR]) : Phillodge, [1979]-. — v. : ill ; 28cm
Annual. — Continues in part: County trades finder. — Absorbed in part: Town & district advertiser, 1979
ISSN 0260-079x = County trades finder. Section 2. Central : £2.75
Primary classification 380.1'025'424 B81-05536

Industrial directory of Wales / Development Corporation for Wales. — 10th ed. (1981). — Cardiff (Pearl Assurance House, Greyfriars Rd, Cardiff CF1 3AG) : The Corporation, [1981]. — 319p
ISSN 0306-185x : £7.50 B81-13412

Kelly's directory of British industry & services in .... Vol.8, The South West & Wales. — 1st ed. (1980/81). — East Grinstead : Kelly's Directories Ltd., 1980-. — v. ; 30cm
Annual
ISSN 0260-616x = Kelly's directory of British industry & services in ... Vol.8. The South West & Wales : £9.00
Primary classification 380.1'025'423 B81-19703

UK Kompass management register. 1, The regional section for Scotland, Wales and Northern Ireland. — 1981/82-. — East Grinstead : Kompass, c1981-. — v. ; 30cm
Annual. — Continues: Company information for Scotland, Wales and N. Ireland
ISSN 0261-5959 = UK Kompass management register. 1. The regional section for Scotland, Wales and Northern Ireland : £15.00 per issue (£12.00 per issue if 7 vols purchased)
Primary classification 380.1'025'411 B81-32281

380.1'03'21 — Commerce — *Encyclopaedias*

Greener, Michael. The Penguin dictionary of commerce / Michael Greener. — 2nd ed. — Harmondsworth : Penguin, 1980. — 329p ; 20cm. — (Penguin reference books)
Previous ed.: 1970
ISBN 0-14-051044-3 (pbk) : £2.50 B81-07510

380.1'03'21 — Commerce — *French & English dictionaries*

Harrap's French and English business dictionary / edited by Françoise Collin, Jane Pratt, Peter Collin. — London : Harrap, 1981. — 514p in various pagings ; 24cm
ISBN 0-245-53455-5 : £15.00 B81-24961

380.1'07'11422 — London & Home Counties. Commerce. Courses — *Directories — Serials*

[Bulletin of special courses *(London and Home Counties Regional Advisory Council for Technological Education)*]. Bulletin of special courses / London and Home Counties Regional Advisory Council for Technological Education. — 1981/82. — London : The Council, 1981. — [33]p
ISBN 0-85394-088-6 : £1.25
Also classified at 607'.11422 ; 658'.007'11422 B81-36306

380.1'076 — Commerce — *Questions & answers — For schools*

Bond, L. C.. Practical assignments in commerce / L.C. Bond. — Harrogate (P.O. Box 54, Harrogate, N. Yorks HG2 0BE) : Bonmar, 1979. — 94p : col.ill,1map,forms,plans ; 25cm
ISBN 0-903791-02-1 (pbk) : Unpriced B81-06360

Thomas, D. J. (Derek John). Commerce (Ordinary Level) / compiled by D.J. Thomas. — 4th ed. — Horsham : Artemis, 1979. — 68p : 1ill ; 22cm. — (General Certificate of Education model answers)
Previous ed.: 1977
ISBN 0-85141-336-6 (pbk) : £1.25 B81-33260

380.1'076 — Commerce — *Questions & answers — For West African students*

Commerce. — London : Macmillan, 1981. — 124p ; 22cm. — (Macmillan certificate model answers)
ISBN 0-333-29165-4 (pbk) : £0.86 B81-40573

380.1'09171'7 — Sovet ékonomicheskoĭ vzaimopomoshchi countries. Trade. Planning. Applications of game theory

Zauberman, Alfred. Topics in trade coordination of planned economies / Alfred Zauberman. — London : Macmillan in association with the Vienna Institute for Comparative Economic Studies, 1980. — 108p ; 22cm
Includes index
ISBN 0-333-30504-3 : £15.00 : CIP rev. B80-10034

380.1'0941 — Great Britain. Commerce

Bond, L. C.. Business today / Cliff Bond with E. Cavalli. — 2nd ed. — London : Pitman, 1981, c1979. — 275p,[16]p of plates : ill(some col.),maps(some col.),facsims,forms ; 25cm
Originally published: Harrogate : Bonmar, 1979. — Includes index
ISBN 0-273-01749-7 (pbk) : Unpriced B81-40384

380.1'0941 — Great Britain. Commerce — *For schools*

Hughes, Henry G.. Textbook of commerce / Henry G. Hughes, John W. Loveridge. — 3rd ed. — London : Butterworth, 1981. — 340p : ill ; 22cm
Previous ed.: 1973. — Includes index
ISBN 0-408-70928-6 (pbk) : Unpriced : CIP rev. B81-02653

Lewis, David, *1938-*. Commerce in Britain / David Lewis. — St Albans : Hart-Davis Educational, 1980. — ix,166p : ill,2maps,2facsims ; 25cm
Includes index
ISBN 0-247-12977-1 (pbk) : £3.40 B81-02404

Skinner, William G.. Commerce today / W.G. Skinner. — 3rd ed. — London : Hodder and Stoughton, 1980. — iv,186p : ill,maps,forms ; 23cm
Previous ed.: 1976. — Includes bibliographies and index
ISBN 0-340-25160-3 (pbk) : £2.45 : CIP rev. B80-02396

380.1'09675'1 — Zaire. Zaire River region. Commerce, *1500-1891 — Sociological perspectives*

Harms, Robert W.. River of wealth, river of sorrow. — London : Yale University Press, Sept.1981. — [288]p
ISBN 0-300-02616-1 : £16.80 : CIP entry B81-30209

380.1′09794 — Archaeology. Applications of obsidian hydration dating — *Study examples: Prehistoric trade — Study regions: California*

Ericson, Jonathon E.. Exchange and production systems in Californian prehistory : the results of hydration dating and chemical characterization of obsidian sources / Jonathon E. Ericson. — Oxford : B.A.R., 1981. — xiii,240p : ill,maps ; 30cm. — (BAR. International series ; 110)
Bibliography: p224-240
ISBN 0-86054-129-0 (pbk) : £10.00 B81-36614

380.1′41′0941 — Great Britain. Agricultural products. Marketing — *Serials*

Report on agricultural marketing schemes for the period ... / Ministry of Agriculture, Fisheries and Food ... [et al.]. — 1978-79. — London : H.M.S.O., 1981. — 91p
ISBN 0-10-224581-9 : £6.00 B81-29444

380.1′41′0973 — United States. Agricultural products trades

Kohls, Richard L.. Marketing of agricultural products. — 5th ed. / Richard L. Kohls, Joseph N. Uhl. — New York : Macmillan ; London : Collier Macmillan, c1980. — xi,612p : ill ; 24cm
Previous ed.: / by Richard L. Kohls, W. David Downey, 1972. — Includes bibliographies and index
ISBN 0-02-979360-2 (pbk) : £5.95 B81-00832

380.1′4131 — Cereals trades. Effects of Common Agricultural Policy of European Economic Community

Debatisse, Michel Louis. EEC organisation of the cereals markets : principles and consequences / by Michel Louis Debatisse. — Ashford : Centre for European Agricultural Studies, Wye College, c1981. — 43,xxxviip : ill ; 30cm. — (Occasional paper / Wye College. Centre for European Agricultural Studies, ISSN 0306-2902 ; no.10)
ISBN 0-905378-27-x (pbk) : £7.50 B81-22135

380.1′4131′0904 — Cereals trades, *ca 1950-1990*

Bastin, Geoffrey. International trade in grain and the world food economy / by Geoffrey Bastin and John Ellis. — London : Economist Intelligence Unit, 1980. — 174p,4p of plates ; col. ill ; 30cm. — (EIU special report ; no.83)
£50.00 (pbk) B81-04435

380.1′41372′0212 — Tea trades — *Statistics — Serials*

Supplement to annual bulletin of statistics / International Tea Committee. — 1980. — London (Sir John Lyon House, High Timber St., Upper Thames St., EC4V 3NH) : The Committee, [1980]. — 14p
Unpriced B81-12422

380.1′414′06041 — Great Britain. Wholesale fruit trades. Organisations: National Federation of Fruit & Potato Trades — *Directories — Serials*

National Federation of Fruit & Potato Trades. Handbook ... including list of members officers and committees / National Federation of Fruit & Potato Trades Ltd. — 1981. — London (308 Seven Sisters Rd, Finsbury Park, N4 2BN) : The Federation, 1981. — lxiii,330p
Unpriced
Also classified at 380.1′415′06041 B81-26597

380.1′414′0943 — West Germany. Fruit trades

Hinton, Lynn. The fruit and vegetable market in West Germany / by Lynn Hinton. — [Cambridge] ([16A Silver St., Cambridge CB3 9FL]) : [University of Cambridge, Department of Land Economy, Agricultural Economics Unit], 1981. — 28leaves : 1map ; 30cm. — (Occasional papers / University of Cambridge. Agricultural Economics Unit ; no.24)
£1.50 (pbk)
Primary classification 380.1′415′0943
B81-38748

380.1′415′06041 — Great Britain. Wholesale horticultural trades. Organisations: National Federation of Fruit & Potato Trades — *Directories — Serials*

National Federation of Fruit & Potato Trades. Handbook ... including list of members officers and committees / National Federation of Fruit & Potato Trades Ltd. — 1981. — London (308 Seven Sisters Rd, Finsbury Park, N4 2BN) : The Federation, 1981. — lxiii,330p
Unpriced
Primary classification 380.1′414′06041
B81-26597

380.1′415′0941 — Great Britain. Horticultural trades & horticultural equipment trades — *Serials*

GTN : garden trade news. — Sept.1978-. — Peterborough (117 Park Rd, Peterborough PE1 2TS) : EMAP National Publications, 1978-. — v. : ill,ports ; 40cm
Monthly. — Continues: Garden equipment and accessories. — Description based on: Mar.1981
ISSN 0261-3816 = GTN. Garden trade news : Unpriced B81-26596

380.1′415′0943 — West Germany. Vegetable trades

Hinton, Lynn. The fruit and vegetable market in West Germany / by Lynn Hinton. — [Cambridge] ([16A Silver St., Cambridge CB3 9FL]) : [University of Cambridge, Department of Land Economy, Agricultural Economics Unit], 1981. — 28leaves : 1map ; 30cm. — (Occasional papers / University of Cambridge. Agricultural Economics Unit ; no.24)
£1.50 (pbk)
Also classified at 380.1′414′0943 B81-38748

380.1′45002′0941 — Great Britain. Radical book trades — *Serials*

The **radical** bookseller. — No.1 (Oct.1980)-. — London (27 Clerkenwell Close, EC1R 0AT) : Radical Bookseller, 1980-. — v. : ill ; 30cm
Ten issues yearly. — With: Radical books of the month
ISSN 0144-1779 = Radical bookseller : £15.00 per year
Primary classification 013′.335 B81-06779

380.1′4562′0009485 — Organisation for Economic Co-operation and Development countries. Engineering trades, *1960-1970.* **Specialisation. Economic aspects** — *Study regions: Sweden*

Ohlsson, Lennart. Engineering trade specialization of Sweden and other industrial countries : a study of trade adjustment mechanisms of factor proportions theory / Lennart Ohlsson. — Amsterdam ; Oxford : North-Holland, 1980. — xvii,284p : ill ; 25cm. — (Studies in international economics ; v.6)
Bibliography: p275-282. — Includes index
ISBN 0-444-86114-9 : £15.56 B81-04891

380.1′45620106′02541 — Great Britain. Fluid power equipment trades — *Directories — Serials*

Directory, U.K. fluid power distributors. — 1981. — New Malden (15 Coombe Rd, New Malden, Surrey) : Applied Technology Publications, [1981]. — 196p
ISSN 0141-7576 : Unpriced B81-32664

380.1′456238 — Great Britain. Boatbuilding materials trades & boatbuilding equipment trades — *Directories — Serials*

Boat equipment buyer′s guide : directory of suppliers. — 10th ed. (1981)-. — Tonbridge (47 High St., Tonbridge, Kent) : Weald of Kent Publications for Castle Books, 1980-. — v. : ill ; 21cm
Annual. — Continues: Boatbuilders′ and chandlers′ directory of suppliers
Unpriced B81-05446

380.1′456292′02341 — Great Britain. Motor vehicle trades — *Career guides*

Moorey, John. Working with cars / John Moorey. — London : Batsford Academic and Educational, 1981. — 112p,[8]p of plates : ill ; 23cm. — ([Careers series])
Includes index
ISBN 0-7134-3563-1 : £5.95 B81-10022

380.1′45629227′02541 — Great Britain. Cycle trades — *Directories — Serials*

Motor cycle and cycle trader year book. — 1981. — Watford (177, Hagden Lane, Watford, Herts WD1 8LW) : Trade Papers, [1980]. — 107p
ISSN 0306-4867 : Unpriced B81-09038

380.1′456632′002541 — Great Britain. Wines trades — *Directories — Serials*

Which? wine guide. — 1981-. — London : Consumers′ Association, 1980-. — v. : ill ; 21cm
Annual
ISSN 0260-7379 = Which? wine guide : £4.95
Primary classification 641.2′2′05 B81-07194

380.1′456641 — Sugar trades — *Forecasts*

Chilvers, Lloyd. The international sugar market : prospects for the 1980s / by Lloyd Chilvers and Robin Foster. — London : E.I.U., 1981. — 113p ; 30cm. — (EIU special report ; no.106)
Bibliography: p112-113
Unpriced (pbk) B81-39595

380.1′456641′0212 — Sugar trades — *Statistics — Serials*

Sugar year book. — 1979. — London (28, Haymarket, SW1Y 4SP) : International Sugar Organization, [1980]. — ix,356p
£7.00 B81-00075

380.1′45669142′025 — Steel trades — *Directories*

Steel traders of the world. — 2nd ed. / edited by Raymond Cordero, compiled by Ruby Packard. — Worcester Park : Metal Bulletin Books, 1980. — 591p : ill ; 23cm
Previous ed.: 1976. — Includes index
ISBN 0-900542-40-3 : £33.00 B81-14565

380.1′45674′02541 — Great Britain. Timber trades — *Directories — Serials*

TTJ telephone address book. — 1981. — London : Benn in association with Timber trades journal & Wood processing, c1981. — 396p
ISBN 0-510-49837-x : £9.60
ISSN 0141-5735
Primary classification 338.7′6748′02541
B81-30866

380.1′456753′0971 — Canada. Fur trades: Hudson′s Bay Company — *Economic relations with North American Indians, to 1763*

Ray, Arthur J.. Give us good measure : an economic analysis of relations between the Indians and the Hudson′s Bay Company before 1763 / Arthur J. Ray and Donald B. Freeman. — Toronto ; London : University of Toronto Press, c1978. — xvi,298p : ill,maps,facsims ; 24cm
Bibliography: p289-294. — Includes index
ISBN 0-8020-5418-8 (cased) : £12.25
ISBN 0-8020-6334-9 (pbk) : £3.40 B81-21959

380.1′456797′0941 — Great Britain. Tobacco trades — *Serials*

Tobacco trade year book and diary. — 1981. — London (c/o International Trade Publications, 21 John Adam St., WC2 6JH) : Tobacco, c1981. — 80,[260]p
ISBN 0-86108-085-8 : £2.00 B81-15160

380.1′45684′00941 — Great Britain. Household furnishings trades, *1975-1980* — *Statistics*

The **Home** furnishings survey / [Euromonitor Publications Limited]. — London : Euromonitor, 1981. — 127p ; 30cm
ISBN 0-903706-56-3 (pbk) : Unpriced
B81-40058

380.1′45′745102541 — Great Britain. Antiques trades - *Directories*

Guide to the antique shops of Britain. — 1982. — Woodbridge : Antique Collectors′ Club, June 1981. — [1000]p
ISBN 0-907462-03-0 : £5.95 : CIP entry
B81-16385

380.1′457451′02541 — Great Britain. Antiques trades — *Directories — Serials*

The **British** art & antiques yearbook. — 1981. — London (72 Broadwick St., W1V 2BP) : Art & Antiques Yearbooks Publications, c1981. — 672p
ISBN 0-900305-24-x : £8.50
ISSN 0140-8763 B81-20065

380.1′457451′05 — Antiques trades — *Serials*

Antiques across the world. — Issue 1 (June 1977)-. — Richmond (111 Mortlake Rd, Kew, Richmond, Surrey, TW9 471) : Michael Davis (Shipping), 1977-. — v. : ill ; 37cm
Quarterly
ISSN 0260-9606 = Antiques across the world : £3.00 per year B81-13217

380.1′457451′0941 — Great Britain. Rural regions. Antiques trades — *Personal observations*

Austen, Peter. The country antique dealer. — Newton Abbot : David & Charles, Jan.1982. — [192]p
ISBN 0-7153-8223-3 : £7.50 : CIP entry B81-33815

380.5 — TRANSPORT

380.5 — Developing countries. Travel time. Evaluation

Banjo, G. Adegboyega. The theoretical basis for travel time savings valuation in developing countries / by G. Adegboyega Banjo. — Liverpool (P.O. Box 147, Liverpool, L69 3BX) : Department of Civic Design, University of Liverpool, 1980. — 34leaves : ill ; 30cm. — (Working paper / University of Liverpool Department of Civic Design, ISSN 0309-8753 ; 15)
Bibliography: leaves 32-34
ISBN 0-906109-06-x (pbk) : £1.55 B81-06157

380.5 — Transport

Du Jonchay, Yvan. The handbook of world transport / by Yvan du Jonchay ; translated by Loren Goldner. — London : Macmillan, 1980. — iii,146p,[27]p of plates : col.ill,col.maps ; 24cm
Translation of: Les grauds transports mondiaux. — Includes index
ISBN 0-333-30097-1 : £20.00 : CIP rev. B80-18212

380.5 — Transport. Economic aspects

Glaister, Stephen. Fundamentals of transport economics / Stephen Glaister. — Oxford : Blackwell, 1981. — xi,194p : ill ; 23cm
Bibliography: p184-190. — Includes index
ISBN 0-631-12526-4 (cased) : £12.50 : CIP rev.
ISBN 0-631-12776-3 (pbk) : £5.95 B81-14950

380.5 — Transport. Economic aspects — *Festschriften*

Changes in the field of transport studies : essays on the progress of theory in relation to policy making in honour of J.P.B. Tissot van Patot / edited and introduced by J.B. Polak & J.B. van der Kamp. — The Hague ; London : Nijhoff in co-operation with The Netherlands Institute of Transport, 1980. — viii,216p : ill ; 25cm. — (Developments in transport studies ; v.1)
Includes bibliographies
ISBN 90-247-2147-4 : Unpriced B81-04601

380.5 — Transport — *For schools*

Punnett, Neil. Transport. — London : Edward Arnold, Apr.1981. — [64]p. — (Systematic secondary series)
ISBN 0-7131-0475-9 (pbk) : £2.00 : CIP entry B81-00833

380.5 — Transport — *Forecasts* — *For children*

Ardley, Neil. Transport on earth. — London : Watts, [1981]. — 37p : col.ill ; 30cm. — (World of tomorrow)
Includes index
ISBN 0-85166-905-0 : £3.99 B81-29018

380.5 — Transport. Human factors — *Conference proceedings*

International Conference on Ergonomics and Transport *(1980 : Swansea).* Human factors in transport research / [based on the proceedings of the International Conference on Ergonomics and Transport held in Swansea from 8-12 September 1980, convened under the auspices of the Ergonomics Society] ; edited by D. J. Oborne, J.A. Levis. — London : Academic Press
Includes index
Vol.1: Vehicle factors : transport systems, workspace, information and safety. — 1980. — xiii,441p : ill ; 24cm
ISBN 0-12-523801-0 : £12.60 : CIP rev. B80-24363

International Conference on Ergonomics and Transport *(1980 : Swansea).* Human factors in transport research / [based on the proceedings of the International Conference on Ergonomics and Transport held in Swansea from 8-12 September, 1980, convened under the auspices of the Ergonomics Society] ; edited by D.J. Oborne, J.A. Levis. — London : Academic Press
Vol.2: User factors : comfort, the environment and behaviour. — 1980. — xiii,427p : ill ; 24cm
Includes bibliographies and index
ISBN 0-12-523802-9 : £12.60 : CIP rev. B80-24364

380.5′03 — Transport — *Polyglot dictionaries*

Dictionary of transport terms in four languages = Fachausdrücke in vier Sprachen aus Handel und Verkehr = Vocabulaire quadrilingue du commerce international. — Downham Market (11 London Rd., Downham Market, Norfolk PE38 9BX) : Ryston & Storck, [1981?]. — 416p : ill ; 22cm
Ill on lining papers
ISBN 0-9507417-0-1 : £12.00 B81-23072

380.5′05 — Transport — *Serials*

Transport reviews : a transnational transdisciplinary journal. — Vol.1, no.1 (Jan.-Mar.1981)-. — London : Taylor & Francis, 1981-. — v.
Quarterly
ISSN 0144-1647 = Transport reviews : £30.00 B81-21932

380.5′068 — Great Britain. Transport. Policies of government

O'Sullivan, Patrick. Transport policy : geographic, economic and planning aspects / Patrick O'Sullivan. — Guildford : Batsford Academic and Educational, 1980. — 313p : ill,maps ; 23cm
Bibliography: p304-308. — Includes index
ISBN 0-7134-1657-2 (cased) : £14.95 : CIP rev.
ISBN 0-7134-1658-0 (pbk) : £7.95 B80-11819

380.5′068 — Great Britain. Transport. Policies of government — *Socialist Environment and Resources Association viewpoints*

Transport politics and the environment / Socialist Environment and Resources Association. — London (9 Poland St., W1V 3DG) : SERA, [1980]. — 23p ; 21cm
Cover title
£0.40 (pbk) B81-33558

380.5′068 — Transport. Policies of governments — *Comparative studies*

Dunn, James A. (James Aloysius). Miles to go : European and American transportation policies / James A. Dunn, Jr. — Cambridge, Mass. ; London : MIT Press, c1981. — 202p ; 24cm. — (MIT Press series in transportation studies ; 6)
Includes index
ISBN 0-262-04062-x : £12.40 B81-29843

380.5′068′4 — Transport services. Management. Applications of operations research — *Conference proceedings*

International Conference on Transportation *(1980 : New Delhi).* Scientific management of transport systems : revised and edited version of selected papers presented at the International Conference on Transportation held at New Delhi, India, November 26-28 1980 / organised by the International Federation of Operational Research Societies and the Operational Research Society of India ; edited by N.K. Jaiswal. — Amsterdam ; Oxford : North-Holland, c1981. — ix,377p : ill,maps ; 23cm
Includes bibliographies and index
ISBN 0-444-86205-6 : Unpriced B81-32850

380.5′07′2 — Transport. Research. Socioeconomic aspects - *Conference proceedings*

World Conference on Transport Research *(1980 : London).* Transport research for social and economic progress. — Farnborough, Hants. : Gower, May 1981
Vol.2. — [700]p
ISBN 0-566-00444-5 : £18.00 : CIP entry B81-04319

380.5′07′2 — Transportation. Research. Socioeconomic aspects - *Conference proceedings*

World Conference on Transport Research *(1980 : London).* Transport research for social and economic progress. — Farnborough, Hants. : Gower, May 1981
Vol.1. — [700]p
ISBN 0-566-00443-7 : £18.00 : CIP entry B81-04318

World Conference on Transport Research *(1980 : London).* Transport research for social and economic progress. — Farnborough, Hants. : Gower, May 1981
Vol.3. — [700]p
ISBN 0-566-00445-3 : £18.00 B81-04320

World Conference on Transport Research *(1980 : London).* Transport research for social and economic progress. — Farnborough, Hants. : Gower, May 1981
Vol 4. — [700]p
ISBN 0-566-00446-1 : £18.00 : CIP entry B81-04321

380.5′072041 — Great Britain. Transport. Research & development by Great Britain. *Department of Transport* — *Serials*

Great Britain. *Department of the Environment.* Report on research and development / Departments of the Environment and Transport. — 1980. — London : H.M.S.O., 1981. — iii,32p
ISBN 0-11-751531-0 : £2.90
Primary classification 607′.2′41 B81-35449

380.5′072041 — Great Britain. Transport. Research organisations: Transport and Road Research Laboratory — *Serials*

Transport and Road Research Laboratory. Transport and road research / Transport and Road Research Laboratory. — 1979. — London : H.M.S.O., 1980. — x,92p
ISBN 0-11-550527-x : £5.70 B81-03998

380.5′09 — Leicestershire. Leicester. Universities. Libraries: University of Leicester. *Library.* **Stock: Documents on transport,** *to 1980*

University of Leicester. *Library.* Guide to the Transport History Collection in Leicester University Library / [compiled] by George Ottley. — [Leicester] ([University Rd, Leicester LE1 7RH]) : Leicester University Library, 1981. — 30p ; 21cm
ISBN 0-906092-01-9 (pbk) : £1.00 B81-11581

380.5′09 — Transport. Geographical aspects — *Conference proceedings*

Transport Geography Study Group. *Conference (1981 : Leicester).* The spirit and purpose of transport geography : papers presented at the Annual Conference of the Transport Geography Study Group (Institute of British Geographers), Leicester, January 1981 / J. Whitelegg (editor). — Lancaster : Transport Geography Study Group, Department of Geography, University of Lancester, [1981]. — 160p : ill,maps ; 21cm
ISBN 0-901989-33-9 (pbk) : Unpriced B81-29869

380.5′09 — Transport, *to 1980* — *For children*

Ward Lock's book of transport / by Jonathan Rutland ... [et al.]. — London : Ward Lock, 1981. — 77p : col.ill,plans,ports ; 28cm
Includes index
ISBN 0-7063-6141-5 : £3.95 : CIP rev. B81-23838

380.5′09181′2 — Western world. Transport. Policies. Formulation

Transport and public policy planning / edited by David Banister and Peter Hall. — London : Mansell, 1981. — 455p : ill,maps ; 25cm
Includes bibliographies and index
ISBN 0-7201-1580-9 : £19.50 : CIP rev. B80-18213

380.5′092′2 — Transport - *Biographies*

These men made transport history. — Cambridge : Stephens, Sept.1981. — [256]p
ISBN 0-85059-542-8 : £25.00 : CIP entry B81-20131

380.5'0941 — Great Britain. *Department of Transport.* **Expenditure. Implications of estimates of public expenditure 1980-1984** — *Inquiry reports*

Great Britain. *Parliament. House of Commons. Transport Committee.* Fifth report from the Transport Committee, session 1980-81 : the transport aspects of the 1981 public expenditure white paper : together with the proceedings of the Committee, minutes of evidence and appendices. — London : H.M.S.O., [1981]. — xix,47p ; 25cm. — ([HC] 299)
ISBN 0-10-229981-1 (pbk) : £3.90 B81-40612

380.5'0941 — Great Britain. *Parliament. House of Commons. Transport Committee.* **Reports** — *Critical studies*

Great Britain. First special report from the Transport Committee, session 1980-81 : Government observations on the First and Second reports of the Committee, session 1979-80. — London : H.M.S.O., [1980]. — ixp ; 25cm. — ([HC] ; 35)
ISBN 0-10-203581-4 (unbound) : £1.40 B81-20357

380.5'0941 — Great Britain. Transport — *Conference proceedings*

Into the '90's *(Conference : 1980 : Liverpool Polytechnic).* Proceedings of transport conference : 'Into the 90's' held at Liverpool Polytechnic 20th October 1980 / edited by Lewis Lesley. — [Liverpool] ([Department of Town and Country Planning, 53 Victoria St. Liverpool L1 6EY]) : Liverpool Polytechnic, 1980
ISBN 0-906442-06-0 : Unpriced B81-25901

380.5'0941 — Great Britain. Transport — *For schools*

Roberts, Frank, *1939-.* On the move / Frank and Bernie Roberts. — Basingstoke : Macmillan Education, 1981. — 31p : ill,maps ; 30cm. — (Looking at Britain ; 4)
ISBN 0-333-28412-7 (pbk) : £1.35 B81-21374

380.5'0941 — Great Britain. Transport services, *1800-1900.* **Social aspects** — *For schools*

Dunning, Richard. Victorian life and transport / Richard Dunning. — Walton-on-Thames : Nelson, 1981. — 48p : ill(some col.),2maps,facsims,ports ; 28cm. — (Keys to the past)
Ill, text on inside covers. — Publisher's no.: NCN 3288-24-0
ISBN 0-17-435023-6 (pbk) : £1.50 B81-29122

380.5'09411 — Scotland. Transport services: Scottish Transport Group — *Serials*

Scottish Transport Group. Annual report and accounts / Scottish Transport Group. — 1980. — Edinburgh (114 George St., Edinburgh EH2 4LX) : The Group, 1981. — 62p
ISBN 0-907181-01-5 : £1.50 B81-29039

380.5'09416 — Northern Ireland. Transport, *1700-ca 1950*

McCutcheon, W. A.. The industrial archaeology of Northern Ireland / W.A. McCutcheon. — Belfast : H.M.S.O., 1980. — xiv,395p,156p of plates : ill,maps(some col.),facsims,plans,ports ; 29cm
At head of title: Department of the Environment for Northern Ireland. — Ill on lining papers. — Includes index
ISBN 0-337-08154-9 : £55.00
Primary classification 338.09416 B81-22222

380.5'09417 — Ireland *(Republic).* **Transport services**

The **Transport** challenge : the opportunity in the 1980s : a report for the Minister for Transport / McKinsey International, Inc.. — Dublin : Stationery Office, 1980. — ii,297p in various pagings : ill ; 30cm
Includes bibliographies
£8.00 (pbk) B81-22228

380.5'09423'3 — Dorset. Transport — *Proposals — Serials*

Dorset. *County Council.* Transport policies and programmes ... submission / Dorset County Council. — 1980/81. — Dorchester (County Hall, Dorchester, Dorset) : The Council, 1979. — 215p in various pagings
ISSN 0260-3446 : £1.50 B81-20036

Dorset. *County Council.* Transport policies and programmes ... submission / Dorset County Council. — 1981/82. — Dorchester (County Hall, Dorchester, Dorset) : The Council, 1980. — 134p in various pagings
ISBN 0-85216-255-3 : £1.50
ISSN 0260-3446 B81-20037

380.5'09423'5 — Devon. Transport — *Proposals — Serials*

Devon. *County Council.* Transport polices and programme / [Devon County Council]. Part 2, Programme. — 1981/82-. — Exeter (County Hall, Topham Rd., Exeter, Devon EX2 4QD) : The Council, 1980-. — v. : ill ; 30cm
Annual. — Continues in part: Transport policies and programme (Devon. County Council)
ISSN 0260-741x = Transport policies and programme - Devon County Council. Part 2. Programme : £1.00 B81-11861

Devon. *County Council.* Transport policies and programme / [Devon County Council]. Part 1, Policies. — 1981/82-. — Exeter County Hall, Topham Rd, Exeter, Devon EX2 4QD : The Council, [1980]-. — v. : ill,maps ; 30cm
Irregular. — Continues in part: Transport policies and programme (Devon. County Council)
ISSN 0260-9401 = Transport polices and programme - Devon County Council. Part 1. Policies : £2.00 B81-11865

Devon. *County Council.* Transport policies and programme / [Devon County Council]. The Public transport plan, draft for consultation. — 1982/83. — [Exeter] ([County Hall, Topsham Rd, Exeter, Devon EX2 4QD]) : [The Council], 1981. — 21p
ISBN 0-86114-318-3 : Unpriced B81-23132

380.5'09424'17 — England. Cotswolds. Transport, *1800-1962 — Illustrations*

Transport in the Cotswolds : from old photographs / [compiled] by D.J. Viner. — Nelson : Hendon Publishing, c1981. — [40]p : chiefly ill,ports ; 21x29cm
Text on inside covers
ISBN 0-86067-066-x (pbk) : £2.50 B81-25997

380.5'09427'1 — Cheshire. Public transport services — *Proposals — Serials*

Cheshire. *Transportation Unit.* Public transport plan for the period ... / [Cheshire County Council, Department of Highways and Transportation, Transportation Unit]. — 1981-86. — Chester (Backford Hall, Chester CH1 6EA) : The Unit, 1980. — iv,88p
Unpriced B81-30857

380.5'09428'3 — Humberside. Public transport services — *Proposals*

Humberside. *County Council.* Public transport plan 1981-1986 / Humberside County Council. — [Beverley] ([Director of Planning, Manor Rd, Beverley, North Humberside, HU17 7BX]) : [The Council], [1981]. — 26p,[2]folded leaves of plates : maps ; 30cm
Unpriced (spiral) B81-18718

380.5'09428'3 — Humberside. Transport — *Proposals — Serials*

Humberside. *County Council.* Transport policy and programme / Humberside County Council. — 1980-81 -. — [Beverley] ([c/o The Planning Department, Manor Rd, Beverley, N. Humberside HU17 7BX]) : The Council, 1979-. — v. : maps ; 30cm
Annual. — Continues: Humberside. County Council. Transport policy and programme submission. — Description based on: 1982-83 issue
ISSN 0262-1509 = Transport policy and programme - Humberside County Council : Unpriced B81-38181

380.5'0947 — Eastern Europe. Transport

East European transport : regions and modes / edited and introduced by Bogdan Mieczkowski. — The Hague ; London : Nijhoff, 1980. — xiv,353p : maps ; 25cm. — (Developments in transport studies ; v.2)
Bibliography: p335-353
ISBN 90-247-2390-6 : Unpriced B81-04570

380.5'0956 — Middle East. Transport services — *Serials*

Middle East industry & transport. — Issue no.34 (Jan./Feb.1981)-. — London (PO Box 261, 63 Long Acre, WC2E 9JH) : IC Magazines, 1981-. — v. : ill
Six issues yearly. — Continues: Middle East transport
ISSN 0261-1473 = Middle East industry & transport (corrected) : £18.00 per year
Primary classification 338.0956 B81-16746

380.5'097292 — Jamaica. Transport. Development. Regulation

Sampson, Cezley I.. The building of institutions for transport development, with special reference to Jamaica / by Cezley I. Sampson. — Liverpool (P.O. 147, Liverpool L69 3BX) : Department of Civic Design, University of Liverpool, 1976. — 37leaves ; 30cm. — (Working paper / University of Liverpool Department of Civic Design ; WP2)
Bibliography: leaves36-37
£1.00 (pbk) B81-05633

380.5'22'0880816 — Great Britain. Transport services for handicapped persons — *Conference proceedings*

Transport for special needs : the report of a conference held on 25 and 26 June 1981 at the Roxburghe hotel, Edinburgh to mark the International Year of Disabled People. — Edinburgh (18 Claremont Cres, Edinburgh EH7 4QD) : Scottish Council on Disability, [1981]. — 38p ; 30cm. — (Planning Exchange forum report ; 28)
Unpriced (pbk) B81-39632

380.5'22'0942 — England. County councils. Public transport plans — *Conference proceedings*

Public transport plans : the impact. — [Oxford] ([Headington, Oxford OX3 0BP]) : Department of Town Planning, Oxford Polytechnic, [1981]
Conference 2 / editors Mervyn Jones and Peter White. — 75p ; 30cm
£2.30 (pbk) B81-18465

380.5'22'094239 — Avon. Public passenger transport services — *Proposals — Serials*

Avon. *County Council.* Public transport plan / Avon County Council. — 1980/1. — Bristol (P.O. Box 11, Avon House, The Haymarket, Bristol BS99 7DE) : County Public Relations and Publicity Dept., [1980]. — [50p]
ISBN 0-86063-088-9 : £1.00 B81-07701

380.5'22'094258 — Hertfordshire. Public transport services — *Proposals — Serials*

Hertfordshire. *Transport Coordination Unit.* Public transport plan / Hertfordshire County Council. — 1979-80-. — [Hertford] ([County Hall, Hertford SG13 8DN]) : The Council, 1979-. — v. : maps ; 30cm
Annual. — Continues in part: Hertfordshire. County Council. Transport policies and programmes. — Final version of: Hertfordshire. Transport Coordination Unit. Public transport plan (draft)
ISSN 0260-5430 = Public transport plan — Hertfordshire County Council : £1.90 B81-20409

Hertfordshire. *Transport Coordination Unit.* Public transport plan / Hertfordshire County Council. — 1981-82. — [Hertford] ([County Hall, Hertford SG13 8Dn]) : The Council, 1981. — 105p in various pagings
ISSN 0260-5430 : Unpriced B81-28386

380.5'22'094264 — Suffolk. Public passenger transport services — *Proposals — Serials*

Suffolk. *Highways Department.* Public passenger transport plan / Suffolk County Council. — 1979/80-. — Ipswich (St Peter's House, Ipswich) : The Council, 1979-. — v. ; 30cm
Annual. — Description based on: 1980/81
ISSN 0144-6142 = Public passenger transport plan — Suffolk County Council : £1.00 B81-02021

380.5′22′094282 — South Yorkshire ***(Metropolitan County).*** **Public transport. Policies —** ***Conference proceedings***

South Yorkshire public transport policies : transcripts of a study conference held at Sheffield City Polytechnic on 26 November 1980 / editor Richard Hammersley. — Sheffield (Sheffield City Polytechnic, Pond St., Sheffield S1 1WB) : URS Publications, [1980?]. — 74p : 1ill ; 30cm. — (Conference transcripts / Sheffield City Polytechnic, Department of Urban & Regional Studies ; 4)
£1.50 (pbk) B81-27042

380.5′24 — Bulk solid materials. Transport — ***Serials***

International bulk journal. — Vol.1, no.1 (Jan.1981)-. — Dorking (40 West St., Dorking, Surrey RH4 1BU) : IBJ Associates, 1981-. — v. : ill,maps,plans ; 30cm
Monthly
ISSN 0260-1087 = International bulk journal : £20.00 per year B81-29077

380.5′24 — Cargo handling. Organisations: International Cargo Handling Co-ordination Association — ***Directories — Serials***

International Cargo Handling Co-ordination Association. Who's who in cargo handling : the directory of members of the International Cargo Handling Co-ordination Association. — 1981. — London : The Association, c1981. — xiv,178p
Unpriced B81-32216

380.5′24 — Freight transport. Containerisation — ***Conference proceedings***

Container Technology Conference ***(1976 : London).*** Conference proceedings / Container Technology Conference, in association with ICHCA. — New Malden (201 High St., New Malden, Surrey KT3 4BW) : C.S. Publications, c1976. — 18v. : ill ; 30cm
Unpriced (pbk) B81-08085

380.5′24 — Freight transport. Containerisation — ***Directories — Serials***

Jane's freight containers. — 13th ed. (1981). — London : Jane's Pub. Co., c1981. — 634p
ISBN 0-7106-0720-2 : £45.00 B81-24692

380.5′24 — Freight transport. Containerisation — ***Serials***

Containerisation international yearbook. — 1981. — London : National Magazine Co., c1981. — 608p
ISBN 0-85223-195-4 : £28.00
ISSN 0305-7402 B81-15450

380.5′24 — Great Britain. Freight transport services: Pickfords Removals Limited, ***to 1947***

Turnbull, Gerard L.. Traffic and transport : an economic history of Pickfords / Gerard L. Turnbull. — London : Allen & Unwin, 1979. — xii,196p : ill,maps,geneal.tables ; 23cm
Includes index
ISBN 0-04-300080-0 : £12.00 : CIP rev.
B79-30618

380.5′24 — International freight transport. Management — ***Serials***

IFM : international freighting management. — Feb. 1980-. — London (30 Old Burlington St., W1X 2AE) : Maclean-Hunter, 1980-. — v. : ill,ports ; 29cm
Monthly. — Description based on: Mar. 1981
ISSN 0261-5886 = IFM. International freighting management : £15.00 per year
B81-31595

380.5′24 — Temperature controlled freight transport services — ***Directories — Serials***

TCS & D directory : temperature controlled storage & distribution. — 1st ed.-. — Redhill (2 Queensway, Redhill, Surrey RH1 1QS) : Retail Journals, [1980]-. — v. : ill ; 30cm
Issued every two years
ISSN 0260-9932 = TCS & D directory : £35.00
Also classified at 338.4′762157 B81-11227

380.5′24′0942511 — Northern Derbyshire. Freight transport, ***ca 1600-1800***

Hey, David. Packmen, carriers and packhorse roads : trade and communications in North Derbyshire and South Yorkshire / David Hey. — [Leicester] : Leicester University Press, 1980. — 279p : ill,maps ; 23cm
Map on lining papers. — Bibliography: p206-269. - Includes index
ISBN 0-7185-1192-1 : £12.50 : CIP rev.
Also classified at 380.5′24′094282 B80-12312

380.5′24′094282 — South Yorkshire ***(Metropolitan County).*** **Freight transport,** ***ca 1600-1800***

Hey, David. Packmen, carriers and packhorse roads : trade and communications in North Derbyshire and South Yorkshire / David Hey. — [Leicester] : Leicester University Press, 1980. — 279p : ill,maps ; 23cm
Map on lining papers. — Bibliography: p206-269. - Includes index
ISBN 0-7185-1192-1 : £12.50 : CIP rev.
Primary classification 380.5′24′0942511
B80-12312

380.5′24′0973 — United States. Freight transport

Bowersox, Donald J.. Introduction to transportation / Donald J. Bowersox, Pat J. Calabro, George D. Wagenheim. — New York : Macmillan ; London : Collier-Macmillan, c1981. — xv,399p : ill,maps,forms ; 24cm
Bibliography: p391-392. — Includes index
ISBN 0-02-313030-x : £11.95 B81-20734

380.5′9 — Transport. Effects of shortages of fuel resources — ***Forecasts***

Wayne, Francis. Energy for future transport / by Francis Wayne. — Hythe ([c/o Secretary, Scottish Association for Public Transport, 351 Kingsway, Dundee DD3 8LG]) : Volturna Press, c1980. — 73p ; 21cm
Cover title
ISBN 0-85606-100-x (pbk) : Unpriced
B81-06971

380.5′90941 — Great Britain. Public transport. Economic aspects

Nash, C. A.. Economics of public transport. — London : Longman, Feb.1982. — [224]p. — (Modern economics)
ISBN 0-582-44631-7 : £6.95 : CIP entry
B81-37600

381 — DOMESTIC TRADE

381′.025 — Distributive trades — ***Directories — For British exporters***

Export courier guide to distributors. — [London] ([21 Montpelier Row SE3 0SR]) : Export Marketors Partnership]
Cover title
Food : Europe. — [1981?]. — 1v.(Loose-leaf) : 1port ; 24cm
£195.00
Also classified at 382′.5′025 B81-19689

381′.06′041 — Great Britain. Trade associations. Linkages

The Sectoral representation of British industry and commerce : a guide to employers' organisations and trade associations in the United Kingdom and links between them. — 7th ed. — London (Centre Point, 103 New Oxford St., WC1A 1DU) : Advice Centre on the Organisation of Industrial and Commercial Representation, [1981]. — 60p in various pagings ; 30cm
Previous ed.: 1979
£5.00 (pbk) B81-33257

381′.09417 — Ireland ***(Republic).*** **Distributive trades —** ***Serials***

IADT news. — Oct.1979-. — Dublin (29 Fitzwilliam Place, Dublin 2) : Irish Association of Distributive Trades, 1979-. — v. : ill ; 31cm
Quarterly. — Description based on: July 1980
Free to retailers and wholesalers only
B81-06107

381′.09421 — London. Goods & services — ***Advertisements — Serials***

Covent guardian & West End advertiser. — CGWE-1(Friday Apr. 3 1981)-. — London (Newspaper House, Winslow Rd, W6 9SF) : London & Westminster Newspapers, 1981-. — v. : ill ; 45cm
Weekly
ISSN 0261-6157 = Covent guardian & West End advertiser : Unpriced B81-32399

Soho & West End advertiser. — SWE-1(Friday Apr. 3 1981)-. — London (Newspaper House, Winslow Rd, W6 9SF) : London & Westminster Newspapers, 1981-. — v. : ill ; 45cm
Weekly
Unpriced B81-32401

Vauxhall & Victoria advertiser. — VV-1(Friday Apr. 3rd 1981)-. — London (Newspaper House, Winslow Rd, W6 9SF) : London & Westminster Newspapers, 1981-. — v. : ill ; 45cm
Weekly
ISSN 0261-6130 = Vauxhall & Victoria advertiser : Unpriced B81-32400

381′.0967′112 — Commodities. Distribution. Traditional techniques. Economic efficiency — ***Study regions: Cameroon. North-West Province***

Hollier, Graham P.. Examining allegations of exploitation in traditional marketing systems : some evidence from West Cameroon / Graham P. Hollier. — [Glasgow] : University of Strathclyde, Department of Geography, 1981. — 20leaves : maps ; 30cm. — (Research seminar series / University of Strathclyde Department of Geography ; no.12)
Some leaves printed on both sides. — Bibliography: leaves 18-20
Unpriced (pbk) B81-29254

381′.1 — Auctioneering firms: Sotheby Parke Bernet Group, ***to 1980***

Herrmann, Frank. Sotheby's : portrait of an auction house / by Frank Herrmann. — London : Chatto & Windus, 1980. — xxvi,468p,[32],viiip of plates : ill(some col.),1plan,facsims,ports ; 25cm
Includes index
ISBN 0-7011-2246-3 : £9.95 : CIP rev.
B80-13767

381′.1 — Great Britain. Gift shops — ***Directories — Serials***

United Kingdom gift shops / [Data Research Group]. — [1981]. — Great Missenden : The Group, 1981. — 177p
ISBN 0-86099-321-3 : Unpriced B81-29065

381′.1 — Great Britain. Hypermarkets & superstores — ***Lists***

List of U.K. hypermarkets & superstores. — 7th ed. — Reading (26 Queen Victoria St., Reading RG1 1TG) : URPI, 1980. — i,63p : 1map ; 30cm
Previous ed.: 1978
£10.00 (pbk) B81-02808

Superstores 1981. — [Watford] ([Letchmore Heath, Watford WD2 8DQ]) : [Institute of Grocery Distribution], [1981]. — ii,63p : 1map ; 30cm
Unpriced (pbk) B81-31674

381′.1 — Great Britain. Supermarkets — ***Directories — Serials***

Large stores directory / [Institute of Grocery Distribution, Research Services]. — July 1980-. — [Watford] ([Letchmore Heath, Watford WD2 8DQ]) : The Institute, 1980-. — v. ; 30cm
Two issues yearly
ISSN 0260-6526 = Large stores directory : £60.00 B81-06684

United Kingdom supermarkets / [Data Research Group]. — [1981]. — Great Missenden : The Group, 1981. — 102leaves
ISBN 0-86099-315-9 : Unpriced B81-29066

381'.1 — Second-hand goods. Purchase - *Manuals*

Ball, Richard. How to buy (almost anything) secondhand. — London : Astragal Books, Sept.1981. — [224]p
ISBN 0-906525-21-7 : £7.95 : CIP entry
B81-20587

381'.1 — Shopping centres. Choice by shoppers. Influence of shoppers' attitudes to shopping centres. Evaluation. Applications of cluster analysis — *Study regions: Buckinghamshire. Milton Keynes*

Expectancy value models in spatial planning : shopping behaviour in Milton Keynes. — Cranfield (Cranfield, Bedford MK43 0AL) : Centre for Transport Studies Cranfield Institute of Technology, 1981. — 26leaves ; 30cm. — (CTS report ; no.17)
Cover title. — Bibliography: leaves 25-26
ISBN 0-902937-60-x (spiral) : Unpriced
B81-30925

381'.1'025 — Retail trades — *Directories* — *Serials*

Stores of the world directory. — 11th ed. (1980-81). — London : Newman Books, [1980?]. — vi,1172p
ISBN 0-7079-6915-8 : Unpriced
ISSN 0081-5829 B81-00076

381'.1'02541 — Great Britain. Department stores — *Directories* — *Serials*

United Kingdom department stores / [Data Research Group]. — [1981]. — Great Missenden : The Group, 1981. — 49leaves
ISBN 0-86099-298-5 : £25.00 B81-37232

381'.1'02541 — Great Britain. Retail trades — *Directories* — *Serials*

Stores, shops, supermarkets retail directory. — 35th ed. (1981). — London : Newman Books, [1980?]. — 1339p
ISBN 0-7079-6916-6 : £31.00
ISSN 0305-4012 B81-00077

381'.1'0941 — Great Britain. Local shopping facilities — *Conference proceedings*

Unit for Retail Planning Information. Local shopping centres and convenience stores : report of an URPI Workshop. — Reading (26 Queen Victoria St., Reading RG1 1TG) : Unit for Retail Planning Information, 1980. — 57p : 3ill ; 26cm. — (URPI report ; U16)
Includes bibliographies
£14.90 (pbk) B81-03850

381'.1'0941 — Great Britain. Retail trades — *Forecasts*

Livesey, Frank. Retailing : developments and prospects to 1985 / by Frank Livesey and Richard J. Hall. — London (42, Colebrook Row, N1 8AF) : Staniland Hall Associates, 1981. — 56p : ill ; 21x30cm
£72.00 (spiral) B81-32818

381'.1'0941 — Great Britain. Retail trades — *Serials*

Independent retailer and caterer. — Vol.15., no.1 (Jan. 1981)-. — London (5, Southwark St., SE1 1RQ) : William Reed, 1981-. — v. : ill ; 40cm
Monthly. — Continues: Cash & carry news
ISSN 0261-0833 = Independent retailer and caterer : £7.00 per year
Also classified at 338.4'76479541'05
B81-15446

381'.1'0941 — Great Britain. Retail trades — *Statistics* — *Serials*

Retailing / Department of Industry, Business Statistics Office. — 1978. — London : H.M.S.O., c1980. — 103p. — (Business monitor ; SDA25)
ISBN 0-11-512872-7 : £5.75 B81-07010

381'.1'0941 — Great Britain. Urban regions. Central areas. Retail trades — *Conference proceedings*

Town centres of the future : report of an URPI conference. — Reading (26 Queen Victoria St., Reading RG1 1TG) : Unit for Retail Planning Information Limited, 1980. — 62p ; 26cm. — (URPI report ; U17)
£14.50 (pbk) B81-05186

381'.1'09421 — London. Shopping areas — *Visitors' guides*

Donald, Elsie Burch. London shopping guide / Elsie Burch Donald. — 4th ed. — Harmondsworth : Penguin, 1981. — 296p : 1form ; 18cm. — (Penguin handbooks)
Previous ed.: 1979. — Includes index
ISBN 0-14-046222-8 (pbk) : £2.50 B81-25440

381.1'09421'34 — London. Kensington and Chelsea *(London Borough).* **Department stores: Harrods Ltd.**

Dale, Tim. Harrods : the store and the legend / Tim Dale. — London : Pan, 1981. — 149p,[16]p of plates : ill,facsims,plans,ports ; 20cm
ISBN 0-330-26344-7 (pbk) : £1.95 B81-23323

381'.1'094226 — West Sussex. Shopping — *For structure planning*

Shopping : consultation document, July 1981 : technical summary / West Sussex County Council. — Chichester (County Planning Officer, County Hall, Chichester, W. Sussex P319 1RL) : [The Council], [1981]. — 15p,3leaves of plates : 3maps ; 30cm
Cover title
ISBN 0-86260-022-7 (spiral) : Unpriced
B81-38950

381'.1'0942338 — Dorset. Bournemouth. Department stores: J. E. Beale Ltd., *to 1905*

Parsons, J. F.. J.E. Beale Ltd. and the growth of Bournemouth : the story of a business enterprise in a growing resort / by J.F. Parsons. — Bournemouth (40 Lowther Rd., Bournemouth) : Bournemouth Local Studies Publications, The Teachers' Centre
Pt 1: 1881-1905. — 1980. — 39p : ill,1map,1port ; 21cm
ISBN 0-906287-31-6 (pbk) : £0.50 B81-08007

381'.1'0942615 — Norfolk. Norwich. Shopping behaviour. Effects of establishment of J. Sainsbury Ltd's supermarket at Bowthorpe

Sainsbury's at Bowthorpe : the impact of a new retailing facility and characteristics of its users / [prepared by M.J. Loveday ... et al.]. — Norwich (County Hall, Martineau Lane, Norwich, NR1 2DH) : County Planning Officer, 1981. — v,54p : ill,maps,forms ; 21x30cm
Cover title
£4.00 (spiral) B81-20851

381'.1'094436 — France. Paris. Department stores: Bon Marché, *1869-1920*

Miller, Michael B.. The Bon Marché. — London : Allen & Unwin, Sept.1981. — [278]p
ISBN 0-04-330316-1 : £12.50 : CIP entry
B81-20140

381'.12 — Great Britain. Non-food multiple shops — *Statistics* — *Serials*

Multiple stores (non-food). — [1981]. — London : Jordan & Sons (Surveys) Ltd., c1981. — xviii,73p
ISBN 0-85938-145-5 : Unpriced B81-24138

381'.14'025 — Mail-order firms — *Directories*

The A to Z of shopping by post. — 2nd ed. / edited by Joy Montague. — Watford : Exley, 1979. — 256p : ill ; 22cm
Previous ed.: / by Angela Lansbury. 1978. — Includes index
ISBN 0-905521-26-9 (cased) : Unpriced
ISBN 0-905521-27-7 (pbk) : £3.50 B81-40159

381'.14'02541 — Great Britain. Mail-order firms — *Directories* — *Serials*

United Kingdom mail order companies / [Data Research Group]. — [1980]. — Great Missenden : The Group, 1980. — 29p
ISBN 0-86099-281-0 : Unpriced B81-06715

381'.14'0941 — Great Britain. Mail-order firms: Empire Stores, *1831-1981*

Beaver, Patrick. A pedlar's legacy : the origins and history of Empire Stores 1831-1981 / by Patrick Beaver. — London (23 Ridgmount St., WC1E 7AH) : Henry Melland, 1981. — 127p : ill(some col.),1map,facsims(some col.),ports (some col.) ; 24cm
ISBN 0-9500730-6-7 : £7.95 B81-27282

381'.14'0941 — Great Britain. Mail-order firms — *Statitics* — *Serials*

Direct marketing : an industry sector analysis. — 1st ed.-. — London : ICC Business Ratios, c1981. — v. ; 30cm. — (ICC Business Ratio report)
Annual
ISSN 0261-3859 = Direct marketing : Unpriced B81-26601

381'.18'02541 — Great Britain. Markets — *Directories* — *Serials*

Markets year book. — 20th [i.e.21st] ed. (1981). — Oldham (Union St., Oldham, Lancs) : World's Fair, [1981?]. — 238p
£3.20 B81-13321

381'.2 — Great Britain. Wholesale fancy goods trades — *Directories* — *Serials*

United Kingdom fancy goods & toy wholesalers / [Data Research Group]. — [1981]. — Great Missenden : The Group, 1981. — 40leaves
ISBN 0-86099-292-6 : £25.00
Primary classification 381'.4568872'02541
B81-37224

381'.2 — Western Europe. Wholesale fancy goods trades — *Directories*

Gifts & novelties trade sources list : a selection of trade sources for the giftware trade. — London : Malcolm Stewart, 1979. — 27p ; 25cm. — (Kingfisher business guides)
ISBN 0-904132-39-0 (pbk) : £0.85 B81-11334

381'.2'0254 — Western Europe. Wholesale trades — *Directories*

Europe trade sources list : a selection of trade suppliers in Europe excluding the UK. — 2nd ed. — London : Malcolm Stewart, 1979. — 28p ; 25cm. — (Kingfisher business guides)
Previous ed.: published as Kingfisher's list of trade sources of Europe. 1972
ISBN 0-904132-42-0 (pbk) : £0.85 B81-11336

381'.2'0941 — Great Britain. Wholesale trades: United Industrial Company Limited

Coles, G. J. K.. The United Industrial Company Limited : investigation under sections 164 and 172 of the Companies Act 1948 : report / by G.J.K. Coles and P.H. Dobson. — London : H.M.S.O., 1981. — ii,139,[74]p ; 30cm
At head of title: Department of Trade
ISBN 0-11-513180-9 (pbk) : £11.90 B81-20971

381'.3 — United States. Consumers. Complaints

No access to law : alternatives to the American judicial system / Laura Nader editor. — New York ; London : Academic Press, c1980. — xxiii,540p : forms ; 24cm
Includes bibliographies and index
ISBN 0-12-513560-2 (cased) : £15.40
ISBN 0-12-513562-9 (pbk) : £8.40 B81-09002

381'.34'06041 — Great Britain. Consumer protection. Organisations: National Consumer Council. *Supports Desk* — *Serials*

[The Clapham omnibus *(London : 1978)*]. The Clapham omnibus / from the Supports Desk of the National Consumer Council. — No.1 (Autumn 1978)-. — London (18 Queen Anne's Gate SW1H 9AA) : The Supports Desk, 1978-. — v. : ill ; 30cm
Quarterly. — Description based on: No.7 (Summer-Autumn 1980)
ISSN 0260-5813 = Clapham omnibus (London. 1978) : Unpriced B81-04826

381'.34'0973 — United States. Consumer protection

Best, Arthur. When consumers complain / Arthur Best. — New York ; Guildford : Columbia University Press, 1981. — xi,232p ; 24cm
Includes index
ISBN 0-231-05124-7 : £9.80 B81-18924

381'.415'02541 — Great Britain. Garden centres — *Directories* — *Serials*

United Kingdom garden centres / [Data Research Group]. — [1981]. — Great Missenden : The Group, 1981. — 101leaves
ISBN 0-86099-305-1 : £25.00 B81-37236

381′.45002 — Great Britain. Antiquarian booksellers & second-hand booksellers — *Directories*

Lewis, Roy Harley. The book browser′s guide. — 2nd ed. — Newton Abbot : David & Charles, Jan.1982. — [256]p
Previous ed.: 1975
ISBN 0-7153-8095-8 : £7.95 : CIP entry
B81-33818

381′.45002 — Great Britain. Antiquarian booksellers & second-hand booksellers — *Directories — Serials*

A **Directory** of dealers in secondhand and antiquarian books in the British Isles. — 1981-83. — London : Sheppard Press, 1981. — xliv,425p
Spine title: Dealers in books, British Isles
ISBN 0-900661-21-6 : £9.00
ISSN 0070-5411 B81-30807

381′.45002′06041 — Great Britain. Bookselling. Organisations: Booksellers Association of Great Britain and Ireland — *Directories — Serials*

Booksellers Association of Great Britain and Ireland. List of members / the Booksellers Association of Great Britian and Ireland. — 1981. — London : The Association, c1981. — [viii],100p
ISBN 0-901690-71-6 : Unpriced
ISSN 0068-0249 B81-31891

381′.45002′068 — Schools. Bookshops. Management — *Manuals*

Hill, Richard, *1944-*. How to set up and run a school bookshop / [written by Richard Hill and Pat Triggs]. — London (1 Effingham Rd, Lee, SE12 8NZ) : School Bookshop Association, 1981. — 42p : ill(some col.),ports ; 30cm
£1.20 (unbound) B81-19745

381′.45002′0941 — Great Britain. Bookselling. Economic aspects — *Serials*

[Economic survey *(Booksellers Association of Great Britain and Ireland. Charter Group)*]. Economic survey / the Booksellers Association Charter Group. — 1979-80. — London : The Association, c1981. — 10p
ISBN 0-901690-70-8 : £6.95
ISSN 0141-917x B81-30722

381′.45070172′0941 — Great Britain. Newsagency trades. Political aspects

Berry, Dave. Where is the other news? : the newstrade & the radical press / [by Dave Berry, Liz Cooper and Charles Landry]. — London : 9 Poland St., W1V 3DG : Minority Press Group, 1980. — 78p : ill,1port ; 22cm. — (Minority Press Group series ; no.2)
ISBN 0-906890-01-2 (cased) : Unpriced
ISBN 0-906890-02-0 (pbk) : £1.25 B81-22208

381′.45070172′0941 — Great Britain. Wholesale newsagency trades. Political aspects

Cooper, Liz. The other secret service : press distributors of press censorship / [by Liz Cooper, Charles Landry and Dave Berry]. — London (9 Poland St., W1V 3DG) : Minority Press Group, 1980. — 32p : ill,port ; 21cm. — (Minority Press Group series ; no.3)
Text on inside cover
ISBN 0-906890-15-2 (pbk) : £0.60 B81-22207

381′.450705′06041 — Great Britain. Bookselling. Organisations: Booksellers Association of Great Britain and Ireland. *Charter Group — Directories — Serials*

Booksellers Association of Great Britain and Ireland. List of charter members / the Booksellers Association of Great Britain and Ireland. — 1980. — London : The Association, c1980. — iv,22p
ISBN 0-901690-67-8 : Unpriced
ISSN 0142-8934 B81-03763

381′.456200028 — Great Britain. Wholesale engineering equipment trades — *Serials*

Engineering distributor : the journal of industrial distribution. — Vol.4, no.8 (Sept.1980)-. — Tonbridge : Benn, 1980-. — v. : ill ; 30cm
Ten issues yearly. — Continues: Engineering distributors journal. — Description based on: Vol.4, no.9 (Oct.1980)
ISSN 0260-4922 = Engineering distributor : £12.00 per year B81-04044

381′.4562131042′02541 — Great Britain. Wholesale electric equipment trades — *Directories — Serials*

United Kingdom electrical wholesalers / [Data Research Group]. — 1981. — Great Missenden : The Group ([1981?]). — 80p
ISBN 0-86099-291-8 : Unpriced B81-13409

381′.456213841′0941 — Great Britain. Retail radio equipment trades — *Serials*

RETRA dealer. — Feb.1980-. — London (57 Newington Causeway, SE1 6BE) : RETRA Ltd, 1980-. — v. : ill,ports ; 30cm
Monthly. — Official organ of: Radio, Electrical and Tevevision Retailers′ Association. — Continues: Electrical & electronic dealer. — Description based on: May 1981 issue
ISSN 0262-0499 = RETRA dealer : Unpriced
Also classified at 381′.45621388′00941
B81-36545

381′.45621388′00941 — Great Britain. Retail television equipment trades — *Serials*

RETRA dealer. — Feb.1980-. — London (57 Newington Causeway, SE1 6BE) : RETRA Ltd, 1980-. — v. : ill,ports ; 30cm
Monthly. — Official organ of: Radio, Electrical and Tevevision Retailers′ Association. — Continues: Electrical & electronic dealer. — Description based on: May 1981 issue
ISSN 0262-0499 = RETRA dealer : Unpriced
Primary classification 381′.456213841′0941
B81-36545

381′.456292 — Great Britain. Car accessories shops — *Directories — Serials*

United Kingdom car accessory shops / [Data Research Group]. — 1980/81. — Great Missenden : The Group, [1981]. — [vii],171p
ISBN 0-86099-272-1 : £26.00 B81-39509

381′.45631 — Great Britain. Agricultural equipment & materials trades — *Directories — Serials*

United Kingdom agricultural merchants / [Data Research Group]. — 1980-81. — Great Missenden : The Group, [1980]. — 235p
ISBN 0-86099-289-6 : £25.00 B81-09694

381′.456413′005 — Retail food trades — *Serials*

Canadean world distribution. — No.01 (5 Nov.1980)-. — London (60 Kingly St., W1R 5LH) : Agra-Canadean Publications, 1980-. — v. ; 30cm
Fortnightly. — Continues in part: Eurofood
£125.00 per year B81-05177

381′.456413′00941 — Great Britain. Grocery trades. Unbranded products

Sheath, Katherine J.. Generics : their development in grocery retailing and the reactions of consumers / by Katherine J. Sheath and Peter J. McGoldrick. — Manchester (P.O. Box 88, Manchester M60 1QD) : Department of Management Sciences, University of Manchester Institute of Science and Technology, 1981. — 103leaves : form ; 30cm
Unpriced (pbk) B81-39876

381′.4564157′0941 — Great Britain. Fast food trades — *Conference proceedings*

Planning for fast foods : report of an URPI conference. — Reading : Unit for Retail Plannning Information, 1980. — 34p : ill ; 30cm. — (URPI. U ; 20)
Unpriced (pbk) B81-16789

381′.456625′0924 — Cleveland. Stockton-on-Tees. Matches. Retailing. Walker, John, *1781-1859 — Accounts*

Walker, John, *1781-1859*. The day-book of John Walker inventor of friction matches : annotated extracts / compiled by Doreen Thomas. — [Cleveland, Middlesborough] : [D. Thomas], 1981. — 31p : ill,1facsim,1port ; 21cm
ISBN 0-9507549-0-0 (pbk) : £0.90 B81-34248

381′.4566402853′02541 — Great Britain. Freezer centres — *Directories — Serials*

United Kingdom freezer centres / [Data Research Group]. — [1980]. — Great Missenden : The Group, 1980. — 103p
ISBN 0-86099-273-x : Unpriced B81-10667

381′.456649′00941 — Great Britain. Meat trades — *Serials*

[UK market review *(Great Britain. Meat and Livestock Commission. Economic Information Service)*]. UK market review / MLC Economic Information Service. — 1981, no.1-. — Bletchley (PO Box 44, Queensway House, Bletchley MK2 2EF) : Meat and Livestock Commission, 1981-. — v. : ill ; 21cm
Three issues yearly. — Continues: UK market survey (Great Britain. Meat and Livestock Commission. Economic Information Service). — Description based on: 1981, no.2
ISSN 0262-1525 = MLC UK market review : Unpriced B81-38182

381′.4566492 — Great Britain. Multiple butchers′ shops — *Directories — Serials*

United Kingdom butchers with 3 or more outlets / [Data Research Group]. — [1981]. — Great Missenden : The Group, 1981. — 45leaves
ISBN 0-86099-307-8 : £24.00 B81-37233

381′.4566494 — Great Britain. Fried fish trades. Organisations: Confederation of Fried Fish Caterers′ Associations — *Serials*

Fried fish caterer / Confederation of Fried Fish Caterers′ Associations. — 1st ed. (Jan.1980) ; No.2 (Feb.1980)-. — Leeds (429 Meanwood Rd, Leeds 7) : G.R. Associates, 1980-. — v. : ill,ports ; 30cm
Monthly
ISSN 0261-2038 = Fried fish caterer : £12.50
B81-20088

381′.4567 — Great Britain. Retail trades. Discounts by manufacturing industries: Discounts on goods — *Inquiry reports*

Great Britain. *Monopolies and Mergers Commission*. Discounts to retailers : a report on the general effect on the public interest of the practice of charging some retailers lower prices than others or providing special benefits to some retailers where the difference cannot be attributed to savings in the supplier′s costs / the Monopolies and Mergers Commission. — London : H.M.S.O., 1981. — viii,239p : ill ; 25cm. — (HC ; 311)
Bibliography: p233-235. — Includes index
ISBN 0-10-231181-1 (pbk) : £7.50 B81-25365

381′.456762823′02541 — Great Britain. Wholesale stationery trades — *Directories*

United Kingdom stationers-wholesale / [Data Research Group]. — [1980]. — Great Missenden : The Group, 1980. — 46p
ISBN 0-86099-285-3 : Unpriced B81-06712

381′.4567731′0924 — London. Wool trades. Heritage, Thomas. Accounts, *1532-1540*

Temple, Peter. Warwickshire grazier and London skinner, 1532-1555. — Oxford : Oxford University Press for the British Academy, Dec.1981. — [240]p. — (Records of social and economic history. New series ; 5)
ISBN 0-19-726008-x : £24.00 : CIP entry
Primary classification 338.7′63′0924 B81-31448

381′.45683′02541 — Great Britain. Wholesale hardware trades — *Directories — Serials*

United Kingdom hardware & ironmongery wholesalers / [Data Research Group]. — [1981]. — Great Missenden : The Group, 1981. — 43leaves
ISBN 0-86099-309-4 : £25.00 B81-37225

381′.4568408′02541 — Great Britain. Do-it-yourself trades — *Directories — Serials*

United Kingdom do-it-yourself shops / [Data Research Group]. — [1981]. — Great Missenden : The Group, 1981. — 177p
ISBN 0-86099-311-6 : £27.00 B81-37228

381′.45687′02541 — Great Britain. Wholesale clothing trades — *Directories — Serials*

United Kingdom clothing wholesalers / [Data Research Group]. — [1981]. — Great Missenden : The Group, 1981. — 28leaves
ISBN 0-86099-308-6 : £24.00 B81-37226

381'.45687'0941 — Great Britain. Clothing shops, *1800-1914*
Adburgham, Alison. Shops and shopping 1800-1914 : where, and in what manner the well-dreesed Englishwoman bought her clothes / Alison Adburgham. — 2nd ed. — London : Allen and Unwin, 1981. — xxiv,304p,[16]p of plates : ill,facsims,1plan ; 25cm
Previous ed.: 1964. — Bibliography: p288-291. - Includes index
ISBN 0-04-942168-9 : £9.95 B81-14292

381'.4568872'02541 — Great Britain. Wholesale toy trades — *Directories* — *Serials*
United Kingdom fancy goods & toy wholesalers / [Data Research Group]. — [1981]. — Great Missenden : The Group, 1981. — 40leaves
ISBN 0-86099-292-6 : £25.00
Also classified at 381'.2 B81-37224

382 — FOREIGN TRADE

382 — Foreign intra-firm trade
Helleiner, G. K.. Intra-firm trade and the developing countries / Gerald K. Helleiner. — London : Macmillan, 1981. — ix,110p : ill ; 23cm
Bibliography: p99-106. — Includes index
ISBN 0-333-27739-2 : £15.00 B81-38730

382 — Foreign trade
International trade : selected readings / edited by Jagdish N. Bhagwati. — Cambridge, Mass. ; London : MIT, c1981. — xxii,414p : ill ; 24cm
Includes bibliographies and index
ISBN 0-262-02160-9 (cased) : £15.50
ISBN 0-262-52060-5 (pbk) : Unpriced
B81-28257

382 — Foreign trade. Effects of industrialisation
Batchelor, R. A.. Industrialisation and the basis for trade / R.A. Batchelor, R.L. Major, A.D. Morgan. — Cambridge : Cambridge University Press, 1980. — xx,347p : ill ; 24cm. — (Economic and social studies ; 32)
Bibliography: p325-336. - Includes index
ISBN 0-521-23302-x : £17.50 : CIP rev.
B80-25461

382 — Foreign trade — *For schools*
Hills, C. A. R.. World trade / C.A.R. Hills. — London : Batsford Educational and Acedemic, 1981. — 72p : ill ; 26cm. — (Today's world)
Includes index
ISBN 0-7134-3472-4 : £5.50 B81-29485

382 — Great Britain. Foreign trade. Finance — *For banking*
Foreign business workbook / Institute of Bankers in Scotland. — 2nd ed. — Edinburgh (20 Rutland Sq., Edinburgh) : [The Institute], 1978. — 73p : ill ; 30cm
Previous ed.: 197-?
£2.25 (pbk) B81-06144

382'.012 — Great Britain. Foreign trade. Commodities — *Classification schedules* — *Serials*
Guide to the classification for overseas trade statistics / published under the authority of the Commissioners of Her Majesty's Customs and Excise. — 1981. — London : H.M.S.O., 1981. — 482p
ISBN 0-11-260464-1 : £12.75 B81-12413

382'.0724 — Foreign trade in intermediate goods & non-traded goods. Mathematical models
Hazari, Bharat R.. Non-traded and intermediate goods and the pure theory of international trade / Bharat R. Hazari, Pasquale M. Sgro, Dong C. Suh. — London : Croom Helm, c1981. — xiii,189p : ill ; 23cm
Includes bibliographies and index
ISBN 0-85664-765-9 : £14.95 : CIP rev.
B80-13329

382'.09'04 — Foreign trade, *1945-1980*
Mégrelis, Christian. Keys for the future : from free trade to fair trade / Christian Mégrelis. — Lexington : Lexington, [1980?] ; [Farnborough, Hants] : Gower [distributor], 1981. — xviii,154p ; 24cm
Translation of: Danger. — Includes index
ISBN 0-669-03705-2 : £12.00 B81-15515

382'.091713'047 — Western bloc countries. Foreign trade with Eastern Europe
Paliwoda, Stanley J.. East-West countertrade arrangements : barter, compensation, buyback and counterpurchase of "parallel" trade / Stanley J. Paliwoda. — Manchester (P.O. Box 88 Manchester M60 1QD) : Department of Management Sciences University of Manchester Institute of Science and Technology, 1981. — 9p : 1 facsim ; 31cm. — (Occasional paper / Department of Management Sciences, University of Manchester Institute of Science and Technology ; no.8105)
Unpriced (pbk)
Also classified at 382'.0947'01713 B81-30914

382'.09171'7 — Sovet ékonomicheskoĭ vzaimopomoshchi countries. Foreign trade — *Statistics*
Comecon foreign trade data 1980 / edited by the Vienna Institute for Comparative Economic Studies (Wiener Institut für Internationale Wirtschaftsvergleiche) ; sponsored by the First Austrian Bank (Die Erste österreichische Spar-Casse). — London : Macmillan, 1981. — 509p : ill ; 20cm
Includes index
ISBN 0-333-30668-6 : £15.00 B81-26507

382'.091812'06 — Western world. Multinational companies. Foreign trade with Africa. Effects of influence of Soviet Union on Africa
Soviet-African trade : the Western business response : ... the outcome of the deliberations of a Study Group organised by the Institute for the Study of Conflict, and of on-the-spot commercial investigations in Africa, Europe and the United States. — London (12 Golden Sq., W1R 3AF) : The Institute, 1980. — 47,[4]p of plates : ill,1map ; 30cm. — (An ISC special report, ISSN 0141-8742)
Cover title. — Text on inside covers. — ISC special report summary (sheet ; [2]p) as insert
£15.00 (pbk)
Also classified at 382'.096'01812 B81-13300

382'.092'4 — France. Foreign trade with Canada & West Indies, *1729-1770.* **Dugard, Robert**
Miquelon, Dale. Dugard of Rouen : French trade to Canada and the West Indies, 1729-1770 / by Dale Miquelon. — Montreal ; London : McGill-Queen's University Press, c1978. — xi,282p : ill ; 24cm
Bibliography: p263-269. - Includes index
ISBN 0-7735-0299-8 : £15.40 B81-05327

382'.094'0417 — Europe. Foreign trade with Ireland *(Republic)* — *Serials*
Trade-links. — Vol.1, no.1 (Summer 1979) ; Vol.2, no.1 (July/Aug.1980)-. — Dublin (P.O. Box 1127, 7 Clare St., Dublin 2) : Libra House, 1979-. — v. : ill,ports ; 30cm
Six issues yearly. — Suspended from Summer 1979 to July/Aug.1980. — Description based on: Vol.2, no.1 (July/Aug.1980)
Unpriced
Also classified at 382'.09417'04 B81-18802

382'.0941 — Great Britain. Foreign trade, *1918-1980* — *For schools*
Anthony, Vivian S.. Britain's overseas trade : the recent history of British trade / Vivian S. Anthony. — 4th ed. — London : Heinemann Educational, 1981. — 112p : ill ; 20cm. — (Studies in the British economy)
Previous ed.: 1976. — Bibliography: p105-108. — Includes index
ISBN 0-435-84583-7 (pbk) : £2.50 : CIP rev.
B81-23782

382'.0941 — Great Britain. Foreign trade. Policies of government. Great Britain. *Parliament. House of Commons. Industry and Trade Committee.* **First report from the Industry and Trade Committee, session 1980-81** — *Critical studies*
Great Britain. *Department of Trade.* Trade policy : the Government's reply to the first report from the Industry and Trade Committee for the session 1980-81 (HC 109) / Department of Trade. — London : H.M.S.O., 1981. — 25p ; 25cm. — (Cmnd. ; 8247)
ISBN 0-10-182470-x (unbound) : £2.40
B81-37019

382'.0941 — Great Britain. Foreign trade — *Statistics* — *Serials*
Statistics of trade through United Kingdom ports . Annual edition / HM Customs and Excise. — 1979. — Southend-on-Sea (Room 603, 27 Victoria Ave., Southend-on-Sea SS2 6AL) : HM Customs and Excise, Statistical Office, 1981. — [356]p in various pagings
ISBN 0-907468-00-4 : £11.00
ISSN 0309-3107 B81-32218

382'.0941 — Great Britain. Ports. Foreign trade — *Statistics* — *Serials*
Port statistics for the foreign trade of the United Kingdom. Part I, Imports and exports at the fifteen principal ports for each division of external trade / British Ports Association. — 1980. — London : The Association, [1981?]. — 45p
Unpriced B81-29042

Port statistics for the foreign trade of the United Kingdom. Part III, Imports and exports at individual ports for each division of external trade / British Ports Assocation. — 1980. — London : The Association, [1981?]. — vii,132p
Unpriced B81-29041

382'.0941 — Great Britain. Seaborne foreign trade, *1480-1914* — *Festschriften*
Shipping, trade and commerce : essays in memory of Ralph Davis / edited by P.L. Cottrell and D.H. Aldcroft. — [Leicester] : Leicester University Press, 1981. — viii,200p : 1port ; 24cm
Bibliography: p7-8. - Includes index
ISBN 0-7185-1195-6 (corrected) : £15.00
Also classified at 387.5'0941 B81-23126

382'.0941'047 — Great Britain. Foreign trade with Soviet Union — *Directories* — *Serials*
Directory of British industry and engineering. — 25th ed. (1981). — London (Walter House, Bedford St., WC2R 0QB) : British Industrial Publicity Overseas, [1981]. — 88p
Cover title: British industry & engineering directory of British firms interested in trade with the USSR. — Spine title: Spravochnik po britanskim firmam
Unpriced
Also classified at 382'.0947'041 B81-35956

382'.0941'05 — Great Britain. Foreign trade with British colonies in Asia. Role of New South Wales, *1776-1811*
Frost, Alan, *1943-*. Convicts and empire : a naval question 1776-1811 / Alan Frost. — Melbourne ; Oxford : Oxford University Press, 1980. — xv,240p : ill,maps,ports ; 23cm
Maps on lining papers. — Bibliography: p227-231. — Includes index
ISBN 0-19-554255-x : £17.50
Also classified at 382'.095'041 B81-18977

382'.0941'054 — Great Britain. Foreign trade with India. Companies: East India Company, *to 1874*
Sutton, Jean. Lords of the east : the East India Company and its ships / Jean Sutton. — London : Conway Maritime, 1981. — 176p : ill,charts,maps,ports ; 27cm
Bibliography: p173. — Includes index
ISBN 0-85177-169-6 : £9.50 B81-40924

382'.0941'05694 — Great Britain. Foreign trade with Israel — *Serials*
British-Israel trade : the journal of the British-Israel Chamber of Commerce. — Vol.23, no.5 (Oct./Nov.1980)-. — London (126-134 Baker St., W1M 1FH) : Designed and produced for the Chamber by Prittie & Nelson Public Relations, 1980-. — v. : ill,ports ; 29cm
Six issues yearly. — Continues: Anglo-Israel trade journal
ISSN 0260-3985 = British-Israel trade : Unpriced
Also classified at 382'.095694'041 B81-06334

382'.09417'04 — Ireland *(Republic).* **Foreign trade with Europe** — *Serials*
Trade-links. — Vol.1, no.1 (Summer 1979) ; Vol.2, no.1 (July/Aug.1980)-. — Dublin (P.O. Box 1127, 7 Clare St., Dublin 2) : Libra House, 1979-. — v. : ill,ports ; 30cm
Six issues yearly. — Suspended from Summer 1979 to July/Aug.1980. — Description based on: Vol.2, no.1 (July/Aug.1980)
Unpriced
Primary classification 382'.094'0417 B81-18802

382′.0947 — Eastern Europe. Foreign trade, *1950-1975*

Matejka, Harriet. The foreign trade system / by Harriet Matejka. — [Oxford] ([62 Woodstock Rd., Oxford]) : [St Antony′s College, Russian and East European Centre], 1980. — 60leaves ; 30cm. — (Papers in East European economics, ISSN 0307-5575 ; no.61)
Unpriced (unbound) B81-10095

382′.0947′01713 — Eastern Europe. Foreign trade with Western bloc countries

Paliwoda, Stanley J.. East-West countertrade arrangements : barter, compensation, buyback and counterpurchase of "parallel" trade / Stanley J. Paliwoda. — Manchester (P.O. Box 88 Manchester M60 1QD) : Department of Management Sciences University of Manchester Institute of Science and Technology, 1981. — 9p : 1 facsim ; 31cm. — (Occasional paper / Department of Management Sciences, University of Manchester Institute of Science and Technology ; no.8105)
Unpriced (pbk)
Primary classification 382′.091713′047
B81-30914

382′.0947′041 — Soviet Union. Foreign trade with Great Britain — *Directories — Serials*

Directory of British industry and engineering. — 25th ed. (1981). — London (Walter House, Bedford St., WC2R 0QB) : British Industrial Publicity Overseas, [1981]. — 88p
Cover title: British industry & engineering directory of British firms interested in trade with the USSR. — Spine title: Spravochnik po britanskim firmam
Unpriced
Primary classification 382′.0941′047 B81-35956

382′.095′041 — Asia. British colonies. Foreign trade with Great Britain. Role of New South Wales, *1776-1811*

Frost, Alan, *1943-*. Convicts and empire : a naval question 1776-1811 / Alan Frost. — Melbourne ; Oxford : Oxford University Press, 1980. — xv,240p : ill,maps,ports ; 23cm
Maps on lining papers. — Bibliography: p227-231. — Includes index
ISBN 0-19-554255-x : £17.50
Primary classification 382′.0941′05 B81-18977

382′.0952 — Japan. Foreign trade

Sinha, Radha. Japan′s options for the 1980s. — London : Croom Helm, Dec.1981. — [288]p
ISBN 0-7099-2311-2 : £14.95 : CIP entry
B81-35868

382′.095694′041 — Israel. Foreign trade with Great Britain — *Serials*

British-Israel trade : the journal of the British-Israel Chamber of Commerce. — Vol.23, no.5 (Oct./Nov.1980)-. — London (126-134 Baker St., W1M 1FH) : Designed and produced for the Chamber by Prittie & Nelson Public Relations, 1980-. — v. : ill,ports ; 29cm
Six issues yearly. — Continues: Anglo-Israel trade journal
ISSN 0260-3985 = British-Israel trade : Unpriced
Primary classification 382′.0941′05694
B81-06334

382′.096′01812 — Africa. Foreign trade with multinational companies of Western world. Effects of influence of Soviet Union on Africa

Soviet-African trade : the Western business response : ... the outcome of the deliberations of a Study Group organised by the Institute for the Study of Conflict, and of on-the-spot commercial investigations in Africa, Europe and the United States. — London (12 Golden Sq., W1R 3AF) : The Institute, 1980. — 47,[4]p of plates : ill,1map ; 30cm. — (An ISC special report, ISSN 0141-8742)
Cover title. — Text on inside covers. — ISC special report summary (sheet ; [2]p) as insert
£15.00 (pbk)
Primary classification 382′.091812′06
B81-13300

382.1 — ECONOMIC RELATIONS

382.1′7 — Great Britain. Foreign trade with Maryland & Virginia. Financing, *1700-1776*

Price, Jacob M.. Capital and credit in British overseas trade : the view from the Chesapeake, 1700-1776. — Cambridge, Mass. ; London : Harvard University Press, 1980. — viii,233p ; 22cm
Bibliography: p205-220. — Includes index
ISBN 0-674-09480-8 : £11.10 B81-16529

382.1′7 — Invisible exports — *Statistics*

Morgan, E. Victor. World invisible trade / prepared for the Committee on Invisible Exports by Economists Advisory Group Limited ; ... report ... prepared by E. Victor Morgan, Alan Doran and Lindsay Milne. — London (7th Floor, The Stock Exchange, EC2N 1HH) : Committee on Invisible Exports, 1981. — 19p ; 26cm
£6.00 (pbk) B81-32316

382.1′7′0941 — Great Britain. Balance of payments — *Statistics — Serials*

United Kingdom balance of payments / Central Statistical Office. — 1980 ed. — London : H.M.S.O., 1980. — 82p
ISBN 0-11-630777-3 : £7.00 B81-02395

382.1′7′0945 — Italy. Balance of payments. Effects of monetary policies, *1945-1978*

Tullio, Giuseppe. The monetary approach to external adjustment : a case study of Italy / Giuseppe Tullio ; foreword by Paolo Baffi. — London : Macmillan, 1981. — xx,127p : ill ; 22cm
Bibliography: p114-123. — Includes index
ISBN 0-333-27651-5 : £15.00
Also classified at 332.4′56′0945 B81-38726

382.3 — FOREIGN TRADE. COMMERCIAL POLICY

382′.3 — Foreign trade. Policies of governments — *Conference proceedings*

International Economics Study Group. *Conference (3rd : 1978 : Isle of Thorns)*. Current issues in commercial policy and diplomacy : papers of the Third Annual Conference of the International Economics Study Group / edited by John Black and Brian Hindley. — London : Macmillan for the Trade Policy Research Centre, 1980. — 148p : ill ; 23cm
Includes bibliographies and index
ISBN 0-333-26170-4 : £20.00 : CIP rev.
B80-08167

382.4 — FOREIGN TRADE. SPECIAL COMMODITIES AND SERVICES

382′.41′091724 — Developing countries. Economic development. Role of exports of cash crops

Ingham, Barbara. Tropical exports and economic development : new perspectives on producer response in three low-income countries / Barbara Ingham. — London : Macmillan, 1981. — xi,123p : ill,1map ; 23cm
Bibliography: p111-118. — Includes index
ISBN 0-333-28569-7 : £12.00 : CIP rev.
B80-13330

382′.41361′0942393 — Avon. Bristol. Cane sugar import trades, *to 1807 — For schools*

Grant, Alison. Bristol and the sugar trade / Alison Grant ; illustrated from contemporary sources. — Harlow : Longman, 1981. — 96p : ill,maps,1plan,ports ; 20cm. — (Then and there series)
Includes index
ISBN 0-582-21724-5 (pbk) : £0.85
Also classified at 972.9′03 B81-35310

382′.41373′0724 — Ivory Coast. Economic development, *1960-1978.* **Role of exports of coffee. Economic models**

Priovolos, Theophilos. Coffee and the Ivory Coast : an econometric study / Theophilos Priovolos. — Lexington, Mass. : Lexington Books ; [Aldershot] : Gower [distributor], 1981. — xv,218p : ill ; 24cm
Bibliography: p209-215. — Includes index
ISBN 0-669-04331-1 : £16.00 B81-39699

382′.4172 — New Zealand. Exports to Great Britain: Butter. Effects of Common Agricultural Policy of European Economic Community

New Zealand′s dairy exports and the EEC : understanding the situation. — London (St. Olaf House, Tooley Street, London SE1) : New Zealand Dairy Board, [1980?]. — [7]p : ill (some col.) ; 22cm
Cover title
Unpriced (pbk) B81-09776

382′.42282 — Organization of the Petroleum Exporting Countries. Conferences. Official resolutions, *1960-1980*

Organization of the Petroleum Exporting Countries. Official resolutions and press releases 1960-1980 / OPEC. — Oxford : Published on behalf of the Organization of the Petroleum Exporting Countries by Pergamon, 1980. — ix,214p ; 30cm
Includes index
ISBN 0-08-027335-1 (pbk) : £18.00 B81-07302

382′.42282 — Organization of the Petroleum Exporting Countries, *to 1980*

Seymour, Ian. OPEC : instrument of change / Ian Seymour. — London : Macmillan, 1980. — ix,306p ; 25cm
Includes index
ISBN 0-333-30667-8 : £15.00 B81-05417

382′.42282 — Petroleum. Foreign trade between United States & Saudi Arabia, 1933-1950

Anderson, Irvine H.. Aramco, the United States and Saudi Arabia : a study of the dynamics of foreign oil policy, 1933-1950 / Irvine H. Anderson. — Princeton ; Guildford : Princeton University Press, c1981. — xiii,259p ; 23cm
Bibliography: p237-251. — Includes index
ISBN 0-691-04679-4 : £11.20 B81-35286

382′.44′096 — Africa. Slave trade with America, *ca 1700-1850 — Readings from contemporary sources*

Hogg, Peter C.. Slavery : the Afro-American experience / Peter Hogg ; illustrated from English sources in the British Library Reference Division. — London : British Library, c1979. — 51p : ill(some col.),1map,facsims,2ports ; 24cm
Text and map on inside covers. — Bibliography: 2p
ISBN 0-904654-28-1 (pbk) : £1.95 : CIP rev.
Also classified at 382′.44′097 B79-17447

382′.44′097 — America. Slave trade with Africa, *ca 1700-1850 — Readings from contemporary sources*

Hogg, Peter C.. Slavery : the Afro-American experience / Peter Hogg ; illustrated from English sources in the British Library Reference Division. — London : British Library, c1979. — 51p : ill(some col.),1map,facsims,2ports ; 24cm
Text and map on inside covers. — Bibliography: 2p
ISBN 0-904654-28-1 (pbk) : £1.95 : CIP rev.
Primary classification 382′.44′096 B79-17447

382′.44′097291 — Cuba. Slave trade. Abolition. Foreign relations between Great Britain & Spain, *1770-1870*

Murray, David R.. Odious commerce : Britain, Spain and the abolition of the Cuban slave trade / David R. Murray. — Cambridge : Cambridge University Press, 1980. — xi,423p ; 23cm. — (Cambridge Latin American studies ; 37)
Bibliography: p400-413. - Includes index
ISBN 0-521-22867-0 : £19.50 : CIP rev.
B80-25464

382′.45574 — Foreign trade in organisms

Inskipp, T. P.. International trade in wildlife / by Tim Inskipp and Sue Wells. — London (10 Percy St., W1P 0DR) : Earthscan, [c1979]. — 104p : ill,facsim ; 21cm
Cover title. — Bibliography: 103-104
ISBN 0-905347-11-0 (pbk) : £2.50 B81-38456

382′.4562147′0941 — Great Britain. Solar energy equipment. Exporting — *Conference proceedings*

. Solar energy export opportunities : conference (C26) at the Royal Institution, London, April 1981. — London (19 Albemarle St., W1X 3HA) : UK Section of the International Solar Energy Society, [c1981]. — 56p : ill ; 30cm. — (UK-ISES conference proceedings ; C26)
Cover title. — Includes bibliographies
ISBN 0-904963-24-1 (pbk) : £8.00 (£3.00 to members of UK ISES) B81-26547

382′.456234 — Weapons trades — *Quotations*

Rodger, Donald. Thus spake Zaharoff : how the 'merchants of death' see themselves and their trade with quotations and comments / Donald Rodger. — London (5 Caledonian Rd., N1 9DX) : Campaign Against Arms Trade, c1980. — 44p : ill ; 21cm
Cover title. — Text on inside covers
ISBN 0-9506922-1-2 (pbk) : Unpriced B81-27311

382′.45664028′0942188 — London. Haringey *(London Borough).* **Wood Green. Preserved food importers: A. Donatantonio & Sons Limited** — *Serials*

[AD ... *(London)*]. AD ... : newsletter of A. Donatantonio & Sons Limited. — 1980, no.1-. — London (105 Mayes Rd, Wood Green, N22 6UP) : Donatantonio, 1980-. — v. : ill,ports ; 30cm
Irregular. — Description based on: 1980, no.2
ISSN 0262-0103 = AD ... (London) : Unpriced B81-38524

382′.456685 — Ancient Arabia. Foreign trade in incense

Groom, Nigel. Frankincense and myrrh : a study of the Arabian incense trade / Nigel Groom. — London : Longman, 1981. — xvi,285p,[16]p of plates : ill,maps ; 23cm. — (Arab background series)
Bibliography: p265-274. - Includes index
ISBN 0-582-76476-9 : £14.95 : CIP rev. B80-34847

382′.45677 — Developed countries. Imports from developing countries: Textiles. Import quotas

Keesing, Donald B.. Textile quotas against developing countries / by Donald B. Keesing and Martin Wolf. — London : Trade Policy Research Centre, 1980. — xii,214p : 1ill ; 19cm. — (Thames essay, ISSN 0306-6991 ; no.23)
ISBN 0-900842-49-0 (pbk) : £6.00 B81-05957

382′.456853′02541 — Great Britain. Footwear industries. Exporters — *Directories* — *Serials*

Directory of British footwear exporters / British Footwear Manufacturers Federation. — 1977-1978. — London (72 Dean St., W1V 5HB) : The Federation, [1977]. — 56p
Unpriced B81-35982

Directory of British footwear exporters / British Footwear Manufacturers Federation. — 1978-1979. — London (72 Dean St., W1V 5HB) : The Federation, [1978]. — 53p
Unpriced B81-35983

Directory of British footwear exporters. — 7th ed. — London (72 Dean St., W1V 5HB) : British Footwear Manufacturers Federation, [1981]. — 46p
Unpriced B81-31561

382′.457 — Great Britain. *Reviewing Committee on the Export of Works of Art* — *Serials*

Great Britain. *Reviewing Committee on the Export of Works of Art.* Export of works of art. — 25th report (1978-79). — London : H.M.S.O., [1980]. — iii,51p
ISBN 0-10-180500-4 : £4.00 B81-04612

Great Britain. *Reviewing Committee on the Export of Works of Art.* Export of works of art. — 26th report (1979-80). — London : H.M.S.O., 1981. — iii,36p. — (Cmnd. ; 8242)
ISBN 0-10-182420-3 : £3.90 B81-29083

382.5 — IMPORTS

382′.5′025 — Importers — *Directories* — *For British exporters*

Export courier guide to distributors. — [London] ([21 Montpelier Row SE3 0SR]) : Export Marketors Partnership]
Cover title
Food : Europe. — [1981?]. — 1v.(Loose-leaf) : 1port ; 24cm
£195.00
Primary classification 381′.025 B81-19689

382′.5′0941 — Great Britain. Import controls

Countering disruptive imports : guide to instruments of commercial defence. — London : Confederation of British Industry, 1979. — 36p : ill ; 21cm
£2.00 (pbk) B81-37962

382′.5′0941 — Great Britain. Import controls — *Free trade viewpoints*

Congdon, Tim. Against import controls / Tim Congdon. — London : Centre for Policy Studies, 1981. — vii,67p ; 21cm
ISBN 0-905880-33-1 : £3.95 B81-39681

382.6 — EXPORTS

382′.6 — Exporting. Prices. Stabilisation. Use of buffer stocks *compared with* **use of forward contracts**

Gemmill, Gordon T.. Forward contracts or international buffer stocks? : a study of their relative efficiencies in stabilising export-earnings / by Gordon T. Gemmill. — [London] : [City University Business School], c1981. — 45 leaves ; 30cm. — (Working paper series / City University Business School, ISSN 0140-1041 ; no.26)
Bibliography: leaf 45
Unpriced (pbk) B81-37616

382′.6′0724 — Great Britain. Exporting, *1955-1973.* **Econometric models**

Winters, L. Alan. An econometric model of the export sector : UK visible exports and their prices 1955-1973 / L. Alan Winters. — Cambridge : Cambridge University Press, 1981. — x,251p : ill ; 24cm. — (Cambridge studies in applied econometrics ; 4)
Bibliography: p239-246. — Includes index
ISBN 0-521-23720-3 : £22.50 : CIP rev. B81-30497

382′.6′091724 — Developing countries. Exports, *1840-1900*

Hanson, John R.. Trade in transition : exports from the Third World, 1840-1900 / John R. Hanson, II. — New York ; London : Academic Press, c1980. — xii,197p : 1ill ; 24cm. — (Studies in social discontinuity)
Bibliography: p183-187. - Includes index
ISBN 0-12-323450-6 : £10.20 B81-03625

382′.6′0941 — Great Britain. Exports to Japan — *Statistics* — *For British businessmen*

Japan buys British : the 1980 details. — London (342 Grand Buildings, Trafalgar Sq., WC2N 5HB) : Anglo-Japanese Economic Institute, c1981. — 23p : ill,ports ; 21cm
Unpriced (pbk) B81-25271

382′.6′09944 — Australia. Economic growth. Role of exports, *1851-1900:* **Primary commodities. Econometric models** — *Study regions: New South Wales*

Tamaschke, H. U.. Exports and economic growth : applications of the staple theory / H.U. Tamaschke. — London : J.K. Publishers, c1980. — ix,160p ; 22cm
Bibliography: p149-157. — Includes index
ISBN 0-906216-90-7 (pbk) : £6.50
Primary classification 382′.6′09945 B81-06961

382′.6′09945 — Australia. Economic growth. Role of exports, *1851-1900:* **Primary commodities. Econometric models** — *Study regions: Australia: Victoria*

Tamaschke, H. U.. Exports and economic growth : applications of the staple theory / H.U. Tamaschke. — London : J.K. Publishers, c1980. — ix,160p ; 22cm
Bibliography: p149-157. — Includes index
ISBN 0-906216-90-7 (pbk) : £6.50
Also classified at 382′.6′09944 B81-06961

382.7 — TARIFF POLICIES

382.7′0972 — Foreign trade. Protection. Policies of Mexican government, *ca 1930-1970*

Kate, Adriaan ten. Protection and economic development in Mexico / Adriaan ten Kate, Robert Bruce Wallace with the co-operation of Antonie Waarts, Maria Delfina Ramírez de Wallace. — Farnborough, Hants. : Gower, c1980. — xii,318p ; 23cm
Includes bibliographies
ISBN 0-566-00409-7 : £17.50 B81-12990

382.9 — TRADE AGREEMENTS

382.9′1 — Customs unions

El-Agraa, A. M.. Theory of customs unions / A.M. El-Agraa & A.J. Jones. — Deddington : Philip Allan, 1981. — ix,134p : ill ; 23cm
Bibliography: p127-131. — Includes index
ISBN 0-86003-031-8 : £6.95 : CIP rev. B80-13771

382.9′142 — European Community — *Practical information* — *For British small firms*

. Big opportunities for small businesses : a starting guide to the European Community / prepared by Conservative and Unionist Members of European Democratic Group ; [compiled by Bill Newton Dunn]. — London (2 Queen Anne's Gate SW1H 9AA) : European Democratic Group, [1981]. — 12p ; 21cm
Unpriced (pbk) B81-27814

382.9′2′09 — General Agreement on Tariffs and Trade *(Organization), to 1970*

Dam, Kenneth W.. The GATT : law and internatioanl economic organization / Kenneth W. Dam. — Chicago ; London : University of Chicago Press, 1977, c1970. — xvii,480p ; 23cm
Includes index
ISBN 0-226-13496-2 (pbk) : £11.20 B81-38562

383 — POSTAL SERVICES

383′.1 — Great Britain. Postal services. Mail. Interception. Procedure — *Inquiry reports*

Diplock, William John Kenneth Diplock, *Baron.* The interception of communications in Great Britain : report / by Lord Diplock. — London : H.M.S.O., [1981]. — 7p ; 25cm. — (Cmnd. ; 8191)
ISBN 0-10-181910-2 (unbound) : £1.10
Also classified at 384 B81-16301

383′.142′09 — International shipping mail transport services — *History*

British maritime postal history. — [Charmouth?] : Published for the author by PHEAS on behalf of Postal History International
Vol.1: The P & O Bombay & Australian lines - 1852-1914 / by R. Kirk. — [1980?]. — 166p : ill,maps,facsims ; 25cm
Unpriced B81-20892

383′.2′0973 — United States. Postal services: United States. *Postal Service.* **Economic aspects**

Sorkin, Alan L.. The economics of the postal system : alternatives and reform / Alan L. Sorkin. — Lexington, Mass. : Lexington Books ; Aldershot : Gower [distributor], c1980. — xii,200p : ill ; 24cm
Includes index
ISBN 0-669-02460-0 : £15.00 B81-30788

383′.42′0942 — England. Rural regions. Post offices — *Proposals*

Taylor, Cliff. Rural post offices : retaining a vital service / by Cliff Taylor ; edited by David Emerson. — London : Bedford Square Press, NCV0, 1981. — vii,36p : 1form ; 30cm
ISBN 0-7199-1056-0 (pbk) : £1.50 B81-29198

383′.4941 — Great Britain. Postal services. Consumer protection services: Post Office Users' National Council — *Serials*

Post Office Users' National Council. Annual report / Pounc. — 1979-80-. — London (Waterloo Bridge House, Waterloo Rd, SE1 8UA) : Post Office Users' National Council, 1980-. — v. ; 21cm
Continues: Post Office Users' National Council. Report on the exercise and performance of its functions for the accounting year ended 31st March ...
ISSN 0261-1317 = Annual report (Post Office Users' National Council) : Unpriced B81-14951

383′.4941′0222 — Great Britain. Postal services — *Illustrations — For children*

Gray, David T.. The post office / illustrated by David T. Gray ; [text by] Constance Milburn. — Glasgow : Blackie, 1981. — 32p : chiefly col.ill ; 21cm. — (Inside story)
Includes index
ISBN 0-216-91035-8 (pbk) : £0.95 B81-29245

383′.4941′05 — Great Britain. ***Post Office*** **—** ***Serials***

Great Britain. *Post Office*. Post Office report and accounts for the year ended 31 March .... — 1980. — London : H.M.S.O., 1980. — 55p
ISBN 0-11-886015-1 : £1.00 B81-00078

383′.49411′05 — Scotland. Postal services — *History — Serials*

The **Postal** history annual. — 1980. — Dumfries (11, Newall Terrace, Dumfries DG1 1LN) : J.A. Mackay, c1980. — 56p
Unpriced B81-10272

383′.494111 — Scotland. Highlands & Islands. Postal services, *to 1980*

Mackay, James A.. The Scottish Highland postal service / James A. Mackay. — Paisley (11, Low Road, Castlehead, Paisley, Scotland, PA2 6AQ) : Gleniffer Press, 1981. — [26]p : ill,1sample ; 6cm
Text and ill. on lining papers. — Limited ed. of 250 copies. — Book in plastic container
ISBN 0-906005-03-5 : £10.00 B81-38420

383′.4942835 — Humberside. Goole & Howden. Postal services, *& 1980*

Sedgewick, William A.. The postal history of Goole, Howden and Selby / by William A. Sedgewick and Ronald Ward. — Sheffield (c/o Hon. Treasurer, 48 Banner Cross Rd., Ecclesall, Sheffield S11 9HR) : Yorkshire Postal History Society, 1981. — 96,(2) p,29leaves of plates : ill,facsims. — (Yorkshire Postal History Society publication ; no.16)
Limited ed. of 250 numbered copies. — Bibliography: p(1)-(2)
Unpriced (pbk)
Also classified at 383′.4942845 B81-25424

383′.4942845 — North Yorkshire. Selby. Postal services, *to 1981*

Sedgewick, William A.. The postal history of Goole, Howden and Selby / by William A. Sedgewick and Ronald Ward. — Sheffield (c/o Hon. Treasurer, 48 Banner Cross Rd., Ecclesall, Sheffield S11 9HR) : Yorkshire Postal History Society, 1981. — 96,(2) p,29leaves of plates : ill,facsims. — (Yorkshire Postal History Society publication ; no.16)
Limited ed. of 250 numbered copies. — Bibliography: p(1)-(2)
Unpriced (pbk)
Primary classification 383′.4942835 B81-25424

383′.49479 — Soviet Union. Transcaucasia. Postal services, *to 1917*

Ashford, P. T.. Imperial Russian stamps used in Transcaucasia / P.T. Ashford. — Ashton (9 Pentre Close, Ashton, Chester CH3 8BR) : British Society of Russian Philately
Pt.5: The Transcausasian Railway. — 1981. — p296-355 : 1map,facsims ; 26cm
Unpriced (pbk) B81-27871

383′.49515 — Tibet. Postal services, *to 1980*

Waterfall, Arnold C.. The postal history of Tibet / Arnold C. Waterfall. — 2nd ed. — London : Published by the Pall Mall Stamp Co. for Robson Lowe, 1981. — 188p : ill,3maps,facsims ; 23cm
Previous ed.: 1965. — Includes index
ISBN 0-85397-199-4 : £12.00 B81-40046

384 — TELECOMMUNICATION SERVICES

384 — Great Britain. Telecommunication services. Interception. Procedure — *Inquiry reports*

Diplock, William John Kenneth Diplock, ***Baron***. The interception of communications in Great Britain : report / by Lord Diplock. — London : H.M.S.O., [1981]. — 7p ; 25cm. — (Cmnd. ; 8191)
ISBN 0-10-181910-2 (unbound) : £1.10
Primary classification 383′.1 B81-16301

384 — Telecommunication services — *Conference proceedings*

International Conference on New Systems and Services in Telecommunications *(1980 : Liège)*. New systems and services in telecommunications : proceedings of the International Conference on New Systems and Services in Telecommunications Liege, Belgium, November 24-26, 1980 / edited by G. Cantraine and J. Destine. — Amsterdam ; Oxford : North-Holland, c1981. — viii,367p : ill ; 27cm
English and French text. — Includes bibliographies
ISBN 0-444-86206-4 : Unpriced B81-32842

384′.041 — Great Britain. Telecommunication services: British Telecom. Charges — *Serials*

British Telecom. British Telecom guide. — Nov. 1980-. — [London] ([2 Gresham St., EC2V 7AG]) : British Telecom, 1980-. — v. ; 30cm
Annual. — Continues in part: Great Britain. Post Office. Post Office guide
ISSN 0261-7153 = British Telecom guide : £0.40 B81-32397

384′.041 — Great Britain. Telecommunication services. Monopolies — *Proposals*

Beesley, Michael E.. Liberalisation of the use of British telecommunications network : report to the Secretary of State / by Michael E. Beesley. — London : H.M.S.O., 1981. — xi,51p : 2ill ; 30cm
At head of title: Department of Industry
ISBN 0-11-513249-x (pbk) : £3.60 B81-24789

384′.0973 — United States. Telecommunication services, *to 1980*

Brock, Gerald W.. The telecommunications industry : the dynamics of market structure / Gerald W. Brock. — Cambridge [Mass.] ; London : Harvard University Press, 1981. — xi,336p : ill ; 24cm. — (Harvard economic studies ; v.151)
Includes index
ISBN 0-674-87285-1 : £17.50 B81-40029

384.54 — United States. Broadcasting services. Audiences. Research — *Manuals*

Handbook of radio and TV broadcasting : research procedures in audience, program and revenues / edited by James E. Fletcher. — New York ; London : Van Nostrand Reinhold, c1981. — viii,336p : ill,maps,facsims,forms ; 29cm
Includes index
ISBN 0-442-22417-6 : £22.95 B81-37780

384.54 — Wales. Broadcasting services in Welsh — *Inquiry reports*

Great Britain. *Parliament. House of Commons. Committee on Welsh Affairs*. Second report from the Committee on Welsh Affairs : together with the proceedings of the Committee thereon, the minutes of evidence and appendices : session 1980-81 : broadcasting in the Welsh language and the implications for Welsh and non-Welsh speaking viewers and listeners. — London : H.M.S.O.. — ([HC] ; 448-1)
Vol.1: Report and proceedings. — [1981]. — ciip ; 25cm
ISBN 0-10-008851-1 (pbk) : £5.45 B81-39633

384.54′06′01 — Commonwealth countries. Broadcasting services. Organisations: Commonwealth Broadcasting Association — *Directories — Serials*

Commonwealth Broadcasting Association. Who's who / Commonwealth Broadcasting Association. — 1980. — London (Broadcasting House, W1A 1AA) : The Association, 1980. — iv,28p
ISSN 0144-6150 : Free B81-13210

384.54′0941 — Great Britain. Broadcasting services: British Broadcasting Corporation. Licences — *Texts*

Great Britain. *Home Office*. Broadcasting : copy of the licence and agreement dated the 2nd day of April 1981 between Her Majesty's Secretary of State for the Home Department and the British Broadcasting Corporation. — London : H.M.S.O., 1981. — 18p ; 25cm. — (Cmnd. ; 8233)
ISBN 0-10-182330-4 (unbound) : £2.10 B81-26090

384.54′0941 — Great Britain. Broadcasting services: British Broadcasting Corporation — *Serials*

British Broadcasting Corporation. BBC annual report and handbook : incorporating the annual report and accounts. — 1981-. — London : BBC, 1980-. — v. ; 21cm
Continues: British Broadcasting Corporation. BBC handbook (1955)
ISSN 0262-0952 = BBC annual report and handbook : £2.50 B81-38989

384.54′0941 — Great Britain. Commercial broadcasting services: Independent Broadcasting Authority — *Serials*

Independent Broadcasting Authority[Annual report and accounts *(Independent Broadcasting Authority)*]. Annual report and accounts / Independent Broadcasting Authority. — 1979-80. — London : The Authority, [1980]. — 142p
ISBN 0-900485-40-x : £2.00 B81-08792

384.54′0941 — Great Britain. Commercial broadcasting services — *Serials*

Television & radio. — 1981. — London : Independent Broadcasting Authority, 1980. — 224p
ISBN 0-900485-39-6 : Unpriced B81-08791

384.54′0973 — United States. Broadcasting services

Bittner, John R.. Professional broadcasting : a brief introduction / John R. Bittner. — Englewood Cliffs ; London : Prentice-Hall, 1981. — xvi,255p : ill,ports ; 23cm
Includes bibliographies and index
ISBN 0-13-725465-2 (pbk) : £8.40 B81-16672

384.54′0973 — United States. Broadcasting services. Policies of government, *1920-1934*

Rosen, Philip T.. The modern stentors : radio broadcasters and the federal government, 1920-1934 / Philip T. Rosen. — Westport, Conn. ; London : Greenwood Press, 1980. — 267p : ill ; 22cm. — (Contributions in economics and economic history ; no.31)
Bibliography: p245-255. — Includes index
ISBN 0-313-21231-7 : £15.95 B81-23463

384.54′43 — Educational broadcasting services

Hawkridge, David. Organizing educational broadcasting. — London : Croom Helm, Nov.1981. — [256]p
ISBN 0-7099-1216-1 : £9.95 : CIP entry B81-30537

384.54′43 — Great Britain. Adolescents' broadcasting services — *Inquiry reports*

Young people & broadcasting : a feasibility study for a young adult unit proposed in the report Broadcasting and youth. — London (98 Portland Place, W1N 4ET) : Calouste Gulbenkian Foundation UK and Commonwealth Branch, 1981. — 32p ; 30cm
ISBN 0-903319-19-5 (pbk) : £1.50 B81-22387

384.54′43 — Great Britain. Broadcasting services: British Broadcasting Corporation. Educational broadcasting services

Howard, George, *1920-*. The BBC, educational broadcasting and the future : a speech given by George Howard at Leeds Polytechnic, Tuesday 3 March 1981. — London : British Broadcasting Corporation, [1981]. — 11p ; 21cm
ISBN 0-563-17976-7 (pbk) : Unpriced B81-30821

384.54′43 — Great Britain. Broadcasting services: British Broadcasting Corporation. ***External Services***

Trethewan, ***Sir*** **Ian**. The BBC and international broadcasting : a speech given by Sir Ian Trethewan to the Royal Overseas League in London, Monday 2 February 1981. — London : British Broadcasting Corporation, [1981]. — 14p ; 21cm
ISBN 0-563-17960-0 (pbk) : Unpriced B81-26833

384.54′52 — Great Britain. Local radio services. Development — *Proposals*

Great Britain. *Local Radio Working Party*. Third report / Home Office Local Radio Working Party. — London (50 Queen Anne's Gate SW1H 9AT) : Home Office, 1980. — 50p : 2maps ; 25cm
Unpriced (unbound) B81-24791

384.54′53 — Great Britain. Commercial radio services — *For advertising — Serials*

The Radio advertisers′ guide. — Ed.1 (July 1980)-. — Totnes (Staverton, Totnes, Devon TQ9 6PG) : Hamilton House, 1980-. — v. : maps ; 30cm
Irregular. — Publication associated with: JICRAR report
ISSN 0260-2423 = Radio advertisers′ guide : £25.00 B81-02336

384.54′53 — London. Commercial radio services: Capital Radio

Capital funbook. — London : Atlas for Capital Radio
No.2 / edited by Angus Allan. — 1979. — 64p : ill(some col.),ports(some col.) ; 28cm
Ill on front inside cover
ISBN 0-900113-48-0 (pbk) : £1.50 B81-16037

384.55′4 — Great Britain. Viewdata services: Prestel

Bird, Emma. The future of Prestel : through the gateway / Emma Bird. — [Slough] ([Clove House, The Broadway, Farnham Common, Slough, Berks. SL2 3PQ]) : Urwick Nexos, [1980]. — ii,23leaves ; 30cm
Bibliography: leaf 23
Unpriced (pbk) B81-16226

384.55′4 — Great Britain. Viewdata services: Prestel — *Serials*

Viewdata and tv user. . — Vol.1, no.1 (Oct.1978)-. — Sutton : IPC Electrical-Electronic Press, 1978-. — v. : ill ; 30cm
Quarterly. — Description based on: Vol.2, no.1 (Oct.1980)
ISSN 0260-6984 = View data and tv user : £4.00 per year B81-07156

384.55′4 — Viewdata services

Woolfe, Roger. Videotex : the new television/telephone information services. — London : Heyden, c1980. — xiii,170p : ill(some col.) ; 26cm. — (Computing sciences series)
ISBN 0-85501-493-8 : £7.00 : CIP rev. B80-11822

384.55′4 — Viewdata services — *Study examples: Prestel*

Viewdata in action : a comparative study of Prestel / editor Rex Winsbury. — London : McGraw-Hill (UK), c1981. — 237p,[8]p of plates : ill(some col.) ; 24cm
Bibliography: p236-237
ISBN 0-07-084548-4 : £14.00 B81-19322

384.55′4′02341 — Great Britain. Television services — *Career guides*

Leeming, Jan. Working in television / Jan Leeming. — London : Batsford Academic and Educational, 1980. — 111p,[8]p of plates : ill,ports ; 23cm
Bibliography: p106. — Includes index
ISBN 0-7134-2248-3 : £5.75 B81-01556

384.55′4′025 — Television services — *Directories — Serials*

Kemps international film & television yearbook. — 26th ed. (1981/82). — London : Kemps, c1981. — 1106p in various pagings
ISBN 0-905255-99-2 : Unpriced
ISSN 0142-0690
Also classified at 384′.8′025 B81-30738

384.55′4′0941 — Great Britain. Commercial television services, *to 1979*

Tinker, Jack. The television barons / Jack Tinker. — London : Quartet, 1980. — xi,222p,[8]p of plates : ill,ports ; 24cm
Bibliography: p215. — Includes index
ISBN 0-7043-2248-x : £7.95 B81-01904

384.55′4′0941 — Great Britain. Television services. Cooperation with cinema industries — *Inquiry reports*

Great Britain. *Interim Action Committee on the Film Industry*. Film and television co-operation : fourth report of the Interim Action Committee on the Film Industry. — London : H.M.S.O., [1981]. — iv,4p ; 25cm. — (Cmnd. ; 8227)
ISBN 0-10-182270-7 (unbound) : £1.40
Also classified at 384′.8′0941 B81-25240

384.55′4′0971 — Canada. Television services, *to 1968.* **Political aspects**

Peers, Frank W.. The public eye : television and the politics of Canadian broadcasting 1952-1968 / Frank W. Peers. — Toronto ; London : University of Toronto Press, c1979. — xvi,459p ; 24cm
Bibliography p441-443. — Includes index
ISBN 0-8020-5436-6 : £17.50 B81-05816

384.55′43 — Great Britain. Commercial television services: Independent Broadcasting Authority. Payments by television companies — *Accounts — Serials*

Independent Broadcasting Authority. Account, additional payments by programme contractors / Independent Broadcasting Authority. — 1979-80. — London : H.M.S.O., 1981-. — 2p
ISBN 0-10-214581-4 : £0.70 B81-20305

384.55′44 — Great Britain. Teletext services: ORACLE — *Codes of conduct*

Independent Broadcasting Authority. The IBA code for teletext transmissions. — [London] ([70 Brompton Rd., SW3 1EY]) : IBA, 1981. — 1folded sheet([5]p) ; 23cm
Cover title
Unpriced (pbk) B81-40881

384.55′455′0973 — United States. Television services. Networks

Network television and the public interest : a preliminary inquiry / edited by Michael Botein, David M. Rice. — Lexington, Mass. : Lexington Books, c1980 ; [Aldershot] : Gower [distributor], 1981. — xvi,223p ; 24cm
Includes index
ISBN 0-669-02927-0 : £13.50 B81-33203

384.6′09426′15 — Norfolk. Norwich. Telephone services, *to 1980*

Clayton, Eric G.. The first 100 years of telephones viewed from Norwich / [Eric G. Clayton]. — [Norwich] ([Norwich Telephone Area, 41 St. Giles St., Norwich NR2 1BA]) : [British Telecom], 1980. — 125p : ill,maps,facsims,plans,ports ; 21cm
ISBN 0-9507298-0-9 (pbk) : Unpriced B81-18221

384.6′5 — Great Britain. Telecommunication services: British Telecom. Telephone exchanges — *Lists — Serials*

British Telecom. List of exchanges / British. Part 1. — 31 March 1980-. — London (2-12 Gresham St., EC2V 7AG) : B.T., 1980-. — v. ; 21cm
Annual. — Continues: List of exchanges (Post Office Telecommuications Management Serivces Department)
ISSN 0260-9649 : £5.50 B81-13211

384.6′5 — United States. Telephone services. Subscribers: Librarians — *Directories — Serials*

The Librarians phone book. — 1979-. — New York ; London : Bowker, 1979-. — v. ; 28cm
Description based on: 1981 ed.
Unpriced B81-10564

384.8 — CINEMA INDUSTRIES

384′.8′025 — Cinema industries — *Directories — Serials*

Kemps international film & television yearbook. — 26th ed. (1981/82). — London : Kemps, c1981. — 1106p in various pagings
ISBN 0-905255-99-2 : Unpriced
ISSN 0142-0690
Primary classification 384.55′4′025 B81-30738

384′.8′02541 — Great Britain. Cinema industries — *Directories — Serials*

[Production *(London : 1976)***]**. Production : a comprehensive guide to Britain′s film and video production companies, with sections on production, film & video facilities, distribution and advertising agencies. — 76-. — London (111a Wardour St., W1V 3TD) : Broadcast, 1976-. — v. : ill ; 30cm
Annual. — Description based on: 81-82
ISSN 0262-0960 = Production (London. 1976) : £3.50
Also classified at 338.7′617785992 B81-38990

384′.8′06542184 — London. Ealing *(London Borough). Sa Cinema industries: Ealing Studios, to 1960*

Perry, George. Forever Ealing. — London (8 Cork St., W1X 2HA) : Pavilion Books, Oct.1981. — [192]p
ISBN 0-907516-06-8 : £8.95 : CIP entry B81-25741

384′.8′0941 — Great Britain. Cinema industries

British film industry / compiled by Linda Wood. — London (127 Charing Cross Rd., WC2 0EA) : BFI Library Services, 1980. — 80p in various pagings ; 30cm. — (BFI information guide ; no.1)
Cover title
Unpriced (pbk) B81-18609

384′.8′0941 — Great Britain. Cinema industries. Cooperation with television services — *Inquiry reports*

Great Britain. *Interim Action Committee on the Film Industry*. Film and television co-operation : fourth report of the Interim Action Committee on the Film Industry. — London : H.M.S.O., [1981]. — iv,4p ; 25cm. — (Cmnd. ; 8227)
ISBN 0-10-182270-7 (unbound) : £1.40
Primary classification 384.55′4′0941 B81-25240

384′.8′0979494 — California. Los Angeles. Hollywood. Cinema industries: Fine Arts Film Company, *to 1917*

Slide, Anthony. The kindergarten of the movies : a history of the Fine Arts Company / by Anthony Slide. — Metuchen ; London : Scarecrow, 1980. — ix,236p : ill,ports ; 23cm
Bibliography: p220-226. — Includes index
ISBN 0-8108-1358-0 : £9.45 B81-05292

384′.83 — Great Britain. Cinema industries. Financial assistance. Organisations: National Film Finance Corporation — *Serials*

National Film Finance Corporation. Annual report and statement of accounts for the year ended 31st March .. / National Film Finance Corporation. — London : H.M.S.O., 1980. — 28p
ISBN 0-10-027939-2 : £2.40 B81-10575

385 — RAILWAY TRANSPORT

385 — Railways — *For children*

Wood, Sydney. The railway revolution. — London : Macmillan, Sept.1981. — [96]p
ISBN 0-333-31307-0 : £4.95 : CIP entry B81-30273

385 — Scotland. Railways. Electrification — *Proposals*

Rail electrification and transport financing : a Scottish strategy. — [Glasgow] ([113 West Regent St., Glasgow G2 2RU]) : Scottish Association for Public Transport], 1981. — [10]leaves : 1map ; 30cm
Bibliography: leaf 10
£0.80 (unbound) B81-36846

385′.025′41 — Great Britain. Preserved railways — *Directories — Serials*

Railways restored : Association of Railway Preservation Societies′ official year book. — 1981. — London : I. Allan, 1981. — 96p
ISBN 0-7110-1102-8 : £1.95
Also classified at 625.1′0074′02 B81-31042

385′.05 — Railway services — *Serials*

Eurail guide. — 11th ed. (1981). — Malibu : Eurail Guide Annual ; London : Distributed by Pitman, c1981. — 816p
ISBN 0-273-01682-2 : £5.95
ISSN 0085-0330 B81-1941

385′.06′041 — Great Britain. Railways. Organisations: Railway Enthusiasts Society — *Serials*

Terminus : journal of the Railway Enthusiasts Society Ltd. — Vol.1, no.1 (Jan.1978)-. — [S.l.] ([c/o 33 High Acres, Abbots Langley, Watford WD5 0JB]) : The Society, 1978-. — v. : ill ; 22cm
Seven issues yearly
ISSN 0260-6844 = Terminus : Unpriced B81-1121

385′.09′034 — Railways, *to ca 1900*

Schivelbusch, Wolfgang. The railway journey : trains and travel in the 19th century / by Wolfgang Schivelbusch ; translated from the German by Anselm Hollo. — Oxford : Blackwell, 1980, c1979. — 213p : ill,maps,facsims,plans,ports ; 28cm
Translation of: Geschichte de Eisenbahnreise. — Originally published: New York : Urizen, 1979
ISBN 0-631-19660-9 : £9.95 : CIP rev. B80-06345

385′.09′04 — Railway services, *1950-1980*

Allen, Geoffrey Freeman. Modern railways / Geoffrey Freeman Allen. — London : Hamlyn, c1980. — 256p : ill(some col),maps ; 31cm
Ill on lining papers. — Includes index
ISBN 0-600-34939-x : £7.95 B81-04059

385′.092′2 — Great Britain. Railway services, *1900-1963 — Personal observations — Collections*

Thomas, Gilbert, *1891-1978*. Double headed : two generations of railway enthusiasm / Gilbert Thomas and David St John Thomas ; drawings by Kenneth Lindley. — Newton Abbot : David & Charles, c1981, c1963. — 200p : ill,facsims,ports ; 23cm
ISBN 0-7153-8184-9 : £5.95 : CIP rev. B81-13544

385′.092′4 — England. Railway services: British Rail. *Western Region, 1946-1961 — Personal observations*

Vaughan, Adrian. Signalman's morning / Adrian Vaughan. — London : John Murray, 1981. — 177p,[12]p of plates : ill,1map,ports ; 23cm
Map on lining papers. — Includes index
ISBN 0-7195-3827-0 : £8.50 : CIP rev. B81-13579

385′.092′4 — England. Railway services: London and North Western Railway, *1921-1966 — Personal observations*

Aland, Harry. Recollections of country station life / by Harry Aland. — Leicester (29 The Fairway, Blaby, Leicester) : Anderson, c1980. — 70p : ill,ports ; 21cm
ISBN 0-9504777-6-1 (pbk) : £2.20 B81-06018

385′.092′4 — North western England. Railway services: British Rail. *London Midland Region.* **London and North Western lines,** *1918-1952 — Personal observations*

Roberts, John Easter. Hazards of the footplate, L.N.W.R. to B.R. : (London & North Western Railway), (London Midland & Scottish), (British Rail) / John Easter Roberts. — Carnforth (3 Grosvenor Place, Carnforth, Lancs., LA5 9DL) : J.E. Roberts, 1980 (1981 [printing]). — 142p : ill,1map ; 21cm
£2.20 (pbk) B81-38672

385′.092′4 — Northern England. Railway services: British Rail. *London Midland Region.* **Settle-Carlisle line,** *1930-1965 — Personal observations*

Fawcett, Dick. Ganger, guard and signalman : working memories of the Settle and Carlisle / Dick Fawcett. — Truro : Barton, c1981. — 112p : ill,1map ; 21cm
ISBN 0-85153-397-3 (pbk) : £2.95 B81-29682

385′.092′4 — Scotland. Fife Region. Railway services: British Rail. *Scottish Region, ca 1930-ca 1970 — Personal observations*

Meacher, Charles. Living with locos / Charlie Meacher. — Truro : Barton, c1980. — 108p : ill ; 22cm
ISBN 0-85153-392-2 (pbk) : £2.95 B81-05999

385′.092′4 — Southern England. Railway services: British Rail. *Southern Region.* **Steam locomotives. Driving,** *1944-1967 — Personal observations*

Evans, Jim. Man of the Southern : Jim Evans looks back / Jim Evans ; edited by Peter Grafton. — London : Allen & Unwin, 1980. — 102p : ill ; 23cm. — (Steam past)
Includes index
ISBN 0-04-385078-2 : £5.50 : CIP rev. B80-10563

385′.0941 — Great Britain. Economic conditions. Effects of railway services, *1830-1914*

Gourvish, T. R.. Railways and the British economy 1830-1914 / prepared for the Economic History Society by T.R. Gourvish. — London : Macmillan, 1980. — 70p ; 22cm. — (Studies in economic and social history)
Bibliography: p62-66. — Includes index
ISBN 0-333-28365-1 (pbk) : £2.25 : CIP rev. B80-24375

385′.0941 — Great Britain. Preserved railways — *Visitors' guides*

Cockman, F. G.. Discovering preserved railways / F.G. Cockman. — Princes Risborough : Shire, 1980. — 80p : ill,maps ; 18cm
Bibliography: p78. — Includes index
ISBN 0-85263-515-x (pbk) : £0.95 B81-05493

385′.0941 — Great Britain. Railway services, *1923-1939*

Bonavia, Michael R.. Railway policy between the wars / Michael R. Bonavia. — Manchester : Manchester University Press, c1981. — x,156p ; 23cm
Includes index
ISBN 0-7190-0826-3 : £11.50 B81-18230

385′.0941 — Great Britain. Railway services, *1975-1979 — Illustrations*

Trains of thought. — London : Allen and Unwin, May 1981. — [128]p
ISBN 0-04-385081-2 : £9.95 : CIP entry B81-04205

385′.0941 — Great Britain. Railway services: British Rail, *to 1972*

Bonavia, Michael R.. British Rail : the first 25 years / Michael R. Bonavia. — Newton Abbot : David & Charles, c1981. — 239p : ill,maps,ports ; 23cm
Bibliography: p233-234. - Includes index
ISBN 0-7153-8002-8 : £7.50 B81-20804

385′.0941 — Great Britain. Railway services: British Railways, *1948-1953*

Bonavia, Michael R.. The birth of British Rail / Michael R. Bonavia. — London : Allen & Unwin, 1979. — 110p : ill,2facsims,ports ; 23cm. — (Steam past)
Bibliography: p105. - Includes index
ISBN 0-04-385071-5 : £3.95 : CIP rev. B78-36776

385′.0941 — Great Britain. Railway services. Disused routes — *Visitors' guides*

Jones, Gareth Lovett. Railway walks : exploring disused railways / Gareth Lovett Jones. — London : Pierrot, 1980. — 285p : ill,maps ; 20cm
Ill on lining papers. — Bibliography: p282-283
ISBN 0-905310-35-7 : £6.50 B81-00079

385′.0941 — Great Britain. Railway services. Effects of policies of government — *Trade union viewpoints*

Iron and Steel Trades Confederation. What is the future? : steel - rail - coal / [Iron & Steel Trades Confederation, National Union of Railwaymen, National Union of Mineworkers]. — [London] ([324 Grays Inn Rd, WC1BX 8DD]) : [The Confederation], [1981]. — 12p ; 21cm
Cover title
Unpriced (pbk)
Primary classification 338.4′7669142′0941 B81-19736

385′.0941 — Great Britain. Railway services: London and North Eastern Railway. Personnel — *Biographies*

Grafton, Peter. Men of the LNER. — London : Allen & Unwin, Oct.1981. — [96]p
ISBN 0-04-385085-5 : £6.95 : CIP entry B81-25106

385′.0941 — Great Britain. Railway services: London, Midland and Scottish Railway, *to 1948*

Hope, S. G.. Reflections of the London, Midland & Scottish Railway ; &, Cameos of life / [S.G. Hope]. — Macclesfield (No.2 Bungalow, Macclesfield Marina, Macclesfield, Cheshire) : S.G. Hope, 1980. — 75p : ill ; 21cm
£1.75 (pbk)
Also classified at 082 B81-23171

385′.0941 — Great Britain. Railway services, *to 1980*

Jones, Edgar, *1953-*. The Penguin guide to the railways of Britain / Edgar Jones. — Harmondsworth : Penguin, 1981. — xx,377p,[16]p of plates : ill,maps ; 20cm. — (A Penguin handbook)
Bibliography: p363-365. - Includes index
ISBN 0-14-046332-1 (pbk) : £2.95 B81-21820

Jones, Edgar, *1953-*. The Penguin guide to the railways of Britain / Edgar Jones. — London : Allen Lane, 1981. — xx,377p,[16]p of plates : ill,maps ; 23cm
Bibliography: p363-365. - Includes index
ISBN 0-7139-1137-9 : £9.95 B81-21819

385′.0941 — Great Britain. Railways

Wrate, C. H.. Into the eighties - with Stephenson / [by C.H. Wrate]. — [England] : [C.H. Wrate], [1980?] (Walsall : Ray). — 13p : ill ; 22cm
Cover title. — Ill on covers
£0.35 (pbk) B81-07003

385′.0941 — Great Britain. Railways, *1920-1939*

Unwin, Philip. Travelling by train in the twenties and thirties. — London : Allen & Unwin, Aug.1981. — [104]p
ISBN 0-04-385086-3 : £6.95 : CIP entry B81-15876

385′.09411 — Scotland. Railway services. Disused routes, *to 1970*

Thomas, John, *1914-*. Scotland / John Thomas. — 2nd ed. — Newton Abbot : David & Charles, 1981. — 224p : ill,maps,facsims ; 23cm. — (Forgotten railways)
Previous ed.: 1976. — Bibliography: p220. — Includes index
ISBN 0-7153-8193-8 : £5.95 : CIP rev. B81-17496

385′.09412′1 — Scotland. Grampian Region. Railway services: Great North of Scotland Railway, *to ca 1960 — Illustrations*

Glen, A. E.. Great North of Scotland Railway album / A.E. Glen, I.A. Glen with A.G. Dunbar. — London : Ian Allan, 1980. — 96p : chiefly ill,2maps ; 25cm
Maps on lining papers
ISBN 0-7110-1054-4 : £7.95 B81-08260

385′.09413′7 — Scotland. Border country. Railway services. Branch lines, *1900-1979 — Illustrations*

Border Country : branch line album / [compiled by] Neil Caplan. — London : Ian Allen, 1981. — 127p : ill,maps ; 25cm
Maps on lining papers
ISBN 0-7110-1086-2 : £5.95
Also classified at 385′.09428′8 B81-18362

385′.09414 — South-west Scotland. Railway services. London, Midland and Scottish Railway: Glasgow & South-Western lines, *1923-1947*

Smith, David L. (David Larmer). Legends of the Glasgow & South Western Railway in LMS days / David L. Smith. — Newton Abbot : David & Charles, c1980. — 176p : ill,maps,ports ; 23cm
Includes index
ISBN 0-7153-7981-x : £5.95 : CIP rev. B80-33394

385′.09415 — Ireland. Railway services, *to 1966*

Middlemass, Tom. Irish standard gauge railways / Tom Middlemass. — Newton Abbot : David & Charles, c1981. — 96p : ill,maps ; 25cm
ISBN 0-7153-8007-9 : £5.95 B81-20805

385′.0942 — England. Great Western Railway, *to 1947.* **Artefacts. Preservation**

Hollingsworth, J. B.. Great Western adventure. — Newton Abbot : David & Charles, Oct.1981. — [160]p
ISBN 0-7153-8108-3 : £5.95 : CIP entry B81-28052

385′.0942 — England. Minor standard gauge railway services, *to ca 1965*

Kidner, R. W.. Minor standard gauge railways / R.W. Kidner. — [Blandford Forum] : Oakwood, 1981. — 64p : ill,maps ; 22cm. — (Locomotion papers ; no.129)
ISBN 0-85361-264-1 (pbk) : Unpriced B81-11546

385′.0942 — England. Railway services: British Rail. Branch lines

Quayle, H. I.. Branch lines into the eighties / H.I. Quayle and Stanley C. Jenkins. — Newton Abbot : David & Charles, 1980. — 96p : ill,maps ; 25cm
Bibliography: p95-96
ISBN 0-7153-7980-1 : £5.50 : CIP rev. B80-18661

385′.0942 — England. Railway services: British Rail. Great Central lines, *to 1966*

Barton, A. J.. From Reddish to Wath / A.J. Barton. — Ilfracombe : Stockwell, 1981. — 116p : ill,maps ; 18cm
ISBN 0-7223-1456-6 : £4.95 B81-37482

385′.0942 — England. Railway services: British Rail. Oxford-Cambridge line, *to 1980*

Simpson, Bill, *1940-*. Oxford to Cambridge railway / by Bill Simpson. — Oxford : Oxford Publishing
Vol.1: Oxford to Bletchley. — c1981. — 152p,[2]p of plates : ill,maps,facsims,plans,1port ; 28cm
ISBN 0-86093-120-x : Unpriced B81-26861

385′.0942 — England. Railway services: British Rail. *Western Region, 1960-1969 — Illustrations*

Western Region in the 1960′s / [compiled by] C.S. Heaps. — London : Ian Allan, 1981. — 112p : chiefly ill ; 25cm
ISBN 0-7110-1126-5 : £5.95 B81-36744

385′.0942 — England. Railway services: London and North Western Railway, *to 1923 — Illustrations*

L. & N.W.R. miscellany / [compiled] by E. Talbot. — Oxford : Oxford Publishing
Vol.2. — c1980. — [103]p : chiefly ill,1map,1facsim,port ; 28cm
Ill on lining papers
ISBN 0-86093-070-x : £5.95 B81-32151

385′.0942 — England. Railway services: London, Midland and Scottish Railway. Branch lines, *1945-1965 — Illustrations*

LMS branch lines 1945-65 / [compiled] by C.J. Gammell. — Oxford : Oxford Publishing, c1980. — [96]p : chiefly ill,maps ; 28cm
Bibliography: p[5]. — Includes index
ISBN 0-86093-062-9 : £4.95 B81-03127

385′.09421′6 — South-east London. Railway services: British Rail. *Southern Region.* **Bexleyheath line,** *to 1979*

Course, Edwin. The Bexleyheath line / Edwin Course. — [Trowbridge] : Oakwood, [1981]. — 40p,[12]p of plates : ill,maps ; 22cm. — (Locomotion papers ; no.130)
ISBN 0-85361-271-4 (pbk) : £1.80
Also classified at 385′.09422′3 B81-15677

385′.09421′86 — London. Harrow *(London Borough).* **Railway services: British Rail.** *London Midland Region.* **Stanmore Branch,** *to 1964*

Scott, Peter G.. The Harrow & Stanmore railway / by Peter G. Scott. — 2nd ed. — Greenhill (11 Duffield Close, Greenhill, Harrow, Middx HA1 2LG) : Hartest Productions, 1981. — 72p : ill,maps,facsims,plans ; 30cm
Previous ed.: 1972. — Bibliography: p68-69. — Includes index
ISBN 0-9506469-1-1 (pbk) : £3.90 B81-37737

385′.09422 — England. Thames River region. Railway services, *to 1980*

Christiansen, Rex. Thames and Severn. — Newton Abbot : David & Charles, Nov.1981. — [224]p. — (A Regional history of the railways of Great Britain ; v.13)
ISBN 0-7153-8004-4 : £8.95 : CIP entry
Also classified at 385′.09424 B81-30369

385′.09422 — South-east England. Railway services: Brighton Belle, *to 1972*

Owen, Nicholas. The Brighton Belle / by Nicholas Owen. — 3rd ed. — Purley : Southern Electric Group, 1981. — 32p : ill,1map,1facsim ; 22cm
Cover title. — Previous ed.: 1974?. — Text and ill. on inside cover
ISBN 0-906988-00-4 (pbk) : £1.30 B81-39814

385′.09422 — South-east England. Railway services: South Eastern & Chatham Railway, *1914-1918*

Gould, David, *1946-*. The South-Eastern & Chatham Railway in the 1914-18 War / David Gould. — [Trowbridge] : Oakwood, [1981]. — 55p,[8]p of plates : ill,plans ; 22cm. — (Locomotion papers ; no.134)
ISBN 0-85361-278-1 (pbk) : £2.70 B81-38647

385′.09422 — Southern England. Railway services: British Rail. *Southern Region, 1948-1981*

The **Changing** Southern scene 1948-1981 / [compiled by] Michael Baker. — London : Ian Allan, 1981. — 110p : all.ill ; 25cm
ISBN 0-7110-1090-0 : £5.95 B81-24853

385′.09422 — Southern England. Railway services: British Rail. *Southern Region.* **Brighton-Portsmouth line,** *to 1980*

Pallant, N.. The Brighton to Portsmouth line / N. Pallant. — [Trowbridge] : Oakwood Press, [1981]. — 44p,[16]p of plates : ill,1map,facsims ; 22cm. — (Locomotion papers ; no.133)
Bibliography: p40
ISBN 0-85361-279-x (pbk) : £2.40 B81-31127

385′.09422′3 — Kent. Railway services: British Rail. *Southern Region.* **Bexleyheath line,** *1979*

Course, Edwin. The Bexleyheath line / Edwin Course. — [Trowbridge] : Oakwood, [1981]. — 40p,[12]p of plates : ill,maps ; 22cm. — (Locomotion papers ; no.130)
ISBN 0-85361-271-4 (pbk) : £1.80
Primary classification 385′.09421′6 B81-15677

385′.09422′64 — West Sussex. Midhurst region. Railway services, *to 1966 — Illustrations*

Branch lines to Midhurst / [compiled by Keith Smith and Vic Mitchell]. — Midhurst (Easebourne La., Midhurst, W. Sussex GU29 9AZ) : Middleton Press, 1981. — [98]p : chiefly ill,maps,facsims,ports ; 25cm
ISBN 0-906520-01-0 : Unpriced B81-23240

385′.09423 — South-west England. Railway services: British Rail. Main lines, *ca 1950- ca 1960*

Rocksborough-Smith, Simon. Main lines to the West / Simon Rocksborough-Smith. — London : Ian Allan, 1981. — 127p : ill ; 25cm
ISBN 0-7110-1117-6 : £6.95 B81-31993

385′.09423 — South-west England. Railway services: Cornish Riviera Express, *to 1978*

Nock, O. S.. The Limited : the story of the Cornish Riviera Express / O.S. Nock. — London : Allen & Unwin, 1979. — 95p : ill ; 23cm. — (Steam past)
Includes index
ISBN 0-04-385073-1 : £3.95 : CIP rev. B78-37630

385′.09423 — South-west England. Railway services, *to 1980*

Thomas, David St John. The West country / by David St John Thomas. — 5th, rev. ed. — Newton Abbot : David & Charles, c1981. — 286p,1leaf of plates : ill,maps,facsims ; 23cm. — (A Regional history of the railways of Great Britain ; v.1)
Previous ed.: 1973. — Map (folded sheet) attached to lining paper. — Bibliography: p272-274. — Includes index
ISBN 0-7153-8152-0 (cased) : £9.50 : CIP rev.
ISBN 0-7153-8210-1 (pbk) : Unpriced B81-07576

385′.09423′72 — Cornwall. Restormel *(District).* **Railway services: Pentewan Railway,** *to 1918*

Lewis, M. J. T.. The Pentewan railway / M.J.T. Lewis. — Rev. and extended ed. — Twelveheads (Chy Mengleth, Twelveheads, Truro, Cornwall) : Twelveheads, 1981. — 92p : ill,maps,ports ; 24cm
Previous ed.: Truro : Barton, 1960. — Includes index
ISBN 0-906294-04-5 (cased) : £4.50
ISBN 0-906294-05-3 (pbk) : £3.00 B81-17716

385′.09423′81 — Somerset. Sedgemoor *(District).* **Railway services: British Rail.** *Western Region.* **Bridgwater Branch,** *to 1954*

Harrison, J. D. (Jem D). The Bridgwater Branch / J.D. Harrison. — [Trowbridge] : Oakwood ; Tisbury : Element [Distributors], 1981. — 40p,[8]p of plates : ill,maps ; 22cm. — (Locomotion papers ; no.132)
ISBN 0-85361-274-9 (pbk) : £1.80 B81-22771

385′.09424 — England. Severn River region. Railway services, *to 1980*

Christiansen, Rex. Thames and Severn. — Newton Abbot : David & Charles, Nov.1981. — [224]p. — (A Regional history of the railways of Great Britain ; v.13)
ISBN 0-7153-8004-4 : £8.95 : CIP entry
Primary classification 385′.09422 B81-30369

385′.09424′13 — Gloucestershire. Forest of Dean *(District).* **Railway services,** *to 1979 — Illustrations*

Forest venturer pictorial : an historic photographic record of railways in the Forest of Dean. — [Lydney] ([Norchard Steam Centre, New Mill, nr. Lydney, Glos GL15 4ET]) : Dean Forest Railway Society
Cover title
Vol.1. — [1981?]. — 2,[24]p : chiefly ill ; 30cm
ISBN 0-9507099-2-1 (pbk) : Unpriced B81-27870

385′.09424′19 — Gloucestershire. Stroud *(District).* **Railway services: British Rail.** *Western Region.* **Dursley branch,** *to 1970*

Smith, Peter, *1955-*. The Dursley branch / Peter Smith. — [Trowbridge] : Oakwood, 1981. — 26p,[8]p of plates : ill,maps ; 22cm. — (Locomotion papers ; no.131)
Bibliography: p26
ISBN 0-85361-270-6 (pbk) : £1.50 B81-15760

385′.09425 — England. Chilterns. Railway services, *ca 1930-1965 — Illustrations*

Railways through the Chilterns / [compiled by] C.R.L. Coles. — London : Ian Allan, 1980. — 126p : chiefly ill,1map ; 25cm
Map on lining papers. — Bibliography: p7
ISBN 0-7110-1067-6 : £5.95 B81-02703

385′.09426 — East Anglia. Railway services: British Rail. *Eastern Region.* **Midland and Great Northern Joint lines,** *to 1980*

Wrottesley, John. The Midland & Great Northern Joint Railway / A.J. Wrottesley. — 2nd ed. — Newton Abbot : David & Charles, 1981. — 221p : ill,maps,1coat of arms,facsims ; 22cm
Previous ed.: 1970. — Bibliography: p206-207. — Includes index
ISBN 0-7153-8173-3 : £6.50 B81-33241

385′.09426 — Eastern England. Railway services: Great Northern Railway, *to 1923*

Wrottesley, John. The Great Northern Railway / John Wrottesley. — London : Batsford
Vol.3: Twentieth century to grouping. — 1981. — 220p : ill,maps,1coat of arms,2facsims,2ports ; 23cm
Bibliography: p206. — Includes index
ISBN 0-7134-2183-5 : £12.50 B81-27836

385′.09426′7 — Essex. Railway services: British Rail. *Eastern Region.* **London, Tilbury & Southend lines,** *to 1961 — Illustrations*

London, Tilbury & Southend album / [compiled by] George Dow. — London : Ian Allan, 1981. — 120p : cheifly ill(some col.),maps,facsims ; 25cm
Maps on lining papers. — Includes index
ISBN 0-7110-1085-4 : £8.95 B81-11358

385′.09426′712 — Essex. Uttlesford *(District).* **Railway services: British Rail.** *Eastern Region.* **Saffron Walden Branch,** *to 1964*

Paye, Peter. The Saffron Walden branch / by P. Paye. — Oxford : Oxford Publishing, c1981. — iv,168p : ill,maps,facsims ; 21cm
ISBN 0-86093-107-2 (pbk) : £3.90 B81-15198

385′.09427 — North-west England. Railway services: British Rail. *London Midland Region.* **Liverpool and Manchester line,** *to 1980*

Rocket 150 : 150th anniversary of the Liverpool & Manchester Railway 1830-1980 : official handbook. — [Bristol] ([9 Poplar Ave., Westbury on Trym, Bristol BS9 2BE]) : British Rail, London Midland Region in association with Avon-Anglia Publications & Services, c1980. — 84p : ill(some col.),maps(some col.) facsims ; 23cm
ISBN 0-905466-27-6 (pbk) : £2.40 B81-07529

385'.09427 — North-West England. Railway services. Disused routes

Marshall, John, *1922 May 1-*. North West England / John Marshall. — Newton Abbot : David & Charles, c1981. — 176p : ill,maps ; 23cm. — (Forgotten railways)
Bibliography: p171-174. — Includes index
ISBN 0-7153-8003-6 : £6.50 B81-19830

385'.09427 — Northern England. Railway services, *1930-1939*

Denton, A. S.. North Midlands trains in the thirties / A.S. Denton. — Trowbridge : Oakwood Press, [1980?]. — 64p : ill ; 22cm. — (Locomotion papers ; no.127)
ISBN 0-85361-267-6 (pbk) : £2.40 B81-13247

385'.09427 — Northern England. Railway services: British Rail. *London Midland Region.* **Settle-Carlisle line,** *1967-1979 — Illustrations*

On the Settle & Carlisle route / [compiled by] T.G. Flinders. — London : Ian Allan, 1981. — 112p : chiefly ill,maps ; 25cm
Map on lining papers. — Bibliography: p112
ISBN 0-7110-1080-3 : £5.95 B81-10547

385'.09427 — Northern England. Railway services: Settle and Carlisle Railway, *to 1979*

Jenkinson, David. Rails in the Fells : a railway case study : an account of the origins, characteristics and contribution of a railway to the landscape, together with an attempt to evaluate its past and present influence on the area through which it passes / David Jenkinson ; with a foreword by Eric Treacy. — 2nd ed., rev. — Seaton : Peco, 1980. — 157p : ill,maps,plans ; 26cm
Previous ed.: 1973. — Bibliography: p154-155. — Includes index
ISBN 0-900586-53-2 : £6.95 B81-08248

385'.09427'3 — Greater Manchester *(Metropolitan County).* **Railway services: Liverpool & Manchester Railway,** *1830 — Illustrations*

Shaw, I.. Views of the most interesting scenery on the line of the Liverpool and Manchester Railway / I. Shaw. — Oldham ([Lees, Oldham OL4 5AL]) : Broadbent, c1980. — 16p,12leaves of plates : ill(some col.) ; 30cm
Facsim. of: 1st ed. Liverpool : I. Shaw, 1831. — Limited ed. of 1000 copies
ISBN 0-904848-05-1 : Unpriced
Also classified at 385'.09427'5 B81-33337

385'.09427'3 — Greater Manchester *(Metropolitan County).* **Railway services: Liverpool & Manchester Railway,** *to 1980*

Ferneyhough, Frank. Liverpool & Manchester Railway 1830-1980 / Frank Ferneyhough ; foreword by Sir Peter Parker. — London : Hale, 1980. — xii,193p,[32]p of plates : ill,3maps,facsims,ports ; 24cm
Bibliography: p180-181. - Includes index
ISBN 0-7091-8137-x : £8.95
Also classified at 385'.09427'5 B81-03949

385'.09427'34 — Greater Manchester *(Metropolitan County).* **Marple region. Railways,** *to 1980*

Burton, Warwick R.. Railways of Marple and district from 1794 / by Warwick R. Burton. — Marple (69 Bowden La., Marple, Cheshire) : M.T. & W.R. Burton, 1980. — iv,56p : ill,1map,plans,1port ; 30cm
Bibliography: p54. — Includes index
ISBN 0-9507288-0-2 (pbk) : £2.50 B81-05271

385'.09427'5 — Merseyside *(Metropolitan County).* **Railway services: Liverpool & Manchester Railway,** *1830 — Illustrations*

Shaw, I.. Views of the most interesting scenery on the line of the Liverpool and Manchester Railway / I. Shaw. — Oldham ([Lees, Oldham OL4 5AL]) : Broadbent, c1980. — 16p,12leaves of plates : ill(some col.) ; 30cm
Facsim. of: 1st ed. Liverpool : I. Shaw, 1831. — Limited ed. of 1000 copies
ISBN 0-904848-05-1 : Unpriced
Primary classification 385'.09427'3 B81-33337

385'.09427'5 — Merseyside *(Metropolitan County).* **Railway services: Liverpool & Manchester Railway,** *to 1980*

Ferneyhough, Frank. Liverpool & Manchester Railway 1830-1980 / Frank Ferneyhough ; foreword by Sir Peter Parker. — London : Hale, 1980. — xii,193p,[32]p of plates : ill,3maps,facsims,ports ; 24cm
Bibliography: p180-181. - Includes index
ISBN 0-7091-8137-x : £8.95
Primary classification 385'.09427'3 B81-03949

385'.09427'8 — Cumbria. Railway services, *to 1979*

Railways of Cumbria / compiled by Peter W. Robinson. — Clapham : Dalesman, 1980. — 96p : ill,maps ; 18x22cm
Bibliography: p96
ISBN 0-85206-602-3 (pbk) : £3.50 B81-02637

385'.09428'1 — Yorkshire. Minor railways, *to 1978*

Redman, Ronald Nelson. Railway byways in Yorkshire / by Ronald Nelson Redman. — Clapham, N. Yorkshire : Dalesman, 1979. — 80p : ill ; 21cm
ISBN 0-85206-556-6 (pbk) : £1.75 B81-13396

385'.09428'17 — West Yorkshire *(Metropolitan County).* **Keighley. Railway services,** *to 1978*

Bairstow, J. M.. Railways of Keighley / by J.M. Bairstow. — Clapham, N. Yorkshire : Dalesman, 1979. — 80p : ill,maps ; 21cm
Bibliography: p80
ISBN 0-85206-527-2 (pbk) : £1.95 B81-17833

385'.09428'47 — North Yorkshire. Scarborough *(District).* **Railway services: Whitby, Redcar & Middlesbrough Union Railway,** *to 1958 — Illustrations*

Hoole, K.. The Whitby, Redcar and Middlesbrough Union Railway / by Ken Hoole. — Nelson, Lancs., Hendon, c1981. — [44]p : chiefly ill,1map,facsims ; 22x29cm
Text on inside cover
ISBN 0-86067-065-1 (pbk) : £2.60
Also classified at 385'.09428'54 B81-22774

385'.09428'54 — Cleveland. Langbaurgh *(District).* **Railway services: Whitby, Redcar & Middlesbrough Union Railway,** *to 1958 — Illustrations*

Hoole, K.. The Whitby, Redcar and Middlesbrough Union Railway / by Ken Hoole. — Nelson, Lancs., Hendon, c1981. — [44]p : chiefly ill,1map,facsims ; 22x29cm
Text on inside cover
ISBN 0-86067-065-1 (pbk) : £2.60
Primary classification 385'.09428'47 B81-22774

385'.09428'8 — England. Border country. Railway services. Branch lines, *1900-1979 — Illustrations*

Border Country : branch line album / [compiled by] Neil Caplan. — London : Ian Allen, 1981. — 127p : ill,maps ; 25cm
Maps on lining papers
ISBN 0-7110-1086-2 : £5.95
Primary classification 385'.09413'7 B81-18362

385'.09429 — Wales. Railway services: British Rail. *Western Region.* **Central Wales line**

Heart of Wales line : the history, route and operation of a fascinating 110-mile railway, and the heartland of Wales it serves / [compiled by Neil Sprinks and Geoffrey Body with the assistance of Mike Tedstone ... et al.]. — Weston-super-Mare (c/o Avon-Anglia Publications & Services, Annesley House, 21 Southside, Weston-super-Mare, Avon BS23 2QM) : British Rail (Western), c1981. — 31p : ill,1map ; 21cm. — (Western at work ; no.3)
Map on inside cover
ISBN 0-905466-41-1 (pbk) : £0.85 B81-34185

385'.09429'4 — South Wales. Railway services, *to 1979*

Barrie, D. S. M.. South Wales / by D.S.M. Barrie. — Newton Abbot : David & Charles, c1980. — 296p : ill,maps ; 23cm. — (A Regional history of the railways of Great Britain ; v.12)
Map (folded sheet) attached to lining paper. — Bibliography: p283-288. - Includes index
ISBN 0-7153-7970-4 : £9.95 : CIP rev.
B80-23166

385'.09429'5 — England. Wye Valley. Railway services: British Rail. *Western Region.* **Ross on Wye-Monmouth line,** *to 1965*

Glover, Mark. The Ross and Monmouth Railway : being a twelve year old boy's research into a small part of our rich railway heritage / by Mark Glover. — [Burford] ([Headmaster's House, Burford School, Burford, Oxford OX8 4PL]) : [M. Glover], [1981]. — 28p : ill,1map ; 21cm
Bibliography: p27
Unpriced (pbk) B81-23391

385'.0952 — Japan. High speed railway services: Nihon Kokuyū Tetsudō. Shinkansen — *Conference proceedings*

The **Shinkansen** high-speed rail network of Japan : proceedings of an IIASA conference, June 27-30, 1977 / A. Straszak, R. Tuch editors. — Oxford : Pergamon, 1980. — xii,452p : ill,maps,plan ; 26cm. — (IIASA proceedings series ; v.7)
ISBN 0-08-024444-0 : £54.00 : CIP rev.
B79-27280

385'.0954 — India. Railways, *to 1914*

Satow, Michael. Railways of the Raj / Michael Satow & Ray Desmond ; with a foreword by Paul Theraux. — London : Scolar, 1980. — 118p : ill(some col.),1map,facsims,ports ; 26x27cm
Bibliography: p50
ISBN 0-85967-533-5 : £15.00 : CIP rev.
B80-03121

Satow Michael. Railways of the Raj. — London : Scolar Press, Feb.1982. — [120]p
Originally published: 1980
ISBN 0-85967-658-7 (pbk) : £7.50 : CIP entry
B81-39230

385'.0973 — United States. Railways, *1960-1980*

Ball, Don. America's railroads : the second generation / Don Ball, Jr. — Cambridge : Stephens, c1980. — 216p : col.ill,maps ; 29cm
Includes index
ISBN 0-85059-515-0 : £16.95 B81-29552

385'.22 — Rail travel

Hollingsworth, J. B.. The atlas of train travel / J.B. Hollingsworth. — London : Sidgwick and Jackson, 1980. — 192p : ill(some col.),maps ; 31cm
Includes index
ISBN 0-283-98706-5 : £6.95 B81-06550

385'.22 — Rail travel, *to 1979*

A **Book** of railway journeys / compiled by Ludovic Kennedy. — London : Collins, 1980. — xxiv,356p : ill,1facsim,ports ; 24cm
ISBN 0-00-216197-4 : £6.95 B81-07013

385'.22'094 — Europe. Railway passenger transport services: Compagnie internationale des wagons-lits et des grands express européens. Orient Express, *to 1976*

Cookridge, E. H.. Orient Express : the life and times of the world's most famous train / E.H. Cookridge. — Large print ed. — Leicester : Ulverscroft, 1981, c1978. — 539p : 1map ; 23cm
Originally published: New York : Random House, 1978 ; London : Allen Lane, 1979. — Map on lining papers. — Bibliography: p529-539
ISBN 0-7089-0629-x : £5.00 : CIP rev.
B81-07441

385'.22'0941 — Great Britain. Railway passenger transport services. Disused routes & stations — *Lists*

Daniels, Gerald. Passengers no more / Gerald Daniels & Les Dench. — 3rd ed. — London : Ian Allen, 1980. — 144p : ill,facsims ; 25cm
Previous ed.: 1973
ISBN 0-7110-0951-1 : £6.95 B81-06432

385'.24'0973 — United States. Railway freight transportation services. Effects of government regulation. Econometric models

Friedlaender, Ann F.. Freight transport regulation : equity, efficiency, and competition in the rail and trucking industries / Ann F. Friedlaender, Richard H. Spady. — Cambridge, Mass. ; London : MIT Press, c1981. — xv,366p : ill ; 24cm. — (MIT Press series on the regulation of economic activity)
Bibliography: p353-359. — Includes index
ISBN 0-262-06072-8 : £18.60
Also classified at 388.3'24'0973 B81-29188

385'.314 — England. Railway services: British Rail. *London Midland Region.* Steam locomotive depots, *1950-1965*

Bolger, Paul. BR steam motive power depots, LMR / Paul Bolger. — London : Ian Allan, 1981. — 144p : ill,1facsim ; 22cm
Includes index
ISBN 0-7110-1019-6 : £6.95 B81-29632

385'.314 — England. Railway services: Great Western Railway. Stations: Halts — *Lists*

Clinker, C. R.. Great Western Railway : a register of halts and platforms 1903-1979 / compiled by C.R. Clinker. — [Weston-super-Mare] ([21 Southside, Weston-super-Mare, Avon BS23 2QU]) : [Avon-Anglia Publications & Services], [c1979]. — 14p ; 30cm. — (Reference aid services ; no.5)
Cover title
ISBN 0-905466-29-2 (pbk) : Unpriced
B81-00080

385'.314 — Great Britain. Railway services: British Rail. Locomotive depots — *Directories*

British Rail locoshed directory. — London : Ian Allen, 1981. — 46p ; 15cm. — (ABC)
ISBN 0-7110-1143-5 (pbk) : £0.50 B81-18364

British Rail traction depot directory. — 1980 ed. — Watford (c/o Termini Enthusiasts, 33 High Acres, Abbots Langley, Watford WD5 0JB) : Railway Enthusiasts Society, [1980]. — 75p : 1ill ; 16cm
ISBN 0-907183-02-6 (pbk) : £0.95 B81-13169

385'.314 — Railways. Stations, *to 1980 — Illustrations*

All stations : a journey through 150 years of railway history / [based on the exhibition Le temps des gares at the Centre Georges Pompidou]. — London : Thames and Hudson, c1981. — 135p,xlp of plates : ill(some col.),maps,1facsim ; 25cm
Translation of: Le temps des gares
ISBN 0-500-01255-5 : £8.50 B81-25407

385'.314'0942165 — London. Lambeth *(London Borough).* Railways. Stations: Waterloo Station, *to 1980*

This is Waterloo / [compiled by] Colin J. Marsden. — London : Ian Allan, 1981. — 53p : ill,1map,plans ; 29cm
ISBN 0-7110-1115-x (pbk) : £1.75 B81-32993

385'.314'09422 — Southern England. Railway services. Stations, *to 1979*

Pryer, G. A.. An historical survey of selected southern stations : layout and illustrations / by G.A. Pryer and G.J. Bowring. — Oxford : Oxford Publishing
Vol.1. — c1980. — [viii],136p : ill,coat of arms,plans ; 31cm
Maps and coat of arms on lining papers. — Bibliography: piv. — Includes index
ISBN 0-86093-016-5 : £7.95 B81-32145

385'.314'09427 — North-west England. Railways. Stations, *to 1980 — Illustrations*

Railway stations in the north west : a pictorial history / compiled by Gordon Biddle ; drawings by Alison Biddle. — Clapham, N. Yorkshire : Dalesman, 1981. — 72p : ill ; 18x22cm
ISBN 0-85206-644-9 (pbk) : £2.95 B81-39593

385'.36 — Southern England. Railway services: British Rail. *Southern Region.* Trains. Two-character headcodes — *Lists*

Beecroft, G. D.. Southern region 2 character headcodes / G.D. Beecroft & B.W. Rayner. — 5th ed. — Purley : Southern Electric Group, 1981. — 29p ; 15cm
Previous ed.: 1978
ISBN 0-906988-02-0 (unbound) : £0.55
B81-39882

385'.361'0941 — Great Britain. Railway services: British Rail. Preserved steam locomotives, *1971-1981*

Siviter, Roger. Steam specials. — Newton Abbot : David & Charles, Sept.1981. — [96]p
ISBN 0-7153-8126-1 (pbk) : £5.95 : CIP entry
B81-21511

385'.5'0941 — Great Britain. Light railways, *to 1978 — Illustrations*

Scott-Morgan, John. British independent light railways / John Scott-Morgan. — Newton Abbot : David & Charles, 1980. — 96p : ill,1map ; 25cm
Bibliography: p96
ISBN 0-7153-7933-x : £5.95 : CIP rev.
B80-13336

385'.5'0942351 — Devon. Light railway services: North Devon and Cornwall Junction Light Railway, *to 1970*

Whetmath, C. F. D.. The North Devon & Cornwall Junction Light Railway : Torrington-Halwill / C.F.D. Whetmath and Douglas Stuckey. — New ed. — Bracknell : Forge, 1980. — 48p : ill,maps,plans ; 21cm
Previous ed.: published as Torrington to Halwill. Lingfield : Oakwood Press, 1963. — Text on inside back cover
£1.95 (pbk) B81-03264

385'.509429'4 — Powys. Montgomery *(District).* Narrow gauge railway services : Welshpool and Llanfair Railway, *1901-1973*

Cartwright, Ralph. The Welshpool & Llanfair light railway. — Newton Abbot : David & Charles, Apr.1981. — [208]p
Previous ed.: 1972
ISBN 0-7153-8151-2 : £6.50 : CIP entry
B81-06889

385'.52'09 — Great Britain. Miniature railways & narrow-gauge railways, *to 1980*

Kichenside, Geoffrey. A source book of miniature & narrow gauge railways / Geoffrey Kichenside. — London : Ward Lock, 1981. — 127p : ill ; 12x17cm
Includes index
ISBN 0-7063-6070-2 : £2.95 : CIP rev.
B81-04281

385'.52'09415 — Ireland. Narrow-gauge railways, *to 1925*

The Irish narrow gauge railway / [compiled by] J.D.C.A. Prideaux. — Newton Abbot : David & Charles, c1981. — 96p : all.ill,1map,facsims ; 25cm
Bibliography: p96
ISBN 0-7153-8071-0 : £5.95 : CIP rev.
B81-17494

385'.52'0942784 — Cumbria. Eskdale. Narrow gauge railway services: Ravenglass & Eskdale Railway, *to 1980*

Davies, W. J. K.. The Ravenglass & Eskdale railway / W.J.K. Davies. — 2nd ed. — Newton Abbot : David & Charles, 1981. — 200p,[22]p of plates : ill,maps,facsims,plans ; 23cm
Previous ed.: 1968. — Includes index
ISBN 0-7153-8194-6 : £5.95 : CIP rev.
B81-14418

385'.52'094292 — Gwynedd. Caernarvonshire. Narrow gauge railway services, *to 1980*

Boyd, James I. C.. Narrow gauge railways in North Caernarvonshire / by James I.C. Boyd ; (in association with J.M. Lloyd and J.S. Wilkinson). — [Trowbridge] : Oakwood
Vol.1: The west. — 1981. — 282p,[36]p of plates : ill,maps ; 23cm. — (The British narrow gauge railway ; no.5)
Map on lining papers. — Includes index
£9.20 (corrected) B81-32727

385'.52'0942923 — Gwynedd. Porthmadog. Narrow gauge railway services: Welsh Highland Light Railway (1964) Ltd, *to 1980*

The **Welsh** Highland Light Railway (1964) Ltd. — Porthmadog (Gelert's Farm Works, Madoc St. West, Porthmadog, Gwynedd) : [Welsh Highland Light Railway (1964) Ltd], [1980?]. — [4]p : ill,1map ; 21cm
Unpriced (unbound) B81-36897

385'.54'09423592 — Devon. South Ham *(District).* China clay industries. Industrial railway services: Lee Moor Tramway, *to 1980*

Hall, R. M. S.. The Lee Moor tramway / by R.M.S. Hall. — Blandford (Old School House, Tarrant Hinton, Nr. Blandford, Dorset) : Oakwood, [1981?]. — 18p,[8]p of plates : ill,maps ; 22cm. — (Locomotion papers ; no.19)
£1.20 (pbk) B81-38160

385'.54'0942819 — West Yorkshire *(Metropolitan County).* Leeds. Tramroads: Lake Lock Rail Road, *to 1853*

Goodchild, John. The Lake Lock Rail Road / by John Goodchild. — [Wakefield] ([Archives Dept., Library H.Q., Balne La., Wakefield W. Yorks]) : Wakefield Metropolitan District Libraries, 1977. — 12p : 1map ; 30cm. — (Archives publication / Wakefield Metropolitan District Libraries ; no.4)
Cover title
ISBN 0-86169-003-6 (pbk) : £0.20 B81-32725

385'54'0942956 — Powys. Brecknock *(District).* Canals: Brecknock and Abergavenny Canal. Tramroads, *to ca 1880*

Rattenbury, Gordon. Tramroads of the Brecknock & Abergavenny canal / Gordon Rattenbury. — Oakham (12 High St., Oakham, Leicestershire, LE15 6AW) : Railway and Canal Historical Society, 1980. — 136p : ill,maps ; 24cm
Includes index
ISBN 0-901461-23-7 (cased) : Unpriced
ISBN 0-901461-24-5 (pbk) : Unpriced
Also classified at 385'.54'094299 B81-07755

385'.54'094299 — Great Britain. Canals: Brecknock and Abergavenny Canal. Tramroads, *to ca 1880*

Rattenbury, Gordon. Tramroads of the Brecknock & Abergavenny canal / Gordon Rattenbury. — Oakham (12 High St., Oakham, Leicestershire, LE15 6AW) : Railway and Canal Historical Society, 1980. — 136p : ill,maps ; 24cm
Includes index
ISBN 0-901461-23-7 (cased) : Unpriced
ISBN 0-901461-24-5 (pbk) : Unpriced
Primary classification 385'54'0942956
B81-07755

385'.6'0941172 — Scotland. Highland Region. Ben Wyvis. Mountain rack railway services — *Proposals*

Murray, John, *1927-*. The Dingwall and Ben Wyvis Railway : a prospectus to build Scotland's first mountain line / by John Murray. — [Bridge of Allan] ([The River Bank, 24 Fishers Green, Bridge of Allan FK9 4PU]) : [J. Murray], [1979]. — 42p,[2]folded leaves of plates : ill(some col),maps,1port ; 15x22cm
Map on cover
£0.75 (pbk) B81-10650

385'90941 — Great Britain. Preserved railways, *to 1980*

Body, Geoffrey. An illustrated history of preserved railways. — Ashbourne : Moorland, May 1981. — [160]p
ISBN 0-86190-018-9 : £6.95 : CIP entry
B81-08864

386 — INLAND WATERWAYS TRANSPORT, FERRY TRANSPORT

386'.0941 — Great Britain. Inland waterways

McKnight, Hugh. The Shell book of inland waterways. — Newton Abbot : David & Charles, Sept.1981. — [528]p
Previous ed.: 1975
ISBN 0-7153-8239-x : £10.00 : CIP entry
B81-21510

386'.09415 — Ireland. Inland waterways. Restoration, *to 1980*

Squires, Roger W.. Inland waterways in Ireland / by Roger W. Squires. — Beckenham (4 Manor Way, Beckenham, Kent) : Waterway Restoration Research, 1981. — 17p : 1map ; 21cm
Cover title. — Map on inside cover
£0.60 (pbk) B81-17289

386'.1 — Scotland. Western Isles. Ferry services. Subsidies by government of Great Britain — *Proposals*

Sea transport to the Scottish islands : a response to the Scottish Office consultative paper of March 1980 / Comhairle Nan Eilean, Western Isles Islands Council. — London (28 Maiden La., WC2E 7JS) : RPT Economic Studies Group, 1980. — [73]p in various pagings ; 30cm
Cover title
Unpriced (pbk) B81-37797

386'.22 — Great Britain. Inland waterways. Boat hire services — *Directories — Serials*

The good boat guide. — 1981. — Harmondsworth : Penguin, 1981. — 296p. — (Penguin handbooks)
ISBN 0-14-046475-1 : £3.50 B81-12417

386'.229 — Great Britain. Inland waterway freight transport. Horse-drawn canal barges, *to 1981*

Smith, D. J. (Donald John). The horse on the cut. — Cambridge : Patrick Stephens, Feb.1982. — [192]p
ISBN 0-85059-514-2 : £9.95 : CIP entry B81-35837

386'.32'09426 — East Anglia. Navigable rivers: Lark Navigation, *1889-1915*

Weston, D. E.. Lord Bristol's amazing steam venture : Victorian and Edwardian riverfolk of Suffolk : as seen by Mr. William Howlett from 1889 to 1915 / by D.E. Weston ; illustrated with contemporary photographs. — Bury St. Edmunds ([13 Minden Drive, Bury St. Edmunds, IP33 3RY]) : D.E. Weston, c1981. — 36p : ill,ports ; 21cm
Ill on inside cover
Unpriced (pbk) B81-18591

386'.32'094271 — Cheshire. Navigable rivers: Mersey and Irwell Navigation, *1720-1887*

Hayman, Alfred. Mersey and Irwell Navigation to Manchester Ship Canal : 1720-1887 / by Alfred Hayman. — [Manchester?] : Federation of Bridgewater Cruising Club, 1981. — 66p : ill,maps ; 21cm + folded sheet(map ; 33x21cm folded to 21x12cm)
Cover title
£0.75 (pbk)
Also classified at 386'.32'094273 B81-25089

386'.32'094273 — Greater Manchester *(Metropolitan County).* **Navigable rivers: Mersey and Irwell Navigation,** *1720-1887*

Hayman, Alfred. Mersey and Irwell Navigation to Manchester Ship Canal : 1720-1887 / by Alfred Hayman. — [Manchester?] : Federation of Bridgewater Cruising Club, 1981. — 66p : ill,maps ; 21cm + folded sheet(map ; 33x21cm folded to 21x12cm)
Cover title
£0.75 (pbk)
Primary classification 386'.32'094271
B81-25089

386'.46'0941 — Great Britain. Canals

Smith, Peter L.. Discovering canals in Britain / Peter L. Smith. — Aylesbury : Shire, 1981. — 96p : ill,maps ; 18cm. — (Discovering series ; no.257)
Bibliography: p95. — Includes index
ISBN 0-85263-549-4 (pbk) : £1.35 B81-40739

386'.46'0941 — Great Britain. Canals, *to 1850*

Hadfield, Charles. The canal age / by Charles Hadfield. — 2nd ed. — Newton Abbot : David & Charles, c1981. — 233p : ill,maps,facsims,ports ; 22cm
Previous ed.: 1968. — Bibliography: p215-220. - Includes index
ISBN 0-7153-8079-6 : £7.50 B81-20809

386'.46'0941 — Great Britain. Lost canals

Russell, Ronald. Lost canals and waterways of Britain. — Newton Abbot : David & Charles, Jan.1982. — [304]p
ISBN 0-7153-8072-9 : £12.50 : CIP entry B81-33823

386'.48'09413 — Scotland. Central Lowlands. Canals: Forth and Clyde Canal — *For environment planning*

Forth and Clyde Canal local (subject) plan : report of survey by working party. — [Glasgow] ([20 India St., Glasgow, G2 4PF]) : [Strathclyde Regional Council, Department of Physical Planning], 1979. — 59p,[31]p of plates (some folded) : ill,plans ; 21x30cm
Unpriced (pbk) B81-12583

386'.48'0941619 — Lisburn *(District).* **Canals: Lagan Canal,** *to 1980*

Blair, May. Once upon the Lagan : the story of the Lagan Canal / May Blair. — Belfast : Blackstaff, c1981. — ix,126p : ill,maps,facsims,ports ; 20x25cm
ISBN 0-85640-245-1 (pbk) : £4.95 : CIP rev. B81-13843

386'.6'0941 — Great Britain. Rivers. Ferry services

Martin, Nancy, *1899-*. River ferries / by Nancy Martin. — Lavenham : Terence Dalton, 1980. — xi,128p : ill ; 23cm
Bibliography: p128. — Includes index
ISBN 0-900963-99-9 : £6.95 B81-00834

386'.6'094112 — Scotland. Islands. Ferry services — *Proposals*

Ferry services for the Scottish Islands : a discussion paper / prepared by the Scottish Consumer Council and G.A. Mackay. — Glasgow (4 Somerset Place, Glasgow GR3 7JT) : The Council, [1981?]. — 15leaves : 1map ; 30cm. — (Report / Scottish Consumer Council)
ISBN 0-907067-01-8 (unbound) : £1.00 B81-36923

387 — WATER TRANSPORT

387 — Water transport — *Conference proceedings*

Inland & maritime waterways & ports = Voies navigables et ports interieurs et maritimes. — Oxford : Pergamon, Dec.1981. — 11v.
ISBN 0-08-026750-5 : £165.00 : CIP entry B81-31375

387.1 — PORTS

387.1'0941 — Great Britain. Ports. Organisations: British Transport Docks Board — *Serials*

British Transport Docks Board. Report and accounts / British Transport Docks Board. — 1980. — [London] ([Melbury House, Melbury Terrace, NW1 6JY]) : The Board, [1981]. — 41p
Unpriced B81-30825

387.1'0941 — Great Britain. Ports — *Statistics — Serials*

Annual digest of port statistics / National Ports Council. — 1979, vol.1. — London : H.M.S.O., [1979]. — 133p
ISBN 0-86073-049-2 : £10.00
ISSN 0305-3156 B81-10313

387.1'09411 — Scotland. Ports — *Practical information — For industries — Serials*

Ports of Scotland. — 1981. — Dundee (13 Albany Terrace, Dundee DD3 6HR) : Town Crier Publications, [1981]. — 84p
ISSN 0142-274x : £2.00 B81-32661

387.1'09412'25 — Scotland. Grampian Region. Peterhead. Harbours: Peterhead Harbour, *to ca 1906*

Buchan, Alex. R.. The port of Peterhead from its establishment to the beginning of the twentieth century / by Alex. R. Buchan. — [Glasgow] ([22 Clochbar Ave., Milngavie, Glasgow G62]) : [A.R. Buchan], [1980]. — 328p : ill,maps,facsims,plans,ports,geneal.tables ; 31cm
Bibliography: p317-322. - Includes index
Unpriced B81-04833

387.1'09412'35 — Scotland. Grampian Region. Aberdeen. Ports: Aberdeen Harbour — *Visitors' guide*

Aberdeen harbour : the official handbook. — London : Published by the authority of the Aberdeen Harbour Board [by] Burrow, [1981]. — 116p : ill(some col.),1map ; 25cm
Folded map on inside cover
£3.50 (pbk) B81-39137

387.1'09421 — London. Ports: Port of London — *Practical information — Serials*

London port handbook : a guide to the docks, wharves and shipping services of London's river. — 1981-. — Downham Market (11 London Rd, Downham Market, Norfolk PE38 9BX) : Charter Publications, 1980-. — v. : ill ; 21cm
Annual. — Continues: London shipping contacts
ISSN 0260-8839 = London port handbook : £2.00 B81-20030

387.1'09422'5 — East Sussex. Coastal regions. Ports. Economic conditions, *1550-1700 — Readings from contemporary sources — Facsimiles*

The **Maritime** economy of Eastern Sussex 1550-1700 / compiled by Colin E. Brent for the East Sussex Record Office. — Lewes ([County Record Office, Pelham House, St. Andrews La., Lewes, E. Sussex BN7 1GW]) : [East Sussex County Council], 1980. — [27]leaves : ill,maps,facsims ; 30cm. — (Local history research unit / East Sussex Record Office ; no.11)
Bibliography: leaf 4
Unpriced (pbk) B81-17383

387.1'09422'792 — Hampshire. Portsmouth. Ports: Port of Portsmouth — *Visitors' guides*

Portsmouth commercial docks official handbook. — London : Burrow, [1979]. — 52p : ill,maps ; 25cm
Unpriced (pbk) B81-09910

387.1'09423'37 — Dorset. Poole. Ports: Port of Poole — *Serials*

Poole ... port yearbook for commercial users. — 1980-81. — Downham Market (11 London Rd, Downham Market, Norfolk PE38 9BX) : Charter Publications [for] the Poole Harbour Commissioners, [1980]. — 36p
ISSN 0260-2547 : Unpriced B81-06287

387.1'09423'93 — Avon. Bristol. Ports: Port of Bristol — *Serials*

Port of Bristol. — 1981. — [Bristol] ([Port Office, St Andrew's Rd, Avonmouth, Bristol BS11 4DQ]) : Published and printed for the Port of Bristol Authority by City of Bristol Printing and Stationery Dept., [1981]. — 104p
Unpriced B81-29665

387.1'09426'49 — Suffolk. Ipswich. Ports: Port of Ipswich — *Serials*

Ipswich Port Authority. Ipswich port handbook. — 1981-. — Downham Market (11 London Rd, Downham Market, Norfolk, PE38 9BX) : Charter Publications for Ipswich Port Authority, 1981-. — v. : ill,maps ; 21cm
Annual. — Continues: Ipswich Port Authority. Handbook
ISSN 0260-9509 = Ipswich port handbook : Unpriced B81-14537

387.1'09495'1 — Greece. Piraeus. Ports: Port of Piraeus — *Serials*

Piraeus shipping handbook : [a guide for the international shipping industry]. — 1980-. — Downham Market (11 London Rd, Downham Market, Norfolk PE38 9BX) : Ryston in conjunction with the Hellenic Shipbrokers Association, 1980-. — v. : ill,ports ; 21cm
Annual. — Supplement to: The Shipbroker
ISSN 0260-5279 = Piraeus shipping handbook : £2.00 (free to subscribers to the Shipbroker) B81-04598

387.1'5 — Gloucestershire. Gloucester. Docks, *to 1980*

Stimpson, Michael. The history of Gloucester Docks and its associated canals and railways / by Michael Stimpson ; with map by Edwin Lambert. — [Potters Bar] ([c/o M. Stimpson, 83 Sunnybank Rd., Potters Bar, Herts.]) : West London Industrial Archaeological Society, 1980. — 24p : ill,1map ; 21cm
ISBN 0-907220-00-2 (pbk) : £0.75 B81-01785

387.1'5 — Gloucestershire. Sharpness. Docks, *to 1976*

Rowles, Wilf. Sharpness / by Wilf Rowles ; edited by Derek Archer. — S.l. : s.n., 1980 (Dursley : Bailey Litho). — 120p : ill,2ports ; 22cm. — (Pages from the past)
Includes index
£5.00 B81-30708

387.1'5 — New York *(City).* **Docks,** *1846-1900 — Illustrations*

Maritime New York : in nineteenth-century photographs / [compiled by] Harry Johnson & Frederick S. Lightfoot. — New York : Dover ; London : Constable, 1980. — xiv,160p : chiefly ill,1map ; 28cm
Includes index
ISBN 0-486-23963-2 (pbk) : £4.65 B81-18585

387.1'53 — Freight transport. Shipping. Terminals *— Conference proceedings*

Terminal operation. — Worcester Park (54 Cheam Common Rd., Worcester Park, Surrey KT4 8RJ) : CS Publications
Vol.2: Proceedings of the 2nd Terminal Operations Conference : organised by Cargo Systems International at Amsterdam on June 18, 19 and 20th 1980 / edited for Cargo Systems by Patrick Finlay. — c1981. — 245p : ill,plans ; 30cm
ISBN 0-907499-12-0 (pbk) : Unpriced
B81-16027

387.2 — WATER TRANSPORT. SHIPS

387.2'0212 — Merchant ships *— Statistics — Serials*

Annual summary of merchant ships completed in the world / Lloyd's Register of Shipping. — 1980. — London : Lloyd's Register of Shipping, c1981. — [14]p
ISSN 0261-2720 : Unpriced B81-20705

387.2'0216 — Ships *— Lists — Serials*

Lloyd's register of shipping. Appendix. — 1980-81. — London : Lloyd's Register of Shipping, c1980. — [903]p
Unpriced B81-16752

Register of ships / Lloyd's Register of Shipping. — 1980-81. — London : Lloyd's Register of Shipping, c1980. — 3v.
ISSN 0141-4909 : Unpriced B81-03571

387.2'045'0216 — Submersibles *— Lists — Serials*

Register of offshore units, submersibles & diving systems / Lloyd's Register of Shipping. — 1980-81. — London : The Register, c1980. — 410p in various pagings
ISSN 0141-4143 : Unpriced
Primary classification 338.2'728 B81-08757

387.2'09 — Merchant ships. Fleets *— History*

Haws, Duncan. Merchant fleets in profile / Duncan Haws. — Cambridge : Stephens
4 / with drawings to 1:1800 scale. — 1980. — 208p : ill ; 24cm
Volume title: The ships of the Hamburg America, Adler and Carr lines
ISBN 0-85059-397-2 : £8.95 : CIP rev.
B80-09162

387.2'09171'7 — Sovet ékonomicheskoĭ vzaimopomoshchi countries. Merchant ships, *1945-1980 — Lists*

Bock, Bruno. Soviet Bloc merchant ships / by Bruno Bock and Klaus Bock ; translated by John A. Broadwin. — London : Jane's, c1981. — 269p : ill ; 29cm
Translation of: Die roten Handelsflotten. — Bibliography: p255. — Includes index
ISBN 0-7106-0143-3 : £12.50 B81-37401

Greenway, Ambrose. Comecon merchant ships / by Ambrose Greenway. — 2nd ed. — Havant : Mason, 1981, c1978. — vi,180p : ill ; 26cm
Previous ed.: 1978. — Includes index
ISBN 0-85937-254-5 (cased) : £6.95
ISBN 0-85932-259-6 (unbound) : Unpriced
B81-15402

387.2'0941 — Great Britain. Shipping, *to 1968.* **Preserved ships**

Elliott, Colin. Maritime heritage : the story of Britain's preserved historic ships and where to see them / by Colin Elliott. — Sulhamstead (13, Wise's Firs, Sulhamstead, Berkshire RG7 4EH) : Tops'l in co-operation with Maritime Trust, 1981. — 64p : ill,ports ; 24cm
Text and ill on inside cover
ISBN 0-906397-07-3 (pbk) : £2.50 : CIP rev.
B81-17537

387.2'0947 — Soviet Union. Merchant ships, *1945-1981 — Lists*

Greenway, Ambrose. Soviet merchant ships / by Ambrose Greenway. — [4th ed]. — Havant : Mason, 1980. — vi,226p : ill ; 26cm
Previous ed.: 1978. — Includes index
ISBN 0-85937-253-7 (cased) : £6.95
ISBN 0-85939-258-8 (unbound) : Unpriced
B81-15403

387.2'09492 — Netherlands. Shipping. Ships, *ca 1550-ca 1850*

Maritime prints by the Dutch masters / selected, introduced and annotated by Irene de Groot and Robert Vorstman ; with 290 illustrations, including 220 in actual size ; translated from the Dutch by Michael Hoyle. — London : Fraser, 1980. — 284p : ill ; 31cm
Translation from the Dutch. — Bibliography: p277-278. — Includes index
ISBN 0-86092-052-6 : £18.00 : CIP rev.
Also classified at 769'.4962382 B80-13773

387.2'23 — Yachts *— Lists — Serials*

Lloyd's register of classed yachts. — 1981-. — London : Lloyd's Register of Shipping, 1981-. — v. ; 18cm
Annual. — Continues: Lloyd's register of yachts
ISSN 0261-6688 = Lloyd's register of classed yachts : Unpriced B81-32270

387.2'432 — Passenger transport. Shipping. Four-funneled steam liners, *to 1980*

Flayhart, William H.. Majesty at sea. — Cambridge : Stephens, Sept.1981. — [160]p
ISBN 0-85059-461-8 : £14.95 : CIP entry
B81-25886

387.2'432'091631 — North Atlantic Ocean. Passenger transport. Shipping. Liners, *1945-1980*

Miller, William H. (William Henry). Transatlantic liners 1945-1980 / William H. Miller. — Newton Abbot : David & Charles, c1981. — 222p : ill ; 26cm
Includes index
ISBN 0-7153-8020-6 : £12.50 B81-33005

387.2'45 — Bulk carrying ships *— Lists — Serials*

The **Bulk** carrier register / compiled ... by H. Clarkson & Company Limited. — 1981. — London : The Company, c1981. — xxxii,555p
ISSN 0305-0122 : £65.00 B81-29115

387.2'45 — Offshore supply ships *— Lists — Serials*

The **Offshore** service vessel register / compiled ... by H. Clarkson & Company Limited. — 1981. — London : The Company, c1981. — 375p
ISSN 0309-040x : £60.00 B81-29114

387.2'45 — Ships: Liquefied gas carriers *— Lists — Serials*

Liquid gas carrier register / compiled ... by H. Clarkson & Company Limited. — 1981. — London : The Company, c1981. — 147p
£40.00 (corrected) B81-29116

387.2'45 — Ships: Tankers *— Lists — Serials*

The **Tanker** register / compiled ... by H. Clarkson & Company Limited. — 1981. — London : The Company, c1981. — xxxi,448p
£65.00 B81-29113

387.5 — OCEAN TRANSPORT

387.5 — Merchant shipping *— Conference proceedings*

Greenwich forum VI : world shipping in the 1990s : records of a conference at the Royal Naval College, Greenwich, 23-25 April 1980 / edited by M.B.F. Ranken. — Guildford, Surrey : Westbury House, c1981. — xii,234p : ill ; 25cm
ISBN 0-86103-049-4 : Unpriced : CIP rev.
B81-04196

387.5 — Merchant ships. Owners *— Directories — Serials*

List of shipowners / Lloyd's Register of Shipping. — 1980-81-. — London : The Register, 1980-. — v. ; 30cm
Annual. — Continues: List of shipowners, index of former names of ships, compound names of ships
ISSN 0260-7387 = List of shipowners : Unpriced B81-06482

387.5 — Shipping

Alderton, Patrick M.. Sea transport : operation and economics / by Patrick M. Alderton. — 2nd ed. — London : Reed, 1980. — 226p : ill,maps ; 22cm
Previous ed.: 1973. — Includes index
ISBN 0-900335-63-7 : £7.95 B81-14120

Branch, Alan E.. The economics of shipping practice and management. — London : Chapman and Hall, July 1981. — [330]p
ISBN 0-412-16350-0 (pbk) : £6.75 : CIP entry
B81-14851

Branch, Alan E.. Elements of shipping. — 5th ed. — London : Chapman & Hall, Nov.1981. — [300]p
Previous ed.: 1977
ISBN 0-412-23700-8 (cased) : £12.00 : CIP entry
ISBN 0-412-23710-5 : pbk : £6.50 B81-30441

387.5'025 — Shipping *— Directories — Serials*

International shipping and shipbuilding directory. Volume 1, ISSD. — 92nd ed. — London : Benn Publications, c1981. — 562p
Spine title: ISSD
ISBN 0-510-49716-0 : £32.00 B81-25502

387.5'028'54044 — Shipping services. Applications of microprocessor systems *— Conference proceedings*

Computers and shipping : an in depth one day seminar on the practical use of the micro-chip on ships and in shipping offices : the Hamburg Plaza Hotel, September 23, 1980 / sponsored by the Institute of Shipping Economics, Bremen and held in conjunction with the Ship Machinery and Marine Technology Exhibition organised by Lloyd's of London Press Ltd., London. — [London] ([c/o Lloyd's, Lime St., EC3M 7HA]) : [Lloyd's of London Press], [1981]. — [105]leaves,[12]leaves of plates : ill ; 31cm
ISBN 0-904093-97-2 : Unpriced B81-15722

387.5'05 — Shipping *— Serials*

Fairplay world shipping year book. — 1981. — London (52 Southwark St., SE1 1UJ) : Fairplay Publications, c1981. — 824p
ISBN 0-905045-26-2 : Unpriced
ISSN 0142-6974 B81-32427

387.5'068 — Shipping services. Management

Stevens, Edward F.. Shipping practice : with consideration of the relevant law. — 11th ed. / Edward F. Stevens and C.S.J. Butterfield ; with a foreword by the late Lord Essendon. — London : Pitman, 1981. — xi,173p : ill,1plan,forms ; 22cm
Previous ed.: 1978. — Includes index
ISBN 0-273-01616-4 (pbk) : Unpriced
B81-38873

387.5'068 — Shipping. Ships. Management *— For British shipmasters*

Kemp, John F.. Business notes for shipmasters / Kemp & Young. — 4th ed. — London : Stanford Maritime, 1980. — 132p : ill,forms ; 21cm
Previous ed.: 1976. — Includes index
ISBN 0-540-07346-6 (pbk) : £2.95 B81-0083

387.5′09163′1 — North Atlantic Ocean. Steam liners: Titanic *(Ship)*. Sinking, *1912*

Lord, Walter. A night to remember / Walter Lord. — Rev. and illustrated ed. — Harmondsworth : Penguin, 1978 (1981 [printing]). — 186p,[16]p of plates : ill,ports ; 18cm
Previous ed.: London : Longmans, Green, 1956. — Includes index
ISBN 0-14-005578-9 (pbk) : £1.75 B81-11531

387.5′092′2 — Cornwall. Fowey. Stephens *(Family)*, *1867-1939*

Ward-Jackson, C. H.. Stephens of Fowey : a portrait of a Cornish merchant fleet 1867-1939 / by C.H. Ward-Jackson. — London : Published by the Trustees of the National Maritime Museum, 1980. — 115p : ill,1map,facsims,ports,geneal.table. — (Maritime monographs and reports, ISSN 0307-8590 ; no.43)
Bibliography: p103-105. — Includes index
ISBN 0-905555-29-5 (pbk) : Unpriced B81-11693

387.5′092′4 — Great Britain. Merchant ships — *Personal observations*

Muir, Ian W.. Dinosaur down below / by Ian W. Muir. — Glasgow (Neilston, Glasgow) : Peveril Publications, c1980. — [88]p : ill,1port ; 22cm
Text, port. on inside covers
Unpriced (pbk) B81-12266

387.5′092′4 — Merchant shipping. Bennetts, John Ray — *Biographies*

Bennetts, John Ray. Far away in Australia / John Ray Bennetts. — Ilfracombe : Stockwell, 1980. — 43p ; 18cm
ISBN 0-7223-1411-6 (pbk) : £1.98 B81-07249

387.5′092′4 — Merchant ships. Sailing. Lewis, Rob — *Biographies — Welsh texts*

Lewis, Rob. Brith yw brethyn bywyd / Rob Lewis ; trosiad gan Dilys Williams. — Llandysul : Gwasg Gomer, 1980. — 163p ; 18cm
ISBN 0-85088-952-9 (pbk) : £2.50 B81-08346

387.5′092′4 — Sailing ships. Sailing. Thomas, Robert, *1843-1903 — Biographies*

Eames, Aled. Ship master : the life and letters of Capt. Robert Thomas of Llandwrog and Liverpool 1843-1903 / Aled Eames. — [Caernarfon] ([County Offices, Caernarfon, Gwynedd LL55 1SH]) : Gwynedd Archives Service, c1980. — 199p,[13]p of plates : ill,facsims,ports ; 22cm
ISBN 0-901337-25-0 (pbk) : £2.95 B81-08356

387.5′092′4 — Shipping. Merchant schooners, *1920-1951 — Personal observations*

England, Richard. Schoonerman / Richard England ; with a foreword by Winston Graham. — London : Hollis & Carter, 1981. — 293p,[16]p of plates : ill,ports ; 23cm
Includes index
ISBN 0-370-30377-6 : £8.95 : CIP rev. B81-03142

387.5′092′4 — Tall ships. Sailing, *ca 1920 — Personal observations*

Brookesmith, Frank. I remember the tall ships / Frank Brookesmith. — Palmerston North, N.Z. : Dunmore ; London : Seafarer, c1980. — 270p,[16]p of plates : ill,ports ; 23cm
Ill on lining papers
ISBN 0-85036-268-7 : £6.00 B81-08280

387.5′0941 — Great Britain. Coastal waters. Shipwrecks, *to 1980*

Larn, Richard. Shipwrecks of Great Britain and Ireland / Richard Larn. — Newton Abbot : David & Charles, 1981. — 208p : ill,maps,facsims,ports ; 23cm
Bibliography: p198-199. — Includes index
ISBN 0-7153-7491-5 : £7.95 B81-15064

387.5′0941 — Great Britain. Merchant shipping, *to 1979*

Hope, Ronald. The Merchant Navy / Ronald Hope. — London : Stanford, 1980. — 132p,[2]p of plates : ill(some col.) ; 25cm
Bibliography: p129-132
ISBN 0-540-07335-0 : £5.95 B81-00836

387.5′0941 — Great Britain. Shipping, *1480-1914 — Festschriften*

Shipping, trade and commerce : essays in memory of Ralph Davis / edited by P.L. Cottrell and D.H. Aldcroft. — [Leicester] : Leicester University Press, 1981. — viii,200p : 1port ; 24cm
Bibliography: p7-8. - Includes index
ISBN 0-7185-1195-6 (corrected) : £15.00
Primary classification 382′.0941 B81-23126

387.5′0941 — Great Britain. Shipping — *Serials*

British shipper. — Vol.0,no.0 (May 1980); Vol.1, no.1 (Oct. 1980)-. — London : National Magazine Co., 1980-. — v. : ill,ports ; 30cm
Monthly. — Introdulctory no., called Vol. 0, no.0, issued May 1980
ISSN 0260-0951 = British shipper : £15.00 per year B81-33282

387.5′0941 — Great Britain. Shipping services: Peninsular and Oriental Line, *to 1939*

Padfield, Peter. Beneath the house flag of the P & O. — London : Hutchinson, Aug.1981. — [160]p
ISBN 0-09-145760-2 : £8.95 : CIP entry B81-20144

387.5′0941 — Great Britain. Shipping — *Statistics — Serials*

British shipping statistics / General Council of British Shipping. — 1979/80. — [London] ([30 St Mary Axe EC3A 8ET]) : The Council, 1980. — 116p
Unpriced B81-07698

387.5′0941 — Great Britain. Shipping, *to 1980*

Simper, Robert. Britain′s maritime heritage. — Newton Abbot : David & Charles, Feb.1982. — [392]p
ISBN 0-7153-8177-6 : £10.95 : CIP entry B81-35826

387.5′09417 — Ireland *(Republic)*. Merchant shipping, *1939-1945*

Forde, Frank. The long watch : the history of the Irish Mercantile Marine in World War Two / Frank Forde. — Dublin : Gill and Macmillan, 1981. — 147p : ill,1chart,2facsims,ports ; 26cm
Bibliography: p134-135. — Includes index
ISBN 0-7171-1126-1 : £15.00 B81-36851

387.5′09423′7 — Cornwall. Coastal waters. Shipwrecks, *to 1966*

Mudd, David. The cruel Cornish sea / David Mudd. — St. Teath : Bossiney, 1981. — 112p : ill,ports ; 21cm
Bibliography: p109
ISBN 0-906456-09-6 (pbk) : £1.75 B81-15312

387.5′09426′7 — Essex. Coastal waters. Sailing boats. Sailing, *1800-1945*

Benham, Hervey. Last stronghold of sail : the story of the Essex sailing-smacks, coasters and barges / by Hervey Benham ; with a chapter on wildfowling by J. Wentworth Day. — London : Harrap, 1948 (1981 printing). — 202p,[31]p of plates : ill,2maps ; 23cm
Maps on lining papers. — Includes index
ISBN 0-245-53784-8 : £7.95 B81-40191

387.5′09429′21 — Gwynedd. Ynys Môn. Shipping, *to 1914*

Eames, Aled. Ships and seamen of Anglesey 1558-1918 : studies in maritime and local history / Aled Eames. — [London] : National Maritime Museum, c1981. — 674p,[32]p of plates,folded leaf : ill,maps,facsims,ports ; 21cm. — (Modern maritime classics reprint, ISSN 0140-9042 ; no.4)
Originally published: Llangefni : Anglesey Antiquarian Society, 1973. — Includes index
ISBN 0-905555-50-3 (pbk) : Unpriced B81-20996

387.5′09438 — Poland. Shipping, *to 1959*. Politico-economic aspects — *Polish texts*

Kowalski, Bronisław. Morskie i terytorialne : aspekty W gospodarce rzeczypospolitey 963-1959 / Bronisław Kowalski. — London : Veritas Foundation, c1980. — 523p,[1]folded leaf + 1map on folded leaf : maps(some col.) ; 21cm
Map on folded leaf in pocket. — Bibliography: p515-523
Unpriced (pbk) B81-21019

387.5′0946′89 — Gibraltar. Shipping services: Bland Ltd, *to 1980*

Somner, Graeme. Bland Gibraltar / by Graeme Somner. — Kendal : World Ship Society, 1981. — 56p : ill,1map,1port ; 21cm
Ill on inside cover. — Includes index
ISBN 0-905617-16-9 (pbk) : £3.00 B81-23206

387.5′0951′25 — Hong Kong. Shipping services — *Serials*

Hong Kong handbook : [guide to the port & shipping services of Hong Kong]. — 1981-. — Downham Market : Ryston, [1980]-. — v. : ill,maps,ports ; 30cm
Annual
ISSN 0260-7786 = Hong Kong handbook : Unpriced B81-09152

387.5′0971 — Canada. Shipping services: Canadian Pacific Steamships, *to 1980*

Musk, George. Canadian Pacific : the story of the famous shipping line / George Musk. — Newton Abbot : David & Charles, c1980. — 272p : ill,maps,facsims,ports ; 26cm
Bibliography: p265. — Includes index
ISBN 0-7153-7968-2 : £15.00 B81-09262

387.5′0973 — United States. Shipping — *Serials*

Seatrade U.S. yearbook. — 2nd ed. (1980). — Colchester (Fairfax House, Colchester CO1 1RJ) : Seatrade Publications, c1980. — 248p
ISBN 0-905597-15-x : Unpriced
ISSN 0142-5056 B81-00837

387.5′1 — English Channel. Hovercraft services: British Rail Hovercraft Limited. Mergers with Hoverlloyd Limited — *Inquiry reports*

Great Britain. *Monopolies and Mergers Commission*. British Rail Hovercraft Limited and Hoverlloyd Limited : a report on the proposed merger / Monopolies and Mergers Commission. — London : H.M.S.O., [1981]. — v,51p : 1ill ; 25cm. — (HC ; 374)
£3.60 (pbk) B81-33093

387.5′1 — Flags of convenience — *National Union of Seamen viewpoints*

National Union of Seamen. Flags of convenience / [by the National Union of Seaman of Great Britain]. — London (Maritime House, Old Town, Clapham, SW4 0JP) : The Union, 1981. — 16p ; 30cm + 1statement sheet(2p ; 34cm)
£1.00 (pbk) B81-26312

387.5′1 — Shipbrokers — *Conference proceedings*

Shipbroking in the 80′s *(Conference : 1980 : Hamburg)*. Shipbroking in the 80′s : a one-day seminar organised by Lloyds of London Press Ltd. and sponsored by the German Shipbrokers Association, the Hamburg Plaza Hotel, September 24, 1980. — [London] : Lloyds of London Press, [1980?]. — 68leaves in various foliations ; 31cm
Includes index
ISBN 0-907432-00-x : Unpriced B81-23309

387.5′1 — Shipping services. Financial aspects — *Conference proceedings*

Money & ships 1981 : Grosvenor House Hotel, London 7-8 April 1981 / conference chairman Adrian Swire ; [edited by David Robinson]. — Colchester (Fairfax House, Colchester CO1 1RJ) : Seatrade Conferences, [1981]. — 161p : ill ; 30cm. — (Seatrade Conferences)
Conference papers
£60.00 (pbk) B81-29139

387.5′42 — Coolies. Transport. Shipping. Sailing ships, *ca 1920*

Lubbock, Basil. Coolie ships and oil sailers / by Basil Lubbock. — Glasgow : Brown, Son & Ferguson, c1981. — x,180p[37]p of plates : ill,ports ; 25cm
Originally published: 1935. — Includes index
ISBN 0-85174-111-8 : £10.50
Also classified at 387.5′448 B81-21233

387.5′42′0941 — Great Britain. Passenger transport services: Shipping services — *Serials*

Trip out. — 1981/82. — London (77 St Mary′s Grove, W4 3LW) : G.P. Hamer, c1981. — 44p
ISBN 0-9506515-2-4 : £1.65 B81-25018

387.5'44 — United States. Freight transport. Shipping. Liners. Management. Conferences

Sletmo, Gunnar K.. Liner conferences in the container age : U.S. policy at sea / Gunnar K. Sletmo and Ernest W. Williams, Jr. ; foreword by Karl E. Bakke. — New York : Macmillan ; London : Collier Macmillan, c1981. — xxxv,343p ; 25cm. — (Studies of the modern corporation)
Bibliography: p321-329. — Includes index
ISBN 0-02-929200-x : £18.95 B81-36125

387.5'44'0681 — Freight transport. Shipping. Costing

Packard, William V.. Voyage estimating / William V. Packard. — London : Fairplay, 1978 (1979 printing). — 79p : ill,2forms ; 25cm. — (Tramp ship series)
Bibliography: p65. — Includes index
ISBN 0-905045-08-4 (pbk) : Unpriced B81-39940

387.5'44'0941 — Great Britain. Freight transport. Shipping — *Statistics* — *Serials*

Nationality of vessels in United Kingdom seaborne trade / Business Statistics Office. — 1979. — London : H.M.S.O., c1980. — 92p. — (Business monitor ; MA8)
ISBN 0-11-512871-9 : £5.50 B81-07800

387.5'44'095 — Far East. Freight transport. Shipping — *Conference proceedings*

Seatrade Hong Kong Conference *(3rd : 1980)*. Far East trade & shipping : seatrade Hong Kong Conference 1980 : Regent Hotel, Kowloon, Hong Kong 19-20 November 1980 : a Seatrade Conference organised in association with Expoship Far East 80, International Maritime Exhibition ... / [edited by Trevor Lones and Hazel Lloyd]. — Colchester (Fairfax House, Colchester CO1 1RJ) : Seatrade Conferences, 1980. — 90p,[18]p : ill,maps ; 30cm
£50.00 (pbk) B81-15480

387.5'442 — Freight transport. Shipping. Roll on/roll off services — *Conference proceedings* — *Serials*

RoRo *(Conference : 4th : 1980 : Monte Carlo)*. RoRo. — 1980. — Rickmansworth (2 Station Rd, Rickmansworth, Hertfordshire WD3 1QP) : BML Business Meetings Limited, c1981. — xiii,221p
'International Conference on Marine Transport using Roll-on/Roll-off Methods, Monte Carlo Convention Centre, 15-17 April 1980' — cover
ISBN 0-904930-14-9 : Unpriced B81-24157

387.5'442 — Freight transport. Shipping. Ships. Freight containers — *Conference proceedings*

Container technology. — Worcester Park (54 Cheam Common Rd., Worcester Park, Surrey KT4 8RJ) : CS Publications
Vol.3: Proceedings of the 3rd Container Technology Conference : organised by Cargo Systems Conferences in London on November 18, 19 & 20, 1980 / edited for Cargo Systems by Patrick Finlay. — c1981. — viii,200p : ill,maps,ports ; 30cm
ISBN 0-907499-13-9 (pbk) : Unpriced B81-16028

387.5'448 — Chemicals. Freight transport. Shipping — *Conference proceedings*

MariChem 80 *(Conference : 3rd : London)*. Conference on the marine transportation, handling and storage of bulk chemicals : London, October 21-23, 1980 / MariChem 80. — Rickmansworth (2 Station Rd., Rickmansworth, Herts. WD3 1QP) : Gastech Ltd, c1981. — xiv,229p : ill(some col.),facsims,ports ; 30cm
ISBN 0-904930-15-7 (pbk) : £40.00 B81-21661

387.5'448 — Petroleum. Freight transport. Shipping. Sailing ships, *to ca 1920*

Lubbock, Basil. Coolie ships and oil sailers / by Basil Lubbock. — Glasgow : Brown, Son & Ferguson, c1981. — x,180p[37]p of plates : ill,ports ; 25cm
Originally published: 1935. — Includes index
ISBN 0-85174-111-8 : £10.50
Primary classification 387.5'42 B81-21233

387.5'448 — Ships: Petroleum products carriers. Demand — *Forecasts* — *Conference proceedings*

Tankers : the new era : a Lloyd's shipping economist conference, the London Press Centre, December 11/12 1980. — [London] : Lloyd's of London Press, [1981]. — 230p in various pagings : ill,maps,plans ; 31cm
ISBN 0-904093-98-0 : Unpriced B81-22148

387.7 — AIR TRANSPORT

387.7 — Airlines: Air America, *to 1978*

Robbins, Christopher. The invisible air force : the story of the CIA's secret airlines / Christopher Robbins. — London : Pan in association with Macmillan, 1981, c1979. — 318p ; 18cm
Originally published: London : Macmillan, 1979. — Bibliography: p311-312. - Includes index
ISBN 0-330-26256-4 (pbk) : £1.75 B81-09724

387.7'065 — Airlines — *Technical data*

Airlines of the world / compiled by Michael J.H. Taylor and David Mondey. — London : Jane's, 1981. — 256p : ill ; 12x19cm. — (Jane's pocket book)
ISBN 0-7106-0014-3 : £4.95 B81-17819

387.7'065'41 — Great Britain. Airlines: British Airways — *Serials*

British Airways. British Airways annual report and accounts. — 1979/80. — London : British Airways Head Office, Speedbird House, Heathrow Airport, TW6 2JA : British Airways Board, 1980. — 72p
ISBN 0-900031-13-1 : £2.00 B81-03762

387.7'09 — Air transport, *to 1978*

Walters, Brian. The illustrated history of air travel / Brian Walters. — London : Marshall Cavendish, 1979. — 185p : ill(some col.),1facsims,ports ; 30cm
Ill on lining papers. — Includes index
ISBN 0-85685-708-4 : £5.95 B81-22790

387.7'09 — Civil aviation, *to 1980*

Wall, Robert, *1929-*. Airliners / Robert Wall. — London : Collins, 1980. — 256p : ill(some col.),facsims,plans,ports ; 31cm
Ill on lining papers. — Includes index
ISBN 0-00-216284-9 : £10.95 B81-04476

387.7'096 — Africa. Air transport — *Serials*

African air transport. — Vol.1, no.1 (Jan./Feb.1980)-. — Winchester (Granville House, St. Peter's St., Winchester Hants.) : Kingswood Publications, 1980-. — v. : ill,ports ; 29cm
Six issues yearly. — Description based on: Vol.1, no.6 (Nov./Dec.1980)
ISSN 0261-2313 = African air transport : £12.00 per year B81-33284

387.7'0998'9 — Antarctic. Mount Erebus. Aeroplanes. Accidents, *1979*

Hickson, Ken. Flight 901 to Erebus / Ken Hickson. — Christchurch [N.Z.] ; London : Whitcoulls, 1980. — 278p,[16]p of plates : ill (come col.),maps,ports ; 22cm
Maps on lining papers
ISBN 0-7233-0641-9 : Unpriced B81-14777

387.7'1 — Air services. Finance — *Serials*

Airfinance journal. — No.1 (Nov.1980)-. — Coggleshall (Stanfield House, 32 Church St., Coggeshall, Essex CO6 1TX) : Hawkins, 1980-. — v. : ill ; 30cm
Monthly
£40.00 per year B81-05590

387.7'1 — Great Britain. Local authority airports. Income & expenditure — *Statistics* — *Serials*

Local authority airports - financial statistics. Estimates / CIPFA Statistical Information Service. — 1981-82 -. — London : Chartered Institute of Public Finance and Accountancy, 1981-. — v. ; 30cm
Annual. — Continues in part: Local authority airports - accounts and statistics, ... (actual) and ... (estimated)
ISSN 0260-9975 = Local authority airports. Financial statistics. Estimates : £6.00 B81-38514

387.7'12 — Europe. International air passenger transport services. Fares — *Inquiry reports*

Great Britain. *Parliament. House of Commons. Industry and Trade Committee.* Fifth report from the Industry and Trade Committee, session 1980-81 : European air fares : together with the proceedings of the Committee relating to the report, the minutes of evidence and appendices. — London : H.M.S.O., [1981]. — xiiip ; 25cm. — ([HC] ; 431)
ISBN 0-10-243181-7 (pbk) : £1.90 B81-4061

Great Britain. *Parliament. House of Commons. Industry and Trade Committee.* Fifth report from the Industry and Trade Committee, session 1980-81 : European air fares. — London : H.M.S.O.
[Vol.2]: Minutes of evidence and appendices. — [1981]. — vi,118p : ill ; 25cm. — ([HC] ; 431-I)
ISBN 0-10-008561-x (pbk) : £5.85 B81-4090

387.7'12 — Great Britain. Domestic air passenger transport services. Fares — *Lists*

Civil Aviation Authority. United Kingdom domestic air tariff / [Civil Aviation Authority] — 9th ed. — London : C.A.A., 1981. — iii,87 ; 30cm. — (CAP ; 397)
Previous ed.: 1980
ISBN 0-86039-108-6 (pbk) : Unpriced B81-1822

387.7'334 — Civil aircraft. Markings — *Lists* — *Serials*

Civil aircraft markings. — 31st ed. (1981). — London : I. Allan, 1981. — 192p
ISBN 0-7110-1104-4 : £1.50 B81-3226

387.7'334023'0216 — Airlines. Aeroplanes — *Lists* — *Serials*

World airline fleets. — 1981. — Hounslow (Noble Corner, Great West Rd, Hounslow, Middlesex TW5 0PA) : Airline Publications & Sales ; London : Distributed by Jane's Publishing Co., c1981. — 592p
ISBN 0-905117-74-3 : £7.50
ISSN 0140-7287 B81-2349

387.7'3340423'0216 — Airlines. Aeroplanes — *Lists* — *Serials*

Airline fleets. — 80-. — Tonbridge : Air-Britain (Historians) Ltd., [1980]-. — v. ; 17cm
Annual. — Continues: World airline fleets handbook
ISSN 0262-1657 = Airline fleets : Unpriced B81-3851

387.7'3340423'0943 — Germany. Civil aircraft — *Lists*

Gerhardt, P-M.. 1980 registers of Germany, D-DM- / compiled by P-M. Gerhardt. — Hornchurch (9 Rook Close, Elm Park, Hornchurch Essex RM12 5QH) : Air-Britain (Historians) Ltd, 1980. — 154p,[8]p of plates : ill ; 24cm
English text, English and German introduction
ISBN 0-85130-080-4 (pbk) : Unpriced B81-0952

387.7'334'094 — Southern Europe. Civil aircraft — *Lists* — *Serials*

Southern Europe and the Middle East civil aircraft registers. — 1976-. — Tonbridge : Air-Britain (Historians), 1976-. — ill,maps ; 24cm
Irregular. — Continues in part: Southern Europe and the Mediterranean civil aircraft registers. — Description based on: 1980 issue
ISSN 0260-9622 = Southern Europe and the Middle East civil aircraft registers : Unpriced
Also classified at 387.7'334'0956 B81-1121

387.7'334'0941 — Great Britain. Civil aircraft — *Lists*

Hoddinott, R.. British civil aircraft register : out of sequence II / compiled by R. Hoddinott. — [Brentwood] : LAAS International, 1981. — [20]p : ill ; 21cm. — (A Laas international publication)
Ill on inside covers
ISBN 0-85075-052-0 (pbk) : Unpriced B81-3935

387.7'334'0941 — Great Britain. Civil aircraft — *Lists* *continuation*

Hoddinott, R.. British civil aircraft register, G-BEAA to G-BEZZ / compiled by R. Hoddinott. — [Brentwood] : LAAS International, 1981. — [20]p : ill ; 21cm. — (A Laas international publication)
Ill on inside covers
ISBN 0-85075-048-2 (pbk) : Unpriced B81-39356

Hoddinott, R.. British civil aircraft register, G-BFAA to G-BFZZ / compiled by R. Hoddinott. — [Brentwood] : LAAS International, 1981. — [20]p : ill ; 21cm. — (A Laas international publication)
Ill on inside covers
ISBN 0-85075-053-9 (pbk) : Unpriced B81-39357

Hoddinott, R.. British Isles civil register / by R.J. Hoddinott & D.S. Seex. — 2nd ed. — [Brentwood] : LAAS International ; West Drayton : The Aviation Hobby Shop [distributor], 1981. — 119p : ill ; 30cm
Previous ed.: 1980. — Ill on inside covers
ISBN 0-85075-049-0 (pbk) : Unpriced B81-20845

387.7'334'0941 — Great Britain. Civil aircraft — *Lists — Serials*

United Kingdom and Ireland civil aircraft registers. — 16th ed. (1980). — Tonbridge : Air-Britain, 1980. — 176p
ISBN 0-85130-079-0 : Unpriced B81-11226

387.7'334'0944 — French aeroplanes, *1979 — Lists*

France. — 8th ed. / [compiled by Norman Harrod]. — [Dagenham] : [LAAS International], 1979. — 144p : ill ; 21cm
Previous ed.: 1977. — Ill on covers
ISBN 0-85075-031-8 (pbk) : Unpriced B81-21362

387.7'334'0956 — Middle East. Civil aircraft — *Lists — Serials*

Southern Europe and the Middle East civil aircraft registers. — 1976-. — Tonbridge : Air-Britain (Historians), 1976-. — ill,maps ; 24cm
Irregular. — Continues in part: Southern Europe and the Mediterranean civil aircraft registers. — Description based on: 1980 issue
ISSN 0260-9622 = Southern Europe and the Middle East civil aircraft registers : Unpriced
Primary classification 387.7'334'094 B81-11216

387.7'3343'0216 — Civil turboprop aeroplanes — *Lists — Serials*

Propjet. — '81. — Wichita : AvCom International ; [London] : Macdonald & Jane's [distributor], c1981. — 173p
£3.95 B81-29109

387.7'36 — Airports

McAllister, Chris. Planes and airports / Chris McAllister. — London : Batsford, 1981. — 64p : ill(some col.),1col.map ; 20cm
Includes index
ISBN 0-7134-3911-4 (pbk) : £1.95
Primary classification 629.133'34 B81-33066

387.7'36 — Great Britain. Local authority airports *— Statistics — Serials*

Local authority airports - accounts and statistics, ... (actual) and ... (estimated) / CIPFA Statistical Information Service. — 1979/80 and 1980/81. — London : Chartered Institute of Public Finance and Accountancy, 1980. — 33p
ISSN 0143-540x : £5.00 B81-20078

387.7'36'025 — Airports — *Directories — Serials*

Airports international directory. — 1981-. — Sutton (Quadrant House, The Quadrant, Sutton, Surrey SM2 5AS) : IPC Transport Press Ltd. for Airports international, c1981-. — v. ; 23cm
ISSN 0261-6513 = Airports international directory : £25.00 B81-33288

387.7'36'02541 — Great Britain. Airports — *Directories — For air services — Serials*

Pooley's flight guide United Kingdom and Ireland / compiled with the assistance of the Civil Aviation Authority. — 1981. — [Boreham Wood] (Elstree Aerodrome, [Boreham Wood], Herts.) : Robert Pooley Ltd., 1981. — 392p
ISSN 0144-7378 : Unpriced B81-21938

387.7'36'0941 — Great Britain. Airports. Conditions of use — *Regulations — Serials*

British Airports Authority. British Airports Authority airports, conditions of use, including aircraft charges from ... — 1st May 1981. — [London] ([2 Buckingham Gate, SW1E 6JL]) : The Authority, [1981]. — [16]p
Unpriced B81-29661

387.7'36'0941 — Great Britain. Airports — *Practical information*

Wright, Alan J.. British airports / Alan J. Wright. — London : Ian Allan, 1980. — 80p : ill,maps ; 19cm
ISBN 0-7110-0967-8 (pbk) : Unpriced B81-00081

387.7'36'0941235 — Scotland. Grampian Region. Aberdeen. Airports: Aberdeen Airport. Development — *Proposals*

The **Development** of Aberdeen airport 1981-1995. — Glasgow ([St Andrews Drive, Glasgow Airport, Paisley PA3 2SW]) : Scottish Airports, 1981. — 28p,[7]p,[5]leaves of plates(3 folded) : ill,maps,plans ; 30cm
Cover title
£2.50 (spiral) B81-37626

387.7'36'09426712 — Essex. Stansted Mountfitchet. Airports: Stansted Airport. Development. Proposals — *Personal observations*

Buchanan, *Sir* **Colin,** *1907-*. No way to the airport / Colin Buchanan. — Harlow : Longman, 1981. — v,121p : ill,maps ; 22cm
Includes index
ISBN 0-582-36123-0 (pbk) : £2.95 B81-38684

387.7'4 — International air services. Political aspects

Gidwitz, Betsy. The politics of international air transport / Betsy Gidwitz. — Lexington, Mass. : Lexington Books ; [Aldershot] : Gower [distributor], 1981, c1980. — xii,259p : maps ; 24cm
Bibliography: p243-246. — Includes index
ISBN 0-669-03234-4 : £16.00 B81-29593

387.7'4042 — London. Hillingdon *(London Borough).* **Airports: Heathrow Airport. Aircraft. Departure routes: Amber 1. Traffic flow,** *1975.* **Analysis**

Coe, G. J.. A study of traffic subject to flow regulations at 'Victor Romeo' on airway Amber 1. Summer 1975 / G.J. Coe, M.G. Goldstein. — London : Civil Aviation Authority, 1976. — vii,39p(4folded),[11]p of plates : ill,1map ; 30cm. — (CAA paper ; 76018) (Dora communication ; 7601)
£5.50 (pbk) B81-07790

387.7'4'0688 — Air services. Marketing

Shaw, S.. Air transport : a marketing perspective. — London : Pitman, Oct.1981. — [288]p
ISBN 0-273-01760-8 (pbk) : £9.95 : CIP entry B81-30255

387.7'42 — Air passenger transport services

Cauter, Gaynor. International airport / Gaynor Cauter ; consultant D.P. Davis. — London : Octopus, 1980. — 127p : ill(some col.),col. plans ; 28cm
Includes index
ISBN 0-7064-1295-8 (pbk) : £3.99 B81-02697

387.7'42 — Air passenger transport services. Great Britain-North America routes — *Practical information*

Combes, Peter. How to fly the Atlantic : a traveller's guide / Peter Combes & John Tiffin. — London : Kogan Page, 1980. — 160p : ill,maps,plans,forms ; 19cm
Includes index
ISBN 0-85038-395-1 (cased) : £5.95
ISBN 0-85038-396-x (pbk) : £2.95 B81-06497

387.7'42 — Air passenger transport services. Physically handicapped passengers — *Practical information*

Cave in the air : advice for handicapped passengers / Air Transport Users Committee. — 2nd ed. — London (129 Kingsway WC2B 6NN) : The Committee, 1979. — 20p : ill ; 21x10cm
Previous ed.: 1977
Unpriced (pbk) B81-36903

387.7'42 — Europe. International air transport services. Fares — *Proposals*

The **New** EEC proposals for European air fares and transport services. — London (6 Stanbrook House, Orchard Grove, Orpington, Kent BR6 OSR) : European Business Publications, Dec.1981. — [88]p. — (European business reports ; no.2)
ISBN 0-907027-05-9 (unbound) : £26.00 : CIP entry B81-38295

387.7'42'05 — Air travel — *Practical information — Serials*

Hickmans world air travel guide. — 1981. — London : Elm Tree Books, 1981. — 624p
ISBN 0-241-10577-3 : £5.95 B81-29074

387.7'44 — Air freight transport

Peak, D. W.. Developments in the air cargo industry : an ICHCA survey / by D.W. Peak. — London : International Cargo Handling Coordination Association, c1981. — iii,97p : ill,maps ; 30cm
Bibliography: p74-75
ISBN 0-906297-17-6 (pbk) : £30.00 (£20.00 for private and library members) B81-13170

387.7'44'094 — European Community countries. Air freight transport

Allen, Roy. Air cargo in the EEC / by Roy Allen. — London : Economist Intelligence Unit, 1981. — 80p,[4]p of plates : ill(some col.) ; 30cm. — (EIU special report ; no.104)
Unpriced (pbk) B81-35673

388 — LAND TRANSPORT

388'.042'0216 — Land passenger transport services *— Lists*

Peschkes, Robert. World gazetteer of tram, trolleybus, and rapid transit systems / by Robert Peschkes. — Exeter : Quail Map. — 55p : maps ; 22cm
Unpriced (pbk)
Also classified at 388.4'6'0216 ; 388.4'13223'0216 ; 388.4'0216 B81-13677

388'.0941 — Great Britain. Land transport — *Serials*

[Newsletter *(National Council on Inland Transport)*]. Newsletter / National Council on Inland Transport. — [1/78]. — London ([5 Pembridge Cres., W11 3DT]) : The Council, 1978-. — v. ; 30cm
Two issues yearly. — Continues: Civilised transport
ISSN 0260-7735 = Newsletter - National Council on Inland Transport : Free to members of the Council only B81-09183

388.1 — ROADS

388.1 — Roads & road traffic. Environmental aspects

Watkins, L. H.. Environmental impact of roads and traffic. — London : Applied Science, Aug.1981. — [256]p
ISBN 0-85334-963-0 : £22.00 : CIP entry B81-17512

388.1'09362'7 — Northern England. Ancient Roman roads: Stanegate

Graham, Frank, *1913-*. The Stanegate : Corbridge, Vindolanda and Carvoran in the days of the Romans / by Frank Graham ; illustrated by Ronald Embleton. — Newcastle upon Tyne : F. Graham, c1981. — 32p : ill (some col.),maps,plans ; 24cm
ISBN 0-85983-181-7 (pbk) : £1.00
Also classified at 936.2'881 B81-21264

388.1'09362'937 — Clwyd. Vale of Clwyd. Ancient Roman roads
Waddelove, E.. A Roman road in the Vale of Clwyd / E. Waddelove. — [Ruthin] ([6 Ffordd Gwynach, Ruthin, Clwyd]) : [E. Waddelove], 1979. — vi,37p : ill,maps(some col.) ; 21cm
ISBN 0-9506803-0-3 (pbk) : £1.00 B81-07995

388.1'0939'2 — Turkey. Ancient Roman roads
French, David, *1933-*. Roman roads and milestones of Asia Minor = Roma cağinda Kücük Asya'daki yollar ve mil taşlari / David French. — Oxford : B.A.R.. — (BAR. International series ; 105) (Monograph / British Institute of Archaeology at Ankara ; no.3)
Fasc.1: The Pilgrim's Road = Fasikül 1: Haci Yolu. — 1981. — 129,65p,[10]p of plates(some folded) : col.maps ; 30cm
English and Turkish text. — Bibliography: p8-12
ISBN 0-86054-123-1 (pbk) : £10.00
Also classified at 625.7'94 B81-36609

388.1'0941 — Great Britain. Roads. Construction. Policies of government. Great Britain. *Parliament. House of Commons. Transport Committee.* **First report from the Transport Committee, session 1980-81** — *Critical studies*
Great Britain. Third special report from the Transport Committee, session 1980-81 : government observations on the first report of the Committee, session 1980-81 (the roads programme). — London : H.M.S.O., 1981. — v,8p ; 25cm. — ([HC] ; 307)
ISBN 0-10-230781-4 (unbound) : £1.70
B81-37016

388.1'0941 — Great Britain. Roads. Construction. Policies of government — *Inquiry reports*
Great Britain. *Parliament. House of Commons. Transport Committee.* First report from the Transport Committee, session 1980-81 : the roads programme : together with the proceedings of the Committee, minutes of evidence and appendices. — London : H.M.S.O.
Vol.1: Report, minutes of proceedings and appendices. — [1980]. — xxxiii,62p ; 25cm. — ([HC] ; 27-I)
ISBN 0-10-270281-0 (pbk) : £4.60 B81-20355

Great Britain. *Parliament. House of Commons. Transport Committee.* First report from the Transport Committee, session 1980-81 : the roads programme : together with the proceedings of the Committee, minutes of evidence and appendices. — London : H.M.S.O.
Vol.2: Minutes of evidence. — [1980]. — v,153p ; 25cm. — ([HC] ; 27-II)
ISBN 0-10-270381-7 (pbk) : £6.30 B81-20356

388.1'0941 — Great Britain. Roads — *Statistics — Serials*
Basic road statistics / British Road Federation. — 1980. — London : British Road Federation, [1980?]. — 32p
ISSN 0309-3638 : £3.00 B81-04539

388.1'09412'1 — Scotland. Grampian Region. Roads. Requirements
Road needs in Grampian / British Road Federation, Transport Action Scotland. — London : The Federation, [1981]. — 11p : 3maps(some col.) ; 30cm
Unpriced (unbound) B81-23340

388.1'0942 — England. Roads, *to 1979*
Addison, *Sir* **William**. The old roads of England / Sir William Addison. — London : Batsford, 1980. — 167p : maps ; 26cm
Bibliography: p155-157. — Includes index
ISBN 0-7134-1714-5 : £8.95 B81-02302

388.1'09427'393 — Greater Manchester *(Metropolitan County).* **Saddlesworth region. Roads & trackways,** *to 1980*
Barnes, Bernard. Passage through time : Saddleworth roads & trackways : a history / Bernard Barnes. — [Greenfield] ([7 Elstead Rd., Greenfield, Oldham]) : Saddleworth Historical Society, 1981. — iv,106p : ill,maps ; 25cm. — (S.H.S. local history series ; 2)
Bibliography: p80-83
ISBN 0-904982-03-3 (pbk) : Unpriced
B81-15686

388.1'09428'49 — North Yorkshire. Hambleton Hills. Trackways: Hambleton Road, *to 1980*
Ellison, D.. The Hambleton Drove Road / [text ... prepared by D. Ellison]. — Helmsley (The Old Vicarage, Helmsley, N. Yorkshire YO6 5BP) : North York Moors National Park Information Service, [1980?]. — 12p : ill,1col.map ; 22cm
Cover title. — Map on inside cover. — Bibliography: p12
Unpriced (pbk) B81-29397

388.1'14 — England. Road bridges: Severn Bridge. Tolls — *Accounts — Serials*
Severn Bridge Tolls Act 1965 account. — 1979-80. — London : H.M.S.O., 1981. — 10p
ISBN 0-10-224481-2 : £1.40 B81-29425

388.1'14 — Hereford and Worcester. Vale of Evesham. Turnpike roads
Cox, Benjamin G.. The Vale of Evesham turnpikes, tollgates, and milestones / by Benjamin G. Cox. — [Evesham] ([Almonry Museum, Evesham, Worcs. WR11 4BD]) : Vale of Evesham Historical Society, c1980. — [35]p : ill,1map,facsims ; 21cm
Bibliography: p[35]
ISBN 0-907353-00-2 (pbk) : Unpriced
B81-10739

388.1'14 — Scotland. Strathclyde Region. Road bridges: Erskine Bridge. Tolls — *Accounts — Serials*
Erskine Bridge Tolls Act, 1968, account. — 1979-80. — London : H.M.S.O., 1981. — 10p
ISBN 0-10-223681-x : £1.80 B81-25485

388.1'2 — Essex. Braintree. Inner relief roads — *Proposals*
Essex. *County Council.* Braintree inner relief road & Bradford Street bypass : action area plan / Essex County Council. — [Chelmsford] ([Planning Department, County Hall, Chelmsford CM1 1LF]) : [The Council], [1981]. — 101p,[16]folded leaves of plates : maps ; 30cm
Two maps (2folded sheets) in pocket. — Includes index
£2.50 (pbk) B81-26637

388.1'2 — Oxfordshire. Oxford. Proposed inner relief roads. Routes. Disputes between Britih government & Oxford. *City Council, 1923-1974*
Newman, Roland. The road and Christ Church Meadow : the Oxford inner relief road controversy 1923-74 : a study of the relationship between central and local government / Roland Newman. — Oxford (Headington, Oxford) : Oxford Polytechnic, 1980. — iii,71p ; 21cm
Unpriced (pbk) B81-15205

388.1'2 — Wales. Trunk roads. Improvement — *Proposals*
Roads in Wales = Ffyrdd yng Nghymru. — [Cardiff] ([Cathays Park, Cardiff CF1 3NQ]) : Welsh Office, 1980. — 35p : maps ; 30cm
English and Welsh text
Unpriced (pbk) B81-12155

388.1'22'0941 — Great Britain. Motorways, *1960-1980 — Conference proceedings*
20 years of British motorways : proceedings of the conference held in London 27-28 February, 1980. — London : Institution of Civil Engineers, 1980. — 133p : ill,maps ; 31cm
ISBN 0-7277-0094-4 : £20.00 B81-10115

388.3 — ROAD TRANSPORT

388.3'023'41 — Great Britain. Road transport industries — *Career guides*
Leeming, David J.. Working with trucks and buses / David J. Leeming. — London : Batsford Academic and Educational, 1981. — 112p,[8]p of plates : ill,1form ; 23cm. — (Careers series)
ISBN 0-7134-3468-6 : £5.75 B81-19644

388.3'068 — Road transport services. Management — *Manuals*
Lowe, David, *1936-*. A study manual of professional competence in road transport management / David Lowe. — 2nd ed. — London : Kogan Page, 1980. — 379p : ill,forms ; 23cm
Previous ed.: 1978. — Includes index
ISBN 0-85038-274-2 : £10.50 B81-00838

388.3'2 — Great Britain. Public road transport services — *Serials*
Annual reports of the Traffic Commissioners to the Minister of Transport ... covering the period 1 April ... to 21 March .... — 1979-1980. — London (2 Marsham St., London SW1 P3EB) : Department of Transport, 1980. — v,118p
£2.60 B81-1027

388.3'22'0254 — Western Europe. Bus services & coach services — *Directories — Serials*
Road passenger transport directory for the British Isles and Western Europe. — 1980/81. — London : I. Allan, c1980. — 280p
Cover title: The Little red book. — Spine title: Passenger transport industry
ISBN 0-7110-1040-4 : £8.95 B81-3101

Road passenger transport directory for the British Isles and western Europe. — 1981/82. — London : Ian Allan, c1980. — 280p
Cover title: The little red book. — Spine title: Passenger transport industry
ISBN 0-7110-1132-x : £9.95 B81-3406

388.3'22'0941 — Great Britain. Bus services
Faulks, R. W.. Urban and rural transport / R.W. Faulks. — London : Ian Allan, 1981. — 188p ill,maps,facsims ; 25cm
Includes index
ISBN 0-7110-1056-0 : £12.95 B81-2486

388.3'22'0942 — England. Bus services, *to 1969*
Crawley, R. J.. The years between / by R.J. Crawley, D.R. MacGregor, F.D. Simpson. — Hedingham ([c/o Hedingham and District Omnibuses Ltd., Wethersfield Rd., Sible Hedingham, Halstead CO9 3LB]) : D.R. MacGregor
Pt.1: National Omnibus and Transport Company. — c1979. — 194p,[4]p of plates : ill (some col.),maps,col.facsims,ports ; 22x30cm
Maps on lining paper. — Bibliography: p194
ISBN 0-9507390-0-6 : £9.00 B81-3148

388.3'22'09421 — North Wales & Cheshire. Bus services: Crosville Motor Services, *to 1980*
Anderson, R. C.. A history of Crosville Motor Services. — Newton Abbot : David & Charles, Nov.1981. — [160]p
ISBN 0-7153-8088-5 : £6.95 : CIP entry
B81-3037

388.3'22'09424 — England. Midlands. Bus services: Birmingham & Midland Motor Omnibus Co., *1940-1970*
Gray, Paul. Midland red : a history of the Company and its vehicles from 1940 to 1970 / by Paul Gray, Malcolm Keeley, John Seale ; on behalf of the Birmingham & Midland Motc Omnibus Trust and the 1685 Group. — Glossop : Transport Publishing Company, [1979]. — 221p : ill(some col.),2plans,1port ; 21x30cm
ISBN 0-903839-27-x : £10.00 B81-1260

388.3'22'09425 — England. East Midlands. Bus services & coach services: United Counties Omnibus Company Limited — *History*
Warwick, Roger M.. An illustrated history of United Counties Omnibus Company Limited / by Roger M. Warwick. — Northampton (101 Broadway East, Northampton NN32 2PP) : R.M. Warwick, c1981
Bibliography: p2
Pt 4: 1938 to 1946. — c1981. — 64p : ill ; 22cm
ISBN 0-9505980-3-8 (pbk) : Unpriced
B81-1897

388.3'22'094276 — Lancashire. Independent bus services, *to 1980*
Dunabin, J. E.. Joint bus services between Leyland and Preston / by J.E. Dunabin. — Bromley Common : Omnibus Society, c1980. — 17p,[4]p of plates : ill,maps ; 26cm
ISBN 0-901307-39-4 (pbk) : £1.10 B81-2186

388.3′228′094231 — Wiltshire. Stagecoaching, *to 1848*
Chandler, John H.. Stagecoach operation through Wiltshire / John H. Chandler. — Salisbury (22 Minster St., Salisbury, Wilts. SP1 1TQ) : South Wilts Industrial Archaeology Society, 1980. — [8]p : ill,maps ; 30cm. — (Historical monograph / South Wiltshire Industrial Archaeology Society ; 8)
Bibliography: p8
ISBN 0-906195-07-1 (unbound) : £0.40
B81-15759

388.3′24′068 — Great Britain. Road freight transport services. Management
Fawcett, P.. The road to transport management / P. Fawcett. — Manchester (Room 20, City Buildings, 69 Corporation St., Manchester M4 2DE) : A.M. Witton (Fleetbooks)
1981 supplement. — c1981. — 44p : ill,forms ; 28cm
ISBN 0-86047-202-7 (pbk) : Unpriced
B81-34251

388.3′24′0941 — Great Britain. Road freight transport services, *1919-1939*
Dunbar, Charles S.. The rise of road transport 1919-1939 / Charles Dunbar. — London : Ian Allan, 1981. — 144p : ill,1map,facsims ; 25cm
Includes index
ISBN 0-7110-1088-9 : £7.95 B81-31989

388.3′24′0941 — Great Britain. Road freight transport services — *Serials*
Haulage and distribution. — Vol.1, no.1 (1980)-. — Dublin ; London (153, Brondesbury Park, NW2 5JL) : Jemma Publications, 1980-. — v. : ill ; 30cm
Monthly. — Continues: Haulage
£7.00 per year B81-13099

388.3′24′0973 — United States. Road freight transport services. Competition. Economic aspects
LaMond, Annette M.. Competition in the general-freight motor-carrier industry / Annette M. LaMond. — Lexington, Mass. : Lexington Books ; [Farnborough, Hants.] : Gower [distributor], 1981, c1980. — xi,123p ; 24cm
Bibliography: p117-118. - Includes index
ISBN 0-669-03308-1 : £12.50 B81-24089

388.3′24′0973 — United States. Road freight transport services. Effects of government regulation. Econometric models
Friedlaender, Ann F.. Freight transport regulation : equity, efficiency, and competition in the rail and trucking industries / Ann F. Friedlaender, Richard H. Spady. — Cambridge, Mass. ; London : MIT Press, c1981. — xv,366p : ill ; 24cm. — (MIT Press series on the regulation of economic activity)
Bibliography: p353-359. — Includes index
ISBN 0-262-06072-8 : £18.60
Primary classification 385′.24′0973 B81-29188

388.3′242 — Great Britain. International road freight transport — *Manuals*
Johnson, J. (Johnny). A transport manager′s guide to international freighting / Johnny Johnson. — London : Kogan Page, 1980. — 118p : maps ; 23cm
ISBN 0-85038-176-2 (cased) : £6.95
ISBN 0-85038-312-9 (pbk) : Unpriced
B81-22867

388.3′4′09493 — Belgium. Urban regions. Public transport services. Vehicles
Bartlett, N. R.. Belgium : the municipal operators / N.R. Bartlett. — Chelmsford (Danbury, Chelmsford, Essex CM3 4PN) : Westbury Marketing, c1981. — 60p : ill,maps ; 15cm
Brussels: a guide to public transport, addenda and corrigenda (ivp) as insert
ISBN 0-907460-01-1 (pbk) : £1.40
ISBN 0-907460-00-3 (Brussels) : Unpriced
B81-26053

388.3′422 — Cars. Use. Implications of shortages of petroleum
Brown, Lester R.. Running on empty : the future of the automobile in an oil-short world / Lester R. Brown, Christopher Flavin, Colin Norman. — New York ; London : W.W. Norton, c1979. — ix,116p : ill ; 22cm. — (A World watch Institute book)
Includes index
ISBN 0-393-01334-0 : £4.50 B81-07897

388.3′422 — Great Britain. Cars. Ownership. Forecasting. Applications of mathematical models
Button, K. J.. Car ownership modelling and forecasting. — Aldershot : Gower, Nov.1981. — [172]p
ISBN 0-566-00320-1 : £12.50 : CIP entry
B81-30968

388.3′422 — Great Britain. Cars. Ownership. Socioeconomic aspects
Bates, John. The factors affecting household car ownership / John Bates in collaboration with Mick Roberts, Steve Lowe and Paul Richards. — Farnborough, Hants. : Gower, c1981. — xvi,168p : ill,2maps ; 23cm
ISBN 0-566-00475-5 : Unpriced : CIP rev.
B81-07446

388.3′4233′09411 — Eastern Scotland. Buses — *Lists*
Buses of Eastern Scotland. — 2nd ed. rev. and enlarged, edited by David G. Wilson. — Manchester : Witton, 1981. — 57p : ill ; 15cm. — (Fleetbook ; no.14)
Previous ed.: / edited by Alan Millar. 1977
ISBN 0-86047-142-x (pbk) : £0.80 B81-19869

388.3′4233′09421 — London. Bus services: London Transport. Buses, *1956-1980* — *Lists*
The Vehicles of London Transport and its predecessors : modern classes from the RM class to date. — London (52 Old Park Ridings, N21 2ES) : published jointly by the P.S.V. Circle and the Omnibus Society, [1981]. — 92p,[8]p of plates : ill ; 30cm. — (Fleet history ; LT9)
Unpriced (pbk) B81-27288

388.3′4233′09422 — England. Home Counties. Buses — *Lists*
Buses of outer London / edited ... by A.M. Witton. — 2nd ed.. — Manchester (Room 20, City Buildings, 69 Corporation St., Manchester M4 2DE) : A. Witton, 1981. — 49p : ill ; 15cm
Previous ed.: 1979
ISBN 0-86047-162-4 (pbk) : £0.80 B81-32546

388.3′4233′094225 — East & West Sussex. Bus services: Southdown Motor Services. Buses — *Lists* — *Serials*
Southdown fleet list. — 10th ed. (1981). — Crowborough (c/o 43 Stone Cross Rd, Crowborough, East Sussex TN6 3DB) : Southdown Enthusiasts′ Club, 1981. — 40p
Cover title: A Complete fleet list of Southdown
£0.60 B81-27134

388.3′4233′094225 — East & West Sussex. Bus services: Southdown Motor Services. Buses. Liveries, *1969-1980*
Changing colours. — [Brighton] ([4 Mile Oak Rd., Southwick, Brighton BN4 4QE]) : Southdown Enthusiasts Club, c1981. — 83p,[6]p of plates : ill ; 30cm
£2.00 (pbk) B81-33678

388.3′4233′09425 — England. East Midlands. Buses — *Lists*
Buses of the East Midlands / edited and published by A.M. Witton. — 3rd ed. — Manchester : Witton, 1981. — 65p : ill ; 15cm. — (Fleetbook ; no.7)
Previous ed.: 1978. — Text on inside cover
ISBN 0-86047-073-3 (pbk) : £0.80 B81-40090

388.3′4233′09428 — North-east England. Buses — *Lists*
Buses of North-East England. — 3rd ed. rev. and enlarged / edited by A.M. Witton. — Manchester : [Witton], 1981. — 65p : ill ; 15cm. — (Fleetbook ; no.8)
Previous ed.: 1978
ISBN 0-86047-083-0 : £0.80 B81-19868

388.3′472′0941 — Great Britain. Bicycles. Use — *Proposals*
Mathew, Don. The bike is back : a bicycles policy for Britain / Don Mathew. — London (9 Poland St., W1V 3DG) : Friends of the Earth, 1980. — 24p ; 21cm
Cover title. — Bibliography on inside cover
ISBN 0-905966-23-6 (pbk) : £0.60 B81-04026

388.4 — LOCAL AND URBAN TRANSPORT

388.4 — Urban regions. Freight transport
Button, K. J.. The economics of urban freight transport / K.J. Button and A.D. Pearman. — London : Macmillan, 1981. — x,218p : ill ; 22cm
Bibliography: p197-210. — Includes index
ISBN 0-333-24808-2 : £20.00 : CIP rev.
B80-01604

388.4 — Urban regions. Transport
Klaassen, Leo H.. Transport and reurbanisation. — Farnborough : Gower, July 1981. — [226]p
ISBN 0-566-00374-0 : £15.00 : CIP entry
B81-14881

388.4′0216 — Rapid transit services — *Lists*
Peschkes, Robert. World gazetteer of tram, trolleybus, and rapid transit systems / by Robert Peschkes. — Exeter : Quail Map. — 55p : maps ; 22cm
Unpriced (pbk)
Primary classification 388′.042′0216 B81-13677

388.4′0724 — Northern England. Urban regions. Transport. Mathematical models
Batey, Peter W. J.. Transport modelling as an aid in structure planning : a new lease of life for the SELNEC model? / by Peter W.J. Batey and John V. Nickson. — Liverpool (P.O. Box 147, Liverpool L69 3BX) : Department of Civic Design, University of Liverpool, 1976. — 25 leaves,[4]leaves of plates : 1ill,3maps ; 30cm. — (Working paper / University of Liverpool Department of Civic Design ; 3)
Bibliography: leaves 24-25
£1.00 (pbk) B81-06198

388.4′09421 — London. Transport — *Proposals*
Greater London Council. Transport policies and programme, 1981-84. — [London] : Greater London Council, [1980]. — 78p : ill,maps ; 30cm
ISBN 0-7168-1159-6 (pbk) : £2.20 B81-34884

388.4′09421 — London. Transport — *Statistics*
Transport facts and figures / [prepared by the Greater London Council]. — [2nd ed.]. — [London] : Greater London Council, 1980. — [32]p : col.ill,maps(some col.) ; 15x21cm
Previous ed.: 1973. — Text and map on inside covers
ISBN 0-7168-1168-5 (pbk) : Unpriced
B81-34885

388.4′09424′91 — West Midlands *(Metropolitan County)*. **Tettenhall. Passenger transport services,** *to 1980*
Williams, Ned, *1944-*. By road and rail to Tettenhall / by Ned Williams. — Wolverhampton (23 Westland Rd., Wolverhampton WV3 9NZ) : Uralia Press, 1980. — [75]p : ill,maps,facsims,ports ; 21cm
Ill, maps on inside covers
ISBN 0-9500533-5-x (pbk) : £1.95 B81-07406

388.4′0944′36 — France. Paris. Public transport services — *Visitors′ guides*
Bartlett, N. R.. Paris transport : the pocket guide / N.R. Barlett. — Chelmsford : Westbury Marketing, c1981. — 64p : ill ; 15cm
Includes index
ISBN 0-907460-02-x (pbk) : £1.60 B81-29936

388.4′09744′61 — United States. Urban regions. Transport, *to 1974* — *Study regions: Massachusetts. Boston*
Schaeffer, K. H.. Access for all : transportation and urban growth / K.H. Schaeffer and Elliott Sclar. — New York ; Guildford : Columbia University Press, 1980. — xi,182p : ill,maps ; 21cm
Originally published: Harmondsworth : Penguin, 1975. — Includes index
ISBN 0-231-05164-6 (cased)
ISBN 0-231-05165-4 (pbk) : £2.75 B81-09519

388.4′0994 — Australia. Urban regions. Journeys to work
Manning, Ian. The journey to work / Ian Manning. — Sydney ; London : Allen & Unwin, 1978. — 194p : ill,maps ; 24cm
Bibliography: p189-191. - Includes index
ISBN 0-86861-192-1 (cased) : £10.50
ISBN 0-86861-200-6 (pbk) : £4.95 B81-08605

388.4'1314'0942337 — Dorset. Poole. Road traffic — *Statistics*
Report of survey roads, traffic & parking : Poole town centre district plan. — [Dorchester] : Dorset County Council, 1981. — 13p,[22]leaves of plates : ill,maps,plans ; 30cm
Cover title
ISBN 0-85216-282-0 (pbk) : £0.40 B81-40631

388.4'1321 — Nottinghamshire. Nottingham. Taxi services. Organisations: Nottingham Licensed Taxi Owners & Drivers Association — *Serials*
Nottingham Licensed Taxi Owners & Drivers Association. Newsletter / Nottingham Licensed Taxi Owners & Drivers Association. — No.1-. — Nottingham (63a Derby Rd., Nottingham) : The Association, [1980]-. — v. ; 33cm
ISSN 0260-8294 = Newsletter — Nottingham Licensed Taxi Owners & Drivers Association : Unpriced B81-09685

388.4'1322'0973 — United States. Urban regions. Bus services. Public bodies — *Case studies*
Hamilton, Neil W.. Governance of public enterprise : a case study of urban mass transit / Neil W. Hamilton, Peter R. Hamilton. — Lexington, Mass. : Lexington Books ; [Aldershot] : Gower [distributor], 1981. — xii,152p
Includes index
ISBN 0-669-03867-9 (24cm) : £12.50 B81-39701

388.4'13223'0216 — Trolleybus services — *Lists*
Peschkes, Robert. World gazetteer of tram, trolleybus, and rapid transit systems / by Robert Peschkes. — Exeter : Quail Map. — 55p : maps ; 22cm
Unpriced (pbk)
Primary classification 388'.042'0216 B81-13677

388.4'1324 — Great Britain. Shops. Goods. Deliveries. Restrictions — *Conference proceedings*
Restricting retail deliveries : the lessons to be learnt : report of an URPI workshop. — Reading (26 Queen Victoria St., Reading RG1 1TG) : Unit for Retail Planning Information, 1980. — 62p : maps ; 30cm. — (URPI : U19)
Bibliography: p61-62
Unpriced (pbk) B81-06485

388.4'2'09421 — London. Railway services — *Illustrations*
Glover, John, *1946-*. London's railways today / John Glover. — Newton Abbot : David & Charles, c1981. — 86p : ill,maps ; 25cm
ISBN 0-7153-8070-2 : £5.95 B81-25404

388.4'28 — London. Southwark *(London Borough)*. **Disused underground railway tunnels**, *to 1975*
Bancroft, Peter, *1953-*. The railway to King William Street and Southwark deep tunnel air-raid shelter / by Peter Bancroft. — Woking (16 Gosden Rd., West End, Woking, Surrey GU24 9LH) : P. Bancroft, 1981. — 29p : ill,maps ; 22cm
Cover title. — Bibliography: p29
ISBN 0-9507416-0-4 (pbk) : £0.95 B81-17892

388.4'6 — North Yorkshire. York. Horse-drawn tram services, *to 1909*
Murray, Hugh. The horse tramways of York 1880-1909 : the birth, life and death of a transport system / by Hugh Murray. — Broxbourne : Light Rail Transit Association, 1980. — 112p,[2]folded leaves of plates : ill,maps ; 23cm
Bibliography: p111
ISBN 0-900433-81-7 : £7.00 B81-26268

388.4'6'0216 — Tram services — *Lists*
Peschkes, Robert. World gazetteer of tram, trolleybus, and rapid transit systems / by Robert Peschkes. — Exeter : Quail Map. — 55p : maps ; 22cm
Unpriced (pbk)
Primary classification 388'.042'0216 B81-13677

388.4'6'0942751 — Merseyside *(Metropolitan County)*. **Wirral** *(District)*. **Tram services: Storeton Tramway**, *to 1980*
Jermy, Roger C.. The Storeton tramway / by Roger C. Jermy. — Weston-super-Mare : AvonAngliA, c1981. — 63p : ill,maps ; 22cm
ISBN 0-905466-43-8 (pbk) : £2.10
ISBN 0-907768-00-8 (Countyvise) B81-40565

388.4'6'0942765 — Lancashire. Blackpool. Tram services, *to 1977*
Palmer, Steve. Blackpool by tram / [Steve Palmer & Brian Turner]. — [New ed.]. — [Glossop] : [Palmer and Turner in association with Transport Publishing], [c1978]. — 111p : ill,maps,1plan,1port ; 29cm
Previous ed.: Blackpool : The authors, 1968. — Maps on lining paper
ISBN 0-903839-32-6 (cased) : £5.95
ISBN 0-903839-35-0 (pbk) : Unpriced B81-03133

388.4'6'0943 — West Germany. Tram services
Pagel, M.. Tramways of Western Germany : including rapid transit. — 3rd ed. / M. Pagel, M.R. Taplin. — Hassocks : Light Rail Transit Association, 1980. — 86p : maps ; 21cm
Previous ed.: / M.R. Taplin. Sidcup : Light Railway Transport League, 1974. — Text on inside covers. — Includes index
ISBN 0-900433-79-5 (pbk) : £1.75 B81-13330

388.4'6'094923 — Netherlands. Amsterdam. Tram services, *to 1980*
Deacon, Ray. Trams in Amsterdam / Ray Deacon. — Sheffield : Sheaf, 1980. — 107p : ill,maps ; 25cm
ISBN 0-9505458-2-1 (pbk) : £5.95 B81-33083

388.4'72'09421 — London. Railways. Stations
Lindsey, C. F.. A directory of London railway stations / compiled by C.F. Lindsey. — London (15 Bournemouth Rd., SW19 3AR) : C.F. Lindsey
Pt.1: Boroughs of Merton and Sutton. — 1981. — 20p : ill ; 21cm
Cover title. — Bibliography: p20
£0.50 (pbk) B81-25387

388.4'74 — Urban regions. Multi-storey car parks — *Conference proceedings*
Multi-storey car parks in shopping centres and office blocks : report of the British Parking Association seminar held in London, October 28, 1980 in conjunction with the Royal Institute of British Architects and of the Open Meeting held on March 27, 1980. — St. Albans (17 The Croft, Chiswell Green, St. Albans, Herts, AL2 3AR) : The Association, [1980]. — 58p : ill,plans ; 30cm
£10.00 (6.00 to members) (pbk) B81-19446

388.4'74'0941 — Great Britain. Car parking facilities. Provision. Environmental factors
Brierley, John. Car parking and the environment / by John Brierley. — 2nd ed. — London : Institution of Municipal Engineers, 1979. — 12p : ill ; 21cm. — (Protection of the environment ; monograph no.2)
Previous ed.: 1971. — Bibliography: p12
£0.75 (pbk) B81-07158

389 — MEASUREMENT AND STANDARDISATION

389'.15'094234 — Channel Islands. Weights & measures — *Early works* — *Facsimiles*
Ansted, D. T.. The Channel Islands : money, weights, and measures / D.T. Ansted. — St. Peter Port : Toucan Press, 1981. — [8]p ; 21cm
Facsim of: edition published 1862
ISBN 0-85694-238-3 (pbk) : Unpriced
Primary classification 332.4'94234 B81-17680

390 — CUSTOMS AND FOLKLORE

390'.094 — European customs, *to 1980*
Pegg, Bob. Rites and riots : folk customs of Britain and Europe / Bob Pegg. — Poole : Blandford Press, 1981. — 144p,[16]p of plates : ill(some col.) ; 26cm
Bibliography: p141. — Includes index
ISBN 0-7137-0997-9 : £8.95 : CIP rev. B81-22531

390'.0941 — British customs — *For children*
Holt, Elizabeth. Customs and ceremonies / Elizabeth Holt and Molly Perham ; illustrated by Ross. — London : Evans, 1980. — 98p : ill ; 19cm. — (Activities nationwide)
Includes index
ISBN 0-237-45507-2 : £3.95 B81-00082

390'.22'0937 — Ancient Rome. Emperors. Ceremonies, *300-600* — *Sources of data: Panegyrics in Latin*
MacCormack, Sabine. Art and ceremony in late antiquity / Sabine G. MacCormack. — Berkeley ; London : University of California Press, c1981. — xvi,417p,[31]p of plates : ill ; 25cm. — (The Transformation of the classical heritage)
Bibliography: p379-399. — Includes index
ISBN 0-520-03779-0 : £27.75 B81-39831

391 — COSTUME AND PERSONAL APPEARANCE

391 — Bedfordshire. Luton. Museums: Luton Museum and Art Gallery. Stock: English smocks — *Catalogues*
Luton Museum and Art Gallery. Smocks in Luton Museum / [compiled] by Marian Nichols. — Luton (Wardown Park Luton [LU2 7HA]) : Borough of Luton Museum and Art Gallery, 1980. — [28]p : ill ; 21cm
Ill on inside cover. — Bibliography: p8
ISBN 0-907106-00-5 (pbk) : Unpriced B81-26251

391'.0089924 — Jewish costume, *to ca 1940*
Rubens, Alfred. A history of Jewish costume / Alfred Rubens ; foreword by James Laver. — Rev. and enl. ed. — London : Owen, c1973 (1981 [printing]). — 221p : ill(some col.),facsims,ports(some col.) ; 33cm
Previous ed.: London : Vallentine, Mitchell, 1967. — Ill on lining papers. — Bibliography: p208-211. — Includes index
ISBN 0-7206-0588-1 : £27.50 B81-21370

391'.009 — Western costume, *to 1979*
Black, J. Anderson. A history of fashion / J. Anderson Black, Madge Garland. — 2nd ed. / updated and rev. by Frances Kennett. — London : Orbis, 1980. — 304p : ill(some col.),ports(some col.) ; 30cm
Previous ed.: 1975. — Ill on lining papers. — Bibliography: p294. - Includes index
ISBN 0-85613-205-5 : £17.50 B81-05198

391'.009 — Western world. Costume, *1000-1980*
Yarwood, Doreen. Costume of the western world : pictorial guide and glossary / Doreen Yarwood ; illustrated by the author. — Guildford : Lutterworth, 1980. — 192p : ill (some col.) ; 22cm
Bibliography: p192
ISBN 0-7188-2405-9 (cased) : £7.95
ISBN 0-7188-2478-4 (pbk) : £4.95 B81-05603

391'.0094 — European costume, *1340-1365*
Newton, Stella Mary. Fashion in the age of the Black Prince : a study of the years 1340-1365 / Stella Mary Newton. — Woodbridge : Boydell, c1980. — vi,151p,[1] leaf of plates : ill(some col.) ; 29cm
Bibliography: p140-145. — Includes index
ISBN 0-85115-125-6 : £20.00 : CIP rev. B80-05857

391'.00941 — British costume, *1100-1947*
Cunnington, Phillis. Costume in pictures / Phillis Cunnington. — Rev. ed. — London (65 Belsize La., NW3 5AU) : Herbert Press, 1981. — 144p : ill,ports ; 24cm
Previous ed.: New York : Dutton ; London : Studio Vista, 1964. — Bibliography: p139. — Includes index
ISBN 0-906969-05-0 : £6.95 B81-26910

391'.00941 — British costume, *1500-1900*
Cumming, Valerie. Exploring costume history 1500-1900 / Valerie Cumming. — London : Batsford Academic and Educational, 1981. — 96p,[4]p of plates : ill(some col.),ports(some col.) ; 26cm
Bibliography: p93-94. — Includes index
ISBN 0-7134-1829-x : £5.95 B81-08612

391'.00942 — English costume, *1485-1603*. **Social aspects** — *For schools*
Freeman, Edith. Tudor life and dress / Edith Freeman. — Walton-on-Thames : Nelson, 1981. — 48p : ill(some col.),2maps(some col.) 2facsims,ports(some col.). — (Keys to the past)
Text, ports on inside covers
ISBN 0-17-435021-x (pbk) : £1.50 B81-37503

391'.00942 — English costume, *ca 1660-1979*
Byrde, Penelope. Museum of Costume / [written and prepared by Penelope Byrde, Myra Mines]. — [Bath] ([Guildhall, Bath, BA1 5AW]) : Bath City Council, c1980. — 41p : col.ill,1plan ; 30cm
Cover title. — Text, plan on inside cover. — Bibliography: p41
ISBN 0-901303-10-0 (pbk) : Unpriced B81-17701

391'.00942 — English fashion, *ca 1550-1980.* **Revivals**
Baines, Barbara Burman. Fashion revivals : from the Elizabethan Age to the present day / Barbara Burman Baines. — London : Batsford, 1981. — 191p,4p of plates : ill(some col.),2facsims,ports(some col.) ; 26cm
Bibliography: p187-188. — Includes index
ISBN 0-7134-1929-6 : £15.00 B81-37842

391'.00945 — Italian costume, *1400-1500*
Herald, Jacqueline. Renaissance dress in Italy 1400-1500. — London : Bell & Hyman, Oct.1981. — [256]p. — (History of dress ; 2)
ISBN 0-7135-1294-6 : £30.00 : CIP entry B81-24653

391'.01 — England. Upper classes. Costume, *1897-1914 — Illustrations*
Stevenson, Pauline. Edwardian fashion / Pauline Stevenson. — London : Ian Allan, 1980. — 127p,[8]p of plates : ill(some col.),facsims,ports ; 30cm
ISBN 0-7110-1013-7 : £7.95 B81-04917

391'.2'0942 — English women's costume, *1730-1930*
Bradfield, Nancy. Costume in detail : women's dress 1730-1930 / written and illustrated by Nancy Bradfield. — New ed. — London : Harrap, 1981. — ix,391 : ill ; 26cm
Previous ed.: 1968. — Ill on lining papers. — Bibliography: p384-385
ISBN 0-245-53608-6 : £13.75 B81-24923

391'.42 — Underwear, *to 1980*
Willett, C.. The history of underclothes. — New rev. ed. — London : Faber, Nov.1981. — [208]p
Previous ed.: London : Michael Joseph, 1951
ISBN 0-571-11747-3 : £11.50 : CIP entry B81-31089

391'.42 — Women's underwear, *1907-1980*
Caldwell, Doreen. And all was revealed : ladies' underwear 1907-1980 / Doreen Caldwell. — London : Arthur Barker, c1981. — 144p : col.ill ; 15x17cm
ISBN 0-213-16797-2 : £4.95 B81-40453

391'.44'09034 — Fashion. Accessories, *1800-1914*
Johnson, Eleanor, *1921-*. Fashion accessories / Eleanor Johnson. — Aylesbury : Shire, 1980. — 32p : ill ; 21cm. — (Shire album ; 58)
Bibliography: p32
ISBN 0-85263-530-3 (pbk) : £0.95 B81-07649

391'.5 — Men. Beards — *Humour*
Stewart, Keith. To my bearded friend : (all you should know about beards) / by Keith Stewart. — Taunton ([K.S. Tinning & Son Ltd.) 2 The Crescent, Taunton, Somerset) : Bolton Fine Arts, c1980. — [48]p : ill ; 21cm
Cover title
ISBN 0-9507277-0-9 (pbk) : Unpriced B81-06439

391'.8 — English wedding dresses, *1735-1970*
Victoria and Albert Museum. Wedding dress 1740-1970 / Madeleine Ginsburg. — London : H.M.S.O., 1981. — 53p : ill,ports ; 21x22cm
At head of title: Victoria and Albert Museum
ISBN 0-11-290328-2 : £3.95 B81-37833

391'.8 — Great Britain. Ceremonial uniforms, *1660-1979*
Mansfield, Alan. Ceremonial costume : court, civil and civic costume from 1660 to the present day / Alan Mansfield. — London : Black, 1980. — xvi,304p : ill,ports ; 25cm
Bibliography: p285-289. - Includes index
ISBN 0-7136-2083-8 : £13.95 : CIP rev. B80-13774

392 — CUSTOMS OF LIFE CYCLE AND DOMESTIC LIFE

392'.1 — Africa. Women. Reproductive system. Mutilation
Female circumcision, excision and infibulation : the facts and proposals for change / edited by Scilla McLean ; with contributions from Marie Assaad ... [et al.]. — London (36 Craven St., Wc2N 5NG) : Minority Rights Group, 1980. — 20p : ill ; 30cm. — (Report / Minority Rights Group, ISSN 0305-6252 ; no.47)
£1.20 (pbk) B81-05033

Sanderson, Lilian Passmore. Against the mutilation of women : the struggle to end unnecessary suffering / by Lilian Passmore Sanderson. — London : Ithaca, 1981. — 117p ; 23cm
ISBN 0-903729-66-0 (cased) : £7.50
ISBN 0-903729-67-9 (pbk) : £2.50 B81-16105

392'.1 — Primitive societies. Reproduction rituals
Paige, Karen Ericksen. The politics of reproductive ritual / Karen Ericksen Paige and Jeffery M. Paige with the assistance of Linda Fuller and Elisabeth Magnus. — Berkeley ; London : University of California Press, c1981. — xii,380p : ill,1geneal.table ; 24cm
Bibliography: p317-371. — Includes index
ISBN 0-520-03071-0 : £15.00 B81-39837

392'.14 — Women. Initiation rites — *Case studies*
Lincoln, Bruce. Emerging from the chrysalis : studies in rituals of women's initiation / Bruce Lincoln. — Cambridge [Mass.] ; London : Harvard University Press, 1981. — xii,153p : ill ; 24cm
Bibliography: p137-147. — Includes index
ISBN 0-674-24840-6 : £12.25 B81-40033

392'.5 — Marriage customs: Bridewealth & dowry — *Conference proceedings*
The **Meaning** of marriage payments / edited by J.L. Comaroff. — London : Academic Press, 1980. — xii,264p : ill,2maps ; 24cm. — (Studies in anthropology)
Conference papers. — Includes bibliographies and index
ISBN 0-12-183450-6 : £12.60 : CIP rev. B80-02407

392'.5'091812 — Western marriage customs, *to 1980*
Walter, Elizabeth. Elizabeth Walter requests the pleasure of your company for a wedding bouquet to celebrate your engagement/marriage/anniversary and those of your friends and relations. — London : Collins, 1981. — [40]p : col.ill ; 21cm
Ill on lining papers
ISBN 0-00-216863-4 : £3.95 : CIP rev. B81-30443

393 — DEATH CUSTOMS

393 — Death customs — *History* — *Conference proceedings*
Mortality and immortality : the anthropology and archaeology of death. — London : Academic Press, Feb.1982. — [300]p
Conference papers
ISBN 0-12-361550-x : CIP entry B81-36061

393'.1'0901 — Ancient burial customs
The **Archaeology** of death. — Cambridge : Cambridge University Press, Oct.1981. — [168] p. — (New directions in archaeology)
ISBN 0-521-23775-0 : £17.50 : CIP entry B81-28822

393'.3 — Mummies — *For children*
Madison, Arnold. Mummies in fact and fiction / by Arnold Madison. — New York ; London : Watts, 1980. — 88p : ill ; 26cm
Bibliography: p84-85. - Includes index
ISBN 0-531-04154-9 : £2.99 B81-03639

393'.3'09 — Mummies, *to ca 1700*
Mummies, disease and ancient cultures / edited by Aidan and Eve Cockburn. — Cambridge : Cambridge University Press, 1980. — x,340p,[4]p of plates : ill(some col.),maps ; 27cm
Includes bibliographies and index
ISBN 0-521-23020-9 : £25.00
Also classified at 616.07 B81-03747

393'.3'0932 — Ancient Egyptian mummies. Investigation. Radiography. Use of x-rays
An **X-ray** atlas of the royal mummies / edited by James E. Harris and Edward F. Wente. — Chicago ; London : University of Chicago Press, 1980. — xxviii,403p : ill ; 25cm
Five microfiches in pocket. — Includes bibliographies and index
ISBN 0-226-31745-5 : £33.00 B81-03095

394 — PUBLIC AND SOCIAL CUSTOMS

394 — Italy. Tuscany. Rural regions. Veglie
Falassi, Alessandro. Folklore by the fireside : text and context of the Tuscan veglia / by Alessandro Falassi ; foreword by Roger D. Abrahams. — London : Scolar, 1980. — xix,377p : ill,music,ports ; 24cm
Originally published: Austin : University of Texas Press, 1980. — Bibliography: p363-372. — Includes index
ISBN 0-85967-600-5 : £12.50 : CIP rev. B80-08175

394.1'0941 — Great Britain. British people. Food habits — *For non-English speaking students — For schools*
Viney, Karen. Food / Karen Viney. — London : Mary Glasgow, c1979. — 32p : ill,1map,ports ; 21cm + 1 teacher's guide(22p : 21cm). — (Project GB ; 8)
ISBN 0-905999-68-1 (pbk) : £0.60
ISBN 0-86158-087-7 (pbk) : Teacher's guide B81-11476

394.1'2'0951 — China. Food, *to 1976 — Anthropological perspectives*
Food in Chinese culture. — London : Yale University Press, Oct.1981. — [448]p
Originally published: 1977
ISBN 0-300-02759-1 : £6.95 : CIP entry B81-31947

394.1'3'09411 — Scottish drinking customs, *to 1955*
McNeill, F. Marian. The Scots cellar : its traditions and lore / F. Marian McNeill. — London : Granada, 1981, c1973. — 351p : music ; 18cm. — (A Mayflower book)
Originally published: Edinburgh : Paterson, 1956. — Includes index
ISBN 0-583-13410-6 (pbk) : £1.95 B81-22277

394.1'5 — Great Britain. Breakfasts, *to 1980*
Read, Jan. The great British breakfast / Jan Read and Maite Manjón. — London : Joseph, 1981. — 128p,[8]p of plates : ill(some col.),facsims(some col.),1port ; 25cm
Facsims on lining papers. — Includes index
ISBN 0-7181-2004-3 : £7.50 B81-36132

394.2 — Anniversaries
Ward, Florence. Florence Ward's Victorian birthday book. — Exeter : Webb & Bower, 1981. — [172]p : col.ill,1col.port ; 14x20cm
ISBN 0-906671-16-7 : Unpriced B81-16661

394.2 — Festivals
Watkins, Peter, *1934-*. Here's the year. — London : Julia MacRae, Nov.1981. — [96]p
ISBN 0-86203-046-3 : £5.25 : CIP entry B81-30341

394.2 — Festivals — *For children*
McFarland, Jeanne. Festivals / Jeanne McFarland. — London : Macdonald Educational, 1981. — 46p : ill(some col.) ; 25cm. — (Macdonald new reference library ; 27)
Text on lining paper. — Bibliography: p44. — Includes index
ISBN 0-356-05827-1 : £2.75 B81-13624

394.2 — Festivals — *For schools*
Purton, Rowland W.. Festivals and celebrations. — Oxford : Blackwell, Nov.1981. — [224]p
ISBN 0-631-91570-2 : £4.50 : CIP entry B81-30167

Rankin, John. Looking at festivals / written by John Rankin ; drawings by Edwin Beecroft. — Guildford : Lutterworth, c1981. — 1portfolio (14 parts) : ill ; 15x21cm + Teacher's guide ([4]p : 15x21cm)
ISBN 0-7188-2321-4 : Unpriced B81-10780

394.2′68282 — Christmas

A **Christmas** book : poems, prose and carols / selected and illustrated by Diane Elson. — Tadworth : World′s Work, 1980. — 108p : ill (some col.) ; 25cm
Includes index
ISBN 0-437-37703-2 : £4.95 B81-00839

Muir, Frank. A treasury of Christmas. — London : Robson, Oct.1981. — [160]p
ISBN 0-86051-154-5 : £6.50 : CIP entry B81-27455

394.2′68282 — Christmas customs. Special subjects: Pets: Cats, *to 1980*

Flick, Pauline. Christmas cats / Pauline Flick. — London : Collins, 1981. — [44]p : ill(some col.) ; 18x25cm
Ill on lining papers
ISBN 0-00-216302-0 : £3.95 : CIP rev. B81-20152

394.2′68282 — Christmas — *For children*

Cox, Lesley. Countdown to Christmas / Lesley Cox and Leslie Foster. — London : Macmillan Education, 1980. — 96p : ill ; 22cm
ISBN 0-333-29136-0 : Unpriced B81-33456

The **Oxford** Christmas book for children / [compiled by] Roderick Hunt. — Oxford : Oxford University Press, 1981. — 160p : ill (some col.),music ; 26cm
ISBN 0-19-278104-9 : £5.95 : CIP rev. B81-22476

Sandak, Cass R.. Christmas / by Cass R. Sandak ; illustrations by Cynthia Pickard. — New York ; London : Watts, 1980. — 48p : col.ill ; 27cm. — (An Easy-read holiday book)
Includes index
ISBN 0-531-04147-6 : £2.99 B81-07131

394.2′68283 — Easter — *For children*

Sandak, Cass R.. Easter / by Cass R. Sandak ; illustrations by Diana Uehlinger. — New York ; London : Watts, 1980. — 48p : col.ill ; 27cm. — (An Easy-read holiday book)
Includes index
ISBN 0-531-04148-4 : £2.99 B81-07132

394.2′683 — Halloween — *For children*

Sandak, Cass R.. Halloween / by Cass R. Sandak ; illustrations by Frank Bozzo. — New York ; London : Watts, 1980. — 32p : col.ill ; 27cm. — (An Easy-read holiday book)
Includes index
ISBN 0-531-04149-2 : £2.99 B81-07130

394.2′683 — London. Wandsworth *(London Borough).* **Colleges of education: Whitelands College. May Queen ceremonies,** *to 1981*

Coe, Malcolm. May Queen Festival / by Malcolm Coe. — [London] ([Putney, SW15 3SN]) : Whitelands College, 1981. — 56p : ill (some col.),ports(some col.) ; 24cm
Cover title
ISBN 0-907456-01-4 (pbk) : Unpriced B81-26972

394.2′683 — St Valentine′s Day — *For children*

Sandak, Cass R.. Valentine′s Day / by Cass R. Sandak ; illustrations by Michael Deas. — New York ; London : Watts, 1980. — 32p : col.ill ; 27cm. — (An Easy-read holiday book)
Includes index
ISBN 0-531-04151-4 : £2.99 B81-07133

394.2′6941 — British calendar customs

Harrowven, Jean. Origins of festivals and feasts / Jean Harrowven. — London : Kaye & Ward, 1980. — 188p : ill ; 23cm
Bibliography: p187-188
ISBN 0-7182-1251-7 : £5.95 B81-00840

394.2′6942 — English calendar customs

Seasons greetings / compiled by Elizabeth Walter. — London : Collins, 1980. — [41]p : col.ill ; 21cm
Ill on lining papers
ISBN 0-00-216728-x : £3.50 B81-06765

394.2′69422 — Southern English calendar customs

Green, Marian. A harvest of festivals / Marian Green ; line drawings by Chris Williamson. — London : Longman, 1980. — 178p : ill,2maps ; 22cm. — (Longman travellers series)
Bibliography: p172. - Includes index
ISBN 0-582-50284-5 : £6.50 : CIP rev. B80-13341

394′.3 — Gloucestershire. Dover′s Hill. Games. Competitions: Robert Dover′s games, *to 1980*

Burns, F. D. A.. Heigh the Cotswold! : a history of Robert Dover′s Olimpick Games / by Francis Burns. — Chipping Campden ([c/o F. Burns, 51 Ridge Rd., Kingswinford, West Midlands DY6 9RE]) : Robert Dover′s Games Society, c1981. — 47p : ill,facsims,1map ; 21cm
ISBN 0-9507487-0-6 (pbk) : Unpriced B81-28916

394′.5′0942 — England. Pageantry, *1558-1603.* **Special subjects: England. Elizabeth I,** *Queen of England*

Wilson, Jean, *1945-*. Entertainments for Elizabeth I / Jean Wilson. — Woodbridge : Brewer, 1980. — 179p : 1ill ; 23cm. — (Studies in Elizabethan and Renaissance culture ; 2)
Bibliography: p171-173. - Includes index. — Includes the text of The four foster children of desire (1581), and those at Cowdray (1591), Elvetham (1591), and Ditchley (1592)
ISBN 0-85991-048-2 : £12.00 : CIP rev.
Primary classification 822′.3′080351 B80-06550

394′.9 — Man. Cannibalism — *Anthropological perspectives*

Arens, W.. The man-eating myth : anthropology & anthropophagy / W. Arens. — Oxford : Oxford University Press, 1979 (1980 [printing]). — vi,206p : ill ; 21cm
Bibliography: p189-201. — Includes index
ISBN 0-19-502793-0 (pbk) : £2.95 B81-25159

395 — ETIQUETTE

395 — Etiquette — *Manuals*

Debrett′s etiquette and modern manners / edited by Elsie Burch Donald ; with a preface by Sir Iain Moncrieffe of that ilk. — London : Debrett′s, c1981. — 400p : ill,facsims ; 23cm
Includes index
ISBN 0-905649-43-5 : £8.95 B81-28501

395′.22 — Weddings. Planning — *For brides*

Beyfus, Drusilla. The bride′s book / Drusilla Beyfus. — London : Allen Lane, 1981. — 239,[16]p of plates : ill(some col.) ; 28cm
Includes index
ISBN 0-7139-1310-x : £9.95 B81-12756

395′.22′0880621 — Royal weddings, *1053-1981*

Cartland, Barbara. Romantic royal marriages / Barbara Cartland. — London : Express Books, 1981. — 128p : ill(some col.),facsims(some col.),ports(some col.) ; 26cm
Includes index
ISBN 0-85079-111-1 (pbk) : £2.95 B81-32856

395′.22′0941 — Great Britain. Weddings. Planning — *Practical information*

Dobson, Sue. The wedding day book / Sue Dobson. — London : Arrow, 1981. — 252p ; 18cm
ISBN 0-09-926660-1 (pbk) : £1.50 B81-40721

395′.4 — Forms of address & titles

Titles : and forms of address : a guide to correct use. — 17th ed. — London : A.C. Black, c1980. — xiii,198p ; 20cm
Previous ed.: 1978. — Includes index
ISBN 0-7136-2072-2 (pbk) : £3.95 B81-22410

398 — FOLKLORE

398′.0941 — British legends. Origins

Senior, Michael. Myths of Britain / Michael Senior. — London : Orbis Publishing, 1979. — 240p : ill(some col.),1map,facsims ; 24cm
Ill on lining papers. — Bibliography: p233. — Includes index
ISBN 0-85613-244-6 : £6.95 B81-17619

398′.09411′35 — Scottish folklore: Shetland folklore

Nicolson, James R.. Shetland folklore / James R. Nicolson ; illustrations by Martin Emslie. — London : Hale, 1981. — 221p : ill,1map ; 23cm
Bibliography: p211-212. — Includes index
ISBN 0-7091-8824-2 : £8.25 B81-26247

398′.09414′23 — Scottish folklore: Strathclyde Region folklore: Islay folklore

Earl, Margaret. Tales of Islay : fact and folklore / by Margaret Earl ; illustrations by Ken Ashfield. — Port Charlotte (Port Charlotte, Islay) : Argyll Reproductions, [1980]. — 62p : ill,map ; cm
Map on inside covers
Unpriced (pbk) B81-08054

398′.09415 — Irish folklore — *Serials*

Sinsear : the folklore journal. — [No.1]-. — Baile Átha Cliath [Dublin] : Roinn Bhéaloideas Éireann, Coláiste na hOllscoile, Baile Átha Cliath, [1979]-. — v. : ill ; 22cm
Irregular. — Text in English and Irish. — Description based on: No.3 (1981)
Unpriced B81-39737

398′.0942 — English folklore — *Collections*

Under the hawthorn : country lore and country saw / [compiled by] Sybil Marshall ; illustrated with wood engravings by George Tute. — London : Dent, 1981. — 64p : ill ; 21cm
ISBN 0-460-04526-1 (corrected) : £2.95 : CIP rev. B81-01839

398′.09429 — Welsh folklore

Rhŷs, *Sir* **John**. Celtic folklore : Welsh and Manx / by John Rhŷs. — London : Wildwood, 1980. — 2v.([32],718p) ; 22cm. — (A Wildwood rediscovery)
Originally published: Oxford : Clarendon, 1901. — Bibliography: p[17]-[32]. — Includes index
ISBN 0-7045-0405-7 (pbk) : Unpriced
ISBN 0-7045-0410-3 (v.2) : £4.95 B81-36526

398′.09747′56 — New York *(State)* **woodsmen′s folklore: St Lawrence County woodsmen′s folklore**

Bethke, Robert D.. Adirondack voices : woodsmen and woods lore / Robert D. Bethke. — Urbana ; London : University of Illinois Press, 1981. — xii,148p : ill,1map,music,ports ; 24cm
Includes index
ISBN 0-252-00829-4 : £7.50 B81-17370

398′.15 — Folklore. Interpretation — *Psychoanalytical perspectives*

Dundes, Alan. Interpreting folklore / Alan Dundes. — Bloomington ; London : Indiana University Press, c1980. — xiv,304p : 1ill,music ; 24cm
Bibliography: p263-287
ISBN 0-253-14307-1 (cased) : Unpriced
ISBN 0-253-20240-x (pbk) : £6.00 B81-02406

398.2 — FOLK LITERATURE

398.2 — Folk plays in Braj Bhasa. Special themes: Hindu myths. Krishna — *Critical studies*

Hawley, John Stratton. At play with Krishna : pilgrimage dramas from Brindavan / John Stratton Hawley in association with Shrivatsa Goswami. — Princeton, N.J. ; Guildford : Princeton University Press, c1981. — xvi,339p : ill ; 23cm
Bibliography: p321-331. — Includes index
ISBN 0-691-06470-9 : £16.80 B81-37735

398.2 — Folk plays in English. Special subjects: Robin Hood — *Critical studies*

Wiles, David. Early plays of Robin Hood. — Woodbridge : D.S. Brewer, Nov.1981. — [128]p
ISBN 0-85991-082-2 : £12.00 : CIP entry B81-30403

398.2 — Mummers′ plays in English — *Critical studies*

Helm, Alex, *b.1920*. The English mummers′ play / Alex Helm ; with a foreword by N. Peacock and E.C. Cawte. — [Woodbridge] : Brewer for the Folklore Society, 1981, c1980. — 116p : ill,maps,music,facsims ; 29cm. — (Mistletoe series)
Bibliography: p101-104. — Includes index
ISBN 0-85991-067-9 : £17.50 : CIP rev. B80-17637

398.2 — Myths & legends — *Anthologies — For children*

Bailey, John, *1940 Nov.4-*. Gods and men : myths and legends from the world's religions / retold by John Bailey, Kenneth McLeish, David Spearman ; illustrated by Derek Collard, Charles Keeping, Jeroo Roy. — Oxford : Oxford University Press, 1981. — 143p : ill ; 23cm
Bibliography: p142-143
ISBN 0-19-278020-4 : £5.95 B81-17667

Oakden, David. The Wheaton book of myths and legends / David Oakden ; illustrated by Peter Stevenson. — Exeter : Wheaton, 1979, c1978. — 119p : col.ill ; 22cm
Contents: Classical and northern stories. Originally published: 1978 — Stories from the East. Originally published: 1978 — Stories from the West. Originally published: 1978
ISBN 0-08-021436-3 : £2.95 B81-06366

398.2 — Tales & legends — *Anthologies — For children*

Mercer, John. Stories of vanishing people. — London : Allison and Busby, Oct.1981. — [128]p
ISBN 0-85031-421-6 (cased) : £5.95 : CIP entry
ISBN 0-85031-422-4 (pbk) : £2.50 B81-28832

398.2'09415 — Irish tales & legends — *Anthologies*

Donegan, Maureen. The bedside book of Irish fables and legends / by Maureen Donegan. — Dublin : Mercier, c1980. — 117p ; 18cm
ISBN 0-85342-635-x (pbk) : £2.30 B81-16082

398.2'09423'5 — Devon tales & legends

Jones, Sally, *1955-*. Legends of Devon / Sally Jones. — Bodmin : Bossiney, 1981. — 102p : ill,ports ; 21cm
Bibliography: p102
ISBN 0-906456-52-5 (pbk) : £1.75 B81-26640

398.2'09427'8 — Lake District tales & legends — *Anthologies*

My favourite stories of Lakeland / edited by Melvyn Bragg ; illustrated by A. Wainwright and by Peter McClure. — Guildford : Lutterworth, 1981. — 126p : ill ; 23cm
ISBN 0-7188-2396-6 : £4.75 B81-03457

398.2'09428'46 — North York Moors tales & legends — *Anthologies*

Atkinson, Marion. Legends of the North York moors : traditions, beliefs, folklore, customs / by Marion Atkinson. — Clapham [N. Yorkshire] : Dalesman, 1981. — 64p : ill,1map ; 22cm
ISBN 0-85206-623-6 (pbk) : £1.50 B81-13393

398.2'0951 — Chinese myths & legends — *Anthologies — For children*

Saunders, Tao Tao. Dragons, gods & spirits from Chinese mythology / text by Tao Tao Liu Sanders ; illustrations by Johnny Pau. — [London] : Peter Lowe, c1980. — 132p : ill (some col.),1col.map ; 28cm
Includes index
ISBN 0-85654-039-0 : £4.95 : CIP rev. B80-24401

398.2'0954 — Hindu tales & legends — *Anthologies*

Amore, Roy C.. Lustful maidens and ascetic kings : Buddhist and Hindu stories of life / Roy C. Amore, Larry D. Shinn ; illustrations by Sharon Wallace. — New York ; Oxford : Oxford University Press, 1981. — xii,198p : ill ; 22cm
Bibliography: p191-198
ISBN 0-19-502838-4 (cased) : £9.95
ISBN 0-19-502839-2 (pbk) : Unpriced
Primary classification 398.2'0954 B81-32978

398.2'0954 — Indian Buddhist tales & legends — *Anthologies*

Amore, Roy C.. Lustful maidens and ascetic kings : Buddhist and Hindu stories of life / Roy C. Amore, Larry D. Shinn ; illustrations by Sharon Wallace. — New York ; Oxford : Oxford University Press, 1981. — xii,198p : ill ; 22cm
Bibliography: p191-198
ISBN 0-19-502838-4 (cased) : £9.95
ISBN 0-19-502839-2 (pbk) : Unpriced
Also classified at 398.2'0954 B81-32978

398.2'096 — African tales & legends — *Anthologies — For children*

Elliot, Geraldine. The hunter's cave : a book of stories based on African folk tales / by Geraldine Elliot ; illustrated by Sheila Hawkins. — London : Routledge & Kegan Paul, 1951 (1981 [printing]). — 174p : ill ; 22cm
ISBN 0-7100-0861-9 (pbk) : £2.95 B81-37649

Elliot, Geraldine. The long grass whispers : a book of African stories / by Geraldine Elliot ; illustrated by Sheila Hawkins. — London : Routledge & Kegan Paul, 1949 (1981 [printing]). — 132p : ill ; 22cm
ISBN 0-7100-0860-0 (pbk) : £2.50 B81-37647

Elliot, Geraldine. The singing chameleon : a book of African stories based on local customs, proverbs and folk-lore / by Geraldine Elliot ; illustrated by Sheila Hawkins. — London : Routledge & Kegan Paul, 1957 (1981 [printing]). — 168p : ill ; 22cm
ISBN 0-7100-0862-7 (pbk) : £2.95 B81-37646

Elliot, Geraldine. Where the leopard passes : a book of African folk tales / by Geraldine Elliot ; illustrated by Sheila Hawkins. — London : Routledge & Kegan Paul, 1949 (1981 [printing]). — 133p : ill ; 21cm
ISBN 0-7100-0863-5 (pbk) : £2.50 B81-37648

398.2'097 — North American Indian myths & legends — *Anthologies — For children*

Wood, Marion. Spirits, heroes and hunters from North American Indian mythology. — London : Peter Lowe, July 1981. — [136]p
ISBN 0-85654-040-4 : £4.50 : CIP entry B81-20620

398.2'09775 — Wisconsin myths & tales: Chippewa myths & tales — *Anthologies*

Wisconsin Chippewa myths & tales and their relation to Chippewa life / based on folktales collected by Victor Barnouw ... [et al.] ; Victor Barnouw. — Madison ; London : University of Wisconsin Press, 1977 (1979 [printing]). — vii,295p : maps ; 23cm
Bibliography: p277-290. — Includes index
ISBN 0-299-07314-9 (cased) : £12.85
ISBN 0-299-07310-6 B81-07506

398.2'1 — Tales — *Anthologies*

Folktales told around the world / edited by Richard M. Dorson. — Chicago ; London : University of Chicago Press, 1978, c1975. — xxv,622p,[12]p of plates : ill,ports ; 23cm
Includes index
ISBN 0-226-15874-8 (pbk) : £7.00 B81-38565

398.2'1 — Tales — *Anthologies — For children*

The **Antelope** and the turtle : from Africa. The crow and the sparrow : from Bangladesh / [retold by Ashraf Siddiqui]. — [London] ([157 Clapham Rd., SW9 0PT]) : Save the Children Fund, 1981. — 16p : ill(some col.) ; 21cm. — (Round the world folk tales)
ISBN 0-333-30755-0 (pbk) : £0.50 B81-38794

Cope, Dawn. Red Riding Hood's favourite fairy tales / Dawn and Peter Cope. — Exeter : Webb & Bower, 1981. — 64p : col.ill,ports ; 26cm
ISBN 0-906671-08-6 : £3.95 B81-35268

Gormless Tom : from Ireland. The tale of the hairy toe : from North America. — [London] ([157 Clapham Rd., SW9 0PT]) : Save the Children Fund, 1981. — 32p : ill(some col.) ; 21cm. — (Round the world folk tales)
ISBN 0-333-30762-3 (pbk) : £0.70 B81-38796

Kincaid, Eric. Eric and Lucy Kincaid's book of classic fairy tales. — Cambridge : Brimax, c1978 (1979 printing). — 77p : col.ill ; 29cm
ISBN 0-904494-88-8 : Unpriced B81-40828

Kruger, Veronica. Storybook international / stories adapted by Veronica Kruger ; line drawings by Patricia Drew. — London : Gollancz, 1981. — 240p : ill(some col.) ; 26cm
ISBN 0-575-03051-8 : £5.95 B81-34174

Manning-Sanders, Ruth. A book of heroes and heroines. — London : Methuen Children's Books, Feb.1982. — [125]p
ISBN 0-416-89310-4 : £4.95 : CIP entry B81-35709

Maui, the stealer of fire : from Polynesia. Prince Wicked : from India. — [London] ([157 Clapham Rd., SW9 0PT]) : Save the Children Fund, 1981. — 32p : ill(some col.) ; 21cm. — (Round the world folk tales)
ISBN 0-333-30766-6 (pbk) : £0.70 B81-38797

My wonderful gift book of fairy tales. — London : Dean, c1979. — 125p : ill ; 29cm
ISBN 0-603-00164-5 : Unpriced B81-17890

Riordan, James. A world of folk tales / James Riordan. — London : Hamlyn, 1981. — 223p : col.ill ; 27cm
Bibliography: p223
ISBN 0-600-33745-6 : £5.50 B81-22093

Riordan, James. A world of folk tales / James Riordan. — London : Hamlyn, 1981. — 5v. : col.ill ; 28cm
In a slip case
ISBN 0-600-36607-3 : £12.50 B81-34859

The **Wise** judge : from Africa. Why the hill is red : from Asia / [retold by Chia Hearn Chek. — [London] ([157 Clapham Rd., SW9 0PT]) : Save the Children Fund, 1981. — 32p : ill (some col.) ; 21cm. — (Round the world folk tales)
ISBN 0-333-30761-5 (pbk) : £0.70 B81-38795

398.2'1'08997 — North American Indian tales — *Anthologies — For children*

Robinson, Gail. Raven the trickster : legends of the North American Indians / retold by Gail Robinson ; introduced by Douglas Hill ; illustrated by Joanna Troughton. — London : Chatto & Windus, 1981. — 124p : ill ; 21cm
ISBN 0-7011-2600-0 : £4.95 : CIP rev. B81-23845

398.2'1'0938 — Ancient Greek tales — *Anthologies — For children*

Green, Roger Lancelyn. Old Greek fairy tales / by Roger Lancelyn Green ; illustrated by Ernest H. Shepard. — London : Bell & Hyman, 1958 (1978 [printing]). — 186p : ill ; 20cm
ISBN 0-7135-1849-9 : £3.95 B81-05472

Marshall, Sybil. Seafarers' quest to Colchis / Sybil Marshall ; [illustrated by Barry Wilkinson]. — St Albans : Hart-Davis Educational, 1981. — 63p : col.ill,1map ; 24cm. — (Tales the Greeks told)
ISBN 0-247-12870-8 (pbk) : £1.35 B81-24768

398.2'1'094 — European tales — *Anthologies — For children*

Leete-Hodge, Lornie. Hamlyn wonderful fairy stories in colour / re-told by Lornie Leete-Hodge ; illustrated by Beverlie Manson. — London : Hamlyn, 1981. — 157p : col.ill ; 31cm
ISBN 0-600-33719-7 : £2.99 B81-31213

Nesbit, E.. The old nursery stories. — London : Hodder & Stoughton, Oct.1981. — [192]p
Originally published: 1975
ISBN 0-340-26598-1 (pbk) : £0.95 : CIP entry B81-26755

398.2'1'0941 — British tales — *Anthologies*

Garner, Alan. The Lad of the Gad / Alan Garner. — London : Collins, 1980. — 116p ; 22cm
ISBN 0-00-184711-2 : £4.95 B81-00083

398.2'1'0941 — British tales — *Anthologies — For children*

Folk tales of the British Isles / edited by Michael Foss ; illustrated by Ken Kiff. — London : Book Club Associates, 1977. — 176p : ill(some col.) ; 25cm
Unpriced B81-37883

398.2′1′0941 — British tales — *Anthologies — For children* *continuation*

The **Jackanory** story book / illustrated by Jo Worth. — London : Book Club Associates, 1979. — 160p : ill ; 24cm
Unpriced B81-37887

398.2′1′09411 — Scottish tales — *Anthologies — For children*

Ratcliff, Ruth. Scottish folk tales / retold by Ruth Ratcliff. — London : Frederick Muller, 1976 (1981 [printing]). — 144p : ill ; 22cm
Bibliography: p10
ISBN 0-584-62400-x (pbk) : £2.95 B81-17670

398.2′1′09411 — Scottish tales — *Anthologies — For schools*

The **Green** man of knowledge and other Scots traditional tales. — Aberdeen : Aberdeen University Press, Oct.1981. — [128]p
ISBN 0-08-025757-7 (cased) : £9.50 : CIP entry
ISBN 0-08-025758-5 (pbk) : £5.00 B81-27360

398.2′1′0941175 — Scottish tales: Highland Region tales: Inverness tales — *Anthologies*

Macnicol, Eona. The jail dancing : and other stories of an old Scottish town (Inverness) / by Eona Macnicol ; illustrated by John Mackay. — Edinburgh : Albyn, c1978. — 126p : ill ; 23cm
ISBN 0-284-98591-0 : £2.75 B81-04884

398.2′1′09415 — Irish tales — *Anthologies — For children*

Haviland, Virginia. Favourite fairy tales told in Ireland / retold from Irish storytellers by Virginia Haviland ; illustrated by Artur Marokvia. — London : Bodley Head, 1967, c1961 (1981 [printing]). — 91p : ill ; 23cm
Originally published: Boston, Mass. : Little, Brown, 1961
ISBN 0-370-01099-x (pbk) : £1.95 B81-40633

398.2′1′0942 — English tales — *Anthologies*

Greig, Francis. The bite and other apocryphal tales. — London : Cape, Sept.1981. — [176]p
ISBN 0-224-01904-x : £5.95 : CIP entry
B81-20623

Marshall, Sybil. Everyman′s book of English folk tales / Sybil Marshall ; illustrated with wood engravings by John Lawrence. — London : Dent, 1981. — 384p : ill ; 25cm
ISBN 0-460-04472-9 : £8.95 B81-22329

398.2′1′09423 — South-west English tales — *Anthologies*

Martyn, Myles. West Country tales / by Myles Martyn ; illustrations by R.G. Pratt. — Dulverton : Breakaway, 1981. — 48p : ill ; 20cm
ISBN 0-907506-02-x (pbk) : £0.75 B81-24084

398.2′1′0942342 — Guernsey tales — *Texts*

Smith, Sidney. The witch′s prophecy of the death of Lady Hatton killed at Castle Cornet, 1672 / by Sidney Smith. — Guernsey : Toucan, 1981. — [4]p ; 20cm. — (Guernsey historical monograph ; no.22)
Cover title
ISBN 0-85694-236-7 (pbk) : Unpriced
B81-18602

398.2′1′094237 — Cornish tales — *Texts — For children*

The **Gay** gown : a Cornish droll. — [Swanage] ([Dunshay Cottage, Haycrafts La., Swanage, Dorset]) : [Rosemorran Press], [1981]. — 6leaves : ill ; 26cm
Unpriced (pbk) B81-17729

398.2′1′09429 — Welsh tales — *Anthologies — For children — Welsh texts*

Palfrey, Eiry. Un tro : chwedlan a straeon cyffrous i blant o Gymru, Cernyw ac Iwerddon / Eiry Palfrey ; arluniwyd y gyfrol gan John Walters. — Llandysul : Gwasg Gomer, 1979. — 96p,[4]leaves of plates : ill,1map ; 21cm
ISBN 0-85088-611-2 (pbk) : £1.50 B81-40402

398.2′1′0943 — German tales — *Anthologies — For children*

Grimm, Jacob. Grimm′s fairy tales / illustrated by Pauline Ellison ; selected and introduced by Richard Adams. — London : Routledge & Kegan Paul, 1981. — 128p : ill(some col.) ; 28cm
ISBN 0-7100-0912-7 : £6.95 : CIP rev.
B81-28152

398.2′1′0943 — German tales — *Texts — For children*

Ash, Jutta. Rapunzel. — London : Andersen Press, Feb.1982. — [32]p
ISBN 0-86264-010-5 : £3.95 : CIP entry
B81-36965

Cinderella / illustrated by Moira Kemp. — London : Hamilton, 1981. — [32]p : col.ill ; 24cm
Based on the story collected by the Brothers Grimm
ISBN 0-241-10636-2 : £3.95 : CIP rev.
B81-25706

Greenway, Shirley. Rapunzel / the Brothers Grimm ; retold by Shirley Greenway ; pictures by Sandy Nightingale. — London : Pan, 1981. — [24]p ; 22cm. — (Piccolo picture classics) (A Piccolo original)
ISBN 0-330-26245-9 (pbk) : £0.80 B81-12624

Grimm, Jacob. The Bremen town musicians / the Brothers Grimm ; translated by Elizabeth Shub ; pictures by Janina Domanska. — London : Macrae, 1981. — [32]p : col.ill ; 24cm
Translation of: Die Bremer Stadtmusikanten
ISBN 0-86203-063-3 : £4.25 : CIP rev.
B81-04304

Grimm, Jacob. Hansel and Gretel / the Brothers Grimm ; pictures by Susan Jeffers. — London : Hamilton, 1981, c1980. — [32]p : col.ill ; 31cm
Originally published: New York : Dial Press, 1980
ISBN 0-241-10531-5 : £4.50 B81-12544

398.2′1′0943 — German tales - *Texts - For children*
Grimm, Jacob. Hansel and Gretel. — London : Kaye & Ward, Apr.1981. — [24]p
ISBN 0-7182-1261-4 : £3.25 : CIP entry
B81-04267

398.2′1′0943 — German tales — *Texts — For children*

Grimm, Jacob. The seven ravens / the Brothers Grimm ; illustrated by Lisbeth Zwerger. — London : Macdonald, 1981. — [24]p : col.ill ; 22x24cm
Translation of: Die sieben Raben
ISBN 0-354-08132-2 : £4.50 B81-22024

Grimm, Jacob. Snow-White and the seven dwarfs : a tale from the Brothers Grimm / translated by Randell Jarrell ; pictures by Nancy Ekholm Burkert. — Harmondsworth : Kestrel, 1974, c1972 (1980 [printing]). — [32]p : col ill ; 32cm
Translation of : Schneewittchen. — Originally published: New York : Farrar, Straus and Giroux, 1972 ; Harmondsworth : Kestrel, 1971
£4.95 B81-03585

The **Twelve** dancing princesses / retold from a story by the Brothers Grimm ; illustrated by Errol Le Cain. — Harmondsworth : Puffin, 1981, c1978. — [32]p : col.ill ; 18x23cm. — (Picture puffins)
Originally published: London : Faber, 1978
ISBN 0-14-050322-6 (pbk) : £0.90 B81-27688

398.2′1′094371 — Czech tales — *Anthologies*
The **Palace** of the moon : and other tales from Czechoslovakia / [translated by] Ruzena Wood ; illustrated by Krystyna Turska. — London : Deutsch, 1981. — 128p : ill ; 24cm
ISBN 0-233-97206-4 : £4.95 B81-13682

398.2′1′0945 — Italian tales — *Anthologies — For children*
Mayo, Margaret. The Italian fairy book / Margaret Mayo ; illustrated by Cara Lockhart Smith. — London : Kaye & Ward, 1981. — 125p : ill ; 23cm
ISBN 0-7182-1283-5 : £4.95 B81-38389

398.2′1′0945 — Italian tales — *Texts — For children*
De Paola, Tomie. The prince of the Dolomites. — London : Methuen, July 1981. — [40]p
ISBN 0-416-21430-4 : £3.95 : CIP entry
B81-14857

398.2′1′0947 — Russian tales — *Anthologies — For children*
. Alyonushka : Russian folk tales / translated from the Russian by Irina Zheleznova ; illustrated by Igor Yershov. — Moscow : Progress ; London : distributed by Central Books, c1980. — 77p : ill(some col.) ; 30cm
Translation of: Alënushka
ISBN 0-7147-1615-4 : £2.50 B81-27826

398.2′1′0947 — Russian tales — *Texts — For children*
Grandfather Frost : from Russia. — [London] ([157 Clapham Rd., SW9 0PT]) : Save the Children Fund, 1981. — 24p : ill(some col.) ; 21cm. — (Round the world folk tales)
ISBN 0-333-30759-3 (pbk) : £0.60 B81-38793

398.2′1′094897 — Finnish tales — *Texts — For children*
Troughton, Joanna. The magic mill : a Finnish folk tale adapted from the Kalevala / Joanna Troughton. — London : Blackie, 1981. — [28]p : chiefly col.ill ; 26cm
ISBN 0-216-91118-4 : £4.95 : CIP rev.
B81-22519

398.2′1′0953 — Arabian tales — *Texts — For children*
Lang, Andrew. [Aladdin]. Aladdin and the wonderful lamp / retold by Andrew Lang ; illustrated by Errol Le Cain. — London : Faber, 1981. — 31p : col.ill ; 31cm
ISBN 0-571-11656-6 : £4.75 : CIP rev.
B81-27941

398.2′1′0954 — Indian tales — *Anthologies — For children*
Crouch, Marcus. [The ivory city and other stories from India and Pakistan. Selections]. The ivory city : and other stories from India and Pakistan / [retold by] Marcus Crouch ; illustrated by William Stobbs. — London : Granada, 1981. — 128p : ill ; 18cm. — (A Dragon book)
Complete ed. originally published : London : Pelham, 1980
ISBN 0-583-30483-4 (pbk) : £0.95 B81-38611

398.2′1′09577 — Nanai tales — *Texts — For children*
Mergen and his friends : a Nanai folktale / [translated by Jim Riordan] ; [drawings by Gennady Pavlishin]. — Moscow : Progress ; [London] : Distributed by Central Books, 1973 (1981 printing). — [20]p : col.ill ; 28cm
Translation of: Mergen i ego druz′ia
ISBN 0-7147-1618-9 (unbound) : £0.60
B81-30811

398.2′1′096 — African tales — *Anthologies*
Fables from Africa / collected by Jan Knappert ; illustrated by Jeroo Ray. — [London] : Evans Brothers, 1981, c1980. — 64p : ill,1map ; 22cm. — (Evans Africa library)
ISBN 0-237-50670-x (pbk) : Unpriced
B81-31876

398.2′1′096 — African tales — *Anthologies — For children*
Auta the giant killer : from Nigeria. Two brothers and two eggs : from the Congo. — [London] ([157 Clapham Rd., SW9 0PT]) : Save the Children Fund, 1981. — 32p : ill (some col.) ; 21cm. — (Round the world folk tales)
ISBN 0-333-30763-1 (pbk) : £0.70 B81-38791

398.2′1′096762 — Masai tales — *Texts — For children*
Aardema, Verna. Who′s in Rabbit′s house? : a Masai tale / retold by Verna Aardema ; pictures by Leo and Diane Dillon. — London : Bodley Head, 1980, c1977. — [32]p : chiefly col.ill ; 26cm
Originally published: New York : Dial Press, 1977
ISBN 0-370-30351-2 : £4.50 : CIP rev.
B80-19726

398.2'1'097 — North American Indian tales — *Anthologies*

Robinson, Gail. Coyote the trickster : legends of the North American Indians / retold by Gail Robinson and Douglas Hill ; illustrated by Peter Stevenson. — [London] : Piccolo, 1981, c1975. — 140p : ill ; 18cm
Originally published: London : Chatto and Windus, 1975
ISBN 0-330-26263-7 (pbk) : £0.95 B81-23697

398.2'1'097 — North American Indian tales — *Anthologies — For children*

Smoking star. The song that comes from the sea. How corn came to the Indians : American Indian. — [London] ([157 Clapham Rd., SW9 0PT]) : Save the Children Fund, 1981. — 32p : ill(some col.) ; 21cm. — (Round the world folk tales)
ISBN 0-333-30765-8 (pbk) : £0.70 B81-38789

398.2'1'0972 — Mexican tales — *Texts — For children*

Mr Wolf and his tail : from Mexico. — [London] ([157 Clapham Rd., SW9 0PT]) : Save the Children Fund, 1981. — 16p : ill(some col.) ; 21cm. — (Round the world folk tales)
ISBN 0-333-30754-2 (pbk) : £0.50 B81-38792

398.2'1'09729 — West Indian tales — *Texts — For children*

Brer Annancy's second bite : from the West Indies. — [London] ([157 Clapham Rd., SW9 0PT]) : Save the Children Fund, 1981. — 24p : ill(some col.) ; 21cm. — (Round the world folk tales)
ISBN 0-333-30756-9 (pbk) : £0.60 B81-38787

398.2'1'097294 — Haitian tales — *Texts — For children*

Uncle Bouki and the horse : from Haiti. — [London] ([157 Clapham Rd., SW9 0PT]) : Save the Children Fund, 1981. — 24p : ill (some col.) ; 21cm. — (Round the world folk tales)
ISBN 0-333-30758-5 (pbk) : £0.60 B81-38786

398.2'1'097295 — Puerto Rican tales — *Texts — For children*

The Tiger and the rabbit : from Puerto Rico. — [London] ([157 Clapham Rd., SW9 0PT]) : Save the Children Fund, 1981. — 24p : ill (some col.) ; 21cm. — (Round the world folk tales)
ISBN 0-333-30757-7 (pbk) : £0.60 B81-38788

398.2'1'0994 — Australian aboriginal tales — *Texts — For children*

The Legend of the frogs : from Australia. — [London] ([157 Clapham Rd., SW9 0PT]) : Save the Children Fund, 1981. — 32p : ill (some col.) ; 21cm. — (Round the world folk tales)
ISBN 0-333-30760-7 (pbk) : £0.70 B81-38790

398.2'1'09969 — Hawaiian tales — *Texts*

Emerson, Nathaniel B.. Pele and Hiiaka : a myth from Hawaii / by Nathaniel B. Emerson ; with an introduction to the new edition by Terence Barrow. — Rutland [Vt.] : Tuttle ; London : Prentice-Hall [distributor], 1978. — xxxii,250p,[9]p of plates : ill,1port ; 24cm
Includes verse in Hawaiian with English translation. — Includes index
ISBN 0-8048-1251-9 : £8.10 B81-24448

398.2'2 — Legends. John, *Prester — Texts*

Ullendorff, Edward. The Hebrew letters of Prester John. — Oxford : Oxford University Press, Feb.1982. — [272]p
ISBN 0-19-713604-4 : £12.00 : CIP entry
B81-35767

398.2'2 — Tales & legends. Special subjects: Saints *— Anthologies — For children*

Saints, birds and beasts / [compiled by] Margaret Mayo ; illustrated by Cara Lockhart Smith. — London : Kaye & Ward, 1980. — 121p : ill ; 23cm
ISBN 0-7182-1236-3 : £4.95 B81-04114

398.2'2'09415 — Irish legends — *Anthologies*

Two death tales from the Ulster Cycle / translated by Maria Tymoczko from the Irish. — Dublin : Dolmen, 1981. — 110p ; 23cm. — (Dolmen texts ; 2)
Bibliography: p109-110. — Contents: The death of Cu Roi — The death of Cu Chulainn
ISBN 0-85105-342-4 : £8.50 B81-28469

398.2'45'095414 — Bengali tales. Special subjects: Animals — *Anthologies*

Raychaudhuri, Upendrakishore. The stupid tiger and other tales / Upendrakishore Raychaudhuri ; translated from the Bengali by William Radice ; illustrated by William Rushton. — London : Deutsch, 1981. — 86p : ill ; 24cm
ISBN 0-233-97256-0 : £3.95 B81-11501

398.2'4528 — Tales. Special subjects: Birds — *Anthologies — For children*

Macdonald, Fiona. Little bird, I have heard— / Fiona Macdonald ; illustrated by Meg Rutherford. — London : Kaye & Ward, 1980. — 62p : ill ; 25cm
ISBN 0-7182-1248-7 : £3.75 B81-02303

398.2'6 — Sayings in English. Special subjects: Weather — *Anthologies*

Wilshere, Jonathan. Leicestershire weather sayings / by Jonathan Wilshere. — Leicester (134 London Rd., Leicester, LE2 1EB) : Leicester Research Section of Chamberlain Music and Books, [1980]. — 24p : ill ; 21cm
Cover title
£1.00 (pbk) B81-10850

398.3/4 — FOLKLORE OF SPECIAL SUBJECTS

398'.329361 — British folklore. Special subjects: Great Britain. Antiquities. Sites

Alexander, Marc. Enchanted Britain / Marc Alexander ; with photographs by the author. — London : Barker, c1981. — 199p,[16]p of plates : ill,2maps ; 23cm
Bibliography: p199. - Includes index
ISBN 0-213-16768-9 : £7.95 B81-11798

398'.32972'1 — Mexico. Sorcery — *Personal observations*

Castaneda, Carlos. The eagle's gift. — London : Hodder & Stoughton, Sept.1981. — [320]p
ISBN 0-340-27086-1 : £6.95 : CIP entry
B81-23933

398'.352 — British legends. Bladud, *King of Britain — Critical studies*

Stewart, Bob. The myth of King Bladud : founder of the hot springs, builder of the temple of Bath, worshipper of Minerva / Bob Stewart. — [Bath] ([Guildhall, Bath BA1 5AW]) : Bath City Council, 1980. — [8]p : ill ; 30x14cm
ISBN 0-901303-11-9 (pbk) : Unpriced
B81-18227

398'.352 — European legends. Characters: Santa Claus. Historicity

Harrison, Shirley. Who is Father Christmas?. — Newton Abbot : David & Charles, Oct.1981. — [64]p
ISBN 0-7153-8222-5 : £3.50 : CIP entry
B81-24661

398'.352 — Legends. Heroes — *For children*

Sproule, Anna. Warriors in myth and legend / by Anna Sproule. — London : Macdonald Educational, 1980. — 46p : ill(some col.) ; 29cm. — (Larger than life)
Includes index
ISBN 0-356-07148-0 : £3.50 B81-00841

398'.352 — Middle Eastern legends. Queen of Sheba — *Critical studies*

Philby, H. St John. The Queen of Sheba / H. St John Philby. — London : Quartet, 1980. — 141p : ill(some col.),ports ; 29cm
Bibliography: p133-134. — Includes index
ISBN 0-7043-2246-3 : £12.50 B81-29550

398'.352 — Tales & myths. Characters: Villains

Sproule, Anna. Villains in myth and legend / by Anna Sproule. — London : Macdonald Educational, 1980. — 46p : ill(some col.) ; 29cm. — (Larger than life)
Includes index
ISBN 0-356-07149-9 : £3.50 B81-08231

398'.369974428 — Folklore. Special subjects: Cats

Briggs, Katharine M.. Nine lives : cats in folklore / Katharine M. Briggs ; with illustrations by John Ward. — London : Routledge & Kegan Paul, 1980. — x,222p : ill ; 25cm
Bibliography: p211-215. — Includes index
ISBN 0-7100-0638-1 : £7.95 : CIP rev.
B80-17638

398'.41 — Superstitions — *Encyclopaedias*

A Dictionary of omens and superstitions / compiled by Philippa Waring. — London : Magnum, 1980, c1978. — 264p ; 18cm
Originally published: London : Souvenir, 1978
ISBN 0-417-04060-1 (pbk) : £1.50 B81-00842

398'.41 — Superstitions — *For children*

Piddock, Helen. The Tiswas book of silly superstitions / compiled by Helen Piddock ; illustrated by Bobbie Craig. — London : Carousel, 1981. — 127p : ill ; 20cm
ISBN 0-552-54185-0 (pbk) : £0.85 B81-24313

398'.42 — Atlantis. Theories, *to 1979*

Forsyth, Phyllis Young. Atlantis : the making of myth / Phyllis Young Forsyth. — Montreal : McGill-Queens University Press ; London : Croom Helm, 1980. — x,209p,[10]p of plates : ill,maps ; 24cm
Bibliography: p199-203. — Includes index
ISBN 0-7099-1000-2 : £12.50 B81-14235

398'.45 — Fabulous beings

Scott, Allan J.. Fantastic people / Allan Scott and Michael Scott Rohan. — London (60 Greek St., Soho Sq., W1V 5LR) : Pierrot, 1980. — 184p : ill(some col.) ; 30cm
ISBN 0-905310-40-3 : £8.95 B81-03515

398'.45 — Fairies

Rodway, Avril. Faries / Avril Rodway. — London : Hutchinson, 1981. — 56p : ill(some col.) ; 18cm. — (The Leprechaun library)
Bibliography: p56
ISBN 0-09-144600-7 : £1.95 : CIP rev.
B81-05119

398'.45 — Great Britain. Fairies, *to 1945*

Spence, Lewis. British fairy origins. — Wellingborough : Aquarian Press, Sept.1981. — [224]p
Originally published: London : Watts, 1946
ISBN 0-85030-262-5 (pbk) : £3.95 : CIP entry
B81-20507

398'.45 — Ireland. Fairies

Logan, Patrick. The old gods : the facts about Irish fairies. — Belfast : Appletree Press, July 1981. — [160]p
ISBN 0-904651-82-7 (cased) : £6.95 : CIP entry
ISBN 0-904651-83-5 (pbk) : £3.95 B81-18069

398'.45'0222 — Fabulous beings — *Illustrations — For children*

O'Brien, John, *1953-*. Elves, gnomes & other little people : coloring book / John O'Brien. — New York : Dover ; London : Constable, 1980. — 38p : chiefly ill ; 28cm. — (Dover coloring book)
Ill on inside covers
ISBN 0-486-24049-5 (pbk) : £1.30 B81-09662

398'.469 — British tales & legends. Special subjects: Dragons — *Critical studies*

Simpson, Jacqueline. British dragons / Jacqueline Simpson. — London : Batsford, 1980. — 160p,[8]p of plates : ill ; 24cm
Bibliography: p153-155. — Includes index
ISBN 0-7134-2559-8 : £9.95 B81-15712

398′.469 — Fabulous beasts

Headon, Deirdre. Mythical beasts / Deirdre Headon ; illustrated by Alan Baker. — London : Hutchinson, 1981. — [56]p : ill(some col.) ; 18cm. — (The Leprechaun library)
Bibliography: p[56]
ISBN 0-09-145560-x : £1.95 : CIP rev. B81-22612

Lurie, Alison. Fabulous beasts / Alison Lurie ; illustrated by Monika Beisner. — London : Cape, 1981. — [32]p : col.ill ; 26cm
ISBN 0-224-01971-6 : £3.95 : CIP rev. B81-27336

398′.469 — Fabulous beasts — *For children*

Fagg, Christopher. Fabulous beasts / by Christopher Fagg ; illustrated by Steve Weston ; edited by Hannah E. Glease. — London (116 Baker St., W.1) : Kingfisher, 1980. — 24p : col.ill ; 23cm. — (Kingfisher explorer books. mysteries)
Bibliography: p24. — Includes index
ISBN 0-7063-6044-3 : £1.95 B81-03555

398.6 — FOLKLORE. RIDDLES

398′.6 — Traditional riddles in Old English — *Anthologies — English texts*

[Exeter book. *Selections*]. Old English riddles : from the Exeter book / [selected and translated by] Michael Alexander. — London : Anvil Press Poetry, 1980. — 71p ; 22cm. — (Poetica ; 11)
ISBN 0-85646-070-2 (pbk) : £2.95 B81-13361

398.8 — FOLKLORE. RHYMES, FOLK SONGS, GAMES

398′.8 — Children's counting-out rhymes in English — *Anthologies*

Counting-out rhymes : a dictionary / edited by Roger D. Abrahams and Lois Rankin. — Austin ; London : University of Texas Press, c1980. — xix,243p ; 24cm. — (Publications of the American Folklore Society. Bibliographical and special series ; v.31)
Bibliography: p223-243
ISBN 0-292-71057-7 : £10.50 B81-04430

398′.8 — Nursery rhymes in English — *Anthologies*

100 nursery rhymes / [illustrators Glynnis i.e., Glenys Ambrus et al.]. — London : Hamlyn, 1980. — 157p : col.ill ; 22cm
Includes index
ISBN 0-600-36462-3 : £2.50 B81-00084

Baa, baa, black sheep and other rhymes. — [London] : Macmillan Children's, c1981. — [12]p : col.ill ; 15x19cm. — (First nursery rhyme books)
Compiled by Lynda Snowdon, illustrated by David Mostyn
ISBN 0-333-30482-9 (unbound) : £0.75 B81-29856

The **Collins** book of nursery rhymes / [illustrations Niki Daly ... et al.]. — London : Collins, 1981. — 122p : col.ill ; 29cm
Includes index
ISBN 0-00-195215-3 : £4.95 B81-37289

Cope, Dawn. Humpty Dumpty's favourite nursery rhymes / Dawn and Peter Cope. — Exeter : Webb & Bower, 1981. — 64p : col.ill,music ; 26cm
ISBN 0-906671-07-8 : £3.95 B81-35270

Doctor Foster and other rhymes. — [London] : Macmillan Children's, c1981. — [12]p : col.ill ; 15x19cm. — (First nursery rhyme books)
Compiled by Lynda Snowdon, illustrated by David Mostyn
ISBN 0-333-28956-0 (unbound) : £0.75 B81-29853

An **Enchanting** book of nursery rhymes / illustrated by Janet & Ann Grahame Johnstone. — London : Dean, c1972 (1980 [printing]). — [116]p : chiefly col.ill ; 28cm
ISBN 0-603-00198-x : £2.50 B81-05866

Hey diddle diddle and other rhymes. — [London] : Macmillan Children's, c1981. — [12]p : col.ill ; 15x19cm. — (First nursery rhyme books)
Compiled by Lynda Snowdon, illustrated by Lynne Cousins
ISBN 0-333-28957-9 (unbound) : £0.75 B81-29854

Jack and Jill and other rhymes. — [London] : Macmillan Children's, c1981. — [12]p : col.ill ; 15x19cm. — (First nursery rhyme books)
Compiled by Lynda Snowdon, illustrated by David Mostyn
ISBN 0-333-30481-0 (unbound) : £0.75 B81-29855

Little tot's nursery rhymes. — London : Dean, c1980. — [24]p : col.ill ; 13cm. — (Dean's little tots' series)
ISBN 0-603-00196-3 (pbk) : £0.15 B81-06341

The **Mother** Goose book / illustrated by Alice and Martin Provensen. — [London] : Beaver, 1981, c1976. — 60p : col.ill ; 28cm
Originally published: New York : Random House, 1976 ; London : Julia MacRae Books, 1980. — Includes index
ISBN 0-600-20478-2 (pbk) : £1.95 B81-34868

Mother Goose comes to Cable Street : nursery rhymes for today / chosen by Rosemary Stones and Andrew Mann ; illustrated by Dan Jones. — Harmondsworth : Puffin, 1980, c1977. — [30]p : col.ill ; 23cm. — (Picture puffins)
Originally published: Harmondsworth : Kestrel, 1977
ISBN 0-14-050313-7 (pbk) : £0.80 B81-00843

398′.8 — Nursery rhymes in English - *Anthologies*

My big book of nursery rhymes. — London : Ward Lock, Apr.1981. — [128]p
ISBN 0-7063-6129-6 : £3.95 : CIP entry B81-07484

398′.8 — Nursery rhymes in English — *Anthologies*

Nicola Bayley's book of nursery rhymes. — Harmondsworth : Puffin, 1981, c1975. — [32]p : col.ill ; 23cm. — (Picture Puffins)
Illustrations by Nicola Bayley. — Originally published: London : Cape, 1975
ISBN 0-14-050371-4 (pbk) : £1.25 B81-27687

Nursery rhymes / illustrated by Hutchings Studio ; edited by Jane Carruth. — Maidenhead : Purnell, 1974 (1981 [printing]). — [28]p : col.ill ; 25cm. — (My first colour library)
Text, ill on lining papers
ISBN 0-361-05048-8 : £0.99 B81-14296

Nursery rhymes / illustrated by Jannat Houston. — London : Pan, 1981. — 24p : col.ill ; 22cm. — (Piccolo picture classics) (A Piccolo original)
ISBN 0-330-26335-8 (pbk) : £8.80 B81-09871

Nursery rhymes / illustrated by Lynn N. Grundy. — Loughborough : Ladybird Books, 1981. — [28]p : col.ill ; 19cm
Text, ill on lining papers
ISBN 0-7214-9511-7 : £0.95 B81-34070

Popular nursery rhymes / edited by Jennifer Mulherin. — London : Granada, 1981. — 160p : ill(some col.),music,facsims,ports ; 29cm
Includes index
ISBN 0-246-11492-4 : £5.95 B81-28620

Tom, Tom, the piper's son and other rhymes. — [London] : Macmillan Children's, c1981. — [12]p : col.ill ; 15x19cm. — (First nursery rhyme books)
Compiled by Lynda Snowdon, illustrated by Lynne Cousins
ISBN 0-333-30480-2 (unbound) : £0.75 B81-29852

Traditional nursery rhymes : and children's verse / collected by Michael Foss ; designed by Leslie & Lorraine Gerry. — London : Book Club Associates, 1976. — 184p : ill(some col.) ; 25cm
Includes index
Unpriced B81-37884

398′.8 — Rhymes in English, *to 1980*. **Origins**

Harrowven, Jean. The origins of rhymes, songs and sayings / Jean Harrowven. — London : Kaye & Ward, 1977 (1980 [printing]). — xi,356p : ill,1port ; 23cm
Bibliography: p333-334. — Includes index
ISBN 0-7182-1267-3 : £6.75
Also classified at 784 B81-04959

398′.8 — Tongue-twisters in English — *Anthologies — For children*

Rogers, Janet. The Beaver book of tongue twisters / Janet Rogers ; illustrated by Graham Thompson. — [London] : Beaver, 1981. — 94p : ill ; 18cm
ISBN 0-600-20385-9 (pbk) : £0.80 B81-37822

398.9 — FOLKLORE. PROVERBS

398′.9 — Proverbs — *Anthologies*

Houghton, Patricia. A world of proverbs / Patricia Houghton. — Poole : Blandford, 1981. — 152p : ill ; 23cm
Includes index
ISBN 0-7137-1114-0 : £4.95 : CIP rev. B81-22536

398′.9′21 — Sayings in English — *Anthologies — For children*

Hughes, Shirley. Over the moon : a book of sayings / chosen and illustrated by Shirley Hughes. — London : Faber, 1980. — [48]p : ill ; 22cm
ISBN 0-571-11594-2 : £3.25 : CIP rev. B80-12323

400 — LANGUAGE

400 — Language

Language and language use : a reader / edited by A.K. Pugh, V.J. Lee and J. Swann. — London : Heinemann Educational in association with The Open University Press, 1980. — viii,406p : ill,2maps ; 23cm
Includes bibliographies and index
ISBN 0-435-10720-8 (cased) : £10.50 : CIP rev.
ISBN 0-435-10721-6 (pbk) : £5.95 B80-25489

Language in use. — Milton Keynes : Open University Press. — (Education studies : a second level course)
At head of title: The Open University
Block 2: Social aspects of language / introduction to block 2 prepared by Peter Griffith for the course team. — 1981. — 110p : ill ; 30cm. — (E263 ; block 2, Parts I-II)
Bibliography: p107-109. — Contents: Part I: The development of social views of language — Part II: Language and social reality — Part III: Linguistic and social determinism
ISBN 0-335-13041-0 (pbk) : Unpriced B81-18012

Language in use / [the E263 Course Team]. — Milton Keynes : Open University Press. — (Educational studies : a second level course)
At head of title: The Open University
Block 3: Language learning and language teaching / introduction to block 3 prepared by Ken Richardson for the Course Team. — 1981. — 152p : ill,maps,facsims ; 30cm. — (E263 ; block 3)
Includes bibliographies. — Contents: Part 1 : Language learning — Part 2 : Language teaching
ISBN 0-335-13042-9 (pbk) : Unpriced B81-25370

Language perspectives. — London : Heinemann Educational, Jan.1982. — [192]p
ISBN 0-435-10910-3 (pbk) : £4.95 : CIP entry B81-34503

Standard languages. — Manchester : Manchester University Press, Oct.1981. — [176]p. — (Mont Follick series ; v.5)
ISBN 0-7190-0774-7 : £10.50 : CIP entry B81-28090

400 — Language. Errors — *Conference proceedings*

Errors in linguistic performance : slips of the tongue, ear, pen, and hand / edited by Victoria A. Fromkin. — New York ; London : Academic Press, 1980. — x,334p : ill ; 24cm
Conference papers. — Includes bibliographies and index
ISBN 0-12-268980-1 : £15.00 B81-17266

400 — Language — *Feminist viewpoints*

Spender, Dale. Man made language / Dale Spender. — London : Routledge & Kegan Paul, 1980. — xi,250p ; 22cm
Bibliography: p236-245. — Includes index
ISBN 0-7100-0675-6 (pbk) : £4.95 : CIP rev. B80-26923

400 — Languages — *For schools*

Introduction to language / T.R.W. Aplin ... [et al.] ; edited by P.J. Downes ; illustrations by Jan Pickett. — London : Hodder and Stoughton, 1981. — 64p : ill,maps ; 25cm
ISBN 0-340-26031-9 (pbk) : £1.25 B81-31860

400′.92′4 — Language. Theories of Harmann, Johann Georg

German, Terence J.. Harmann on language and religion. — Oxford : Oxford University Press, Oct.1981. — [216]p. — (Oxford theological monographs)
ISBN 0-19-826717-7 : £12.50 : CIP entry
Primary classification 200′.92′4 B81-26752

401 — Language — *Philosophical perspectives*

Dilman, Ilham. Studies in language and reason / Ilham Dilman. — London : Macmillan, 1981. — x,218p ; 23cm
Bibliography: p211-213. — Includes index
ISBN 0-333-28445-3 : £15.00 B81-23263

Katz, Jerrold J.. Language and other abstract objects. — Oxford : Blackwell, Nov.1981. — [272]p
ISBN 0-631-12946-4 : £13.50 : CIP entry B81-30171

401 — Language — *Philosophical perspectives — Conference proceedings*

Philosophy and grammar : papers on the occasion of the Quincentennial of Uppsala University / edited by Stig Kanger and Sven Öhman. — Dordrecht ; London : Reidel, c1981. — 158p : ill ; 23cm. — (Synthese library ; v.143)
Includes one chapter in German. — Includes bibliographies and index
ISBN 90-277-1091-0 : Unpriced B81-04730

401 — Language. Pragmatics

Radical pragmatics / edited by Peter Cole. — New York ; London : Academic Press, c1981. — xiv,328p : ill ; 24cm
Includes bibliographies and index
ISBN 0-12-179660-4 : £19.40 B81-34433

Speech act theory and pragmatics / edited by John R. Searle, Ferenc Kiefer and Manfred Bierwisch. — Dordrecht ; London : Reidel, c1980. — xii,317p : ill ; 23cm. — (Synthese language library ; v.10)
Includes bibliographies and index
ISBN 90-277-1043-0 : Unpriced
ISBN 90-277-1045-7 (pbk) : Unpriced
Primary classification 410 B81-14686

401′.9 — Autistic children. Language

Fay, Warren H.. Emerging language in autistic children / by Warren H. Fay and Adriana Luce Schuler. — London : Edward Arnold, c1980. — xiii,216p ; 24cm. — (Language intervention series ; v.5)
Originally published: Baltimore : University Park Press, 1980. — Bibliography: p191-209. — Includes index
ISBN 0-7131-6329-1 : £10.50 : CIP rev. B80-33414

401′.9 — Children, 7 to 14 years. Language skills. Development. Assessment

Assessing language development / Andrew Wilkinson ... [et al.]. — Oxford : Oxford University Press, 1980. — ix,246p : ill ; 21cm. — (Oxford studies in education)
Bibliography: p241-246
ISBN 0-19-911102-2 (pbk) : £3.50 B81-03628

401′.9 — Children. Language skills. Acquisition

The **child's** construction of language. — London : Academic Press, Jan.1982. — [370]p
ISBN 0-12-213580-6 : CIP entry B81-34117

401′.9 — Children. Language skills. Acquisition. Phonological aspects — *Conference proceedings*

Child phonology / edited by Grace H. Yeni-Komshian, James F. Kavanagh, Charles A. Ferguson. — New York ; London : Academic Press. — (Perspectives in neurolinguistics, neuropsychology and psycholinguistics)
Vol.1: Production. — 1980. — xiv,304p : ill ; 24cm
Conference papers. — Includes bibliographies and index
ISBN 0-12-770601-1 : £15.20 B81-17000

401′.9 — Children. Language skills. Acquisition. Psychological aspects

Karmiloff-Smith, Annette. A functional approach to child language : a study of determiners and reference / Annette Karmiloff-Smith. — Cambridge : Cambridge University Press, 1979 (1981 [printing]). — vi,258p : ill ; 23cm
Bibliography: p242-251. — Includes index
ISBN 0-521-28549-6 (pbk) : £6.50 B81-40809

401′.9 — Children. Language skills. Acquisition — *Serials*

First language. — Vol.1, pt.1, no.1 (Feb.1980)-. — Chalfont St Giles (Halfpenny Furze, Mill Lane, Chalfont St Giles, Buckinghamshire HP8 4NR) : Alpha Academic, 1980-. — v. ; 21cm
Three issues yearly
ISSN 0142-7237 = First language : £12.50 per year B81-02341

401′.9 — Children. Language skills. Development

Children's language. — New York : Gardner ; New York ; London : Distributed by Halsted
Includes bibliographies and index
Vol.2 / edited by Keith E. Nelson. — [c1980]. — xvi,607p : ill ; 24cm
ISBN 0-470-26716-x : £18.70 B81-09787

Elliot, Alison J.. Child language. — Cambridge : Cambridge University Press, 1981. — vi,194p ; 24cm. — (Cambridge textbooks in linguistics)
Bibliography: p176-190. - Includes index
ISBN 0-521-22518-3 (cased) : £12.50 : CIP rev.
ISBN 0-521-22556-4 (pbk) : £4.50 B81-13533

Hastings, Phyllis. Encouraging language development. — London : Croom Helm, June 1981. — [96]p. — (Croom Helm special education series)
ISBN 0-7099-0286-7 (cased) : £8.95 : CIP entry
ISBN 0-7099-0287-5 (pbk) : £4.50 B81-12877

Reynell, Joan. Language development and assessment / Joan Reynell. — Lancaster : MTP, 1980. — 176p : ill ; 23cm. — (Studies in development paediatrics ; v.1)
Bibliography: p165-167. — Includes index
ISBN 0-85200-300-5 : £7.95 : CIP rev. B79-31144

Wood, Barbara S.. Children and communication : verbal and nonverbal language development / Barbara S. Wood. — 2nd ed. — Englewood Cliffs ; London : Prentice-Hall, c1981. — viii,296p : ill ; 24cm
Previous ed.: 1976. — Includes bibliographies and index
ISBN 0-13-131920-5 : £10.35 B81-25054

401′.9 — Children. Language skills. Development — *Conference proceedings*

Language and learning in home and school. — London : Heinemann Educational, Jan.1982. — [224]p. — (Language and learning series)
Conference papers
ISBN 0-435-10192-7 : £7.50 : CIP entry B81-34502

401′.9 — Children. Language skills. Development — *Manuals — For teaching*

Moyle, Donald. Children's words : a practical guide to helping children overcome difficulties in learning to read, write, speak and spell. — London : Grant McIntyre, Feb.1982. — [192]p
ISBN 0-86216-032-4 (cased) : £10.95 : CIP entry
ISBN 0-86216-033-2 (pbk) : £3.95 B81-40239

401′.9 — Children, to 7 years. Language skills. Development

Wells, Gordon. Learning through interaction : the study of language development / Gordon Wells, with contributions by Allayne Bridges ... [et al.]. — Cambridge : Cambridge University Press, 1981. — viii,304p : ill ; 23cm. — (Language at home and at school ; 1)
Bibliography: p283-298. - Includes index
ISBN 0-521-23774-2 (cased) : £20.00
ISBN 0-521-28219-5 (pbk) : £6.50 B81-15984

401′.9 — Children, to 8 years. Language skills. Development — *For teaching*

Flood, James. Language/reading instruction for the young child / James Flood, Diane Lapp. — New York : Macmillan ; London : Collier Macmillan, c1981. — viii,535p : ill,plan ; 26cm
Includes bibliographies and index
ISBN 0-02-338470-0 : £10.95 B81-15623

401′.9 — Foreign language skills. Acquisition. Psychological aspects

McDonough, Steven H.. Psychology in foreign language teaching / Steven H. McDonough. — London : Allen & Unwin, 1981. — 168p : ill ; 23cm
Bibliography: p157-166. — Includes index
ISBN 0-04-418002-0 : £10.00 (pbk) : £3.95 B81-16049

401′.9 — Great Britain. Hotel & catering industries. Personnel. Language skills

'Qué?' : how to identify communications training needs in the multi-racial workplace. — [Wembley] ([Ramsey House, Central Sq., Wembley, Middx HA9 7AP]) : [Hotel and Catering Industry Training Board], [1981?]. — 27p ; 30cm
Cover title
Unpriced (pbk) B81-33183

401′.9 — Language. Comprehension. Thought processes — *Conference proceedings*

Elements of discourse understanding / edited by Aravind K. Joshi, Bonnie L. Webber, Ivan A. Sag. — Cambridge : Cambridge University Press, 1981. — ix,341p : ill ; 24cm
Conference papers. — Includes bibliographies and index
ISBN 0-521-23327-5 : £22.50 B81-38004

401′.9 — Language. Psychological aspects

Paivio, Allan. Psychology of language / Allan Paivio, Ian Begg. — Englewood Cliffs ; London : Prentice-Hall, c1981. — xiv,417p : ill ; 24cm
Bibliography: p378-405. — Includes index
ISBN 0-13-735951-9 : £12.95 B81-22717

401′.9 — Language. Social aspects

Steiner, George, *1929-*. On difficulty : and other essays / George Steiner. — Oxford : Oxford University Press, 1978 (1980 [printing]). — xi,209p ; 21cm. — (Oxford paperbacks)
Originally published: 1978. — Includes index
ISBN 0-19-281314-5 (pbk) : £2.95 B81-29364

401′.9 — Language. Social psychology — *Conference proceedings*

International Conference on Social Psychology and Language *(1st : 1979 : University of Bristol)*.
Language : social psychological perspectives : selected papers from the first International Conference on Social Psychology and Language held at the University of Bristol, England July 1979 / edited by Howard Giles, W. Peter Robinson and Philip M. Smith. — Oxford : Pergamon, 1980. — xv,442p : ill ; 26cm
Includes bibliographies and index
ISBN 0-08-024696-6 : £25.00 : CIP rev. B80-22907

401′.9 — Man. Spoken language *related to* **thought processes. Research**

Kreckel, M.. Communicative acts and shared knowledge in natural discourse. — London : Academic Press, Aug.1981. — [350]p
ISBN 0-12-426180-9 : CIP entry B81-18128

401′.9 — Pre-school children. Speech. Development. Role of mothers

Howe, Christine. Acquiring language in a conversational context / Christine Howe. — London : Academic Press, 1981. — xiii,149p : ill ; 24cm. — (Behavioural development)
Bibliography: p135-141. — Includes index
ISBN 0-12-356920-6 : £10.20 : CIP rev. B81-11932

401′.9 — Psycholinguistics

Loar, Brian. Mind and meaning. — Cambridge : Cambridge University Press, Dec.1981. — [268]p. — (Cambridge studies in philosophy)
ISBN 0-521-22959-6 : £22.00 : CIP entry
Primary classification 128′.2 B81-37004

Miller, George A.. Language and speech / George A. Miller. — Oxford : W.H. Freeman, c1981. — viii,150p : ill(some col.) ; 25cm
Bibliography: p146. — Includes index
ISBN 0-7167-1297-0 (cased) : £8.20
ISBN 0-7167-1298-9 (pbk) : £3.50 B81-38412

Speech, place, and action. — Chichester : Wiley, Jan.1982. — [384]p
ISBN 0-471-10045-5 : £15.00 : CIP entry B81-34475

401′.9 — Psycholinguistics — *Conference proceedings*

Mutual knowledge. — London : Academic Press, Feb.1982. — [250]p
Conference papers
ISBN 0-12-652980-9 : CIP entry B81-35909

401′.9 — Sociolinguistics

Saville-Troike, Muriel. The ethnography of communication. — Oxford : Blackwell, Jan.1982. — [240]p. — (Language in society ; no.3)
ISBN 0-631-12781-x (cased) : £12.50 : CIP entry
ISBN 0-631-12725-9 (pbk) : £6.50 B81-34294

401′.9 — Speech acts — *Sociolinguistic perspectives*

Burton, Deirdre. Dialoque and discourse : a sociolinguistic approach to modern drama dialogue and naturally occurring conversation / Deirdre Burton. — London : Routledge & Kegan Paul, 1980. — xi,210p : ill ; 23cm
Bibliography: p190-202. - Includes index
ISBN 0-7100-0560-1 : £12.50 : CIP rev.
Primary classification 822′.914′0926 B80-17940

401′.9 — Twins, 1-3 years. Language skills. Acquisition — *Study examples: Serbo-Croatian language*

Savić, Svenka. How twins learn to talk : a study of the speech development of twins from 1 to 3 / Svenka Savić ; translated into English by Vladislaua Felbabov. — London : Academic Press, 1980. — xiv,195p : ill ; 24cm
Bibliography: p182-190. - Includes index
ISBN 0-12-619580-3 : £15.00 : CIP rev. B80-11000

401′.9 — Verbal deficit

Gordon, J. C. B.. Verbal deficit. — London : Croom Helm, July 1981. — [176]p
ISBN 0-85664-990-2 : £8.95 : CIP entry B81-13744

401′.9 — Wales. Children. Language skills. Influence of bilingual mothers

Harrison, Godfrey. Bilingual mothers in Wales and the language of their children. — Cardiff : University of Wales Press, Nov.1981. — [101] p. — (Social science monographs ; no.6)
ISBN 0-7083-0794-9 (pbk) : £5.00 : CIP entry B81-30900

405 — Language — *Serials*

Speech and language. — Vol.3. — New York ; London : Academic Press, 1980. — xiii,311p
ISBN 0-12-608603-6 : £19.40
ISSN 0193-3434
Primary classification 612′.78′05 B81-16747

Speech and language. — Vol.4. — New York ; London : Academic Press, 1980. — xii,392p
ISBN 0-12-608604-4 : Unpriced
ISSN 0193-3434
Primary classification 612′.78′05 B81-30758

Studies of meaning, language & change. — No.9 (June 1980)-. — Bristol (6 Carmarthen Rd, Westbury-on-Trym, Bristol) : Rain Publications, 1980-. — v. ; 21cm
Three issues yearly. — Continues: Acid rain. — Description based on: No.10-11 (Oct.1980-Feb.1981)
ISSN 0261-3212 = Studies of meaning, language & change : £1.20 per year B81-23137

405 — Modern languages — *Serials*

The **Year's** work in modern language studies. — Vol.41 (1979). — London : The Modern Humanities Research Association, 1980. — 1260p
ISBN 0-900547-73-1 : Unpriced
ISSN 0084-4152
Also classified at 809 B81-09113

407 — Language. Learning by children — *Conference proceedings*

Language acquisition and linguistic theory / edited by Susan L. Tavakolian. — Cambridge, Mass. ; London : M.I.T., c1981. — ix,233p : ill ; 24cm
Conference papers. — Bibliography: p210-222. — Includes index
ISBN 0-262-20039-2 : £12.40 B81-38136

407 — Languages. Teaching. Applications of linguistics

Gannon, Peter. Using linguistics : an educational focus / Peter Gannon and Pam Czerniewska. — London : Edward Arnold, 1980. — 220p ; 22cm
Bibliography: p207-214. — Includes index
ISBN 0-7131-6294-5 (pbk) : £5.75 : CIP rev. B80-19161

Leontiev, A. A.. Psychology and the language learning process / A.A. Leontiev ; edited by C.V. James. — Oxford : Pergamon, 1981. — xi,159p ; 22cm. — (Language teaching methodology series)
ISBN 0-08-024601-x (cased) : Unpriced : CIP rev. B81-38614

407 — Languages. Teaching — *For language teaching*

Johnson, Keith. Communicative language teaching. — Oxford : Pergamon, Nov.1981. — [160]p. — (Language teaching methodology series)
ISBN 0-08-025355-5 : £4.95 : CIP entry B81-28799

407′.8 — England. Secondary schools. Curriculum subjects: Languages. Teaching. Use of Audio-visual aids. Research projects. Schools Council. Communication and Social Skills Project

Lorac, Carol. Communication and social skills. — Exeter : Wheaton, Apr.1981. — [206]p
ISBN 0-08-026427-1 (cased) : £8.00 : CIP entry
ISBN 0-08-026426-3 (pbk) : £4.75 B81-11946

407′.8 — Schools. Curriculum subjects: Languages. Teaching. Use of audio-visual aids: Video equipment

Video in the language classroom. — London : Allen & Unwin, Aug.1981. — [208]p. — (Practical language teaching ; no.7)
ISBN 0-04-371079-4 (pbk) : £3.50 : CIP entry B81-15880

409′.2′4 — Language. Philosophical perspectives. Theories of Frege, Gottlob

Dummett, Michael. Frege : philosophy of language / Michael Dummett. — 2nd ed. — London : Duckworth, 1981. — xliii,708p ; 25cm
Previous ed.: 1973. — Bibliography: p685-693. — Includes index
ISBN 0-7156-1568-8 : £28.00 B81-26021

409′.39′4 — Ancient Middle East. Languages — *Festschriften*

Societies and languages of the ancient Near East. — Warminster : Aris and Phillips, Feb.1982. — [368]p
ISBN 0-85668-205-5 (pbk) : £15.00 : CIP entry B81-35723

409′.47 — Soviet Union. Languages

Comrie, Bernard. The languages of the Soviet Union / Bernard Comrie. — Cambridge : Cambridge University Press, 1981. — xx,317p : 1map ; 24cm. — (Cambridge language surveys)
Bibliography: p290-300. — Includes index
ISBN 0-521-23230-9 (cased) : £27.50
ISBN 0-521-29877-6 (pbk) : £8.50 B81-25934

409′.678 — Tanzania. Languages

Language in Tanzania / editors Edgar C. Polomé, C.P. Hill ; foreword by N.A. Kuhanga. — Oxford : Published for the International African Institute by Oxford University Press, 1980. — xiii,428p : ill,maps,form ; 23cm. — (Ford Foundation language surveys)
Includes bibliographies and index
ISBN 0-19-724205-7 (corrected) : £10.00 B81-19921

409′.73 — United States. Languages, *to 1980*

Language in the USA / edited by Charles A. Ferguson Shirley Brice Heath with the assistance of David Hwang ; foreword by Dell H. Hymes. — Cambridge : Cambridge University Press, 1981. — xxxviii,592p : ill,maps ; 24cm
Bibliography: p534-575. — Includes index
ISBN 0-521-23140-x : £30.00
ISBN 0-521-29834-2 (pbk) : £12.50 B81-38288

410 — LINGUISTICS

410 — Contrastive linguistics

Contrastive linguistics and the language teacher. — Oxford : Pergamon, Aug.1981. — [160]p. — (Language teaching methodology series)
ISBN 0-08-027230-4 (pbk) : £6.00 : CIP entry B81-16400

410 — Linguistics

Essays on linguistics : language systems & structures / by members of the Institute of Linguistics, USSR Academy of Science ; [translated from the Russian] by Christopher English. — Moscow : Progress Publishers ; [London] : Distributed by Central Books, 1980. — iv,298p ; 21cm
Translation of: Ocherki po lingvistike
£4.95 B81-03288

Kress, Gunther. Language as ideology / Gunther Kress and Robert Hodge. — London : Routledge & Kegan Paul, 1979 (1981 [printing]). — x,163p : 1ill ; 22cm
Bibliography: p152-158. - Includes index
ISBN 0-7100-0795-7 (pbk) : £3.75 B81-09549

Lyons, John. Language and linguistics : an introduction / John Lyons. — Cambridge : Cambridge University Press, 1981. — 356p : ill ; 23cm
Bibliography: p333-350. — Includes index
ISBN 0-521-23034-9 (cased) : £15.00 : CIP rev.
ISBN 0-521-29775-3 (pbk) : £4.50 B81-10505

410 — Linguistics — *Festschriften*

Crossing the boundaries in linguistics : studies presented to Manfred Bierwisch / edited by Wolfgang Klein and Willem Levelt. — Dordrecht ; London : Reidel, c1981. — x,292p : ill,1port ; 23cm. — (Synthese language library ; v.13)
Includes bibliographies and index
ISBN 90-277-1259-x : Unpriced B81-33275

Linguistic studies in honour of Paul Christophersen / edited by Robin Thelwall. — Coleraine : New University of Ulster, 1980. — viii,191p : maps ; 21cm. — (Occasional papers in linguistics and language learning, ISSN 0308-2075 ; no.7)
Includes bibliographies
£2.50 (pbk) B81-15377

410 — Speech acts

Speech act theory and pragmatics / edited by John R. Searle, Ferenc Kiefer and Manfred Bierwisch. — Dordrecht ; London : Reidel, c1980. — xii,317p : ill ; 23cm. — (Synthese language library ; v.10)
Includes bibliographies and index
ISBN 90-277-1043-0 : Unpriced
ISBN 90-277-1045-7 (pbk) : Unpriced
Also classified at 401 B81-14686

410 — Texts. Linguistic aspects

Beaugrande, Robert-Alain de. Introduction to text linguistics / Robert-Alain de Beaugrande, Wolfgang Ulrich Dressler. — London : Longman, 1981. — xv,270p : ill ; 22cm. — (Longman linguistics library ; no.26)
Translation of: Einführung in die Textlinguistik. — Bibliography: p225-254. — Includes index
ISBN 0-582-55486-1 (cased) : Unpriced
ISBN 0-582-55485-3 (pbk) : £5.50 B81-38267

410'.28'54 — Linguistics. Applications of digital computer systems — *Serials*

ALLC journal. — Vol.1, no.1 (Summer 1980)-. — Cambridge (Dr J.L. Dawson, University of Cambridge Literary and Linguistic Computing Centre, Sidgwick Site, Cambridge, CB3 9DA) : Association of Literary and Linguistic Computing, 1980-. — v. : ill ; 30cm
Two issues yearly
Unpriced
Also classified at 802'.8'54 B81-06192

410'.3'21 — Linguistics — *Encyclopaedias*

Ducrot, Oswald. Encyclopedic dictionary of the sciences of language / by Oswald Ducrot and Tizvetan Todorov ; translated by Catherine Porter. — Oxford : Blackwell Reference, 1981. — xiii,380p : ill ; 24cm
Translation of: Dictionnaire encyclopédique des sciences du langage. — Includes index
ISBN 0-631-12793-3 : £15.00 : CIP rev.
B80-20548

410'.5 — Linguistics — *Serials*

Language & communication : an interdisciplinary journal. — Vol.1, no.1 (1981)-. — Oxford : Pergamon, 1981-. — v. ; 25cm
Three issues yearly
Unpriced
Also classified at 001.51'05 B81-13320

410'.9 — Linguistics, *1632-1980*

Aarsleff, Hans. From Locke to Saussure. — London : Athlone Press, Aug.1981. — [380]p
ISBN 0-485-30001-x : £18.00 : CIP entry
B81-18038

411 — Runes

Elliott, Ralph W. V.. Runes : an introduction / by Ralph W.V. Elliott. — Repr. with minor corrections. — Manchester : Manchester University Press, 1963, c1959 (1980 [printing]). — xvi,124p,xxivp of plates : ill,2maps ; 22cm
Bibliography: p110-116. - Includes index
ISBN 0-7190-0787-9 (pbk) : £3.95 B81-04434

Howard, Michael, *1948-*. The runes and other magical alphabets / by Michael Howard. — Wellingborough : Aquarian Press, 1978 (1981 [printing]). — 96p : ill,ports ; 22cm
Bibliography: p96
ISBN 0-85030-244-7 (pbk) : £2.50 B81-14772

411 — Writing systems

Nakanishi, Akira. Writing systems of the world : alphabets, syllabaries, pictograms / by Akira Nakanishi. — Rutland, Vt. : Tuttle ; London : Prentice-Hall [distributor], 1980. — 122p : ill,maps(some col.),facsims ; 27cm
Translation from the Japanese. — Col. maps on lining papers. — Bibliography: p117-118. — Includes index
ISBN 0-8048-1293-4 : Unpriced B81-18627

412 — Functional semantics

Dick, Simon C.. Studies in functional grammar / Simon C. Dick. — London : Academic Press, 1980. — xi,245p : ill ; 24cm
Bibliography: p230-238. — Includes index
ISBN 0-12-216350-8 : £16.40 : CIP rev.
Primary classification 415 B80-26929

412 — Language. Origins

Gans, Eric. The origin of language : a formal theory of representation / Eric Gans. — Berkeley ; London : University of California Press, c1981. — xiii,314p ; 24cm
ISBN 0-520-04202-6 : £12.00 B81-27505

412 — Semantics

Baldinger, Kurt. Semantic theory : towards a modern semantics / Kurt Baldinger ; translated by William C. Brown and edited by Roger Wright. — Oxford : Blackwell, 1980. — xxiv,320p : ill ; 22cm
Translation of: Teoría semántica. — Translation of: 'Teoria semantica, hacia una semantica moderna'. 2nd ed. Madrid : Ediciones Alcala, 1977. — Includes index
ISBN 0-631-10891-2 (cased) : £16.00 : CIP rev.
ISBN 0-631-11491-2 (pbk) : £6.50 B80-11387

Kates, Carol A.. Pragmatics and semantics : an empiricist theory / Carol A. Kates. — Ithaca ; London : Cornell University Press, 1980. — 253p ; 23cm
Bibliography: p237-247. — Includes index
ISBN 0-8014-1288-9 : £10.50 B81-10955

Palmer, F. R.. Semantics / F.R. Palmer. — 2nd ed. — Cambridge : Cambridge University Press, 1981. — vi,221p : ill ; 21cm
Previous ed.: 1976. — Bibliography: p208-213. — Includes index
ISBN 0-521-23966-4 (cased) : £12.50 : CIP rev.
ISBN 0-521-28376-0 (pbk) : £4.50 B81-21564

Wierzbicka, Anna. Lingua mentalis : the semantics of natural language / Anna Wierzbicka. — Sydney ; London : Academic Press, 1980. — xi,367p ; 24cm
Bibliography: p349-360. — Includes index
ISBN 0-12-750050-2 : £28.90 B81-16641

412 — Semantics — *Serials*

Syntax and semantics. — Vol.13. — New York ; London : Academic Press, c1980. — xv,403p
ISBN 0-12-613513-4 : £20.60
ISSN 0092-4563
Primary classification 415 B81-16737

Syntax and semantics. — Vol.14. — New York ; London : Academic Press, c1981. — xvii,301p
ISBN 0-12-613514-2 : £16.00
ISSN 0092-4563
Primary classification 415 B81-35088

412 — Semantics. Theories of Montague, Richard

Dowty, David R.. Introduction to Montague semantics / by David R. Dowty, Robert E. Wall and Stanley Peters. — Dordrecht ; London : Reidel, c1981. — xi,313p ; 23cm. — (Synthese language library ; v.11)
Includes bibliographies and index
ISBN 90-277-1141-0 (cased) : Unpriced
ISBN 90-277-1142-9 (pbk) : Unpriced
B81-07301

413'.028 — Indo-European languages. Lexicology

Beard, Robert, *1938-*. The Indo-European lexicon : a full synchronic theory / Robert Beard. — Amsterdam ; Oxford : North-Holland, c1981. — xvi,389p : ill ; 23cm. — (North-Holland linguistic series ; 44)
Bibliography: p357-374. — Includes index
ISBN 0-444-86214-5 : £21.75 B81-35332

413'.1 — Abbreviations — *Dictionaries*

De Sola, Ralph. Abbreviations dictionary : abbreviations, acronyms, anonyms, appellations, computer terminology ... / Ralph De Sola. — Expanded international 6th ed. — New York ; Oxford : Elsevier, c1981. — xvi,966p ; 23cm
Previous ed.: 1978
ISBN 0-444-00380-0 : Unpriced B81-38109

Paxton, John. Everyman's dictionary of abbreviations / by John Paxton. — Reprinted with revisions and supplement. — London : Dent, 1981. — xiii,384,[8]p ; 23cm. — (Everyman's reference library)
Originally published: 1974
ISBN 0-460-04538-5 : £7.95 B81-15482

413'.1 — Abbreviations - *Encyclopaedias*

Pugh, Eric. Pugh's dictionary of acronyms and abbreviations. — 4th ed. — London : Bingley, July 1981. — [344]p
Previous ed.: 1977
ISBN 0-85157-292-8 : £38.00 : CIP entry
B81-13758

414 — Man. Voice. Quality. Phonetic description

Laver, John. The phonetic description of voice quality / John Laver. — Cambridge : Cambridge University Press, 1980. — ix,186p : ill ; 24cm. — (Cambridge studies in linguistics, ISSN 0068-676x ; 31)
Bibliography: p166-180. - Includes index
ISBN 0-521-23176-0 : £15.00 : CIP rev.
B80-25494

414 — Phonetics

Catford, John Cunnison. Fundamental problems in phonetics. — Edinburgh : Edinburgh University Press, Jan.1982. — [278]p
Originally published: 1977
ISBN 0-85224-437-1 (pbk) : £12.00 : CIP entry
B81-39215

414'.01 — Phonology. Theories, *1950-1979*

Jones, Charles, *1939-*. Current issues in phonological theory : an inaugural lecture / by Charles Jones. — [Durham] : University of Durham, 1980. — 22p ; 22cm
Bibliography: p21-22
£0.60 (pbk) B81-05076

414'.02461 — Phonology — *For medicine*

Grunwell, Pamela. Clinical phonology. — London : Croom Helm, Oct.1981. — [208]p
ISBN 0-7099-1109-2 (pbk) : £7.95 : CIP entry
B81-25713

414'.09 — Phonetics, *to 1980 — Festschriften*

Towards a history of phonetics / edited by R.E. Asher and Eugénie J.A. Henderson. — Edinburgh : Edinburgh University Press, 1981. — xi,317p : ill,facsims,ports ; 24cm
Includes bibliographies and index
ISBN 0-85224-374-x : Unpriced B81-36318

415 — Functional grammar

Dick, Simon C.. Studies in functional grammar / Simon C. Dick. — London : Academic Press, 1980. — xi,245p : ill ; 24cm
Bibliography: p230-238. — Includes index
ISBN 0-12-216350-8 : £16.40 : CIP rev.
Also classified at 412 B80-26929

Predication and expression in functional grammar . — London : Academic Press, Dec.1981. — [250]p
ISBN 0-12-111350-7 : CIP entry B81-31333

415 — Language. Determiners. Semantic aspects — *Conference proceedings*

The **Semantics** of determiners / edited by Johan van der Auwera. — London : Croom Helm, c1980. — 309p : ill ; 23cm
Conference papers. — Includes bibliographies and index
ISBN 0-7099-0240-9 : £15.95 : CIP rev.
B80-11001

415 — Language. Intension. Ambiguity — *Conference proceedings*

Ambiguities in intensional contexts / edited by Frank Heny. — Dordrecht ; London : Reidel, c1981. — 1vii,285p : ill ; 23cm. — (Synthese language library ; v.12)
Includes bibliographies and index
ISBN 90-277-1167-4 (cased) : Unpriced
B81-05564

415 — Language. Morphology

Comrie, Bernard. Language universals and linguistic typology. — Oxford : Blackwell, Sept.1981. — [256]p
ISBN 0-631-12971-5 (cased) : £12.50 : CIP entry
ISBN 0-631-12618-x (pbk) : £6.50 B81-22616

415 — Languages. Grammar. Arc Pair theory

Johnson, David E.. Arc pair grammar / David E. Johnson, Paul M. Postal. — Princeton ; Guildford : Princeton University Press, c1980. — xii,739p : ill ; 25cm
Bibliography: p715-723. - Includes index
ISBN 0-691-08270-7 : £19.50 B81-05860

415 — Languages. Questions

Questions / edited by Henry Hiz. — Dordrecht ; London : Reidel, c1979. — xvii,366p : ill ; 24cm. — (Synthese language library ; v.1)
Originally published: 1978. — Includes bibliographies and index
ISBN 90-277-0813-4 (cased) : Unpriced
ISBN 90-277-1035-x (pbk) : Unpriced B81-14687

415 — Languages. Surface structure. Transformational-generative theories

Fiengo, Robert. Surface structure : the interface of autonomous components / Robert Fiengo. — Cambridge, Mass. ; London : Harvard University Press, 1980. — 213p ; 24cm. — (The Language and thought series)
Bibliography: p205-209. — Includes index
ISBN 0-674-85725-9 : £13.50 B81-16568

415 — Man. Syntactic skills. Acquisition

Moulton, Janice. The organization of language / Janice Moulton & George M. Robinson. — Cambridge : Cambridge University Press, 1981. — xvi,389p : ill ; 24cm
Includes index
ISBN 0-521-23129-9 (cased) : £25.00
ISBN 0 521-53126-6 (pbk) : £7.95 B81-19007

415 — Spoken language. Discourse. Analysis

Edmondson, Willis. Spoken discourse. — London : Longman, June 1981. — [240]p. — (Longman linguistics library ; no.27)
ISBN 0-582-29120-8 (cased) : £9.95 : CIP entry
ISBN 0-582-29121-6 (pbk) : £5.95 B81-13793

Studies in discourse analysis / edited by Malcolm Coulthard and Martin Montgomery. — London : Routledge & Kegan Paul, 1981. — ix,198p ; 24cm
Bibliography: p184-192. — Includes index
ISBN 0-7100-0510-5 : £5.95 : CIP rev. B81-00844

415 — Syntax

Miller, J. E.. Syntax. — London : Hutchinson, Sept.1981. — [224]p
ISBN 0-09-144110-2 (cased) : £12.95 : CIP entry
ISBN 0-09-144111-2 (pbk) : £5.95 B81-22573

415 — Syntax — *Serials*

Syntax and semantics. — Vol.13. — New York ; London : Academic Press, c1980. — xv,403p
ISBN 0-12-613513-4 : £20.60
ISSN 0092-4563
Also classified at 412 B81-16737

Syntax and semantics. — Vol.14. — New York ; London : Academic Press, c1981. — xvii,301p
ISBN 0-12-613514-2 : £16.00
ISSN 0092-4563
Also classified at 412 B81-35088

415 — Syntax. Transformational-generative theories

Binding and filtering. — London : Croom Helm, May 1981. — [320]p. — (Croom Helm linguistics series)
ISBN 0-7099-0386-3 : £15.95 : CIP entry B81-06881

417′.2 — Creole languages — *Conference proceedings*

Theoretical orientations in Creole studies : [proceedings of a symposium on theoretical orientations in Creole studies, held at St. Thomas, U.S. Virgin Islands, March 28-April 1, 1979] / edited by Albert Valdman, Arnold Highfield. — New York ; London : Academic Press, 1980. — xi,449p : ill ; 24cm
Includes bibliographies and index
ISBN 0-12-710160-8 : £16.60 B81-19328

417′.2 — Dialectology

Chambers, J. K.. Dialectology / J.K. Chambers, Peter Trudgill. — Cambridge : Cambridge University Press, 1980. — 218p : ill,maps ; 24cm. — (Cambridge textbooks in linguistics)
Bibliography: p209-214. - Includes index
ISBN 0-521-22401-2 (cased) : £15.00 : CIP rev.
ISBN 0-521-29473-8 (pbk) : £4.95 B80-25496

418 — Applied linguistics

Bell, Roger T.. An introduction to applied linguistics : approaches and methods in language teaching / Roger T. Bell. — London : Batsford Academic, 1981. — 270p : ill ; 23cm
Bibliography: p258-264. — Includes index
ISBN 0-7134-3683-2 (cased) : Unpriced
ISBN 0-7134-3684-0 (pbk) : £5.95 B81-33069

Crystal, David. Directions in applied linguistics / David Crystal. — London : Academic Press, 1981. — vii,179p : forms ; 24cm. — (Applied language studies)
Bibliography: p163-169. — Includes index
ISBN 0-12-198420-6 : £10.40 : CIP rev. B81-11931

418 — Idioms

Fernando, Chitra. On idiom : critical views and perspectives / by Chitra Fernando and Roger Flavell. — [Exeter] : University of Exeter, 1981. — iii,94p ; 21cm. — (Exeter linguistic studies ; v.5)
Bibliography: p89-94
ISBN 0-85989-137-2 (pbk) : £1.50 B81-26354

418 — Language. Usage

Language in use. — Milton Keynes : Open University Press. — (Educational studies : a second level course)
At head of title: The Open University
Block 1: Language variation and diversity / prepared by David Graddol for the Course Team. — 1981. — 125p : ill,col.maps,facsims,1port ; 30cm. — (E263 ; block 1)
Bibliography: p123-124
ISBN 0-335-13040-2 (pbk) : Unpriced B81-14596

418 — Language. Variety

Locating language in time and space / edited by William Labov. — New York ; London : Academic Press, c1980. — xx,271p : ill,maps ; 24cm. — (Quantitative analyses of linguistic structure ; v.1)
Includes bibliographies and index
ISBN 0-12-432101-1 : £13.80 B81-22206

418′.007 — Educational institutions. Curriculum subjects: Modern languages. Teaching. Use of drama

Holden, Susan. Drama in language teaching / Susan Holden. — Harlow : Longman, 1981. — ix,84p : ill ; 22cm. — (Longman handbooks for language teachers)
Bibliography: p81-83. - Includes index
ISBN 0-582-74600-0 (pbk) : Unpriced B81-19054

418′.007 — Foreign languages. Teaching — *Conference proceedings*

Pergamon Institute of English. *Seminar (1st : 1979 : Oxford).* Foreign language teaching : meeting individual needs : papers form the first Pergamon Institute of English Seminar Oxford, 1979 / edited by Howard B. Altman and C. Vaughan James. — Oxford : Pergamon, 1980. — x,135p : ill ; 21cm. — (Pergamon Institute of English (Oxford) Symposia)
Includes bibliographies
ISBN 0-08-024604-4 (pbk) : £3.95 : CIP rev. B80-05861

418′.007 — Foreign languages. Teaching. Methodology - *For industries*

Language incorporated. — Oxford : Pergamon, June 1981. — [128]p. — (Pergamon Institute of English (Oxford) symposia)
ISBN 0-08-024578-1 : £4.95 : CIP entry B81-09995

418′.007 — Schools. Curriculum subjects: Foreign languages. Reading — *For teaching*

Kellermann, Marcelle. The forgotten third skill : reading a foreign language / Marcelle Kellermann. — Oxford : Pergamon, 1981. — x,129p ; 22cm. — (Language teaching methodology series)
Bibliography: p127
ISBN 0-08-024599-4 (cased) : £5.95
ISBN 0-08-024598-6 (pbk) : £3.95 B81-11445

418′.007′1041 — Great Britain. Schools. Curriculum subjects: Foreign languages

Hawkins, Eric. Modern languages in the curriculum / Eric W. Hawkins. — Cambridge : Cambridge University Press, 1981. — xiv,322p ; 23cm
Bibliography: p309-319. - Includes index
ISBN 0-521-23211-2 (cased) : £9.50
ISBN 0-521-29871-7 (pbk) : £4.95 B81-17929

418′.007′1241 — Great Britain. Secondary schools. Curriculum subjects: Modern languages. Courses. Use of graded objectives

Harding, Ann. Graded objectives in modern languages / Ann Harding, Brian Page, Sheila Rowell. — London (20 Carlton House Terrace, SW1Y 5AP) : Centre for Information on Language Teaching and Research, 1980. — 137p ; 21cm
Bibliography: p129-137
ISBN 0-903466-28-7 (pbk) : £3.75 B81-05762

418′.007′1241 — Great Britain. Secondary schools. Curriculum subjects: Modern languages. Teaching

New objectives in modern language teaching / Oxfordshire Modern Languages Advisory Committee. — London : Hodder and Stoughton, c1981. — vi,90p ; 22cm
ISBN 0-340-24592-1 (pbk) : £3.25 : CIP rev. B80-19162

418′.007′15 — Adult education. Curriculum subjects: Foreign languages. Self-directed learning

Holec, Henri. Autonomy and foreign language learning / prepared for the Council of Europe by Henri Holec. — Oxford : Published for and on behalf of the Council of Europe by Pergamon, 1981, c1979. — v,51p : forms ; 25cm
Bibliography: p50-51. — Papers from the Council of Europe Modern Languages Project
ISBN 0-08-025357-1 (pbk) : £2.50 B81-27809

418′.007′15 — Europe. Adult education. Curriculum subjects: Foreign languages. European unit/credit system

Trim, J. L. M.. Developing a unit/credit scheme of adult language learning / prepared for the Council of Europe by J.L.M. Trim. — Oxford : Published for and on behalf of the Council of Europe by Pergamon, 1980. — v,74p : ill ; 26cm
Papers on the Council of Europe Modern Languages Project. — Previous ed.: 1978. — Bibliography: p73-74
ISBN 0-08-024596-x (pbk) : £4.75 : CIP rev. B80-12806

418′.02′01 — Languages. Translation. Theories

Newmark, Peter, *1916-*. Approaches to translation / Peter Newmark. — Oxford : Pergamon, 1981. — xiii,200p ; 26cm. — (Language teaching methodology series) (Pergamon Institute of English (Oxford))
Bibliography: p191-195. — Includes index
ISBN 0-08-024603-6 (cased) : Unpriced : CIP rev.
ISBN 0-08-024602-8 (pbk) : £4.95 B80-26930

419 — Deaf persons. Sign languages: British Sign Language. Manual signs — *Illustrations*

Sutcliffe, T. H.. Sign and say / T.H. Sutcliffe. — London : R.N.I.D., c1981. — 89p : chiefly ill ; 15x21cm
Text on inside cover
£1.25 (pbk) B81-36857

419 — Deaf persons. Sign languages: British Sign Language. Manual signs. Structure

Brennan, Mary. Words in hand : a structural analysis of the signs of British sign language / Mary Brennan, Martin D. Colville, Lilian K. Lawson. — Edinburgh (Moray House, Edinburgh) : British Sign Language Research Project, [1980]. — 262p : ill ; 30cm
Ill on inside covers. — Bibliography: p251-254. - Includes index
Unpriced (spiral) B81-19055

419 — Deaf persons. Sign languages: British Sign Language. Psycholinguistic aspects

Perspectives on British Sign Language and deafness / edited by B. Woll, J. Kyle and M. Deuchar. — London : Croom Helm, c1981. — 268p : ill ; 23cm
Bibliography: p247-262. — Includes index
ISBN 0-7099-2703-7 : £14.95 : CIP rev. B81-07921

420 — ENGLISH LANGUAGE

420 — English language

Hewett, Peter. English language & literature O Level : a course leading to the special NEC O Level examinations set by the Associated Examining Board in English Language O Level and English literature O Level / Peter Hewett and Jack Roberts. — Cambridge : National Extension College, c1979. — 3v. : ill ; 30cm. — (National Extension College correspondence texts ; course no. E18)
ISBN 0-86082-141-2 (pbk) : Unpriced
Also classified at 820.9 B81-13942

Partridge, Eric. Eric Partridge in his own words / with tributes by Anthony Burgess ... [et al.] ; edited by David Crystal. — London : Deutsch, 1980. — 251p ; 23cm
Bibliography: p239-244. - Includes index
ISBN 0-233-97300-1 : £6.50 : CIP rev.
B80-24405

Sparrow, John. Good English / by John Sparrow. — London : English Association, 1980. — 16p ; 22cm. — (Presidential address / English Association ; 1980)
ISBN 0-900232-07-2 (pbk) : Unpriced
B81-14618

420 — English language — *Festschriften*

Studies in English linguistics for Randolph Quirk / edited by Sidney Greenbaum, Geoffrey Leech & Jan Svartvik. — London : Longman, 1980, c1979. — xvi,304p,fold leaf : ill ; 23cm
Bibliography: p294-304
ISBN 0-582-55079-3 : £18.00 : CIP rev.
B80-07326

420 — English language. Variety

O'Donnell, W. R.. Variety in contemporary English / W.R. O'Donnell and Loreto Todd. — London : Allen & Unwin, 1980. — x,156p : ill,1map ; 23cm
Includes bibliographies and index
ISBN 0-04-421005-1 (cased) : £10.00 : CIP rev.
ISBN 0-04-421006-x (pbk) : £4.50 B80-12322

420'.1'9 — English language. Usage. Social aspects

Bolinger, Dwight. Language, the loaded weapon : the use and abuse of language today / Dwight Bolinger. — London : Longman, 1980. — ix,214p : ill ; 23cm
Bibliography: p202-204. — Includes index
ISBN 0-582-29107-0 (cased) : £9.95 : CIP rev.
ISBN 0-582-29108-9 (pbk) : £4.95 B80-25167

420'.7'1 — Schools. Curriculum subjects: English language. Teaching

Evans, Tricia. Teaching English. — London : Croom Helm, Nov.1981. — [224]p
ISBN 0-7099-0901-2 (cased) : £11.95 : CIP entry
ISBN 0-7099-0902-0 (pbk) : £5.95 B81-30985

420'.7'104121 — Scotland. Grampian Region. Schools. Curriculum subjects: English language. Teaching — *Serials*

GEV : Grampian English views : language and communication. — Vol.1, no.1 [1977?]-. — [Aberdeen] (c/o W. Hall, Aberdeen Grammar School [Skene St., Aberdeen]) : Grampian Regional Council, [1977?]. — v. : ill ; 21cm
Three issues yearly. — Description based on: Vol.3, no.3 (Mar.'80)
£1.40 per year B81-06455

420'.7'1042 — England. Schools. Curriculum subjects: English language. Teaching

Rosen, Harold. Neither Bleak House nor Liberty Hall : English in the curriculum / Harold Rosen. — London : University of London Institute of Education, c1981. — 24p ; 21cm
'An inaugural lecture delivered at the University of London Institute of Education on Wednesday, 4 March 1981'. — At head of title: University of London Institute of Education
ISBN 0-85473-109-1 (pbk) : £0.80 B81-28229

420'.7'1242 — England. Middle schools. Curriculum subjects: English language. Teaching

Haigh, Gerald. English 8 to 13 / Gerald Haigh. — London : Temple Smith, 1980. — 175p ; 23cm. — (Teaching in practice)
Includes index
ISBN 0-85117-195-8 (cased) : £9.95
ISBN 0-85117-206-7 (pbk) : £3.95
Also classified at 820'.7'1242 B81-00845

420'.7'1242 — England. Secondary schools. Curriculum. Role of English language — *Case studies*

Schools Council. *Language across the Curriculum Project*. Language across the curriculum : four case studies : the report of the School Council Language across the Curriculum Project / Irene Robertson ; edited with an introduction by Richard Choat ; foreword by Michael Marland. — London : Methuen Educational, 1980. — 175p : 1ill ; 21cm. — (Schools Council working paper, ISSN 0533-1668 ; 67)
Bibliography: p172-173
ISBN 0-423-50790-7 (pbk) : £6.25 : CIP rev.
B80-25498

420'.7'1242 — England. Secondary schools. Curriculum subjects: English language. Continuous assessment

Scott, Patrick, *1949-*. Coursework in English : principles and assessment / [written by Patrick Scott on behalf of the NATE working party]. — [Huddersfield] ([10B Thornhill Rd., Edgerton, Huddersfield HD3 3AU]) : National Association for the Teaching of English, 1980. — 25p ; 21cm. — (NATE examinations booklet ; no.3)
£0.60 (pbk)
Also classified at 820'.7'1242 B81-19575

420'.7'1242 — England. Secondary schools. Curriculum subjects: English language. C.S.E. examinations & G.C.E. (O level) examinations

Barnes, Douglas. Seals of approval : an analysis of English examinations at sixteen plus / Douglas Barnes and John Seed. — [Leeds] : University of Leeds School of Education, c1981. — 36p ; 30cm
Cover title
Unpriced (spiral)
Also classified at 820'.7'1242 B81-14176

420'.9 — English language, *to 1905*

Jespersen, Otto. Growth and structure of the English language. — 10th ed. — Oxford : Blackwell, Feb.1982. — [256]p
Previous ed.: 1938
ISBN 0-631-12986-3 (cased) : £12.00 : CIP entry
ISBN 0-631-12987-1 (pbk) : £4.95 B81-37595

420'.9 — English language, *to 1977*

Clark, Cecily. An introduction to the history of the English language / Georges Bourcier ; English adaptation by Cecily Clark. — Cheltenham : Thornes, 1981. — viii,230p : ill,2maps ; 24cm
Translation and adaptation of: Histoire de la langue anglaise du Moyen Age à nos jours. — Includes bibliographies and index
ISBN 0-85950-482-4 (cased) : £12.50
ISBN 0-85950-487-5 (pbk) : £7.25 B81-29146

421 — ENGLISH LANGUAGE. WRITTEN AND SPOKEN CODES

421'.076 — English language. Punctuation — *Questions & answers*

De Larrabeiti, Michael. Full marks : the Papermate guide to punctuation / Michael de Larrabeiti. — London : Macmillan Education, 1981. — 32p : ill ; 21cm
ISBN 0-333-31585-5 (pbk) : £0.65 B81-39089

421'.076 — English language. Punctuation — *Questions & answers — For schools*

William, Eric, *1942-*. Punctuation patterns in practice / Eric Williams. — London : Edward Arnold, 1981. — 71p : ill ; 22cm
ISBN 0-7131-0511-9 (pbk) : £1.60 : CIP rev.
B81-12875

421'.1 — English language. Alphabets — *For children*

Curry, Peter. Peter Curry's abc. — Tadworth : World's Work, c1981. — [32]p : chiefly col.ill ; 18cm
ISBN 0-437-32938-0 : £2.95 B81-18840

Fior, Jane. ABC / Jane Fior ; pictures by Gill Chapman. — London : Collins, c1981. — [48]p : col.ill ; 15cm. — (Let's read ; 1) (Collins colour cubs)
ISBN 0-00-196035-0 (pbk) : Unpriced
B81-18844

Fowler, Richard, *1944-*. The bean abc / by Richard Fowler. — Harlow : Longman, 1980. — 28p : chiefly col.ill ; 28cm
ISBN 0-582-39094-x : £2.95 B81-19790

Little tot's abc and counting. — London : Dean, c1980. — [24]p : col.ill ; 13cm. — (Dean's little tots' series)
ISBN 0-603-00194-7 (pbk) : £0.15
Also classified at 513'.5 B81-18850

Lobel, Anita. On Market Street / pictures by Anita Lobel ; words by Arnold Lobel. — London : Ernest Benn, 1981. — [40]p : col.ill ; 26cm
ISBN 0-510-00118-1 : £3.95 B81-23196

Pieńkowski, Jan. ABC / Jan Pieńkowski. — London : Heinemann, 1980. — [28]p : of col.ill ; 18cm. — (Concept books)
Text, ill on inside covers
ISBN 0-434-95642-2 : £2.95 B81-18839

Woodward, Ken. Ken Woodward's ABC parade / Ken Woodward. — Maidenhead : Purnell, 1974 (1981 [printing]). — [28]p : chiefly col.ill ; 25cm
Text, ill on lining papers
ISBN 0-361-05050-x : £0.99 B81-18841

421'.1 — English language. Alphabets. Special subjects: Agricultural industries. Farms — *For children*

Miller, Jane, *1925-*. Farm alphabet book / Jane Miller. — London : Dent, 1981. — [32]p : of col.ill ; 23cm
ISBN 0-460-06979-9 : £3.50 B81-24256

421'.1 — English language. Alphabets. Special subjects: Animals — *For children*

A peaceable kingdom : the Shaker abecedarius / illustrated by Alice and Martin Provensen ; afterword by Richard Meran Barsam. — Harmondsworth : Penguin, 1981, c1978. — [42]p : chiefly col.ill ; 17x26cm. — (Picture puffin)
Originally published: New York : Viking ; London : Kestrel, 1978. — Text originally published: as Rhymes of animals in Shaker Manifesto of July 1882
ISBN 0-14-050370-6 (pbk) : £1.25 B81-27827

Youldon, Gillian. Alphabet / [designed by Gillian Youldon and illustrated by James Hodgson]. — [London] : Watts, [1981]. — [14]p : chiefly col.ill ; 21cm. — (All a-board story books)
Cover title. — Ill and text on lining papers
ISBN 0-85166-893-3 : £1.99 B81-10600

421'.1 — English language. Alphabets. Special subjects: Animals — *Illustrations — For children*

Craig, Bobbie. A comic and curious collection of animals, birds and other creatures / by Bobbie Craig. — Loughborough : Ladybird, c1981. — 57p : chiefly col.ill ; 31cm
Ill and text on lining papers
ISBN 0-7214-7515-9 : £1.95 B81-28746

Stevenson, Peter. Ward Lock's animal ABC / illustrated by Peter Stevenson. — London : Ward Lock, 1980. — [32]p : chiefly col.ill ; 21x26cm
ISBN 0-7063-5968-2 : £1.95 B81-19956

421'.1 — English language. Alphabets. Special subjects: Occupations — *For children*

Campbell, Rod. ABC / Rod Campbell. — London : Abelard, 1980. — [32]p : all col.ill ; 17x22cm
ISBN 0-200-72703-6 (cased) : £2.95 : CIP rev.
ISBN 0-200-72702-8 (pbk) : £0.95 B80-12808

421'.1 — English language. Alphabets. Special subjects: Personal names — *For children — Facsimiles*

Ewen, Doris. An ABC of children's names / by Doris & Mary Ewen. — London : Macmillans Children's, 1980. — [28] leaves : col.ill ; 17cm
Facsim of: edition published London : Henry Frowde, 1912. — Leaves are concertina folded
ISBN 0-333-28518-2 : £1.95 B81-07076

421'.1'0222 — English language. Alphabets — *Illustrations — For children*

Anno, Mitsumasa. Anno's magical abc : an anamorphic alphabet / Mitsumasa Anno & Masaichiro Anno. — London : Bodley Head, 1981. — [64]p : chiefly col.ill,ill,1port ; 26cm
Translated from the Japanese. — 2 sheets of mirror paper in pocket
ISBN 0-370-30405-5 : £5.95 B81-37921

421'.5 — English language. Phonetics — *For Spanish speaking students*

Finch, Diana F.. A course in English phonetics for Spanish speakers. — London : Heinemann Educational, Jan.1982. — [192]p
ISBN 0-435-28078-3 (pbk) : £5.50 : CIP entry B81-35887

421'.5 — English language. Sounds *compared with* **sounds of Dutch language** — *For Dutch speaking students*

Collins, Beverley. The sounds of English and Dutch / Beverley Collins and Inger Mees. — The Hague ; London : Leiden University Press, 1981. — 293p : ill ; 25cm
Bibliography: p278-279
ISBN 90-602-1477-3 (cased) : Unpriced
ISBN 90-602-1477-3 (pbk) : Unpriced
Also classified at 439.3'115 B81-15514

421'.6 — Spoken English language. Intonation

Ladd, D. Robert. The structure of intonational meaning : evidence from English / D. Robert Ladd, Jr. — Bloomington ; London : Indiana University Press, c1980. — xi,239p : ill ; 25cm
Bibliography: p221-228. — Includes index
ISBN 0-253-15864-8 : £11.00 B81-01884

422 — ENGLISH LANGUAGE. ETYMOLOGY

422 — English language. Verbs. Semantics

Dowty, David R.. Word meaning and Montague grammar : the semantics of verbs and times in generative semantics and in Montague's PTQ / David R. Dowty. — Dordrecht ; London : Reidel, c1979. — xvii,415p : ill ; 23cm. — (Synthese language library ; v.7)
Bibliography: p396-407. - Includes index
ISBN 90-277-1008-2 (cased) : Unpriced
ISBN 90-277-1009-0 (pbk) : Unpriced B81-07300

422 — English language. Words & phrases. Etymology

Radford, Edwin. To coin a phrase : a dictionary of origins / Edwin Radford and Alan Smith. — Rev. ed. — London : Macmillan, 1981. — ix,281p ; 20cm. — (Papermac)
Originally published: London : Hutchinson, 1973
ISBN 0-333-31643-6 (pbk) : £2.95 B81-38639

423 — ENGLISH LANGUAGE. DICTIONARIES

423 — English language — *Dictionaries*

Chambers mini dictionary / edited by E.M. Kirkpatrick ; pronunciation under the direction of David Abercrombie and Alan Kemp. — Edinburgh : Chambers, c1978 (1981 [printing]). — vi,634p ; 12cm
ISBN 0-550-10701-0 : £1.15 B81-29179

Collins double book encyclopedia & dictionary : with 293 colour photographs. — Rev. ed. — London : Collins, 1981. — 575,444p,[32]p of plates : ill(some col.),maps,ports ; 22cm
Previous ed.: 1968
ISBN 0-00-434337-9 : £6.95
Also classified at 032 B81-39289

Collins minigem English dictionary. — London : Collins, 1981. — v,249p ; 14cm
ISBN 0-00-458375-2 (pbk) : £0.85 B81-41014

Harrap's easy English dictionary / editor P.H. Collin. — London : Harrap, 1980. — 542p ; 23cm
ISBN 0-245-53660-4 (cased) : £3.95
ISBN 0-245-53624-8 (pbk) : £2.50 B81-02235

Kirkpatrick, E. M.. Chambers family dictionary / edited by E.M. Kirkpatrick ; illustrations by David Brogan. — Edinburgh : Chambers, c1981. — xii,980,16p : ill,col.maps ; 26cm
ISBN 0-550-10615-4 : £9.95 B81-26180

Longman new generation dictionary / [editor-in-chief Paul Procter]. — Harlow : Longman, 1981. — 15a,798p : ill ; 21cm
Text on lining papers
ISBN 0-582-55626-0 : £3.95 B81-32556

McArthur, Tom. Longman lexicon of contemporary English / Tom McArthur. — Harlow : Longman, 1981. — xiii,910p : ill ; 22cm
Text on inside covers. — Includes index
ISBN 0-582-55527-2 (pbk) : £4.95 B81-29374

The **Oxford** dictionary for writers and editors / compiled by the Oxford English Dictionary Department. — Oxford : Clarendon Press, 1981. — xiv,448p ; 18cm
'... successor to eleven editions of the Authors' and printers' dictionary first published under the editorship of F. Howard Collins ...' Publisher's note
ISBN 0-19-212970-8 : £4.95 : CIP rev. B80-19165

The **World** book dictionary. — 1979 ed., edited by Clarence L. Barnhart, Robert K. Barnhart / prepared in cooperation with World Book-Childcraft International, Inc. — Chicago ; London : Published for World Book-Childcraft International [by] Doubleday, c1979. — 2v.(2430p) : ill ; 29cm. — (A Thorndike-Barnhart dictionary)
Previous ed.: published as The World book encyclopedia dictionary / Clarence L. Barnhart, editor in chief : prepared in cooperation with the staff of the World book encyclopedia. Chicago : Field Enterprises Educational Corp., 1963
ISBN 0-7166-0279-2 : Unpriced B81-15566

423 — English language — *Dictionaries — Early works*

Johnson, Samuel, *1709-1784*. Johnson's dictionary : a modern selection. — London : Gollancz, Feb.1982. — [480]p
Originally published: 1963
ISBN 0-575-03098-4 : £8.95 : CIP entry B81-40240

423 — English language - *Dictionaries - For children*

Manley, Deborah. The Kingfisher dictionary. — London (Elsley Court, 20 Great Titchfield St., W1P 7AD) : Kingfisher Books, Sept.1981. — [192]p
ISBN 0-86272-023-0 : £3.95 : CIP entry B81-20491

423 — English language — *Dictionaries — For children*

Manley, Deborah. The piccolo illustrated dictionary / compiled by Deborah Manley and John Paton. — London : Pan, 1981. — 189p : ill,maps ; 20cm. — (A Piccolo book)
ISBN 0-330-26621-7 (pbk) : £2.50 B81-38098

Mr. Men picture dictionary. — London : Thurman, c1981. — 252p : col.ill ; 29cm
ISBN 0-85985-171-0 : £4.95 B81-40123

423 — English language — *Dictionaries — For non-English speaking students*

Oxford basic English dictionary / edited by Shirley Burridge. — Oxford : Oxford University Press, 1981. — 297p : ill ; 18cm
Text on inside covers
ISBN 0-19-431261-5 (pbk) : £1.00 B81-36462

Oxford elementary learner's dictionary of English / edited by Shirley Burridge. — Oxford : Oxford University Press, 1981. — 297p : ill ; 21cm
Text on inside covers
ISBN 0-19-431253-4 (pbk) : £1.95 B81-18587

423 — English language — *Dictionaries — For schools*

Augarde, A. J.. The Oxford dictionary / compiled by A.J. Augarde. — Oxford : Oxford University Press, c1981. — 316p ; 22cm
ISBN 0-19-910218-x : £1.65
ISBN 0-19-910217-1 (school ed.) : Unpriced B81-12943

Hawkins, Joyce M.. The Oxford senior dictionary. — Oxford : Oxford University Press, Jan.1982. — [768]p
ISBN 0-19-910222-8 (pbk) : £3.95 : CIP entry
ISBN 0-19-910221-x : £2.50(non-net) B81-40258

Mackenzie, Dorothy C.. The Oxford school dictionary / compiled by Dorothy C. Mackenzie. — 4th ed. / rev. by A.J. Augarde. — Oxford : Oxford University Press, 1981. — x,356p ; 21cm
Previous ed.: 1974
ISBN 0-19-910220-1 : £2.95 : CIP rev.
ISBN 0-19-910219-0 (non-net) : Unpriced B81-13856

Witty, F. R.. Nelson first English dictionary / F.R. Witty. — Walton-on-Thames : Nelson, 1981. — 112p : ill,maps ; 25cm + Workbook (32p: ill,maps; 28cm)
ISBN 0-17-424393-6 (pbk) : £1.10
ISBN 0-17-424392-8 (Workbook) : £0.50 B81-12939

Wright, Walter D.. A first dictionary / Walter D. Wright. — Rev. ed. — Welwyn : Nisbet, 1981. — iii,220p : ill ; 19cm
Previous ed.: 1952
ISBN 0-7202-0936-6 (cased) : Unpriced
ISBN 0-7202-0935-8 (pbk) : £1.15 B81-39619

423 — English language. Usage — *Dictionaries*

McArthur, Tom. Longman lexicon of contemporary English / Tom McArthur. — Harlow : Longman, 1981. — xiii,910p : ill ; 23cm
Includes index
ISBN 0-582-55636-8 : £6.95 B81-36285

423 — English language. Usage — *Dictionaries — For Nigerian students*

A **First** sentence dictionary. — Amersham : Hulton Educational in association with Spectrum, 1979. — 203p : ill(some col.) ; 21cm
ISBN 0-7175-0807-2 (pbk) : Unpriced B81-11590

423 — English language. Usage — *Dictionaries — For non-English speaking students*

Chambers universal learners' dictionary / edited by E.M. Kirkpatrick ; pronunciation under the direction of David Abercrombie and Alan Kemp. — Edinburgh : Chambers, c1980. — xx,907p ; 20cm
ISBN 0-550-10634-0 (pbk) : £2.50 B81-24041

423'.1 — English language. Antonyms & synonyms — *Dictionaries*

A **Dictionary** of synonyms and antonyms. — New rev. ed. / edited by Laurence Urdang and Martin Manser. — Newton Abbot : David & Charles, 1980. — v,345p ; 19cm
ISBN 0-7153-8080-x : £5.95 B81-00846

Room, Adrian. Room's dictionary of distinguishables / Adrian Room. — Boston ; London : Routlegde & Kegan Paul, 1981. — 132p : ill ; 24cm
ISBN 0-7100-0775-2 : £5.95 : CIP rev. B81-14960

423'.1 — English language. Homonyms — *Dictionaries — For schools*

Blaney, David. Sounds similar / by David Blaney. — London (Romford Rd., W15 4LZ) : Nelpress, c1980. — 64p : ill ; 30cm
ISBN 0-901987-34-4 (pbk) : Unpriced B81-17956

423'.1 — English language. Idioms — *Dictionaries*

Brewer, E. Cobham. Brewer's dictionary of phrase and fable. — Rev. ed. / by Ivor H. Evans. — London : Cassell, c1981. — xvi,1213p ; 23cm
Previous ed.: [i.e. Centenary ed.]: 1970
ISBN 0-304-30706-8 : £9.95 B81-36189

423'.1 — English language — *Thesauri*

Roget, Peter. Everyman's thesaurus of English words and phrases / revised from Peter Roget by D.C. Browning. — Rev. ed. — London : Sphere, 1981. — ix,556p ; 20cm
Previous ed.: 1952. — Includes index
ISBN 0-7221-1914-3 (pbk) : £2.10 B81-38466

Thesaurus of English words / edited by M.H. Manser. — London : Hamlyn, 1979 (1981 [printing]). — 214p ; 22cm
Includes index
ISBN 0-600-33213-6 : £5.00 B81-25452

423'.1 — English language. Words & phrases — *Lists — For crossword puzzles*

Pulsford, Norman G.. The modern crossword dictionary / compiled by Norman G. Pulsford. — London : Pan, 1967 (1981 printing). — 555p ; 18cm
ISBN 0-330-26521-0 (pbk) : £1.95 B81-23563

424.2'4927 — English language — *For Saudi-Arabian students*

Saudi Arabian schools' English. — London : Macmillan
Intermediate second grade
Pupils book / [writer and adviser John Field]. — 1981. — 128p : col.ill,1col.map ; 24cm
Cover title
ISBN 0-333-31130-2 (pbk) : Unpriced B81-36928

Saudi Arabian schools' English. — [London] : Macmillan
Secondary first grade
Reader 2 / writer and adviser Colin Swatridge. — 1980. — 46p : ill ; 24cm
ISBN 0-333-29221-9 (pbk) : Unpriced B81-36925

Saudi Arabian schools' English. — London : Macmillan
Secondary second grade
Pupils book / [writer and adviser John Field]. — 1981. — 190p : ill(some col.),col.maps ; 24cm
Includes index
ISBN 0-333-31586-3 (pbk) : Unpriced B81-36927

Saudi Arabian schools' English. — [London] : Macmillan
Secondary second grade
Teachers book / [writer and adviser John Field]. — 1981. — 124p ; 22cm
ISBN 0-333-31590-1 (pbk) : Unpriced B81-36926

425 — ENGLISH LANGUAGE. GRAMMAR

425 — English language. Aspectual verbs. Complementation

Freed, Alice F.. The semantics of English aspectual complementation / Alice F. Freed. — Dordrecht ; London : Reidel, c1979. — x,172p ; 23cm. — (Synthese language library ; v.8)
Bibliography: p163-165. - Includes index
ISBN 90-277-1010-4 (cased) : Unpriced
ISBN 90-277-1011-2 (pbk) : Unpriced B81-14692

425 — English language. Clauses

Young, David J.. The structure of English clauses / David J. Young. — London : Hutchinson, 1980. — xiii,373p : ill ; 23cm
Bibliography. p309-311. - Includes index
ISBN 0-09-141450-4 (cased) : £12.00 : CIP rev.
(pbk) : £5.95 B80-06865

425 — English language. Grammar. Theories

Stageberg, Norman C.. An introductory English grammar / Norman C. Stageberg. — 4th ed. — New York ; London : Holt, Rinehart and Winston, c1981. — xiv,370p : ill ; 24cm
Previous ed.: 1977. — Includes index
ISBN 0-03-049381-1 (pbk) : £7.95 B81-23054

425 — English language. Grammar. Transformational-generative theories

Radford, Andrew. Transformational syntax. — Cambridge : Cambridge University Press, Nov.1981. — [402]p. — (Cambridge textbooks in linguistics)
ISBN 0-521-24274-6 (cased) : £22.50 : CIP entry
ISBN 0-521-28574-7 (pbk) : £7.50 B81-38810

425 — English language. Quantifiers

Aldridge, M. V.. English quantifiers. — Amersham : Avebury Publishing, Nov.1981. — [276]p
ISBN 0-86127-208-0 (pbk) : £15.00 : CIP entry B81-30397

425 — English language. Syntax

Matthews, P. H.. Syntax / P.H. Matthews. — Cambridge : Cambridge University Press, 1981. — xix,306p : ill ; 24cm. — (Cambridge textbooks in linguistics)
Includes index
ISBN 0-521-22894-8 (cased) : £19.50
ISBN 0-521-29709-5 (pbk) : £6.50 B81-32622

425 — Spoken English language. Syntax

Cooper, William E.. Syntax and speech / William E. Cooper, Jeanne Paccia-Cooper. — Cambridge, Mass. ; London : Harvard University Press, 1980. — ix,275p : ill ; 25cm. — (Cognitive science series ; 3)
Bibliography: p251-265. — Includes index
ISBN 0-674-86075-6 : £12.60 B81-16565

427 — ENGLISH LANGUAGE. EARLY FORMS, SLANG, DIALECTS

427'.02 — English language, *1066-1400 — Festschriften*

So meny people longages and tonges : philological essays in Scots and mediaeval English presented to Angus McIntosh / edited by Michael Benskin and M.L. Samuels. — Edinburgh (Middle English Dialect Project, 2 Buccleuch Pl., Edinburgh EH8 9LW) : M. Benskin and M.L. Samuels, 1981. — xli,460p : ill,maps,1port ; 21cm
Bibliography: p379-414. — Includes index
ISBN 0-9506938-2-0 (pbk) : Unpriced B81-27723

427'.02 — English language, *1066-1625 — Samplers*

Partridge, A. C.. A companion to Old and Middle English. — London : Deutsch, Oct.1981. — [352]p
ISBN 0-233-97308-7 (cased) : £12.95 : CIP entry
ISBN 0-233-97410-3 (pbk) : £6.95
Also classified at 429 B81-26747

427'.09 — English language. Slang, *to 1811 — Dictionaries — Facsimiles*

Grose, Francis. [Lexicon balatronicum]. 1811 dictionary of the vulgar tongue : a dictionary of buckish slang, university wit, and pickpocket eloquence : unabridged from the original 1811 edition / with a foreword by Max Harris. — Adelaide : Bibliophile ; London : Papermac, 1981, c1971. — [238]p ; 21cm
Facsim of: Lexicon balatronicum / compiled originally by Captain Grose. London : printed for C. Chappel, 1811
ISBN 0-333-31502-2 (pbk) : £1.95 B81-24325

427'.1 — English language. Cockney dialect

Barltrop, Robert. The muvver tongue / Robert Barltrop & Jim Wolveridge. — London : Journeyman, 1980. — 135p ; 23cm
ISBN 0-904526-63-1 (cased) : Unpriced
ISBN 0-904526-46-1 (pbk) : £2.95 B81-04156

Wright, Peter, *1923-*. Cockney dialect and slang / Peter Wright. — London : Batsford, 1981. — 184p : ill ; 23cm
Bibliography: p174-175. - Includes index
ISBN 0-7134-2242-4 : £8.95 B81-15959

427'.44'03 — English language. Hereford and Worcester dialect: Worcestershire dialect — *Dictionaries*

Words of old Worcestershire. — Kidderminster : Kenneth Tomkinson, [1981]. — 92p ; 22cm
ISBN 0-907083-04-8 (pbk) : Unpriced B81-36151

427'.45 — English language. Shropshire dialect

Kilford, Valerie. Shropshire words and dialect / Valerie Kilford. — Telford (2 Edward Terrace, Trench Rd., Trench, Telford, Salop TF2 6PJ) : V. Kilford, 1981. — ii,28p,[7]p of plates : ill,map ; 27cm
Cover title. — Bibliography: p28
Unpriced (pbk) B81-24275

427'.64 — English language. Suffolk dialect

Claxton, A. O. D.. The Suffolk dialect of the 20th century / A.O.D. Claxton. — 3rd ed. — Woodbridge : Boydell, 1968 (1981 [printing]). — xvi,122p : music ; 22cm. — ([The Suffolk library])
Previous ed.: Ipswich : Norman Adlard, 1960
ISBN 0-85115-144-2 (pbk) : £3.50 B81-14666

427'.941135'03 — English language. Shetland dialect — *Dictionaries*

Graham, John J.. The Shetland dictionary / John J. Graham. — Stornoway : Thule, 1979. — xxvii,124p ; 23cm
ISBN 0-906191-33-5 : £4.95 B81-17121

427'.9416 — English language. Northern Irish dialect

Pepper, John. Catch yourself on! / John Pepper ; illustrations by Rowel Friers. — Belfast : Blackstaff, c1980. — 59p : ill ; 21cm
ISBN 0-85640-237-0 (pbk) : £2.50 B81-02879

427'.9416'03 — English language. Northern Irish dialect — *Dictionaries*

Pepper, John. John Pepper's Ulster-English dictionary. — Belfast : Appletree Press, Oct.1981. — [80]p
ISBN 0-904651-88-6 (pbk) : £2.50 : CIP entry B81-30998

427'.9416'7 — English language. Belfast dialect. Words. Pronunciation

Milroy, James. Regional accents of English : Belfast. — Belfast : Blackstaff Press, Nov.1981. — [128]p
ISBN 0-85640-241-9 (pbk) : £5.50 : CIP entry B81-34963

427'.9595 — English language. Malaysian usage & Singaporean usage

Platt, John T.. English in Singapore and Malaysia : status, features, functions / John Platt and Heidi Weber. — Kuala Lumpur ; Oxford : Oxford University Press, 1980. — xviii,292p,[4]p of plates : ill,maps ; 26cm
Map on lining papers. — Bibliography: p277-286. — Includes index
ISBN 0-19-580438-4 (cased) : £16.00
ISBN 0-19-580444-9 (pbk) : Unpriced B81-25976

427'.97292 — English language. Jamaican dialect. Usage by West Indians in Great Britain. Sociolinguistic aspects

Sutcliffe, David. British black English. — Oxford : Blackwell, Jan.1982. — [192]p
ISBN 0-631-12711-9 : £9.95 : CIP entry B81-34293

427'.97292'0321 — English language. Jamaican dialect — *Dictionaries*

Dictionary of Jamaican English / edited by F.G. Cassidy and R.B. Le Page. — 2nd ed. — Cambridge : Cambridge Unversity Press, 1980. — lxvi,509p ; 24cm
Previous ed.: 1967. — Bibliography: pxvii-xxix
ISBN 0-521-22165-x : £30.00 B81-00847

427'.973 — Spoken English language. American usage. Sounds. Transcription — *Questions & answers*

Dew, Donald. Phonetic transcription : an audio-tutorial program / Donald Dew, Paul J. Jensen. — 2nd ed. — Columbus [Ohio] ; London : Merrill, c1979. — vi,122p : forms ; 25cm
Previous ed.: Columbus, Ohio : Merrill, 1974. — Text on inside cover. — Bibliography: p121-122
ISBN 0-675-08309-5 (pbk) : £4.95 B81-13985

427′.973′03 — English language. American usage — *Dictionaries*

Oxford American dictionary / [compiled by] Eugene Ehrlich ... et al.. — New York ; Oxford : Oxford University Press, 1980. — 816p ; 24cm
ISBN 0-19-502795-7 : £9.95 B81-18192

428 — ENGLISH LANGUAGE USAGE

428 — English language — *For schools*

Adams, Anthony. English skills / Anthony Adams, Norman Butterworth, Esmor Jones. — London : Harrarp
3. — 1980. — 72p : ill,1map,facsims,1form ; 25cm
ISBN 0-245-53245-5 (pbk) : Unpriced
B81-08099

Adams, Anthony. English skills / Anthony Adams, Norman Butterworth, Esmor Jones. — London : Harrap
Teachers' book. — 1980. — 15p ; 25cm
ISBN 0-245-53246-3 (unbound) : £1.95
B81-38620

Brindley, D. J.. Excellence in English. — London : Hodder & Stoughton, Sept.1981
Book 5. — [240]p
ISBN 0-340-24449-6 (pbk) : £3.25 : CIP entry
B81-22605

Finn, F. E. S.. In your own words. — London : J. Murray
Pupils' book. — Oct.1981. — [96]p
ISBN 0-7195-3878-5 (pbk) : £1.10 : CIP entry
B81-27405

Finn, F. E. S.. In your own words. — London : J. Murray
Teachers' book. — Oct.1981. — [120]p
ISBN 0-7195-3879-3 (pbk) : £1.50 : CIP entry
B81-27408

Framework English. — Walton-on-Thames : Nelson
Bk.3 / Don Shiach. — 1981. — 144p : ill,facsims,ports ; 28cm + 1 teachers' book(31p : 25cm)
ISBN 0-17-433353-6 : £2.20 B81-13324

Gregg, Joan Young. Communication and culture : a reading-writing text / Joan Young Gregg. — New York ; London : D. Van Nostrand, c1981. — xvi,236p : ill,1map ; 24cm
ISBN 0-442-23895-9 (pbk) : £6.70 B81-09009

Hapgood, Michael. English lessons. — London : Heinemann Educational, Apr.1981
1: Teachers' notes. — [32]p
ISBN 0-435-10403-9 (pbk) : £1.25 : CIP entry
B81-08928

Hapgood, Michael. English lessons one / Michael Hapgood. — London : Heinemann Educational, 1981. — 90p : ill ; 25cm + Teacher's book(28 : 22cm)
ISBN 0-435-10400-4 (pbk) : Unpriced
B81-27081

Healy, Maura. Your language / [compiled by] Maura Healy. — Basingstoke : Macmillan Education
1. — 1981. — 96p : ill,facsims,1map ; 25cm
ISBN 0-333-28167-5 (pbk) : Unpriced
B81-31303

Healy, Maura. Your language / Maura Healy. — Basingstoke : Macmillan Education
2. — 1981. — 96p : ill ; 25cm
ISBN 0-333-28168-3 (pbk) : £1.95 : CIP rev.
B81-13791

Healy, Maura. Your language / Maura Healy. — Basingstoke : Macmillan Education
3. — 1981. — 103p : ill ; 25cm
ISBN 0-333-28169-1 : £1.95 : CIP rev.
B81-13901

Hurst, Keith. Network two : an English course-book for secondary schools / Keith Hurst, John Simes. — London : Hodder and Stoughton, 1981. — 152p : ill,facsims,ports ; 24cm
Includes index
ISBN 0-340-25769-5 (pbk) : £2.50 : CIP rev.
B81-13808

Jones, Barry. Basics of English. — London : Bell & Hyman, July 1981. — [64]p
ISBN 0-7135-1271-7 (pbk) : £1.95 : CIP entry
B81-16391

Munro, M.. Early English skills / [M. Munro, E.J. Bell] ; [illustrator S. Aspey]. — Glasgow : Collins
Workbook 1. — 1981, c1980. — 29p : ill ; 30cm
ISBN 0-00-312230-1 (unbound) : £0.40
B81-12936

Owen, Christopher. English workshop. — London : Hodder and Stoughton Educational, June 1981
2. — [160]p
ISBN 0-340-24296-5 (pbk) : £2.45 : CIP entry
B81-13567

Richmond, John. Investigating our language. — London : Edward Arnold, Feb.1982. — [112]p
ISBN 0-7131-0610-7 (pbk) : £2.75 : CIP entry
B81-36392

Ridout, Ronald. Openings in English / Ronald Ridout and J.R.C. Yglesias. — London : Hutchinson
Book 1. — 1981. — 64p : ill(some col.),2maps (some col.) ; 24cm
Includes index
ISBN 0-09-142201-9 (pbk) : Unpriced : CIP rev. B80-13344

Ridout, Ronald. Openings in English. — London : Hutchinson
Bk.2 / Ronald Ridout and J.R.C. Yglesias. — 1981. — 64p : ill(some col.) ; 24cm
Includes index
ISBN 0-09-142771-1 (pbk) : Unpriced
B81-32514

Self, David. An English course : for secondary schools / David Self. — London : Ward Lock Educational
Bk.1. — 1978. — vi,169p : ill ; 22cm
Includes bibliographies and index
ISBN 0-7062-3699-8 (pbk) : Unpriced
B81-28716

Self, David. An English course : for secondary schools / David Self. — London : Ward Lock Educational
Bk.2. — 1978. — ix,198p : ill ; 22cm
Includes bibliographies and index
ISBN 0-7062-3700-5 (pbk) : Unpriced
B81-28717

Taylor, Boswell. First English / Boswell Taylor. — London : Hodder and Stoughton, 1980
2 / illustrated by Margaret Chamberlain and Lesley Smith. — 96p : ill(some col.) ; 25cm
ISBN 0-340-23047-9 (pbk) : £1.65 : CIP rev.
B80-12810

Taylor, Boswell. First English. — London : Hodder & Stoughton Educational
3. — Sept.1981. — [96]p
ISBN 0-340-26225-7 : £1.95 : CIP entry
B81-30210

428 — English language — *Questions & answers*

English through practice. — Thirsk (Breckenbrough, Thirsk, N. Yorkshire, YO7 4EN) : Crakehill Press
Grammar
Pt.1 / Alexandar Reid. — c1981. — 60p : ill ; 21cm
ISBN 0-907105-05-x (pbk) : Unpriced
B81-25573

Focal English / [compiled by] Alwyn Jones, Andrew Burgen and Ian Hosker. — Cheltenham : Thornes, 1980. — ix,170p : ill ; 22cm
ISBN 0-85950-478-6 (pbk) : £2.20 : CIP rev.
B80-10046

428 — English language - *Questions & answers*

Lucas, Michael Arthur. English in fact. — London : Heinemann Educational, May 1981
Students' book. — [96]p
ISBN 0-435-28420-7 (pbk) : £1.75 : CIP entry
B81-07479

Lucas, Michael Arthur. English in fact. — London : Heinemann Educational, May 1981
Teachers' book. — [64]p
ISBN 0-435-28421-5 (pbk) : £2.50 : CIP entry
B81-07480

428 — English language — *Questions & answers — For children*

Epps, Peter. Sense or nonsense? : a reading for meaning split book / developed by Peter Epps. — Ilminster (25 East St., Ilminster, Somerset TA19 0AN) : Creative Teaching Aids, 1980. — 3v.([12];[12]p,[6]leaves) ; 30x11cm
In plastic wallet
ISBN 0-907093-03-5 (spiral) : £2.80
ISBN 0-907093-00-0 (1st level (sentences))
ISBN 0-907093-02-7 (1st level (sentences))
ISBN 0-907093-01-9 (2nd level (stories))
B81-29801

Pemberton, Gordon. Basic workbooks for every day / Gordon Pemberton. — Exeter : Wheaton
Bk.1. — 1981. — 32p : ill ; 28cm
Cover title
ISBN 0-08-024181-6 (pbk) : £0.50
Primary classification 510′.76 B81-34596

Pemberton, Gordon. Basic workbooks for every day / Gordon Pemberton. — Exeter : Wheaton
Bk.2. — 1981. — 32p : ill,1plan ; 28cm
Cover title
ISBN 0-08-024182-4 (pbk) : £0.50
Primary classification 510′.76 B81-34597

Pemberton, Gordon. Basic workbooks for every day / Gordon Pemberton. — Exeter : Wheaton
Bk.3. — 1981. — 32p : ill,1map,1plan ; 28cm
Cover title
ISBN 0-08-024183-2 (pbk) : £0.50
Primary classification 510′.76 B81-34598

Pemberton, Gordon. Basic workbooks for every day / Gordon Pemberton. — Exeter : Wheaton
Bk.4. — 1981. — 32p : ill,1map ; 28cm
Cover title
ISBN 0-08-024184-0 (pbk) : £0.50
Primary classification 510′.76 B81-34599

Pemberton, Gordon. Basic workbooks for every day / Gordon Pemberton. — Exeter : Wheaton
Bk.6. — 1981. — 32p : ill,2maps ; 28cm
Cover title
ISBN 0-08-024186-7 (pbk) : £0.50
Primary classification 510′.76 B81-34600

Pemberton, Gordon. Basic workbooks for every day / Gordon Pemberton. — Exeter : Wheaton
Bk.7. — 1981. — 32p : ill,1map ; 28cm
Cover title
ISBN 0-08-024187-5 (pbk) : £0.50
Primary classification 510′.76 B81-34601

Pemberton, Gordon. Basic workbooks for every day / Gordon Pemberton. — Exeter : Wheaton
Bk.8. — 1981. — 32p : ill ; 28cm
Cover title
ISBN 0-08-024188-3 (pbk) : £0.50
Primary classification 510′.76 B81-34602

428 — English language — *Questions & answers — For Irish students*

Jennings, Barry. Work with words 3 / Barry Jennings. — Dublin : Educational Co., 1981. — 80p : ill ; 21cm
Unpriced (pbk) B81-29571

Work with words. — Dublin : Educational Company of Ireland, 1981
2 / Barry Jennings. — 63p : ill ; 21cm
Text on inside covers
Unpriced (pbk) B81-22777

428 — English language — *Questions & answers — For Irish students* *continuation*

Work with words. — Dublin : Educational Company of Ireland
4 / Barry Jennings. — 1981. — 96p : ill,facsims ; 21cm
Unpriced (pbk) B81-34803

428 — English language — *Questions & answers — For school leavers*

Abbott, A.. English for life / A. Abbott. — Glasgow : Collins, 1981. — 64p : ill,maps,facsims,forms ; 26cm. — (A Ready for work record book)
Text on inside covers
ISBN 0-00-197018-6 (pbk) : £0.85 B81-22745

428 — English language — *Questions & answers — For schools*

Abbs, Brian. Authentic English for reading / Brian Abbs, Vivian Cook and Mary Underwood. — Oxford : Oxford University Press
2. — 1981. — [71]p : ill,1map,ports ; 25cm
ISBN 0-19-454111-8 (pbk) : £1.95 B81-18279

Brandling, Redvers. What's your opinion? / Redvers Brandling. — Leeds : E. J. Arnold, 1981. — 40pamphlets : ill(some col.) ; 22cm
ISBN 0-560-00885-6 : £6.95 B81-37961

Cooper, Malcolm. Senior English reading / Malcolm Cooper, Jane Cooper. — London : Longman, 1980. — x,121p : ill,forms ; 25cm
ISBN 0-582-60139-8 (pbk) : Unpriced B81-08744

Evans, Tony. Extend your English / Tony Evans. — London : Edward Arnold, 1981. — 78p : ill,1form ; 25cm
ISBN 0-7131-0532-1 (pbk) : £2.25 : CIP rev. B81-13703

Hope, D. H.. Start with English / D.H. Howe. — Oxford : Oxford University Press
4. — 1981. — 100p : col.ill ; 26cm
ISBN 0-19-433642-5 (pbk) : £1.95 B81-38587

Howe, D. H.. Start with English / D.H. Howe. — Oxford : Oxford University Press
6 / [illustrations by Jonnie Ata Mak]. — c1981. — 108p : col.ill ; 26cm
ISBN 0-19-433644-1 (pbk) : £1.95 B81-40567

Howe, D. H.. Start with English. — Oxford : Oxford University Press
Cover title
Workbook 2 / D.H. Howe. — 1980. — 48p : ill ; 26cm
ISBN 0-19-433637-9 (pbk) : £0.65 B81-27146

Hurst, Keith. Network one : an English course-book for secondary schools / Keith Hurst, John Simes. — London : Hodder and Stoughton, 1981. — 152p : ill,facsims ; 24cm
Includes index
ISBN 0-340-25768-7 (pbk) : Unpriced B81-17841

Jenkins, John P.. English practice / John P. Jenkins and Vivian Summers. — Exeter : Wheaton, 1979 (1980 [printing]). — 74p ; 21cm
ISBN 0-08-022896-8 (pbk) : £0.85 B81-09649

Jenkins, John P.. Further English practice / John P. Jenkins and Vivian Summers. — Exeter : Wheaton, 1979 (1980 [printing]). — 71p ; 21cm
ISBN 0-08-022897-6 (pbk) : £0.85 B81-09648

Jenkins, John P.. Put it across : exercises in communication / John P. Jenkins. — London : Edward Arnold, 1981. — 48p : ill,maps,1geneal.table ; 25cm
ISBN 0-7131-0524-0 (pbk) : £1.75 : CIP rev. B81-13704

John, Roland. Collins graded English tests / Roland John. — Glasgow : Collins. — (Collins English library. Level 5)
Bk.5. — 1981. — 45p ; 27cm
ISBN 0-00-370310-x (pbk) : £0.60 B81-12935

John, Roland. Collins graded English tests / Roland John. — Glasgow : Collins, 1981. — (Collins English library. Level L)
Bk.6. — 1981. — 45p ; 27cm + 1 teacher's book((19p ; 27cm))
ISBN 0-00-370311-8 (pbk) : £0.60
ISBN 0-00-370312-6 (teacher's book : pbk) : £0.60 B81-12934

Ledgard, T. G.. Basic English revision / T.G. Ledgard and C.J.S. Garner. — London : Cassell, 1981. — 160p ; 22cm
ISBN 0-304-30777-7 (pbk) : Unpriced B81-29386

McLullich, Helen H.. Wordpower / Helen H. McLullich ; [illustrated by Ray Mutimer]. — Edinburgh : Oliver & Boyd
1. — 1981. — 64p : ill(some col.),1map ; 25cm
Cover title
ISBN 0-05-003193-7 (pbk) : £1.35 B81-24483

McLullich, Helen H.. Wordpower / Helen H. McLullich ; illustrated by Ray Mutimer. — Edinburgh : Oliver & Boyd
Starter. — 1981. — 31p : col.ill ; 25cm
ISBN 0-05-003375-1 (pbk) : £0.95 B81-24484

Meyer, Maricelle. Action English / Maricelle Meyer and Robert Sugg ; illustrated by Andrea Cameron. — London : Evans Bros
Workbook 3. — 1981. — 62p : ill ; 25cm
ISBN 0-237-50471-5 (pbk) : Unpriced B81-26005

Pemberton, Gordon. Basic workbooks for every day / Gordon Pemberton. — Exeter : Wheaton
Cover title
Book 5. — 1981. — 32p : ill,1map ; 28cm
ISBN 0-08-024185-9 (pbk) : £0.50
Also classified at 513'.076 B81-36644

Poulton, Mike. Word play / by Mike Poulton. — Exeter : Wheaton, 1979. — 4v. : ill ; 21cm
ISBN 0-08-021907-1 (pbk) : £2.10
ISBN 0-08-021908-x (Bk 2) : £0.45
ISBN 0-08-021909-8 (Bk 3) : £0.60
ISBN 0-08-021910-1 (Bk 4) : 0.60 B81-15060

Rixon, Shelagh. My English workbook / Shelagh Rixon. — London : Macmillan. — (Macmillan junior workbooks)
Cover title
1. — 1980. — 32p : chiefly ill ; 30cm
ISBN 0-333-30089-0 (pbk) : £0.50 B81-09850

Rowe, Albert. Language skills / Albert Rowe ; illustrated by Maurice Hutching Associates. — Exeter : Wheaton, 1981. — v,164p : ill ; 21cm
ISBN 0-08-024978-7 (pbk) : £1.90 B81-16101

428 — English language — *Questions & answers — For slow learning adolescents — For schools*

Ridgway, Bill. Setting out / Bill Ridgway. — London : Edward Arnold, 1981. — 96p : ill ; 25cm. — (Twelve to sixteen ; v.1)
ISBN 0-7131-0440-6 (pbk) : £2.50 : CIP rev. B80-23187

Ridgway, Bill. Setting out: word-bank and handwriting / Bill Ridgway. — London : Edward Arnold, 1981. — 32p : ill ; 25cm. — (Twelve to sixteen ; v.1)
ISBN 0-7131-0490-2 (pbk) : £1.50 : CIP rev. B80-23188

428 — English language. Usage

Brook, G. L.. Words in everyday life / G.L. Brook. — London : Macmillan, 1981. — 207p ; 23cm. — (St Antony's/Macmillan series)
Bibliography: p177-180. — Includes index
ISBN 0-333-21939-2 : £15.00 B81-40731

428'.001'9 — English language. Usage. Social aspects

Sociolinguistic patterns in British English / edited by Peter Trudgill. — Repr. with corrections. — London : Edward Arnold, 1979, c1978. — 186p : ill,2maps ; 23cm
Bibliography: p173-182. - Includes index
ISBN 0-7131-6232-5 (pbk) : £4.50 : CIP rev. B79-20654

428'.0024624 — English language — *For construction*

Waterhouse, Graham. English for the construction industry / Graham and Celia Waterhouse. — London : Macmillan, 1981. — xii,203p : ill ; 23cm
ISBN 0-333-31254-6 (pbk) : £3.95 B81-38733

428'.002465 — English language — *For business practices*

Gartside, L.. English for business studies : a practical course for use in secondary schools and colleges / L. Gartside. — 3rd ed. — Plymouth : Macdonald and Evans, 1981. — x,406p : ill ; 22cm
Previous ed.: 1975. — Bibliography: p389-390. — Includes index
ISBN 0-7121-0582-4 (pbk) : £3.95 B81-39555

Scott, John F.. English for secretarial and business students / John F. Scott. — Dublin : Gill and Macmillan, 1981. — 154p : ill ; 22cm
ISBN 0-7171-0949-6 (pbk) : £2.70 B81-36875

428'.002465 — English language — *Programmed instructions — For business practices*

Smith, Leila R.. Personal learning guide for English for careers trio : business, professional and technical, second edition / Leila R. Smith. — New York ; Chichester : Wiley, c1981. — 89p ; 28cm
ISBN 0-471-09191-x (pbk) : £3.65 B81-21968

428'.01'9 — English language. Usage. Social aspects — *For schools*

Cole, Ruth. Keeping in touch / Ruth Cole and John Wyatt. — London : Macmillan Education, 1981. — 71p : ill,1form ; 25cm
ISBN 0-333-28977-3 (pbk) : Unpriced : CIP rev. B80-18171

428'.02 — English language. Translation from foreign languages

Duff, Alan, *1942-*. The third language : recurrent problems of translation into English / Alan Duff. — Oxford : Pergamon, 1981. — xiii,138p,[1]leaf of plates : ill ; 26cm. — (Language teaching methodology series)
Bibliography: p127. - Includes index
ISBN 0-08-027248-7 (cased) : Unpriced
ISBN 0-08-025334-2 (pbk) : £5.95 B81-27803

428'.02465 — English language — *For business practices*

Pincott, Millie. English for business students. — 2nd ed. — London : Longman, Jan.1982. — [150]p
ISBN 0-582-41261-7 : £2.95 : CIP entry B81-34324

428.1 — ENGLISH LANGUAGE USAGE. WORDS

428.1 — English language. Antonyms — *For children*

Allington, Richard. Opposites / by Richard Allington and Kathleen Krull ; illustrated by Eulala Conner. — Oxford : Blackwell Raintree, c1981. — 32p : col.ill ; 24cm. — (Beginning to learn about)
Originally published: Milwaukee : Raintree Childrens, c1979
ISBN 0-86256-011-x : £2.50 B81-17353

Opposites / illustrated by Derek Collard. — London : Hamlyn, 1981. — [42]p : col.ill ; 26cm. — (I can learn)
ISBN 0-600-36480-1 : £1.99 B81-24060

428.1 — English language. Obsolete words

Hook, J. N.. The grand panjandrum : & 1,999 other rare, useful, and delightful words and expressions / J.N. Hook. — New York : Macmillan ; London : Collier Macmillan, c1980. — xiii,392p ; 22cm
Includes index
ISBN 0-02-553620-6 : £7.95 B81-20735

428.1 — English language. Pronunciation — *For non-English speaking students*

Hooke, Robert. A handbook of English pronunciation. — London : Edward Arnold, Aug.1981. — [256]p
ISBN 0-7131-8022-6 (pbk) : £2.50 : CIP entry B81-20610

428.1 — English language. Pronunciation — *For non-English speaking students* *continuation*

Ponsonby, Mimi. How now, brown cow?. — Oxford : Pergamon, Dec.1981. — [128]p. — (English language courses)
ISBN 0-08-025354-7 (pbk) : £3.95 : CIP entry
B81-31517

428.1 — English language. Pronunciation. Teaching

Tench, Paul. Pronunciation skills / by Paul Tench. — London : Macmillan, 1981. — 124p : ill ; 19cm. — (Essential language teaching series)
Bibliography: p117-118. — Includes index
ISBN 0-333-27178-5 (pbk) : £2.50 B81-38645

428.1 — English language. Sounds — *For pre-school children*

Cassin, S.. Sounds fun / S. Cassin & D. Smith ; illustrated by A. Rodger. — Glasgow : Collins. — (First steps) (Collins help your child series)
1. — 1980. — 34p : chiefly ill ; 26cm
ISBN 0-00-197010-0 (pbk) : £0.65 B81-14168

Cassin, S.. Sounds fun / S. Cassin & D. Smith ; illustrated by A. Rodger. — Glasgow : Collins. — (First steps) (Collins help your child series)
2. — 1981. — 34p : chiefly ill ; 26cm
ISBN 0-00-197021-6 (pbk) : £0.65 B81-14169

428.1 — English language. Sounds — *Questions & answers — For schools*

Parker, Andrew, *19---*. Sound practice / [by Andrew Parker and Jane Stamford]. — Huddersfield : Schofield & Sims, 1981. — 5v. : ill ; 30cm
£1.75 (unbound) B81-13143

428.1 — English language. Sounds. Recall & recognition

Welford, A. T.. Comparing recall and recognition in signal detection terms / A.T. Welford. — Cardiff (c/o R. Slater, Department of Applied Psychology, UWIST, Llwyn-y-Grant, Penylan, Cardiff CF3 7UX) : [UWIST Department of Applied Psychology], 1981. — 35p : ill ; 30cm. — (Occasional paper / UWIST Department of Applied Psychology ; no.9)
Bibliography: p32-34
£0.50 (spiral)
Also classified at 513'.2'019 B81-24797

428.1 — English language. Spelling — *Dictionaries*

Kirkpatrick, E. M.. Chambers spell well! / compiled by E.M. Kirkpatrick and C.M. Schwarz. — Edinburgh : W & R Chambers, 1980. — viii,247p ; 16cm
ISBN 0-550-11821-7 (cased) : £1.95 (pbk) : £1.25 B81-02463

Maxwell, Christine. The Pergamon dictionary of perfect spelling / Christine Maxwell. — 2nd ed. — Exeter : Wheaton, 1978. — 335p : 2maps ; 22cm
Previous ed.: 1977. — Text on lining paper. — Bibliography: p335
ISBN 0-08-022866-6 (cased) : £3.50 : CIP rev.
ISBN 0-08-022865-8 (pbk) : £2.50
ISBN 0-08-022864-x (cased) : (non-net) (pbk) : (non-net) B78-19111

Schoenheimer, H. P.. Compact speller / H.P. Schoenheimer. — London : Longman, 1981, c1967. — x,110p ; 12cm
Originally published: London : F. Warne, 1967
ISBN 0-582-68045-x : £0.70 B81-24079

428.1 — English language. Spelling — *For schools*

Henderson, E. E.. Spell-well / E.E. Henderson. — [Glasgow] : [Blackie]
Workbook 3. — [1981]. — 47p : ill ; 25cm
ISBN 0-216-90800-0 (unbound) : £0.85
B81-19500

Henderson, E. E.. Spell-well / E.E. Henderson. — [Glasgow] : Blackie
Workbook 3. — [1981]. — 47p : ill ; 25cm
ISBN 0-216-91059-5 (pbk) : £0.85 B81-22934

Henderson, E. E.. Spell-well / E.E. Henderson. — [Glasgow] : [Blackie]
Workbook 4. — [1981]. — 47p : ill ; 25cm
ISBN 0-216-90801-9 (unbound) : £0.85
B81-19501

Ridout, C. J.. The new spell-well / C.J. Ridout. — Glasgow : Blackie
Book 6. — 1981. — 64p : 2ill ; 19cm
ISBN 0-216-90618-0 (pbk) : Unpriced
B81-09277

Wood, Elizabeth. Exercise your spelling. — London : Edward Arnold
Bk.1. — Dec.1981. — [50]p
ISBN 0-7131-0625-5 (pbk) : £0.50 : CIP entry
B81-31538

428.1 — English language. Spelling — *Questions & answers*

The **Old** fashioned rules of spelling book : the no-nonsense, proudly old-fashioned rules of spelling, which if they are followed, will help you to spell correctly. — London : Ward Lock Educational, 1980. — 24p ; 31x13cm
ISBN 0-7062-4085-5 (pbk) : £0.50 B81-00086

428.1 — English language. Spelling — *Questions & answers — For schools*

Hedley, John. Spelling practice / by John Hedley. — Huddersfield : Schofield & Sims
3. — 1981. — 30p : col.ill ; 26cm
ISBN 0-7217-0381-x (pbk) : £0.60 B81-32366

Hedley, John. Spelling practice / by John Hedley. — Huddersfield : Schofield & Sims
4. — 1981. — 30p : col.ill ; 26cm
ISBN 0-7217-0382-8 (pbk) : Unpriced
B81-16606

Hedley, John. Spelling practice / [by John Hedley]. — Huddersfield : Schofield & Sims
4. Teacher's book. — 1981. — 24p ; 23cm
ISBN 0-7217-0386-0 (pbk) : £0.85 B81-19605

Wood, Elizabeth. Exercise your spelling. — London : Edward Arnold
Book 2. — Dec.1981. — [32]p
ISBN 0-7131-0626-3 (pbk) : £0.50 : CIP entry
B81-31554

Wood, Elizabeth. Exercise your spelling. — London : Edward Arnold
Book 3. — Dec.1981. — [32]p
ISBN 0-7131-0627-1 (pbk) : £0.50 : CIP entry
B81-31555

428.1 — English language. Vocabulary — *For slow learning adolescents*

Quillian, Susan. Which word? / Susan Quillian. — [Welwyn Garden City] : Nisbet, [1981]. — 48p : ill ; 21cm
ISBN 0-7202-0838-6 (pbk) : £0.70 B81-16963

428.1 — English language. Words

Brandreth, Gyles. Wordplay. — London : Severn House, Oct.1981. — [300]p
ISBN 0-7278-2017-6 : £6.95 : CIP entry
B81-24664

428.1 — English language. Words. Analysis — *Programmed instructions — For teaching reading in schools*

Wilson, Robert M.. Programmed word attack for teachers / Robert M. Wilson, MaryAnne Hall. — 3rd ed. — Columbus ; London : Merrill, c1979. — x,77p ; 28cm
Previous ed.: 1974. — Bibliography: p75-77
£3.75 (spiral) B81-12500

428.1 — English language. Words — *For children*

Mayer, Mercer. Little Monster at work / by Mercer Mayer. — London : Dean, 1980, c1978. — 45p : col.ill ; 27cm. — (A New gold medal book)
Originally published: New York : Golden Press, 1978
ISBN 0-603-00201-3 : £1.25 B81-32159

Mayer, Mercer. Little Monster's word book / by Mercer Mayer. — London : Dean, 1980, c1977. — 45p : col.ill ; 26cm. — (A New gold medal book)
Originally published: New York : Golden Press, 1977
ISBN 0-603-00200-5 : £1.25 B81-32160

The **New** gold medal book of words. — London : Dean, c1980. — 45p : chiefly col.ill ; 26cm
ISBN 0-603-00203-x : £1.25 B81-06494

428.1 — English language. Words — *For pre-school children*

Cassin, S.. Word fun / S. Cassin & D. Smith ; illustrated by A. Rodger. — Glasgow : Collins. — (First steps) (Collins help your child series)
1. — 1980. — 34p : chiefly ill ; 26cm
ISBN 0-00-197012-7 (pbk) : £0.65 B81-14172

Cassin, S.. Word fun / S. Cassin & D. Smith ; illustrated by A. Rodger. — Glasgow : Collins. — (First steps) (Collins help your child series)
2. — 1981. — 34p : chiefly ill ; 26cm
ISBN 0-00-197023-2 (pbk) : £0.65 B81-14173

428.1 — English language. Words — *Illustrations — For non-English speaking students*

The **Oxford-Duden** pictorial English dictionary / [edited by John Pheby]. — Oxford : Oxford University Press, 1981. — 820p : ill(some col.),music ; 20cm
Includes index
ISBN 0-19-864140-0 : £7.50 : CIP rev.
B81-08850

428.1 — English language. Words — *Lists — For children*

Solomons, Gerald. Words we need / Gerald Solomons. — London : A & C Black, [1981]. — 71p ; 18cm
ISBN 0-7136-2150-8 (pbk) : £0.95
ISBN 0-7136-2151-6 (non-net) : £0.85
B81-38879

428.1 — English language. Words — *Questions & answers — For schools*

Bromley, J.. Now to work / J. Bromley and R. Callow. — Andover : Philograph
4. — c1980. — 31p : ill ; 20cm
ISBN 0-85370-506-2 (pbk) : £1.85 (for pack of 10 copies) B81-16197

428.1 — English language. Words. Roots — *Questions & answers*

Glazier, Teresa Ferster. The least you should know about vocabulary building : word roots / Teresa Ferster Glazier. — New York ; London : Holt, Rinehart and Winston, c1981. — vii,179p ; 24cm
Includes index
ISBN 0-03-056121-3 (pbk) : £5.25 B81-22860

428.1 — English language. Words. Special subjects: Young vertebrates — *For children*

Broomfield, Robert. The baby animal ABC / drawn by Robert Broomfield. — Harmondsworth : Puffin in association with the Bodley Head, 1981, c1964. — [31]p : chiefly col.ill ; 17x23cm. — (Picture Puffins)
Originally published: London : Bodley Head, 1964. — Text on inside cover
ISBN 0-14-050006-5 (pbk) : £0.95 B81-27654

428.1 — English language. Words. Usage

Howard, Philip. New words for old / Philip Howard. — London : Unwin, 1980, c1977. — xv,127p : ill ; 18cm
Originally published: London : H. Hamilton, 1977. — Includes index
ISBN 0-04-421004-3 (pbk) : £1.75 : CIP rev.
B80-13345

Howard, Philip. Words fail me / Philip Howard. — London : Hamilton, 1980. — 181p ; 23cm
Includes index
ISBN 0-241-10491-2 : £5.95 : CIP rev.
B80-21751

428.1 — English language. Words. Usage — *Questions & answers*

Wenborn, Neil. Word power : a test yourself guide / Neil Wenborn. — London : Kogan Page, 1981. — 125p : forms ; 19cm
ISBN 0-85038-432-x : £5.95 B81-25411

428.1'022'2 — English language. Words — *For children — Illustrations*

Fay, Hermann. [Big pictures little words]. My big picture word book / pictures by Hermann Fay. — London : Collins, 1981. — [96]p : chiefly col.ill ; 27cm
Translation from the German. — Originally published: 1973
ISBN 0-00-138208-x (pbk) : Unpriced
B81-11443

428.1′022′2 — English language. Words — *For children — Illustrations* *continuation*

Phonic blends. — London : Methuen Educational. — 1979
Emerald set. — 6v. : col.ill ; 15cm
ISBN 0-7055-0692-4 (unbound) : Unpriced
B81-19615

Phonic blends. — London : Methuen Educational. — 1979
Gold set. — 6v. : col.ill ; 15cm
ISBN 0-7055-0691-6 (unbound) : Unpriced
B81-19614

428.1′076 — English language. Vocabulary - *Questions & answers - For non-English speaking students*

Berman, Michael. Key to Playing with words and Working with words. — Oxford : Pergamon, Apr.1981. — [16]p. — (Materials for language practice)
ISBN 0-08-025353-9 (pbk) : £1.00 : CIP entry
B81-03813

Berman, Michael. Playing and working with words. — Oxford : Pergamon, Apr.1981. — [96]p. — (Materials for language practice)
ISBN 0-08-025352-0 (pbk) : £2.95 : CIP entry
B81-04266

Berman, Michael. Playing with words. — Oxford : Pergamon, Apr.1981. — [48]p. — (Materials for language practice)
ISBN 0-08-025351-2 (pbk) : £1.50 : CIP entry
B81-04265

428.1′076 — English language. Vocabulary — *Questions & answers — For non-English speaking students*

Yorkey, Richard. Checklist for vocabulary study / Richard Yorkey. — New York : Harlow : Longman, 1981. — ix,117p : ill ; 26cm
Includes index
ISBN 0-582-79767-5 (pbk) : £1.75 B81-27236

428.1′076 — English language. Vocabulary — *Questions & answers — For schools*

Richards, Haydn. One thousand harder vocabulary exercises / W. Haydn Richards. — New ed.. — Exeter : Wheaton, 1979. — 40p ; 21cm + teacher′s ed.(40p ; 21cm)
Previous ed.: 1951
ISBN 0-08-022873-9 (pbk) : £0.60
ISBN 0-08-022874-7 (teacher′s ed.) : £0.80
B81-32334

Richards, Haydn. One thousand vocabulary exercises / W. Haydn Richards. — New ed. — Exeter : Wheaton, 1977. — 40p ; 21cm + teacher′s ed.(40p ; 21cm)
Previous ed.: 1966
ISBN 0-08-022216-1 (pbk) : £0.60
ISBN 0-08-022565-9 (teacher′s ed.) : £0.80
B81-32335

428.2 — ENGLISH LANGUAGE USAGE. GRAMMAR

428.2 — English language. Comprehension. Cloze procedure tests — For slow learning students — For schools

Hutchinson, Lynn. Which word?. — London : Hodder and Stoughton, Sept.1981. — [64]p
ISBN 0-340-27001-2 (pbk) : £0.95 : CIP entry
B81-21584

428.2 — English language. Comprehension — *For slow-learning adolescents — For schools*

Footsteps. — Edinburgh : Holmes McDougall
2 / Alec Webster & Anne Webster. — [1980]. — 47p : ill(some col.),col.maps,1plan ; 26cm
Cover title
ISBN 0-7157-1479-1 (pbk) : £2.15 B81-11701

428.2 — English language. Comprehension — *Questions & answers — For schools*

Comprehension, interpretation and criticism : in four stages / [compiled by] G.R. Halson. — Harlow : Longman, 1981
Stage 1. — 2nd ed. — x,108p ; 22cm
Previous ed.: 1963
ISBN 0-582-24260-6 (pbk) : £1.45 B81-10221

Comprehension, interpretation and criticism : in four stages / [compiled by] G.R. Halson. — Harlow : Longman, 1981
Stage 2. — 2nd ed. — x,110p ; 22cm
Previous ed.: 1963
ISBN 0-582-24261-4 (pbk) : £1.45 B81-10228

Comprehension, interpretation and criticism : in four stages / [compiled by] G.R. Halson. — Harlow : Longman, 1981
Stage 3. — 2nd ed. — x,118p ; 22cm
Previous ed.: 1963
ISBN 0-582-24262-2 (pbk) : £1.45 B81-10229

Comprehension, interpretation and criticism : in four stages / [compiled by] G. R. Halson. — Harlow : Longman, 1981
Introductory bk. — 2nd ed. — x,86p ; 22cm
Previous ed.: 1964
ISBN 0-582-24263-0 (pbk) : £1.35 B81-10230

Finn, F. E. S.. Comprehension and composition / F.E.S. Finn. — London : Murray, c1980. — 88p : ill ; 22cm + Teachers′ book(88, T12p : ill ; 22cm)
ISBN 0-7195-3755-x (pbk) : £0.95
ISBN 0-7195-3761-4 (Teachers′ book) : : £1.50
Also classified at 808′.042′076 B81-32380

Mann, F. F.. Englishcraft / F.F. Mann and A.J. Smith. — Slough : University Tutorial Press
3. — 1981. — ix,145p : ill ; 23cm
ISBN 0-7231-0790-4 (pbk) : Unpriced
Also classified at 808′.042′076 B81-19603

Niven, Cyril. Understanding the information / C. Niven. — Glasgow : Collins
Study skills 3. — 1981. — 29p : ill ; 26cm + Answer book(29p: ill ; 26cm)
ISBN 0-00-314222-1 (pbk) : £0.40
ISBN 0-00-314224-8 (Answer book) : £1.00
B81-22746

Proud, Alan. Improve your comprehension. — London : Edward Arnold, Sept.1981. — [96]p
ISBN 0-7131-0584-4 (pbk) : £2.50 : CIP entry
B81-22453

. Reading with purpose. — Walton-on-Thames : Nelson
4 / [compiled by] Christopher Walker. — 1980. — 96p : ill(some col.),col.1map,col.coat of arms,1facsim ; 25cm
ISBN 0-17-422454-0 (pbk) : £1.75 B81-13988

Ridgway, Bill. Newsmakers. — London : Edward Arnold, Sept.1981
1. — [64]p
ISBN 0-7131-0564-x (pbk) : £1.50 : CIP entry
B81-23747

Ridgway, Bill. Newsmakers. — London : Edward Arnold, Sept.1981
2. — [64]p
ISBN 0-7131-0565-8 (pbk) : £1.50 : CIP entry
B81-23748

Self, David. Developing comprehension skills / David Self. — London : Ward Lock Educational, 1978 (1981 [printing]). — 69p ; 23cm
ISBN 0-7062-3701-3 (pbk) : Unpriced
B81-28714

428.2 — English language. Comprehension. Special subjects: Communication — *Questions & answers*

Cooper, Alan, *1941-*. Matters of fact : comprehension exercises in communication skills / Alan Cooper, Peter Leggott, Cyril Sprenger. — London : Edward Arnold, 1980. — vii,55p : ill,maps,facsims,forms,1 geneal.table ; 25cm
ISBN 0-7131-0507-0 (pbk) : £1.75 : CIP rev.
B80-33427

428.2 — English language. Comprehension. Special subjects: Residences. Accidental fires. Safety aspects — *For schools*

English : Fire at flat 3. — London : Macmillan Education for the Home Office, 1981. — 1portfolio : ill(some col.) ; 30cm. — (11 to 16+ project fire)
A Home Office/Schools Council project
ISBN 0-333-31771-8 : £12.95 B81-38634

428.2 — English language. Comprehension. Special subjects: Work — *Questions & answers — For slow readers — For schools*

Ridgway, Bill. Words about work / Bill Ridgway. — London : Edward Arnold, 1981. — 48p : ill,facsims ; 25cm
ISBN 0-7131-0568-2 (pbk) : £1.75 : CIP rev.
B81-16381

428′.2 — English language. Extracts from newspapers. Adaptations. Comprehension — *Questions & answers — For slow learning adolescents — For schools*

Brandling, Redvers. What the papers said / Redvers Brandling. — London : Edward Arnold, 1980. — 64p : ill,facsims ; 25cm
ISBN 0-7131-0419-8 (pbk) : £1.95 : CIP rev.
B80-04157

428.2 — English language. Grammar

Garrett, Malcolm. English corrected / Malcolm Garrett. — Rev. ed. — London : Heinemann Educational, 1980. — 88p ; 22cm
Previous ed.: published as Coded corrections. 1979
ISBN 0-435-10140-4 (pbk) : £1.30 : CIP rev.
B80-13348

Neuman, D. M.. English grammar for proficiency / D.M. Neuman. — Walton-on-Thames : Nelson, 1980. — 172p ; 22cm
Includes index
ISBN 0-17-555135-9 (pbk) : £1.95 B81-00848

Trudgill, Peter. International English. — London : Edward Arnold, Feb.1982. — [112]p
ISBN 0-7131-6361-5 (cased) : £10.00 : CIP entry
ISBN 0-7131-6362-3 (pbk) : £4.95 B81-37565

Winter, Michael, *1955-*. Harrap′s pocket English grammar / Michael Winter. — London : Harrap, 1981. — 79p ; 18cm
Includes index
ISBN 0-245-53717-1 (pbk) : £1.75 B81-37656

428.2 — English language. Grammar — *For children*

Davidson, Jessica. How to improve your grammar / by Jessica Davidson. — New York ; London : Watts, 1980. — 66p : ill ; 25cm. — (A language skills concise guide)
Includes index
ISBN 0-531-04131-x : £2.99 B81-03008

428.2 — English language. Grammar — *Questions & answers*

Groves, Paul. Smudge and chewpen sentence book / Paul Groves and Nigel Grimshaw. — London : Edward Arnold, 1981. — 96p ; 22cm
ISBN 0-7131-0510-0 (pbk) : £1.60 B81-09592

428.2 — English language. Grammar — *Questions & answers — For schools*

Davies, G. C.. Master your English / G.C. Davies, S.M. Dillon, C. Egerton-Chesney ; illustrated by G.C. Davies. — Oxford : Blackwell, 1981
Adverbs and adjectives. — 32p : ill ; 20cm
ISBN 0-631-92080-3 (pbk) : £0.60 B81-29699

Davies, G. C.. Master your English / G.C. Davies, S.M. Dillon, C. Egerton-Chesney ; illustrated by G.C. Davies. — Oxford : Blackwell, 1981
Common mistakes. — 32p : ill ; 20cm
ISBN 0-631-92060-9 (pbk) : £0.60 B81-29696

Davies, G. C.. Master your English / G.C. Davies, S.M. Dillon, C. Egerton-Chesney ; illustrated by G.C. Davies. — Oxford : Blackwell, 1981
Nouns and pronouns. — 32p : ill ; 20cm
ISBN 0-631-92100-1 (pbk) : £0.60 B81-29694

Davies, G. C.. Master your English / G.C. Davies, S.M. Dillon, C. Egerton-Chesney ; illustrated by G.C. Davies. — Oxford : Blackwell, 1981
Punctuation. — 32p : ill ; 20cm
ISBN 0-631-92070-6 (pbk) : £0.60 B81-29698

428.2 — English language. Grammar — *Questions & answers — For schools* *continuation*

Davies, G. C.. Master your English / G.C. Davies, S.M. Dillon, C. Egerton-Chesney ; illustrated by G.C. Davies. — Oxford : Blackwell, 1981
Sentences and capital letters. — 32p : ill ; 20cm
ISBN 0-631-92110-9 (pbk) : £0.60 B81-29697

Davies, G. C.. Master your English / G.C. Davies, S.M. Dillon, C. Egerton-Chesney ; illustrated by G.C. Davies. — Oxford : Blackwell, 1981
Verbs. — 32p : ill ; 20cm
ISBN 0-631-92090-0 (pbk) : £0.60 B81-29695

Davis, John. Handling language / John Davis ; illustration ideas by John Davis and drawn by Graham Humphreys. — London : Hutchinson
Bk.1. — 1981. — 60p : col.ill ; 21cm
ISBN 0-09-143281-2 (pbk) : Unpriced : CIP rev. B80-21752

428.2 — English language. Phrasal verbs & prepositional verbs — *Questions & answers*

Stone, Linton. Phrasal and prepositional verbs / Linton Stone. — London : Harrap, 1981. — 46p ; 22cm. — (Contemporary grammar units ; 2)
ISBN 0-245-53771-6 (pbk) : £1.00 B81-32731

428.2 — English language. Précis. Writing — *Questions & answers — For schools*

Banks, R. A.. Summary and directed writing / R.A. Banks and F.D.A. Burns. — London : Hodder and Stoughton, c1980. — 126p : ill,maps ; 22cm
ISBN 0-340-25608-7 (pbk) : Unpriced : CIP rev. B80-13778

Twenty more summaries in English language for GCE / [compiled by] Brian Rowe. — London : Hodder and Stoughton, 1980. — 46p ; 22cm
ISBN 0-340-25607-9 (pbk) : £0.75 : CIP rev. B80-12811

428.2 — English language. Prepositions — *Questions & answers*

Stone, Linton. Prepositions / Linton Stone. — London : Harrap, 1981. — 47p ; 22cm. — (Contemporary grammar units ; 1)
ISBN 0-245-53770-8 (pbk) : £1.00 B81-32730

428.2′02438 — English language — *Questions & answers — For commerce*

Andrews, R. G. H.. English for commerce : elementary stage / R.G.H. Andrews. — Amersham : Hulton Educational, 1981. — 96p ; 24cm
ISBN 0-7175-0886-2 (pbk) : £1.50 B81-27085

428.2′0248 — English language. Grammar — *For authors & public speaking*

Brush up your grammar : a pocket guide for professional writers and speakers. — [St. Neots] ([105 Great North Rd., Eaton Socon, St. Neots, Cambs. PE19 3EL]) : Solo, [1981?]. — iii,32p : ill ; 22cm
ISBN 0-9507623-1-8 (pbk) : £1.20 B81-34981

428.24 — ENGLISH LANGUAGE. FOR FOREIGN STUDENTS

428.2′4 — English language. Colloquialisms — *For non-English speaking students*

Coe, Graham. Colloquial English / Graham Coe. — London : Routledge & Kegan Paul, 1981. — xii,236p : ill,maps,forms,1plan ; 19cm. — (Colloquial series)
Includes index
ISBN 0-7100-0740-x (pbk) : £3.50 : CIP rev. B81-10419

428.2′4 — English language. Comprehension — *Questions & answers — For Caribbean students*

Wheatley, J. N.. Comprehension for Caribbean examinations : multiple choice and other exercises / J.N. Wheatley, T.B. Parris, C.H. Wheatley. — London : Macmillan Caribbean, 1979 (1980 [printing]). — viii,118p : ill,1map ; 25cm
ISBN 0-333-25897-5 (pbk) : Unpriced B81-13915

428.2′4 — English language. Comprehension — *Questions & answers — For non-English speaking students*

Archer, Margaret. Practice tests for first certificate English / Margaret Archer, Enid Nolan-Woods. — Walton-on-Thames : Nelson
Book 4. — 1981. — 68p : ill,1map,forms ; 25cm
ISBN 0-17-555304-1 (pbk) : £1.45 B81-22098

Archer, Margaret. Practice tests for first certificate English / Margaret Archer, Enid Nolan-Woods. — Walton-on-Thames : Nelson
Book 4. Teacher′s ed., with answers. — 1981. — 68p : ill,1map,forms ; 25cm
ISBN 0-17-555305-x (pbk) : £1.60 B81-22097

Crossbird, David. Accurate reading and listening / David Crossbird, Robert Cameron. — London : Cassell, 1981. — 123p ; 22cm + Answer key(28p : 22cm)
ISBN 0-304-30780-7 (pbk) : Unpriced : CIP rev. B81-15844

Davies, Evelyn, *1931-*. Strategies for reading / Evelyn Davies and Norman Whitney. — London : Heinemann Educational
Students′ book. — c1981. — iv,75p : ill,maps,facsims ; 30cm
ISBN 0-435-28940-3 (pbk) : £2.25 : CIP rev. B81-04260

Davies, Evelyn, *1931-*. Strategies for reading. — London : Heinemann Educational. — (Reading comprehension course ; 2)
Teachers′ guide. — Feb.1982. — [96]p
ISBN 0-435-28941-1 (pbk) : £2.50 : CIP entry B81-35697

English comprehension passages / [edited by] Margaret Russell. — London : Collins
Book 2. — 1977. — 64p ; 21cm
ISBN 0-00-325351-1 (pbk) : Unpriced B81-23222

Grellet, Françoise. Developing reading skills. — Cambridge : Cambridge University Press, Oct.1981. — [256]p
ISBN 0-521-28364-7 (pbk) : £5.50 : CIP entry B81-31951

428.2′4 — English language. Extracts from newspapers. Comprehension — *Questions & answers — For non-English speaking students*

Land, Geoffrey. What the papers say? : a selection of newspaper extracts for language practice / Geoffrey Land. — Harlow : Longman, 1981. — 128p : ill,facsims,ports ; 23cm
ISBN 0-582-79317-3 (pbk) : £1.45
ISBN 0-582-79318-1 (Key to the exercises) : £1.20 B81-32961

428.2′4 — English language — *For Caribbean students*

Jones, Rhodri. New English for the Caribbean / by Rhodri Jones and Daphne Heywood. — London : Heinemann Educational
Bk.2. — 1981. — vi,138p : ill ; 25cm
Includes index
ISBN 0-435-10487-x (corrected : pbk) : £2.60 B81-38694

Keane, Leila. Junior language arts for the Caribbean / Leila Keane, Evan Jones. — [Port of Spain] : Longman Caribbean ; London : Longman
Language book
Year 3 / [illustrated by Doffy Weir]. — 1980. — 128p : ill(some col.) ; 25cm
Includes index
ISBN 0-582-75045-8 (pbk) : £1.50 B81-17758

428.2′4 — English language — *For non-English speaking students*

Contemporary English / R. Rossner ... [et al.]. — London : Macmillan
Pupil′s book 4. — 1981. — vi,121p : ill ; 25cm
ISBN 0-333-28729-0 (pbk) : £1.75 B81-21857

Contemporary English / R. Rossner ... [et al.]. — London : Macmillan
Pupils book 4
Teacher′s book. — 1981. — xvi,48p ; 22cm
ISBN 0-333-30037-8 (pbk) : £1.95 B81-22742

Curtin, John. Survival English : an intensive course for adults / John Curtin & Peter Viney. — London : Glasgow
In plastic case
Keybook. — 1979. — 40p ; 30cm
ISBN 0-86158-105-9 (pbk) : Unpriced B81-36931

Curtin, John. Survival English : an intensive course for adults / John Curtin, Peter Viney. — [London] : Glasgow
In plastic case
[Workbook]. — 1979. — 103p : ill,1map ; 30cm
ISBN 0-86158-104-0 (pbk) : Unpriced B81-36930

Fitzpatrick, Anthony. English for international conferences. — Oxford : Pergamon, Dec.1981. — [61]p. — (Material for language practice)
ISBN 0-08-027277-0 (pbk) : £2.50 : CIP entry B81-33857

Granger, Colin. Play games with English. — London : Heinemann Educational
Teachers′ book 2. — Jan.1982. — [80]p
ISBN 0-435-28063-5 (pbk) : £2.20 : CIP entry B81-34499

Gray, Joanna. Discovering English. — London : Cassell. — (Cassell′s foundation English ; 2)
Students′ book. — Nov.1981. — [144]p
ISBN 0-304-30669-x (pbk) : CIP entry B81-31074

Gray, Joanna. Discovering English. — London : Cassell. — (Cassell′s foundation English ; 2)
Teacher′s book. — Dec.1981. — [72]p
ISBN 0-304-30670-3 (pbk) : £3.95 : CIP entry B81-36988

Maclin, Alice. Reference guide to English : a handbook of English as a second language / Alice Maclin. — New York ; London : Holt, Rinehart and Winston, c1981. — xii,405p ; 24cm
Includes index
ISBN 0-03-053226-4 (pbk) : £6.95 B81-23094

428′.2′4 — English language - *For non-English speaking students*

Romijn, Elizabeth. Live action English. — Oxford : Pergamon, May 1981. — [96]p. — (Materials for language practice)
ISBN 0-08-025361-x (pbk) : £1.95 : CIP entry B81-05145

428.2′4 — English language — *For non-English speaking students*

Schmid-Schönbein, Gisela. English for Mopsy and me. — Oxford : Pergamon. — (English language courses)
Teachers′ book 1. — Oct.1981. — [64]p
ISBN 0-08-027226-6 (pbk) : £1.95 : CIP entry B81-25853

Schmid-Schönbein, Gisela. English for Mopsy and me. — Oxford : Pergamon. — (English language courses)
Pupils′ workbook 1. — Oct.1981. — [40]p
ISBN 0-08-027227-4 (pbk) : £1.95 : CIP entry B81-25852

Schmid-Schönbein, Gisela. English for Mopsy and me. — Oxford : Pergamon. — (English language courses)
Pupils′ workbook 2. — Oct.1981. — [40]p
ISBN 0-08-027228-2 (pbk) : £1.95 : CIP entry B81-25851

Schmid-Schönbein, Gisela. English for Mopsy and me. — Oxford : Pergamon. — (English language courses)
Teachers′ book 2. — Oct.1981. — [64]p
ISBN 0-08-027229-0 (pbk) : £1.95 : CIP entry B81-25850

Stone, Linton. New Cambridge First Certificate English / Linton Stone. — London : Macmillan, 1981. — iv,204p : ill,1map ; 25cm
ISBN 0-333-30852-2 (pbk) : £2.95 B81-38802

428.2'4 — English language — *For non-English speaking students — For schools*

Exchanges. — London : Heinemann Educational, July 1981. — (Main course English)
Part B
Teachers' book. — [96]p
ISBN 0-435-28467-3 (pbk) : £3.95 : CIP entry
B81-14821

428.2'4 — English language. Grammar — *For non-English speaking students*

Azar, Betty Schrampfer. Understanding and using English grammar / Betty Schrampfer Azar. — Englewood Cliffs ; London : Prentice-Hall, c1981. — xvi,400p ; 24cm
Includes index
ISBN 0-13-936492-7 (pbk) : £7.65 B81-34952

Carrier, Michael. Take 5 : games and activities for the language learner / Michael Carrier and The Centre for British Teachers. — London : Harrap, 1980. — 96p : ill ; 25cm
Bibliography: p89. - Includes index
ISBN 0-245-53630-2 (pbk) : £2.95 B81-14631

Close, R. A.. English as a foreign language : its constant grammatical problems / R.A. Close. — 3rd ed. — London : Allen & Unwin, 1981. — 219p : ill ; 22cm
Previous ed.: 1977. — Bibliography: p205-207. — Includes index
ISBN 0-04-425025-8 (pbk) : £4.50 B81-22741

Coe, Norman. A learner's grammar of English / Norman Coe. — Walton-on-Thames : Nelson, 1980. — xv,238p : ill ; 22cm
ISBN 0-17-555281-9 (pbk) : Unpriced : CIP rev. B80-11006

English for adults / M. Bianchi ... [et al.]. — Oxford : Oxford University Press, 1981
3: Coursebook. — 164p : ill ; 24cm
Adaptation of English für Erwachsene. Bd. 3.
ISBN 0-19-433367-1 : £2.95 B81-15672

Lennox Cook, John. A new way to proficiency in English : a comprehensive guide to English as a foreign language / John Lennox Cook, Amorey Gethin, Keith Mitchell. — 2nd ed. — Oxford : Blackwell, 1980. — xiii,305p ; 22cm
Previous ed.: 1967. — Includes index
ISBN 0-631-12642-2 (cased) : Unpriced : CIP rev.
ISBN 0-631-12652-x (pbk) : £3.95 B80-20552

Swan, Michael. Practical English usage / Michael Swan. — Oxford : Oxford University Press, 1980. — xxiv,639p ; 23cm
Includes index
ISBN 0-19-431186-4 : £5.95
ISBN 0-19-431185-6 (pbk) : £2.95 B81-00850

Woodford, Protase E.. Bridges to English / Protase E. Woodford, Doris Kernan. — New York ; London : McGraw-Hill
ISBN 0-07-034481-7 (pbk) : £4.75 B81-19687

428.2'4 — English language. Grammar — *Questions & answers — For non-English speaking students*

Harkess, Shiona. Cue for communication / Shiona Harkess and John Eastwood. — Oxford : Oxford University Press, 1981. — 128p : ill,facsims,ports ; 22cm
Includes index
ISBN 0-19-432781-7 (pbk) : £2.25 B81-38369

Kench, A. B.. Essential grammar practice / by A.B. Kench. — London : Macmillan, 1981. — viii,223p : ill ; 23cm
Includes index
ISBN 0-333-28730-4 (pbk) : £2.95 B81-38728

Lennox Cook, John. The student's book of English : a complete coursebook and grammar to advanced intermediate level / John Lennox Cook, Amorey Gethin, Barry Unsworth. — Oxford : Blackwell, 1981. — vi,408p ; 22cm
Includes index
ISBN 0-631-12812-3 (pbk) : £3.95 B81-11468

Seidl, Jennifer. Grammar in practice / Jennifer Seidl. — Oxford : Oxford University Press
1. — 1981. — iv,156p : ill ; 22cm
Includes index
ISBN 0-19-432719-1 (pbk) : £1.75 B81-22793

Spankie, Greig M.. Extensions : a grammar workbook / G.M. Spankie. — London : Evans, 1981. — 85p ; 22cm
Includes index
ISBN 0-237-50623-8 (pbk) : Unpriced
B81-36501

428.2'4 — English language. Proficiency of non-English speaking students. Assessment. Use of cloze procedure tests

Moller, Alan. Cloze in class. — Oxford : Pergamon, July 1981. — (Pergamon Institute of English (Oxford) materials for language practice)
Teacher's booklet. — [32]p
ISBN 0-08-027268-1 (pbk) : £1.00 : CIP entry
B81-13846

Moller, Alan. Cloze in class. — Oxford : Pergamon, July 1981. — (Pergamon Institute of English (Oxford) materials for language practice)
Workbook. — [64]p
ISBN 0-08-025350-4 (pbk) : £2.95 : CIP entry
B81-13454

428.2'4 — English language — *Questions & answers — For Caribbean students*

Craig, Dennis, *1929-*. New world English / Dennis Craig, Grace Walker Gordon ; advisers Belle Tyndall, Desmond Clarke, Clive Borely. — Trinidad : Longman Caribbean ; Harlow : Longman
Students' book 1. — 1981. — 146p : ill ; 25cm
ISBN 0-582-76556-0 (pbk) : Unpriced
B81-12157

Craig, Dennis, *1929-*. New world English / Dennis Craig, Grace Walker Gordon ; advisers Belle Tyndall, Desmond Clark, Clive Borely. — Trinidad : Longman Caribbean ; Harlow : Longman
Students' book 2. — 1981. — 145p : ill,1map,ports ; 25cm
ISBN 0-582-76558-7 (pbk) : £1.85 B81-40307

Craig, Dennis, *1929-*. New world English / Dennis Craig, Grace Walker Gordon ; advisers Belle Tyndall, Desmond Clarke, Clive Borely. — [Port of Spain] : Longman Caribbean ; London : Longman
Teacher's book 2. — [1981]. — iv,44p ; 30cm
Cover title
ISBN 0-582-76559-5 (spiral) : £1.00
B81-34917

Gray, Cecil, *1923-*. English for life : a basic proficiency course for Caribbean secondary schools / Cecil Gray. — Walton-on-Thames : Nelson Caribbean
Phase 2. — 1981. — v,202p : ill,ports ; 25cm
ISBN 0-17-566247-9 (pbk) : £2.40 B81-38966

The **Ibis** workbooks. — [Glasgow] : Collins
Book 2 / E.E. Mejias & O.N. Stanford. — 1981. — 30p : ill ; 26cm
ISBN 0-00-319811-1 (unbound) : £0.55
B81-12166

Jones, Rhodri. New English for the Caribbean / Rhodri Jones and Ceronne Prevatt-Miller. — London : Heinemann Educational
Bk.1. — 1981. — ix,150p : ill,1chart,facsims ; 25cm
Includes index
ISBN 0-435-10486-1 (pbk) : £2.60 B81-31789

Narinesingh, Roy. Nelson CXC practice tests: English / Roy and Clifford Narinesingh. — Walton-on-Thames : Nelson Caribbean, 1981. — 94p : ill ; 19cm
ISBN 0-17-566132-4 (pbk) : £1.00 B81-36792

Rowe, Brian. Multiple choice questions for CXC English Basic. — London : Hodder and Stoughton, Jan.1982. — [64]p
ISBN 0-340-27028-4 (pbk) : £0.95 : CIP entry
B81-34649

Rowe, Brian. Multiple choice questions for CXC English General. — London : Hodder and Stoughton, Jan.1982. — [64]p
ISBN 0-340-27029-2 (pbk) : £0.95 : CIP entry
B81-34653

428.2'4 — English language — *Questions & answers — For Caribbean students — For schools*

Parker, T. H.. English for common entrance / T.H. Parker and G. King. — London : Longman, 1980. — v,97p ; 25cm
ISBN 0-582-75019-9 (pbk) : £1.10 B81-05837

428.2'4 — English language — *Questions & answers — For non-English speaking students*

Active context English. — London : Macmillan
1: Workbook. — 1981. — 48p : ill ; 25cm
ISBN 0-333-31852-8 (pbk) : Unpriced
B81-36844

Active context English. — London : Macmillan
2: Workbook. — 1981. — 52p : ill,1map ; 25cm
ISBN 0-333-31853-6 (pbk) : Unpriced
B81-36845

Alexander, L. G.. Follow me : English for beginners / by L.G. Alexander, Roy Kingsbury. — [London] : Longman
Bk.2. — [1981]. — v,131p : ill,maps,facsims ; 25cm
ISBN 0-582-51668-4 (pbk) : £2.00 B81-21438

Alexander, L. G.. Follow me : English for beginners / by L.G. Alexander, Roy Kingsbury. — [London] : Longman
Teacher's bk.2. — c1981. — 191p ; 22cm
Includes index
ISBN 0-582-51669-2 (pbk) : £2.50 B81-21436

Alexander, L. G.. Follow me : English for beginners / by L.G. Alexander, Roy Kingsbury. — [London] : Longman
Workbook 2. — 1981. — 30p : ill,facsims ; 24cm
ISBN 0-582-51670-6 (pbk) : £0.70 B81-21437

Archer, Margaret. Practice tests for Cambridge preliminary English / Margaret Archer, Enid Nolan-Woods. — Walton-on-Thames : Nelson
[Pupils book]. — 1981. — [52]p : ill,1map,1plan ; 25cm
Cover title
ISBN 0-17-555313-0 (pbk) : £1.30 B81-38964

Archer, Margaret. Practice tests for Cambridge preliminary English / Margaret Archer, Enid Nolan-Woods. — Walton-on-Thames : Nelson
Teacher's notes. — 1981. — [58]p : ill,1map,1plan ; 25cm
Cover title
ISBN 0-17-555314-9 (pbk) : £1.45 B81-38965

Archer, Margaret. Working with English : a course in general and technical English / M. Archer and Nolan-Woods. — London : Cassell. — (Cassell EFl)
Bk.2. — 1981. — 114p : ill,1map,forms ; 25cm
ISBN 0-304-30541-3 (pbk) : Unpriced : CIP rev. B80-10568

Archer, Margaret. Working with English : a course in general and technical English / M. Archer and E. Nolan-Woods. — London : Cassell. — (Cassell EFL)
Bk.2. — 1981
Teacher's book. — 86p : 1map ; 25cm
ISBN 0-304-30542-1 (pbk) : Unpriced : CIP rev. B80-11005

Archer, Margaret. Working with English : a course in general and technical English / M. Archer and E. Nolan-Woods. — London : Cassell
Book 3. — 1981. — 115p : ill ; 25cm
ISBN 0-304-30615-0 (pbk) : Unpriced : CIP rev. B81-00849

Archer, Margaret. Working with English : a course in general and technical English / M. Archer and E. Nolan-Woods. — London : Cassell
Teacher's book 3. — 1981. — 78p ; 25cm
ISBN 0-304-30616-9 (pbk) : Unpriced : CIP rev. B81-03361

428.2'4 — English language — *Questions & answers — For non-English speaking students*
continuation

Archer, Margaret. Working with English. — London : Cassell, Sept.1981
4: Student's book. — [128]p
ISBN 0-304-30618-5 (pbk) : £2.75 : CIP entry
B81-22679

Archer, Margaret. Working with English. — London : Cassell, Sept.1981
4: Teacher's book. — [80]p
ISBN 0-304-30619-3 (pbk) : £2.95 : CIP entry
B81-23955

Berer, Marge. Mazes : a problem-solving reader / Marge Berer and Mario Rinvolucri. — London : Heinemann Educational, 1981. — 98p : ill ; 15x21cm
ISBN 0-435-28719-2 (pbk) : £1.40 : CIP rev.
B81-14964

Byrne, Donn, *1929-*. Going places : an integrated skills course for post-elementary students / Donn Byrne and Susan Holden. — Harlow : Longman, 1981, c1980. — 80p : ill(some col.),maps(some col.),music,forms ; 30cm
ISBN 0-582-51549-1 (pbk) : Unpriced
B81-08406

Dunlop, Ian, *1925 Nov. 8-*. In and about English / by Ian Dunlop and Heinrich Schrand. — Oxford : Pergamon, 1981. — s1981 : ill,maps,facsims,forms ; 24cm. — (Materials for language practice)
ISBN 0-08-024570-6 (pbk) : £2.50 : CIP rev.
B80-07329

English for adults. — Oxford : Oxford University Press
3: Progress book / M. Bianchi ... [et al.]. — 1981. — 136p : ill,1map,1form ; 24cm
ISBN 0-19-433368-x (pbk) : £1.95 B81-21391

Ferguson, Nicolas. English by objectives / Nicolas Ferguson, Máire O'Reilly. — London : Evans
Preliminary units [Student's book]. — 1978, c1977. — 77p : ill ; 21cm
Originally published: Geneva : Centre for the Experimentation and Evaluation of Language Learning Techniques, 1977
ISBN 0-237-50282-8 (pbk) : Unpriced
B81-09021

Fowler, W. S. (William Scott). Proficiency English / W.S. Fowler. — Walton-on-Thames : Nelson
5: Interview / W.S. Fowler, John Pidcock, Robin Rycroft. — 1981. — 60p : ill ; 25cm
ISBN 0-17-555145-6 (pbk) : £1.75 B81-22091

Fowler, W. S. (William Scott). Test your English / W.S. Fowler and Norman Coe. — Walton-on-Thames : Nelson
Book 1: Beginners to intermediate. — 1977 (1980 [printing]). — 28p ; 25cm
ISBN 0-17-555247-9 (pbk) : Unpriced
B81-15264

Fowler, W. S. (William Scott). Test your English / W.S. Fowler and Norman Coe. — Walton-on-Thames : Nelson
Book 2: Intermediate to First Certificate. — 1978 (1980 [printing]). — 45p ; 25cm
ISBN 0-17-555248-7 (pbk) : Unpriced
B81-15263

Fowler, W. S. (William Scott). Test your English / W.S. Fowler and Norman Coe. — Walton-on-Thames : Nelson
Teachers guide : to books 1, 2 and 3. — 1980. — 76p ; 25cm
ISBN 0-17-555249-5 (pbk) : £1.50 B81-22092

Granger, Colin. Play games with English / Colin Granger ; illustrated by John Plumb. — London : Heinemann Educational
Book 2. — 1981. — 73p : ill ; 21cm
Includes index
ISBN 0-435-28062-7 (pbk) : £0.95 : CIP rev.
B81-12383

Gray, Joanna. Starting English : a new beginner's course / Joanna Gray. — London : Cassell, 1981. — 129p : ill,1map,facsims ; 25cm + Teacher's book(79p: ill ; 25cm). — (Cassell's foundation English ; book 1)
Teacher's book by Susan Henderson & Joanna Gray
ISBN 0-304-30621-5 (pbk) : £2.35 : CIP rev.
ISBN 0-304-30622-3 (Teacher's book) : £3.95
B81-05148

Hartley, Bernard. Streamline English connections : an intensive English course for pre-intermediate students / Bernard Hartley & Peter Viney. — Oxford : Oxford University Press
Workbook A, Unit 1-40. — 1981. — [48]p : ill,forms ; 30cm
ISBN 0-19-432235-1 (pbk) : £1.00 B81-14279

Holiday English. — Rev. version. — London (140 Kensington Church St., W8 4BN) : Mary Glasgow Publications
Level 4. — 1979
Previous ed.: i.e. Pilot ed., 1978
Student's workbook / Hannah Charlton. — 79p : ill ; 30cm
Cover title
ISBN 0-905999-39-8 (pbk) : £1.95 B81-28542

Holiday English. — Rev. version. — London (140 Kensington Church St., W8 4BN) : Mary Glasgow Publications
Level 4. — 1979
Previous ed.: i.e. Pilot ed., 1978
Teacher's handbook / Hannah Charlton. — 20p ; 30cm + supplement(15p:ill;29cm)
ISBN 0-905999-44-4 (pbk) : £1.50 B81-28541

Holiday English. — Rev. version. — London (140 Kensington Church St., W8 4BN) : Mary Glasgow Publications
Level 5. — 1979
Previous ed.: i.e. Pilot ed., 1978
Student's workbook / Patricia Mugglestone. — 79p : ill,1map,2ports ; 30cm
Cover title
ISBN 0-905999-49-5 (pbk) : £1.95 B81-28544

Holiday English. — Rev. version. — London (140 Kensington Church St., W8 4BN) : Mary Glasgow Publications
Level 5. — 1979
Previous ed.: i.e. Pilot ed., 1978
Teacher's handbook / Patricia Mugglestone. — 28p ; 30cm + Supplement(15p:map;29cm)
ISBN 0-905999-54-1 (pbk) : £1.50 B81-28543

Holiday English. — Rev. version. — London (140 Kensington Church St., W8 4BN) : Mary Glasgow Publications
Level 6. — 1979
Previous ed.: i.e. Pilot ed., 1978
Student's workbook / Richard Young. — 79p : ill,2maps,facsims,1port ; 30cm
Cover title
ISBN 0-905999-59-2 (pbk) : £1.95 B81-28540

Holiday English. — Rev. version. — London (140 Kensington Church St., W8 4BN) : Mary Glasgow Publications
Level 6. — 1979
Previous ed.: i.e. Pilot ed., 1978
Teacher's handbook / Richard Young. — 26p ; 30cm + Supplement(15p:ill;29cm)
ISBN 0-905999-64-9 (pbk) : £1.50 B81-28545

Kassem, Maureen J. E.. Tests in English for overseas students. — Cheltenham : Thornes, Aug.1981. — [224]p
ISBN 0-85950-464-6 (pbk) : £4.50 : CIP entry
B81-20147

Kassem, Maureen J. E.. Tests in English for overseas students. — Cheltenham : Thornes, Aug.1981
Teacher's guide. — [96]p
ISBN 0-85950-318-6 (pbk) : £1.50 : CIP entry
B81-16903

Kay, Christian. Preliminary English practice tests / Christian Kay, Frances Simmonds. — [Glasgow] : Collins, [1981]. — 80p : ill,1map,plans ; 22cm + Key(24p ; 22cm)
ISBN 0-00-370030-5 (pbk) : £1.50
ISBN 0-00-370031-3 (Key) : £0.85 B81-12161

Meredith-Parry, John. Getting through / by John Meredith-Parry and Lorraine Weller. — London : Edward Arnold. — 1981
Workbook. — 63p : ill ; 25cm
ISBN 0-7131-8068-4 (pbk) : £1.35 : CIP rev.
B81-18109

Network / John Eastwood ... [et al.]. — Oxford : Oxford University Press
1. — 1981
Workbook. — 104p : ill,1map,1geneal.table ; 25cm
ISBN 0-19-457053-3 (pbk) : £1.50 B81-11535

Network / John Eastwood ... [et al.]. — Oxford : Oxford University Press
2. — 1981
Student's book. — 200p : ill,maps ; 25cm
ISBN 0-19-457056-8 (pbk) : £2.50 B81-29880

Network / John Eastwood ... [et al.]. — Oxford : Oxford University Press
2. — 1981
Teacher's book. — 164p ; 25cm
ISBN 0-19-457057-6 (pbk) : £4.50 B81-31400

Network / John Eastwood ...[et al.]. — Oxford : Oxford University Press
2. — 1981
Wordbook. — 10'2p : ill ; 25cm
ISBN 0-19-457058-4 (pbk) : £1.50 B81-31399

Prowse, Philip. Exchanges / Philip Prowse, Judy Garton-Sprenger ; project adviser T.C. Jupp. — Complete ed. — London : Heinemann Educational. — (Main course English. Level 2)
Students' book. — 1981. — 153p : ill(some col.),forms ; 30cm
ISBN 0-435-28470-3 (pbk) : £2.95 : CIP rev.
B81-13478

Prowse, Philip. Exchanges / Philip Prowse, Judy Garton-Sprenger ; project adviser T.C. Jupp. — London : Heinemann Educational. — (Main course English. Level 1)
Students' book
Part B. — 1981. — p73-149 : ill(some col.),facsims ; 30cm
ISBN 0-435-28468-1 (pbk) : £1.95 : CIP rev.
B81-13486

Skills for learning. — Walton-on-Thames : Nelson. — 1980
Development. — International ed. — 226p : ill ; 25cm
ISBN 0-17-580092-8 (pbk) : £2.95
ISBN 0-17-580093-6 (Teachers' book) : £2.25
B81-17086

Swan, H. A.. English for yourself / H.A. Swan ; illustrations by Barney Aldridge. — Amersham : Hulton, 1981. — 157p : ill,maps,facsims,form ; 24cm
ISBN 0-7175-0874-9 (pbk) : £2.40 B81-21153

Thorn, Michael. Exploring English / Michael Thorn. — London : Cassell. — (Cassell's foundation English ; bk.3)
Teacher's book / Michael Thorn, Joanna Gray. — Rev. ed. / revised by Susan Henderson. — 1981. — iv,91p ; 25cm
Previous ed.: 1979
ISBN 0-304-30786-6 (pbk) : £3.95 B81-35413

Yorio, Carlos A.. Who did/done it? : a crime reader for students of English / Carlos A. Yorio, L.A. Morse. — Englewood Cliffs ; London : Prentice-Hall, c1981. — viii,184p : ill ; 23cm
The word 'done' in the title is crossed out
ISBN 0-13-958207-x (pbk) : £4.50 B81-16671

428.2'4 — English language — *Questions & answers — For non-English speaking students — For schools*

Hartley, Bernard. Streamline English connection : an intensive English course for pre-intermediate students. — Oxford : Oxford University Press
Workbook B, units 41-80. — 1981. — [48]p : ill ; 30cm
ISBN 0-19-432236-x (pbk) : Unpriced
B81-29390

428.2′4 — English language. Special subjects: Great Britain. Social life — *For non-English speaking students*

Bulger, Anthony. Explorations / Anthony Bulger ; conceived by Anthony Bulger and Michel Bellity ; cover and illustrations by Y. Primault. — Oxford : Pergamon for and on behalf of the British European Centre, 1981. — xiv,164p : ill,1map,facsims ; 23cm. — (English language courses)
At head of half-title: Pergamon Institute of English (Oxford). — Originally published: 1979. — Bibliography: pxi
ISBN 0-08-025358-x (pbk) : £2.95 B81-19551

428.2′4 — Trinity College, London. Non-English speaking students. Curriculum subjects: Spoken English language. Syllabuses

Maddock, Vivienne. Getting through Trinity College English. — Oxford : Pergamon, June 1981. — [160]p. — (Pergamon Institute of English (Oxford) materials for language practice)
ISBN 0-08-024574-9 (pbk) : £2.50 : CIP entry B81-12390

428.2′4′0245 — English language — *Questions & answers* — *For science* — *For non-English speaking students*

Chaplen, Frank. A course in intermediate scientific English / Frank Chaplen. — London : Evans, 1981. — 149p : ill ; 25cm
ISBN 0-237-50418-9 (pbk) : Unpriced B81-19862

Chaplen, Frank. A course in intermediate scientific English / Frank Chaplen. — London : Evans
Teacher's book. — 1981. — 99p : ill ; 25cm
ISBN 0-237-50514-2 (pbk) : Unpriced B81-19861

428.2′4′0246 — English language — For technology — For non-English speaking students

Moore, C. J.. Craft in English. — London : Heinemann Educational
Craft reader. — Nov.1981. — [72]p
ISBN 0-435-28560-2 (pbk) : £1.95 : CIP entry B81-30306

428.2′4′0246 — English language — *For technology* — *For non-English speaking students*

Moore, C. J.. Craft in English. — London : Heinemann Educational
Language workbook. — Nov.1981. — [88]p
ISBN 0-435-28561-0 (pbk) : £1.60 : CIP entry B81-30163

Moore, C. J.. Craft in English. — London : Heinemann
Teachers' book. — Nov.1981. — [64]p
ISBN 0-435-28562-9 (pbk) : £3.00 : CIP entry B81-30161

428.2′4′024647 — English language - *For non-English speaking hotel personnel*

Binham, Philip. Hotel English. — Oxford : Pergamon, June 1981. — [128]p. — (Materials for language practice)
ISBN 0-08-025340-7 (pbk) : £2.90 : CIP entry B81-12316

428.2′4′07 — Non-English speaking students. Education. Curriculum subjects: English language — *For teaching*

Towards the creative teaching of English / Maggie Melville ... [et al.] ; edited by Lou Spaventa. — London : Allen & Unwin, 1980. — 94p : ill ; 25cm
ISBN 0-04-371074-3 (pbk) : £4.50 : CIP rev. B80-12328

428.2′4′07 — Non-English speaking students. Education. Curriculum subjects: English language. Teaching

Lewis, Michael, *1945-*. Source book for teaching English overseas : a practical guide for language assistants / Michael Lewis and Jimmie Hill. — London : Heinemann Educational, 1981. — 119p : ill ; 25cm
Bibliography: p116-117
ISBN 0-435-28992-6 (pbk) : £4.95 B81-31964

Strevens, Peter, *1922--*. Teaching English as an international language : from practice to principle / Peter Strevens. — Oxford : Pergamon, 1980. — xi,163p : 1map ; 21cm. — (Language teaching methodology series)
Bibliography: p151-160. — Includes index
ISBN 0-08-025333-4 (pbk) : £4.95 : CIP rev. B80-12812

428.2′4′07 — Non-English speaking students. Education. Curriculum subjects: English language. Teaching. Communication

Communication in the classroom : applications and methods for a communicative approach / edited by Keith Johnson and Keith Morrow. — Harlow : Longman, 1981. — vi,152p : ill ; 22cm. — (Longman handbooks for language teachers)
Bibliography: p147-152
ISBN 0-582-74605-1 (pbk) : Unpriced B81-19052

428.2′4′07 — Non-English speaking students. Education. Curriculum subjects: English language. Teaching — *Manuals*

Nicholls, Sandra. Teaching English as a second language / by Sandra Nicholls and Julia Naish. — London : British Broadcasting Corporation, 1981. — 96p : ill,forms ; 21cm
Bibliography: p95-96
ISBN 0-563-16444-1 (pbk) : £2.95 B81-07973

428.2′4′07 — Non-English speaking students. Education. Curriculum subjects: English language. Teaching — *Serials*

Practical English teaching : a magazine for teachers of English as a foreign language. — Vol., no.1 (Oct.1980)-. — London : Mary Glasgow Publications, 1980-. — v. : ill ; 30cm
Quarterly
ISSN 0260-4752 = Practical English teaching : £5.50 per year B81-04094

428.2′4′071 — Schools. Non-English speaking students. Curriculum subjects: English language. Teaching

Ellis, Rod. Teaching secondary English : a guide to the teaching of English as a second language / Rod Ellis, Brian Tomlinson. — London : Longman, 1980. — v,330p : ill,1map ; 21cm
Bibliography: p328. - Includes index
ISBN 0-582-60170-3 (pbk) : £2.90 B81-03891

428.2′4′0715 — Adult education institutions. Non-English speaking students. Curriculum subjects: English language. Syllabuses. Development

Munday, John. Communicative syllabus design : a sociolinguistic model for defining the content of purpose-specific language programmes / John Mundy. — Cambridge : Cambridge University Press, 1981, c1978. — vi,232p : ill ; 23cm
Bibliography: p219-228. — Includes index
ISBN 0-521-28294-2 (pbk) : £4.95 B81-15336

428.2′4′076 — Non-English speaking students. Curriculum subjects: English language. Examinations set by University of Cambridge. First Certificate in English & Certificate of Proficiency in English. Techniques — *Manuals*

Gethin, Anthony. How to pass Cambridge First Certificate and Proficiency in English. — Oxford : Blackwell, Oct.1981. — [128]p
ISBN 0-631-12904-9 : £2.95 : CIP entry B81-28069

428.2′4′078 — English language. Teaching aids: Word puzzles — *For non-English speaking students*

Jones, Lewis, *1924-*. Graded English puzzles / Lewis Jones ; illustrations by Willie Rodger. — Glasgow : Collins
Book 4. — 1981. — 48p : ill ; 18cm. — (Collins English library. Level 4)
ISBN 0-00-370303-7 (pbk) : £0.60 B81-34767

Jones, Lewis, *1924-*. Graded English puzzles / Lewis Jones ; illustrations by Willie Rodger. — Glasgow : Collins
Book 5. — 1981. — 48p : ill ; 18cm. — (Collins English library. Level 5)
ISBN 0-00-370304-5 (pbk) : £0.60 B81-34768

Jones, Lewis, *1924-*. Graded English puzzles / Lewis Jones ; illustrations by Willie Rodger. — Glasgow : Collins
Book 6. — 1981. — 48p : ill ; 18cm. — (Collins English library. Level 6)
ISBN 0-00-370305-3 (pbk) : £0.60 B81-34769

428.2′4′078 — Non-English speaking students. Education. Curriculum subjects: English language. Teaching materials

Lewis, Michael. Source book for teaching English overseas. — London : Allen & Unwin, Aug.1981. — [128]p
ISBN 0-04-371086-7 (pbk) : £6.95 : CIP entry B81-15879

428.2′4′078 — Non-English speaking students. Education. Curriculum subjects: English language. Teaching. Use of blackboards

Mugglestone, Patricia. Planning and using the blackboard / Patricia Mugglestone. — London : Allen & Unwin, 1980. — 95p : ill,maps ; 20cm. — (Practical language teaching ; no.1)
Bibliography: p94-95
ISBN 0-04-371062-x (pbk) : £2.50 : CIP rev. B79-36289

Shaw, Peter, *19---*. Using blackboard drawing / Peter Shaw and Thérèse de Vet. — London : Allen & Unwin, 1980. — 128p : ill ; 20cm. — (Practical language teaching ; no.5)
ISBN 0-04-371075-1 (pbk) : £3.50 : CIP rev. B80-18225

428.2′441 — English language. Grammar - *For French students*

Culhane, Terry. English alone. — Oxford : Pergamon, June 1981. — [160]p. — (Pergamon Institute of English (Oxford) English language courses)
ISBN 0-08-025308-3 (pbk) : £15.00 : CIP entry B81-12315

428.2′489 — English language. Phrasal verbs — *For Greek students*

Tsekouras, Dimitri. English phrasal verbs in Greek / Dimitri Tsekiuras. — London : Hodder and Stoughton, c1980. — 184p ; 22cm
ISBN 0-340-24482-8 (pbk) : £2.10 : CIP rev. B80-04158

428.2′4927 — English language — *For Arabic speaking students*

Allen, W. Stannard. Progressive living English for the Arab world / W. Stannard Allen, [J.M. Morgan, Alan C. McLean]. — Harlow : Longman
Teacher's bk.3 / W. Stannard Allen, Alan C. McLean. — c1976 (1981 [printing]). — xiii,154p ; 22cm
ISBN 0-582-76492-0 (pbk) : £1.38 B81-32959

McLean, Alan C.. Gateway : a first English course for Arab students / Alan C. McLean. — Harlow : Longman
Teachers guide 1. — 1980. — x,156p : ill ; 24cm
Includes index
ISBN 0-582-76284-7 (pbk) : £2.50 B81-24482

428.2′4927 — English language — *For Saudi-Arabian students*

Saudi Arabian schools' English. — [London] : Macmillan
Secondary second grade. — 1981
Reader 2 / [writers and advisers Norman Cook and Colin Swatridge]. — 46p : ill ; 24cm
ISBN 0-333-31589-8 (pbk) : Unpriced B81-40108

428.2′496 — English language. Comprehension — *Questions & answers. For East African students*

Bracey, N. W.. Comprehension and summary for O-level / N.W. Bracey. — Harlow : Longman, 1981. — viii,87p ; 22cm
ISBN 0-582-60194-0 (pbk) : £1.10 B81-37404

428.2′496 — English language — *For African students* — *For schools*

Crew, C. C.. Seek and find English / C.C. Crew. — Teacher's ed. — Exeter : Wheaton, 1960 (1978 [printing]). — 80,15p ; 24cm
ISBN 0-08-022875-5 (pbk) : £1.00 B81-26560

428.2′496 — English language — *For Sudanese students*

Bates, Martin, *1949-*. The NILE course for the Sudan / Martin Bates. — London : Longman. — (New integrated Longman English)
Pupils' bk.2 / Martin Bates, Michael Palmer. — 1981. — 160p : col.ill,col.maps,col.facsims ; 24cm
Text on inside covers
ISBN 0-582-76457-2 (pbk) : £1.68 B81-21434

Bates, Martin, *1949-*. The Nile course for the Sudan / Martin Bates. — Harlow : Longman
Teacher's book 2. — 1981. — 338p ; 22cm
ISBN 0-582-76458-0 (pbk) : £2.10 B81-40701

The **NILE** course for the Sudan. — Harlow : Longman. — (New integrated Longman English)
Student's book 5 / Julian Corbluth. — 1981. — 152p : ill ; 24cm
ISBN 0-582-76460-2 (pbk) : £1.90 B81-24480

428.2′496 — English language — *For West African students*

Hyde, Elizabeth, *1924-*. New Evans primary English / [Elizabeth Hyde and Michael Kelly]. — London : Evans. — 48p : col.ill ; 25cm
ISBN 0-237-50591-6 (pbk) : Unpriced B81-23541

Hyde, Elizabeth, *1924-*. New Evans primary English / Elizabeth Hyde, Michael Kelly. — London : Evans
1
Teacher's bk. — 1981. — 98p : ill ; 25cm
ISBN 0-237-50592-4 (pbk) : Unpriced B81-29165

428′.2′496 — English language — *Questions & answers — For Cameroon students*

Ndangam, Augustine. Evans Cameroon primary English : pupil's book for the final year / Augustine Ndangam and David Weir. — London : Evans, 1980. — viii,135p : ill,maps ; 25cm
ISBN 0-237-50447-2 (pbk) : Unpriced B81-32362

428.2′496 — English language — *Questions & answers — For East African students*

Grant, Neville J. H.. English in use : an English course for secondary schools / Neville J.H. Grant, C.R. Wang'ombe with the advice of K. Barasa. — [London] : Longman
[Students'] bk.3. — 1980. — v,187p : ill,1map,1form ; 25cm
ISBN 0-582-60176-2 (pbk) : £1.75 B81-15240

428.2′4963 — English language — *For Nigerian students*

Nation-wide English : a course for primary schools / Ronald Ridout ... [et al.]. — London : Evans
5
Teacher's bk. — 1981. — 115p ; 22cm
ISBN 0-237-50463-4 (pbk) : Unpriced B81-29167

428.2′4963 — English language — *Questions & answers — For Nigerian students*

Montgomery, Michael, *1940-*. Effective English / Michael Montgomery. — London : Evans Bros, 1981
Practice book 4 / [illustrated by Annette Olney]. — 47p : ill ; 25cm
ISBN 0-237-50493-6 (unbound) : Unpriced B81-20859

428.3 — ENGLISH LANGUAGE. SPOKEN EXPRESSION

428.3 — Spoken English language — *For teaching non-English speaking students*

English for adults / M. Bianchi ... [et al.]. — Oxford : Oxford University Press
3: Course leader's handbook. — 1981. — x,130p : ill
Adaptation of English für Erwachsene. Bd.3
ISBN 0-19-433369-8 (pbk) : £4.50 B81-14499

428.3 — Spoken English language. Grammar

Lennox Cook, John. The student's book of English : transcript of recordings / John Lennox Cook, Amorey Gethin, Barry Unsworth. — Oxford : Blackwell, 1981. — 64p ; 15cm
ISBN 0-631-12589-2 (unbound) : Unpriced B81-11333

428.3 — Spoken English language. Role-playing exercises

Lamb, Michael. Factions and fictions. — Oxford : Pergamon, Jan.1982. — [128]p. — (Materials for language practice)
ISBN 0-08-028612-7 (pbk) : £4.50 : CIP entry B81-34473

428.3 — Spoken English language. Teaching aids: Board games

Benson, Bryan. Wordways boards. — Oxford : Pergamon. — (Materials for language practice)
Teacher's guide. — Nov.1981. — [16]p
ISBN 0-08-025362-8 (pbk) : £3.50 : CIP entry B81-28797

428.3 — Spoken English language. Usage by students of schools in Great Britain

Language in school and community / edited by Neil Mercer. — London : Edward Arnold, 1981. — vii,248p : ill ; 22cm
Includes bibliographies and index
ISBN 0-7131-6347-x (pbk) : £5.75 : CIP rev. B81-16359

428.3′07′8 — Spoken English language. Teaching aids: Longman sound cassette tape recordings — *For teaching*

How to make the most of graded readers on cassette / compiled and edited by Janet Tadman. — Harlow : Longman, 1980. — 29p ; 20cm
ISBN 0-582-52785-6 (pbk) : Unpriced B81-12242

428.3′4 — Spoken English language. Comprehension — *Questions & answers — For non-English speaking students*

Todd, Frances. Focus listening / Frances Todd. — London : Macmillan
ISBN 0-333-30751-8 (pbk) : Unpriced B81-26341

Todd, Frances. Focus listening / Frances Todd. — London : Macmillan
Teacher's book. — 1981. — 85p : ill,maps,plans ; 24cm
ISBN 0-333-30752-6 (pbk) : Unpriced B81-26340

428.3′4 — Spoken English language. Dialogues — *For non-English speaking students*

Hargreaves, Roger. Arguing and discussing / Roger Hargreaves and Mark Fletcher. — London : Evans, 1981. — 70p : ill ; 21cm. — (Evans functional units)
ISBN 0-237-50423-5 (pbk) : Unpriced B81-16135

428.3′4 — Spoken English language — *For non-English speaking students*

Byrne, John, *19---*. Zig zag : an activity course for children / John Byrne & Anne Waugh. — Oxford : Oxford University Press
Student's book year 3 / illustrated by Annabel Spenceley ... [et al.] ; location photographs by Terry Williams. — 1981. — 96p : ill,maps,ports ; 30cm
ISBN 0-19-433338-8 (pbk) : £1.95 B81-38588

Byrne, John, *19---*. Zigzag : an activity course for children / John Byrne & Anne Waugh. — Oxford : Oxford University Press
Teacher's book year 3. — 1981. — 103p : 1map ; 30cm
ISBN 0-19-433340-x (spiral) : £3.00 B81-38372

428.3′4 — Spoken English language - *For non-English speaking students*

Cook, Vivian. English for life. — International ed. — Oxford : Pergamon, May 1981. — (Pergamon Institute of English (Oxford) English language courses)
Vol.2: Meeting people
Students' book. — [160]p
ISBN 0-08-024608-7 (pbk) : £2.95 : CIP entry B81-08836

428.3′4 — Spoken English language — *For non-English speaking students*

Cook, Vivian. People and places. — International ed. — Oxford : Pergamon, Dec.1981. — (English for life ; v.1)
Key. — [32]p
ISBN 0-08-027233-9 (pbk) : £1.00 : CIP entry B81-36985

Cook, Vivian. People and places / V.J. Cook ; designed and illustrated by Rowan Barnes-Murphy. — International ed. — (English for life ; v.1)
Students' book. — Oxford : Pergamon, 1980. — vii,133p : ill,maps,facsims,1plan,forms,ports ; 25cm
ISBN 0-08-024564-1 (pbk) : £1.95 : CIP rev. B80-00157

Cook, Vivian. People and places. — International ed. — Oxford : Pergamon, Dec.1981. — (English for life ; v.1)
Workbook. — [96]p
ISBN 0-08-027231-2 (pbk) : £2.00 : CIP entry B81-36986

Keltner, Autumn. English for adult competency / Autumn Keltner, Leann Howard, Frances Lee, with Virginia Kellner ... [et al.] ; illustrations by Mark Neyndorff. — Englewood Cliffs ; London : Prentice-Hall
Bk.2 / Autumn Keltner and Gretchen Bitterlin with Sandra Coler, Joan Lindgren, Selma Myers. — c1981. — xi,188p : ill,forms ; 28cm
ISBN 0-13-279752-6 (pbk) : £3.85 B81-12963

McDowell, John. Basic listening. — London : Edward Arnold
Student's book. — Jan.1982. — [32]p
ISBN 0-7131-8069-2 (pbk) : £1.50 : CIP entry B81-34585

McDowell, John. Basic listening. — London : Edward Arnold
Teacher's book. — Jan.1982. — [80]p
ISBN 0-7131-8075-7 (pbk) : £3.50 : CIP entry B81-34586

Smith, Bernard. In your own words. — London : Hodder & Stoughton Educational, Oct.1981. — [144]p
ISBN 0-340-25319-3 (pbk) : £2.95 : CIP entry B81-31161

428.3′4 — Spoken English language. Grammar — *Questions & answers — For non-English speaking students*

Molinsky, Steven J.. Side by side : English grammar through guided conversations / Steven J. Molinsky, Bill Bliss ; illustrated by Richard E. Hill. — Englewood Cliffs ; London : Prentice-Hall
Includes index
ISBN 0-13-809855-7 (pbk) : £4.50 B81-09293

428.3′4 — Spoken English language — *Questions & answers — For non-English speaking students*

Watcyn-Jones, Peter. Pair work : activities for effective communication / Peter Watcyn-Jones. — Harmondsworth : Penguin, 1981. — 2v.(126p) : ill,maps,forms ; 25cm. — (Penguin functional English)
ISBN 0-14-081320-9 (pbk) : Unpriced
ISBN 0-14-081321-7 (Student B) B81-17028

428.3′4 — Spoken English language. Role-playing exercises — *For non-English speaking students — For schools*

Cripwell, K. R.. On the line / [compiled by] K. Cripwell. — Oxford : Oxford University Press, 1981. — [96]p : chiefly ill,maps,facsim,forms ; 20x21cm
ISBN 0-19-432782-5 (pbk) : £1.95 B81-36460

428.3′4′024372 — Spoken English language — *For teaching non-English speaking students*

Ur, Penny. Discussions that work. — Cambridge : Cambridge University Press, Nov.1981. — [122]p. — (Cambridge handbooks for English language teachers. New series)
ISBN 0-521-28169-5 (pbk) : £2.95 : CIP entry B81-38814

428.3′4′024642 — Spoken English language. Dialogues — *For non-English speaking restaurant personnel*

Binham, Philip. Restaurant English. — Oxford : Pergamon, July 1981. — [128]p. — (Pergamon Institute of English (Oxford) materials for language practice)
ISBN 0-08-025339-3 (pbk) : £2.90 : CIP entry
B81-13442

428.3′407 — Non-English speaking students. Education. Curriculum subjects: English language — *For teaching*

Winn Bell Olsen, Judy E.. Communication starters. — Oxford : Pergamon, Sept.1981. — [96]p. — (Language teaching methodology)
ISBN 0-08-025360-1 (pbk) : £3.25 : CIP entry
B81-21573

428.4 — ENGLISH LANGUAGE. READING

428.4 — Children. Reading skills. Development

Clay, Marie M.. Reading : the patterning of complex behaviour / Marie M. Clay. — 2nd ed. — Auckland ; London : Heinemann Educational, 1979. — 276p : ill ; 22cm
Previous ed.: 1972. — Includes bibliographies and index
ISBN 0-435-80234-8 (pbk) : £3.95 B81-25257

428.4 — Reading. Learning by children

Meek, Margaret. Learning to read. — London : Bodley Head, Sept.1981. — [192]p
ISBN 0-370-30154-4 : £4.95 : CIP entry
B81-25134

428.4′01′9 — English language. Reading. Psycholinguistic aspects — *Conference proceedings*

United Kingdom Reading Association. *Conference (17th : 1980 : University of Warwick)*. The reader and the text : proceedings of the seventeenth annual course and conference of the United Kingdom Reading Association, University of Warwick, 1980 / editor L. John Chapman. — London : Heinemann Educational, 1981. — 172p : ill ; 22cm
Includes bibliographies
ISBN 0-435-10908-1 (pbk) : £5.95 B81-36252

428.4′01′9 — Reading. Learning by man. Psychological aspects

Sanford, A. J.. Understanding written language : explorations in comprehension beyond the sentence / A.J. Sanford and S.C. Garrod. — Chichester : Wiley, c1981. — xiv,224 : ill ; 24cm
Bibliography: p214-220. — Includes index
ISBN 0-471-27842-4 : £11.30 B81-14761

428.4′01′9 — Reading. Psychological aspects

Neuropsychological and cognitive processes in reading / edited by Francis J. Pirozzolo, Merlin C. Wittrock. — New York ; London : Academic Press, 1981. — xvii,344p : ill ; 24cm. — (Perspectives in neurolinguistics, neuropsychology, and psycholinguistics)
Includes bibliographies and index
ISBN 0-12-557360-x : £16.60 B81-35747

428.4′01′9 — Reading. Psychological aspects — *Conference proceedings*

Processing of visible language. — New York ; London : Published in cooperation with NATO Scientific Affairs Division [by] Plenum. — (NATO conference series. III, Human factors ; v13)
Includes bibliographies and index
2 / edited by Paul A. Kolers, Merald E. Wrolstad and Herman Bouma. — 1980. — xvii,616p : ill ; 26cm
Conference papers
ISBN 0-306-40576-8 : Unpriced B81-09285

428.4′05 — Reading skills — *Serials*

[Reading research *(New York)*]. Reading research. — Vol.2. — New York ; London : Academic Press, 1981. — x,233p
ISBN 0-12-572302-4 : £12.40 B81-33320

428.4′07′1042 — England. Schools. Curriculum subjects: Reading. Teaching

Towards a language policy. — [Coventry] (Mile Lane, Coventry CV1 2NN) : [Elm Bank Teachers Centre], [1981]. — 85p : 1ill,2forms ; 30cm
ISBN 0-901606-30-8 (spiral) : Unpriced
B81-14736

428.4′07′12417 — Ireland *(Republic)*. Secondary schools. Students, 12-13 years. Reading skills

Swan, T. Desmond. Reading standards in Irish schools : a national survey of reading standards and related aspects of first year pupils in post-primary schools in the Republic of Ireland, 1971-72 / by T. Desmond Swan. — Dublin : Educational Company of Ireland, 1978. — iii,97p : ill,1form ; 21cm
Bibliography: p91-97
ISBN 0-904916-76-6 (pbk) : Unpriced
B81-37768

428.4′076 — English language. Reading — *Questions & answers — For non-English speaking students*

Barr, Pauline. Advanced reading skills / Pauline Barr, John Clegg and Catherine Wallace. — Harlow : Longman, 1981. — vii,191p : ill,forms,ports ; 25cm
ISBN 0-582-55904-9 (pbk) : £2.75 B81-29688

Sonka, Amy L.. Skillful reading : a text and workbook for students of English as a second language / Amy L. Sonka ; with editorial assistance by Elizabeth Whalley. — Englewood Cliffs ; London : Prentice-Hall, c1981. — xix,278p : ill,plans,forms ; 28cm
Includes index
ISBN 0-13-812404-3 (pbk) : £5.15 B81-12525

428.4′076 — English language. Reading — *Questions & answers — For schools*

Jennaway, Lorna. Reading is easy / Lorna Jennaway. — Sydney ; London : McGraw-Hill Bk.1. — c1980. — xv,207p : ill ; 28cm
Includes index
ISBN 0-07-093507-6 (pbk) : £4.25 B81-10366

Jennaway, Lorna. Reading is easy / Lorna Jennaway. — Sydney ; London : McGraw-Hill Bk.2. — c1980. — xv,203p : ill ; 28cm
Includes index
ISBN 0-07-093508-4 (pbk) : £4.25 B81-10373

428.4′2 — Reading disordered children. Reading skills. Assessment & development — *For teaching*

Clay, Marie M.. The early detection of reading difficulties : a diagnostic survey with recovery procedures / Marie M. Clay. — 2nd ed. — Auckland, N.Z. ; London : Heinemann Educational, 1979. — 118p : ill,forms ; 26cm
Previous ed.: 1972. — Bibliography: p90. — Includes index
ISBN 0-435-80239-9 (pbk) : £2.95 B81-02857

Dechant, Emerald. Diagnosis and remediation of reading disabilities / Emerald Dechant. — Englewood Cliffs ; London : Prentice-Hall, c1981. — xiv,410p : ill,forms ; 25cm
Bibliography: p387-402. — Includes index
ISBN 0-13-208454-6 : £11.65 B81-22709

Harris, Albert J.. How to increase reading ability : a guide to developmental and remedial methods / Albert J. Harris and Edward R. Sipay. — 7th ed. rev. and enl. — New York ; London : Longman, c1980. — xix,763p : ill,forms ; 25cm
Previous ed.: New York : D. McKay, 1975. — Bibliography: p583-676. — Includes index
ISBN 0-582-28066-4 : £12.95 B81-23677

428.4′2 — Schools. Reading disordered students. Reading skills. Teaching. Use of phonics — *For teaching*

Ekwall, Eldon E.. Diagnostic-prescriptive phonics lessons : a corrective-remedial approach for disabled readers : student puzzle pages and worksheets / Eldon E. Ekwall. — Boston, Mass. ; London : Allyn and Bacon, c1981. — ix,150p : ill,forms ; 28cm + Teacher's manual (62p ; ill,forms ; 24cm)
ISBN 0-205-07227-5 (pbk) : £18.95
ISBN 0-205-07225-9 (teacher's manual) : £17.95 B81-24238

428.4′2′071073 — United States. Schools. Curriculum subjects: Reading. Remedial teaching

Bader, Lois A.. Reading diagnosis and remediation in classroom and clinic : a guide to becoming an effective diagnostic-remedial teacher of reading and language skills / Lois A. Bader. — New York : Macmillan ; London : Collier Macmillan, c1980. — xii,300p : ill,forms ; 26cm
Bibliography: p293-295. - Includes index
ISBN 0-02-305100-0 (pbk) : £6.95 B81-02223

428.4′3 — Reading skills. Self-development — *Manuals — For students in American higher education institutions*

Rubin, Dorothy. Reading and learning power / Dorothy Rubin. — New York : Macmillan ; London : Collier Macmillan, c1980. — xiv,476p : ill,forms ; 26cm
Includes index
ISBN 0-02-404290-0 (pbk) : £5.95
Primary classification 378′.17028′120973
B81-00830

428.4′3′0240431 — Children. Reading skills. Development — *For parents*

Ervin, Jane. Reading with your child : number one priority / Jane Ervin. — Boston [Mass.] ; London : Allyn and Bacon, c1981. — [16]p : col. ill ; 14x22cm. — (Your child CAN read and YOU can help series)
Text on inside cover
ISBN 0-205-07554-1 (pbk) : Unpriced
B81-31421

McKenzie, Moira. Helping your child with reading / Moira McKenzie. — London : Watts, c1980. — 80p : ill ; 18cm.. — (Parents′ guides)
Bibliography: p73-79. — Includes index
ISBN 0-85166-865-8 : £2.95 B81-07208

428.4′3′071242817 — West Yorkshire *(Metropolitan County)*. Bradford. Middle schools. Students. Reading skills. Development. Projects: Bradford Book Flood Experiment

Ingham, Jennie. Books and reading development : the Bradford Book Flood Experiment / Jennie Ingham. — London : Heinemann Educational on behalf of the British National Bibliography, 1981. — xvi,318p : 1form ; 23cm
Experiment funded by the British National Bibliography Research Fund. — Bibliography: p316-318
ISBN 0-435-10450-0 : £16.50 : CIP rev.
B81-20463

428.6 — ENGLISH LANGUAGE. READING BOOKS

428.6 — English language. Reading books — *Christian viewpoints — For pre-school children*

Doney, Meryl. Now I am big / Meryl Doney ; pictures by D′reen Neeves. — Tring : Lion Publishing, 1981. — [16]p : chiefly col.ill ; 19cm. — (Little Lions under fives)
ISBN 0-85648-222-6 (pbk) : £0.35 B81-26998

428.6 — English language. Reading books — *For children*

You and me : for young children : the first you and me book / [editor Philip Clark] ; [contributors Susan Baker, Diane Wilmer] ; [illustrators Peter Bailey, Lynne Cousins]. — London : British Broadcasting Corportation, 1981. — 64p : ill(some col.) ; 30cm
Cover title. — Based on the BBC Television series
ISBN 0-563-31681-0 (pbk) : £2.85 B81-36421

428.6 — English language. Reading books — *For pre-school children*

Berg, Leila. The hot, hot day / Leila Berg ; photographs by John Walmsley. — London : Methuen Children′s, 1981. — [24]p : chiefly col.ill ; 16cm. — (Methuen chatterbooks)
ISBN 0-416-88790-2 : £1.25 B81-29803

Berg, Leila. In a house I know / Leila Berg ; photographs by John Walmsley. — London : Methuen Children′s, 1981. — [24]p : chiefly col.ill ; 16cm. — (Methuen chatterbooks)
ISBN 0-416-88800-3 : £1.25 B81-29802

428.6 — English language. Reading books — *For pre-school children* *continuation*

Berg, Leila. Our walk / Leila Berg ; photographs by John Walmsley. — London : Methuen Children's, 1981. — [24]p : chiefly col.ill ; 16cm. — (Methuen chatterbooks)
ISBN 0-416-88810-0 : £1.25 B81-29805

Berg, Leila. A tickle / Leila Berg ; photographs by John Walmsley. — London : Methuen Children's, 1981. — [24]p : chiefly col.ill ; 16cm. — (Methuen chatterbooks)
ISBN 0-416-88780-5 : £1.25 B81-29804

Bruna, Dick. My meals / [illustrations by Dick Bruna]. — London : Methuen Children's, 1980, c1979. — 1folded sheet([16]p) : all col.ill ; 14cm. — (A Dick Bruna zig zag book)
ISBN 0-416-89930-7 : £1.50 B81-07866

Bruna, Dick. My toys / [illustrations by Dick Bruna]. — London : Methuen Children's, 1980, c1979. — 1folded sheet([16]p) : all col.ill ; 14cm. — (A Dick Bruna zig zag book)
ISBN 0-416-89920-x : £1.50 B81-07864

Bruna, Dick. Out and about / [illustrations by Dick Bruna]. — London : Methuen Children's, 1980, c1979. — 1folded sheet([16]p) : all col.ill ; 14cm. — (A Dick Bruna zig zag book)
ISBN 0-416-89940-4 : £1.50 B81-07865

Bruna, Dick. When I'm big / Dick Bruna. — London : Methuen, 1981. — [26]p : col.ill ; 16cm
ISBN 0-416-20860-6 : £1.35 B81-19740

Docherty, Maura. The lost mouse / by Maura Docherty ; illustrated by Anne Boyd. — Andover : Philograph, c1980. — 16p : col.ill ; 21cm. — (A Read and talk book)
ISBN 0-85370-416-3 (pbk) : £2.30 B81-27850

Docherty, Maura. The park / by Maura Docherty ; illustrated by Anne Boyd. — Andover : Philograph, c1980. — 16p : col.ill ; 21cm. — (A Read and talk book)
ISBN 0-85370-417-1 (pbk) : £2.30 B81-27852

Docherty, Maura. Washday / by Maura Docherty ; illustrated by Anne Boyd. — Andover : Philograph, c1980. — 16p : col.ill ; 21cm. — (A Read and talk book)
ISBN 0-85370-419-8 (pbk) : £2.30 B81-27851

Docherty, Maura. 'What are you going to do?' / by Maura Docherty ; illustrated by Anne Boyd. — Andover : Philograph, c1980. — 16p : col.ill ; 21cm. — (A Read and talk book)
ISBN 0-85370-418-x (pbk) : £2.30 B81-27849

East, Helen. Henry's house / by Helen East ; illustrated by Maggie Ling. — London : Macdonald, 1981. — 20p : col.ill ; 21cm. — (First starters)
ISBN 0-356-06922-2 : £1.00 B81-37292

East, Helen. Louisa's garden / by Helen East ; illustrated by Glynis Porter. — London : Macdonald Educational, 1981. — 20p : col.ill ; 21cm. — (First starters)
ISBN 0-356-06921-4 : £1.00 B81-37193

East, Helen. Maria goes to work / by Helen East ; illustrated by Terry Burton. — London : Macdonald Educational, 1981. — [20]p : col.ill ; 21cm. — (First starters)
ISBN 0-356-06923-0 : £1.00 B81-37928

East, Helen. Michael goes shopping / by Helen East ; illustrated by Corinne Burrows. — London : Macdonald Educational, 1981. — 17p : col.ill ; 21cm. — (First starters)
ISBN 0-356-06924-9 : £1.00 B81-37192

East, Helen. Sara by the seashore / by Helen East ; illustrated by Joanna Stubbs. — London : Macdonald Educational, 1981. — 20p : col.ill ; 21cm. — (First starters)
ISBN 0-356-06925-7 : £1.00 B81-37929

Fior, Jane. The pet show / Jane Fior ; pictures by Gill Chapman. — London : Collins, c1981. — [48]p : col.ill ; 15cm. — (Let's read ; 3) (Collins colour cubs)
ISBN 0-00-196036-9 (pbk) : Unpriced B81-13058

Fior, Jane. The toy cupboard / Jane Fior ; pictures by Gill Chapman. — London : Collins, c1981. — [48]p : col.ill ; 15cm. — (Let's read ; 4) (Collins colour cubs)
ISBN 0-00-196037-7 (pbk) : Unpriced B81-13120

First picture-word book / illustrated by Kersti Chaplet ... [et al.]. — London : Pelham, 1981. — 221p : chiefly col.ill ; 21cm
Translated from the French. — Includes index
ISBN 0-7207-1310-2 (pbk) : £2.95 B81-09890

Gleeson, Joan. Lets go! / [text by Joan Gleeson] ; [illustrated by Ann Kennedy]. — Dublin : Gill and Macmillan
Stage 1. — 1981
Approach book. — 24p : col.ill ; 22cm
Cover title. — Text on inside covers
ISBN 0-7171-1117-2 (pbk) : £0.50 B81-20944

Gleeson, Joan. Lets go! / [text by Joan Gleeson] ; [illustrated by Ann Kennedy]. — Dublin : Gill and Macmillan
Stage 1. — 1981
Basic A. — 24p : col.ill ; 22cm
Cover title. — Text on inside covers
ISBN 0-7171-1118-0 (pbk) : £0.65 B81-20945

Gleeson, Joan. Let's go! / [text Joan Gleeson] ; [illustrated by Ann Kennedy]. — Dublin : Gill and Macmillan
Cover title. — Text on inside covers
Stage 1. — 1981
Basic B. — 24p : col.ill ; 22cm
ISBN 0-7171-1120-2 (pbk) : £0.65 B81-29966

Gleeson, Joan. Lets go! / [text by Joan Gleeson] ; [illustrated by Ann Kennedy]. — Dublin : Gill and Macmillan
Stage 1. — 1981
Extension A. — 24p : col.ill ; 22cm
Cover title. — Text on inside covers
ISBN 0-7171-1119-9 (pbk) : £0.65 B81-20947

Gleeson, Joan. Lets go! / [text by Joan Gleeson] ; [illustrated by Ann Kennedy]. — Dublin : Gill and Macmillan
Stage 1. — 1981
Extension B. — 24p : col.ill ; 22cm
Cover title. — Text on inside covers
ISBN 0-7171-1121-0 (pbk) : £0.65 B81-20948

Hawke, Kathleen, *1935-*. I love butterflies / words by Kathleen Hawke, Margaret Roc ; illustrations by Allan Stomann. — London : Evans, 1981, c1979. — [16]p : chiefly col.ill ; 15x21cm. — (Say what you like!)
Originally published: Sydney : Methuen of Australia, 1979
ISBN 0-237-29286-6 (pbk) : Unpriced B81-08105

Hawke, Kathleen, *1935-*. I love chairs that are big and soft / words by Kathleen Hawke, Margaret Roc ; illustrations by Allan Stomann. — London : Evans, 1981, c1979. — [16]p : chiefly col.ill ; 15x21cm. — (Say what you like!)
Originally published: Sydney : Methuen of Australia, 1979
ISBN 0-237-29288-2 (pbk) : Unpriced B81-08103

Hawke, Kathleen, *1935-*. I love going to the beach / words by Kathleen Hawke, Margaret Roc ; illustrations by Allan Stomann. — London : Evans, 1981, c1979. — [16]p : chiefly col.ill ; 15x21cm. — (Say what you like!)
Originally published: Sydney : Methuen of Australia, 1979
ISBN 0-237-29287-4 (pbk) : Unpriced B81-08102

Hawke, Kathleen, *1935-*. I love running when I take off my shoes / words by Kathleen Hawke, Margaret Roc ; illustrations by Allan Stomann. — London : Evans, 1981, c1979. — [16]p : chiefly col.ill ; 15x21cm. — (Say what you like!)
Originally published: Sydney : Methuen of Australia, 1979
ISBN 0-237-29289-0 (pbk) : Unpriced B81-08104

Hay, Dean. Look at me / Dean Hay. — Glasgow : Collins, 1981. — [12]p : chiefly col.ill ; 20cm
Previous ed.: 1977
ISBN 0-00-126150-9 (unbound) : £0.95 B81-24533

Hay, Dean. My friends / Dean Hay. — Glasgow : Collins, 1981. — [12]p : chiefly col.ill ; 20cm
Previous ed.: 1977
ISBN 0-00-126151-7 (unbound) : £0.95 B81-24538

Jessel, Camilla. Away for the night / Camilla Jessel. — London : Methuen Children's, 1981. — [24]p : chiefly col.ill ; 16cm. — (Methuen chatterbooks)
ISBN 0-416-88870-4 : £1.25 B81-29811

Jessel, Camilla. Going to the doctor / Camilla Jessel. — London : Methuen Children's, 1981. — [24]p : chiefly col.ill ; 16cm. — (Methuen chatterbooks)
ISBN 0-416-88890-9 : £1.25 B81-29810

Jessel, Camilla. Moving house / Camilla Jessel. — London : Methuen Children's, 1981. — [24]p : chiefly col.ill ; 16cm. — (Methuen chatterbooks)
ISBN 0-416-88880-1 : £1.25 B81-29813

Jessel, Camilla. The new baby / Camilla Jessel. — London : Methuen Children's, 1981. — [24]p : chiefly col.ill ; 16cm. — (Methuen chatterbooks)
ISBN 0-416-88860-7 : £1.25 B81-29812

Piers, Helen. Animal babies / Helen Piers. — London : Methuen Children's, 1981. — [24]p : chiefly col.ill ; 16cm. — (Methuen chatterbooks)
ISBN 0-416-88850-x : £1.25 B81-29806

Piers, Helen. Animal homes / Helen Piers. — London : Methuen Children's, 1981. — [24]p : chiefly col.ill ; 16cm. — (Methuen chatterbooks)
ISBN 0-416-88840-2 : £1.25 B81-29808

Piers, Helen. Animal noises / Helen Piers. — London : Methuen Children's, 1981. — [24]p : chiefly col.ill ; 16cm. — (Methuen chatterbooks)
ISBN 0-416-88830-5 : £1.25 B81-2980[illegible]

Piers, Helen. Eat up! / Helen Piers. — London : Methuen Children's, 1981. — [24]p : chiefly col.ill ; 16cm. — (Methuen chatterbooks)
ISBN 0-416-88820-8 : £1.25 B81-2980[illegible]

Price, Alan. An ABC adventure in Toyland / written and illustrated by Alan and Sabine Price. — London : Dean, c1969 (1980 [printing]). — [28]p : col.ill ; 32cm. — (An Everyday picture book)
ISBN 0-603-00211-0 : £1.25 B81-3215[illegible]

Price, Alan. Baby's first picture book / by Alan and Sabine Price. — London : Dean, c1968 (1980 [printing]). — [28]p : chiefly col.ill ; 32cm. — (An Everyday picture book)
ISBN 0-603-00210-2 : £1.25 B81-3215[illegible]

428.6 — English language. Reading books — *For schools*

Ahlberg, Allen. Master Money the millionaire / by Allan Ahlberg ; with pictures by Andre Amstutz. — Harmondsworth : Puffin, 1981. — [24]p : col.ill ; 21cm. — (Happy families)
ISBN 0-7226-5667-x (cased) : £2.50
ISBN 0-14-031246-3 (pbk) : £0.80 B81-1292[illegible]

428.6 — English language. Reading books — *For schools* *continuation*

Ahlberg, Allen. Miss Brick the builder's baby / by Allan Ahlberg ; with pictures by Colin McNaughton. — Harmondsworth : Puffin, 1981. — [24]p : col.ill ; 21cm. — (Happy families)
ISBN 0-7226-5663-7 (cased) : £2.50
ISBN 0-14-031242-0 (pbk) : £0.80 B81-12920

Ahlberg, Allen. Mr and Mrs Hay the horse / by Allan Ahlberg ; with pictures by Colin McNaughton. — Harmondsworth : Puffin, 1981. — [24]p : col.ill ; 21cm. — (Happy families)
ISBN 0-7226-5668-8 (cased) : £2.50
ISBN 0-14-031247-1 (pbk) : £0.80 B81-12922

Ahlberg, Allen. Mr Buzz the beeman / by Allan Ahlberg ; with pictures by Faith Jaques. — Harmondsworth : Puffin, 1981. — [24]p : col.ill ; 21cm. — (Happy families)
ISBN 0-7226-5665-3 (cased) : £2.50
ISBN 0-14-031247-4 (pbk) : £0.80 B81-12924

Ahlberg, Allen. Mr Tick the teacher / by Allan Ahlberg ; with pictures by Faith Jaques. — Harmondsworth : Puffin, 1981. — [24]p : col.ill ; 21cm. — (Happy families)
ISBN 0-7226-5666-1 (cased) : £2.50
ISBN 0-14-031245-5 (pbk) : £0.80 B81-12923

Ahlberg, Allen. Mrs Lather's laundry / by Allan Ahlberg ; with pictures by Andre Amstutz. — Harmondsworth : Puffin, 1981. — [24]p : col.ill ; 21cm. — (Happy families)
ISBN 0-7226-5664-5 (cased) : £2.50
ISBN 0-14-031243-9 (pbk) : £0.80 B81-12921

Ball, Brian, *1932-*. Dennis and the flying saucer / Brian Ball ; pictures by Margaret Chamberlain. — London : Heinemann, 1980. — 28p : col.ill ; 21cm. — (A Heinemann easy-to-read book)
ISBN 0-434-92830-5 : £2.95 B81-13164

Border, Rosemary. Daredevils / Rosemary Border. — London : Macmillan, 1981. — 60p : ill ; 21cm. — (Ranger. Range 8, Fact)
ISBN 0-333-31479-4 (pbk) : £0.80 B81-37291

Boyce, E. R.. At school / E.R. Boyce. — London : Macmillan Education, 1981. — [12]p : col.ill ; 16x21cm. — (The Gay way introductory series. Second set)
Cover title
ISBN 0-333-31169-8 (pbk) : Unpriced
B81-39319

Boyce, E. R.. At the pictures / E.R. Boyce. — London : Macmillan Education, 1981. — [12]p : col.ill ; 16x21cm. — (The Gay way introductory series. Second set)
Cover title
ISBN 0-333-31169-8 (pbk) : Unpriced
B81-39313

Boyce, E. R.. At the shops / E.R. Boyce. — London : Macmillan Education, 1981. — [12]p : col.ill ; 16x21cm. — (The Gay way introductory series. Second set)
Cover title
ISBN 0-333-31169-8 (pbk) : Unpriced
B81-39318

Boyce, E. R.. A birthday / E.R. Boyce. — London : Macmillan Education, 1981. — [12]p : col.ill ; 16x21cm. — (The Gay way introductory series. Second set)
Cover title
ISBN 0-333-31169-8 (pbk) : Unpriced
B81-39316

Boyce, E. R.. Cowboys and Indians / [E.R. Boyce] ; [illustrated by John Lobban]. — London : Macmillan, 1981. — 32p : ill(some col.) ; 21cm. — (The Gay way series. The fifth yellow book)
Includes: The monkey, the mice and the cheese / illustrated by Pat Nessling
ISBN 0-333-27325-7 (pbk) : £0.65 B81-37202

Boyce, E. R.. A day out / E.R. Boyce. — London : Macmillan Education, 1981. — [12]p : col.ill ; 16x21cm. — (The Gay way introductory series. Second set)
Cover title
ISBN 0-333-31169-8 (pbk) : Unpriced
B81-39314

Boyce, E. R.. Holidays / E.R. Boyce. — London : Macmillan Education, 1981. — [12]p : col.ill ; 16x21cm. — (The Gay way introductory series. Second set)
Cover title
ISBN 0-333-31169-8 (pbk) : Unpriced
B81-39317

Boyce, E. R.. A picnic / E.R. Boyce. — London : Macmillan Education, 1981. — [12]p : col.ill ; 16x21cm. — (The Gay way introductory series. Second set)
Cover title
ISBN 0-333-31169-8 (pbk) : Unpriced
B81-39320

Boyce, E. R.. The three friends / [E.R. Boyce] ; [illustrated by Pat Nessling]. — London : Macmilln, 1981. — 32p : ill(some col.) ; 21cm. — (The Gay way series. The fourth yellow book)
Includes: The three wishes / illustrated by Maureen Williams
ISBN 0-333-27324-9 (pbk) : £0.65 B81-37203

Boyce, E. R.. A visit / E.R. Boyce. — London : Macmillan Education, 1981. — [12]p : col.ill ; 16x21cm. — (The Gay way introductory series. Second set)
Cover title
ISBN 0-333-31169-8 (pbk) : Unpriced
B81-39315

Brandenberg, Franz. Leo and Emily. — London : Bodley Head, Feb.1982. — [64]p. — (Bodley beginners)
ISBN 0-370-30915-4 : £3.25 : CIP entry
B81-36976

Douglas, N.. The iron horse : and other stories / by N. Douglas. — Glasgow : Gibson, 1981. — 192p : ill ; 21cm. — (World wide adventures)
ISBN 0-7169-5514-8 (pbk) : Unpriced
B81-35655

Flavell, L.. Paul and Claire at home / L. Flavell, R.H.C. Fice and F.S. Claxton. — London : Macmillan, 1980. — 24p : ill(some col.) ; 22cm. — (Ranger satellites)
Translation of: Jacques et Claire à la maison. — Cover title
ISBN 0-333-28726-6 (pbk) : £0.55 B81-10537

Flavell, L.. Paul, Claire and the duck / L. Flavell, R.H.C. Fice and F.S. Claxton. — London : Macmillan, 1980. — 24p : ill(some col.) ; 22cm. — (Ranger satellites)
Translation of: Jacques, Claire et le canard. — Cover title
ISBN 0-333-28728-2 (pbk) : £0.55 B81-10540

Flavell, L.. Paul, Claire and the ghost / L. Flavell, R.H.C. Fice and F.S. Claxton. — London : Macmillan, 1980. — 24p : ill(some col.) ; 22cm. — (Ranger satellites)
Translation of: Jacques, Claire et le fantôme. — Cover title
ISBN 0-333-28272-8 (pbk) : £0.55 B81-10539

Flavell, L.. Paul, Claire and the rabbit / L. Flavell, R.H.C. Fice and F.S. Claxton. — London : Macmillan, 1980. — 24p : ill(some col.) ; 22cm. — (Ranger satellites)
Translation of: Jacques, Claire et le lapin. — Cover title
ISBN 0-333-28727-4 (pbk) : £0.55 B81-10538

Flowerdew, Phyllis. Reading on / Phyllis Flowerdew and Sam Stewart. — Edinburgh : Oliver & Boyd
Red book 1. — 1981. — 192p : ill,maps,facsims,ports ; 21cm
Previous ed.: 1958. — Text on inside cover
ISBN 0-05-003356-5 (pbk) : £1.75 B81-07809

Flowerdew, Phyllis. Reading on / Phyllis Flowerdew and Sam Stewart. — Edinburgh : Oliver & Boyd
Yellow book 1. — New ed. — 1981. — 191p : ill,maps,ports ; 21cm
Previous ed.: 1962
ISBN 0-05-003358-1 (pbk) : £1.75 B81-07808

Flowerdew, Phyllis. Reading on / Phyllis Flowerdew and Sam Stewart. — Edinburgh : Oliver & Boyd
Yellow book 2. — 2nd ed. — 1981. — 192p : ill,maps,facsims,ports ; 21cm
Previous ed.: 1963
ISBN 0-05-003359-x (pbk) : £1.75 B81-07807

Francis, Dick. Knock down / Dick Francis ; abridged by J.R.C. and G.M. Yglesias. — Walton-on-Thames : Nelson, 1981. — 138p ; 18cm. — (Getaway)
ISBN 0-17-432185-6 (pbk) : £0.95 B81-35038

Francis, Dick. Rat race / Dick Francis ; abridged by J.R.C. and G.M. Yglesias. — Walton-on-Thames : Nelson, 1981. — 151p ; 18cm. — (Getaway)
ISBN 0-17-432182-1 (pbk) : £0.95 B81-35037

From plank to plank : appreciation and skills of English / compiled and edited by Liam Bell ... [et al.]. — Dublin : Gill and Macmillan, 1976 (1980 [printing]). — 140p : ill ; 14x28cm
Includes index
ISBN 0-7171-0785-x (pbk) : Unpriced
B81-28399

Gage, Wilson. Mrs. Gaddy and the ghost / by Wilson Gage ; pictures by Marylin Hafner. — London : Bodley Head, 1981, c1979. — 55p : col.ill ; 22cm. — (Bodley beginners)
Originally published: New York : Greenwillow, c1979
ISBN 0-370-30410-1 : £3.25 : CIP rev.
B81-02098

Gilroy, Beryl. In for a penny / Beryl Gilroy ; illustrated by Simon Willby. — London : Cassell, 1980. — 94p : ill ; 19cm. — (Cassell compass books)
ISBN 0-304-30369-0 (pbk) : £1.50 B81-11894

Groves, Paul. Miss Willow and the river boat / Paul Groves. — London : Edward Arnold, 1981. — 23p ; 22cm. — (Oh, Miss!)
ISBN 0-7131-0573-9 (pbk) : 0.75 : CIP rev.
B81-07933

Groves, Paul. Miss Willow goes camping / Paul Groves. — London : Edward Arnold, 1981. — 23p ; 22cm. — (Oh, Miss!)
ISBN 0-7131-0574-7 (pbk) : 0.75 : CIP rev.
B81-07931

Groves, Paul. Miss Willow goes to the zoo / Paul Groves. — London : Edward Arnold, 1981. — 23p ; 22cm. — (Oh, Miss!)
ISBN 0-7131-0572-0 (pbk) : 0.75 : CIP rev.
B81-07932

Groves, Paul. The smuggler and other stories. — London : J. Murray, Sept.1981. — [96]p
ISBN 0-7195-3867-x (pbk) : £1.10(non-net) : CIP entry B81-21520

Hogg, Gordon. Twists. — London : Edward Arnold, Dec.1981. — [80]p
ISBN 0-7131-0613-1 (pbk) : £1.00 : CIP entry
B81-33874

Hooper, Mary. Only the beginning / Mary Hooper ; edited by J.R.C. and G.M. Yglesias. — Walton-on-Thames : Nelson, 1981. — 94p ; 18cm. — (Getaway)
ISBN 0-17-432183-x (pbk) : £0.95 B81-35040

Johnson, Barrie. The bullfighter / by Barrie Johnson ; illustrated by Ray Mutimer. — Huddersfield : Schofield & Sims, 1981. — 16p : ill ; 21cm. — (The Relay readers. Yellow book ; 3)
ISBN 0-7217-0406-9 (pbk) : £0.35 B81-38924

428.6 — English language. Reading books — *For schools continuation*

Johnson, Barrie. Christmas shopping / by Barrie Johnson ; illustrated by Ray Mutimer. — Huddersfield : Schofield & Sims, 1981. — 16p : ill ; 21cm. — (The relay readers. Green book ; 2)
ISBN 0-7217-0411-5 (pbk) : Unpriced
B81-17562

Johnson, Barrie. A fair cop! / by Barrie Johnson ; illustrated by Ray Mutimer. — Huddersfield : Schofield & Sims, 1981. — 16p : ill ; 21cm. — (The relay readers. Green book ; 1)
ISBN 0-7217-0410-7 (pbk) : Unpriced
B81-17566

Johnson, Barrie. Gone fishing! / by Barrie Johnson ; illustrated by Ray Mutimer. — Huddersfield : Schofield & Sims, 1981. — 16p : ill ; 21cm. — (The relay readers. Green book ; 3)
ISBN 0-7217-0412-3 (pbk) : Unpriced
B81-17563

Johnson, Barrie. A mad scramble? / by Darrie Johnson ; illustrated by Ray Mutimer. — Huddersfield : Schofield & Sims, 1981. — 16p : ill ; 21cm. — (The Relay readers. Red book ; 1)
ISBN 0-7217-0398-4 (pbk) : £0.35 B81-38925

Johnson, Barrie. A near thing! / by Barrie Johnson ; illustrated by Ray Mutimer. — Huddersfield : Schofield & Sims, 1981. — 16p : ill ; 21cm. — (The Relay readers. Yellow book ; 2)
ISBN 0-7217-0405-0 (pbk) : £0.35 B81-38923

Johnson, Barrie. No hiding-place / by Barrie Johnson ; illustrated by Ray Mutimer. — Huddersfield : Schofield & Sims, 1981. — 16p : ill ; 21cm. — (The Relay readers. Yellow book ; 1)
ISBN 0-7217-0404-2 (pbk) : £0.35 B81-38922

Johnson, Barrie. Not a leg to stand on! / by Barrie Johnson illustrated ; by Ray Mutimer. — Huddersfield : Schofield & Sims, 1981. — 16p : ill ; 21cm. — (The relay readers. Blue book ; 3)
ISBN 0-7217-0418-2 (pbk) : Unpriced
B81-17561

Johnson, Barrie. Pit stop! / by Barrie Johnson ; illustrated by Ray Mutimer. — Huddersfield : Schofield & Sims, 1981. — 16p : ill ; 21cm. — (The relay readers. Blue book ; 2)
ISBN 0-7217-0417-4 (pbk) : Unpriced
B81-17565

Johnson, Barrie. Pot shots / by Barrie Johnson ; illustrated by Ray Mutimer. — Huddersfield : Schofield & Sims, 1981. — 16p : ill ; 21cm. — (The Relay readers. Red book ; 3)
ISBN 0-7217-0400-x (pbk) : £0.35 B81-38927

Johnson, Barrie. Strange meeting / by Barrie Johnson : illustrated by Ray Mutimer. — Huddersfield : Schofield & Sims, 1981. — 16p : ill ; 21cm. — (The relay readers. Blue book ; 1)
ISBN 0-7217-0416-6 (pbk) : Unpriced
B81-17564

Johnson, Barrie. What a catch! / by Barrie Johnson ; illustrated by Ray Mutimer. — Huddersfield : Schofield & Sims, 1981. — 16p : ill ; 21cm. — (The Relay readers. Red book ; 2)
ISBN 0-7217-0399-2 (pbk) : £0.35 B81-38926

Kemp, Marion. All together / Marion Kemp, Sheila Lane and David Mackay ; illustrated by Rowan Barnes-Murphy ... [et al.] ; cover illustration by Peter Firman. — Harlow : Longman, 1981. — 63p : ill(some col.),coat of arms ; 24cm. — (Whizz bang. Bumper book)
ISBN 0-582-18259-x (cased) : Unpriced
ISBN 0-582-18258-1 (pbk) : £1.95 B81-27234

Lip, Evelyn. The fairy princess / written and illustrated by Evelyn Lip. — Singapore : Macmillan Southeast Asia ; London : Macmillan, 1981. — 16p : col.ill ; 19x21cm. — (Ranger satellites ; 6)
Text on inside cover
ISBN 0-333-31241-4 (pbk) : £0.60 B81-35222

Lip, Evelyn. The green monster / written and illustrated by Evelyn Lip. — Singapore : Macmillan Southeast Asia ; London : Macmillan, 1981. — 16p : col.ill ; 19x21cm. — (Ranger satellites ; 9)
Text on inside cover
ISBN 0-333-31244-9 (pbk) : £0.60 B81-35220

Lip, Evelyn. The lazy fly / written and illustrated by Evelyn Lip. — Singapore : Macmillan Southeast Asia ; London : Macmillan, 1981. — 16p : col.ill ; 19x21cm. — (Ranger satellites ; 2)
Text on inside cover
ISBN 0-333-31237-6 (pbk) : £0.60 B81-35219

Lip, Evelyn. The magic bowl / written and illustrated by Evelyn Lip. — Singapore : Macmillan Southeast Asia ; London : Macmillan, 1981. — 16p : col.ill ; 19x21cm. — (Ranger satellites ; 5)
Text on inside cover
ISBN 0-333-31240-6 (pbk) : £0.60 B81-35225

Lip, Evelyn. The playful donkey / written and illustrated by Evelyn Lip. — Singapore : Macmillan Southeast Asia ; London : Macmillan, 1981. — 16p : col.ill ; 19x21cm. — (Ranger satellites ; 1)
Text on inside cover
ISBN 0-333-31236-8 (pbk) : £0.60 B81-35218

Lip, Evelyn. Rashid's bow and arrow / written and illustrated by Evelyn Lip. — Singapore : Macmillan Southeast Asia ; London : Macmillan, 1981. — 16p : col.ill ; 19x21cm. — (Ranger satellites ; 8)
Text on inside cover
ISBN 0-333-31243-0 (pbk) : £0.60 B81-35221

Lip, Evelyn. Ten little chicks / written and illustrated by Evelyn Lip. — Singapore : Macmillan Southeast Asia ; London : Macmillan, 1981. — 16p : col.ill ; 19x21cm. — (Ranger satellites ; 3)
Text on inside cover
ISBN 0-333-31238-4 (pbk) : £0.60 B81-35223

Lip, Evelyn. The waterfall / written and illustrated by Evelyn Lip. — Singapore : Macmillan Southeast Asia ; London : Macmillan, 1981. — 16p : col.ill ; 19x21cm. — (Ranger satellites ; 4)
Text on inside cover
ISBN 0-333-31239-2 (pbk) : £0.60 B81-35224

Lip, Evelyn. The wishing book / written and illustrated by Evelyn Lip. — Singapore : Macmillan Southeast Asia ; London : Macmillan, 1981. — 16p : col.ill ; 19x21cm. — (Ranger satellites ; 7)
Text on inside cover
ISBN 0-333-31242-2 (pbk) : £0.60 B81-35226

McCullagh, Sheila K.. Sita and the little old woman / [author Sheila McCullagh] ; [artist Ferelith Eccles Williams]. — St. Albans : Granada, 1981. — 8p : col.ill ; 19cm. — (One two three and away!. Blue book ; 7) (Platform readers. Level 1)
Cover title
ISBN 0-247-12918-6 (pbk) : Unpriced
ISBN 0-247-13169-5 (set) : £1.30 B81-21223

McCullagh, Sheila K.. The big man, the witch and the donkey / [author Sheila McCullagh] ; [artist Caroline Sharpe]. — St. Albans : Granada, 1981. — 16p : col.ill ; 22cm. — (One two three and away!. Green book ; 6) (Platform readers. Level 1)
Cover title
ISBN 0-247-13212-8 (pbk) : Unpriced
ISBN 0-247-13188-1 (set) : £3.25 B81-21224

McCullagh, Sheila K.. Billy Blue-hat and the frog / [author Sheila McCullagh] ; [artist Ferelith Eccles Williams]. — St. Albans : Granada, 1981. — 8p : col.ill ; 19cm. — (One two three and away!. Blue book ; 8) (Platform readers. Level 1)
Cover title
ISBN 0-247-12927-5 (pbk) : Unpriced
ISBN 0-249-13169-5 (set) : £1.30 B81-21222

McCullagh, Sheila K.. Sita climbs the wall / [author Sheila McCullagh] ; [artist Eccles Williams]. — St. Albans : Granada, 1981. — 16p : col.ill ; 22cm. — (One two three and away!. Green book ; 4) (Green platform readers)
Cover title
ISBN 0-247-13209-8 (pbk) : Unpriced
ISBN 0-247-13188-1 (set) : £3.25 B81-21226

McCullagh, Sheila K.. The little old man and the little black cat / [author Sheila McCullagh] ; [artist Robert Geary. — St. Albans : Granada, 1981. — 16p : col.ill ; 22cm. — (One two three and away!. Green book ; 2) (Green platform readers)
Cover title
ISBN 0-247-13206-3 (pbk) : Unpriced
ISBN 0-247-13188-1 (set) : £3.25 B81-21228

McCullagh, Sheila K.. The little old woman and the grandfather clock / [author Sheila McCullagh] ; [artist Robert Geary]. — St. Albans : Granada, 1981. — 16p : col.ill ; 22cm. — (One two three and away!. Green book ; 3) (Green platform readers)
Cover title
ISBN 0-247-13207-1 (pbk) : Unpriced
ISBN 0-247-13188-1 (pbk) : £3.25 B81-21227

McCullagh, Sheila K.. The magic wood / [author Sheila McCullagh] ; [artist Caroline Sharpe]. — At. Albans : Granada, 1981. — 8p : col.ill ; 19cm. — (One two three and away!. Blue book ; 9) (Platform readers. Level 1)
Cover title
ISBN 0-247-12928-3 (pbk) : Unpriced
ISBN 0-247-13169-5 (set) : £1.30 B81-21221

McCullagh, Sheila K.. Roger and the school bus / [author Sheila McCullagh] ; [artist Ferelith Eccles Williams]. — St. Albans : Granada, 1981. — 16p : col.ill ; 22cm. — (One two three and away!. Green book ; 1) (Green platform readers)
Cover title
ISBN 0-247-13205-5 (pbk) : Unpriced
ISBN 0-247-13188-1 (set) : £3.25 B81-21229

McCullagh, Sheila K.. When the school door was shut / [author Sheila McCullagh] ; [artist Ferelith Eccles Williams]. — St. Albans : Granada, 1981. — 16p : col.ill ; 22cm. — (One two three and away!. Green book ; 5) (Green platform readers)
Cover title
ISBN 0-247-13210-1 (pbk) : Unpriced
ISBN 0-247-13188-1 (set) : £3.25 B81-2122[illegible]

McCullagh, Sheila K.. The witch and the donkey / [author Sheila McCullagh] ; [artist Caroline Sharpe]. — At. Albans : Granada, 1981. — 8p : col.ill ; 19cm. — (One two three and away!. Blue book ; 10) (Platform readers. Level 1)
Cover title
ISBN 0-247-12929-1 (pbk) : Unpriced
ISBN 0-247-13169-5 (set) : £1.30 B81-21220

Mackay, David, *1920-*. The blue breakthrough book / David Mackay and Pamela Schaub. — London : Longman, 1980. — 16,16,16,16p : col.ill ; 20cm. — (Breakthrough books)
Contents: Fire! - Old houses - Crocodiles are dangerous - The football book
ISBN 0-582-25039-0 : £2.75 B81-0850[illegible]

Mackay, David, *1920-*. Dressing up / [written by David Mackay, Brian Thompson and Pamela Schaub] ; [illustrated by Edward McLachlan]. — London : Longman, 1980, c1970. — 16p : col.ill ; 19cm. — (Breakthrough books)
Cover title
ISBN 0-582-25031-5 (pbk) : £0.35 B81-0587[illegible]

428.6 — English language. Reading books — *For schools* *continuation*

Mackay, David, *1920-*. The football book / [written by David Mackay] ; [illustrated by Simon Stern]. — London : Longman, 1980, c1972. — 16p : col.ill ; 19cm. — (Breakthrough books)
Cover title
ISBN 0-582-25035-8 (pbk) : £0.35 B81-05874

Mackay, David, *1920-*. The loose tooth / [David Mackay, Brian Thompson and Pamela Schaub wrote this book] ; [Posy Simmonds did the pictures]. — London : Longman, 1970 (1980 [printing]). — 16p chiefly col.ill ; 19cm. — (Breakthrough books)
Cover title. — Originally published: London : Longman for the Schools Council, 1970. — Text on inside cover
ISBN 0-582-25029-3 (pbk) : £0.35 B81-05561

Mackay, David, *1920-*. The red breakthrough book / David Mackay, Brian Thompson, Pamela Schaub. — London : Longman, 1980. — 16,16,16,16p : col.ill ; 20cm. — (Breakthrough books)
Contents: Our baby — The loose tooth — People in stories — Dressing up
ISBN 0-582-25038-2 : £2.75 B81-08503

Marshall, Edward. Three by the sea. — London : Bodley Head, Feb.1982. — [64]p. — (Bodley beginners)
ISBN 0-370-30455-1 : £3.25 : CIP entry
B81-36977

Marshall, Edward. Troll country / by Edward Marshall ; pictures by James Marshall. — London : Bodley Head, 1980. — 56p : col.ill ; 22cm. — (Bodley beginners)
Originally published: New York : Dial Press, 1980
ISBN 0-370-30408-x : £3.25 : CIP rev.
B81-00610

Mayer, Mercer. Little Monster at home / by Mercer Mayer. — London : Dean, 1980, c1978. — [24]p : col.ill ; 21cm
Originally published: New York : Golden Press, 1978
ISBN 0-603-00222-6 (pbk) : £0.30 B81-07869

Mayer, Mercer. Little Monster at school / by Mercer Mayer. — London : Dean, 1980, c1978. — [24]p : col.ill ; 21cm
Originally published: New York : Golden Press, 1978
ISBN 0-603-00221-8 (pbk) : £0.30 B81-07868

Mayer, Mercer. Little Monster's alphabet book / by Mercer Mayer. — London : Dean, 1980, c1978. — [24]p : col.ill ; 21cm
Originally published: New York : Golden Press, 1978
ISBN 0-603-00223-4 (pbk) : £0.30 B81-07871

Mayer, Mercer. Little Monster's bedtime book / by Mercer Mayer. — London : Dean, 1980, c1978. — [24]p : col.ill ; 21cm
Originally published: New York : Golden Press, 1978
ISBN 0-603-00224-2 (pbk) : £0.30 B81-07870

Mayer, Mercer. Little Monster's counting book / by Mercer Mayer. — London : Dean, 1980, c1978. — [24]p : col.ill ; 21cm
Originally published: New York : Golden Press, 1978
ISBN 0-603-00220-x (pbk) : £0.30 B81-07872

Mayer, Mercer. Little Monster's neighbourhood / by Mercer Mayer. — London : Dean, 1980, c1978. — [24]p : col.ill ; 21cm
Originally published: New York : Golden Press, 1978
ISBN 0-603-00225-0 (pbk) : £0.30 B81-07867

Message and medium. — London : Hodder and Stoughton, Sept.1981. — [176]p
ISBN 0-340-26903-0 (pbk) : £1.95 : CIP entry
B81-20518

Morpurgo, Michael. The day I took the bull by the horn / Michael Morpurgo. — London : Ward Lock Educational, c1979. — 24p : ill ; 21cm. — (WLE library graded reading series 10-14. level 4)
Text on inside cover
ISBN 0-7062-3818-4 (pbk) : Unpriced
B81-09668

Morpurgo, Michael. The ghost-fish / Michael Morpurgo. — London : Ward Lock Educational, c1979. — 28p : ill ; 21cm. — (WLE library graded reading series 10-14. level 4)
Text on inside cover
ISBN 0-7062-3820-6 (pbk) : Unpriced
B81-09667

Morpurgo, Michael. Love at first sight / Michael Morpurgo. — London : Ward Lock Educational, c1979. — 24p : ill ; 21cm. — (WLE library graded reading series 10-14. level 4)
Text on inside cover
ISBN 0-7062-3817-6 (pbk) : Unpriced
B81-08061

Morpurgo, Michael. That's how / Michael Morpurgo. — London : Ward Lock Educational, c1979. — 24p : ill ; 21cm. — (WLE library graded reading series 10-14. Level 4)
Text on inside cover
ISBN 0-7062-3819-2 (pbk) : Unpriced
B81-09666

Nothing to fear : and other stories / selected and edited by D'Arcy Adrian-Vallance ; illustrated by Geoff Appleton. — Harlow : Longman, c1981. — 44p : ill ; 20cm. — (Longman structural readers. Stage 4. Fiction)
ISBN 0-582-53109-8 (pbk) : £0.60 B81-18934

O'Neill, Robert. The sheriff / Robert O'Neill. — Harlow : Longman, 1981. — 16p : col.ill ; 20cm. — (Longman structural readers. Stage 1. Fiction)
Cover title
ISBN 0-582-52518-7 (pbk) : Unpriced
B81-24549

Oxford junior readers. — [Oxford] : Oxford University Press
1: Red series / Roderick Hunt ; [illustrated by Victor Ambrus et al.]. — c1981. — 127p : ill (some col.) ; 22cm
Cover title
ISBN 0-19-918128-4 (pbk) : Unpriced
B81-17155

Oxford junior readers. — [Oxford] : Oxford University Press
2: Red series / Roderick Hunt ; [illustrated by Victor Ambrus et al.]. — c1981. — 128p : ill (some col.) ; 22cm
Cover title
ISBN 0-19-918129-2 (pbk) : £1.25 B81-23129

Oxford junior readers. — [Oxford] : Oxford University Press
3: Orange series / Mike Samuda ; [illustrated by Martin Cottam et al.]. — [1980]. — 128p : ill(some col.) ; 22cm
Cover title
ISBN 0-19-917030-4 (pbk) : Unpriced
B81-17156

Oxford junior readers. — Oxford : Oxford University Press
Cover title
3: Red series / Roderick Hunt ; [illustrated by Priscilla Barrett et al.]. — 1981. — 128p : ill (some col.) ; 22cm
ISBN 0-19-918130-6 (pbk) : £1.25 B81-18795

Oxford junior readers. — Oxford : Oxford University Press
Cover title
4: Orange series / Mike Samuda ; [illustrated by Robert Ayton et al.]. — 1980. — 128p : ill (some col.),1facsim,ports(some col.) ; 22cm
ISBN 0-19-917031-2 (pbk) : £1.25 B81-19439

Oxford junior readers. — [Oxford] : Oxford University Press
4: Red series / Roderick Hunt ; [illustrated by Victor Ambrus et al.]. — c1981. — 128p : ill (some col.) ; 22cm
Cover title
ISBN 0-19-918131-4 (pbk) : £1.25 B81-25952

Oxford junior readers. — Oxford : Oxford University Press
Cover title
5: Green series / Roderick Hunt ; [illustrated by Victor Ambrus et al.]. — 1981. — 128p : ill (some col.) ; 22cm
ISBN 0-19-918132-2 (pbk) : £1.25 B81-18794

Oxford junior readers. — Oxford : Oxford University Press
5: Orange series / Mike Samuda ; [illustrated by Martin Cottam ... et al.]. — c1980. — 128p : ill(some col.),maps ; 22cm
Cover title
ISBN 0-19-917032-0 (pbk) : £1.25 B81-36461

Oxford Junior Readers. — [Oxford] : Oxford University Press
6: Red series / Roderick Hunt ; [illustrated by Victor Ambrus ... et al.]. — c1981. — 128p : ill(some col.) ; 22cm
Cover title
ISBN 0-19-918133-0 (pbk) : £1.25 B81-22792

Pearson, Susan. Molly moves out / by Susan Pearson ; pictures by Steven Kellogg. — London : Bodley Head, 1981. — 64p : col.ill ; 22cm. — (Bodley beginners)
ISBN 0-370-30411-x : £3.25 : CIP rev.
B81-00087

Rose, Christine. The snow goose and other stories / Paul Gallico ; simplified by Christine Rose. — Harlow : Longman, 1981. — 58p : ill ; 19cm. — (NMSR. Stage 3)
ISBN 0-582-52653-1 (pbk) : £0.60 B81-39603

Schaub, Pamela. Fire! / [Pamela Schaub wrote this book] ; [David McKee did the pictures]. — London : Longman, 1980, c1972. — 16p : col.ill ; 19cm. — (Breakthrough books)
Cover title
ISBN 0-582-25032-3 (pbk) : £0.35 B81-07863

The **Screaming** plant : and other horror stories / edited by J.R.C. and G.M. Yglesias. — Walton-on-Thames : Nelson, 1981. — 96p ; 18cm. — (Getaway)
ISBN 0-17-432186-4 (pbk) : £0.95 B81-35039

Stagg, S. A.. Carry on reading / by S.A. Stagg and J.A. Wynne. — Huddersfield : Schofield & Sims
1st introductory book / illustrated by Lesley Bellamy. — 1980. — 96p : ill ; 21cm
ISBN 0-7217-0422-0 (pbk) : £0.95
ISBN 0-7217-0425-5 (net ed.) : £1.25
B81-29027

Stagg, S. A.. Carry on reading / by S.A. Stagg and J.A. Wayne. — London : Hale, 1981
3rd introducory book / illustrated by Lesley Bellamy. — 112p : ill(some col.) ; 20cm
ISBN 0-7217-0427-1 (pbk) : £1.40 B81-21310

Stagg, S. A.. Carry on reading / by S.A. Stagg and J.A. Wynne. — Huddersfield : Schofield & Sims, 1981
Second introductory book / illustrated by Margaret Helen Sherry. — 96p : ill(some col.) ; 20cm
ISBN 0-7217-0423-9 (pbk) : £0.95
ISBN 0-7217-0426-3 (net ed.) : Unpriced
B81-19521

Thackray, Derek. Reading readiness workbooks / Derek and Lucy Thackray. — Sevenoaks : Hodder and Stoughton
1: Visual training. — 1980. — [24]p : ill ; 22x28cm
ISBN 0-340-24232-9 (unbound) : Unpriced
B81-33086

428.6 — English language. Reading books — *For schools* *continuation*

Thackray, Derek. Reading readiness workbooks / Derek and Lucy Thackray. — Sevenoaks : Hodder and Stoughton
2: Auditory training. — 1980. — [24]p : ill ; 22x28cm
ISBN 0-340-24233-7 (unbound) : Unpriced
B81-33087

Van Leeuwen, Jean. Tales of Oliver pig / Jean Van Leeuwen ; pictures by Arnold Lobel. — London : Bodley Head, 1981, c1979. — 64p : col.ill ; 22cm. — (Bodley beginners)
Originally published: New York : Dial Press, c1979
ISBN 0-370-30409-8 : £3.25 : CIP rev.
B81-02097

Wood, David, *1950-*. The glass prison / David Wood and Phyllis Edwards. — London : Edward Arnold, 1980. — 32p ; 22cm. — (Vardo ; 7)
ISBN 0-7131-0466-x (pbk) : £0.80 : CIP rev.
B80-19487

Wood, David, *1950-*. The invaders / David Wood and Phyllis Edwards. — London : Edward Arnold, 1980. — 32p ; 22cm. — (Vardo ; 5)
ISBN 0-7131-0464-3 (pbk) : £0.80 : CIP rev.
B80-19488

Wood, David, *1950-*. The last rays of the sun / David Wood and Phyllis Edwards. — London : Edward Arnold, 1980. — 32p ; 22cm. — (Vardo ; 6)
ISBN 0-7131-0465-1 (pbk) : £0.80 : CIP rev.
B80-19489

The **Yellow** breakthrough book / David Mackay ... [et al.]. — London : Longman, 1980. — 16,16,16,16p : col.ill ; 20cm. — (Breakthrough books)
Contents: Reading - The cat, the bird and the tree - Eating - Helping
ISBN 0-582-25037-4 : £2.75 B81-08504

428.6 — English language. Reading books: One, two, three and away! — *For teaching*

McCullagh, Sheila K.. Teacher's handbook / Sheila McCullagh. — 2nd ed. — St. Albans : Hart-Davis Educational, 1981. — 128p : ill ; 22cm. — (One, two, three and away!)
Previous ed.: 1975. — Flow chart (folded sheet) attached to inside cover
ISBN 0-247-13083-4 (pbk) : £3.50 B81-24298

428.6 — English language. Reading books: Poetry — *For pre-school children*

PM readalongs : rhymes for beginners. — London : Methuen Educational, 1980. — 7v. : col.ill ; 30cm. — (Methuen's resources for reading. Early reading)
Contents: Mrs Hen - Teddy bear - Out to play - Farmyard talk - The bear - One two - Sounds around
ISBN 0-7055-0753-x (pbk) : £4.00 B81-12621

428.6 — English language. Reading books. Special subjects: Animals — *For children*

Murray, Philippa. Life lines / Philippa Murray, Alison Sinclair and Susan Quilliam. — Welwyn : Nisbet, 1981. — 94p : col.ill ; 21cm
ISBN 0-7202-1013-5 (pbk) : £1.40 B81-29024

428.6 — English language. Reading books. Special subjects: Association football. Competitions: World Cup, *to 1982*

Capel, Will. The story of the World Cup / Will Capel. — London : Heinemann Educational, 1981. — 29p : ill,ports ; 18cm. — (Heinemann guided readers. Beginners level)
ISBN 0-435-27083-4 (pbk) : £0.45 B81-24397

428.6 — English language. Reading books. Special subjects: Babies — *Christian viewpoints* — *For pre-school children*

Doney, Meryl. Now we have a new baby / Meryl Doney ; pictures by Jane Fort. — Tring : Lion Publishing, 1981. — [16]p : chiefly col.ill ; 19cm. — (Little Lions under fives)
ISBN 0-85648-199-8 (pbk) : £0.35 B81-26999

428.6 — English language. Reading books. Special subjects: Cars — *For schools*

Hoare, Stephen. Car mad! / Stephen Hoare. — London : Harrap, 1980. — 39p : ill,ports ; 19cm. — (The Reporters series)
ISBN 0-245-53573-x (pbk) : £0.80 B81-08114

428.6 — English language. Reading books. Special subjects: Children. Adoption — *For schools*

Althea. Jane is adopted / by Althea ; illustrated by Isabel Pearce. — London : Souvenir, c1980. — [24]p : col.ill ; 19cm. — (Althea's brightstart books)
ISBN 0-285-62457-1 : £1.50 B81-07141

428.6 — English language. Reading books. Special subjects: Colour

Shapiro, Arnold. Squiggly Wiggly's surprise / written by Arnold Shapiro ; designed and illustrated by Charles Murphy. — [Croydon] : Pied Piper, [1981]. — [22]p : col.ill ; 20cm + 1finger puppet
ISBN 0-7166-5602-7 : Unpriced B81-08476

428.6 — English language. Reading books. Special subjects: Days & months — *For children*

Eccles Williams, Ferelith. The Oxford Ox's calendar / Ferelith Eccles Williams. — Tadworth : World's Work, c1980. — [32]p : chiefly col.ill ; 19x25cm
ISBN 0-437-86008-6 : £3.50 B81-12618

428.6 — English language. Reading books. Special subjects: Escapes

Great escapes / L.M. Arnold and Alice E. Varty general editors ; [illustrated by Tim Marwood]. — London : Macmillan, 1980. — 46p : ill ; 19cm. — (Activity readers. 5)
Text on inside cover
ISBN 0-333-25415-5 (pbk) : £0.50 B81-09931

428.6 — English language. Reading books. Special subjects: Exploration

Arnold, L. M.. Explorers on top of the world / L.M. Arnold and Alice E. Varty ; [illustrated by Jill Fenwick]. — London : Macmillan, 1980. — 46p : col.ill,1port ; 19cm. — (Activity readers. 5)
Text on inside cover
ISBN 0-333-25412-0 (pbk) : £0.50 B81-12499

428.6 — English language. Reading books. Special subjects: Fire stations

Spier, Peter. Fire station / by Peter Spier. — London : Collins, 1981. — [12]p : col.ill ; 23cm. — (Peter Spier's village books)
Cover title
ISBN 0-00-140137-8 : £1.50 B81-25630

428.6 — English language. Reading books. Special subjects: Garages

Spier, Peter. Bill's garage / by Peter Spier. — London : Collins, 1981. — [10]p : col.ill ; 16x23cm. — (Peter Spier's village books)
Cover title
ISBN 0-00-140136-x : £1.50 B81-25631

428.6 — English language. Reading books. Special subjects: Great Britain. Agricultural industries: Farms — *For schools*

Milburn, Constance. Reading round the farm / Constance Milburn ; [illustrated by Linda Birch]. — Glasgow : Blackie, 1981. — 16p : chiefly col.ill ; 21cm. — (Reading round books ; bk.7)
Cover title. — Text on inside covers. — Includes index
ISBN 0-216-90913-9 (pbk) : £0.50 B81-13397

428.6 — English language. Reading books. Special subjects: Grocery shops

Spier, Peter. Food market / by Peter Spier. — London : Collins, 1981. — [12]p : col.ill ; 23cm. — (Peter Spier's village books)
Cover title
ISBN 0-00-140139-4 : £1.50 B81-25628

428.6 — English language. Reading books. Special subjects: Hearing — *For schools*

Kincaid, Doug. Ears and hearing / Doug Kincaid and Peter Coles. — Exeter : Wheaton, c1981. — 24p : col.ill ; 21x22cm. — (Read and do)
ISBN 0-08-026409-3 (pbk) : Unpriced
B81-38128

428.6 — English language. Reading books. Special subjects: Historical events — *For children*

Hutchings. Purnell's adventures in time : word book / by Hutchings. — Maidenhead : Purnell, 1981. — 61p : chiefly col.ill ; 30cm
ISBN 0-361-05059-3 : £3.99 B81-27178

428.6 — English language. Reading books. Special subjects: Length — *For children*

Marshall, Sybil. The mouse with the longest tail / by Sybil Marshall and John Coop ; drawings by Pete Beard. — St. Albans : Hart-Davis Educational for Granada Television, c1981. — 15p : col.ill ; 22cm. — (Sam and Squeak stories. Set two)
With: The summer fair / by Ursula Daniels
ISBN 0-247-13203-9 (unbound) : Unpriced
ISBN 0-247-13157-1 (set) : Unpriced
Also classified at 428.6 B81-22172

428.6 — English language. Reading books. Special subjects: Manufacture — *For schools*

Althea. How was it made? / by Althea ; illustrated by the author. — London : Souvenir, c1980. — [24]p : col.ill ; 19cm. — (Althea's brightstart books)
ISBN 0-285-62458-x : £1.50 B81-07140

428.6 — English language. Reading books. Special subjects: Markets — *For schools*

Milburn, Constance. Reading round the market / Constance Milburn ; [illustrated by David Brogan]. — Glasgow : Blackie, 1980. — 16p : chiefly col.ill ; 24cm. — (Reading round books ; bk.8)
Cover title. — Text on inside covers. — Includes index
ISBN 0-216-90914-7 (pbk) : £0.50 B81-13399

428.6 — English language. Reading books. Special subjects: Money — *For children*

Daniels, Ursula. Scarecrow Sam / by Ursula Daniels and John Coop ; drawings by Pete Beard. — St. Albans : Hart-Davis Educational for Granada Television, c1981. — 15p : col.ill ; 22cm. — (Sam and Squeak stories. Set two)
With: The three o'clock cake / by Ursula Daniels
ISBN 0-247-13202-0 (unbound) : Unpriced
ISBN 0-247-13157-1 (set) : Unpriced
Also classified at 428.6 B81-22174

428.6 — English language. Reading books. Special subjects: Numeration — *For children*

Daniels, Ursula. Presents for Grandma / by Ursula Daniels and John Coop ; drawings by Pete Beard. — St. Albans : Hart-Davis Educational for Granada Television, c1981. — 15p : col.ill ; 22cm. — (Sam and Squeak stories. Set two)
With: Sam's rocket / by Ursula Daniels
ISBN 0-247-13204-7 (unbound) : Unpriced
ISBN 0-247-13157-1 (set) : Unpriced
Primary classification 428.6 B81-22173

Daniels, Ursula. Rabbits don't eat lupins / by Ursula Daniels ; drawings by Pete Beard. — St. Albans : Hart-Davis Educational for Granada Television, c1981. — 15p : col.ill ; 22cm. — (Sam and Squeak stories. Set two)
With: The pet show / by Ursula Daniels
ISBN 0-247-13201-2 (unbound) : Unpriced
ISBN 0-247-13157-1 (set) : Unpriced
Primary classification 428.6 B81-22171

428.6 — English language. Reading books. Special subjects: Olympic Games, *to 1980* — *For schools*

Baguley, Nigel. The Olympic Games / Nigel Baguley. — London : Harrap, 1980. — 48p : ill,ports ; 19cm. — (The Reporters series)
ISBN 0-245-53572-1 (pbk) : £0.80 B81-24329

428.6 — English language. Reading books. Special subjects: Opposites — *For children*

Hoban, Tana. Push-pull-empty-full : a book of opposites / by Tana Hoban. — Harmondsworth : Kestrel, 1974, c1972 (1981 [printing]). — [34]p : chiefly ill ; 21cm
Originally published: New York : Macmillan, 1972
ISBN 0-7226-6265-3 : £3.50 B81-35282

428.6 — English language. Reading books. Special subjects: Ordinal numbers — *For children*

Daniels, Ursula. Rabbits don't eat lupins / by Ursula Daniels ; drawings by Pete Beard. — St. Albans : Hart-Davis Educational for Granada Television, c1981. — 15p : col.ill ; 22cm. — (Sam and Squeak stories. Set two)
With: The pet show / by Ursula Daniels
ISBN 0-247-13201-2 (unbound) : Unpriced
ISBN 0-247-13157-1 (set) : Unpriced
Also classified at 428.6 B81-22171

428.6 — English language. Reading books. Special subjects: Parks — *For schools*

Milburn, Constance. Reading round the park / Constance Milburn ; [illustrated by David Brogan]. — Glasgow : Blackie, 1980. — 16p : chiefly col ill ; 24cm. — (Reading round books ; bk.5)
Cover title. — Text on inside covers. — Includes index
ISBN 0-216-90911-2 (pbk) : £0.50 B81-15140

428.6 — English language. Reading books. Special subjects: Pet shops

Spier, Peter. The pet shop / by Peter Spier. — London : Collins, 1981. — [12]p : col.ill ; 23cm. — (Peter Spier's village books)
Cover title
ISBN 0-00-140135-1 : £1.50 B81-25629

428.6 — English language. Reading books. Special subjects: Pirates — *For schools*

Swan, D. K.. Pirates / D.K. Swan. — Harlow : Longman, 1981. — 44p : ill(some col.),3col.maps ; 19cm. — (NMSR. Stage 2)
ISBN 0-582-53541-7 (pbk) : £0.60 B81-35367

428.6 — English language. Reading books. Special subjects: Places — *For children*

Murray, Philippa. Landscapes / Philippa Murray, Alison Sinclair and Susan Quilliam. — Welwyn : Nisbet, 1981. — 95p : ill(some col.),1map ; 21cm
ISBN 0-7202-1014-3 (pbk) : £1.40 B81-29025

428.6 — English language. Reading books. Special subjects: Schools

Spier, Peter. My school / by Peter Spier. — London : Collins, 1981. — [12]p : col.ill ; 23cm. — (Peter Spier's village books)
Cover title
ISBN 0-00-140138-6 : £1.50 B81-25632

428.6 — English language. Reading books. Special subjects: Seaside resorts — *For schools*

Milburn, Constance. Reading round the seaside / Constance Milburn ; [illustrated by Kirsty Kirkwood]. — Glasgow : Blackie, 1981. — 16p : chiefly col.ill ; 24cm. — (Reading round books ; bk.6)
Cover title. — Text on inside covers. — Includes index
ISBN 0-216-90912-0 (pbk) : £0.50 B81-13398

428.6 — English language. Reading books. Special subjects: Shapes — *For children*

Daniels, Ursula. Presents for Grandma / by Ursula Daniels and John Coop ; drawings by Pete Beard. — St. Albans : Hart-Davis Educational for Granada Television, c1981. — 15p : col.ill ; 22cm. — (Sam and Squeak stories. Set two)
With: Sam's rocket / by Ursula Daniels
ISBN 0-247-13204-7 (unbound) : Unpriced
ISBN 0-247-13157-1 (set) : Unpriced
Also classified at 428.6 B81-22173

428.6 — English language. Reading books. Special subjects: Sight — *For schools*

Kincaid, Doug. Eyes and looking / Doug Kincaid and Peter Coles. — Exeter : Wheaton, c1981. — 24p : col.ill ; 21x22cm. — (Read and do)
ISBN 0-08-026411-5 (pbk) : Unpriced B81-38127

428.6 — English language. Reading books. Special subjects: Smell & taste — *For schools*

Kincaid, Doug. Taste and smell / Doug Kincaid and Peter Coles. — Exeter : Wheaton, c1981. — 24p : col.ill ; 21x22cm. — (Read and do)
ISBN 0-08-026410-7 (pbk) : Unpriced B81-38130

428.6 — English language. Reading books. Special subjects: Sorting — *For children*

Marshall, Sybil. The mouse with the longest tail / by Sybil Marshall and John Coop ; drawings by Pete Beard. — St. Albans : Hart-Davis Educational for Granada Television, c1981. — 15p : col.ill ; 22cm. — (Sam and Squeak stories. Set two)
With: The summer fair / by Ursula Daniels
ISBN 0-247-13203-9 (unbound) : Unpriced
ISBN 0-247-13157-1 (set) : Unpriced
Primary classification 428.6 B81-22172

428.6 — English language. Reading books. Special subjects: Space flight

All about space / L.M. Arnold and Alice E. Varty general editors. — London : Macmillan, 1980. — 46p : col.ill ; 19cm. — (Activity readers. 4)
ISBN 0-333-25413-9 (pbk) : £0.50 B81-21654

428.6 — English language. Reading books. Special subjects: Time

Shapiro, Arnold. Mr. Cuckoo's clock shop / written by Arnold Shapiro ; designed and illustrated by Linda Griffith. — [Croydon] : Pied Piper, [1981]. — [22]p : col.ill ; 20cm
ISBN 0-7166-5601-9 : Unpriced B81-08477

428.6 — English language. Reading books. Special subjects: Time — *For children*

Daniels, Ursula. Scarecrow Sam / by Ursula Daniels and John Coop ; drawings by Pete Beard. — St. Albans : Hart-Davis Educational for Granada Television, c1981. — 15p : col.ill ; 22cm. — (Sam and Squeak stories. Set two)
With: The three o'clock cake / by Ursula Daniels
ISBN 0-247-13202-0 (unbound) : Unpriced
ISBN 0-247-13157-1 (set) : Unpriced
Primary classification 428.6 B81-22174

428.6 — English language. Reading books. Special subjects: Touch — *For schools*

Kincaid, Doug. Touch and feel / Doug Kincaid and Peter Coles. — Exeter : Wheaton, c1981. — 24p : col.ill ; 21x22cm. — (Read and do)
ISBN 0-08-026408-5 (pbk) : Unpriced B81-38129

428.6 — English language. Reading books. Special subjects: Toy shops

Spier, Peter. The toy shop / by Peter Spier. — London : Collins, 1981. — [12]p : col.ill ; 23cm. — (Peter Spier's village books)
Cover title
ISBN 0-00-140134-3 : £1.50 B81-25627

428.6 — English language. Reading books. Special subjects: Vehicles

Wheels go round. — London : Methuen, 1981. — [24]p : col.ill ; 22x24cm
Cover title
ISBN 0-416-20840-1 (spiral) : £3.25 B81-19608

428.6 — English language. Reading books. Special subjects: Veterinary medicine — *For schools*

Herriot, James. Let sleeping vets lie / James Herriott ; abridged by J.R.C. and G.M. Yglesias. — Walton-on-Thames : Nelson, 1981. — 105p ; 18cm. — (Getaway)
ISBN 0-17-432181-3 (pbk) : £0.95 B81-37507

428.6 — English language. Reading books. Special subjects: Wildlife conservation — *For schools*

Body, Wendy. Wildlife in danger / Wendy Body. — London : Harrap, 1980. — 38p : ill ; 19cm. — (The Reporters series)
ISBN 0-245-53525-x (pbk) : £0.80 B81-01539

428.6 — English language. Reading books: Strip cartoons — *For schools*

Cobb, David, *1926-*. Dino the dinosaur / [text and exercises by David Cobb]. — London : Longman, 1981. — 8p : ill(some col.) ; 29cm. — (The adventures of Billy and Lilly)
Cover title
ISBN 0-582-53107-1 (pbk) : £0.40 B81-14039

Cobb, David, *1926-*. Football in space / [text and exercises by David Cobb]. — London : Longman, 1981. — 8p : ill(some col.) ; 29cm. — (The adventures of Billy and Lilly)
Cover title
ISBN 0-582-53106-3 (pbk) : £0.40 B81-14040

Cobb, David, *1926-*. Lilly's flying horse / [text and exercises by David Cobb]. — London : Longman, 1981. — 8p : ill(some col.) ; 29cm. — (The adventures of Billy and Lilly)
Cover title
ISBN 0-582-53104-7 (pbk) : £0-40 B81-14041

Cobb, David, *1926-*. Tennis star! / [text and exercises by David Cobb]. — London : Longman, 1981. — 8p : ill(some col.) ; 29cm. — (The adventures of Billy and Lilly)
Cover title
ISBN 0-582-53105-5 (pbk) : £0.40 B81-17672

428.6'2 — English language. Reading books — *For slow learning adolescents*

Anchor action. — London : Cassell, c1981. — (Cassell reading development scheme)
1 / [edited by] John Blanchard. — 30p : ill ; 22cm
ISBN 0-304-30103-5 (pbk) : Unpriced B81-14161

Anchor action. — London : Cassell, c1981. — (Cassell reading development scheme)
2 / [edited by] Joan Tate. — 30p : ill ; 22cm
ISBN 0-304-30104-3 (pbk) : Unpriced B81-14162

Banjo action. — London : Cassell, c1981. — (Cassell reading development scheme)
1 / [edited by] John Blanchard. — 30p : ill ; 22cm
ISBN 0-304-30105-1 (pbk) : Unpriced B81-14163

Banjo action. — London : Cassell, c1981. — (Cassell reading development scheme)
2 / [edited by] John Blanchard. — 30p : ill ; 22cm
ISBN 0-304-30106-x (pbk) : Unpriced B81-14164

Banjo action. — London : Cassell, c1981. — (Cassell reading development scheme)
3 / [edited by] John Blanchard. — 30p : ill ; 22cm
ISBN 0-304-30107-8 (pbk) : Unpriced B81-14166

Banjo action. — London : Cassell, c1981. — (Cassell reading development scheme)
4 / [edited by] Joan Tate. — 30p : ill ; 22cm
ISBN 0-304-30649-5 (pbk) : Unpriced B81-14167

Carew, Jan. Dark night, deep water / Jan Carew. — Harlow : Longman, 1981. — 96p ; 19cm. — (Knockouts)
ISBN 0-582-39097-4 (cased) : £2.95
ISBN 0-582-20076-8 (pbk) : £10.50 B81-38585

Carew, Jan. Dead Man's Creek : two stories / by Jan Carew. — Harlow : Longman, 1981. — 62p : ill ; 19cm. — (Knockouts)
Contents: Dead Man's Creek - City of the Tobors
ISBN 0-582-20091-1 (pbk) : £0.65 B81-10079

Carew, Jan. House of fear : two stories / by Jan Carew. — London : Longman, 1981. — 64p ; 19cm. — (Knockouts)
ISBN 0-582-20090-3 (pbk) : £0.65 B81-12578

Chilton, Irma. Flash. — London : Cassell, July 1981. — [64]p. — (Red Lion books ; 23)
ISBN 0-304-30704-1 (pbk) : £0.95 : CIP entry B81-13884

Crosher, G. R.. The dogs of the marsh. — London : Cassell, July 1981. — [64]p. — (Red Lion books ; 15)
ISBN 0-304-30628-2 (pbk) : £0.95 : CIP entry B81-13875

Crosher, G. R.. Journey into danger. — London : Cassell, July 1981. — [64]p. — (Red Lion books ; 16)
ISBN 0-304-30629-0 (pbk) : £0.95 : CIP entry B81-13876

428.6'2 — English language. Reading books — *For slow learning adolescents continuation*

Duberley, Susan. The ring / Susan Duberley. — London : Hutchinson, 1981. — 32p ; 21cm. — (Spirals)
ISBN 0-09-144881-6 (pbk) : Unpriced : CIP rev. B81-20487

Edwards, Cliff. Hair raisers / Cliff Edwards ; illustrations by Michael Strand. — Harlow : Longman, 1981. — 4v. : ill,ports ; 27cm
ISBN 0-582-20158-6 (pbk) : £2.95 B81-28629

Eisenberg, Lisa. Falling star / Lisa Eisenberg. — London : Murray, c1980. — 57p : ill ; 18cm. — (A Laura Brewster book)
ISBN 0-7195-3818-1 (pbk) : £0.75 B81-11382

Eisenberg, Lisa. Fast-food king / Lisa Eisenberg. — London : Murray, c1980. — 58p : ill ; 18cm. — (A Laura Brewster book)
ISBN 0-7195-3817-3 (pbk) : £0.75 B81-11384

Eisenberg, Lisa. Golden idol / Lisa Eisenberg. — London : Murray, c1980. — 59p : ill ; 18cm. — (A Laura Brewster book)
ISBN 0-7195-3819-x (pbk) : £0.75 B81-11381

Eisenberg, Lisa. House of laughs / Lisa Eisenberg. — London : Murray, c1980. — 57p : ill ; 18cm. — (A Laura Brewster book)
ISBN 0-7195-3814-9 (pbk) : £0.75 B81-11196

Eisenberg, Lisa. Killer music / Lisa Eisenberg. — London : Murray, c1980. — 60p : ill ; 18cm. — (A Laura Brewster book)
ISBN 0-7195-3815-7 (pbk) : £0.75 B81-11385

Eisenberg, Lisa. Tiger rose / Lisa Eisenberg. — London : Murray, c1980. — 59p : ill ; 18cm. — (A Laura Brewster book)
ISBN 0-7195-3816-5 (pbk) : £0.75 B81-11383

Escott, John. The ghost of Genny Castle. — London : Cassell, July 1981. — [64]p. — (Red Lion books ; 21)
ISBN 0-304-30702-5 (pbk) : £0.95 : CIP entry B81-13881

Hill, L. A.. Stories from Ancient Greece / by L.A. Hill. — Oxford : Oxford University Press, 1981. — 32p : ill(some col.) ; 20cm. — (Oxford graded readers. 1,000 headwords. Senior level)
ISBN 0-19-421810-4 (pbk) : £0.50 B81-24723

Hughes, George, *19---*. Adventure in Tokyo / by George Hughes ; pictures by Kenzo Sato. — Oxford : Oxford University Press, 1981. — 48p : ill(some col.) ; 20cm. — (Oxford graded readers. 1,000 headwords. Senior level)
ISBN 0-19-421807-4 (pbk) : £0.60 B81-24722

Into the future : a collection of sci-fi / edited by J.R.C. and G.M. Yglesias. — Walton-on-Thames : Nelson, 1981. — 105p ; 18cm
ISBN 0-17-432188-0 (pbk) : £0.95 B81-38424

Jones, Geraldine. Adventure in New York / by Geraldine Jones ; pictures by Cynthia Back. — Oxford : Oxford University Press, 1981. — 48p : ill(some col.) ; 20cm. — (Oxford graded readers. 1,000 headwords. Senior level)
ISBN 0-19-421809-0 (pbk) : £0.60 B81-24721

Jones, John, *19---*. Fame and misfortune / John Jones ; illustrations by Elizabeth Honey. — Melbourne : Longman Cheshire ; Aylesbury : Ginn [distributor], 1979. — 63p : ill ; 18cm. — (Trendset)
ISBN 0-602-22414-4 (pbk) : Unpriced B81-18359

King, Clive. First day out / Clive King ; illustrated by Jacqueline Atkinson. — London : Benn, 1976. — 46p : ill ; 19cm. — (An Inner ring hipster. Green circle hipsters)
ISBN 0-510-07743-9 (pbk) : £0.75 B81-28356

King, Clive. High jacks, low jacks / Clive King ; illustrated by Jacqueline Atkinson. — London : Benn, 1976 (1980 [printing]). — 46p : ill ; 19cm. — (Inner ring hipsters. Green circle hipsters)
ISBN 0-510-07739-0 (pbk) : £0.75 B81-24719

Levine, Josie. Vet in a spin / James Herriot ; adapted by Josie Levine ; illustrations by Larry. — Harlow : Longman, 1981. — 106p : ill ; 19cm. — (Knockouts)
ISBN 0-582-20099-7 (pbk) : £0.80 B81-34935

Loxton, Margaret. The dark shadow / Margaret Loxton. — London : Hutchinson, 1981. — 32p ; 21cm. — (Spirals)
ISBN 0-09-144891-3 (pbk) : Unpriced : CIP rev. B81-20486

McLeish, Kenneth. Hostages / Kenneth McLeish. — Harlow : Longman, 1981. — 75p : ill,facsims ; 19cm. — (Knockouts)
ISBN 0-582-39100-8 : £2.95 B81-07680

Mays, Dennis. The knight of the road. — London : Cassell, July 1981. — [48]p. — (Red Lion books ; 19)
ISBN 0-304-30632-0 (pbk) : £0.95 : CIP entry B81-13879

Parker, Richard. Digging for treasure / Richard Parker ; illustrated by Trevor Stubley. — London : Benn, 1976 (1979 [printing]). — 44p : ill ; 19cm. — (Inner ring hipsters. Red circle hipsters)
ISBN 0-510-07728-5 (pbk) : £0.75 B81-24716

Parker, Richard. Flood / Richard Parker ; illustrated by Trevor Stubley. — London : Benn, 1976 (1979 [printing]). — 46p : ill ; 19cm. — (Inner ring hipsters. Red circle hipsters)
ISBN 0-510-07729-3 (pbk) : £0.75 B81-24718

Parker, Richard. Sausages on the shore / Richard Parker ; illustrated by Trevor Stubley. — London : Benn, 1976 (1979 [printing]). — 45p : ill ; 19cm. — (Inner ring hipsters. Red circle hipsters)
ISBN 0-510-07727-7 (pbk) : £0.75 B81-24715

Parker, Richard. The Sunday papers / Richard Parker ; illustrated by Trevor Stubley. — London : Benn, 1976 (1979 [printing]). — 45p : ill ; 19cm. — (Inner ring hipsters. Red circle hipsters)
ISBN 0-510-07736-6 (pbk) : £0.75 B81-24717

Pasakarnis, Ernest. The sweet secret. — London : Cassell, July 1981. — [64]p. — (Red Lion books ; 20)
ISBN 0-304-30633-9 (pbk) : £0.95 : CIP entry B81-13880

Pepper, Ann. Comanche / Harold Keith ; adapted by Ann Pepper. — Oxford : Oxford University Press, c1979. — 96p ; 18cm. — (Alpha western)
ISBN 0-19-424270-6 (pbk) : £0.70 B81-23574

Philbin, Kevin. The stone of Gan. — London : Cassell, July 1981. — [48]p. — (Red Lion books ; 17)
ISBN 0-304-30630-4 (pbk) : £0.95 : CIP entry B81-13877

Philbin, Kevin. A time gone by. — London : Cassell, July 1981. — [64]p. — (Red Lion books ; 18)
ISBN 0-304-30631-2 (pbk) : £0.95 : CIP entry B81-13878

Real English : a practical guide to reading, talking and writing today. — Huddersfield : Schofield & Sims
2 by Glyn Edwards and Frank Hayes. — 1981. — 96p : ill(some col.),maps,facsims,forms ; 30cm
ISBN 0-7217-0354-2 (pbk) : £1.75 B81-14177

Townson, Hazel. Walk over my grave. — London : Cassell, July 1981. — [48]p. — (Red Lion books ; 22)
ISBN 0-304-30703-3 (pbk) : £0.95 : CIP entry B81-13882

Townson, Hazel. Who is Sylvia?. — London : Cassell, July 1981. — [48]p. — (Red Lion books ; 24)
ISBN 0-304-30794-7 (pbk) : £0.95 : CIP entry B81-13883

Yglesias, J. R. C.. Means of escape / Spencer Dunmore ; abridged by J.R.C. and G.M. Yglesias. — Walton-on-Thames : Nelson, 1981. — 133p ; 18cm. — (Getaway)
Full ed. originally published : London : P. Davies, 1978
ISBN 0-17-432187-2 (pbk) : £0.95 B81-38423

428.6'2 — English language. Reading books for slow learning adolescents: Cassell reading development scheme — *For teaching*

Blanchard, John, *1947-*. Cassell reading development scheme : teacher's book / John Blanchard, Joan Tate. — London : Cassell, c1981. — 12p ; 22cm
Bibliography: p12
ISBN 0-304-30112-4 (unbound) : Unpriced B81-14165

428.6'2 — English language. Reading books for slow learning adolescents: Laura Brewster books — *For teaching*

Laura Brewster teacher's guide. — London : Murray, c1981. — 89p ; 23cm
Originally published: Belmont : Fearon Pitman, c1979
ISBN 0-7195-3820-3 (pbk) : Unpriced B81-14591

428.6'2 — English language. Reading books — *For slow learning children* — *For schools*

Chilton, Irma. The soul ship / by Irma Chiltern ; illustrations by Sophie Kittredge. — London : Cassell, 1980. — 64p : ill ; 18cm. — (Red lion books)
ISBN 0-304-30511-1 (pbk) : £0.95 : CIP rev. B80-05313

Deary, Terry. Hope Street / by Terry Deary ; illustrations by Andy Carroll. — London : Cassell, 1980. — 62p : ill ; 18cm — (Red lion books)
ISBN 0-304-30514-6 (pbk) : £0.95 : CIP rev. B80-05314

Escott, John. The bandstand / by John Escott ; illustrations by Dilys Jones. — London : Cassell, 1980. — 64p : ill ; 18cm. — (Cassell red lion books)
ISBN 0-304-30510-3 (pbk) : £0.95 : CIP rev. B80-05315

Gee, Sue. The great escape / adapted by Sue Gee from The great escape by Paul Brickhill. — London : Hutchinson, 1981. — 124p : ill,1map,1plan ; 19cm. — (The Bulls-eye series)
ISBN 0-09-141021-5 (pbk) : Unpriced : CIP rev. B81-20164

Holt, Maurice. Winged escort. — London : Hutchinson Education, Feb.1982. — [128p]. — (Bulls-eye)
ISBN 0-09-141011-8 (pbk) : £0.85 : CIP entry B81-38325

McBratney, Sam. The pigeon killer / by Sam McBratney ; illustrations by Bruce Symons. — London : Cassell, 1980. — 48p : ill ; 18cm. — (Red lion books)
ISBN 0-304-30261-9 (pbk) : £0.95 CIP rev. B80-05319

Nobes, Jean. Modesty Blaise / adapted by Jean Nobes from Modesty Blaise by Peter O'Donnell. — London : Hutchinson, 1981. — 128p ; 19cm. — (The Bulls-eye series)
ISBN 0-09-144371-7 (pbk) : Unpriced B81-19821

428.6′2 — English language. Reading books — *For slow learning children — For schools*
continuation

Nobes, Jean. Slay ride / adapted by Jean Nobes from the Slay ride by Dick Francis. — London : Hutchinson, 1981. — 128p ; 19cm. — (The Bulls-eye series)
ISBN 0-09-143661-3 (pbk) : Unpriced
B81-19820

Nobes, Patrick. Walkabout. — London : Hutchinson, Feb.1982. — [96]p. — (Bulls-eye)
ISBN 0-09-146891-4 (pbk) : £0.85 : CIP entry
B81-38326

Philbin, Kevin. Bonfire robbery / by Kevin Philbin ; illustrations by Richard Appleby. — London : Cassell, 1980. — 31p : ill ; 18cm. — (Red lion books)
ISBN 0-304-30270-8 (pbk) : £0.95 : CIP rev.
B80-05321

Welchman, Dorothy. Ring of bright water / adapted by Dorothy Welchman from Ring of bright water by Gavin Maxwell. — London : Hutchinson, 1981. — 95p : 1map ; 19cm. — (The Bulls-eye series)
ISBN 0-09-144871-9 (pbk) : Unpriced : CIP rev. B81-20489

428.6′2 — English language. Reading books — *For slow learning students*

Duberley, Susan. Snake / Susan Duberley. — London : Hutchinson, 1981. — 40p ; 21cm. — (Spirals)
ISBN 0-09-144261-3 (pbk) : £0.65 : CIP rev.
B81-00602

Falk, Ian. Running scared / Ian Falk ; illustrations by Greg Aznar. — Melbourne : Longman Cheshire ; Aylesbury : Ginn [distributor], 1979. — 67p : ill ; 18cm. — (Trendset)
ISBN 0-602-22411-x (pbk) : Unpriced
B81-09529

Gee, Sue. Loves me, loves me not / Sue Gee. — London : Hutchinson, 1981. — 38p ; 21cm. — (Spirals)
ISBN 0-09-144271-0 (pbk) : £0.65 : CIP rev.
B81-00851

Taylor, James P.. A price to pay. — London : Edward Arnold, Dec.1981. — [64]p. — (Taken from life)
ISBN 0-7131-0560-7 (pbk) : £1.50 : CIP entry
B81-31550

428.6′2 — English language. Reading books: Plays — *For slow-learning students*

Walke, David. Package holiday / David Walke. — London : Hutchinson, 1980. — 40p ; 21cm. — (Spirals)
Contents: The travel agent′s — The plane — The island
ISBN 0-09-144031-9 (pbk) : £0.60 B81-02175

428.6′2 — English language. Reading books. Special subjects: Animals — *For slow learning students — For schools*

Taylor, James P.. How to catch a dragon. — London : Edward Arnold, Dec.1981. — [64]p. — (Taken from life)
ISBN 0-7131-0559-3 (pbk) : £1.50 : CIP entry
B81-31549

428.6′2 — English language. Reading books. Special subjects: Construction industries — *For illiterate adults*

Gibbons, Patrick. Steel fixing : my job as a chippie and a steel fixer / Patrick Gibbons. — London : Macmillan Education, 1979. — 16p : ill ; 22cm. — (Brighton books)
ISBN 0-333-25773-1 (pbk) : £0.45 : CIP rev.
B79-12857

428.6′2 — English language. Reading books. Special subjects: Racing motorcycles. Racing. Sheene, Barry — *For slow learning adolescents*

The Sheene machine / edited by Andrew Marriott. — Harlow : Longman, 1981. — 103p,[8]p of plates : ports ; 19cm. — (Knockouts)
Originally published: London : Pelham, 1979
ISBN 0-582-20008-3 (pbk) : £0.80 B81-27616

428.6′4 — English language. Reading books — *For non-English speaking students*

Allman, Kate. A question of reading / Kate Allman ; photographs by Bas Parfitt ; illustrations by John May. — Leeds : E.J. Arnold
Bk.1. — c1981. — 47p : ill ; 21cm
ISBN 0-560-00944-5 (pbk) : Unpriced
B81-26163

Allman, Kate. A question of reading / Kate Allman ; photographs by Bas Parfitt ; illustrations by John May. — Leeds : E.J. Arnold
Bk.2. — c1981. — 47p : ill ; 21cm
ISBN 0-560-00945-3 (pbk) : Unpriced
B81-26164

Allsop, Jake. The plot / Jake Allsop. — London : Cassell, 1981. — 63p : ill ; 18cm. — (Cassell English programme)
ISBN 0-304-30658-4 (pbk) : Unpriced
B81-28500

Anderson, Jane. Flambards / K.M. Peyton ; adapted by Jane Anderson. — Oxford : Oxford University Press, c1980. — 96p ; 18cm. — (Alpha general fiction)
ISBN 0-19-424169-6 (pbk) : Unpriced
B81-00852

Body, Wendy. Storyline / Wendy Body, Derek Cheshire. — Leeds : E.J. Arnold
1. — c1981. — 61p : ill ; 21cm
ISBN 0-560-03590-x (pbk) : Unpriced
B81-26161

Body, Wendy. Storyline / Wendy Body, Derek Cheshire. — Leeds : E.J. Arnold
2. — c1981. — 61p : ill ; 21cm
ISBN 0-560-03591-8 (pbk) : Unpriced
B81-26162

Dahl, Roald. The way up to heaven and other stories / Roald Dahl. — Copenhagen : Grafisk Forlag ; London : Murray, c1980. — 80p : ill ; 19cm. — (Easy readers. B)
ISBN 0-7195-3767-3 (pbk) : £0.90 B81-15026

Doyle, *Sir* Arthur Conan. The hound of the Baskervilles / Sir Arthur Conan Doyle. — Copenhagen : Grafisk Forlag ; London : Murray, c1980. — 96p : ill ; 19cm. — (Easy readers. C)
ISBN 0-7195-3807-6 (pbk) : £0.90 B81-15027

Doyle, *Sir* Arthur Conan. The speckled band / Sir Arthur Conan Doyle. — Rev. ed / revised by Robert Dewsnap. — Copenhagen : Grafisk Forlag ; London : Murray, c1980. — 45p : ill ; 19cm. — (Easy readers. A)
ISBN 0-7195-3802-5 (pbk) : £0.60 B81-15028

Kaleidoscope : an anthology of English varieties for upper-intermediate and more advanced students / [compiled by] Michael Swan. — Cambridge : Cambridge University Press, 1979. — xi,212p : ill,facsims,maps ; 20cm. — (Cambridge English language learning ; 7)
ISBN 0-521-21621-4 (pbk) : £1.95 B81-00088

Lowe, Sally. The African child / Camara Laye ; abridged and simplified by Sally Lowe ; illustrations by Anne Rodger. — London : Collins, 1980. — 80p : ill ; 19cm. — (Collins English library. Level 4) (A Collins graded reader)
ISBN 0-00-370142-5 (pbk) : £0.65 B81-11285

Machin, Noel. Roller coaster : a novel / by Burton Wohl ; based on a screenplay by Richard Levinson & William Link ; story by Sanford Sheldon and Richard Levinson & William Link ; suggested by a story by Tommy Cook ; abridged and simplified by Noel Machin. — Harlow : Longman, 1980, c1977. — 70p ; 19cm. — (Longman simplified English series)
ISBN 0-582-53335-x (pbk) : £0.70 B81-07753

Matthews, Geoffrey, *1930-*. The space invaders / Geoffrey Matthews ; illustrated by Chris Evans. — London : Heinemann Educational, 1980. — 58p : ill ; 18cm. — (Heinemann guided readers. Intermediate level ; no.24)
ISBN 0-435-27072-9 (pbk) : £0.65 B81-05555

Moggach, Tony. I, Lucifer / Peter O′Donnell ; adapted by Tony Moggach. — Oxford : Oxford University Press, c1980. — 96p ; 18cm. — (Alpha thriller)
ISBN 0-19-424282-x (pbk) : £0.65 B81-02505

More modern short stories : for students of English / selected and edited by Peter J.W. Taylor. — Oxford : Oxford University, 1981. — 130p ; 22cm
Bibliography: p127-130
ISBN 0-19-416708-9 (pbk) : £1.95 B81-37089

Morris, Margery. The Valentine generation and other stories : John Wain, John Updike, Doris Lessing and others / selected and simplified by Margery Morris ; photographs by Francis Azemard. — Harlow : Longman, c1980. — 52p : ill ; 20cm. — (Longman structural readers. Fiction. Stage 5)
ISBN 0-582-53108-x (pbk) : £0.55 B81-00853

Morris, Marjery. The lovely lady and other stories / D.H. Lawrence ; abridged and simplified by Marjery Morris ; illustrations by Maureen and Gordon Gray. — London : Collins, 1981. — 64p : ill ; 19cm. — (Collins English library. Level 4) (A Collins graded reader)
ISBN 0-00-370129-8 (pbk) : £0.65 B81-11284

Pearson, Christopher. The two million dollar loan / Christopher Pearson ; illustrated by Garry Rees. — London : Heinemann Educational, 1981. — 58p : ill ; 18cm. — (Heinemann guided readers. Intermediate level ; 24)
ISBN 0-435-27076-1 (pbk) : £0.65 B81-05554

Stevenson, Robert Louis. The bottle imp / Robert Louis Stevenson. — Rev. ed. / by Robert Dewsnap. — Copenhagen : Grafisk Forlag ; London : Murray, 1980. — 46p : ill ; 19cm. — (Easy readers)
ISBN 0-7195-3804-1 (pbk) : £0.60
ISBN 87-429-7391-0 (Denmark)
ISBN 0-88436-894-7 (U.S.)
ISBN 82-05-12607-0 (Norway)
ISBN 91-243-1068-9 (Sweden)
ISBN 90-01-27510-9 (Holland)
ISBN 3-12-534131-0 (Germany) B81-34839

Stewart, Mary. The castle of danger / Mary Stewart ; abridged and simplified by Celia Turvey. — Harlow : Longman, 1981. — 126p ; 18cm. — (Longman simplified English series)
ISBN 0-582-52688-4 (pbk) : £0.70 B81-20684

Tarner, Margaret. My cousin Rachel / Daphne du Maurier ; retold by Margaret Tarner ; illustrated by Kay Mary Wilson. — London : Heinemann Educational, 1980. — 74p : ill ; 18cm. — (Heinemann guided readers. Intermediate level ; 26)
ISBN 0-435-27074-5 (pbk) : Unpriced : CIP rev. B80-11842

Wagner, Rosemary. The Poseidon adventure / Paul Gallico ; adapted by Rosemary Wagner. — Oxford : Oxford University Press, 1980. — 96p ; 18cm. — (Alpha thriller)
ISBN 0-19-424281-1 (pbk) : £0.65 B81-05809

Warrener, Barry. ′Shock′ / by Barry Warrener. — Bradford (Bolton Royd, Manningham La., Bradford 8) : Bradford Literacy Group, c1981. — 17p : ill ; 22cm. — (BLG ; no.002)
£0.50 (pbk) B81-35279

428.6'4 — English language. Reading books — *For non-English speaking students* *continuation*

Wilde, Oscar. The Canterville ghost / Oscar Wilde. — Rev. ed. / Robert Dewsnap. — Copenhagen : Grafisk Forlag ; London : Murray, 1980, c1981. — 46p : ill ; 19cm. — (Easy readers. A)
ISBN 0-7195-3803-3 (pbk) : £0.60
ISBN 87-429-7441-0 (Denmark)
ISBN 0-88436-892-0 (U.S.)
ISBN 82-05-12605-4 (Norway)
ISBN 91-243-1067-0 (Sweden)
ISBN 90-01-27504-4 (Holland)
ISBN 3-12-534121-3 (Germany) B81-34840

Wymer, Norman. Lucky to be alive / Norman Wymer. — Harlow : Longman, 1981. — 51p : ill,2maps,ports ; 19cm. — (Books in easy English. Stage 2)
ISBN 0-582-53211-6 (pbk) : £0.50 B81-27233

428.6'4 — English language. Reading books: Poetry — *For non-English speaking students*

Easy English poems / [compiled by] Norah Woollard ; illustrations by Willie Rodger. — London : Collins, 1981. — 47p : ill ; 18cm. — (Collins English library. Level 3) (A Collins graded reader)
ISBN 0-00-370137-9 (pbk) : £0.60 B81-11280

428.6'4 — English language. Reading books. Special subjects: Association football — *For non-English speaking students*

Dean, Michael. Spotlight on football. — London : Cassell, Sept.1981. — [64]p. — (Spotlight readers)
ISBN 0-304-30595-2 (pbk) : £0.80 : CIP entry B81-23940

428.6'4 — English language. Reading books. Special subjects: Boxing. Muhammad Ali — *For non-English speaking students*

Milton, Peter. Spotlight on Muhammad Ali. — London : Cassell, Sept.1981. — [32]p
ISBN 0-304-30591-x (pbk) : £0.65 : CIP entry B81-25680

428.6'4 — English language. Reading books. Special subjects. British tales & legends — *For non-English speaking students*

Robinson, Philip. Spotlight on strange stories. — London : Cassell, Sept.1981. — [64]p
ISBN 0-304-30567-7 (pbk) : £0.80 : CIP entry B81-25677

428.6'4 — English language. Reading books. Special subjects: Cars. Racing — *For non-English speaking students*

Price, Roger. Spotlight on motor racing. — London : Cassell, Sept.1981. — [64]p. — (Cassell graded readers ; level 3)
ISBN 0-304-30565-0 (pbk) : £0.80 : CIP entry B81-25679

428.6'4 — English language. Reading books. Special subjects: Computer systems. Applications — *For non-English speaking students*

Humby, Edward. Computer applications / Edward Humby and Philip Bedford Robinson. — London : Cassell, 1980. — 125p : ill ; 22cm. — (Special English)
ISBN 0-304-30553-7 (pbk) : £2.65 : CIP rev. B80-08717

428.6'4 — English language. Reading books. Special subjects: Disasters, *1883-1976* — *For non-English speaking students*

Evans, Michael, *1945-*. Great disasters / Michael Evans. — London : Macmillan, 1981. — 75p : ill ; 21cm. — (Range 5, Fact)
ISBN 0-333-30830-1 (pbk) : £0.80 B81-23017

428.6'4 — English language. Reading books. Special subjects: Drama in English. Shakespeare, William — *For non-English speaking students*

Barnaby, David. Spotlight on Shakespeare. — London : Cassell, Sept.1981. — [64]p. — (Cassell graded readers ; level 4)
ISBN 0-304-30597-9 (pbk) : £0.80 : CIP entry B81-25671

428.6'4 — English language. Reading books. Special subjects: England, *1642-1660* — *For non-English speaking students*

Newhouse, Julia. Spotlight on the English Revolution. — London : Cassell, Sept.1981. — [96]p. — (Spotlight readers)
ISBN 0-304-30571-5 (pbk) : £1.00 : CIP entry B81-23937

428.6'4 — English language. Reading books. Special subjects: European Economic Community — *For non-English speaking students*

Haines, Simon. Spotlight on the Common Market. — London : Cassell, Sept.1981. — [64]p. — (Spotlight readers)
ISBN 0-304-30596-0 (pbk) : £0.80 : CIP entry B81-23941

428.6'4 — English language. Reading books. Special subjects: General knowledge — *For non-English speaking students*

Giese, Diana. What's new? / Diana Giese. — 2nd ed. — London : Evans, 1981. — 32p : ill,1port ; 19cm. — (Evans graded reading. grade 1)
Previous ed.: 1975
ISBN 0-237-50342-5 (pbk) : Unpriced B81-36503

428.6'4 — English language. Reading books. Special subjects: Great Britain. Churchill, Winston S. (Winston Spencer), *1874-1965* — *For non-English speaking students*

Newhouse, Julia. Spotlight on Winston Churchill. — London : Cassell, Sept.1981. — [96]p. — (Cassell graded readers ; level 6)
ISBN 0-304-30572-3 (pbk) : £1.00 : CIP entry B81-25653

428.6'4 — English language. Reading books. Special subjects: Great Britain. Food — *For non-English speaking students*

Smerdon, Sue. A taste of Britain / Sue Smerdon, Margaret Harvey. — Harlow : Longman, 1981. — 76p : ill(some col.),1facsim ; 14x22cm. — (Longman structural readers. Stage 4. Background)
ISBN 0-582-53683-9 (pbk) : £0.60 B81-32956

West, Christine. Spotlight on British food. — London : Cassell, Sept.1981. — [64]p
ISBN 0-304-30564-2 (pbk) : £0.60 : CIP entry B81-25678

428.6'4 — English language. Reading books. Special subjects: Humour in English — *For non-English speaking students*

The Book of British humour / compiled by Judith King, Ronald Ridout, D.K. Swan. — Harlow : Longman, c1981. — 58p : ill ; 20cm. — (Longman structural readers. Stage 4. Background)
ISBN 0-582-53695-2 (pbk) : £0.60 B81-05962

428.6'4 — English language. Reading books. Special subjects: Illusions — *For non-English speaking students*

Haines, Simon. Spotlight on illusions. — London : Cassell, Sept.1981. — [32]p. — (Spotlight readers)
ISBN 0-304-30561-8 (pbk) : £0.65 : CIP entry B81-23859

428.6'4 — English language. Reading books. Special subjects: Inventions — *For non-English speaking students*

Border, Rosemary. Spotlight on inventions. — London : Cassell, Sept.1981. — [32]p
ISBN 0-304-30563-4 (pbk) : £0.65 : CIP entry B81-23861

428.6'4 — English language. Reading books. Special subjects: London. Westminster *(London Borough).* **Waxworks: Madame Tussaud's** — *For non-English speaking students*

Jones, Lewis, *1924-*. The story of Madame Tussaud's / Lewis Jones. — London : Collins, 1980. — 48p : ill,ports ; 18cm. — (Collins English library. Level 2) (A Collins graded reader)
ISBN 0-00-370133-6 (pbk) : £0.48 B81-12754

428.6'4 — English language. Reading books. Special subjects: Medicine — *For non-English speaking students*

Border, Rosemary. Spotlight on a doctor's day. — London : Cassell, Sept.1981. — [32]p
ISBN 0-304-30562-6 (pbk) : £0.65 : CIP entry B81-23860

428.6'4 — English language. Reading books. Special subjects: News — *For non-English speaking students*

Badger, Charles. It's in the news / Charles Badger, S.H. Hartman ; drawings Sam Thompson. — Amersham : Hilton Educational, 1981, c1978. — 160p : ill,maps ; 24cm + Teacher's book(16p; 23cm)
Originally published: Culemborg, Netherlands : Educaboek, 1978
ISBN 0-7175-0971-0 (pbk) : £2.25
ISBN 0-7175-0985-0 (Teacher's book) : £0.90 B81-35620

428.6'4 — English language. Reading books. Special subjects: Paranormal phenomena — *For non-English speaking students*

West, Christine. Spotlight on surprises of nature. — London : Cassell, Sept.1981. — [64]p
ISBN 0-304-30568-5 (pbk) : £0.80 : CIP entry B81-25674

428.6'4 — English language. Reading books. Special subjects: Pop music industries — *For non-English speaking students*

Carrier, Michael. Spotlight on the pop industry. — London : Cassell, Sept.1981. — [96]p. — (Spotlight readers)
ISBN 0-304-30570-7 (pbk) : £1.00 : CIP entry B81-23862

428.6'4 — English language. Reading books. Special subjects: Preventive medicine — *For non-English speaking students*

Howard, Joanna. Preventive medicine / Joanna Howard. — London : Heinemann Educational, 1981. — 32p : ill ; 19cm. — (Heinemann science and technical readers. Elementary level)
Includes index
ISBN 0-435-29945-x (pbk) : Unpriced B81-16429

428.6'4 — English language. Reading books. Special subjects: Radio stations — *For non-English speaking students*

Goodman-Stephens, Pamela. Spotlight on a radio station. — London : Cassell, Sept.1981. — [32]p. — (Spotlight readers)
ISBN 0-304-30592-8 (pbk) : £0.65 : CIP entry B81-23938

428.6'4 — English language. Reading books. Special subjects: Radio, *to ca 1920* — *Non-English speaking students*

Border, Rosemary. Spotlight on the beginning of radio. — London : Cassell, Sept.1981. — [32]p
ISBN 0-304-30593-6 (pbk) : £0.65 : CIP entry B81-23939

428.6'4 — English language. Reading books. Special subjects: Social sciences — *For non-English speaking students*

Stevenson, Jane L.. Reading the social sciences in English / Jane L. Stevenson, Susan Sprachman. — London : Longman, 1981. — 117p : ill,3maps ; 22cm
ISBN 0-582-74809-7 (pbk) : £1.30 : CIP rev. B81-07924

428.6'4 — English language. Reading books. Special subjects: Social security benefits — *For non-English speaking students*

Mohammed, *19---*. National insurance number / by Mohammed. — Bradford (Bolton Royd, Manningham La., Bradford 8) : Bradford Literacy Group, c1981. — 16p : ill ; 22cm. — (BLG ; no.001)
£0.50 (pbk) B81-36574

428.6'4 — English language. Reading books. Special subjects: Superstitions — *For non-English speaking students*

Woods, Edward G.. Superstition / Edward G. Woods. — 2nd ed. — London : Evans, 1981. — 30p : ill ; 19cm. — (Evans graded reading. grade 2)
Previous ed.: 1976
ISBN 0-237-50346-8 (pbk) : Unpriced B81-36502

428.6′4 — English language. Reading books. Special subjects: Tales — *For non-English speaking students*

Janssen, Arlo T.. International stories : a conversation-reader to improve your English / Arlo T. Janssen ; illustrations by Rosa Lopez with Ahmed Al-Sager, Rosa Maria Trevi n o and Ofelia Trevi n o Janssen. — Englewood Cliffs ; London : Prentice-Hall, c1981. — viii,151p : ill ; 23cm
ISBN 0-13-470856-3 (pbk) : £3.85 B81-12609

428.6′4 — English language. Reading books. Special subjects: Tennis — *For non-English speaking students*

Slater, Steven. Spotlight on tennis. — London : Cassell, Sept.1981. — [32]p
ISBN 0-304-30594-4 (pbk) : £0.60 : CIP entry B81-25654

428.6′4 — English language. Reading books. Special subjects: United States. Politics. Kennedy *(Family)* — *For non-English speaking students*

Haines, Simon. Spotlight on the Kennedys. — London : Cassell, Sept.1981. — [64]p. — (Cassell graded readers ; level 3)
ISBN 0-304-30566-9 (pbk) : £0.80 : CIP entry B81-25675

428.6′4 — English language. Reading books. Special subjects: Washington, D.C., *to 1980* — *For non-English speaking students*

Pennink, Betsy. This is Washington / Betsy Pennink. — London : Heinemann Educational, 1981. — 29p : ill,maps,ports ; 18cm. — (Heinemann guided readers. Beginner level ; B15)
ISBN 0-435-27079-6 (pbk) : £0.45 B81-25621

428.6′4927 — English language. Reading books — *For Arabic speaking students*

Rimmer, J. A.. The search / J.A. Rimmer ; illustrated by John Fraser. — Harlow : Longman, 1981. — iii,56p : ill ; 20cm. — (Longman graded structural readers for the Arab world. Stage 4)
ISBN 0-582-76479-3 (pbk) : £0.65 B81-40309

428.6′496 — English language. Reading books — *For African students*

Chisungo, Jefurio. The big radio mystery / Jefurio Chisungo ; illustrated by Maureen and Gordon Gray. — Harlow : Longman, 1981. — 39p : col.ill ; 20cm. — (Action books. Level two)
ISBN 0-582-59593-2 (pbk) : £0.55 B81-20688

Chisungo, Jefurio. Call Mr Africa / Jefurio Chisungo ; illustrated by Maureen and Gordon Gray. — Harlow : Longman, 1981. — 48p : col.ill ; 19cm. — (Action book / Level three)
ISBN 0-582-59591-6 (pbk) : £0.58 B81-20689

428.6′496 — English language. Reading books — *For African students — For schools*

Dibba, Ebou. Olu and the smugglers / Ebou Dibba ; illustrated by Maureen and Gordon Gray. — [Harlow] : Longman, 1980. — 40p : col.ill ; 20cm. — (Action books. Level 2)
ISBN 0-582-59592-4 (pbk) : £0.55 B81-01653

Sweetman, David. The amulet / David Sweetman ; illustrated by Maureen and Gordon Gray. — [London] : Longman, 1980. — 47p : col.ill ; 20cm. — (Action books. Level 2)
ISBN 0-582-59584-3 (pbk) : £0.58 B81-08066

Sweetman, David. The Moyo Kids / David Sweetman ; illustrated by Maureen and Gordon Gray. — [Harlow] : Longman, 1980. — 32p : col.ill ; 20cm. — (Action books. Level 1)
ISBN 0-582-59553-3 (pbk) : Unpriced B81-08490

Sweetman, David. Skyjack over Africa / David Sweetman ; illustrated by Maureen and Gordon Gray. — [Harlow] : Longman, 1980. — 30p : col.ill ; 20cm. — (Action books. Level 1)
ISBN 0-582-59585-1 (pbk) : £0.50 B81-08475

428.6′496 — English language. Reading books — *For Nigerian students*

Fulani, Dan. God′s case : no appeal. — London : Hodder & Stoughton Educational, Nov.1981. — [96]p
ISBN 0-340-27578-2 (pbk) : £1.50 : CIP entry B81-30144

Fulani, Dan. The price of liberty. — London : Hodder & Stoughton Educational, Dec.1981. — [96]p
ISBN 0-340-27771-8 (pbk) : £1.50 : CIP entry B81-31468

428.6′496 — English language. Reading books - *For Nigerian students*

Fulani, Dan. Sauna, secret agent. — London : Hodder & Stoughton, June 1981. — [96]p
ISBN 0-340-27051-9 (pbk) : £1.35 : CIP entry B81-16862

429 — OLD ENGLISH LANGUAGE

429 — Old English language — *Samplers*

Partridge, A. C.. A companion to Old and Middle English. — London : Deutsch, Oct.1981. — [352]p
ISBN 0-233-97308-7 (cased) : £12.95 : CIP entry
ISBN 0-233-97410-3 (pbk) : £6.95
Primary classification 427′.02 B81-26747

433 — GERMAN LANGUAGE. DICTIONARIES

433′.21 — German language. Figurative usage — *German & English dictionaries*

Spalding, Keith. An historical dictionary of German figurative usage / by Keith Spalding with the assistance of Kenneth Brooke. — Oxford : Basil Blackwell
German and English text
Fasc.34: Lage-Lippe. — c1981. — p1577-1624 ; 26cm
ISBN 0-631-04040-4 (pbk) : £6.50 B81-31784

433′.21 — German language — *German & English dictionaries*

Berlinka, Jane. Get by on your own in German : a situational vocabulary / Jane Berlinka and José Berlinka. — London : Edward Arnold, 1981. — 59p ; 18cm
ISBN 0-7131-0526-7 (pbk) : £1.25 B81-21376

433′.51 — German language — *Italian & German dictionaries*

Collins gem dictionary : tedesco-italiano, italiano-tedesco = Deutsch-Italienisch, Italienisch-Deutsch. — London : Collins, 1981. — x,630p ; 12cm
ISBN 0-00-458683-2 (pbk) : Unpriced
Also classified at 453′.31 B81-12217

437 — GERMAN LANGUAGE. EARLY FORMS, SLANG, DIALECTS

437′.947 — Yiddish language

Feinsilver, Lillian Mermin. The taste of Yiddish : a warm and humorous guide to a fascinating language / by Lillian Mermin Feinsilver. — South Brunswick : Barnes ; London : Yoseloff, c1970 (1980 printing). — 437p ; 24cm
Bibliography: p379-391. — Includes index
ISBN 0-498-02515-2 (cased) : Unpriced
ISBN 0-498-02427-x (pbk) : £4.95 B81-03395

437′.947′09 — Yiddish language, *to ca 1950*

Weinreich, Max. History of the Yiddish language / Max Weinreich ; translated by Shlomo Noble with the assistance of Joshua A. Fishman. — Chicago ; London : University of Chicago Press, 1980. — x,833p : ill,maps ; 24cm
Translation of: Geshikhte fun der yidisher shprakh. — Includes index
ISBN 0-226-88604-2 : £14.00 B81-05066

438 — GERMAN LANGUAGE USAGE

438 — German language — *For schools*

Berlinka, Jane. Deutsch in Wort und Bild. — London : Arnold, Sept.1981
Book 3. — [176]p
ISBN 0-7131-0541-0 (pbk) : £3.50 : CIP entry B81-23807

Kilborn, Richard W.. Themen und Variationen : practice in German styles and registers : Lehrerheft / Richard W. Kilborn, Peter H. Meech. — London : Harrap, 1980. — 63p ; 22cm
ISBN 0-245-53473-3 (pbk) : £3.50 B81-32469

Paxton, N.. Zielpunkt Deutsch : a complete course for advanced students / N. Paxton, B.A. Brentnall. — 2nd ed. — London : Hodder and Stoughton, 1981. — 342p : ill,ports ; 25cm
Previous ed.: London : English Universities Press, 1975. — Includes index
ISBN 0-340-26117-x (pbk) : £4.75 : CIP rev. B80-23198

438 — German language — *Questions & answers*

Meinhof, Ulrike Hanna. Die verlorene Ehre der Katharina Blum : Arbeitsmaterialien für den fortgeschrittenen Deutschunterricht / Ulrike Hanna Meinhof and Ruth Rach. — London : Harrap, 1981. — 72p : ill,1map,facsims ; 30cm. — (Textlupe)
German text
ISBN 0-245-53548-9 (pbk) : £2.95 B81-37710

438.2′421 — German language. Comprehension - *For schools*

Shotter, David. Panorama. — London : Heinemann Educational, July 1981. — (Deutscher Sprachkurs)
Pupil′s book. — [152]p
ISBN 0-435-38848-7 (pbk) : £5.95 : CIP entry B81-13477

Shotter, David. Panorama. — London : Heinemann Educational, July 1981. — (Deutscher Sprachkurs)
Teacher′s book. — [456]p
ISBN 0-435-38847-9 (pbk) : £7.50 : CIP entry B81-13476

438.2′421 — German language. Comprehension — *Questions & answers*

Coggle, Paul. Study supplement / Paul Coggle and Ingrid K.J. Williams. — Harlow : Longman, 1981, c1980. — 64p : ill,maps,facsims,2plans,forms ; 24cm. — (Ealing course in German)
English and German text. — Text on inside covers
ISBN 0-582-35253-3 (pbk) : £1.75 B81-40306

438.2′421 — German language. Comprehension — *Questions & answers — For schools*

Cumming, Gisela. Kommissar Schlaufuchs / Gisela Cumming ; illustrations by John Edwards. — Amersham : Hulton, 1981. — 93p ; 22cm
German and English text
ISBN 0-7175-0869-2 (pbk) : £1.25 B81-25391

438.2′421 — German language. Grammar

Hammond, Robin T.. A German reference grammar / Robin Hammond. — Oxford : Oxford University Press, 1981. — 256p ; 19cm
Includes index
ISBN 0-19-912048-x (pbk) : £3.50 B81-24966

438.3′421 — Spoken German language — *Phrase books*

Ellis, D. L.. Travellers′ German / D.L. Ellis, A. Cheyne ; pronunciation J. Baldwin. — London : Pan, 1981. — 158p : ill,1map ; 17cm. — (Pan languages)
Includes index
ISBN 0-330-26293-9 (pbk) : £1.00 B81-22891

438.3′421 — Spoken German language - *Phrase books*

Sutton, P. J.. German conversation topics. — London : Hodder & Stoughton, Aug.1981. — [96]p
ISBN 0-340-26143-9 (pbk) : £1.65 : CIP entry B81-20603

438.3′421 — Spoken German language — *Questions & answers*

Richards, Donald. Bei uns in Deutschland : a German language course for beginners / by Donald Richards. — London : Cassell
German and English text
2
Pupil's book. — 1981. — 215p : ill,1map ; 22cm
ISBN 0-304-30774-2 (pbk) : Unpriced
B81-27024

Richards, Donald. Bei uns in Deutschland 2 / by Donald Richards. — London : Cassell
Teacher's book. — 1981. — 64p ; 22cm
ISBN 0-304-30775-0 (pbk) : £2.25 B81-29205

438.6′421 — German language. Reading books

Noack, Barbara. Die Zürcher Verlobung / Barbara Noack. — Kopenhagen : Grafisk Forlag ; London : Murray, c1978. — 90p : ill ; 19cm. — (Easy readers = Leicht zu lesen. C)
ISBN 0-7195-3765-7 (pbk) : £0.90 B81-15025

Zuckmayer, Carl. Der Seelenbräu / Carl Zuckmayer. — Kopenhagen : Grafisk Forlag ; London : Murray, c1978. — 76p : ill ; 19cm. — (Easy readers = Leicht zu lesen. D)
ISBN 0-7195-3764-9 (pbk) : £0.90 B81-15024

438.6′421 — German language. Reading books — *For schools*

Craig, David, *1935-*. Otto 1 : Otto ist geizig / David Craig ; illustrated by Peter MacKarell. — London : Edward Arnold, 1981. — 48p : ill ; 22x15cm
ISBN 0-7131-0542-9 (pbk) : £1.25 B81-21656

Craig, David, *1935-*. Otto 2 : Otto ist gierig / David Craig ; illustrated by Peter MacKarell. — London : Edward Arnold, 1981. — 48p : ill ; 22x15cm
ISBN 0-7131-0543-7 (corrected : pbk) : £1.25
B81-29948

Craig, David, *1935-*. Otto 3 : Otto ist großzügig / David Craig ; illustrated by Peter MacKarell. — London : Edward Arnold, 1981. — 18p : ill ; 21x15cm
ISBN 0-7131-0544-5 (pbk) : £1.25 B81 21655

Joseph, Inga. Deutsche Kinder schreiben / Inga Joseph. — Basingstoke : Macmillan Education, 1980. — 44p : 2ill ; 21cm
German text, English introduction and exercises
ISBN 0-333-26201-8 (pbk) : £0.80 : CIP rev.
B80-05881

Kurze Krimis / [herausgegeben von] Dennis Mueller. — New York ; London : Holt, Rinehart and Winston, c1981. — 163p : ill ; 24cm
German text with preface and some vocabulary in English
ISBN 0-03-056719-x : £4.50 B81-22859

Schnurre, Wolfdietrich. Stories. — London : Bell & Hyman, June 1981. — [144]p
ISBN 0-7135-1247-4 (pbk) : £2.95 : CIP entry
B81-15895

Von Hofe, Harold. Die Mittelstufe / Harold von Hofe. — 4th ed. — New York ; London : Holt, Rinehart and Winston, c1981. — vi,249 ; 24cm
Previous ed.: 1971
ISBN 0-03-057864-7 (pbk) : £5.50 B81-22875

Walbruck, Harry A.. Lustige Geschichten : a graded reader for beginning students / Harry A. Walbruck, Astrid Henschel. — London : Bell and Hyman in association with National Textbook Company, 1979. — 179p : ill ; 23cm
German text, English introduction, notes & vocabulary
ISBN 0-7135-1127-3 (pbk) : Unpriced
B81-20890

Walbruck, Harry A.. Spannende Geschichten : a graded reader for intermediate students / Harry A. Walbruck. — London : Bell & Hyman in association with National Textbook Company, 1979. — 87p : ill ; 23cm
German text, English introduction, notes & vocabulary
ISBN 0-7135-1128-1 (pbk) : Unpriced
B81-20891

438.6′421 — German language. Reading books. Special subjects: Germany. Political events, *1945-1961* — *For schools*

Cumming, Gisela. Flucht nach Western / Gisela Cumming. — London : Edward Arnold, 1981. — 78p : ill,maps ; 22cm
English and German text
ISBN 0-7131-0498-8 (pbk) : £1.50 B81-20380

439.31 — DUTCH LANGUAGE

439.3′115 — Dutch language. Sounds *compared with* **sounds of English language** — *For Dutch speaking students*

Collins, Beverley. The sounds of English and Dutch / Beverley Collins and Inger Mees. — The Hague ; London : Leiden University Press, 1981. — 293p : ill ; 25cm
Bibliography: p278-279
ISBN 90-602-1477-3 (cased) : Unpriced
ISBN 90-602-1477-3 (pbk) : Unpriced
Primary classification 421′.5 B81-15514

439.3′182421 — Dutch language — *For schools*

Smit, Jacob. Dutch grammar and reader : with exercises / by Jacob Smit, Reinder P. Meijer. — 2nd ed. — Cheltenham : Thornes, 1978. — xiii,201p : 1map ; 22cm
English and Dutch text. — Originally published: 1976
ISBN 0-85950-022-5 (pbk) : £3.75 B81-37762

439.3′1′82421 — Dutch language — *For schools*

Williams, Jelly K.. A Dutch reader and grammar. — Cheltenham : Thornes, Nov.1981. — [112]p
ISBN 0-85950-349-6 : £3.95 : CIP entry
B81-34207

439.3′183421 — Spoken Dutch language — *Phrase books*

Ellis, D. L.. Travellers' Dutch / D.L. Ellis, D. van der Luit ; pronunciation J. Baldwin. — London : Pan, 1981. — 157p : ill,1map ; 17cm. — (Pan languages)
Includes index
ISBN 0-330-26380-3 (pbk) : £1.00 B81-22892

Schoenmakers, Anneke. Praatpaal : een cursus Nederlands voor beginners / Samengesteld door Anneke Schoenmakers ; geïllustreerd door Christopher Heywood. — Cheltenham : Thornes, 1981. — xv,144p : ill,2maps ; 25cm
Dutch text, English notes and wordlist
ISBN 0-85950-474-3 (pbk) : £3.95 : CIP rev.
B80-34899

439.5 — SCANDINAVIAN LANGUAGES

439′.5 — Scandinavian languages — *Conference proceedings*

International Conference of Nordic and General Linguistics *(4th : 1980 : Oslo)*. The Nordic languages and modern linguistics : proceedings of the Fourth International Conference of Nordic and General Linguistics in Oslo 1980 / edited by Even Hovdhaugen. — Oslo : Universitetsforlaget, c1980 ; London : Global Book Resources [distributor]. — viii,392p : ill,1map ; 22cm
Includes bibliographies
ISBN 82-00-05569-8 (pbk) : £20.50 B81-27022

439′.65 — Old Norse language. Grammar

Valfells, Sigrid. Old Icelandic. — Oxford : Clarendon Press, Sept.1981. — [368]p
ISBN 0-19-811172-x (cased) : £15.00 : CIP entry
ISBN 0-19-811173-8 (pbk) : £7.50 B81-23885

439′.6915 — Spoken Icelandic language. Sounds. Quantity, *to 1980*

Árnason, Kristján. Quantity in historical phonology : Icelandic and related cases / Kristján Arnason. — Cambridge : Cambridge University Press, 1980. — 234p : ill,music ; 24cm. — (Cambridge studies in linguistics, ISSN 0068-676x ; no.30)
Bibliography: p219-228. - Includes index
ISBN 0-521-23040-3 : £8.50 : CIP rev.
B80-25523

439.9 — EAST GERMANIC LANGUAGES

439′.9 — Gothic language. Grammar

Wright, Joseph, *1855-1930*. Grammar of the Gothic language : and the Gospel of St. Mark : selections from the other Gospels and the Second Epistle to Timothy with notes and glossary / by Joseph Wright. — 2nd ed. / with a supplement to the grammar by O.L. Sayce. — Oxford : Clarendon Press, 1954 (1981 [printing]). — ix,383p ; 19cm
Previous ed.: 1910. — Bibliography: p382-383
ISBN 0-19-811185-1 (pbk) : £8.50 : CIP rev.
B81-06592

440 — ROMANCE LANGUAGES

440′.76 — England. Educational institutions. Curriculum subjects: French language. Academic achievement of students, 16-19 years. Assessment — *For teaching*

French 16-19 Study Group. French 16-19 : a new perspective : a report of the French 16-19 Study Group. — London : Hodder and Stoughton, c1981. — v,101p : ill,1map ; 24cm
Text in English and French
ISBN 0-340-25528-5 (pbk) : £3.75 B81-22099

441 — FRENCH LANGUAGE. WRITTEN AND SPOKEN CODES

441′.5 — French language. Generative phonology

Tranel, Bernard. Concreteness in generative phonology : evidence form French / by Bernard Tranel. — Berkeley [Calif.] ; London : University of California Press, c1981. — xiii,324p ; 24cm
Bibliography: p315-324
ISBN 0-520-04165-8 : £20.75 B81-39774

442 — FRENCH LANGUAGE. ETYMOLOGY

442′.4 — Romance languages. Words. Borrowing by other Romance languages, *500-1500*

Rothwell, William. Lexical borrowing in a medieval context / by William Rothwell. — Manchester : John Rylands University Library of Manchester, 1980. — p118-143 ; 25cm
£1.30 (pbk) B81-35541

443 — FRENCH LANGUAGE. DICTIONARIES

443′.21 — French language. English false friends — *French & English dictionaries*

Kirk-Greene, C. W. E.. French false friends / C.W.E. Kirk-Greene. — London : Routledge & Kegan Paul, 1981. — vi,197p ; 23cm
ISBN 0-7100-0741-8 : £7.95 : CIP rev.
B81-03704

443′.21 — French language — *French & English dictionaries*

Collins Robert concise French English English French dictionary / by Beryl T. Atkins ... [et al.] ; based on the Collins Robert French-English English-French dictionary = Robert Collins junior dictionnaire français-anglais anglais-français / par Beryl T. Atkins ... [et al.] ; établi d'après le texte abrégé et remanié du Dictionnaire français-anglais anglais-français le Robert & Collins. — London : Collins, 1981. — xii,411,535p ; 22cm
ISBN 0-00-433486-8 : £5.95 B81-26318

443′.21 — French language — *French & English dictionaries* *continuation*

The **Concise** Oxford French dictionary. — 2nd ed. / French-English edited by H. Ferrar ; English-French edited by J.A. Hutchinson and J.-D. Biard. — Oxford : Clarendon, 1980. — xxvi,596,ix,267p ; 23cm
Concise Oxford French-English dictionary / edited by Abel and Marguerite Chevalley, originally published: 1934 ; Concise Oxford English-French dictionary / edited by G.W.F.R. Goodridge, originally published: 1940
ISBN 0-19-864126-5 : £7.50 B81-02401

Harrap's new pocket French and English dictionary. — Rev. ed. / abridged by Patricia Forbes and Margaret Ledésert from Harrap's new shorter French and English dictionary. — London : Pan, 1981, c1969. — 525p ; 18cm. — (Pan reference)
Previous ed.: London : Harrap, 1951
ISBN 0-330-26488-5 (pbk) : £1.95 B81-14122

Mansion, J. E.. Grand Harrap : dictionnaire français-anglajs et anglais-français / J.E. Mansion. — Ed atlas / édition revu par R.P.L. Ledésert et Margaret Ledésert. — London : Harrap, 1981. — 4v. : col.maps ; 29cm
Previous ed.: published as Harrap's standard French and English dictionary. — Includes bibliographies
ISBN 0-245-53773-2 : £95.00 B81-36606

443′.21 — French language — *Vocabularies*

Wildbore, Alison M.. Comment ça se dit. — London : Edward Arnold, Dec.1981. — [48]p
ISBN 0-7131-0451-1 (pbk) : £1.50 : CIP entry B81-31547

443′.9634 — French language — *Bambara & French dictionaries*

Bailleul, Charles. Petit dictionnaire bambara-français, français-bambara / par Charles Bailleul. — [Amersham] : Avebury, 1981. — xii,339p ; 24cm
ISBN 0-86127-220-x : £20.00
Primary classification 496′.34 B81-37488

447 — FRENCH LANGUAGE. EARLY FORMS, SLANG, DIALECTS

447′.01 — Anglo-Norman language — *Anglo-Norman & English dictionaries*

Anglo-Norman dictionary / edited by Louise W. Stone, William Rothwell and T.B.W. Reid. — London : Modern Humanities Research Association
Fasc.2: D-E. — 1981. — p139-289 ; 25cm. — (Publications of the Modern Humanities Research Association ; v.8)
At head of title: The Modern Humanities Research Association in conjunction with the Anglo-Norman Text Society
ISBN 0-900547-80-4 (pbk) : Unpriced B81-29844

448 — FRENCH LANGUAGE USAGE

448 — French language — *For schools*

Downes, P. J.. French for today. — London : Hodder & Stoughton
Workbook B1. — Jan.1982. — [48]p
ISBN 0-340-23365-6 (pbk) : £0.95 : CIP entry B81-34131

Downes, P. J.. French for today. — London : Hodder & Stoughton Educational
Pupil's book B. — Sept.1981. — [128]p
ISBN 0-340-23368-0 (pbk) : £1.85 : CIP entry B81-28169

Fyfe, James. 'O' grade French. — London : Hodder & Stoughton, July 1981
Pupil's book. — [64]p
ISBN 0-340-26288-5 (pbk) : £1.35 : CIP entry B81-19150

Fyfe, James. 'O' grade French. — London : Hodder & Stoughton, July 1981
Teacher's book. — [40]p
ISBN 0-340-26752-6 (pbk) : £1.85 : CIP entry B81-19149

Gilbert, Mark. Le francais par l'image. — London : Hodder and Stoughton, May 1981
Book 4. — [128]p
ISBN 0-340-24388-0 (pbk) : £2.75 : CIP entry B81-04217

Gilbert, Mark. Le francais par l'image. — London : Hodder & Stoughton Educational
Teacher's book 4. — Oct.1981. — [48]p
ISBN 0-340-24389-9 (pbk) : £0.95 : CIP entry B81-31162

Honnor, Sylvia. Tricolore / Sylvia Honnor and Heather Mascie-Taylor. — Leeds : E.J. Arnold
2
Flash cards / illustrated by Marc Lillo. — c1981. — 48flashcards : col.ill ; 25x20cm
ISBN 0-560-20543-0 : £14.50 B81-40818

Honnor, Sylvia. Tricolore / Sylvia Honnor and Heather Mascie-Taylor. — Leeds : E.J. Arnold
2
Games cards. — c1981. — 12games cards : ill (some col.) ; 22x23cm
ISBN 0-560-20545-7 : £2.75 B81-40816

Honnor, Sylvia. Tricolore / Sylvia Honnor and Heather Mascie-Taylor. — Leeds : E.J. Arnold
2
Pupil's book. — c1981. — 192p : ill,maps ; 25cm
Text in English and French
ISBN 0-560-20540-6 (pbk) : £2.50 B81-40814

Honnor, Sylvia. Tricolore / Sylvia Honnor and Heather Mascie-Taylor. — Leeds : E.J. Arnold
2
Reading cards. — c1981. — 8reading cards : ill,maps ; 25x20cm
ISBN 0-560-20544-9 : £2.00 B81-40817

Honnor, Sylvia. Tricolore / Sylvia Honnor and Heather Mascie-Taylor. — Leeds : E.J. Arnold
2
Spirit duplicating masters. — c1981. — [69]p : ill ; 28cm
Text in French and English
ISBN 0-560-20542-2 (pbk) : Unpriced B81-40815

Honnor, Sylvia. Tricolore / Sylvia Honnor and Heather Mascie-Taylor. — Leeds : E.J. Arnold
2
Teacher's book. — c1981. — 135p : ill ; 25cm
Text in English and French
ISBN 0-560-20541-4 (pbk) : £4.95 B81-40813

Sanderson, David. Échanges : wide ability French course / David Sanderson. — London : Harrap
English and French text
Pt.2
Activity book. — 1981. — 122p : ill ; 18x22cm
ISBN 0-245-53539-x (pbk) : £2.50 B81-29248

Sanderson, David. Échanges : wide ability French course / David Sanderson. — London : Murray
Pt.2. — 1980
Pupil's book. — 80p : ill ; 28cm
English and French text
ISBN 0-245-53537-3 (pbk) : £2.50 B81-18849

Sanderson, David. Échanges : wide ability French course / David Sanderson. — London : Harrap
Pt.2. — 1980
Teacher's book. — 147p ; 28cm
English and French text
ISBN 0-245-53538-1 (pbk) : £6.50 B81-18837

Sprake, David. Communications / David Sprake ; [illustrations by Graham Higgins and Klim Forster]. — Oxford : Oxford University Press, 1981. — 216p : ill(some col.),1map,forms ; 26cm
English and French text. — Includes index
ISBN 0-19-832385-9 (pbk) : £3.25
ISBN 0-19-840312-7 (cassette) B81-21165

Tour de France / Scottish Central Committee on Modern Languages. — London : Heinemann Educational
1. — c1981. — 64p : ill,1map,ports ; 25cm
ISBN 0-435-37752-3 (pbk) : £1.40 : CIP rev. B81-13863

Tour de France. — London : Heinemann Educational
1: Teacher's book. — Oct.1981. — [192]p
ISBN 0-435-37754-x (pbk) : £6.50 : CIP entry B81-30510

448 — French language — *Questions & answers — For schools*

Redstone, Sylvia C.. De jour en jour / by Sylvia C. Redstone. — Rev. ed. — London : Cassell
1. — 1981. — x,182p : ill,music ; 21cm
English and French text. — Previous ed.: 1969
ISBN 0-304-30758-0 (pbk) : Unpriced : CIP rev. B81-08874

Vivent les différences : an intermediate reader for communication / Gilbert A. Jarvis ... [et al.]. — 2nd ed. — New York ; London : Holt, Rinehart and Winston, c1981. — x,205p : ill,1map,facsims,ports ; 23cm
French text with preface and some vocabulary in English. — Previous ed.: 1977
ISBN 0-03-058117-6 (pbk) : £4.50 B81-22865

448 — French language - *Questions & answers - For schools*

Whitmore, P. C.. French for CSE. — 3rd ed. — London : Bell and Hyman, June 1981. — [246]p
Previous ed.: London : Bell, 1977
ISBN 0-7135-1265-2 (pbk) : £3.50 : CIP entry B81-14966

448 — French language — *Questions & answers — For schools*

Wildbore, Alison M.. Débrouillez-vous! / Alison M. Wildbore ; illustrations by Marian Jeremiah. — London : Edward Arnold, 1980. — 63p : ill,maps,facsims ; 28cm
English and French text
ISBN 0-7131-0442-2 (pbk) : £1.95 : CIP rev. B80-05333

448′.002465 — French language - *For business enterprise*

Bower, Malcolm. French for business. — 2nd ed. — London : Hodder and Stoughton, July 1981. — [160]p
Previous ed.: 1977
ISBN 0-340-26920-0 (pbk) : £2.15 : CIP entry B81-13763

448.1 — French language. Vocabulary — *For schools*

Moore, S.. French exam revision : grammar and vocabulary / S. Moore, A.L. Antrobus, G.F. Pugh. — Harlow : Longman, 1981. — 123p ; 18cm
Text in English and French
ISBN 0-582-35351-3 (pbk) : £1.50
Primary classification 448.2′421 B81-38263

448.2′421 — French language. Comprehension - *Questions & answers - For schools*

Albani, Alex. En l'an 2000. — London : Heinemann Educational, May 1981. — [64]p
ISBN 0-435-37030-8 (pbk) : £1.80 : CIP entry B81-04254

448.2′421 — French language. Comprehension — *Questions & answers — For schools*

MacDonald, Ian, *1947-*. Dans les journaujx / Ian MacDonald. — London : Edward Arnold, 1981. — 48p : facsims,1form ; 22cm
Mostly French text, preface and some text in English
ISBN 0-7131-0540-2 (pbk) : £1.50 : CIP rev. B81-03366

448.2′421 — French language. Crossword puzzles — *Collections — For schools*

Barnes, Carole. French topic crosswords / Carole Barnes ; illustrated by Val Saunders. — London : Edward Arnold, 1981. — 48p : ill,maps ; 20x27cm
ISBN 0-7131-0448-1 (pbk) : £1.50 B81-29169

448.2′421 — French language — *For slow learning students — For schools*

Johnson, Christopher. D'accord. — London : Hodder & Stoughton
1: Pupils' book. — Jan.1982. — [64]p
ISBN 0-340-24951-x (pbk) : £1.35 : CIP entry B81-34146

448.2'421 — French language — *For slow learning students — For schools* *continuation*

Johnson, Christopher. D'accord. — London : Hodder and Stoughton
2: Pupils' book. — Jan.1982. — [64]p
ISBN 0-340-27709-2 (pbk) : £1.25 : CIP entry
B81-34147

448.2'421 — French language. Grammar

Astington, Eric. French structures : a manual for advanced students : systems and structures in contemporary French / Eric Astington. — London : Collins, 1980. — 218p ; 23cm
English and French text. — Includes index
ISBN 0-00-433449-3 : £4.95 B81-00089

448.2'421 — French language. Grammar — *For schools*

Creighton, N. W.. Mille et un points / Neil Creighton. — New ed. — London : Harrap, 1981. — 75p ; 22cm. — (Harrap's French grammar revision)
Previous ed.: Stockport : Portrea Publications, 1978. — Includes index
ISBN 0-245-53776-7 (pbk) : £1.50
ISBN 0-245-53777-5 (non-net) : £1.25
B81-19679

Moore, S.. French exam revision : grammar and vocabulary / S. Moore, A.L. Antrobus, G.F. Pugh. — Harlow : Longman, 1981. — 123p ; 18cm
Text in English and French
ISBN 0-582-35351-3 (pbk) : £1.50
Also classified at 448.1 B81-38263

448.2'421 — French language. Grammar — *French texts*

Barson, John. La grammaire a l'oeuvre / John Barson. — 3rd ed. — New York ; London : Holt, Rinehart and Winston, 1981. — xv,249p ; 24cm
French text, English introduction and notes
ISBN 0-03-050891-6 (pbk) : £7.50 B81-29484

448.2'421 — French language. Grammar — *Questions & answers — For schools*

Coffman, Mary E.. Schaum's outline of French grammar / Mary E. Coffman. — 2nd ed. — New York ; London : McGraw-Hill, c1981. — 307p ; 28cm. — (Schaum's outline series)
Previous ed.: 1973. — Includes index
ISBN 0-07-011553-2 : £3.45 B81-24281

448.2'421 — French language. Verbs. Imperfect tense & perfect tense — *For schools*

Mountjoy, M. E.. Getting to know the perfect and imperfect tenses / M.E. Mountjoy ; illustrated by Val Saunders. — London : Edward Arnold, 1980. — 60p : ill ; 23cm
ISBN 0-7131-0446-5 (pbk) : £1.50 : CIP rev.
B80-13352

448.3'421 — Spoken French language

Humphreys, R. A. (Robert Ashton). Colloquial French / R.A. Humphreys. — London : Routledge & Kegan Paul, 1980. — viii,166p ; 19cm. — (Colloquial series)
English and French text
ISBN 0-7100-0450-8 (pbk) : £2.95 : CIP rev.
B80-26940

448.3'421 — Spoken French language. Comprehension — *Questions & answers*

Campagna, Andrew F.. Points de vue / Andrew F. Campagna, Philip Grundlehner. — New York ; London : Holt, Rinehart and Winston, c1981. — ix,228p : ill,maps,forms ; 28cm
French text, English preface. — Includes index
ISBN 0-03-055546-9 (pbk) : £6.50 B81-22965

448.3'421 — Spoken French language — *Phrase books*

Ellis, D. L.. Travellers' French / D.L. Ellis, F. Clarke ; pronunciation J. Baldwin. — London : Pan, 1981. — 153p : ill,1map ; 17cm. — (Pan languages)
Includes index
ISBN 0-330-26292-0 (pbk) : £1.00 B81-22889

448.3'421 — Spoken French language — *Questions & answers — For schools*

Buckley, Michael. Action: graded French / Michael Buckby. — Walton-on-Thames : Nelson
Bk. 2. — 1981. — 191p : ill(some col.),maps ; 25cm + 1teacher's book(161p : ill ; 25cm)
ISBN 0-17-439037-8 (pbk) : £2.95
ISBN 0-17-439024-2 (teacher's book) : £2.95
B81-14776

448.6'421 — French language. Reading books

Dubois, Claude. L'affaire des tableaux volés / Claude Dubois ; illustrated by George Armstrong. — London : Bell & Hyman in association with National Textbook Company, 1979, c1976. — 128p : ill ; 23cm. — (A Monsieur Maurice mystery)
Originally published: Skokie, Ill. : National Textbook Company, 1976
ISBN 0-7135-1130-3 (pbk) : £1.65 B81-05843

Mélange littéraire / [edité par] Josette Smetana, Marie-Rose Myron. — 2e éd. — New York ; London : Holt, Rinehart and Winston, c1981. — vii,196p ; 24cm
French text, English preface and appendix. — Previous ed.: 1970
ISBN 0-03-058171-0 (pbk) : £4.95 B81-34430

Robbe-Grillet, Alain. Le rendez-vous / Alain Robbe-Grillet, Yvone Lenard. — New York ; London : Holt, Rinehart and Winston, c1981. — xi,184p ; 24cm
French text, English introduction and notes
ISBN 0-03-056248-1 (pbk) : £4.50 B81-23056

448.6'421 — French language. Reading books — *For schools*

Dubois, Claude. L'affaire du cadavre vivant / Claude Dubois ; illustrated by George Armstrong. — London : Bell & Hyman in association with National Textbook Co., 1979, c1975. — 107p : ill ; 23cm. — (A Monsieur Maurice mystery) (Bell & Hyman modern language texts)
Originally published: Skokie, Ill. : National Textbook Co., 1973
ISBN 0-7135-1129-x (pbk) : £1.80 B81-07205

MacDonald, Ian. Catastrophe!. — London : Edward Arnold, Sept.1981. — [48]p. — (Faut le croire!)
ISBN 0-7131-0545-3 (pbk) : £1.25 : CIP entry
B81-23808

Pivot, Agnès. Les adventures en mer. — London : Edward Arnold, Sept.1981. — [48]p. — (Faut le croire!)
ISBN 0-7131-0546-1 (pbk) : £1.25(non-net) : CIP entry B81-21472

448.6'421 — French language. Reading books: Plays — *For schools*

Roussy de Sales, Richard de. Rions encore! / Richard de Roussy de Sales. — London : Bell & Hyman in association with National Textbook Company, 1979, c1972. — 48p ; 23cm
French text, introduction in English. — Originally published: Skokie : National Textbook Company, 1972. — Contents: Chez le coiffeur — Aux Galeries Lafayette — Chez l'antiquaire — Au lycée
ISBN 0-7135-1133-8 (pbk) : Unpriced
B81-11849

448.6'421 — French language. Reading books. Special subjects: France. Resistance movements, *1940-1944 — For schools*

Roper, John. Les héros et les héroïnes de la Résistance. — London : Edward Arnold, Sept.1981. — [48]p. — (Faut le croire!)
ISBN 0-7131-0547-x (pbk) : £1.25 : CIP entry
B81-21488

448.6'421 — French language. Reading books. Special subjects: France. Social life — *For schools*

Bonneau, Michel. A la découverte de la France / Michel et Elisabeth Bonneau. — Amersham : Hulton, 1981. — 77p : ill,facsims,maps ; 23cm
French text, English foreword. — French text originally published: Stuttgart : Klett, 1979. — Map on cover
ISBN 0-7175-0904-4 (pbk) : £1.60 B81-31137

Rogus, Timothy. Lettres de France : impressions of contemporary France for beginning students / Timothy Rogus. — London : Bell & Hyman in association with National Textbook Company, 1979, c1976. — 62p : ill ; 23cm
French text, introduction in English. — Originally published: Skokie : National Textbook Company, 1976. — Includes index
ISBN 0-7135-1132-x (pbk) : Unpriced
B81-11846

448.6'421 — French language. Reading books. Special subjects: Work — *For schools*

Chafer, Anthony. Le monde du travail. — London : Edward Arnold, June 1981. — [16]p. — (En l'etat actuel des choses)
ISBN 0-7131-0549-6 (pbk) : £1.25 : CIP entry
B81-12891

453 — ITALIAN LANGUAGE. DICTIONARIES

453'.21 — Italian language — *Italian & English dictionaries*

The **Cambridge** Italian dictionary / general editor Barbara Reynolds. — Cambridge : Cambridge University Press
Vol.2: English-Italian. — 1981. — xix,843p ; 29cm
ISBN 0-521-08708-2 : Unpriced : CIP rev.
B81-13536

453'.31 — Italian language — *German & Italian dictionaries*

Collins gem dictionary : tedesco-italiano, italiano-tedesco = Deutsch-Italienisch, Italienisch-Deutsch. — London : Collins, 1981. — x,630p ; 12cm
ISBN 0-00-458683-2 (pbk) : Unpriced
Primary classification 433'.51 B81-12217

458 — ITALIAN LANGUAGE USAGE

458.1 — Italian language. Vocabulary — *For schools*

Falaschi, A.. Essential modern Italian vocabulary : by A. Falaschi. — London : Harrap, 1981. — 64p : ill ; 22cm
ISBN 0-245-53640-x (pbk) : £1.75 B81-23156

458.2'421 — Italian language. Comprehension — *Questions & answers — For schools*

Clay, Kay. Uno sguardo all'Italia / Kay Clay and Annamaria Favret. — London : Harrap, 1981. — 79p : ill ; 22cm
ISBN 0-245-53558-6 (pbk) : £1.95 B81-29672

458.2'421 — Italian language. Grammar

Speroni, Charles. Basic Italian / Charles Speroni, Carlo L. Golino. — 5th ed. — London : Holt, Rinehart and Winston, c1981. — xv,441p,[8]p of plates : ill(some col.),1map,forms ; 25cm
Previous ed.: 1977. — Map on lining papers
ISBN 0-03-058174-5 : £12.50 B81-25533

Valgimigli, Maria. Living Italian. — 3rd ed. — London : Hodder and Stoughton, July 1981. — [352]p
Previous ed.: 1971
ISBN 0-340-26030-0 (pbk) : £2.45 : CIP entry
B81-13887

458.3'421 — Spoken Italian language — *Phrase books*

Ellis, D. L.. Travellers' Italian / D.L. Ellis, C. Mariella ; pronunciation J. Baldwin. — London : Pan, 1981. — 155p : ill,1map ; 17cm. — (Pan languages)
Includes index
ISBN 0-330-26295-5 (pbk) : £1.00 B81-22887

Powell, Bob. Get by in Italian : a quick beginners' course for holidaymakers and business people / course writer : Bob Powell. — London : British Broadcasting Corporation, 1981. — 72p : ill ; 18cm
ISBN 0-563-16469-7 (pbk) : £1.75 B81-17912

467 — SPANISH LANGUAGE. EARLY FORMS, SLANG, DIALECTS

467.97295'019 — Spanish language. Puerto Rican dialects. Usage. Sociolinguistic aspects
Morris, Marshall. Saying and meaning in Puerto Rico : some problems in the ethnography of discourse / by Marshall Morris. — Oxford : Pergamon, 1981. — xiv,152p ; 24cm. — (Language & communication library ; v.1)
Bibliography: p139-141. - Includes index
ISBN 0-08-025822-0 : £8.25 : CIP rev. B80-26522

468 — SPANISH LANGUAGE USAGE

468 — Spanish language — *For schools*
Pride, John C.. School Spanish course / John C. Pride. — 2nd ed. — Slough : University Tutorial, 1930. — xiv,448p : ill,maps,facsims ; 21cm
Previous ed.: 1968. — Includes index
ISBN 0-7231-0811-0 (pbk) : £3.65 B81-03411

468 — Spanish language — *Questions & answers*
Allen, Edward David. ¿Habla español? : an introductory course. — 2nd ed. / Edward David Allen ... [et al.]. — New York ; London : Holt, Rinehart and Winston, c1981. — xvi,502p,[8]p of plates : ill(some col.),col.map ; 25cm
English and Spanish text. — Previous ed.: 1976. — Includes index
ISBN 0-03-057196-0 : £10.25 B81-22879

468 — Spanish language — *Questions & answers — For schools*
Bawcutt, G. J.. Señales de España : reading comprehension activities / G.J. Bawcutt and P. Jeffery. — London : Harrap, 1981. — 60p : ill,facsims,forms ; 21cm
Spanish text, English introduction and notes. — Includes index
ISBN 0-245-53378-8 (pbk) : £1.95 B81-26178

468 — Spanish language - *Questions & answers - For schools*
Bennett, A. J.. Buenos días. — London : Hodder and Stoughton, May 1981
Part 3
Pupil's book. — [128]p
ISBN 0-340-24363-5 (pbk) : £1.95 : CIP entry B81-04223

468 — Spanish language — *Questions & answers — For schools*
Bennett, A. J.. ¡Buenos días!. — London : Hodder & Stoughton
Part 3: Teacher's book. — Oct.1981. — [64]p
ISBN 0-340-24361-9 (pbk) : £1.95 : CIP entry B81-28149

Lewis, Heloise. Vamos amigos / Heloise Lewis in association with Marjorie Bodden ... [et al.] ; consultant editor José Amodia. — [Port of Spain] : Longman Caribbean ; London : Longman
Pupils' bk.2. — New ed. / illustrated by Martina Selway. — 1981. — 137p : ill,1map,music ; 25cm
Text in English and Spanish. — Previous ed.: / illustrated by David McKee. 1971. — Map on inside cover
ISBN 0-582-76576-5 (pbk) : £1.75 B81-18936

468.2'4 — Spanish language — *For non-Spanish speaking students*
Jackson, Eugene. Spanish made simple / Eugene Jackson and Antonio Rubio ; advisory editor Irene Hart. — 2nd ed. (completely revised). — London : Heinemann, 1981. — xiv,354p : 1map ; 22cm. — (Made simple books)
English and Spanish text. — Previous ed.: New York : Made Simple Books, 1955 ; W.H. Allen, 1969
ISBN 0-434-98451-5 (pbk) : £2.75 B81-23208

Pfeiffer, Rubin. Cuentitos simpáticos : a graded reader for beginning students / Rubin Pfeiffer. — London : Bell & Hyman in association with National Textbook Co., 1978. — v,172p : ill ; 23cm
Unpriced (pbk) B81-08998

Pfeiffer, Rubin. Cuentitos simpáticos : a graded reader for intermediate students / Rubin Pfeiffer. — London : Bell & Hyman in association with National Textbook Co., 1978. — v,180p : ill ; 23cm
Unpriced (pbk) B81-08997

468.2'421 — Spanish language. Comprehension — *For schools*
Zollo, M. A.. ¿Vale?. — London : Edward Arnold, Nov.1981. — [96]p
ISBN 0-7131-0606-9 (pbk) : £1.85 : CIP entry B81-30604

468.2'421 — Spanish language. Comprehension — *Questions & answers — For Caribbean students*
Ariza, Julio de. Ambiente Latinoamericano : a reader for Caribbean secondary schools / Julio & Mireille de Ariza. — Harlow : Longman Caribbean, 1981. — 58p : ill ; 21cm
ISBN 0-582-76535-8 (pbk) : £1.20 B81-22938

468.2'421 — Spanish language. Comprehension — *Questions & answers — For schools*
Davies, John Grey. ¡Estamos en Espana! : a survival guide to everyday situations / John Grey Davies ; illustrations by Val Saunders. — London : Edward Arnold, 1981. — 62p : ill ; 23cm
ISBN 0-7131-0502-x (pbk) : £1.75 B81-09594

468.2'421 — Spanish language. Grammar
Copeland, John G.. Intermediate Spanish / John G. Copeland, Ralph Kite, Lynn Sandstedt. — 2nd ed. — New York ; London : Holt, Rinehart and Winston
Conversación y repaso. — 1981. — xii,288p : ill ; 24cm
Includes index
ISBN 0-03-057601-6 (pbk) : £6.00 B81-29480

Iglesias, Mario. Spanish for oral and written review / Mario Iglesias ; Walter Meiden. — 2nd ed. — New York ; London : Holt, Rinehart and Winston, 1981. — xiii,504p ; 24cm
Includes index
ISBN 0-03-057724-1 (pbk) : £9.00 B81-29479

Neale-Silva, Eduardo. El español en síntesis / Eduardo Neale-Silva, John M. Lipski. — New York ; London : Holt, Rinehart and Winston, c1980. — xiv,393p : ill ; 24cm
Text in Spanish and English
ISBN 0-03-058133-8 : £10.95 B81-34431

468.2'421 — Spanish language. Grammar — *For schools*
Taylor, R. J. (Robert John). A simple Spanish grammar : with exercises / R.J. Taylor and C.E. Alberry. — London : Edward Arnold, 1981. — 96p ; 22cm
English text, examples and exercises in Spanish. — Includes index
ISBN 0-7131-0548-8 (pbk) : £1.95 : CIP rev. B81-14959

468.2'421 — Spanish language. Grammar — *Spanish texts*
Michalson, Dorothy. Spanish grammar : un buen repaso / Dorothy Michalson, Charlotte Aires. — Englewood Cliffs ; London : Prentice-Hall, c1981. — xx,276p : ill,1map ; 23cm
Includes index
ISBN 0-13-824334-4 (pbk) : £7.10 B81-17298

468.3'421 — Spanish language. Idioms — *Lists*
Pierson, Raymond H.. Guide to Spanish idioms. — Cheltenham : Stanley Thornes, Aug.1981. — [180]p
ISBN 0-85950-334-8 (pbk) : £2.75 : CIP entry B81-23803

468.3'421 — Spoken Spanish language — *Phrase books*
Ellis, D. L.. Travellers' Spanish / D.L. Ellis, ; pronunciation J. Baldwin. — London : Pan, 1981. — 157p : ill,1map ; 17cm. — (Pan languages)
Includes index
ISBN 0-330-26294-7 (pbk) : £1.00 B81-22890

468.3'421 — Spoken Spanish language — *Questions & answers — For schools*
Mannion Watson, C. A.. ¿Qué se dice? : Spanish situational dialogues / C.A. Mannion Watson. — Leeds : E.J. Arnold, 1978 (1979 [printing]). — 80p : ill,maps,facsims ; 15x21cm
English and Spanish text
ISBN 0-560-02719-2 (pbk) : £1.40 B81-13021

Roberts, Christine. Destination Spain : survival language course / Christine Roberts, Rosemary Hunt. — London : Harrap
Activities book. — 1980. — 57p : ill,1map,facsims,forms ; 21cm
English text with examples in Spanish
ISBN 0-245-53401-6 (pbk) : £2.25 B81-14630

Roberts, Christine. Destination Spain : survival language course / Christine Roberts, Rosemary Hunt. — London : Harrap
Student's book. — 1980. — 120p : ill,maps,facsims,1form,ports ; 21cm
ISBN 0-245-53364-8 (pbk) : £2.95 B81-14629

Roberts, Christine. Destination Spain : survival language course / Christine Roberts, Rosemary Hunt. — London : Harrap
Teacher's book / Christine Roberts. — 1980. — 63p : ill ; 21cm
ISBN 0-245-53365-6 (pbk) : £3.75 B81-14628

468.6'421 — Spanish language. Reading books
Lecturas básicas : a literary reader. — 2nd ed. / [edited by] Guillermo I. Castillo-Feliú, Edward J. Mullen. — New York ; London : Holt, Rinehart and Winston, c1981. — vii,81p : ill ; 24cm
English and Spanish text. — Previous ed.: 1980
ISBN 0-03-058108-7 (pbk) : £3.75 B81-25589

Viaje por la literatura española : journey through Spanish literature : representative texts / edited by Salvador Ortiz-Carboneres. — Leamington Spa (24 Binswood Ave., Leamington Spa, Warwickshire) : Berg, 1981. — 75p : ill,1facsim ; 21cm
Spanish text, English preface and notes
ISBN 0-907582-00-1 (pbk) : £2.95 B81-36856

468.6'421 — Spanish language. Reading books — *For schools*
Agüera, Helen C.. Lectures básicas : a cultural reader / Helen C. Agüera, Modesto M. Díaz. — 2nd ed. — New York ; London : Holt, Rinehart and Winston, c1981. — vii,75p : ill ; 24cm
Previous ed.: 197-?
ISBN 0-03-058109-5 (pbk) : £3.75 B81-22871

Copeland, John G.. Intermediate Spanish / John G. Copeland Ralph Kite, Lynn Sandstedt. — 2nd ed. — New York ; London : Holt, Rinehart and Winston, c1981
Previous ed.: 1977
Civilización y cultura. — viii,206p : ill ; 24cm
ISBN 0-03-057606-7 (pbk) : £5.00 B81-22870

Copeland, John G.. Intermediate Spanish / John G. Copeland, Ralph Kite, Lynn Sandstedt. — 2nd ed. — New York ; London : Holt, Rinehart and Winston, c1981
Previous ed.: 1977
Literatura y arte. — viii,261p : ill ; 224cm
ISBN 0-03-057604-0 (pbk) : £5.00 B81-22869

468.6'421 — Spanish language. Reading books. Special subjects: Spain, *to 1980*
Cirre, José F.. España y los españoles / José F. Cirre, Manuela M. Cirre. — 2nd ed. — New York ; London : Holt, Rinehart and Winston, c1981. — vii,190, xlvip,[2]leaves of plates : ill,1map,facsims,ports ; 24cm
Spanish text, Preface and notes in English. — Previous ed.: 1970. — Includes index
ISBN 0-03-058051-x (corrected : pbk) : £5.00 B81-27046

468.6'421 — Spanish language. Reading books. Special subjects: Spanish America, *to 1980*
Ortiz-Carboneres, Salvador. Latin American history : selected texts from the beginning to modern times. — Leamington Spa (24 Binswood Ave., Leamington Spa, Warwickshire CV32 5SQ) : Berg, Sept.1981. — [128]p
ISBN 0-907582-02-8 (pbk) : £2.95 : CIP entry B81-24624

468.6'421 — Spanish language. Reading books. Special subjects: Spanish civilization, *to 1980*
Valdés, Joaquín. Lecturas básicas : a civilization reader. — 2nd ed. / Joaquín Valdés. — New York ; London : Holt, Rinehart and Winston, c1981. — vii,96p : ill ; 24cm
Text in English and Spanish. — Previous ed.: / Frederick J. Zierten. c1976
ISBN 0-03-058201-6 (pbk) : £3.75 B81-25553

469 — PORTUGUESE LANGUAGE

469.3′421 — Spoken Portuguese language — *Phrasebooks*

Swinglehurst, *Edmund.* Portuguese phrase book / Edmund Swinglehurst ; Portuguese translation and phonetic transcription by Teresa de Paiva-Raposa. — London : Hamlyn, 1981. — 224p ; 15cm
Parallel English and Portuguese text, introduction and notes in English. — Includes index
ISBN 0-600-37263-4 (pbk) : £0.95 B81-22056

469.83′421 — Portuguese language — *Phrase books*

Canavarro, A.. Portuguese phrase book / A. Canavarro, L. Coleman and R. Nash Newton. — London : Hodder and Stoughton, 1980. — 163p ; 15cm. — (Teach yourself books)
ISBN 0-340-23697-3 (pbk) : £0.95 : CIP rev. B80-00683

469.83′421 — Spoken Portuguese language — *Phrase books*

Ellis, D. L.. Travellers′ Portuguese / D.L. Ellis, K. Sandeman McLaughlin ; pronunciation J. Baldwin. — London : Pan, 1981. — 156p : ill,1map ; 17cm. — (Pan languages)
Includes index
ISBN 0-330-26379-x (pbk) : £1.00 B81-22893

470 — ITALIC LANGUAGES

470′.7′1042 — England. Educational institutions. Curriculum subjects: Latin language

Goodyear, F. R. D.. The future of Latin studies in English education : an inaugural lecture / by F.R. D. Goodyear. — London ([Regent′s Park, NW1 4NS]) : Bedford College, University of London, [1981?]. — 14p ; 26cm
Delivered Nov.21, 1967
Unpriced (pbk)
Also classified at 870′.7′1042 B81-35416

473 — LATIN LANGUAGE. DICTIONARIES

473′.21 — Latin language — *Latin-English dictionaries*

Oxford Latin dictionary. — Oxford : Clarendon
Facs.8: Sopor-Z y thum. — Feb.1982. — [260]p
ISBN 0-19-864221-0 (pbk) : £20.00 : CIP entry B81-36303

475 — LATIN LANGUAGE. GRAMMAR

475 — Great Britain. Latin language. Grammar. Teaching, *ca 600-ca 800*

Law, Vivien. The insular Latin grammarians. — Woodbridge : Boydell Press, Dec.1981. — [128]p. — (Studies in Celtic history ; 3)
ISBN 0-85115-147-7 : £15.00 : CIP entry B81-33878

477 — LATIN LANGUAGE. OLD, POSTCLASSICAL, VULGAR LATIN

477 — Latin language, *1000-1500 — Latin & English dictionaries*

Dictionary of medieval Latin from British sources . — London : Published for the British Academy by Oxford University Press, 1981
Fasc.IIC / prepared by R.E. Latham ; under the direction of a committee appointed by the British Academy. — xii,551p ; 31cm
Bibliography: pix-xii
ISBN 0-19-725968-5 (pbk) : £76.00 B81-24263

480 — CLASSICAL LANGUAGES AND MODERN GREEK

480 — Greek language

Palmer, Leonard R.. The Greek language / Leonard R. Palmer. — London : Faber, 1980. — xii,355p : 2maps ; 23cm. — (The Greek languages)
Bibliography: p316-320. — Includes index
ISBN 0-571-11390-7 : £25.00 : CIP rev. B79-30039

480′.05 — Classical languages — *Serials*

Harvard studies in classical philology. — Vol.84. — Cambridge, Mass. ; London : Harvard University Press, 1980. — viii,341p
ISBN 0-674-37931-4 : £18.00
ISSN 0073-0688 B81-17462

481 — GREEK LANGUAGE. WRITTEN AND SPOKEN CODES

481′.7 — Inscriptions in Greek, *B.C.500-ca A.D.250*

Woodhead, A. G.. The study of Greek inscriptions / by A.G. Woodhead. — 2nd ed. — Cambridge : Cambridge University Press, 1981. — 150p,4p of plates : ill ; 23cm
Previous ed.: 1959. — Includes index
ISBN 0-521-23188-4 (cased) : £15.00 : CIP rev.
ISBN 0-521-29860-1 (pbk) : £5.50 B81-19115

485 — GREEK LANGUAGE. GRAMMAR

485 — Greek language. Inflexion — *Lists*

Usher, H. J. K.. An outline of Greek accidence / H.J.K. Usher. — London : Duckworth, 1981. — 48p ; 26cm
Text in English and Greek
ISBN 0-7156-1456-8 (pbk) : £2.95 B81-21917

488 — GREEK LANGUAGE. CLASSICAL GREEK USAGE

488 — Greek language — *For schools*

A **New** Greek course for schools / [Greek Course Committee]. — Glasgow (c/o W.A. Williams, Jordanhill College of Education, 70 Southbrae Drive, Glasgow G13 1PP) : The Committee
Bk.3. — c1977. — 67p : ill,maps ; 30cm
Cover title
Unpriced (spiral) B81-10171

488.2′421 — Greek language. Grammar — *Questions & answers — For schools*

Hillard, A. E.. Elementary Greek exercises / A.E. Hillard and C.G. Botting. — London : Duckworth, 1981. — vii,157p ; 20cm. — (Paperduck)
″An introduction to North and Hillard′s Greek prose composition″. — Originally published: London : Rivingtons, 1909
ISBN 0-7156-1524-6 (pbk) : £4.95 B81-04315

488.3′421 — Greek language — *Phrase books — For schools*

Auden, H. W.. [Greek prose phrase-book]. Greek phrase book : based on the writings of Thucydides, Xenophon, Demosthenes, Plato / H.W. Auden. — London : Duckworth, 1981. — ix,112p ; 20cm. — (Paperduck)
Facsim of: Greek prose phrase-book, published: Edinburgh : W. Blackwood, 1899. — Includes index
ISBN 0-7156-1467-3 (cased) : Unpriced
ISBN 0-7156-1498-1 (pbk) : £4.95 B81-34536

489.3 — MODERN GREEK LANGUAGE

489′.3′321 — Modern Greek language — *Modern Greek & English dictionaries*

Pring, J. T.. The Oxford dictionary of modern Greek : English-Greek. — Oxford : Clarendon Press, Sept.1981. — [300]p
ISBN 0-19-864136-2 : £4.25 : CIP entry B81-23876

Pring, J. T.. The Oxford dictionary of modern Greek : Greek-English and English-Greek. — Oxford : Clarendon Press, Sept.1981. — [520]p
Includes the text of The Oxford dictionary of modern Greek (Greek-English), originally published: 1965
ISBN 0-19-864137-0 : £6.95 : CIP entry B81-23877

489′.383421 — Spoken Modern Greek language — *Phrase books*

Ellis, D. L.. Travellers′ Greek / D.L. Ellis, B. Rapi ; pronunciation J. Baldwin. — London : Pan, 1981. — 157p : ill,1map ; 17cm. — (Pan languages)
Includes index
ISBN 0-330-26296-3 (pbk) : £1.00 B81-22886

Swinglehurst, Edmund. Greek phrase book / Edmund Swinglehurst ; Greek translation by Maria Waring ; phonetic transcription by Henry Waring. — London : Hamlyn, 1981. — 224p ; 15cm
English text, examples in Greek. — Includes index
ISBN 0-600-34137-2 (pbk) : £0.95 B81-22074

491.2/4 — INDIC LANGUAGES

491′.25′0924 — Sanskrit language. Grammar. Theories of Pāṇini

Kiparsky, Paul. Pāṇini as a variationist / Paul Kiparsky ; edited by S.D. Joshi. — Cambridge, Mass. ; London : MIT Press in collaboration with the Centre of Advanced Study in Sanskrit, University of Poona, Ganeshkhind, Pune (India), 1979. — x,304p ; 26cm. — (Current studies in linguistics series ; 7) (Publications of the Centre of Advanced Study in Sanskrit. Class B ; no.6)
Bibliography: p250-255. — Includes index
ISBN 0-262-11070-9 (corrected) : £15.50 B81-05519

491′.4383′421 — Spoken Hindi & Urdu languages. Grammar

Russell, Ralph. A new course in Hindustani for learners in Britain. — London : University of London, School of Oriental & African Studies, July 1981
Part 2: An outline of grammar and common usage. — [102]p
ISBN 0-7286-0085-4 (pbk) : £2.00 : CIP entry B81-14789

Russell, Ralph. A new course in Hindustani for learners in Britain. — London : University of London, School of Oriental & African Studies, July 1981
Part 3: Rapid readings. — [180]p
ISBN 0-7286-0086-2 (pbk) : £2.50 : CIP entry B81-14790

Russell, Ralph. A new course in Hindustani for learners in Britain. — London : University of London, School of Oriental and African Studies
Pt.4: The Urdu script. — Feb.1982. — [132]p
ISBN 0-7286-0093-5 (pbk) : £2.50 : CIP entry B81-35841

491.6 — CELTIC LANGUAGES

491.6′05 — Celtic languages — *Serials*

Studia celtica. — Vol.14/15 (1979/80). — Cardiff : University of Wales Press on behalf of the Board of Celtic Studies of the University of Wales, [1981]. — 462p
ISSN 0081-6353 : Unpriced B81-13200

491.6′2 — Irish language

Ó Siadhail, Micheál. Learning Irish : an introductory self-tutor / Micheál Ó Siadhail. — [Dublin] ([10 Burlington Rd., Dublin 4]) : Dublin Institute for Advanced Studies, 1980. — 331p ; 21cm + 3sound cassettes
Includes index
£10.00 (pbk) B81-12620

491.6′2′060415 — Ireland. Irish language. Organisations: Gaelic League, *to 1914 — Irish texts*

Ó Súilleabháin, Donnchadh. An Piarsach agus Conradh na Gaeilge / Donnchadh Ó Súilleabháin. — Baile′ Atha Cliath (6 Sráid Fhearchair, Baile Átha Cliath 2) : Clódhanna, 1981. — viii,200p : facsims ; 22cm
Text in Irish and English. — Bibliography: p198-200
£3.00 (pbk) B81-26826

491.6′2′06041825 — Louth *(County).* **Dundalk. Irish language. Organisations: Gaelic League.** *Craobh Dhún Dealgan, to 1976 — Irish texts*

Céitinn, Séamas. Cracbh den Chonradh : scéal Chraobh Dhún Dealgan de Chonradh na Gaeilge 1899-1976 / Séamas Céitinn. — Dún Dealgan ([40 Páirc Ghleann na Gaorchaibh, Dún Laoghaine, Eine]) : Coiste Mhuirtheimhne, c1980. — 79p : ill,ports ; 22cm
Unpriced B81-2778

491.6′2′0924 — Ireland. Irish language. Promotion. Ó Dubhda, Peadar — *Biographies*

Ó Néill, Padraig. Peadar Ó Dubhda : ′the forgotten man′. — [Dún Laoghaire] ([40 Páirc Ghleann na Gaorthaibh, Dún Laoghaire]) : [Éigse Oirialla], [1981]. — 63p : ill,1coat of arms,music,facsims,ports ; 19cm
Written by Padraig Ó Néill
Unpriced (pbk) B81-2104

491.6′23 — Irish language — *Dictionaries*

De Bhaldraithe, Tomás. Innéacs Nua-Ghaeilge : don Dictionary of the Irish language / Tomás De Bhaldraithe. — Baile Átha Cliath : Acadamh Ríoga Na héireann, 1981. — iv,78p ; 25cm. — (Deascán Foclóireachta ; 1)
ISBN 0-901714-18-6 (pbk) : Unpriced
B81-29610

491.6′25 — Syntax. Transformational-generative theories *related to* semantic theories of Montague, Richard — *Study examples: Irish language*

McCloskey, James. Transformational syntax and model theoretic semantics : a case study in modern Irish / by James McCloskey. — Dordrecht ; London : Reidel, c1979. — ix,258p : ill ; 24cm. — (Synthese language library ; v.9)
Bibliography: p248-254. - Includes index
ISBN 90-277-1025-2 (cased) : Unpriced
ISBN 90-277-1026-0 (pbk) : Unpriced
B81-07298

491.6′27 — Old Irish language. Grammar — *Irish texts*

Ó Fiannachta, Pádraig. Seanghaeilge ga dua / Pádraig Ó Fiannachta. — 2 eagrán. — Má Nuad [ie Maynooth] ([St Patricks College, Maynooth, Co. Kildare, Irish Republic]) : Am Sagart, 1981. — 174p ; 22cm
Previous ed.: 1974
Unpriced (pbk) B81-37865

491.6′282 — Irish language. Comprehension — *Questions & answers — For Irish speaking students — For schools*

Ó Maonaigh, Tomás. Sraith oibre don ardteist / Tomás ó Maonaigh. — Baile Uailcín [i.e. Walkinstown] (Bóther Bhaile an Aird, Baile Uailcín, Baile Átha Cliath 12) : Helicon Teoranta
Unpriced (pbk) B81-16706

Ó Riain, Clement. Caisleáin óir / Clement Ó Riain. — Baile Uailcín [i.e. Walkinstown] (Bóthar Bhaile an Aird, Baile Uailcín Baile Átha Cliath 12) : Helicon Teoranta, [1980?]. — 40p ; 21cm. — (Nótai Helicon)
Text on inside cover
Unpriced (pbk) B81-16704

491.6′282 — Irish language. Grammar — *Irish texts*

Úrchúsa Gaeilge : cúrsa leasaithe dírithe ar laigí áirithe i scríobh na Gaeilge / [edited by] Dónall P. Ó Baoill, Conchúr Ó Rónáin. — Baile Átha Cliath (31 Plás Mhic Liam, Baile Átha Cliath 2) : Institiúid teangeolaíochta Éireann, 1980. — vi,153p ; 24cm. — (Foilseachán / Institiúid Teangeolaíochta Éireann ; 21 (G))
Conference papers
Unpriced (pbk) B81-10023

491.6′283421 — Irish language — *Phrase books*

Nugent, M.. Siolta / le M. Nugent. — [Tallaght] : Folens, c1981. — 144p ; 18cm
Irish and English text
ISBN 0-86121-157-x (pbk) : Unpriced
B81-37612

491.6′286 — Irish language. Reading books — *For Irish speaking pre-school children*

Ní Mhaoláin, Páraicín. Ríró agus Óró / Páraicín Ní Mhaoláin, Treasa NíAilpín. — Baile Átha Cliath (Bóthar Bhaile an Aird, Baile Vailcín, Baile Átha Cliath 12) : An Comhlacht Oideachais, c1981. — 24p : chiefly col.ill ; 21cm
Unpriced (pbk) B81-23049

491.6′286 — Irish language. Reading books — *For Irish speaking students*

Ní Mhaoláin, Páraicín. Lionta / Páraicín Ní Mhaoláin, Treasa Ní Ailpín. — Bgaile Átha Cliath [i.e. Dublin] (Bóthar Bhaile an Aird, Biale Vailcín, Baile Átha Cliath 12) : Comhlacht Oideachais na hÉireann Teoranta, c1981. — 32p : col.ill ; 21cm
Unpriced (pbk) B81-25937

491.6′382421 — Gaelic language. Comprehension — *Questions & answers — For schools*

Maciver, Donald J. M.. Gaelic language practice : exercises in language practice for learners of Gaelic at Ordinary Grade / Donald J.M. Maciver. — [Stornoway?] :
Buidheann-foillseachaidh nan Eilean an Iar, 1980. — [103]p ; 20cm
ISBN 0-906437-07-5 (pbk) : Unpriced
B81-32734

491.6′63′0924 — Welsh language. Lexicography. Thomas, R. J. — *Biographies — Welsh texts*

Phillips, Vincent H.. R.J. Thomas 1908-1976 : agweddau ar ei fywyd a'i waith / gan Vincent H. Phillips, Elfyn Jenkins. — [St. Fagans] : Amgueddfa Werin Cymru (1980). — 38p ; 22cm
ISBN 0-85485-045-7 (pbk) : Unpriced
B81-10934

491.6′67 — Welsh language. Dialects. Spatial distribution. Analysis. Applications of digital computer systems

Thomas, Alan R. (Alan Richard). Areal analysis of dialect data by computer : a Welsh example / by Alan R. Thomas ; [flow charts of computational procedures by Dafydd Roberts]. — Cardiff : Published on behalf of the Board of Celtic Studies [by the] University of Wales Press, 1980. — vii,126p : ill,maps ; 32cm
Bibliography: p125-126
ISBN 0-7083-0783-3 : £14.95 B81-02797

491.6′681 — Welsh language. Words. Special subjects. Houses — *For children*

Watson, Carol. Y ty = The house / cynlluniwyd gan Carol Watson ; lluniau gan Colin King ; ymgynghorwr Maxwell Evans. — Caerdydd : Gwasg y Dref Wen, 1980. — 24p : colill ; 21cm. — (Cyfres gair a llun = Works and pictures series)
Text on inside covers
£0.95 (pbk) B81-05538

491.6′681 — Welsh language. Words. Special subjects: Shops — *For children*

Watson, Carol. Y siop = The shop / cynlluniwyd gan Carol Watson ; lluniau gan Colin King ; ymgynghorwr Maxwell Evans. — Caerdydd : Gwasg y Dref Wen, 1980. — 24p : col.ill ; 21cm. — (Cyfres gair a llun = Words and pictures series)
Text on inside covers
£0.95 (pbk) B81-05540

491.6′681 — Welsh language. Words. Special subjects: Towns — *For children*

Watson, Carol. Y dref = The town / cynlluniwyd gan Carol Watson ; lluniau gan Colin King ; ymgynghorwr Maxwell Evans. — Caerdydd : Gwasg y Dref Wen, 1980. — 24p : col.ill ; 21cm. — (Cyfres gair a llun = Words and pictures series)
Text on inside covers
£0.95 (pbk) B81-05539

491.6′682 — Welsh language. Grammar — *Welsh texts*

Davies, W. Beynon. Grym gramadeg / W. Beynon Davies. — Llandysul : Gwasg Gomer, 1981. — 77p ; 22cm
ISBN 0-85088-974-x (pbk) : £1.50 B81-38339

Williams, Stephen J. (Stephen Joseph), *1896-*. Elfennau gramadeg Cymraeg / gan Stephen J. Williams. — 2 argraffiad gyda chyfnewidiadau. — Caerdydd : Gwasg Prifysgol Cymru, 1980. — xii,246p ; 20cm
Previous ed.: 1959. — Includes index
ISBN 0-7083-0780-9 : £6.95 : CIP rev.
B80-13354

491.6′686 — Welsh language. Reading books — *For Welsh speaking pre-school children*

Evans, Dilwen M.. Y crydd a'r ddau goblyn / addaswyd y stori wreiddiol gan Lucy Kincaid ; addasiad Cymraeg gan Dilwen M. Evans ; darluniwyd gan Gillian Embleton. — Llandysul : Gwasg Gomer, 1981. — [24]p : col.ill ; 27cm. — (Nawr gellwch chi ddarllen)
ISBN 0-85088-594-9 : Unpriced B81-40352

Evans, Dilwen M.. Yr hwyaden fach hyll / addaswyd y stori wreiddiol gan Lucy Kincaid ; addasiad Cymraeg gan Dilwen M. Evans ; darluniwyd gan Gillian Embleton. — Llandysul : Gwasg Gomer, 1981. — [24]p : col.ill ; 27cm. — (Nawr gellwch chi ddarllen)
ISBN 0-85088-614-7 : Unpriced B81-40353

Evans, Dilwen M.. Yr iâr fach goch / addaswyd y stori wreiddiol gan Lucy Kincaid ; addasiad Cymraeg gan Dilwen M. Evans ; darluniwyd gan Belinda Lyon. — Llandysul : Gwasg Gomer, 1981. — [24]p : col.ill ; 27cm. — (Nawr gellwch chi ddarllen)
ISBN 0-85088-604-x : Unpriced B81-40347

Evans, Dilwen M.. Y tri mochyn bach / addaswyd y stori wreiddiol gan Lucy Kincaid ; addasiad Cymraeg gan Dilwen M. Evans ; darluniwyd gan Eric Rowe. — Llandysul : Gwasg Gomer, 1981. — [24]p : col.ill ; 27cm. — (Nawr gellwch chi ddarllen)
ISBN 0-85088-574-4 : Unpriced B81-40351

Evans, Dilwen M.. Y dywysoges hir ei chwsg / addaswyd y stori gan Lucy Kincaid ; addasiad Cymraeg gan Dilwen M. Evans ; darluniwyd gan Gillian Embleton. — Llandysul : Gwasg Gomer, 1981. — [24]p : col.ill ; 27cm. — (Nawr gellwch chi ddarllen)
ISBN 0-85088-584-1 : Unpriced B81-40350

Strange, Morfudd. Elen Benfelen a'r tri arth / addaswyd y stori gan Lucy Kincaid ; addasiad Cymraeg gan Morfudd Strange ; darluniwyd gan Belinda Lyon. — Llandysul : Gwasg Gomer, 1981. — [24]p : col.ill ; 27cm. — (Nawr gellwch chi ddarllen)
ISBN 0-85088-534-5 : Unpriced B81-40346

Strange, Morfudd. Jac a'i goeden ffa / addaswyd y stori gan Lucy Kincaid ; addasiad Cymraeg gan Morfudd Strange ; darluniwyd gan Eric Rowe. — Llandysul : Gwasg Gomer, 1981. — [24]p : col.ill ; 27cm. — (Nawr gellwch chi ddarllen)
ISBN 0-85088-544-2 : Unpriced B81-40349

Strange, Morfudd. Rapynsel / addaswyd y stori gan Lucy Kincaid ; addasiad Cymraeg gan Morfudd Strange ; darluniwyd gan Georgina Hargreaves. — Llandysul : Gwasg Gomer, 1981. — [24]p : col.ill ; 27cm. — (Nawr gellwch chi ddarllen)
ISBN 0-85088-554-x : Unpriced B81-40348

Strange, Morfudd. Y dywysoges a'r broga / addaswyd y stori wreiddiol gan Lucy Kincaid ; addasiad Cymraeg gan Morfudd Strange ; darluniwyd gan Pamela Storey. — Llandysul : Gwasg Gomer, 1981. — [24]p : col.ill ; 27cm. — (Nawr gellwch chi ddarllen)
ISBN 0-85088-564-7 : Unpriced B81-40345

491.6′686 — Welsh language. Reading books — *For Welsh speaking students*

Huws, Emily. Stori a chwedl : cyfres ddarllen i blant o 7 i 11 oed / Emily Huws, Elfyn Pritchard ; darluniwyd y gyfrol gan Roger Jones. — Llandysul : Gwasg Gomer
Lefel 1. — 1980
Llyfr 1. — 37p : col.ill ; 21cm
ISBN 0-85088-813-1 (pbk) : £0.95 B81-40067

Huws, Emily. Stori a chwedl : cyfres ddarllen i blant o 7 i 11 oed / Emily Huws, Elfyn Pritchard ; darluniwyd y gyfrol gan Roger Jones. — Llandysul : Gwasg Gomer
Lefel 1. — 1980
Llyfr 2. — 39p : col.ill ; 21cm
ISBN 0-85088-823-9 (pbk) : £0.95 B81-40066

Huws, Emily. Stori a chwedl : cyfres ddarllen i blant o 7 i 11 oed / Emily Huws, Elfyn Pritchard ; darluniwyd y gyfrol gan Roger Jones. — Llandysul : Gwasg Gomer
Lefel 2. — 1980
Llyfr 1. — 44p : col.ill ; 21cm
ISBN 0-85088-833-6 (pbk) : £0.95 B81-40069

491.6′686 — Welsh language. Reading books — *For Welsh speaking students* *continuation*
Huws, Emily. Stori a chwedl : cyfres ddarllen i blant o 7 i 11 oed / Emily Huws, Elfyn Pritchard ; darluniwyd y gyfrol gan Roger Jones. — Llandysul : Gwasg Gomer
Lefel 2. — 1980
Llyfr 2. — 43p : col.ill ; 21cm
ISBN 0-85088-843-3 (pbk) : £0.95 B81-40068

Huws, Emily. Stori a chwedl : cyfres ddarllen i blant o 7 i 11 oed / Emily Huws, Elfyn Pritchard ; darluniwyd y gyfrol gan Roger Jones. — Llandysul : Gwasg Gomer
Lefel 3. — 1980
Llyfr 1. — 34p : col.ill ; 21cm
ISBN 0-85088-853-0 (pbk) : £0.95 B81-40070

Huws, Emily. Stori a chwedl : cyfres ddarllen i blant o 7 i 11 oed / Emily Huws, Elfyn Pritchard ; darluniwyd y gyfrol hon gan Roger Jones. — Llandysul : Gwasg Gomer
Lefel 3. — 1980
Llyfr 2. — 34p : col.ill ; 21cm
ISBN 0-85088-863-8 (pbk) : £0.95 B81-40075

Huws, Emily. Stori a chwedl : cyfres ddarllen i blant o 7 i 11 oed / Emily Huws, Elfyn Pritchard ; darluniwyd y gyfrol gan Roger Jones. — Llandysul : Gwasg Gomer
Lefel 4. — 1981
Llyfr 1. — 43p : col.ill ; 21cm
ISBN 0-85088-784-4 (pbk) : £0.95 B81-40076

Huws, Emily. Stori a chwedl : cyfres ddarllen i blant o 7 i 11 oed / Emily Huws, Elfyn Pritchard ; darluniwyd y gyfrol gan Roger Jones. — Llandysul : Gwasg Gomer
Lefel 4. — 1981
Llyfr 2. — 41p : col.ill ; 21cm
ISBN 0-85088-794-1 (pbk) : £0.95 B81-40077

Huws, Emily. Stori a chwedl : cyfres ddarllen i blant o 7 i 11 oed / Emily Huws, Elfyn Pritchard ; darluniwyd y gyfrol gan Roger Jones. — Llandysul : Gwasg Gomer
Lefel 5. — 1980
Llyfr 1. — 37p : col.ill ; 21cm
ISBN 0-85088-804-2 (pbk) : £0.95 B81-40071

Huws, Emily. Stori a chwedl : cyfres ddarllen i blant o 7 i 11 oed / Emily Huws, Elfyn Pritchard ; darluniwyd y gyfrol gan Roger Jones. — Llandysul : Gwasg Gomer
Lefel 5. — 1980
Llyfr 2. — 39p : col.ill ; 21cm
ISBN 0-85088-814-x (pbk) : £0.95 B81-40072

Huws, Emily. Stori a chwedl : cyfres ddarllen i blant o 7 i 11 oed / Emily Huws, Elfyn Pritchard ; darluniwyd y gyfrol gan Roger Jones. — Llandysul : Gwasg Gomer
Lefel 6. — 1981
Llyfr 1. — 40p : col.ill ; 21cm
ISBN 0-85088-824-7 (pbk) : £0.95 B81-40073

Huws, Emily. Stori a chwedl : cyfres ddarllen i blant o 7 i 11 oed / Emily Huws, Elfyn Pritchard ; darluniwyd y gyfrol gan Roger Jones. — Llandysul : Gwasg Gomer
Lefel 6. — 1981
Llyfr 2. — 36p : col.ill ; 21cm
ISBN 0-85088-834-4 (pbk) : £0.95 B81-40074

491.6′686421 — Welsh language. Reading books — *For children*
Boore, Roger. Gwen ac Alun am fod yn gerddorion / Juan Capdevila ; lluniau gan Violeta Denou ; addasiad gan Roger Boore ; ymgynghorwr D. Gwynfor Evans. — [Caerdydd] : Gwasg y Dref Wen, c1981. — 29p : col.ill ; 27cm. — (Cyfres Gwen ac Alun)
Translation and adaptation of: Nico y Ana quieren ser músicos
£1.95 B81-36188

Boore, Roger. Siôn yn yr eira / Juan Capdevila ; lluniau gan Violeta Denou ; addasiad gan Roger Boore ; ymgyrghorwr D. Gwynfor Evans. — [Caerdydd] : Gwasg y Dref Wen, c1981. — [30]p : col.ill ; 27cm. — (Cyfres Siôn yn darganfod)
Translation and adaptation of: Teo en la nieve
ISBN 84-401-0646-7 : £1.95 B81-36140

491.6′78 — Cornish language — *For schools*
Fudge, Crysten. Kernewek mar plek! / gans Crysten Fudge ; delynyasow gans Rex Vinson. — Redruth (Trewolsta, Trewirgie, Redruth, [Cornwall]) : Dyllansow Truran, [1980?]. — 76p : ill,maps ; 32cm
Cornish and English text. — Includes index
Unpriced (pbk) B81-39686

491.6′88249166 — Breton language. Grammar — *Welsh texts*
Williams, Rita. Cyflwyno′r Llydaweg / cyfaddasiad Rita Williams o Brezhoneg buan hag aes [gan] Per Denez. — Caerdydd : Cyhoeddwyd ar ran Bwydd Gwybodau Celtaidd Prifysgol Cymru [gan] Wasg Prifysgol Cymru, 1981. — xviii,315p : ill ; 21cm
ISBN 0-7083-0746-9 (pbk) : Unpriced B81-22751

491.7 — RUSSIAN LANGUAGE

491.73′21 — Russian language — *Russian & English dictionaries*
Coulson, Jessie. The pocket Oxford Russian dictionary. — Oxford : Clarendon Press, Sept.1981. — [844]p
Includes the text of The pocket Oxford Russian English dictionary / compiled by Jessie Coulson, originally published 1975
ISBN 0-19-864122-2 : £5.95 : CIP entry B81-23875

Harrison, W. (William). Russian-English and English-Russian dictionary / by W. Harrison and Svetlana Le Fleming. — London : Routledge & Kegan Paul, 1973 (1981 [printing]). — xii,568p ; 16cm
ISBN 0-7100-0800-7 (pbk) : £4.50 B81-35603

Scanlan, George. Harrap′s Russian vocabulary. — [Rev ed.] / George Scanlan, Peter Collin. — London : Harrap, 1980. — 103p ; 14cm
Previous ed.: published as A classified Russian vocabulary / P.H. Collin. 1962
ISBN 0-245-53699-x (cased) : £2.95
ISBN 0-245-53623-x (pbk) : £2.00 B81-07077

Wilson, Elizabeth A. M.. Conversational Russian dictionary for English speakers. — Oxford : Pergamon, Oct.1981. — [1440]p
ISBN 0-08-020554-2 : £25.00 : CIP entry B81-30203

491.75 — Russian language. Predicates. Agreement
Corbett, G. G.. Predicate agreement in Russian / G.G. Corbett. — Birmingham : Department of Russian Language & Literature, University of Birmingham, c1979. — xii,111p : ill ; 21cm. — (Birmingham Slavonic monographs, ISSN 0141-3805 ; no.7)
Bibliography: p105-111
ISBN 0-7044-0349-8 (pbk) : £2.80 B81-10091

491.75 — Russian language. Prepositions: ′do′
Wade, Terence L. B.. The Russian preposition do and the concept of extent / Terence L.B. Wade. — Birmingham : Department of Russian Language & Literatre, University of Birmingham, c1980. — ix,148p ; 21cm. — (Birmingham Slavonic monographs, ISSN 0141-3805 ; no.9)
Bibliography: p141-148
ISBN 0-7044-0375-7 (pbk) : £3.60 B81-10089

491.78′02 — Science & technology. Documents on science & documents on technology: Documents in Russian. Translation
Heron, Patricia A.. Reading Russian : a course for complete beginners who wish to acquire the ability to translate scientific texts : and to accompany the Russian-English dictionary / by P.A. Heron. — Birmingham : University of Aston in Birmingham, c1977. — 57leaves : 1ill ; 30cm. — (Occasional publication / University of Aston in Birmingham. Modern Languages Department ; no.5)
ISBN 0-903807-54-8 (pbk) : Unpriced B81-39489

491.782′421 — Russian language. Grammar
Norman, Peter. Russian for today / Peter Norman. — Letchworth : Prideaux, 1978, c1965 (1980 [printing]). — 351p ; 20cm. — (Russian texts for students ; no.7)
Originally published: London : University of London Press, 1965. — Includes index
£2.95 (pbk) B81-09338

491.799 — BELORUSSIAN LANGUAGE

491.7′99 — Belorussia. Belorussian language — *Correspondence, diaries, etc.*
[Pismo russkomu drugu. *English*]. Letter to a Russian friend : a ′samizdat′ publication from Soviet Byelorussia. — London (52, Penn Road, N7 9RE) : Association of Byelorussians in Great Britain, 1979. — 64p ; 25cm
Parallel Belorussian text and English translation. — Cover title
£1.00 (pbk) B81-39616

491.8 — SLAVIC LANGUAGES

491.8′283421 — Spoken Serbo-Croatian language — *Phrase books*
Ellis, D. L.. Travellers′ Serbo-Croat / D.L. Ellis, E. Spong ; pronunciation J. Baldwin. — London : Pan, 1981. — 155p : ill,1map ; 17cm. — (Pan languages)
Includes index
ISBN 0-330-26381-1 (pbk) : £1.00 B81-22888

491.8′515 — Generative phonology. Abstractness. Theories — *Study examples: Polish language*
Gussmann, Edmund. Studies in abstract phonology / Edmund Gussmann. — Cambridge, Mass. ; London : MIT Press, c1980. — xii,160p ; 25cm. — (Linguistic inquiry monographs ; 4)
Bibliography: p147-149. — Includes index
ISBN 0-262-07081-2 (cased) : £13.50
ISBN 0-262-57057-2 (pbk) : Unpriced B81-29172

491.8′582421 — Polish language. Grammar
Swan, Oscar. A concise grammar of Polish / Oscar Swan. — London : Orbis Books, 1980, c1978. — x,87p : 1port ; 20cm
Originally published: Washington, D.C. : University Press of America, 1978
ISBN 0-901149-14-4 (pbk) : Unpriced B81-19604

492 — SEMITIC LANGUAGES

492 — Western Semitic languages. Grammar
Robinson, Theodore H.. Paradigms and exercises in Syriac grammar. — 4th ed. — Oxford : Clarendon Press, Jan.1982. — [168]p
Originally published: 1962
ISBN 0-19-815458-5 (pbk) : £5.50 : CIP entry B81-33826

492.7 — ARABIC LANGUAGE

492′.7′321 — Arabic language — *Arabic & English dictionaries*
The **Concise** Oxford English-Arabic dictionary of current usage. — Oxford : Oxford University Press, Jan.1982. — [544]p
ISBN 0-19-864321-7 (pbk) : £4.50 : CIP entry B81-3399

492′.7′82 — Arabic language, *to ca 700.* **Grammar** *— Sources of data: Papyri in Arabic*
Hopkins, Simon. Studies in the grammar of early Arabic. — Oxford : Oxford University Press, Nov.1981. — [312]p. — (London oriental serie ; v.37)
ISBN 0-19-713603-6 : £28.00 : CIP entry B81-30338

492′.782421 — Arabic language. Grammar
Ayyad, A. T.. Teach yourself Arabic. — London (68a Delancy St., NW1 7RY) : Ta Ha Publishers, Dec.1981
Part 1: Rules of reading and writing. — [128]p
ISBN 0-907461-13-1 (pbk) : £2.75 : CIP entry B81-3923

492′.783421 — Spoken Arabic language. Grammar
McLoughlin, Leslie J.. Colloquial Arabic (Levantine). — London : Routledge and Kegan Paul, Aug.1981. — [145]p
ISBN 0-7100-0668-3 (pbk) : £3.50 : CIP entry B81-1815

492.9 — SOUTH ARABIAN LANGUAGES

492′.9 — Jibbāli language — *Jibbāli & English dictionaries*
Johnstone, T. M.. Jibbāli lexicon. — Oxford : Oxford University Press, Jan.1982. — [320]p
ISBN 0-19-713602-8 : £24.00 : CIP entry B81-3441

493 — HAMITIC AND CHAD LANGUAGES

493'.1 — Egypt. Wadi el-Hudi. Amethyst mines. Rock engravings: Inscriptions in Middle Egyptian, *ca B.C.2000-B.C.1700 — Collections*
The **Amethyst** mining inscriptions of Wadi el-Hudi / [edited by] ; Ashraf I. Sadek. — Warminster : Aris & Phillips
Part 1: Text. — c1980. — 120p : maps ; 30cm
Includes index
ISBN 0-85668-162-8 (pbk) : £12.00 : CIP rev.
B80-33473

493'.1 — Inscribed Ancient Egyptian stones: Rosetta Stone
Andrews, Carol. The Rosetta stone. — New ed. — London : British Museum Publications, Sept.1981. — [32]p
Previous ed.: 1950
ISBN 0-7141-0931-2 (pbk) : £1.25 : CIP entry
B81-28702

493'.7286 — Hausa language. Reading books
Fulani, Dan. Sauna, dan sandan ciki. — London : Hodder & Stoughton Educational, Dec.1981. — [128]p
ISBN 0-340-27466-2 (pbk) : £1.50 : CIP entry
B81-31469

495 — LANGUAGES OF EAST AND SOUTHEAST ASIA

495 — Sino-Tibetan languages. Etymological aspects
Luce, G. H.. A comparative word-list of Old Burmese, Chinese and Tibetan. — London (Malet St., WC1E 7HP) : School of Oriental and African Studies, June 1981. — [120]p
ISBN 0-7286-0084-6 (pbk) : £3.00 : CIP entry
B81-10506

495.1 — CHINESE LANGUAGE

495.1 — Chinese language
Chang, Raymond. Speaking of Chinese / Raymond Chang, Margaret Scrogin Chang. — London : Deutsch, 1980. — x,198p : ill ; 22cm. — (The Language library)
Originally published: New York : Norton, 1978. — Bibliography: p195-198
ISBN 0-233-97176-9 : £7.95 : CIP rev.
B80-18228

495.1'11 — Chinese language. Characters
Miaoling, Lin. Everyday Chinese characters. — London : Duckworth, Apr. 1981. — [80]p
ISBN 0-7156-1552-1 (cased) : £1.50 : CIP entry
ISBN 0-7156-1553-x (pbk) : £1.50 B81-00090

495.1'11'0321 — Chinese language. Characters — *Dictionaries*
Leon, N. H.. Character indexes of modern Chinese = Xian dai han yu hanzi jian zi / N.H. Leon. — London : Curzon, 1981, c1980. — xv,508p ; 23cm
ISBN 0-7007-0134-6 (pbk) : £9.50 B81-11052

495.1'82421 — Chinese language. Grammar
Birch, Ivan J.. Introduction to Chinese / by Ivan J. Birch. — Halifax, W. Yorkshire (234 Long La., Wheatley, Halifax, W. Yorkshire HX3 5JS) : I.J. Birch, 1980
Pt.2. — 32p ; 22cm
Cover title
ISBN 0-905406-02-8 (pbk) : £1.50 B81-10527

495.1'83421 — Spoken Chinese language. Mandarin — *Phrase books*
Lay, Nancy Duke S.. Say it in Chinese : (Mandarin) / by Nancy Duke Lay. — New York : Dover ; London : Constable, 1980. — xix,187p ; 14cm. — (Dover "Say it" series)
Text in English and Chinese. — Includes index
ISBN 0-486-23325-1 (pbk) : £1.75 B81-18484

495.6 — JAPANESE LANGUAGE

495.6 — Japanese language
Kindaichi, Haruhiko. The Japanese language / Haruhiko Kindaichi ; translated and annotated by Umeyo Hirano. — Rutland, Vt : Tuttle, 1978 ; London : Prentice-Hall [distributor]. — 295p ; 20cm
Translation of: Nippongo
ISBN 0-8048-1185-7 : £9.90 B81-25173

495.6'11 — Japanese language. Characters. Radicals
Anderson, Olov Bertil. Bushu : a key to the radicals of the Japanese script / Olov Bertil Anderson. — London : Curzon, 1981, c1980. — xii,87p ; 22cm
ISBN 0-7007-0127-3 (pbk) : £3.50 : CIP rev.
B81-13782

495.6'2 — Japanese language. Origins
Miller, Roy Andrew. Origins of the Japanese language : lectures in Japan during the academic year 1977-78 / Roy Andrew Miller. — Seattle ; London : University of Washington Press, c1980. — xiii,217p : 3maps ; 24cm. — (Publications on Asia of the School of International Studies ; no.34)
Bibliography: p183-206. — Includes index
ISBN 0-295-95766-2 : £10.50 B81-23006

495.6'82421 — Japanese language. Grammar
Clarke, H. D. B.. Colloquial Japanese / H.D.B. Clarke and Motoko Hamamura. — London : Routledge & Kegan Paul, 1981. — vii,337p ; 19cm
English and Japanese text
ISBN 0-7100-0595-4 (pbk) : £4.50 : CIP rev.
B81-00091

495.6'82421'05 — Japanese language. Grammar — *Serials*
Sheffield studies in Japanese. Scientific and technical Japanese series 031. — 1-. — Sheffield ([Sheffield S10 2TN]) : University of Sheffield Centre of Japanese Studies, 1979-. — v. : ill ; 31cm
Irregular. — Text in English, appendices in Japanese
Unpriced B81-06154

495.8 — BURMESE LANGUAGE

495'.8321 — Burmese language — *Burmese & English dictionaries*
A **Burmese-English** dictionary / compiled under the direction of the late J.A. Stewart and of C.W. Dunn from material supplied by a large number of contributors. — [London] : School of Oriental and African Studies, University of London
Pt.6.: 'asā" B-'am' C / revised and edited by Hla Pe, A.J. Allott and J.W.A. Okell. — 1981. — p361-373 ; 32cm
ISBN 0-7286-0083-8 (pbk) : £10.00 : CIP rev.
B81-21517

496.3 — NIGER-CONGO LANGUAGES

496'.34 — Bambara language — *French & Bambara dictionaries*
Bailleul, Charles. Petit dictionnaire bambara-français, français-bambara / par Charles Bailleul. — [Amersham] : Avebury, 1981. — xii,339p ; 24cm
ISBN 0-86127-220-x : £20.00
Also classified at 443'.9634 B81-37488

496'.392321 — Swahili language — *Swahili & English dictionaries*
Learner's Swahili-English, English-Swahili dictionary / [compiled by] Ali Ahmed Jahadhmy. — London : Evans, 1981. — xix,106p ; 22cm
ISBN 0-237-50467-7 (pbk) : Unpriced
B81-26006

496'.39282421 — Swahili language. Grammar
Mīachina, E. N.. The Swahili language : a descriptive grammar / E.N. Myachina ; translated by G.L. Campdell. — London : Routledge & Kegan Paul, 1981. — vi,86p ; 22cm. — (Languages of Asia and Africa, ISSN 0261-0116)
Translation of: Lazyk Suahili. — Bibliography: p84-86. — Includes index
ISBN 0-7100-0849-x (pbk) : £7.00 B81-40136

496'.39286 — Swahili language. Reading books — *For Swahili speaking students*
Zaidi, Noor H.. Simba wa Tsavo / Noor H. Zaidi. — London : Macmillan, 1980. — 92p ; 19cm
Adaptation of: The man-eaters of Tsavo. — Text on inside cover
£0.95 (pbk) B81-09893

497 — NORTH AMERICAN INDIAN LANGUAGES

497'.4 — Maya language. Phonological aspects. Learning by children in Pustunich, Mexico
Straight, H. Stephen. The acquisition of Maya phonology : variation in Yucatec child language / H. Stephen Straight. — New York ; London : Garland, 1976. — xxiii,255p : 3maps ; 21cm. — (Garland studies in American Indian linguistics)
Bibliography: p221-226
ISBN 0-8240-1973-3 : Unpriced B81-26934

497'.5 — Wichita language. Grammar
Rood, David S.. Wichita grammar / David S. Rood. — New York ; London : Garland, c1976. — xix,310p ; 21cm. — (Garland studies in American Indian linguistics)
Bibliography: p275. — Includes index
ISBN 0-8240-1972-5 : Unpriced B81-27501

499.1 — NONAUSTRONESIAN LANGUAGES OF OCEANIA

499'.15 — Diyari language. Grammar
Austin, Peter. A grammar of Diyari, South Australia / Peter Austin. — Cambridge : Cambridge University Press, 1981. — xv,269p : 2maps ; 24cm. — (Cambridge studies in linguistics, ISSN 0068-676x ; 32)
Bibliography: p264-269. - Includes index
ISBN 0-521-22849-2 : £30.00 : CIP rev.
B81-14978

499'.15 — Ngiyambaa language
Donaldson, Tamsin. Ngiyambaa : the language of the Wangaaybuwan / Tamsin Donaldson. — Cambridge : Cambridge University Press, 1980. — xxx,345p,4p of plates : ill,2maps,ports ; 24cm. — (Cambridge studies in linguistics, ISSN 0068-676x ; 29)
Bibliography: p337-342. - Includes index
ISBN 0-521-22524-8 : £26.00 B81-07739

499.2 — AUSTRONESIAN LANGUAGES, MALAY LANGUAGES

499'.22 — Indonesian languages — *Conference proceedings*
Papers on Indonesian languages and literatures / edited by Nigel Phillips and Khaidir Anwar. — London (School of Oriental and African Studies, Malet St. WC1E 7HP) : Indonesian Etymological Project, 1981. — x,155p : ill,2facsims,maps ; 25cm
Conference papers. — Includes a chapter in French. — Includes bibliographies and index
ISBN 0-9507474-0-8 (pbk) : Unpriced : CIP rev.
Also classified at 899'.22 B81-08855

499.9 — MINOR LANGUAGES (INCLUDING ARTIFICIAL LANGUAGES)

499'.96 — Georgian language. Syntax
Harris, Alice C.. Georgian syntax : a study in relational grammar / Alice C. Harris. — Cambridge : Cambridge University Press, 1981. — xxii,327p : ill ; 24cm. — (Cambridge studies in linguistics ; 33)
Bibliography: p309-318. — Includes index
ISBN 0-521-23584-7 : £35.00 B81-32080

500 — SCIENCE

500 — Nature *related to* culture. Sexual aspects
Nature, culture and gender / edited by Carol P. MacCormack and Marilyn Strathern. — Cambridge : Cambridge Unviersity Press, 1980. — ix,227p : ill ; 22cm
Includes bibliographies and index
ISBN 0-521-23491-3 (cased) : £12.00
ISBN 0-521-28001-x (pbk) : £3.95
Primary classification 306 B81-09919

500 — Science
Living with technology : a foundation course. — Milton Keynes : Open University Press. — (T101 ; block 1H)
At head of title: The Open University
Block 1[H]: Heat / prepared by the Course Team. — 27p : ill(some col.) ; 30cm
ISBN 0-335-08955-0 (pbk) : Unpriced (available 1982)
Also classified at 600 B81-10904

500 — Science *continuation*

Living with technology : a foundation course. — Milton Keynes : Open University Press. — (T101 ; block 1)
At head of title: The Open University
Block 1: Home / prepared by the Course Team. — 96p : ill(some col.),plans(some col.) ; 30cm
ISBN 0-335-08952-6 (pbk) : Unpriced (available 1982)
Also classified at 600 B81-10903

Living with technology : a foundation course. — Milton Keynes : Open University Press. — (T101 ; block 1N)
At head of title: The Open University
Block 1[N]: Numeracy / prepared by the Course Team. — 1979. — 68p : ill(some col.) ; 30cm
ISBN 0-335-08953-4 (pbk) : Unpriced (available 1982)
Also classified at 600 B81-10905

Living with technology : a foundation course. — Milton Keynes : Open University Press. — (T101 ; block 1SC)
At head of title: The Open University
Block 1[SC]: Space and comfort / prepared by the Course Team. — 1979. — 32p : ill(some col.),plans(some col.) ; 30cm
ISBN 0-335-08954-2 (pbk) : Unpriced (available 1982)
Also classified at 600 B81-10906

Living with technology : a foundation course. — Milton Keynes : Open University Press
At head of title: The Open University
Block 1[SM]: Structures and materials / prepared by the Course Team. — 1979. — 32p : ill(some col.) ; 30cm. — (T101 ; block 1SM)
ISBN 0-335-08956-9 (pbk) : Unpriced (available 1982)
Also classified at 600 B81-10907

Living with technology : a foundation course. — Milton Keynes : Open University Press
At head of title: The Open University
Block 2: Communication / prepared by the Course Team. — 1980. — 102p : ill(some col.) ; 30cm. — (T101 ; block 2)
ISBN 0-335-08957-7 (pbk) : Unpriced (available 1982)
Also classified at 600 B81-10908

Living with technology : a foundation course. — Milton Keynes : Open University Press
At head of title: The Open University
Block 2[E]: Electricity / prepared by the Course Team. — 1980. — 32p : ill(some col.) ; 30cm. — (T101 ; block 2E)
ISBN 0-335-08959-3 (pbk) : Unpriced (available 1982)
Also classified at 600 B81-10910

Living with technology : a foundation course. — Milton Keynes : Open University Press
At head of title: The Open University
Block 2[F]: Feedback / prepared by the Course Team. — 1980. — 25p : col.ill ; 30cm. — (T101 ; block 2F)
ISBN 0-335-08961-5 (pbk) : Unpriced (available 1982)
Also classified at 600 B81-10911

Living with technology : a foundation course. — Milton Keynes : Open University Press
At head of title: The Open University
Block 2[N]: Numeracy / prepared by the Course Team. — 1980. — 45p : ill(some col.) ; 30cm. — (T101 ; block 2N)
ISBN 0-335-08958-5 (pbk) : Unpriced (available 1982)
Also classified at 600 B81-10913

Living with technology : a foundation course. — Milton Keynes : Open University Press
At head of title: The Open University
Block 2[S]: Signals / prepared by the Course Team. — 1980. — 30p : ill(some col.) ; 30cm. — (T101 ; block 2S)
ISBN 0-335-08960-7 (pbk) : Unpriced (available 1982)
Also classified at 600 B81-10912

Living with technology : a foundation course. — Milton Keynes : Open University Press
At head of title: The Open University
Block 2[C]: Computers / prepared by the Course Team. — 1980. — 17p : ill(some col.) ; 30cm. — (T101 ; block 2C)
ISBN 0-335-08962-3 (pbk) : Unpriced (available 1982)
Also classified at 600 B81-10909

Living with technology : a foundation course. — Milton Keynes : Open University Press
At head of title: The Open University
Block 3[EC]: Energy conversion / prepared by the Course Team. — 1980. — 60p : ill(some col.) ; 30cm. — (T101 ; block 3EC)
ISBN 0-335-08965-8 (pbk) : Unpriced (available 1982)
Also classified at 600 B81-10914

Living with technology : a foundation course. — Milton Keynes : Open University Press
At head of title: The Open University
Block 4[N]: Numeracy / prepared by the Course Team. — 1980. — 44p : col.ill ; 30cm. — (T101 ; block 4N)
ISBN 0 335-08967-4 (pbk) : Unpriced (available 1982)
Also classified at 600 B81-10918

Living with technology : a foundation course. — Milton Keynes : Open University Press
At head of title: The Open University
Block 4: Resources / prepared by the Course Team. — 1980. — 107p : ill(some col.),2col.maps,1facsim ; 30cm. — (T101 ; block 4)
ISBN 0-335-08966-6 (pbk) : Unpriced (available 1982)
Also classified at 600 B81-10915

Living with technology : a foundation course. — Milton Keynes : Open University Press
At head of title: The Open University
Block 4[C]: Chemistry / prepared by the Course Team. — 1980. — 45p : ill(some col.) ; 30cm. — (T101 ; block 4C)
ISBN 0-335-08968-2 (pbk) : Unpriced (available 1982)
Also classified at 600 B81-10916

Living with technology : a foundation course. — Milton Keynes : Open University Press
At head of title: The Open University
Block 4[M]: Materials / prepared by the Course Team. — 1980. — 30p : ill(some col.) ; 30cm. — (T101 ; block 4M)
ISBN 0-335-08969-0 (pbk) : Unpriced (available 1982)
Also classified at 600 B81-10917

Living with technology : a foundation course. — Milton Keynes : Open University Press
At head of title: The Open University
Block 5[B]: Biology / prepared by the Course Team. — 1980. — 39p : ill(some col.) ; 30cm. — (T101 ; block 5B)
ISBN 0-335-08971-2 (pbk) : Unpriced (available 1982)
Also classified at 600 B81-10920

Living with technology : a foundation course. — Milton Keynes : Open University Press
At head of title: The Open University
Block 5: Food / prepared by the Course Team. — 1980. — 142 : ill(some col.),col.maps,facsims ; 30cm. — (T101 ; block 5)
ISBN 0-335-08970-4 (pbk) : Unpriced (available 1982)
Also classified at 600 B81-10919

Living with technology : a foundation course. — Milton Keynes : Open University Press
At head of title: The Open University
Block 5[C]: Chemistry / prepared by the Course Team. — 1980. — 15p : ill(some col.) ; 30cm. — (T101 ; block 5C)
ISBN 0-335-08972-0 (pbk) : Unpriced (available 1982)
Also classified at 600 B81-10921

Living with technology : a foundation course. — Milton Keynes : Open University Press
At head of title: The Open University
Block 6: Health / prepared by the Course Team. — 1980. — 120p : col.ill ; 30cm. — (T101 ; block 6)
ISBN 0-335-08973-9 (pbk) : Unpriced (available 1982)
Also classified at 600 B81-10922

Living with technology : a foundation course. — Milton Keynes : Open University Press. — (T101 ; block 6N)
At head of title: The Open University
Block 6[N]: Numeracy / prepared by the Course Team. — 48p : col.ill ; 30cm
ISBN 0-335-08974-7 (pbk) : Unpriced (available 1982)
Also classified at 600 B81-10902

Pournelle, Jerry. A step farther out / by Jerry Pournelle. — London : Star
Originally published: in 1 vol. London : W.H. Allen, 1980
Pt.1 / preface by Larry Niven ; foreword by A.E. van Vogt. — 1981, c1979. — 197p : ill ; 18cm
ISBN 0-352-30883-4 (pbk) : £1.50 B81-23584

Pournelle, Jerry. A step farther out / by Jerry Pournelle ; preface by Larry Niven ; foreword by A.E. van Vogt. — London : Star
Originally published: in 1 vol. London : W.H. Allen, 1979
Pt.2. — 1981, c1979. — 200p : ill ; 18cm
ISBN 0-352-30906-7 (pbk) : £1.50 B81-29311

Pyke, Magnus. Everyman's book of scientific facts and feats. — London : Dent, Oct.1981. — [288]p
ISBN 0-460-04540-7 : £8.95 : CIP entry
B81-28031

Vergara, William C.. Science in everyday life / William C. Vergara. — London : Souvenir, 1980. — viii,306p : ill ; 23cm
Originally published: New York : Harper & Row, 1980. — Includes index
ISBN 0-285-62470-9 : £6.95
Also classified at 600 B81-10901

500 — Science — *For Caribbean students*

Owen, Michael, *19---*. Caribbean primary science / Michael Owen. — [Glasgow] : Collins
Book 2. — [1981]. — 63p : ill,1chart ; 23cm
ISBN 0-00-317822-6 (pbk) : £1.05 B81-12165

500 — Science — *For children*

Wicks, Keith. Science can be fun. — London : Macmillan Children's Books, Feb.1982. — [32] p. — (Help yourself)
ISBN 0-333-30860-3 : £2.50 : CIP entry
B81-35783

500 — Science — *For Nigerian students*

Longman integrated science / R.O. Alabi ... [et al.]. — Harlow : Longman
Teacher's guide 2. — 1981. — 110p : ill ; 25cm
ISBN 0-582-65514-5 (pbk) : £2.00 B81-40305

Universal primary science. — Ibadan ; London : Evans
Year 6: Moving on earth / A.E. Ashworth, J.O. Ryan, J.A. Sofolahan
Teacher's guide. — 1981. — 49p ; 22cm
ISBN 0-237-50111-2 (pbk) : Unpriced
B81-37700

500 — Science — *For schools*

Henly, Randal L.. Investigating science in school / by Randal L. Henly, Anthony J. Fox, Danielle Mooney. — Tallaght : Folens, [1981]. — (Intermediate certificate)
Originally published: 1977. — Includes index
£6.60 B81-18619

Jackson, Sylvia. Introducing science / Sylvia Jackson. — Glasgow : Blackie
3: Energy. — 1980. — 32p : col.ill ; 25cm
Cover title
ISBN 0-216-90828-0 (pbk) : £1.35
ISBN 0-216-90839-6 (Teacher's guide 3/4) : £1.80 B81-07810

500 — Science — *For schools* *continuation*

Jackson, Sylvia. Introducing science / Sylvia Jackson. — Glasgow : Blackie
4: Light. — 1980. — 32p : ill(some col.) ; 25cm
Cover title
ISBN 0-216-90829-9 (pbk) : £1.35
ISBN 0-216-90839-6 (Teacher's guide 3/4) : £1.80 B81-07811

Jackson, Sylvia. Introducing science / Sylvia Jackson. — Glasgow : Blackie
Cover title
5: Change / [illustrated by Dorothy Hamilton]. — 1981. — 31p : col.ill ; 25cm
ISBN 0-216-90830-2 (pbk) : £1.35 B81-25335

Jackson, Sylvia. Introducing science / Sylvia Jackson. — Glasgow : Blackie
Cover title
6: Heat / [illustrated by Dorothy Hamilton]. — 1981. — 32p : col.ill ; 25cm
ISBN 0-216-90831-0 : £1.35 B81-25334

Jackson, Sylvia. Introducing science / Sylvia Jackson. — Glasgow : Blackie
Teacher's guide 5/6. — 1981. — 29p : ill ; 21cm
ISBN 0-216-90840-x : £1.80 B81-25333

Marchant, Don. Science : for first examinations / Don Marchant. — Edinburgh : Holmes McDougall, c1981. — 256p : ill(some col.) ; 28cm. — (Holmes McDougall science series)
Includes index
ISBN 0-7157-1991-2 (pbk) : £2.95 B81-28729

Mee, A. J.. Science 2000. — London : Heinemann Educational, Sept.1981
Book 2. — [128]p
ISBN 0-435-57567-8 (pbk) : £2.50 : CIP entry B81-22577

Ryan, Kieran. A structured course in intermediate science / Kieran Ryan. — [Dublin] : Helicon, [1981]. — 118p : ill ; 21cm
Unpriced (pbk) B81-34446

500 — Science. Manuscripts: Leonardo, *da Vinci*. **Codex Hammer** — *Critical studies*

Roberts, Jane, *1949-*. Leonardo da Vinci, the Codex Hammer, formerly the Codex Leicester / catalogue by Jane Roberts ; introduction by Carlo Pedretti. — [London] : Royal Academy of Arts, 1981. — 126p : ill,facsims ; 28cm
In slip case with: Leonardo da Vinci nature studies from the Royal Library at Windsor Castle / catalogue by Carlo Pedretti. — Bibliography: p126
ISBN 0-384-20590-9 (pbk) : Unpriced B81-36101

500 — Science. Policies of governments

Tisdell, C. A.. Science and technology policy. — London : Chapman and Hall, Oct.1981. — [250]p
ISBN 0-412-23320-7 : £12.00 : CIP entry
Also classified at 600 B81-28835

500 — Science. Projects — *For schools*

Wood, R. S.. Projects in general science / R.S. Wood ; illustrated by David and Maureen Embry. — London : Routledge & Kegan Paul, 1981. — ix,118p : ill ; 25cm. — (Secondary science series)
ISBN 0-7100-0793-0 (pbk) : £4.95 : CIP rev. B81-04324

500 — Science *related to* **belief** — *Early works*

Darwin to Einstein : primary sources on science and belief / edited by Noel G. Coley and Vance M.D. Hall. — Harlow : Longman in association with The Open University Press, 1980. — ix,358p : ill ; 23cm. — (Open University set book)
Includes index
ISBN 0-582-49158-4 (cased) : Unpriced : CIP rev.
ISBN 0-582-49159-2 (pbk) : £5.95
Primary classification 121'.6 B80-25084

500.2 — Physical sciences

Garden, Janet E.. Physical science : a basis for understanding / Janet E. Garden, Marion J. Gadsby. — Toronto ; Chichester : Wiley, 1981. — 384p : ill(some col.) ; 25cm
Includes index
ISBN 0-471-99843-5 : £8.25 B81-30793

Turk, Jonathan. Physical science : with environmental and other practical applications / Jonathan Turk, Amos Turk. — 2nd ed. — Philadelphia ; London : Saunders College, c1981. — viii,643p : ill,charts, maps ; 27cm. — (Saunders golden sunburst series)
Previous ed.: Philadelphia ; London : Saunders, 1977. — Text on lining paper. — Includes index
ISBN 0-03-057782-9 : £13.95 B81-22884

500.2 — Physical sciences. Named effects & laws — *Encyclopaedias*

Ballentyne, D. W. G.. A dictionary of named effects and laws : in chemistry, physics and mathematics / D.W.G. Ballentyne and D.R. Lovett. — 4th ed. — London : Chapman and Hall, 1980. — viii,346p : ill ; 22cm. — (Science paperbacks)
Previous ed.: 1970
ISBN 0-412-22380-5 (cased) : £15.00 : CIP rev.
ISBN 0-412-22390-2 (pbk) : £7.95 B80-08199

500.2'0246 — Physical sciences — *Questions & answers* — *For technicians*

Feeley, T. M.. Objective tests in engineering and physical science / T.M. Feeley, D.T. Rees. — Cheltenham : Thornes, 1980. — xv,92p : ill ; 23cm + sample answer sheet
ISBN 0-85950-473-5 (pbk) : £1.75 B81-12031

500.2'072041 — Physical sciences. Research in British institutions — *Directories* — *Serials*

Research in British universities, polytechnics and colleges. Vol.1, Physical sciences. — 2nd ed. (1981). — Boston Spa : RBUPC Office, British Library, c1981. — xiv,885p
Spine title: RBUPC. Vol.1, Physical sciences
ISBN 0-900220-87-2 : Unpriced
ISSN 0142-2472 B81-20726

500.5 — Space sciences - *Conference proceedings*

International Astronautical Congress *(31st : 1980 : Tokyo)*. Applications of space developments. — Oxford : Pergamon, July 1981. — [360]p
Conference papers
ISBN 0-08-026729-7 : £30.00 : CIP entry B81-17538

500.5'05 — Space sciences. Terrestrial applications — *Serials*

Advances in earth oriented applications of space technology : an international journal. — Vol.1, no.1 (1981)-. — Oxford : Pergamon, 1981-. — v. : ill,maps ; 28cm
Quarterly
Unpriced B81-11215

500.5'07 — Education. Curriculum subjects: Space science — *Serials*

Space education / publication of the British Interplanetary Society. — Vol.1, no.1 (July 1981)-. — London (27 South Lambert Rd, SW8 1S7) : The Society, 1981-. — v. : ill ; 30cm
Two issues yearly. — Supplement to: Spaceflight
ISSN 0261-1813 = Space education : Unpriced B81-39740

500.5'072 — Space sciences. Research — *Directories*

Aerospace research index : a guide to world research in aeronautics, meteorology, astronomy and space science / consultant editors A.P. Willmore and S.R. Willmore. — [Guernsey] : Hodson, c1981. — 597p ; 24cm. — (Reference on research)
Includes index
ISBN 0-582-90009-3 : Unpriced B81-08587

500.507'2 — Space sciences. Research. Use of balloons - *Conference proceedings*

Scientific ballooning - II. — Oxford : Pergamon, Apr.1981. — [274]p. — (Advances in space research ; v.1, no.11)
ISBN 0-08-028390-x : £14.50 : CIP entry B81-08934

500.9'422'74 — Hampshire. Selborne. Natural history — *Early works*

White, Gilbert. Portrait of a tortoise. — London : Virago, Sept.1981. — [64]p
Originally published: London : Chatto & Windus, 1946
ISBN 0-86068-218-8 : £3.50 : CIP entry B81-22480

501 — Philosophy of science

Giedymin, Jerzy. Science and convention. — Oxford : Pergamon, Nov.1981. — [260]p. — (Foundations & philosophy of science & technology)
ISBN 0-08-025790-9 : £12.50 : CIP entry B81-28843

Munévar, Gonzalo. Radical knowledge. — Amersham : Avebury, Sept.1981. — [144]p
ISBN 0-86127-109-2 (cased) : £12.00 : CIP entry
ISBN 0-86127-114-9 (pbk) : £5.95 B81-21553

Scientific revolutions. — Oxford : Oxford University Press, June 1981. — [180]p. — (Oxford readings in philosophy)
ISBN 0-19-875051-x (pbk) : £3.95 : CIP entry B81-08866

Smith, Peter James. Realism and the progress of science. — Cambridge : Cambridge University Press, Nov.1981. — [135]p. — (Cambridge studies in philosophy)
ISBN 0-521-23937-0 : £12.50 : CIP entry B81-32526

Wisdom, J. O.. Challengeability in modern science. — Amersham : Avebury, Dec.1981. — [240]p
ISBN 0-86127-106-8 : £16.00 : CIP entry B81-31635

501 — Philosophy of science. Theories

Stove, David Charles. Popper and after. — Oxford : Pergamon [May 1981]. — [192]p. — (Pergamon international library)
ISBN 0-08-026792-0 (cased) : £7.95 : CIP entry
ISBN 0-08-026791-2 (pbk) : £4.95 B81-07605

501 — Science — *Philosophical perspectives*

Reduction, time and reality : studies in the philosophy of the natural sciences / edited by Richard Healey. — Cambridge : Cambridge University Press, 1981. — xi,202p : ill ; 24cm
Includes bibliographies and index
ISBN 0-521-23708-4 : £12.50 : CIP rev. B81-10448

Scientific explanation. — Oxford : Clarendon, Sept.1981. — [150]p. — (Herbert Spencer lectures)
ISBN 0-19-858214-5 : £6.95 : CIP entry B81-28129

Simon, Herbert A.. The sciences of the artificial / Herbert A. Simon. — 2nd ed. — Cambridge, Mass. ; London : MIT Press, c1981. — xiii,247p : ill ; 21cm
Previous ed.: 1969. — Includes index
ISBN 0-262-19193-8 (cased) : Unpriced
ISBN 0-262-69073-x (pbk) : Unpriced B81-28445

501 — Science. Relations with belief. Theories, *ca 1800-ca 1930*

Darwin to Einstein : historical studies on science and belief / edited by Colin Chant and John Fauvel at the Open University. — Harlow : Longman in association with The Open University Press, 1980. — x,335p : ill ; 23cm
Includes index
ISBN 0-582-49156-8 (cased) : Unpriced : CIP rev.
ISBN 0-582-49157-6 (pbk) : £5.65
Primary classification 121'.6 B80-25083

501 — Science. Relations with belief. Theories, *ca 1800-ca 1930* *continuation*

Science and belief : from Darwin to Einstein. — Milton Keynes : Open University Press. — (Arts : a third level course)
At head of title: The Open University
Block 1 (Unit 1): Beliefs in science : an introduction / prepared for the Course Team by James R. Moore. — 1981. — 44p : ill,ports ; 30cm. — (A381 ; block 1(1))
Bibliography: p42-44
ISBN 0-335-11000-2 (pbk) : Unpriced
Primary classification 121′.6 B81-27594

Science and belief : from Darwin to Einstein. — Milton Keynes : Open University Press. — (Arts : a third level course)
At head of title: The Open University
Block 2: Science and metaphysics in Victorian Britain / prepared for the Course Team by James R. Moore ... [et al.]. — 1981. — 73p : ill,facsim,ports ; 30cm. — (A381 ; block II (2,3))
Includes bibliographies. — Contents: Unit 2: The metaphysics of evolution - Unit 3: Scientists and the spiritual world
ISBN 0-335-11001-0 (pbk) : Unpriced
Primary classification 121′.6 B81-13179

Science and belief : from Darwin to Einstein. — Milton Keynes : Open University Press. — (Arts : a third level course)
At head of title: The Open University
Block 3: Time, chance and thermodynamics / prepared for the Course Team by Colin A. Russell. — 1981. — 74p : ill,ports ; 30cm. — (A381 ; block 3)
Includes bibliographies. — Contents: Unit 4 : Thermodynamics and time — Unit 5 : Thermodynamics and chance
ISBN 0-335-11002-9 (pbk) : Unpriced
Primary classification 121′.6 B81-27593

501 — Science. Sexual aspects — *Philosophical perspectives*

Ruse, Michael. Is science sexist? : and other problems in the biomedical sciences / Michael Ruse. — Dordrecht ; London : Reidel, c1981. — xix,299p : ill,maps,1facsim ; 23cm. — (The University of Western Ontario series in philosophy of science ; 17)
Bibliography: p273-290. — Includes index
ISBN 90-277-1249-2 (cased) : Unpriced
ISBN 90-277-1250-6 (pbk) : Unpriced
B81-34682

501 — Science. Theories. Applications of general systems theory — *French texts*

Laszlo, Ervin. Le systémisme. — Oxford : Pergamon, Dec.1981. — [116]p
ISBN 0-08-027051-4 (pbk) : £4.50 : CIP entry
B81-31720

501 — Science. Theories. Development, *to 1979 — Philosophical perspectives*

Krige, John. Science, revolution and discontinuity / John Krige. — Brighton : Harvester, 1980. — 231p ; 23cm. — (Harvester studies in philosophy ; 10)
Bibliography: p221-228. — Includes index
ISBN 0-85527-625-8 : £18.95 : CIP rev.
B80-13787

501 — Science. Theories of Marxists

Nowak, Leszek. The structure of idealization : towards a systematic interpretation of the Marxian idea of science / by Leszek Nowak. — Dordrecht ; London : Reidel, c1980. — xi,277p : ill ; 23cm. — (Synthese library ; v.139)
Bibliography: p266-271. - Includes index
ISBN 90-277-1014-7 : Unpriced B81-06110

501 — Science. Theories, *to ca 1950 — Philosophical perspectives — Conference proceedings*

Probabilistic thinking, thermodynamics and the interaction of the history and philosophy of science : proceedings of the 1978 Pisa conference on the history and philosophy of science, vol.II / edited by Jaakko Hintikka, David Gruender and Evandro Agazzi. — Dordrecht ; London : Reidel, c1981. — xiv,326p ; 23cm. — (Synthese library ; v.146)
Includes bibliographies and index
ISBN 90-277-1127-5 : Unpriced B81-20763

Theory change, ancient axiomatics, and Galileo's methodology : proceedings of the 1978 Pisa conference on the history and philosophy of science, vol.1 / edited by Jaakko Hintikka, David Gruender and Evandro Agazzi. — Dordrecht ; London : Reidel, c1981. — xiv,354p ; 23cm. — (Synthese library ; v.145)
Includes bibliographies and index
ISBN 90-277-1126-7 : Unpriced B81-16462

501 — Scientific knowledge — *Sociological perspectives*

Knorr-Cetina, Karin D.. The manufacture of knowledge : an essay on the constructivist and contextual nature of science / by Karin D. Knorr-Cetina ; preface by Rom Harré. — Oxford : Pergamon, 1981. — xiv,189p : ill,facsims ; 26cm
Bibliography: p173-181. — Includes index
ISBN 0-08-025777-1 : £12.50 B81-38279

501 — Western Europe. Science. Theories, *1200-1600*

Grant, Edward. Studies in medieval science and natural philosophy / Edward Grant. — London : Variorum Reprints, 1981. — 378p in various pagings : ill,1facsim,1port ; 24cm. — (Collected studies series ; CS142)
Facsimile reprints of: 16 articles originally published between 1962 and 1979. — Includes index
ISBN 0-86078-089-9 : £24.00 : CIP rev.
B81-21526

501′.8 — Science. Methodology

Wójcicki, Ryszard. Topics in the formal methodology of empirical sciences / Ryszard Wójcicki ; [translated from Polish by Ewa Jansen]. — Dordrecht ; London : Reidel, c1979. — 290p ; 23cm. — (Synthese library ; v.135)
Translation of: Metodologia fomalna nauk empirycznych. — Bibliography: p275-279. — Includes index
ISBN 90-277-1004-x : Unpriced B81-03518

501′.8 — Science. Methodology — *Philosophical perspectives*

Feyerabend, Paul K.. Philosophical papers. — Cambridge : Cambridge University Press
Vol.1: Realism, rationalism and scientific method. — Sept.1981. — [354]p
ISBN 0-521-22897-2 : £22.50 : CIP entry
B81-25775

Feyerabend, Paul K.. Philosophical papers. — Cambridge : Cambridge University Press
Vol.2: Problems of empiricism. — Sept.1981. — [256]p
ISBN 0-521-23964-8 : £17.50 : CIP entry
B81-25774

502′.3 — Science. Research — *Career guides*

Medawar, P. B.. Advice to a young scientist / P.B. Medawar. — London : Pan, 1981, c1979. — xiii,109p ; 20cm. — (Pan scientific affairs)
Originally published: London : Harper & Row, 1979. — Includes index
ISBN 0-330-26325-0 (pbk) : £1.50 B81-19695

502′.469 — Science — *For building construction*

Basic building craft science / Alf Fulcher ... [et al.]. — London : Granada, 1981. — 164p : ill ; 23cm. — (Granada building crafts series)
Includes index
ISBN 0-246-11223-9 : Unpriced
ISBN 0-246-11265-4 (pbk) B81-24461

502′.8 — Science. Laboratory techniques — *For schools*

Beginning science. — St. Albans : Hart-Davis Educational, 1981, c1980. — 31p : ill ; 21cm. — (Centre science)
ISBN 0-247-13139-3 (unbound) : £0.40
B81-24295

502′.8′2 — Microscopes. Use

Marmasse, Claude. Microscopes and their uses / Claude Marmasse. — New York ; London : Gordon and Breach, c1980. — xiii,329p : ill ; 24cm
Bibliography: p321-322. — Includes index
ISBN 0-677-05510-2 : Unpriced B81-02299

502′.8′25 — Electron microscopy — *Conference proceedings*

Electron microscopy and analysis, 1981. — Bristol : Institute of Physics, Jan.1982. — [560] p. — (Conference series / Institute of Physics, ISSN 0305-2346 ; no.61)
ISBN 0-85498-152-7 : £34.00 : CIP entry
B81-34575

502′.8′25 — High resolution electron microscopy

Spence, John C. H.. Experimental high-resolution electron microscopy / John C.H. Spence. — Oxford : Clarendon Press, 1981. — xii,370p : ill ; 23cm. — (Monographs on the physics and chemistry of materials)
Includes bibliographies and index
ISBN 0-19-851365-8 : £35.00 : CIP rev.
B80-01166

502′.8′25 — Scanning electron microscopy — *Conference proceedings*

Scanned image microscopy / edited by Eric A. Ash. — London : Academic Press, 1980. — xv,461p : ill,1port ; 24cm. — (The Rank Prize Funds opto-electronic biennial symposia ; 1980)
Includes bibliographies and index
ISBN 0-12-065180-7 : £20.40 : CIP rev.
B80-29555

502′.8′51 — Science. Applications of systems analysis

Mattessich, Richard. Instrumental reasoning and systems methodology : an epistemology of the applied and social sciences / Richard Mattessich. — Dordrecht ; London : Reidel, c1978. — xxii,396p : ill ; 23cm. — (Theory and decision library ; v.15)
Bibliography: p324-352. - Includes index
ISBN 90-277-0837-1 (cased) : Unpriced
ISBN 90-277-1081-3 (pbk) : Unpriced
B81-05646

503′.21 — Science — *Encyclopaedias*

Godman, A.. Longman illustrated science dictionary : all fields of scientific language explained and illustrated / Arthur Godman. — Harlow : Longman, 1981. — 256p : col.ill ; 20cm
Ill on lining papers. — Includes index
ISBN 0-582-55645-7 : £2.95 B81-39653

503′.21 — Science — *Encyclopaedias — For children*

Kerrod, Robin. Purnell's first dictionary of science / written by Robin Kerrod ; illustrated by Bryan Foster. — Maidenhead : Purnell, c1981. — 61p : col.ill ; 30cm
ISBN 0-361-05057-7 : £3.99 B81-26342

503′.31 — Science - *German-English dictionaries*

Dorian, A. F.Dictionary of science and technology : German-English. — 2nd rev. ed. — Oxford : Elsevier Scientific, Aug.1981. — [1250]p
ISBN 0-444-41997-7 : CIP entry
Also classified at 603′.31 B81-16866

505 — Science — *Serials*

General science journal. — Vol.1, no.1 (Mar. 1978). — [Warrington] ([32 Beechwood Ave., Padgate, Warrington, Cheshire) : Newart Visual Aids, 1978. — 1v. ; 30cm
One issue only published
Unpriced B81-09135

McGraw-Hill yearbook of science and technology . — 1980. — New York ; London : McGraw-Hill, c1981. — 433p
ISBN 0-07-045488-4 : Unpriced
Also classified at 605 B81-34063

505 — Science - *Serials*

Royal Institution of Great Britain. Proceedings of the Royal Institution of Great Britain. — Vol.53 (1981). — Northwood : Science Reviews, Aug.1981. — 1v.
ISBN 0-905927-71-0 (pbk) : £16.50 : CIP entry
B81-19124

506′.041 — Great Britain. Science. Organisations: British Association for the Advancement of Science, *to 1900*

Morrell, Jack. Gentleman of science : early years of the British Association for the Advancement of Science / Jack Morrell & Arnold Thackray. — Oxford : Clarendon, 1981. — xxiii,592p,[16]p of plates : ill,2facsims,ports ; 24cm
Ill on lining papers. — Bibliography: p559-573. — Includes index
ISBN 0-19-858163-7 : £30.00 : CIP rev. B81-13873

506′.041 — Great Britain. Science. Organisations: British Association for the Advancement of Science, *to 1981*

The **Parliament** of science. — London : Science Reviews, Aug.1981. — 1v.
ISBN 0-905927-66-4 (pbk) : £12.25 : CIP entry B81-18057

506′.041 — Great Britain. Science. Organisations: Royal Society — *Serials*

Royal Society. Royal Society News. — Issue 1 (Jan.1980)-. — London : Information Department of the Royal Society, 1980-. — v. : ill ; 30cm
Six issues yearly. — Description based on: Issue 4 (July 1980)
ISSN 0260-2725 = Royal Society news : Free B81-04636

Royal Society. The Year book of the Royal Society of London. — 1981. — London : Royal Society, [1981]. — 339p
ISBN 0-85403-154-5 : Unpriced B81-20723

506′.041 — Great Britain. Young scientists. Organisations: BAYS, *to 1979*

Tribute to BAYS, 1969-1979 : a special issue of BAYSNEWS. — London : British Association for the Advancement of Science, [1980?]. — 84p : ill,ports ; 22cm
Cover title
£2.00 (pbk) B81-39278

507 — Physics teachers. Professional education

Davies, Brian. The education and training of physics teachers worldwide. — London : Murray, Dec.1981. — [256]p
ISBN 0-7195-3922-6 (pbk) : £4.90 : CIP entry B81-33872

507 — Science. Information sources — *Conference proceedings*

International CODATA Conference *(7th : 1980 : Kyoto)*. Data for science and technology : proceedings of the Seventh International, CODATA Conference Kyoto, Japan, 8-11 October 1980 : at the invitation of the Science Council of Japan, the Chemical Society of Japan and the Japan Society for CODATA / edited by Phyllis S. Glaeser. — Oxford : Pergamon, 1981. — xxii,615p : ill(some col.),maps,1port ; 31cm
Festschrift in honour of Professor Takehiko Shimanouchi. — Includes bibliographies and index
ISBN 0-08-026201-5 : £62.50 : CIP rev.
Also classified at 607 B81-12314

507 — Science. Information sources — *Manuals*

Davidge, R.. The use of scientific information services / R. Davidge and E.R. Wooding. — 4th ed. — [Englefield Green] ([Englefield Green, Surrey]) : Royal Holloway College Library and Physics Department, 1980. — 43p : 1ill ; 30cm
Cover title. — Previous ed.: 1978. — Includes index
£2.00 (spiral) B81-02024

507′.1 — Schools. Curriculum subjects: Science. Teaching

Solomon, Joan, *1932-*. Teaching children in the laboratory / Joan Solomon. — London : Croom Helm, c1980. — 156p : ill ; 22cm
Includes index
ISBN 0-7099-2304-x (cased) : £9.95 : CIP rev.
ISBN 0-7099-2305-8 (pbk) : £5.50 B80-13356

507′.10171241 — Commonwealth countries. Educational institutions. Curriculum subjects: Science. Teaching — *Serials*

CASME journal. — Vol.1, no.1 (Nov. & Dec. 1980)-. — London (36 Craven St., WC2N 5NG) : Junior Club Publications for the Commonwealth Association of Science and Mathematics Educators, 1980-. — v. : ill ; 30cm
Three issues yearly. — Continues: Science teacher (London)
ISSN 0261-5916 = CASME journal (corrected) : £3.57 per year B81-31564

507′.10174927 — Arab countries. Schools. Curriculum subjects: Science. Teaching

Arrayed, J. E.. A critical analysis of school science teaching in Arab countries / J.E. Arrayed. — London : Longman, 1980. — viii,254p : ill,forms ; 23
Includes an appendix in Arabic
ISBN 0-582-78317-8 : £11.75 B81-05918

507′.1017671 — Islamic countries. Educational institutions. Curriculum subjects: Science. Teaching — *Islamic viewpoints*

Social and natural sciences : the Islamic perspective / edited by Isma′il R. Al-Faruqi and Abdullah Omar Nasseef. — [London] : Hodder and Stoughton, 1981. — viii,177p ; 24cm. — (Islamic education series)
Conference papers
ISBN 0-340-23613-2 : £6.95 : CIP rev.
Primary classification 300′.7′1017671 B80-11317

507′.1042 — England. Schools. Curriculum subjects: Science

Ingle, Richard. Science in schools : which way now? / Richard Ingle and Arthur Jennings ; foreword by Sir Norman Lindop. — London : University of London Institute of Education, 1981. — 185p : ill ; 22cm. — (Studies in education (new series), ISSN 0458-2101 ; 8)
Includes index
ISBN 0-85473-100-8 (pbk) : Unpriced B81-33327

507′.1042 — England. Schools. Curriculum subjects: Science. Choice. Equality of opportunity — *Case studies*

Everley, Barry. We can do it now! : (ages 4-16) : a report on some good practices in science, technology and crafts in schools / by Barry Everley. — Manchester : Equal Opportunities Commission
Part 1. — Manchester : Equal Opportunities Commission. — 41p : ill ; 22cm
ISBN 0-905829-43-3 (pbk) : Unpriced B81-39680

507′.11′42132 — London. Westminster *(London Borough)*. **Universities. Colleges: Imperial College of Science and Technology** — *Serials*

Imperial College of Science and Technology. Calendar / Imperial College of Science and Technology. — 1980-81. — London : The College, c1980. — v,628p
Unpriced B81-06823

507′.11422 — London & Home Counties. Higher education institutions. Curriculum subjects: Science. Courses — *Serials*

[Science education in the region *(London and Home Counties Regional Advisory Council for Technological Education)*]. Science education in the region / London and Home Counties Regional Advisory Council for Technological Education. — 1981/83. — London : The Council, 1981. — [26]p
ISBN 0-85394-084-3 : £0.70 B81-36305

507′.12 — Middle schools & secondary schools. Curriculum subjects: Science. Teaching

Simpson, Ronald D.. Science, students, and schools : a guide for the middle and secondary school teacher / Ronald D. Simpson, Norman D. Anderson. — New York ; Chichester : Wiley, c1981. — xiii,558p : ill,forms ; 25cm
Bibliography: p520-523. — Includes index
ISBN 0-471-02477-5 : £10.50 B81-23320

507′.12 — Secondary schools. Curriculum subjects: Science. Resource-based activities

Foster, Don. Resource-based learning in science / Don Foster with contributions from Philip Walker, Geoffrey Crabb, Bill Harrison ; illustrations by Anne Blevins ... [et al.]. — Hatfield (College La., Hatfield, Herts) : Association for Science Education, c1979. — 121p : ill ; 30cm. — (Study series / Association for Science Education ; no.14)
Bibliography: p118-121. — Includes index
ISBN 0-902786-52-0 (pbk) : £1.75 B81-10733

507′.1241 — Great Britain. Secondary schools. Curriculum subjects: Science — *For teaching*

Teacher′s guide 1 / general editors Colin Terry and Tony Loosmore. — St. Albans : Hart-Davis Educational, 1981. — 29p ; 22cm. — (Centre science)
Cover title
ISBN 0-247-13185-7 (pbk) : £0.95 B81-39610

507′.1241 — Great Britain. Secondary schools. Mixed ability groups. Curriculum subjects: Science. Teaching. Implications of assessment of cognitive development of students

Shayer, Michael. Towards a science of science teaching : cognitive development and curriculum demand / Michael Shayer and Philip Adey. — London : Heinemann Educational, 1981. — xii,159p : ill ; 22cm
Bibliography: p152-155. - Includes index
ISBN 0-435-57825-1 (pbk) : £3.95 B81-09526

507′.1241 — Great Britain. Secondary schools. Students: Girls. Curriculum subjects: Science

The **Missing** half : girls and science education / edited by Alison Kelly. — Manchester : Manchester University Press, c1981. — x,320p : ill,2facsims ; 22cm
Includes bibliographies and index
ISBN 0-7190-0831-x (cased) : Unpriced : CIP rev.
ISBN 0-7190-0753-4 (pbk) : £6.95 B81-08036

507′.124252 — Nottinghamshire. Secondary schools. Curriculum subjects: Science. Teaching

Brown, Peter, *1934-*. Organisation of science teaching in the age group 11-14 in Nottinghamshire schools / Peter Brown and David Lomax. — [Nottingham] ([University Park, Nottingham NG7 2RD]) : University of Nottingham School of Education, 1980. — 37,[11]p ; 30cm
Bibliography: p37
ISBN 0-85359-078-8 (spiral) : Unpriced B81-11520

507′.2 — Science. Historiography, *1700-1800*

The **Ferment** of knowledge : studies in the historiography of eighteenth-century science / edited by G.S. Rousseau and Roy Porter. — Cambridge : Cambridge University Press, 1980. — xiii,500p ; 24cm
Includes index
ISBN 0-521-22599-x : £25.00 : CIP rev. B80-36032

507′.2041 — Great Britain. *Science Research Council* — *Serials*

Great Britain. *Science Research Council*. Report of the Council for the year ... / Science Research Council. — 1979-80. — London : H.M.S.O., [1980]. — 115p
ISBN 0-10-027909-0 : £7.10 B81-11760

507′.2041 — Science. Research in British Institutions — *Directories*

Research in British universities, polytechnics and colleges : Vol.2, Biological sciences. — 2nd ed. (1981). — Boston Spa (RBUPC Office, British Library Lending Division, Boston Spa, Wetherby, W.Yorks., LS23 7B9) : British Library, June 1981. — [655]p
ISBN 0-900220-88-0 (pbk) : £20.00 : CIP entry
ISSN 0143-0734
Also classified at 300′.7′2041 B81-13546

507′.20417 — Science. Research in Irish higher education institutions — *Directories*

Colgan, John, *1939-*. Science and engineering in Irish higher education : a directory of the research and professional interests of personnel in the science and technology departments of Irish colleges / John Colgan and Brendan Finucane. — Dublin (Shelbourne House, Shelbourne Rd., Dublin 4) : National Board for Science and Technology, 1981. — iv,111p in various pagings ; 30cm
Includes index
ISBN 0-86282-002-2 (pbk) : Unpriced
Also classified at 607′.2′417 B81-23238

507′.2042132 — London. Westminster *(London Borough)*. **Universities. Colleges: Imperial College of Science and Technology. Research projects** — *Serials*

Imperial College of Science and Technology. Research report / Imperial College of Science and Technology, University of London. — 1977-80. — [London] : [The College], [1981?]. — [x],331p
ISSN 0307-885x : Unpriced B81-31033

507′.24 — Science. Experiments, *to ca 1975*

Harré, Rom. Great scientific experiments : 20 experiments that changed our view of the world / Rom Harré. — Oxford : Phaidon, 1981. — 222p : ill,facsims,ports ; 26cm
Includes bibliographies and index
ISBN 0-7148-2096-2 : £8.95 B81-36514

507′.24 — Science. Research. Use of laboratory animals

Animals in research : new perspectives in animal experimentation / edited by David Sperlinger. — Chichester : Wiley, c1981. — x,373p : ill ; 24cm
Includes bibliographies and index
ISBN 0-471-27843-2 : £16.50 B81-21696

507′.24 — Science. Research. Use of laboratory animals — *Serials*

FRAME technical news. — No.1 (June 1979)-. — London (312a Worple Rd, Wimbledon, SW20 8QU) : Fund for the Replacement of Animals in Medical Experiments, 1979-. — v. : ill ; 30cm
Two issues yearly. — Description based on: No.4 (Mar.1981)
ISSN 0143-8352 = FRAME technical news : Unpriced B81-33936

507′.24 — Testing laboratories. Accreditation — *Serials*

ILAC : international directory of laboratory accreditation systems and other schemes for assessment of testing laboratories : répertoire international des organisations d′essais et des systèmes d′agrément de laboratoires d′essais : directorio internacional de sistemas d′acreditamiento de laboratorios y otras disposiciones para el reconocimiento de pruebas. — 1981-. — London (37 Queen Sq., WC1N 3BL) : IMSWORLD Publications, 1981-. — v. ; 30cm
ISSN 0262-0995 = ILAC. International Laboratory Accreditation Conference : Unpriced B81-37248

507′.6 — Science — *Exercises, worked examples — For technicians*

Browning, D. R.. Science facts and formulae for TEC courses. — London : Longman, Dec.1981. — [24]p
ISBN 0-582-41234-x (pbk) : £0.80 : CIP entry B81-31822

507′.6 — Science — *Questions & answers — For schools*

O′Dea, John. Objective tests in science : to intermediate level / John O′Dea. — Dublin : Folens, c1979. — 120p : ill ; 25cm. — (Folens objective tests)
ISBN 0-86121-064-6 (pbk) : Unpriced B81-19425

Perkins, E. J. (Elizabeth Joan). Integrated science / by E.J. Perkins ; general editor A.J.B. Robertson. — Walton-on-Thames : Celtic Revision Aids, 1981. — 73p : ill ; 19cm. — (Model answers O Level)
ISBN 0-17-751123-0 (pbk) : £1.10 B81-12661

Perkins, E. J. (Elizabeth Joan). Integrated science / E.J. Perkins ; general editor A.J.B. Robertson. — Walton-on-Thames : Celtic Revision Aids, 1981. — 106p : ill ; 19cm. — (Multiple choice O Level)
ISBN 0-17-751191-5 (pbk) : £1.10 B81-12662

507′.8 — Education. Curriculum subjects: Science. Teaching aids: Games & simulations

Ellington, Henry. Games and simulations in science education / Henry Ellington, Eric Addinall and Fred Percival. — London : Kogan Page, 1981. — 216p : ill ; 23cm
Bibliography: p209-211. — Includes index
ISBN 0-85038-338-2 : £10.95 B81-08122

507′.9 — Ireland *(Republic)*. **Scientists. Awards** — *Directories*

Gillick, Mary. Fellowships and scholarships available to Irish scientists and technologists / compiled by Mary Gillick. — Dublin (Shelbourne House, Shelbourne Rd., Dublin 4) : National Board for Science and Technology, c1981. — vii,105p ; 21cm
Includes index
ISBN 0-86282-004-9 (pbk) : £1.00
Also classified at 607′.39 B81-23161

508.3164 — Pacific Ocean. Scientific expeditions. Voyages by ships, *1768-1771:* **Endeavour** *(Ship) — Correspondence, diaries, etc.*

Banks, *Sir* **Joseph**. The journal of Joseph Banks in the Endeavour / with a commentary by A.M. Lysaght. — Guildford : Genesis in association with Rigby, 1980. — 2v. : ill,1map,facsims,ports ; 25cm
Facsim of ms, in Mitchell Library. Sydney. - Limited ed. of 500 numbered copies. — Includes index
ISBN 0-904351-05-x : £230.00
ISBN 0-904351-03-3 (Vol.1)
ISBN 0-904351-04-1 (Vol.2) B81-18985

508.7 — America. Pacific coastal regions. Spanish scientific expeditions, *1787-1803*

Engstrand, Iris H. W.. Spanish scientists in the new world : the eighteenth-century expeditions / Iris H.W. Engstrand. — Seattle ; London : University of Washington Press, c1981. — xiv,220p,[38]p of plates : ill(some col.),maps,plans,ports ; 24cm
Bibliography: p200-209. — Includes index
ISBN 0-295-95764-6 : Unpriced B81-39805

509 — SCIENCE. HISTORICAL AND GEOGRAPHICAL TREATMENT

509 — Science. Creativity, *to 1979*

Judson, Horace Freeland. The search for solutions / Horace Freeland Judson ; introduction by Lewis Thomas. — London : Hutchinson, c1980. — ix,211p : ill(some col.),facsims,maps(some col.),music,ports(some col.) ; 23x28cm
Originally published: New York : Holt, Rinehart and Winston, 1980. — Bibliography: p205. — Includes index
ISBN 0-09-141700-7 : £7.95 : CIP rev. B80-13358

509 — Science, *to 1979*

Sagan, Carl. Cosmos / Carl Sagan. — London : Macdonald Futura, 1981, c1980. — xvi,365p : ill(some col.),maps,facsims(some col.),ports (some col.) ; 27cm
Originally published: New York : Random House, c1980. — Bibliography: p350-355. - Includes index
ISBN 0-354-04531-8 : £12.50 B81-15197

509 — Science, *to 1980 — Festschriften*

The **Analytic** spirit : essays in the history of science in honor of Henry Guerlac / edited by Harry Woolf. — Ithaca ; London : Cornell University Press, 1981. — 363p : ill,1port ; 25cm
Includes index
ISBN 0-8014-1350-8 : £15.00 B81-36458

509′.2′2 — France. Science. Organisations: Académie des sciences. Members. Eulogies, *1699-1791 — Critical studies*

Paul, Charles B.. Science and immortality : the éloges of the Paris Academy of Sciences (1699-1791) / Charles B. Paul. — Berkeley ; London : University of California Press, c1980. — x,202p ; 24cm
Bibliography: p181-197. - Includes index
ISBN 0-520-03986-6 : £11.75 B81-06932

509′.2′2 — Great Britain. Science — *Biographies — Serials*

Who′s who of British scientists. — 3rd ed. (1980/81). — Dorking (Executive House, 136 South St., Dorking, Surrey) : Simon Books, 1980. — xv,589p
ISBN 0-86229-001-5 : £27.50 B81-09232

509′.2′4 — Science. Darwin, Erasmus — *Correspondence, diaries, etc*

Darwin, Erasmus. The letters of Erasmus Darwin. — Cambridge : Cambridge University Press, Aug.1981. — [364]p
ISBN 0-521-23706-8 : £45.00 : CIP entry B81-20504

509′.2′4 — Science. Galilei, Galileo — *Biographies*

Drake, Stillman. Galileo / Stillman Drake. — Oxford : Oxford University Press, 1980. — 100p ; 19cm. — (Past masters)
Bibliography: p94-96. - Includes index
ISBN 0-19-287527-2 (cased) : £4.50 : CIP rev.
ISBN 0-19-287526-4 (pbk) : £0.95 B80-23201

Suggett, Martin. Galileo and the birth of modern science / Martin Suggett. — Hove : Wayland, 1981. — 72p : ill,ports ; 25cm. — (Pioneers of science and discovery)
Bibliography: p70. — Includes index
ISBN 0-85340-821-1 : £3.95 B81-37695

509′.2′4 — Science. Hales, Stephen — *Biographies*

Allan, D. G. C.. Stephen Hales : scientist and philanthropist / D.G.C. Allan and R.E. Schofield. — London : Scolar Press, 1980. — 220p ; 25cm
Bibliography: p202-215. - Includes index
ISBN 0-85967-482-7 : £17.50 : CIP rev. B80-07337

509′.2′4 — Science. Krebs, Hans — *Biographies*

Krebs, Hans. Reminiscences and reflections. — Oxford : Clarendon Press, Sept.1981. — [250]p
ISBN 0-19-854702-1 : £10.00 : CIP entry B81-21606

509′.2′4 — Science. Pyke, Magnus — *Biographies*

Pyke, Magnus. The six lives of Pyke / Magnus Pyke. — London : Dent, 1981. — 213p,[8]p of plates : ill,ports ; 22cm
ISBN 0-460-04542-3 : £5.95 : CIP rev. B81-25860

509′.2′4 — Science. Theories of Galilei, Galileo. Influence of scientific theories, *1250-1600*

Wallace, William A. (William Augustine). Prelude to Galileo : essays on medieval and sixteenth-century sources of Galileo′s thought / William A. Wallace. — Dordrecht ; London : Reidel, c1981. — xvi,369p ; 23cm. — (Boston studies in the philosophy of science ; v.62)
Bibliography: p349-357. - Includes index
ISBN 90-277-1215-8 (cased) : Unpriced
ISBN 90-277-1216-6 (pbk) : Unpriced B81-20832

509′.2′4 — Science. Theories of Leonardo, *da Vinci*

Zammattio, Carlo. Leonardo the scientist / Carlo Zammattio, Augusto Marinoni, Anna Maria Brizio. — London : Hutchinson, 1981, c1980. — 192p : ill(some col.),col.maps,facsims,ports ; 22cm
Includes index
ISBN 0-09-142651-0 : £4.95 B81-32444

509′.38 — Ancient Greece. Science, *B.C.600-A.D.199*

Farrington, Benjamin. Greek science : its meaning for us / Benjamin Farrington. — Nottingham : Spokesman, 1980. — 320p : ill ; 22cm
Originally published: in 2 vols. Harmondsworth : Penguin, 1944, 1949. — Includes bibliographies and index
ISBN 0-85124-287-1 (cased) : Unpriced
ISBN 0-85124-288-x (pbk) : £4.50 B81-14735

509′.4 — Europe. Science, *1500-1600*
Schmitt, Charles B.. Studies in Renaissance philosophy and science / Charles B. Schmitt. — London : Variorum Reprints, 1981. — 342p in various pagings : ill,1port ; 24cm. — (Collected studies series ; CS146)
Includes 1 paper in Italian and 1 in French. — Includes index
ISBN 0-86078-093-7 : £24.00 : CIP rev.
Primary classification 190′.9′031 B81-21551

509′.4 — Western Europe. Science, *ca 1785-1850 — Conference proceedings*
Epistemological and social problems of the sciences in the early nineteenth century / edited by H.N. Jahnke and M. Otte. — Dordrecht ; London : Reidel, c1981. — xlii,430p ; 25cm
Conference papers. — Includes bibliographies and index
ISBN 90-277-1223-9 : Unpriced B81-14061

509′.41 — Great Britain. Science. Policies of government
Budworth, D. W.. Public science — private view / D. W. Budworth. — Bristol : Hilger, c1981. — xv,183p : ill ; 23cm
ISBN 0-85274-449-8 (cased) : £9.95 : CIP rev.
ISBN 0-85274-452-8 (pbk) : £5.95 B81-08882

509′.51 — China. Science, *to ca 1800*
Ronan, Colin A.. The shorter Science and civilisation in China. — Cambridge : Cambridge University Press
Vol.2. — Nov.1981. — [480]p
ISBN 0-521-23582-0 : £15.00 : CIP entry
Also classified at 609′.51 B81-31189

509′.73 — United States. Science. Policies of government
Science, technology, and national policy / edited by Thomas J. Kuehn, Alan L. Porter. — Ithaca ; London : Cornell University Press, 1981. — 530p ; 24cm
Bibliography: p515-524. — Includes index
ISBN 0-8014-1343-5 (cased) : £21.00
ISBN 0-8014-9876-7 (pbk) : Unpriced
Also classified at 609′.73 B81-27263

510 — MATHEMATICS

510 — Applied mathematics
Handbook of applicable mathematics / chief editor Walter Ledermann. — Chichester : Wiley
Vol.2: Probability / Emlyn Lloyd. — 1980. — xix,450p : ill ; 25cm
Bibliography: p439-442. — Includes index
ISBN 0-471-27821-1 : £27.50 : CIP rev.
B80-20574

Handbook of applicable mathematics / chief editor Walter Ledermann. — Chichester : Wiley
Vol.3: Numerical methods / edited by Robert F. Churchhouse. — c1981. — xvii,565p : ill ; 25cm
Includes bibliographies and index
ISBN 0-471-27947-1 : £27.50 : CIP rev.
B81-25894

510 — Applied mathematics — *Festschriften*
Special topics of applied mathematics : functional analysis, numerical analysis and optimization : proceedings of the seminar held at the GMD, Bonn, 8-10 October, 1979 / dedicated to Heinz Unger ; managing editors J. Frehse, D. Pallaschke, U. Trottenberg. — Amsterdam ; Oxford : North-Holland, 1980. — viii,248p : ill ; 23cm
Includes bibliographies
ISBN 0-444-86035-5 : £17.69
Also classified at 515.7 ; 519.4 ; 515
B81-03637

510 — Applied mathematics — *For schools*
Plumpton, Charles. New tertiary mathematics / C. Plumpton, P.S.W. MacIlwaine. — Oxford : Pergamon. — (Pergamon international library)
Vol.2
Includes index
Pt. 2: Further applied mathematics. — 1981. — p231-452,xiip : ill ; 25cm
ISBN 0-08-025037-8 (cased) : Unpriced : CIP rev.
ISBN 0-08-025026-2 (pbk) : £6.90
ISBN 0-08-025036-x (pbk : non-net) : Unpriced
ISBN 0-08-021646-3 (set) : Unpriced
B80-18677

510 — Mathematics
Balla, M. Y.. Basic mathematics / M.Y. Balla, R.A. Zepp. — London : Macmillan, 1981. — vii,199p : ill ; 25cm. — (Macmillan intermediate student texts)
ISBN 0-333-30557-4 (pbk) : £3.15 B81-22252

Devlin, Keith J.. Sets, functions and logic. — London : Chapman and Hall, Apr.1981. — [96]p
ISBN 0-412-22660-x : £6.00 : CIP entry
ISBN 0-412-22670-7 (pbk) : £2.95 B81-02370

Introduction to pure mathematics. — Milton Keynes : Open University Press. — (Mathematics : a second level course)
At head of title: The Open University
Unit 2: Introduction II, maps and flows / prepared by the Course Team. — New ed. — 1980. — 47p : ill(some col.) ; 30cm. — (M203 ; 2)
Previous ed.: 1979. — Includes index
ISBN 0-335-05791-8 (pbk) : Unpriced
B81-11348

Introduction to pure mathematics. — Milton Keynes : Open University Press. — (Mathematics : a second level course)
At head of title: The Open University
Unit 3: Geometry I, plane geometry / prepared by the Course Team. — New ed. — 1980. — 66p : ill(some col.) ; 30cm. — (M203 ; 3)
Previous ed.: 1979. — Includes index
ISBN 0-335-05792-6 (pbk) : Unpriced
B81-11352

Introduction to pure mathematics. — Milton Keynes : Open University Press. — (Mathematics : a second level course)
At head of title: The Open University
Unit 4: Group theory I, groups and subgroups / prepared by the Course Team. — New ed. — 1980. — 59p : ill(some col.) ; 30cm. — (M203 ; 4)
Previous ed.: 1979. — Includes index
ISBN 0-335-05794-2 (pbk) : Unpriced
B81-13183

Introduction to pure mathematics. — Milton Keynes : Open University Press. — (Mathematics : a second level course)
At head of title: The Open University
Unit 5: Linear algebra I, linear independence and bases / prepared by the Course Team. — New ed. — 1980. — 57p : ill(some col.) ; 30cm. — (M203 ; 5)
Previous ed.: 1979. — Includes index
ISBN 0-335-05793-4 (pbk) : Unpriced
B81-11351

Introduction to pure mathematics. — Milton Keynes : Open University Press. — (Mathematics : a second level course)
At head of title: The Open University
Unit 7: Linear algebra II, matrices / prepared by the Course Team. — New ed. — 1980. — 58p : ill(some col.) ; 30cm. — (M203 ; 7)
Previous ed.: 1979. — Includes index
ISBN 0-335-05796-9 (pbk) : Unpriced
B81-11353

Introduction to pure mathematics. — Milton Keynes : Open University Press. — (Mathematics : a second level course)
At head of title: The Open University
Unit 8: Analysis I, the real numbers and other number systems / prepared by the Course Team. — New ed. — 1980. — 64p : ill(some col.) ; 30cm. — (M203 ; 8)
Previous ed.: 1979. — Includes index
ISBN 0-335-05935-x (pbk) : Unpriced
B81-11354

Introduction to pure mathematics. — Milton Keynes : Open University Press. — (Mathematics : a second level course)
At head of title: The Open University
Unit 9: Analysis II, functions and continuity / prepared by the Course Team. — New ed. — 1980. — 54p : ill(some col.) ; 30cm. — (M203 ; 9)
Previous ed.: 1979. — Includes index
ISBN 0-335-05936-8 (pbk) : Unpriced
B81-11350

Introduction to pure mathematics. — Milton Keynes : Open University Press. — (Mathematics : a second level course)
At head of title: The Open University
Unit 10: Analysis III, properties of continuous functions / prepared by the Course Team. — New ed. — 1980. — 52p : ill(some col.) ; 30cm. — (M203 ; 10)
Previous ed.: 1979. — Includes index
ISBN 0-335-05937-6 (pbk) : Unpriced
B81-11349

Introduction to pure mathematics. — Milton Keynes : Open University Press. — (Mathematics : a second level course)
At head of title: The Open University
Unit 11: Linear algebra III, linear equations / prepared by the Course Team. — New ed. — 1980. — 52p : ill ; 30cm. — (M203 ; 11)
Previous ed.: 1979. — Includes index
ISBN 0-335-05797-7 (pbk) : Unpriced
B81-27801

Introduction to pure mathematics. — Milton Keynes : Open University Press. — (Mathematics : a second level course)
At head of title: The Open University
Unit 12: Linear algebra IV, eigenvectors / prepared by the Course Team. — New ed. — 1980. — 52p : ill ; 30cm. — (M203 ; 12)
Previous ed.: 1979. — Includes index
ISBN 0-335-05798-5 (pbk) : Unpriced
B81-27799

Introduction to pure mathematics. — Milton Keynes : Open University Press. — (Mathematics : a second level course)
At head of title: The Open University
Unit 13: Linear algebra V, vector spaces / prepared by the Course Team. — New ed. — 1980. — 55p : ill ; 30cm. — (M203 ; 13)
Previous ed.: 1979. — Includes index
ISBN 0-335-05799-3 (pbk) : Unpriced
B81-27794

Introduction to pure mathematics. — Milton Keynes : Open University Press. — (Mathematics : a second level course)
At head of title: The Open University
Unit 14: Group theory III, conjugacy / prepared by the Course Team. — New ed. — 1980. — 59p : ill ; 30cm. — (M203 ; 14)
Previous ed.: 1979. — Text on inside cover. — Includes index
ISBN 0-335-05800-0 (pbk) : Unpriced
B81-27800

Introduction to pure mathematics. — Milton Keynes : Open University Press. — (Mathematics : a second level course)
At head of title: The Open University
Unit 15: Group theory IV, homomorphisms / prepared by the Course Team. — 1979 (1980 [printing]). — 53p : ill(some col.) ; 30cm. — (M203 ; 15)
Includes index
ISBN 0-335-05801-9 (pbk) : Unpriced
B81-27793

Introduction to pure mathematics. — Milton Keynes : Open University Press. — (Mathematics : a second level course)
At head of title: The Open University
Unit 16: Geometry II, conics, quadrics and quadratic forms / prepared by the Course Team. — 1980. — 42p : ill ; 30cm. — (M203 ; 16)
Includes index
ISBN 0-335-05938-4 (pbk) : Unpriced
B81-27792

Introduction to pure mathematics. — Milton Keynes : Open University Press. — (Mathematics : a second level course)
At head of title: The Open University
Unit 18: Analysis IV, differentiation / prepared by the Course Team. — 1980. — 61p : ill ; 30cm. — (M203 ; 18)
Includes index
ISBN 0-335-05940-6 (pbk) : Unpriced
B81-27802

510 — Mathematics *continuation*

Introduction to pure mathematics. — Milton Keynes : Open University. — (Mathematics : a second level course)
Unit 21: Geometry IV, projective geometry / prepared by the course team. — New ed. — 1980. — 61p : ill(some col.) ; 30cm. — (M203 ; unit 21)
At head of title: The Open University. — Previous ed.: 1979. — Includes index
ISBN 0-335-05802-7 (pbk) : Unpriced
B81-28604

Introduction to pure mathematics. — Milton Keynes : Open University. — (Mathematics : a second level course)
Unit 22: Geometry V, non-Euclidean geometry / prepared by the course team. — New ed. — 1980. — 43p : ill ; 30cm. — (M203 ; unit 22)
At head of title: The Open University. — Previous ed.: 1979. — Includes index
ISBN 0-335-05803-5 (pbk) : Unpriced
B81-28603

Introduction to pure mathematics. — Milton Keynes : Open University. — (Mathematics : a second level course)
Unit 23: Axioms / prepared by the course team. — 1980. — 46p : ill ; 30cm. — (M203 ; unit 23)
At head of title: The Open University. — Includes index
ISBN 0-335-05943-0 (pbk) : Unpriced
B81-28602

Introduction to pure mathematics. — Milton Keynes : Open University. — (Mathematics : a second level course)
Unit 24: Group theory V, actions / prepared by the course team. — New ed. — 1980. — 44p : ill(some col.) ; 30cm. — (M203 ; unit 24)
At head of title: The Open University. — Previous ed.: 1979. — Includes index
ISBN 0-335-05804-3 (pbk) : Unpriced
B81-28601

Introduction to pure mathematics. — Milton Keynes : Open University. — (Mathematics : a second level course)
Unit 25: Geometry VI, the Kleinian view / prepared by the course team. — New ed. — 1980. — 55p : ill(some col.) ; 30cm. — (M203 ; unit 25)
At head of title: The Open University. — Previous ed.: 1979. — Text on inside covers. — Includes index
ISBN 0-335-05805-1 (pbk) : Unpriced
B81-28600

Introduction to pure mathematics. — Milton Keynes : Open University. — (Mathematics : a second level course)
Unit 26: Analysis VII, integration / prepared by the course team. — 1980. — 59p : ill(some col.) ; 30cm. — (M203 ; unit 26)
At head of title: The Open University. — Text on inside covers. — Includes index
ISBN 0-335-05944-9 (pbk) : Unpriced
B81-28599

Introduction to pure mathematics. — Milton Keynes : Open University. — (Mathematics : a second level course)
Unit 27: Topology I, homeomorphisms / prepared by the course team. — 1980. — 54p : ill(some col.) ; 30cm. — (M203 ; unit 27)
At head of title: The Open University. — Text on inside covers. — Includes index
ISBN 0-335-05945-7 (pbk) : Unpriced
B81-28598

Introduction to pure mathematics. — Milton Keynes : Open University. — (Mathematics : a second level course)
Unit 28: Analysis VIII, line and double integrals / prepared by the course team. — 1980. — 62p : ill ; 30cm. — (M203 ; unit 28)
At head of title: The Open University. — Includes index
ISBN 0-335-05946-5 (pbk) : Unpriced
B81-28597

Introduction to pure mathematics. — Milton Keynes : Open University. — (Mathematics : a second level course)
Unit 29: Topology II, connectedness and compactness / prepared by the course team. — 1980. — 56p : ill(some col.) ; 30cm. — (M203 ; unit 29)
At head of title: The Open University. — Includes index
ISBN 0-335-05947-3 (pbk) : Unpriced
B81-28596

Introduction to pure mathematics. — Milton Keynes : Open University. — (Mathematics : a second level course)
Unit 30: Analysis IX, sequences and series / prepared by the course team. — 1980. — 69p : ill(some col.) ; 30cm. — (M203 ; unit 30)
At head of title: The Open University. — Includes index
ISBN 0-335-05948-1 (pbk) : Unpriced
B81-28595

Introduction to pure mathematics. — Milton Keynes : Open University. — (Mathematics : a second level course)
Unit 31: Topology III, pancakes and ham sandwiches / prepared by the course team. — 1980. — 53p : ill(some col.) ; 30cm. — (M203 ; unit 31)
At head of title: The Open University. — Includes index
ISBN 0-335-05949-x (pbk) : Unpriced
B81-28594

Introduction to pure mathematics. — Milton Keynes : Open University. — (Mathematics : a second level course)
Unit 32: Analysis X, sequences of functions / prepared by the course team. — 1980. — 44p : ill ; 30cm. — (M203 ; unit 32)
At head of title: The Open University. — Includes index
ISBN 0-335-05950-3 (pbk) : Unpriced
B81-28593

Littlewood, J. E.. Collected papers of J.E. Littlewood. — Oxford : Clarendon Press, Sept.1981
Vol.1. — [750]p
ISBN 0-19-853353-5 : £40.00 : CIP entry
B81-20530

Newbury, J.. Basic numeracy skills and practice / J. Newbury. — London : Macmillan, 1981. — viii,151p : ill ; 22cm
ISBN 0-333-29336-3 (pbk) : £2.95 B81-38803

Studies in pure mathematics. — Milton Keynes : Open University Press. — (Mathematics ; a third level course)
At head of title: The Open University
Logic
Includes index
Unit 1-4 / prepared by the [M335 Logic Option Course Team]. — 1981. — 94p : ill ; 30cm. — (M335 ; L 1-4)
ISBN 0-335-14012-2 (pbk) : Unpriced
B81-14599

Studies in pure mathematics. — Milton Keynes : Open University Press. — (Mathematics : a third level course)
At head of title: The Open University
Number theory. — (M335 ; NT 1-4)
Units 1-4 / prepared by the Course Team. — 1981. — 84p : ill ; 30cm
ISBN 0-335-14010-6 (pbk) : Unpriced
B81-13184

510 — Mathematics. Applications

Dunning-Davies, J.. Mathematical methods for mathematicians, physical scientists and engineers. — Chichester : Ellis Horwood, Nov.1981. — [424]p. — (Ellis Horwood series in mathematics and its applications)
ISBN 0-85312-367-5 : £19.50 : CIP entry
B81-35876

510 — Mathematics. Concepts

Sondheimer, Ernst. Numbers and infinity. — Cambridge : Cambridge University Press, Oct.1981. — [184]p
ISBN 0-521-24091-3 (cased) : £7.50 : CIP entry
ISBN 0-521-28433-3 (pbk) : £3.75 B81-31282

Stewart, Ian, *1945-*. Concepts of modern mathematics / Ian Stewart. — Harmondsworth : Penguin, 1975 (1981 [printing]). — viii,339p : ill ; 20cm
Includes index
ISBN 0-14-021849-1 (pbk) : £3.50 B81-29161

510 — Mathematics — *Early works*

Newton, *Sir* Isaac. The mathematical papers of Isaac Newton. — Cambridge : Cambridge University Press
Vol.8: 1697-1722 / edited by D.T. Whiteside with the assistance in publication of A. Prag. — 1981. — lv,704p,[1],ivleaves of plates : ill,facsims ; 29cm
Parallel Latin text and English translation. — Includes index
ISBN 0-521-20103-9 : £85.00 : CIP rev.
B81-10444

510 — Mathematics — *For Caribbean students*

Singh, M. P.. Oxford mathematics for the Caribbean / M.P. Singh, V. Bentt, S. Bynoe. — Oxford : Oxford University Press
4. — 1981. — 174p : ill,1plan ; 25cm
ISBN 0-19-914082-0 (pbk) : £2.75 B81-38589

510 — Mathematics — *For children*

Kelsey, Edward. Mrs Witchitt works it out!. — Cambridge : Cambridge University Press, Dec.1981. — [14]p. — (Maths with a story!)
ISBN 0-521-28606-9 (pbk) : £0.65 : CIP entry
B81-34005

Snell, Gordon. Max — the Muddleville millionaire. — Cambridge : Cambridge University Press, Dec.1981. — [14]p. — (Maths with a story!)
ISBN 0-521-28607-7 (pbk) : £0.65 : CIP entry
B81-34004

Snell, Gordon. Muddleville olympics. — Cambridge : Cambridge University Press, Dec.1981. — [14]p. — (Maths with a story!)
ISBN 0-521-28609-3 (pbk) : £0.65 : CIP entry
B81-34003

Ward, Peter. Pirate gold. — Cambridge : Cambridge University Press, Dec.1981. — [14] p. — (Maths with a story!)
ISBN 0-521-28608-5 (pbk) : £0.65 : CIP entry
B81-34002

Wood, Leslie. Ride with us on the big red bus : a mathematical adventure with shapes, patterns, comparisons, measuring and sets / by Leslie Wood and Roy Burden. — [Exeter] : Wheaton, 1978. — [120]p : col.ill ; 20x21cm
Cover title
ISBN 0-08-024191-3 : £4.95 B81-09646

510 — Mathematics — *For Irish students*

Holland, Frederick J.. Checkpoint maths 3 / F.J. Holland. — Dublin : Educational Company, 1981. — 235p : ill ; 21cm
Unpriced (pbk) B81-34766

510 — Mathematics — *For Kenyan students*

Singh, Malkiat. Revision mathematics : a course for primary school leavers / Malkiat Singh. — London : Evans
Bk.2. — 1980. — 68p : ill ; 25cm
ISBN 0-237-50403-0 (pbk) : Unpriced
B81-32361

510 — Mathematics — *For schools*

Benharbit, Adbelali. Basic mathematics : a pre-calculus course for science and engineering. — Chichester : Wiley, Oct.1981. — [240]p
ISBN 0-471-27941-2 (cased) : £14.75 : CIP entry
ISBN 0-471-27942-0 (pbk) : £5.50 B81-28070

Bostock, L.. Mathematics. — Cheltenham : Thornes, Aug.1981. — [512]p
ISBN 0-85950-306-2 (pbk) : £5.75 : CIP entry
B81-16902

Celia, C. W.. Advanced mathematics. — Basingstoke : Macmillan Education
2. — Feb.1982. — [400]p
ISBN 0-333-23193-7 (pbk) : £5.95 : CIP entry
B81-35800

510 — Mathematics — *For schools*
continuation

Chester, Joyce. Maths matters / Joyce Chester, Eon Harper, Gerry Price. — London : Addison-Wesley, c1980-1981
4-6. — 3v : ill(some col.) ; 28cm
ISBN 0-201-03585-5 (pbk) : £3.50
ISBN 0-201-03586-3 (5)
ISBN 0-201-03587-1 (6) B81-07837

Fletcher, Alexander J.. Structured mathematics / Alexander J. Fletcher, Helen M. Faulkner. — London : Hodder and Stoughton
Bk. 5. — c1981. — 56p : ill ; 24cm
ISBN 0-340-24964-1 (pbk) : £0.85 : CIP rev. B80-08723

Fletcher, Alexander J.. Structured mathematics / Alexander J. Fletcher, Helen M. Faulkner. — London : Hodder & Stoughton
Bk. 6. — c1981. — 56p : ill ; 24cm
ISBN 0-340-24965-x (pbk) : £0.85 : CIP rev. B80-12336

Fox, R. W.. A basic examination course in mathematics / R.W. Fox and E. Kitney. — London : Edward Arnold
Bk.1. — 1981. — viii,245p : ill ; 25cm + 1 answer book(63p : ill ; 23cm)
ISBN 0-7131-0430-9 (pbk) : £3.25 : CIP rev.
ISBN 0-7131-0432-5 (answer book) B80-13360

Fox, R. W.. A basic examination course in mathematics / R.W. Fox and E. Kitney. — London : Edward Arnold
Bk.2. — 1981. — 232p : ill ; 25cm + 1 answer book(71p : ill ; 23cm)
ISBN 0-7131-0431-7 (pbk) : £3.25 : CIP rev.
ISBN 0-7131-0433-3 (answer book) B80-13361

Goddard, T. R.. Time for maths / compiled by T.R. Goddard, J.W. Adams and R.P. Beaumont. — Huddersfield : Schofield & Sims
5: Teacher's notes. — c[1981]. — 32p : ill ; 30cm
Cover title
ISBN 0-7217-2296-2 (pbk) : Unpriced B81-16608

Graham, Duncan. Maths for you / Duncan and Christine Graham. — London : Hutchinson
Bk.1. — 1981. — 233p : ill ; 24cm
ISBN 0-09-140881-4 (pbk) : £2.50 : CIP rev. B80-06897

Greer, A.. Revision practice in new mathematics / A. Greer. — Cheltenham : Thornes, 1981. — 83p : ill ; 19cm. — (ST(P) revision notes series)
ISBN 0-85950-323-2 (pbk) : £1.25 : CIP rev. B81-03186

Individualised mathematics. — Cambridge : Cambridge University Press
Geometry 1
Symmetry and trigonometry. — Nov.1981. — [112]p
ISBN 0-521-28377-9 (pbk) : £2.60 : CIP entry B81-31230

Infant mathematics. — London : Heinemann Educational
First stage: Teacher's notes. — Nov.1981. — [288]p
ISBN 0-435-02945-2 (pbk) : £4.95 : CIP entry B81-34206

Kenwood, H. M.. Mathematics : an integrated approach / H.M. Kenwood, G.M. Staley ; consultant editor C. Plumpton. — Basingstoke : Macmillan Education, 1980. — x,438p : ill ; 24cm
ISBN 0-333-24581-4 (pbk) : £3.95 : CIP rev. B80-12830

Latham, Paul. Nuffield maths 3 / [Paul Latham, Percy Truelove]. — Harlow : Longman. — (Nuffield maths 5-11)
Pupils' book. — 112p : ill(some col.) ; 25cm
ISBN 0-582-19173-4 (pbk) : Unpriced B81-24258

Latham, Paul. Nuffield maths 3 / [Paul Latham, Percy Truelove]. — Harlow : Published for the Nuffield Foundation by Longman. — (Nuffield maths 5-11)
Teachers' handbook / [contributing authors Eric Albany, Raymond Bull] ; [illustrator Chris Williamson]. — xii,162p : ill ; 26cm
Includes index
ISBN 0-582-19177-7 (pbk) : Unpriced B81-24259

Latham, Paul. Nuffield maths 4 / Paul Latham and Percy Truelove. — London : Longman
Cover title
Pupils book. — 1981. — 96p : ill ; 25cm
ISBN 0-582-19174-2 (pbk) : £1.75 B81-40200

Latham, Paul. Nuffield maths 4 / [Paul Latham, Percy Truelove]. — Harlow : Published for the Nuffield Foundation by Longman. — (Nuffield maths 5-11)
Includes index
Teachers' handbook / [contributory authors Eric A. Albany, Raymond J. Bull] ; [illustrator Chris Williamson]. — 1981. — 158p : ill ; 26cm
ISBN 0-582-19178-5 (pbk) : Unpriced B81-40297

Lewis, Barry, *1946-*. Diversions in modern mathematics / Barry Lewis. — London : Heinemann Educational, 1981. — 135p : ill ; 22cm
Includes index
ISBN 0-435-51600-0 (pbk) : £1.75 : CIP rev. B81-06887

Modern mathematics for schools / Scottish Mathematics Group. — Glasgow : Blackie
Extra questions to accompany mathsheets 2. — 1981. — 80p : ill ; 30cm
ISBN 0-216-91030-7 (unbound) : Unpriced
ISBN 0-550-75964-6 (Chambers) B81-37504

Modern mathematics for schools / Scottish Mathematics Group. — Glasgow : Blackie
Extra questions to accompany mathsheets 2. — 1981
Teachers ed.. — 80p : ill(some col.) ; 30cm
ISBN 0-216-91031-5 (unbound) : Unpriced
ISBN 0-550-75965-4 (Chambers) B81-37505

Perkins, Martin. Advanced maths. — London : Bell and Hyman
Book 1. — Feb.1982. — [573]p
ISBN 0-7135-1272-5 (pbk) : £5.95 : CIP entry B81-38316

Schools Mathematics Project. Individualised mathematics. — Cambridge : Cambridge University Press, June 1981
Matrix algebra and isometric transformations. — [96]p
ISBN 0-521-28265-9 (pbk) : £2.60 : CIP entry B81-19165

Stead, Jeffrey. Core mathematics. — Cambridge : Cambridge University Press
Book 1. — Dec.1981. — [320]p
ISBN 0-521-23232-5 (pbk) : £2.95 : CIP entry B81-30897

Stead, Jeffrey. Core mathematics. — Cambridge : Cambridge University Press, Dec.1981
Book 2. — [304]p
ISBN 0-521-23233-3 (pbk) : £2.95 : CIP entry B81-32599

Step by step maths. — Dublin : Gill and Macmillan
1 / Clare Martin. — 1981. — 108p : ill ; 21cm
ISBN 0-7171-1113-x (pbk) : £1.50 B81-21900

510 — Mathematics — *For secondary school teaching*

Wheeler, Roger F.. Rethinking mathematical concepts / Roger F. Wheeler. — Chichester : Horwood, 1981. — 314p : ill ; 24cm. — (Ellis Horwood series in mathematics and its applications)
Includes index
ISBN 0-85312-284-9 : £17.50 B81-21697

510 — Mathematics — *For slow learning children — For schools*

Stanfield, Jan. Impact maths / Jan Stanfield, Jerzy Cwirko-Godycki ; illustrated by Anna Clarke. — London : Evans
Pupils book 1. — 1981. — 64p : ill ; 26cm
ISBN 0-237-50225-9 (pbk) : Unpriced B81-16136

Stanfield, Jan. Impact maths / Jan Stanfield, Jerzy Cwirko-Godycki ; illustrated by Anna Clarke. — London : Evans
Teachers book 1. — 1981. — 31p : ill ; 25cm
ISBN 0-237-50227-5 (pbk) : Unpriced B81-16137

510 — Mathematics — *For users of pocket electronic calculators*

King, David, *1932-*. Daily telegraph calculator book / by David King ; drawings by Holland. — 2nd (rev.) ed. — [London] : [Daily Telegraph], 1980. — 127p : ill ; 20cm
Previous ed.: 1979
ISBN 0-901684-44-9 (pbk) : £1.25 B81-01782

510 — Mathematics — *For West African students*

New general mathematics for West Africa. — New ed. / J.B. Channon ... [et al.]. — Harlow : Longman
Previous ed.: i.e. New ed. / by J.B. Channon, A. McLeish Smith, H.C. Head. 1971-78
1. — 1981. — 188p : ill ; 25cm
Includes index
ISBN 0-582-60644-6 (pbk) : £2.40 B81-16204

510 — Mathematics. Problem solving

Solving real problems with mathematics. — Cranfield (Cranfield Institute of Technology, Cranfield, Bedford MK43 0AL) : CIT Press
Vol.1. — Nov.1981. — [105]p
ISBN 0-902937-62-6 (pbk) : £4.50 : CIP entry B81-40266

510 — Mathematics. Problem solving — *Manuals — For teaching*

Polya, George. Mathematical discovery : on understanding, learning, and teaching problem solving / George Polya. — Combined ed. — New York ; Chichester : Wiley, c1981. — xxv,212,220p : ill ; 23cm
Originally published: in 2 vols. 1962-1965. — Ill on inside covers. — Bibliography: p207-209. — Includes index
ISBN 0-471-08975-3 (pbk) : £10.50 B81-23431

510 — Periodical articles on mathematics - *Collections*

The **Best** of Manifold. — Orpington (9 Clareville Rd, Orpington, Kent BR5 1RU) : Shiva, May 1981. — [100]p
ISBN 0-906812-07-0 : £5.50 : CIP entry B81-10008

510'.1 — Mathematics. Formalism. Implications of incompleteness theorems in metamathematics

Webb, Judson Chambers. Mechanism, mentalism, and metamathematics : an essay on finitism / Judson Chambers Webb. — Dordrecht ; London : Reidel, c1980. — xiii,277p : ill ; 23cm. — (Synthese library ; v.137)
Bibliography: p248-263. — Includes index
ISBN 90-277-1046-5 : Unpriced
Also classified at 150'.1 B81-07824

510'.1 — Mathematics — *Philosophical perspectives*

Davis, Philip J.. The mathematical experience / Philip J. Davis, Reuben Hersh ; with an introduction by Gian-Carlo Rota. — Brighton : Harvester Press, 1981. — xix,440p : ill,facsims,ports ; 24cm
Originally published: Boston, Mass.: Birkhäuser, 1981. — Bibliography: p417-434. — Includes index
ISBN 0-7108-0364-8 : £12.95 : CIP rev. B81-31106

510'.212 — Mathematics — *Tables*

Mathematical and statistical tables / [compiled by] Ahmad, Fox and Shaw. — London : African Universities Press in association with Edward Arnold, 1981. — 32p : 2ill ; 23cm
Cover title. — Text, ill on inside covers
ISBN 0-7131-0624-7 (pbk) : £0.70 B81-36876

510′.212 — Mathematics - *Tables - For schools*

Fox, R. W.. Mathematical tables and data. — 3rd ed. — London : Edward Arnold, June 1981. — [32]p
Previous ed.: 1970
ISBN 0-7131-0594-1 (pbk) : £1.25(non-net) : CIP entry B81-14868

510′.24301 — Mathematics — *For social sciences*

Emerson, Lloyd S.. Fundamental mathematics for the management and social sciences / Lloyd S. Emerson, Laurence R. Paguette. — Alternate ed. — Boston, Mass. ; London : Allyn and Bacon, c1981. — x,576p : ill(some col.) ; 25cm
Previous ed. i.e. 2nd ed.: 1978. — Includes index
Unpriced (corrected cased)
ISBN 0-205-07352-2 (Study guide and computer supplement) : Unpriced
Also classified at 510′.24658 B81-21095

Whipkey, Kenneth L.. The power of mathematics : applications to management and the social sciences / Kenneth L. Whipkey, Mary Nell Whipkey, George W. Conway, Jr. — 2nd ed. — New York ; Chichester : Wiley, c1981. — x,622p : ill(some col.) ; 26cm
Previuos ed.: 1978. — Text on lining papers. — Includes index
ISBN 0-471-07709-7 : £11.50
Also classified at 510′.24658 B81-18680

Williams, Gareth, *1939-*. Mathematics with applications in the management, natural, and social sciences / Gareth Williams. — Boston [Mass.] ; London : Allyn and Bacon, c1981. — xiii,658p : ill ; 25cm
Text on lining papers. — Includes index
ISBN 0-205-07188-0 : Unpriced
Also classified at 510′.24658 B81-26209

510′.2433 — Mathematics — *For economics*

Kennedy, Gavin. Mathematics for innumerate economists. — London : Duckworth, Oct.1981. — [144]p
ISBN 0-7156-1564-5 (cased) : £18.00 : CIP entry
ISBN 0-7156-1609-9 (pbk) : £6.95 B81-30356

Khoury, Sarkis J.. Mathematical methods in finance and economics / Sarkis J. Khoury, Torrence D. Parsons. — New York ; Oxford : North Holland, c1981. — xii,295p : ill ; 24cm
Includes index
ISBN 0-444-00425-4 : £23.67 B81-36755

510′.2433 — Mathematics — *For economics — For African students*

Onimode, Bade. Basic mathematics for economists / Bade Onimode, Iz. Osayimwese. — London : Allen & Unwin, 1980. — x,247p : ill ; 22cm
Includes bibliographies and index
ISBN 0-04-330304-8 (pbk) : £4.90 : CIP rev. B80-19176

510′.24372 — Applied mathematics - *For teaching*

Evyatar, A.. Motivated mathematics. — Cambridge : Cambridge University Press, June 1981. — [280]p
ISBN 0-521-23308-9 (spiral) : £18.00 : CIP entry B81-19117

510′.245 — Mathematics — *For natural sciences*

Applicable mathematics of non-physical phenomena. — Chichester : Ellis Horwood, Jan.1982. — [310]p. — (Ellis Horwood series in mathematics and its applications)
ISBN 0-85312-366-7 : £19.50 : CIP entry B81-39212

510′.245 — Mathematics — *For science*

Chirgwin, Brian H.. A course of mathematics for engineers and scientists / Brian H. Chirgwin and Charles Plumpton. — 1st ed., reprinted (with corrections). — Oxford : Pergamon. — (Pergamon international library)
Includes index
Vol.4. — 1977, c1964 (1981 [printing]). — viii,353p : ill ; 21cm
ISBN 0-08-026494-8 (pbk) : £7.50
Primary classification 510′.2462 B81-16114

510′.24541 — Mathematics — *For physical chemistry*

Mortimer, Robert G.. Mathematics for physical chemistry / Robert G. Mortimer. — New York : Macmillan ; London : Collier Macmillan, c1981. — x,405p : ill ; 24cm
Includes bibliographies and index
ISBN 0-02-384000-5 (pbk) : £6.95 B81-33404

510′.24574 — Mathematics — *For biochemistry*

Cornish-Bowden, Athel. Basic mathematics for biochemists. — London : Chapman and Hall, Nov.1981. — [200]p
ISBN 0-412-23000-3 (cased) : £7.50 : CIP entry
ISBN 0-412-23010-0 (pbk) : £3.95 B81-30440

510′.24574 — Mathematics — *For biology*

Newby, J. C.. Mathematics for the biological sciences : from graphs through calculus to differential equations / J.C. Newby. — Oxford : Clarendon Press, 1980. — xv,319p : ill ; 23cm. — (Oxford applied mathematics and computing science series)
Includes index
ISBN 0-19-859623-5 : £20.00 : CIP rev.
ISBN 0-19-859624-3 (pbk) : £8.95 B80-02743

510′.246 — Mathematics — *For technicians*

Bird, J. O.. Engineering mathematics & science 3 checkbook. — London : Butterworths, Jan.1982. — [156]p
ISBN 0-408-00670-6 (cased) : £6.95 : CIP entry
ISBN 0-408-00625-0 (pbk) : £3.95 B81-34114

Bird, J. O.. Mathematics 4 checkbook. — London : Butterworths, Sept.1981. — [256]p
ISBN 0-408-00660-9 (cased) : £6.00 : CIP entry
ISBN 0-408-00612-9 (pbk) : £3.80 B81-23915

Bird, J. O.. Technician mathematics / J.O. Bird and A.J.C. May. — London : Longman. — (Longman technician series. Mathematics and sciences)
Levels 4 and 5. — 1981. — 413p : ill ; 22cm
Includes index
ISBN 0-582-41762-7 (pbk) : £7.95 B81-22179

Buchan, R. B.. Mathematics for technicians / R.B. Buchan, A. Greer, G.W. Taylor. — Scotec ed. — Cheltenham : Thornes. — (Technology today series)
Includes index
Level III: Engineering mathematics. — 1981. — ix,254p : ill ; 23cm
ISBN 0-85950-443-3 (pbk) : £4.50 : CIP rev. B80-33490

Dyball, George E.. Mathematics for technician engineers : a third-level course / George E. Dyball. — London : McGraw-Hill, c1980. — xii,358p : ill ; 23cm
Includes index
ISBN 0-07-084636-7 (pbk) : £4.95 : CIP rev. B80-12337

Kettlewell, J. B.. Mathematics : level 1 / J.B. Kettlewell. — Walton-on-Thames : Nelson, 1981. — 287p : ill ; 22cm. — (Nelson TEC books)
Includes index. — Publisher′s no.: NCN 5844 45 0
ISBN 0-17-741122-8 (pbk) : £3.50 B81-32853

Perry, Owen. Mathematics I / Owen Perry, Joyce Perry. — London : Macmillan, 1981. — (Macmillan technician series)
1. — Sept. 1980. — viii,182p : ill ; 21x24cm
ISBN 0-333-28171-3 (pbk) : Unpriced : CIP rev. B80-13362

Pocock, K. A.. Mathematics 1 / K.A. Pocock. — London : Keith Dickson, c1980. — 59p : ill ; 17cm. — (TEC student′s pocketbook ; no.1)
ISBN 0-85380-126-8 (pbk) : £1.50 B81-40930

Stroud, K. A.. Mathematics for engineering techniques / K.A. Stroud. — Cheltenham : Thornes. — (S.T. (P) technology today series)
Includes index
Book 2a: Practical applications. — 1981. — 267p : ill ; 25cm
ISBN 0-85950-469-7 (pbk) : £3.25 : CIP rev. B80-34912

Walker, Eric. Mathematics level 1 / Eric Walker. — London : Holt, Rinehart and Winston, c1981. — xii,387p : ill ; 22cm. — (Holt technician texts)
ISBN 0-03-910314-5 (pbk) : £3.50 : CIP rev. B81-00855

Walker, Eric. Mathematics level 2 : analytical. — Eastbourne : Holt-Saunders, Jan.1982. — [173]p
ISBN 0-03-910343-9 (pbk) : £2.55 : CIP entry B81-33999

Walker, Eric. Mathematics level 2 : mensuration. — Eastbourne : Holt-Saunders, Jan.1982. — 1v.
ISBN 0-03-910344-7 (pbk) : £2.55 : CIP entry B81-34000

Walker, Eric. Mathematics level 2. — Eastbourne : Holt-Saunders, Jan.1982. — 1v.
ISBN 0-03-910345-5 (pbk) : £1.95 : CIP entry B81-33998

510′.246 — Mathematics — *Programmed instructions — For technicians*

Carman, Robert A.. Mathematics for trades : a guided approach / Robert A. Carman, Hal M. Saunders. — New York ; Chichester : Wiley, c1981. — xii,580p : ill(some col.),forms ; 28cm
Includes index
ISBN 0-471-13481-3 (pbk) : £8.00 B81-09664

510′.246 — Mathematics — *Questions & answers — For technicians*

Bird, J. O.. Mathematics 1 checkbook / J.O. Bird, A.J.C. May. — London : Butterworths, 1981. — viii,172p : ill ; 20cm. — (Butterworths technical and scientific checkbooks. Level 1)
Includes index
ISBN 0-408-00632-3 (cased) : Unpriced : CIP rev.
ISBN 0-408-00609-9 (pbk) : Unpriced B81-00856

Bird, J. O.. Mathematics 2 checkbook / J.O. Bird, A.J.C. May. — London : Butterworths, 1981. — x,224p : ill ; 20cm. — (Butterworths technical and scientific checkbooks. Level 2)
Includes index
ISBN 0-408-00633-1 (cased) : Unpriced : CIP rev.
ISBN 0-408-00610-2 (pbk) : Unpriced B81-03370

Bird, J. O.. Mathematics 3 checkbook. — London : Butterworth, July 1981. — [196]p. — (Butterworths checkbook series)
ISBN 0-408-00634-x (pbk) : £3.95 : CIP entry B81-14852

510′.2462 — Mathematics — *For engineering*

Bajpai, A. C.. Specialist techniques in engineering mathematics / A.C. Bajpai, L.R. Mustoe, D. Walker. — Chichester : Wiley, c1980. — ix,401p : ill
Bibliography: p387-388. — Includes index
ISBN 0-471-27907-2 (cased) : £19.50 : CIP rev.
ISBN 0-471-27908-0 (pbk) : £8.75 B80-34913

Chirgwin, Brian H.. A course of mathematics for engineers and scientists / Brian H. Chirgwin and Charles Plumpton. — 1st ed., reprinted (with corrections). — Oxford : Pergamon. — (Pergamon international library)
Includes index
Vol.4. — 1977, c1964 (1981 [printing]). — viii,353p : ill ; 21cm
ISBN 0-08-026494-8 (pbk) : £7.50
Also classified at 510′.245 B81-16114

510′.2462 — Mathematics - *For engineering*

Garlick, F. J.. Technical mathematics : a second level course. — London : McGraw-Hill, June 1981. — [384]p
ISBN 0-07-084644-8 (pbk) : £4.50 : CIP entry B81-10004

510′.2462 — Mathematics — *For engineering*

Gottfried, Byron S.. Schaum′s outline of theory and problems of introduction to engineering calculations / by Byron S. Gottfried. — New York ; London : McGraw-Hill, c1979. — 233p : ill ; 28cm. — (Schaum′s outline series)
Includes index
ISBN 0-07-023837-5 (pbk) : £5.25 B81-26660

510'.2462 — Mathematics — *For engineering continuation*

Meadows, R. G.. Electrical and engineering mathematics / Richard Meadows. — London : Pitman
Vol.2. — 1981. — xii,300p : ill ; 25cm
Includes index
ISBN 0-273-01408-0 (pbk) : £5.25 B81-21840

Morris, Jack. Mathematics for mechanical and production engineering, Level IV / Jack Morris. — New York ; London : Van Nostrand Reinhold, 1981. — x,323p : ill ; 24cm
Includes index
ISBN 0-442-30459-5 (cased) : £13.00
ISBN 0-442-30460-9 (pbk) : £5.95 B81-31862

510'.2462 — Mathematics — *For engineering — Conference proceedings*

Workshop on the Information Linkage between Applied Mathematics and Industry *(2nd : 1979 : Monterey)*. Information linkage between applied mathematics and industry II / [proceedings of the Second Annual Workshop on the Information Linkage between Applied Mathematics and Industry, Naval Postgraduate School, Monterey, California, February 22-24, 1979] ; edited by Arthur L. Schoenstadt ... [et al.]. — New York ; London : Academic Press, 1980. — xii,293p : ill,charts ; 24cm
ISBN 0-12-628750-3 : £11.20 B81-16198

510'.246213 — Mathematics — *For electrical technicians*

Bird, J. O.. Mathematics for electrical technicians, levels 4 and 5 / J.O. Bird, A.J.C. May. — London : Longman, 1981. — 384p : ill ; 22cm. — (Longman technician series. Mathematics and sciences)
Includes index
ISBN 0-582-41760-0 (pbk) : 6.95 B81-18939

510'.24642 — Mathematics — *For catering industries*

Hughes, Janet. Costing and calculations for catering / Janet Hughes and Brian Ireland. — Cheltenham : Thornes, 1981. — vi,170p : ill,forms ; 24cm
ISBN 0-85950-493-x (pbk) : £2.75 : CIP rev.
Also classified at 647'.95'0681 B81-03356

510'.24658 — Mathematics — *For business studies*

Edwards, Barry. The readable maths and statistics book / Barry Edwards. — London : Allen & Unwin, 1980. — ix,328p : ill ; 22cm
Includes index
ISBN 0-04-310007-4 (corrected : cased) : Unpriced : CIP rev.
ISBN 0-04-310008-2 (pbk) : £6.95 B80-19178

510'.24658 — Mathematics — *For management*

Emerson, Lloyd S.. Fundamental mathematics for the management and social sciences / Lloyd S. Emerson, Laurence R. Paguette. — Alternate ed. — Boston, Mass. ; London : Allyn and Bacon, c1981. — x,576p : ill(some col.) ; 25cm
Previous ed. i.e. 2nd ed.: 1978. — Includes index
Unpriced (corrected cased)
ISBN 0-205-07352-2 (Study guide and computer supplement) : Unpriced
Primary classification 510'.24301 B81-21095

Whipkey, Kenneth L.. The power of mathematics : applications to management and the social sciences / Kenneth L. Whipkey, Mary Nell Whipkey, George W. Conway, Jr. — 2nd ed. — New York ; Chichester : Wiley, c1981. — x,622p : ill(some col.) ; 26cm
Previuos ed.: 1978. — Text on lining papers. — Includes index
ISBN 0-471-07709-7 : £11.50
Primary classification 510'.24301 B81-18680

Williams, Gareth, *1939-*. Mathematics with applications in the management, natural, and social sciences / Gareth Williams. — Boston [Mass.] ; London : Allyn and Bacon, c1981. — xiii,658p : ill ; 25cm
Text on lining papers. — Includes index
ISBN 0-205-07188-0 : Unpriced
Primary classification 510'.24301 B81-26209

510'.24658 — Mathematics — *Questions & answers — For business studies*

Lipscombe, Stan. Business calculations / Stan Lipscombe ; illustrated by Janet Payne. — Stockport : Polytech, 1979. — 138p : ill,forms ; 22cm. — (A Business Education Council course. General level)
ISBN 0-85505-031-4 (pbk) : Unpriced B81-09347

510'.28 — Electronic calculators — *Questions & answers — For schools*

Green, D. R.. Can you calculate? / David Green. — London : Edward Arnold, 1981. — iv,36p : ill ; 23cm
Bibliography: p36
ISBN 0-7131-0489-9 (pbk) : £1.10 : CIP rev. B80-13788

510'.3 — Mathematics — *Polyglot dictionaries*

Eisenreich, Günther. Dictionary of mathematics in four languages. — Oxford : Elsevier Scientific, Feb.1982. — [1500]p
ISBN 0-444-99706-7 : £40.00 : CIP entry B81-36209

510'.3'21 — Mathematics — *Encyclopaedias*

The **Universal** encyclopedia of mathematics / with a foreword by James R. Newman. — London : Pan, 1976, c1964 (1980 printing). — 714p : ill ; 20cm. — (Pan reference books)
This translation originally published: London : Allen and Unwin, 1964. — Translation of: Meyers Rechenduden
ISBN 0-330-24396-9 (pbk) : £2.95 B81-00093

510'.3'21 — Mathematics — *Encyclopaedias — For schools*

Kaner, Peter. A basic dictionary of maths. — London : Bell & Hyman, Oct.1981. — [64]p
ISBN 0-7135-1269-5 (pbk) : £1.75 : CIP entry B81-30191

510'.5 — Mathematics — *Serials*

Bulletin of mathematics. — Issue no.1 (Apr./May 1981)-. — London ([Flat No.160, 16 Newport Court, WC2H 7JS) : Okikiolu Scientific and Industrial Organization, 1981-. — v. ; 21cm
Quarterly
ISSN 0261-1023 = Bulletin of mathematics : £2.90 per issue B81-33292

510'.7 — Education. Curriculum subjects: Mathematics. Teaching

Freudenthal, Hans. Weeding and sowing : preface to a science of mathematical education / Hans Freudenthal. — Dordrecht ; London : Reidel, 1978 (1980 [printing]). — ix,315p : ill ; 23cm
Includes index
ISBN 90-277-1072-4 (pbk) : Unpriced B81-03234

510'.7 — Great Britain. Mathematics teachers. Professional education — *Conference proceedings*

Mathematics, education and teachers. — [Southend-on-Sea] ([Maitland House, Warrior Sq., Southend-on-Sea, Essex SS1 2JY]) : Institute of Mathematics and its Applications, [1978?]. — 83p ; 20cm. — (Symposium proceedings series / Institute of Mathematics and its Applications ; no.18)
Conference papers. — Cover title
Unpriced (spiral) B81-13273

510'.71 — Schools. Curriculum subjects: Mathematics. Curriculum. Development, *1960-1980*

Howson, Geoffrey. Curriculum development in mathematics / Geoffrey Howson, Christine Keitel, Jeremy Kilpatrick. — Cambridge : Cambridge University Press, 1981. — viii,288p : forms ; 24cm
Bibliography: p271-281. — Includes index
ISBN 0-521-23767-x : £19.50 : CIP rev. B81-19194

510'.71 — Schools. Curriculum subjects: Mathematics. Learning by students. Psychological aspects

Buxton, Laurie. Do you panic about maths? : coping with maths anxiety / Laurie Buxton. — London : Heinemann Educational, 1981. — 168p : ill ; 24cm
Bibliography: p166. — Includes index
ISBN 0-435-50101-1 (corrected : pbk) : £3.95 B81-13365

510'.71041 — Great Britain. Schools. Curriculum subjects: Mathematics. Teaching

Dean, Peter G.. Teaching and learning mathematics. — London : Woburn Press, Jan.1982. — [280]p
ISBN 0-7130-0168-2 : £11.00 : CIP entry B81-34570

Mathematics across the curriculum : a second level course / prepared by the Course Team. — Milton Keynes : Open University Press. — (Post experience/mathematics/education : an inter-faculty second level course)
At head of title: The Open University
Unit 2: Planning. — 1980. — 48p : ill,facsims,plans ; 21x30cm. — (PME233 ; unit 2)
ISBN 0-335-00456-3 (pbk) : Unpriced B81-07975

Mathematics across the curriculum : a second level course / prepared by the course team. — Milton Keynes : Open University Press. — (Post experience/mathematics/education : an inter-faculty second level course)
At head of title: The Open University
Unit 5: Getting started. — 1980. — 47p : ill ; 21x30cm. — (PME233 ; unit 5)
Bibliography: p47
ISBN 0-335-00459-8 (pbk) : Unpriced B81-39149

Mathematics across the curriculum : a second level course / prepared by the course team. — Milton Keynes : Open University Press. — (Post experience/mathematics/education : an inter-faculty second level course)
At head of title: The Open University
Unit 6: Making plans. — 1980. — 48p : ill ; 21x30cm. — (PME233 ; unit 6)
ISBN 0-335-00465-2 (pbk) : Unpriced B81-39150

Mathematics across the curriculum : a second level course / prepared by the Course Team. — Milton Keynes : Open University Press. — (Post experience/mathematics/education : an inter-faculty second level course)
At head of title: The Open University
Unit 7: Finding answers. — 1980. — 45p : ill,plans ; 21x30cm. — (PME233 ; unit 7)
ISBN 0-335-00466-0 (pbk) : Unpriced B81-07977

Mathematics across the curriculum : a second level course / prepared by the Course Team. — Milton Keynes : Open University Press. — (Post experience/mathematics/education : an inter-faculty second level course)
At head of title: The Open University
Unit 8: Finishing off. — 1980. — 30p : ill ; 21x30cm. — (PME233 ; unit 8)
ISBN 0-335-00467-9 (pbk) : Unpriced B81-07978

Mathematics across the curriculum : a second level course / prepared by the Course Team. — Milton Keynes : Open University Press. — (Post experience/mathematics/education : an inter-faculty second level course)
At head of title: The Open University
Unit 9: Project write-up. — 1980. — 14p : ill ; 21x30cm. — (PME233 ; unit 9)
ISBN 0-335-00468-7 (pbk) : Unpriced B81-07976

Mathematics across the curriculum : a second level course / prepared by the Course Team. — Milton Keynes : Open University Press. — (Post experience/mathematics/education : an inter faculty second level course)
At head of title: The Open University
Unit 10: Seeking out relationships. — 1980. — 47p : ill,facsims ; 21x30cm. — (PME233 ; unit 10)
ISBN 0-335-00469-5 (pbk) : Unpriced B81-07974

Mathematics across the curriculum : a second level course / prepared by the Course Team. — Milton Keynes : Open University Press. — (Post experience/mathematics/education : an inter-faculty second level course)
At head of title: The Open University
Unit 14: Mathematical aspects. — 1980. — 25p : ill ; 21x30cm. — (PME233 ; unit 14)
ISBN 0-335-00478-4 (pbk) : Unpriced B81-07980

510'.7'1041 — Great Britain. Schools. Curriculum subjects: Mathematics. Teaching *continuation*

Mathematics across the curriculum : a second level course / prepared by the Course Team. — Milton Keynes : Open University Press. — (Post experience/mathematics/education : an inter-faculty second level course)
At head of title: The Open University
Unit 15: Overview. — 1980. — 27p : ill ; 21x30cm. — (PME233 ; unit 15)
ISBN 0-335-00479-2 (pbk) : Unpriced B81-07979

510'.7'1041 — Great Britain. Schools. Curriculum subjects: Mathematics. Teaching. Cooperation between schools & employers

Bird, David, *19---*. Mathematics in school and employment : a study of liaison activities / David Bird and Michael Hiscox. — London : Methuen Educational, 1981. — 141p ; 21cm. — (Schools Council working paper ; no.68)
ISBN 0-423-50830-x (pbk) : Unpriced : CIP rev. B81-02102

510'.7'1041 — Great Britain. Schools. Curriculum subjects: Mathematics. Teaching. Implications of requirements by school leavers of mathematical skills — *Conference proceedings*

Mathematical needs of school leavers entering employment II / [Proceedings of a conference organised by the Institute of Mathematics and its Applications in association with the Shell Centre for Mathematical Education, University of Nottingham held in Nottingham in July 1975]. — [Southend-on-Sea] ([Maitland House, Warrior Sq., Southend-on-Sea, Essex SS1 2JY]) : The Institute, [c1975]. — ix,110p : ill ; 21cm. — (Symposium proceedings series / Institute of Mathematics and its Applications ; no.11)
Cover title
Unpriced (spiral) B81-13265

Mathematical needs of school leavers entering employment III : the way forward / [Proceedings of a conference organised by the Institute of Mathematics and its Applications in association with Brunel University Education Liaison Centre held at Brunel University in September, 1976]. — [Southend-on-Sea] ([Maitland House, Warrior Sq., Southend-on-Sea, Essex SS1 2JY]) : The Institute, [c1976]. — vi,182p : ill ; 20cm. — (Symposium proceedings series / Institute of Mathematics and its Applications ; no.14)
Cover title
Unpriced (spiral) B81-13264

510'.7'1241 — Great Britain. Secondary schools. Curriculum subjects: Mathematics. Understanding by students

Children's understanding of mathematics: 11-16 / the CSMS Mathematics Team [i.e.] K.M. Hart ... [et al.]. — London : John Murray, c1981. — 231p : ill ; 24cm
Bibliography: p225-226. — Includes index
ISBN 0-7195-3772-x (pbk) : £6.95 B81-32442

510'.76 — Applied mathematics — *Questions & answers — For schools*

Ridgway, Bill. Where's the maths in print / Bill Ridgway. — London : Edward Arnold, 1981. — 48p : ill,1map,facsim,ports ; 25cm
Text on inside covers
ISBN 0-7131-0480-5 (pbk) : £1.70 B80-23205

510'.76 — England. Secondary schools. Curriculum subjects: Mathematics. N level examinations & F level examinations. Proposals — *Conference proceedings*

The N and F proposals in relation to mathematics : proceedings of a symposium organised by the Institute of Mathematics and its Applications held in London on 1st July, 1978. — Southend-on-Sea (Maitland House, Warrior Sq., Southend-on-Sea, Essex SS1 2JY) : The Institute, c1979. — v,79p : ill ; 20cm. — (Symposium proceedings series / Institute of Mathematics and its Applications ; no.20)
Bibliography: p47
Unpriced (spiral) B81-13262

510'.76 — Great Britain. Schools. Curriculum subjects: Mathematics. Academic achievement of students. Tests: Profile of Mathematical Skills — *For teaching*

France, Norman. Profile of mathematical skills : (levels 1 & 2) : teacher's book and tables of norms / by Norman France. — Sunbury-on-Thames : Nelson, 1979. — 31p ; 28cm
ISBN 0-17-420193-1 (pbk) : £2.30 B81-38014

510'.76 — Mathematics — *Questions & answers*

Williams, Gareth, *1939-*. Instructor's manual to accompany Mathematics with applications in the management, natural, and social sciences / Gareth Williams. — Boston [Mass.] ; London : Allyn and Bacon, c1981. — 299p : ill ; 22cm
ISBN 0-205-07189-9 (pbk) : £1.00 B81-26396

510'.76 — Mathematics — *Questions & answers — For African students*

Jarman, E. A.. Certificate notes : modern mathematics / E.A. Jarman. — London : Longman, 1980. — 153p : ill ; 22cm. — (Study for success)
ISBN 0-582-60654-3 (pbk) : Unpriced B81-08456

510'.76 — Mathematics — *Questions & answers — For Caribbean students*

Greer, Alex. Multiple-choice tests in mathematics for Caribbean schools. — Cheltenham : Thornes, Feb.1982. — [96]p
ISBN 0-85950-448-4 (pbk) : £1.95 : CIP entry B81-35722

510'.76 — Mathematics — *Questions & answers — For Caribbean students — For schools*

Caribbean primary mathematics. — Aylesbury : Ginn
2. — Metric
1st part. — 1979 (1980 [printing]). — 80p : ill,forms ; 28cm
Cover title. — Previous ed.: 1973
ISBN 0-85474-075-9 (pbk) : Unpriced B81-09816

Caribbean primary mathematics. — Aylesbury : Ginn
2. — Metric
2nd part. — 1979 (1980 [printing]). — 80p : ill,forms ; 28cm
Cover title. — Previous ed.: 1973
ISBN 0-85474-076-7 (pbk) : Unpriced B81-09815

510'.76 — Mathematics — *Questions & answers — For children*

Pemberton, Gordon. Basic workbooks for every day / Gordon Pemberton. — Exeter : Wheaton
Bk.1. — 1981. — 32p : ill ; 28cm
Cover title
ISBN 0-08-024181-6 (pbk) : £0.50
Also classified at 428 B81-34596

Pemberton, Gordon. Basic workbooks for every day / Gordon Pemberton. — Exeter : Wheaton
Bk.2. — 1981. — 32p : ill,1plan ; 28cm
Cover title
ISBN 0-08-024182-4 (pbk) : £0.50
Also classified at 428 B81-34597

Pemberton, Gordon. Basic workbooks for every day / Gordon Pemberton. — Exeter : Wheaton
Bk.3. — 1981. — 32p : ill,1map,1plan ; 28cm
Cover title
ISBN 0-08-024183-2 (pbk) : £0.50
Also classified at 428 B81-34598

Pemberton, Gordon. Basic workbooks for every day / Gordon Pemberton. — Exeter : Wheaton
Bk.4. — 1981. — 32p : ill,1map ; 28cm
Cover title
ISBN 0-08-024184-0 (pbk) : £0.50
Also classified at 428 B81-34599

Pemberton, Gordon. Basic workbooks for every day / Gordon Pemberton. — Exeter : Wheaton
Bk.6. — 1981. — 32p : ill,2maps ; 28cm
Cover title
ISBN 0-08-024186-7 (pbk) : £0.50
Also classified at 428 B81-34600

Pemberton, Gordon. Basic workbooks for every day / Gordon Pemberton. — Exeter : Wheaton
Bk.7. — 1981. — 32p : ill,1map ; 28cm
Cover title
ISBN 0-08-024187-5 (pbk) : £0.50
Also classified at 428 B81-34601

Pemberton, Gordon. Basic workbooks for every day / Gordon Pemberton. — Exeter : Wheaton
Bk.8. — 1981. — 32p : ill ; 28cm
Cover title
ISBN 0-08-024188-3 (pbk) : £0.50
Also classified at 428 B81-34602

510'.76 — Mathematics — *Questions & answers — For East African students*

Modern mathematics for East Africa / edited by E.A. Jarman. — Harlow : Longman
"Adapted from 'Joint schools project mathematics' edited by M.C. Mitchelmore and B. Raymor"
Textbook 4. — 1980. — 284p : ill,maps ; 25cm
Includes index
ISBN 0-582-60651-9 (pbk) : £2.85 B81-34939

510'.76 — Mathematics — *Questions & answers — For Irish students*

Slevin, Tom. Step by step maths / Tom Slevin. — Dublin : Gill and Macmillan
4. — 1981. — 120p : ill(some col.) ; 21x22cm
ISBN 0-7171-1087-7 (pbk) : £1.70 B81-39803

Step by step maths. — Dublin : Gill and Macmillan
3 / Tom Slevin. — 1981. — 120p : ill(some col.) ; 21x22cm
ISBN 0-7171-1086-9 (pbk) : £1.70 B81-33661

510'.76 — Mathematics — *Questions & answers — For Irish students — For schools*

Step by step maths. — Dublin : Gill & Macmillan
2 / Clare Martin. — 1981. — 108p : ill(some col.) ; 21x22cm
ISBN 0-7171-1114-8 (pbk) : £1.40 B81-25564

510'.76 — Mathematics — *Questions & answers — For schools*

Bass, Doris. Link mathematics / Doris Bass, Ann Farnham. — London : Cassell
Bk.1. — 1981. — 138p : ill ; 23cm
ISBN 0-304-30741-6 (pbk) : Unpriced
ISBN 0-304-30742-4 (answers) : Unpriced B81-27027

Bass, Doris. Link mathematics / Doris Bass, Ann Farnham. — London : Cassell
Bk.2. — 1981. — 176p : ill ; 23cm
ISBN 0-304-30743-2 (pbk) : Unpriced
ISBN 0-304-30744-0 (answers) : Unpriced B81-27026

Bass, Doris. Link mathematics / Doris Bass, Ann Farnham. — London : Cassell
Bk.3. — 1981. — 178p : ill ; 23cm
ISBN 0-304-30745-9 (pbk) : Unpriced
ISBN 0-304-30746-7 (answers) B81-27025

Chuter, C. F.. Essentials of mathematics : a one volume course for O'Level / C.F. Chuter and R.W. Fox. — London : Edward Arnold, 1981. — vi,266p : ill ; 25cm
ISBN 0-7131-0418-x (pbk) : £3.50 : CIP rev. B80-00692

Clayton, B.. Practical mathematics / by B. Clayton. — Huddersfield : Schofield & Sims
3 / by Brian Clayton and Margaret Knight. — 1981. — 92p : ill(some col.),col.maps ; 28cm
ISBN 0-7217-2274-1 (pbk) : £1.25 B81-24189

Connah, P.. Revision maths / Peter Connah. — Basingstoke : Macmillan
ISBN 0-333-28860-2 (pbk) : £1.50 : CIP rev. B80-13364

Cox, Christopher J.. Practice papers in mathematics / Christopher J. Cox. — Cheltenham : Thornes
Bk. 1. — 1981. — 156p : ill ; 22cm + 1pamphlet(4p : ill, 22cm)
ISBN 0-85950-479-4 (pbk) : £1.95 B81-26806

510'.76 — Mathematics — *Questions & answers — For schools* *continuation*

Cox, Christopher J. Practice papers in mathematics / Christopher J. Cox. — Cheltenham : Thornes
Book 2. — 1981. — 177p : ill ; 22cm + answer book(6p : ill ; 22cm)
ISBN 0-85950-484-0 (pbk) : £1.95 : CIP rev. B81-03355

Derham, H. M.. Objective tests, O-level modern mathematics / H.M. Derham. — New ed. — London : Longman, 1980. — 78p : ill ; 22cm. — (Study for success)
Previous ed.: published as Multiple choice questions in modern mathematics. 1977
ISBN 0-582-65077-1 (pbk) : £0.95 B81-38172

Edwards, Suzanne. Numberland / Suzanne Edwards & Cherrie Wild. — Glasgow : Collins, c1981. — 3v. : ill ; 30cm + 1storybook(([24]p : ill ; 39cm))
ISBN 0-00-315332-0 (unbound) : £1.20
ISBN 0-00-315333-9 (v.2) : £0.40
ISBN 0-00-315334-7 (v.3) : £0.40
ISBN 0-00-315330-4 (story book) : £1.95 B81-12933

Exercises for certificate mathematics / Modular Mathematics Organization. — London : Heinemann Educational. — (Modular mathematics)
Book 2. — 1981. — 108p : ill ; 22cm
ISBN 0-435-50953-5 (pbk) : £1.95 B81-23370

Goddard, T. R.. Time for maths / compiled by T.R. Goddard, J.W. Adams and R.P. Beaumont. — Huddersfield : Schofield & Sims
5. — 1981. — 40p : ill(some col.) ; 30cm
ISBN 0-7217-2290-3 (pbk) : Unpriced B81-16607

Goddard, T. R.. Time for maths / compiled by T.R. Goddard, J.W. Adams and R.P. Beaumont. — Huddersfield : Schofield & Sims
6: [Pupil's book]. — 1981. — 40p : ill(some col.) ; 30cm
ISBN 0-7217-2291-1 (pbk) : £0.75 B81-29337

Goddard, T. R.. Time for maths / compiled by T.R. Goddard, J.W. Adams and R.P. Beaumont. — Huddersfield : Schofield & Sims
6: Teacher's notes and answers. — c1981. — 40p : ill(some col.) ; 30cm
ISBN 0-7217-2297-0 : £0.95 B81-35668

Haigh, A. M.. Keynote maths / Alan Haigh. — Slough : University Tutorial Press, 1981
Book 3. — 198p : ill ; 21cm
ISBN 0-7231-0796-3 (pbk) : £1.95 B81-27070

Hastie, B. R.. Worked examples in ordinary mathematics : paper 2 / B.R. Hastie. — Glasgow : Gibson, c1981. — 71p : ill ; 21cm. — (Pass books)
Text on inside covers
ISBN 0-7169-3117-6 (pbk) : Unpriced B81-21964

I can solve it : primary maths work cards. — Dublin : Folens
Bk.1 / [by] Bernadette McWey ; [illustration by Lynne Loftus]. — c1981. — 79p : ill ; 25cm
ISBN 0-86121-149-9 (pbk) : Unpriced B81-39126

I can solve it : primary maths work cards. — Dublin : Folens
Bk.2 / [by Bernadette McWey] ; [illustration by Lynne Loftus]. — c1981. — 96p : ill ; 24cm
Cover title. — Text on inside cover
ISBN 0-86121-150-2 (pbk) : Unpriced B81-40281

I can solve it : primary maths work cards. — Dublin : Folens
Bk.6 / J.J. O'Neill ; [illustration by Lynne Loftus]. — [1981?]. — 80p : ill ; 24cm
ISBN 0-86121-155-3 (pbk) : Unpriced B81-40282

Irwin, J. R.. Essentials of pure mathematics. — London : Edward Arnold, May 1981. — [320]p
ISBN 0-7131-0551-8 (pbk) : £4.00 : CIP entry B81-11917

Plumpton, Charles. Multiple-choice mathematics : an examination test books / C. Plumpton ; advisory editor N. Warwick. — Basingstoke : Macmillan, 1981. — 107p : ill ; 30cm
ISBN 0-333-28663-4 (pbk) : £1.95 B81-13630

Smith, R. L. (Ronald Levington). Practice questions in pure mathematics / R. L. Smith and C. Denton. — London : Edward Arnold, 1981. — ix,146p ; 23cm
ISBN 0-7131-0434-1 (pbk) : £2.95 B81-24953

Taylor, David C.. Essential mathematics for A Level / David C. Taylor, Ivor S. Atkinson. — Walton-on-Thames : Nelson, 1981. — 388p : ill ; 25cm
Includes index
ISBN 0-17-431280-6 (pbk) : £5.75 B81-36260

Wakeling, E.. Mechanical mathematics to O level / E. Wakeling and A.J. Raven. — London : Heinemann Educational, 1981. — 2v. : ill ; 22cm + Answer book(63p:ill;22cm)
ISBN 0-435-50776-1 (pbk) : Unpriced
ISBN 0-435-50777-x (v.2) : £1.50
ISBN 0-435-50778-8 (Answer book) : £2.75 B81-19348

Wright, Walter D.. Maths for living / Walter D. Wright. — Welwyn Garden City : Nisbet, 1981. — 64p : ill(some col.) ; 21cm + teacher's book(16p : ill;20cm)
Includes index
ISBN 0-7202-0933-1 (pbk) : £1.00 B81-10353

Young, D. (Dennis). Group mathematics test / D. Young. — 2nd ed.. — Sevenoaks : Hodder and Stoughton, c1980. — 2sheets(4p) : ill ; 24x31cm + Manual(23p ; 22cm ; pbk)
Previous ed.: 1970
ISBN 0-340-11620-x
ISBN 0-340-11621-8 (Form B) : £1.50
ISBN 0-340-26310-5 (Manual) : £1.25 B81-10803

510'.76 — Mathematics — *Questions & answers — For slow learning children — For schools*

Court, R. A.. Simple modern maths 3 / R.A. Court, A.M. Court ; with advice from M.B. Godsen. — Walton-on-Thames : Nelson
ISBN 0-17-431012-9 (pbk) : £1.50 B81-26943

Stanfield, Jan. Impact maths / Jan Stanfield, Jerzy Cwirko-Godycki ; illustrated by Anna Clarke. — London : Evans
Pupil's book 2. — 1981. — 64p : ill ; 25cm
ISBN 0-237-50226-7 (pbk) : Unpriced B81-37741

510'.76 — Mathematics — *Questions & answers — For Southern African students*

Bicknell, E. D.. Revision mathematics for Junior Certificate / E.D. Bicknell, J.E. Hay and M.W. Hay. — Harlow : Longman, 1980. — 160p : ill ; 25cm
ISBN 0-582-60695-0 (pbk) : £2.00 B81-37407

510'.76 — Mathematics — *Questions & answers — For users of pocket electronic calculators — For schools*

Birtwistle, C.. Maths with a calculator. — London : Edward Arnold, Feb.1982. — [48]p
ISBN 0-7131-0642-5 (pbk) : £1.60 : CIP entry B81-37561

Rothery, Andrew. Calculator maths / Andrew Rothery. — London : Harrap, 1980. — 68p : ill ; 21cm
ISBN 0-245-53496-2 (pbk) : £1.95 B81-06867

510'.76 — Mathematics — *Questions & answers — For West African students*

Kalejaiye, A. O.. New general mathematics for West Africa 2 / A.O. Kalejaiye, M.F. Macrae. — London : Longman, 1981
Cover title
Students' practice book. — 59p : ill,2maps ; 25cm
ISBN 0-582-65059-3 (pbk) : £0.70 B81-37403

510'.76 — Mathematics — *Study examples: Mathematics associated with occupations — Questions & answers — For schools*

MATCH : math applied to career highlights / written by Learning Achievement Corporation. — New York ; London : Gregg Division, McGraw-Hill
1: Number systems and addition : personal communications ; Subtraction : recreation. — c1981. — 127p : ill ; 28cm
ISBN 0-07-037111-3 (pbk) : £3.70 B81-19685

510'.7'8 — Schools. Curriculum subjects: Mathematics. Activities using pocket electronic calculators — *For teaching*

Moursurd, David G.. Calculators in the classroom : with applications for elementary and middle school teachers / David G. Moursurd ; contributing editor Douglas L. Shult. — New York ; Chichester : Wiley, c1981. — vi,202p : ill ; 23cm
Bibliography: p174-177
ISBN 0-471-08113-2 (pbk) : Unpriced B81-37489

510'.7'8 — Schools. Curriculum subjects: Mathematics. Learning by students. Applications of digital computer systems

Papert, Seymour. Mindstorms : children, computers and powerful ideas / Seymour Papert. — Brighton : Harvester, 1980. — viii,230p : ill ; 24cm. — (Harvester studies in cognitive science ; 14)
Includes index
ISBN 0-85527-163-9 : £8.50 : CIP rev. B80-06378

510'.9 — Mathematics, *to 1980*

Ashurst, F. Gareth. Founders of modern mathematics. — London : Muller, Feb.1982. — [144]p
ISBN 0-584-10380-8 : £7.50 : CIP entry B81-37578

Young, Laurence. Mathematicians and their times : history of mathematics and mathematics of history / Laurence Young. — Amsterdam ; Oxford : North-Holland, 1981. — x,344p ; 24cm. — (North-Holland mathematics studies ; 48) (Notas de matemática ; 76)
Includes index
ISBN 0-444-86135-1 (pbk) : £14.43 B81-16605

510'.92'2 — Mathematics. Von Neumann, John & Wiener, Norbert — *Biographies*

Heims, Steve J.. John von Neumann and Norbert Wiener : from mathematics to the technologies of life and death / Steve J. Heims. — Cambridge, Mass. ; London : MIT, c1980. — xviii,547p : ill,ports ; 24cm
Includes index
ISBN 0-262-08105-9 : £12.40 B81-02898

510'.92'4 — Mathematics. Babbage, Charles — *Biographies*

Hyman, Anthony. Charles Babbage. — Oxford : Oxford University Press, Jan.1982. — [350]p
ISBN 0-19-858170-x : £12.50 : CIP entry B81-34413

510'.92'4 — Mathematics. Hamilton, *Sir* William Rowan — *Biographies*

Hankins, Thomas L.. Sir William Rowan Hamilton / Thomas L. Hankins. — Baltimore ; London : Johns Hopkins University Press, c1980. — xxi,474p : ill,facsim,ports ; 24cm
Bibliography: p455-464. — Includes index
ISBN 0-8018-2203-3 : £19.50 B81-34184

510'.92'4 — Mathematics. MacLaurin, Colin — *Correspondence, diaries, etc.*

MacLaurin, Colin. The collected letters of Colin MacLaurin. — Nantwich : Shiva, Jan.1982. — [420]p
ISBN 0-906812-08-9 : £15.00 : CIP entry B81-37547

510'.92'4 — Mathematics. Peano, Giuseppe — *Biographies*

Kennedy, Hubert C.. Peano : life and works of Giuseppe Peano / Hubert C. Kennedy. — Dordrecht ; London : Reidel, c1980. — xii,230p : 1port ; 23cm. — (Studies in the history of modern science ; v.4)
Bibliography: p211-215. — Includes index
ISBN 90-277-1067-8 (cased) : Unpriced
ISBN 90-277-1068-6 (pbk) : Unpriced B81-02937

510'.92'4 — Mathematics. Philosophical perspectives. Philosophy of mathematics. Theories of Frege, Gottlob

Resnik, Michael D.. Frege and the philosophy of mathematics / Michael D. Resnik. — Ithaca ; London : Cornell University Press, c1980. — 244p ; 23cm
Bibliography: p235-240. - Includes index
ISBN 0-8014-1293-5 : £9.00 B81-05475

511 — MATHEMATICS. GENERALITIES

511'.024624 — Mathematics. Numerical methods — *For civil engineering*

Majid, K. I.. Introduction to matrix and numerical methods for civil engineers / by K.I. Majid. — Oxford : Woodstock Publishing, 1980. — iv,248p : ill ; 21cm
Includes index
ISBN 0-907300-00-6 (pbk) : Unpriced
Primary classification 512.9'434'024624
B81-03896

511'.11024054 — Motion — *Questions & answers — For children*

Watson, Philip. Super motion. — London : Methuen/Walker, Sept.1981. — [48]p. — (Science club)
ISBN 0-416-24260-x : £3.95 : CIP entry
B81-23775

511'.2 — Intuitionistic mathematics

Brouwer, L. E. J.. Brouwer's Cambridge lectures on intuitionism / edited by D. Van Dalen. — Cambridge : Cambridge University Press, 1981. — xii,109p : ill,1port ; 23cm
Bibliography: p103-105. — Includes index
ISBN 0-521-23441-7 : £9.50 : CIP rev.
B81-22696

511'.2 — Intuitionistic mathematics. Predicate calculus. Semantic aspects

Gabbay, Dov M.. Semantical investigations in Heyting's intuitionistic logic / Dov M. Gabbay. — Dordrecht ; London : Reidel, c1981. — x,287p : ill ; 23cm. — (Synthese library ; v.148)
Bibliography: p280-284. — Includes index
ISBN 90-277-1202-6 : Unpriced B81-26221

511.3 — Formal languages — *Conference proceedings*

Formal language theory : perspectives and open problems / edited by Ronald V. Book. — New York ; London : Academic Press, 1980. — xiii,454p : ill ; 24cm
Conference papers. — Includes bibliographies and index
ISBN 0-12-115350-9 : £14.00 B81-22003

511.3 — Lambda calculus

Barendregt, H. P.. The lambda calculus : its syntax and semantics / H.P. Barendregt. — Amsterdam ; Oxford : North-Holland, c1981. — xiv,615p : ill,ports ; 23cm. — (Studies in logic and the foundations of mathematics ; v.103)
Bibliography: p580-591. - Includes index
ISBN 0-444-85490-8 : £42.61 B81-23641

511.3 — Mathematical logic

Boolos, George. Computability and logic / George Boolos, Richard Jeffrey. — 2nd ed. — Cambridge : Cambridge University Press, 1980. — x,285p : ill ; 24cm. — ([Open University set book])
Previous ed.: 1974. — Includes index
ISBN 0-521-23479-4 (cased) : £17.50
ISBN 0-521-29967-5 (pbk) : £5.95 B81-06659

Grandy, Richard E.. Advanced logic for applications / Richard E. Grandy. — Dordrecht ; London : Reidel, c1979. — xi,167p ; 23cm. — (A Pallas paperback ; 13)
Originally published: 1977. — Includes index
ISBN 90-277-1034-1 (pbk) : Unpriced
B81-02774

Hofstadter, Douglas R.. Gödel, Escher, Bach : an eternal golden braid / Douglas R. Hofstadter. — Harmondsworth : Penguin, 1980, c1979. — xxi, : ill,music,ports ; 24cm
Originally published: Brighton : Harvester Press, 1979. — Bibliography: p746-756. - Includes index
ISBN 0-14-005579-7 (pbk) : £5.95 B81-00857

Reichenbach, Hans. Elements of symbolic logic / Hans Reichenbach. — New York : Dover ; London : Constable, 1980, c1975. — xiii,444p ; 22cm
Originally published: New York : Macmillan Co., 1947. — Includes index
ISBN 0-486-24004-5 (pbk) : £4.05 B81-18785

Wang, Hao. Popular lectures on mathematical logic / Wang Hao. — New York ; London : Van Nostrand Reinhold, c1981. — ix,273p : ill ; 24cm
Includes index
ISBN 0-442-23109-1 : £18.70 B81-11442

511.3 — Mathematical logic — *Festschriften*

To H.B. Curry : essays on combinatory logic, lambda calculus and formalism / edited by J.P. Seldin, J.R. Hindley. — London : Academic Press, 1980. — xxv,606p : ill,1port ; 24cm
Includes bibliographies
ISBN 0-12-349050-2 : £26.60 : CIP rev.
B80-11011

511.3 — Mathematics. Recursive functions — *For computer sciences*

Péter, Rózsa. Recursive functions in computer science. — Chichester : Horwood, May 1981. — [160]p. — (Ellis Horwood series in computers and their applications)
ISBN 0-85312-164-8 : £16.50 : CIP entry
B81-08822

511.3 — Propositional calculus

Segerbery, Krister. The essence of classical propositional operators. — Oxford : Clarendon, Apr.1981. — [150]p. — (Oxford logic guides)
ISBN 0-19-853173-7 : £10.00 : CIP entry
B81-00858

511.3'2 — Mathematics. Analytic sets — *Conference proceedings*

Analytic sets / by C.A. Rogers ... [et al.] ; [developed from lectures given at the London Mathematical Society Instructional Conference on Analytic Sets, University College London, July 1978]. — London : Academic Press, 1980p. — x,499p : ill ; 24cm
Includes 1 section in French. — Includes bibliographies and index
ISBN 0-12-593150-6 : £48.00 : CIP rev.
B80-10580

511.3'2 — Mathematics. Fuzzy sets

Dubois, Didier. Fuzzy sets and systems : theory and applications / Didier Dubois, Henri Prade. — New York ; London : Academic Press, 1980. — xvii,393p : ill ; 24cm. — (Mathematics in science and engineering ; v.144)
Includes bibliographies and index
ISBN 0-12-222750-6 : £27.80 B81-07340

511.3'2 — Mathematics. Fuzzy sets. Applications

Fuzzy reasoning and its applications / edited by E.H. Mamdani, B.R. Gaines. — London : Academic Press, 1981. — xviii,381p : ill ; 26cm. — (Computers and people series)
Includes bibliographies
ISBN 0-12-467750-9 : £12.60 : CIP rev.
B81-13549

511.3'22 — Axiomatic set theory

Chuaqui, R.. Axiomatic set theory : impredicative theories of classes / Rolando Basim Chuaqui. — Amsterdam ; Oxford : North-Holland, c1981. — xv,388p ; 24cm. — (North-Holland mathematical studies) (Notas de matemática ; (78))
Bibliography: p377-379. — Includes index
ISBN 0-444-86178-5 (pbk) : Unpriced
B81-29847

511.3'24 — Algebra. Ordered sets. Combinatorial optimisation & linear optimisation

Zimmermann, U.. Linear and combinatorial optimization in ordered algebraic structures / U. Zimmermann. — Amsterdam ; Oxford : North-Holland, c1981. — ix,380p : ill ; 25cm. — (Annals of discrete mathematics ; 10)
Bibliography: p339-368. - Includes index
ISBN 0-444-86153-x : £24.22 B81-21385

511'.4 — Applied mathematics. Approximation

Approximation theory and applications / [proceedings of a workshop on approximation theory and applications, Technion, Haifa, Israel May 5- June 25, 1980] ; edited by Zvi Ziegler. — New York ; London : Academic Press, 1981. — xi,358p : ill ; 24cm
Includes bibliographies
ISBN 0-12-780650-4 : £17.20 B81-39565

511'.4 — Mathematics. Approximation

Powell, M. J. D.. Approximation theory and methods / M.J.D. Powell. — Cambridge : Cambridge University Press, 1981. — x,339p : ill ; 24cm
Includes index
ISBN 0-521-22472-1 : £25.00 B81-24290

511'.4 — Mathematics. Approximation — *Conference proceedings*

Quantitative approximation : proceedings of a Symposium on Quantitative Approximation, held in Bonn, West Germany, August 20-24, 1979 / edited by Ronald A. Devore, Karl Scherer. — New York ; London : Academic Press, 1980. — xi,324p : ill ; 24cm
Includes bibliographies
ISBN 0-12-213650-0 : £12.40 B81-05692

511'.4'028542 — Mathematics. Approximation. Applications of digital computer systems. Programs. Optimal algorithms

Traub, J. F.. A general theory of optimal algorithms / J.F. Traub, H. Woźniakowski. — New York ; London : Academic Press, 1980. — xiv,341p : ill ; 24cm. — (ACM monograph series)
Includes bibliographies and index
ISBN 0-12-697650-3 : £20.20 B81-06004

511'.42 — Mathematics. Spline functions

Schumaker, Larry L.. Spline functions : basic theory / Larry L. Schumaker. — New York ; Chichester : Wiley, c1981. — xiv,553p : ill ; 24cm. — (Pure and applied mathematics, ISSN 0079-8185)
Bibliography: p524-547. — Includes index
ISBN 0-471-76475-2 : £26.40 B81-23430

511'.5 — Graph theory

Swamy, M. N. S.. Graphs, networks, and algorithms / M.N.S. Swamy, K. Thulasiraman. — New York ; Chichester : Wiley, c1981. — xviii,592p : ill ; 24cm
Includes index
ISBN 0-471-03503-3 : £23.50 B81-23332

511'.5 — Graph theory. Applications

Graphs, networks and design. — Milton Keynes : Open University Press. — (Technology/Mathematics : a third level interfaculty course)
[Unit 4]: Selections and distributions. — 1980. — 51p : ill,2facsims,3ports ; 30cm. — (TM361 ; 4)
At head of title: The Open University. — Bibliography: p50. — Includes index
ISBN 0-335-17058-7 (pbk) : Unpriced
B81-40820

511'.5 — Graph theory. Applications of algebra — *Conference proceedings*

Algebraic methods in graph theory / edited by L. Lovász and Vera T. Sós. — Amsterdam ; Oxford : North-Holland, 1981. — 2v.(847p) : ill ; 25cm. — (Colloquia mathematica Societatis János Bolyai, ISSN 0139-3383 ; 25)
Conference papers. — Includes bibliographies
ISBN 0-444-85442-8 : Unpriced B81-35559

511'.5 — Graphs

Temperley, H. N. V.. Graph theory and applications. — Chichester : Ellis Horwood, Nov.1981. — [166]p. — (Ellis Horwood series in mathematics and its applications)
ISBN 0-85312-252-0 : £15.00 : CIP entry
B81-30375

511'.5 — Graphs — *For children*

Wood, Leslie. A graph we make from the big red bus / Leslie Wood and Roy Burden. — [Exeter] : Wheaton, c1981. — [24]p : col.ill ; 20x21cm
ISBN 0-08-026433-6 (cased) : Unpriced
ISBN 0-08-026432-8 (pbk) : £0.85 B81-33422

511'.5 — Graphs. Spectral theory

Cvetković, Dragoš M.. Spectra of graphs : theory and application / Dragoš M. Cvetković, Michael Doob, Horst Sachs. — New York ; London : Academic Press, 1980, c1979. — 368p : ill ; 24cm. — (Pure and applied mathematics)
Bibliography: p324-359. — Includes index
ISBN 0-12-195150-2 : £25.20 B81-20858

511'.5 — Zero-symmetric graphs

Coxeter, H. S. M.. Zero-symmetric graphs : trivalent graphical regular representations, of groups / H.S.M. Coxeter, Roberto Frucht, David L. Powers. — New York ; London : Academic Press, 1981. — ix,170p : ill ; 24cm
Bibliography: p165-168. — Includes index
ISBN 0-12-194580-4 : £10.00 B81-38700

511'.5'076 — Graphs — *Questions & answers — For schools*

Hollands, Roy. Graphs and charts / Roy Hollands and Howell Moses. — St. Albans : Hart-Davis Educational, 1981. — (Basic maths)
[Pupils book]. — 31p : ill ; 25cm + Answer book(31p : ill ; 25cm)
ISBN 0-247-13066-4 (unbound) : £0.48
ISBN 0-247-13079-6 (Answer book) : £0.95
B81-24392

511'.6 — Combinatorial analysis. Applications of matroids

Bryant, Victor. Independence theory in combinations : an introductory account with applications to graphs and transversals / Victor Bryant and Hazel Perfect. — London : Chapman and Hall, 1980. — xii,144p : il! ; 23cm. — (Chapman and Hall mathematics series)
Bibliography: p139. — Includes index
ISBN 0-412-16220-2 (cased) : £10.00 : CIP rev.
ISBN 0-412-22430-5 (pbk) : unpriced
B80-03614

511'.6 — Combinatorial analysis — *Conference proceedings*

Combinatorics 79 / edited by M. Deza and I.G. Rosenberg. — Amsterdam ; Oxford : North-Holland, 1980
Conference papers. — Papers in English or French
Part 1. — xxii,309p : ill,ports ; 25cm. — (Annals of discrete mathematics ; 8)
Reprinted from the journal Annals of Discrete Mathematics, Vol.8, 1980. — Includes bibliographies
ISBN 0-444-86110-6 : £26.78
ISBN 0-444-86112-2 (set) : Unpriced
B81-19964

Combinatorics 79 / edited by M. Deza and I.G. Rosenberg. — Amsterdam ; Oxford : North-Holland, 1980
Conference papers. — Papers in English or French
Part 2. — vii,309p : ill ; 25cm. — (Annals of discrete mathematics ; 9)
Reprinted from the journal Annals of Discrete Mathematics, Vol.9, 1980. — Includes bibliographies
ISBN 0-444-86111-4 : £26.78
ISBN 0-444-86112-2 (set) : Unpriced
B81-19965

511'.6 — Combinatorial optimisation — *Conference proceedings*

Combinatorial mathematics, optimal designs and their applications / edited by J. Srivastava. — Amsterdam ; Oxford : North-Holland, 1980. — viii,391p : ill ; 25cm. — (Annals of discrete mathematics ; 6)
Conference papers. — Includes bibliographies
ISBN 0-444-86048-7 : £28.34 B81-06509

511'.6 — Ramsey theory

Graham, Ronald L.. Ramsey theory / Ronald L. Graham, Bruce L. Rothschild, Joel H. Spencer. — New York ; Chichester : Wiley, c1980. — ix,174p : ill ; 24cm. — (Wiley-Interscience series in discrete mathematics)
Bibliography: p465-169. — Includes index
ISBN 0-471-05997-8 : £11.75 B81-03899

511'.8 — Dynamical systems. Mathematical models

Modelling of dynamical systems / edited by H. Nicholson. — Stevenage : Peregrinus on behalf of the Institution of Electrical Engineers. — (IEE control engineering series ; 13)
Vol.2. — 1981. — xiv,264p : ill ; 24cm
Includes bibliographies and index
ISBN 0-906048-45-1 : Unpriced B81-12145

511'.8 — Mathematical models. Applications

Saaty, Thomas L.. Thinking with models : mathematical models in the physical, biological, and social sciences / by Thomas L. Saaty and Joyce M. Alexander. — Oxford : Pergamon, 1981. — xi,181p : ill ; 25cm. — (International series in modern applied mathematics and computer science ; v.2) (Pergamon international library)
Includes bibliographies and index
ISBN 0-08-026475-1 (cased) : Unpriced : CIP rev.
ISBN 0-08-026474-3 (pbk) : £6.80 B81-18156

511'.8 — Mathematical models. Applications — *Case studies*

Case studies in mathematical modeling / edited by William E. Boyce. — Boston [Mass.] ; London : Pitman, 1981. — xiii,386p : ill,maps ; 25cm. — ([Applicable mathematics series])
Includes bibliographies and index
ISBN 0-273-08486-0 : £22.00 B81-18453

511'.8 — Mathematical models - *Case studies*

Case studies in mathematical modelling. — Cheltenham : Thornes, Aug.1981. — [300]p
ISBN 0-85950-304-6 : £5.95 : CIP entry
B81-16901

511'.8 — Mathematical models. Design & applications — *Conference proceedings*

Polymodel 2 *(Conference : 1979 : Teeside Polytechnic)*. Modelling and simulation in practice /2 : proceedings of Polymodel 2, the Second Annual Conference of the North East Polytechnics Mathematical Modeling and Computer Simulation Group, held at Teeside Polytechnic in May 1979 / edited by M.J. O'Carroll ... [et al.]. — Northallerton (Garden House, Welbury, Northallerton, Yorkshire, DL6 2SE) : Emjcc, 1980. — 350p : ill ; 25cm
Includes bibliographies
ISBN 0-9506994-0-3 : Unpriced B81-15655

511'.8'05 — Mathematical models. Design & applications — *Conference proceedings — Serials*

Modeling and simulation. — Vol.11, pt.1 (1980). — Research Triangle Park : Instrument Society of America ; Chichester : Wiley [distributors], c1980. — 335p
ISBN 0-87664-495-7 : £16.50 B81-29998

Modeling and simulation. — Vol.11, pt.2 (1980). — Research Triangle Park : Instrument Society of America ; Chichester : Wiley [distributors], c1980. — p337-801
ISBN 0-87664-496-5 : £16.50 B81-29999

Modeling and simulation. — Vol.11, pt.3 (1980). — Research Triangle Park : Instrument Society of America ; Chichester : Wiley [distributors], c1980. — p803-1213
ISBN 0-87664-497-3 : £16.50 B81-30000

Modeling and simulation. — Vol.11, pt.4 (1980). — Research Triangle Park : Instrument Society of America ; Chichester : Wiley [distributors], c1980. — p1215-1672
ISBN 0-87664-498-1 : £16.50 B81-30001

511'.8'05 — Mathematical models — *Serials*

Mathematical modelling : an international journal. — Vol.1, no.1 (1980)-. — New York ; Oxford : Pergamon, 1980-. — v. : ill ; 26cm
Quarterly
Unpriced B81-06106

512 — ALGEBRA

512 — Algebra

Auvil, Daniel L.. Intermediate algebra / Daniel L. Auvil. — Reading, Mass. ; London : Addison-Wesley, c1979. — xi,494p : ill(some col.) ; 23cm
Text on lining papers. — Includes index
ISBN 0-201-00135-7 : £10.50 B81-40414

Drooyan, Irving. Elementary algebra : structure and skills. — 5th ed. / Irving Drooyan, Walter Hadel. — New York ; Chichester : Wiley, c1981. — ix,351p : ill ; 25cm
Previous ed.: / by Irving Drooyan, Walter Hadel, Frank Fleming. 1977. — Text, ill on lining papers. — Includes index
ISBN 0-471-08286-4 : £11.20 B81-17242

Kolman, Bernard. College algebra / Bernard Kolman, Arnold Shapiro. — New York ; London : Academic Press, c1981. — xvi,384,[72]p : ill(some col.) ; 26cm
Includes index
ISBN 0-12-417884-7 : £12.00 B81-40771

Schlichting, Marvin. Intermediate algebra / Marvin Schlichting. — New York ; London : Van Nostrand Reinhold, c1981. — x,573p : ill ; 24cm
Includes index
ISBN 0-442-21214-3 : £11.95 B81-25384

Wright, D. Franklin. Intermediate algebra / D. Franklin Wright, Bill D. New. — Boston, Mass. ; London : Allyn and Bacon, c1981. — x,494p : ill ; 25cm
Text on lining papers. — Includes index
ISBN 0-205-07185-6 : £11.25 B81-16298

Zuckerman, Martin M.. Intermediate algebra : a straightforward approach for college students / Martin M. Zuckerman. — New York ; London : Norton, c1976. — xiii,596p,A64,I6p : ill(some col.) ; 25cm
Text on lining papers. — Includes index
ISBN 0-393-09207-0 : £9.95 B81-23428

Zuckerman, Martin M.. Intermediate algebra : a straightforward approach / Martin M. Zuckerman. — Alternate ed. — New York ; Chichester : Wiley, c1981. — xvi,354,[43]p : ill (some col.) ; 26cm
Previous ed.: New York : Norton, 1976. — Ill. and text on lining papers. — Includes index
ISBN 0-471-09385-8 : £10.45 B81-24049

512 — Universal algebra

Cohn, P. M.. Universal algebra / P.M. Cohn. — Rev. ed. — Dordrecht ; London : Reidel, c1981. — xv,412p : ill ; 23cm. — (Mathematics and its applications ; v.6)
Previous ed.: New York : Harper & Row, 1965. — Bibliography: p381-400. — Includes index
ISBN 90-277-1213-1 (cased) : Unpriced
ISBN 90-277-1254-9 (pbk) : Unpriced
B81-24977

512'.00246 — Algebra — *Programmed instructions — For technicians*

King, Kenneth E.. Introductory algebra : and related topics for technicians / Kenneth E. King. — Englewood Cliffs ; London : Prentice-Hall, c1979. — [317]p : ill ; 28cm
ISBN 0-13-501585-5 : £6.45 B81-24399

512'.0076 — Algebra — *Questions & answers*

Groza, Vivian Shaw. Elementary algebra / Vivian Shaw Groza. — 3rd ed.. — Philadelphia ; London : Saunders, c1981. — ix,659p : ill ; 28cm
Previous ed.: 1978. — Text on inside front cover. — Includes index
ISBN 0-03-057719-5 (pbk) : Unpriced
B81-33138

Groza, Vivian Shaw. Intermediate algebra / Vivian Shaw Groza, Gene Sellers. — 2nd ed. — Philadelphia ; London : Saunders, c1981. — [842]p in various pagings : ill(some col.) ; 28cm
Previous ed.: 1978. — Includes index
ISBN 0-03-057722-5 (pbk) : Unpriced
B81-33139

Lewis, Harry. Elementary algebra skills for college / Harry Lewis. — New York ; London : D. Van Nostrand, c1981. — ix,350p : ill ; 28cm
Includes index
ISBN 0-442-20396-9 (pbk) : £11.20 B81-03744

512'.0076 — Algebra — *Questions & answers continuation*

Lewis, Harry. Intermediate algebra skills for college / Harry Lewis. — New York ; London : D. Van Nostrand, c1981. — vii,504p : ill ; 28cm
Text on inside back cover. — Includes index
ISBN 0-442-23163-6 : £12.10 B81-26432

McKeague, Charles P.. Intermediate algebra : a text/workbook / Charles P. McKeague. — New York ; London : Academic Press, c1981. — xvi,518,A55p : ill(some col.) ; 28cm
Includes index
ISBN 0-12-484763-3 (pbk) : £11.20 B81-39574

Marshall, A. Robert. Study guide to accompany Elementary algebra, second edition / A. Robert Marshall. — New York ; London : Academic Press, c1981. — iii,317p : ill ; 28cm
ISBN 0-12-484764-1 (pbk) : £4.00 B81-39575

Wright, D. Franklin. Introductory algebra / D. Franklin Wright, Bill D. New. — Boston [Mass.] ; London : Allyn and Bacon, c1981. — xiv,366p : ill(some col.) ; 25cm
Text on lining papers. — Includes index
ISBN 0-205-07310-7 : Unpriced B81-26207

512'.0076 — Algebra — *Questions & answers — For teaching*

McKeague, Charles P.. Instructor's manual for Elementary algebra / Charles P. McKeague. — New York ; London : Academic Press, [1981?]. — v,49p : ill ; 23cm
ISBN 0-12-484752-8 (unbound) : £1.80 B81-32786

512'.02 — Abstract algebra

Gardiner, C. F.. Modern algebra : a natural approach, with applications / C.F. Gardiner. — Chichester : Horwood, 1981. — 288p : ill ; 24cm. — (Ellis Horwood series in mathematics and its applications)
Bibliography: p283. - Includes index
ISBN 0-85312-285-7 : £12.50
ISBN 0-85312-303-9 (students ed.)
ISBN 0-470-27115-9 (Halsted Press) B81-24055

512'.13 — Algebra & trigonometry

Kolman, Bernard. College algebra and trigonometry / Bernard Kolman, Arnold Shapiro. — New York ; London : Academic Press, c1981. — xvi,506p,[96]p : ill(some col.) ; 26cm
Includes index
ISBN 0-12-417840-5 : £11.20 B81-35432

512'.13'076 — Algebra & trigonometry — *Questions & answers*

Barnett, Raymond A.. College algebra with trigonometry / Raymond A. Barnett. — 2nd ed. — New York ; London : McGraw-Hill, c1979. — xvi,523p : ill ; 25cm
Previous ed.: 1974. — Text and ill on lining papers. — Includes index
ISBN 0-07-003809-0 : £13.75 B81-12109

512'.13'077 — Algebra & trigonometry — *Programmed instructions*

Kolman, Bernard. Introduction to algebra and trigonometry / Bernard Kolman, Arnold Shapiro. — New York ; London : Academic Press, c1981. — xvi,602p in various pagings : ill(some col.) ; 26cm
Includes index
ISBN 0-12-417830-8 (pbk) : £7.40 B81-29767

512'.2 — Finite groups — *Conference proceedings*

Finite simple groups II / [proceedings of a London Mathematical Society Research Symposium in Finite Simple Groups held at the University of Durham in July-August 1978] ; edited by Michael J. Collins. — London : Academic Press, 1980. — xv,345p : ill ; 24cm
Includes bibliographies
ISBN 0-12-181480-7 : £25.00 : CIP rev. B80-09201

512'.2 — One-parameter semigroups

Davies, E. B.. One-parameter semigroups / E.B. Davies. — London : Academic Press, 1980. — viii,230p ; 24cm. — (L.M.S. monographs, ISSN 0076-0560 ; 15)
Bibliography: p221-226. - Includes index
ISBN 0-12-206280-9 : £19.80 : CIP rev. B80-11012

512'.2 — Semigroups — *Conference proceedings*

Monash University Conference on Semigroups *(1979 : Monash University)*. Semigroups : proceedings of the Monash University Conference on Semigroups held at the Monash University, Clayton, Victoria, Australia, October, 1979 / edited by T.E. Hall, P.R. Jones, G.B. Preston. — New York ; London : Academic Press, 1980. — x,255p : ill ; 24cm
Includes bibliographies
ISBN 0-12-319450-4 : £10.20 B81-03890

512'.2'0212 — Algebra. Groups — *Tables*

Thomas, A. D. (Alan David). Group tables / A.D. Thomas and G.V. Wood. — Orpington (9 Clareville Rd, Orpington, Kent BR5 1RV) : Shiva, c1980. — 184p : ill ; 24cm. — (Shiva mathematics series ; 2)
ISBN 0-906812-04-6 (cased) : £12.50 : CIP rev.
ISBN 0-906812-02-x (pbk) : £6.50 B80-05891

512'.22 — Group theory

Hiller, H.. Geometry of coxeter groups. — London : Pitman, Jan.1982. — [221]p. — (Research notes in mathematics ; 54)
ISBN 0-273-08517-4 : £8.50 : CIP entry B81-34157

512'.22 — Group theory *expounded by* **permutations**

Glass, A. M. W.. Ordered permutation groups. — Cambridge : Cambridge University Press, Jan.1982. — [336]p. — (London Mathematical Society lecture notes series, ISSN 0076-0552 ; 55)
ISBN 0-521-24190-1 (pbk) : £12.50 : CIP entry B81-33996

512'.4 — Non-commutative rings with chain conditions

Chatters, A. W.. Rings with chain conditions / A.W. Chatters & C.R. Hajarnavis. — Boston [Mass.] ; London : Pitman Advanced Publishing, c1980. — 197p ; 25cm. — (Research notes in mathematics ; 44)
Bibliography: p183-195. — Includes index
ISBN 0-273-08446-1 (pbk) : £7.50 B81-03198

512'.5 — Linear algebra

Anton, Howard. Elementary linear algebra / Howard Anton. — 3rd ed. — New York ; Chichester : Wiley, c1981. — xvii,339,A1-A28, I1-I7p : ill(some col.) ; 24cm
Previous ed.: 1977. — Includes index
ISBN 0-471-05338-4 : £11.45 B81-18976

Daniel, James W.. Elementary linear algebra and its applications / James W. Daniel. — Englewood Cliffs ; London : Prentice-Hall, c1981. — xii,310,A27p : ill ; 25cm
Text on lining papers. — Includes index
ISBN 0-13-258293-7 : £12.30 B81-25172

512'.55 — Algebraic K-theory

Silvester, John R.. Introduction to algebraic K-theory / John R. Silvester. — London : Chapman and Hall, 1981. — xi,255p ; 22cm. — (Chapman and Hall mathematics series)
Bibliography: p251. — Includes index
ISBN 0-412-22700-2 (cased) : Unpriced : CIP rev.
ISBN 0-412-23740-7 (pbk) : Unpriced B81-16402

512'.55 — Hopf algebras

Abe, Eiichi. Hopf algebras / Eiichi Abe ; translated by Hisae Kinoshita and Hiroko Tanaka. — Cambridge : Cambridge University Press, 1980. — xii,284p : ill ; 23cm. — (Cambridge tracts in mathematics ; [74])
Includes index
ISBN 0-521-22240-0 : £16.00 B81-04727

512'.55 — Mathematics. Category theory

Krishnan, V. Sankrithi. An introduction to category theory / V. Sankrithi Krishnan. — New York ; Oxford : North Holland, c1981. — x,173p : ill ; 24cm
Bibliography: p167-168. - Includes index
ISBN 0-444-00383-5 : £16.04 B81-11293

512'.55 — Semisimple Lie groups. Representations — *Conference proceedings*

NATO Advanced Study Institute on Representations of Lie Groups and Harmonic Analysis *(1977 : Liège)*. Harmonic analysis and representations of semisimple Lie groups : lectures given at the NATO Advanced Study Institute on Representations of Lie Groups and Harmonic Analysis, held at Liège, Belgium, September 5-17, 1977 / edited by J.A. Wolf, M. Cahen and M. De Wilde. — Dordrecht ; London : Reidel, c1980. — viii,495p : ill ; 23cm. — (Mathematical physics and applied mathematics ; v.5)
Includes bibliographies and index
ISBN 90-277-1042-2 : Unpriced B81-05650

512'.55 — Topological algebras. K-theory

Berrick, A. J.. An approach to algebraic K-theory. — London : Pitman, Feb.1982. — [116]p. — (Research notes in mathematics ; 56)
ISBN 0-273-08529-8 (pbk) : £8.50 : CIP entry B81-35775

512'.55 — Von Neumann algebras

Stratila, Serban. Modular theory in operator algebras. — Tunbridge Wells : Abacus, Sept.1981. — [492]p
ISBN 0-85626-190-4 : £12.00 : CIP entry B81-22510

512'.7 — Number theory

Cohn, Harvey. [A second course in number theory]. Advanced number theory / Harvey Cohn. — Corr. republication. — New York : Dover ; London : Constable, 1980, c1962. — xi,276p : ill ; 21cm
Originally published: New York : Wiley, 1962. — Bibliography: p243-246. - Includes index
ISBN 0-486-64023-x (pbk) : £2.90 B81-18489

512'.73 — Additive number theory. Hardy-Littlewood method

Vaughan, R. C.. The Hardy-Littlewood method / R.C. Vaughan. — Cambridge : Cambridge University Press, 1981. — vii,172p ; 23cm. — (Cambridge tracts in mathematics)
Bibliography: p152-168. — Includes index
ISBN 0-521-23439-5 : £15.00 : CIP rev. B81-14983

512'.73 — Analytic number theory — *Conference proceedings*

Recent progress in analytic number theory / edited by H. Halberstam and C. Hooley. — London : Academic Press, 1981. — 2v.(xii,628p) ; 24cm
Conference papers. — Includes bibliographies
ISBN 0-12-318201-8 : Unpriced : CIP rev.
ISBN 0-12-318202-6 (v.2) B81-12373

512.9 — Algebra — *For schools*

Greer, A.. Revision practice in algebra / A. Greer. — Cheltenham : Thornes, 1981. — 82p : ill ; 19cm. — (ST(P) revision notes series)
ISBN 0-85950-321-6 (pbk) : £1.25 : CIP rev. B81-03184

McKeague, Charles P.. Elementary algebra / Charles P. McKeague. — 2nd ed. — New York ; London : Academic Press, c1981. — xiv,386p : ill(some col.) ; 25cm
Previous ed.: 1978. — Text on lining papers. — Includes index
ISBN 0-12-484755-2 : £9.00 B81-35436

512.9'0024372 — Algebra — *For teaching*

Halford, Nancy. Instructor's manual to accompany Wright and New's Introductory algebra / Nancy Halford. — Boston, Mass. ; London : Allyn and Bacon, c1981. — 257p : ill ; 24cm
ISBN 0-205-07311-5 (pbk) : Unpriced B81-26212

512.9'0024372 — Algebra — *For teaching*
continuation

Johnson, Carol. Instructor's manual to accompany Wright and New's Intermediate algebra / Carol Johnson. — Boston, Mass. ; London : Allyn and Bacon, c1981. — 270p : ill ; 24cm
ISBN 0-205-07186-4 (pbk) : Unpriced
B81-26211

Johnson, Carol. Study guide to accompany Wright and New's Intermediate algebra / Carol Johnson with Nancy Halford. — Boston, Mass. ; London : Allyn and Bacon, c1981. — x,231p : ill ; 24cm
ISBN 0-205-07187-2 (pbk) : Unpriced
B81-40106

512.9'0076 — Algebra — *Questions & answers — For schools*

Bolt, R. L.. Revision and practice in algebra / R.L. Bolt. — London : Edward Arnold, 1981. — 58p ; 23cm + Answer book(21p ; 23cm)
ISBN 0-7131-0506-2 (pbk) : £1.25
ISBN 0-7131-0515-1 (Answer book) : £1.25
B81-25401

Halford, Nancy. Study guide to accompany Wright and New's Introductory algebra / Nancy Halford with Carol Johnson. — Boston [Mass.] ; London : Allyn and Bacon, c1981. — x,330p : ill ; 24cm
ISBN 0-205-07312-3 (pbk) : £2.50 B81-40667

Hollands, Roy. Basic algebra / Roy Hollands and Howell Moses. — St. Albans : Hart-Davis Educational, 1981. — (Basic maths)
[Pupils book]. — 31p : ill ; 25cm + Answer book(31p : ill ; 25cm)
ISBN 0-247-13067-2 (unbound) : £0.48
ISBN 0-247-13081-8 (Answer book) : £0.95
B81-24393

512.9'434 — Algebra. Large scale matrices

Large scale matrix problems / edited by Åke Björck, Robert J. Plemmons, Hans Schneider. — New York ; Oxford : North Holland, c1981. — 404p : ill ; 24cm
Includes bibliographies and index
ISBN 0-444-00563-3 : Unpriced B81-30678

512.9'434 — Algebra. Matrices

Eves, Howard. Elementary matrix theory / Howard Eves. — New York : Dover ; London : Constable, 1980, c1966. — xvi,325p : ill ; 21cm
Originally published: Boston, Mass. : Allyn and Bacon, 1966. — Bibliography: p310-314. — Includes index
ISBN 0-486-63946-0 (pbk) : £3.45 B81-00094

512.9'434 — Algebra. Sparse matrices. Applications — *Conference proceedings*

IMA Numerical Analysis Group. *Conference (1980 : University of Reading)*. Sparse matrices and their uses : based on the proceedings of the IMA Numerical Analysis Group Conference, organised by the Institute of Mathematics and its Applications and held at the University of Reading, 9th-11th July, 1980 / edited by Iain S. Duff. — London : Academic Press, 1981. — xii,387p : ill ; 24cm. — (The Institute of Mathematics and its Applications conference series)
Includes bibliographies and index
ISBN 0-12-223280-1 : £18.00 : CIP rev.
B81-06062

512.9'434 — Algebra. Sparse matrices. Solution. Applications of digital computer systems

George, Alan, *1943-*. Computer solution of large sparse positive definite systems / Alan George, Joseph W-H Liu. — Englewood Cliffs ; London : Prentice-Hall, c1981. — xii,324p : ill ; 24cm. — (Prentice-Hill series in computational mathematics)
Bibliography: p314-320. — Includes index
ISBN 0-13-165274-5 : £17.45 B81-28220

12.9'434 — Linear algebra. Matrices

Graham, Alexander. Kronecker products and matrix calculus. — Chichester : Ellis Horwood, Nov.1981. — [160]p. — (Ellis Horwood series in mathematics and its applications)
ISBN 0-85312-391-8 : £14.95 : CIP entry
B81-31065

512.9'434 — Linear algebra. Matrices — *For engineering & science*

Deif, Assem. Advanced matrix theory for scientists and engineers. — Tunbridge Wells : Abacus, Feb.1982. — [250]p
ISBN 0-85626-327-3 : £12.50 : CIP entry
B81-39225

512.9'434 — Linear equations. Solution. Algebra. Matrices. Applications of digital computer systems. Programs

Rice, John R.. Matrix computations and mathematical software / John R. Rice. — New York ; London : McGraw-Hill, c1981. — xii,248p : ill,facsims ; 25cm. — (McGraw-Hill computer science series)
Bibliography: p241-242. — Includes index
ISBN 0-07-052145-x : £16.75 B81-39821

512.9'434 — Matrix algorithms. Rounding errors. Analysis. Applications of digital computer systems

Miller, Webb. Software for roundoff analysis of matrix algorithms / Webb Miller, Celia Wrathall. — New York ; London : Academic Press, 1980. — x,151p : ill ; 24cm. — (Computer science and applied mathematics)
Bibliography: p143-147. — Includes index
ISBN 0-12-497250-0 : £10.40 B81-22002

512.9'434'02433 — Algebra. Matrices — *For economics*

Rau, Nicholas. Matrices and mathematical programming : an introduction for economists / Nicholas Rau. — London : Macmillan, 1981. — xiii,236p : ill ; 23cm
Bibliography: p231-232. — Includes index
ISBN 0-333-27768-6 : £20.00 B81-22373

512.9'434'024624 — Algebra. Matrices — *For civil engineering*

Majid, K. I.. Introduction to matrix and numerical methods for civil engineers / by K.I. Majid. — Oxford : Woodstock Publishing, 1980. — iv,248p : ill ; 21cm
Includes index
ISBN 0-907300-00-6 (pbk) : Unpriced
Also classified at 511'.024624 B81-03896

513 — ARITHMETIC

513 — Arithmetic — *For schools*

Greer, A.. Revision practice in arithmetic / A. Greer. — Cheltenham : Thornes, 1981. — 54p : ill ; 19cm. — (ST(P) revision notes series)
ISBN 0-85950-320-8 (pbk) : £1.00 : CIP rev.
B81-03183

Sharples, J. B.. Arithmetic : a complete course for first examinations / J.B. Sharples. — Glasgow : Collins, 1981. — 126p : ill ; 26cm
Text on inside cover
ISBN 0-00-322005-2 (pbk) : £1.75 B81-20857

Sharples, J. B.. Arithmetic : a complete course for first examinations / J.B. Sharples. — S.C.E. 'O' grade. — Glasgow : Collins, 1981. — 126p : ill ; 26cm
Text on inside cover
ISBN 0-00-322006-0 (pbk) : £1.75 B81-20856

513'.0212 — Arithmetic — *Tables — For schools*

Whitehead, Geoffrey. Arithmetical tables : for junior, middle and secondary schools / by Geoffrey Whitehead. — Huddersfield (P.O. Box 1, Holmfirth, Huddersfield HD7 2RP) : Vyner, c1981. — 16p : ill ; 24cm. — (The SIMPLEX educational series ; ESI)
Cover title. — Text on inside covers
ISBN 0-906628-03-2 (pbk) : £0.60 B81-19451

513'.024613 — Arithmetic — *Questions & answers — For nursing*

McHenry, Ruth W.. Self-teaching tests in arithmetic for nurses. — 10th ed. / Ruth W. McHenry. — St. Louis ; London : Mosby, 1980. — x,184p : ill ; 27cm + 1 answers pamphlet(18p ; 27cm)
Previous ed.: / Ruth W. Jessee, Ruth W. McHenry. 1975
ISBN 0-8016-2505-x (pbk) : Unpriced
B81-08164

513'.076 — Arithmetic — *Questions & answers — For children*

Griffiths, A. L.. Basic 5 a day / A.L. Griffiths ; [illustrations by Peter Joyce] ; [diagrams by Hamish Gordon]. — Edinburgh : Oliver & Boyd, 1981. — 60p : ill(some col.) ; 25cm + Answers([8]p;21cm)
ISBN 0-05-003433-2 (pbk) : £1.10
ISBN 0-05-003439-1 (Answers) : Unpriced
B81-15239

Griffiths, A. L.. Basic 6 a day / A.L. Griffiths. — Edinburgh : Oliver & Boyd, 1981. — 76p : ill(some col.) ; 25cm
ISBN 0-05-003434-0 (pbk) : Unpriced
B81-37840

513'.076 — Arithmetic — *Questions & answers — For schools*

Arithmetic : revision and practice / M. Bowman ... [et al.]. — Oxford : Oxford University Press, 1981. — 212p : ill ; 25cm
ISBN 0-19-914087-1 (pbk) : £2.75 B81-25408

Bullock, G. V.. Foundation / G.V. Bullock. — Andover : Philograph
Number book 4: Division, hundreds, tens and units : Style U. — [1981?]. — 16p ; 18cm
ISBN 0-85370-312-4 (pbk) : £1.20 (for pack of 5 copies) B81-16199

Pemberton, Gordon. Basic workbooks for every day / Gordon Pemberton. — Exeter : Wheaton
Cover title
Book 5. — 1981. — 32p : ill,1map ; 28cm
ISBN 0-08-024185-9 (pbk) : £0.50
Primary classification 428 B81-36644

Smith, Ewart. Examples in arithmetic : for CSE/O/CS / Ewart Smith. — Cheltenham : Thornes, 1981. — 107p : ill ; 22cm
ISBN 0-85950-301-1 (pbk) : £1.30 : CIP rev.
B81-06029

513'.076 — Arithmetic — *Questions & answers — For users of electronic calculators — For schools*

Shelton, J.. Calculator mathematics / J. Shelton. — Glasgow : Collins, 1981. — 48p : ill ; 23cm
ISBN 0-00-318735-7 (pbk : non-net) : £0.75
ISBN 0-00-197016-x (pbk : net) : £0.95
B81-20918

Watson, F. R.. BAC pac : basic arithmetic with a calculator / F.R. Watson. — [Keele] : University of Keele, [1981]. — 61p : ill ; 30cm. — (Keele mathematical education publications)
£1.00 (unbound) B81-19700

Wroe, Geoffrey. Try the electronic calculator / Geoffrey Wroe. — London : Harrap, 1980. — 32p : col.ill ; 21cm. — (Maths takes off. Level 3. Arithmetic)
ISBN 0-245-53756-2 (pbk) : £0.75 B81-07778

513'.076 — Records of achievement. Arithmetical calculations — *Questions & answers*

Marsh, L. G.. The Guinness mathematics book / by Leonard Marsh. — Enfield (2 Cecil Court, London Rd., Enfield, Middx) : GBR Educational, c1980. — 93p : ill(some col.) ; 21cm
ISBN 0-85112-630-8 (pbk) : £2.50 : CIP rev.
B81-01840

513'.077 — Arithmetic — *Programmed instructions*

Carman, Robert A.. Basic mathematical skills : a guided approach / Robert A. Carman, Marilyn J. Carman. — 2nd ed. — New York ; Chichester : Wiley, c1981. — xii,576p : ill (some col.) ; 28cm
Previous ed. : 1975. — Includes index
ISBN 0-471-03608-0 (pbk) : £10.90 B81-18440

513'.12 — Algebra & arithmetic

Engelsohn, Harold S.. Basic mathematics : arithmetic and algebra / Harold S. Engelsohn, Joseph Feit. — New York ; Chichester : Wiley, c1980. — xi,532p : ill(some col.),1map,2plans ; 28cm
Includes index
ISBN 0-471-24145-8 (pbk) : £10.10 B81-02612

513′.2 — Arithmetic. Addition — *For pre-school children*

Bruna, Dick. I know about numbers / Dick Bruna. — London : Methuen, 1981. — [26]p : col.ill ; 16cm
ISBN 0-416-20880-0 : £1.35 B81-19742

513′.2 — Numbers — *For children*

Bown, Derick. Numbers and colours / illustrated by Derick Bown ; edited by Jane Carruth. — Maidenhead : Purnell, 1975 (1981 [printing]). — [26]p : chiefly col.ill ; 25cm. — (My first colour library)
ISBN 0-361-05049-6 : £0.99
Also classified at 535.6 B81-18847

Curry, Peter. Peter Curry's 123. — Tadworth : World's Work, c1981. — [32]p : chiefly col.ill ; 18cm
ISBN 0-437-32939-9 : £2.95 B81-12957

Dugan, Michael. Nonsense numbers / text by Michael Dugan ; pictures by Jack Newnham. — [London] : Angus & Robertson, 1980. — [32]p : col.ill ; 21x29cm
Originally published: Melbourne : Nelson, 1980
ISBN 0-207-95962-5 : £3.95 B81-08339

Fior, Jane. 123 / Jane Fior ; pictures by Gill Chapman. — London : Collins, c1981. — [48]p : col.ill ; 15cm. — (Let's read ; 2) (Collins colour cubs)
ISBN 0-00-196034-2 (pbk) : Unpriced B81-15721

Fowler, Richard, *1944-*. The bean 123 / by Richard Fowler. — Harlow : Longman, 1981. — 28p : chiefly col.ill ; 28cm
ISBN 0-582-39124-5 : £2.95 B81-22326

The **New** gold medal book of numbers, shapes and colours. — London : Dean, c1980. — 45p : chiefly col.ill ; 26cm
ISBN 0-603-00204-8 : £1.25
Primary classification 516 B81-13259

Wood, Leslie. Numbers we make from the big red bus / Leslie Wood and Roy Burden. — [Exeter] : Wheaton, c1981. — [24]p : col.ill ; 20x21cm
ISBN 0-08-026435-2 (cased) : Unpriced
ISBN 0-08-026434-4 (pbk) : £0.85 B81-32868

513′.2 — Numbers — *For pre-school children*

Cassin, S.. Number fun / S. Cassin & D. Smith ; illustrated by A. Rodger. — Glasgow : Collins. — (First steps) (Collins help your child series)
1. — 1980. — 34p : chiefly ill ; 26cm
ISBN 0-00-197011-9 (pbk) : £0.65 B81-14170

Cassin, S.. Number fun / S. Cassin & D. Smith ; illustrated by A. Rodger. — Glasgow : Collins. — (First steps) (Collins help your child series)
2. — 1981. — 34p : chiefly ill ; 26cm
ISBN 0-00-197022-4 (pbk) : £0.65 B81-14171

Stobbs, Joanna. One sun, two eyes, and a million stars / Joanna and William Stobbs. — Oxford : Oxford University Press, c1981. — [26]p : chiefly col.ill ; 22x23cm
ISBN 0-19-279747-6 : £4.25 B81-39615

513′.2′019 — Numbers. Recall & recognition

Welford, A. T.. Comparing recall and recognition in signal detection terms / A.T. Welford. — Cardiff (c/o R. Slater, Department of Applied Psychology, UWIST, Llwyn-y-Grant, Penylan, Cardiff CF3 7UX) : [UWIST Department of Applied Psychology], 1981. — 35p : ill ; 30cm. — (Occasional paper / UWIST Department of Applied Psychology ; no.9)
Bibliography: p32-34
£0.50 (spiral)
Primary classification 428.1 B81-24797

513′.2′0222 — Numbers — *Illustrations* — *For children*

Crowther, Robert. The most amazing hide-and-seek counting book / by Robert Crowther. — [Harmondsworth] : Kestrel, c1981. — [12]p : chiefly col.ill ; 23x31cm
Originally published: 1977
ISBN 0-7226-5598-3 : £4.50 B81-19403

One green frog. — London : Methuen Children's Books, 1981. — [24]p : chiefly col.ill ; 22cm
Captions translated from the Italian
ISBN 0-416-20850-9 (spiral) : £3.25 B81-18251

Woolcock, Peter. One, two, three book of numbers. — London : Hodder and Stoughton Children's Books, Sept.1981. — [48]p
ISBN 0-340-26646-5 : £2.50 : CIP entry B81-23928

513′.2′076 — Arithmetic. Addition & subtraction — *Questions & answers* — *For schools*

Hesse, K. A.. Adding & subtracting : hundreds of sums carefully selected and graded to give extra practice to children of all ages / K.A. Hesse. — Harlow : Longman, 1980 (1981 [printing]). — 32p ; 25cm. — (Basic arithmetic practice ; 1)
ISBN 0-582-39170-9 (pbk) : £0.60 B81-39673

Wroe, Geoffrey. Addition and subtraction problems / Geoffrey Wroe. — London : Harrap, 1980. — 32p : ill ; 21cm. — (Maths takes off. Level 3. Number)
ISBN 0-245-53750-3 (pbk) : £0.75 B81-07775

513′.2′076 — Arithmetic. Addition — *Questions & answers*

The **Old** fashioned adding-up book : the no-nonsense book of practice in basic addition (with answers). — London : Ward Lock Educational, 1981. — 11 leaves ; 32x13cm
ISBN 0-7062-4086-3 (pbk) : £0.50 B81-13965

513′.2′076 — Arithmetic. Multiplication & division — *Questions & answers* — *For schools*

Hesse, K. A.. Multiplying & dividing : hundreds of sums, carefully selected and graded to give extra practice to children of all ages / K.A. Hesse. — Harlow : Longman, 1980 (1981 [printing]). — 32p ; 25cm. — (Basic arithmetic practice ; 2)
ISBN 0-582-39171-7 (pbk) : £0.60 B81-39674

Millinship, L. P.. Master your tables / L.P. Millinship, D.R. Howells. — Oxford : Basil Blackwell
2. — 1981. — [24]p ; 20cm
ISBN 0-631-92330-6 (pbk) : £0.55 B81-17547

Millinship, L. P.. Master your tables / L.P. Millinship, D.R. Howells. — Oxford : Basil Blackwell
3. — 1981. — [24]p ; 20cm
ISBN 0-631-92320-9 (pbk) : £0.55 B81-17544

Millinship, L. P.. Master your tables / L.P. Millinship, D.R. Howells. — Oxford : Basil Blackwell
4. — 1981. — [24]p ; 20cm
ISBN 0-631-92310-1 (pbk) : £0.55 B81-17546

Millinship, L. P.. Master your tables / L.P. Millinship, D.R. Howells. — Oxford : Basil Blackwell
5. — 1981. — [24]p : 20cm
ISBN 0-631-92300-4 (pbk) : £0.55 B81-17545

Millinship, L. P.. Master your tables / L.P. Millinship, D.R. Howells. — Oxford : Basil Blackwell
10. — 1981. — [24]p ; 20cm
ISBN 0-631-92250-4 (pbk) : £0.55 B81-17548

Wroe, Geoffrey. Multiplication and division problems / Geoffrey Wroe. — London : Harrap, 1980. — 32p : ill ; 21cm. — (Maths takes off. Level 3. Number)
ISBN 0-245-53751-1 (pbk) : £0.75 B81-07785

513′.2′076 — Arithmetic. Multiplication — *Questions & answers* — *For schools*

Multiplication. — Ely (Resource and Technology Centre, Back Hill, Ely, Cambs.) : EARO, c1979. — 36p : ill ; 15x22cm. — (Access)
ISBN 0-904463-56-7 (pbk) : Unpriced B81-20983

Wroe, Geoffrey. Buying in bulk / Geoffrey Wroe. — London : Harrap, 1980. — 32p : col.ill ; 21cm. — (Maths takes off. Level 3. Arithmetic)
ISBN 0-245-53752-x (pbk) : £0.75 B81-07783

513′.24 — Arithmetic. Percentages — *Questions & answers* — *For schools*

Wroe, Geoffrey. Discount / Geoffrey Wroe. — London : Harrap, 1980. — 32p : col.ill ; 21cm. — (Maths takes off. Level 3. Arithmetic)
ISBN 0-245-53755-4 (pbk) : £0.75 B81-07782

513′.24 — Arithmetic. Ratios — *Questions & answers* — *For schools*

Hollands, Roy. Percentage, ratio, proportion / Roy Hollands and Howell Moses. — St. Albans : Hart-Davis Educational, 1981. — (Basic maths)
[Pupils book]. — 31p : ill ; 25cm + Answer book(31p : ill ; 25cm)
ISBN 0-247-13068-0 (unbound) : £0.48
ISBN 0-247-13082-6 (Answer book) : £0.95 B81-24391

513′.26′076 — Arithmetic. Fractions. Addition & subtraction — *Questions & answers* — *For schools*

Wroe, Geoffrey. Addition and subtraction of fractions / Geoffrey Wroe. — London : Harrap, 1980. — 32p : col.ill ; 21cm. — (Maths takes off. Level 3. Arithmetic)
ISBN 0-245-53753-8 (pbk) : £0.75 B81-07784

513′.26′076 — Arithmetic. Fractions — *Questions & answers* — *For schools*

Wroe, Geoffrey. Make a fraction / Geoffrey Wroe. — London : Harrap, 1980. — 32p : col.ill ; 21cm. — (Maths takes off. Level 3. Arithmetic)
ISBN 0-245-53754-6 (corrected : pbk) : £0.75 B81-13029

513′.5 — Numeration — *For children*

Allington, Richard. Numbers / by Richard Allington and Kathleen Krull ; illustrated by Tom Garcia. — Oxford : Blackwell Raintree, c1981. — 31p : col.ill ; 24cm. — (Beginning to learn about)
Originally published: Milwaukee : Raintree Childrens, c1979
ISBN 0-86256-010-1 : £2.50 B81-17350

Campbell, Rod. Grand parade counting book / Rod Campbell. — London : Abelard, 1980. — [32]p : all col.ill ; 17x22cm
ISBN 0-200-72705-2 (cased) : £2.95 : CIP rev.
ISBN 0-200-72704-4 (pbk) : £0.95 B80-12835

Little tot's abc and counting. — London : Dean, c1980. — [24]p : col.ill ; 13cm. — (Dean's little tots' series)
ISBN 0-603-00194-7 (pbk) : £0.15
Primary classification 421′.1 B81-18850

Stevenson, Peter, *1953-*. Ward Lock's counting book / illustrated by Peter Stevenson. — London : Ward Lock, 1980. — [32]p : chiefly col.ill ; 21x26cm
ISBN 0-7063-5969-0 : £1.95 B81-00095

513′.93 — Business arithmetic

Cleaves, Cheryl S.. Mathematics of the business world / Cheryl S. Cleaves, Margie J. Hobbs, Janice H. Van Dyke. — Reading, Mass. ; London : Addison-Wesley, c1979. — xii,434p : ill ; 28cm
Includes index
ISBN 0-201-02773-9 (pbk) : £9.10 B81-39717

Miller, Paul S.. Business math / Paul S. Miller. — New York ; London : McGraw-Hill, 1980. — xi,626p : ill(some col.),forms ; 28cm
Includes index
ISBN 0-07-042157-9 (pbk) : £8.35 B81-00096

513′.93 — Business arithmetic — *For African students*

Newcomb, V. N.. Practical calculations for business studies. — Chichester : Wiley, Sept.1981. — [152]p
ISBN 0-471-27966-8 (cased) : £9.00 : CIP entry
ISBN 0-471-27967-6 (pbk) : £3.50 B81-23740

513'.93'076 — Business arithmetic — *Questions & answers*

Felton, James J.. Instructor's manual to accompany Business mathematics : a basic course / James J. Felton. — Boston [Mass.] ; London : Allyn and Bacon, c1981. — 433p ; 24cm
ISBN 0-205-07324-7 (pbk) : £1.00 B81-26394

Funk, Jerry. Sportset : a business math practice set / Jerry Funk. — Boston, Mass. ; London : Allyn and Bacon, c1982. — iii,121p : form ; 28cm
ISBN 0-205-07670-x (pbk) : Unpriced
B81-40100

Warren, Michael J. R.. Business calculations / Michael J.R. Warren ; advisory editor Patricia Callender. — Amersham : Hulton Educational, 1980, c1979. — 128p : ill ; 24cm. — (Hulton BEC books)
ISBN 0-7175-0834-x (pbk) : £2.10 B81-07184

513'.93'077 — Business arithmetic — *Programmed instructions*

Cain, Jack. Mathematics for business careers / Jack Cain, Robert A. Carman. — New York ; Chichester : Wiley, c1981. — viii,616p : ill (some col),forms ; 28cm
Includes index
ISBN 0-471-03163-1 (pbk) : £8.50 B81-09663

Felton, James J.. Business mathematics : a basic course / James J. Felton. — Boston [Mass.] ; London : Allyn and Bacon, c1981. — viii,535p : ill ; 28cm
Includes index
ISBN 0-205-07323-9 (pbk) : Unpriced
B81-26203

514 — TOPOLOGY

514 — Topological geometry

Porteous, Ian R.. Topological geometry / Ian R. Porteous. — 2nd ed. — Cambridge : Cambridge University Press, 1981. — 486p : ill ; 24cm
Previous ed.: London : Van Nostrand Reinhold, 1969. — Includes index
ISBN 0-521-23160-4 (cased) : £25.00
ISBN 0-521-29839-3 (pbk) : £9.95 B81-09820

514'.2 — Algebraic topology

Kosniowski, Czes. A first course in algebraic topology / Czes Kosniowski. — Cambridge : Cambridge University Press, 1980. — viii,269p : ill ; 24cm
Bibliography: p260-261. - Includes index
ISBN 0-521-23195-7 (cased) : £18.00 : CIP rev.
ISBN 0-521-29864-4 (pbk) : £6.96 B80-25545

Maunder, C. R. F.. Algebraic topology / C.R.F. Maunder. — Cambridge : Cambridge University Press, 1980. — ix,375p : ill ; 24cm
Originally published: London : Van Nostrand Reinhold, 1970. — Bibliography: p361-368. — Includes index
ISBN 0-521-23161-2 (cased) : £20.00 : CIP rev.
ISBN 0-521-29840-7 (pbk) : £8.50 B80-25546

514'.223 — Topological spaces: Manifolds. Tensor analysis

Bishop, Richard L.. Tensor analysis on manifolds / Richard L. Bishop, Samuel I. Goldberg. — Corr. republication. — New York : Dover ; London : Constable, 1980. — viii,280p : ill ; 21cm
Originally published: New York : Macmillan ; London : Collier-Macmillan, 1968. — Bibliography: p273-274. — Includes index
ISBN 0-486-64039-6 (pbk) : £3.60 B81-28883

514'.23 — Algebraic topology. Homology theory

Bauer, Hans Joachim. Commutator calculus and groups of homotopy classes. — Cambridge : Cambridge University Press, Oct.1981. — [161] p. — (London Mathematical Society lecture note series, ISSN 0076-0552 ; 50)
ISBN 0-521-28424-4 (pbk) : £11.25 : CIP entry
B81-31237

514'.233 — Topological spaces: Compact complex manifolds

Sundararaman, D.. Moduli, deformations and classifications of compact complex manifolds / D. Sundararaman. — Boston [Mass.] ; London : Pitman, c1980. — 261p : ill ; 25cm. — (Research notes in mathematics ; 45)
Bibliography: p203-261
ISBN 0-273-08458-5 (pbk) : £9.00 B81-04622

514'.3 — Topological spaces: Surfaces

Griffiths, H. B.. Surfaces / H.B. Griffiths. — 2nd ed. — Cambridge : Cambridge University Press, 1981. — xii,128p : ill ; 24cm
Previous ed.: 1976. — Bibliography: p124. — Includes index
ISBN 0-521-23570-7 (cased) : £12.50
ISBN 0-521-29977-2 (pbk) : £4.95 B81-37132

514'.32 — Topological spaces. Fixed points

Istrăţescu, Vasile I.. Fixed point theory : an introduction / Vasile I. Istrăţescu. — Dordrecht ; London : Reidel, c1981. — xv,466p ; 23cm. — (Mathematics and its applications ; v.7)
Bibliography: p419-457. — Includes index
ISBN 90-277-1224-7 : Unpriced B81-29175

514'.32 — Topological spaces. Fixed points. Theories — *Conference proceedings*

Analysis and computation of fixed points : proceedings of a symposium conducted by the Mathematics Research Center, the University of Wisconsin-Madison, May 7-8, 1979 / edited by Stepen M Robinson. — New York ; London : Academic Press, 1980. — ix,413p : ill ; 24cm. — (Publication no.4 of the Mathematics Research Center, the University of Wisconsin-Madison)
Includes bibliographies and index
ISBN 0-12-590240-9 : £14.60 B81-14749

514'.7 — Differential topology

Arnold, V. I.. Singularity theory. — Cambridge : Cambridge University Press, Oct.1981. — [272] p. — (London Mathematical lecture note series, ISSN 0076-0552 ; 53)
ISBN 0-521-28511-9 (pbk) : £12.50 : CIP entry
Primary classification 516.3'6 B81-31284

514'.72 — Catastrophe theory — *For science & engineering*

Gilmore, Robert. Catastrophe theory for scientists and engineers / Robert Gilmore. — New York ; Chichester : Wiley, c1981. — xvii,666p : ill ; 24cm
Includes index
ISBN 0-471-05064-4 : £32.15 B81-33368

514'.72 — Differential topology

Dodson, C. T. J.. Categories, bundles and spacetime topology / C.T.J. Dodson. — Orpington (9 Clareville Rd, Orpington, Kent BR5 1RU) : Shiva, c1980. — xiii,223p : ill ; 24cm. — (Shiva mathematics series ; 1)
Bibliography: p207-214. — Includes index
ISBN 0-906812-01-1 (pbk) : £8.50 : CIP rev.
B80-06382

514'.74 — Mathematics. Global analysis

Kahn, Donald W.. Introduction to global analysis / Donald W. Kahn. — New York ; London : Academic Press, 1980. — ix,336p : ill ; 24cm. — (Pure and applied mathematics)
Bibliography: p327-331. — Includes index
ISBN 0-12-394050-8 : £19.40 B81-00859

515 — CALCULUS

515 — Calculus

Amazigo, John C.. Advanced calculus : and its applications to the engineering and physical sciences / John C. Amazigo, Lester A. Rubenfeld. — New York ; Chichester : Wiley, 1980. — vii,407p : ill ; 24cm
Bibliography: p362-364. — Includes index
ISBN 0-471-04934-4 : £10.25 B81-00097

Anton, Howard. Calculus : with analytic geometry / Howard Anton. — Brief ed. — New York ; Chichester : Wiley, c1981. — xxiv,753,A1-A93,I1-I6p : ill(some col.) ; 25cm
Previous ed.: 1980. — Text and ill on lining papers. — Includes index
ISBN 0-471-09443-9 : £14.00 B81-24888

Arya, Jagdish C.. Applied calculus for business and economics / Jagdish C. Arya, Robin W. Lardner. — Englewood Cliffs ; London : Prentice-Hall, c1981. — xii,356p,A38p : ill ; 25cm
Text on lining papers. — Includes index
ISBN 0-13-039255-3 : £13.25 B81-34956

Binmore, K. G.. The foundations of analysis : a straightforward introduction / K.T. Binmore. — Cambridge : Cambridge University Press
Bk. 1: Logic, sets and number. — 1980. — x,131p : ill ; 24cm
Includes index
ISBN 0-521-23322-4 (cased) : £10.00
ISBN 0-521-59915-2 (pbk) : £4.95 B81-16422

Binmore, K. G.. The foundations of analysis : a straight-forward introduction / K.G. Binmore. — Cambridge : Cambridge University Press
Book 2: Topological ideas. — 1981. — xii,249p : ill ; 24cm
Includes index
ISBN 0-521-23350-x (cased) : £15.00
ISBN 0-521-29930-6 (pbk) : £6.95 B81-37131

Burkill, J. C.. A second course in mathematical analysis / by J.C. Burkill, and H. Burkill. — Cambridge : Cambridge University Press, 1970 (1980 [printing]). — vi,526p ; 24cm
Bibliography: p522. - Includes index
ISBN 0-521-07519-x (cased) : Unpriced
B81-04182

Dixon, Charles, *1935-*. Advanced calculus / Charles Dixon. — Chichester : Wiley, c1981. — ix,147p ; 24cm
Includes index
ISBN 0-471-27913-7 : £10.75 : CIP rev.
ISBN 0-471-27914-5 (pbk) : Unpriced
B81-13797

Grossman, Stanley I.. Calculus / Stanley I. Grossman. — 2nd ed. — International ed. — New York ; London : Academic Press, 1981. — xviii,1020,A129p : ill(some col.) ; 26cm
Previous ed.: 1977. — Includes index
ISBN 0-12-304370-0 : £8.40 B81-22396

Grossman, Stanley I.. Calculus / Stanley I. Grossman. — New York ; London : Academic Press
Part 1: The calculus of one variable. — c1981. — xvii,667,A1-A116p : col.ill ; 26cm
Includes index
ISBN 0-12-304301-8 : £11.20 B81-29819

An **Introduction** to calculus / prepared by the course team. — Milton Keynes : Open University Press. — (Mathematics/science : an inter-faculty second level course)
At head of title: The Open University
[Block 2]: Functions & numbers
Unit 1: Graphs & inequalities. — 1979. — 78p : ill(some col.) ; 30cm + 7sheets(ill ; 21x30cm folded to 21x15cm) + 6 actetate overlays(ill ; 21x15cm). — (MS283 ; 2, unit 1)
Sheets and overlays in envelope
ISBN 0-335-05878-7 (pbk) : Unpriced
B81-39148

An **Introduction** to calculus / prepared by the course team. — Milton Keynes : Open University Press. — (Mathematics/science : an inter-faculty second level course)
At head of title: The Open University
[Block 2]: Functions & numbers
Unit 3: Approximations. — 1979. — 63p : ill (some col.) ; 30cm. — (MS283 ; 2, unit 3)
ISBN 0-335-05879-5 (pbk) : Unpriced
B81-39147

An **Introduction** to calculus / prepared by the course team. — Milton Keynes : Open University Press. — (Mathematics/science : an inter-faculty second level course)
At head of title: The Open University
[Block 2]: Functions & numbers
Unit 4: Numbers from nature. — 1979. — 53p : ill(some col.) ; 30cm. — (MS283 ; 2, unit 4)
ISBN 0-335-05880-9 (pbk) : Unpriced
B81-39146

515 — Calculus *continuation*

An **Introduction** to calculus / prepared by the course team. — Milton Keynes : Open University. — (Mathematics/Science : an inter-faculty second level course)
At head of title: The Open University
[Block 3]: Calculus
Unit 3: Integration. — 1979. — 70p : ill(some col.) ; 30cm. — (MS283 ; 3, unit 3)
ISBN 0-335-05883-3 (pbk) : Unpriced
B81-38865

An **Introduction** to calculus / prepared by the course team. — Milton Keynes : Open University. — (Mathematics/Science : an inter-faculty second level course)
At head of title: The Open University
[Block 3]: Calculus
Unit 4: Taylor series. — 1979. — 51p : ill (some col.) ; 30cm. — (MS283 ; 3, unit 4)
ISBN 0-335-05884-1 (pbk) : Unpriced
B81-38194

An **Introduction** to calculus prepared by the course team. — Milton Keynes : Open University. — (Mathematics/Science : an inter-faculty second level course)
At head of title: The Open University
[Block 1]: Beginnings
Unit 1: Computation. — 1979. — 48p : ill ; 30cm. — (MS283 ; 1, unit 1)
ISBN 0-335-05874-4 (pbk) : Unpriced
B81-38857

An **Introduction** to calculus prepared by the course team. — Milton Keynes : Open University. — (Mathematics/Science : an inter-faculty second level course)
At head of title: The Open University
[Block 1]: Beginnings
Unit 2: Algebra. — 1979. — 64p : ill(some col.) ; 30cm. — (MS283 ; 1, unit 2)
ISBN 0-335-05875-2 (pbk) : Unpriced
B81-38858

An **Introduction** to calculus prepared by the course team. — Milton Keynes : Open University. — (Mathematics/Science : an inter-faculty second level course)
At head of title: The Open University
[Block 1]: Beginnings
Unit 3: Transformations & trigonometry. — 1979. — 53p : ill(some col.) ; 30cm. — (MS283 ; 1, unit 3)
ISBN 0-335-05876-0 (pbk) : Unpriced
B81-38859

An **Introduction** to calculus prepared by the course team. — Milton Keynes : Open University. — (Mathematics/Science : an inter-faculty second level course)
At head of title: The Open University
[Block 1]: Beginnings
Unit 4: Functions. — 1979. — 51p : ill(some col.) ; 30cm. — (MS283 ; 1, unit 4)
ISBN 0-335-05877-9 (pbk) : Unpriced
B81-38860

An **Introduction** to calculus prepared by the course team. — Milton Keynes : Open University. — (Mathematics/Science : an inter-faculty second level course)
At head of title: The Open University
[Block 1]: Calculus
Unit 1: Differentiation. — 1979. — 60p : ill (some col.) ; 30cm. — (MS283 ; 3, unit 1)
ISBN 0-335-05881-7 (pbk) : Unpriced
B81-38861

An **Introduction** to calculus prepared by the course team. — Milton Keynes : Open University. — (Mathematics/Science : an inter-faculty second level course)
At head of title: The Open University
[Block 1]: Calculus
Unit 2: Differentiation in action. — 1979. — 63p : ill(some col.) ; 30cm. — (MS283 ; 3, unit 2)
ISBN 0-335-05882-5 (pbk) : Unpriced
B81-38862

An **Introduction** to calculus prepared by the course team. — Milton Keynes : Open University. — (Mathematics/Science : an inter-faculty second level course)
At head of title: The Open University
[Block 3]: Calculus
Unit 5: The exponential & logarithmic functions. — 1979. — 32p : ill(some col.) ; 30cm. — (MS283 ; 3, unit 5)
ISBN 0-335-05885-x (pbk) : Unpriced
B81-38863

Kolman, Bernard. Calculus for the management, life, and social sciences / Bernard Kolman. — New York ; London : Academic Press, c1981. — xiii,514p : ill ; 25cm
Text on lining papers. — Includes index
ISBN 0-12-417890-1 (cased) : £11.20
B81-35355

Mulholland, H.. Calculus made simple / H. Mulholland. — London : Heinemann, 1981. — ix,326p : ill ; 22cm. — (Made simple books)
Originally published: London : W.H. Allen, 1976. — Includes index
ISBN 0-434-98461-2 (pbk) : £2.50 B81-23210

Murphy, Ian S.. Basic mathematical analysis : the facts / Ian S. Murphy. — Stirling (64 Murray Place, Stirling FK8 2BX) : Arklay, 1980. — 245p : ill ; 24cm
Bibliography: p221. — Includes index
ISBN 0-9507126-0-4 (pbk) : £4.95 B81-00861

Sherlock, A. J.. Calculus. — London : Edward Arnold, Oct.1981. — [512]p
ISBN 0-7131-3446-1 (pbk) : £8.50 : CIP entry
B81-27937

515 — Location. Optimisation. Mathematical models

Optimisation in locational and transport analysis. — Chichester : Wiley, Jan.1982. — [288]p
ISBN 0-471-28005-4 : £19.60 : CIP entry
B81-34561

515 — Mathematics. Optimisation

Gill, Philip E.. Practical optimization / Philip E. Gill, Walter Murray, Margaret H. Wright. — London : Academic Press, 1981. — xvi,401p : ill ; 26cm
Bibliography: p363-387. — Includes index
ISBN 0-12-283950-1 : £19.20 : CIP rev.
B81-08909

515 — Mathematics. Optimisation. Applications

Fletcher, R.. Practical methods of optimization. — Chichester : Wiley
Vol.2: Constrained optimization. — Jan.1982. — [200]p
ISBN 0-471-27828-9 : £14.00 : CIP entry
B81-34559

515 — Mathematics. Optimisation. Applications of digital computer systems

Schwefel, Hans-Paul. Numerical optimization of computer models / Hans-Paul Schwefel. — Chichester : Wiley, c1981. — vii,389p : ill ; 24cm
Translation of: Numerische Optimierung von Computer-Modellen mittels der Evolutionsstrategie. — Bibliography: p248-290. — Includes index
ISBN 0-471-09988-0 : £12.50 : CIP rev.
B81-13893

515 — Mathematics. Optimisation — *Festschriften*

Special topics of applied mathematics : functional analysis, numerical analysis and optimization : proceedings of the seminar held at the GMD, Bonn, 8-10 October, 1979 / dedicated to Heinz Unger ; managing editors J. Frehse, D. Pallaschke, U. Trottenberg. — Amsterdam ; Oxford : North-Holland, 1980. — viii,248p : ill ; 23cm
Includes bibliographies
ISBN 0-444-86035-5 : £17.69
Primary classification 510 B81-03637

515′.02433 — Calculus — *For economics*

Sydsæter, Knut. Topics in mathematical analysis for economics / Knut Sydsæter. — London : Academic Press, 1981. — x,445p : ill ; 24cm
Bibliography: p419-421. — Includes index
ISBN 0-12-679980-6 : £16 40 : CIP rev.
B81-13447

515′.024658 — Calculus — *For business studies*

Arya, Jagdish C.. Mathematical analysis for business and economics / Jagdish C. Arya, Robin W. Lardner. — Englewood Cliffs ; London : Prentice-Hall, c1981. — xi,641-A50p : ill ; 25cm
Text on lining papers. — Includes index
ISBN 0-13-561019-2 : £13.60 B81-25508

Byrkit, Donald R.. Calculus for business and economics / Donald R. Byrkit, Shawky E. Shamma. — New York ; London : Van Nostrand, c1981. — xi,372p : ill ; 24cm
Includes index
ISBN 0-442-21305-0 : £17.80 B81-36814

515′.028′5424 — Calculus. Applications of digital computer systems. Programming languages: Basic language

Christensen, Mark J.. Computing for calculus / by Mark J. Christensen. — New York ; London : Academic Press, c1981. — iv,236p : ill ; 28cm
ISBN 0-12-304365-4 (pbk) : Unpriced
B81-39879

515′.09′033 — Calculus, *ca 1750-1850*

Grabiner, Judith V.. The origins of Cauchy′s rigorous calculus / Judith V. Grabiner. — Cambridge, Mass. ; London : M.I.T. Press, c1981. — 252p ; 24cm
Bibliography: p225-240. — Includes index
ISBN 0-262-07079-0 : £24.50 B81-39643

515′.13 — Calculus & topology

Introduction to analysis and topology. — Milton Keynes : Open University Press. — (Mathematics : a second level course)
At head of title: The Open University. — Also published: as Introduction to pure mathematics. Unit 8, 1980
Unit 1: Analysis I, the real number and other number systems / prepared by the course team. — 1980. — 64p : ill(some col.) ; 30cm. — (M212 ; [unit 1])
ISBN 0-335-05935-x (pbk) : Unpriced
B81-39485

515′.13 — Calculus & topology — *Festschriften*

General topology and modern analysis : [proceedings of a conference on general topology and modern analysis held at the University of California, Riverside, May 28-31, 1980, in honor of F. Burton Jones] / edited by L.F. McAuley, M.M.Rao. — New York ; London : Academic Press, 1981. — xv,514p : ill,1port ; 25cm
Includes index
ISBN 0-12-481820-x : £20.20 B81-35746

515′.14 — Calculus & linear algebra

Michel, Anthony N.. Mathematical foundations in engineering and science : algebra and analysis / Anthony N. Michel, Charles J. Herget. — Englewood Cliffs ; London : Prentice-Hall, c1981. — xi,484p : ill ; 24cm
Includes bibliographies and index
ISBN 0-13-561035-4 : £18.15 B81-12520

515′.15 — Calculus & analytic geometry

Leithold, Louis. The calculus : with analytic geometry / Louis Leithold. — 4th ed. — New York ; London : Harper & Row, c1981. — xvi,1140,A60p ; 25cm
Previous ed.: 1976. — Text on lining papers. — Includes index
ISBN 0-06-043935-1 : £18.95 B81-23669

515′.223 — Topological spaces: Riemannian manifolds. Conformal mappings

Cohn, Harvey. Conformal mapping on Riemann surfaces / Harvey Cohn. — Corr. republication. — New York : Dover ; London : Constable, 1980, c1967. — xiv,325p : ill ; 21cm
Originally published: London : McGraw-Hill, 1967. — Bibliography: p316-317. - Includes index
ISBN 0-486-64025-6 (pbk) : £3.50 B81-18491

515′.243 — Infinite series. Convergence. Acceleration. Techniques

Halliday, A. S. M.. A review of methods for the acceleration of convergence of infinite series / by A.S.M. Halliday. — Cardiff (King Edward VII Ave., Cardiff) : Department of Mathematics, University of Wales Institute of Science and Technology, c1980. — 38p ; 30cm. — (Math report ; 80-3)
Bibliography: p37-38
Unpriced (pbk) B81-15098

515′.2432 — Calculus. Singular perturbations. Asymptotic theory — *Conference proceedings*

Singular perturbations and asymptotics : proceedings of an advanced seminar conducted by the Mathematics Research Center, the University of Wisconsin-Madison, May 28-30, 1980 / edited by Richard E. Meyer, Seymour V. Parter. — New York ; London : Academic Press, 1980. — ix,409p : ill ; 24cm. — (Publication no.45 of the Mathematics Research Center, the University of Wisconsin-Madison)
Includes index
ISBN 0-12-493260-6 : Unpriced B81-23000

515′.2432 — Calculus. Singular perturbations. Numerical solution

Miranker, Willard L.. Numerical methods for stiff equations : and singular perturbation problems / Willard L. Miranker. — Dordrecht ; London : Reidel, c1981. — xiii,202p : ill ; 23cm. — (Mathematics and its applications ; v.5)
Bibliography: p194-196. - Includes index
ISBN 90-277-1107-0 : Unpriced
Primary classification 515.3′52 B81-07571

515′.2433 — Nonharmonic Fourier series

Young, Robert M.. An introduction to nonharmonic Fourier series / Robert M. Young. — New York ; London : Academic Press, 1980. — x,246p ; 24cm. — (Pure and applied mathematics)
Bibliography: p225-234. - Includes index
ISBN 0-12-772850-3 : £20.60 B81-15010

515′.25 — Mathematics. Polylogarithmic functions

Lewin, Leonard, *1919-*. Polylogarithms and associated functions / Leonard Lewin. — New York ; Oxford : North-Holland, c1981. — xvii,359p : ill ; 24cm
Bibliography: p349-353. — Includes index
ISBN 0-444-00550-1 : £29.64 B81-35333

515.3′5 — Bifurcation theory

Hassard, B. D.. Theory and applications of Hopf bifurcation / B.D. Hassard, N.D. Kazarinoff and Y.-H. Wan. — Cambridge : Cambridge University Press, 1981. — 311p : ill ; 23cm + 1microfiche; 11x15cm. — (London Mathematical Society lecture note series, ISSN 0076-0552 ; 41)
Microfiche in pocket. — Bibliography: p300-309. — Includes index
ISBN 0-521-23158-2 (pbk) : £15.00 B81-27868

515.3′5 — Boundary value problems & initial value problems. Uniform numerical methods

Doolan, E. P.. Uniform numerical methods for problems with initial and boundary layers / E.P. Doolan, J.J.H. Miller, W.H.A. Schilders. — Dublin (P.O. Box 5, 51 Sandycove Rd., Dun Laoire, Co. Dublin) : Boole, 1980. — xv,324p : ill ; 25cm
Bibliography: p293-318. - Includes index
ISBN 0-906783-02-x : £28.00 B81-16495

515.3′5 — Differential equations

Arrowsmith, D. K.. Ordinary differential equations. — London : Chapman and Hall, Feb.1982. — [300]p. — (Chapman and Hall mathematics series)
ISBN 0-412-22600-6 (cased) : £12.00 : CIP entry
ISBN 0-412-22610-3 (pbk) : £6.00 B81-36378

Differential equations and numerical mathematics . — Oxford : Pergamon, Jan.1982. — [130]p
Conference papers
ISBN 0-08-026491-3 : £21.00 : CIP entry B81-34470

Rainville, Earl D.. Elementary differential equations / Earl D. Rainville, Phillip E. Bedient. — 6th ed. — New York : Macmillan ; London : Collier Macmillan, c1981. — xiv,529p : ill ; 25cm
Previous ed.: 1974. — Includes bibliographies and index
ISBN 0-02-397770-1 (cased) : £10.50
ISBN 0-02-979480-1 (pbk) : £7.95 B81-20736

Spiegel, Murray R.. Applied differential equations / Murray R. Spiegel. — 3rd ed. — Englewood Cliffs ; London : Prentice-Hall, c1981. — xvi,654,[63]p : ill ; 25cm
Previous ed.: Englewood Cliffs : Prentice-Hall, 1967. — Text on lining papers. — Bibliography: 2p. - Includes index
ISBN 0-13-040097-1 : £14.25 B81-17295

515.3′5 — Differential equations. Asymptotic theory

Delves, L. M.. Analysis of global expansion methods : weakly asymptotically diagonal systems / L.M. Delves and T.L. Freeman. — London : Academic Press, 1981. — x,275p ; 24cm. — (Computational mathematics and applications)
Bibliography: p270-272. — Includes index
ISBN 0-12-208880-8 : £20.40 B81-35426

515.3′5 — Differential equations. Asymptotic theory — *Conference proceedings*

Conference on Analytical and Numerical Approaches to Asymptotic Problems rk1980 *(University of Nijmegen)*. Analytical and numerical approaches to asymptotic problems in analysis : proceedings of the Conference on Analytical and Numerical Approaches to Asymptotic Problems, University of Nijmegen, The Netherlands, June 9-13 1980 / edited by O. Axelsson, L.S. Frank and A. Van Der Sluis. — Amsterdam ; Oxford : North-Holland, 1981. — xvi,381p : ill ; 24cm. — (North-Holland mathematics studies, ISSN 0304-0208 ; 47)
Includes bibliographies
ISBN 0-444-86131-9 (pbk) : £20.30 B81-20835

515.3′5 — Differential equations. Boundary value problems. Solution. Variational methods

Rektorys, Karel. Variational methods in mathematics, science and engineering / Karel Rektorys. — 2nd ed. — Dordrecht ; London : Reidel, 1980. — 571p : ill ; 28cm
Previous ed.: 1977. — Bibliography: p565-566. — Includes index
ISBN 90-277-1060-0 : Unpriced B81-07517

515.3′5 — Differential equations — *Conference proceedings*

Conference on Differential Equations *(8th : 1979 : Oklahoma State University)*. Differential equations : proceedings of the Eighth Fall Conference on Differential Equations held at Oklahoma State University, October 1979 / edited by Shair Ahmad, Marvin Keener, A.C. Lazer. — New York ; London : Academic Press, 1980. — ix,278p : ill ; 24cm
Includes bibliographies
ISBN 0-12-045550-1 : £11.20 B81-00862

515.3′5 — Functional differential equations. Solution. Cauchy's theorem — *Conference proceedings*

Abstract Cauchy problems and functional differential equations / [edited by] F. Kappel & W. Schappacher. — Boston, Mass. ; London : Pitman Advanced Publishing, c1981. — 238p : ill ; 25cm. — (Research notes in mathematics ; 48)
Conference papers. — Includes bibliographies
ISBN 0-273-08494-1 (pbk) : Unpriced B81-16202

515.3′5 — Mathematical models: Differential equations

Burghes, D. N.. Modelling with differential equations / D.N. Burghes and M.S. Borrie. — Chichester : Horwood, 1981. — 172p : ill ; 24cm. — (Ellis Horwood series in mathematics and its applications)
Bibliography: p169-170. - Includes index
ISBN 0-85312-286-5 (cased) : £12.50
ISBN 0-85312-296-2 (pbk) : Unpriced B81-21694

515.3′5 — Perturbation theory

Nayfeh, Ali Hasan. Introduction to perturbation techniques / Ali Hasan Nayfeh. — New York ; Chichester : Wiley, c1981. — xiv,519p : ill ; 24cm
Bibliography: p501-505. — Includes index
ISBN 0-471-08033-0 : £16.00 B81-10643

515.3′5 — Small parameter differential equations. Solution. Asymptotic expansions

Mishchenko, E. F.. Differential equations with small parameters and relaxation oscillations / E.F. Mishchenko and N.Kh. Rozov ; translated from Russian by F.M.C. Goodspeed. — New York ; London : Plenum, c1980. — x,228p : ill ; 24cm. — (Mathematical concepts and methods in science and engineering ; 13)
Translation of: Differentsial′nye uravneniia s malym parametrom i relaksatsionnye kolebaniia. — Includes index
ISBN 0-306-39253-4 : Unpriced B81-09829

515.3′5 — System identification

Trends and progress in system indentification / edited by Pieter Eykhoff. — Oxford : Pergamon, 1981. — xvi,402p : ill,ports ; 31cm. — (IFAC series for graduates, research workers & practising engineers ; v.1)
Includes bibliographies and index
ISBN 0-08-025683-x : £30.00 B81-25418

515.3′52 — Ordinary differential equations

Rao, M. Rama Mohana. Ordinary differential equations. — London : Edward Arnold, Sept.1981. — [256]p
ISBN 0-7131-3452-6 (pbk) : £6.95 : CIP entry B81-21500

515.3′52 — Ordinary differential equations. Periodic solution & stability

Rouche, N.. Ordinary differential equations : stability and periodic solutions / N. Rouche, J. Mawhin ; R.E. Gaines (translator). — Boston [Mass.] ; London : Pitman Advanced Publishing Program, 1980. — viii,260p : ill ; 25cm. — (Surveys and reference works in mathematics)
Translation of: Equations différentielles ordinaires. Tome 2. Stabilités et solutions périodiques. — Bibliography: p233-258. - Includes index
ISBN 0-273-08419-4 : £15.00 B81-03730

515.3′52 — Ordinary differential equations. Stiff systems. Numerical solution

Miranker, Willard L.. Numerical methods for stiff equations : and singular perturbation problems / Willard L. Miranker. — Dordrecht ; London : Reidel, c1981. — xiii,202p : ill ; 23cm. — (Mathematics and its applications ; v.5)
Bibliography: p194-196. - Includes index
ISBN 90-277-1107-0 : Unpriced
Also classified at 515′.2432 B81-07571

515.3′53 — Linear evolution equations. Boundary value problems. Singularities — *Conference proceedings*

Singularities in boundary value problems : proceedings of the NATO Advanced Study Institute held at Maratea, Italy, September 22-October 3, 1980 / edited by H.G. Garnir. — Dordrecht ; London : Reidel published in cooperation with NATO Scientific Affairs Division, c1981. — xvi,377p : ill ; 25cm. — (NATO advanced study institutes series. Series C, Mathematical and physical sciences ; v.65)
Includes bibliographies and index
ISBN 90-277-1240-9 : Unpriced B81-26219

515.3′53 — Mathematics. Boundary element methods - *Serials*

Progress in boundary element methods. — Vol.1-. — London (4 Graham Lodge, Graham Rd., NW4 3DG) : Pentech, July 1981. — [285]p
ISBN 0-7273-1610-9 : £28.00 : CIP entry
ISSN 0260-7018 B81-14799

515.3′53 — Mathematics. Finite element methods

Becker, Eric B.. Finite elements : an introduction / Eric B. Becker, Graham F. Carey and J. Tinsley Oden. — Englewood Cliffs ; London : Prentice-Hall
Vol.1. — 1981. — xii,258p : ill ; 24cm
Includes index
ISBN 0-13-317057-8 : £17.45 B81-26906

515.3'53 — Mathematics. Finite element methods — *Conference proceedings*

Numerical methods in coupled problems. — Swansea (91 West Cross La., West Cross, Swansea, W. Glamorgan) : Pineridge Press, Aug.1981. — [1000]p
Conference papers
ISBN 0-906674-13-1 : £44.00 : CIP entry B81-22584

515.3'53 — Nonlinear evolution equations. Solution. Bäcklund transformation. Applications of jet bundle theory

Pirani, F. A. E.. Local jet bundle formulation of Bäcklund transformations : with applications to non-linear evolution equations / by F.A.E. Pirani, D.C. Robinson and W.F. Shadwick. — Dordrecht ; London : Reidel, c1979. — viii,132p : ill ; 24cm. — (Mathematical physics studies ; v.1)
Bibliography: p125-129. - Includes index
ISBN 90-277-1036-8 (pbk) : Unpriced B81-04604

515.3'53 — Nonlinear partial differential equations

Recent contributions to nonlinear partial differential equations / H. Berestycki & H. Brezis (editors). — Boston (Mass.) ; London : Pitman Advanced Publishing Program, c1981. — 226p : ill ; 25cm. — (Research notes in mathematics ; 50)
English and French text. — Includes bibliographies
ISBN 0-273-08492-5 : Unpriced B81-38251

515.3'53 — Nonlinear partial differential equations. Applications — *Conference proceedings*

Nonlinear partial differential equations and their applications : Collège de France seminar. — Boston [Mass.] ; London : Pitman. — (Research notes in mathematics ; 53)
Vol.1 / H. Brezis & J.L. Lions, editors ; D. Cioranescu, coordinator. — [1981]. — 388p : ill ; 25
Includes 11 papers in French. — Includes bibliographies and index
ISBN 0-273-08491-7 (pbk) : Unpriced B81-40143

515.3'53 — Nonlinear partial differential equations. Sequential solution

Rosinger, Elemer E.. Nonlinear partial differential equations : sequential and weak solutions / Elemer E. Rosinger. — Amsterdam ; Oxford : North-Holland, 1980. — xix,317p : ill ; 14cm. — (North-Holland mathematics studies ; 44) (Notas de matemática ; (73))
Bibliography: p305-317
ISBN 0-444-86055-x (pbk) : £15.90 B81-03929

515.3'53 — Partial differential equations. Numerical solution. Maximum principles

Sperb, René P.. Maximum principles and their applications / René P. Sperb. — New York ; London : Academic Press, 1981. — ix,224p : ill ; 24cm. — (Mathematics in science and engineering ; v.157)
Bibliography: p217-221. — Includes index
ISBN 0-12-656880-4 : Unpriced B81-38749

515.3'53 — Partial differential equations. Solution. Hilbert space methods

Showalter, R. E.. Hilbert space methods for partial differential equations / R.E. Showalter. — San Francisco ; London : Pitman, 1977, c1979 (1979 [printing]). — 196p ; 24cm. — (Pitman advanced publishing program)
Bibliography: p187-190. — Includes index
ISBN 0-273-08440-2 (pbk) : Unpriced B81-40368

515.3'53 — Second order elliptic partial differential equations. Boundary value problems. Solution

Clements, David L.. Boundary value problems governed by second order elliptic systems / David L. Clements. — Boston ; London : Pitman Advanced Publishing Program, 1981. — viii,162p : ill ; 24cm. — (Monographs and studies in mathematics ; 12)
Bibliography: p158-160. — Includes index
ISBN 0-273-08502-6 : Unpriced B81-38248

515.3'53 — Solitons

Eckhaus, Wiktor. The inverse scattering transformation and the theory of solitons : an introduction / Wiktor Eckhaus, Aart van Harten. — Amsterdam ; Oxford : North-Holland, c1981. — xi,222p : 1ill ; 24cm. — (North-Holland mathematics studies ; 50)
Bibliography: p217-222
ISBN 0-444-86166-1 (pbk) : £12.31 B81-23649

Lamb, G. L.. Elements of soliton theory / G.L. Lamb, Jr. — New York ; Chichester : Wiley, c1980. — xii,289p : ill ; 24cm. — (Pure and applied mathematics)
Text on lining papers. — Bibliography: p279-283. — Includes index
ISBN 0-471-04559-4 : £16.00 B81-05622

515.3'53'076 — Partial differential equations. Solution — *Questions & answers*

Bitsadze, A. V.. A collection of problems on the equations of mathematical physics / A.V. Bitsadze, D.F. Kalinichenko ; translated from the Russian by V.M. Volosov and I.G. Volosova. — Moscow : MIR ; [London] : Distributed by Central Books, 1980. — 334p ; 21cm
Translation of: Sbornik zadach po uravneniiam matematicheskoĭ fiziki
£3.50 B81-06479

515.3'55 — Nonlinear differential equations & boundary value problems. Numerical solution

Baker, Christopher T. H.. The numerical solution to nonlinear problems. — Oxford : Clarendon Press, Jan.1982. — [384]p
ISBN 0-19-853354-3 : £15.00 : CIP entry B81-34384

Fučík, Svatopluk. Solvability of nonlinear equations and boundary value problems / Svatopluk Fučík. — Dordrecht ; London : Reidel, c1980. — 390p ; 23cm. — (Mathematics and its applications ; v.4)
Bibliography: p373-381. - Includes index
ISBN 90-277-1077-5 : Unpriced B81-15254

515.3'55 — Nonlinear differential equations — *Conference proceedings*

Nonlinear differential equations : invariance, stability and bifurcation : proceedings of a symposium ... held in Villa Madruzzo, Trento, Italy from May 25-30, 1980 / edited by Piero de Mottoni, Luigi Salvadori. — New York ; London : Academic Press, c1981. — xi,357p : ill ; 24cm
ISBN 0-12-508780-2 : £12.40 B81-35360

515.3'6 — Mathematics. Differential random inequalities

Ladde, G. S.. Random differential inequalities / G.S. Ladde and V. Lakshmikantham. — New York ; London : Academic Press, 1980. — xi,211p ; 24cm. — (Mathematics in science and engineering ; v.150)
Bibliography: p202-205. — Includes index
ISBN 0-12-432750-8 : £16.80 B81-15057

515.4'2 — Ergodic theory

Parry, William. Topics in ergodic theory / William Parry. — Cambridge : Cambridge University Press, 1981. — x,110p : ill ; 23cm. — (Cambridge tracts in mathematics ; 75)
Bibliography: p98-107. — Includes index
ISBN 0-521-22986-3 : £10.00 B81-14645

515.4'2 — Ergodic theory. Applications of dynamical systems theory

Furstenberg, H.. Recurrence in ergodic theory and combinatorial number theory / H. Furstenberg. — Princeton ; Guildford : Princeton University Press, c1981. — vii,202p ; 24cm. — (M.B. Porter lectures)
Bibliography: p195-199. — Includes index
ISBN 0-691-08269-3 : £19.50 B81-22145

515.4'2 — Measure & integration

De Barra, G.. Measure theory and integration. — Chichester : Ellis Horwood, July 1981. — [260] p. — (Ellis Horwood series in mathematics and its applications)
ISBN 0-85312-337-3 : £21.50 : CIP entry B81-20592

515.4'2 — Measure theory & integration

Aliprantis, Charalambos D.. Principles of real analysis / Charalambos D. Aliprantis and Owen Burkinshaw. — London : Edward Arnold, c1981. — xii,285p : ill ; 24cm
Originally published: New York : North Holland, 1981. — Includes bibliographies and index
ISBN 0-7131-3434-8 : £16.00 B81-29170

515.4'3 — Calculus. Cubature & quadrature

Engels, H.. Numerical quadrature and cubature / H. Engels. — London : Academic Press, 1980. — xiv,441p : ill ; 24cm. — (Computational mathematics and applications)
Includes index
ISBN 0-12-238850-x : £32.00 B79-34133

515'.63 — Differential calculus. Vector analysis

Differential vector calculus. — London : Longman, July 1981. — [288]p. — (Longman mathematical texts)
ISBN 0-582-44193-5 : £9.95 : CIP entry B81-14981

515'.63 — Tensor analysis

Goodbody, A. M.. Cartesian tensors : with applications to mechanics, fluid mechanics and elasticity. — Chichester : Ellis Horwood, Dec.1981. — [336]p. — (The Ellis Horwood series in mathematics and its applications)
ISBN 0-85312-220-2 : £22.50 : CIP entry B81-31379

515'.63 — Vector analysis

Marsden, Jerrold E.. Vector calculus / Jerrold E. Marsden, Anthony J. Tromba with the assistance of Michael Hoffman and Joanne Seitz. — 2nd ed. — Oxford : W.H. Freeman, c1981. — xviii,591p : ill ; 24cm
Previous ed.: 1976. — Includes index
ISBN 0-7167-1244-x : £13.95 B81-36488

515'.64 — Applied mathematics. Variational inequalities. Numerical analysis

Numerical analysis of variational inequalities / Roland Glowinski, Jacques-Louis Lions, Raymond Trémolières. — English version / edited, prepared and produced by Trans-Inter-Scientia. — Amsterdam ; Oxford : North-Holland, c1981. — xxix,776p : ill ; 23cm. — (Studies in mathematics and its applications ; v.8)
Previous ed.: published as Analyse numérique des inéquations variationelles. Paris : Bordas, 1976. — Bibliography: p767-776
ISBN 0-444-86199-8 : £44.46 B81-35329

515'.64 — Calculus of variations

Leitmann, George. The calculus of variations and optimal control : an introduction / George Leitmann. — New York ; London : Plenum, c1981. — xvi,311p : ill ; 24cm. — (Mathematical concepts and methods in science and engineering ; v.24)
Bibliography: p305-307. — Includes index
ISBN 0-306-40707-8 : Unpriced
Also classified at 629.8'312 B81-32646

515.7 — Applied mathematics. Functional analysis

Griffel, D. H.. Applied functional analysis. — Chichester : Ellis Horwood, July 1981. — [416] p. — (Ellis Horwood series in mathematics and its applications)
ISBN 0-85312-226-1 : £25.00 : CIP entry B81-20560

515.7 — Calculus. Continuous functions. Approximation

Rivlin, Theodore J.. An introduction to the approximation of functions / Theodore J. Rivlin. — New York : Dover ; London : Constable, 1981, c1969. — viii,150p : ill ; 21cm
Originally published: Waltham, Mass. : Blaisdell, 1969. — Bibliography: p143-147. — Includes index
ISBN 0-486-64069-8 (pbk) : £2.40 B81-39072

515.7 — Mathematics. Functional analysis

Heuser, Harro. Functional analysis. — Chichester : Wiley, Jan.1982. — [464]p
Translation of: Funktionanalysis
ISBN 0-471-28052-6 (cased) : £25.00 : CIP entry
ISBN 0-471-10069-2 (pbk) B81-34646

515.7 — Mathematics. Functional analysis *continuation*

Kantorovich, L. V.. Functional analysis. — 2nd ed. — Oxford : Pergamon, June 1981. — [800]p
Previous ed.: published as Functional analysis in normed spaces. 1964
ISBN 0-08-023036-9 (cased) : £45.00 : CIP entry
ISBN 0-08-026486-7 (pbk) : £15.00 B81-13534

515.7 — Mathematics. Functional analysis — *Festschriften*

Special topics of applied mathematics : functional analysis, numerical analysis and optimization : proceedings of the seminar held at the GMD, Bonn, 8-10 October, 1979 / dedicated to Heinz Unger ; managing editors J. Frehse, D. Pallaschke, U. Trottenberg. — Amsterdam ; Oxford : North-Holland, 1980. — viii,248p : ill ; 23cm
Includes bibliographies
ISBN 0-444-86035-5 : £17.69
Primary classification 510 B81-03637

515.7 — Nuclear & conuclear spaces

Hogbe-Nlend, Henri. Nuclear and conuclear spaces : introductory course on nuclear and conuclear spaces in the light of the duality 'topology-bornology' / Henri Hogbe-Nlend and Vincenzo Bruno Moscatelli. — Amsterdam ; Oxford : North-Holland, c1981. — x,275p ; 24cm. — (North-Holland mathematics studies ; 52) (Notas de matemática ; 79)
Bibliography: p263-275
ISBN 0-444-86207-2 (pbk) : £29.64 B81-35334

515.7'02462 — Applied mathematics. Functional analysis — *For engineering*

Nowinski, J. L.. Application of functional analysis in engineering / J.L. Nowinski. — New York ; London : Plenum, c1981. — xv,304p : ill ; 24cm. — (Mathematical concepts and methods in science and engineering ; .22)
Includes index
ISBN 0-306-40693-4 : Unpriced B81-32647

515.7'09 — Mathematics. Functional analysis, *to 1980*

Dieudonné, Jean. History of functional analysis / Jean Dieudonné. — Amsterdam ; Oxford : North-Holland, 1981. — vi,312p ; 24cm. — (North-Holland mathematics studies ; 49) (Notas de matemática ; 77)
Bibliography: p280-298. - Includes index
ISBN 0-444-86148-3 (pbk) : £12.42 B81-16601

515.7'2 — Operational calculus

Mikusinski, Jan. Operational calculus. — 2nd ed. — Oxford : Pergamon, June 1981. — (International series in pure and applied mathematics ; v.109)
Previous ed.: 1959
Vol.1. — [320]p
ISBN 0-08-025071-8 : £12.00 : CIP entry
B81-11921

515.7'23 — Calculus. Laplace transforms

Watson, E. J.. Laplace transforms and applications / E.J. Watson. — New York ; London : Van Nostrand Reinhold, c1981. — viii,205p : ill ; 23cm. — (VNR new mathematics library ; 10)
Bibliography: p189-190
ISBN 0-442-30176-6 (cased) : £8.50
ISBN 0-442-30428-5 (pbk) : £3.95 B81-29186

515.7'23 — Mathematics. Fourier integral operators

Treves, François. Introduction to pseudodifferential and Fourier integral operators / François Treves. — New York ; London : Plenum, c1980. — (The University series in mathematics)
Bibliography: pxxix-xxxiv. — Includes index
Vol.1: Pseudodifferential operators. — xxxix,299p ; 24cm
ISBN 0-306-40403-6 : Unpriced
Also classified at 515.7'242 B81-10028

Treves, François. Introduction to pseudodifferential and Fourier integral operators / François Treves. — New York ; London : Plenum, c1980. — (The University series in mathematics)
Bibliography: pxv-xx. — Includes index
Vol.2: Fourier integral operators. — xxv,p301-649 ; 24cm
ISBN 0-306-40404-4 : Unpriced
Also classified at 515.7'242 B81-10027

515.7'24 — Mathematics. Operators. Inequalities

Schröder, Johann. Operator inequalities / Johann Schröder. — New York ; London : Academic Press, 1980. — xvi,367p ; 24cm. — (Mathematics in science and engineering ; v.147)
Bibliography: p343-357. - Includes index
ISBN 0-12-629750-9 : £22.20 B81-06833

515.7'242 — Mathematics. Differential operators. Spectral theory

Müller-Pfeiffer, Erich. Spectral theory of ordinary differential operators / Erich Müller-Pfeiffer ; translation editor: M.S.P. Eastham. — Chichester : Horwood, 1981. — 246p ; 24cm. — (Ellis Horwood series in mathematics and its applications)
Translation of: Spektraleigenschaften singularer gewohnlicher Differentialoperatoren. — Includes index
ISBN 0-85312-189-3 : £16.50 B81-10604

515.7'242 — Mathematics. Hyperbolic differential operators

Chaillon, Jacques. Hyperbolic differential polynomials : and their singular perturbations / Jacques Chaillon ; translated from the French by J.W. Nienhuys. — Dordrecht ; London : Reidel, c1979. — xv,168p : ill ; 23cm. — (Mathematics and its applications ; v.3)
Translation of: Les polynômes différentiels hyperboliques et leurs perturbations singulières. — Bibliography: p164-166. - Includes index
ISBN 90-277-1032-5 : Unpriced B81-07270

515.7'242 — Mathematics. Pseudodifferential operators

Taylor, Michael E.. Pseudodifferential operators / Michael E. Taylor. — Princeton ; Guildford : Princeton University Press, c1981. — xi,451p : ill ; 25cm. — (Princeton mathematical series ; 34)
Bibliography: p424-445. — Includes index
ISBN 0-691-08282-0 : £21.30 B81-37158

Treves, François. Introduction to pseudodifferential and Fourier integral operators / François Treves. — New York ; London : Plenum, c1980. — (The University series in mathematics)
Bibliography: pxxix-xxxiv. — Includes index
Vol.1: Pseudodifferential operators. — xxxix,299p ; 24cm
ISBN 0-306-40403-6 : Unpriced
Primary classification 515.7'23 B81-10028

Treves, François. Introduction to pseudodifferential and Fourier integral operators / François Treves. — New York ; London : Plenum, c1980. — (The University series in mathematics)
Bibliography: pxv-xx. — Includes index
Vol.2: Fourier integral operators. — xxv,p301-649 ; 24cm
ISBN 0-306-40404-4 : Unpriced
Primary classification 515.7'23 B81-10027

515.7'3 — Sequence spaces

Ruckle, William H.. Sequence spaces / William H. Ruckle. — Boston (Mass.) ; London : Pitman Advanced Publishing Program, c1981. — 198p : ill ; 25cm. — (Research notes in mathematics ; 49)
Bibliography: p195-198
ISBN 0-273-08507-7 (pbk) : Unpriced
B81-38250

515.7'3 — Topological spaces: Radon measures

Tjur, Tue. Probability based on Radon measures / Tue Tjur. — Chichester : Wiley, c1980. — xi,232p : ill ; 24cm. — (Wiley series on probability and mathematical statistics)
Bibliography: p225-227. — Includes index
ISBN 0-471-27824-6 : £18.50 B81-02790

515.7'32 — Banach spaces. Nonlinear differential equations

Lakshmikantham, V.. Nonlinear differential equations in abstract spaces / by V. Lakshmikantham and S. Leela. — Oxford : Pergamon, 1981. — x,258p ; 26cm. — (International series in nonlinear mathematics ; v.2)
Bibliography: p244-255. — Includes index
ISBN 0-08-025038-6 : £18.75 B81-25250

515.7'33 — Hilbert spaces. Linear systems & linear operators

Fuhrmann, Paul A.. Linear systems and operators in Hilbert space / Paul A. Fuhrmann. — New York ; London : McGraw-Hill, c1981. — x,325p : ill ; 25cm
Bibliography: p318-322. — Includes index
ISBN 0-07-022589-3 : £19.25 : CIP rev.
B79-07238

515.8'4 — Calculus. Fuctions of several variables

Craven, B. D.. Functions of several variables. — London : Chapman and Hall, Aug.1981. — [120]p
ISBN 0-412-23330-4 (cased) : £12.00 : CIP entry
ISBN 0-412-23340-1 (pbk) : £6.00 B81-19186

515.88 — Calculus. Convex functions

Giles, John R.. Convex analysis with application in differentiation of convex functions. — Oxford : Oxford University Press, Feb.1982. — [292]p. — (Research notes in mathematics ; 58)
ISBN 0-273-08537-9 (pbk) : £10.50 : CIP entry
B81-35774

515.9 — Calculus. Functions of complex variables

Segal, Sanford L.. Nine introductions in complex analysis / Sanford L. Segal. — Amsterdam ; Oxford : North-Holland Publishing, c1981. — xvi,715p : ill ; 25cm. — (Notas de matemática ; 80) (North-Holland mathematical studies ; 53)
Bibliography: p713-715
ISBN 0-444-86226-9 (pbk) : Unpriced
B81-38239

515.9 — Calculus. Functions of complex variables — *Conference proceedings*

Aspects of contemporary complex analysis : proceedings of an instructional conference organised by the London Mathematical Society at the University of Durham (A Nato Advanced Study Institute) / edited by D.A. Brannan, J.G. Clunie. — London : Academic Press, 1980. — xiii,572p : ill ; 24cm
Includes bibliographies
ISBN 0-12-125950-1 : £45.00 B81-11260

515.9'02462 — Calculus. Functions of complex variables — *For engineering*

LePage, Wilbur R.. Complex variables and the Laplace transform for engineers / Wilbur R. LePage. — New York : Dover ; London : Constable, 1980, c1961. — xvii,475p : ill ; 21cm
Originally published: New York : McGraw-Hill, 1961. — Bibliography: p469-470. — Includes index
ISBN 0-486-63926-6 (pbk) : £3.80 B81-04956

515.9'83 — Mathematics. Elliptic functions

Alling, Norman L.. Real elliptic curves / Norman L. Alling. — Amsterdam ; Oxford : North-Holland, c1981. — xi,349p ; 24cm. — (North-Holland mathematics studies ; 54) (Notas de matemática ; 81)
Bibliography: p335-339. — Includes index
ISBN 0-444-86233-1 (pbk) : Unpriced
B81-38108

516 — GEOMETRY

516 — Finite geometry — *Conference proceedings*

Finite geometries and designs : proceedings of the second Isle of Thorns conference 1980 / edited by P.J. Cameron, J.W.P. Hirschfeld, D.R. Hughes. — Cambridge : Cambridge University Press, 1981. — 371p : ill ; 23cm. — (London Mathematical Society lecture note series, ISSN 0076-0522 ; 49)
Includes bibliographies and index
ISBN 0-521-28378-7 (pbk) : £15.00 B81-18760

516 — Geometry

Blumenthal, Leonard M.. A modern view of geometry / Leonard M. Blumenthal. — New York : Dover ; London : Constable, 1980, c1961. — xii,191p : ill ; 21cm
Originally published: San Francisco : London : Freeman, 1961. — Includes index
ISBN 0-486-63962-2 (pbk) : £2.50 B81-00098

516 — Geometry *continuation*
Efimov, N. V.. Higher geometry / N.V. Efimov ; translated from the Russian by P.C. Sinha. — Moscow : Mir ; [London] : Distributed by Central Books, 1980. — 560p : ill ; 22cm
Translation of: Vysshaia geometriia. — Includes index
ISBN 0-7147-1600-6 : £4.95 B81-23600

516 — Shapes — *For children*
Allington, Richard. Shapes / by Richard Allington and Kathleen Krull ; illustrated by Lois Ehlert. — Oxford : Blackwell Raintree, c1981. — 32p : col.ill ; 24cm. — (Beginning to learn about)
Originally published: Milwaukee : Raintree Childrens, c1979
ISBN 0-86256-014-4 : £2.50 B81-17346

Bradbury, Lynne. Colours and shapes / written by Lynne Bradbury ; illustrated by Lynn N. Grundy. — Loughborough : Ladybird Books, 1981. — [28]p : col.ill ; 19cm
Text, ill on lining papers
ISBN 0-7214-9509-5 : £0.95
Primary classification 535.6 B81-34073

The **New** gold medal book of numbers, shapes and colours. — London : Dean, c1980. — 45p : chiefly col.ill ; 26cm
ISBN 0-603-00204-8 : £1.25
Also classified at 513'.2 ; 535.6 B81-13259

Shapes and colours / illustrated by David Mostyn. — London : Hamlyn, 1981. — [42]p : col.ill ; 26cm. — (I can learn)
ISBN 0-600-36481-x : £1.99
Also classified at 535.6 B81-24061

516 — Sizes — *For children*
Woolcock, Peter. Big and small. — Sevenoaks : Hodder & Stoughton, Sept.1981. — [48]p
ISBN 0-340-26647-3 : £2.50 : CIP entry B81-23929

516'.15 — Spirals. Aesthetic aspects
Cook, Theodore Andrea. The curves of life : being an account of spiral formations and their application to growth in nature, to science and to art : with special reference to the manuscripts of Leonardo da Vinci / by Theodore Andrea Cook. — New York : Dover ; London : Constable, 1979. — xxx,479p : ill,facsims,plans ; 22cm
Facsimile of: 1st ed. London : Constable, 1914. — Includes index
ISBN 0-486-23701-x (pbk) : £3.50 B81-33384

516.2 — Geometry — *For schools*
Greer, A.. Revision practice in geometry and trigonometry / A. Greer. — Cheltenham : Thornes, 1981. — 98p : ill,1map ; 19cm. — (ST(P) revision notes series)
ISBN 0-85950-322-4 (pbk) : £1.75 : CIP rev. B81-03185

516.2 — Geometry. Theorems — *For schools*
Shortt, John. Geometry theorems and problems for the intermediate certificate / John Shortt and Jim Tully. — Dublin : Helicon Ltd
Book 1: Lower and higher course (theorems 1-15). — 1981. — 34p : ill ; 21cm
Unpriced (unbound) B81-29568

516'.2 — Incommensurable quantities. Theories of Euclid. Origins
Knorr, Wilbur Richard. The evolution of the Euclidean elements : a study of the theory of incommensurable magnitudes and its significance for early Greek geometry / Wilbur Richard Knorr. — Dordrecht ; London : Reidel, c1975. — ix,374p : ill ; 23cm. — (Synthese historical library ; v.15)
Bibliography: p353-365. - Includes index
ISBN 90-277-0509-7 (cased) : Unpriced
ISBN 90-277-1192-5 (pbk) : Unpriced B81-05842

516.2'0076 — Geometry. Measurement — *Questions & answers — For schools*
Wroe, Geoffrey. Measurement problems / Geoffrey Wroe. — London : Harrap, 1980. — 32p : col.ill ; 21cm. — (Maths takes off. Level 3. Geometry and measurement)
ISBN 0-245-53759-7 (pbk) : £0.75 B81-07777

516.2'0076 — Geometry — *Questions & answers — For schools*
Hollands, Roy. Simple geometry / Roy Hollands and Howell Moses. — St. Albans : Hart-Davis Educational, 1981. — (Basic maths)
[Pupil's book]. — 31p : ill ; 25cm + Answer book(31p : ill(some col.) ; 25cm)
ISBN 0-247-13065-6 (unbound) : £0.48
ISBN 0-247-13078-8 (Answer book) : £0.95 B81-24296

516.2'15 — Geometry. Angles — *For schools*
Angles. — Ely (Resource and Technology Centre, Back Hill, Ely, Cambs.) : EARO, c1979. — 22p : ill,2ports ; 21x30cm + 2overlays. — (Access)
ISBN 0-904463-61-3 (unbound) : Unpriced B81-20982

516.2'15 — Polygons — *Questions & answers — For schools*
Wroe, Geoffrey. Geometry / Geoffrey Wroe. — London : Harrap, 1980. — 32p : col.ill ; 21cm. — (Maths takes off. Level 3. Geometry and measurement)
ISBN 0-245-53761-9 (pbk) : £0.75 B81-07781

516.2'2 — Area. Measurement — *Questions & answers — For schools*
Wroe, Geoffrey. Area / Geoffrey Wroe. — London : Harrap, 1980. — 32p : col.ill ; 21cm. — (Maths takes off. Level 3. Geometry and measurement)
ISBN 0-245-53757-0 (pbk) : £0.75 B81-07776

516.2'2 — Pi. Determination. Geometrical techniques
Jarnecki, T. S.. [Pi] — a new value / by T.S. Jarnecki. — [Rev. ed]. — London : [Hettena Associates], c1981. — 24p,[5]p of plates : ill ; 31cm
Previous ed.: London : Polytechnic of Central London, Civil Engineering Department, 1978
£10.00 (pbk) B81-32821

516.2'3 — Cubes. Volume. Measurement — *Questions & answers — For schools*
Wroe, Geoffrey. Volume / Geoffrey Wroe. — London : Harrap, 1980. — 32p : col.ill ; 21cm. — (Maths takes off. Level 3. Geometry and measurement)
ISBN 0-245-53758-9 (pbk) : £0.75 B81-07780

516.2'3 — Volume. Measurement — *Questions & answers — For schools*
Holland, Roy. Weight, volume, capacity / Roy Hollands and Howell Moses. — St Albans : Hart-Davis Educational, 1980. — 31p : ill ; 25cm + answer book(31p : ill ; 25cm). — (Basic maths)
Cover title
ISBN 0-247-12996-8 : £0.48
ISBN 0-247-13075-3 (answer bk) : £0.95
Also classified at 531'.14'076 B81-16578

516.2'3'076 — Solid figures — *Questions & answers*
Giles, Geoff. 3-D sketching / Geoff Giles. — [Edinburgh] : Oliver & Boyd. — (DIME mathematical aids)
5: Wedges. — 1979. — 10p : ill ; 21cm
ISBN 0-05-003214-3 (unbound) : £3.00 B81-21972

516.2'4 — Spherical trigonometry — *For navigation*
Clough-Smith, J. H.. An introduction to spherical trigonometry : with practical examples, for students of navigation, hydrographic surveying and nautical astronomy / by J.H. Clough-Smith. — 2nd ed. — Glasgow : Brown, Son & Ferguson, 1978. — viii,114p : ill ; 22cm
Previous ed.: 1966. — Bibliography: pviii
ISBN 0-85174-320-x : £6.00 B81-05070

516.2'4 — Spherical trigonometry — *For surveying*
Jackson, J. E.. Sphere, spheroid and projections for surveyors / J.E. Jackson. — London : Granada, 1980. — xiv,138p : ill ; 24cm. — (Aspects of modern land surveying)
Bibliography: p133. — Includes index
ISBN 0-246-11340-5 : £15.00 B81-07215

516.3 — Analytic geometry
Carico, Charles C.. Analytic geometry / Charles C. Carico, Irving Drooyan. — New York ; Chichester : Wiley, c1980. — xiv,310p : ill ; 25cm
Text on lining paper. — Includes index
ISBN 0-471-06435-1 : £8.30 B81-00099

516.3 — Geometry. Nonlinear analysis — *Conference proceedings*
Nonlinear problems of analysis in geometry and mechanics / [edited by] M. Atteia, D. Bancel & I. Gumowski. — Boston [Mass.] ; London : Pitman, c1981. — 208p : ill ; 25cm. — (Research notes in mathematics ; 46)
Conference papers. — Includes bibliographies
ISBN 0-273-08493-3 (pbk) : £8.50
Primary classification 531'.01'515 B81-05452

516.3'5 — Algebraic geometry. Nash functions
Tognoli, A.. Algebraic geometry and Nash functions / A. Tognoli. — London : Academic Press, 1978. — 60p ; 24cm. — (Institutiones mathematicae ; v.3)
At head of title: Istituto nazionale di alta matematica. — Bibliography: p60
Unpriced (pbk) B81-17622

516.3'52 — Algebraic curves
Clemens, C. Herbert. A scrapbook of complex curve theory / C. Herbert Clemens. — New York ; London : Plenum, c1980. — ix,186p : ill ; 24cm. — (The University series in mathematics)
Bibliography: p181. — Includes index
ISBN 0-306-40536-9 : Unpriced B81-09914

516.3'6 — Differential geometry
Arnold, V. I.. Singularity theory. — Cambridge : Cambridge University Press, Oct.1981. — [272] p. — (London Mathematical lecture note series, ISSN 0076-0552 ; 53)
ISBN 0-521-28511-9 (pbk) : £12.50 : CIP entry
Also classified at 514'.7 B81-31284

Hsiung, Chua-Chih. A first course in differential geometry / Chua-Chih Hsiung. — New York ; Chichester : Wiley, c1981. — xvi,343p : ill ; 24cm. — (Pure and applied mathematics)
Text on lining papers. — Bibliography: p313-315. — Includes index
ISBN 0-471-07953-7 : £18.75 B81-23531

Kock, Anders. Synthetic differential geometry. — Cambridge : Cambridge University Press, Feb.1982. — [328]p. — (London Mathematical lecture note series, ISSN 0076-0552 ; 51)
ISBN 0-521-24138-3 (pbk) : £13.00 : CIP entry B81-36241

516.3'6 — Topological spaces: Differentiable manifolds
Michor, P. W.. Manifolds of differentiable mappings / P.W. Michor. — Orpington (9 Clareville Rd, Orpington, Kent BR5 1RU) : Shiva, c1980. — iv,158p ; 24cm. — (Shiva mathematics series ; 3)
Bibliography: p144-151. — Includes index
ISBN 0-906812-03-8 (pbk) : £8.00 : CIP rev. B80-06384

516.3'6'002453 — Differential geometry — *For physics*
Schutz, Bernard F.. Geometrical methods of mathematical physics / Bernard F. Schutz. — Cambridge : Cambridge University Press, 1980. — xii,250p : ill ; 24cm
Includes bibliographies and index
ISBN 0-521-23271-6 (cased) : £18.00
ISBN 0-521-29887-3 (pbk) : £7.50 B81-00863

516.3'62 — Integral geometry
Ambartzumian, R. V.. Combinatorial integral geometry. — Chichester : Wiley, Nov.1981. — [250]p. — (Wiley series in probability and mathematical statistics)
ISBN 0-471-27977-3 : £15.00 : CIP entry B81-31203

516'.5 — Projective geometry
Garner, Lynn E.. An outline of projective geometry / Lynn E. Garner. — New York ; Oxford : North Holland, c1981. — vi,220p : ill ; 24cm
Bibliography: p214-215. - Includes index
ISBN 0-444-00423-8 : £16.35 B81-18488

516′.5 — Projective geometry — *Conference proceedings*

Geometry - von Staudt′s point of view : proceedings of the NATO Advanced Study Institute held at Bad Windsheim, West Germany, July 21-August 1, 1980 / edited by Peter Plaumann and Karl Strambach. — Dordrecht ; London : Reidel in cooperation with NATO Scientific Affairs Division, c1981. — xi,430p : ill ; 25cm. — (NATO advanced study institutes series. Series C, Mathematical and physical sciences ; v.70)
Includes bibliographies and index
ISBN 90-277-1283-2 : Unpriced B81-27726

516′.5 — Synthetic geometry — *Anthroposophical viewpoints*

Adams, George, *1894-1963*. The lemniscatory ruled surfaces in space and counterspace / George Adams. — London : Steiner, 1979. — 83p : ill ; 29cm
£3.50 (pbk) B81-18418

519 — PROBABILITIES AND APPLIED MATHEMATICS

519.2 — Calculus. Stochastic integration

Metivier, Michel. Stochastic integration / Michel Metivier, J. Pellaumail. — New York ; London : Academic Press, 1980. — xii,196p ; 24cm. — (Probability and mathematical statistics)
Bibliography: p188-194. — Includes index
ISBN 0-12-491450-0 : £14.00 B81-01532

519.2 — Point processes — *Conference proceedings*

Point processes and queuing problems / edited by P. Bártfai, J. Tomkó. — Amsterdam ; Oxford : North-Holland, c1981. — 426p ; 25cm. — (Colloquia mathematica societatis Jánes Bolyai, ISSN 0139-3383 ; 24)
Conference papers
ISBN 0-444-85432-0 : £25.19
Also classified at 519.8′2 B81-21442

519.2 — Probabilities

Bauer, H.. Probability theory and elements of measure theory. — 2nd ed. — London : Academic Press, May 1981. — [500]p. — (Probability & mathematical statistics)
Translation of: Wahrscheinlichkeitstheorie und Grundzuge der Masstheorie. — Previous ed.: New York ; London : Holt, Rinehart and Winston, 1972
ISBN 0-12-082820-0 : CIP entry B81-04332

Haight, Frank A.. Applied probability / Frank A. Haight. — New York ; London : Plenum, c1981. — xi,290p : ill ; 24cm. — (Mathematical concepts and methods in science and engineering ; 23)
Includes index
ISBN 0-306-40699-3 : Unpriced B81-36184

Moore, P. G. (Peter Gerald). Principles of statistical techniques : a first course, from the beginnings, for schools and universities : with many examples and solutions / P.G. Moore. — 2nd ed. — Cambridge : Cambridge University Press, 1969 (1979 [printing]). — viii,288p : ill ; 22cm
Previous ed.: 1958. — Bibliography: p285. — Includes index
ISBN 0-521-29055-4 (pbk) : £4.95 B81-01650

Probabilistic analysis and related topics. — New York ; London : Academic Press
Vol.2 / edited by A.T. Bharucha-Reid. — 1979. — ix,207pp : ill ; 24cm
Includes index
ISBN 0-12-095602-0 : £15.40 B81-22160

Ross, Sheldon M.. Introduction to probability models / Sheldon M. Ross. — 2nd ed. — New York ; London : Academic Press, c1980. — xi,376p : ill ; 25cm. — (Probability and mathematical statistics)
Previous ed.: 1972. — Includes bibliographies and index
ISBN 0-12-598460-x : £12.40 B81-17712

519.2 — Probabilities & statistical mathematics

Maritz, J. S.. Distribution-free statistical methods. — London : Chapman and Hall, Aug.1981. — [250]p. — (Monographs on applied probability and statistics)
ISBN 0-412-15940-6 : £12.00 : CIP entry B81-18153

519.2 — Probabilities & statistical mathematics — *Festschriften*

Contributions to statistics : Jaroslav Hájek memorial volume / editor Jana Jurečková. — Dordrecht ; London : Reidel, c1979. — 317p : ill,1port ; 25cm
Includes bibliographies and index
ISBN 90-277-0883-5 : Unpriced B81-02080

519.2 — Probabilities — *Festschriften*

Contributions to probability : a collection of papers dedicated to Eugene Lukacs / edited by J. Gani ; V.K. Rohatgi. — New York ; London : Academic Press, 1981. — xxi,311p : 1port ; 24cm
ISBN 0-12-274460-8 : £26.40 B81-39785

519.2 — Probabilities — *For schools*

On the ball / [Schools Council Project on Statistical Education]. — Slough : Published for the Schools Council by Foulsham Educational, c1980. — 15p : ill ; 21cm + teachers′ notes(14p ; 21cm). — (Statistics in your world. [Level 2])
ISBN 0-572-01074-5 (pbk) : Unpriced
ISBN 0-572-01101-6 (teachers′ notes) : Unpriced B81-16714

Probability games / [Schools Council Project on Statistical Education]. — Slough : Published for the Schools Council by Foulsham Educational, c1980. — 16p : ill ; 21cm + teachers′ notes(18p : ill ; 21cm). — (Statistics in your world. [Level 1])
ISBN 0-572-01071-0 (pbk) : Unpriced
ISBN 0-572-01098-2 (teachers′ notes) : Unpriced B81-16712

519.2 — Random fields. Geometric aspects

Adler, Robert J.. The geometry of random fields / Robert J. Adler. — Chichester : Wiley, c1981. — xi,280p : ill ; 24cm. — (Wiley series in probability and mathematical statistics)
Bibliography: p263-272. — Includes index
ISBN 0-471-27844-0 : £17.50 B81-19001

519.2 — Stochastic differential equations

Ikeda, Nobuyuki. Stochastic differential equations and diffusion processes / by Nobuyuki Ikeda, Shinzo Watanabe. — Amsterdam ; Oxford : North-Holland, 1981. — xiv,464p ; 24cm. — (North-Holland mathematical library ; v.24)
Bibliography: p453-460. — Includes index
ISBN 0-444-86172-6 : £34.52 B81-36751

Schuss, Zeev. Theory and applications of stochastic differential equations / Zeev Schuss. — New York ; Chichester : Wiley, c1980. — xiii,321p : ill ; 24cm. — (Wiley series in probability and mathematical statistics)
Text on lining papers. — Bibliography: p315-318. — Includes index
ISBN 0-471-04394-x : Unpriced B81-08443

519.2 — Stochastic dynamical systems — *Conference proceedings*

International Conference on Analysis and Optimisation of Stochastic Systems *(1978 : University of Oxford)*. Analysis and optimisation of stochastic systems : based on the proceedings of the International Conference on Analysis and Optimisation of Stochastic Systems held at the University of Oxford from 6-8 September, 1978, organised by the Institute of Mathematics and its Applications / edited by O.L.R. Jacobs ... [et al.]. — London : Academic Press, 1980. — xiv,573p : ill ; 24cm. — (The Institute of Mathematics and its Applications conference series)
Includes bibliographies and index
ISBN 0-12-378680-0 : £20.00 : CIP rev. B80-11016

519.2 — Stochastic processes

Karlin, Samuel. A second course in stochastic processes / Samuel Karlin, Howard M. Taylor. — New York ; London : Academic Press, c1981. — xviii,542p : ill ; 24cm
Includes index
ISBN 0-12-398650-8 : £19.60 B81-34432

519.2 — Stochastic processes — *Conference proceedings*

Applied Stochastic Processes Conference *(1978 : University of Georgia)*. Applied stochastic processes / edited by G. Adomian ; proceedings of the Applied Stochastic Processes Conference held at the Center for Applied Mathematics, University of Georgia, Athens, Georgia May 15-19 1978. — New York ; London : Academic Press, 1980. — ix,301pp : ill ; 24cm
ISBN 0-12-044380-5 : £13.60 B81-15127

519.2′0245 — Probabilities — *For science*

Soong, T. T.. Probabilistic modeling and analysis in science and engineering / T.T. Soong. — New York ; Chichester : Wiley, c1981. — xiii,384p : ill ; 24cm
Includes index
ISBN 0-471-08061-6 : £16.60
Also classified at 519.2′02462 B81-39799

519.2′02462 — Probabilities — *For engineering*

Soong, T. T.. Probabilistic modeling and analysis in science and engineering / T.T. Soong. — New York ; Chichester : Wiley, c1981. — xiii,384p : ill ; 24cm
Includes index
ISBN 0-471-08061-6 : £16.60
Primary classification 519.2′0245 B81-39799

519.2′0724 — Probabilities. Simulations — *For schools*

If at first - / [Schools Council Project on Statistical Education]. — Slough : Published for the Schools Council by Foulsham Educational, c1980. — 15p : ill ; 21cm + teachers′ notes(22p : ill ; 21cm). — (Statistics in your world. [Level 1])
ISBN 0-572-01072-9 (pbk) : Unpriced
ISBN 0-572-01099-0 (teachers′ notes) : Unpriced B81-16713

519.2′076 — Probabilities & statistical mathematics — *Questions & answers*

Problems in probability theory, mathematical statistics and theory of random functions / edited by A.A. Sveshnikov ; translated by Scripta Technica, Inc. ; edited by Bernard R. Gelbaum. — New York : Dover ; London : Constable, 1978, c1968. — ix,481p : ill ; 24cm
Translation of: Zbornik zadach po teorii veroi͡atnosteĭ, matematicheskoĭ statistike i teorii sluchaĭnykh funkt͡siĭ. — Originally published: Philadelphia : Eastbourne : Saunders, 1968. — Bibliography: p475-477. — Includes index
ISBN 0-486-63717-4 (pbk) : £4.10 B81-40720

Skipworth, G. E.. Exercises and worked examples in statistics / G.E. Skipworth. — 2nd ed. — London : Heinemann Educational, 1980. — vii,149p ; 22cm
Previous ed.: 1971
ISBN 0-435-53791-1 (pbk) : £2.95 B81-01893

519.2′82 — Applied mathematics. Approximation. Monte Carlo methods

Rubinstein, Reuven Y.. Simulation and the Monte Carlo method / Reuven Y. Rubinstein. — New York ; Chichester : Wiley, c1981. — xv,278p : ill ; 24cm. — (Wiley series in probability and mathematical statistics)
Text on lining papers. — Includes bibliographies and index
ISBN 0-471-08917-6 : £23.00 B81-33072

519.2′87 — Probabilities. Limit theory. Applications of discrete martingales

Hall, P.. Martingale limit theory and its applications / P. Hall, C.C. Heyde. — New York ; London : Academic Press, 1980. — xii,308p ; 24cm. — (Probability and mathematical statistics)
Bibliography: p285-297. — Includes index
ISBN 0-12-319350-8 : £20.20 B81-16617

519.3 — Differential games

Basar, T.. Dynamic noncooperative game theory. — London : Academic Press, Jan.1982. — [480]p
ISBN 0-12-080220-1 : CIP entry B81-34120

519.3 — Game theory

Rosenmüller, J.. The theory of games and markets / J. Rosenmüller. — Amsterdam ; Oxford : North-Holland, c1981. — viii,554p : ill ; 23cm
Bibliography: p551-554
ISBN 0-444-85482-7 : Unpriced B81-39207

519.3 — Search games

Gal, Shmuel. Search games / Shmuel Gal. — New York ; London : Academic Press, 1980. — xiv,216p : ill ; 24cm. — (Mathematics in science and engineering ; v.149)
Bibliography: p209-213. - Includes index
ISBN 0-12-273850-0 : £11.20 B81-05838

519.4 — Digital computers. Arithmetic operations

Kulisch, Ulrich W.. Computer arithmetic in theory and practice / Ulrich W. Kulisch, Willard L. Miranker. — New York ; London : Academic Press, 1981. — xiii, 249p : ill,1port ; 24cm. — (Computer science and applied mathematics)
Bibliography: p239-243. — Includes index
ISBN 0-12-428650-x : Unpriced B81-29791

519.4 — Mathematics. Interval analysis — *Conference proceedings*

Interval mathematics 1980 / edited by Karl L.E. Nickel. — New York ; London : Academic Press, 1980. — xv,554p : ill ; 24cm
Conference papers. — Includes bibliographies
ISBN 0-12-518850-1 : £16.60 B81-16616

519.4 — Numerical analysis

Watson, W. A.. Numerical analysis : the mathematics of computing / W.A. Watson, T. Philipson, P.J. Oates. — 2nd ed. — London : Edward Arnold, 1981. — vi,216p : ill ; 24cm
Previous ed.: 1969. — Bibliography: p214. — Includes index
ISBN 0-7131-2817-8 (pbk) : £5.95 : CIP rev. B80-23207

519.4 — Numerical analysis — *Conference proceedings*

The **Contribution** of Dr. J.H. Wilkinson to numerical analysis : proceedings of a symposium organised by the Institute of Mathematics and its Applications held in London on July 6th, 1977. — Southend-on-Sea (Maitland House, Warrior Sq., Southend-on-Sea, Essex SS1 2JY) : The Institute, c1978. — viii,91p ; 21cm. — (Symposium proceedings series / Institute of Mathematics and its Applications ; no.19)
Includes bibliographies
Unpriced (spiral) B81-13272

519.4 — Numerical analysis — *Festschriften*

Special topics of applied mathematics : functional analysis, numerical analysis and optimization : proceedings of the seminar held at the GMD, Bonn, 8-10 October, 1979 / dedicated to Heinz Unger ; managing editors J. Frehse, D. Pallaschke, U. Trottenberg. — Amsterdam ; Oxford : North-Holland, 1980. — viii,248p : ill ; 23cm
Includes bibliographies
ISBN 0-444-86035-5 : £17.69
Primary classification 510 B81-03637

519.4'05 — Numerical analysis — *Serials*

IMA journal of numerical analysis. — Vol.1, no.1 (Jan. 1981)-. — London : Academic Press on behalf of the Institute of Mathematics and its Applications, 1981-. — v. : ill ; 26cm
Quarterly. — Continues in part: Journal of the Institute of Mathematics and its Applications. — Description based on: Vol.1, no.2 (Apr. 1981)
ISSN 0272-4974 = IMA journal of numerical analysis : £48.00 per year B81-39733

519.5 — Categorical data. Dual scaling

Nishisato, Shizuhiko. Analysis of categorical data : dual scaling and its applications / Shizuhiko Nishisato. — Toronto ; London : University of Toronto Press, c1980. — xiii,276p : ill ; 25cm. — (Mathematical expositions, ISSN 0076-5333 ; no.24)
Bibliography: p259-270. — Includes index
ISBN 0-8020-5489-7 : £16.50 B81-27495

519.5 — Categorical data. Statistical analysis

Palckett, R. L.. The analysis of categorical data / R.L. Palckett. — 2nd ed. — London : Griffin, 1981. — xii,207p : ill ; 22cm. — (Griffin's statistical monograph series ; no.35)
Previous ed.: 1974. — Bibliography: p176-196. — Includes index
ISBN 0-85264-265-2 (pbk) : £7.95 B81-40018

519.5 — Centrography — *For geography*

Kellerman, Aharon. Centrographic measures in geography / by Aharon Kellerman. — Norwich : Geo Abstracts, c1981. — 32p : ill ; 22cm. — (Concepts and techniques in modern geography, ISSN 0306-6142 ; no.32)
Bibliography: p29-32
ISBN 0-86094-091-8 (pbk) : Unpriced B81-40799

519.5 — Linear statistical models

Arnold, Steven F.. The theory of linear models and multivariate analysis / Steven F. Arnold. — New York ; Chichester : Wiley, c1981. — xv,475p ; 24cm. — (Wiley series in probability and mathematical statistics)
Bibliography: p464-469. — Includes index
ISBN 0-471-05065-2 : £21.70
Primary classification 519.5'35 B81-23348

519.5 — Nonparametric statistical mathematics

Conover, W. J.. Practical nonparametric statistics / W.J. Conover. — 2nd ed. — New York ; Chichester : Wiley, 1980. — xiv,493p : ill ; 24cm. — (Wiley series in probability and mathematical statistics)
Previous ed.: 1971. — Text on lining papers. — Bibliography: p394-426. — Includes index
ISBN 0-471-02867-3 : £13.50 B81-00865

519.5 — Qualitative data. Statistical analysis. Applications of loglinear models — *For social sciences*

Gilbert, G. Michael. Modeiling society. — London : Allen & Unwin, Nov.1981. — [160]p. — (Contemporary social research series ; 2)
ISBN 0-04-312009-1 (cased) : £12.95 : CIP entry
ISBN 0-04-312000-5 (pbk) : £5.95 B81-28787

519.5 — Statistical analysis

Cox, D. R.. Applied statistics. — London : Chapman and Hall, Sept.1981. — [220]p
ISBN 0-412-16560-0 (cased) : £15.00 : CIP entry
ISBN 0-412-16570-8 (pbk) : £8.50 B81-23907

Wetherill, G. Barrie. Intermediate statistical methods / G. Barrie Wetherill. — London : Chapman and Hall, 1981. — xv,390p : ill ; 24cm + Solutions to exercises(74p; 24cm). — (Science paperbacks ; 172)
Bibliography: p354-359. — Includes index
ISBN 0-412-16440-x (cased) : Unpriced: CIP rev.
ISBN 0-412-16450-7 (pbk) : Unpriced
ISBN 0-412-23520-x (Solutions to exercises) : Unpriced B81-03687

519.5 — Statistical mathematics

Developments in statistics. — New York ; London : Academic Press, 1980
Includes bibliographies and index
Vol.3 / edited by Paruchuri R. Krishnaiah. — xiv,254p : ill ; 24cm
ISBN 0-12-426603-7 : £19.60 B81-14751

Erricker, B. C.. Elementary statistics / B.C. Erricker. — 3rd ed. / revised by W.T. Ellis and Pat Davies. — London : Hodder and Stoughton, 1981. — 319p : ill ; 22cm
Previous ed.: London : English University Press, 1970. — Includes index
ISBN 0-340-25683-4 (pbk) : £2.95 B81-26002

Folks, J. Leroy. Ideas of statistics / J. Leroy Folks. — New York ; Chichester : Wiley, c1981. — xiii,368p : ill,1map,ports ; 24cm
Includes bibliographies and index
ISBN 0-471-02099-0 : £8.80 B81-14763

Freund, John E.. Statistics : a first course / John E. Freund. — 3rd ed. — Englewood Cliffs ; London : Prentice-Hall, c1981. — xiv,466p : ill (some col.) ; 24cm
Previous ed.: 1976. — Text on lining papers. — Bibliography: p415-416. — Includes index
ISBN 0-13-845958-4 : £11.65 B81-12516

Gilbert, Norma. Statistics / Norma Gilbert. — 2nd ed. — Philadelphia ; London : Saunders, c1981. — xi,434p : ill ; 25cm
Previous ed.: 1976. — Text on lining papers. — Includes index
ISBN 0-03-058091-9 : Unpriced B81-33140

Kendall, *Sir* Maurice. The advanced theory of statistics / Sir Maurice Kendall and Alan Stuart. — London : Griffin
Previous ed.: 1973. — Bibliography: p671-716. — Includes index
Vol.2: Inference and relationship. — 4th ed. — 1979. — x,748p : ill ; 26cm
ISBN 0-85264-255-5 : £25.00 B81-27520

Larsen, Richard J.. An introduction to mathematical statistics and its applications / Richard J. Larsen, Morris L. Marx. — Englewood Cliffs ; London : Prentice-Hall, c1981. — xii,536,A60p : ill ; 25cm
Bibliography: pA45-A56. — Includes index
ISBN 0-13-487744-6 : £14.90 B81-16643

Lindgren, Bernard W.. Elementary statistics / Bernard W. Lindgren, Donald A. Berry. — New York : Macmillan ; London : Collier Macmillan, c1981. — xi,530p : ill ; 25cm
Includes index
ISBN 0-02-370790-9 : Unpriced B81-21451

Mattson, Dale E.. Statistics : difficult concepts, understandable explanations / Dale E. Mattson. — St. Louis ; London : Mosby, 1981. — xiii,482p : ill ; 24cm
Includes index
ISBN 0-8016-3173-4 (pbk) : £11.25 B81-30124

Rowntree, Derek. Statistics without tears : a primer for non-mathematicians / Derek Rowntree. — Harmondsworth : Penguin, 1981. — 199p ; 19cm. — (A Pelican book)
Bibliography: p191-195. - Includes index
ISBN 0-14-022326-6 (pbk) : £1.95 B81-11530

Sprent, Peter. Quick statistics : an introduction to non-parametric methods / Peter Sprent. — Harmondsworth : Penguin, 1981. — 364p : ill ; 20cm. — (Pebguin handbooks)
Bibliography: p251-252. — Includes index
ISBN 0-14-080438-2 (pbk) : £3.95 B81-21035

Stoodley, Keith D. C.. Applied statistical techniques / K.D.C. Stoodley, T. Lewis, C.L.S. Stainton. — Chichester : Horwood, 1980. — 310p : ill ; 24cm. — (Ellis Horwood series in mathematics & its applications)
Includes index
ISBN 0-85312-157-5 : £16.50 : CIP rev. B80-02757

Wetherill, G. Barrie. Elementary statistical methods. — 3rd ed. — London : Chapman and Hall, Jan.1982. — [348]p. — (Science paperbacks)
Previous ed.: 1972
ISBN 0-412-24000-9 (pbk) : £6.95 : CIP entry B81-34403

519.5 — Statistical mathematics. Accuracy — *For schools*

Getting it right / [Schools Council Project on Statistical Education]. — Slough : Published for the Schools Council by Foulsham Educational, c1981. — 19p : ill ; 21cm + teachers' notes(16p : ill ; 21cm). — (Statistics in yuor world. [Level 2])
ISBN 0-572-01078-8 (pbk) : Unpriced
ISBN 0-572-01105-9 (teachers' notes) : Unpriced B81-16720

519.5 — Statistical mathematics — *Conference proceedings*

International Conference in Statistics *(1979 : Tokyo)*. Recent developments in statistical inference and data analysis : proceedings of the International Conference in Statistics in Tokyo / edited by K. Matusita. — Amsterdam ; Oxford : North-Holland, 1980. — 364p : ill ; 23cm
Includes bibliographies
ISBN 0-444-86104-1 : £20.87 B81-00864

519.5 — Statistical mathematics — *For comparative studies*

Statistical methods for comparative studies : techniques for bias reduction / Sharon Anderson ... [et al.] with contributions from Anthony S. Bryk, Joel Kleinman. — New York ; Chichester : Wiley, c1980. — xiii,289p : ill ; 24cm. — (Wiley series in probability and mathematical statistics)
Includes bibliographies and index
ISBN 0-471-04838-0 : £13.50 B81-00100

519.5 — Statistical mathematics — *For schools*

Devine, F.. Basic statistics : a step by step guide / F. Devine. — London : Harrap, 1981. — 282p : ill ; 24cm
ISBN 0-245-53495-4 (pbk) : £3.95 B81-29249

Greer, A.. Revision practice in statistics / A. Greer. — Cheltenham : Thornes, 1981. — 126p : ill ; 19cm. — (ST(P) revision notes series)
ISBN 0-85950-324-0 (pbk) : £1.95 : CIP rev. B81-03187

Practice makes perfect / [Schools Council Project on Statistical Education]. — Slough : Published for the Schools Council by Foulsham Educational, c1980. — 16p : ill ; 21cm + teachers' notes(20p : ill ; 21cm). — (Statistics in your world. [Level 1])
ISBN 0-572-01070-2 (pbk) : Unpriced
ISBN 0-572-01097-4 (teachers' notes) : Unpriced B81-16711

519.5 — Statistical mathematics. Graphs — *For schools*

Figuring the future / [Schools Council Project on Statistical Education]. — Slough : Published for the Schools Council by Foulsham Educational, c1981. — 20p : ill ; 21cm + teachers' notes(16p ; 21cm). — (Statistics in your world. [Level 4])
ISBN 0-572-01089-3 (pbk) : Unpriced
ISBN 0-572-01116-4 (teachers' notes) : Unpriced B81-16718

Leisure for pleasure / [Schools Council Project on Statistical Education]. — Slough : Published for the Schools Council by Foulsham Educational, c1980. — 16p : ill ; 21cm + teachers' notes(20p : ill ; 21cm). — (Statistics in your world. [Level 1])
ISBN 0-572-01066-4 (pbk)
ISBN 0-572-01093-1 (teachers' notes) : Unpriced B81-16716

519.5 — Statistical mathematics. Limits

Serfling, Robert J.. Approximation theorems of mathematical statistics / Robert J. Serfling. — New York ; Chichester : Wiley, c1980. — xiv,371p ; 24cm. — (Wiley series in probability and mathematical statistics)
Bibliography: p353-363. — Includes index
ISBN 0-471-02403-1 : £18.70 B81-10644

519.5 — Statistical mathematics. Outliers

Hawkins, D. M.. Identification of outliers / D.M. Hawkins. — London : Chapman and Hall, 1980. — x,188p ; 23cm. — (Monographs on applied probability and statistics)
Bibliography: p128-135 — Includes index
ISBN 0-412-21900-x : £10.00 : CIP rev. B80-00700

519.5'02415 — Statistical mathematics — *For psychology*

Levine, Gustav. Introductory statistics for psychology : the logic and the methods / Gustav Levine. — International ed. — New York ; London : Academic Press, c1981. — xv,496p : ill ; 24cm
Includes index
ISBN 0-12-445470-4 (pbk) : £6.80 B81-33160

Levine, Gustav. Introductory statistics for psychology : the logic and the methods / Gustav Levine. — New York ; London : Academic Press, c1981. — xv,496p : ill ; 24cm
Text on lining papers. — Includes index
ISBN 0-12-445480-1 : £10.20 B81-35434

519.5'02415 — Statistical mathematics — *For psychometrics*

Ferguson, George A.. Statistical analysis in psychology and education / George A. Ferguson. — 5th ed. — New York ; London : McGraw-Hill, c1981. — x,549p : ill ; 25cm
Bibliography: p514-517. - Includes index
ISBN 0-07-020482-9 (cased) : £14.95
ISBN 0-07-066282-7 (pbk) : £6.50 B81-10370

519.5'0243 — Statistical mathematics — *For behavioural sciences*

Shavelson, Richard J.. Instructor's manual to accompany Statistical reasoning for the behavioral sciences / Richard J. Shavelson. — Boston, Mass. ; London : Allyn and Bacon, c1981. — 100p : ill ; 24cm
ISBN 0-205-06934-7 (pbk) : £1.00 B81-40105

Shavelson, Richard J.. Statistical reasoning for the behavioral sciences / Richard J. Shavelson. — Boston [Mass.] ; London : Allyn and Bacon, c1981. — 673p : ill ; 25cm
Bibliography: p671-673. — Includes index
ISBN 0-205-06935-5 : £18.95 B81-12099

Young, Robert K.. Introductory statistics for the behavioral sciences / Robert K. Young, Donald J. Veldman. — 4th ed. — New York ; London : Holt, Rinehart and Winston, c1981. — x,687p : ill ; 24cm
Previous ed.: 1977. — Includes index
ISBN 0-03-043051-8 : £10.75 B81-23057

519.5'024301 — Statistical analysis — *For social sciences*

Morris, Carl N.. Introduction to data analysis and statistical inference / Carl N. Morris, John E. Rolph. — Englewood Cliffs ; London : Prentice-Hall, c1981. — xx,389p : ill ; 24cm
Bibliography: p373-377. — Includes index
ISBN 0-13-480582-8 : £9.75 B81-33750

519.5'024301 — Statistical mathematics — *For social sciences*

Champion, Dean J.. Basic statistics for social research / Dean J. Champion. — 2nd ed. — New York : Macmillan ; London : Collier Macmillan, c1981. — xii,452p : ill ; 24cm
Previous ed.: Scranton : Chandler, 1970. — Includes bibliographies and index
ISBN 0-02-320600-4 : £12.50 B81-36165

Hays, William L.. Statistics / William L. Hays. — 3rd ed. — New York ; London : Holt, Rinehart and Winston, c1981. — xi,713p : ill ; 25cm
Previous ed.: published as Statistics for the social sciences. 1973. — Bibliography: p669-672. — Includes index
ISBN 0-03-056706-8 : £13.95 B81-25281

Pfeiffer, Kenneth. Basic statistics for the behavioral sciences / Kenneth Pfeiffer and James N. Olson. — New York ; London : Holt, Rinehart and Winston, c1981. — xv,444p : ill ; 25cm
Text and ill on lining papers. — Includes index
ISBN 0-03-049866-x : £10.25 B81-22864

519.5'024309 — Statistical mathematics — *For sociology*

Startup, Richard. Introducing social statistics. — London : Allen and Unwin, Jan.1982. — [224] p. — (Studies in sociology ; 12)
ISBN 0-04-310012-0 (cased) : £10.95 : CIP entry
ISBN 0-04-310013-9 (pbk) : £4.95 B81-33922

519.5'02433 — Statistical mathematics — *For economics*

Hebden, Julia. Statistics for economists. — Oxford : Philip Allan, Aug.1981. — [224]p
ISBN 0-86003-036-9 (cased) : £12.00 : CIP entry
ISBN 0-86003-134-9 (pbk) : £5.95 B81-23900

Kazmier, Leonard J.. Basic statistics for business and economics / Leonard J. Kazmier. — International student ed. — Auckland ; London : McGraw-Hill, c1979. — xiv,457p : ill ; 21cm
Includes index
ISBN 0-07-066369-6 (pbk) : £7.50 B81-31682

Mansfield, Edwin. Statistics for business and economics : methods and applications / Edwin Mansfield. — New York ; London : Norton, c1980. — xviii,580,A94p : col.ill ; 25cm
Text on lining papers. — Includes index
ISBN 0-393-95057-3 : £9.95
Primary classification 519.5'024658 B81-19878

519.5'024372 — Statistical mathematics — *For teaching*

Crocker, A. C.. Statistics for the teacher / A.C. Crocker. — 3rd ed. — Windsor : NFER-Nelson, 1981. — 158p : ill ; 22cm
Previous ed.: 1974. — Includes index
ISBN 0-85633-220-8 (pbk) : £4.75 B81-24215

519.5'024574 — Statistical mathematics — *For biology*

Bailey, Norman T. J.. Statistical methods in biology / Norman T.J. Bailey. — 2nd ed. — London : Hodder and Stoughton, 1981. — viii,216p : 2ill ; 22cm
Previous ed.: London : English Universities Press, 1959. — Bibliography: p173-174. — Includes index
ISBN 0-340-24756-8 (pbk) : £3.95 : CIP rev. B80-18684

Bishop, O. N.. Statistics for biology : a practical guide for the experimental biologist / O.N. Bishop. — 3rd ed. — Harlow : Longman, 1980. — viii,215p : ill ; 22cm
Previous ed.: 1971. — Bibliography: p205. - Includes index
ISBN 0-582-35330-0 (pbk) : Unpriced B81-12228

Finney, D. J.. Statistics for biologists / D.J. Finney. — London : Chapman and Hall, 1980. — viii,165p : ill ; 21cm. — (Science paperbacks)
Includes index
ISBN 0-412-21540-3 (pbk) : £3.75 : CIP rev. B80-08725

519.5'0246 — Statistical mathematics — *For technicians*

Bird, J. O.. Statistics for technicians / J.O. Bird, A.J.C. May. — London : Longman, 1981. — 124p : ill ; 22cm. — (Longman technician series. Mathematics and sciences)
Includes index
ISBN 0-582-41576-4 (pbk) : £3.50 B81-18948

Walker, Eric. Statistics Level 3. — London : Holt, Rinehart and Winston, Feb.1982. — [160]p. — (Holt technician texts)
ISBN 0-03-910356-0 (pbk) : £3.95 : CIP entry B81-40250

519.5'02461 — Statistical mathematics - *For medicine*

Strike, Paul W.. Medical laboratory statistics. — Bristol : J. Wright, Sept.1981. — [176]p
ISBN 0-7236-0582-3 : £5.50 : CIP entry B81-20573

519.5'0246177 — Statistical mathematics — *For ophthalmology*

Sommer, Alfred. Epidemiology and statistics for the ophthalmologist / Alfred Sommer. — New York ; Oxford : Oxford University Press, 1980. — x,86p : ill ; 21cm
Bibliography: p83. - Includes index
ISBN 0-19-502656-x (pbk) : £7.95
Also classified at 614.4'0246177 B81-07727

519.5'0246238 — Statistical mathematics — *For shipping*

Goodwin, E. M.. Marine statistics : theory and practice / E.M. Goodwin, J.F. Kemp. — London : Stanford Maritime, 1979. — 336p : ill ; 24cm
Includes index
ISBN 0-540-07379-2 : £12.50 : CIP rev. B79-20053

519.5'02465 — Statistical mathematics — *For business enterprise*

Wheldon, Harold J.. Wheldon's business statistics and statistical method. — 9th ed / G.L. Thirkettle. — Plymouth : Macdonald and Evans, 1981. — ix,278p : ill,maps,forms ; 22cm
Previous ed.: 1976. — Includes index
ISBN 0-7121-2324-5 (pbk) : £3.75 B81-17828

519.5'02465 — Statistical mathematics — *Questions & answers — For business enterprise*

Innes, Alexander E.. Business statistics by example / Alexander E. Innes. — Rev. ed. — London : Macmillan, 1979. — vii,271p : ill ; 24cm
Previous ed.: 1974. — Bibliography: p268. - Includes index
ISBN 0-333-26928-4 (pbk) : £5.50 : CIP rev. B79-17510

519.5'024657 — Statistical mathematics — *For accounting*

Bancroft, G.. Maths and statistics for accounting and business studies. — London : McGraw-Hill, Sept.1981. — [320]p
ISBN 0-07-084564-6 (pbk) : £7.95 : CIP entry B81-21639

519.5'024658 — Statistical mathematics — *For business studies*

Mansfield, Edwin. Statistics for business and economics : methods and applications / Edwin Mansfield. — New York ; London : Norton, c1980. — xviii,580,A94p : col.ill ; 25cm
Text on lining papers. — Includes index
ISBN 0-393-95057-3 : £9.95
Also classified at 519.5'02433 B81-19878

519.5'024658 — Statistical mathematics — *For management*

Ashford, John, *1929-*. Statistics for management / John Ashford. — 2nd ed. — London : Institute of Personnel Management, 1980. — 458 : ill ; 22cm. — (Management in perspective)
Previous ed.: 1977. — Includes index
ISBN 0-85292-271-x (pbk) : £9.95 : CIP rev. B81-06091

Levin, Richard I.. Statistics for management / Richard I. Levin. — 2nd ed. — London : Prentice-Hall, c1981. — viii,792p : ill(some col.) ; 24cm. — (Prentice-Hall international series in management)
Previous ed.: 1978. — Bibliography: p788. - Includes index
ISBN 0-13-845388-8 (pbk) : £7.50 B81-17292

519.5'02491 — Statistical mathematics — *For geography*

Matthews, John A.. Quantitative and statistical approaches to geography : a practical manual / John A. Matthews. — Oxford : Pergamon, 1981. — xii,204p : ill,maps ; 26cm. — (Pergamon Oxford geographies)
Bibliography: p180-182. — Includes index
ISBN 0-08-024296-0 (cased) : £15.50
ISBN 0-08-024295-2 (pbk) : £6.50 B81-35755

519.5'028'54 — Statistical analysis. Applications of digital computer systems — *Conference proceedings*

International Symposium on Data Analysis and Informatics *(2nd : 1979 : Versailles)*. Data analysis and informatics : proceedings of the Second International Symposium on Data Analysis and Informatics, organised by the Institut de recherche d'informatique, Versailles, October 17-19, 1979 / edited by F. Diday ... [et al.]. — Amsterdam ; Oxford : North-Holland, 1980. — viii,790p : ill,1map ; 23cm
English and French text. — Includes bibliographies
ISBN 0-444-86005-3 : £31.80 B81-05958

519.5'028'5404 — Statistical analysis. Applications of digital computer systems

Cooke, D.. Basic statistical computing. — London : Edward Arnold, Dec.1981. — [208]p
ISBN 0-7131-3441-0 (pbk) : £5.95 : CIP entry B81-32047

519.5'028'542 — Statistical analysis. Applications of digital computer systems. Programs: IDA program — *Manuals*

Ling, Robert F.. User's manual for IDA / Robert F. Ling, Harry V. Roberts. — [Palo Alto] ; London : Scientific Press/McGraw-Hill, c1980. — [218]p in various pagings ; 28cm
Includes index
ISBN 0-07-037905-x (pbk) : £8.75 B81-19534

519.5'028'5424 — Statistical mathematics. Applications of programs written in Basic language on small digital computer systems

Van Tassel, Dennie. Basic-pack statistics programs for small computers / Dennie Van Tassel. — Englewood Cliffs ; London : Prentice-Hall, c1981. — x,230p ; 28cm. — (Prentice-Hall series in personal computing)
Includes index
ISBN 0-13-066381-6 (pbk) : £11.00 B81-17300

519.5'028'5425 — Statistical mathematics. Applications of digital computer systems. Software packages: STATLIB — *Manuals*

Brelsford, William M.. STATLIB : a statistical computing library / William M. Brelsford, Daniel A. Relles. — Englewood Cliffs ; London : Prentice-Hall, c1981. — xviii,427p : ill ; 28cm. — (A Bell Laboratories/Rand Corporation book)
Bibliography: p399-400. — Includes index
ISBN 0-13-846220-8 (pbk) : £11.40 B81-26007

519.5'06'041 — Great Britain. Statistical mathematics. Organisations: Institute of Statisticians — *Directories — Serials*

Institute of Statisticians. List of members / the Institute of Statisticians. — Jan.1974. — Bury St. Edmunds (St. Edmunds House, Lower Baxter St., Bury St. Edmunds, Suffolk IP33 1LP) : The Institute, 1974. — 39p
£0.50 B81-12432

Institute of Statisticians. List of members / the Institute of Statisticians. — Jan.1976. — Bury St Edmunds (36, Churchgate St., Bury St Edmunds, Suffolk IP33 1RD) : The Institute, 1976. — 47p
£1.00 B81-06634

. List of members / the Institute of Statisticians. — Jan.1975. — Bury St. Edmunds (St. Edmunds House, Lower Baxter St., Bury St. Edmunds, Suffolk IP33 1LP) : The Institute, 1975. — 41p
£0.75 B81-12433

519.5'07 — Statistical mathematics - *Questions & answers*

Wetherill, G. Barrie. Solution to exercises in Intermediate statistical methods. — London : Chapman and Hall, Apr.1981. — [80]p
ISBN 0-412-23520-x (pbk) : £2.00: CIP entry B81-03688

519.5'07'1242 — England. Secondary schools. Curriculum subjects: Statistical mathematics

Holmes, Peter. Statistics in schools 11-16. — London : Methuen, July 1981. — [100]p. — (Working papers / Schools Council, ISSN 0533-1668 ; 69)
ISBN 0-423-50840-7 (pbk) : £5.00 : CIP entry B81-13500

519.5'07'7 — Statistical mathematics — *Programmed instructions*

Stahl, Sidney M.. Reading and understanding applied statistics : a self-learning approach / Sidney M. Stahl, Janies D. Hennes. — 2nd ed. — St. Louis ; London : Mosby, 1980. — xvii,374p : ill ; 23cm
Previous ed.: 1975. — Bibliography: p370-371. — Includes index
ISBN 0-8016-4754-1 (pbk) : £8.50 B81-08540

519.5'2 — Statistical mathematics. Circular distribution - *For biology*

Batschelet, Edward. Circular statistics in biology. — London : Academic Press, Aug.1981. — [300]p. — (Mathematics in biology)
ISBN 0-12-081050-6 : CIP entry B81-17521

519.5'3 — Cluster analysis

Everitt, Brian. Cluster analysis / Brian Everitt. — 2nd ed. — London : Published on behalf of the Social Science Research Council by Heinemann Educational, 1980. — 136p : ill ; 22cm. — (Reviews of current research ; 11)
Previous ed.: 1974. — Bibliography: p119-132. — Includes index
ISBN 0-435-82296-9 (pbk) : £5.50 : CIP rev. B81-01217

519.5'3 — Discriminant analysis

Abassi, Boulem. A mathematical programming method of discriminant analysis / by Boulem Abassi and Albert H. Russell. — London (Basinghall St., EC2V 5AH) : Gresham College, c1981. — 24 leaves : ill ; 30cm. — (Working paper series / City University Business School, ISSN 0140-1041 ; no.20)
Bibliography: p24
Unpriced (pbk) B81-11321

Hand, D. J.. Discrimination and classification. — Chichester : Wiley, Dec.1981. — [224]p. — (Wiley series in probability and mathematical statistics)
ISBN 0-471-28048-8 : £15.50 : CIP entry B81-34017

519.5'3 — Statistical analysis. Spatial analysis

Ripley, Brian D.. Spatial statistics / Brian D. Ripley. — New York ; Chichester : Wiley, c1981. — x,252p : ill ; 24cm. — (Wiley series in probability and mathematical statistics)
Bibliography: p214-241. — Includes index
ISBN 0-471-08367-4 : £18.75 B81-23316

519.5'32 — Statistical mathematics. Cumulative frequencies — *For schools*

Equal pay / [Schools Council Project on Statistical Education]. — Slough : Published for the Schools Council by Foulsham Educational, c1981. — 19p : ill ; 21cm + teachers' notes(16p ; 21cm). — (Statistics in your world. [Level 4])
ISBN 0-572-01091-5 (pbk) : Unpriced
ISBN 0-572-01118-0 (teachers' notes) : Unpriced B81-16721

519.5'32 — Statistical mathematics. Finite mixture distributions

Everitt, Brian. Finite mixture distributions / B.S. Everitt and D.J. Hand. — London : Chapman and Hall, 1981. — ix,143p : ill ; 23cm. — (Monographs on applied probability and statistics)
Bibliography: p129-138. - Includes index
ISBN 0-412-22420-8 : Unpriced B81-28989

519.5'35 — Multivariate analysis

Arnold, Steven F.. The theory of linear models and multivariate analysis / Steven F. Arnold. — New York ; Chichester : Wiley, c1981. — xv,475p ; 24cm. — (Wiley series in probability and mathematical statistics)
Bibliography: p464-469. — Includes index
ISBN 0-471-05065-2 : £21.70
Also classified at 519.5 B81-23348

Chatfield, Christopher. Introduction to multivariate analysis / Christopher Chatfield, Alexander J. Collins. — London : Chapman and Hall, 1980. — x,246p : ill ; 24cm. — (Science paperbacks)
Bibliography: p231-234. — Includes index
ISBN 0-412-16030-7 (cased) : £13.00 : CIP rev.
ISBN 0-412-16040-4 (pbk) : £7.50 B80-23218

Gordon, A. D.. Classification. — London : Chapman and Hall, Aug.1981. — [250]p. — (Monographs on applied probability and statistics)
ISBN 0-412-22850-5 : £10.00 : CIP entry B81-18150

519.5'35 — Multivariate analysis — *Conference proceedings*

Looking at Multivariate Data *(1980 : University of Sheffield)*. Interpreting multivariate data. — Chichester : Wiley, Dec.1981. — [360]p. — (Wiley series in probability and mathematical statistics : applied probability and statistics section)
Conference papers
ISBN 0-471-28039-9 : £25.00 : CIP entry B81-31826

519.5'352 — Analysis of variance

Analysis of variance / edited by P.R. Krishnaiah. — Amsterdam ; Oxford : North-Holland, 1980. — xvii,1002p : ill,port ; 25cm. — (Handbook of statistics ; v.1)
Includes bibliographies and index
ISBN 0-444-85335-9 : £54.35 B81-07321

519.5'352 — Categorial data. Analysis of variance
Fleiss, Joseph L.. Statistical methods for rates and proportions / Joseph L. Fleiss. — 2nd ed. — New York ; Chichester : Wiley, c1981. — xviii,321p ; 24cm. — (Wiley series in probability and mathematical statistics)
Previous ed.: 1973. — Includes bibliographies and index
ISBN 0-471-06428-9 : £18.00 B81-24052

519.5'352'0243 — Analysis of covariance — *For behavioural sciences*
Huitema, Bradley E.. The analysis of covariance and alternatives / Bradley E. Huitema. — New York ; Chichester : Wiley, c1980. — xiv,445p : ill ; 24cm
Bibliography: p431-439. - Includes index
ISBN 0-471-42044-1 : £14.75
Primary classification 519.5'352'024574
B81-05919

519.5'352'024574 — Analysis of covariance — *For biology*
Huitema, Bradley E.. The analysis of covariance and alternatives / Bradley E. Huitema. — New York ; Chichester : Wiley, c1980. — xiv,445p : ill ; 24cm
Bibliography: p431-439. - Includes index
ISBN 0-471-42044-1 : £14.75
Also classified at 519.5'352'0243 B81-05919

519.5'352'02491 — Analysis of variance — *For geography*
Silk, John. The analysis of variance / by John Silk. — Norwich : Geo Abstacts, c1981. — 57p : ill ; 21cm. — (Concepts and techniques in modern geography, ISSN 0306-6142 ; no.30)
Bibliography: p54-57
ISBN 0-86094-071-3 (pbk) : Unpriced
B81-35340

519.5'36 — Design. Optimisation. Applications of linear regression analysis
Silvey, S. D.. Optimal design : an introduction to the theory for parameter estimation / S.D. Silvey. — London : Chapman and Hall, 1980. — viii,86p ; 22cm. — (Monographs on applied probability and statistics)
Bibliography: p82-84. — Includes index
ISBN 0-412-22910-2 : £6.50 : CIP rev.
B80-18685

519.5'36 — Linear regression analysis
Toutenberg, Helge. Prior information in linear models. — Chichester : Wiley, Jan.1982. — [192]p. — (Wiley series in probability and mathematical statistics)
ISBN 0-471-09974-0 : £14.00 : CIP entry
B81-38305

519.5'36 — Linear regression analysis. Applications
Weisberg, Sanford. Applied linear regression / Sanford Weisberg. — New York ; Chichester : Wiley, c1980. — xii,283p : ill ; 24cm. — (Wiley series in probability and mathematical statistics)
Bibliography: p269-275. — Includes index
ISBN 0-471-04419-9 : £13.25 B81-02416

519.5'36 — Regression analysis
Draper, N. R.. Applied regression analysis / N.R. Draper, H. Smith. — 2nd ed. — New York ; Chichester : Wiley, c1981. — xiv,709p : ill ; 24cm. — (Wiley series in probability and mathematical statistics)
Previous ed.: 1966. — Bibliography: p675-699. - Includes index
ISBN 0-471-02995-5 : £15.50 B81-23385

Wonnacott, Thomas H.. Regression : a second course in statistics / Thomas H. Wonnacott, Ronald J. Wonnacott. — New York ; Chichester : Wiley, c1981. — xix,556p : ill ; 24cm. — (Wiley series in probability and mathematical statistics)
Bibliography: p545-548. — Includes index
ISBN 0-471-95974-x : Unpriced B81-10040

519.5'4 — Abstract spaces. Statistical inference
Grenander, Ulf. Abstract inference / Ulf Grenander. — New York ; Chichester : Wiley, c1981. — ix,526p : ill ; 24cm. — (Wiley series in probability and mathematical statistics)
Bibliography: p511-521. — Includes index
ISBN 0-471-08267-8 : £19.95 B81-17249

519.5'4 — Order statistics. Methodology
David, H. A.. Order statistics / H.A. David. — 2nd ed. — New York ; London : Wiley, c1981. — xiii,360p : ill ; 24cm. — (Wiley series in probability and mathematical statistics) (A Wiley publication in applied statistics)
Previous ed.: 1970. — Bibliography: p299-352. — Includes index
ISBN 0-471-02723-5 : £18.75 B81-16450

519.5'4 — Statistical inference
Barnett, Vic. Comparative statistical inference. — 2nd ed. — Chichester : Wiley, Dec.1981. — [300]p. — (Wiley series in probability and mathematical statistics : applied probability and statistics section)
Previous ed.: 1973
ISBN 0-471-10076-5 : £18.00 : CIP entry
B81-31611

Huntsberger, David V.. Elements of statistical inference / David V. Huntsberger, Patrick Billingsley. — 5th ed. — Boston [Mass.] ; London : Allyn and Bacon, c1981. — xiv,505p : col.ill ; 24cm + Instructor's manual(151p: ill;22cm) + Study guide(136p: ill;24cm)
Previous ed.: 1977. — Includes index
ISBN 0-205-07305-0 : £16.95
ISBN 0-205-07380-8 (International students ed.) : £16.95
ISBN 0-205-07306-9 (Instructor's manual) : Unpriced
ISBN 0-205-07307-7 (Study guide) : Unpriced
B81-29020

Zacks, Shelemyahu. Parametric statistical inference : basic theory and modern approaches / by Shelemyahu Zacks. — Oxford : Pergamon, 1981. — xvi,387p ; 26cm. — (International series in nonlinear mathematics ; v.4) (Pergamon international library)
Bibliography: p364-379. — Includes index
ISBN 0-08-026468-9 : £20.00 B81-17239

519.5'4 — Statistical inference. Robustness
Huber, Peter J.. Robust statistics / Peter J. Huber. — New York ; Chichester : Wiley, c1981. — ix,308p : ill ; 24cm. — (Wiley series in probability and mathematical statistics)
Bibliography: p294-300. — Includes index
ISBN 0-471-41805-6 : £18.00 B81-23344

519.5'4 — Statistical mathematics. Forecasting
Bennett, R. J.. Statistical forecasting / by R.J. Bennett. — Norwich : Geo Abstracts, 1981, c1980. — 43p : ill ; 22cm. — (Concepts and techniques in modern geography, ISSN 0306-6142 ; no.28)
Bibliography: p38-40
ISBN 0-86094-064-0 (pbk) : £1.00 B81-11343

519.5'4'01 — Statistical inference — *Philosophical perspectives*
Seidenfeld, Teddy. Philosophical problems of statistical inference : learning from R.A. Fisher / Teddy Seidenfeld. — Dordrecht ; London : Reidel, c1979. — xiii,245p : ill ; 23cm. — (Theory and decision library ; v.22)
Bibliography: p239-242. - Includes index
ISBN 90-277-0965-3 : Unpriced B81-04417

519.5'42 — Decision making. Change. Detection. Mathematical models
Rapoport, Amnon. Response models for detection of change / Amnon Rapoport, William E. Stein and Graham J. Burkheimer. — Dordrecht ; London : Reidel, 1979. — viii,200p : ill ; 23cm. — (Theory and decision library ; v.18)
Bibliography: p180-183. - Includes index
ISBN 90-277-0934-3 : Unpriced B81-06467

519.5'42 — Decision theory
Kmietowicz, Z. W.. Decision theory and incomplete knowledge. — Farnborough, Hants. : Gower Press, Apr.1981. — [136]p
ISBN 0-566-00327-9 : £10.00 : CIP entry
B81-02658

519.5'42 — Decision theory. Concepts: Utility. Theories
Expected utility hypotheses and the Allais Paradox : contemporary discussions of decisions under uncertainty with Allais' rejoinder / edited by Maurice Allais and Ole Hagen. — Dordrecht ; London : Reidel, c1979. — vii,714p : ill ; 23cm. — (Theory and decision library ; v.21)
Bibliography: p664-681. - Includes index
ISBN 90-277-0960-2 : Unpriced B81-03955

519.5'5 — Time series. Analysis
Chatfield, Christopher. The analysis of time series : an introduction / C. Chatfield. — 2nd ed. — London : Chapman and Hall, 1980. — xiv,268p : ill ; 22cm
Previous ed.: 1975. — Bibliography: p245-255. — Includes index
ISBN 0-412-22460-7 (pbk) : £6.50 : CIP rev.
B80-11854

519.5'5 — Time series. Analysis — *Conference proceedings*
Time series analysis : proceedings of the international conference held at Houston, Texas, August 1980 / edited by O.D. Anderson and M. Ray Perryman. — Amsterdam ; Oxford : North-Holland, c1981. — ix,661p : ill ; 24cm
Includes bibliographies
ISBN 0-444-86177-7 : Unpriced B81-30038

519.5'5 — Time series. Spectral analysis
Priestley, M. B.. Spectral analysis and time series / M.B. Priestley. — London : Academic Press, 1981. — 2v. : (xvii,890,(45)p) : ill ; 24cm. — (Probability and mathematical statistics)
Bibliography: pRi-Rxxi. — Includes index
ISBN 0-12-564901-0 : Unpriced
ISBN 0-12-569402-9 (V.2) : Unpriced
B81-29735

519.5'5'024301 — Time series. Analysis — *For social sciences*
McCleary, Richard. Applied time series analysis for the social sciences / Richard McCleary, Richard A. Hay, Jr. with Errol E. Meidinger and David McDowall ; foreword by Kenneth C. Land. — Beverly Hills ; London : Sage, c1980. — 331p : ill ; 23cm
Bibliography: p321-326. — Includes index
ISBN 0-8039-1205-6 (cased) : £12.50
ISBN 0-8039-1206-4 (pbk) : £6.25 B81-03942

519.5'5'05 — Time series. Analysis — *Serials*
Journal of time series analysis : a journal sponsored by the Bernoulli Society for Mathematical Statistics and Probability. — Vol.1, no.1 (1980)-. — Clevedon (4 Bellevue Mansions, Bellevue Rd, Clevedon, Avon BS21 7NU) : Tieto, 1980-. — v. : ill ; 25cm
Quarterly
ISSN 0143-9782 = Journal of time series analysis : £22.00 per year to institutions (£7.50 to individuals) B81-39732

TSA & F flyer : the Times series analysis and forecasting monthly information bulletin. — No.1 (June 1980)-. — Nottingham (9 Ingham Grove, Lenton Gardens, Nottingham NG7 2LQ) : O.D. Anderson, 1980-. — v. ; 30cm
Monthly. — Description based on: No.2 (July 1980)
ISSN 0260-9053 : £2.00 per year B81-27908

519.7 — Mathematical programming
Arthanari, T. S.. Mathematical programming in statistics / T.S. Arthanari, Yadolah Dodge. — New York ; Chichester : Wiley, c1981. — xviii,413p : ill ; 24cm. — (Wiley series in probability and mathematical statistics)
Includes bibliographies and index
ISBN 0-471-08073-x : £18.00 B81-23329

519.7 — Mathematical programming — *Conference proceedings*
Mathematical programming at Oberwolfach / edited by H. König, B. Korte and K. Ritter ; [contributors] A. Bachem ... [et al.]. — Amsterdam ; Oxford : North-Holland, 1981. — viii,257p : ill ; 24cm. — (Mathematical programming study)
Conference papers. — Includes bibliographies
ISBN 0-444-86136-x (pbk) : £11.88 B81-15047

519.7′03 — Dynamic programming

Cooper, Leon. Introduction to dynamic programming / by Leon Cooper and Mary W. Cooper. — Oxford : Pergamon, 1981. — ix,289p : ill ; 26cm. — (International series in modern applied mathematics and computer science ; v.1) (Pergamon international library)
Includes index
ISBN 0-08-025065-3 (cased) : Unpriced
ISBN 0-08-025064-5 (pbk) : £8.50 B81-27711

519.7′2 — Linear programming

Murtagh, Bruce A.. Advanced linear programming : computation and practice / Bruce A. Murtagh. — New York ; London : McGraw-Hill, c1981. — xii,202p : ill ; 24cm
Bibliography: p197-199. — Includes index
ISBN 0-07-044095-6 : £16.95 : CIP rev.
B80-08727

Vajda, S.. Linear programming. — London : Chapman and Hall, Apr.1981. — [120]p. — (Science paperbacks ; 167)
ISBN 0-412-16430-2 (pbk) : £3.95 : CIP entry
B81-03686

519.7′2′024658 — Linear programming — *For management*

Wu, Nesa. Linear programming and extensions / Nesa Wu, Richard Coppins. — New York ; London : McGraw-Hill, c1981. — xvi,475p : ill ; 25cm. — (McGraw-Hill series in industrial engineering and management science)
Includes bibliographies and index
ISBN 0-07-072117-3 : £17.95 B81-36515

519.7′6 — Optimisation. Nonlinear programming

Ben-Israel, Adi. Optimality in nonlinear programming : a feasible directions approach / A. Ben-Israel, A. Ben-Tal, S. Zlobec. — New York ; Chichester : Wiley, c1981. — xii,144p : ill ; 24cm. — (Pure and applied mathematics, ISSN 0079-8185)
Bibliography: p135-140. - Includes index
ISBN 0-471-08057-8 : £12.50 B81-17085

519.8′2 — Queueing theory

Cooper, Robert B.. Introduction to queueing theory / Robert B. Cooper. — 2nd ed. — New York ; Oxford : North Holland, c1981. — xv,347p : ill ; 24cm
Previous ed.: New York : Macmillan. London : Collier-Macmillan, 1972. — Bibliography: p325-339. — Includes index
ISBN 0-444-00379-7 : £14.00 B81-24854

Queues and point processes. — Chichester : Wiley, Dec.1981. — [150]p. — (Wiley series in probability and mathematical statistics)
ISBN 0-471-10074-9 : £12.00 : CIP entry
B81-30899

519.8′2 — Queuing theory — *Conference proceedings*

Point processes and queuing problems / edited by P. Bártfai, J. Tomkó. — Amsterdam ; Oxford : North-Holland, c1981. — 426p ; 25cm. — (Colloquia mathematica societatis Jánes Bolyai, ISSN 0139-3383 ; 24)
Conference papers
ISBN 0-444-85432-0 : £25.19
Primary classification 519.2 B81-21442

519.8′2′0212 — Queues. Statistical models — *Technical data*

Hillier, Frederick S.. Queueing tables and graphs / Frederick S. Hillier, Oliver S. Yu with David M. Amis ... [et al.]. — New York ; Oxford : North Holland, c1981. — 231p : ill ; 29cm. — (Publications in operations research series ; 3)
ISBN 0-444-00582-x : £17.17 B81-24022

520 — ASTRONOMY

520 — Amateur astronomy — *Manuals*

Sidgwick, J. B.. Observational astronomy for amateurs. — 4th ed. — London : Pelham, Nov.1981. — [500]p
Previous ed.: 1971
ISBN 0-7207-1378-1 : £12.50 : CIP entry
B81-30395

520 — Astronomy

Burrus, Thomas L.. Earth in crisis : an introduction to the earth sciences / Thomas L. Burrus, Herbert J. Spiegel ; original drawings by George Ondricek, Jr.. — 2nd ed. — St Louis ; London : Mosby, 1980. — xi,549p : ill,charts,maps ; 26cm
Previous ed.: 1976. — Includes index
ISBN 0-8016-0902-x : Unpriced
Primary classification 550 B81-13255

Harwit, Martin. Cosmic discovery : the search, scope and heritage of astronomy / Martin Harwit. — Brighton : Harvester Press, 1981. — xi,334p : ill ; 24cm
Originally published: New York : Basic Books, 1981. — Includes index
ISBN 0-7108-0089-4 : £12.95 : CIP rev.
B81-12805

Jefferys, William H.. Discovering astronomy / William H. Jefferys, R. Robert Robbins. — New York ; Chichester : Wiley, c1981. — xi,466p : ill,charts,ports ; 29cm
Instrument package (2 sheets) in pocket. — Includes index
ISBN 0-471-44125-2 : £15.85 B81-35617

Pasachoff, Jay M.. Contemporary astronomy / Jay M. Pasachoff. — 2nd ed. — Philadelphia ; London : Saunders College, c1981. — xiv,545,A58,xviip,[32]p of plates : ill(some col.),col.charts,maps,facsims,ports ; 26cm. — (Saunders golden sunburst series)
Previous ed.: Philadelphia ; London : Saunders, 1977. — Charts on lining papers. — Bibliography: pA45-A58. — Includes index
ISBN 0-03-057861-2 : £14.50 B81-22881

Reports on astronomy / International Council of Scientific Unions, International Astronomical Union ; edited by Edith A. Müller. — Dordrecht ; London : Reidel, c1979. — vii,228p : ill ; 26cm. — (Transactions of the International Astronomical Union ; v.17A ; pt.2)
Includes bibliographies
ISBN 90-277-1006-6 : £56.00 B81-20240

Reports on astronomy / International Council of Scientific Unions, International Astronomical Union ; edited by Edith A. Müller. — Dordrecht ; London : Reidel, c1979. — vii,246p ; 26cm. — (Transactions of the International Astronomical Union ; v.17A ; pt.2)
Includes bibliographies
ISBN 90-277-1007-4 : £56.00 B81-20239

Wyatt, Stanley P.. Instructor's manual to accompany Principles of astronomy : a short version, 2nd ed. / Stanley P. Wyatt, James B. Kaler. — Boston, Mass. ; London : Allyn and Bacon, c1981. — 20p ; 22cm
ISBN 0-205-07316-6 (unbound) : Unpriced
B81-16296

Wyatt, Stanley P.. Principles of astronomy : a short version / Stanley P. Wyatt, James B. Kaler. — 2nd ed.. — Boston [Mass.] ; London : Allyn and Bacon, c1981. — xii,516,[28] p,[16]p of plates : ill(some col.) ; 24cm
Previous ed.: Boston : Allyn and Bacon, 1974. — Bibliography: 5p. — Includes index
ISBN 0-205-07315-8 (pbk) : Unpriced
B81-26205

520 — Astronomy — *Early works*

Ptolemaeus, Claudius. [Almagest. English]. Ptolemy's Almagest. — London : Duckworth, Nov.1981. — [720]p
Translated from the Greek
ISBN 0-7156-1588-2 : £42.00 : CIP entry
B81-31175

520 — Astronomy — *For children*

Astronomy / edited by John Paton. — London : Pan, 1981. — 93p : ill(some col.),charts(some col.) ; 18cm. — (A Piccolo factbook)
Text on inside cover. — Includes index
ISBN 0-330-26415-x (pbk) : £1.25 B81-38773

Astronomy / edited by John Paton. — London : Kingfisher, 1981. — 93p : ill(some col.) ; 19cm. — (A Kingfisher factbook)
Includes index
ISBN 0-86272-013-3 : £2.50 : CIP rev.
B81-14405

Couper, Heather. Heavens above / Heather Couper and Terence Murtagh. — London : Watts, c1981. — 64p : col.ill,col.charts,col.maps ; 30cm
Bibliography: p62. - Includes index
ISBN 0-85166-909-3 : £3.99 B81-12163

520 — Outer space

Feldman, Anthony. Secrets of space / Anthony Feldman. — London : Aldus, 1980. — 336p : ill(some col.),charts(some col.),1facsim,1map,ports(some col.) ; 30cm
Ill on lining papers. — Includes index
ISBN 0-490-00462-8 : £10.95 B81-01596

520′.3′21 — Astronomy — *Encyclopaedias*

Hopkins, Jeanne. Glossary of astronomy and astrophysics / Jeanne Hopkins ; foreword by S. Chandrasekhar. — 2nd ed. rev. and enl. — Chicago ; London : University of Chicago Press, 1980. — ix,196p ; 24cm
Previous ed.: 1976
ISBN 0-226-35171-8 : £10.50 B81-06562

Maddison, R. E. W.. A dictionary of astronomy / Robert E.W. Maddison ; editor Valerie Illingworth. — London : Hamlyn, 1980. — 208p : ill ; 25cm
Bibliography: p208
ISBN 0-600-32996-8 : £5.95 B81-02621

Mitton, Jacqueline. Key definitions in astronomy / Jacqueline Mitton. — London : Muller, 1980. — 168p : ill ; 21cm. — (A Language of its own)
Spine title: Astronomy
ISBN 0-584-10547-9 (cased) : £6.95 : CIP rev.
ISBN 0-584-10565-7 (pbk) : £4.50 B80-24443

520′.5 — Astronomy — *Serials*

[Handbook for ... *(British Astronomical Association)*]. Handbook for ... / British Astronomical Association. — 1981. — Hailsham (Burlington House, Piccadilly, W1V 0NL) : The Association, 1980. — 108.xii p
ISSN 0068-130x : £2.50 B81-01999

[Newsletter *(Darlington Astronomical Society)*]. Newsletter / the Darlington Astronomical Society. — No.1 (Oct.1980)-. — Darlington (c/o Paul Tate, 59 Eden Cres., Darlington, Co. Durham DL1 5TN) : The Society, 1980-. — v. : ill ; 30cm
Quarterly
ISSN 0260-7794 = Newsletter - Darlington Astronomical Society : Unpriced B81-12426

Vistas in astronomy. — Vol.24. — Oxford : Pergamon, Oct.1981. — [377]p
ISBN 0-08-028437-x : £50.00 : CIP entry
B81-28123

520′.5 — Astronomy — *Serials* — *For children*

[Popular astronomy *(Ilford)*]. Popular astronomy. — Vol.28 no.1 (Jan.1981)-. — Ilford (c/o V.L. Tibbott, 58 Vaughan Gardens, Ilford, Essex IG1 3PD) : Junior Astronomical Society, 1981-. — ill,ports ; 30cm
Quarterly. — Continues: Hermes (Ilford)
ISSN 0261-0892 = Popular astronomy (Junior Astronomical Society) : Unpriced B81-16836

520′.7′1142659 — Cambridgeshire. Cambridge. Universities: University of Cambridge. *Institute of Astronomy* — *Serials*

. Annual report / University of Cambridge, Institute of Astronomy. — 1979-1980. — Cambridge (The Observatories, Madingley Rd., Cambridge CB3 0HA) : The Institute, [1980]. — 41p
ISSN 0306-0489 : Unpriced B81-12406

520′.9 — Astronomy, ***to 1979***

Apfel, Necia H.. Architecture of the universe / Necia H. Apfel, J. Allen Hynek. — Rev. ed. — Menlo Park ; London : Benjamin/Cummings, c1979. — xii,499p,[8]p of plates : ill(some col.),charts ; 24cm
Previous ed.: published as Astronomy one / by J. Allen Hynek, Necia H. Apfel. Menlo Park : W. A. Benjamin, 1972. — Includes index
ISBN 0-8053-4747-x (pbk) : £10.60 B81-02431

520′.9′01 — Astronomy, ***to 1000.*** **Archaeological sources**

Cornell, James. The first stargazers : an introduction to the origins of astronomy / James Cornell. — London : Athlone, 1981. — ix,262p : ill,plans ; 24cm
Bibliography: p247-255. — Includes index
ISBN 0-485-30004-4 : £7.95 : CIP rev. B81-15897

520′.92′4 — Astronomy. Herschel, William — ***Biographies***

Moore, Patrick. William Herschel : astronomer and musician of 19 New King Street, Bath / Patrick Moore. — Sidcup (95 Walton Rd., Sidcup, Kent DA14 4LL) : P.M.E. Erwood in association with the William Herschel Society, 1981. — vii,26p,[7]leaves of plates : ill,facsims,plans,ports ; 21cm
Bibliography: p25
ISBN 0-907322-06-9 (pbk) : £1.50 B81-21047

520′.92′4 — Netherlands. Astronomy. Oort, Jan Hendrik — ***Festschriften***

Oort and the universe : a sketch of Oort′s research and person : liber amicorum presented to Jan Kendrik Oort on the occasion of his 80th birthday 28 April 1980 / edited by Hugo Van Woerden, Willem N. Brouw and Henk C. Van de Hulst. — Dordrecht ; London : Reidel, c1980. — viii,210p : ill,2facsims,ports ; 25cm
Includes bibliographies and index
ISBN 90-277-1180-1 (cased) : Unpriced
ISBN 90-277-1209-3 (pbk) : Unpriced B81-05277

520′.9361 — Great Britain. Astronomy, ***B.C.4000-B.C.1500***

Astronomy and society in Britain during the period 4000-1500 B.C. / edited by C.L.N. Ruggles & A.W.R. Whittle. — Oxford : B.A.R., 1981. — 342p : ill,maps,plans ; 30cm. — (BAR. British series ; 88)
Includes bibliographies
ISBN 0-86054-130-4 (pbk) : £12.00 B81-36631

520′.972 — Pre-Columbian Mexico. Astronomy

Aveni, Anthony F.. Skywatchers of ancient Mexico / by Anthony F. Aveni ; foreword by Owen Gingerich. — Austin ; London : University of Texas Press, c1980. — x,355p : ill (some col.),maps,plans ; 27cm. — (The Texas Pan American series)
Bibliography: p331-344. — Includes index
ISBN 0-292-77557-1 : £19.50 B81-32509

521 — THEORETICAL ASTRONOMY

521′.5′09 — Astronomy. Theories, ***to 1980***

Moore, Patrick. The development of astronomical thought / by Patrick Moore. — 2nd ed. — Hornchurch : Ian Henry, 1981. — vi,108p,[6]p of plates : ill,charts ; 20cm
Previous ed.: Edinburgh : Oliver & Boyd, 1969
ISBN 0-86025-841-6 : £4.95 B81-36874

521′.542′0924 — Venus. Origins. Theories of Velikovsky, Immanuel

Forrest, Bob. Velikovsky′s sources / Bob Forrest. — [Manchester] ([53 Bannerman Ave., Prestwich, Manchester M25 5DR]) : [B. Forrest]
Pt.1. — c1981. — 80p ; 30cm
Text on inside cover
Unpriced (pbk) B81-36193

522 — PRACTICAL AND SPHERICAL ASTRONOMY

522 — Astronomy — ***Amateurs′ manuals***

Ridpath, Ian. The young astronomer′s handbook / Ian Ridpath. — London : Hamlyn, 1981. — 224p : col.ill,maps,ports ; 19cm
Bibliography: p214. - Includes index
ISBN 0-600-36423-2 : £3.50 B81-22279

Ronan, Colin A.. The practical astronomer / Colin A. Ronan. — London : Pan, 1981. — 205p : ill(some col.),charts(some col.),facsims (some col.) ; 30cm
Bibliography: p200. — Includes index
ISBN 0-330-26231-9 (pbk) : £5.95 B81-03478

522′.028′54 — Astronomy. Calculations. Use of pocket electronic calculators

Duffett-Smith, Peter. Practical astronomy with your calculator. — 2nd ed. — Cambridge : Cambridge University Press, Nov.1981. — [200]p
Previous ed.: 1979
ISBN 0-521-24059-x : £15.00 : CIP entry
ISBN 0-521-28411-2 (pbk) : £4.95 B81-32528

522′.194134′05 — Edinburgh. Astronomical observatories: Royal Observatory, Edinburgh — ***Serials***

Royal Observatory, Edinburgh. Annual report for the year ended 30 September ... / Royal Observatory Edinburgh. — 1979. — Edinburgh (Blackford Hill, Edinburgh) : The Observatory, c1980. — 36p
ISBN 0-902553-23-2 : Unpriced B81-03351

522′.1942251 — East Sussex. Herstmonceux. Astronomical observatories: Royal Greenwich Observatory — ***Serials***

Royal Greenwich Observatory. The Report of the Royal Greenwich Observatory for the period ... October 1 to ... September 30. — 1979-1980. — Hailsham (Herstmonceux Castle, Hailsham, East Sussex BN27 1RP) : The Observatory, 1981. — 51p
£3.00 B81-32428

522′.294134 — Edinburgh. Radiotelescopes. Organisations: Royal Observatory, Edinburgh. ***U.K. Infrared Telescope Unit — Serials***

UKIRT newsletter / U.K. Infrared Telescope Unit of the Royal Observatory, Edinburgh. — No.1 (Apr.1979)-. — Edinburgh ([Blackford Hill, Edinburgh EH9 3HJ]) : The Unit, 1979-. — v. : ill ; 28cm
Irregular. — Description based on: No.4 (Sept.1980)
ISSN 0143-0599 = UKIRT newsletter : Unpriced B81-05832

522′.4 — Planispheric astrolabes

National Maritime Museum. ***Department of Navigation and Astronomy***. The planispheric astrolabe / Department of Navigation and Astronomy, National Maritime Museum Greenwich. — Amended impression. — [London] : National Maritime Museum, 1979. — 56p ; 25cm
Previous ed.: 1976. — Bibliography: p55. — Includes index
£1.00 (corrected : pbk) B81-06524

522′.67 — Astronomical spectrometers

Meaburn, John. Detection and spectrometry of faint light / by John Meaburn. — Dordrecht ; London : Reidel, c1976. — viii,270p : ill ; 25cm. — (Astrophysics and space science library ; v.56)
Includes index
ISBN 90-277-0678-6 : Unpriced B81-02887

522′.686 — Gamma ray astronomy

Gamma-ray astronomy : a Royal Society discussion held on 27 and 28 November 1980 / arranged by the British National Committee on Space Research under the leadership of Sir Harrie Massey, A.W. Wolfendale and R.D. Wills. — London : Royal Society, 1981. — ix,211p : ill ; 31cm
Originally published: in Philosophical transactions of the Royal Society of London, series A, vol.301(no.1462), p489-703. — Includes bibliographies
ISBN 0-85403-170-7 : £22.90 B81-31990

522′.686 — United States. X-ray astronomy. Use of artificial satellites: Einstein Observatory — ***Conference proceedings***

X-ray astronomy with the Einstein satellite : proceeding of the High Energy Astrophysics Division of the American Astronomical Society meeting on x-ray astronomy held at the Harvard/Smithsonian Center for Astrophysics, Cambridge, Massachusetts, U.S.A., January 28-30, 1980 / edited by Riccardo Giacconi. — Dordrecht ; London : Reidel, c1981. — viii,330p : ill ; 25cm. — (Astrophysics and space science library ; v.87)
Includes bibliographies and index
ISBN 90-277-1261-1 : Unpriced B81-29560

522′.686 — X-ray astronomy

Culhane, J. Leonard. X-ray astronomy / J. Leonard Culhane and Peter W. Sanford. — London : Faber, 1981. — 192p,[16]p of plates : ill,1port ; 23cm
Bibliography: p185. — Includes index
ISBN 0-571-11550-0 : £10.00 : CIP rev. B81-11948

522′.686 — X-ray astronomy — ***Conference proceedings***

Galactic x-ray sources. — Chichester : Wiley, Apr.1981. — [400]p
Conference papers
ISBN 0-471-27963-3 : £25.00 : CIP entry B81-03354

X-ray astronomy : proceedings of the NATO Advanced Study Institute held at Erice, Sicily, July 1-14, 1979 / edited by Riccardo Giacconi and Giancarlo Setti. — Dordrecht ; London : Reidel in cooperation with NATO Scientific Affairs Division, c1980. — vii,406p : ill ; 25cm. — (NATO advanced study institutes series : Series C, Mathematical and physical sciences ; v.60)
Includes bibliographies and index
ISBN 90-277-1156-9 : Unpriced B81-01783

522′.7′0151 — Spherical astronomy. Mathematical aspects

Taff, Laurence G.. Computational spherical astronomy / Laurence G. Taff. — New York ; Chichester : Wiley, c1981. — x,233p : ill ; 24cm
Bibliography: p227-229. - Includes index
ISBN 0-471-06257-x : £18.00 B81-23394

522′.9 — Astronomy. Implications of refraction of electromagnetic radiation

International Astronomical Union. ***Symposium (89th : 1978 : Uppsala)***. Refractional influences in astrometry and geodesy / International Astronomical Union = Union astronomique internationale symposium no.89 organized by IAU in cooperation with IAG and IUGG, held in Uppsala, Sweden, 1-5 August 1978 ; edited by Erik Tengström and George Teleki with the cooperation of I. Ohlsson. — Dordrecht ; London : Reidel, c1979. — xxiv,394p : ill ; 25cm
Includes bibliographies and index
ISBN 90-277-1037-6 (cased) : Unpriced
ISBN 90-277-1038-4 (pbk) : Unpriced
Also classified at 526′.1 B81-07135

523 — DESCRIPTIVE ASTRONOMY

523 — Astronomical bodies

Dutton, A. M.. Journey to the stars / A.M. Dutton. — Bognor Regis : New Horizon, c1978. — 107p,[10]p,[10]leaves of plates : ill ; 22cm
Includes index
ISBN 0-86116-013-4 : £2.95 B81-21830

523 — Astronomical bodies: Singularities

Davies, P. C. W.. The edge of infinity : naked singularities and the destruction of spacetime / Paul Davies. — London : Dent, 1981. — viii,194p : ill ; 24cm
Includes index
ISBN 0-460-04490-7 : £7.95 : CIP rev. B81-02105

523 — Outer space — ***For children***

Simon, Seymour. The long view into space / Seymour Simon. — London : Julia MacRae, 1980, c1979. — [48]p : ill ; 28cm
Originally published: New York : Crown, 1979
ISBN 0-86203-086-2 : £4.50 : CIP rev. B80-17650

523 — Pulsars — *Conference proceedings*
Pulsars : held in Bonn, Federal Republic of Germany, August 26-29, 1980 / edited by W. Sieber and R. Wielebinski. — Dordrecht ; London : Reidel, 1981. — xv,475p : ill,ports ; 25cm. — (Symposium / International Astronomical Union ; no.95)
Conference proceedings. — Includes bibliographies and index
ISBN 90-277-1280-8 (cased) : Unpriced
ISBN 90-277-1282-4 (pbk) : Unpriced
B81-26894

523 — Quasi-stellar objects
Hoyle, Fred. Quasar controversy resolved. — Cardiff : University College Cardiff Press, Oct.1981. — [80]p
ISBN 0-906449-28-6 (pbk) : £3.25 : CIP entry
B81-30972

523 — Science. Research. Information. Communication. Social aspects — *Study examples: Research on black holes*
Jones, Pat, *1954-*. Some social aspects of information transfer : an investigation of social networks and the communication of ideas in relation to research into black holes / by Pat Jones. — London (207 Essex Rd., N1 3PN) : Polytechnic of North London School of Librarianship, 1981, c1980. — 117p : ill ; 30cm. — (Research report / Polytechnic of North London. School of Librarianship, ISSN 0143-8549 ; no.4)
Bibliography: p114-117
ISBN 0-900639-15-6 (pbk) : £4.80 B81-31135

523'.005 — Astronomical data — *Serials*
Astronomical phenomena for the year ... / prepared jointly by the Nautical Almanac Office, United States Naval Observatory and Her Majesty's Nautical Almanac Office, Royal Greenwich Observatory. — 1982. — Washington : U.S.G.P.O. ; London : H.M.S.O., 1979. — 73p
ISBN 0-11-886903-5 : £1.75
ISSN 0083-2421 B81-04911

523'.005 — Outer space — *Conference proceedings — Serials*
Advances in space research : the official journal of the Committee on Space Research (COSPAR). — Vol.1,no.1 (1981)-. — Oxford : Pergamon, 1981-. — v. : ill ; 25cm
ISSN 0273-1177 : Unpriced B81-24134

523.01 — Astrophysics
Kourganoff, V.. Introduction to advanced astrophysics / by V. Kourganoff. — Dordrecht ; London : Reidel, c1980. — xiii,479p : ill ; 25cm. — (Geophysics and astrophysics monographs ; v.17)
Includes bibliographies and index
ISBN 90-277-1002-3 (cased) : Unpriced
ISBN 90-277-1003-1 (pbk) : Unpriced
B81-01835

523'.01 — Relativistic astrophysics
Demianski, Marek. Relativistic astrophysics. — Oxford : Pergamon, Dec.1981. — [300]p. — (International series in natural philosophy ; v.110)
ISBN 0-08-025042-4 : £25.00 : CIP entry
B81-31803

523.01'072 — Astrophysics. Research. Role of Spacelab Programme — *Conference proceedings*
Astrophysics from spacelab / edited by Pier Luigi Bernacca and Remo Ruffini. — Dordrecht ; London : Reidel, c1980. — xi,664p : ill,maps ; 25cm. — (Astrophysics and space science library ; v.81)
Conference papers. — Includes bibliographies and index
ISBN 90-277-1064-3 : Unpriced B81-03808

523.01'5012 — Infrared astronomy — *Conference proceedings*
Infrared astronomy / edited by C.G. Wynn-Williams and D.P. Cruikshank with the assistance of Deborah Weiner. — Dordrecht ; London : Reidel, c1981. — xvi,376p : ill ; 25cm. — (Symposium / International Astronomical Union ; no.96)
Conference papers. — Includes bibliographies and index
ISBN 90-277-1227-1 (cased) : Unpriced
ISBN 90-277-1228-x (pbk) : Unpriced
B81-09284

523.01'584 — Galaxies. Radiation. Redshifts. Interpretation — *Conference proceedings*
International Astronomical Union. *Symposium (92nd : 1979 : Los Angeles)*. Objects of high redshift / International Astronomical Union = Union astronomique internationale, symposium no.92 held in Los Angeles, U.S.A., August 28-31, 1979 ; edited by G.O. Abell and P.J.E. Peebles. — Dordrecht ; London : Reidel, c1980. — xvi,340p : ill,ports ; 25cm
Includes bibliographies and index
ISBN 90-277-1118-6 : Unpriced
ISBN 90-277-1119-4 (pbk) : Unpriced
B81-03978

523.01'88 — Dynamo theory
Krause, F.. Mean-field magnetohydrodynamics and dynamo theory / by F. Krause and K.-H. Rädler. — Oxford : Pergamon, 1980. — 271p : ill ; 22cm
Bibliography: p254-269. — Includes index
ISBN 0-08-025041-6 : £15.00 : CIP rev.
Primary classification 538'.6 B79-34858

523.01'9 — High energy astrophysics - *Conference proceedings*
High energy astrophysics. — Oxford : Pergamon, Apr.1981. — [300]p. — (Advances in space research ; v.1, no.13)
Conference papers
ISBN 0-08-028395-0 : £17.00 : CIP entry
B81-10433

523.01'92 — Astronomical bodies. Radio frequency radiation. Recombination lines — *Conference proceedings*
Radio recombination lines : proceedings of a workshop held in Ottawa, Ontario, Canada, August 24-25, 1979 / edited by P.A. Shaver. — Dordrecht ; London : Reidel, c1980. — x,284p : ill ; 25cm. — (Astrophysics and space science library ; v.80)
Includes index
ISBN 90-277-1103-8 : Unpriced B81-03235

523.01'97 — Nuclear astrophysics
Audouze, Jean. An introduction to nuclear astrophysics : the formation and the evolution of maths in the universe / Jean Audouze and Sylvie Vauclair. — Dordrecht ; London : Reidel, c1980. — xxiv,167p : ill ; 25cm. — (Geophysics and astrophysics monographs ; v.18)
Includes bibliographies and index
ISBN 90-277-1012-0 (cased) : Unpriced
ISBN 90-277-1053-8 (pbk) : Unpriced
B81-05829

523.01'97223 — Outer space. Cosmic rays — *Conference proceedings*
Origin of cosmic rays : [conference held] jointly with International Union of Pure and Applied Physics held in Bologna, Italy, June 11-14, 1980 / International Astronomical Union = Union Astronomique Internationale / edited by Giancarlo Setti, Gianfranco Spada, Arnold W. Wolfendale. — Dordrecht ; London : Reidel, c1981. — xv,409p : ill ; 25cm. — (Symposium / International Astronomical Union ; no.94)
Includes bibliographies
ISBN 90-277-1271-9 (cased) : Unpriced
ISBN 90-277-1272-7 (pbk) : Unpriced
B81-26893

523.01'97'6 — High energy astrophysics
Longair, M. S.. High energy astrophysics. — Cambridge : Cambridge University Press, Dec.1981. — [420]p
ISBN 0-521-23513-8 (cased) : £24.00 : CIP entry
ISBN 0-521-28013-3 (pbk) : £8.95 B81-32533

523.1 — ASTRONOMY. UNIVERSE

523.1 — Astronomy. Cosmology
Harrison, Edward R.. Cosmology : the science of the universe / Edward R. Harrison. — Cambridge : Cambridge University Press, 1981. — xi,430p : ill ; 26cm
Includes bibliographies and index
ISBN 0-521-22981-2 : £15.00 B81-26193

Sciama, D. W.. Modern cosmology. — Cambridge : Cambridge University Press, Nov.1981. — [210]p
Originally published: 1971
ISBN 0-521-28721-9 (pbk) : £5.95 : CIP entry
B81-38809

523.1 — Astronomy. Cosmology — *Conference proceedings*
Cosmology : proceedings of a symposium organised by the Institute of Mathematics and its Applications held in London in June 1975. — Southend-on-Sea (Maitland House, Warrior Sq., Southend-on-Sea, Essex SS1 2JY) : The Institute, c1976. — v,84p : ill ; 20cm. — (Symposium proceedings series / Institute of Mathematics and its Applications ; no.13)
Includes bibliographies
Unpriced (spiral) B81-13271

523.1 — Cosmology
Raine, D. J.. The isotropic universe : an introduction to cosmology / D.J. Raine. — Bristol : Hilger, c1981. — xiv,253p : ill ; 26cm. — (Monographs on astronomical subjects, ISSN 0141-1128 : 7)
Bibliography: p247-250. — Includes index
ISBN 0-85274-370-x : £19.50 : CIP rev.
B81-12873

523.1 — Universe
Rowan-Robinson, Michael. Cosmology / Michael Rowan-Robinson. — 2nd ed. — Oxford : Clarendon, 1981. — xii,152p : ill,maps ; 23cm. — (Oxford physics series)
Previous ed.: 1977. — Bibliography: p140-141. — Includes index
ISBN 0-19-851857-9 (cased) : £12.50
ISBN 0-19-851858-7 (pbk) : £5.95 B81-29575

523.1 — Universe — *For children*
Bergh, Catherine de. Discovering the sky / Catherine de Bergh, Jean-Pierre Verdet ; [translated from the French by Anthea Bell] ; [illustrated by Gérald Eveno, Puig Rosado, Wolker Theinhardt]. — St. Albans : Hart-Davis, 1981. — 62p : ill(some col.) ; 27cm. — (Signposts series)
Translation of: A la découverte du ciel. — Includes index
ISBN 0-247-13034-6 : £3.50 B81-11572

523.1 — Universe — *Mystic viewpoints*
Talbot, Michael, *1953-*. Mysticism and the new physics / Michael Talbot. — London : Routledge & Kegan Paul, 1981, c1980. — 209p : ill ; 22cm
Bibliography: p199-204. — Includes index
ISBN 0-7100-0831-7 (pbk) : £3.95 : CIP rev.
B81-10508

523.1'01 — Universe. Theories
Ahmed, Shafi. The absolute theory of the universe / Shafi Ahmed. — Bognor Regis : New Horizon, c1980. — 30p : ill ; 21cm
ISBN 0-86116-400-8 : £3.50 B81-21776

Johnston, Alan. The cosmic ecosystem : a revised view of cosmology / Alan Johnston. — London : Wildwood House, 1980. — vii,194p : ill ; 23cm
Bibliography: p188. - Includes index
ISBN 0-7045-3044-9 : £7.95 B81-00866

523.1'01 — Universe. Theories — *Early works*
Kant, Immanuel. Universal natural history and theory of the heavens / Immanuel Kant ; translated with introduction and notes by Stanley L. Jaki. — Edinburgh : Scottish Academic Press, 1981. — 302p ; 24cm
Translation of: Allgemeine Naturgeschichte und Theorie des Himmels. — Bibliography: p209-210. — Includes index
ISBN 0-7073-0294-3 : £12.50 B81-36841

523.1'01574 — Astronomy. Cosmology. Biological aspects
Hoyle, Fred. Space travellers. — Cardiff : University College Cardiff Press, May 1981. — [192]p
ISBN 0-906449-27-8 : £8.95 : CIP entry
B81-13555

523.1'022'2 — Universe — *Illustrations*
Marten, Michael. The radiant universe : electronic images from space / Michael Marten, John Chesterman. — Poole : Blandford, 1980. — 128p : chiefly ill(some col.),col.maps ; 31cm
Includes index
ISBN 0-7137-1116-7 : £8.95 B81-01559

523.1′09 — Astronomy. Cosmology, *to 1980*

Lovell, *Sir* **Bernard**. Emerging cosmology / Bernard Lovell. — New York ; Guildford : Columbia University Press, 1981. — 208p ; 24cm. — (Convergence)
Includes index
ISBN 0-231-05304-5 : £10.20 B81-31877

523.1′1 — Universe. Structure

Peebles, P. J. E.. The large-scale structure of the universe / by P.J.E. Peebles. — Princeton ; Guildford : Princeton University Press, c1980. — xiii,422p : ill ; 25cm. — (Princeton series in physics)
Bibliography: p402-416. - Includes index
ISBN 0-691-08239-1 (cased) : £16.50
ISBN 0-691-08240-5 (pbk) : Unpriced
B81-03950

523.1′11 — Outer space. Plasmas

Alfvén, Hannes. Cosmic plasma / by Hannes Alfvén. — Dordrecht ; London : Reidel, c1981. — xi,164p : ill ; 25cm. — (Astrophysics and space science library ; v.82)
Bibliography: p153-159. - Includes index
ISBN 90-277-1151-8 : Unpriced B81-15253

523.1′12 — Galaxies. Images. Measurement. Organisations: COSMOS Facility — *Serials*

COSMOS newsletter. — Issue 77/1 (1977 Nov.15)-. — Edinburgh (Royal Observatory, Blackford Hill, Edinburgh RH9 3HJ) : COSMOS Facility, 1977-. — v. ; 30cm
Irregular
ISSN 0143-2028 = COSMOS newsletter : Private circulation B81-05320

523.1′12 — Galaxies. Physical properties — *Conference proceedings*

The **Structure** and evolution of normal galaxies. — Cambridge : Cambridge University Press, Sept.1981. — [278]p
Conference papers
ISBN 0-521-23907-9 : £15.00 : CIP entry
B81-23749

523.1′12 — Outer space. Dusts — *Conference proceedings*

International Astronomical Union. *Symposium (90th : 1979 : Ottawa)*. Solid particles in the solar system / International Astronomical Union, Symposium no. 90 ; organized by the IAU in cooperation with COSPAR, held at Ottawa, Canada, August 27-30, 1979 ; edited by Ian Halliday and Bruce A. McIntosh. — Dordrecht ; London : Reidel, c1980. — xii,441p : ill,ports ; 25cm
Includes bibliographies and index
ISBN 90-277-1164-x (cased) : Unpriced
ISBN 90-277-1165-8 (pbk) : Unpriced
Also classified at 523.5′1 B81-02719

523.1′2 — Cosmogony

Heidmann, Jean. Extragalactic adventure. — Cambridge : Cambridge University Press, Feb.1982. — [174]p
Translation of: Au-delà de notre Voie Lactée
ISBN 0-521-23571-5 (cased) : £12.50 : CIP entry
ISBN 0-521-28045-1 (pbk) : £4.95 B81-40267

523.1′8 — Galaxies. Radiation. Redshifts. Interpretation

Parish, Leonard. The theory of cosmic aberration : a new interpretation of the Hubble red-shifts / Leonard Parish. — Luton (Windmill Rd., Luton LU1 3XS) : Cortney, 1981. — v,44p : ill ; 24cm
ISBN 0-904378-11-x (pbk) : £3.50 B81-18769

523.2 — ASTRONOMY. SOLAR SYSTEM

523.2 — Solar system

The **New** solar system / edited by J. Kelly Beatty, Brian O'Leary, Andrew Chaikin ; introduction by Carl Sagan. — Cambridge : Cambridge University Press, 1981. — 224p : ill (some col.),charts,col.maps,facsims ; 29cm
Bibliography: p213-218. — Includes index
ISBN 0-521-23881-1 : £9.95 : CIP rev.
B81-39909

523.2 — Solar systems. Dynamics — *Conference proceedings*

International Astronomical Union. *Symposium (81st : 1978 : Tokyo)*. Dynamics of the solar system : proceedings of the 81st Symposium of the International Astronomical Union held in Tokyo, Japan, 23-26 May, 1978 / edited by Raynor L. Dunscombe. — Dordrecht ; London : Reidel, c1979. — xiv,330p : ill,ports ; 25cm
'This volume is dedicated to Yusuke Hagihara ... 1897-1979' - half title page verso. — Includes bibliographies and index
ISBN 90-277-0976-9 (cased) : Unpriced
ISBN 90-277-0977-7 (pbk) : Unpriced
B81-15257

523.2′0724 — Solar system. Simulation. Use of Stonehenge

Saunders, Mike, *1935-*. Saturn, Uranus and Neptune, at Stonehenge / Mike Saunders. — Caterham (Caterham, Surrey) : Downs, 1981. — 2leaves : 1plan ; 21x30cm
Unpriced (pbk) B81-19448

Saunders, Mike, *1942-*. Solar system / Mike Saunders. — Caterham (Caterham, Surrey) : Downs Books, c1980. — 1sheet : charts ; 23x32cm
In transparent envelope
Unpriced B81-26990

523.3 — ASTRONOMY. MOON

523.3 — Moon

Cadogan, Peter H.. The moon : our sister planet / Peter H. Cadogan. — Cambridge : Cambridge University Press, 1981. — viii,391p : ill,maps ; 26cm
Bibliography: p387-389. — Includes index
ISBN 0-521-23684-3 (cased) : £27.50
ISBN 0-521-28152-0 (pbk) : £12.50 B81-36680

523.3 — Moon. Surface features

Murray, Bruce. Earthlike planets : surfaces of Mercury, Venus, Earth, Moon, Mars / Bruce Murray, Michael C. Malin, Ronald Greeley. — Oxford : W.H. Freeman, c1981. — xiv,387p,8p of plates : ill(some col.) ; 24cm
Includes bibliographies and index
ISBN 0-7167-1148-6 (cased) : £16.70
ISBN 0-7167-1149-4 (pbk) : £8.95
Primary classification 523.4 B81-36487

523.4 — ASTRONOMY. PLANETS

523.4 — Solar system. Planets

Francis, Peter. The planets : a decade of discovery / Peter Francis. — Harmondsworth : Penguin, 1981. — 411p : ill,maps,2facsims,2ports ; 20cm. — (Pelican books)
Bibliography: p399-401. - Includes index
ISBN 0-14-022053-4 (pbk) : £3.95 B81-10411

Jackson, Joseph H.. Pictorial guide to the planets. — 3rd ed. / Joseph H. Jackson & John H. Baumert. — New York ; London : Harper & Row, c1981. — viii,246p[4]p of plates : ill(some col.),charts ; 28cm
Previous ed.: New York : Crowell, 1973. — Includes index
ISBN 0-06-014869-1 : £9.50 B81-33752

523.4 — Solar system. Planets — *For children*

Ridpath, Ian. Stars and planets / by Ian Ridpath ; illustrated by Ron Jobson. — London : Granada, 1981. — 63p : col.ill,col.charts ; 19cm. — (Granada guides)
Includes index
ISBN 0-246-11627-7 : £1.95
Also classified at 523.8 B81-39307

523.4 — Solar system. Planets. Structure & physical properties

Cook, A. H.. Interiors of the planets / A.H. Cook. — Cambridge : Cambridge University Press, 1980. — xi,348p : ill ; 24cm
Bibliography: p324-342. — Includes index
ISBN 0-521-23214-7 : £25.00 B81-03397

523.4 — Solar system. Terrestrial planets. Surface features

Murray, Bruce. Earthlike planets : surfaces of Mercury, Venus, Earth, Moon, Mars / Bruce Murray, Michael C. Malin, Ronald Greeley. — Oxford : W.H. Freeman, c1981. — xiv,387p,8p of plates : ill(some col.) ; 24cm
Includes bibliographies and index
ISBN 0-7167-1148-6 (cased) : £16.70
ISBN 0-7167-1149-4 (pbk) : £8.95
Also classified at 523.3 B81-36487

523.4′3 — Mars. Surface features. Observation, *to 1980*

Firsoff, V. A.. The new face of Mars / V.A. Firsoff. — Hornchurch : Henry, 1980. — 162p : ill ; 20cm
Bibliography: p160-162. — Includes index
ISBN 0-86025-818-1 : £4.95 B81-01962

523.4′5 — Jupiter. Observation — *Amateurs' manuals*

Peek, Bertrand M.. The planet Jupiter. — 2nd ed. — London : Faber, Sept.1981. — [256]p
Previous ed.: 1958
ISBN 0-571-18026-4 : £9.50 : CIP entry
B81-21466

523.4′6′09 — Saturn. Observation, *to 1960*

Alexander, A. F. O'D.. The planet Saturn : a history of observation theory and discovery / A.F.O'D. Alexander. — New York : Dover ; London : Constable, 1980, c1962. — 474p,22p of plates : ill,facsims ; 21cm
Originally published: London : Faber, 1962. — Includes index
ISBN 0-486-23927-6 (pbk) : £5.00 B81-05275

523.4′82 — Pluto. Discovery — *Personal observations*

Tombaugh, Clyde W.. Out of the darkness : the planet Pluto / Clyde W. Tombaugh, Patrick Moore. — Harrisburg, Pa. : Stackpole Books ; Guildford : Lutterworth, 1980. — 221p : ill,ports ; 24cm
Includes index
ISBN 0-7188-2500-4 : £7.95 B81-02428

523.5 — ASTRONOMY. METEORS, SOLAR WIND, ZODIACAL LIGHT

523.5′1 — Meteors & meteorites — *Conference proceedings*

International Astronomical Union. *Symposium (90th : 1979 : Ottawa)*. Solid particles in the solar system / International Astronomical Union, Symposium no. 90 ; organized by the IAU in cooperation with COSPAR, held at Ottawa, Canada, August 27-30, 1979 ; edited by Ian Halliday and Bruce A. McIntosh. — Dordrecht ; London : Reidel, c1980. — xii,441p : ill,ports ; 25cm
Includes bibliographies and index
ISBN 90-277-1164-x (cased) : Unpriced
ISBN 90-277-1165-8 (pbk) : Unpriced
Primary classification 523.1′12 B81-02719

523.6 — ASTRONOMY. COMETS

523.6 — Comets

Calder, Nigel. The comet is coming! : the feverish legacy of Mr Halley / Nigel Calder. — London : British Broadcasting Corporation, 1980. — 160p.[8]p of plates : ill(some col.),facsims,1map,ports ; 24cm
Bibliography: p152. — Includes index
ISBN 0-563-17859-0 : £8.75 B81-00867

Comets : readings from Scientific American / [edited by] John C. Brandt. — Oxford : W.H. Freeman, c1981. — xxxi,92p : ill(some col.),charts,facsims,1port ; 30cm
Facsim. reprints. — Bibliography: p89-90. — Includes index
ISBN 0-7167-1319-5 (cased) : £7.50
ISBN 0-7167-1320-9 (pbk) : £3.50 B81-38411

523.7 — ASTRONOMY. SUN

523.7 — Sun

Mitton, Simon. Daytime star : the story of our sun / Simon Mitton. — London : Faber & Faber, 1981. — xv,191p : ill,1plan ; 22cm
Bibliography: p184-185. — Includes index
ISBN 0-571-11659-0 : £10.00 : CIP rev.
B81-24597

523.7 — Sun. Evolution

Gribbin, John. The strangest star : a scientific account of the life and death of the sun / John Gribbin. — London : Athlone in association with Fontana, 1980. — 184p : ill ; 23cm
Bibliography: p180-184
ISBN 0-485-11207-8 : £6.95 : CIP rev. B80-04174

523.7'028 — Solar radioastronomy, *to 1978*

Krüger, A.. Introduction to solar radio astronomy and radio physics / by A. Krüger. — Dordrecht ; London : Reidel, c1979. — xiii,330p : ill ; 24cm. — (Geophysics and astrophysics monographs ; v.16)
ISBN 90-277-0957-2 (cased) : Unpriced
ISBN 90-277-0997-1 (pbk) : Unpriced B81-10310

523.7'5 — Solar flares. Magnetohydrodynamic properties

Solar flare magnetohydrodynamics / edited by E.R. Priest. — New York ; London : Gordon and Breach Science, 1981. — xii,563p : ill ; 24cm. — (The Fluid mechanics of astrophysics and geophysics, ISSN 0260-4353 ; v.1)
Includes bibliographies and index
ISBN 0-677-05530-7 : Unpriced B81-20801

523.8 — ASTRONOMY. STARS

523.8 — O stars — *Conference proceedings*

International Astronomical Union. *Symposium (83rd : 1978 : Vancouver Island)*. Mass loss and evolution of O-type stars / edited by P.S. Conti and C.W.H. De Loore. — Dordrecht ; London : Reidel, c1979. — xix,501p : ill,ports ; 25cm
At head of title: International Astronomical Union, Union astronomique internationale, Symposium no.83, held at Vancouver Island, Canada June 5-9, 1978. — Includes bibliographies and index
ISBN 90-277-0988-2 (cased) : Unpriced
ISBN 90-277-0989-0 (pbk) : Unpriced B81-15258

523.8 — Stars — *Conference proceedings*

Solar phenomena in stars and stellar systems : proceedings of the NATO Advanced Study Institute held at Bonas, France, August 25-September 5, 1980 / edited by Roger M. Bonnet and Andrea K. Dupree. — Dordrecht ; London : Reidel, published in cooperation with NATO Scientific Affairs Division, c1981. — x,591p : ill ; 25cm. — (NATO advanced study institutes series. Series C, Mathematical and physical sciences, ISSN 0377-2071 ; v.68)
Includes index
ISBN 90-277-1275-1 : Unpriced B81-25606

523.8 — Stars. Evolution — *Conference proceedings*

Fundamental problems in the theory of stellar evolution : symposium no.93, held at Kyoto University, Kyoto, Japan, July 22-25, 1980 / edited by Daiichiro Sugimoto, Donald Q. Lamb and David N. Schramm. — Dordrecht ; London : Reidel, c1981. — xv,347p : ill ; 25cm. — (IAU symp. ; no.93)
At head of title: International Astronomical Union. — Includes bibliographies and index
ISBN 90-277-1273-5 (cased) : Unpriced
ISBN 90-277-1274-3 (pbk) B81-25626

523.8 — Stars. Evolution. Effects of mass loss

International Astronomical Union. *Colloquium (59th : 1980 : Miramare)*. Effects of mass loss on stellar evolution : IAU Colloquium no.59 held in Miramare, Trieste, Italy, September 15-19, 1980 / edited by C. Chiosi and R. Stalio. — Dordrecht ; London : Reidel, c1981. — xxi,566p : ill ; 25cm. — (Astrophysics and space science library ; v.89)
Includes bibliographies and index
ISBN 90-277-1292-1 B81-36867

523.8 — Stars — *For children*

Kraske, Robert. Riddles of the stars : white dwarfs, red giants, and black holes / Robert Kraske. — New York ; London : Harcourt Brace Jovanovich, c1979. — 95p : ill,1port ; 22cm
Includes index
ISBN 0-15-266907-8 : £3.95 B81-17272

Ridpath, Ian. Stars and planets / by Ian Ridpath ; illustrated by Ron Jobson. — London : Granada, 1981. — 63p : col.ill,col.charts ; 19cm. — (Granada guides)
Includes index
ISBN 0-246-11627-7 : £1.95
Primary classification 523.4 B81-39307

523.8'2 — Stars: Red giants — *Conference proceedings*

Physical processes in red giants : proceedings of the second workshop, held at the Ettore Majorana Centre for Scientific Culture, Advanced School of Astronomy, in Erice, Sicily, Italy, September 3-13, 1980 / edited by Icko Iben, Jr. and Alvio Renzini. — Dordrecht ; London : Reidel, c1981. — xv,488p : ill,ports ; 25cm. — (Astrophysics and space science library ; v.88)
Includes bibliographies and index
ISBN 90-277-1284-0 : Unpriced B81-27869

523.8'41 — Binary stars. Photometry & spectroscopy — *Conference proceedings*

Photometric and spectroscopic binary systems : proceedings of the NATO Advanced Study held at Maratea, Italy, June 1-14, 1980 / edited by Ellen B. Carling and Zdeněk Kopal. — Dordrecht ; London : Reidel, published in cooperation with NATO Scientific Affairs Division, c1981. — xi,572p : ill ; 25cm. — (NATO advanced study institutes series. Series C, Mathematical and physical sciences, ISSN 0377-2071 ; v.69)
Includes bibliographies and index
ISBN 90-277-1281-6 : Unpriced B81-25603

523.8'444 — Eclipsing binary stars. Light. Variation

Kopal, Zdeněk. Language of the stars : a discourse on the theory of the light changes of eclipsing variables / Zdeněk Kopal. — Dordrecht ; London : Reidel, c1979. — vii,280p : ill ; 25cm. — (Astrophysics and space science library ; v.77)
Includes index
ISBN 90-277-1001-5 : Unpriced
ISBN 90-277-1044-9 (pbk) : Unpriced B81-04466

523.8'55 — Globular clusters — *Conference proceedings*

Globular clusters : based on the proceedings of a Nato Advanced Study Institute held at the Institute of Astronomy University of Cambridge, August 1978 / edited by D. Hanes & B. Madore. — Cambridge : Cambridge University Press, 1980. — 390p : ill ; 24cm. — (Cambridge astrophysics series)
Includes bibliographies and index
ISBN 0-521-22861-1 : £27.50 : CIP rev. B80-25556

525 — ASTRONOMY. PLANETS. EARTH

525'.35 — Earth. Nutation. Effects of elasticity of earth's core — *Conference proceedings*

Internal Astronomical Union. *Symposium (78th : 1977 : Kiev)*. Nutation and the earth's rotation / International Astronomical Union = Union astronomique internationale symposium no.78 held in Kiev, U.S.S.R., 23-28 May, 1977 ; edited by E.P. Fedorov and M.L. Smith and P.L. Bender. — Dordrecht ; London : Reidel, c1980. — xvi,266p : ill ; 25cm
Includes two chapters in French. — Includes bibliographies and index
ISBN 90-277-1113-5 (cased) : Unpriced
ISBN 90-277-1114-3 : Unpriced B81-06516

525'.35 — Earth. Rotation. Measurement. Techniques

Project Merit : a review of the techniques to be used during Project Merit to monitor the rotation of the Earth / International Astronomical Union, International Union of Geodesy and Geophysics, Joint Working Group on the Rotation of the Earth ; editor George A. Wilkins. — Hailsham (Herstmonceux Castle, Hailsham, E. Sussex BN27 1RP) : Royal Greenwich Observatory, 1980. — vii,77p : ill ; 30cm
Bibliography: p67-74
Unpriced (pbk) B81-19517

525'.35 — Earth. Rotation. Variation

Warlow, P.. The reversing earth. — London : Dent, Jan.1982. — [220]p
ISBN 0-460-04478-8 : £8.95 : CIP entry B81-38303

525'.35'0287 — Earth. Rotation. Measurement. Projects: MERIT — *Serials*

MERIT newsletter / International Astronomical Union [and] International Union of Geodesy and Geophysics. — No.1 (Nov.1979)-. — Hailsham (c/o Dr G.A. Wilkins, Royal Greenwich Observatory, Herstmonceux Castle, Hailsham, East Sussex BN27 1RP) : IAU/IUGG Joint Working Group on the Rotation of the Earth, 1979-. — v. ; 30cm
Irregular. — Description based on: No.3 (Mar.1981)
Unpriced B81-29402

525'.69'0916337 — Bristol Channel. Tides — *Tables — Serials*

Arrowsmith's Bristol Channel tide table. — 1981. — Bristol : Arrowsmith, [1980]. — 73p
£0.75p B81-10264

525'.69'09164 — Pacific Ocean. Coastal waters. Tides — *Tables — Serials*

Admiralty tide tables. Volume 3, Pacific Ocean and adjacent seas including tidal stream tables, parts I&II. — 1982. — [Taunton] ([Hydrographic Department, Ministry of Defence, Taunton, Somerset TA1 2DN]) : Hydrographer of the Navy, 1981. — 469p in various pagings
£6.50 B81-31601

525'.69'0941 — Great Britain. Coastal waters. Tides — *Tables — Serials*

Tide, distance and speed tables. — 1981. — Glasgow : Brown, Son & Ferguson, [1980?]. — 284p
ISBN 0-85174-399-4 : Unpriced B81-04681

525'.69'0942276 — Hampshire. Southampton. Ports: Port of Southampton. Tides — *Tables — Serials*

Port of Southampton tide tables / British Transport Docks Board. — 1981. — Southampton (Dock House, Canute Road, Southampton SO9 1PZ) : The Board, [1980?]. — 59p
Unpriced B81-08571

525'.69'09427682 — Lancashire. Fleetwood. Ports: Port of Fleetwood. Tides — *Tables — Serials*

Tide tables. Fleetwood. — 1981. — [London] : British Transport Docks Board, [1980]. — 40p
Unpriced B81-09193

525'.69'0942781 — Cumbria. Barrow-in-Furness. Ports: Port of Barrow-in-Furness. Tides — *Tables — Serials*

Tide tables ... Barrow & Silloth British Transport Docks Board. — 1981. — London ([Melbury House, Melbury Terr., NW1]) : The Board, [1980?]. — 44p
Unpriced
Also classified at 525'.69'0942787 B81-10291

525'.69'0942787 — Cumbria. Silloth. Ports: Port of Silloth. Tides — *Tables — Serials*

Tide tables ... Barrow & Silloth British Transport Docks Board. — 1981. — London ([Melbury House, Melbury Terr., NW1]) : The Board, [1980?]. — 44p
Unpriced
Primary classification 525'.69'0942781 B81-10291

525'.69'094283 — Humberside. Humber Estuary. Tides — *Tables — Serials*

Tide tables ... Hull, Immingham, Grimsby, Goole, Keadby / British Transport Docks Board. — 1981. — [London] ([Melbury House, Melbury Terr., NW1]) : [The Board], [1980?]-. — 89p
Unpriced B81-06191

526 — GEODESY, CARTOGRAPHY

526 — Cartography — *For developing countries*

Loxton, John. Practical map production / John Loxton. — Chichester : Wiley, c1980. — xiii,137p : ill,1 map ; 24cm
Bibliography: p128. — Includes index
ISBN 0-471-27782-7 (cased) : £8.50
ISBN 0-471-27783-5 (pbk) : £4.50 B81-00101

526'.028'5 — Cartography. Data processing — *Conference proceedings*

NATO Advanced Study Institute on Map Data Processing *(1979 : Maratea).* Map data processing / [proceedings of a NATO Advanced Study Institute on Map Data Processing, held in Maratea, Italy, June 18-29, 1979] ; edited by Herbert Freeman, Goffredo G. Pieroni. — New York ; London : Academic Press, 1980. — ix,374p : ill,2maps ; 24cm
Includes bibliographies and index
ISBN 0-12-267180-5 : £14.60 B81-16636

526'.05 — Cartography — *Serials*

International yearbook of cartography / edited ... in cooperation with the International Cartographic Association. — 19 (1979). — Bonn : Kirschbaum ; London : George Philip & Son Ltd., 1979. — 163p
ISBN 3-7812-1030-8 : Unpriced B81-17486

International yearbook of cartography / edited ... in cooperation with the International Cartographic Association. — 20 (1980). — Bonn : Kirschbaum ; London : George Philip & Son Ltd., 1980. — 219p
ISBN 3-7812-1054-5 : Unpriced B81-17485

526'.092'2 — Cartography, *to ca 1970.* **Research. Research personnel** — *Directories — Serials*

International directory of research in the history of cartography and in carto-bibliography. — No.3 (1981). — [London] ([c/o Professor E.M.J. Campbell, Geography Department, Birkbeck College, 7 Gresse St, W1P 1PA]) : [International directory of current research in the history of cartography and in carto-bibliography], [1981]. — 87p
ISBN 0-9504616-2-8 : Unpriced
ISSN 0307-6113 B81-30871

526'.0941 — Great Britain. Cartography. Organisations: Ordnance Survey, *to 1977*

A History of the Ordnance Survey / edited by W.A. Seymour ; with contributions by J.H. Andrews ... [ed al.]. — Folkestone : Dawson, 1980. — xiv,394p,[28]p of plates : ill(some col.),maps(some col.),2plans ; 31cm
Includes index
ISBN 0-7129-0979-6 : £35.00 : CIP rev.
B80-18692

526'.1 — Geodesy

Cross, P. A.. Geodetic appreciation / P.A. Cross, J.R. Hollwey and L.G. Small. — London ([Forest Rd., E17 4JB]) : North East London Polytechnic, Department of Land Surveying, 1980. — xiii,185p : ill,charts,1map ; 30cm. — (Working paper / North East London Polytechnic Department of Land Surveying ; no.2)
Bibliography: p182-185
ISBN 0-907382-01-0 (pbk) : Unpriced
B81-10036

Theory of the earth's shape. — Oxford : Elsevier Scientific, Feb.1982. — [694]p. — (Developments in solid earth geophysics ; 13)
Translation of: Teoria figurii pămîntului
ISBN 0-444-99705-9 : £50.00 : CIP entry
ISBN 0-444-41799-0 (set) B81-36208

526'.1 — Geodesy. Implications of refraction of light

International Astronomical Union. *Symposium (89th : 1978 : Uppsala).* Refractional influences in astrometry and geodesy / International Astronomical Union = Union astronomique internationale symposium no.89 organized by IAU in cooperation with IAG and IUGG, held in Uppsala, Sweden, 1-5 August 1978 ; edited by Erik Tengström and George Teleki with the cooperation of I. Ohlsson. — Dordrecht ; London : Reidel, c1979. — xxiv,394p : ill ; 25cm
Includes bibliographies and index
ISBN 90-277-1037-6 (cased) : Unpriced
ISBN 90-277-1038-4 (pbk) : Unpriced
Primary classification 522'.9 B81-07135

526.8'6 — Maps. Proofing. Techniques

Dixon-Gough, R. W.. Proofing : the requirements of the mapmaker and some current techniques / R.W. Dixon-Gough. — London (Forest Rd., E17 4JB) : Department of Land Surveying, North East London Polytechnic, c1980. — iv leaves,37p : ill ; 30cm. — (Working paper / North East London Polytechnic Department of Land Surveying)
Bibliography: p37
ISBN 0-907382-00-2 (pbk) : Unpriced
B81-10029

526.9 — SURVEYING

526.9 — Land. Surveying. Quantitative methods

Robinson, Carl. Quantitative methods for surveyors. — Lancaster : Construction Press, May 1981. — [224]p
ISBN 0-86095-891-4 (pbk) : CIP entry
B81-12816

526.9 — Surveying

Surveying : theory and practice. — 6th ed. / Raymond E. David ... [et al.]. — New York ; London : McGraw-Hill, c1981. — xv,992p : ill (some col.),charts,maps(some col.) ; 25cm
Previous ed.: 1967. — Ill, maps on lining papers. — Includes bibliographies and index
ISBN 0-07-015790-1 : £20.95 B81-39591

526.9 — Surveying. Measurement. Analysis & adjustment

Mikhail, Edward M.. Analysis and adjustment of survey measurements / Edward M. Mikhail, Gordon Gracie. — New York ; London : Van Nostrand Reinhold, c1981. — xii,340p : ill ; 24cm
Bibliography: p333-335. — Includes index
ISBN 0-442-25369-9 : £21.40 B81-08708

526.9'024624 — Surveying — *For construction*

Whyte, W. S.. Site surveying and levelling 2. — London : Butterworth, Oct.1981. — [160]p
ISBN 0-408-00532-7 (pbk) : £5.00 : CIP entry
B81-25310

526.9'06'041 — Great Britain. Surveying. Organisations: Faculty of Architects and Surveyors — *Serials*

Faculty of Architects and Surveyors. Year book and list of members / the Faculty of Architects and Surveyors Limited. — 1981. — London (86, Edgware Rd, W2 2YW) : Sterling Publications, [1981?]. — 224p
Spine title: FAS yearbook/list of members
ISSN 0141-8823 : Unpriced
Also classified at 720'.6'041 B81-21341

526.9'06'041 — Great Britain. Surveying. Organisations: Incorporated Association of Architects & Surveyors — *Directories — Serials*

[Reference book & list of members *(Incorporated Association of Architects & Surveyors)***].** Reference book & list of members / the Incorporated Association of Architects & Surveyors. — 1981. — London (25 Catherine St., WC2B 5JW) : Millbank Publications, [1981]. — 316p
Unpriced
Primary classification 720'.6'041 B81-32276

526.9'06'041 — Great Britain. Surveying. Organisations: Royal Institution of Chartered Surveyors — *Directories — Serials*

Royal Institution of Chartered Surveyors. Year book / the Royal Institution of Chartered Surveyors. — 1981. — East Grinstead : T. Skinner, c1981. — lii,1733p
ISSN 0308-1451 : £22.00 B81-29110

526.9'07'1141 — Great Britain. Chartered surveyors. In-service training. Courses — *Directories — Serials*

A Directory of continuing professional development courses of interest to chartered surveyors / the Royal Institution of Chartered Surveyors. — 1980/81-. — [London] : The Institution, 1980-. — v. ; 30cm
Annual. — Continues: Directory of post-qualification courses of interest to chartered surveyors
ISSN 0260-4981 = Directory of continuing professional development courses of interest to chartered surveyors : £0.60 B81-07366

526.9'09172'4 — Developing countries. Land. Surveying — *Conference proceedings*

The **Role** of the surveyor in developing countries : with particular reference to Central and Southern Africa : report of the proceedings of a CASLE regional seminar held in Malawi on 31 March-3 April, 1981 / Commonwealth Association of Surveying and Land Economy. — London (12 Great George St., SW1P 3AD) : Casle, 1981. — 134p : 2maps ; 30cm
ISBN 0-903577-22-4 (pbk) : £5.00 B81-35751

526.9'9 — Underwater surveying

Milne, P. H.. Underwater engineering surveys / P.H. Milne. — London : Spon, 1980. — ix,366p : ill ; 26cm
Includes bibliographies and index
ISBN 0-419-11310-x : £19.50 : CIP rev.
B80-04767

526.9'9'0941 — Great Britain. *Hydrographic Department — Serials*

Great Britain. *Hydrographic Department.* Report by the Hydrographer of the Navy .... — 1978. — Taunton : [Hydrographer of the Navy], 1979. — 42p
Unpriced B81-10572

529 — TIME

529 — Time

Gribbin, John. Timewarps / John Gribbin. — London : Sphere, c1979. — xii,180p,[8]p of plates : ill,ports ; 18cm
Originally published: London : Dent, 1979. — Bibliography: p166-171. - Includes index
ISBN 0-7221-4078-9 (pbk) : £1.25 B81-05552

529'.7 — Time. Measurement — *For children*

Bradbury, Lynne. Tell me the time / written by Lynne Bradbury ; illustrated by Lynn N. Grundy. — Loughborough : Ladybird Books, 1981. — [28]p : col.ill ; 19cm
Text, ill on lining papers
ISBN 0-7214-9508-7 : £0.95 B81-34072

Brook, Judy. Around the clock / Judy Brook. — Kingswood : World's Work, c1980. — [32]p : chiefly col.ill ; 21cm
ISBN 0-437-29211-8 : £2.95 B81-05233

Wood, Leslie. Time we see from the big red bus / Leslie Wood and Roy Burden. — [Exeter] : Wheaton, c1981. — [24]p : col.ill ; 20x21cm
ISBN 0-08-026431-x (cased) : Unpriced
ISBN 0-08-026430-1 (pbk) : £0.85 B81-32867

529'.7'076 — Time. Measurement — *Questions & answers — For schools*

Hollands, Roy. Time, distance, speed / Roy Hollands and Howell Moses. — St Albans : Hart-Davis Educational, 1981. — 31p : ill ; 25cm + answer book(31p : ill ; 25cm). — (Basic maths)
Cover title
ISBN 0-247-12997-6 (pbk) : £0.48
ISBN 0-247-13076-1 (answer bk) : £0.95
B81-16579

Wroe, Geoffrey. The digital clock / Geoffrey Wroe. — London : Harrap, 1980. — 32p : ill (some col.) ; 21cm. — (Maths takes off. Level 3. Geometry and measurement)
ISBN 0-245-53760-0 (pbk) : £0.75 B81-07779

530 — PHYSICS

530 — Matter

The **Nature** of matter. — Oxford : Clarendon Press, June 1981. — [200]p
ISBN 0-19-851151-5 : £8.95 : CIP entry
B81-15837

530 — Physics

Buckman, William G.. College physics : principles and applications / William G. Buckman. — New York ; London : D. Van Nostrand, c1981. — xvi,559p : ill(some col.) ; 24cm
Text on lining papers. — Includes bibliographies and index
ISBN 0-442-20844-8 : £17.20 B81-26431

530 — Physics *continuation*

Duncan, Tom. Advanced physics : materials and mechanics / T. Duncan. — 2nd ed. — London : Murray, 1981. — viii,374p : ill ; 23cm
Previous ed.: 1973. — Includes index
ISBN 0-7195-3854-8 (pbk) : £3.75 : CIP rev. B81-08902

Eisberg, Robert M.. Physics : foundations and applications / Robert M. Eisberg, Lawrence S. Lerner. — New York ; London : McGraw-Hill
Vol.1. — c1981. — xii,711p : ill ; 26cm
Text on lining papers. — Includes index
ISBN 0-07-019091-7 : £13.25 B81-36276

Halliday, David, *1916-*. Fundamentals of physics / David Halliday, Robert Resnick with the assistance of W. Farrell Edwards, John Merrill. — 2nd ed. — New York ; Chichester : Wiley, c1981. — xv,816p,[32]p : ill(some col.) ; 27cm
Previous ed.: 1970. — Text on lining papers. — Includes index
ISBN 0-471-03363-4 : £15.50 B81-11405

Halliday, David, *1916-*. Fundamentals of physics / David Halliday, Robert Resnick with the assistance of W. Farrall Edwards, John Merrill. — 2nd ed., extended version. — New York ; Chichester : Wiley, c1981. — xv,947,A24,I-13p : ill(some col.) ; 26cm
Previous ed.: 1970. — Text on lining papers. — Includes index
ISBN 0-471-08005-5 : £17.00 B81-18681

Marion, Jerry B.. Physics in the modern world / Jerry B. Marion. — 2nd ed. — New York ; London : Academic Press, c1981. — viii,648p : ill(some col.),1facsim,ports ; 25cm
Previous ed.: 1975. — Text on lining papers. — Includes bibliographies and index
ISBN 0-12-472280-6 : £11.80 B81-19051

A **Perspective** of physics : selections from 1979 Comments on modern physics. — New York ; London : Gordon and Breach
Vol.4 / introduced and put into perspective by Sir Harrie Massey. — c1980. — xxxiv,349p : ill ; 24cm
Includes index
ISBN 0-677-16190-5 : Unpriced B81-16178

Robertson, Barry C.. Modern physics for applied science / Barry C. Robertson. — New York ; Chichester : Wiley, c1981. — 271p : ill ; 24cm
Text on lining papers. — Includes index
ISBN 0-471-05343-0 : £13.40 B81-37109

Savel'ev, I. V.. Physics : a general course / I.V. Savelyev. — Moscow : Mir ; [London] (Central) [distributor], 1980
Translation of: Kurs obshcheĭ fiziki
Vol.1: Mechanics, molecular physics / translated from the Russian by G. Leib. — 439p : ill ; 23cm
Includes index
ISBN 0-7147-1597-2 : £45.50 B81-23402

Savel'ev, I. V.. Physics : a general course / I.V. Savelyev. — Moscow : Mir ; [London] (Central) [distributor], 1980
Translation of: Kurs obshcheĭ fiziki
Vol.2: Electricity and magnetism, waves, optics / translated from the Russian by G. Leib. — 508p : ill ; 23cm
Includes index
ISBN 0-7147-1598-0 : £4.50 B81-23405

Schwinger, Julian. Selected papers (1937-1976) of Julian Schwinger / edited by M. Flato, C. Fronsdal and K.A. Milton. — Dordrecht ; London : Reidel, c1979. — xxvii,413p : ill,1port ; 23cm. — (Mathematical physics and applied mathematics ; v.4)
ISBN 90-277-0974-2 : Unpriced
ISBN 90-277-0975-0 (pbk) : Unpriced B81-16291

Williams, Dudley, *1912-*. Physics for science and engineering / Dudley Williams, John Spangler. — New York ; London : Van Nostrand, c1981. — xiii,974p : ill(some col.) ; 24cm
Includes index
ISBN 0-442-26155-1 : £17.20 B81-26035

530 — Physics — *For schools*

Beiser, Arthur. Modern technical physics / Arthur Beiser. — 3rd ed. — Menlo Park ; London : Benjamin/Cummings, c1979. — 866p : ill ; 24cm
Previous ed.: 1973. — Text on lining papers. — Includes index
ISBN 0-8053-0680-3 : £14.70 B81-00868

Bishop, O. N.. Physics : a practical approach / O.N. Bishop. — London : Macmillan Educational, 1981. — vii,407p : ill ; 28cm
Includes index
ISBN 0-333-22593-7 (pbk) : £3.95 B81-22744

Casserly, Brendan. Physics : a basic course / Brendan Casserly and Bernard Horgan. — Dublin : Educational Company, 1981. — vi,263p : ill ; 21cm
Includes index
Unpriced (pbk) B81-34350

Deeson, Eric. Diagnostic testing in advanced physics. — Sevenoaks : Hodder and Stoughton
Complete volume. — Oct.1981. — [192]p
ISBN 0-340-26281-8 (pbk) : £3.95 : CIP entry B81-25788

Deeson, Eric. Diagnostic testing in advanced physics. — Sevenoaks : Hodder and Stoughton
Test volume. — Oct.1981. — [96]p
ISBN 0-340-26282-6 (pbk) : £2.25 : CIP entry B81-25787

Duncan, Tom. Advanced physics : fields, waves and atoms / T. Duncan. — 2nd ed. — London : Murray, 1981. — vii,552p : ill ; 23cm
Previous ed.: 1975. — Includes index
ISBN 0-7195-3845-9 (pbk) : £4.75 : CIP rev. B81-08903

Duncan, Tom. Advanced physics. — London : J. Murray, Jan.1982. — [700]p
ISBN 0-7195-3889-0 (pbk) : £8.50 : CIP entry B81-33845

Gardner, D. J.. Physics around us. — London : Edward Arnold, Sept.1981. — [48]p
ISBN 0-7131-0536-4 (pbk) : £1.75 : CIP entry B81-25697

Geddes, S. M.. Advanced physics / S.M. Geddes. — Basingstoke : Macmillan Education, 1981. — viii,368p : ill,1map ; 24cm
Includes index
ISBN 0-333-27063-0 (pbk) : £5.95 B81-30674

An **Illustrated** coursebook physics / consultant Martin Hollins ; translated by David Turton. — London : Macdonald Educational, 1981. — 179p : ill(some col.) ; 23cm
Translation from the German. — Includes index
ISBN 0-356-06313-5 (pbk) : Unpriced B81-36800

Jackson, B. H.. Physics matters / by B.H. Jackson. — Slough : University Tutorial Press
Book 3. — 1981. — 266p : ill ; 20x21cm
Includes index
ISBN 0-7231-0786-6 (pbk) : Unpriced B81-14637

Muncaster, Roger. A-level physics / Roger Muncaster. — Cheltenham : Thornes, 1981. — 792p : ill ; 23cm
Includes index
ISBN 0-85950-483-2 (pbk) : £7.50 : CIP rev. B81-07427

Nelkon, M.. Advanced Level physics. — 5th ed. — London : Heinemann Educational, Jan.1982. — [928]p
Previous ed.: 1977
ISBN 0-435-68666-6 (pbk) : £9.50 : CIP entry B81-35869

Nelkon, M.. Principles of physics / M. Nelkon. — 8th ed. — St. Albans : Hart-Davis Educational, 1981. — ix,626p : ill ; 24cm
Previous ed.: 1977. — Includes index
ISBN 0-247-13120-2 (pbk) : £4.50 B81-24521

Nelkon, M.. Revision book in ordinary level physics / M. Nelkon. — 4th ed. — London : Heinemann Educational, 1981. — vi,218p : ill ; 22cm
Previous ed.: 1973
ISBN 0-435-67663-6 (pbk) : £2.25 B81-03060

Reid, Alistair. O-grade physics / Alistair Reid. — London : Edward Arnold, 1980. — 92p : ill ; 25cm
Includes index
ISBN 0-7131-0435-x (pbk) : £2.75 : CIP rev. B80-08730

Swartz, Clifford E.. Phenomenal physics / Clifford E. Swartz. — New York ; Chichester : Wiley, c1980. — x,741p : ill(some col.) ; 27cm
Text on lining papers. — Includes index
ISBN 0-471-83880-2 : £12.25 B81-11406

Warren, Peter. Physics alive. — London : Murray, Aug.1981. — [256]p
ISBN 0-7195-3782-7 (pbk) : £3.50 : CIP entry B81-19162

530 — Physics. Projects — *For schools*

Campbell, L. J.. Projects in physics / L.J. Campbell and R.J. Carlton ; illustrated by David and Maureen Embry. — London : Routledge Kegan Paul, 1981. — xi,116p : ill ; 25cm. — (Secondary science series)
ISBN 0-7100-0802-3 (pbk) : £4.95 : CIP rev. B81-07584

530'.01'8 — Physics. Qualitative methods

Gitterman, M.. Qualitative analysis of physical problems / M. Gitterman, V. Halpern. — New York ; London : Academic Press, 1981. — xiv,274p : ill ; 24cm
Includes index
ISBN 0-12-285150-1 : £13.80 B81-33027

530'.0243633 — Physics — *For fire fighting*

Sheen, P. A. D.. Fire technology calculations / by P.A.D. Sheen, A. Gray. — [Leicester] ([148 New Walk, Leicester LE1 7QB]) : Institution of Fire Engineers, c1980. — v,98p : ill ; 22cm
£5.50 B81-10302

530'.024574 — Physics — *For biology*

Kane, Joseph W.. [Life science physics]. Physics / Joseph W. Kane, Morton M. Sternheim. — S.I. version. — New York ; Chichester : Wiley, c1980. — xviii,664p : ill(some col.),ports ; 26cm
Originally published: 1978. — Text on lining papers. — Includes index
ISBN 0-471-08036-5 : £13.00 B81-02053

530'.0246 — Physics — *For technicians*

Schofield, Walter. Physical science for technician engineers. — London : McGraw-Hill, Aug.1981. — [272]p
ISBN 0-07-084642-1 (pbk) : £5.45 : CIP entry B81-16884

530'.02461 — Physics — *For medicine*

Brown, B. H.. Medical physics and physiological measurement. — Oxford : Blackwell Scientific, Nov.1981. — [544]p
ISBN 0-632-00704-4 : £12.00 : CIP entry B81-30473

530'.024613 — Physics — *For tropical nursing*

Duckworth, F. O.. Physics and chemistry / F.O. Dosekun. — London : Macmillan, 1980. — 260p : ill ; 25cm. — (Macmillan Tropical nursing and health sciences series)
Includes index
ISBN 0-333-28441-0 (pbk) : £4.95 : CIP rev.
Also classified at 540'.24613 B80-29589

530'.024616 — Physics — *For radiography*

Wilks, Robin J.. Principles of radiological physics / Robin J. Wilks ; foreword by June P. Smalley. — Edinburgh : Churchill Livingstone, 1981. — x,542p : ill ; 24cm
Includes index
ISBN 0-443-02035-3 (pbk) : £15.00 B81-17756

530'.024617 — Physics — *For anaesthesia*

Hill, D. W.. Physics applied to anaesthesia / D.W. Hill. — 4th ed. — London : Butterworths, 1980. — xi,484p : ill ; 23cm
Previous ed.: 1976. — Includes bibliographies and index
ISBN 0-407-00188-3 : £19.95 : CIP rev. B80-12839

530'.028 — Physics. Experiments — *Manuals*

Hatheway, Jean P.. Laboratory manual to accompany Physics in the modern world. 2nd ed. by Jerry Marion / Jean P. Hatheway, Stephen M. Burroughs. — New York ; London : Academic Press, c1981. — vi,138p : ill,forms ; 28cm
ISBN 0-12-472286-5 (pbk) : £3.40 B81-22395

530'.028 — Physics. Experiments — *Manuals — For African students*

Okeke, P. N.. Preliminary practical physics : a manual of experimental physics for developing countries / P.N. Okeke. — Chichester : Wiley, c1981. — x,244p : ill ; 24cm
Includes index
ISBN 0-471-27852-1 (cased) : £10.00 : CIP rev.
ISBN 0-471-27851-3 (pbk) : Unpriced B81-03149

530'.028'54 — Physics. Applications of programmable electronic calculators — *Questions & answers*

Christian, J. Richard, *1916-*. Physics problems for programmable calculators : mechanics and electromagnetism / J. Richard Christman. — New York ; Chichester : Wiley, c1981. — 299p : ill ; 28cm
Supplement to: Physics. 3rd ed. / Robert Resnick, David Halliday, and Fundamentals of physics. 2nd ed / by David Halliday and Robert Resnick
ISBN 0-471-08212-0 (pbk) : £4.20 B81-16950

530'.03'21 — Physics — *Encyclopaedias*

Encyclopedia of physics / edited by Rita G. Lerner, George L. Trigg ; foreword by Walter Sullivan. — Reading, Mass. ; London : Addison-Wesley, c1981. — xvi,1157p : ill ; 29cm
Includes bibliographies and index
ISBN 0-201-04313-0 : £49.95 B81-21355

530'.07'11 — Physics. Postgraduate education — *Conference proceedings*

International Conference on Postgraduate Education of Physicists *(1980 : Prague)*. Proceedings of the International Conference on Postgraduate Education of Physicists, Prague, 24th-30th August 1980 / editors P.J. Kennedy, K. Vacek. — Edinburgh (Physics Departmart, University of Edinburgh, Edinburgh EH9 3JZ) : International Commission on Physics Education, [1981]. — 303p : ill,facsims,ports ; 22cm
ISBN 0-9507510-0-6 (pbk) : £7.00 B81-28237

530'.072041 — Great Britain. *Science Research Council. Physics Committee — Serials*

Great Britain. *Science Research Council. Physics Committee*. Annual review / Science Research Council Physics Committee. — 1979/80. — Swindon : The Council, [1981]. — 39p
Unpriced B81-32684

530'.072041 — Physics. Research in British institutions — *Directories*

Research fields in physics at United Kingdom universities and polytechnics. — 6th ed. — Bristol : Institute of Physics, c1981. — xviii,420p ; 25cm
Previous ed.: 1978. — Includes index
ISBN 0-85498-038-5 (pbk) : £20.00 : CIP rev. B81-05117

530'.0724 — Physics. Experiments

Bernard, Cicero H.. Laboratory experiments in college physics / Cicero H. Bernard, Chirold D. Epp. — 5th ed. — New York ; Chichester : Wiley, c1980. — viii,437p : ill,forms ; 28cm
Previous ed.: Lexington : Xerox College Publishing, 1972
ISBN 0-471-05441-0 (pbk) : £6.60 B81-06981

530'.076 — Physics — *Questions & answers*

Cronin, Jeremiah A.. University of Chicago graduate problems in physics : with solutions / Jeremiah A. Cronin, David F. Greenberg, Valentine L. Telegdi. — Chicago ; London : University of Chicago Press, 1979, c1967. — 263p : ill ; 23cm. — (A Phoenix book)
Originally published: Reading, Mass. ; London : Addison-Wesley, 1967
ISBN 0-226-12109-7 (pbk) : £4.90 B81-32873

Pinskiĭ, A. A.. Problems in physics / A.A. Pinsky ; translated from the Russian by Mark Samokhvalov. — Moscow : MIR ; [London] : Distributed by Central Books, 1980. — 333p : ill ; 21cm
Translation of: Zadachi po fizike
£3.25 B81-05636

530'.076 — Physics — *Questions & answers — For schools*

Harrison, D. A.. Understanding physics. — London : Heinemann Educational
Vol.1. — Jan.1982. — [88]p
ISBN 0-435-67300-9 (pbk) : £2.50 : CIP entry B81-33986

Harrison, D. A.. Understanding physics. — London : Heinemann Educational
Vol.2. — Jan.1982. — [112]p
ISBN 0-435-67301-7 (pbk) : £2.95 : CIP entry B81-33987

Hinson, Don. Physics exercises for year 3 / Don Hinson. — London : Harrap, 1981. — iv,92p : ill ; 22cm
Includes index
ISBN 0-245-53554-3 (pbk) : £1.95 B81-18986

Hinson, Don. Physics exercises for year 4 / Don Hinson. — London : Harrap, 1981. — vi,90p : ill ; 22cm
Includes index
ISBN 0-245-53555-1 (pbk) : Unpriced B81-40325

Neill, R. H. C.. Upgrade your physics / R.H.C. Neill, G. Sydserff. — London : Edward Arnold, 1981. — iv,92p : ill ; 23cm
Includes index
ISBN 0-7131-0496-1 (pbk) : £1.95 B81-21375

Nelkon, M.. Exercises in O-Level physics with worked examples / M. Nelkon. — 4th ed. — St. Albans : Hart-Davis Educational, 1981. — 154p : ill ; 24cm
Previous ed.: St. Albans : Chatto and Windus Educational, 1974
ISBN 0-247-13182-2 (pbk) : £1.60 B81-24303

Smith, Barry A.. A question of physics / Barry A. Smith. — Thirsk (Breckenbrough, Thirsk, N. Yorkshire YO7 4EN) : Crakehill. — (The Question of science series)
Part 1: 750 multiple choice questions. — c1981. — 40p : ill ; 21cm
ISBN 0-907105-03-3 (pbk) : Unpriced B81-06358

530'.076 — Physics — *Questions & answers — For teaching*

Marion, Jerry B.. Instructor's manual for Physics in the modern world, second edition / by Jerry B. Marion. — New York ; London : Academic Press, c1981. — vii,63p : ill ; 24cm
ISBN 0-12-472282-2 (pbk) : Unpriced B81-39570

530'.092'2 — Physicists: Nobel prizewinners — *Biographies*

Weber, Robert L.. Pioneers of science : Nobel prize winners in physics / Robert L. Weber ; edited by J.M.A. Lenihan. — Bristol : Institute of Physics, c1980. — xviii,272p : ports ; 24cm
Bibliography: p267-268. — Includes index
ISBN 0-85498-036-9 : £9.50 : CIP rev. B80-13371

530'.092'4 — Physics. Dyson, Freeman J. — *Biographies*

Dyson, Freeman J.. Disturbing the universe / Freeman Dyson. — London : Pan, 1981, c1979. — viii,280p ; 20cm. — (Pan scientific affairs)
Originally published: New York ; London : Harper & Row, 1979. — Includes index
ISBN 0-330-26324-2 (pbk) : £2.50 B81-19699

530'.092'4 — Physics. Einstein, Albert — *Personal observations*

Einstein / Louis de Broglie, Louis Armand, Pierre-Henri Simon ... [et al.]. — New York ; London : Peebles Press, 1979. — 219p : ill,ports ; 24cm
Translation of: Einstein
ISBN 0-85690-070-2 : £7.50 B81-25344

530'.092'4 — Physics. Newton, *Sir* **Isaac** — *Biographies*

Westfall, Richard S.. Never at rest : a biography of Isaac Newton / Richard S. Westfall. — Cambridge : Cambridge University Press, 1980. — xviii,908p : ill,ports ; 24cm
Bibliography: p875-884. — Includes index
ISBN 0-521-23143-4 : £25.00 B81-14661

530'.092'4 — Physics. Theories of Einstein, Albert

Wheeler, John Archibald. Albert Einstein : his strength and his struggle / by J.A. Wheeler. — [Leeds] : Leeds University Press, 1980. — 14p ; 21cm. — (The twentieth Selig Brodetsky memorial lecture)
£0.95 (pbk) B81-19399

530.1 — PHYSICS. THEORIES

530.1 — Physics. Theories

Ash, David A.. The Tower of Truth / presented by David Ash ; illustrated by Anna Ash. — 2nd rev. impression. — [Hove] ([5 Westbourne Pl., Hove, E. Sussex]) : Camspress, 1981. — [52]p : ill ; 17x21cm
Previous ed.: Dolsdon : D. & A. Ash, 1977
ISBN 0-906186-01-3 (pbk) : Unpriced B81-29206

Toraldo di Francia, G.. The investigation of the physical world / G. Toraldo di Francia. — Cambridge : Cambridge University Press, 1981. — xii,466p : ill ; 24cm
Translation of: L'indagine del mondo fisico. — Bibliography: p449-456. — Includes index
ISBN 0-521-23338-0 (cased) : £30.00
ISBN 0-521-29925-x (pbk) : £10.95 B81-34529

530.1 — Universal media: Ether. Theories, *1740-1900*

Conceptions of ether : studies in the history of ether theories, 1740-1900 / edited by G.N. Cantor and M.J.S. Hodge. — Cambridge : Cambridge University Press, 1981. — x,351p : ill ; 24cm
Bibliography: p341-246. — Includes index
ISBN 0-521-22430-6 : £30.00 B81-34523

530.1'1 — Fourth dimension

Hinton, Charles Howard. Speculations on the fourth dimension : selected writings of Charles H. Hinton / edited by Rudolf v.B. Rucker. — New York : Dover ; London : Constable, c1980. — xix,204p : ill ; 22cm
Bibliography: pxvii-xix. — Includes index
ISBN 0-486-23916-0 (pbk) : £2.20 B81-06177

530.1'1 — Physics. General theory of relativity — *Festschriften*

Essays in general relativity : a festschrift for Abraham Taub / edited by Frank J. Tipler. — New York ; London : Academic Press, 1980. — xviii,236p : ill,1port ; 24cm
List of works: p233-236
ISBN 0-12-691380-3 : £16.80 B81-16640

530.1'1 — Physics. Relativity

Lilley, Sam. Discovering relativity for yourself / with some help from Sam Lilley. — Cambridge : Cambridge University Press, 1981. — xi,425p : ill ; 24cm
Includes index
ISBN 0-521-23038-1 (cased) : 17.50
ISBN 0-521-29780-x (pbk) : £7.95 B81-37930

530.1'1 — Physics. Relativity *continuation*
Rindler, Wolfgang. Introduction to special relativity. — Oxford : Clarendon Press, Feb.1982. — [150]p
ISBN 0-19-853181-8 (cased) : £15.00 : CIP entry
ISBN 0-19-853182-6 (pbk) : £6.95 B81-36966

530.1'1 — Physics. Special theory of relativity
Ugarov, V. A.. Special theory of relativity / V.A. Ugarov ; translated from the Russian by Yuri Atanov. — Moscow : MIR ; [London] : Distributed by Central Books, 1979. — 406p : ill ; 23cm
Translation of: Spet͡sial'nai͡a teorii͡a otnositel'nosti. — Added t.p. in Russian. — Includes index
£5.95 B81-03603

Winterflood, A. H.. Einstein's error / A.H. Winterflood. — [London] ([9 Grosvenor Gardens, N10 3TB]) : [A.H. Winterflood], 1980. — 54p : ill ; 21cm
Limited ed. of 100 copies. — Includes index
£3.00 (pbk) B81-20054

530.1'1 — Space & time
Understanding space and time. — Milton Keynes : Open University Press. — (Science : a third level course)
At head of title: The Open University
Block 6: Topics in space and time. — 1979. — 28,44,23p : ill,1facsim ; 30cm. — (S354 ; block 6)
Contents: Part A: Signals from the creation - Part B: Black holes - Part C: The direction of time
ISBN 0-335-08005-7 (pbk) : Unpriced B81-14715

530.1'1 — Space. Theories, *to ca 1720*
Grant, Edward. Much ado about nothing : theories of space and vacuum from the Middle Ages to the scientific revolution / Edward Grant. — Cambridge : Cambridge University Press, 1981. — xii,456p : 3ill ; 24cm
Bibliography: p419-437. — Includes index
ISBN 0-521-22983-9 : £30.00 B81-32077

530.1'1'01 — Physics. Relativity — *Philosophical perspectives*
Angel, Roger B.. Relativity : the theory and its philosophy / by Roger B. Angel. — Oxford : Pergamon, 1980. — xi,259p : ill ; 26cm. — (Foundations & philosophy of science & technology) (Pergamon international library)
Includes bibliographies and index
ISBN 0-08-025197-8 (cased) : £20.00 : CIP rev. (pbk) : £8.50 B80-06904

530.1'1'0924 — Physics. Relativity. Theories of Einstein, Albert
Reichenbach, Hans. From Copernicus to Einstein / Hans Reichenbach ; translated by Ralph B. Winn. — Corrected republication. — New York : Dover ; London : Constable, 1980, c1970. — 123p : ill ; 22cm
Translation of: Von Kopernikus bis Einstein. — Originally published: New York : Philosophical Library, 1942
ISBN 0-486-23940-3 (pbk) : £1.25 B81-03745

530.1'2 — Physics. Quantum theory
Fromhold, Albert Thomas. Quantum mechanics for applied physics and engineering / Albert Thomas Fromhold, Jr. — New York ; London : Academic Press, 1981. — xvi,430p : ill ; 24cm
Bibliography: p414-415. — Includes index
ISBN 0-12-269150-4 : Unpriced B81-29820

Liboff, Richard L.. Introductory quantum mechanics / Richard L. Liboff. — San Francisco ; London : Holden-Day, c1980. — xv,653p : ill ; 24cm
Includes index
ISBN 0-8162-5172-x : £15.00 B81-02708

Sproull, Robert L.. Modern physics : the quantum physics of atoms, solids, and nuclei. — 3rd ed. / Robert L. Sproull, W. Andrew Phillips. — New York ; Chichester : Wiley, c1980. — xi,682p : ill ; 24cm
Previous ed.: / by Robert L. Sproull. 1963. — Includes index
ISBN 0-471-81840-2 : £16.00 B81-00869

530.1'2 — Physics. Quantum theory. Applications of mathematics. Operators
Schechter, Martin. Operator methods in quantum mechanics / Martin Schechter. — New York ; Oxford : North Holland, c1981. — xx,324p ; 24cm
Bibliography: p319-321. - Includes index
ISBN 0-444-00410-6 : £16.98 B81-11292

530.1'2 — Physics. Quantum theory — *Conference proceedings*
Workshop on Quantum Logic *(1979 : Ettore Majorana Center for Scientific Culture).* Current issues in quantum logic / [proceedings of the Workshop on Quantum Logic, held December 2-9, 1979, at the Ettore Majorana Center for Scientific Culture, Erice, Sicily] ; edited by Enrico G. Beltrametti and Bas C. van Fraassen. — New York ; London : Plenum, c1981. — ix,492p : ill ; 26cm. — (Ettore Majorana international science series. Physical sciences ; v.8)
Includes index
ISBN 0-306-40652-7 : Unpriced B81-33677

530.1'2 — Physics. Quantum theory — *Philosophical perspectives*
Logic and probability in quantum mechanics / edited by Patrick Suppes. — Dordrecht ; London : Reidel, c1976. — xv,541p : ill ; 23cm. — (Synthese library ; v.78)
Includes bibliographies and index
ISBN 90-277-0570-4 (cased) : Unpriced
ISBN 90-277-1200-x (pbk) : Unpriced B81-15255

530.1'2 — Physics. Quantum theory. Rotation groups. Representations
Normand, Jean-Marie. A Lie group : rotations in quantum mechanics / Jean-Marie Normand. — Amsterdam ; Oxford : North-Holland, 1980. — xvii,486p : ill ; 27cm
Bibliography: p471-473. - Includes index
ISBN 0-444-86125-4 : £24.70 B81-07396

530.1'2 — Physics. Relativistic quantum theory
Berestetskiĭ, V. B.. Quantum electrodynamics. — 2nd ed. — Oxford : Pergamon, Feb.1982. — [550]p. — (Course of theoretical physics ; v.4)
Translation of: Kvantovaya elektrodinamika. — Previous ed. published as: Relativistic quantum theory. 1974
ISBN 0-08-026503-0 (cased) : £28.75 : CIP entry
ISBN 0-08-026504-9 (pbk) : £12.00 B81-35908

530.1'2 — Quantum theory
Dirac, P. A. M.. The principles of quantum mechanics. — 4th ed. — Oxford : Clarendon Press, Nov.1981. — [328]p. — (The International series of monographs on physics ; 27)
Previous ed.: 1947
ISBN 0-19-852011-5 (pbk) : £7.95 : CIP entry B81-33642

Martin, John Legat. Basic quantum mechanics. — Oxford : Oxford University Press, June 1981. — [200]p. — (Oxford physics series)
ISBN 0-19-851815-3 (cased) : £17.50 : CIP entry
ISBN 0-19-851815-1 (pbk) : £7.95 B81-11918

Rae, Alastair I. M.. Quantum mechanics. — London : McGraw-Hill, Sept.1981. — [256]p
ISBN 0-07-084127-6 (pbk) : £6.25 : CIP entry B81-23881

530.1'2 — Quantum theory. Time dependent methods
Amrein, Werner O. Non-relativistic quantum dynamics / by W.O. Amrein. — Dordrecht ; London : Reidel, c1981. — 237p ; 24cm. — (Mathematical physics studies ; V.2)
Includes index
ISBN 90-277-1324-3 (pbk) : Unpriced B81-38409

530.1'2 — Uncertainty principle — *For civil engineering*
Ditlevsen, Ove. Uncertainty modeling : with applications to multidimensional civil engineering systems / Ove Ditlevsen. — New York ; London : McGraw-Hill, c1981. — xv,412p : ill ; 24cm
Bibliography: p403-404. — Includes index
ISBN 0-07-017046-0 : £33.95 : CIP rev. B80-18694

530.1'3 — Relativistic statistical mechanics. Theories
Groot, S. R. de. Relativistic kinetic theory : principles and applications / S.R. de Groot, W.A. van Leeuwen, Ch.G. van Weert. — Amsterdam ; Oxford : North-Holland, 1980. — xvii,417p ; 23cm
Bibliography: p391-405. - Includes index
ISBN 0-444-85453-3 : £29.23 B81-03993

530.1'3 — Statistical mechanics
Akhiezer, A. I.. Methods of statistical physics. — Oxford : Pergamon, Sept.1981. — [462]p. — (International series in natural philosophy ; v.104)
ISBN 0-08-025040-8 : £22.50 : CIP entry B81-28198

Bowler, M. G.. Lectures on statistical mechanics. — Oxford : Pergamon, Jan.1982. — [125]p
ISBN 0-08-026516-2 (cased) : £9.00 : CIP entry
ISBN 0-08-026515-4 (pbk) : £4.50 B81-34471

Rumer, I͡U. B.. Thermodynamics, statistical physics and kinetics / Yu. B. Rumer, M. Sh. Ryvkin ; translated from the Russian by S. Semyonov. — Moscow : Mir ; [London] (Central) [distributor], 1980. — 600p : ill ; 23cm
Translation of: Termodinamika, statisticheskai͡a fizika i kinetika. — Includes index
ISBN 0-7147-1599-9 : £5.95
Also classified at 539'.7 B81-23403

530.1'3 — Statistical mechanics — *Conference proceedings*
International Solvay Conference on Physics *(17th : 1978 : Université Libre de Bruxelles).* Order and fluctuations in equilibrium and nonequilibrium statistical mechanics : XVIIth international Solvay Conference on Physics / edited by G. Nicolis, G. Dewel and J.W. Turner. — New York ; Chichester : Wiley, c1981. — xix,374p : ill ; 24cm. — (Nonequilibrium problems in the physical sciences and biology ; v.1)
Includes bibliographies and index
ISBN 0-471-05927-7 : £31.50 B81-18756

International Summer School on Fundamental Problems in Statistical Mechanics *(5th : 1980 : Enschede).* Fundamental problems in statistical mechanics V : proceedings of the Fifth International Summer School on Fundamental Problems in Statistical Mechanics, Enschede, the Netherlands, June 23-July 5, 1980 / editor E.G.D. Cohen. — Amsterdam ; Oxford : North-Holland, 1980. — ix,387p : ill ; 27cm
Includes index
ISBN 0-444-86137-8 : £25.09 B81-09438

530.1'3 — Statisticl mechanics
Rosser, W. G. V.. An introduction to statistical physics. — Chichester : Ellis Horwood, June 1981. — [356]p. — (Ellis Horwood series in physics in medicine and biology)
ISBN 0-85312-272-5 : £25.00 : CIP entry B81-12918

530.1'3'05 — Statistical mechanics — *Serials*
Studies in statistical mechanics. — Vol.9. — Amsterdam ; Oxford : North-Holland, c1981. — xxviii,367p
ISBN 0-444-86026-6 : Unpriced B81-31884

530.1'41 — Electromagnetic fields
Buckley, Ruth V.. Electromagnetic fields : theory, worked examples and problems / Ruth V. Buckley. — London : Macmillan, 1981. — 163p : ill ; 24cm
Bibliography: p163
ISBN 0-333-30664-3 (pbk) : £4.50 B81-21800

Eyges, Leonard. The classical electromagnetic field / Leonard Eyges. — New York : Dover ; London : Constable, 1980, c1972. — xvii,413p : ill ; 21cm
Originally published: Reading, Mass. : London : Addison-Wesley, 1972. — Bibliography: p406-407. — Includes index
ISBN 0-486-63947-9 (pbk) : £4.40 B81-00102

530.1′41 — Electromagnetic fields
continuation
Konopinski, Emil J.. Electromagnetic fields and relativistic particles / Emil J. Konopinski. — New York ; London : McGraw-Hill, c1981. — xi,626p : ill ; 25cm
Bibliography: p610. — Includes index
ISBN 0-07-035264-x : £21.95 B81-39590

530.1′41 — Electromagnetic waves. Theories. Applications
Research topics in electromagnetic wave theory / edited by J.A. Kong. — New York ; Chichester : Wiley, c1981. — 355p : ill ; 25cm
Includes index
ISBN 0-471-08782-3 : £20.00 B81-24223

530.1′41 — Electromagnetic waves. Transmission & propagation
Gekker, I. R.. Interactions of strong electromagnetic fields with plasmas. — Oxford : Clarendon Press, July 1981. — [350]p. — (Oxford studies in physics)
Translation of: Vzaimodeĭstvie sil͡n͡y kh élektromagnitn͡y kh poleĭ s plazmoĭ
ISBN 0-19-851467-0 : £30.00 : CIP entry
B81-20600

530.1′41 — Viscoelastic materials. Electromagnetic waves. Propagation — *Conference proceedings*
Wave propagation in viscoelastic media. — London : Pitman, Jan.1982. — [300]p. — (Research notes in mathematics ; 52)
Conference papers
ISBN 0-273-08511-5 (pbk) : £10.50 : CIP entry
B81-34156

530.1′41′02462 — Electromagnetism. Theories — *For engineering*
Hayt, William H.. Engineering electromagnetics / William H. Hayt, Jr. — 4th ed. — New York ; London : McGraw Hill, c1981. — xiii,527p : ill ; 25cm. — (McGraw-Hill series in electical engineering)
Previous ed.: 1974. — Text on lining papers. — Includes index
ISBN 0-07-027395-2 : £23.95 B81-16134

530.1′42 — Physics. Unified field theory
Prasad, Ramon. Fundamental constants / by Ramon Prasad. — London (25 City Rd., EC1Y 2DE) : Geometrica, 1981. — 117p ; 21cm
ISBN 0-904377-01-6 (pbk) : £2.50 B81-07074

530.1′43 — Einstein′s field equations. Exact solution
Exact solutions of Einstein′s field equations / D. Kramer ... [et al.] ; edited by E. Schmutzer. — Cambridge : Cambridge University Press, 1980. — 425p ; 24cm. — (Cambridge monographs on mathematical physics ; [6])
Bibliography: p386-416. - Includes index
ISBN 0-521-23041-1 : £30.00 B81-11202

530.1′43 — Physics. Quantum field theory — *Festschriften*
Field theory, quantization and statistical physics : in memory of Bernard Jouvet / edited by E. Tirapegui. — Dordrecht ; London : Reidel ; London, c1981. — xxii,322p : ill,1port ; 23cm. — (Mathematical physics and applied mathematics ; v.6)
Includes index
ISBN 90-277-1128-3 : Unpriced B81-09275

530.1′43 — Physics. Relativistic quantum field theory
Barut, A. O.. Electrodynamics and classical theory of fields & particles / A.O. Barut. — Corr. republication. — New York : Dover ; London : Constable, 1980. — xv,235p : ill ; 21cm
Originally published: London : Collier Macmillan, 1964. — Bibliography: p221. - Includes index
ISBN 0-486-64038-8 (pbk) : £2.60
Also classified at 539.7′21 B81-18494

530.1′5 — Physics. Mathematics
Reed, Michael, *1942-*. Methods of modern mathematical physics / Michael Reed, Barry Simon. — New York ; London : Academic Press
1: Functional analysis. — Rev. and enl. ed. — 1980. — xv,400p : ill ; 24cm
Previous ed.: 1972. — Includes index
ISBN 0-12-585050-6 : Unpriced B81-17001

530.1′5 — Physics. Mathematics — *For schools*
Avery, J. H.. Mathematics of physics / by J.H. Avery and M. Nelkon. — 4th ed. — London : Heinemann Educational, 1980. — ix,338p : ill ; 22cm
Previous ed.: 1973. — Includes index
ISBN 0-435-68047-1 (pbk) : £4.20 B81-01545

530.1′5′01 — Physics. Mathematics. Theories — *Philosophical perspectives*
Sneed, Joseph D.. The logical structure of mathematical physics / Joseph D. Sneed. — 2nd ed., rev. — Dordrecht ; London : Reidel, c1979. — xxv,320p : ill ; 23cm. — (Synthese library ; v.35)
Previous ed.: 1971. — Bibliography: p308-312. - Includes index
ISBN 90-277-1056-2 (cased) : Unpriced
ISBN 90-277-1059-7 (pbk) : Unpriced
B81-10839

530.1′55 — Physics. Nonlinear analysis — *Conference proceedings*
Applications of nonlinear analysis in the physical sciences : invited papers presented at a workshop at Bielefeld, Federal Republic of Germany, 1-10 October 1979 / edited by H. Amann, N. Bazley, K. Kirchgässner. — Boston ; London : Pitman Advanced Publishing Program, 1981. — x,325p : ill ; 25cm. — (Surveys and reference works in mathematics ; 6)
Conference papers. — Includes index
ISBN 0-273-08501-8 : Unpriced B81-38249

530.1′55353 — Physics. Linear partial differential equations
Bit͡sadze, A. V.. Equations of mathematical physics / A.V. Bitsadze ; translated from the Russian by V.M. Volosov and I.G. Volosova. — Moscow : MIR ; [London] : Distributed by Central Books, 1980. — 318p : ill ; 21cm
Translation of: Uravnenii͡a matematicheskoĭ fiziki. — Includes index
£3.95
Also classified at 530.1′5545 B81-06518

530.1′55353 — Physics. Mathematics. Bifurcation theory — *Conference proceedings*
Bifurcation phenomena in mathematical physics and related topics : proccedings of the NATO Advanced Study Institute held at Cargèse, Corsica, France, June 24-July 7, 1979 / edited by Claude Bardos and Daniel Bessis. — Dordrecht ; London : Reidel in cooperation with NATO Scientific Affairs Division, c1980. — ix,596p : ill ; 25cm. — (NATO advanced study institutes series. Series C, Mathematical and physical sciences ; v.54)
Includes bibliographies
ISBN 90-277-1086-4 : Unpriced B81-06503

530.1′5543 — Physics. Applications of path integrals
Schulman, L. S.. Techniques and applications of path integration / L.S. Schulman. — New York ; Chichester : Wiley, c1981. — xv,359p : ill ; 24cm
Includes index
ISBN 0-471-76450-7 : £18.50 B81-18998

530.1′5545 — Physics. Linear integral equations
Bit͡sadze, A. V.. Equations of mathematical physics / A.V. Bitsadze ; translated from the Russian by V.M. Volosov and I.G. Volosova. — Moscow : MIR ; [London] : Distributed by Central Books, 1980. — 318p : ill ; 21cm
Translation of: Uravnenii͡a matematicheskoĭ fiziki. — Includes index
£3.95
Primary classification 530.1′55353 B81-06518

530.1′557 — Physics. Applications of functional integration — *Conference proceedings*
Colloquium on Functional Integration *(1979 : Louvain-la-Neuve)*. Functional integration theory and applications / [proceedings of the Colloquium on Functional Integration : Theory and Applications, held in Louvain-la-Neuve, Belgium, November 6-9, 1979] ; edited by Jean Pierre Antoine and Enrique Tirapegui. — New York ; London : Plenum, c1980. — x,355p : ill ; 26cm
Includes index
ISBN 0-306-40573-3 : Unpriced B81-20004

530.1′5636 — Physics. Mathematics. Differential forms
Westenholz, C. von. Differential forms in mathematical physics / C. von Westenholz. — Rev. ed. — Amsterdam ; Oxford : North-Holland, 1981. — xv,563p : ill ; 23cm. — (Studies in mathematics and its applications ; v.3)
Previous ed.: 1978. — Bibliography: p557-558. — Includes index
ISBN 0-444-85435-5 (cased) : £34.52
ISBN 0-444-85437-1 (pbk) : Unpriced
B81-36761

530.4 — PHYSICS. STATES OF MATTER

530.4 — Condensed matter. Applications of Green′s functions
Rickayzen, G.. Green′s functions and condensed matter / G. Rickayzen. — London : Academic Press, 1980. — x,357p : ill ; 24cm. — (Techniques of physics ; 5)
Includes bibliographies and index
ISBN 0-12-587950-4 : £22.80 : CIP rev.
B80-18244

530.4 — Condensed matter — *Conference proceedings*
European Physical Society. *Condensed Matter Division. General Conference (1st : 1980 : Antwerp)*. Recent developments in condensed matter physics / [presented at the First General Conference of the European Physical Society held April 9-11, 1980, at the University of Antwerp (RUCA and UIA), Antwerp, Belgium] ; edited by J.T. Devreese ; associate editors L.F. Lemmens, V.E. van Doren, J. van Royen. — New York ; London : Pelham
Vol.1: Invited papers. — 1981. — xvii,856p : ill ; 25cm
Includes bibliographies and index
ISBN 0-306-40646-2 : Unpriced B81-40065

530.4′1 — Crystalline solids. Phase transitions
Bruce, A. D.. Structural phase transitions / A.D. Bruce and R.A. Cowley. — London : Taylor & Francis, 1981. — 326p : ill ; 26cm. — (Taylor & Francis monographs on physics)
Includes bibliographies and index
ISBN 0-85066-206-0 : £15.00 B81-08617

530.4′1 — Metals. Electrons. Interactions with phonons
Grimvall, Göran. The electron-phonon interaction in metals / Göran Grimvall. — Amsterdam ; Oxford : North-Holland, c1981. — xiv,304p : ill ; 23cm. — (Selected topics in solid state physics ; v.16)
Bibliography: p273-288. — Includes index
ISBN 0-444-86105-x : Unpriced B81-29845

530.4′1 — Metals. Fermi surfaces. Electrons — *Festschriften*
Electrons at the Fermi surface / edited by M. Springford. — Cambridge : Cambridge University Press, 1980. — xv,541p : ill,1port ; 24cm
′...a festschrift to honour Professor David Shoenberg, FRS...′ — Preface. — Bibliography: p509-528. — Includes index
ISBN 0-521-22337-7 : £35.00 B81-02419

530.4′1 — Molecular solids. Phase transitions — *Conference proceedings*
Phase transitions in molecular solids. — London : Faraday Division, Chemical Society, 1980, c1981. — 298p,[2]p of plates : ill ; 25cm. — (Faraday discussions of the Chemical Society, ISSN 0301-7249 ; no.69)
Conference papers. — Includes index
ISBN 0-85186-748-0 (pbk) : Unpriced
B81-26114

530.4′1 — One-dimensional solids — *Conference proceedings*
The Physics and chemistry of low dimensional solids : proceedings of the NATO Advanced Study Institute held at Tomar, Portugal, August 26-September 7, 1979 / edited by Luis Alcacer. — Dordrecht ; London : Reidel in cooperation with NATO Scientific Affairs Division, c1980. — ix,436p : ill ; 25cm. — (NATO advanced study institutes series. Series C, Mathematical and physical sciences ; v.56)
Includes index
ISBN 90-277-1144-5 : Unpriced B81-06504

530.4'1 — Solid state physics

Harrison, Walter A.. Solid state theory / Walter A. Harrison. — Unabridged and corr. republication. — New York : Dover ; London : Constable, 1980, c1979. — xviii,554p : ill ; 21cm
Originally published: New York : Maidenhead : McGraw-Hill, 1970. — Includes index
ISBN 0-486-63948-7 (pbk) : £5.65 B81-00103

530.4'1 — Solid-state physics. Many-body problem. Solution. Applications of Green's functions

Mahan, Gerald D.. Many-particle physics / Gerald D. Mahan. — New York ; London : Plenum, c1981. — xiv,1003p : ill ; 24cm. — (Physics of solids and liquids)
Bibliography: p987-998. — Includes index
ISBN 0-306-40411-7 : Unpriced B81-25958

530.4'1 — Solids. Elections

Bube, Richard H.. Electrons in solids : an introductory survey / Richard H. Bube. — New York ; London : Academic Press, c1981. — xii,229p : ill, ; 24cm
Includes index
ISBN 0-12-138650-3 : £14.00 B81-16635

530.4'1 — Solids. Internal friction. Measurement. Use of ultrasonic waves — *Conference proceedings*

Internal friction and ultrasonic attenuation in solids : proceedings of the third European Conference University of Manchester, England, 18-20 July 1980 / edited by C.C. Smith ; sponsored by the Institute of Physics Materials and Testing Group. — Oxford : Pergamon, 1980. — xiii,415p : ill ; 26cm
Includes bibliographies and index
ISBN 0-08-024771-7 : £20.00 : CIP rev.
B80-18695

530.4'1 — Solids. Magnetic properties

Chakravarty, A. S.. Introduction to the magnetic properties of solids / A.S. Chakravarty. — New York ; Chichester : Wiley, c1980. — xv,696p : ill ; 24cm
Includes index
ISBN 0-471-07737-2 : Unpriced B81-08441

530.4'1 — Solids. Properties. Determination. Use of thermally stimulated processes

Chen, R.. Analysis of thermally stimulated processes / by R. Chen and Y. Kirsh. — Oxford : Pergamon, 1981. — xv,361p : ill ; 26cm. — (International series on the sciences of the solid state ; v.15)
Includes bibliographies and index
ISBN 0-08-022930-1 : £25.00 B81-18761

530.4'1 — Solids. Structure & physical properties

Bacon, G. E.. The architecture of solids / George E. Bacon. — London : Taylor & Francis, 1981. — viii,140p : ill ; 22cm. — (The Wykeham science series)
Bibliography: p135. — Includes index
ISBN 0-85109-850-9 (pbk) : £5.50 : CIP rev.
B81-15913

530.4'1 — Solids. Surfaces. Adsorption of gases — *Technical data*

Saxena, S. C.. Thermal accommodation and adsorption coefficients of gases / written by S.C. Saxena, R.K. Joshi. — New York ; London : McGraw-Hill, c1981. — xxxxvi,412p : ill ; 29cm. — (McGraw-Hill/CINDAS data series on material properties ; v.II—1)
Includes index
ISBN 0-07-065031-4 : £29.75
Also classified at 530.4'1 B81-32462

530.4'1 — Solids. Surfaces. Properties — *Conference proceedings*

Physics of solid surfaces. — Oxford : Elsevier Scientific, Jan.1982. — [300]p. — (Studies in surface science and catalysis ; 9)
Conference papers
ISBN 0-444-99716-4 : £35.00 : CIP entry
B81-35882

530.4'1 — Solids. Surfaces. Thermal accomodation of gases — *Technical data*

Saxena, S. C.. Thermal accommodation and adsorption coefficients of gases / written by S.C. Saxena, R.K. Joshi. — New York ; London : McGraw-Hill, c1981. — xxxxvi,412p : ill ; 29cm. — (McGraw-Hill/CINDAS data series on material properties ; v.II—1)
Includes index
ISBN 0-07-065031-4 : £29.75
Primary classification 530.4'1 B81-32462

530.4'1 — Solids. Surfaces. Two-dimensional ordering — *Conference proceedings*

Ordering in two dimensions : proceedings of an international conference held at Lake Geneva, Wisconsin, U.S.A. May 28-30 1980 / editor : Sunil K. Sinha. — New York ; Oxford : North Holland, c1980. — xix,497p : ill ; 27cm
Includes index
ISBN 0-444-00581-1 : £27.99 B81-09432

530.4'1 — Superionic solids

Chandra, Suresh. Superionic solids : principles and applications / Suresh Chandra. — Amsterdam ; Oxford : North-Holland, c1981. — xi,404p : ill ; 23cm
Bibliography: p371-387. — Includes index
ISBN 0-444-86039-8 : £31.56 B81-36764

530.4'1 — Thin films. Structures & physical properties — *Serials*

Physics of thin films. — Vol.11 (1980). — New York ; London : Academic Press, c1980. — xv,336p
ISBN 0-12-533011-1 : £27.00
ISSN 0079-1970 B81-16841

530.4'1'05 — Solids. Structure & physical properties — *Serials*

Solid state physics. — Vol.35. — New York ; London : Academic Press, 1980. — vii,404p
ISBN 0-12-607735-5 : Unpriced
ISSN 0081-1947 B81-02397

530.4'2 — Liquids. Atoms, ions & molecules. Dynamics

Boon, Jean Pierre. Molecular hydrodynamics / Jean Pierre Boon, Sidney Yip. — New York ; London : McGraw-Hill, c1980. — xvii,417p : ill ; 24cm
Bibliography: p405-414. — Includes index
ISBN 0-07-006560-8 : £21.15 B81-00870

530.4'3'0212 — Gases. Physical properties — *Technical data*

Properties of nonmetallic fluid elements / edited by Y.S. Touloukian, C.Y. Ho. — New York ; London : McGraw-Hill, c1981. — xvi,208p : ill ; 29cm. — (McGraw-Hill/CINDAS data series on material properties ; v.III—2)
ISBN 0-07-065033-0 : £23.50 B81-32461

530.4'4 — Magnetically confined plasmas. Fusion

Stacey, Weston M.. Fusion plasma analysis / Weston M. Stacey, Jr. — New York ; Chichester : Wiley, c1981. — xv,376p : ill ; 24cm
Includes index
ISBN 0-471-08095-0 : £18.80 B81-17088

530.4'4 — Plasmas

Lifshits, E. M.. Physical kinetics. — Oxford : Pergamon, Nov.1981. — [625]p. — (Course of theoretical physics ; v.10) (Pergamon international library)
ISBN 0-08-020641-7 (cased) : £18.00 : CIP entry
ISBN 0-08-026480-8 (pbk) : £9.00 B81-31072

530.4'4 — Plasmas - *Conference proceedings*

Physics of plasmas close to thermonuclear conditions. — Oxford : Pergamon, June 1981. — 2v. [(750)p.]
ISBN 0-08-024475-0 : £31.00 : CIP entry
B81-17528

530.4'4 — Plasmas — *Conference proceedings*

Relation between laboratory and space plasmas : proceedings of the international workshop held at Gakushi-Kaikan (University Alumni Association) Tokyo, Japan, April 14-15, 1980 / edited by Hiroshi Kikuchi. — Dordrecht ; London : Reidel, c1981. — xii,414p : ill,1map,ports ; 25cm. — (Astrophysics and space science library ; v.84)
Includes bibliographies and index
ISBN 90-277-1248-4 : Unpriced B81-27728

530.4'4 — Plasmas. Effects of lasers

Hora, Heinrich. Physics of laser driven plasmas / Heinrich Hora. — New York ; Chichester : Wiley, c1981. — xiv,317p : ill ; 24cm
Includes index
ISBN 0-471-07880-8 : £27.50 B81-40152

530.4'4 — Plasmas. Electromagnetic fields. Oscillations

Lominadze, D. G.. Cyclotron waves in plasma / by D.G. Lominadze ; translated by A.N. Dellis ; edited by S.M. Hamberger. — Oxford : Pergamon, 1981. — xii,206p : ill ; 24cm. — (International series in natural philosophy ; v.102)
Translation of: T͡Siklotronnye volny v plazme
ISBN 0-08-021680-3 : £15.00 : CIP rev.
B81-15866

530.4'4 — Plasmas. Nonlinear effects

Sitenko, A. G.. Fluctuations and non-linear wave interactions in plasmas. — Oxford : Pergamon, Dec.1981. — [250]p. — (International series in natural philosophy ; v.107)
ISBN 0-08-025051-3 : £17.50 : CIP entry
B81-31373

530.4'4'05 — Plasmas — *Serials*

Reviews of plasma physics. — Vol.8. — New York ; London ([Black Arrow House, 2 Chandos Rd, NW10 6NR]) : Consultants Bureau, c1980. — 460p
Unpriced B81-12424

530.8 — PHYSICAL UNITS, DIMENSIONS, CONSTANTS

530.8 — Dimensional analysis

Staicu, C. I.. Restricted and general dimensional analysis. — Tunbridge Wells : Abacus Press, Sept.1981. — [220]p
ISBN 0-85626-300-1 : £17.50 : CIP entry
B81-25893

530.8 — Measurement — *Conference proceedings*

Nelex 80 : 7-9 October international : metrology conference. — East Kilbride (East Kilbride, Glasgow [G75 0QU]) : National Engineering Laboratory, c1980. — 464p in various pagings : ill ; 29cm
Includes bibliographies
Unpriced (pbk) B81-23654

530.8'0212 — Measures — *Tables* — *For children*

Paull, Dorothy. The ladybird book of tables : and other measures / compiled by Dorothy Paull ; designed and illustrated by Hurlston Design Ltd. — Loughborough : Ladybird, c1981. — 51p : col.ill,1col.map ; 18cm
Text, ill on lining papers
ISBN 0-7214-0663-7 : £0.50 B81-29961

530.8'02462 — Measurement — *For engineering*

Galyer, J. F. W.. Metrology for engineers / by J.F.W. Galyer and C.R. Shotbolt. — 4th ed. — London : Cassell, 1980. — vii,243p : ill ; 25cm
Previous ed.: 1969. — Bibliography: p237-238. - Includes index
ISBN 0-304-30612-6 (pbk) : £4.95 B81-04850

530.8'028 — Science. Measurement. Experiments — *Manuals* — *For schools*

Measuring. — St. Albans : Hart-Davis Educational, 1981, c1980. — 63p : ill ; 21cm. — (Centre science)
ISBN 0-247-13124-5 (unbound) : £0.72
B81-24515

530.8′0724 — Science. Measurement. Experiments — *For schools*

Measurement. — London : Harrap, 1981. — 48p : ill ; 25cm. — (Access to science)
Cover title. — Text on inside cover
ISBN 0-245-53659-0 (pbk) : £1.50
ISBN 0-245-53701-5 (Teacher′s notes and tests) : £1.25 B81-37435

531 — MECHANICS

531 — Classical mechanics

Ramsey, A. S.. [An introduction to the theory of Newtonian attraction]. Newtonian attraction. — Cambridge : Cambridge University Press, Nov.1981. — [184]p
Originally published: 1940
ISBN 0-521-09193-4 (pbk) : £6.95 : CIP entry B81-38808

531 — Continuous media. Mechanics. Partial differential equations — *Conference proceedings*

International Symposium on Continuum Mechanics and Partial Differential Equations *(1977 : Rio de Janeiro)*. Contemporary developments in continuum mechanics and partial differential equations : proceedings of the International Symposium on Continuum Mechanics and Partial Differential Equations, Rio de Janeiro, August 1977 / edited by Guilherme M. de la Penha and Luiz Adauto J. Medeiros. — Amsterdam ; Oxford : North-Holland, 1978. — viii,613p : ill ; 24cm. — (North-Holland mathematics studies ; 30)
Includes index
ISBN 0-444-85166-6 (pbk) : Unpriced B81-05803

531 — Mechanics

Abbot, P.. Mechanics. — New ed. — London : Hodder & Stoughton, Dec.1981. — [320]p. — (Teach yourself books)
Previous ed.: 1971
ISBN 0-340-26953-7 (pbk) : £1.50 : CIP entry B81-30906

Fetter, Alexander L.. Theoretical mechanics of particles and continua / Alexander L. Fetter, John Dirk Walecka. — New York ; London : McGraw-Hill, c1980. — xvii,570p : ill ; 25cm. — (International series in pure and applied physics)
Bibliography: p556. — Includes index
ISBN 0-07-020658-9 : £13.80 B81-00871

Greenspan, Donald. Computer-oriented mathematical physics / by Donald Greenspan. — Oxford : Pergamon, 1981. — viii,170p : ill ; 26cm. — (International series in nonlinear mathematics ; v.3)
Bibliography: p165-166. — Includes index
ISBN 0-08-026471-9 (cased) : Unpriced : CIP rev.
ISBN 0-08-026470-0 (pbk) : £4.00 B81-07420

Irodov, I. E.. Fundamental laws of mechanics / I.E. Irodov ; translated from the Russian by Yuri Atanov. — Moscow : Mir, 1981 ; [London] : Distributed by Central Books. — 271p : ill ; 20cm
Translation of: Osnovnye zakony mekhaniki. — Includes index
ISBN 0-7147-1601-4 (pbk) : £1.95 B81-23487

Medley, D. G.. An introduction to mechanics and modelling. — London : Heinemann Educational, Jan.1982. — [320]p
ISBN 0-435-52560-3 (pbk) : £6.95 : CIP entry B81-34500

Nikitin, E. M.. Theoretical mechanics : for technical schools / E.M. Nikitin ; translated from the Russian by George Yankovsky. — Moscow : Mir ; [London] : distributed by Central Books, 1980. — 446p : ill ; 21cm
Translation and revision of: Teoreticheskaīa mekhanika. — Includes index
ISBN 0-7147-1588-3 : £3.95 B81-23519

Spiegel, Murray R.. Schaum′s outline of theory and problems of theoretical mechanics : with an introduction to Lagrange′s equations and Hamiltonian theory / by Murray R. Spiegel. — SI (Metric) ed. / adapted for SI Units by Y. Proykova. — New York ; London : MacGraw-Hill, c1980. — 368p : ill ; 28cm. — (Schaum′s outline series)
Includes index
ISBN 0-07-084357-0 (pbk) : £4.95 : CIP rev. B80-07350

531 — Mechanics — *Conference proceedings*

International Congress of Theoretical and Applied Mechanics *(15th : 1980 : University of Toronto)*. Theoretical and applied mechanics : proceedings of the XVth International Congress of Theoretical and Applied Mechanics, University of Toronto, Canada, August 17-23, 1980 / edited by F.P.J. Rimrott and B. Tabarrok. — Amsterdam ; Oxford : North-Holland, 1980. — xxxi,457p : ill,ports ; 27cm
Includes bibliographies and index
ISBN 0-444-85411-8 : £30.53
Also classified at 620.1 B81-23606

531 — Mechanics — *For schools*

Holt, P. J.. Mechanics : essential theory and exercises / P.J. Holt. — London : Hodder and Stoughton, 1980. — iv,203p : ill ; 24cm
ISBN 0-340-25022-4 (pbk) : £2.95 : CIP rev. B80-12840

531 — Mechanics. Newton, *Sir* Isaac. Philosophiae naturalis principia mathematica — *Critical studies*

Cohen, I. Bernard. The Newtonian revolution : with illustrations of the transformation of scientific ideas / I. Bernard Cohen. — Cambridge : Cambridge University Press, 1980. — xv,404p : ill ; 24cm
Bibliography: p361-395. - Includes index
ISBN 0-521-22964-2 : £18.00 B81-11189

531′.01′51 — Mechanics. Mathematics — *Conference proceedings*

Trends in applications of pure mathematics to mechanics. — Boston ; London : Pitman Advanced Publishing Program published on behalf of the International Society for the Interaction of Mechanics and Mathemtics. — (Monographs and studies in mathematics ; 11)
Conference papers
Vol.III: A collection of invited papers presented at a symposium at Heriot-Watt University in September 1979 / edited by R.J. Knops. — 1981. — v,234p : ill ; 24cm
Includes bibliographies and index
ISBN 0-273-08487-9 : Unpriced B81-38252

531′.01′512523 — Rigid bodies. Mechanics. Vector analysis. Applications of matrices — *For engineering*

Crouch, T.. Matrix methods applied to engineering rigid body mechanics / T. Crouch. — Oxford : Pergamon, 1981. — xviii,339p : ill ; 26cm. — (Pergamon international libray)
ISBN 0-08-024245-6 (cased) : £19.00 : CIP rev.
ISBN 0-08-024246-4 (pbk) : £7.50 B80-26986

531′.01′515 — Mechanics. Nonlinear analysis — *Conference proceedings*

Nonlinear problems of analysis in geometry and mechanics / [edited by] M. Atteia, D. Bancel & I. Gumowski. — Boston [Mass.] ; London : Pitman, c1981. — 208p : ill ; 25cm. — (Research notes in mathematics ; 46)
Conference papers. — Includes bibliographies
ISBN 0-273-08493-3 (pbk) : £8.50
Also classified at 516.3 B81-05452

531′.0246 — Mechanics — *For technicians*

Bacon, D. H.. Mechanical science for higher technicians 4/5 / D.H. Bacon and R.C. Stephens. — London : Butterworth, 1981. — 250p : ill ; 24cm. — (Butterworths technician series)
ISBN 0-408-00570-x (pbk) : Unpriced B81-24962

531.1 — DYNAMICS, STATICS, PARTICLE MECHANICS

531′.11 — Linear systems. Vibration

Thureau, Pierre. An introduction to the principles of vibrations of linear systems / by Pierre Thureau and Daniel Lecler ; adapted and translated by J. Grosjean. — English ed. — Cheltenham : Thornes, 1981. — ix,131p : ill ; 23cm
Translation of: Vibrations. — Bibliography: p129. — Includes index
ISBN 0-85950-465-4 (pbk) : £3.95 B81-29117

531′.11 — Motion — *For schools*

Fairbrother, Bob. Getting around / Bob Fairbrother. — Glasgow : Blackie, 1981. — 32p : ill ; 17x25cm. — (Modular science)
ISBN 0-216-90590-7 (pbk) : £1.40 B81-39186

531′.112 — Speed — *For children*

Hardcastle, Michael. Top speed / Michael Hardcastle. — London : Harrap, 1981. — 34p : ill,ports ; 19cm. — (The Reporters series)
ISBN 0-245-53390-7 (pbk) : £0.80 B81-19680

531′.1133 — Nonlinear waves

Bhatnagar, P. L.. Nonlinear waves in one-dimensional dispersive systems / by P.L. Bhatnagar. — Oxford : Clarendon Press, 1979. — xii,142p : ill ; 25cm. — (Oxford mathematical monographs)
Includes indexes
ISBN 0-19-853531-7 : £7.50 : CIP rev. B79-24432

Solitons and nonlinear wave equations. — London : Academic Press, July 1981. — [350]p
ISBN 0-12-219120-x : CIP entry B81-13847

531′.1133 — Waves — *For middle schools*

Bolton, W. (William), *1933-*. Rays, waves and oscillations / [W. Bolton]. — London : Butterworths, 1980. — 96p : ill ; 25cm. — (Study topics in physics ; bk.6)
Bibliography: p95. - Includes index
ISBN 0-408-10657-3 (pbk) : £1.60
Also classified at 535 B81-07551

531′.1133 — Waves — *For schools*

Parkhouse, P. G. J. T.. Waves and oscillations / P.G.J.T. Parkhouse. — Exeter : Wheaton, 1979. — 63p : ill ; 25cm. — (Selected topics in physics)
Bibliography: p63. — Includes index
ISBN 0-08-022192-0 (pbk) : £1.70 B81-07526

531′.1133′0151 — Waves. Motion. Mathematics

Baldock, G. R.. Mathematical theory of wave motion / G.R. Baldock and T. Bridgeman. — Chichester : Ellis Horwood, 1981. — 261p : ill ; 24cm. — (Ellis Horwood series in mathematics and its applications)
Bibliography: p255. — Includes index
ISBN 0-85312-225-3 : £19.50 : CIP rev. B80-33531

531′.1137 — Multiphase transport phenomena — *Conference proceedings*

Multi-Phase Flow and Heat Transfer Symposium-Workshop *(1979 : Miami Beach)*. Multiphase transport : fundamentals, reactor safety, applications / [proceedings of the Multi-Phase Flow and Heat Transfer Symposium-Workshop held in Miami Beach, Florida, U.S.A., on 16-18 April 1979] ; edited by T. Nejat Veziroğlu. — Washington ; London : Hemisphere, c1980 ; London : McGraw-Hill [Distributor]. — 5v.(xvi,2932p) : ill ; 25cm
Includes index
ISBN 0-89116-159-7 : £170.25 B81-10124

531′.14 — Gravitation — *Conference proceedings*

Cosmology and gravitation : spin, torsion, rotation, and supergravity / edited by Peter G. Bergmann and Venzo De Sabbata. — New York ; London : Plenum in cooperation with NATO Scientific Affairs Division, c1980. — ix,510p : ill ; 26cm. — (NATO advanced study institutes series. Series B, Physics ; v.58)
Conference papers. — Includes index
ISBN 0-306-40478-8 : Unpriced B81-04921

531′.14 — Gravitation. General theory of relativity

Fundamental principles of general relativity theories : local and global aspects of gravitation and cosmology / Hans-Jürgen Treder ... [et al.]. — New York ; London : Plenum, c1980. — 216p ; 24cm
Bibliography: p199-208. - Includes index
ISBN 0-306-40405-2 : Unpriced B81-04431

531′.14 — Gravitation. Theories

Nicolson, Iain. Gravity, black holes and the universe / Iain Nicolson. — Newton Abbot : David & Charles, c1981. — 264p : ill,charts,ports ; 24cm
Bibliography: p258-260. - Includes index
ISBN 0-7153-7849-x : £10.95 B81-13072

Wesson, Paul S.. Gravity, particles and astrophysics : a review of modern theories of gravity and G-variability and their relation to elementary particle physics and astrophysics / Paul S. Wesson. — Dordrecht ; London : Reidel, c1980. — viii,188p ; 25cm. — (Astrophysics and space science library ; v.79)
Bibliography: p162-186. — Includes index
ISBN 90-277-1083-x : Unpriced B81-01677

531′.14 — Gravitational waves

Davies, P. C. W.. The search for gravity waves / P.C.W. Davies. — Cambridge : Cambridge University Press, 1980. — viii,144p : ill,ports ; 22cm
Includes index
ISBN 0-521-23197-3 : £5.95 : CIP rev.
B80-29595

531′.14′076 — Weight. Measurement — *Questions & answers — For schools*

Holland, Roy. Weight, volume, capacity / Roy Hollands and Howell Moses. — St Albans : Hart-Davis Educational, 1980. — 31p : ill ; 25cm + answer book(31p : ill ; 25cm). — (Basic maths)
Cover title
ISBN 0-247-12996-8 : £0.48
ISBN 0-247-13075-3 (answer bk) : £0.95
Primary classification 516.2′3 B81-16578

531′19 — Solids. Mechanics - *Festschriften*

Mechanics of solids. — Oxford : Pergamon, May 1981. — [720]p
ISBN 0-08-025443-8 : £40.00 : CIP entry
B81-05167

531.3 — SOLIDS. DYNAMICS

531′.32 — Mechanical vibration

Hutton, David V.. Applied mechanical vibrations / David V. Hutton. — New York ; London : McGraw-Hill, c1981. — xiii,336p : ill ; 25cm
Bibliography: p325. - Includes index
ISBN 0-07-031549-3 : £20.75 B81-10593

531′.32 — Vibration

Thomson, William T.. Theory of vibration : with applications / William T. Thomson. — [2nd ed.]. — London : Allen & Unwin, 1981. — x,467p : ill ; 25cm
Previous ed.: published as Mechanical vibrations. New York : Prentice-Hall, 1948 ; London : Allen & Unwin, 1950. — Includes index
ISBN 0-04-620008-8 : £9.95 : CIP rev.
B81-00104

Thomson, William T.. Theory of vibration with applications / William T. Thomson. — 2nd ed. — Englewood Cliffs ; London : Prentice-Hall, c1981. — xvi,493p : ill ; 24cm
Previous ed.: 1972. — Includes bibliographies and index
ISBN 0-13-914523-0 : £17.50 B81-12677

531′.33 — Solids. Elastic waves. Excitation & propagation

Dieulesaint, E.. Elastic waves in solids : applications to signal processing / E. Dieulesaint, D Royer ; translated by A. Bastin and M. Motz. — Chichester : Wiley, c1980. — xix,511p : ill ; 24cm
Translation of: Ondes elastiques dans les solides. — Includes index
ISBN 0-471-27836-x : Unpriced : CIP rev.
B80-20613

531′.382 — Solids. Deformation

Billington, E. W.. The physics of deformation and flow / E.W. Billington and A. Tate. — New York ; London : McGraw-Hill, c1981. — xx,626p : ill ; 24cm
Includes bibliographies and index
ISBN 0-07-005285-9 : £25.25 : CIP rev.
Also classified at 532′.051 B80-18246

531′.3823′0924 — Elasticity theory. Germain, Sophie

Bucciarelli, Louis L.. Sophie Germain : an essay in the history of the theory of elasticity / Louis L. Bucciarelli and Nancy Dworsky. — Dordrecht ; London : Reidel, c1980. — xi,147p : ill,facsim,ports ; 23cm. — (Studies in the history of modern science ; v.6)
Includes index
ISBN 90-277-1134-8 (cased) : Unpriced
ISBN 90-277-1135-6 (pbk) : Unpriced
B81-03236

531′.3825 — Plasiticity. Mathematics

Nečas, Jindřich. Mathematical theory of elastic and elasto-plastic bodies : an introduction / Jindřich Nečas and Ivan Hlaváček. — Amsterdam ; Oxford : Elsevier Scientific, 1981. — 342p : ill ; 25cm. — (Studies in applied mechanics ; 3)
Bibliography: p335-339. — Includes index
ISBN 0-444-99754-7 : £27.42 : CIP rev.
B80-20614

531.5 — SOLIDS. MASS, GRAVITY, BALLISTICS

531′.5 — Gravitation. Quantum theory — *Conference proceedings*

Quantum gravity 2. — Oxford : Clarendon Press, Sept.1981. — [800]p
Conference papers
ISBN 0-19-851952-4 : £35.00 : CIP entry
B81-25763

531′.5 — Supergravity — *Conference proceedings*

Superspace and supergravity : proceedings of the Nuffield Workshop, : Cambridge June 16-July 12, 1980 / edited by S.W. Hawking & M. Roček. — Cambridge : Cambridge University Press, 1981. — xii,527p : ill ; 24cm
Includes bibliographies
ISBN 0-521-23908-7 : £24.00 : CIP rev.
B81-10482

531.6 — ENERGY

531′.6 — Energy. Chemical aspects — *Conference proceedings*

Energy and chemistry. — London : Royal Society of Chemistry, Dec.1981. — [368]p. — (Special publication / Royal Society of Chemistry, ISSN 0260-6291 ; no.41)
Conference papers
ISBN 0-85186-845-2 (pbk) : CIP entry
B81-38853

531′.6 — Energy — *For children*

Satchwell, John. Energy at work. — London (17 Hanway House, Hanway Place, W.1) : Walker Books, Apr.1981. — [48]p. — (All about earth)
ISBN 0-416-05660-1 : £3.50 : CIP entry
B81-02100

531′.6 — Energy. Grading & degrading

Moore, Desmond F.. Thermodynamic principles of energy degrading / Desmond F. Moore. — London : Macmillan, 1981. — xv,155p : ill ; 25cm
Bibliography: p152. — Includes index
ISBN 0-333-29504-8 (cased) : £15.00
ISBN 0-333-29506-4 (pbk) : Unpriced
B81-38643

532 — FLUIDS. MECHANICS

532′.002462 — Fluids. Mechanics — *For engineering*

Granet, Irving. Fluid mechanics for engineering technology / Irving Granet. — 2nd ed. — Englewood Cliffs ; London : Prentice-Hall, c1981. — xiv,385p : ill ; 24cm
Previous ed.: 1971. — Includes index
ISBN 0-13-322610-7 : £12.95 B81-22714

Mott, Robert L.. Applied fluid mechanics / Robert L. Mott. — 2nd ed. — Columbus, Ohio ; London : Merrill, c1979. — xvi,405p : ill ; 26cm
Previous ed.: Columbus, Ohio : Merrill, 1972. — Includes index
ISBN 0-675-08305-2 : £14.25 B81-28499

532′.05 — Fluids. Dynamics

Fluid dynamics / edited by R.J. Emrich. — New York ; London : Academic Press, 1981. — xx,403,29p : ill ; 24cm. — (Methods of experimental physics ; v.18, Pt.A)
Includes index
ISBN 0-12-475960-2 : £33.00 B81-39568

532′.05′0151 — Fluids. Dynamics. Mathematics — *For geophysics*

Friedlander, Susan. An introduction to the mathematical theory of geophysical fluid dynamics / Susan Friedlander. — Amsterdam ; Oxford : North-Holland, 1980. — x,272p : ill ; 24cm. — (Notas de matemática ; 70) (North-Holland mathematics studies ; 41)
Bibliography: p263-268. - Includes index
ISBN 0-444-86032-0 : £13.92 B81-06838

532′.05′02854 — Fluids. Dynamics. Applications of digital computer systems

Computational fluid dynamics / edited by Wolfgang Kollman. — Washington ; London : Hemisphere ; London : McGraw-Hill [Distributor]. — (A Von Karman Institute book)
Vol.2 / with contributions by H. Hollanders ... [et al.]. — c1980. — vi,265p : ill ; 26cm
Includes index
ISBN 0-89116-192-9 : £19.50 B81-10120

532′.051 — Fluids. Flow

Billington, E. W.. The physics of deformation and flow / E.W. Billington and A. Tate. — New York ; London : McGraw-Hill, c1981. — xx,626p : ill ; 24cm
Includes bibliographies and index
ISBN 0-07-005285-9 : £25.25 : CIP rev.
Primary classification 531′.382 B80-18246

532′.051′01511 — Fluids. Flow. Mathematics. Numerical methods — *Serials*

International journal for numerical methods in fluids. — Vol.1, no.1 (Jan.-Mar. 1981)-. — Chichester ; New York : Wiley, 1981-. — v. : ill ; 26cm
Quarterly
ISSN 0271-2091 : £37.50 per year B81-24126

532′.051015′117 — Fluids. Flow. Mathematics. Numerical methods - *Conference proceedings*

Numerical methods in laminar and turbulent flow . — Swansea (91 West Cross Lane, West Cross, Swansea, W. Glam.) : Pineridge, June 1981. — [1200]p
Conference papers
ISBN 0-906674-15-8 : £43.00 : CIP entry
B81-10512

532′.051′01515353 — Fluids. Flow. Mathematics. Finite element methods

Taylor, C.. Finite element programming in fluids. — Swansea (91 West Cross La., West Cross, Swansea, W. Glam.) : Pineridge Press, July 1981. — [240]p
ISBN 0-906674-16-6 : £11.50 : CIP entry
B81-13465

532′.051028′5 — Fluids. Flow. Mathematics. Numerical methods. Applications of digital computer systems

Computational techniques in transient and turbulent fluid flow. — Swansea (91 West Cross Lane, West Cross, Swansea, West Glam.) : Pineridge, May 1981. — [350]p
ISBN 0-906674-17-4 : £19.00 : CIP entry
B81-10514

532′.051′072 — Fluids. Flow. Analysis. Numerical methods

Patankar, S. V.. Numerical heat transfer and fluid flow / Suhas V. Patankar. — Washington ; London : Hemisphere, c1980. — xiii,197p : ill ; 24cm. — (Series in computational methods in mechanics and thermal sciences)
Bibliography: p189-193. - Includes index
ISBN 0-07-048740-5 : £13.50
Primary classification 536.2′072 B81-04512

532'.052 — Porous media. Multiphase flow — *For petroleum engineering*

Marle, Charles M.. Multiphase flow in porous media / Charles M. Marle. — Paris : Technip ; London : Distributed by Graham & Trotman, 1981. — xii,257p : ill ; 24cm. — (Institut français du pétrole publications)
At head of title: Institut français du pétrole, École nationale supérieure du pétrole et des moteurs. — Includes index
ISBN 2-7108-0404-2 (pbk) : £30.00 B81-34077

532'.0527'01515353 — Fluids. Dynamics. Turbulence. Partial differential equations

Bradshaw, Peter. Engineering calculation methods for turbulent flow / Peter Bradshaw, Tuncer Cebeci, James H. Whitelaw. — London : Academic Press, 1981. — xii,331p ; 24cm
Bibliography: p310-325. — Includes index
ISBN 0-12-124550-0 : £18.60 : CIP rev. B80-29604

532'.0527'0724 — Fluids. Turbulent flow. Mathematical models

Prediction methods for turbulent flows / edited by Wolfgang Kollmann. — Washington ; London : Hemisphere ; London : McGraw-Hill [distributor], c1980. — vii,468p : ill ; 27cm. — (A Von Karman Institute book)
Includes bibliographies and index
ISBN 0-89116-178-3 : £25.25 B81-39369

532'.053 — Fluids. Flow. Measurement — *Conference proceedings*

Advances in flow measurement techniques. — Cranfield : BHRA Fluid Engineering, Sept.1981. — [350]p
Conference papers
ISBN 0-906085-58-6 (pbk) : £33.00 : CIP entry B81-24648

532'.053'05 — Fluids. Flow. Measurement — *Serials*

Developments in flow measurement. — 1. — London : Applied Science, Dec.1981. — [320]p. — (The Developments series)
ISBN 0-85334-976-2 : £30.00 : CIP entry B81-31513

532'.0532'028 — Fluids. Flow. Velocity. Measurement. Applications of hot-wire anemometry

Perry, A. E.. Hot-wire anemometry. — Oxford : Clarendon Press, Feb.1982. — [200]p
ISBN 0-19-856327-2 : £30.00 : CIP entry B81-36231

532'.0532028 — Fluids. Flow. Velocity. Measurement. Applications of laser doppler anemometry

Durst, F.. Principles and practice of laser-doppler anemometry. — 2nd ed. — London : Academic Press, May 1981. — [450]p
Previous ed.: 1976
ISBN 0-12-225260-8 : CIP entry B81-09971

532'.0593 — Fluids. Waves

Lighthill, *Sir* James. Waves in fluids / James Lighthill. — Cambridge : Cambridge University Press, 1978 1980 [printing]. — xv,504p : ill ; 23cm
Bibliography: p470-486. — Includes index
ISBN 0-521-29233-6 (pbk) : £9.95 B81-36258

532.5 — HYDRODYNAMICS

532'.51 — Liquids. Flow. Stability

Chandrasekhar, S. (Subrahmonyan). Hydrodynamic and hydromagnetic stability / by S. Chandrasekhar. — New York : Dover ; London : Constable, 1981, c1961. — xix,652p : ill ; 21cm
Originally published: Oxford : Clarendon Press, 1961. — Includes index
ISBN 0-486-64071-x (pbk) : £7.60 B81-39073

Drazin, P. G.. Hydrodynamic stability / P.G. Drazin, W.H. Reid. — Cambridge : Cambridge University Press, 1981. — xiv,525p : ill ; 22cm. — (Cambridge monographs on mechanics and applied mathematics)
Bibliography: p479-513. - List of films: p515-516. - Includes index
ISBN 0-521-22798-4 : £35.00 B81-17930

532'.56 — Liquids. Pressure. Surges — *Conference proceedings*

International Conference on Pressure Surges *(3rd : 1980 : University of Kent at Canterbury)*. Proceedings of the Third International Conference on Pressure Surges : Canterbury, England, March 25-27, 1980 / organised by BHRA Fluid Engineering in conjunction with The City University, London ; [editors, H.S. Stephens, J.A. Hanson]. — Cranfield : BHRA Fluid Engineering, c1980. — 2v.(vii,645p) : ill ; 30cm
Includes index
ISBN 0-906085-24-1 (pbk) : Unpriced : CIP rev. B80-03630

533.1 — GASES. STATICS AND OTHER PHENOMENA

533'.13 — Gases. Diffusion

Cunningham, R. E.. Diffusion in gases and porous media / R.E. Cunningham and R.J.J. Williams. — New York ; London : Plenum, c1980. — xxiii,275p : ill ; 24cm
Includes index
ISBN 0-306-40537-7 : Unpriced B81-08207

533.6 — AEROMECHANICS

533'.62 — Aerodynamics

Allen, John E. (John Elliston). Aerodynamics. — 2nd ed. — London : Granada, Jan.1982. — 1v.
Previous ed.: London : Hutchinson, 1963
ISBN 0-246-11300-6 : £8.95 : CIP entry B81-33983

533.7 — KINETIC THEORY OF GASES

533'.7 — Gases. Kinetic theory

Hesketh, R. V.. Paradigm regained : a basis for a kinetic theory of gas mixtures / R.V. Hesketh. — Berkeley (Lower Stone, Berkeley, Glos. GL13 9DP) : Institute for Retarded Study, 1981. — 63 leaves ; 30cm
ISBN 0-9506963-1-5 (pbk) : Unpriced B81-13293

534 — SOUND AND RELATED VIBRATIONS

534 — Acoustics

Pierce, Allan D.. Acoustics : an introduction to its physical principles and application / Allan D. Pierce. — New York ; London : McGraw-Hill, c1981. — xxii,642p : ill ; 25cm. — (McGraw-Hill series in mechanical engineering)
Includes index
ISBN 0-07-049961-6 : £20.25 B81-32118

534 — Sound waves

Temkin, Samuel. Elements of acoustics / Samuel Temkin. — New York ; Chichester : Wiley, c1981. — xii,515p : ill ; 24cm
Bibliography: p478-489. — Includes index
ISBN 0-471-05990-0 : £15.40 B81-23251

534'.05 — Acoustics — *Serials*

Physical acoustics. — Vol.4. — New York ; London : Academic Press, 1979. — xii,561p
ISBN 0-12-477914-x : Unpriced
ISSN 0079-1873 B81-13319

534.5'5 — Ultrasonic waves — *Conference proceedings*

Ultrasonics International 79 *(conference : Graz)*. Ultrasonics International 79 : Kongress Zentrum Stefaniensaal, Graz, Austria 15-17 May, conference proceedings / conference organizer : Z. Novak ; assistant conference organizer : S.L. Bailey ; local organizer: B. Langenecker ; scientific panel E.E. Aldridge ... [et al.] ; sponsored by the journal Ultrasonics. — Guildford : IPC Science and Technology Press, c1979. — 648p : ill ; 24cm
Includes bibliographies and index
ISBN 0-86103-012-5 (pbk) : Unpriced B81-36098

535 — LIGHT AND PARAPHOTIC PHENOMENA

535 — Inhomogeneous media. Optical properties

Egan, Walter G.. Optical properties of inhomogeneous materials : applications to geology, astronomy, chemistry, and engineering / Walter G. Egan and Theodore W. Hilgeman. — New York ; London : Academic Press, 1979. — xi,235p : ill ; 24cm
Bibliography: p221-226. — Includes index
ISBN 0-12-232650-4 : £19.60 B81-11268

535 — Light — *For children*

Crews, Donald. Light / Donald Crews. — London : Bodley Head, 1981. — [30]p : chiefly col.ill ; 21cm
ISBN 0-370-30907-3 : £3.95 : CIP rev. B81-28160

535 — Light — *For schools*

Bolton, W. (William), *1933-*. Rays, waves and oscillations / [W. Bolton]. — London : Butterworths, 1980. — 96p : ill ; 25cm. — (Study topics in physics ; bk.6)
Bibliography: p95. - Includes index
ISBN 0-408-10657-3 (pbk) : £1.60
Primary classification 531'.1133 B81-07551

535 — Optics

Born, Max. Principles of optics : electromagnetic theory of propagation, interference and diffraction of light / by Max Born and Emil Wolf with contributions by A.B. Bhatia ... [et al.]. — 6th ed. — Oxford : Pergamon, 1980. — xxviii,808p,[21]p of plates : ill ; 25cm
Previous ed.: 1975. — Includes index
ISBN 0-08-026482-4 (cased) : £22.00 : CIP rev.
ISBN 0-08-026481-6 (pbk) : £12.00 B80-24444

Fincham, W. H. A.. Optics. — 9th ed. / W.H.A. Fincham, M.H. Freeman. — London : Butterworths, 1980. — vii,498p,[12]p of plates : ill(some col.) ; 24cm
Previous ed.: 1974. — Includes index
ISBN 0-407-93422-7 : £15.00 : CIP rev. B80-06386

Welford, W. T.. Optics / W.T. Welford. — 2nd ed. — Oxford : Oxford University Press, 1981. — 150p : ill ; 23cm. — (Oxford physics series) (Oxford science publications)
Previous ed.: 1976. — Bibliography: p143. — Includes index
ISBN 0-19-851846-3 (cased) : £12.50
ISBN 0-19-851847-1 (pbk) : Unpriced B81-17067

535 — Optics — *Conference proceedings*

ICO-12 Meeting *(1981 : Graz)*. Current trends in optics : invited papers from the ICO-12 Meeting, Graz, Austria, 1981 / edited by F.T. Arecchi and F.R. Aussenegg. — London : Taylor & Francis, 1981. — vii,190p : ill ; 23cm
Includes bibliographies and index
ISBN 0-85066-222-2 (pbk) : £12.00 B81-36924

535'.4 — Light. Scattering in liquids & solutions of polymers — *Conference proceedings*

Workshop on Quasielastic Light Scattering Studies of Fluids and Macromolecular Solutions *(1979 : Milan)*. Light scattering in liquids and macromolecular solutions / [proceedings of the Workshop on Quasielastic Light Scattering Studies of Fluids and Macromolecular Solutions, held at the Centro Informazioni Studi Esperienze (CISE), Segrate, Milan, Italy, May 11-13, 1979] ; edited by V. Degiorgio, M. Corti and M. Giglio. — New York ; London : Plenum, c1980. — lx,295p : ill ; 26cm
Includes index
ISBN 0-306-40558-x : Unpriced B81-06510

535'.012 — Infrared radiation

Infrared and millimeter waves / edited by Kenneth J. Button. — New York ; London : Academic Press. — xi,428p : ill ; 24cm
ISBN 0-12-147703-7 : £28.00
Primary classification 537.5'344 B81-17002

Infrared and millimeter waves. — New York ; London : Academic Press
Includes bibliographies and index
Millimeter systems / edited by Kenneth J. Button, James C. Wiltse. — 1981. — xii,364p : ill ; 24cm
ISBN 0-12-147704-5 : £30.40
Primary classification 537.5'344 B81-39571

535'.05 — Optics — *Serials*
Progress in optics. — Vol.19. — Amsterdam ; Oxford : North-Holland, 1981. — xvi,393p
ISBN 0-444-85444-4 : Unpriced B81-30735

535'.07'1041 — Great Britain. Schools. Students, 5-14 years. Curriculum subjects: Light — *For teaching*
Richards, Jenny, *1939-*. Light and colour / Jenny Richards. — Basingstoke (Houndmills, Basingstoke RG21 2XS) : Globe Education [for] West Sussex County Council, 1981. — 47p : ill,forms ; 30cm. — (Science horizons. Level 2a)
Bibliography: p10. — List of films: p10
ISBN 0-333-28539-5 (pbk) : £3.95 B81-31304

535'.15 — Light. Quantum theory
Haken, H.. Light / H. Haken. — Amsterdam ; Oxford : North-Holland
Vol.1: Waves, photons, atoms. — c1981. — xvi,353p : ill ; 23cm
Bibliography: p339-340. - Includes index
ISBN 0-444-86020-7 : £13.41 B81-22449

535'.2 — Physical optics
Lipson, S. G.. Optical physics / S.G. Lipson and H. Lipson. — 2nd ed. — Cambridge : Cambridge University Press, 1981. — xiii,463p : ill ; 24cm
Previous ed.: 1969. — Bibliography: p450-452. — Includes index
ISBN 0-521-22630-9 : £25.00 B81-19012

535'.35 — Thermoluminescence dosimetry - *Conference proceedings*
Applied thermoluminescence dosimetry. — Bristol, Hilger, June 1981. — [400]p
Conference papers
ISBN 0-85274-544-3 : £36.00 : CIP entry B81-12788

535.5'8 — Lasers. Theories — *Conference proceedings*
New Zealand Summer School in Laser Physics *(2nd : 1980 : University of Waikato)*. Laser physics : proceedings of the Second New Zealand Summer School in Laser Physics / edited by D.F. Walls, J.D. Harvey. — Sydney ; London : Academic Press, c1980. — xi,287p : ill ; 24cm
Includes index
ISBN 0-12-733280-4 : £16.90 B81-24971

535.6 — Colour
Chamberlin, G. J.. Colour : its measurement, computation and application / G.J. Chamberlin and D.G. Chamberlin. — London : Heyden, c1980. — xii,137p : ill(some col.) ; 25cm. — (Heyden international topics in science)
Bibliography: p131. — Includes index
ISBN 0-85501-222-6 : Unpriced : CIP rev. B80-02430

535.6 — Colour — *For children*
Allington, Richard. Colours / by Richard Allington and Kathleen Krull ; illustrated by Noel Spangler. — Oxford : Blackwell Raintree, c1981. — 32p : col.ill ; 24cm. — (Beginning to learn about)
Originally published: Milwaukee : Raintree Childrens, c1979
ISBN 0-86256-012-8 : £2.50 B81-17347

535.6 — Colours — *For children*
Bown, Derick. Numbers and colours / illustrated by Derick Bown ; edited by Jane Carruth. — Maidenhead : Purnell, 1975 (1981 [printing]). — [26]p : chiefly col.ill ; 25cm. — (My first colour library)
ISBN 0-361-05049-6 : £0.99
Primary classification 513'.2 B81-18847

Bradbury, Lynne. Colours and shapes / written by Lynne Bradbury ; illustrated by Lynn N. Grundy. — Loughborough : Ladybird Books, 1981. — [28]p : col.ill ; 19cm
Text, ill on lining papers
ISBN 0-7214-9509-5 : £0.95
Also classified at 516 B81-34073

The **New** gold medal book of numbers, shapes and colours. — London : Dean, c1980. — 45p : chiefly col.ill ; 26cm
ISBN 0-603-00204-8 : £1.25
Primary classification 516 B81-13259

Shapes and colours / illustrated by David Mostyn. — London : Hamlyn, 1981. — [42]p : col.ill ; 26cm. — (I can learn)
ISBN 0-600-36481-x : £1.99
Primary classification 516 B81-24061

535.6'02474 — Colour — *For design*
Ellinger, Richard G.. Color structure and design / Richard G. Ellinger. — New York ; London : Van Nostrand Reinhold, 1980, c1963. — 137p : ill(some col.) ; 23cm
Originally published: Scranton : International Textbook Co., 1963. — Includes index
ISBN 0-442-23941-6 (pbk) : £7.45 B81-17149

535.8'4 — Fluorescence spectroscopy
Standards in fluorescence spectrometry. — London : Chapman and Hall, Nov.1981. — [160]p. — (Techniques in visible and ultraviolet spectrometry ; v.2)
ISBN 0-412-22500-x : £10.00 : CIP entry B81-30384

535.8'4 — High resolution spectroscopy
Holas, J. M.. High resolution spectroscopy. — London : Butterworths, Oct.1981. — [864]p
ISBN 0-408-10605-0 : £60.00 : CIP entry B81-28819

535.8'4 — Molecular spectroscopy. Semiclassical theory — *Conference proceedings*
Semiclassical methods in molecular scattering and spectroscopy : proceedings of the NATO ASI held in Cambridge, England in September 1979 / edited by M. S. Child. — Dordrecht ; London : Reidel published in cooperation with NATO Scientific Affairs Division, c1980. — xi,332p : ill ; 25cm. — (NATO advanced study institutes series. Series C, Mathematical and physical sciences ; v.53)
Includes index
ISBN 90-277-1082-1 : Unpriced
Primary classification 539'.6 B81-05610

535.8'4 — Spectral lines. Broadening
Breene, R. G.. Theories of spectral line shape / R.G. Breene, Jr. — New York ; Chichester : Wiley, c1981. — xiii,344p : ill ; 24cm
Bibliography: p324-331. — Includes index
ISBN 0-471-08361-5 : £20.50 B81-23528

535.8'4 — Spectroscopy
Spectrometric techniques / edited George A. Vanasse. — New York ; London : Academic Press, 1981
Vol.2. — xi,303p : ill,1port ; 24cm
Includes bibliographies and index
ISBN 0-12-710402-x : £28.40 B81-39569

535.8'42 — Infrared fourier transform spectroscopy — *Conference proceedings*
Analytical applications of FT-IR to molecular and biological systems : proceedings of the NATO Advanced Study Institute held at Florence, Italy, August 31 to September 12, 1979 / edited by James R. Durig. — Dordrecht ; London : Reidel in cooperation with NATO Scientific Affairs Division, c1980. — x,607p : ill ; 25cm. — (NATO advanced study institutes series. Series C, Mathematical and physical sciences ; v.57)
Includes index
ISBN 90-277-1145-3 : Unpriced B81-07414

535.8'42 — Infrared spectroscopy
Wilson, E. Bright. Molecular vibrations : the theory of infrared and Raman vibrational spectra / E. Bright Wilson, Jr., J.C. Decius, Paul C. Cross. — Corrected republication. — New York : Dover ; London : Constable, 1980, c1955. — xi,388p : ill ; 21cm
Originally published: New York ; London : McGraw Hill, 1955. — Includes index
ISBN 0-486-63941-x (pbk) : £3.80
Also classified at 535.8'46 B81-05229

535.8'42 — Infrared spectroscopy. Spectra. Interpretation
Socrates, G.. Infrared characteristic group frequencies / G. Socrates. — Chichester : Wiley, c1980. — xi,153p ; 24x27cm
Bibliography: p148-149. - Includes index
ISBN 0-471-27592-1 : £24.00 B81-04537

535.8'42 — Vibration spectroscopy — *Serials*
Vibrational spectra and structure. — Vol.10. — Amsterdam ; Oxford : Elsevier Scientific, 1981. — xvi,498p
ISBN 0-444-42001-0 : £56.21 : CIP rev. B81-20596

Vibrational spectra and structure. — Vol.9. — Amsterdam ; Oxford : Elsevier, 1981
Vol.9. — Dec. 1980. — xv,519p
ISBN 0-444-41943-8 : £52.10 : CIP rev. B80-31512

535.8'42'0222 — Infrared spectroscopy. Spectra — *Illustrations — For schools*
Infrared spectra for Certificate of Sixth Year Studies / Scottish Curriculum Development Service, Dundee Centre. — [Dundee] ([College of Education, Gardyne Rd., Broughty Ferry, Dundee DD5 1NY]) : [The Centre], [1980]. — 1portfolio : (chiefly ill) ; 23x33cm. — (Memorandum / Scottish Curriculum Development Service, Dundee Centre ; no.44)
At head of title: Consultative Committee on the Curriculum
£1.60 B81-34434

535.8'42'05 — Infrared spectroscopy — *Serials*
Advances in infrared and Raman spectroscopy. — Vol.8. — London : Heyden, c1981. — xv,368p
ISBN 0-85501-188-2 : Unpriced : CIP rev.
ISSN 0309-426x
Also classified at 535.8'46'05 B80-33535

535.8'46 — Coherent Raman spectroscopy
Eesley, G. L.. Coherent Raman spectroscopy / G.L. Eesley. — Oxford : Pergamon, 1981. — x,142p : ill ; 26cm
Includes index
ISBN 0-08-025058-0 : £17.00 B81-19104

535.8'46 — Raman spectroscopy
Wilson, E. Bright. Molecular vibrations : the theory of infrared and Raman vibrational spectra / E. Bright Wilson, Jr., J.C. Decius, Paul C. Cross. — Corrected republication. — New York : Dover ; London : Constable, 1980, c1955. — xi,388p : ill ; 21cm
Originally published: New York ; London : McGraw Hill, 1955. — Includes index
ISBN 0-486-63941-x (pbk) : £3.80
Primary classification 535.8'42 B81-05229

535.8'46'05 — Raman spectroscopy — *Serials*
Advances in infrared and Raman spectroscopy. — Vol.8. — London : Heyden, c1981. — xv,368p
ISBN 0-85501-188-2 : Unpriced : CIP rev.
ISSN 0309-426x
Primary classification 535.8'42'05 B80-33535

535.8'9 — Optical waveguides
Adams, M. J.. An introduction to optical waveguides. — Chichester : Wiley, Dec.1981. — [384]p
ISBN 0-471-27969-2 : £22.50 : CIP entry B81-31363

536 — HEAT

536 — Heat — *For schools*
Kernaghan, Ingleby. Heat & insulation / Ingleby Kernaghan. — Glasgow : Blackie, 1981. — 32p : ill ; 17x21cm. — (Modular science)
ISBN 0-216-90586-9 (pbk) : £1.30 B81-10776

536'.2 — Heat transfer
Holman, J. P.. Heat transfer / J.P. Holman. — 5th ed. — New York ; London : McGraw-Hill, c1981. — xv,570p : ill ; 24cm
Previous ed.: 1976. — Includes index
ISBN 0-07-029618-9 : £20.50 B81-30647

Incropera, Frank P.. Fundamentals of heat transfer / Frank P. Incropera, David P. DeWitt. — New York ; Chichester : Wiley, c1981. — xxiii,819p : ill ; 24cm
Text on lining paper. — Includes index
ISBN 0-471-42711-x : £13.70 B81-20965

Lienhard, John H.. A heat transfer textbook / John H. Lienhard, with Chapter 6 by Roger Eichhorn. — Englewood Cliffs ; London : Prentice-Hall, c1981. — xi,516p : ill ; 25cm
Includes index
ISBN 0-13-385112-5 : £17.50 B81-12521

536′.2′001511 — Heat transfer. Mathematics. Numerical methods — *Conference proceedings*

Numerical methods in heat transfer / edited by R.W. Lewis, K. Morgan, O.C. Zienkiewicz. — Chichester : Wiley, c1981. — xv,536p : ill ; 24cm. — (Wiley series in numerical methods in engineering)
Includes index
ISBN 0-471-27803-3 : £28.00 B81-19002

536′.201511 — Heat transfer. Mathematics. Numerical methods - *Conference proceedings*

Numerical methods in thermal problems. — Swansea (91 West Cross La., West Cross, Swansea, W. Glam.) : Pineridge Press, June 1981. — [1400]p
Conference papers
ISBN 0-906674-12-3 : £46.00 : CIP entry B81-10424

536′.2′015194 — Heat transfer. Mathematics. Numerical methods

Hausen, Helmuth. Heat transfer in counterflow, parallel-flow and cross-flow. — London : McGraw-Hill, Dec.1981. — [576]p
Translation of: Warmeubertragung im Gegenstrom, Gleichstrom und Kreuzstrom
ISBN 0-07-027215-8 : CIP entry B81-31531

536.2′072 — Heat transfer. Analysis. Numerical methods

Patankar, S. V.. Numerical heat transfer and fluid flow / Suhas V. Patankar. — Washington ; London : Hemisphere, c1980. — xiii,197p : ill ; 24cm. — (Series in computational methods in mechanics and thermal sciences)
Bibliography: p189-193. - Includes index
ISBN 0-07-048740-5 : £13.50
Also classified at 532′.051′072 B81-04512

536′.25 — Two-phase flow. Heat transfer — *For engineering*

Two-phase flow and heat transfer in the power and process industries / A.E. Bergles ... [et al.]. — Washington ; London : Hemisphere, c1981. — xvi,707p : ill ; 24cm
Includes bibliographies and index
ISBN 0-07-004902-5 : £38.95 B81-39115

536′.33 — Heat transfer. Radiation

Siegel, Robert. Thermal radiation heat transfer / Robert Siegel, John R. Howell. — 2nd ed. — Washington ; London : Hemisphere, c1981. — xvi,862p : ill ; 25cm. — (Series in thermal and fluids engineering)
Previous ed.: New York : Maidenhead : McGraw-Hill, 1972. — Includes index
ISBN 0-07-057316-6 : £25.95 B81-12051

536′.401 — Phase transitions. Mathematics

Sinai, IA. G.. Mathematical problems in the theory of phase transitions. — Oxford : Pergamon, July 1981. — [128]p
ISBN 0-08-026469-7 : £11.00 : CIP entry B81-14472

536′.41 — Explosions. Flash radiographs — *Illustrations*

LASL PHERMEX data. — Berkeley ; London : University of California Press
Vol.3 / editor Charles L. Mader. — c1980. — 527p : chiefly ill ; 26cm. — (Los Alamos series on dynamic material properties)
Bibliography: p4-6. - Includes index
ISBN 0-520-04011-2 : £25.50 B81-27901

536′.41 — High pressure. Information sources — *Lists*

Guide to sources of information on research and technology at high pressures / High Pressure Technology Association. — Leeds (c/o J.L. Sturges, Hon. Secretary, Department of Mechanical Engineering, University of Leeds, Leeds LS2 9JT) : HPTA, c1980. — 18p ; 21cm
£1.50 (pbk) B81-04166

536′.5 — Extreme temperature

Zemansky, Mark W.. Temperatures very low and very high / Mark W. Zemansky. — New York : Dover ; London : Constable, 1981, c1964. — viii,127p : ill ; 21cm
Originally published: New York : Van Nostrand, 1964. — Bibliography: p123. — Includes index
ISBN 0-486-24072-x (pbk) : £2.05 B81-39074

536′.5′028 — Temperature. Measurement. Experiments — *Manuals* — *For schools*

Measuring temperature. — St. Albans : Hart-Davis Educational, 1981, c1980. — 31p ; 21cm. — (Centre science)
ISBN 0-247-13131-8 (unbound) : £0.40 B81-24297

536′.7 — Fluids. Thermodynamic properties — *Conference proceedings*

Chemistry and geochemistry of solutions at high temperatures and pressures. — Oxford : Pergamon, Dec.1981. — [600]p. — (Physics and chemistry of the earth ; v.13) (International series in earth sciences ; v.37)
Conference papers
ISBN 0-08-026285-6 : £90.00 : CIP entry B81-31359

536′.7 — Non-equilibrium thermodynamics. Statistical mechanics

Kreuzer, H. J.. Nonequilibrium thermodynamics and its statistical foundations / H.J. Kreuzer. — Oxford : Clarendon, 1981. — xx,438p : ill ; 22cm. — (Monographs on the physics and chemistry of materials) ([Oxford science publications])
Bibliography: p403-423. — Includes index
ISBN 0-19-851361-5 : £45.00 : CIP rev. B80-18248

536′.7 — Thermodynamics — *Arabic texts*

Van Wylen, Gordon J.. Asāsiyyāt ad-dinamīkā l-harāriyyah al kilāsikiyyah / ta'lāf Gūrdūn Ğ. Fān Waylin, Rītšard A. Sūntāğ ; tarğamah Muḥsin Sālim Riḍwān ; murāğa'ah 'Abd ar-Rāziq 'Abd al-Fattāh. — Niyū Yūrk [i.e. New York] ; Siyašstir [i.e. Chichester] : Waylī [i.e. Wiley], c1981. — 864p,[1]folded leaf of plates : ill ; 23cm
Translation of: Fundamentals of classical thermodynamics. 2nd ed. SI version
ISBN 0-471-04504-7 (pbk) : £11.50 B81-37421

536′.7′02462 — Thermodynamics — *For engineering*

Todd, James P.. An introduction to thermodynamics for engineering technologists / James P. Todd, Herbert B. Ellis. — New York ; Chichester : Wiley, c1981. — x,469p : ill ; 25cm
Includes index
ISBN 0-471-05300-7 : £11.75 B81-14768

537 — ELECTRICITY

537 — Electricity

Duffin, W. J.. Electricity and magnetism / W.J. Duffin. — 3rd ed. — London : McGraw-Hill, c1980. — xxvi,467p : ill ; 23cm
Previous ed.: 1973. — Bibliography: p443-445. - Includes index
ISBN 0-07-084111-x (pbk) : Unpriced : CIP rev.
Also classified at 538 B80-18249

537 — Electricity — *For children*

Jardine, Jim. Electricity / Jim Jardine. — London : Heinemann Educational, 1981. — 31p : ill ; 19cm. — (Heinemann science and technical readers. Elementary level)
ISBN 0-435-29007-x (pbk) : £0.85 B81-29933

537 — Electromagnetism

Electromagnetism. — Milton Keynes : Open University Press. — (Science/Mathematics : a third level course)
At head of title: The Open University
Block 2: The electric field. — 1980. — 80p in various pagings : ill ; 30cm. — (SM325 ; block 2)
Contents: Unit 2: Coulomb's law of electrostatic forces — Unit 3: The electric field — Unit 4: The electric potential — Unit 5: Capacitance — Unit 6: Dielectrics
ISBN 0-335-08106-1 (pbk) : Unpriced
ISBN 0-335-08105-3 B81-31145

Electromagnetism. — Milton Keynes : Open University Press. — (Science/mathematics : a third level course)
At head of title: The Open University
Block 4: Electromagnetic waves. — 1980. — 34,32,38p : ill ; 30cm. — (SM352 ; block 4)
Contents: Units 13/14. Maxwell's equations and electromagnetic waves — Unit 15. Electromagnetic waves : boundaries — Unit 16. Electromagnetic waves : media
ISBN 0-335-08108-8 (pbk) : Unpriced B81-39478

Rossiter, V.. Electromagnetism / V. Rossiter. — London : Heyden, c1979. — xi,168p : ill ; 24cm
Bibliography: p147-148. - Includes index
ISBN 0-85501-456-3 (pbk) : £7.00 B81-12987

537 — Electromagnetism. Applications

Booker, Henry G.. Energy in electromagnetism. — Stevenage : Peregrinus, Dec.1981. — [384]p. — (IEE electromagnetic waves series ; 13)
ISBN 0-906048-59-1 : £25.00 : CIP entry B81-31807

537 — Nonlinear electromagnetism

Nonlinear electromagnetics / edited by Piergiorgio L.E. Uslenghi. — New York ; London : Academic Press, 1980. — x,426p : ill ; 24cm
ISBN 0-12-709660-4 : £16.80 B81-03775

537′.0212 — Electricity — *Technical data*

Scaddan, Brian. Electrical formulae for technical students / Brian Scaddan. — Guildford : Westbury House, 1981. — 30p : ill ; 15x21cm
Includes index
ISBN 0-86103-048-6 (pbk) : Unpriced : CIP rev. B80-33538

537′.0246 — Electricity — *For technicians*

Morris, Noel M.. Electrical and electronic principles / Noel M. Morris. — London : Pitman, 1980. — ix,230p : ill ; 25cm
Includes index
ISBN 0-273-01329-7 (pbk) : £4.95 B81-05689

537′.028 — Electricity. Experiments — *Manuals* — *For schools*

Magnetism and electricity. — St. Albans : Hart-Davis Educational, 1981, c1980. — 30p : ill ; 21cm. — (Centre science)
ISBN 0-247-13125-3 (unbound) : £0.40
Also classified at 538′.028 B81-24517

537′.0724 — Electricity. Experiments — *Manuals* — *For children*

Catherall, Ed. Electric power / Ed Catherall. — Hove : Wayland, 1981. — 32p : col.ill ; 24cm. — (Young scientist)
ISBN 0-85340-871-8 : £2.95 B81-40623

537.2 — ELECTROSTATICS

537′.24 — Dielectrics. High-field phenomena — *Conference proceedings*

Dielectrics Society. *Meeting (1981 : Oxford)*. High field phenomena in dielectrics : the Dielectrics Society 1981 Meeting, 7-9 April, 1981, Lady Margaret Hall and the Physical Chemistry Laboratory, Oxford. — [Salford] ([c/o C.W. Smith, Department of Electrical Engineering, University of Salford, Salford M5 4WT]) : [The Society], [1981]. — 53p : ill ; 30cm
Cover title
Unpriced (spiral) B81-31315

537.2′4 — Dielectrics. Physical properties — *Conference proceedings*

Conference on Physics of Dielectric Solids *(1980 : University of Kent)*. Physics of dielectric solids, 1980 : invited papers presented at the Conference on Physics of Dielectric Solids held at the University of Kent at Canterbury, 8-11 September 1980 / edited by C.H.L. Goodman. — Bristol : Institute of Physics, c1980. — 151p : ill ; 24cm. — (Conference series, ISSN 0305-2346 ; no.58)
Includes bibliographies
ISBN 0-85498-149-7 : £23.00 : CIP rev. B81-05130

537.5 — ELECTRONICS

537.5 — Electronics
Thomson, Charles M.. Fundamentals of electronics / Charles M. Thomson. — Englewood Cliffs ; London : Prentice-Hall, c1979. — xvi,600p : ill ; 25cm
Includes index
ISBN 0-13-338103-x : £12.30 B81-25162

537.5 — Electronics - *For schools*
Sladdin, M.. Elementary electronics. — London : Hodder & Stoughton, June 1981. — [192]p
ISBN 0-340-24643-x (pbk) : £3.95 : CIP entry B81-09997

537.5 — Quantum electronics — *Serials*
Progress in quantum electronics. — Vol.6. — Oxford : Pergamon, Oct.1981. — [294]p
ISBN 0-08-028387-x : £31.50 : CIP entry B81-31102

537.5′05 — Electronics — *Serials*
Advances in electronics and electron physics. — Vol.51. — New York ; London : Academic Press, 1980. — xi,455p
ISBN 0-12-014651-7 : Unpriced
ISSN 0065-2539 B81-03772

. Advances in electronics and electron physics. — vol.53. — New York ; London : Academic Press, 1980. — xi,322p
ISBN 0-12-014653-3 : Unpriced
ISSN 0065-2539 B81-12442

Advances in electronics and electron physics. — Vol.55. — New York ; London : Academic Press, 1981. — ix,403p
ISBN 0-12-014655-x : Unpriced
ISSN 0065-2539 B81-32669

Advances in electronics and electron physics. Supplement. — 13B. — New York ; London : Academic Press, 1980. — xvii,392p
ISBN 0-12-014574-x : Unpriced
ISSN 0065-2547 B81-20423

537.5′2 — Glow discharges
Chapman, Brian. Glow discharge processes : sputtering and plasma etching / Brian Chapman. — New York ; Chichester : Wiley, c1980. — xv,406p : ill ; 24cm
Includes bibliographies and index
ISBN 0-471-07828-x : £16.85 B81-04503

537.5′34 — Gyrotropic waveguides
Hlawiczka, P.. Gyrotropic waveguides. — London : Academic Press, Dec.1981. — [100]p
ISBN 0-12-349940-2 : CIP entry B81-31338

537.5′344 — Millimetre waves
Infrared and millimeter waves / edited by Kenneth J. Button. — New York ; London : Academic Press. — xi,428p : ill ; 24cm
ISBN 0-12-147703-7 : £28.00
Also classified at 535′.012 B81-17002

Infrared and millimeter waves. — New York ; London : Academic Press
Includes bibliographies and index
Millimeter systems / edited by Kenneth J. Button, James C. Wiltse. — 1981. — xii,364p : ill ; 24cm
ISBN 0-12-147704-5 : £30.40
Also classified at 535′.012 B81-39571

537.5′352 — Extended x-ray absorption fine structure spectroscopy
EXAFS spectroscopy : techniques and applications / [based on the proceedings of a symposium on the Applications of EXAFS to Materials Science, held at the 1979 meeting of the Materials Research Society, November 26-30, 1979, in Boston, Massachusetts] ; edited by B.K. Teo and D.C. Joy. — New York ; London : Plenum, c1981. — viii,275p : ill,plan ; 26cm
Includes index
ISBN 0-306-40654-3 : Unpriced B81-24231

537.5′352 — Mössbauer spectroscopy. Applications
Applications of Mossbauer spectroscopy / edited by Richard L. Cohen. — New York ; London : Academic Press
Vol.2. — 1980. — xiii,439p : ill ; 24cm
Includes bibliographies and index
ISBN 0-12-178402-9 : £29.80 B81-16999

537.5′352 — Neutron capture gamma-ray spectroscopy — *Conference proceedings*
International Symposium on Neutron-Capture Gamma-Ray Spectroscopy and Related Topics *(4th : 1981 : Grenoble)*. Neutron-capture gamma-ray spectroscopy and related topics 1981. — Bristol : Institute of Physics, Feb.1982. — [600]p. — (Conference series / Institute of Physics, ISSN 0305-2346 ; no.62)
ISBN 0-85498-153-5 : £35.00 : CIP entry B81-39237

537.6 — ELECTRODYNAMICS AND THERMOELECTRICITY

537.6 — Electrodynamics
Griffiths, David J.. Introduction to electrodynamics / David J. Griffiths. — Englewood Cliffs ; London : Prentice-Hall, c1981. — x,479p : ill ; 24cm
Text on lining papers. — Includes index
ISBN 0-13-481374-x : £15.55 B81-14681

537.6′2 — Electricity. Conductors. Thermoelectric properties — *For electrical engineering*
Tslaf, Avraham. Combined properties of conductors : an aid for calculation of thermal processes in electrical and heat engineering / Avraham Tslaf. — Amsterdam ; Oxford : Elsevier Scientific, 1981. — xiv,596p : ill ; 25cm. — (Physical sciences data ; 9)
Includes index
ISBN 0-444-41959-4 : £49.24 B81-35341

537.6′2 — Electron bombardment conductivity
Ehrenberg, W.. Electron bombardment induced conductivity and its applications. — London : Academic Press, 1981. — [360]p
ISBN 0-12-233350-0 : CIP entry B81-08912

537.6′22 — Electromagnetism. Hall effect — *Conference proceedings*
Commemorative Symposium on the Hall Effect and its Applications *(1979 : Baltimore)*. The Hall effect and its applications / [proceedings of the Commemorative Symposium on the Hall Effect and its Applications, held at the Johns Hopkins University, Baltimore, Maryland, November] ; edited by C.L. Chien and C.R. Westgate. — New York ; London : Plenum, c1980. — x,550p : ill,facsims ; 26cm
Includes index
ISBN 0-306-40556-3 : Unpriced B81-02286

537.6′22 — Gallium arsenide semiconductors — *Conference proceedings — Serials*
Gallium arsenide and related compounds. — 1980. — Bristol : The Institute of Physics, c1981. — xv,753p. — (Conference series / The Institute of Physics, ISSN 0305-2346 ; no.56)
ISBN 0-85498-147-0 : Unpriced B81-28713

537.6′22 — Organic semiconductors. Electrical properties
Kao, Kwan C.. Electrical transport in solids : with particular reference to organic semiconductors / by Kwan C. Kao and Wei Hwang. — Oxford : Pergamon, 1981. — xx,663p : ill ; 26cm. — (International series in the science of the solid state ; v.14)
Bibliography: p569-653. - Includes index
ISBN 0-08-023973-0 : £50.00 : CIP rev. B79-36303

537.6′22 — Semiconductors
Ridley, B. K.. Quantum processes in semiconductors. — Oxford : Clarendon Press, Nov.1981. — [300]p
ISBN 0-19-851150-7 : £35.00 : CIP entry B81-31069

537.6′22 — Semiconductors. Defects - *Conference proceedings*
International Conference on Defects and Radiation Effects in Semiconductors *(1980 : Oiso)*. Defects and radiation effects in semiconductors, 1980. — Bristol : Institute of Physics, June 1981. — [760]p. — (Conference series / Institute of Physics, ISSN 0305-2346 ; no.59)
ISBN 0-85498-150-0 : £40.00 : CIP entry B81-15834

537.6′22 — Semiconductors. Defects — *Conference proceedings*
Materials Research Society. *Annual Meeting (1980 : Boston, Mass.)*. Defects in semiconductors : proceedings of the Materials Research Society Annual Meeting, November 1980, Copley Plaza Hotel, Boston, Massachusetts, U.S.A. / editors J. Narayan and T.Y. Tan. — New York ; Oxford : North Holland, c1981. — xi,537p : ill ; 24cm. — (Materials Research Society symposia proceedings ; v.2)
Includes index
ISBN 0-444-00596-x : Unpriced B81-29848

537.6′22 — Semiconductors. Electro-optical properties — *Conference proceedings*
Semiconductor optoelectronics / edited by Marian A. Herman. — Chichester : Wiley, c1980. — xii,648p : ill ; 24cm
Conference papers
ISBN 0-471-27589-1 : £19.50 B81-21083

537.6′22 — Semiconductors. Microscopy — *Conference proceedings*
Microscopy of semiconducting materials, 1981. — Bristol : Institute of Physics, Oct.1981. — [450] p. — (Conference series / Institute of Physics, ISSN 0305-2346 ; no.60)
Conference papers
ISBN 0-85498-151-9 : £32.00 : CIP entry B81-28136

537.6′22 — Semiconductors. Plasmas
Pozhela, Juras. Plasma and current instabilities in semiconductors / by Juras Pozhela ; translated by O.A. Germogenova. — Oxford : Pergamon, 1981. — xv,301p : ill ; 26cm. — (International series in the science of the solid state ; v.18)
Translation from the Lithuanian. — Includes index
ISBN 0-08-025048-3 : £27.00 B81-25419

537.6′22 — Semiconductors: Silicon. Defects & impurities
Ravi, K. V.. Imperfections and impurities in semiconductor silicon / K.V. Ravi. — New York ; Chichester : Wiley, c1981. — xiv,379p : ill ; 24cm
Includes index
ISBN 0-471-07817-4 : £24.50 B81-23530

537.6′23 — Non-equilibrium superconductivity
Nonequilibrium superconductivity, phonons, and Kapitza boundaries / [based on the proceedings of a NATO Advanced Study Institute on Nonequilibrium Superconductivity, Phonons, and Kapitza Boundaries, held August 25-September 5, 1980, in Acquafredda di Maratea, Italy] ; edited by Kenneth E. Gray. — New York ; London : Plenum in cooperation with Nato Scientific Affairs Division, c1981. — x,699p : ill ; 26cm. — (NATO advanced study institutes series. Series B, physics ; v.65)
Includes bibliographies and index
ISBN 0-306-40720-5 : Unpriced B81-36677

537.6′23 — Superconductivity
Van Duzer, T.. Principles of superconductive devices and circuits / T. van Duzer, C.W. Turner. — London : Edward Arnold, 1981. — xii,369p : ill ; 24cm
Text on lining papers. — Includes index
ISBN 0-7131-3432-1 : £2.00 : CIP rev. B81-15944

537.6′23 — Ternary superconductors — *Conference proceedings*
International Conference on Ternary Superconductors *(1980 : Lake Geneva, Wis.)*. Ternary superconductors : proceedings of the International Conference on Ternary Superconductors held September 24-26, 1980, Lake Geneva, Wisconsin, USA / editors G.K. Shenoy, B.D. Dunlap and F.Y. Fradin. — New York ; Oxford : North-Holland, c1981. — xviii,322p : ill ; 27cm
Includes index
ISBN 0-444-00626-5 : Unpriced B81-27086

537.7′092′4 — Nuclear physics. Heisenberg, Werner *- Biographies*

Heisenberg, Werner. Physics and beyond. — London : Allen & Unwin, June 1981. — [264] p. — (World perspectives ; no.23)
Translation of: Der teil und das Ganze. — This translation originally published: New York : Harper & Row, 1971
ISBN 0-04-925020-5 (pbk) : £7.50 : CIP entry B81-09494

538 — MAGNETISM

538 — Magnetism

Duffin, W. J.. Electricity and magnetism / W.J. Duffin. — 3rd ed. — London : McGraw-Hill, c1980. — xxvi,467p : ill ; 23cm
Previous ed.: 1973. — Bibliography: p443-445. - Includes index
ISBN 0-07-084111-x (pbk) : Unpriced : CIP rev.
Primary classification 537 B80-18249

538 — Strong magnetic fields — *Conference proceedings*

International Conference on Megagauss Magnetic Field Generation and Related Topics *(2nd : 1979 : Washington, D.C.)*. Megagauss physics and technology / [proceedings of the Second International Conference on Megagauss Magnetic Field Generation and Related Topics, held in Washington, D.C., May 30-June 1, 1979] ; edited by Peter J. Turchi. — New York ; London : Plenum, c1980. — xiv,683p : ill ; 26cm
Includes index
ISBN 0-306-40461-3 : Unpriced B81-03782

538′.028 — Magnetism. Experiments — *Manuals — For schools*

Magnetism and electricity. — St. Albans : Hart-Davis Educational, 1981, c1980. — 30p : ill ; 21cm. — (Centre science)
ISBN 0-247-13125-3 (unbound) : £0.40
Primary classification 537′.028 B81-24517

538′.3 — Magneto-optics — *Conference proceedings*

NATO Advanced Study Institute on Theoretical Aspects and New Developments in Magneto-Optics *(1979 : University of Antwerp)*. Theoretical aspects and new developments in magneto-optics : [proceedings of the NATO Advanced Study Institute on Theoretical Aspects and New Developments in Magneto-Optics, held at the University of Antwerp, Antwerp, Belgium, July 16-28, 1979] / edited by Jozef T. Devreese. — New York ; London : Plenum, c1980. — xi,626p : ill ; 26cm. — (NATO advanced study institutes series. Series B, Physics ; v.60)
Includes index
ISBN 0-306-40555-5 : Unpriced B81-18201

538′.362 — High resolution nuclear magnetic resonance spectroscopy

Becker, Edwin D.. High resolution NMR : theory and chemical applications / Edwin D. Becker. — 2nd ed. — New York ; London : Academic Press, 1980. — xiv,354p : ill ; 24cm
Previous ed.: 1969. — Includes index
ISBN 0-12-084660-8 : £13.60 B81-22151

538′.362 — Nuclear magnetic resonance

Abragam, A.. Nuclear magnetism. — Oxford : Clarendon Press, Nov.1981. — [600]p. — (International series of monographs in physics)
ISBN 0-19-851294-5 : £50.00 : CIP entry B81-31071

538′.362′05 — Nuclear magnetic resonance spectroscopy — *Serials*

Nuclear magnetic resonance. — Vol.10. — London : Royal Society of Chemistry, c1981. — xlix,322p. — (Specialist periodical report / Royal Society of Chemistry)
ISBN 0-85186-332-9 : Unpriced : CIP rev.
ISSN 0305-9804 B81-19179

538′.364 — Electron spin resonance spectroscopy — *Serials*

Electron spin resonance. — Vol.6. — London : The Royal Society of Chemistry, c1981. — xiii,359p. — (Specialist periodical report / Royal Society of Chemistry)
ISSN 0305-9758 : Unpriced B81-32221

538′.44 — Ferromagnetic materials. Domains

O′Dell, T. H.. Ferromagnetodynamics : the dynamics of magnetic bubbles, domains and domain walls / T.H. O′Dell. — London : Macmillan, 1981. — vii,230p : ill ; 25cm
Bibliography: p207-227. — Includes index
ISBN 0-333-26413-4 : Unpriced B81-33665

538.6 — MAGNETOHYDRODYNAMICS

538′.6 — Mean-field magnetohydrodynamics

Krause, F.. Mean-field magnetohydrodynamics and dynamo theory / by F. Krause and K.-H. Rädler. — Oxford : Pergamon, 1980. — 271p : ill ; 22cm
Bibliography: p254-269. — Includes index
ISBN 0-08-025041-6 : £15.00 : CIP rev.
Also classified at 523.01′88 B79-34858

538.7 — GEOMAGNETISM AND RELATED PHENOMENA

538′.72 — Earth. Palaeozoic magnetic field — *Conference proceedings*

Global Reconstruction and the Geomagnetic Field during the Palaeozoic *(Symposium : 1979 : Canberra)*. Global reconstruction and the geomagnetic field during the palaeozoic : proceedings of IUGG Symposium ′Global Reconstruction and the Geomagnetic Field during the Palaeozoic′ Canberra, 1979, December / edited by M.W. McElhinny ... [et al.]. — Tokyo : Center for Academic Publications Japan ; Dordrecht ; London : Reidel, c1981. — 142p : ill,maps ; 27cm. — (Advances in earth and planetary sciences ; 10)
′Supplement issue to Journal of geomagnetism and geoelectricity′. — Includes bibliographies
ISBN 90-277-1231-x : Unpriced B81-36719

538′.766 — Earth. Magnetosphere. Ultra low frequency pulsations — *Conference proceedings*

ULF pulsations in the magnetosphere : reviews from the special sessions on geomagnetic pulsations at xvii General Assembly of the International Union for [i.e. of] Geodesy and Geophysics, Canberra, 1979, December / edited by D.J. Southwood. — Tokyo : Center for Academic Publications Japan ; Dordrecht ; London : Reidel, c1981. — 145p : ill ; 27cm. — (Advances in earth and planetary sciences ; 11)
′Supplement issue to Journal of geomagnetism and geoelectritiy′. — Includes bibliographies
ISBN 90-277-1232-8 : Unpriced B81-36718

539 — MODERN PHYSICS

539 — Atoms & molecules — *For schools*

Lambert, Andrew. Atoms, molecules & crystals / Andrew Lambert. — Glagow : Blackie, 1980. — 32p : ill ; 17x21cm. — (Modular science)
ISBN 0-216-90583-4 (pbk) : £1.30
Also classified at 548 B81-10727

539 — Atoms & molecules. Structure & properties

Bransden, B. H.. Physics of atoms and molecules. — London : Longman, Aug.1981. — [640]p
ISBN 0-582-44401-2 (pbk) : £13.95 : CIP entry B81-18161

539 — Modern physics

Beiser, Arthur. Concepts of modern physics / Arthur Beiser. — 3rd ed. — New York ; London : McGraw-Hill, 1981. — viii,533p : ill ; 25cm
Previous ed.: 1973. — Includes index
ISBN 0-07-004382-5 : £17.25 B81-32372

Gautreau, Ronald. Schaum′s outline of theory and problems of modern physics / by Ronald Gautreau and William Savin. — New York ; London : McGraw-Hill, c1978. — 309p : ill ; 28cm. — (Schaum′s outline series)
Includes index
ISBN 0-07-023062-5 (pbk) : £4.50 B81-00872

539.1 — STRUCTURE OF MATTER

539′.1 — Matter. Structure

Smith, Cyril Stanley. A search for structure : selected essays on science, art and history / Cyril Stanley Smith. — Cambridge, Mass. ; London : MIT Press, c1981. — x,410p : ill ; 27cm
Bibliography: p390-399. — Includes index
ISBN 0-262-19191-1 : £21.50 B81-39646

539′.14 — Atoms. Structure

Ratcliffe, D. H.. Particulate configuration of the elements : revelations concerning the atom / D.H. Ratcliffe. — Ilfracombe : Stockwell, 1981. — 32p ; 18cm
Originally serialised in Telicom by International Society for Philosophical Enquiry
ISBN 0-7223-1437-x (pbk) : £1.38 B81-16768

Woodgate, G. K.. Elementary atomic structure / G.K. Woodgate. — 2nd ed. — Oxford : Clarendon, 1980. — ix,228p : ill ; 24cm
Previous ed.: Maidenhead : McGraw-Hill, 1970. — Includes index
ISBN 0-19-851146-9 : £9.95 : CIP rev. B80-06908

539.2 — RADIATION

539.2 — Diffraction

Cowley, John M.. Diffraction physics / by John M. Cowley. — 2nd rev. ed. — Amsterdam ; Oxford : North-Holland, 1981. — xiv,430p : ill ; 23cm
Previous ed.: 1975. — Bibliography: p411-424. — Includes index
ISBN 0-444-86121-1 : Unpriced B81-39199

539.2 — Electromagnetic radiation

Olijnychenko, P.. Electromagnetic radiation / by P. Olijnychenko. — London ([76 Gorefield House, Alpha Place, N.W.6]) : [P. Olijnychenko]
Section 1.5. — Rev. ed. — 1981. — [8]p ; 21cm
Previous ed.: 1965
Unpriced (unbound) B81-29266

Read, F. H.. Electromagnetic radiation / F.H. Read. — Chichester : Wiley, c1980. — xiv,331p : ill ; 24cm. — (The Manchester physics series)
Text on lining papers. — Includes index
ISBN 0-471-27718-5 (cased) : £19.50 : CIP rev.
ISBN 0-471-27714-2 (pbk) : £7.95 B80-11416

539.6 — MOLECULAR PHYSICS

539′.6 — Molecules. Dynamics & structure - *Conference proceedings*

. Molecular ions, molecular structure and interaction with matter. — Bristol : Hilger, June 1981. — [450]p. — (Annals of the Israel Physical Society, ISSN 0309-8710 ; v.4)
Conference papers
ISBN 0-85274-441-2 : £25.00 : CIP entry B81-12791

539′.6 — Molecules. Dynamics. Quantum theory — *Conference proceedings*

NATO Advanced Study Institute on Quantum Dynamics of Molecules : the New Experimental Challenge to Theorists *(1979 : Cambridge)*. Quantum dynamics of molecules : the new experimental challenge to theorists / [proceedings of the NATO Advance Study Institute on Quantum Dynamics of Molecules : the New Experimental Challenge to Theorists, held at Trinity Hall, Cambridge, United Kingdom, September 15-29, 1979] ; edited by R.G. Woolley. — New York ; London : Plenum in cooperation with NATO Scientific Affairs Division, c1980. — xiv,557p : ill ; 26cm. — (NATO advanced study institutes series. Series B, Physics ; v.57)
Includes bibliographies and index
ISBN 0-306-40462-1 : Unpriced B81-06962

539′.6 — Molecules. Scattering. Semiclassical theory — *Conference proceedings*

Semiclassical methods in molecular scattering and spectroscopy : proceedings of the NATO ASI held in Cambridge, England in September 1979 / edited by M. S. Child. — Dordrecht ; London : Reidel published in cooperation with NATO Scientific Affairs Division, c1980. — xi,332p : ill ; 25cm. — (NATO advanced study institutes series. Series C, Mathematical and physical sciences ; v.53)
Includes index
ISBN 90-277-1082-1 : Unpriced
Also classified at 535.8′4 B81-05610

539′.6 — Polyatomic molecules. Vibration spectroscopy. Spectra. Measurement & interpretation
Papoušek, D.. Molecular vibrational-rotational spectra. — Oxford : Elsevier Scientific, Dec.1981. — [350]p. — (Studies in physical and theoretical chemistry ; 17)
ISBN 0-444-99737-7 : £40.00 : CIP entry B81-31832

539′.6′05 — Molecules. Interactions — *Serials*
Molecular interactions. — Vol.2. — Chichester : Wiley, c1981. — xxii,627p
ISBN 0-471-27681-2 : £39.00 B81-29430

539.7 — NUCLEAR PHYSICS

539.7 — Atoms. Interactions with electric fields & magnetic fields
Fraga, Serafin. Atoms in external fields / Serafin Fraga and Janina Muszyńska. — Amsterdam ; Oxford : Elsevier Scientific, 1981. — ix,557p : ill ; 25cm. — (Physical sciences data ; 8)
Bibliography: p555-557
ISBN 0-444-41936-5 : £46.23 B81-11138

539.7 — Atoms. Structure & physical properties — *For schools*
Bolton, W. (William), *1933-*. Atoms and quanta / W. Bolton. — London : Butterworths, 1980. — 96p : ill ; 25cm. — (Study topics in physics ; bk.7)
Bibliography: p.95. - Includes index
ISBN 0-408-10658-1 (pbk) : £1.60 B81-03437

539.7 — Nuclear physics
Growth points in nuclear physics. — Oxford : Pergamon
Vol.3. — Dec.1981. — [200]p
ISBN 0-08-026485-9 (cased) : £8.95 : CIP entry
ISBN 0-08-026484-0 (pbk) : £4.45 B81-31374

539′.7 — Thermodynamics
Rumer, IU. B.. Thermodynamics, statistical physics and kinetics / Yu. B. Rumer, M. Sh. Ryvkin ; translated from the Russian by S. Semyonov. — Moscow : Mir ; [London] (Central) [distributor], 1980. — 600p : ill ; 23cm
Translation of: Termodinamika, statisticheskaia fizika i kinetika. — Includes index
ISBN 0-7147-1599-9 : £5.95
Primary classification 530.1′3 B81-23403

539.7′02461 — Nuclear physics - *For medicine*
Dyson, N. A.. An introduction to nuclear physics, with applications in medicine and biology. — Chichester : Ellis Horwood, Sept.1981. — [256] p. — (Ellis Horwood series in physics in medicine & biology)
ISBN 0-85312-265-2 : £19.50 : CIP entry B81-20517

539.7′05 — Nuclear physics — *Conference proceedings — Serials*
Atomic physics. — 7. — New York ; London : Plenum, c1981. — x,573p
ISBN 0-306-40650-0 : Unpriced
ISSN 0090-6360 B81-35968

539.7′072 — Nuclear physics. Research organisations - *Directories - Serials*
World nuclear directory. — 6th ed. — London : Longman, Apr.1981. — 1v
Previous ed.: published as 'Nuclear research index'. St. Peter Port : Hodgson, 1976
ISBN 0-582-90010-7 : £70.00 : CIP entry B81-04302

539.7′072 — Nuclear physics. Research, *to 1955*
Snow, C. P.. The physicists / C.P. Snow ; introduction by William Cooper. — London : Macmillan, 1981. — 192p : ill,facsims,ports ; 25cm
Includes index
ISBN 0-333-32228-2 : £8.95 B81-40733

539.7′072042576 — Oxfordshire. Abingdon. Nuclear physics laboratories: Culham Laboratory — *Serials*
Culham Laboratory. Annual report / Culham Laboratory. — 1979. — Abingdon (UKAEA, Culham Laboratory, Abingdon, Oxon.) : The Laboratory, 1980. — vi,69p
ISSN 0309-7692 : £2.00 B81-06929

539.7′092′4 — Nuclear physics. Oppenheimer, J. Robert — *Biographies*
Goodchild, Peter, *1939-*. J. Robert Oppenheimer : Shatterer of Worlds / Peter Goodchild. — London : British Broadcasting Corporation, 1980. — 301p : ill,facsims,1map,ports ; 26cm
Bibliography: p291-292. — Includes index
ISBN 0-563-17781-0 : £9.95 B81-03108

539.7′2 — High energy physics
Orbis Scientiae *(1980 : Coral Gables)*. Recent developments in high-energy physics / [proceedings of Orbis Scientiae 1980 [held by the Center for Theoretical Studies, University of Miami, Coral Gables, Florida, January 14-17, 1980] ; Chairman Behram Kursunoglu ; editors Arnold Perlmutter, Linda F. Scott. — New York ; London : Plenum, c1980. — viii,311p : ill ; 26cm. — (Studies in the natural sciences ; v.17)
Includes index
ISBN 0-306-40565-2 : Unpriced B81-03533

539.7′2 — High energy physics — *Conference proceedings*
NATO Advanced Study Institute on Techniques and Concepts of High-Energy Physics *(1980 : Faile Conference Center)*. Techniques and concepts of high-energy physics / [proceedings of a NATO Advanced Study Institute on Techniques and Concepts of High-Energy Physics, held July 2-13, 1980, at the Faile Conference Center, St. Croix, US Virgin Islands] ; edited by Thomas Ferbel. — New York ; London : Plenum in cooperation with NATO Scientific Affairs Division, c1981. — xi,541p : ill ; 26cm. — (NATO advanced study institute series. Series B, Physics ; v.66)
Includes bibliographies and index
ISBN 0-306-40721-3 : Unpriced B81-40089

539.7′2 — High energy physics. Gauge theories
Lopes, J. Leite. Gauge field theories. — Oxford : Pergamon, Oct.1981. — [450]p
ISBN 0-08-026501-4 : £17.00 : CIP entry B81-24600

539.7′21 — Electric fields & magnetic fields. Charged particles. Motion
Artsimovich, L. A.. Motion of charged particles in electric and magnetic fields / L.A. Artsimovich and S. Yu Lukyanov ; translated from the Russian by Oleg Glebov. — Moscow : Mir, 1980 ; [London] : Distributed by Central Books. — 224p,[1]leaf of plates : ill(some col.) ; 21cm
Translation of: Dvizhenie zariazhennykh chastits v ėlektricheskikh i magnitnykh poliakh
ISBN 0-7147-1596-4 : £3.95 B81-23480

539.7′21 — Elementary particles
Cheng, David C.. Elementary particle physics : an introduction / David C. Cheng, Gerard K. O'Neill. — Reading, Mass. ; London : Addison-Wesley, 1979. — viii,423p : ill ; 25cm
Includes index
ISBN 0-201-05463-9 : £13.95 B81-05801

Progress in particle and nuclear physics. — Oxford : Pergamon
Vol.6: Nuclear astrophysics : proceedings of the International School of Nuclear Physics, Erice, 25 March-6 April, 1980 / edited by Sir Denys Wilkinson. — 1981. — 349p : ill ; 26cm
Includes index
ISBN 0-08-027117-0 : Unpriced B81-26165

Trefil, James S.. From atoms to quarks : an introduction to the strange world of particle physics / James S. Trefil. — London : Athlone, 1980. — xi,225p : ill ; 24cm
ISBN 0-485-11204-3 : £7.50 B80-08211

539.7′21 — Elementary particles — *Conference proceedings*
Guangzhou Conference on Theoretical Particle Physics *(1980 : Conghua)*. Proceedings of the 1980 Guangzhou Conference on Theoretical Particle Physics. — Beijing : Science Press ; London : Van Nostrand Reinhold [distributor], 1980. — 2v(xiv,1765p) : ill ; 25cm
English text, English and Chinese foreword
ISBN 0-442-20273-3 : £67.15 B81-10188

International School of Subnuclear Physics *(16th : 1978 : Erice)*. The new aspects of subnuclear physics : [proceedings of the Sixteenth International School of Subnuclear Physics, held in Erice, Sicily, July 31-August 11, 1978] / edited by Antonino Zichichi. — New York ; London : Plenum, c1980. — viii,805p : ill ; 26cm. — (The Subnuclear series ; v.16)
Includes index
ISBN 0-306-40459-1 : Unpriced B81-24477

539.7′21 — Elementary particles. Gauge theories
Aitchison, Ian J. R.. Gauge theories in particle physics. — Bristol : Hilger, Dec.1981. — [366]p
ISBN 0-85274-534-6 : £14.50 : CIP entry B81-31510

539.7′21 — Elementary particles. Quantum theory. Density matrices
Blum, Karl. Density matrix theory and applications / Karl Blum. — New York ; London : Plenum, c1981. — xii,217p : ill ; 24cm. — (Physics of atoms and molecules)
Bibliography: p213-214. — Includes index
ISBN 0-306-40819-8 : Unpriced B81-38259

539.7′21 — Elementary particles. Symmetry
Gibson, W. M.. Symmetry principles in elementary particle physics / W.M. Gibson, B.R. Pollard. — Cambridge : Cambridge University Press, 1976 (1980 [printing]). — xi,386p : ill ; 22cm. — (Cambridge monographs on physics)
Bibliography: p373-378. — Includes index
ISBN 0-521-29964-0 (pbk) : £9.95 : CIP rev. B80-11417

539.7′21 — Excitons
Reynolds, Donald C.. Excitons : their properties and uses / Donald C. Reynolds, Thomas C. Collins. — New York ; London : Academic Press, c1981. — x,291p : ill ; 24cm
Includes index
ISBN 0-12-586580-5 : £20.20 B81-19044

539.7′21 — Particles. Relativistic quantum theory
Barut, A. O.. Electrodynamics and classical theory of fields & particles / A.O. Barut. — Corr. republication. — New York : Dover ; London : Constable, 1980. — xv,235p : ill ; 21cm
Originally published: London : Collier Macmillan, 1964. — Bibliography: p221. - Includes index
ISBN 0-486-64038-8 (pbk) : £2.60
Primary classification 530.1′43 B81-18494

539.7′21 — Particles. Superposition. Quantum theory
Schlegel, Richard. Superposition & interaction : coherence in physics / Richard Schlegel. — Chicago ; London : University of Chicago Press, 1980. — xii,302p : ill ; 24cm
Includes index
ISBN 0-226-73841-8 : £13.50 B81-12684

539.7′21 — Quarks — *Conference proceedings*
Cargèse Summer Institute on Quarks and Leptons *(1979)*. Quarks and leptons : Cargèse 1979 / [proceedings of the 1979 Cargèse Summer Institute on Quarks and Leptons, held in Cargèse, Corsica, July 9-29, 1979] ; edited by Maurice Lévy ... [et al.]. — New York ; London : Plenum published in cooperation with NATO Scientific Affairs Division, c1980. — xvi,720p : ill ; 26cm. — (NATO advanced study institutes series. Series B, Physics ; vol.61)
Includes index
ISBN 0-306-40560-1 : Unpriced
Also classified at 539.7′211 B81-13383

539.7′21 — Quarks. Statistical mechanics — *Conference proceedings*
Statistical mechanics of quarks and hadrons : proceedings of an international symposium, held at the University of Bielefeld, F.R.G., August 24-31, 1980 / edited by Helmut Satz. — Amsterdam ; Oxford : North-Holland, c1981. — xii,479p : ill ; 23cm
ISBN 0-444-86227-7 : Unpriced
Primary classification 539.7′216 B81-39202

539.7′21′028 — Many-Fermion systems. Statistical analysis. Moment methods — *Conference proceedings*

International Conference on Theory and Applications of Moment Methods in Many-Fermion Systems-Spectral Distribution Methods *(1979 : Iowa State University)*. Theory and applications of moment methods in many-Fermion systems / [proceedings of the International Conference on Theory and Applications of Moment Methods in Many-Fermion Systems-Spectral Distribution Methods, held at Iowa State University, Ames, Iowa, September 10-14, 1979] ; edited by B.J. Dalton ... [et al.]. — New York ; London : Plenum, c1980. — ix,511p : ill ; 25cm
Includes index
ISBN 0-306-40463-x : Unpriced B81-06005

539.7′21′05 — Elementary particles — *Serials*

Progress in particle and nuclear physics. — Vol.5. — Oxford : Pergamon, 1981. — 285p
ISBN 0-08-027109-x : Unpriced : CIP rev.
ISSN 0146-6410 B80-28325

Progress in particle and nuclear physics. — Vol.7. — Oxford : Pergamon, 1981. — v, 316p
ISBN 0-08-027152-9 : Unpriced : CIP rev.
ISSN 0146-6410 B81-07471

Progress in particle and nuclear physics. — Vol.8. — Oxford : Pergamon, Feb.1982. — [420]p
ISBN 0-08-029103-1 : £45.00 : CIP entry B81-38331

539.7′211 — Leptons — *Conference proceedings*

Cargèse Summer Institute on Quarks and Leptons *(1979)*. Quarks and leptons : Cargèse 1979 / [proceedings of the 1979 Cargèse Summer Institute on Quarks and Leptons, held in Cargèse, Corsica, July 9-29, 1979] ; edited by Maurice Lévy ... [et al.]. — New York ; London : Plenum published in cooperation with NATO Scientific Affairs Division, c1980. — xvi,720p : ill ; 26cm. — (NATO advanced study institutes series. Series B, Physics ; vol.61)
Includes index
ISBN 0-306-40560-1 : Unpriced
Primary classification 539.7′21 B81-13383

539.7′2112 — Electron spectroscopy - *Serials*

Electron spectroscopy. — London : Academic Press, Apr.1981
Vol.4. — [500]p
ISBN 0-12-137804-7 : CIP entry B81-06066

539.7′2112 — Electron transfer reactions

Cannon, Roderick D.. Electron transfer reactions / R.D. Cannon. — London : Butterworths, 1980. — xi,351p : ill ; 24cm
Bibliography: p315-338. — Includes index
ISBN 0-408-10646-8 : £32.00 : CIP rev. B79-36798

539.7′213 — Neutrons. Scattering — *Conference proceedings*

Neutron scattering in biology, chemistry and physics : a Royal Society discussion / organized by Sir Ronald Mason, E.W.J. Mitchell and J.W. White, held on 26 and 27 September 1979. — London : Royal Society, 1980. — viii,201p : ill ; 31cm
Includes bibliographies
ISBN 0-85403-151-0 : £19.50 B81-07134

539.7′213 — Pulsed neutrons. Scattering

Windsor, C. G.. Pulsed neutron scattering. — London : Taylor and Francis, Sept.1981. — [440]p
ISBN 0-85066-195-1 : £25.00 : CIP entry B81-20509

539.7′216 — Hadrons. Statistical mechanics — *Conference proceedings*

Statistical mechanics of quarks and hadrons : proceedings of an international symposium, held at the University of Bielefeld, F.R.G., August 24-31, 1980 / edited by Helmut Satz. — Amsterdam ; Oxford : North-Holland, c1981. — xii,479p : ill ; 23cm
ISBN 0-444-86227-7 : Unpriced
Also classified at 539.7′21 B81-39202

539.7′222 — Accidental x-rays

Martin, E. B. M.. Adventitious X-rays. — Northwood : Science Reviews, Dec.1981. — [120]p. — (Occupational hygiene monographs, ISSN 0141-7568 ; 7)
ISBN 0-905927-90-7 (pbk) : £5.00 : CIP entry B81-36995

539.7′3 — Particle accelerators — *Conference proceedings*

Adriatic Summer Meeting on Particle Physics *(3rd : 1980 : Dubrovnik)*. Particle physics 1980 : proceedings of the 3rd Adriatic Summer Meeting on Particle Physics, Dubrovnik, Yugoslavia, September 3-13, 1980 / edited by Ivan Andri′c, Ivan Dadi′c, Nikola Zovko. — Amsterdam ; Oxford : North-Holland, c1981. — viii,499p : ill ; 23cm
Includes index
ISBN 0-444-86174-2 : Unpriced B81-25515

539.7′4 — Atoms. Nuclei. Structure & properties

Lawson, R. D.. Theory of the nuclear shell model / R.D. Lawson. — Oxford : Clarendon Press, 1980. — xii,534p : ill ; 24cm. — (Oxford studies in nuclear physics)
Bibliography: p509-518. - Includes index
ISBN 0-19-851516-2 : £45.00 : CIP rev. B79-15387

539.7′5 — Kaons. Interactions with nucleons — *Conference proceedings*

Low and intermediate energy kaon-nucleon physics : proceedings of the Workshop held at the Institute of Physics of the University of Rome, March 24-28, 1980 / edited by E. Ferrari and G. Violini. — Dordrecht ; London : Reidel, c1981. — xi,428p : ill ; 25cm
Includes index
ISBN 90-277-1183-6 : Unpriced B81-13325

539.7′5 — Nuclear reactions, *1896-1979*

Transmutation. — London : Heyden, Aug.1981. — [130]p. — (Nobel prize topics in chemistry)
ISBN 0-85501-685-x (cased) : £12.00 : CIP entry
ISBN 0-85501-686-8 (pbk) : 5.50 B81-22594

539.7′54 — Atoms. Nuclei. Interactions with elementary particles

Strong and electromagnetic interactions of elementary particles and nuclei / edited by N.G. Basov ; translated from the Russian by Harold H. McFaden. — New York ; London : Consultants Bureau, c1980. — 206p : ill ; 28cm. — (Proceedings (Trudy) of the P.N. Lebedev Physics Institute ; v.95)
Translation of: Sil′nye i elektromagnitye vzaimodeĭstviīa elementarnykh chastits i īader
ISBN 0-306-10965-4 (pbk) : Unpriced B81-19758

539.7′54 — Elementary particles. Interactions — *Conference proceedings*

Europhysics Study Conference on Unification of the Fundamental Particle Interactions *(1980 : Erice)*. Unification of the fundamental particle interactions / [proceedings of the Europhysics Study Conference on Unification of the Fundamental Particle Interactions held in Erice, Sicily, March 17-24, 1980] ; edited by Sergio Ferrara, John Ellis and Peter van Nieuwenhuizen. — New York ; London : Plenum, c1980. — xii,727p : ill,1port ; 26cm. — (Ettore Majorana international science series. Physical sciences ; v.7)
Includes index
ISBN 0-306-40575-x : Unpriced B81-17157

539.7′54 — Leptons. Interactions with hadrons — *Conference proceedings*

Seminar on Probing Hadrons with Leptons *(4th : 1979 : Erice)*. Probing hadrons with leptons / [proceedings of the Fourth Seminar on Probing Hadrons with Leptons, held in Erice, Sicily, in March, 1979] ; edited by Giuliano Preparata and Jean-Jacques Aubert. — New York ; London : Plenum, c1980. — x,507p : ill ; 26cm. — (Ettore Majorana international science series. Physical sciences ; v.5)
Includes index
ISBN 0-306-40438-9 : Unpriced B81-03309

539.7′62 — Atoms. Nuclei. Fission

Nuclear fission and neutron-induced fission cross-sections / G.D. James ... [et al.]. — Oxford : Pergamon, 1981. — xv,277p : ill ; 26cm. — (Neutron physics and nuclear data in science and technology ; v.1)
Bibliography: p227-248. — Includes index
ISBN 0-08-026125-6 : £25.00 B81-17238

539.7′62′072044 — France. Nuclear fission. Research. Political aspects, *to 1950*

Weart, Spencer R.. Scientists in power / Spencer R. Weart. — Cambridge, Mass. ; London : Harvard University Press, 1979. — xiii,343,[8]p of plates : ill,1map,ports ; 25cm
Bibliography: p279-291. - Includes index
ISBN 0-674-79515-6 : £12.95 B81-11313

539.7′62′0904 — Nuclear fission. Research, *1919-1979*

Clark, Ronald W.. The greatest power on earth : the story of nuclear fission / Ronald W. Clark ; foreword by Lord Zuckerman. — London : Sidgwick & Jackson, 1980. — xii,342p,[16]p of plates : ill,1facsim,ports ; 24cm
Bibliography: p299-04. - Includes index
ISBN 0-283-98715-4 : £8.95 B81-04150

539.7′7 — Solids. Nuclear tracks. Detection — *Conference proceedings*

Solid state nuclear track detectors. — Oxford : Pergamon, Jan.1982. — [990]p
Conference papers
ISBN 0-08-026509-x : £100.00 : CIP entry B81-39234

539.7′7′05 — Dosimetry — *Serials*

Radiation protection dosimetry. — Vol.1, no.1 (1981)-. — Ashford (P.O. Box No.7, Ashford, Kent) : Nuclear Technology Publishing, 1981-. — v. : ill ; 25cm
Quarterly
ISSN 0144-8420 = Radiation protection dosimetry : £30.00 per year B81-30008

540 — CHEMISTRY(INCLUDING CRYSTALLOGRAPHY, MINERALOGY)

540 — Chemistry

Abrash, Henry I.. Chemistry / Henry I. Abrash, Kenneth I. Hardcastle. — Encino : Glencoe ; London : Collier Macmillan, c1981. — xxvi,676p : ill(some col.) ; 29cm
Text on lining papers. — Includes index
ISBN 0-02-471100-4 : £11.95 B81-15615

Brady, James E.. Fundamentals of chemistry / James E. Brady, John R. Holum. — New York ; Chichester : Wiley, c1981. — xvii,797p,[8]p of plates : ill(some col.),ports ; 26cm
Text and ill. on lining papers. — Includes index
ISBN 0-471-05816-5 : £13.75 B81-18444

Brown, Theodore L.. Chemistry : the central science / Theodore L. Brown, H. Eugene LeMay, Jr. — 2nd ed. — Englewood Cliffs ; London : Prentice Hall, c1981. — xxii,843p : ill(some col.),ports ; 27cm
Previous ed.: 1977. — Text on lining papers. — Includes index
ISBN 0-13-128504-1 : £14.90 B81-16542

Chemistry with inorganic qualitative analysis / Therald Moeller ... [et al.]. — New York ; London : Academic Press, c1980. — xxx,1085,[36]p : ill(some col.) ; 27cm
Text on lining papers. — Includes index
ISBN 0-12-503350-8 : Unpriced B81-00873

Malone, Leo J.. Basic concepts of chemistry / Leo J. Malone. — New York ; Chichester : Wiley, c1981. — xiv,454p : ill(some col.) ; 25cm
Text on lining papers. — Includes index
ISBN 0-471-06381-9 : £9.50 B81-16339

Seese, William S.. Basic chemistry / William S. Seese, Guido H. Daub. — 3rd ed. — Englewood Cliffs ; London : Prentice Hall, c1981. — xiv,596,I12p : ill(some col.) ; 24cm
Previous ed.: c1977. — Text on lining papers. — Includes bibliographies and index
ISBN 0-13-057653-0 : £12.95 B81-16540

540 — Chemistry *continuation*

Selvaratnam, M.. Problem solving in general chemistry. — London : Heinemann Educational, Jan.1982. — [240]p
ISBN 0-435-65257-5 (pbk) : £4.95 : CIP entry B81-34498

Stine, William R.. Applied chemistry / William R. Stine ; contributors, Owen D. Faut, Mary Rees, Edward B. Stockham. — 2nd ed. — Boston, Mass. ; London : Allyn and Bacon, c1981. — xvi,558p : ill(some col.),col.maps,1port ; 25cm
Previous ed.: published as Chemistry for the consumer. 1978. — Text on lining papers. — Includes index
ISBN 0-205-07313-1 : £8.95 B81-16297

Widom, Joanne M.. Chemistry : an introduction to general, organic, and biological chemistry / Joanne M. Widom, Stuart J. Edelstein. — Oxford : W.H. Freeman, c1981. — xiv,743,A-36,I-20p : ill(some col.) ; 25cm
Text on lining papers. — Includes index
ISBN 0-7167-1224-5 : £13.95
ISBN 0-7167-1314-4 (Study guide) : £4.95 B81-33652

540 — Chemistry — *For schools*

Buttle, J. W.. Chemistry. — 4th ed. — London : Butterworths, July 1981. — [652]p
Previous ed.: 1974
ISBN 0-408-70938-3 (pbk) : £6.95 : CIP entry B81-19143

Combined chemistry / J. Brockington ... [et al.]. — Harlow : Longman, 1981. — xviii,684p : ill ; 25cm
Includes index
ISBN 0-582-35183-9 (pbk) : £7.95 B81-29750

Focus on chemistry : a course for first examinations / edited by R.T. Allsop, R.S. Lowrie. — Exeter : Wheaton, 1981. — 130p : ill ; 24cm
Includes index
ISBN 0-08-024977-9 (pbk) : £3.60 B81-11452

Hughes, A. M. (Andrew Michael). Chemistry in balance / A.M. Hughes. — Slough : University Tutorial Press, 1981. — 199p : ill ; 20x21cm
Includes index
ISBN 0-7231-0814-5 (pbk) : £2.60 B81-27072

An **Illustrated** coursebook chemistry / consultant Kenneth Murfitt ; translated by Bob Wright. — London : Macdonald Educational, c1981. — 160p : chiefly col.ill,1map ; 23cm
Translation from the German. — Includes index
ISBN 0-356-06314-3 (pbk) : Unpriced B81-36801

Investigating chemistry. — 2nd ed. — London : Heinemann Educational, July 1981
Previous ed.: / by L. Davies and others. 1973
Pupil's book. — [576]p
ISBN 0-435-64166-2 (pbk) : £3.75 : CIP entry B81-13821

Johnstone, A. H.. Chemistry about us / A.H. Johnstone, T.I. Morrison, N. Reid. — London : Heinemann Educational, 1981. — xii,260p : ill ; 24cm
Includes index
ISBN 0-435-64499-8 (pbk) : £3.80 B81-09531

Ramsden, E. N.. Revision notes in chemistry / E.N. Ramsden. — Cheltenham : Thornes, 1981. — 113p : ill(some col) ; 19cm. — (ST(P) revision notes series)
ISBN 0-85950-498-0 (pbk) : £1.95 : CIP rev. B80-36060

Slater, Bryan. A foundation course in chemistry. — Basingstoke : Macmillan Education, Feb.1982. — [160]p
ISBN 0-333-25515-1 (pbk) : £2.65 : CIP entry B81-35799

Underwood, D. N.. Chemistry / D.N. Underwood, D.E. Webster. — 5th ed. — London : Edward Arnold, 1981. — viii,540p : ill ; 23cm
Previous ed.: 1976. — Includes index
ISBN 0-7131-0516-x (pbk) : £4.50 B81-31870

540 — Chemistry. Projects — *For schools*

Stone, R. H. (Robert Henry). Projects in chemistry / R.H. Stone and D.W.H. Tripp ; illustrated by David and Maureen Embry. — London : Routledge & Kegan Paul, 1981. — xi,106p : ill ; 25cm. — (Secondary science series)
ISBN 0-7100-0801-5 (pbk) : £4.95 : CIP rev. B81-06617

540′.1′12 — Alchemy

Coudert, Allison. Alchemy : the philosophers stone / Allison Coudert. — London : Wildwood, 1980. — 239p : ill,facsims ; 26cm
Bibliography: p222-230. - Includes index
ISBN 0-7045-0413-8 (pbk) : £5.95 B81-00874

540′.1′12 — Alchemy — *Early works*

[**Rosarium philosophorum.** *English*]. The rosary of the philosophers / edited with a commentary by Adam McLean. — Edinburgh (12 Antigua St., Edinburgh) : [A. McLean], c1980. — 130p : ill(some col.) ; 22cm. — (Magnum opus hermetic sourceworks ; no.6)
Translation of: Rosarium philosophorum, from a ms. in the Ferguson Collection of Glasgow University. — Limited ed. of 250 copies. — Bibliography: p5
Unpriced B81-34440

540.1′41 — Electromagnetic waves. Scattering

Bayvel, L. P.. Electromagnetic scattering and its applications. — London : Applied Science, Aug.1981. — [304]p
ISBN 0-85334-955-x : £24.00 : CIP entry B81-17510

540′.1′51 — Chemistry. Calculations — *For schools*

Ramsden, E. N.. Calculations for A-Level chemistry. — Cheltenham : Thornes, Dec.1981. — [296]p
ISBN 0-85950-309-7 (pbk) : £3.50 : CIP entry B81-31813

Ramsden, E. N.. Calculations for O-level chemistry / E.N. Ramsden. — Cheltenham : Thornes, c1981. — v,151p : ill ; 22cm
Includes index
ISBN 0-85950-312-7 (pbk) : £2.25 : CIP rev. B81-11963

540′.1′51 — Chemistry. Calculations — *Questions & answers*

Solutions manual for Fundamentals of chemistry, 4th ed. / Brescia ... [et al.]. — New York ; London : Academic Press, c1980. — 197p : ill ; 23cm
ISBN 0-12-132396-x (pbk) : £0.60 B81-14603

540′.1′51 — Chemistry. Calculations — *Questions & answers — For schools*

Holderness, A.. A class book of problems in chemistry : to Advanced level : with answers / A. Holderness and John Lambert. — 4th ed. — London : Heinemann Educational, 1980. — iv,56p ; 22cm. — (Heinemann books for advanced level chemistry)
Previous ed.: 1971
ISBN 0-435-65439-x (pbk) : £1.50 B81-06364

540′.1′51 — Chemistry. Numerical methods

Norris, A. C.. Computational chemistry : an introduction to numerical methods / A.C. Norris. — Chichester : Wiley, c1981. — xiii,454p : ill ; 24cm
Includes index
ISBN 0-471-27949-8 (cased) : £19.75
ISBN 0-471-27950-1 (pbk) : Unpriced B81-39797

540′.23′41 — Great Britain. Chemists — *Codes of conduct*

Royal Society of Chemistry. Guidance on standards of conduct / [Royal Society of Chemistry. — London : The Society, c1981. — 28p ; 20cm
£5.00 (free to members) (pbk) B81-37661

540′.23′41 — Great Britain. Consultant chemists — *Codes of conduct*

Royal Society of Chemistry. Guide for consultancy / [Royal Society of Chemistry. — 3rd rev. ed. — London : The Society, c1981. — 9p ; 20cm
£1.00 (free to members) (pbk) B81-37660

540′.24574 — Chemistry — *For ecology*

Hay, R. K. M.. Chemistry for agriculture and ecology : a foundation course / R.K.M. Hay. — Oxford : Blackwell Scientific, 1981. — xi,243p : ill ; 22cm
Includes bibliographies and index
ISBN 0-632-00699-4 (pbk) : £5.50
Also classified at 540′.2463 B81-18891

540′.246 — Chemistry — *For technicians*

Brockington, John. Technician chemistry, Level 1. — London : Longman, June 1981. — [224] p. — (Longman technician series)
ISBN 0-582-41593-4 (pbk) : £4.95 : CIP entry B81-14942

Hawkins, M. D.. Technician chemistry 2 / M.D. Hawkins. — London : Cassell, 1981. — xiv,334p : ill ; 22cm. — (Cassell's TEC series)
Includes index
ISBN 0-304-30549-9 (pbk) : Unpriced B81-40566

540′.246 — Chemistry — *Questions & answers — For technicians*

Chivers, P. J.. Chemistry 2 checkbook / P.J. Chivers. — London : Butterworths, 1981. — vi,161p : ill ; 20cm. — (Butterworths technical and scientific checkbooks. Level 2)
Previous control number ISBN 0-408-00622-6. — Includes index
ISBN 0-408-00637-4 (cased) : Unpriced
ISBN 0-408-00622-6 (pbk) : Unpriced B81-36187

540′.2461 — Chemistry — *For medicine*

Taylor, J. B.. Introductory medicinal chemistry. — Chichester : Ellis Horwood, Aug.1981. — [224]p
ISBN 0-85312-207-5 : £20.00 : CIP entry B81-20516

540′.24613 — Chemistry — *For tropical nursing*

Duckworth, F. O.. Physics and chemistry / F.O. Dosekun. — London : Macmillan, 1980. — 260p : ill ; 25cm. — (Macmillan Tropical nursing and health sciences series)
Includes index
ISBN 0-333-28441-0 (pbk) : £4.95 : CIP rev.
Primary classification 530′.024613 B80-29589

540′.2463 — Chemistry — *For agriculture*

Hay, R. K. M.. Chemistry for agriculture and ecology : a foundation course / R.K.M. Hay. — Oxford : Blackwell Scientific, 1981. — xi,243p : ill ; 22cm
Includes bibliographies and index
ISBN 0-632-00699-4 (pbk) : £5.50
Primary classification 540′.24574 B81-18891

540′.3 — Chemistry — *Polyglot dictionaries*

Dictionary of chemical terminology : in five languages : English, German, French, Polish, Russian / edited by Dobromiła Kryt. — Amsterdam ; Oxford : Elsevier Scientific, 1980. — 600p ; 25cm
Includes index
ISBN 0-444-99788-1 : Unpriced B81-04132

540′.3′21 — Chemistry — *Encyclopaedias*

The **Condensed** chemical dictionary. — 10th ed. / revised by Gessner G. Hawley. — New York ; London : Van Nostrand Reinhold, 1981. — xi,1135p ; 25cm
Previous ed.: 1977. — Text on lining papers
ISBN 0-442-23244-6 : £27.50 B81-25381

Miall's dictionary of chemistry. — 5th ed. / edited by D.W.A. Sharp. — Harlow : Longman, 1981. — ix,501p : ill ; 24cm
Previous ed.: published as A New dictionary of chemistry. 1968
ISBN 0-582-35152-9 : £25.00 B81-23678

540′.5 — Chemistry — *Serials*
Survey of progress in chemistry. — Vol.9. — New York ; London : Academic Press, 1980. — x,271p
ISBN 0-12-610509-x : Unpriced B81-02995

540′.6′041 — Great Britain. Chemistry. Organisations: Royal Society of Chemistry — *Directories — Serials*
Royal Society of Chemistry. Register of members / the Royal Society of Chemistry. — 1980-. — London : The Society, c1980-. — v. ; 30cm
Irregular. — Spine title: RSC register. — Continues: Register of members (Chemical Society)
ISSN 0260-3039 = Register of members - Royal Society of Chemistry : Unpriced
B81-00875

540′.7 — Chemistry. Information sources — *Serials*
[**Newsletter** *(Royal Society of Chemistry. Information Services)*]. Newsletter / Royal Society of Chemistry Information Services. — No.8 (Nov.1980)-. — Nottingham (The University, Nottingham NG7 2RD) : The Society, 1980-. — v. ; 30cm
Three issues yearly. — Continues: UKCIS newsletter
ISSN 0260-4140 = Newsletter — Royal Society of Chemistry. Information Services : Unpriced B81-06683

540′.72041 — Chemistry. Research projects supported by Great Britain. *Science Research Council — Directories — Serials*
Current grants in chemistry. — 1 May 1980. — Swindon : Science Research Council, 1981. — 156p
Unpriced B81-13213

540′.76 — Chemistry — *Questions & answers*
Jenkins, E. W.. Resource book of test items in chemistry / E.W. Jenkins. — London : Murray, 1981. — vi,106p : ill ; 29cm
Bibliography: p15
ISBN 0-7195-3849-1 (pbk) : £3.50 : CIP rev.
B81-03707

Sorum, C. H.. How to solve general chemistry problems. — 6th ed. / C.H. Sorum, R.S. Boikess. — Englewood Cliffs ; London : Prentice-Hall, c1981. — ix,326p : ill ; 23cm
Previous ed.: 1976. — Text on inside covers. — Includes index
ISBN 0-13-434126-0 (pbk) : £7.10 B81-17281

Stine, William R.. Instructor′s manual to accompany Applied chemistry. 2nd ed / William R. Stine, Joseph G. Helinski. — Boston [Mass.] ; London : Allyn and Bacon, c1981. — I-50,II-106p ; 22cm
ISBN 0-205-07314-x (pbk) : £1.00 B81-26434

540′.76 — Chemistry — *Questions & answers — For schools*
Brown, Peter. Questions in ′A′ level chemistry. — London : Edward Arnold, Sept.1981. — [96]p
ISBN 0-7131-0578-x (pbk) : CIP entry
B81-22485

Brown, Peter. Solutions in ′A′ level chemistry. — London : Edward Arnold, Sept.1981. — [128]p
ISBN 0-7131-0579-8 (pbk) : CIP entry
B81-22513

Crawley, S.. Objective tests in chemistry : higher and advanced level / by S. Crawley. — Glasgow : Gibson, 1980. — 48p : ill ; 21cm
ISBN 0-7169-6950-5 (pbk) : Unpriced
B81-13052

Pandit, V.. Model answers G.C.E. Advanced Level chemistry : London board / V. Pandit. — London (9, Ellerslie Rd, W12 7BN) : V. Pandit, c1981. — 124p : ill ; 22cm
ISBN 0-9507233-2-0 (pbk) : £2.50 B81-38551

Stebbens, Derek. Multiple-choice questions for A-Level chemistry / Derek Stebbens. — London : Butterworths, 1980. — vii,184p : ill ; 25cm
ISBN 0-408-10644-1 (pbk) : £2.95 : CIP rev.
B80-00178

Wood, C. A.. Questions in chemistry to O and H grade. — London : Heinemann Educational, Oct.1981. — [112]p
ISBN 0-435-64970-1 (pbk) : £1.95 : CIP entry
B81-28166

540′.92′4 — Chemistry. Curie, Marie — *Biographies — For children*
Brandon, Ruth. Marie Curie. — London : Hodder and Stoughton, Sept.1981. — [128]p. — (Twentieth century people)
ISBN 0-340-25951-5 : £4.95 : CIP entry
B81-25669

540′.92′4 — Chemistry. Pasteur, Louis — *Biographies — For children*
Le Guevellou, Jean-Marie. Louis Pasteur / Jean-Marie Le Guevellou ; illustrated by Pierre Brochard ; [translated by Merle Philo]. — St. Albans : Hart-Davis, 1981. — 30p : col.ill ; 25cm. — (Junior histories)
Translation of the French
ISBN 0-247-13216-0 : £2.95 B81-39465

541 — PHYSICAL AND THEORETICAL CHEMISTRY

541′.042′1 — Solid state materials. Reactivity — *Conference proceedings*
International Symposium on the Reactivity of Solids *(9th : 1980 : Cracow)*. Reactivity of solids. — Oxford : Elsevier Scientific, Jan.1982. — 2v. ([1500]p.). — (Materials science monographs ; 10)
ISBN 0-444-99707-5 : £100.00 : CIP entry
B81-34564

541′.0421 — Solids. Nuclear magnetic resonance spectroscopy — *Conference proceedings*
Nuclear magnetic resonance spectroscopy in solids : a Royal Society discussion / organized by Sir Rex Richards and K.J. Packer, held on 18 and 19 June 1980. — London : Royal Society, 1981. — iv,p477-686 : ill ; 31cm
Originally published in Philosophical transactions of the Royal Society of London, Series A, v.299, no.1452, 1981. — Includes bibliographies
ISBN 0-85403-160-x : £20.00 B81-22057

541′.0421 — Solids. Valency. Variation — *Conference proceedings*
Santa Barbara Institute for Theoretical Physics. *Conference (1981)*. Valence fluctuations in solids : Santa Barbara Institute for Theoretical Physics Conference, Santa Barbara, California, January 27-30, 1981 / edited by L.M. Falicov, W. Hanke, M.B. Maple. — Amsterdam ; Oxford : North-Holland, c1981. — xi,465p : ill ; 27cm
ISBN 0-444-86204-8 : Unpriced B81-35562

541′.0421′05 — Solids. Chemical properties — *Serials*
Chemical physics of solids and their surfaces. — Vol.8. — London (Burlington House, W1V 0BN) : Royal Society of Chemistry, c1980. — x, 250p. — (Specialist periodical report / Royal Society of Chemistry)
ISBN 0-85186-740-5 : Unpriced : CIP rev.
ISSN 0142-3401
Primary classification 541.3′453′05 B80-19761

541′.0422 — Liquids. High pressure chemistry
Isaacs, Neil S.. Liquid phase high pressure chemistry / Neil S. Isaacs. — Chichester : Wiley, c1981. — vii,414p : ill ; 24cm
Text on inside covers. — Bibliography: p404. - Includes index
ISBN 0-471-27849-1 : £33.00 B81-13074

541.0′95 — Catalysis — *Conference proceedings*
Jerusalem Symposium on Quantum Chemistry and Biochemistry *(12th : 1979)*. Catalysis in chemistry and biochemistry : theory and experiment : proceedings of the Twelth Jerusalem Symposium on Quantum Chemistry and Biochemistry held in Jerusalem, Israel, April 2-4, 1979 / edited by Bernard Pullman. — Dordrecht ; London : Reidel, c1979. — vii,390p : ill ; 25cm. — (The Jerusalem symposium on quantum chemistry and biochemistry ; v.12)
Includes index
ISBN 90-277-1039-2 : Unpriced B81-01676

541.2 — THEORETICAL CHEMISTRY

541.2 — Atoms & molecules. Chemical properties. Determination. Use of electric potentials — *Conference proceedings*
Chemical applications of atomic and molecular electrostatic potentials : reactivity, structure, scattering and energetics of organic, inorganic, and biological systems / edited by Peter Politzer and Donald G. Truhlar. — New York ; London : Plenum, c1981. — ix,472p : ill ; 26cm
Conference papers. — Includes index
ISBN 0-306-40657-8 : Unpriced B81-24217

541.2′05 — Theoretical chemistry — *Serials*
[**Theoretical chemistry** *(London : 1974)*].
Theoretical chemistry. — Vol.4. — London : Royal Society of Chemistry, c1981. — x,177. — (Specialist periodical report / Royal Society of Chemistry)
ISBN 0-85186-784-7 : Unpriced : CIP rev.
ISSN 0305-9995 B81-10435

[**Theoretical chemistry** *(New York : 1975)*].
Theoretical chemistry. — Vol.5. — New York ; London : Academic Press, 1980. — xiii,267p
ISBN 0-12-681905-x : Unpriced
ISSN 0361-0551 B81-04937

[**Theoretical chemistry** *(New York : 1975)*].
Theoretical chemistry. — Vol.6, pt.A. — New York ; London : Academic Press, 1981. — xiii,299p
ISBN 0-12-681906-8 : £25.20
ISSN 0361-0551 B81-35100

541.2′2 — Molecules. Structure. Determination. Physicochemical techniques
Wheatley, P. J.. The determination of molecular structure / by P.J. Wheatley. — 2nd ed. — New York : Dover ; London : Constable, 1981, c1968. — vi,264p : ill ; 21cm
Originally published: Oxford : Clarendon Press, 1968. — Includes index
ISBN 0-486-64068-x (pbk) : £3.45 B81-39075

541.2′23 — Inorganic compounds. Stereochemistry
Burdett, Jeremy K.. Molecular shapes : theoretical models of inorganic stereochemistry / Jeremy K. Burdett. — New York ; Chichester : Wiley, c1980. — xi,287p : ill ; 24cm
Bibliography: p276-282. - Includes index
ISBN 0-471-07860-3 : £15.75 B81-02956

541.2′23′01516 — Stereochemistry. Applications of distance geometry
Crippen, G. M.. Distance geometry and conformational calculations / G.M. Crippen. — Chichester : Research Studies Press, c1981. — 58p : ill ; 29cm. — (Chemometrics research studies series ; 1)
Bibliography: p55. — Includes index
ISBN 0-471-27991-9 (pbk) : £10.00 : CIP rev.
B81-07615

541.2′23′05 — Stereochemistry — *Serials*
Topics in stereochemistry. — Vol.12. — New York ; Chichester : Wiley, c1981. — x,352p
ISBN 0-471-05292-2 : £37.50
ISSN 0082-500x B81-24100

541.2′24 — Chemical compounds. Mixed valency — *Conference proceedings*
NATO Advanced Study Institute *(1979 : Oxford)*
Mixed-valence compounds : theory and applications in chemistry, physics, geology, and biology : proceedings of the NATO Advanced Study Institute held at Oxford, England, September 9-21, 1979 / edited by David B. Brown. — Dordrecht ; London : Reidel, c1980. — viii,519p : ill ; 25cm. — (NATO advanced study institutes series. Series C, Mathematical and physical sciences ; v.58)
Includes index
ISBN 90-277-1152-6 : Unpriced B81-03810

541.2′24 — Free radicals
Scott, P. R.. Odd-electron species. — Cambridge : Cambridge University Press, Oct.1981. — [128]p
ISBN 0-521-28177-6 (pbk) : £2.85 : CIP entry
B81-31279

541.2'24 — Free radicals — *Conference proceedings*

Frontiers of Free Radical Chemistry *(Conference : 1979 : Louisiana State University)*. Frontiers of free radical chemistry : ... based on papers prepared by speakers in a symposium entitled 'Frontiers of Free Radical Chemistry', held at Louisiana State University in Baton Rouge, Louisiana, in April 10-11, 1979, and sponsored by Exxon Education Foundation / edited by William A. Pryor. — New York ; London : Academic Press, 1980. — xiii,385p : ill ; 24cm
Includes index
ISBN 0-12-566550-4 : £15.20 B81-05382

541.2'24 — Valency

Theory of valency in progress / edited by V.I. Kuznetsov ; translated from the Russian by Alexander Rosinkin. — Moscow : Mir ; [London] : distributed by Central Books, 1980. — 262p : ill ; 23cm
Translation and revision of: Razvitie uchenii͡a o valentnosti. — Includes index
ISBN 0-7147-1591-3 : £4.95 B81-23522

541.2'242 — Coordination compounds — *Conference proceedings*

International Conference on Coordination Chemistry *(21st : 1980 : Toulouse)*. Coordination chemistry-21 : proceedings of the 21st International Conference on Coordination Chemistry, Toulouse, France, 7-11 July 1980 / [organised by the] International Union of Pure and Applied Chemistry (Inorganic and Organic Chemistry Divisions) in conjunction with Centre national de la recherche scientifique, Laboratoire de chimie de coordination, Toulouse, Université Paul Sabatier, Toulouse ; editor J.P. Laurent. — Oxford : Pergamon, 1981. — x,190p : ill ; 28cm
Includes index
ISBN 0-08-025300-8 : £21.00 : CIP rev. B81-05134

541.2'26 — Intermolecular forces

Intermolecular forces : their origin and determination / by Geoffrey C. Maitland ... [et al.]. — Oxford : Clarendon, 1981. — xiv,616p : ill ; 24cm. — (The International series of monographs on chemistry)
Includes index
ISBN 0-19-855611-x : £39.50 B81-32497

541.2'8 — Chemistry. Nuclear magnetic resonance spectroscopy — *Serials*

Annual reports on NMR spectroscopy. — Vol.10B. — London : Academic Press, 1980. — vii,511p
ISBN 0-12-505348-7 : Unpriced : CIP rev.
ISSN 0066-4103 B81-03774

Annual reports on NMR spectroscopy. — Vol.11A. — London : Academic Press, 1981. — vii,282p
ISBN 0-12-505311-8 : Unpriced
ISSN 0066-4103 B81-32690

Annual reports on NMR spectroscopy. — Vol.11B. — London : Academic Press, Jan.1982. — [400]p
ISBN 0-12-505349-5 : CIP entry B81-34119

541.2'8 — Chemistry. Quantum theory

Zahradník, Rudolf. Elements of quantum chemistry / Rudolf Zahradník, Rudolf Polák ; [translated by Jiři Horký]. — New York ; London : Plenum, 1980. — 462p : ill ; 24cm
Translation from the Czech. — Includes index
ISBN 0-306-31093-7 : Unpriced B81-18561

541.2'8 — Chemistry. Quantum theory — *Conference proceedings*

International Congress of Quantum Chemistry *(3rd : 1979 : Kyoto)*. Horizons of quantum chemistry : proceedings of the Third International Congress of Quantum Chemistry held at Kyoto, Japan, October 29-November 3, 1979 / edited by Kenichi Fukui and Bernard Pullman. — Dordrecht ; London : Reidel, c1980. — xviii,292p : ill ; 25cm
At head of title: International Academy of Quantum Molecular Science. — Includes index
ISBN 90-277-1105-4 : Unpriced B81-01867

541.2'8 — Inorganic compounds. Spectroscopy — *Serials*

Spectroscopic properties of inorganic and organometallic compounds. — Vol.13. — London : Royal Society of Chemistry, c1980. — xv,413p. — (Specialist periodical report / Royal Society of Chemistry)
ISBN 0-85186-113-x : Unpriced B81-29655

Spectroscopic properties of inorganic and organometallic compounds. — Vol.14. — London : Royal Society of Chemistry, Dec.1981. — [400]p. — (Specialist periodical report / Royal Society of Chemistry)
ISBN 0-85186-123-7 : CIP entry
ISSN 0584-8555
Also classified at 547'.05 B81-32050

541.2'8 — Molecules. Excited states

The **Excited** state in chemical physics / edited by J. Wm. McGowan. — New York ; London : Wiley. — (Advances in chemical physics ; vol.45)
Pt.2. — c1981. — xi,609p : ill ; 24cm
Includes index
ISBN 0-471-05119-5 : £42.00 B81-33224

541.2'8 — Molecules. Spin-orbit coupling

Richards, W. G.. Spin-orbit coupling molecules / by W.G. Richards, H.P. Trivedi and D.L. Cooper. — Oxford : Clarendon, 1981. — viii,105p ; 24cm + 1microfiche(11x15cm). — (The International series of monographs on chemistry) (Oxford science publications)
1 microfiche in pocket. — Bibliography: p95-102. — Includes index
ISBN 0-19-855614-4 : £13.00 B81-23543

541.2'8 — Molecules. Structure. Determination. Nuclear magnetic resonance spectroscopy — *Serials*

Nuclear magnetic resonance. — Vol.9. — London (Burlington House, W1V 0BN) : Royal Society of Chemistry, c1980. — xiii,336p. — (Specialist periodical report / Royal Society of Chemistry)
ISBN 0-85186-960-2 : Unpriced : CIP rev.
ISBN 0-85404-960-6 (Society members)
ISSN 3305-9804 B80-19198

541.2'8'05 — Chemistry. Quantum theory — *Serials*

Advances in quantum chemistry. — Vol.12 (1980). — New York ; London : Academic Press, c1980. — x,325p
ISBN 0-12-034812-8 : Unpriced
ISSN 0065-3276 B81-21941

541.3 — PHYSICAL CHEMISTRY

541.3 — Physical chemistry

Adamson, Arthur W.. A textbook of physical chemistry / Arthur W. Adamson. — 2nd ed. — New York ; London : Academic Press, c1979. — xxv,953,23p : ill ; 26cm
Previous ed.: 1973. — Text on lining papers. — Includes bibliographies and index
ISBN 0-12-044260-4 : £16.00 B81-00876

Chang, Raymond. Physical chemistry : with applications to biological systems / Raymond Chang. — 2nd ed. — New York : Macmillan ; London : Collier Macmillan, c1981. — viii,659p : ill ; 27cm
Previous ed.: published as Physical chemistry with applications to biological systems. 1977. — Text on lining papers. — Includes index
ISBN 0-02-321040-0 (cased) : £14.95
ISBN 0-02-979050-x (pbk) : £7.95 B81-20731

Experiments in physical chemistry. — 4th ed. / David P. Shoemaker ... [et al.]. — New York ; London : McGraw-Hill, c1981. — xii,787p : ill ; 25cm
Previous ed.: 1974. — Text on lining paper. — Includes bibliographies and index
ISBN 0-07-057005-1 : £16.95 B81-31958

Liptrot, G. F.. Modern physical chemistry. — London : Bell & Hyman, Aug.1981. — [480]p
ISBN 0-7135-2231-3 (pbk) : £6.95 : CIP entry B81-18067

541.3 — Physical chemistry — *For schools*

Wilson, D. E.. Essential ideas in physical chemistry. — London : Hodder and Stoughton, June 1981. — [144]p
ISBN 0-340-20830-9 (pbk) : £2.95 : CIP entry B81-11915

541.3'024574 — Physical chemistry — *For biology*

Barrow, Gordon M.. Physical chemistry for the life sciences / Gordon M. Barrow. — New York ; London : McGraw-Hill, c1981. — xi,468p : ill ; 25cm
Previous ed.: 1974. — Text on lining papers. — Includes bibliographies and index
ISBN 0-07-003858-9 : £16.95 B81-24282

541.3'05 — Physical chemistry — *Serials*

Advances in chemical physics. — Vol.47, pt.2. — New York ; Chichester : Wiley, c1981. — xii,718p
ISBN 0-471-06274-x : £43.60
ISSN 0065-2385 B81-25028

Advances in chemical physics. — Vol.47, pt.1. — New York ; Chichester : Wiley, c1981. — xiii,769p
ISBN 0-471-06275-8 : £50.00
ISSN 0065-2385 B81-25027

Advances in chemical physics. — Vol.48. — New York ; Chichester : Wiley, c1981. — vii,549
ISBN 0-471-08294-5 : £45.00
ISSN 0065-2385 B81-33944

Advances in chemical physics. — Vol.46. — New York ; Chichester : Wiley, c1981. — ix,430p
ISBN 0-471-08295-3 : £37.50
ISSN 0065-2385 B81-24151

Annual reports on the progress of chemistry. Section C, Physical chemistry. — Vol.76 (1979). — London : Royal Society of Chemistry, 1980-. — v. ; 22cm
Continues in part: Annual reports on the progress of chemisty. Section A, Physical and inorganic chemistry
ISBN 0-85186-812-6 : Unpriced
ISSN 0260-1826 = Annual reports on the progress of chemistry. Section C. Physical chemistry B81-20083

International reviews in physical chemistry. — Vol.1, no.1 (Apr.1981). — Sevenoaks : Butterworths, 1981-. — v. : ill ; 25cm
Three issues yearly. — Continues: MTP international review of science. Physical chemistry
ISSN 0144-235x = International reviews in physical chemistry : £45.00 per year B81-38189

541.3'076 — Physical chemistry — *Questions & answers*

Atkins, P. W.. Solutions manual for physical chemistry. — 2nd ed. — Oxford : Oxford University Press, Jan.1982. — [[450]p
Previous ed.: 1979
ISBN 0-19-855156-8 (pbk) : £7.50 : CIP entry B81-37524

541.3'4 — Solutions — *Conference proceedings*

International Symposium on Solute-Solute-Solvent Interactions *(5th : 1980 : Florence)*. Advances in solution chemistry / [a part of the proceedings of the Fifth International Symposium on Solute-Solute-Solvent Interactions, held June 2-6, 1980, in Florence, Italy] ; edited by I. Bertini, L. Lunazzi and A. Dei. — New York ; London : Plenum, c1981. — ix,387p : ill ; 26cm
Includes index
ISBN 0-306-40638-1 : Unpriced B81-31871

541.3'41 — Binary solutions. Dielectric properties

Akhadov, I͡A. I͡U. Dielectric properties of binary solutions / by Y.Y. Akhadov. — Oxford : Pergamon, 1981. — 475p : ill ; 25cm
Includes index
ISBN 0-08-023600-6 : £47.00 : CIP rev. B80-12346

541.3'41 — Solutions. Equilibrium constraints — *Technical data — For solvent extraction*

Wisniak, Jaime. Liquid-liquid equilibrium and extraction. — Oxford : Elsevier Scientific. — (Physical sciences data ; 7)
Part B. — Oct.1981. — [600]p
ISBN 0-444-42023-1 : CIP entry B81-28177

541.3′423 — Non-aqueous solvents
Popovych, Orest. Nonaqueous solution chemistry / Orest Popovych, Reginald P.T. Tompkins. — New York ; Chichester : Wiley, 1981. — xiii,500p : ill ; 25cm
Includes bibliographies and index
ISBN 0-471-02673-5 : £36.75 B81-33014

541.3′45 — Colloids & surface phenomena
Shaw, Duncan J.. Introduction to colloid and surface chemistry / Duncan J. Shaw. — 3rd ed. — London : Butterworths, 1980. — viii,273p : ill ; 22cm
Previous ed.: 1970. — Bibliography: p257-265. — Includes index
ISBN 0-408-71049-7 (pbk) : £5.95 : CIP rev. B80-11857

541.3′451 — Colloids & surface phenomena
Hunter, R. J.. Zeta potential in colloid science. — London : Academic Press, Apr.1981. — [400]p. — (Colloid science, ISSN 0305-9723)
ISBN 0-12-361960-2 : CIP entry B81-06031

541.3′453 — Adhesion — *Conference proceedings — Serials*
[Adhesion *(London)*]. Adhesion. — 5. — London : Applied Science, c1981. — viii,160
ISBN 0-85334-929-0 : £18.00
ISSN 0260-4450 B81-11874

541.3′453 — Adsorption
Ościk, J.. Adsorption. — Chichester : Ellis Horwood, June 1981. — [256]p. — (Ellis Horwood series in physical chemistry)
Translation of: Adsorpcja
ISBN 0-85312-166-4 : £19.50 : CIP entry B81-10016

541.3′453 — Molecular sieves: Zeolites — *Serials*
Zeolites : the international journal of molecular sieves. — Vol.1, no.1 (Apr.1981)-. — Guildford : IPC Science and Technology Press, 1981-. — v. : ill,ports ; 30cm
Quarterly
ISSN 0144-2449 = Zeolites : £70.00 per year B81-30829

541.3′453 — Surface phenomena
Jaycock, M. J.. Chemistry of interfaces / M.J. Jaycock and G.D. Parfitt. — Chichester : Horwood, 1981. — 279p : ill ; 24cm. — (Ellis Horwood series in chincal science)
Includes index
ISBN 0-85312-028-5 : £27.50 : CIP rev.
ISBN 0-85312-298-9 (Student ed.) : Unpriced B80-11858

Somorjai, Gabor A.. Chemistry in two dimensions : surfaces / by Gabor A. Somorjai. — Ithaca ; London : Cornell University Press, 1981. — 575p : ill ; 24cm
Includes index
ISBN 0-8014-1179-3 : £29.00 B81-27508

541.3′453′05 — Surface phenomena — *Serials*
Chemical physics of solids and their surfaces. — Vol.8. — London (Burlington House, W1V 0BN) : Royal Society of Chemistry, c1980. — x, 250p. — (Specialist periodical report / Royal Society of Chemistry)
ISBN 0-85186-740-5 : Unpriced : CIP rev.
ISSN 0142-3401
Also classified at 541′.0421′05 B80-19761

541.3′5 — Chemical reactions. Initiation. Use of high energy lasers
Laser-induced chemical processes / edited by Jeffrey I. Steinfeld. — New York ; London : Plenum, c1981. — xii,276p : ill ; 24cm
Includes bibliographies and index
ISBN 0-306-40587-3 : Unpriced B81-15062

541.3′5 — Chemiluminescence — *Conference proceedings*
Bioluminescence and chemiluminescence : basic chemistry and analytical applications / edited by Marlene A. DeLuca, William D. McElroy. — New York ; London : Academic Press, c1981. — xxviii,782p : ill,maps,ports ; 24cm
Conference papers. — Includes index
ISBN 0-12-208820-4 : £24.80
Primary classification 574.19′125 B81-35357

541.3′5 — Molecules. Radiationless transitions — *Conference proceedings*
NATO Advanced Study Institute on Radiationless Processes *(1979 : Erice)*. Radiationless processes / [proceedings of the NATO Advanced Study Institute on Radiationless Processes held at the Ettore Majorana Centre for Scientific Culture, Erice, Sicily, Italy, November 18-December 1, 1979] ; edited by Baldassare DiBartolo ; assistant editor Velda Goldera. — New York ; London : Plenum, c1980. — xix,545p : ill ; 26cm. — (NATO advanced study institute series. Series B, Physics ; v.62)
Includes index
ISBN 0-306-40577-6 : Unpriced B81-17005

541.3′5′05 — Photochemistry — *Serials*
Photochemical and photobiological reviews. — Vol.6. — New York ; London ([Black Arrow House, Chandos Rd, NW10]) : Plenum, c1981. — ix,203p
ISBN 0-306-40662-4 : Unpriced
Primary classification 574.19′153′05 B81-20456

541.3′5′05 — Photochemistry - *Serials*
Photochemistry. — Vol.11. — London : Royal Society of Chemistry, Aug.1981. — [650]p. — (Specialist periodical report)
ISBN 0-85186-095-8 : CIP entry
ISSN 0556-3860 B81-15932

541.3′5′05 — Photochemistry — *Serials*
Photochemistry. — Vol.12. — London : Royal Society of Chemistry, Feb.1982. — [600]p. — (Specialist periodical report / Royal Society of Chemistry)
ISBN 0-85186-105-9 : CIP entry
ISSN 0556-3860 B81-39251

541.3′6 — Thermochemistry
Mortimer, C. T.. Chemistry, calorimetry, metals and medicine : an inaugural lecture / by C.T. Mortimer ; given in the University of Keele on Tuesday 1st November 1977. — [Keele] : [University of Keele], [1978]. — 24p : ill ; 22cm
Unpriced (pbk) B81-09131

541.3′63 — Phase transitions. Thermochemistry
Oonk, H. A. J.. Phase theory. — Oxford : Elsevier Scientific, Sept.1981. — [285]p. — (Studies in modern thermodynamics ; 3)
ISBN 0-444-42019-3 : CIP entry B81-28195

541.3′69 — Inorganic chemistry. Thermodynamics
Johnson, D. A.. Some thermodynamic aspects of inorganic chemistry. — 2nd ed. — Cambridge : Cambridge University Press, Feb.1982. — [280] p. — (Cambridge texts in chemistry and biochemistry)
Previous ed.: 1968
ISBN 0-521-24204-5 (cased) : £18.00 : CIP entry
ISBN 0-521-28521-6 (pbk) : £6.95 B81-36954

541.3′7 — Electrochemical techniques
Bard, Allen J.. Electrochemical method : fundamentals and applications / Allen J. Bard, Larry R. Faulkner. — New York ; Chichester : Wiley, c1980. — xviii,718p : ill ; 24cm
Text on lining papers. — Bibliography: p38-41. — Includes index
ISBN 0-471-05542-5 : £14.70 B81-02290

541.3′7 — Electrochemistry
Comprehensive treatise of electrochemistry. — New York ; London : Plenum
Vol.2: Electrochemical processing / edited by J.O′M. Bockris ... [et al.]. — c1981. — xxii,616p : ill ; 26cm
Includes index
ISBN 0-306-40503-2 : Unpriced B81-33167

Comprehensive treatise of electrochemistry. — New York ; London : Plenum
Vol.3: Electrochemical energy conversion and storage / edited by J. O′M. Bockris ... [et al.]. — c1981. — xxii,540p : ill ; 26cm
Includes bibliographies and index
ISBN 0-306-40590-3 : Unpriced B81-36674

541.3′7 — Electrochemistry — *Conference proceedings*
Australian Electrochemistry Conference *(5th : 1980 : Perth)*. Progress in electrochemistry : proceedings of the Fifth Australian Electrochemistry Conference, Perth, Western Australia 18-22 August 1980 / edited by D.A.J. Rand, G.P. Power, I.M. Ritchie. — Amsterdam ; Oxford : Elsevier Scientific, 1981. — x,470p : ill,ports ; 25cm. — (Studies in physical and theoretical chemistry ; 15)
Includes index
ISBN 0-444-41955-1 : £40.22 B81-22288

541.3′7 — Electrophoresis
Andrews, Andrew T.. Electrophoresis. — Oxford : Clarendon Press, Nov.1981. — [400]p
ISBN 0-19-854626-2 : £28.00 : CIP entry B81-31070

541.3′7 — Photoelectrochemistry — *Conference proceedings*
Photoelectrochemistry. — London : Faraday Division, Royal Society of Chemistry, 1980, [c1981]. — 438p,[4]p of plates : ill ; 26cm. — (Faraday discussions of the Chemical Society, ISSN 0301-7249 ; no.70)
Conference papers. — Includes index
ISBN 0-85186-738-3 (pbk) : Unpriced B81-36915

541.3′72 — Ions. Hydration
Conway, B. E.. Ionic hydration in chemistry and biophysics / B.E. Conway. — Amsterdam ; Oxford : Elsevier Scientific, 1981. — xxx,774p : ill ; 25cm. — (Studies in physical and theoretical chemistry ; 12)
Includes index
ISBN 0-444-41947-0 : £51.13 B81-23637

541.3′72 — Liquids. Electrical conductivity
Smedley, Stuart I.. The interpretation of ionic conductivity in liquids / Stuart I. Smedley. — New York ; London : Plenum, c1980. — xvi,195p : ill ; 24cm
Includes index
ISBN 0-306-40529-6 : Unpriced B81-08261

541.3′724 — Conductive metal oxide electrodes
Electrodes of conductive metallic oxides / edited by Sergio Trasatti. — Amsterdam ; Oxford : Elsevier Scientific. — (Studies in physical and theoretical chemistry ; 11)
Includes index
Pt.B. — 1981. — xiii,367-702p : ill ; 25cm
ISBN 0-444-41988-8 : Unpriced : CIP rev. B81-12375

541.3′724 — Metal oxide electrodes. Chemical reactions
Morrison, S. Roy. Electrochemistry at semiconductor and oxidized metal electrodes / S. Ray Morrison. — New York ; London : Plenum, c1980. — xiv,401p : ill ; 24cm
Bibliography: p374-377. - Includes index
ISBN 0-306-40524-5 : Unpriced
Also classified at 541.3′77 B81-08211

541.3′724 — Selective ion sensitive electrodes
Ion-selective electrode reviews. — Oxford : Pergamon, Aug.1981
Vol.2. — [270]p
ISBN 0-08-028434-5 : £24.00 : CIP entry B81-22671

541.3′724 — Selective ion sensitive electrodes — *Conference proceedings*
Ion-selective electrodes. — Oxford : Elsevier Scientific, Dec.1981. — [428]p. — (Analytical chemistry symposia series ; v.8)
Conference papers
ISBN 0-444-99714-8 : £40.00 : CIP entry B81-31619

541.3′77 — Semiconductor electrodes. Chemical reactions
Morrison, S. Roy. Electrochemistry at semiconductor and oxidized metal electrodes / S. Ray Morrison. — New York ; London : Plenum, c1980. — xiv,401p : ill ; 24cm
Bibliography: p374-377. - Includes index
ISBN 0-306-40524-5 : Unpriced
Primary classification 541.3′724 B81-08211

541.3′8′05 — Radiochemistry — *Serials*

Advances in inorganic chemistry and radiochemistry. — Vol.22 (1979). — New York ; London : Academic Press, c1979. — ix,457p
ISBN 0-12-023622-2 : Unpriced
ISSN 0065-2792
Also classified at 546′.05 B81-33699

Advances in inorganic chemistry and radiochemistry. — Vol.23. — New York ; London : Academic Press, 1980. — ix,441p
ISBN 0-12-023623-0 : Unpriced
ISSN 0065-2792
Primary classification 546′.05 B81-04015

. Amersham research news / the Radiochemical Centre. — [No.1] (Apr.1980)-. — Amersham ([White Lion Rd,] Amersham, [Bucks. HP7 9LL]) : The Centre, 1980-. — v. ; 21cm
Monthly. — Description based on: No.4 (July/Aug.1980)
ISSN 0260-1451 = Amersham research news : Free B81-00877

541.3′884′028 — Radioisotopes. Use. Laboratory techniques

Faires, R. A.. Radioisotope laboratory techniques. — 4th ed. / by R.A. Faires, G.G.J. Boswell. — London : Butterworths, 1981. — xiii,335p,[8]p of plates : ill ; 24cm
Previous ed.: / by R.A. Faires and B.H. Parks. 1973. — Includes bibliographies and index
ISBN 0-408-70940-5 : Unpriced : CIP rev. B80-23245

541.3′9 — Chemical reactions. Equilibria & kinetics

Meites, Louis. An introduction to chemical equilibrium and kinetics / by Louis Meites. — Oxford : Pergamon, 1981. — xiii,549p : ill. — (Pergamon international library) (Pergamon series in analytical chemistry ; v.1)
Includes index
ISBN 0-08-023802-5 (cased) : Unpriced : CIP rev.
ISBN 0-08-023803-3 (pbk) : £8.75 B80-05348

541.3′9 — Chemical reactions. Kinetics - *Serials*

Progress in reaction kinetics. — Vol.10. — Oxford : Pergamon, Apr.1981. — [406]p
ISBN 0-08-027155-3 : £36.00 : CIP entry B81-04201

541.3′9 — Fast chemical reactions in solutions — *Conference proceedings*

NATO Advanced Study Institute on New Applications of Chemical Relaxation Spectrometry and Other Fast Reaction Methods in Solution *(1978 : Aberystwyth)*. Techniques and applications of fast reactions in solution : proceedings of the NATO Advanced Study Institute on New Applications of Chemical Relaxation Spectrometry and Other Fast Reaction Methods in Solution, held at the University College of Wales, Aberystwyth, September 10-20, 1978 / edited by W.J. Gettins and E. Wyn-Jones. — Dordrecht ; London : Published in cooperation with NATO Scientific Affairs Division [by] Reidel, c1979. — xi,608p : ill ; 25cm. — (NATO advanced study institutes series. Series C, Mathematical and physical sciences ; v.50)
Includes index
ISBN 90-277-1022-8 : Unpriced B81-06569

541.3′9 — Gases. Chemical reactions. Energy transfer & kinetics — *Serials*

Gas kinetics and energy transfer. — Vol.4. — London : The Royal Society of Chemistry, c1981. — x,242p. — (Specialist periodical report / Royal Society of Chemistry)
ISBN 0-85186-786-3 : Unpriced
ISSN 0309-6890 B81-28712

541.3′9 — Inorganic compounds. Chemical reactions

Burns, D. T.. Inorganic reaction chemistry / D.T. Burns, A. Townshend and A.H. Carter. — Chichester : Horwood. — (Ellis Horwood series in analytical chemistry)
Vol.2: Reactions of the elements and their compounds
Part A: Alkali metals to nitrogen. — 1981. — 300p ; 24cm
ISBN 0-85312-119-2 : £27.50 : CIP rev. B81-06598

Inorganic reaction chemistry. — Chichester : Horwood. — (Ellis Horwood series in analytical chemistry)
Vol.2: Reactions of the elements and their compounds / D.T. Burns, A. Townshend and A.H. Carter
Osmium to zirconium. — 1981. — p306-580 ; 24cm
Bibliography: p554-559. — Includes index
ISBN 0-85312-352-7 : £27.50 : CIP rev. B81-08940

541.3′9′05 — Inorganic compounds. Chemical reactions — *Serials*

Inorganic reaction mechanisms. — Vol.7. — London : Royal Society of Chemistry, c1981. — xxi,442p. — (Specialist periodical report / Royal Society of Chemistry)
ISBN 0-85186-315-9 : Unpriced
ISSN 0305-8255 B81-30721

541.3′92 — Chemical reactions. Equilibria

Denbigh, K. G.. The principles of chemical equilibrium : with applications in chemistry and chemical engineering / by Kenneth Denbigh. — 4th ed. — Cambridge : Cambridge University Press, 1981. — xxi,494p : ill ; 24cm
Previous ed.: 1971. — Includes index
ISBN 0-521-23682-7 (cased) : £22.00 B81-17024

541.3′94 — Chemical reactions. Kinetics & mechanisms

Espenson, James H.. Chemical kinetics and reaction mechanisms / James H. Espenson. — New York ; London : McGraw-Hill, c1981. — x,218p : ill ; 25cm. — (McGraw-Hill series in advanced chemistry)
Includes index
ISBN 0-07-019667-2 : £17.45 B81-17052

541.3′94 — Fast chemical reactions — *Conference proceedings*

Fast reactions in energetic systems : proceedings of the NATO Advanced Study Institute held at Preveza, Greece, July 6-19, 1980 / edited by Christos Capellos and Raymond F. Walker. — Dordrecht ; London : Reidel in cooperation with NATO Scientific Affairs Division, c1981. — x,759p : ill,1map ; 25cm. — (NATO advanced study institutes series. Series C, Mathematical and physical sciences ; v.71)
Includes index
ISBN 90-277-1299-9 : Unpriced B81-33343

541.3′95 — Catalysis. Chemical compounds: Complexes

Yermakov, Yu. I.. Catalysis by supported complexes. — Oxford : Elsevier Scientific, Sept.1981. — [540]p. — (Studies in surface science and catalysis ; 8)
ISBN 0-444-42014-2 : CIP entry B81-24609

541.3′95 — Catalysts. Research - *Conference proceedings*

International Congress on Catalysis *(7th : 1980 : Tokyo)*. New horizons in catalysis. — Oxford : Elsevier Scientific, Apr.1981. — [1600]p. — (Studies in surface science and catalysis ; v.7)
ISBN 0-444-99750-4 : £95.00 : CIP entry
ISBN 0-444-99740-70-444-99739-3 (v.7A) (v.7B) B81-11922

541.3′95 — Catalysts: Zeolites. Structure & physical properties — *Conference proceedings*

Catalysis by zeolites : proceedings of an international symposium / organized by the Institut de recherches sur la catalyse, CNRS, Villeurbanne and sponsored by Centre national de la recherche scientifique, Ecully (Lyon), September 9-11, 1980 ; editors B. Imelik ... [et al.]. — Amsterdam ; Oxford : Elsevier Scientific, 1980. — xii,351p : ill ; 25cm. — (Studies in surface science and catalysis ; 5)
Conference papers. — English text, English and French prefaces. — Includes index
ISBN 0-444-41916-0 : £28.90 : CIP rev. B80-13799

541.3′95 — Homogeneous catalysis by transition metal compounds

Masters, Christopher, *1947-*. Homogeneous transition metal catalysis : a gentle art / Christopher Masters. — London : Chapman and Hall, 1981. — x,277p : ill ; 22cm
Includes index
ISBN 0-412-22110-1 (cased) : £20.00
ISBN 0-412-22120-9 (pbk) : £9.50 B81-06796

541.3′95 — Homogeneous catalysis — *Serials*

Aspects of homogeneous catalysis. — Vol.4. — Dordrecht ; London : D. Reidel, c1981. — 204p
ISBN 90-277-1139-9 : Unpriced B81-24129

541.3′95′05 — Catalysis — *Serials*

Advances in catalysis. — Vol.29. — New York ; London : Academic Press, 1980. — xiv,367p
ISBN 0-12-007829-5 : Unpriced
ISSN 0360-0564 B81-20711

541.3′95′05 — Catalysis - *Serials*

Catalysis. — Vol.4. — London : Royal Society of Chemistry, July 1981. — [265]p. — (A Specialist periodical report)
ISBN 0-85186-554-2 : CIP entry
ISSN 0140-0568 B81-14899

542 — CHEMISTRY. LABORATORIES, APPARATUS, EQUIPMENT

542 — Chemistry. Experiments — *For schools*

Akonta, Wisdom K.. Practical chemistry : for school certificate / Wisdom K. Akonta, Stephen A. Afolayan. — London : Macmillan Education, 1980. — ix,61p : ill ; 25cm
ISBN 0-333-29296-0 (ppk) : £0.92 B81-23125

542 — Chemistry. Laboratory techniques

Integrated experimental chemistry / David A. Aikens ... [et al.]. — Boston, Mass. ; London : Allyn and Bacon. — (The Allyn and Bacon chemistry series)
Vol.1: Principles and techniques. — c1978. — xxii,413p,viiip : ill,1form ; 24cm
Includes index
ISBN 0-205-05923-6 : £10.35 B81-11820

542 — Chemistry. Laboratory techniques — *Manuals*

Chemical technicians′ ready reference handbook. — 2nd ed. / Gershon J. Shugar ... [et al.]. — New York ; London : McGraw-Hill, c1981. — xxii,867p : ill ; 25cm
Previous ed.: 1973. — Includes index
ISBN 0-07-057176-7 : £27.95 B81-27529

Frantz, Harper W.. Frantz, Malm′s chemistry in the laboratory. — [3rd ed.], [condensed and updated] / James B. Ifft, Julian L. Roberts, Jr. — Oxford : W.H. Freeman, c1981. — x,257p : ill ; 28cm
Previous ed.: 1968. — Text on inside cover
ISBN 0-7167-1238-5 (pbk) : £5.60 B81-37378

542 — Chemistry. Research. Use of lasers

Chemical and biochemical applications of lasers. — Vol.5 1980. — London : Academic Press, c1980. — 281p
ISBN 0-12-505405-x : [£13.00] B81-09711

542′.4 — Distillation. Laboratory techniques

Krell, Erich. Handbook of laboratory distillation. — 2nd ed., rev. — Oxford : Elsevier Scientific, Sept.1981. — [576]p. — (Techniques and instrumentation in analytical chemistry ; 2)
Translation of: Handbuch der Laboratoriumsdestillation
ISBN 0-444-99723-7 : £40.00 : CIP entry B81-24630

542′.8 — Chemistry. Applications of computer systems - *Conference proceedings*

Data processing in chemistry. — Oxford : Elsevier Scientific, Apr.1981. — [300]p. — (Studies in physical and theoretical chemistry ; 16)
Conference papers
ISBN 0-444-99744-x : £45.00 : CIP entry B81-03694

542′.8 — Chemistry. Applications of minicomputer systems — *Conference proceedings*

Personal computers in chemistry / edited by Peter Lykos. — New York ; Chichester : Wiley, c1981. — xi,262p : ill ; 24cm
Conference papers. — Includes index
ISBN 0-471-08508-1 : £14.75 B81-14767

542'.8 — Chemistry laboratories. Applications of computer system networks — *Conference proceedings*

Computer networks in the chemical laboratory : presented in part as a symposium at the 179th national meeting of the American Chemical Society, Houston, Texas, March, 1980 / edited by George C. Levy, Dan Terpstra. — New York ; Chichester : Wiley, c1981. — xv,221p : ill ; 24cm
Includes index
ISBN 0-471-08471-9 : £17.00 B81-23326

543 — CHEMICAL ANALYSIS

543 — Chemical analysis

Schenk, George H.. Introduction to analytical chemistry / George H. Schenk, Richard B. Hahn, Arleigh V. Hartkopf. — 2nd ed.. — Boston [Mass.] ; London : Allyn and Bacon, c1981. — xii,523p : ill ; 25cm
Previous ed.: published as Quantitative analytical chemistry. Boston, Mass. : Allyn and Bacon, 1977. — Text on lining papers. — Includes index
ISBN 0-205-07236-4 : Unpriced B81-26204

Treatise on analytical chemistry / [edited by I.M. Kolthoff and Philip J. Elving]
Part 2: Analytical chemistry of inorganic and organic compounds
Vol.15. — New York ; London : Wiley, c1976. — xxi,509p : ill ; 25cm
Text on inside covers. — Includes bibliographies and index
ISBN 0-471-50009-7 : £36.15 B81-27715

Wilson and Wilson's comprehensive analytical chemistry. — Amsterdam ; Oxford : Elsevier Scientific
Vol.11: The application of mathematical statistics in analytical chemistry ; mass spectrometry ; ion selective electrodes edited by G. Svehla / contributors to volume XI J. Grimshaw, P.Móritz, W.E. van der Linden. — 1981. — xiv,407p : ill ; 24cm
Includes index
ISBN 0-444-41886-5 B81-13025

543 — Chemical analysis — *For teaching*

Baiulescu, G. E.. Education and teaching in analytical chemistry. — Chichester : Ellis Horwood, Nov.1981. — [160]p. — (Ellis Horwood series in analytical chemistry)
ISBN 0-85312-384-5 : £12.50 : CIP entry B81-30492

543 — Chemical analysis. Physical methods

Physcial methods in modern chemical analysis / edited by Theodore Kuwana. — New York ; London : Academic Press
Vol.2. — 1980. — xi,411p : ill ; 24cm
Includes bibliographies and index
ISBN 0-12-430802-3 : £29.00 B81-14610

543 — Chemical analysis. Quality control

Kateman, G.. Quality control in analytical chemistry / G. Kateman, F.W. Pijpers. — New York ; Chichester : Wiley, c1981. — xii,276p : ill ; 24cm. — (Chemical analysis, ISSN 0069-2883 ; v.60)
Includes bibliographies and index
ISBN 0-471-46020-6 : £25.00 B81-24194

543 — Chemical analysis. Use of immobilised enzymes

Carr, Peter W.. Immobilized enzymes in analytical and clinical chemistry : fundamentals and applications / Peter W. Carr, Larry D. Bowers. — New York ; Chichester : Wiley, c1980. — xvii,460p : ill ; 24cm. — (Chemical analysis ; v.56)
Includes index
ISBN 0-471-04919-0 : £24.00 B81-03963

543 — Inorganic compounds. Chemical analysis. Separation & preconcentration. Laboratory techniques

Minczewski, J.. Separation and preconcentration methods in inorganic trace analysis. — Chichester : Ellis Horwood, Dec.1981. — [538] p. — (Ellis Horwood series in analytical chemistry)
Translation of: Analiza śladowa - metody rozdzielania i zagęszczania
ISBN 0-85312-165-6 : £31.50 : CIP entry B81-31511

543'.0028 — Chemical analysis — *Laboratory manuals*

Huskins, D. J.. On-line process analysers. — Chichester : Ellis Horwood. — (Ellis Horwood series in analytical chemistry)
Vol.1: General handbook. — Jan.1982. — [312]p
ISBN 0-85312-329-2 : £27.50 : CIP entry B81-35881

543'.0028 — Chemical analysis. Laboratory techniques

Chalmers, R. A.. Quantitative chemical analysis. — Chichester : Ellis Horwood, July 1981. — [416]p. — (Ellis Horwood series in analytical chemistry)
ISBN 0-85312-192-3 : £25.00 : CIP entry B81-18173

Methodicum chimicum : a critical survey of proven methods and their application in chemistry, natural science and medicine / editor-in-chief Friedhelm Korte. — New York ; London : Academic Press
Vol.11: Natural compounds
Pt.2: Antibiotics, vitamins and hormones / edited by F. Korte and M. Goto ; contributions from R.E. Burgess ... [et al.]. — 1977. — ix,304p : ill ; 28cm
ISBN 0-12-460746-2 : £33.60 B81-29740

Methodicum chimicum / editor-in-chief Friedhelm Korte. — New York ; London : Academic Press
Vol.11: Natural compounds
Part 3: Steroids, terpenes and alkaloids / edited by F. Korte and M. Goto ; contributions from Ch. Baumann ... [et al.]. — 1978. — viii,244p : ill ; 28cm
Includes index
ISBN 0-12-460747-0 : £33.60 B81-14560

543'.005 — Chemical analysis — *Serials*

TrAC : trends in analytical chemistry. — Vol.1 no.1 (1981)-. — Amsterdam ; Cambridge : Elsevier Scientific Pub. Co., 1981-. — v. : ill ; 29cm
Monthly
Unpriced B81-39741

543'.0076 — Chemical analysis — *Questions & answers*

Schenk, George H.. Solutions manual to accompany Introduction to analytical chemistry, second edition / George H. Schenk, Richard B. Hahn, Arleigh V. Hartkopf. — Boston [Mass.] ; London : Allyn and Bacon, c1981. — 64p ; 22cm
ISBN 0-205-07237-2 (unbound) : £1.00 B81-26401

543'.00941 — Chemical analysis by Laboratory of the Government Chemist — *Serials*

Laboratory of the Government Chemist. Report of the Government Chemist. — 1979. — London : H.M.S.O., 1980. — 197p : ill
ISBN 0-11-512919-7 : £6.50
ISSN 0307-6814 B81-00107

543'.08 — Chemical analysis. Flow injection

Růžička, Jaromír. Flow injection analysis / Jaromír Růžička, Elo Harald Hansen. — New York ; Chichester : Wiley, c1981. — xi,207p : ill ; 24cm. — (Chemical analysis ; v.62)
Includes index
ISBN 0-471-08192-2 : £20.00 B81-33152

543'.08 — Chemical analysis. Separation. Experiments — *Manuals* — *For schools*

Separating things. — St. Albans : Hart-Davis Educational, 1981, c1980. — 30p : ill ; 21cm. — (Centre science)
ISBN 0-247-13122-9 (unbound) : £0.40 B81-24519

543'.08 — Instrumental chemical analysis systems

Instrumental methods of analysis. — 6th ed. / Hobart H. Willard ... [et al.]. — New York ; London : Van Nostrand, 1981. — xxiv,1030p : ill ; 25cm
Previous ed.: / Hobart H. Willard, Lynne L. Merritt Jr., John A. Dean. 1974
ISBN 0-442-24502-5 : £21.70 B81-26040

543'.08 — Materials. Separation. Experiments — *For schools*

Separating substances. — London : Harrap, 1981. — 48p : ill ; 25cm. — (Access to science)
Cover title. — Text on inside cover
ISBN 0-245-53661-2 (pbk) : £1.50
ISBN 0-245-53702-3 (Teacher's notes and tests) : £1.25 B81-37434

543'.0812 — Electron probe microanalysis

Heinrich, Kurt F. J.. Electron beam x-ray microanalysis / Kurt F. J. Heinrich. — New York ; London : Van Nostrand Reinhold, c1981. — xxiii,578p,[8]p of plates : ill(some col.) ; 24cm
Includes index
ISBN 0-442-23286-1 : £31.90 B81-10187

543'.0858 — Chemical analysis. Absorption spectroscopy. Standards

Standards in absorption spectrometry / Ultraviolet Spectrometry Group ; edited by C. Burgess and A. Knowles. — London : Chapman and Hall, 1981. — x,142p : ill ; 24cm. — (Techniques in visible and ultraviolet spectrometry ; v.1)
Includes index
ISBN 0-412-22470-4 : £9.50 B81-08188

543'.0858 — Chemical analysis. Atomic absorption spectroscopy. Techniques

Van Loon, J. C.. Analytical atomic absorption spectroscopy : selected methods / Jon C. Van Loon. — New York ; London : Academic Press, 1980. — xi,337p : ill ; 24cm
Includes index
ISBN 0-12-714050-6 : £19.60 B81-22150

543'.0858 — Chemical analysis. Atomic spectroscopy — *Serials*

Annual report on analytical atomic spectroscopy. — Vol.9 reviewing 1979. — London (Burlington House, W1V 0BN) : Royal Society of Chemistry, c1980. — xii,345p
ISBN 0-85186-727-8 : Unpriced
ISSN 0306-1353 B81-03797

Annual reports on analytical atomic spectroscopy. — Vol.10. — London : Royal Society of Chemistry, Nov.1981. — [350]p
ISBN 0-85186-717-0 : CIP entry
ISSN 0306-1353 B81-31186

Progress in analytical atomic spectroscopy. — Vol.3. — Oxford : Pergamon, Oct.1981. — [390]p
ISBN 0-08-029081-7 : £43.00 : CIP entry B81-30205

543'.0858 — Chemical analysis. Photoacoustic spectroscopy

Rosencwaig, Allan. Photoacoustics and photoacoustic spectroscopy / Allan Rosencwaig. — New York ; Chichester : Wiley, c1980. — xii,309p : ill ; 24cm
Text on lining papers. — Includes bibliographies and index
ISBN 0-471-04495-4 : Unpriced B81-10172

543'.08586 — Chemical analysis. X-ray diffractometry & x-ray spectroscopy — *Conference proceedings* — *Serials*

Advances in X-ray analysis. — Vol.24. — New York ; London ([88 Middlesex St., E1 7EX]) : Plenum Press, c1981. — xx,428p
ISBN 0-306-40734-5 : Unpriced
ISSN 0376-0308 B81-35465

543'.086 — Thermal analysis

Thermal analysis / W.W. Wendlandt (advisory editor). — Amsterdam ; Oxford : Elsevier Scientific. — (Wilson and Wilson's comprehensive analytical chemistry ; v.12)
Pt.A: Simultaneous thermoanalytical examinations by means of the derivatograph / by J. Paulik and F. Paulik. — 1981. — xviii,277p : ill ; 24cm
Bibliography: p211-258. — Includes index
ISBN 0-444-41949-7 : Unpriced : CIP rev. B80-34948

543'.086 — Thermal analysis - *Conference proceedings*

European Symposium on Thermal Analysis *(2nd : 1981 : University of Aberdeen).* Proceedings of the Second European Symposium on Thermal Analysis, ESTA2, University of Aberdeen, UK, 1-4 September 1981, organized by the Thermal Methods Group of the Analytical Division of the Chemical Society. — London : Heyden, Aug.1981. — [600]p
ISBN 0-85501-705-8 : £26.00 : CIP entry B81-20526

543'.0871 — Chemical analysis. Electrochemical techniques. Applications — *Conference proceedings*

International Symposium on Electroanalysis in Clinical, Environmental and Pharmaceutical Chemistry *(1981 : University of Wales Institute of Science and Technology).* Programme and abstracts of papers / International Symposium on Electronalysis in Clinical, Environmental and Pharmaceutical Chemistry, 13-16 April 1981, held at Traherne Hall, The University of Wales Institute of Science and Technology, Cardiff, Wales ; [organised by] The Electroanalytical Group, Analytical Division, The Royal Society of Chemistry. — Cardiff ([King Edward VII Ave., Cardiff CF1 3NU]) : UWIST, [1981]. — 156p in various pagings : ill ; 30cm
Includes index
Unpriced (pbk) B81-23299

543'.0871 — Chemical analysis. Isotachophoresis — *Conference proceedings*

International Symposium on Isotachophoresis *(2nd : 1980 : EIndhoven).* Analytical isotachophoresis : proceedings of the 2nd International Symposium on Isotachophoresis, Eindhoven, September 9-11, 1980 / editor F.M. Everaerts ; co-editors F.E.P. Mikkers and Th. P.E.M. Verheggen. — Amsterdam ; Oxford : Elsevier Scientific, 1981. — xi,234p : ill ; 25cm. — (Analytical chemistry symposia series ; v.6)
Includes index
ISBN 0-444-41957-8 : £23.08 B81-19278

543'.0871 — Chemical analysis. Use of selective ion sensitive electrodes

Ion-selective electrodes in analytical chemistry / edited by Henry Freiser. — New York ; London : Plenum. — (Modern analytical chemistry)
Vol.2. — c1980. — xi,291p : ill ; 24cm
Includes index
ISBN 0-306-40500-8 : Unpriced B81-19961

543'.0873 — Trace elements. Chemical analysis. Applications of mass spectrometry — *Conference proceedings*

Applications of mass spectrometry to trace analysis. — Oxford : Elsevier Scientific, Jan.1982. — [450]p
Conference papers
ISBN 0-444-42042-8 : CIP entry B81-37525

543'.0882 — Non-destructive neutron activation analysis

Nondestructive activation analysis : with nuclear reactors and radioactive neutron sources / edited by Saadia Amiel. — Amsterdam ; Oxford : Elsevier Scientific, 1981. — xvi,369p : ill,1port ; 25cm. — (Studies in analytical chemistry ; 3)
Includes index
ISBN 0-444-41942-x : £31.37 B81-15496

543'.089'028 — Chromatography. Experiments — *Manuals — For schools*

Separating colours. — St. Albans : Hart-Davis Educational, 1981, c1980. — 31p : ill ; 22cm. — (Centre science)
ISBN 0-247-13121-0 (unbound) : £0.40 B81-24518

543'.0892 — Affinity chromatography

Scouten, William H.. Affinity chromatography : bioselective adsorption on inert matrices / William H. Scouten. — New York ; Chichester : Wiley, c1981. — xiii,348p : ill ; 24cm. — (Chemical analysis, ISSN 0069-2883 ; v.59)
Includes index
ISBN 0-471-02649-2 : £26.50 B81-24193

543'.0894 — High performance liquid chromatography — *Serials*

. High-performance liquid chromatography. — Vol.2 (1980). — New York ; London : Academic Press, 1980. — xiii,341p
ISBN 0-12-312202-3 : £22.20 B81-29443

High-performance liquid chromatography : advances and perspectives. — Vol.1 (1980)-. — New York ; London : Academic Press, 1980-. — v. ; 24cm
Irregular
Unpriced B81-20309

543'.08956 — Thin-layer chromatography — *Conference proceedings*

Thin layer chromatography : quantitative environmental and clinical applications / edited by Joseph C. Touchstone, Dexter Rogers. — New York ; Chichester : Wiley, c1980. — xix,561p : ill,maps ; 24cm
Includes index
ISBN 0-471-07958-8 : £21.50 B81-10642

543'.0896 — Gas chromatography. Use of derivatives of organic compounds

Drozd, J.. Chemical derivatization in gas chromatography / J. Drozd with a contribution by J. Novák. — Amsterdam ; Oxford : Elsevier Scientific, 1981. — xiii,232p : ill ; 25cm. — (Journal of chromatography library ; v.19)
Includes index
ISBN 0-444-41917-9 : Unpriced : CIP rev. B81-09967

543'.0896 — Headspace analysis: Gas chromatography — *Conference proceedings*

Applied headspace gas chromatography / edited by Bruno Kolb. — London : Heyden, c1980. — x,185p : ill ; 25cm
Conference papers. — Includes bibliographies and index
ISBN 0-85501-488-1 : £13.00 : CIP rev. B79-36306

545 — QUANTITATIVE ANALYSIS

545'.33 — Mass spectrometry

Beynon, J. H.. An introduction to mass spectrometry. — Cardiff : University of Wales Press, Oct.1981. — [66]p
ISBN 0-7083-0810-4 (pbk) : £3.95 : CIP entry B81-28823

545'.33'05 — Mass spectrometry — *Serials*

Dynamic mass spectrometry. — Vol.6. — London : Heyden, Sept.1981. — [384]p
ISBN 0-85501-499-7 : £35.00 : CIP entry B81-24607

Mass spectrometry. — Vol.6. — London : Royal Society of Chemistry, Nov.1981. — [330]p. — (Specialist periodical report / Royal Society of Chemistry)
ISBN 0-85186-308-6 : CIP entry
ISSN 0305-9987 B81-31187

546 — INORGANIC CHEMISTRY

546 — Inorganic chemistry

Sharpe, A. G.. Inorganic chemistry / Alan G. Sharpe. — London : Longman, 1981. — xv,682p : ill ; 23cm
Includes bibliographies and index
ISBN 0-582-45064-0 (cased) : Unpriced : CIP rev.
ISBN 0-582-45080-2 (pbk) : £11.95 B81-07591

546 — Inorganic chemistry - *For schools*

Liptrot, G. F.. Modern inorganic chemistry. — 3rd ed. — London : Bell & Hyman, June 1981. — [471]p. — (Modern chemistry series)
Previous ed.: 1974
ISBN 0-7135-2183-x (pbk) : £4.95 : CIP entry B81-15918

546 — Inorganic chemistry — *For schools*

Mackay, K. M.. Introduction to modern inorganic chemistry / K.M. Mackay, R.A. Mackay. — 3rd ed. — London : International Textbook Co., 1981. — xiv,349p : ill ; 28cm
Previous ed.: 1972. — Bibliography: p322-328. — Includes index
ISBN 0-7002-0278-1 (pbk) : £9.95 : CIP rev. B81-05116

546 — Inorganic compounds

Inorganic chemistry : concepts and case studies / [S247 Course Team]. — Milton Keynes : Open University Press. — (Science : a second level course)
At head of title: The Open University
Block 1: Thermodynamics and the reactions of metals / written by David Johnson and Kiki Warr in collaboration with the Course Team. — 1981. — 116p : ill ; 30cm. — (S247 ; block 1)
ISBN 0-335-17020-x (pbk) : Unpriced B81-14720

Inorganic chemistry : concepts and case studies / [S247 Course Team]. — Milton Keynes : Open University Press. — (Science : a second level course)
At head of title: The Open University
Block 2: The crystalline state / written by Lesley Smart and Stuart Bennett in collaboration with the Course Team ; [Block 3] : [Metals and coordination compounds] / [written by Stuart Bennett in collaboration with the Course Team]. — 1981. — 62,51p : ill (some col.) ; 30cm. — (S247 ; books 2 and 3)
ISBN 0-335-17021-8 (corrected : pbk) : Unpriced B81-27789

Kauffman, George B.. Inorganic chemical compounds. — London : Heyden, Apr.1981. — 1v.. — (Fundamentals of chemistry)
ISBN 0-85501-683-3 (cased) : CIP entry
ISBN 0-85501-684-1 (pbk) : Unpriced B81-06597

546 — Inorganic compounds — *Conference proceedings*

Speciality inorganic chemicals. — London : Royal Society of Chemistry, Sept.1981. — [506]p. — (Special publication / Royal Society of Chemistry, ISSN 0260-6291 ; no.40)
Conference papers
ISBN 0-85186-835-5 (pbk) : £18.00 : CIP entry B81-30208

546'.05 — Inorganic chemistry — *Serials*

Annual reports on the progress of chemistry. Section A, Inorganic chemistry. — Vol.77 (1980). — London : Royal Society of Chemistry, Nov.1981. — [300]p
ISBN 0-85186-120-2 : £36.50 : CIP entry
ISSN 0260-1818 B81-30364

546'.05 — Inorganic compounds — *Serials*

Advances in inorganic chemistry and radiochemistry. — Vol.22 (1979). — New York ; London : Academic Press, c1979. — ix,457p
ISBN 0-12-023622-2 : Unpriced
ISSN 0065-2792
Primary classification 541.3'8'05 B81-33699

Advances in inorganic chemistry and radiochemistry. — Vol.23. — New York ; London : Academic Press, 1980. — ix,441p
ISBN 0-12-023623-0 : Unpriced
ISSN 0065-2792
Also classified at 541.3'8'05 B81-04015

Comments on modern chemistry. Part A, Comments on inorganic chemistry : a journal of critical discussion of the current literature. — Vol.1, no.1 (1981)-. — New York : Gordon and Breach ; London : Gordon and Breach [Distributor], 1981-. — v. : ill ; 22cm
Six issues yearly. — CODEN: COICDZ
ISSN 0260-3594 = Comments on inorganic chemistry : £42.00 per year B81-35815

Progress in inorganic chemistry. — Vol.28. — New York ; Chichester : Wiley, c1981. — v,463p
ISBN 0-471-08310-0 : £28.00
ISSN 0079-6379 B81-24095

546'.2'0212 — Hydrogen & deuterium. Solubility - *Tables*

Hydrogen and deuterium. — Oxford : Pergamon, Aug.1981. — [670]p. — (Solubility data series, ISSN 0191-5622)
ISBN 0-08-023927-7 (pbk) : £100.00 : CIP entry B81-19154

546'.22 — Water. Molecules. Structure. Determination. Spectroscopy — *Tables*

Flaud, J. M.. Water vapour line parameters from microwave to medium infrared. — Oxford : Pergamon, Nov.1981. — [259]p. — (International tables of selected constants ; 19)
ISBN 0-08-026181-7 : £31.25 : CIP entry
B81-28793

546'.24'028 — Acids. Experiments — *Manuals — For schools*

Acids and alkalis. — St. Albans : Hart-Davis Educational, 1981, c1980. — 31p : ill ; 22cm. — (Centre science)
ISBN 0-247-13123-7 (unbound) : £0.40
Also classified at 546'.3 B81-24520

546'.3 — Alkalies. Experiments — *Manuals — For schools*

Acids and alkalis. — St. Albans : Hart-Davis Educational, 1981, c1980. — 31p : ill ; 22cm. — (Centre science)
ISBN 0-247-13123-7 (unbound) : £0.40
Primary classification 546'.24'028 B81-24520

546'.3 — Transition metal clusters

Transition metal clusters / editor B.F.G. Johnson. — Chichester : Wiley, c1980. — 681p : ill ; 24cm
Includes index
ISBN 0-471-27817-3 : £33.00 : CIP rev.
B80-11422

546'.34 — Ionic liquids

Ionic liquids / edited by Douglas Inman and David G. Lovering. — New York ; London : Plenum, c1981. — x,450p : ill ; 24cm
Includes index
ISBN 0-306-40412-5 : Unpriced B81-17163

546'.4 — Rare earth elements — *Conference proceedings*

Indo-U.S. Conference on Science and Technology *(1980 : Cochin)*. Science and technology of rare earth materials : [proceedings of the Indo-U.S. Conference on Science and Technology held at Cochin, India, on March 3-8, 1980] / edited by E.C. Subbarao, W.E. Wallace. — New York ; London : Academic Press, 1980. — xiv,439p : ill ; 24cm
Includes index
ISBN 0-12-675640-6 : £16.40 B81-19334

546'.431 — Uranium. Disequilibrium. Environmental aspects

Uranium series disequilibrium. — Oxford : Clarendon Press, Jan.1982. — [550]p
ISBN 0-19-854423-5 : £45.00 : CIP entry
B81-34383

546'.6 — Transition metals. Physical properties — *Conference proceedings*

International Conference on the Physics of Transition Metals *(1980 : University of Leeds)*. Physics of transition metals, 1980 : invited and contributed papers from the International Conference on the Physics of Transition Metals held at the University of Leeds, 18-22 August 1980 / edited by P. Rhodes. — Bristol : Institute of Physics, c1981. — xvii,692p : ill ; 24cm. — (Conference series / Institute of Physics, ISSN 0305-2346 ; no.55)
Includes bibliographies and index
ISBN 0-85498-146-2 : Unpriced B81-13243

546'.681 — Carbon — *Conference proceedings*

London International Carbon and Graphite Conference *(5th : 1978)*. Proceedings of the Fifth London International Carbon and Graphite Conference. — London : Society of Chemical Industry
Vol.1: Papers read at the conference held at Imperial College, London, 18-22 September 1978. — 1978. — 531p : ill ; 31cm
ISBN 0-901001-54-6 : Unpriced B81-39190

London International Carbon and Graphite Conference *(5th : 1978)*. Proceedings of the Fifth London International Carbon and Graphite Conference. — London : Society of Chemical Industry
Vol.2: Papers read at the conference held at Imperial College, London, 16-22 September 1978. — 1978. — iii,p532-986 : ill ; 31cm
Includes index
ISBN 0-901001-55-4 : Unpriced B81-39191

London International Carbon and Graphite Conference *(5th : 1978)*. Proceedings of the Fifth London International Carbon and Graphite Conference. — London (Society of Chemical Industry)
Vol.3. — 1979. — ii,189p : ill ; 30cm
ISBN 0-901001-60-0 (pbk) : Unpriced
B81-39192

546'.7 — Nonmetals. Photometric analysis & fluorimetric analysis

Snell, Foster Dee. Photometric and Fluorometric methods of analysis : nonmetals / Foster Dee Snell. — New York ; Chichester : Wiley, c1981. — xii,818p : ill,1port ; 26cm
Includes index
ISBN 0-471-81023-1 : £56.00 B81-33429

546'.711'2 — Nitrogen oxides. Solubility

Oxides of nitrogen. — Oxford : Pergamon, Nov.1981. — [390]p. — (Solubility data series, ISSN 0191-5622 ; v.8)
ISBN 0-08-023924-2 : £50.00 : CIP entry
B81-31064

546'.71159 — Nitrogen. Fixation

New trends in the chemistry of nitrogen fixation / edited by J. Chatt, L.M. da Câmara Pina, R.L. Richards. — London : Academic Press, 1980. — x,284p : ill ; 24cm
Conference papers. — Includes index
ISBN 0-12-169450-x : £22.40 : CIP rev.
B80-08739

546'.71159 — Nitrogen. Fixation — *Conference proceedings*

International Symposium on Nitrogen Fixation *(4th : 1980 : Canberra)*. Current perspectives in nitrogen fixation : proceedings of the Fourth International Symposium on Nitrogen Fixation held in Canberra, Australia, 1 to 5 December 1980 / editorial committee Alan H. Gibson, William E. Newton. — Amsterdam ; Oxford : Elsevier, 1981. — x,534p : ill ; 26cm
Includes bibliographies and index
ISBN 0-444-80291-6 : £38.46 B81-36765

546'.7122 — Phosphorus compounds

Goldwhite, Harold. Introduction to phosphorus chemistry / Harold Goldwhite. — Cambridge : Cambridge University Press, 1981. — xiv,113p : ill ; 24cm. — (Cambridge texts in chemistry and biochemistry)
Bibliography: p106-110. — Includes index
ISBN 0-521-22978-2 (cased) : £12.50
ISBN 0-521-29757-5 (pbk) : £5.95 B81-34527

546'.721542 — Oxygen & ozone. Solubility — *Tables*

Oxygen and ozone. — Oxford : Pergamon, Nov.1981. — [540]p. — (Solubility data series, ISSN 0191-5622 ; v.7)
ISBN 0-08-023915-3 : £50.00 : CIP entry
B81-30381

547 — ORGANIC CHEMISTRY

547 — Organic chemistry

Bailey, Philip S.. Study guide to accompany Organic chemistry : a brief survey of concepts and applications / Philip S. Bailey, Jr and Christina A. Bailey. — Boston, [Mass.] ; London : Allyn and Bacon, c1981. — 181p : ill ; 24cm
Previous ed.: 1978
ISBN 0-205-07235-6 (pbk) : Unpriced
B81-18892

Hawkins, M. D.. Success in organic chemistry / Malcolm D. Hawkins. — London : Murray, 1981. — xv,318p : ill ; 22cm. — (Success studybooks)
Bibliography: p289. — Includes index
ISBN 0-7195-3795-9 (pbk) : £3.50 B81-25165

Hunt, C. B.. Organic chemistry / C.B. Hunt, A.K. Holliday. — London : Butterworths, 1981. — xv,453p : ill ; 24cm. — (Butterworth intermediate chemistry)
Includes index
ISBN 0-408-70915-4 (pbk) : £5.95 B81-22413

Tetrahedron reports on organic chemistry / chairman of the board of editors Sir Derek Barton ; executive editors J.E. Baldwin, W.D. Ollis ; administrative editor T. Stephen. — Oxford : Pergamon
Vol.1. — c1976. — 275p in various pagings : ill ; 28cm
ISBN 0-08-021154-2 : £33.00 B81-14259

Tetrahedron reports on organic chemistry / chairman of the board of editors Sir Derek Barton ; executive editors J.E. Baldwin, W.D. Ollis ; administrative editor T. Stephen. — Oxford : Pergamon
Vol.4. — c1978. — 336p in various pagings : ill ; 28cm
ISBN 0-08-022093-2 : £33.00 B81-14260

547 — Organic compounds

Bailey, Philip S.. Organic chemistry : a brief survey of concepts and applications / Philip S. Bailey, Jr., and Christina A. Bailey. — 2nd ed. — Boston, Mass. ; London : Allyn and Bacon, c1981. — xvi,429p : ill(some col.) ; 25cm
Previous ed.: 1978. — Text on lining papers. — Includes index
ISBN 0-205-07233-x : £19.95 B81-25957

Norman, R.O.C.. Modern organic chemistry. — 3rd ed. — London : Bell & Hyman, June 1981. — [366]p
Previous ed.: London : Mills and Boon, 1975
ISBN 0-7135-2185-6 (pbk) : £4.75 : CIP entry
B81-15912

Organic chemistry / [S246 Course Team]. — Milton Keynes : Open University Press. — (Science : a second level course)
At head of title: The Open University
Block 1: Organic compounds : classification and structure / prepared by an Open University Course Team. — 1980. — 56,28,20p : ill(some col.) ; 30cm. — (S264 ; units 1-3)
Contents: Unit 1: An introduction to organic chemistry - Unit 2: The shapes of molecules - Unit 3: The search for new drugs
ISBN 0-335-16000-x (pbk) : Unpriced
B81-11459

Organic chemistry. — Milton Keynes : Open University Press. — (Science : a second level course)
At head of title: The Open University. — Contents: Unit 4: Molecular separation and identification - Unit 5: Spectroscopic identification - Unit 6: Molecular bonding and chemical reactions
Block 2: Molecular identification and bonding / prepared by an Open University Course Team. — 1980, c1981. — 25,42,12p : ill(some col.) ; 30cm. — (S246 ; block 2, unit 4-6)
ISBN 0-335-16001-8 (pbk) : Unpriced
B81-18013

Organic chemistry. — Milton Keynes : Open University Press. — (Science : a second level course)
At head of title: The Open University
Block 3: Reaction mechanisms : an introduction / prepared by an Open University Course team. — 1980. — 50,35,23p : ill ; 30cm. — (S246 ; block 3, unit 7-9)
Contents: Unit 7: Substitution reactions - Unit 8: Elimination and addition reactions - Unit 9: Terpene biosynthesis
ISBN 0-335-16002-6 (pbk) : Unpriced
B81-18014

Solomons, T. W. Graham. Organic chemistry / T.W. Graham Solomons. — 2nd ed. — New York ; Chichester : Wiley, c1980. — xii,1066,[44]p : ill(some col.) ; 27cm
Previous ed.: 1978. — Text on lining papers. — Bibliography: pB1-B5. - Includes index
ISBN 0-471-04213-7 : £15.25 B81-07645

547 — Organic compounds *continuation*

Streitwieser, Andrew. Introduction to organic chemistry / Andrew Streitwieser, Jr., Clayton H. Heathcock. — 2nd ed. — New York : Macmillan ; London : Collier Macmillan, c1981. — xxii,1258p : ill ; 26cm + 1solution manual and study guide(iv,661p : ill ; 26cm : pbk)
Solution manual and study guide prepared by Paul A. Bartlett. — Previous ed.: 1976. — Text on lining papers. — Includes index
ISBN 0-02-418050-5 (cased) : £17.95
ISBN 0-02-978310-8 (pbk) : £9.95
ISBN 0-02-418060-2 (Solution manual and study guide) : £9.50 B81-29335

Vogel, Arthur Israel. Vogel's elementary practical organic chemistry. — London : Longman
1: Preparations. — 3rd ed. / revised by B.V. Smith, N.M. Waldron. — 1980. — xvii,407p : ill ; 24cm
Previous ed.: published as Elementary practical organic chemistry. 1966. — Bibliography: p394. — Includes index
ISBN 0-582-47009-9 : £9.95 : CIP rev. B79-21741

Wingrove, Alan S.. Organic chemistry / Alan S. Wingrove, Robert L. Caret. — New York ; London : Harper & Row, c1981. — xxiv,1334p : ill(some col.) ; 27cm
Text and ill on lining papers. — Bibliography: p1321-1334. — Includes index
ISBN 0-06-163400-x : £15.00 B81-28451

547'.0014 — Organic chemistry. Terminology

The **Vocabulary** of organic chemistry / Milton Orchin ... [et al.]. — New York ; Chichester : Wiley, c1980. — ix,609p : ill ; 24cm
Includes index
ISBN 0-471-04491-1 : £18.75 B81-10645

547'.0028 — Organic chemistry. Experiments — *Manuals*

Lehman, John W.. Instructor's manual to accompany Operational organic chemistry : a laboratory course / John W. Lehman. — Boston [Mass.] ; London : Allyn and Bacon, c1981. — 107p : ill ; 22cm
ISBN 0-205-07147-3 (pbk) : £1.00 B81-26399

547'.0028'54 — Organic chemistry. Applications of digital computer systems — *Conference proceedings*

Computational theoretical organic chemistry : proceedings of the NATO Advanced Study Institute held at Menton, France, June 29-July 13, 1980 / edited by I.G. Csizmadia and R. Daudel. — Dordrecht ; London : Reidel, published in cooperation with NATO Scientific Affairs Division, c1981. — vii,426p : ill ; 25cm. — (NATO advanced study institutes series. Series C, Mathematical and physical sciences, ISSN 0377-2071 ; v.67)
Includes index
ISBN 90-277-1270-0 : Unpriced B81-25602

547'.0028'5425 — Organic chemistry. Applications of digital computer systems. Programs: Dendral program

Applications of artificial intelligence for organic chemistry : the DENDRAL project / Robert K. Lindsay ... [et al.]. — New York ; London : McGraw-Hill, c1980. — xii,194p : ill ; 24cm. — (McGraw-Hill advanced computer science series)
Bibliography: p179-186. - Includes index
ISBN 0-07-037895-9 : £14.60 B81-04517

547'.005 — Organic chemistry — *Serials*

Annual reports on the progress of chemistry. Section B, Organic chemistry. — Vol.76 (1979). — London : Royal Society of Chemistry, c1980. — xix,519p
ISBN 0-85186-111-3 : Unpriced : CIP rev.
ISSN 0069-3030 B80-34952

Annual reports on the progress of chemistry. Section B, Organic chemistry. — Vol.77 (1980). — London : Royal Society of Chemistry, Oct.1981. — [410]p
ISBN 0-85186-121-0 : £40.50 : CIP entry
ISSN 0069-3030 B81-24669

547'.00724 — Organic chemistry. Experiments

Lehman, John W.. Operational organic chemistry : a laboratory course / John W. Lehman. — Boston [Mass.] ; London : Allyn and Bacon, c1981. -- xi,671p : ill ; 25cm
Bibliography: p648-658. - Includes index
ISBN 0-205-07146-5 : £19.95 B81-18893

547'.0076 — Organic chemistry — *Questions & answers*

Bailey, Philip S.. Instructor's manual to accompany Organic chemistry : a brief survey of concepts and applications. 2nd ed / Philip S. Bailey, Jr, Christina A. Bailey. — Boston [Mass.] ; London : Allyn and Bacon, c1981. — 42p ; 22cm
ISBN 0-205-07234-8 (unbound) : £1.00 B81-26435

Ryles, A. P.. Worked examples in essential organic chemistry. — Chichester : Wiley, Aug.1981. — [192]p
ISBN 0-471-27972-2 (cased) : £14.50 : CIP entry
ISBN 0-471-27975-7 (pbk) : £6.50 B81-19170

547'.03 — Organic hydroxyl compounds

The **Chemistry** of ethers, crown ethers, hydroxyl groups and their sulphur analogues / edited by Saul Patai. — Chichester : Wiley, 1980. — 2v.(xiv,1142p) : ill ; 24cm. — (The Chemistry of functional groups. Supplement E)
Includes index
ISBN 0-471-27618-9 : £98.00
ISBN 0-471-27771-1 (pt.1£49.00)
ISBN 0-471-27772-x (pt.2) : £49.00
Also classified at 547'.035 ; 547'.061 ; 547'.063 B81-10778

547'.035 — Crown-ethers

Jong, F. de. Stability and reactivity of crown-ether complexes. — London : Academic Press, Sept.1981. — [180]p
ISBN 0-12-208780-1 (pbk) : CIP entry B81-30303

547'.035 — Ethers

The **Chemistry** of ethers, crown ethers, hydroxyl groups and their sulphur analogues / edited by Saul Patai. — Chichester : Wiley, 1980. — 2v.(xiv,1142p) : ill ; 24cm. — (The Chemistry of functional groups. Supplement E)
Includes index
ISBN 0-471-27618-9 : £98.00
ISBN 0-471-27771-1 (pt.1£49.00)
ISBN 0-471-27772-x (pt.2) : £49.00
Primary classification 547'.03 B81-10778

547'.036 — Carbonyl compounds

Oxocarbons / edited by Robert West. — New York ; London : Academic Press, 1980. — xi,235p : ill ; 24cm
Includes index
ISBN 0-12-744580-3 : £18.00 B81-21837

547'.043 — Diazo compounds

Ershov, Vladimir V.. Quinonediazides. — Oxford : Elsevier, Aug.1981. — [302]p. — (Studies in organic chemistry ; v.7)
ISBN 0-444-41737-0 : CIP entry B81-25108

547'.05 — Organometallic compounds. Spectroscopy — *Serials*

Spectroscopic properties of inorganic and organometallic compounds. — Vol.14. — London : Royal Society of Chemistry, Dec.1981. — [400]p. — (Specialist periodical report / Royal Society of Chemistry)
ISBN 0-85186-123-7 : CIP entry
ISSN 0584-8555
Primary classification 541.2'8 B81-32050

547'.05'05 — Organometallic compounds — *Serials*

Advances in organometallic chemistry. — Vol.19. — New York ; London : Academic Press, 1981. — ix,318p
Unpriced B81-32668

Organometallic chemistry. — Vol.9. — London : Royal Society of Chemistry, c1981. — xviii,539p. — (Specialist periodical report / Royal Society of Chemistry)
ISBN 0-85186-571-2 : Unpriced B81-29057

547'.054 — Organic rare earth compounds & organic actinide compounds — *Conference proceedings*

Organometallics of the f-elements : proceedings of the NATO Advanced Study Institute held at Sogesta, Urbino, Italy, September 11-22, 1978 / edited by Tobin J. Marks and R. Dieter Fischer. — Dordrecht ; London : Reidel, c1979. — xv,517p : ill ; 25cm. — (Nato advanced study institutes series. Series C, Mathematical and Physical Sciences ; v.44)
Includes index
ISBN 90-277-0990-4 : Unpriced B81-15268

547'.0568 — Organic group IV compounds — *Serials*

Organometallic chemistry reviews. — Oxford : Elsevier Scientific, Oct.1981. — [300]p. — (Journal of Organometallic Chemistry library ; 12)
ISBN 0-444-42025-8 : CIP entry B81-27379

547'.0568'05 — Organic Group IV compounds — *Serials*

Organometallic chemistry reviews, annual surveys, silicon-tin-lead. — 1981. — Amsterdam ; Oxford : Elsevier Scientific, 1981. — [vi],566p. — (Journal of organometallic chemistry library ; 11)
ISBN 0-444-41985-3 : Unpriced : CIP rev. B81-12306

547'.0572'05 — Organic selenium compounds & organic tellurium compounds - *Serials*

Organic compounds of sulphur, selenium, and tellurium. — Vol.6. — London : Royal Society of Chemistry, Sept.1981. — [350]p. — (A Specialist periodical report)
ISBN 0-85186-299-3 : CIP entry
ISSN 0305-9812
Primary classification 547'.06'05 B81-20502

547'.06 — Organic sulphur compounds — *Conference proceedings*

International Symposium on Organic Sulfur Chemistry *(9th : 1980 : Riga)*. Organic sulfur chemistry : invited lectures presentd at the 9th International Symposium on Organic Sulfur Chemistry, Riga, USSR, 9-14 June 1980 / edited by R. Kh. Freidlina and A.E. Skorova. — Oxford : Pergamon, 1981. — vii,230p : ill ; 28cm
At head of title: International Union of Pure and Applied Chemistry (Organic Chemistry Division)
ISBN 0-08-026180-9 : £27.00 B81-33447

547'.06'05 — Organic sulphur compounds - *Serials*

Organic compounds of sulphur, selenium, and tellurium. — Vol.6. — London : Royal Society of Chemistry, Sept.1981. — [350]p. — (A Specialist periodical report)
ISBN 0-85186-299-3 : CIP entry
ISSN 0305-9812
Also classified at 547'.0572'05 B81-20502

547'.061 — Organic sulphides

The **Chemistry** of ethers, crown ethers, hydroxyl groups and their sulphur analogues / edited by Saul Patai. — Chichester : Wiley, 1980. — 2v.(xiv,1142p) : ill ; 24cm. — (The Chemistry of functional groups. Supplement E)
Includes index
ISBN 0-471-27618-9 : £98.00
ISBN 0-471-27771-1 (pt.1£49.00)
ISBN 0-471-27772-x (pt.2) : £49.00
Primary classification 547'.03 B81-10778

547'.063 — Organic sulfhydryl compounds

The **Chemistry** of ethers, crown ethers, hydroxyl groups and their sulphur analogues / edited by Saul Patai. — Chichester : Wiley, 1980. — 2v.(xiv,1142p) : ill ; 24cm. — (The Chemistry of functional groups. Supplement E)
Includes index
ISBN 0-471-27618-9 : £98.00
ISBN 0-471-27771-1 (pt.1£49.00)
ISBN 0-471-27772-x (pt.2) : £49.00
Primary classification 547'.03 B81-10778

547'.065 — Sulphonium compounds

The **Chemistry** of the sulphonium group / edited by C.J.M. Stirling. — Chichester : Wiley, 1981. — 2v.(xiii,847p) : ill ; 24cm. — (The Chemistry of functional groups)
Includes index
ISBN 0-471-27655-3 : Unpriced : CIP rev.
ISBN 0-471-27769-x (v.1) : £35.00
ISBN 0-471-27770-3 (v.2) : £40.00 B80-31528

547'.07'05 — Organic phosphorus compounds - *Serials*

Organophosphorus chemistry. — Vol.12. — London : Royal Society of Chemistry, Sept.1981. — [300]p. — (A Specialist periodical report)
ISBN 0-85186-106-7 : CIP entry
ISSN 0306-0713 B81-20565

547'.08046 — Organic silicon compounds. Chemical analysis

Colvin, Ernest. Silicon in organic synthesis. — London : Butterworths, Aug.1981. — [348]p. — (Butterworths monographs in chemistry and chemical engineering)
ISBN 0-408-10619-0 : £15.00 : CIP entry B81-18175

547.1'3 — Organic compounds. Physical chemistry

Lowry, Thomas H.. Mechanism and theory in organic chemistry / Thomas H. Lowry, Kathleen Schueller Richardson. — 2nd ed. — New York ; London : Harper & Row, c1981. — x,991p : ill ; 25cm
Previous ed.: 1976. — Includes index
ISBN 0-06-044083-x : £16.25 B81-28265

547.1'3'05 — Physical organic chemistry — *Serials*

Progress in physical organic chemistry. — Vol.13. — New York ; Chichester : Wiley, c1981. — ix,638p
ISBN 0-471-06253-7 : £46.75
ISSN 0079-6662 B81-25481

547.1'3723 — Organic acids & bases. Ionisation. Thermodynamic properties

Perrin, D. D.. pKa prediction for organic acids and bases. — London : Chapman and Hall, Nov.1981. — [150]p
ISBN 0-412-22190-x : £10.00 : CIP entry B81-31266

547.1'39 — Hammett equation

Johnson, C. D.. The Hammett equation / C.D. Johnson. — Cambridge : Cambridge University Press, 1981, c1973. — vii,196p : ill ; 22cm. — (Cambridge texts in chemistry and biochemistry)
Originally published: 1973. — Includes index
ISBN 0-521-29970-5 (pbk) : £5.95 B81-24512

547.1'39 — Organic compounds. Chemical reactions. Mechanisms

Sykes, Peter. A guidebook to mechanism in organic chemistry / Peter Sykes. — 5th ed. — London : Longman, 1981. — xii,397p : ill ; 22cm
Previous ed.: 1975. — Bibliography: p379-381. — Includes index
ISBN 0-582-44121-8 (pbk) : £6.95 : CIP rev. B81-03357

547.1'394'05 — Organic compounds. Chemical reactions. Mechanisms — *Serials*

Organic reaction mechanisms. — 1979. — Chichester : Wiley, c1981. — 759p
ISBN 0-471-27818-1 : £58.00
ISSN 0474-4772 B81-12416

547.2 — Halogenated hydrocarbons

Hála, Slavoj. Analysis of complex hydrocarbon mixtures. — Oxford : Elsevier Scientific. — (Wilson and Wilson's comprehensive analytical chemistry ; v.13)
Part A: Separation methods. — Oct.1981. — [425]p
ISBN 0-444-99736-9 : £45.00 : CIP entry
ISBN 0-444-99734-2 (set) : £90.00 B81-25293

Hála, Slavoj. Analysis of complex hydrocarbon mixtures. — Oxford : Elsevier Scientific. — (Wilson and Wilson's comprehensive analytical chemistry ; v.13)
Part B: Group analysis and detailed analysis. — Oct.1981. — [425]p
ISBN 0-444-99735-0 : £45.00 : CIP entry
ISBN 0-444-99734-2 (set) : £90.00 B81-25292

547'.2 — Organic compounds. Synthesis

De la Mare, P. B. D.. Electrophilic additions to unsaturated systems. — 2nd ed. — Oxford : Elsevier Scientific, Nov.1981. — [392]p. — (Studies in organic chemistry ; 9)
Previous ed.: 1966
ISBN 0-444-42030-4 : CIP entry B81-31233

Mackie, Raymond K.. Guidebook to organic synthesis. — London : Longman, Nov.1981. — [256]p
ISBN 0-582-45592-8 (pbk) : £8.00 : CIP entry B81-30153

Wade, Leroy G.. Compendium of organic synthetic methods. — New York ; Chichester : Wiley
Vol.4 / Leroy G. Wade, Jr. — c1980. — xvi,497p : ill ; 24cm
ISBN 0-471-04923-9 : Unpriced B81-08440

547'.2 — Organic compounds. Synthesis — *Conference proceedings*

IUPAC Symposium on Organic Synthesis *(3rd : 1980 : Madison)*. Organic synthesis today and tomorrow : proceedings of the 3rd IUPAC Symposium on Organic Synthesis Madison, Wisconsin, USA, 15-20 June 1980 / [organised by] International Union of Pure and Applied Chemistry (Organic Division) University of Wisconsin (Department of Chemistry) ; edited by Barry M. Trost and C. Richard Hutchinson. — Oxford : Pergamon, 1981. — x,354p : ill ; 28cm
Includes index
ISBN 0-08-025268-0 : £37.50 B81-25338

547'.2 — Organic compounds. Synthesis. Electrochemical techniques

Kyriacou, Demetrios K.. Basics of electroorganic synthesis / Demetrios K. Kyriacou. — New York ; Chichester : Wiley, c1981. — xiii,153p : ill ; 24cm
Bibliography: p147-148. — Includes index
ISBN 0-471-07975-8 : £17.00 B81-23432

547'.2 — Organic compounds. Synthesis. Protection of functional groups. Protective groups

Greene, Theodora W.. Protective groups in organic synthesis / Theodora W. Greene. — New York ; Chichester : Wiley, c1981. — xiii,349p : ill ; 24cm
Includes index
ISBN 0-471-05764-9 : £26.25 B81-33225

547'.2 — Organic compounds. Synthesis. Reagents: Organic copper compounds

Posner, Gary H.. An introduction to synthesis using organocopper reagents / Gary H. Posner. — New York ; Chichester : Wiley, c1980. — xvii,140p : ill ; 24cm
Includes bibliographies and index
ISBN 0-471-69538-6 : £12.50 B81-04690

547'.2 — Organic compounds. Synthesis. Reagents — *Serials*

Reagents for organic synthesis. — Vol.9. — New York ; Chichester : Wiley, c1981. — [vii],596p
Also entitled: Fieser and Fieser's reagents for organic synthesis
ISBN 0-471-05631-6 : £28.00
ISSN 0271-6747 B81-35444

Synthetic reagents. — Vol.4. — Chichester : Ellis Horwood, 1981. — 426p
ISBN 0-85312-309-8 : £32.50 : CIP rev.
ISBN 0-470-27133-7 (Halsted Press) B80-36063

547'.2 — Organic compounds. Synthesis. Use of stable isotopes

Ott, Donald G.. Syntheses with stable isotopes of carbon, nitrogen and oxygen / Donald G. Ott. — New York ; Chichester : Wiley, c1981. — vii,224p : ill ; 24cm
Includes index
ISBN 0-471-04922-0 : £15.25 B81-11300

547'.2'05 — Organic compounds. Synthesis — *Serials*

Annual reports in organic synthesis. — 1979. — New York ; London : Academic Press, 1980. — xiii,461p
ISBN 0-12-040810-4 : Unpriced
ISSN 0066-409x B81-03773

General and synthetic methods. — Vol.4. — London : Royal Society of Chemistry, c1981. — xiii,376. — (Specialist periodical report / Royal Society of Chemistry)
ISBN 0-85186-854-1 : Unpriced
ISSN 0141-2140 B81-29058

Journal of synthetic methods : the journal of the Chemical Reactions Documentation Service. — Vol.4, no.1 (Jan.1978)-. — London (128 Theobalds Rd, WC1X 8RP) : Derwent, 1978-. — v. ; 21cm
Monthly. — Continues: CRDS abstracts journal. — Description based on: Vol.6, no.1 (Jan.1980)
ISSN 0260-8847 = Journal of synthetic methods : £110.00 per year to academic institutions only B81-09195

547'.23 — Organic compounds. Oxidation. Catalysis. Palladium compounds. Mechanisms

Henry, Patrick M.. Palladium catalyzed oxidation of hydrocarbons / Patrick M. Henry. — Dordrecht ; London : Reidel, c1980. — xv,435p ; 23cm. — (Catalysis by metal complexes ; v.2)
Includes index
ISBN 90-277-0986-6 : Unpriced B81-04689

547'.28 — Polymerisation

Odian, George. Principles of polymerization / George Odian. — New York ; Chichester : Wiley, c1981. — xxvi,731p : ill ; 25cm
Previous ed.: New York : McGraw-Hill, 1970. — Includes index
ISBN 0-471-05146-2 : £26.25 B81-33012

547'.29'05 — Fermentation — *Serials*

Annual reports on fermentation processes. — Vol.4. — New York ; London : Academic Press, 1980. — xiv,319p
ISBN 0-12-040304-8 : Unpriced
ISSN 0140-9115 B81-33279

547.3'02 — Organic compounds. Chemical analysis. Sampling — *Conference proceedings*

Trace-organic sample handling / edited by Eric Reid. — Chichester : Horwood, 1981. — 383p : ill ; 24cm. — (Methodological surveys. Sub-series (A), Analysis ; v.10)
Includes index
ISBN 0-85312-187-7 : Unpriced B81-17415

547.3'05 — Physical chemistry — *Serials*

Annual reports on the progress of chemistry. Section C, Physical chemistry. — Vol.77 (1980). — London : Royal Society of Chemistry, Sept.1981. — [230]p
ISBN 0-85186-822-3 : £36.50 : CIP entry
ISSN 0260-1826 B81-23892

547.3'0873 — Organic compounds. Mass spectrometry

Howe, Ian. Mass spectrometry : principles and applications. — 2nd ed / Ian Howe, Dudley H. Williams, Richard D. Bowen. — New York ; London : McGraw-Hill, c1981. — xii,276p : ill ; 24cm
Previous ed.: published as Principles of organic mass spectrometry. 1972. — Includes index
ISBN 0-07-070569-0 : £20.75 B81-40644

Schlunegger, Urs P.. Advanced mass spectrometry : applications in organic and analytical chemistry / Urs P. Schlunegger ; translation editor T.R. Crompton. — Oxford : Pergamon, 1980. — xii,143p : ill ; 22cm
Includes index
ISBN 0-08-023842-4 : £12.25 : CIP rev. B80-12847

547.3'0877 — Organic compounds. Carbon-13 nuclear resonance

Mann, B. E.. 13C nmr data for organometallic compounds. — London : Academic Press, July 1981. — [450]p
ISBN 0-12-469150-1 : CIP entry B81-13848

547.3'4 — Organic compounds. Qualitative analysis & preparation of derivatives to confirm analysis — *Laboratory manuals*

Criddle, W. J.. Spectral and chemical characterization of organic compounds : a laboratory handbook / W.J. Criddle and G.P. Ellis. — 2nd ed. — Chichester : Wiley, c1980. — xi,115p : ill ; 26cm
Previous ed.: 1976. — Includes index
ISBN 0-471-27813-0 (cased) : £13.00 : CIP rev.
ISBN 0-471-27812-2 (pbk) : £4.50 B80-25586

547.3′4 — Organic compounds. Qualitative analysis — *Laboratory manuals — For schools*

Davies, D. G.. Organic reactions at Advanced Level. — 2nd ed. — London : Bell & Hyman, Jan.1982. — [52]p
ISBN 0-7135-2197-x (pbk) : £1.50 : CIP entry B81-34291

547.3′46 — Organic compounds. Qualitative analysis. Spectroscopy

Silverstein, Robert M.. Spectrometric identification of organic compounds. — 4th ed, Robert M. Silverstein, G. Clayton Bassler, Terence C. Morrill. — New York ; Chichester : Wiley, c1981. — 442p : ill,forms ; 29cm
Previous ed.: 1974. — Includes bibliographies and index
ISBN 0-471-02990-4 : £14.40 B81-24944

547′.4 — Alkynes, allenes & cumulenes. Synthesis. Laboratory techniques — *Manauls*

Brandsma, L.. Synthesis of acetylenes, allenes and cumulenes : a laboratory manual / L. Brandsma and H.D. Verkruijsse. — Amsterdam ; Oxford : Elsevier Scientific. — ix,276p : ill ; 25cm. — (Studies in organic chemistry ; 8)
ISBN 0-444-42009-6 : £32.48 B81-39265

547′.5 — Macrocyclic compounds — *Serials*

Progress in macrocyclic chemistry. — Vol.2. — New York ; Chichester : John Wiley, c1981. — ix,347p
ISBN 0-471-05178-0 : £31.00 B81-25493

547′.5 — Polycyclic aromatic compounds. Chemical analysis

Lee, Milton L.. Analytical chemistry of polycyclic aromatic compounds / Milton L. Lee, Milos v. Novotny, Keith D. Bartle. — New York ; London : Academic Press, c1981. — xi,462p : ill ; 24cm
Includes index
ISBN 0-12-440840-0 : £33.60 B81-35359

547′.59 — Chromans

Chromans and tocopherols / edited by G.P. Ellis, I.M. Lockhart. — New York ; Chichester : Wiley, c1981. — xii,469p : ill ; 24cm. — (The chemistry of heterocyclic compounds ; v.36)
Includes index
ISBN 0-471-03038-4 : £77.80 B81-24192

547′.59 — Heterocyclic compounds. Toxic effects. Environmental aspects — *Conference proceedings*

Chlorinated dioxins and related compounds. — Oxford : Pergamon, Dec.1981. — [624]p. — (Pergamon series on environmental science ; v.5)
Conference papers
ISBN 0-08-026256-2 : £37.50 : CIP entry B81-32043

547′.59 — Heterocyclic phosphorus compounds

Quin, Louis D.. The heterocyclic chemistry of phosphorus : systems based on the phosphorus-carbon bond / Louis D. Quin. — New York ; Chichester : Wiley, c1981. — xiii,434p : ill ; 24cm
Includes index
ISBN 0-471-06461-0 : £25.00 B81-16449

547′.59′05 — Heterocyclic compounds — *Serials*

Advances in heterocyclic chemistry. — Vol.24. — New York ; London : Academic Press, 1979. — xi,461p
ISBN 0-12-020624-2 : £32.80
ISSN 0065-2725 B81-16843

Advances in heterocyclic chemistry. — Vol.26. — New York ; London : Academic Press, c1980. — ix,247p
ISBN 0-12-020626-9 : Unpriced
ISSN 0065-2725 B81-04934

Advances in heterocyclic chemistry. — Vol.27. — New York ; London : Academic Press, 1980. — ix,331p
ISBN 0-12-020627-7 : Unpriced
ISSN 0065-2725 B81-32693

Heterocyclic chemistry : a review of the literature abstracted between ... and ... — Vol.1-. — London (Burlington House, W1V 3BN) : Royal Society of Chemistry, 1980-. — v. ; 22cm. — (Specialist periodical report / Royal Society of Chemistry)
Annual. — Merger of: Saturated heterocyclic chemistry ; and, Aromatic and heteroaromatic chemistry. — Continues in part: Organic compounds of sulphur, selenium and tellurium
ISSN 0144-8773 = Heterocyclic chemistry : Unpriced B81-12402

547′.593 — 1,2,3-triazoles

Finley, K. Thomas. Triazoles- 1, 2, 3 / K. Thomas Finley ; Volume editor John A. Montgomery. — New York ; Chichester : Wiley, c1980. — ix,349p ; 24cm. — (The Chemistry of heterocyclic compounds, ISSN 0069-3154 ; v.39)
Includes index
ISBN 0-471-07827-1 : Unpriced B81-09272

547′.593 — 1,2,4-triazoles

Temple, Carroll. Triazoles 1,2,4 / Carroll Temple, Jr. ; edited by John A. Montgomery. — New York ; Chichester : Wiley, c1981. — xiv,791p : ill ; 24cm. — (The Chemistry of heterocyclic compounds, ISSN 0069-3154 ; v.37)
Includes index
ISBN 0-471-04656-6 : £95.00 B81-11696

547′.593 — Benzimadazoles

Benzimidazoles and congeneric tricyclic compounds / edited by P.N. Preston. — New York ; Chichester : Wiley, c1981. — 2v. : ill ; 24cm. — (The Chemistry of heterocyclic compounds, ISSN 0069-3154 ; v.40)
Includes index. — Contents: Pt.1 / with contributions by D. M. Smith, G. Tennant — Pt.2 / with contributions by M. F. G. Stevens, G. Tennant
ISBN 0-471-03792-3 : Unpriced
ISBN 0-471-08189-2 (v.2) : £98.00 B81-33223

547′.593 — Porphyrins. Coordination compounds

Berezin, B. D.. Coordination compounds of porphyrins and phthalocyanines / B.D. Berezin ; translation by V.G. Vopian. — Chichester : Wiley, 1981. — xiii,286p : ill ; 24cm
Translation of: Koordinat͡sionnye soedineni͡ia porfirinov i ftalot͡sianina. — Includes index
ISBN 0-471-27857-2 : £19.15 : CIP rev
Also classified at 547.8′6 B81-14830

547′.596 — Isoquinolines

Isoquinolines / edited by Guenter Grethe. — New York ; Chichester : Wiley. — (The Chemistry of heterocyclic compounds, ISSN 0069-3154 ; v.38)
Pt. 1. — 1981. — xv,561p : ill ; 24cm
Includes index
ISBN 0-471-37481-4 : Unpriced B81-24023

547′.604593 — Aromatic compounds. Nitration

Schofield, K.. Aromatic nitration / K. Schofield. — Cambridge : Cambridge University Press, 1980. — v,376p : ill ; 24cm
Includes index
ISBN 0-521-23362-3 : £27.50 : CIP rev. B80-39368

547′.610457 — Aromatic hydrocarbons. Electronic properties

Pope, Martin. Electronic processes in organic crystals. — Oxford : Clarendon Press, Jan.1982. — [800]p. — (Monographs on the physics and chemistry of materials)
ISBN 0-19-851334-8 : £50.00 : CIP entry B81-34563

547′.611 — Indandiones

Pharmacochemistry of 1,3-Indandiones. — Oxford : Elsevier Scientific, Sept.1981. — [350] p. — (Pharmacochemistry library ; v.3)
ISBN 0-444-41976-4 : CIP entry B81-22640

547′.611 — Tetraphenylborates. Solubility — *Tables*

Popovych, Orest. Tetraphenylborates / volume editor Orest Popovych ; evaluator and compiler Orest Popovych. — Oxford : Pergamon, c1981. — xii,242p ; 28cm. — (Solubility data series, ISSN 0191-5622 ; v.18)
Includes index
ISBN 0-08-023928-5 : £50.00 B81-18759

547′.636 — Quinonediazides

Ershov, Vladimir. Quinonediazides / Vladimir V. Ershov and Gregory A. Nikiforov, Cornelis R.H.I. de Jonge ; [translated from Russian into English by Dimitri I. Paschenko]. — Amsterdam ; Oxford : Elsevier Scientific, 1981. — 301p : ill ; 25cm
Includes index
ISBN 0-444-42008-8 : £34.45 B81-39266

547.7 — Graft copolymers

Sperling, L. H.. Interpenetrating polymer networks and related materials / L.H. Sperling. — New York ; London : Plenum, c1981. — xi,265p : ill ; 24cm
Bibliography: p243-261. — Includes index
ISBN 0-306-40539-3 : Unpriced B81-29909

547.7 — Marine organisms. Natural products — *Serials*

Marine natural products. — Vol.4. — London : Academic Press, 1981. — xiv,199p
ISBN 0-12-624004-3 : £18.00
ISSN 0163-8572 B81-35102

547.7 — Optically active polymers — *Conference proceedings*

Optically active polymers / edited by Eric Selegny. — Dordrecht ; London : Reidel, c1979. — xi,417p : ill ; 25cm. — (Charged and reactive polymers ; v.5)
Conference papers. — Includes index
ISBN 90-277-0904-1 : Unpriced B81-04148

547.7 — Polymer science

Young, Robert J.. Introduction to polymeric materials. — London : Chapman and Hall, Aug.1981. — [250]p
ISBN 0-412-22170-5 (cased) : £12.00 : CIP entry
ISBN 0-412-22180-2 (pbk) : £5.00 B81-18159

547.7 — Polymers

Allcock, Harry R.. Contemporary polymer chemistry / Harry R. Allcock, Frederick W. Lampe. — Englewood Cliffs ; London : Prentice-Hall, c1981. — vii,599p : ill ; 25cm
Bibliography: p581-587. — Includes index
ISBN 0-13-170258-0 : £21.40 B81-20022

547.7 — Polymers — *Conference proceedings*

China-U.S. Bilateral Symposium on Polymer Chemistry and Physics *(1979 : Beijing)*. Proceedings of China-U.S. Bilateral Symposium on Polymer Chemistry and Physics : October 5-10, 1979, Beijing. — Beijing : Science Press ; New York ; London : distributed by Van Nostrand Reinhold, 1981. — vii,434p,[1]leaf of plates : ill ; 27cm
Includes index
ISBN 0-442-20073-0 : £27.65 B81-31302

Hearle, J. W. S.. Polymers and their properties. — Chichester : Ellis Horwood
Vol.1: Fundamentals of structure and mechanics. — Nov.1981. — [384]p
ISBN 0-85312-033-1 : £30.00 : CIP entry B81-32027

International Symposium on Macromolecular Chemistry *(1978 : Tashkent)*. International symposium on macromolecular chemistry, IUPAC, Tashkent, 1978 : proceedings of the International Symposium on Macromolecular Chemistry held in Tashkent, USSR under the auspices of the International Union of Pure and Applied Chemistry, 17-21 October 1978 / editors V. Kabanov, C.G. Overberger. — New York ; [Chichester] : Wiley, c1980. — 207p : ill ; 23cm. — (Polymer symposia, ISSN 0360-8905 ; 67)
Includes index
ISBN 0-471-09013-1 (pbk) : £11.50 B81-21149

547.7 — Stereoregular polymers

Preparation and properties of stereoregular polymers : based upon the proceedings of the NATO Advanced Study Institute held at Tirrennia, Pisa, Italy, October 3-14, 1978 / edited by Robert W. Lenz and Francesco Ciardelli. — Dordrecht ; London : Published in cooperation with NATO Scientific Affairs Division [by] Reidel, c1980. — xvii,472p : ill ; 25cm. — (NATO Advanced study institutes series. Series C, Mathematical and physical sciences ; v.51)
Includes index
ISBN 90-277-1055-4 : Unpriced B81-05852

547.7'044 — Polymers. Structure — *Conference proceedings*

International Symposium on Macromolecules *(1980 : Florence)*. Structural order in polymers : lectures presented at the International Symposium on Macromolecules, Florence, Italy, 7-12 September 1980 / edited by Francesco Ciardelli and Paolo Giusti. — Oxford : Pergamon, 1981. — xiv,247p : ill ; 28cm
At head of title: International Union of Pure and Applied Chemistry (Macromolecular Division)
ISBN 0-08-025296-6 : £30.00 : CIP rev.
Also classified at 574.19'24 B81-10421

547.7'044 — Polymers. Structure. Determination

Koenig, Jack L.. Chemical microstructure of polymer chains / Jack L. Koenig. — New York ; Chichester : Wiley, c1980. — xviii,414p : ill ; 24cm
Includes index
ISBN 0-471-07725-9 : Unpriced B81-08446

547.7'0442 — Polymers. Structure

Bassett, D. C.. Principles of polymer morphology / D.C. Bassett. — Cambridge : Cambridge University Press, 1981. — ix,251p : ill ; 21cm. — (Cambridge solid state science series)
Bibliography: p243-245. — Includes index
ISBN 0-521-23270-8 (cased) : £25.00
ISBN 0-521-29886-5 (pbk) : £8.95 B81-37633

547.7'04426 — Polymers. Molecules. Dynamics

Bailey, R. T.. Molecular motion in high polymers / by R.T. Bailey, Alastair M. North and Richard A. Pethrick. — Oxford : Clarendon, 1981. — xvi,415p : ill ; 24cm. — (The International series of monographs on chemistry)
Includes index
ISBN 0-19-851333-x : £42.50 : CIP rev.
B81-10469

547.7'045453 — Polymers. Surfaces

Cherry, B. W.. Polymer surfaces / B.W. Cherry. — Cambridge : Cambridge University Press, 1981. — x,161p : ill ; 23cm. — (Cambridge solid state science series)
Bibliography: p145-152. - Includes index
ISBN 0-521-23082-9 (cased) : £14.00
ISBN 0-521-29792-3 (pbk) : £6.95 B81-09925

547.7'0455'05 — Polymers. Photochemistry — *Serials*

Developments in polymer photochemistry. — 2. — London : Applied Science, c1981. — x,278p. — (Developments series)
ISBN 0-85334-936-3 : £30.00 B81-24102

Developments in polymer photochemistry. — 3. — London : Applied Science, Oct.1981. — [368]p. — (The Developments series)
ISBN 0-85334-978-9 : £29.00 : CIP entry
B81-27954

Polymer photochemistry : an international journal. — Vol.1, no.1 (Jan.1981)-. — Barking : Applied Science, 1981-. — v. : ill ; 24 cm
Quarterly
ISSN 0144-2880 = Polymer photochemistry : Unpriced B81-15072

547.7'04561 — Polymers. Combustion

Cullis, C. F.. The combustion of organic polymers / by C.F. Cullis and M.M. Hirschler. — Oxford : Clarendon, 1981. — x,419p : ill ; 24cm. — (International series of monographs on chemistry)
Bibliography: p347-389. — Includes index
ISBN 0-19-851351-8 : Unpriced : CIP rev.
B81-04253

547.7'0457 — Polymers. Electrical properties

Blythe, A. R.. Electrical properties of polymers / A.R. Blythe. — Cambridge : Cambridge University Press, c1979 (1980 [printing]). — x,191p : ill ; 22cm. — (Cambridge solid state science series)
Bibliography: p181-183. — Includes index
ISBN 0-521-29825-3 (pbk) : £4.95 B81-25190

547.7'04572 — Solutions of polymers. Electro-optical properties — *Conference proceedings*

NATO Advanced Study Institute on Molecular Electro-optics *(1980 : New York)*. Molecular electro-optics : electro-optic properties of macromolecules and colloids in solution : [proceedings of a NATO Advanced Study Institute on Molecular Electro-optics, held July 14-24, 1980, at Rensselaer Polytechnic Institute, Troy, New York] / edited by Sonja Krause. — New York ; London : Plenum published in cooperation with NATO Scientific Affairs Division, c1981. — viii,520p : ill ; 26cm. — (NATO advanced study institutes series. Series B, Physics ; v.64)
Includes index
ISBN 0-306-40659-4 : Unpriced B81-24474

547.7'0459'05 — Natural products. Synthesis — *Serials*

The **total** synthesis of natural products. — Vol.4. — New York ; Chichester : Wiley, c1981. — ix,610p
ISBN 0-471-05460-7 : £42.00 B81-33310

547.7'04595 — Polymers. Synthesis. Catalysis — *Conference proceedings*

Polymer catalysts and affinants-polymers in chromatography : proceedings of the 18th Prague IUPAC Microsymposium on Macromolecules, 10-13 July 1978, sixth discussion conference, 17-21 July 1978, Prague, Czechoslovakia, held under the auspices of the International Union of Pure and Applied Chemistry, the Czechoslovak Academy of Sciences, and the Czechoslovak Chemical Society Re editors B. Sedlacek, C.G. Overberger, H.F. Mark. — New York ; [Chichester] : Wiley, c1980. — vi,251p : ill ; 23cm. — (Polymer symposia, ISSN 0360-8905 ; 68)
Includes index
ISBN 0-471-09014-x (pbk) : £14.50
Also classified at 547.7'046 B81-21150

547.7'046 — Polymers. Chromatography — *Conference proceedings*

Polymer catalysts and affinants-polymers in chromatography : proceedings of the 18th Prague IUPAC Microsymposium on Macromolecules, 10-13 July 1978, sixth discussion conference, 17-21 July 1978, Prague, Czechoslovakia, held under the auspices of the International Union of Pure and Applied Chemistry, the Czechoslovak Academy of Sciences, and the Czechoslovak Chemical Society Re editors B. Sedlacek, C.G. Overberger, H.F. Mark. — New York ; [Chichester] : Wiley, c1980. — vi,251p : ill ; 23cm. — (Polymer symposia, ISSN 0360-8905 ; 68)
Includes index
ISBN 0-471-09014-x (pbk) : £14.50
Primary classification 547.7'04595 B81-21150

547.7'046 — Vegetable fibres. Identification

Catling, Dorothy M.. Identification of vegetable fibres. — London : Chapman & Hall, Dec.1981. — [150]p
ISBN 0-412-22300-7 : £12.50 : CIP entry
B81-31729

547.7'05 — Polymers — *Serials*

Journal of polymer science. Macromolecular reviews. — Vol.15. — New York ; Chichester : Wiley, c1980. — iii,486p
ISBN 0-471-08889-7 : Unpriced
ISSN 0076-2083 B81-20092

Macromolecular chemistry : a review of the literature published during .... — Vol.1-. — London (Burlington House, W1V 0BN) : The Royal Society of Chemistry, 1980-. — v. ; 22cm. — (Specialist periodical report / Royal Society of Chemistry)
Annual
ISSN 0144-2988 = Macromolecular chemistry : Unpriced B81-10563

547.7'1 — Essential oils. Carbon-13 nuclear magnetic resonance spectroscopy

Kubeczka, K. -H.. Essential oils analysis by carbon-13 NMR spectroscopy. — London : Heyden, July 1981. — [360]p
ISBN 0-85501-704-x : CIP entry B81-20191

547.7'1'0321 — Terpenoids — *Encyclopaedias*

Glasby, John S.. Encyclopaedia of the terpenoids. — Chichester : Wiley, Dec.1981. — [1000]p
ISBN 0-471-27986-2 : £85.00 : CIP entry
B81-31364

547.7'1'05 — Terpenoids — *Serials*

Terpenoids and steroids. — Vol.10. — London : Royal Society of Chemistry, c1981. — xi,284p. — (Specialist periodical report / Royal Society of Chemistry)
ISBN 0-85186-336-1 : Unpriced : CIP rev.
Also classified at 547.7'3'05 B81-04335

547.7'2 — Alkaloids

Cordell, Geoffrey A.. Introduction to alkaloids : a biogenetic approach / Geoffrey A. Cordell. — New York ; Chichester : Wiley, c1981. — xvi,1055p ; 24cm
Includes bibliographies and indexes
ISBN 0-471-03478-9 : £92.50 B81-40212

Hesse, Manfred. Alkaloid chemistry / Manfred Hesse ; translated from the German edition by I. Ralph C. Bick. — New York ; Chichester : Wiley, c1981. — xii,231p : ill ; 24cm
Translation of: Alkaloidchemie. —
Bibliography: p203-215. — Includes index
ISBN 0-471-07973-1 : £20.00 B81-33071

547.7'2'05 — Alkaloids — *Serials*

The **alkaloids**. — Vol.10. — London : Royal Society of Chemistry, c1981. — xii,263p. — (Specialist periodical report / Royal Society of Chemistry)
ISBN 0-85186-337-x : Unpriced
ISSN 0305-9707 B81-20716

The **alkaloids**. — Vol.11. — London : Royal Society of Chemistry, Dec.1981. — [265]p. — (Specialist periodical report / Royal Society of Chemistry)
ISBN 0-85186-347-7 : CIP entry
ISSN 0305-9707 B81-30890

547.7'3 — Steroids

Witzmann, Rupert F.. Steroids : keys to life / Rupert F. Witzmann ; translated by Rosemarie Peter ; foreword by Hans Selye. — New York ; London : Van Nostrand Reinhold, c1981. — xiii,256p[16]p of plates : ill(some col.),ports ; 25cm
Translation of: Schlüssel des Lebens. —
Bibliography: p245-249. — Includes index
ISBN 0-442-29590-1 : £24.25 B81-39885

547.7'3 — Steroids. Chemical analysis — *Conference proceedings*

Symposium on the Analysis of Steroids *(1981 : Eger)*. Advances in steroid analysis. — Oxford : Elsevier Scientific, Jan.1982. — [464]p. — (Analytical chemistry symposia series ; v.10)
ISBN 0-444-99711-3 : £40.00 : CIP entry
B81-34494

547.7'3'05 — Steroids — *Serials*

Terpenoids and steroids. — Vol.10. — London : Royal Society of Chemistry, c1981. — xi,284p. — (Specialist periodical report / Royal Society of Chemistry)
ISBN 0-85186-336-1 : Unpriced : CIP rev.
Primary classification 547.7'1'05 B81-04335

547.7'34 — Prostaglandins & thromboxanes

Prostaglandins and thromboxanes. — London : Butterworths, Jan.1982. — [176]p. — (Butterworths monographs in chemistry)
ISBN 0-408-10773-1 : £14.00 : CIP entry
B81-37533

547.7'34 — Prostaglandins — *Conference proceedings*

Essential fatty acids and prostaglandins. — Oxford : Pergamon, Dec.1981. — [949]p. — (Progress in lipid research ; v.20)
ISBN 0-08-028011-0 : £56.00 : CIP entry
B81-33858

547.7'342 — Gibberellins — *Conference proceedings*

Gibberellins : chemistry, physiology and use : proceedings of a meeting organised jointly by the Society for Experimental Biology and the British Plant Growth Regulator Group, held at Imperial College, London on 25th March, 1980 / edited by J.R. Lenton. — Wantage ([c/o] M.B. Jackson, ARC Letcombe Laboratory, Wantage, Oxon. OX12 9JT) : British Plant Growth Regulator Group, 1980. — vii,143p : ill ; 21cm. — (Monongraph / British Plant Growth Regulator Group ; no.5)
Unpriced (pbk) B81-12461

547.7'5 — Amino acids, peptides & proteins — *Serials*

Amino-acids, peptides and proteins. — Vol.12. — London : Royal Society of Chemistry, Dec.1981. — [630]p. — (Specialist periodical report / Royal Society of Chemistry)
ISBN 0-85186-104-0 : CIP entry
ISSN 0306-0004 B81-32051

547.7'5 — Proteins

The **Proteins.** — New York ; London : Academic Press
Previous ed.: / edited by Hans Neurath. 1964-1970
Vol.4. — 3rd ed. / edited by Hans Neurath, Robert L. Hill, assisted by Carol-Leigh Boeder. — 1979. — xiv,679p : ill ; 24cm
ISBN 0-12-516304-5 : £33.60 B81-11265

547.7'5 — Proteins — *Conference proceedings*

Conference on Protein Chemistry *(1979 : Honolulu).* Frontiers in protein chemistry : proceedings of the Conference on Protein Chemistry, University of Hawaii, Honolulu, Hawaii, U.S.A., July 2-6, 1979 / editors Teh-Yung Liu, Gunji Mamiya, Kerry T. Yasunobu. — New York ; Oxford : Elsevier/North-Holland, c1980. — xiii,569p : ill ; 25cm. — (Developments in biochemistry ; v.10)
Includes index
ISBN 0-444-00414-9 : Unpriced B81-07267

Nucleic acids and proteins : the proceedings of Symposium on nucleic acids and proteins / edited by Shen Zhao-Wen. — Beijing : Science Press ; London : Van Nostrand Reinhold, 1980. — xiv,662p : ill ; 25cm
ISBN 0-442-20072-2 : £35.70
Primary classification 547.7'9 B81-37028

547.7'5 — Proteins. Microstructure. Research. Applications of electron microscopy

Electron microscopy of proteins. — London : Academic Press
Vol.1. — Oct.1981. — [350]p
ISBN 0-12-327601-2 : CIP entry B81-25847

Electron microscopy of proteins. — London : Academic Press
Vol.2. — Feb.1982. — [320]p
ISBN 0-12-327602-0 : CIP entry B81-36063

547.7'5 — Proteins. Molecules. Amino acid sequence. Determination

Croft, L. R.. Introduction to protein sequence analysis / L.R. Croft. — Chichester : Wiley, c1980. — xi,157p : ill ; 23cm
Bibliography: p141-152. - Includes index
ISBN 0-471-27710-x (pbk) : £4.95 : CIP rev. B80-13379

547.7'5 — Proteins. Molecules. Amino acid sequence — *Lists*

Croft, L. R.. Handbook of protein sequence analysis : a compilation of amino acid sequences of proteins with an introduction to the methodology / L.R. Croft. — 2nd ed. — Chichester : Wiley, c1980. — xiv,628p : ill ; 24cm
Previous ed.: published as Handbook of protein sequences. Oxford : Joynson-Bruvvers, 1973. — Bibliography: p141-152. - Includes index
ISBN 0-471-27703-7 : £38.00 : CIP rev. B80-13378

547.7'5 — Proteins. Post-translational modification. Role of enzymes

The **Enzymology** of post-translational modification of proteins / edited by Robert B. Freedman and Hilary C. Hawkins. — London : Academic Press. — (Molecular biology)
Vol.1. — 1980. — viii,515p : ill ; 24cm
Includes bibliographies and index
ISBN 0-12-266501-5 : £40.00 : CIP rev. B80-29624

547.7'5 — Proteins. Sulfhydryl groups

Torchinskiĭ, ĬU. M.. Sulfur in proteins / Yu. M. Torchinsky ; translator W. Wittenberg ; translation editor D. Metzler. — Oxford : Pergamon, 1981. — xv,294p : ill ; 26cm
Translation of: Sera v belkakh. — Bibliography: p237-277. - Includes index
ISBN 0-08-023778-9 : £40.00 : CIP rev. B80-12849

547.7'5044 — Proteins. Structure

Walton, Alan G.. Polypeptides and protein structure / Alan G. Walton. — New York ; Oxford : Elsevier, c1981. — x,393p : ill ; 26cm
Includes bibliographies and index
ISBN 0-444-00407-6 : Unpriced B81-32387

547.7'5046 — Amino acids. Chemical analysis

Amino acid analysis / editor J.M. Rattenbury. — Chichester : Ellis Horwood ; New York ; Chichester : Wiley, 1981. — 380p : ill ; 24cm
Includes index
ISBN 0-85312-194-x : £27.50 : CIP rev.
ISBN 0-470-27141-8 (Wiley) B81-08924

547.7'5046 — Proteins. Chemical analysis. Gel electrophoresis - *Laboratory manuals*

Gel electrophoresis of proteins. — London (1 Falconberg Court, W1V 5FG) : IRL Press, Aug.1981. — [300]p
ISBN 0-904147-22-3 (pbk) : £7.50 : CIP entry B81-18170

547.7'5'05 — Amino acids, peptides & proteins — *Serials*

Amino-acids, peptides, and proteins. — Vol.11. — London : Royal Society of Chemistry, c1981. — xxi,552p. — (Specialist periodical report / Royal Society of Chemistry)
ISBN 0-85186-880-0 : Unpriced
ISSN 0306-0004 B81-26583

547.7'56 — Peptides

The **Peptides** : analysis, synthesis, biology. — New York ; London : Academic Press
Vol.1: Major methods of peptide bond formation / edited by Erhard Gross, Johannes Meienhofer. — 1979. — xvii,435p : ill ; 24cm
Includes index
ISBN 0-12-304201-1 : £27.20 B81-22161

547.7'56 — Peptides — *Festschriften*

Perspectives in peptide chemistry / editors A. Eberle, R. Geiger and T. Wieland. — Basel ; London : Karger, 1981. — xi,444p : ill ; 25cm
Includes bibliographies and index
ISBN 3-8055-1297-x : £38.00 B81-13075

547.7'58 — Enzymes

Palmer, Trevor. Understanding enzymes / Trevor Palmer. — Chichester, Horwood, 1981. — 405p : ill ; 24cm
Includes bibliographies and index
ISBN 0-85312-202-4 (cased) : £25.00 : CIP rev.
ISBN 0-85312-307-1 (pbk) : Unpriced B81-08925

547.7'58 — Immobilised enzymes

Trevan, Michael D.. Immobilized enzymes : an introduction and applications in biotechnology / Michael D. Trevan. — Chichester : Wiley, c1980. — xiv,138p : ill ; 24cm
Bibliography: p133-134. — Includes index
ISBN 0-471-27826-2 : £8.75 : CIP rev. B80-25588

547.7'580442 — Enzymes. Molecules. Structure & chemical properties

Wharton, Christopher W.. Molecular enzymology / Christopher W. Wharton, Robert Eisenthal. — Glasgow : Blackie, 1981. — ix,326p : ill ; 21cm. — (Tertiary level biology)
Bibliography: p310-317. — Includes index
ISBN 0-216-91012-9 : Unpriced : CIP rev. B81-15922

547.7'5804594 — Enzymes. Chemical reactions. Kinetics

Engel, Paul C.. Enzyme kinetics. — 2nd ed. — London : Chapman and Hall, Feb.1982. — [96] p. — (Outline studies in biology)
Previous ed.: 1977
ISBN 0-412-23970-1 (pbk) : £2.45 : CIP entry B81-36379

547.7'5804594'0724 — Enzymes. Chemical reactions. Kinetics. Mathematical models — *Conference proceedings*

Kinetic data analysis : design and analysis of enzyme and pharmacokinetic experiments / [proceedings of a satellite symposium on design and analysis of enzyme and pharmacokinetic experiments, organized in conjunction with the XIth International Congress of Biochemistry, and held July 14, 1979, in Toronto, Canada] ; edited by Laszlo Endrenyi. — New York ; London : Plenum, c1981. — ix,427p : ill ; 26cm
Includes index
ISBN 0-306-40724-8 : Unpriced B81-28961

547.7'8 — Carbohydrates

The **Carbohydrates** : chemistry and biochemistry. — New York ; London : Academic Press
Vol.1B. — 2nd ed. / edited by Ward Pigman, Derek Horton ; assistant editor Joseph D. Wander. — 1980. — xxiii,643-1627p : ill ; 24cm
Previous ed.: in 1 vol. / edited by Ward Pigman, 1957. — Includes index
ISBN 0-12-556351-5 : £45.15 B81-17007

547.7'8 — Carbohydrates - *Serials*

Carbohydrate chemistry. — Vol.12. — London : Royal Society of Chemistry, May 1981. — [500]p. — (A Specialist periodical report)
ISBN 0-85186-940-8 : CIP entry
ISSN 0576-7172 B81-08839

547.7'9 — DNA. Research — *Philosophical perspectives*

Cavalieri, Liebe F.. The double-edged helix : science in the real world / Liebe F. Cavalieri. — New York ; Guildford : Columbia University Press, 1981. — 196p ; 24cm. — (Convergence)
Includes index
ISBN 0-231-05306-1 : £10.20 B81-3187

547.7'9 — DNA. Structure. Determination, *1953* — *Personal observations*

Watson, James D.. The double helix : a personal account of the discovery of the structure of DNA / James D. Watson. — New critical ed., including text, commentary, reviews, original papers / edited by Gunther S. Stent. — London : Weidenfeld and Nicolson, c1981. — xxv,298p : ill,facsims, ports ; 22cm
Includes index
ISBN 0-297-77899-4 : £10.00 B81-1563

547.7'9 — Nucleic acids — *Conference proceedings*

Nucleic acids and proteins : the proceedings of Symposium on nucleic acids and proteins / edited by Shen Zhao-Wen. — Beijing : Science Press ; London : Van Nostrand Reinhold, 1980. — xiv,662p : ill ; 25cm
ISBN 0-442-20072-2 : £35.70
Also classified at 547.7'5 B81-3702

Symposium on Nucleic Acids Chemistry *(9th : 1981 : Tokyo).* Ninth Symposium on Nucleic Acids Chemistry held in Tokyo Japan October 28th-30th 1981. — Eynsham (1 Abbey St., Oxford OX8 1JJ) : IRL Press, Nov.1981. — [200]p. — (Nucleic acids symposium series, ISSN 0261-3166 ; no.10)
ISBN 0-904147-32-0 (pbk) : £9.00 : CIP entry B81-3110

547.7'90442 — Nucleic acids. Structure

Topics in nucleic acid structure / edited by Stephen Neidle. — London : Macmillan, 1981. — x,221p : ill ; 24cm. — (Topics in molecular and structural biology ; 1)
Includes bibliographies and index
ISBN 0-333-26678-1 : £20.00 B81-3067

547.7′904572 — Nucleic acids. Gel electrophoresis. Laboratory techniques
Gel electrophoresis of nucleic acids. — Eynsham (1 Abbey St., Oxford OX8 1JJ) : IRL Press, Dec.1981. — [200]p
ISBN 0-904147-24-x (pbk) : £7.50 : CIP entry
B81-31369

547.8′4 — Polymers. Structure, chemical & physical properties
Brydson, J. A.. Flow properties of polymer melts. — 2nd ed. — London : Godwin, May 1981. — [288]p
Previous ed.: London: Iliffe, 1970
ISBN 0-7114-5681-x : £22.00 : CIP entry
B81-10443

547.8′427′09 — Synthetic polymers, *to 1978*
McMillan, Frank M.. The chain straighteners : fruitful innovation : the discovery of linear and stereoregular synthetic polymers / Frank M. McMillan. — London : Macmillan, 1979. — xx,207p ; 22cm
Includes index
ISBN 0-333-25929-7 : £17.00 : CIP rev.
B79-19196

547.8′6 — Phthalocyanines. Coordination compounds
Berezin, B. D.. Coordination compounds of porphyrins and phthalocyanines / B.D. Berezin ; translation by V.G. Vopian. — Chichester : Wiley, 1981. — xiii,286p : ill ; 24cm
Translation of: Koordinat͡sionnye soedinenii͡a porfirinov i ftalot͡sianina. — Includes index
ISBN 0-471-27857-2 : £19.15 : CIP rev
Primary classification 547′.593 B81-14830

547.8′69 — Carotenoids — *Conference proceedings*
International Symposium on Carotenoids *(5th : 1978 : Madison)*. Carotenoids-5 : contributed papers presented at the Fifth International Symposium on Carotenoids Madison, Wisconsin, USA, 23-28 July 1978 / [organizing committee, the Graduate School, and the Department of Physiological Chemistry of the University of Wisconsin-Madison and Medical Research Service, William S. Middleton Memorial Veterans Medical Center, Madison, Wisconsin USA ; Symposium editor, T.W. Goodwin. — Oxford : Pergamon, c1979. — p435-886 : ill(some col.) ; 28cm
At head of title: International Union of Pure and Applied Chemistry (Organic Chemistry Division)
ISBN 0-08-022359-1 : £21.75 B81-17235

548 — CRYSTALLOGRAPHY

548 — Crystallography
Whittaker, E. J. W.. Crystallography : an introduction for earth science (and other solid state) students / by E.J.W. Whittaker. — Oxford : Pergamon, 1981. — xii,254p : ill ; 26cm. — (Pergamon international library)
Bibliography: p249. — Includes index
ISBN 0-08-023805-x (cased) : Unpriced
ISBN 0-08-023804-1 (pbk) : £8.35 B81-33434

548 — Crystals — *For schools*
Lambert, Andrew. Atoms, molecules & crystals / Andrew Lambert. — Glagow : Blackie, 1980. — 32p : ill ; 17x21cm. — (Modular science)
ISBN 0-216-90583-4 (pbk) : £1.30
Primary classification 539 B81-10727

548′.2 — Crystals. Surfaces. Structure & physical properties
The **Chemical** physics of solid surfaces and heterogeneous catalysis. — Oxford : Elsevier Scientific, Apr.1981
Vol.1: Clean solid surfaces. — [350]p
ISBN 0-444-41924-1 : CIP entry B81-12378

548′.5′05 — Crystals. Growth - *Serials*
Progress in crystal growth and characterization. — Vol.3. — Oxford : Pergamon, July 1981. — [394]p
ISBN 0-08-028405-1 : £51.00 : CIP entry
B81-16852

548′.8 — Intercalated layered compounds
Intercalated layered materials / edited by F. Lévy. — Dordrecht ; London : Reidel, c1979. — 578p : ill ; 25cm. — (Physics and chemistry of materials with layered structures ; v.6)
Includes index
ISBN 90-277-0967-x : Unpriced B81-06292

548′.81′028 — Crystals. Structure. Determination. Methods
Giacovazzo, Carmelo. Direct methods in crystallography / Carmelo Giacovazzo. — London : Academic Press, c1980. — xiv,432p : ill ; 24cm
Bibliography: p417-428. — Includes index
ISBN 0-12-282450-4 : £37.80 : CIP rev.
B80-10063

Theory and practice of direct methods in crystallography / edited by M.F.C. Ladd and R.A. Palmer. — New York ; London : Plenum, c1980. — xiv,421p : ill ; 24cm
Includes bibliographies and index
ISBN 0-306-40223-8 : Unpriced B81-27865

548′.83 — Crystals. Defects. X-ray crystallography — *Conference proceedings*
NATO Advanced Study Institute on Characterization of Crystal Growth Defects by X-ray Methods *(1979 : University of Durham)*. Characterisation of crystal growth defects by X-ray methods / [proceedings of the NATO Advanced Study Institute on Characterization of Crystal Growth Defects by X-ray Methods, held August 29-September 10, 1979, at Durham University, Durham, United Kingdom] ; edited by Brian K. Tanner and D. Keith Bowen. — New York ; London : Plenum published in cooperation with NATO Scientific Affairs Division, c1980. — xxvi,589p : ill ; 26cm. — (NATO advanced study institutes series. Series B, Physics ; v.63)
Includes index
ISBN 0-306-40628-4 (corrected) : Unpriced
B81-15143

548′.83 — Electron diffraction, *to 1980*
Fifty years of electron diffraction / general editor, P. Goodman ; regional and special subject editors M.J. Whelan ... [et al.]. — Dordrecht ; London : Published for the International Union of Crystallography by Reidel, c1981. — xiv,440p : ill,ports ; 25cm
Includes bibliographies and index
ISBN 90-277-1246-8 (cased) : Unpriced
ISBN 90-277-1331-6 (pbk) : Unpriced
B81-34846

548′.83 — X-ray diffraction
Hukins, David W. L.. X-ray diffraction by disordered and ordered systems. — Oxford : Pergamon, Jan.1982. — [173]p
ISBN 0-08-023976-5 : £11.95 : CIP entry
B81-34489

548′.9 — Crystals. Optical properties. Determination. Spindle-stage techniques
Bloss, F. Donald. The spindle stage : principles and practice / F. Donald Bloss. — Cambridge : Cambridge University Press, 1981. — xii,340p : ill ; 24cm
Bibliography: p330-335. — Includes index
ISBN 0-521-23292-9 : £35.00 B81-28317

548′.9 — Crystals. Photoelastic properties & electro-optical properties
Narasimhamurty, T. S.. Photoelastic and electro-optic properties of crystals / T.S. Narasimhamurty. — New York ; London : Plenum, c1981. — xxix,514p : ill ; 24cm
Bibliography: p421-501. — Includes index
ISBN 0-306-31101-1 : Unpriced B81-30810

548′.9 — Liquid crystals — *Conference proceedings*
Liquid crystals : proceedings of an international conference held at the Raman Research Institute, Bangalore, December 3-8, 1979 / edited by S. Chandrasekhar. — London : Heyden, c1980. — x,605p,[28]p of plates : ill ; 25cm
Includes index
ISBN 0-85501-163-7 : £35.00 B81-01828

549 — MINERALOGY

549 — Gemmology
Read, Peter G.. Gems / P.G. Read. — London : Newnes Technical, 1981. — 107p : ill ; 17cm. — (Questions & answers)
Includes index
ISBN 0-408-00546-7 (pbk) : Unpriced : CIP rev. B81-20609

549 — Mineralogy
Battey, M. H.. Mineralogy for students / M.H. Battey. — 2nd ed. — London : Longman, 1981. — xii,355p : ill ; 25cm
Previous ed.: 1972. — Includes bibliographies and index
ISBN 0-582-44005-x (pbk) : £8.95 : CIP rev.
B81-16384

549′.0212 — Minerals — *Technical data*
Sinkankas, John. Gemstone & mineral data book : a compilation of data, recipes, formulas and instructions for the mineralogist, gemologist, lapidary, jeweler, craftsman and collector / John Sinkankas. — New York ; London : Van Nostrand Reinhold, 1981, c1972. — 352p ; 23cm
Originally published: New York : Winchester, c1972. — Includes index
ISBN 0-442-24709-5 (pbk) : £5.90 B81-36882

549′.112 — Chondrites. Metals. Separation from sulphides & silicates. Use of chlorine — *Manuals*
Easton, A. J.. Analysis of chondritic material using selective attack by chlorine / A.J. Easton, V.K. Din and C.J. Elliott. — London : British Museum (Natural History), 1981. — v,36p : ill ; 30cm. — (Publication / British Museum (Natural History) ; no.837)
Bibliography: p35-36
ISBN 0-565-00837-4 (spiral) : Unpriced
B81-26950

549′.12′0212 — Minerals. Physical properties — *Technical data*
Physical properties of rocks and minerals / edited by Y.S. Touloukian, W.R. Judd, R.F. Roy. — New York ; London : McGraw-Hill, c1981. — xx,548p : ill,maps ; 29cm. — (McGraw-Hill/CINDAS data series on material properties ; v.II—2)
Includes bibliographies
ISBN 0-07-065032-2 : £31.25
Also classified at 552′.06 B81-32463

549′.125 — Opaque minerals. Identification. Use of reflected light microscopes
Craig, James R. (James Roland). Ore microscopy and ore petrography / James R. Craig, David J. Vaughan. — New York ; Chichester : Wiley, c1981. — xii,406p : ill ; 24cm
Includes bibliographies and index
ISBN 0-471-08596-0 : £17.95 B81-33369

549′.27 — Graphite. Physical properties
Kelly, B. T.. The physics of graphite. — London : Applied Science, July 1981. — [432]p. — (RES mechanica monographs)
ISBN 0-85334-960-6 : £30.00 : CIP entry
B81-14445

549′.6 — Rock-forming minerals
Deer, W. A.. Rock-forming minerals. — 2nd ed. — London : Longman
Vol.1A: Orthosilicates. — Feb.1982. — [928]p
Previous ed.: 1962
ISBN 0-582-46526-5 : £50.00 : CIP entry
B81-36347

549′.67 — Clay minerals. Crystals. Structure. Determination. Applications of x-ray diffraction
Crystal structures of clay minerals and their X-ray identification / edited by G.W. Brindley and G. Brown. — [New ed.]. — London (41 Queen′s Gate, SW7 5HR) : Mineralogical Society, 1980. — 495p,[7]leaves of plates : ill ; 25cm. — (Mineralogical Society monograph, ISSN 0144-1485 ; no.5)
Previous ed.: i.e. 2nd ed. published as The X-ray identification and crystal structures of clay minerals. 1961. — Includes bibliographies and index
ISBN 0-903056-08-9 : £28.00 B81-15979

549′.67 — Clay minerals. Electron microscopy. Specimens — *Sources of data: Japan*
Electron micrographs of clay minerals / Toshio Sudo ... [et al.]. — Tokyo : Kodansha ; Amsterdam ; Oxford : Elsevier Scientific, 1981. — x,203p : ill,1map ; 27cm. — (Developments in sedimentology, ISSN 0070-4571 ; 31)
Map on lining papers. — Includes bibliographies and index
ISBN 0-444-99751-2 : £27.69 B81-15497

549'.67 — Clay minerals. Structure & properties. Analysis. Laboratory techniques - *Conference proceedings*

Advanced techniques for clay mineral analysis. — Oxford : Elsevier Scientific, Aug.1981. — [350] p. — (Developments in sedimentology ; v.34)
Conference papers
ISBN 0-444-42002-9 : CIP entry B81-20593

550 — EARTH

550 — Earth — *Early works*

Hobbs, William, *fl.1715*. The earth generated and anatomized / by William Hobbs ; an early eighteenth century theory of the earth edited with an introduction by Roy Porter. — [London] : British Museum (Natural History), c1981. — 157p : ill,maps,facsims ; 26cm
ISBN 0-8014-1366-4 : £24.50 B81-39834

550 — Earth — *For children*

Amazing facts about our earth : wonders of our earth / [illustrated by Penny Simon]. — London : Transworld, 1980. — [32]p : col.ill ; 28cm. — (A Carousel book)
ISBN 0-552-57047-8 (pbk) : £0.95 B81-12539

Corretti, Gilberto. Let's look at planet earth / [text by Gilberto Corretti] ; [illustrations by Dario Bartolini and Gilberto Corretti] ; [translated by Jo Zweng]. — Hove : Wayland, 1979. — 98p : ill(some col.),col.charts,col.maps ; 31cm. — (Let's look at series)
Includes index
ISBN 0-85340-659-6 : £3.75 B81-12538

Thackray, John. The story of the earth / John Thackray. — London : Ward Lock, 1980. — 96p : ill(some col.),col.maps ; 29cm
Includes index
ISBN 0-7063-5801-5 : £3.95 B81-02526

550 — Earth sciences

Burrus, Thomas L.. Earth in crisis : an introduction to the earth sciences / Thomas L. Burrus, Herbert J. Spiegel ; original drawings by George Ondricek, Jr.. — 2nd ed. — St Louis ; London : Mosby, 1980. — xi,549p : ill,charts,maps ; 26cm
Previous ed.: 1976. — Includes index
ISBN 0-8016-0902-x : Unpriced
Also classified at 520 B81-13255

Tarbuck, Edward J.. Earth science / Edward J. Tarbuck and Frederick K. Lutgens. — 2nd ed. — Columbus ; London : Merrill, c1979. — xvi,544p,[20]p of plates : ill(some col.),charts,maps,ports ; 27cm
Previous ed.: 1976. — Includes index
ISBN 0-675-08303-6 : £13.50 B81-02796

550'.3'21 — Earth sciences — *Encyclopaedias*

The **Cambridge** encyclopedia of earth sciences. — Cambridge : Cambridge University Press, Nov.1981. — [496]p
ISBN 0-521-23900-1 : £19.95 : CIP entry B81-30182

551 — GEOLOGY

551 — Earth. Dynamics. Frames of reference — *Conference proceedings*

International Astronomical Union. *Colloquium (56th : 1980 : Warsaw)*. Reference coordinate systems for earth dynamics : proceedings of the 56th Colloquium of the International Astronomical Union held in Warsaw, Poland, September 8-12, 1980 / edited by E.M. Gaposchkin and B. Kołaczek. — Dordrecht ; London : Reidel, 1981. — xiii,396p : ill ; 25cm. — (Astrophysics and space science library ; v.86)
Includes bibliographies and index
ISBN 90-277-1260-3 : Unpriced B81-22132

551 — Earth. Evolution

Dott, Robert H.. Evolution of the earth / Robert H. Dott, Jr., Roger L. Batten ; maps and diagrams by Ranall D. Sale. — 3rd ed. — New York ; London : McGraw-Hill, c1981. — vii,113p : ill(some col.),maps(some col.) ; 26cm
Previous ed.: 1976. — Ill, map on lining papers. — Includes bibliographies and index
ISBN 0-07-017625-6 : £16.05 B81-10126

The **Evolving** earth / editor L.R.M. Cocks. — London : British Museum (Natural History), 1981. — vii,264p,[1]leaf of plate : ill(some col.),maps(some col.) ; 29cm. — (Chance, change & challenge)
Cover title. — Includes index
ISBN 0-521-23810-2 : £30.00 : CIP rev. B81-10510

Ozima, Minoru. The earth: its birth and growth / Minoru Ozima ; translated by Judy Wakabayashi. — Cambridge : Cambridge University Press, 1981. — x,117p : ill,maps ; 22cm
Translation of : Chikyu-shi. — Includes index
ISBN 0-521-23500-6 : £10.50
ISBN 0-521-28005-2 (pbk) : £3.95 B81-38097

Stierlin, Réne G.. The south wind : an essay on the evolution of the earth's features and attitude / by René G. Stierlin. — London : Regency, [1980]. — 57p : ill,charts ; 23cm
ISBN 0-7212-0645-x : £3.00 B81-05709

551 — Environmental geology

Coates, Donald R.. Environmental geology / Donald R. Coates. — New York ; Chichester : Wiley, c1981. — 701p : ill,maps,plans ; 25cm
Text on lining paper. — Includes bibliographies and index
ISBN 0-471-06379-7 : £11.50 B81-18442

Costa, John E.. Surficial geology : building with the earth / John E. Costa, Victor R. Baker. — New York ; London : Wiley, c1981. — ix,498p : ill,maps ; 29cm
Includes bibliographies and index
ISBN 0-471-03229-8 : £14.25 B81-17730

Keller, Edward A.. Environmental geology / Edward A. Keller, with assistance from E.M. Burt. — 2nd ed. — Columbus ; London : Merrill, c1979. — xii,548p,[20]p of plates : ill (some col.),maps ; 26cm
Previous ed.: 1976. — Text, map on lining paper. — Includes index
ISBN 0-675-08296-x : £13.50 B81-05234

551 — Geology

The **Earth** : structure, composition and evolution / [the S237 Course Team]. — Milton Keynes : Open University Press. — (Science : a second level course)
At head of title: The Open University
Block 3: Igneous processes : phase relations and geochemistry. — 1981. — 105p : ill(some col.),1map ; 30cm. — (S237 ; Block 3)
Bibliography: p89
ISBN 0-335-16057-3 (pbk) : Unpriced B81-25368

551 — Geology — *For schools*

Study the earth. — London : Hodder and Stoughton
Unit 4: Useful materials from the earth. — Jan.1982. — [80]p
ISBN 0-340-24188-8 (pbk) : £1.95 : CIP entry B81-34126

551 — Geophysical processes

Sanders, John E.. Principles of physical geology / John E. Sanders. — New York ; Chichester : Wiley, c1981. — xi,624p : ill(some col.),col.charts,maps(some col.),port ; 29cm
Maps on lining papers. — Includes bibliographies and index
ISBN 0-471-08424-7 : £12.65 B81-23979

551 — Geophysical processes — *For schools*

Horrocks, N. K.. Physical geography and climatology / N.K. Horrocks ; with a foreword by the late S.W. Wooldridge. — 3rd ed. (metric). — Harlow : Longman, 1981. — xiv,370p : ill,maps ; 22cm
Previous ed.: 1964. — Includes index
ISBN 0-582-35322-x (pbk) : £3.20 B81-20058

551 — Geophysical processes. Influence of man

Man and environmental processes : a physical geography perspective / edited by K.J. Gregory, D.E. Walling. — London : Butterworths, 1981. — xiv,276p : ill,charts,maps ; 26cm. — (Studies in physical geography, ISSN 0142-6389)
Originally published: Folkestone : Dawson, 1979. — Includes bibliographies and index
ISBN 0-408-10736-7 (cased) : £12.50
ISBN 0-408-10740-5 (pbk) : £6.95 B81-11449

551 — Geothermal processes

Elder, John, *1933-*. Geothermal systems / John Elder. — London : Academic Press, 1981. — ix,508p : ill,maps ; 24cm
Bibliography: p495-502. - Includes index
ISBN 0-12-236450-3 : £20.60 B81-19323

551 — Physical geology

Strahler, Arthur N.. Physical geology / Arthur N. Strahler. — New York ; London : Harper & Row, c1981. — xviii,612p,[8]p of plates : ill (some col.),col.maps ; 29cm
Text and maps on lining papers. — Includes index
ISBN 0-06-046462-3 : £15.95 B81-28450

551'.012 — Geology. Classification

Murray, John W.. A guide to classification in geology / J.W. Murray. — Chichester (Market Cross House, Cooper St., Chichester, W. Sussex PO19 1EB) : Ellis Horwood, 1981. — 112p : ill ; 19cm. — (Ellis Horwood series in geology)
Includes bibliographies and index
ISBN 0-85312-193-1 : £10.00 : CIP rev.
ISBN 0-85312-319-5 (Student ed) : Unpriced B80-19207

551'.028 — Geology. Applications of remote sensing

Remote sensing in geology / edited by Barry S. Siegal, Alan R. Gillespie. — New York ; Chichester : Wiley, c1980. — xviii,702p,[32]p of plates : ill(some col.),maps,plans ; 29cm
Includes index
ISBN 0-471-79052-4 : £22.60 B81-02291

551'.03 — Geology — *Polyglot dictionaries*

Geological nomenclature / edited by W.A. Visser — The Hague ; London : Nijhoff, 1980. — xxvi,540p ; 28cm
At head of title: Royal Geological and Mining Society of the Netherlands. — Includes index
ISBN 90-247-2403-1 : Unpriced B81-04062

551'.05 — Geophysical processes — *Serials*

Advances in geophysics. — Vol.22. — New York ; London : Academic Press, 1980. — xiv,424p
ISBN 0-12-018822-8 : Unpriced
ISSN 0065-2687 B81-20414

551'.06'041 — Great Britain. Geology. Organisations: Institute of Geological Sciences — *Serials*

Institute of Geological Sciences. Annual report for ... / Institute of Geological Sciences. — 1979. — London : The Institute, 1981. — 126p in various pagings
ISBN 0-85272-071-8 : £6.50
ISSN 0073-9308 B81-2349

551'.07'1041 — Great Britain. Schools. Students, 5-14 years. Curriculum subjects: Geology — *For teaching*

Hudson, Christine. Beneath our feet / Christine Hudson and Alan Taylor. — Basingstoke (Houndmills, Basingstoke RG21 2XS) : Globe Education [for] West Sussex County Council, 1981. — 38p : ill,forms ; 30cm. — (Science horizons. Level 2a)
Bibliography: p10-11. — List of films: p11
ISBN 0-333-28538-7 (pbk) : £3.95 B81-3130

551'.07'11421 — London. Universities: University of London. Geology departments — *Serials*

University of London. Geological newsletter / University of London. — No.13 (1981). — [London] ([c/o F.J. Fitch, Department of Geology, Birkbeck College, 7 Gresse St., W1P 1PA]) : University of London Board of Studies in Geology, c1980. — 170p in various pagings
ISSN 0144-0039 : Unpriced B81-1681

551'.0724 — Geology. Data. Statistical analysis

Koch, George S.. Statistical analysis of geological data / George S. Koch, Jr. and Richard F. Link. — Corr. republication. — New York : Dover ; London : Constable, 1980, c1971. — ix,375,438p : ill,maps ; 21cm
Originally published: in 2v. New York : Chichester : Wiley, 1970-1971. — Includes bibliographies and indexes
ISBN 0-486-64040-x (pbk) : Unpriced
B81-28887

551.1 — Earth. Structure & physical properties

The Earth : structure, composition and evolution / [the S237 Course Team]. — Milton Keynes : Open University Press. — (Science : a second level course)
At head of title: The Open University
Block 1: Earth composition : elements, minerals and rocks. — 1981. — 99p : ill(some col.) ; 30cm. — (S237 ; block 1)
Bibliography: p85
ISBN 0-335-16055-7 (pbk) : Unpriced
B81-27790

551.1'05 — Earth. Structure & physical properties — *Serials*

Advances in earth and planetary sciences. — 1-. — Japan : Center for Academic Publications ; London : D. Reidel, 1977-. — v. : ill,maps ; 27cm
Irregular. — Some issues are supplementary to: Journal of geomagnetism and geolectricity ; Journal of physics of the earth ; and, Geochemical journal. — Description based on: 9
Unpriced B81-30723

551.1'1 — Earth. Interior

Brown, G. C.. The inaccessible earth / G.C. Brown and A.E. Mussett. — London : Allen & Unwin, 1981. — xii,235p : ill ; 25cm
Text on lining papers. — Bibliography: p219-227. - Includes index
ISBN 0-04-550027-4 (cased) : Unpriced : CIP rev.
ISBN 0-04-550028-2 (pbk) : Unpriced
B80-23252

551.1'1 — Earth. Transition zone. Structure

Structure of transition zone / edited by S. Asano. — Tokyo : Center for Academic Publications Japan ; Dordrecht ; London : Reidel, c1980. — x,184p : ill ; 27cm. — (Advances in earth and planetary sciences ; 8)
Includes bibliographies and index
ISBN 90-277-1149-6 : Unpriced B81-39182

551.1'16'0722 — Earth. Mantle. Geophysical processes — *Case studies*

Crustal and mantle processes. — Milton Keynes : Open University Press. — (Science : a third level course)
At head of title: The Open University
Dalradian case study : orogenic processes. — 1980. — 91p : ill(some col.),maps(some col.) ; 30cm. — (S336 ; DA)
Bibliography: p90-91
ISBN 0-335-16010-7 (pbk) : Unpriced
Also classified at 551.1'4'0722 B81-39480

Crustal and mantle processes. — Milton Keynes : Open University Press. — (Science : a third level course)
At head of title: The Open University
Red Sea case study : an embryonic ocean basin. — 1980. — 142p : ill(some col.),maps(some col.) ; 30cm + 1sheet(col.map ; 30x20cm). — (S336 ; RS)
Includes bibliographies
ISBN 0-335-16011-5 (pbk) : Unpriced
Also classified at 551.1'4'0722 B81-39481

551.1'3 — Lithosphere. Deformation. Role of gravity. Dynamic models

Ramberg, Hans. Gravity, deformation and the earth's crust : in theory, experiments and geological application / Hans Ramberg. — 2nd ed. — London : Academic Press, 1981. — xii,452p : ill,maps ; 24cm
Previous ed.: 1967. — Bibliography: p424-436. — Includes index
ISBN 0-12-576860-5 : £32.80 B81-29814

551.1'3 — Lithosphere. Evolution — *Conference proceedings*

The Origin and evolution of the earth's continental crust : a Royal Society discussion held on 21 and 22 February 1980 / organized by S. Moorbath and B.F. Windley. — London : Royal Society, 1981. — viii,303p : ill,maps ; 31cm
Conference papers. — Includes bibliographies
ISBN 0-85403-162-6 : £32.95 B81-29202

551.1'36 — Extensional plate tectonics — *Conference proceedings*

Extensional tectonics associated with convergent plate boundaries : a Royal Society discussion held on 19 and 20 March 1980 / organized by F.J. Vine and A.G. Smith. — London : Royal Society, 1981. — vi,224p,[16]p of plates : ill,maps ; 31cm
Originally published: in Philosphical Transactions of the Royal Society of London, series A, vol.300 (no.1454). — Pages also numbered 219-442. — Includes bibliographies
ISBN 0-85403-161-8 : £29.75 B81-20276

551.1'36 — Lithosphere. Plates. Motion — *Conference proceedings*

IUGG Interdisciplinary Symposium *(9th : 1979 : Canberra)*. Recent crustal movements, 1979 : proceedings of the IUGG Interdisciplinary Symposium No. 9, 'Recent Crustal Movements', Canberra, A.C.T., Australia, December 13-14, 1979 / edited by P. Vyskočil, R. Green and H. Mälzer. — Amsterdam ; Oxford : Elsevier Scientific, 1981. — x,355p : ill,maps ; 25cm. — (Developments in geotectonics ; 16)
Includes bibliographies
ISBN 0-444-41953-5 : £31.13 B81-11143

Mechanisms of continental drift and plate tectonics / edited by P.A. Davies and S.K. Runcorn. — London : Academic Press, 1980. — xiii,362p : ill,maps ; 24cm
Conference papers. — Includes bibliographies and index
ISBN 0-12-206160-8 : £33.00 : CIP rev.
B80-29628

551.1'36 — Malay archipelago. Geological features: Wallace's line

Wallace's line and plate tectonics. — Oxford : Clarendon Press, Sept.1981. — [200]p. — (Oxford monographs on biogeography)
ISBN 0-19-854545-2 : £15.00 : CIP entry
B81-21605

551.1'36 — Pre-Cambrian era. Lithosphere. Plates. Motion

Precambrian plate tectonics / edited by A. Kröner. — Amsterdam ; Oxford : Elsevier Scientific, 1981. — xxi,781p(4folded) : ill,maps ; 25cm. — (Developments in Precambrian geology ; 4)
Includes bibliographies and index
ISBN 0-444-41910-1 : Unpriced
ISBN 0-444-41690-0
ISBN 0-444-41863-6 B81-31793

551.1'36 — Tectonics

Trench-forearc geology. — Oxford : Blackwell Scientific, Sept.1981. — [530]p
ISBN 0-632-00708-7 : £40.00 : CIP entry
B81-30410

551.1'36 — Tectonics — *For schools*

Weymann, Darrell. Tectonic processes / Darrell Weyman. — London : Allen & Unwin, 1981. — viii,102p : col.ill,col.maps ; 25cm. — (Processes in physical geography ; v.4)
Bibliography: p96. — Includes index
ISBN 0-04-551044-x (pbk) : Unpriced : CIP rev. B81-02545

551.1'4'0722 — Lithosphere. Geophysical processes — *Case studies*

Crustal and mantle processes. — Milton Keynes : Open University Press. — (Science : a third level course)
At head of title: The Open University
Dalradian case study : orogenic processes. — 1980. — 91p : ill(some col.),maps(some col.) ; 30cm. — (S336 ; DA)
Bibliography: p90-91
ISBN 0-335-16010-7 (pbk) : Unpriced
Primary classification 551.1'16'0722 B81-39480

Crustal and mantle processes. — Milton Keynes : Open University Press. — (Science : a third level course)
At head of title: The Open University
Red Sea case study : an embryonic ocean basin. — 1980. — 142p : ill(some col.),maps(some col.) ; 30cm + 1sheet(col.map ; 30x20cm). — (S336 ; RS)
Includes bibliographies
ISBN 0-335-16011-5 (pbk) : Unpriced
Primary classification 551.1'16'0722 B81-39481

551.2'1 — Volcanoes

Francis, Peter. Volcanoes / Peter Francis. — Harmondsworth : Penguin, 1976 (1981 [printing]). — 368p : ill,maps ; 20cm. — (Pelican books)
Includes index
ISBN 0-14-021897-1 (pbk) : £2.95 B81-21115

551.2'1'0945813 — Italy. Mount Etna. Research by British institutions, *1977-1979*

United Kingdom research on Mount Etna 1977-1979 / prepared on behalf of the Etna Research Subcommittee of the Royal Society's Volcanological and Seismological Committee ; edited by A.T. Huntingdon, J.E. Guest and E.H. Francis. — London : Royal Society, 1980. — 56p,[1] folded leaf of plates : ill,maps ; 30cm
Includes summaries in Italian. — Bibliography: p53-56
ISBN 0-85403-153-7 (pbk) : £2.75 B81-05385

551.2'2 — Earth. Free oscillations

Lapwood, E. R.. Free oscillations of the earth / E.R. Lapwood, T. Usami. — Cambridge : Cambridge University Press, 1981. — xii,243p : ill ; 22cm. — (Cambridge monographs on mechanics and applied mathematics)
Bibliography: p225-232. - Includes index
ISBN 0-521-23536-7 : £25.00 : CIP rev.
B81-08948

551.2'2 — Earthquakes. Forecasting

Current research in earthquake prediction I / edited by Tsuneji Rikitake. — Tokyo : Center for Academic Publications Japan ; Dordrecht ; London : Reidel, c1981. — xiii,383p : ill,maps ; 24cm. — (Developments in earth and planetary sciences ; 2)
Includes bibliographies
ISBN 90-277-1133-x : Unpriced B81-36722

551.2'2 — Earthquakes. Mechanics

Kasahara, K.. Earthquake mechanics / K. Kasahara. — Cambridge : Cambridge University Press, 1981. — xiii,248p : ill,maps ; 24cm. — (Cambridge earth science series)
Bibliography: p224-241. — Includes index
ISBN 0-521-22736-4 : £25.00 B81-37138

551.2'2'0924 — Seismology. Milne, John, *1850-1913* — *Biographies*

Herbert-Gustar, A. L.. John Milne : father of modern seismology / A.L. Herbert-Gustar & P.A. Nott. — Tenterden (Caxton House, High St., Tenterden, Kent) : Norbury, 1980. — xvi,196p,[12]p of plates : ill(some col.),2maps,ports ; 23cm
Ill on lining papers. — Bibliography: p189-196
ISBN 0-904404-34-x : £9.50 B81-05087

551.3'00722 — Earth. Surface. Geophysical processes — *Case studies*

Surface and sedimentary processes. — Milton Keynes : Open University Press. — (Science : a third level course)
At head of title: The Open University
Changing sea-levels : a Jurassic case study. — 1980. — 120p : ill,maps ; 30cm. — (S335 ; CH)
Includes bibliographies
ISBN 0-335-16013-1 (pbk) : Unpriced
B81-39482

Surface and sedimentary processes. — Milton Keynes : Open University Press. — (Science : a third level course)
At head of title: The Open University
Palaeoclimatology case study : glaciation and the Ice Age. — 1980. — 124p : ill(some col.),maps(some col.),facsims ; 30cm. — (S335 ; PA)
Bibliography: p120
ISBN 0-335-16012-3 (pbk) : Unpriced
B81-39483

551.3'04 — Sedimentology

Leeder, M. R.. Sedimentology. — London : Allen & Unwin, Feb.1982. — [528]p
ISBN 0-04-551053-9 (cased) : £20.00 : CIP entry
ISBN 0-04-551054-7 (pbk) : £11.00 B81-35919

551.3'04 — Strata. Mobile belts. Oblique-slip faults. Sedimentation — *Conference proceedings*

Sedimentation in oblique-slip mobile zones / edited by Peter F. Ballance and Harold G. Reading. — Oxford : Blackwell Scientific, 1980. — vi,265p : ill,maps ; 25cm. — (Special publication / International Association of Sedimentologists, ISSN 0141-3600 ; no.4)
Includes bibliographies
ISBN 0-632-00607-2 (pbk) : £14.50 : CIP rev. B80-18712

551.3'04028 — Soils & sediments. Analysis. Use of electron microscopy

Smart, P.. Electron microscopy of soils and sediments. — Oxford : Clarendon Press, Sept.1981. — [400]p
ISBN 0 19-857574-2 : £35.00 : CIP entry B81-21622

551.3'1 — Glaciation — *Conference proceedings*

Glacial geomorphology. — London : Allen & Unwin, Dec.1981. — [304]p. — (The 'Binghamton' symposia in geomorphology : international series ; no.5)
Conference proceedings
ISBN 0-04-551045-8 : £12.00 : CIP entry B81-31530

551.3'1'05 — Glaciology — *Serials*

Annals of glaciology / [International Glaciological Society]. — Vol.1 (1980)-. — [Cambridge] ([Lensfield Rd, Cambridge CB2 1ER]) : The Society, 1980-. — v. : ill ; 30cm
Annual
ISSN 0260-3055 = Annals of glaciology : Unpriced B81-27133

Annals of glaciology / [International Glaciological Society]. — Vol.2 (1981). — Cambridge ([Lensfield Rd], Cambridge CB2 1ER) : The Society, [1981]. — vi,192p
ISBN 0-9502484-3-6 : Unpriced
ISSN 0260-3055 B81-33941

551.3'12 — Glaciers. Physical properties

Paterson, W. S. B.. The physics of glaciers / by W.S.B. Paterson. — 2nd ed. — Oxford : Pergamon, 1981. — vii,380p : ill,maps ; 24cm. — (Pergamon international library)
Previous ed.: 1969. — Bibliography: p351-372. — Includes index
ISBN 0-08-024005-4 (cased) : £7.25 : CIP rev.
ISBN 0-08-024006-2 (pbk) : £7.25 B81-10429

551.3'5 — Fluvial processes — *Conference proceedings*

Fluvial geomorphology. — London : Allen & Unwin, Nov.1981. — [304]p. — (The 'Binghampton' symposia in geomorphology : international series ; no.4)
Conference papers
ISBN 0-04-551046-6 : £12.00 : CIP entry B81-30215

551.3'54 — Continental shelf. Sedimentation

Sedimentary dynamics of continental shelves. — Oxford : Elsevier Scientific, July 1981. — [400] p. — (Developments in sedimentology, ISSN 0070-4571 ; 32)
ISBN 0-444-41962-4 : CIP entry B81-19139

551.3'55 — Alluvial fans. Formation

Rachocki, Andrzej. Alluvial fans : an attempt at an empirical approach / Andrzej Rachocki. — Chichester : Wiley, c1981. — x,161p : ill,maps ; 24cm
Bibliography: p153-157. — Includes index
ISBN 0-471-27999-4 : £14.00 : CIP rev. B81-24593

551.4 — GEOMORPHOLOGY AND GENERAL HYDROLOGY

551.4 — Deserts. Geomorphology

Goudie, Andrew. Desert geomorphology / Andrew Goudie and Andrew Watson. — Basingstoke : Macmillan Education, 1980. — 28p : ill,maps ; 22cm. — (Aspects of geography)
Bibliography: p28
ISBN 0-333-28659-6 (pbk) : £1.30 : CIP rev. B80-13380

551.4 — Geomorphological processes

Derbyshire, Edward. Geomorphological processes / E. Derbyshire, K.J. Gregory, J.R. Hails. — London : Butterworths, 1981, c1979. — 312p : ill,charts,maps ; 26cm. — (Studies in physical geography, ISSN 0142-6389)
Originally published: Folkestone : Dawson, 1979. — Bibliography: p290-305. - Includes index
ISBN 0-408-10735-9 (cased) : £12.50
ISBN 0-408-10739-1 (pbk) : £6.95 B81-11453

551.4 — Geomorphology

Gerrard, John. Soils and landforms. — London : Allen & Unwin, Oct.1981. — [256]p
ISBN 0-04-551048-2 (cased) : £15.00 : CIP entry
ISBN 0-04-551049-0 (pbk) : £7.95
Also classified at 631.4 B81-26737

Stephens, Nicholas, *1926-*. Geomorphology in the service of man : inaugural lecture delivered at the College on 11 December 1979 / by Nicholas Stephens. — Swansea : University College of Swansea, 1980. — 40p : ill,maps ; 22cm
Bibliography: p38-40
ISBN 0-86076-021-9 (pbk) : Unpriced B81-05982

551.4 — Natural resources: Water. Chemical reactions. Equilibria

Stumm, Werner. Aquatic chemistry : an introduction emphasizing chemical equilibria in natural waters / Werner Stumm, James J. Morgan. — [2nd ed.]. — New York ; Chichester : Wiley, c1981. — xiv,780p : ill ; 24cm
Previous ed.: 1970. — Includes bibliographies and index
ISBN 0-471-04831-3 : £24.75 B81-33019

551.4'01 — Landforms. Formation. Theories. Implications of motion of lithospheric plates

Ollier, Cliff. Tectonics and landforms / Cliff Ollier. — London : Longman, 1981. — 324p : ill,maps ; 25cm. — (Geomorphology texts ; 6)
Bibliography: p311-322. - Includes index
ISBN 0-582-30032-0 (cased) : Unpriced : CIP rev.
ISBN 0-582-30033-9 (pbk) : £9.95 B80-29631

551.4'09426'725 — Essex. Colne Point. Landforms

Butler, R. J. (Robert John). Shingle spits and salt marshes in the Colne Point area of Essex : a geomorphological study / R.J. Butler, J.T. Greensmith, L.W. Wright. — London (Mile End Rd., E1 4NS) : Department of Geography, Queen Mary College, 1981. — 51p : ill,maps ; 30cm. — (Occasional paper / Queen Mary College. Department of Geography, ISSN 0306-2740 ; no.18)
Bibliography: p47-51
ISBN 0-904791-18-1 (pbk) : Unpriced B81-33334

551.4'09681'1 — Botswana. Surface features — *Sources of data: Aerial photographs*

Mallick, D. I. J. A geological interpretation of Landsat imagery and air photography of Botswana / D.I.J. Mallick, F. Habgood and A.C. Skinner. — London : H.M.S.O., 1981. — iv,36p : ill,maps(some col.) ; 28cm. — (Overseas geology and mineral resources ; no.56)
One map on two folded leaves in pocket. — Bibliography: p34-35
ISBN 0-11-884138-6 (pbk) : £5.00 B81-36658

551'.4'1 — Continental shelf. Geological features

Boillot, G.. Geology of the continental margins / G. Boillot ; translated by A. Scarth. — London : Longman, 1981. — xi,115p : ill,maps ; 24cm
Translation of: Géologie des marges continentales. — Bibliography: p109-111. - Includes index
ISBN 0-582-30036-3 (pbk) : £4.95 B81-19059

551.4'1 — South-west England. Coastal waters. Bed. Cretaceous strata

Aptian-Cenomanian stratigraphy in boreholes from offshore south-west England / G.K. Lott ... [et al.]. — London : H.M.S.O., 1980. — ii,12p : ill,maps ; 30cm. — (Report / Institute of Geological Sciences ; 80/8)
Bibliography: p11-12
ISBN 0-11-884185-8 : £1.00 B81-05189

551.4'36 — Derbyshire. Wolfscotedale. Hills. Slopes. Terracettes

Gerrard, John. Terracettes in Wolfscotedale, Derbyshire : a deductive approach / John Gerrard and Martin Webster. — [Birmingham] : [Department of Geography, University of Birmingham], [1979]. — 56p : ill ; 30cm. — (Occasional publication / Department of Geography, University of Birmingham ; no.7)
Bibliography: p52-56
ISBN 0-7044-0358-7 (pbk) : £1.00 B81-39706

551.4'36 — Hills. Slopes. Analysis

Finlayson, Brian. Hillslope analysis / Brian Finlayson, Ian Statham. — London : Butterworths, 1980. — 230p : ill,maps ; 15x22cm. — (Sources and methods in geography)
Bibliography: p224-227. — Includes index
ISBN 0-408-10622-0 (pbk) : £3.25 : CIP rev. B80-11427

551.4'36 — South Wales. Rock slopes. Stability — *Conference proceedings*

Cliff and slope stability : South Wales / editor John W. Perkins. — Cardiff (38 Park Place, Cardiff CF1 3BB) : Department of Extra-Mural Studies University College, Cardiff, [1980]. — 206p : ill,maps ; 30cm
Conference papers. — Includes bibliographies
Unpriced (pbk) B81-22779

551.4'57'094125 — Scotland. Tayside Region. Beaches

Wright, Robert, *1943-*. The beaches of Tayside / R. Wright ; commissioned by the Countryside Commission for Scotland, 1978. — [Aberdeen] ([c/o Department of Geography, University of Aberdeen, Aberdeen]) : [R. Wright], 1981. — 66p,[56]p of plates : ill,maps(some col.) ; 30cm
One folded leaf attached to inside cover. — Bibliography: p65-66
Unpriced (pbk) B81-32455

551.4'57'0942 — England. Coastal regions. Landforms

Steers, J. A.. Coastal features of England and Wales : eight essays / J.A. Steers ; with an appreciation by D.R. Stoddart and a complete checklist of the published writings of J.A. Steers. — Cambridge : Oleander, c1981. — 206p : ill,maps ; 22cm
Bibliography: p188-195. - Includes index
ISBN 0-900891-70-x : £15.00 : CIP rev. B80-21846

551.46 — Oceanographic instruments, *1670-1903*

McConnell, Anita. No sea too deep : the history of oceanographic instruments. — Bristol : Hilger, Jan.1982. — [200]p
ISBN 0-85274-416-1 : £23.00 : CIP entry B81-34568

551.46 — Oceanography

Anikouchine, William A.. The world ocean : an introduction to oceanography / William A. Anikouchine, Richard W. Sternberg. — 2nd ed. — Englewood Cliffs ; London : Prentice-Hall, c1981. — xiii,513p : ill,maps ; 25cm
Previous ed.: 1973. — Maps on lining papers. — Includes bibliographies and index
ISBN 0-13-967778-x : £13.95 B81-3718[illegible]

Dietrich, Günter. General oceanography : an introduction. — 2nd ed. / Günter Dietrich ... [et al.] ; translated by Susanne and Hans Ulrich Roll. — New York ; Chichester : Wiley, c1980. — xxi,626p,8fold. p of plates : ill(some col.),maps(some col.) ; 25cm
Translation of: Allgemeine Meereskunde. — Previous ed.: / Günter Dietrich with contributions by Kurt Kalle ; translated by Feodor Ostapoff. New York : Interscience Publishers, 1963. — Bibliography: p571-604. — Includes index
ISBN 0-471-02102-4 : Unpriced B81-0844[illegible]

551.46 — Oceanography *continuation*

Study of the sea. — Farnham : Fishing News Books, July 1981. — [272]p
ISBN 0-85238-112-3 : £25.00 : CIP entry
Also classified at 639'.22 B81-16893

551.46 — Oceans

Barton, Robert. Secrets of the oceans / Robert Barton. — London : Aldus, 1980. — 336p : ill (some col.),maps(some col.),ports ; 30cm
Ill on lining papers. — Includes index
ISBN 0-490-00461-x : £10.95 B81-00879

551.46'0028 — Oceanography. Applications of remote sensing

Remote sensing in meteorology, oceanography and hydrology / [based on material presented at a postgraduate summer school sponsored by the European Association of Remote Sensing Laboratories (EARSel) and held at the University of Dundee in September 1980] ; editor A.P. Cracknell. — Chichester : Horwood, 1981. — 542p,[8]p of plates : ill (some col.),charts,maps(some col.) ; 24cm
Includes bibliographies and index
ISBN 0-85312-212-1 : £35.00 : CIP rev.
Also classified at 551.48'028 ; 551.5'028 B81-09968

551.46'0028 — Oceans. Remote sensing. Data. Interpretation — *Conference proceedings*

Interactive Workshop on Interpretation of Remotely Sensed Data *(1979 : Williamburg).* Remote sensing of atmospheres and oceans / [proceedings of the Interactive Workshop on Interpretation of Remotely Sensed Data held in Williamsburg, Virginia, May 23-25 1979] ; edited by Adarsh Deepak. — New York ; London : Academic Press, 1980. — xiv,614p : ill,1map ; 24cm
Includes index
ISBN 0-12-208460-8 : £25.20
Primary classification 551.5'028 B81-22001

551.46'005 — Oceanography — *Serials*

Oceanography and marine biology. — Vol.18. — Aberdeen : Aberdeen University Press, 1980. — 528p
ISBN 0-08-025732-1 : £35.00 : CIP rev.
ISSN 0079-3218
Also classified at 574.92'05 B80-12853

551.46'005 — Oceanography - *Serials*

Oceanography and marine biology. — Vol.19. — Aberdeen : Aberdeen University Press, Sept.1981. — [655]p
ISBN 0-08-028439-6 : CIP entry
ISSN 0078-3218
Also classified at 574.92'05 B81-20511

551.4'6'005 — Oceanography — *Serials*

Progress in oceanography. — Vol.9. — Oxford : Pergamon, Oct.1981. — [258]p
ISBN 0-08-027116-2 : £38.00 : CIP entry B81-30982

551.46'005 — Oceans — *Serials*

Ocean yearbook / sponsored by the International Ocean Institute. — 2. — Chicago ; London : University of Chicago Press, c1980. — ix,713p
ISBN 0-226-06603-7 : Unpriced B81-27906

551.46'0072 — Marine sciences. Research

Scott, Desmond P. Dehany. The importance of marine scientific research for the future of mankind : a public lecture to inaugurate the second M.Sc. course in Sea use - law, economics and policy making / Desmond P. Dehany Scott. — [London] : The London School of Economics and Political Science, 1981. — 26p ; 21cm
ISBN 0-85328-070-3 (pbk) : Unpriced B81-16039

551.46'0072041 — Great Britain. Oceanography. Research organisations: Institute of Oceanographic Sciences — *Serials*

Institute of Oceanographic Sciences. Annual report / Institute of Oceanographic Sciences. — 1979. — Wormley (Wormley, Godalming, Surrey GU8 5UB) : The Institute, c1980. — 103p
ISBN 0-904175-10-3 : £4.00
ISSN 0309-4472 B81-24989

551.46'01 — Oceans. Electrochemical properties

Marine electrochemistry. — Chichester : Wiley, Oct.1981. — [528]p
ISBN 0-471-27976-5 : £30.00 : CIP entry B81-28041

551.46'01 — Oceans. Organic compounds

Marine organic chemistry : evolution, composition, interactions and chemistry of organic matter in seawater / edited by E.K. Duursma and R. Dawson. — Amsterdam ; Oxford : Elsevier Scientific, 1981. — xiv,521p(4 fold.) : ill(some col.),maps ; 25cm. — (Elsevier oceanography series ; 31)
Includes bibliographies and index
ISBN 0-444-41892-x : Unpriced B81-16023

551.46'01 — Physical oceanography

Evolution of physical oceanography : scientific surveys in honor of Henry Stommel / edited by Bruce. A. Warren and Carl Wunsch. — Cambridge, Mass. ; London : MIT Press, c1981. — xxxiii,623p : ill,charts,maps,ports ; 29cm
Ill on 1 folded sheet in pocket. — Bibliography: p554-611. — Includes index
ISBN 0-262-23104-2 : £23.25 B81-28355

551.46'08 — Oceans. Bed. Geological features

The **Ocean** basins and margins. — New York ; London : Plenum
Vol.5: The Arctic Ocean / edited by Alan E.M. Nairn, Michael Churkin, Jr. and Francis G. Stehli. — c1981. — xiv,672p,[6]p of plates : ill,maps ; 26cm
Includes bibliographies and index
ISBN 0-306-37775-6 : Unpriced B81-25597

551.46'08 — Oceans. Bed. Interactions with sound waves — *Conference proceedings*

Bottom-interacting ocean acoustics / edited by William A. Kuperman and Finn B. Jensen. — New York ; London : Published in co-operation with NATO Scientific Affairs Division by Plenum, c1980. — xiv,717p : ill,charts,maps ; 26cm. — (NATO conference series. IV Marine sciences ; v.5)
Includes bibliographies and index
ISBN 0-306-40624-1 : Unpriced B81-23411

551.46'083 — Oceans. Bed. Phosphorite

Baturin, G. N.. Phosphorite on the sea floor. — Oxford : Elsevier Scientific, Jan.1982. — [300] p. — (Developments in sedimentology, ISSN 0070-4571 ; 33)
Translation of: Fosfority na dne okeanov
ISBN 0-444-41990-x : CIP entry B81-34495

551.46'083'336 — North Sea. Marine sediments

Holocene marine sedimentation in the North Sea basin. — Oxford : Blackwell Scientific, Nov.1981. — [524]p. — (Special publication / International Association of Sedimentologists, ISSN 0141-3600 ; 5)
ISBN 0-632-00858-x (pbk) : £20.00 : CIP entry B81-30979

551.46'084'337 — Malin Sea. Bed. Geological features

The **Geology** of the Malin Sea / D. Evans ... [et al.] ; contributors P.L. Barber, G.P. Durant and D.C. Pendlebury. — London : H.M.S.O., 1980. — iii,44p : ill,charts,maps ; 30cm + charts(5 folded sheets ; 30x 24cm. folded to 18x16cm). — (Report / Institute of Geological Sciences ; 79/15)
Five folded sheets (col.charts) in pocket. — Includes bibliographies
ISBN 0-11-884127-0 (pbk) : £6.00 B81-12767

551.46'09 — Coastal regions. Lagoons

Barnes, R. S. K.. Coastal lagoons : the natural history of a neglected habitat / R.S.K. Barnes. — Cambridge : Cambridge University Press, 1980. — xi,106p : ill,maps ; 23cm. — (Cambridge studies in modern biology ; 1)
Bibliography: p95-102. — Includes index
ISBN 0-521-23422-0 (cased) : £12.00
ISBN 0-521-29945-4 (pbk) : £4.95 B81-02614

551.46'09 — Estuaries — *Conference proceedings*

International Estuarine Research Conference *(5th : 1979 : Jekyll Island).* Estuarine perspectives / [proceedings of the fifth biennial International Estuarine Research Conference, Jekyll Island, Georgia, October 7-12, 1979] ; edited by Victor S. Kennedy. — New York ; London : Academic Press, 1980. — xxi,533p : ill,maps ; 24cm
Includes bibliographies and index
ISBN 0-12-404060-8 : £19.20 B81-14752

551.46'137 — England. Solent

The **Solent** estuarine system : an assessment of present knowledge. — Swindon (Polaris House, North Star Ave., Swindon SN1 1EU) : Natural Environment Research Council, c1980. — iv,100p : ill,maps ; 30cm. — (The Natural Environment Research Council publications. Series C, ISSN 0140-9611 ; no.22)
Includes bibliographies
Unpriced (pbk) B81-04943

551.46'57 — South-west Pacific Ocean. Geophysical processes — *Conference proceedings*

Geodynamics in south-west Pacific = Géodynamique du sud-ouest Pacifique : Symposium International Noumea - Nouvelle Calédonie, 27 août-2 septembre, 1976 / sous le patronage de Office de la recherche scientifique et technique outre-mer ... [et al.]. — Paris : Technip ; London : Distributed by Graham & Trotman, c1977. — xi,413p,[3]folded leaves of plates : maps ; 27cm
Includes parallel French text and English translation of foreword and one chapter in French. — Includes bibliographies and index
ISBN 2-7108-0317-8 (pbk) : £41.00 B81-34080

551.47 — Coastal waters. Hydrodynamics

Wood, A. M. Muir. Coastal hydraulics. — 2nd ed. / A.M. Muir Wood, C.A. Fleming. — London : Macmillan, 1981. — xv,280p : ill ; 25cm
Previous ed.: 1969. — Includes index
ISBN 0-333-26129-1 : £25.00 B81-39088

551.47 — Oceans. Interactions with atmosphere. Measurement

Air-sea interaction : instruments and methods / edited by F. Dobson, L. Hasse and R. Davis. — New York ; London : Plenum, c1980. — xii,801p : ill ; 26cm
Includes bibliographies and index
ISBN 0-306-40543-1 : Unpriced B81-03201

551.48 — Fresh waters. Mechanics — *For geology*

Chapman, Richard E.. Geology and water : an introduction to fluid mechanics for geologists / by Richard E. Chapman. — The Hague ; London : Nijhoff, 1981. — xvi,228p : ill,maps ; 25cm. — (Developments in applied earth sciences ; v.1)
Includes bibliographies and index
ISBN 90-247-2455-4 : Unpriced B81-17113

551.48 — Hydrology

Dinkele, Geoff. An excursion into hydrology / Geoff Dinkele. — London : Harrap, 1981. — 31p : ill,maps ; 30cm. — (Harrap's advanced geography topics)
Bibliography: p31
ISBN 0-245-53520-9 (pbk) : £1.10 B81-24958

551.48 — Peatlands. Water cycle

Ivanov, K. E.. Water movement in mirelands / K.E. Ivanov ; translated from the Russian by Arthur Thomson and H.A.P. Ingram. — London : Academic Press, 1981. — xxviii,276p : ill,maps ; 24cm
Translation of: Vodoobmen v bolontnykh landshaftakh. — Bibliography: p258-267. — Includes index
ISBN 0-12-376460-2 : £24.60 B81-23547

551.48'028 — Hydrology. Applications of remote sensing

Remote sensing in meteorology, oceanography and hydrology / [based on material presented at a postgraduate summer school sponsored by the European Association of Remote Sensing Laboratories (EARSel) and held at the University of Dundee in September 1980] ; editor A.P. Cracknell. — Chichester : Horwood, 1981. — 542p,[8]p of plates : ill (some col.),charts,maps(some col.) ; 24cm
Includes bibliographies and index
ISBN 0-85312-212-1 : £35.00 : CIP rev.
Primary classification 551.46'0028 B81-09968

551.48'05 — Hydrology — *Serials*

Advances in hydroscience. — Vol.12 (1981). — New York ; London : Academic Press, c1981. — x,440p
ISBN 0-12-021812-7 : £28.60
ISSN 0065-2768 B81-35101

551.48'0724 — Hydrology. Mathematical models — *Conference proceedings*

International Symposium on Logistics and Benefits of Using Mathematical Models of Hydrologic and Water Resource Systems *(1978 : Pisa)*. Logistics and benefits of using mathematical models of hydrologic and water resource systems : selected papers with summary of discussions from The International Symposium on Logistics and Benefits of Using Mathematical Models of Hydrologic and Water Resource Systems, Pisa, Italy, 24-26 October 1978 / convened by The International Institute for Applied Systems Analysis and cosponsored by The World Meteorological Organization and the IBM Scientific Center (Pisa) ; A.J. Askew, F. Greco, and J. Kindler, editors. — Oxford : Pergamon, 1981. — viii,258p : ill,maps ; 26cm. — (IIASA proceedings series ; v.13)
Includes bibliographies
ISBN 0-08-025662-7 : £23.00 : CIP rev. B81-23806

551.48'0724 — Hydrology. Simulations. Applications of digital computer systems

Abbott, M. B.. Engineering applications of computational hydraulics. — London : Pitman Vol.1. — Feb.1982. — [288]p. — (Monographs and surveys in water resources engineering ; 5)
ISBN 0-273-08512-3 : £27.50 : CIP entry B81-35776

551.48'3 — Streams. Junctions. Playfair's law

Kennedy, Barbara A.. On Playfair's Law / by Barbara A. Kennedy. — Oxford (Mansfield Rd., Oxford OX1 3TB) : School of Geography, [1981?]. — 19p : ill ; 30cm. — (Working papers / School of Geography University of Oxford ; no.1)
Bibliography: p19
Unpriced (pbk) B81-13969

551.48'3'0941 — Great Britain. Rivers

British rivers. — London : Allen & Unwin, Sept.1981. — [228]p
ISBN 0-04-551047-4 : £20.00 : CIP entry B81-20483

551.48'3'0941 — Great Britain. Rivers, *to 1980*

Burton, Anthony. The changing river. — London : Gollancz, Feb.1982. — [192]p
ISBN 0-575-02967-6 : £10.95 : CIP entry B81-38315

551.48'3'094577 — Semi-arid regions. Streams. Channels — *Study regions: Italy. Basento River Valley*

Alexander, David, *1953-*. Observations on the regularity of ephemeral channel form / David Alexander. — London (26 Bedford Way, WC1H 0AP) : Department of Geography, University College London, 1980. — 24,[18]p : ill,1map ; 30cm. — (Occasional papers / University College, London. Department of Geography ; no.36)
Bibliography: p22-24
Unpriced (pbk) B81-39038

551.48'9 — Great Britain. Floods. Forecasting. Applications of mathematical models — *Conference proceedings*

Floods due to high winds and tides. — London : Academic Press, Nov.1981. — [100]p
Conference proceedings
ISBN 0-12-551820-x : CIP entry B81-28138

551.48'9'0941 — Great Britain. Flooding — *Conference proceedings*

Flood studies report — five years on : proceedings of a conference organized by the Institution of Civil Engineers and held in Manchester, 22-24 July, 1980. — London : Telford, 1981. — vii,159p : ill,maps ; 31cm
ISBN 0-7277-0120-7 : £20.00 B81-28960

551.49 — Ground water

Todd, David Keith. Groundwater hydrology / David Keith Todd. — 2nd ed. — New York ; Chichester : Wiley, c1980. — xiii,535p : ill,maps ; 24cm
Previous ed.: New York : Wiley ; London : Chapman and Hall, 1959. — Map and text on lining papers. — Includes bibliographies and index
ISBN 0-471-87616-x : £13.00 B81-02054

551.49 — Ground water. Chemical analysis. Laboratory techniques

Cook, J. M. (Jennifer Mary). Methods for the chemical analysis of groundwater / J.M. Cook and D.L. Miles. — London : H.M.S.O., 1980. — iii,55p : ill ; 30cm. — (Report / Institute of Geological Sciences ; 80/5)
Includes bibliographies
ISBN 0-11-884183-1 (pbk) : £3.50 B81-13156

551.49 — Ground water. Geochemical aspects — *Conference proceedings*

Geochemistry of groundwater. — Oxford : Elsevier Scientific, Nov.1981. — [260]p. — (Developments in water science ; 16)
ISBN 0-444-42036-3 : CIP entry B81-34008

551.49 — Ground water. Seepage

Kovács, György. Seepage hydraulics / by György Kovács ; [translated by Katalin Kovács]. — Amsterdam ; Oxford : Elsevier Scientific, 1981. — 730p : ill ; 25cm. — (Developments in water science ; 10)
Translation of: A szivágás hidraulikája. — Includes bibliographies and index
ISBN 0-444-99755-5 : £54.24 : CIP rev. B80-18715

Marino, Miguel A.. Seepage and groundwater. — Oxford : Elsevier Scientific, Aug.1981. — [400] p. — (Developments in water sciences ; 13)
ISBN 0-444-41975-6 : CIP entry B81-18078

551.49'0941 — Great Britain. Hydrogeology

A **Survey** of British hydrogeology 1980. — London : Royal Society, 1981. — 190p : ill,maps ; 30cm
Includes bibliographies
ISBN 0-85403-177-4 (pbk) : Unpriced B81-40060

551.5 — METEOROLOGY

551.5 — Atmosphere. Physical properties

Fleagle, Robert G.. An introduction to atmospheric physics / Robert G. Fleagle, Joost A. Businger. — 2nd ed. — New York ; London : Academic Press, 1980. — xiv,432p : ill ; 24cm. — (International geophysics series ; v.25)
Previous ed.: 1963. — Bibliography: p417-419. — Includes index
ISBN 0-12-260355-9 : £16.60 B81-16192

Iribarne, J. V.. Atmospheric physics / J.V. Iribarne and H.-R. Cho. — Dordrecht ; London : Reidel, c1980. — xii,212p : ill,charts ; 25cm
Bibliography: p199-200. - Includes index
ISBN 90-277-1033-3 : Unpriced B81-01774

551.5 — Meteorology

Dynamical meteorology. — London : Methuen, Sept.1981. — [200]p
ISBN 0-416-73830-3 (cased) : £10.00 : CIP entry
ISBN 0-416-73840-0 (pbk) : £4.95 B81-30295

551.5 — Weather

Forsdyke, A. G.. The weather guide / A.G. Forsdyke ; illustrated by Angus McBride. — London : Hamlyn, 1969 (1980 [printing]). — 159p : col.ill,col.charts,col.maps ; 19cm
Bibliography: p156. — Includes index
ISBN 0-600-35377-x : £2.50 B81-02197

Miller, Albert. Elements of meteorology / Albert Miller, Jack C. Thompson. — 3rd ed. — Columbus [Ohio] ; London : Merrill, c1979. — xv,383p,[16]p of plates : ill(some col.),charts,maps ; 26cm
Previous ed.: 1975. — Bibliography: p365-367. - Includes index
ISBN 0-675-08293-5 : £12.75 B81-12643

Roth, Günter D.. Collins guide to the weather / Gunter D. Roth ; translated by E.M. Yates. — London : Collins, c1981. — 256p : ill(some col.),charts(some col.), maps(some col.),forms ; 20cm
Translation of: Wetterkunde für alle. — Maps on lining papers. — Includes index
ISBN 0-00-219010-9 : £6.95 B81-22142

551.5 — Weather — *For children*

Ford, Adam. Weather watch / written by Adam Ford. — London (11 New Fetter La., EC4P 4EE) : Methuen / Walker Books, 1981. — 41p : col.ill,col.maps ; 28cm. — (All about earth)
Maps on lining papers. — Includes index
ISBN 0-416-05670-9 : £3.95 : CIP rev. B81-25880

Weihmann, Götz. Weather / Götz Weihmann ; [translated by Patricia Green]. — St. Albans : Hart-Davis, c1981. — 32p : col.ill,2col.maps ; 26cm. — (Natural science series)
Translation from the German. — Includes index
ISBN 0-247-13154-7 : £2.95 B81-39612

551.5 — Weather — *For schools*

Atherton, M. A.. Air and earth / Michael Atherton & Roger Robinson. — 80p : ill(some col.),col.charts,col.maps,facsims ; 25cm. — (Study the earth)
Cover title
ISBN 0-340-23946-8 (pbk) : £1.95 : CIP rev. B80-11025

Crisp, Tony, *1940-*. Weather / Tony Crisp. — Walton-on-Thames : Nelson, 1981. — 48p : ill (some col.),col.charts,col.maps ; 22x27cm. — (The active earth)
ISBN 0-17-434215-2 (pbk) : £1.45 B81-36255

551.5'0246238 — Meteorology — *For seafaring*

Sanderson, Roy. Meteorology at sea. — London : Stanford Maritime, Dec.1981. — [232]p
ISBN 0-540-07405-5 : £8.50 : CIP entry B81-34220

551.5'028 — Atmosphere. Remote sensing. Data. Interpretation — *Conference proceedings*

Interactive Workshop on Interpretation of Remotely Sensed Data *(1979 : Williamburg)*. Remote sensing of atmospheres and oceans / [proceedings of the Interactive Workshop on Interpretation of Remotely Sensed Data held in Williamsburg, Virginia, May 23-25 1979] ; edited by Adarsh Deepak. — New York ; London : Academic Press, 1980. — xiv,614p : ill,1map ; 24cm
Includes index
ISBN 0-12-208460-8 : £25.20
Also classified at 551.46'0028 B81-22001

551.5'028 — Meteorology. Applications of remote sensing

Remote sensing in meteorology, oceanography and hydrology / [based on material presented at a postgraduate summer school sponsored by the European Association of Remote Sensing Laboratories (EARSel) and held at the University of Dundee in September 1980] ; editor A.P. Cracknell. — Chichester : Horwood, 1981. — 542p,[8]p of plates : ill (some col.),charts,maps(some col.) ; 24cm
Includes bibliographies and index
ISBN 0-85312-212-1 : £35.00 : CIP rev.
Primary classification 551.46'0028 B81-09968

551.5'05 — Weather — *Serials*

Jet stream. — Vol.0, no.0 ; Vol.1, nos.1-2 (Mar.1981)-. — Reading (60 Talfourd Ave., Reading RG6 2BP) : Westwind Services, 1981-. — v : ill,charts ; 24cm
Six issues yearly. — Introductory no., called v.0, no.0, issued Jan.1981
ISSN 0261-0787 = Jet stream : £19.00 per year B81-24696

551.5'07'1041 — Great Britain. Schools. Students, 5-14 years. Curriculum subjects: Weather — *For teaching*

Hudson, Jim. Understanding the weather / Jim and Christine Hudson. — Basingstoke (Houndmills, Basingstoke RG21 2XS) : Globe Education [for] West Sussex County Council, 1981. — 60p : ill,forms,1map ; 30cm. — (Science horizons. Level 2b)
Bibliography: p10. — List of films: p10-11
ISBN 0-333-31301-1 (pbk) : £3.95 B81-31309

551.5'099 — Solar system. Planets. Atmosphere — *Comparative studies*
Kondratyev, K. Y.. Weather and climate on planets. — Oxford : Pergamon, Nov.1981. — [750]p
ISBN 0-08-026493-x : £43.00 : CIP entry B81-30983

551.5'1'0724 — Air. Experiments — *For children*
Kincaid, Doug. In the air / Doug Kincaid, Peter S. Coles ; designed & illustrated by John Hill. — [Amersham] : Hulton, 1981. — 64p : ill (some col.) ; 25cm. — (Science in a topic)
Text, ill on inside covers. — Bibliography: 1p
ISBN 0-7175-0877-3 (pbk) : £1.85 B81-14338

551.5'1'0724 — Air. Experiments — *For schools*
Air. — London : Harrap, 1981. — 48p : ill ; 25cm. — (Access to science)
Cover title. — Text on inside cover
ISBN 0-245-53663-9 (pbk) : £1.50
ISBN 0-245-53704-x (Teacher's notes and tests) : £1.25 B81-37432

551.5'14 — Mesosphere - *Conference proceedings*
The **Mesosphere** and thermosphere. — Oxford : Pergamon, Apr.1981. — [238]p. — (Advances in space research ; v.1, no.12)
Conference papers
ISBN 0-08-028393-4 : £13.00 : CIP entry
Also classified at 551.5'14 B81-09972

551.5'14 — Middle atmosphere. Research — *Proposals*
U.K. research studies proposed for the Middle Atmosphere Programme 1982-85 / prepared on behalf of the British National Committee for Solar-Terrestrial Physics. — London : Royal Society, 1981. — 38p : ill,1map ; 22cm
ISBN 0-85403-173-1 (pbk) : Unpriced B81-37963

551.5'14 — Thermosphere - *Conference proceedings*
The **Mesosphere** and thermosphere. — Oxford : Pergamon, Apr.1981. — [238]p. — (Advances in space research ; v.1, no.12)
Conference papers
ISBN 0-08-028393-4 : £13.00 : CIP entry
Primary classification 551.5'14 B81-09972

551.5'14'0911 — Polar regions. Upper atmosphere — *Conference proceedings*
Exploration of the Polar upper atmosphere : proceedings of the NATO Advanced Study Institute held at Lillehammer, Norway, May 5-16, 1980 / edited by C.S. Deehr and J.A. Holtet. — Dordrecht ; London : Reidel published in cooperation with NATO Scientific Affairs Division, c1981. — xvi,498p : ill,music ; 25cm. — (NATO advanced study institutes series. Series C, Mathematical and physical sciences ; v.64)
Includes bibliographies and index
ISBN 90-277-1225-5 : Unpriced B81-13653

551.5'14'098 — South America. Upper atmosphere. Meteorological conditions — *Statistics*
An **Aeroclimatic** handbook of South America / edited by Z.I. Gavrilova ; translated by Brian D. Giles and Denis J.B. Shaw. — [Birmingham] : [Department of Geography, University of Birmingham], [1976]. — xviii,[138]p : 1map ; 30cm. — (Occasional publication / Department of Geography - Edgbaston Meteorological Observatory ; no.1)
Translation of: Aéroklimaticheskiĭ spravochnik Iūzhnoĭ Ameriki
ISBN 0-7044-0352-8 (pbk) : £1.00 B81-39709

551.5'17 — Atmosphere. Circulation
Atkinson, B. W.. Meso-scale atmospheric circulations. — London : Academic Press, May 1981. — [450]p
ISBN 0-12-065960-3 : CIP entry B81-08802

551.5'17'098 — Southern South America. Atmosphere. Circulation. Analysis. Applications of synoptic climatology
Sturman, Andrew P.. Aspects of the synoptic climatology of the southern South American sector / Andrew P. Sturman. — [Birmingham] : [Department of Geography, University of Birmingham], 1978. — 18p,[8]leaves of plates : ill ; 30cm. — (Occasional publication / Department of Geography, University of Birmingham ; no.5)
Bibliography: p16-18
ISBN 0-7044-0356-0 (pbk) : £0.50 B81-39710

551.5'27 — Atmosphere. Radiation
Liou, Kuo-Nan. An introduction to atmosphere radiation / Kuo-Nan Liou. — New York ; London : Academic Press, 1980. — xii,392p : ill ; 24cm. — (International geophysics series ; v.26)
Bibliography: p378-383. — Includes index-
ISBN 0-12-451450-2 : £21.00 B81-15058

551.5'52 — Hurricanes
Simpson, Robert H.. The hurricane and its impact / Robert H. Simpson and Herbert Riehl. — Oxford : Blackwell, 1981. — xxvii,398p : ill,charts,maps ; 24cm
Includes index
ISBN 0-631-12738-0 : £19.50 B81-39949

551.5'54 — Thunderstorms
Magono, Chōji. Thunderstorms / by Choji Magono. — Amsterdam ; Oxford : Elsevier, 1980. — x,261p : ill,1chart ; 25cm. — (Developments in atmospheric science ; 12)
Bibliography: p229-253. — Includes index
ISBN 0-444-41882-2 : £26.15 : CIP rev. B80-25599

551.5'6 — Light. Propagation in atmosphere
Greenler, Robert. Rainbows, halos, and glories / Robert Greenler. — Cambridge : Cambridge University Press, 1980. — x,195p,[32]p of plates : ill(some col.) ; 27cm
Bibliography: p187. - Includes index
ISBN 0-521-23605-3 : £15.00 B81-09825

551.5'634 — Ball lightning & bead lightning
Barry, James Dale. Ball lightning and bead lightning : extreme forms of atmospheric electricity / James Dale Barry. — New York ; London : Plenum, c1980. — x,298p : ill ; 24cm
Bibliography: p203-291. — Includes index
ISBN 0-306-40272-6 : Unpriced B81-00881

551.57'6 — Clouds. Particles
Pruppacher, Hans R.. Microphysics of clouds and precipitation / by Hans R. Pruppacher and James D. Klett. — Dordrecht ; London : Reidel, 1980. — xiv,714p : ill ; 24cm
Originally published: 1978. — Bibliography: p656-697. - Includes index
ISBN 90-277-1106-2 (pbk) : Unpriced B81-04133

551.57'6 — Clouds. Structure & optical properties
Clouds : their formation, optical properties, and effects / edited by Peter V. Hobbs, Adarsh Deepak. — New York ; London : Academic Press, 1981. — xiv,497p : ill,maps,facsims ; 24cm
Conference papers. — Includes index
ISBN 0-12-350720-0 : £32.20 B81-40804

551.57'73 — Drought
Garcia, Rolando V.. Drought and man : the 1972 case history / by Rolando V. Garcia. — Oxford : Pergamon
Vol.1: Nature pleads not guilty / with a section of climatic variability by J. Smagorinsky and special contributions from M. Ellman ... [et al.]. — 1981. — xiv,300p : ill,charts ; 26cm
Includes bibliographies and index
ISBN 0-08-025823-9 : £25.00 B81-38271

551.57'81241'0212 — Great Britain. Rainfall — *Statistics — Serials*
Monthly and annual totals of rainfall ... for the United Kingdom. — 1972. — Bracknell (London Rd., Bracknell, Berks. RG12 2SZ) : Meteorological Office, c1980. — xi,106p
ISBN 0-86180-046-x : Unpriced B81-17484

551.57'81254 — South Asia. Monsoons — *Conference proceedings*
Monsoon dynamics / edited by Sir James Lighthill & R.P. Pearce. — Cambridge : Cambridge University Press, 1981. — xxii,735p : ill,charts,maps ; 24cm
Conference papers. — Includes bibliographies and index
ISBN 0-521-22497-7 (cased) : £55.00 (pbk) : Unpriced B81-14662

551.57'848'0247965 — Avalanches — *Conference proceedings — For mountaineering*
Avalanche : proceedings of a symposium for skiers, ski-mountaineers and mountaineers, with accounts of experiences of avalanches in Scotland, Europe and the Himalayas / edited by John Harding, Michael Baker, Edward Williams with special assistance from André Roch and Fred Harper. — London (74 South Audley St., W1Y 5FF) : Alpine Club, c1980. — 62p : ill ; 21cm
ISBN 0-900523-43-3 (pbk) : Unpriced
Also classified at 551.57'848'0247969 B81-08311

551.57'848'0247969 — Avalanches — *Conference proceedings — For skiing*
Avalanche : proceedings of a symposium for skiers, ski-mountaineers and mountaineers, with accounts of experiences of avalanches in Scotland, Europe and the Himalayas / edited by John Harding, Michael Baker, Edward Williams with special assistance from André Roch and Fred Harper. — London (74 South Audley St., W1Y 5FF) : Alpine Club, c1980. — 62p : ill ; 21cm
ISBN 0-900523-43-3 (pbk) : Unpriced
Primary classification 551.57'848'0247965 B81-08311

551.6 — CLIMATE AND WEATHER

551.6 — Applied climatology
Hobbs, John E.. Applied climatology : a study of atmospheric resources / John E. Hobbs. — London : Butterworths, 1981, c1980. — 218p : ill,charts,maps ; 26cm. — (Studies in physical geography, ISSN 0142-6389)
Originally published: Folkestone : Dawson, 1980. — Includes bibliographies and index
ISBN 0-408-10737-5 : £12.50 B81-11448

Oliver, John E.. Climatology : selected applications / John E. Oliver. — [Washington D.C.] : Winston ; London : Edward Arnold, 1981. — ix,260p : ill,charts ; 24cm. — (Scripta series in geography)
Bibliography: p245-250. — Includes index
ISBN 0-7131-6303-8 : £14.95 : CIP rev. B80-23255

551.6 — Climate
Trewartha, Glenn T.. The earth's problem climates / Glenn T. Trewartha. — 2nd ed. — Madison ; London : University of Wisconsin Press, 1981. — xi,371p : ill,charts,maps ; 26cm
Previous ed.: 1961. — Maps on lining papers. — Bibliography: p349-366. — Includes index
ISBN 0-299-08230-x : £13.50 B81-25647

551.6 — Climate. Changes — *Conference proceedings*
International School of Climatology *(1st : 1980 : Ettore Majorcana Center for Scientific Culture)*. Climatic variations and variability : facts and theories : NATO Advanced Study Institute First Course of the International School of Climatology, Ettore, Majorcana Centre for Scientific Culture, Erice, Italy, March 9-21 1980 / edited by A. Berger. — Dordrecht ; London : Reidel in co-operation with NATO Scientific Affairs Division, c1981. — xxvi,795p : ill,maps ; 25cm. — (NATO advanced study institutes series. Series C, Mathematical and physical sciences ; v.72)
Includes index
ISBN 90-277-1300-6 : Unpriced B81-33338

551.6 — Climate. Changes. Effects — *Conference proceedings*
Consequences of climate change / edited by Catherine Delano Smith and Martin Parry. — Nottingham : Department of Geography, University of Nottingham, 1981. — 143p : ill,maps ; 21cm
Conference papers. — Includes bibliographies
ISBN 0-85358-022-7 (pbk) : £3.50 B81-34818

551.6 — Climate. Changes — *For schools*
Barry, R. G.. Climatic change / R.G. Barry. — Basingstoke : Macmillan Education, 1981. — v,34p : ill,charts ; 22cm. — (Aspects of geography)
Bibliography: p32-33
ISBN 0-333-30563-9 (pbk) : £1.30 B81-31907

551.6 — Climate. Changes. Theories
Hoyle, Fred. Ice / Fred Hoyle. — London : Hutchinson, 1981. — 190p,[8]p of plates : ill,charts,maps ; 23cm
Includes index
ISBN 0-09-145320-8 : £7.95 : CIP rev.
B81-12322

551.6 — Climate. Effects of man — *Conference proceedings*
Interactions of energy and climate : proceedings of an international workshop held in Münster, Germany, March 3-6, 1980 / edited by W. Bach, J. Pankrath and J. Williams. — Dordrecht ; London : Reidel, c1980. — xl,569p : ill,charts,maps ; 25cm
Includes index
ISBN 90-277-1179-8 (cased) : Unpriced
ISBN 90-277-1177-1 (pbk) : Unpriced
B81-31224

551.6 — Climate. Influence of changes in solar radiation — *Conference proceedings*
Solar-terrestrial influences on weather and climate : proceedings of a symposium/workshop held at the Fawcett Center for Tomorrow, The Ohio State University, Columbus, Ohio, 24-28 August, 1978 / edited by Billy M. McCormac, Thomas A. Seliga. — Dordrecht ; London : Reidel, c1979. — xiii,346p : ill,maps,ports ; 25cm
Includes bibliographies and index
ISBN 90-277-0978-5 : Unpriced B81-15207

551.6 — Climatology
General climatology, 3 / edited by H.E. Landsberg. — Amsterdam ; Oxford : Elsevier Scientific, 1981. — xi,408p : ill,1map ; 30cm. — (World survey of climatology ; no.3)
Includes bibliographies and index
ISBN 0-444-41776-1 : £46.13 : CIP rev.
B80-19209

551.6 — Dendroclimatology — *Conference proceedings*
International Workshop on Global Dendroclimatology *(2nd : 1980 : University of East Anglia)*. Report and recommendations / Second International Workshop on Global Dendroclimatology July 1980 / edited by M.K. Hughes ... [et al.], assisted by D.A. Campbell. — Belfast (c/o Dr. J. Pilcher, Palaeoecology Laboratory, Queen's University of Belfast, Belfast BT7 1NN) : Organising Committee of The Workshop, 1980. — 68p ; 21cm
ISBN 0-9507344-0-3 (pbk) : £2.50 B81-12021

551.6 — Man. Effects of climatic change
Gribbin, John. Climate and mankind / by John Gribbin. — London (10 Percy St., W1P 0DR) : Earthscan, [c1979]. — 56p : ill,2maps ; 21cm
Cover title. — Bibliography: p56
ISBN 0-905347-12-9 (pbk) : £2.50 B81-38454

551.6 — Quaternary climate
Quaternary paleoclimate / edited by W.C. Mahaney. — Norwich : Geo Abstracts, [1981?]. — xv,464p : ill,maps ; 24cm
Conference papers. — Includes bibliographies and index
ISBN 0-86094-076-4 (pbk) : Unpriced
B81-24902

551.6'028 — Climatology. Statistical methods — *Conference proceedings*
International Conference on Statistical Climatology *(1st : 1979 : Tokyo)*. Statistical climatology : proceedings of the First International Conference on Statistical Climatology (a Satellite Meeting to the 1979 Session of the ISI), held at the Inter-University Seminar House, Hachioji, Tokyo (Japan), November 29-December, 1979 / edited by S. Ikeda (editor-in-chief) ; E. Zuki, E. Uchida and M.M. Yoshino. — Amsterdam ; Oxford : Elsevier Scientific, 1980. — x,388p : ill,maps ; 25cm. — (Developments in atmospheric science ; 13)
Includes bibliographies
ISBN 0-444-41923-3 : £29.85 : CIP rev.
B80-24452

551.6'09 — Climate. Changes. Influence of man — *Conference proceedings*
Climate and history. — Cambridge : Cambridge University Press, Oct.1981. — [531]p
Conference papers
ISBN 0-521-23902-8 : £30.00 : CIP entry
B81-32521

551.6'3'0247971 — Weather. Forecasting — *For yachting*
Singleton, Frank. Weather forecasting for sailors / Frank Singleton ; illustrations by J.R. Nicholas. — London : Hodder and Stoughton, 1981. — xii,146p,[4]p of plates : ill,charts,1facsim ; 20cm. — (Teach yourself books)
Bibliography: p142-143. - Includes index
ISBN 0-340-25977-9 (pbk) : £1.95 : CIP rev.
B81-09998

551.6'31 — Weather. Forecasting. Traditional techniques
Page, Robin. Weather forecasting : the country way / Robin Page ; with wood engravings by Thomas Bewick. — Harmondsworth : Penguin, 1981, c1977. — 70p : ill ; 18cm
Originally published: London : Davis-Poynter, 1977. — Includes index
ISBN 0-14-005154-6 (pbk) : £1.00 B81-25201

Weather wise : folklore, country sayings and predictions about Britain's climate / [edited and designed by the Reader's Digest Association]. — London : Reader's Digest Association, c1980. — 48p : ill(some col.),1map ; 14x20cm
£0.50 (pbk) B81-10846

551.6'6'0245474 — Microclimate. Measurement — *For ecology*
Unwin, D. M.. Microclimate measurement for ecologists / D.M. Unwin. — London : Academic Press, 1980. — viii,97p : ill ; 24cm. — (Biological techniques series ; 3)
Bibliography: p94-95. — Includes index
ISBN 0-12-709150-5 : £9.80 : CIP rev.
B80-31543

551.68'781273 — United States. Rainmaking, *1800-1946*
Spence, Clark C.. The rainmakers : American pluviculture to World War II / Clark C. Spence. — Lincoln [Neb.] ; London : University of Nebraska Press, c1980. — x,181p,[8]p of plates : ill ; 23cm
Includes index
ISBN 0-8032-4117-8 : £9.60 B81-05456

551.6914'3 — Climate & weather. Influence of mountains
Barry, Roger G.. Mountain weather and climate. — London : Methuen, Sept.1981. — [300]p
ISBN 0-416-73730-7 : £15.00 : CIP entry
B81-23771

551.69162 — Tropical regions. Oceans. Climate — *Conference proceedings*
Meteorology over the tropical oceans : the main papers presented at a joint conference held 21 to 25 August 1978 in the Rooms of the Royal Society, London, by the Royal Meteorological Society, the American Meteorological Society, the Deutsche Meteorologische Gesellschaft and the Royal Society / edited by D.B. Shaw. — Bracknell (James Glaisher House, Grenville Place, Bracknell, Berkshire RG12 1BX) : Royal Meteorological Society, [1981]. — 278p,[1]p of plates : ill,maps,ports ; 27cm
Includes bibliographies
£15.00 B81-37657

551.6941 — Great Britain. Weather
Stirling, Robin. The weather of Britain. — London : Faber, Nov.1981. — [288]p
ISBN 0-571-11695-7 : £12.50 : CIP entry
B81-30955

551.695 — Southern & western Asia. Climate
Climates of southern and western Asia / edited by K. Takahashi and H. Arakawa. — Amsterdam ; Oxford : Elsevier Scientific, 1981. — xiii,333p : maps ; 30cm. — (World survey of climatology ; v.9)
Includes bibliographies and index
ISBN 0-444-41861-x : Unpriced : CIP rev.
B81-06043

551.7 — STRATIGRAPHY

551.7 — Sedimentary basins. Stratigraphy
Conybeare, C. E. B.. Lithostratigraphic analysis of sedimentary basins / C.E.B. Conybeare. — New York ; London : Academic Press, 1979. — xii,555p : ill,maps ; 24cm
Bibliography: p498-531. — Includes index
ISBN 0-12-186050-7 : £31.80 B81-11264

551.7 — Stratigraphy. Applications of facies analysis
Hallam, A.. Facies interpretation and the stratigraphic record / A. Hallam. — Oxford : W.H. Freeman, c1981. — xii,291p : ill,maps ; 24cm
Bibliography: p245-270. — Includes index
ISBN 0-7167-1291-1 : £10.95 B81-37379

551.7'01 — Geological time
Thackray, John. The age of the earth / [John Thackray]. — London : HMSO for the Institute of Geological Sciences, c1980. — 34p : ill(some col.),col.maps,ports(some col.) ; 20x21cm
Cover title
ISBN 0-11-884077-0 (pbk) : £0.90 B81-04716

551.7'1 — Pre-Cambrian strata. Formation
Mel'nik, Y. P.. Precambrian banded iron-formations. — Oxford : Elsevier Scientific, Feb.1982. — [316]p. — (Developments in Precambrian geology ; 5)
ISBN 0-444-41934-9 : CIP entry B81-35706

551.7'1'091814 — Southern hemisphere. Pre-Cambrian strata
. Precambrian of the Southern Hemisphere / edited by D.R. Hunter. — Amsterdam ; Oxford : Elsevier Scientific, 1981. — xxiii,882p : ill,maps ; 25cm. — (Developments in Precambrian geology ; 2)
Includes bibliographies and index
ISBN 0-444-41862-8 : £67.04 : CIP rev.
B80-25600

551.7'12 — Archaean greenstone strata
Condie, Kent C.. Archean greenstone belts / Kent C. Condie. — Amsterdam ; Oxford : Elsevier, 1981. — viii,434p : ill,maps ; 23cm. — (Developments in Precambrian geology ; 3)
Bibliography: p384-423. - Includes index
ISBN 0-444-41854-7 : £46.72 : CIP rev.
B80-10596

551.7'6'094283 — Humberside. Mesozoic strata
Mesozoic rocks proved by IGS boreholes in the Humber and Acklam areas / G.D. Gaunt ... [et al.]. — London : H.M.S.O., 1980. — 11,34p : ill,maps ; 30cm. — (Report / Institute of Geological Sciences ; no.79/13)
Summaries in French and German. — Bibliography: p33-34
ISBN 0-11-884125-4 (pbk) : £2.50
Also classified at 551.7'6'0942843 B81-10031

551.7'6'0942843 — North Yorkshire. Acklam region. Mesozoic strata
Mesozoic rocks proved by IGS boreholes in the Humber and Acklam areas / G.D. Gaunt ... [et al.]. — London : H.M.S.O., 1980. — 11,34p : ill,maps ; 30cm. — (Report / Institute of Geological Sciences ; no.79/13)
Summaries in French and German. — Bibliography: p33-34
ISBN 0-11-884125-4 (pbk) : £2.50
Primary classification 551.7'6'094283
B81-10031

551.7'7 — Mid Cretaceous strata
Aspects of mid-Cretaceous regional geology / edited by R.A. Reyment and P. Bengtson. — London : Academic Press, 1981. — ix,327p,[4] folded leaves of plates : ill,maps ; 24cm
IGCP Project 58. — Includes bibliographies and index
ISBN 0-12-587040-x : £30.00 : CIP rev.
B81-06623

551.7'9'05 — Quaternary strata — *Serials*
Quaternary studies. — Vol.1 (1981)-. — London (Geography Section, Calcutta House, Old Castle St., E1 7NT) : City of London Polytechnic, 1981-. — v. : ill,maps ; 30cm
Issued every two years
ISSN 0261-9784 = Quaternary studies : £2.50
B81-36537

551.7′9′0941 — Great Britain. Quaternary strata — *Festschriften*

The **Quaternary** in Britain : essays, reviews and original work on the Quaternary published in honour of Lewis Penny on his retirement / edited by John Neale and John Flenley. — Oxford : Pergamon, 1981. — xi,267p,[1]leaf of plates : ill,maps,1port ; 24cm
Includes index
ISBN 0-08-026254-6 : £14.50 : CIP rev.
B81-10422

551.7′9′09425 — England. East Midlands. Quaternary strata — *For field studies*

Field handbook, annual field meeting, Leicester, 1981 / Quaternary Research Association ; edited by T.D. Douglas. — Newcastle upon Tyne (Ellison Place, Newcastle upon Tyne Polytechnic, Newcastle upon Tyne NE1 8ST) : PETRAS, 1981. — v,59p : ill,maps ; 21cm
Cover title: Field guide to the East Midlands region. — Bibliography: p56-59
Unpriced (pbk) B81-26113

551.7′92 — Earth. Glacial epoch ice sheets

The **Last** great ice sheets / edited by George H. Denton, Terence J. Hughes. — New York ; Chichester : Wiley, c1981. — xvii,484p,[6]p of plates : ill(some col.),maps(some col.) ; 29cm + 27sheets(chiefly maps(some col.) ; 110x79cm folded to 29x22cm)
In slip case. — Includes bibliographies and index
ISBN 0-471-06006-2 : £59.00 B81-23533

551.7′92′0941 — Great Britain. Ice ages

Sparks, B. W.. The Ice Age in Britain. — London : Methuen, Oct.1981. — [320]p. — (Methuen library reprints)
ISBN 0-416-32160-7 : £17.50 : CIP entry
B81-25727

551.7′92′0941172 — Scotland. Highland Region. Inner Cromarty Firth. Lateglacial strata

Peacock, J. D.. Late and post-glacial marine environments in part of the Inner Cromarty Firth, Scotland / J.D. Peacock, D.K. Graham and D.M. Gregory. — London : H.M.S.O., 1980. — 11p : ill,map ; 30cm. — (Report / Institute of Geological Sciences ; 80/7)
Bibliography: p10-11
ISBN 0-11-884160-2 (pbk) : £1.00
Also classified at 551.7′93′0941172 B81-13278

551.7′92′094723 — Russia *(RSFSR)*. Kola peninsula. Upper Pleistocene strata

Gudina, V. I.. The stratigraphy and foraminifera of the upper Pleistocene in the Kola peninsula / V.I. Gudina, V.Ya Evzerov ; translated by E. Lees ; edited by M. Hughes. — Boston Spa : British Library Lending Division, c1981. — 192p : ill,1map ; 30cm
Translation of: Stratigrafiia i foraminifery verkhnego pleistoťsena Kol′skogo poluostrova. — Bibliography: p158-166
ISBN 0-85350-181-5 (pbk) : £10.00 B81-36880

551.7′93 — France. Périgord. Stone Age rock shelters. Stratigraphy

Laville, Henri. Rock shelters of the Perigord : geological stratigraphy and archaeological succession / Henri Laville, Jean-Philippe Rigaud, James Sackett. — New York ; London : Academic Press, c1980. — xii,371p : ill,maps ; 25cm. — (Studies in archaeology)
Bibliography: p357-366. - Includes index
ISBN 0-12-438750-0 : £19.20 B81-15016

551.7′93′0941172 — Scotland. Highland Region. Inner Cromarty Firth. Holocene strata

Peacock, J. D.. Late and post-glacial marine environments in part of the Inner Cromarty Firth, Scotland / J.D. Peacock, D.K. Graham and D.M. Gregory. — London : H.M.S.O., 1980. — 11p : ill,map ; 30cm. — (Report / Institute of Geological Sciences ; 80/7)
Bibliography: p10-11
ISBN 0-11-884160-2 (pbk) : £1.00
Primary classification 551.7′92′0941172
B81-13278

551.8 — STRUCTURAL GEOLOGY

551.8 — Geological features. Mapping

Barnes, John W.. Basic geological mapping. — Milton Keynes : Open University Press, Nov.1981. — [128]p. — (Geological Society of London handbook series ; 1)
ISBN 0-335-10035-x (pbk) : £4.95 : CIP entry
B81-30284

551.8 — Geological structure

Wilson, Gilbert. Introduction to small-scale geological structures. — London : Allen & Unwin, Feb.1982. — [160]p
ISBN 0-04-551051-2 (cased) : £10.00 : CIP entry
ISBN 0-04-551052-0 (pbk) : £4.95 B81-35928

551.8′7 — Grabens. Formation

Mechanism of graben formation : selected papers of an ICG Symposium held during the 17th IUGG General Assembly, Canberra, Australia, December 5, 1979 / edited by J.H. Illies. — Amsterdam ; Oxford : Elsevier Scientific, 1981. — vii,266p : ill,maps ; 25cm. — (Inter-Union Commission on Geodynamics scientific report ; no. 63) (Developments in geotectonics ; 17)
Includes bibliographies
ISBN 0-444-41956-x : £25.96 B81-19279

551.8′7 — Thrusts & nappes — *Conference proceedings*

Thrust and nappe tectonics / edited by K.R. McClay, N.J. Price. — Oxford : Published for the Geological Society of London by Blackwell Scientific, 1981. — vi,539p,[6]p of plates : ill,maps ; 26cm
Conference papers. — Includes bibliographies and index
ISBN 0-632-00614-5 : £45.00 B81-18860

551.8′961′2 — Libya. Structural geology - *Conference proceedings*

The **Geology** of Libya. — London : Academic Press, Apr.1981
Vol.1. — [461]p
ISBN 0-12-615501-1 : CIP entry B81-03680

The **Geology** of Libya. — London : Academic Press, Apr.1981
Vol.2. — [461]p
ISBN 0-12-615502-x : CIP entry B81-03681

The **Geology** of Libya. — London : Academic Press, Apr.1981
Vol.3. — [461]p
ISBN 0-12-615503-8 : CIP entry B81-03682

551.9 — GEOCHEMISTRY

551.9 — Geochemistry — *Conference proceedings*

Geochemical exploration, 1980. — Oxford : Elsevier Scientific, Sept.1981. — [690]p. — (Developments in economic geology ; 15) (Special publication / Association of Exploration Geochemists ; no.1)
Conference papers
ISBN 0-444-42012-6 : CIP entry B81-28197

552 — PETROLOGY

552 — Rocks

Derry, Duncan R.. World atlas of geology and mineral deposits / Duncan R. Derry assisted by Laurence Curtis ... [et al.]. — London (15 Wilson St., EC2M 2TR) : Mining Journal Books, 1980. — 110p : ill,maps(some.col) ; 26x34cm
ISBN 0-470-26996-0 : £20.00
Also classified at 553 B81-01693

552′.06 — Rocks. Constituents: Trace metals. Chemical analysis. X-ray spectrometry

Bevan, Sheila A.. Determination of trace amounts of niobium, yttrium, zirconium, rubidium and strontium in rock powders by x-ray spectrometry / Sheila A. Bevan and Joyce M. Griffiths. — London (Cornwall House, Stamford St., SE1 9NQ) : Laboratory of the Government Chemist, 1981. — 16p : ill ; 30cm. — (Occasional paper / Laboratory of the Government Chemist ; no.1)
Cover title
Unpriced (pbk) B81-39857

552′.06 — Rocks. Physical properties — *Technical data*

Physical properties of rocks and minerals / edited by Y.S. Touloukian, W.R. Judd, R.F. Roy. — New York ; London : McGraw-Hill, c1981. — xx,548p : ill,maps ; 29cm. — (McGraw-Hill/CINDAS data series on material properties ; v.II—2)
Includes bibliographies
ISBN 0-07-065032-2 : £31.25
Primary classification 549′.12′0212 B81-32463

552′.06 — Rocks. Quantitative analysis — *Manuals*

Jeffery, P. G.. Chemical methods of rock analysis / by P.G. Jeffery and D. Hutchison. — 3rd ed. — Oxford : Pergamon, 1981. — xvi,379p : ill ; 24cm. — (Pergamon series in analytical chemistry ; vol.4)
Previous ed: 1975. — Includes index
ISBN 0-08-023806-8 : £25.00 B81-33199

552′.06′0287 — Rocks. Structure & properties. Testing & monitoring. Techniques

Rock characterization testing & monitoring : ISRM suggested methods / editor E.T. Brown. — Oxford : Published for the Commission on Testing Methods, International Society for Rock Mechanics by Pergamon, 1981. — x,211p : ill,forms ; 28cm
Includes bibliographies
ISBN 0-08-027308-4 (cased) : Unpriced
ISBN 0-08-027309-2 (pbk) : £8.00 B81-27805

552.0941 — Great Britain. Rocks — *Field guides*

Johansson, Folke. Rocks and minerals / photographs by Folke Johansson and Per H. Lundegårdh. — Poole : Blandford, c1981. — 126p : col. ill ; 12cm. — (A Blandford mini-guide)
These illustrations originally published: in Lilla stenboken/per H. Lundegårdh Stockholm : Almqvist & Wiksell Forlag, 1978. — Includes index
ISBN 0-7137-1208-2 (pbk) : £0.95
Also classified at 553′.0941 B81-31420

552.095 — Asia. Rocks. Metamorphism

Metamorphic complexes of Asia. — Oxford : Pergamon, Sept.1981. — [350]p
Translation of: Metamorficheskie kompleksy Azii
ISBN 0-08-022854-2 : £20.00 : CIP entry
B81-22570

552′.1 — Igneous rocks. Petrology

Sood, Mohan K.. Modern igneous petrology / Mohan K. Sood. — New York ; Chichester : Wiley, c1981. — xviii,244p ; ill ; 24cm
Bibliography: p205-227. — Includes indexes
ISBN 0-471-08915-x : £20.50 B81-40210

552′.1 — Magma. Physical properties — *Conference proceedings*

Physics of magnetic processes / R.B. Hargraves, editor. — Pinceton ; Guildford : Princeton University Press, 1980. — vii,585p : ill,maps ; 25cm
Conference papers. — Includes bibliographies and index
ISBN 0-691-08259-6 (cased) : £21.90
ISBN 0-691-08261-8 (pbk) : £8.40 B81-04568

552′.1942162 — London. Greenwich *(London Borough)*. Astronomical observations: Royal Greenwich Observatory, *to 1946*

National Maritime Museum. The Old Royal Observatory : a brief history / by P.S. Laurie. — Revised. — [London] : The Museum, 1972 (1977 printing). — 17p,[4]p of plates : ill,1plan,1port ; 25cm
Previous ed.: 1960
ISBN 0-905555-04-x (pbk) : Unpriced
B81-07009

552′.2 — Andesites

Andesites. — Chichester : Wiley, Jan.1982. — [640]p
ISBN 0-471-28034-8 : £35.00 : CIP entry
B81-34647

552′.5 — Sedimentary rocks — *For field studies*

Tucker, Maurice E.. The field description of sedimentary rocks. — Milton Keynes : Open University Press, Nov.1981. — [128]p. — (Geological Society of London handbook series ; 2)
ISBN 0-335-10036-8 (pbk) : £4.95 : CIP entry
B81-30221

552′.5 — Sedimentary rocks. Petrology
Tucker, Maurice E.. Sedimentary petrology : an introduction / M.E. Tucker. — Oxford : Blackwell Scientific, 1981. — viii,252p : ill,maps ; 24cm. — (Geoscience texts ; v.3)
Bibliography: p229-248. — Includes index
ISBN 0-632-00074-0 (pbk) : £8.50 : CIP rev.
B81-03698

552′.5 — Sedimentary rocks: Red beds
Turner, P.. Continental red beds / P. Turner. — Amsterdam ; Oxford : Elsevier Scientific, 1980. — xiii,562p : ill,maps ; 25cm. — (Developments in sedimentology ; 29)
Bibliography: p493-536. — Includes index
ISBN 0-444-41908-x : £32.07 : CIP rev.
B80-13382

552′.5 — Sedimentary rocks. Sedimentation
Allen, John R. L.. Sedimentary structures. — Oxford : Elsevier Scientific. — (Developments in sedimentology, ISSN 0070-4571 ; 30A)
Vol.1. — Oct.1981. — [650]p
ISBN 0-444-41935-7 : CIP entry
ISBN 0-444-41946-2 (set) : Unpriced
B81-27380

Allen, John R. L.. Sedimentary structures. — Oxford : Elsevier Scientific. — (Developments in sedimentology, ISSN 0070-4571 ; 30B)
Vol.2. — Feb.1982. — [650]p
ISBN 0-444-41945-4 : CIP entry
ISBN 0-444-41946-2 (set) : Unpriced
B81-35708

552′.5 — Tillites
Earth's pre-pleistocene glacial record : international geological correlation programme project 38 — pre-pleistocene tillites / edited and collated by M.J. Hambrey and W.B. Harland ; asssociate editors N.M. Chumakov ... [et al.]. — Cambridge : Cambridge University Press, 1981. — xv,1004p : ill,maps ; 31cm. — (Cambridge earth science series)
Includes bibliographies and index
ISBN 0-521-22860-3 : £98.00
B81-38289

553 — ECONOMIC GEOLOGY

553 — Economic geology. Role of tectonics
Economic geology and geotectonics / edited by D.H. Tarling. — Oxford : Blackwell Scientific, 1981. — x,213p : ill,maps ; 24cm
Includes bibliographies and index
ISBN 0-632-00738-9 : £15.00 : CIP rev.
B81-03161

553 — Mineral deposits
Derry, Duncan R.. World atlas of geology and mineral deposits / Duncan R. Derry assisted by Laurence Curtis ... [et al.]. — London (15 Wilson St., EC2M 2TR) : Mining Journal Books, 1980. — 110p : ill,maps(some.col) ; 26x34cm
ISBN 0-470-26996-0 : £20.00
Primary classification 552
B81-01693

Jensen, Mead L.. Economic mineral deposits. — 3rd ed., rev. printing, Mead L. Jensen, Alan M. Bateman. — New York ; Chichester : Wiley, c1981. — vii,593p : ill,maps ; 29cm
Previous ed.: / A.M. Bateman. London : Chapman and Hall, 1950. — Includes index
ISBN 0-471-09043-3 : £14.20
B81-16945

553 — Minerals — *Conference proceedings*
'Industrial Minerals' International Congress *(4th : 1980 : Atlanta).* Industrial minerals : proceedings of the 4th 'Industrial Minerals' International Congress : held at the Hilton Hotel, Atlanta, Georgia, USA on 28-30 May 1980 / edited by B.M. Coope ; organized by 'Industrial minerals' — London : Metal Bulletin PLC, 1981. — 239p : ill,maps ; 30cm
Includes bibliographies and index
ISBN 0-900542-53-5 (pbk) : Unpriced
B81-30108

553 — Stratabound ore deposits & stratiform ore deposits
Handbook of strata-bound and stratiform ore deposits. — Oxford : Elsevier Scientific, June 1981
Part 3
Vol.10: Bibliography and ore occurrence data Indexes volumes 8-10. — 1v.
ISBN 0-444-41825-3 : CIP entry
B81-12785

Handbook of strata-bound and stratiform ore deposits / edited by K.H. Wolf. — Amsterdam ; Oxford : Elsevier Scientific
Pt.III. v.8: General studies. — c1981. — xix,592p : ill,maps ; 25cm
Includes bibliographies
ISBN 0-444-41823-7 : Unpriced
B81-35555

Handbook of strata-bound and stratiform ore deposits / edited by K.H. Wolf. — Amsterdam ; Oxford : Elsevier Scientific
Regional studies and specific deposits. — 1981. — xiv,771p(16fold.) : ill,maps ; 25cm
Includes bibliographies and index
ISBN 0-444-41824-5 : Unpriced : CIP rev.
B80-31545

553′.0941 — Great Britain. Minerals — *Field guides*
Johansson, Folke. Rocks and minerals / photographs by Folke Johansson and Per H. Lundegårdh. — Poole : Blandford, c1981. — 126p : col. ill ; 12cm. — (A Blandford mini-guide)
These illustrations originally published: in Lilla stenboken/per H. Lundegårdh Stockholm : Almqvist & Wiksell Forlag, 1978. — Includes index
ISBN 0-7137-1208-2 (pbk) : £0.95
Primary classification 552.0941
B81-31420

553′.1 — Mineral deposits. Strata. Effects of tectonics
Mitchell, A. H. G.. Mineral deposits and global tectonic settings. — London : Academic Press, Dec.1981. — [420]p
ISBN 0-12-499050-9 : CIP entry
B81-31344

553.2′1′0941 — Great Britain. Peat bogs
Godwin, SirHarry. The archives of the peat bogs / Sir Harry Godwin. — Cambridge : Cambridge University Press, 1981. — viii,229p : ill,maps,plans ; 26cm
Bibliography: p219-221. — Includes index
ISBN 0-521-23784-x : £25.00
B81-39904

553.2′4 — Coal
Krevelen, D. W. Van. Coal : typology, chemistry, physics, constitution / D.W. Van Krevelen. — Amsterdam ; Oxford : Elsevier scientific, 1961 (1981 [printing]). — xviii,514p : ill ; 25cm. — (Coal science and technology ; 3)
Bibliography: p495-496. — Includes index
ISBN 0-444-40600-x : Unpriced
B81-38113

553.2′4 — Coal — *For children*
Gunston, Bill. Coal. — London : Watts, 1981. — 38p : col.ill,1col.map,1port ; 30cm. — (Energy)
Ill on lining papers. — Includes index
ISBN 0-85166-871-2 : £3.99
B81-13686

553.2′4 — Coal. Geochemical aspects
Bouška, Vladimír. Geochemistry of coal. — Oxford : Elsevier Scientific, Nov.1981. — [260]p. — (Coal science and technology ; v.1)
Translation and revision of: Geochemi uhlí
ISBN 0-444-99738-5 : £30.00 : CIP entry
B81-30522

553.2′4′05 — Coal. Serials. Titles — *Abbreviations — Serials*
Serial title abbreviations / IEA Coal Research, Technical Information Service. — 1981. — London (14/15 Lower Grosvenor Place, SW1W 0EX) : IEA Coal Research, c1980. — 37p
ISBN 92-902906-4-1 : Unpriced
B81-15147

553.2′8′094 — North-western Europe. Continental shelf. Natural gas & petroleum deposits — *Conference proceedings*
Conference on Petroleum Geology of the Continental Shelf of North-West Europe *(2nd : 1980 : London).* Petroleum geology of the continental shelf of North-West Europe : proceedings of the Second Conference on Petroleum Geology of the Continental Shelf of North-West Europe organised by the Institute of Petroleum and held in London 4-6 March 1980 / edited by L.V. Illing and G.D. Hobson. — London : Heyden on behalf of the Institute of Petroleum, 1981. — xviii,521p,[6]leaves of plates : ill(some col.),maps(some col.) ; 30cm
Includes bibliographies and index
ISBN 0-85501-656-6 : Unpriced
B81-19397

553.2′82 — Kerogen
Kerogen : insoluble organic matter from sedimentary rocks / edited by Bernard Durand. — Paris : Technip ; London : Distributed by Graham & Trotman, 1980. — xxviii,519p : ill (some col.),maps ; 25cm
Includes three chapters in French. — Includes bibliographies and index
ISBN 2-7108-0371-2 : £53.00
B81-37745

553.2′82 — Petroleum — *Conference proceedings*
Karcher Symposium *(3rd : 1979 : Oklahoma).* Origin and chemistry of petroleum : proceedings of the third annual Karcher Symposium, Oklahoma, May 4 1979 / edited by Gordon Atkinson and Jerry J. Zuckerman. — Oxford : Pergamon, 1981. — ix,116p : ill,maps ; 26cm
Includes bibliographies and index
ISBN 0-08-026179-5 : £12.50 : CIP rev.
B81-04308

World Petroleum Congress *(10th : 1979 : Bucharest).* Proceedings of the Tenth World Petroleum Congress. — London : Heyden. — 59p ; 29cm
English and French text
ISBN 0-85501-476-8 : Unpriced
ISBN 0-85501-470-9 (set of 6 vols.) : Unpriced
B81-10110

World Petroleum Congress *(10th : 1979 : Bucharest).* Proceedings of the Tenth World Petroleum Congress. — London : Heyden
Vol.1: General. — c1980. — v,162p : ill,map,ports ; 29cm
English and French text. — Added t.p. in French
ISBN 0-85501-471-7 : Unpriced
ISBN 0-85501-470-9 (set of 6 vols.) : Unpriced
B81-10111

World Petroleum Congress *(10th : 1979 : Bucharest).* Proceedings of the Tenth World Petroleum Congress. — London : Heyden, c1980
Vol.2: Exploration, supply and demand. — vii,441p : ill,maps ; 29cm
Includes four papers in French. — Includes index
ISBN 0-85501-472-5 : Unpriced
B81-10756

World Petroleum Congress *(10th : 1979 : Bucharest).* Proceedings of the Tenth World Petroleum Congress. — London : Heyden, c1980
Vol.3: Production. — vii,413p : ill,maps ; 29cm
Includes six papers in French. — Includes index
ISBN 0-85501-473-3 : Unpriced
B81-10757

World Petroleum Congress *(10th : 1979 : Bucharest).* Proceedings of the Tenth World Petroleum Congress. — London : Heyden, c1980
Vol.4: Storage, transport, processing. — vii,459p : ill,maps ; 29cm
Includes four papers in French. — Includes index
ISBN 0-85501-474-1 : Unpriced
B81-10754

World Petroleum Congress *(10th : 1979 : Bucharest).* Proceedings of the Tenth World Petroleum Congress. — London : Heyden, c1980
Vol.5: Conservation, environment, safety and training. — vii,359p : ill,maps ; 29cm
Includes six papers in French. — Includes index
ISBN 0-85501-475-x : Unpriced
B81-10755

553.2′82 — Petroleum deposits
Hobson, G. D.. Introduction to petroleum geology / by G.D. Hobson and E.N. Tiratsoo. — 2nd ed. — Beaconsfield ([4 Burkes Parade, Beaconsfield, Bucks. HP9 1WS]) : Scientific Press, 1981. — viii,352p : ill,maps ; 25cm
Previous ed.: 1975. — Includes bibliographies and index
ISBN 0-901360-12-0 : Unpriced
B81-12562

553.2'82 — Petroleum deposits *continuation*

Wheeler, Robert R.. Oil : from prospect to pipeline / Robert R. Wheeler, Maurine Whited. — 4th ed. — Houston ; London : Gulf Publishing, 1981. — xi,146p : ill,1map,1form ; 21cm
Previous ed.: 1975
ISBN 0-87201-635-8 (pbk) : Unpriced
B81-38947

553.2'82 — Petroleum deposits. Formation — *Conference proceedings*

Organic maturation studies and fossil fuel exploration / [based on the proceedings of a symposium held at the Fifth International Palynological Conference, Cambridge, England, 3-5 July 1980] ; edited by J. Brooks. — London : Academic Press, 1981. — xiii,441p : ill,2maps ; 24cm
Includes bibliographies and index
ISBN 0-12-135760-0 : £25.00 : CIP rev.
B81-02646

553.2'82 — Petroleum deposits. Reservoirs. Rocks. Properties

Monicard, Robert P.. Properties of reservoir rocks : core analysis / Robert P. Monicard ; translation from the French by David Berley. — Paris : Technip ; London : Distributed by Graham & Trotman, 1980. — xii,168p : ill ; 24cm. — (Institut français du pétrole publications)
At head of title: Institut français du pétrole, École nationale supérieure du pétrole et des moteurs. — Bibliography: p163-165. — Includes index
ISBN 2-7108-0387-9 (pbk) : £19.00 B81-34075

553.4'629 — Manganese deposits

Roy, Supriya. Manganese deposits / Supriya Roy. — London : Academic Press, 1981. — x,458p : ill,maps ; 24cm
Bibliography: p393-451. — Includes index
ISBN 0-12-601080-3 : £40.00 : CIP rev.
B80-18270

553.4'92 — Karsts. Bauxite deposits

Bárdossy, György. Karst bauxites. — Oxford : Elsevier Scientific, Dec.1981. — [500]p. — (Developments in economic geology ; 14)
Translation of: Karsztbauxitok
ISBN 0-444-99727-x : £45.00 : CIP entry
B81-31622

553.6'2'0941292 — Scotland. Fife Region. Newport-on-Tay region. Sand & gravel deposits

Laxton, J. L.. The sand and gravel resources of the country around Newport-on-Tay, Fife Region : description of 1:25000 sheet no 42 and parts of no.32 and 52 / J.L. Laxton and D.L. Ross. ; contributor M.A.E. Browne. — Edinburgh : H.M.S.O., 1981. — iv,97p : ill,maps(some col.) ; 30cm. — (Mineral assessment report ; 89)
At head of title: Institute of Geological Sciences, Natural Environment Research Council. — Folded sheet (map) in pocket. — Bibliography: p97
ISBN 0-11-887413-6 (pbk) : £12.75 B81-40395

553.6'2'09422723 — Hampshire. Loddon Valley region. Sand & gravel deposits

Clarke, M. R.. The sand and gravel resources of the Loddon Valley area : description of 1:25000 sheets SU75, 76 and parts of SU64, 65, 66 and 74 / M.R. Clarke, E.J. Raynor and R.A. Sobey. — London : H.M.S.O., 1980. — iii,111p : ill,maps ; 30cm. — (Mineral assessment report ; 48)
Folded sheet (col. map) in pocket. — Bibliography: p111
ISBN 0-11-884109-2 (pbk) : £8.75 B81-08374

553.6'2'0942275 — Hampshire. Fordingbridge region. Sand & gravel deposits

Kubala, M.. The sand and gravel resources of the country around Fordingbridge, Hampshire : description of 1:25000 resource sheet SU11 and parts of SU00, SU01, SU10, SU20 and SU21 / M. Kubala. — London : H.M.S.O., 1980. — iv,98p : ill,maps ; 30cm. — (Mineral assessment report ; 50)
Folded sheet (col. map) in pocket. — Bibliography: p98
ISBN 0-11-884111-4 (pbk) : £7.75 B81-03091

553.6'2'09426715 — Essex. Pebmarsh region. Sand & gravel deposits

Marks, R. J.. The sand and gravel resources of the country north-east of Halstead, Essex : description of 1:25000 resource sheet TL 83 / R.J. Marks and J.W. Merritt. — London : H.M.S.O., 1981. — iii,118p : ill,maps(some col.) ; 30cm. — (Mineral assessment report ; 68)
At head of title: Institute of Geological Sciences, Natural Environment Research Council. — Folded Sheet (map) in pocket. — Bibliography: p118
ISBN 0-11-884168-8 (pbk) : £13.25 B81-40396

553.6'3 — Evaporites

Evaporite deposits : illustration and interpretation of some environmental sequences. — Paris : Technip ; London : Marketed and distributed by Graham & Trotman, 1980. — xvi,266p : ill,maps ; 27cm
At head of title: Chambre syndicale de la recherche et de la production du pétrole et du gaz naturel, Comité des techniciens, Commission exploration, Sous-Commission laboratoires de géologie. — Includes bibliographies and index
ISBN 2-7108-0385-2 (pbk) : £31.00 B81-34457

553.6'32 — Salt — *For children*

Gibbs, Richard. Salt / Richard Gibbs. — Hove : Wayland, 1980. — 72p : ill,maps ; 20x22cm. — (World resources)
Bibliography: p70. - Includes index
ISBN 0-85340-740-1 : £3.75 B81-05545

553.6'36 — Potash deposits

Rüping, G.. Potash deposits outside of North America : paper read before the Fertiliser Society of London on the 16th October 1980 / by G. Rüping. — London (93 Albert Embankment, SE1 7TU) : [The Society], [1980]. — 52p : ill ; 21cm. — (Proceedings / Fertiliser Society ; no.193)
Unpriced (pbk) B81-04586

553.6'4 — Phosphate deposits

World survey of phosphate deposits / editor M.C. Mew. — 4th ed. — London (25 Wilton Rd, SW1V 1NH) : British Sulphur Corporation, 1980. — ix,238p : ill(some col.),col.maps ; 31cm
Previous ed.: 1971. — Includes index
£185.00 B81-04696

553.7'07'1041 — Great Britain. Schools. Students, 5-14 years. Curriculum subjects: Water — *For teaching*

Gordon-Smith, Catherine. From rain to tap / Catherine Gordon-Smith. — Basingstoke (Houndmills, Basingstoke RG21 2XS) : Globe Education [for] West Sussex County Council, 1981. — 48p : ill,forms ; 30cm. — (Science horizons. Level 1)
Bibliography: p11. — List of films: p11
ISBN 0-333-31299-6 (pbk) : £3.95 B81-31305

553.7'0724 — Water. Experiments — *For schools*

Water. — London : Harrap, 1981. — 48p : ill ; 25cm. — (Access to science)
Cover title. — Text on inside cover
ISBN 0-245-53662-0 (pbk) : £1.50
ISBN 0-245-53703-1 (Teacher's notes and tests) : £1.25 B81-37433

553.8'09427 — Northern England. Gemstones — *Collectors' guides*

Rodgers, Peter R.. Gemstones of Northern England / by Peter R. Rodgers. — Clapham [N. Yorkshire] : Dalesman, 1981. — 72p : ill,maps ; 21cm
Bibliography: p70-71. — Includes index
ISBN 0-85206-628-7 (pbk) : £1.95 B81-22922

554/559 — GEOLOGY OF SPECIAL LOCALITIES

554 — Europe. Geological features

Ager, Derek V.. The geology of Europe / Derek V. Ager. — London : McGraw-Hill, c1980. — xix,535p : ill,maps ; 25cm
Includes bibliographies and index
ISBN 0-07-084115-2 : £16.00 : CIP rev.
B80-18272

554 — Western Europe. Geological features

Geology of the European countries. — [Paris] : Dunod in cooperation with the Comité nátional français de géologie ; [London] : distributed by Graham & Trotman
'Published ... on the occasion of the 26th International Geological Congress'
Austria, Federal Republic of Germany, Ireland, The Netherlands, Switzerland, United Kingdom. — 1980. — xxii,432p,[2]leaves of plates : ill,maps(some col.) ; 28cm
Includes bibliographies
ISBN 0-86010-261-0 : £30.00 B81-19627

Geology of the European countries. — [Paris] : Dunod in cooperation with the Comité national français de géologie ; [London] : distributed by Graham and Trotman
'Published ... on the occasion of the 26th International Geological Congress'
Denmark, Finland, Iceland, Norway, Sweden. — c1980. — xxii,455p : ill,maps ; 28cm
Includes bibliographies
ISBN 0-86010-262-9 : £30.00 B81-19628

554.1 — Great Britain. Geological features

Anderson, J. G. C.. The structure of the British Isles / by J.G.C. Anderson and T.R. Owen. — 2nd ed. — Oxford : Pergamon, 1980. — xiii,251p : ill,maps ; 25cm. — (Pergamon international library)
Previous ed.: 1968. — Bibliography: p225-243. - Includes index
ISBN 0-08-023998-6 (cased) : £12.50 : CIP rev.
ISBN 0-08-023997-8 (pbk) : £5.95 B80-17680

554.1 — Great Britain. Strata

Rayner, Dorothy H.. The stratigraphy of the British Isles / Dorothy H. Rayner. — 2nd ed. — Cambridge : Cambridge University Press, 1981. — xix,460p : ill,maps ; 24cm
Previous ed.: 1967. — Bibliography: p430-447. — Includes index
ISBN 0-521-23452-2 (cased) : £32.50 : CIP rev.
ISBN 0-521-29961-6 (pbk) : £12.50 B81-20534

554.11'072 — Scotland. Geological features. Research by Institute of Geological Sciences

Institute of Geological Sciences. The Institute of Geological Sciences in Scotland and Northern Ireland. — London : The Institute, c1981. — 24p : ill,maps ; 20x21cm
Cover title. — Text and map on inside covers
ISBN 0-85272-074-2 (pbk) : Unpriced
Also classified at 554.16'072 B81-40000

554.16'072 — Northern Ireland. Geological features. Research by Institute of Geological Sciences

Institute of Geological Sciences. The Institute of Geological Sciences in Scotland and Northern Ireland. — London : The Institute, c1981. — 24p : ill,maps ; 20x21cm
Cover title. — Text and map on inside covers
ISBN 0-85272-074-2 (pbk) : Unpriced
Primary classification 554.11'072 B81-40000

554.22'33 — Kent. Faversham region. Geological features

Holmes, S. C. A.. Geology of the country around Faversham : memoir for 1:50,000 geological sheet 273 / S.C.A. Holmes ; contributors G. Bisson ... [et al.]. — London : H.M.S.O., 1981. — xii,117p : ill,maps ; 29cm. — (Geological survey of Great Britain. England and Wales)
Includes bibliographies and index
ISBN 0-11-884141-6 : Unpriced B81-39870

554.22'5 — England. Weald. Geological features — *For field studies*

Gibbons, Wes. The Weald / Wes Gibbons. — London : Unwin Paperbacks, 1981. — 116p : ill,maps ; 20cm. — (Rocks and fossils ; 2)
Text on inside cover. — Bibliography: p110. - Includes index
ISBN 0-04-554004-7 (pbk) : £3.95 B81-19384

554.22'62 — West Sussex. Chichester region. Geological features

Bone, David, *1953-*. Geology around Chichester : a brief guide / by David Bone. — [Chichester] ([29 Little London, Chichester PO19 1PB]) : Chichester District Museum, c1980. — [8]p : ill,2maps ; 22cm
Bibliography: p8
£0.20 (unbound) B81-37219

554.24′9′05 — West Midlands *(Metropolitan County)*. Black Country. Geological features — *Serials*

The **Black** Country geologist / Black Country Geological Society. — No.1-. — Birmingham (c/o Hon. Secretary, 16 St. Nicholas Gardens, Kings Norton, Birmingham B38 8TW) : The Society, 1981-. — v. : ill ; 30cm
Annual
ISSN 0260-714x = Black Country geologist : Unpriced B81-38197

554.26 — Eastern England. Geological features

Kent, *Sir* **Peter,** *1913-*. Eastern England from the Tees to the Wash. — 2nd ed. / by Sir Peter Kent with contributions by G.D. Gaunt and C.J. Wood ; based on the 1st ed. by Vernon Wilson. — London : H.M.S.O., 1980. — vii,155p,[1]folded leaf of plates : ill(some col.),maps(some col.) ; 25cm. — (British regional geology)
At head of title: Institute of Geological Sciences. Natural Environment Research Council. — Previous ed.: published as East Yorkshire and Lincolnshire, 1948. — Bibliography: p137-146. — Includes index
ISBN 0-11-884121-1 (pbk) : £4.50 B81-37873

554.27′8 — Eastern Cumbria. Geological features — *For field studies*

Eastern Cumbria field meeting : 15-18 May 1981 / contributors C. Bendelow ... [et al.] ; compiled and edited by John Boardman. — [London] ([c/o J. Rose, Department of Geography, Birkbeck College, University of London, 7 Gesse St., W1P 1PA]) : Quaternary Research Association, 1981. — 128p : ill,maps ; 21cm
Cover title: Field guide to Eastern Cumbria. — Bibliography: p123-128
Unpriced (pbk) B81-26059

554.29′21 — Gwynedd. Ynys Môn. Geological features — *For field studies*

Bates, D. E. B.. Anglesey / by D.E.B. Bates and J.R. Davies. — London (Burlington House, Picadilly, London W1 0JU) : Geologists′ Association, 1981. — 31p : ill,maps ; 21cm. — (Geologists′ Association guide ; no.40)
Cover title. — Text on inside covers. — Bibliography: p31
Unpriced (pbk) B81-38528

554.29′23 — Gwynedd. Lleyn Peninsula. Geological features — *For field studies*

Cattermole, Peter. Lleyn Peninsula / by P.J. Cattermole and M. Romano. — London (Burlington House, Picadilly, London, W1 0JU) : Geologists′ Association, 1981. — 39p : ill,maps ; 21cm. — (Geologists′ Association guide ; no.39)
Cover title. — Text on inside covers. — Bibliography: p38-39
Unpriced (pbk) B81-38527

554.29′67 — Dyfed. Llanelli *(District)*. Geological features

Bowen, D. Q.. The Llanelli landscape : the geology and geomorphology of the country around Llanelli / D.Q. Bowen. — Llanelli (Public Library, [Vaughan St.], Llanelli, [Dyfed]) : Llanelli Borough Council, c1980. — xvii,280p : ill,maps ; 24cm. — (Llanelli Public Library Local History Resaarch Group series ; no.2)
Bibliography: p262-267. - Includes index
ISBN 0-906821-01-0 : Unpriced B81-05985

555.98 — Eastern Indonesia. Geological features — *Conference proceedings*

CCOP-IOC SEATAR Working Group Meeting *(1979 : Bandung)*. The geology and tectonics of eastern Indonesia. — Oxford : Pergamon, Sept.1981. — [356]p. — (Special publication / Geological Research and Development Centre ; no.2)
ISBN 0-08-028732-8 : £22.00 : CIP entry B81-25112

556.1′2 — Libya. Geological features — *Conference proceedings*

Symposium on the Geology of Libya *(2nd : 1978 : Tripoli)*. The geology of Libya : Second Symposium on the Geology of Libya, held at Tripoli, September 16-21 1978 / editors M.J. Salem and M.T. Busrewil. — London : Academic Press, 1980. — 3v.(xiv,1155p,[17] folded leaves of plates) : ill,maps ; 28cm
English text, English and Arabic abstracts. — Includes bibliographies and index
ISBN 0-12-615501-1 : Unpriced
ISBN 0-12-615502-x (v.2) : £20.00
ISBN 0-12-615503-8 (v.3) : £20.00 B81-35427

556.6′4 — Northern Sierra Leone. Geological features

The **geology** and mineral resources of northern Sierra Leone / A. Macfarlane ... [et al.] ; revised by H. Colley with contributions from R.D. Beckinsale, R.J. Pankhurst and N.J. Snelling. — London : H.M.S.O., 1981. — 103p : ill,maps(some col.) ; 29cm. — (Overseas memoir ; 7)
At head of title: Institute of Geological Sciences, Natural Environment Research Council. — Six maps on folded leaves in pocket. — Includes bibliographies and index
ISBN 0-11-884136-x : £18.00 B81-39869

557.91′3 — Northern Arizona. Geological features — *Field guides*

Perkins, John W.. Utah and Northern Arizona : a field guidebook / by John W. Perkins. — Cardiff (38, Park Place, Cardiff CF1 3BB) : Dept. of Extra-Mural Studies, University College, Cardiff, c1981. — 129p : ill,maps ; 21cm
Bibliography: p127-129
Unpriced (pbk)
Primary classification 557.92 B81-23076

557.91′32 — Arizona. Grand Canyon. Geological features

Redfern, Ron. Corridors of time : a spectacular view of 1,700,000,000 years of earth′s history as exposed in the Grand Canyon / unique panoramic photography and narrative by Ron Redfern ; illustrations by Gary Hincks ; introduction by Carl Sagan. — London : Orbis, c1980. — 198p : ill,maps ; 32cm
Ill on lining papers. — Bibliography: p194-195. - Includes index
ISBN 0-85613-316-7 : £25.00 B81-14261

557.92 — Utah. Geological features — *Field guides*

Perkins, John W.. Utah and Northern Arizona : a field guidebook / by John W. Perkins. — Cardiff (38, Park Place, Cardiff CF1 3BB) : Dept. of Extra-Mural Studies, University College, Cardiff, c1981. — 129p : ill,maps ; 21cm
Bibliography: p127-129
Unpriced (pbk)
Also classified at 557.91′3 B81-23076

558.5′1 — Peru. Western Cordillera. Geological features

The **geology** of the Western Cordillera of northern Peru / E.J. Cobbing ... [et al.]. — London : H.M.S.O, 1981. — iii,143p : ill(some col.),maps(some col.) ; 29cm. — (Overseas memoir ; 5)
At head of title: Institute of Geological Sciences, Natural Environment Research Council. — Two maps on 2 folded leaves in pocket. — Bibliography: p130-134. — Includes index
ISBN 0-11-884118-1 : £26.00 B81-25582

559.31 — New Zealand. Geological features

Fleming, C. A.. The geological history of New Zealand and its life / C.A. Fleming. — [Auckland N.Z.] : Auckland University Press ; [Oxford] : Oxford University Press, c1979. — 141p : ill,maps ; 21cm
Bibliography: p115-127. — Includes index
ISBN 0-19-647975-4 (pbk) : Unpriced B81-39125

560 — PALAEONTOLOGY

560 — Fossil microorganisms

Microfossils from recent and fossil shelf seas. — Chichester : Ellis Horwood, June 1981. — [352]p. — (Ellis Horwood series in geology)
ISBN 0-85312-338-1 : £35.00 : CIP entry B81-13852

560 — Prehistoric animals

Moody, Richard, *1939-*. Prehistoric world / Richard Moody ; artists John Barber ... [et al.]. — London : Hamlyn, c1980. — 320p : ill(some col.),maps,ports ; 31cm
Bibliography: p314. — Includes index
ISBN 0-600-37255-3 : £12.95 B81-00108

560 — Prehistoric animals — *For children*

Amazing facts about prehistoric animals : astonishing facts / illustrated by Bobbie Craig. — [London] : Carousel, 1980. — [32]p : col.ill ; 28cm
ISBN 0-552-57046-x (pbk) : £0.95 B81-08971

Goodenough, Simon. Purnell′s book of dinosaurs and prehistoric animals / written by Simon Goodenough ; photography by Ardea London ... [et al.] ; illustrations by Wilcock, Riley Graphic Art Limited. — Maidenhead : Purnell, 1977 (1981 [printing]). — 45p : ill(some col.) ; 32cm
Ill on lining papers
ISBN 0-361-03960-3 : £2.50 B81-20659

Lambert, David, *1932-*. Dinosaur world / by David Lambert. — London ; Pan, 1981. — 91p : ill(some col.),maps(some col.),ports ; 16cm. — (A Piccolo factbook)
Text on inside cover. — Includes index
ISBN 0-330-26358-7 (pbk) : £1.25 B81-38772

560′.45 — Palaeo-ecology

Dodd, J. Robert. Paleoecology : concepts and applications / J. Robert Dodd, Robert J. Stanton, Jr. — New York ; Chichester : Wiley, c1981. — xiv,559p : ill,maps ; 24cm
Bibliography: p513-546. — Includes index
ISBN 0-471-04171-8 : £25.00 B81-23714

560.9423′31 — Dorset. Lyme Bay. Fossils — *Collectors′ guides*

Clarke, Nigel J.. Lyme Bay fossils : beach guide / by Nigel J. Clarke. — Charmouth (The Holt, The Street, Charmouth, Dorset) : N.J. Clarke, [1981?]. — 28p : ill ; 19cm
Cover title
ISBN 0-907683-01-0 (pbk) : Unpriced B81-33107

561 — FOSSIL PLANTS

561 — Fossil plants

Taylor, Thomas N. (Thomas Norwood). Paleobotany : an introduction to fossil plant biology / Thomas N. Taylor. — New York ; London : McGraw-Hill, c1981. — xiii,589p : ill,ports ; 25cm
Bibliography: p500-555. — Includes index
ISBN 0-07-062954-4 : £20.95 B81-31961

561′.09 — Palaeobotany, *to ca 1950*

Andrews, Henry N.. The fossil hunters : in search of ancient plants / Henry N. Andrews. — Ithaca ; London : Cornell University Press, 1980. — 241p : ill,ports ; 25cm
Bibliography: p399-416. - Includes index
ISBN 0-8014-1248-x : £17.00 B81-00882

561′.2 — Fossil flowering plants. Evolution

Hughes, Norman F.. Palaeobiology of angiosperm origins. — Cambridge : Cambridge University Press, Nov.1981. — [242]p. — (Cambridge earth science series)
Originally published: 1976
ISBN 0-521-28726-x (pbk) : £9.95 : CIP entry B81-38811

562 — FOSSIL INVERTEBRATES

563′.12 — Palaeogene strata. Fossil Foraminiferdia

Stratigraphical atlas of fossil foraminifera. — Chichester : Ellis Horwood, May 1981. — [256]p. — (Ellis Horwood series in geology)
ISBN 0-85312-210-5 : £25.00 : CIP entry B81-13851

564′.53 — Ammonoids
The **Ammonoidea** : the evolution, classification, mode of life and geological usefulness of a major fossil group : proceedings of an International Symposium held at the University of York / edited by M.R. House, J.R. Senior. — London : Published for the Systematics Association by Academic Press. — xiv,593p : ill,maps ; 24cm. — (The Systematics Association special volume ; no.18)
Includes bibliographies and index
ISBN 0-12-356780-7 : £36.00 B81-21783

565′.2′07402134 — London. Kensington and Chelsea *(London Borough).* Museums: British Museum (Natural History). Stock: Fossil Arthropoda. Type-specimens — *Catalogues*
British Museum (Natural History). Catalogue of the type and figured specimens of fossil crustacea (excl. Ostracoda), Chelicerata, Myriapoda and Pycnogonida in the British Museum (Natural History) / compiled by S.F. Morris. — [London] : The Museum, c1980. — 53p,[6]p of plates : ill ; 30cm. — (Publication / British Museum (Natural History) ; no.828)
Bibliography: p49-53
ISBN 0-565-00828-5 (pbk) : £5.00 B81-04953

565′.33 — Fossil Ostracoda
Neale, John W.. The Ostracoda : religion, sex and mystery! / by J.W. Neale. — [Hull] : University of Hull, 1981. — 12p ; 21cm. — (Inaugural lectures / University of Hull)
ISBN 0-85958-432-1 (pbk) : £0.75 B81-35752

565′.7′0942827 — South Yorkshire *(Metropolitan County).* Thorne Moors. Fossil insects
Buckland, P. C.. Thorne Moors : a palaeoecological study of a bronze age site : a contribution to the history of the British insect fauna / P.C. Buckland. — [Birmingham] : [Department of Geography, University of Birmingham], [1979]. — 173p : ill,maps ; 30cm. — (Occasional publication / Department of Geography, University of Birmingham ; no.8)
Bibliography: p157-173
ISBN 0-7044-0359-5 (pbk) : £2.00 B81-39704

566 — FOSSIL VERTEBRATES

566 — Fossil vertebrates. Anatomy *related to* evolution of vertebrates
Jarvik, Erik. Basic structure and evolution of vertebrates / Erik Jarvik. — London : Academic Press
Vol.2. — 1980. — xiii,337p : ill ; 26cm
Bibliography: p269-326. - Includes index
ISBN 0-12-380802-2 : £27.00 : CIP rev.
Also classified at 596′.038 B80-27009

567.9′1 — Dinosaurs
Halstead, L. B.. Dinosaurs / L.B. Halstead, Jenny Halstead. — Poole : Blandford, 1981. — 170p : ill(some col.) ; 20cm
Includes index
ISBN 0-7137-1017-9 (cased) : £4.95 : CIP rev.
ISBN 0-7137-1154-x (pbk) : £2.95 B81-25676

567.9′1 — Dinosaurs — *For children*
Lambert, David, *1932-*. Dinosaur world. — London : Ward Lock, Apr.1981. — [96]p. — (Kingfisher factbook)
ISBN 0-7063-6107-5 : £2.50 : CIP entry
B81-03166

Lambert, David, *1932-*. Dinosaur world / by David Lambert ; editor Jacqui Bailey. — London : Kingfisher, 1981. — 91p : ill(some col.),maps(some col.),ports ; 19cm. — (A Kingfisher factbook)
Includes index
ISBN 0-86272-009-5 : £2.50 : CIP rev.
B81-14402

Lambert, David, *1932-*. Dinosaurs / by David Lambert ; illustrated by Ross Wardle. — London : Granada, 1981. — 64p : col.ill ; 19cm. — (Granada guides)
Includes index
ISBN 0-246-11566-1 : £1.95 B81-39304

Taylor, Ron, *1927-*. The wonder book of dinosaurs / [Ron Taylor]. — London : Ward Lock, 1981. — 37p : ill(some col.),ports ; 27cm
Includes index
ISBN 0-7063-6132-6 : £2.50 B81-39962

567.9′1 — Dinosaurs — *For children* — *Welsh texts*
Lambert, David, *1932-*. [Exploring the age of dinosaurs. Welsh]. Oes y deinosoriaid / David Lambert ; ymgynghorwr Berian Williams ; cynlluniwyd gan David Nash ; arlunwyr John Francis, Bernard Robinson, Ross Wardle. — Caerdydd : Gwasg y Dref Wen, c1980. — [24]p : col.ill ; 23cm. — (Darganfod)
Translation of: Exploring the age of dinosaurs
£1.95 B81-09034

567.9′1 — Fossil dinosaurs — *For children*
Aliki. Digging up dinosaurs : and putting them together again / by Aliki. — London : Bodley Head, 1981. — 40p : ill(some col.) ; 21x23cm
Originally published: New York : Crowell, 1981. — Includes index
ISBN 0-370-30441-1 : £3.95 : CIP rev.
B81-27432

567.9′1′0222 — Dinosaurs — *Illustrations*
Ovenden, Denys. Dinosaurs : a colour guide to the dinosaurs of the prehistoric world, all principal types illustrated / [painted by Denys Ovenden ; text by Barry Cox]. — [London] : Fontana, 1979. — 1folded sheet([12]p) : col.ill ; 25cm. — (Domino ; 18)
ISBN 0-00-685458-3 : £0.85 B81-20260

569′.09499 — Greece. Samos. Turolian strata. Fossil mammals
Solounias, Nikos. The turolian fauna from the island of Samos, Greece : with special emphasis on the hyaenids and the bovids / Nikos Solounias. — Basel ; London : Karger, 1981. — xvi,232p : ill,maps ; 23cm. — (Contributions to vertebrate evolution ; v.6)
Bibliography: p220-232
ISBN 3-8055-2692-x (pbk) : £13.00 B81-38095

569′.9 — China. Fossil man. Bones — *Illustrations*
Zhong guo gu ren lei hua ji = Atlas of primitive man in China / compiling group of the atlas [organized by] Institute of Vertebrate Paleontology and Paleoanthropology, Chinese Academy of Sciences. — Beiging : Science Press ; New York ; London : distributed by Van Nostrand Reinhold, 1980. — 174p : chiefly ill(some col.),col.maps ; 30cm
Chinese title transliterated. — Maps on lining papers
ISBN 0-442-20013-7 : £24.95
Primary classification 931′.01 B81-37693

569′.9 — Fossil man
Reader, John. Missing links : the hunt for earliest man / John Reader. — London : Collins, 1981. — 272p : ill(some col.),1map,facims(some col.),ports(some col.) ; 25cm
Includes index
ISBN 0-00-216091-9 : £9.95 B81-11424

569′.9 — Man. Evolution. Sources of evidence: Fossils
Poirier, Frank E.. Fossil evidence : the human evolutionary journey / Frank E. Poirier. — 3rd ed. — St. Louis ; London : Mosby, 1981. — xv,428p : ill,maps,plans ; 24cm
Previous ed.: 1977. — Includes bibliographies and index
ISBN 0-8016-3952-2 (pbk) : £9.75 B81-25046

569′.9′09632 — Ethiopia. Hadar. Fossil hominids
Johanson, Donald C.. Lucy : the beginnings of humankind / Donald C. Johanson and Maitland A. Edey. — London : Granada, 1981. — 409p,[8]p of plates : ill(some col.),col.maps,ports(some col.) ; 24cm
Maps on lining papers. — Bibliography: p385-389. - Includes index
ISBN 0-246-11362-6 : £9.95 B81-21680

569′.9′0967627 — Kenya. Lake Turkana region. Fossil hominids
Leakey, Richard E.. People of the Lake : man, his origins, nature and future / Richard Leakey and Roger Lewin. — Harmondsworth : Penguin, 1981, c1978. — 234p,8p of plates : ill,maps,ports ; 20cm. — (Pelican books)
Originally published: Garden City, N.Y. : Anchor Press, 1978; London : Collins, 1979. — Includes index
ISBN 0-14-022333-9 (pbk) : £1.95
Primary classification 573.2 B81-05547

570 — LIFE SCIENCES

571.57′81 — Rainfall. Measurement. Use of meteorological satellites
Barrett, E. C.. The use of satellite data in rainfall monitoring. — London : Academic Press, Oct.1981. — [320]p
ISBN 0-12-079680-5 : CIP entry B81-26773

573 — PHYSICAL ANTHROPOLOGY

573 — Environment. Adaptation of man
Frisancho, A. Roberto. Human adaptation : a functional interpretation / A. Roberto Frisancho. — St. Louis ; London : Mosby, 1979. — xi,209p : ill,maps ; 25cm
Includes index
ISBN 0-8016-1693-x : Unpriced B81-08659

573′.028 — Biology. Use of radioactive isotopes
Ayrey, E.. The use of radioactive isotopes in life sciences. — London : Allen & Unwin, Sept.1981. — [176]p
ISBN 0-04-570011-7 (cased) : £4.95 : CIP entry
ISBN 0-04-570012-5 (pbk) : £4.95 B81-20554

573.2 — Man. Evolution
Aspects of human evolution. — London : Taylor and Francis, Apr.1981. — [230]p. — (Symposia / The Society for the Study of Human Biology, ISSN 0081-153x ; 21)
ISBN 0-85066-209-5 : £12.00 : CIP entry
B81-04279

Bokum, Branko. Man : the fallen ape / Branko Bokum. — [London] : Abacus, 1979, c1977. — ix,229p,[8]p of plates : ill ; 18cm
Originally published: New York : Doubleday, 1977. — Bibliography: p218-229
ISBN 0-349-10339-9 (pbk) : £1.75 B81-10811

Leakey, Richard E.. The making of mankind / Richard E. Leakey. — London : Joseph, 1981. — 256p : ill(some col.),col.maps,ports(some col.) ; 26cm
Includes index
ISBN 0-7181-1931-2 : £9.95 B81-18700

Leakey, Richard E.. People of the Lake : man, his origins, nature and future / Richard Leakey and Roger Lewin. — Harmondsworth : Penguin, 1981, c1978. — 234p,8p of plates : ill,maps,ports ; 20cm. — (Pelican books)
Originally published: Garden City, N.Y. : Anchor Press, 1978; London : Collins, 1979. — Includes index
ISBN 0-14-022333-9 (pbk) : £1.95
Also classified at 569′.9′0967627 B81-05547

Tanner, Nancy Makepeace. On becoming human / Nancy Makepeace Tanner. — Cambridge : Cambridge University Press, 1981. — xviii,373p : ill,maps ; 24cm
Bibliography: p278-360. — Includes index
ISBN 0-521-23554-5 (cased) : £20.00
ISBN 0-521-28028-1 (pbk) : £6.95 B81-38913

Wilson, Peter J.. Man, the promising primate : the conditions of human evolution / Peter J. Wilson. — New Haven ; London : Yale University Press, c1980. — xiii,185p ; 22cm
Bibliography: p171-177. - Includes index
ISBN 0-300-02514-9 : £8.20 : CIP rev.
B80-31547

573.2 — Man. Evolution — *Conference proceedings*
The **Emergence** of man : a joint symposium of the Royal Society and the British Academy held on 12 and 13 March 1980 / organized by J.Z. Young, E.M. Jope and K.P. Oakley. — London : The Royal Society : The British Academy, 1981. — 216p : ill ; 31cm
Includes bibliographies
ISBN 0-85403-158-8 : £21.00 B81-29757

573.2 — Man. Evolution — *For children*
Man′s place in evolution. — London : British Museum (Natural History), 1980. — 108p : ill (some col.),maps ; 23cm
Published to accompany the exhibition Man′s place in evolution at the Natural History Museum. — Bibliography: p103. — Includes index
ISBN 0-521-23177-9 (cased) : £12.00 : CIP rev.
ISBN 0-521-29849-0 (pbk) : £3.95 B80-33557

573.2 — Man. Evolution. Natural selection. Aesthetic factors

Goulstone, J.. Human evolution through aesthetic selection / by J. Goulstone. — Bexleyheath (10 Haslemere Rd., Bexleyheath, Kent DA7 4WG) : J. Goulstone, c1981. — [14]p,[8]leaves of plates : ill ; 26cm
Unpried (pbk) B81-25417

573.2 — Man. Evolution. Role of feeding behaviour

Omnivorous primates : gathering and hunting in human evolution / edited by Robert S.O. Harding and Geza Teleki. — New York ; Guildford : Columbia University Press, 1981. — vi,673p : ill,maps ; 24cm
Bibliography: p595-667. — Includes index
ISBN 0-231-04024-5 : £24.75 B81-24010

573.2'01 — Man. Evolution. Theories

Collyns, Robin. Prehistoric germ warfare / by Robin Collyns. — London : Star, 1980. — 146p ; 18cm
ISBN 0-352-30700-5 (pbk) : £1.25 B81-01825

573.2'1 — Man. Genetics

Winchester, A. M.. Human genetics / A.M. Winchester. — 3rd ed. — Columbus ; London : Merrill, c1979. — vi,226p : ill,1map ; 23cm
Previous ed.: 1975. — Includes index
ISBN 0-675-08314-1 (pbk) : £4.95 B81-03331

573.2'1'05 — Man. Genetics — *Serials*

Advances in human genetics. — 11. — New York ; London ([88 Middlesex St., E1 7EX]) : Plenum Press, c1981. — xix,385p
ISBN 0-306-40688-8 : Unpriced
ISSN 0065-275x B81-35105

573.2'15 — Man. Population genetics

Cannings, C.. Genealogical and genetic structure. — Cambridge : Cambridge University Press, Nov.1981. — [151]p. — (Cambridge studies in mathematical biology ; 3)
ISBN 0-521-23946-x (cased) : £17.50 : CIP entry
ISBN 0-521-28363-9 (pbk) : £6.95 B81-32527

573.3 — Piltdown man

Weiner, J. S.. The piltdown forgery / J.S. Weiner. — New York : Dover ; London : Constable, 1981, c1980. — xii,214p,[8]p of plates : ill,ports ; 21cm
Originally published: Oxford : Oxford University Press, 1955. — Includes index
ISBN 0-486-24075-4 (pbk) : £2.75 B81-39076

573'.691 — Man. Maxillofacial region. Anthropometric features

Farkas, Leslie G.. Anthropometry of the head and face in medicine / Leslie G. Farkas. — New York ; Oxford : Elsevier, c1981. — xxii : ill ; 26cm
Bibliography: p103-106. — Includes index
ISBN 0-444-00557-9 : £31.16 B81-36749

574 — BIOLOGY

574 — Biology

Baker, Jeffrey J. W.. A course in biology / Jeffrey J.W. Baker, Garland E. Allen. — 3rd ed. — Reading, Mass. ; London : Addison-Wesley, c1979. — xi,592,I1-18p,iip of plates : ill(some col.),ports ; 24cm. — (Addison-Wesley series in the life sciences)
Previous ed.: 1972. — Includes bibliographies and index
ISBN 0-201-00308-2 : £12.60 B81-40415

Biological science : an introductory study / William A. Andrews ... [et al.]. — Scarborough, Ont. ; London : Prentice-Hall, c1980. — ix,784p : ill(some col.) ; 26cm. — (Prentice-Hall intermediate science series)
Includes index
ISBN 0-13-076562-7 : £14.25 B81-15579

Biology in profile : a guide to the many branches of biology / edited by P.N. Campbell ; sponsored by the Committee on the Teaching of Science of the International Council of Scientific Unions. — Oxford : Pergamon, 1981. — xi,128p : ill ; 26cm
Includes bibliographies
ISBN 0-08-026846-3 (cased) : Unpriced
ISBN 0-08-026845-5 (pbk) : £3.95 B81-27808

Keeton, William T.. Biological science / William T. Keeton ; illustrated by Paula di Santo Bensadoun. — 3rd ed. — New York ; London : Norton, c1980. — xv,1080,A51p : ill(some col.),col.maps ; 26cm
Previous ed.: 1972. — Includes bibliographies and index
ISBN 0-393-95021-2 : £10.65 B81-03485

574 — Biology — *For schools*

Foster, R. M.. Biology / R.M. Foster. — London : Longman, 1970 (1980 [printing]). — iv,96p : ill ; 20cm. — (Longman certificate notes)
ISBN 0-582-69575-9 (pbk) : £0.95 B81-00883

Mackean, D. G.. Life study : a textbook of biology / D.G. Mackean. — London : John Murray, c1981. — 266p : ill(some col.) ; 29cm
Includes index
ISBN 0-7195-3861-0 (cased) : Unpriced : CIP rev.
ISBN 0-7195-3783-5 (pbk) : Unpriced B81-10454

Riley, Peter D.. Life science : groundwork in biology / Peter D. Riley. — Amersham : Hulton Educational, 1981. — 160p : ill,forms ; 26cm
Includes index
ISBN 0-7175-0865-x (pbk) : £2.95 B81-31141

Soper, R.. Modern biology : for first examinations / R. Soper, S. Tyrell Smith. — Basingstoke : Macmillan Education, 1979. — 360p : ill,maps,plans,forms ; 25cm
Includes index
ISBN 0-333-26304-9 (pbk) : £2.65 : CIP rev. B79-15971

Torrance, James. Ordinary biology. — London : Edward Arnold, Sept.1981. — [128]p
ISBN 0-7131-0576-3 (pbk) : £2.50 : CIP entry B81-22486

574 — Biology. Projects — *For schools*

Ewington, E. J.. Projects in biology / E.J. Ewington and J. Spencer ; illustrated by David and Maureen Embry. — London : Routledge & Kegan Paul, 1981. — xii,107p : ill ; 25cm. — (Secondary science series)
ISBN 0-7100-0769-8 (pbk) : £4.95 : CIP rev. B81-07628

574 — Natural history. Activities — *For children*

Willson, Robina Beckles. Eyes wide open : natural history activities for the very young / [compiled by] Robina Beckles Willson ; illustrated by Kate Penayre. — London : Heimemann, 1981. — 95p : ill ; 23cm
Bibliography: p91. — Includes index
ISBN 0-434-97259-2 : £3.95 B81-35370

574 — Natural history — *Amateurs manuals*

Brown, Vinson. The amateur naturalist's handbook / Vinson Brown. — Englewood Cliffs ; London : Prentice-Hall, c1980. — xii,420p : ill,maps,1plan,2ports ; 21cm. — (A Spectrum book)
Bibliography: p399-410. — Includes index
ISBN 0-13-023739-6 (cased) : Unpriced
ISBN 0-13-023721-3 (pbk) : £4.50 B81-16674

574 — Organisms

Attenborough, David. Life on earth : a natural history / David Attenborough. — London : Fontana, 1981, c1979. — 319p : col.ill ; 20cm
Originally published: London : Collins, 1979. — Includes index
ISBN 0-00-636184-6 (pbk) : £3.95 B81-17740

Camp, Pamela S.. Exploring biology / Pamela S. Camp, Karen Arms. — Philadelphia ; London : Saunders College, c1981. — xii,484p : ill (some col.),maps(some col.),ports ; 27cm
Text, ill on lining papers. — Includes bibliographies and index
ISBN 0-03-047701-8 : £12.50 B81-23053

Hendrickson, Herbert T.. Essential biology / Herbert T. Hendrickson. — New York ; London : Harper & Row, c1981. — xiii,329p : ill(some col.),2col.maps ; 24cm
Includes index
ISBN 0-06-042792-2 : Unpriced B81-26199

574 — Organisms — *For children*

Althea. Day by day / written and illustrated by Althea Braithwaite. — Cambridge : Published for the National Trust by Dinosaur, c1977 (1981 [printing]). — [63]p : col.ill ; 15cm
ISBN 0-85122-296-x (cased) : £1.95
ISBN 0-85122-135-1 (pbk) : Unpriced B81-26255

Ardley, Neil. Our world of nature : a first picture encyclopedia / Neil Ardley ; illustrated by Chris Shields. — Maidenhead : Purcell, 1981. — 61p : col.ill ; 33cm
Includes index
ISBN 0-361-04360-0 : £3.99 B81-26343

Bellini, Francesca. Let's look at life on earth / [text by Francesca Bellini and Gilberto Corretti] ; [illustrations by Gilberto Corretti] ; [translated by Jo Zweng]. — Hove : Wayland, 1979. — 98p : ill(some col.),maps(some col.) ; 31cm. — (Let's look at series)
Includes index
ISBN 0-85340-660-x : £3.75 B81-09940

[St Michael encyclopedia of natural history]. Children's nature encyclopaedia / consultant editor Joyce Pope ; foreword by Gerald Durrell. — [London] : Octopus, [1980]. — 253p : col.ill ; 29cm
Originally published: London : Sundial, 1978. — Includes index
ISBN 0-7064-0676-1 : £4.99 B81-05991

Ward Lock's nature book. — London : Ward Lock, Apr.1981. — [224]p
ISBN 0-7063-6136-9 : £5.95 : CIP entry B81-02575

574 — Organisms — *For schools*

Basic biology. — Huddersfield : Schofield & Sims
1: The body / by A. Lawson and A. Nicholson ; illustrated by Edward Taylor. — 1980. — 88p : ill(some col.) ; 26cm
ISBN 0-7217-3565-7 (pbk) : £1.65 B81-39030

Jenking, C. Mary. The diversity of life / C. Mary Jenking, Ann Boyce. — Basingstoke : Macmillan Education, 1979. — viii,200p : ill ; 24cm. — (Foundations of biology)
Bibliography: p196-197. — Includes index
ISBN 0-333-24193-2 (pbk) : £3.95 : CIP rev. B79-23861

McCahill, T.. S.C.E. 'O' grade biology : a concise approach / T. McCahill. — Glasgow : Collins, 1981. — 192p ; 22cm
Text on inside covers. — Includes index
ISBN 0-00-327748-8 (pbk) : £1.75 B81-20853

Reid, Donald. Biology for the individual. — London : Heinemann Educational
Teachers' guide to Books 1-7. — Jan.1982. — [128]p
ISBN 0-435-59765-5 : £6.50 : CIP entry B81-34395

Roberts, M. B. V.. Biology for life / M.B.V. Roberts. — Walton-on-Thames : Nelson, 1981. — vii,407p : ill,ports ; 28cm
Includes index
ISBN 0-17-448081-4 (pbk) : £3.95 B81-29785

Robson, M. D.. Biology today : a course for first examination / M.D. Robson, A.G. Morgan. — Basingstoke : Macmillan Education, 1980. — 175p : ill ; 30cm
ISBN 0-333-22359-4 (pbk) : £2.75 : CIP rev. B79-20083

Smallman, Clare. Biology for you / Clare Smallman. — London : Hutchinson
Bk 1. — c1981. — 143p : ill,maps ; 24cm
Includes index
ISBN 0-09-140891-1 (pbk) : Unpriced : CIP rev. B80-06917

Smallman, Clare. Biology for you. — London : Hutchinson, Apr.1981
2. — [176]p
ISBN 0-09-141131-9 (pbk) : £2.25 : CIP entry B81-00884

574 — Organisms — *For students in tropical regions*

Stone, R. H. (Robert Henry). New biology for tropical schools / by R.H. Stone and A.B. Cozens with the advice of F. Commissiong and J. Omange. — 3rd ed. — Harlow : Longman, 1981. — viii,343p : ill ; 25cm
Previous ed.: published as New biology for West African schools. 1975. — Includes index
ISBN 0-582-60643-8 (pbk) : £3.80 B81-40702

574 — Organisms — *For students in tropical regions — For schools*

Ewusie, J. Yanney. Tropical biology for 'O' Level and School Certificate / by J. Yanney Ewusie. — 4th ed., rev. and enl. — London : African Universities Press in association with Harrap, 1980. — 338p : ill ; 25cm
Previous ed.: London : Harrap, 1974. — Includes index
ISBN 0-245-53551-9 (pbk) : £3.00 B81-00109

574 — Organisms — *For West African students*

Iloeje, S. O.. Certificate practical biology / S.O. Iloeje. — 2nd ed. — Harlow : Longman, 1981. — iv,108p : ill ; 25cm
Previous ed.: 1973
ISBN 0-582-65068-2 (pbk) : £1.70 B81-40311

574 — Organisms — *For West African students — For schools*

Mackean, D. G.. Introduction to biology. — West African ed., 2nd ed. — London : J. Murray, Oct.1981. — [256]p
Previous ed.: 1977
ISBN 0-7195-3887-4 (pbk) : £2.75 : CIP entry B81-28007

574 — Organisms — *New Church viewpoints*

Swedenborg, Emanuel. Life in animals and plants : a translation of extracts from chapter nineteen of The apocalypse explained by Emanuel Swedenborg. — London : Swedenborg Society, 1981. — 35p ; 19cm
Translation of: Apocalypsis explicata
Unpriced (pbk) B81-29708

574'.01 — Biology - *Philosophical perspectives*

Against biological determinism. — London : Allison & Busby, Sept.1981. — [192]p
ISBN 0-85031-423-2 (cased) : £9.95 : CIP entry
ISBN 0-85031-424-0 (pbk) : £4.95 B81-20129

574'.01 — Biology — *Philosophical perspectives*

Towards a liberatory biology. — London : Allison and Busby, Sept.1981. — [192]p
ISBN 0-85031-425-9 (pbk) : £9.95 : CIP entry
ISBN 0-85031-426-7 (pbk) : £4.95 B81-25111

574'.01028 — Biology. Statistics

Powell, F. C.. Statistical tables for the social, biological and physical sciences. — Cambridge : Cambridge University Press, Feb.1982. — [96]p
ISBN 0-521-24141-3 (cased) : £7.50 : CIP entry
ISBN 0-521-28473-2 (pbk) : £2.95
Primary classification 310 B81-40268

574'.012 — Chemotaxonomy — *Conference proceedings*

Chemosystematics : principles and practice / [proceedings of an International Symposium held at the University of Southampton] ; edited by F.A. Bisby, J.G. Vaughan, C.A. Wright. — London : Published for the Systematics Association by Academic Press, 1980. — xii,449p : ill ; 24cm. — (The Systematics Association special volume, ISSN 0309-2593 ; no.16)
Includes bibliographies and index
ISBN 0-12-101550-5 : Unpriced B81-12144

574'.012 — Organisms. Classification — *Questions & answers — For schools*

Classification. — St. Albans : Hart-Davis Educational, 1981, c1980. — 38p : ill,forms ; 21cm. — (Centre science)
ISBN 0-247-13126-1 (unbound) : £0.50 B81-24516

574'.01'51 — Biology. Mathematics — *For schools*

Mathematics in biology / D.C. Carter ... [et al.]. — Walton-on-Thames : Nelson, 1981. — ix,205p : ill ; 22cm. — (Selected topics in biology)
Includes index. — Publisher's no.: NCN 3208-21-0
ISBN 0-17-448091-1 (pbk) : £2.50 B81-29121

574'.01'5195 — Biology. Applications of statistical mathematics — *Case studies*

Biostatistics casebook / edited by Rupert G. Miller, Jr ... [et al.]. — New York ; Chichester : Wiley, c1980. — xii,238p : ill ; 23cm. — (Wiley series in probability and mathematical statistics)
Includes bibliographies
ISBN 0-471-06258-8 (pbk) : £7.95 B81-04022

574'.028 — Biology. Centrifugation

Sheeler, Phillip. Centrifugation in biology and medical science / Phillip Sheeler. — New York ; Chichester : Wiley, c1981. — xiv,269p : ill ; 24cm
Includes bibliographies and index
ISBN 0-471-05234-5 : £21.70 B81-23342

574'.028 — Biology. Nuclear magnetic resonance spectroscopy

Gadian, David G.. Nuclear magnetic resonance and its applications to living systems. — Oxford : Clarendon, Nov.1981. — [250]p
ISBN 0-19-854627-0 : £15.00 : CIP entry B81-30527

574'.028 — Biology. Use of lasers — *Conference proceedings*

NATO Symposium on Lasers in Biology and Medicine *(1979 : Lucca).* Lasers in biology and medicine / [proceedings of the NATO Symposium on Lasers in Biology and Medicine, Camaiore, Lucca, Italy, August 19-31, 1979] ; edited by F. Hillenkamp, R. Pratesi and C.A. Sacchi. — New York ; London : Plenum, published in cooperation with NATO Scientific Affairs Division, c1980. — xi,463p : ill ; 26cm. — (NATO advanced study institutes series. Series A, Life sciences ; v.34)
Includes index
ISBN 0-306-40470-2 : Unpriced
Also classified at 610'.28 B81-14642

574'.028 — Natural history. Use of magnifying glasses

Headstrom, Richard. [Nature in miniature]. Nature discoveries with a hand lens / Richard Headstrom. — New York : Dover ; London : Constable, 1981, c1968. — xviii,412,xiiip : ill ; 21cm
Originally published: New York : Knopf, 1968. — Bibliography: p403-412. — Includes index
ISBN 0-486-24077-0 (pbk) : £4.15 B81-39077

574'.03 — Biology — *Polyglot dictionaries*

Haensch, Günther. Dictionary of biology : English-German-French-Spanish / by Günther Haensch and Gisela Haberkamp de Antón. — 2nd rev. and enl. ed. — Amsterdam ; Oxford : Elsevier Scientific, 1981. — xii,680p ; 23cm
Previous ed.: 1976
ISBN 0-444-41968-3 : £45.45 B81-23608

574'.03'21 — Biology. Concepts — *Encyclopaedias*

Roe, Keith E.. Dictionary of theoretical concepts in biology / Keith E. Roe & Richard G. Frederick. — Metuchen ; London : Scarecrow, 1981. — xli,267p ; 23cm
ISBN 0-8108-1353-x : £12.25 B81-13912

574'.03'21 — Natural environment — *Encyclopaedias*

Octopus big book of nature / foreword by Maurice Burton. — London : Octopus, 1981. — 320p : col.ill,maps ; 31cm
Translation from the Czech. — Includes index
ISBN 0-7064-1275-3 : £6.95 B81-18197

574'.05 — Natural environment — *Serials*

The North western naturalist. — 1980. — [Cheadle Hulme, Cheshire] : [North Western Naturalists' Union], [1980]. — 17p
ISSN 0307-7888 : Unpriced B81-09036

574'.06'041 — Great Britain. Biology. Standardisation. Organisations: National Biological Standards Board — *Accounts — Serials*

National Biological Standards Board. Account / National Biological Standards Board. — 1979-80. — London : H.M.S.O., 1981. — 2p
ISBN 0-10-219181-6 : £0.70 B81-26595

574'.06'042823 — South Yorkshire *(Metropolitan County).* **Rotherham** *(District).* **Organisms. Organisations: Rotherham Naturalists' Society,** *to 1980*

Rotherham Naturalists Society 1880-1980. — [Worksop] ([c/o D.Bailey, 57 New Rd., Firbeck, Worksop, Notts. S81 8JY]) : [The Society], [1981]. — [20]p : col.ill,1map ; 21cm
Cover title. — Text, map on inside covers
£0.50 (pbk) B81-21427

574'.07 — Community development. Role of biology education

Biological education for community development / edited by P.J. Kelly and G. Schaefer on behalf of the International Union of Biological Sciences (IUBS) and in cooperation with the Institute for Science Education (ISN) at the University of Kiel, West Germany. — London : Taylor & Francis, 1980. — ix,191p : ill ; 23cm
Includes bibliographies and index
ISBN 0-85066-214-1 (pbk) : £9.50 B81-05827

574'.07'041 — Great Britain. Biology. Information sources — *Lists*

Wyatt, H. V.. A directory of information resources in biology in the UK / [compiled by] H.V. Wyatt. — [London] : British Library ; Boston Spa : Distributed by Publications, British Library Lending Division, 1981. — v,83p ; 30cm. — (British Library research & development reports, ISSN 0308-2385 ; no.5606)
Includes index
ISBN 0-905984-65-x (pbk) : Unpriced B81-29261

574'.07'1 — Schools. Curriculum subjects: Biology. Teaching

Dowdeswell, W. H.. Teaching and learning biology / W.H. Dowdeswell. — London : Heinemann Educational, 1981. — 245p : ill ; 22cm
Bibliography: p235. - Includes index
ISBN 0-435-59261-0 (pbk) : £5.95 B81-19356

574'.07'1241 — Secondary schools. Curriculum subjects: Biology. Teaching

Dallas, Dorothy M.. Teaching biology today / Dorothy Dallas. — London : Hutchinson, 1980. — 179p : ill ; 24cm
Bibliography: p167-176. - Includes index
ISBN 0-09-141091-6 (pbk) : £4.95 : CIP rev. B80-13384

574'.072041 — Great Britain. Natural environment. Research organisations: Natural Environment Research Council — *Serials*

Natural Environment Research Council. Report of the Council for the period 1 April ... — 31 March ... / the Natural Environment Research Council. — 1979-1980. — London : H.M.S.O., 1980. — vi,142p
Cover title: The Natural Environment Research Council report for ...
ISBN 0-10-027899-x : £6.30
ISSN 0072-7008 B81-03524

574'.072041 — Great Britain. *Science Research Council. Biological Sciences Committee — Serials*

Great Britain. *Science Research Council. Biological Sciences Committee.* Annual report / Science Research Council, Science Board, Biological Sciences Committee. — 1979/80. — Swindon : The Council, [1980?]. — 22p
Unpriced B81-37243

574'.0723 — Great Britain. Biology. Field studies

A Handbook for naturalists / edited by Mark R.D. Seaward assisted by Susan Joy and Frank H. Brightman ; foreword by H.R.H. The Duke of Edinburgh. — London : Constable in association with Council For Nature/Council for Environmental Conservation, 1981. — 202p : ill,maps,2facsims,1port ; 18cm
Includes bibliographies and index
ISBN 0-09-462390-2 : £4.95 B81-10738

574'.074'02 — Great Britain. Museums. Stock: Natural history specimens — *Statistics*
A **Survey** of zoological and botanical material in museums and other institutions of Great Britain / editors E.G. Hancock, P.J. Morgan. — [s.l.] : Biology Curators Group, 1980. — 31p ; 30cm. — (Report / Biology Curators Group ; no.1)
ISBN 0-9507092-0-4 (pbk) : Unpriced
B81-04854

574'.074'02134 — London. Kensington & Chelsea *(London Borough).* **Museums: British Museum (Natural History),** *to 1900*
Gunther, A. E.. The founders of science at the British Museum 1753-1900 : a contribution to the centenary of the opening of the British Museum (Natural History) on 18th April 1981 / by A.E. Gunther. — Halesworth (17 Thoroughfare, Halesworth, Suffolk IP19 8AH) : Halesworth Press, c1980. — ix,219p : ill,2maps,plans,ports,1geneal.table ; 25cm
Maps on lining papers. — Bibliography: p196-209. - Includes index
ISBN 0-9507276-0-1 : £7.90 B81-05477

574'.074'02134 — London. Kensington and Chelsea *(London Borough).* **Museums: British Museum (Natural History),** *to 1980*
British Museum (Natural History). The Natural History Museum at South Kensington : a history of the British Museum (Natural History) 1753-1980 / William T. Stearn. — London : Heinemann in association with the British Museum (Natural History), 1981. — xxiii,414p,[48]p of plates : ill,1plan,ports ; 25cm
Ill on lining papers. — Includes index
ISBN 0-434-73600-7 : £15.00 B81-23232

British Museum (Natural History). Nature stored nature studied : collections, conservation and allied research at the British Museum (Natural History). — [London] : The Museum, 1981. — 64p : ill,maps,facsims,ports ; 25cm. — (Publication / British Museum (Natural History) ; no.835)
Bibliography: p64
ISBN 0-565-00835-8 (pbk) : Unpriced
B81-18838

574'.076 — Biology — *Questions & answers — For African students*
Stone, R. H. (Robert Henry). Revision biology for tropical schools / R.H. Stone. — Oxford : Oxford University Press, 1981. — 190p : ill ; 26cm
Includes index
ISBN 0-19-914060-x (pbk) : £2.75 B81-18278

574'.076 — Biology — *Questions & answers — For schools*
Clegg, C. J.. Test your biology. — London : Murray, Jan.1982. — [128]p
ISBN 0-7195-3863-7 (pbk) : £1.80 : CIP entry
B81-33850

Interpretation tests in biology. — London : Edward Arnold, Sept.1981. — [112]p
ISBN 0-7131-0550-x (pbk) : £2.50 : CIP entry
B81-21489

Thomas, B. L.. Biology : a concise guide for first examinations / B.L. Thomas. — Exeter : Wheaton, 1979. — vii,72p : ill ; 27cm
Includes index
ISBN 0-08-022879-8 (pbk) : £1.75 B81-16582

574'.09 — Biology — *History — Serials*
Studies in history of biology. — 4. — Baltimore ; London : Johns Hopkins University Press, c1980. — 198p
ISBN 0-8018-2362-5 : £13.20 B81-00885

574'.09'034 — Biology, *1840-1940*
Biology, medicine and society 1840-1940. — Cambridge : Cambridge University Press, Nov.1981. — [344]p. — (Past and present publications)
ISBN 0-521-23770-x : £22.50 : CIP entry
Also classified at 610'.09'034 B81-30183

574'.092'2 — Biologists — *Case studies*
Pettifer, Julian. Nature watch / Julian Pettifer and Robin Brown. — London : Joseph, c1981. — 207p : col.ill,maps(some col.),ports(some col.) ; 26cm
Includes bibliographies and index
ISBN 0-7181-1994-0 : £9.95 B81-10635

574'.092'4 — Austria. Natural history. Schauberger, Viktor — *Biographies*
Alexanderson, Olof. Living water. — Wellingborough : Turnstone Press, July 1981. — [160]p
Translation of: Det levande vattnet
ISBN 0-85500-111-9 (cased) : £6.95 : CIP entry
ISBN 0-85500-112-7 (pbk) : £3.50 B81-14952

574'.092'4 — Hampshire. Selborne. Natural history. White, Gilbert — *Biographies*
Johnson, Walter. Gilbert White / Walter Johnson. — London : Macdonald Futura, 1981, c1928. — 331p : ill,maps ; 18cm. — (Heritage)
Originally published: London : Murray, 1928. — Includes index
ISBN 0-7088-2067-0 (pbk) : £1.95 B81-33405

574.1 — ORGANISMS. PHYSIOLOGY

574.1 — Organisms. Physiology
Biology : form and function. — Milton Keynes : Open University Press. — (Science : a second level course)
At head of title: The Open University
Cell biology I / prepared by the S202 Course Team. — 1981. — 23,61p : ill(some col.) ; 30cm. — (S202 ; units 4 & 5)
Includes bibliographies. — Contents: Unit 4: Cell structure - Unit 5: Macromolecules and membranes
ISBN 0-335-16031-x (pbk) : Unpriced
B81-27795

Biology : form and function. — Milton Keynes : Open University Press. — (Science : a second level course)
At head of title: The Open University
The diversity of organisms / prepared by the S202 Course Team. — 1981. — vii,51,60,55p : ill(some col.) ; 30cm. — (S202 ; units 1-3)
Includes bibliographies. — Contents: Unit 1: Marine organisms - Unit 2: From sea to land, plants and arthropods - Unit 3: From sea to land, vertebrates
ISBN 0-335-16030-1 (corrected : pbk) : Unpriced B81-11355

Biology : form and function. — Milton Keynes : Open University Press. — (Science : a second level course)
At head of title: The Open University
The S202 picture book / prepared by the S202 Course Team. — 1981. — 50p : chiefly ill (some col.) ; 30cm. — (S202 ; PB)
Includes index
ISBN 0-335-16042-5 (pbk) : Unpriced
B81-19490

574.1'33 — Organisms. Metabolism. Effects of cyanides
Cyanide in biology. — London : Academic Press, July 1981. — [500]p
ISBN 0-12-716980-6 : CIP entry B81-14871

574.1'33 — Organisms. Metabolism — *For schools*
Boyce, Ann. Metabolism, movement and control / A. Boyce, C.M. Jenking. — Basingstoke : Macmillan Education, 1980. — viii,280p : ill ; 24cm. — (Foundations of biology)
Bibliography: p274-276. — Includes index
ISBN 0-333-26779-6 (pbk) : £4.50 : CIP rev.
B80-10600

574.1'6 — Organisms. Reproductive cycle. Biological rhythms — *Conference proceedings*
Colston Research Society. *Symposium (32nd : 1980 : University of Bristol).* Biological clocks in seasonal reproductive cycles : proceedings of the Thirty-second Symposium of the Colston Research Society held in the University of Bristol March-April 1980 / editors B.K. Follett and D.E. Follett. — Bristol : Scientechnica, 1981. — xii,292p : ill ; 25cm. — (Colston papers ; v.32)
ISBN 0-85608-032-2 : £22.50 : CIP rev.
B81-06616

574.1'66 — Sex. Evolution
Bell, Graham. The masterpiece of nature. — London : Croom Helm, Sept.1981. — [544]p
ISBN 0-85664-753-5 : £29.50 : CIP entry
B81-22541

574.1'7 — Organisms. Cells. Differentiation - *Conference proceedings*
Cellular controls in differentiation. — London : Academic Press, Aug.1981. — [300]p
Conference papers
ISBN 0-12-453580-1 : CIP entry B81-19209

574.1'8 — Organisms. Virus receptors
Virus receptors. — London : Chapman and Hall. — (Receptors and recognition. Series B ; v.8)
Pt.2: Animal viruses / edited by K. Lonberg-Holm and L. Philipson. — 1981. — xii,217p : ill ; 24cm
Includes bibliographies and index
ISBN 0-412-16410-8 : Unpriced B81-15980

574.1'88 — Organisms. Regulation
Biological regulation and development. — New York ; London : Plenum
Molecular organization and cell function / edited by Robert F. Goldberger. — c1980. — xvi,620p : ill ; 27cm
Includes bibliographies and index
ISBN 0-306-40486-9 : Unpriced B81-08193

574.1'882 — Organisms. Biological rhythms
Biological rhythms / edited by Jurgen Aschoff. — New York ; London : Plenum, c1981. — xix,563p : ill ; 26cm. — (Handbook of behavioral neurobiology ; v.4)
Includes bibliographies and index
ISBN 0-306-40585-7 : Unpriced B81-26233

574.19 — Biology. Quantum theory
Davydov, A. S.. Biology and quantum mechanics. — Oxford : Pergamon, Dec.1981. — [250]p. — (International series in natural philosophy ; v.109)
ISBN 0-08-026392-5 : £18.70 : CIP entry
B81-31360

574.19'1 — Biophysics
Developments in biophysical research / edited by Antonio Borsellino ... [et al.] ; [proceedings of a congress on developments in biophysical methods sponsored by the Italian Society for Pure and Applied Biophysics and held October 8-11, 1979, in Parma, Italy]. — New York ; London : Plenum, c1980. — xi,365p : ill ; 26cm
Includes index
ISBN 0-306-40627-6 : Unpriced B81-19715

Stanford, A. L.. Foundations of biophysics / A.L. Stanford, Jr. — New York ; London : Academic Press
Exercise booklet. — [198-?]. — 23p ; 23cm
ISBN 0-12-663352-5 (unbound) : £2.80
B81-14608

574.19'1'05 — Biophysics - *Serials*
Progress in biophysics and molecular biology. — 36. — Oxford : Pergamon, June 1981. — [146]p
ISBN 0-08-028394-2 : £29.50 : CIP entry
B81-16854

574.19'12 — Biological materials. Mechanical properties — *Conference proceedings*
The **mechanical** properties of biological materials. — Cambridge : Cambridge University Press for the Society for Experimental Biology, 1980. — ix,513p : ill ; 24cm. — (Symposia of the Society for Experimental Biology ; no.34)
Conference papers. — Edited by J.F.V. Vincent and J.D. Currey. — Includes bibliographies and index
ISBN 0-521-23478-6 : £30.00 B81-08063

574.19'121 — Autotrophs. Bioenergetics *compared with* **bioenergetics of heterotrophs**
Anderson, John W.. Bioenergetics of autotrophs and heterotrophs / John W. Anderson. — London : Edward Arnold, 1980. — 60p : ill ; 22cm. — (The Institute of Biology's studies in biology, ISSN 0537-9024 ; no.126)
Bibliography: p60
ISBN 0-7131-2807-0 (pbk) : £2.50 : CIP rev.
B80-20640

574.19′121 — Bioenergetics

Jones, C. W.. Biological energy conservation : oxidative phosphorylation / C.W. Jones. — 2nd ed. — London : Chapman and Hall, 1981. — 78p : ill ; 21cm. — (Outline studies in biology)
Previous ed.: 1976. — Bibliography: p76-77. — Includes index
ISBN 0-412-23360-6 (pbk) : Unpriced : CIP rev. B81-15826

Nicholls, D. G.. Bioenergetics. — London : Academic Press, Feb.1982. — [180]p
ISBN 0-12-518120-5 (cased) : CIP entry
ISBN 0-12-518122-1 (pbk) : Unpriced B81-36062

574.19′121′05 — Bioenergetics — *Serials*

Topics in bioelectrochemistry and bioenergetics. — Vol.4. — Chichester : Wiley, c1981. — xiv,342p
ISBN 0-471-27904-8 : £35.00 : CIP rev.
ISSN 0160-3183
Also classified at 574.19′283 B81-19158

574.19′125 — Bioluminescence — *Conference proceedings*

Bioluminescence and chemiluminescence : basic chemistry and analytical applications / edited by Marlene A. DeLuca, William D. McElroy. — New York ; London : Academic Press, c1981. — xxviii,782p : ill,maps,ports ; 24cm
Conference papers. — Includes index
ISBN 0-12-208820-4 : £24.80
Also classified at 541.3′5 B81-35357

574.19′153′05 — Photobiology — *Serials*

Photochemical and photobiological reviews. — Vol.6. — New York ; London ([Black Arrow House, Chandos Rd, NW10]) : Plenum, c1981. — ix,203p
ISBN 0-306-40662-4 : Unpriced
Also classified at 541.3′5′05 B81-20456

574.19′2 — Biochemistry

Borek, Ernest. The atoms within us / Ernest Borek. — Rev. ed. — New York ; Guildford : Columbia University Press, 1980. — xi,238p : ill ; 22cm
Previous ed.: London : Oxford University Press, 1961. — Includes index
ISBN 0-231-04386-4 (cased) : £11.05 B81-09518

Campbell, Peter N.. Biochemistry illustrated. — Edinburgh : Churchill Livingstone, July 1981. — [216]p
ISBN 0-443-02176-7 (pbk) : £8.50 : CIP entry B81-14946

Comprehensive biochemistry / edited by Marcel Florkin and Elmer H. Stotz. — Amsterdam ; Oxford : Elsevier Scientific
Vol.19A: Amino acid metabolism and sulphur metabolism / [edited by] Albert Newberger, Laurens L. M. Van Deenen. — 1981. — xviii,481p : ill ; 23cm
Includes index
ISBN 0-444-80257-6 : £33.46 B81-19271

Kilgour, Gordon L.. Fundamentals of biochemistry / Gordon L. Kilgour. — New York ; London : Van Nostrand Reinhold, c1981. — xiv,380p : ill(some col.) ; 24cm
Text on lining papers. — Includes index
ISBN 0-442-25756-2 : £16.45 B81-17185

Steiner, Robert F.. The chemistry of living systems / Robert F. Steiner, Seymour Pomerantz. — New York ; London : Van Nostrand, c1981. — xii,540p : ill(some col.) ; 25cm
Includes bibliographies and index
ISBN 0-442-28128-5 : £18.70 B81-26038

Suckling, Keith E.. Biological chemistry : the molecular approach to biological systems / K.E. Suckling, C.J. Suckling. — Cambridge : Cambridge University Press, 1980. — xii,381p : ill ; 23cm. — (Cambridge texts in chemistry and biochemistry)
Bibliography: p370-376. - Includes index
ISBN 0-521-22852-2 (cased) : £25.00 : CIP rev.
ISBN 0-521-29678-1 (pbk) : £9.95 B80-25607

Yudkin, Michael. A guidebook to biochemistry. — 4th ed. / Michael Yudkin, Robin Offord. — Cambridge : Cambridge University Press, 1980, c1965. — xi,261p : ill ; 23cm
Previous ed.: 1979. — Includes index
ISBN 0-521-23084-5 (cased) : £18.00 : CIP rev.
ISBN 0-521-29794-x (pbk) : £6.95 B80-25608

574.19′2 — Biological materials — *Conference proceedings*

World Biomaterials Congress *(1st : 1980 : Baden)*. Biomaterials 1980. — Chichester : Wiley, Jan.1982. — [800]p. — (Advances in biomaterials ; v.3)
ISBN 0-471-10126-5 : £40.00 : CIP entry B81-34477

574.19′2 — Biological materials. Cooperative phenomena

Cooperative phenomena in biology / edited by George Karreman. — New York ; Oxford : Pergamon, c1980. — ix,246p : ill ; 24cm
Includes bibliographies and index
ISBN 0-08-023186-1 : £21.25 B81-21816

574.19′2 — Pollutants. Biochemistry

Ottaway, J. H.. The biochemistry of pollution / J.H. Ottaway. — London : Edward Arnold, 1980. — 60p : ill,maps ; 22cm. — (The Institute of Biology′s studies in biology, ISSN 0537-9024 ; no.123)
Bibliography: p60
ISBN 0-7131-2784-8 (pbk) : £2.50 : CIP rev. B80-18276

574.19′2′014 — Biochemistry. Terminology

Biochemical nomenclature and related documents / International Union of Biochemistry. — London (c/o Biochemical Society, 7 Warwick Court, WC1R 5DP) : IUB, 1978. — vi,223p : ill ; 28cm
Unpriced (pbk) B81-33402

574.19′2′02461 — Biochemistry — *For medicine*

Toporek, Milton. Basic chemistry of life / Milton Toporek. — St Louis ; London : Mosby, 1981. — 521p : ill ; 24cm
Originally published: New York : Appleton-Century-Crofts, 1968. — Includes bibliographies and index
ISBN 0-8016-5002-x (pbk) : £12.00 B81-02480

574.19′2′028 — Biochemistry. Laboratory techniques

A Biologists guide to principles and techniques of practical biochemistry / edited by Bryan L. Williams and Keith Wilson. — 2nd ed. — London : Edward Arnold, 1981. — xiii,318p : ill ; 22cm. — (Contemporary biology)
Previous ed.: 1975. — Includes bibliographies and index
ISBN 0-7131-2829-1 : £8.50 : CIP rev. B81-16358

Laboratory techniques in biochemistry and molecular biology. — Vol.9, Sequencing of proteins and peptides. — Amsterdam ; Oxford : North-Holland, 1981. — xviii,327p
ISBN 0-444-80275-4 : £30.75
ISSN 0075-7535 B81-11230

574.19′2′028 — Biochemistry. Laboratory techniques. Quantitative methods

Dawes, Edwin A.. Quantitative problems in biochemistry / Edwin A. Dawes. — 6th ed. — London : Longman, 1980. — ix,335p : ill ; 24cm
Previous ed.: Edinburgh : Churchill Livingstone, 1972. — Includes bibliographies and index
ISBN 0-582-44402-0 : £12.95 B81-02793

574.19′2′05 — Biochemistry — *Serials*

Advances in enzymology and related areas of molecular biology. — Vol.51. — New York ; Chichester : Wiley, 1980. — v,317p
ISBN 0-471-05653-7 : Unpriced
ISSN 0065-258x B81-16825

Advances in enzymology and related areas of molecular biology. — Vol.52. — New York ; Chichester : Wiley, c1981. — v,408p
ISBN 0-471-08120-5 : £20.50
ISSN 0065-258x B81-25483

Essays in biochemistry. — Vol.16. — London : Published for the Biochemical Society by Academic Press, c1980. — xi,183p
ISBN 0-12-158116-0 : Unpriced
ISSN 0071-1365 B81-07346

Essays in biochemistry. — Vol.17. — London : Academic Press, Nov.1981. — 1v.
ISBN 0-12-158117-9 : CIP entry
ISSN 0071-1365 B81-28139

574.19′2′05 — Organisms. Effects of pesticides. Biochemical aspects — *Serials*

Progress in pesticide biochemistry. — Vol.1-. — Chichester : Wiley, c1981-. — v. : ill ; 24cm
£24.00 B81-29986

574.19′2′0711 — Higher education institutions. Curriculum subjects: Biochemistry. Teaching

Biochemical education / edited by Charles F.A. Bryce. — London : Croom Helm, c1981. — 219p : ill ; 23cm
Bibliography: p195-207. - Includes index
ISBN 0-7099-0600-5 : £12.95 B81-20782

574.19′2′0924 — Biochemistry. Warburg, Otto — *Biographies*

Krebs, *Sir* Hans. Otto Warburg : cell physiologist, biochemist and eccentric / by Hans Krebs in collaboration with Roswitha Schmid ; translated by Hans Krebs and Anne Martin. — Oxford : Clarendon Press, 1981. — x,141p,[21]p of plates : ill,facsims,ports ; 23cm
Translation of: Otto Warburg, Zellphysiologe - Biochemiker - Mediziner 1883-1970. — Includes bibliographies and index
ISBN 0-19-858171-8 : £10.00 : CIP rev. B81-11920

574.19′214 — Animals. Inorganic compounds. Crystals. Growth

Inorganic biological crystal growth. — Oxford : Pergamon, Oct.1981. — [280]p. — (Progress in crystal growth and characterization)
ISBN 0-08-028420-5 : £26.00 : CIP entry B81-30176

574.19′214 — Organisms. Metal ions

Hughes, M. N.. The inorganic chemistry of biological processes / M.N. Hughes. — 2nd ed. — Chichester : Wiley, c1981. — ix,338p : ill ; 23cm
Previous ed.: 1972. — Includes index
ISBN 0-471-27815-7 (pbk) : £9.90 B81-23350

574.19′214 — Organisms. Metals

Harrison, P. M.. Metals in biochemistry / P.M. Harrison, R.J. Hoare. — London : Chapman and Hall, 1980. — 48p : ill ; 21cm. — (Outline studies in biology)
Bibliography: p76-78. - Includes index
ISBN 0-412-13160-9 (pbk) : £2.45 : CIP rev. B80-08749

574.19′214 — Organisms. Oxygen — *Conference proceedings*

BOC Priestley Conference *(2nd : 1980 : Birmingham)*. Oxygen and life : lectures delivered at the Second BOC Priestley Conference, sponsored by the BOC Gases Division Trust and organised by the Royal Society of Chemistry in conjunction with the University of Birmingham, Birmingham, September 15th-18th 1980. — London : Royal Society of Chemistry, c1981. — xii,224p : ill ; 21cm. — (Special publication / Royal Society of Chemistry, ISSN 0260-6291 ; 39)
ISBN 0-85186-825-8 (pbk) : Unpriced : CIP rev. B81-04333

574.19′214′05 — Inorganic biochemistry — *Serials*

Advances in inorganic biochemistry. — 1-. — New York ; Oxford : Elsevier/North-Holland, 1979. — v. : ill ; 25cm
Irregular
ISSN 0190-0218 = Advances in inorganic biochemistry : Unpriced B81-13096

574.19′214′05 — Inorganic compounds. Biochemistry — *Serials*

Inorganic biochemistry. — Vol.2. — London : Royal Society of Chemistry, c1981. — xiv,347p. — (Specialist periodical report / Royal Society of Chemistry)
ISBN 0-85186-555-0 : Unpriced
ISSN 0142-9698 B81-29053

574.19'24 — Biopolymers
MacGregor, E. A.. Polymers in nature / E.A. MacGregor and C.T. Greenwood. — Chichester : Wiley, c1980. — ix,391p : ill ; 24cm
Includes index
ISBN 0-471-27762-2 : £19.50 : CIP rev. B80-25610

574.19'24 — Biopolymers - *Conference proceedings*
International Symposium on Macromolecules *(1980 : Florence)*. Structural order in polymers : lectures presented at the International Symposium on Macromolecules, Florence, Italy, 7-12 September 1980 / edited by Francesco Ciardelli and Paolo Giusti. — Oxford : Pergamon, 1981. — xiv,247p : ill ; 28cm
At head of title: International Union of Pure and Applied Chemistry (Macromolecular Division)
ISBN 0-08-025296-6 : £30.00 : CIP rev.
Primary classification 547.7'044 B81-10421

574.19'24 — Biopolymers. Physical properties. Measurement
Spragg, S. P.. The physical behaviour of macromolecules with biological functions / S.P. Spragg. — Chichester : Wiley, c1980. — xv,202p : ill ; 24cm. — (Monographs in molecular biophysics and biochemistry)
Includes index
ISBN 0-471-27784-3 : £13.50 : CIP rev. B80-29645

574.19'2431 — Organisms. Sterols
Pollak, O. J.. Sitosterol / O.J. Pollak, David Kritchevsky. — Basel ; London : Karger, c1981. — viii,219p ; 25cm. — (Monographs on atherosclerosis ; v.10)
Bibliography: p167-214. — Includes index
ISBN 3-8055-0568-x : £37.00 B81-26227

574.19'245 — Organisms. Kinins — *Conference proceedings*
Current concepts in kinin research : proceedings of the satellite symposium of the 7th International Congress of Pharmacology, Paris, 22 July, 1978 / editors Gert L. Haberland, Ulla Hamberg. — Oxford : Pergamon, 1979. — vii,285p : ill ; 26cm. — (Advances in the biosciences ; v.17)
Includes bibliographies and index
ISBN 0-08-023761-4 : £23.00 : CIP rev. B79-07262

574.19'245 — Organisms. Proteins. Interactions
Protein-protein interactions / edited by C. Frieden, L.W. Nichol. — New York ; Chichester : Wiley, c1981. — xl,403p : ill ; 24cm
Includes index
ISBN 0-471-04979-4 : £33.45 B81-28309

574.19'245 — Organisms. Proteins. Interactions with nucleic acids — *Conference proceedings*
Biological implications of protein-nucleic acid interactions / edited by J. Augustyniak. — Amsterdam ; Oxford : Elsevier/North Holland Biomedical, 1980. — xiv,667p,[5]p of plates : ill ; 22cm
Conference papers. — Includes index
ISBN 0-444-80292-4 : £27.39
Primary classification 574.87'328 B81-22443

574.19'247 — Organisms. Lipids
Furth, Anna J.. Lipids and polysaccharides in biology / Anna J. Furth. — London : Edward Arnold, 1980. — 66p : ill ; 22cm. — (The Institute of Biology's studies in biology, ISSN 0537-9024 ; no.125)
Biliography: p66
ISBN 0-7131-2805-4 (pbk) : £2.60 : CIP rev.
Also classified at 574.19'2482 B80-18280

Gurr, M. I.. Lipid biochemistry : an introduction / M.I. Gurr, A.T. James. — 3rd ed. — London : Chapman and Hall, 1980. — vii,247p : ill ; 22cm
Previous ed.: 1975. — Includes index
ISBN 0-412-22620-0 (cased) : £12.50 : CIP rev.
ISBN 0-412-22630-8 (pbk) : £6.50 B80-25611

Progress in lipid research. — Vol.18. — Oxford : Pergamon, Aug.1981. — [243]p
ISBN 0-08-027129-4 : £32.00 : CIP entry B81-23789

574.19'24'705 — Organisms. Lipids — *Serials*
Progress in lipid research. — Vol.19. — Oxford : Pergamon, Dec.1981. — [230]p
ISBN 0-08-021000-7 : £38.00 : CIP entry B81-34221

574.19'248 — Organisms. Carbohydrates
Candy, David J.. Biological functions of carbohydrates / David J. Candy. — Glasgow : Blackie, 1980. — ix,197p : ill ; 21cm. — (Tertiary level biology)
Bibliography: p187-190. - Includes index
ISBN 0-216-91010-2 (cased) : £16.95 : CIP rev.
ISBN 0-216-91011-0 (pbk) : £7.95 B80-18281

574.19'248 — Organisms. Carbohydrates. Metabolism. Regulation
Carbohydrate metabolism : quantitative physiology and mathematical modelling / edited by C. Cobelli and R.N. Bergman. — Chichester : Wiley, c1981. — xvi,440p,[1]leaf of plates : ill,ports ; 24cm. — (A Wiley-Interscience publication)
Conference papers. — Includes bibliographies and index
ISBN 0-471-27912-9 : £26.50 : CIP rev. B81-16885

574.19'248'05 — Organisms. Carbohydrates — *Serials*
Biology of carbohydrates. — Vol.1-. — New York ; Chichester : Wiley, 1981-. — v. : ill ; 24cm
£34.75 B81-33698

574.19'2482 — Organisms. Polysaccharides
Furth, Anna J.. Lipids and polysaccharides in biology / Anna J. Furth. — London : Edward Arnold, 1980. — 66p : ill ; 22cm. — (The Institute of Biology's studies in biology, ISSN 0537-9024 ; no.125)
Biliography: p66
ISBN 0-7131-2805-4 (pbk) : £2.60 : CIP rev.
Primary classification 574.19'247 B80-18280

574.19'25 — Organisms. Enzymes. Chemical reactions. Kinetics. Mathematical models
Lam, Chan F.. Techniques for the analysis and modelling of enzyme kinetic mechanisms / Chan F. Lam. — Chichester : Research Studies, c1981. — xv,396p : ill ; 24cm. — (Medical computing series ; 4)
Includes bibliographies and index
ISBN 0-471-09981-3 : £21.00 : CIP rev. B81-13760

574.19'25 — Organisms. Enzymes. Regulation by reversible phosphorylation
Recently discovered systems of enzyme regulation by reversible phosphorylation / edited by P. Cohen. — Amsterdam ; Oxford : Elsevier/North-Holland Biomedical, 1980. — xv,273p : ill ; 25cm. — (Molecular aspects of cellular regulation ; v.1)
Includes index
ISBN 0-444-80226-6 : £27.13 B81-04535

574.19'25 — Organisms. Glycolytic enzymes
The **Enzymes** of glycolysis : structure, activity and evolution : a Royal Society discussion held on 16 and 17 October 1980 / organised by Sir David Phillips, C.C.F. Blake and H.C. Watson. — London : Royal Society, 1981. — v,214p,2p of plates : ill(some col.) ; 31cm
Originally published: in Philosophical transactions of the Royal Society of London, series B, vol.293(no.1063) p1-214. — Includes bibliographies
ISBN 0-85403-169-3 : £21.45 B81-31987

574.19'25 — Organisms. Isoenzymes
Rider, C. C.. Isoenzymes / C.C. Rider, C.B. Taylor. — London : Chapman and Hall, 1980. — 78p : ill ; 21cm. — (Outline studies in biology)
Includes index
ISBN 0-412-15640-7 (pbk) : £2.45 : CIP rev. B80-23259

574.19'256 — Organisms. Proteinases - *Conference proceedings*
Proteinases and their inhibitors. — Oxford : Pergamon, June 1981. — [500]p
Conference papers
ISBN 0-08-027377-7 : £33.00 : CIP entry B81-09490

574.19'258 — Biochemistry. Oxidation & reduction — *Conference proceedings*
International Symposium on Oxidases and Related Redox Systems *(3rd : 1979 : State University of New York)*. Oxidases and related redox systems. — Oxford : Pergamon, Oct.1981. — 2v.[(1250p.)]. — (Advances in the biosciences ; v.33 and 34)
ISBN 0-08-024421-1 : £125.00 : CIP entry B81-28187

574.19'258 — Organisms. Cytochrome oxidases
Wikström, M.. Cytochrome oxidase. — London : Academic Press, Dec.1981. — [200]p
ISBN 0-12-752020-1 : CIP entry B81-31352

574.19'258 — Organisms. Cytochrome P-450
Cytochrome P-450 / edited by Ryo Sato and Tsuneo Omura. — Tokyo : Kodansha ; New York ; London : Academic Press, c1978. — xii,233p : ill ; 24cm
Includes index
ISBN 0-12-619850-0 : £18.00 B81-14604

574.19'258 — Organisms. Cytochrome P-450 — *Conference proceedings*
European Meeting on Cytochrome P-450 *(3rd : 1980 : Saltsjöbaden)*. Biochemistry, biophysics and regulation of cytochrome P-450 : proceedings of the Third European Meeting on Cytochrome P-450 held in Saltsjöbaden, Sweden, June 16-19, 1980 / editors Jan-Ake Custafsson ... [et al.]. — Amsterdam ; Oxford : Elsevier/North-Holland Biomedical, 1980. — xiv,626p : ill ; 2350 £32.40. — (Developments in biochemistry, ISSN 0165-1714 ; v.13)
Includes index
ISBN 0-444-80282-7 B81-05378

574.19'27 — Organisms. Hormone receptors. Development
Csaba, G.. Ontogeny and phylogeny of hormone receptors / G. Csaba. — Basel ; London : Karger, 1981. — xi,172p : ill ; 25cm. — (Monographs in developmental biology ; v.15)
Bibliography: p156-169. — Includes index
ISBN 3-8055-2174-x : £38.50 B81-38744

574.19'27'05 — Organisms. Hormones — *Serials*
Biochemical actions of hormones. — Vol.8. — New York ; London : Academic Press, 1981. — xi,545p
ISBN 0-12-452808-2 : Unpriced B81-32404

574.19'283 — Bioelectrochemistry — *Serials*
Topics in bioelectrochemistry and bioenergetics. — Vol.4. — Chichester : Wiley, c1981. — xiv,342p
ISBN 0-471-27904-8 : £35.00 : CIP rev.
ISSN 0160-3183
Primary classification 574.19'121'05 B81-19158

574.19'283 — Organisms. Chemical reactions. Thermodynamics. Models: Thermodynamics of macrocyclic ligands & polymers
Bioenergetics and thermodynamics : model systems : synthetic and natural chelates and macrocycles as models for biological and pharmaceutical studies : proceedings of the NATO Advance Study Institute held at Tabiano, Parma, Italy, May 21-June 1, 1979 / edited by A. Braibanti. — Dordrecht ; London : Reidel in cooperation with NATO Scientific Affairs Division, 1980. — ix,474p : ill ; 25cm. — (NATO advanced study institutes series. Series C, Mathematical and physical sciences ; v.55)
Includes index
ISBN 90-277-1115-1 : Unpriced B81-08366

574.19'285 — Biochemistry. Affinity chromatography — *Conference proceedings*
Affinity chromatography and related techniques. — Oxford : Elsevier Scientific, Nov.1981. — [450]p. — (Analytical chemistry symposia series ; v.9)
Conference papers
ISBN 0-444-42031-2 : CIP entry B81-33644

574.19'285 — Biochemistry. Mass spectrometry — *Conference proceedings*

International Symposium on Mass Spectrometry in Biochemistry and Medicine *(6th : 1979).* Recent developments in mass spectrometry in biochemistry and medicine, 6 : proceedings of the 6th International Symposium on Mass Spectrometry in Biochemistry and Medicine, Venice, 21 and 22 June 1979 / edited by Alberto Frigerio and Malcolm McCamish. — Amsterdam ; Oxford : Elsevier Scientific, 1980. — ix,553p : ill ; 25cm. — (Analytical chemistry symposia series ; v.4)
Includes index
ISBN 0-444-41870-9 : £32.82 : CIP rev. B80-05910

International Symposium on Mass Spectrometry in Biochemistry, Medicine and Environmental Research *(7th : 1980 : Milan).* Recent developments in mass spectrometry in biochemistry, medicine and environmental research, 7. — Oxford : Elsevier Scientific, Oct.1981. — 1v.. — (Analytical chemistry symposia series ; v.7)
ISBN 0-444-42029-0 : CIP entry B81-30197

Soft ionization biological mass spectrometry. — London : Heyden, Dec.1981. — [160]p
Conference papers
ISBN 0-85501-706-6 : £16.00 : CIP entry B81-36990

574.19'285'05 — Biochemistry. Chemical analysis — *Serials*

Methods of biochemical analysis. — Vol.27. — New York ; Chichester : Wiley, c1981. — vii,537p
ISBN 0-471-06503-x : £29.75 B81-33318

574.19'29 — Natural products. Biosynthesis. Mechanisms

Manitto, Paolo. Biosynthesis of natural products / Paolo Manitto ; translation editor P.G. Sammes. — Chichester : Horwood, 1981. — 548p : ill ; 24cm
Translation from the Italian. — Includes index
ISBN 0-85312-062-5 : £35.00 : CIP rev. B80-36077

574.19'29 — Secondary metabolites. Biosynthesis

Herbert, R. B.. The biosynthesis of secondary metabolites. — London : Chapman and Hall, July 1981. — [250]p
ISBN 0-412-16370-5 (pbk) : £15.00 : CIP entry
ISBN 0-412-16380-2 (pbk) : £6.50 B81-14855

574.19'29'05 — Biosynthesis — *Serials*

Biosynthesis. — Vol.6. — London : Royal Society of Chemistry, c1980. — x,295p. — (Specialist periodical report / Royal Society of Chemistry)
ISBN 0-85186-990-4 : Unpriced : CIP rev. B80-33566

574.19'294 — Organisms. Polysaccharides. Biosynthesis & degradation — *Conference proceedings*

Mechanisms of saccharide polymerization and depolymerization / edited by J. John Marshall. — New York ; London : Academic Press, 1980. — xiv,442p : ill ; 24cm
Conference papers. — Includes index
ISBN 0-12-474150-9 : £18.00 B81-21838

574.2 — ORGANISMS. DISEASES

574.2 — Organisms. Tumours. Growth

Neoplasms : comparative pathology of growth in animals, plants, and man / Hans E. Kaiser, editor. — Baltimore ; London : Williams & Wilkins, c1981. — xxxii,908p : ill ; 29cm
Includes bibliographies and index
ISBN 0-683-04503-2 : £114.00 B81-24347

574.2'322 — Organisms. Pathogens: Bacteria. Endotoxins — *Conference proceedings*

International Congress of Immunology Satellite Workshop *(4th : 1980 : Paris).* Bacterial endotoxins and host response : proceedings of the 4th International Congress of Immunology Satellite Workshop held in Paris, France, on 26 July, 1980 / M.K. Agarwal editor. — Amsterdam ; Oxford : Elsevier/North-Holland, 1980. — ix,436p : ill ; 25cm
Includes index
ISBN 0-444-80301-7 : £26.28 B81-05072

574.2'9 — Cellular immunity

McConnell, Ian. The immune system : a course on the molecular and cellular basis of immunity. — 2nd ed. / I. McConnell, A. Munro, H. Waldmann. — Oxford : Blackwell Scientific, 1981. — xvii,319p : ill ; 24cm
Previous ed.: / edited by M.J. Hobart, Ian McConnell. 1975. — Includes bibliographies and index
ISBN 0-632-00626-9 (pbk) : £10.50 : CIP rev. B80-34981

574.2'9 — Immunogenetics

Hildemann, W. H.. Comprehensive immunogenetics / W.H. Hildemann, E.A. Clark, R.L. Raison. — Oxford : Blackwell Scientific, c1981. — xi,368p : ill ; 24cm
Includes bibliographies and index
ISBN 0-632-00788-5 : £18.75 B81-25908

574.2'9 — Immunogenetics — *Conference proceedings*

Genetic control of natural resistance to infection and malignancy / [proceedings of an international symposium of the Canadian Society for Immunology held in Montreal, Quebec, March 18-20, 1980] ; edited by Emil Skamene, Patricia A.L. Kongshavn, Maurice Landy. — London : Academic Press, 1980. — xxi,598p : ill ; 24cm. — (Perspectives in immunology)
Includes bibliographies and index
ISBN 0-12-647680-2 : £18.60 B81-16783

574.2'9 — Immunology

Cooper, Edwin. General immunology. — Oxford : Pergamon, Aug.1981. — [300]p
ISBN 0-08-026368-2 (cased) : £25.00 : CIP entry
ISBN 0-08-026369-0 (pbk) : £8.75 B81-20617

Eisen, Herman N.. Immunology : an introduction to molecular and cellular principles of the immune responses / Herman N. Eisen. — 2nd ed. — Hagerstown ; London : Harper & Row, 1980. — p290-547,xxxvip : ill ; 26cm
Previous ed.: 1974. — Originally published in : Microbiology. 3rd ed. / B.D. Davis ... [et al.]. — Includes index
ISBN 0-06-140781-x (pbk) : £10.75 B81-20238

Inchley, Christopher J.. Immunobiology / Christopher J. Inchley. — London : Edward Arnold, 1981. — 82p : ill ; 22cm. — (The Institute of Biology's studies in biology, ISSN 0537-9024 ; no.128)
Bibliography: p81-82
ISBN 0-7131-2808-9 (pbk) : £2.50 B81-29283

574.2'9 — Immunology — *Conference proceedings*

International Congress of Immunology *(4th : 1980 : Paris).* Immunology 80 : Fourth International Congress of Immunology / edited by M. Fougereau and J. Dausset. — London : Academic Press, 1980. — xxxii,1279p : ill ; 23cm. — (Progress in immunology ; 4)
Includes biblographies and index
ISBN 0-12-262940-x (pbk) : Unpriced : CIP rev.
ISBN 0-12-262901-9 (v.1 : cased) : £28.60
ISBN 0-12-262902-7 (v.2 : cased) : £28.60
ISBN 0-12-262903-5 (v.3 : cased) : £28.60 B80-29647

Molecules, cells and parasites in immunology / edited by Carlos Larralde ... [et al.] ; Marcella W. Vogt, editorial assistant. — New York ; London : Academic Press, 1980. — xiii,231p : ill,1map ; 24cm
Conference papers. — Includes index
ISBN 0-12-436840-9 : £11.00 B81-21843

574.2'9 — Molecular immunology — *Serials*

Contemporary topics in molecular immunology. — Vol.8. — New York ; London ([88 Middlesex St., E1 7EX]) : Plenum Press, c1981. — xiv,226p
ISBN 0-306-40661-6 : Unpriced
ISSN 0090-8800 B81-32257

574.2'9 — Organisms. Liposomes. Immunological aspects — *Conference proceedings*

Liposomes and immunobiology : proceedings of a national symposium held March 14-15, 1980, in Houston, Texas / edited by Baldwin H. Tom, Howard R. Six. — New York ; Oxford (256 Banbury Rd, Oxford OX2 7DE) : Elsevier/North-Holland, c1980. — xv,333p : ill,ports ; 24cm
Conference papers. — Includes bibliographies and index
ISBN 0-444-00441-6 : £18.27 B81-01896

574.2'9 — Organisms. Liposomes. Immunological aspects - *Conference proceedings*

Liposomes, drugs and immunocompetent cell functions. — London : Academic Press, June 1981. — [200]p
Conference papers
ISBN 0-12-518660-6 : CIP entry B81-14885

574.2'9'028 — Immunology. Laboratory techniques

Immunological methods. — New York ; London : Academic Press
Vol.2 / edited by Ivan Lefkovits, Benvenuto Pernis. — 1981. — 316p : ill ; 24cm
Includes bibliographies and index
ISBN 0-12-442702-2 : £23.20 B81-38905

574.2'9'05 — Immunology — *Serials*

Advances in immunology. — Vol.30. — New York ; London : Academic Press, c1980. — xi,344p
ISBN 0-12-000430-5 : Unpriced
ISSN 0065-2776 B81-29976

Advances in immunology. — Vol.29. — New York ; London : Academic Press, 1980. — xiii,341p
ISBN 0-12-022429-1 : Unpriced
ISSN 0065-2776 B81-09233

574.2'92 — Antigens

Antibody production / edited by L.E. Glynn and M.W. Steward. — Chichester : Wiley, c1981. — ix,231p : ill ; 23cm
Includes bibliographies
ISBN 0-471-27916-1 (pbk) : £4.50 : CIP rev. B80-34983

The **Antigens** / edited by Michael Sela. — New York ; London : Academic
Includes bibliographies and index
Vol.5 / [contributors Joseph P. Brown et al.]. — 1979. — xiii,410p : ill ; 24cm
ISBN 0-12-635505-3 : £24.40 B81-14267

Structure and function of antibodies / edited by L.E. Glynn and M.W. Steward. — Chichester : Wiley, c1981. — ix,306p : ill ; 23cm
Includes bibliographies
ISBN 0-471-27917-x (pbk) : £4.50 : CIP rev. B80-34984

574.2'95 — Immune reactions. Role of lymphokines — *Serials*

Lymphokines : a forum for iommunoregulatory cell products. — Vol.2-. — New York ; London : Academic Press, 1981-. — v. : ill ; 24cm
Continues: Lymphokine reports
£23.20
Primary classification 612'.11822 B81-37249

574.3 — ORGANISMS. DEVELOPMENT

574.3 — Organisms. Development

Biology : form and function. — Milton Keynes : Open University Press. — (Science : a second level course)
At head of title: The Open University prepared by the S202 Course Team. — 1981. — 52p : ill(some col.) ; 30cm. — (S202 ; units 11-13)
Bibliography: p51. — Contents: Unit 11: Development : the component processes — Units 12-13: Cellular differentiation
ISBN 0-335-16034-4 (pbk) : Unpriced B81-25369

Ham, Richard G.. Mechanisms of development / Richard G. Ham, Marilyn J. Veomett. — St. Louis ; London : Mosby, v 1980. — xii,843p : ill ; 24cm
Includes index
ISBN 0-8016-2022-8 : Unpriced B81-08672

574.3 — Organisms. Development *continuation*

Karp, Gerald. Development / Gerald Karp, N.J. Berrill. — 2nd ed. — New York ; London : McGraw-Hill, c1981. — viii,692p : ill ; 25cm
Authors' names in reverse order in previous ed. — Previous ed.: 1976. — Includes bibliographies and index
ISBN 0-07-033340-8 : £15.25 B81-23727

574.3 — Organisms. Development. Genetic aspects

The **Molecular** genetics of development / edited by Terrance Leighton, William F. Loomis. — New York ; London : Academic Press, 1980. — xii,478p : ill ; 24cm. — (Molecular biology)
Includes bibliographies and index
ISBN 0-12-441960-7 : £27.80 B81-21836

Stewart, Alistair D.. The genetic basis of development. — Glasgow : Blackie, Oct.1981. — [230]p. — (Tertiary level biology)
ISBN 0-216-91161-3 (cased) : £17.95 : CIP entry
ISBN 0-216-91160-5 (pbk) : £8.95 B81-27429

574.3'05 — Organisms. Development — *Serials*

Current topics in developmental biology. — Vol.14. — New York ; London : Academic Press, 1980. — ix,381p
ISBN 0-12-153114-7 : Unpriced
ISSN 0070-2153 B81-02396

Current topics in developmental biology. — Vol.15, pt.1. — New York ; London : Academic Press, 1980. — xii,427p
ISBN 0-12-153115-5 : £22.00
ISSN 0070-2153 B81-16736

Current topics in developmental biology. — Vol.16, pt.2. — New York ; London : Academic Press, 1980. — xi,410p
ISBN 0-12-153116-3 : Unpriced
ISSN 0070-2153 B81-20419

574.3'0724 — Organisms. Development. Mathematical models

Ransom, Robert. Computers and embryos : models in developmental biology / Robert Ransom. — Chichester : Wiley, c1981. — xii,212p : ill ; 24cm
Includes bibliographies and index
ISBN 0-471-09972-4 : £14.00 : CIP rev. B81-30521

574.4 — ORGANISMS. ANATOMY

574.4'028 — Organisms. Morphometrics. Use of stereology

Weibel, Ewald R.. Stereological methods / Ewald R. Weibel. — London : Academic Press
Vol.2: Theoretical foundations. — 1980. — xiv,340p : ill ; 24cm
Bibliography: p317-325. — Includes index
ISBN 0-12-742202-1 : £26.00 : CIP rev. B80-20644

574.5 — ECOLOGY

574.5 — Ecology

Budyko, M. I.. Global ecology / M.I. Budyko. — Moscow : Progress Publishers ; [London] : Central Books [distributor], 1980. — 323p : ill,maps ; 21cm
Translation of: Global'naîa ekologiîa. — Bibliography: p313-323
ISBN 0-200-10500-0 : £3.25 B81-03308

Colinvaux, Paul. Why big fierce animals are rare / Paul Colinvaux. — Harmondsworth : Penguin, 1980. — 224p : ill ; 20cm. — (Pelican books)
Originally published: London : Allen and Unwin, 1980. — Bibliography: p210-216. - Includes index
ISBN 0-14-022257-x (pbk) : £1.95 B81-12634

Grant, W. D.. Environmental microbiology. — Glasgow : Blackie, Sept.1981. — [207]p. — (Tertiary level biology)
ISBN 0-216-91153-2 (cased) : £17.95 : CIP entry
ISBN 0-216-91152-4 (pbk) : £8.95 B81-22491

Nebel, Bernard J.. Environmental science : the way the world works / Bernard J. Nebel ; with editorial assistance by Edward J. Kormondy. — Englewood Cliffs ; London : Prentice-Hall, c1981. — xvii,715p : ill,maps ; 25cm
Includes bibliographies and index
ISBN 0-13-283002-7 : £12.30 B81-12960

574.5 — Ecology. Biochemical aspects

Harborne, J. B.. Introduction to ecological biochemistry. — 2nd ed. — London : Academic Press, Feb.1982. — [200]p
Previous ed.: 1977
ISBN 0-12-324680-6 (cased) : CIP entry
ISBN 0-12-324682-2 (pbk) : Unpriced B81-36066

574.5 — Ecology — *For African students*

Ecological biology. — Harlow : Longman
Teacher's guide 2 / D.W. Ewer, J.B. Hall. — 1981. — 352p : ill ; 25cm
Includes index
ISBN 0-582-65053-4 (pbk) : £6.00 B81-37405

574.5 — Ecology — *For children*

Arnold, Neil, *1939-*. The young ecologist / Neil Arnold ; foreword by Tony Soper. — London : Ward Lock, 1981. — 48p : ill(some col.) ; 29cm
Bibliography: p47
ISBN 0-7063-5802-3 : Unpriced : CIP rev.

574.5 — Ecosystems

Anderson, J. M. (Jonathan Michael). Ecology for environmental sciences : biosphere, ecosystems and man / J.M. Anderson. — London : Edward Arnold, 1981. — viii,175p : ill ; 22cm. — (Resource and environmental sciences series)
Bibliography: p160-170. — Includes index
ISBN 0-7131-2814-3 (pbk) : £5.95 : CIP rev. B81-14962

Itô, Y.. Comparative ecology / Y. Itô ; edited and translated by Jiro Kikkawa. — English language ed. — Cambridge : Cambridge University Press, 1980. — xl,436p : ill ; 24cm
Translation of: Hikaku Seitaigaku. 2nd ed. — Bibliography: p373-403. - Includes index
ISBN 0-521-22977-4 (cased) : £20.00
ISBN 0-521-29845-8 (pbk) : £8.95 B81-14496

574.5 — Ecosystems. Assessment — *For environmental conservation*

Spellerberg, Ian F.. Ecological evaluation for conservation / Ian F. Spellerberg. — London : Edward Arnold, 1981. — 60p : ill,2maps ; 22cm. — (The Institute of Biology's studies in biology, ISSN 0537-9024 ; no.133)
Bibliography: p60
ISBN 0-7131-2823-2 (pbk) : £1.95 : CIP rev. B81-13737

574.5 — Ecosystems — *For African students*

Ecological biology. — Harlow : Longman
2: The inter-relations of organisms / editors D.W. Ewer, J.B. Hall
Practical bk. / D.W. Ewer, J.B. Hall. — 1980. — 137p : ill ; 25cm
ISBN 0-582-65046-1 (pbk) : Unpriced B81-26447

574.5 — Organisms. Behaviour. Implications of economic aspects of resource allocation

Limits to action : the allocation of individual behaviour / edited by J.E.R. Staddon. — New York ; London : Academic Press, 1981. — xix,308p : ill ; 24cm
Includes bibliographies and index
ISBN 0-12-662650-2 : £13.60 B81-35748

574.5'01'51 — Ecology. Mathematics

Vandermeer, John. Elementary mathematical ecology / John Vandermeer. — New York ; Chichester : Wiley, c1981. — x,294p : ill ; 24cm
Includes bibliographies and index
ISBN 0-471-08131-0 : £20.00 B81-24224

574.5'02462 — Ecology — *For engineering*

Camougis, George. Environmental biology for engineers : a guide to environmental assessment / George Camougis. — New York ; London : McGraw-Hill, c1981. — viii,214p : ill,1map ; 25cm
Bibliography: p193-211. — Includes index
ISBN 0-07-009677-5 : £17.50 B81-10121

574.5'06'0421 — Ecology action groups: London Greenpeace Group — *Serials*

[Newsletter *(London Greenpeace Group)*]. Newsletter / London Greenpeace Group. — [No.1]-. — London (Endsleigh St., WC1) : Greenpeace (London), [197?]-. — v. : ill ; 30cm
Five issues yearly. — Description based on: April 1979 issue
ISSN 0260-7395 = Newsletter — London Greenpeace Group : Unpriced B81-05588

574.5'0724 — Ecology. Mathematical models

Theoretical ecology : principles and applications / edited by Robert M. May. — 2nd ed. — Oxford : Blackwell Scientific, 1981. — ix,489p : ill ; 25cm
Previous ed.: 1976. — Bibliography: p419-468. — Includes index
ISBN 0-632-00768-0 (cased) : £20.00
ISBN 0-632-00762-1 (pbk) : £10.80 B81-26838

574.5'0998'9 — Antarctic. Ecosystems — *Conference proceedings*

Ecology in the Antarctic : papers presented at a meeting held on 11 October 1979 organised by the Linnean Society of London / edited by W.N. Bonner and R.J. Berry. — London : Published for the Linnean Society of London [by] Academic Press, c1980. — vii,150p,[1] folded leaf of plates : ill,maps ; 26cm
'Reprinted from the Biological journal of the Linnean Society, v.14, no.1, 1980'. — Includes bibliographies
ISBN 0-12-114950-1 (pbk) : £9.60 B81-14602

574.5'2 — Earth. Carbon cycle. Mathematical models — *Conference proceedings*

Carbon cycle modelling. — Chichester : Wiley, Sept.1981. — [404]p. — (SCOPE ; 16)
Conference papers
ISBN 0-471-10051-x : £20.00 : CIP entry B81-20564

574.5'222 — Biogeochemical cycles

Some perspectives of the major biogeochemical cycles / edited by Gene E. Likens. — Chichester : Published on behalf of the Scientific Committee on Problems of the Environment (SCOPE) of the International Council of Scientific Unions by Wiley, c1981. — xiii,175p : ill,maps ; 24cm. — (SCOPE ; 17)
Conference papers. — Includes bibliographies and index
ISBN 0-471-27989-7 : £11.00 : CIP rev. B81-23737

574.5'222 — Ecosystems. Bioenergetics

Miller, David H. (David Hewitt). Energy at the surface of the earth : an introduction to the energetics of ecosystems / David H. Miller. — New York ; London : Academic Press, c1981. — xvii,516p : ill ; 24cm. — (International geophysics series ; v.27)
Includes bibliographies and index
ISBN 0-12-497150-4 : Unpriced B81-40478

574.5'222 — Ecosystems. Effects of stress — *Conference proceedings*

Stress effects on natural ecosystems. — Chichester : Wiley, Apr.1981. — [256]p. — (Environmental monographs and symposia)
ISBN 0-471-27834-3 : £20.00 : CIP entry B81-02106

574.5'222 — Great Britain. Organisms. Effects of agriculture

Mellanby, Kenneth. Farming and wildlife / Kenneth Mellanby. — London : Collins, 1981. — 178p,24p of plates : ill,maps ; 23cm. — (The New naturalist ; 67)
Bibliography: p169-174. — Includes index
ISBN 0-00-219239-x : £9.50 B81-23589

574.5'222 — Organisms. Effects of natural disasters — *Conference proceedings*

Spring Systematics Symposium *(3rd : 1980 : Field Museum of Natural History)*. Biotic crises in ecological and evolutionary time / [proceedings of the third Annual Spring Systematics Symposium held at the Field Museum of Natural History, Chicago, Illinois, May 10, 1980] ; edited by Matthew H. Nitecki. — New York ; London : Academic Press, 1981. — xi,301p : ill,maps ; 24cm
Includes bibliographies and index
ISBN 0-12-519640-7 : Unpriced B81-29790

574.5′223 — Ecosystems. Influence of man — *For schools*
Tivy, Joy. Human impact on the ecosystem. — Edinburgh : Oliver and Boyd, Oct.1981. — [244]p. — (Conceptual frameworks in geography)
ISBN 0-05-003424-3 (cased) : £7.50 : CIP entry
ISBN 0-05-003203-8 (pbk) : £4.75 B81-25786

574.5′223 — Environment. Role of microorganisms
Burdick, Eric. Invisible life. — London : Macmillan, Sept.1981. — [192]p
ISBN 0-333-29142-5 : £6.95 : CIP entry B81-23943

574.5′24 — Organisms. Competition
Pontin, A. J.. Competition and coexistence of species. — London : Pitman, Feb.1982. — [105]p
ISBN 0-273-08489-5 : £8.95 : CIP entry B81-35777

574.5′24′094 — Europe. Wall ecosystems
Darlington, Arnold. Ecology of walls. — London : Heinemann Educational, Sept.1981. — [128]p
ISBN 0-435-60222-5 (pbk) : £8.50 : CIP entry
ISBN 0-435-60223-3 (pbk) : £3.95 B81-22635

574.5′248 — Organisms. Population. Dynamics
Berryman, Alan A.. Population systems : a general introduction / Alan A. Berryman. — New York ; London : Plenum, c1981. — xv,222p : ill ; 24cm. — (Population ecology)
Includes index
ISBN 0-306-40589-x : Unpriced B81-24236

574.5′248 — Organisms. Population. Dynamics. Mathematical models
Nisbet, R. M.. Modelling fluctuating populations. — Chichester : Wiley, Jan.1982. — [416]p
ISBN 0-471-28058-5 : £22.50 : CIP entry B81-34412

574.5′248 — Organisms. Population. Effects of environment
Begon, Michael. Population ecology : a unified study of animals and plants / Michael Begon, Martin Mortimer. — Oxford : Blackwell Scientific, 1981. — vii,200p : ill ; 25cm
Bibliography: p185-192. — Includes index
ISBN 0-632-00812-1 (cased) : £15.00 : CIP rev.
ISBN 0-632-00667-6 (pbk) : £7.00 B81-13481

574.5′248′0724 — Organisms. Population. Dynamics. Mathematical models — *Conference proceedings*
The **Mathematical** theory of the dynamics of biological populations II : based on the proceedings of a conference on The Mathematical theory of the dynamics of biological populations organised by the Institute of Mathematics and its Applications and held in Oxford, 1st-3rd July 1980 / edited by R.W. Hiorns, D. Cooke. — London : Academic Press, 1981. — xii,327p : ill ; 24cm
Includes bibliographies and index
ISBN 0-12-348780-3 : £14.50 : CIP rev. B81-06063

574.5′249 — Parasitology
Schmidt, Gerald D.. Foundations of parasitology / Gerald D. Schmidt, Larry S. Roberts. — 2nd ed. — St. Louis ; London : Mosby, 1981. — x,795p : ill(some col.),maps,facsims ; 24cm
Previous ed.: 1977. — Includes bibliographies and index
ISBN 0-8016-4344-9 (pbk) : £16.25 B81-32996

Trends and perspectives in parasitology. — Cambridge : Cambridge University Press
1 / edited by D.W.T. Crompton and B.A. Newton. — 1981. — 101p,6,3p of plates : ill ; 27cm
Includes bibliographies
ISBN 0-521-23821-8 (cased) : £9.50 : CIP rev.
ISBN 0-521-28242-x (pbk) : £4.50 B81-16354

574.5′2621 — Polar ecosystems
Money, D. C.. Polar ice and periglacial lands / D.C. Money. — London : Evans, 1980. — 48p : ill,maps ; 21cm. — (Environmental systems)
Bibliography: p46-47
ISBN 0-237-29266-1 (pbk) : £1.20 B81-00110

574.52′63 — Aquatic ecosystems. Effects of toxic materials — *Conference proceedings*
Ecotoxicology and the aquatic environment. — Oxford : Pergamon, Dec.1981. — [100]p. — (Water science and technology)
Conference papers
ISBN 0-08-029092-2 : £17.50 : CIP entry B81-32040

574.5′263′0724 — Aquatic ecosystems. Mathematical models
Beyer, Jan E.. Aquatic ecosystems : an operational research approach / Jan E. Beyer. — Seattle ; London : University of Washington Press, c1981. — ix,317p : ill,maps ; 22cm
Bibliography: p301-315
ISBN 0-295-95719-0 : £14.00 B81-39804

574.5′2632 — Freshwater ecosystems
The **functioning** of freshwater ecosystems / edited by E.D. Le Cren and R.H. Lowe-McConnell. — Cambridge : Cambridge University Press, 1980. — xxix,588p : ill,maps ; 24cm. — (International Biological Programme ; 22)
English text, English, French, Russian and Spanish contents pages. — Maps on lining papers. — Bibliography: p505-570. — Includes index
ISBN 0-521-22507-8 : £40.00 B81-00886

574.5′2632′0941 — Great Britain. Freshwater ecosystems
Maitland, Peter S.. Synoptic limnology : the analysis of British freshwater ecosystems / Peter S. Maitland. — Edinburgh (78 Craighall Rd, Edinburgh) : Institute of Terrestrial Ecology, 1979. — 28p : ill,maps ; 30cm
At head of title: Natural Environment Research Council. Institute of Terrestrial Ecology. — Bibliography: p28
ISBN 0-904282-30-9 (pbk) : £3.00 B81-38370

574.5′2632′0967 — Africa. Tropical regions. Freshwater ecosystems
Beadle, L. C.. The inland waters of tropical Africa. — 2nd ed. — London : Longman, Nov.1981. — [448]p
Previous ed.: 1974
ISBN 0-582-46341-6 : £28.00 : CIP entry B81-30154

574.5′26322 — Hypertrophic lakes — *Conference proceedings*
S.I.L. Workshop on Hypertrophic Ecosystems *(1979 : Växjö)*. Hypertrophic ecosystems : S.I.L. Workshop on Hypertrophic Ecosystems held at Vaxjo, September 10-14, 1979 / edited by J. Barica and L.R. Mur. — The Hague ; London : Junk, 1980. — xv,348p : ill,maps ; 27cm. — (Developments in hydrobiology ; 2)
Includes bibliographies
ISBN 90-619-3752-3 : Unpriced
ISBN 90-619-3751-5 B81-22133

574.5′26322′09411 — Scotland. Large lochs. Lake ecosystems
The **Ecology** of Scotland′s largest lochs : Lomond, Awe, Ness, Morar and Shiel / edited by Peter S. Maitland. — The Hague ; London : Junk, 1981. — xiv,297p : ill,maps ; 25cm. — (Monographiae biologicae ; v.44)
Includes bibliographies and index
ISBN 90-619-3097-9 : Unpriced B81-36726

574.5′26325 — South-eastern United States. Bottomland hardwood forests. Wetlands. Ecology — *Conference proceedings*
Wetlands of bottomland hardwood forests. — Oxford : Elsevier Scientific, Sept.1981. — [450] p. — (Developments in agricultural and managed forest ecology ; v.11)
Conference proceedings
ISBN 0-444-42020-7 : CIP entry B81-28179

574.5′2636 — Coastal ecosystems
Mann, K. H.. Ecology of coastal waters. — Oxford : Blackwell Scientific, Jan.1982. — [320]p. — (Studies in ecology ; v.8)
ISBN 0-632-00669-2 : £13.00 : CIP entry B81-38291

574.5′2636 — Environment. Adaptation of marine organisms
Functional adaptations of marine organisms / edited by F. John Vernberg, Winona B. Vernberg. — New York ; London : Academic Press, c1981. — xi,347p : ill,maps ; 24cm. — (Physiological ecology)
Includes bibliographies and index
ISBN 0-12-718280-2 : £22.20 B81-35362

574.5′2636 — Marine benthic organisms. Ecology
Gray, John S.. The ecology of marine sediments / John S. Gray. — Cambridge : Cambridge University Press, 1981. — xi,185p : ill ; 23cm. — (Cambridge studies in modern biology ; 2)
Bibliography: p172-177. — Includes index
ISBN 0-521-23553-7 (cased) : £15.00 : CIP rev.
ISBN 0-521-28027-3 (pbk) : £6.95 B81-13805

574.5′2636 — Marine ecosystems
Analysis of marine ecosystems / [edited by] A.R. Longhurst. — London : Academic Press, 1981. — xxii,741p : ill,charts,maps ; 24cm
Includes bibliographies and index
ISBN 0-12-455560-8 : £52.00 : CIP rev. B80-27014

Estuaries and enclosed seas. — Oxford : Elsevier Scientific, Dec.1981. — [350]p. — (Ecosystems of the world ; v.26)
ISBN 0-444-41921-7 : CIP entry
Primary classification 574.5′26365 B81-31621

Marine ecology. — Chichester : Wiley
Vol.5: Ocean management
Pt.1. — Feb.1982. — [576]p
ISBN 0-471-27997-8 : £33.00 : CIP entry B81-35922

Tait, R. V.. Elements of marine ecology : an introductory course / R.V. Tait. — 3rd ed. — London : Butterworths, 1981. — 356p : ill,maps ; 24cm
Previous ed.: 1972. — Includes bibliographies and index
ISBN 0-408-71054-3 (pbk) : Unpriced : CIP rev. B80-29654

574.5′2636 — Marine ecosystems. Effects of ocean hydrodynamics — *Conference proceedings*
International Liège Colloquium on Ocean Hydrodynamics *(12th : 1980)*. Ecohydrodynamics : proceedngs of the 12th International Liège Colloquium on Ocean Hydrodynamics / edited by Jacques C.J. Nihoul. — Amsterdam ; Oxford : Elsevier, 1981. — xii,359p : ill,maps ; 25cm. — (Elsevier oceanography series ; 32)
Includes index
ISBN 0-444-41969-1 : Unpriced : CIP rev. B81-08927

574.5′2636 — Marine ecosystems. Effects of pollution of oceans by petroleum
Neff, Jerry M.. Response of marine animals to petroleum and specific petroleum hydrocarbons / Jerry M. Neff and Jack W. Anderson. — London : Applied Science, c1981. — x,177p : ill ; 23cm
Bibliography: p155-170. — Includes index
ISBN 0-85334-953-3 : £15.00 : CIP rev. B81-12799

574.5′2636 — Marine ecosystems. Effects of pollution of oceans by petroleum — *Conference proceedings*
Petroleum and the marine environment : PETROMAR 80 / Eurocean ; under the high patronage of HSH Prince Rainier III of Monaco. — London : Graham & Trotman, 1981. — vi,788p : ill,maps ; 30cm
Conference papers
ISBN 0-86010-215-7 (pbk) : £35.00 B81-34081

574.5′2636 — Marine organisms. Effects of pollution of oceans. Biological monitoring — *Conference proceedings*
Pollution and Physiology of Marine Organisms *(Conference : 1979 : Milford, Conn.)*. Biological monitoring of marine pollutants / [proceedings of a symposium on Pollution and Physiology of Marine Organisms, held in Milford, Connecticutt, November 7-9, 1979] ; edited by F. John Vernberg ... [et al.]. — New York ; London : Academic Press, 1981. — xiii,559p : ill,maps ; 24cm
Includes bibliographies and index
ISBN 0-12-718450-3 : £22.80 B81-38696

574.5'2636 — Organisms. Effects of pollution of oceans by petroleum
Oil pollution and wildlife / Nature Conservancy Council. — London (19 Belgrave Sq., SW1X 8PY) : The Council, c1979. — 1folded sheet (([6]p)) : col.ill ; 21cm
ISBN 0-86139-014-8 : Unpriced B81-01965

574.5'2636'072041 — Marine ecosystems. Research organisations: Institute for Marine Environmental Research — *Serials*
Institute for Marine Environmental Research. Report / Institute for Marine Environmental Research. — 1973-1974. — Plymouth (67, Citadel Rd., Plymouth, Devon PL1 3DH) : The Institute, 1974. — 71p
Unpriced B81-09080

Institute for Marine Environmental Research. Report / Institute for Marine Environmental Research. — 1974-1975. — Plymouth (67, Citadel Rd., Plymouth, Devon PL1 3DH) : The Institute, 1975. — 85p
Unpriced B81-09081

574.5'26365 — Estuary ecosystems
Estuaries and enclosed seas. — Oxford : Elsevier Scientific, Dec.1981. — [350]p. — (Ecosystems of the world ; v.26)
ISBN 0-444-41921-7 : CIP entry
Also classified at 574.5'2636 B81-31621

McLusky, Donald S.. The estuarine ecosystem / Donald S. McLusky. — Glasgow : Blackie, 1981. — viii,150p : ill,maps ; 21cm. — (Tertiary level biology)
Bibliography: p132-143. - Includes index
ISBN 0-216-91115-x (cased) : £12.75 : CIP rev.
ISBN 0-216-91116-8 (pbk) : £6.25 B81-06596

574.5'2638 — Rocky seashore. Ecology
Brehaut, Roger N.. Ecology of rocky shores. — London : Edward Arnold, Dec.1981. — [64]p. — (The Institute of Biology's studies in biology, ISSN 0537-9024 ; no.139)
ISBN 0-7131-2839-9 (pbk) : £1.95 : CIP entry B81-30996

574.5'2638 — Seashore. Benthic ecosystems — *Conference proceedings*
The **Shore** environment / edited by J.H. Price, D.E.G. Irvine and W.F. Farnham. — London : Published for the Systematics Association by Academic Press, 1980. — 2v.(xx,945p) : ill,maps ; 24cm. — (The Systematics Association special volume, ISSN 0309-2593 ; no.17)
Conference papers. — Includes bibliographies and index
ISBN 0-12-564701-8 : Unpriced : CIP rev.
ISBN 0-12-564702-6 (v.2) : £48.20 B80-23261

574.5'264 — Heathland ecosystems & shrubland ecosystems
Heathlands and related shrublands : analytical studies / edited by R.L. Specht. — Amsterdam ; Oxford : Elsevier Scientific, 1981. — xvi,385p : ill,maps ; 27cm. — (Ecosystems of the world ; 9B)
Map on lining papers. — Includes bibliographies and index
ISBN 0-444-41809-1 : £31.37
ISBN 0-444-41810-5 (set) B81-15498

574.5'264 — Land ecosystems. Radioisotopes. Distribution
Bocock, K. L.. Radionuclides in terrestrial ecosystems : a review of their distribution and movement / K.L. Bocock. — Cambridge (68 Hills Rd., Cambridge CB2 1LA) : Institute of Terrestrial Ecology, 1981. — ix,27p : 1ill ; 30cm
At head of title: Natural Environment Research Council, Institute of Terrestrial Ecology. — Bibliography: p24-27
ISBN 0-904282-49-x (pbk) : £2.00 B81-25390

574.5'264 — Mediterranean climatic regions. Shrubland ecosystems
Mediterranian-type shrublands / edited by Francesco di Castri, David W. Goodall and Raymond L. Specht. — Amsterdam ; Oxford : Elsevier Scientific, 1981. — xii,643p : ill,maps ; 27cm. — (Ecosystems of the world ; 11)
Maps on lining papers. — Includes bibliographies and index
ISBN 0-444-41858-x : Unpriced : CIP rev. B80-25613

574.5'264'072041 — Great Britain. Land ecosystems. Research organizations: Institute of Terrestrial Ecology — *Serials*
Institute of Terrestrial Ecology. Annual report / Natural Environment Research Council, Institute of Terrestrial Ecology. — 1979. — Cambridge (68 Hills Rd, Cambridge CB2 1LA) : The Institute, 1980. — 154p
ISBN 0-904282-43-0 : £5.00
ISSN 0308-1125 B81-04954

574.5'2642 — Forest ecosystems
Dynamic properties of forest ecosystems / edited by D.E. Reichle. — Cambridge : Cambridge University Press, 1981. — xxvi,683p : ill,1map ; 24cm. — (International biological programme ; 23)
Includes contents lists in French, Russian and Spanish. — Includes bibliographies and index
ISBN 0-521-22508-6 : £50.00 B81-16287

574.5'2642 — Jungle ecosystems
Jungles / edited by Edward S. Ayensu. — London : Cape, 1980. — 200p : ill(some col.),col.maps,ports ; 32cm
Includes index
ISBN 0-224-01881-7 : £16.00 : CIP rev. B80-18726

574.5'2642 — North America. Taiga. Ecosystems
Larsen, James A.. The boreal ecosystem / James A. Larsen. — New York ; London : Academic Press, 1980. — xvi,500p : ill,maps ; 24cm. — (Physiological ecology)
Includes bibliographies and index
ISBN 0-12-436880-8 : £29.00 B81-15123

574.5'2642 — Tropical rain forest ecosystems — *For children*
Eden, Michael. Rain-forests. — London : Bodley Head, Oct.1981. — [24]p. — (The Young geographers)
ISBN 0-370-30369-5 : £2.75 : CIP entry B81-25769

574.5'2642'0913 — Tropical rain forest ecosystems
Money, D. C.. Tropical rainforests / D.C. Money. — London : Evans, 1980. — 48p : ill,maps ; 21cm. — (Environmental systems)
Bibliography: p45
ISBN 0-237-29272-6 (pbk) : £1.20 B81-00111

574.5'2643 — Cumbria. Hampsfell. Bracken. Primary productivity
Chen, Ling-zhi. Primary production, decomposition and nutrient cycling in a bracken grassland ecosystem / by Ling-Zhi Chen and D.K. Lindley. — Grange-over-Sands (Merlewood Research Station, Grange-over-Sands, Cumbria LA11 6JU) : Institute of Terrestrial Ecology, 1981. — i,66p : ill ; 30cm. — (Merlewood research and development paper, ISSN 0308-3675 ; no.80)
Bibliography: p64-66
Unpriced (pbk) B81-13157

574.5'2643'0722 — Cornwall. North Cornwall *(District).* **Field ecosystems** — *Case studies*
Allaby, Michael. A year in the life of a field / Michael Allaby. — Newton Abbot : David & Charles, c1981. — 208p : ill,ports ; 24cm
Bibliography: p205-206. — Includes index
ISBN 0-7153-7889-9 : £7.95 B81-08704

574.5'2644 — Tundra ecosystems
Tundra ecosystems : a comparative analysis / edited by L.C. Bliss, O.W. Heal, J.J. Moore [i.e. Moor]. — Cambridge : Cambridge University Press, 1981. — xxxvi,813p : ill ; 24cm. — (The International Biological Programme ; 25)
Includes bibliographies and index
ISBN 0-521-22776-3 : £55.00 : CIP rev. B81-03151

574.5'265 — Arid region ecosystems
Arid-land ecosystems : structure, functioning and management / edited by D.W. Goodall, R.A. Perry with the assistance of K.M.W. Howes. — Cambridge : Cambridge University Press. — (International Biological Programme ; 17)
Vol.2. — 1981. — xvii,605p : ill ; 24cm
Includes bibliographies and index
ISBN 0-521-22988-x : £50.00 B81-11200

574.5'2652'0912 — Temperate regions. Desert ecosystems
Temperate deserts and semi-deserts. — Oxford : Elsevier Scientific, Nov.1981. — [250]p. — (Ecosystems of the world ; 5)
ISBN 0-444-41931-4 : CIP entry B81-31195

574.5'2652'0966 — Sahara Desert. Ecology, *to 1980* — *Conference proceedings*
The **Sahara** : ecological change and early economic history / edited by J.A. Allan ; with contributions by G. Barker ... [et al.] ; the proceedings of a conference convened by the Centre of African Studies in association with the Centre of Middle Eastern Studies, the School of Oriental & African Studies, University of London. — Outwell : Middle East and North African Studies, 1981. — xii,146p : ill,maps ; 21cm. — (Menas monograph ; no.1)
Includes bibliographies
ISBN 0-906559-04-9 (pbk) : £4.50
Also classified at 330.966 B81-31132

574.5'267'099435 — Island ecosystems — *Study regions: Queensland. Great Barrier Reef. One-Tree Island*
Heatwole, Harold. Community ecology of a coral cay : a study of One-Tree Island, Great Barrier Reef, Australia / Harold Heatwole, Terence Done, Elizabeth Cameron. — The Hague ; London : Junk, 1981. — xiv,379p : ill,1map ; 25cm. — (Mongraphiae biologicae ; v.43)
Bibliography: p363-375. — Includes index
ISBN 90-619-3096-0 : Unpriced B81-36727

574.5'3 — Organisms. Feeding & nutrition. Evolutionary aspects
Physiological ecology. — Oxford : Blackwell Scientific, Aug.1981. — [416]p
ISBN 0-632-00555-6 (cased) : £18.00 : CIP entry
ISBN 0-632-00617-x (pbk) : £8.50 B81-20590

574.5'43 — Autumn — *For children*
Allington, Richard L.. Beginning to learn about autumn. — Oxford : Blackwell Raintree, Oct.1981. — [32]p
ISBN 0-86256-047-0 : £2.50 : CIP entry B81-30564

574.5'43 — Great Britain. Organisms. Winter life — *School texts*
Bishop, O. N.. Winter biology. — Cambridge : Cambridge University Press, Oct.1981. — [64]p
ISBN 0-521-28176-8 : £1.95 : CIP entry B81-30481

574.5'43 — Great Britain. Woodlands. Autumn life & winter life — *For children*
Imrie, Jean. Woodland in autumn & winter / Jean Imrie. — London : Adam & Charles Black, c1981. — 48p : ill(some col.) ; 21cm. — (Black's picture information books)
Adaptation of: Bos in herbst en winter / by G. den Hoed. — Bibliography: p45. — Includes index
ISBN 0-7136-2117-6 : £3.50 : CIP rev. B81-10475

574.5'43 — Great Britain. Woodlands. Spring life & summer life — *For children*
Imrie, Jean. Woodland in spring & summer / Jean Imrie. — London : Adam & Charles Black, c1981. — 48p : ill(some col.) ; 21cm. — (Black's picture information books)
Adaptation of: Bos in lente en zomer / by G. den Hoed. — Bibliography: p45. — Includes index
ISBN 0-7136-2116-8 : £3.50 B81-33659

574.5'43 — Seasons — *For children*
Leutscher, Alfred. A walk through the seasons / written by Alfred Leutscher ; [illustrations Graham Allen ... et al.] ; [editor Sue Tarsky]. — London : Methuen/Walker, 1981. — 137p : col.ill,1map ; 28cm
Bibliography: p130. — Includes index
ISBN 0-416-05710-1 : £7.95 B81-21444

574.5'43 — Spring — *For children*
Allington, Richard L.. Beginning to learn about spring. — Oxford : Blackwell Raintree, Oct.1981. — [32]p
ISBN 0-86256-045-4 : £2.50 : CIP entry B81-30562

574.5'43 — Summer — *For children*
Allington, Richard L.. Beginning to learn about summer. — Oxford : Blackwell Raintree, Oct.1981. — [32]p
ISBN 0-86256-046-2 : £2.50 : CIP entry
B81-30563

574.5'43 — Winter — *For children*
Allington, Richard L.. Beginning to learn about winter. — Oxford : Blackwell Raintree, Oct.1981. — [32]p
ISBN 0-86256-044-6 : £2.50 : CIP entry
B81-30439

574.5'43'0222 — Seasons — *Illustrations — For children*
Craig, Helen. The months of the year / by Helen Craig. — [London] : Aurum, c1981. — 1folded sheet ; 168x6cm folded to 6x6cm : col.ill
In slip case
ISBN 0-906053-18-8 (unbound) : £1.95
B81-16036

574.5'43'0941 — Great Britain. Organisms. Seasonal variation — *Personal observations*
Hatton, Austin. The nature year : once around the sun - / by Austin Hatton ; illustrations by N.W. Cusa. — [London] : Sunday telegraph, c1979. — 123p : ill ; 19cm
£1.95 (pbk) B81-04439

574.5'43'09422 — South-east England. Rural regions. Seasons
Clucas, Philip. Country seasons / written, photographed, illustrated and designed by Philip Clucas. — Leicester : Windward, c1978. — 155p : ill(some col.) ; 33cm
Includes index
ISBN 0-904681-39-4 : £5.95 B81-11563

574.8 — ORGANISMS. HISTOLOGY AND CYTOLOGY

574.8'21 — Histochemistry
Histochemistry. — Chichester : Wiley, Nov.1981. — [312]p
ISBN 0-471-10010-2 : £25.00 : CIP entry
B81-30519

574.87 — Cytology
Advanced cell biology / Lazar M. Schwartz and Miguel M. Azar, editors. — New York ; London : Van Nostrand Reinhold, c1981. — xix,1175p : ill ; 24cm
Includes index
ISBN 0-442-27471-8 : £29.65 B81-29555

574.87 — Organisms. Cells
Avers, Charlotte J.. Cell biology / Charlotte J. Avers. — 2nd ed. — New York ; London : D. Van Nostrand, c1981. — xvi,485p : ill(some col.) ; 24cm
Previous ed.: 1976. — Text on lining papers. — Includes bibliographies and index
ISBN 0-442-25770-8 : £18.70 B81-26430

De Robertis, E. D. P.. Essentials of cell and molecular biology / E.D.P. De Robertis, E.M.F. De Robertis, Jr.. — Philadelphia ; London : Saunders College, c1981. — xi,395p : ill(some col.) ; 25cm
Includes bibliographies and index
ISBN 0-03-057713-6 : £11.95 B81-31690

574.87 — Organisms. Cells. Evolution. Role of symbiosis
Margulis, Lynn. Symbiosis in cell evolution : life and its environment on the early earth / Lynn Margulis. — Oxford : W.H. Freeman, c1981. — xxii,419p : ill ; 24cm
Bibliography: p365-392. — Includes index
ISBN 0-7167-1255-5 (cased) : £16.40
ISBN 0-7167-1256-3 (pbk) : £9.20 B81-33656

574.87 — Organisms. Eukaryotic cells. Evolution
Tribe, Michael A.. The evolution of eukaryotic cells / Michael Tribe, Andrew Morgan, Peter Whittaker. — London : Edward Arnold, 1981. — 60p : ill ; 22cm. — (The Institute of Biology's studies in biology, ISSN 0537-9024 ; no.131)
Bibliography: p59-60
ISBN 0-7131-2821-6 (pbk) : £1.95 : CIP rev.
B81-25693

574.87'028 — Cytology. Laboratory techniques — *Serials*
Methods in cell biology. — Vol.21. — New York ; London : Academic Press, 1980. — xvii,512p
ISBN 0-12-564140-0 : Unpriced B81-08251

574.87'028 — Organisms. Cells. Experiments — *Manuals — For schools*
Units of life. — St. Albans : Hart-Davis Educational, 1981, c1980. — 31p : ill ; 21cm. — (Centre science)
ISBN 0-247-13129-6 (unbound) : £0.40
B81-24514

574.87'05 — Cytology — *Serials*
International review of cytology. — Vol.69. — New York ; London : Academic Press, 1981. — ix,339p
ISBN 0-12-364469-0 : Unpriced
ISSN 0074-7696 B81-24154

International review of cytology. — Vol.70. — New York ; London : Academic Press, 1981. — ix,351p
ISBN 0-12-364470-4 : Unpriced
ISSN 0074-7696 B81-32670

International review of cytology. Supplement. — 11B. — New York ; London : Academic Press, 1980. — xix,257p
ISBN 0-12-364372-4 : Unpriced
ISSN 0074-770x B81-20031

574.87'072 — Organisms. Cells. Mathematical models
Mathematical models in molecular and cellular biology / edited by Lee A. Segel. — Cambridge : Cambridge University Press, 1980. — ix,757p : ill ; 24cm
Includes bibliographies and index
ISBN 0-521-22925-1 : £45.00
Primary classification 574.8'8'072 B81-09822

574.87'2 — Organisms. Cells. Structure
Steer, Martin W.. Understanding cell structure / Martin W. Steer. — Cambridge : Cambridge University Press, 1981. — viii,126p : ill ; 24cm
Bibliography: p117-124. - Includes index
ISBN 0-521-23745-9 (cased) : £12.50
ISBN 0-521-28198-9 (pbk) : £4.95 B81-14498

574.87'2 — Organisms. Cells. Structure. Evolutionary aspects
Dillon, Lawrence S.. Ultrastructure, macromolecules and evolution / Lawrence S. Dillon. — New York ; London : Plenum, c1981. — viii,708p : ill ; 24cm
Bibliography: p567-699. — Includes index
ISBN 0-306-40528-8 : Unpriced B81-37467

574.87'3 — Organisms. Cells. Microtubules — *Conference proceedings*
International Symposium on Microtubules and Microtubule Inhibitors *(2nd : 1980 : Beerse)*. Microtubules and microtubule inhibitors 1980 : proceedings of the 2nd International Symposium on Microtubules and Microtubule Inhibitors, Beerse, Belgium, 26-29 August, 1980 / organized by the Janssen Research Foundation under the auspices of the Belgian Society for Cell Biology ; chaired by P. Dustin and K.R. Porter ; editors M. De Brabander and J. De May. — Amsterdam ; Oxford : Elsevier/North Holland Biomedical, 1980. — x,576p : ill ; 25cm. — (Janssen Research Foundation series ; v.3)
Includes index
ISBN 0-444-80305-x : £31.27 B81-09437

574.87'3'0222 — Organisms. Cells. Ultrastructure — *Illustrations*
Fawcett, Don W.. [The cell, its organelles and inclusions]. The cell / Don W. Fawcett. — 2nd ed. — Philadelphia ; London : Saunders, 1981. — viii,862p : ill ; 27cm
Previous ed.: published as The cell, its organelles and inclusions, 1966. — Includes bibliographies and index
ISBN 0-7216-3584-9 : £22.75 B81-26961

574.87'32 — Organisms. Cells. Nuclei
The Cell nucleus / edited by Harris Busch. — New York ; London : Academic Press
Vol.8: Nuclear particles
Pt.A. — 1981. — xxi,401p : ill ; 24cm
Includes bibliographies and index
ISBN 0-12-147608-1 : £31.40 B81-38920

574.87'32 — Organisms. Chromatin
Bradbury, E. Morton. DNA, chromatin and chromosomes / E. Morton Bradbury, Norman Maclean, Harry R. Matthews. — Oxford : Blackwell Scientific, 1981. — xvii,281p : ill ; 24cm
Includes bibliographies and index
ISBN 0-632-00355-3 (pbk) : £9.80 B81-40186

Bradbury, E. Morton. DNA, chromatin and chromosomes. — Oxford : Blackwell Scientific Publications, June 1981. — [224]p
ISBN 0-632-00554-8 (pbk) : £8.50 : CIP entry
B81-09497

574.87'32 — Organisms. Recombinant DNA — *Conference proceedings*
Cleveland Symposium on Macromolecules *(3rd : 1981)*. Recombinant DNA. — Oxford : Elsevier Scientific, Dec.1981. — [316]p
ISBN 0-444-42039-8 : CIP entry B81-33862

574.87'322 — Chromosomes — *Conference proceedings*
International Chromosome Conference *(7th : 1980 : Oxford)*. Chromosomes today. — London : Allen & Unwin
Vol.7: Proceedings of the Seventh International Chromosome Conference held in Oxford, England, 26-31 August 1980 / editors M.D. Bennett, M. Bobrow, G. Hewitt. — 1981. — xxiii,310p : ill ; 24cm
Includes bibliographies and index
ISBN 0-04-575021-1 : Unpriced : CIP rev.
B81-15875

574.87'322 — Gene expression
Lewin, Benjamin. Gene expression / Benjamin Lewin. — New York ; Chichester : Wiley. — xv,1160p : ill ; 25cm
ISBN 0-471-01977-1 (cased) : £25.65
ISBN 0-471-01976-3 (pbk) : £13.25 B81-18757

574.87'322 — Genetic information. Organisation — *Conference proceedings*
Miami Winter Symposium *(1980)*. Mobilization and reassembly of genetic information : proceedings of the Miami Winter Symposium, January 1980 : sponsored by the Department of Biochemistry, University of Miami School of Medicine, Miami, Florida and by the Papanicolaou Cancer Research Institute, Miami, Florida / edited by Walter A. Scott ... [et al.]. — New York ; London : Academic Press, 1980. — xx,459p : ill ; 24cm
ISBN 0-12-633360-2 : £22.40 B81-14561

574.87'322 — Organisms. Cells. Chromosomes. Analysis. Laboratory techniques
Sharma, Arun Kumar. Chromosome techniques : theory and practice / Arun Kumar Sharma and Archana Sharma. — 3rd ed. — London : Butterworths, 1980. — xii,711p : ill ; 24cm
Previous ed.: 1972. — Includes bibliographies and index
ISBN 0-408-70942-1 : £50.00 : CIP rev.
B80-04789

574.87'322 — Organisms. Cells. Genes. Molecular biology — *Serials*
Gene amplification and analysis. — Vol.1-. — New York ; New York ; Oxford : Elsevier/North-Holland, c1981. — v. : ; 25cm
Annual
Unpriced B81-30734

574.87'322 — Organisms. Eukaryotic cells. Gene expression — *Conference proceedings*
Sigrid Jusélius Foundation Symposium *(8th : 1980 Helsinki)*. Expression of eukaryotic viral and cellular genes : Eighth Sigrid Jusélius Foundation Symposium Helsinki, Finland June 1980 / edited by Ralf F. Pettersson ... [et al.]. — London : Academic Press, 1981. — xi,324p : ill ; 24cm
Includes bibliographies
ISBN 0-12-553120-6 : £20.40
Also classified at 576'.64 B81-12361

574.87′3223 — Organisms. Cells. Genetics

Swanson, Carl P.. Cytogenetics : the chromosome in division, inheritance and evolution / Carl P. Swanson, Timothy Merz, William J. Young. — 2nd ed. — Englewood Cliffs ; London : Prentice-Hall, c1981. — xiv,577p : ill,1map ; 24cm
Previous ed.: 1967. — Includes bibliographies and index
ISBN 0-13-196618-9 : £15.55 B81-09294

574.87′3224 — Genetics. Biochemical aspects

Woods, R. A.. Biochemical genetics / R.A. Woods. — 2nd ed. — London : Chapman and Hall, 1980. — 80p : ill ; 21cm. — (Outline studies in biology)
Previous ed.: 1973. — Bibliography: p77-78. - Includes index
ISBN 0-412-22400-3 (pbk) : £2.45 : CIP rev. B80-08754

574.87′328 — Molecular genetics

Mays, Laura Livingston. Genetics : a molecular approach / Laura Livingston Mays. — New York : Macmillan ; London : Collier Macmillan, c1981. — xxii,693p : ill(some col.),maps(some col.) ; 24cm
Includes bibliographies and index
ISBN 0-02-378320-6 : £14.95 B81-29312

574.87′328 — Organisms. Nucleic acids. Biochemistry

Davidson, J. N.. Davidson′s The biochemistry of the nucleic acids. — 9th ed. — London : Chapman and Hall, July 1981. — [450]p
Previous ed.: 1976
ISBN 0-412-22680-4 (cased) : £12.00 : CIP entry
ISBN 0-412-22690-1 (pbk) : £6.00 B81-15916

574.87′328 — Organisms. Nucleic acids. Interactions with proteins — *Conference proceedings*

Biological implications of protein-nucleic acid interactions / edited by J. Augustyniak. — Amsterdam ; Oxford : Elsevier/North Holland Biomedical, 1980. — xiv,667p,[5]p of plates : ill ; 22cm
Conference papers. — Includes index
ISBN 0-444-80292-4 : £27.39
Also classified at 574.19′245 B81-22443

574.87′328 — Organisms. Nucleic acids. Sequences

Nucleic acid sequences handbook. — Eastbourne : Praeger
Vol.1. — Nov.1981. — [320]p
ISBN 0-03-060626-8 : £8.00 : CIP entry B81-31231

Nucleic acid sequences handbook. — Eastbourne : Praeger
Vol.2. — Nov.1981. — [320]p
ISBN 0-03-060627-6 : £8.00 : CIP entry B81-31232

574.87′328′05 — Organisms. Nucleic acids - *Serials*

Progress in nucleic acid research and molecular biology. — Vol.24 (1980). — New York ; London : Academic Press, c1980. — xii,279p
ISBN 0-12-540024-1 : £21.00
ISSN 0079-6603 B81-16842

574.87′328′05 — Organisms. Nucleic acids — *Serials*

Progress in nucleic acid research and molecular biology. — Vol.25 (1981). — New York ; London : Academic Press, c1981. — xiii,256p
ISBN 0-12-540025-x : Unpriced
ISSN 0079-6603 B81-32692

574.87′3282 — Organisms. DNA. Replication & recombination — *Conference proceedings*

ICN-UCLA Symposia on Mechanistic Studies of DNA and Genetic Recombination *(1980 : Keystone)*. Mechanistic studies of DNA replication and genetic recombination / [proceedings of the 1980 ICN-UCLA Symposia on Mechanistic Studies of DNA and Genetic Recombination held in Keystone, Colorado, March 16-21, 1980] ; edited by Bruce Alberts. — New York ; London : Academic Press, 1980. — xxix,1003p : ill ; 24cm. — (ICN-UCLA symposia on molecular and cellular biology ; v.19)
Includes index
ISBN 0-12-048850-7 : Unpriced B81-31129

574.87′3282 — Organisms. Eukaryotic cells. DNA. Mutagenesis & repair — *Conference proceedings*

Symposium on DNA Repair and Mutagenesis in Eukaryotes *(1979 : Atlanta)*. DNA repair and mutagenesis in eukaryotes / [proceedings of the Symposium on DNA Repair and Mutagenesis in Eukaryotes sponsored by the National Institute of Environmental Health Sciences, and held in Atlanta, Georgia, June 25-29, 1979] ; edited by W.M. Generoso, M.D. Shelby and F.J. de Serres. — New York ; London : Plenum, c1980. — xii,458p : ill ; 26cm. — (Basic life sciences ; v.15)
Includes bibliographies and index
ISBN 0-306-40552-0 : Unpriced B81-04783

574.87′3283 — Organisms. RNA polymerases & transfer RNA — *Conference proceedings*

Oji International Seminar on Genetic and Evolutionary Aspects of Transcriptional and Translational Apparatus *(1979 : Hokkaido)*. Genetics and evolution of polymerase, tNRA and ribosomes / [proceedings of the Oji International Seminar on Genetic and Evolutionary Aspects of Transcriptional and Translational Apparatus held at Hokkaido, 1979] ; [sponsored by Japan Society of the Promotion of Science] ; edited by Syozo Osawa ... [et al.]. — Amsterdam ; Oxford : University of Tokyo Press, 1980. — ix,669p : ill ; 24cm
Includes index
ISBN 0-444-80288-6 : £23.17
Primary classification 574.87′34 B81-09433

574.87′34 — Organisms. Ribosomes — *Conference proceedings*

Oji International Seminar on Genetic and Evolutionary Aspects of Transcriptional and Translational Apparatus *(1979 : Hokkaido)*. Genetics and evolution of polymerase, tNRA and ribosomes / [proceedings of the Oji International Seminar on Genetic and Evolutionary Aspects of Transcriptional and Translational Apparatus held at Hokkaido, 1979] ; [sponsored by Japan Society of the Promotion of Science] ; edited by Syozo Osawa ... [et al.]. — Amsterdam ; Oxford : University of Tokyo Press, 1980. — ix,669p : ill ; 24cm
Includes index
ISBN 0-444-80288-6 : £23.17
Also classified at 574.87′3283 B81-09433

574.87′342 — Organisms. Cells. Mitochondria. DNA — *Conference proceedings*

International Bari Conference on the Organization and Expression of the Mitochondrial Genome *(12th : 1980 : Martina Franca)*. The organization and expression of the mitochondrial genome : proceedings of the 12th International Bari Conference on the Organization and Expression of the Mitochondrial Genome held in Martina Franca, Italy, 23-28 June, 1980 / editors A.M. Kroon and C. Saccone. — Amsterdam ; Oxford : Elsevier/North-Holland Biomedical, 1980. — xi,451p : ill ; 25cm. — (Developments in genetics ; v.2)
Includes index
ISBN 0-444-80276-2 : £28.43 B81-04083

574.87′5 — Organisms. Cells. Membranes. Bioenergetics — *Conference proceedings*

Membrane bioenergetics : based on the International Workshop held at Cranbrook School, Bloomfield Hills, Michigan, July 5-7, 1979 : in honor of Efraim Racker / edited by C.P. Lee, G. Schatz, L. Ernster. — Reading, Mass. ; London : Addison-Wesley, 1979. — xxxiv,609p : ill,1port ; 24cm
Includes index
ISBN 0-201-03999-0 (pbk) : Unpriced B81-37965

574.87′5 — Organisms. Cells. Membranes — *Conference proceedings*

Membranes et communication intercellulaire = Membranes and intercellular communication : Les Houches, Session XXXIII, 30 juillet-30 août 1979 / édité par Roger Balian, Marc Chabre, Philippe F. Devaux. — Amsterdam ; Oxford : North-Holland, c1981. — xxxii,657p : ill ; 23cm
Conference papers. — English text with preface in French and English. — At head of title: USMG. NATO ASI
ISBN 0-444-85469-x : £48.08 B81-18483

574.87′5 — Organisms. Cells. Membranes. Fluorescence spectroscopy — *Conference proceedings*

Fluorescent probes / [based on a meeting, Fluorescent probes in proteins and membranes, held at the Royal Institution of Great Britain, Thursday 8 November 1979] ; edited by G.S. Beddard and M.A. West. — London : Academic Press, 1981. — x,235p : ill ; 24cm
Includes bibliographies
ISBN 0-12-084680-2 : £15.20 : CIP rev. B81-15915

574.87′5 — Organisms. Cells. Membranes. Immobilized enzymes. Mathematical models

Kernevez, Jean-Pierre. Enzyme mathematics / Jean-Pierre Kernevez. — Amsterdam : Oxford : North-Holland, 1980. — xiii,262p : ill ; 23cm. — (Studies in mathematics and its applications ; v.10)
ISBN 0-444-86122-x : £17.21 B81-06742

574.87′5 — Organisms. Cells. Membranes. Physiology

Membrane structure / editors, J.B. Finean and R.H. Michell. — Amsterdam ; Oxford : Elsevier/North-Holland Biomedical, 1981. — xi,271p : ill ; 25cm. — (New comprehensive biochemistry ; v.1)
Includes index
ISBN 0-444-80304-1 : £27.56 B81-39267

574.87′5 — Organisms. Cells. Membranes. Receptors. Characterisation & purification. Methods

Membrane receptors : methods for purification and characterization / edited by S. Jacobs and P. Cuatrecasas. — London : Chapman and Hall, 1981. — xii,240p : ill ; 24cm. — (Receptors and recognition. Series B ; v.11)
Includes bibliographies and index
ISBN 0-412-21740-6 : Unpriced : CIP rev. B81-03363

574.87′5 — Organisms. Cells. Membranes. Transport phenomena

Höfer, M.. Transport across biological membranes / M. Höfer ; translated by J.G. Hoggett. — Boston ; London : Pitman Advanced Publishing Program, c1981. — xiii,184p : ill ; 24cm. — (The Pitman international series in cellular and developmental biology)
Translation of: Transport durch biologische Membranen. — Bibliography: p168-179. - Includes index
ISBN 0-273-08480-1 : £15.00 B81-16162

Membrane transport / editors S.L. Bonting and J.J.H.H.M. de Pont. — Amsterdam ; Oxford : Elsevier-North-Holland Biomedical, 1981. — 362p : ill ; 25cm. — (New comprehensive biochemistry ; v.2)
Includes index
ISBN 0-444-80307-6 : Unpriced B81-39349

574.87′5 — Organisms. Excitable cells. Membranes. Physiology

Hendry, Bruce. Membrane physiology and cell excitation / Bruce Hendry. — London : Croom Helm, c1981. — 159p : ill ; 22cm. — (Croom Helm biology in medicine series)
Includes bibliographies and index
ISBN 0-7099-0148-8 (cased) : £9.95
ISBN 0-7099-0149-6 (pbk) : £4.50 B81-06242

574.87′5 — Organisms. Membranes. Electrical noise. Analysis

DeFelice, Louis J.. Introduction to membrane noise / Louis J. DeFelice. — New York ; London : Plenum, c1981. — xiv,500p : ill ; 24cm
Bibliography: p473-490. - Includes index
ISBN 0-306-40513-x : Unpriced B81-27112

574.87′5 — Organisms. Receptors. Biochemical aspects

Boeynaems, J. M.. Outlines of receptor theory / by J.M. Boeynaems and J.E. Dumont. — Amsterdam ; London : Elsevier/North-Holland Biomedical, 1980. — vii,226p : ill ; 25cm
Includes index
ISBN 0-444-80131-6 : £24.25 B81-03972

574.8'75 — Organisms. Receptors. Biochemical aspects
Receptor regulation. — London : Chapman and Hall, Dec.1981. — [250]p. — (Receptors and recognition. Series B ; v.13)
ISBN 0-412-15930-9 : £20.00 : CIP entry
B81-31749

574.87'5'05 — Organisms. Cells. Membranes — *Serials*
Membrane structure and function. — Vol.4. — New York ; Chichester : Wiley, c1981. — vii,246p
ISBN 0-471-08774-2 : £23.50 B81-24097

Membrane structure and function / edited by E. Edward Bittar. — New York ; Chichester : Wiley
Vol.2. — c1980. — vii,373p : ill ; 24cm
Includes index
ISBN 0-471-03817-2 : £22.75 B81-09828

574.87'5'05 — Organisms. Membranes. Transport phenomena — *Serials*
Current topics in membranes and transport. — Vol.14. — New York ; London : Academic Press, 1980. — xv,477p
ISBN 0-12-153314-x : Unpriced
ISSN 0070-2161 B81-09234

574.87'6 — Organisms. Cancer. Cells. Organelles
Cancer-cell organelles. — Chichester : Ellis Horwood, Aug.1981. — [320]p. — (Methodological surveys ; v.11)
ISBN 0-85312-344-6 : £22.50 : CIP entry
B81-21548

574.87'6 — Organisms. Liver. Microsomes. Enzymes
Hepatic cytochrome P-450 monooxygenase system. — Oxford : Pergamon, Sept.1981. — [756]p. — (International encyclopaedia of pharmacology and therapeutics ; section 108)
ISBN 0-08-027381-5 : £73.00 : CIP entry
B81-21559

574.87'6041 — Organisms. Cells. Ions. Measurement. Use of micorelectrodes
Purves, R. D.. Microelectrode methods for intracellular recording and ionophoresis / R.D. Purves. — London : Academic Press, 1981. — x,146p : ill ; 24cm. — (Biological techniques series)
Bibliography: p137-144. — Includes index
ISBN 0-12-567950-5 : £9.80 B81-20861

574.87'6041'05 — Organisms. Cells. Biophysics — *Serials*
Comments on modern biology. Part A, Comments on molecular and cellular biophysics : a journal of critical discussion of the current literature. — Vol.1, no.1 (1980)-. — New York : Gordon and Breach ; London : Gordon and Breach [Distributor], 1980-. — v. : ill ; 21cm
Six issues yearly. — CODEN: CMCBDM
ISSN 0143-8123 = Comments on modern biology. Part A. Comments on molecular and cellular biophysics : £42.00 per year
B81-08763

574.87'6042 — Organisms. Cells. Hormone receptors. Interactions with toxins — *Conference proceedings*
Receptor-mediated binding and internalization of toxins and hormones / edited by John L. Middlebrook, Leonard D. Kohn ; [proceedings of a symposium based on the conference on receptor-mediated binding and internalization of toxins and hormones, held in Frederick, Maryland, on March 24-26, 1980 sponsored by The U.S. Army Medical Research Institute for Infectious Diseases]. — New York ; London : Academic Press, 1981. — xiv,374p : ill ; 24cm
Includes bibliographies and index
ISBN 0-12-494850-2 : £19.20
Also classified at 574.87'6042 B81-39578

574.87'6042 — Organisms. Cells. Ions. Measurement. Use of selective ion sensitive microelectrodes
The **Application** of ion-selective microelectrodes / editor Thomas Zeuthen. — Amsterdam ; Oxford : Elsevier/North Holland, 1981. — xiii,284p : ill ; 25cm. — (Research monographs in cell and tissue physiology ; v.4)
Includes bibliographies and index
ISBN 0-444-80268-1 : £38.63 B81-23635

574.87'6042 — Organisms. Cells. Liquid crystals. Physical properties
Brown, Glenn H.. Liquid crystals and biological structures / Glenn H. Brown, Jerome J. Wolken. — New York ; London : Academic Press, 1979. — xi,187p : ill ; 24cm
Bibliography: p181-182. — Includes index
ISBN 0-12-136850-5 : £14.40 B81-11267

574.87'6042 — Organisms. Cells. Toxins. Interactions with hormone receptors — *Conference proceedings*
Receptor-mediated binding and internalization of toxins and hormones / edited by John L. Middlebrook, Leonard D. Kohn ; [proceedings of a symposium based on the conference on receptor-mediated binding and internalization of toxins and hormones, held in Frederick, Maryland, on March 24-26, 1980 sponsored by The U.S. Army Medical Research Institute for Infectious Diseases]. — New York ; London : Academic Press, 1981. — xiv,374p : ill ; 24cm
Includes bibliographies and index
ISBN 0-12-494850-2 : £19.20
Primary classification 574.87'6042 B81-39578

574.87'6042'05 — Organisms. Cells. Biochemistry — *Serials*
Bioscience reports : communications and reviews in molecular and cellular biology. — Vol.1, no.1 (Jan.1981)-. — London (7 Warwick Court, High Holborn, WC1R 5DP) : The Biochemical Society, 1981-. — v. : ill,ports ; 26cm
Monthly
ISSN 0144-8463 = Bioscience reports : £85.00 per year
Primary classification 574.8'8'05 B81-27922

574.87'61 — Organisms. Cells. Development. Mechanisms
McLaren, Anne. Germ cells and soma. — London : Yale University Press, July 1981. — [128]p. — (Mrs. Hepsa Ely Silliman memorial lectures ; 45)
ISBN 0-300-02694-3 : £9.45 : CIP entry
B81-22683

574.87'61 — Organisms. Cells. Energy metabolism
Reich, J. G.. Energy metabolism of the cell. — London : Academic Press, Aug.1981. — [300]p
ISBN 0-12-585920-1 : CIP entry B81-18127

574.87'61 — Organisms. Cells. Enzymes & proteins. ADP-ribosylation — *Conference proceedings*
Fogarty International Conference on Novel ADP-Ribosylations of Regulatory Enzymes and Proteins *(1979 : National Institutes of Health, Bethesda, Md)*. Novel ADP-ribosylations of regulatory enzymes and proteins : proceedings of the Fogarty International Conference on Novel ADP-Ribosylations of Regulatory Enzymes and Proteins, National Institutes of Health, Bethesda, Maryland, U.S.A., October 22-24, 1979 / editors: Mark E. Smulson, Takashi Sugimura. — New York ; Oxford : Elsevier/North-Holland, c1980. — xi,452p : ill ; 25cm. — (Developments in cell biology ; 6)
Includes index
ISBN 0-444-00403-3 : £21.42 B81-04845

574.87'61 — Organisms. Cells. Metabolism. Regulation. Role of calcium
Calcium and cell function. — New York ; London : Academic Press
Vol. 1: Calmodulin / edited by Wai Yiu Cheung. — 1980. — 395p : ill ; 24cm. — (Molecular biology)
Includes bibliographies and index
ISBN 0-12-171401-2 : £26.20 B81-21990

574.87'61 — Organisms. Cells. Metabolism. Regulation. Role of hormones — *Conference proceedings*
INSERM European Symposium on Hormones and Cell Regulation *(5th : 1980 : Bischoffsheim)*. Hormones and cell regulation : proceedings of the Fifth INSERM European Symposium on Hormones and Cell Regulation, held at Le Bischenberg, Bischoffsheim (France), 1-4 October, 1980, sponsored by Institut National de la Santé et de la Recherche Médicale / edited by J.E. Dumont and J. Nunez. — Amsterdam ; Oxford : Elsevier/North-Holland Biomedical, 1981. — xii,266p : ill ; 25cm. — (European symposium ; v.5)
Includes index
ISBN 0-444-80322-x : £22.88 B81-19274

574.87'61 — Organisms. Cells. Polyproteins. Synthesis — *Conference proceedings*
Biosynthesis, modification, and processing of cellular and viral polyproteins / [proceedings of the conference held on May 27-31, 1980 at Hamburg-Blankenese, West Germany] ; edited by Gebhard Koch, Dietmar Richter. — New York ; London : Academic Press, 1980. — xvii,341p : ill ; 24cm
Includes bibliographies and index
ISBN 0-12-417560-0 : £16.40 B81-17588

574.87'61 — Organisms. Cells. Proteins. Phosphorylation — *Conference proceedings*
Protein phosphorylation and bio-regulation / Friedrich-Miescher-Institut and European Molecular Biology Organization workshop, Basel, December 10-12, 1979 ; editors G. Thomas, E.J. Podesta and J. Gordon. — Basel ; London : Karger, 1980. — viii,232p : ill ; 25cm
Includes bibliographies
ISBN 3-8055-1168-x : £24.60 B81-04536

574.87'612 — Organisms. Cells. Differentiation
Bownes, Mary. Differentiation in cells. — London : Chapman and Hall, Sept.1981. — [80]p. — (Outline studies in biology)
ISBN 0-412-22830-0 (pbk) : £2.45 : CIP entry
B81-25776

574.87'612 — Organisms. Cells. Differentiation — *Conference proceedings*
Differentiation in vitro. — Cambridge : Cambridge University Press, Jan.1982. — [286] p. — (Symposium of the British Society for Cell Biology ; 4th)
Conference papers
ISBN 0-521-23926-5 : £30.00 : CIP entry
B81-39254

574.87'62 — Organisms. Cells. Cycles. Control systems
The **Cell** cycle. — Cambridge : Cambridge University Press, Dec.1981. — [288]p. — (Society for Experimental Biology seminar series ; 10)
ISBN 0-521-23912-5 (cased) : £20.00 : CIP entry
ISBN 0-521-28342-6 (pbk) : £8.95 B81-34016

574.87'62 — Organisms. Cells. Cycles. Control systems. Mechanisms
Nuclear-cytoplasmic interactions in the cell cycle / edited by Gary L. Whitson. — London : Academic Press, 1980. — xiii,342p : ill ; 24cm. — (Cell biology)
Includes bibliographies and index
ISBN 0-12-747750-0 : £22.00 B81-16780

574.87'62 — Organisms. Cells. Division
Lloyd, D.. The cell division cycle. — London : Academic Press, Feb.1982. — [420]p
ISBN 0-12-453760-x : CIP entry B81-35914

574.87'64 — Organisms. Cells. Motility
Biology of the chemotactic response. — Cambridge : Cambridge University Press, Dec.1981. — [192]p. — (Society for Experimental Biology seminar series ; 12)
ISBN 0-521-23305-4 (cased) : £20.00 : CIP entry
ISBN 0-521-29897-0 (pbk) : £8.95 B81-37002

574.88 — Molecular biology
Ninio, J.. Molecular approaches to evolution. — London : Pitman, Jan.1982. — [138]p
Translation of: Approches moléculaires de l'évolution
ISBN 0-273-08521-2 (pbk) : £5.95 : CIP entry
B81-34158

574.8'8 — Molecular biology — *Festschriften*
Structural studies on molecules of biological interest : a volume in honour of Professor Dorothy Hodgkin / edited by Guy Dodson, Jenny P. Glusker, and David Sayre. — Oxford : Clarendon Press, 1981. — xviii,610p : ill,ports ; 25cm
Includes bibliographies and index
ISBN 0-19-855362-5 : £39.00 : CIP rev.
B80-09680

574.88 — Organisms. Membranes. Effects of low temperature — *Conference proceedings*

Effects of low temperature on biological membranes. — London : Academic Press, Oct.1981. — [350]p
Conference papers
ISBN 0-12-507650-9 : CIP entry B81-27369

574.8'8 — Organisms. Molecules. Structure. Determination. Infrared & Raman spectroscopy — *Conference proceedings*

Infrared and Raman spectroscopy of biological molecules : proceedings of the NATO Advanced Study Institute held at Athens, Greece, August 22-31, 1978 / edited by Theo M. Theophanides. — Dordrecht ; London : Reidel, published in cooperation with NATO Scientific Affairs Division, c1979. — lx,372p : ill ; 25cm. — (NATO advanced study institutes series. Series C - Mathematical and physical sciences ; v.43)
Includes index
ISBN 90-277-0966-1 : Unpriced B81-16321

574.8'8'05 — Molecular biology — *Serials*

Bioscience reports : communications and reviews in molecular and cellular biology. — Vol.1, no.1 (Jan.1981)-. — London (7 Warwick Court, High Holborn, WC1R 5DP) : The Biochemical Society, 1981-. — v. : ill,ports ; 26cm
Monthly
ISSN 0144-8463 = Bioscience reports : £85.00 per year
Also classified at 574.87'6042'05 B81-27922

Molecular aspects of medicine. — Vol.3. — Oxford : Pergamon, Dec.1981. — [562]p
ISBN 0-08-028871-5 : £47.00 : CIP entry B81-32039

574.8'8'072 — Organisms. Molecules. Mathematical models

Mathematical models in molecular and cellular biology / edited by Lee A. Segel. — Cambridge : Cambridge University Press, 1980. — ix,757p : ill ; 24cm
Includes bibliographies and index
ISBN 0-521-22925-1 : £45.00
Also classified at 574.87'072 B81-09822

574.9 — BIOLOGY. GEOGRAPHICAL TREATMENT

574.9 — Biogeography

Jones, R. L.. Biogeography : structure, process, pattern and change within the bioshpere / R.L. Jones. — Amersham : Hulton, 1980. — 192p : ill,maps ; 26cm
Bibliography: p182. - Includes index
ISBN 0-7175-0872-2 (pbk) : £5.20 B81-05425

Simmons, Ian. Biogeographical processes. — London : Allen and Unwin, Jan.1982. — [136] p. — (Processes in physical geography ; 5)
ISBN 0-04-574016-x (pbk) : £4.25 : CIP entry B81-33912

Tivy, Joy. Biogeography. — 2nd ed. — London : Longman, Oct.1981. — [416]p
Previous ed.: Edinburgh : Oliver & Boyd, 1971
ISBN 0-582-30009-6 (pbk) : £6.95 : CIP entry B81-28110

574.9 — Organisms. Distribution. Geographical aspects

Rapoport, Eduardo H.. Areography : geographical strategies of species. — Oxford : Pergamon, Feb.1982. — [250]p. — (Publications of the Fundación Bariloche ; v.1) (Pergamon international library)
Translation of: Areografia
ISBN 0-08-028914-2 : £16.00 : CIP entry B81-35947

574.909'46 — Seashore. Organisms — *For schools*

Jennings, Terry. Sea and seashore / Terry Jennings ; illustrated by Karen Daws, Ann Winterbotham ; map by Rudolph Britto. — Oxford : Oxford University Press, 1981. — 32p : ill(some col.),1col.map ; 29cm. — (The young scientist investigates)
ISBN 0-19-917050-9 : £2.50 B81-24408

574.909'52 — Woodlands. Organisms — *For children*

Waters, John. The wildlife of woodlands / John Waters. — London : Macdonald Educational, c1981. — 45p : ill(some col.) ; 29cm. — (Nature in focus)
Ill on lining papers. — Bibliography: p44. - Includes index
ISBN 0-356-07122-7 : £3.50 B81-17166

574.909'54 — Deserts. Organisms

Wagner, Frederic H.. Wildlife of the deserts / Frederic H. Wagner. — [London] : Windward, [1981]. — 231p : ill(some col.),1col.map ; 27cm
Includes index
ISBN 0-7112-0024-6 : £7.95 B81-19996

574.92'05 — Marine biology — *Serials*

Advances in marine biology. — Vol.18. — London : Academic Press, 1980. — x,681p
ISBN 0-12-026118-9 : Unpriced
ISSN 0065-2881 B81-12431

Oceanography and marine biology. — Vol.18. — Aberdeen : Aberdeen University Press, 1980. — 528p
ISBN 0-08-025732-1 : £35.00 : CIP rev.
ISSN 0079-3218
Primary classification 551.46'005 B80-12853

574.92'05 — Marine biology - *Serials*

Oceanography and marine biology. — Vol.19. — Aberdeen : Aberdeen University Press, Sept.1981. — [655]p
ISBN 0-08-028439-6 : CIP entry
ISSN 0078-3218
Primary classification 551.46'005 B81-20511

574.92'134 — Baltic Sea. Natural environment

The **Baltic** Sea / edited by Aarno Voipio. — Amsterdam ; Oxford : Elsevier Scientific, 1981. — xiv,418p : ill,maps ; 25cm. — (Elsevier oceanography series ; 30)
Includes bibliographies and index
ISBN 0-444-41884-9 : £50.57 B81-23639

574.92'9'06041 — Great Britain. Freshwater biology. Organisations: Freshwater Biological Association, *to 1979*

Fogg, G. E.Freshwater Biological Association 1929-1979 : the first fifty years / by G.E. Fogg. — Ambleside : The Association, 1979. — 39p,[16]p of plates : ill(some col.),ports ; 22cm
ISBN 0-900386-36-3 (pbk) : £1.00 B81-08297

574.92'9'4 — Europe. Freshwater organisms — *Field guides*

Pott, Eckart. Rivers and lakes : plants and animals illustrated and identified with colour photographs / Eckart Pott ; translated and edited by Gwynne Vevers. — London : Chatto & Windus, c1980. — 144p : col.ill ; 19cm. — (Chatto nature guides)
Translation of: Bach-Fluss-See. — Includes index
ISBN 0-7011-2543-8 (cased) : £4.95 : CIP rev.
ISBN 0-7011-2544-6 (pbk) : £2.50 B80-25620

574.92'9'41 — Great Britain. Freshwater organisms

Young, Geoffrey. Ponds and streams / [written by Geoffrey Young]. — Norwich : Jarrold, 1981. — 31p : col.ill ; 19cm. — (WATCH outdoor guide ; 8)
Cover title. — Text on inside cover. — Includes index
ISBN 0-85306-974-3 (pbk) : Unpriced B81-37061

574.92'9'41 — Great Britain. Freshwater regions. Organisms — *For children*

Aston, Oliver. Life in ponds & streams / Oliver Aston. — London : Macdonald Educational, c1980. — 45p : col.ill ; 29cm. — (Nature in focus)
Ill on lining papers. — Bibliography: p43-44. — Includes index
ISBN 0-356-07121-9 : £2.95 B81-03907

574.94 — Europe. Seashore. Organisms

Jackman, Leslie. The seashore naturalist's handbook / Leslie Jackman. — London : Hamlyn, 1981. — 224p : col.ill ; 19cm
Bibliography: p216-217. — Includes index
ISBN 0-600-36447-x : £3.50 B81-25453

574.94 — North-western Europe. Coastal waters. Natural environment — *For yachting*

Drummond, Maldwin. The yachtsman's naturalist / by Maldwin Drummond and Paul Rodhouse ; with foreword by Sir Peter Scott ; illustrated by John Rignall. — London : Angus & Robertson, 1980. — 224p,[48]p of plates : ill (some col.),1map,1plan ; 24cm
Bibliography: p217-218. — Includes index
ISBN 0-207-95808-4 : £8.95 B81-01735

574.941 — Great Britain. Coastal regions. Organisms — *Field guides*

Ovenden, Denys. Collins handguide to the sea coast / painted by Denys Ovenden ; text by John Barrett. — London : Collins, 1981. — 128p : ill(some col.) ; 20cm
Bibliography: p124-125. — Includes index
ISBN 0-00-219781-2 (cased) : £4.95
ISBN 0-00-219780-4 (pbk) : £2.50 B81-33106

574.941 — Great Britain. Gardens. Organisms

Bellamy, David. Bellamy's backyard safari : a primer to the study of evolution, right in your own backyard / David J. Bellamy, Thomas J. Bellamy ; illustrations by David Greene ; edited by Mike Weatherley. — London : British Broadcasting Corporation, 1981. — 120p : ill(some col.) ; 25cm
Bibliography: p118
ISBN 0-563-16468-9 (pbk) : £4.50 B81-29773

574.941 — Great Britain. Marine organisms — *For schools*

Jennings, Terry. Sea and seashore / Terry Jennings ; illustrated by Karen Daws, Ann Winterbotham ; map by Rudolph Britto. — Oxford : Oxford University Press, 1981. — 32p : ill(some col.) ; 28cm. — (The Young scientist investigates)
ISBN 0-19-917041-x (pbk) : £1.50 B81-19094

574.941 — Great Britain. Natural environment — *Field guides*

Leutscher, Alfred. A field guide to the British countryside / Alfred Leutscher ; edited by Nigel Sitwell. — London : New English Library, c1981. — 319p : col.ill ; 20cm. — (A Charles Herridge book)
Bibliography: p313. — Includes index
ISBN 0-450-04818-7 (cased) : £7.95
ISBN 0-450-05055-6 (pbk) : £4.95 B81-07524

574.941 — Great Britain. Natural history, *ca 1820-ca 1870*

Barber, Lynn. The heyday of natural history 1820-1870 / by Lynn Barber. — London : Cape, 1980. — 320p,[14]p of plates : ill(some col.),facsims(some col.),ports ; 26cm
Includes index
ISBN 0-224-01448-x : £9.50 : CIP rev. B80-04763

574.941 — Great Britain. Organisms

Harris, Jeanette. The Kingfisher nature handbook / Jeanette Harris. — London : Kingfisher, 1981. — 192p : ill(some col.) ; 20cm
Includes index
ISBN 0-7063-6098-2 : £3.95 : CIP rev. B81-00112

The **Living** countryside : a weekly nature guide to the British Isles. — London : Orbis Publishing, [1981]-. — v. : ill(some col.),col.maps,lports ; 30cm
To be completed in 120-150? parts
£0.60(per issue) (pbk) B81-30058

The **Natural** history of Britain and Ireland / photographs by Heather Angel ; text by Heather Angel ... [et al.]. — London : Joseph, 1981. — 256p : col.ill,col.maps ; 30cm
Bibliography: p246. — Includes index
ISBN 0-7181-1989-4 : £12.50 B81-23704

574.941 — Great Britain. Organisms — *Field guides*

Arlott, Norman. The complete guide to British wildlife / illustrations Norman Arlott ; text Richard Fitter and Alastair Fitter. — London : Collins, 1981. — 287p : ill (some col.) ; 22cm
Bibliography: p262-263. — Includes index
ISBN 0-00-219224-1 (cased) : £7.95 (pbk) : Unpriced B81-21853

574.941 — Great Britain. Organisms — *For children*

Whitehead, Pamela K.. Countryside notebook / written by Pamela K. Whitehead ; photographs by Michael M. Whitehead. — Loughborough : Ladybird, c1981. — 50p : col.ill ; 18cm. — (Nature series)
Ill on lining paper. — Includes index
ISBN 0-7214-0665-3 : £0.50 B81-26636

574.941 — Great Britain. Seashore. Organisms

Angel, Heather. The Guinness book of seashore life / Heather Angel ; illustrations by Vanessa Luff ; photographs by Heather Angel. — Enfield : Guinness Superlatives, 1981. — 160p : ill(some col.),maps(some col.) ; 21cm. — (Britain's natural heritage)
Includes index
ISBN 0-85112-304-x : £4.50 B81-11569

Young, Geoffrey. By the sea / [written by Geoffrey Young]. — Norwich : Jarrold, 1981. — 31p : col.ill ; 20cm. — (WATCH outdoor guide ; 7)
Cover title. — Text on inside cover. — Includes index
ISBN 0-85306-973-5 (pbk) : Unpriced B81-37064

574.941 — Great Britain. Seashore. Organisms — *For children*

Whitehead, Pamela K.. Seaside notebook / written by Pamela K. Whitehead ; photographs by Michael M. Whitehead. — Loughborough : Ladybird, c1981. — 51p : col.ill ; 18cm. — (Nature series)
Ill on lining papers. — Includes index
ISBN 0-7214-0666-1 : £0.50 B81-26635

574.941 — Great Britain. Seashore. Organisms — *Questions & answers — For children*

Saville, Malcolm. The seashore quiz / Malcolm Saville ; illustrated by Robert Micklewright. — London : Carousel, 1981. — 128p : ill,1map ; 20cm
ISBN 0-552-54176-1 (pbk) : £0.75 B81-27824

574.941 — Great Britain. Towns. Organisms — *For children*

Carter, Graham. Wildlife in towns / Graham Carter. — London : Macdonald Educational, c1980. — 45p : col.ill ; 29cm. — (Nature in focus)
Ill on lining papers. — Bibliography: p43. — Includes index
ISBN 0-356-07120-0 : £2.95 B81-04060

574.941 — Great Britain. Woodlands. Organisms

Young, Geoffrey. Woods / [written by Geoffrey Young]. — Norwich : Jarrold, 1981. — 31p : col.ill ; 19cm. — (WATCH outdoor guide ; 6)
Cover title. — Text on inside cover. — Includes index
ISBN 0-85306-972-7 (pbk) : Unpriced B81-37063

574.9411'022'2 — Scotland. Organisms — *Illustrations*

Brockie, Keith. Keith Brockie's wildlife sketchbook. — London : Dent, 1981. — 130p : ill(some col.) ; 27cm
ISBN 0-460-04514-8 : £9.50 : CIP rev. B81-18088

574.9411'72 — Scotland. Highland Region. Kinlochewe. Nature reserves: Beinn Eighe National Nature Reserve — *Visitors' guides*

Nature Conservancy Council. Beinn Eighe : National Nature Reserve : Glas Leitire : nature trail / Nature Conservancy Council. — Inverness : Nature Conservancy Council, North West Scotland Region, c1979. — [16]p : ill (some col.),1col.map ; 21cm
ISBN 0-86139-056-3 (unbound) : £0.25 B81-39625

574.9411'85 — Scotland. Highland Region. Eilean Shona. Organisms — *Personal observations*

Tomkies, Mike. Between earth and paradise / Mike Tomkies ; with photographs in black and white and colour by the author. — London : Heinemann, 1981. — 214p,[4]p of plates : ill (some col.) ; 25cm
ISBN 0-434-78800-7 : £7.95 B81-23235

574.9414'23 — Scotland. Strathclyde Region. Bute. Organisms — *Serials*

Transactions of the Buteshire Natural History Society. — Vol.21 (1980). — [Rothesay] ([c/o The Museum, Stuart St., Rothesay, Buteshire]) : [The Society], [1980]. — 115p
ISBN 0-905812-02-6 : Unpriced
Also classified at 936.1'423 B81-25500

574.9414'86 — Scotland. Dumfries and Galloway Region. Nithsdale *(District)*. **Nature reserves: Caerlaverock National Nature Reserve** — *Visitors' guides*

Nature Conservancy Council. Caerlaverock : National Nature Reserve / Nature Conservancy Council. — Balloch : [The Council] Southwest Scotland Region, c1979. — [4]p : 1map ; 21cm
ISBN 0-86139-070-9 (unbound) : Unpriced B81-39626

574.9415'03'21 — Ireland. Organisms — *Encyclopaedias*

Hickin, Norman E.. Irish nature / Norman Hickin. — Dublin : O'Brien, 1980. — 240p : ill ; 25cm
Bibliography: p239-240. — Index
ISBN 0-905140-39-7 : £11.50 B81-02319

574.9417 — Ireland *(Republic)*. **Sites of special scientific interest** — *Lists*

Areas of scientific interest in Ireland / sponsored by the Heritage Trust. — Dublin (St. Martin's House, Waterloo Rd., Dublin 4) : An Foras Forbartha, 1981. — ii,166p : ill ; 30cm(pbk). — (National heritage inventory)
Bibliography: p165-166
ISBN 0-906120-50-0 : £3.00 B81-38036

574.942 — England. Organisms — *Personal observations*

Hudson, W. H.. The book of a naturalist / by W.H. Hudson. — London : Wildwood, 1980. — 360p ; 22cm
Includes index
ISBN 0-7045-0408-1 (pbk) : £3.50
ISBN 0-7045-3055-9 B81-06087

574.9422'51 — East Sussex. Rotherfield region. Organisms — *Personal observations*

Thornhill, Alan. Three mile man : a countryman's view of nature / text by Alan Thornhill ; photographs by Peter Warnett ; introduction by Malcolm Muggeridge ; with drawings by Lawrence Easden. — London : Collins, 1980. — 144p : ill(some col.),1map ; 22x25cm
Includes index
ISBN 0-00-219094-x : £8.95 B81-08777

574.9422'56 — East Sussex. Woodingdean. Nature reserves: Castle Hill National Nature Reserve — *Visitors' guides*

Nature Conservancy Council. Castle Hill : National Nature Reserve / Nature Conservancy Council. — Ashford, Kent : Nature Conservancy Council - South East Region, c1978. — [4]p : 1ill,1map ; 21cm
ISBN 0-86139-031-8 (unbound) : Unpriced B81-39624

574.9422'7 — Hampshire. Natural environment, *ca 1900 — Personal observations*

Hudson, W. H.. Hampshire days / W.H. Hudson. — Oxford : Oxford University Press, 1980. — 250p : ill ; 20cm
Originally published: London : Longman, 1903. — Includes index
ISBN 0-19-281298-x (pbk) : £1.95 : CIP rev. B80-02421

574.9422'74 — Hampshire. Selborne. Natural history — *Early works*

White, Gilbert. The illustrated natural history of Selborne. — Exeter : Webb & Bower, Oct.1981. — [256]p
Originally published: London : B. White and Son, 1789 [i.e. 1788]
ISBN 0-906671-47-7 : £12.50 : CIP entry B81-30485

574.9423'1'05 — Wiltshire. Natural history — *Serials*

[Bulletin *(Wiltshire Archaeological and Natural History Society. Natural History Section : 1978)*]. Bulletin / Wiltshire Archaeological & Natural History Society Natural History Section. — No.9 (Feb.1978)-. — Bradford-on-Avon (c/o Mrs E. Stephens, 95 Leigh Park Rd, Bradford-on-Avon, [Wilts.]) : The Section, 1978-. — v. ; 30cm
Two issues yearly. — Continues: Biannual bulletin (Wiltshire Archaeological and Natural History Society. Natural History Section). — Description based on: No.15 (Feb.1981)
ISSN 0262-1665 = Bulletin - Wiltshire Archaeological & Natural History Society. Natural History Section (1978) : Unpriced B81-38512

574.9423'13 — Wiltshire. Cole River region. Organisms, *ca 1870*

Jefferies, Richard. By the brook / by Richard Jefferies ; edited and with an introduction by George Miller. — London (74 Fortune Green Rd., West Hampstead, NW6 1DS) : Eric & Joan Stevens, 1981, c1980. — 14p : 1ill ; 19cm
Limited ed. of 170 numbered copies of which the first 20 are specially bound
£12.60 B81-17036

574.942'319 — Wiltshire. East Avon River. Organisms — *Personal observations*

Pease, Richard. The river keeper. — Newton Abbot : David & Charles, Jan.1982. — [168]p
ISBN 0-7153-8248-9 : £6.95 : CIP entry B81-33820

574.9423'5 — Devon. Exe Estuary. Natural environment — *Conference proceedings*

Essays on the Exe Estuary / edited by G.T. Boalch. — Exeter : Devonshire Association for the Advancement of Science, Literature and Art, 1980. — 185p : ill,maps ; 22cm. — (Special volume / Devonshire Association for the Advancement of Science, Literature and Art ; no.2)
Conference papers. — Includes bibliographies and index
£7.50 (pbk) B81-09562

574.9423'85 — England. Exmoor. National parks: Exmoor National Park. Organisms

Allen, N. V.. Exmoor's wildlife : mammals, birds, reptiles, fish, butterflies, woods, flowers / N.V. Allen. — South Molton (South Molton, N. Devon) : Quest (Western) Publications, 1979. — 64p : ill ; 20cm
ISBN 0-905297-12-1 (pbk) : Unpriced B81-12981

574.9424'41 — Hereford and Worcester. Chaddesley Corlett. Nature reserves: Chaddesley Woods National Nature Reserve — *Walkers' guides*

Nature Conservancy Council. Chaddesley Woods : National Nature Reserve : Jubilee Walk / Nature Conservancy Council. — Shrewsbury : Nature Conservancy Council, West Midland Region, c1977 (1978 [printing]). — [4]p : 1map ; 21cm
ISBN 0-86139-016-4 (unbound) : Unpriced B81-39627

574.9425'11 — England. Peak District. Organisms

Nature in the Peak District / Nature Conservancy Council. — Shrewsbury (Attingham Park, Shrewsbury, Shropshire SYJ 4TW) : Nature Conservancy Council, West Midland Region, c.1981. — 20p : ill(some col.),col.maps ; 22cm
Cover title. — Text on inside cover
ISBN 0-86139-106-3 (pbk) : Unpriced B81-37494

574.9425'6'02471 — Bedfordshire. Organisms — *For environment planning*

A **Bedfordshire** wildlife review, 1979 / prepared by Bedfordshire Natural History Society ; for Bedfordshire County Council. — [Luton] ([51 Wychwood Ave., Luton LU2 7HT]) : [Scientific Committee, Bedfordshire Natural History Society], [1979]. — 89,[49]p,[24] of plates(some col.) : maps ; 30cm
Includes index
Unpriced (spiral)

574.9426 — East Anglia. Organisms

The **Jarrold** book of the countryside of East Anglia / with text by E.A. Ellis. — Norwich : Jarrold, c1979. — [64]p : chiefly col.ill ; 19cm
Bibliography: p[4]
ISBN 0-85306-835-6 (pbk) : Unpriced B81-23672

574.9427'51 — Merseyside *(Metropolitan County).* Wirral *(District).* Hilbre. Natural history

Hilbre, the Cheshire island. — Liverpool : Liverpool University Press, Jan.1982. — [300]p
ISBN 0-85323-314-4 : £15.00 : CIP entry B81-33788

574.9428'21 — South Yorkshire *(Metropolitan County).* Sheffield region. Organisms — *Serials*

The **Sorby** record. — No.18 (1980). — Sheffield (c/o D. Whiteley, City of Sheffield Museums Department, Weston Park, Sheffield S10 2TP) : Sorby Natural History Society, [1980?]. — 94p
Unpriced B81-15089

574.9428'41 — North Yorkshire. Horton-in-Ribblesdale. Nature reserves: Ling Gill National Nature Reserve — *Visitors' guides*

Nature Conservancy Council. Ling Gill : National Nature Reserve / Nature Conservancy Council. — Newcastle upon Tyne : Nature Conservancy Council - North East Region, c1979. — [4]p : 1ill,1map ; 21cm
ISBN 0-86139-065-2 (unbound) : Unpriced B81-39622

574.9428'41 — North Yorkshire. Ribblesdale. Nature reserves: Colt Park Wood National Nature Reserve — *Visitors' guides*

Nature Conservancy Council. Colt Park Wood : National Nature Reserve / Nature Conservancy Council. — Newcastle upon Tyne : Nature Conservancy Council - North East Region, c1979. — [4]p : 1ill,1map ; 21cm
ISBN 0-86139-067-9 (unbound) : Unpriced B81-39629

574.9428'48 — North Yorkshire. Hawes. Nature reserves: Scar Close National Nature Reserve — *Visitors' guides*

Nature Conservancy Council. Scar Close : National Nature Reserve / Nature Conservancy Council. — Newcastle upon Tyne : Nature Conservancy Council - North East Region, c1979. — [4]p : 1ill,1map ; 21cm
ISBN 0-86139-066-0 (unbound) : Unpriced B81-39628

574.9428'6 — Durham *(County).* Magnesian limestone regions. Natural environment

The **Magnesian** limestone of Durham County / edited by T.C. Dunn. — Darlington (1 Abbey Rd., Darlington, Co. Durham DL3 7RA) : Durham County Conservation Trust, 1980. — 77p : ill,maps ; 30cm
Includes bibliographies
ISBN 0-905362-01-2 (pbk) : £2.75 B81-08373

574.9428'61 — Durham *(County).* Upper Teesdale. Organisms, *to 1980*

Bellamy, David. The great seasons / presented in words by David Bellamy and in pictures by Sheila Mackie. — London : Hodder & Stoughton in association with Oriel, 1981. — 153p,70 leaves of plates : col.ill ; 25cm
ISBN 0-340-25720-2 : £9.95 B81-17916

574.9428'67 — Durham *(County).* Castle Eden Dene. Natural environment — *Visitors' guides*

Monck, Bill. Castle Eden Dene : an illustrated guide / [writ[illegible] by Bill Monck]. — [Peterlee] ([Estates [illegible]ent, Lee House, Yoden Way, Pete[illegible]am]) : Peterlee Development [illegible] — 48p : ill(some
[illegible]
B81-06445

[illegible] istory of Wales / [illegible] Collins, 1981. — [illegible] cm. — (The [illegible] index
B81-16018

574.9429'29 — Gwynedd. Cadair Idris. Nature reserves: Cadair Idris National Nature Reserve — *Visitors' guides*

Nature Conservancy Council. Cadair Idris National Nature Reserve / Cyngor Gwarchod Natur = Nature Conservancy Council. — Bangor, Gwynedd (Ffordd Penrhos, Bangor, Gwynedd LL57 2LQ) : Nature Conservancy Council, North Wales Region, c1978. — 1folded sheet([4]p) : 1ill,1map ; 21cm
ISBN 0-86139-036-9 : Unpriced B81-08774

574.9429'29 — Gwynedd. Morfa Dyffryn. Nature reserves: Morfa Dyffryn National Nature Reserve — *Visitors' guides*

Nature Conservancy Council. Morfa Dyffryn National Nature Reserve / Cyngor Gwarchod Natur = Nature Conservancy Council. — Bangor, Gwynedd (Ffordd Penrhos, Bangor, Gwynedd LL57 2LQ) : Nature Conservancy Council, North Wales Region, c1978. — 1folded sheet([4]p) : 1ill,1map ; 21cm
ISBN 0-86139-033-4 : Unpriced B81-08609

574.9484'5 — Norway. Andoya. Natural environment

Grant, William M. B. A report on a Royal Air Force scientific expedition of exploration to the island of Andoya in Arctic Norway / by Corporal William M.B. Grant. — [Findhorn] ([69 Findhorn Bay Caravan Park, Findhorn, Morayshire]) : [W.M.B. Grant], [1981]. — 40p : ill,1map,ports ; 23cm
Cover title
For private distribution (pbk) B81-27838

574.969'1 — Madagascar. Organisms

Jolly, Alison. A world like our own : man and nature in Madagascar / Alison Jolly ; photographs by Russ Kinne. — New Haven ; London : Yale University Press, 1980. — xvi,272p,[4]p of plates : ill(some col.),1map,ports ; 29cm
Bibliography: p257-266. - Includes index
ISBN 0-300-02478-9 : £18.90 B81-05647

574.9764'94 — Texas. Guadalupe Mountains. Natural environment

Allender, Michael. The Guadalupe Mountains of Texas / photographs and drawings by Michael Allender ; text by Alan Tennant. — Austin ; London : University of Texas Press, c1980. — 166p : ill(some col.) ; 32cm
ISBN 0-292-72720-8 : £19.45 B81-32505

574.9776 — Minnesota. Forests. Organisms — *Personal observations*

Hoover, Helen. The long-shadowed forest / Helen Hoover. — South Yarmouth, Mass. : Curley ; [Long Preston] : Distributed by Magna Print, [1981?], c1963. — xi,516p ; 23cm
Originally published: New York : Crowell ; London : Souvenir, 1963. — Published in large print. — Bibliography: p492-498. — Includes index
ISBN 0-89340-328-8 : Unpriced B81-37970

574.993'2 — New Caledonia. Organisms

Holloway, J. D.. A survey of the lepidoptera, biogeography and ecology of New Caledonia / by J.D. Holloway. — The Hague ; London : Junk, 1979. — xii,588p : ill,maps ; 25cm. — (Series entomologica ; v.15)
Bibliography: p547-560. - Includes index
ISBN 90-619-3125-8 : Unpriced B81-19392

574.994 — Australia. Natural environment — *For children*

Butler, Harry, *1930-*. Looking at the wild with Harry Butler. — Sydney ; London : Hodder and Stoughton
At the river / illustrated by Tony Oliver. — 1980. — 63p : ill,1map ; 12x18cm
ISBN 0-340-23855-0 (pbk) : £1.25 B81-11977

Butler, Harry, *1930-*. Looking at the wild with Harry Butler. — Sydney ; London : Hodder and Stoughton
On the farm / illustrated by Tony Oliver. — 1980. — 63p : ill,1map ; 12x18cm
ISBN 0-340-23860-7 (pbk) : £1.25 B81-12243

574.994 — Australia. Organisms. Distribution. Geographical aspects

Ecological biogeography of Australia / edited by Allen Keast. — The Hague ; London : Junk, 1981. — 2v.(2142p) : ill,maps ; 25cm + 1map : col. ; 82x99cm. — (Monographiae biologicae ; v.41)
In slip case. — Includes bibliographies and index
ISBN 90-619-3092-8 : Unpriced B81-26173

574.998'9'0723 — Antarctic. Natural environment. British research organisations: British Antarctic Survey — *Serials*

British Antarctic Survey. Annual report / British Antarctic Survey. — 1976-77. — Cambridge : The Survey, 1977. — 64p
ISBN 0-85665-061-7 : Unpriced
ISSN 0141-3325 B81-15166

574.999 — Extraterrestrial life

Asimov, Isaac. Extraterrestrial civilizations / Isaac Asimov. — London : Pan, 1981, c1979. — 316p ; 18cm
Originally published: New York : Crown, 1979 ; London : Robson, 1980. — Includes index
ISBN 0-330-26249-1 (pbk) : £1.50 B81-09721

574.999 — Intelligent extraterrestrial life

Bracewell, Ronald N.. The galactic club : intelligent life in outer space / Ronald N. Bracewell. — New York ; London : Norton, 1979, c1976. — viii,141p : ill ; 21cm
Originally published: San Francisco : San Francisco Book Co., 1976. — Includes index
ISBN 0-393-95022-0 (pbk) : £2.50 B81-03925

575 — EVOLUTION AND GENETICS

575 — Evolution

Evolution / [S364 Course Team]. — Milton Keynes : Open University Press. — (Science : a third level course)
At head of title: The Open University
Unit 1: The nature of evolution ; Unit 2: The beginnings of life / prepared by an Open University Course Team. — 1981. — 37,50p : ill(some col.) ; 30cm. — (S364 ; units 1 and 2)
Includes bibliographies
ISBN 0-335-16085-9 (pbk) : Unpriced B81-27591

The **Evolving** biosphere / editor P.L. Forey. — London : British Museum [Natural History), 1981. — viii,311p : ill(some col.),maps(some col.) ; 29cm. — (Chance, change & challenge)
Includes index
ISBN 0-521-23811-0 : £32.50 : CIP rev. B81-10504

575 — Evolution — *For children*

Taylor, Ron, *1927-*. The story of evolution / Ron Taylor. — London : Ward Lock, 1980. — 77p : ill(some col.),col.maps ; 33cm
Col. ill on lining papers. — Includes index
ISBN 0-7063-5926-7 : £4.95 : CIP rev. B80-28348

575 — Organisms. Evolution

Day, William. Genesis on planet Earth. — Nantwich : Shiva, Oct.1981. — [408]p
Originally published: East Lansing, Mich. : House of Talos Publishers, 1979
ISBN 0-906812-09-7 : £9.95 : CIP entry B81-28182

575 — Organisms. Evolution. Biochemical aspects

Biochemical evolution / edited by H. Gutfreund. — Cambridge : Cambridge University Press, 1981. — vii,368p : ill ; 24cm
Includes bibliographies and index
ISBN 0-521-23549-9 : £30.00 : CIP rev.
ISBN 0-521-28025-7 (pbk) : £12.50 B81-08900

575 — Organisms. Evolution *expounded by* organisms, *1978*

Attenborough, David. Life on earth : a natural history / David Attenborough. — Augmented and enl. ed. — London : Reader's Digest Association in conjunction with Collins and the British Broadcasting Corporation, 1980 (1981 [printing]). — 368p : ill(some col.) ; 27cm
Previous ed.: London : Collins : British Broadcasting Corporation, 1979. — Includes index
ISBN 0-00-219092-3 : £14.95 B81-18499

575 — Organisms. Evolution *expounded by* **organisms,** *1978* *continuation*
Attenborough, David. Life on earth : a natural history / David Attenborough. — Augm. and enl. ed. — London : Reader's Digest Association in conjunction with Collins and the British Broadcasting Corporation, c1980 (1981 [printing]). — 368p : ill (some col.) ; 27cm
Previous ed.: London : Collins; British Broadcasting Corporations, 1979. — Includes index
ISBN 0-00-219092-3 : £14.95 B81-31385

575 — Organisms. Evolution — *Festschriften*
Evolution and speciation : essays in honor of M.J.D. White / editors William R. Atchley, David S. Woodruff. — Cambridge : Cambridge University Press, 1981. — ix,536p : ill,maps,1port ; 24cm
Includes bibliographies and index
ISBN 0-521-23823-4 : £30.00 B81-37999

575 — Organisms. Speciation. Effects of continental drift — *Conference proceedings*
Systematics Discussion Group. Vicariance biogeography : a critique : symposium of the Systematics Discussion Group of the American Museum of Natural History May 2-4, 1979 / edited by Gareth Nelson and Donn E. Rosen. — New York ; Guildford : Columbia University Press, 1981. — xvi,593p : ill,maps ; 24cm
Bibliography: p539-584. — Includes index
ISBN 0-231-04808-4 : £21.65 B81-24011

575'.0092'4 — Evolution. Darwin, Charles — *Biographies*
Stonehouse, Bernard. Charles Darwin and evolution / Bernard Stonehouse. — Hove : Wayland, 1981. — 72p : ill,1map,ports ; 24cm. — (Pioneers of science and discovery)
Bibliography: p70. — Includes index
ISBN 0-85340-667-7 (corrected) : £3.95 B81-37696

575.01 — Evolution. Theories — *Conference proceedings*
The **Evolutionary** synthesis : perspectives on the unification of biology / edited by Ernest Mayr and William B. Provine. — Cambridge, Mass. ; London : Harvard University Press, 1980. — xi,487p ; 24cm
Conference papers. — Includes bibliographies and index
ISBN 0-674-27225-0 : £15.00 B81-16563

575.01'6 — Science. Theories. Influence of ideology — *Study examples: Theories of evolution, 1800-1980*
Greene, John C.. Science, ideology, and world view : esssays in the history of evolutionary ideas / John C. Greene. — Berkeley ; London : University of California Press, c1981. — x,202p ; 23cm
Includes index
ISBN 0-520-04217-4 : £11.50 B81-39838

575.01'62 — Evolution. Natural selection
Origin of species. — London : British Museum (Natural History), 1981. — 120p : ill(some col.),geneal.table,maps,ports ; 22cm
Includes index
ISBN 0-521-23878-1 (cased) : £12.00 : CIP rev.
ISBN 0-521-28276-4 (pbk) : £3.95 B81-19163

575.01'62 — Evolution. Natural selection. Theories
Brownlee, A.. Biological complementariness : a study of evolution / A. Brownlee. — [Midlothian] ([509 Lanark Rd., Juniper Green, Midlothian, EH14 5DQ]) : A. Brownlee, c1981. — viii,133p,[8]p of plates : ill ; 22cm
Bibliography: p127-130. — Includes index
£3.00 (cased) (pbk) : £1.50 B81-33457

575.1 — Genetic engineering
Old, R. W.. Principles of gene manipulation. — 2nd ed. — Oxford : Blackwell Scientific, Nov.1981. — [180]p. — (Studies in microbiology ; v.2)
Previous ed.: 1980
ISBN 0-632-00856-3 (pbk) : £6.50 : CIP entry B81-31082

575.1 — Genetic engineering — *Serials*
[Genetic engineering *(London)*]. Genetic engineering. — 1-. — London : Academic Press, 1981-. — v. : ill ; 23cm
Unpriced B81-33316

[Genetic engineering *(New York)*]. Genetic engineering. — Vol.3. — New York ; London : Plenum Press, c1981. — x,346p
ISBN 0-306-40729-9 : Unpriced
ISSN 0196-3716 B81-30861

575.1 — Genetics
Avers, Charlotte J.. Genetics / Charlotte J. Avers. — Rev. ed. — New York ; London : Van Nostrand, c1980. — xi,659p : ill(some col.),1port ; 24cm
Previous ed.: 1980. — Includes bibliographies and index
ISBN 0-442-30463-3 (pbk) : £17.20 B81-21321

Fristrom, James W.. Principles of genetics / James W. Fristrom and Philip T. Spieth ; illustrations by Dianne K. Fristrom. — New York : Chiron Press ; Oxford : Blackwell Scientific [distributor], c1980. — x,687p : ill ; 24cm
Bibliography: p662-673. — Includes index
ISBN 0-632-00647-1 : £11.50 B81-00887

Gardner, Eldon J.. Principles of genetics. — 6th ed. / Eldon J. Gardner, D. Peter Snustad. — New York ; Chichester : Wiley, c1981. — x,611,[74]p : ill,maps,1facsim,ports ; 25cm
Previous ed.: 1975. — Ill on lining papers. — Includes bibliographies and index
ISBN 0-471-04412-1 : £13.50 B81-15120

Levine, Louis, *1921-*. Biology of the gene / Louis Levine. — 3rd ed. — St. Louis ; London : Mosby, 1980. — xvii,542p : ill,maps ; 24cm
Previous ed.: 1973. — Includes bibliographies and index
ISBN 0-8016-2988-8 (pbk) : £12.75 B81-08039

Pai, Anna C.. Genetics : its concepts and implications / Anna C. Pai, Helen Marcus-Roberts. — Englewood Cliffs ; London : Prentice-Hall, c1981. — xxi,711p : ill ; 25cm
Includes bibliographies and index
ISBN 0-13-351007-7 : £16.20 B81-22724

Suzuki, David T.. An introduction to genetic analysis. — 2nd ed. / David T. Suzuki, Anthony J.F. Griffiths, Richard C. Lewontin. — Oxford : W.H. Freeman, c1981. — xv,911,[75]p : ill ; 25cm
Previous ed.: 1976. — Bibliography: pR1-R8. — Includes index
ISBN 0-7167-1263-6 : £15.95 B81-33655

575.1'05 — Genetic engineering — *Serials*
Genetic engineering. — Vol.2. — London : Academic Press, Oct.1981. — [180]p
ISBN 0-12-270302-2 : CIP entry B81-27368

575.1'076 — Genetics — *Questions & answers*
Robbins, Robert J.. Solutions manual for An introduction to genetic analysis : second edition David T. Suzuki, Anthony J.F. Griffiths, Richard C. Lewontin / prepared by Robert J. Robbins. — Oxford : W.H. Freeman, c1981. — 114p : ill ; 23cm
ISBN 0-7167-1304-7 (pbk) : £1.00 B81-36485

575.1'0941 — Great Britain. Rural regions. Organisms. Genetic aspects
Ford, E. B.. Taking genetics into the countryside / E.B. Ford. — London : Weidenfeld and Nicolson, c1981. — x,150p,[12]p of plates : ill ; 23cm
Bibliography: p139-140. - Includes index
ISBN 0-297-77932-x : £9.95 B81-15629

575.1'2'076 — Organisms. Genes — *Questions & answers — For schools*
Fourth report : S6. Genetics problems / Southern Regional Council for Further Education, Science Teachers' Study Group, Biology Working Party. — Reading (26 Bath Rd., Reading RG1 6NT) : [The Council], [1981]. — 34 leaves : ill ; 30cm
Unpriced (unbound) B81-25064

575.1'5 — Population genetics
Falconer, D. S.. Introduction to quantitative genetics. — 2nd ed. — London : Longman, July 1981. — [384]p
Previous ed.: Edinburgh: Oliver and Boyd, 1960
ISBN 0-582-44195-1 : £7.95 : CIP entry B81-15941

Wallace, Bruce. Basic population genetics / Bruce Wallace. — New York ; Guildford : Columbia University Press, 1981. — xii,688p : ill ; 24cm
Bibliography: p645-677. — Includes index
ISBN 0-231-05042-9 : £16.25 B81-29269

Wills, Christopher. Genetic variability / Christopher Wills. — Oxford : Clarendon Press, 1981. — xiii,312p : ill ; 25cm. — (Oxford science publications)
Bibliography: p282-304. — Includes index
ISBN 0-19-857570-x : Unpriced : CIP rev. B80-23266

575.1'5 — Population genetics. Ecological aspects
Merrell, David John. Ecological genetics. — Harlow : Longman, Oct.1981. — [500]p
ISBN 0-582-46349-1 : £14.00 : CIP entry B81-30280

575.2 — Evolution. Role of phenocopy
Piaget, Jean. Adaptation and intelligence : organic selection and phenocopy / Jean Piaget ; translated by Stewart Eames ; foreword by Terrance A. Brown. — Chicago ; London : University of Chicago Press, 1980. — 124p : ill ; 25cm
Translation of: Adaptation vitale et psychologie de l'intelligence. — Includes index
ISBN 0-226-66777-4 : £6.60 B81-06982

575.2 — Genes. Variation. Quantitative methods
Quantitative genetic variation / edited by James N. Thompson, Jr, J.M. Thoday. — New York ; London : Academic Press, 1979. — x,305p : ill ; 24cm
Includes bibliographies and index
ISBN 0-12-688850-7 : £14.60 B81-11263

575.9422'67 — West Sussex. Pagham Harbour. Organisms
The **Natural** history of Pagham Harbour. — 2nd ed. — Bognor Regis ([11 Coniston Close, Felpham, W. Sussex PO22 8ND]) : Bognor Regis Natural Science Society
Pt.2: Plants and animals other than birds and mammals / edited by R.W. Rayner. — 1981. — 69p : ill,maps ; 24cm
Previous ed.: 1975. — Includes bibliographies
Unpriced (pbk) B81-39019

576 — MICROORGANISMS

576 — Microbiology
Anderson, Dean A.. Introduction to microbiology / Dean A. Anderson, Rodney J. Sobieski. — 2nd ed. — St. Louis ; London : Mosby, 1980. — xv,518p : ill ; 24cm
Previous ed.: 1973. — Text on inside cover. — Includes bibliographies and index
ISBN 0-8016-0206-8 (pbk) : £12.75 B81-08203

Pelczar, Michael J.. Elements of microbiology / Michael J. Pelczar Jr., E.C.S. Chan, with the assistance of Merna Foss Pelczar. — New York ; London : McGraw-Hill, c1981. — vi,698p : ill(some col.),col.maps,ports ; 25cm
Col. ill on lining papers. — Includes bibliographies and index
ISBN 0-07-049240-9 : £16.25 B81-36480

576 — Microbiology. Applications of genetics — *Conference proceedings*
Society for General Microbiology. *Symposium (31st : 1981 : University of Cambridge)*. Genetics as a tool in microbiology : thirty-first symposium of the Society for General Microbiology held at the University of Cambridge, April 1981 / edited by S.W. Glover and D.A. Hopwood. — Cambridge : published for the Society for General Microbiology [by] Cambridge University Press, 1981. — 427p : ill ; 24cm
Includes bibliographies and index
ISBN 0-521-23748-3 : £27.50 : CIP rev.
B81-075

576 — Microorganisms. Cells. M
Rogers, H. J.. Microbial
membranes / H.J.
Ward. — Lo
— x,564
In

576 — Microorganisms — *For schools*

Singleton, Paul. Introduction to bacteria. — Chichester : Wiley, Dec.1981. — [166]p
ISBN 0-471-10034-x (cased) : £9.50 : CIP entry
ISBN 0-471-10035-8 (pbk) : £4.75 B81-33885

Williams, J. I.. Micro-organisms. — 2nd ed. — London : Bell & Hyman, Jan.1982. — [176]p
Previous ed.: London : Mills and Boon, 1976
ISBN 0-7135-1321-7 (pbk) : £3.75 : CIP entry
B81-38841

576'.028 — Microbiology. Laboratory techniques. Applications of gas chromatography

Drucker, D. B.. Microbiological applications of gas chromatography / D.B. Drucker. — Cambridge : Cambridge University Press, 1981. — viii,478p : ill ; 24cm
Bibliography: p425-469. — Includes index
ISBN 0-521-22365-2 : £45.00 B81-37137

576'.028 — Microbiology. Laboratory techniques — *Manuals*

Seeley, Harry W.. Microbes in action : a laboratory manual of microbiology / Harry W. Seeley, Jr., Paul J. VanDemark. — 3rd ed. — Oxford : W.H. Freeman, 1981. — xii,385p : ill ; 28cm
Previous ed.: 1972. — Includes index
ISBN 0-7167-1259-8 (pbk) : £6.80 B81-37386

Seeley, Harry W.. Selected exercises from Microbes in action : a laboratory manual of microbiology / Harry W. Seeley, Jr., Paul J. VanDemark. — 3rd ed. — Oxford : W.H. Freeman, c1981. — x,268p : ill ; 28cm
Previous ed.: 1972. — Includes index
ISBN 0-7167-1260-1 (pbk) : £6.80 B81-37387

Smith, Alice Lorraine. Microbiology : laboratory manual and workbook / Alice Lorraine Smith. — 5th ed. — St. Louis ; London : Mosby, 1981. — viii,199p : ill,forms ; 24cm
Previous ed.: 1977. — Bibliography: p8-9
ISBN 0-8016-4707-x (pbk) : £7.00 B81-31152

576'.03 — Microbiology - *Encyclopedias*

Singleton, Paul. Dictionary of microbiology. — Chichester : Wiley, June 1981. — [496]p
Originally published: 1978
ISBN 0-471-28036-4 (pbk) : £4.95 : CIP entry
B81-09978

576'.11 — Microorganisms. Physiology — *Serials*

Advances in microbial physiology. — Vol.22. — London : Academic Press, Sept.1981. — [250]p
ISBN 0-12-027722-0 : CIP entry
ISSN 0065-2911 B81-21610

576'.118 — Surfaces. Adhesion of microorganisms — *Conference proceedings*

Adhesion and microorganism pathogenicity. — London : Pitman Medical, 1981. — x,346p : ill ; 24cm. — (Ciba Foundation symposium ; 80)
Conference paper... — Includes bibliographies and index
ISBN 0-272... Unpriced B81-19829

Mi... editors R.C.W. ... : Published ...y, London ...cm ...aphies ...68

576'.11925 — Microorganisms of economic importance. Enzymes

Microbial enzymes and bioconversions / edited by A.H. Rose. — London : Academic Press, 1980. — xviii,693p : ill,1port ; 24cm. — (Economic microbiology ; v.5)
Includes bibliographies and index
ISBN 0-12-596555-9 : £50.00 : CIP rev.
B80-20651

576'.1334 — Microorganisms. Cells. Cycles

Edwards, C. A.. The microbial cell cycle / Clive Edwards. — Walton-on-Thames : Nelson, 1981. — 88p : ill ; 22cm. — (Aspects of microbiology)
Includes bibliographies and index
ISBN 0-17-771103-5 (pbk) : £2.75 B81-21847

576'.138 — Microorganisms. Evolution — *Conference proceedings*

Society for General Microbiology. *Symposium (32nd : 1981 : University of Edinburgh)*. Molecular and cellular aspects of microbial evolution : thirty-second symposium of the Society for General Microbiology held at the University of Edinburgh, September 1981 / edited by M.J. Carlile, J.F. Collins and B.E.B. Moseley. — Cambridge : Cambridge University Press for the Society for General Microbiology, 1981. — x,368p : ill ; 24cm
Includes bibliographies and index
ISBN 0-521-24108-1 : £27.50 : CIP rev.
B81-21565

576'.139 — Microorganisms. Genetics

Molecular breeding and genetics of applied microorganisms / edited by Kenji Sakaguchi and Masanori Okanishi. — Tokyo : Kodansha ; New York ; London : Academic Press, c1981. — xii,160p : ill ; 24cm
Includes index
ISBN 0-12-615050-8 : £15.20 B81-29770

576'.16 — Applied microbiology

Essays in applied microbiology. — Chichester : Wiley, Jan.1982. — [380]p
ISBN 0-471-27998-6 : £19.50 : CIP entry
B81-34562

576'.16 — Applied microbiology — *Conference proceedings*

GIAM VI *(Conference : 1980 : Lagos)*. Global impacts of applied microbiology : GIAM VI : sixth international conference / edited by S.O. Emejuaiwe, O. Ogunbi, S.O. Sanni. — London : Academic Press, 1981. — xlii,652p : ill ; 23cm. — (International conferences on global impacts of applied microbiology)
Includes bibliographies
ISBN 0-12-238280-3 (pbk) : £20.60 : CIP rev.
B81-04328

576'.16'05 — Applied microbiology — *Serials*

Advances in applied microbiology. — Vol.26 (1980). — New York ; London : Academic Press, c1980. — xii,271p
ISBN 0-12-002626-0 : £16.60
ISSN 0065-2164 B81-16840

576'.163 — Food. Contaminants: Microorganisms. Ecology

Microbial ecology of foods / by the International Commission on Microbiological Specifications for Foods ; Editorial Committee J.H. Silliker ... [et al.]. — New York ; London : Academic Press. — (Microorganisms in foods ; 3)
Vol.2: Food commodities. — 1980. — xxii,p333-997 : ill ; 24cm
Bibliography: p862-911. — Includes index
ISBN 0-12-363502-0 : £38.40 B81-19835

576'.163 — Food. Contaminants: Psychrophillic microorganisms — *Conference proceedings*

Psychrotrophic microorganisms in spoilage and pathogenecity. — London : Academic Press, Jan.1982. — [550]p
Conference papers
ISBN 0-12-589720-0 : CIP entry B81-35910

...63'05 — Food. Contaminants: Microorganisms ...*ials*

...**ments** in food microbiology. — 1. — ... : Applied Science, Feb.1982. — [224]p. ...Developments series)
...34-999-1 : £21.00 : CIP entry
B81-35855

576'.165 — Microorganisms. Growth. Control measures

Principles and practice of disinfection, preservation and sterilisation. — Oxford : Blackwell Scientific, Nov.1981. — [640]p
ISBN 0-632-00547-5 : £27.50 : CIP entry
B81-32023

576'.192 — Aquatic microorganisms

Rheinheimer, G.. Aquatic microbiology / G. Rheinheimer. — 2nd ed / [translated from German by Norman Walker]. — Chichester : Wiley, c1980. — 235p : ill ; 25cm
Translation of: Mikrobiologie der Gewässer. — Previous ed.: 1974. — Bibliography: p209-225. — Includes index
ISBN 0-471-27643-x : £10.00 : CIP rev.
B79-17551

576'.64 — Non-Arthopoda borne togaviruses

Horzinek, M. C.. Non-arthropod-borne togaviruses / M.C. Horzinek. — London : Academic Press, 1981. — ix,200p : ill ; 24cm. — (Experimental virology)
Bibliography: p163-193. — Includes index
ISBN 0-12-356550-2 : £16.40 B81-23548

576'.64 — Viruses

Comprehensive virology / edited by Heinz Fraenkel-Conrat and Robert R. Wagner. — New York ; London : Plenum
17: Methods used in the study of viruses. — c1981. — xvi,463p : ill ; 26cm
Includes bibliographies and index
ISBN 0-306-40418-4 : Unpriced B81-19272

576'.64 — Viruses. Genetics — *Conference proceedings*

Sigrid Jusélius Foundation Symposium *(8th : 1980 Helsinki)*. Expression of eukaryotic viral and cellular genes : Eighth Sigrid Jusélius Foundation Symposium Helsinki, Finland June 1980 / edited by Ralf F. Pettersson ... [et al.]. — London : Academic Press, 1981. — xi,324p : ill ; 24cm
Includes bibliographies
ISBN 0-12-553120-6 : £20.40
Primary classification 574.87'322 B81-12361

576'.64'0321 — Virology — *Encyclopaedias*

Rowson, K. E. K.. A dictionary of virology / K.E.K. Rowson, T.A.L. Rees, B.W.J. Mahy. — Oxford : Blackwell Scientific, 1981. — v,230p : ill ; 22cm
ISBN 0-632-00697-8 (cased) : Unpriced : CIP rev.
ISBN 0-632-00784-2 (pbk) : £9.80 B81-03828

576'.6483 — Plants. Pathogens: Viruses

Gibbs, Adrian. Plant virology : the principles / Adrian Gibbs, Bryan Harrison. — London : Edward Arnold, 1976 (1980 [printing]). — x,292p : ill ; 25cm
Bibliography: p257-278. — Includes index
ISBN 0-7131-2764-3 (pbk) : £10.50 B81-40561

576'.6484 — Togaviruses

The **Togaviruses** : biology, structure, replication / edited by R. Walter Schlesinger ; contributors Walter E. Brandt ... [et al.]. — New York ; London : Academic Press, c1980. — xv,687p : ill ; 24cm
Includes bibliographies and index
ISBN 0-12-625380-3 : £37.40 B81-15121

576'.6484 — Vertebrates. Pathogens: Viruses. Genetics — *Conference proceedings*

ICN-UCLA Symposia on Animal Virus Genetics *(1980 : Keystone)*. Animal virus genetics / edited by Bernard N. Fields, Rudolf Jaenisch ; proceedings of the 1980 ICN-UCLA Symposia on Animal Virus Genetics, held in Keystone, Colorado, March 9-14, 1980. — New York ; London : Academic Press, 1980. — xxvi,830p : ill ; 24cm. — (ICN-UCLA symposia on molecular and cellular biology ; vol. xviii, 1980)
Includes index
ISBN 0-12-255850-2 : £25.20 B81-21989

577 — BIOLOGY. PROPERTIES OF LIFE

577 — Life. Origin
Gribbin, John. Genesis : the origins of man and the universe / John Gribbin. — London : Dent, c1981. — xvi,360p : ill,maps,2ports ; 24cm
Bibliography: p342-345. — Includes index
ISBN 0-460-04505-9 : £7.95 B81-21999

Sheldrake, Rupert. A new science of life : the hypothesis of formative causation / Rupert Sheldrake. — London : Blond & Briggs, 1981. — 229p : ill ; 24cm
Bibliography: p209-218. — Includes index
ISBN 0-85634-115-0 : £12.50 : CIP rev. B81-10497

577 — Life. Origin. Astronomical aspects
Hoyle, Fred. Evolution from space / Fred Hoyle, Chandra Wickramasinghe. — London : Dent, 1981. — xii,176p : ill ; 24cm
Includes index
ISBN 0-460-04535-0 : £7.95 : CIP rev. B81-12846

578 — BIOLOGY. MICROSCOPY

578′.45 — Biology. Electron microscopy
Hayat, M. A.. Principles and techniques of electron microscopy : biological applications / M.A. Hayat. — [Rev. ed.]. — London : Edward Arnold, 1981. — xv,522p : ill ; 24cm
Previous ed.: in 9 Vols. New York ; London : Van Nostrand Reinhold, 1970-78. — Bibliography: p457-505. — Includes index
ISBN 0-7131-2830-5 : £27.50 : CIP rev. B81-06061

578′.45 — Biology. Electron probe microanalysis — *Conference proceedings*
Microbeam analysis in biology / edited by Claude P. Lechene, Ronald R. Warner. — New York ; London : Academic Press, 1979. — xx,672p : ill ; 24cm
Conference papers. — Includes bibliographies and index
ISBN 0-12-440340-9 : £22.20 B81-34986

578′.45 — Biology. Transmission electron microscopy
Weakley, Brenda S.. A beginner's handbook in biological transmission electron microscopy / Brenda S. Weakley. — [2nd ed.]. — Edinburgh : Churchill Livingstone, 1981. — xi,252p : ill ; 24cm
Previous ed.: published as A beginner's handbook in biological electron microscopy. 1972. — Includes bibliographies and index
ISBN 0-443-02091-4 (pbk) : £9.75 : CIP rev. B81-07912

578′.45′05 — Biology. Electron microscopy — *Serials*
Electron microscopy in biology. — Vol.1-. — New York ; Chichester : Wiley, 1981-. — v. : ill ; 24cm
Annual
ISSN 0275-5262 = Electron microscopy in biology : £30.50 B81-33947

578′.6 — Biological specimens. Preparation. Histology. Laboratory techniques — *For optical microscopy*
Kiernan, J. A.. Histological and histochemical methods : theory and practice / J.A. Kiernan. — Oxford : Pergamon, 1981. — xii,344p : ill ; 25cm. — (Pergamon international library)
Bibliography: p309-324. — Includes index
ISBN 0-08-024936-1 (cased) : Unpriced : CIP rev.
ISBN 0-08-024935-3 (pbk) : £10.50 B80-23330

579 — BIOLOGICAL SPECIMENS. COLLECTION AND PRESERVATION

579 — Living matter. Preservation. Cryogenic techniques
Morris, G. J.. Cryopreservation : an introduction to cryopreservation in culture collections / G.J. Morris. — Cambridge (68 Hills Rd., Cambridge CB2 1LA) : Institute of Terrestrial Ecology, 1981. — 27p,[8]p of plates : ill(some col.) ; 30cm
At head of title: Natural Environment Research Council, Institute of Terrestrial Ecology. — Bibliography: p27
ISBN 0-904282-45-7 (pbk) : £2.00 B81-25393

579 — Microlepidoptera. Collecting — *Amateurs' manuals*
Sokoloff, Paul. Practical hints for collecting and studying the microlepidoptera / by Paul Sokoloff. — [Feltham, Middx] : The Amateur Entomologists' Society, [1980]. — 40p : ill ; 22cm. — (The Amateur entomologist ; v.16)
Cover title. — Bibliography: p33-37
Unpriced (pbk) B81-02820

579′.1 — Vertebrates. Skull. Collecting — *Amateurs' manuals*
Steel, Richard. Skulls! / Richard Steel ; illustrated by Gerry Gaston. — London : Heinemann, 1980. — 87p : ill ; 21cm
Includes index
ISBN 0-434-96450-6 : £3.95 B81-06556

579′.4 — Fish. Taxidermy — *Manuals*
Migdalski, Edward C.. Fish mounts and other fish trophies : the complete book of fish taxidermy / Edward C. Migdalski. — 2nd ed. — New York ; Chichester : Wiley, c1981. — xii,212p : ill ; 24cm
Previous ed.: published as How to make fish mounts. New York : Ronald Press, 1960. — Includes index
ISBN 0-471-07990-1 : £11.20 B81-33156

579′.4 — Taxidermy — *Amateurs' manuals*
Metcalf, John C.. Taxidermy : a complete manual / John C. Metcalf. — London : Duckworth, 1981. — 166p,[8]p of plates : ill (some col.) ; 27cm
Bibliography: p138. — Includes index
ISBN 0-7156-1051-1 (cased) : Unpriced
ISBN 0-7156-1565-3 (pbk) : £9.95 B81-17927

580 — BOTANICAL SCIENCES

580′.74′442195 — London. Richmond upon Thames *(London Borough).* **Botanical gardens: Royal Botanic Gardens** *(Kew).* **Plants mentioned in Bible —** *Visitors' guides*
Hepper, F. Nigel. Bible plants at Kew / F. Nigel Hepper. — London : H.M.S.O., 1981. — 63p : ill(some col.),1map ; 19cm
At head of title: Royal Botanic Gardens, Kew. — Bibliography: p51-53. — Includes index
ISBN 0-11-241171-1 (pbk) : £2.95 B81-37139

580′.74′442659 — Cambridgeshire. Cambridge. Universities. Botanical gardens: Cambridge University Botanic Garden. Stock: Plants — *Catalogues*
Cambridge University Botanic Garden. Catalogue of plants in the Cambridge University Botanic Garden / [compiled] by P.F. Yeo and C.J. King. — [Cambridge] : Cambridge University Botanic Garden, 1981. — 132 : ill ; 23cm
Bibliography: [3]p
Unpriced (pbk) B81-09330

581 — BOTANY

581 — Great Britain. Carnivorous plants — *Serials*
The **Carnivorous** Plant Society journal. — Vol.4 (Spring 1980)-. — [London] (c/o Mr T. Clifton, 31 Barclay Rd, Walthamstow, E17) : The Society, 1980-. — v. : ill ; 21cm
Continues: Carnivorous Plant Society
ISSN 0260-440x = Carnivorous Plant Society journal : Unpriced B81-31566

581 — Plants
The **Encyclopedia** of the plant kingdom / [botanical editor Anthony Huxley]. — London : Salamander, 1981, c1977. — 240p : ill(some col.) ; 31cm
Originally published: London : Hamlyn, 1977. — Ill on lining papers. — Includes index
ISBN 0-86101-095-7 : £7.95 B81-39856

581 — Plants — *For children*
Wilson, Ron. The life of plants / Ron Wilson. — London : Ward Lock, 1980. — 96p : col.ill ; 28cm
Includes index
ISBN 0-7063-5800-7 : £3.95 B81-025

581 — Plants — *For schools*
Booth, Philip, *1940-*. The life of p
Booth. — London : Heinem
1981. — 75p : ill ; 25cm
individual ; bk.11)
ISBN 0-435-59769

Gosden, Sheila. Plant science / Sheila Gosden. — Glasgow : Blackie, 1981. — 32p : ill ; 17x25cm. — (Modular science)
ISBN 0-216-90589-3 (pbk) : £1.40 B81-39187

581 — Rare plants
Threatened plants. — [London] : British Museum (Natural History), c1981. — [12]p : ill ; 15x21cm. — (Publication / British Museum (Natural History) ; no.836)
ISBN 0-565-00836-6 (unbound) : £0.30 B81-26126

581′.012 — Plants. Taxonomy
Stace, Clive A.. Plant taxonomy and biosystematics / Clive A. Stace. — London : Edward Arnold, 1980. — viii,279p : ill,maps ; 22cm. — (Contemporary biology)
Bibliography: p252-268. — Includes index
ISBN 0-7131-2802-x (pbk) : £8.95 : CIP rev. B80-18287

581′.03 — Botany — *Polyglot dictionaries*
Macura, Paul. Elsevier's dictionary of botany. — Oxford : Elsevier Scientific
2: General terms. — Oct.1981. — 1v.
ISBN 0-444-41977-2 : CIP entry B81-31197

581′.05 — Botany — *Serials*
Advances in botanical research. — Vol.8. — London : Academic Press, 1980. — xii,285p
ISBN 0-12-005908-8 : Unpriced
ISSN 0065-2296 B81-32698

Advances in botanical research. — Vol.9. — London : Academic Press, Feb.1982. — [280]p
ISBN 0-12-005909-6 : CIP entry
ISSN 0065-2296 B81-36037

581′.05 — Plants — *Serials*
Commentaries in plant science. — Vol.2. — Oxford : Pergamon Press, 1981. — ix,261p
ISBN 0-08-025898-0 : £23.00 : CIP rev. B80-27018

581′.07′1142659 — Cambridgeshire. Cambridge. Universities: University of Cambridge. *School of Botany, to 1981*
Walters, S. M.. The shaping of Cambridge botany : a short history of whole-plant botany in Cambridge from the time of Ray into the present century : published on the occasion of the sesquicentenary of Henslow's New Botanic Garden, 1831-1981 / by S.M. Walters. — Cambridge : Cambridge University Press, 1981. — xv,121p : ill,facsims,2plans,ports ; 26cm
Bibliography: p111-116. — Includes index
ISBN 0-521-23795-5 : £17.50 B81-26266

581′.0724 — Plants. Cells & tissues. Culture — *Conference proceedings*
Plant tissue culture : methods and applications in agriculture : [proceedings of a symposium based on the UNESCO training course on plant tissue culture : methods and applications in agriculture, sponsored by UNESCO and held in Campinas, Sao Paulo, Brazil, on November 8-22, 1978] / edited by Trevor A. Thorpe. — New York ; London : Academic Press, 1981. — x,379p : ill ; 24cm
Includes bibliographies and index
ISBN 0-12-690680-7 : £13.20 B81-354

Plant tissue culture. — Boston ; Londo
Advanced Publishing Program, c1
531p,[50]p of plates : ill ; 27cm
Pitman international series
Conference papers. — I
ISBN 0-273-08488-7

581′.0724 — Pl
Tissue cu
edit

581.1 — Plants. Physiology — *Conference proceedings*

The **Plant** cuticle. — London : Academic Press, Dec.1981. — [320]p. — (Linnean Society symposium series, ISSN 0161-6366 ; no.10)
Conference papers
ISBN 0-12-199920-3 : CIP entry B81-32049

581.1 — Plants. Physiology. Ecological aspects

Fitter, A. H.. Environmental physiology of plants / A.H. Fitter and R.K.M. Hay. — London : Academic Press, 1981. — xii,355p : ill,1map ; 24. — (Experimental botany ; v.15)
Bibliography: p297-338. — Includes index
ISBN 0-12-257760-4 (cased) : Unpriced
ISBN 0-12-257762-0 (pbk) : Unpriced
B81-29734

581.1 — Plants. Physiology. Effects of diseases — *Conference proceedings*

Effects of disease on the physiology of growing plants. — Cambridge : Cambridge University Press, Nov.1981. — [230]p. — (Society for Experimental Biology seminar series ; 11)
Conference papers
ISBN 0-521-23306-2 (cased) : £20.00 : CIP entry
ISBN 0-521-29898-9 (pbk) : £8.95 B81-34013

581.1'072 — Plants. Physiology. Mathematical models - *Conference proceedings*

Mathematics and plant physiology. — London : Academic Press, June 1981. — [300]p
Conference papers
ISBN 0-12-596880-9 : CIP entry B81-12356

581.1'21 — Plants. Stomata. Physiology

Stomatal physiology / edited by P.G. Jarvis and T.A. Mansfield. — Cambridge : Cambridge University Press, 1981. — 295p : ill ; 24cm. — (Society for Experimental Biology : Seminar series ; 8)
Includes bibliographies and index
ISBN 0-521-23683-5 (cased) : £22.00
ISBN 0-521-28151-2 (pbk) : £10.95 B81-37811

581.1'33 — Plants. Secondary metabolism

Vickery, Margaret L.. Secondary plant metabolism / Margaret L. Vickery and Brian Vickery. — London : Macmillan, 1981. — xii,335p : ill ; 25cm
Includes bibliographies and index
ISBN 0-333-27017-7 (cased) : Unpriced
ISBN 0-333-27018-5 (pbk) : Unpriced
B81-34198

581.1'3304207'2 — Plants. Photosynthesis. Research. Applications of mathematical models

Charles-Edwards, D. A.. The ... matics of photosynthesis and ... London : Academic Pres... Experim...
...-13461

581.1'3354 — Plants. Water. Deficiency. Adaptation of plants

Adaptation of plants to water and high temperature stress / edited by Neil C. Turner, Paul J. Kramer. — New York ; Chichester : Wiley, c1980. — xiii,482p : ill ; 24cm
Conference papers. — Includes index
ISBN 0-471-05372-4 : £21.50
Also classified at 581.19'162 B81-04525

581.1'66 — Plants. Sexual reproduction

Bristow, Alec. The sex life of plants : a study of the secrets of reproduction / Alec Bristow. — London : New English Library, 1980, c1978. — 223p : ill ; 19cm
Originally published: New York : Holt, Rinehart and Winston, 1978 ; London : Barrie and Jenkins, 1979. — Includes index
ISBN 0-450-04667-2 (pbk) : £1.25 B81-00888

581.19'162 — High temperature. Adaptation of plants

Adaptation of plants to water and high temperature stress / edited by Neil C. Turner, Paul J. Kramer. — New York ; Chichester : Wiley, c1980. — xiii,482p : ill ; 24cm
Conference papers. — Includes index
ISBN 0-471-05372-4 : £21.50
Primary classification 581.1'3354 B81-04525

581.19'2 — Plants. Biochemistry

The **Biochemistry** of plants : a comprehensive treatise. — New York ; London : Academic Press
Vol.4: Lipids : structure and function / P.K. Stumpf, editor. — 1980. — xv,693p : ill ; 25cm
Includes bibliographies and index
ISBN 0-12-675404-7 : £36.40 B81-33739

The **Biochemistry** of plants : a comprehensive treatise / P.K. Stumpf and E.E. Conn editors-in-chief. — New York ; London : Academic Press
Vol.6: Proteins and nucleic acids / Abraham Marcus editor. — 1981. — xiii,652p : ill ; 25cm
Includes bibliographies and index
ISBN 0-12-675406-3 : £44.60 B81-38908

The **Biochemistry** of plants : a comprehensive treatise / P.K. Stumpf and E.E. Conn, editors-in-chief. — New York ; London : Academic Press
Photosynthesis / M.D. Hatch and N.K. Boardman, editors. — 1981. — xvii,521p : ill ; 25cm
Includes bibliographies and index
ISBN 0-12-675408-x : £43.00 B81-39572

581.19'2'05 — Plants. Biochemistry — *Serials*

Progress in phytochemistry. — Vol.7. — Oxford : Pergamon Press, 1981. — xii,344p
ISBN 0-08-026362-3 : Unpriced
ISSN 0079-6689 B81-23509

Recent advances in phytochemistry. — Vol.14. — New York ; London : Plenum Press, c1980. — xiii,215p
...BN 0-306-40572-5 : Unpriced
...N 0006-1530 B81-18807

...Plants. Nitrogen & carbon. ... *Conference proceedings*

...bon metabolism : proceedings of ... the physiology and ... nt productivity held in ... ly 14-17, 1980 / edited by ... The Hague ; London : ... p : ill ; 25cm. — ... d soil sciences ; v.3)
...d B81-17114

... lts / ... 2nd ed. ... : ill ... in

581.19'24 — Plants. Organic compounds. Qualitative analysis. Laboratory techniques

Harborne, J. B.. Phytochemical methods : a guide to modern techniques of plant analysis / J.B. Harborne. — London : Chapman and Hall, 1973 (1976 [printing]). — x,278p : ill ; 25cm
Includes bibliographies and index
ISBN 0-412-10540-3 : £9.50 B81-10026

581.19'242 — Plants. Indole alkaloids — *Conference proceedings*

Indole and biogenetically related alkaloids / edited by J.D. Phillipson and M.H. Zenk. — London : Academic Press, 1980. — xvii,379p : ill ; 24cm. — (Annual proceedings of the Phytochemical Society of Europe, ISSN 0309-9393 ; no.17)
Includes bibliographies and index
ISBN 0-12-554450-2 : £32.60 : CIP rev.
B80-02778

581.19'247 — Plants. Lipids — *Conference proceedings*

Symposium on Recent Advances in the Biogenesis and Function of Plant Lipids *(1980 : Paris)*. Biogenesis and function of plant lipids : proceedings of the Symposium on Recent Advances in the Biogenesis and Function of Plant Lipids, held in Paris, June 4-7, 1980 / editors P. Mazliak ... [et al.]. — Amsterdam ; Oxford : Elsevier/North-Holland Biomedical Press, 1980. — xiv,451p : 1ill,1port ; 25cm. — (Developments in plant biology ; v.6)
Includes index
ISBN 0-444-80273-8 : £27.83 B81-00889

581.2 — PLANTS. DISEASES

581.2 — Plants. Phytoalexins

Phytoalexins. — Glasgow : Blackie, Dec.1981. — [320]p
ISBN 0-216-91162-1 : £28.00 : CIP entry
B81-3145

581.2'09 — Plants. Pathology, *to 1980*

Ainsworth, G. C.. Introduction to the history of plant pathology / G.C. Ainsworth. — Cambridge : Cambridge University Press, 1981. — xii,315p : ill(some col.),1map,facsims,ports ; 24cm
Bibliography: p252-293. — Includes index
ISBN 0-521-23032-2 : £27.50 B81-3713

581.2'3 — Plants. Diseases. Vectors

Plant diseases and vectors : ecology and epidemiology / edited by Karl Maramorosch, Kerry F. Harris. — New York ; London : Academic Press, c1981. — xii,368p : ill ; 24cm
Includes bibliographies and index
ISBN 0-12-470240-6 : £21.40 B81-3535

581.2'3 — Plants. Leaves. Surfaces. Pathogens: Microorganisms — *Conference proceedings*

Microbial ecology of phylloplane / edited by J.P. Blakeman. — London : Academic Press, 1981. — xiii,502p : ill ; 24cm
Conference papers. — Includes bibliographies and index
ISBN 0-12-103750-9 : £20.40 : CIP rev.
B81-1342

581.2'3 — Plants. Vectors

Vectors of plant pathogens / edited by Kerry F. Harris, Karl Maramorosch. — New York ; London : Academic Press, 1980. — xiv,467p : ill ; 24cm
Includes bibliographies and index
ISBN 0-12-326450-2 : £27.00 B81-2215

581.2'326 — Plants. Parasites: Fungi

Deverall, Brian J.. Fungal parasitism. — 2nd ed. — London : Edward Arnold, Nov.1981. — [72]p. — (The Institute of Biology's studies in biology, ISSN 0537-9024 ; no.7)
Previous ed.: 1969
ISBN 0-7131-2832-1 (pbk) : £2.40 : CIP entry
B81-3061

581.2'34 — Plants. Virus diseases

Handbook of plant virus infections : comparative diagnosis / edited by Edouard Kurstak. — Amsterdam ; Oxford : Elsevier/North-Holland Biomedical Press, 1981. — xiii,943p : ill ; 25cr
Includes bibliographies and index
ISBN 0-444-80309-2 : Unpriced B81-3003

581.3 — PLANTS. DEVELOPMENT

581.3'1 — Plants. Effects of daylight — *Conference proceedings*

Plants and the daylight spectrum. — London : Academic Press, Dec.1981. — [400]p
Conference papers
ISBN 0-12-650980-8 : CIP entry B81-31347

581.3'1 — Plants. Growth. Analysis. Quantitative methods

Causton, David R.. The biometry of plant growth / David R. Causton, Jill C. Venus. — London : Edward Arnold, 1981. — xii,307p : ill ; 24cm
Bibliography: p284-299. — Includes index
ISBN 0-7131-2812-7 : £25.00 : CIP rev. B80-33575

581.3'1 — Plants. Growth. Effects of light

Whatley, Jean M.. Light and plant life / Jean M. Whatley, F.R. Whatley. — London : Edward Arnold, 1980. — 92p : ill ; 22cm. — (The Institute of Biology's studies in biology, ISSN 0537-9024 ; no.124)
Bibliography: p92
ISBN 0-7131-2785-6 (pbk) : £3.40 : CIP rev. B80-18289

581.3'1 — Plants. Growth. Effects of soil properties

Davidescu, David. Evaluation of fertility by plant and soil analysis. — Tunbridge Wells : Abacus, Jan.1982. — [488]p
Translation of: Testarea stării de fertilitate prin plantă şi sol
ISBN 0-85626-123-8 : £24.95 : CIP entry B81-40261

581.3'1 — Plants. Leaves. Growth

Dale, John E.. The growth of leaves. — London : Edward Arnold, Dec.1981. — [64]p. — (The Institute of Biology's studies in biology, ISSN 0537-9024 ; no.137)
ISBN 0-7131-2836-4 (pbk) : £1.95 : CIP entry B81-31631

581.3'8 — Plants. Evolution

Thomas, Barry, *1940-*. The evolution of plants and flowers / by Barry Thomas ; with eight double-page paintings by Tony Swift. — [London] : Peter Lowe, c1981. — 116p : col.ill,col.maps ; 28cm
Bibliography: p114. — Includes index
ISBN 0-85654-024-2 : £5.96 : CIP rev. B79-16663

581.3'8 — Plants. Evolution. Effects of environmental pollution

Bradshaw, A. D.. Evolution and pollution / A.D. Bradshaw, T. McNeilly. — London : Edward Arnold, 1981. — 76p : ill ; 22cm. — (The Institute of Biology's studies in biology, ISSN 0537-9024 ; no.130)
Bibliography: p74-76
ISBN 0-7131-2818-6 (pbk) : £2.50 B81-32822

581.4 — PLANTS. ANATOMY

581.4 — Plants. Anatomy

Fahn, A.. Plant anatomy. — 3rd ed. — Oxford : Pergamon, Feb.1982. — [400]p. — (Pergamon international library)
Previous ed.: 1974
ISBN 0-08-028030-7 (cased) : £27.00 : CIP entry
ISBN 0-08-028029-3 (pbk) : £12.50 B81-35943

581.4 — Plants. Anatomy — *Anthropological viewpoints*

Adams, George, *1894-1963*. The plant between sun and earth : and the science of physical and ethereal spaces / George Adams, Olive Whicher ; preface by Ehrenfried Pfeiffer. — 2nd ed. (rev. and enl.). — London : Steiner, 1980. — 224p,xx p of plates : ill(some col.) ; 25cm
Previous ed.: Stourbridge : Goethean Science Foundation, 1952. — Includes index
ISBN 0-85440-360-4 (pbk) : £14.00 B81-06108

581.5 — PLANTS. ECOLOGY

581.5 — Plants. Ecology — *Conference proceedings*

British Ecological Society. *Symposium (21st : 1979 : Edinburgh)*. Plants and their atmospheric environment : the 21st Symposium of the British Ecological Society Edinburgh 1979 / edited by J. Grace, E.D. Ford and P.G. Jarvis. — Oxford : Blackwell Scientific, 1981. — vii,417p : ill ; 25cm
Includes bibliographies and index
ISBN 0-632-00525-4 : £18.50 B81-25600

581.5 — Plants. Productivity. Effects of radiation

Ross, Juhan. The radiation regime and architecture of plant stands / Juhan Ross. — The Hague ; London : Junk, 1981. — xxvii,391p : ill ; 25cm. — (Tasks for vegetation sciences ; 3)
Bibliography: p363-381. — Includes index
ISBN 90-619-3607-1 : Unpriced B81-27727

581.5'222 — Plants. Toxic effects of heavy metals

Effects of heavy metal pollution on plants. — London : Applied Science Publishers, July 1981. — (Pollution monitoring series)
Vol.1: Effects of trace metals on plant function. — [360]p
ISBN 0-85334-959-2 : £25.00 : CIP entry B81-14811

Effects of heavy metal pollution on plants. — London : Applied Science Publishers, July 1981. — (Pollution monitoring series)
Vol.2: Metals in the environment. — [256]p
ISBN 0-85334-923-1 : £20.00 : CIP entry B81-14812

581.5'247 — Plants. Ecological communities. Distribution

Kellman, Martin C.. Plant geography / Martin C. Kellman. — 2nd ed. — London : Methuen, 1980. — xii,181p,[8]p of plates : ill,maps ; 24cm
Previous ed.: 1975. — Bibliography: p152-171. - Includes index
ISBN 0-416-73850-8 (cased) : £4.95 : CIP rev.
ISBN 0-416-73860-5 (pbk) : £3.50 B80-08755

581.5'248 — Plants. Population

Harper, John L.. Population biology of plants / John L. Harper. — London : Academic Press, 1977 (1981 printing). — xxiv,892p : ill ; 23cm
Bibliography: p779-828. — Includes index
ISBN 0-12-325852-9 (pbk) : Unpriced B81-30039

581.5'2642'09667 — Ghana. Forests. Vascular plants. Ecology

Hall, J. B.. Distribution and ecology of vascular plants in a tropical rain forest : forest vegetation in Ghana / J.B. Hall and M.D. Swaine. — The Hague ; London : Junk, 1981. — xv,382p : ill,maps ; 27cm + 1transparency (3 overlays)(b & w ; 19x24cm). — (Geobotany ; 1)
Transparency in pocket. — Bibliography: p357-364. — Includes index
ISBN 90-619-3681-0 : Unpriced
Primary classification 581.9667 B81-36866

581.6 — ECONOMIC BOTANY

581.6'1 — Plants useful to man

De Bray, Lys. Midsummer silver / Lys de Bray. — London : Dent, 1980. — 64p : ill ; 21cm
Includes index
ISBN 0-460-04512-1 : £2.95 B81-00114

Gordon, Lesley. A country herbal / Lesley Gordon. — Exeter : Webb & Bower, 1980. — 208p : ill(some col.),facsims ; 26cm
Bibliography: p203-204. — Includes index
ISBN 0-906671-09-4 : £9.95 : CIP rev. B80-21893

581.6'1'0973 — United States. Plants useful to man

Coon, Nelson. Using wild and wayside plants / Nelson Coon. — [Rev. ed.], [Repr. with expanded bibliography]. — New York : Dover ; London : Constable, 1980. — 284p : ill,maps ; 22cm
Originally published: New York : Hearthside, 1969. — Bibliography: p271-278. — Includes index
ISBN 0-486-23936-5 (pbk) : £2.50 B81-00890

581.6'3'094 — North-western Europe. Edible plants & medicinal plants — *Field guides*

Launert, Edmund. The Hamlyn guide to edible and medicinal plants of Britain and Northern Europe / Edmund Launert ; illustrated by Roger Gorringe and Anne Davies. — London : Hamlyn, c1981. — 288p : col.ill ; 20cm
Bibliography: p277. — Includes index
ISBN 0-600-37216-2 (cased) : £5.95
ISBN 0-600-35281-1 (pbk) : £3.95 B81-37329

581.6'34 — Medicinal plants

Hamilton, Edward. The Flora Homoeopathica. — London : Homoeopathic Trust, Aug.1981. — [626]p
Facsim. of: 1st ed. London : Bailliere, 1852
ISBN 0-9507629-0-3 : £40.00 : CIP entry B81-24627

Pahlow, Mannfried. Living medicine : the healing properties of plants / by Mannfried Pahlow ; introduction by Karl Heinz Caspers ; translated from the German by Linda Sonntag. — Wellingborough : Thorsons, 1980. — 96p,[8]p of plates : ill(some col.) ; 23cm
Translation of: Heilpflanzen heute. — Includes index
ISBN 0-7225-0605-8 (cased) : £5.95
ISBN 0-7225-0592-2 (pbk) : £2.95 B81-03503

581.6'52'03 — Western Europe. Weeds — *Polyglot dictionaries*

Williams, Gareth. Dictionary of weeds of western Europe. — Oxford : Elsevier Scientific, Oct.1981. — 1v.
ISBN 0-444-41978-0 : CIP entry B81-31196

581.8 — PLANTS. HISTOLOGY AND CYTOLOGY

581.87'322 — Plants. Genetic information. Modification. Use of cell culture

Chaleff, R. S.. Genetics of higher plants : applications of cell culture / R.S. Chaleff ; foreword by John G. Torrey. — Cambridge : Cambridge Unviersity Press, 1981. — xii,184p : ill ; 25cm. — (Developmental and cell biology series ; 9)
Bibliography: p157-176. — Includes index
ISBN 0-521-22731-3 : £16.00 B81-25599

581.87'33 — Plants. Cells. Chloroplasts

Tribe, Michael. Chloroplasts and mitochondria. — 2nd ed. — London : Edward Arnold, Nov.1981. — [64]p. — (The Institute of Biology's studies in biology, ISSN 0537-9024 ; no.31)
Previous ed: 1972
ISBN 0-7131-2828-3 (pbk) : £2.40 : CIP entry
Also classified at 581.87'34 B81-30607

581.87'33 — Plants. Cells. Chloroplasts. Biochemistry

Halliwell, Brian. Chloroplast metabolism. — Oxford : Clarendon Press, Nov.1981. — [250]p
ISBN 0-19-854549-5 : £18.00 : CIP entry B81-30337

581.87'33 — Plants. Cells. Plastids

Kirk, John T. O.. The plastids : their chemistry, structure, growth and inheritance / John T.O. Kirk, Richard A.E. Tilney-Bassett. — Rev. 2nd ed. — Amsterdam ; Oxford : Elsevier North-Holland Biomedical Press, 1978. — xx,960p : ill ; 25cm
Previous ed.: London : W.H. Freeman, 1967. — Includes bibliographies and index
ISBN 0-444-80022-0 : Unpriced B81-02414

581.87'34 — Plants. Cells. Mitochondria

Tribe, Michael. Chloroplasts and mitochondria. — 2nd ed. — London : Edward Arnold, Nov.1981. — [64]p. — (The Institute of Biology's studies in biology, ISSN 0537-9024 ; no.31)
Previous ed: 1972
ISBN 0-7131-2828-3 (pbk) : £2.40 : CIP entry
Primary classification 581.87'33 B81-30607

581.87'5 — Plants. Lignins. Biodegradation

Crawford, Ronald L.. Lignin biodegradation and transformation / Ronald L. Crawford. — New York ; Chichester : Wiley, c1981. — xvi,154p : ill ; 24cm
Bibliography: p119-137. — Includes index
ISBN 0-471-05743-6 : £18.75 B81-23246

581.87′6042 — Plants. Cells. Glycoproteins — *Conference proceedings*

The phytochemistry of cell recognition and cell surface interactions / edited by Frank A. Loewus and Clarence A. Ryan. — New York ; London : Plenum Press, c1981. — x,277p : ill ; 24cm. — (Recent advances in phytochemistry ; vol.15)
Conference papers. — Includes index
ISBN 0-306-40758-2 : Unpriced B81-37956

581.9 — BOTANY. GEOGRAPHICAL TREATMENT

581.9 — Plants. Distribution. Geographical aspects

Stott, P. A.. Historical plant geography : an introduction / Philip Stott. — London : Allen & Unwin, 1981. — xii,151p : ill,maps,ports ; 24cm
Bibliography: p133-144. — Includes index
ISBN 0-04-580010-3 (cased) : £12.00
ISBN 0-04-580011-1 (pbk) : £5.95 B81-23964

581.92′9′41 — Great Britain. Running water. Plants

Haslam, S. M.. River vegetation : its identification, assessment and management : a field guide to the macrophytic vegetation of British watercourses / S.M. Haslam, P.A. Wolseley. — Cambridge : Cambridge University Press, 1981. — vi,154p,[1]leaf of plates : ill,maps ; 31cm
Includes index
ISBN 0-521-23186-8 (cased) : £18.00 : CIP rev.
ISBN 0-521-23187-6 (pbk) : £6.95 B81-13825

581.938 — Ancient Greece. Vegetation. Literary sources

Dicks, T. R. B.. Vegetation changes in ancient Greece : the literary evidence / T.R.B. Dicks. — [Glasgow] ([George St., Glasgow, G1 1XW]) : University of Strathclyde, Department of Geography, [1980]. — 11 leaves ; 30cm. — (Research seminar series / University of Strathclyde Department of Geography ; no.9)
Cover title
Unpriced (pbk) B81-06532

581.941 — Great Britain. Plants — *Field guides*

Clapham, A. R.. Excursion flora of the British Isles / by A.R. Clapham, T.G. Tutin and E.F. Warburg. — 3rd ed. — Cambridge : Cambridge University Press, 1981. — xxxiii,499p : ill ; 24cm
Previous ed.: 1968. — Includes index
ISBN 0-521-23290-2 : £12.50 B81-08183

581.941 — Great Britain. Plants in danger of extinction & rare plants

Perring, Franklyn. Britain's endangered plants / text by Franklyn Perring and Roland E. Randall. — Norwich : Jarrold, c1981. — [32]p : col.ill ; 19cm. — (The Jarrold nature series)
Text on inside covers. — Includes index
ISBN 0-85306-908-5 (pbk) : Unpriced B81-19351

581.941 — Great Britain. Vascular plants — *Field guides*

Wigginton, M. J.. Guide to the identification of some of the more difficult vascular plant species : with particular application to the Watsonian vice-counties 66-70, Durham, Northumbria and Cumbria / M.J. Wigginton, G.G. Graham. — Banbury (Calthorpe House, Calthorpe St., Banbury, Oxon OX16 8EX) : Nature Conservancy Council, 1981. — 145p : ill ; 30cm. — (Occasional paper / Nature Conservancy Council. England Field Unit ; no.1)
Includes index
ISBN 0-86139-133-0 (spiral) : Unpriced B81-39040

581.9412′6 — Scotland. Tayside Region. Angus *(District).* **Plants**

Ingram, Ruth. The flora of Angus : (Forfar, V.C.90) / Ruth Ingram, Henry J. Noltie. — [Dundee] ([Albert Sq., Dundee DD1 1DA]) : Dundee Museums and Art Galleries, 1981. — liv,270p,[1]leaf of plates : 1col.ill,maps ; 21cm
Bibliography: p236-241. — Includes index
ISBN 0-900344-45-8 (pbk) : Unpriced B81-35323

581.9418′22 — Meath *(County).* **Duleek. Common land. Plants**

Synnott, Donal M.. A Common Green : Duleek : the botany and history of a Meath Commonage / by Donal Synnott ; illustrations by Simon Coleman ; historical account by Michael Ward. — [Duleek] (["Endevere", Duleek, Co. Meath]) : Duleek Historical Society, 1980. — 28p : ill ; 22x29cm
£1.00 (pbk)
Primary classification 333.2 B81-21734

581.9425′11 — England. Peak District. Plants

Anderson, Penny. Wild flowers and other plants of the Peak District : an ecological study / Penny Anderson & David Shimwell. — Ashbourne : Moorland, c1981. — 192p : ill,maps ; 22cm
Bibliography: p178-180. — Includes index
ISBN 0-86190-017-0 : £6.95 : CIP rev. B81-08870

581.9667 — Ghana. Forests. Vascular plants. Distribution

Hall, J. B.. Distribution and ecology of vascular plants in a tropical rain forest : forest vegetation in Ghana / J.B. Hall and M.D. Swaine. — The Hague ; London : Junk, 1981. — xv,382p : ill,maps ; 27cm + 1transparency (3 overlays)(b & w ; 19x24cm). — (Geobotany ; 1)
Transparency in pocket. — Bibliography: p357-364. — Includes index
ISBN 90-619-3681-0 : Unpriced
Also classified at 581.5′2642′09667 B81-36866

581.994 — Australia. Plants

Australian vegetation / edited by R.H. Groves. — Cambridge : Cambridge University Press, 1981. — xiii,449p : ill,maps ; 24cm
Includes bibliographies and index
ISBN 0-521-23436-0 : £27.50 : CIP rev. B81-15942

Beadle, Noel C. W.. The vegetation of Australia / Noel C.W. Beadle. — Cambridge : Cambridge University Press, 1981. — xxvii,690p,[1]folded leaf of plates : ill,maps ; 25cm
Bibliography: p639-656. — Includes index
ISBN 0-521-24195-2 : £50.00 B81-36683

582 — SPERMATOPHYTES

582 — Plants. Classification

Whittle, Tyler. Curtis's flower garden displayed. — Oxford : Oxford University Press, Oct.1981. — [264]p
ISBN 0-19-217715-x : £19.50 : CIP entry B81-28020

582′.0014 — Seed plants. Terminology - *Lists*

Index Kewensis plantarum phanerogamarum. — Oxford : Clarendon Press, July 1981
Supplementum sextum decimum: Nomina et synonyma omnium familiarum et graduum infrafamiliarum ab initio anni MDCCCCLXXI ad finem anni MCCCCCLXXV nonnulla etiam antea edita complectens. — [250]p
ISBN 0-19-854531-2 : £14.00 : CIP entry B81-13872

582′.0463 — North-western Europe. Seed plants. Pollen grains

The Northwest European pollen flora. — Amsterdam ; Oxford : Elsevier Scientific [for] the Royal Botanical Society of the Netherlands III, parts 21-28 / editors W. Punt, G.C.S. Clarke. — 1981
Includes bibliographies and index
Parts 21-28. — 138p : ill ; 25cm
ISBN 0-444-41996-9 : Unpriced : CIP rev. B81-16865

582′.0463 — Pollen — *Identification manuals — For bee-keeping*

Sawyer, R. W.. Pollen identification for beekeepers. — Cardiff : University College Cardiff Press, Oct.1981. — [112]p
ISBN 0-906449-29-4 (pbk) : £5.95 : CIP entry B81-30174

582′.0464 — Great Britain. Berries — *Field guides*

Ostern, Hedvig Wright. Berries / illustrations by Hedvig Wright Ostern. — Poole : Blandford, c1981. — 127p : col. ill ; 12cm. — (A Blandford mini-guide)
These illustrations originally published: in Der lille baerbogen/Eva Maehre Lauritzen. Oslo : Aschehoug, 1981. — Includes index
ISBN 0-7137-1209-0 (pbk) : £0.95 B81-3141

582′.0467 — Seeds & seedlings — *For schools*

Jennings, Terry. Seeds and seedlings / Terry Jennings ; illustrated by Karen Daws ... [et al.] — Oxford : Oxford University Press, 1981. — 32p : ill(some col.) ; 28cm. — (The Young scientist investigates)
ISBN 0-19-917040-1 (pbk) : Unpriced B81-2539

582′.0467 — Seeds — *For children*

Jennings, Terry. Seeds and seedlings / Terry Jennings ; illustrated by Karen Daws ... [et al.] — Oxford : Oxford University Press, 1981. — 32p : ill(some col.) ; 29cm. — (The young scientist investigates)
ISBN 0-19-917049-5 : £2.50 B81-2440

582′.0467′07402659 — Cambridgeshire. Cambridge. Universities. Botanical gardens: Cambridge University Botanic Garden. Seeds — *Lists — Serials*

Delectus seminum, sporarum et plantarum ex horto Cantabrigiensis Academiae. — Mense Decembri (1980). — Cambridge (Cambridge CB2 1JF) : University Botanic Garden, [1981]. — 7p
Unpriced B81-1330

582.13 — Flowering plants

Hickey, Michael. 100 families of flowering plants / Michael Hickey & Clive King ; foreword by S.M. Walters. — Cambridge : Cambridge University Press, 1981. — xix,567p : ill ; 24cm
Bibliography: p554. - Includes index
ISBN 0-521-23283-x (cased) : £27.50
ISBN 0-521-29891-1 (pbk) : £8.95 B81-0818

582.13 — Flowering plants — *For children*

Jennings, Terry. Flowers / Terry Jennings ; illustrated by Karen Daws, Peter Willmot. — Oxford : Oxford University Press, 1981. — 32p : ill(some col.) ; 29cm. — (The young scientist investigates)
ISBN 0-19-917048-7 : £2.50 B81-2440

582.13 — Flowering plants — *Personal observation*

Grace, *Princess, consort of Rainier III, Prince of Monaco.* My book of flowers / by Princess Grace of Monaco with Gwen Robyns. — London : Sidgwick and Jackson, 1980. — 224p : ill(some col.),facsims,ports(some col.) ; 29cm
Originally published: Garden City, N.Y. : Doubleday, 1980. — Bibliography: p220. — Includes index
ISBN 0-283-98466-x : £10.00 B81-0290

582.13′012 — Flowering plants. Families. Identification — *Algorithms*

Thonner, Franz. Thonner's analytical key to the families of flowering plants. — Translated and revised ed., R. Geesink ... [et al.]. — Wageningen : PUDOC ; The Hague ; London Leiden University Press, 1981. — xxvi,231p : ill,1facsim,1port ; 24cm. — (Leiden botanical series ; v.5)
Previous ed.: published as Anleitung zum Bestimmen der Familien der Blütenpflanzen. 2 Aufl. Berlin : Friedländer, 1917. —
Bibliography: pxiv-xv. - Includes index
ISBN 90-602-1461-7 (cased) : Unpriced
ISBN 90-602-1479-x (pbk) : Unpriced B81-2714

582.13′012 — Flowering plants. Taxonomic groups

Cronquist, Arthur. An integrated system of classification of flowering plants / Arthur Cronquist. — New York ; Guildford : Columbia University Press, 1981. — xviii,1262p : ill ; 24cm
Includes bibliographies and index
ISBN 0-231-03880-1 : £72.00 B81-397

582.13′022′2 — Flowering plants — *Illustrations — For children*

Wrigley, Elsie. Colours of flowers / by Elsie Wrigley ; illustred by the author. — Cambridge : Dinosaur, c1980. — 24p : chiefly col.ill ; 16x19cm. — (Althea′s nature series)
ISBN 0-85122-233-1 (cased) : £1.85 : CIP rev.
ISBN 0-85122-206-4 (pbk) : Unpriced
B80-06401

582.1′3041662 — Flowering plants. Pollination by insects - *For children*

. Finding out about flowers and insects. — Poole : Blandford Press, Apr.1981. — [32]p. — (Japanese nature series)
ISBN 0-7137-1152-3 : £2.95 : CIP entry
B81-04355

582.13′044 — Flowering plants. Anatomy

Roland, Jean-Claude. Atlas of flowering plant structure / Jean-Claude Roland and Françoise Roland ; translated [sic] by Dennis Baker. — London : Longman, 1980. — 103p : ill ; 26cm
Translation of: Atlas de biologie végétale. — Bibliography: p101. — Includes index
ISBN 0-582-45589-8 (pbk) : £6.25 : CIP rev.
B80-04189

582.13′094 — Europe. Flowering plants - *Field guides*

Halliday, G.. Wild flowers. — London : Lowe, July 1981. — [184]p
ISBN 0-85654-618-6 : £5.95 : CIP entry
B81-13834

582.13′094 — Europe. Mountainous regions. Flowering plants — *Visitors′ guides*

Bacon, Lionel. Mountain flower holidays in Europe / by Lionel Bacon ; hon. editor J.A. Kelly. — [Woking] : Alpine Garden Society, [1979]. — 293p : ill(some col.),maps ; 23cm
Bibliography: p20. - Includes index
ISBN 0-900048-31-x : £8.00 B81-01764

582.13′094 — North-western Europe. Flowering plants — *Field guides*

Rose, Francis, *1921-*. The wild flower key : a guide to plant identification in the field, with and without flowers / over 1400 species compiled and described by Francis Rose ; illustrated by R.B. Davis ... [et al.]. — London : Warne, 1981. — 480p : ill(some col.) ; 20cm
Includes index
ISBN 0-7232-2418-8 (cased) : £8.95
ISBN 0-7232-2419-4 (pbk) : £5.95 B81-20962

582.13′094 — North-western Europe. Flowering plants — *Identification manuals*

Jones, Marilyn. Wild flowers / [Marilyn Jones] ; [illustrator Wendy Bramall]. — London : Kingfisher, 1980. — 125p : col.ill,1col.map ; 20cm
Includes index
ISBN 0-7063-5998-4 : £2.50 : CIP rev.
B80-17690

582.13′0941 — Great Britain. Flowering plants

Mabey, Richard. The flowering of Britain / Richard Mabey and Tony Evans. — London : Hutchinson, 1980. — 173p : col.ill ; 25cm
Bibliography: p163-167. - Includes index
ISBN 0-09-142690-1 : £9.95 : CIP rev.
B80-13391

582.13′0941 — Great Britain. Flowering plants — *Field guides — For children*

Flowers of the hedgerow and wayside / [Joe Firmin, editor] ; [illustrations by Elizabeth Graham-Yoo′ll i.e. Graham-Yool]. — Cambridge : Dinosaur in association with Theorem, 1976 (1978 [printing]). — 32p : col.ill ; 21x10cm. — (National Trust children′s series) (Nature notebooks ; 1)
Cover title
ISBN 0-85122-118-1 (pbk) : £0.75 B81-26865

Wrigley, Elsie. Flowers in the garden / by Elsie Wrigley ; illustrated by the author. — Cambridge : Dinosaur, c1981. — 24p : col.ill ; 16x19cm. — (Althea′s nature series)
ISBN 0-85122-273-0 (cased) : £1.85 : CIP rev.
ISBN 0-85122-257-9 (pbk) : £0.70 B81-02670

582.13′0941 — Great Britain. Flowering plants — *For children*

Björk, Gun. Small flowers in the fields / text, Gun Björk ; illustrations, Ingvar Björk ; English version, Pamela Holt. — London : Hodder and Stoughton, 1981. — [26]p : chiefly col.ill ; 16cm
Translation from the Swedish
ISBN 0-340-25960-4 : £1.25 B81-12246

Jennings, Terry. Flowers / Terry Jennings ; illustrated by Karen Daws, Peter Willmott. — Oxford : Oxford University Press, 1981. — 32p : ill(some col.) ; 28cm. — (The Young scientist investigates)
ISBN 0-19-917039-8 (pbk) : £1.50 B81-22795

582.13′0941 — Great Britain. Seashore. Flowering plants — *For children*

Björk, Gun. Small flowers on the seashore / text, Gun Björk ; illustrations, Ingvar Björk ; English version, Pamela Holt. — London : Hodder and Stoughton, 1981. — [26]p : chiefly col.ill ; 16cm
Translation from the Swedish
ISBN 0-340-25961-2 : £1.25 B81-12247

582.13′09425′11 — England. Peak District. National parks: Peak District National Park. Flowering plants

Anthony, Stewart. Wild flowers in the Peak National Park / [words Stewart Anthony] ; [design, cover photograph and diagrams Shelagh Gregory] ; [drawings Denise Miller]. — Bakewell (Aldern House, Baslow Rd., Bakewell, Derbyshire DE4 1AE) : Peak Park Joint Planning Board, c1980. — 32p : ill(some col.) ; 14x19cm. — (A Peak National Park handbook)
Cover title. — Bibliography: p32
ISBN 0-901428-66-3 (pbk) : Unpriced
B81-09168

582.13′09496 — Balkan Peninsula. Flowering plants — *Field guides*

Polunin, Oleg. Flowers of Greece and the Balkans : a field guide / Oleg Polunin ; photographs taken by the author and others ; line drawings by Barbara Everard and Ann Davies, Pat Halliday and maps by John Callow. — Oxford : Oxford University Press, 1980. — xv,592p,[80]p of plates : ill(some col.),maps(some col.) ; 23cm
Col. map on lining papers. — Bibliography: p583-592. - Includes index
ISBN 0-19-217626-9 : £40.00 : CIP rev.
B80-04794

582.13′0994 — Australia. Flowering plants — *Field guides*

Fairley, Alan. The Observer′s book of wildflowers of Australia / Alan Fairley. — Sydney : Methuen Australia ; London : Warne, 1981. — 128p : col.ill ; 15cm. — (A8)
Bibliography: p122-123. — Includes index
ISBN 0-454-00242-4 : £2.50 B81-32974

582.1′4 — Succulents

Bechtel, Helmut. Cactus identifier : including succulent plants / by Helmut Bechtel ; with photographs by the author ; [translated by Manly Bannister] ; [adapted by E.W. Egan]. — Poole : Blandford Press, 1981. — 256p : col.ill ; 14cm
Translation of: Bunte Welt der Kakteen. — Originally published: New York : Stirling ; London : Distributed by Ward Lock, 1977. — Includes index
ISBN 0-7137-1147-7 (pbk) : £2.95 B81-16653

Říha, J.. The illustrated encyclopedia of cacti & other succulents / by J. Říha and R. Šubík ; edited by Gillian and Kenneth A. Beckett ; [translated by D. Hábová]. — London : Octopus, 1981. — 352p : ill(some col.),maps ; 24cm
Translation from the Czech. — Bibliography: p345. — Includes index
ISBN 0-7064-1492-6 : £4.95 B81-28249

Succulent scene one. — Burgess Hill (11 Wingle Tye Rd., Burgess Hill, West Sussex RH15 9HR) : Southern Reprographics, Oct.1981. — [80]p
ISBN 0-907678-00-9 (pbk) : £2.95 : CIP entry
B81-30904

582.1′4 — Succulents — *Field guides*

Rowley, G. D.. Name that succulent : keys to the families and genera of succulent plants in cultivation / Gordon D. Rowley ; with illustrations by the author. — Cheltenham : Thornes, 1980. — 268p : ill ; 21cm
Bibliography: p259. — Includes index
ISBN 0-85950-447-6 : £8.75 : CIP rev.
B80-17691

582.1′4 — Succulents. Names — *Indexes — Serials*

Repertorium plantarum succulentarum. — 29 (1978). — Richmond, Surrey (67 Gloucester Court, Kew Rd, Richmond, Surrey TW9 3EA) : International Organization for Succulent Plant Study, 1980. — 16p
£1.90 B81-07005

582.16 — Great Britain. Deciduous trees — *Illustrations*

Wilkinson, John, *1934-*. Trees. — [London] : Fontana, 1979
2 : a colour guide to broadleaved trees of British towns, parks and country / [painted by John Wilkinson ; text by Alan Mitchell]. — 1folded sheet([12]p) : col.ill ; 25cm. — (Domino ; 8)
ISBN 0-00-685466-4 : £0.85 B81-20747

582.16 — Great Britain. Evergreen trees — *Illustrations*

Wilkinson, John, *1934-*. Trees. — [London] : Fontana, 1979
1 : a colour guide to conifers and other evergreen trees in Britain / [... painted by John Wilkinson ; text by Alan Mitchell]. — 1folded sheet([12]p) : col.ill ; 25cm. — (Domino ; 2)
ISBN 0-00-685442-7 : £0.85 B81-20744

582.16 — Trees — *For children*

Jennings, Terry. Trees / Terry Jennings ; illustrated by Norma Burgin, Karen Daws, David More. — Oxford : Oxford University Press, 1981. — 32p : ill(some col.),col.plan ; 29cm. — (The young scientist investigates)
ISBN 0-19-917047-9 : £2.50 B81-24406

582.16′003′21 — Trees — *Encyclopaedias*

The **Oxford** encyclopedia of trees of the world / consultant editor Bayard Hora. — Oxford : Oxford University Press, 1981. — 288p : ill (some col.),col.maps ; 29cm
Bibliography: p277. — Includes index
ISBN 0-19-217712-5 : £12.50 : CIP rev.
B80-18730

582.16′005 — Trees — *Serials*

International Dendrology Society. International Dendrology Society year book. — 1980. — London (c/o Mrs A.M. Eustace, Whistley Green Farmhouse, Hurst, Reading, Berkshire RG10 0DU) : The Society, 1981. — 144p
ISSN 0307-322x : Unpriced B81-33465

582.1609182′1 — Caribbean region. Trees

Seddon, S. A.. Trees of the Caribbean / S.A. Seddon and G.W. Lennox. — [London] : Macmillan Caribbean, c1980. — v,74p : col.ill ; 21cm
ISBN 0-333-28793-2 (pbk) : £1.60 B81-06538

582.16094 — Europe. Trees

Gorer, Richard. Illustrated guide to trees / by Richard Gorer. — London : Kingfisher, 1980. — 196p : ill(some col.) ; 27cm
Bibliography: p192. - Includes index
ISBN 0-7063-6003-6 : £6.95 : CIP rev.
B80-17692

582.16094 — Europe. Trees — *Field guides*

Harz, Kurt. Trees and shrubs / Kurt Harz ; illustrated and identified with colour photographs ; translated and edited by Gwynne Vevers. — London : Chatto & Windus, c1980. — 144p : col.ill ; 19cm. — (Chatto nature guides)
Translation of: Bäume und Straücher. — Includes index
ISBN 0-7011-2541-1 (cased) : £4.95 : CIP rev.
ISBN 0-7011-2542-x (pbk) : £2.50
Also classified at 582.1′7′094 B80-25628

582.16094 — Europe. Trees — *Field guides continuation*

Humphries, C. J.. The Hamlyn guide to trees of Britain and Europe / C.J. Humphries, J.R. Press, D.A. Sutton ; illustrated by I. Garrard, T. Hayward, D. More. — London : Hamlyn, 1981. — 320p : ill(some col.),1col.map ; 20cm
Bibliography: p310. — Includes index
ISBN 0-600-38777-1 (cased) : £5.95
ISBN 0-600-35278-1 (pbkUnpriced) B81-22310

582.16094 — Europe. Trees — *For children*

Bartos-Höppner, Barbara. My favourite trees / Barbara Bartos-Höppner ; pictures by Monika Laingruber. — Glasgow : Blackie, 1980. — [26]p : col.ill ; 29cm
Translation of: Meine allerliebsten Baume
ISBN 0-216-91051-x : £3.95 : CIP rev.
B80-18731

582.160941 — Great Britain. Trees

Harris, Esmond. The Guinness book of trees / Esmond & Jeanette Harris ; illustrations by Vanessa Luff. — Enfield : Guinness Superlatives, 1981. — 160p : ill(some col.),maps(some col.) ; 21cm. — (Britain's natural heritage)
Includes index
ISBN 0-85112-303-1 : £4.50 B81-11570

Wilkinson, Gerald. A history of Britain's trees. — London : Hutchinson, Oct.1981. — [160]p
ISBN 0-09-146000-x : £8.95 : CIP entry
B81-26793

582.160941 — Great Britain. Trees — *Encyclopaedias*

Bean, W. J.. Trees and shrubs : hardy in the British Isles / W.J. Bean. — 8th ed. rev. / chief editor D.L. Clarke ; general editor Sir George Taylor. — London : Murray
Previous ed.: 1950. — Includes index
Vol.4: Ri-Z. — 1980. — xv,808p,[64]p of plates : ill ; 23cm
ISBN 0-7195-2428-8 : £40.00
Also classified at 582.1′7′0941 B81-31221

582.160941 — Great Britain. Trees — *Field guides*

Fairhurst, Alan. The Blandford guide to trees of the British countryside / Alan Fairhurst and Eric Soothill. — Poole : Blandford, 1981. — 159p : ill(some col.) ; 25cm
Bibliography: p147. — Includes index
ISBN 0-7137-0938-3 : £9.95 : CIP rev.
B81-02664

582.160941 — Great Britain. Trees — *For children*

Jennings, Terry. Trees / Terry Jennings ; illustrated by Norma Burgin, Karin Daws, David More. — Oxford : Oxford University Press, 1981. — 32p : ill(some col.),1col.plan ; 28cm. — (The Young scientist investigates)
ISBN 0-19-917038-x (pbk) : £1.50 B81-22791

582.1609412′32 — Scotland. Grampian Region. Ellon. Country parks: Haddo House Country Park. Trees — *Walkers' guides*

Haddo House Country Park Tree Trail / [illustrations drawn by Morgan Fisher]. — Aberdeen (Woodhill House, [Ashgrove Rd. West], Aberdeen [AB9 2LU]) : The Ranger Service, Department of Leisure, Recreation & Tourism, Grampian Regional Council, [1981]. — 16p : ill,2maps ; 20x21cm
£0.35 (pbk) B81-18634

582.16097 — Western North America. Trees

Peattie, Donald Culross. A natural history of western trees / by Donald Culross Peattie ; illustrated by Paul Landacre. — Lincoln [Neb.] ; London : University of Nebraska Press, 1980, c1953. — xiv,751p : ill ; 23cm. — (A Bison book)
Originally published: Boston : Houghton Mifflin, 1953. — Includes index
ISBN 0-8032-8701-1 (pbk) : £7.50 B81-17373

582.1′7′094 — Europe. Shrubs — *Field guides*

Harz, Kurt. Trees and shrubs / Kurt Harz ; illustrated and identified with colour photographs ; translated and edited by Gwynne Vevers. — London : Chatto & Windus, c1980. — 144p : col.ill ; 19cm. — (Chatto nature guides)
Translation of: Bäume und Sträucher. — Includes index
ISBN 0-7011-2541-1 (cased) : £4.95 : CIP rev.
ISBN 0-7011-2542-x (pbk) : £2.50
Primary classification 582.16094 B80-25628

582.1′7′0941 — Great Britain. Shrubs — *Encyclopaedias*

Bean, W. J.. Trees and shrubs : hardy in the British Isles / W.J. Bean. — 8th ed. rev. / chief editor D.L. Clarke ; general editor Sir George Taylor. — London : Murray
Previous ed.: 1950. — Includes index
Vol.4: Ri-Z. — 1980. — xv,808p,[64]p of plates : ill ; 23cm
ISBN 0-7195-2428-8 : £40.00
Primary classification 582.160941 B81-31221

583 — DICOTYLEDONS

583′.152 — Lithops

Fearn, Brian. Lithops : an introduction to a fascinating group of plants / by Brian Fearn. — Oxford : National Cactus & Succulent Society, c1981. — 69p : ill ; 19cm. — (Handbook / National Cactus and Succulent Society ; no.4)
Bibliography: p65-66. — Includes index
ISBN 0-902099-06-x (pbk) : Unpriced
B81-36463

583′.32′012 — Legumes. Taxonomy — *Conference proceedings*

International Legume Conference *(1978 : Royal Botanic Gardens, Kew)*. Advances in legume systematics : volume 2 of the proceedings of the International Legume Conference, Kew, 24-29 July 1978, held under the auspices of the Royal Botanic Gardens, Kew, the Missouri Botanical Garden, and the University of Reading / edited by R.M. Polhill and P.H. Raven. — Kew : Royal Botanic Gardens, c1981. — 2v.(xvi,1049p) : ill,maps ; 25cm
In slip case. — Three microfiche in pocket. — Includes bibliographies and index
ISBN 0-85521-224-1 (pbk) : £30.00 B81-38704

583′.47 — Mammillaria — *Collectors' guides*

Pilbeam, John. Mammillaria : a collector's guide / John Pilbeam ; photography by Bill Weightman. — London : Batsford, 1981. — 165p,[8]p of plates : ill(some col.) ; 26cm
Bibliography: p155-157. — Includes index
ISBN 0-7134-3897-5 : £17.50 B81-37846

583′.48′0941 — Great Britain. Umbelliferae — *Field guides*

Tutin, T. G.. Umbellifers of the British Isles / T.G. Tutin ; illustrated by Ann Davies. — London (c/o British Museum (Nat. Hist.), Cromwell Rd., S.W.7) : Botanical Society of the British Isles, 1980. — 197p : ill ; 19cm. — (B.S.B.I. handbook ; no.2)
Bibliography: p189-190. - Includes index
ISBN 0-901158-02-x (pbk) : Unpriced
B81-11137

583′.95 — Australia. Platylobeae

Shaw, H. K. Airy. A partial synopsis of the Euphorbiacae-Platylobeae of Australia (excluding Phyllanthus, Euphorbia and Calycopeplus) / H.K. Airy Shaw. — [Richmond] ([The Herbarium, Royal Botanic Gardens, Kew, Richmond, Surrey TW9 3AE]) : Kew Bulletin, 1980. — p577-700 : ill ; 25cm
Reprinted from Kew bulletin v.35 no.3. — Includes index
£6.00 (pbk) B81-15349

584 — MONOCOTYLEDONS

584 — Monocotyledons

Dahlgren, R. M. T.. The monocotyledons. — London : Academic Press, Nov.1981. — [400]p
ISBN 0-12-200680-1 : CIP entry B81-28142

584′.04 — Monocotyledons. Anatomy

Tomlinson, P. B.. Anatomy of the monocotyledons. — Oxford : Pergamon
Vol.7: Helobiae (Alismatidae). — Dec.1981. — [550]p
ISBN 0-19-854502-9 : £40.00 : CIP entry
B81-31738

584′.094 — Europe. Flowering bulbs — *Field guides*

Grey-Wilson, Christopher. Bulbs : the bulbous plants of Europe and their allies / Christopher Grey-Wilson, Brian Mathew ; illustrated by Marjorie Blamey ; line drawings by Christopher Grey-Wilson. — London : Collins, 1981. — 285p,48p plates : ill(some col) ; 25cm
Bibliography: p273. — Includes index
ISBN 0-00-219211-x : £9.95 B81-34764

584′.15 — Orchids

Dressler, Robert L.. The orchids : natural history and classification / Robert L. Dressler. — Cambridge, Mass. ; London : Harvard University Press, 1981. — 332p,[16]p of plates : ill(some col.),maps ; 25cm
Bibliography: p283-301. — Includes index
ISBN 0-674-87525-7 : £16.50 B81-38275

584′.15′09495 — Greece. Orchids

Lepper, J. D.. Orchids of Greece / J.D. Lepper ; with a foreword by Mary Briggs. — Ilfracombe : Stockwell, 1981. — 56p,[8]p of plates : col.ill ; 18cm
Bibliography: p56. — Includes index
ISBN 0-7223-1450-7 (pbk) : £2.50 B81-16775

584′.324 — Haworthia — *Illustrations*

Bates, John Thomas. The Haworthia drawings of John Thomas Bates / introduced by Gordon D. Rowley. — Reading (Cactusville, Reading) : G.D. Rowley, 1980. — 43p : chiefly ill,1 facsims,ports ; 30cm
Limited ed. of 50 copies. — Bibl.: p42. - Includes index
Private circulation (pbk) B81-06450

588 — BRYOPHYTES

588′.0941 — Great Britain. Bryophytes

Watson, E. V.. British mosses and liverworts : an introductory work, with full descriptions and figures of over 200 species, and keys for identification of all except the very rare species / written and illustrated by E. Vernon Watson ; with a foreword by Paul Richards. — 2nd ed. — Cambridge : Cambridge University Press, 1968 (1980 [printing]). — xvi,498p : ill ; 22cm
Previous ed.: 1955. — Includes index
ISBN 0-521-29472-x (cased) : Unpriced
ISBN 0-521-06741-3 B81-30940

588′.2 — Mosses

Richardson, D. H. S.. The biology of mosses / by D.H.S. Richardson. — Oxford : Blackwell Scientific, 1981. — xii,220p : ill ; 24cm
Includes bibliographies and index
ISBN 0-632-00782-6 (pbk) : £9.80 : CIP rev.
B81-13458

588′.20941 — Great Britain. Mosses — *Field guides*

Watson, E. Vernon. British mosses and liverworts. — 3rd ed. — Cambridge : Cambridge University Press, Nov.1981. — [519]p
Previous ed.: 1968
ISBN 0-521-24004-2 (cased) : £25.00 : CIP entry
ISBN 0-521-28536-4 (pbk) : £12.95
Also classified at 588′.33′0941 B81-34014

588′.2′097 — Eastern North America. Mosses

Crum, Howard A.. Mosses of Eastern North America / Howard A. Crum and Lewis E. Anderson. — New York ; Guildford : Columbia University Press, 1981. — 2v.(1328p) : ill ; 27cm
Bibliography: p1301-1314. — Includes index
ISBN 0-231-04516-6 : £30.20 B81-14737

588′.33′0941 — Great Britain. Liverworts — *Field guides*
Watson, E. Vernon. British mosses and liverworts. — 3rd ed. — Cambridge : Cambridge University Press, Nov.1981. — [519]p
Previous ed.: 1968
ISBN 0-521-24004-2 (cased) : £25.00 : CIP entry
ISBN 0-521-28536-4 (pbk) : £12.95
Primary classification 588′.20941 B81-34014

589 — THALLOPHYTES

589′.04133 — Plants. Nitrogen. Fixation
Nitrogen fixation. — Oxford : Oxford University Press
Vol.2: Rhizobium. — Feb.1982. — [400]p
ISBN 0-19-854552-5 : £28.00 : CIP entry B81-36230

589.1′012 — Australia. Lichens. Genera
Rogers, Roderick W.. The genera of Australian lichens : (lichenized fungi) / Roderick W. Rogers. — St. Lucia, Qld. ; London : University of Queensland Press, c1981. — 124p : ill ; 26cm
Bibliography: p108-115. — Includes index
ISBN 0-7022-1579-1 : £12.95 B81-40173

589.1′09425′3 — Lincolnshire. Lichens
Seaward, M. R. D.. Lichen flora of Lincolnshire / by M.R.D. Seaward. — Lincoln (c/o M.R.D. Seaward, School of Environmental Science, University of Bradford) : Lincolnshire Naturalists′ Union, 1980. — 18p : 2maps ; 21cm. — (Lincolnshire natural history brochure ; no.8)
Bibliography: p17-18
ISBN 0-9500353-6-x (pbk) : £1.25 B81-04427

589.2 — Fungi
Cooke, Roderic. Fungi / Roderic Cooke ; line drawings by Bob Parker. — London : Collins, 1981. — 159p,[16]p of plates : ill,2maps,1port ; 22cm. — (Collins countryside series ; 8)
Bibliography: p153-154. — Includes index
ISBN 0-00-219063-x : £4.95 B81-14027

589.2′0415 — Fungi. Genetics — *Conference proceedings*
The **Fungal** nucleus. — Cambridge : Cambridge University Press, Feb.1982. — [358]p. — (Symposium of the British Mycological Society ; no.5)
Conference papers
ISBN 0-521-23492-1 : £32.50 : CIP entry B81-36244

589.2′0419247 — Organisms. Lipids. Biochemistry — *Study examples: Fungi*
Weete, John D.. Lipid biochemitry of fungi and other organisms / John D. Weete with contributions by Darrell J. Weber. — New York ; London : Plenum, c1980. — xii,388p : ill ; 24cm
Bibliography: p317-357. - Includes index
ISBN 0-306-40570-9 : Unpriced B81-05093

589.2′041929 — Fungi. Secondary metabolites: Toxins. Biosynthesis
The **Biosynthesis** of mycotoxins : a study in secondary metabolism / edited by Pieter S. Steyn ; contributors John A. Anderson ... [et al.]. — New York ; London : Academic press, 1980. — xv,432p : ill ; 24cm
Includes bibliographies and index
ISBN 0-12-670650-6 : £24.80 B81-02841

589.2′0452482′0913 — Tropical regions. Mycorrhizas — *Conference proceedings*
Tropical mycorrhiza research / edited by Peitsa Mikola. — Oxford : Clarendon, 1980. — xii,270p : ill ; 24cm
Includes bibliographies and index
ISBN 0-19-854553-3 : £15.00 : CIP rev. B80-06923

589.2′0914′8 — Soil fungi
Domsch, K. H.. Compendium of soil fungi / K.H. Domsch, W. Gams, Traute-Heidi Anderson. — London : Academic Press, 1980. — 2v.([1264]p) : ill ; 26cm
Bibliography: [371]p. - Includes index
ISBN 0-12-220401-8 : Unpriced
ISBN 0-12-220402-6 (v.2) : £23.00 B81-23194

Garrett, S. D.. Soil fungi and soil fertility : an introduction to soil mycology / S.D. Garrett. — 2nd ed. — Oxford : Pergamon, 1981. — ix,150p[3]p of plates : ill ; 22cm. — (Pergamon international library)
Previous ed.: 1963. — Bibliography: p141-145. - Includes index
ISBN 0-08-025507-8 (cased) : £7.90
ISBN 0-08-025506-x (pbk) : £4.00 B81-19101

589.2′094 — Europe. Fungi — *Field guides*
Klán, Jaroslav. Mushrooms and fungi / by Jaroslav Klán ; illustrated by Bohumil Vančura ; [translated by Daniela Coxon]. — London : Hamlyn, [1981]. — 224p : ill(some col.),22cm. — (A Hamlyn colour guide)
Includes index
ISBN 0-600-35288-9 : £2.95 B81-22767

Phillips, Roger, *1932-*. Mushrooms : and other fungi of Great Britain and Europe / by Roger Phillips assisted by Lyndsay Shearer ; editor Derek Reid ; Russula and Lactarius editor Ronald Rayner. — London : Ward Lock, 1981. — 287p : col.ill ; 30cm
Bibliography: p282. — Includes index
ISBN 0-7063-6128-8 : £10.95 B81-39900

589.2′094 — North-western Europe: Fungi — *Field guides*
Reid, Derek. Mushrooms and toadstools / [Derek Reid] ; [illustrator Bernard Robinson]. — London : Kingfisher, 1980. — 124p : col.ill ; 20cm. — (A Kingfisher guide)
Includes index
ISBN 0-7063-5999-2 : £2.50 : CIP rev. B80-28357

589.2′09424′8 — Warwickshire. Fungi — *Lists*
A **Fungus** flora of Warwickshire / edited by M.C. Clark on behalf of the Committee for the Fungus Survey of Warwickshire ; with a section on lichens by D.C. Lindsay. — London : Published for the Birmingham Natural History Society by the British Mycological Society, 1980. — 272p : maps ; 24cm
Includes bibliographies and index
ISBN 0-903130-05-x (pbk) : £8.00 B81-04433

589.2′22′094 — Europe. Agaricales — *Illustrations*
Wilkinson, John, *1934-*. Mushrooms & toadstools : all the main edible and poisonous fungi of Britain and Europe / [painted by John Wilkinson ; text by David Pegler and Brian Spooner]. — [London] : Fontana, 1979. — 1folded sheet([12]p) : col.ill ; 25cm. — (Domino ; 3)
ISBN 0-00-685443-5 : £0.85 B81-20743

589.2′22′0941 — Great Britain. Agaricales — *Field guides*
Hahnewald, Edgar. Mushrooms and toadstools / illustrations by Edgar Hahnewald. — Poole : Blandford, c1981. — 128p : col. ill ; 12cm. — (A Blandford mini-guide)
These illustrations originally published: in Lilla svampboken/Jens Stordal. Stockholm : Almqvist & Wiskell Forlag, 1977. — Includes index
ISBN 0-7137-1211-2 (pbk) : £0.95 B81-31417

589.2′3 — Conidial fungi
Biology of conidial fungi / edited by Garry T. Cole, Bryce Kendrick. — New York ; London : Academic Press, 1981
Vol.1. — xviii,486p : ill ; 24cm
Includes bibliographies and index
ISBN 0-12-179501-2 : £32.60 B81-37712

Biology of conidial fungi / edited by Garry T. Cole, Bryce Kendrick. — New York ; London : Academic Press, 1981
Vol.2. — xx,660p : ill ; 24cm
Includes bibliographies and index
ISBN 0-12-179502-0 : £45.40 B81-37713

589.2′33 — Yeasts
Berry, David R.. Biology of yeasts. — London : Edward Arnold, Dec.1981. — [64]p. — (The Institute of Biology′s studies in biology, ISSN 0537-9024 ; no.140)
ISBN 0-7131-2838-0 (pbk) : £1.95 : CIP entry B81-30995

Biology and activities of yeasts / edited by F.A. Skinner, Susan M. Passmore and R.R. Davenport. — London : Academic Press, 1980. — xvi,310p : ill ; 24cm. — (The Society for Applied Bacteriology symposium series ; no.9)
Conference papers. — Includes bibliographies and index
ISBN 0-12-648080-x : £15.80 : CIP rev. B80-31565

589.2′4 — Botrytis
The **Biology** of Botrytis / J.R. Coley-Smith, K. Verhoeff, W.R. Jarvis. — London : Academic Press, 1980. — xiv,318p : ill(somecol.) ; 24cm
Includes bibliographies and index
ISBN 0-12-179850-x : £26.00 : CIP rev. B80-27026

589.3 — Algae
Lee, Robert Edward. Phycology / Robert Edward Lee. — Cambridge : Cambridge University Press, 1980. — x,478p : ill ; 25cm
Includes bibliographies and index
ISBN 0-521-22530-2 (cased) : £27.50
ISBN 0-521-29541-6 (pbk) : £9.95 B81-02247

589.3′52636 — Marine algae. Primary productivity — *Conference proceedings*
Primary productivity in the sea / edited by Paul G. Falkowski. — New York ; London : Plenum [c1980]. — ix,531p : ill ; 26cm. — (Brookhaven symposia in biology ; no.31) (Environmental science research ; v.19)
Conference papers. — Includes index
ISBN 0-306-40623-3 : Unpriced B81-09830

589.392 — Seaweeds
The **Biology** of seaweeds. — Oxford : Blackwell Scientific, Sept.1981. — [816]p. — (Botanical monographs ; v.17)
ISBN 0-632-00672-2 : £45.00 : CIP entry B81-22644

589.392 — Seaweeds. Use
Chapman, V. J.. Seaweeds and their uses / V.J. Chapman. — 3rd ed. / with chapters by D.J. Chapman. — London : Chapman and Hall, 1980. — ix,334p : ill,maps ; 23cm
Previous ed.: London : Methuen, 1970. — Bibliography: p279-312. - Includes index
ISBN 0-412-15740-3 : £17.50 : CIP rev. B80-11440

589.4 — Phytoplankton. Physiology. Ecological aspects
The **Physiological** ecology of phytoplankton / edited by I. Morris. — Oxford : Blackwell Scientific, 1980. — x,625p : ill ; 25cm. — (Studies in ecology ; vol.7) (Studies in ecology ; v.7)
Includes bibliographies and index
ISBN 0-632-00395-2 : £32.00 : CIP rev. B80-09221

589.4′6′09162 — Marine blue-green algae
Humm, Harold J.. Introduction and guide to the marine bluegreen algae / Harold J. Humm, Susanne R. Wicks. — New York ; Chichester : Wiley, c1980. — x,194p : ill ; 24cm
Bibliography: p178-188, — Includes index
ISBN 0-471-05217-5 : £12.50 B81-01694

589.4′7 — Cumbria. Lake District. Desmids — *Field guides*
Lind, Edna M.. A Key to the commoner desmids of the English Lake District / by Edna M. Lind and Alan J. Brook ; illustrated by Joanna Langhorne, D. Williamson and A.J. Brook. — Ambleside : Freshwater Biological Association, 1980. — 123p : ill ; 21cm. — (Scientific publication / Freshwater Biological Association, ISSN 0367-1887 ; no.42)
Text on inside covers. — Bibliography: p120. — Includes index
ISBN 0-900386-40-1 (pbk) : Unpriced B81-13299

589.4′7 — Desmids
Brook, Alan J.. The biology of desmids / Alan J. Brook. — Oxford : Blackwell Scientific, 1981. — ix,276p : ill ; 24cm. — (Botanical monographs, ISSN 0068-0389 ; v.16)
Bibliography: p242-264. — Includes index
ISBN 0-632-00253-0 : £23.50 : CIP rev. B80-04795

589.9 — Mycoplasmas
The **Mycoplasmas**. — New York ; London : Academic Press
Vol.2: Human and animal mycoplasmas / edited by J.G. Tully and R.F. Whitcomb. — 1979. — xiv,509p : ill ; 24cm
Includes bibliographies and index
ISBN 0-12-078402-5 : £29.00 B81-10867

Plant and insect mycoplasma techniques. — London : Croom Helm, Oct.1981. — [384]p
ISBN 0-7099-0272-7 : £22.50 : CIP entry B81-24656

589.9'05222 — Bacteria. Denitrification & nitrification. Environmental aspects
Denitrification, nitrification, and atmospheric nitrous oxide / edited by C.C. Delwiche. — New York ; Chichester : Wiley, c1981. — xi,286p : ill ; 24cm
Bibliography: p241-277. — Includes index
ISBN 0-471-04896-8 : £25.00 B81-23404

589.9'2 — Mycobacterium. Culture. Laboratory techniques
Chadwick, Maureen V.. Mycobacteria. — Bristol : J. Wright, Sept.1981. — [128]p. — (Monographs in medical laboratory science series)
ISBN 0-7236-0595-5 (pbk) : £5.00 : CIP entry B81-21588

589.9'4 — Gram negative rods
Haemophilus, pasteurella and actinobacillus. — London : Academic Press, Aug.1981. — [300]p
ISBN 0-12-406780-8 : CIP entry B81-20591

589.9'5 — Endospore-forming aerobic bacteria — *Conference proceedings*
The **Aerobic** endospore-forming bacteria : classification and identification / edited by R.C.W. Berkeley and M. Goodfellow. — London : Published for the Society for General Microbiology by Academic Press, 1981. — xv,373p : ill ; 24cm. — (Special publications of the Society for General Microbiology ; v.4)
Conference papers. — Includes bibliographies and index
ISBN 0-12-091250-3 : £15.00 : CIP rev. B80-23271

589.9'504133 — Microorganisms. Nitrogen. Fixation — *Conference proceedings*
Phytochemical Society of Europe. *Symposium (1979 : Sussex)*. Nitrogen fixation : proceedings of the Phytochemical Society of Europe Symposium Sussex, September, 1979 / edited by W.D.P. Stewart and J.R. Gallon. — London : Academic Press, 1980. — xviii,451p : ill,ports ; 24cm. — (Annual proceedings of the Phytochemical Society of Europe, ISSN 0309-9393 ; no.18)
Includes bibliographies and index
ISBN 0-12-669450-8 : £27.00 : CIP rev. B80-20654

589.9'504133 — Microorganisms. Nitrogen. Fixation. Measurement
Methods for evaluating biological nitrogen fixation / edited by F.J. Bergerson. — Chichester : Wiley, c1980. — x,702p : ill ; 24cm
Bibliography: p637-680. — Includes index
ISBN 0-471-27759-2 : £3,.00 : CIP rev. B80-31548

590 — ZOOLOGICAL SCIENCES

590'.74'4 — Zoos. Animals — *For children*
Stemmler, Carl. Zoo animals / [translated from the original German text of Carl Stemmler by Brenda F. Groth]. — St. Albans : Hart-Davis, 1981. — 35p : col.ill ; 15x16cm. — (Questions answered)
ISBN 0-247-13160-1 : £1.50 B81-39469

590'.74'442614 — Norfolk. Kilverstone. Wildlife parks: Kilverstone Wildlife Park — *Personal observations*
Fisher, Rosamund. My jungle babies / Rosamund Fisher. — London : Arrow, 1981, c1979. — 181p,[8]p of plates : col.ill,col.ports ; 18cm
Originally published: London : Allen & Unwin, 1979
ISBN 0-09-926000-x (pbk) : £1.50 B81-18708

591 — ZOOLOGY

591 — Animals
The **Encyclopedia** of wild life. — London : Corgi, 1981, c1974. — 255p : col.ill,col.maps ; 30cm
Originally published: London : Spring Books, 1974. — Includes index
ISBN 0-552-98207-5 (pbk) : £5.95 B81-40208

The **Encyclopedia** of wild life / [editors Eve Harlow and Iain Parsons]. — London : Salamander, 1981, c1974. — 255p : ill(some col.),col.maps ; 31cm
Originally published: London : Spring Books, 1974. — Ill on lining papers. — Includes index
ISBN 0-86101-096-5 : £6.95 B81-39858

Kilpatrick, Cathy. The Hamlyn all-colour animal encyclopedia / Cathy Kilpatrick and John Hard. — London : Hamlyn, 1981. — 320p : col.ill,col.maps ; 29cm
Ill on lining papers. — Includes index
ISBN 0-600-30370-5 : £6.95 B81-22061

591 — Animals associated with British royal families, *to 1980*
Brown, Michele. The Royal animals / Michele Brown. — London : W.H. Allen, 1981. — 94p : ill(some col.),ports(some col.) ; 28cm
ISBN 0-491-02913-6 : £6.95 B81-14000

591 — Animals — *For children*
Amazing facts about animals : wonders of the animal world / [illustrated by Bobbie Craig]. — [London] : Carousel, 1980. — [32]p : col.ill ; 28cm
ISBN 0-552-57044-3 (pbk) : £0.95 B81-08973

Animal acrobats / illustrations by David Nockels. — London : Methuen/Walker, c1981. — [12]p : col.ill ; 15cm. — (Animals in action) (A Methuen/Walker pop-up book)
ISBN 0-416-05900-7 : £1.50 B81-19734

Animal athletes / illustrations by David Nockels. — London : Methuen/Walker, c1981. — [12]p : col.ill ; 15cm. — (Animals in action) (A Methuen/Walker pop-up book)
ISBN 0-416-05880-9 : £1.50 B81-19739

Animal builders / illustrations by David Nockels. — London : Methuen/Walker, c1981. — [12]p : col.ill ; 15cm. — (Animals in action) (A Methuen/Walker pop-up book)
ISBN 0-416-05890-6 : £1.50 B81-19737

Animal surprises / illustrations by David Nockels. — London : Methuen/Walker, c1981. — [10]p : col.ill ; 15cm. — (Animals in action) (A Methuen/Walker pop-up book)
ISBN 0-416-05870-1 : £1.50 B81-19625

Animals / illustrated by Susan Neale. — London : Hamlyn, 1981. — [42]p : col.ill ; 26cm. — (I can learn)
ISBN 0-600-36483-6 : £1.99 B81-24057

Lambert, David, *1932-*. Animal life / by David Lambert. — London : Pan, 1981. — 91p : ill (some col.),col.maps ; 18cm. — (A Piccolo factbook)
Text on inside cover. — Includes index
ISBN 0-330-26360-9 (pbk) : £1.25 B81-38776

Lambert, David, *1932-*. Animal life / by David Lambert ; editor Jacqui Bailey. — London : Kingfisher, 1981. — 91p : ill(some col.) ; 19cm. — (A Kingfisher factbook)
Includes index
ISBN 0-86272-010-9 : £2.50 : CIP rev. B81-14398

Lambert, David, *1932-*. Animal wonders. — London : Ward Lock, Apr.1981. — [96]p. — (Kingfisher factbook)
ISBN 0-7063-6106-7 : £2.50 : CIP entry B81-03165

Swallow, Su. Animal record breakers / Su Swallow. — London : Macdonald, 1981. — 32p : col.ill,1col.map ; 29cm. — (Eye openers!)
Includes index
ISBN 0-356-07093-x : £2.50 B81-20275

Taylor, Ron, *1927-*. The wonder book of animals / [Ron Taylor]. — London : Ward Lock, 1981. — 37p : col.ill ; 27cm
Includes index
ISBN 0-7063-6131-8 : £2.50 B81-39963

591 — Animals — *For schools*
Wood-Robinson, Valerie. Man & other animals / Valerie Wood-Robinson. — Glasgow : Blackie, 1981. — 32p : ill ; 17x21cm. — (Modular science)
ISBN 0-216-90588-5 (pbk) : £1.40 B81-10730

591 — Animals — *Stories, anecdotes — For children*
Manning-Sanders, Ruth. Animal stories / Ruth Manning-Sanders ; illustrated by Annette Macarthur-Onslow. — Harmondsworth : Puffin in association with Oxford University Press, 1980, c1961. — 156p : ill ; 18cm
Originally published: London : Oxford University Press, 1961
ISBN 0-14-031219-6 (pbk) : £0.85 B81-02277

591 — Nocturnal animals — *For children*
Vevers, Gwynne. Animals of the dark / Gwynne Vevers ; illustrated by Wendy Bramall. — London : Bodley Head, 1980. — 23p : col.ill ; 22cm. — (A Bodley Head young naturalist)
Includes index
ISBN 0-370-30331-8 : £2.75 : CIP rev. B80-18293

591 — Zoology
Boolootian, Richard A.. College zoology. — 10th ed. / Richard A. Boolootian, Karl A. Stiles. — New York : Macmillan ; London : Collier Macmillan, c1981. — x,803p : ill,maps ; 25cm
Previous ed.: 1976. — Includes bibliographies and index
ISBN 0-02-311990-x : £14.50 B81-2931

591'.022'2 — Animals — *Illustrations — For children*
Stobbs, William. Animal pictures / William Stobbs. — London : Bodley Head, 1981. — 28p : chiefly col.ill ; 27cm
ISBN 0-370-30341-5 : £3.95 B81-1610

591'.023 — Occupations involving animals — *For children*
Mountfield, Anne. Working with animals / Anne Mountfield. — London : Harrap, 1980. — 39p : ill ; 19cm. — (The Reporters series)
ISBN 0-245-53393-1 (pbk) : £0.80 B81-0390

591'.023'41 — Great Britain. Occupations involving animals — *Career guides*
Jennings, Kenneth N.. Working with animals / Kenneth N. Jennings. — London : Batsford Academic and Educational, 1981. — 112p,[8]p of plates : ill ; 23cm. — (Careers series)
Includes index
ISBN 0-7134-3306-x : £5.75 B81-1964

Young, Helen, *1938-*. Careers working with animals / Helen Young. — London : Kogan Page, 1981. — 112p ; 19cm
ISBN 0-85038-435-4 (cased) : £5.95
ISBN 0-85038-436-2 (pbk) : £2.50 B81-2603

591'.028 — Zoology. Laboratory techniques
Hickman, Frances M.. Laboratory studies in integrated zoology. — 5th ed. / Frances M. Hickman. — St Louis ; London : Mosby, 1979. — xi,508p : ill ; 26cm + 1sheet(96x57cm folded to 24x19cm)
Previous ed.: 1974. — Pages perforated at inside edge and pierced for binder. — Includes index
ISBN 0-8016-2177-1 (pbk) : £8.50 B81-1665

591'.042'09162 — Oceans. Animals in danger of extinction — *For children*
Disappearing animals of the seas / compiled by Gill Gould with Michael M. Scott (wildlife adviser) ; illustrations by Alan R. Thomson, John Butler and Stephen Adams. — Edinburgh : Chambers, c1980. — [28]p : ill(some col.),col.maps ; 20cm. — (Animals in danger)
Produced in association with the World Wildlife Fund
ISBN 0-550-32004-0 : £2.25 B81-0468

591′.042′096 — Africa. Tropical rain forests. Animals in danger of extinction — *For children*

. Disappearing animals of the forests of Africa / compiled by Gill Gould ; wildlife adviser Michael M. Scott ; illustrations by John Butler, Sheila Smith and Alan R. Thomson. — Edinburgh : Chambers, c1980. — [28]p : ill (some col.),col.maps ; 20cm. — (Animals in danger)
Produced in association with the World Wildlife Fund
ISBN 0-550-32001-6 : £2.25 B81-04691

591′.042′097 — North America. Animals in danger of extinction — *For children*

Disappearing animals of North America / compiled by Gill Gould ; wildlife adviser Michael M. Scott ; illustrations by Graham Berry ... [et al.]. — Edinburgh : Chambers, c1980. — [28]p : ill(some col.),col.maps ; 20cm. — (Animals in danger)
Produced in association with the World Wildlife Fund
ISBN 0-550-32005-9 : £2.25 B81-04607

591′.076 — Animals — *Questions & answers*

Wildlife : questions and answers / edited by Dilys Breese. — London : British Broadcasting Corporation, 1981. — 144p : ill ; 20cm
ISBN 0-563-17171-5 (pbk) : £2.50 B81-37716

591′.092′4 — Zoology. Durrell, Gerald — *Biographies*

Durrell, Gerald. My family and other animals ; The Bafut beagles ; The drunken forest ; Encounters with animals ; A zoo in my luggage ; The whispering land ; Menagerie manor / Gerald Durrell. — London : Heinemann, 1981. — 812p ; 24cm
ISBN 0-905712-56-0 : £6.95 B81-34734

Durrell, Gerald. The picnic : and suchlike pandemonium / Gerald Durrell. — Large print ed. — Bath : Chivers, c1979. — 286p ; 23cm. — (A Lythway autobiography)
Originally published: London : Collins, 1979
ISBN 0-85119-700-0 : £5.25 B81-12969

Durrell, Gerald. The picnic : and suchlike pandemonium / Gerald Durrell. — [London] : Fontana, 1981, c1979. — 193p ; 18cm
Originally published: London : Collins, 1979
ISBN 0-00-636312-1 (pbk) : £1.25 B81-32916

Durrell, Gerald. A zoo in my luggage / Gerald Durrell ; with illustrations by Ralph Thompson. — Harmondsworth : Penguin, 1964, c1960 (1980 [printing]). — 190p : ill ; 18cm
Originally published: London : Hart-Davis, 1960
ISBN 0-14-002084-5 (pbk) : £0.95 B81-04778

591.1 — ANIMALS. PHYSIOLOGY

591.1 — Animals. Physiology — *Conference proceedings*

International Congress of Physiological Sciences *(28th : 1980 : Budapest)*. Advances in physiological sciences : proceedings of the 28th International Congress of Physiological Sciences, Budapest 1980. — Oxford : Pergamon, c1981. — 36v. : ill ; 25cm
Subtitle of v.22-36: Satellite symposium of the 28th International Congress of Physiological Sciences ... Hungary 1980. — Includes bibliographies and index
ISBN 0-08-026407-7 : £270.00 v.1-21, £280.00 v.22-36 B81-19606

591.1 — Animals. Physiology — *For children*

Cooper, Gale. Inside animals / written and illustrated by Gale Cooper. — London : Hodder and Stoughton, 1981, c1978. — 64p : ill(some col.) ; 26cm
Originally published: Boston, Mass. : Little, Brown, 1978. — Includes index
ISBN 0-340-25872-1 : £3.95 B81-03435

591.1′13 — Animals. Blood

Sanderson, J. H.. An atlas of laboratory animal haematology. — Oxford : Clarendon, Apr.1981. — [200]p
ISBN 0-19-857520-3 : £75.00 : CIP entry B81-07455

591.1′16 — Animals. Heart

Hearts and heart-like organs. — New York ; London : Academic Press
Vol.1: Comparative anatomy and development / edited by Geoffrey H. Bourne. — 1980. — xiv,415p : ill ; 24cm
Includes bibliographies and index
ISBN 0-12-119401-9 : £32.80 B81-14562

Hearts and heart-like organs. — New York ; London : Academic Press
Vol.2: Physiology / edited by Geoffrey H. Bourne. — 1980. — xiv,573p : ill ; 24cm
Includes bibliographies and index
ISBN 0-12-119402-7 : £36.40 B81-14563

591.1′16 — Animals. Heart — *Serials*

Hearts and heart-like organs. — Vol.3. — New York ; London : Academic Press, 1980. — xiv,431p
ISBN 0-12-119403-5 : £29.80 B81-29442

591.1′16 — Animals. Peripheral arteries. Chemoreceptors. Physiology - *Conference proceedings*

Arterial chemoreceptors. — Leicester : Leicester University Press, Apr.1981. — [554]p
Conference papers
ISBN 0-7185-1205-7 : £20.00 : CIP entry B81-05129

591.1′2 — Animals. Respiration

Dejours, Pierre. Principles of comparative respiratory physiology / Pierre Dejours. — 2nd rev. ed. — Amsterdam ; Oxford : Elsevier/Holland Biomedical, 1981. — xvi,265p : ill ; 25cm
Previous ed.: 1975. — Bibliography: p231-254. - Includes index
ISBN 0-444-80279-7 : £13.25 B81-23607

591.1′3 — Animals. Nutrition. Biochemicl aspects

Georgievskii, V. I.. Mineral nutrition of animals. — London : Butterworths, Dec.1981. — [416] p. — (Studies in the agricultural and food sciences)
Translation of Mineral′noe pitanie zhivotnykh
ISBN 0-408-10770-7 : £45.00 : CIP entry B81-31716

591.1′3′05 — Animals. Nutrition — *Serials*

[Nutrition research *(New York)*]. Nutrition research : the international medium for rapid publication of communications in the nutritional sciences. — Vol.1, no.1 (1981)-. — New York ; Oxford : Pergamon, 1981-. — v. : ill ; 26cm
Six issues yearly
ISSN 0271-5317 = Nutrition research (Elmsford) : Unpriced B81-36540

591.1′32 — Animals. Digestive system. Hormones — *Conference proceedings*

Cellular basis of chemical messengers in the digestive system / edited by Morton I. Grossman, Mary A.B. Brazier, Juan Lechago. — New York ; London : Academic Press, 1981. — xvii,359p : ill ; 26cm. — (UCLA forum in medical sciences ; no.23)
Conference papers. — Includes bibliographies and index
ISBN 0-12-304420-0 : £18.60 B81-38910

591.1′3′2 — Animals. Intestines. Anatomy — *Conference proceedings*

International Conference on Intestinal Adaptation *(2nd : 1981 : Titisee)*. Intestinal adaptation and its mechanisms. — Lancaster : MTP Press, Jan.1982. — [500]p
ISBN 0-85200-442-7 : £29.00 : CIP entry B81-38818

591.1′4 — Animals. Endocrine system — *Serials*

Oxford reviews of reproductive biology. — Vol.3 (1981). — Oxford : Clarendon Press, Sept.1981. — [325]p
ISBN 0-19-857536-x : £30.00 : CIP entry
Primary classification 591.1′6 B81-21621

591.1′42 — Animals. Behaviour. Control by neuroendocrine system — *Conference proceedings*

International Symposium of Hormonal Control of Behavior *(1978 : Acapulco)*. Comparative aspects of neuroendocrine control of behavior / International Symposium of Hormonal Control of Behavior, Acapulco, December 10-13, 1978 ; volume editors C. Valverde-Rodriguez, H. Aréchiga. — Basel ; London : Karger, c1980. — x,250p : ill ; 25cm. — (Frontiers of hormone research ; v.6)
Includes bibliographies
ISBN 3-8055-0571-x : £29.50 B81-03054

591.1′42 — Animals. Endocrine system

Goldsworthy, Graham J.. Endocrinology / Graham J. Goldsworthy, John Robinson, William Mordue. — Glasgow : Blackie, 1981. — xiv,184p : ill ; 21cm. — (Tertiary level biology)
Bibliography: p173-177. - Includes index
ISBN 0-216-91008-0 (cased) : £16.95 : CIP rev.
ISBN 0-216-91009-9 (pbk) : £7.95 B80-20656

591.1′42 — Animals. Endocrine system. Physiology

Tepperman, Jay. Metabolic and endocrine physiology : an introductory text / Jay Tapperman. — 4th ed. — Chicago ; London : Year Book Medical Publishers, c1980. — xii,335p : ill ; 26cm. — (Physiology textbook series)
Previous ed.: 1973. — Includes bibliographies and index
ISBN 0-8151-8755-6 : £19.75
ISBN 0-8151-8756-4 (pbk) : £16.00 B81-02973

591.1′42 — Animals. Endocrine system. Regulation. Effects of olfactory perception — *Conference proceedings*

Olfaction and endocrine regulation. — Eynsham (1 Abbey St., Eynsham, Oxford OX8 1JJ) : IRL Press, Jan.1982. — [350]p
Conference papers
ISBN 0-904147-35-5 (pbk) : £12.00 : CIP entry B81-37540

591.1′58 — Animals. Variation

Fingerman, Milton. Animal diversity / Milton Fingerman. — 3rd ed. — New York ; London : Saunders College, 1981. — vii,310p : ill ; 24cm. — (Modern biology series)
Previous ed.: New York ; London : Holt, Rinehart and Winston, 1976. — Includes bibliographies and index
ISBN 0-03-049611-x (pbk) : £5.25 B81-25274

591.1′6 — Animals. Reproductive system — *Serials*

Oxford reviews of reproductive biology. — Vol.3 (1981). — Oxford : Clarendon Press, Sept.1981. — [325]p
ISBN 0-19-857536-x : £30.00 : CIP entry
Also classified at 591.1′4 B81-21621

591.1′6′05 — Animals. Reproductive system — *Serials*

Oxford reviews of reproductive biology. — Vol.2 (1980). — Oxford : Clarendon Press, 1980. — 273p,[8]p of plates
ISBN 0-19-857535-1 : £20.00 : CIP rev.
ISSN 0260-0854 B81-07426

591.1′82 — Animals. Neurotransmitter receptors

Neurotransmitter receptors. — London : Chapman and Hall. — (Receptors and recognition. Series B ; v.10)
Includes bibliographies and index
Pt.2: Biogenic amines / edited by H.I. Yamamura and S.J. Enna. — 1981. — xi,273p : ill ; 24cm
ISBN 0-412-23130-1 : Unpriced B81-34627

591.1′82 — Animals. Sensory organs

Sense organs / general editors M.S. Laverack and D.J. Cosens. — Glasgow : Blackie, 1981. — xvi,394p : ill ; 24cm
Includes bibliographies and index
ISBN 0-216-91094-3 : £29.75 B81-17859

591.1′823 — Animals. Eyes — *Serials*

Current eye research. — Vol.1, no.1 (1981)-. — London (1 Falconberg Court, W1V 5FG) : IRL Press, 1981-. — v. ; 28cm
Monthly. — CODEN: CEYRDM
ISSN 0271-3683 = Current eye research : £80.00 per year B81-33321

591.1'852 — Animals. Collagen. Genetic aspects
Gene families of collagen and other proteins : proceedings of a conference held at the College of Medicine and Dentistry of New Jersey - Rutgers Medical School, Piscataway, New Jersey, U.S.A., April 27-May 2, 1980 / editors : Darwin J. Prockop, Pamela C. Champe. — New York ; Oxford : Elsevier/North-Holland, c1980. — x,242p : ill ; 25cm. — (Developments in biochemistry, ISSN 0165-1714 ; v.15)
Includes index
ISBN 0-444-00567-6 : £14.82 B81-05848

591.1'852 — Animals. Flight & swimming. Dynamics. Mathematical models
Childress, Stephen. Mechanics of swimming and flying / Stephen Childress. — Cambridge : Cambridge University Press, 1981. — 155p : ill ; 23cm. — (Cambridge studies in mathematical biology ; 2)
Bibliography: p149-152. — Includes index
ISBN 0-521-23613-4 (cased) : £17.50
ISBN 0-521-28071-0 (pbk) : £7.50 B81-36895

591.1'852 — Animals. Locomotion — *For schools*
Alexander, R. McNeill. Locomotion of animals. — Glasgow : Blackie, Feb.1982. — [176]p. — (Tertiary level biology)
ISBN 0-216-91159-1 (cased) : £14.00 : CIP entry
ISBN 0-216-91158-3 (pbk) : £7.00 B81-36035

591.1'852 — Animals. Movement. Mechanics — *Conference proceedings*
Aspects of animal movement / edited by H.Y. Elder and E.R. Trueman. — Cambridge : Cambridge University Press, 1980. — viii,250p : ill ; 24cm. — (Seminar series / Society for Experimental Biology ; 5)
Conference papers. — Includes bibliographies and index
ISBN 0-521-23086-1 (cased) : £18.00 : CIP rev.
ISBN 0-521-29795-8 (pbk) : £6.95 B80-25639

591.1'852 — Animals. Muscles. Nerves. Electrical activity
Stein, Richard B.. Nerve and muscle : membranes, cells and systems / Richard B. Stein. — New York ; London : Plenum, c1980. — ix,265p : ill ; 24cm
Bibliography: p233-254. — Includes index
ISBN 0-306-40512-1 : Unpriced B81-02686

591.1'852 — Animals. Voluntary muscles. Development
Development and specialization of skeletal muscle / edited by D.F. Goldspink. — Cambridge : Cambridge University Press, 1980. — 155p : ill ; 24cm. — (Seminar series / Society for Experimental Biology ; 7)
Includes bibliographies and index
ISBN 0-521-23317-8 (cased) : £18.00
ISBN 0-521-29907-1 (pbk) : £8.95 B81-14640

591.1'852 — Aquatic animals. Skeletal system. Growth
Skeletal growth of aquatic organisms : biological records of environmental change / edited by Donald C. Rhoads and Richard A. Lutz. — New York ; London : Plenum, c1980. — xiii,750p : ill ; 26cm. — (Topics in geobiology ; v.1)
Includes bibliographies and index
ISBN 0-306-40259-9 : Unpriced
Primary classification 594'.01852 B81-03988

591.1'88 — Animals. Brain. Energy metabolism — *Conference proceedings*
Animal models and hypoxia : proceedings of an international symposium on animal models and hypoxia, held at Wiesbaden Federal Republic of Germany, 19 November 1979 / editor V. Stefanovich. — Oxford : Pergamon, 1981. — viii, 126p : ill ; 26cm
Includes bibliographies and index
ISBN 0-08-025911-1 : £12.50 : CIP rev. B81-06583

591.1'88 — Animals. Central nervous system. Physiology
Integrative control functions of the brain / editorial board Masao Ito ... [et al.]. — Toyko : Kodansha ; Amsterdam ; Oxford : Elsevier/North-Holland Biomedical Press
Vol.3 / section editors Masanori Otsuka ... [et al.]. — 1980. — xiii,402p : ill ; 27cm
Includes bibliographies and index
ISBN 0-444-80314-9 : Unpriced B81-30032

591.1'88 — Animals. Nervous system
Biology, brain and behaviour / [SD286 Course Team]. — [Milton Keynes] : [Open University Press]
At head of title: The Open University
Module B3: Brain and spinal cord ; Module B4: Comparative motor systems / prepared by a Course Team from the Faculties of Science and Social Sciences. — 1981. — 72,39p : ill (some col.) ; 30cm. — (SD286 ; block B, [3 and 4])
Includes bibliographies
ISBN 0-335-16067-0 (pbk) : Unpriced
Also classified at 591.51 B81-30797

Biology, brain and behaviour / [SD286 Course Team]. — [Milton Keynes] : [Open University Press]
At head of title: The Open University
Module A: An introduction to brain and behaviour / prepared by a Course Team from the Faculties of Science and Social Sciences. — [1981]. — 70p : ill(some col.) ; 30cm. — (SD286)
ISBN 0-335-16066-2 (pbk) : Unpriced
Also classified at 591.51 B81-27754

Commentaries in the neurosciences / editors A.D. Smith, R. Llinás, P.G. Kostyuk. — Oxford : Pergamon, 1980. — ix,668p,[22]p of plates : ill (some col.) ; 28cm
Includes bibliographies and index
ISBN 0-08-025501-9 : £30.00 : CIP rev. B80-09222

591.1'88 — Animals. Nervous system. Neuroactive peptides — *Conference proceedings*
Royal Society. *Discussion Meeting (1980)*.
Neuroactive peptides : a Royal Society Discussion Meeting held on 30 and 31 January 1980 / organized by Sir Arnold Burgen, H.W. Kosterlitz and L.L. Iversen. — London : The Society, 1980. — 195p,[6]p of plates : ill ; 26cm
Originally published: in Proceedings of the Royal Society of London. Series B, Vol.210. — Includes bibliographies
ISBN 0-85403-149-9 : £11.40 B81-06160

591.1'88 — Animals. Nervous system. Synapses. Neurotransmitters — *Conference proceedings*
Symposium on Regulatory Mechanisms of Synaptic Transmission *(1980 : Mexico City)*.
Regulatory mechanisms of synaptic transmission / [proceedings of a Symposium on Regulatory Mechanisms of Synaptic Transmission, held April 14-16, 1980, in Mexico City, Mexico, and sponsored by Universidad Nacional Autónoma de México] ; edited by Ricardo Tapia and Carl W. Cotman. — New York ; London : Plenum in cooperation with Universidad Nacional Autónoma de México, c1981. — viii,422p : ill ; 26cm
Includes bibliographies and index
ISBN 0-306-40740-x : Unpriced B81-36675

591.1'88 — Animals. Non-impulse neurons — *Conference proceedings*
Neurones without impulses : their significance for vertebrate and invertebrate nervous systems / edited by Alan Roberts and Brian M.W. Bush. — Cambridge : Cambridge University Press, 1981. — x,290p : ill ; 24cm. — (Seminar series / Society for Experimental Biology ; 6)
Conference papers. — Includes bibiliographies and index
ISBN 0-521-23364-x (cased) : £25.00
ISBN 0-521-29935-7 (pbk) : £10.95 B81-10361

591.1'88 — Drug receptors — *Conference proceedings*
Drug receptors and their effectors / edited by Nigel J.M. Birdsall. — London : Macmillan, 1981. — 182p : ill ; 25cm
Conference papers. — At head of title: Biological Council, The Co-ordinating Committee for Symposia on Drug Action. — Includes bibliographies and index
ISBN 0-333-29327-4 : £30.00 B81-23085

591.1'88 — Neurobiology
Jones, D. G.. Neurons and synapses. — London : Edward Arnold, Nov.1981. — [64]p. — (The Institute of Biology's studies in biology, ISSN 0537-9024 ; no.135)
ISBN 0-7131-2825-9 (pbk) : £2.40 : CIP entry B81-30609

Mill, Peter J.. Comparative neurobiology. — London : Edward Arnold, Dec.1981. — [224]p. — (Contemporary biology)
ISBN 0-7131-2810-0 : £8.95 : CIP entry B81-31556

591.1'88 — Neurobiology — *Conference proceedings*
Theoretical approaches in neurobiology : based on a work session of the Neurosciences Research Program / edited by Werner E. Reichardt and Tomaso Poggio. — Cambridge, Mass. ; London : MIT, c1981. — x,252p : ill ; 24cm
Conference papers. — Bibliography: p215-239. — Includes index
ISBN 0-262-18100-2 : £12.40 B81-16626

591.1'88 — Neurobiology. Laboratory techniques
Methods in neurobiology / edited by Robert Lahue. — New York ; London : Plenum
Vol.1. — c1981. — xiii,600p : ill ; 26cm
Includes bibliographies and index
ISBN 0-306-40517-2 : Unpriced B81-40688

591.1'88'05 — Neurobiology — *Serials*
Progress in neurobiology. — Vol.15. — Oxford : Pergamon, Nov.1981. — [350]p
ISBN 0-08-029084-1 : £43.00 : CIP entry B81-31078

591.19'135 — High altitudes. Adaptation of animals — *Conference proceedings*
Life, Heat, and Altitude Conference *(1979 : University of Nevada)*. Environmental physiology : aging, heat and altitude : proceedings of Life, Heat and Altitude Conference held on May 15-17, 1979 at the University of Nevada, Las Vegas, Nevada, U.S.A. / editors Steven M. Horvath and Mohamed K. Yousef. — New York ; Oxford : Elsevier/North-Holland, c1981. — 468p : ill ; 24cm
Includes bibliographies and index
ISBN 0-444-00583-8 : Unpriced
Also classified at 591.19'162 B81-25534

591.19'162 — High temperatures. Adaptation of animals — *Conference proceedings*
Life, Heat, and Altitude Conference *(1979 : University of Nevada)*. Environmental physiology : aging, heat and altitude : proceedings of Life, Heat and Altitude Conference held on May 15-17, 1979 at the University of Nevada, Las Vegas, Nevada, U.S.A. / editors Steven M. Horvath and Mohamed K. Yousef. — New York ; Oxford : Elsevier/North-Holland, c1981. — 468p : ill ; 24cm
Includes bibliographies and index
ISBN 0-444-00583-8 : Unpriced
Primary classification 591.19'135 B81-25534

591.19'212 — Animals. Osmoregulation
Rankin, J. C.. Animal osmoregulation / J.C Rankin, J. Davenport. — Glasgow : Blackie, 1981. — vi,202p : ill ; 21cm. — (Tertiary level biology)
Bibliography: p185-196. — Includes index
ISBN 0-216-91014-5 (cased) : £16.75 : CIP rev.
ISBN 0-216-91015-3 (pbk) : £8.25 B81-11908

591.19'214 — Animals. Copper. Metabolism — *Conference proceedings*
Biological roles of copper. — Amsterdam ; Oxford : Excerpta Medica, 1980. — viii,343p : ill,maps ; 25cm. — (Ciba Foundation symposium. (new series) ; 79)
Confernce papers. — Includes bibliographies and index
ISBN 90-219-4085-x : £22.95 B81-05459

591.19'214 — Animals. Iron. Metabolism
Bezkorovainy, Anatoly. Biochemistry of nonheme iron / Anatoly Bezkorovainy with a chapter contributed by Dorice Narins. — New York ; London : Plenum, c1980. — xviii,435p : ill ; 24cm. — (Biochemistry of the elements ; v.1)
Bibliography: p421. - Includes index
ISBN 0-306-40501-6 : Unpriced B81-13379

Iron in biochemistry and medicine, II / edited by A. Jacobs and M. Worwood. — London : Academic Press, 1980. — xii,706p : ill ; 24cm
Includes bibliographies and index
ISBN 0-12-378980-x : £41.00 : CIP rev. B80-12870

591.19'245 — Animals. Calcium-binding proteins — *Conference proceedings*
Calcium-binding proteins : structure and function : proceedings of an international symposium on calcium-binding proteins and calcium function in health and disease, held June 8-12, 1980 at the Wisconsin Center, Madison, Wisconsin, U.S.A. / editors Frank L. Siegel ... [et al.]. — New York ; Oxford : Elsevier/North-Holland, c1980. — xx,511p : ill ; 25cm. — (Developments in biochemistry, ISSN 0165-1714 ; v.14)
Includes index
ISBN 0-444-00565-x : £21.57 B81-15045

591.19'245 — Animals. Glutamines — *Conference proceedings*
International Symposium on Glutamine: Metabolism, Enzymology, and Regulation *(1979 : Querétaro).* Glutamine : metabolism, enzymology, and regulation / [proceedings of the International Symposium on Glutamine: Metabolism, Enzymology and Regulation, sponsored by the Universidad Naciónal Autónoma de México held in La Mansión Galindo, Querétaro, México, November 25-28, 1979] ; edited by Jaime Mora, Rafael Palacios. — New York ; London : Academic Press, 1980. — xix,334p : ill ; 24cm
Includes index
ISBN 0-12-506040-8 : £15.80 B81-16637

591.19'245 — Animals. Tryptophan. Metabolism — *Conference proceedings*
International Study Group for Tryptophan Research. *International Meeting (3rd : 1980 : Kyoto).* Biochemical and medical aspects of tryptophan metabolism : proceedings of the third International Meeting of the International Study Group for Tryptophan Research held in Kyoto, Japan, August 4-7, 1980 / editors Osamu Hayaishi, Yuzuru Ishimura, Ryo Kido. — Amsterdam ; Oxford : Elsevier/North-Holland Biomedical, 1980. — ix, 373p : ill ; 25cm. — (Developments in biochemistry, ISSN 0165-1714 ; v.16)
Includes index
ISBN 0-444-80297-5 : Unpriced B81-13968

591.19'27'05 — Animals. Hormones — *Serials*
Recent progress in hormone research. — Vol.36. — New York ; London : Academic Press, 1980. — xvii,629p
ISBN 0-12-571136-0 : Unpriced
ISSN 0079-9963 B81-06948

591.2 — ANIMALS. DISEASES

591.2'3'05 — Animals. Parasitic diseases — *Serials*
Advances in parasitology. — Vol.19. — London : Academic Press, Oct.1981. — [360]p
ISBN 0-12-031719-2 : CIP entry
ISSN 0065-308x B81-28141

591.2'33 — Animals. Babesiosis — *Conference proceedings*
Babesiosis / edited by Miodrag Ristic, Julius P. Kreier. — New York ; London : Academic Press, 1981. — xv,589p : ill ; 24cm
Conference papers. — Includes bibliographies and index
ISBN 0-12-588950-x : £29.80 B81-38870

591.2'9 — Animals. Immunology — *Conference proceedings*
Congress of Developmental and Comparative Immunology *(1st : 1980 : Aberdeen).* Aspects of developmental and comparative immunology 1 : proceedings of the 1st Congress of Developmental and Comparative Immunology, 27 July-1 August 1980, Aberdeen / editor J.B. Solomon. — Oxford : Pergamon, 1981. — xvii,572p : ill ; 26cm
Includes bibliographies and index
ISBN 0-08-025922-7 : £46.00 : CIP rev. B80-27027

591.2'93 — Animals. B-cells & T-cells — *Conference proceedings*
T and B lymphocytes : recognition and function / edited by Fritz H. Bach ... [et al.]. — New York ; London : Academic Press, 1979. — xxvi,709p : ill ; 24cm. — (ICN-UCLA symposia on molecular and cellular biology ; v.16)
Conference papers. — Includes index
ISBN 0-12-069850-1 : Unpriced B81-13165

591.2'95 — Animals. Immune reactions
Animal models of immunological processes. — London : Academic Press, Dec.1981. — [200]p
ISBN 0-12-333520-5 : CIP entry B81-33869

591.2'95 — Animals. Immune reactions. Role of nutrition — *Conference proceedings*
Diet and resistance to disease / [proceedings of the symposium on diet and resistance to disease held at the American Chemical Society Agricultural and Food Division meeting, held March 26, 1980, in Houston, Texas] ; edited by Marshall Phillips and Albert Baetz. — New York ; London : Plenum, c1981. — vii,220p : ill ; 26cm. — (Advances in experimental medicine and biology ; v.135)
Includes bibliographies and index
ISBN 0-306-40636-5 : Unpriced B81-19276

591.3 — ANIMALS. DEVELOPMENT

591.3'3 — Embryos. Development
Oppenheimer, Steven B.. Introduction to embryonic development / Steven B. Oppenheimer. — Boston, Mass. ; London : Allyn and Bacon, c1980. — 404p : ill ; 24cm
Includes bibliographies and index
ISBN 0-205-07348-4 (pbk) : £7.50 B81-11240

591.3'3'09033 — Embryology, *1700-1800*
Roe, Shirley A.. Matter, life, and generation : eighteenth-century embryology and the Haller-Wolff debate / Shirley A. Roe. — Cambridge : Cambridge University Press, 1981. — 214p : ill,ports ; 24cm
Bibliography: p 184-204. — Includes index
ISBN 0-521-23540-5 : £16.00 B81-32076

591.3'6 — Animals. Sex differences
Mechanisms of sex differentiation in animals and man / edited by C.R. Austin and R.G. Edwards. — London : Academic Press, 1981. — xv,603p : ill ; 24cm
Includes bibliographies and index
ISBN 0-12-068540-x : £37.00 : CIP rev.
Also classified at 612'.6 B81-11936

591.3'8 — Animals. Evolution. Ecological aspects
Colombo, Federica. Animal evolution. — London : Burke, Oct.1981. — 1v.. — (Animal behaviour ; 3)
Translation of: Les animaux et les environnement
ISBN 0-222-00822-9 : £4.95 : CIP entry B81-30301

Shvarts, S. S.. The evolutionary ecology of animals / S.S. Shvarts ; translated from the Russian and edited by Ayesha E. Gill ; with new material by the author and editor. — New York ; London : Consultants Bureau, c1977. — vii,292p : ill ; 24cm. — (Studies in Soviet science. Life sciences)
Translation of: Évolîutsionnaîa ékologiîa zhivotnykh. — Includes bibliographies
ISBN 0-306-10920-4 : Unpriced B81-03200

591.3'9 — Young animals — *For children*
Carruth, Jane. Animal babies / by Jane Carruth ; illustrated by John Francis. — Maidenhead : Purnell, 1974 (1980 [printing]). — [28]p : col.ill ; 25cm. — (My first colour library)
Ill on lining papers
ISBN 0-361-05051-8 : £0.99 B81-14297

Shapiro, Larry. Baby animals / [written by Larry Shapiro] ; [designed and illustrated by Linda Griffith ; paper engineering by Tor Lokvig]. — [Swindon] : Child's Play, c1979. — [10]p : chiefly col.ill ; 18cm. — (A Kaleidoscope book ; bk.2)
Cover title. — Originally published: Los Angeles : Visual Communications, 1979. — Text, ill on lining papers
ISBN 0-85953-097-3 : Unpriced B81-32882

591.3'9'0222 — Young animals — *Illustrations*
The World of young animals / conceived and edited by Ann Guilfoyle ; with text by Roger A. Caras and Steve Graham. — London : Allen & Unwin, 1981, c1980. — 173p : chiefly ill(some col.) ; 26cm
Originally published: New York : Macmillan, 1980
ISBN 0-04-591019-7 : £9.56 B81-09339

591.3'9'0222 — Young animals — *Illustrations — For children*
Little tot's baby animals. — London : Dean, c1980. — [24]p : col.ill ; 13cm. — (Dean's little tots' series)
ISBN 0-603-00195-5 (pbk) : £0.15 B81-06344

591.4 — ANIMALS. ANATOMY

591.4'8 — Vertebrates. Autonomic nervous system - *Conference proceedings*
Development of the autonomic nervous system. — London : Pitman Medical, June 1981. — [320]p. — (CIBA Foundations symposium ; 83)
ISBN 0-272-79619-0 : £19.50 : CIP entry B81-09464

591.5 — ANIMALS. ECOLOGY

591.5 — Animals. Ecology
Dasmann, Raymond F.. Wildlife biology / Raymond F. Dasmann. — 2nd ed. — New York ; Chichester : Wiley, c1981. — ix,212p : ill ; 24cm
Previous ed.: 1964. — Ill on lining paper. — Bibliography: p195-203. - Includes index
ISBN 0-471-08042-x : £9.00 B81-11305

591.5 — Animals. Health. Effects of lead pollutants — *Conference proceedings*
International Symposium on Environmental Lead Research *(2nd : 1978 : Cincinnati).* Environmental lead / [proceedings of the Second International Symposium on Environmental Lead Research held in Cincinnati, Ohio, December 5-7, 1978] ; edited by Donald R. Lynam, Lillian G. Piantanida, Jerome F. Cole. — New York ; London : Academic Press, 1981. — xi,358p : ill,maps ; 24cm. — (Ecotoxicology and environmental quality series)
Includes bibliographies and index
ISBN 0-12-460520-6 : £20.60 B81-40774

591.5 — Animals. Social behaviour
Broom, Donald. Biology of behaviour. — Cambridge : Cambridge University Press, Nov.1981. — [304]p
ISBN 0-521-23316-x (cased) : £20.00 : CIP entry
ISBN 0-521-29906-3 (pbk) : £7.95 B81-33622

591.5 — Environment. Adaptation of animals — *For children*
Jenkins, Alan Charles. Secrets of nature. — London : Hodder and Stoughton, Apr.1981. — [128]p
ISBN 0-340-26526-4 (pbk) : £1.25 : CIP entry B81-02563

591.5 — Europe. Animals. Tracks, droppings & marks — *Illustrations*
Ovenden, Denys. Animal tracks & signs : what animal went there? a detective's guide to European wild and domestic animal tracks, droppings and other signs / [painted by Denys Ovenden]. — [London] : Fontana, 1980. — 1folded sheet([12]p) : col.ill ; 25cm. — (Domino ; 24)
ISBN 0-00-685460-5 : £0.95 B81-20258

591.5'09676 — East Africa. Animals. Ecology
Burton, Jane. Animals of the African year : the ecology of East Africa / by Jane Burton ; photographs by Jane Burton. — [London] : Peter Lowe, 1979. — 141p : col.ill,1col.map ; 28cm
Originally published: 1972. — Bibliography: p137. — Includes index
ISBN 0-85654-626-7 : £4.95 B81-18226

591.51 — Animals. Behaviour
Biology, brain and behaviour / [SD286 Course Team]. — [Milton Keynes] : [Open University Press]
At head of title: The Open University
Module B3: Brain and spinal cord ; Module B4: Comparative motor systems / prepared by a Course Team from the Faculties of Science and Social Sciences. — 1981. — 72,39p : ill (some col.) ; 30cm. — (SD286 ; block B, [3 and 4])
Includes bibliographies
ISBN 0-335-16067-0 (pbk) : Unpriced
Primary classification 591.1'88 B81-30797

591.51 — Animals. Behaviour *continuation*

Biology, brain and behaviour / [SD286 Course Team]. — [Milton Keynes] : [Open University Press]
At head of title: The Open University
Module A: An introduction to brain and behaviour / prepared by a Course Team from the Faculties of Science and Social Sciences. — [1981]. — 70p : ill(some col.) ; 30cm. — (SD286)
ISBN 0-335-16066-2 (pbk) : Unpriced
Primary classification 591.1′88 B81-27754

The **Oxford** companion to animal behaviour. — Oxford : Oxford University Press, June 1981. — [600]p
ISBN 0-19-866120-7 : £15.00 : CIP entry
B81-11942

Toates, Frederick M.. Animal behaviour : a systems approach / Frederick M. Toates. — Chichester : Wiley, c1980. — xi,299p : ill ; 24cm
Bibliography: p271-290. — Includes index
ISBN 0-471-27724-x (cased) : £17.00 : CIP rev.
ISBN 0-471-27723-1 (pbk) : £6.40 B80-11441

591.51 — Animals. Behaviour. Ecological aspects

Morse, Douglass H.. Behavioral mechanisms in ecology / Douglass H. Morse. — Cambridge, Mass. ; London : Harvard University Press, 1980. — viii,383p : ill ; 25cm
Bibliography: p315-371. - Includes index
ISBN 0-674-06460-7 : £12.00 B81-09351

591.51 — Animals. Behaviour. Evolution. Ecological aspects

Krebs, J. R.. An introduction to behavioural ecology / J.R. Krebs, N.B. Davies ; drawings by Jan Parr. — Oxford : Blackwell Scientific, 1981. — x,292p : ill ; 24cm
Bibliography: p265-278. — Includes index
ISBN 0-632-00666-8 (cased) : Unpriced : CIP rev. B81-16876

591.51 — Animals. Behaviour — *For children*

Lambert, David, *1932-*. First picture book of animals / written by David Lambert ; designed by Dave Nash ; illustrated by Mike Atkinson ... [et al.]. — London : Kingfisher, 1981. — 61p : col.ill ; 31cm
Ill on lining papers. — Includes index
ISBN 0-86272-008-7 : £2.95 : CIP rev.
B81-27449

591.51 — Animals. Behaviour. Genetic factors

Ehrman, Lee. Behavior genetics and evolution / Lee Ehrman, Peter A. Parsons. — New York ; London : McGraw-Hill, c1981. — xiv,450p : ill,maps ; 25cm
Previous ed.: published as The genetics of behavior. Sunderland, Mass. : Sinauer Associates, 1976. — Bibliography: p392-429. — Includes index
ISBN 0-07-019276-6 : £15.95 B81-36273

591.51 — Animals. Behaviour. Predictability

Predictability, correlation, and contiguity / edited by Peter Harzem and Michael D. Zeiler. — Chichester : Wiley, c1981. — xiii,417p : ill ; 24cm. — (Advances in analysis of behaviour ; v.2)
Includes bibliographies and index
ISBN 0-471-27847-5 : £20.50 : CIP rev.
B81-00115

591.51 — Animals. Social behaviour

Colombo, Federica. Animal society. — London : Burke, Oct.1981. — 1v.. — (Animal behaviour ; 4)
Translation of: Les animaux en societe
ISBN 0-222-00823-7 : £4.95 : CIP entry
B81-30188

591.51 — Animals. Social behaviour. Evolution. Natural selection — *Conference proceedings*

Natural selection and social behavior : recent research and new theory / edited by Richard D. Alexander and Donald W. Tinkle. — New York : Chiron ; Oxford : Distributed by Blackwell Scientific, c1981. — xii,532p : ill ; 25cm
Includes bibliographies and index
ISBN 0-632-00624-2 : £35.00 B81-36195

591.51 — Ethology

McFarland, David. Quantitative ethology. — London : Pitman, Oct.1981. — [300]p. — (Pitman series in neurobiology and behaviour)
ISBN 0-273-08417-8 : £17.50 : CIP entry
B81-28781

Perspectives in ethology. — New York ; London : Plenum
Vol.4: Advantages of diversity / edited by P.P.G. Bateson and Peter H. Klopfer ; [contribution, Peter G. Caryl ... et al.]. — c1981. — xiii,249p : ill ; 24cm
Includes bibliographies and index
ISBN 0-306-40511-3 : Unpriced B81-17910

591.51′05 — Animals. Behaviour — *Serials*

Advances in the study of behavior. — Vol.11. — New York ; London : Academic Press, 1980. — xi,377p
ISBN 0-12-004511-7 : Unpriced
ISSN 0065-3454 B81-29967

591.51′072 — Animals. Behaviour. Research. Quantitative methods — *Conference proceedings*

. Quantitative analysis of behavior. — Cambridge, Mass. : Ballinger ; New York ; London ; Harper and Row
Vol.1: Discriminative properties of reinforcement schedules / edited by Michael L. Commons, John A. Nevin. — c1981. — xxvii,437p : ill ; 24cm
Includes bibliographies and index
ISBN 0-88410-377-3 : £27.75 B81-38458

591.52′48 — Animals. Population

Elseth, Gerald D.. Population biology / Gerald D. Elseth, Kandy D. Baumgardner. — New York ; London : Van Nostrand, c1981. — xvi,623p : ill ; 24cm
Bibliography: p585-606. — Includes index
ISBN 0-442-26235-3 : £15.70 B81-01895

591.52′48′072 — Animals. Population. Research. Statistical methods

Blower, J. Gordon. Estimating the size of animal populations / J. Gordon Blower, Laurence M. Cook, James A. Bishop. — London : Allen & Unwin, 1981. — 128p : ill ; 24cm
Includes index
ISBN 0-04-591017-0 (cased) : Unpriced : CIP rev. B80-09224

591.52′49 — Parasites: Animals. Biochemistry — *Conference proceedings*

The **Biochemistry** of parasites : proceedings of the satellite conference of the 13th Meeting of the Federation of European Biochemical Societies (FEBS) held in Jerusalem, August 1980 / editor Gerald M. Slutzky. — Oxford : Pergamon, 1981. — vii,228p : ill ; 26cm
Includes index
ISBN 0-08-026381-x : £16.70 : CIP rev.
B81-05152

591.52′5 — Animals. Migration

Animal migration, orientation, and navigation / edited by Sidney A. Gauthreaux, Jr.. — New York ; London : Academic Press, 1980. — xii,387p : ill ; 24cm. — (Physiological ecology)
Includes bibliographies and index
ISBN 0-12-277750-6 : £22.00 B81-19047

Colombo, Federica. Animal migration / Federica Colombo ; adapted by Paul-Henry Plantain ; translated by R.D. Martin, and A.-E. Martin. — London : Burke, 1981. — 94p : col.ill,col.maps ; 28cm. — (Animal behaviour)
Translation of: Les animaux et leurs migrations. — Ill on lining paper. — Includes index
ISBN 0-222-00791-5 : £4.95 : CIP rev.
B80-09683

591.52′5 — Animals. Migration. Evolutionary aspects

Baker, R. Robin. Migration. — London : Hodder & Stoughton, Jan.1982. — [208]p
ISBN 0-340-26079-3 (pbk) : £4.95 : CIP entry
B81-34149

591.5′25 — Animals. Migration — *For children*

Vevers, Gwynne. Animals that travel. — London : Bodley Head, July 1981. — [24]p
ISBN 0-370-30399-7 : £2.95 : CIP entry
B81-14940

591.52′5 — Animals. Migration — *For children — Welsh texts*

Rowland-Entwistle, Theodore. [Exploring animal journeys. Welsh]. Teithiau anifeiliaid / Theodore Rowland-Entwistle ; ymgynghorwr Berian Williams ; cynlluniwyd gan David Nash ; arlunwyr Graham Allen ... [et al.]. — Caerdydd : Gwasg y Dref Wen, c1980. — [24]p : col.ill,col.maps ; 23cm. — (Darganfod)
Translation of: Exploring animal journeys
£1.95 B81-04983

591.52′632 — Freshwater ecosystems. Predation by predatory animals

Zaret, Thomas M.. Predation and freshwater communities / Thomas M. Zaret ; foreword by G. Evelyn Hutchinson. — New Haven ; London : Yale University Press, c1980. — xiv,187p : ill ; 22cm
Bibliography: p155-180. - Includes index
ISBN 0-300-02349-9 : £9.50 B81-08159

591.53 — Food. Storage by animals — *For children*

Vevers, Gwynne. Animals that store food / Gwynne Vevers ; illustrated by Joyce Bee. — London : Bodley Head, 1980. — 23p : col.ill ; 22cm. — (Bodley Head young naturalists) (A Bodley Head young naturalist)
Includes index
ISBN 0-370-30330-x : £2.75 : CIP rev.
B80-13819

591.53 — Predatory animals — *For children*

Hatley, Jan. Killers in the wild / Jan Hatley. — Basingstoke : Macmillan, 1981. — 96p : ill (some col.),col.maps ; 30cm. — (Macmillan feature books)
Includes index
ISBN 0-333-30684-8 : £4.95 : CIP rev.
B81-30290

591.53′022′2 — Animals. Food — *Illustrations — For children*

What do animals eat?. — [London] : British Museum (Natural History), c1979. — [8]p : ill ; 22x30cm
Cover title
ISBN 0-565-00808-0 (pbk) : Unpriced
B81-14123

591.59 — Animals. Communication

Schauenberg, Paul. Animal communication / Paul Schauenberg ; translated by R.D. Martin, and A.-E. Martin. — London : Burke, 1981. — 94p : col.ill ; 28cm. — (Animal behaviour)
Translation of: Les animaux et leurs langages. — Ill on lining paper. — Includes index
ISBN 0-222-00792-3 : £4.95 : CIP rev.
B80-09684

591.6 — ECONOMIC ZOOLOGY

591.6 — Animals. Relationships with man — *For children*

Briquebec, John. Animals & man / author John Briquebec ; design Louise Burston. — Maidenhead : Purnell, 1981. — 57p : ill(some col.) ; 30cm
Ill on lining papers. — Includes index
ISBN 0-361-04654-5 : £3.99
Primary classification 304.2 B81-27769

591.8 — ANIMALS. HISTOLOGY AND CYTOLOGY

591.8′2 — Animals. Tissue fluids — *Conference proceedings*

Tissue fluid pressure and composition / edited by Alan R. Hargens. — Baltimore ; London : Williams & Wilkins, c1981. — xiv,275p : ill,port ; 26cm
Conference papers. — Includes bibliographies and index
ISBN 0-683-03891-5 : £40.75 B81-20754

591.87 — Mononuclear phagocytes — *Conference proceedings*

Heterogeneity of mononuclear phagocytes / [proceedings of an international workshop held in Baden/Vienna, July 15-19, 1980] ; edited by Othmar Förster, Maurice Landy. — London : Academic Press, 1981. — xxviii,538p : ill ; 24cm
Includes bibliographies and index
ISBN 0-12-262360-6 : £16.40 : CIP rev.
B81-08910

591.87′6041 — Animals. Glands. Cells. Electrical activity
Peterson, O. H.. The electrophysiology of gland cells / O.H. Petersen. — London : Academic Press, 1980. — ix,253p : ill ; 24cm. — (Monographs of the Physiological Society, ISSN 0079-2020 ; no.36)
Bibliography: p219-244. — Includes index
ISBN 0-12-552150-2 : £19.20 : CIP rev.
B80-06928

591.87′62 — Animals. Gastrointestinal tract. Cells. Reproduction
Cell proliferation in the gastrointestinal tract / edited by D.R. Appleton, J.P. Sunter, A.J. Watson. — Tunbridge Wells : Pitman Medical, 1980. — xxvii,428p : ill ; 24cm
Conference papers. — Bibliography: p383-428
ISBN 0-272-79597-6 : £25.00 : CIP rev.
B80-24472

591.9 — ZOOLOGY. GEOGRAPHICAL TREATMENT

591.909′43 — Mountainous regions. Animals
Perry, Richard. Mountain wildlife / Richard Perry. — London : Croom Helm, c1981. — 179p,[16]p of plates : ill ; 23cm
Bibliography: p171-177. — Includes index
ISBN 0-7099-0247-6 : £6.95 B81-25154

591.909′43 — Mountainous regions. Animals — *For children*
Cuisin, Michel. Mountain animals / edited by Michael Chinery ; written by Michel Cuisin ; illustrated by Pierre Probst ; translated by Anne-Marie Moore. — London : Ward Lock, 1980. — 44p : ill(some col.),maps(some col.) ; 28cm. — (Nature hidden world) (A Kingfisher book)
Translation of: Dans les montagnes
ISBN 0-7063-5947-x : £2.95 : CIP rev.
B80-01645

591.92 — Marine animals — *For children*
Under the sea. — [London] : Sparrow, 1980. — [24]p : ill(some col.],col.maps ; 29cm. — (Discoverers)
Adaptation of: The superbook of the underwater world. — Bibliography: p24
ISBN 0-09-923550-1 (pbk) : £0.70 B81-07985

591.92 — Tropical regions. Marine animals — *For children*
Sakharnov, S.. Who lives in the warm sea? / S. Shakharnov ; drawings by N. Ustinov ; translated into English by Eve Manning. — Moscow : Progress ; [London] : Central Books [distributor], 1975 (1980 printing). — [18]p : col.ill ; 25cm
Translation of: Kto zhivet v tëplom more
£0.45 (pbk) B81-14012

591.92′733 — Red Sea. Coral reefs. Marine animals
Bemert, Gunnar. Red Sea coral reefs / Gunnar Bemert, Rupert Ormond. — London : Kegan Paul, 1981. — 192p : col.ill,col.maps ; 28cm
Bibliography: p185. — Includes index
ISBN 0-7103-0007-7 : £25.00 B81-23074

591.941 — Great Britain. Animals
Young, Geoffrey. Looking at wildlife / [written by Geoffrey Young]. — Norwich : Jarrold, 1981. — 31p : col.ill ; 19cm. — (WATCH outdoor guide ; 5)
Cover title. — Text on inside cover. — Includes index
ISBN 0-85306-971-9 (pbk) : Unpriced
B81-37062

591.941 — Great Britain. Animals — *For children*
Grimes, Brian. British wild animals. — Sevenoaks : Hodder & Stoughton, Oct.1981. — [128]p
ISBN 0-340-26888-3 : £7.95 : CIP entry
B81-28849

591.9424′6 — Staffordshire. Animals — *Personal observations*
Drabble, Phil. Country wise / Phil Drabble. — London : Joseph, 1980. — 191p : ill,ports ; 22cm
Includes index
ISBN 0-7181-1952-5 : £6.95 B81-00116

591.95 — Asia. Animals — *For children — Poems*
Spence, Peter. Professor Potts meets the animals in Asia / words by Peter Spence ; pictures by Gillian Chapman ; authenticated by Gillian Standing. — London : Watts, c1981. — [32]p : col.ill ; 28cm
ISBN 0-85166-897-6 : £2.99 B81-11089

591.96 — Africa. Animals
Felix, Jiří. Animals of Africa / Jiří Felix ; illustrated by Jaromír Knotek and Libuše Knotková ; [translated by Dana Hábová]. — London : Hamlyn, 1981. — 314p : col.ill,col.maps ; 28cm
Translation from the Czech. — Maps on lining papers. — Includes index
ISBN 0-600-36488-7 : £4.50 B81-27777

591.96 — Africa. Animals — *For children — Poems*
Wright, Kit. Professor Potts meets the animals in Africa / words by Peter Spence [i.e. Kit Wright] ; pictures by Gillian Chapman ; authenticated by Gillian Standing. — London : Watts, c1981. — [32]p : col.ill ; 28cm
ISBN 0-85166-895-x : £2.99 B81-14128

591.96 — Africa. Savanna regions. Animals — *For children*
Cuisin, Michel. Animals of the African plains / edited by Michael Chinery ; written by Michel Cuisin ; illustrated by Alexis Oussenko ; translated by Anne-Marie Moore. — London : Kingfisher, 1980. — 44p : ill(some col.) ; 29cm. — (Nature's hidden world)
Translation of: Dans la savane
ISBN 0-7063-6034-6 : £2.95 : CIP rev.
B80-28359

591.967′112 — West Cameroon. Animals. Collecting — *Personal observations*
Durrell, Gerald. The Bafut beagles / Gerald Durrell ; with illustrations by Ralph Thompson. — Harmondsworth : Penguin, 1958, c1954 (1981 [printing]). — 202p : ill ; 18cm
Originally published: London : Hart Davis, 1954
ISBN 0-14-001266-4 (pbk) : £1.25 B81-17344

591.968′022′2 — South Africa. Nature reserves: National parks. Animals — *Illustrations*
Morris, Jean, *1931-*. South African wildlife / Jean Morris. — Aylesbury : Timmins, 1980. — [144]p : all col.ill ; 29cm
ISBN 0-86978-170-7 : £10.95 B81-17130

591.97 — Eastern North America. Animals — *Field guides*
Collins, Henry Hill. Harper & Row's complete field guide to North American wildlife. — New York ; London : Harper & Row
Eastern ed. / assembled by Henry Hill Collins, Jr ; illustrations by Paul Donahue ... [et al.]. — c1981. — xi,714p,110p of plates : ill(some col.),1map ; 23cm
Map on lining paper. — Includes bibliographies and index
ISBN 0-690-01969-6 : Unpriced B81-30803

591.97 — North America. Animals — *For children — Poems*
Spence, Peter. Professor Potts meets the animals in North America / words by Peter Spence ; pictures by Gillian Chapman ; authenticated by Gillian Standring. — London : Watts, c1981. — [32]p : col.ill ; 28cm
ISBN 0-85166-896-8 : £2.99 B81-11094

591.97 — Western North America. Animals — *Field guides*
Ransom, Jay Ellis. Harper & Row's complete field guide to North American wildlife. — New York ; London : Harper & Row
Western ed. / assembled by Jay Ellis Ransom ; illustrations by Biruta Akerbergs ... [et al.]. — 1981. — xi,809p,129p of plates : ill(some col.),1map ; 23cm
Map on lining paper. — Includes bibliographies and index
ISBN 0-690-01971-8 : Unpriced B81-27701

591.982′7 — Argentina. Patagonia. Animals. Collecting — *Personal observations*
Durrell, Gerald. The whispering land / Gerald Durrell ; with illustrations by Ralph Thompson. — Harmondsworth : Penguin, 1964, c1961 (1979 [printing]). — 216p : ill ; 18cm
Originally published: London : Hart-Davis, 1961
ISBN 0-14-002083-7 (pbk) : £0.95 B81-00891

591.994′022′2 — Australia. Animals — *Illustrations — For children*
Niland, Kilmeny. Feathers, fur and frills / Kilmeny Niland. — Sydney ; London : Hodder and Stoughton, 1980. — [32]p : chiefly ill(some col.) ; 29cm
ISBN 0-340-25781-4 : £4.50 B81-12245

592 — INVERTEBRATES

592 — Great Britain. Hypolithic invertebrates — *For children*
Free, John B.. Life under stones / John B. Free. — London : Adam & Charles Black, 1981. — 25p : col.ill ; 22cm. — (Nature in close-up)
Includes index
ISBN 0-7136-2121-4 : £2.95 : CIP rev.
B81-04286

592 — Invertebrates
Calow, Peter. Invertebrate biology : a functional approach / P. Calow. — London : Croom Helm, c1981. — 183p : ill ; 22cm
Bibliography: p166-176. — Includes index
ISBN 0-7099-0000-7 (cased) : £11.95 : CIP rev.
ISBN 0-7099-0001-5 (pbk)
ISBN 0-470-27238-4 (U.S.) B81-12830

Hegner, Robert W.. Invertebrate zoology. — 3rd ed. / Joseph G. Engemann, Robert W. Hegner. — New York : Macmillan ; London : Collier Macmillan, c1981. — xxi,746p : ill,1map ; 26cm
Previous ed.: 1968. — Includes bibliographies and index
ISBN 0-02-333780-x : £12.95 B81-21445

592 — Zooplankton — *Conference proceedings*
Evolution and ecology of zooplankton communities / [proceedings of a symposium on the structure of zooplankton communities held at Dartmouth College on 20-25 August 1978, sponsored by the American Society of Limnology and Oceanography, the National Science Foundation, and Dartmouth College] ; W. Charles Kerfoot, editor. — Hanover, N.H. ; London : University Press of New England, 1980. — xxiii,793p : ill,maps ; 26cm. — (Special symposium / American Society fo Limnology and Oceanography ; v.3)
Includes bibliographies and index
ISBN 0-87451-180-1 : £22.50 B81-13173

592′.01′028 — Invertebrates. Physiology. Experiments — *Manuals*
Practical invertebrate zoology : a laboratory manual for the study of the major groups of invertebrates, excluding protochordates / compiled and edited by R.P. Dales ; contributors F.E.G. Cox ... [et al.]. — 2nd ed. — Oxford : Blackwell Scientific, 1981. — xii,356p : ill ; 25cm
Previous ed.: London : Sidgwick & Jackson, 1969. — Bibliography: p343-349. - Includes index
ISBN 0-632-00755-9 (pbk) : £9.50 : CIP rev.
B80-34999

592′.01′09162 — Marine invertebrates. Physiology — *Comparative studies*
Hammen, Carl S.. Marine invertebrates : comparative physiology / Carl S. Hammen. — Hanover, N.H. ; London : Published for University of Rhode Island by University Press of New England, 1980. — xii,127p : ill ; 22cm
Bibliography: p115-123. — Includes index
ISBN 0-87451-188-7 : £7.25 B81-27570

592′.0113 — Invertebrates. Blood. Cells
Invertebrate blood cells / edited by N.A. Ratcliffe and A.F. Rowley. — London : Academic Press, 1981
Vol.1: General aspects, animals without true circulatory systems to cephalopods. — 323,[57p] : ill ; 24cm
Includes bibliographies and index
ISBN 0-12-582101-8 : £33.00 B81-36329

592'.0113 — Invertebrates. Blood. Cells *continuation*

Invertebrate blood cells / edited by N.A. Ratcliffe and A.F. Rowley. — London : Academic Press
Vol.2: Arthropods to urochordates, invertebrates and vertebrates compared. — 1981. — xii,p327-641,xlvp : ill ; 24cm
Includes bibliographies and index
ISBN 0-12-582102-6 : £33.00 B81-38866

592'.012 — Invertebrates. Respiration

Wells, Rufus M. G.. Invertebrate respiration / Rufus M.G. Wells. — London : Edward Arnold, 1980. — 72p : ill ; 22cm. — (The Institute of Biology's studies in biology, ISSN 0537-9024 ; no.127)
Bibliography: p72
ISBN 0-7131-2806-2 (pbk) : £2.25 : CIP rev. B80-33585

592'.016 — Invertebrates. Reproduction — *Conference proceedings*

International Society of Invertebrate Reproduction. *International Symposium (2nd : 1979 : Davis, Calif.)*. Advances in invertebrate reproduction : proceedings of the Second International Symposium of the International Society of Invertebrate Reproduction (ISIR) held in Davis, California, on August 27-31, 1979 / editors Wallis H. Clark, Jr, Terrance S. Adams. — New York ; Oxford : Elsevier/North-Holland, c1981. — ix,400p : ill ; 25cm. — (Developments in endocrinology ; v.11)
Includes index
ISBN 0-444-00594-3 : £22.14 B81-15494

592'.03'2 — Invertebrates. Primordial germ cells

Primordial germ cells in the invertebrates. — Cambridge : Cambridge University Press, Nov.1981. — [258]p. — (Developmental and cell biology)
ISBN 0-521-22189-7 : £30.00 : CIP entry B81-33618

592.0909'732 — Gardens. Invertebrates — *For children*

Jennings, Terry. Small garden animals / Terry Jennings ; illustrated by John Barber, Karen Daws. — Oxford : Oxford University Press, 1981. — 32p : chiefly col.ill ; 28cm. — (The Young scientist investigates)
ISBN 0-19-917036-3 (pbk) : £1.50 B81-17127

592.092'9 — Still waters. Invertebrates

Price, Taff. Taff Price's stillwater flies : a modern account of natural history, flydressing and fishing technique. — London : Ernest Benn
Bk. 2. — 1981. — p91-185,4p of plates : ill (some col.) ; 25cm
ISBN 0-510-22542-x (pbk) : £5.95
Primary classification 799.1'755 B81-12744

592.092'942821 — South Yorkshire *(Metropolitan County)*. **Sheffield** *(District)*. **Freshwater invertebrates. Distribution**

Freshwater invertebrates of the Sheffield district / edited by Krys A. Zasada and Eluned H. Smith ; compiled by Tim H. Riley ; illustrations by Steven Garland, Jeremy Lee ; map production by Derek Whiteley. — Sheffield ([17 Winchester Ave., Sheffield S10 4EA]) : Sorby Natural History Society, 1981. — 88p : ill,maps ; 21cm. — (Sorby record special series, ISSN 0260-2032 ; no.4)
Bibliography: p6-7
ISBN 0-9500396-5-9 (pbk) : Unpriced B81-30918

592.0941 — Great Britain. Gardens. Invertebrates — *For children*

Jennings, Terry. Small garden animals / Terry Jennings ; illustrated by John Barber, Karen Daws. — Oxford : Oxford University Press, 1981. — 32p : ill(some col.) ; 29cm. — (The young scientist investigates)
ISBN 0-19-917045-2 : £2.50 B81-24405

592.79'6 — Ants - *For children*

Finding out about ants. — Poole : Blandford Press, Apr.1981. — [32]p. — (Japanese nature series)
ISBN 0-7137-1153-1 : £2.95 : CIP entry B81-04330

593.1 — Protozoa

Farmer, John N.. The protozoa : introduction to protozoology / John N. Farmer. — St. Louis ; London : Mosby, 1980. — ix,732p : ill ; 24cm
Includes bibliographies and index
ISBN 0-8016-1550-x (pbk) : £18.00 B81-00982

593.1'041 — Protozoa. Physiology

Biochemistry and physiology of protozoa. — 2nd ed. / edited by M. Levandowsky, S.H. Hutner ; consulting editor Luigi Provasoli. — New York ; London : Academic Press
Previous ed.: / edited by A. Lwoff. New York : Academic Press, 1951-1964
Vol.4. — 1981. — xvii,574p : ill ; 24cm
Includes bibliographies and index
ISBN 0-12-444604-3 : £32.60 B81-33255

593.1'041'88 — Protozoa. Nervous system

Electrical conduction and behaviour in 'simple' invertebrates. — Oxford : Clarendon Press, Jan.1982. — [400]p
ISBN 0-19-857171-2 : £30.00 : CIP entry B81-34554

593.1'0724 — Schools. Laboratory organisms: Protozoa

Page, F. C.. The culture and use of free-living protozoa in teaching / Frederick Page. — Cambridge (68 Hill Rd., Cambridge CB2 1LA) : Institute of Terrestrial Ecology, 1981. — 54p : ill ; 21cm
At head of title: Institute of Terrestrial Ecology, Natural Environment Research Council. — Bibliography: p49-50. — Includes index
ISBN 0-904282-52-x (pbk) : £2.10 B81-25386

593.1'8 — Phytoflagellata — *Conference proceedings*

Phytoflagellates / editor Elenor R. Cox. — New York ; Oxford ([256 Banbury Rd, Oxford OX2 7DE]) : Elsevier/North-Holland, c1980. — ix,473p : ill ; 25cm. — (Developments in marine biology, ISSN 0163-6995 ; vol.2)
Includes bibliographies and index
ISBN 0-444-00363-0 : £21.95 B81-00893

593.6'0941 — Great Britain. Coastal waters. Anthozoa

Manuel, R. L.. British anthozoa : keys and notes for the identification of the species / R.L. Manuel. — London : Published for the Linnean Society of London and the Estuarine and Brackish-water Sciences Association by Academic Press, 1981. — 241p,2 leaves of plates : ill ; 22cm. — (Synopses of the British fauna. New series ; no.18)
Bibliography: p230-236. — Includes index
ISBN 0-12-470050-0 (pbk) : Unpriced : CIP rev. B80-29678

593.7 — Scyphozoa. Life cycle — *Illustrations — For children*

Jellyfish. — London : Deutsch, Oct.1981. — [36]p
ISBN 0-233-97379-6 : £2.50 : CIP entry B81-26744

594 — Molluscs

Boyle, P. R.. Molluscs and man. — London : Edward Arnold, Nov.1981. — [64]. — (The Institute of Biology's studies in biology, ISSN 0537-9024 ; no.134)
ISBN 0-7131-2824-0 (pbk) : £2.40 : CIP entry B81-30606

594'.01852 — Molluscs. Skeletal system. Growth

Skeletal growth of aquatic organisms : biological records of environmental change / edited by Donald C. Rhoads and Richard A. Lutz. — New York ; London : Plenum, c1980. — xiii,750p : ill ; 26cm. — (Topics in geobiology ; v.1)
Includes bibliographies and index
ISBN 0-306-40259-9 : Unpriced
Also classified at 591.1'852 B81-03988

594'.0471 — Marine molluscs. Shells — *Collectors' guides*

Eisenberg, Jerome M.. A collector's guide to seashells of the world / Jerome M. Eisenberg ; consulting editor William E. Old, Jr ; with photographs and drawings by the author. — New York ; London : McGraw-Hill, 1981. — 237p : chiefly ill(some col.) ; 27cm
Bibliography: p214-217. - Includes index
ISBN 0-07-019140-9 : £12.50 B81-10066

594'.0471'095353 — Oman. Marine molluscs. Shells — *Field guides*

Bosch, Donald. Seashells of Oman. — London : Longman, July 1981. — [208]p
ISBN 0-582-78309-7 : £14.70 : CIP entry B81-1494[illegible]

594'.051'0973 — United States. Shellfish. Behaviour. Effects of power stations — *Conference proceedings*

Power plants : effects on fish and shellfish behavior / editors Charles H. Hocutt ... [et al.] — New York ; London : Academic Press, 1980. — xiii,346p : ill ; 24cm
Includes bibliographies and index
ISBN 0-12-350950-5 : £16.00
Primary classification 597'.051'0973 B81-1475[illegible]

594.0953'8 — Saudi Arabia. Marine molluscs. Shells

Sharabati, Doreen. Saudi Arabian seashells. — London (8 Welbeck Way, W1M 8HA) : VNU Books International, Oct.1981. — [120]p
ISBN 0-9507641-0-8 : £16.00 : CIP entry B81-2574[illegible]

594'.3'02461 — Africa. Freshwater gastropoda — *For medicine*

Brown, D. S.. Freshwater snails of Africa and their medical importance / D.S. Brown. — London : Taylor & Francis, 1980. — x,487p : ill ; maps ; 24cm
Includes bibliographies and index
ISBN 0-85066-145-5 : £25.00 CIP rev. B80-0640[illegible]

594'.32 — Strombidae & Harpidae

Walls, Jerry G.. Conchs, tibias and harps / Jerry G. Walls. — Neptune ; Reigate : T.F.H., c1980. — 191p : ill(some col.),maps ; 23cm
Bibliography: p180-181. - Includes index
ISBN 0-87666-629-2 : £6.95 B81-1068[illegible]

594'.5'05 — Cephalopoda — *Serials*

Cephalopod newsletter. — Part 1 (1977)-. — London (Dr. Marion Nixon, Wellcome Institute for the History of Medicine, 183 Euston Rd, NW1 2BP) : [s.n.], 1977-. — v. ; 30cm
Two issues yearly
ISSN 0260-681x = Cephalopod newsletter : Unpriced B81-1321[illegible]

595.1'045249 — Animals. Parasites: Worms. Biochemistry

Barrett, John, *1943-*. Biochemistry of parasitic helminths / John Barrett. — London : Macmillan, 1981. — ix,308p : ill ; 25cm
Includes index
ISBN 0-333-25668-9 : £25.00 : CIP rev. B80-2447[illegible]

595.1'21 — Hymenolepis diminuta

Biology of the tapeworm Hymenolepis diminuta / edited by Hisao P. Arai. — New York ; London : Academic Press, 1980. — xii,733p : ill ; 24cm
Includes bibliographies and index
ISBN 0-12-058980-x : £25.20 B81-1661[illegible]

595.1'23'0941 — Flatworms — *Study regions: Great Britain*

Ball, Ian R.. British planarians. — Cambridge : Cambridge University Press, Nov.1981. — [160]p. — (Synopes of the British fauna ; 19)
ISBN 0-521-23875-7 (cased) : £16.00 : CIP entry
ISBN 0-521-28272-1 (pbk) : £6.95 B81-3881[illegible]

595'.146'0872 — Oligochaeta. Cells. Ultrastructure

Jamieson, B. G. M.. The ultrastructure of the Oligochaeta. — London : Academic Press, Oct.1981. — [520]p
ISBN 0-12-380180-x : CIP entry B81-2677[illegible]

595.1'82045249 — Plants. Parasites: Roundworms

Dropkin, Victor H.. Introduction to plant nematology / Victor H. Dropkin. — New York ; Chichester : Wiley, c1980. — xiii,293p : ill,2maps ; 24cm
Includes bibliography and index
ISBN 0-471-05578-6 : £14.00 B81-0175[illegible]

595.1'82045249'094 — Europe. Plants. Parasites: Round worms. Distribution. Surveys — *Standards*
Brown, D. J. F.. European plant parasitic nematode survey : instructions for participants / compiled by D.J.F. Brown, B. Boag and C.E. Taylor. — [Dundee] ([Invergowrie, Dundee DD2 5DA]) : Scottish Horticultural Research Institute, [1979]. — 16p : maps,forms ; 21cm. — (Occasional publication / Scottish Horticultural Research Institute ; no.3)
Bibliography: p14-16
Unpriced (pbk) B81-22165

595.3'72 — Wood lice
Sutton, Stephen. Woodlice / by Stephen Sutton ; key written in collaboration with Paul Harding, David Burn. — Oxford : Pergamon, 1980, c1972. — 143p,8p of plates : ill(some col.),1form,col.maps ; 23cm. — (Invertebrate types)
Originally published: Aylesbury : Ginn, 1972. — Bibliography: p135-140. — Includes index
ISBN 0-08-025942-1 : £4.90 : CIP rev.
B80-20663

595.3'841 — Lobsters
The **Biology** and management of lobsters / edited by J. Stanley Cobb, Bruce F. Phillips. — New York ; London : Academic Press
Includes bibliographies and index
Vol.1: Physiology and behavior. — c1980. — xv,463p : ill ; 24cm
ISBN 0-12-177401-5 : £30.80 B81-14030

The **Biology** and management of lobsters / edited by J. Stanley Cobb, Bruce F. Phillips. — New York ; London : Academic Press
Includes bibliographies and index
Vol.2: Ecology and management. — c1980. — xii,390p : ill,maps ; 24cm
ISBN 0-12-177402-3 : £29.00 B81-14029

595.4'2'041 — Ticks
Physiology of ticks. — Oxford : Pergamon, Feb.1982. — [450]p. — (Current themes in tropical science ; v.1)
ISBN 0-08-024937-x : £62.50 : CIP entry
B81-35907

595.6'2 — Centipedes
Lewis, J. G. E.. The biology of centipedes / J.G.E. Lewis. — Cambridge : Cambridge University Press, 1981. — 476p : ill ; 23cm
Bibliography: p429-455. — Includes index
ISBN 0-521-23413-1 : £33.00 : CIP rev.
B81-19118

595.7 — Entomology
Elzinga, Richard J.. Fundamentals of entomology / Richard J. Elzinga. — 2nd ed. — Englewood Cliffs ; London : Prentice-Hall, c1981. — x,422p : ill ; 25cm
Previous ed.: 1978. — Bibliography: p401-410. - Includes index
ISBN 0-13-338194-3 : £12.95 B81-17307

Romoser, William S.. The science of entomology / William S. Romoser. — 2nd ed. — New York : Macmillan ; London : Collier Macmillan, c1981. — xiv,575p : ill ; 27cm
Previous ed.: 1973. — Bibliography: p491-528. — Includes index
ISBN 0-02-403410-x : £13.95 B81-36118

595.7 — Insects
Borror, Donald J.. An introduction to the study of insects. — 5th ed. / Donald J. Borror, Dwight M. De Long, Charles A. Triplehorn. — Philadelphia ; London : Saunders College, c1981. — x,827p : ill ; 25cm
Previous ed.: New York ; London : Holt, Rinehart and Winston, 1976. — Includes bibliographies and index
ISBN 0-03-043531-5 : £15.95 B81-34427

Gillott, Cedric. Entomology / Cedric Gillott. — New York ; London : Plenum, c1980. — xviii,729p : ill,maps ; 26cm
Includes bibliographies and index
ISBN 0-306-40366-8 : Unpriced B81-00117

The **Oxford** book of insects. — Oxford : Oxford University Press, June 1981. — [224]p
Originally published: 1968
ISBN 0-19-217725-7 (pbk) : £2.50 : CIP entry
B81-16856

595.7 — Insects — *Festschriften*
Insect biology in the future : 'VBW 80' / edited by Michael Locke, David S. Smith. — New York ; London : Academic Press, 1980. — xv,977pp : ill,facsims ; 24cm
Facsims on lining papers. — Bibliography: p947-961. — Includes index
ISBN 0-12-454340-5 : £32.00 B81-14753

595.7 — Insects — *For schools*
Sully, Nina. Looking at insects. — London : Batsford, Jan.1982. — [48]p. — (Looking at science)
ISBN 0-7134-3990-4 : £3.95 : CIP entry
B81-33837

595.7'01 — Insects. Physiology
Insect physiology / W. Mordue ... [et al.]. — Oxford : Blackwell Scientific, 1980. — viii,108p : ill ; 24cm
Includes bibliographies and index
ISBN 0-632-00385-5 (pbk) : £5.75 : CIP rev.
B80-03645

595.7'01'05 — Insects. Physiology — *Serials*
Advances in insect physiology. — Vol.15. — London : Academic Press, c1980. — 624p
ISBN 0-12-024215-x : Unpriced : CIP rev.
ISSN 0065-2806 B80-12875

595.7'013 — Insects. Nutrition — *Conference proceedings*
Current topics in insect endocrinology and nutrition : a tribute to Gottfried S. Fraenkel / edited by Govindan Bhaskaran, Stanley Friedman and J.G. Rodriguez ; [proceedings of the symposium honoring Gottfried S. Fraenkel held at the Annual Meeting of the Entomological Society of America, November 1979, in Denver, Colorado]. — New York ; London : Plenum, c1981. — vi,362p : ill,port ; 26cm
Includes bibliographies and index
ISBN 0-306-40621-7 : Unpriced
Also classified at 595.7'0142 B81-17161

595.7'0142 — Insects. Endocrine system — *Conference proceedings*
Current topics in insect endocrinology and nutrition : a tribute to Gottfried S. Fraenkel / edited by Govindan Bhaskaran, Stanley Friedman and J.G. Rodriguez ; [proceedings of the symposium honoring Gottfried S. Fraenkel held at the Annual Meeting of the Entomological Society of America, November 1979, in Denver, Colorado]. — New York ; London : Plenum, c1981. — vi,362p : ill,port ; 26cm
Includes bibliographies and index
ISBN 0-306-40621-7 : Unpriced
Primary classification 595.7'013 B81-17161

595.7'01912 — Insects. Temperature. Regulation — *Conference proceedings*
Insect thermoregulation / edited by Bernd Heinrich. — New York ; Chichester : Wiley, c1981. — ix,328p : ill ; 24cm
Includes bibliographies and index
ISBN 0-471-05144-6 : £18.75 B81-14765

595.7'0334 — Insects. Eggs
Hinton, H. E.. Biology of insect eggs / H.E. Hinton. — Oxford : Pergamon, 1981. — 3v.(xxiv,1125p) : ill ; 26cm
Bibliography: p779-999. — Includes index
ISBN 0-08-021539-4 : £125.00 : CIP rev.
B78-16232

595.7'038 — Insects. Evolution
Hennig, Willi. Insect phylogeny / Willi Hennig ; translated and edited by Adrian C. Pont ; revisionary notes by Dieter Schlee with the collaboration of Michael Achtelig ... [et al.]. — Chichester : Wiley, c1981. — xxii,514p : ill ; 24cm
Translation of: Die Stammesgeschichte der Insekten. — Bibliography: p445-488. — Includes index
ISBN 0-471-27848-3 : £28.00 : CIP rev.
B81-00118

595.7'05249 — Parasites: Insects
Marshall, A. G.. The ecology of ectoparasitic insects. — London : Academic Press, Dec.1981. — [550]p
ISBN 0-12-474080-4 : CIP entry B81-33870

595.7'0873223 — Insects. Cells. Genetics — *Conference proceedings*
Insect cytogenetics / edited on behalf of the Society by R.L. Blackman, G.M. Hewitt & M. Ashburner. — Oxford : Blackwell Scientific for the Royal Entomological Society, 1980. — viii,278p : ill ; 27cm. — (Symposia of the Royal Entomological Society of London ; no.10)
Conference papers. — Includes bibliographies and index
ISBN 0-632-00552-1 : £22.50 : CIP rev.
B81-02373

595.70909'3 — Tropical regions. Insects — *Serials*
Insect science and its application : the international journal of tropical insect science / [sponsored by the International Centre of Insect Physiology and Ecology (ICIPE) and the African Association of Insect Scientists (AAIS)]. — Vol.1, no.1 (1980)-. — Oxford : Pergamon, 1980-. — v. : ill,maps ; 28cm
Quarterly
ISSN 0191-9040 = Insect science and its application : Unpriced B81-05312

595.70994 — Australia. Insects — *Field guides*
Goode, John, *1927-*. Insects of Australia / John Goode ; with illustrations from the classic The insects of Australia and New Zealand by R.J. Tillyard. — London : Angus & Robertson, 1980. — x,260p,[8]p of plates : ill(some col.) ; 20cm
Text on lining papers. — Bibliography: p241-242. — Includes index
ISBN 0-207-13531-2 : £5.95 B81-17921

595.7'22 — American cockroaches
The **American** cockroach. — London : Chapman and Hall, Dec.1981. — [400]p
ISBN 0-412-16140-0 : £20.00 : CIP entry
B81-31750

595.7'22 — Cockroaches. Physiology. Research. Laboratory techniques
Bell, William J.. The laboratory cockroach. — London : Chapman and Hall, Dec.1981. — [164]p
ISBN 0-412-23990-6 (pbk) : £6.95 : CIP entry
B81-31712

595.7'4504334 — Great Britain. Caddis flies. Larvae — *Field guides*
Edington, John M.. A key to the caseless caddis larvae of the British Isles, with notes on their ecology / by J.M. Edington and A.G. Hildrew. — Ambleside : Freshwater Biological Association, 1981. — 91p,4p of plates : ill ; 21cm. — (Scientific publication / Freshwater Biological Association, ISSN 0367-1887 ; no.43)
Bibliography: p86-91. - Includes index
ISBN 0-900386-41-x (pbk) : Unpriced
B81-18008

595.76 — Beetles
Crowson, R. A.. The biology of the coleoptera / R.A. Crowson. — London : Academic Press, 1981. — xii,802p,1folded leaf of plates : ill ; 24cm
Bibliography: p699-745. — Includes index
ISBN 0-12-196050-1 : £58.00 : CIP rev.
B80-20665

595.76'9 — Ladybirds. Life cycle — *For children*
Wootton, Anthony. Life of the ladybird. — London : Dent, Sept.1981. — [48]p
Translation of: Marienkaefer
ISBN 0-460-06085-6 : £3.95 : CIP entry
B81-22632

595.77 — Flies — *For children* — *Welsh texts*
Hope, Ffransis. Y gleren / [gan Ffransis Hope] ; [addaswyd o Holandeg Francis Brewer ; lluniau gan Jan van Wijngaarden]. — Caerdydd : Gwasg y Dref Wen, c1980. — 16p : col.ill,1map ; 22cm. — (Cyfres y seren)
Text, map on inside covers
£0.80 (pbk) B81-07498

595.77'1 — Simulium damnosum. Control measures. Biological aspects
Blackflies. — London : Academic Press, July 1981. — [400]p
ISBN 0-12-434060-1 : CIP entry B81-13443

595.77'4 — Drosophila. Genetics
The **genetics** and biology of drosophila. — London : Academic Press, June 1981
Vol.3a. — [450]p
ISBN 0-12-064945-4 : CIP entry B81-08914

595.77'4 — Drosophila. Genetics — *Conference proceedings*
International Conference on Development and Behavior of Drosophila melanogaster *(1979 : Tata Institute of Fundamental Research).*
Development and neurobiology of Drosophila / [proceedings of the International Conference on Development and Behavior of Drosophila melanogaster, held at the Tata Institute of Fundamental Research, Bombay, India, December 19-22, 1979] ; edited by O. Siddiqi ... [et al.]. — New York ; London : Plenum, c1980. — x,496p : ill,ports ; 26cm. — (Basic life sciences ; v.16)
Includes bibliographies and index
ISBN 0-306-40559-8 : Unpriced B81-04574

595.77'5'07402132 — London. Kensington and Chelsea (London Borough). Museums: British Museum (Natural History). Stock: Fleas. Collection: Rothschild Collection - *Catalogues*
Mardon, D. K.. An illustrated catalogue of the Rothschild collection of fleas (siphonaptera) in the British Museum (Natural History). — London : British Museum (Natural History), May 1981
Vol.6: Pygiopsyllidae. — [298]p
ISBN 0-565-00820-x : CIP entry B81-07939

595.78 — Butterflies & moths — *For children*
Butterflies and moths / illustrated by Norman Weaver, Tony Swift, Phil Weare. — London : Hamilton, 1980. — 28p : col.ill ; 20cm. — (Small world)
Includes index
ISBN 0-241-10502-1 : £1.95 B81-07125

595.78'094 — Europe. Butterflies & moths — *Field guides*
Hargreaves, Brian. Butterflies and moths / Brian Hargreaves, Michael Chinery. — London : Collins, 1981. — 240p : col.ill ; 12cm. — (Collins gem guides)
Includes index
ISBN 0-00-458808-8 (pbk) : £1.75 B81-39618

595.78'1 — Female noctuidae. Reproductive system
Pierce, F. N.. The genitalia of the group Noctuidae of the lepidoptera of the British Islands : an account of the morphology of the female reproductory organs / by F.N. Pierce ; illustrated by the author. — Oxford : Classey, 1978. — 62p,xvp of plates ; 22cm
Originally published: Oundle : F.N. Pierce, 1942
ISBN 0-86096-003-x (pbk) : £4.50 B81-07161

595.78'1'0924 — Moths — *Personal observations*
Allan, P. B. M.. Leaves from a moth-hunter's notebooks / by P.B.M. Allan ; edited and with an introduction by R.S. Wilkinson. — Faringdon : Classey, 1980. — 281p : 1port ; 21cm
Includes index
ISBN 0-900848-89-8 : £9.00 B81-04565

595.78'1'094267 — Essex. Moths
Emmet, A. M.. The smaller moths of Essex / by A.M. Emmet. — London (Passmore Edwards Museum, Romford Rd., E15 4LZ) : Essex Field Club, c1981. — 158p : ill,maps ; 21cm. — (Essex naturalist, ISSN 0071-1489 ; no.6)
ISBN 0-905637-11-9 (pbk) : £7.00 B81-37412

595.78'9 — Butterflies
Goodden, Robert. Butterflies / Robert Goodden ; illustrated by Joyce Bee. — London : Hamlyn, 1972, c1971 (1979 printing). — 159p : ill (chiefly col.),col.maps ; 18cm. — (Hamlyn all-colour paperbacks)
Bibliography: p156. — Includes index
ISBN 0-600-00073-7 (pbk) : £0.95 B81-26542

Smart, Paul. The illustrated encyclopedia of the butterfly world / Paul Smart. — London : Corgi, 1981, c1976. — 274p : col.ill + 1map,1facsim,1port ; 30cm
Originally published: London : Hamlyn, 1976. — Includes index
ISBN 0-552-98206-7 (pbk) : £5.95 B81-40209

595.78'9 — Meadow brown butterflies. Life cycle
Dawdeswell, W. H.. The life of the meadow brown. — London : Heinemann Educational, Sept.1981. — [176]p
ISBN 0-435-60224-1 (pbk) : £6.50 : CIP entry B81-30258

595.78'9'094 — Europe. Butterflies
Watson, Allan. Butterflies / [author Allan Watson] ; [illustrators Alan Male, Bernard Robinson, David Wright] ; [designed and edited by Eric Inglefield]. — London : Kingfisher, 1981. — 124p : ill(some col.) ; 20cm. — (Kingfisher guides)
Includes index
ISBN 0-7063-6100-8 : £2.50 : CIP rev. B81-03829

595.78'9'094 — Northern Europe. Butterflies — *Identification manuals*
Dal, Björn. The butterflies of northern Europe. — London : Croom Helm, Jan.1982. — [128]p
ISBN 0-7099-0810-5 : £5.95 : CIP entry B81-34315

595.78'9'0941 — Great Britain. Butterflies — *Field guides*
Fekjan, Jan. Butterflies / illustrations by Jan Fekjan. — Poole : Blandford, c1981. — 127p : col. ill ; 12cm. — (A Blandford mini-guide)
These illustrations originally published: in Den lilla sommerfuglboken/Nils Petter Thuesen. Oslo : Aschehoug. 1981. — Includes index
ISBN 0-7137-1210-4 (pbk) : £0.95 B81-31414

595.78'9'0941 — Great Britain. Butterflies — *For children*
Chinery, Michael. A child's book of butterflies & flowers / by Michael Chinery ; illustrations by Michael Atkinson. — London : Granada, 1981. — [27]p : col.ill ; 26cm
ISBN 0-246-11550-5 : £2.95 B81-18392

595.78'9'0941 — Great Britain. Butterflies — *Illustrations*
Beningfield, Gordon. Beningfield's butterflies / paintings and drawings by Gordon Beningfield ; text by Robert Goodden. — Harmondsworth : Penguin, 1981, c1978. — 92p : ill(some col.) ; 30cm
Originally published: London : Chatto and Windus, 1978
ISBN 0-14-006026-x (pbk) : £4.95 B81-40482

595.78'9'09411 — Scotland. Butterflies
Thomson, George, *1943-*. The butterflies of Scotland : a natural history / George Thomson. — London : Croom Helm, c1980. — xvii,267p,[27]p of plates : ill(some col.),maps,ports ; 24cm
Bibliography: p243-256. — Includes index
ISBN 0-7099-0383-9 : £19.95 : CIP rev. B80-04192

595.78'9'096 — Africa. Butterflies — *Field guides*
Carcasson, R. H.. Collins handguide to the butterflies of Africa / written and illustrated by R.H. Carcasson. — London : Collins, 1981, c1980. — xix,188p : ill(some col.),3maps(some col.) ; cm
Includes index
ISBN 0-00-219783-9 (cased) : £7.95
ISBN 0-00-219784-7 (pbk) : £4.95 B81-39769

595.79 — Great Britain. Sawflies — *Field guides*
Quinlan, John, *1925-*. Symphyta : (except Tenthredinidae) Hymenoptera / by J. Quinlan and I.D. Gauld. — New ed. — London : Royal Entomological Society of London, 1981. — 67p : ill ; 23cm. — (Handbooks for the identification of British insects ; vol.VI, pt.2(a))
Previous ed.: published as Hymenoptera (Symphyta). 1951. — Bibliography: p40-41. — Includes index
Unpriced (pbk) B81-31314

595.79'045 — Social insect sociobiology - *Conference proceedings*
Biosystematics of social insects. — London : Academic Press, Aug.1981. — [280]p. — (The Systematics Association special volume ; no.19)
Conference papers
ISBN 0-12-357180-4 : CIP entry B81-18129

595.79'6 — Ants — *For children*
Ants / consultant editor Henry Pluckrose ; illustrated by Tony Swift and David Cook. — London : Hamilton, 1981. — 28p : col.ill ; 21cm. — (Small world)
Includes index
ISBN 0-241-10539-0 : £2.25 B81-16727

595.79'60451 — Ants. Social behaviour
Dumpert, Klaus. The social biology of ants / Klaus Dumpert ; translated by C. Johnson. — Boston ; London : Pitman, 1981. — vi,298p : ill ; 25cm. — (The Pitman international series in neurobiology and behaviour)
Translation of: Das Sozialleben der Ameisen. — Bibliography: p264-292. — Includes index
ISBN 0-273-08479-8 : Unpriced B81-38440

595.79'8 — Great Britain. Scolioidea, Vespoidea & Sphecoidea — *Field guides*
Richards, O. W.. Scolioidea, Vespoidea and Sphecoidea : Hymenoptera, Aculeata / by O.W. Richards. — [London] : Royal Entomological Society of London, 1980. — 118p : ill ; 23cm. — (Handbooks for the identification of British insects ; v.V1, pt 3(b))
Bibliography: p85-88
£8.30 (pbk) B81-06535

595.79'8 — Wasps — *For children*
Bees and wasps / consultant editor Henry Pluckrose ; illustrated by Tony Swift and Norman Weaver. — London : Hamilton, 1981. — 28p : col.ill ; 21cm. — (Small world)
Includes index
ISBN 0-241-10540-4 : £2.25
Primary classification 595.79'9 B81-16728

Clay, Pat. Wasps. — London : A & C Black, Sept.1981. — [26]p. — (Nature in close-up ; 14)
ISBN 0-7136-2153-2 : £2.95 : CIP entry B81-22530

595.79'9 — Bees
Teale, Edwin Way. The golden throng : a book about bees / by Edwin Way Teale ; illustrated from eighty-five photographs by the author. — Sherborne : Alphabooks, 1981, c1968. — 160p,[64]p of plates : ill ; 25cm
Originally published: New York : Dodd, Mead, 1940 ; London : Hale, 1942. — Bibliography: p155-156. — Includes index
ISBN 0-906670-20-9 : £9.50 B81-29528

595.79'9 — Bees — *Early works*
Hill, Thomas. A profitable instruction of the perfect ordering of bees. — Gerrards Cross : International Bee Research Association, Sept.1981. — [46]p. — (Texts of early bee books ; no.4)
Previous ed.: London : B.L., 1579
ISBN 0-86098-092-8 : £12.00 : CIP entry B81-21552

595.79'9 — Bees — *For children*
Bees and wasps / consultant editor Henry Pluckrose ; illustrated by Tony Swift and Norman Weaver. — London : Hamilton, 1981. — 28p : col.ill ; 21cm. — (Small world)
Includes index
ISBN 0-241-10540-4 : £2.25
Also classified at 595.79'8 B81-16728

596 — VERTEBRATES

596 — Extinct vertebrates — *Illustrations* — *For children*
Rice, Shawn. As dead as a dodo. — London : Methuen, Oct.1981. — [32]p
ISBN 0-416-21420-7 : £4.95 : CIP entry B81-25840

596 — Vertebrates
Grey, Chris. Purnell's illustrated world atlas of animals / by Chris Grey. — Maidenhead : Purnell, 1981. — 61p : col.ill,col.maps ; 33cm
Ill, text on lining papers. — Includes index
ISBN 0-361-04911-0 : £2.99 B81-22962

Pearson, Ronald. Lecture notes on vertebrate zoology / Ronald Pearson and John N. Ball. — Oxford : Blackwell Scientific, 1981. — viii,180p : ill ; 24cm
Includes bibliographies and index
ISBN 0-632-00729-x (pbk) : £7.50 B81-29574

596 — Vertebrates *continuation*

Young, J. Z.. The life of vertebrates / J.Z. Young. — 3rd ed. — Oxford : Clarendon Press, 1981. — xv,645p : ill,maps ; 24cm
Previous ed.: 1962. — Bibliography: p586-606. — Includes index
ISBN 0-19-857172-0 (cased) : £25.00 : CIP rev.
ISBN 0-19-857173-9 (pbk) : £14.00 B81-12883

596 — Vertebrates — *For children*

Charushin, Evgeniĭ Ivanovich. My animal book / Yevgeny Charushin ; translated from the Russian by Olga Shartse ; drawings by Nikita Charushin. — Moscow : Progress ; [London] : Central Books [distributor], 1980. — 68p : col.ill ; 29cm
Translation of: Moi͡a pervai͡a zoologii͡a
ISBN 0-7147-1581-6 : £1.95 B81-20237

My favourite book of animals. — London : Dean, 1980, c1978. — [16]p : col.ill ; 29cm
ISBN 0-603-00216-1 : £0.75 B81-38488

596'.0028 — Vertebrates. Autoradiography

Curtis, C. G.. Whole-body autoradiography / C.G. Curtis ... [et al.]. — London : Academic Press, 1981. — xi,125p,[4]leaves of plates : ill (some col.) ; 24cm. — (Biological techniques series)
Bibliography: p109-118. — Includes index
ISBN 0-12-199660-3 : £12.40 B81-23552

596'.0074 — Zoos. Vertebrates — *Illustrations* — *For children*

My first book of the zoo. — London : Dean, [1980]. — [8]p : all col.ill ; 15cm. — (A Dean board book)
ISBN 0-603-00236-6 (pbk) : £0.25 B81-06343

596'.01 — Chordates. Physiology

Alexander, R. McNeill. The chordates / R. McNeill Alexander. — 2nd ed. — Cambridge : Cambridge University Press, 1981. — 510p : ill ; 24cm
Previous ed.: 1975. — Includes bibliographies and index
ISBN 0-521-23658-4 (cased) : £35.00
ISBN 0-521-28141-5 (pbk) : £12.50 B81-34522

596'.01 — Vertebrates. Physiology

Marshall, P. T.. Physiology of mammals and other vertebrates / P.T. Marshall, G.M. Hughes. — 2nd ed. — Cambridge : Cambridge University Press, 1980. — xvi,343p : ill ; 26cm
Previous ed.: 1965. — Includes index
ISBN 0-521-22633-3 (cased) : Unpriced : CIP rev.
ISBN 0-521-29586-6 (pbk) : £7.95 B80-25645

596'.0113 — Vertebrates. Blood. White cells — *Conference proceedings*

International Leukocyte Culture Conference *(12th : 1978 : Ben Gurion University of the Negev)*. Cell biology and immunology of leukocyte function : proceedings of the Twelfth International Leukocyte Culture Conference held at the Ben Gurion University of the Negev, Beer Sheva, Israel, June 25-30, 1978 / edited by Michael R. Quastel. — New York ; London : Academic Press, 1979. — xxix,959p : ill ; 24cm
Includes bibliographies and index
ISBN 0-12-569650-7 : £31.20 B81-04014

596'.012 — Vertebrates. Respiratory system. Evolution — *Comparative studies*

The **Evolution** of air breathing invertebrates / David J. Randall ... [et al.]. — Cambridge : Cambridge University Press, 1981. — 133p : ill ; 24cm
Bibliography: p120-129. — Includes index
ISBN 0-521-22259-1 : £15.00 B81-16420

596'.0142 — Vertebrates. Endocrine system

Norris, David O.. Vertebrate endocrinology / David O. Norris. — Philadelphia : Lea & Febiger ; London : Baillière Tindall, 1980. — xii,524p : ill ; 27cm
Includes bibliographies and index
ISBN 0-8121-0699-7 : £13.75 B81-16097

596'.01'8 — Vertebrates. Locomotion — *Conference proceedings*

Vertebrate locomotion. — London : Academic Press, Nov.1981. — [450]p. — (Symposia of the Zoological Society of London, ISSN 0084-5612 ; no.48)
Conference papers
ISBN 0-12-613348-4 : CIP entry B81-28140

596'.01823 — Vertebrates. Eyes. Lenses. Cells & molecules. Structure & properties

Molecular and cellular biology of the eye lens / edited by Hans Bloemendal. — New York ; Chichester : Wiley, c1981. — xv,469p : ill ; 24cm
Includes index
ISBN 0-471-05171-3 : £48.00 B81-33371

596'.01852 — Vertebrates. Muscles. Contraction — *Conference proceedings*

The **Regulation** of muscle contraction : excitation-contraction coupling / edited by Alan D. Grinnell, Mary A.B. Brazier. — New York ; London : Academic Press, 1981. — xvii,380p : ill ; 27cm. — (UCLA forum in medical sciences ; no.22)
Conference papers. — Includes bibliographies and index
ISBN 0-12-303780-8 : £19.80 B81-40772

596'.0188 — Lower vertebrates. Behaviour. Neurophysiological aspects

Brain mechanisms of behaviour in lower vertebrates / edited by P.R. Laming. — Cambridge : Cambridge University Press, 1981. — ix,318p : ill ; 24cm. — (Seminar series / Society for Experimental Biology ; 9)
Includes bibliographies and index
ISBN 0-521-23702-5 (cased) : £25.00 : CIP rev.
ISBN 0-521-28168-7 (pbk) : £11.50 B81-19145

596'.0188 — Vertebrates. Brain. Biochemistry

Bachelard, H. S.. Brain biochemistry / H.S. Bachelard. — 2nd ed. — London : Chapman and Hall, 1981. — 79p : ill ; 21cm. — (Outline studies in biology)
Previous ed.: 1974. — Includes index
ISBN 0-412-23470-x (pbk) : Unpriced : CIP rev. B81-15939

596'.0188 — Vertebrates. Brain — *Comparative studies*

Macphail, E. M.. Brain and intelligence in vertebrates. — Oxford : Clarendon Press, Nov.1981. — [450]p
ISBN 0-19-854550-9 (cased) : £20.00 : CIP entry
ISBN 0-19-854551-7 (pbk) : £9.95 B81-30528

596'.0188 — Vertebrates. Nervous system

Nathan, Peter. The nervous system. — 2nd ed. — Oxford : Oxford University Press, Aug.1981. — [400]p
Previous ed.: Harmondsworth : Penguin, 1969
ISBN 0-19-261344-8 : £12.50 : CIP entry B81-18125

596'.0188 — Vertebrates. Nervous system. Development

Studies of normal and abnormal development of the nervous system / volume editors W. Lierse, F. Beck. — Basel ; London : Karger, 1981. — viii,325p : ill ; 24cm. — (Bibliotheca anatomica ; no.19)
Includes bibliographies
ISBN 3-8055-1039-x (pbk) : £49.00 B81-10094

596'.0188 — Vertebrates. Nervous system. Development — *Conference proceedings*

Development in the nervous system. — Cambridge : Cambridge University Press, Nov.1981. — [407]p
Conference papers
ISBN 0-521-23493-x : £40.00 : CIP entry B81-31276

596'.0188 — Vertebrates. Nervous system. Peptides — *Conference proceedings*

Neuropeptides : biochemical and physiological studies / editor R.P. Millar. — Edinburgh : Churchill Livingstone, 1981. — 380p : ill,1port ; 24cm
Conference papers. — Includes bibliographies and index
ISBN 0-443-02265-8 : £20.00 B81-16138

596'.0188 — Vertebrates. Nervous system. Peptides — *Serials*

[**Neuropeptides** *(Edinburgh)*]. Neuropeptides : an international journal. — Vol.1, no.1 (July 1980)-. — Edinburgh : Churchill Livingstone, 1980-. — v. : ill ; 25cm
Six issues yearly
ISSN 0143-4179 = Neuropeptides (Edinburgh) : £55.00 per year B81-01996

596'.0188 — Vertebrates. Sensory perception. Role of dorsal horn of spinal cord — *Conference proceedings*

Spinal cord sensation : sensory processing in the dorsal horn / the proceedings of a satellite symposium of the International Congress of Physiological Sciences held at Keszthely, Hungary, July 9-12, 1980 ; edited by A.G. Brown and M. Réthelyi. — Edinburgh : Scottish Academic Press, 1981. — xvi,341p,[13]p of plates : ill ; 24cm
Includes bibliographies and index
ISBN 0-7073-0295-1 : £15.00 B81-40285

596'.019214 — Vertebrates. Calcium. Metabolism. Regulation. Role of hormones — *Conference proceedings*

International Conference on Calcium Regulating Hormones *(7th : 1980 : Estes Park, Colo.)*. Hormonal control of calcium metabolism : proceedings of the Seventh International Conference on Calcium Regulating Hormones (Seventh Parathyroid Conference) Estes Park, Colorado, U.S.A., September 5-9, 1980 / editors David V. Cohn, Roy V. Talmage, J. Les Matthews. — Amsterdam ; Oxford : Excerpta Medica, 1981. — xviii,506p : ill,2ports ; 25cm. — (International congress series ; 511)
Includes index
ISBN 90-219-0478-0 : £37.79
ISBN 0-444-90893-0 (Elsevier North-Holland) B81-21384

596'.02 — Vertebrates. Cancer. Genetic factors — *Conference proceedings*

Genetic origins of tumor cells / edited by F.J. Cleton and J.W.I.M. Simons. — The Hague ; London : Nijhoff, 1980. — xvi,128p : ill ; 25cm. — (Developments in oncology ; v.1)
Includes bibliographies and index
ISBN 90-247-2272-1 : Unpriced B81-02773

596'.02 — Vertebrates. Tumours. Role of viruses — *Conference proceedings*

Munich Symposium on Microbiology *(5th : 1980)*. Leukaemias, lymphomas and papillomas : comparative aspects / [proceedings of the 5th Munich Symposium on Microbiology, held on 3-4 June 1980 and organized by the WHO Collaborating Centre for Collection and Evaluation of Data on Comparative Virology] ; edited by Peter A. Bachmann. — London : Taylor & Francis, 1980. — 273p : ill ; 23cm. — (Munich symposia on microbiology)
Includes index
ISBN 0-85066-213-3 (pbk) : £9.50 B81-03958

596'.029 — Vertebrates. Major histocompatibility system — *Conference proceedings*

International Convocation on Immunology *(7th : 1980 : Niagara Falls)*. Immunobiology of the major histocompatibility complex : 7th International Convocation on Immunology, Niagara Falls, N.Y., July 7-10, 1980 / editors M.B. Zaleski, C.J. Abeyounis and K. Kano. — Basel ; London : Karger, 1981. — xii,396p : ill ; 25cm
Includes bibliographies and index
£52.70 B81-39026

596'.0292 — Vertebrates. Organs. Isoantigens — *Conference proceedings*

Organ specific alloantigens / edited by Parviz Lalezari and Henry Krakauer. — New York ; London : Grune & Stratton, c1980. — iv,150p : ill ; 26cm
Transplantation proceedings reprint, V.12, no.3, suppl. 1, Sept. 1980. — Includes index
ISBN 0-8089-1324-7 : £13.80 B81-21832

596'.0295 — Vertebrates. Immune reactions. Regulation

Strategies of immune regulation / edited by Eli Sercarz, Alastair J. Cunningham. — New York ; London : Academic Press, 1980. — xix,537p : ill ; 24cm
Includes bibliographies and index
ISBN 0-12-637140-7 : £22.20 B81-06352

596′.031 — Vertebrates. Limbs. Regeneration

Wallace, H.. Vertebrate limb regeneration / H. Wallace. — Chichester : Wiley, c1981. — xii,276p : ill ; 24cm
Bibliography: p237-270. — Includes index
ISBN 0-471-27877-7 : £19.50 B81-09781

596′.038 — Vertebrates. Evolution

Jarvik, Erik. Basic structures and evolution of vertebrates / Erik Jarvik. — London : Academic Press, 1980
Bibliography: p505-562. — Includes index
Vol.1. — xvi,575p : ill ; 26cm
ISBN 0-12-380801-4 : £41.00 : CIP rev.
B80-10598

596′.038 — Vertebrates. Evolution *related to* **anatomy of fossil vertebrates**

Jarvik, Erik. Basic structure and evolution of vertebrates / Erik Jarvik. — London : Academic Press
Vol.2. — 1980. — xiii,337p : ill ; 26cm
Bibliography: p269-326. - Includes index
ISBN 0-12-380802-2 : £27.00 : CIP rev.
Primary classification 566 B80-27009

596′.039′0222 — Young vertebrates — *Illustrations — For children*

Baby animals. — Maidenhead : Purnell, 1981. — [28]p : chiefly col.ill ; 27cm. — (All in colour picture books)
ISBN 0-361-05067-4 : £1.25 B81-19308

596′.087 — Vertebrates. Nervous system. Cells — *Serials*

Advances in cellular neurobiology. — Vol.1 (1980)-. — New York ; London : Academic Press, 1980. — v. : ill ; 24cm
Irregular
Unpriced B81-08365

596′.0875 — Vertebrates. Excitable cells. Membranes. Culture. Laboratory techniques: In vitro methods. Applications

Excitable cells in tissue culture / edited by Phillip G. Nelson and Melvyn Lieberman. — New York ; London : Plenum, c1981. — xvii,422p : ill ; 24cm
Includes bibliographies and index
ISBN 0-306-40516-4 : Unpriced B81-32816

596′.087612 — Vertebrates. Blood. Cells. Differentiation — *Conference proceedings*

Microenvironments in haemopoietic and lymphoid differentiation : Ciba Foundation symposium 84 in honour of John Humphrey / [editors: Ruth Porter and Julie Whelan]. — London : Pitman, 1981. — xi,348p : ill,port ; 24cm. — (Ciba Foundation symposium ; 84)
Includes bibliographies and index
ISBN 0-272-79636-0 : Unpriced : CIP rev.
B81-13426

596.0942 — England. Vertebrates — *Personal observations*

Drabble, Phil. A weasel in my meatsafe / Phil Drabble ; drawings by Ralph Thompson. — Large print ed. — Leicester : Ulverscroft, 1980, c1977. — 259p : ill ; 23cm. — (Ulverscroft large print series)
Originally published: London : Collins, 1957
ISBN 0-7089-0531-5 : £4.25 : CIP rev.
B80-23279

597′.0012 — Fish. Taxonomy

Webb, J. E.. Guide to living fishes / J.E. Webb, J.A. Wallwork, J.H. Elgood. — London : Macmillan, 1981. — ix,181p : ill,maps ; 23cm
Includes index
ISBN 0-333-30680-5 (cased) : £10.00
ISBN 0-333-23330-1 (pbk) : Unpriced
B81-21770

597′.0022′2 — Fish, reptiles & amphibians — *Illustrations*

Fishes, reptiles and amphibians : a picture sourcebook / edited and arranged by Don Rice. — New York ; London : Van Nostrand Reinhold, c1981. — 154p : all.ill ; 28cm
Includes index
ISBN 0-442-21196-1 (pbk) : £8.45 B81-31779

597′.01 — Fish. Physiology. Environmental factors — *Conference proceedings*

NATO Advanced Study Institute on Environmental Physiology of Fishes *(1979 : Bishop′s University)*. Environmental physiology of fishes / [lectures presented at the 1979 NATO Advanced Study Institute on Environmental Physiology of Fishes, held at Bishop′s University, Lennoxville, Quebec, Canada, August 12-25, 1979] ; edited by M.A. Ali. — New York ; London : Plenum, published in cooperation with NATO Scientific Affairs Division, c1980. — xi,723p : ill,maps ; 26cm. — (NATO advanced study institutes series. Series A, Life sciences ; v.35)
Includes bibliographies and index
ISBN 0-306-40574-1 : Unpriced B81-14641

597′.01826 — Fish. Chemoreception

Chemoreception in fishes. — Oxford : Elsevier Scientific, Jan.1982. — [500]p. — (Developments in aquaculture and fisheries science ; 8)
ISBN 0-444-42040-1 : CIP entry B81-34479

597′.02 — Fish. Stress

Stress and fish. — London : Academic Press, Oct.1981. — [350]p
Conference papers
ISBN 0-12-554550-9 : CIP entry B81-27351

597′.05 — Fish. Ecology — *Conference proceedings*

Symposium on the Ethology and Behavioral Ecology of Fishes *(2nd : 1979 : Normal, Ill.)*. Ecology and ethology of fishes : proceedings of the 2nd Biennial Symposium on the Ethology and Behavioral Ecology of Fishes, held at Normal, Ill., U.S.A., October 19-22, 1979 / edited by David L.G. Noakes and Jack A. Ward. — The Hague ; London : Junk, 1981. — 142p : ill,maps,ports ; 27cm. — (Developments in environmental biology of fishes ; 1)
Includes bibliographies
ISBN 90-619-3821-x : Unpriced B81-29286

597′.05′09811 — Brazil. Amazon River Basin. Flood plains. Freshwater fish. Ecology

Goulding, Michael, *19---*. The fishes and the forest : explorations in Amazonian natural history / Michael Goulding. — Berkeley ; London : University of California Press, c1980. — xii,280p : ill,2maps,1port ; 24cm
Bibliography: p259-264. - Includes index
ISBN 0-520-04131-3 : £12.00 B81-27270

597′.051′0973 — United States. Fish. Behaviour. Effects of power stations — *Conference proceedings*

Power plants : effects on fish and shellfish behavior / editors Charles H. Hocutt ... [et al.]. — New York ; London : Academic Press, 1980. — xiii,346p : ill ; 24cm
Includes bibliographies and index
ISBN 0-12-350950-5 : £16.00
Also classified at 594′.051′0973 B81-14758

597′.05248 — Marine fish. Population. Dynamics

Cushing, D. H.. Fisheries biology : a study in population dynamics / D.H. Cushing. — 2nd ed. — Madison ; London : University of Wisconsin Press, 1981. — xvi,295p : ill,maps ; 24cm
Previous ed.: 1968. — Bibliography: p259-280. — Includes index
ISBN 0-299-08110-9 : £11.35 B81-29542

597′.05248′094141 — Scotland. Strathclyde Region. Clyde Estuary. Fish. Population, *1978*

Walker, Callum R.. An investigation of the fish population of the Clyde Estuary : January-November 1978 / by Callum R. Walker. — [Paisley] ([High St., Paisley, Renfrewshire PA1 2BE]) : Department of Biology, Paisley College of Technology, 1979. — 20p : ill,1map ; 30cm
Bibliography: p20
Unpriced (spiral) B81-12030

597′.053 — Fish. Feeding behaviour — *For angling*

Walker, Richard. Catching fish. — Newton Abbot : David & Charles, Sept.1981. — [160]p
ISBN 0-7153-8198-9 : £6.50 : CIP entry
B81-28175

597′.0875 — Fish. Ions. Transport — *Conference proceedings*

Epithelial transport in the lower vertebrates = Transports épithéliaux chez les vertébrés inférieurs : Jean Maetz symposium : proceedings of the memorial symposium to Jean Maetz held at the Station zoologique of Billefranche-sur-Mer, 26-27 June 1978 / edited by B. Lahlau. — Cambridge : Cambridge University Press, 1980. — xiv,366p : ill,1port ; 24cm
Includes five papers in French. — Includes bibliographies and index
ISBN 0-521-22748-8 : £25.00 B81-03548

597.092′735 — Persian Gulf. Inshore fish — *Field guides*

Relyea, Kenneth. Inshore fishes of the Arabian Gulf / Kenneth Relyea ; with illustrations by Robert Charles. — London : Allen & Unwin, 1981. — 149p,8p of plates : ill(some col.) ; 21cm. — (The Natural history of the Arabian Gulf)
Map on lining papers. — Bibliography: p135-137. - Includes index
ISBN 0-04-597003-3 : Unpriced B81-19098

597.092′94 — Europe. Freshwater fish — *Illustrations — For angling*

Nicholls, James. Freshwater fishes : an angler′s guide in colour to British and N. European freshwater fishes of rivers, canals, lakes, reservoirs / [painted by James Nicholls]. — [London] : Fontana, 1979. — 1folded sheet ([12]p) : col.ill ; 25cm. — (Domino ; 17)
ISBN 0-00-685470-2 : £0.85 B81-20257

597.092′941 — Great Britain. Freshwater fish — *Early works — Facsimiles*

Houghton, W.. British fresh-water fishes / W. Houghton ; illustrated by A.F. Lydon ; engraved by Benjamin Fawcett. — Redesigned one-vol. ed. with additional material / foreword by Lord Hardinge of Penshurst. — Exeter (33 Southernhay East, Exeter, Devon EX1 1NS) : Webb & Bower, 1981. — 256p : ill (some col.) ; 32cm
Facsim. of ed. published in 2 vols. London : s.n., 1879. — Includes index
ISBN 0-906671-06-x : £20.00 B81-12160

597.094 — Europe. Fish — *Field guides*

Fekjan, Jan. Fish / illustrations by Jan Fekjan. — Poole : Blandford, c1981. — 127p : col. ill ; 12cm. — (A Blandford mini-guide)
These illustrations originally published: in Den lille fiskeboken/Nils Petter Thuesen. Oslo : Aschehoug, 1981. — Includes index
ISBN 0-7137-1207-4 (pbk) : £0.95 B81-31415

597.097 — North America. Deserts. Fish

Fishes in North American deserts / edited by Robert J. Naiman and David L. Soltz. — New York ; Chichester : Wiley, c1981. — x,552p : ill,maps ; 24cm
Conference papers. — Includes index
ISBN 0-471-08523-5 : £29.75 B81-37111

597′.2 — Agnatha: Cyclostomata

Biology of lampreys. — London : Academic Press
Vol.3. — Feb.1982. — [450]p
ISBN 0-12-324803-5 : CIP entry B81-36064

597′.31 — Sharks — *For children*

Stonehouse, Bernard. Sharks / Bernard Stonehouse. — Hove : Wayland, 1981. — 60p : col.ill ; 24cm. — (Animals of the world)
Col. ill on lining papers. — Includes index
ISBN 0-85340-833-5 : £3.50 B81-22043

597′.53 — Sticklebacks — *For children*

Lane, Margaret, *1907-*. The stickleback. — London : Methuen/Walker, Oct.1981. — [32]p. — (Animal lives ; 4)
ISBN 0-416-05830-2 : £3.50 : CIP entry
B81-30461

597′.58 — African Cichlidae. Colour. Patterns. Behavioural aspects

Voss, J.. Color patterns of African cichlids / by J. Voss. — Neptune, N.J. ; Reigate : T.F.H., c1980. — 123p : ill(some col.),1map ; 21cm
Ill on lining paper
ISBN 0-87666-503-2 : £3.95 B81-05769

597.6 — Amphibians in danger of extinction — *Lists*

Groombridge, Brian, *1946-*. World checklist of endangered amphibians and reptiles / Brian Groombridge. — [Rev. 2nd. ed.]. — London : Wildlife Advisory Branch, Nature Conservancy Council, [1981]. — 63p ; 30cm
Previous ed.: 1979. — Bibliography: p53-59. — Includes index
ISBN 0-86139-095-4 (pbk) : Unpriced
Primary classification 597.9 B81-38707

597.6 — Herpetology — *Conference proceedings*

European Herpetological Symposium *(1980 : Department of Zoology, University of Oxford).* European Herpetological Symposium 1980 / edited by John Coborn. — Burford ([c/o Cotswold District Council, 5 Dyer St., Cirencester, Glos., GL7 2PT]) : Cotswold Wild Life Park, [1980?]. — x,140p : ill,maps ; 30cm
Preface in English, Dutch, French, Spanish, German and Swedish. — Includes bibliographies
Unpriced (pbk) B81-40653

597.6'012 — Amphibians. Taxonomy

Webb, J. E.. Guide to living amphibians / J.E. Webb, J.A. Wallwork, J.H. Elgood. — London : Macmillan, 1981. — viii,144p,[8]p of plates : ill,maps ; 23cm
Includes index
ISBN 0-333-30749-6 (cased) : £10.00
ISBN 0-333-30601-5 (pbk) : Unpriced
B81-24030

597.6'0482 — Amphibians. Embryos. Tissues. Transplantation. Immunological aspects

Volpe, E. Peter. The amphibian embryo in transplantation immunity / E. Peter Volpe. — Basel ; London : Karger, 1980. — ix,148p : ill ; 25cm. — (Monographs in developmental biology ; v.14)
Bibliography: p135-145. - Includes index
ISBN 3-8055-1087-x : £32.55 B81-09624

597.6'05 — Herpetology — *Serials*

[Bulletin *(British Herpetological Society : 1980)*]. Bulletin / the British Herpetological Society. — No.1 (June 1980)-. — London (c/o Zoological Society of London, Regent's Park, NW1) : The Society, 1980-. — v. : ill ; 24cm
Two issues yearly. — Continues: Newsletter (British Herpetological Society)
ISSN 0260-5805 = Bulletin - British Herpetological Society (1980) : Free to Society members only B81-04444

597.8 — Frogs

Sonntag, Linda. Frogs / Linda Sonntag. — London : Hutchinson, 1981. — 54p : ill(some col.) ; 18cm. — (The Leprechaun library)
ISBN 0-09-144590-6 : £1.95 : CIP rev.
B81-05118

597.8 — Frogs & toads — *For children*

Clay, Pat. Frogs and toads. — London : A & C Black, Sept.1981. — [26]p. — (Nature in close-up ; 13)
ISBN 0-7136-2152-4 : £2.95 : CIP entry
B81-22529

597.8 — Frogs — *For children*

Lane, Margaret, *1907-*. The frog. — London : Methuen, Sept.1981. — [32]p
ISBN 0-416-05780-2 : £3.50 : CIP entry
B81-25864

597.9 — Reptiles

Biology of the Reptilia / edited by Carl Gans. — London : Academic Press
Vol.11: Morphology F / coeditor for this volume Thomas S. Parsons. — 1981. — xi,475p : ill ; 24cm
Includes bibliographies and index
ISBN 0-12-274611-2 : Unpriced B81-29737

597.9 — Reptiles — *For children*

Reptiles / illustrated by Gary Hincks, Alan Male, Phil Weare. — London : Hamilton, 1980. — 28p : col.ill ; 20cm. — (Small world)
Includes index
ISBN 0-241-10504-8 : £1.95 B81-07124

597.9 — Reptiles in danger of extinction — *Lists*

Groombridge, Brian, *1946-*. World checklist of endangered amphibians and reptiles / Brian Groombridge. — [Rev. 2nd. ed.]. — London : Wildlife Advisory Branch, Nature Conservancy Council, [1981]. — 63p ; 30cm
Previous ed.: 1979. — Bibliography: p53-59. — Includes index
ISBN 0-86139-095-4 (pbk) : Unpriced
Also classified at 597.6 B81-38707

597.9'042 — Reptiles. Diseases

Diseases of the reptilia. — London : Academic Press, Aug.1981
Vol.1. — [250]p
ISBN 0-12-187901-1 : CIP entry B81-15804

597.9'094 — Great Britain. Reptiles & amphibians — *Illustrations*

Ovenden, Denys. Reptiles & amphibians : a colour guide to all the lizards, snakes, frogs, toads, newts and salamanders of Britain and Northern Europe / [painted by Denys Ovenden ; text by Nicholas Arnold]. — [London] : Fontana, 1979. — 1folded sheet([12]p) : col.ill ; 25cm. — (Domino ; 4)
ISBN 0-00-685444-3 : £0.85 B81-20745

597.92 — Northern Greece. Tortoises

Expedition to Greece 1980 / D. Stubbs ... [et al.]. — London : University of London Union, Malet St., W.C.1 : University of London, Natural History Society, [1980]. — 136p : ill,maps ; 30cm
Cover title. — Bibliography: p133-136. — Includes index
ISBN 0-9507556-0-5 (spiral) : £5.00
B81-21330

597.96'0469 — Venomous snakes

Phelps, Tony. Poisonous snakes / Tony Phelps. — Poole : Blandford, 1981. — viii,237p,[16]p of plates : ill(some col.),maps,ports ; 23cm
Bibliography: p224-225. - Includes index
ISBN 0-7137-0877-8 : £10.95 : CIP rev.
B81-00895

597.96'0469 — Venomous snakes — *For children*

Stonehouse, Bernard. Venomous snakes / Bernard Stonehouse. — Hove : Wayland, 1981. — 60p : col.ill ; 24cm. — (Animals of the world)
Ill on lining papers. — Includes index
ISBN 0-85340-846-7 : £3.50 B81-40619

598 — Birds

Michelet, Jules. The bird. — London : Wildwood House, Sept.1981. — [356]p
Translation of: L'oiseau
ISBN 0-7045-0444-8 (pbk) : £3.50 : CIP entry
B81-23796

Robiller, Franz. Birds throughout the world / Franz Robiller ; [translated from the German by Ilse Lindsay]. — Old Woking : Gresham Books, c1979. — 218p : col.ill,maps ; 25cm
Translation of: Vögel in aller Welt. — Bibliography: p215-218
ISBN 0-905418-39-5 : £8.50 B81-12630

598 — Birds — *Festschriften*

A Bundle of feathers : proffered to Sálim Ali : for his 75th birthday in 1971 / edited by Sidney Dillon Ripley II ; sponsored by the Bombay Natural History Society. — Delhi ; London : Oxford University Press, c1978. — x,241p,[9] pofplates : ill,maps,ports ; 24cm
Includes bibliographies and index
ISBN 0-19-560811-9 : Unpriced B81-34937

598 — Birds — *For children*

Boorer, Wendy. Know your birds / written by Wendy Boorer ; illustrated by Sean Milne. — London : Methuen, 1980. — 41p : ill(some col.) ; 27cm. — (Animal friends)
Bibliography: p40. — Includes index
ISBN 0-416-89070-9 : £2.95 : CIP rev.
B80-18304

Jennings, Terry. Birds / Terry Jennings ; illustrated by Karen Daws ... [et al.]. — Oxford : Oxford University Press, 1981. — 32p : ill(some col.),2col.maps ; 29cm. — (The young scientist investigates)
ISBN 0-19-917046-0 : £2.50 B81-24407

Lambert, David, *1932-*. Birds / by David Lambert. — London : Pan, 1981. — 93p : ill (some col.),col.maps ; 18cm. — (A Piccolo factbook)
Text on inside cover. — Includes index
ISBN 0-330-26417-6 (pbk) : £1.25 B81-38771

Lambert, David, *1932-*. Birds / by David Lambert ; editor Jacqui Bailey. — London : Kingfisher, 1981. — 93p : ill(some col.) ; 19cm. — (A Kingfisher factbook)
Includes index
ISBN 0-86272-015-x : £2.50 : CIP rev.
B81-14389

598 — Birds — *For schools*

Jennings, Terry. Birds / Terry Jennings ; illustrated by Karen Daws, Diane Rosher, Mike Woodhatch ; maps by Rudolph Britto. — Oxford : Oxford University Press, 1981. — 32p : ill(some col.),2col.maps ; 28cm. — (The Young scientist investigates)
ISBN 0-19-917037-1 (pbk) : Unpriced
B81-25396

598 — Naturalised birds

Long, John L.. Introduced birds of the world : the worldwide history, distribution and influence of birds introduced to new enviroments / John L. Long ; illustrated by Susan Tingay. — Newton Abbot : David & Charles, 1981. — 528p : ill,maps ; 27cm
Based on work carried out for The Agricultural Protection Board of Western Australia. — Bibliography: p495-518. — Includes index
ISBN 0-7153-8180-6 : £15.00 B81-36853

598'.0142 — Birds. Latin names. Etymology

Gotch, A. F.. Birds : their Latin names explained / A.F. Gotch. — Poole : Blandford, 1981. — 348p : ill ; 22cm
Bibliography: p325. — Includes index
ISBN 0-7137-1175-2 : £10.95 : CIP rev.
B81-30450

598'.0216 — Birds — *Lists*

Howard, Richard, *1936-*. A complete checklist of the birds of the world / Richard Howard, Alick Moore ; with a foreword by Leslie Brown. — Oxford : Oxford University Press, 1980. — viii,701p ; 23cm
Includes index
ISBN 0-19-217681-1 : £17.50 : CIP rev.
B80-04799

598'.022'2 — Birds — *Illustrations*

Birds : a picture sourcebook / edited and arranged by Don Rice. — New York ; London : Van Nostrand Reinhold, 1980. — x,150p : chiefly ill ; 28cm
Includes index
ISBN 0-442-20395-0 (pbk) : £6.70 B81-00896

598'.03'21 — Birds — *Encyclopaedias*

Walters, Michael. The complete birds of the world / [text by] Michael Walters. — Illustrated ed. — Newton Abbot : David & Charles, c1981. — xii,367p,320p of plates : ill (some col.) ; 29cm
Previous ed.: 1980. — Bibliography: p326-328. - Includes index
ISBN 0-7153-8170-9 : £45.00 B81-19708

598'.042'0941 — Great Britain. Rare birds — *Field guides*

Hollom, P. A. D.. The popular handbook of rarer British birds / P.A.D. Hollom. — 2nd ed. (rev.). — London : Witherby, 1980. — 190p,56 p of plates : ill(some col.) ; 22cm
Previous ed.: 1960. — Includes index
ISBN 0-85493-129-5 : £12.00 B81-02310

598'.07'234 — Birds. Observation. Sites — *Visitors' guides*

Alden, Peter. Finding birds around the world / Peter Alden and John Gooders. — London : Deutsch, 1981. — xxviii,683p : maps ; 22cm
Bibliography: p561-576. — Includes index
ISBN 0-233-97381-8 : £8.95 B81-36579

598'.07'2340941 — Great Britain. Birds. Observation, *1970-1979*

Wallace, Ian. Bird watching in the seventies. — London : Macmillan, Sept.1981. — [192]p
ISBN 0-333-30026-2 : £7.95 : CIP entry
B81-23944

598'.07'2344 — Europe. Birds. Observation — *Manuals*

Ardley, Neil. Illustrated guide to birds and birdwatching / by Neil Ardley. — London : Kingfisher, 1980. — 197p : ill(some col.),maps (some col.) ; 27cm
Bibliography: p194. - Includes index
ISBN 0-7063-6002-8 : £6.95 : CIP rev. B80-17703

598'.07'23441 — Great Britain. Birds. Observation — *Humour*

Oddie, Bill. Bill Oddie's little black bird book. — London : Eyre Methuen, 1980. — viii,148p : ill,1map,ports ; 23cm
Bibliography: p146-147
ISBN 0-413-47820-3 : £4.95 B81-02412

598'.07'23441 — Great Britain. Birds. Observation — *Serials*

Birdwatcher's yearbook. — 1981-. — Buckingham (Rostherne, Hall Close, Maids Moreton, Buckingham MK18 1RH) : Buckingham Press, 1980-. — v. : ill,maps,ports ; 22cm
ISSN 0144-364x = Birdwatcher's yearbook : Unpriced B81-00897

Birdwatcher's yearbook. — 1982. — Buckingham (Rostheme, Hall Close, Maids Moreton, Buckingham MK18 1RH) : Buckingham Press, Oct.1981. — [320]p
ISBN 0-9506478-2-9 (pbk) : £5.95 : CIP entry
ISSN 0144-364x B81-31950

598'.07'23441 — Great Britain. Birds. Observation. Sites

Gooders, John. The bird seeker's guide / John Gooders. — London : Deutsch, 1980. — 208p,[12]p of plates : ill ; 21cm
Includes index
ISBN 0-233-97297-8 (cased) : £6.95
ISBN 0-233-97380-x (pbk) : £3.50 B81-13594

598'.07'23442617 — Norfolk. Hickling. Birds. Observation, *1911 — Correspondence, diaries, etc.*

Vincent, Jim, *1884-1944*. A season of birds : a Norfolk diary, 1911 / Vincent and Lodge. — London : Weidenfeld and Nicolson, c1980. — 152p : col.ill,2maps,1facsim,ports ; 19x21cm
Map on lining papers. — Includes index
ISBN 0-297-77830-7 : £7.50 B81-03047

598.2'07'23441 — Great Britain. Birds. Observation — *Correspondence, diaries, etc.*

Millington, Richard. A twitcher's diary : the birdwatching year of Richard Millington. — Poole : Blandford Press, 1981. — 192p : ill (some col.),1map ; 24cm
Includes index
ISBN 0-7137-1174-4 (pbk) : £8.95 : CIP rev. B81-23827

598.2'1 — Birds. Physiology

Form and function in birds / edited by A.S. King, J. McLelland. — London : Academic Press
Vol.2. — 1981. — xi,496p : ill ; 27cm
Includes index
ISBN 0-12-407502-9 : £42.00 : CIP rev. B80-13821

598.2'142 — Birds. Endocrine system — *Conference proceedings*

International Symposium on Avian Endocrinology *(2nd : 1980 : Benalmadena)*. Avian endocrinology / [proceedings of the Second International Symposium on Avian Endocrinology held in Benalmadena, Spain in May 1980] ; edited by August Epple, Milton H. Stetson with the assistance of Barbara J. Nibbio. — New York ; London : Academic Press, 1980. — xv,577p : ill ; 24cm
Includes bibliographies and index
ISBN 0-12-240250-2 : £19.20 B81-16639

598.2'38 — Birds. Evolution

Feduccia, Alan. The age of birds / Alan Feduccia. — Cambridge, Mass. ; London : Harvard University Press, 1980. — 196p : ill,2maps ; 29cm
Bibliography: p183-187. — Includes index
ISBN 0-674-00975-4 : £12.00 B81-02795

598.25 — Birds. Adaptation

Goodwin, Derek. Birds of man's world / Derek Goodwin ; line illustrations by Robin Prytherch. — Ithaca : Cornell University Press ; London : British Museum (Natural History), 1978. — viii,183p : ill ; 22cm
Includes index
ISBN 0-8014-1167-x : £6.95 B81-22070

598.252'5 — Birds. Migration — *For children*

Ruge, Klaus. Migrating birds / Klaus Ruge ; [translated by Patricia Green]. — St. Albans : Hart-Davis, c1981. — 30p : col.ill,col.maps ; 26cm. — (Natural science series)
Translation from the German. — Includes index
ISBN 0-247-13153-9 : £2.95 B81-39613

598.2'543 — Great Britain. Birds. Winter life

Your winter birds. — Sandy (The Lodge, Sandy, Beds., SG19 2DL) : Royal Society for the Protection of birds, c1980. — 15p : col.ill,col.2maps ; 21cm
Unpriced (unbound) B81-27602

598.29'24 — Marine birds

Saunders, David, *1937-*. Seabirds / David Saunders ; illustrated by Ken Lilly. — London : Hamlyn, 1971 (1980 printing). — 159p : col.ill,col.maps ; 19cm
Bibliography: p156. — Includes index
ISBN 0-600-35376-1 : £2.50 B81-02469

598.294 — Europe. Birds — *Illustrations*

Burton, Philip, *1936-*. Small birds : a colour guide to common small birds of Britain and Northern Europe / [painted by Philip Burton]. — [London] : Fontana, 1979. — 1folded sheet ([12]p) : col.ill ; 25cm. — (Domino ; 1)
ISBN 0-00-685441-9 : £0.85 B81-20748

598.294 — Western Europe. Birds — *Field guides*

Hayman, Peter. The Mitchell Beazley birdwatcher's pocket guide / Peter Hayman. — London : Mitchell Beazley in association with the Royal Society for the Protection of Birds, c1979. — 192p : col.ill ; 20cm
ISBN 0-85533-148-8 : £3.95 B81-01574

598.2941 — Great Britain. Birds

A Notebook of birds 1907-1980 / with a commentary by Jim Flegg ; and illustrations by Norman Arlott, Robert Gillmor and Laurel Tucker. — London : Macmillan, 1981. — vii,184p : ill ; 23cm
Selections from British birds. — Includes index
ISBN 0-333-30880-8 : £6.95 : CIP rev. B81-13809

598.2941 — Great Britain. Birds — *Correspondence, diaries, etc.*

Hudson, W. H.. Birds of a feather : unpublished letters of W.H. Hudson / edited and introduced by Dennis Shrubsall ; with wood engravings by Marcus Beaver. — Bradford-on-Avon : Moonraker, c1981. — 108p : ill ; 23cm
Includes index
ISBN 0-239-00205-9 : £6.95 B81-24559

598.2941 — Great Britain. Birds — *Early works — Facsimiles*

Morris, F. O.. [A history of British birds. Selections]. British birds / F.O. Morris ; a selection from the original work edited and with an introduction by Tony Soper ; illustrated by A.F. Lydon ; engraved by Benjamin Fawcett. — Exeter : Webb & Bower, 1981. — 240p : col.ill ; 32cm
Full ed. published: in 6v. London : Groombridge and Sons, 1851-1857. — Includes index
ISBN 0-906671-37-x : £20.00 : CIP rev. B81-13790

598.2941 — Great Britain. Birds — *Field guides*

Holland, John, *19---*. Bird spotting / John Holland ; illustrated by Rein Stuurman. — 5th rev. ed. — Poole : Blandford, 1979 (1980 [printing]). — 291p : ill(some col.) ; 15cm
Includes index
ISBN 0-7137-1148-5 (pbk) : £2.95 B81-08466

Tinggaard, Karl Aage. Birds / illustrations by Karl Aage Tinggaard. — Poole : Blandford, c1981. — 127p : col. ill ; 12cm. — (A Blandford mini-guide)
These illustrations originally published: in Lilla fågelboken/Sigfrid Durango. Stockholm : Almqvist & Wiksell Forlag, 1977. — Includes index
ISBN 0-7137-1212-0 (pbk) : £0.95 B81-31416

598.2941 — Great Britain. Birds — *For children*

Chinery, Michael. A child's book of birds & flowers / by Michael Chinery ; illustrations by Michael Atkinson. — London : Granada, 1981. — [26]p : col.ill ; 26cm
ISBN 0-246-11549-1 : £2.95 B81-18393

598.2941 — Great Britain. Birds. Names

Greenoak, Francesca. All the birds of the air : the names, lore and literature of British birds / Francesca Greenoak ; illustrated by Alastair Robertson. — Rev. ed. — Harmondsworth : Penguin, 1981. — 333p : ill ; 20cm
Previous ed.: London : Deutsch, 1979. — Bibliography: p297-299. — Includes index
ISBN 0-14-005532-0 (pbk) : £3.95 B81-37918

598.2941 — Great Britain. Freshwater regions & marshes. Water birds — *For children*

Richards, Alan. Waterside birds / Alan Richards. — London : Adam & Charles Black, 1981. — 25p : col.ill ; 22cm. — (Nature in close-up)
Includes index
ISBN 0-7136-2122-2 : £2.95 : CIP rev. B81-01856

598.2941 — Great Britain. Gardens. Birds — *For children*

Gill, Peter, *1924-*. Birds in the garden / by Peter Gill ; illustrated by the author. — Cambridge : Dinosaur, c1981. — 24p : col.ill ; 16x19cm. — (Althea's nature series)
ISBN 0-85122-274-9 (cased) : £1.85 : CIP rev.
ISBN 0-85122-258-7 (pbk) : £0.70 B81-02671

598.2941'022'2 — Great Britain. Gardens. Birds — *Illustrations*

Lambert, Terence. The bird table : attracting birds to garden or balcony, how to recognize and feed them / [painted by Terence Lambert ; ... written by Hermann Heinzel]. — [London] : Fontana, 1979. — 1folded sheet([12]p) : col.ill ; 25cm. — (Domino ; 5)
ISBN 0-00-685445-1 : £0.85 B81-20740

598.29411'35 — Scotland. Shetland. Birds

Tulloch, Bobby. A guide to Shetland birds / by Bobby Tulloch and Fred Hunter. — Rev. ed., Repr. with minor amendments. — Lerwick ([Prince Alfred St.], Lerwick, Shetland [ZE1 0EP]) : Shetland Times, 1981, c1979. — 45,[16]p of plates : ill ; 22cm
Previous ed.: i.e. Rev. ed. 1972
Unpriced (pbk) B81-27603

598.29412'8'05 — Scotland. Tayside Region. Perthshire. Birds — *Serials*

Perthshire bird report. — '80. — [Perth] ([George St., Perth]) : [Perth Museum and Art Gallery], [1981]. — 15p
ISSN 0144-3208 : Unpriced B81-35459

598.29422'1'05 — Surrey. Birds — *Serials*

Surrey bird report. — No.27 (1979). — Wallington, c/o 15, Bond Gardens, Wallington, Surrey : Surrey Bird Club, [1980?]. — 108p
ISSN 0491-6255 : £2.50 B81-15085

598.29422'7'05 — Hampshire. Birds — *Serials*

The Hampshire bird report. — 1979. — Andover (c/o L.F. Weatherly, 6 Duncan Court, Admirals Way, Andover, Hampshire) : Hampshire Ornithological Society, 1981. — 59p
ISSN 0438-4903 : £1.50 B81-31896

598.29422'9'05 — Berkshire. Birds — *Serials*

Reading Ornithological Club. The Birds of Berkshire. — 1978. — [South Ascot] (c/o Siskins, 7 Llanvair Drive, South Ascot, Berks. SL5 9HS) : Reading Ornithological Club, 1979. — 40p
Cover title: Annual report (Reading Ornithological Club)
ISSN 0140-3192 : £0.90 B81-25496

598.29422'9'05 — Berkshire. Birds — *Serials* *continuation*
Reading Ornithological Club. The Birds of Berkshire. — 1979. — [South Ascot] (c/o Siskins, 7 Llanvair Drive, South Ascot, Berks. SL5 9HS) : Reading Ornithological Club, 1980. — 36p
Cover title: Annual report (Reading Ornithological Club)
ISSN 0140-3192 : £1.00 B81-25497

598.29424'62 — Staffordshire. Keele. Universities: University of Keele. Woodlands. Birds
Emley, David W.. The bird life of Keele University / David W. Emley. — Keele : [Keele University Library], 1980. — 22p : ill,1map ; 21cm. — (Keele University Library occasional publication ; no.16)
Map on inside back cover. — Bibliography: p2
Unpriced (pbk) B81-19873

598.29425'3'05 — Lincolnshire. Birds — *Serials*
[Lincolnshire bird report *(Lincolnshire Bird Club)*]. Lincolnshire bird report : including the Gibraltar Point Observatory report. — 1979-. — Brigg (c/o Mr R.N. Goodall, 3 Kettleby View, Brigg [Lincs.]) : Lincolnshire Bird Club, [1980?]-. — v. : ill ; 21cm
Annual. — Description based on: 1980 issue
ISSN 0261-5525 = Lincolnshire bird report (Lincolnshire Bird Club) : Unpriced
B81-30869

598.29425'4'05 — Leicestershire. Birds — *Serials*
The **Birds** of Leicestershire and Rutland / The Leicestershire and Rutland Ornithological Society. — 1976. — Leicester (c/o 76 Lorne Rd, Leicester) : The Society, 1978. — 52p
Unpriced B81-21339

The **Birds** of Leicestershire and Rutland / Leicestershire and Rutland Ornithological Society. — 1978. — Leicester (c/o 76, Lorne Rd, Leicester) : The Society, 1979. — 48p
Unpriced B81-21340

The **Birds** of Leicestershire and Rutland. — 1979. — Leicester (c/o H.G. Cherry, 26 Scraptoft La., Leicester) : Leicestershire and Rutland Ornithological Society, 1980. — 48p
Unpriced B81-15281

598.29425'49 — Leicestershire. Hinckley and Bosworth *(District)*. **Birds**, *1915-1979*
Peacock, D. A.. Then and now : birds of Hinckley and district, 1915-79 : a comparison of the present day distribution of birds with some historical records in and around the district of Hinckley / D.A. Peacock. — Leicester ([96 New Walk, Leicester, LE1 6TD]) : Published on behalf of the Society [Hinckley and District Natural History Society] by Leicestershire Museums Service, 1980. — 25p ; 30cm
Bibliography: p25
ISBN 0-85022-078-5 (spiral) : £0.50
B81-05812

598.29425'7 — Oxfordshire. Birds — *Personal observations*
Christie, Clifford. And then they fly away / Clifford Christie ; photographs by Ian Buchanan ; drawings by Harry Williams. — [London] : Corgi, 1981, c1976. — 175p,[8]p of plates : ill,ports ; 18cm
Originally published: London : Constable, 1976
ISBN 0-552-11728-5 (pbk) : £1.25 B81-37271

598.29425'9'05 — Buckinghamshire. Birds — *Serials*
Buckinghamshire bird report. — 1980. — Grendon Underwood (c/o C. Fisher, Fairings, High St., Grendon Underwood, Aylesbury, Bucks. HP18 0SL) : Buckinghamshire Bird Club, Feb.1982. — [32]p
ISBN 0-907823-00-9 (pbk) : £2.00 : CIP entry
ISSN 0262-0561 B81-38824

598.29426'5 — Cambridgeshire. Eastern Cambridgeshire. Birds — *Lists*
A **Checklist** of the birds of Cambridgeshire / Research Committee, Cambridge Bird Club ; [drawing: G.M.S. Easy ... et al.]. — [Cambridge] ([c/o Town Secretary, 178 Nuns Way, Cambridge CBL 2NS]) : [The Committee], [1981]. — 33p : ill ; 21cm
Cover title
Unpriced (pbk) B81-17638

598.29426'5'05 — Cambridgeshire. Birds — *Serials*
[Report for ... *(Cambridge Bird Club)*]. Report for ... / Cambridge Bird Club. — No.35 (1979). — [Cambridge] ([c/o B. Harrup, 49 Priam's Way, Stapleford, Cambridge CB2 5DT]) : The Club, 1981. — 48p
Cover title: Cambridgeshire bird report
£1.15 B81-21947

598.29428'1'05 — Yorkshire. Birds — *Serials*
[Ornithological report for the years ... *(Yorkshire Naturalists' Union)*]. Ornithological report for the years ... / Yorkshire Naturalists' Union. — 1967, 1968, 1969. — Knaresborough (c/o John R. Mather, 44 Aspin La., Knaresborough) : Yorkshire Naturalists' Union, Ornithological Section, 1980. — 53p
ISSN 0306-3925 : £1.00 B81-10554

598.29428'21 — South Yorkshire *(Metropolitan County)*. **Sheffield region. Birds** — *Serials*
[The Magpie *(Sheffield)*]. The Magpie : [journal of the Sheffield Bird Study Group]. — No.1 (1977)-. — Sheffield ([c/o J. Hornbuckle, 30 Hartington Rd, Sheffield S7 2LF]) : Published by the Group in conjunction with Sheffield University Dept. of Zoology, 1977-. — v. : ill ; 30cm
Irregular
ISSN 0261-0868 = Magpie (Sheffield) : Unpriced B81-17489

Sheffield bird report. — 1979. — [Sheffield] ([c/o J. Hornbuckle, 30 Hartington Rd, Sheffield S7 2LF]) : Sheffield Bird Study Group, [1980]. — 76p
Unpriced B81-17464

598.29428'6'05 — Durham *(County)*. **Birds. Distribution** — *Serials*
Birds in Durham. — 1979. — [Sunderland] ([57 Park Ave., Roker, Sunderland]) : Durham Bird Club, [1981]. — 89p
ISSN 0144-3151 : £1.75 B81-33313

598.29428'89 — Northumberland. Farne Islands. Birds — *Serials*
Birds on the Farne Islands. — 1980. — Alnwick (Narrowgate House, Alnwick, [Northumbria]) : Farne Islands Local Committee of the National Trust, [1981?]. — 7p
ISSN 0144-3925 : Unpriced B81-35114

598.29429'6'05 — Dyfed. Birds — *Serials*
Dyfed bird report / West Wales Naturalists' Trust. — 1972-76. — Haverfordwest (7 Market St., Haverfordwest, Dyfed) : The Trust, [197?]. — 27p
Unpriced B81-31895

598.2953'6 — Arabia. Gulf States. Birds
Jennings, Michael C.. Birds of the Arabian Gulf. — London : Allen & Unwin, Sept.1981. — [176]p
ISBN 0-04-598009-8 : £9.95 : CIP entry
B81-20482

598.2953'8'0216 — Saudi Arabia. Birds — *Lists*
Jennings, Michael C.. The birds of Saudi Arabia : a check-list / Michael C. Jennings ; with some line drawings by C.J.F. Coombs. — Cambridge (10 Mill La., Whittlesford, Cambridge) : M.C. Jennings, c1981. — 112p : ill,maps ; 21cm
Bibliography: p68-73. — Includes index
ISBN 0-9507405-0-0 (pbk) : Unpriced
B81-31325

598.2954 — India. Hilly regions. Birds
Ali, Sálim. Indian hill birds / by Sálim Ali ; illustrated by G.M. Henry. — Delhi ; Oxford : Oxford University Press, 1949 (1979 [printing]). — lvi,188p,[72]p of plates : ill(some col.),2col.maps ; 19cm
Maps on lining papers. — Includes index
£11.95 B81-03611

598.2956'05 — Middle East. Birds — *Serials*
Sandgrouse / the Ornithological Society of the Middle East. — No.1-. — Sandy (c/o The Lodge, Sandy, Bedfordshire SG19 2DL) : The Editorial Committee of the Society, 1980-. — v. ; 22cm
Annual. — Continues: Turkish bird report
ISSN 0260-4736 = Sandgrouse : £5.00
B81-30011

598.296'022'2 — Africa. Birds — *Illustrations*
Amuchástegui, Axel. Some birds and mammals of Africa / by Axel Amuchástegui ; with a descriptive text by Hilary Hook. — London : Tryon Gallery, c1979. — [41]p,xivleaves of plates : col.ill ; 54cm
Limited ed. of 505 copies, of which 500 are numbered 1-500 and bound in quarter leather, and five are lettered A-E and bound in full vellum
Unpriced
Also classified at 599.096 B81-36406

598.2966 — West & Central Africa. Birds — *Field guides*
Mackworth-Praed, C. W.. Birds of West Central and Western Africa. — London : Longman. — (African handbook of birds. Series 3)
Vol.1. — Oct.1981. — 1v.
Originally published: 1970
ISBN 0-582-46086-7 : £30.00 : CIP entry
B81-28774

Mackworth-Praed, C. W.. Birds of West Central and Western Africa. — London : Longman. — (African handbook of birds. Series 3)
Vol.2. — Oct.1981. — [818]p
Originally published: 1973
ISBN 0-582-46087-5 : £30.00 : CIP entry
B81-28775

598.29676 — East Africa. Birds
Karmali, John. Birds of Africa : a bird photographer in East Africa / John Karmali ; foreword by Roger Tory Peterson. — London : Collins, 1980. — 191p : ill(some col.),maps (some col.) ; 33cm
Bibliography: p187. - Includes index
ISBN 0-00-219031-1 : £12.50 B81-00898

598.29676 — East Africa. Birds — *Field guides*
Williams, John G. (John George). A field guide to the birds of East Africa / John G. Williams ; foreword by Roger Tony Peterson. — [Completely rev. ed.] / with over 600 species illustrated in full colour by Norman Arlott. — London : Collins, c1980. — 415p : col.ill,1map ; 20cm
Previous ed.: published as A field guide to the birds of East and Central Africa. 1963. — Bibliography: p400-401. - Includes index
ISBN 0-00-219179-2 : £7.95 B81-03770

598.2968 — Southern Africa. Birds — *Field guides*
Mackworth-Praed, C. W.. Birds of the southern third of Africa. — London : Longman. — (African handbook of birds. Series 2)
Vol.1. — Oct.1981. — [688]p
Originally published: 1962
ISBN 0-582-46084-0 : £30.00 : CIP entry
B81-28111

Mackworth-Praed, C. W.. Birds of the southern third of Africa. — London : Longman. — (African handbook of birds. Series 2)
Vol.2. — Oct.1981. — [716]p
Originally published: 1963
ISBN 0-582-46085-9 : £30.00 : CIP entry
B81-28004

598.29931'022'2 — New Zealand. Birds — *Illustrations*
Moon, Geoff. The birds around us : New Zealand birds, their habits and habitats / Geoff Moon. — Rev. ed. — Auckland ; London : Heinemann, 1980. — 207p : chiefly col.ill ; 30cm
Previous ed.: 1979. — Includes index
ISBN 0-908592-03-5 : £20.00 B81-00899

598.2994 — Australia. Birds — *Field guides*
Pizzey, Graham. A field guide to the birds of Australia / Graham Pizzey ; illustrated by Roy Doyle. — Sydney ; London : Collins, 1980. — 460p,88p of plates : ill(some col.),col.maps ; 22cm
Col. map on lining papers. — Includes index
ISBN 0-00-219201-2 : £12.50 B81-03720

598'.33 — Great Britain. Birds: Waders
Hale, W. G.. Waders / W.G. Hale. — London : Collins, 1980. — 320p,24p of plates : ill,maps ; 23cm. — (The New naturalist ; [65])
Bibliography: p297-307. - Includes index
ISBN 0-00-219727-8 : £9.50 B81-00900

598′.33 — Great Britain. Coastal regions. Birds

Lloyd, Clare. Birdwatching on estuaries, coast and sea / Clare Lloyd ; with drawings by Norman Arlott. — London : Severn House, c1981. — 160p : ill(some col.),1chart,maps ; 22cm. — (Severn House naturalist′s library)
Bibliography: p155-157. - Includes index
ISBN 0-7278-2003-6 : £7.75 : CIP rev. B80-23280

598′.338 — Black-headed gulls. Life cycle — *For children*

Stidworthy, John. Black-headed gull / John Stidworthy ; illustrated by John Thompson-Steinkrauss. — London : Heinemann ... in association with the British Museum (Natural History), 1981. — 32p : col.ill ; 24cm
Bibliography: p32. — Includes index
ISBN 0-434-96495-6 : £4.95 B81-35371

598.4′1 — Ducks — *For children*

Sheehan, Angela. The duck / by Angela Sheehan ; illustrated by Maurice Pledger and Bernard Robinson. — London : Angus & Robertson, c1979. — [25]p : col.ill ; 22cm. — (Eye-view library)
ISBN 0-207-95832-7 : Unpriced B81-38446

598.4′1 — Geese

Owen, Myrfyn. Wild geese of the world : their life history and ecology / Myrfyn Owen ; with a foreword by Sir Peter Scott ; illustrated by Joe Blossom. — London : Batsford, 1980. — 236p,8p of plates : ill(some col.),maps ; 26cm
Bibliography: p217-230. — Includes index
ISBN 0-7134-0831-6 : £15.00 B81-02798

598.4′1 — Greenland. White-fronted geese

Greenland white-fronted goose / [Greenland White-fronted Goose Study] ; [written by ADF and APF]. — [Aberystwyth] ([School of Biological Sciences, University College of Wales, Aberystwyth, Dyfed]) : [The Society], [1978]. — 16p : ill,maps ; 22cm
Cover title
Unpriced (pbk) B81-12289

Greenland White-fronted Goose Study. Report of the 1979 Greenland White-fronted Goose Study expedition to Eqalungmiut Nunât, West Greenland. — Aberystwyth (Dept. of Zoology, University College of Wales, Aberystwyth) : The Study, Aug.1981. — [200]p
ISBN 0-9507667-0-4 (pbk) : £5.00 : CIP entry B81-24642

Greenland White-fronted Goose Study : preliminary report : Eqalungmiut Nunat, 5th May-20th August 1979. — [Aberystwyth] ([School of Biological Sciences, University College of Wales, Penglais, Aberystwyth, Dyfed]) : [The Society], [1979]. — [8]p : 3maps ; 30cm
£0.20 (unbound) B81-12288

598.4′1 — Manitoba. Delta Marsh. Canvasbacks

Hochbaum, H. Albert. The canvasback on a prairie marsh / by H. Albert Hochbaum ; drawings by the author. — Lincoln, [Neb.] ; London : University of Nebraska Press, c1981. — xxii,207p : ill ; 22cm
Originally published: Washington D.C. : American Wildlife Institute, 1944. — Includes index
ISBN 0-8032-2300-5 (cased) : £2.30
ISBN 0-8032-7200-6 (pbk) : £2.30 B81-38247

598.4′1 — North America. Trumpeter swans

Banko, Winston E.. The trumpeter swan : its history, habits and population in the United States / by Winston E. Banko. — Lincoln [Neb.] ; London : University of Nebraska Press, 1980. — x,214p : ill,maps ; 23cm. — (A Bison book ; BB731)
Originally published: Washington, D.C. : U.S. Fish and Wildlife Service, 1960. — Bibliography: p189-197. - Includes index
ISBN 0-8032-6057-1 (pbk) : £3.60 B81-14689

598.4′41 — Penguins — *For children* — *Welsh texts*

Hope, Ffransis. Y pengwin / [gan Ffransis Hope] ; [addaswyd o Holandeg Francis Brewer ; lluniau gan Jan van Wijngaarden]. — Caerdydd : Gwasg y Dref Wen, c1980. — 16p : col.ill,1map ; 22cm. — (Cyfres y seren)
Text, map on inside covers
£0.80 (pbk) B81-07493

598.4′41′0998 — British Antarctic Territory. Antarctic Peninsula. Penguins. Distribution

Croxall, J. P.. The distribution of penguins on the Antarctic peninsula and islands of the Scotia Sea / by J.P. Croxall and E.D. Kirkwood. — Cambridge : British Antarctic Survey, 1979. — 186p : col.maps ; 30cm
Bibliography: p182-186
ISBN 0-85665-071-4 (pbk) : Unpriced
Also classified at 598.4′41′0998 B81-15216

598.4′41′0998 — Scotia Sea. Islands. Penguins. Distribution

Croxall, J. P.. The distribution of penguins on the Antarctic peninsula and islands of the Scotia Sea / by J.P. Croxall and E.D. Kirkwood. — Cambridge : British Antarctic Survey, 1979. — 186p : col.maps ; 30cm
Bibliography: p182-186
ISBN 0-85665-071-4 (pbk) : Unpriced
Primary classification 598.4′41′0998 B81-15216

598′.51 — Ostriches — *For children*

Wootton, Anthony. Ostriches / Anthony Wootton. — Hove : Wayland, 1981. — 60p : col.ill ; 24cm. — (Animals of the world)
Ill on lining papers. — Includes index
ISBN 0-85340-849-1 : £3.50 B81-40621

598′.65 — Columbidae

Delacour, Jean. Wild pigeons and doves / Jean Delacour. — New ed. — Neptune, N.J. ; Reigate : T.F.H., c1980. — 189p : ill(some col.) ; 21cm
Previous ed.: Fond du Lac, Wis. : All-Pets Books, 1959. — Ill, text on lining papers. — Includes index
ISBN 0-87666-968-2 : £4.95 B81-05530

598′.71 — Parrots — *For children*

Stonehouse, Bernard. Parrots / Bernard Stonehouse. — Hove : Wayland, 1981. — 61p : col.ill ; 24cm. — (Animals of the world)
Ill on lining papers. — Includes index
ISBN 0-85340-802-5 : £3.50 B81-07558

598.8′83 — Sparrows - *For children*

Finding out about sparrows. — Poole : Blandford Press, Apr.1981. — [32]p. — (Japanese nature series)
ISBN 0-7137-1151-5 : £2.95 : CIP entry B81-04327

598′.91 — Birds of prey

Weick, Friedhelm. Birds of prey of the world / Friedhelm Weick in collaboration with Leslie H. Brown. — London : Collins, 1980. — 159p : ill(some col.) ; 29cm
English and German text. — Bibliography: p156-159. — Includes index
ISBN 0-00-219277-2 : £15.00 B81-00901

598′.91 — Birds of prey — *For children*

Cuisin, Michel. Birds of prey / illustrated by Carl Brenders ; edited by Michael Chinery ; written by Michel Cuisin ; translated by Anne-Marie Moore. — London : Kingfisher, 1980. — 44p : ill(some col.) ; 29cm. — (Nature′s hidden world)
Translation of: Les rapaces d′Europe
ISBN 0-7063-6033-8 : £2.95 : CIP rev. B80-28365

598′.91 — Golden eagles. Life cycle — *For children*

Riley, Terry, *1941-*. Year of the golden eagle / devised and illustrated by Terry Riley ; written by John Andrews. — London : Dent, 1981. — 32p : col.ill,1col.map ; 28cm
ISBN 0-460-06919-5 : £3.95 B81-11491

598′.91′094 — Europe. Birds of prey — *Field guides*

Flight identification of European raptors / R.F. Porter ... [et al.]. — 3rd ed. — Calton : Poyser, 1981. — 180p,[96]p of plates : ill ; 25cm
Material first appeared in the journal ′British birds′ vols 64-66, 1971-1973. — Previous ed.: 1976. — Includes index
ISBN 0-85661-027-5 : £9.60 B81-36883

598′.91′0941 — Great Britain. Birds of prey

Parry, Gareth. The Country Life book of birds of prey / Gareth Parry and Rory Putman. — [London] : Country Life Books, 1979. — 120p : chiefly ill(some col.),maps ; 36cm
ISBN 0-600-31531-2 : £20.00 B81-00902

598′.916 — Eagles — *For children*

Clarkson, Ewan. Eagles / Ewan Clarkson. — Hove : Wayland, 1981. — 60p : col.ill ; 24cm. — (Animals of the world)
Col. ill on lining papers. — Includes index
ISBN 0-85340-512-3 : £3.50 B81-22046

598′.916 — North America. Hawks — *Field guides*

Heintzelman, Donald S.. A guide to hawk watching in North America / Donald S. Heintzelman. — University Park, [Pa.] ; London : Pennsylvania State University Press, c1979. — xii,284p : ill,maps,forms ; 23cm. — (Keystone books)
Bibliography: p279-280. — Includes index
ISBN 0-271-00212-3 : £4.45 B81-32852

598′.916 — Nottinghamshire. Honey buzzards

Irons, Anthony. Breeding of the Honey Buzzard (Pernis apivorus) in Nottinghamshire : a contribution to the ornithology of Nottinghamshire / by Anthony Irons. — [Nottingham] ([19 Woodland Grove, Chilwell, Nottingham NG9 5BP]) : Trent Valley Bird Watchers, 1980. — 15p : ill ; 21cm
Bibliography: p15
Unpriced (pbk) B81-21074

598′.918 — Great Britain. Peregrine falcons

Ratcliffe, Derek. The peregrine falcon / by Derek Ratcliffe ; with illustrations by Donald Watson. — Calton : Poyser, 1980. — 416p,iv,32p of plates : ill(some col.) ; 24cm
Bibliography: p366-373 — Includes index
ISBN 0-85661-026-7 : £12.00 B81-01716

598′.97 — Barn owls. Life cycle — *For children*

Riley, Terry, *1941-*. Year of the barn owl / devised and illustrated by Terry Riley ; written by John Andrews. — London : Dent, 1981. — 32p : col.ill,1col.map ; 28cm
ISBN 0-460-06958-6 : £3.95 : CIP rev. B80-07374

598′.97 — Kenya. Lake Naivasha region. Verreaux′s eagle owls — *Personal observations*

Adamson, Joy. Friends from the forest / Joy Adamson ; foreword by Juliette Huxley ; drawing by Norman Arlott. — London : Collins, 1981. — 86p : ill ; 22cm
ISBN 0-00-262458-3 : £4.95
Primary classification 599.8′2 B81-13621

598′.97′0222 — Owls — *Illustrations* — *For children*

García Sánchez, J. L.. Funny facts about the owl / pictures by Nella Bosnia ; idea by J.L. García Sánchez and M.A. Pacheco ; translated by Ricard Whitecross. — London : Evans, 1981. — [22]p : chiefly col.ill ; 23cm. — (Funny facts series)
Translation of: El buho. — Ill on lining paper
ISBN 0-237-45565-x : £2.95 B81-12472

598′.97′094233 — Dorset. Owls — *Personal observations*

Rome, Claire. An owl came to stay / Claire Rome ; with illustrations by the author. — Large print ed.. — Bath : Chivers Press, 1981, c1979. — 168p : ill ; 23cm. — (A Lythway autobiography)
Originally published: London : Elek, 1979
ISBN 0-85119-710-8 : Unpriced B81-11639

598'.97'0942538 — Lincolnshire. Hough-on-the-Hill. Owls — *Personal observations*

Burkett, Molly. Take an owl or two : the story of Boz and Owly / Molly Burkett ; illustrated by Julie Stiles. — London : Pan, 1981, c1979. — 125p : ill ; 18cm. — (Piccolo books)
Originally published: London : Deutsch, 1979
ISBN 0-330-26467-2 (pbk) : £1.10 B81-38170

598'.97'0942585 — Hertfordshire. Harpenden. Animals in danger of extinction. Breeding. Organisations: Wildlife Breeding Centre. Owls - *For children*

Goldsmith, John, *1947-*. The Rajah of Bong : and other owls / John Goldsmith ; illustrations by Ken Turner. — London : Pelham, 1981. — 44p : ill(some col.) ; 24cm. — (Graham Dangerfield's animals)
ISBN 0-7207-1293-9 : £4.95 B81-15232

599 — MAMMALS

599 — Mammals

Eisenberg, John F.. The mammalian radiations. — London : Athlone Press, Nov.1981. — [597]p
ISBN 0-485-30008-7 : £32.00 : CIP entry B81-30558

O'Hanlon, Maggie. Wild animals of the world / Maggie O'Hanlon, Doreen Edmond. — Poole : Blandford, 1981. — 168p : col.ill ; 20cm
Bibliography: p158. — Includes index
ISBN 0-7137-1139-6 (cased) : £4.95 : CIP rev.
ISBN 0-7137-1145-0 (pbk) : £2.95 B81-22543

599 — Mammals — *For children*

Wild animals. — [London] : Sparrow, 1980. — [24]p : col.ill,col.maps ; 29cm. — (Discoverers)
Adaptation of: The Superbook of wild animals. — Bibliography: p24
ISBN 0-09-923560-9 (pbk) : £0.70 B81-19528

599'.0072041 — Great Britain. Mammals. Observation — *Manuals*

Clark, Michael, *1943-*. Mammal watching / Michael Clark ; with drawings by the author. — London : Severn House, 1981. — 175p : ill (some col.) ; 22cm. — (Severn House naturalist's library)
Bibliography: p170-173. — Includes index
ISBN 0-7278-2010-9 : £7.95 : CIP rev. B81-14900

599.01 — Mammals. Physiology

Progress in anatomy / editors R.J. Harrison & R.L. Holmes assisted by F. Beck ... [et al.]. — Cambridge : Cambridge University Press
Vol.1. — 1981. — x,250p : ill ; 26cm
At head of title: The Anatomical Society of Great Britain and Ireland. — Includes bibliographies and index
ISBN 0-521-23603-7 : £27.50 : CIP rev. B81-14828

599.01'1 — Mammals. Cardiovascular system. Regulation. Role of adrenergic neurons of central nervous system — *Conference proceedings*

Central adrenaline neurons : basic aspects and their role in cardiovascular functions : proceedings of an international symposium held at the Wenner-Gren Center, Stockholm August 27-28, 1979 / edited by Kjell Fuxe ... [et al.]. — Oxford : Pergamon, 1980. — xiv,347p : ill ; 26cm. — (Wenner-Gren Center international symposium series ; v.33)
Includes bibliographies and index
ISBN 0-08-025927-8 : £22.00 : CIP rev. B80-09688

599.01'1 — Mammals. Circulatory system. Physiology

Structure and function of the circulation / edited by Colin J. Schwartz, Nicholas T. Werthessen and Stewart Wolf. — New York ; London : Plenum
Vol.2. — 1981. — x,848p : ill ; 26cm
Includes bibliographies and index
ISBN 0-306-40620-9 : Unpriced B81-15038

Structure and function of the circulation / edited by Colin J. Schwartz, Nicholas T. Werthessen and Stewart Wolf. — New York ; London : Plenum
Vol.3. — c1981. — xii,551p : ill ; 26cm
Includes bibliographies and index
ISBN 0-306-40751-5 : Unpriced B81-36679

599.01'13 — Mammals. Blood. Lymphocytes. Mitogenesis

Hume, David A.. Mitogenic lymphocyte transformation : a general model for the control of Mammalian cell proliferation and differentiation / David A. Hume and Maurice J. Weidemann. — Amsterdam ; Oxford : Elsevier/North-Holland Biomedical, 1980. — xi,251p : ill ; 25cm. — (Research monographs in immunology ; v.2)
Includes bibliographies and index
ISBN 0-444-80219-3 : £24.70 B81-07219

599.01'21 — Mammals. Lungs. Gases. Transfer — *Conference proceedings*

Gas exchange function of normal and diseased lungs / volume editors J. Piiper and P. Scheid. — Basel ; London : Karger, 1981. — xvi,318p : ill ; 25cm. — (Progress in respiration research ; v.16)
Conference papers. — Includes bibliographies and index
ISBN 3-8055-1638-x : £49-50 B81-21441

599.01'32 — Mammals. Large intestine. Homeostasis & nutritional aspects

Wrong, O. M.. The large intestine : its role in mammalian nutrition and homeostasis / O.M. Wrong, C.J. Edmonds, V.S. Chadwick. — Lancaster : MTP, 1981. — xiii,217p : ill ; 25cm
Bibliography: p175-212. — Includes index
ISBN 0-85200-351-x : £16.95 B81-27066

599.01'33 — Mammals. Xenobiotics. Metabolism. Role of enzymes

Enzymatic basis of detoxication / edited by William B. Jakoby. — New York ; London : Academic Press. — (Biochemical pharmacology and toxicology)
Vol.2. — 1980. — xiv,369p : ill ; 24cm
Includes index
ISBN 0-12-380002-1 : £24.80 B81-15007

599.01'33 — Newborn mammals. Energy metabolism — *Conference proceedings*

Metabolic adaptation to extrauterine life : the antenatal role of carbohydrates and energy metabolism : proceedings of a workshop held in Brussels, December 19-21, 1979 / sponsored by the Commission of the European Communities, as advised by the Committee on Medical and Public Health Research ; R. de Meyer (editor). — The Hague ; London : Nijhoff for the Commission of the European Communities, 1981. — xii,371p : ill ; 25cm. — (Developments in perinatal medicine ; v.1)
ISBN 90-247-2484-8 : Unpriced B81-22129

599.01'3305 — Mammals. Xenobiotics. Metabolism - *Serials*

Foreign compound metabolism in mammals. — Vol.6. — London : Royal Society of Chemistry, Aug.1981. — [480]p. — (A Specialist periodical report)
ISBN 0-85186-058-3 : CIP entry
ISSN 0300-3493 B81-18083

599.01'49 — Mammals. Kidneys. Glomeruli. Basement membranes — *Conference proceedings*

International Symposium on the Glomerular Basement Membrane *(1st : 1980 : Vienna)*. The glomerular basement membrane : proceedings of the First International Symposium on the Glomerular Basement Membrane, Vienna September 8-12, 1980 / editor Gert Lubec. — Basel ; London : Karger, 1981. — vii,434p : ill ; 24cm
Originally published: as Renal physiology, Vol.3, no.1-6 (1980). — Includes bibliographies and index
ISBN 3-8055-2952-x (pbk) : £41.50 B81-38416

599.01'6 — Mammals. Ovaries

Biology of the ovary / edited by P.M. Motta and E.S.E. Hafez. — The Hague ; London : Nijhoff, 1980. — x,344p : ill ; 28cm. — (Developments in obstetrics and gynecology ; v.2)
Includes bibliographies and index
ISBN 90-247-2316-7 : Unpriced B81-07762

599.01'6 — Mammals. Reproduction — *Conference proceedings*

Reproductive processes and contraception / edited by Kenneth W. McKerns. — New York ; London : Plenum, c1981. — xxi,731p : ill ; 24cm. — (Biochemical endocrinology)
Conference papers. — Includes bibliographies and index
ISBN 0-306-40534-2 : Unpriced B81-38019

599.01'6 — Mammals. Reproduction. Environmental factors

Environmental factors in mammal reproduction / edited by Desmond Gilmore and Brian Cook. — London : Macmillan, 1981. — x,330p ; 25cm. — (Biology and environment)
Includes bibliographies and index
ISBN 0-333-24150-9 : £25.00 B81-22250

599.01'6 — Mammals. Reproduction. Neuroendocrinological aspects

Neuroendocrinology of reproduction : physiology and behavior / edited by Norman T. Adler. — New York ; London : Plenum, c1981. — xxi,555p,[8]p of plates : ill(some col.) ; 25cm
Includes bibliographies and index
ISBN 0-306-40600-4 (cased) : Unpriced
ISBN 0-306-40611-x (pbk) : Unpriced B81-33164

599.01'6 — Mammals. Reproduction. Regulation

Bioregulators of reproduction / edited by Georgiana Jagiello, Henry J. Vogel. — New York ; London : Academic Press, 1981. — xxv,584p : ill ; 24cm. — (P & S Biomedical sciences symposia series)
Conference papers. — Includes bibliographies and index
ISBN 0-12-379980-5 : £39.40 B81-39583

599.01'6 — Mammals. Reproduction. Regulation. Role of gonads

Intragonadal regulation of reproduction / edited by Paul Franchimont and Cornelia P. Channing. — London : Academic Press, 1981. — xiii,429p : ill ; 24cm
Includes bibliographies and index
ISBN 0-12-265280-0 : £19.60 : CIP rev.
Also classified at 612'.4 B81-08908

599.01'6 — Mammals. Testes

Descended and cryptorchid testis / edited by E.S.E. Hafez. — The Hague ; London : Nijhoff, 1980. — vi,191p : ill ; 28cm. — (Clinics in andrology ; v.3)
Includes bibliographies and index
ISBN 90-247-2299-3 : Unpriced B81-01675

599.01'825 — Mammals. Auditory nervous system. Physiology — *Conference proceedings*

Neuronal mechanisms of hearing / [proceedings of a symposium on 'neuronal mechanisms of hearing', organised by the Czechoslovak Academy of Sciences as a satellite symposium to the 28th International Congress of Physiological Sciences, held July 20-23, 1980, in Prague Czechoslovakia] ; edited by Josef Syka and Lindsay Aitkin. — New York ; London : Plenum, c1981. — xii,443p : ill ; 26cm
Includes bibliographies and index
ISBN 0-306-40656-x : Unpriced B81-34977

599.01'826 — Mammals. Olfactory perception — *Conference proceedings*

Olfaction in mammals : (the proceedings of a symposium held at the Zoological Society of London on 24 and 25 November 1978) / edited by D. Michael Stoddart. — London : Published for the Zoological Society of London by Academic Press, 1980. — xv,368p : ill ; 24cm. — (Symposia of the Zoological Society of London ; no.45)
Includes bibliography and index
ISBN 0-12-613345-x : £27.40 : CIP rev. B80-11885

599.01'852 — Mammals. Elastic tissues. Elastin

Biology and pathology of elastic tissues / volume editors A.M. Robert and L. Robert. — Basel ; London : Karger, c1980. — viii,230p : ill ; 25cm. — (Frontiers of matrix biology ; v.8)
Includes bibliographies and index
ISBN 3-8055-3078-1 : £32.60 B81-06122

599.01′852 — Placental mammals. Skull

Moore, W. J. (William James). The mammalian skull / W.J. Moore. — Cambridge : Cambridge University Press, 1981. — xi,369p : ill ; 25cm. — (Biological structure and function, ISSN 0308-5384 ; 8)
Bibliography: p324-343. — Includes index
ISBN 0-521-23318-6 : £40.00 B81-13028

599.01′88 — Mammals. Brain. Isolated specimens. Preparation — *For electrophysiology*

Electrophysiology of isolated mammalian CNS preparations / edited by G.A. Kerkut and H.V. Wheal. — London : Academic Press, 1981. — 402p : ill ; 24cm
Includes bibliographies and index
ISBN 0-12-404680-0 : £27.80 B81-29763

599.01′88 — Mammals. Brain. Steroid hormone receptors — *Conference proceedings*

Steroid hormone regulation of the brain : proceedings of an international symposium held at the Wenner-Gren Center, Stockholm, 27-28 October 1980 / edited by Kjell Fuxe, Jan-Åke Gustafsson, Lennart Wetterberg. — Oxford : Pergamon, c1981. — xviii,406p : ill ; 26cm. — (Wenner-Gren Center international sysmposium series ; 34)
Includes bibliographies and index
ISBN 0-08-026864-1 : £33.00 : CIP rev.
B81-16397

599.01′88 — Mammals. Central nervous system. Neurotransmitters. Turnover

Central neurotransmitter turnover / edited by C.J. Pycock and P.V. Taberner. — London : Croom Helm, c1981. — 197p : ill ; 23cm
Includes bibliographies and index
ISBN 0-7099-0471-1 : £11.95 : CIP rev.
B80-21927

599.01′88 — Mammals. Central nervous system. Synapses. Neurotransmitters: Glutamate

Glutamate : transmitter in the central nervous system / edited by P.J. Roberts, J. Storm-Mathisen, G.A.R. Johnston. — Chichester : Wiley, c1981. — xii,226p,[11]p of plates : ill ; 24cm
Includes bibliographies and index
ISBN 0-471-27951-x : £16.50 : CIP rev.
B81-20125

599.01′88 — Mammals. Cerebral cortex — *Conference proceedings*

The **Organization** of the cerebral cortex : proceedings of a neurosciences research program colloquium / editors Francis O. Schmitt ... [et al.] ; contributing editors Floyd E. Bloom ... [et al.]. — Cambridge, Mass. ; London : MIT, c1981. — xxi,592p : ill ; 26cm
Includes bibliographies and index
ISBN 0-262-19189-x : £31.00 B81-28256

599.01′88 — Mammals. Nervous system. Taurine — *Conference proceedings*

A.N. Richards Symposium *(21st : 1979 : Valley Forge).* The effects of taurine on excitable tissues : proceedings of the 21st A.N. Richards Symposium of the Physiological Society of Philadelphia, Valley Forge, Pennsylvania, April 23-24, 1979 / edited by S.W. Schaffer Steven J. Baskin James J. Kocsis. — Lancaster : MTP Press, c1981. — 446p : ill ; 24cm. — (Monographs of the Physiological Society of Philadelphia ; v.7)
Includes bibliographies and index
ISBN 0-85200-562-8 : £35.50 B81-38101

599.01′88 — Mammals. Neurotransmitter receptors — *Conference proceedings*

Neurotransmitters and their receptors : based on a workshop sponsored by the European Molecular Biology Organisation and the Weizmann Institute of Science, Rehovot February 1980 / edited by U.Z. Littauer ... [et al.]. — Chichester : Wiley, c1980. — viii,570p : ill ; 25cm
Includes index
ISBN 0-471-27893-9 : £15.00 : CIP rev.
B80-18742

Psychopharmacology and biochemistry of neurotransmitter receptors : proceedings of an international conference held on April 11-13, 1980 in Tucson, Arizona, U.S.A. / editors Henry I. Yamamura, Richard W. Olsen, Earl Usdin. — New York ; Oxford : Elsevier/North-Holland, c1980. — xiv,676p : ill ; 25cm. — (Developments in neuroscience ; v.11)
ISBN 0-444-00568-4 : £29.25 B81-11139

599.01′88 — Mammals. Purinergic receptors

Purinergic receptors / edited by G. Burnstock. — London : Chapman and Hall, 1981. — ix,365p : ill ; 24cm. — (Receptors and recognition. Series B ; v.12)
Includes bibliographies and index
ISBN 0-412-15840-x : Unpriced B81-34710

599.01′88 — Mammals. Synapses. Adrenergic transmitters & cholinergic transmitters — *Conference proceedings*

OHOLO Biological Conference on Neuroactive Compounds and their Cell Receptors *(1979 : Zichron Ya′acov).* Neurobiology of cholinergic and adrenergic transmitters / volume editors E. Heldman ... [et al.] ; technical editor S.R. Smith. — Basel ; London : Karger, 1980. — xiv,197p : ill ; 23cm. — (Monographs in neural sciences ; v.7)
At head of title: 24th annual OHOLO Biological Conference on Neuroactive Compounds and their Cell Receptors, Zichron Ya′acov, April 1-4, 1979. — Includes bibliographies and index
ISBN 3-8055-0828-x (pbk) : £22.25 B81-28312

599.01′92 — Mammals. Biochemistry

White, Abraham. Principles of biochemistry. — 6th ed. / Abraham White ... [et al.], International student ed. — Tokyo ; London : McGraw-Hill, c1978. — xi,1492p : ill ; 25cm
Previous ed.: 1973. — Text on lining papers. — Includes bibliographies and index
ISBN 0-07-085844-6 : £14.95 B81-40409

599.01′924 — Mammals. Branched chain ketoacids — *Conference proceedings*

International Symposium on Metabolism and Clinical Implications of Branched Chain Amino and Ketoacids *(1980 : Kiawah Island Conference Center).* Metabolism and clinical implications of branched chain amino and ketoacids : proceedings of the International Symposium on Metabolism and Clinical Implications of Branched Chain Amino and Ketoacids held at the Kiawah Island Conference Center, Charleston, South Carolina, U.S.A., November 15-16, 1980 / editors Mackenzie Walser and John R. Williamson. — New York ; Oxford : Elsevier/North-Holland, c1981. — xxiii,631p : ill,ports ; 25cm. — (Developments in biochemistry, ISSN 0165-1714 ; v.18)
Includes index
ISBN 0-444-00622-2 : £40.80
Primary classification 599.01′9245 B81-22299

599.01′9245 — Mammals. Branched chain amino acids — *Conference proceedings*

International Symposium on Metabolism and Clinical Implications of Branched Chain Amino and Ketoacids *(1980 : Kiawah Island Conference Center).* Metabolism and clinical implications of branched chain amino and ketoacids : proceedings of the International Symposium on Metabolism and Clinical Implications of Branched Chain Amino and Ketoacids held at the Kiawah Island Conference Center, Charleston, South Carolina, U.S.A., November 15-16, 1980 / editors Mackenzie Walser and John R. Williamson. — New York ; Oxford : Elsevier/North-Holland, c1981. — xxiii,631p : ill,ports ; 25cm. — (Developments in biochemistry, ISSN 0165-1714 ; v.18)
Includes index
ISBN 0-444-00622-2 : £40.80
Also classified at 599.01′924 B81-22299

599.01′92456 — Mammals. Melanocyte stimulating hormone peptides

Thody, A. J.. The MSH peptides / A.J. Thody. — London : Academic Press, 1980. — viii,162p : ill ; 24cm
Bibliography: p129-154. - Includes index
ISBN 0-12-687850-1 : £16.00 B81-11375

599.01′9248 — Mammals. Carbohydrates. Metabolism

Carbohydrate metabolism and its disorders. — London : Academic Press
Vol.3 / edited by P.J. Randle, D.F. Steiner, W.J. Whelan. — 1981. — 530p,[1]leaf of plates : ill(some col.) ; 24cm
Includes bibliographies and index
ISBN 0-12-579703-6 : £34.60 : CIP rev.
B81-08795

599.01′927 — Mammals. Prolactin

Prolactin / edited by Robert B. Jaffe. — New York ; Oxford : Elsevier, c1981. — xiv,228p : ill ; 24cm. — (Current endocrinology)
Includes bibliographies and index
ISBN 0-444-00555-2 : £15.81 B81-35331

599.01′927 — Mammals. Prolactin — *Conference proceedings*

Advances in prolactin : proceedings of the Satellite Symposium to the 6th International Congress of Endocrinology, Adelaine [i.e. Adelaide], February 18-19, 1980 / volume editors M. L′Hermite, S.J. Judd. — Basel ; London : Karger, 1980. — vii,266p : ill ; 25cm. — (Progress in reproductive biology ; v.6)
Includes bibliographies
ISBN 3-8055-0859-x : £24.50 B81-17234

599.01′927 — Mammals. Prostaglandins — *Conference proceedings*

The **Prostaglandin** system : endoperoxides, prostacyclin, and thromboxanes / [proceedings of a NATO Advanced Study Institute on Advances in Endoperoxide, Prostacyclin and Thromboxanes Research held September 2-13, 1979 in Erice, Sicily] ; edited by F. Berti and G.P. Velo. — New York ; London : Plenum published in cooperation with NATO Scientific Affairs Division, c1981. — ix,428p : ill ; 26cm. — (NATO advanced study institutes series. Series A, Life sciences ; v.36)
Includes index
ISBN 0-306-40645-4 : Unpriced B81-24394

599.01′927 — Mammals. Prostaglandins. Measurement — *Conference proceedings*

Prostaglandins, prostacyclin, and thromboxanes measurement : a workshop symposium on prostaglandins, prostacyclin and thromboxanes measurement : methodological problems and clinical prospects, Nivelles, Belgium, November 15-16, 1979 / sponsored by the Commission of the European Communities, as advised by the Committee on Medical and Public Health Research ; edited by J.M. Boeynaems and A.G. Herman. — The Hague ; London : Nijhoff for the Commission of the European Communities, 1980. — x,201p : ill ; 25cm. — (Developments in pharmacology ; v.1)
ISBN 90-247-2417-1 : Unpriced B81-07268

599.02 — Mammals. Diseases. Sex differences

Glucksmann, Alfred. Sexual dimorphism in human and mammalian biology and pathology / A. Glucksmann. — London : Academic Press, 1981. — xi,356p : ill ; 24cm
Bibliography: p305-345. — Includes index
ISBN 0-12-286960-5 : £18.80 : CIP rev.
B81-06624

599.02′3 — Developing countries. Mammals. Parasitic diseases. Biochemical aspects — *Conference proceedings*

International Symposium on the Biochemistry of Parasites and Host-Parasite Relationships *(3rd : 1980 : Beerse).* The host-invader interplay : proceedings of the Third International Symposium on the Biochemistry of Parasites and Host-Parasite Relationships. Beerse, Belgium, 30 June-3 July, 1980 / organized by the Janssen Research Foundation ; editor H. Van den Bossche. — Amsterdam ; Oxford : Elsevier/North-Holland, 1980. — xv,766p : ill ; 25cm. — (Janssen Research Foundation series ; V.2)
Includes index
ISBN 0-444-80284-3 : £33.07 B81-06310

599.02'34 — Mammals. Slow virus diseases. Pathology — *Conference proceedings*

Aspects of slow and persistent virus infections : proceedings of the European Workshop sponsored by the Commission of the European Communities on the advice of the Committee on Medical and Public Health Research, held in London (U.K.), April 5-6, 1979 / edited by D.A.J. Tyrrell. — The Hague ; London : Nijhoff for the Commission of the European Communities, 1979. — xii,286p : ill ; 25cm. — (New perspectives in clinical microbiology ; v.2)
Includes index
Unpriced (corrected)
ISBN 90-247-2329-9 B81-07710

599.02'9 — Mammals. Immunoassay. Use of enzymes — *Conference proceedings*

Immunoenzymatic assay techniques : proceedings of a European workshop sponsored by the Commission of the European Communities, as advised by the Committee on Medical and Public Health Research and held in Tirrenia (Pisa), Italy, April 23-27, 1979 / edited by R. Malvano. — The Hague ; London : Nijhoff for the Commission of the European Communities, 1980. — xv,272p : ill ; 25cm. — (Developments in clinical biochemistry ; v.1)
ISBN 90-247-2314-0 : Unpriced B81-07289

599.02'93 — Mammals. B-cells — *Conference proceedings*

International Conference on B Lymphocytes in the Immune Response *(2nd : 1980 : Scottsdale, Ariz.)*. B lymphocytes in the immune response : functional, developmental, and interactive properties : proceedings of the Second International Conference on B Lymphocytes in the Immune Response, Scottsdale, Arizona, U.S.A., October 18-22, 1980 / editors: Norman Klinman ... [et al.]. — New York ; Oxford : Elsevier/North Holland, c1981. — xvii,540p : ill ; 25cm. — (Developments in immunology, ISSN 0163-5921 ; v.15)
Includes index
ISBN 0-444-00611-7 : £35.22 B81-23640

.02'95 — Mammals. Endocytosis & exocytosis. Immunological aspects — *Conference proceedings*

Endocytosis and exocytosis in host defence : symposium in celebration of the 10th anniversary of the University of Linköping, Linköping May 27-28, 1980 / volume editors L.B. Edebo, L. Enerbäck and O.I. Stendahl. — Basel ; London : Karger, c1981. — viii,272p : ill ; 25cm. — (Monographs in allergy ; v.17)
Includes bibliographies
ISBN 3-8055-1865-x : Unpriced B81-36176

99.03'3 — Mammals. Embryology

Patten, Bradley Merrill. Patten's foundations of embryology. — 4th ed. / Bruce M. Carlson. — New York ; London : McGraw-Hill, c1981. — xv,672p,[16]p of plates : ill(some col.) ; 25cm. — (McGraw-Hill series in organismic biology)
Previous ed.: published as Foundations of embrlyology. 1974. — Ill on lining papers. — Bibliography: p615-653. — Includes index
ISBN 0-07-009875-1 : £15.25 B81-29829

99.03'3 — Mammals. Embryos & foetuses. Development — *Conference proceedings*

The Fetus and independent life. — London : Pitman, Dec.1981. — [320]p. — (CIBA Foundation symposium ; 86)
Conference papers
ISBN 0-272-79650-6 : £22.50 : CIP entry B81-31461

99.03'33 — Mammals. Ova. Implantation — *Conference proceedings*

Cellular and molecular aspects of implantation / edited by Stanley R. Glasser and David W. Bullock. — New York ; London : Plenum, c1981. — xxi,497p : ill ; 26cm
Conference papers. — Includes bibliographies and index
ISBN 0-306-40581-4 : Unpriced B81-24232

599.03'33 — Mammals. Placenta. Maternal-foetal transfer — *Conference proceedings*

Placental transfer : methods and interpretations / [based on a satellite meeting of the International Congress of Physiological Sciences] ; edited by M. Young ... [et al.]. — London : Saunders, 1981. — 250p,[4]p of plates : ill(some col.) ; 25cm. — (Placenta. Supplement ; 2)
Includes bibliographies and index
ISBN 0-7216-9661-9 : £20.00 B81-29931

599.03'33 — Mammals. Placental transfer

Transfer across the primate and non-primate placenta / edited by H.C.S. Wallenburg, B.K. van Kreel and J.P. van Dijk. — London : Saunders, 1981. — ix,189p : ill ; 26cm. — (Placenta. Supplement ; 1)
Includes bibliographies and index
ISBN 0-7216-9106-4 : Unpriced B81-11692

599.051 — Adult mammals. Influence of young mammals

Bell, Richard Q.. Child effects on adults / Richard Q. Bell, Lawrence V. Harper. — Lincoln [Neb.] ; London : University of Nebraska Press, 1980, c1977. — xii,253p ; 23cm. — (Bison Books in clinical psychology)
Orginally published: Hillsdale, N.J. : Erlbaum, 1977. — Bibliography: p215-236. - Includes index
ISBN 0-8032-6058-x (pbk) : £3.30 B81-12717

599.051 — Mammals. Behaviour. Effects of endocrine system

Neuroendocrine regulation and altered behaviour / edited by Pavel D. Hrdina and Radhey L. Singhal. — London : Croom Helm, c1981. — 409p : ill ; 25cm
Includes bibliographies and index
ISBN 0-7099-0457-6 : £25.00 : CIP rev. B81-06584

599.051 — Young mammals. Relationships with mothers. Behavioural aspects

Maternal influences and early behavior / edited by Robert W. Bell and William P. Smotherman. — Lancaster : MTP, c1980. — 442p : ill ; 24cm
Includes bibliographies and index
ISBN 0-85200-537-7 : £24.91 B81-06542

599.052'48 — Small mammals. Population. Dynamics

Finerty, James Patrick. The population ecology of cycles in small mammals : mathematical theory and biological fact / James Patrick Finerty. — New Haven ; London : Yale University Press, c1980. — xiv,234p : ill,maps ; 25cm
Bibliography: p205-228. — Includes index
ISBN 0-300-02382-0 : £11.70 B81-18210

599.053 — Young mammals. Suckling — *For children*

Nakatani, Chiyoko. Feeding babies / Chiyoko Nakatani. — London : Bodley Head, 1981. — 28p : col.ill ; 22cm
Translated from the Japanese
ISBN 0-370-30404-7 : £2.95 : CIP rev. B81-12866

599.08 — Mammals. Cells & tissues. Microstructure. Scanning electron microscopy — *Conference proceedings*

Symposium on Three Dimensional Microanatomy *(1980 : Mexico City)*. Three dimensional microanatomy of cells and tissue surfaces : proceedings of the Symposium on Three Dimensional Microanatomy held in Mexico City, Mexico, August 17-23, 1980 / editors Delmas J. Allen, Pietro M. Motta, Liberato J.A. DiDio. — New York ; Oxford : Elsevier/North-Holland, c1981. — x,372p : ill ; 24cm
Includes index
ISBN 0-444-00607-9 : £32.76 B81-23605

599.08'24'076 — Mammals. Tissues - *Questions & answers*

Wheater, Paul R.. Self-assessment in histology. — Edinburgh : Churchill Livingstone, July 1981. — [176]p
ISBN 0-443-02109-0 (pbk) : £3.50 : CIP entry B81-14984

599.08'73 — Mammals. Kidneys. Cells. Ultrastructure. Physiology

Functional ultrastructure of the kidney / edited by Arvid B. Maunsbach, T. Steen Olsen, Erik Ilsø Christensen. — London : Academic Press, 1980. — xvi,485p : ill ; 24cm
Conference papers. — Includes index
ISBN 0-12-481250-3 : £40.00 : CIP rev. B80-29701

599.08'7612 — Mammals. Epidermis. Keratinocytes. Differentiation

Epidermal keratinocyte differentiation and fibrilogenesis / volume editor M. Pruniéras. — Basel ; London : Karger, 1981. — viii,190p : ill ; 25cm. — (Frontiers of matrix biology ; v.9)
Includes index
ISBN 3-8055-0893-x : £30.00 B81-21439

599.08'7612 — Mammals. Epidermis. Keratinocytes. Differentiation. Biochemical aspects — *Conference proceedings*

Biochemistry of normal and abnormal epidermal differentiation : proceedings of the U.S.-Japan seminar, Boyne Mountain Lodge, Boyne Falls, Michigan, July 29-August 2, 1979 / editors I.A. Bernstein and Makoto Seiji. — London : Karger, 1980. — x,440p : ill ; 23cm. — (Current problems in dermatology ; v.10)
Includes index
ISBN 3-8055-1915-x (pbk) : £36.15 B81-34535

599'.08'765 — Mammals. Cells. Ultrastructure. Pathology

Ghadially, Feroze N.. Ultrastructural pathology of the cell and matrix. — 2nd ed. — London : Butterworths, Nov.1981. — [920]p
Previous ed.: 1975
ISBN 0-407-00166-2 : £65.00 : CIP entry B81-33636

599.092 — Marine mammals

Handbook of marine mammals. — London : Academic Press, Apr.1981
Vol.2: Seals. — [350]p
ISBN 0-12-588502-4 : CIP entry B81-05120

599.092 — Marine mammals — *Conference proceedings*

Mammals in the seas. — Rome : Food and Agriculture Organization of the United Nations ; London : HMSO [distributor]. — (FAO fisheries series ; no.5)
Vol.2: Pinniped species summaries and report on sirenians : being the annex B appendices VI and VII of the report of the FAO Advisory Committee on Marine Resources Research Working Party on Marine Mammals with the cooperation of the United Nations Environment Programme. — 1979. — xiii,151p : ill ; 28cm
Conference papers. — Ill on lining papers
ISBN 92-510-0512-5 (pbk) : £6.00 B81-37394

599.094 — Europe. Mammals

Corbet, G. B.. The mammals of Britain and Europe / text by Gordon Corbet ; illustrated by Denys Ovenden. — London : Collins, 1980. — 253p : ill(some col.),col.maps ; 20cm
Bibliography: p247. — Includes index
ISBN 0-00-219772-3 (cased) : £6.95
ISBN 0-00-219774-x (pbk) : £3.95 B81-15404

599.0941 — Great Britain. Mammals

The **RSPCA** book of British mammals / edited by Leofric Boyle ; illustrated by Priscilla Barrett. — London : Collins, 1981. — 242p,[16]p of plates : ill(some col.) ; 24cm
Bibliography: p231-234. — Includes index
ISBN 0-00-219118-0 : £8.95 B81-40663

599.0941 — Great Britain. Rural regions. Mammals

Smith, Guy N.. Animals of the countryside / by Guy N. Smith ; with drawings by Pat Lakin and other artists, past and present ; paintings for coloured plates by Martin Pettinger. — Hindhead : Saiga, c1980. — xi,180p,12p of plates : ill(some col.) ; 25cm
ISBN 0-904558-58-4 : £7.50 B81-04781

599.09428′21 — South Yorkshire *(Metropolitan County).* **Sheffield region. Mammals. Distribution**
Clinging, Valerie. Mammals of the Sheffield area / by Valerie Clinging and Derek Whiteley ; illustrations by: Steven Garland, Jeremy Lee, Derek Whiteley. — Sheffield : Sorby Natural History Society, [1980]. — 48p : ill,maps ; 21cm. — (Sorby record special series ; no.3)
Bibliography: p44-47. - Includes index
Unpriced (pbk) B81-07263

599.0953′6 — Persian Gulf countries. Mammals — *Field guides*
Harrison, David L. (David Lakin). Mammals of the Arabian Gulf / David L. Harrison. — London : Allen & Unwin, 1981. — 92p,12p of plates : ill(some col.),1map ; 21cm. — (The Natural history of the Arabian Gulf)
Map on lining papers. — Bibliography: p87. — Includes index
ISBN 0-04-599007-7 : Unpriced B81-29956

599.096 — Africa. Mammals — *Field guides*
Haltenorth, Theodor. A field guide to the mammals of Africa : including Madagascar / Theodor Haltenorth, Helmut Diller ; translated by Robert W. Hayman. — London : Collins, c1980. — 400p : col.ill,maps ; 20cm
Translation of: Säugetiere Afrikas und Madagaskars. — Bibliography: p391-392. — Includes index
ISBN 0-00-219778-2 : £8.95 B81-04084

599.096 — Africa. Mammals — *Illustrations*
Amuchástegui, Axel. Some birds and mammals of Africa / by Axel Amuchástegui ; with a descriptive text by Hilary Hook. — London : Tryon Gallery, c1979. — [41]p,xivleaves of plates : col.ill ; 54cm
Limited ed. of 505 copies, of which 500 are numbered 1-500 and bound in quarter leather, and five are lettered A-E and bound in full vellum
Unpriced
Primary classification 598.296′022′2 B81-36406

599′.09676 — East Africa. Mammals
Kingdom, Jonathan. East African mammals. — London : Academic Press
Vol.3. — Dec.1981
Part C: (Bovids). — [400]p
ISBN 0-12-408344-7 : CIP entry B81-39219

Kingdom, Jonathan. East African mammals. — London : Academic Press
Vol.3. — Dec.1981
Part D: (Bovids). — [400]p
ISBN 0-12-408345-5 : CIP entry B81-39220

599.097 — North America. Mammals
Hall, E. Raymond. The mammals of North America. — 2nd ed. / E. Raymond Hall. — New York ; Chichester : Wiley, 1981. — 2v.(1181,90p) : ill,maps ; 29cm
Previous ed.: New York : Ronald Press, 1959. — Bibliography: p1138-1175. — Includes index
ISBN 0-471-05595-6 : £50.00
ISBN 0-471-05443-7 (v.1) : £28.50
ISBN 0-471-05444-5 (v.2) : £28.50 B81-24881

599.09778 — Missouri. Mammals
Schwartz, Charles W.. The mammals of Missouri / Charles W. Schwartz and Elizabeth R. Schwartz. — Rev. ed. — Columbia, Mo. ; London : University of Missouri Press and Missouri Department of Conservation, 1981. — viii,356p : ill,maps ; 29cm
Previous ed.: 1959-. — Includes bibliographies and index
ISBN 0-8262-0324-8 : £16.90 B81-29589

599.2 — Kangaroos — *Illustrations — For children*
García Sánchez, J. L.. Funny facts about the kangaroo / pictures by Nella Bosnia ; idea by J.L. García Sánchez and M.A. Pacheco ; translated by Richard Whitecross. — London : Evans, 1981. — [22]p : chiefly.ill ; 23cm. — (Funny facts series)
Translation of: El canguro. — Ill on lining paper
ISBN 0-237-45566-8 : £2.95 B81-12470

599.2 — Koalas — *For children*
Gray, Patricia. Hello koala / written by Patricia Gray ; illustrated by Martina Selway. — London : Longman, 1981. — 18p : col.ill ; 18cm
ISBN 0-582-39079-6 : £1.75 B81-29352

599.32′2 — Rabbits & hares — *For children*
Clarke, Anne. Rabbit / Anne Clarke ; illustrated by John Thompson-Steinkrauss. — London : Heinemann in association with the British Museum (National History), London, 1981. — 32p : col.ill ; 25cm. — (British Museum (Natural History)picture books)
Bibliography: p32. — Includes index
ISBN 0-434-93275-2 : £4.95 B81-32356

599.32′3′0994 — Australia. Rodents
Watts, C. H. S.. The rodents of Australia / C.H.S. Watts & H.J. Aslin. — London : Angus & Robertson, 1981. — xi,321p,16p of plates : ill(some col.),maps ; 25cm
Map on lining papers. — Bibliography: p289-305. - Includes index
ISBN 0-207-14235-1 : £10.00 B81-17738

599.32′32 — Beavers — *For children*
Lane, Margaret, *1907-*. The beaver. — London : Methuen/Walker, Oct.1981. — [32]p. — (Animal lives ; 3)
ISBN 0-416-05800-0 : £3.50 : CIP entry B81-30455

599.32′32 — Beavers — *For children — Welsh texts*
Hope, Ffransis. Yr afanc / [gan Ffransis Hope] ; [addaswyd o Holandeg Francis Brewer ; lluniau gan Kees de Kiefte]. — Caerdydd : Gwasg y Dref Wen, c1980. — 16p : col.ill,1map ; 22cm. — (Cyfres y seren)
Text, map on inside covers
£0.80 (pbk) B81-07500

599.32′32 — Squirrels — *For children*
Lane, Margaret, *1907-*. The squirrel. — London : Methuen, Sept.1981. — [32]p
ISBN 0-416-05820-5 : £3.50 : CIP entry B81-25865

599.32′33 — Hamsters — *For children*
Laurey, Harriet. The life of a hamster. — London : Hutchinson, Sept.1981. — [32]p. — (Animal lives)
ISBN 0-09-145430-1 : £2.95 : CIP entry B81-25667

599.32′33 — Hamsters. Immune reactions — *Conference proceedings*
Hamster immune responses in infectious and oncologic diseases / edited by J. Wayne Streilein ... [et al.] ; [proceedings of a conference ... held June 3-5, 1980, in Dallas, Texas]. — New York ; London : Plenum, 1981. — xii,474p : ill ; 26cm. — (Advances in experimental medicine and biology ; v.134)
Includes index
ISBN 0-306-40642-x : Unpriced B81-23408

599.32′33 — Harvest mice. Life cycle — *Illustrations — For children*
The Harvest mouse. — London : Deutsch, Oct.1981. — [36]p
ISBN 0-233-97378-8 : £2.50 : CIP entry B81-26745

599.32′33 — House mice — *Conference proceedings*
Biology of the house mouse : (the proceedings of a symposium held at the Zoological Society of London on 22 and 23 November 1979) / edited by R.J. Berry. — London : Published for the Society by Academic Press, 1981. — xxx,715p : ill,maps ; 24cm. — (Symposia of the Zoological Society of London, ISSN 0084-5612 ; no.47)
Includes bibliographies and index
ISBN 0-12-613347-6 : £36.80 : CIP rev. B81-06032

599.3′3041825 — Insectivores. Ears. Development
MacPhee, R. D. E.. Auditory regions of primates and eutherian insectivores : morphology, ontogeny, and character analysis / R.D.E. MacPhee. — Basel ; London : Karger, c1981. — xv,282p : ill ; 23cm. — (Contributions to primatology ; v.18)
Bibliography: p270-282
ISBN 3-8055-1963-x (pbk) : £16.50
Primary classification 599.8′041825 B81-26352

599.5 — Marine mammals
Handbook of marine mammals / edited by Sam H. Ridgway and Richard J. Harrison. — London : Academic Press
Vol.1: The walrus, sea lions, fur seals and sea otter. — 1981. — 235p : ill,maps ; 24cm
Includes bibliographies and index
ISBN 0-12-588501-6 : £14.60 B81-38918

599.5 — Whales
Bonner, W. Nigel. Whales / W. Nigel Bonner. — Poole : Blandford, 1980. — x,278p,[8]p of plates : ill(some col.) ; 23cm. — (Blandford mammal series)
Bibliography: p263-270. - Includes index
ISBN 0-7137-0887-5 : £10.95 : CIP rev. B80-19232

Watson, Lyall. Sea guide to whales of the world. — London : Hutchinson, Oct.1981. — [304]p
ISBN 0-09-146600-8 : £12.50 : CIP entry B81-24611

599.5 — Whales — *For children*
Simon, Noel. Whalers. — London : Dent, Oct.1981. — [48]p. — (Animal families)
ISBN 0-460-06957-8 : £2.25 : CIP entry B81-28057

599.5 — Whales. Population. Assessment
Allen, K. Radway. Conservation and management of whales / K. Radway Allen. — Seattle : Washington Sea Grant ; London : Butterworths, 1980. — ix,107p : ill ; 24cm
Bibliography: p101-103. - Includes index
ISBN 0-408-10725-1 : £10.00
Primary classification 639.9′795 B81-03738

599.5′0451 — Cetacea. Behaviour
Cetacean behavior : mechanisms and functions / edited by Louis M. Herman. — New York ; Chichester : Wiley, c1980. — xiii,463p : ill,maps ; 24cm
Includes bibliographies and index
ISBN 0-471-37315-x : Unpriced B81-08447

599.5′1 — Newfoundland. Burgeo. Coastal waters. Fin whales — *Personal observations*
Mowat, Farley. A whale for the killing / Farley Mowat. — London : Pan in association with Heinemann, 1979, c1972. — 191p : 3maps ; 19cm
Originally published: Boston, Mass. : Little, Brown, 1972 ; London : Heinemann, 1973
ISBN 0-330-25889-3 (pbk) : £1.00 B81-01589

599.5′3 — British Columbia. Killer whales
Jeune, Paul. Killer whale : the saga of Miracle / by Paul Jeune. — Toronto : McClelland and Stewart ; Edinburgh : Macdonald [distributor], c1979. — 190p : ill ; 22cm
ISBN 0-7710-4416-x : £5.95 B81-37719

599.5′3 — Dolphins
Alpers, Anthony. Dolphins / Antony Alpers. — 2nd ed. — Milton Keynes : Robin Clark, 1979, c1963. — 247p,[43]p of plates ; 18cm
Originally published: London : John Murray, 1963. — Includes index
ISBN 0-86072-024-1 (pbk) : £1.75 B81-3796

599.5′304372 — Toothed whales. Age. Determination — *Conference proceedings*
International Conference on Determining Age of Odontocete Cetaceans and Sirenians *(1978 : La Jolla).* Age determination of toothed whales and sirenians / [proceedings of the International Conference on Determining Age of Odontocete Cetaceans and Sirenians, La Jolla, California, September 5-19, 1978] ; [edited by W.F. Perrin and A.C. Myrick, Jr.]. — Cambridge ([Red House, Station Rd., Histon, Cambridge CB4 4NP]) : International Whaling Commission, 1980. — viii,229p : ill ; 31cm. — (Reports / International Whaling Commission ; special issue 3)
Includes bibliographies and index
Unpriced
Also classified at 599.5′504372 B81-2917

599.5′504372 — Sirenia. Age. Determination — *Conference proceedings*

International Conference on Determining Age of Odontocete Cetaceans and Sirenians *(1978 : La Jolla)*. Age determination of toothed whales and sirenians / [proceedings of the International Conference on Determining Age of Odontocete Cetaceans and Sirenians, La Jolla, California, September 5-19, 1978] ; [edited by W.F. Perrin and A.C. Myrick, Jr.]. — Cambridge ([Red House, Station Rd., Histon, Cambridge CB4 4NP]) : International Whaling Commission, 1980. — viii,229p : ill ; 31cm. — (Reports / International Whaling Commission ; special issue 3)
Includes bibliographies and index
Unpriced
Primary classification 599.5′304372 B81-29171

599.6′1 — Elephants

Freeman, Dan. Elephants : the vanishing giants / Dan Freeman. — London : Hamlyn, 1980. — 192p : ill(some col.),col.maps,ports ; 32cm. — (A Bison book)
Bibliography: p190. - Includes index
ISBN 0-600-33190-3 : £6.95 B81-03327

599.6′1 — Elephants — *For children*

Coleman, Jill. The elephant / story by Jill Coleman ; pictures by Michael Atkinson. — London : Angus & Robertson, c1979. — [21]p : col.ill ; 23cm. — (Wildlife library)
Text on lining paper
ISBN 0-207-95845-9 : Unpriced B81-33672

Gray, Patricia. Hello elephant / written by Patricia Gray ; illustrated by Martina Selway. — London : Longman, 1981. — 18p : col.ill ; 18cm
ISBN 0-582-39078-8 : £1.75 B81-29355

599.6′1 — Elephants — *For children — Welsh texts*

Hope, Ffransis. Yr eliffant / [gan Ffransis Hope] ; [addaswyd o Holandeg Francis Brewer ; lluniau gan C. Teeuwisse]. — Caerdydd : Gwasg y Dref Wen, c1980. — 16p : col.ill,1map ; 22cm. — (Cyfres y seren)
Text, map on inside covers
£0.80 (pbk) B81-07499

599.6′1 — Kenya. Wildlife reserves: National parks: Tsavo National Park. African elephants — *Personal observations*

Sheldrick, Daphne. An elephant called Eleanor / Daphne Sheldrick. — London : Dent, 1980. — 128p : ill,ports ; 25cm
ISBN 0-460-06900-4 : £5.95 : CIP rev. B80-03651

599.72′5 — Zebras — *For children*

The **Zebra** / translated by Dominique Vouillemin ; illustrated by Tony Graham. — London : Macdonald Educational, 1981. — 19p : col.ill,1col.map ; 24cm. — (Animal world)
Translation from the French. — Map on lining paper
ISBN 0-356-07160-x : Unpriced B81-37476

599.72′8 — Rhinoceroses — *For children*

Simon, Noel. Rhinos. — London : Dent, Oct.1981. — [32]p. — (Animal families)
ISBN 0-460-06065-1 : £3.50 : CIP entry B81-30452

599.73′57 — Deer — *For children*

Townsend, Anita. The deer / story by Anita Townsend ; pictures by Bernard Robinson. — London : Angus & Robertson, c1979. — [22]p : col.ill ; 23cm. — (Wildlife library)
ISBN 0-207-95846-7 : Unpriced B81-38444

599.73′57 — Giraffes — *For children*

Simon, Noel. Giraffes. — London : Dent, Oct.1981. — [32]p. — (Animal families)
ISBN 0-460-06066-x : £3.50 : CIP entry B81-30453

599.73′57 — North America. Mule deer & black-tailed deer. Ecology

Mule and black-tailed deer of North America / compiled and edited by Olof C. Wallmo ; illustrated by Dean Rocky Barrick. — Lincoln [Neb.] ; London : University of Nebraska Press, c1981. — xvii,605p : ill,maps ; 021. — (A Wildlife Management Institute book)
Bibliography: p556-598. — Includes index
ISBN 0-8032-4715-x : £19.45 B81-34455

599.73′57 — Reindeer — *For children*

Clarkson, Ewan. Reindeer. — Hove : Wayland, 1981. — 61p : col.ill ; 24cm. — (Animals of the world)
Ill on lining papers. — Includes index
ISBN 0-85340-803-3 : £3.50 B81-07555

599.73′58 — Buffaloes — *For children*

Stonehouse, Bernard. Buffaloes / Bernard Stonehouse. — Hove : Wayland, 1981. — 61p : col.ill ; 24cm. — (Animals of the world)
Ill on lining papers. — Includes index
ISBN 0-85340-801-7 : £3.50 B81-07556

599.73′6 — Camels

Gauthier-Pilters, Hilde. The camel : its evolution, ecology, behavior and relationship to man / Hilde Gauthier-Pilters and Anne Innis Dagg ; photographs by Hilde Gauthier-Pilters. — Chicago ; London : University of Chicago Press, 1981. — xii,208p : ill,maps ; 24cm
Bibliography: p173-200. — Includes index
ISBN 0-226-28453-0 : £15.60 B81-38134

599.74′427 — Hyenas — *For children*

Whitlock, Ralph. Hyenas & jackals / Ralph Whitlock. — Hove : Wayland, 1981. — 60p : col.ill ; 24cm. — (Animals of the world)
Ill on lining papers. — Includes index
ISBN 0-85340-847-5 : £3.50
Also classified at 599.74′442 B81-40622

599.74′428 — Leopards — *For children*

Kilpatrick, Cathy. Leopards / Cathy Kilpatrick. — Hove : Wayland, 1981. — 61p : col.ill ; 24cm. — (Animals of the world)
Ill on lining papers. — Includes index
ISBN 0-85340-800-9 : £3.50 B81-07553

599.74′428 — North-eastern India. Wildlife reserves: Tiger Haven Reserve. Tigers - *Personal observations*

Singh, Arjan. Tara the tigress. — London : Quartet, July 1981. — 1v.
ISBN 0-7043-2282-x : £9.95 : CIP entry B81-16869

599.74′428 — Northern Kenya. Leopards — *Personal observations*

Adamson, Joy. Queen of Shaba : the story of an African leopard / Joy Adamson. — [London] : Fontana, 1981, c1980. — 253p,[8]p of plates : ill,ports ; 18cm
Originally published: London : Collins ; Harvill Press, 1980
ISBN 0-00-636311-3 (pbk) : £1.75 B81-28410

599.74′428 — South Africa. Transvaal. Wildlife reserves: Timbavati Nature Reserve. White lions — *Personal observations*

McBride, Chris. Operation white lion / Chris McBride. — London : Collins, 1981. — 159p,[32]p of plates : col.ill,2maps,col.ports ; 26cm
ISBN 0-00-262611-x : £8.50 B81-31769

599.74′428 — Tigers

Courtney, Nicholas. The tiger : symbol of freedom / Nicholas Courtney. — London : Quartet, 1980. — 110p,[32]p of plates : ill(some col.),maps,coats of arms,ports ; 29cm
Bibliography: p105-110
ISBN 0-7043-2245-5 : £9.95 B81-14017

Mountfort, Guy. Saving the tiger / Guy Mountfort ; with a foreword by Sir Peter Scott. — London : Joseph, c1981. — 119p : ill(some col.),1facsim,ports(some col.) ; 28cm
Bibliography: p118. - Includes index
ISBN 0-7181-1991-6 : £7.95 B81-10222

599.74′428 — Tigers — *For children*

Gray, Patricia. Hello tiger / written by Patricia Gray ; illustrated by Martina Selway. — London : Longman, 1981. — 18p : col.ill ; 18cm
ISBN 0-582-39076-1 : £1.75 B81-29353

The **Tiger** / translated by Nicole Lagneau ; illustrated by Tony Graham. — London : Macdonald Educational, 1981. — 20p : col.ill,1col.map ; 24cm. — (Animal world)
Translation from the French. — Map on lining papers
ISBN 0-356-07161-8 : Unpriced B81-37475

599.74′428′05 — Felidae — *Serials*

[Wild cat *(Welwyn)***]**. Wild cat : the journal of the Cat Survival Trust. — Vol.1, no.1 (Oct.1977)-. — Welwyn (Marlind Centre, Codicote Rd, Welwyn, Hertfordshire AL6 9TU) : [The Trust], 1977-. — v. : ill ; 21cm
Two issues yearly. — Description based on: Vol.2, no.1 (May 1980)
ISSN 0260-7492 = Wild cat (Welwyn) : Free to Trust members B81-17474

599.74′442 — Jackals — *For children*

Whitlock, Ralph. Hyenas & jackals / Ralph Whitlock. — Hove : Wayland, 1981. — 60p : col.ill ; 24cm. — (Animals of the world)
Ill on lining papers. — Includes index
ISBN 0-85340-847-5 : £3.50
Primary classification 599.74′427 B81-40622

599.74′442 — Wolves. Behaviour & ecology — *Personal observations*

Zimen, Erik. The wolf : his place in the natural world / Erik Zimen ; translated from the German by Eric Mosbacher. — London : Souvenir, 1981. — vi,373p,[16]p of plates : ill (some col.) ; 24cm
Translation of: Der Wolf. — Bibliography: p361-368. — Includes index
ISBN 0-285-62411-3 : £9.95 B81-21742

599.74′442 — Wolves — *For children*

Simon, Noel. Wolves. — London : Dent, Oct.1981. — [48]p. — (Animal families)
ISBN 0-460-06975-6 : £2.50 : CIP entry B81-30451

Townsend, Anita. The wolf / story by Anita Townsend pictures by Michael Atkinson. — London : Angus and Robertson, 1979. — [21]p : col.ill ; 23cm. — (Wildlife library)
ISBN 0-207-95843-2 : Unpriced B81-35581

599.74′443 — Giant pandas

Morris, Ramona. The giant panda / Ramona and Desmond Morris. — Rev. ed / revised by Jonathan Barzdo. — London : Macmillan, 1981. — 192p : ill,ports ; 20cm. — (Papermac)
Previous ed.: published as Men and pandas. London : Hutchinson, 1966. — Bibliography: p183-189. — Includes index
ISBN 0-333-32473-0 (pbk) : £2.50 B81-38637

Morris, Ramona. The giant panda. — Revised ed. — London : Kegan Page, Aug.1981. — [192]p
Previous ed. published as: Men and pandas. London : Hutchinson, 1966
ISBN 0-85038-489-3 : £7.95 : CIP entry B81-20462

599.74′443 — Giant pandas — *For children*

Gray, Patricia. Hello panda / written by Patricia Gray ; illustrated by Martina Selway. — London : Longman, 1981. — 18p : col.ill ; 18cm
ISBN 0-582-39077-x : £1.75 B81-29354

Wang, Zhongyi. Giant pandas / Wang Zhongyi. — Hove : Wayland, 1981. — 60p : col.ill ; 24cm. — (Animals of the world)
Ill on lining papers. — Includes index
ISBN 0-85340-848-3 : £3.50 B81-40620

599.74′443 — Giant pandas — *Illustrations*

Belson, Jenny. The giant panda book. — London : Collins, Dec.1981. — [80]p
ISBN 0-00-216392-6 (pbk) : £3.95 : CIP entry B81-36991

599.74′443 — Giant pandas — *Illustrations*
continuation

Da Xiong Mao = The giant panda / editors Zhu Jing and Li Yangwen. — Beijing : Science Press ; New York ; London : distributed by Van Nostrand Reinhold, 1981, c1980. — 171p : chiefly ill(some col.),col.maps ; 29cm
ISBN 0-442-20064-1 : Unpriced B81-37472

599.74′443 — Pandas - *For children*

Finding out about pandas. — Poole : Blandford Press, Apr.1981. — [32]p. — (Japanese nature series)
ISBN 0-7137-1150-7 : £2.95 : CIP entry
B81-04325

599.74′446 — Bears — *For children*

Sheehan, Angela. The bear / story by Angela Sheehan ; pictures by Michael Atkinson. — London : Angus & Robertson, c1979. — [22]p : col.ill ; 23cm. — (Wildlife library)
ISBN 0-207-95844-0 : Unpriced B81-38445

599.74′446 — Peninsular Malaysia. Malayan bears — *Personal observations* — *Polish texts*

Lasocki, Wiesław A.. Ali Baba : malajski nied'zwied'z / W.A. Lasocki, M.W. Dąbrowska ; układ graficzny ilustracje i okładka Irena Ludwig. — [Poland] : Gryf ; [London] ([364 Uxbridge Rd., W3 9SL]) : [W.A. Lasocki], [c1979]. — 140p : ill ; 24cm
Unpriced (pbk) B81-14725

599.74′447 — Great Britain. Otters

Laidler, Liz. Otters in Britain. — Newton Abbot : David & Charles, Feb.1982. — [168]p. — (British mammals ; 2)
ISBN 0-7153-8069-9 : £6.95 : CIP entry
B81-36395

599.74′447 — Great Britain. Otters. Distribution, *1977-1979*

Lenton, E. J.. Otter survey of England 1977-79 / E.J. Lenton, P.R.F. Chain, D.J. Jefferies. — Shrewsbury : Interpretative Branch, Nature Conservancy Council, [1981?]. — 75p : maps,1form ; 30cm
Bibliography: p69-70
ISBN 0-86139-111-x (spiral) : Unpriced
B81-38706

599.74′447 — Great Britain. Pine martens — *Personal observations*

Hurrell, H. G.. Fling : the pine marten / H.G. Hurrell ; illustrations by Mike Frost in collaboration with the author. — Plymouth (203 Elburton Rd., Plymstock, Plymouth, Devon) : Westway, 1981. — 55p : ill,maps ; 21cm
Bibliography: p55
ISBN 0-901474-07-x (pbk) : £1.50 B81-34996

599.74′447 — Hertfordshire. Harpenden. Animals in danger of extinction. Breeding. Organisations: Wildlife Breeding Centre. Otters — *For children*

Goldsmith, John, *1947-*. Tarkina the otter / John Goldsmith ; illustrations by Ken Turner. — London : Pelham, 1981. — 44p : ill(some col.) ; 24cm. — (Graham Dangerfield's animals)
ISBN 0-7207-1292-0 : £4.95 B81-15231

599.74′447 — Otters — *For children*

Sheehan, Angela. The otter / by Angela Sheehan ; illustrated by Bernard Robinson. — London : Angus & Robertson, c1979. — [28]p : col.ill ; 23cm. — (Eye-view library)
ISBN 0-207-95833-5 : £2.95 B81-37938

Simon, Noel. Otters. — London : Dent, Oct.1981. — [48]p. — (Animal families)
ISBN 0-460-06974-8 : £2.25 : CIP entry
B81-30454

599.74′447 — Otters — *Stories, anecdotes*

Williamson, Henry. Tarka the otter : his joyful water-life and death in the country of the two rivers / Henry Williamson ; illustrated by C.F. Tunnicliffe. — Basingstoke : Macmillan Education, 1981. — 240p : ill,1map ; 21cm. — (M books)
For adolescents
ISBN 0-333-30602-3 : £1.50 B81-21818

Williamson, Henry. Tarka the otter : his joyful water-life and death in the country of the two rivers / Henry Williamson ; with an introduction by Richard Williamson. — Large print ed. — Leicester : Ulverscroft, 1981. — 380p ; 23cm. — (Ulverscroft large print series)
Originally published: London : Putnam, 1927
ISBN 0-7089-0545-5 : £5.00 B81-12612

599.74′447 — Weasels — *Stories, anecdotes*

Biggins, Dorothy. The savage whisper / by Dorothy Biggins. — Wilmslow (Animals' Convalescent Home, Newgate, Wilmslow, Cheshire, SK9 5LN) : Humane Education Society, [1981]. — 8p : ill ; 22cm
Unpriced (pbk) B81-16509

599.74′5 — Mammals: Seals — *For children*

Cloudsley-Thompson, J. L.. Seals and sea lions / John Cloudsley-Thompson. — Hove : Wayland, 1981. — 60p : col.ill ; 24cm. — (Animals of the world)
Col. ill on lining papers. — Includes index
ISBN 0-85340-832-7 : £3.50 B81-22047

599.8 — Primates — *Festschriften*

Perspectives in primate biology : (the proceedings of a symposium held at the Zoological Society of London on 31 May and 1 June 1979) / edited by E.H. Ashton and R.L. Holmes. — London : Pubished for the Society by Academic Press, 1981. — xvii,424p,[1]leaf of plates : ill(some col.),ports ; 24cm. — (Symposia of the Zoological Society of London, ISSN 0084-5612 ; no.46)
"... held to mark the 75th birthday of Professor Lord Zuckerman ..." - Half t.p. verso. — Includes bibliographies and index
ISBN 0-12-613346-8 : £28.40 : CIP rev.
B81-12333

599.8′041825 — Primates. Ears. Development

MacPhee, R. D. E.. Auditory regions of primates and eutherian insectivores : morphology, ontogeny, and character analysis / R.D.E. MacPhee. — Basel ; London : Karger, c1981. — xv,282p : ill ; 23cm. — (Contributions to primatology ; v.18)
Bibliography: p270-282
ISBN 3-8055-1963-x (pbk) : £16.50
Also classified at 599.3′3041825 B81-26352

599.8′0436 — Primates. Sex differences

Mitchell, G. (Gary). Human sex differences : a primatologist's perspective / G. Mitchell. — New York ; London : Van Nostrand Reinhold, c1981. — ix,220p ; 24cm
Includes bibliographies and index
ISBN 0-442-23865-7 : £14.20 B81-29558

599.8′0451 — Primates. Social behaviour

Zuckerman, Solly Zuckerman, *Baron*. The social life of monkey and apes / S. Zuckerman. — 2nd ed. — London : Routledge & Kegan Paul, 1981. — xx,511p,[24]p of plates : ill ; 23cm
Previous ed.: London : Kegan Paul & Co., 1932. — Bibliography: p317-340. — Includes index
ISBN 0-7100-0691-8 : £17.50 : CIP rev.
B80-27043

599.8′0451′095951 — Peninsular Malaysia. Tropical rain forests. Primates. Behaviour

Malayan forest primates : ten years' study in tropical rain forest / edited by David J. Chivers. — New York ; London : Plenum, c1980. — xxiv,364p : ill,maps ; 26cm
Bibliography: p339-356. - Includes index
ISBN 0-306-40626-8 : Unpriced B81-05666

599.8′074′02134 — London. Kensington and Chelsea *(London Borough).* **Museums: British Museum (Natural History). Stock: Primates. Type-specimens** — *Catalogues*

British Museum (Natural History). Catalogue of primates in the British Museum (Natural History) and elsewhere in the British Isles / [compiled by] Prudence Hero Napier. — London : British Museum (Natural History)
Part 2: Family Cercopithecidae, subfamily Cercopithecinae. — 1981. — x,203p ; 30cm
Bibliography: p186-199. - Includes index
ISBN 0-565-00815-3 (pbk) : Unpriced
B81-11329

599.8′1 — Environment. Adaptation of hips & thighs of lorises

McArdle, John E.. Functional morphology of the hip and thigh of the lorisiformes / John E. McArdle. — Basel ; London : Karger, 1981. — 132p : ill ; 23cm. — (Contributions to primatology ; v.17)
Bibliography: p126-132
ISBN 3-8055-1767-x (pbk) : Unpriced
B81-11538

599.8′1 — Madagascar. Nocturnal lemurs

Nocturnal Malagasy primates : ecology, physiology and behavior / P. Charles-Dominique ... [et al.]. — New York ; London : Academic Press, 1980. — xii,215p : ill,maps ; 24cm. — (Communication and behavior)
Includes bibliographies and index
ISBN 0-12-169350-3 : £15.40 B81-04532

599.8′2 — Cornwall. Seaton. Woolly monkeys — *Personal observations*

Williams, Leonard. Samba / Leonard Williams. — Rev. ed. — London : Allison & Busby, 1980. — 127p,[16]p of plates : ill,plan,ports ; 23cm
Previous ed.: published as Samba & the monkey mind. London : Bodley Head, 1965
ISBN 0-85031-339-2 (cased) : £6.95 : CIP rev.
ISDN 0 85031-340-6 (pbk) : £2.95 B80-09232

599.8′2 — Kenya. Lake Naivasha region. Colobus monkeys — *Personal observations*

Adamson, Joy. Friends from the forest / Joy Adamson ; foreword by Juliette Huxley ; drawing by Norman Arlott. — London : Collins, 1981. — 86p : ill ; 22cm
ISBN 0-00-262458-3 : £4.95
Also classified at 598′.97 B81-13621

599.8′2 — New world monkeys. Evolution. Theories. Implications of continental drift — *Conference proceedings*

Evolutionary biology of the New World monkeys and continental drift / [expanded proceedings of a Symposium at the Seventh Congress of the International Primatological Society, held at Bangalore, India 1979] ; edited by Russell L. Ciochon and A. Brunetto Chiarelli. — New York ; London : Plenum, c1980. — xvi,528p : ill,maps ; 26cm. — (Advances in primatology)
Includes bibliographies and index
ISBN 0-306-40487-7 : Unpriced B81-17954

599.8′2 — Panama. Barro Colorado Island. Mantled howler monkeys. Foraging behaviour

Milton, Katharine. The foraging strategy of howler monkeys : a study in primate economics / Katharine Milton. — New York ; Guildford : Columbia University Press, 1980. — xiv,165p : ill,maps ; 24cm
Bibliography: p151-159. - Includes index
ISBN 0-231-04850-5 : £11.10 B81-04843

599.88′2′09598 — Indonesia. Siberut. Beelow gibbons. Social behaviour — *Personal observations*

Whitten, Anthony. The gibbons of Siberut. — London : Dent, Feb.1982. — [224]p
ISBN 0-460-04476-1 : £8.95 : CIP entry
B81-36199

599.88′40416 — Great apes. Reproduction

Reproductive biology of the great apes : comparative and biomedical perspectives / edited by Charles E. Graham. — New York ; London : Academic Press, c1981. — xviii,437p : ill ; 24cm
Includes bibliographies and index
ISBN 0-12-295020-8 : £32.20 B81-39581

599.88′46 — Gorillas

Dixson, A. F.. The natural history of the gorilla / A.F. Dixson ; with a foreword by R.D. Martin. — London : Weidenfeld and Nicolson, 1981. — xviii,202p,[16]p of plates : ill,maps ; 25cm. — (The World naturalist)
Bibliography: p180-198. — Includes index
ISBN 0-297-77895-1 : £16.50 B81-09591

599.88′46 — Gorillas — *For children*

Wootton, Anthony, *1935-*. Gorillas / Anthony Wootton. — Hove : Wayland, 1981. — 61p : col.ill ; 24cm. — (Animals of the world)
Col. ill on lining papers. — Includes index
ISBN 0-85340-831-9 : £3.50 B81-22044

599.9 — Man. Biology

Practical human biology. — London : Academic Press, July 1981. — [380]p
ISBN 0-12-741960-8 : CIP entry B81-13484

599.9 — Man. Biology — *For schools*

Robson, M. D.. Human biology today. — Basingstoke : Macmillan Education, Feb.1982. — [176]p
ISBN 0-333-27879-8 (pbk) : £2.95 : CIP entry B81-35798

600 — TECHNOLOGY

600 — Appropriate technology

Reddy, Amulya K. N.. Technology, development and the environment : a re-appraisal / Amulya Kumar N. Reddy. — Nairobi : United Nations Environment Programme ; Oxford : Pergamon, 1979. — vii,52p : ill ; 21cm. — (Elements ; 1)
ISBN 0-08-025693-7 (corrected : pbk) : £2.25 B81-20048

600 — Technology

Living with technology : a foundation course. — Milton Keynes : Open University Press. — (T101 ; block 1H)
At head of title: The Open University
Block 1[H]: Heat / prepared by the Course Team. — 27p : ill(some col.) ; 30cm
ISBN 0-335-08955-0 (pbk) : Unpriced (available 1982)
Primary classification 500 B81-10904

Living with technology : a foundation course. — Milton Keynes : Open University Press. — (T101 ; block 1)
At head of title: The Open University
Block 1: Home / prepared by the Course Team. — 96p : ill(some col.),plans(some col.) ; 30cm
ISBN 0-335-08952-6 (pbk) : Unpriced (available 1982)
Primary classification 500 B81-10903

Living with technology : a foundation course. — Milton Keynes : Open University Press. — (T101 ; block 1N)
At head of title: The Open University
Block 1[N]: Numeracy / prepared by the Course Team. — 1979. — 68p : ill(some col.) ; 30cm
ISBN 0-335-08953-4 (pbk) : Unpriced (available 1982)
Primary classification 500 B81-10905

Living with technology : a foundation course. — Milton Keynes : Open University Press. — (T101 ; block 1SC)
At head of title: The Open University
Block 1[SC]: Space and comfort / prepared by the Course Team. — 1979. — 32p : ill(some col.),plans(some col.) ; 30cm
ISBN 0-335-08954-2 (pbk) : Unpriced (available 1982)
Primary classification 500 B81-10906

Living with technology : a foundation course. — Milton Keynes : Open University Press
At head of title: The Open University
Block 1[SM]: Structures and materials / prepared by the Course Team. — 1979. — 32p : ill(some col.) ; 30cm. — (T101 ; block 1SM)
ISBN 0-335-08956-9 (pbk) : Unpriced (available 1982)
Primary classification 500 B81-10907

Living with technology : a foundation course. — Milton Keynes : Open University Press
At head of title: The Open University
Block 2: Communication / prepared by the Course Team. — 1980. — 102p : ill(some col.) ; 30cm. — (T101 ; block 2)
ISBN 0-335-08957-7 (pbk) : Unpriced (available 1982)
Primary classification 500 B81-10908

Living with technology : a foundation course. — Milton Keynes : Open University Press
At head of title: The Open University
Block 2[E]: Electricity / prepared by the Course Team. — 1980. — 32p : ill(some col.) ; 30cm. — (T101 ; block 2E)
ISBN 0-335-08959-3 (pbk) : Unpriced (available 1982)
Primary classification 500 B81-10910

Living with technology : a foundation course. — Milton Keynes : Open University Press
At head of title: The Open University
Block 2[F]: Feedback / prepared by the Course Team. — 1980. — 25p : col.ill ; 30cm. — (T101 ; block 2F)
ISBN 0-335-08961-5 (pbk) : Unpriced (available 1982)
Primary classification 500 B81-10911

Living with technology : a foundation course. — Milton Keynes : Open University Press
At head of title: The Open University
Block 2[N]: Numeracy / prepared by the Course Team. — 1980. — 45p : ill(some col.) ; 30cm. — (T101 ; block 2N)
ISBN 0-335-08958-5 (pbk) : Unpriced (available 1982)
Primary classification 500 B81-10913

Living with technology : a foundation course. — Milton Keynes : Open University Press
At head of title: The Open University
Block 2[S]: Signals / prepared by the Course Team. — 1980. — 30p : ill(some col.) ; 30cm. — (T101 ; block 2S)
ISBN 0-335-08960-7 (pbk) : Unpriced (available 1982)
Primary classification 500 B81-10912

Living with technology : a foundation course. — Milton Keynes : Open University Press
At head of title: The Open University
Block 2[C]: Computers / prepared by the Course Team. — 1980. — 17p : ill(some col.) ; 30cm. — (T101 ; block 2C)
ISBN 0-335-08962-3 (pbk) : Unpriced (available 1982)
Primary classification 500 B81-10909

Living with technology : a foundation course. — Milton Keynes : Open University Press
At head of title: The Open University
Block 3[EC]: Energy conversion / prepared by the Course Team. — 1980. — 60p : ill(some col.) ; 30cm. — (T101 ; block 3EC)
ISBN 0-335-08965-8 (pbk) : Unpriced (available 1982)
Primary classification 500 B81-10914

Living with technology : a foundation course. — Milton Keynes : Open University Press
At head of title: The Open University
Block 4[N]: Numeracy / prepared by the Course Team. — 1980. — 44p : col.ill ; 30cm. — (T101 ; block 4N)
ISBN 0-335-08967-4 (pbk) : Unpriced (available 1982)
Primary classification 500 B81-10918

Living with technology : a foundation course. — Milton Keynes : Open University Press
At head of title: The Open University
Block 4: Resources / prepared by the Course Team. — 1980. — 107p : ill(some col.),2col.maps,1facsim ; 30cm. — (T101 ; block 4)
ISBN 0-335-08966-6 (pbk) : Unpriced (available 1982)
Primary classification 500 B81-10915

Living with technology : a foundation course. — Milton Keynes : Open University Press
At head of title: The Open University
Block 4[C]: Chemistry / prepared by the Course Team. — 1980. — 45p : ill(some col.) ; 30cm. — (T101 ; block 4C)
ISBN 0-335-08968-2 (pbk) : Unpriced (available 1982)
Primary classification 500 B81-10916

Living with technology : a foundation course. — Milton Keynes : Open University Press
At head of title: The Open University
Block 4[M]: Materials / prepared by the Course Team. — 1980. — 30p : ill(some col.) ; 30cm. — (T101 ; block 4M)
ISBN 0-335-08969-0 (pbk) : Unpriced (available 1982)
Primary classification 500 B81-10917

Living with technology : a foundation course. — Milton Keynes : Open University Press
At head of title: The Open University
Block 5[B]: Biology / prepared by the Course Team. — 1980. — 39p : ill(some col.) ; 30cm. — (T101 ; block 5B)
ISBN 0-335-08971-2 (pbk) : Unpriced (available 1982)
Primary classification 500 B81-10920

Living with technology : a foundation course. — Milton Keynes : Open University Press
At head of title: The Open University
Block 5: Food / prepared by the Course Team. — 1980. — 142 : ill(some col.),col.maps,facsims ; 30cm. — (T101 ; block 5)
ISBN 0-335-08970-4 (pbk) : Unpriced (available 1982)
Primary classification 500 B81-10919

Living with technology : a foundation course. — Milton Keynes : Open University Press
At head of title: The Open University
Block 5[C]: Chemistry / prepared by the Course Team. — 1980. — 15p : ill(some col.) ; 30cm. — (T101 ; block 5C)
ISBN 0-335-08972-0 (pbk) : Unpriced (available 1982)
Primary classification 500 B81-10921

Living with technology : a foundation course. — Milton Keynes : Open University Press
At head of title: The Open University
Block 6: Health / prepared by the Course Team. — 1980. — 120p : col.ill ; 30cm. — (T101 ; block 6)
ISBN 0-335-08973-9 (pbk) : Unpriced (available 1982)
Primary classification 500 B81-10922

Living with technology : a foundation course. — Milton Keynes : Open University Press. — (T101 ; block 6N)
At head of title: The Open University
Block 6[N]: Numeracy / prepared by the Course Team. — 48p : col.ill ; 30cm
ISBN 0-335-08974-7 (pbk) : Unpriced (available 1982)
Primary classification 500 B81-10902

Vergara, William C.. Science in everyday life / William C. Vergara. — London : Souvenir, 1980. — viii,306p : ill ; 23cm
Originally published: New York : Harper & Row, 1980. — Includes index
ISBN 0-285-62470-9 : £6.95
Primary classification 500 B81-10901

600 — Technology — *Forecasts*

Goodwin, Peter. Future world / Peter Goodwin. — London : Hamlyn, c1979. — 156p : ill(some col.) ; 33cm
Col. ill on lining papers. — Includes index
ISBN 0-600-39432-8 : £6.50 B81-22048

Panati, Charles. Breakthroughs : astonishing advances in your lifetime in medicine, science and technology / Charles Panati ; illustrations by Stan Fedinick. — London : Pan in association with Macmillan London, 1980. — 351p : ill ; 18cm
Originally published: Boston, Mass. : Houghton Mifflin, 1980. — Includes index
ISBN 0-330-26199-1 (pbk) : £1.95 B81-03477

Panati, Charles. Breakthroughs : astonishing advances in your lifetime in medicine, science and technology / Charles Panati ; illustrations by Stan Fedinick. — London : Macmillan, 1980. — 351p : ill ; 23cm
Originally published: Boston, Mass. : Houghton Mifflin, 1980. — Includes index
ISBN 0-333-28799-1 : £7.95 B81-03480

600 — Technology. Policies of governments

Tisdell, C. A.. Science and technology policy. — London : Chapman and Hall, Oct.1981. — [250]p
ISBN 0-412-23320-7 : £12.00 : CIP entry
Primary classification 500 B81-28835

600 — Workmanship
Pye, David, *1914-*. The art of workmanship / David Pye. — London : Royal College of Art, 1980, c1979. — 10p ; 30cm. — (RCA papers ; no.10)
ISBN 0-902490-48-6 (pbk) : Unpriced B81-04853

601 — Technology. Philosophical perspectives
Rapp, Friedrich. Analytical philosophy of technology / Friedrich Rapp ; translated by Stanley R. Carpenter and Theodor Langenbruch. — Dordrecht ; London : Reidel, c1981. — xiv,199p ; 23cm. — (Boston studies in the philosophy of science ; v.63)
Translation of: Analytische technikphilosophie. — Bibliography: p187-194. — Includes index
ISBN 90-277-1221-2 (cased) : Unpriced
ISBN 90-277-1222-0 (pbk) : Unpriced B81-27725

602.1′06 — Fluid power - *Conference proceedings*
International Symposium on Fluid Power *(6th : 1981 : Cambridge)*. Papers presented at the Sixth International Symposium on Fluid Power. — Cranfield : B.H.R.A. Fluid Engineering, Apr.1981. — 1v.
ISBN 0-906085-53-5 (pbk) : £27.00 : CIP entry B81-04352

603′.21 — Technology — *Encyclopaedias*
Evans technical dictionary. — London : Evans, 1981. — 138p : ill ; 19cm
ISBN 0-237-50561-4 (cased) : Unpriced
ISBN 0-237-50498-7 (pbk) : Unpriced B81-29166

603′.21 — Technology — *Encyclopaedias — For children*
Vincent, Hugh. A basic dictionary of technical terms. — London : Bell and Hyman, June 1981. — [48]p
ISBN 0-7135-1270-9 (pbk) : £1.60 : CIP entry B81-10478

603′.31 — Technology - *German-English dictionaries*
Dorian, A. F.Dictionary of science and technology : German-English. — 2nd rev. ed. — Oxford : Elsevier Scientific, Aug.1981. — [1250]p
ISBN 0-444-41997-7 : CIP entry
Primary classification 503′.31 B81-16866

604.2 — Technical drawings
Collier, P.. Engineering drawing, Second Level. — London : Hutchinson, Sept.1981. — [256]p
ISBN 0-09-146611-3 (pbk) : £6.50 : CIP entry B81-22581

604.2′076 — Engineering. Design. Technical drawings — *Questions & answers*
Mochel, Edward V.. Problems in engineering design graphics / Edward V. Mochel, Leroy S. Fletcher. — Englewood Cliffs ; London : Prentice-Hall, c1981. — [90]leaves : chiefly ill ; 28cm
ISBN 0-13-716274-x (pbk) : £7.45 B81-39910

604.2′4 — Illustrations: Technical drawings. Draftsmanship — *Manuals*
Dezart, Louis. Drawing for publication : a manual for technical illustrators / Louis Dezart. — London : Architectural Press, 1980. — vii,79p : ill,plans ; 26cm
ISBN 0-85139-185-0 (cased) : £8.95
ISBN 0-85139-184-2 (pbk) : £4.95 B81-07332

604.2′4 — Technical drawings. Draftsmanship
Holmes, Clive. Beginner′s guide to technical illustrations. — Sevenoaks : Newnes, Jan.1982. — [160]p
ISBN 0-408-00582-3 (pbk) : £3.60 : CIP entry B81-34161

604.2′4 — Technical drawings. Draftsmanship
Engineering graphics / Frederick E. Giesecke ... [et al.]. — 3rd ed. — New York : Macmillan ; London : Collier Macmillan, c1981. — vi,888p : ill(some col.) ; 26cm
Previous ed.: 1975. — Text on lining papers. — Bibliography: p806-814. — Includes index
ISBN 0-02-342620-9 : £15.95 B81-33454

Luzadder, Warren J.. Fundamentals of engineering drawing for design, product development, and numerical control / Warren J. Luzadder. — 8th ed. — Englewood Cliffs ; London : Prentice-Hall, c1981. — xv,638p : ill,facsims,plans,forms ; 29cm
Previous ed.: Englewood Cliffs : Prentice-Hall, 1977. — Bibliography: p613-617. — Includes index
ISBN 0-13-338350-4 : £14.25 B81-12674

Mechanical drawing. — 9th ed. / Thomas E. French ... [et al.]. — New York ; London : McGraw-Hill, c1980. — 568p : ill(some col.),maps,plans ; 27cm
Previous ed.: 1974. — Includes index
ISBN 0-07-022313-0 : £14.50 B81-32708

Nelson, John A.. Handbook of drafting technology / John A. Nelson. — New York ; London : Van Nostrand Reinhold, c1981. — xi,353p : ill ; 29cm
Includes index
ISBN 0-442-28661-9 (cased) : £17.20
ISBN 0-442-28662-7 (pbk) : £11.20 B81-21405

Pickup, F.. Engineering drawing with worked examples. — 3rd ed. / M.A. Parker and F. Pickup. — London : Hutchinson
2. — 1981. — 271p : chiefly ill ; 22cm
Previous ed.: 1970
ISBN 0-09-144681-3 (pbk) : £3.95 B81-21415

Simms, K.. Graphic communication for technical design / K. Simms. — London : Macmillan, 1981. — 264p : ill ; 25cm
Includes index
ISBN 0-333-29181-6 (pbk) : £5.95 B81-21796

Technical drawing / Frederick E. Giesecke ... [et al.]. — 7th ed. / revised by Ivan Leroy Hill and John Thomas Dygdon. — New York : Macmillan ; London : Collier Macmillan, c1980. — vii,868p : ill(some col.),maps ; 26cm
Previous ed.: / revised by Henry Cecil Spencer and Ivan Leroy Hill. 1974. — Bibliography: p794-802. - Includes index
ISBN 0-02-342610-1 (cased) : £14.25
ISBN 0-02-978750-5 (pbk) : £7.50 B81-00119

604.2′4 — Technical drawings. Draftsmanship — *For technicians*
Davies, K. M.. Technician engineering drawing and design 2 / K.M. Davies. — London : Cassell, 1981. — 191p : ill ; 25cm. — (Cassell′s TEC series)
ISBN 0-304-30291-0 (pbk) : £5.50 B81-27772

Jeary, L. N.. Engineering drawing 1 checkbook. — London : Butterworths, Jan.1982. — [156]p
ISBN 0-408-00667-6 (cased) : £6.95 : CIP entry (pbk) : £3.95 B81-34113

Luzadder, Warren J.. Problems in engineering drawing : for design, product development, and numerical control. — [Englewood Cliffs] ; [London] : [Prentice-Hall]
Vol.1. — 8th ed., Warren J. Luzadder, K.E. Botkin. — [c1981]. — 77leaves : ill,plans ; 28cm + 1instruction pamphlet(10p ; 28cm)
Cover title. — Previous ed.: published as Fundamentals of engineering drawings / by Warren J. Luzadder. 1977
ISBN 0-13-716373-8 (pbk) : £5.80 B81-17309

Luzadder, Warren J.. Problems in engineering drawing : for design, product development, and numerical control. — [Englewood Cliffs] ; [London] : [Prentice-Hall]
Vol.2 / Larry D. Goss, Warren J. Luzadder. — [c1981]. — 80leaves : ill,plans ; 28cm + 1instruction pamphlet(10p ; 28cm)
Cover title
ISBN 0-13-716381-9 (pbk) : £5.80 B81-17308

Ostrowsky, O.. Engineering drawing for technicians / O. Ostrowsky. — London : Edward Arnold
Vol.2. — 1981. — 94p : ill ; 22x28cm
Includes index
ISBN 0-7131-3429-1 (pbk) : £3.95 : CIP rev. B81-03367

604.2′4′076 — Technical drawings. Draftsmanship — *Questions & answers — For schools*
Donaldson, Stanley S.. Test papers in technical drawing. — 2nd ed. — Freeland : Technical Press, July 1981. — [104]p
Previous ed.: 1972
ISBN 0-291-39488-4 (pbk) : £3.95 : CIP entry B81-22575

Forrest, Douglas. Engineering drawing exam papers / compiled by Douglas Forrest. — 2nd ed. — Edinburgh : Holmes McDougall
Previous ed.: 1971
Book 1: ′O′ grade. — c1978. — [40]p : ill ; 30cm
ISBN 0-7157-1832-0 (pbk) : Unpriced B81-08707

604.6 — Great Britain. Household waste materials. Recycling
Holmes, J. R.. The recovery of useful material from refuse / by J.R. Holmes. — London : Institution of Municipal Engineers, 1975. — 24p : ill ; 21cm. — (Protection of the environment ; monograph no.27)
£1.00 (pbk) B81-06099

604.6 — Waste materials. Recycling
Holmes, J. R.. Refuse recycling and recovery / John R. Holmes. — Chichester : Wiley, c1981. — ix,186p : ill,plans ; 24cm. — (The Institution of Environmental Science series)
Bibliography: p181. — Includes index
ISBN 0-471-27902-1 (cased) : £13.00 : CIP rev.
ISBN 0-471-27903-x (pbk) : Unpriced B81-13572

604.6′09181′2 — Western world. Waste materials. Recycling
Kut, David. Waste recycling for energy conservation / David Kut and Gerard Hare. — London : Architectural Press, 1981. — vii,326p,[32]p of plates : ill ; 24cm
Includes bibliographies and index
ISBN 0-85139-707-7 : £25.00 B81-29265

604.6′0941 — Great Britain. Industrial waste materials — *Serials*
Materials reclamation weekly. Directory & handbook. — 1980. — London : Maclaren on behalf of Distinctive Publications, c1980. — 508p
Unpriced B81-00903

604.6′09417 — Ireland *(Republic)*. **Solid waste materials. Recycling by local authorities**
O′Rourke, C.. Refuse disposal : recovery potential for local authorities / C. O′Rourke. — Dublin (St. Martin′s House, Waterloo Rd., Dublin 4) : An Foras Forbartha, 1980. — xii,30p ; 30cm
ISBN 0-906120-34-9 (pbk) : £2.00 B81-05432

604.6′09417 — Ireland *(Republic)*. **Waste materials. Recycling**
Daly, Irene M. T.. Today′s wastes, tomorrow′s energy / Irene M.T. Daly. — [Dublin] ([Confederation House, Kildare St., Dublin 2]) : [Confederation of Irish Industry], [1981?]. — 16p : col.ill,1col.port ; 30cm
Unpriced (pbk) B81-14527

Hopkins, Les. Recycling for what it′s worth : recovering waste for profit / by Les Hopkins and Dermot Malone. — Dublin (Ballymun Rd, Dublin 9) : Institute for Industrial Research and Standards, c1980. — 62p : ill,1port ; 21cm
ISBN 0-900450-50-9 (pbk) : £1.10 B81-02881

604.6′0973 — United States. Solid waste materials. Recovery
Veselind, Aarne P.. Unit operations in resource recovery engineering / P. Aarne Veselind, Alan E. Rimer. — Englewood Cliffs ; London : Prentice-Hall, c1981. — x,452p : ill ; 24cm
Includes index
ISBN 0-13-937953-3 : £8.80 B81-12512

604.7′01′54 — Dangerous materials. Chemistry — *For fire fighting*
Turner, Charles F.. The chemistry of fire and hazardous materials / Charles F. Turner, Joseph W. McCreary. — Boston [Mass.] ; London : Allyn and Bacon, c1981. — x,292p : ill ; 25cm
Includes index
ISBN 0-205-06912-6 : £11.25 B81-03195

605 — Technology — *Serials*

McGraw-Hill yearbook of science and technology. — 1980. — New York ; London : McGraw-Hill, c1981. — 433p
ISBN 0-07-045488-4 : Unpriced
Primary classification 505 B81-34063

Yearbook of science and the future. — 1981. — Chicago ; London : Encyclopaedia Britannica, c1980. — 445p
ISBN 0-85229-375-5 : Unpriced
ISSN 0096-3291 B81-15074

606'.042733 — Greater Manchester *(Metropolitan County)*. Manchester. Technology. Organisations: Manchester Technology Association — *Serials*

[Year book *(Manchester Technology Association)*]. Year book / Manchester Technology Association. — 1980. — Manchester (The University of Manchester Institute of Science and Technology, P.O. Box 88, Sackville St., Manchester M60 1QD) : The Association, [1980]. — 32p
ISSN 0308-4302 : Unpriced B81-23133

607 — Developing countries. Technical education. Foreign assistance. British organisations: Technical Education and Training Organisation for Overseas Countries — *Serials*

Technical Education and Training Organisation for Overseas Countries. Annual report / Technical Education and Training Organisation for Overseas Countries. — 1979-80. — London (17 Dacre St., SW1H 0DJ) : TETOC, [1980?]. — 48p
Unpriced B81-14546

607 — Education. Curriculum subjects: Crafts, design & technology — *Serials*

The **Stanley** link in craft design and technology : [a magazine for teachers, employees and parents]. — No.3 (Oct.1979)-. — Sheffield (Woodside, Sheffield S3 9DP) : Educational Service of Stanley Tools, 1979-. — v. : ill (some col.) ; 30cm
Annual. — Continues: The Stanley link in design and craft education. — Supplement: The Stanley link in craft design and technology. Bulletin
£2.00 per year B81-06149

607 — Technology. European information sources — *Directories*

European sources of scientific and technical information. — 5th ed. — London : Longman, Dec.1981. — [496]p
Previous ed.: 1976
ISBN 0-582-90108-1 : £75.00 : CIP entry B81-32048

607 — Technology. Information sources — *Conference proceedings*

International CODATA Conference *(7th : 1980 : Kyoto)*. Data for science and technology : proceedings of the Seventh International, CODATA Conference Kyoto, Japan, 8-11 October 1980 : at the invitation of the Science Council of Japan, the Chemical Society of Japan and the Japan Society for CODATA / edited by Phyllis S. Glaeser. — Oxford : Pergamon, 1981. — xxii,615p : ill(some col.),maps,1port ; 31cm
Festschrift in honour of Professor Takehiko Shimanouchi. — Includes bibliographies and index
ISBN 0-08-026201-5 : £62.50 : CIP rev.
Primary classification 507 B81-12314

607'.11422 — London & Home Counties. Technology. Courses — *Directories* — *Serials*

[Bulletin of special courses *(London and Home Counties Regional Advisory Council for Technological Education)*]. Bulletin of special courses / London and Home Counties Regional Advisory Council for Technological Education. — 1981/82. — London : The Council, 1981. — [33]p
ISBN 0-85394-088-6 : £1.25
Primary classification 380.1'07'11422 B81-36306

607'.1142853 — Cleveland. Middlesbrough. Technical colleges: Constantine College, *1916-1970*

Leonard, James W.. Constantine College / by James W. Leonard. — [Middlesbrough] : Teesside Polytechnic, 1981. — xiv,211p : ill,maps,1port ; 22cm
Includes index
ISBN 0-907550-00-2 : £5.00 B81-32490

607'.1241 — Great Britain. Secondary schools. Curriculum subjects: Technology. Syllabuses. Planning — *For teaching*

Teacher's master manual / Ray Page ... [et al.]. — Nottingham : National Centre for School Technology, Trent Polytechnic in association with Oliver & Boyd, 1981. — 100p : ill,1plan ; 24cm. — (Schools Council modular courses in technology)
Bibliography: p100
ISBN 0-05-003414-6 (pbk) : £3.50 B81-38010

607'.12411 — Scotland. Secondary schools. Technical education — *For teaching*

Teacher's guide. — London : Heinemann Educational, 1981. — ix,116p : ill ; 25cm. — (Scottish technical education modules)
ISBN 0-435-75934-5 (pbk) : £6.50 B81-36343

607'.2'41 — Great Britain. Consultants scientists. Organisations: Association of Consulting Scientists — *Directories* — *Serials*

Association of Consulting Scientists. Members and services / Association of Consulting Scientists. — 1979-1980-. — Buntingford (Owles Hall, Buntingford, Herts.) : The Association, 1979-. — v. ; 30cm
Issued every two years. — Continues: Association of Consulting Scientists. List of members, including the Testing Laboratories Group [and] services offered
ISSN 0261-1864 = Members and services - Association of Consulting Scientists : £2.00 B81-16822

607'.2'41 — Great Britain. *Department of Industry*. Research organisations — *Serials*

Great Britain. *Department of Industry.* Department of Industry research establishments review / prepared by the Department of Industry and the Central Office of Information. — 1980. — London (Abell House, John Islip St., SW1P 4LN) : The Department, 1980. — 20p
ISSN 0142-2871 : Unpriced B81-05185

607'.2'41 — Great Britain. Research & development by Great Britain. *Department of the Environment* — *Serials*

Great Britain. *Department of the Environment.* Report on research and development / Departments of the Environment and Transport. — 1980. — London : H.M.S.O., 1981. — iii,32p
ISBN 0-11-751531-0 : £2.90
Also classified at 380.5'072041 B81-35449

607'.2'417 — Technology. Research in Irish higher education institutions — *Directories*

Colgan, John, *1939-*. Science and engineering in Irish higher education : a directory of the research and professional interests of personnel in the science and technology departments of Irish colleges / John Colgan and Brendan Finucane. — Dublin (Shelbourne House, Shelbourne Rd., Dublin 4) : National Board for Science and Technology, 1981. — iv,111p in various pagings ; 30cm
Includes index
ISBN 0-86282-002-2 (pbk) : Unpriced
Primary classification 507'.20417 B81-23238

607'.34'42132 — London. Westminster *(London Borough)*. Exhibitions: Great Exhibition *(1851 : London)*

The **Great** Exhibition of 1851 / [compiled by] C.H. Gibbs-Smith. — 2nd ed. — London : H.M.S.O., 1981. — 96p : chiefly ill,ports ; 20x21cm
At head of title: Victoria & Albert Museum. — Previous ed.: 1950. — Bibliography: p29
ISBN 0-11-290344-4 (pbk) : £3.95 B81-38951

607'.36 — Commonwealth developing countries. Technical education. Examinations

Examinations in technical and commercial subjects : problems and prospects for Commonwealth developing countries. — London : Commonwealth Secretariat, Education Division, c1980. — 75p ; 30cm
Bibliography: p75
ISBN 0-85092-185-6 (pbk) : £2.00
Primary classification 378'.166'091724 B81-37497

607'.39 — Ireland *(Republic)*. Technologists. Awards — *Directories*

Gillick, Mary. Fellowships and scholarships available to Irish scientists and technologists / compiled by Mary Gillick. — Dublin (Shelbourne House, Shelbourne Rd., Dublin 4) : National Board for Science and Technology, c1981. — vii,105p ; 21cm
Includes index
ISBN 0-86282-004-9 (pbk) : £1.00
Primary classification 507'.9 B81-23161

607'.41 — Great Britain. Technical education — *Conference proceedings*

The **New** technician education : proceedings of a joint conference of the Further Education Research Association and the Society for Research into Higher Education, January 1979 / editor John Heywood. — Guildford : The Society, 1980. — 157p : ill ; 22cm. — (SHRE proceedings ; 2)
Bibliography: p149-157
ISBN 0-900868-78-3 (pbk) : £8.25 B81-13343

607'.52 — Japan. Technology. Information sources — *Manuals*

Gibson, Robert W.. Japanese scientific and technical literature. — Aldershot : Gower, Jan.1982. — [576]p
ISBN 0-566-00505-0 : £65.00 : CIP entry B81-34286

608 — Great Britain. Patent agents — *Directories* — *Serials*

Chartered Institute of Patent AgentsThe Register of Patent Agents. — Mar.1981. — London (Staple Inn Buildings, WC1V 7PZ) : Chartered Institute of Patent Agents, [1981]. — 80p
£1.00 B81-25014

608 — Inventions — *Proposals*

Pawlicki, T. B.. How to build a flying saucer : and other proposals in speculative engineering / T.B. Pawlicki. — Englewood Cliffs ; London : Prentice-Hall, c1981. — 152p : ill
Includes index
ISBN 0-13-402461-3 (pbk) : £4.15 B81-28478

608'.05 — Patents. Information — *Serials*

World patent information : the international journal for patent information and industrial innovation / a joint periodical of the Commission of the European Communities and the World Intellectual Property Organization. — Vol.1, no.1 (Jan.1979)-. — Oxford : Pergamon, 1979-. — v. : ill ; 30cm
Quarterly. — Description based on: Vol.3, no.1 (Jan.1981)
Unpriced B81-27914

608.7492 — Benelux countries. Patents

Rimmer, Brenda M.. Guide to official industrial property literature : the Netherlands, Belgium, Luxembourg, Benelux / Brenda M. Rimmer. — London : British Library, Science Reference Library, c1981. — 28p : ill,facsims,forms ; 25cm
Includes index
ISBN 0-902914-60-x (pbk) : Unpriced : CIP rev. B81-08797

609 — TECHNOLOGY. HISTORICAL AND GEOGRAPHICAL TREATMENT

609 — Great Britain. Educational institutions. Curriculum subjects: Industrial archaeology — *Serials*

AIA education newsletter / Association for Industrial Archaeology [Education Group]. — 1[(1980?)]-. — Norwich (c/o D. Alderton, Keswick Hall College of Education, Norwich NR4 6TL) : [The Group], [1980?]-. — v. : ill ; 30cm
Description based on: 2(Autumn 1980)
ISSN 0262-0081 = AIA education newsletter : Unpriced B81-38521

609 — Industrial archaeology — *For children*

Vialls, Christine. Your book of industrial archaeology / Christine Vialls. — London : Faber, 1981. — 76p : ill,1map,plans ; 16x22cm
Bibliography: p73-74. - Includes index
ISBN 0-571-11633-7 : £3.25 : CIP rev. B81-04287

609 — Inventions, *to 1966*

De Bono, Edward. Eureka! : how and when the greatest inventions were made : an illustrated history of inventions from the wheel to the computer / edited by Edward de Bono. — London : Thames and Hudson, 1979, c1974. — 248p : ill(some col.),ports(some col.) ; 30cm
Includes index
ISBN 0-500-27156-9 (pbk) : £3.95 B81-33754

609 — Inventions, *to 1978* — *For children*

Storer, J. D.. The Beaver book of great inventions / J.D. Storer ; illustrated by Rosalind Lobb. — London : Beaver, 1980. — 142p : ill ; 18cm
Includes index
ISBN 0-600-34923-3 (pbk) : £0.85 B81-06349

609 — Inventions, *to 1980*

Wymer, Norman. Inventors / Norman Wymer. — London : Hamlyn, 1981. — 93p : ill(some col.),ports (some col.) ; 28cm. — (History eye-witness)
Ill on lining papers. — Includes index
ISBN 0-600-34927-6 : £2.95 B81-24162

609 — Technological development. Role of employment policies of governments

Kidd, Charles V.. Manpower policies for the use of science and technology in development / Charles V. Kidd. — New York ; Oxford : Pergamon, c1980. — xii,183p ; 24cm. — (Pergamon policy studies on socio-economic development)
Bibliography: p171-177. - Includes index
ISBN 0-08-025124-2 : £10.00 B81-05330

609 — Technology — *History* — *Serials*

History of technology. — 5th annual vol.. — London : Mansell, 1980. — 160p
ISBN 0-7201-1585-x : £18.50 : CIP rev.
ISSN 0307-5451 B80-23286

History of technology. — 6th annual volume (1981). — London : Mansell, Dec.1981. — [192]p
ISBN 0-7201-1634-1 : £18.00 : CIP entry B81-31535

609 — Technology, *to 1979*

Birdsall, Derek. The technology of man : a visual history / Derek Birdsall & Carlo M. Cipolla. — London : Wildwood House, 1980, c1979. — 264p : ill(some col.),maps(some col.),facsims (some col.) ; 26cm
Ill on lining papers. — Includes index
ISBN 0-7045-3035-x : £16.95 B81-21366

609′.047 — Appropriate technology, *1965-1979*

McRobie, George. Small is possible / George McRobie ; with a foreword by Verena Schumacher. — London : Cape, 1981. — xv,331p ; 23cm
Bibliography: p316-318. — Includes index
ISBN 0-224-01858-2 : £7.95 B81-06958

609′.172′4 — Developing countries. Technological development — *Conference proceedings*

The **Panchgani** dialogue on development : Asia and the Pacific meet the West in India. — Bombay : Moral Re-Armament ; London : Grosvenor Books [distributor], [1980?]. — 18p : ill,ports ; 28cm
Conference papers. — Cover title
Unpriced (pbk) B81-17681

609′.2′4 — Italy. Inventions. Leonardo, *da Vinci* — *Critical studies*

Heydenreich, Ludwig H.. Leonardo the inventor / Ludwig H. Heydenreich, Bern Dibner, Ladislao Reti. — London : Hutchinson, 1981, c1980. — 192p : ill,maps(some col.),facsims,ports ; 22cm
Includes index
ISBN 0-09-142661-8 : £4.95 B81-32445

609′.2′4 — Technology. Theories of Heidegger, Martin

Loscerbo, John. Being and technology : a study in the philosophy of Martin Heidegger / John Loscerbo. — The Hague ; London : Nijhoff, 1981. — xii,286p ; 25cm. — (Phaenomenologica ; 82)
Bibliography: p271-278. — Includes index
ISBN 90-247-2411-2 : Unpriced B81-36728

609′.2′4 — United States. Inventions. Tesla, Nikola — *Biographies*

O'Neill, John J. (John Joseph), *1889-*. Prodigal genius : the life of Nikola Tesla / John J. O'Neill. — London : Granada, 1980, c1968. — 349p ; 18cm. — (A Panther book)
Originally published: New York : Washburn, 1944 ; London : Spearman, 1968. — Includes index
ISBN 0-586-05000-0 (pbk) : £2.95 B81-14307

609′.41 — Great Britain. Industrial antiquities

Wailes, Rex. A source book of the industrial past / Rex Wailes. — London : Ward Lock, 1980. — 128p : ill ; 12x17cm. — (Source books)
Includes index
ISBN 0-7063-5885-6 : £2.95 : CIP rev. B80-17707

609′.41 — Great Britain. Industrial antiquities, *ca 1000-ca 1500* — *Conference proceedings*

Medieval industry. — London : Council for British Archaeology, Sept.1981. — [166]p. — (Research report / Council for British Archaeology, ISSN 0589-9036 ; no.40)
Conference papers
ISBN 0-906780-07-1 (pbk) : £11.00 : CIP entry B81-28204

609′.41 — Great Britain. Industrial antiquities — *Directories* — *Serials*

Light railways, canals, steamers and industrial preservation. — 20th ed. (1981-82). — Weston-super-Mare (21 Southside, Weston-super-Mare, Avon BS23 2QU) : Avon-Anglia Publications and Services, c1981. — 64p
Cover title: AAA guide to light railways, canals, steamers and industrial preservation
ISBN 0-905466-38-1 : £0.90 B81-25482

609′.41 — Great Britain. Industrial archaeology, *1900-1980*

Hudson, Kenneth. The archaeology of the consumer society. — London : Heinemann, Apr.1981. — [144]p
ISBN 0-435-32959-6 : £12.50 : CIP entry B81-03690

609′.41 — Great Britain. Technological development. Role of education

The **Next** frontier : a venture with frontier groups in Sheffield. — [Sheffield] ([Sheffield City Polytechnic, 55 Broomgrove Rd., Sheffield S10 2NA]) : Sheffield Region Centre for Science & Technology, 1980. — 34p : 1form ; 30cm. — (Paper / Sheffield Region Centre for Science & Technology ; 20)
Cover title
ISBN 0-903761-23-8 (pbk) : Unpriced B81-27718

609′.424′13 — Gloucestershire. Forest of Dean *(District)*. **Industrial antiquities** — *Visitors' guides*

Paar, H. W.. An industrial tour of the Wye Valley & Forest of Dean / by H.W. Paar ; with illustrations and map by Edwin Lambert. — [Potters Bar] ([c/o M. Stimpson, 83 Sunnybank Rd., Potters Bar, Herts.]) : West London Industrial Archaeological Society, 1980. — 24p : ill,1map ; 21cm
Bibliography: p22-24
ISBN 0-907220-01-0 (pbk) : £0.75 B81-08337

609′.425′892 — Hertfordshire. Watford. Industrial antiquities — *Serials*

Journal of the Watford and District Industrial History Society. — No.10 (1980). — Watford (c/o G.J. Child, 13 Cromer Rd, Watford) : The Society, [1980]. — 68p
ISSN 0307-5281 : Unpriced B81-24155

609.427 — North-west England. Industrial antiquities — *Identification manuals*

Ashmore, Owen. The industrial archaeology of North-west England. — Manchester : Manchester University Press, Sept.1981. — [272]p
ISBN 0-7190-0820-4 : £9.50 : CIP entry B81-22509

609′.51 — China. Technological development *compared with* **technological development in India** *(Republic)*

India-China comparative research : technology and science for development / edited by Erik Baark and Jon Sigurdson. — London : Curzon, 1981, c1980. — ix,154p : ill ; 22cm. — (Studies on Asian topics, ISSN 0142-6028 ; no.3)
Bibliography: p147-151
ISBN 0-7007-0138-9 (pbk) : £4.00
Also classified at 609′.54 B81-16176

609′.51 — China. Technology, *to ca 1800*

Ronan, Colin A.. The shorter Science and civilisation in China. — Cambridge : Cambridge University Press
Vol.2. — Nov.1981. — [480]p
ISBN 0-521-23582-0 : £15.00 : CIP entry
Primary classification 509′.51 B81-31189

609′.54 — India *(Republic)*. **Technological development** *compared with* **technological development in China**

India-China comparative research : technology and science for development / edited by Erik Baark and Jon Sigurdson. — London : Curzon, 1981, c1980. — ix,154p : ill ; 22cm. — (Studies on Asian topics, ISSN 0142-6028 ; no.3)
Bibliography: p147-151
ISBN 0-7007-0138-9 (pbk) : £4.00
Primary classification 609′.51 B81-16176

609′.6 — Africa. Alternative technology — *Serials*

Popular technology : a magazine devoted to the development and application of relevant technologies in Africa. — Vol.1, no.1-. — London (49 Great Cumberland Place, W1H 7LH) : Wenca, 1980-. — v. : ill ; 28cm
Six issues yearly
£4.50 per year B81-05930

609′.73 — United States. Technology. Policies of government

Science, technology, and national policy / edited by Thomas J. Kuehn, Alan L. Porter. — Ithaca ; London : Cornell University Press, 1981. — 530p ; 24cm
Bibliography: p515-524. — Includes index
ISBN 0-8014-1343-5 (cased) : £21.00
ISBN 0-8014-9876-7 (pbk) : Unpriced
Primary classification 509′.73 B81-27263

609′.99 — Outer space. Colonisation — *Forecasts* — *For children*

Ardley, Neil. Out into space / Neil Ardley. — London : Watts, [1981]. — 36p : col.ill ; 30cm. — (World of tomorrow)
Includes index
ISBN 0-85166-906-9 : £3.99
Primary classification 919.9′04 B81-26677

610 — MEDICINE

610 — Man. Adaptation. Medical aspects

Dubos, René. Man adapting / by René Dubos. — [Enl. ed.] / with a new chapter by the author. — New Haven ; London : Yale University Press, c1980. — xxii,538p : ill ; 21cm. — (Yale University Mrs. Hepsa Ely Silliman memorial lectures)
Previous ed.: 1965. — Bibliography: p467-519. - Includes index
ISBN 0-300-02580-7 (cased) : Unpriced : CIP rev.
ISBN 0-300-02581-5 (pbk) : £5.00 B81-06498

610 — Medicine

Essential sciences for clinicians. — Oxford : Blackwell Scientific, Aug.1981. — [432]p
ISBN 0-632-00733-8 : £18.00 : CIP entry B81-22689

610 — Medicine *continuation*

Wallace, William F. M.. Science and medicine : an inaugural lecture delivered before the Queen's University of Belfast on 16 April 1980 / William F.M. Wallace. — [Belfast] : Queen's University of Belfast, c1980. — 21p : ill,1facsim,ports ; 21cm. — (New lecture series / Queen's University of Belfast ; no.122)
ISBN 0-85389-185-0 (pbk) : £0.40 B81-05873

610 — Medicine. Applications of behavioural sciences

The **Comparative** handbook of behavioral medicine. — Lancaster : MTP
Vol.2: Syndromes & special areas / edited by James M. Ferguson and C. Barr Taylor. — c1981. — 289p : ill ; 24cm
Includes index
ISBN 0-85200-541-5 : £15.50 B81-29467

610 — Medicine. Decision making — *Conference proceedings*

Trans-Disciplinary Symposium on Philosophy and Medicine *(5th : 1977 : Los Angeles)*. Clinical judgement : a critical appraisal : proceedings of the Fifth Trans-disciplinary Symposium on Philosophy and Medicine held at Los Angeles, California, April 4-16, 1977 / edited by H. Tristram Engelhardt, Jr, Stuart F. Spicker, Bernard Towers. — Dordrecht ; London : Reidel, c1979. — xxvi,278p ; 23cm. — (Philosophy and medicine ; v.6)
Includes bibliographies and index
ISBN 90-277-0952-1 : Unpriced B81-15250

610 — Medicine. Information systems. Machine-readable files. Security measures — *Conference proceedings*

Data protection in health information systems : considerations and guidelines / edited by G.G. Griesser ... [et al.] on behalf of Working Group 4 of the International Medical Informatics Association (IMIA), Special Interest Group of the International Federation for Information Processing (IFIP). — Amsterdam ; Oxford : North-Holland, 1980. — xxvi,217p : ill ; 23cm
Bibliography: p179-202. - Includes index
ISBN 0-444-86052-5 : £19.18 B81-04025

610'.09'034 — Medicine, *1840-1940*

Biology, medicine and society 1840-1940. — Cambridge : Cambridge University Press, Nov.1981. — [344]p. — (Past and present publications)
ISBN 0-521-23770-x : £22.50 : CIP entry
Primary classification 574'.09'034 B81-30183

610'.1 — Medicine — *Philosophical perspectives*

Downie, R. S.. Caring and curing : a philosophy of medicine and social work / R.S. Downie and Elizabeth Telfer. — London : Methuen, 1980. — x,174p ; 22cm
Bibliography: p169-170. - Includes index
ISBN 0-416-71800-0 (cased) : £8.50 : CIP rev.
ISBN 0-416-71810-8 (pbk) : £3.95
Primary classification 361'.001 B80-18203

Murphy, Edmond A.. Skepsis, dogma, and belief : uses and abuses in medicine / Edmond A. Murphy. — Baltimore ; London : Johns Hopkins University Press, c1981. — x,176p ; 24cm
Includes index
ISBN 0-8018-2510-5 : £10.50 B81-40031

610'.14 — Medicine. Terminology

Chabner, Davi-Ellen. The language of medicine : a write-in text explaining medical terms / Davi-Ellen Chabner. — 2nd ed. — Philadelphia ; London : Saunders, 1981. — xii,706p,xxxip : ill ; 27cm
Previous ed.: 1976. — Includes index
ISBN 0-7216-2479-0 (pbk) : £9.95 B81-12746

Roberts, Ffrangcon. Ffrangcon Roberts' Medical terms : their origin and construction. — 6th ed. / extensively rev. and enl. by Bernard Lennox. — London : Heinemann Medical, 1980. — x,132p ; 19cm
Previous ed.: published as Medical terms, 1971. — Includes index
ISBN 0-433-19151-1 (pbk) : £4.50 B81-02454

610'.14 — Medicine. Terminology — *Programmed instructions*

Birmingham, Jacqueline Joseph. Medical terminology : a self-learning module / Jacqueline Joseph Birmingham. — New York ; London : McGraw-Hill, c1981. — ix,436p : ill (some col.) ; 24cm
Bibliography: p141-415. - Includes index
ISBN 0-07-005386-3 (spiral) : £8.35 B81-17958

Smith, Genevieve Love. Medical terminology : a progammed text / Genevieve Love Smith, Phyllis E. Davis. — 4th ed. — New York ; Chichester : Wiley, c1981. — xvi,325p : ill (some col) ; 26cm
Previous ed.: 1976. — Includes index
ISBN 0-471-05827-0 (spiral) : £7.00 B81-09659

610'.14 — Medicine. Terminology — *Questions & answers*

Rickards, Ralph. Understanding medical terms : a self-instructional course / Ralph Rickards. — Edinburgh : Churchill Livingstone, 1980. — 106p : ill ; 30cm
Includes index
ISBN 0-443-02029-9 (pbk) : £2.35 : CIP rev. B80-13823

610'.1'51 — Medicine. Laboratory techniques. Mathematics

Campbell, June Blankenship. Laboratory mathematics : medical and biological applications / June Blankenship Campbell, Joe Bill Campbell. — 2nd ed. — St. Louis ; London : Mosby, 1980. — viii,285p : ill ; 26cm
Previous ed.: under the names of June Blankenship, Joe Bill Campbell. 1976. — Bibliography: p272. - Includes index
ISBN 0-8016-0702-7 (pbk) : Unpriced B81-08204

610'.1'53 — Medicine. Applications of physics

Damask, A. C.. Medical physics / A.C. Damask. — New York ; London : Academic Press
Vol.2: External senses. — 1981. — xiii,274p : ill ; 24cm
Includes bibliographies and index
ISBN 0-12-201202-x : £19.60 B81-37707

610'.1'9 — Medicine. Psychological aspects

Medical psychology : contributions to behavioral medicine / edited by Charles K. Prokop, Laurence A. Bradley. — New York ; London : Academic Press, 1981. — xiv,530p : ill ; 25cm
Includes bibliographies and index
ISBN 0-12-565960-1 : £16.60 B81-35435

Psychological factors in health care : a practitioner's manual / edited by Michael Jospe, Joseph Nieberding, Barry D. Cohen. — Lexington, Mass. : Lexington Books, c1980 ; [Aldershot] : Gower [distributor], 1981. — xxx,482p ; 24cm
Includes bibliographies and index
ISBN 0-669-02076-1 : £18.50 B81-33141

610'.21'2 — Medicine. Statistics — Conference proceedings

Perspectives in medical statistics. — London : Academic Press, Feb.1982. — [300]p
ISBN 0-12-102520-9 : CIP entry B81-36059

610'.212 — Medicine — *Technical data*

Exacta medica : reference tables and data for the medical and nursing profession / [compiled by Ian Reid Entwistle]. — Birkenhead (c/o 10 Westwood Court, Birkenhead, Merseyside L43 6XF) : Exacta, [1980]. — 34p : 1ill ; 9x17cm
Cover title. — Originally published: Birkenhead : Picturettes, 1973
ISBN 0-9503701-2-6 (spiral) : Unpriced B81-10708

610'.24055 — Medicine — *Encyclopaedias — For adolescents*

Baldwin, Dorothy. Know your body / Dorothy Baldwin ; illustrated by Julia Rout. — Harmondsworth : Puffin, 1981, c1979. — 149p : ill ; 18cm. — (Puffin plus)
Originally published: Harmondsworth : Kestrel Books, 1979
ISBN 0-14-031340-0 (pbk) : £0.90 B81-25200

610'.24613 — Medicine — *Encyclopaedias — For nursing*

Morten, Honnor. The nurse's dictionary / originally compiled by Honnor Morten. — 29th ed. / revised by Joan M. Martin. — London : Faber, 1980. — 392p : ill ; 16cm
Previous ed.: / revised by P. Jean Cunningham. 1976
ISBN 0-571-18007-8 (pbk) : £1.30 : CIP rev. B80-04203

610'.24613 — Medicine - *For nursing*

Burton, J. L.. Essential medicine. — Edinburgh : Churchill Livingstone, Aug.1981. — [224]p
ISBN 0-443-02438-3 (pbk) : £4.95 : CIP entry B81-18079

610'.28 — Bioengineers. Professional education — *Conference proceedings*

Education, training and careers in biomedical engineering in the 1980's. — London (Royal College of Surgeons of England, Lincoln's Inn Fields, WC2A 3PN) : Biological Engineering Society, 1981. — 122p : ill ; 21cm
Conference papers
ISBN 0-904716-22-8 (pbk) : £5.00 B81-21963

610'.28 — Electronic medical equipment

Carr, Joseph J. Introduction to biomedical equipment technology / Joseph J. Carr, John M. Brown. — New York ; Chichester : Wiley, c1981. — xiii,430p : ill ; 25cm
Includes index
ISBN 0-471-04143-2 : £11.75 B81-14762

610'.28 — Electronic medical equipment. Applications of microprocessor systems — *Conference proceedings*

IFIP-IMIA (TC4) Working Conference on Changes in Health Care Instrumentation due to Microprocessor Technology *(1980 : Rome)*. Changes in health care instrumentation due to microprocessor technology : proceedings of the IFIP-IMIA (TC4) Working Conference on Changes in Health Care Instrumentation due to Microprocessor Technology, Rome, Italy, 6-8 February, 1980 / edited by Francesco Pinciroli and John Anderson. — Amsterdam ; Oxford : North-Holland, 1981. — ix,326p : ill ; 23cm
Includes index
ISBN 0-444-86138-6 : Unpriced B81-14156

610'.28 — Electronic medical equipment. Use

Bergveld, P.. Electromedical instrumentation : a guide for medical personnel / P. Bergveld. — Cambridge : Cambridge University Press, 1980. — x,134p : ill ; 24cm. — (Techniques of measurement in medicine ; 2)
Includes index
ISBN 0-521-21892-6 (cased) : £14.00
ISBN 0-521-29305-7 (pbk) : £4.50 B81-01648

610'.28 — Medical equipment: Automatic radioactive sample counters

An **Introduction** to automatic radioactive sample counters / the Hospital Physicists' Association Radionuclide Topic Group. — London (47 Belgrave Sq., SW1X 8QX) : [The Association], c1980. — 65p : ill ; 21cm. — (Topic Group report ; 33)
Bibliography: p64-65
ISBN 0-904181-18-9 (pbk) : Unpriced B81-24793

610'.28 — Medical equipment — *Serials*

Clinica : world medical device news. — Special issue (Sept.5th 1980) ; Oct.31st 1980-. — Richmond (18a Hill St., Richmond, Surrey TW9 1TN) : George Street, 1980-. — v. ; 32cm
Fortnightly
ISSN 0144-7777 = Clinica : £169.00 per year B81-32706

610'.28 — Medicine. Illustrations. Rymsdyk, Jan van — *Biographies*

Thornton, John Leonard. Jan van Rymsdyk. — Cambridge : Oleander Press, Dec.1981. — [86]p
ISBN 0-906672-02-3 : £9.95 : CIP entry B81-31519

610'.28 — Medicine. Laboratory techniques — *Manuals*

Basic medical laboratory technology. — 2nd ed. — Tunbridge Wells : Pitman Medical, Jan.1982. — [384]p
Previous ed.: 1975
ISBN 0-272-79630-1 : £14.95 : CIP entry
B81-34159

610'.28 — Medicine. Laboratory techniques — *Manuals — For tropical medicine*

Cheesbrough, Monica. Medical laboratory manual for tropical countries / Monica Cheesbrough. — Doddington (14 Bevills Close, Doddington, Cambs. PE15 0TT) : M. Cheesbrough
Vol.1. — 1981. — xii,519p : ill(some col.),maps ; 27cm
Eleven sheets (1 folded) as inserts. — Includes index
ISBN 0-9507434-1-0 (pbk) : £7.60 : CIP rev.
ISBN 0-9507434-0-2 (set) : Unpriced
B81-16855

610'.28 — Medicine. Techniques

Procedures in practice : articles published in the British medical journal. — London : British Medical Association, c1981. — 74p : ill ; 30cm
ISBN 0-7279-0075-7 (pbk) : Unpriced
B81-26988

610'.28 — Medicine. Use of lasers — *Conference proceedings*

NATO Symposium on Lasers in Biology and Medicine *(1979 : Lucca).* Lasers in biology and medicine / [proceedings of the NATO Symposium on Lasers in Biology and Medicine, Camaiore, Lucca, Italy, August 19-31, 1979] ; edited by F. Hillenkamp, R. Pratesi and C.A. Sacchi. — New York ; London : Plenum, published in cooperation with NATO Scientific Affairs Division, c1980. — xi,463p : ill ; 26cm. — (NATO advanced study institutes series. Series A, Life sciences ; v.34)
Includes index
ISBN 0-306-40470-2 : Unpriced
Primary classification 574'.028 B81-14642

610'.28 — Medicine. Use of polymers — *Conference proceedings*

Biomedical and dental applications of polymers / [based on an American Chemical Society symposium on biomedical and dental applications of polymers, held March 23-28, 1980, at the 179th national meeting in Houston, Texas] ; edited by Charles G. Gebelein and Frank F. Koblitz. — New York ; London : Plenum, c1981. — xii,792p : ill ; 26cm. — (Polymer science and technology ; v.14)
Includes index
ISBN 0-306-40632-2 : Unpriced B81-19275

Symposium on Polymeric Materials and Pharmaceuticals for Biomedical Use *(1979 : Honolulu).* Biomedical polymers : polymeric materials and pharmaceuticals for biomedical use : proceedings from the Symposium on Polymeric Materials and Pharmaceuticals for Biomedical Use presented April 4-6, 1979 at the First Joint Congress of the American Chemical Society and the Chemical Society of Japan in Honolulu, Hawaii / edited by Eugene P. Goldberg, Akio Nakajima. — New York ; London : Academic Press, 1980. — xii,457p : ill ; 24cm
Includes index
ISBN 0-12-287580-x : £18.00 B81-07522

610'.28 — Medicine. Use of ultrasonic waves

Wyn-Jones, E.. 'Seeing' events with sound : inaugural lecture / by E. Wyn-Jones. — [Salford] ([Salford, Lancs M5 4WT]) : University of Salford, [1980?]. — [15]p : ill ; 21cm
Cover title
Unpriced (pbk) B81-05731

610'.28 — Medicine. Use of ultrasonic waves — *Conference proceedings*

European Congress on Ultrasonics in Medicine *(4th : 1981 : Dubrovnik-Cavtat).* 4th European Congress on Ultrasonics in Medicine : Dubrovnik-Cavtat, Yugoslavia, May 17-24, 1981 : abstracts / under the auspices of the Federal Executive Council of Yugoslavia (Savezno izvršno vijeće) ; organized by the Yugoslav Association of Societies for Ultrasound in Medicine and Biology in association with the Ultrasonic Center, Dr J. Kajfeš Hospital, Zagreb, Yugoslavia ; sponsored by the European Federation of Societies for Ultrasound in Medicine and Biology ; editor V. Latin. — Amsterdam ; Oxford : Excerpta Medica, 1981. — 146p ; 24cm
ISBN 90-219-1246-5 (pbk) : Unpriced
B81-26891

610'.28 — United States. Medical technology. Evaluation — *Conference proceedings*

Methods for evaluating health services / edited by Paul M. Wortman. — Beverly Hills ; London : Published in cooperation with the Evaluation Research Society [by] Sage, c1981. — 143p : 1ill ; 22cm. — (Sage research progress series in evaluation ; v.8)
Conference papers. — Includes bibliographies
ISBN 0-8039-1531-4 (cased) : Unpriced
ISBN 0-8039-1532-2 (pbk) : Unpriced
B81-26981

610'.28'5 — Medicine. Data processing

Data in medicine : collection, processing and presentation : a physical-technical introduction for physicians and biologists / edited by Robert S. Reneman, Jan Strackee. — The Hague ; London : Nijhoff, 1979. — xiv,330p : ill(some col.),facsims ; 25cm. — (Instrumentation and techniques in clinical medicine ; v.1)
Includes bibliographies and index
ISBN 90-247-2150-4 : Unpriced B81-16292

610'.28'54 — Medicine. Applications of digital computer systems

Greenfield, Tony. Computers and health / Tony Greenfield ; an inaugural lecture delivered before the Queen's University of Belfast on 2 December 1980. — [Belfast] ([University Rd., Belfast BT7 1NN]) : Queen's university of Belfast, c1980. — 29p : ill ; 21cm. — (New lecture series / Queen's University of Belfast)
ISBN 0-85389-190-7 (pbk) : £0.40 B81-11554

610'.28'54404 — Medicine. Real time image processing. Applications of real time computer systems

Real-time medical image processing / edited by Morio Onoe, Kendall Preston, Jr. and Azriel Rosenfeld. — New York ; London : Plenum, c1980. — xiii,244p,[8]p of plates : ill(some col.) ; 26cm
Includes bibliographies and index
ISBN 0-306-40551-2 : Unpriced B81-09912

610'.3'21 — Medicine — *Encyclopaedias*

Black's medical dictionary. — 33rd ed. / William A.R. Thomson. — London : A.C. Black, 1981. — 982p : ill ; 23cm
Previous ed: 1979
ISBN 0-7136-2128-1 : £9.95 : CIP rev.
B81-22524

Carding, David Kellett. The family medical handbook : an A-Z guide / David Kellett Carding. — 2nd ed. — London : Unwin Paperbacks, 1981. — 263p : ill ; 18cm
Previous ed.: published as The home medical guide. London : Pan, 1970
ISBN 0-04-616020-5 (pbk) : £1.95 B81-11592

Concise medical dictionary / [editor, Elizabeth A. Martin]. — Oxford : Oxford University Press, 1980. — vii,695p : ill ; 21cm. — (Oxford medical publications)
ISBN 0-19-261295-6 : £8.95 B81-02678

Playfair, A. S.. The Hamlyn pocket medical dictionary / A.S. Playfair. — London : Hamlyn, 1980. — 256p : ill ; 15cm
ISBN 0-600-36311-2 (pbk) : £1.25 B81-00904

610'.5 — Medicine — *Conference proceedings — Serials*

Symposia reporter. — [Vol.1, no.1 (1979)?]-. — Macclesfield (Sunderland House, Sunderland St., Macclesfield, Cheshire SK11 6JF) : Professional Postgraduate Services, [1979?]-. — v. : ill,ports ; 28cm
ISSN 0261-2100 = Symposia reporter : Unpriced B81-21946

610'.5 — Medicine - *Serials*

Advanced medicine. — 17. — Tunbridge Wells : Pitman Medical, July 1981. — [330]p
ISBN 0-272-79633-6 (pbk) : £16.50 : CIP entry
ISSN 0308-3888 B81-14784

610'.5 — Medicine — *Serials*

The **Medical** annual. — 98th year (1980/81). — Bristol : J. Wright, c1980. — xxxvi,325p
ISBN 0-7236-0561-0 : Unpriced : CIP rev.
B80-12360

The **Medical** annual. — 99th year (1981/82). — Bristol : J. Wright, 1981. — xxv,311p
ISBN 0-7236-0602-1 : Unpriced : CIP rev.
B81-17536

[Medicine international *(Monthly add-on journal : UK edition)***].** Medicine international : [the monthly add-on journal]. — UK ed. — Vol.1, no.1 (Jan.1981)-. — Oxford (52 New Inn Hall St., Oxford OX1 2BS) : Medical Education (International), 1981-. — v. : ill ; 28cm
Monthly. — Continues: Medicine (Monthly add-on journal). — Supplement: medicine in practice
ISSN 0144-0403 = Medicine international. The monthly add-on journal. UK edition : £12.00 per year B81-13693

[Recent advances in medicine *(Edinburgh)***].** Recent advances in medicine. — No.18. — Edinburgh : Churchill Livingstone, 1981. — ix,404p
ISBN 0-443-02077-9 : Unpriced
ISSN 0143-6791 B81-17471

Wrexham medical journal. — No.8 (1980). — Wrexham (Maelor General Hospital, Wrexham LL13 7TD) : Wrexham Postgraduate Medical Centre, [1980?]. — 103p
ISSN 0306-9966 : Unpriced B81-16824

610'.5 — Medicine — *Serials — For general practice*

Medicine in practice : general practice supplement. — Vol.1, no.1 (1981)-. — Oxford (52 New Inn Hall St., Oxford OX1 2BS) : Medical Education (International), 1981-. — v. : ill ; 28cm
Six issues yearly. — Supplement to: Medicine international (Monthly add-on journal : UK edition). — Description based on: Vol.1, no.3 (June 1981)
ISSN 0260-2342 = Medicine in practice : Free to subscribers to Medicine international
B81-32795

610'.5 — Medicine — *Serials — For medical students*

Student update : a new educational journal for the clinical medical student. — Vol.1, no.1 (Nov./Dec. 1979)-. — London (33 Alfred Place, WC1E 7DP) : Update Publications, 1979-. — v. : ill ; 28cm
Six issues yearly. — Description based on: Vol.2, no.5 (Sept./Oct. 1980)
ISSN 0260-5163 = Student update (corrected) : £7.00 per year B81-03592

610'.6 — Medicine. Organisations — *Directories*

Directory of international and national medical societies. — Oxford : Pergamon, Sept.1981. — [350]p
ISBN 0-08-027991-0 : £29.00 : CIP entry
B81-21585

610.69'0973 — United States. Medicine — *Career guides*

Introduction to health professions / edited by Anne S. Allen. — 3rd ed. — St. Louis ; London : Mosby, 1980. — xvi,248p : ill ; 22cm
Previous ed.: 1979. — Includes bibliographies and index
ISBN 0-8016-0113-4 (pbk) : £8.25 B81-08038

610.69'52'02541 — Great Britain. Doctors — *Directories — Serials*

The **Medical** register. — 1981. — London (44 Hallam St., W1N 6AE) : General Medical Council, c1981. — 2v.
Unpriced B81-28388

610.69'52'060421 — England. Physicians. Organisations: Royal College of Physicians of London — *Directories — Serials*

Royal College of Physicians of London. List of the fellows and members of the Royal College of Physicians of London. — 1981. — London : The College, [1981]. — 319p
ISBN 0-900596-49-x : Unpriced
ISSN 0307-8841 B81-31007

610.69'53 — Medical assistants. Duties

Lawton, M. Murray. Lawton and Foy's textbook for medical assistants / M. Murray Lawton ... [et al.]. — 4th ed. — St. Louis ; London : Mosby, 1980. — ix,460p : ill,facsims,forms ; 25cm
Previous ed.: published as A textbook for medical assistants. 1975. — Includes bibliographies and index
ISBN 0-8016-2893-8 : £13.50 B81-10340

Zakus, Sharron M.. Clinical skills and assisting techniques for the medical assistant / Sharron M. Zakus. — St. Louis ; London : Mosby, 1981. — xiv,351p : ill,forms ; 28cm
Bibliography: p337-339. — Includes index
ISBN 0-8016-5672-9 (pbk) : £11.25 B81-25052

610.69'53'02541 — Great Britain. Medical laboratory technician — *Directories — Serials*

The **Medical** laboratory scientific officers register. — 1981. — [London] ([The Council for Professions Supplementary to Medicine, 184 Kennington Park Rd, SE11 4BU]) : Medical Laboratory Technicians Board, [1981]. — 327p
Unpriced B81-33297

610.69'6 — Doctors. Visits by children — *For children*

Snell, Nigel. Kate visits the doctor / Nigel Snell. — London : Hamilton, 1981. — [25]p : col.ill ; 16x17cm
ISBN 0-241-10640-0 : £2.50 : CIP rev.
B81-25758

610.69'6 — Ireland *(Republic).* **Doctors. Professional conduct**

Medical Council. Constitution and functions : a guide to ethical conduct and behaviour and to fitness to practise / The Medical Council. — Dublin ([c/o The Registrar, Brian V. Lea, 6 Kildare St, Dublin, 2]) : The Council, 1981. — 27p ; 22cm
Unpriced (pbk) B81-35007

610.69'6 — Patients. Care. Cultural aspects & religious aspects

Sampson, A. C. M.. The neglected ethic : cultural and religious factors in the care of patients. — London : McGraw-Hill, Jan.1982. — [144]p. — (McGraw-Hill nursing studies series)
ISBN 0-07-084645-6 (pbk) : £3.25 : CIP entry
B81-34488

610'.7 — Medicine. Information sources

Chen, Ching-Chih. Health sciences information sources / Ching-Chih Chen. — Cambridge, Mass. ; London : MIT, c1981. — xxxviii, ; 24cm
Includes index
ISBN 0-262-03074-8 : £31.00 B81-28258

Cook, Audrey. Health studies : a guide to sources of information / prepared by Audrey Cook, Pam Bailey and Anne Ramsay. — Newcastle upon Tyne (Ellison Building, Ellison Place, Newcastle upon Tyne NE1 8ST) : Travelling Workshops Experiment, Newcastle upon Tyne Polytechnic Products Ltd, [1981?]. — 109p : ill ; 30cm
Bibliography: p87-96. — Includes index
ISBN 0-906471-05-2 (spiral) : Unpriced
B81-31408

610'.7'1141 — Great Britain. Doctors. Professional education. Postgraduate courses — *Directories — Serials*

Summary of postgraduate diplomas and courses in medicine / Councils for Postgraduate Medical Education National Advice Centre. — 1981. — [London] ([7 Marylebone Rd, NW1 5HH]) : Council for Postgraduate Medical Education in England and Wales on behalf of the three Councils of the United Kingdom, [1981]. — 67p
ISSN 0302-3494 : £3.50 B81-20727

610'.7'1141 — Great Britain. General practitioners. Continuing professional education

Maintaining standards in general practice. — Edinburgh (8 Queen St., Edinburgh EH2 1JE) : Scottish Council for Postgraduate Medical Education, c1981. — 37p ; 21cm
ISBN 0-905830-04-0 (pbk) : Unpriced
B81-10935

610'.7'1141 — Great Britain. General practitioners. Professional education. Vocational courses — *Serials*

Trainee : preparing for general practice. — Vol.1, no.1 (Mar.1981)-. — London : Update Publications, 1981-. — v. : ill ; 28cm
Quarterly. — Supplement to: Update (London)
ISSN 0260-3896 = Trainee : Unpriced
B81-30831

610'.7'1141 — Great Britain. Medical personnel. Professional education. Social aspects

Atkinson, Paul. The clinical experience : the construction and reconstruction of medical reality / Paul Atkinson. — Farnborough, Hants. : Gower, c1981. — vi,142p ; 23cm
Bibliography: p139-142
ISBN 0-566-00413-5 : £11.50 B81-11605

610'.7'1141 — Great Britain. Medical schools. Curriculum subjects: Medicine. Postgraduate courses — *Conference proceedings*

Parkhouse, James. Feasibility study on postgraduate medical education / James Parkhouse and Cynthia McLaughlin. — Southend-on-Sea (Maitland House, Warrior Sq., Southend-on-Sea, Essex SS1 2JY) : Institute of Mathematics and its Applications, c1975. — ii,83p : 1ill ; 20cm. — (Proceedings series / Institute of Mathematics and its Applications ; no.10)
Bibliography: p83
Unpriced (spiral) B81-13267

610'.7'1151156 — China. Peking. Medical schools: Peking Union Medical College, *to 1977*

Bullock, Mary Brown. An American transplant : the Rockefeller Foundation and Peking Union Medical College / Mary Brown Bullock. — Berkeley ; London : University of California Press, c1980. — xxvii,280p : ill,maps,ports ; 24cm
Bibliography: p241-257. — Includes index
ISBN 0-520-03559-3 : £10.50 B81-16632

610'.7'1173 — United States. Primary health services. Medical personnel. Professional education

Approaches to teaching primary health care / edited by Harry J. Knopke, Nancy L. Diekelmann. — St. Louis ; London : Mosby, 1981. — xxii,322p : ill
Includes bibliographies and index
ISBN 0-8016-2732-x : £13.50 B81-33046

610'.72 — Medicine. Research — *Conference proceedings*

Basic research and clinical medicine / editor S. Philip Bralow ; coeditors and awardees Rosalyn S. Yalow ... [et al.]. — Washington [D.C.] ; London : Hemisphere Publishing, c1981. — xiii,280p : ill ; 25cm
Includes bibliographies and index
ISBN 0-07-007150-0 : £23.50 B81-23724

610'.7'204 — Europe. Medicine. Research

Collaboration in medical research in Europe. — London : Pitman, Oct.1981. — [160]p
ISBN 0-272-79634-4 (pbk) : £8.95 : CIP entry
B81-28121

610'.72041 — Great Britain. *Medical Research Council — Serials*

Great Britain. *Medical Research Council.* Annual report, April ... March ... / Medical Research Council. — 1979-1980. — London : H.M.S.O., [1980]. — x,80p
ISBN 0-10-027759-4 : £4.65
ISSN 0141-2256 B81-01794

610'.72041 — Great Britain. Medicine. Research. Projects. Grants from Great Britain. *Medical Research Council*

Great Britain. *Medical Research Council.* Project grants : purpose of scheme and conditions (1981) / Medical Research Council. — London (20 Park Cres., W1N 4AL) : The Council, 1981. — 26p ; 21cm
Unpriced (pbk) B81-21048

610'.72042733 — Greater Manchester *(Metropolitan County).* **Manchester. Hospitals: University Hospital of South Manchester. Research projects —** *Lists — Serials*

University Hospital of South Manchester. Research report / University Hospital of South Manchester. — 1978-80. — [Manchester] ([Mauldeth House, Mauldeth Rd, Manchester]) : Manchester Area Health Authority (Teaching), South District, 1980. — 82p
Unpriced B81-30711

610.73 — Medicine. Nursing

Beland, Irene L.. Clinical nursing : pathophysiological and psychosocial approaches. — 4th ed. / Irene L. Beland, Joyce Y. Passos. — New York : Macmillan ; London : Collier-Macmillan, c1981. — xiv,1279p : ill ; 29cm
Previous ed.: 1975. — Includes bibliographies and index
ISBN 0-02-307890-1 : £20.95 B81-38917

Blattner, Barbara. Holistic nursing / Barbara Blattner. — Englewood Cliffs ; London : Prentice-Hall, c1981. — x,502p : ill,forms ; 24cm
Includes bibliographies and index
ISBN 0-13-392571-4 (cased) : Unpriced
ISBN 0-13-392563-3 (pbk) : £9.95 B81-33146

Current issues in nursing / edited by Lisbeth Hockey. — Edinburgh : Churchill Livingstone, 1981. — xiv,159p ; 22cm. — (Recent advances in nursing, ISSN 0144-6592 ; 1)
Includes bibliographies
ISBN 0-443-02186-4 (pbk) : £5.50 B81-16207

Handbook of nursing procedures. — Oxford : Blackwell Scientific, Jan.1982. — [320]p
ISBN 0-632-00687-0 (pbk) : £5.00 : CIP entry
B81-34783

Hood, Gail H.. Total patient care : foundations and practice. — 5th ed. / Gail H. Hood, Judith R. Dincher. — St.Louis ; London : Mosby, 1980. — viii,915p : ill ; 25cm
Previous ed.: / by Dorothy F. Johnston and Gail H. Hood. 1976. — Includes bibliographies and index
ISBN 0-8016-2574-2 : £9.75 B81-08090

Introduction to nursing practice / [edited by] Lillie M. Shortridge, E. Juanita Lee. — New York ; London : McGraw-Hill, c1980. — xv,588p : ill ; 25cm
Includes bibliographies and index
ISBN 0-07-057056-6 : £10.15 B81-09778

Juneau, Patricia S.. Medical-surgical nursing / Patricia S. Juneau. — New York : Macmillan ; London : Collier Macmillan, c1980. — viii,702p : ill ; 24cm
Includes index
ISBN 0-02-361570-2 (pbk) : £10.50 B81-05946

Mosby's comprehensive review of nursing / [editor Dolores F. Saxton] ; [associate editors Patricia M. Nugent, Phyllis K. Pelikan]. — 10th ed. — St. Louis ; London : Mosby, 1981. — xi,672p : forms ; 24cm
Previous ed.: 1977. — Bibliography: p628-630. — Includes index
ISBN 0-8016-3530-6 (pbk) : £9.75 B81-25053

610.73 — Medicine. Nursing *continuation*

Process in clinical nursing / [edited by] Beverly J. Leonard, Alice R. Redland. — Englewood Cliffs ; London : Prentice-Hall, c1981. — xvi,448p : ill ; 24cm
Includes bibliographies and index
ISBN 0-13-723205-5 (pbk) : Unpriced B81-36498

Roper, Nancy. Learning to use the process of nursing / Nancy Roper, Winifred W. Logan, Alison J. Tierney. — Edinburgh : Churchill Livingstone, 1981. — 119p : ill,forms ; 28cm
ISBN 0-443-02234-8 (pbk) : £4.50 B81-37100

Shafer's medical-surgical nursing. — 7th ed. / [edited by] Wilma J. Phipps, Barbara C. Long, Nancy Fugate Woods. — St. Louis ; London : Mosby, 1980. — xix,991p : ill ; 29cm
Previous ed.: published as: Medical-surgical nursing / edited by Kathleen Newton Shafer et al. 1975. — Includes bibliographies and index
ISBN 0-8016-3934-4 : Unpriced B81-08152

Spencer, May. Introduction to nursing. — 5th ed. — Oxford : Blackwell Scientific, Oct.1981. — [544]p
Previous ed.: 1976
ISBN 0-632-00705-2 (pbk) : £7.50 : CIP entry B81-30999

Tabbner, A. R.. Nursing care : theory and practice / A.R. Tabbner ; foreword by Michael Drake. — Melbourne ; Edinburgh : Churchill Livingstone, 1981. — x,524p : ill ; 25cm
Bibliography: p515-516. — Includes index
ISBN 0-443-02239-9 (pbk) : £7.50 : CIP rev. B81-08875

Tucker, Susan MartinPatient care standards / Susan Martin Tucker ... [et al.]. — 2nd ed. — St. Louis ; London : Mosby, 1980. — xii,562p : ill ; 24cm
Previous ed.: 1975. — Bibliographies: p514-519. - Includes index
ISBN 0-8016-5122-0 (pbk) : £12.75 B81-08045

610.73 — Medicine. Nursing. Change. Implementation

Mauksch, Ingeborg G.. Implementing change in nursing / Ingeborg G. Mauksch, Michael H. Miller. — St. Louis ; London : Mosky, 1981. — xii,195p : ill ; 24cm
Bibliography: p186-191. - Includes index
ISBN 0-8016-3476-8 (pbk) : £7.75 B81-05755

610.73 — Medicine. Nursing — *Conference proceedings*

Gunpowder, treason and plot : report of a day spent studying the nursing process in Dumfries and Galloway / contributors Elizabeth A. Edwards ... [et al.] ; editors Valerie A. Head ... [et al.]. — [Dumfries] : [Dumfries and Galloway Health Board], [1981]. — 32p : ill,forms ; 21cm
Includes bibliographies
Unpriced (pbk) B81-23371

610.73 — Medicine. Nursing. Decision making

Aspinall, Mary Jo. Decision making for patient care : applying the nursing process / Mary Jo Aspinall, Christine A. Tanner. — New York : Appleton-Century-Crofts ; London : Prentice-Hall, c1981. — ix,374p : ill ; 24cm
Includes bibliographies and index
ISBN 0-8385-1555-x (pbk) : £11.95 B81-37690

610.73 — Medicine. Nursing — *For nursing auxiliaries*

Hutton, Shirley W.. Basic nursing care : a guide for nursing auxiliaries. — 2nd ed / Shirley W. Hutton, Yvonne Nielsen. — London : Baillière Tindall, 1981. — vi,126p ; 21cm
Previous ed.: 1974. — Includes index
ISBN 0-7020-0857-5 (pbk) : £2.25 B81-17797

610.73 — Medicine. Nursing — *For student nurses*

Mitchell, Pamela Holsclaw. Concepts basic to nursing / Pamela Holsclaw Mitchell, Anne Loustau. — New York ; London : McGraw-Hill, c1981. — xi,688p : ill ; 25cm
Previous ed.: 1977. — Includes bibliographies and index
ISBN 0-07-042582-5 : £13.25 B81-27185

610.73 — Medicine. Nursing. Leadership

Yura, Helen. Nursing leadership : theory and process / Helen Yura, Dorothy Ozimek, Mary B. Walsh. — 2nd ed. — New York ; [London] : Appleton-Century-Crofts, c1981. — xiii,240p : ill ; 23cm
Previous ed.: 1976. — Bibliography: p215-231. — Includes index
ISBN 0-8385-7028-3 (pbk) : £7.75 B81-16521

610.73 — Medicine. Nursing — *Manuals*

Adam, Evelyn. To be a nurse / Evelyn Adam. — Toronto ; Eastbourne : Saunders, c1980. — x,118p : 2ill ; 22cm
Bibliography: p107-115
ISBN 0-7216-1032-3 (pbk) : £4.75 B81-06771

Billing, Hazel. Practical procedures for nurses. — 3rd ed. / Hazel Billing. — London : Baillière Tindall, 1981. — x,162p : ill ; 19cm. — (Nurses' aids series)
Previous ed.: / by Doris H.M. Billing, 1976. — Includes index
ISBN 0-7020-0865-6 (pbk) : £3.25 : CIP rev. B81-16404

Britten, Jessie D.. Practical notes on nursing procedures / Jessie D. Britten. — 7th ed. / serviced by Margery A. Priest ; foreword by George H. Marshall. — Edinburgh : Churchill Livingstone, 1979 (1980 [printing]). — x,218p : ill ; 22cm. — (Churchill Livingstone nursing texts)
Previous ed.: 1971. — Includes index
ISBN 0-443-01758-1 (pbk) : £2.95 B81-12761

Jackson, Jane. The whole nurse catalog / Jane Jackson. — New York ; Edinburgh : Churchill Livingstone, 1980. — xxii,743p : ill ; 26cm
Includes bibliographies and index
ISBN 0-443-08062-3 (pbk) : Unpriced B81-12230

610.73 — Medicine. Practical nursing

Forrest, Jane. Practical nursing and anatomy for pupil nurses. — 4th ed / Jane Forrest, Margaret Watson. — London : Edward Arnold, 1981. — 259p : ill,1form ; 22cm
Previous ed.: 1974. — Includes index
ISBN 0-7131-4392-4 (pbk) : £4.95 : CIP rev. B81-10477

610.73 — Nursing

Roper, Nancy. Principles of nursing. — 3rd ed. — Edinburgh : Churchill Livingstone, Jan.1982. — [352]p. — (Churchill Livingstone nursing texts)
Previous ed.: 1973
ISBN 0-443-02343-3 (pbk) : £4.25 : CIP entry B81-34001

610.73 — Patients. Lifting & carrying — *Manuals*

Downie, Patricia A.. Lifting, handling and helping patients / by Patricia A. Downie and Pat Kennedy ; with a foreword by Theodora Turner. — London : Faber, 1981. — 143p : ill ; 21cm
Bibliography: p139-140. - Includes index
ISBN 0-571-11630-2 (cased) : £6.50
ISBN 0-571-11631-0 (pbk) : Unpriced B81-13043

Fresen Rantz, Marilyn. Lifting, moving, and transferring patients : a manual / Marilyn Fresen Rantz, Donald Courtial. — 2nd ed, with 322 illustrations by Richard Pearce. — St. Louis ; London : Mosby, 1981. — viii,182p : ill ; 25cm
Previous ed.: 1977. — Includes index
ISBN 0-8016-4087-3 (spiral) : £7.00 B81-24229

Hollis, Margaret. Safer lifting for patient care. — Oxford : Blackwell Scientific, Nov.1981. — [144]p
ISBN 0-632-00825-3 (pbk) : £4.25 : CIP entry B81-32024

610.73'01 — Medicine. Nursing — *Philosophical perspectives*

King, Imogene M.. A theory for nursing : systems, concepts, process / Imogene M. King. — New York ; Chichester : Wiley, c1981. — xii,181p : ill,forms ; 22cm
Includes bibliographies and index
ISBN 0-471-07795-x : £9.00 B81-30791

Parse, Rosemarie Rizzo. Man-living-health : a theory of nursing / Rosemarie Rizzo Parse. — New York ; Chichester : Wiley, c1981. — xix,202p : ill ; 22cm. — (A Wiley medical publication)
Bibliography: p181-196. — Includes index
ISBN 0-471-04443-1 (pbk) : £8.40 B81-33421

610.73'01 — Medicine. Nursing. Theories. Construction

Roy, Callista. Theory construction in nursing : an adaptation model / Callista Roy, Sharon L. Roberts. — Englewood Cliffs ; London : Prentice-Hall, c1981. — xv,299p : ill ; 24cm
Includes bibliographies and index
ISBN 0-13-913657-6 : £11.65 B81-22752

610.73'01'9 — Medicine. Nursing. Psychological aspects

Nurse-client interaction : implementing the nursing process / Sandra J. Sundeen ... [et al.]. — 2nd ed. — St. Louis ; London : Mosby, 1981. — xii,252p : ill ; 24cm
Previous ed.: 1976. — Includes bibliographies and index
ISBN 0-8016-4844-0 (pbk) : £8.50 B81-25050

610.73'01'9 — Nurses. Stress

Living with stress and promoting well-being : a handbook for nurses / edited by Karen E. Claus, June T. Bailey. — St. Louis ; London : Mosby, 1980. — xii,171p : ill ; 24cm
Includes bibliographies and index
ISBN 0-8016-1148-2 (pbk) : £6.75 B81-02875

610.73'05 — Medicine. Nursing — *Serials*

Recent advances in nursing. — 3. — Edinburgh : Churchill Livingstone, Feb.1982. — [256]p
ISBN 0-443-01935-5 : £7.00 : CIP entry
ISSN 0144-6592 B81-35717

610.73'06'0416 — Northern Ireland. Medicine. Nursing. Organisations: Northern Ireland Council for Nurses and Midwives — *Accounts — Serials*

Northern Ireland Council for Nurses and Midwives. Statement of accounts ... for the year ended 31 March ... / Northern Ireland Council for Nurses and Midwives. — 1980. — Belfast : H.M.S.O., 1980. — 9p
ISBN 0-337-02325-5 : £1.60 B81-30718

610.73'068 — England. Nursing services. Management

Armstrong, Mary. Practical nursing management / Mary Armstrong. — London : Edward Arnold, 1981. — 228p : ill,1map ; 23cm
Includes index
ISBN 0-7131-4375-4 (pbk) : £8.00 : CIP rev. B81-12901

610.73'068 — Nursing services. Management

Blake, Robert R.. Grid approaches for managerial leadership in nursing / Robert R. Blake, Jane Srygley Mouton, Mildred Tapper. — St. Louis ; London : Mosby, 1981. — vii,158p : ill ; 24cm
Includes index
ISBN 0-8016-0696-9 (pbk) : £7.00 B81-14994

Douglass, Laura Mae. The effective nurse : leader and manager / Laura Mae Douglass. — St. Louis ; London : Mosby, 1980. — xvi,237p : ill,forms ; 24cm
Includes bibliographies and index
ISBN 0-8016-1448-1 (pbk) : £7.50 B81-08189

Stevens, Warren F.. Management and leadership in nursing / Warren F. Stevens. — New York ; London : McGraw-Hill, c1978. — x,270p : ill ; 24cm
Includes bibliographies and index
ISBN 0-07-061260-9 : £11.20 B81-00905

610.73'068 — Nursing services. Management. Statistical mathematics

Goldstone, Leonard A.. Statistics in the management of nursing services / Leonard A. Goldstone. — Tunbridge Wells : Pitman Medical, 1980. — 272p : ill,forms ; 23cm
Bibliography: p253-254. - Includes index
ISBN 0-272-79598-4 (pbk) : £12.00 B81-03431

610.73'068 — United States. Medicine. Nursing. Management

McQuillan, Florence L.. The realities of nursing management : how to cope / Florence L. McQuillan. — London : Prentice-Hall, c1978. — viii,372p : ill,forms ; 24cm
Includes bibliographies and index
ISBN 0-87618-991-5 : £12.95 B81-24230

The **Nurse** as manager / [edited by] Joyce L. Schweiger. — New York ; Chichester : Wiley, c1980. — xii,194p : ill,forms ; 23cm
Includes bibliographies and index
ISBN 0-471-04343-5 (pbk) : £6.50 B81-03787

610.73'068 — United States. Nursing services. Management

Arndt, Clara. Nursing administration : theory for practice with a systems approach / Clara Arndt, Loucine M. Daderian Huckabay. — 2nd ed. — St Louis ; London : Mosby, 1980. — xii,350p : ill ; 25cm
Previous ed.: 1975. — Includes bibliographies and index
ISBN 0-8016-0305-6 : £10.75 B81-00906

Langford, Teddy L.. Managing and being managed : preparation for professional nursing practice / Teddy L. Langford. — Englewood Cliffs ; London : Prentice-Hall, c1981. — ix,294p : ill ; 23cm
Includes bibliographies and index
ISBN 0-13-550525-9 (cased) : Unpriced
ISBN 0-13-550517-8 (pbk) : £10.45 B81-39906

610.73'068'3 — South Wales. Nurses. Job satisfaction

Wallis, D.. Job satisfaction among professional workers : discussion of a project : some theories and a model / D. Wallis & D. Cope. — Cardiff (c/o R. Slater, Department of Applied Psychology, UWIST, Llwyn-y-Grant, Penylan, Cardiff CF3 7UX) : [UWIST Department of Applied Psychology], 1977. — 19leaves : ill ; 30cm. — (Occasional paper / UWIST Department of Applied Psychology ; no.5)
Bibliography: leaves 16-19
£0.50 (spiral) B81-24802

610.73'06'9 — England. Medicine. Nursing. Attitudes of ward sisters

Redfern, Sally J.. Hospital sisters. — London (Henrietta Place, W1M 0AB) : Royal College of Nursing, July 1981. — [123]p
ISBN 0-902606-65-4 : £4.00 : CIP entry B81-20644

610.73'06'9 — Great Britain. Nurses. Professional conduct

Pyne, Reginald H.. Professional discipline in nursing : theory and practice / Reginald H. Pyne. — Oxford : Blackwell Scientific, 1981. — xi,160p : ill ; 22cm
Includes index
ISBN 0-632-00728-1 (pbk) : Unpriced : CIP rev. B81-05154

610.73'06'9 — Medicine. Nursing — *Career guides*

Napier, K. Barry. So you want to be an angel? : the nurses' survival guide / K. Barry Napier. — London (13 Golden Sq., W1R 3AG) : Settle Bendall, 1981. — 130p : 2ill ; 22cm
Includes index
ISBN 0-907070-02-7 (cased) : Unpriced
ISBN 0-907070-03-5 (pbk) : Unpriced B81-32789

610.73'06'9 — United States. Medicine. Nursing — *Career guides*

DeYoung, Lillian. Dynamics of nursing / Lillian DeYoung. — 4th ed. — St. Louis ; London : Mosby, 1981. — xi,235p : ill ; 24cm
Previous ed.: published as The foundations of nursing as conceived, learned and practiced in professional nursing. 1976. — Includes bibliographies and index
ISBN 0-8016-1283-7 (pbk) : £9.75 B81-33044

610.73'06'980973 — United States. Nursing auxiliaries. Duties

Caldwell, Esther. Health assistant / Esther Caldwell, Barbara Hegner. — New York ; London : Van Nostrand Reinhold, c1981. — vi,279p : ill(some col.) ; 27cm
Includes index
ISBN 0-442-21850-8 : £10.45 B81-29629

610.73'06'99 — Great Britain. Hospitals. Intensive care units. Patients. Communication with nurses — *Study regions: North-west England*

Ashworth, Pat M.. Care to communicate : an investigation into problems of communication between patients and nurses in intensive therapy units / Pat Ashworth. — London (Henrietta Place, Cavendish) : Royal College of Nursing, c1980. — 123p : ill ; 22cm
Bibliography: p115-123
ISBN 0-902606-60-3 (pbk) : £4.00 B81-06464

610.73'06'99 — Hospitals. Patients. Interpersonal relationships with nurses. Psychosocial aspects

Preston, Ronald Philip. The dilemmas of care : social and nursing adaptions to the deformed, the disabled and the aged / Ronald Philip Preston. — New York ; Oxford : Elsevier, c1979. — 220p ; 24cm
ISBN 0-444-99068-2 : £6.42 B81-11290

610.73'06'99 — Medicine. Nursing. Communication

Edwards, Barba Jean. Communication in nursing practice / Barba Jean Edwards, John K. Brilhart. — St. Louis ; London : Mosby, 1981. — vii,245p : ill,forms ; 24cm
Includes bibliographies and index
ISBN 0-8016-0786-8 (pbk) : £7.00 B81-40359

610.73'06'99 — Nurses. Communication with patients

Communication in nursing care / edited by Will Bridge and Jill Macleod Clark with 8 contributors ; foreword by Dame Phyllis Friend. — London : HM & M, c1981. — viii,167p ; 20cm. — (Education for care)
Includes bibliographies
ISBN 0-85602-083-4 (pbk) : Unpriced B81-27703

610.73'06'99 — United States. Medicine. Nursing. Leadership

Bernhard, Linda Anne. Leadership : the key to the professionalization of nursing / Linda Anne Bernhard, Michelle Walsh. — New York ; London : McGraw-Hill, c1981. — xii,195p : ill ; 24cm
Includes bibliographies and index
ISBN 0-07-004936-x (pbk) : £6.25 B81-23725

Kron, Thora. The management of patient care : putting leadership skills to work / Thora Kron with contributions by Ellen Durbin. — 5th ed. — Philadelphia ; London : Saunders, 1981. — x,238p : ill ; 26cm
Includes bibliographies and index
ISBN 0-7216-5529-7 (pbk) : £5.95 B81-12751

610.73'07'11 — Nurses. Lifelong professional education

Austin, Eileen Kay. Guidelines for the development of continuing education offerings for nurses / Eileen Kay Austin. — New York : Appleton-Century-Crofts ; London : Prentice-Hall, c1981. — 191p : ill,forms ; 23cm
Includes bibliographies and index
ISBN 0-8385-3524-0 (pbk) : £7.45 B81-37685

610.73'07'11 — Nurses. Professional education. Nursing practice. Teaching

Huckabay, Loucine M. Daderian. Conditions of learning and instruction in nursing modularized / Loucine M. Daderian Huckabay. — St. Louis ; London : Mosby, 1980. — xiii,497p : ill ; 25cm
Includes bibliographies and index
ISBN 0-8016-2304-9 : Unpriced B81-08200

Robertson, Catherine M.. Clinical teaching / Catherine M. Robertson. — Tunbridge Wells : Pitman Medical, 1980. — 70p ; 22cm
Bibliography: p69-70
ISBN 0-272-79599-2 (pbk) : £4.95 B81-00907

610.73'07'1141 — Great Britain. Nurses. Professional education — *For teaching*

Quinn, Francis M.. The principles and practice of nurse education / Francis M. Quinn. — London : Croom Helm, c1980. — 336p : ill,forms ; 22cm
Includes bibliographies and index
ISBN 0-85664-891-4 (cased) : £13.95 : CIP rev.
ISBN 0-7099-0363-4 (pbk) : £7.95 B80-12363

610.73'07'1141 — Great Britain. Nurses. Professional education — *Serials*

Nurse education today. — Vol.1, no.1 (Apr.1981)-. — Edinburgh : Churchill Livingstone, 1981-. — v. : ill,ports ; 30cm
Six issues yearly
ISSN 0260-6917 = Nurse education today : £10.00 per year B81-33052

610.73'07'1142 — England. Nurses. Professional education. Organisations: Joint Board of Clinical Nursing Studies, *to 1980*

Joint Board of Clinical Nursing Studies. Review of the work of the Joint Board of Clinical Nursing Studies 1970-1980. — [London] ([178/202 Great Portland St., W1N 5TB]) : The Board, [1980]. — 82p : ill ; 21cm
Cover title. — Report by Marjorie Gardener
Unpriced (pbk) B81-14548

610.73'071'142 — Great Britain. Hospitals. Wards. Student nurses. Professional education. Role of head nurses

Orton, Helen D.. Ward learning climate. — London : Royal College of Nursing, Nov.1981. — [95]p
ISBN 0-902606-67-0 (pbk) : £4.00 : CIP entry B81-34958

610.73'072 — Medicine. Nursing. Research

Dempsey, Patricia Ann. The research process in nursing / Patricia Ann Dempsey, Arthur D. Dempsey. — New York ; London : Van Nostrand, c1981. — viii,272p : ill ; 24cm
Includes bibliographies and index
ISBN 0-442-20884-7 : £10.45 B81-02459

Readings for nursing research / edited by Sydney D. Krampitz, Natalie Pavlovich. — St. Louis ; London : Mosby, 1981. — xii,285p : ill,forms ; 28cm
Includes bibliographies and index
ISBN 0-8016-2747-8 (pbk) : £7.00 B81-09768

Readings on the research process in nursing / [compiled by] David J. Fox, Ilse R. Leeser. — New York ; [London] : Appleton-Century-Crofts, c1981. — viii,232p : ill,forms ; 24cm
Includes bibliographies
ISBN 0-8385-8266-4 (pbk) : £10.75 B81-16517

610.73'072 — Medicine. Nursing. Research. Methodology

Ackerman, Winona B.. Research methods for nurses / Winona B. Ackerman, Paul R. Lohnes. — New York ; London : McGraw-Hill, c1981. — xii,270p : ill ; 25cm
Includes bibliographies and index
ISBN 0-07-000182-0 : £13.75 B81-10203

Research methodology and its application to nursing / edited by Yvonne M. Williamson. — New York ; Chichester : Wiley, c1981. — xvi,325p : ill ; 24cm
Includes bibliographies and index
ISBN 0-471-03313-8 : £9.50 B81-23713

610.73'076 — Medicine. Nursing — *Questions & answers*

Gillies, Dee Ann. Saunders tests for self-evaluation of nursing competence / Dee Ann Gillies, Irene Barrett Alyn. — 3rd ed, rev. reprint. — Philadelphia ; London : Saunders, 1980. — viii,496,147,249p ; 26cm
Previous ed.: 1973. — Bibliography: p491-494. — Includes index
ISBN 0-7216-4157-1 (pbk) : £6.95 B81-05804

Hood, Gail H.. Medical-surgical nursing : a workbook for nurses. — 5th ed. / Gail H. Hood, Judith R. Dincher. — St. Louis ; London : Mosby, 1980. — vii,225p : ill ; 24cm
Previous ed.: / Dorothy F. Johnston, Gail H. Hood. 1976. — Includes bibliographies
ISBN 0-8016-2567-x (pbk) : £5.75 B81-08199

Hull, E. J.. Do-it-yourself revision for nurses. — 2nd ed. — London : Baillière Tindall, Feb.1982
Previous ed.: 1970
Book 1. — [160]p
ISBN 0-7020-0911-3 (pbk) : £1.95 : CIP entry B81-37567

610.73'076 — Medicine. Nursing — *Questions & answers* *continuation*

Hull, E. J.. Do-it-yourself revision for nurses. — 2nd ed. — London : Baillière Tindall, Feb.1982
Previous ed.: 1970
Book 2. — [160]p
ISBN 0-7020-0912-1 (pbk) : £1.95 : CIP entry
B81-37568

Hull, E. J.. Do-it-yourself revision for nurses. — 2nd ed. — London : Baillière Tindall, Feb.1982
Previous ed.: 1970
Book 3. — [160]p
ISBN 0-7020-0913-x (pbk) : £1.95 : CIP entry
B81-37569

Hull, E. J.. Do-it-yourself revision for nurses. — 2nd ed. — London : Baillière Tindall
Previous ed.: 1970
Book 4. — Feb.1982. — [160]p
ISBN 0-7020-0914-8 (pbk) : £1.95 : CIP entry
B81-35816

Riddle, Janet T. E.. Objective tests for nurses / Janet T.E. Riddle, Joan Dinner. — Edinburgh : Churchill Livingstone
Bibliography: pvi
Bk.2: The skeletal system and the muscular system / foreword by Margaret W. Thomson. — 1981. — viii,102p : ill ; 25cm
ISBN 0-443-01740-9 (pbk) : Unpriced : CIP rev.
B80-25666

610.73'092'4 — Australia. Medical services: Royal Flying Doctor Service. Nursing services. Miller, Robin, *1940-1975 — Correspondence, diaries, etc.*

Miller, Robin, *1940-1975*. Sugarbird lady / Robin Miller ; compiled and edited by Harold Dicks. — Large print ed. — Leicester : Ulverscroft, 1981, c1979. — 317p ; 22cm
Originally published: Adelaide : Rigby, 1979 ; London : Hale, 1980
ISBN 0-7089-0615-x : £5.00 : CIP rev.
B81-03368

610.73'092'4 — England. Medicine. Nursing. Harker, Cassy M. — *Biographies*

Harker, Cassy M.. Call me matron / by Cassy M. Harker with Jack Glattbach. — Large print ed. — Leicester : Ulverscroft, 1981, c1980. — 358p ; 23cm
Originally published: London : Heinemann, 1980
ISBN 0-7089-0671-0 : £5.00 : CIP rev.
B81-19161

610.73'0924 — Medicine. Nursing. Nightingale, Florence — *Biographies*

Smith, F. B.. Florence Nightingale. — London : Croom Helm, Jan.1982. — [192]p
ISBN 0-7099-2314-7 : £9.95 : CIP entry
B81-33890

610.73'092'4 — Medicine. Nursing. Prentis, Evelyn, *1934-1937 — Biographies*

Prentis, Evelyn. A nurse in time / Evelyn Prentis ; with decorations by Douglas Hall. — London : Arrow, 1979, c1977. — 207p : ill ; 18cm
Originally published: London : Hutchinson, 1977
ISBN 0-09-919450-3 (pbk) : £0.85 B81-15308

610.73'092'4 — Medicine. Nursing. Prentis, Evelyn, *1946-1963 — Biographies*

Prentis, Evelyn. A nurse in parts / Evelyn Prentis ; with decorations by Douglas Hall. — London : Arrow, 1981, c1980. — 200p : ill ; 18cm
Originally published: London : Hutchinson, 1980
ISBN 0-09-924920-0 (pbk) : £1.25 B81-03894

610.73'092'4 — Medicine. Nursing. Prentis, Evelyn — *Biographies*

Prentis, Evelyn. A nurse near by / Evelyn Prentis ; with decorations by Douglas Hall. — London : Hutchinson, 1981. — 198p : ill ; 23cm
ISBN 0-09-144560-4 : £5.95 B81-11562

610.73'0941 — Great Britain. Medicine. Nursing — *Manuals*

Long, Rosemary. Systematic nursing care / Rosemary Long ; with a foreword by Baroness McFarlane of Llandaff. — London : Faber, 1981. — 95p : ill ; 21cm
Bibliography: p92-94. — Includes index
ISBN 0-571-11615-9 (cased) : £6.95
ISBN 0-571-11616-7 (pbk) : Unpriced
B81-08740

610.73'0941 — Great Britain. Medicine. Nursing, *to 1979*

Rewriting nursing history / edited by Celia Davies. — London : Croom Helm, 1980. — 226p : ill ; 23cm
Includes index
ISBN 0-85664-956-2 (cased) : £11.95
B81-07547

610.73'0973 — United States. Medicine. Nursing

Current issues in nursing / [edited by] Joanne Comi McCloskey, Helen K. Grace. — Oxford : Blackwell Scientific, c1981. — xxi,793p : ill ; 24cm
Includes bibliographies and index
ISBN 0-86542-005-x (pbk) : Unpriced
B81-38782

Kelly, Lucie Young. Dimensions of professional nursing. — 4th ed. / Lucie Young Kelly. — New York : Macmillan ; London : Collier Macmillan, c1981. — x,689p ; 25cm
Previous ed.: 1975. — Includes bibliographies and index
ISBN 0-02-362270-9 : £11.95 B81-33394

610.73'43'0941 — Great Britain. Medicine. District nursing

Illing, Margaret. District nursing / Margaret Illing, Brian Donovan ; foreword by Lisbeth Hockey. — London : Baillière Tindall, 1981. — ix,243p : ill ; 22cm
Includes bibliographies and index
ISBN 0-7020-0878-8 (pbk) : £6.50 : CIP rev.
B81-13462

610.73'43'0941 — Great Britain. Medicine. District nursing — *Serials*

Community view : a journal for nurses working in the community. — [No.1], (July 1979)-. — Welwyn Garden City (Bessemer Rd, Welwyn Garden City, Herts. AL7 1HF) : Smith & Nephew, 1979-. — v. : ill ; 30cm
Quarterly. — Description based on: No.7 (Sept.1980)
Unpriced B81-07365

610.73'43'0973 — United States. Medicine. District nursing

Friedman, Marilyn M.. Family nursing : theory & assessment / Marilyn M. Friedman. — New York : Appleton-Century-Crofts ; London : Prentice-Hall, c1981. — xi,338p : ill ; 28cm
Includes index
ISBN 0-8385-2532-6 (pbk) : £70.75 B81-09292

610.73'46 — Industrial health. Nursing. Counselling

Williams, M. Margaret Durrant. Counselling in occupational health nursing. — London (Henrietta Place, W1M 0AB) : Royal College of Nursing, Sept.1981. — [102]p
ISBN 0-902606-66-2 : £4.00 : CIP entry
B81-28809

610.73'6 — Patients. Rehabilitation. Nursing

Comprehensive rehabilitation nursing / edited by Nancy Martin, Nancye B. Holt, Dorothy Hicks. — New York ; London : McGraw-Hill, c1981. — xviii,792p : ill,forms ; 25cm
Includes bibliographies and index
ISBN 0-07-040611-1 : £13.80 B81-05853

610.73'61 — Medicine. Emergency treatment. Nursing

Emergency procedures and first aid for nurses / edited by Muriel Skeet. — Oxford : Blackwell Scientific, 1981. — viii,288p,[7]p of plates : ill (some col.) ; 19cm
Bibliography: p276. — Includes index
ISBN 0-632-00594-7 (pbk) : £6.50 : CIP rev.
B81-13547

Lanros, Nedell E.. Assessment & intervention in emergency nursing / Nedell E. Lanros. — Bowie [Md.] : Brady ; London : Prentice-Hall, c1978. — viii,486p : ill ; 26cm
Includes bibliographies and index
ISBN 0-87618-990-7 : £14.25 B81-25161

610.73'61 — Medicine. Intensive care. Nursing. Psychological aspects

The **Psychological** aspects of intensive care nursing / Nathan M. Simon, editor. — Bowie, Md. : Brady ; London : Prentice-Hall, c1980. — xiv,305p ; 24cm
Includes index
ISBN 0-87619-663-6 : £11.00 B81-04687

610.73'61 — Medicine. Nursing. Emergency treatment

Bradley, David, *1945-*. Accident and emergency nursing / David Bradley. — London : Baillière Tindall, 1980. — x,294p,[4]p of plates : ill (some col.),1plan ; 20cm. — (Nurses' aid series. Special interest texts)
Bibliography: p288. — Includes index
ISBN 0-7020-0751-x (pbk) : £6.75 : CIP rev.
B80-07376

Budassi, Susan A.. Emergency nursing : principles and practice / Susan A. Budassi, Janet M. Barber. — St. Louis ; London : Mosby, 1981. — xiv,775p : ill,forms ; 25cm
Includes bibliographies and index
ISBN 0-8016-0451-6 : £17.50 B81-14996

610.73'61 — United States. Chronically sick persons. Long-term care. Nursing

Walston, Betty J.. The nurse assistant in long-term care : a new era / Betty J. Walston, Keith E. Walston. — St. Louis ; London : Mosby, 1980. — xiii,204p : ill ; 24cm
Includes index
ISBN 0-8016-5355-x (pbk) : £6.50 B81-08161

610.73'62 — Children. Intensive care. Nursing — *Manuals*

Pediatric critical care nursing / edited by Katherine W. Vestal. — New York ; Chichester : Wiley, c1981. — xiv,450p : ill,forms ; 24cm. — (A Wiley medical publication)
Includes bibliographies and index
ISBN 0-471-05674-x : £12.50 B81-23383

610.73'62 — Children. Nursing — *Manuals*

Brunner, Lillian S.. Lippincott manual of paediatric nursing. — London : Harper and Row, Oct.1981. — [760]p
ISBN 0-06-318183-5 (pbk) : £8.95 : CIP entry
B81-30202

Evans, Marilyn Lang. Guide to pediatric nursing : a clinical reference / Marilyn Lang Evans, Beverly Desmond Hansen. — New York : Appleton-Century-Crofts ; London : Prentice-Hall, c1980. — xiii,284p : 2forms ; 28cm
Bibliography: p251-258
ISBN 0-8385-3533-x (pbk) : £9.70 B81-04455

Handbook of comprehensive pediatric nursing / Martha Underwood Barnard ... [et al.]. — New York ; London : McGraw-Hill, c1981. — xiv,578p,[2]folded p of plates : ill,forms ; 15cm
Ill on inside covers. — Includes bibliographies and index
ISBN 0-07-003740-x (pbk) : Unpriced
B81-31960

Thompson, Eleanor Dumont. [Pediatrics for practical nurses]. Pediatric nursing : an introductory text / Eleanor Dumont Thompson. — 4th ed. — Philadelphia ; London : Saunders, 1981. — x,429p : ill ; 26cm
Previous ed.: published as Pediatrics for practical nurses. 1976. — Includes bibliographies and index
ISBN 0-7216-8843-8 (pbk) : £8.95 B81-26964

Wong, Donna L.. Clinical handbook of pediatric nursing / Donna L. Wong, Lucille F. Whaley. — St. Louis ; London : Mosby, 1981. — xi,304p : ill,2forms ; 28cm
ISBN 0-8016-5545-5 (spiral) : £7.75
B81-24247

610.73'62 — Hospitals. Patients: Children — *For nursing*
Jolly, June. The other side of paediatrics : a guide to the everyday care of sick children / June Jolly ; illustrated by Gillian Simmonds. — London : Macmillan, 1981. — xx,164p : ill ; 22cm. — (New approaches to care)
Includes bibliographies
ISBN 0-333-29448-3 (cased) : £10.00
ISBN 0-333-29449-1 (pbk) : £4.95 B81-15034

610.73'62 — Newborn babies. Intensive care. Nursing — *Manuals*
The **Expanding** role of the nurse in neonatal intensive care / edited by Roger E. Sheldon, Pati Sellers Dominiak. — New York ; London : Grune & Stratton, c1980. — xix,320p : ill ; 24cm. — (Monographs in neonatalogy)
Includes index
ISBN 0-8089-1270-4 : £9.80 B81-07363

Halliday, Henry L.. Handbook of neonatal intensive care. — London : Baillière Tindall, Oct.1981. — [224]p
ISBN 0-7020-0884-2 (pbk) : £6.95 : CIP entry B81-25834

Kelnar, C. J. H.. The newborn sick baby. — London : Baillière Tindall, Sept.1981. — [256]p
ISBN 0-7020-0728-5 (pbk) : £8.00 : CIP entry B81-23813

610.73'65 — Old persons. Nursing
Ebersole, Priscilla. Toward healthy aging : human needs and nursing response / Priscilla Ebersole, Patricia Hess. — St. Louis ; London : Mosby, 1981. — xx,697p : ill ; 27cm
Includes bibliographies and index
ISBN 0-8016-1491-0 : £13.50 B81-25051

Flaherty, Maureen O'Brien. The care of the elderly person : a guide for the licensed practical nurse / Maureen O'Brien Flaherty. — 3rd ed. — St. Louis ; London : Mosby, 1980. — x,218p : ill,port ; 24cm
Previous ed.: / written under the name of Maureen J. O'Brien 1975. — Bibliography: p202-208. - Includes index
ISBN 0-8016-3706-6 (pbk) : Unpriced B81-08139

Storrs, Alison M. F.. Geriatric nursing / Alison M.F. Storrs. — 2nd ed. — London : Baillière Tindall, 1980. — viii,253p,[16]p of plates : ill ; 19cm. — (Nurses' aids series)
Previous ed.: 1976. — Includes index
ISBN 0-7020-0815-x (pbk) : Unpriced : CIP rev. B80-11451

610.73'65'0973 — United States. Old persons. Nursing
Nursing care of the older adult : in the hospital, nursing home, and community / edited by Mildred O. Hogstel. — New York ; Chichester : Wiley, c1981. — xv,587p : ill,forms ; 24cm. — (A Wiley medical publication)
Includes bibliographies and index
ISBN 0-471-06022-4 : £11.25 B81-24056

610.73'677 — Man. Aorta. Surgery. Nursing
Aspinall, Mary Jo. Aortic arch surgery / Mary Jo Aspinall. — New York ; [London] : Appleton-Century-Crofts, c1980. — 106p : ill ; 23cm. — (Continuing education in cardiovascular nursing. Series 2, Surgical aspects of cardiovascular disease - nursing intervention ; unit 4)
ISBN 0-8385-0171-0 (pbk) : £4.50 B81-17414

610.73'678 — Gynaecology & obstetrics. Nursing
McNall, Leota KesterContemporary obstetric and gynecologic nursing / edited by Leota Kester McNall. — St. Louis ; London : Mosby, 1980. — x,265p : ill,forms ; 24cm
Includes bibliographies and index
ISBN 0-8016-3325-7 (pbk) : Unpriced B81-08568

610.73'678 — Obstetrics. Nursing
Bash, Deborah Blumenthal. The nurse and the childbearing family / Deborah Blumenthal Bash, Winifred Atlas Gold. — New York ; Chichester : Wiley, c1981. — v,718p,[2]p of plates : ill(some col.),forms ; 25cm
Includes bibliographies and index
ISBN 0-471-05520-4 : £12.00 B81-17250

Jensen, Margaret Duncan. Maternity care : the nurse & the family / Margaret Duncan Jensen, Ralph C. Benson, Irene M. Bobak. — 2nd ed. — St Louis ; London : Mosby, 1981. — xxiii,1013p : ill(some col.),forms ; 29cm
Previous ed.: 1977. — Includes bibliographies and index
ISBN 0-8016-2492-4 : £16.75 B81-30116

610.73'678 — United States. Midwifery
Varney, Helen. Nurse-midwifery / Helen Varney. — Boston [Mass.] ; Oxford : Blackwell Scientific, c1980. — xiii,654p : ill ; 27cm
Includes bibliographies and index
ISBN 0-86542-001-7 : £24.50 B81-01722

610.73'68 — Patients with mental disorders. Nursing
Burgess, Ann Wolbert. Psychiatric nursing in the hospital and the community. — 3rd ed. / Ann Wolbert Burgess. — Englewood Cliffs ; London : Prentice Hall, c1981. — xviii,670p : ill ; 24cm
Previous ed.: 1976. — Includes bibliographies and index
ISBN 0-13-731927-4 : £12.95 B81-16538

Burr, Joan. Nursing the psychiatric patient. — 4th ed. / Joan Burr, John Andrews ; with illustrations by Sylvia Treadgold. — London : Baillièrte Tindall, 1981. — 311p : ill ; 22cm
Previous ed.: 1976. — Includes index
ISBN 0-7020-0855-9 (pbk) : £6.50 : CIP rev. B81-12878

610.73'68 — Psychiatric nursing — *Manuals*
Darcy, P. T.. Theory and practice of psychiatric care. — London : Hodder & Stoughton, Nov.1981. — [224]p
ISBN 0-340-26564-7 (pbk) : £4.95 : CIP entry B81-30133

610.73'68'076 — Patients with mental disorders. Nursing — *Questions & answers*
Jalim, M.. Psychiatric nursing objective test / M. Jalim. — London : Faber, 1980. — 112p ; 19cm
ISBN 0-571-11582-9 (pbk) : £1.95 : CIP rev. B80-17709

610.73'68'0924 — England. Psychiatric hospitals. Nursing — *Personal observations*
Beavis, Gwladys. Oh, my feet! : life in a mental hospital / Gwladys Beavis. — Cardiff (43 Lower Cathedral Rd., Cardiff) : Cleglen Publishing, 1980. — 72p : 1port ; 22cm
ISBN 0-905041-04-6 : £3.90 B81-11055

610.73'68'0926 — United States. Mentally ill persons. District nursing — *Case studies*
Rowan, Frances Power. The chronically distressed client : a model for intervention in the community / Frances Power Rowan. — St. Louis ; London : Mosby, 1980. — xiii,217p : 1ill ; 24cm
Includes bibliographies and index
ISBN 0-8016-4204-3 (pbk) : Unpriced B81-08558

610.73'698 — Cancer patients. Nursing
Bouchard-Kurtz, Rosemary. Nursing care of the cancer patient / Rosemary Bouchard-Kurtz, Norma Speese-Owens. — 4th ed. — St. Louis ; London : Mosby, 1981. — xvi,503p : ill,ports ; 24cm
Previous ed.: 1976. — Includes bibliographies and index
ISBN 0-8016-0720-5 (pbk) : £14.00 B81-25045

Concepts of oncology nursing / Donna L. Vredevoe ... [et al.] with contribution by Carol A. Brainerd. — Englewood Cliffs ; London : Prentice-Hall, c1981. — xii,401p : ill ; 24cm
Includes bibliographies and index
ISBN 0-13-166587-1 : £12.30 B81-25060

610'.76 — Great Britain. Foreign doctors. PLAB examinations — *Manuals*
Moulds, A. J.. A guide to PLAB / Alistair Moulds, Tommy Bouchier Hayes, Ken Young. — London : Heinemann Medical, 1981. — 131p : forms ; 22cm
ISBN 0-433-22601-3 (pbk) : £6.50 B81-24894

610'.76 — Medicine — *Questions & answers*
Anderson, Digby C.. Self-assessment in clinical medicine / D.C. Anderson, D.M. Large. — Oxford : Blackwell Scientific, 1981. — viii,120p ; 22cm
Includes index
ISBN 0-632-00676-5 (pbk) : £3.75 B81-21413

Bell, P.. Multiple choice questions in medicine for the MRCP examinations. — Bristol : Wright, Oct.1981. — [176]p
ISBN 0-7236-0630-7 (pbk) : £5.50 : CIP entry B81-27422

Medicine : PreTest self-assessment and review / edited by John M. Dwyer. — New York ; London : McGraw-Hill, c1978. — ix,221p : ill ; 22cm. — (PreTest series)
Originally published: Wallingford, Conn. : PreTest Service, 1978. — Bibliography: p215-221
ISBN 0-07-051601-4 (pbk) : £6.95 B81-19483

Moulds, A. J.. MCQ tutor for the MRCGP exam / A.J. Moulds and T.A.I. Bouchier Hayes. — London : Heinemann Medical, 1981. — 153p : 1ill,1form ; 22cm
ISBN 0-433-22600-5 (pbk) : £4.50 B81-08209

610'.76 — Medicine — *Questions & answers — For general practice*
The **MRCGP** study book : tests and self-assessment exercises devised by MRCGP examiners for those preparing for the exam / by T.A.I. Bouchier Hayes ... [et al.]. — London : Update, 1981. — 175p : forms ; 25cm
ISBN 0-906141-13-3 (cased) : Unpriced : CIP rev.
ISBN 0-906141-31-1 (pbk) : Unpriced B80-21940

610'.76 — Medicine — *Questions & answers — For physicians*
Corke, C. F.. Self-assessment for MRCP (Part 1) / C.F. Corke. — Oxford : Blackwell Scientific, 1981. — x,239p ; 22cm
Bibliography: pix-x
ISBN 0-632-00819-9 (pbk) : £7.50 : CIP rev. B81-19144

610'.76 — Medicine — *Questions & answers — For schools*
Godman, A.. Objective tests : O-Level health science / A. Godman, Anne C. Gutteridge. — Harlow : Longman, 1981. — vi,90p : ill ; 22cm. — (Study for success)
ISBN 0-582-60627-6 (pbk) : £1.10 B81-34938

610'.76 — Medicine — *Questions & answers — For student nurses*
Harrison, R. J. (Richard John). Multiple choice questions and answers with explanatory notes on medicine, surgery and nursing, including relevant physiology and anatomy / R.J. Harrison. — London : Hodder and Stoughton, 1981. — vii,107p ; 22cm
Cover title: Medicine, surgery and nursing
ISBN 0-340-24707-x (pbk) : £1.95 : CIP rev. B81-06081

610'.92'4 — Medicine. Hodgkin, Thomas, *1798-1866* — *Biographies*
Rose, Michael, *1937 Oct.31-*. Curator of the dead : Thomas Hodgkin (1798-1866) / Michael Rose. — London : Owen, 1981. — 148p,[4]p of plates : ill,ports ; 23cm
Bibliography: p141-142. — Includes index
ISBN 0-7206-0527-x : £9.50 B81-27044

610'.92'4 — Scotland. Medicine. Young, Thomas — *Biographies*
Scott, Sheila A.. Thomas Young of Rosetta / [compiled by Sheila Scott]. — [Peebles] ([43 Rosetta Rd., Peebles EH45 8HH]) : S. Scott, 1980. — 7p : 1ill,1port ; 22cm
£0.20 (pbk) B81-09243

610'.92'4 — Somerset. Rural regions. Medicine — *Personal observations*
Clifford, Robert. Oh dear, Doctor! / Robert Clifford ; illustrated by Nick Baker. — London : Pelham, 1981. — 191p : ill ; 23cm
ISBN 0-7207-1308-0 : £6.50 B81-08485

610'.92'4 — Somerset. Rural regions. Medicine — *Personal observations* *continuation*
Clifford, Robert. What next, doctor? / Robert Clifford ; illustrated by Nick Baker. — London : Sphere, 1981, c1979. — 159p : ill ; 18cm
Originally published: London : Pelham, 1979
ISBN 0-7221-2381-7 (pbk) : £1.00 B81-12627

610'.92'4 — Tanzania. Medicine, *1959-1962 — Personal observations*
Jilek-Aall, Louise. Call Mama Doctor : African notes of a young woman doctor / Louise Jilek-Aall. — London : Allen & Unwin, 1980. — 219p,[32]p of plates : ill(some col.),2 maps,ports(some col.) ; 23cm
Originally published: Saanichton, B.C. : Hancock House, 1979. — Maps on lining papers
ISBN 0-04-925018-3 : £5.95 B81-05520

610'.931 — Taoist medicine, *ca 320 — Early works*
Ke, Hong. Alchemy, medicine and religion in the China of A.D. 320 : the Nei P'ien of Ko Hung (Pao-p'u tzu) / translated & edited by James R. Ware. — New York : Dover ; London : Constable, 1981, c1966. — xiv,388p ; 21cm
Translation from the Chinese. — Originally published: Cambridge, Mass. : M.I.T. Press, 1966. — Includes index
ISBN 0-486-24088-6 (pbk) B81-40028

610'.941 — Great Britain. Medicine
Todd, John W.. The state of medicine : a critical review / by John W. Todd. — Lancaster : MTP, 1981. — vii,235p ; 23cm
Includes index
ISBN 0-85200-384-6 : £11.95 B81-38029

610'.9411 — Scotland. Medicine — *Serials*
Scottish medicine : a bimonthly journal distributed free of charge to all general practitioners in Scotland. — Vol.1, no.1 (Apr.1981)-. — Edinburgh (11 Woodall Terrace, Edinburgh EH14 5BR) : Hermiston Publications, 1981-. — v. : ill,ports ; 30cm
Six issues yearly
ISSN 0261-3921 = Scottish medicine : Unpriced B81-33325

610'.9411 — Scotland. Medicine, *to 1980*
Hamilton, David, *1939-*. The healers : a history of medicine in Scotland / David Hamilton. — Edinburgh : Canongate, 1981. — xiii,318p : ill ; 23cm
Ill on lining papers. — Bibliography: p275-280. — Includes index
ISBN 0-903937-99-9 : £12.95 B81-26471

610'.9413'4 — Edinburgh. Medicine — *Serials*
Edinburgh medicine. — No.1 (Mar.1980)-. — Edinburgh (11 Woodhall Terrace, Edinburgh EH14 5BR) : Edinburgh Medicine Associates, 1980-. — v. : ill,ports ; 30cm
Six issues yearly
ISSN 0260-3934 = Edinburgh medicine : Unpriced B81-02334

610'.9425'81 — Hertfordshire. North Hertfordshire *(District).* **Medicine —** *Serials*
North Herts medical journal : the quarterly publication of North Hertfordshire Medical Society. — Vol.1, no.1 (Summer 1980)-. — Hitchin (Marshall House, Bancroft, Hitchin) : The Society, 1980-. — v. : ill,chart, ports ; 21cm
ISSN 0260-3241 = North Herts medical journal : Unpriced B81-04596

610'.945 — Italy. Medicine, *1260-1327*
Siraisi, Nancy G.. Taddeo Alderotti and his pupils : two generations of Italian medical learning / Nancy G. Siraisi. — Princeton ; Guildford : Princeton University Press, c1981. — xxiii461p ; 25cm
Bibliography: p416-443. — Includes index
ISBN 0-691-05313-8 : £17.80 B81-26184

610'.95 — Asia. Medicine — *Serials*
[Postgraduate doctor *(Asian edition)***].**
Postgraduate doctor : the journal of prevention, diagnosis and treatment. — [Asian ed.]. — Vol.1, no.1 (Jan.1981)-. — Richmond (19 The Green, Richmond, Surrey TW9 1PX) : Barker Publications, 1981-. — v. : ill ; 28cm
Monthly
ISSN 0144-8455 = Postgraduate doctor. Asia : £12.00 per year B81-23144

610'.952 — Japan. European medicine, *1870-1980*
Bowers, John Z.. When the twain meet : the rise of western medicine in Japan / John Z. Bowers. — Baltimore ; London : Johns Hopkins University Press, c1980. — xi,173p ; 24cm. — (The Henry E. Sigerist supplements to the Bulletin of the history of medicine. New series ; no.5)
Bibliography: p161-168. — Includes index
ISBN 0-8018-2432-x : £8.50 B81-34421

610'.96 — Africa. Medicine — *Serials*
Africa health. — Vol.1, no.1 (Oct.1978)-. — Sutton, Surrey (Surrey House, 1 Throwley Way, Sutton, Surrey SM1 4QQ) : IPC Middle East Publishing Company, c1978-. — v. : ill (some col.),ports ; 30cm
Eleven issues yearly. — Supplement: Laboratory equipment international
ISSN 0141-9536 = Africa health : £21.00 per year B81-28382

610'.973 — United States. Medicine, *1730-1930 — Illustrations*
Images of healing : a portfolio of American medical & pharmaceutical practice in the 18th, 19th & early 20th centuries / edited by Ann Novotny & Carter Smith ; with an introduction by William D. Sharpe. — New York : Macmillan ; London : Collier Macmillan, c1980. — 144p : ill(some col.),facsims,ports (some col.) ; 26cm. — (A Media Projects Incorporated book)
Bibliography: p142. - Includes index
ISBN 0-02-590820-0 : £9.95 B81-20988

611 — MAN. ANATOMY

611 — Man. Anatomy
Cunningham, D. J.. Cunningham's textbook of anatomy. — 12th ed. / edited by G.J. Romanes. — Oxford : Oxford University Press, 1981. — ix,1078p : ill(some col.) ; 29cm. — (Oxford medical publications)
Previous ed.: 1972. — Includes bibliographies and index
ISBN 0-19-263134-9 : £25.00 : CIP rev. B80-20688

The **Johns** Hopkins atlas of human functional anatomy / original illustrations, with descriptive legends by Leon Schlossberg ; text edited by Geroge D. Zuidema. — 2nd ed. rev. and expanded. — Baltimore ; London : Johns Hopkins University Press, 1980. — x,115p : ill (some col.) ; 28cm
Previous ed.: Baltimore : The Johns Hopkins University Press ; London : Bailliere Tindall, 1977. — Includes index
ISBN 0-8018-2363-3 (cased) : Unpriced
ISBN 0-8018-2364-1 (pbk) : Unpriced B81-11288

Lumley, J. S. P.. Essential anatomy : and some clinical applications / J.S.P. Lumley, J.L. Craven, J.T. Aitken. — 3rd ed. — Edinburgh : Churchill Livingstone, 1980. — xi,480p : ill ; 22cm
Previous ed.: 1975. — Includes index
ISBN 0-443-02003-5 (pbk) : £7.95 : CIP rev. B80-05926

Mizeres, Nicholas James. Human anatomy : a synoptic approach / Nicholas James Mizeres. — New York ; Oxford : Elsevier, c1981. — 341p : ill ; 26cm
Bibliography: p313-314. — Includes index
ISBN 0-444-00438-6 (cased) : Unpriced
ISBN 0-444-00608-7 (pbk) : Unpriced B81-30035

Murphy, T. R.. Practical human anatomy : laboratory handbook and pictorial guide / T.R. Murphy. — London : Lloyd-Luke
Section 1: Thorax. — 1981. — 153p : ill ; 19cm
Includes index
ISBN 0-85324-155-4 (pbk) : Unpriced B81-39132

611 — Man. Anatomy — *Early works*
French, R. K.. Anatomical education in a Scottish University, 1620 : an annotated translation of the lecture notes of John Moir / R.K. French. — Aberdeen (26 Carden Place, Aberdeen) : Equipress, 1975. — xix,86p : ill,1facsim ; 21cm. — (Texts in the history of medicine ; no.1)
Includes index
Unpriced (pbk) B81-17004

611'.0022'2 — Man. Anatomy — *Illustrations*
The **New** atlas of the human body / edited by Vanio Vannini and Giuliano Pogliani ; translated and revised for the English edition by Richard T. Jolly. — [London] : Corgi, 1980. — 107p : chiefly ill(some col.) ; 28cm
Translation of: Nuovo atlante del corpo umano. — Includes index
ISBN 0-552-98115-x (pbk) : £4.95 B81-17167

611'.0028 — Man. Dissection — *Manuals*
Shearer, Edwin Morrill. Shearer's manual of human dissection. — 6th ed. / edited by Charles E. Tobin, John J. Jacobs. — New York ; London : McGraw-Hill, c1981. — xvii,282p : ill ; 24cm
Previous ed.: 1967. — Includes index
ISBN 0-07-064926-x (spiral) : £14.75 B81-10067

611'.013'0222 — Man. Embryos. Anatomy — *Illustrations*
Stephens, Trent D.. Atlas of human embryology / Trent D. Stephens. — New York : Macmillan ; London : Collier Macmillan, c1980. — xiii,98p : ill ; 28cm
Bibliography: p79. - Includes index
ISBN 0-02-417150-6 (pbk) : £6.50 B81-04452

611'.018 — Man. Cells & tissues. Structure
Han, Seong S.. Human microscopic anatomy / Seong S. Han, Jan O.V. Holmstedt. — New York ; London : McGraw-Hill, 1981. — xi,641p : illl ; 25cm
Includes bibliographies and index
ISBN 0-07-025961-5 : £21.00 B81-17769

Leeson, Thomas S.. Histology / Thomas S. Leeson, C. Roland Leeson. — 4th ed. — Philadelphia ; London : Saunders, 1981. — viii,600p : ill ; 26cm
Previous ed.: 1976. — Includes bibliographies and index
ISBN 0-7216-5704-4 (pbk) : £12.95 B81-33142

611'.018 — Man. Diseases caused by fungi. Histopathology
Chandler, Francis W.. A colour atlas and textbook of the histopathology of mycotic diseases / Francis W. Chandler, William Kaplan, Libero Ajello. — London : Wolfe Medical, 1980. — 333p : col.ill ; 27cm
Bibliography: p319-320. — Includes index
ISBN 0-7234-0754-1 : £35.00 B81-02306

611'.018 — Man. Tissues. Regeneration
Tissue repair and regeneration / editor L.E. Glynn. — Amsterdam ; Oxford : Elsevier/North-Holland Biomedical, 1981. — xxi,597p : ill ; 25cm. — (Handbook of inflammation ; v.3)
Includes bibliographies and index
ISBN 0-444-80278-9 : Unpriced B81-32390

611'.018 — Man. Tissues. Specimens. Preparation — *Manuals*
Sheehan, Dezna C.. Theory and practice of histotechnology / Dezna C. Sheehan, Barbara B. Hrapchak. — 2nd ed. — St. Louis ; London : Mosby, 1980. — xiii,481p,[2]p of plates : ill (some col.),forms ; 26cm
Previous ed.: 1973. — Includes bibliographies and index
ISBN 0-8016-4573-5 : £21.00 B81-13935

611'.018 — Medicine. Histopathology
Recent advances in histopathology. — Edinburgh : Churchill Livingstone
No.11 / edited by Peter P. Anthony and Roderick N.M. MacSween. — 1981. — xi,287p : ill ; 24cm
Includes bibliographies and index
ISBN 0-443-02386-7 (pbk) : Unpriced B81-24472

611'.018 — Medicine. Histopathology — *Serials*

Diagnostic histopathology. — Vol.4, no.1 (Jan. - Mar. 1981)-. — Chichester : Wiley in association with the Pathological Society of Great Britain and Ireland, 1981-. — v. ; 26cm
Quarterly. — Continues: Investigative & cell pathology
ISSN 0272-7749 = Diagnostic histopathology : £65.00 per year B81-20326

611'.018'05 — Man. Cells & tissues. Physiology — *Serials*

Research monographs in cell and tissue physiology. — Vol.5. — Amsterdam ; Oxford : Elsevier/North-Holland Biomedical Pres, 1981. — xviii,511p
ISBN 0-444-80308-4 : £38.31 B81-27323

611'.0181 — Man. Cells. Cytoplasm. Ageing

Age pigments / editor R.S. Sohal. — Amsterdam ; Oxford : Elservier/North-Holland Biomedical, 1981. — xvi,394p : ill ; 25cm
Includes bibliographies and index
ISBN 0-444-80277-0 : Unpriced B81-32848

611'.0181 — Man. Cells. Revitalisation

Abbott, David. New life for old : therapeutic immunology / David Abbott. — London : Muller, 1981. — xiv,155p : ill,ports ; 24cm
Includes index
ISBN 0-584-10399-9 : £8.95 : CIP rev.
B80-21942

611'.0181 — Man. DNA. Repair. Mechanisms *related to* **effects of ionising radiation on human lymphocytes** — *Conference proceedings*

Lymphocyte stimulation : differential sensitivity to radiation : biochemical and immunological processes / [papers presented at the European Molecular Biology Organization lecture course]. — New York ; London : Plenum, c1980. — viii,188p : ill ; 26cm
Includes index
ISBN 0-306-40475-3 : Unpriced
Primary classification 612'.1122 B81-06566

611'.0181 — Man. Liver. Cells — *Conference proceedings*

Falk Symposium *(27th : 1979 : Basel).* Communications of liver cells : proceedings of the 27 Falk Symposium on the occasion of the 5th International Congress of Liver Deseases held at Basel, Switzerland, October 5-7, 1979 / edited by H. Popper... [et al.]. — Lancaster : MTP, c1980. — xxv,430p : ill ; 25cm
Includes index
ISBN 0-85200-350-1 : £24.95 B81-02711

611'.0181'028 — Man. Normal cells in vitro *compared with* **tumour cells in vitro**

Vasiliev, J. M.. Neoplastic and normal cells in culture / J.M. Vasiliev, I.M. Gelfand. — Cambridge : Cambridge University Press, 1981. — xiii,372p : ill ; 24cm. — (Developmental and cell biology series)
Bibliography: p272-346. — Includes index
ISBN 0-521-23149-3 : £36.00
Primary classification 616.99'2'0028 B81-37136

611'.01816 — Man. Genetics. Biochemical aspects

Harris, Harry, *1919-*. The principles of human biochemical genetics / Harry Harris. — 3rd rev. ed. — Amsterdam ; Oxford : Elsevier/North-Holland, 1980. — xv,554p : ill ; 25cm
Previous ed.: 1975. — Bibliography: p473-545. - Includes index
ISBN 0-444-80264-9 : £26.67
ISBN 0-444-80256-8 (pbk) : Unpriced
B81-05476

611'.0185 — Man. Blood. Lymphocytes. Circulation

De Sousa, Maria. Lymphocyte circulation : experimental and clinical aspects / Maria de Sousa with contributions by A.S.G. Curtis, D.M.V. Parrott. — Chichester : Wiley, c1981. — xii,259p,[16]p of plates : ill ; 24cm
Bibliography: p218-252. — Includes index
ISBN 0-471-27854-8 : £19.50 : CIP rev.
B81-02107

611.'0187 — Epithelia. Hydrogen ions. Transport — *Conference proceedings*

International Conference on Hydrogen Ion Transport in Epithelia *(1980 : Frankfurt am Main).* Hydrogen ion transport in epithelia : proceedings of the International Conference on Hydrogen Ion Transport in Epithelia held in Frankfurt am Main (German Federal Republic), July 8-12, 1980 / editors Irene Schulz ... [et al.]. — Amsterdam ; Oxford : Elsevier/North Holland Biomedical, 1980. — x,474p : ill ; 25cm. — (Developments in bioenergetics and biomembranes ; v.4)
Includes index
ISBN 0-444-80290-8 : £28.65
ISBN 0-444-80015-8 B81-05420

611'.018931 — Man. Mouth. Histology

Ten Cate, A. R.. Oral histology : development, structure and function / A.R. Ten Cate with contributions from A.C. Dale ... [et al.] ; [illustrations by J.G. Dale]. — Saint Louis ; London : Mosby, 1980. — xi,2-472p : ill ; 29cm
Bibliography: p450-465. - Includes index
ISBN 0-8016-4886-6 : £21.25 B81-00908

611'.018966 — Women. Uterus. Endometrium. Histopathology

Robertson, William B.. The endometrium / William B. Robertson. — London : Butterworths, 1981. — xii,201p : ill ; 25cm. — (Postgraduate pathology series)
Includes bibliographies and index
ISBN 0-407-00171-9 : Unpriced B81-13670

611.4 — MAN. ANATOMY. LYMPHATIC AND GLANDULAR SYSTEMS

611'.47 — Man. Intermediate pituitary gland. Intermediate lobe peptides - *Conference proceedings*

. Peptides of the pars intermedia. — London : Pitman Medical, May 1981. — [320]p. — (Ciba Foundation symposium ; 81)
Conference papers
ISBN 0-272-79617-4 : £19.50 : CIP entry
B81-04375

611.8 — MAN. ANATOMY. NERVOUS SYSTEM

611'.8 — Man. Nervous system. Anatomy

Brodel, A.. Neurological anatomy : in relation to clinical medicine / A. Brodal. — 3rd ed. — New York ; Oxford : Oxford University Press, 1981. — xvii,1053p : ill ; 24cm
Translation from the Norwegian. — Previous ed.: 1969. — Bibliography: p853-1035. — Includes index
ISBN 0-19-502694-2 : £25.00 B81-24536

611'.81 — Man. Brain. Anatomy

Montemurro, Donald G.. The human brain in dissection / Donald G. Montemurro, J. Edward Bruni. — Philadelphia ; London : Saunders, 1981. — ix,123p : ill ; 22x29cm
Bibliography: p117-118. — Includes index
ISBN 0-7216-6438-5 (spiral) : Unpriced
B81-25220

611'.85 — Man. Temporal bone. Anatomy — *For surgery*

Anson, Barry J.. Surgical anatomy of the temporal bone / Barry J. Anson, James A. Donaldson. — 3rd ed. — Philadelphia ; London : Saunders, 1981. — xvi,734p : ill(some col.) ; 26cm
Previous ed.: 1973. — Bibliography: p711-718. - Includes index
ISBN 0-7216-1292-x : £47.50 B81-12749

611.9 — MAN. REGIONAL ANATOMY

611'.9 — Man. Back & limbs. Anatomy

Hollinshead, W. Henry. Functional anatomy of the limbs and back. — 5th ed. / W. Henry Hollinshead, David B. Jenkins. — Philadelphia ; London : Saunders, 1981. — vi,399p : ill ; 26cm
Previous ed.: 1976. — Includes index
ISBN 0-7216-4755-3 : £12.00 B81-12652

611'.9 — Man. Ears & vocal tract. Anatomy

Singh, Roderick P.. Anatomy of hearing and speech / Roderick P. Singh. — New York ; Oxford : Oxford University Press, 1980. — xii,153p : ill ; 24cm
Includes bibliographies and index
ISBN 0-19-502665-9 (cased) : Unpriced
ISBN 0-19-502666-7 (pbk) : Unpriced
B81-01792

611'.9 — Man. Regional anatomy

Abrahams, Peter H.. The pocket examiner in regional and clinical anatomy. — London : Pitman Medical, Sept.1981. — [288]p
ISBN 0-272-79621-2 (pbk) : £4.95 : CIP entry
B81-23856

611'.9'0222 — Man. Regional anatomy — *Illustrations*

Jamieson, Edward Bald. Jamieson's illustrations of regional anatomy. — 10th ed. — Edinburgh : Churchill Livingstone
Previous ed.: 1972
Section 2: Head and neck. — Nov.1981. — [80]p
ISBN 0-443-02266-6 (pbk) : £3.25 : CIP entry
B81-30486

611'.91 — Man. Head & neck. Anatomy

Montgomery, Royce L.. Head and neck anatomy with clinical corrections / Royce L. Montgomery ; clinical consultants Ernest W. Small, Stephen R. Matteson ; medical illustrator Robert L. Blake, Sr. — New York ; London : McGraw-Hill, c1981. — ix,339p : ill ; 25cm
Includes index
ISBN 0-07-042853-0 : £12.50 B81-25150

611'.91 — Man. Head. Anatomy

Sicher, Harry. Sicher's oral anatomy. — 7th ed. / E. Lloyd DuBrul. — St. Louis ; London : Mosby, 1980. — ix,572p : ill(some col.) ; 26cm
Previous ed.: published as Oral anatomy. 1975. — Bibliography: p541-549. - Includes index
ISBN 0-8016-4605-7 : £20.75 B81-15002

611'.91'0222 — Man. Head & neck. Anatomy — *Illustrations*

Correlative sectional anatomy of the head and neck : a color atlas / [edited by] Joseph R. Thompson, Anton N. Hasso. — St. Louis ; London : Mosby, 1980. — xi,445p : chiefly ill (some col.) ; 31cm
Includes index
ISBN 0-8016-4934-x : £138.00 B81-08150

McMinn, R. M. H.. A colour atlas of head and neck anatomy / R.M.H. McMinn, R.T. Hutchings, B.M. Logan. — London : Wolfe Medical, c1981. — 240p : col.ill ; 27cm
Includes index
ISBN 0-7234-0755-x : Unpriced B81-24568

612 — MAN. PHYSIOLOGY

612 — Man. Body — *For schools*

Manton, Lynne. My body / authors Lynne and Roger Manton ; consultant Lorna Ridgway ; design Ray Carpenter ; illustration Cathie Felstead. — London : Ward Lock Educational, c1979. — 7v. : col.ill ; 21cm + booklet(15p : 21cm). — (Zig-zag pack ; 1)
Bibliography: [2]p
ISBN 0-7062-3812-5 : Unpriced B81-32553

612 — Man. Physiology

Barrass, Robert. Human biology made simple / Robert Barrass. — London : Heinemann, c1981. — xv,303p : ill ; 23cm. — (Made simple books)
Bibliography: p275. — Includes index
ISBN 0-434-98463-9 (cased) : £5.95
ISBN 0-434-98464-7 (pbk) : £2.95 B81-23211

The **Body** machine : your health in perspective / Christiaan Barnard, consultant editor ; John Illman, co-ordinating editor. — London : Hamlyn, 1981. — 256p : ill(some col.),ports (some col.) ; 30cm
Includes index
ISBN 0-600-33212-8 : £9.95 B81-40752

612 — Man. Physiology *continuation*

Brooks, Stewart M.. The human body : structure and function in health and disease. — 2nd ed. / Stewart M. Brooks, Natalie Paynton-Brooks. — St. Louis ; London : Mosby, 1980. — xvii,532p : ill ; 24cm
Previous ed.: published as Basic science and the human body / Stewart M. Brooks. 1975. — Bibliography: p512-513. — Includes index
ISBN 0-8016-0808-2 (pbk) : Unpriced B81-08536

Deamer, David W.. Being human / David W. Deamer. — Philadelphia ; London : Sanders College Publishing, c1981. — viii,508p,[8]p of plates : ill(some col.) ; 25cm
Includes index
ISBN 0-03-022076-9 : £12.95 B81-26339

Griffiths, Mary, *1916-*. Introduction to human physiology / Mary Griffiths. — 2nd ed. / with new and revised line drawings by Iris J. Nichols. — New York : Macmillan ; London : Collier Macmillan, c1981. — xiv,524p : ill (some col.) ; 25cm
Previous ed.: 1974. — Includes bibliographies and index
ISBN 0-02-347230-8 : £12.50 B81-29333

Guyton, Arthur C.. Textbook of medical physiology / Arthur C. Guyton. — 6th ed. — Philadelphia ; London : Saunders, 1981. — xxxiv,1074p : ill(some col.) ; 28cm
Previous ed.: 1976. — Includes bibliographies and index
ISBN 0-7216-4394-9 : £19.50 B81-13938

Human biology : an exhibition of ourselves. — 2nd ed. — Cambridge : Cambridge University Press, Jan.1982. — [124]p
Previous ed.: 1977
ISBN 0-521-23832-3 (cased) : £12.00 : CIP entry
ISBN 0-521-28247-0 (pbk) : £3.95 B81-34418

Medical physiology / edited by Vernon B. Mountcastle. — 14th ed. — St. Louis ; London : Mosby, 1980. — 2v.((xiv,1999,73p.)) : ill ; 28cm
Previous ed.: 1974. — Includes bibliographies and index
ISBN 0-8016-3560-8 : Unpriced B81-08177

The **Principles** and practice of human physiology / editors O.G. Edholm, J.S. Weiner. — London : Academic Press, 1981. — xiii,672p,[1]leaf of plates : ill(some col.) ; 24cm
Includes bibliographies and index
ISBN 0-12-231650-9 : £36.80 : CIP rev. B80-20690

Scratcherd, T.. Aids to physiology. — Edinburgh : Churchill Livingstone, Dec.1981. — [328]p
ISBN 0-443-01959-2 (pbk) : £6.00 : CIP entry B81-31841

Tortora, Gerard J.. Principles of anatomy and physiology / Gerard J. Tortora, Nicholas P. Anagnostakos. — 3rd ed. — New York ; London : Harper & Row, c1981. — xiv,826p : ill(some col.) ; 29cm
Previous ed.: 1978. — Bibliography: p795-801. — Includes index
ISBN 0-06-046642-1 : £ 7.95 B81-27785

Vander, Arthur J.. Human physiology : the mechanisms of body function / Arthur J. Vander, James H. Sherman, Dorothy S. Luciano. — 3rd ed. — New York ; London : McGraw-Hill, c1980. — x,724p : ill(some col.) ; 25cm
Previous ed.: 1975. — Bibliography: p684-696. - Includes index
ISBN 0-07-066961-9 : £8.95 B81-00120

612 — Man. Physiology — *For children*

Amazing facts about the body : stunning facts / illustrated by Bobbie Craig. — [London] : Carousel, 1980. — [32]p : col.ill ; 28cm
ISBN 0-552-57045-1 (pbk) : £0.95 B81-08974

612 — Man. Physiology — *For schools*

Mackean, D. G.. Study guides in human physiology. — London : J. Murray
Series C. — Oct.1981. — 1v.
ISBN 0-7195-3780-0 (pbk) : £14.00 : CIP entry B81-30317

Soper, R.. Modern human and social biology / R. Soper, S. Tyrell Smith. — Basingstoke : Macmillan Education, 1981. — 348p : ill ; 25cm
Includes index
ISBN 0-333-31653-3 (pbk) : Unpriced B81-26509

612 — Man. Physiology — *For students in tropical regions*

Soper, R.. Modern human and social biology : for the tropics / R. Soper, S. Tyrell Smith. — London : Macmillan, 1981. — 348p : ill,maps,ports ; 25cm
Includes index
ISBN 0-333-31026-8 (pbk) : Unpriced B81-26508

612'.0014 — Man. Physiology. Terminology

Squires, Bruce P.. Basic terms of anatomy and physiology / Bruce P. Squires. — Toronto ; London : Saunders, c1981. — vii,165p : ill ; 28cm
ISBN 0-7216-8537-4 (pbk) : £4.75 B81-33385

612'.0024613 — Man. Physiology — *For nursing*

Gibson, John, *1907-*. Modern physiology and anatomy for nurses / John Gibson. — 2nd ed. — Oxford : Blackwell Scientific, 1981. — vii,338p : ill ; 24cm
Previous ed.: 1975. — Bibliography: p326. — Includes index
ISBN 0-632-00795-8 (pbk) : £7.50 : CIP rev. B81-12903

Ross, Janet S.. Foundations of anatomy & physiology / Ross and Wilson. — 5th ed. / revised by Kathleen J.W. Wilson. — Edinburgh : Churchill Livingstone, 1981. — 291p : ill(some col.) ; 28cm
Previous ed.: 1973. — Includes index
ISBN 0-443-01681-x (pbk) : £7.50 B81-20001

Taverner, Deryck. Taverner's physiology. — 4th ed. — London : Hodder & Stoughton, Jan.1982. — [256]p
Previous ed.: published as: Physiology for nursing. London : English Universities Press, 1972
ISBN 0-340-23763-5 (pbk) : £3.95 : CIP entry B81-34121

612'.0028'7 — Man. Physiology. Measurement

Sykes, M. K.. Principles of clinical measurement. — 2nd ed. / M.K. Sykes, M.D. Vickers, C.J. Hull, with an additional chapter by P.J. Winterburn. — Oxford : Blackwell Scientific, 1981. — x,325p : ill ; 26cm
Previous ed.: published as Principles of measurement for anaesthetists. 1970. — Includes bibliographies and index
ISBN 0-632-00044-9 : £21.00 : CIP rev. B80-13830

612'.007 — Man. Physiology — *Questions & answers*

Forsling, Mary. Pocket examiner in physiology. — London : Pitman, Sept.1981. — [224]p
ISBN 0-272-79635-2 (pbk) : £4.95 : CIP entry B81-23858

612'.0072 — Man. Physiology. Research by graduates of University of Oxford, *1628-1674*

Frank, Robert G. (Robert Gregg). Harvey and the Oxford physiologists : a study of scientific ideas / by Robert G. Frank, Jr. — Berkeley ; London : University of California Press, c1680. — xviii,368p,[12]p of plates : ill,plan,ports ; 26cm
Ill on lining papers. — Includes index
ISBN 0-520-03906-8 : £16.50 B81-11246

612'.00724 — Man. Physiology. Mathematical models — *For bioengineering*

Bahill, A. Terry. Bioengineering : biomedical, medical and clinical engineering / A. Terry Bahill. — Englewood Cliffs ; London : Prentice-Hall, c1981. — xiv,304p : ill ; 24cm
Includes bibliographies and index
ISBN 0-13-076380-2 : £18.15 B81-17205

612'.007'7 — Man. Physiology — *Programmed instructions*

Anthony, Catherine Parker. Basic concepts in anatomy and physiology : a programmed presentation. — 4th ed. / Catherine Parker Anthony, Gary A. Thibodeau. — St Louis ; London : Mosby, 1980. — viii,214p : ill ; 26cm
Previous ed.: / by Catherine Parker Anthony. 1974. — Template in pocket
ISBN 0-8016-0260-2 (spiral) : £6.25 B81-08093

612'.009 — Medicine. Physiology, *to ca 1900*

Knight, Bernard, *1931-*. Discovering the human body : how pioneers of medicine solved the mysteries of anatomy and physiology / Bernard Knight. — London : Heinemann, 1980. — 192p : ill,facsims,ports ; 29cm
Bibliography: p192. — Includes index
ISBN 0-434-39350-9 : £9.50 B81-01691

612'.014 — Man. Circadian rhythms

Minors, D. S.. Circadian rhythms and the human. — Bristol : J. Wright, Sept.1981. — [248]p
ISBN 0-7236-0592-0 : £12.00 : CIP entry B81-23849

612'.014 — Man. Effects of mechanical vibration - *Conference proceedings*

International CISM-IFToMM Symposium *(1979 : Udine)*. Man under vibration. — Oxford : Elsevier Scientific, Apr.1981. — [350]p. — (Studies in environmental science ; 13)
ISBN 0-444-99743-1 : £50.00 : CIP entry B81-03825

612'.01426 — Man. Thermoreception

Hensel, H.. Thermoreception and temperature regulation / H. Hensel. — London : Academic Press, 1981. — x,321p : ill ; 24cm. — (Monographs of the Physiological Society ; no.38)
Bibliography: p254-308. — Includes index
ISBN 0-12-341260-9 : £20.20 B81-26357

612'.01444 — Man. Effects of light

Tibbs, Hardwin. The future of light / Hardwin Tibbs. — London : Watkins, 1981. — iv,103p : ill ; 20cm
Bibliography: p93-103
ISBN 0-7224-0196-5 (pbk) : £3.95 : CIP rev. B81-05135

612'.01446 — Man. Physiology. Effects of temperature — *For ergonomics — Conference proceedings*

Bioengineering, thermal physiology and comfort / edited by K. Cena and J.A. Clark. — Amsterdam ; Oxford : Elsevier Scientific, 1981. — 289p : ill ; 25cm. — (Studies in environmental science ; 10)
Conference papers. — Includes bibliographies and index
ISBN 0-444-99761-x : £23.90 : CIP rev. B80-10620

612'.01448 — Medicine. Dosimetry

Greening, J. R.. Fundamentals of radiation dosimetry / J.R. Greening. — Bristol : Hilger in collaboration with the Hospital Physicists' Association, c1981. — xii,160p : ill ; 22cm. — (Medical physics handbooks, ISSN 0143-0203 ; 6)
Bibliography: p149-155. - Includes index
ISBN 0-85274-519-2 : £10.95 B81-08187

612'.01448 — Medicine. Thermoluminescence dosimetry

McKinlay, A. F.. Thermoluminescence dosimetry / A.F. McKinlay. — Bristol : Hilger in collaboration with the Hospital Physicists' Association, c1981. — x,170p : ill ; 22cm. — (Medical physics handbooks, ISSN 0143-0203 ; 5)
Bibliography: p159-165. - Includes index
ISBN 0-85274-520-6 : £11.95 B81-19759

612'.014486 — United States. Man. Foetuses & babies. Effects of low-level ionising radiation, *to 1980*

Sternglass, Ernest J.[Low-level radiation]. Secret fallout : low-level radiation from Hiroshima to Three Mile Island / Ernest J. Sternglass. — Expanded [ed]. — New York ; London : McGraw-Hill, 1981. — xvii,306p ; 21cm
Previous ed.: New York : Ballantine, 1972 ; London : Earth Island Ltd, 1973. — Bibliography: p277-293. — Includes index
ISBN 0-07-061242-0 (pbk) : £4.50 B81-26658

612'.015 — Man. Organic acids

Chalmers, R. A.. Organic acids in man. — London : Chapman and Hall, Jan.1982. — [400]p
ISBN 0-412-14890-0 : £27.50 : CIP entry
B81-34402

612'.015'05 — Medicine. Biochemistry — *Serials*

Clinical biochemistry reviews. — Vol.2-. — New York ; Chichester : Wiley, 1981-. — v. ; 26cm
Annual. — Continues: Annual review of clinical biochemistry
£16.50 B81-24992

612'.015'05 — Medicine. Biochemistry - *Serials*

Recent advances in clinical biochemistry. — No.2. — Edinburgh : Churchill Livingstone, Aug.1981. — [302]p
ISBN 0-443-02005-1 : £20.00 : CIP entry
ISSN 0143-6767 B81-16411

612'.015'0924 — Medicine. Biochemistry. De Ropp, Robert S. — *Biographies*

De Ropp, Robert S.. Warrior's way / Robert S. de Ropp. — London : Allen & Unwin, 1980, c1979. — x,405p : 1port ; 21cm
Originally published: New York : Delacorte Press/S. Lawrence, 1979. — Includes index
ISBN 0-04-921026-2 : £6.95 : CIP rev.
B79-34893

612'.0151 — Urokinase — *Conference proceedings*

Urokinase : basic and clinical aspects. — London : Academic Press, Jan.1982. — [250]p. — (Serono symposia ; no.48)
Conference papers
ISBN 0-12-469280-x : CIP entry B81-33981

612'.01513 — Man. Leukotrienes — *Conference proceedings*

Institute of Basic Medical Sciences. *Symposium (1980 : London)*. SRS-A and leukotrienes : proceedings of the Annual Symposium of the Institute of Basic Medical Sciences, Royal College of Surgeons of England, 24th September 1980 / edited by Priscilla J. Piper. — Chichester : Research Studies Press, c1981. — xiii,282p : ill ; 24cm. — (Prostaglandins research studies series)
Includes bibliographies and index
ISBN 0-471-27959-5 : £16.00 B81-18758

612'.01522 — Man. Acid-base balance, electrolyte balance & fluid balance

Li, Arthur K. C.. Fluid, electrolytes, acid-base and nutrition / Arthur K.C. Li, Michael R. Wills, Gillian C. Hanson. — London : Academic Press, 1980. — ix,80p : ill ; 22cm
Includes index
ISBN 0-12-448150-7 (pbk) : £3.40 : CIP rev.
B80-11036

Stewart, Peter A.. How to understand acid-base : a quantitative acid-base primer for biology and medicine / Peter A. Stewart. — London : Edward Arnold, 1981. — xii,186p : ill ; 24cm
Includes index
ISBN 0-7131-4390-8 : £14.00 B81-21377

612'.01522 — Man. Body fluids

Burke, Shirley R.. The composition and function of body fluids / Shirley R. Burke. — 3rd ed. — St. Louis ; London : Mosby, 1980. — xii,208p : ill ; 23cm
Previous ed.: 1976. — Includes index
ISBN 0-8016-0903-8 (pbk) : Unpriced
B81-08166

612'.01522 — Man. Body fluids. Electrolytes — *Programmed instructions* — *For nursing*

Weldy, Norma Jean. Body fluids and electrolytes : a programmed presentation / Norma Jean Weldy. — 3rd ed. — St Louis ; London : Mosby, 1980. — xi,131p : ill ; 24cm
Previous ed.: 1976. — Template in pocket. — Bibliography: p118. — Includes index
ISBN 0-8016-5383-5 (spiral) : £5.95
B81-08094

612'.01522 — Man. Body fluids. Pressure. Monitoring — *Manuals*

Cywinski, Jozef. The essentials in pressure monitoring : blood and other body fluids / Jozef Cywinski and Bernard Tardieu ; foreword by J. Warren Harthorne. — The Hague ; London : Nijhoff Medical Division, 1980. — 117p : col.ill ; 25cm
Includes index
ISBN 90-247-2385-x (pbk) : Unpriced
B81-04552

612'.01524 — Man. Effects of mineral fibres — *Conference proceedings*

Biological effects of mineral fibres = Effets biologiques des fibres minérales : proceedings of a symposium organized by IARC, l'Institut national de la santé et de la recherche médicale (National Institute of Health and Medical Research), and the MRC Pneumoconiosis Unit, Penarth, UK, held at the International Agency for Research on Cancer, Lyon, France 25-27 September 1979 / editor-in-chief J.C. Wagner ; technical editor for IARC W. Davis. — Lyon : International Agency for Research on Cancer ; [London] : [H.M.S.O.], 1980. — 2v.(xxxix,1007p) : ill ; 25cm. — (IARC scientific publications ; no.30) (INSERM symposia series ; v.92)
Includes bibliographies and index
ISBN 92-8321-130-8 : Unpriced B81-20814

612'.01524 — Man. Magnesium

Wacker, Warren E. C.. Magnesium and man / Warren E.C. Wacker. — Cambridge, Mass. ; London : Harvard University Press, 1980. — 171p : ill ; 24cm. — (A Commonwealth Fund book)
Bibliography: p117-158. — Includes index
ISBN 0-674-54225-8 : £10.50 B81-16562

612'.01524 — Man. Magnesium — *Conference proceedings*

International Symposium on Magnesium *(2nd : 1976 : Montreal)*. Magnesium in health and disease : proceedings of the 2nd International Symposium on Magnesium, Montreal, Quebec, May 30-June 1, 1976 / edited by Marc Cantin and Mildred S. Seeling. — Lancaster : MTP, c1980. — 965p : ill ; 24cm. — (Monographs of the American College of Nutrition ; v.4)
Includes bibliographies and index
ISBN 0-85200-535-0 : £95.00 B81-04581

612'.0157 — Man. Insulin receptors — *Conference proceedings*

Current news on insulin receptors. — London : Academic Press, Jan.1982. — [600]p. — (Proceedings of the Serono symposia, ISSN 0308-5503 ; v.41)
Conference papers
ISBN 0-12-058620-7 : CIP entry B81-34116

612'.0157 — Man. Purines. Metabolism — *Conference proceedings*

International Symposium on Purine Metabolism in Man *(3rd : 1979 : Madrid)*. Purine metabolism in man - III / edited by Aurelio Rapado, R.W.E. Watts, Chirs H.M.M. De Bruyn. — New York ; London : Plenum Press
Clinical and therapeutic aspects / [proceedings of the first half of the Third International Symposium on Purine Metabolism in Man, held in Madrid, Spain, June 11-15, 1979]. — c1980. — xxii,444p : ill ; 26cm. — (Advances in experimental medicine and biology ; v.122A)
Includes bibliographies and index
ISBN 0-306-40310-2 : Unpriced B81-39033

612'.044 — Man. Exercise. Physiological aspects

Bassey, E. J.. Exercise : the facts / E.J. Bassey and P.H. Fentem. — Oxford : Oxford University Press, 1981. — x,97p ; 21cm
Bibliography: p94. — Includes index
ISBN 0-19-217716-8 (pbk) : Unpriced
B81-15669

Burke, Edmund J.. Fit to exercise. — London : Pelham, Oct.1981. — [208]p
ISBN 0-7207-1224-6 : £7.50 : CIP entry
B81-27932

612'.044 — Physical fitness. Exercises. Physiological aspects

McArdle, William D.. Exercise physiology : energy, nutrition, and human performance / William D. McArdle, Frank I. Katch, Victor L. Katch. — Philadelphia : Lea & Febiger ; London : Kimpton, 1981. — xi,508p : ill(some col.) ; 27cm
Includes bibliographies and index
ISBN 0-8121-0682-2 : £8.50 B81-16095

612'.044 — Sports & games. Physiological aspects

Fox, Edward L.. The physiological basis of physical education and athletics / Edward L. Fox, Donald K. Mathews ; illustrated by Nancy Allison Close. — 3rd ed. — Philadelphia ; London : Saunders College, c1981. — xvi,677p : ill ; 25cm
Previous ed.: 1976. — Text on lining papers. — Includes bibliographies and index
ISBN 0-03-057676-8 : £12.50 B81-25591

612.1 — MAN. PHYSIOLOGY. CARDIOVASCULAR SYSTEM

612'.1 — Man. Cardiovascular system. Effects of prostaglandins — *Conference proceedings*

A.N. Richards Symposium *(20th : 1978 : King of Prussia, Pa.)*. Prostaglandins in cardiovascular and renal function : proceedings of the 20th annual A.N. Richards Symposium of the Physiological Society of Philadelphia, King of Prussia, Pennsylvania, May 8-9, 1978 / edited by Alexander Scriabine, Allan M. Lefer and Frederick A. Kuehl. — Lancaster : MTP, c1980. — 498p : ill ; 24cm. — (Monographs of the Physiological Society of Philadelphia ; v.6)
Includes bibliographies and index
ISBN 0-85200-532-6 : £29.95
Also classified at 612'.463 B81-04661

612'.1 — Man. Cardiovascular system. Physiology

Berne, Robert M.. Cardiovascular physiology / Robert M. Berne, Matthew N. Levy. — 4th ed. — St. Louis ; London : Mosby, 1981. — ix,286p : ill ; 24cm
Previous ed.: 1977. — Includes bibliographies and index
ISBN 0-8016-0655-1 : £14.00 B81-40363

Heller, Lois Jane. Cardiovascular physiology / Lois Jane Heller, David E. Mohrman. — New York ; London : McGraw-Hill, c1981. — vi,169p : ill ; 23cm
Bibliography: p153-156. — Includes index
ISBN 0-07-027973-x (pbk) : £7.95 B81-10119

612'.1 — Man. Cardiovascular system. Prostaglandins — *Conference proceedings*

International Symposium on Prostaglandins and Thromboxanes in the Cardiovascular System *(3rd : 1980 : Halle)*. Prostaglandins and thromboxanes. — Oxford : Pergamon, May 1981. — [500]p
ISBN 0-08-027369-6 : £33.00 : CIP entry
B81-09986

612'.1 — Man. Cardiovascular system. Psychophysiological aspects

Obrist, Paul A.. Cardiovascular psychophysiology : a perspective / Paul A. Obrist. — New York ; London : Plenum, c1981. — x,236p : ill ; 24cm
Bibliography: p211-231. — Includes index
ISBN 0-306-40599-7 : Unpriced B81-24214

612'.1 — Man. Cardiovascular system. Regulation

Gardiner, Sheila M.. Cardiovascular homeostasis : intrarenal and extrarenal mechanisms / Sheila M. Gardiner and Terence Bennett. — Oxford : Oxford University Press, 1981. — viii,158p : ill ; 22cm. — (Oxford medical publications)
Includes bibliographies and index
ISBN 0-19-261178-x : £12.50 : CIP rev.
B81-13583

612′.1 — Man. Circulatory system. Control by nervous system — *Conference proceedings*

Neural control of circulation / edited by Maysie J. Hughes, Charles D. Barnes. — New York ; London : Academic Press, 1980. — xii,175p : ill ; 24cm. — (Research topics in physiology ; 2)
Includes bibliographies and index
ISBN 0-12-360850-3 : £13.60 B81-03193

612′.1 — Man. Circulatory system. Role of smooth muscles of heart

Ba sar, Erol. Vasculature and circulation : the role of myogenic reactivity in the regulation of blood flow / Erol Ba sar, Christoph Weiss. — Amsterdam ; Oxford : Elsevier/North Holland Biomedical, 1981. — xviii,272p : ill ; 25cm
Bibliography: p255-263. — Includes index
ISBN 0-444-80271-1 : £37.79 B81-21428

612′.112 — Man. Blood. Eosinophils — *Conference proceedings*

The **Eosinophil** in health and disease / proceedings of the Eosinophil centennial, Brook Lodge, Augusta, Michigan September 24-28, 1979 ; edited by Adel A.F. Mahmoud, K. Frank Austen ; technical editor Arlene Stolper Simon. — New York ; London : Grune & Stratton, c1980. — xxii,364p : ill,2ports ; 24cm
Includes index
ISBN 0-8089-1274-7 : £22.20 B81-13936

612′.1122 — Man. Blood. Lymphocytes. Effects of ionising radiation ***related to*** **DNA repair mechanisms** — *Conference proceedings*

Lymphocyte stimulation : differential sensitivity to radiation : biochemical and immunological processes / [papers presented at the European Molecular Biology Organization lecture course]. — New York ; London : Plenum, c1980. — viii,188p : ill ; 26cm
Includes index
ISBN 0-306-40475-3 : Unpriced
Also classified at 611′.0181 B81-06566

612′.115 — Heparin — *Conference proceedings*

International Conference on the Chemistry and Biology of Heparin *(1980 : Chapel Hill, N.C.)*. Chemistry and biology of heparin : proceedings of the International Conference on the Chemistry and Biology of Heparin held in Chapel Hill, North Carolina, U.S.A. on March 20-22, 1980 / editors Roger L. Lundblad ... [et al.]. — New York ; Oxford : Elsevier/North-Holland, c1981. — xv,667p : ill ; 25cm. — (Developments in biochemistry, ISSN 0165-1714 ; v.12)
Includes index
ISBN 0-444-00445-9 : £41.27 B81-21389

612′.115 — Man. Fibrinolysis

Marsh, N. A.. Fibrinolysis. — Chichester : Wiley, Sept.1981. — [272]p
ISBN 0-471-28029-1 : £16.50 : CIP entry B81-20126

612′.115 — Man. Fibrinolysis. Role of urokinase — *Conference proceedings*

Fibrinolysis and urokinase / edited by Volkmar Tilsner, Heidemarie Lenau. — London : Academic Press, 1980. — x,432p : ill ; 24cm. — (Proceedings of the Serono symposia, ISSN 0308-5503 ; v.31)
Includes bibliographies and index
ISBN 0-12-691150-9 : £26.20 : CIP rev.
ISSN 0308-5503 B80-20693

612′.115 — Man. Fibrinolysis — *Serials*

Progress in fibrinolysis. — Vol.5-. — Edinburgh : Churchill Livingstone, 1981-. — v. : ill ; 24cm
Irregular. — Continues: Progress in chemical fibrinolysis and thrombolysis
ISSN 0262-0790 = Progress in fibrinolysis : £30.00 B81-37245

612′.116 — Man. Blood plasma. Lipids. Optimisation — *Conference proceedings*
Conference on Health Effects of Blood Lipids *(1979 : New York, N.Y.)*. Plasma lipids : optimal levels for health / [proceedings of the Conference on Health Effects of Blood Lipids : Optimal Distributions for Populations] ; [edited and held by] American Health Foundation ; Ernest L. Wynder conference chairman ; Henry Blackburn, Barry Lewis, Robert Wissler, workshop chairmen. — New York ; London : Academic Press, 1980. — ix,187p : ill ; 25cm
Includes bibliographies and index
ISBN 0-12-103450-x : £8.40 B81-22000

612′.116 — Man. Blood plasma. Proteins. Fractionation. Techniques
Methods of plasma protein fractionation / edited by J.M. Curling. — London : Academic Press, 1980. — xiii,326p : ill ; 24cm
Includes bibliographies and index
ISBN 0-12-199550-x : £23.20 : CIP rev. B80-09691

612′.1181 — Haemorrheology — *Serials*
Clinical hemorheology : a companion journal of Biorheology. — Vol.1, no.1 (1981)-. — New York ; Oxford : Pergamon, 1981-. — v. : ill ; 26cm
Six issues yearly
ISSN 0271-5198 = Clinical hemorheology : Unpriced B81-26586

612′.1181 — Man. Blood. Flow. Measurement
Measurement of blood flow : applications to the splanchnic circulation / edited by D. Neil Granger, Gregory B. Bulkley. — Baltimore ; London : Williams & Wilkins, c1981. — xvi,537p : ill(some col.) ; 26cm
Includes bibliographies and index
ISBN 0-683-03730-7 : £57.50 B81-27493

612′.1181 — Man. Blood. Flow. Measurement. Applications of physics
Rowan, J. O.. Physics and the circulation / J.O. Rowan. — Bristol : Hilger in association with Hospital Physicists′ Association, c1981. — 122p : ill ; 22cm. — (Medical physics handbooks ; 9)
Includes bibliographies and index
ISBN 0-85274-508-7 : £11.95 : CIP rev. B81-12790

612′.1181 — Man. Blood. Rheology
Blood viscosity in heart disease and cancer. — Oxford : Pergamon, Dec.1981. — [192]p
ISBN 0-08-024954-x : £18.00 : CIP entry B81-31518

Chmiel, Horst. On the rheology of blood and synovial fluids / Horst Chmiel and Eckehard Walitza. — Chichester : Research Studies Press, c1980. — xii,166p : ill ; 24cm. — (Chemical engineering aspects of biomedicine research studies series ; 1)
Bibliography: p147-163. — Includes index
ISBN 0-471-27858-0 : £14.50 : CIP rev.
Also classified at 612′.75 B80-35019

612′.11822 — Man. Blood. Lymphokines
Lymphokines : a forum for immunoregulatory cell products. — New York ; London : Academic Press
Vol.3: Lymphokines in macrophage activation / edited by Edgar Pick ; advisory editor Maurice Landy. — 1981. — xviii,450p : ill ; 24cm
Includes bibliographies and index
ISBN 0-12-432003-1 : £32.80 B81-40777

612′.11822 — Man. Blood. Lymphokines — *Serials*
Lymphokines : a forum for iommunoregulatory cell products. — Vol.2-. — New York ; London : Academic Press, 1981-. — v. : ill ; 24cm
Continues: Lymphokine reports
£23.20
Also classified at 574.2′95 B81-37249

612′.118223 — Man. Blood. Lymphocytes. Immunoglobulins
Lymphocytic regulation by antibodies / edited by Constantin Bona, Pierre-André Cazenave. — New York ; Chichester : Wiley, c1981. — x,324p : ill ; 24cm
Includes bibliographies and index
ISBN 0-471-05693-6 : £28.25 B81-17087

612′.11825 — Man. Blood groups. Distribution — *Statistics*
Tills, D.. The distribution of the human blood groups and other polymorphisms. Supplement 1. — Oxford : Oxford University Press, Feb.1982. — [300]p. — (Oxford monographs on medical genetics)
ISBN 0-19-261129-1 : £30.00 : CIP entry B81-35773

612′.11825 — Man. Blood groups. Racial aspects
Pearson, Roger. Blood groups and race / by Roger Pearson. — 2nd ed. (rev.). — London (BCM-Thule, WC1V 6XX) : Folk and Race, 1966 (1980 [printing]). — 30p : ill,2maps ; 21cm
Previous ed.: 1959
£0.65 (pbk) B81-04445

612′.12 — Man. Blood. Angiotensin. Formation. Role of renin — *Serials*
Renin. — Vol.5. — Westmount, Quebec : Eden Press ; Edinburgh : Churchill Livingstone, c1980. — 368p. — (Annual research reviews)
ISBN 0-443-02479-0 : Unpriced
ISSN 0703-2986 B81-20722

612′.13 — Man. Blood vessels. Physiology
Humphreys, P.. Physiology of the arterial and venous systems / by P. Humphreys. — [London] : University of London Board of Studies in Physiology ; London (B.M.A. House, Tavistock Sq., WC1H 9JP) : Distributed by the B.L.A.T. Centre for Health and Medical Education, [1980]. — 21p : ill ; 15x22cm. — (Individual study of medical physiology. Secton 4. Unit 2 ; session 2)
Unpriced (pbk) B81-15666

612′.13 — Man. Cardiovascular system. Blood. Circulation
Oka, Syoten. Cardiovascular hemorheology. — Cambridge : Cambridge University Press, Nov.1981. — [214]p
ISBN 0-521-23650-9 : £20.00 : CIP entry B81-33620

612′.13 — Man. Microcirculatory system — *Conference proceedings*
European Conference on Microcirculation *(11th : 1980 : Garmisch-Partenkirchen)*. Recent advances in microcirculatory research : 11th European Conference on Microcirculation, Garmisch-Partenkirchen, September 15-19, 1980 / volume editor P. Gaehtgens. — Basel ; London : Karger, c1981. — xiv,737p : ill ; 25cm. — (Bibliotheca anatomica ; no.20)
Includes bibliographies and index
ISBN 3-8055-2272-x : Unpriced B81-36086

612′.133 — Man. Head & neck. Arteries
Lasjaunias, Pierre L.. Craniofacial and upper cervical arteries : functional, clinical and angiographic aspects / Pierre L. Lasjaunias with collaboration of Alex Berenstein. — Baltimore ; London : Williams & Wilkins, c1981. — xiii,199p : ill(some col.) ; 29cm
Bibliography: p193-195. — Includes index
ISBN 0-683-04900-3 : £68.50 B81-20758

612′.14 — Man. Blood. Pressure. Regulation
Coleman, Thomas G.. Blood pressure control / Thomas G. Coleman. — St. Albans, Vt. : Eden ; Lancaster : MTP
Vol.1. — c1980. — 248p ; 22cm
Bibliography: p150-245. — Includes index
ISBN 0-88831-088-9 : £14.95 B81-16038

612′.14 — Man. Blood pressure. Regulation. Biochemical aspects
Biochemical regulation of blood pressure / edited by Richard L. Soffer. — New York ; Chichester : Wiley, c1981. — viii,456p : ill ; 24cm
Includes index
ISBN 0-471-05600-6 : £34.65 B81-33372

612′.14′0287 — Man. Blood pressure. Measurement
O′Brien, Eoin. Essentials of blood pressure measurement / Eoin O′Brien, Kevin O′Malley ; with a foreword by George E. Burch. — Edinburgh : Churchill Livingstone, 1981. — x,69p : ill ; 19cm
Bibliography: p63-64. — Includes index
ISBN 0-443-02336-0 (pbk) : £2.25 : CIP rev. B81-15842

612'.171 — Man. Heart. Dynamics — *Conference proceedings*

Cardiac dynamics / edited by Jan Baan, Alexander C. Arntzenius and Edward L. Yellin. — The Hague ; London : Nijhoff, 1980. — xxii,549p : ill ; 25cm. — (Developments in cardiovascular medicine ; v.2)
Includes index
ISBN 90-247-2212-8 : Unpriced B81-04480

612.2 — MAN. PHYSIOLOGY. RESPIRATORY SYSTEM

612'.2 — Man. Lungs. Blood. Circulation — *Conference proceedings*

Symposium on the Pulmonary Circulation *(1979 : Erice, Sicily).* Pulmonary circulation in health and disease / [proceedings of the Symposium on the Pulmonary Circulation, held at the Ettore Majorana Center for Scientific Culture, Erice, Sicily, Italy, July 16-21, 1979] ; edited by G. Cumming and G. Bonsignore. — New York ; London : Plenum, c1980. — ix,442p : ill ; 26cm. — (Ettore Majorana international science series. Life sciences ; v.3)
Includes index
ISBN 0-306-40473-7 : Unpriced B81-05068

612'.22 — Man. Lungs. Metabolism — *Conference proceedings*

Metabolic activities of the lung. — Amsterdam ; Oxford : Excerpta Medica, 1980. — ix,401p : ill ; 25cm. — (Ciba Foundation symposium. New series ; 78)
Conference papers. — Includes bibliographies and index
ISBN 90-219-4084-1 : £2m.53 B81-02987

612.3 — MAN. PHYSIOLOGY. DIGESTIVE SYSTEM

612'.3 — Children. Nutrition. Health aspects

Textbook of paediatric nutrition. — 2nd ed. — Edinburgh : Churchill Livingstone, Oct.1981. — [448]p
Previous ed.: 1976
ISBN 0-443-02285-2 (pbk) : £15.00 : CIP entry B81-25300

612'.3 — Man. Digestive system. Physiology

Hawker, Ross Wilson. Notebook of medical physiology : gastrointestinal : with aspects of total parenteral nutrition : a revision text for candidates preparing for examinations in basic medical sciences ; includiong multiple choice questions / Ross Wilson Hawker. — Edinburgh : Churchill Livingstone, 1981. — 246p : ill ; 22cm
Includes bibliographies and index
ISBN 0-443-02144-9 (pbk) : £4.95 : CIP rev. B80-31602

Sanford, Paul A.. Digestive system physiology. — London : Edward Arnold, Nov.1981. — [192] p. — (Physiological principles in medicine, ISSN 0260-2946 ; 3)
ISBN 0-7131-4380-0 (pbk) : £5.00 : CIP entry B81-30593

612'.3 — Man. Nutrition. Medical aspects

Nutrition of man / edited by J.C. Waterlow. — London : Published for the British Council by Churchill Livingstone, c1981. — 104p : ill ; 28cm
Cover title
ISBN 0-443-02449-9 (pbk) : £9.50 B81-12725

Weinsier, Roland L.. Handbook of clinical nutrition : clinician's manual for the diagnosis and management of nutritional problems / Roland L. Weinsier, C.E. Butterworth, Jr. — St. Louis ; London : Mosby, 1981. — xiv,231p : ill,forms
Includes bibliographies and index
ISBN 0-8016-5406-8 (pbk) : £8.25 B81-19513

612'.3 — Man. Nutrition, Medical aspects - *Conference proceedings - Serials*

Recent advances in clinical nutrition. — 1st (9-11 July 1980). — London (80 Bondway, SW8 2JF) : John Libbey, Apr.1981. — [312]p
Conference papers
ISBN 0-86196-009-2 : £18.00 : CIP entry
ISSN 0260-8170 B81-07459

612'.3'088042 — Pregnant women & lactating women. Nutrition. Physiology

Worthington-Roberts, Bonnie S.. Nutrition in pregnancy and lactation / Bonnie S. Worthington-Roberts, Joyce Vermeersch, Sue Rodwell Williams. — 2nd ed. — St. Louis ; London : Mosby, 1981. — ix,309p : ill ; 24cm
Previous ed.: 1977. — Includes bibliographies and index
ISBN 0-8016-5626-5 (pbk) : £8.50 B81-25607

612'.31 — Man. Mouth. Stratified epithelia

Schroeder, Hubert E.. Differentiation of human oral stratified epithelia / Hubert E. Schroeder with technical assistance of Margrit Amstad-Jossi. — Basel ; London : Karger, 1981. — x,306p : ill ; 25cm
Bibliography: p269-291. — Includes index
ISBN 3-8055-1462-x : £39.75 B81-26121

612'.31 — Man. Periodontium

The **Periodontal** ligament in health and disease. — Oxford : Pergamon, Feb.1982. — [464]p
ISBN 0-08-024412-2 (cased) : £38.00 : CIP entry
ISBN 0-08-024411-4 (pbk) : £19.00 B81-35905

612'.311 — Man. Mastication. Physiology

Watt, David M.. Gnathosonic diagnosis and occlusal dynamics. — Eastbourne : Holt-Saunders, June 1981. — [224]p
ISBN 0-03-059624-6 : £18.00 : CIP entry B81-14823

612'.311 — Man. Teeth. Surface interactions — *Conference proceedings*

Tooth surface interactions and preventive dentistry : proceedings of a workshop on tooth surface interactions and preventive dentistry held at the Hotel Lysebu, Voksenlia, Oslo 3, Norway on December 4-6th 1980 / edited by Gunnar Rølla, Torleif Sønju, Graham Embery ; organised by the Research Group on Surface and Colloid Phenomena in the Oral Cavity under the auspices of the Council of Europe. — London : Information Retrieval, c1981. — 217p : ill ; 23cm
ISBN 0-904147-29-0 (pbk) : £15.00 B81-22231

612'.32 — Man. Gastrointestinal tract. Physiology

Gastrointestinal physiology / edited by Leonard R. Johnson. — 2nd ed. — St. Louis ; London : Mosby, 1981. — xi,173p : ill ; 24cm
Previous ed.: 1977. — Includes bibliographies and index
ISBN 0-8016-2532-7 (pbk) : £10.50 B81-24245

612'.33 — Man. Intestines. Hormones

Gut hormones. — 2nd ed. / edited by Stephen R. Bloom and Julia M. Polak. — Edinburgh : Churchill Livingstone, 1981. — xxv,605p : ill,2ports ; 24cm
Previous ed.: 1978. — Includes index
ISBN 0-443-02323-9 : £24.00 : CIP rev. B81-05125

612'.34 — Man. Pancreas. Glucagon. Physiology

Glucagon : physiology, pathophysiology, and morphology of the pancreatic A-cells / edited by Roger H. Unger, Lelio Orci. — New York ; Oxford : Elsevier, c1981. — xix,451p : ill(some col.) ; 24cm. — (Current endocrinology)
Includes bibliographies and index
ISBN 0-444-00435-1 : Unpriced B81-32845

612'.34 — Pancreas. Exocrine cells — *Conference proceedings*

International Symposium on the Biology of Exocrine Pancreatic Cells *(1st : 1980 : Toulouse).* Biology of normal cancerous exocrine pancreatic cells : proceedings of the 1st International Symposium on the Biology of Exocrine Pancreatic Cells held in Toulouse (France), 7-9 May, 1980 / sponsored by the Institut National de la Santé et de la Recherche Médicale ; editors A. Ribet, L. Pradayrol, C. Susini. — Amsterdam ; Oxford : Elsevier/North-Holland Biomedical, 1980. — xix,336p : ill ; 25cm. — (INSERM symposium ; no.15)
Includes index
ISBN 0-444-80269-x : £19.88 B81-05955

612'.35 — Man. Bile acids. Metabolism — *Conference proceedings*

Bile Acid Meeting *(6th : 1980 : Freiburg im Breisgau).* Bile acids and lipids : proceedings of the 6th Bile Acid Meeting (Falk Symposium 29) held at Freiburg in Breslau, West Germany, October 9-11, 1980 / edited by G. Paumgartner A. Stiehl W. Gerok. — Lancaster : MTP Press, c1981. — xx,384p : ill,1port ; 24cm. — (Falk symposium ; 29)
Includes bibliographies and index
ISBN 0-85200-389-7 : £24.95
Also classified at 612'.397 B81-38100

612'.39 — Man. Energy metabolism

Atkins, Gordon L.. An outline of energy metabolism in man / Gordon L. Atkins. — London : Heinemann Medical, 1981. — 96p : ill ; 25cm
Bibliography: p92. — Includes index
ISBN 0-433-00950-0 (1pbk) : £4.95 B81-17884

612'.3924 — Calcitonin — *Conference proceedings*

Calcitonin 1980 : chemistry, physiology, pharmacology and clinical aspects : proceedings of an international symposium held in Milan, October 15-17, 1980 / editor A. Pecile. — Amsterdam ; Oxford : Excerpta Medica, 1981. — xi,388p : ill ; 25cm. — (International congress series ; no.540)
Includes bibliographies and index
ISBN 90-219-0480-2 : Unpriced
ISBN 0-444-90195-7 (Elsevier) B81-26948

612'.3924 — Man. Iron. Metabolism

Iron / edited by James D. Cook. — New York ; Edinburgh : Churchill Livingstone, 1980. — 180p : ill ; 24cm. — (Methods in hematology ; v.1)
Includes index
ISBN 0-443-08118-2 : Unpriced B81-13245

612'.397 — Man. Lipids. Metabolism — *Conference proceedings*

Bile Acid Meeting *(6th : 1980 : Freiburg im Breisgau).* Bile acids and lipids : proceedings of the 6th Bile Acid Meeting (Falk Symposium 29) held at Freiburg in Breslau, West Germany, October 9-11, 1980 / edited by G. Paumgartner A. Stiehl W. Gerok. — Lancaster : MTP Press, c1981. — xx,384p : ill,1port ; 24cm. — (Falk symposium ; 29)
Includes bibliographies and index
ISBN 0-85200-389-7 : £24.95
Primary classification 612'.35 B81-38100

612'.398 — Man. Nitrogen. Metabolism — *Conference proceedings*

Nitrogen metabolism in man. — London : Applied Science, Dec.1981. — [512]p
Conference papers
ISBN 0-85334-991-6 : £38.00 : CIP entry B81-31515

612'.399 — Man. Vitamin B6 — *Conference proceedings*

Methods in vitamin B-6 nutrition : analysis and status assessment / edited by James E. Leklem and Robert D. Reynolds. — New York ; London : Plenum, c1981. — xi,401p : ill ; 26cm
Conference papers. — Includes index
ISBN 0-306-40640-3 : Unpriced B81-24233

612'.399 — Man. Vitamin C

Mervyn, Leonard. Vitamin C. — Wellingborough : Thorsons, Oct.1981. — [96]p
ISBN 0-7225-0717-8 (pbk) : £0.95 : CIP entry B81-30279

612'.399 — Man. Vitamin C — *Conference proceedings*

Vitamin C. — London : Applied Science Publishers, Dec.1981. — [400]p
Conference papers
ISBN 0-85334-109-5 : £30.00 : CIP entry B81-33876

612'.399 — Man. Vitamin C. Functions & metabolism

Nobile, S.. Vitamin C. — Lancaster : MTP Press, June 1981. — [175]p
ISBN 0-85200-419-2 : £9.95 : CIP entry B81-18177

612.4 — MAN. PHYSIOLOGY. LYMPHATIC, EXOCRINE, ENDOCRINE SYSTEMS

612′.4 — Man. Endocrine system

Hardy, Richard Neville. Endocrine physiology. — London : Edward Arnold, July 1981. — [160]p. — (Physiological principles in medicine, ISSN 0260-2946)
ISBN 0-7131-4378-9 : £6.00 : CIP entry B81-14856

Perspectives in clinical endocrinology / edited by Walter B. Essman. — Lancaster : MTP Press, c1980. — 425p : ill ; 24cm
Includes bibliographies and index
ISBN 0-85200-554-7 : £23.50 B81-03467

612′.4 — Man. Endocrine system *related to* **reproductive system**

Intragonadal regulation of reproduction / edited by Paul Franchimont and Cornelia P. Channing. — London : Academic Press, 1981. — xiii,429p : ill ; 24cm
Includes bibliographies and index
ISBN 0-12-265280-0 : £19.60 : CIP rev.
Primary classification 599.01′6 B81-08908

612′.405 — Man. Hormones

Kutsky, Roman J.. Handbook of vitamins, minerals and hormones / Roman J. Kutsky. — 2nd ed. — New York ; London : Von Nostrand Reinhold, c1981. — xvi,492p : ill ; 24cm
Previous ed.: published as Handbook of vitamins and hormones. 1973. — Bibliography: p458-459. — Includes index
ISBN 0-442-24557-2 : £20.85
Primary classification 613.2′8 B81-36077

612′.43 — Man. Thymus — *Conference proceedings*

The **Thymus** gland. — London : Academic Press, Nov.1981. — [200]p
Conference papers
ISBN 0-12-404180-9 : CIP entry B81-30213

612′.46 — Man. Defecation & urination. Social aspects — *Humour*

Are you sitting comfortably? : a scatological scrapbook of sh- and all about it / [compiled by] Susan Stranks & Don Grant. — London : Macdonald Futura, c1980. — [96]p : ill ; 18x20cm
ISBN 0-354-04580-6 : £3.95 B81-06545

612′.463 — Man. Kidneys

The **Kidney** / edited by Barry M. Brenner, Floyd C. Rector Jr. ; with contributions by 93 authorities. — 2nd ed. — Philadelphia ; London : Saunders, 1981. — 2v. : ill(some col.) ; 27cm
Previous ed.: 1976. — Includes index
ISBN 0-7216-1969-x : £74.50
ISBN 0-7216-1967-3 (Vol.1) : £37.25
ISBN 0-7216-1968-1 (Vol.2) : £37.25 B81-13937

612′.463 — Man. Kidneys. Effects of prostaglandins — *Conference proceedings*

A.N. Richards Symposium *(20th : 1978 : King of Prussia, Pa.)*. Prostaglandins in cardiovascular and renal function : proceedings of the 20th annual A.N. Richards Symposium of the Physiological Society of Philadelphia, King of Prussia, Pennsylvania, May 8-9, 1978 / edited by Alexander Scriabine, Allan M. Lefer and Frederick A. Kuehl. — Lancaster : MTP, c1980. — 498p : ill ; 24cm. — (Monographs of the Physiological Society of Philadelphia ; v.6)
Includes bibliographies and index
ISBN 0-85200-532-6 : £29.95
Primary classification 612′.1 B81-04661

612′.463 — Man. Kidneys. Hormones — *Conference proceedings*

Kanematsu Conference on the Kidney *(6th : 1980 : Sydney)*. Hormones and the kidney : proceedings of the 6th Kanematsu Conference on the Kidney, Sydney, Feb. 4-5, 1980 / volume editors G.S. Stokes and J.F. Mahony. — Basel ; London : Karger, 1980. — vii,267p : ill ; 25cm. — (Progress in biochemical pharmacology ; v.17)
Includes bibliographies and index
ISBN 3-8055-1090-x : £43.00 B81-11537

612′.463 — Man. Kidneys. Physiology

Catto, Graeme R. D.. Clinical aspects of renal physiology. — London : Baillière Tindall, Nov.1981. — [144]p
ISBN 0-7020-0893-1 : £6.50 : CIP entry B81-30166

Lote, Christopher J.. Principles of renal physiology. — London : Croom Helm, Jan.1982. — [192]p
ISBN 0-7099-0078-3 (cased) : £11.95 : CIP entry
ISBN 0-7099-0079-1 (pbk) : £5.95 B81-34305

612′.467 — Man. Lower urinary tract. Physiology

Griffiths, D. J. (Derek John). Urodynamics : the mechanics and hydrodynamics of the lower urinary tract / D.J. Griffiths. — Bristol : Hilger in collaboration with the Hospital Physicists Association, c1980. — ix,139p : ill ; 22cm. — (Medical physics handbooks ; 4)
Includes index
ISBN 0-85274-507-9 : £11.95 : CIP rev. B80-08228

612′.492 — Man. Corticotrophin & lipotrophin

ACTH and LPH in health and disease / volume editors Tj.B. van Wimersma Greidanus, L.H. Rees. — London : Karger, 1981. — ix,210p : ill ; 25cm. — (Frontiers of hormone research ; v.8)
Includes bibliographies and index
ISBN 3-8055-1977-x : £35.10 B81-34534

612′.492 — Man. Pituitary gland. Hormones. Secretion. Role of biological rhythms — *Conference proceedings*

Human pituitary hormones : circadian and episodic variations : a workshop symposium held in Brussels, Belgium, November 29-30, 1979 / sponsored by the Commission of the European Community, as advised by the Committee on Medical and Public Health Research ; edited by E. van Cauter and G. Copinschi. — The Hague ; London : Nijhoff for The Commission of the European Communities, 1981. — ix,352p : ill ; 25cm. — (Developments in endocrinology ; v.1)
ISBN 90-247-2481-3 : Unpriced B81-27019

612′.492 — Man. Posterior pituitary gland. Hormones: Peptides — *Conference proceedings*

International Symposium on Neurohypophyseal Peptide Hormones and other Biologically Active Peptides *(1980 : University of Illinois, Chicago)*. Neurohypophyseal peptide hormones and other biologically active peptides : proceedings of the International Symposium on Neurohypophyseal Peptide Hormones and other Biologically Active Peptides held September 1980 at the University of Illinois, Chicago, Illinois, U.S.A., in memory of Dr. Roderich Walter / editor David H. Schlesinger. — New York ; Oxford : Elsevier/North-Holland, c1981. — xiv,293p : ill ; 25cm. — (Developments in endocrinology ; 13)
Bibliography: p271-290. — Includes index
ISBN 0-444-00605-2 : Unpriced B81-39196

612.6 — MAN. PHYSIOLOGY. REPRODUCTIVE SYSTEM AND DEVELOPMENT

612′.6 — Man. Chorionic gonadotropins — *Conference proceedings*

Conference on Human Chorionic Gonadotropin *(1979 : Bellagio)*. Chorionic gonadotropin / edited by Sheldon J. Segal ; [proceedings of the Conference on Human Chorionic Gonadotropin, held at the Rockefeller Foundation Conference and Study Center, Bellagio, Italy, November 14-16, 1979]. — New York ; London : Plenum, c1980. — ix,507p : ill ; 26cm
Includes bibliographies and index
ISBN 0-306-40563-6 : Unpriced B81-13350

612′.6 — Man. Fertility

Research on fertility and sterility. — Lancaster : MTP Press, July 1981. — [450]p
ISBN 0-85200-357-9 : £29.95 : CIP entry
Also classified at 616.6′92 B81-19146

Silber, Sherman J.. How to get pregnant / Sherman J. Silber. — London : Owen, 1981, c1980. — viii,229p : ill ; 23cm
Originally published: New York : Scribner, 1980. — Includes index
ISBN 0-7206-0589-x : £8.95 B81-34367

612′.6 — Man. Fertility — *Conference proceedings*

Eugenics Society. *Symposium (16th : 1979 : London)*. Changing patterns of conception and fertility : proceedings of the Sixteenth Annual Symposium of the Eugenics Society, London 1979 / edited by D.F. Roberts, R. Chester. — London : Academic Press, 1981. — xii,211p : ill ; 24cm
Includes bibliographies and index
ISBN 0-12-589640-9 : £10.40 B81-37704

612.6 — Man. Fertility. Regulation — *Conference proceedings*

Research frontiers in fertility regulation / [proceedings of an International Workshop on Research Frontiers in Fertility Regulation February 11 to 14, 1980 Mexico City, Mexico] ; [sponsored by the Program for Applied Research of Fertility Regulation Northwestern University, Chicago, Illinois] ; edited by Gerald I. Zatuchni, Miriam H. Labbok, John J. Sciarra ; prepared with the technical assistance of Carolyn K. Osborn ; with 74 contributors. — Hagerstown ; London : Harper & Row, c1980. — x,459p : ill ; 24cm. — (PARFR series on fertility regulation)
Includes bibliographies and index
ISBN 0-06-142902-3 : £16.25 B81-21450

612′.6 — Man. Reproduction

Page, Ernest W.. Human reproduction : essentials of reproductive and perinatal medicine / Ernest W. Page, Claude A. Villee, Dorothy B. Villee. — 3rd ed. — Philadelphia ; London : Saunders, 1981. — xvii,526p : ill ; 25cm
Previous ed.: 1976. — Includes bibliographies and index
ISBN 0-7216-7053-9 : Unpriced
Also classified at 618 B81-33221

612′.6 — Man. Reproduction — *For children*

Althea. A baby in the family / by Althea ; illustrated by Ljiljana Rylands. — 2nd ed. — Cambridge : Dinosaur, c1981. — [32]p : col.ill,1port ; 16x19cm. — (Dinosaur′s Althea books)
Previous ed.: 1975
ISBN 0-85122-284-6 (cased) : £1.85
ISBN 0-85122-283-8 (pbk) : £0.70 B81-26335

612′.6 — Man. Reproduction. Role of prostaglandins

Roger, Norman L.. Prostaglandins in reproduction / Norman L. Payser. — Chichester : Research Studies, c1981. — xii,260p : ill ; 24cm. — (Prostaglandins research studies series ; 2)
Includes bibliographies and index
ISBN 0-471-09986-4 : £17.75 : CIP rev. B81-18124

612′.6 — Man. Reproductive system. Role of hormone receptors — *Conference proceedings*

Conference on Functional Correlates of Hormone Receptors in Reproduction *(1980 : Augusta)*. Functional correlates of hormone receptors in reproduction : proceedings of the Conference on Functional Correlates of Hormone Receptors in Reproduction held on October 13-15, 1980 in Augusta, Georgia, U.S.A. / editors Virendra B. Mahesh ... [et al.]. — New York ; Oxford : Elsevier, c1980. — viii,594p : ill ; 25cm. — (Developments in endocrinology)
Includes bibliographies and index
ISBN 0-444-00604-4 : £43.59 B81-36757

612′.6 — Man. Sex differences

Mechanisms of sex differentiation in animals and man / edited by C.R. Austin and R.G. Edwards. — London : Academic Press, 1981. — xv,603p : ill ; 24cm
Includes bibliographies and index
ISBN 0-12-068540-x : £37.00 : CIP rev.
Primary classification 591.3′6 B81-11936

612′.6 — Women. Sexuality — *Feminist viewpoints*

Love your enemy? : the debate between heterosexual feminism and political lesbianism. — London : Onlywomen Press, 1981. — 68p : ill ; 21cm
ISBN 0-906500-08-7 (pbk) : £1.75 B81-35172

612′.6′001 — Man. Growth. Theories, *to 1979*
Tanner, J. M.. A history of the study of human growth / J.M. Tanner. — Cambridge : Cambridge University Press, 1981. — xi,499, : ill,facsims ; 24cm
Bibliography: p403-454. — Includes index
ISBN 0-521-22488-8 : £30.00 B81-35601

612′.6′00704 — Europe. Adolescents. Sex education
Kozakiewicz, Mikołaj. Sex education and adolescence in Europe : sexuality, marriage and the family / Mikołaj Kozakiewicz. — London : [IPPF Europe], 1981. — 118p : 1ill ; 21cm
Cover title. — At head of title: IPPF Europe. — Bibliography: p107-118
ISBN 0-904983-07-2 (pbk) : £4.50
Also classified at 612′.6′0094 B81-28328

612′.6′0094 — Europe. Adolescents. Sexuality
Kozakiewicz, Mikołaj. Sex education and adolescence in Europe : sexuality, marriage and the family / Mikołaj Kozakiewicz. — London : [IPPF Europe], 1981. — 118p : 1ill ; 21cm
Cover title. — At head of title: IPPF Europe. — Bibliography: p107-118
ISBN 0-904983-07-2 (pbk) : £4.50
Primary classification 612′.6′00704 B81-28328

612′.61 — Men. Penis. Enlargement
Grange, Felix. The male genital organs / by Felix Grange. — London (225 Putney Bridge Rd., SW15 2PY) : Roberts, [1981]. — 60p ; 19cm. — (Body image problems series ; no.4)
ISBN 0-906185-13-0 (pbk) : £2.00 B81-15716

612′.61 — Men. Sex
Llewellyn-Jones, Derek. Everyman / Derek Llewellyn-Jones. — Oxford : Oxford University Press, 1981. — viii,302p : ill ; 23cm
Bibliography: p293-298. — Includes index
ISBN 0-19-217724-9 : £8.50 : CIP rev. B81-30484

612′.61 — Men. Testes. Effects of drugs — *Serials*
Effects of hormones, drugs and chemicals on testicular function. — Vol.1-. — Westmount : Eden Press ; Edinburgh : Churchill Livingstone, 1980-. — v ; 22cm. — (Annual research reviews)
Annual
Unpriced B81-04702

612′.61′072 — Men. Reproductive system. Research — *Conference proceedings*
Goals in male reproductive research / editors Saul Boyarsky, Kenneth Polakoski. — Oxford : Pergamon, c1981. — xv,139p : ill ; 26cm
Conference papers. — Includes bibliographies and index
ISBN 0-08-025910-3 : £12.50 : CIP rev. B81-03814

612′.62 — Women. Fertility. Role of endocrine system
Reproductive endocrinology and infertility / edited by Shawky Z.A. Badawy. — Miami : Symposia Specialists ; London : Year Book Medical [[distributor]], c1980. — vii,183p : ill ; 24cm
ISBN 0-8151-0406-5 : Unpriced B81-08206

612.62 — Women. Gonadotrophins — *Conference proceedings*
The **Gonadotropins** : basic science and clinical aspects in females. — London : Academic Press, Feb.1982. — [550]p. — (Proceedings of the Serono symposia, ISSN 0308-5503 ; v.42)
Conference papers
ISBN 0-12-258550-x : CIP entry B81-38310

612′.62 — Women. Ovaries
Horský, Jan. Ovarian function and its disorders / Jan Horský, Jiří Presl. — The Hague ; London : Nijhoff, 1981. — xvii,423p : ill ; 25cm. — (Developments in obstetrics and gynecology ; v.3)
Translated from the Czech. — Bibliography: p379-406. - Includes index
ISBN 90-247-2326-4 : Unpriced B81-17116

12′.62 — Women. Ovaries. Physiology
Functional morphology of the human ovary / edited by J.R.T. Coutts. — Lancaster : MTP, 1981. — xiv,266p : ill ; 24cm
Includes bibliographies and index
ISBN 0-85200-358-7 : £19.95 B81-23684

612′.62 — Women. Reproductive system
Taylor-Grant, G.. The female zone and problems of pelvic floor sag / by G. Taylor-Grant. — London (225 Putney Bridge Rd., SW15 2PY) : Roberts, [1981]. — 61p : ill ; 19cm. — (The body perfect & body image problems series ; no.3)
ISBN 0-906185-12-2 (pbk) : £2.00 B81-15717

612′.62 — Women. Reproductive system. Self-examination
Laws, Sophie. Down there : an illustrated guide to self-exam / [written and compiled by Sophie Laws]. — London (38 Mount Pleasant, W.C.1) : Onlywomen Press, 1981. — 28p : ill ; 22cm
Form on inside cover
ISBN 0-906500-05-2 (pbk) : £0.50 B81-17733

612′.62 — Women. Uterus. Endometrium. Effects of hormones — *Conference proceedings*
The **Endometrium** : hormonal impacts / [proceedings of a symposium on the physiology and pathophysiology of the menstrual cycle, held April 22-23, 1980, in Paris, France] ; edited by Jean de Brux, Rodrigue Mortel, Jean Pierre Gautray. — New York ; London : Plenum, c1981. — viii,167p : ill ; 26cm
Includes bibliographies and index
ISBN 0-306-40749-3 : Unpriced B81-36676

612′.62 — Women. Uterus. Endometrium. Relationship with blastocysts
Seminar on Reproductive Physiology and Sexual Endocrinology *(7th : 1980 : Brussels).* Blastocyst-endometrium relationships / 7th Seminar on Reproductive Physiology and Sexual Endocrinology, Brussels, May 21-24, ; volume editors F. Leroy ... [et al.]. — Basel ; London : Karger, 1980. — x,336p : ill ; 25cm. — (Progress in reproductive biology ; v.7)
Includes bioliographies
ISBN 3-8055-0988-x : £52.00 B81-09169

612′.62′05 — Women. Sex — *Serials*
Curious woman : all that′s feminine & personal to you. — Part 1-. — Llandderfel (Bwlch yn Horeb, Llandderfel LL23 7RN, Gwynedd) : Rufus Wilson ; London (31 Corsica St., N5 1JT) : Moore Harness [distributor], 1980-. — v. : ill,ports ; 30cm
Monthly
ISSN 0261-0558 = Curious woman : £0.45 per issue B81-15152

612′.64 — Man. Embryos & foetuses. Development
Balinsky, B. I.. An introduction to embryology. — 5th ed. / B.I. Balinsky assisted by B.C. Fabian. — Philadelphia ; London : Saunders College, c1981. — xiv,768p : ill ; 25cm
Previous ed.: 1976. — Bibliography: p716-746. — Includes index
ISBN 0-03-057712-8 : £14.95 B81-25590

Langman, Jan. Medical embryology / Jan Langman ; original illustrations by Jill Leland. — 4th ed. — Baltimore ; London : Williams & Wilkins, c1981. — xi,384p : ill(some col.) ; 24cm
Previous ed.: 1975. — Ill on lining papers. — Includes index
ISBN 0-683-04858-9 : £22.00 B81-24374

612′.64 — Man. Embryos & foetuses. Development — *For children*
The **Baby** in the bubble : our story / by George and Sybil ; [illustrated by Frances Flynn]. — Witney (Bridge House, Witney, Oxon. OX8 6HY) : Oxford School Publications, c1980. — [12]p : ill ; 30cm
Cover title. — Text, ill on inside covers
ISBN 0-905697-03-0 (pbk) : £1.00 B81-14485

How you grew before birth. — Witney (Bridge House, Witney, Oxon. OX8 6HY) : Oxford School Publications, c1980. — 1sheet : ill ; 42x59cm folded to 21x30cm
ISBN 0-905697-04-9 : £0.40 B81-14486

612′.64014 — Man. Foetuses. Endocrine system. Development
Jirásek, Jan E.. Human fetal endocrines / Jan E. Jirásek. — The Hague ; London : Nijhoff, 1980. — xiv,245p : ill ; 25cm. — (Developments in obstetrics and gynaecology ; v.1)
Bibliography: p204-239. - Includes index
ISBN 90-247-2325-6 : Unpriced B81-13651

612′.6401715 — Man. Foetuses. Cranium. Development — *Conference proceedings*
Current research trends in prenatal craniofacial development : proceedings of an international conference on current research trends in prenatal craniofacial development, held at the National Institutes of Health, Bethesda, Maryland, U.S.A. April 8-10, 1980 / editors Robert M. Pratt, Richard L. Christiansen. — New York ; Oxford : Elsevier/North-Holland, c1980. — 456p : ill ; 24cm
Includes bibliographies and index
ISBN 0-444-00572-2 : £33.52 B81-21430

612′.640191 — Man. Foetuses. Skull. Development — *Illustrations*
Shapiro, Robert. The embryogenesis of the human skull : an anatomic and radiographic atlas / Robert Shapiro, Franklin Robinson. — Cambridge, Mass. ; London : Harvard University Press, 1980. — 101p : chiefly ill (some col.) ; 29cm. — (A Commonwealth Fund book)
ISBN 0-674-24790-6 : £27.00 B81-03644

612′.640191′0246176 — Man. Embryos & foetuses. Head. Development — *For dentistry*
Sperber, Geoffrey H.. Craniofacial embryology / Geoffrey H. Sperber ; with a foreword by Phillip V. Tobias. — 3rd ed. — Bristol : Wright, 1981. — xiv,204p : ill(some col.) ; 23cm. — (A Dental practitioner handbook ; no.15)
Previous ed: 1976. — Includes bibliographies and index
ISBN 0-7236-0552-1 (pbk) : Unpriced : CIP rev. B81-07949

612′.646 — Man. Trophoblast — *Conference proceedings*
Placenta : receptors, pathology & toxicology. — Eastbourne : Praeger, Sept.1981. — [336]p
Conference papers
ISBN 0-7216-6353-2 : £26.00 : CIP entry B81-26693

612′.647 — Man. Foetuses. Physiology — *Conference proceedings*
Studies in perinatal physiology / edited by Elsie M. Widdowson ; contributors Pauline Alexander ... [et al.]. — Tunbridge Wells : Pitman Medical, 1980. — vi,186p : ill,1port ; 29cm
Conference papers
ISBN 0-272-79586-0 : £20.00 : CIP rev.
Also classified at 612′.652 B80-05378

612′.647 — Man. Placenta — *Conference proceedings*
The **Human** placenta : proteins and hormones / edited by Arnold Klopper, Andrea Genazzani, Pier Giorgio Crosignani. — London : Academic Press, 1980. — xiv,478p : ill ; 24cm. — (Proceedings of the Serono symposia ; v.35)
Includes bibliographies
ISBN 0-12-416150-2 : £28.40 : CIP rev. B80-13834

612′.65 — Scotland. Strathclyde Region. Glasgow. Immigrant children. Growth
Goel, K. M.. Growth of immigrant children in Glasgow / K.M. Goel with the collaboration of E.M. Sweet, R.B. Thomson, S. Halliday. — Oxford : Oxfam, 1980?. — 38p : ill,forms ; 30cm
Unpriced (pbk) B81-09855

612′.652 — Newborn babies. Physiology — *Conference proceedings*
Studies in perinatal physiology / edited by Elsie M. Widdowson ; contributors Pauline Alexander ... [et al.]. — Tunbridge Wells : Pitman Medical, 1980. — vi,186p : ill,1port ; 29cm
Conference papers
ISBN 0-272-79586-0 : £20.00 : CIP rev.
Primary classification 612′.647 B80-05378

612′.664 — Babies. Breast feeding. Medical aspects
Lawrence, Ruth A.. Breast-feeding : a guide for the medical profession / Ruth A. Lawrence. — St. Louis ; London : Mosby, 1980. — xiv,367p : ill,forms ; 25cm
Includes bibliographies and index
ISBN 0-8016-2897-0 (pbk) : £13.00 B81-08027

612'.664 — Nursing mothers. Milk. Effects of drugs

Wilson, John T.. Drugs in breast milk / John T. Wilson. — Lancaster : MTP, c1981. — ix,110p : ill ; 25cm
Bibliography: p87-103. — Includes index
ISBN 0-85200-575-x : £11.95 B81-23686

612'.664 — Women. Breasts

Harris, Anthony, *1937-*. The breast book : a practical guide to health and beauty / Anthony Harris. — London : Sphere, 1980. — 242p : ill ; 18cm
ISBN 0-7221-4244-7 (pbk) : £1.50 B81-12944

Holt, Marcus. The breast and bust improvement / by Marcus Holt. — London (225 Putney Bridge Rd., SW15 2PY) : Roberts Publications, 1981. — 63p : ill ; 19cm. — (Body image problem series ; no.2)
ISBN 0-906185-15-7 (pbk) : £2.50 B81-36410

612'.664 — Women. Lactation

Jelliffe, D. B.. Human milk in the modern world : psychosocial, nutritional and economic significance / Derrick B. Jelliffe, E.F. Patrice Jelliffe. — Oxford : Oxford University Press, 1978 (1979 [printing]). — 500p : ill,facsims ; 24cm. — (Oxford medical publications)
Bibliography: p414-488. — Includes index
ISBN 0-19-264921-3 (pbk) : £12.50 B81-39274

612'.665 — Women. Menopause

Coope, Jean. Your menopause questions / Jean Coope. — London : British Medical Association, [1981]. — 31p ; 19cm. — (A Family doctor booklet)
£0.50 (unbound) B81-23535

Lloyd, Mollie. The change of life / Mollie Lloyd. — Updated ed. — Dublin : Arlen House, 1979. — 160p ; 18cm
Previous ed.: Brighton : Owl Publications, 1974. — Includes index
ISBN 0-905223-06-3 (pbk) : £1.70 B81-17639

Reitz, Rosetta. Menopause : a positive approach / Rosetta Reitz. — London : Unwin Paperbacks, 1981, c1979. — ix,276p ; 20cm
Originally published: Radnor, Pa. : Chilton Book Co., 1977 ; Hassocks : Harvester Press, 1979. — Bibliography: p257-265. — Includes index
ISBN 0-04-612031-9 (pbk) : £2.95 : CIP rev. B81-00121

Studd, John W. W.. The menopause / John W.W. Studd, Margaret Thom ; illustrated by the Hayward Art Group. — Feltham : Hamlyn Paperbacks, 1981. — 47p : ill ; 17cm. — (Pocket health guides)
ISBN 0-600-20314-x (pbk) : £0.85 B81-40888

612'.67 — Gerontology — *Conference proceedings*

British Society of Gerontology. *Conference (1980 : Aberdeen).* Current trends in British gerontology. — Aldershot : Gower, Dec.1981. — [240]p
ISBN 0-566-00495-x : £11.50 : CIP entry B81-31608

612'.67 — Man. Ageing

Aging : a challenge to science and society. — Oxford : Published on behalf of l'Institut de la Vie and the World Health Organization Regional Office for Europe by Oxford University Press. — (Oxford medical publications)
Vol.1: Biology / edited by D. Danon, N.W. Shock and M. Marois. — 1981. — xv,346p : ill ; 24cm
Includes bibliographies and index
ISBN 0-19-261254-9 : £25.00 : CIP rev. B80-11040

Aging. — Oxford : Oxford University Press. — (Oxford medical publications)
Conference papers
Vol.3: Behavioural sciences and conclusions. — Dec.1981. — [350]p
ISBN 0-19-261256-5 : £30.00 : CIP entry B81-31353

612'.68 — Man. Longevity — *Manuals*

Richards, Dick, *1930-*. Live to be a hundred / by Dick Richards. — London (225 Putney Bridge Rd., SW15 2PY) : Roberts Publications, [1981?]. — 80p : ill ; 19cm. — (Body perfect and body image problem series ; no.6)
ISBN 0-906185-14-9 (pbk) : £2.50 B81-36411

612.7 — MAN. PHYSIOLOGY. MOTOR AND INTEGUMENTARY SYSTEMS

612'.7 — Man. Musculoskeletal system

Poland, James L.. The musculoskeletal system / James L. Poland, Donald J. Hobart, Otto D. Payton ; illustrated by Carol L. Fairchild. — 2nd ed. — Bern : Huber ; London : Kimpton, c1981. — 373p : ill ; 22cm
Previous ed.: Flushing, N.Y. : Medical Examination Pub. Co., 1977. — Includes bibliographies and index
ISBN 0-87488-667-8 (pbk) : £8.50 B81-16125

Rosse, Cornelius. The musculoskeletal system in health and disease / Cornelius Rosse, D. Kay Clawson with 10 additional contributors. — Hagerstown ; London : Harper & Row, c1980. — xiii,447p : ill ; 27cm
Includes bibliographies and index
ISBN 0-06-142287-8 : £22.75 B81-02225

Scientific foundations of orthopaedics and traumatology / edited by Robert Owen, John Goodfellow and Peter Bullough. — London : Heinemann Medical, 1980. — xii,531p : ill ; 29cm
Includes bibliographies and index
ISBN 0-433-24320-1 : £42.00 B81-13011

612'.7 — Man. Musculoskeletal systems — *For children*

Ward, Brian. The skeleton and movement / Brian R. Ward. — London : Watts, 1981. — 48p : col.ill ; 26cm. — (The Human body)
Includes index
ISBN 0-85166-908-5 : £3.99 B81-26072

612'.7 — Newborn babies. Posture

Wenham, Agnes. Lend baby a hand : an illustrated guide to early posture care / by Agnes Wenham ; photographs by Bob Cnoops. — London : Heinemann Medical, 1980. — xii,127p : ill ; 14x20cm
ISBN 0-433-35400-3 (pbk) : £5.25 B81-02784

612'.74 — Man. Muscles. Fatigue

Human muscle fatigue. — London : Pitman Medical, May 1981. — [362]p. — (Ciba Foundation symposium ; 82)
ISBN 0-272-79618-2 : £19.50 : CIP entry B81-07472

612'.74 — Man. Muscles. Physiology

Keynes, R. D.. Nerve and muscle. — Cambridge : Cambridge University Press, Nov.1981. — [169]p. — (Cambridge texts in the physiological sciences ; 2)
ISBN 0-521-23945-1 : £15.00 : CIP entry
ISBN 0-521-28362-0 (pbk) : £4.95
Primary classification 612'.8 B81-31190

612'.74 — Man. Smooth muscles

Smooth muscle : an assessment of current knowledge / edited by Edith Bülbring ... [et al.]. — London : Edward Arnold, 1981. — xii,563p : ill ; 26cm
Bibliography: p459-549. - Includes index
ISBN 0-7131-4348-7 : £45.00 : CIP rev. B80-18753

612'.75 — Man. Bones. Physiology

Vaughan, Janet. The physiology of bone / Janet Vaughan. — 3rd ed. — Oxford : Clarendon Press, 1981. — xx,265p : ill ; 24cm. — (Oxford science publications)
Previous ed.: 1975. — Bibliography: p214-253. — Includes index
ISBN 0-19-857584-x : £25.00 : CIP rev. B81-23874

612'.75 — Man. Joints. Physiology

Kapandji, I. A.. The physiology of the joints. — 2nd ed. — Edinburgh : Churchill Livingstone
Translation of: Physiologie articulaire
Vol.1: Upper limb. — Dec.1981. — [208]p
Previous ed. of this translation: London : Livingstone, 1970
ISBN 0-443-02504-5 (pbk) : £6.50 : CIP entry B81-31833

612'.75 — Man. Skeletal system. Mechanics - *Conference proceedings*

Mechanical factors and the skeleton. — London (80 Bondway, SW8 1SF) : John Libbey, Apr.1981. — [224]p
Conference papers
ISBN 0-86196-006-8 : £14.00 : CIP entry B81-07458

612'.75 — Man. Synovial fluid. Rheology

Chmiel, Horst. On the rheology of blood and synovial fluids / Horst Chmiel and Eckehard Walitza. — Chichester : Research Studies Press, c1980. — xii,166p : ill ; 24cm. — (Chemical engineering aspects of biomedicine research studies series ; 1)
Bibliography: p147-163. — Includes index
ISBN 0-471-27858-0 ; £14.50 : CIP rev.
Primary classification 612'.1181 B80-35019

612'.76 — Kinesiology

Piscopo, John. Kinesiology : the science of movement / John Piscopo, James A. Baley. — New York ; Chichester : Wiley, c1981. — xx,619p : ill,1form ; 25cm
Includes index
ISBN 0-471-03483-5 : £11.50 B81-23393

612'.76 — Man. Exercise. Bioenergetics & biomechanics

Ghista, Dhanjoo N.. Human body dynamics. — Oxford : Clarendon Press, Jan.1982. — [350]p. — (Oxford medical engineering series)
ISBN 0-19-857548-3 : £30.00 : CIP entry B81-34415

612'.76 — Man. Exercise. Bioenergetics & biomechanics — *Conference proceedings*

International Symposium on Exercise Bioenergetics and Gas Exchange *(1980 : Milan).* Exercise bioenergetics and gas exchange : proceedings of the International Symposium on Exercise Bioenergetics and Gas Exchange held in Milan, Italy, July 7-9, 1980 : a satellite of the XXVIII International Congress of Physiological Sciences / editors Paolo Cerretelli and Brian J. Whipp. — Amsterdam ; Oxford : Elsevier/North Holland, 1980. — ix,362p : ill,2 ports ; 25cm. — (Symposia of the Giovanni Lorenzini Foundation ; v.9)
Includes index
ISBN 0-444-80295-9 : £23.71 B81-05495

612'.76 — Man. Movement

Thompson, Clem W.. Manual of structural kinesiology / Clem W. Thompson. — 9th ed. — St. Louis ; London : Mosby, 1981. — vii,142p : ill(some col.) ; 28cm
Previous ed.: 1977. — Bibliography: p140. — Includes index
ISBN 0-8016-4940-4 (pbk) : £9.75 B81-33002

612'.76 — Sports. Techniques. Biomechanics

Simonian, Charles. Fundamentals of sports biomechanics / Charles Simonian. — Englewood Cliffs ; London : Prentice-Hall, c1981. — xv,221p : ill ; 24cm
Includes bibliographies and index
ISBN 0-13-344499-6 : £10.45 B81-26905

612'.76'02479 — Man. Movement — *For performing arts*

King, Nancy R.. A movement approach to acting / Nancy R. King. — Englewood Cliffs ; London : Prentice Hall, 1981. — xiii,240p : ill ; 24cm
Bibliography: p230-232. — Includes index
ISBN 0-13-604637-1 : £9.05 B81-16530

612'.78'05 — Man. Speech — *Serials*

Speech and language. — Vol.3. — New York ; London : Academic Press, 1980. — xiii,311p
ISBN 0-12-608603-6 : £19.40
ISSN 0193-3434
Also classified at 405 B81-16747

612′.78′05 — Man. Speech — *Serials*
continuation

Speech and language. — Vol.4. — New York ; London : Academic Press, 1980. — xii,392p
ISBN 0-12-608604-4 : Unpriced
ISSN 0193-3434
Also classified at 405 B81-30758

612′.79 — Man. Skin. Microorganisms

Noble, W. C.. Microbiology of human skin / (Noble and Somerville). — 2nd ed. / W.C. Noble. — London : Lloyd-Luke, 1981. — xii,433p : ill ; 24cm. — (Major problems in dermatology ; v.2)
Previous ed.: London : Saunders, 1974. — Includes bibliographies and index
ISBN 0-85324-150-3 : Unpriced B81-19396

612′.799 — Man. Nails

Zaias, Nardo. The nail in health and disease / Nardo Zaias. — Lancaster : MTP, c1980. — 260p : ill ; 27cm
Includes index
ISBN 0-85200-534-2 : £35.00 B81-05856

612.8 — MAN. PHYSIOLOGY. NERVOUS SYSTEM

612′.8 — Learning by man. Neurophysiological aspects — *Conference proceedings*

Neural mechanisms of goal-directed behavior and learning / edited by Richard F. Thompson, Leslie H. Hicks, V.B. Shvyrkov. — New York ; London : Academic Press, 1980. — xvii,639p : ill ; 24cm
Conference papers. — Includes bibliographies and index
ISBN 0-12-688980-5 : £31.80
Primary classification 612′.8 B81-14754

612′.8 — Man. Behaviour. Neurophysiological aspects

Heiniger, Margot C.. Neurophysiological concepts in human behavior : the tree of learning / Margot C. Heiniger, Shirley L. Randolph. — St. Louis ; London : Mosby, 1981. — xiii,350p : ill ; 24cm
Includes index
ISBN 0-8016-2203-4 : £17.50 B81-33041

612′.8 — Man. Motivation. Neurophysiological aspects — *Conference proceedings*

Neural mechanisms of goal-directed behavior and learning / edited by Richard F. Thompson, Leslie H. Hicks, V.B. Shvyrkov. — New York ; London : Academic Press, 1980. — xvii,639p : ill ; 24cm
Conference papers. — Includes bibliographies and index
ISBN 0-12-688980-5 : £31.80
Also classified at 612′.8 B81-14754

612′.8 — Man. Nervous system

Jensen, David. The human nervous system / David Jensen ; illustrated by Barbara Jensen. — New York : Appleton-Century-Crofts ; London : Prentice-Hall, c1980. — xv,349p : ill ; 28cm
Bibliography: p333-336. - Includes index
ISBN 0-8385-3944-0 (pbk) : £9.70 B81-05658

612′.8 — Man. Nervous system — *For auxiliary personnel in health services*

Brown, Donald R.. Neurosciences for allied health therapies / Donald R. Brown. — St. Louis ; London : Mosby, 1980. — xiv,358p : ill ; 25cm
Includes bibliographies and index
ISBN 0-8016-0827-9 : Unpriced B81-08195

612′.8 — Man. Nervous system. Physiology

Keynes, R. D.. Nerve and muscle. — Cambridge : Cambridge University Press, Nov.1981. — [169]p. — (Cambridge texts in the physiological sciences ; 2)
ISBN 0-521-23945-1 : £15.00 : CIP entry
ISBN 0-521-28362-0 (pbk) : £4.95
Also classified at 612′.74 B81-31190

Newman, P. P.. Neurophysiology / P.P. Newman. — Lancaster : MTP, c1980. — 525p : ill ; 24cm. — (Monographs in modern neurobiology)
Includes bibliographies and index
ISBN 0-85200-544-x : £14.95 B81-03508

Noback, Chrales R.. The human nervous system : basic priciples of neurobiology / text by Charles R. Noback ; illustrated by Robert J. Demarest. — 3rd ed. — New York ; London : McGraw-Hill, c1981. — xii,591p : ill ; 25cm
Previous ed.: 1975. — Includes bibliographies and index
ISBN 0-07-046851-6 : £16.75 B81-29832

Stratton, Donald B.. Neurophysiology / Donald B. Stratton. — New York ; London : McGraw-Hill, c1981. — xii,387p : ill ; 24cm
Bibliography: p357-360. — Includes index
ISBN 0-07-062151-9 : £13.95 B81-12053

Willis, William D.. Medical neurobiology : neuroanatomical and neurophysiological principles basic to clinical neuroscience / William D. Willis Jr., Robert G. Grossman. — St. Louis ; London : Mosby, 1981. — ix,593p : ill ; 29cm
Previous ed.: 1977. — Includes bibliographies and index
ISBN 0-8016-5584-6 : £26.00 B81-40357

612′.8 — Man. Nervous system. Synapses. Research. Use of horseradish peroxidase

Tracing neural connections with horseradish peroxidase. — Chichester : Wiley, Jan.1982. — [280]p. — (IBRO handbook series : methods in the neurosciences)
ISBN 0-471-10028-5 : £22.00 : CIP entry B81-34510

612′.8 — Man. Sensory nerves. Conductation

Sinclair, David. Mechanisms of cutaneous sensation. — 2nd ed. — Oxford : Oxford University Press, Nov.1981. — [325]p. — (Oxford medical publications)
Previous ed.: 1967
ISBN 0-19-261174-7 : £15.00 : CIP entry B81-28854

612′.8 — Medicine. Psychophysiology

Gale, Anthony. Psychophysiology : a bridge between disciplines : an inaugural lecture delivered at the University 30 January, 1979 / by Anthony Gale ; under the chairmanship of H.J. Eysenck. — [Southampton] : University of Southampton, 1979. — 30p : ill ; 21cm
Bibliography: p29-30
ISBN 0-85432-207-8 (pbk) : Unpriced B81-04553

612′.8 — Neurophysiology

Feldberg, W. S.. Fifty years on : looking back on some developments in neurohumoral physiology. — Liverpool : Liverpool University Press, Nov.1981. — [120]p. — (The Sherrington lectures ; 16)
ISBN 0-85323-364-0 (pbk) : £4.50 : CIP entry B81-30630

612′.8′024372 — Man. Nervous system. Physiology — *For teaching*

Jensen, Robert A.. Behavioral neuroscience : an instructor′s guide : for use with Behavioral neuroscience - an introduction, by Carl Cotman and James L. McGaugh / Robert A. Jensen. — New York ; London : Academic Press, c1979. — 111p ; 23cm
Cover title
ISBN 0-12-191655-3 (pbk) : £0.60 B81-31767

612′.8′024613 — Man. Nervous system — *For nursing*

Bickerton, J.. Neurology for nurses / J. Bickerton, J. Small. — London : Heinemann Medical, 1981. — 205p : ill ; 25cm
ISBN 0-433-02830-0 (pbk) : £6.50 B81-24919

612′.8042 — Man. Catecholamines. Effects of stress — *Conference proceedings*

International Symposium on Catecholamines and Stress *(2nd : 1979 : Smolenice Castle)*.
Catecholamines and stress : recent advances : proceedings of the Second International Symposium on Catecholamines and Stress, held in Smolenice Castle, Czechoslovakia, September 12-16, 1979 / editors Earl Usdin, Richard Kvetňanský, Irwin J. Kopin. — New York ; Oxford : Elsevier/North-Holland, c1980. — xxv,618p : ill ; 25cm. — (Developments in neuroscience ; v.8)
Includes index
ISBN 0-444-00402-5 : £20.04 B81-06116

612′.8042 — Medicine. Neurochemistry

Green, A. Richard. Pharmacology and biochemistry of psychiatric disorders. — Chichester : Wiley, Oct.1981. — [200]p
ISBN 0-471-09998-8 (cased) : £13.00 : CIP entry
ISBN 0-471-10000-5 (pbk) : £5.90
Also classified at 615′.78 B81-28044

612′.8042 — Medicine. Neurochemistry — *Conference proceedings*

Chemisms of the brain. — Edinburgh : Churchill Livingstone, Sept.1981. — [408]p
Conference papers
ISBN 0-443-02409-x : £20.00 : CIP entry B81-22597

612′.8042′05 — Medicine. Neurochemistry — *Serials*

Essays in neurochemistry and neuropharmacology. — Vol.5. — Chichester ; New York : Wiley, c1981. — xv,153p
ISBN 0-471-27879-3 : £16.50
ISSN 0147-0205
Also classified at 615′.78′05 B81-24997

612′.8042′072 — Medicine. Neurochemistry. Research. Methodology — *Serials*

Research methods in neurochemistry. — Vol.5. — New York ; London ([88 Middlesex St., E1 7EX]) : Plenum Press, c1981. — xvi,318p
ISBN 0-306-40583-0 : Unpriced
ISSN 0096-2902 B81-32403

612′.813 — Man. Nervous system. Biophysics

Vasilescu, V.. Introduction to neurobiophysics. — Tunbridge Wells : Abacus Press, Dec.1981. — [267]p
Translation of: Introducere in neurobiofizica
ISBN 0-85626-302-8 : £22.50 : CIP entry B81-31651

612′.82 — Man. Brain. Ageing — *Conference proceedings*

International School of Physiopathology and Clinic of the Third Age *(2nd : 1980 : Ettore Majorana Center for Scientific Culture)*. The aging brain : neurological and mental disturbances / [proceedings of the second course of the International school of Physiopathology and Clinic of the Third Age, held at the Ettore Majorana Center for Scientific Culture, Erice, Sicily, Italy, March 3-8, 1980] ; edited by G. Barbagallo-Sangiorgi and A.N. Exton-Smith. — New York ; London : Plenum, c1980. — xiii,393p : ill ; 26cm. — (Ettore Majorana international science series. Life sciences ; vol.5)
Includes index
ISBN 0-306-40625-x : Unpriced B81-13380

612′.82 — Man. Brain. Development. Role of hormones — *Conference proceedings*

Hormones and brain development : proceedings of an international symposium held in Berlin, German Democratic Republic on September 6-8, 1978 / G. Dörner and M. Kawakami, editors. — Amsterdam ; Oxford : North-Holland Biomedical, 1978. — xiii,473p ; 25cm. — (Developments in endocrinology ; v.3)
Includes index
ISBN 0-444-80091-3 : Unpriced B81-02415

612′.82 — Man. Brain. Effects of environment

Walsh, Roger. Towards an ecology of brain / Roger Walsh. — Lancaster : MTP, c1981. — 192p : ill ; 24cm
Bibliography: p157-188. — Includes index
ISBN 0-85200-570-9 : £12.95 B81-33078

612′.82 — Man. Brain. Neurophysiological aspects — *Festschriften*

The **Warsaw** colloquium on instrumental conditioning and brain research : proceedings of the symposium to honour the memory of Jerzy Konorski and 60 years of the Nencki Institute, held in Jabłonna near Warsaw, 1-5 May 1979 / edited by Bogusław Zernicki and Kazimierz Zieliński. — The Hague ; London : Nijhoff, 1980. — xii,736p,[12]p of plates : ill ; 25cm
Includes bibliographies and index
ISBN 90-247-2412-0 : Unpriced B81-20987

612′.82 — Man. Brain. Neurophysiological aspects — *For children*

Ward, Brian. The brain and nervous system / Brian R. Ward. — London : Watts, 1981. — 48p : col.ill ; 26cm. — (The Human body)
Includes index
ISBN 0-85166-907-7 : £3.99 B81-26073

612′.82 — Man. Brain. Physiology

Russell, Peter, *1946-*. The brain book / Peter Russell. — London : Routledge & Kegan Paul, 1979 (1980 [printing]). — x,270p : ill(some col.) ; 24cm
Bibliography: p256-259. - Includes index
ISBN 0-7100-0706-x (pbk) : £3.95 : CIP rev. B80-27060

612′.82 — Man. Brain. Psychophysiological aspects

Powell, Graham E.. Brain function therapy. — Farnborough, Hants. : Gower, June 1981. — [324]p
ISBN 0-566-00315-5 : £10.00 : CIP entry B81-12913

Psychophysiology : today and tomorrow / editor N.P. Bechtereva. — Oxford : Pergamon, 1981. — viii,263p : ill ; 26cm
Includes bibliographies and index
ISBN 0-08-025930-8 : £25.00 : CIP rev. B80-23963

Young, J. Z.. Programs of the brain / J.Z. Young. — Oxford : Oxford University Press, 1978 (1981 [printing]). — 325p : ill ; 23cm. — (Oxford paperbacks)
'Based on the Gifford Lectures, 1975-7'. — Includes bibliographies and index
ISBN 0-19-286019-4 (pbk) : £4.95 : CIP rev. B80-12211

612′.82 — Man. Brain *related to* **mind**

Taylor, Gordon Rattray. The natural history of the mind : an exploration / Gordon Rattray Taylor. — London : Granada, 1980, c1979. — x,370p ; 20cm. — (A Paladin book)
Originally published: London : Secker and Warburg, 1979. — Bibliography: p341-357. — Includes index
ISBN 0-586-08386-3 (pbk) : £2.50
Primary classification 128′.2 B81-02750

612′.82 — Man. Central nervous system. Neurotransmission — *Conference proceedings*

Chemical neurotransmission 75 years. — London : Academic Press, Jan.1982. — [500]p
Conference papers
ISBN 0-12-671480-0 : CIP entry B81-34410

612′.821 — Man. Sleep

Mellor, Isha. Sleep / Isha Mellor. — London : W.H. Allen, 1981. — 80p : ill ; 21cm
ISBN 0-491-02715-x : £3.95 B81-40903

612′.821 — Man. Sleep. Neurophysiological aspects

Cohen, David B.. Sleep and dreaming : origins, nature and functions / by David B. Cohen. — Oxford : Pergamon, 1980, c1979. — xii,315p : ill ; 26cm. — (International series in experimental psychology ; v.23)
Bibliography: p283-300. — Includes index
ISBN 0-08-021467-3 (cased) : Unpriced
ISBN 0-08-027400-5 (pbk) : £7.00 B81-16265

612′.821 — Man. Sleep. Physiological aspects

Physiology in sleep / edited by John Orem, Charles D. Barnes. — New York ; London : Academic Press, 1980. — xiv,347p : ill ; 24cm. — (Research topics in physiology ; 3)
Includes bibliographies and index
ISBN 0-12-527650-8 : £19.40 B81-16788

612′.821′0880565 — Old persons. Sleep patterns. Variation — *Study regions: Switzerland. Basel*

Spiegel, René. Sleep and sleeplessness in advanced age / René Spiegel. — Lancaster : MTP, c1981. — 272p : ill,forms ; 24cm. — (Advances in sleep research ; v.5)
Bibliography: p249-268. - Includes index
ISBN 0-85200-546-6 : £17.95 B81-10327

612′.822 — Man. Brain. Auditory evoked & visual evoked electric potentials. Laboratory techniques

Evoked potentials in clinical testing. — Edinburgh : Churchill Livingstone, Oct.1981. — [250]p. — (Clinical neurology and neurosurgery monographs ; v.3)
ISBN 0-443-01791-3 : £15.00 : CIP entry B81-30629

612′.822 — Man. Brain. Effects of hormones — *Conference proceedings*

Hormones and the brain : papers presented at a workshop organised and sponsored by the International Health Foundation on the theme The brain as an endocrine target organ in health and disease. The workshop was held in Bordeaux, France under the auspices of the Université de Bordeaux 11 and the Unité d'Enseignement et de Recherche de Médecine 1 / edited by David de Wied and Pieter A. van Keep assisted by Pamela Freebody. — Lancaster : MTP, 1980. — xiv,337p : ill ; 25cm
Includes bibliographies and index
ISBN 0-85200-313-7 : £16.90 B81-03970

612′.822 — Man. Brain. Electric potentials associated with motivation & electric potentials associated with sensormotor activities — *Conference proceedings*

International Symposium on Electrical Potentials Related to Motivation, Motor and Sensory Processes of the Brain *(5th : 1979 : Ulm-Reisensburg)*. Motivation, motor and sensory processes of the brain : electrical potentials behaviour and clinical use : proceedings of the Fifth International Symposium on Electrical Potentials Related to Motivation, Motor and Sensory Processes of the Brain (Moss V), held at Ulm-Reisensburg, May 14-18, 1979 / edited by H.H. Kornhuber and L. Deecke. — Amsterdam ; Oxford : Elsevier/North Holland Biomedical, 1980. — xxv,811p : ill,ports ; 27cm. — (Progress in brain research ; V.5A)
Includes bibliographies and index
ISBN 0-444-80196-0 : Unpriced B81-15374

612′.822 — Man. Brain. Electroencephalography *related to* **evoked electric potentials**

Bazar, Erol. EEG- brain dynamics : relation between EEG and brain evoked potentials / Erol Bazar. — Amsterdam ; Oxford : Elsevier/North-Holland Biomedical, 1980. — xxi,411p : ill ; 25cm
Bibliography: p393-403. — Includes index
ISBN 0-444-80249-5 : £39.40 B81-04663

612′.822 — Man. Brain. Tissues. Biochemistry — *Conference proceedings*

Transmitter biochemistry of human brain tissue : proceedings of the symposium held at the 12th CINP Congress, Göteborg, Sweden, June 1980 / edited by Peter Riederer and Earl Usdin. — London : Macmillan, 1981. — 332p : ill ; 24cm
Includes bibliographies and index
ISBN 0-333-31089-6 : £22.00 B81-40516

612′.825 — Man. Brain. Hemispheres. Asymmetry

Springer, Sally P.. Left brain, right brain / Sally P. Springer, Georg Deutsch. — Oxford : W.H. Freeman, c1981. — xii,243p : ill ; 25cm
Includes index
ISBN 0-7167-1269-5 (cased) : £10.70
ISBN 0-7167-1270-9 (pbk) : £4.95 B81-37382

612′.825 — Man. Brain. Right hemisphere. Psychophysiological aspects

Blakeslee, Thomas R.. The right brain : a new understanding of the unconscious mind and its creative powers / Thomas R. Blakeslee. — London : Macmillan, 1980. — x,275p : ill ; 23cm
Originally published: Garden City, N.Y. : Anchor Press / Doubleday, 1980. — Bibliography: p224-263. - Includes index
ISBN 0-333-29089-5 (cased) : £10.00 : CIP rev.
ISBN 0-333-29090-9 (pbk) : £2.95 B80-21956

612′.825 — Man. Cerebral cortex. Neurophysiology

Bindman, Lynn. The neurophysiology of the cerebal cortex / Lynn Bindman and Olof Lippold. — London : Edward Arnold, 1981. — xii,495p : ill ; 26cm
Bibliography: p413-462. — Includes index
ISBN 0-7131-4360-6 : £47.50 : CIP rev. B80-23296

612′.8252 — Man. Motor activities. Neurophysiological aspects

Motor unit types, recruitment and plasticity in health and disease / editor John E. Desmedt. — Basel ; London : Karger, 1981. — viii,416p : ill ; 25cm. — (Progress in clinical neurophysiology ; v.9)
Bibliography: p368-410. — Includes index
ISBN 3-8055-1929-x : £39.35 B81-38092

612′.84 — Children. Sight. Assessment

Gardiner, P. A.. The development of vision. — Lancaster : MTP Press, Sept.1981. — [150]p
ISBN 0-85200-303-x : £8.95 : CIP entry B81-22681

612′.84 — Man. Colour vision. Theories, *1830-1900*

Sherman, Paul D.. Colour vision in the nineteenth century. — Bristol : Hilger, Aug.1981. — [260]p
ISBN 0-85274-376-9 : £35.00 : CIP entry B81-18081

612′.84 — Man. Eyes

Eden, John. The eye book / John Eden ; illustrations by Laszlo Kubinyi. — Harmondsworth : Penguin, 1981, c1978. — vii,215p : ill ; 20cm. — (Penguin handbooks)
Originally published: New York : Viking Press, 1978 ; Newton Abbot : David & Charles, 1979. — Includes index
ISBN 0-14-046449-2 (pbk) : £1.95 B81-16977

612′.84 — Man. Eyes. Physiology

Adler, Francis Heed. Adler's physiology of the eye : clinical application / edited by Robert A. Moses. — 7th ed. — St. Louis ; London : Mosby, 1981. — xii,747p : ill ; 26cm
Previous ed.: 1975. — Includes bibliographies and index
ISBN 0-8016-3541-1 : £33.00 B81-24265

612′.84 — Man. Sight — *For children*

Allington, Richard. Looking / by Richard Allington and Kathleen Krull ; illustrated by Bill Bober. — Oxford : Blackwell Raintree, c1981. — 31p : col.ill ; 24cm. — (Beginning to learn about)
Originally published: Milwaukee : Raintree Childrens, c1980
ISBN 0-86256-015-2 : £2.50 B81-17345

612′.84 — Man. Sight. Neurophysiological aspects — *Conference proceedings*

ISCEV Symposium *(18th : 1980 : Amsterdam)*. Visual pathways : electrophysiology and pathology : proceedings of the 18th I.S.C.E.V. Symposium, Amsterdam, May 18-22, 1980 / edited by H. Spekreijse and P.A. Apkarian. — The Hague ; London : Junk, 1981. — xviii,453p : ill ; 24cm. — (Documenta ophthalmologica. Proceedings series ; v.27)
Includes bibliographies and index
ISBN 90-619-3723-x : Unpriced B81-27021

612′.841 — Man. Eyes. Anterior chamber — *Festschriften*

Progress in anterior eye segment : research and practice : volume in honour of John E. Harris / edited by O. Hockwin & W.B. Rathbun. — The Hague ; London : Junk, 1979. — ix,370p : ill,1port ; 24cm. — (Documenta ophthalmologica. Proceedings series ; v.18)
Includes bibliographies
ISBN 90-619-3158-4 : Unpriced B81-19393

612′.85 — Man. Hearing — *For children*

Allington, Richard. Hearing / by Richard Allington and Kathleen Krull ; illustrated by Wayne Dober. — Oxford : Blackwell Raintree, c1981. — 32p : col.ill ; 24cm. — (Beginning to learn about)
Originally published: Milwaukee : Raintree Childrens, c1980
ISBN 0-86256-013-6 : £2.50 B81-17352

612′.85 — Man. Hearing. Physiology & psychophysiology

Gelfand, Stanley A.. Hearing : an introduction to psychological and physiological acoustics / Stanley A. Gelfand. — New York : Dekker ; London : Butterworths, c1981. — xi,379p : ill ; 24cm
Includes index
ISBN 0-8247-1189-0 : £16.00 B81-18275

612'.86 — Smell — *For children*

Allington, Richard. Smelling / by Richard Allington and Kathleen Krull ; illustrated by Rick Thrun. — Oxford : Blackwell Raintree, 1981. — 32p : col.ill ; 24cm. — (Beginning to learn about)
Originally published: / by Richard L. Allington and Kathleen Cowles. Milwaukee : Raintree Children's, 1980
ISBN 0-86256-016-0 : £2.50
ISBN 0-8265-6016-0 B81-28665

612'.87 — Taste — *For children*

Allington, Richard. Tasting / by Richard Allington and Kathleen Krull ; illustrated by Noel Spangler. — Oxford : Blackwell Raintree, 1981. — 32p : col.ill ; 24cm. — (Beginning to learn about)
Originally published: / by Richard L. Allington and Kathleen Cowles. Milwaukee : Raintree Children's, 1980
ISBN 0-86256-018-7 : £2.50
ISBN 0-8265-6018-7 B81-28664

612'.88 — Touch — *For children*

Allington, Richard. Touching / by Richard Allington and Kathleen Krull ; illustrated by Yoshi Miyake. — Oxford : Blackwell Raintree, 1981. — 32p : col.ill ; 24cm. — (Beginning to learn about)
Originally published: / by Richard L. Allington and Kathleen Cowles. Milwaukee : Raintree Children's, 1980
ISBN 0-86256-017-9 : £2.50
ISBN 0-8265-6017-9 B81-28667

612.9 — MAN. REGIONAL PHYSIOLOGY

612'.92 — Man. Oral region — *For dentistry*

Adams, David. Essentials of oral biology / David Adams. — Edinburgh : Churchill Livingstone, 1981. — 132p : ill ; 22cm. — (Churchill Livingstone dental books)
Includes bibliographies and index
ISBN 0-443-02095-7 (pbk) : £3.15 B81-37098

612'.94'01 — Man. Thorax. Physiology. Theories, *to 1978*

French, R. K.. The history of the heart : thoracic physiology from ancient to modern times / R.K. French. — Aberdeen (26 Carden Place, Aberdeen) : Equipress, 1979. — 77p : ill ; 26cm. — (Texts in the history of medicine ; no.2)
Unpriced (pkb) B81-17003

612'.97 — Man. Hands

The **Hand** / edited by Raoul Tubiana. — Philadelphia ; London : Saunders
ISBN 0-7216-8907-8 : £49.50 B81-26960

613 — HYGIENE

613 — England. Population. Health. Inequalities. Influence of social class

Inequalities in health : report of a research working group. — [London] ([Alexander Fleming House, Elephant and Castle, SE1 6BY]) : Department of Health and Social Security, 1980. — 417p : ill ; 30cm
Cover title
£8.00 (pbk) B81-15354

613 — Executives. Health — *Serials*

Executive fitness newsletter. — Vol.1, no.1-. — Aylesbury : Rodale Press, [1981?]-. — v. ; 30cm
Fortnightly
ISSN 0261-5371 = Executive fitness newsletter : £10.00 per year B81-32262

613 — Families. Health

Skeet, Muriel. Family care : how to look after yourself and your family / Muriel Skeet. — London : Macmillan, 1981. — 126p : ill ; 25cm. — (Macmillan tropical community health manuals)
Includes index
ISBN 0-333-32164-2 (pbk) : £1.95 B81-39955

The **Which?** guide to family health / editor Michael Leitch ; consultant editor A.S. Playfair. — London : Consumer's Association : Hodder & Stoughton, c1980. — 215p : ill(some col.) ; 25cm
Includes index
ISBN 0-340-25051-8 : £7.95 B81-19875

613 — Man. Health

A **Handbook** of health. — London : MTP Press, Oct.1981. — [275]p
ISBN 0-85200-308-0 : £9.95 : CIP entry B81-27424

The **Harvard** Medical School health letter book / edited by G. Timothy Johnson, Stephen E. Goldfinger. — Cambridge, Mass. ; London : Harvard University Press, 1981. — 444p : ill ; 24cm
Includes index
ISBN 0-674-37725-7 : £9.60 B81-28259

Williamson, G. Scott. Science, synthesis and sanity : an inquiry into the nature of living / G. Scott Williamson and Innes H. Pearse. — Edinburgh : Scottish Academic, 1980. — 352p,[1] leaf of plates : 1port ; 22cm
Originally published: London : Collins, 1965. — Includes index
ISBN 0-7073-0259-5 (pbk) : £5.25 B81-08580

613 — Man. Health — *For schools*

Gadd, P.. Human biology / P. Gadd. — London : Macmillan, 1981. — 91p : ill ; 28cm. — (Certificate revision series)
Includes index
ISBN 0-333-29525-0 (pbk) : £1.40 B81-40734

Johnson, Vaughan. Good health / Vaughan Johnson and Trefor Williams. — Walton-on-Thames : Nelson
4. — 1981. — 64p : ill(some col.) ; 25cm
Publisher's no.: NCN 0528-12-0
ISBN 0-17-423094-x (pbk) : £1.30 B81-33378

613 — Man. Health — *For West African students*

Godman, A.. Certificate notes : O-level Health Science / A. Godman, Anne C. Gutteridge. — Harlow : Longman, 1981. — vi,122p : ill ; 22cm. — (Study for success)
ISBN 0-582-60621-7 (pbk) : £1.15 B81-40700

613 — Man. Health. Holism

Flynn, Patricia Anne Randolph. Holistic health : the art and science of care / Patricia Anne Randolph Flynn. — Bowie : Brady ; London : Prentice-Hall, c1980. — xvi,239p : ill,forms ; 24cm
Bibliography: p217-227. - Includes index
ISBN 0-87619-626-1 (pbk) : £8.40 B81-05771

613 — Man. Health — *Humour*

Le Poste, Pierre. Rude health. — London : Macmillan, Oct.1981. — [48]p
ISBN 0-333-32570-2 : £3.95 : CIP entry B81-27366

613 — Man. Health. Improvement — *Conference proceedings*

Kellogg Nutrition Symposium *(5th)*. Good health : is there a choice? : fifth Kellogg Nutrition Symposium / edited by P.H. Fentem. — London : Macmillan, 1981. — viii,79p : ill ; 23cm
Includes bibliographies
ISBN 0-333-31139-6 : £8.95 B81-24261

613 — Man. Health. Improvement — *Manuals*

Bennett, Paul, *1953-*. Picture of health / Paul Bennett. — Bognor Regis (Horizon House, Victoria Drive, Bognor Regis, W. Sussex) : New Horizon, 1981. — 117p : ill ; 21cm
ISBN 0-86116-657-4 : £4.75 B81-23172

Norfolk, Donald. Fit for life / Donald Norfolk. — Feltham : Hamlyn Paperbacks, 1981, c1980. — 288p : ill ; 18cm
Originally published: Feltham : Hamlyn, 1980. — Includes index
ISBN 0-600-20048-5 (pbk) : £1.50 B81-23173

Sorochan, Walter D.. Promoting your health / Walter D. Sorochan. — New York ; Chichester : Wiley, c1981. — x,577p : ill(some col.),col.maps,facsims,forms,ports ; 28cm
Includes bibliographies and index
ISBN 0-471-04681-7 (pbk) : £7.85 B81-18441

613 — Man. Health. Self-care

Murray, Al. Towards total health : a realistic approach to better living / Al Murray & Mike Bettsworth. — London : Batsford, 1981. — 119p : ill ; 26cm
Includes index
ISBN 0-7134-3413-9 : £6.95 B81-33362

Stoppard, Miriam. [Miriam Stoppard's healthcare]. Healthcare : with an A-Z of common medical complaints and how to treat them / Miriam Stoppard. — London : Macdonald Futura, 1981, c1980. — 208p : ill ; 22cm
Originally published: London : Weidenfeld and Nicolson, 1980. — Includes index
ISBN 0-7088-2001-8 (pbk) : £2.50 B81-17432

613 — Man. Health. Self-care — *Manuals*

Benjamin, Harry. Everybody's guide to nature cure / by Harry Benjamin. — 2nd ed. — Wellingborough : Thorsons, 1961 (1981 [printing]). — 481p : ill ; 22cm
Previous ed.: London : Health for All Publishing Co., 1936. — Includes index
ISBN 0-7225-0703-8 (pbk) : £4.95 B81-29182

613 — Yemen *(Arab Republic)*. **Population. Health. Effects of promotion of developed countries' pharmaceutical products**

Melrose, Dianna. The great health robbery : baby milk and medicines in Yemen / by Dianna Melrose. — Oxford : Oxfam, 1981. — 50,ivp : ill,1map,facsim ; 21cm
Bibliography: p50. - List of films: p.50
ISBN 0-85598-054-0 (pbk) : £1.30 B81-17640

613'.024613 — Man. Health — *For nursing*

Jackson, Sheila M.. Personal and community health / Sheila M. Jackson and Susan Lane. — 2nd ed. — London : Baillière Tindall, 1981. — viii,293p : ill ; 18cm. — (Nurses' aids series)
Previous ed.: 1975. — Includes bibliographies and index
ISBN 0-7020-0846-x (pbk) : Unpriced B81-24914

613'.0246467 — Man. Health & hygiene — *For hairdressing*

Salter, Mary. Health for hairdressers : notes for hairdressing students and apprentices / by Mary Salter and Doreen Sturtivant ; illustrated by Yvonne Sturtivant. — Oxford : Technical, 1981. — v,138p : ill ; 21cm
Includes index
ISBN 0-291-39501-5 (pbk) : £4.50 : CIP rev. B81-14395

613'.04244 — Pregnant women & mothers. Health — *Practical information*

Gardner, Mary. People want healthy babies / [text by Mary Gardner, Jean Macdougall and Allan Thomson] ; [designed and illustrated by Pat McNeill]. — Hamilton (Board Office, 14 Beckford St., Hamilton ML3 OTA) : Lanarkshire Health Board, [1981?]. — [16]p : col.ill ; 21cm. — (Health education booklets)
Unpriced (unbound) B81-33582

613'.04244 — Women, 40 years -. Ageing. Effects. Prevention — *Manuals*

Lloyd-Jones, Vernon. Why grow old? / Vernon Lloyd-Jones. — Swansea : Christopher Davies, 1980. — 100p ; 22cm
ISBN 0-7154-0554-3 (pbk) : £1.95 B81-37146

613'.04244 — Women. Health — *For women*

Cherry, Sheldon H.. [For women of all ages]. The women's guide to health / S.H. Cherry. — London : Granada, 1981, c1979. — xii,207p : ill ; 24cm
Originally published: New York : Macmillan, 1979. — Includes index
ISBN 0-246-11440-1 : £6.95 B81-15628

613'.04244 — Women. Health — *For women continuation*

Cooke, Cynthia W.. The good health guide for women / Cynthia W. Cooke and Susan Dworkin. — Rev. British ed. / by Jill Turner and Wendy Savage. — Feltham : Hamlyn, 1981. — 422p ; 20cm
Previous ed.: published as Ms. guide to woman's health. New York : Doubleday, 1979. — Bibliography: p393-407. — Includes index
ISBN 0-600-20278-x : £2.95 B81-38435

613'.0432 — Children. Health

Macfarlane, J. A.. Child health / J.A. Macfarlane. — London : Grant McIntyre, 1980. — 208p : ill ; 19cm. — (Pocket consultant)
Cover title. — Bibliography: p197-198. - Includes index
ISBN 0-86216-010-3 (pbk) : £4.95 : CIP rev. B80-19254

613'.0432 — Great Britain. Primary schools. Students. Health — *For parents*

Forsythe, Elizabeth. Preparation for school : a medical guide for parents / Elizabeth Forsythe. — London : Faber, 1981. — 160p : ill ; 20cm
Includes index
ISBN 0-571-11739-2 (pbk) : £3.25 B81-24590

613'.0432 — Great Britain. Socially disadvantaged children. Health

Blaxter, Mildred. The health of the children : a review of research on the place of health in cycles of disadvantage / Mildred Blaxter. — London : Heinemann Educational, 1981. — xiii,272p : ill,1map ; 23cm. — (Studies in deprivation and disadvantage ; 3)
Bibliography: p226-265. — Includes index
ISBN 0-435-82034-6 : £14.95 : CIP rev. B81-03691

613'.0432 — United States. Primary schools. Students. Health — *For teaching*

Elementary school health : education and service / Richard L. Rhodes ... [et al.]. — Boston, Mass. ; London : Allyn and Bacon, c1981. — vii,483p : ill,forms ; 25cm
Previous ed.: i.e. Preliminary ed. published as Health and the elementary teacher. c1977. — Includes bibliographies and index
ISBN 0-205-06979-7 : £19.95 B81-01929

613'.0432 — United States. Schools. Students. Health

Schaller, Warren E.. The school health program. — 5th ed. / Warren E. Schaller. — Philadelphia ; London : Saunders, c1981. — xiii,574p : ill,forms ; 25cm
Previous ed.: / by the late Alma Nemir and Warren E. Schaller, 1975. — Includes bibliographies and index
ISBN 0-03-057702-0 : £12.75
Primary classification 371.7'1'0973 B81-23092

613'.0432'0941 — Great Britain. Paediatrics. Preventive medicine — *Conference proceedings*

Study day report : (International Year of the Child) : the preventive aspects of child health : 28 November 1979. — Edinburgh : Scottish Health Service Centre, [1980?]. — 28p : ill,1form,ports ; 30cm
Unpriced (pbk) B81-18218

613'.0433 — Nottinghamshire. Sutton-in-Ashfield. Health. Attitudes of school leavers

Perkins, Elizabeth R.. School leavers in Sutton-in-Ashfield : health knowledge and attitudes / Elizabeth R. Perkins. — [Nottingham] : University of Nottingham, 1976. — 19,[21]leaves : ill ; 30cm. — (Occasional paper / Leverhulme Health Education Project ; no.2)
Unpriced (pbk) B81-22824

613'.0438 — Old persons. Hygiene — *Polish texts*

Tarnawski, Apolinary. Hygiena starości i starzenia si e / Apolinary Tarnawski. — Londyn : Polska fundacja kulturalna, 1980. — 144p : ill,1port ; 22cm
Unpriced (pbk) B81-02329

613'.07 — Health education — *Conference proceedings*

Anderson, Digby C.. Who knows best in health education? : proceedings of the Study Day, May 2nd 1979 / Digby C. Anderson, Elizabeth R. Perkins, Nicholas J. Spencer. — [Nottingham] : University of Nottingham, 1979. — 36leaves : facsims ; 30cm. — (Occasional paper / Leverhulme Health Education Project ; no.19)
Includes bibliographies
Unpriced (pbk) B81-22738

International Conference on Health Education *(10th : 1979 : London)*. 10th International Conference on Health Education : 'health education in action ; achievements and priorities' : London 2-7 September 1979 : report / [prepared for the Health Education Council and the Scottish Health Education Unit by K.A. Dunn]. — London : Health Education Council, 1980. — 167p ; 30cm
Text in English and French. — Cover title
£4.50 (free to conference delegates) (pbk) B81-14555

613'.07 — Health education. Role of mass media — *Conference procedings*

Health education and the media. — Oxford : Pergamon, Oct.1981. — [606]p
Conference papers
ISBN 0-08-027982-1 : £40.00 : CIP entry B81-30204

613'.07 — Nottinghamshire. Sutton-in-Ashfield. Pre-school children. Mothers. Health education

Perkins, Elizabeth R.. Health education and preschool provision in Sutton-in-Ashfield / Elizabeth R. Perkins. — Rev. — [Nottingham] : University of Nottingham, 1978. — 13,ivp ; 30cm. — (Occasional paper / Leverhulme Health Education Project ; no.3)
Previous ed.: 1976
Unpriced (pbk) B81-22823

613'.07 — Patients. Health education

Redman, Barbara Klug. Issues and concepts in patient education / Barbara Klug Redman, contributors Nancy Lloyd Rothman, Daniel A. Rothman. — New York : Appleton-Century-Crofts ; London : Prentice-Hall, c1981. — xi,129p ; 24cm. — (Appleton patient education series)
Includes index
ISBN 0-8385-4405-3 (pbk) : £5.80 B81-25919

613'.07 — Patients. Health education — *For nursing*

Redman, Barbara Klug. The process of patient teaching in nursing : Barabara Klug Redman. — 4th ed. — St. Louis ; London : Mosby, 1980. — x,291p : ill,forms ; 24cm
Previous ed.: 1976. — Includes bibliographies and index
ISBN 0-8016-4100-4 (pbk) : £8.50 B81-05422

613'.07'041 — Great Britain. Health education — *Proposals*

Practical prospects for health education in the 1980s : a report of the Leverhulme Health Education Project, University of Nottingham, April 1980 / edited by Digby C. Anderson and Elizabeth R. Perkins. — [Nottingham] : [University of Nottingham], [1980]. — 88p ; 30cm
Bibliography: p70-72
Unpriced (pbk) B81-11311

613'.07'04252 — Nottinghamshire. Health education. Role of health visitors

Perkins, Elizabeth R.. Group health education by health visitors / Elizabeth R. Perkins. — [Nottingham] : University of Nottingham, 1978. — 9,14,2leaves ; 30cm. — (Occasional paper / Leverhulme Health Education Project ; no.7)
Unpriced (pbk) B81-22818

613'.07'1041 — Great Britain. Schools. Curriculum subjects: Health education

Anderson, Digby C.. Curricula as implicative descriptions of classrooms : a case of conspicuous formal irrelevance / Digby C. Anderson. — [Nottingham] : University of Nottingham, 1978. — 12leaves ; 30cm. — (Occasional paper / Leverhulme Health Education Project ; no.11)
Unpriced (pbk) B81-22728

Anderson, Digby C.. Systematic and modest schemes for health education in schools / Digby C. Anderson. — [Nottingham] : University of Nottingham, 1979. — 19leaves ; 30cm. — (Occasional paper / Leverhulme Health Education Project ; no.15)
Bibliography: p19
Unpriced (pbk) B81-22729

Health education in schools / edited by James Cowley, Kenneth David and Trefor Williams. — London : Harper & Row, 1981. — 352p : ill ; 22cm. — (Harper education series)
Bibliography: p336-340. — Includes index
ISBN 0-06-318178-9 (cased) : Unpriced : CIP rev.
ISBN 0-06-318179-7 (pbk) : Unpriced B81-13565

613'.07'124252 — Nottinghamshire. Secondary schools. Health education

Burrows, L.. Health education in Nottinghamshire secondary schools : a survey of the current organisation of health education in Nottinghamshire secondary schools and the attitudes of head teachers towards it / L. Burrows with Sally D. Snell. — [Nottingham] : University of Nottingham, 1975. — 5,2,4leaves ; 30cm. — (Occasional paper / Leverhulme Health Education Project ; no.1)
Unpriced (pbk) B81-22825

613'.07'15 — Nottinghamshire. Sutton-in-Ashfield. Adult health education

Perkins, Elizabeth R.. Health and community involvement : adult education and health education in Sutton / Elizabeth R. Perkins. — [Nottingham] : University of Nottingham, 1977. — 9leaves ; 30cm. — (Occasional paper / Leverhulme Health Education Project ; no.4)
Unpriced (pbk) B81-22821

613'.076 — Man. Health — *Questions & answers — For West African students*

Usua, E. J.. Questions and answers : O-level health science / E.J. Usua, C.V. Adophy. — Harlow : Longman, 1981, c1980. — 91p : ill ; 22cm. — (Study for success)
ISBN 0-582-60652-7 (pbk) : £0.95 B81-40197

613'.088658 — Executives. Health — *Serials*

Executive Health Club. — No.99 (Feb.1981)-. — London (2 Palace Rd N8) : United Health Promotion, 1981-. — v. : ill,ports ; 28x12cm
Monthly. — Continues: Survival kit
ISSN 0261-8230 = Executive Health Club : Unpriced B81-33724

613'.0887928 — Ballet dancers. Health — *Manuals*

Vincent, L. M.. The dancer's book of health / L.M. Vincent. — London : Dance, 1980. — 151p : ill ; 22cm
ISBN 0-903102-60-9 (pbk) : £3.00 B81-13622

613'.0941 — Great Britain. Man. Health & safety — *For schools*

Picton, Margaret. Understanding health and safety / Margaret Picton ; illustrated by Doreen Lang. — Glasgow : Blackie, 1981. — 124p : col.ill ; 22cm
ISBN 0-216-90873-6 (pbk) : £3.30 B81-29726

613.1 — HYGIENE. ENVIRONMENTAL FACTORS

613'.1 — Colour. Health aspects — *Spiritualist viewpoints*

Hylton, *Dr.*. Colour in health and disease : a series of lectures / by Dr. Hylton through his medium Irene Edouin. — 8th ed. — London : Greater World Association, 1979. — 49p ; 19cm
Previous ed.: 1978
£0.85 (pbk) B81-28941

613'.122'0941 — Great Britain. Spas. Development — *Conference proceedings*

The **Future** of British spas and health and pleasure resorts : a report of the conference held at Bath on November 1st, 1979, sponsored by the British Tourist Authority in cooperation with the British Spas Federation and the British Resorts Association. — London : British Tourist Authority, [1980]. — 28p ; 30cm
£5.00 (pbk) B81-04548

613'.19 — Man. Health. Effects of atmospheric pollution. Psychosocial factors

Harris, Anthony H.. Economics and epidemiology : a critical review of the state of the art / by A.H. Harris. — [Aberdeen] : [University of Aberdeen, Department of Political Economy], [1981]. — 33,[11]p ; 30cm. — (Discussion paper / University of Aberdeen Department of Political Economy ; 81-06)
Bibliography: p33
Unpriced (pbk) B81-20675

613'.192 — Pranayama

Iyengar, B. K. S.. Light on pr a n a y a ma : pr a n a y a ma d ı pik a / B.K.S. Iyengar. — London : Allen & Unwin, 1981. — xxiv,294p : ill,ports ; 21cm
Includes index
ISBN 0-04-149057-6 : Unpriced B81-17273

613'.194 — Europe. Naturist beaches — *Directories — Serials*

[Free-sun *(Europe's beaches)***]**. Free-sun : nude sea bathing : the complete book : Europe's beaches ... : includes 56 pages reprinted as the booklet 'Nude sea bathing in Britain'. — 1979-. — March (37 West End, March, Cambridgeshire, PE15 8DN) : Free-Sun Books, 1979-. — v. : ill,port ; 21cm
Annual. — Description based on: 1980 issue
ISSN 0260-6038 = Free-sun (Europe's beaches) : £5.00 B81-04646

613'.194 — Great Britain. Naturist beaches — *Directories — Serials*

[Free-sun *(nude sea bathing in Britain)***]**. Free-sun : nude sea bathing in Britain. — 1979-. — March (37 West End, March, Cambridgeshire, PE15 8DN) : Free-sun Books, 1979-. — v. : ill ; 21cm
Annual. — Description based on: 1980 issue
ISSN 0260-6046 = Free-sun (nude sea bathing in Britain) : £1.50 B81-04165

613'.194'02541 — Great Britain. Nudist camps — *Directories*

British naturism handbook / [Alan McCombe editor]. — Orpington ([Sheepcote, Orpington, Kent BR5 4ERT]) : Central Council for British Naturism, c1981. — 88p : ill,maps ; 21cm
Cover title. — New ed. of title last published 1978
ISBN 0-906248-03-5 (pbk) : £2.00 B81-23180

613.2 — HYGIENE. DIETETICS

613.2 — Babies & pregnant women. Health. Effects of diet

Davis, Adelle. Let's have healthy children. — New expanded and rev. ed. — London : Unwin Paperbacks, Oct.1981. — [400]p
Previous ed.: 1974
ISBN 0-04-612032-7 (pbk) : £1.95 : CIP entry B81-30883

613.2 — Clinical dietetics

American Dietetic Association. Handbook of clinical dietetics / American Dietetic Association. — New Haven ; London : Yale University Press, c1981. — 507p in various pagings : ill,1form ; 28cm
Includes index
ISBN 0-300-02256-5 (pbk) : £12.60 B81-16159

613.2 — Food. Health aspects — *Conference proceedings*

Soil, food and health in a changing world / edited by Kenneth Barlow and Peter Bunyard. — Berkhamstead (P.O. Box 97, Berkhamstead, Herts., HP4 2PX) : A.B. Academic, c1981. — 107p : ill ; 25cm
Conference papers. — Includes bibliographies
ISBN 0-907360-00-9 (pbk) : Unpriced B81-37066

613.2 — Man. Health. Effects of diet — *Politics of Health Group viewpoints*

Food and profit : it makes you sick / The Politics of Health Group. — London (c/o BSSRS, 9 Poland St., W.1) : The Group, [1981]?. — 28p : ill ; 21cm. — (Pamphlet / Politics of Health Group ; no.1)
£0.50 (pbk) B81-36693

613.2 — Man. Nutrition

Calloway, Doris Howes. Nutrition & health / Doris Howes Calloway, Kathleen Oliver Carpenter. — Philadelphia ; London : Saunders College, c1981. — vii,341p : ill(some col.) ; 25cm
Includes bibliographies and index
ISBN 0-03-057711-x : £11.50 B81-31687

Fleck, Henrietta. Introduction to nutrition / Henrietta Fleck. — 4th ed. — New York : Macmillan ; London : Collier Macmillan, c1981. — viii,580p : ill ; 27cm
Previous ed.: 1976. — Includes bibliographies and index
ISBN 0-02-338280-5 : £10.95 B81-29331

Gates, June C.. Basic foods / June C. Gates. — 2nd ed. — New York ; London : Holt, Rinehart and Winston, c1981. — xi,636p : ill ; 25cm
Previous ed.: 1976. — Includes bibliographies and index
ISBN 0-03-049846-5 : £10.95 B81-22872

Hafen, Brent Q.. Nutrition, food and weight control. — Expanded ed. / Brent Q. Hafen with contributions from Laren R. Robison ... [et al.]. — Boston, Mass. ; London : Allyn and Bacon, c1981. — 371p in various pagings : ill ; 25cm
Previous ed.: 1981. — Bibliography: pD1-D3. - Includes index
ISBN 0-205-06825-1 : £17.95 B81-13004

Hafen, Brent Q.. Nutrition, food, and weight control / Brent Q. Hafen with contributions from Laren R. Robinson, Brenda Peterson, Katherine G. Elliott. — Boston, Mass. ; London : Allyn and Bacon, c1981. — 293p in various pagings : ill ; 24cm
Bibliography: pD1-D3. - Includes index
ISBN 0-205-06825-1 (pbk) : £9.95 B81-13006

Hildreth, E. M.. Elementary science of food. — 2nd ed. — London : Bell & Hyman, Aug.1981. — [306]p
Previous ed.: London : Allman, 1952
ISBN 0-7135-2059-0 (pbk) : £4.25 : CIP entry B81-20650

Hutchin, Kenneth C.. Food and your body / by Kenneth C. Hutchin. — London (National Dairy Centre, John Princes St., W1M 0AP) : National Dairy Council, 1980. — 24p : ill ; 26cm
Ill and text on inside covers
ISBN 0-902748-26-2 (pbk) : Unpriced B81-21073

McLaren, Donald S.. Nutrition and its disorders / Donald S. McLaren. — 3rd ed. — Edinburgh : Churchill Livingstone, 1981. — viii,277p : ill ; 22cm. — (Churchill Livingstone medical texts)
Previous ed.: 1976. — Includes bibliographies and index
ISBN 0-443-02158-9 (pbk) : £5.95 : CIP rev. B80-07428

Mowry, Lillian. Mowry's basic nutrition and diet therapy. — 6th ed. / Sue Rodwell Williams. — St. Louis ; London : Mosby, 1980. — xii,213p : ill ; 24cm
Previous ed.: 1975. — Includes bibliographies and index
ISBN 0-8016-5556-0 (pbk) : £6.75 B81-14522

Muller, H. G.. Nutrition and food processing / H.G. Muller, G. Tobin. — London : Croom Helm, c1980. — 302p : ill ; 23cm
Bibliography: p287-296. — Includes index
ISBN 0-85664-540-0 : £15.95 : CIP rev. B80-11961

Pyke, Magnus. Food for all the family / Magnus Pyke ; illustrated by Bill Tidy. — London : Pan, 1981, c1980. — 256p : ill ; 18cm
Originally published: London : J. Murray, 1980. — Includes index
ISBN 0-330-26373-0 (pbk) : £1.50 B81-26331

Salmon, Jenny. Balancing your diet : how to eat sensibly and well / Jenny Salmon. — Cambridge : Published for J. Sainsbury Limited by Woodhead-Faulkner, 1980. — 32p : ill ; 21cm. — (Sainsbury's food guides ; no.2)
Cover title. — Text on inside cover
£0.30 (pbk) B81-37264

Stare, Fredrick J.. Living nutrition / Fredrick J. Stare, Margaret McWilliams. — 3rd ed. — New York ; Chichester : Wiley, c1981. — 580p : ill(some col.),2maps ; 26cm
Previous ed.: 1977. — Includes bibliographies and index
ISBN 0-471-04940-9 : £10.50 B81-13082

Sumner, Margaret. Thought for food / Margaret Sumner. — Oxford : Oxford University Press, 1981. — 168p ; 19cm
Includes index
ISBN 0-19-217690-0 (cased) : £5.95 : CIP rev.
ISBN 0-19-286003-8 (pbk) : £2.25 B80-23294

Williams, Sue Rodwell. Nutrition and diet therapy / Sue Rodwell Williams ; including original drawings by George Straus. — 4th ed. — St. Louis ; London : Mosby, 1981. — xix,840p : ill ; 25cm
Previous ed.: 1977. — Includes bibliographies and index
ISBN 0-8016-5554-4 : £14.00 B81-25612

Winick, Myron. Nutrition in health and disease / Myron Winick. — New York ; Chichester : Wiley, c1980. — viii,261p : ill ; 24cm
Includes bibliographies and index
ISBN 0-471-05713-4 : £10.25 B81-00909

Worthington-Roberts, Bonnie S.. Contemporary developments in nutrition / Bonnie S. Worthington-Roberts. — St. Louis ; London : Mosby, 1981. — x,603p : ill ; 24cm
Includes index
ISBN 0-8016-5627-3 (pbk) : £12.75 B81-09771

613.2 — Man. Nutrition — *Conference proceedings*

International Congress on Nutrition *(11th : 1978 : Rio de Janeiro)*. Nutrition and food science : present knowledge and utilization / [proceedings of the Eleventh International Congress on Nutrition held in Rio de Janeiro, Brazil, August 27-September 1, 1978] ; edited by Walter Santos ... [et al.]. — New York ; London : Plenum, c1980
Vol.1: Food and nutrition policies and programs. — xiii,808p : ill ; 26cm
Includes bibliographies and index
ISBN 0-306-40342-0 : Unpriced B81-13001

International Congress on Nutrition *(11th : 1978 : Rio de Janeiro)*. Nutrition and food science : present knowledge and utilization / [proceedings of the Eleventh International Congress on Nutrition held in Rio de Janeiro, Brazil, August 27-September 1, 1978] ; edited by Walter Santos ... [et al.]. — New York ; London : Plenum, c1980
Vol.2: Nutrition education and food science and technology. — xvii,950p : ill ; 26cm
Includes bibliographies and index
ISBN 0-306-40343-9 : Unpriced B81-13002

International Congress on Nutrition *(11th : 1978 : Rio de Janeiro)*. Nutrition and food science : present knowledge and utilization / [proceedings of the Eleventh International Congress on Nutrition held in Rio de Janeiro, Brazil, August 27-September 1, 1978] ; edited by Walter Santos ... [et al.]. — New York ; London : Plenum, c1980
Vol.3: Nutritional biochemistry and pathology. — xvi,815p : ill ; 26cm
Includes bibliographies and index
ISBN 0-306-40344-7 : Unpriced B81-13003

Symposium on nutrition : held on 6th and 7th December 1979 in the Hall of the Royal College of Physicians of Edinburgh / edited by S.H. Davies. — Edinburgh : Royal College of Physicians of Edinburgh, 1980. — 123p : ill ; 21cm. — (Publication / Royal College of Physicians of Edinburgh ; n.53)
ISBN 0-85405-036-1 (pbk) : Unpriced B81-06117

613.2 — Man. Nutrition - *For adolescents*
Creese, Angela[Guide to nutrition]. The young homemaker guide to nutrition. — London : Bell & Hyman, Aug.1981. — [96]p. — (The Young homemaker series)
Originally published as: Guide to nutrition. London : Mills & Boon, 1969
ISBN 0-7135-2065-5 (pbk) : CIP entry B81-16362

613.2 — Man. Nutrition — *For medical students*
Bender, A. E.. Nutrition for medical students. — Chichester : Wiley, Feb.1982. — [352]p
ISBN 0-471-28041-0 : £16.00 : CIP entry B81-36234

613.2 — Man. Nutrition. Health aspects
Food safety / edited by Howard R. Roberts. — New York ; Chichester : Wiley, c1981. — xiii,339p ; 25cm
Includes index
ISBN 0-471-06458-0 : £24.50
Primary classification 363.1′92 B81-23425

613′.2 — Man. Nutrition. Health aspects
Nutritional problems in modern society. — London (80 Broadway, Vauxhall, SW8 1SF) : Libbey, Apr.1981. — [160]p
ISBN 0-86196-007-6 : £9.50 : CIP entry B81-04273

613.2 — Patients. Interviewing by dieticians
Anderson, Digby C.. The details of dietetic interviews : an initial assessment / Digby C. Anderson and Cheryl Stephen. — [Nottingham] : University of Nottingham, 1980. — 26leaves ; 30cm. — (Occasional paper / Leverhulme Health Education Project ; no.20)
Bibliography: p26
Unpriced (pbk) B81-22736

613.2′024613 — Man. Health. Effects of diet — *For nursing*
Huskisson, Joan M.. Nutrition and dietetics in health and disease : a practical handbook for nurses / Joan M. Huskisson ; forward by Elizabeth M.H. Janes. — London : Baillière Tindall, 1981. — xii,318p : ill ; 20cm. — (Nurses′ aids series. Special interest text)
Includes bibliographies and index
ISBN 0-7020-0814-1 (pbk) : £5.75 B81-11637

613.2′024613 — Man. Nutrition — *For nursing*
Green, Marilyn L.. Nutrition in contemporary nursing practice / Marilyn L. Green, Joann Harry. — New York ; Chichester : Wiley, c1981. — xvii,864p,[2]p of plates : ill(some col.),1map,forms ; 24cm. — (A Wiley medical publication)
Text on lining papers. — Includes bibliographies and index
ISBN 0-471-03892-x : £15.95 B81-24886

Uddoh, Caroline K. O.. Nutrition / Caroline K.O. Uddoh. — London : Macmillan, 1980. — 204p : ill ; 22cm. — (Macmillan tropical nursing and health sciences series)
Bibliography: p197-198. - Includes index
ISBN 0-333-28437-2 (pbk) : £4.50 : CIP rev. B80-24599

613.2′0246176 — Man. Nutrition — *For dentistry*
Randolph, Patricia M.. Diet, nutrition, and dentistry / Patricia M. Randolph, Carol I. Dennison ; illustrations by J. Douglas Walter. — St. Louis ; London : Mosby, 1981. — vi,358p : ill ; 26cm
Includes bibliographies and index
ISBN 0-8016-4088-1 (pbk) : £11.25 B81-18968

613.2′025′41 — Great Britain. Dieticians — *Directories — Serials*
The **Dietitians** register. — 1980. — [London] ([Park House, 184 Kennington Park Rd., SE11 4BU]) : Printed and published under the direction of the Dietitians Board, [1980]. — 61 leaves
ISSN 0305-3989 : Unpriced B81-06692

613.2′03′21 — Man. Nutrition — *Encyclopaedias*
Tver, David F.. Nutrition and health encyclopedia / David F. Tver and Percy Russell. — New York ; London : Van Nostrand Reinhold, c1981. — v,569p : ill ; 24cm
ISBN 0-442-24859-8 : £22.55 B81-36815

613.2′05 — Man. Nutrition — *Serials*
[Digest *(Heinz Baby Food Advisory Service)*].
Digest : a quarterly newssheet on nutritional matters / [Heinz Baby Food Advisory Service]. — Nov.1980-. — Hayes (Dept. D, H.J. Heinz Co. Ltd., Hayes Park, Hayes, Middlesex) : The Service, 1980-. — v. ; 24cm
ISSN 0261-202x = Digest (Heinz Baby Food Advisory Service) : Unpriced B81-20089

World review of nutrition and dietetics. — Vol.36. — Basel ; London : Karger, 1981. — x,226p
ISBN 3-8055-1347-x : £50.50
ISSN 0084-2230 B81-11872

613.2′072 — Man. Nutrition. Research — *Conference proceedings*
Problems in nutrition research today / edited by H.E. Aebi, G.B. Brubacher, M.R. Turner ; [proceedings of a symposium held in Bern, Switzerland in October 1979, organized by the Swiss Nutrition Foundation]. — London : Academic Press, 1981. — x,151p : ill ; 24cm
Includes bibliographies and index
ISBN 0-12-044420-8 : £12.00 : CIP rev. B81-09488

613.2′088042 — Pregnant women. Nutrition — *Conference proceedings*
Maternal nutrition in pregnancy - eating for two? : based on a workshop sponsored by Nestlé Nutrition, held at the Chateau de Rochegude, Vaucluse, France, 1-4 June 1980 / edited by John Dobbing. — London : Academic Press, 1981. — x,197p : ill,ports ; 24cm
Includes bibliographies and index
ISBN 0-12-218850-0 : £13.80 B81-19335

613.2′088054 — Children. Nutrition
Infant and child feeding / edited by Jenny T. Bond ... [et al.]. — New York ; London : Academic Press, c1981. — xxiv,502p : ill ; 24cm. — (The Nutrition foundation)
Ill. on lining papers. — Includes bibliographies and index
ISBN 0-12-113350-8 : £32.80 B81-39582

Pipes, Peggy L.. Nutrition : in infancy and childhood / Peggy L. Pipes. — 2nd ed. — St. Louis ; London : Mosby, 1981. — ix,317p : ill,forms ; 24cm
Previous ed.: 1977. — Includes bibliographies and index
ISBN 0-8016-3941-7 (pbk) : £8.50 B81-24243

613.2′0880542 — Babies. Diet
Mac Keith, Ronald Charles. Mac Keith′s infant feeding and feeding difficulties. — Edinburgh : Churchill Livingstone, Apr.1981. — [344]p
Previous ed.: 1977
ISBN 0-443-01945-2 (pbk) : £9.00 : CIP entry B81-00122

613.2′0880542 — Babies: Vegetarians. Nutrition — *For parents*
Yntema, Sharon. The vegetarian baby : a complete and valuable source book for vegetarian parents / by Sharon Yntema. — Wellingborough : Thorsons, 1981, c1980. — 160p : 2ill ; 22cm
Originally published: Ithaca, N.Y. : McBooks, 1980. — Bibliography: p155-156. - Includes index
ISBN 0-7225-0688-0 (pbk) : £3.50 : CIP rev. B81-14796

613.2′092′4 — Man. Nutrition. Theories of Graham, Sylvester
Nissenbaum, Stephen. Sex, diet, and debility in Jacksonian America : Sylvester Graham and health reform / Stephen Nissenbaum. — Westport, Conn. ; London : Greenwood Press, 1980. — xvii,198p ; 22cm. — (Contributions in medical history, ISSN 0147-1058 ; no.4)
Bibliography: p175-189. - Includes index
ISBN 0-313-21415-8 : Unpriced B81-05749

613.2′0941 — Great Britain. Man. Nutrition
Dietary goals for the UK in the 1980′s : the 1980 Nutrition Award prize-winning papers / sponsored by Van dan Berghs & Jurgens Limited. — Burgess Hill (Sussex House, Burgess Hill, W. Sussex RH15 9AW) : Van den Berghs & Jurgens Limited, c1981. — 94p : ill,ports ; 18cm
Includes bibliographies
Unpriced (pbk) B81-26277

613.2′0943′46 — West Germany. Heidelberg. Persons, 20-40 years. Health. Effects of diet — *German texts*
Arab, L.. Ernährung und Gesundheit : eine Untersuchung bei jungen Frauen und Männern in Heidelberg / L. Arab, B. Schellenberg und G. Schlierf unter Mitarbeit von M. Blum ... [et al.]. — Basel ; London : Karger, c1981. — xi,203p : ill ; 23cm. — (Beiträge zu Infusionstherapie und klinische Ernährung ; Bd.7)
Includes index
ISBN 3-8055-2384-x (pbk) : £10.40 B81-30694

613.2′5 — Physical fitness. Slimming
Burton, Penny. Slimmers Mirror : diet, fitness and fun for all the family / [written by Penny Burton]. — London : Mirror, 1981. — 26p + 1folded sheet : ill(some col.),ports(some col.) ; 36cm
′Daily Mirror Slimmers Club calorie counter′ (1 folded sheet) as insert
ISBN 0-85939-248-1 (unbound) : £0.50 B81-19417

Slimming workshop / [editor Brenda Marshall]. — London : Marshall Cavendish, c1979. — 80p : ill(some col.) ; 28cm. — (Your body)
Includes index
ISBN 0-85685-352-6 (pbk) : £0.99 B81-09273

Weekend slimming for all / edited by Janet Crumbie. — London ([Carmelite House, Carmelite St., E.C.4.]) : Harmsworth Publications for Associated Newspapers, c1981. — 64p : ill(some col.),ports ; 27cm
Includes index
£0.90 (pbk) B81-18909

613.2′5 — Physical fitness. Slimming. Diet
Eyton, Audrey. The dieter′s guide to success : 100 ways to beat temptation and get slim / Audrey Eyton and Henry Jordan. — [London] : Fontana Paperbacks, 1981. — 126p ; 19cm
ISBN 0-00-636239-7 (pbk) : £1.25 B81-19349

The **My** weekly guide to slimming. — London : D.C. Thomson, c1981. — 66p : ill(some col.) ; 31cm
£0.45 (unbound) B81-17751

Parriott, Sara. Calories don′t count when - / Sara Parriott. — London : Sphere, 1981, c1979. — [105]p : ill ; 20cm
ISBN 0-7221-6714-8 (pbk) : £1.00 B81-09847

Pinkus, Susan. Slimming diets. — Havant : Mason, Aug.1981. — [32]p
Originally published: 1973
ISBN 0-85937-102-6 (pbk) : £0.20 : CIP entry B81-18049

Trimmer, Eric. The complete book of slimming and diets. — Loughton : Piatkus, Sept.1981. — [160]p
ISBN 0-86188-081-1 : £6.95 : CIP entry B81-21523

613.2′5 — Physical fitness. Slimming. Diet. Group therapy — *Personal observations*
Tribe, Pauline. I just grow′d / Pauline Tribe. — Bognor Regis : New Horizon, c1979. — 245,xvp : ill ; 21cm
ISBN 0-86116-259-5 : £3.90 B81-21828

613.2′6 — Man. Health. Effects of edible plants
Peterson, Vicki. Eat your way to health / Vicki Peterson ; illustrated by Yvonne Skargon. — London : Allen Lane, 1981. — 208p : ill ; 23cm
Includes index
ISBN 0-7139-1401-7 : £6.95 B81-29362

613.2′6 — Man. Health. Improvement. Use of natural food
Kunz-Bircher, Ruth. The health guide / by Ruth Kunz-Bircher ; translated from the French by Rosemary Sheed. — London : Allen & Unwin, 1981. — 166p ; 23cm
Translation of: Le guide de Santé Bircher. — Bibliography: p166
ISBN 0-04-613040-3 : £6.95 B81-25915

613.2'62'05 — Vegetarianism — *Serials*
[**Vegetarian** *(Altrincham : 1980)*]. The Vegetarian. — Sept./Oct. 1980-. — Altrincham : Vegetarian Society (UK) Ltd., 1980-. — v. : ill ; 27cm
Six issues yearly. — Continues: Alive
ISSN 0260-3233 = Vegetarian (Altrincham. 1980) : £0.35 per issue B81-03588

613.2'62'06 — Vegetarianism. Organisations — *Directories* — *Serials*
The **International** vegetarian health food handbook. — 1981/82. — Altrincham : The Vegetarian Society of the United Kingdom, [1981]. — 311p
£1.75 B81-13201

613.2'8 — Man. Health. Effects of fats — *Butter Information Council viewpoints* — *Serials*
Diet and health. — No.1 (1981)-. — Tunbridge Wells (2 Nevill St., Tunbridge Wells, Kent TN2 5TT) : Butter Information Council, 1981-. — v. : ill,ports ; 41cm
Irregular
ISSN 0261-5320 = Diet and health : Unpriced B81-33942

613.2'8 — Man. Health. Effects of vitamin B complex
Mervyn, Leonard. The B vitamins : their major role in maintaining your health / by Leonard Mervyn. — Wellingborough : Thorsons, 1981. — 96p ; 18cm. — (Nature's way)
Includes index
ISBN 0-7225-0667-8 (pbk) : £0.95 : CIP rev. B81-02387

613.2'8 — Man. Health. Effects of vitamin C
Basu, T. K.. Vitamin C in health and disease. — London : Croom Helm, Jan.1982. — [160]p
ISBN 0-7099-0445-2 : £10.95 : CIP entry B81-34307

613.2'8 — Man. Health. Effects of vitamins
Gildroy, Ann. Vitamins and your health. — London : Allen & Unwin, Jan.1982. — [144]p
ISBN 0-04-641039-2 : £6.95 : CIP entry B81-33909

613.2'8 — Man. Nutrients: Minerals
Kutsky, Roman J.. Handbook of vitamins, minerals and hormones / Roman J. Kutsky. — 2nd ed. — New York ; London : Von Nostrand Reinhold, c1981. — xvi,492p : ill ; 24cm
Previous ed.: published as Handbook of vitamins and hormones. 1973. — Bibliography: p458-459. — Includes index
ISBN 0-442-24557-2 : £20.85
Also classified at 613.2'8 ; 612'.405 B81-36077

613.2'8 — Man. Nutrients: Vitamins
Kutsky, Roman J.. Handbook of vitamins, minerals and hormones / Roman J. Kutsky. — 2nd ed. — New York ; London : Von Nostrand Reinhold, c1981. — xvi,492p : ill ; 24cm
Previous ed.: published as Handbook of vitamins and hormones. 1973. — Bibliography: p458-459. — Includes index
ISBN 0-442-24557-2 : £20.85
Primary classification 613.2'8 B81-36077

613.2'8 — Man. Nutrition. Role of minerals
Mervyn, Leonard. Minerals and your health / Len Mervyn. — London : Unwin Paperbacks, 1981, c1980. — 129p : ill ; 18cm
Originally published: 1980. — Bibliography: p124. — Includes index
ISBN 0-04-641038-4 (pbk) : £1.75 : CIP rev. B81-20553

613.2'8 — Man. Nutrition. Trace elements & vitamins
Pfeiffer, Carl C.. [Dr. Pfeiffer's total nutrition]. Total nutrition. — St. Albans : Granada, Feb.1982. — [160]p
Originally published as: Dr. Pfeiffer's total nutrition. New York : Simon and Schuster, 1980
ISBN 0-246-11686-2 : £4.50 : CIP entry B81-35797

613.4 — HYGIENE. CARE OF PERSON

613'.4 — Man. Personal hygiene — *For schools*
Moses, Howell. Look good — feel good / Howell Moses & Ann Salway. — St. Albans : Hart-Davis Educational, 1981. — 96p : ill,facsims ; 25cm. — (New learning for living ; 1)
Text on inside cover. — Includes index
ISBN 0-247-12979-8 (pbk) : £2.15 B81-18202

613.5/6 — HYGIENE. ARTIFICIAL ENVIRONMENTS

613.6'2 — European Community countries. Man. Health. Effects of shiftwork — *Case studies*
The **Effects** of shiftwork on health, social and family life. — [Dublin] ([Loughlinstown House, Shankill, Co. Dublin]) : European Foundation for the Improvement of Living and Working Conditions, [1980]. — 451p in various pagings : ill ; 29cm
Conference papers. — Includes bibliographies
Unpriced (pbk)
Primary classification 306'.3 B81-09832

613.6'2 — European Community countries. Man. Health. Effects of shiftwork — *Case studies* — *French texts*
Effets du travail posté sur la santé, la vie sociale et la vie familiale / [Fondation européenne pour l'amélioration des conditions de vie et de travail]. — [Shankill] ([Loughlinstown House, Shankill, Co. Dublin]) : [European Foundation for the Improvement of Living and Working Conditions], [1980]. — [507]p : ill ; 30cm
Conference papers. — Includes bibliographies
£5.00 (pbk)
Primary classification 306'.3 B81-05314

613.6'2 — European Community countries. Man. Health. Effects of shiftwork — *Case studies* — *Italian texts*
Gli **Effetti** del lavoro a turni sulla salute e sulla vita sociale e familiare / [Fondazione europea per il miglioramento delle condizioni di vita e di lavoro]. — [Shankill] ([Loughlinstown House, Shankill, Co. Dublin]) : [European Foundation for the Improvement of Living and Working Conditions], [1980]. — [501]p : ill ; 30cm
Conference papers. — Includes bibliographies
£5.00 (pbk)
Primary classification 306'.3 B81-05785

613.6'2 — Industrial health — *Serials*
Recent advances in occupational health. — No.1. — Edinburgh : Churchill Livingstone, Oct.1981. — [259]p
ISBN 0-443-02300-x : £16.00 : CIP entry
ISSN 0261-1449 B81-25301

613.6'2 — Personnel. Health. Effects of shiftwork & night work — *Conference proceedings*
International Symposium on Night and Shift Work *(5th : 1980 : Rouen)*. Night and shift work. — Oxford : Pergamon, June 1981. — [516]p. — (Advances in the biosciences ; v.30)
ISBN 0-08-025516-7 : £33.00 : CIP entry B81-13510

613.6'9 — Shipwrecks. Survival — *Manuals*
Lee, E. C. B.. Safety and survival at sea / E.C.B. Lee and Kenneth Lee. — Rev. and expanded ed. — New York ; London : Norton, c1980. — viii,315p,[8]p of plates : ill ; 24cm. — (A Giniger book)
Previous ed.: London : Cassell, 1971. — Bibliography: p301-303. — Includes index
ISBN 0-393-03242-6 : £11.25 B81-03484

613.6'9 — Shipwrecks. Survival — *Manuals* — *For yachting*
Robin, Bernard. Survival at sea : a practical manual of survival and advice to the shipwrecked, assembled from an analysis of thirty-one survival stories / Bernard Robin ; translated and edited by Richard Simpkin. — London : Paul, 1981. — 238 : ill,charts,maps ; 23cm
Translated from the French. — Bibliography: p235. — Includes index
ISBN 0-09-143090-9 (cased) : £7.95
ISBN 0-09-143091-7 (pbk) : £4.95 B81-21417

613.6'9 — Survival. Techniques — *Manuals* — *For children*
Eldin, Peter. The explorer's handbook / Peter Eldin ; with drawings by Roger Smith. — [London] : Armada, 1980. — 127p : ill ; 18cm
ISBN 0-00-691709-7 (pbk) : £0.75 B81-06983

613.7 — PHYSICAL FITNESS

613.7 — Physical education, *to 1980*
Landmarks in the history of physical education / P.C. McIntosh ... [et al.]. — 3rd ed. — London : Routledge & Kegan Paul, 1981. — ix,262p,[7]p of plates : ill ; 22cm
Previous ed.: (ie. 1st ed.) 1957. — Includes bibliographies and index
ISBN 0-7100-0796-5 (pbk) : £4.95 : CIP rev. B81-07585

613.7 — Physical fitness — *Manuals*
Hockey, Robert V.. Physical fitness : the pathway to healthful living / Robert V. Hockey. — 4th ed. — St. Louis ; London : Mosby, 1981. — vii,151p : ill,forms ; 24cm
Previous ed.: 1977. — Includes bibliographies and index
ISBN 0-8016-2216-6 (pbk) : £6.50 B81-31148

Roy, Harcourt. Fitness in the firm's time / by Harcourt Roy. — Saffron Walden : C.W. Daniel, c1981. — 149p : ill ; 23cm
ISBN 0-85207-150-7 : £4.50 B81-37116

Thomas, Vaughan. Book of fitness & exercise / Vaughan Thomas. — Poole : Blandford, [1981]. — 95p : ill(some col.),1 port ; 15cm. — ('How to')
Includes index
ISBN 0-7137-1047-0 (pbk) : £1.95 B81-08468

613.7 — Physical fitness. Tai-keg — *Manuals*
Chan. Tai-Keg : Kung Fu manual / by Chan. — Banbury (P.O. Box 39, Banbury, Oxon. OX16 0NT) : Jomacast, c1981. — 31p : ill,2ports ; 30cm
Unpriced (unbound) B81-39275

613.7 — United States. Physical education
Bucher, Charles A.. Physical education and sport : change and challenge / Charles A. Bucher, Nolan A. Thaxton. — St. Louis ; London : Mosby, 1981. — vii,243p : ill ; 24cm
Includes index
ISBN 0-8016-0876-7 (pbk) : £7.75 B81-24286

613.7 — United States. Physical education — *Career guides*
Parks, Janet B.. Physical education : the profession / Janet B. Parks. — St. Louis ; London : Mosby, 1980. — x,147p : ill ; 24cm
Includes bibliographies and index
ISBN 0-8016-3759-7 (pbk) : Unpriced B81-08140

613.7'046 — Physical fitness. Hatha-yoga
Choudhury, Bikram. Bikram's beginning yoga class / by Bikram Choudhury with Bonnie Jones Reynolds ; photographs by Guy Webster ; illustrations by Bonnie Jones Reynolds with Judy Markham. — London : Unwin Paperbacks, 1981. — 211p : ill,ports ; 25cm
Originally published: Los Angeles : J.P. Tarcher, c1978
ISBN 0-04-149058-4 (pbk) : £4.95 B81-24532

Volin, Michael. Challenging the years : Yoga wisdom and modern knowledge for healthier and longer life / Michael Volin. — London : Sphere
Originally published: in 1v. London : Pelham, 1979
Vol.1. — 1981, c1979. — xv,141p,[4]p of plates : ill ; 18cm
ISBN 0-7221-8749-1 (pbk) : £1.25 B81-28982

613.7'046 — Pregnant women. Physical fitness. Hatha-yoga
Berg, Vibeke. Yoga in pregnancy / Vibeke Berg. — London : Watkins, 1981. — viii,42p : ill ; 23cm
Translation of: Yoga for gravide. — Bibliography: p133. — Includes index
ISBN 0-7224-0186-8 (pbk) : £3.95 B81-17046

613.7'07 — Physical education. Evaluation
Verducci, Frank M.. Measurement concepts in physical education / Frank M. Verducci. — St. Louis ; London : Mosby, 1980. — xii,367p : ill,forms ; 26cm
Includes bibliographies and index
ISBN 0-8016-5225-1 (pbk) : £11.25 B81-04127

613.7'07'073 — United States. Educational institutions. Curriculum subjects: Physical education. Teaching. Assessment

Anderson, William G.. Analysis of teaching physical education / William G. Anderson. — St. Louis ; London : Mosby, 1980. — xvi,128p : forms ; 24cm
Bibliography: p120-121. — Includes index
ISBN 0-8016-0179-7 (pbk) : Unpriced B81-08561

613.7'07'1 — Schools. Curriculum subjects: Physical education. Performance of students. Assessment

Safrit, Margaret J.. Evaluation in physical education / Margaret J. Safrit. — Englewood Cliffs ; London : Prentice-Hall, c1981. — xv,398p : ill ; 24cm
Previous ed.: 1973. — Includes bibliographies and index
ISBN 0-13-292250-9 : £9.70 B81-12671

613.7'07'1141 — Great Britain. Further education institutions. Curriculum subjects: Physical education

National Association of Teachers in Further and Higher Education. *Physical Education Section. Conference (1980 : Wentworth).* Physical education in further education : report of the N.A.T.F.H.E. Physical Education Section 1980 Annual Conference, held at Sheffield Polytechnic, Wentworth Site, Wentworth, Nr. Rotherham / edited by Irene K. Glaister. — Milton-under-Wychwood (Mrs. I.K. Glaister, Fardon House, Frog La., Milton-under-Wychwood, Oxon) : National Association of Teachers in Further and Higher Education, Physical Education Section, [1980]. — 64p ; 21cm
£3.20 (pbk) B81-32472

613.7'07'12 — Secondary schools. Curriculum subjects: Physical education. Syllabuses. Planning — *Manuals*

Lawson, Hal A.. Physical education in secondary schools : curricular alternatives / Hal A. Lawson, Judith H. Placek. — Boston, Mass. ; London : Allyn and Bacon, c1981. — xi,258p : ill ; 24cm
Includes bibliographies and index
ISBN 0-205-07156-2 (pbk) : £6.95 B81-11242

613.7'1 — Association footballers. Physical fitness — *Manuals* — *For training*

Muckle, David Sutherland. Get fit for soccer : training, diet, travel, environment factors ... / David Sutherland Muckle. — London : Pelham, 1981. — 151p : ill,ports ; 23cm
Bibliography: p143-144. — Includes index
ISBN 0-7207-1342-0 : £6.95 B81-36286

613.7'1 — Cyclists. Physical fitness. Exercises

Woodland, Les. Cycle racing : training to win / Les Woodland. — [London] : Selpress, 1981, c1975. — 144p : ill ; 21cm
Originally published: London : Pelham, 1975. — Bibliography: p140-141. — Includes index
ISBN 0-900654-44-9 (pbk) : Unpriced B81-17806

613.7'1 — Lawn tennis players. Physical fitness - *Manuals - For training*

Bolliger, A.. Get fit for tennis. — London : Pelham, Aug.1981. — [176]p
Translation of: Top fit im Tennis
ISBN 0-7207-1350-1 : £5.95 : CIP entry B81-17505

613.7'1 — Man. Hips & thighs. Muscles. Exercises — *Manuals*

Everroad, Jim. How to trim your hips and shape your thighs / Jim Everroad and Lonna Mosow. — London : Pan, 1981, c1979. — 47p : ill ; 20cm
ISBN 0-330-26317-x (pbk) : £0.80 B81-19697

613.7'1 — Physical fitness. Exercises

The **Complete** head to toe exercise book : get fitter — feel better / [edited by Linda Fox]. — London : Marshall Cavendish, 1977 (1979 printing). — 178p : col.ill ; 29cm
ISBN 0-85685-756-4 (pbk) : £1.99 B81-19569

Fairfax, Esther. The reluctant keep-fitter / by Esther Fairfax. — Weybridge : Whittet, 1981. — 96p : ill ; 26cm
ISBN 0-7112-0095-5 (cased) : £5.95
ISBN 0-7112-0097-1 (pbk) : £2.95 B81-16099

Lillee, Dennis. Dennis Lillee's book of family fitness. — London : Angus & Robertson, 1981, c1980. — 144p : ill,ports ; 22cm
Originally published in Australia. 1980
ISBN 0-207-14277-7 : £3.95 B81-17728

Martin, Trisha. Keep fit in confined spaces / by Trisha Martin. — Henley-on-Thames : Ellis, 1980. — 32p : ill ; 11cm
ISBN 0-85628-093-3 (pbk) : Unpriced : CIP rev. B80-06421

Walsh, Barry. Getting fit the hard way / Barry Walsh & Peter Douglas. — Poole : Blandford, 1981. — 123p : ill ; 23cm
Includes index
ISBN 0-7137-1086-1 : £4.95 B81-08130

613.7'1 — Physical fitness. Stretching exercises — *Manuals*

Anderson, Bob, *1945-*. Stretching / by Bob Anderson ; illustrated by Jean Anderson ; cricket section contributed by Bernard Thomas. — London : Pelham, 1981, c1980. — 192p : ill ; 27cm
Originally published: Bolinas : Shelter Publications, 1980. — Includes index
ISBN 0-7207-1351-x (pbk) : £5.95 B81-34425

613.7'1 — Physical fitness. T'ai chi ch'üan

Liu, Da. T'ai Chi Ch'uan and I Ching / Da Liu. — 2nd ed. — London : Routledge & Kegan Paul, 1981. — xii,105p : ill ; 22cm
Previous ed.: New York : Harper and Row, 1972 ; London : Routledge and Kegan Paul, 1974
ISBN 0-7100-0848-1 (pbk) : £3.25 B81-28151

613.7'1'088042 — Women. Physical fitness. Exercises

Schwarzenegger, Arnold. Arnold's bodyshaping for women / Arnold Schwarzenegger with Douglas Kent Hall. — London : Pelham, 1980, c1979. — 160p : ill,ports ; 29cm
Originally published: New York : Simon & Schuster, 1979
ISBN 0-7207-1291-2 : £6.50 B81-00910

613.7'1'0880565 — Old persons. Physical fitness. Exercises

Gibbs, Russell. Exercises for the elderly. — London : Jill Norman, July 1981. — [152]p
ISBN 0-906908-52-3 (cased) : £6.95 : CIP entry
ISBN 0-906908-53-1 (pbk) : £3.50 B81-13504

613.7'8'0924 — Physical fitness. Posture. Theories of Alexander, F. Matthias

Barlow, Wilfred. The Alexander principle / Wilfred Barlow. — London : Arrow, 1975 (1981 [printing]). — 223p,[24]p of plates : ill ; 18cm
Originally published: London : Gollancz, 1973. — Includes index
ISBN 0-09-910160-2 (pbk) : £1.75 B81-15432

613.7'9 — Physical fitness. Massage — *Manuals*

Inkeles, Gordon. The new massage : total body conditioning for people who exercise / by Gordon Inkeles ; photography by Greg Peterson. — London : Unwin Paperbacks, 1981, c1980. — 190p : ill ; 25cm
Originally published: New York : Putnam, 1980
ISBN 0-04-613043-8 (pbk) : £4.25 B81-19365

613.8 — ADDICTIONS AND HEALTH

613.8'1 — Alcoholic drinks. Consumption. Health aspects

Booth, Peter G.. Drink, drinking & drinking problems / by Peter G. Booth. — [Prescot] (Windsor Clinic, Rainhill Hospital, Prescot, Merseyside) : P.G. Booth, c1980. — 20p : ill ; 21x22cm
£0.75 (pbk) B81-00123

Linn, Robert. You can drink and stay healthy : a guide for the social drinker / Robert Linn. — London : Sphere, 1981, c1979. — xii,179p : ill ; 18cm
Originally published: New York : F. Watts, 1979. — Includes index
ISBN 0-7221-5563-8 (pbk) : £1.25 B81-26829

Rutherford, Derek. Alcohol : an information booklet for the purpose of alcohol education / by Derek Rutherford. — Rev. ed. — Manchester (1 North Parade, Deansgate, Manchester M3 2WD) : Independent Order of Rechabites (Salford Unity) Friendly Society, 1980. — 48p : ill (some col.) ; 21cm
Previous ed. i.e. rev.ed., 1975
Unpriced (pbk) B81-31409

613.8'3 — Solvent sniffing. Health aspects — *For drug abuse education*

Teaching about a volatile situation : suggested health education strategies for minimising casualties associated with solvent sniffing / prepared by ISDD's Evaluation Research Unit. — London (3 Blackburn Rd., NW16 1XA) : Institute for the Study of Drug Dependence, 1980. — [6]p ; 30cm
£0.20 (unbound) B81-18710

613.8'5 — Cigarette smoking. Health aspects

. Smoking and arterial disease. — Tunbridge Wells : Pitman Medical, Apr.1981. — [336]p
ISBN 0-272-79604-2 (pbk) : £20.00 : CIP entry B81-06073

613.8'5 — Cigarette smoking. Stopping — *Manuals*

Stop : a guide to non-smoking. — Harmondsworth : Penguin, 1981. — 163p : ill ; 9cm
ISBN 0-14-006000-6 (pbk) : £0.95 B81-23524

613.8'5 — Tobacco smoking

Ashton, Heather. Smoking : psychology and pharmacology. — London : Tavistock, Feb.1982. — [250]p
ISBN 0-422-77700-5 : £10.00 : CIP entry B81-35728

613.8'5'05 — Tobacco smoking. Health aspects — *Serials*

[Information bulletin *(ASH)***]**. Information bulletin / ASH. — Issue no.1 (Apr.1978)-. — London (27 Mortimer St., W1N 7RJ) : ASH, 1978. — v. ; 30cm
Fortnightly
ISSN 0261-0590 = Information bulletin — ASH : £5.00 per year B81-15154

613.8'5'0941 — Great Britain. Tobacco smoking. Attitudes of society

Attitudes towards smoking : indications for further research : report of the Panel on Attitudes towards Smoking (Sub-Committee of the Joint MRC-SSRC Committee on Research into Smoking) / prepared on behalf of the Panel by Robert J. Merriman. — London : Social Science Research Council, c1981. — 63p : ill ; 30cm
Bibliography: p56-63
ISBN 0-86226-030-2 (unbound) : Unpriced B81-14328

613.9 — BIRTH CONTROL AND SEX HYGIENE

613.9'0880564 — Persons, 40 years-. Sex relations — *Manuals*

Felstein, Ivor. Sex in later life / Ivor Felstein. — London : Granada, 1980. — 238p ; 18cm. — (A Mayflower book)
Includes index
ISBN 0-583-13072-0 (pbk) : £1.95 B81-04085

613.9'4 — Babies. Gender. Choice — *Manuals* — *For parents*

Rorvik, David M.. Your baby's sex : now you can choose / by David M. Rorvik with handrum B. Shettles. — Toronto ; London : Bantam, 1971, c1970 (1980- [priniting]). — xxiii,114p ; 18cm
Originally published: New York : Dodd, Mead, 1970. — Includes index
ISBN 0-553-17719-2 (pbk) : £0.95 B81-05557

613.9'4 — Contraception

Cowper, Ann. Family planning : fundamentals for health professionals. — London : Croom Helm, 1981. — 160p : ill ; 22cm
Bibliography: p155-157. — Includes index
ISBN 0-85664-907-4 (cased) : £11.95 : CIP rev.
ISBN 0-85664-908-2 (pbk) : Unpriced
Also classified at 362.8'286 B81-13747

613.9'4 — Family planning — *Manuals* — *Spanish texts*

Manual de planificacion familiar para medicos / editado para la IPPF por Ronald L. Kleinman ; traducido al español por Ana Attwood. — London : [International Planned Parenthood Federation], 1981. — 262p : ill ; 21cm
Translation from the English. — At head of title: Federación Internacional de Planificación de la Familia. — Bibliography: p255-256. — Includes index
ISBN 0-86089-042-2 (pbk) : £5.50 B81-33374

613.9'4 — Great Britain. Family Planning Association approved contraceptives — *Lists*

Approved list of contraceptives : based on available data on efficacy and acceptability. — London (27 Mortimer St., W1N 7RJ) : Family Planning Association, 1981. — 16p : ill ; 15x21cm
Cover title
£1.00 (pbk) B81-17677

613.9'4 — Man. Artificial insemination. Use of frozen semen — *Conference proceedings*

Frozen human semen : a Royal College of Obstetricians and Gynaecologists Workshop on the cryobiology of human semen, and its role in artificial insemination by donor March 22 and 23, 1979 / edited by D.W. Richardson, D. Joyce, E.M. Symonds. — The Hague ; Lonson : Nijhoff for The Royal College of Obstetricians and Gynaecologists, 1980. — 272p : ill,2maps ; 25cm. — (Developments in obstetrics and gynecology ; v.4)
Conference papers. — Includes bibliographies
ISBN 90-247-2370-1 : Unpriced B81-05713

613.9'4 — Man. Contraception. Immunological aspects

Talwar, G. P.. Immunology of contraception / G.P. Talwar. — London : Edward Arnold, 1980. — xiii,149p : ill ; 24cm. — (Current topics in immunology, ISSN 0305-8204 ; 13)
Includes index
ISBN 0-7131-4369-x : £13.50 : CIP rev. B80-33628

613.9'4 — Man. Contraception. Political aspects

Djerassi, Carl. The politics of contraception / Carl Djerassi. — New York ; London : Norton, 1980, c1979. — 274p : ill,facsims ; 22cm
Originally published: Stanford, Calif. : Stanford Alumni Association, 1979. — Includes index
ISBN 0-393-01264-6 (corrected) : £6.50 B81-15144

613.9'4 — Man. Homologous artificial insemination

Homologous artificial insemination (AIH) / edited by J.C. Emperaire, A. Audebert and E.S.E. Hafez. — The Hague ; London : Nijhoff, 1980. — x,235p : ill ; 25cm. — (Clinics in andrology ; v.1)
Includes bibliographies and index
ISBN 90-247-2269-1 : Unpriced B81-02642

613.9'4024055 — Man. Contraception — *Manuals* — *For adolescents*

Mayle, Peter. We're not pregnant : an illustrated guide to birth control / by Peter Mayle & Arthur Robins. — London : Macmillan, 1981. — [56]p : col.ill ; 26cm
ISBN 0-333-31849-8 (pbk) : £3.95 B81-38799

613.9'42 — Great Britain. Man. Sterilisation

Sterilisation and the National Health Service : a report / by the Birth Control Trust. — London : The Trust (27 MOrtimer St., W1N 7RJ), 1981. — 36p : forms ; 21cm
Cover title
£0.90 (pbk) B81-19283

613.9'432 — Oral contraceptives — *Conference proceedings*

The development of a new triphasic oral contraceptive : the proceedings of a special symposium held at the 10th World Congress on fertility and sterility, Madrid, July 1980 / co-ordinating editors J. Cortés-Prieto and A. Campos-da-Paz ; edited by R.B. Greenblatt. — Lancaster : MTP Press, 1980. — 128p : ill ; 23cm
ISBN 0-85200-376-5 : £9.95 B81-31501

613.9'434 — Man. Contraception. Natural methods — *Catholic viewpoints*

Johnson, Jean, *1926-*. Natural family planning / Jean Johnson. — London : Catholic Truth Society, 1981. — 24p : ill ; 19cm
ISBN 0-85183-382-9 (pbk) : £0.30 B81-15314

613.9'435 — Intrauterine devices

IUD technology. — Lancaster : MTP Press, Nov.1981. — [250]p. — (Progress in contraceptive delivery systems ; v.4)
ISBN 0-85200-356-0 : £18.95 : CIP entry B81-30634

613.9'435 — Intrauterine devices. Complications

Edelman, david A.. Intrauterine devices and their complications / David A. Edelman, Gary S. Berger, Louis Keith. — The Hague ; London : Nijhoff, 1979. — xviii,263p : ill,1port ; 25cm
Includes bibliographies and index
ISBN 90-247-2218-7 : Unpriced B81-02772

613.9'435 — Intrauterine devices — *Conference proceedings*

Medicated intrauterine devices : physiological and clinical aspects / edited by E.S.E. Hafez and W.A.A. van Os. — The Hague ; London : Nijhoff, 1980. — x,236p : ill ; 28cm. — (Developments in obstetrics and gynecology ; v.5)
Includes bibliographies and index
ISBN 90-247-2371-x : Unpriced B81-07266

613.9'5'07 — Sex education

Pickering, Lucienne. Boys talk. — London : Geoffrey Chapman, Sept.1981. — [80]p
ISBN 0-225-66309-0 (pbk) : £1.95 : CIP entry B81-20123

Pickering, Lucienne. Girls talk. — London : Geoffrey Chapman, Sept.1981. — [80]p
ISBN 0-225-66310-4 (pbk) : £1.95 : CIP entry B81-20122

613.9'507 — Sex education

Szasz, Thomas. [Sex by prescription]. Sex : facts, frauds and follies / Thomas Szasz. — Oxford : Basil Blackwell, 1981, c1980. — xii,194p ; 22cm
Originally published: Garden City, N.Y. : Anchor Press/Doubleday, 1980. — Includes index
ISBN 0-631-12736-4 (cased) : £8.50 : CIP rev.
ISBN 0-631-12737-2 (pbk) : £3.50
Primary classification 616.6'906 B81-04356

613.9'6 — Sexual intercourse - *Early works*

Vatsyayana. The Kama Sutra. — London : Allen and Unwin, June 1981. — [304]p
Originally published: 1963
ISBN 0-04-891049-x (cased) : £5.95 : CIP entry
ISBN 0-04-891048-1 (pbk) : £1.95 B81-09492

614 — PUBLIC HEALTH

614'.092'4 — Great Britain. Public health. Chadwick, *Sir. Edwin* — *Biographies*

Finer, S. E.. The life and times of Sir Edwin Chadwick / by S.E. Finer. — London : Methuen, 1980. — x,555p,[1] leaf of plates : 1 ill,,2ports ; 23cm
Originally published: 1952. — Bibliography: p516-540. - Includes index
ISBN 0-416-17350-0 : £19.50 B81-03600

614.1 — FORENSIC MEDICINE

614'.1 — Forensic psychiatry

Tennent, T. G.. Forensic psychiatry. — London : Pitman, Nov.1981. — [224]p
ISBN 0-272-79637-9 : £14.95 : CIP entry B81-30344

614'.1 — Great Britain. Forensic psychology

Haward, L. R. C.. Forensic psychology / L.R.C. Haward. — London : Batsford Academic and Educational, 1981. — 324p : ill,forms ; 23cm
Includes index
ISBN 0-7134-2475-3 : £15.00 B81-12561

614'.1'0973 — United States. Forensic medicine — *Serials*

Legal medicine. — 1980-. — Philadelphia ; London : Saunders, c1980-. — v. : ill ; 24cm
Annual. — Continues: Legal medicine annual
£15.75
Also classified at 347.304'41'05 B81-00911

614.4 — PUBLIC HEALTH. INCIDENCE, DISTRIBUTION AND CONTROL OF DISEASE

614.4 — Man. Diseases. Epidemiology. Social factors

Changing disease patterns and human behaviour / edited by N.F. Stanley and R.A. Joske. — London : Academic Press, 1980. — xiii,666p : ill,maps ; 24cm
Includes bibliographies and index
ISBN 0-12-663560-9 : £41.00 : CIP rev. B80-20720

614.4'0246177 — Epidemiology — *For ophthalmology*

Sommer, Alfred. Epidemiology and statistics for the ophthalmologist / Alfred Sommer. — New York ; Oxford : Oxford University Press, 1980. — x,86p : ill ; 21cm
Bibliography: p83. - Includes index
ISBN 0-19-502656-x (pbk) : £7.95
Primary classification 519.5'0246177 B81-07727

614.4'05 — Man. Epidemics — *Serials*

Epidemiologic reviews. — Vol.1 (1979)-. — Baltimore ; London : Johns Hopkins University Press, 1979-. — v. : ill ; 26cm
Sponsored by: Society for Epidemiologic Research and International Epidemiological Association. — Description based on: Vol.2 (1980)
ISSN 0193-936x = Epidemiologic reviews : £8.00 B81-11860

614.4'072042 — England. Public health laboratories: Public Health Laboratory Service Board — *Accounts* — *Serials*

Public Health Laboratory Service Board. Accounts / Public Health Laboratory Service Board. — 1979-80. — London : H.M.S.O., 1981. — 6p
ISBN 0-10-230481-5 : £1.10 B81-31597

614.4'072042 — England. Public health laboratories: Public Health Laboratory Service Board — *Directories* — *Serials*

[Directory *(Public Health Laboratory Service Board)*]. Directory / Public Health Laboratory Service. — 1980. — [London] (61 Colindale Ave., NW9 5EQ) : The Service, [1980]. — xii,59p
ISSN 0141-9692 : Unpriced B81-06520

614.4'072042 — England. Public health laboratories: Public Health Laboratory Service Board — *Serials*

Public Health Laboratory Service Board. Public Health Laboratory Service annual report. — 1979/80. — London (61 Colindale Ave., NW9 5EQ) : Public Health Laboratory Service Board, [1980]. — iii,81p
ISBN 0-901144-08-8 : Unpriced
ISSN 0142-3517 B81-26382

614.4'09 — Man. Epidemics. Control measures, *to ca 1940*

Winslow, Charles-Edward Amory. The conquest of epidemic disease : a chapter in the history of ideas / Charles-Edward Amory Winslow. — Madison ; London : University of Wisconsin Press, 1980, c1971. — viii,411p ; 22cm
Originally published: Princeton : Princeton University Press, 1943 ; West Drayton : Hafner, 1967. — Bibliography: p384-397. - Includes indexes
ISBN 0-299-08240-7 (cased) : £15.00
ISBN 0-299-08244-x (pbk) : £4.50 B81-02949

614.4'2 — Man. Diseases. Epidemiology. Geographical aspects

Inglis, Brian. The diseases of civilization. — London : Hodder & Stoughton, Aug.1981. — [448]p
ISBN 0-340-21717-0 : £9.95 : CIP entry B81-17532

614.4′2 — Man. Diseases. Epidemiology. Geographical aspects - *Conference proceedings*

International Geographical Congress *(24th : 1980 : Tokyo)*. The geography of health. — Oxford : Pergamon, July 1981. — [270]p
ISBN 0-08-027434-x : £8.50 : CIP entry
B81-16851

614.4′273 — United States. Morbidity. Effects of air pollution control. Economic aspects. Methods development for assessing air pollution control benefits — *Critical studies*

Air pollution control and morbidity - a critical commentary on the morbidity study in 'Methods development for assessing air pollution control benefits vol.1' by T.D. Crocker et al / R.L. Akehurst ... [et al.]. — [Aberdeen] : University of Aberdeen, Department of Political Economy, 1981. — 22leaves ; 30cm. — (Discussion paper / University of Aberdeen. Department of Political Economy ; 81-08)
Unpriced (pbk) B81-28291

614.4′4 — Hospitals. Patients. Nosocomial infections. Control

Castle, Mary. Hospital infection control : principles and practice / Mary Castle ; [illustrated by Molly Ross]. — New York ; Chichester : Wiley, c1980. — xiv,251p : ill,forms ; 25cm
Includes index
ISBN 0-471-05395-3 : £8.90 B81-04846

Control of hospital infection. — 2nd ed. — London : Chapman and Hall, Oct.1981. — [350]p
Previous ed.: / Working Party on Control of Hospital Infection. 1975
ISBN 0-412-16300-4 : £15.00 : CIP entry
B81-30462

614.4′4′0973 — United States. Preventive medicine

Bloom, Martin. Primary prevention : the possible science / Martin Bloom. — Englewood Cliffs ; London : Prentice-Hall, c1981. — xi,242p : ill ; 23cm
Bibliography: p215-232. — Includes index
ISBN 0-13-700062-6 (pbk) : £7.65
Primary classification 362′.0424′0973

614.4′7 — Man. Communicable diseases. Aerosol vaccination

Lebedinskiĭ, V. A.. The inhalation (aerosol) method of vaccination / V.A. Lebedinskii ; translated by B. Haigh ; edited by H.T. Zwartouw. — Boston Spa : British Library Lending Division, c1981. — vi,182p : ill ; 30cm
Translation of: Ingali͡at͡sionnyĭ (azrogennyĭ) metod Vakt͡sinat͡sii. — Bibliography: p162-182
ISBN 0-85350-179-3 (pbk) : Unpriced
B81-07367

614.4′8 — Disinfectants — *Conference proceedings*

Disinfectants : their use and evaluation of effectiveness / edited by C. H. Collins ... [et al.]. — London : Academic Press, 1981. — xvi,229p : ill(some col.) ; 24cm. — (The Society for Applied Bacteriology technical series ; no.16)
Includes bibliographies and index
ISBN 0-12-181380-0 : Unpriced B81-22300

614.5′21 — Man. Smallpox. Vaccination. Role of Jenner, Edward

Baxby, Derrick. Jenner's smallpox vaccine : the riddle of vaccinia virus and its origin / Derrick Baxby. — London : Heinemann Educational, 1981. — xiv,214p : ill,ports ; 23cm
Bibliography: p197-209. — Includes index
ISBN 0-435-54057-2 : £8.50 B81-25261

614.5′23′094912 — Man. Diseases. Epidemiology. Geographical aspects — *Study examples: Measles. Epidemics — Study regions: Iceland*

Spatial diffusion : an historical geography of epidemics in an island community / A.D. Cliff ... [et al.]. — Cambridge : Cambridge University Press, 1981. — xi,238p : ill,maps ; 26cm. — (Cambridge geographical studies ; 14)
Bibliography: p231-236. — Includes index
ISBN 0-521-22840-9 : £19.50 : CIP rev.
B81-15857

614.5′32′094 — Europe. Man. Malaria. Epidemiology & public health measures, *to 1975*

Bruce-Chwatt, Leonard Jan. The rise and fall of malaria in Europe : a historico-epidemiological study / Leonard Jan Bruce-Chwatt and Julian de Zulueta. — Published on behalf of the Regional Office for Europe of the World Health Organisation by Oxford : Oxford University Press, 1980. — 240p,[49]p of plates : ill,maps,facsims,ports ; 25cm
Bibliography: p183-211. - Includes index
ISBN 0-19-858168-8 : £12.00 : CIP rev.
B80-09696

614.5′7 — Man. Legionnaires' disease. Causes

Thomas, Gordon. Trauma : the search for the cause of legionnaires' disease. — London : H. Hamilton, Oct.1981. — [384]p
ISBN 0-241-10366-5 : £9.95 : CIP entry
B81-25705

614.5′732′00945 — Italy. Man. Plague. Public health measures, *1576-1657*

Cipolla, Carlo M.. Fighting the plague in seventeenth-century Italy / Carlo M. Cipolla. — Madison ; London : University of Wisconsin Press, 1981. — xi,123p : ill,2map,2facsims ; 22cm. — (The Curti lectures ; 1978)
Bibliography: p117-119. — Includes index
ISBN 0-299-08340-3 (cased) : £8.65
ISBN 0-299-08344-6 (pbk) : £3.20 B81-29378

614.5′9132 — Man. Blood. Hypertension. Epidemiology

Epidemiology of arterial blood pressure / edited by H. Kesteloot and J.V. Joossens. — The Hague ; London : Nijhoff, 1980. — xvi,515p : ill,maps ; 25cm. — (Developments in cardiovascular medicine ; v.8)
Includes index
ISBN 90-247-2386-8 : Unpriced B81-04603

614.5′9136′0097444 — Man. Arteries. Atherosclerosis. Epidemiology — *Study regions: Massachusetts. Framingham*

Dawber, Thomas Royle. The Framingham study : the epidemiology of atherosclerotic disease / Thomas Royle Dawber. — Cambridge, Mass. ; London : Harvard University Press, 1980. — viii,257p : ill ; 25cm. — (A Commonwealth Fund book)
Bibliography: p233-238. - Includes index
ISBN 0-674-31730-0 : £5.40 B81-04120

614.5′93′9 — Preventive medicine. Role of nutrition

Preventive nutrition and society. — London : Academic Press, Nov.1981. — [220]p
ISBN 0-12-704450-7 : CIP entry B81-28783

614.5′939′00973 — United States. Preventive medicine. Role of nutrition

Caliendo, Mary Alice. Nutrition and preventive health care / Mary Alice Caliendo. — New York : Macmillan ; London : Collier Macmillan, c1981. — xiii,705p : ill ; 26cm
Ill on lining papers. — Includes index
ISBN 0-02-318330-6 : £12.95 B81-33401

614.5′9462 — Man. Diabetes. Epidemiology

West, Kelly M.. Epidemiology of diabetes and its vascular lesions / Kelly M. West. — New York ; Oxford : Elsevier, c1978. — xi,579p : ill ; 26cm
Bibliography: p441-555. - Includes index
ISBN 0-444-00254-5 : Unpriced B81-10384

614.5′996 — Great Britain. Water supply. Fluoridation. Public health aspects

Grant, Doris. The fluoridation fallacy : and fluoridation of water supplies and corrosion : a statement to water engineers in Great Britain / by Doris Grant. — Sudbury : Bloomfield Books, c1979. — 16p ; 21cm
Cover title
£0.40 (pbk) B81-04704

615 — PHARMACOLOGY AND THERAPEUTICS

615 — Pharmacology & therapeutics — *Conference proceedings*

International Congress of Pharmacology *(8th : 1981 : Tokyo)*. Advances in pharmacology & therapeutics II. — Oxford : Pergamon
Vol.1: CNS pharmacology / neuropeptides. — Feb.1982. — [300]p
ISBN 0-08-028021-8 : £32.00 : CIP entry
B81-39244

International Congress of Pharmacology *(8th : 1981 : Tokyo)*. Advances in pharmacology & therapeutics II. — Oxford : Pergamon
Vol.2: Neurotransmitters — receptors. — Feb.1982. — [340]p
ISBN 0-08-028022-6 : £32.00 : CIP entry
B81-38330

International Congress of Pharmacology *(8th : 1981 : Tokyo)*. Advances in pharmacology & therapeutics II. — Oxford : Pergamon
Vol.3: Cardio-renal & cell pharmacology. — Feb.1982. — [346]p
ISBN 0-08-028023-4 : £32.00 : CIP entry
B81-37592

International Congress of Pharmacology *(8th : 1981 : Tokyo)*. Advances in pharmacology & therapeutics II. — Oxford : Pergamon
Vol.4: Biochemical-immunological pharmacology. — Feb.1982. — [210]p
ISBN 0-08-028024-2 : £32.00 : CIP entry
B81-38333

International Congress of Pharmacology *(8th : 1981 : Tokyo)*. Advances in pharmacology & therapeutics II. — Oxford : Pergamon
Vol.5: Toxicology & experimental models. — Feb.1982. — [380]p
ISBN 0-08-028025-0 : £32.00 : CIP entry
B81-39239

International Congress of Pharmacology *(8th : 1981 : Tokyo)*. Advances in pharmacology & therapeutics II. — Oxford : Pergamon
Vol.6: Clinical pharmacology — teaching in pharmacology. — Feb.1982. — [310]p
ISBN 0-08-028026-9 : £32.00 : CIP entry
B81-38307

615′.01524 — Calcium. Action. Role of transport phenomena across cell membranes

Membrane transport of calcium. — London : Academic Press, Jan.1982. — [290]p
ISBN 0-12-159320-7 : CIP entry B81-34118

615′.03 — Pharmacology & therapeutics — *Encyclopaedias*

International encyclopedia of pharmacology and therapeutics. — Oxford : Pergamon, Sept.1981
Section 107: Inhibitors of mitochondrial function. — [324]p
ISBN 0-08-027380-7 : £29.00 : CIP entry
B81-22565

615.1 — DRUGS

615′.1 — Controlled release drugs — *Conference proceedings*

Controlled release of bioactive materials : based on the Symposium at the 6th International Meeting of the Controlled Release Society in New Orleans, Louisiana, August 1979 / edited by Richard Baker. — New York ; London : Academic Press, 1980. — xiii,473p : ill ; 24cm
Includes index
ISBN 0-12-074450-3 : £19.40
Also classified at 668′.65 B81-05968

International Symposium on Controlled Release of Bioactive Materials *(7th : 1980 : Ft. Lauderdale)*. Controlled release of pesticides and pharmaceuticals / [proceedings of the Seventh International Symposium on Controlled Release of Bioactive Materials, held July 27-30, 1980, in Ft. Lauderdale, Florida] ; edited by Danny H. Lewis. — New York ; London : Plenum, c1981. — ix,340p : ill ; 26cm
Includes index
ISBN 0-306-40743-4 : Unpriced
Also classified at 668′.65 B81-34690

615'.1 — Drugs

Burger's medicinal chemistry. — 4th ed. — New York ; Chichester : Wiley
Previous ed.: published in 2 vols as Medicinal chemistry. — Includes index
Part 3 / edited by Manfred E. Wolff. — c1981. — xiv,1354p : ill ; 26cm
ISBN 0-471-01572-5 : £63.35 B81-24941

Eadie, Mervyn J.. Introduction to clinical pharmacology / Mervyn J. Eadie, John H. Tyrer, Felix Bochner. — Lancester : MTP, c1981. — vi,142p : ill ; 24cm
Includes bibliographies and index
ISBN 0-85200-594-6 (pbk) : £5.95 B81-38026

Manual of clinical pharmacology / editors David Robertson, Craig R. Smith. — Baltimore ; London : Williams & Wilkins, c1981. — xv,350p ; 26cm
Includes index
ISBN 0-683-07300-1 (pbk) : £19.50 B81-21918

Penn, R. G.. Pharmacology / R.G. Penn. — 3rd ed. — London : Baillière Tindall, 1980. — x,320p : ill ; 20cm. — (Concise medical textbooks)
Previous ed.: 1974. — Bibliography: p305-306. - Includes index
ISBN 0-7020-0822-2 (pbk) : £4.75 : CIP rev. B80-24499

615'.1 — Drugs — *Conference proceedings*

International Symposium on Medicinal Chemistry *(7th : 1980 : Torremolinos)*. Medicinal chemistry advances : proceedings of the Seventh International Symposium on Medicinal Chemistry, Torremolinos, Spain, 2-5 September 1980 / edited by Federico G. de las Heras and Salvador Vega. — Oxford : Pergamon, 1981. — xiii,512p : ill ; 24cm
Includes index
ISBN 0-08-025297-4 : £33.00 : CIP rev. B81-15833

615'.1 — Drugs. Design

Drug design. — Vol.10. — New York ; London : Academic Press, 1980. — xi,432p. — (Medicinal chemistry ; v.11)
ISBN 0-12-060310-1 : Unpriced B81-20421

615'.1 — Drugs. Design & development — *Conference proceedings*

Strategy in drug research. — Oxford : Elsevier Scientific, Jan.1982. — [600]p. — (Pharmacochemistry library ; v.4)
Conference papers
ISBN 0-444-42053-3 : CIP entry B81-38828

615'.1 — Pharmacology

Asperheim, Mary K.. Pharmacology : an introductory text / Mary Kaye Asperheim. — 5th ed. — Philiadelphia ; London : Saunders, 1981. — viii,237p : ill ; 26cm
Previous ed.: published as Pharmacology for practical nurses. 1975. — Bibliography: p223. — Includes index
ISBN 0-7216-1446-9 (pbk) : £5.75 B81-27105

Basic pharmacology / editors R.W. Foster and B. Cox with J.R. Carpenter ... [et al.]. — London : Butterworths, 1980. — xvii,348p : ill ; 24cm
Bibliography: p326. - Includes index
ISBN 0-407-00170-0 (pbk) : £6.95 : CIP rev. B80-12890

Gerald, Michael C.. Pharmacology : an introduction to drugs / Michael C. Gerald. — 2nd ed. — Englewood Cliffs ; London : Prentice-Hall, c1981. — xiv,686p : ill ; 24cm
Previous ed.: 1974. — Includes bibliographies and index
ISBN 0-13-662098-1 : Unpriced B81-36494

Lewis, J. J.. Lewis's pharmacology. — 5th ed. / James Crossland. — Edinburgh : Churchill Livingstone, 1980. — ix,969p : ill ; 25cm
Previous ed.: 1970. — Includes bibliographies and index
ISBN 0-443-02190-2 (cased) : £29.00
ISBN 0-443-01173-7 (pbk) : £19.50 B81-13012

Schmidt, R. Marilyn. Harper's handbook of therapeutic pharmacology / R. Marilyn Schmidt, Solomon Margolin. — Philadelphia ; Cambridge : Harper & Row, c1981. — xiii,752p ; 24cm
Bibliography: p706. — Includes index
ISBN 0-397-54264-x (pbk) : Unpriced B81-26137

615'.1 — Pharmacology — *Conference proceedings*

World Conference on Clinical Pharmacology & Therapeutics *(1st : 1980 : London)*. Clinical pharmacology & therapeutics : proceedings of plenary lectures symposia and therapeutic sessions of the First World Conference on Clinical Pharmacology & Therapeutics London, UK, 3-9 August 1980 / [sponsored by the International Union of Pharmacology and the British Pharmacological Society] ; edited by P. Turner ; executive editors C. Padgham, A. Hedges. — London : Macmillan, 1980. — xvi,576p : ill ; 24cm
Includes bibliograhies
ISBN 0-333-31229-5 (cased) : £40.00
ISBN 0-333-31230-9 (pbk) : Unpriced B81-09932

615'.1 — Pharmacology — *For respiratory therapy*

Mathewson, Hugh S.. Pharmacology : for respiratory therapists / Hugh S. Mathewson. — 2nd ed. — St. Louis ; London : Mosby, 1981. — xi,97p : ill ; 23cm
Previous ed.: 1977. — Includes index
ISBN 0-8016-3161-0 (pbk) : £7.75 B81-24244

615'.1 — Solid drugs

Carstensen, Jens Thurø. Solid pharmaceutics : mechanical properties and rate phenomena / Jens Thurø Carstensen. — New York ; London : Academic Press, 1980. — xii,259p : ill ; 24cm
Includes bibliographies and index
ISBN 0-12-161150-7 : £22.40 B81-15125

615'.1'024613 — Drugs — *For nursing*

Skelley, Esther G.. Medications and mathematics for the nurse / Esther G. Skelley. — New York ; London : Van Nostrand Reinhold, c1981. — vi,282p : ill ; 27cm
Includes index
ISBN 0-442-21882-6 : £10.45
Also classified at 615'.4'01513 B81-29630

Squire, Jessie E.. Basic pharmacology for nurses. — 7th ed. / Jessie E. Squire, Bruce D. Clayton. — St. Louis ; London : Mosby, 1981. — vii,296p : ill ; 28cm + Answer book(4p : 26cm)
Previous ed.: 1977. — Text on inside covers. — Bibliography: p272-280. — Includes index
ISBN 0-8016-4743-6 (pbk) : £10.00 B81-25466

Trounce, J. R.. Clinical pharmacology for nurses / J.R. Trounce. — 9th ed. / chapter on anaesthetic drugs by J.M. Hall .... — Edinburgh : Churchill Livingstone, 1981. — vi,426p : ill ; 19cm
Previous ed.: 1979. — Includes index
ISBN 0-443-02333-6 (pbk) : £4.25 B81-19090

615'.1'024613 — Pharmacology — *Case studies* — *For nursing*

Marion, Mildred Francis. Pharmacology learning guide / Mildred Francis Marion, Constance A. Hoyt, Sheila LaFortune Fredette. — St. Louis ; London : Mosby, 1981. — ix,117p : ill ; 26cm
Bibliography: p100-102. — Includes index
ISBN 0-8016-3109-2 : £6.00 B81-24241

615'.1'0246176 — Pharmacology — *For dentistry*

. Pharmacology and therapeutics for dentistry / [edited by] Enid A. Neidle, Donald C. Kroeger, John A. Yagiela in collaboration with James W. Smudski. — St. Louis ; London : Mosby, 1980. — xi,749p : ill ; 25cm
Includes bibliographies and index
ISBN 0-8016-3635-3 : £21.75 B81-07521

615'.1'025 — Pharmacologists — *Directories*

Pharmacology and pharmacologists : an international directory. — Oxford : Oxford University Press, 1981. — xxii,387p ; 26cm
Includes index
ISBN 0-19-200101-9 : £40.00 B81-35311

615'.1'04613 — Drugs — *For nursing*

Gibson, John, *1907-*. The nurse's materia medica / John Gibson. — 5th ed. — Oxford : Blackwell Scientific, 1980. — xx,268p ; 19cm
Previous ed.: 1976. — Includes index
ISBN 0-632-00685-4 (pbk) : £4.00 : CIP rev. B80-13407

615'.1'05 — Drugs — *Serials*

Advances in pharmaceutical sciences. — Vol.5. — London : Academic Press, Dec.1981. — [220]p
ISBN 0-12-032305-2 : CIP entry B81-31330

Annual reports in medicinal chemistry. — Vol.15. — New York ; London : Academic Press, 1980. — xiii,346p
ISBN 0-12-040515-6 : Unpriced
ISSN 0065-7743 B81-04606

Pharma projects. — Vol.2 (May 1981)-. — Richmond (53A George St., Richmond, Surrey TW9 1HE) : V & O Publications, 1981-. — v. ; 30cm
Monthly. — Continues: Pharma prospects
ISSN 0261-2623 = Pharma projects : Unpriced B81-29975

Pharma prospects. — Vol.1 (May 1980)- Vol.1, no.11 (Apr.1981). — [Richmond] ([53a George St., Richmond, Surrey TW9 1HE]) : [V & O Publications], 1980-1981. — 1v. ; 30cm
Monthly. — Continued by: Pharma projects. — Description based on: Vol.1, no.7 (Dec.1980)
ISSN 0260-8375 = Pharma prospects : Unpriced B81-08765

615'.1'05 — Pharmaceutical products — *Serials*

International journal of pharmaceutical technology & product manufacture. — Vol.1, no.1 (Autumn 1979)-. — London (P.O. Box 78, NW11 0PG) : Childwall University Press, 1979-. — v. : ill ; 28cm
Quarterly
£25.00 B81-06193

615'.1'05 — Pharmacology — *Serials*

Reviews in pure & applied pharmacological sciences. — Vol.1, no.1 (Jan.-Mar.1980)-. — London (Suite 500, 150 Regent St., W1R 5FA) : Freund Pub. House, 1980-. — v. : ill ; 24cm
Quarterly
ISSN 0197-2839 = Reviews in pure & applied pharmacological sciences : £32.00 per year B81-29990

615'.1'068 — United States. Pharmacies. Management

Smith, Harry A., *1925-*. Principles and methods of pharmacy management / Harry A. Smith. — 2nd ed. — Philadelphia : Lea & Febiger ; London : Kimpton, 1980. — xiv,413p : ill,plans ; 25cm
Previous ed.: 1975. — Includes index
ISBN 0-8121-0765-9 : £9.00 B81-16094

615'.1'0684 — Pharmaceutical industries. Management. Long-range planning

Levitt, Ruth, *1950-*. Planning systems in the pharmaceutical industry / by Ruth Levitt. — Richmond (53A George St., Richmond, Surrey TW9 1HE) : PJB, 1980. — iii,59leaves : ill ; 31cm
Bibliography: p50-52
Unpriced (spiral) B81-21324

615'.1'072073 — United States. Research & development by pharmaceutical industries

Bezold, Clement. The future of pharmaceuticals : the changing environment for new drugs / Clement Bezold ; foreword by Alvin Toffler. — New York ; Chichester : Wiley, c1980. — xiii,142p : ill ; 23cm
Includes index
ISBN 0-471-08343-7 : £6.50 B81-09755

615'.1'076 — Drugs — *Questions & answers*

Robinson, Bryan V.. Multiple choice questions in pharmacology / Bryan V. Robinson. — Tunbridge Wells : Pitman Medical, 1980. — viii,277p : ill ; 23cm
Bibliography: p11
ISBN 0-272-79590-9 (pbk) : £5.50 : CIP rev. B80-11044

615'.1'076 — Pharmacology — *Questions & answers*

1200 multiple choice questions in pharmacology / R.W. Foster (editor) ... [et al.]. — London : Butterworths, 1980. — xi,176p : ill ; 22cm
ISBN 0-407-00192-1 (pbk) : £3.50 : CIP rev. B80-03662

615'.1'0941 — Great Britain. Non-prescription drugs — *For pharmaceutical trades — Serials*

O.T.C. medication. — Oct. 1980-. — [London] (2 Drayson Mews, Kensington, W8) : Joint Marketing & Publishing Services, 1980-. — v. : ill,ports ; 30cm
Three issues yearly
ISSN 0260-518x = O.T.C. medication : Unpriced B81-04443

615'.1'0941 — Great Britain. Non-prescription drugs — *For self-treatment*

Coleman, Vernon. The home pharmacy : the consumer's guide to over-the-counter medicine / Vernon Coleman. — London : Macmillan, 1980. — 206p ; 23cm
Includes index
ISBN 0-333-27506-3 : £6.95 B81-01688

615'.19 — Drugs. Physicochemical aspects

Florence, A. T.. Physicochemical principles of pharmacy / A.T. Florence and D. Attwood. — London : Macmillan, 1981. — x,509p : ill ; 25cm
Includes index
ISBN 0-333-23404-9 (cased) : Unpriced
ISBN 0-333-23405-7 (pbk) : Unpriced B81-33669

615'.19 — Pharmaceutics

Progress in pharmaceutical research. — Oxford : Blackwell Scientific, Sept.1981. — [184]p. — (Clinical reports on applied chemistry ; v.4)
ISBN 0-632-00787-7 : £8.00 : CIP entry B81-30470

615'.19'005 — Drugs. Structure & chemical properties — *Serials*

Analytical profiles of drug substances. — Vol.9. — New York ; London : Academic Press, 1980. — ix,618p
ISBN 0-12-260809-7 : £19.20 B81-27923

615'.1901 — Drugs. Analysis. Use of ion-selective membrane electrodes

Coşofreţ, Vasile V.. Membrane electrodes in drug-substances analysis. — Oxford : Pergamon, Dec.1981. — [376]p
Translated from the Romanian
ISBN 0-08-026264-3 : £29.50 : CIP entry B81-34218

615'.19015 — Drugs. Infrared spectroscopy. Spectra — *Technical data*

Infra-red reference spectra : published on the recommendation of the Medicines Commission pursuant to the Medicines Act 1968 : effective date : 1 December 1980. — London : HMSO, 1980. — xiv,273,[37]p : chiefly ill ; 22x31cm
Companion volume to: British pharmacopœia 1980. — Includes index
ISBN 0-11-320303-9 : Unpriced B81-09878

615'.1901'5 — Pharmaceutics. Research. Applications of radioisotopes

Radionuclide imaging in drug research. — London : Croom Helm, Oct.1981. — [256]p
ISBN 0-7099-2716-9 : £16.95 : CIP entry B81-31098

615.3 — ORGANIC DRUGS

615'.3 — Drugs: Anionic polymers

Anionic polymeric drugs / edited by L. Guy Donaruma, Raphael M. Ottenbrite, Otto Vogl. — New York ; Chichester : Wiley, c1980. — xii,356p : ill ; 24cm. — (Polymers in biology and medicine ; v.1)
Includes index
ISBN 0-471-05530-1 : £21.15 B81-05206

615'.3142 — Cimetidine — *Conference proceedings*

Cimetidine in the 80s. — Edinburgh : Churchill Livingstone, Jan.1982. — [256]p
Conference papers
ISBN 0-443-02540-1 : £16.00 : CIP entry B81-38820

615'.3142 — Histamine H2-receptor antagonists — *Conference proceedings*

Further experience with H2-receptor antagonists in peptic ulcer disease and progress in histamine research : European symposium Capri, October 18-20, 1979 / editors A. Torsoli, P.E. Lucchelli, R.W. Brimblecombe. — Amsterdam ; Oxford : Excerpta Medica, 1980. — 370p : ill ; 25cm
Spine title: H2-antogonists
ISBN 90-219-9467-4 : £27.83 B81-00912

615'.315684 — Medicine. Drug therapy. Germanium

Asai, Kazuhiko. Miracle cure : organic germanium / Kazuhiko Asai. — Tokyo : Japan Publications ; Hemel Hempstead : International Book Distributors [distributor], 1980. — 171p : ill,1port ; 22cm
Includes index
ISBN 0-87040-474-1 : £9.90 B81-28474

615'.32 — Medicine. Natural remedies: Aromatic plant essential oils

Arnould-Taylor, W. E.. Aromatherapy for the whole person : phys-essential therapy / by W.E. Arnould-Taylor. — Cheltenham : Thornes, 1981. — vii,88p : ill ; 23cm
ISBN 0-85950-337-2 (pbk) : £4.25 : CIP rev. B81-15901

615'.32 — Medicine. Natural remedies: Raw juices

Charmine, Susan E.. The complete raw juice therapy. — Wellingborough : Thorsons, Oct.1981. — [128]p
Originally published: 1977
ISBN 0-7225-0732-1 (pbk) : £1.00 : CIP entry B81-28181

615'.32 — Medicine. Plant remedies

Mességué, Maurice. Health secrets of plants and herbs / Maurice Mességué. — London : Pan in association with Collins, 1981, c1979. — 335p : ill ; 20cm
Translation of: Mon herbier de sante. — Originally published: London : Collins, 1979
ISBN 0-330-26343-9 (pbk) : £1.95 B81-22894

615'.321 — England. Medicine. Herbal remedies

Harmer, Juliet. The magic of herbs & flowers : an illuminated manuscript celebrating their healing properties / by Juliet Harmer. — [London] : Macmillan, [1980]. — [68]p : col.ill ; 16cm
Includes index
ISBN 0-333-29375-4 : £2.95 B81-05204

615'.321 — Medicine. Herbal remedies

Griggs, Barbara. Green pharmacy : a history of herbal medicine. — London : Jill Norman & Hobhouse, Oct.1981. — [384]p
ISBN 0-906908-64-7 : £7.95 : CIP entry B81-27418

615'.321 — Medicine. Herbal remedies — *Manuals*

Wickham, Cynthia. Common plants as natural remedies / Cynthia Wickham. — London : Muller, 1981. — 144p : col.ill ; 24cm
Bibliography: p143. — Includes index
ISBN 0-584-10475-8 : £7.50 : CIP rev. B81-07922

615'.324324 — Medicine. Herbal remedies: Garlic, *to 1979*

Simons, Paul. Garlic : the powerful panacea / by Paul Simons. — Wellingborough : Thorsons, 1980. — 96p : 1facsim ; 18cm
Includes index
ISBN 0-7225-0626-0 (pbk) : £0.95 : CIP rev. B80-23314

615'.329 — Antibiotics. Action. Molecular biology

The Molecular basis of antibiotic action / E.F. Gale ... [et al.]. — 2nd ed. — London : Wiley, c1981. — xxiii,646p : ill ; 24cm
Previous ed.: 1972. — Includes bibliographies and index
ISBN 0-471-27915-3 : £35.00 B81-38741

615'.329 — Beta-lactam antibiotics. Chemical properties — *Conference proceedings*

Recent advances in the chemistry of β-Lactam antibiotics : the proceedings of the Second International Symposium arranged by the Fine Chemicals and Medicinals Group of the Industrial Division of the Royal Society of Chemistry, Cambridge, England 30th June-2nd July 1980 / edited by G.I. Gregory. — London : Royal Society of Chemistry, c1981. — ix,378p : ill ; 21cm. — (Special publication / Royal Society of Chemistry, ISSN 0260-6291 ; no.38)
ISBN 0-85186-815-0 (pbk) : Unpriced B81-18722

615'.329 — Beta-lactam antibiotics — *Conference proceedings*

β-lactam antibiotics : mode of action, new developments, and future prospects / edited by Milton R.J. Salton, Gerald David Shockman. — New York ; London : Academic Press, 1981. — xv,604p : ill ; 24cm
Conference papers. — Includes bibliographies and index
ISBN 0-12-616050-3 : £26.20 B81-38695

615'.329 — Medicine. Drug therapy. Antibiotics

Garrod, Lawrence P.. Antibiotic and chemotherapy. — 5th ed. / Lawrence P. Garrod, Harold P. Lambert, Francis O'Grady ; with a chapter on laboratory methods by Pamela M. Waterworth. — Edinburgh : Churchill Livingstone, 1981. — 514p : ill ; 24cm
Previous ed.: 1973. — Includes bibliographies and index
ISBN 0-443-02143-0 : £18.50 B81-27519

615'.329 — Medicine. Drug therapy. Antibiotics — *Conference proceedings*

The **Future** of antibiotherapy research / [based on the proceedings of the Second Rhône-Poulenc Round Table Conference entitled Antibiotics of the Future, held in Paris from 13-15 February, 1980] ; edited by L. Ninet ... [et al.]. — London : Academic Press, 1981. — xx,508p : ill,1port ; 24cm
Includes bibliographies and index
ISBN 0-12-519780-2 : £25.00 B81-38408

International Symposium on New Trends in Antibiotics: Research and Therapy *(1980 : Milan)*. New trends in antibiotics : research and therapy : proceedings of the International Symposium on New Trends in Antibiotics: Research and Therapy, held in Milan, Italy, October 29-31, 1980 / editors G. Gialdroni Grassi and L.D. Sabath. — Amsterdam ; Oxford : Elsevier, 1981. — x,354p : ill ; 25cm. — (Symposia of the Giovanni Lorenzini Foundation ; vol.10)
Includes index
ISBN 0-444-80326-2 : Unpriced B81-25517

615'.329'028 — Medicine. Drug therapy. Antibacterials. Testing. Laboratory techniques

Bryant, M. C.. Laboratory control of antibacterial chemotherapy. — Bristol : John Wright, Nov.1981. — [96]p. — (Institute of Medical Laboratory Sciences monographs)
ISBN 0-7236-0594-7 (pbk) : £5.50 : CIP entry B81-32026

615'.32924 — Ceftriaxone

Reports on ceftriaxone (Rocephin). — Basel ; London : Karger, 1981. — 103p : ill ; 26cm
Originally published: as Chemotherapy Vol.27, Supplement 1, 1981. — Includes bibliographies
ISBN 3-8055-3034-x (pbk) : £7.70 (free to subscribers) B81-38415

615'.32992 — Nystatin. Discovery

Baldwin, Richard S.. The fungus fighters : two women scientists and their discovery / Richard S. Baldwin ; with a foreword by Gilbert Dalldorf. — Ithaca ; London : Cornell University Press, 1981. — 212p : ill,ports ; 23cm
Includes index
ISBN 0-8014-1355-9 : £9.00 B81-36449

615'.32992 — Sisomicin — *Conference proceedings*

Sisomicin : an international round-table discussion / [proceedings of an international round-table discussion held on 14 March in Lucerne, Switzerland, sponsored by Schering Corporation USA and its affiliates, the Essex Group of Companies] ; edited by P. Noone. — London : Royal Society of Medicine : Academic Press, 1980. — viii,72p,[13]p of plates : ill,ports ; 24cm. — (Royal Society of Medicine series. International congress and symposium series, ISSN 0142-2367 ; no.35)
ISBN 0-12-793125-2 (pbk) : £12.20
ISBN 0-8089-1349-2 (U.S.) B81-31226

615'.32995 — Augmentin — *Conference proceedings*

Augmentin : clavulanate-potentiated amoxycillin : proceedings of the first symposium, 3 and 4 July, 1980 / editors G.N. Rolinson, A. Watson. — Amsterdam, ; Oxford : Excerpta Medica, 1980. — viii,308p : ill ; 25cm. — (International congress series ; no.544)
Includes index
ISBN 90-219-9487-9 : £21.02 B81-15048

615'.35 — Medicine. Enzyme therapy

Enzymes as drugs / edited by John S. Holcenberg, Joseph Roberts. — New York ; Chichester : Wiley, c1981. — x,455p : ill ; 25cm
Includes index
ISBN 0-471-05061-x : £41.50 B81-33020

615'.36 — Medicine. Drug therapy. Hormones

Bentley, P. J.. Endocrine pharmacology : physiological basis and therapeutic applications / P.J. Bentley. — Cambridge : Cambridge University Press, 1980. — xvi,496p : ill ; 26cm
Bibliography: p435-484. — Includes index
ISBN 0-521-22673-2 : £40.00 B81-38978

615'.36 — Medicine. Natural remedies: Oysters

Lewis, Alan. The Japanese oyster. — Wellingborough : Thorsons, Sept.1981. — [64]p
ISBN 0-7225-0721-6 (pbk) : £0.75 : CIP entry B81-28183

615'.366 — Drugs: Oestrogens. Action

Chaudhury, Ranjit Roy. Pharmacology of estrogens. — Oxford : Pergamon, Aug.1981. — [180]p. — (International encyclopedia of pharmacology and therapeutics ; section 106)
ISBN 0-08-026869-2 : £21.00 : CIP entry B81-16398

615'.37 — Medicine. Drug therapy. Antivirals — *Conference proceedings*

Developments in antiviral therapy / [based on the proceedings of a symposium held at the London Hospital Medical College on 30 Novermber, 1979, by the British Society for Antimicrobial Chemotherapy] ; edited by L.H. Collier, J. Oxford. — London : Academic Press, 1980. — xvii,291p : ill ; 24cm
Includes bibliographies and index
ISBN 0-12-181150-6 : £18.60 : CIP rev. B80-23315

615'.37 — Medicine. Drug therapy. Ribavirin — *Conference proceedings*

Ribavirin : a broad spectrum antiviral agent / edited by Roberts A. Smith, William Kirkpatrick. — New York ; London : Academic Press, 1980. — xiii,237p : ill ; 24cm
Conference papers. — Includes bibliographies and index
ISBN 0-12-652350-9 : £11.80 B81-01533

615'.39 — Medicine. Drug therapy. Immunoglobulin — *Conference proceedings*

Immunohemotherapy. — London : Academic Press, Dec.1981. — [500]p
Conference papers
ISBN 0-12-523280-2 : CIP entry B81-34010

615.4 — PHARMACY

615'.4 — Pharmacy — *Conference proceedings*
European Symposium on Clinical Pharmacy *(9th : 1980 : Helsinki)*. Progress in clinical pharmacy III : proceedings of the Ninth European Symposium on Clinical Pharmacy held in Helsinki, Finland, 13-16 August 1980 / editors H. Turakka and E. van der Kleijn. — Amsterdam ; Oxford : Elsevier/North-Holland Biomedical, 1981. — xiv,358p : ill,forms ; 25cm
Includes index
ISBN 0-444-80338-6 : £25.47 B81-22447

615'.4'01513 — Drugs. Dosage. Arithmetical calculations — *For nursing*
Dison, Norma. Simplified drugs and solutions for nurses : including arithmetic / Norma Dison. — 7th ed. — St. Louis ; London : Mosby, 1980. — vii,139p : ill ; 22cm
Previous ed.: 1976
ISBN 0-8016-1311-6 (pbk) : £6.00 B81-08542

Skelley, Esther G.. Medications and mathematics for the nurse / Esther G. Skelley. — New York ; London : Van Nostrand Reinhold, c1981. — vi,282p : ill ; 27cm
Includes index
ISBN 0-442-21882-6 : £10.45
Primary classification 615'.1'024613 B81-29630

615'.4'01513 — Drugs. Dosage. Arithmetical calculations — *Programmed instructions*
Zatz, Joel L.. Pharmaceutical calculations / Joel L. Zatz. — 2nd ed. — New York ; Chichester : Wiley, c1981. — ix,388p ; 26cm
Previous ed.: 1973. — Includes index
ISBN 0-471-07757-7 (pbk) : £10.00 B81-21084

615'.4'01513 — Drugs. Dosage. Arithmetical calculations — *Questions & answers — For nursing*
Hart, Laura K.. The arithmetic of dosages and solutions : a programmed presentation / Laura K. Hart. — 5th ed. — St. Louis ; London : Mosby, 1981. — vii,68p : ill ; 26cm
Previous ed.: St. Louis : Mosby ; London : Distributed by Kimpton, 1977. — Template in pocket
ISBN 0-8016-2076-7 (spiral) : £6.50 B81-25463

Radcliff, Ruth K.. Calculation of drug dosages : a workbook / Ruth K. Radcliff, Sheila J. Ogden. — 2nd ed. — St. Louis ; London : Mosby, 1980. — ix,289p ; 28cm
Previous ed.: 1977. — Text on inside covers
ISBN 0-8016-4067-9 (pbk) : £7.00 B81-02971

Vervoren, Thora M.. Workbook of solutions and dosage of drugs : including arithmetic. — 11th ed., Thora M. Vervoren, Joan E. Oppeneer. — St. Louis ; London : Mosby, 1980. — ix,201p : ill ; 27cm
Previous ed.: 1976. — Bibliography: p201
ISBN 0-8016-0236-x (pbk) : £7.25 B81-08141

615'.4'02541 — Great Britain. Pharmaceutical chemists — *Directories — Serials*
Pharmaceutical Society of Great Britain. Annual register of pharmaceutical chemists. — 1981. — London : The Society, c1981. — 901p
ISBN 0-85369-150-9 : Unpriced
ISSN 0260-955x B81-26385

615'.4'0922 — Great Britain. Pharmacy. Organisations: Society of Apothecaries. Officials — *Biographies*
Whittet, T. D.. Clerks, bedels and chemical operators of the Society of Apothecaries : the Gideon De Laune lecture for 1977 / by T.D. Whittet. — [Twickenham] ([Regal House, Twickenham, Middx]) : [E.R. Squibb and Sons Ltd], [1980?]. — 88p : ill,1coat of arms,ports ; 21cm
£2.00 (pbk) B81-22969

615'.4'0941 — Great Britain. Pharmacy — *Serials*
British journal of pharmaceutical practice : the journal of postgraduate pharmacy. — Vol.1, no.1 (Apr.1979)-. — London (1 Bedford St., WC2E 9HD) : Medical News-Tribune, 1979-. — v. : ill,ports ; 27cm
Monthly. — Description based on: Vol.2, no.2 (May 1980)
ISSN 0144-8803 = British journal of pharmaceutical practice : £14.00 per year B81-08223

615.5 — MEDICINE. THERAPY

615.5 — Alternative medicine
Drury, Nevill. The healing power. — London : Muller, Sept.1981. — [224]p
ISBN 0-584-97078-1 (cased) : £7.95 : CIP entry
ISBN 0-584-97106-0 (pbk) : £5.95 B81-28107

Law, Donald. A guide to alternative medicine / Donald Law. — Rev. ed. — London : Turnstone, 1979. — 212p : ill ; 20cm
Previous ed.: 1974. — Bibliography: p200-207. — Includes index
ISBN 0-85500-107-0 (pbk) : £2.50 B81-40373

615.5 — Alternative medicine, *to 1978*
Inglis, Brian. Natural medicine / Brian Inglis. — [London] : Fontana, 1980, c1979. — 259p ; 18cm
Originally published: London : Collins, 1979. — Bibliography: p205-211. - Includes index
ISBN 0-00-635602-8 (pbk) : £1.75 B81-00125

615.5'05 — Medicine. Therapy — *Serials*
Today's treatment. — 4. — London : British Medical Association, c1981. — x,178p
ISBN 0-7279-0076-5 : Unpriced B81-30836

615.5'32 — Medicine. Homeopathy
Blackie, Margery G.. [The patient, not the cure]. The challenge of homoeopathy : the patient, not the cure / Margery G. Blackie. — London : Unwin Paperbacks, 1981, c1976. — 247p,[4]p of plates : ill,2ports ; 20cm
Originally published: London : Macdonald and Jane's, 1975. — Includes index
ISBN 0-04-613042-x (pbk) : £2.50 : CIP rev. B80-27078

Boyd, Hamish W.. Introduction to homoeopathic medicine / Hamish W. Boyd. — Beaconsfield : Beaconsfield, 1981. — xii,239p ; 22cm. — (Beaconsfield homoeopathic library)
Bibliography: p227-228. — Includes index
ISBN 0-906584-05-1 (pbk) : £10.50 B81-25640

615.5'32 — Medicine. Homeopathy. Remedies
Borland, Douglas M.. Homoeopathy in practice. — Beaconsfield : Beaconsfield Publishers, Nov.1981. — [208]p. — (Beaconsfield homoeopathic library)
ISBN 0-906584-06-x (pbk) : £4.95 : CIP entry B81-30619

615.5'32 — Medicine. Homeopathy. Remedies — *Encyclopaedias*
Pratt, Noel J.. Homoeopathic prescribing / Noel J. Pratt ; with an appendix on the constitutional remedies by Marion Gray. — Beaconsfield : Beaconsfield Publishers, 1980. — xvp,79leaves ; 22cm. — (The Beaconsfield homoeopathic library)
ISBN 0-906584-03-5 (pbk) : £5.95 : CIP rev. B80-13843

615.5'32 — Medicine. Homeopathy. Remedies — *For pharmacy*
The **Pharmacist** and homoeopathic medicines / British Homoeopathic Association. — London (27A Devonshire St., W1N 1RJ) : The Association, c1981. — 37p ; 21cm
Cover title. — Bibliography: p37
Unpriced (pbk) B81-17924

615.5'32'05 — Medicine. Homeopathy — *Serials*
The **Homoeopathic** alternative : a quarterly publication of the Association for Homoeopathic Medicine. — Vol.1 no.1 (Autumn 1980)-. — Hexham (20a Shaftoe Leazes, Hexham, Northumberland) : The Association, 1980-. — v. : ill ; 21cm
ISSN 0260-6356 : £2.00 per year B81-02822

Homoeopathy today : journal of the Hahnemann Society for the Promotion of Homoeopathy. — Spring 1980-. — London (Humane Education Centre, Avenue Lodge, Bounds Green Rd, N22 4EU) : The Society, 1980-. — v. : ill ; 25cm
Quarterly. — Continues: Hahnemann newsletter. — Description based on: Autumn 1980
ISSN 0261-2828 = Homoeopathy today : £3.00 per year B81-20432

615.5'32'0924 — Medicine. Homeopathy. Hahnemann, Samuel — *Biographies*

Cook, Trevor M.. Samuel Hahnemann. — Wellingborough : Thorsons, Nov.1981. — [160]p
ISBN 0-7225-0689-9 : £5.95 : CIP entry
B81-30488

615.5'33 — Medicine. Osteopathy

Scofield, Arthur G.. Chiropractice. — Wellingborough : Thorsons, June 1981. — [224]p
ISBN 0-7225-0702-x (pbk) : £3.95 : CIP entry
B81-12909

615.5'33'02541 — Great Britain. Osteopaths — *Directories — Serials*

Register of Osteopaths. Directory of members / the Register of Osteopaths. — 1981. — London (1 Suffolk St., SW1Y 4HG) : General Council and Register of Osteopaths, [1981]. — 54p
ISSN 0306-803x : Unpriced B81-20437

615.5'8 — Hospitals. Patients. Drug therapy — *For pharmacists*

Clinical pharmacy and hospital drug management. — London : Chapman and Hall, Nov.1981. — [300]p
ISBN 0-412-22760-6 : £15.00 : CIP entry
B81-30355

615.5'8 — Medicine. Drug therapy

Lewis, J. G.. Therapeutics / J.G. Lewis. — 4th ed. — London : Hodder and Stoughton, 1980. — viii,302p : ill ; 23cm
Previous ed: 1978. — Bibliography: p268-269. - Includes indexes
ISBN 0-340-25166-2 (cased) : £7.95 : CIP rev.
ISBN 0-340-25167-0 (pbk) : £4.95 B79-36834

Rogers, H. J.. A textbook of clinical pharmacology / H.J. Rogers, R.G. Spector, J.R. Trounce. — London : Hodder and Stoughton, 1981. — vii,853p : ill ; 24cm
Bibliography: p826-842. — Includes index
ISBN 0-340-22358-8 (pbk) : £12.95 : CIP rev.
B80-12893

615.5'8 — Medicine. Drug therapy. Evaluation. Use of medical records — *For nursing*

. Systematic patient medication record review : a manual for nurses / Timothy H. Self, Questin M. Srnka, Ingeborg G. Mauksch. — St. Louis ; London : Mosby, 1980. — vii.132p : forms ; 24cm
Bibliography: p132
ISBN 0-8016-4479-8 (spiral) : £6.50
B81-08160

615.5'8'024613 — Drug therapy - *For district nursing*

Anderson, David J.. Drugs and the community nurse. — London (Henrietta Place, W1M 0AB) : Royal College of Nursing, May 1981. — [180]p
ISBN 0-902606-64-6 (pbk) : £4.00 : CIP entry
B81-09980

615.5'8'024613 — Medicine. Drug therapy — *For nursing*

Asperheim, Mary K.. The pharmacologic basis of patient care / Mary K. Asperheim, Laurel A. Eisenhauer. — 4th ed. — Philadelphia ; London : Saunders, 1981. — viii,650p : ill ; 28cm
Text on lining papers. — Includes bibliographies and index
ISBN 0-7216-1438-8 : £11.25 B81-26959

Gerald, Michael C.. Nursing : pharmacology and therapeutics / Michael C. Gerald, Freda V. O'Bannon. — Englewood Cliffs ; London : Prentice-Hall, c1981. — xiii,528p : ill ; 25cm
Includes bibliographies and index
ISBN 0-13-627505-2 : £12.95 B81-25056

615.5'8'05 — Medicine. Drug therapy — *Serials*

Advances in pharmacology and chemotherapy. — Vol.17 (1980). — New York ; London : Academic Press, c1980. — x,326p
ISBN 0-12-032917-4 : £23.40
ISSN 0065-3144 B81-16844

Drug therapeutics : concepts for physicians. — 1980-. — Edinburgh : Churchill Livingstone, 1980-. — v. : ill ; 23cm
Annual. — Description based on: 1981 ed
ISSN 0163-1705 = Drug therapeutics : Unpriced B81-15082

Drugs of choice. — 1980-1981. — St. Louis ; London : C.V. Mosby, 1980. — xv,773p
ISBN 0-8016-3444-x : Unpriced B81-12425

The **Year** book of drug therapy. — 1980. — Chicago ; London : Year Book Medical Publishers, c1980. — 456p
ISBN 0-8151-4618-3 (corrected) : Unpriced
ISSN 0084-3733 B81-03506

615.5'8'088054 — Children. Drug therapy — *Manuals*

Benitz, William E.. The pediatric drug handbook / William E. Benitz, David S. Tatro. — Chicago ; London : Year Book Medical Publishers, c1981. — xiv,475p ; 17cm
Includes index
ISBN 0-8151-0663-7 (pbk) : Unpriced
B81-40355

615.6 — DRUG THERAPY. MEDICATION

615'.63 — Medicine. Intravenous therapy — *Manuals — For nursing*

Coco, Charlene Dianne. Intravenous therapy : a handbook for practice / Charlene Dianne Coco. — St. Louis ; London : Mosby, 1980. — xi,170p : ill,forms ; 24cm
Bibliography: p158-160. — Includes index
ISBN 0-8016-0995-x (spiral) : Unpriced
B81-08539

615'.63 — Medicine. Intravenous therapy — *Serials*

British journal of intravenous therapy. — Vol.1, no.1 (July 1980)-. — London (1 Bedford St., WC2E 9HD) : Medical News Tribune, 1980-. — v. : ill ; 30cm
Quarterly
ISSN 0144-879x = British journal of intravenous therapy : £2.50 per year
B81-00913

615'.65 — Man. Blood. Autotransfusion — *Conference proceedings*

International Autotransfusion Symposium *(1st : 1980 : University of Maryland, School of Medicine)*. Autotransfusion : proceedings of the First International Autotransfusion Symposium, held April 24-25, 1980 at the Blood Bank Laboratories, University of Maryland, School of Medicine, Maryland, USA / editors Jerome M. Hauer, Robert L. Thurer and R. Ben Dawson. — New York ; Oxford : Elsevier/North-Holland, c1981. — 152p : ill,forms ; 24cm
Includes bibliographies and index
ISBN 0-444-00599-4 : Unpriced B81-28932

615'.65 — Man. Blood. White cells. Separation & transfusion — *German texts*

Kretschmer, Volker. Leukozytenseparation und -transfusion / Volker Kretschmer. — Basel ; London : Karger, c1981. — viii,189p : ill ; 23cm. — (Beiträge zu Infusionstherapie und klinische Ernährung ; Bd.6)
Bibliography: p169-189
£15.60 (pbk) B81-33269

615.7 — PHARMACODYNAMICS

615'.7 — Anti-inflammatory drugs: Non-steroid hormones - *Conference proceedings*

Are all non-steroidal anti-inflammatory drugs the same?. — Oxford (52 New Inn Hall St., Oxford OX1 2BS) : Medicine Publishing Foundation, May 1981. — [12]p. — (Medicine forum, ISSN 0260-9312 ; 1)
Conference papers
ISBN 0-906817-11-0 (pbk) : £2.50 : CIP entry
B81-12902

615'.7 — Antimicrobials. Biochemistry

Franklin, T. J.. Biochemistry of antimicrobial action. — 3rd ed. — London : Chapman and Hall, Apr.1981. — [256]p
Previous ed.: 1975
ISBN 0-412-22440-2 (cased) : £15.00 : CIP entry
ISBN 0-412-22450-x (pbk) : £6.95 B81-00126

615'.7 — Clinical trials. Methodology

Weiner, John M.. Issues in the design and evaluation of medical trials / John M. Weiner. — The Hague ; London : Nijhoff, c1980. — ix,206p : ill ; 25cm
Includes index
ISBN 90-247-2377-9 : Unpriced B81-10827

615'.7 — Drugs. Action

Curry, Stephen H.. Drug disposition and pharmacokinetics : with a consideration of pharmacological and clinical relationships / Stephen H. Curry. — 3rd ed. — Oxford : Blackwell Scientific, 1980. — x,330p,[1]folded leaf : ill ; 24cm
Previous ed.: 1977. — Includes bibliographies and index
ISBN 0-632-00639-0 (pbk) : £12.80 : CIP rev.
B80-11455

Lancaster, Richard. Pharmacology in clinical practice / Richard Lancaster. — London : Heinemann Medical, 1980. — vi,604p : ill ; 24cm
Includes bibliographies and index
ISBN 0-433-19052-3 : £25.00 B81-30776

Lewis, Peter. Essential clinical pharmacology. — Lancaster : MTP Press, Sept.1981. — [150]p
ISBN 0-85200-372-2 : £5.95 : CIP entry
B81-21546

Principles of medicinal chemistry / edited by William O. Foye. — 2nd ed. — Philadelphia : Lea & Febiger ; London : Kimpton, 1981. — xiii,931p : ill ; 27cm
Previous ed.: 1974. — Includes bibliographies and index
ISBN 0-8121-0722-5 : £22.50 B81-16120

Ryan, Sheila A.. Handbook of practical pharmacology / Sheila A. Ryan, Bruce D. Clayton. — 2nd ed. — St. Louis ; London : Mosby, 1980. — xvii,350p : ill ; 22cm
Previous ed.: 1977. — Bibliography: p341. - Includes index
ISBN 0-8016-4240-x (spiral) : Unpriced
B81-12596

615'.7 — Drugs. Action — *For paediatrics*

Pediatric pharmacology : therapeutic principles in practice / edited by Sumner J. Yaffe. — New York ; London : Grune & Stratton, c1980. — xiv,493p : ill ; 27cm
Includes index
ISBN 0-8089-1251-8 : £25.00 B81-15020

615'.7 — Drugs. Action. Role of structure & properties of drug molecules — *Conference proceedings*

International Symposium on Molecular Basis of Drug Action *(1980 : Querétaro)*. Molecular basis of drug action : proceedings of the International Symposium on Molecular Basis of Drug Action held in Querétaro, Mexico, October 13-16, 1980 / editors Thomas P. Singer and Raul N. Ondarza. — New York ; Oxford : Elsevier/North Holland, c1981. — xix,408p : ill,1port ; 25cm. — (Developments in biochemistry ; v.19)
Includes bibliographies and index
ISBN 0-444-00632-x : Unpriced B81-35564

615'.7 — Drugs. Monitoring

Therapeutic drug monitoring / edited by Alan Richens and Vincent Marks. — Edinburgh : Churchill Livingstone, 1981. — xii,528p : ill ; 24cm
Includes bibliographies and index
ISBN 0-443-02162-7 : £20.00 : CIP rev.
B81-16407

615'.7 — Immunopharmacology — *Conference proceedings*

International Conference on Immunopharmacology *(1st : 1980 : Brighton)*. Advances in immunopharmacology : proceedings of the First International Conference on Immunopharmacology, July 1980, Brighton, England / editors J. Hadden ... [et al.]. — Oxford : Pergamon, 1981. — ix,517p : ill ; 25cm
Includes bibliographies and index
ISBN 0-08-026384-4 (cased) : Unpriced : CIP rev.
ISBN 0-08-027974-0 (pbk) : £14.50 B81-04276

615'.7 — Man. Drug therapy. Immunosuppressive drugs

Immunosuppressive therapy / edited by J.R. Salaman. — Lancaster : MTP, 1981. — xi,257p : ill ; 25cm. — (Current status of modern therapy ; v.7)
Includes index
ISBN 0-85200-338-2 : £16.95 B81-06332

615'.7 — Man. Effects of drugs

Liska, Ken. Drugs and the human body : with implications for society / Ken Liska. — New York : Macmillan ; London : Collier Macmillan, c1981. — xiv,318p : ill,facsims,1port ; 24cm
Includes index
ISBN 0-02-370960-x : £6.25 B81-21448

Plant, Martin A.. Drugs in perspective / Martin A. Plant. — [Sevenoaks] : Teach Yourself Books, 1981. — xi,210p : ill,1map ; 18cm. — (Care and welfare)
Bibliography: p195-203. — Includes index
ISBN 0-340-25976-0 (pbk) : £1.95 : CIP rev. B81-08811

Schild, H. O.. Applied pharmacology / H.O. Schild. — 12th ed. — Edinburgh : Churchill Livingstone, 1980. — 519p : ill ; 25cm
Previous ed.: by Andrew Wilson, H.O. Schild, Walter Modell. 1975. — Includes bibliographies and index
ISBN 0-443-02199-6 (pbk) : £11.95 : CIP rev. B80-13845

615'.7 — Pharmacodynamics

Goodman, Louis S.. Goodman and Gilman's The pharmacological basis of therapeutics. — 6th ed. / editors Alfred Goodman Gilman, Louis S. Goodman, Alfred Gilman ; associate editors Steven E. Mayer, Kenneth L. Melmon. — New York : Macmillan ; London : Baillière Tindall, c1980. — xvi,1843p,[1]fold.leaf of plates : ill (some col.) ; 27cm
Previous ed.: published as The pharmacological basis of therapeutics / editors Louis S. Goodman, Alfred Gilman, associate editors Alfred G. Gilman, George B. Koelle. New York : Macmillan, 1975. — Includes bibliographies and index
ISBN 0-7020-0826-5 : £28.50 B81-00914

615'.7 — Pharmacokinetics

Clark, Bruce. An introduction to pharmacokinetics / Bruce Clark, Dennis A. Smith. — Oxford : Blackwell Scientific, 1981. — vii,75p : ill ; 19cm
Bibliography: p74-75
ISBN 0-632-00743-5 (pbk) : £2.80 : CIP rev. B81-00915

Rowland, Malcolm. Clinical pharmacokinetics : concepts and applications / Malcolm Rowland, Thomas N. Tozer. — Philadelphia : Lea & Febiger ; London : Kimpton, 1980. — x,331p : ill(some col.) ; 27cm
Bibliography: p283-286. — Includes index
ISBN 0-8121-0681-4 : £13.75 B81-16096

Shargel, Leon. Applied biopharmaceutics and pharmacokinetics / Leon Shargel, Andrew B.C. Yu. — New York ; [London] : Appleton-Century-Crofts, c1980. — viii,253p : ill ; 24cm
Bibliography: p244. — Includes index
ISBN 0-8385-0206-7 (pbk) : Unpriced B81-08619

615'.7 — Pharmacokinetics — *Conference proceedings*

Pharmacokinetics : proceedings of a course organised by the Institute of Mathematics and its Applications held in London in September 1974. — Southend-on-Sea (Maitland House, Warrior Sq., Southend-on-Sea, Essex SS1 2JY) : The Institute, c1975. — viii,182p : ill ; 20cm. — (Symposium proceedings series / Institute of Mathematics and its Applications ; no.7)
Unpriced (spiral) B81-13263

615'.7 — Selective toxins. Biochemistry

Albert, Adrien. Selective toxicity : the physico-chemical basis of therapy / Adrien Albert. — 6th ed. — London : Chapman and Hall, 1979 (1981 [printing]). — xiii,662p : ill ; 24cm. — (Science paperbacks ; 176)
Previous ed.: 1973. — Bibliography: p577-631. — Includes index
ISBN 0-412-23650-8 : Unpriced : CIP rev. B81-13860

615'.704 — Drugs. Interactions

Stockley, Ivan H.. Drug interactions. — Oxford : Blackwell Scientific, Oct.1981. — [512]p
ISBN 0-632-00843-1 (pbk) : £15.00 : CIP entry B81-28016

615'.7042 — Man. Diseases caused by drugs

Iatrogenic diseases. — 2nd ed., update 1981. — Oxford : Oxford University Press, June 1981. — [200]p. — (Oxford medical publications)
Second ed. originally published: 1978
ISBN 0-19-261263-8 : £15.00 : CIP entry B81-12870

615'.7042'05 — Drugs. Side effects — *Serials*

Side effects of drugs annual. — 5. — Amsterdam ; Oxford : Excerpta Medica, 1981. — xxiv,476p
ISBN 90-219-3055-2 : Unpriced
ISSN 0378-6080 B81-24685

615'.705 — Man. Drugs. Metabolism — *Serials*

Progress in drug metabolism. — Vol.6. — Chichester : Wiley, Nov.1981. — [320]p
ISBN 0-471-28023-2 : £20.50 : CIP entry B81-30523

615'.7'0724 — Man. Drugs & toxins. Metabolism. Mathematical models

O'Flaherty, Ellen J.. Toxicants and drugs : kinetics and dynamics / Ellen J. O'Flaherty. — New York ; Chichester : Wiley, c1981. — xvi,398p : ill ; 24cm
Includes bibliographies and index
ISBN 0-471-06047-x : £26.40 B81-23322

615'.71 — Aldosterone. Antagonists — *Conference proceedings*

Aldosterone antagonists in clinical medicine : proceedings of the Searle symposium, Nice, April 13-15, 1978 / editorial board G.M. Addison ... [et al.]. — Amsterdam ; Oxford : Excerpta Medica, 1978. — 527p : ill ; 25cm. — (International congress series ; no.460)
Includes bibliographies and index
ISBN 90-219-0387-3 : Unpriced B81-04922

615'.71 — Anti-hypertensive drugs

Doyle, Austin. Anti-hypertensive drugs. — Oxford : Pergamon, Feb.1982. — [260]p. — (International encyclopaedia of pharmacology and therapeutics ; section 109)
ISBN 0-08-028849-9 : £29.50 : CIP entry B81-35945

615'.71 — Man. Beta adrenergic receptors. Blocking agents

Frishman, William H.. Clinical pharmacology of the beta-adrenoceptor blocking drugs / William H. Frishman ; foreword by Edmund H. Sonnenblick. — New York : Appleton-Century-Crofts ; London : Prentice-Hall, 1980. — xiv,221p : ill ; 24cm
Includes index
ISBN 0-8385-1143-0 : £11.00 B81-04428

615'.71 — Man. Beta adrenergic receptors. Blocking agents — *Conference proceedings*

The **Clinical** impact of beta-adrenoceptor blockade : proceedings of an international symposium, Berlin, May 1980 / editors, D.M. Burley and G.F.B. Birdwood. — Horsham ([Wimblehurst Rd., Horsham, W. Sussex RH12 4AB]) : CIBA Laboratories, 1980. — 287p ; 24cm
Unpriced (pbk) B81-29514

615'.71 — Man. Cardiovascular system. Drug therapy

Clinical applications of cardiovascular drugs / edited by Leonard S. Dreifus and Albert N. Brest. — The Hague ; London : Nijhoff, 1980. — 257p : ill ; 25cm. — (Developments in cardiovascular medicine ; v.5)
Includes index
ISBN 90-247-2295-0 : Unpriced
ISBN 90-247-2369-8 (pbk) : Unpriced B81-00916

615'.71 — Man. Cardiovascular system. Drug therapy. Drugs. Interactions

Cardiovascular and respiratory disease therapy / edited by J.C. Petrie. — Amsterdam ; Oxford : Elsevier/North-Holland Biomedical, 1980. — ix,243p : ill ; 25cm. — (Clinically important adverse drug reactions ; v.1)
Includes bibliographies and index
ISBN 0-444-80233-9 : £18.68 B81-11140

615'.71 — Man. Vascular diseases. Drug therapy. Hydroxyethylrutosides — *Conference proceedings*

Hydroxyethylrutosides in vascular disease / [condensed proceedings of an international symposium] ; [organised by Zyma (United Kingdom) Limited and held at the Manor House Hotel, Moretonhampstead, Devon on 18th and 19th April 1980] ; edited by T.B. Pulvertaft, J.S. Lyons and C.A.S. Wink. — London (1 Wimpole St., W1M 8AE) : Royal Society of Medicine, 1981. — ix,66p : ill ; 25cm. — (International congress and symposium series / Royal Society of Medicine ; no.42)
At head of title: Royal Society of Medicine. — Includes bibliographies
ISBN 0-12-793395-6 (pbk) : Unpriced : CIP rev.
ISBN 0-8089-1378-6 (U.S.) B81-04353

615'.71 — Medicine. Drug therapy. Nadolol — *Conference proceedings*

International experience with nadolol : a long acting β-blocking agent / [proceedings of a symposium held by Squibb Europe Limited at the Grand Hotel, Paris on 5, 6 and 7 December 1980] ; edited by F. Gross. — London : Royal Society of Medicine : Academic Press, 1981. — 229p : ill ; 25cm. — (Royal Society of Medicine international congress and symposium series, ISSN 0142-2367 ; no.37)
Includes bibliographies
ISBN 0-12-791743-8 (pbk) : Unpriced
ISBN 0-8089-1368-9 (Grune & Stratton) : Unpriced B81-14601

615'.71 — Prazosin — *Conference proceedings*

Prazosin : pharmacology, hypertension and congestive heart failure / edited by M.D. Rawlins, P. Lund-Johansen and T.D. Lawrie. — London : Royal Society of Medicine, 1981. — xii,143p : ill ; 24cm. — (Royal Society of Medicine series. International congress and symposium series ; no.41)
Conference papers. — Includes bibliographies
ISBN 0-12-793528-2 (pbk) : Unpriced B81-16785

615'.718 — Anticoagulants & fibrinolytics

Chazov, E. I.. Anticoagulants and fibrinolytics / E.I. Chazov, K.M. Lakin ; translated by E.P. Fadeev, G.S. Vats, A.P. Bermont. — Chicago ; London : Year Book Medical, 1980. — vii,358p : ill ; 22cm
Translation from the Russian. — Bibliography: p303-352. - Includes index
ISBN 0-8151-1649-7 : £28.50 B81-09760

615'.72 — Man. Respiratory system. Drug therapy. Antibiotics — *Conference proceedings*

Round Table Conference on Developments in Antibiotic Treatment of Respiratory Infections in the Hospital and General Practice *(1980 : Scheveningen)*. Developments in antibiotic treatment of respiratory infections : proceedings of the Round Table Conference on Developments in Anti-biotic Treatment of Respiratory Infections in the Hospital and General Practice, held in the Kurhaus, Scheveningen, The Netherlands, June 15-16, 1980 / edited by Ralph van Furth. — The Hague ; London : Nijhoff, c1981. — 251p : ill ; 25cm. — (New perspectives in clinical microbiology ; 4)
Includes index
ISBN 90-247-2493-7 : Unpriced B81-37479

615′.72 — Man. Respiratory system. Effects of drugs. Measurement

Respiratory system / edited by J.B.L. Howell & A.E. Tattersfield. — London : Macmillan, 1981. — 94p : ill ; 26cm. — (Methods in clinical pharmacology ; 2)
'Reprinted from British journal of clinical pharmacology, vol.8. 1979, vol.9. 1980'. — Includes bibliographies
ISBN 0-333-31186-8 : £17.50 B81-38732

615′.73 — Man. Gastrointestinal tract. Drugs. Absorption — *Conference proceedings*

International Conference on Drug Absorption *(1979 : Edinburgh).* Drug absorption / [proceedings of the International Conference on Drug Absorption, Edinburgh, September 1979] ; edited by L.F. Prescott and W.S. Nimmo. — Lancaster : MTP Press, c1981. — xi,353p : ill ; 25cm
Includes bibliographies and index
ISBN 0-85200-528-8 : £24.95 B81-08255

615′.73 — Man. Gastrointestinal tract. Effects of domperidone — *Conference proceedings*

Progress with domperidone : a gastrokinetic and anti-emetic agent / [proceedings of an international symposium sponsored by the Janssen Research Foundation at the 11th International Congress of Gastroenterology, Hamburg, on 10 June 1980] ; edited by G. Towse. — London : Royal Society of Medicine, 1981. — xi,110p : ill,ports ; 24cm. — (Royal Society of Medicine series. International congress and symposium series, ISSN 0142-2367 ; no.36)
Includes bibliographies
ISBN 0-12-794643-8 (pbk) : Unpriced B81-11088

615′.739 — Man. Lipids. Metabolism. Effects of drugs — *Conference proceedings*

International Symposium On Drugs Affecting Lipid Metabolism *(7th : 1980 : Milan).* Drugs affecting lipid metabolism : proceedings of the VIIth International Symposium on Drugs Affecting Lipid Metabolism held in Milan, Italy, 28-31 May, 1980 / editors Remo Fumagalli, David Kritchevsky and Rodolfo Paoletti. — Amsterdam ; Oxford : Elsevier/North-Holland, 1980. — x,394p : ill ; 25cm. — (Symposia of the Giovanni Lorenzini Foundation ; v.7)
Includes index
ISBN 0-444-80283-5 : £25.29 B81-02789

615′.766 — Aphrodisiacs — *Encyclopaedias*

The **Biodisiac** book. — London (3 Clifford St., W1) : Biodisiac Institute, Oct.1981. — [64]p
ISBN 0-85140-548-7 : £3.95 : CIP entry B81-28161

615′.766 — Women. Health. Effects of sex hormone drugs

Seaman, Barbara. Women and the crisis in sex hormones / Barbara Seaman and Gideon Seaman. — Toronto ; London : Bantam, 1978, c1977 (1979 printing). — xv,621p ; 18cm
Originally published: New York : Rawson Associates, 1977 ; Hassocks : Harvester Press, 1978. — Includes index
ISBN 0-553-13415-9 (pbk) : £1.95 B81-04933

615′.778 — Man. Skin. Effects of systemic drugs — *German texts*

Zürcher, Kaspar. Cutaneous side effects of systemic drugs : a commentated synopsis of today's drugs = Hautnebenwirkungen interner Arzneimittel : eine kommentierte Synopsis der heutigen Medikamente / Kaspar Zürcher, Alfred Krebs, with a contribution by Otmar Widmer. — Basel ; London : Karger, 1980. — xi,370p ; 26cm
German text, English summary and drug index. — Includes bibliographies and index
ISBN 3-8055-0019-x : £32.30 B81-13076

615′.778 — Man. Skin. Steroid hormones. Absorption — *Conference proceedings*

Percutaneous absorption of steroids / edited by P. Mauvais-Jarvis, C.F.H. Vickers, J. Wepierre. — London : Academic Press, 1980. — xviii,294p : ill,1 port ; 24cm
Conference papers. — Includes index
ISBN 0-12-480680-5 : £15.60 : CIP rev. B80-09246

615′.78 — Canada. Psychotropic drugs — *Conference proceedings*

Canadian College of Neuropsychopharmacology. *Meeting (2nd : 1979 : Hamilton, Ont.).* Recent advances in Canadian neuropsychopharmacology : selected proceedings of the 2nd Annual Meeting of the Canadian College of Neuropsychopharmacology, Hamilton, Ont., April 1979 / editors Paul Grof and Bishan Saxena. — Basel ; London : Karger, 1980. — 237p : ill ; 23cm
Includes bibliographies
ISBN 3-8055-1459-x (pbk) : £24.50 B81-26326

615′.78 — Man. Autonomic nervous system. Effects of drugs — *Serials*

Journal of autonomic pharmacology. — Vol.1, no.1 (Nov.1980)-. — North Ferriby (P.O. Box 2, North Ferriby, North Humberside HU14 3AA) : Galen, 1980-. — v. : ill ; 25cm
Quarterly
ISSN 0144-1795 = Journal of autonomic pharmacology : £35.00 per year B81-06473

615′.78 — Man. Behaviour. Effects of drugs

Iversen, Susan D. Behavioral pharmacology / Susan D. Iversen, Leslie L. Iversen. — 2nd ed. — New York ; Oxford : Oxford University Press, 1981. — xii, 305p : ill ; 23cm
Previous ed.: 1975. — Bibliography: p278-298. — Includes index
ISBN 0-19-502778-7 (cased) : Unpriced
ISBN 0-19-502779-5 (pbk) : £7.95 B81-31401

615′.78 — Man. Central nervous system. Neuropharmacological aspects

Neuropharmacology of central nervous system and behavioral disorders / edited by Gene C. Palmer. — New York ; London : Academic Press, 1980, c1981. — xxiv,672p : ill ; 24cm. — (Psychologic and pharmacologic bases of drug therapy)
Includes bibliographies and index
ISBN 0-12-544760-4 : £33.20 B81-33033

615′.78 — Man. Hearing. Effects of drugs

Pharmacology of hearing : experimental and clinical bases / co-editors R. Don Brown, Ernest A. Daigneault. — New York ; Chichester : Wiley, c1981. — ix,353p : ill ; 24cm
Includes index
ISBN 0-471-05074-1 : £39.00 B81-38578

615′.78 — Monoamine oxidase inhibitors. Action — *Conference proceedings*

Monoamine oxidase inhibitors : the state of the art : based on a Symposium of the 12th Congress of the Collegium Internationale Neuro-Psychopharmacologicum Gothenberg, 22-26 June, 1980 / edited by M.B.H. Youdim, E.S. Paykel. — Chichester : Wiley, c1981. — xviii,214p : ill ; 24cm
Includes bibliographies and index
ISBN 0-471-27880-7 : £13.00 B81-11691

615′.78 — Neuropharmacology

Green, A. Richard. Pharmacology and biochemistry of psychiatric disorders. — Chichester : Wiley, Oct.1981. — [200]p
ISBN 0-471-09998-8 (cased) : £13.00 : CIP entry
ISBN 0-471-10000-5 (pbk) : £5.90
Primary classification 612′.8042 B81-28044

615′.78 — Neuropsychopharmacology — *Conference proceedings*

Collegium Internationale Neuro-Psychopharmacologicum. *Congress (12th : 1980 : Göteborg).* Recent advances in neuro-psychopharmacology. — Oxford : Pergamon, Apr.1981. — [422]p
ISBN 0-08-026382-8 : £33.00 : CIP entry B81-00917

615′.78 — Psychopharmacology

Clinical pharmacology in psychiatry / edited by Earl Usdin with the assistance of John M. Davis ... [et al.]. — New York ; Oxford : Elsevier, c1981. — xvi,352p : ill ; 27cm
Includes bibliographies and index
ISBN 0-444-00556-0 : £26.17 B81-35337

Current developments in psychopharmacology / editors Walter B. Essman, L. Valzelli. — Lancaster : MTP
Vol.6. — c1981. — 226p : ill ; 24cm
Includes bibliographies and index
ISBN 0-85200-551-2 : £29.50 B81-33077

Theory in psychopharmacology. — London : Academic Press
Vol.1. — Dec.1981. — [320]p
ISBN 0-12-188000-1 : CIP entry B81-31334

615′.78 — Psychotropic drugs. Action. Effects of human ageing

Psychopharmacology of aging / edited by Carl Eisdorfer and William E. Fann. — Lancaster : MTP, c1980. — 271p : ill ; 24cm. — (Aging)
Includes index
ISBN 0-85200-549-0 : £20.50 B81-05065

615′.78′05 — Neuropharmacology — *Serials*

Essays in neurochemistry and neuropharmacology. — Vol.5. — Chichester ; New York : Wiley, c1981. — xv,153p
ISBN 0-471-27879-3 : £16.50
ISSN 0147-0205
Primary classification 612′.8042′05 B81-24997

615′.7827′09 — Cannabis, *to 1979*

Abel, Ernest L. Marihuana : the first twelve thousand years / Ernest L. Abel. — New York ; London : Plenum, c1980. — xi,289p ; 24cm
Bibliography: p273-282. - Includes index
ISBN 0-306-40496-6 : Unpriced B81-04101

615′.7827′0924 — Cannabis — *Personal observations*

Lindsay, Michael, *d.197-.* Mind-sprung / Michael Lindsay. — London (111 High Holborn WC1V 6JS) : Nold Jonson, 1981. — 141p ; 23cm
ISBN 0-907538-00-2 : £4.50 B81-19771

615′.7828 — Man. Effects of alcohol — *Conference proceedings*

Alcohol tolerance and dependence / edited by Henk Rigter an John C. Crabbe, Jr.. — Amsterdam ; Oxford : Elsevier/North-Holland Biomedical, 1980. — 455p : ill ; 25cm
Includes bibliographies and index
ISBN 0-444-80212-6 : £38.01 B81-04145

615′.783 — Medicine. Drug therapy. Aspirin — *Conference proceedings*

Aspirin symposium 1980 / [proceedings of an International Symposium held by The Aspirin Foundation at the Royal College of Surgeons, London on Thursday 5th June, 1980] ; edited by Jean Hallam, L. Goldman and G.R. Fryers. — London (1 Wimpole St. W1N 8AE) : Royal Society of Medicine, 1981. — vii,72p : ill ; 25cm. — (Royal Society of Medicine international congress and symposium series ; 39)
Includes bibliographies
ISBN 0-12-791845-0 (pbk) : Unpriced B81-15683

615′.788 — Psychotropic drugs

DuQuesne, J. T. A handbook of psychoactive medicines. — London : Quartet, Nov.1981. — [512]p
ISBN 0-7043-2270-6 (pbk) : £6.95 : CIP entry B81-30353

615′.7882 — Benzodiazepines — *Conference proceedings*

International Symposium on Benzodiazepines *(1st : 1979 : Rio de Janeiro).* Benzodiazepines today and tomorrow : proceedings of the 1st International Symposium on Benzodiazepines in Rio de Janeiro, 28-30 September 1979 / edited by R.G. Priest ... [et al.]. — Lancaster : MTP, 1980. — xvi,293p : ill ; 24cm
Includes bibliographies and index
ISBN 0-85200-368-4 : £14.95 : CIP rev. B80-12369

615.8 — PHYSICAL AND OTHER THERAPIES

615.8 — Medicine. Homeopathy. Remedies. Electronic potentisers — *Manuals*
Copen, Bruce. Electronic homoeopathic medicine / by Bruce Copen. — Haywards Heath : Academic Publications, 1981. — 58p : ill ; 21cm
£2.00 (pbk) B81-06282

615.8 — Non-medical healing
Coddington, Mary. In search of the healing energy. — Wellingborough (Denington Estate, Wellingborough, Northants NN8 2RQ) : Excalibur Books, Aug.1981. — [192]p
ISBN 0-85454-078-4 (pbk) : £3.50 : CIP entry B81-15926

Corvo, Joseph. The miracle of you / Joseph Corvo. — London (7 Belsize Square NW3 4HT) : Corvoline, c1981. — 112p : ill ; 22cm
ISBN 0-9507433-0-5 (pbk) : £2.75 B81-38972

615.8′043 — Man. Resuscitation — *Manuals*
Ellis, Patricia Diane. Cardiopulmonary resuscitation : procedures for basic and advanced life support / Patricia Diane Ellis, Diane M. Billings. — St. Louis ; London : Mosby, 1980. — xii,239p : ill ; 24cm
Includes bibliographies and index
ISBN 0-8016-1557-7 (pbk) : Unpriced B81-08566

615.8′2′023 — Physiotherapists. Interpersonal relationships with patients. Psychological aspects
Bourne, Stanford. Under the doctor : studies in the psychological problems of physiotherapists, patients and doctors / Stanford Bourne. — [Amersham] : Avebury, 1981. — 211p ; 23cm
ISBN 0-86127-601-9 (cased) : £12.00 : CIP rev.
ISBN 0-86127-602-7 (pbk) : £7.50 B80-21978

615.8′2′02341 — Great Britain. Medicine. Physiotherapy — *Career guides*
Physiotherapy : the career for you?. — London (14 Bedford Row, WC1R 1ED) : The Chartered Society of Physiotherapy, [1981]. — 18p : ill ; 21cm
Cover title
Unpriced (pbk) B81-15118

615.8′2′02541 — Great Britain. Physiotherapists — *Directories — Serials*
The **Physiotherapists** register. — 1980. — [London] ([Park House, 184 Kennington Park Rd., SE11 4BU]) : Printed and published under the direction of the Physiotherapists Board, [1980]. — 310p
Unpriced B81-06691

615.8′22 — Do-in — *Manuals*
Rofidal, Jean. Do.In : eastern massage and yoga techniques / by Jean Rofidal ; translated from the French by Transcript. — Wellingborough : Thorsons, 1981. — 160p : ill ; 22cm
Translation of: Do.In. — Includes index
ISBN 0-7225-0651-1 (pbk) : Unpriced B81-08720

615.8′22 — Man. Shiatzu. Use of pressure points of ears
Chan, Pedro. Ear acupressure. — Wellingborough : Thorsons, Nov.1981. — [112]p
Originally published: Los Angeles : Price, Stern, Sloan, 1977
ISBN 0-7225-0727-5 (pbk) : £2.95 : CIP entry B81-30587

615.8′22 — Man. Soft tissues. Manipulation. Techniques
Chaitow, Leon. Neuro-muscular technique : a practitioner′s guide to soft tissue manipulation / by Leon Chaitow ; illustrated by Bevil Roberts. — Wellingborough : Thorsons, 1980. — 144p : ill(some col.),ports ; 26cm
Bibliography: p141-142. — Includes index
ISBN 0-7225-0586-8 : £15.00 : CIP rev. B80-12370

15.8′22 — Man. Therapy. Massage
Jackson, Richard, *1948-*. [Holistic massage]. Massage therapy : the holistic way to physical and mental health / by Richard Jackson ; photographs by Selby Smith ; illustrations by Bonnie Timmons. — Wellingborough : Thorsons, 1980, c1977. — 128p : ill ; 22cm
Originally published: New York : Drake, 1977
ISBN 0-7225-0646-5 (pbk) : £2.95 B81-01565

615.8′22 — Medicine. Physiotherapy. Massage — *Manuals*
Beard, Gertrude. Beard′s massage. — 3rd ed. / Elizabeth C. Wood, Paul D. Becker. — Philadelphia ; London : Saunders, 1981. — xiii,166p : ill ; 26cm
Previous ed.: 1974. — Bibliography: p146-148. — Includes index
ISBN 0-7216-9592-2 (spiral) : £10.75 B81-31861

615.8′22 — Medicine. Self-treatment. Use of neuromuscular technique — *Manuals*
Chaitow, Leon. Instant pain control : trigger point self-treatment / by Leon Chaitow ; line drawings by Bevil Roberts ; photographs by Paul Turner. — Wellingborough : Thorsons, 1981. — 95p : ill ; 22cm
Includes index
ISBN 0-7225-0671-6 (pbk) : £2.95 : CIP rev. B81-14903

615.8′22 — Medicine. Self-treatment. Use of Shiatzu — *Manuals*
Dalet, Roger. Safeguard your health and beauty with finger massage / Roger Dalet ; translated by Linda Zuck. — London : Hutchinson, 1980. — 157p : ill(some col.) ; 24cm
Translation of: Sauvegardez vous-même votre santé et votre beauté par simple pression d′un doigt
ISBN 0-09-143461-0 (pbk) : £4.95 : CIP rev. B80-13410

615.8′22 — Shiatzu — *Manuals*
Namikoshi, Toru. The complete book of shiatsu therapy / Toru Namikoshi. — Tokyo : Japan Publications ; Hemel Hempstead : International Book Distributors [distributor], 1981. — 256p : ill ; 26cm
Includes index
ISBN 0-87040-461-x (pbk) : £7.75 B81-28472

615.8′24 — Medicine. Physiotherapy. Exercises
Hollis, Margaret. Practical exercise therapy / Margaret Hollis with contributions by Barbara Sanford, Patricia J. Waddington. — 2nd ed. — Oxford : Blackwell Scientific, 1981. — ix,253p : ill ; 24cm
Previous ed.: 1976. — Bibliography: p249. — Includes index
ISBN 0-632-00806-7 (pbk) : £9.80 : CIP rev. B81-11952

615.8′24′02541 — Great Britain. Remedial gymnasts — *Directories — Serials*
Remedial Gymnasts Board. The Remedial gymnasts register. — 1981. — [London] ([184 Kennington Park Rd, SE11 4BU]) : Remedial Gymnasts Board, [1981]. — 37leaves
Unpriced B81-32894

615.8′31 — Medicine. Chromotherapy
Wilson, Annie. What colour are you? the way to health through colour / by Annie Wilson and Lilla Bek. — Wellingborough : Turnstone, 1981. — 159p : ill ; 22cm
ISBN 0-85500-146-1 (pbk) : £3.75 : CIP rev. B81-12840

615.8′36 — Respiratory therapy equipment
McPherson, Steven P.. Respiratory therapy equipment / Steven P. McPherson with contributions by Charles B. Spearman. — 2nd ed. — St. Louis ; London : Mosby, 1981. — xii,514p : ill ; 25cm
Previous ed.: 1977. — Includes index
ISBN 0-8016-3313-3 : £17.50 B81-15004

615.8′42 — Medicine. Actinotherapy
Clayton, Edward Bellis. Clayton′s electrotherapy. — 8th ed. — London : Baillière Tindall, Feb.1982. — [240]p
Previous ed.: 1975
ISBN 0-7020-0902-4 (pbk) : £6.50 : CIP entry
Primary classification 615.8′45 B81-35929

615.8′42 — Medicine. Radiotherapy
Mould, R. F.. Radiotherapy treatment planning / R.F. Mould. — Bristol : Hilger in collaboration with the Hospital Physicists′ Association, c1981. — 204p : ill ; 22cm. — (Medical physics handbooks, ISSN 0143-0203 ; 7)
Bibliography: p185. — Includes index
ISBN 0-85274-504-4 : £12.95 B81-09560

615.8′42′028 — Europe. Medicine. Radiotherapy. Applications of computerised tomography scanners — *Conference proceedings*
Computerized tomographic scanners in radiotherapy in Europe : proceedings of a workshop meeting held at the World Health Organization, Geneva, Switzerland, March 28-30, 1979 / edited by Roger J. Berry. — London (32 Welbeck St., W1M 7PG) : British Institute of Radiology, 1981. — 216p : ill ; 27cm. — (British journal of radiology supplement, ISSN 0007-1285 ; 15)
Conference papers. — Bibliography: p213-216
Unpriced (pbk) B81-26117

615.8′42′02854 — Medicine. Radiotherapy. Applications of digital computer systems
Wood, Raymond G.. Computers in radiotherapy planning. — Chichester : Wiley, Aug.1981. — [156]p. — (Medical computing series ; 5)
ISBN 0-471-09994-5 : £10.00 : CIP entry B81-18123

615.8′424 — Great Britain. Hospitals. Radiopharmaceutical products. Quality control
Quality assurance of radio-pharmaceuticals : a guide to hospital practice : a special issue of Nuclear medicine communications / edited by M. Frier and S.R. Hesslewood. — London : Chapman and Hall in association with the British Nuclear Medicine Society, 1980. — i,57p : 1ill ; 24cm
Cover title
ISBN 0-412-23270-7 (pbk) : Unpriced : CIP rev. B80-20713

615.8′424 — Medicine. Applications of radiopharmaceutical products — *Conference proceedings*
European Symposium on Radiopharmacology *(2nd : 1980 : Noordwijkerhout)*. Progress in radiopharmacology : selected topics : proceedings of the Second European Symposium on Radiopharmacology held at Noordwijkerhout, The Netherlands, November 6-8, 1980 / editor Peter H. Cox. — Amsterdam ; Oxford : Elsevier/North-Holland Biomedical Press, 1981. — x,339p : ill ; 25cm. — (Progress in radiopharmacology ; v.2)
Includes index
ISBN 0-444-80323-8 : £27.32 B81-21443

615.8′424 — Radiopharmaceutical products — *Conference proceedings*
Radiopharmaceuticals : structure-activity relationships / edited by Richard P. Spencer. — New York ; London : Grune & Stratton, c1981. — ix,843p : ill ; 27cm
Conference papers. — Includes index
ISBN 0-8089-1387-5 : £25.20 B81-35419

615.8′45 — Medicine. Electrotherapy
Clayton, Edward Bellis. Clayton′s electrotherapy. — 8th ed. — London : Baillière Tindall, Feb.1982. — [240]p
Previous ed.: 1975
ISBN 0-7020-0902-4 (pbk) : £6.50 : CIP entry
Also classified at 615.8′42 B81-35929

615.8′51 — Medicine. Biodynamic psychology
Biodynamic psychology : the collected papers. — [London] ([Institute of Biodynamic Psychology, Acacia House, Centre Ave., The Vale, Acton Park, W3 7JX]) : Biodynamic Psychology
Vol.1 & 2. — 1980. — 160p : 1port ; 21cm
ISBN 0-9506313-3-7 (pbk) : Unpriced B81-16191

615.8′512 — Medicine. Hypnotherapy
Chertok, Léon. Sense and nonsense in psychotherapy : the challenge of hypnosis / by Léon Chertok ; translated by R.H. Ahrenfeldt ; and revised by the author. — Oxford : Pergamon, 1981. — xvii,244p ; 22cm
Translation of: Le non-savoir des psy. — Bibliography: p213-232. — Includes index
ISBN 0-08-026793-9 (cased) : Unpriced
ISBN 0-08-026813-7 (pgk) : £7.50 B81-27689

615.8'512 — Medicine. Hypnotherapy — *Conference proceedings*

Scientific Meeting on Clinical Hypnosis. Clinical hypnosis in medicine / [selected papers from the Annual Scientific Meeting on Clinical Hypnosis] ; [sponsored by the American Society of Clinical Hypnosis and cosponsored by the American Society of Clinical Hypnosis Education and Research Foundation] ; edited by Harold J. Wain. — Miami : Symposia Specialists ; London : Distributed by Year Book Medical, c1980. — 254,xvp : ill ; 23cm
Includes bibliographies and index
ISBN 0-8151-9067-0 : £27.25 B81-40509

615.8'512 — Medicine. Hypnotherapy — *Manuals*

Waxman, David. Hypnosis : a guide for patients and practitioners / by David Waxman. — London : Allen and Unwin, 1981. — xvi,160p : ill,ports ; 23cm. — (The Medicine today series)
Bibliography: p152-155. — Includes index
ISBN 0-04-616021-3 : Unpriced : CIP rev.
B81-15873

615.8'5152'02541 — Great Britain. Occupational therapists — *Directories — Serials*

Occupational Therapists Board. The Occupational therapists register. — 1981. — London (184 Kennington Park Rd, SE11 4BU) : The Board, [1981]. — 136p
Unpriced B81-24141

615.8'52 — Buddhism. Spiritual healing

Birnbaum, Raoul. The healing Buddha / Raoul Birnbaum ; foreword by John Blofeld. — London : Rider, 1980, c1979. — xviii,253p,[12]p of plates : ill ; 22cm
Bibliography: p238-243. — Includes index. — Includes translations from the Chinese Buddhist Canon
ISBN 0-09-142451-8 (pbk) : £4.50 : CIP rev.
B80-05937

615.8'52 — Man. Therapy. Metamorphic technique — *Serials*

The **Metamorphic** Association newsletter. — No.1 (Jan. 1981)-. — [London] ([26 Chalcot Sq., NW1]) : The Association, 1981-. — v. ; 21cm
Description based on: No.2 (May 1981)
ISSN 0262-1533 = Metamorphic Association newsletter : £2.50 per year B81-38180

615.8'52 — Spiritual healing. Communication — *Texts*

Matron *(Spirit).* Messages and instructions from the Healing Guides / transmitted by 'Matron' and Les Stratmeyer from beyond the Veil ; and received and transcribed by Ronald Alford. — London : Regency Press, c1980. — 39p,[2] leaves of plates : ports ; 23cm
ISBN 0-7212-0660-3 : £2.40 B81-07188

615.8'52 — Spiritual healing — *Manuals*

Wallace, Amy. The psychic healing book : how to develop your psychic potential safety simply, effectively / by Amy Wallace and Bill Henkin. — Wellingborough : Turnstone Press, 1981, c1978. — xiv,205p ; 22cm
Originally published: New York : Delacorte, 1978. — Bibliography: p203-205
ISBN 0-85500-144-5 (pbk) : £3.50 B81-14778

615.8'52'05 — Spiritual healing — *Serials*

Journal of the Unity Teaching and Healing Trust . — Vol.1, no.1 (Jan.1981)-. — Holsworthy (The Priory, Thornbury, Holsworthy, Devon EX22 7DA) : The Trust, 1981-. — v. ; 21cm
Quarterly
ISSN 0260-9371 = Journal of the Unity Teaching and Healing Trust : Unpriced
B81-13689

615.8'52'0924 — Christianity. Spiritual healing. Cain, John — *Biographies*

Sykes, Pat. You don't know John Cain? / by Pat Sykes ; with an introduction by Alan Whittaker. — Gerrards Cross : Van Duren, 1979. — 128p : ill,facsim,ports ; 23cm
ISBN 0-905715-10-1 : £5.50 B81-01776

615.8'52'0924 — Christianity. Spiritual healing. Cain, John — *Personal observations*

Wooding, Valerie. John Cain healing guide / by Valerie Wooding. — Gerrards Cross (P.O. Box 1, Gerrards Cross, Bucks. SL9 7AE) : V.D.C.P., 1980. — 62p ; 22cm
ISBN 0-905715-19-5 (pbk) : Unpriced
B81-22940

615.8'52'0924 — Christianity. Spiritual healing — *Personal observations*

Sanford, Agnes. Healing gifts of the spirit / by Agnes Sanford. — Evesham : James, 1966 (1980 [printing]). — 176p ; 20cm. — (Golden gift books)
ISBN 0-85305-210-7 (pbk) : £3.25 B81-12778

Stapleton, Ruth Carter. In his footsteps : the healing ministry of Jesus — then and now / Ruth Carter Stapleton. — London : Hodder and Stoughton, 1980, c1979. — 116p ; 18cm
Originally published: San Francisco : Harper and Row, c1979
ISBN 0-340-25886-1 (pbk) : £1.25 : CIP rev.
B80-12719

615.8'54 — Man. Therapy. Diet. Fibre

Medical aspects of dietary fiber / edited by Gene A. Spiller and Ruth McPherson Kay. — New York ; London : Plenum Medical, c1980. — xix,299p : ill ; 24cm. — (Topics in gastroenterology)
Includes index
ISBN 0-306-40507-5 : Unpriced B81-03992

615.8'54 — Medicine. Therapy. Diet

Robinson, Corinne H.. Basic nutrition and diet therapy / Corinne H. Robinson. — 4th ed. — New York : Macmillan ; London : Collier Macmillan, c1980. — ix,383p : ill ; 24cm
Previous ed.: New York : Macmillan, 1975. — Includes bibliographies and index
ISBN 0-02-402450-3 (pbk) : £5.75 B81-01844

615.8'54 — Medicine. Therapy. Diet — *Manuals*

Mayo clinic diet manual : a handbook of dietry practices / prepared by the dietetic staffs of the Mayo Clinic Rochester Methodist Hospital and St. Marys Hospital of Rochester Minnesota ; [editors Cecilia M. Pemberton, Clifford F. Gastineau ; editorial committee Carl F. Anderson ... et al.]. — 5th ed. — Philadelphia ; London : Saunders, 1981. — x,320p : 1form ; 26cm
Previous ed.: 1971. — Includes bibliographies and index
ISBN 0-7216-6212-9 (pbk) : £10.50 B81-29301

615.8'.54 — Medicine. Therapy. Honey — *Early works*

Hill, John. The virtues of honey. — 2nd ed. — Gerrards Cross : International Bee Research Association, July 1981. — [26]p. — (Texts of early bee books ; no.3)
Previous ed.: s.l: s.n., 17--?
ISBN 0-86098-099-5 : £6.00 : CIP entry
B81-21601

615.8'82'088042 — Folk medicine. Role of women, *to 1980*

Chamberlain, Mary. Old wives' tales : their history, remedies and spells / Mary Chamberlain. — London : Virago, c1981. — 284p : ill ; 21cm
Bibliography: p270-276. — Includes index
ISBN 0-86068-015-0 (cased) : £7.50 : CIP rev.
ISBN 0-86068-016-9 (pbk) : £4.50
Also classified at 615.8'82'09 B81-22504

615.8'82'09 — Folk medicine. Remedies, *to 1800 — Collections*

Chamberlain, Mary. Old wives' tales : their history, remedies and spells / Mary Chamberlain. — London : Virago, c1981. — 284p : ill ; 21cm
Bibliography: p270-276. — Includes index
ISBN 0-86068-015-0 (cased) : £7.50 : CIP rev.
ISBN 0-86068-016-9 (pbk) : £4.50
Primary classification 615.8'82'088042
B81-22504

615.8'82'094 — Europe. Folk medicine

Hand, Wayland D.. Magical medicine : the folkloric component of medicine in the folk belief, custom and ritual of the peoples of Europe and America : selected essays / of Wayland D. Hand ; foreword by Lloyd G. Stevenson. — Berkeley ; London : University of California Press, c1980. — xxvii,345p : ill,1port ; 24cm
Bibliography: pxiii-xxii. - Includes index
ISBN 0-520-04129-1 : £13.50
Also classified at 615.8'82'0973 B81-27511

615.8'82'09415 — Ireland. Folk medicine

Logan, Patrick. [Making the cure]. Irish country cures / Patrick Logan. — Belfast : Appletree, 1981. — xi,180p : ill ; 22cm
Originally published: Dublin : Talbot Press, 1972. — Includes index
ISBN 0-904651-80-0 (cased) : Unpriced : CIP rev.
ISBN 0-904651-81-9 (pbk) : Unpriced
B81-1807

615.8'82'0973 — United States. Folk medicine

Hand, Wayland D.. Magical medicine : the folkloric component of medicine in the folk belief, custom and ritual of the peoples of Europe and America : selected essays / of Wayland D. Hand ; foreword by Lloyd G. Stevenson. — Berkeley ; London : University of California Press, c1980. — xxvii,345p : ill,1port ; 24cm
Bibliography: pxiii-xxii. - Includes index
ISBN 0-520-04129-1 : £13.50
Primary classification 615.8'82'094 B81-2751

615.8'92 — Acupuncture

Austin, Mary, *1914-.* Acupuncture therapy : the philosophy, principles and methods of Chinese acupuncture / by Mary Austin ; illustrations by Denis Lawson-Wood. — [Abridged and rev. ed]. — Wellingborough : Turnstone, 1981. — 192p ; 22cm
Previous ed.: 1974. — Includes index
ISBN 0-85500-142-9 (pbk) : £3.75 B81-1783

Roberts, Michael J. (Michael John), *1945-.* Acupuncture therapy : its mode of action / by Michael J. Roberts. — Leicester (69 Desford Rd., Newbold Verdon, Leicester LE9 9LG) : Eresus Publications, c1981. — 17p ; 21cm
ISBN 0-9507758-0-0 (pbk) : £2.00 B81-3839

615.8'92 — Moxibustion

Low, Royston H.. The principles and practice of moxibustion. — Wellingborough : Thorsons, Sept.1981. — [96]p
ISBN 0-7225-0675-9 : £5.95 : CIP entry
B81-2151

615.8'92'06041 — Great Britain. Acupuncture. Organisations: British Acupuncture Association — *Directories — Serials*

British Acupuncture Association. Register and year book / British Acupuncture Association. — 1980/1982. — [Manchester] ([37 Peter St., Manchester M2 5QD]) : The Association, [1980?]. — 64p
£1.15 B81-3545

615.8'92'06041 — Great Britain. Acupuncture. Organisations: British Acupuncture Association — *Serials*

[Newsletter *(British Acupuncture Association)***].** Newsletter / the British Acupuncture Association. — Manchester (c/o Harvester House, 37 Peter St., Manchester M2 5QD) : The Association, 1976-. — v. ; 21cm
Three issues yearly. — Continues: Newsletter (Acupuncture Association)
ISSN 0260-5996 = Newsletter — British Acupuncture Association (corrected) : Unpriced B81-102

615.8'92'09 — Acupuncture, *to 1979*

Lu, Gwei-djen. Celestial lancets : a history and rationale of acupuncture and moxa / by Lu Gwei-djen and Joseph Needham. — Cambridge : Cambridge University Press, 1980. — xxi,427p : ill,facsims ; 26cm
Bibliography: p324-381. — Includes index
ISBN 0-521-21513-7 : £45.00 B81-016

615.8'92'0951 — China. Acupuncture, *1979*

Lewith, G. T.. Modern Chinese acupuncture / by G.T. Lewith and N.R. Lewith. — Wellingborough : Thorsons, 1980. — 12mp : ill ; 23cm
Includes index
ISBN 0-7225-0662-7 : £5.95 : CIP rev. B80-23323

615.9 — TOXICOLOGY

615.9 — Chemicals. Toxic effects — *Conference proceedings*

Symposium on Chemical Indices and Mechanisms of Organ-Directed Toxicity *(1981 : Barcelona)*. Organ-directed toxicity chemical indices and mechanisms. — Oxford : Pergamon, Oct.1981. — [400]p. — (IUPAC symposium series)
ISBN 0-08-026197-3 : £33.50 : CIP entry B81-28178

615.9 — Man. Acute poisoning

Proudfoot, Alexander T.. Diagnosis and management of acute poisoning. — Oxford : Blackwell Scientific, Sept.1981. — [150]p
ISBN 0-632-00584-x (pbk) : £5.00 : CIP entry B81-22618

615.9 — Man. Health. Toxic effects of environmental pollutants. Nutritional factors

Calabrese, Edward J.. Nutrition and environmental health : the influence of nutritional status on pollutant toxicity and carcinogenicity / Edward J. Calabrese. — New York ; Chichester : Wiley, c1981
Vol.2: Minerals and macronutrients. — xvi,468p : ill ; 24cm
Includes bibliographies and index
ISBN 0-471-08207-4 : £28.00 B81-23318

615.9 — Man. Liver. Toxic effects of drugs

Drug reactions and the liver. — Tunbridge Wells : Pitman Medical, May 1981. — [376]p
ISBN 0-272-79620-4 (pbk) : £25.00 : CIP entry B81-08843

615.9 — Man. Physiology. Toxic effects of anaesthetics

Bruce, David L.. Functional toxicity of anesthesia / David L. Bruce. — New York ; London : Grune & Stratton, c1980. — x,125p : ill ; 24cm. — (The Scientific basis of clinical anesthesia)
Includes index
ISBN 0-8089-1276-3 : £8.80 B81-04575

615.9 — Man. Poisoning

Poisoning : diagnosis and treatment / edited by J.A. Vale and T.J. Meredith. — London : Update, 1981. — 220p,[8]p of plates : ill(some col.) ; 26cm
Bibliography: p210-211. — Includes index
ISBN 0-906141-81-8 (cased) : Unpriced : CIP rev.
ISBN 0-906141-82-6 (pbk) : Unpriced B80-27081

615.9 — Medicine. Toxicology. Biochemical aspects

Reviews in biochemical toxicology. — New York ; Oxford : Elsevier
3 / editors Ernest Hodgson, John R. Bend, Richard M. Philpot. — c1981. — ix,368p : ill ; 25cm
ISBN 0-444-00436-x : Unpriced B81-25521

615.9 — Medicine. Toxicology — *Conference proceedings*

International Congress on Toxicology *(2nd : 1980 : Brussels)*. Mechanisms of toxicity and hazard evaluation : proceedings of the Second International Congress on Toxicology held in Brussels, Belgium, July 6-11, 1980 / editors B. Holmstedt ... [et al.]. — Amsterdam ; Oxford : Elsevier/North-Holland, 1980. — xiv,665p : ill ; 25cm
Includes index
ISBN 0-444-80293-2 : £32.79 B81-03390

615.9'0028 — Medicine. Toxicology. Laboratory techniques — *Manuals*

Standard operating procedures : analytical chemistry and metabolism / edited by I.P. Sword and A.W. Waddell. — Lancaster : MTP, c1981. — xv,295p : ill,forms ; 31cm
ISBN 0-85200-371-4 : £39.00 B81-23683

615.9'005 — Applied toxicology — *Serials*

Journal of applied toxicology : an international forum devoted to research and methods emphasizing direct clinical and industrial applications. — Vol.1, no.1 (Feb.1981)-. — Philadelphia, Pa. ; London : Heyden, 1981-. — v. : ill,maps ; 30cm
Six issues yearly. — 'Official medium of publication of the Genetic Toxicology Association'
ISSN 0260-437x = JAT. Journal of applied toxicology : £65.00 yearly B81-28385

615.9'005 — Medicine. Toxicology — *Serials*

[Toxicology *(New York)***]**. Toxicology : principles and practice. — Vol.1-. — New York ; Chichester : Wiley, 1981-. — v. ; 24cm
£13.50 B81-23504

615.9'02 — Industrial medicine. Toxicology

Patty, Frank Arthur. Patty's industrial hygiene and toxicology. — 3rd rev. ed. / George D. Clayton, Florence E. Clayton editors. — New York ; Chichester : Wiley
Vol.2A: Toxicology / contributors R.R. Beard ... [et al.]. — c1981. — xviiip,p1467-2878 : ill ; 24cm
Includes index
ISBN 0-471-16042-3 : £62.00
Primary classification 363.1'1'0973 B81-23243

615.9'02 — Xenobiotics. Biodegradation — *Conference proceedings*

Microbial degradation of xenobiotics and recalcitrant compounds. — London : Academic Press, Dec.1981. — [400]p
Conference papers
ISBN 0-12-442920-3 : CIP entry B81-31341

615.9'02'0941 — Great Britain. Industries. Materials. Toxic effects

Specimen safety data sheets for products of interest to BACS. — London (93 Albert Embankment SE1 TTU) : British Association for Chemical Specialities, 1981. — [47]leaves ; 31cm
Unpriced (pbk) B81-34703

615.9'07 — Chemicals. Toxic effects. Analysis

Testing for toxicity. — Basingstoke : Taylor and Francis, Sept.1981. — [400]p
ISBN 0-85066-218-4 : £18.00 : CIP entry B81-21587

615.9'08 — Man. Poisoning. Emergency treatment — *Manuals*

Czajka, Peter A.. Poisoning emergencies : a guide for emergency medical personnel / Peter A. Czajka, James P. Duffy. — St. Louis ; London : Mosby, 1980. — xiv,174p : ill ; 19cm
Text on inside cover. — Includes bibliographies and index
ISBN 0-8016-1205-5 (pbk) : Unpriced B81-08562

615.9'25 — Man. Toxic effects of mineral dusts. Research. Laboratory techniques. In vitro methods

The In vitro effects of mineral dusts / edited by R.C. Brown ... [et al.]. — London : Academic Press, 1980. — xx,373p : ill ; 24cm
Conference papers. — Includes bibliographies and index
ISBN 0-12-137240-5 : £20.00 : CIP rev. B80-09701

615.9'25625 — Man. Toxic effects of nickel — *Conference proceedings*

International Conference on Nickel Toxicology *(2nd : 1980 : Swansea)*. Nickel toxicology / [proceedings of the Second International Conference on Nickel Toxicology held from 3-5 September, 1980, in Swansea, Wales organised by the Subcommittee on Environmental and Occupational Toxicology of Nickel, Commission on Toxicology, International Union of Pure and Applied Chemistry, and the Association of Clinical Scientists] ; edited by Stanley S. Brown and F. William Sunderman, Jr. — London : Academic Press, 1980. — xx,193p : ill ; 24cm
Includes bibliographies and index
ISBN 0-12-137680-x : £15.00 B81-11376

615.9'5 — Naturally occurring toxins — *Conference proceedings*

International Symposium on Animal, Plant and Microbial Toxins *(6th : 1979 : Uppsala)*. Natural toxins : proceedings of the 6th International Symposium on Animal, Plant and Microbial Toxins, Uppsala, August 1979 / editors D. Eaker and T. Wadström. — Oxford : Pergamon, 1980. — xii,719p : ill ; 26cm
Includes bibliographies and index
ISBN 0-08-024952-3 : £45.00 : CIP rev. B80-12895

615.9'511 — Environment. Contamination by tetrachlorodibenzodioxin. Toxic effects — *Study regions: Italy. Seveso*

Whiteside, Thomas. The pendulum and the toxic cloud : the course of dioxin contamination / Thomas Whiteside. — New Haven ; London : Yale University Press, 1979. — 205p : ill ; 21cm
Bibliography: p187-200. - Includes index
ISBN 0-300-02274-3 (cased) : £9.45
ISBN 0-300-02283-2 (pbk) : Unpriced B81-09387

615.9'512 — Aromatic halogen compounds. Toxic effects. Environmental aspects

Halogenated biphenyls, terphenyls, napthalenes, dibenzodioxins and related products / editor Renate D. Kimbrough. — Amsterdam ; Oxford : Elsevier / North-Holland, 1980. — xi,406 : ill,maps ; 25cm. — (Topics in environmental health ; v.4)
Includes bibliographies and index
ISBN 0-444-80253-3 : £38.54 B81-07326

616 — MAN. DISEASES

616 — Adolescents. Medical aspects — *Conference proceedings*

Adolescent medicine : present and future concepts / editors C. Andrew Rigg, Robert B. Shearin. — Miami : Symposia Specialists ; Chicago ; London : Distributed by Year Book Medical, c1980. — 348,xvp : ill,1map,1plan ; 24cm. — (A Home study textbook program)
Includes bibliographies and index
ISBN 0-8151-7341-5 : £37.25 B81-09764

616 — Great Britain. Hospitals. House physicians. Duties — *Manuals*

Birch, C. Allan. The house physician's handbook. — 5th ed. / C. Allan Birch, S.J. Surtees, Richard Wray. — Edinburgh : Churchill Livingstone, 1980. — xiv,299p : ill ; 22cm
Previous ed.: / by C. Allan Birch, 1977. — Includes index
ISBN 0-443-02117-1 (pbk) : £4.95 : CIP rev. B80-08231

616 — Internal medicine — *Conference proceedings*

International Congress of Internal Medicine *(15th : 1980 : Hamburg)*. XVth International Congress of Internal Medicine, Hamburg, 18-22nd August 1980 : abstracts / editors H. Hornbostel, G. Strohmeyer, E. Schmidt. — Amsterdam ; Oxford : Excerpta medica, 1980. — 112p ; 25cm. — (International congress series ; no.536)
Includes index
ISBN 90-219-1245-7 (pbk) : £9.59 B81-01834

616 — Man. Acute diseases. Recovery. Psychological factors

Cousins, Norman. Anatomy of an illness as perceived by the patient : reflections on healing and regeneration / by Norman Cousins ; introduction by René Dubos. — New York ; London : Norton, c1979. — 173p ; 22cm
Bibliography: p163-173
ISBN 0-393-01252-2 : £5.75 B81-06350

Cousins, Norman. Anatomy of an illness as perceived by the patient : reflections on healing and regeneration / by Norman Cousins ; introduction by René Dubos. — Toronto ; London : Bantam, 1981, c1979. — 173p ; 21cm
Originally published: New York : London : Norton, c1979. — Bibliography: p163-173
ISBN 0-553-01293-2 (pbk) : £1.95 B81-27835

616 — Man. Acute diseases. Treatment. Psychosocial aspects

Stress and survival : the emotional realities of life-threatening illness / edited by Charles A. Garfield. — St. Louis ; London : Mosby, 1979. — xviii,388p : ill ; 27cm
Includes bibliographies and index
ISBN 0-8016-1743-x : £10.50 B81-12000

616 — Man. Diseases

Boyd, William, *1885-1979*. Introduction of the study of disease / William Boyd, Huntingdon Sheldon. — Philadelphia : Lea & Febiger ; London : Kimpton, 1980. — 660p : ill,maps,ports ; 27cm
Previous ed.: 1977. — Text, ill on lining papers. — Includes bibliographies and index
ISBN 0-8121-0729-2 : £9.00 B81-16118

Controversies in clinical care / edited by Victor M. Rosenoer and Marcus Rothschild. — Lancaster : MTP, c1981. — 234p : ill ; 24cm
Includes bibliographies and index
ISBN 0-85200-565-2 : £17.75 B81-38032

Davidson, *Sir* **Stanley**. Davidson's principles and practice of medicine : a textbook for students and doctors. — 13th ed. / edited by John Macleod. — Edinburgh : Churchill Livingstone, 1981. — xiii,943p,iip of plates : ill (some col.) ; 24cm
Previous ed.: 1977. — Includes bibliographies and index
ISBN 0-443-02487-1 (cased) : Unpriced
ISBN 0-443-02489-8 (pbk) : £11.50 B81-32989

Family guide to common ailments / medical advisor Joan Gomez ; additional contributions Nicola McClure and Nigel Perryman. — London : Hamlyn, c1981. — 240p : col.ill ; 28cm
Includes index
ISBN 0-600-33210-1 : £6.95 B81-38670

Houston, J. C.. A short textbook of medicine. — 7th ed. — London : Hodder & Stoughton, Oct.1981. — [760]p. — (University medical texts)
Previous ed.: 1979
ISBN 0-340-26758-5 (pbk) : £7.45 : CIP entry B81-24629

Reese, A. J. M.. The principles of pathology. — 2nd ed. — Bristol : J. Wright, Oct.1981. — [256]p
Previous ed.: 1974
ISBN 0-7236-0603-x (pbk) : £7.50 : CIP entry B81-24638

Rubenstein, David. Lecture notes on clinical medicine / David Rubenstein, David Wayne. — 2nd ed. — Oxford : Blackwell Scientific, 1980. — xii,323p : ill ; 24cm
Previous ed.: 1976. — Bibliography: p301-303. - Includes index
ISBN 0-632-00545-9 (pbk) : £6.50 : CIP rev. B80-09251

616 — Man. Diseases & injuries

Bevan, James. The pocket medical encyclopedia and first aid guide : emergencies, symptoms, treatments / James Bevan. — London : Mitchell Beazley, c1979. — 144p : ill(some col.),1col.plan ; 20cm
Includes index
ISBN 0-85533-151-8 (pbk) : Unpriced B81-09955

616 — Man. Diseases. Psychosocial aspects

Kimball, Chase Patterson. The biopsychosocial approach to the patient / Chase Patterson Kimball. — Baltimore ; London : Williams & Wilkins, 1981. — xvi,381p ; 23cm
Includes index
ISBN 0-683-04616-0 (pbk) : £21.00 B81-13667

616 — Man. High risk diseases. Nutritional aspects

Nutrition and the killer diseases / edited by Myron Winick. — New York ; Chichester : Wiley, c1981. — viii,191p : ill ; 24cm. — (Current concepts in nutrition ; 10)
Includes index
ISBN 0-471-09130-8 : £22.75 B81-33151

616'.001'9 — Man. Sickness. Psychological aspects

Lewis, S. A.. Psychology applied to medicine : old wine in new bottles : an inaugural lecture delivered before the Queen's University of Belfast on 6 February 1980 / S.A. Lewis. — [Belfast] : Queen's University of Belfast, c1980. — 22p : ill ; 21cm. — (New lecture series / Queen's University of Belfast ; no.123)
ISBN 0-85389-187-7 (pbk) : £0.40 B81-05765

616'.001'9 — Medicine. Diagnosis & therapy. Decision making

Weinstein, Milton C.. Clinical decision analysis / Milton C. Weinstein, Harvey V. Fineberg [with] Arthur S. Elstein ... [et al.]. — Philadelphia ; London : Saunders, 1980. — xiii,351p : ill ; 27cm
Bibliography: p305-315. - Includes index
ISBN 0-7216-9166-8 : £14.25 B81-04627

616'.0024613 — Man. Diseases — *For nursing*

Toohey, M.. Toohey's medicine for nurses. — 13th ed., by Arnold Bloom. — Edinburgh : Churchill Livingstone, 1981. — 522p : ill(some col.),1port ; 22cm
Previous ed.: 1978. — Includes index
ISBN 0-443-02201-1 (pbk) : £6.95 B81-15243

Understanding nursing care / edited by Anne M. Chilman, Margaret Thomas. — 2nd ed. — Edinburgh : Churchill Livingstone, 1981. — 595p : ill(some col.) ; 29cm
Previous ed.: 1978. — Includes bibliographies and index
ISBN 0-443-02563-0 (cased) : Unpriced
ISBN 0-443-02160-0 (pbk) : £11.95 B81-35613

616'.0024613 — Man. Diseases — *Questions & answers — For nursing*

SEN review book : objective test questions for pupil nurses / edited and compiled by Lynn Copcutt. — Hemel Hempstead (P.O. Box 81, Hemel Hempstead, Herts.) : Pastest Service, 1981. — viii,104p ; 22cm
ISBN 0-906896-02-9 (pbk) : Unpriced B81-23967

SRN review book : objective test questions for student nurses / edited and compiled by Lynn Copcutt. — Hemel Hempstead (P.O. Box 81, Hemel Hempstead, Herts.) : Pastest Service, 1981. — x,102p ; 22cm
ISBN 0-906896-01-0 (pbk) : Unpriced B81-23966

616'.0024617 — Man. Diseases - *For anaesthesia*

Vickers, M. D.. Medicine for anaesthetists. — 2nd ed. — Oxford : Blackwell Scientific, Aug.1981. — [616]p
Previous ed.: 1977
ISBN 0-632-00737-0 : £26.00 : CIP entry B81-16934

616'.00246171 — Man. Diseases — *Questions & answers — For surgery*

Kelly, M. J.. Questions and answers in surgery for students / M.J. Kelly, Gill Kelly, H.P. Henderson ; with a foreword by R.Y. Calne. — Bristol : Wright, 1981. — xiv,319p ; 19cm
Includes index
ISBN 0-7236-0601-3 (pbk) : Unpriced : CIP rev. B81-13754

616'.00246176 — Man. Diseases - *For dentistry*

Human disease for dental students. — London : Pitman Medical, Apr.1981. — [368]p
ISBN 0-272-79608-5 (pbk) : £9.95 : CIP entry B81-03685

616'.003'21 — Man. Diseases — *Encyclopaedias*

Carding, David Kellett. The family medical handbook : an A-Z guide / David Kellett Carding. — 2nd ed. — London : Faber, 1981. — 263p : ill ; 19cm
Previous ed. published as: The home medical guide, 1976
ISBN 0-571-18027-2 : £4.95 B81-13040

Smiddy, F. G.. Dictionary of general pathology / F.G. Smiddy. — Tunbridge Wells : Pitman Medical, 1980. — 326p ; 21x10cm
ISBN 0-272-79585-2 (pbk) : £4.95 : CIP rev. B80-05388

616'.005 — Internal medicine — *Serials*

Advances in internal medicine. — Vol.26 (1980). — Chicago ; London : Year Book Medical Publishers, c1980. — xxviii,599p
ISBN 0-8151-8296-1 : Unpriced
ISSN 0065-2822 B81-25499

616'.005 — Man. Diseases — *Serials*

Clinical Research Centre. Biennial report / Clinical Research Centre. — 1976/1977. — London ([20 Park Cres., W1N 4AL]) : Medical Research Council, 1978. — 285p
ISSN 0141-2108 : Unpriced B81-34060

Clinical Research Centre. Biennial report / Clinical Research Centre. — 1976/1977. — London ([20 Park Cres., W1N 4AL]) : Medical Research Council, 1979. — 224p
ISSN 0141-2108 : Unpriced B81-34065

616'.0072 — Man. Diseases. Research — *Serials*

Clinical research reviews / editors: Janssen Pharmaceutical Ltd. — Vol.1 (1981)-. — Marlow ([Janssen House, Marlow, Bucks. SL7 1ET]) : Janssen Pharmaceutical Ltd., 1981-. — v. : ; 24cm
Six issues yearly
ISSN 0260-8367 = Clinical research reviews : Unpriced B81-33289

616'.0076 — Man. Diseases — *Questions & answers*

MRCP Part 1 review book : multiple choice questions / compiled and edited by B. I. Hoffbrand in collaboration with teaching staff from the Academic Centre, Whittington Hospital, London, the Medical School, University of Newcastle-upon-Tyne ; foreword by J. Anderson. — 2nd ed. — Hemel Hempstead (P.O. Box 81, Hemel Hempstead, Herts.) : Pastest Service, 1981. — x,150p ; 22cm
Previous ed.: 1980
ISBN 0-906896-03-7 (pbk) : Unpriced B81-23965

616'.00880625 — Virginia. Negro slaves. Diseases, *1770-1860*

Savitt, Todd L.. Medicine and slavery : the diseases and health care of blacks in an antebellum Virginia / Todd L. Savitt. — Urbana ; London : University of Illinois Press, c1978. — 332p : ill,maps ; 24cm. — (Blacks in the New World)
Includes index
ISBN 0-252-00653-4 : £9.00 B81-11256

616'.01 — Man. Immune reactions. Microbiological aspects — *Conference proceedings*

Microbial perturbation of host defences. — London : Academic Press, Sept.1981. — [250]p
Conference papers
ISBN 0-12-524750-8 : CIP entry B81-23873

616'.01 — Man. Pathogens: Microorganisms

Smith, Alice Lorraine. Microbiology and pathology / Alice Lorraine Smith. — 12th ed. — St. Louis ; London : Mosby, 1980. — xii,851p,[3] leaves of plates : ill(some col.) ; 25cm
Previous ed.: 1976. — Includes bibliographies and index
ISBN 0-8016-4673-1 : £14.00
Also classified at 616.07 B81-08040

616.01 — Medicine. Microbiology

Collee, J. G.. Applied medical microbiology. — 2nd ed. — Oxford : Blackwell Scientific, Aug.1981. — [144]p. — (Basic microbiology ; v.3)
Previous ed.: 1976
ISBN 0-632-00853-9 (pbk) : £4.50 : CIP entry B81-19218

616'.01 — Medicine. Microbiology

Grüneberg, R. N.. Microbiology for clinicians / R.N. Grüneberg. — Lancaster : MTP, 1981. — 179p : ill ; 25cm
Bibliography: p173-174. — Includes index
ISBN 0-85200-386-2 : £11.95 B81-27091

Smith, Alice Lorraine. Principles of microbiology / Alice Lorraine Smith. — 9th ed. — St. Louis ; London : Mosby, 1981. — x,723p : ill ; 25cm
Previous ed.: 1977. — Includes bibliographies and index
ISBN 0-8016-4682-0 : £12.50 B81-28921

616'.014 — Man. Pathogens: Anaerobic bacteria

Willis, A. T.. Management of anaerobic infections : prevention and treatment / A.T. Willis, P.H. Jones and S. Reilly. — Chichester : Research Studies Press, 1981. — viii,97p ; 24cm. — (Antimicrobial chemotherapy research studies series ; 1)
Bibliography: p59-91. — Includes index
ISBN 0-471-28037-2 : £9.50 : CIP rev. B81-09966

616'.014 — Man. Pathogens: Bacteria. Toxins

Stephen, J.. Bacterial toxins / J. Stephen, R.A. Pietrowski. — Walton-on-Thames : Nelson, 1981. — 104p : ill ; 22cm. — (Aspects of microbiology)
Includes bibliographies and index
ISBN 0-17-771102-7 (pbk) : £2.75 B81-12659

616'.014 — Medicine. Anaerobic bacteriology — *Manuals*

Silver, Sylvia. Anaerobic bacteriology for the clinical laboratory / Sylvia Silver. — St. Louis ; London : Mosby, 1980. — x,118p : ill ; 23cm
Includes bibliographies and index
ISBN 0-8016-4625-1 (pbk) : £6.75 B81-08042

Sutter, Vera L.. Wadsworth anaerobic bacteriology manual / Vera L. Sutter, Diane M. Citron, Sidney M. Finegold, with a chapter on gas-liquid chromatography by Kenneth S. Bricknell. — 3rd ed. — St. Louis ; London : Mosby, 1980. — xi,131p : ill ; 24cm
Previous ed.: Los Angeles : UCLA School of Medicine, 1975. — Bibliographies: p116-124. - Includes index
ISBN 0-8016-4848-3 (pbk) : £6.75 B81-08041

616'.014 — Medicine. Bacteriology

Notes on medical bacteriology. — Edinburgh : Churchill Livingstone, Sept.1981. — [320]p. — (Churchill Livingstone medical text)
ISBN 0-443-02264-x (pbk) : £5.95 : CIP entry B81-22639

616'.014'2 — Man. Staphylococci - *Conference proceedings*

The **Staphylococci**. — Aberdeen : Aberdeen University Press, Apr.1981. — [152]p
Conference papers
ISBN 0-08-025749-6 : CIP entry B81-04351

616'.014'5 — Man. Pathogens: Escherichia coli

Glass, Robert E.. Gene function. — London : Croom Helm, Oct.1981. — [448]p
ISBN 0-7099-0081-3 (cased) : £19.95 : CIP entry
ISBN 0-7099-0082-1 (pbk) : £9.95 B81-24658

616'.015 — Man. Pathogens: Fungi. Identification. Laboratory techniques

Campbell, Mary C.. The medical mycology handbook / Mary C. Campbell, Joyce L. Stewart ; foreword by Howard W. Larsh. — New York ; Chichester : Wiley, c1980. — xvi,436p : ill(some col.) ; 23cm
Includes bibliographies and index
ISBN 0-471-04728-7 (spiral) : £13.30 B81-04463

616'.0194 — Man. Pathogens: Viruses

Principles of animal virology / edited by Wolfgang K. Joklik. — New York : Appleton-Century-Crofts ; London : Prentice-Hall, c1980. — x,373p,1 leaf of plates : ill(some col.),2maps ; 27cm
Includes bibliographies and index
ISBN 0-8385-7920-5 : £14.25 B81-03343

616'.0194 — Tropical medicine. Virology

Metselaar, D.. Practical virology for medical students and practitioners in tropical countries. — Oxford : Oxford University Press, Feb.1982. — [400]p. — (Oxford medical publications)
ISBN 0-19-261317-0 (pbk) : £6.95 : CIP entry B81-35771

616'.0194'05 — Medicine. Virology — *Serials*

Progress in medical virology. — Vol.27. — Basel ; London : Karger ; [Chichester] : [Wiley] [distributor], 1981. — 210p
ISBN 3-8055-1784-x : £31.25 B81-29984

616'.025 — Medicine. Emergency treatment

Birch's emergencies in medical practice. — 11th ed. / edited by Colin Ogilvie. — Edinburgh : Churchill Livingstone, 1981. — xv,351p : ill ; 26cm
Previous ed.: published as Emergencies in medical practice. 1976. — Includes bibliographies and index
ISBN 0-443-01983-5 : £18.95 : CIP rev. B80-31649

Textbook of basic emergency medicine. — 2nd ed. / [edited by] Robert H. Miller. — St. Louis ; London : Mosby, 1980. — x,283p : ill ; 24cm
Previous ed.: 1975. — Includes index
ISBN 0-8016-3449-0 (pbk) : Unpriced B81-21262

616'.025 — Medicine. Emergency treatment — *Conference proceedings*

International Congress on Immediate Care *(1980 : Brighton)*. Immediate prehospital care : the proceedings of the International Congress on Immediate Care, Brighton, England, 22nd-25th October 1980 / edited by Peter J.F. Baskett. — Chichester : Wiley, c1981. — xiv,290p : ill,maps ; 24cm. — (A Wiley medical publication)
Includes bibliographies and index
ISBN 0-471-28035-6 : £16.00 : CIP rev. B81-06619

616'.025 — Medicine. Emergency treatment — *Manuals*

Emergency medicine / [edited by] Roger Evans. — London : Butterworths, 1981. — x,465p : ill ; 24cm
Includes bibliographies and index
ISBN 0-407-00172-7 : Unpriced : CIP rev. B81-14974

Hardy, R. H.. Accidents and emergencies : a practical handbook for personal use / R.H. Hardy. — 3rd ed. — Oxford : Oxford University Press, 1981. — xiii,177leaves : ill ; 19cm. — (Oxford medical publications)
Previous ed.: 1978. — Bibliography: p166-169. — Includes index
ISBN 0-19-261321-9 (pbk) : £5.50 B81-36154

Wilson, Frank. Essential accident and emergency care. — Lancaster : MTP Press, July 1981. — [300]p
ISBN 0-85200-307-2 : £7.95 : CIP entry B81-19208

616'.025 — Medicine. Emergency treatment — *Manuals — For paramedics*

Copass, Michael K.. The paramedic manual / Michael K. Copass, Mickey S. Eisenberg. — Philadelphia ; London : Saunders, 1980. — xvii,283p : ill ; 20cm. — (W.B. Saunders red books)
Text on inside covers. — Includes index
ISBN 0-7216-2716-1 (spiral) : £7.00 B81-03408

Wasserberger, Jonathan. Practical paramedic procedures / Jonathan Wasserberger, David H. Eubanks. — 2nd ed. — St. Louis ; London : Mosby, 1981. — xvi,222p : ill,forms ; 24cm
Previous ed.: published as Advanced paramedic procedures. 1977. — Bibliography: p213-215. — Includes index
ISBN 0-8016-5353-3 (pbk) : £8.50 B81-31149

616'.025 — Medicine. Emergency treatment. Triage

Rund, Douglas A.. Triage / Douglas A. Rund, Tondra S. Rausch. — St. Louis ; London : Mosby, 1981. — ix,255p : ill,plans,forms ; 24cm
Includes index
ISBN 0-8016-4221-3 (pbk) : £9.75 B81-24239

616'.025'076 — Medicine. Emergency treatment — *Questions & answers — For paramedics*

Wills, Sheryle L.. Paramedic review : a manual for examination preparation / Sheryle L. Wills, Sharyn A. Tremblay. — St. Louis ; London : Mosby, 1981. — xi,260p : ill ; 24cm
ISBN 0-8016-5688-5 (pbk) : £7.75 B81-31150

616.02'52 — First aid — *For children*

Winch, Brenda. First aid. — London : Macmillan Children's Books, Feb.1982. — [32]p. — (Help yourself)
ISBN 0-333-30861-1 : £2.50 : CIP entry B81-35781

616.02'52 — First aid — *For industries*

Great Britain. *Health and Safety Commission*. Health and Safety (First-Aid) Regulations 1981. — London : Health & Safety Executive, Aug.1981. — [20]p
ISBN 0-11-883447-9 (pbk) : CIP entry B81-25132

Great Britain. *Health and Safety Executive*. First aid at work. — London : Health and Safety Executive, Aug.1981. — [50]p. — (Health & safety series booklet ; HS(R)11)
ISBN 0-11-883446-0 (pbk) : CIP entry B81-24608

Taylor, Stephen James Lake Taylor, *Baron*. First aid in the factory : and on the building site and farm, in the shop, office and warehouse, with a new chapter on first aid in the home / Lord Taylor of Harlow ; with a foreword by A. Austin Eagger. — 5th ed. / with the assistance of Prudence D. Wright and Evelyn Craven. — London : Longman, 1981. — xiii,174p : ill,1facsim ; 22cm
Previous ed.: / with the assistance of Prudence D. Wright. 1973. — Includes index
ISBN 0-582-41587-x (pbk) : £4.95 B81-07063

616.02'52 — First aid — *Manuals*

Andrew, Robert. The Hamlyn family first aid book / Robert Andrew ; foreword by David Delvin ; line drawings by David Farris. — London : Hamlyn Paperbacks, 1981. — 158p ; 18cm
Includes index
ISBN 0-600-20011-6 (pbk) : £1.50 B81-12594

Jeffery, Mervyn. Nuttall's first aid / by Mervyn Jeffery. — London : Warne, 1979. — 47p : ill ; 15cm
Bibliography: p46. — Includes index
ISBN 0-7232-2252-5 (pbk) : £0.35 B81-17899

Paterson-Brown, P. N.. A matter of life or death / by P.N. Paterson-Brown. — New ed. — [S.l.] ; [Scotland] : [P.N. Paterson-Brown] ; Hawick (Carnarvon St., Hawick, Scotland) : Buccleuch Printers Ltd. [distributor], 1977 (1980 [printing]). — 16p : ill ; 21cm
Previous ed.: 1975
£0.40 (pbk) B81-00919

616.02'52 — First aid — *Manuals — For outdoor activities*

Breyfogle, Newell D.. The common sense medical guide and outdoor reference / Newell D. Breyfogle ; medical advisors Sherman C. Meschter, John A. Reyburn, Jr. ; illustrated by Allan Parker. — New York ; London : McGraw-HIll, c1981. — xv,413p : ill ; 18cm
Text on inside covers. — Bibliography: p394-399. — Includes index
ISBN 0-07-007672-3 (cased) : Unpriced
ISBN 0-07-007673-1 (pbk) : £4.95 B81-27887

616.02'52'0243694 — First aid — *Manuals — For Girl Guides*

Field, Lynette. Health & first aid : for camps & holidays / Lynette Field. — London (17 Buckingham Palace Rd., SW1W 0PT) : Girl Guides Association, 1981. — 32p : ill ; 21cm
£0.50 (pbk) B81-22247

616.02'52'024649 — First aid - *Manuals - For housewives*

Creese, Angela. Safety for your family. — 2nd ed. — London : Bell & Hyman, Aug.1981. — [281]p
Previous ed.: London : Mills & Boon, 1968
ISBN 0-7135-2070-1 (pbk) : CIP entry
Primary classification 643'.028'9 B81-16361

616'.028 — Critically ill patients. Intensive care

Current practice in critical care. — St. Louis ; London : Mosby. — (Mosby's current practice and perspectives in nursing series)
Vol.1. — 1979. — xx,267p : ill ; 26cm
Includes bibliographies
ISBN 0-8016-3521-7 (cased) : Unpriced
ISBN 0-8016-3522-5 (pbk) : Unpriced
B81-09606

Mosby's comprehensive review of critical care / edited by Donna A. Zschoche. — 2nd ed. — St. Louis ; London : Mosby, 1981. — xxii,961p : ill,forms ; 25cm
Previous ed.: 1976. — Includes index
ISBN 0-8016-5697-4 : £18.25 B81-09609

616'.028 — Critically ill patients. Intensive care — *Conference proceedings*

Emergency management of the critically ill / editors Arnold Aberman, Alexander G. Logan. — Miami : Symposia Specialists ; Chicago ; London : Distributed by Year Book Medical, c1980. — 404,xvi p : ill ; 24cm
Includes bibliographies and index
ISBN 0-8151-0003-5 : £37.75 B81-09770

Panamerican Congress on Critical Care Medicine *(1st : 1979 : Mexico City)*. Critical care medicine : proceedings of the first Panamerican Congress on Critical Care Medicine, Mexico City, September 23-27, 1979 / editors: Alberto Villazón ... [et. al]. — Amsterdam ; Oxford : Excerpta Medica, 1980. — vi,230p : ill ; 25cm. — (International congress series ; 503)
Includes indexes
ISBN 0-444-90128-0 : £22.96 B81-00920

616'.028 — Critically ill patients. Intensive care — *Manuals*

Atkinson, R. S.. Handbook of intensive care / R.S. Atkinson, J.J. Hamblin and J.E.C. Wright. — London : Chapman and Hall, 1981. — ix,386p : ill ; 24cm
Includes bibliographies and index
ISBN 0-412-14010-1 : Unpriced: CIP rev.
B81-14415

Standards for critical care / Brenda Crispell Johanson ... [et al.]. — St. Louis ; London : Mosby, 1981. — xii,535p : ill ; 26cm
Bibliography: p517-522. — Includes index
ISBN 0-8016-2527-0 (pbk) : £11.25 B81-18967

616'.028 — Medicine. Intensive care

Intensive care. — Lancaster : MTP Press, Nov.1981. — [525]p
ISBN 0-85200-340-4 : £14.95 : CIP entry
B81-33647

616'.028 — Medicine. Intensive care — *Manuals*

Intensive care therapeutics / edited by Joseph M. Civetta. — New York : Appleton-Century-Crofts ; London : Prentice-Hall, c1980. — xii,402p : ill ; 23cm
Includes index
ISBN 0-8385-4305-7 (pbk) : £11.40 B81-04124

616'.028'024613 — Medicine. Intensive care — *For nursing*

AACN's clinical reference for critical-care nursing / editor-in-chief Marguerite Rodgers Kinney ; editors Cynthia Boyd Dear, Donna Rogers Packa, Dorothy M. Nagelhout Voorman. — New York ; London : McGraw-Hill, c1981. — xviii,1229p : ill ; 26cm
Col. ill on lining papers. — Includes bibliographies and index
ISBN 0-07-001133-8 : £34.50 B81-10207

Hamilton, Ardith J.. [Selected subjects for critical care nurses]. Critical care nursing skills / Ardith J. Hamilton. — New York : Appleton-Century-Crofts ; London : Prentice-Hall, c1981. — ix,277p : ill ; 24cm
Originally published: Missoula : Mountain Press Publishing, 1975. — Includes bibliographies and index
ISBN 0-8385-1242-9 (pbk) : Unpriced
B81-33363

Intensive care for nurses / edited by D.B. Clarke and A.D. Barnes. — 3rd ed. — Oxford : Blackwell Scientific, 1980. — ix,197p : ill ; 22cm
Previous ed.: 1975. — Inlcudes index
ISBN 0-632-00696-x (pbk) : £6.75 B81-00921

616'.042 — Isolated communities. Genetic disorders — *Conference proceedings*

Sigrid Jusélius Foundation. *Symposium (7th : 1978 : Mariehamn)*. Population structure and genetic disorders : Seventh Sigrid Jusélius Foundation Symposium, Mariehamn, Aland Islands, Finland, August 1978 / edited by Aldur W. Eriksson ... [et al.]. — London : Academic Press, 1980. — xvii,690p : ill,maps,1port ; 24cm
Includes bibliographies and index
ISBN 0-12-241450-0 : £55.00 : CIP rev.
B80-09702

616'.042 — Man. Diseases. Genetic factors — *For counselling*

Harper, Peter S.. Practical genetic counselling / by Peter S. Harper. — Bristol : Wright, 1981. — ix,285p : ill ; 23cm
Includes index
ISBN 0-7236-0567-x : £12.50 B81-09859

616'.042 — Man. Genetic disorders

Milunsky, Aubrey. Know your genes / Aubrey Milunsky. — Harmondsworth : Penguin, 1980, c1977. — 320p : ill ; 20cm. — (Pelican books)
Originally published: Boston : Houghton Mifflin, 1977. — Includes index
ISBN 0-14-022286-3 (pbk) : £2.50 B81-00922

616'.042 — Man. Genetics. Medical aspects

Kelly, Thaddeus E.. Clinical genetics and genetic counseling / Thaddeus E. Kelly. — Chicago ; London : Year Book Medical, c1980. — xi,425p : ill ; 24cm
Includes bibliographies and index
ISBN 0-8151-5011-3 : £24.50 B81-15003

616'.043 — Man. Congenital abnormalities

Cardiovascular, respiratory, gastrointestinal and genitourinary malformations. — Lancaster : MTP Press, Aug.1981. — [240]p. — (Advances in the study of birth defects ; v.6)
ISBN 0-85200-397-8 : £18.50 : CIP entry
B81-22580

Developmental toxicology. — London : Croom Helm, Sept.1981. — [352]p
ISBN 0-7099-2306-6 : £18.95 : CIP entry
B81-28059

Genetic disorders, syndromology and prenatal diagnosis. — Lancaster : MTP Press, Aug.1981. — [270]p. — (Advances in the study of birth defects ; v.5)
ISBN 0-85200-396-x : £18.50 : CIP entry
B81-22682

616'.047 — Immunocompromised patients. Infection

International Symposium on Infections in the Immunocompromised Host *(1st : 1980 : Veldhoven)*. Infections in the immunocompromised host : pathogenesis, prevention and therapy : proceedings of the First International Symposium on Infections in the Immunocompromised Host held in Veldhoven, The Netherlands, 1-5 June, 1980 / editors Jan Verhoef, Phillip K. Peterson, Paul G. Quie. — Amsterdam ; Oxford : Elsevier, 1980. — viii,315p : ill ; 25cm. — (Developments in immunology ; v.11)
Includes index
ISBN 0-444-80287-8 : £15.56 B81-04479

616'.047 — Man. Diseases. Neuropsychological aspects

Jefferson, James W.. Neuropsychiatric features of medical disorders / James W. Jefferson and John R. Marshall. — New York ; London : Plenum Medical, c1981. — xx,383p : ill ; 26cm. — (Critical issues in psychiatry)
Includes bibliographies and index
ISBN 0-306-40674-8 : Unpriced B81-34971

616'.047 — Man. Head. Headaches

Wilkinson, Marcia. Headaches and migraine. — London : Martin Dunitz, Aug.1981. — [96]p. — (Positive health guides)
ISBN 0-906348-17-x (pbk) : £5.95 : CIP entry
ISBN 0-906348-18-8 (pbk) : £2.50 B81-16918

616'.0472 — Man. Chronic pain. Therapy

Pawl, Ronald Phillip. Chronic pain primer / Ronald Phillip Pawl. — Chicago ; London : Year Book Medical, c1979. — xv,206p : ill,forms ; 21cm
Includes bibliographies and index
ISBN 0-8151-6650-8 (pbk) : £12.75 B81-07303

The **Therapy** of pain / edited by Mark Swerdlow. — Lancaster : MTP, 1981. — xix,250p : ill ; 25cm. — (Current status of modern therapy ; v.6)
Includes index
ISBN 0-85200-259-9 : £16.95 : CIP rev.
B80-33652

616'.0472 — Man. Head. Headaches. Therapy. Diet

Nightingale, Michael. Diets to help headaches / by Michael Nightingale. — Wellingborough : Thorsons, 1981. — 47p ; 18cm
ISBN 0-7225-0649-x (pbk) : Unpriced
B81-08534

616'.0472 — Man. Pain. Drug therapy. Buprenorphine — *Conference proceedings*

A **New** route to pain relief. — Oxford (52 New Inn Hall St., Oxford OX1 2BS) : Medicine Publishing Foundation, Dec.1981. — [16]p. — (Medicine forum, ISSN 0260-9312 ; 2)
Conference papers
ISBN 0-906817-16-1 (pbk) : £2.50 : CIP entry
B81-32046

616'.0472 — Man. Pain. Relief

Persistent pain. — London : Academic Press, June 1981
Vol.3. — [220]p
ISBN 0-12-792573-2 : CIP entry B81-12330

616'.0472 — Man. Pain. Relief — *Conference proceedings*

Pain, discomfort and humanitarian care : proceedings of the national conference held at the National Institutes of Health, Bethesda, Maryland, U.S.A., February 15-16, 1979 / editors Lorenz K.Y. Ng, John J. Bonica. — New York ; Oxford : Elsevier/North-Holland, c1980. — xv,371p : ill ; 25cm. — (Developments in neurology ; v.4)
Includes bibliographies and index
ISBN 0-444-00399-1 : £20.44 B81-02191

616.07 — Clinical medicine. Reference values

Reference values in laboratory medicine. — Chichester : Wiley, Jan.1982. — [360]p
Conference papers
ISBN 0-471-28025-9 : £16.50 : CIP entry
B81-34662

616.07 — Man. Cells. Diseases

Dixon, K. C.. Cellular defects in disease. — Oxford : Blackwell Scientific, July 1981. — [464]p
ISBN 0-632-00734-6 : £16.50 : CIP entry
B81-15919

616.07 — Man. Diseases. Anatomical aspects

Sandritter, Walter. Color atlas & textbook of macropathology / by Walter Sandritter and C. Thomas ; translated and edited by W.H. Kirsten. — 3rd English ed. — Chicago ; London : Year Book Medical, c1979. — xvi,379p : ill(some col.) ; 26cm
Translation of: Makropathologie. 4.Aufl. — Bibliography: p342-348.— Includes index
ISBN 0-8151-7549-3 : £53.50 B81-06356

616.07 — Man. Diseases. Biochemical aspects

Applied biochemistry of clinical disorders / edited by Allan G. Gornall. — Hagerstown ; London : Harper & Row, c1980. — xvi,444p : ill ; 26cm
Includes bibliographies and index
ISBN 0-06-141010-1 : £19.50 B81-22986

616.07 — Man. Diseases. Physiological aspects

Kelman, G. R.. Physiology : a clinical approach / G.R. Kelman. — 3rd ed. / with chapters 14 and 15 by T.J. Crow. — Edinburgh : Churchill Livingstone, 1980. — 211p : ill ; 22cm. — (Churchill Livingstone medical texts)
Previous ed.: 1975
ISBN 0-443-01820-0 (pbk) : £3.95 : CIP rev.
B80-17724

616.07 — Man. Diseases. Physiological aspects *continuation*

Stephens, Gwen J.. Pathophysiology for health practitioners / Gwen J. Stephens. — New York : Macmillan ; London : Collier Macmillan, c1980. — xiii,657p : ill ; 26cm
Includes bibliographies and index
ISBN 0-02-417120-4 : £13.75 B81-02775

616.07 — Man. Diseases. Role of lysosomes & plasma membranes — *Conference proceedings*

Cell biological aspects of disease : the plasma membrane and lysosomes / edited by W. Th. Daems, E.H. Burger, B.A. Afzelius. — The Hague ; London : Leiden University Press, 1981. — xi,337p : ill ; 25cm. — (Boerhaave series for postgraduate medical education ; v.19)
Conference papers. — Includes index
ISBN 90-602-1466-8 : Unpriced B81-14651

616.07 — Medicine. Pathology

Dixon, Michael F.. Aids to pathology / Michael F. Dixon. — 2nd ed.. — Edinburgh : Churchill Livingstone, 1981. — 252p : ill ; 22cm
Previous ed.: 1978. — Includes bibliographies and index
ISBN 0-443-02383-2 (pbk) : £4.95 B81-40196

Dixon, Michael F.. Aids to pathology / Michael F. Dixon. — 2nd ed. — Edinburgh : Churchill Livingstone, 1981. — 252p : ill ; 22cm
Previous ed.: 1978. — Bibliography: p249. — Includes index
ISBN 0-443-02549-5 (pbk) : £1.95 B81-38264

Govan, Alasdair D. T.. Pathology illustrated / Alasdair D.T. Govan, Peter S. Macfarlane, Robin Callander. — Edinburgh : Churchill Livingstone, 1981. — 866p : ill ; 25cm
Includes index
ISBN 0-443-01647-x (pbk) : £13.95 B81-15247

Govan, Alasdair D. T.. Pathology illustrated / Alasdair D.T. Govan, Peter S. Macfarlane, Robin Callander. — International student ed. — Edinburgh : Churchill Livingstone, 1981. — 866p : ill ; 25cm
Includes index
ISBN 0-443-02511-8 (pbk) : £8.00 B81-25611

Progress in clinical pathology. — New York ; London : Grune & Stratton ; London : Distributed by Academic Press
The University of Minnesota issue / editors Mario Stefanini, Ellis S. Bensen ; coeditors M. Desmond Burke, Donald P. Connelly, Roslyn A.K. Yomtovian. — c1981. — xvi,324p : ill ; 27cm
Includes bibliographies and index
ISBN 0-8089-1310-7 : £29.40 B81-39576

Smith, Alice Lorraine. Microbiology and pathology / Alice Lorraine Smith. — 12th ed. — St. Louis ; London : Mosby, 1980. — xii,851p,[3] leaves of plates : ill(some col.) ; 25cm
Previous ed.: 1976. — Includes bibliographies and index
ISBN 0-8016-4673-1 : £14.00
Primary classification 616'.01 B81-08040

Spector, W. G.. An introduction to general pathology / W.G. Spector. — 2nd ed. — Edinburgh : Churchill Livingstone, 1980. — 300p : ill ; 22cm. — (Churchill Livingstone medical text)
Previous ed.: 1977. — Includes bibliographies and index
ISBN 0-443-01970-3 (pbk) : £4.95 : CIP rev. B80-13848

616.07 — Mummies. Pathology

Mummies, disease and ancient cultures / edited by Aidan and Eve Cockburn. — Cambridge : Cambridge University Press, 1980. — x,340p,[4]p of plates : ill(some col.),maps ; 27cm
Includes bibliographies and index
ISBN 0-521-23020-9 : £25.00
Primary classification 393'.3'09 B81-03747

616.07'0246176 — Medicine. Pathology — *For dentistry*

Walter, J. B.. Principles of pathology for dental students / J.B. Walter, Margaret C. Hamilton, M.S. Israel. — 4th ed. — Edinburgh : Churchill Livingstone, 1981. — 668p : ill ; 24cm
Previous ed.: 1974. — Includes bibliographies and index
ISBN 0-443-02243-7 (pbk) : £15.00 B81-19997

616.07'05 — Man. Diseases. Physiological aspects — *Serials*

[Clinical physiology *(Oxford)***]**. Clinical physiology. — Vol.1, no.1 (Feb.1981)-. — Oxford : Blackwell Scientific for the Scandinavian Society of Clinical Physiology, 1981-. — v. ; 25cm
Six issues yearly. — Continues in part: Scandinavian journal of clinical & laboratory investigation
ISSN 0144-5979 = Clinical physiology (Oxford) : £60.00 per year B81-20703

616.07'05 — Medicine. Pathology — *Serials*

International review of experimental pathology. — Vol.22 (1980). — New York ; London : Academic Press, c1980. — vii,261p
ISBN 0-12-364922-6 : Unpriced
ISSN 0074-7718 B81-22404

Pathology annual. — Vol.15, pt.2 (1980). — New York : Appleton-Century-Crofts ; London : Prentice-Hall International, c1980. — x,452p
ISBN 0-8385-7762-8 : £23.75 B81-23151

The **year** book of pathology and clinical pathology. — 1979. — Chicago ; London : Year Book Medical Publishers, c1979. — 456p
ISBN 0-8151-1439-7 : Unpriced B81-20431

The **Year** book of pathology and clinical pathology. — 1980. — Chicago ; London : Year Book Medical Publishers, c1980. — 458p
ISBN 0-8151-1440-0 : Unpriced B81-09067

616.07'05 — Medicine. Pathology. Serials: Pathology annual — *Indexes*

Pathology annual cumulative index 1966-1979 / series editors Sheldon C. Sommers, Paul Peter Rosen. — New York : Appleton-Century-Crofts ; London : Prentice-Hall, 1981. — viii,184p ; 25cm
ISBN 0-8385-7766-0 : Unpriced B81-26118

616.07'1 — Man. Diseases. Aetiology

Hoy, Ronald. Nature and causation of disease / Ronald Hoy. — London : McGraw-Hill, c1981. — 188p : ill ; 25cm. — (McGraw-Hill nursing studies series)
Bibliography: p180-181. — Includes index
ISBN 0-07-084617-0 (pbk) : £3.95 B81-37717

616.07'1 — Man. Diseases. Environmental factors

Western diseases : their emergence and prevention / edited by H.C. Trowell, D.P. Burkitt ; foreword by John R.K. Robson. — London : Edward Arnold, 1981. — xix,456p : ill,maps ; 24cm
Includes bibliographies and index
ISBN 0-7131-4373-8 : £28.50 B81-15648

616.07'1 — Man. Diseases. Role of interactions of enzymes with chemical pollutants of environment — *Conference proceedings*

Environmental chemicals, enzyme function and human disease. — Amsterdam ; Oxford : Excerpta Medica, 1980. — x,380p : ill,1map ; 25cm. — (Ciba Foundation symposium. New series ; 76)
Conference papers. — Includes bibliographies and index
ISBN 90-219-4082-5 : £27.71 B81-16271

616.07'1 — Man. Diseases. Role of receptors

Blecher, Melvin. Receptors and human disease / Melvin Blecher and Robert S. Bar. — Baltimore ; London : Williams & Wilkins, c1981. — vi,344p : ill ; 26cm
Includes index
ISBN 0-683-00609-6 : £42.75 B81-24340

616.07'2 — Man. Diseases. Syndromes: Eye manifestations — *Conference proceedings*

The **Eye** and systemic disease / edited by Frederick A. Mausolf. — 2nd ed. — St. Louis ; London : Mosby, 1980. — xiv,496p : ill ; 26cm
Conference papers. — Previous ed.: 1975. — Includes bibliographies and index
ISBN 0-8016-3159-9 : Unpriced B81-08665

616.07'2 — Man. Diseases. Syndromes: Oral manifestations

Oral manifestations of systemic disease / edited by J. Harold Jones and David K. Mason. — London : Saunders, 1980. — x,559p : ill ; 27cm
Includes bibliographies and index
ISBN 0-7216-5213-1 : £32.50 : CIP rev. B80-21988

616.07'2 — Man. Systemic diseases. Symptoms: Skin disorders

Cutaneous aspects of internal disease / [edited by] Jeffrey P. Callen. — Chicago ; London : Year Book Medical, c1981. — xv,682p : ill(some col.),1map ; 26cm
Includes index
ISBN 0-8151-1411-7 : £66.00 B81-14155

616.07'2 — Man. Tissues. Inflammation — *Conference proceedings*

International Meeting on Future Trends in Inflammation *(4th : 1980 : London)*.
Inflammation : mechanisms and treatment : proceedings of the Fourth International Meeting on Future Trends in Inflammation organized by the European Biological Research Association and held in London 18th-22nd February 1980 / edited by D.A. Willoughby, J.P. Giroud. — Lancaster : MTP Press, 1980. — xxxiii,873p : ill ; 24cm
Includes index
ISBN 0-85200-362-5 : £39.95 B81-13592

616.07'5 — Man. Diagnosis. Imaging systems

Evans, A. Ll.. The evaluation of medical images / A.Ll. Evans. — Bristol : Hilger in collaboration with the Hospital Physicists' Association, c1981. — xi,130p : ill ; 22cm. — (Medical physics handbooks, ISSN 0143-0203 ; 10)
Bibliography: p123-127. — Includes index
ISBN 0-85274-518-4 : £11.95 : CIP rev. B81-12789

The **Physical** basis of medical imaging / edited by Craig M. Coulam ... [et al.]. — New York : Appleton-Century-Crofts ; London : Prentice-Hall, c1981. — ix,354p : ill,plans ; 29cm
Includes index
ISBN 0-8385-7844-6 : £34.65 B81-37173

Scientific basis of medical imaging. — Edinburgh : Churchill Livingstone, Dec.1981. — [320]p
ISBN 0-443-01986-x : £18.00 : CIP entry B81-31348

616.07'5 — Man. Prognosis

Prognosis : contemporary outcomes of disease / James F. Fries and George E. Ehrlich editors. — Bowie : Charles Press ; London : Prentice-Hall, c1981. — xxxii,565p : ill ; 25cm
Includes index
ISBN 0-89303-005-8 : £22.70 B81-08528

616.07'5 — Medicine. Diagnosis

Bouchier, Ian A. D.. Clinical skills. — 2nd ed. — Eastbourne : Holt-Saunders, Jan.1982. — [735]p
Previous ed.: London : Saunders, 1976
ISBN 0-7216-1893-6 : £9.50 : CIP entry B81-34656

Clinical diagnostic manual for the house officer / edited by Kenneth L. Baughman, Bruce M. Greene. — Baltimore ; London : Williams & Wilkins, c1981. — xi,159p : ill ; 19cm
Includes index
£9.95 (pbk) B81-17041

Notes on clinical method. — Manchester : Manchester University Press, Jan.1982. — [120]p
Previous ed.: 1971
ISBN 0-7190-0851-4 (pbk) : £4.95 : CIP entry B81-33828

616.07'5 — Medicine. Diagnosis *continuation*

Wulff, Henrik R.. Rational diagnosis and treatment : an introduction to clinical decision-making / Henrik R. Wulff ; with a foreword by J.E. Lennard-Jones. — 2nd ed. — Oxford : Blackwell Scientific, 1981. — xi,209p : ill ; 22cm
Previous ed.: 1976. — Includes index
ISBN 0-632-00713-3 (pbk) : £7.25 : CIP rev. B81-13496

616.07'5 — Medicine. Diagnosis. Applications of ophthalmology

Chumbley, Lee C.. Ophthalmology in internal medicine / Lee C. Chumbley. — Philadelphia ; London : Saunders, 1981. — xii,280p : ill,1port ; 26cm
Includes index
ISBN 0-7216-2578-9 : £18.00 B81-05469

616.07'5 — Medicine. Diagnosis. Imaging - *Conference proceedings*

Physical effects of medical imaging. — Chicester : Wiley, Aug.1981. — [336]p
Conference papers
ISBN 0-471-10039-0 : £15.00 : CIP entry B81-16880

616.07'5 — Medicine. Differential diagnosis

Gunn, Alexander. Differential diagnosis. — Lancaster : MTP Press, Sept.1981. — [300]p
ISBN 0-85200-399-4 : £13.95 : CIP entry B81-21598

616.07'5 — Medicine. Immunodiagnosis. Laboratory techniques

Aloisi, Ralph Michael. Principles of immunodiagnostics / Ralph Michael Aloisi. — St. Louis ; London : Mosby, 1979. — x,172p : ill ; 25cm
Includes bibliographies and index
ISBN 0-8016-0118-5 (pbk) : £11.25 B81-12593

Metals in immunodiagnosis / edited by Noel R. Rose, Pierluigi E. Bigazzi. — 2nd ed. — New York ; Chichester : Wiley, c1980. — xii,269p : ill ; 26cm
Previous ed.: 1973. — Includes bibliographies and index
ISBN 0-471-02208-x (spiral) : £11.00 B81-04962

616.07'5 — Oriental medicine. Diagnosis

Kushi, Michio. How to see your health : book of Oriental diagnosis / Michio Kushi. — Tokyo : Japan Publications ; Hemel Hempstead : International Book Distributors [distributor], 1980. — 160p : ill ; 26cm
Includes index
ISBN 0-87040-467-9 (pbk) : £7.15 B81-28476

616.07'5'024613 — Man. Diagnosis — *For nursing*

Block, Gloria J.. Health assessment for professional nursing : a developmental approach / Gloria J. Block, JoEllen Wilbur Nolan, Mary K. Dempsey with contributions by Susan K. Pennington, Toni Tripp-Reimer. — New York ; Appleton-Century-Crofts ; London : Prentice-Hall, c1981. — xix,361p : ill,forms ; 29cm
Includes bibliographies and index
ISBN 0-8385-3660-3 : £14.85 B81-37684

616.07'5'024613 — Medicine. Diagnosis — *For nursing*

Health assessment / Lois Malasanos ... [et al.]. — 2nd ed. — St.Louis ; London : Mosby, 1981. — x,723p : ill(some col.),forms ; 29cm
Previous ed.: 1977. — Includes bibliographies and index
ISBN 0-8016-3073-8 : £17.50 B81-30117

616.07'5'024613 — Medicine. Diagnosis. Laboratory techniques — *For nursing*

Strand, Marcella M.. Clinical laboratory tests : a manual for nurses / Marcella M. Strand, Lucille A. Elmer. — 2nd ed. — St. Louis ; London : Mosby, 1980. — ix,155p ; 22cm
Previous ed.: 1976. — Bibliography: p154-155
ISBN 0-8016-4827-0 (spiral) : £5.25 B81-08167

616.07'5'028 — Medicine. Diagnosis. Laboratory techniques

Evans, D. M. D.. Special tests and their meanings / D.M.D. Evans. — 12th ed. — London : Faber, 1981. — 270p : ill ; 19cm
Previous ed.: 1978. — Includes index
ISBN 0-571-18034-5 (pbk) : £2.50 : CIP rev. B81-25303

Oppenheim, Irwin A.. Textbook for laboratory assistants / Irwin A. Oppenheim. — 3rd ed. — St. Louis ; London : Mosby, 1981. — xiii,187p : ill ; 23cm
Previous ed.: 1976. — Includes bibliographies and index
ISBN 0-8016-3722-8 (pbk) : £9.50 B81-25047

616.07'5'076 — Medicine. Diagnosis. Data interpretation — *Questions & answers*

Gabriel, Roger. Medical data interpretation for MRCP. — 2nd ed. — London : Butterworths, Nov.1981. — [216]p
Previous ed.: 1978
ISBN 0-407-00217-0 (pbk) : £3.95 : CIP entry B81-30549

616.07'5'0903 — Medicine. Diagnosis. Technological development, *1600-1977*

Reiser, Stanley Joel. Medicine and the reign of technology / Stanley Joel Reiser. — Cambridge : Cambridge University Press, 1981, c1978. — xi,317p : ill,1facsim ; 23cm
Bibliography: p279-307. — Includes index
ISBN 0-521-28223-3 (pbk) : £5.95 B81-19009

616.07'54 — Man. Ambulatory monitoring

Clinical ambulatory monitoring / edited by W.A. Littler. — London : Chapman and Hall, 1980. — ix,174p : ill ; 24cm
Includes bibliographies and index
ISBN 0-412-15830-2 : £12.50 : CIP rev. B80-23327

616'.07'54 — Man. Diagnosis. Applications of radiesthesia

Mermet, *Abbé*. Principles & practice of radiesthesia. — Dulverton : Watkins, Nov.1981. — [232]p
Translation of: Comment j'opère
ISBN 0-7224-0140-x (pbk) : £4.00 : CIP entry B81-30371

616.07'54 — Man. Diagnosis. Physical examination

Burnside, John W.. Physical diagnosis : an introduction to clinical medicine. — 16th ed. / John W. Burnside. — Baltimore ; London : Williams & Wilkins, c1981. — xiii,256p : ill (some col.),1facsim ; 26cm
Previous ed.: published as Adam's physical diagnosis. — Bibliography: p24-25. — Includes index
ISBN 0-683-01137-5 : £18.50 B81-20761

Major, Ralph H.. Major's physical diagnosis : an introduction to the clinical process. — 9th ed / Mahlon H. Delp, Robert T. Manning. — Philadelphia ; London : Saunders, 1981. — xiv,574p : ill ; 25cm
Previous ed.: 1975. — Includes bibliographies and index
ISBN 0-7216-3002-2 (pbk) : £13.95 B81-22974

616.07'54 — Man. Diagnosis. Physical examination — *For auxiliary personnel in health services of developing countries*

Essex, B. J.. Diagnostic pathways in clinical medicine / B.J. Essex ; foreword by W.J. Makene ; illustrations by A. Barrett. — 2nd ed. — Edinburgh : Churchill Livingstone, 1980. — xiv,168p : ill(some col.),forms ; 30cm. — (Medicine in the tropics series)
Previous ed.: 1977. — Includes index
ISBN 0-443-02059-0 (pbk) : £7.50 : CIP rev. B80-08235

616.07'54 — Man. Diagnosis. Physical examination. Techniques

Clinical skills : interviewing, history taking, and physical diagnosis / Robert St. Hillman ... [et al.]. — New York ; London : McGraw-Hill, c1981. — x,422p : ill ; 21cm
Bibliography: p403-404. — Includes index
ISBN 0-07-028910-7 (pbk) : £9.25 B81-17883

616.07'54'024613 — Man. Diagnosis. Physical examination — *For nursing*

Thompson, June M.. Clinical manual of health assessment / June M. Thompson, Arden C. Bowers ; illustrated by Ann L. Schreck. — St. Louis ; London : Mosby, 1980. — ix,476p : forms ; 28cm
Includes bibliographies and index
ISBN 0-8016-4935-8 (pbk) : £12.75 B81-08035

616.07'543 — Man. Diagnosis. Ultrasonography

Diagnostic ultrasound : text and cases / edited by Dennis A. Sarti, W. Frederick Sample. — The Hague ; London : Nijhoff, c1980. — xiv,707p : ill ; 29cm
Includes index
ISBN 90-247-2262-4 : Unpriced B81-02433

McDicken, W. N.. Diagnostic ultrasonics : principles and use of instruments / W.N. McDicken. — 2nd ed. — New York ; Chichester : Wiley, c1981. — x,381p : ill ; 27cm. — (A Wiley medical publication)
Previous ed.: 1976. — Includes bibliographies and index
ISBN 0-471-05740-1 : £24.50 B81-23397

Medical ultrasonic images : formation, display, recording and perception : based on papers presented at a European Symposium held in Brussels, January 31-February 1, 1981 organized by the European Federation of Societies for Ultrasound in Medicine and Biology in association with Polaroid Corporation / editors C.R. Hill, A. Kratochwil. — Amsterdam ; Oxford : Excerpta Medica, 1981. — xi,173p : ill ; 25cm. — (International congress series ; no.541)
Includes index
ISBN 90-219-0483-7 : Unpriced B81-29846

New techniques and instrumentation in ultrasonography / edited by P.N.T. Wells and C. Ziskin. — New York ; Edinburgh : Churchill Livingstone, 1980. — 245p : ill ; 25cm. — (Clinics in diagnostic ultrasound ; v.5)
Includes index
ISBN 0-443-08075-5 : Unpriced B81-12153

616.07'543 — Man. Diagnosis. Use of ultrasonic waves - *Conference proceedings*

Investigative ultrasonology. — Tunbridge Wells : Pitman Medical, June 1981
Conference papers
2: Clinical advances. — [340]p
ISBN 0-272-79576-3 : £18.00 : CIP entry B81-13559

616.07'543'05 — Medicine. Ultrasonography — *Serials*

Progress in medical ultrasound. — Vol.2 (1981). — Amsterdam ; Oxford : Excerpta Medica, c1981. — xi,282p
ISBN 90-219-3057-9 : Unpriced B81-32911

616.07'545 — Medicine. Diagnosis. Infrared thermography

Woodrough, R. E.. Medical infra-red thermography. — Cambridge : Cambridge University Press, Dec.1981. — [256]p. — (Techniques of measurement in medicine)
ISBN 0-521-23879-x (cased) : £27.50 : CIP entry
ISBN 0-521-28277-2 (pbk) : £12.50 B81-38815

616.07'56 — Man. Ambulatory monitoring. Chemical analysis. Laboratory techniques

Fleming, Rita A.. Primary care techniques : laboratory tests in ambulatory facilities / Rita A. Fleming ; with 101 illustrations by Kathleen Gatto Johnson. — St. Louis ; London : Mosby, 1980. — ix,116p : ill ; 23cm
Includes bibliographies and index
ISBN 0-8016-1592-5 (spiral) : Unpriced B81-08560

616.07'56 — Man. Peptides. Radioimmunoassay — *Conference proceedings*
International Symposium on Radioimmunology *(5th : 1981 : Lyon)*. Physiological peptides and new trends in radioimmunology : proceedings of the Vth International Symposium on Radioimmunology held in Lyon (France) 9-11 April 1981 / sponsored by Institut National de la Recherche Médicale et Delegation Générale à la Recherche Scientifique et Technique ; scientific committee: M. Jouvet ... [et al.] ; organizing committee : Ch. A. Bozollin ... [et al.] ; edited by Ch. A. Bozollin. — Amsterdam ; Oxford : Elsevier/North-Holland Biomedical, 1981. — xii,370p : ill ; 24cm
Includes bibliographies and index
ISBN 0-444-80358-0 : Unpriced B81-38111

616.07'56 — Medicine. Diagnosis. Chemical analysis
Baron, D. N.. A short textbook of chemical pathology. — 4th ed. — London : Hodder & Stoughton, July 1981. — [288]p. — (University medical texts)
Previous ed.: London : English Universities Press, 1972
ISBN 0-340-26522-1 (pbk) : £4.95 : CIP entry B81-14914

Richterich, R.. Clinical chemistry : theory, practice, and interpretation / the late R. Richterich and J.P. Colombo, with contributions from C. Bachmann ... [et al.]. — Chichester : Wiley, c1981. — xxiv,766p : ill,1plan ; 24cm
Translation of: Klinische Chemie. 4. Aufl.. — Includes index
ISBN 0-471-27809-2 : £31.50 B81-16335

616.07'56 — Medicine. Diagnosis. Chemical analysis - *Questions & answers*
Whitby, L. G.. Multiple choice questions on clinical chemistry. — Oxford : Blackwell Scientific, May 1981. — [80]p
ISBN 0-632-00694-3 (pbk) : £2.25 : CIP entry B81-08801

616.07'56 — Medicine. Diagnosis. High pressure liquid chromatography, gas chromatography & mass spectrometry — *Conference proceedings*
Current developments in the clinical applications of HPLC, GC and MS / [proceedings of a symposium held at the Clinical Research Centre, Watford Road, Harrow, Middlesex, UK, on May 30, 31 and June 1, 1979] ; editors A.M. Lawson, C.K. Lim and W. Richmond. — London : Academic Press, 1980. — xv,301p : ill ; 24cm. — (Clinical Reseach Centre symposium ; no.1)
Includes bibliographies and index
ISBN 0-12-439650-x : £21.40 : CIP rev. B80-18330

616.07'56 — Medicine. Immunoassay
Immunoassays for the 80s / edited by A. Voller, A. Bartlett and D. Bidwell. — Lancaster : MTP, 1981. — xiii,508p : ill ; 25cm
Includes index
ISBN 0-85200-374-9 : £24.95 B81-29468

616.07'56 — Medicine. Radioimmunoassay — *Conference proceedings*
Radioimmunoassay of hormones, proteins and enzymes : proceedings of the international symposium Gardone Riviera, May 8-10, 1980 / editor A. Albertini. — Amsterdam ; Oxford : Excerpta Medica, 1980. — xi,272p : ill ; 25cm. — (International congress series ; no.528)
Includes index
ISBN 90-219-0454-3 : £22.86 B81-01674

616.07'56'0321 — Medicine. Diagnosis. Chemical analysis — *Encyclopaedias*
Hood, W.. A-Z of clinical chemistry : a guide for the trainee / W. Hood. — Lancaster : MTP Press, 1980. — vii,386p : ill ; 23cm
Bibliography: p382-383
ISBN 0-85200-311-0 : £7.95 : CIP rev. B80-00743

616.07'56'076 — Medicine. Diagnosis. Chemical analysis — *Questions & answers*
Fleming, P. R.. Multiple-choice questions on Clinical chemistry in diagnosis and treatment / P.R. Fleming, P.H. Sanderson. — London : Lloyd-Luke, 1981. — 112p : ill ; 19cm
ISBN 0-85324-153-8 (pbk) : £3.75 B81-23162

616.07'561 — Man. Blood. Diagnosis. Radiography. Use of radioisotopes
Bowring, C. S.. Radionuclide tracer techniques in haematology / C.S. Bowring. — London : Butterworths, 1981. — vii,140p : ill ; 22cm
Includes bibliographies and index
ISBN 0-407-00183-2 (pbk) : Unpriced : CIP rev. B81-02570

616.07'561 — Man. Blood. Testing. Laboratory techniques. Quality control
Quality control. — Edinburgh : Churchill Livingstone, Feb.1982. — [180]p. — (Methods in hematology ; 3)
ISBN 0-443-02229-1 : £10.00 : CIP entry B81-36212

616.07'57 — Forensic medicine. Radiology
Evans, K. T.. Forensic radiology. — Oxford : Blackwell Scientific, Aug.1981. — [212]p
ISBN 0-632-00587-4 : £15.00 : CIP entry B81-21595

616.07'57 — Man. Diagnosis. Radiography. Positioning
Clark, K. C.. Clark's positioning in radiography. — 10th ed. — London : Heinemann Medical [for] Ilford
Previous ed.: published as Positioning in radiography / revised by James McInnes. 1974
Vol.2 / edited by Louis Kreel. — 1981. — p486-916 : ill ; 30cm
Includes index
ISBN 0-433-18833-2 : £22.50 B81-19683

616.07'57 — Man. Diagnosis. Radiography — *Questions & answers*
Carter, P. H.. Objective tests in diagnostic radiography. — Edinburgh : Churchill Livingstone, Feb.1982. — [128]p
ISBN 0-443-02408-1 (pbk) : £2.95 : CIP entry B81-36211

616.07'57 — Medicine. Radiology
Chapman, Stephen. A guide to radiological procedures. — London : Baillière Tindall, Oct.1981. — [156]p
ISBN 0-7020-0885-0 (pbk) : £6.00 : CIP entry B81-25835

616.07'57'024613 — Man. Diagnosis. Radiography *— For nursing*
Ehrlich, Ruth Ann. Patient care in radiography / Ruth Ann Ehrlich, Ellen McCloskey Givens ; photographs by Rebecca A. Kruse. — St. Louis ; London : Mosby, 1981. — xiv,191p : ill,forms ; 24cm
Bibliography: p160. - Includes index
ISBN 0-8016-1507-0 (pbk) : £9.25 B81-25049

616.07'57'02541 — Great Britain. Radiographers — *Directories — Serials*
Radiographers Board. The Radiographers register. — 1981. — [London] ([184 Kennington Park Rd, SE11 4BU]) : Radiographers Board, [1981]. — 270p
Unpriced B81-32893

616.07'57'028 — Radiologic equipment. Inspection & maintenance
McLemore, Joy M.. Quality assurance in diagnostic radiology / Joy M. McLemore. — Chicago ; London : Year Book Medical Publishers, c1981. — xii,225p : ill ; 24cm
Includes bibliographies and index
ISBN 0-8151-5832-7 : £16.50 B81-40354

616.07'57'0289 — Medicine. Radiology. Safety measures
Shapiro, Jacob. Radiation protection : a guide for scientists and physicians / Jacob Shapiro. — 2nd ed. — Cambridge, Mass. ; London : Harvard University Press, 1981. — xxi,480p : ill,1form ; 25cm
Previous ed.: 1972. — Bibliography: p441-471. — Includes index
ISBN 0-674-74584-1 : £17.50 B81-38900

616.07'57'05 — Man. Diagnosis. Radiography — *Serials*
Diagnostic radiology. — 1980. — New York ; London : Academic Press, c1980. — xiii,846p
£50.20 B81-27333

The **Year** book of diagnostic radiology. — 1981. — Chicago ; London : Year Book Medical Publishers, 1981. — 480p
ISBN 0-8151-9328-9 : Unpriced
ISSN 0098-1672 B81-24998

616.07'57'09 — Medicine. Radiology, *to 1937*
Mould, R. F.. A history of X-rays and radium with a chapter on radiation units: 1895-1937 / by Richard F. Mould. — Sutton : IPC Building & Contract Journals, c1980. — 100p : ill,facsims,ports ; 30cm
Bibliography: p62-69. - Includes index
ISBN 0-617-00355-6 (pbk) : £12.75
Also classified at 621.36'73'09 B81-04855

616.07'57'0926 — Man. Diagnosis. Radiography — *Case studies*
Rosenbaum, Harold D.. Pearls in diagnostic radiology / Harold D. Rosenbaum. — New York ; Edinburgh : Churchill Livingstone, 1980. — vii,240p : ill ; 26cm
Includes bibliographies
ISBN 0-443-08151-4 : Unpriced B81-12226

616.07'572 — Man. Diagnosis. Computerised tomography
Herman, Gabor T.. Image reconstruction from projections : the fundamentals of computerized tomography / Gabor T. Herman. — New York ; London : Academic Press, 1980p. — xiv,316p : ill ; 24cm. — (Computer science and applied mathematics)
Bibliography: p297-305. — Includes index
ISBN 0-12-342050-4 : £19.20 B81-14750

616.07'572 — Man. Diagnosis. Computerised tomography. Contrast media — *Conference proceedings*
Contrast media in computed tomography : international workshop Berlin, January 14-17, 1981 / editors R. Felix, E. Kazner, O.H. Wegener ; editorial board C.D. Claussen ... [et al.]. — Amsterdam ; Oxford : Excerpta Medica, 1981. — viii,302p : ill ; 25cm. — (International congress series ; 561)
Includes summaries in German. — Includes index
ISBN 90-219-0502-7 : £23.67 B81-36748

616.07'572 — Man. Diagnosis. Radiography. Use of x-rays
Armstrong, Peter, *1940-*. X-ray diagnosis / Peter Armstrong, Martin L. Wastie with contributions on ultrasound by Anthony J. Buschi and A. Norman A.G. Brenbridge. — Oxford : Blackwell Scientific, 1981. — viii,344p : ill ; 25cm
Includes index
ISBN 0-632-00173-9 : £19.75 : CIP rev. B80-18758

Paul, Lester W.. Paul and Juhl's Essentials of roentgen interpretation. — 4th ed. / John H. Juhl. — Hagerstown ; London : Harper & Row, c1981. — xii,1213p : ill ; 27cm
Previous ed.: published as The essentials of roentgen interpretation. 1972. — Includes bibliographies and index
ISBN 0-06-142143-x : £44.00 B81-28267

616.07'572 — Man. Diagnosis. Radiography. Use of x-rays. Techniques
Plaats, G. J. van der. Medical X-ray techniques in diagnostic radiology : a textbook for radiographers and radiological technicians / G.J. van der Plaats with the assistance of P. Vijlbrief. — 4th ed. — The Hague ; London : Nijhoff, 1980. — viii,463p : ill ; 24cm
Previous ed.: London : Macmillan, 1972. — Includes index
ISBN 90-247-2155-5 : Unpriced B81-19876

616.07'572 — Medical x-ray equipment
Bushong, Stewart C.. Radiologic science for technologists : physics, biology, and protection / Stewart C. Bushong. — 2nd ed. — St. Louis ; London : Mosby, 1980. — xi,503p : ill,plans ; 25cm + workbook and laboratory manual (x,260p : ill,forms;28cm)
Previous ed.: 1975. — Includes index
ISBN 0-8016-0928-3 : £15.50
ISBN 0-8016-0927-5 (workbook and laboratory manual) : £8.50 B81-05777

616.07'575 — Man. Diagnosis. Radiography. Use of radioisotope scanning. Techniques

CLifton, Nancy Ann. Basic imaging procedures in nuclear medicine / Nancy Ann Clifton, Pamela J. Simmons. — New York : Appleton-Century-Crofts ; London : Prentice-Hall, c1981. — xii,59p : ill ; 23cm
Bibliography: p147. — Includes index
ISBN 0-8385-0578-3 (spiral) : £9.75
B81-36600

616.07'575 — Man. Diagnosis. Radiography. Use of radioisotopes

Chackett, K. F.. Radionuclide technology : an introduction to quantitative nuclear medicine / K.F. Chackett. — New York ; London : Van Nostrand Reinhold, 1981. — xiv,426p : ill ; 25cm
Bibliography: p391-415. — Includes index
ISBN 0-442-30170-7 (cased) : £17.00
ISBN 0-442-30171-5 (pbk) : £8.50 B81-28408

Radionuclide section scanning. — London : Chapman & Hall, Dec.1981. — [200]p
ISBN 0-412-23200-6 : £25.00 : CIP entry
B81-31730

616.07'575 — Nuclear medicine

Ell, Peter Josef. Nuclear medicine : an introductory text / Peter Josef Ell, Edward Sydney Williams ; foreword by R.E. Steiner. — Oxford : Blackwell Scientific, c1981. — xv,208p : ill(some col.) ; 25cm
Includes bibliographies and index
ISBN 0-632-00682-x : £21.50 B81-35439

Nuclear medicine technology and techniques / edited by Donald R. Bernier, James K. Langan, L. David Wells. — St. Louis ; London : Mosby, 1981. — xiii,538p : ill ; 26cm
Includes index
ISBN 0-8016-0662-4 : £26.75 B81-30118

616.07'575 — Nuclear medicine. Laboratory techniques

Mosby's manual of nuclear medicine procedures / [edited by] D. Bruce Sodee, Paul J. Early. — 3rd ed. / with the technical assistance of Sharon Wike Pry. — St. Louis (London) : Mosby, 1981. — xii, 601p : ill ; 26cm
Previous ed. published as: Technology and interpretation of nuclear medicine procedures. 1975. — Includes bibliographies and index
ISBN 0-8016-4729-0 (pbk) : £25.25 B81-31403

616.07'575'05 — Nuclear medicine — *Serials*

The **Year** book of nuclear medicine. — 1981. — Chicago ; London : Year Book Medical Publishers, c1981. — 404p
ISBN 0-8151-4525-x : Unpriced
ISSN 0084-3903 B81-33464

616.07'58 — Medicine. Diagnosis. Electron microscopy - *Reviews of research*

Electron microscopy in human medicine. — Maidenhead : McGraw-Hill, May 1981
Vol.4: Soft tissues, bones and joints. — [352]p
ISBN 0-07-032504-9 : £36.78 : CIP entry
B81-09969

616.07'582 — Man. Diagnosis. Applications of cytology

Advances in clinical cytology / [edited by] Leopold G. Koss, Dulcie V. Coleman. — London : Butterworths, 1981. — xi,355p : ill (some col.) ; 25cm
Includes bibliographies and index
ISBN 0-407-00174-3 : Unpriced : CIP rev.
B80-11908

616.07'582 — Man. Diagnosis. Applications of fine needle aspiration biopsy cytology

Kline, Tilde S.. Handbook of fine needle aspiration biopsy cytology / Tilde S. Kline. — St. Louis ; London : Mosby, 1981. — xi,319p : ill ; 26cm
Includes bibliographies and index
ISBN 0-8016-2701-x : £27.75 B81-40361

616.07'583 — Medicine. Diagnosis. Histology

Carleton, Harry Montgomerie. Carleton's histological technique. — 5th ed. / by R.A.B. Drury, E.A. Wallington. — Oxford : Oxford University Press, 1980. — vi,520p : ill ; 24cm. — (Oxford medical publications)
Previous ed.: 1967. — Includes bibliographies and index
ISBN 0-19-261310-3 : £24.00 : CIP rev.
B80-01217

616.07'76 — Medicine. Pathology — *Questions & answers*

Smiddy, F. G.. Multiple choice questions in general pathology. — London : Pitman Medical, Oct.1981. — [320]p
ISBN 0-272-79631-x (pbk) : £5.95 : CIP entry
B81-23857

616.07'9 — Man. Immunological deficiency

Asherson, G. L.. Diagnosis and treatment of immunodeficiency diseases / G.L. Asherson, A.D.B. Webster ; with a foreword by J.H. Humphrey. — Oxford : Blackwell Scientific, 1980. — x,390p : ill ; 25cm
Includes bibliographies and index
ISBN 0-632-00183-6 : £25.00 : CIP rev.
B80-03181

616.07'9 — Man. Interferons

Friedman, Robert M.. Interferons : a primer / Robert M. Friedman. — New York ; London : Academic Press, 1981. — xii,151p : ill ; 24cm
Bibliography: p7. — Includes index
ISBN 0-12-268280-7 : £11.60 B81-39580

616.07'9 — Man. Interferons — *Conference proceedings*

International Meeting on the Biology of the Interferon System *(1981 : Rotterdam)*. The biology of the interferon system : proceedings of the International Meeting on the Biology of the Interferon System, held in Rotterdam, The Netherlands on 21-24 April 1981 / organized by TNO ; editors Edward de Maeyer, George Galasso and Huub Schellekens. — Amsterdam ; Oxford : Elsevier/North-Holland Biomedical, 1981. — xvi,470p : ill,1port ; 24cm
Includes bibliographies and index
ISBN 0-444-80360-2 : Unpriced B81-38110

616.07'9 — Man. Interferons — *Serials*

Interferon. — London : Academic Press, 1980. — x,99p
ISBN 0-12-302251-7 : Unpriced : CIP rev.
B80-27055

Interferon. — Vol.3 (1981). — London : Academic Press, Dec.1981. — [150]p
ISBN 0-12-302252-5 : CIP entry B81-31001

616.07'9 — Man. Primary immunological deficiency — *Conference proceedings*

International Symposium on Primary Immunodeficiencies *(1980 : Abbaye de Royaumont)*. Primary immunodeficiencies : proceedings of the International Symposium on Primary Immunodeficiencies held in Abbaye de Royaumont (France), 18-20 July, 1980 / sponsored by the Institut National de la Santé et de la Recherche Médicale ; editors M. Seligmann, W.H. Hitzig. — Amsterdam ; Oxford : Elsevier/North-Holland Biomedical, 1980. — xiii,577p : ill ; 25cm. — (INSERM symposium ; no.16)
Includes index
ISBN 0-444-80296-7 : Unpriced B81-14287

616.07'9 — Medicine. Immunology

Amos, W. M. G.. Basic immunology / W.M.G. Amos. — London : Butterworths, 1981. — viii,188p : ill ; 24cm
Bibliography: p179. — Includes index
ISBN 0-407-00178-6 (pbk) : Unpriced : CIP rev. B81-23919

Barrett, James T.. Basic immunology and its medical application / James T. Barrett. — 2nd ed. — St. Louis ; London : Mosby, 1980. — xiv,303p : ill ; 24cm
Previous ed.: 1976. — Includes index
ISBN 0-8016-0495-8 (pbk) : £11.25 B81-12639

Clark, William R.. The experimental foundations of modern immunology / William R. Clark. — New York ; Chichester : Wiley, c1980. — ix,372p : ill ; 24cm
Includes bibliographies and index
ISBN 0-471-04088-6 : £9.30 B81-00923

Clinical aspects of immunology. — 4th ed. — Oxford : Blackwell Scientific, Jan.1982. — 2v. [1800]p
Previous ed.: 1975
ISBN 0-632-00702-8 : £95.00 : CIP entry
B81-34637

Immunologic fundamentals. — 2nd ed. / Nancy J. Bigley ... [et al.] ; with electronmicroscopy by Raoul Fresco. — Chicago ; London : Year Book Medical, 1981. — xiii,341p : ill ; 23cm
Previous ed.: / by Nancy J. Bigley. Chicago : Year Book Medical, 1975. — Includes bibliographies and index
ISBN 0-8151-0801-x (pbk) : £13.00 B81-14157

Playfair, J. H. L.. Immunology at a glance. — 2nd ed. — Oxford : Blackwell Scientific, Dec.1981. — [80]p
Previous ed.: 1979
ISBN 0-632-00805-9 (pbk) : £3.00 : CIP entry
B81-31646

Roitt, Ivan M.. Essential immunology / Ivan M. Roitt. — 4th ed. — Oxford : Blackwell Scientific, 1980. — xvi,358p : ill(some col.) ; 24cm
Previous ed.: 1977. — Includes index
ISBN 0-632-00739-7 (pbk) : £6.00 : CIP rev.
B80-20724

616.07'9'028 — Medicine. Immunology. Laboratory techniques

Hudson, Leslie. Practical immunology / Leslie Hudson, Frank C. Hay. — 2nd ed. — Oxford : Blackwell Scientific, 1980. — xvi,359p : ill ; 24cm
Previous ed.: 1976. — Ill, text on inside covers. — Includes bibliographies and index
ISBN 0-632-00353-7 (pbk) : £10.00 : CIP rev.
B80-18721

Peacock, Julia E.. Manual of laboratory immunology / Julia E. Peacock and Russsell H. Tomar. — Philadelphia : Lea & Febiger ; London : Kimpton, 1980. — xii,228p : ill ; 24cm
Includes bibliographies
£8.00 (pbk) B81-16117

Techniques in clinical immunology / edited by R.A. Thompson. — 2nd ed. — Oxford : Blackwell Scientific, 1981. — 339p : ill ; 24cm
Previous ed.: 1977. — Includes bibliographies and index
ISBN 0-632-00723-0 (pbk) : £15.00 : CIP rev.
B81-10432

616.07'9'05 — Man. Diseases. Immunological aspects — *Serials*

Clinical immunology update. — 1981 ed.. — Edinburgh : Churchill Livingstone, c1981. — xiii,427p
ISBN 0-443-02431-6 : £16.00 B81-07891

616.07'9'05 — Medicine. Immunology — *Serials*

Clinical immunobiology. — Vol.4. — New York ; London : Academic Press, 1980. — xxii,198p
ISBN 0-12-070004-2 : Unpriced
ISSN 0097-1014 B81-20708

616.07'93 — Man. Phagocytes. Immunology. Laboratory techniques — *Manuals*

Investigation of phagocytes in disease / [edited by] Steven D. Douglas, Paul G. Quie. — Edinburgh : Churchill Livingstone, 1981. — x,79p : ill ; 25cm. — (Practical methods in clinical immunology series ; v.3)
Includes bibliographies and index
ISBN 0-443-02046-9 : £12.00 B81-25594

616.07'95 — Man. Immune reactions. Role of histocompatibility gene complex

The **Role** of the major histocompatibility complex in immunobiology. — Chichester : Wiley, Nov.1981. — [406]p
ISBN 0-471-10124-9 : £25.00 : CIP entry
B81-32021

616.07'95 — Man. Immune reactions. Role of lymphocytes. Research — *Personal observations*

Goodfield, June. An imagined world : a story of scientific discovery / by June Goodfield. — London : Hutchinson, 1981. — 240p : ill ; 24cm
ISBN 0-09-145480-8 : £8.95 : CIP rev. B81-17517

616.07'95 — Man. Immune reactions. Role of T-cells — *Conference proceedings*

Regulatory T lymphocytes / edited by Benvenuto Pernis, Henry J. Vogel. — New York ; London : Academic Press, 1980. — xxii,449p : ill ; 24cm. — (P & S biomedical sciences symposia series)
Conference papers. — Includes index
ISBN 0-12-551860-9 : £26.60 B81-02276

616.08 — Man. Diseases. Effects of personality

Arehart-Triechel, Joan. Bio types : the critical link between your personality and your health / Joan Arehart-Triechel. — London : W.H. Allen, 1981, c1980. — 245p ; 22cm
Originally published: New York : Times Books, 1980. — Includes index
ISBN 0-491-02674-9 : £7.50 B81-08208

616.08 — Man. Psychosomatic diseases

Foundations of psychosomatics. — Chichester : Wiley, Oct.1981. — [432]p
ISBN 0-471-27855-6 : £14.90 : CIP entry B81-27951

616.08 — Man. Psychosomatic diseases — *Conference proceedings*

European Conference on Psychosomatic Research *(12th : 1978 : Bodø)*. Strategies in psychosomatic practice and research : proceedings of the 12th European Conference on Psychosomatic Research, Bodø, July 9-13, 1978 / editor H. Freyberger. — Basel ; London : Karger, 1979. — vii,321p : ill,1map ; 25cm
Includes bibliographies and index
ISBN 3-8055-3044-7 : £39.00 B81-00127

Society for Psychosomatic Research. *Conference 21st (1977 : London)*. The coming age of psychosomatics : proceedings of the Twenty-first Annual Confernce of the Society for Psychosomatic Research held at the Royal College of Physicians, St. Andrew's Place, Regent's Park, London, N.W.1 21st and 22nd November 1977 / edited by Malcolm Carruthers and Peter Mellett. — Oxford : Pergamon, 1979. — viiip,p227-385 : ill ; 26cm
Includes bibliographies
ISBN 0-08-023736-3 : £11.50 : CIP rev. B79-05742

616.08 — Man. Psychosomatic diseases. Role of stress — *Conference proceedings*

Society, stress, and disease. — Oxford : Oxford University Press. — (Oxford medical publications)
Vol.4: Working life / edited by Lennart Levi. — 1981. — xvii,370p : ill ; 25cm
Papers from a conference sponsored by the University of Uppsala and the World Health Organization. — Includes bibliographies and index
ISBN 0-19-264421-1 : £40.00 : CIP rev. B79-27485

616.1 — MAN. DISEASES OF CARDIOVASCULAR SYSTEM

616.1 — Man. Cardiovascular system. Diseases

The **heart**, arteries and veins / editor-in-chief J. Willis Hurst ; edtors ... [others]. — 4th ed. — New York ; London : McGraw-Hill
Previous ed.: 1974
Update 4: The heart / editor J. Willis Hurst. — c1981. — xiii,286p : ill ; 29cm
ISBN 0-07-031493-4 : £25.95 B81-27574

Zoob, Max. Cardiology for students / Max Zoob ; foreword by J.F. Goodman. — Edinburgh : Churchill Livingstone, 1979, c1977. — 319p : ill ; 19cm. — (Livingstone medical text)
Includes bibliographies and index
ISBN 0-443-01530-9 (pbk) : £4.95 B81-40107

616.1 — Patients with cardiovascular disease. Health education. Teaching

Manual of patient education for cardiopulmonary dysfunctions / [edited by] Barbara Shelden Czerwinski. — St. Louis ; London : Mosby, 1980. — xvii,253p : ill,forms ; 25cm
Includes bibliographies and index
ISBN 0-8016-1197-0 (pbk) : £10.00 B81-08196

616.1'001'9 — Man. Cardiovascular system. Diseases. Psychological factors

Steptoe, Andrew. Psychological factors in cardiovascular disorders / Andrew Steptoe. — London : Academic Press, 1981. — xi,286p : ill ; 24cm
Bibliography: p231-280. — Includes index
ISBN 0-12-666450-1 : Unpriced B81-20864

616.1'001'9 — Man. Cardiovascular system. Diseases. Psychosocial aspects

Psychosocial aspects of cardiovascular disease : the life-threatened patient, the family, and the staff / edited by James Reiffel ... [et al.] ; with the editorial assistance of Lillian G. Kutscher. — New York ; Guildford : Columbia University Press, 1980. — xviii,363p : 1ill,forms ; 24cm. — (Foundation of Thanatology series)
Bibliography: p351-352. — Includes index
ISBN 0-231-04354-6 : £13.80 B81-01537

616.1'0028 — Patients with cardiovascular diseases. Blood pressure. Monitoring

Daily, Elaine Kiess. Techniques in bedside hemodynamic monitoring. — 2nd ed. / Elaine Kiess Daily, John Speer Schroeder. — St. Louis ; London : Mosby, 1980. — xi,198p : ill ; 24cm
Previous ed.: / John Speer Schroeder, Elaine Kiess Daily. 1976. — Includes bibliographies and index
ISBN 0-8016-4363-5 (pbk) : £8.50 B81-08165

616.1'024613 — Man. Circulatory system. Diseases — *For nursing*

Riddle, Janet T. E.. The circulatory system and the respiratory system. — Edinburgh : Churchill Livingstone, Sept.1981. — [104]p. — (Objective tests for nurses ; book 3)
ISBN 0-443-01741-7 (pbk) : £2.50 : CIP entry
Also classified at 616.2'024613 B81-21570

616.1'028 — Critically ill patients. Blood pressure. Monitoring

Hemodynamic monitoring in the critically ill / edited by Paul W. Armstrong, Ronald S. Baigrie ; 15 contributors. — Hagerstown ; London : Harper & Row, c1980. — xxiv,159p : ill ; 22cm
Includes bibliographies and index
ISBN 0-06-140268-0 : £9.75 B81-04692

616.1'028'024613 — Patients with cardiovascular diseases. Intensive care — *Questions & answers — For nursing*

Jackle, Mary. Cardiovascular problems : a critical care nursing focus / Mary Jackle, Marney Halligan. — Bowie : Robert J. Brady ; London : Prentice-Hall, c1980. — xiii,513p : ill,forms ; 26cm. — (Critical issues in critical care)
Includes index
ISBN 0-87619-667-9 (pbk) : £11.00 B81-04538

616.1'06'05 — Man. Cardiovascular system. Therapy — *Serials*

Advances in the management of cardiovascular disease. — Vol.1. (1980)-. — Chicago ; London : Year Book Medical publishers, 1980-. — v. : ill,ports ; 24cm
Annual
£74.00 B81-04161

616.1'062 — Man. Cardiovascular system. Therapy. Intra-aortic balloon counterpulsation — *For nursing*

Rose, Alycia T. Kurylo. Circulatory assist : intra-aortic balloon pumping / Alycia T. Kurylo Rose ; test questions prepared by Raymond D. Lams. — New York : Appleton-Century-Crofts ; London : Prentice-Hall, c1981. — viii,53p : ill ; 23cm. — (Continuing education in cardiovascular nursing. Series 2, Surgical aspects of cardiovascular disease-nursing intervention ; unit 6)
Includes bibliographies
ISBN 0-8385-1125-2 (pbk) : £4.85 B81-34680

616.1'0624 — Man. Cardiovascular system. Physiotherapy. Exercises. Prescription & testing

Guidelines for graded exercise testing and exercise prescription / American College of Sports Medicine. — 2nd ed. — Philadelphia : Lea & Febiger ; London : Kimpton, 1980. — 151p ; 20cm
Previous ed.: 1975
ISBN 0-8121-0769-1 (pbk) : £3.50 B81-16122

Wilson, Philip K.. Cardiac rehabilitation, adult fitness, and exercise testing / Philip K. Wilson, Paul S. Fardy, Victor F. Froelicher. — Philadelphia : Lea & Febiger ; London : Kimpton, 1981. — xii,462p : ill,map,plans,forms ; 27cm
Includes index
ISBN 0-8121-0687-3 : £13.75 B81-16123

616.1'0624 — Patients with cardiovascular diseases. Rehabilitation. Physical activities — *Conference proceedings*

Physical conditioning and cardiovascular rehabilitation / edited by Lawrence S. Cohen, Michael B. Mock, Ivar Ringqvist. — New York ; Chichester : Wiley, 1981. — xv,324p : ill ; 27cm
Conference papers
ISBN 0-471-08713-0 : Unpriced B81-08689

616.1'0636 — Man. Blood. Artificial oxygenation. Effects — *Conference proceedings*

Workshop Symposium on Basic Aspects of Blood Trauma in Extracorporeal Oxygenation *(1978 : Stolberg)*. Basic aspects of blood trauma : a Workshop Symposium on Basic Aspects of Blood Trauma in Extracorporeal Oxygenation held at Stolberg near Aachen, Federal Republic of Germany, November 21-23, 1978 / sponsored by the Commission of the European Communities, as advised by the Committee on Medical and Public Health Research ; edited by H. Schmid Schonbein, P. Teitel. — The Hague ; London : Nijhoff for the Commission of the European Communities, 1979. — 404p,[1]leaf of plates : ill(some col.) ; 25cm
Includes bibliographies
ISBN 90-247-2279-9 : Unpriced B81-05651

616.1'071 — Man. Cardiovascular system. Diseases. Role of diet

Holmes, David, *1927-*. Recommendations for the prevention and after-care of cardio-vascular disease in humans : based on the results of recent research / David Holmes. — [Emsworth] ([1 Western Parade, Emsworth, Hants. PO10 7HS]) : [D. Holmes], [1981]. — 54p : ill ; 21cm
Bibliography: p53-54
Unpriced (pbk) B81-31967

616.1'075'024613 — Man. Cardiovascular system. Diagnosis — *Programmed instructions — For nursing*

Thompson, Donald A.. Cardiovascular assessment : guide for nurses and other health professionals / Donald A. Thompson. — St. Louis ; London : Mosby, 1981. — x,238p : ill,froms ; 24cm
Ill. on inside cover. — Bibliography: p206-208. — Includes index
ISBN 0-8016-4954-4 (pbk) : £8.50 B81-25613

616.1'07575 — Man. Cardiovascular system. Diagnosis. Radiography. Use of radioisotope scanning

Nuclear cardiology : principles and methods / edited by Aldo N. Serafini, Albert J. Gilson, and William M. Smoak. — New York ; London : Plenum Medical, c1977. — xv,249p,[1] leaf of plates : ill(some col.) ; 24cm. — (Topics in cardiovascular disease)
Includes index
ISBN 0-306-30952-1 : Unpriced B81-00924

Strauss, H. WilliamCardiovascular nuclear medicine / edited by H. William Strauss, Bertram Pitt. — 2nd ed. — St. Louis ; London : Mosby, 1979. — xii,429p : ill ; 27cm
Previous ed.: 1974. — Includes bibliographies and index
ISBN 0-8016-2409-6 : Unpriced B81-08168

616.1'2 — Man. Heart. Diseases

Advances in heart disease / edited by Dean T. Mason. — New York ; London : Grune & Stratton. — (Clinical cardiology monographs)
Includes index
Vol.3. — c1980. — xx,811p : ill ; 24cm
ISBN 0-8089-1284-4 : £27.80 B81-13617

Fowler, Noble O.. Cardiac diagnosis and treatment / Noble O. Fowler ; foreword by J. Willis Hurst. — 3rd ed. / authors of contributed chapters Robert J. Adolph ... [et al.]. — Hagerstown ; London : Harper & Row, c1980. — xxi,1301p : ill ; 27cm
Previous ed.: 1976. — Includes bibliographies and index
ISBN 0-06-140818-2 : £43.95 B81-03089

Introduction to cardiology / edited by Robert H. Eich. — Hagerstown ; London : Harper & Row, c1980. — xiii,346p,[2]p of plates : ill (some col.) ; 24cm
Includes bibliographies and index
ISBN 0-06-140770-4 (pbk) : Unpriced B81-17016

Joseph, Simon. Heart trouble / Simon Joseph ; illustrated by the Hayward Art Group. — Feltham : Hamlyn Paperbacks, 1981. — 48p : ill ; 17cm. — (Pocket health guides)
ISBN 0-600-20311-5 (pbk) : £0.85 B81-40892

Lee, Won R.. Essentials of clinical cardiology / Won R. Lee. — Bowie : Charles Press ; London : Prentice-Hall, c1980. — x,463p : ill ; 21cm. — (The Charles Press series on cardiology and critical care)
Includes index
ISBN 0-89303-008-2 (pbk) : £16.20 B81-02078

Schrire, Velva. Schrire's clinical cardiology. — 4th ed. / by Elliot Chester. — Bristol : John Wright, 1981. — vii,344p : ill ; 25cm
Previous ed.: published as Clinical cardiology / Velva Schrire. St. Albans : Staples, 1972. — Includes bibliographies and index
ISBN 0-7236-0600-5 (pbk) : £17.50 : CIP rev. B81-04376

616.1'2 — Man. Heart. Diseases — *Conference proceedings*

Cardiac ischemia and arrhythmias : an international congress / sponsored by International Medical Education Corporation, Englewood, Colorado, U.S.A. ; edited by Ezra A. Amsterdam, William E. James. — Miami : Symposia Specialists ; Chicago ; London : Distributed by Year Book Medical, c1980. — xvi,368p : ill,facsims ; 24cm
Includes index
ISBN 0-8151-4848-8 : £29.50 B81-13258

Conference On Cardiovascular Disease *(10th : 1979 : Snowmass-at-Aspen)*. Current concepts in clinical cardiology : 10th Conference on Cardiovascular Disease in Snowmass-at-Aspen, Aspen, Cola, January 15-19, 1979 / editor John H.K. Vogel. — Basel ; London : Karger, c1980. — vii,360p : ill ; 25cm. — (Advances in cardiology ; v.27)
Includes bibliographies
ISBN 3-8055-0098-x : £52.00 B81-02221

616.1'2 — Man. Heart. Diseases — *For children*

Tully, Mary-Alice. Heart disease / by Mary-Alice and Marianne Tully. — New York ; London : Watts, 1980. — 64p : ill ; 23cm. — (A First book)
Bibliography: p61. - Includes index
ISBN 0-531-04163-8 : £2.99 B81-03640

616.1'2'0024613 — Medicine. Cardiology — *For nursing*

Karch, Amy Morrison. Cardiac care : a guide for patient education / Amy Morrison Karch ; with a contribution by Susanna Cunningham ; foreword by Nina T. Argondizzo. — New York : Appleton-Century-Crofts ; London : Prentice-Hall, c1981. — xiii,161p : ill ; 24cm. — (Appleton patient education series)
Includes index
ISBN 0-8385-1041-8 (pbk) : Unpriced B81-33365

616.1'2'005 — Man. Heart. Diseases — *Serials*

Progress in cardiology. — 9. — Philadelphia : Lea & Febiger ; London : Kimpton, c1980. — xi,193p
ISBN 0-8121-0728-4 : £7.50
ISSN 0097-109x B81-20311

616.1'2'005 — Medicine. Cardiology — *Serials*

Advances in cardiology. — Vol.28. — Basel ; London : Karger, c1981. — ix,247p
ISBN 3-8055-1185-x : £39.25
ISSN 0065-2326 B81-25484

Cardiology update. — 1981 ed. — Edinburgh : Churchill Livingstone, c1981. — 392p
ISBN 0-443-02434-0 : Unpriced
ISSN 0163-1675 B81-12409

Recent advances in cardiology. — No.8. — Edinburgh : Churchill Livingstone, 1981
8. — Dec. 1980. — ix,348p
ISBN 0-443-01995-9 : £20.00 : CIP rev.
ISSN 0143-2435 B80-31661

616.1'2043 — Man. Heart. Congenital abnormalities

Becker, Anton E.. Pathology of congenital heart disease. — London : Butterworths, Sept.1981. — [363]p. — (Postgraduate pathology series)
ISBN 0-407-00137-9 : £35.00 : CIP entry B81-23918

616.1'205 — Man. Heart. Diseases. Prevention

Kezdi, Paul. You and your heart : how to take care of your heart for a long and healthy life / Paul Kexdi. — Rev. ed., With further revisions. — Harmondsworth : Penguin, 1981. — 222p : ill ; 19cm. — (Pelican books)
Previous ed.: New York : Atheneum, 1977. — Includes index
ISBN 0-14-022298-7 (pbk) : £1.75 B81-11534

616.1'2071 — Man. Heart. Diseases. Role of drugs

Drug-induced heart disease / edited by M.R. Bristow. — Amsterdam ; Oxford : Elsevier/North-Holland Biomedical Press, 1980. — 476p : ill ; 25cm. — (Meyler and Peck's drug-induced diseases ; v.5)
Includes bibliographies and index
ISBN 0-444-80206-1 : £36.44 B81-15664

616.1'2075 — Man. Heart. Diagnosis

Winwood, R. S.. Essentials of clinical diagnosis in cardiology. — London : Edward Arnold, June 1981. — [256]p
ISBN 0-7131-4388-6 (pbk) : £10.00 : CIP entry B81-12858

616.1'207543 — Man. Heart. Diagnosis. Echocardiography

The **Essentials** in echocardiography. — The Hague ; London : Nijhoff. — (The Tardieu series)
1 / J.-L. Laurenceau, M.-C. Malergue ; Bernard Tardieu medical illustrator ; foreword by A.J. Tajik. — 1981. — 151p : ill(some col.) ; 25cm
Bibliography: p139-148. — Includes index
ISBN 90-247-2482-1 (pbk) : Unpriced B81-23228

Reigenbaum, Harvey. Echocardiography / Harvey Feigenbaum. — Philadelphia : Lea & Febiger ; London : Kimpton, 1981. — xiii,580p : ill ; 27cm
Previous ed.: 1977. — Includes index
ISBN 0-8121-0758-6 : £12.00 B81-16121

616.1'207543 — Man. Heart. Diagnosis. Echocardiography — *Conference proceedings*

Echocardiology / edited by Hans Rijsterborgh. — The Hague ; London : Nijhoff, 1981. — xx,476p : ill ; 25cm. — (Developments in cardiovascular medicine ; v.13)
Conference papers. — Includes index
ISBN 90-247-2491-0 : Unpriced B81-33342

616.1'207543 — Man. Heart. Diagnosis. Two-dimensional echocardiography

Two-dimensional echocardiography / edited by Joseph A. Kisslo. — New York ; Edinburgh : Churchill Livingstone, 1980. — xii,204p : ill ; 25cm. — (Clinics in diagnostic ultrasound ; v.4)
Includes index
ISBN 0-443-08076-3 : £11.00 B81-09610

616.1'207547 — Man. Heart. Ambulatory monitoring by electrocardiography

Ambulatory ECG monitoring : a monograph / edited by Shlomo Stern. — Chicago ; London : Year Book Medical, c1978. — x,197p : ill ; 24cm
Includes index
ISBN 0-8151-8213-9 : £19.25 B81-06355

Wenger, Nanette Kass. Ambulatory electrocardiographic recording / Nanette Kass Wenger, Michael B. Mock, Ivar Ringqvist. — Chicago ; London : Year Book Medical, c1981. — xx,456p : ill ; 24cm
Includes index
ISBN 0-8151-9220-7 : £43.50 B81-30121

616.1'207547 — Man. Heart. Cardiac output. Measurement. Electrical impedance techniques

Mohapatra, Surya. Non-invasive cardiovascular monitoring by electrical impedance technique. — London : Pitman Medical, July 1981. — [304]p
ISBN 0-272-79612-3 : £26.00 : CIP entry B81-13903

616.1'207547 — Man. Heart. Diagnosis. Electrocardiograms. Interpretation — *Manuals*

Rowlands, Derek J.. Understanding the electrocardiogram : a new approach / by Derek J. Rowlands. — [Edinburgh] : [Churchill Livingstone]
Section 1: The normal ECG. — [1980]. — 104p : col.ill ; 31cm
Originally published: Macclesfield : Pharmaceutical Divisions I.C.I., 1980
ISBN 0-443-02506-1 (spiral) : Unpriced B81-17434

616.1'207547 — Man. Heart. Diagnosis. Electrocardiography

Chou, Te-Chuan. Electrocardiography in clinical practice / Te-Chuan Chou. — New York ; London : Grune & Stratton, c1979. — xiv,500p : ill ; 26cm
Includes bibliographies and index
ISBN 0-8089-1138-4 : £24.80 B81-13056

Conover, Mary Boudreau. Understanding electrocardiography : physiological and interpretive concepts. — 3rd ed. / Mary Boudreau Conover, contributor Edward L. Conover. — St. Louis ; London : Mosby, 1980. — xv,287p : ill ; 24cm
Previous ed.: / Mary H. Conover, Edwin G. Zallis, contributor Edward L. Conover. 1976. — Includes index
ISBN 0-8016-5676-1 (pbk) : £8.75 B81-08202

Goldberger, Ary Louis. Clinical electrocardiography : a simplified approach / Ary Louis Goldberger, Emanuel Goldberger. — 2nd ed. — St. Louis ; London : Mosby, 1981. — xi,307p : ill ; 26cm
Previous ed.: 1977. — Bibliography: p300-301. — Includes index
ISBN 0-8016-1865-7 : £12.25 B81-31154

What's new in electrocardiography / edited by H.J.J. Wellens and H.E. Kulbertus. — The Hague ; London : Nijhoff, 1981. — xi,384p : ill ; 25cm
Includes index
ISBN 90-247-2450-3 (cased) : Unpriced
ISBN 90-247-2452-x (pbk) B81-36865

616.1'207547 — Man. Heart. Diagnosis. Electrocardiography - *Conference proceedings*

International Congress on Electrocardiology *(7th : 1980 : Lisbon)*. New frontiers of electrocardiology. — Chichester : Wiley, Aug.1981. — [456]p
ISBN 0-471-10041-2 : £20.00 : CIP entry B81-18058

616.1'207547'024613 — Man. Heart. Diagnosis. Electrocardiography — *For nursing*

Kernicki, Jeanette G.. Electrocardiography for nurses : physiological correlates / Jeanette G. Kernicki, Kathi M. Weiler. — New York ; Chichester : Wiley, c1981. — vii,262p : ill ; 27cm. — (A Wiley medical publication)
Includes index
ISBN 0-471-05752-5 : £11.00 B81-23978

616.1'2079 — Man. Heart. Diseases. Immunological aspects

Clinical immunology of the heart / [edited by] John B. Zabriskie, Mary Allen Engle, Herman Villarreal, Jr. — New York ; Chichester : Wiley, c1981. — xiii,238p : ill ; 27cm. — (Wiley series in clinical immunology)
Includes index
ISBN 0-471-02676-x : Unpriced B81-08661

616.1'22 — Man. Heart. Angina pectoris — *Conference proceedings*

Unstable angina : a rational approach to its recognition and management / edited by Allen G. Adelman and Bernard S. Goldman. — The Hague ; London : Nijhoff, 1981. — xxi,336p : ill ; 25cm
Includes index
ISBN 90-247-2486-4 : Unpriced B81-32371

616.1'23 — Man. Heart. Coronary diseases

Anderson, Ian, *1939-*. Heart attacks understood / Ian Anderson ; illustrated by Chris Evans. — London : Pan in association with Macmillan, 1981, c1980. — 154p : ill ; 18cm
Originally published: London : Macmillan, 1980. — Includes index
ISBN 0-330-26318-8 (pbk) : £1.50 B81-19694

Coronary heart disease : the modern epidemic. — 2nd ed. — [London] ([5 John Princes St., W1M 0AP]) : National Dairy Council in association with the Eggs Authority, 1980. — 24p : col.ill ; 22cm
Cover title. — Previous ed.: 1978
ISBN 0-902748-25-4 (pbk) : Unpriced
B81-09321

Hampton, John R.. All about heart attacks / J.R. Hampton. — Edinburgh : Churchill Livingstone, 1981. — 74p : ill ; 19cm. — (Churchill Livingstone patient handbook ; 8)
ISBN 0-443-02221-6 (pbk) : £1.25 B81-37096

Maclean, Una. Heart attack : survival, recovery, prevention / Una Maclean. — London : Granada, 1981. — 142p ; 21cm
Bibliography: p137-139. - Includes index
ISBN 0-246-11126-7 : £6.95 B81-21682

616.1'23 — Man. Heart. Coronary diseases. Effects of exercise

Shephard, Roy J.. Ischaemic heart disease and exercise / Roy J. Shephard. — London : Croom Helm, c1981. — 428p : ill ; 23cm
Bibliography: p324-418. - Includes index
ISBN 0-7099-0325-1 : £19.95 B81-17851

616.1'23'0024613 — Man. Heart. Coronary diseases — *Programmed instructions — For nursing*

Vinsant, Marielle Ortiz. Commonsense approach to coronary care : a program. — 3rd ed. / Marielle Ortiz Vinsant, Martha I. Spence. — St. Louis ; London : Mosby, 1981. — xiii,349p : ill ; 26cm
Previous ed.: 1975. — Template in pocket. — Bibliography: p326-348
ISBN 0-8016-5235-9 (spiral) : £10.00
B81-09767

616.1'23028'028 — Man. Heart. Coronary diseases. Intensive care. Instrumentation

Grandis, S. L.. Instrumentation for coronary care / S.L. Grandis. — Cambridge : Cambridge University Press, 1981. — vii,138p : ill ; 24cm. — (Techniques of measurement in medicine ; 5)
Includes bibliographies and index
ISBN 0-521-23548-0 (cased) : £16.00 : CIP rev.
ISBN 0-521-28024-9 (pbk) : £5.50 B81-28011

616.1'2305 — Man, Heart. Coronary diseases. Prevention. Role of diet & exercise

Passwater, Richard. Supernutrition for healthy hearts. — Wellingborough : Thorsons, June 1981. — [416]p
ISBN 0-7225-0690-2 (pbk) : £4.50 : CIP entry
B81-09481

616.1'2305 — Man. Heart. Coronary diseases. Prevention. Role of exercise

Kavanagh, Terence. The healthy heart program / Terence Kavanagh. — Updated and expanded ed.. — Toronto ; London : Van Nostrand Reinhold, c1980. — x,318p : ill ; 22cm
Previous ed.: published as Heart attack? counterattack!, 1976. — Bibliography: p310-313. - Includes index
ISBN 0-442-29768-8 (pbk) : £5.20 B81-09020

616.1'23706 — Man. Heart. Muscles. Infarction. Therapy

Coronary care / editor Joel S. Karliner ; associate editor Gabriel Gregoratos. — New York ; Edinburgh : Churchill Livingstone, 1981. — xxv,1108p : ill ; 27cm
Includes index
ISBN 0-443-08061-5 : Unpriced B81-12225

616.1'23707575 — Man. Heart. Muscles. Acute infarction. Diagnosis. Use of radioisotope scanning: Thallium-201 imaging & technetium-99m-pyrophosphate imaging

Myocardial imaging in the coronary care unit : thallium-201 and technetium-99m-pyrophosphate / edited by Frans J.Th. Wackers. — The Hague ; London : Nijhoff, 1980. — xii,255p : ill ; 25cm. — (Developments in cardiovascular medicine ; v.9)
Includes index
ISBN 90-247-2396-5 : Unpriced B81-07277

616.1'24 — Man. Heart. Muscles. Degradation

Degradative processes in heart and skeletal muscle / editor K. Wildenthal. — Amsterdam ; Oxford : Elsevier/North-Holland Biochemical Press, 1980. — xvii,461p : ill ; 25cm. — (Research monographs in cell and tissue physiology ; v.3)
Includes bibliographies and index
ISBN 0-444-80235-5 : £41.75
Also classified at 616.7'4 B81-05268

616.1'25 — Man. Heart. Mitral valve. Diseases

Fitzmaurice, Joan B.. Rheumatic heart disease and mitral valve disease / Joan B. Fitzmaurice. — New York ; London : Appleton-Century-Crofts, c1980. — viii,71p : ill ; 23cm. — (Continuing education in cardiovascular nursing. Series 2, Surgical aspects of cardiovascular disease - nursing intervention ; unit 3)
Includes bibliographies
ISBN 0-8385-8439-x (pbk) : £4.50
Primary classification 616.1'27 B81-12158

616.1'27 — Man. Heart. Rheumatic diseases

Fitzmaurice, Joan B.. Rheumatic heart disease and mitral valve disease / Joan B. Fitzmaurice. — New York ; London : Appleton-Century-Crofts, c1980. — viii,71p : ill ; 23cm. — (Continuing education in cardiovascular nursing. Series 2, Surgical aspects of cardiovascular disease - nursing intervention ; unit 3)
Includes bibliographies
ISBN 0-8385-8439-x (pbk) : £4.50
Also classified at 616.1'25 B81-12158

616.1'28 — Man. Heart. Arrhythmia

Arrhythmias of the heart / editor J. Nieveen. — Amsterdam ; Oxford : Excerpta Medica, 1981. — x,256p : ill ; 25cm. — (The Jonxis lectures ; v.6)
Includes bibliographies and index
ISBN 90-219-6006-0 : Unpriced B81-35561

Bellet, Samuel. Bellet's essentials of cardiac arrhythmias. — 2nd ed. / Richard H. Helfant. — Philadelphia ; London : Saunders, 1980 c1979. — xi,389p : ill,1port ; 26cm
Previous ed.: published as Essentials of cardiac arrhythmias. 1972. — Includes bibliographies and index
ISBN 0-7216-4626-3 : £13.25 B81-00925

Bennett, David H.. Cardiac arrhythmias : practical notes on interpretation and treatment / David H. Bennett. — Bristol : John Wright, 1981. — viii,164p : ill ; 24cm
Includes index
ISBN 0-7236-0590-4 (pbk) : £8.50 : CIP rev.
B81-03177

Schamroth, Leo. The disorders of cardiac rhythm / Leo Schamroth. — 2nd ed. — Oxford : Blackwell Scientific, 1980. — 2v.(xx,736,lvp) : ill ; 29cm
Previous ed.: in 1v. 1977. — Bibliography: pi-xl — Includes index
ISBN 0-632-00619-6 : £56.00 : CIP rev.
B80-07800

616.1'28 — Man. Heart. Arrhythmia — *Conference proceedings*

Diagnosis and treatment of cardiac arrhythmias : proceedings of an international symposium on diagnosis and treatment of cardiac arrhythmias held at Barcelona, Spain, on 5-8 October 1977 / editors A. Bayes and J. Cosin. — Oxford : Pergamon, 1980. — xxiii,1003p : ill ; 26cm
Translation of: Diagnostico y tratamiento de las arritmias cardiacas. — Includes index
ISBN 0-08-024426-2 : £90.00 : CIP rev.
B79-18413

616.1'28061 — Man. Heart. Arrhythmia. Drug therapy

Pharmacology of antiarrhythmic agents / section editor L. Szekeres. — Oxford : Pergamon, 1981. — ix,383p : ill ; 28cm. — (International encyclopedia of pharmacology and therapeutics ; Section 105)
Includes bibliographies and index
ISBN 0-08-025897-2 : £35.40 : CIP rev.
B80-09256

616.1'28061 — Man. Heart. Arrhythmia. Drug therapy — *Conference proceedings*

Prognosis and pharmacotherapy of life-threatening arrhythmias. — London : Academic Press, Nov.1981. — [250]p. — (International congress and symposium series / Royal Society of Medicine ; no.49)
Conference papers
ISBN 0-12-794635-7 (pbk) : CIP entry
B81-30340

616.1'28061 — Man. Heart. Arrhythmia. Drug therapy. Evaluation — *Conference proceedings*

Symposium on How to Evaluate a New Antiarrhythmic Drug *(1980 : Philadelphia)*. The evaluation of new antiarrhythmic drugs : proceedings of the Symposium on How to Evaluate a New Antiarrhythmic Drug : the evaluation of new antiarrhythmic agents for the treatment of ventricular arrhythmias held at Philadelphia, Pennsylvania, October 8-9, 1980 / edited by Joel Morganroth ... [et al.]. — The Hague ; London : Nijhoff, 1981. — xiv,323p : ill ; 25cm. — (Developments in cardiovascular medicine ; v.11)
ISBN 90-247-2474-0 : Unpriced B81-17112

616.1'2807 — Man. Heart. Arrhythmia. Electrophysiology

The **Slow** inward current and cardiac arrhythmias / edited by Douglas P. Zipes, John C. Gailey, Victor Elharrar. — The Hague ; London : Nijhoff, 1980. — xiii,521p : ill,facsims ; 25cm. — (Developments in cardiovascular medicine ; vol.7)
Includes index
ISBN 90-247-2380-9 : Unpriced B81-03418

616.1'2807547 — Man. Heart. Arrhythmia. Diagnosis. Electrocardiograms. Interpretation — *For nursing*

Gardiner, J.. The ECG - what does it tell? / J. Gardiner. — Cheltenham : Thornes, 1981. — 60p : ill ; 16x32cm
Includes index
ISBN 0-85950-302-x (pbk) : £1.95 : CIP rev.
B81-13745

616.1'29 — Man. Heart. Heart failure — *Conference proceedings*

Sudden death / edited by H.E. Kulbertus and H.J.J. Wellens. — The Hague ; London : Nijhoff, 1980. — xvi,404p : ill,1map ; 26cm. — (Developments in cardiovascular medicine ; v.4)
Conference papers. — Includes index
ISBN 90-247-2290-x : Unpriced B81-03806

616.1'29 — Man. Heart. Heart failure — *Early works*

The Concept of heart failure : from Avicenna to Albertini / translations, commentaries, and an essay by Saul Jarcho. — Cambridge, Mass. ; London : Harvard University Press, 1980. — ix,407p ; 29cm. — (A Commonwealth Fund book)
Includes index
ISBN 0-674-15635-8 : £27.00 B81-09356

616.1'290252 — Man. Heart. Heart failure. First aid. Resuscitation — *Manuals*

Seymour, Rogers James. The heart attack survival manual : a guide to using CPR (Cardiopulmonary Resuscitation) in a crisis / Rogers James Seymour. — Englewood Cliffs ; London : Prentice-Hall, c1981. — ix,115p : ill ; 24cm. — (A Spectrum book)
Bibliography: p111-115
ISBN 0-13-385740-9 (cased) : Unpriced
ISBN 0-13-385732-8 (pbk) : £3.85 B81-22716

616.1'290252 — Man. Heart. Heart failure. Resuscitation

Safar, Peter. Cardiopulmonary cerebral resuscitation / by Peter Safar ; prepared for the World Federation of Societies of Anaesthesiologists. — Stavenger : Laerdal ; Philadelphia ; London : Saunders [distributor], 1981. — 240p : ill(some col.) ; 21cm
Bibliography: p220-230. — Includes index
ISBN 82-990738-0-4 (pbk) : £5.50 B81-34829

616.1'3 — Man. Blood vessels. Inflammation

Vasculitis / edited by Klaus Wolff, Richard K. Winkelmann. — London : Lloyd-Luke, 1980. — xiv,338p : ill ; 26cm. — (Major problems in dermatology ; v.10)
Conference papers. — Includes bibliographies and index
ISBN 0-85324-151-1 : £20.00
Also classified at 616.4'2 B81-00926

616.1'3 — Man. Blood vessels. Thrombosis

Pitney, W. R.. Venous and arterial thrombosis. — Edinburgh : Churchill Livingstone, Nov.1981. — [264]p
ISBN 0-443-01973-8 : £9.00 : CIP entry
B81-30379

616.1'3 — Man. Cardiovascular system. Occlusion — *Conference proceedings*

Vascular occlusion : epidemiological, pathophysiological and therapeutic aspects / edited by M. Tesi, J.A. Dormandy. — London : Academic Press, 1981. — xii,473p : ill ; 24cm. — (Proceedings of the Serono Symposia, ISSN 0308-5503 ; v.37)
Includes bibliographies
ISBN 0-12-685380-0 : £28.80 : CIP rev.
B81-06626

616.1'305'0941 — Great Britain. Man. Arteries. Diseases. Prevention — *For general practice*

Prevention of arterial disease in general practice : report of a sub-committee of the Royal College of General Practitioners' Working Party on Prevention. — London : The College, 1981. — 19p ; 28cm. — (Report from general practice ; 19)
Bibliography: p17-19
ISBN 0-85084-076-7 (pbk) : £3.00 B81-13334

616.1'3071 — Man. Vascular diseases. Role of hormones

Hormones and vascular disease. — Tunbridge Wells : Pitman Medical, June 1981. — [360]p
ISBN 0-272-79622-0 : £20.00 : CIP entry
B81-13558

616.1'3075 — Man. Blood vessels. Diagnosis

Methods in angiology : a physical-technical introduction written for clinicians by physicians / edited by Marc Verstraete ; introduced by D.E. Strandness, Jr. ; with additional expert commentary. — The Hague ; London : Nijhoff, 1980. — xii,411p : ill,1port ; 25cm. — (Instrumentation and techniques in clinical medicine ; v.2)
Includes index
ISBN 90-247-2376-0 : Unpriced B81-06123

616.1'307572 — Man. Blood vessels. Emergency diagnosis. Angiography

Ben-Menachem, Yoram. Angiography in trauma : a work atlas / Yoram Ben-Menachem with neuroradiological contributions by Stanley F. Handel ; graphic designs by Sherry Alexander. — Philadelphia ; London : Saunders, 1981. — x,476p : ill(some col.) ; 29cm
Includes bibliographies and index
ISBN 0-7216-1733-6 : Unpriced B81-17092

616.1'32 — Man. Blood. Hypertension

Knapton, James. High blood pressure / James Knapton ; illustrated by Jennie Smith. — Feltham : Hamlyn Paperbacks, 1981. — 47p : ill ; 17cm. — (Pocket health guides)
ISBN 0-600-20312-3 (pbk) : £0.85 B81-40890

Lewis, Peter J.. High blood pressure / Peter J. Lewis. — Edinburgh : Churchill Livingstone, 1981. — 55p ; 19cm. — (Churchill Livingstone patient handbook ; 7)
ISBN 0-443-02301-8 (pbk) : £1.00 : CIP rev.
B81-14980

O'Brien, Eoin. High blood pressure. — London : Martin Dunitz, Feb.1982. — [112]p. — (Positive health guides)
ISBN 0-906348-23-4 (cased) : £5.95 : CIP entry
ISBN 0-906348-24-2 (pbk) : £2.50 B81-37585

616.1'32 — Man. Blood. Hypertension — *Conference proceedings*

Colloquium on New Trends in Arterial Hypertension - Cellular Pharmacology and Physiopathology *(1980 : Deauville).* New trends in arterial hypertension : proceedings of the Colloquium on New Trends in Arterial Hypertension — Cellular Pharmacology and Physiopathology, held in Deauville (France), 30 October-1 November, 1980 : sponsored by the Institut National de la Santé et de la Recherche Médicale / editors M. Worcel ... [et al.]. — Amsterdam ; Oxford : Elsevier/North-Holland, 1981. — xvii,362p : ill ; 25cm. — (INSERM symposia ; no.17)
Introduction in English and French. — Includes index
ISBN 0-444-80324-6 : £27.20 B81-22290

Hypertension : a round table : proceedings of a panel discussion held at the Royal Society of Medicine London on 10 April 1980 / edited by Clive Wood and Yvonne Rue. — London (1 Wimpole St.) : The Society with financial support form Merck, Sharp and Dohme, c1980. — 20p ; 25cm. — (Forum series / Royal Society of Medicine, ISSN 0144-5618 ; no.1)
Unpriced (pbk) B81-09613

International Symposium of Nephrology *(2nd : 1980 : Montecatini Terme).* Secondary forms of hypertension : current diagnosis and management / [the Second International Symposium of Nephrology, Montecatini Terme, Italy May 6-8, 1980] ; edited M. Donald Blaufox, Claudio Bianchi. — New York ; London : Grune & Stratton, c1981. — xvi,341p : ill ; 24cm
Includes index
ISBN 0-8089-1384-0 : £11.20 B81-35403

616.1'32 — Man. Blood. Hypertension — *For general practice*

ABC of hypertension : articles published in the British Medical Journal. — London : British Medical Association, c1981. — 44p : ill,facsims,forms,1port ; 30cm
ISBN 0-7279-0074-9 (pbk) : Unpriced
B81-30040

616.1'3206 — Man. Blood. Hypertension. Therapy — *Conference proceedings*

The Therapeutics of hypertension / [proceedings of a symposium held in the Babbage Lecture Theatre, Cambridge, 1st-2nd October 1979, sponsored by Merck, Sharp and Dohme] ; edited by J.I.S. Robertson, G.W. Pickering and A.D.S. Caldwell. — London : Royal Society of Medicine, 1980. — xiii,264p : ill ; 24cm. — (Royal Society of Medicine series. International congress and symposium series, ISSN 0142-2367 ; no.26)
Includes bibliographies
ISBN 0-12-793568-1 (pbk) : £12.00 : CIP rev.
B80-09704

616.1'32061 — Man. Blood. Hypertension. Drug therapy. Captopril — *Conference proceedings*

Captopril and hypertension / edited by David B. Case, Edmund H. Sonnenblick and John H. Laragh. — New York ; London : Plenum Medical, c1980. — xi,236p : ill ; 24cm. — (Topics in cardiovascular disease)
Conference papers. — Includes bibliographies and index
ISBN 0-306-40532-6 : Unpriced B81-08212

616.1'32071 — Man. Hypertension. Role of renal medulla

The Renal papilla and hypertension / edited by Anil K. Mandal and Sven-Olof Bohman. — New York ; London : Plenum Medical, c1980. — xxiv,237p,[36]p of plates : ill ; 24cm
Includes bibliographies and index
ISBN 0-306-40506-7 : Unpriced B81-0657[?]

616.1'35 — Man. Blood vessels. Thrombosis

Haemostasis and thrombosis / edited by Arthur L. Bloom and Duncan P. Thomas. — Edinburgh : Churchill Livingstone, 1981. — xii,868p : ill ; 26cm
Includes bibliographies and index
ISBN 0-443-01991-6 : £35.00 : CIP rev.
Primary classification 616.1'57 B81-3032[?]

616.1'36 — Man. Arteries. Atherosclerosis — *Conference proceedings*

Prostaglandins, platelets, lipids : new developments in atherosclerosis / editors Hadley L. Conn, Jr., Eugene De Felice, Peter T. Kuo. — Miami : Symposia Specialists ; New York ; Oxford : Distributed by Elsevier, c1981. — xii,152p : ill ; 24cm
Conference papers. — Includes index
ISBN 0-444-00566-8 : £15.98 B81-3675[?]

616.1'36071 — Man. Arteries. Atherosclerosis. Role of lipoprotein metabolism

Lipoproteins, atherosclerosis and coronary heart disease / edited by N.E. Miller and B. Lewis. — Amsterdam ; Oxford : Elsevier/North-Holland Biomedical, 1981. — xiv,214p : ill ; 25cm. — (Metabolic aspects of cardiovascular disease ; v.1)
Includes bibliographies and index
ISBN 0-444-80265-7 : £13.61 B81-3675[?]

616.1'4 — Man. Abdomen & pelvis. Veins. Disease — *Conference proceedings*

Pelvic Vein Symposium *(1980 : Igls-Innsbruck).* Pelvic and abdominal veins : progress in diagnostics and therapy : proceedings of the Pelvic Vein Symposium, Igls-Innsbruck, Austria, October 11-12, 1980 / editors Robert May, Jürgen Weber. — Amsterdam ; Oxford : Excerpta Medica, 1981. — xvi,374p : ill(some col.) ; 25cm. — (International congress series ; no.550)
Includes bibliographies and index
ISBN 90-219-0494-2 : Unpriced B81-3555[?]

616.1'4 — Man. Legs & pelvis. Veins. Diseases. Diagnosis. Phlebography

Lee Thomas, M.. Phlebography of the lower limb. — Edinburgh : Churchill Livingstone, Feb.1982. — [232]p
ISBN 0-443-01841-3 : £22.00 : CIP entry
B81-3571[?]

616.1'5 — Man. Blood. Diseases

Blood and its diseases / I. Chanarin ... [et al.]. — 2nd ed. — Edinburgh : Churchill Livingstone, 1980. — 287p : ill ; 22cm
Previous ed.: 1976. — Includes bibliographies and index
ISBN 0-443-02191-0 (pbk) : £6.95 : CIP rev.
B80-1063[?]

Fundamentals of hematology / Richard A. Rifkind ... [et al.]. — 2nd ed. — Chicago ; London : Year Book Medical, c1980. — ix,204p : ill ; 25cm. — (Internal medicine series)
Previous ed.: Chicago : Year Book Medical, 1976. — Includes bibliographies and index
ISBN 0-8151-7336-9 (pbk) : Unpriced
B81-1415[?]

616.1'5 — Man. Blood. Diseases
continuation

Postgraduate haematology / edited by A.V. Hoffbrand and S.M. Lewis. — 2nd ed. — London : Heinemann Medical, 1981. — x,774p : ill ; 23cm
Previous ed.: published as Haematology 1972. — Includes bibliographies and index
ISBN 0-433-15051-3 : £28.00 B81-36317

616.1'5 — Medicine. Haematology

Child, J. A.. Aids to clinical haematology. — Edinburgh : Churchill Livingstone, Dec.1981. — [112]p
ISBN 0-443-01984-3 (pbk) : £2.95 : CIP entry B81-31362

Hoffbrand, A. V.. Essential haematology / A.V. Hoffbrand, J.E. Pettit. — Oxford : Blackwell Scientific, 1980. — vii,236p : ill ; 24cm
Includes bibliographies and index
ISBN 0-632-00679-x (pbk) : £7.50 : CIP rev. B80-35062

616.1'5 — Medicine. Haematology — *Conference proceedings*

Experimental hematology today, 1981 / editors Siegmund J. Baum, G. David Ledney, Amanullah Khan. — Basel ; London : Karger, c1981. — xiv,248p : ill ; 28cm
Conference papers. — Includes bibliographies
ISBN 3-8055-2255-x : £41.00 B81-28311

616.1'5'005 — Medicine. Haematology — *Serials*

Current hematology. — Vol.1-. — New York ; Chichester : Wiley, 1981-. — v. : ill ; 27cm
Annual
ISSN 0272-085x = Current hematology : Unpriced B81-38183

Experimental hematology today. — 1977-. — Basel ; London : Karger, 1977-. — v. : ill ; 28cm
Annual. — Description based on: 1980 issue
£43.00 B81-12415

616.1'5'0076 — Medicine. Haematology — *Questions & answers*

Pegrum, G. D.. Multiple choice questions in haematology : with answers and explanatory comments / G.D. Pegrum and T.R. Mitchell. — London : Edward Arnold, 1981. — 63p ; 22cm
ISBN 0-7131-4393-2 (pbk) : £1.95 : CIP rev. B81-13868

616.1'51 — Man. Blood. Red cells. Metabolic disorders. Related to disorders of lenses of eyes — *Conference proceedings*

International Symposium on Red Blood Cell and Lens Metabolism *(2nd : 1979 : University of Texas Medical Branch)*. Red blood cell and lens metabolism : proceedings of the Second International Symposium on Red Blood Cell and Lens Metabolism, University of Texas Medical Branch, Galveston, Texas, U.S.A., October 27-29, 1979 / editor : Satish K. Srivastava. — New York ; Oxford : Elsevier/North-Holland, c1980. — xiv,508p : ill ; 25cm. — (Developments in biochemistry, ISSN 0165-1714 ; v.9)
Includes index
ISBN 0-444-00388-6 : £24.19
Also classified at 617.7'42 B81-03987

616.1'52 — Man. Sickle cell disease

Sickle-cell disease. — Edinburgh : Churchill Livingstone, Feb.1982. — [192]p. — (Medicine in the tropics series)
ISBN 0-443-02037-x (pbk) : £4.95 : CIP entry B81-35720

616.1'52042 — Man. Blood. Thalassaemia

Weatherall, D. J.. The thalassaemia syndromes / D.J. Weatherall & J.B. Clegg. — 3rd ed. — Oxford : Blackwell Scientific, 1981. — xii,875p : ill,1port ; 26cm
Previous ed.: 1972. — Bibliography: p781-858. - Includes index
ISBN 0-632-00084-8 : £42.00 : CIP rev. B81-06586

616.1'57 — Man. Blood. Haemostatic disorders

Haemostasis and thrombosis / edited by Arthur L. Bloom and Duncan P. Thomas. — Edinburgh : Churchill Livingstone, 1981. — xii,868p : ill ; 26cm
Includes bibliographies and index
ISBN 0-443-01991-6 : £35.00 : CIP rev.
Also classified at 616.1'35 B81-30327

616.1'57 — Man. Haemophilia — *Conference proceedings*

International Haemophilia Conference *(1st : 1980 : Bonn)*. The haemophiliac in the eighties : proceedings of the 1st International Haemophilia Conference, 14th World Federation of Hemophilia General Assembly, Bonn, October 3-7 1980 / editors H. Egli, M.J. Inwood. — Basel ; London : Karger, 1981. — xii,310p : ill,ports ; 26cm
Originally published: as Haemostasis Vol.10, Supplement 1, 1981. — Includes bibliographies and index
ISBN 3-8055-2885-x (pbk) : £25.50 (free to subscribers) B81-38417

616.1'57'005 — Man. Blood. Coagulation disorders — *Serials*

Recent advances in blood coagulation. — No.3. — Edinburgh : Churchill Livingstone, 1981. — viii,350p
ISBN 0-443-02182-1 : Unpriced : CIP rev.
ISSN 0143-6740 B81-21569

616.1'57061 — Man. Blood. Coagulation. Inhibitors — *Conference proceedings*

The **Physiological** inhibitors of blood coagulation and fibrinolysis : proceedings of a round-table conference held at the University of Leuven, Belgium, July 22-23, 1978 / editors D. Collen, B. Wiman, and M. Verstraete. — Amsterdam ; Oxford : Elsevier/North-Holland Biomedical, 1979. — viii,295p : ill ; 25cm
Includes index
ISBN 0-444-80092-1 : Unpriced B81-10112

616.1'572 — Man. Haemophilia — *Conference proceedings*

Unresolved problems in haemophilia. — Lancaster : MTP Press, Dec.1981. — [250]p
Conference papers
ISBN 0-85200-388-9 : £12.00 : CIP entry B81-36998

616.2 — MAN. DISEASES OF RESPIRATORY SYSTEM

616.2 — Man. Respiratory system. Diseases

Clinical investigation of respiratory disease. — London : Chapman and Hall, Dec.1981. — [350]p
ISBN 0-412-15780-2 : £15.20 : CIP entry B81-31748

Crofton, *Sir* John. Respiratory diseases / Sir John Crofton and Andrew Douglas. — 3rd ed.. — Oxford : Blackwell Scientific, 1981. — xvi,819p : ill ; 25cm
Previous ed.: 1975. — Includes index
ISBN 0-632-00577-7 : £35.00 B81-24289

Flenley, David C.. Respiratory medicine / David C. Flenley. — London : Baillière Tindall, 1981. — 263p : ill ; 22cm. — (Concise medical textbooks)
Includes bibliographies and index
ISBN 0-7020-0840-0 (pbk) : £6.50 : CIP rev. B81-16937

Forgacs, Paul. Problems in respiratory medicine / Paul Forgacs. — Lancaster : MTP, 1981. — 158p : ill ; 24cm. — (Problems in practice series)
Bibliography: p147. — Includes index
ISBN 0-85200-318-8 : £7.95 B81-38030

Scientific foundations of respiratory medicine / edited by J.G. Scadding and Gordon Cumming ; associate editor W.M. Thurlbeck. — London : Heinemann Medical, 1981. — xii,746p : ill ; 29cm
Includes bibliographies and index
£63.00 (corrected) B81-29955

White, Roger. Respiratory infections and tumours / Roger White. — Lancaster : Published, in association with Update, by MTP Press, 1981. — 92p,[8]p of plates : ill(some col.) ; 20cm. — (Topics in respiratory disease)
Bibliography: p89. — Includes index
ISBN 0-85200-428-1 : £5.95 B81-39380

616.2'0046 — Man. Respiratory system. Therapy

Rarey, Kanute P.. Respiratory patient care / Kanute P. Rarey, John W. Youtsey. — Englewood Cliffs ; London : Prentice-Hall, c1981. — xvi,400p : ill ; 25cm
Includes index
ISBN 0-13-774604-0 : £16.05 B81-26904

616.2'0047 — Man. Respiratory system. Diseases. Physiological aspects

Pathophysiology of respiration / edited by Meir H. Kryger. — New York ; Chichester : Wiley, c1981. — xvi,352p : ill ; 24cm. — (Wiley pathophysiology series)
Includes bibliographies and index
ISBN 0-471-05923-4 (pbk) : £12.95 B81-40207

616.2'00471 — Man. Respiratory system. Disorders. Role of surface-active agents — *Conference proceedings*

International Symposium on Clinical Importance of Surfactant Defects *(1979 : Hamburg)*. Clinical importance of surfactant defects / International Symposium on Clinical Importance of Surfactant Defects, Hamburg, October 31-November 2, 1979 ; volume editor P. von Wichert. — Basel ; London : Karger, 1981. — vii,319p : ill ; 25cm. — (Progress in respiration research ; v.15)
Includes bibliographies and index
ISBN 3-8055-1011-x : £43.00 B81-11542

616.2'004757 — Man. Respiratory system. Diagnosis. Radiography

Flower, Christopher. Radiology of the respiratory system / Christopher Flower. — Lancaster : Published, in association with Update, by MTP Press, 1981. — 122p : ill ; 20cm. — (Topics in respiratory disease)
Includes index
ISBN 0-85200-429-x : £5.95 B81-39379

616.2'02068 — Man. Hay fever. Self-treatment

Knight, Allan. Asthma & hay fever : how to relieve wheezing and sneezing / Allan Knight. — London : Dunitz, 1981. — 123p : ill(some col.) ; 23cm. — (Positive health guide)
Includes index
ISBN 0-906348-16-1 (cased) : Unpriced : CIP rev.
ISBN 0-906348-14-5 (pbk) : £2.50
Also classified at 616.2'38068 B81-08897

616.2'024613 — Man. Respiratory system. Diseases — *For nursing*

Riddle, Janet T. E.. The circulatory system and the respiratory system. — Edinburgh : Churchill Livingstone, Sept.1981. — [104]p. — (Objective tests for nurses ; book 3)
ISBN 0-443-01741-7 (pbk) : £2.50 : CIP entry
Primary classification 616.1'024613 B81-21570

616.2'2'005 — Otolaryngology — *Serials*

The **Year** book of otolaryngology. — 1980. — Chicago ; London : Year Book Medical Publishers, c1980. — 357p
ISBN 0-8151-6644-3 : Unpriced B81-09066

616.2'307'54 — Man. Bronchi. Diagnosis. Bronchoscopy

Stradling, Peter. Diagnostic bronchoscopy. — 4th ed. — Edinburgh : Churchill Livingstone, July 1981. — [180]p
Previous ed.: 1976
ISBN 0-443-02277-1 : £35.00 : CIP entry B81-13762

616.2'307545 — Man. Bronchi. Diagnosis. Fibre-optic bronchoscopy — *Manuals*

Oho, Kenkichi. Practical fiberoptic bronchoscopy / Kenkichi Oho, Ryuta Amemiya. — Tokyo : Igaku-Shoin ; London : Chapman and Hall, 1980. — x,112p : ill(some col.) ; 27cm
Bibliography: p105-107. - Includes index
ISBN 0-412-16480-9 : £20.00 B81-07151

616.2'34061 — Man. Bronchi. Bronchitis. Herbal remedies

Gosling, Nalda. Herbs for bronchial troubles. — Wellingborough : Thorsons, Dec.1981. — [64]p
ISBN 0-7225-0714-3 (pbk) : £0.75 : CIP entry B81-32053

616.2'38 — Man. Bronchi. Asthma

Bronchial asthma : principles of diagnosis and treatment / edited by M. Eric Gershwin. — New York ; London : Grune & Stratton ; London : Distributed by Academic Press, c1981. — xvii,456p : ill ; 24cm
Includes bibliographies and index
ISBN 0-8089-1331-x : £26.20 B81-39788

616.2'38 — Man. Bronchi. Asthma — *Conference proceedings*

International Congress on Respiratory Diseases *(1979 : Basel)*. Asthma / International Congress on Respiratory Diseases, Basel, October 10-13, 1979, 6th General Meeting of the European Society for Clinical Respiratory Physiology (SEPCR) ; volume editor H. Herzog ; co-editors D.W. Empey ... [et al.]. — Basel ; London : Karger, 1980. — viii,314p : ill ; 25cm. — (Progress in respiration research ; v.14)
Includes bibliographies and index
ISBN 3-8055-0991-x : £23.75 B81-09611

616.2'3806 — Man. Bronchi. Asthma. Therapy

Roberts, R. A.. Asthma and its relief / R.A. Roberts. — Hornchurch : Henry, c1980. — vii,78p : ill ; 17cm
Includes index
ISBN 0-86025-849-1 : £3.95 B81-27188

616.2'38061 — Man. Bronchi. Asthma. Drug therapy. Sodium cromoglycate — *Conference proceedings*

Charles Blackley Symposium *(4th : 1981 : Nottingham)*. New approaches to Intal therapy / presented at the fourth Charles Blackley Symposium 5-10 July 1981 Cripp's Hall University of Nottingham. — [Oxford] : Medical Education Services, [1981]. — [12]p : ill ; 28cm
ISBN 0-906817-13-7 (unbound) : Unpriced B81-39679

616.2'38068 — Man. Bronchi. Asthma. Self-treatment

Knight, Allan. Asthma & hay fever : how to relieve wheezing and sneezing / Allan Knight. — London : Dunitz, 1981. — 123p : ill(some col.) ; 23cm. — (Positive health guide)
Includes index
ISBN 0-906348-16-1 (cased) : Unpriced : CIP rev.
ISBN 0-906348-14-5 (pbk) : £2.50
Primary classification 616.2'02068 B81-08897

616.2'4 — Man. Lungs. Diseases

Assessment of a patient with lung disease / edited by Jonathan R. Webb. — Lancaster : Published, in association with Update, by MTP Press, 1981. — 92p,[8]p of plates : ill(some col.) ; 20cm. — (Topics in respiratory disease)
Bibliography: p89. — Includes index
ISBN 0-85200-426-5 : £5.95 B81-39381

616.2'4 — Man. Lungs. Effects of aerosols

Aerosols, airways and asthma / edited by Joseph J. Trautlein. — Lancaster : MTP, c1981. — 102p : ill ; 24cm
Includes index
ISBN 0-85200-569-5 : £11.95 B81-33073

616.2'4 — Man. Lungs. Failure. Effects of shock

Schneus, Günther. Shock : acute progressive lung failure. — Oxford (52 New Inn Hall St., Oxford OX1 2BS) : Medical Publishing Foundation, Oct.1981. — [56]p
ISBN 0-906817-10-2 (pbk) : £14.95 : CIP entry B81-30632

616.2'4 — Man. Lungs. Interstitial diseases

Pickering, C. A. C.. Interstitial lung disease / C.A.C. Pickering, L. Doyle, K.B. Carroll. — Lancaster : Published, in association with Update, by MTP Press, 1981. — 116p,[3]p of plates : ill(some col.) ; 20cm. — (Topics in respiratory disease)
Includes bibliographies and index
ISBN 0-85200-427-3 : £5.95 B81-39382

616.2'4 — Man. Lungs. Obstructive diseases

Geddes, Duncan M.. Airways obstruction / Duncan M. Geddes. — Lancaster : Published, in association with Update, by MTP Press, 1981. — 92p,[8]p of plates : ill(some col.) ; 20cm. — (Topics in respiratory disease)
Bibliography: p88. — Includes index
ISBN 0-85200-425-7 : £5.95 B81-39383

616.2'4'0024613 — Man. Lungs. Diseases - *For nursing*

Sexton, Dorothy L.. Chronic obstructive pulmonary disease : care of the child and adult / Dorothy L. Sexton. — St. Louis ; London : Mosby, 1981. — xiii,292p : ill ; 24cm
Bibliography: p269-271. - Includes index
ISBN 0-8016-4490-9 : £12.00 B81-15000

616.2'4'005 — Man. Lungs. Diseases — *Serials*

Current pulmonology. — Vol.1-. — New York ; Chichester : Wiley, 1979-. — v. : ill ; 26cm
Annual. — Description based on: Vol.3
ISSN 0163-7800 = Current pulmonology : £35.00 B81-33697

Pulmonary disease reviews. — Vol.1-. — New York ; Chichester : Wiley, 1980-. — v. : ill ; 27cm
Annual. — Description based on: Vol.2
ISSN 0272-7900 = Pulmonary disease reviews : £31.00 B81-34022

616.2'406 — Man. Lungs. Therapy — *Manuals*

Manual of pulmonary procedures / edited by Stephen J. Jay, Robert B. Stonehill. — Philadelphia ; London ; Saunders, 1980. — xii,187p : ill ; 20cm
Includes index
ISBN 0-7216-5116-x (spiral) : £7.00 B81-06491

616.2'407 — Man. Lungs. Pathology

Gibbs, A. R.. Atlas of pulmonary pathology. — Lancaster : MTP Press, Dec.1981. — [136]p. — (Current histopathology series ; v.3)
ISBN 0-85200-331-5 : £30.00 : CIP entry B81-38817

616.2'4075 — Man. Lungs. Diagnosis. Techniques

Pulmonary diagnosis : imaging and other techniques / edited by Charles E. Putman. — New York : Appleton-Century-Crofts ; London : Prentice-Hall, c1981. — viii,323p : ill ; 29cm
Includes index
ISBN 0-8385-8058-0 : £34.90 B81-40137

616.2'4075 — Man. Lungs. Diagnosis. Tests

Hughes, D. T. D.. Lung function for the clinician / D.T.D. Hughes and D.W. Empey. — London : Academic Press, 1981. — ix,122p : ill ; 23cm
Includes bibliographies and index
ISBN 0-12-792078-1 (pbk) : £6.80 : CIP rev. B81-12329

616.2'44 — Man. Lungs. Coccidioidomycosis

Coccidioidomycosis : a text / edited by David A. Stevens. — New York ; London : Plenum Medical, c1980. — xvii,279p : ill ; 24cm. — (Current topics in infectious disease)
Includes index
ISBN 0-306-40410-9 : Unpriced B81-04582

616.2'48 — Man. Lungs. Emphysema — *Conference proceedings*

Biochemistry, pathology and genetics of pulmonary emphysema : proceedings of an international symposium held in Sassari, Italy, 27-30 April 1980 / editors J. Bignon and G.L. Scarpa. — Oxford : Pergamon, 1981. — 428p : ill ; 25cm
English text, French résumé. — Also available in pbk. as Vol.16, Supplement No.1, 1981 to the journal Bulletin Européen de physiopathologie respiratoire. — Includes index
ISBN 0-08-027379-3 : £27.00 : CIP rev. B81-06614

616.2'49 — Man. Lungs. Blood vessels. Embolism — *Conference proceedings*

International Symposium on Pulmonary Circulation *(3rd : 1979 : Prague)*. Pulmonary embolism : selected papers of the International Symposium on Pulmonary Circulation III, Prague, July 2-4, 1979 / volume editor J. Widímský. — Basel ; London : Karger, 1980. — vii,189p : ill ; 25cm. — (Progress in respiration research ; v.13)
Includes index
ISBN 3-8055-0487-x : £43.50 B81-04029

616.3 — MAN. DISEASES OF DIGESTIVE SYSTEM

616.3 — Man. Digestive system. Diseases

Hobsley, Michael. Disorders of the digestive system. — London : Edward Arnold, Nov.1981. — [192]p. — (Physiological principles in medicine, ISSN 0260-2946)
ISBN 0-7131-4381-9 : £6.50 : CIP entry B81-30594

Palmer, Eddy D.. Practical points in gastroenterology / by Eddy D. Palmer. — 3rd ed. — Bern : Huber ; London : Kimpton, 1980. — 279p : ill ; 22cm
Previous ed.: 1975. — Includes index
ISBN 0-87488-733-x (pbk) : £9.00 B81-05228

Read, Alan E.. Basic gastroenterology : including diseases of the liver. — 3rd ed / Alan E. Read, R.F. Harvey and J.M. Naish with chapters by L.R. Celestin, K.T. Evans and G.M. Roberts. — Bristol : John Wright, 1981. — vii,558p : ill ; 22cm
Previous ed.: / by J.M. Naish and Alan E. Read with chapters by L.R. Celestin and K.T. Evans, 1974. — Includes bibliographies and index
ISBN 0-7236-0551-3 (pbk) : Unpriced B81-17655

616.3'005 — Man. Digestive system. Diseases — *Serials*

Developments in digestive diseases. — 3. — Philadelphia : Lea & Febiger ; London : Kimpton, 1980. — xx,258p
ISBN 0-8121-0754-3 : £11.25
ISSN 0149-7235 B81-15547

616.3'075 — Man. Digestive system. Diagnosis

Clinical diagnosis of gastrointestinal diseases / edited by Allan Kerr Grant, Alan Skyring ; foreword by Harold O. Conn. — Oxford : Blackwell Scientific, 1981. — xxi,401p : ill ; 24cm
Includes bibliographies and index
ISBN 0-632-00603-x : £18.50 B81-14497

616.3'1075 — Man. Mouth. Lesions. Differential diagnosis

Differential diagnosis of oral lesions / [edited by] Norman K. Wood, Paul W. Goaz. — 2nd ed. — St. Louis ; London : Mosby, 1980. — xv,663p,[4]p of plates : ill(some col.),forms ; 27cm
Previous ed.: 1975. — Includes bibliographies and index
ISBN 0-8016-5617-6 : £27.75 B81-08146

616.3'1079 — Man. Mouth. Diseases. Immunological aspects

Dolby, A. E.. Introduction to oral immunology. — London : Edward Arnold, Dec.1981. — [96]p
ISBN 0-7131-4404-1 (pbk) : £6.00 : CIP entry B81-31633

616.3'16 — Man. Salivary glands. Sialadenosis & sialadenitis

Sialadenosis and sialadenitis : pathophysiological and diagnostic aspects / volume editors C.R. Pfaltz, R. Chilla. — Basel ; London : Karger, 1981. — 249p : ill ; 25cm. — (Advances in oto-rhino-laryngology ; v.26)
Bibliography: p210-234. — Includes index
ISBN 3-8055-1669-x : £42.00 B81-38090

616.3'2 — Man. Oesophagus. Diseases

Foregut / edited by J.H. Baron and Frank G. Moody. — London : Butterworths, 1981. — 324p : ill ; 24cm. — (Gastroenterology ; 1) (Butterworths international medical reviews, ISSN 0260-0110)
Includes bibliographies and index
ISBN 0-407-02287-2 : Unpriced : CIP rev. B81-09460

616.3'3 — Man. Gastrointestinal tract. Communicable diseases

DuPont, Herbert L.. Infections of the gastrointestinal tract : microbiology, pathophysiology, and clinical features / Herbert L. DuPont and Larry K. Pickering. — New York ; London : Plenum Medical, c1980. — xvi,173p : ill,1map ; 24cm. — (Current topics in infectious disease)
Includes index
ISBN 0-306-40409-5 : Unpriced B81-00927

616.3'3 — Man. Gastrointestinal tract. Haemorrhages

Gastrointestinal haemorrhage / edited by Peter W. Dykes and Michael R.B. Keighley ; with a foreword by Sir Francis Avery Jones. — Bristol : John Wright, c1981. — xvi,472p : ill ; 25cm
Includes index
ISBN 0-7236-0584-x : Unpriced : CIP rev. B81-14798

616.3'3 — Man. Gastrointestinal tract. Haemorrhages — *Conference proceedings*

Gastrointestinal hemorrhage / edited by Richard G. Fiddian-Green, Jeremiah G. Turcotte. — London : Grune & Stratton, c1980. — xvi,429p : ill ; 24cm
Conference papers. — Includes bibliographies and index
ISBN 0-8089-1267-4 : £25.00 B81-01712

616.3'3 — Medicine. Gastroenterology — *For nursing*

Aspects of gastroenterology for nurses. — London : Pitman Medical, Oct.1981. — [288]p
ISBN 0-272-79607-7 : £15.00 : CIP entry B81-25778

616.3'3'005 — Medicine. Gastroenterology — *Serials*

Topics in gastroenterology. — 8. — Oxford : Blackwell Scientific, 1980. — xi,305p
ISBN 0-632-00725-7 : £16.00
ISSN 0307-6598 B81-08579

Topics in gastroenterology. — 9. — Oxford : Blackwell Scientific, Dec.1981. — [336]p
ISBN 0-632-00898-9 (pbk) : £18.00 : CIP entry B81-40260

616.3'3'007 — Patients. Health education. Special subjects: Man. Gastrointestinal tract. Diseases — *For nursing*

Gastrointestinal care : a guide for patient education / edited by Beverly H. Bonaparte. — New York : Appleton-Century-Crofts ; London : Prentice-Hall, c1981. — xii,132p : ill,forms ; 24cm : forms. — (Appleton patient education series)
Includes bibliographies and index
ISBN 0-8385-3096-6 (pbk) : £7.40 B81-36602

616.3'3042 — Man. Gastrointestinal tract. Diseases. Genetic aspects — *Conference proceedings*

Genetics and heterogeneity of common gastrointestinal disorders / [proceedings of an international workshop held in Indian Wells, California, March 17-19, 1980] ; edited by Jerome I. Rotter, I. Michael Samloff, David L. Rimoin. — New York ; London : Academic Press, 1980. — xviii,582p : ill ; 24cm
Includes index
ISBN 0-12-598760-9 : £19.60 B81-16633

616.3'3075 — Man. Gastrointestinal tract. Diagnosis

Bouchier, Ian A. D.. Clinical investigation of gastrointestinal function. — 2nd ed. — Oxford : Blackwell Scientific, July 1981. — [240]p
Previous ed.: / by Ian A. D. Bouchier. 1969
ISBN 0-632-00742-7 (pbk) : £8.00 : CIP entry B81-13456

616.3'307545 — Man. Gastrointestinal tract. Fibre-optic endoscopy

Therapeutic endoscopy and radiology of the gut / edited by John R. Bennett. — London : Chapman and Hall, 1981. — xii,271p : ill ; 24cm
Includes bibliographies and index
ISBN 0-412-22070-9 : £20.00
Also classified at 616.3'30757 B81-19839

616.3'30757 — Man. Gastrointestinal tract. Radiology

Bartram, Clive I. Clinical radiology in gastroenterology. — Oxford : Blackwell Scientific, July 1981. — [288]p
ISBN 0-632-00213-1 : £12.50 : CIP entry B81-13455

Therapeutic endoscopy and radiology of the gut / edited by John R. Bennett. — London : Chapman and Hall, 1981. — xii,271p : ill ; 24cm
Includes bibliographies and index
ISBN 0-412-22070-9 : £20.00
Primary classification 616.3'307545 B81-19839

616.3'307572 — Man. Gastrointestinal tract. Diagnosis. Radiography. Biphasic contrast

Orth, J. Odo op den. The standard biphasic-contrast examination of the stomach and duodenum : method, results, and radiological atlas / by J. Odo op den Orth. — Hague ; London : Nijhoff, 1979. — viii,182p : ill ; 28cm. — (Series in radiology ; v.1)
Bibliography: p169-179. - Includes index
ISBN 90-247-2159-8 : Unpriced B81-16323

616.3'4 — Man. Colon. Colonoscopy

Colonoscopy : techniques, clinical practice and colour atlas / edited by Richard H. Hunt and Jerome D. Waye. — London : Chapman and Hall, 1981. — xii,412p,[32]p of plates : ill(some col.) ; 24cm
Includes bibliographies and index
ISBN 0-412-22710-x : Unpriced : CIP rev. B81-14864

616.3'4 — Man. Colon. Diagnosis. Radiography

Radiographic atlas of colon disease / [edited by] Edward I. Greenbaum. — Chicago ; London : Year Book Medical Publishers, c1980. — xv,664p : ill ; 27cm
Includes bibliographies and index
ISBN 0-8151-3923-3 : £71.25 B81-06245

616.3'4 — Man. Colon. Diverticular disease

Painter, N.S.. Diverticular disease of the colon / by N.S. Painter. — 7th ed. — London : Norgine, c1981. — 28p : ill ; 21cm. — (The Present state of knowledge ; no.1)
Previous ed.: 1977. — Bibliography: p27-28
ISBN 0-901210-19-6 (pbk) : Unpriced B81-35682

616.3'4 — Man. Intestines. Coeliac disease. Genetic factors — *Conference proceedings*

The Genetics of coeliac disease / edited by R.B. McConnell. — Lancaster : MTP, 1981. — xxxi,301p : ill,ports ; 24cm
Conference papers. — Includes index
ISBN 0-85200-363-3 (corrected) : £24.95 : CIP rev. B80-17732

616.3'4 — Man. Intestines. Inflammatory diseases — *Conference proceedings*

Inflammatory disease of the bowel / edited by Bryan N. Brooke and Andrew W. Wilkinson. — Tunbridge Well : Pitman Medical, 1980. — 244p : ill ; 24cm
Conference papers. — Includes index
ISBN 0-272-79556-9 : £20.00 : CIP rev. B80-13416

616.3'427 — Tube-fed patients. Diarrhoea — *For nursing*

Reducing diarrhea in tube-fed patients / CURN Project ; principal investigator Jo Anne Horsley. — New York ; London : Grune & Stratton, c1981. — xvii,99p : ill ; 23cm. — (Using research to improve nursing practice)
Bibliography: p93-94. — Includes index
ISBN 0-8089-1326-3 (spiral) : Unpriced B81-37753

616.3'43 — Man. Gastrointestinal tract. Peptic ulcers

Peptic ulcer : a guide for the practicing physician / by members of the staff of the Center for Ulcer Research and Education (CURE) ; Morton I. Grossman, editor ; ; Janet D. Elashoff ... [et al.]. — Chicago ; London : Year Book Medical, c1981. — xvi,179p : ill ; 24cm
Bibliography: p132-164. — Includes index
ISBN 0-8151-4009-6 : £17.75 B81-30122

616.3'43 — Man. Gastrointestinal tract. Peptic ulcers — *Conference proceedings*

Advances in ulcer disease : proceedings of a symposium on the pathogenesis and therapy of ulcer disease : Munich March 13-14, 1980 / editors: K.-H. Holtermüller, J.-R. Malagelada. — Amsterdam ; Oxford : Excerpta Medica, 1980. — x,558p : ill ; 25cm. — (International congress series ; no.537)
Includes index
ISBN 90-219-9504-2 : £43.44 B81-09436

616.3'44 — Man. Intestines. Inflammatory diseases

Inflammatory bowel disease / edited by Joseph B. Kirsner, Roy G. Shorter. — Philadelphia : Lea & Febiger ; London : Kimpton, 1980. — xiv,693p : ill(some col.) ; 27cm
Previous ed.: 1975. — Includes bibliographies and index
ISBN 0-8121-0698-9 : £33.50 B81-16119

616.3'445 — Man. Colon. Crohn's disease — *Conference proceedings*

International Workshop on Crohn's Disease *(2nd : 1980 : Noordwijk/Leiden)*. Recent advances in Crohn's disease : proceedings of the 2nd International Workshop on Crohn's Disease, Noordwijk/Leiden, 25-28 June 1980 / edited by A.S. Peña ... [et al.]. — The Hague ; London : Nijhoff, 1981. — xviii,549p : ill ; 25cm. — (Developments in gastroenterology ; v.1)
Includes index
ISBN 90-247-2475-9 : Unpriced B81-15265

616.3'447 — Man. Colon. Colitis

Goulston, S. J. M.. Fundamentals of colitis / by S.J.M. Goulston and V.J. McGovern. — Oxford : Pergamon, 1981. — xi,133p : ill ; 22cm. — (Pergamon international library)
Includes index
ISBN 0-08-026862-5 (cased) : Unpriced
ISBN 0-08-026861-7 (pbk) : £5.00 B81-33344

616.3'5 — Man. Haemorrhoids

The **Haemorrhoid** syndrome. — Tunbridge Wells : Abacus, July 1981. — [200]p
ISBN 0-85626-306-0 : £20.00 : CIP entry B81-13741

616.3'6 — Man. Biliary tract. Diseases

Sherlock, Sheila. Diseases of the liver and biliary system / Sheila Sherlock. — 6th ed. — Oxford : Blackwell Scientific, 1981. — xiv,537p,[8]p of plates : ill(some col.) ; 26cm
Previous ed.: 1975. — Includes bibliographies and index
ISBN 0-632-00766-4 : £24.00 B81-18496

616.3'62 — Man. Blood. Portal hypertension — *Conference proceedings*

Medical and surgical problems of portal hypertension / edited by Marshall J. Orloff, Sergio Stipa, Vincenzo Ziparo. — London : Academic Press, 1980. — ix,351p : ill,2forms ; 24cm. — (Proceedings of the Serono symposia, ISSN 0308-5503 ; v.34)
Conference papers. — Includes bibliographies
ISBN 0-12-528380-6 : £20.40 : CIP rev. B80-23336

616.3'62 — Man. Liver. Bilirubin. Metabolic disorders - *Conference proceedings*

Familial hyperbilirubinemia : proceedings of the Workshop of Familial Disorders of Hepatic Bilirubin Metabolism held in Venice, Italy, 23rd-24th May 1980 / edited by L. Okoliscanyi. — Chichester : Wiley, c1980. — xi,263p : ill ; 24cm
Includes bibliographies and index
ISBN 0-471-27927-7 : £15.50 B81-09780

616.3′62 — Man. Liver. Diseases

Triger, David R.. Practical management of liver disease / David R. Triger. — Oxford : Blackwell Scientific, 1981. — v,249p : ill ; 23cm
Includes index
ISBN 0-632-00719-2 : £9.00 : CIP rev. B81-12357

616.3′62061 — Man. Liver. Drug therapy. (+)-Cyanidanol-3 — *Conference proceedings*

International Workshop on (+)-Cyanidanol-3 in Diseases of the Liver *(1981 : Crans-Montana)*. International Workshop on (+)-Cyanidanol-3 in Diseases of the Liver. — London : Academic Press, Oct.1981. — [350]p. — (International congress and symposium series / Royal Society of Medicine ; no.47)
ISBN 0-12-790898-6 (pbk) : CIP entry B81-25110

616.3′620654 — Man. Liver. Diseases. Therapy. Diet

Gosling, Nalda. Diets to help liver troubles / by Nalda Gosling. — Wellingborough : Thorsons, 1981. — 48p ; 18cm
ISBN 0-7225-0657-0 (pbk) : Unpriced B81-08526

616.3′6207583 — Man. Liver. Diagnosis. Needle aspiration biopsy

Patrick, R. S.. Biopsy pathology of the liver / R.S. Patrick and J.O'D. McGee. — London : Chapman and Hall, 1980. — vii,335p : ill ; 25cm. — (Biopsy pathology series)
Includes bibliographies and index
ISBN 0-412-00030-x : £15.00 : CIP rev. B80-04814

616.3′623 — Man. Liver. Viral hepatitis — *Conference proceedings*

Falk Symposium *(28th : 1979 : Basel)*. Virus and the liver : proceedings of the 28th Falk Symposium on the occasion of the 5th International Congress of Liver Diseases held at Basel, Switzerland, October 5-7 1979 / edited by L. Bianchi ... [et al.]. — Lancaster : MTP, c1980. — xviii,424p : ill ; 24cm
Includes index
ISBN 0-85200-349-8 : £24.95 : CIP rev. B80-13851

616.3′6230792 — Man. Hepatitis virus B. Vaccines — *Conference proceedings*

International Symposium on Hepatitis B Vaccine *(1st : 1980 : Paris)*. Hepatitis B vaccine : proceedings of the International Symposium on Hepatitis B Vaccine held in Paris (France), 8-9 December, 1980 / sponsored by the Institut National de la Santé et de la Recherche Médicale, the Institut Pasteur de Paris and the Institut de Virologie de Tours ; editors Philippe Maupas, Pierre Guesry. — Amsterdam ; Oxford : Elsevier/North-Holland Biomedical, 1981. — xiii,318p : ill,maps ; 25cm. — (INSERM symposium ; no.18)
Includes index
ISBN 0-444-80325-4 : £25.77 B81-21386

616.3′65 — Man. Gall bladder. Gallstones

Rose, G. A.. Urinary stones. — Lancaster : MTP Press, Oct.1981. — [300]p
ISBN 0-85200-342-0 : £16.95 : CIP entry B81-28023

616.3′650654 — Man. Gall bladder. Therapy. Diet

Gosling, Nalda. Diets to help gall bladder troubles / by Nalda Gosling. — Wellingborough : Thorsons, 1980. — 48p ; 18cm
ISBN 0-7225-0637-6 (pbk) : £0.60 : CIP rev. B80-18767

616.3′7 — Man. Pancreas. Diseases

The **Pancreas** / edited by W. Milo Keynes and Roger G. Keith. — London : Heinemann Medical, c1981. — xii,371p : ill ; 22cm. — (Tutorials in postgraduate medicine)
Includes bibliographies and index
ISBN 0-433-18274-1 : £18.00 B81-36446

Pancreatic disease : diagnosis and therapy / editor Thomas L. Dent ; associate editors Frederic E. Eckhauser, Aaron I. Vinik, Jeremiah G. Turcotté ; editorial associate Jeanne H. Tashian. — New York ; London : Grune & Stratton, c1981. — xvii,553p : ill ; 24cm
Conference papers. — Includes index
ISBN 0-8089-1376-x : £39.00 B81-39558

616.3′7 — Man. Pancreas. Diseases — *Conference proceedings*

Pancreatic disease in clinical practice. — London : Pitman Medical, Jan.1982. — [448]p
Conference papers
ISBN 0-272-79605-0 : £30.00 : CIP entry B81-34153

616.3′9 — Man. Body fluids. Electrolytes. Disorders — *Programmed instructions*

Berlyne, Geoffrey M.. A course in clinical disorders of the body fluids and electrolytes / Geoffrey M. Berlyne. — Oxford : Blackwell Scientific, 1980. — viii,240p : ill ; 22cm
Includes index
ISBN 0-632-00356-1 (pbk) : £6.80 : CIP rev. B80-03184

616.3′9 — Man. Electrolyte balance. Neuropsychiatric aspects

Electrolytes and neuropsychiatric disorders / edited by Paul E. Alexander. — Lancaster : MTP, c1981. — 313p : ill ; 24cm
Includes bibliographies and index
ISBN 0-85200-557-1 : £26.50 B81-38027

616.3′9 — Man. Metabolic disorders

Endocrinology and metabolism / editors Philip Felig ... [et al.]. — New York ; London : McGraw-Hill, c1981. — xiv,1388p : ill(some col.) ; 26cm
Includes index
ISBN 0-07-020387-3 : £52.50
Primary classification 616.4 B81-39592

616.3′9 — Man. Nutritional disorders — *Conference proceedings*

National Academy of Clinical Biochemistry. *Meeting (3rd : 1979 : New Orleans)*. Nutritional elements and clinical biochemistry / [proceedings of the Third Annual Meeting of the National Academy of Clinical Biochemistry, held in New Orleans, Louisiana, July 13-14, 1979] ; edited by Marge A. Brewster and Herbert K. Naito. — New York ; London : Plenum, c1980. — xiii,463p : ill,forms ; 26cm
Includes bibliographies and index
ISBN 0-306-40569-5 : Unpriced B81-01588

616.3′9 — Man. Nutritional disorders. Role of gastrointestinal tract — *Conference proceedings*

Nutrition and gastroenterology / edited by Myron Winick. — New York ; Chichester : Wiley, c1980. — x,221p : ill ; 24cm. — (Current concepts in nutrition ; v.9)
Includes index
ISBN 0-471-08173-6 : £17.50 B81-03105

616.3′9072′0222 — Man. Nutritional disorders. Symptoms — *Illustrations*

McLaren, Donald S.. A colour atlas of nutritional disorders / Donald S. McLaren. — London : Wolfe Medical, 1981. — 109p : ill (some col.) ; 27cm. — (Wolfe medical atlases)
Bibliography: p106. — Includes index
ISBN 0-7234-0757-6 : £12.00 B81-15324

616.3′950654 — Great Britain. Man. Osteomalacia. Prevention & treatment. Vitamin D

Great Britain. *Working Party on Fortification of Food with Vitamin D*. Rickets and osteomalacia / report of the Working Party on Fortification of Food with Vitamin D. Committee on Medical Aspects of Food Policy. — London : H.M.S.O., 1980. — xii,66p : ill ; 25cm. — (Report on health and social subjects ; 19)
At head of title: Department of Health and Social Security. — Bibliography: p54-66
ISBN 0-11-320747-6 (pbk) : £3.90
Primary classification 618.92′3950654 B81-10030

616.3′98 — Man. Obesity

Garrow, J. S.. Treat obesity seriously : a clinical manual / J.S. Garrow. — Edinburgh : Churchill Livingstone, 1981. — 246p : ill ; 23cm
Ill on lining papers. — Bibliography: p210-229. — Includes index
ISBN 0-443-02306-9 : £10.00 : CIP rev. B81-16406

616.3′98 — Man. Obesity — *Conference proceedings*

Obesity : pathogenesis and treatment / edited by G. Enzi ... [et al.]. — London : Academic Press, 1981. — ix,338p : ill ; 24cm. — (Proceedings of the Serono symposia, ISSN 0308-5503 ; v.28)
Includes bibliographies and index
ISBN 0-12-240150-6 : £12.00 B81-17427

616.3′980651 — Man. Obesity. Behaviour therapy

LeBow, Michael D.. Weight control : the behavioural strategies / Michael D. LeBow. — Chichester : Wiley, c1981. — xi,346p : ill,facsims,forms ; 24cm
Bibliography: p303-328. — Includes index
ISBN 0-471-27745-2 : £11.75 : CIP rev. B80-20727

616.3′99 — Man. Metabolic acidosis

Metabolic acidosis. — London : Pitman, Feb.1982. — [320]p. — (Ciba Foundation symposium ; 87)
Conference papers
ISBN 0-272-79651-4 : £22.50 : CIP entry B81-35780

616.3′99 — Man. Recurrent polyserositis

Eliakim, Marcel. Recurrent polyserositis : (familial Mediterranean fever, periodic disease) / Marcel Eliakim, Micha Levy and Michael Ehrenfeld. — Amsterdam ; Oxford : Elsevier/North-Holland Biomedical, 1981. — x,227p : ill ; 25cm
Bibliography: p183-203. — Includes index
ISBN 0-444-80331-9 : £27.56 B81-39203

616.3′995 — Man. Metabolic disorders. Role of enzymes

Belfiore, Francesco. Enzyme regulation and metabolic diseases / Francesco Belfiore. — Basel ; London : Karger, 1980. — xxiii,877p : ill ; 25cm
Bibliography: p541-793. - Includes index
ISBN 3-8055-0005-x : £62.25 B81-18999

616.3′9970654 — Man. Blood. Hyperlipidaemia. Therapy. Diet

Fat chance : a diet workbook for cholesterol and calorie control / Neil J. Stone ... [et al.]. — Chicago ; London : Year Book Medical, c1980. — viii,88p ; 16cm
ISBN 0-8151-8417-4 (pbk) : Unpriced B81-14216

616.4 — MAN. DISEASES OF BLOOD-FORMING, LYMPHATIC, ENDOCRINE SYSTEMS

616.4 — Man. Endocrine system. Diseases

Dillon, Richard S.. Handbook of endocrinology : diagnosis and management of endocrine and metabolic disorders / Richard S. Dillon. — Philadelphia : Lea & Febiger ; London : Kimpton, 1980. — viii,760p : ill ; 27cm
Previous ed.: 1973. — Includes bibliographies and index
ISBN 0-8121-0642-3 : £25.00 B81-16116

Endocrinology and metabolism / editors Philip Felig ... [et al.]. — New York ; London : McGraw-Hill, c1981. — xiv,1388p : ill(some col.) ; 26cm
Includes index
ISBN 0-07-020387-3 : £52.50
Also classified at 616.3′9 B81-39592

Management of endocrine disorders / [edited by] Jerome M. Hershman. — Philadelphia : Lea & Febiger ; London : Kimpton, 1980. — xi,259p : ill ; 24cm
Includes bibliographies and index
ISBN 0-8121-0715-2 (pbk) : £7.25 B81-01664

616.4 — Man. Endocrine system. Diseases *continuation*

Practical endocrinology / edited by Jerome M. Hershman. — Chichester : Wiley, c1981. — xiv,284p : ill ; 22cm + pamphlet(15p ; 21cm). — (Postgraduate medicine for the primary care physician) (A Wiley medical publication)
Includes bibliographies and index
ISBN 0-471-09502-8 : £17.00 B81-34533

Thomson, John A.. An introduction to clinical endocrinology / John A. Thomson. — 2nd ed. — Edinburgh : Churchill Livingstone, 1981. — 184p : ill ; 22cm. — (Churchill Livingstone medical text)
Previous ed.: 1976. — Includes bibliographies and index
ISBN 0-443-02307-7 (pbk) : £4.25 B81-15245

616.4 — Medicine. Endocrinology

Clinical endocrinology. — London : Butterworths, Aug.1981. — (Butterworths international medical reviews, ISSN 0260-0072)
1: The pituitary. — [320]p
ISBN 0-407-02272-4 : £13.50 : CIP entry B81-16921

616.4 — Medicine. Endocrinology, *to 1980*

Medvei, Victor Cornelius. A history of endocrinology. — Lancaster : MTP Press, Jan.1982. — [900]p
ISBN 0-85200-245-9 : £29.95 : CIP entry B81-33793

616.4'005 — Medicine. Endocrinology — *Serials*

The Year book of endocrinology. — 1980. — Chicago ; London : Year Book Medical Publishers, c1980. — 384p
ISBN 0-8151-7608-2 : Unpriced
ISSN 0084-3741 B81-03796

616.4'07 — Man. Endocrine system. Diseases. Physiological aspects

Endocrine control of growth / edited by William H. Doughaday. — New York ; Oxford : Elsevier, c1981. — xii,275p : ill ; 24cm. — (Current endocrinology)
Includes index
ISBN 0-444-00434-3 : £15.64 B81-23609

Ryan, Will G.. Endocrine disorders : a pathophysiologic approach / Will G. Ryan. — 2nd ed. — Chicago ; London : Year Book Medical Publishers, c1980. — xv,148p : ill ; 25cm. — (Internal medicine series)
Previous ed.: 1975. — Includes bibliographies and index
ISBN 0-8151-7487-x (pbk) : £13.75 B81-06251

616.4'075 — Man. Endocrine system. Diagnosis

Toft, Anthony D.. Diagnosis and management of endocrine diseases. — Oxford : Blackwell Scientific, Aug.1981. — [368]p
ISBN 0-632-00553-x (pbk) : £6.50 : CIP entry B81-16933

616.4'075 — Man. Endocrine System. Diagnosis. Laboratory techniques

Jeffcoate, S. L.. Efficiency and effectiveness in the endocrine laboratory. — London : Academic Press, July 1981. — [230]p
ISBN 0-12-382160-6 : CIP entry B81-13444

616.4'0756 — Man. Endocrine system. Diagnosis. Biochemical techniques

Ismail, Adel A. A.. Biochemical investigations in endocrinology : methods and interpretations / Adel A. Ismail. — London : Academic Press, 1981. — xi,275p : ill ; 24cm
Includes bibliographies and index
ISBN 0-12-374850-x : £14.20 B81-23551

616.4'2 — Man. Lymphatic system. Inflammation

Vasculitis / edited by Klaus Wolff, Richard K. Winkelmann. — London : Lloyd-Luke, 1980. — xiv,338p : ill ; 26cm. — (Major problems in dermatology ; v.10)
Conference papers. — Includes bibliographies and index
ISBN 0-85324-151-1 : £20.00
Primary classification 616.1'3 B81-00926

616.4'2 — Man. Lymphomas. Diagnosis

Lymphomas other than Hodgkin's disease. — Oxford : Oxford University Press, Apr.1981. — [75]p. — (Oxford medical publications)
ISBN 0-19-261296-4 : £10.00 : CIP entry B81-02358

616.4'2 — Man. Lymphomas. Lymphoid cells. Classification. Use of cell surface markers — *Conference proceedings*

Leukemia Marker Conference *(1981 : Vienna)*. Leukemia markers : proceedings of the Leukemia Marker Conference held in Vienna, February 15-18, 1981 / edited by W. Knapp. — London : Academic Press, 1981. — xv,574p : ill ; 24cm
Includes index
ISBN 0-12-416750-0 : £20.00 : CIP rev.
Primary classification 616.99'419'0012 B81-11933

616.4'207583 — Man. Lymph nodes. Diagnosis. Biopsy

Robb-Smith, A. H. T.. Lymph node biopsy / by A.H.T. Robb-Smith and C.R. Taylor. — London : Heyden, c1981. — 308p : ill(some col.) ; 31cm
Bibliography: p283-296. — Includes index
ISBN 0-905203-99-2 : Unpriced B81-24424

616.4'4 — Man. Low T3 syndrome — *Conference proceedings*

The "low T3 syndrome" / edited by R.-D. Hesch. — London : Academic Press, 1981. — viii,263p : ill ; 24cm. — (Proceedings of the Serono symposia, ISSN 0308-5503 : v.40)
Includes bibliographies
ISBN 0-12-344350-4 : Unpriced B81-25592

616.4'62 — Man. Diabetes

Diabetes mellitus. — Bowie, Md. : Brady ; London : Prentice-Hall
Vol.5 / Harold Rifkin, Philip Raskin editors. — c1981. — xvi,391p : ill ; 24cm
Includes index
ISBN 0-87619-747-0 : £14.90 B81-15483

Gunn, Alexander D. G.. Diabetes / Alexander D.G. Gunn ; illustrated by the Hayward Art Group. — Feltham : Hamlyn Paperbacks, 1981. — 48p : ill ; 17cm. — (Pocket health guides)
ISBN 0-600-20313-1 (pbk) : £0.85 B81-40887

Handbook of diabetes mellitus. — Chichester : Wiley, Aug.1981
Vol.1: Etiology/Hormone physiology. — [366]p
ISBN 0-471-10017-x : £30.00 : CIP entry B81-18090

Handbook of diabetes mellitus. — Chichester : Wiley, Aug.1981
Vol.2: Islet cell function/Insulin action. — [225]p
ISBN 0-471-10016-1 : £15.00 : CIP entry B81-18163

Handbook of diabetes mellitus. — Chichester : Wiley
Vol.3: Intermediary metabolism and its regulation. — Oct.1981. — [317]p
ISBN 0-471-10015-3 : £23.00 : CIP entry B81-25821

Handbook of diabetes mellitus. — Chichester : Wiley
Vol.4: Biochemical pathology. — Oct.1981. — [297]p
ISBN 0-471-10018-8 : £20.00 : CIP entry B81-25822

Handbook of diabetes mellitus. — Chichester : Wiley
Vol.5: Current and future therapies. — Oct.1981. — [420]p
ISBN 0-471-10019-6 : £27.00 : CIP entry B81-25823

616.4'62 — Man. Diabetes. Complications: Renal failures & retinal diseases — *Conference proceedings*

Conference on Diabetic Renal-Retinal Syndrome *(1979 : Brooklyn)*. Diabetic renal-retinal syndrome : Conference on Diabetic Renal-Retinal Syndrome, Brooklyn, November 12-13, 1979 / sponsored by Division of Renal Diseases, Department of Medicine and The Office of Continuing Education of the State University of New York Downstate Medical Center, co-sponsored by the Department of Ophthalmology, College of Physicians and Surgeons, Columbia University ; Eli A. Friedman, Francis A. L'Esperance, Jr., editors. — New York ; London : Grune & Stratton, c1980. — xv,451p : ill,ports ; 24cm
Includes index
ISBN 0-8089-1302-6 : £22.20 B81-03757

616.4'62 — Man. Diabetes. Complications: Retinal diseases

L'Esperance, Francis A.. Diabetic retinopathy : clinical evaluation and management / Francis A. L'Esperance, Jr., William A. James Jr. — St. Louis ; London : Mosby, 1981. — xv,294p : ill(some col.) ; 27cm
Includes bibliographies and index
ISBN 0-8016-2948-9 : £35.25
Primary classification 617.7'3 B81-15001

616.4'62 — Man. Diabetes — *For children*

Riedman, Sarah R.. Diabetes / by Sarah R. Riedman. — New York ; London : Watts, 1980. — 62p : ill ; 23cm. — (A First book)
Bibliography: p58-59. — Includes index
ISBN 0-531-04162-x : £2.99 B81-03210

616.4'62 — Man. Diabetes - *For diabetics*

Anderson, James W.. Diabetes. — London (Flat 5, 25 Cleveland Sq., W2 6DD) : Martin Dunitz, Aug.1981. — [160]p
ISBN 0-906348-21-8 (cased) : £5.95 : CIP entry
ISBN 0-906348-22-6 (pbk) : £2.50 B81-16919

Tattersall, Robert. Diabetes. — Edinburgh : Churchill Livingstone, July 1981. — [64]p. — (Patient handbooks)
ISBN 0-443-02318-2 (pbk) : £1.00 : CIP entry B81-14982

616.4'62 — Man. Diabetes. Nutritional aspects - *Conference proceedings*

Nutrition and diabetes. — London (80 Bondway, SW8 1SF) : John Libbey, June 1981. — [160]p
Conference papers
ISBN 0-86196-008-4 : £9.00 : CIP entry B81-12882

616.4'62'00321 — Man. Diabetes — *Encyclopaedias* — *For diabetics*

Jorgensen, Caryl Dow. The ABC of diabetes / Caryl Dow Jorgensen and John E. Lewis. — U.K. ed. / edited by Peter Daggett. — London : New English Library, 1981, c1979. — 287p : ill ; 23cm
Originally published: as The ABCs of diabetes. New York : Crown, 1979. — Bibliography: p268-271. — Includes index
ISBN 0-450-04838-1 : £6.50 B81-27010

616.4'62061 — Man. Diabetes. Drug therapy. Biguanides — *Conference proceedings*

Biguanide therapy today / edited by A. van der Kuy and S.G. Th. Hulst. — London : Royal Society of Medicine, 1981. — vi,73p : ill ; 25cm. — (International congress and symposium series / Royal Society of Medicine, ISSN 0142-2367 ; no.48)
Conference papers. — Includes bibliographies
ISBN 0-12-794687-x (pbk) : Unpriced B81-27062

616.4'62061 — Man. Diabetes. Drug therapy. Insulin — *Conference proceedings*

Vienna-Lainz Diabetes Symposium *(2nd : 1980)*. New approaches to insulin therapy : proceedings of the 2nd Vienna-Lainz Diabetes Symposium Vienna, Austria April 23-26 1980 / edited by Karl Irsigler .. [et al.] ; sponsored by the Ludwig Boltzmann Research Institute for Metabolic Disease and Nutrition. — Lancaster : MTP, 1981. — xvii,569p : ill,ports ; 24cm
Includes index
ISBN 0-85200-377-3 : £27.95 B81-38025

616.4′66 — Man. Hypoglycaemia

Budd, Martin. Low blood sugar : (hypoglycaemia) : the 20th century epidemic? / by Martin Budd. — Wellingborough : Thorsons, 1981. — 127p : ill ; 22cm
Includes index
ISBN 0-7225-0589-2 (pbk) : £2.95 B81-24171

Marks, Vincent. Hypoglycaemia. — 2nd ed. — Oxford : Blackwell Scientific, July 1981. — [500]p
Previous ed.: 1964
ISBN 0-632-00673-0 : £27.00 : CIP entry B81-14968

616.5 — MAN. DISEASES OF INTEGUMENTARY SYSTEM

616.5 — Man. Epidermis. Diseases — *Conference proceedings*

European Society for Dermatological Research. *Symposium (1979 : Cardiff)*. The epidermis disease : based on the proceedings of the European Society for Dermatological Research Symposium, held at the Welsh National School of Medicine, Cardiff, on April 18-20, 1979 / edited by R. Marks, E. Christopher. — Lancaster : MTP, 1981. — xii,597p : ill ; 24cm
Includes bibliographies and index
ISBN 0-85200-370-6 : £24.95 : CIP rev. B80-19237

616.5 — Man. Skin. Diseases

Callen, Jeffrey P.. Manual of dermatology : introduction to diagnosis and treatment / Jeffrey P. Callen, Marek A. Stawiski, John J. Voorhees. — Chicago ; London : Year Book Medical, c1980. — xi,294p : ill ; 21cm
Includes bibliographies and index
ISBN 0-8151-1410-9 (pbk) : £17.00 B81-12965

Okoro, Anezi N.. Pictorial handbook of common skin diseases / Anezi N. Okoro. — London : Macmillan, 1981. — 200p,[16]p of plates : ill (some col.) ; 22cm. — (Concise clinical medicine in the tropics)
Bibliography: p193. - Includes index
ISBN 0-333-28611-1 (cased) : Unpriced : CIP rev.
ISBN 0-333-28613-8 (pbk) : £14.00 B80-36112

Rorsman, Hans. Dermatology / Hans Rorsman ; [translated from Swedish by Marcia Skogh]. — 2nd ed. — Lund : Studentlitteratur ; [London] : Wolfe Medical [distributor], 1979, c1976. — 252p : ill ; 23cm
Previous ed.: 1976. — Includes index
ISBN 0-7234-0747-9 (pbk) : £8.00 B81-15320

Steigleder, Gerd Klaus. Dermatology / Gerd Klaus Steigleder and Howard I. Maibach ; translated by Dora Wirth (Languages) Ltd. — Chicago ; London : Year Book Medical, 1980. — xii,467p : ill ; 19cm. — (Thieme flexibooks)
Translation of: Dermatologie und Venerologie. 2 Ausg. — Bibliography: p454-456. - Includes index
ISBN 0-8151-8176-0 (pbk) : £12.50 B81-05880

616.5 — Man. Skin. Effects of psoralens

Psoralens in cosmetics and dermatology. — Oxford : Pergamon, Nov.1981. — [350]p
Conference papers
ISBN 0-08-027057-3 : £25.00 : CIP entry B81-35026

616.5 — Medicine. Dermatology

Dermatology. — 3rd ed. — London : Butterworths, Aug.1981. — [320]p
Previous ed.: London : Crosby Lockwood Staples, 1973
ISBN 0-407-00208-1 (pbk) : £15.00 : CIP entry B81-16920

Mackie, Rona M.. Clinical dermatology. — Oxford : Oxford University Press, July 1981. — [250]p. — (Oxford medical publications)
ISBN 0-19-261271-9 (pbk) : £9.95 : CIP entry B81-13501

616.5 — Medicine. Dermatology — *For developing countries*

Canizares, Orlando. A manual of dermatology for developing countries. — Oxford : Oxford University Press, Feb.1982. — [350]p. — (Oxford medical publications)
ISBN 0-19-261366-9 (cased) : £15.00 : CIP entry
ISBN 0-19-261185-2 (pbk) : £5.00 B81-35770

616.5′0024613 — Man. Skin. Diseases — *For nursing*

Seville, R. H.. Dermatological nursing and therapy / R.H. Seville, E. Martin. — Oxford : Blackwell Scientific, 1981. — ix,226p,[12]p of plates : ill(some col.) ; 22cm
Includes index
ISBN 0-632-00549-1 (pbk) : £7.50 B81-08967

616.5′075 — Man. Skin. Diagnosis

Pinkus, Hermann. A guide to dermatohistopathology / Hermann Pinkus, Amir H. Mehregan. — 3rd ed. — New York ; London : Appleton-Century-Crofts, c1981. — xv,591p : ill ; 29cm
Previous ed.: 1976. — Includes index
ISBN 0-8385-3151-2 : £43.80 B81-33147

616.5′079 — Man. Skin. Diseases. Immunological aspects

Dahl, Mark V.. Clinical immunodermatology / Mark V. Dahl. — Chicago ; London : Year Book Medical, c1981. — xii,280p : ill ; 24cm
Includes bibliographies and index
ISBN 0-8151-2246-2 : £22.75 B81-25608

Fellner, Michael J.. Immunology of skin diseases / Michael J. Fellner. — New York ; Oxford : Elsevier, c1980. — xvi,174p : ill ; 24cm
Includes bibliographies and index
ISBN 0-444-00364-9 : £12.37 B81-05828

Immunodermatology / edited by Bijan Safai and Robert A. Good. — New York ; London : Plenum, c1981. — xlii,717p,[2]p of plates : ill (some col.) ; 26cm. — (Comprehensive immunology ; 7)
Includes bibliographies and index
ISBN 0-306-40380-3 : Unpriced B81-19270

616.5′2606 — Man. Skin. Psoriasis. Therapy

Marks, Ronald. Psoriasis. — London (Flat 5, 25 Cleveland Sq., W2) : Martin Dunitz, Aug.1981. — [96]p. — (Positive health guides)
ISBN 0-906348-19-6 (cased) : £5.95 : CIP entry
ISBN 0-906348-20-x (pbk) : £2.50 B81-16917

616.5′260654 — Man. Skin. Psoriasis. Therapy. Diet

Clements, Harry. Diets to help psoriasis. — Wellingborough : Thorsons, Sept.1981. — [48]p
ISBN 0-7225-0708-9 (pbk) : £0.60 : CIP entry B81-21515

616.5′3 — Man. Skin. Acne — *For adolescents*

Murray, David, *1943-*. The anti-acne book / David Murray. — London : Arlington, 1981. — 64p : ill ; 13cm. — (Arlington pocket books)
ISBN 0-85140-282-8 (pbk) : £0.75 B81-21913

616.5′44 — Man. Skin. Warts

Bunney, Mary H.. Viral warts. — Oxford : Oxford University Press, Dec.1981. — [92]p. — (Oxford medical publications)
ISBN 0-19-261335-9 : £8.50 : CIP entry B81-31354

616.5′45 — Man. Pressure sores

Preventing decubitus ulcers / CURN Project ; principal investigator: Jo Anne Horsley ; director: Joyce Crane ; the protocol manuscript ... prepared by Karen B. Haller, Janet D. Bingle. — New York ; London : Grune & Stratton, c1981. — xvii,174p : ill,forms ; 23cm. — (Using research to improve nursing practice)
Includes bibliographies and index
ISBN 0-8089-1328-x (spiral) : £9.60 B81-39559

616.5′45 — Man. Skin. Pressure sores — *For nursing*

Barton, Anthony, *1925-*. The management and prevention of pressure sores / Anthony Barton and Mary Barton ; in association with the Multiple Sclerosis Society of Great Britain and Northern Ireland. — London : Faber, 1981. — 96p,[4]p of plates : ill(some col.) ; 21cm
Bibliography: p92-93. — Includes index
ISBN 0-571-11672-8 (cased) : £7.25 : CIP rev.
ISBN 0-571-11673-6 (pbk) : Unpriced B81-11924

616.5′46 — Man. Hair & scalp. Diseases

Rook, Arthur. Diseases of the hair and scalp. — Oxford : Blackwell Scientific, Jan.1982. — [576]p
ISBN 0-632-00822-9 : £28.50 : CIP entry B81-37544

616.5′46 — Men. Baldness. Prevention

Drabble, D. J.. Baldness and hair care / D. J. Drabble. — London (225 Putney Bridge Rd., SW15 2PY) : Roberts Publications, [1980]. — 56p : ill ; 19cm. — (Body perfect-body image problem series ; no.1)
ISBN 0-906185-11-4 (pbk) : £2.00 B81-08302

616.5′47 — Man. Nails. Diseases

The Nail. — Edinburgh : Churchill Livingstone, July 1981. — [160]p. — (GEM monographs)
Translation of: L′ongle
ISBN 0-443-02102-3 : £24.00 : CIP entry B81-15843

616.6 — MAN. DISEASES OF UROGENITAL SYSTEM

616.6 — Man. Urinary tract. Diseases

Asscher, A. W.. The challenge of urinary tract infections / A.W. Asscher. — London : Academic Press, 1980. — x,209p : ill,2facsims ; 24cm
Includes index
ISBN 0-12-790220-1 : £15.20 : CIP rev. B80-09708

Walls, John. Urinary tract infections, calculi and tubular disorders / John Walls. — Lancaster : In association with Update by MTP, 1981. — 90p,[10]p of plates : ill(some col.) ; 20cm. — (Topics in renal disease)
Bibliography: p86-87. — Includes index
ISBN 0-85200-424-9 : £5.95 B81-29463

616.6 — Man. Urogenital system. Diseases

Brooks, David. Renal medicine and urology. — Edinburgh : Churchill Livingstone, Dec.1981. — [296]p
ISBN 0-443-01718-2 (pbk) : £7.50 : CIP entry B81-31842

Newsam, J. E.. Urology and renal medicine. — 3rd ed. — Edinburgh : Churchill Livingstone, May 1981. — [304]p
Previous ed.: 1975
ISBN 0-443-02391-3 (pbk) : £6.50 : CIP entry B81-0741?

616.6 — Medicine. Urology

Blandy, John P.. Lecture notes on urology. — 3rd ed. — Oxford : Blackwell Scientific, Jan.1982. — [350]p
Previous ed.: 1977
ISBN 0-632-00688-9 (pbk) : £8.50 : CIP entry B81-3463-

Essentials of basic science in urology / edited by Salah Al- Askari, Mircea Golimbu, Pablo Morales. — New York ; London : Grune & Stratton, 1981. — xiii,322p : ill ; 26cm
Includes index
ISBN 0-8089-1299-2 : £22.00 B81-1393-

616.6′0024613 — Medicine. Urology — *For nursin*

Stirling, Margaret W. A.. Urology / Margaret W.A. Stirling, Roy Scott. — 2nd ed. — London : Heinemann Medical, 1981. — vii,81p : ill ; 19cm. — (Modern practical nursing serie ; 5)
Previous ed.: 1971. — Includes index
ISBN 0-433-31701-9 (pbk) : £2.95 B81-2497

16.6'005 — Medicine. Urology — *Serials*

Current trends in urology. — Vol.1-. — Baltimore ; London : Williams & Wilkins, 1981-. — v. : ill ; 26cm
£31.25 B81-27135

Recent advances in urology/andrology. — No.3-. — Edinburgh : Churchill Livingstone, 1981-. — v. : ill ; 24cm
Irregular. — Continues: Recent advances in urology
ISSN 0261-8788 = Recent advances in urology, andrology : Unpriced B81-34057

The **Year** book of urology. — 1980. — Chicago ; London : Year Book Medical Pulishers, c1980. — 366p
ISBN 0-8151-3470-3 : Unpriced
ISSN 0084-4071 B81-10242

16.6'0088055 — Man. Pubertal disorders. Physiological aspects — *Conference proceedings*

Pathophysiology of puberty / edited by E. Cacciari, A. Prader. — London : Academic Press, 1980. — x,453p : ill ; 24cm. — (Proceedings of the Serono symposia, ISSN 0308-5503 ; v.36)
Includes bibliographies and index
ISBN 0-12-154160-6 : £26.40 : CIP rev. B80-23338

16.6'06 — Men. Urogenital system. Therapy

Current urologic therapy / [edited by] Joseph J. Kaufman. — Philadelphia ; London : Saunders, 1980. — xxxv,517p : ill ; 27cm
Includes index
ISBN 0-7216-5304-9 : £24.25 B81-03983

16.6'07545 — Man. Urinary tract. Diagnosis. Endoscopy

Mitchell, J. P.. Endoscopic operative urology / J.P. Mitchell. — Bristol : Wright, 1981. — xiii,461p,[24]p of plates : ill(some col.) ; 24cm
Bibliography: p434-449. — Includes index
ISBN 0-7236-0532-7 : Unpriced : CIP rev. B81-10502

16.6'0757 — Man. Urinary tract. Diagnosis. Radiography

Urinary tract and adrenal glands / editor Ernest J. Ferris, associate editor Joanna J. Seibert. — New York ; London : Grune & Stratton, c1980. — ix,535p : ill ; 26cm. — (Multiple imaging procedures ; v.4)
Includes index
ISBN 0-8089-1296-8 : £33.40 B81-14028

16.6'07572 — Man. Urogenital system. Diagnosis. Imaging

Lalli, Anthony F.. Tailored urologic imaging / Anthony F. Lalli. — Chicago ; London : Year Book Medical, c1980. — xi,323p : ill ; 24cm
Includes bibliographies and index
ISBN 0-8151-5276-0 : £33.00 B81-09758

6.6'1 — Man. Kidneys. Diseases

Cameron, Stewart. Kidney disease : the facts / Stewart Cameron. — Oxford : Oxford University Press, 1981. — 323p,[16]p of plates : ill ; 23cm. — (Oxford medical publications)
Includes index
ISBN 0-19-261329-4 : £6.95 : CIP rev. B81-13811

Davison, Alex M.. A synopsis of renal diseases / A.M. Davison. — Bristol : John Wright, 1981. — v,186p : ill ; 19cm
Includes index
ISBN 0-7236-0569-6 (pbk) : Unpriced B81-17654

Gabriel, Roger. Renal medicine / Roger Gabriel. — 2nd ed. — London : Baillière Tindall, 1981. — 266p : ill ; 22cm. — (Concise medical textbooks)
Previous ed.: 1977. — Bibliography: p256. - Includes index
ISBN 0-7020-0847-8 (pbk) : £5.50 B81-18787

Manual of clinical nephrology : of the Rogosin Kidney Center / edited by Jhoong S. Cheigh, Kurt H. Stenzel, Albert L. Rubin. — The Hague ; London : Nijhoff, 1981. — xxi,491p : ill ; 25cm. — (Developments in nephrology ; v.1)
Includes bibliographies and index
ISBN 90-247-2397-3 (pbk) : Unpriced B81-20837

Practical nephrology / edited by Stanley S. Franklin. — New York ; Chichester : Wiley, c1981. — xiv,498p : ill ; 22cm + 1 pamphlet (15p ; 21cm). — (Postgraduate medicine for the primary care physician)
Includes bibliographies and index
ISBN 0-471-09512-5 : £22.00 B81-24226

Williams, D. Gwyn. Renal disease : an illustrated guide / D. Gwyn Williams. — Lancaster : In association with Update by MTP, 1981. — 87p : ill(some col.) ; 20cm. — (Topics in renal disease)
ISBN 0-85200-421-4 : £5.95 B81-29461

616.6'1 — Man. Kidneys. Diseases. Haematological aspects

Hematologic problems in renal disease / edited by Joanne H. Jepson. — Reading, Mass. ; London : Addison-Wesley, c1979. — vii,351p : ill ; 25cm
Includes bibliographies and index
ISBN 0-201-03481-6 : £27.00 B81-05479

616.6'1 — Man. Kidneys. Diseases — *Illustrations*

Asscher, A. W.. Nephrology illustrated. — London (173 Great Portland St., W.1) : Gower Medical, Oct.1981. — [240]p
ISBN 0-906923-01-8 : £40.00 : CIP entry B81-26702

616.6'1 — Man. Kidneys. Effects of general diseases

The **Kidney** in systemic disease / edited by Wadi N. Suki, Garabed Eknoyan. — 2nd ed. — New York ; Chichester : Wiley, c1981. — xv,660p : ill ; 27cm. — (A Wiley medical publication)
Previous ed.: 1976. — Includes index
ISBN 0-471-02632-8 : £31.456 B81-24936

616.6'1'0024613 — Man. Kidneys. Diseases — *For nursing*

Brundage, Dorothy J.. Nursing management of real problems / Dorothy J. Brundage. — 2nd ed. — St. Louis ; London : Mosby, 1980. — vii,232p : ill ; 24cm
Previous ed.: 1976. — Includes index
ISBN 0-8016-0849-x (pbk) : Unpriced B81-08201

616.6'1'005 — Man. Kidneys. Diseases — *Serials*

Contemporary nephrology. — Vol.1-. — New York ; London ([2 Chandos Rd, NW10 6NR]) : Plenum Medical, 1981-. — v. ; 24cm
Issued every two years
Unpriced B81-35457

616.6'1'008042 — Pregnant women. Kidneys. Diseases — *Conference proceedings*

Symposium on Nephrology *(8th : 1980 : Hannover)*. Kidney and pregnancy : 8th Symposium on Nephrology, Hannover, June 20 and 21, 1980 / volume editors G.M. Eisenbach and J. Brod. — Basel ; London : Karger, c1981. — vi,167p : ill ; 23cm. — (Contributions to nephrology ; v.25)
Includes bibliographies and index
ISBN 3-8055-1798-x (pbk) : £23.75 B81-26229

616.6'12 — Man. Kidneys. Glomeruli. Diseases

Sharpstone, Paul. Renal glomerular diseases / Paul Sharpstone and J.A.P. Trafford. — Lancaster : In association with Update by MTP, 1981. — 83p,[11]p of plates : ill(some col.) ; 20cm. — (Topics in renal disease)
Bibliography: p76. — Includes index
ISBN 0-85200-422-2 : £5.95 B81-29464

616.6'14 — Man. Kidneys. Acute renal failure

Acute renal failure / edited by Antoine Chapman. — Edinburgh : Churchill Livingstone, 1980. — vi,178p : ill ; 24cm. — (Clinics in critical care medicine ; 1)
Includes bibliographies and index
ISBN 0-443-01930-4 : £15.00 : CIP rev. B80-09709

Acute renal failure / edited by Barry M. Brenner and Jay H. Stein. — New York ; Edinburgh : Churchill Livingstone, 1980. — viii,296p : ill ; 24cm. — (Contemporary issues in nephrology ; v.6)
Includes bibliographies and index
ISBN 0-443-08116-6 : Unpriced B81-12152

Treatment of renal failure. — Lancaster : MTP Press, July 1981. — [200]p
ISBN 0-85200-336-6 : £14.95 : CIP entry B81-21544

616.6'14 — Man. Kidneys. Renal failure

Boulton-Jones, Michael. Acute and chronic renal failure / Michael Boulton-Jones. — Lancaster : In association with Update by MTP, 1981. — 108p,[4]p of plates : ill(some col.) ; 20cm
Includes index
ISBN 0-85200-420-6 : £5.95 B81-29462

616.6'22 — Man. Kidneys. Nephrolithiasis

Nephrolithiasis / guest editor Fredric L. Coe. — New York ; Edinburgh : Churchill Livingstone, 1980. — x,275p : ill ; 24cm. — (Contemporary issues in nephrology ; v.5)
Includes bibliographies and index
ISBN 0-443-08048-8 : £19.00 B81-02788

616.6'22 — Man. Urinary tract. Calculi — *Conference proceedings*

International Symposium on Urolithiasis Research *(4th : 1980 : Williamsburg, Va.)*. Urolithiasis : clinical and basic research / [proceedings of the Fourth International Symposium on Urolithiasis Research, held June 22-26, 1980, in Williamsburg, Virginia] ; edited by Lynwood H. Smith, William G. Robertson, and Birdwell Finlayson. — New York ; London : Plenum, c1981. — xxvi,1035p : ill ; 26cm
Includes index
ISBN 0-306-40635-7 : Unpriced B81-24237

616.6'3 — Man. Incontinence

Incontinence and its management / edited by Dorothy Mandelstam. — London : Croom Helm, c1980. — 233p : ill,forms ; 23cm
Bibliography: p225. - Includes index
ISBN 0-7099-0088-0 : £9.95 B81-06939

616.6'3 — Man. Proteinuria — *Conference proceedings*

International Meeting on Urinary Proteins *(1980 : Parma)*. Urinary proteins : International Meeting on Urinary Proteins, Parma, June 21, 1980 / volume editor L. Migone ; co-editors L. Scarpioni, V. Cambi. — Basel ; London : Karger, c1981. — viii,123p : ill ; 23cm. — (Contributions to nephrology ; v.26)
Includes bibliographies and index
ISBN 3-8055-1848-x (pbk) : £22.00 B81-40151

Symposium on Experimental and Clinical Aspects of Proteinuria *(1980 : Giessen)*. Experimental and clinical aspects of proteinuria / volume editor M. Weise. — Basel ; London : Karger, 1981. — ix,166p : ill,1port ; 23cm. — (Contributions to nephrology ; v.24)
At head of title: Symposium on Experimental and Clinical Aspects of Proteinuria, Giessen, March 22-23, 1980. — Includes bibliographies and index
ISBN 3-8055-1655-x (pbk) : £20.75 B81-22988

616.6'5 — Man. Prostate gland. Benign enlargement. Self-treatment. Use of mind — *Personal observations*

Shattock, E. H.. Mind your body : a practical method of self-healing / E.H. Shattock. — Wellingborough : Turnstone, 1979 (1980 [printing]). — x,117p : ill ; 22cm
ISBN 0-85500-099-6 (pbk) : Unpriced : CIP rev.
Primary classification 616.7'22 B80-07803

616.6'5 — Man. Reproductive system. Skin. Diseases

Korting, G. W.. Practical dermatology of the genital region / by G.W. Korting ; translated by William Curt and Helen Ollendorff Curth. — Philadelphia ; London : Saunders, 1981. — ix,190p : col.ill ; 26cm
Translation of: Praktische Dermatologie der Genitalregion. — Includes index
ISBN 0-7216-5498-3 : £34.50 B81-37456

616.6′5075 — Men. Diagnosis

Diagnosis in andrology / edited by J. Bain and E.S.E. Hafez. — The Hague ; London : Nijhoff, 1980. — vi,261p : ill ; 28cm. — (Clinics in andrology ; v.4)
Includes bibliographies and index
ISBN 90-247-2365-5 : Unpriced B81-06353

616.6′906 — Man. Sexual disorders. Therapy

Kaplan, Helen Singer. The illustrated manual of sex therapy / Helen Singer Kaplan ; drawings by David Passalacqua. — London : Granada, 1981, c1975. — x,181p : ill ; 30cm. — (A Mayflower book)
Originally published: New York : Quadrangle ; New York Times Book Co, 1975 ; London : Souvenir Press, 1976
ISBN 0-583-13183-2 (pbk) : £3.95 B81-25096

Kaplan, Helen Singer. The new sex therapy : active treatment of sexual dysfunctions / Helen Singer Kaplan. — Harmondsworth : Penguin, 1978, c1974 (1981 [printing]). — 589p : ill ; 20cm. — (A Pelican book)
Originally published: New York : Brunner/Mazel ; London : Baillière Tindall, 1974. — Includes bibliographies and index
ISBN 0-14-022345-2 (pbk) : £5.95 B81-25210

Szasz, Thomas. [Sex by prescription]. Sex : facts, frauds and follies / Thomas Szasz. — Oxford : Basil Blackwell, 1981, c1980. — xii,194p ; 22cm
Originally published: Garden City, N.Y. : Anchor Press/Doubleday, 1980. — Includes index
ISBN 0-631-12736-4 (cased) : £8.50 : CIP rev.
ISBN 0-631-12737-2 (pbk) : £3.50
Also classified at 613.9′507 B81-04356

616.6′9061 — Man. Sexual disorders. Drug therapy

Drug treatment of sexual dysfunction / volume editors Th.A. Ban and F.A. Freyhan. — Basel ; London : Karger, c1980. — 194p : ill ; 25cm. — (Modern problems of pharmacopsychiatry ; v.15)
Includes bibliographies
ISBN 3-8055-2906-6 : £29.50 B81-03898

616.6′92 — Man. Infertility

The **Infertile** couple / edited by R.J. Pepperell, Bryan Hudson, Carl Wood. — Edinburgh : Churchill Livingstone, 1980. — vii,252p : ill ; 25cm
Includes bibliographies and index
ISBN 0-443-01727-1 : £10.00 : CIP rev. B80-09717

Infertility : a textbook based on the work of the Royal Northern Hospital Philip Hill Parenthood Clinic / edited by Elliot E. Philipp and G. Barry Carruthers. — London : Heinemann Medical, 1981. — vi,268p : ill,1form ; 25cm
Includes bibliographies and index
ISBN 0-433-25102-6 : £25.00 B81-09858

Research on fertility and sterility. — Lancaster : MTP Press, July 1981. — [450]p
ISBN 0-85200-357-9 : £29.95 : CIP entry
Primary classification 612′.6 B81-19146

616.6′92 — Man. Infertility. Role of endocrine system — *Conference proceedings*

Endocrinology of human infertility : new aspects / edited by P.G. Crosignani, B.L. Rubin. — London : Academic Press, c1981. — viii,454p : ill ; 23cm. — (Proceedings of the Sereno Clinical Colloquia on Reproduction ; no.2)
Conference papers. — Includes bibliographies and index
ISBN 0-12-790949-4 (pbk) : £28.00 : CIP rev. B81-13551

616.7 — MAN. DISEASES OF MUSCULOSKELETAL SYSTEM

616.7′1 — Man. Bones. Diseases

Radiology, pathology, and immunology of bones and joints : a review of current concepts / edited by Frieda Feldman. — New York : Appleton-Century-Crofts ; London : Prentice Hall, c1978. — 388p : ill ; 29cm
Includes index
ISBN 0-8385-8254-0 (cased) : £28.95
ISBN 0-8385-8253-2 (pbk) : Unpriced
Also classified at 616.7′2 B81-25164

616.7′1075 — Man. Bones. Diagnosis

Resnick, Donald. Diagnosis of bone and joint disorders : with emphasis on articular abnormalities / Donald Resnick, Gen Niwayama. — Philadelphia ; London : Saunders, 1981. — 3v(lxviii,3277,xlvip) : ill (some col.) ; 29cm
Includes index
ISBN 0-7216-7564-6 : Unpriced
ISBN 0-7216-7561-1 (v.1) : £60.00
ISBN 0-7216-7562-x (v.2) : £75.75
ISBN 0-7216-7563-8 (v.3) : £75.75
Also classified at 616.7′2075 B81-34741

616.7′107572 — Man. Bones. Diagnosis. Radiography. Use of x-rays

Griffiths, Harry J.. Basic bone radiology / Harry J. Griffiths. — New York ; [London] : Appleton-Century-Crofts, c1981. — xi,191p : ill ; 24cm
Includes bibliographies and index
ISBN 0-8385-0535-x (pbk) : £10.10 B81-16522

616.7′107575 — Man. Bones. Diagnosis. Scintigraphy

Bone scintigraphy / edited by Ernest K.J. Pauwels, Henri E. Schütte, Wybren K. Taconis ; associate editor Peter J. Ell. — The Hague ; London : Leiden University Press, 1981. — viii,210p : ill ; 25cm. — (Boerhaave series for postgraduate medical education ; v.20)
Includes index
ISBN 90-602-1476-5 B81-29174

616.7′12 — Man. Bones. Paget′s disease

Hamdy, R. C.. Paget′s disease of bone : assessment and management / R.C. Hamdy. — Eastbourne : Praeger, 1981. — 203p,[15]p of plates : ill(some col.) ; 26cm. — (Endocrinology and metabolism series ; v.1) (Praeger special studies)
Bibliography: p168-198. — Includes index
ISBN 0-03-059177-5 : £13.50 : CIP rev. B80-31671

616.7′15061 — Man. Bones. Osteomyelitis. Local drug therapy. Antibiotics — *Conference proceedings*

Local Antibiotic Therapy in Osteomyelitis and Soft-tissue Infections *(Conference : 1980 : Amsterdam).* Local antibiotic treatment in osteomyelitis and soft-tissue infections : proceedings of a symposium, Amsterdam, October 25, 1980 / editors Th.J.G. van Rens, F.H. Kayser. — Amsterdam ; Oxford : Excerpta Medica, 1981. — viii,196p : ill(some col.) ; 25cm. — (International congress series ; 556)
Includes summaries in German. — Includes index
ISBN 90-219-9511-5 : Unpriced B81-29008

616.7′2 — Man. Arthritis & rheumatic diseases

Fox, William W.. Arthritis : is your suffering really necessary? / by William W. Fox. — London : Hale, 1981. — 127p : ill ; 23cm
ISBN 0-7091-9150-2 : £5.95 B81-34732

Golding, Douglas N.. Problems of arthritis and rheumatism. — Lancaster : MTP Press, Sept.1981. — [160]p. — (Problems in practice series)
ISBN 0-85200-394-3 : £7.95 : CIP entry B81-21604

616.7′2 — Man. Joints. Diseases

Radiology, pathology, and immunology of bones and joints : a review of current concepts / edited by Frieda Feldman. — New York : Appleton-Century-Crofts ; London : Prentice Hall, c1978. — 388p : ill ; 29cm
Includes index
ISBN 0-8385-8254-0 (cased) : £28.95
ISBN 0-8385-8253-2 (pbk) : Unpriced
Primary classification 616.7′1 B81-25164

616.7′2 — Man. Knees. Joints. Diagnosis. Arthroscopy

Johnson, Lanny L.. Diagnostic and surgical arthroscopy : the knee and other joints / Lanny L. Johnson. — 2nd ed. — St. Louis ; London : Mosby, 1981. — xv,432p : ill(some col.) ; 29cm
Previous ed.: published as Comprehensive arthroscopic examination of the knee. 1977. — Includes bibliographies and index
ISBN 0-8016-2535-1 : £77.00 B81-15006

616.7′2′00222 — Man. Rheumatic diseases — *Illustrations*

A **Colour** atlas of rheumatology / [compiled] A.C. Boyle. — New and enl. ed. — London : Wolfe Medical, 1980. — 176p : chiefly ill(som col.) ; 20cm. — (Wolfe medical atlas ; 10)
Previous ed.: 1974. — Includes index
ISBN 0-7234-0753-3 : £12.00 B81-035C

616.7′2′005 — Man. Joints. Diseases — *Serials*

Studies in joint disease. — 1-. — Tunbridge Wells : Pitman Medical, 1980-. — v. : ill ; 24cm
Annual
ISSN 0260-9320 = Studies in joint disease : Unpriced B81-1025

616.7′2065 — Man. Joints. Arthritis & rheumatic diseases. Naturopathy

Quick, Clifford. Why endure rheumatism and arthritis?. — London : Allen & Unwin, Jan.1982. — [208]p
Originally published: 1980
ISBN 0-04-616022-1 (pbk) : £2.25 : CIP entry B81-339

616.7′2068 — Man. Joints. Arthritis & rheumatic diseases. Self-treatment

Hart, F. Dudley. Overcoming arthritis : a guide to coping with stiff or aching joints / Frank Dudley Hart. — London : Dunitz, c1981. — 122p : ill(some col.) ; 23cm. — (Positive healt guide)
Includes index
ISBN 0-906348-15-3 (cased) : Unpriced : CIP rev.
ISBN 0-906348-13-7 (pbk) : £2.50 B80-233

616.7′2075 — Man. Joints. Diagnosis

Resnick, Donald. Diagnosis of bone and joint disorders : with emphasis on articular abnormalities / Donald Resnick, Gen Niwayama. — Philadelphia ; London : Saunders, 1981. — 3v(lxviii,3277,xlvip) : ill (some col.) ; 29cm
Includes index
ISBN 0-7216-7564-6 : Unpriced
ISBN 0-7216-7561-1 (v.1) : £60.00
ISBN 0-7216-7562-x (v.2) : £75.75
ISBN 0-7216-7563-8 (v.3) : £75.75
Primary classification 616.7′1075 B81-347

616.7′207572 — Man. Joints. Diagnosis. Arthrography

Arndt, Rolf-D.. Clinical arthrography / Rolf-D. Arndt, John W. Horns, Richard H. Gold wit a special contribution on temporomandibular joint arthrography by Donald D. Blaschke. — Baltimore ; London : Williams & Wilkins, c1981. — xi,212p : ill ; 26cm
Includes bibliographies and index
ISBN 0-683-00253-8 : £36.00 B81-106

616.7′22 — Man. Hips. Osteoarthritis. Self-treatment. Use of mind — *Personal observations*

Shattock, E. H.. Mind your body : a practical method of self-healing / E.H. Shattock. — Wellingborough : Turnstone, 1979 (1980 [printing]). — x,117p : ill ; 22cm
ISBN 0-85500-099-6 (pbk) : Unpriced : CIP rev.
Also classified at 616.6′5 B80-078

616.7′22 — Man. Joints. Rheumatoid arthritis — *Conference proceedings*

International Congress on Rheumatoid Arthritis *(1980 : Hakone).* New horizons in rheumatoid arthritis : proceedings of the International Congress on Rheumatoid Arthritis, Hakone, 24-26 August 1980 / editors Yuichi Shiokawa Tohru Abe, Yasuo Yamauchi. — Amsterdam Oxford : Excerpta Medica, 1981. — xii,309p ill(some col.),1 col.port ; 25cm. — (International congress series ; no.535)
Includes index
ISBN 90-219-0460-8 : Unpriced B81-298

616.7′22′00924 — Man. Joints. Arthritis — *Personal observations*

Bratley, Bertha Harlington. Fifty arthritic years Bertha Harlington Bratley. — Ilfracombe : Stockwell, 1981. — 128p ; 19cm
ISBN 0-7223-1488-4 : £4.35 B81-355

16.7′2205 — Man. Joints. Arthritis. Prevention. Use of Pantothenic acid
Barton-Wright, E. C.. Arthritis : its cause and control / by E.C. Barton-Wright. — 2nd ed. — London (225 Putney Bridge Rd., SW15 2PY) : Roberts Publications, 1978. — 17p ; 19cm
Cover title. — Previous ed.: 1975
ISBN 0-906185-04-1 (pbk) : £0.60 B81-06549

16.7′220654 — Man. Arthritis. Therapy. Diet — *Recipes*
Laver, Mary. Diet for life : a cookbook for arthritics / Mary Laver and Margaret Smith ; foreword by Collin H. Dong ; with illustrations by Lila Quaife. — London : Pan, 1981. — 239p : ill ; 20cm
Includes index
ISBN 0-330-26303-x (pbk) : £1.95 B81-09716

16.7′22068 — Man. Joints. Osteoarthritis. Self-treatment
Crabbe, Buster. Buster Crabbe′s arthritis exercise book / by Buster Crabbe with Raphael Cilento. — London : Angus & Robertson, 1981, c1980. — 159p : ill ; 22cm
Originally published: New York : Simon and Schuster, 1980. — Includes index
ISBN 0-207-14190-8 (cased) : £4.95
ISBN 0-207-14198-3 (pbk) : £2.95 B81-24566

16.7′23 — Man. Rheumatic diseases
Mason and Currey′s clinical rheumatology. — 3rd ed. / edited by H.L.F. Curry. — Tunbridge Wells : Pitman Medical, 1980. — ix,372p : ill ; 24cm
Previous ed.: published as An introduction to clinical rheumatology. 1975. — Includes bibliographies and index
ISBN 0-272-79595-x : Unpriced : CIP rev. B80-36115

Textbook of rheumatology / William N. Kelley ... [et al.]. — Philadelphia ; London : Saunders, 1981. — xlv,2054,xlii p : ill(some col.) ; 29cm
Includes index
ISBN 0-7216-5352-9 : £56.00 B81-01815

.6.7′23 — Man. Rheumatic diseases — *Conference proceedings*
International Seminar on Treatment of Rheumatic Diseases *(2nd : 1980 : Israel)*. Progress in rheumatology. — Bristol : Wright, Feb.1982. — [224]p
ISBN 0-7236-7007-2 : £12.50 : CIP entry B81-35843

6.7′23 — Medicine. Rheumatology *- For general practice*
Rogers, Michael. Rheumatology in general practice. — Edinburgh : Churchill Livingstone, Aug.1981. — [128]p. — (Library of general practice)
ISBN 0-443-01720-4 (pbk) : £8.00 : CIP entry B81-16412

6.7′23′005 — Rheumatology — *Periodicals*
Recent advances in rheumatology. — No.2. — Edinburgh : Churchill Livingstone, 1981. — vi,137p
ISBN 0-443-02066-3 : Unpriced : CIP rev.
ISSN 0309-2283 B80-20733

6.7′23061 — Man. Arthritis & rheumatic diseases. Drug therapy. Piroxicam — *Conference proceedings*
Practical problems of rheumatology / [sponsored by Pfizer] ; edited by Robert G. Richardson. — London : Royal Society of Medicine : Academic Press, 1980. — viii,36p : ill ; 24cm. — (Royal Society of Medicine series. International congress and symposium series, ISSN 0142-2367 ; no.32)
Conference papers
ISBN 0-12-793532-0 (pbk) : £4.20 : CIP rev. B80-18336

6.7′23061 — Man. Rheumatic diseases. Drug therapy — *Conference proceedings*
Current themes in rheumatology : condensed report of a Geigy symposium Albufeira, Portugal, February 1981 / editors R.J. Chiswell and G.F.B. Birdwood. — Northampton : Cambridge Medical, c1981. — 33p : ill ; 25cm
Includes bibliographies
ISBN 0-904052-09-5 (pbk) : Unpriced B81-21075

616.7′23079 — Man. Rheumatic diseases. Immunological aspects
Immunological aspects of rheumatology. — Lancaster : MTP Press, June 1981. — [270]p
ISBN 0-85200-164-9 : £24.95 : CIP entry B81-18176

616.7′2309 — Man. Rheumatic diseases *- Case studies*
Golding, Douglas N.. Tutorials in clinical rheumatology. — Tunbridge Wells : Pitman Medical, May 1981. — [128]p
ISBN 0-272-79611-5 : £6.95 : CIP entry B81-06035

616.7′3 — Man. Back. Backache
Evans, David. Backache : its evolution and conservative treatment. — Lancaster : MTP Press, Sept.1981. — [300]p
ISBN 0-85200-430-3 : £9.95 : CIP entry B81-28130

Hall, Hamilton. The back doctor : lifetime relief for your aching back / Hamilton Hall. — London : Gollancz, 1981, c1980. — xi,194p : ill ; 24cm
Originally published: New York : McGraw-Hill, 1980. — Includes index
ISBN 0-575-02952-8 : £4.95 B81-11793

Jayson, Malcolm I. V.. Back pain : the facts / Malcolm I.V. Jayson ; line drawings by Richard Neave. — Oxford : Oxford University Press, 1981. — xi,180p,[8]p of plates : ill ; 23cm. — (Oxford medical publications)
Includes index
ISBN 0-19-261285-9 : £4.95 : CIP rev. B81-22477

616.7′3 — Man. Spine. Ankylosing spondylitis
Ankylosing spondylitis / edited by J.M.H. Moll. — Edinburgh : Churchill Livingstone, 1980. — x,301p : ill,2facsims,ports ; 26cm
Includes bibliographies and index
ISBN 0-443-01830-8 : £30.00 : CIP rev. B80-13852

616.7′3 — Man. Spine. Degenerative diseases
Maurice-Williams, R. S.. Spinal degenerative disease / by R.S. Maurice-Williams ; with a foreword by R. Campbell Connolly. — Bristol : John Wright, 1981. — xiii,341p ; 23cm
Bibliography: p314-333. — Includes index
ISBN 0-7236-0583-1 : Unpriced B81-12679

616.7′3 — Man. Spine. Slipped discs
Cyriax, James. The slipped disc / James Cyriax. — 3rd ed. — Farnborough, Hants. : Gower, 1980. — xvii,236p,[8]p of plates : ill,1facsim ; 23cm
Previous ed.: 1975. — Bibliography: p231-232. - Includes index
ISBN 0-566-02218-4 : £9.50 : CIP rev. B80-11462

616.7′30682 — Man. Back. Backache. Therapy. Use of hatha-yoga
Zebroff, Kareen. Back fitness the yoga way : exercises and hints for a strong, supple back / by Kareen Zebroff. — Wellingborough : Thorsons, 1980, c1979. — 96p : ill ; 22cm
Originally published: Vancouver : Fforbez, 1979
ISBN 0-7225-0685-6 (pbk) : £2.50 B81-14774

616.7′4 — Man. Movement disorders
Movement disorders. — London : Butterworths, Feb.1982. — [320]p. — (Butterworths international medical reviews. Neurology, ISSN 0260-0137 ; 2)
ISBN 0-407-02295-3 : £13.50 : CIP entry B81-36373

616.7′4 — Man. Muscles. Spasticity — *Conference proceedings*
Spasticity / disordered motor control ; [from an international symposium sponsored by Ciba-Geigy Corporation] ; edited by Robert G. Feldman, Robert R. Young, Werner P. Koella. — Miami : Symposia Specialists ; Chicago ; London ; Distributed by Year Book, c1980. — xviii,510p : ill ; 24cm
Includes index
ISBN 0-88372-128-7 : £46.50 B81-10842

616.7′4 — Man. Voluntary muscles. Degradation
Degradative processes in heart and skeletal muscle / editor K. Wildenthal. — Amsterdam ; Oxford : Elsevier/North-Holland Biochemical Press, 1980. — xvii,461p : ill ; 25cm. — (Research monographs in cell and tissue physiology ; v.3)
Includes bibliographies and index
ISBN 0-444-80235-5 : £41.75
Primary classification 616.1′24 B81-05268

616.7′4 — Man. Voluntary muscles. Diseases
Disorders of voluntary muscle / edited by Sir John Walton. — 4th ed. — Edinburgh : Churchill Livingstone, 1981. — 1069p : ill ; 26cm
Previous ed.: 1974. — Includes bibliographies and index
ISBN 0-443-01847-2 : £48.00 B81-23681

616.7′406 — Man. Movement disorders. Therapy
Disorders of movement / edited by A. Barbeau. — Lancaster : MTP, 1981. — xi,227p : ill ; 25cm. — (Current status of modern therapy ; v.8)
Includes index
ISBN 0-85200-212-2 : £14.95 B81-14657

616.7′4061 — Man. Muscles. Nerves. Drug therapy
Bowman, W. C.. Pharmacology of neuromuscular function : with special reference to anaesthetic practice / W.C. Bowman. — Bristol : John Wright, 1980. — xi,186p : ill ; 23cm
Bibliography: p134-180. - Includes index
ISBN 0-7236-0558-0 : £10.50 : CIP rev. B80-17733

616.7′407547 — Man. Muscles. Electromyography. Data processing — *Conference proceedings*
International Conference on EEG and EMG Data Processing *(1981 : Kanazawa)*. Recent advances in EEG and EMG data processing : the proceedings of the International Conference on EEG and EMG Data Processing, held in Kanazawa, Japan, September 10-12, 1981 / edited by Nariyoshi Yamaguchi, Kiyoshi Fujisawa. — Amsterdam ; Oxford : Elsevier/North-Holland Biomedical, 1981. — xiii,421p : ill ; 25cm
Includes index
ISBN 0-444-80356-4 : Unpriced
Primary classification 616.8′047547 B81-32846

616.7′48 — Man. Muscular dystrophy — *Conference proceedings*
Muscular dystrophy research : advances and new trends : proceedings of an international symposium on muscular dystrophy research, Venice, Italy, April 10-12, 1980 / editors: C. Angelini, G.A. Danieli, D. Fontanari. — Amsterdam ; Oxford : Excerpta Medica, 1980. — xi,332p : ill,1map ; 25cm. — (International congress series ; no.527)
Includes index
ISBN 90-219-0453-5 : £27.23 B81-02542

616.7′48 — Man. Muscular dystrophy. Smith, Christine — *Biographies*
Smith, Christine. Clouds got in my way. — London : Eyre & Spottiswoode, Oct.1981. — [272]p
ISBN 0-413-80240-x : £6.00 : CIP entry B81-25288

616.7′7079′028 — Man. Connective tissues. Diseases. Immunology. Laboratory techniques — *Manuals*
Glynn, L. E.. Immunological investigation of connective tissue diseases / L.E. Glynn, C.A. Reading. — Edinburgh : Churchill Livingstone, 1981. — x,98p : ill ; 25cm. — (Practical methods in clinical immunology series ; v.4)
Bibliography: p84-94. — Includes index
ISBN 0-443-01850-2 : £15.00 B81-25593

616.8 — MAN. DISEASES OF NERVOUS SYSTEM, PSYCHIATRIC DISORDERS

616.8 — Deviance. Medical aspects
Conrad, Peter, *1945-*. Deviance and medicalization / Peter Conrad, Joseph W. Schneider ; foreword by Joseph R. Gusfield. — St. Louis ; London : Mosby, 1980. — xvi,311p : ill ; 26cm
Bibliography: p277-294. — Includes index
ISBN 0-8016-1025-7 (pbk) : Unpriced B81-08557

616.8 — Man. Hands. Nerves. Therapy

Dellon, A. Lee. Evaluation of sensibility and re-education of sensation in the hand / A. Lee Dellon. — Baltimore ; London : Williams & Wilkins, c1981. — xiv,263p : ill(some col.) ; 26cm
Bibliography: p246-258. — Includes index
ISBN 0-683-02427-2 : £42.00 B81-24346

616.8 — Man. Nervous system. Chronic diseases

Seiden, Margaret R.. Practical management of chronic neurologic problems / Margaret R. Seiden. — New York : Appleton-Century-Crofts ; London : Prentice-Hall, 1981. — x,405p : ill ; 24cm
Includes bibliographies and index
ISBN 0-8385-7871-3 : £19.90 B81-37687

616.8 — Man. Nervous system. Diseases

Adams, Raymond D.. Principles of neurology / Raymond D. Adams, Maurice Victor. — 2nd ed. — New York ; London : McGraw-Hill, c1981. — x,1094p : ill ; 25cm
Previous ed.: 1977. — Includes bibliographies and index
ISBN 0-07-000294-0 : £31.50 B81-39796

Reeves, Alexander G.. Disorders of the nervous system : a primer / Alexander G. Reeves with contributions by Edward Valenstein, José L. Ochoa, John E. Woodford. — Chicago ; London : Year Book Medical, c1981. — xi,240p : ill ; 25cm. — (Internal medicine series)
Includes bibliographies and index
ISBN 0-8151-7136-6 (pbk) : £19.00 B81-17091

Sutherland, John M.. Fundamentals of neurology / John M. Sutherland. — Lancaster : MTP Press, c1981. — vii,272p : ill ; 24cm
Includes bibliographies and index
ISBN 0-85200-529-6 (pbk) : £7.95 B81-06092

616.8 — Man. Nervous system. Disorders. Neuropsychological aspects

Brain-behaviour relationships / edited by James R. Merikangas. — Lexington, Mass. : Lexington Books ; [Aldershot] : Gower [distributor], 1981. — x,217p : ill ; 24cm
Includes bibliographies and index
ISBN 0-669-03082-1 : £15.00 B81-38603

616.8 — Man. Nervous system. Effects of blood diseases

Davies-Jones, G. A. B.. Neurological complications in clinical haematology / G.A.B. Davies-Jones, F.E. Preston, W.R. Timperley. — Oxford : Blackwell Scientific, 1980. — xii,241p : ill ; 25cm
Includes bibliographies and index
ISBN 0-632-00064-3 : £18.50 : CIP rev. B80-07806

616.8 — Man. Nervous system. Effects of toxins — *Conference proceedings*

International Congress on Neurotoxicology *(1979 : Varese).* Advances in neurotoxicology : proceedings of the International Congress on Neurotoxicology, Varses, Italy, 27-30 September 1979 / editor L. Manzo ; associate editors N. Léry, Y. Lacasse, L. Roche. — Oxford : Pergamon, 1980. — xxxvi,405p : ill ; 26cm
Includes bibliographies and index
ISBN 0-08-024953-1 : £26.50 : CIP rev. B80-07388

616.8 — Man. Nervous system. Metabolic disorders — *Conference proceedings*

Metabolic disorders of the nervous system. — London : Pitkin, Dec.1981. — [524]p. — (Progress in neurology series, ISSN 0260-0013 ; 7)
Conference papers
ISBN 0-272-79624-7 : £35.00 : CIP entry B81-31367

616.8 — Man. Stress

Kutash, Irwin L.. Handbook on stress and anxiety / Irwin L. Kutash, Louis B. Schlesinger and associates. — San Francisco ; London : Jossey-Bass, 1980. — xx,580p : ill ; 24cm. — (The Jossey-Bass social and behavioral science series)
Bibliography: p474-550. - Includes index
ISBN 0-87589-478-x : Unpriced
Also classified at 616.85′223 B81-18270

Mulry, Ray. Tension management & relaxation : an approach to a balanced way of living / Ray Mulry. — St. Louis ; London : Mosby, 1981. — 1v(xii, 115p) ; 21cm + 1 pamphlet([4]p: 1 ill; 27cm) + 4 round cassettes(240 min: 3-3/4ips:mono)
In plastic case
ISBN 0-8016-3596-9 (pbk) : £27.50 B81-31402

Text book of stress / [edited] by R.P. Saxena. — Laindon (9 Suffolk Drive, Laindon, Essex SS15 6PL) : International Society for the Prevention of Stress, c1980. — 278p : ill ; 27cm
Includes bibliographies and index
ISBN 0-906482-06-2 : £29.00 B81-08794

616.8 — Man. Stress. Role of social change

Uprooting and development : dilemmas of coping with modernization / edited by George V. Coelho and Paul I. Ahmed with the assistance of Ying-Ying T. Yuan. — New York ; London : Plenum, c1980. — xxviii,538p ; 24cm. — (Current topics in mental health)
Includes bibliographies and index
ISBN 0-306-40509-1 : Unpriced B81-06507

616.8 — Man. Stress. Self-treatment

Cooper, Cary L.. The stress check : coping with the stresses of life and work / Cary L. Cooper. — Englewood Cliffs ; London : Prentice Hall, c1981. — x,211p : ill,forms ; 21cm. — (A Spectrum book)
Bibliography: p192-207. - Includes index
ISBN 0-13-852640-0 (cased) : Unpriced B81-11750

616.8 — Man. Stress — *Serials*

The **new** Welsh journal of medicine. — Vol,no.1 (Jan. 1980)-. — Cardiff (19 Hawfinch Close, Cardiff, South Wales) : Institute of Stress, 1980. — 1v. : ill ; 25cm
Only one issue published. — Vol.1, no.1 called also vol.1, no.1-4
ISSN 0143-8638 = New Welsh journal of medicine : Unpriced B81-05353

616.8 — Man. Stress. Therapy

Everly, George S.. The nature and treatment of the stress response : a practical guide for clinicians / George S. Everly, Jr. and Robert Rosenfeld with Roger J. Allen ... [et al.]. — New York ; London : Plenum, c1981. — xvii,215p : ill ; 24cm
Bibliography: p195-205. - Includes index
ISBN 0-306-40677-2 : Unpriced B81-23356

616.8 — Man. Stress. Therapy. Applications of astrology

Sewell, Rupert J.. Stress and the sun signs : an astrological approach to the self-treatment of tension / by Rupert J. Sewell. — Wellingborough : Aquarian, 1981. — 96p : 1ill ; 22cm
Bibliography: p93-94. — Includes index
ISBN 0-85030-241-2 (pbk) : Unpriced B81-08527

616.8 — Man. Stress. Therapy — *Theosophical viewpoints*

Baker, Douglas, *1922-*. Esoteric healing / by Douglas Baker. — Essendon ('Little Elephant', High Rd., Essendon, Herts.) : D. Baker. — (The seven pillars of ancient wisdom ; v.3)
Part 2. — c1976. — 260p,[3] folded leaves of plates : ill(some col.),col.ports ; 29cm
Includes index
Unpriced (pbk) B81-08396

616.8 — Medicine. Neurology

Davidson, D. L. W.. Neurological therapeutics. — London : Pitman Medical, Apr.1981. — [264]p
ISBN 0-272-79616-6 : £15.00 : CIP entry B81-08827

616.8 — Medicine. Neurology — *For psychiatry*

Kaufman, David Myland. Clinical neurology for psychiatrists / David Myland Kaufman. — New York ; London : Grune & Stratton, c1981. — xii,366p : ill,forms ; 27cm
Includes bibliographies and index
ISBN 0-8089-1321-2 : £16.50 B81-35422

616.8 — Medicine. Neurology — *Serials*

Recent advances in clinical neurology. — 3. — Edinburgh : Churchill Livingstone, Oct.1981. — [272]p
ISBN 0-443-02121-x : £14.00 : CIP entry
ISSN 0307-7403 B81-2529

616.8 — Medicine. Neuropsychology

Handbook of clinical neuropsychology / edited b Susan B. Filskov, Thomas J. Boll. — New York ; Chichester : Wiley, c1981. — xvii,806p ill ; 27cm. — (A Wiley-Interscience publication) (Wiley series on personality processes, ISSN 0195-4008)
Text on lining papers. — Includes bibliographies and index
ISBN 0-471-04802-x : £19.95 B81-1843

616.8 — Medicine. Psychoneuroendocrinology — *Conference proceedings*

International Society of Psychoneuroendocrinology. *Congress (11th : 198 : Florence).* Progress in psychoneuroendocrinology : proceedings of the XI Congress of the International Society of Psychoneuroendocrinology held in Florence, Italy, 16-20 June, 1980 / editors : Francesca Brambilla, Giorgio Racagni and David de Wied. — Amsterdam ; Oxford : Elsevier/North-Holland, 1980. — xi,669p : ill 25cm. — (Symposia of the Giovanni Lorenzin Foundation ; v.8)
Includes index
ISBN 0-444-80294-0 : £41.50 B81-0725

616.8 — Neuropsychiatry

Trimble, Michael R.. Neuropsychiatry / Michael R. Trimble. — Chichester : Wiley, c1981. — xiv,287p : ill ; 24cm
Includes index
ISBN 0-471-27827-0 : £13.60 : CIP rev. B81-0012

616.8′041 — Man. Nervous system. Diseases caus by microorganisms

Brown, W. Jann. Neuropathology of parasitic infections. — Oxford : Oxford University Pres Jan.1982. — [200]p. — (Oxford medical publications)
ISBN 0-19-261246-8 : £15.00 : CIP entry B81-3437

616.8′0427 — Man. Nervous system. Diseases. Research. Use of laboratory animals

Animal models of neurological disease / edited b F. Clifford Rose, P.O. Behan. — Tunbridge Wells : Pitman Medical, 1980. — xiv,479p : il ; 24cm. — (Progress in neurology series, ISSN 0260-0013)
Includes index
ISBN 0-272-79591-7 : £30.00 : CIP rev. B80-2451

616.8′0428′024613 — Patients with neurological diseases. Intensive care — *Programmed instructions — For nursing*

Snyder, Mariah. Neurologic problems : a critica care nursing focus / Mariah Snyder, Mary Jackle. — Bowie : Brady ; London : Prentice-Hall, c1981. — x,437p : ill,1form ; 26cm
Includes index
ISBN 0-87619-713-6 (pbk) : £11.00 B81-152

616.8′0442 — Man. Myelination. Disorders. Genetic aspects — *Conference proceedings*

International Symposium on Neurological Mutations Affecting Myelination : Research Tools in Neurobiology — Correlations to Huma Neurological Diseases *(1980 : Seillac).* Neurological mutations affecting myelination research tools in neurobiology : correlations t human neurological diseases : proceedings of the International Symposium on Neurological Mutations Affecting Myelination : Research Tools in Neurobiology - Correlations to Human Neurological Diseases, held in Seillac (France), 13-17 April, 1980 / sponsored by th Institut national de la santé et de la recherch médicale, the European Molecular Biology Organization and the European Society for Neurobiology ; editor: Nicole Baumann. — Amsterdam ; Oxford : Elsevier/North-Hollan Biomedical Press, 1980. — xvii,565p : ill ; 25cm. — (INSERM symposium ; no.14)
Includes index
ISBN 0-444-80270-3 : £36.74 B81-047

616.8′0442 — Man. Nervous system. Genetic disorders

Neurogenetic directory / edited by Ntinos C. Myrianthopoulos. — Amsterdam ; Oxford : North-Holland. — (Handbook of clinical neurology ; v.42)
Pt.1. — c1981. — xix,772p : ill ; 27cm
Includes bibliographies
ISBN 0-7204-7242-3 : Unpriced
ISBN 0-7204-7200-8 (set) : Unpriced
B81-29702

616.8′0443 — Man. Central nervous system. Congenital abnormalities

Warkany, Josef. Mental retardation and congenital malformations of the central nervous system / Josef Warkany, Ronald J. Lemire, M. Michael Cohen, Jr. — Chicago ; London : Year Book Medical, c1981. — x,459p : ill ; 26cm
Includes bibliographies and index
ISBN 0-8151-9096-4 : £47.50 B81-40510

616.8′0461 — Man. Nervous system. Drug therapy

Eadie, Mervyn J.. Neurological clinical pharmacology / Mervyn J. Eadie, John H. Tyrer. — Lancaster : MTP, c1980. — x,470p : ill ; 24cm
Bibliography: p402-448. - Includes index
ISBN 0-85200-527-x : £24.95 B81-00129

616.8′047 — Clinical neurophysiology

Clinical neurophysiology / edited by Eric Stålberg and Robert R. Young. — London : Butterworths, 1981. — 417p : ill ; 24cm. — (Butterworths international medical reviews. Neurology, ISSN 0260-0137 ; 1)
Includes bibliographies and index
ISBN 0-407-02294-5 : Unpriced : CIP rev.
B81-04329

616.8′047 — Man. Nervous system. Diseases. Physiological aspects

Lance, James W.. A physiological approach to clinical neurology. — 3rd ed. / James W. Lance, James G. McLeod. — London : Butterworths, 1981. — xiii,380p : ill ; 24cm
Previous ed.: 1975. — Includes bibliographies and index
ISBN 0-407-00196-4 : Unpriced : CIP rev.
B80-18768

616.8′047 — Medicine. Neuropathology

The **Molecular** basis of neuropathology. — London : Edward Arnold, Oct.1981. — [650]p
ISBN 0-7131-4374-6 : £50.00 : CIP entry
B81-30313

Weller, Roy O.. Moving parts in medicine : an inaugural lecture : delivered at the University 22 January, 1981 / by Roy O. Weller. — [Southampton] : University of Southampton, 1981. — 15p ; 21cm
Bibliography: p15
ISBN 0-85432-216-7 (pbk) : £0.50 B81-33341

616.8′0472 — Man. Nervous system. Diseases. Syndromes: Face manifestations

Dyken, Paul R.. Facial features of neurologic syndromes / Paul R. Dyken, Max D. Miller ; with illustrations by Karen Waldo and John Hagan. — St. Louis ; London : Mosby, 1980. — xii,449p : ill,1port ; 27cm
Bibliography: p423-433. - Includes index
ISBN 0-8016-1485-6 : Unpriced B81-08662

616.8′0475 — Man. Nervous system. Diagnosis

Bickerstaff, Edwin R.. Neurological examination in clinical practice / Edwin R. Bickerstaff. — 4th ed. — Oxford : Blackwell Scientific, 1980. — xii,360p : ill ; 25cm
Previous ed.: 1973. — Includes index
ISBN 0-632-00548-3 : £18.00 : CIP rev.
B80-08238

616.8′0475 — Man. Nervous system. Diagnosis — *Case studies*

Tyrer, John H.. Exercises in neurological diagnosis. — 3rd ed. — Edinburgh : Churchill Livingstone, Sept.1981. — [416]p
Previous ed.: 1975
ISBN 0-443-01785-9 (pbk) : £9.95 : CIP entry
B81-25767

616.8′0475 — Man. Nervous system. Differential diagnosis

Patten, John, *1935-*. Neurological differential diagnosis : an illustrated approach with 288 figures / John Patten. — Rev. reprint. — London : Starke, 1978, c1977. — x,292p : ill ; 30cm
Includes index
ISBN 0-287-66988-2 : £16.50 B81-11187

616.8′04754 — Man. Nervous system. Tests — *Manuals*

Van Allen, Maurice W.. Pictorial manual of neurologic tests : a guide to the performance and interpretation of the neurologic examination / illustrated by George Buckley. — 2nd ed. / Maurice W. Van Allen, Robert L. Rodnitzky. — Chicago ; London : Year Book Medical, 1981. — xi,227p : ill ; 16x24cm
Previous ed.: 1969. — Bibliography: p211. — Includes index
ISBN 0-8151-8960-5 : Unpriced B81-14218

616.8′047547 — Man. Brain. Electroencephalography. Data processing — *Conference proceedings*

International Conference on EEG and EMG Data Processing *(1981 : Kanazawa)*. Recent advances in EEG and EMG data processing : the proceedings of the International Conference on EEG and EMG Data Processing, held in Kanazawa, Japan, September 10-12, 1981 / edited by Nariyoshi Yamaguchi, Kiyoshi Fujisawa. — Amsterdam ; Oxford : Elsevier/North-Holland Biomedical, 1981. — xiii,421p : ill ; 25cm
Includes index
ISBN 0-444-80356-4 : Unpriced
Also classified at 616.7′407547 B81-32846

616.8′047547 — Man. Brain. Electroencephalography. Techniques

Kiloh, L. G.. Clinical electroencephalography. — 4th ed. — London : Butterworths, July 1981. — [320]p
Previous ed.: 1972
ISBN 0-407-00160-3 : £19.50 : CIP entry
B81-14887

616.8′047572 — Man. Brain. Diagnosis. Computerised tomography — *Manuals*

Valentine, A. R.. A practical introduction to cranial CT / A.R. Valentine, P. Pullicino, E. Bannan ; with a foreword by G.H. du Boulay. — London : Heinemann Medical, 1981. — 149p : ill ; 22cm
Includes index
ISBN 0-433-33602-1 (pbk) : £8.00 B81-12103

616.8′047583 — Man. Brain. Diagnosis. Tissue biopsy. Smear techniques

Adams, J. Hume. Brain biopsy : the smear technique for neurosurgical biopsies / J. Hume Adams, David I. Graham, David Doyle. — London : Chapman and Hall, 1981. — x,124p : ill ; 24cm. — (Biopsy pathology series)
Includes bibliographies and index
ISBN 0-412-22270-1 : Unpriced: CIP rev.
B81-02099

616.8′0479 — Man. Nervous system. Diseases. Immunological aspects

Aarli, Johan A.. Immunological aspects of neurological diseases / Johan A. Aarli and Olav Tönder. — Basel ; London : Karger, c1980. — ix,189p : ill ; 23cm. — (Monographs in neural sciences ; v.6)
Includes bibliographies and index
ISBN 3-8055-0814-x (pbk) : £25.75 B81-07265

616.8′05 — Medicine. Neurology — *Serials*

Current neurology. — Vol.1-. — New York ; Chichester : Wiley, 1978-. — v. : ill ; 27cm
Annual. — Description based on: Vol.3
ISSN 0161-780x = Current neurology : £35.00
B81-34056

616.8′1 — Man. Brain. Blood vessels. Diseases

Current concepts in cerebrovascular disease / edited by Fletcher H. McDowell, Edmund H. Sonnenblick, Michael Lesch. — New York ; London : Grune & Stratton, c1980. — v,94p : ill ; 29cm
′Progress in cardiovascular diseases reprint, March/April and May/June 1980′ Vol.xxii, numbers 5 and 6. — Includes index
ISBN 0-8089-1353-0 : £11.00 B81-22004

616.8′1 — Man. Brain. Blood vessels. Diseases — *Conference proceedings*

International Salzburg Conference *(10th : 1980)*. Cerebral vascular disease 3 : proceedings of the 10th International Salzburg Conference, September 24-27, 1980 / editors J.S. Meyer ... [et al.]. — Amsterdam ; Oxford : Excerpta Medica, 1981. — 351p : ill ; 25cm. — (International congress series ; no.532)
Includes index
ISBN 90-219-0481-0 : £26.82
ISBN 0-444-90197-3 (Elsevier/North-Holland)
B81-22293

616.8′1 — Man. Brain. Metabolic disorders — *Conference proceedings*

International Symposium on the Pathophysiology of Cerebral Energy Metabolism *(2nd : 1979 : Belgrade)*. Circulatory and developmental aspects of brain metabolism / [proceedings of the second International Symposium on the Pathophysiology of Cerebral Energy Metabolism, organized and sponsored by the Serbian Academy of Sciences and Art and held in Belgrade, Yugoslavia, September 16-20, 1979] ; edited by Maria Spatz ... [et al.]. — New York ; London : Plenum, c1980. — x,446p : ill ; 26cm
Includes bibliographies and index
ISBN 0-306-40542-3 : Unpriced B81-08240

616.8′1 — Man. Brain. Strokes

Rose, F. Clifford. Stroke : the facts / by F. Clifford Rose and Rudy Capildeo ; with a foreword by Sir Peter Medawar. — Oxford : Oxford University Press, 1981. — 143p,[8]p of plates : ill ; 23cm. — (Oxford medical publications)
Includes index
ISBN 0-19-261170-4 : £4.95 : CIP rev.
B81-12337

Sessler, Gloria Jean. Stroke : how to prevent it/how to survive it / Gloria Jean Sessler. — Englewood Cliffs ; London : Prentice-Hall, c1981. — 278p ; 24cm. — (A Spectrum book)
Includes index
ISBN 0-13-852913-2 (cased) : Unpriced
ISBN 0-13-852905-1 (pbk) : £4.50 B81-22711

616.8′1 — Man. Brain. Strokes. Physiotherapy

Dardier, Esmé L.. The early stroke patient : positioning and movement / Esmé L. Dardier ; drawings by Judy Stoker. — London : Baillière Tindall, 1980. — 116p : ill(some col.) ; 25cm
Bibliography: p111-112. — Includes index
ISBN 0-7020-0729-3 (spiral) : £5.95 : CIP rev.
B79-34910

616.8′1 — Stroke patients. Speech therapy

Coles, Ruth. Practical activities for stroke groups : a manual for speech therapists / by Ruth Coles, Andrea Miller. — [Wheathampstead] ([Castle Farm, Lea Valley, Wheathampstead, Herts.]) : [R. Coles], c1981. — 99p : ill,maps,facsims ; 23cm
Bibliography: p94-95
ISBN 0-9507507-0-0 (pbk) : Unpriced
B81-24184

616.8′107543 — Man. Brain. Blood vessels. Diagnosis. Doppler ultrasonography

Spencer, Merrill P.. Cerebrovascular evaluation with Doppler ultrasound / by Merrill P. Spencer, John M. Reid with contributions by Edwin C. Brockenbrough ... [et al.]. — The Hague ; London : Nijhoff, 1981. — x,245p : ill (some col.) ; 25cm. — (Developments in cardiovascular medicine ; v.6)
Bibliography: p223-237. - Includes index
ISBN 90-247-2384-1 : Unpriced B81-15262

616.8′107572 — Man. Brain. Blood vessels. Diagnosis. Angiography

Osborn, Anne G.. Introduction to celebral angiography / Anne G. Osborn with Julian G. Maack and Bradley R. Nelson, Thomas C. Caswell ; cover illustration adapted from drawing by Anne G. Osborn. — Hagerstown ; London : Harper & Row, c1980. — xi,436p : ill ; 26cm
Includes bibliographies and index
ISBN 0-06-141829-3 : £28.00 B81-08376

616.8′3 — Man. Tardive dyskinesia

Tardive dyskinesia. — Bristol : Wright, Feb.1982. — [256]p
ISBN 0-7236-7006-4 : £15.00 : CIP entry
B81-35844

616.8'33 — Man. Parkinson's disease
Research progress in Parkinson's disease / edited by F. Clifford Rose, Rudy Capildeo. — Tunbridge Wells : Pitman Medical, 1981. — xiii,428p : ill ; 23cm. — (Progress in neurology series, ISSN 0260-0013)
Includes index
ISBN 0-272-79601-8 : Unpriced B81-40843

Stern, Gerald. Parkinson's disease. — Oxford : Oxford University Press, Feb.1982. — [90]p. — (Oxford medical publications)
ISBN 0-19-261293-x : £4.50 : CIP entry B81-35772

616.8'34 — Man. Multiple sclerosis
Multiple sclerosis : the facts. — [Dublin] (14 Merrion Sq., Dublin 2) : Multiple Sclerosis Society of Ireland, [1981?]. — 15p : ill ; 22cm
Unpriced (unbound) B81-21923

616.8'34068 — Man. Multiple sclerosis. Self-treatment
Graham, Judy. Multiple sclerosis : a self-help guide to its management / by Judy Graham. — Wellingborough : Thorsons, 1981. — 160p : ill,1port ; 22cm
Bibliography: p150-153. — Includes index
ISBN 0-7225-0625-2 (cased) : Unpriced : CIP rev.
ISBN 0-7225-0624-4 (pbk) : £3.50 B81-12856

616.8'37062 — Man. Quadriplegia & paraplegia. Physiotherapy
Bromley, Ida. Tetraplegia and paraplegia : a guide for physiotherapists / Ida Bromley ; illustrated by Janet Plested ; foreword by Sir Ludwig Guttman. — 2nd ed. — Edinburgh : Churchill Livingstone, 1981. — x,256p : ill ; 25cm
Previous ed.: 1976. — Bibliography: p251-252. - Includes index
ISBN 0-443-01992-4 (pbk) : Unpriced : CIP rev. B80-09711

616.8'41 — Man. Vertigo
Evaluation and clinical management of dizziness and vertigo. — Bristol : Wright, Jan.1982. — [240]p
ISBN 0-7236-7003-x : £12.50 : CIP entry B81-34779

616.8'49 — Man. Brain. Oedema
Brain edema / edited by Marinus de Vlieger, Samuel A. de Lange, Jan W.F. Beks. — New York ; Chichester : Wiley, 1981. — xii,176p : ill ; 26cm. — (A Wiley medical publication)
Includes index
ISBN 0-471-04477-6 : £22.75 B81-35619

616.8'49 — Man. Hypersomnia & narcolepsy
Roth, Bedřich. Narcolepsy and hypersomnia / Bedřich Roth ; translated by Margaret Schierlová ; English translation edited and 5 chapters co-authored by Roger Broughton. — London : Karger, 1980. — xv,310p : ill ; 25cm
Translation from the Czech. — Bibliography: p270-303. - Includes index
ISBN 3-8055-0490-x : £24.50 B81-21691

616.8'5 — Brain damaged patients — *Case studies*
Luriîa, A. R.. The man with a shattered world : a history of a brain wound / A.R. Luria ; translated from the Russian by Lynn Solotaroff. — Harmondsworth : Penguin, 1975, c1972 (1981 printing). — 130p ; 20cm. — (Penguin education) (Penguin modern psychology)
Translation of: Poterîannyĭ i vozvrashchennyĭ mir. — Originally published: New York : Basic Books, 1972 ; London : Cape, 1973. — Includes index
ISBN 0-14-080579-6 (pbk) : £1.95 B81-40435

616.8'5 — Man. Neuroses
Trimble, Michael R.. Post-traumatic neurosis. — Chichester : Wiley, Nov.1981. — [100]p
ISBN 0-471-09975-9 : £10.00 : CIP entry
Primary classification 617'.21 B81-30520

616.85'2 — Man. Anorexia nervosa — *Personal observations*
MacLeod, Sheila. The art of starvation / Sheila MacLeod. — London : Virago, 1981. — 193p ; 21cm
ISBN 0-86068-164-5 (cased) : £5.95
ISBN 0-86068-169-6 (pbk) : £2.95 B81-10180

616.8'5206 — Man. Neuroses. Behaviour therapy
Caine, T. M.. Personal styles in neurosis : implications for small group psychotherapy and behaviour therapy / T.M. Caine, O.B.A. Wijesinghe, D.A. Winter. — London : Routledge & Kegan Paul, 1981. — xi,219p : ill ; 23cm. — (The International library of group psychotherapy and group process)
Bibliography: p193-210. — Includes index
ISBN 0-7100-0617-9 : £11.50 B81-17257

616.85'206 — Man. Neuroses. Behaviour therapy
Marks, Isaac M.. Cure and care of neuroses : theory and practice of behavioral psychotherapy / Isaac Marks. — New York ; Chichester : Wiley, c1981. — xiii,331p : ill ; 24cm
Bibliography: p289-316. — Includes index
ISBN 0-471-08808-0 : £17.50 B81-23341

616.8'5206 — Man. Neuroses. Psychotherapy. Bioenergetics
Lowen, Alexander. Fear of life / Alexander Lowen. — New York : Macmillan ; London : Collier Macmillan, c1980. — 274p ; 22cm
ISBN 0-02-575880-2 : £5.95 B81-19597

616.85'21 — Hallucinations. Psychotherapy — *Case studies*
Schatzman, Morton. The story of Ruth / Morton Schatzman. — London : Duckworth, 1980. — 306p : ill ; 23cm
Originally published: New York : Putnam, 1980
ISBN 0-7156-1504-1 : £6.95 B81-06183

616.85'22 — Man. Agoraphobia
Mathews, Andrew M.. Agoraphobia. — London : Tavistock, Oct.1981. — [220]p
ISBN 0-422-78060-x : £14.00 : CIP entry B81-28061

616.85'22 — Man. Agoraphobia — *Personal observations*
Vose, Ruth Hurst. Agoraphobia. — London : Faber, Sept.1981. — [208]p
ISBN 0-571-11752-x (cased) : £7.95 : CIP entry
ISBN 0-571-11753-8 (pbk) : £3.50 B81-23758

616.85'223 — Man. Neuroses: Anxiety
Graham, Arthur. Depression and anxiety / Arthur Graham ; illustrated by the Hayward Art Group. — Feltham : Hamlyn Paperbacks, 1981. — 48p : ill ; 17cm. — (Pocket health guides)
ISBN 0-600-20315-8 (pbk) : £0.85
Primary classification 616.85'27 B81-40891

Handbook of studies on anxiety / edited by Graham D. Burrows and Brian Davies. — Amsterdam ; Oxford : Elsevier/North-Holland, 1980. — xiii,405p : ill ; 25cm
Includes bibliographies and index
ISBN 0-444-80224-x : £32.20 B81-02244

Kutash, Irwin L.. Handbook on stress and anxiety / Irwin L. Kutash, Louis B. Schlesinger and associates. — San Francisco ; London : Jossey-Bass, 1980. — xx,580p : ill ; 24cm. — (The Jossey-Bass social and behavioral science series)
Bibliography: p474-550. - Includes index
ISBN 0-87589-478-x : Unpriced
Primary classification 616.8 B81-18270

616.85'223 — Man. Neuroses: Anxiety. Neuropsychological aspects
Gray, Jeffrey A.. The neuropsychology of anxiety. — Oxford : Clarendon Press, Oct.1981. — [500]p. — (Oxford psychology series)
ISBN 0-19-852109-x : £29.00 : CIP entry B81-26762

616.85'225 — Man. Agoraphobia. Self-treatment
Peel, R.. Agoraphobia : (fear & anxiety) : self help brochure / by R. Peel. — Halifax (3 Acacia Drive, Lightcliffe, Halifax, West Yorkshire HX3 8UF) : R. Peel, c1981. — 36p : facsim ; 22cm
Cover title. — Text on inside covers
£1.00 (pbk) B81-40883

616.85'232 — Man. Korsakoff's syndrome
Butters, Nelson. Alcoholic Korsakoff's syndrome : an information-processing approach to amnesia / Nelson Butters, Laird S. Cermak. — New York ; London : Academic Press, 1980. — xiv,188p : ill ; 24cm
Bibliography: p170-181. — Includes index
ISBN 0-12-148380-0 : £9.40 B81-0227

616.85'25 — Man. Hypochondria
Meister, Robert. Hypochondria : towards a bette understanding / by Robert Neister [i.e. Meister]. — London : Owen, 1981, c1980. — 194p ; 23cm
Originally published: New York : Taplinger, 1980. — Bibliography: p181-190. — Includes index
ISBN 0-7206-0590-3 : £8.95 B81-293C

616.85'27 — Man. Depression
Arieti, Silvano. Severe and mild depression : the psychotherapeutic approach / Silvano Arieti and Jules Bemporad. — London : Tavistock Publications, 1980, c1978. — x,453p ; 24cm
Originally published: New York : Basic Books, 1978. — Bibliography: p431-441. - Includes index
ISBN 0-422-77340-9 : Unpriced : CIP rev. B80-0367

Graham, Arthur. Depression and anxiety / Arthur Graham ; illustrated by the Hayward Art Group. — Feltham : Hamlyn Paperbacks, 1981. — 48p : ill ; 17cm. — (Pocket health guides)
ISBN 0-600-20315-8 (pbk) : £0.85
Also classified at 616.85'223 B81-4089

Winokur, George. Depression : the facts / by George Winokur. — Oxford : Oxford University Press, 1981. — viii,166p : ill ; 23cm — (Oxford medical publications)
Includes index
ISBN 0-19-261315-4 : £5.95 : CIP rev. B81-1446

616.85'27 — Man. Depression. Psychobiological aspects — *Conference proceedings*
Pfizer Symposium on Depression *(1980 : Boca Raton)*. The psychobiology of affective disorders : Pfizer Symposium on Depression, Boca Raton, Florida, February 28-29, 1980 / edited by Joseph Mendels, Jay D. Amsterdam. — Basel ; London : Karger, c1980. — 220p : ill ; 23cm
Includes index
ISBN 3-8055-1400-x (pbk) : £9.75 B81-262

616.85'2706 — Man. Depression. Behaviour therap
Behavior therapy for depression : present status and future directions / edited by Lynn P. Rehm ; with a foreword by Irene Elkin Waskow. — New York ; London : Academic Press, c1981. — 389p : ill ; 24cm
Includes bibliographies and index
ISBN 0-12-585880-9 : £16.60 B81-177

616.85'27061 — Man. Depression. Drug therapy — *Conference proceedings*
New directions in antidepressant therapy : an international review of the triazolopyridine derivatives / [proceedings of an International symposium held at the Royal College of Physicians, London, on 8th January 1981] ; edited by S. Gershon, M.H. Lader and A.D.S. Caldwell. — London : published jointly by Th Royal Society of Medicine, Academic Press, 1981. — viii,107p : ill ; 24cm. — (Internationa congress and symposium series / Royal Societ of Medicine, ISSN 0142-2367 ; no.46)
Includes bibliographies
ISBN 0-12-791549-4 (pbk) : Unpriced : CIP rev. B81-123

616.8'53 — Man. Epilepsy
Hopkins, Anthony. Epilepsy : the facts / Anthony Hopkins. — Oxford : Oxford University Press, 1981. — 158p, 2p of plates : ill ; 23cm
Includes index
ISBN 0-19-261257-3 : £4.95 : CIP rev. B81-134

616.8'53 — Man. Epilepsy *continuation*

Laidlaw, Mary V.. Epilepsy explained / Mary V. Laidlaw, John Laidlaw. — Edinburgh : Churchill Livingstone, 1980. — 83p : ill ; 19cm. — (A Churchill Livingstone patient handbook)
Bibliography: p79
ISBN 0-443-01962-2 (pbk) : £1.20 : CIP rev. B80-13854

Sutherland, John M.. The epilepsies : modern diagnosis and treatment / John M. Sutherland, Mervyn J. Eadie ; foreword by Henry Miller. — 3rd ed.. — Edinburgh : Churchill Livingstone, 1980. — x,156p : ill ; 22cm
Previous ed.: 1974. — Includes bibliographies and index
ISBN 0-443-02184-8 (pbk) : £3.95 : CIP rev. B80-10636

616.8'53 — Man. Epilepsy — *Conference proceedings*

Epilepsy updated : causes and treatment / editor Preston Robb. — Miami : Symposia Specialists, c1980 ; Chicago ; London : Year Book Medical [distributor]. — xix,314p : ill,1map ; 24cm
Conference papers. — Includes index
ISBN 0-88372-127-9 : £22.50 B81-07069

616.8'53 — Man. Epilepsy. Psychiatric aspects

Epilepsy and psychiatry. — Edinburgh : Churchill Livingstone, Dec.1981. — [416]p
ISBN 0-443-02311-5 : £22.00 : CIP entry B81-31834

616.8'53'0072 — Man. Epilepsy. Research. Grants from British Epilepsy Association — *Lists*

British Epilepsy Association. Epilepsy research fund 1968-1980 / British Epilepsy Association. — [Wokingham] ([Crowthorne House, Bigshotte, New Wokingham Rd., Wokingham, Berks. RG11 3AY]) : British Epilepsy Association, 1981. — 32p : ill,1port ; 21cm
Cover title. — Port, ill on inside cover
Unpriced (pbk) B81-23362

616.8'53061 — Man. Epilepsy. Drug therapy

The **Treatment** of epilepsy / edited by J.H. Tyrer. — Lancaster : MTP Press, 1980. — xii,386p : ill ; 25cm. — (Current status of modern therapy ; v.5)
Includes index
ISBN 0-85200-253-x : £17.95 : CIP rev. B79-31795

616.8'53061 — Man. Epilepsy. Drug therapy. Phenytoin. Side effects

Hassell, Thomas Michael. Epilepsy and the oral manifestations of phenytoin therapy / Thomas Michael Hassell. — Basel ; London : Karger, c1981. — xiv,205p : ill,1port ; 25cm. — (Monographs in oral science ; v.9)
Includes bibliographies and index
ISBN 3-8055-1008-x : £37.25 B81-26224

616.8'53061 — Man. Epilepsy. Drug therapy. Sodium valproate — *Conference proceedings*

The **Place** of sodium valproate in the treatment of epilepsy / [proceedings of an international symposium sponsored by Reckitt-Labaz held at the Metropole Hotel, Birmingham, on the 8th-9th, November 1979] ; edited by M.J. Parsonage and A.D.S. Caldwell. — London : Royal Society of Medicine, 1980. — xii,208p : ill ; 24cm. — (Royal Society of Medicine series. International congress and symposium series, ISSN 0142-2367 ; no.30)
Includes bibliographies
ISBN 0-12-793248-8 (pbk) : £12.00 : CIP rev.
ISBN 0-8089-1293-3 (U.S.) B80-18339

616.85'5 — Man. Articulation disorders

Bernthal, John E.. Articulation disorders / John E. Bernthal, Nicholas W. Bankson. — Englewood Cliffs ; London : Prentice-Hall, c1981. — vi,329p : ill ; 24cm
Includes bibliographies and index
ISBN 0-13-049072-5 : £13.25 B81-36572

616.85'5 — Man. Articulation disorders. Therapy

Weiss, Curtis E.. Clinical management of articulation disorders / Curtis E. Weiss, Herold S. Lillywhite, Mary E. Gordon. — St. Louis ; London : Mosby, 1980. — xi,303p : ill,forms ; 24cm
Includes bibliographies and index
ISBN 0-8016-5391-6 (pbk) : £8.50 B81-31112

616.85'5 — Man. Communication disorders

Communication disorders / edited by R.W.Rieber. — New York ; London : Plenum, c1981. — ix,356p : ill ; 24cm. — (Applied psycholinguistics and communication disorders)
Includes bibliographies and index
ISBN 0-306-40527-x : Unpriced B81-32648

616.85'506 — Man. Speech disorders. Therapy

Brown, Betty Byers. Speech therapy : principles & practice / Betty Byers Brown. — Edinburgh : Churchill Livingstone, 1981. — x,262p : ill ; 22cm
Bibliography: p248-256. — Includes index
ISBN 0-443-02099-x (pbk) : £5.95 B81-33742

616.85'5075 — Man. Language disorders & speech disorders. Diagnosis

Peterson, Harold A.. Appraisal and diagnosis of speech and language disorders / Harold A. Peterson, Thomas P. Marquardt. — Englewood Cliffs ; London : Prentice-Hall, c1981. — x,340p : ill ; 24cm
Includes bibliographies and index
ISBN 0-13-043505-8 : £12.30 B81-12721

616.85'5075 — Mentally ill persons. Speech disorders. Diagnosis

Speech evaluation in psychiatry / edited by John K. Darby ; principal scientific consultant Michael H. L. Hecker, scientific consultants Gavin Andrews ... [et al.]. — New York ; London : Grune & Stratton, c1981. — xii,416p : ill ; 24cm
Includes bibliographies and index
ISBN 0-8089-1315-8 : £19.40 B81-18185

616.85'5075'0926 — Man. Speech disorders. Diagnosis — *Case studies*

Emerick, Lon L.. A casebook of diagnosis and evaluation in speech pathology and audiology / Lon L. Emerick. — Englewood Cliffs ; London : Prentice-Hall, 1981. — viii,182p : ill,facsims,forms ; 23cm
Includes bibliographies and index
ISBN 0-13-117358-8 (pbk) : £7.75 B81-16678

616.85'52 — Man. Jargon aphasia

Jargonaphasia / edited by Jason W. Brown. — New York ; London : Academic Press, 1981. — xviii,329p : ill,1port ; 24cm. — (Perspectives in neurolinguistics, neuropsychology and psycholinguistics)
Includes bibliographies and index
ISBN 0-12-137580-3 : £19.60 B81-37708

616.85'5206 — Man. Aphasia. Therapy

Language intervention strategies in adult aphasia / edited by Roberta Chapey. — Baltimore ; London : Williams & Wilkins, 1981. — xviii,383p : ill,forms ; 26cm
Includes bibliographies and index
ISBN 0-683-01511-7 : £33.50 B81-17770

616.85'53 — Dyslexia — *Conference proceedings*

Dyslexia. — Oxford : Pergamon, Jan.1982. — [180]p. — (Wenner-Gren Center international symposium series ; v.35)
Conference papers
ISBN 0-08-026863-3 : £18.00 : CIP entry B81-34472

616.85'53'00924 — Dyslexia — *Personal observations*

Simpson, Eileen. Reversals : a personal account of victory over dyslexia / Eileen Simpson ; with a foreword and a commentary by Macdonald Critchley and an epilogue by Marion Welchman. — London : Gollancz, 1981, c1979. — xiii,248p ; 22cm
Originally published: Boston, Mass. : Houghton Mifflin, 1979 ; London : Gollancz, 1980. — Bibliography: p247-248
ISBN 0-575-03003-8 (pbk) : £2.95 B81-22267

616.85'54'001 — Great Britain. Man. Stuttering. Theories, *1800-1900*

Rockey, Denyse. Speech disorder in nineteenth century Britain : the history of stuttering / Denyse Rockey. — London : Croom Helm, c1980. — 280p : ill,facsims,1map ; 23cm
Bibliography: p258-267. — Includes index
ISBN 0-85664-809-4 : £19.95 : CIP rev. B79-20144

616.85'5406 — Man. Stuttering. Therapy — *Conference proceedings*

Maintenance of fluency : proceedings of the Banff conference, Banff, Alberta, Canada, June 1979. — New York ; Oxford : Elsevier, c1981. — xviii,284p : ill ; 24cm
Includes bibliographies and index
ISBN 0-444-00415-7 : £17.00 B81-06354

616.85'7 — Man. Migraine

Progress in migraine research. — Tunbridge Wells : Pitman
1. — Oct.1981. — [232]p. — (Progress in neurology, ISSN 0260-0013 ; 6)
ISBN 0-272-79627-1 : £20.00 : CIP entry B81-25752

616.8'57 — Man. Migraine

Sacks, Oliver. Migraine : the natural history of a common disorder / Oliver Sacks ; with a foreword by William Gooddy. — Completely rev. and expanded ed. — London : Pan, 1981. — 281p ; 18cm
Previous ed.: London : Faber, 1970. — Bibliography: p265-269. — Includes index
ISBN 0-330-26237-8 (pbk) : £1.95 B81-03383

616.8'57071 — Man. Migraine. Role of diet

Wentworth, Josie A.. The migraine guide & cookbook / Josie A. Wentworth ; introduction by Katharina Dalton. — London : Sidgwick & Jackson, 1981. — 237p : ill,forms ; 23cm
Bibliography: p228-231. - Includes index
ISBN 0-283-98741-3 : £6.95
Primary classification 641.5'631 B81-17649

616.85'72071 — Women. Psychoses: Depression. Social factors — *Study regions: London. Southwark (London Borough). Camberwell*

Brown, George W. (George William), *1930-*. Social origins of depression : a study of psychiatric disorder in women / George W. Brown and Tirril Harris. — London : Tavistock Publications, 1978 (1979 [printing]). — xi,399p : ill ; 24cm
Bibliography: p375-389. — Includes index
ISBN 0-422-77000-0 (pbk) : £5.50 B81-01646

616.85'8 — Man. Personality disorders

Millon, Theodore. Disorders of personality : DSM-111 : Axis II / Theodore Millon. — New York ; Chichester : Wiley, c1981. — xi,458p : ill ; 24cm
Bibliography: p430-441. — Includes index
ISBN 0-471-06403-3 : £17.00 B81-23982

616.85'88 — Man. Mental handicaps — *For youth groups*

Growing together : a CMS action pack on mental handicap for youth groups and house groups. — [London] : CMS, [1981]. — 1portfolio : ill ; 31cm
£1.00 B81-37071

616.85'88 — Man. Mental retardation

International review of research in mental retardation. — New York ; London : Academic Press
Includes bibliographies and index
Vol.10 / edited by Norman R. Ellis. — 1981. — xiv,184p : ill ; 24cm
ISBN 0-12-366210-9 : £14.60 B81-40776

616.85'88'005 — Man. Mental retardation — *Serials*

Applied research in mental retardation. : a multidisciplinary journal. — Vol.1, no.1/2 (1980)-. — New York ; Oxford : Pergamon, 1980-. — v. : ill ; 23cm
Quarterly
Unpriced B81-32237

616.85'880651 — Mentally handicapped persons. Behaviour therapy — *For nursing*

Bailey, Roy D.. Therapeutic nursing for the mentally handicapped. — Oxford : Oxford University Press, Nov.1981. — [150]p. — (Oxford medical publications)
ISBN 0-19-261314-6 (pbk) : £4.95 : CIP entry B81-30531

616.85′8806515 — Mentally handicapped persons. Drama therapy

Warren, Bernie. Drama games : for mentally handicapped people / Bernie Warren. — London : National Society for Mentally Handicapped Children and Adults, c1981. — 28p ; 21cm
Cover title. — Text on inside cover. — Bibliography: p27-28
ISBN 0-85537-062-9 (pbk) : £1.00 B81-22104

616.85′884 — Man. Brain dysfunction. Neuropsychological aspects

De Renzi, Ennio. Disorders of space exploration and cognition. — Chichester : Wiley, Jan.1982. — [272]p
ISBN 0-471-28024-0 : £12.50 : CIP entry B81-38338

616.86 — Addiction. Medical aspects *related to* **schizophrenia** — *Conference proceedings*

Biochemistry of schizophrenia and addiction : in search of a common factor / edited by Gwynneth Hemmings. — Lancaster : MTP Press, c1980. — xvi,344p : ill ; 24cm
Includes bibliographies and index
ISBN 0-85200-310-2 : £17.95 : CIP rev.
Primary classification 616.89′82 B80-04227

616.86 — Man. Brain. Brain damage. Role of alcoholism & drug addiction. Biochemical aspects — *Conference proceedings*

Addiction and brain damage / edited by Derek Richter. — London : Croom Helm, c1980. — 305p : ill ; 23cm
Conference papers. — Includes bibliographies and index
ISBN 0-7099-0254-9 : £15.95 : CIP rev. B80-11912

616.86′1 — Alcoholism. Medical aspects

Glatt, Max. Alcoholism. — London : Hodder & Stoughton, Jan.1982. — [256]p. — (Teach yourself books)
ISBN 0-340-26817-4 (pbk) : £2.25 : CIP entry B81-34127

Medical consequences of alcohol abuse / [edited by] P.M.S. Clark and L.J. Kricka. — Chichester : Horwood, 1980. — 282p : ill ; 24cm. — (Ellis Horwood series in chemical science)
Includes index
ISBN 0-85312-195-8 : £27.50 : CIP rev. B80-19246

616.86′1075′024613 — Alcoholism. Identification & assessment — *For nursing*

Estes, Nada J.. Nursing diagnosis of the alcoholic person / Nada J. Estes, Kathleen Smith-DiJulio, M. Edith Heinemann. — St. Louis ; London : Mosby, 1980. — ix,251p : ill,forms ; 23cm
Includes bibliographies and index
ISBN 0-8016-1558-5 (pbk) : £7.00 B81-14987

616.86′3 — Opiate addiction. Medical aspects

Wikler, Abraham. Opioid dependence : mechanisms and treatment / Abraham Wikler. — New York ; London : Plenum, c1980. — xiv,255p : ill ; 24cm
Includes bibliographies and index
ISBN 0-306-40591-1 : Unpriced B81-08585

616.8′7 — Man. Cranium. Diseases. Treatment. Use of osteopathy

Brookes, Denis. Lectures on cranial osteopathy. — Wellingborough : Thorsons, Oct.1981. — [128]p
ISBN 0-7225-0698-8 : £7.95 : CIP entry B81-24666

616.8′707 — Man. Peripheral nervous system. Diseases. Physiological aspects

The **Physiology** of peripheral nerve disease / [edited by] Austin J. Sumner. — Philadelphia ; London : Saunders, 1980. — viii,504p : ill ; 24cm
Includes bibliographies and index
ISBN 0-7216-8639-7 : £20.00 B81-07233

616.89 — Man. Behavioural disorders

Grant, Igor. Behavioral disorders : understanding clinical psychopathology / by Igor Grant. — New York ; London : SP, c1979. — ix,317p : ill ; 24cm
Includes bibliographies and index
ISBN 0-89335-061-3 : £7.95 B81-06548

616.89 — Man. Mental disorders

Curran, Desmond. Psychological medicine : an introduction to psychiatry. — 9th ed. / Desmond Curran, Maurice Partridge, Peter Storey. — Edinburgh : Churchill Livingstone, 1980. — 449p : ill ; 22cm
Previous ed.: 1976. — Bibliography: p438-440. — Includes index
ISBN 0-443-02192-9 (pbk) : £8.50 : CIP rev. B80-20737

New perspectives in abnormal psychology / edited by Alan E. Kazdin, Alan S. Bellack, Michel Hersen. — New York ; Oxford : Oxford University Press, 1980. — x,586p : ill,1facsim,ports ; 25cm
Bibliography: p511-563. - Includes index
ISBN 0-19-502652-7 : £12.00 B81-00928

Readings in psychiatry : compiled from Medicine, the monthly add-on journal. — [Oxford] ([52 New Inn Hall St., Oxford OX1 2BS]) : Medical Education, c1980. — iii,114p : ill ; 30cm
ISBN 0-906817-09-9 (pbk) : £5.00 B81-17050

616.89 — Man. Mental disorders — *Early works* — *Facsimiles*

Maudsley, Henry. The pathology of mind : a study of its distempers, deformities and disorders / Henry Maudsley ; introduced by Sir Aubrey Lewis. — London : Friedman, 1979. — 571p ; 22cm
Facsim of: 2nd ed. London : Macmillan, 1895. — Includes index
ISBN 0-904014-42-8 : Unpriced B81-29210

616.89 — Man. Mental disorders. Ethnopsychological aspects

Devereux, George. Basic problems of ethnopsychiatry / George Devereux ; translated by Basia Miller Gulati and by George Devereux. — Chicago ; London : University of Chicago Press, 1980. — xiii,366p ; 24cm
Translation of: Essais d′ethnopsychiatrie générale. — Bibliography: p336-356. - Includes index
ISBN 0-226-14355-4 : £13.50 B81-04560

616.89 — Man. Mental disorders. Role of brain damage

Freemon, Frank R.. Organic mental disease / Frank R. Freemon. — Lancaster : MTP, c1981. — 211p : ill ; 24cm
Bibliography: p185-208. — Includes index
ISBN 0-85200-560-1 : £17.75 B81-38034

616.89 — Man. Mental illness — *For general practice*

Psychiatric illness in general practice. — 2nd ed. — Oxford : Oxford University Press, Nov.1981. — [260]p. — (Oxford medical publications)
Previous ed.: 1966
ISBN 0-19-261243-3 : £15.00 : CIP entry B81-28853

616.89 — Man. Somatopsychic diseases

Psychiatric presentations of medical illness : somatopsychic disorders / edited by Richard C.W. Hall. — Lancaster : MTP, c1980. — 421p ; 24cm
Includes bibliographies and index
ISBN 0-85200-533-4 : £18.95 B81-07072

616.89 — Medicine. Psychiatry

Critical psychiatry : the politics of mental health / edited by David Ingleby. — Harmondsworth : Penguin, 1981. — 228p ; 20cm. — (Penguin education)
ISBN 0-14-080308-4 (pbk) : £2.95 B81-17034

Divergent views in psychiatry / edited by Maurice Dongier, Eric D. Wittkower ; 17 contributors. — Hagerstown ; London : Harper & Row, 1981. — xiii,336p ; 25cm
Includes bibliographies and index
ISBN 0-06-140695-3 : £13.00 B81-26056

Hughes, Jennifer. An outline of modern psychiatry. — Chichester : Wiley, Dec.1981. — [160]p
ISBN 0-471-10073-0 (cased) : £11.50 : CIP entry
ISBN 0-471-10024-2 (pbk) : £6.75 B81-3388[illegible]

Ingram, I. M.. Notes on psychiatry / I.M. Ingram, G.C. Timbury, R.M. Mowbray. — 5th ed. — Edinburgh : Churchill Livingstone, 1981. — viii,137p ; 22cm. — (Churchill Livingstone medical text)
Previous ed.: 1976. — Bibliography: p127. — Includes index
ISBN 0-443-02339-5 (pbk) : £3.95 B81-3286[illegible]

Models for clinical psychopathology / edited by Carl Eisdorfer ... [et al.]. — Lancaster : MTP, c1981. — xii,276p : ill ; 24cm
Includes bibliographies and index
ISBN 0-85200-559-8 : £14.95 B81-3307[illegible]

Sim, Myre. Guide to psychiatry / Myre Sim ; with a chapter on legal aspects of psychiatry in the United States of America by John Donnelly. — 4th ed. — Edinburgh : Churchill Livingstone, 1981. — 765p : ill ; 25cm
Previous ed.: 1974. — Bibliography: p707-747. — Includes index
ISBN 0-443-02334-4 (pbk) : £15.00 : CIP rev. B81-2812[illegible]

616.89 — Mentally handicapped persons. Psychiatry

Reid, Andrew H.. The psychiatry of mental handicap. — Oxford : Blackwell Scientific, Jan.1982. — [160]p
ISBN 0-632-00929-2 (pbk) : £4.50 : CIP entry B81-3921[illegible]

616.8′9001′8 — Medicine. Psychiatry. Methodology — *Conference proceedings*

Learning theory approaches to psychiatry. — Chichester : Wiley, Feb.1982. — [250]p
ISBN 0-471-28042-9 : £17.60 : CIP entry B81-3623[illegible]

616.89′0024613 — Man. Mental disorders — *For nursing*

Koshy, Tharayil Koshy. Revision notes on psychiatry. — 2nd ed. — London : Hodder and Stoughton, Dec.1981. — [192]p. — (Modern nursing series)
Previous ed.: 1977
ISBN 0-340-27049-7 (pbk) : £3.25 : CIP entry B81-3144[illegible]

616.89′005 — Medicine. Psychiatry — *Serials*

Psychiatric medicine update. — 1981 ed. — Edinburgh : Churchill Livingstone, 1981. — 235p
ISBN 0-443-02433-2 : Unpriced B81-1310[illegible]

The **Year** book of psychiatry and applied mental health. — 1980. — Chicago ; London : Year Book Medical Publishers, 1980. — 378p
ISBN 0-8151-3326-x : Unpriced B81-0906[illegible]

The **Year** book of psychiatry and applied mental health. — 1981. — Chicago ; London : Year Book Medical Publishers, 1981. — 374p
ISBN 0-8151-3328-6 : Unpriced B81-2499[illegible]

616.89′0072 — Medicine. Psychiatry. Research

Psychiatric research in practice : biobehavioral themes / edited by E.A. Serafetinides. — New York ; London : Grune & Stratton, c1981. — xii,244p : ill ; 24cm. — (Seminars in psychiatry)
Includes index
ISBN 0-8089-1316-6 : £13.80 B81-2086[illegible]

616.89′0072 — Medicine. Psychiatry. Research. Methodology

What is a case? : the problem of definition in psychiatric community surveys / edited by J.K. Wing, Paul Bebbington and Lee N. Robins. — London : Grant McIntyre, 1981. — xv,250p : ill ; 24cm
Bibliography: p223-236. — Includes index
ISBN 0-86286-003-2 : £21.00 B81-2634[illegible]

616.89'0072 — Medicine. Psychiatry. Research. Methodology. Study examples: Community surveys

What is a case?. — London : Grant McIntyre, May 1981. — [352]p
ISBN 0-86216-050-2 : £20.00 : CIP entry B81-07916

616.89'00722 — Man. Mental disorders. Longitudinal studies

Prospective longitudinal research : an empirical basis for the primary prevention of psychosocial disorders / edited by Sarnoff A. Mednick and André E. Baert ; assistant editor Barbara Phillips Bachmann. — Oxford : Published on behalf of the World Health Organization Regional Office for Europe [by] Oxford University Press, 1981. — xiii,382p : ill ; 29cm. — (Oxford medical publications)
Bibliography: p343-367. — Includes index
ISBN 0-19-261184-4 : £50.00 : CIP rev. B80-02800

616.89'0076 — Medicine. Psychiatry — *Questions & answers*

Glew, Geoffrey. Multiple choice questions in psychiatry. — 2nd ed. — London : Butterworths, Oct.1981. — [144]p
Previous ed.: 1978
ISBN 0-407-00225-1 (pbk) : £4.25 : CIP entry B81-30491

Psychiatry : PreTest self-assessment and review / edited by J. Craig Nelson. — New York ; London : McGraw-Hill, c1977. — x,196p ; 22cm. — (PreTest series)
Originally published: Wallingford, Conn. : PreTest Service, 1977. — Bibliography: p193-196
ISBN 0-07-051604-9 (pbk) : £6.95 B81-19484

616.89'0092'4 — England. Midlands. Medicine. Psychiatry — *Personal observations*

Delaney, Joyce. It's my nerves, doctor / Joyce Delaney. — London : Sphere, 1980. — 214p ; 18cm
ISBN 0-7221-2995-5 (pbk) : £1.10 B81-12941

616.89'0094 — North-western Europe. Medicine. Psychiatry, *1600-1900*

Doerner, Klaus. Madmen and the bourgeoisie : a social history of insanity and psychiatry / Klaus Doerner ; translated by Joachim Neugroschel and Jean Steinberg. — Oxford : Blackwell, 1981. — vi,361p ; 24cm
Translation of: Bürger und Irre. — Includes index
ISBN 0-631-10181-0 : £15.00 : CIP rev.
Primary classification 362.2'042'094 B81-20187

616.89'022'05 — Adolescents. Psychiatry — *Serials*

Adolescent psychiatry : developmental and clinical studies. — Vol.8. — Chicago ; London : University of Chicago Press, 1980. — x,567p
ISBN 0-226-24053-3 : £15.00 B81-30852

616.89'024613 — Man. Mental disorders — *For nursing*

Dally, Peter. Psychology and psychiatry. — 5th ed. — London : Hodder & Stoughton, Nov.1981. — [304]p. — (Modern nursing series)
Previous ed.: London : English Universities Press, 1975
ISBN 0-340-27126-4 (pbk) : £3.95 : CIP entry B81-28804

616.89'025 — Man. Mental disorders. Emergency treatment

Soreff, Stephen M.. Management of the psychiatric emergency / Stephen M. Soreff. — New York ; Chichester : Wiley, c1981. — xiii,290p ; 23cm
Includes index
ISBN 0-471-06012-7 (pbk) : £8.50 B81-13077

616.89'025 — Man. Mental disorders. Emergency treatment — *Manuals*

Mitchell, Jeffrey T.. Emergency response to crisis : a crisis intervention guidebook for emergency service personnel / Jeffrey T. Mitchell and H.L.P. Resnik. — Bowie : Brady ; London : Prentice-Hall, c1981. — xxv,218p : ill ; 23cm
Bibliography: p69-71. — Includes index
ISBN 0-87619-828-0 (pbk) : £13.95 B81-36653

Slaby, Andrew Edmund. Handbook of psychiatric emergencies / Andrew E. Slaby, Julian Lieb, Laurence R. Tancredi. — 2nd ed. — Garden City, N.Y. : Medical Examination Publishing Co. ; London : Kimpton, 1981. — 338p : forms ; 22cm
Previous ed.: 1975. — Bibliography: p307-334. — Includes index. — Publisher's no.: MEPC645
ISBN 0-87488-655-4 (cased) : Unpriced
ISBN 0-87488-645-7 (pbk) : £8.00 B81-16092

616.89'025 — Medicine. Psychiatry. Emergency treatment — *For house physicians*

Dubin, William R.. Emergency psychiatry for the house officer / William R. Dubin and Robert Stolberg. — Lancaster : MTP Press, c1981. — 166p : ill ; 21cm
Includes bibliographies and index
ISBN 0-85200-580-6 (pbk) : £8.95 B81-38099

616.89'05 — Preventive psychiatry

Symposium on Psychiatric Prevention *(1979 : Athens)*. Aspects of preventive psychiatry / Symposium on Psychiatric Prevention, organized by the Center for Mental Health, Athens, December 14-16, 1979 ; volume editor G.N. Christodoulou. — Basel ; London : Karger, 1981. — vi,116p,[1]p of plates : ill (some col.) ; 24cm. — (Bibliotheca psychiatrica ; n.160)
Includes bibliographies
ISBN 3-8055-1218-x (pbk) : £17.00 B81-11539

616.89'05'0941 — Great Britain. Man. Mental disorders. Prevention — *For general practice*

Prevention of psychiatric disorders in general practice : report of a Sub-committee of the Royal College of General Practitioners' Working Party on Prevention. — London : The Collge, 1981. — iv,17p ; 28cm. — (Report from general practice ; 20)
Bibliography: p17
ISBN 0-85084-079-1 (pbk) : £3.00 B81-13338

616.89'07 — Man. Mental disorders. Biochemical aspects — *Conference proceedings*

The **Biochemistry** of psychiatric disturbances / edited by G. Curzon. — Chichester : Wiley, c1980. — xii,144p : ill ; 24cm
Conference papers. — Includes bibliographies and index
ISBN 0-471-27814-9 : £13.00 B81-02613

Biological markers in psychiatry & neurology. — Oxford : Pergamon, Feb.1982. — [544]p
Conference papers
ISBN 0-08-027987-2 : £37.50 : CIP entry B81-38332

616.89'07 — Man. Mental disorders. Neurophysiological aspects — *Conference proceedings*

International Symposium on Clinical Neurophysiological Aspects of Psychopathological Conditions *(1st : 1979 : Umeå)*. Clinical neurophysiological aspects of psychopathological conditions / First International Symposium on Clinical Neurophysiological Aspects of Psychopathological Conditions, Umea, May 30-June 1, 1979 ; volume editors C. Perris and L. von Knorring, D. Kemali. — Basel ; London : Karger, c1980. — vi,192p : ill ; 23cm. — (Advances in biological psychiatry ; v.4)
Includes bibliographies and index
ISBN 3-8055-0604-x (pbk) : £18.50 B81-06839

616.89'07 — Man. Mental disorders. Role of enzymes & neurotransmitters — *Conference proceedings*

Enzymes and neurotransmitters in mental disease : based on a symposium held at the Technion Faculty of Medicine, Haifa, Israel, August 28-30, 1979 / edited by Earl Usdin, Theodore L. Sourkes, Moussa B.H. Youdim. — Chichester : Wiley, c1980. — xvi,650p : ill ; 24cm
Includes bibliographies and index
ISBN 0-471-27791-6 : £33.50 : CIP rev. B80-17734

616.89'07'05 — Medicine. Psychopathology — *Serials*

Psychobiology and psychopathology. — Vol.1-. — Pacific Grove, Calif. : Boxwood Press ; Amsterdam ; Oxford : [Distributed by] Elsevier/North-Holland Biomedical Press, 1981-. — v. : ill ; 24cm
Unpriced
Primary classification 156'.2'05 B81-39508

616.89'071 — Man. Mental disorders. Role of neuroendocrine system — *Conference proceedings*

Psychoneuroendocrinology and abnormal behavior / volume editors J. Mendlewicz and H.M. van Praag. — Basel ; London : Karger, 1980. — 128p : ill ; 23cm. — (Advances in biological psychiatry ; v.5)
Conference papers. — Includes bibliographies and index
ISBN 3-8055-0599-x (pbk) : £15.25 B81-04464

616.89'075 — Man. Mental disorders. Diagnosis

Leff, J. P.. Psychiatric examination in clinical practice. — 2nd ed. — Oxford : Blackwell Scientific, Oct.1981. — [160]p
Previous ed.: 1978
ISBN 0-632-00818-0 : £5.50 : CIP entry B81-27381

616.89'1 — Man. Mental disorders. Therapy — *Conference proceedings*

Current trends in treatment in psychiatry / edited by T.G. Tennent. — Tunbridge Wells : Pitman Medical, 1980. — 258p : ill ; 24cm
Conference papers. — Includes bibliographies
ISBN 0-272-79596-8 : £9.95 B81-02780

616.89'1'024613 — Man. Mental disorders. Therapy — *For nursing*

Mental health nursing : a bio-psycho-cultural approach / Elaine Anne Pasquali ... [et al.]. — St. Louis ; London : Mosby, 1981. — xviii,723p ; 25cm
Includes bibliographies and index
ISBN 0-8016-3758-9 : £15.50 B81-28920

616.89'1'05 — Man. Mental disorders. Therapy — *Serials*

Current psychiatric therapies. — Vol.19 (1980). — New York ; London : Grune & Stratton, c1980. — x,218p
ISBN 0-8089-1300-x : Unpriced B81-24149

616.89'122 — Man. Mental disorders. Electroconvulsive therapy

Electroconvulsive therapy : an appraisal / edited by Robert L. Palmer. — Oxford : Oxford University Press, 1981. — x,316p : ill ; 23cm
Includes bibliographies and index
ISBN 0-19-261266-2 : £20.00 B81-18305

616.89'13 — Man. Mental disorders. Therapy. Physical methods

Dally, Peter. An introduction to physical methods & treatment in psychiatry. — 6th ed. — Edinburgh : Churchill Livingstone, Apr.1981. — [212]p
Previous ed.: / by William Sargant, Eliot Slater ; assisted by Desmond Kelly. 1972
ISBN 0-443-02019-1 (pbk) : £6.00 : CIP entry B81-03147

616.89'14 — Medicine. Existential psychotherapy

Bergantino, Len. Psychotherapy, insight and style : the existential moment / Len Bergantino. — Boston ; London : Allyn and Bacon, c1981. — xii,288p : ill ; 25cm
Includes bibliographies and index
ISBN 0-205-07281-x : £18.95 B81-32641

616.89'14 — Medicine. Psychotherapy

Dubovsky, Steven L.. Psychotherapeutics in primary care / Steven L. Dubovsky. — New York ; London : Grune & Stratton, 1981. — xi,213p ; 24cm
Includes bibliographies and index
ISBN 0-8089-1337-9 : £11.00 B81-23554

Handbook of innovative psychotherapies / edited by Raymond Corsini. — New York ; Chichester : Wiley, c1981. — xxviii,969p : ill ; 26cm : pbk. — (Wiley series on personality processes, ISSN 0195-4008)
Includes bibliographies and index
ISBN 0-471-06229-4 : £28.00 B81-33428

616.89'14 — Medicine. Psychotherapy *continuation*

Lomas, Peter. The case for personal psychotherapy / Peter Lomas. — Oxford : Oxford University Press, 1981. — 152p ; 22cm
Includes index
ISBN 0-19-217680-3 : £9.50 : CIP rev. B81-14383

U'Ren, Richard C.. The practice of psychotherapy : a guide for the beginning therapist / Richard C. U'Ren. — New York ; London : Grune & Stratton, c1980. — x,171p ; 24cm
Includes index
ISBN 0-8089-1242-9 : £11.00 B81-00929

616.89'14 — Medicine. Psychotherapy. Counselling

George, Rickey L.. Theory, methods, & processes of counseling & psychotherapy / Rickey L. George, Therese Stridde Cristiani. — Englewood Cliffs ; London : Prentice-Hall, c1981. — xvi,336p : ill,ports ; 25cm. — (Prentice-Hall series in counseling and human development)
Includes bibliographies and index
ISBN 0-13-913905-2 : £13.25 B81-26909

616.89'14 — Medicine. Psychotherapy. Crisis intervention

Burgess, Anne Wolbert. Crisis intervention theory and practice : a clinical handbook / Anne Wolbert Burgess, Bruce A. Baldwin. — Englewood Cliffs ; London : Prentice-Hall, c1981. — xvii,333p ; 24cm
Includes bibliographies and index
ISBN 0-13-193466-x (cased) : Unpriced
ISBN 0-13-193458-9 (pbk) : £9.05 B81-28421

616.89'14 — Medicine. Psychotherapy. Effectiveness. Evaluation

Smith, Mary Lee. The benefits of psychotherapy / Mary Lee Smith, Gene V. Glass, Thomas I. Miller. — Baltimore ; London : Johns Hopkins University Press, c1980. — xvi,269p : ill ; 24cm
Bibliography: p221-261. - Includes index
ISBN 0-8018-2352-8 : £13.50 B81-11320

616.89'14 — Medicine. Psychotherapy. Effects

Rachman, Stanley J.. The effects of psychological therapy / by S.J. Rachman and G.T. Wilson. — 2nd enl. ed. — Oxford : Pergamon, 1980. — v,302p : ill ; 26cm. — (International series in experimental psychology ; vol.24)
Previous ed.: published as The effects of psychotherapy. 1971. — Bibliography: p265-287. — Includes index
ISBN 0-08-024675-3 (cased) : £22.00 : CIP rev.
ISBN 0-08-024674-5 (pbk) : £8.00 B80-09714

616.89'14 — Medicine. Psychotherapy. Long-term effectiveness

Improving the long-term effects of psychotherapy : models of durable outcome / edited by Paul Karoly and John J. Steffen. — New York : Gardner Press ; New York ; London : Halsted [distributor], c1980. — xiii,492p ; 24cm
Includes index
ISBN 0-470-26854-9 : Unpriced B81-08590

616.89'14 — Medicine. Psychotherapy — *Manuals*

Bockar, Joyce A.. Primer for the psychotherapist / Joyce A. Bockar. — 2nd ed. — Lancaster : MTP, 1981. — 149p : ill ; 24cm
Previous ed.: published as Primer for the nonmedical psychotherapist. New York : Spectrum Publications, 1976. — Bibliography: p140. — Includes index
ISBN 0-85200-573-3 : £8.95 B81-38033

616.89'14 — Medicine. Psychotherapy. Rational-emotive therapy

Wessler, Ruth A.. The principles of rational-emotive therapy / Ruth A. Wessler, Richard L. Wessler ; foreword by Albert Ellis. — San Francisco ; London : Jossey-Bass, 1980. — xx,274p ; 24cm. — (The Jossey-Bass social and behavioral science series)
Bibliography: p261-268. — Includes index
ISBN 0-87589-473-9 : Unpriced B81-16434

616.89'14 — Medicine. Psychotherapy. Reality therapy

Glasser, William. Stations of the mind : new directions for reality therapy / William Glasser. — New York ; London : Harper & Row, c1981. — xx,288p : ill,1port ; 22cm
Ill on lining paper. — Includes index
ISBN 0-06-011478-9 : £6.95 B81-30809

616.89'14 — Medicine. Psychotherapy. Systems — *Comparative studies*

Clare, Anthony W.. Let's talk about me : a critical examination of the new psychotherapies / Anthony W. Clare with Sally Thompson. — London : British Broadcasting Corporation, 1981. — 253p ; 22cm
Includes index
ISBN 0-563-17887-6 (pbk) : £4.50 B81-26822

616.89'14 — Medicine. Psychotherapy. Use of imagination — *Conference proceedings* — *Serials*

Imagery. — Vol.2. — New York ; London : Plenum, c1981. — xi,397p
ISBN 0-306-40748-5 : Unpriced B81-35969

616.89'14'05 — Medicine. Psychotherapy — *Serials*

Comprehensive psychotherapy. — Vol.2. — New York ; London : Gordon and Breach, c1981. — [viii],121p
Unpriced (corrected) B81-35813

616.89'14'08808162 — Deaf persons. Psychotherapy

Deafness and mental health / edited by Laszlo K. Stein, Eugene D. Mindel, Theresa Jabaley. — New York ; London : Grune & Stratton ; London : Distributed by Academic Press, c1981. — xiii,256p ; 27cm
Includes bibliographies and index
ISBN 0-8089-1347-6 : £19.60 B81-39789

616.89'14'0924 — Medicine. Psychotherapy — *Personal observations*

Kopp, Sheldon. The hanged man / Sheldon Kopp. — London : Sheldon, 1981, c1974. — 254p : ill ; 21cm
Originally published: Palo Alto : Science and Behavior Books, 1974. — Bibliography: p253-254
ISBN 0-85969-334-1 (pbk) : £3.95 B81-25907

616.89'14'0973 — United States. Psychotherapy

Psychotherapy : practice, research, policy / edited by Gary R. VandenBos. — Beverly Hills ; London : Sage, c1980. — 288p : ill ; 23cm. — (Sage studies in community mental health ; 1)
ISBN 0-8039-1536-5 (cased) : Unpriced
ISBN 0-8039-1537-3 (pbk) : £6.25 B81-14615

616.89'142 — Medicine. Behaviour therapy

Clinical procedures for behavior therapy / C. Eugene Walker ... [et al.]. — Englewood Cliffs ; London : Prentice-Hall, c1981. — xv,400p : ill,forms ; 24cm
Includes bibliographies and index
ISBN 0-13-137794-9 : £12.95 B81-19650

Handbook of clinical behavior therapy / edited by Samuel M. Turner, Karen S. Calhoun, Henry E. Adams. — New York ; Chichester : Wiley, c1981. — xv,765p : ill ; 26cm. — (Wiley series on personality processes)
Includes bibliographies and index
ISBN 0-471-04178-5 : £16.85 B81-13081

616.89'142 — Medicine. Cognitive behaviour therapy

Assessment strategies for cognitive-behavioral interventions / edited by Philip C. Kendall, Steven D. Hollon. — New York ; London : Academic Press, c1981. — xiv,425p ; 24cm. — (Personality and psychopathology ; 24)
Includes bibliographies and index
ISBN 0-12-404460-3 : £16.60 B81-17264

616.89'142 — Medicine. Cognitive behaviour therapy. Techniques

McMullin, Rian E.. Cognitive-behavior therapy : a restructuring approach / Rian E. McMullin, Thomas R. Giles. — New York ; London : Grune & Stratton, c1981. — xi,132p : ill,forms ; 24cm. — (Current issues in behavioral psychology)
Bibliography: p103-108. — Includes index
ISBN 0-8089-1362-x (pbk) : £8.40 B81-35428

616.89'152 — Medicine. Group therapy — *Festschriften*

Mullan, Hugh. Group psychotheray : theory and practice / Hugh Mullan and Max Rosenbaum. — 2nd ed. — New York : Free Press ; London : Collier Macmillan, c1978. — xiv,418p : ill ; 24cm
Previous ed.: New York : Free Press of Glencoe, 1962. — Bibliography: p400-409. — Includes index
ISBN 0-02-922080-7 : £11.95 B81-00930

616.89'1523 — Medicine. Drama therapy

Allen, Robert D.. Psychotheatrics : the new art of self-transformation / Robert D. Allen and Nina Krebs. — New York ; London : Garland STPM, c1979. — xiii,216p : ill ; 24cm
Bibliography: p211-212. — Includes index
ISBN 0-8240-7007-0 : £24.75 B81-25949

616.89'156 — Married couples. Psychotherapy

The **Handbook** of marriage and marital therapy / edited by G. Pirooz Sholevar. — Lancaster : MTP, 1981. — 552p ; 24cm
Includes bibliographies and index
ISBN 0-85200-567-9 : £23.75 B81-39386

616.89'156 — Medicine. Family therapy

Barker, Philip, *1929-*. Basic family therapy / Philip Barker. — London : Granada, 1981. — x,214p : ill ; 25cm
Bibliography: p197-208. — Includes index
ISBN 0-246-11249-2 (cased) : £12.00 : CIP rev.
ISBN 0-246-11482-7 (pbk) : Unpriced B81-06070

Developments in family therapy. — London : Routledge, Aug.1981. — [366]p
ISBN 0-7100-0812-0 (pbk) : £6.95 : CIP entry B81-17540

Sedgwick, Rae. Family mental health : theory and practice / Rae Sedgwick. — St. Louis ; London : Mosby, 1981. — x,296p : ill,forms ; 24cm
Includes bibliographies and index
ISBN 0-8016-4447-x (pbk) : £7.00 B81-09765

616.89'156 — Medicine. Family therapy. Techniques

Minuchin, Salvador. Family therapy techniques / Salvador Minuchin, H. Charles Fishman. — Cambridge, Mass. ; London : Harvard University Press, 1981. — 303p ; 25cm
Includes index
ISBN 0-674-29410-6 : £9.00 B81-38241

616.89'156 — Medicine. Family therapy. Techniques — *Comparative studies*

Jones, Susan L.. Family therapy : a comparison of approaches / Susan L. Jones. — Bowie : Brady ; London : Prentice-Hall, c1980. — xii,220p ; 25cm
Bibliography: p184-220
ISBN 0-87619-625-3 : £9.70 B81-03979

616.89'156'0926 — Medicine. Family therapy. Techniques — *Case studies*

Madanes, Cloé. Strategic family therapy / Cloé Madanes. — San Francisco ; London : Jossey-Bass, 1981. — xxx,240p ; 24cm. — (The Jossey-Bass social and behavioural science series)
Bibliography: p229-233. — Includes index
ISBN 0-87589-487-9 : £11.95 B81-26094

616.89'156'0973 — United States. Medicine. Family therapy

Family therapy and major psychopathology / edited by Melvin R. Lansky. — New York ; London : Grune & Stratton, c1981. — xvi,431p : ill ; 24cm. — (Seminars in psychiatry)
Includes index
ISBN 0-8089-1360-3 : £15.40 B81-35425

616.89'16 — Man. Mental disorders. Social therapy

Clark, David H.. Social therapy in psychiatry / David H. Clark ; foreword by G.M. Carstairs. — 2nd ed. — Edinburgh : Churchill Livingstone, 1981. — vii,126p ; 22cm
Previous ed.: 1974. — Bibliography: p121-122. — Includes index
ISBN 0-443-02107-4 (pbk) : £2.95 B81-15326

616.89'16 — Man. Mental disorders. Social therapy *continuation*

Taylor, Christine M.. Returning to mental health. — Cheltenham : Thornes, Aug.1981. — [160]p
ISBN 0-85950-307-0 : £4.50 : CIP entry B81-19207

616.89'162 — Man. Mental disorders. Hypnotherapy

Erickson, Milton H.. Hypnotic investigation of psychodynamic processes / by Milton H. Erickson. — New York : Irvington ; New York ; London : Halsted [distributor], c1980. — xi,367p : ill,2ports ; 24cm. — (The Collected papers of Milton H. Erickson on hypnosis)
Bibliography: p556-559. — Includes index
ISBN 0-470-26723-2 : £16.00 B81-03546

Erickson, Milton H.. Innovative hypnotherapy / by Milton H. Ericson. — New York : Irvington ; New York ; London : Halsted [distributor], c1980. — xxii,561p : 2ports ; 24cm. — (The Collected papers of Milton H. Erickson on hypnosis ; v.4)
Bibliography: p543-548. — Includes index
ISBN 0-470-26724-0 : £18.75 B81-03547

616.89'1656 — Man. Mental disorders. Therapy. Role of arts

Feder, Elaine. The expressive arts therapies / Elaine & Bernard Feder. — Englewood Cliffs ; London : Prentice Hall, c1981. — vi,249p : ill ; 24cm. — (A Spectrum book)
Includes index
ISBN 0-13-298059-2 (cased) : Unpriced
ISBN 0-13-298042-8 (pbk) : £4.50 B81-16526

616.89'17 — Medicine. Psychoanalysis. Brief therapy

Alexander, Franz. Psychoanalytic therapy : principles and application / by Franz Alexander and Thomas Morton French with Catherine Lillie Bacon ... [et al.]. — Lincoln [Neb.] ; London : University of Nebraska Press, 1980, c1974. — xiii,353p : ill ; 21cm. — (Bison books in clinical psychology)
Originally published: New York : Ronald Press, 1946
ISBN 0-8032-1007-8 (cased) : £11.00
ISBN 0-8032-5903-4 (pbk) : £3.00 B81-04580

616.89'17 — Medicine. Psychoanalysis. Group therapy

Agazarian, Yvonne. The visible and invisible group : two perspectives on group psychotherapy and group process / co-therapists Yvonne Agazarian, Richard Peters. — London : Routledge & Kegan Paul, 1981. — x,292p : ill ; 22cm. — (The International library of group psychotherapy and group process)
ISBN 0-7100-0692-6 : £13.50 B81-17258

616.89'17 — Medicine. Psychoanalysis. Role of interpretation of language of patients with mental disorders

Forrester, John. Language and the origins of psychoanalysis / John Forrester. — London : Macmillan, 1980. — xvi,285p ; 23cm
Bibliography: p256-281. - Includes index
ISBN 0-333-25946-7 : £15.00 : CIP rev. B80-03671

616.89'18 — Man. Mental disorders. Drug therapy. Clobazam — *Conference proceedings*

Clobazam / edited by I. Hindmarch and P.D. Stonier. — London : Royal Society of Medicine, 1981. — xiii,198p : ill ; 25cm. — (International congress and symposium series, ISSN 0142-2367 ; no.43)
Proceedings of an International Symposium on Clobazam held at Wentworth College, University of York on 13-15 April, 1981. — Includes bibliographies
ISBN 0-12-791985-6 (pbk) : Unpriced : CIP rev.
ISBN 0-8089-1426-x (U.S) B81-24610

616.89'18 — Man. Mental disorders. Drug therapy. Lithium compounds — *Conference proceedings*

Aktuelle Perspektiven der Lithiumprophylaxe *(Conference : 1979 : Vienna)*. Current perspectives in lithium prophylaxis : international symposium on 'Aktuelle Perspektiven der Lithiumprophylaxe', Vienna, October 19-20, 1979 / volume editors P. Berner, G. Lenz and R. Wolf. — Basel ; London : Karger, 1981. — vi,248p : ill ; 24cm. — (Bibliotheca psychiatrica ; no.161)
Papers in German or English. — Includes bibliographies
ISBN 3-8055-1753-x (pbk) : £23.50 B81-38747

616.89'18 — Man. Mental disorders. Drug therapy. Role of neuroreceptors

Neuroreceptors : basic and clinical aspects : based on symposia held at the American College of Neuropsychopharmacology Annual Meeting, December 1979 / edited by Earl Usdin, William E. Bunney, Jr., and John M. Davis. — Chichester : Wiley, c1981. — 279p ; 24cm
Includes bibliographies and index
ISBN 0-471-27876-9 : £21.50 : CIP rev. B81-07908

616.89'5 — Man. Affective disorders - *Manuals*

Handbook of affective disorders. — Edinburgh : Churchill Livingstone, Aug.1981. — [480]p
ISBN 0-443-02036-1 (pbk) : £40.00 : CIP entry B81-16410

616.89'5 — Man. Psychoses: Depression

Freden, Lars. Psychosocial aspects of depression. — Chichester : Wiley, Jan.1982. — [240]p
ISBN 0-471-10023-4 : £12.50 : CIP entry B81-34509

616.89'5 — Man. Psychoses: Manic depression

Mania : an evolving concept / edited by Robert H. Belmaker and H.M. van Praag. — Lancaster : MTP Press, c1980. — 403p : ill ; 24cm
Includes bibliographies and index
ISBN 0-85200-538-5 : £18.95 B81-13593

616.89'509 — Women. Psychoses: Depression — *Case studies*

Scarf, Maggie. Unfinished business : pressure points in the lives of women / Maggie Scarf. — Shorter ed.. — [London] : Fontana, 1981, c1980. — xvi,491p ; 18cm
Previous ed.: Covent Garden, N.Y. : Doubleday, 1980. — Bibliography: p467-475. — Includes index
ISBN 0-00-636268-0 (pbk) : £1.95 B81-27087

616.89'82 — Man. Schizophrenia

Coping with schizophrenia / the National Schizophrenia Fellowship ; edited by Henry R. Rollin ; preface by Lady Wakehurst. — London : Burnett Books in association with Deutsch, 1980. — 231p ; 23cm
Includes index
ISBN 0-233-97245-5 : £8.95 : CIP rev. B80-08786

Strauss, John S.. Schizophrenia / John S. Strauss and William T. Carpenter. — New York ; London : Plenum Medical, c1981. — xi,220p : ill ; 24cm. — (Critical issues in psychiatry)
Includes index
ISBN 0-306-40704-3 : Unpriced B81-37469

616.89'82 — Man. Schizophrenia — *For families of schizophrenics*

Arieti, Silvano. Understanding and helping the schizophrenic : a guide for family and friends / Silvano Arieti. — British ed. / revised and adapted by Justin Schlicht. — Harmondsworth : Penguin, 1981, c1979. — 222p ; 20cm. — (A Pelican book)
Originally published: New York : Basic Books, 1979. — Includes index
ISBN 0-14-022328-2 (pbk) : £2.75 B81-25211

616.89'82 — Man. Schizophrenia. Neurobiological aspects

Oades, Robert D.. Attention and schizophrenia. — London : Pitman, Jan.1982. — [350]p
ISBN 0-273-08490-9 : £20.00 : CIP entry B81-34155

616.89'82 — Man. Schizophrenia *related to* **addiction** — *Conference proceedings*

Biochemistry of schizophrenia and addiction : in search of a common factor / edited by Gwynneth Hemmings. — Lancaster : MTP Press, c1980. — xvi,344p : ill ; 24cm
Includes bibliographies and index
ISBN 0-85200-310-2 : £17.95 : CIP rev.
Also classified at 616.86 B80-04227

616.89'82'001 — Man. Schizophrenia. Theories, *to 1980*

Shapiro, Sue A.. Contemporary theories of schizophrenia : review and synthesis / Sue A. Shapiro. — New York ; London : McGraw-Hill, c1981. — xii,289p : ill ; 24cm
Bibliography: p257-276. - Includes index
ISBN 0-07-056423-x : £15.25 B81-19467

616.89'8209 — Man. Schizophrenia — *Case studies*

Rokeach, Milton. The three Christs of Ypsilanti : a psychological study / by Milton Rokeach. — New York ; Guildford : Columbia University Press, 1981. — xii,338p,ivp ; 21cm
Originally published: New York : Knopf, 1964. — Includes index
ISBN 0-231-05271-5 (pbk) : £4.95 B81-25617

616.9 — MAN. GENERAL DISEASES

616.9 — Man. Communicable diseases

Notes on infectious diseases. — Edinburgh : Churchill Livingstone, Dec.1981. — [288]p. — (Churchill Livingstone medical text)
ISBN 0-443-02424-3 : £4.50 : CIP entry B81-31623

Welsby, P. D.. Infectious diseases / by Philip D. Welsby. — Lancaster : MTP, 1981. — ix,297p : ill ; 24cm
Includes bibliographies and index
ISBN 0-85200-385-4 : £14.95 B81-38028

616.9 — Man. Diseases. Microbiological aspects

Edmond, R. T. D.. Infection. — London : Grant McIntyre, Jan.1982. — [288]p. — (Pocket consultants)
ISBN 0-86286-008-3 (pbk) : £5.95 : CIP entry B81-34652

616.9 — Man. Granuloma — *Conference proceedings*

Workshop on Basic and Clinical Aspects of Granulomatous Diseases *(1980 : Bethesda, Md.)*. Basic and clinical aspects of granulomatous diseases : proceedings of the Workshop on Basic and Clinical Aspects of Granulomatous Diseases held June 18-20, 1980 Bethesda, Maryland / editors Dov L. Boros and Tekeshi Yoshida. — New York ; Oxford : Elsevier/North-Holland, c1980. — xv,348p : ill ; 24cm
Includes bibliographies and index
ISBN 0-444-00587-0 : £27.86 B81-27119

616.9 — Man. Sarcoidosis — *Conference proceedings*

International Conference on Sarcoidosis and Other Granulomatous Diseases *(8th : 1978 : Cardiff)*. Eighth International Conference on Sarcoidosis and Other Granulomatous Diseases / editors W. Jones Williams, Brian H. Davies. — Cardiff (College Buildings, University Place, Cardiff [CF1 1SA]) : Alpha Omega, c1980. — xxxii,774p : ill,1port ; 23cm
Includes bibliographies
ISBN 0-900663-10-3 : £35.00 B81-13298

616.9024613 — Man. Communicable diseases. Immunological aspects & microbiological aspects - *For nursing*

Blackwell, C. Caroline. Principles of infection and immunity in patient care. — Edinburgh : Churchill Livingstone, June 1981. — [160]p. — (Churchill Livingstone nursing texts)
ISBN 0-443-01906-1 (pbk) : £3.95 : CIP entry B81-14466

616.9'05 — Man. Communicable diseases — *Serials*

Current clinical topics in infectious diseases. — 1-. — New York ; London : McGraw-Hill, 1980-. — v. : ill ; 25cm
Annual. — Description based on: 2
£24.25 B81-32267

616.9'07 — Medical schools. Curriculum subjects: Paediatrics. Examinations. Use of multiple-choice questions

Uttley, W. S.. MCQs in paediatrics. — Edinburgh : Churchill Livingstone, Sept.1981. — [208]p
ISBN 0-443-02185-6 (pbk) : £4.00 : CIP entry B81-21567

616.9'09172'2 — Developed countries. Population. Exotic communicable diseases

Westwood, John C. N.. The hazard from dangerous exotic diseases / by John C.N. Westwood. — London : Macmillan, 1980. — x,223p : ill,maps ; 23cm
Bibliography: p213-223
ISBN 0-333-28360-0 : £17.50 B81-07232

616.9'2'079 — Man. Virus diseases. Immunological aspects — *Conference proceedings*

Biological products for viral diseases. — London : Taylor and Francis, Nov.1981. — [260]p. — (Munich symposia on microbiology ; 6)
Conference papers
ISBN 0-85066-226-5 (pbk) : £12.00 : CIP entry B81-32006

616.9'25 — Man. Rift Valley fever — *Conference proceedings*

Rift Valley fever : proceedings of a workshop on Rift Valley fever, Herzlia, Israel, March 18-21, 1980 / volume editors T.A. Swartz, M.A. Klingberg, N. Goldblum ; associate editor C.M. Papier. — Basel ; London : Karger, c1981. — xii,196p : ill,maps ; 23cm. — (Contributions to epidemiology and biostatistics ; v.3)
Includes bibliographies and index
ISBN 3-8055-1770-x (pbk) : £22.00
Also classified at 636.089'6925 B81-36175

616.9'2507572 — Man. Virus diseases. Diagnosis. Use of immunofluorescence

Gardner, P. S.. Rapid virus diagnosis : application of immunofluorescence / P.S. Gardner and J. McQuillin. — 2nd ed. / assisted by M. Grandien. — London : Butterworths, 1980. — xiii,312p : ill ; 24cm
Previous ed.: 1974. — Includes bibliographies and index
ISBN 0-407-38441-3 : £25.00 : CIP rev. B80-11469

616.9'362 — Man. Malaria

Malaria. — New York ; London : Academic Press
Includes bibliographies and index
Vol.1: Epidemiology, chemotherapy, morphology and metabolism. — 1980. — xvii,416p : ill,maps ; 24cm
ISBN 0-12-426101-9 : £31.40 B81-15009

Malaria. — New York ; London : Academic Press
Vol.2: Immunology and immunization / edited by Julius P. Kreier. — 1980. — xvii,346p : ill ; 24cm
Includes bibliographies and index
ISBN 0-12-426103-5 : £22.20 B81-22205

Malaria / edited by Julius P. Kreier. — New York ; London : Academic Press
Vol.2: Pathology, vector studies and culture. — 1980. — xvii,328p : ill ; 24cm
Includes bibliographies and index
ISBN 0-12-426102-7 : £24.80 B81-15008

616.95'1 — Man. Venereal diseases

Hjorth, Neils. Venereology in practice : the sexually committed diseases / by Neils Hjorth and Henning Schmidt ; English language edition edited by Howard I. Maibach. — Chicago ; London : Year Book Medical, c1979. — 108p : col.ill ; 20cm
Translation of: Praktisk venerologi. — Includes index
ISBN 0-8151-5728-2 (pbk) : £11.25 B81-12999

King, Ambrose. Venereal diseases. — 4th ed. / Ambrose King, Claude Nicol, Philip Rodin. — London : Baillière Tindall, 1980. — x,419p,v leaves of plates : ill(some col.) ; 24cm
Previous ed.: / by Ambrose King and Claude Nicol, 1975. — Includes index
ISBN 0-7020-0816-8 : £14.00 : CIP rev. B80-10096

Willcox, R. R.. Venereological medicine. — London : Grant McIntyre, July 1981. — [300] p. — (Pocket consultants)
ISBN 0-86286-001-6 (pbk) : £7.95 : CIP entry B81-14459

616.95'1'005 — Man. Sexually transmitted diseases — *Serials*

Recent advances in sexually transmitted diseases. — No.2. — Edinburgh : Churchill Livingstone, 1981. — xii,281
ISBN 0-443-01817-0 : Unpriced : CIP rev. B80-25718

616.95'109 — Man. Venereal diseases — *Case studies*

Sava, George. Crusader's clinic : sex, sin and prejudice / George Sava. — Bognor Regis : New Horizon, c1977. — 206p ; 23cm
ISBN 0-86116-094-0 : £1.25 B81-21713

616.95'13'0072076149 — Alabama. Tuskegee region. Negroes. Untreated syphilis. Research projects: Tuskegee Syphilis Experiment, *to 1972*

Jones, James H.. Bad blood : the Tuskegee Syphilis Experiment / James H. Jones. — New York : Free Press ; London : Collier Macmillan, 1981. — xii,272p,[16]p of plates : ill,ports ; 24cm
Bibliography: p256-262. — Includes index
ISBN 0-02-916670-5 : £8.95 B81-38653

616.9'6 — Man. Parasitic diseases

Beck, J. Walter. Medical parasitology. — 3rd ed. / J. Walter Beck, John E. Davies. — St. Louis ; London : Mosby, 1981. — vii,355p,[8]p of plates : ill(some col.) ; 24cm
Previous ed.: 1976. — Includes index
ISBN 0-8016-0552-0 (pbk) : £16.50 B81-24285

Knight, Richard. Parasitic disease in man. — Edinburgh : Churchill Livingstone, Dec.1981. — [264]p
ISBN 0-443-01952-5 (pbk) : £8.00 : CIP entry B81-31840

616.9'6061 — Man. Parasitic diseases. Drug therapy

Antiparasitic chemotherapy / volume editor H. Schönfeld. — Basel ; London : Karger, 1981. — 287p,[1]leaf of plates : ill(some col.) ; 25cm. — (Antibiotics and chemotherapy ; v.30)
Includes bibliographies
ISBN 3-8055-2160-x : £60.75 B81-38745

616.9'6075 — Man. Parasitic diseases. Diagnosis. Laboratory techniques

Desowitz, Robert S.. Ova and parasites : medical parasitology for the laboratory technologist / Robert S. Desowitz. — Hagerstown ; London : Harper & Row, c1980. — x,307p,[3]p of plates : ill(some col.) ; 24cm
Includes bibliographies and index
ISBN 0-06-140688-0 (pbk) : £14.75 B81-05468

616.9'6079'0913 — Tropical regions. Man. Parasitic diseases. Immunological aspects

Houba, Václav. Immunological investigation of tropical parasitic diseases / Vaclav Houba. — Edinburgh : Churchill Livingstone, 1980. — viii,170p : ill ; 25cm. — (Practical methods in clinical immunology series ; v.2)
Includes bibliographies and index
ISBN 0-443-01900-2 : £16.00 : CIP rev. B80-12382

616.9'63 — Man. Parasites: Schistosomes. Immunological aspects

McLaren, Diane J.. Schistosoma mansoni : the parasite surface in relation to host immunity / Diane J. McLaren. — Chichester : Research Studies Press, c1980. — xv,229p : ill ; 24cm. — (Tropical medicine research studies series ; 1)
Bibliography: p195-229
ISBN 0-471-27869-6 : £18.00 : CIP rev. B80-35074

616.9'654 — Man. Trichinellosis — *Conference proceedings*

International Conference on Trichinellosis *(5th : 1980 : Noordwijk aan Zee)*. Trichinellosis : proceedings of the Fifth International Conference on Trichinellosis, September 1-5 1980, Noordwijk aan Zee, The Netherlands / edited by Charles W. Kim, E. Joost Ruitenberg and Jacob S. Teppema ; in association with W.C. Campbell ... [et al.]. — Chertsey : Reedbooks, 1981. — xviii,434p : ill ; 24cm
Includes index
ISBN 0-906544-04-1 : Unpriced : CIP rev. B81-13865

616.9'69061 — Man. Systemic mycoses. Intravenous drug therapy. Miconazole

The **Role** of intravenous miconazole in the treatment of systemic mycoses / edited by G. Towse. — London (1 Wimpole St., W1M 8AL) : Royal Society of Medicine, 1981. — 52p : ill,ports ; 25cm. — (International congress and symposium series / Royal Society of Medicine, ISSN 0142-2367 ; no.45)
Conference papers. — Includes bibliographies
ISBN 0-12-794641-1 (pbk) : Unpriced B81-23730

616.97 — Man. Allergies

Evaluation and management of allergic and asthmatic diseases / edited by M. Eric Gershwin and Stephen M. Nagy, Jr. — New York ; London : Grune & Stratton, c1979. — xii,284p : ill ; 24cm
Includes bibliographies and index
ISBN 0-8089-1206-2 : £12.60 B81-39560

Randolph, Theron G.. Allergies : your hidden enemy. — Wellingborough : Turnstone Press, Oct.1981. — [288]p
Originally published: New York : Lippincott and Crowell, 1980
ISBN 0-85500-151-8 (cased) : £7.95 : CIP entry B81-28124

616.97 — Man. Allergies — *For patients*

Frazier, Claude Albee. Coping & living with allergies : a complete guide to help allergy patients of all ages / Claude A. Frazier. — Englewood Cliffs ; London : Prentice-Hall, c1980. — xii,240p : ill ; 21cm. — (A Spectrum book)
Bibliography: p228-229. — Includes index
ISBN 0-13-172304-9 (cased) : Unpriced
ISBN 0-13-172296-4 (pbk) : £3.85 B81-16650

616.97'005 — Man. Allergies — *Serials*

Progress in allergy. — Vol.28. — Basel ; London : Karger ; [Chichester] : [Distributed by Wiley], 1981. — [1v.]
ISBN 3-8055-1834-x : £36.25
ISSN 0079-6034 B81-30853

616.97'079 — Man. Allergies. Immunological aspects

Immunological and clinical aspects of allergy / edited by M.H. Lessof. — Lancaster : MTP, 1981. — ix,443p : ill,facsim ; 25cm
Includes index
ISBN 0-85200-244-0 : £24.95 : CIP rev. B80-11914

616.97'079 — Man. Allergies. Immunological aspects — *Conference proceedings*

American Society of Ophthalmologic and Otolaryngologic Allergy. *Meeting (37th : 1980?)*. Allergy : immunology and medical treatment / [from the 37th Annual Meeting of the American Society of Ophthalmologic and Otolaryngologic Allergy] ; edited by Fordyce Johnson, James T. Spencer Jr. — Miami : Symposia Specialists ; London : Distributed by Year Book Medical, c1980. — ix,302p : ill ; 24cm. — (A Home study textbook program)
Includes index
ISBN 0-8151-4904-2 : £24.75 B81-18971

616.97′079 — Man. Allergies. Immunological aspects — *Conference proceedings*
continuation

European Academy of Allergology and Clinical Immunology. *Congress (11th : 1980 : Vienna)*. Clinical immunology and allergology : proceedings of the symposia at the XIth Congress of the European Academy of Allergology and Clinical Immunology held in Vienna, Austria, 6-13 October, 1980 / editors C. Steffen and H. Ludwig. — Amsterdam ; Oxford : Elsevier/North-Holland Biomedical, 1981. — xii,421p ; 25cm. — (Developments in immunology ; v.14)
Includes index
ISBN 0-444-80312-2 : £24.34 B81-13055

Symposium on Chronobiology in Allergy and Immunology *(1979 : Jerusalem)*. Recent advances in the chronobiology of allergy and immunology : proceedings of the Symposium on Chronobiology in Allergy and Immunology, Xth International Congress of Allergology, Jerusalem, Israel, November 11th 1979 / editors M.H. Smolensky, A Reinberg, J.P. McGovern. — Oxford : Pergamon, 1980. — ix,358p : ill ; 26cm. — (Advances in the biosciences ; v.28)
ISBN 0-08-025891-3 : £27.00 : CIP rev.
B80-23257

616.97′3 — Man. Skin. Contact dermatitis

Cronin, Etain. Contact dermatitis / Etain Cronin. — Edinburgh : Churchill Livingstone, 1980. — 915p : ill ; 24cm
Includes bibliographies and index
ISBN 0-443-02014-0 : £28.00 : CIP rev.
B79-35369

616.97′5 — Man. Allergens: Food

Greer, Rita. Food allergy : a practical, easy guide / Rita Greer, Robert Woodward. — London (225 Putney Bridge Rd., SW15 2PY) : Roberts Publications, 1981. — 80p : ill ; 19cm
Bibliography: p74-77
ISBN 0-906185-16-5 (pbk) : £2.50 B81-36408

616.97′5 — Man. Allergens: Food — *Conference proceedings*

Food Allergy Workshop *(1st : 1980 : Haslemere)*. The proceedings of the First Food Allergy Workshop, held at Lythe Hill Hotel, Haslemere, Surrey, 20-23 January 1980 / [sponsored by Fisons Limited Pharmaceutical Division, Loughborough]. — Oxford (52 New Inn Hall St., Oxford OX1 2BS) : Medical Education Services Ltd., 1980. — xii,108p : ill ; 24cm
Includes bibliographies
ISBN 0-906817-07-2 (pbk) : £3.50 B81-04508

616.9′78061 — Man. Autoimmune diseases. Drug therapy. D-penicillamine — *Conference proceedings*

Modulation of autoimmunity and disease : the penicillamine experience / edited by R.N. Maini and H. Berry. — Eastbourne : Praeger, 1981. — xiv,310p : ill ; 25cm. — (Clinical pharmacology and therapeutics series ; v.1)
Conference papers. — Includes bibliographies and index
ISBN 0-03-059627-0 : £12.00 : CIP rev.
B81-13452

616.9′803 — Industrial medicine

Developments in occupational medicine / edited by Carl Zenz. — Chicago ; London : Year Book Medical Publishers, c1980. — xi,477p : ill ; 26cm
Includes bibliographies and index
ISBN 0-8151-9862-0 : £37.50 B81-07890

616.9′803′02341 — Great Britain. Industrial medical services. Doctors. Duties

The **Occupational** physician / developed by the Occupational Health Committee of the British Medical Association from the original pamphlet The doctor in industry. — London : BMA, c1980. — 23p : 1form ; 30cm
ISBN 0-7279-0066-8 (pbk) : Unpriced
Primary classification 331.2′0416169803′0941
B81-19330

616.9′88 — Man. Hypothermia - *Conference proceedings*

International 'Action for Disaster' Conference *(3rd : 1979 : Aberdeen)*. Hypothermia - ashore and afloat. — Aberdeen : Aberdeen University Press, May 1981. — [216]p
Conference papers
ISBN 0-08-025750-x : £18.00 : CIP entry
B81-14824

616.9′88′3 — Developing countries. Tropical regions. Medicine

Nwokolo, Chukwuedu. An introduction to clinical medicine in a tropical environment. — Edinburgh : Churchill Livingstone, Feb.1982. — [224]p. — (Medicine in the tropics series)
ISBN 0-443-02127-9 (pbk) : £5.00 : CIP entry
B81-35719

616.9′88′3 — Tropical medicine

Bell, Dion R.. Lecture notes on tropical medicine / Dion R. Bell. — Oxford : Blackwell Scientific, 1981. — vii,324p : maps ; 22cm. — (Lecture notes)
Bibliography: p315. - Includes index
ISBN 0-632-00546-7 (pbk) : £8.50 : CIP rev.
B81-08800

616.9′88′3 — Tropical medicine. Immunology

Greenwood, B. M.. Immunology of medicine in the tropics. — London : Edward Arnold, Apr.1981. — [400]p. — (Current topics in immunology, ISSN 0141-3368 ; 14)
ISBN 0-7131-4368-1 : £15.00 : CIP entry
B81-03169

616.9′88′3 — Tropical regions. Man. Diseases

Manson, *Sir* **Patrick**. Manson′s tropical diseases. — 18th ed. — London : Baillière Tindall, Aug.1981. — [768]p
Previous ed.: 1972
ISBN 0-7020-0830-3 : £25.00 : CIP entry
B81-20618

616.9′88′306041 — Tropical medicine. Organisations: Royal Society of Tropical Medicine and Hygiene — *Serials*

Royal Society of Tropical Medicine and Hygiene. Year book of the Royal Society of Tropical Medicine and Hygiene. — 1980. — London (Manson House, 26 Portland Place, W1N 4EY) : The Society, [1980]. — 109p
Unpriced B81-06821

616.9′893 — Man. High attitude disorders

Hackett, Peter H.. Mountain sickness : prevention, recognition & treatment / Peter H. Hackett. — New York : American Alpine Club ; Leicester : Cordee [distributor], 1980. — 75p : 1ill ; 17cm. — (American Alpine Club climber′s guide)
Bibliography: p73-75
ISBN 0-930410-10-6 (pbk) : £2.50 B81-04549

616.9′89307 — Man. High altitude disorders. Physiological aspects

Heath, Donald. Man at high altitude : the pathophysiology of acclimatization and adaptation / Donald Heath, David Reid Williams ; foreword by Sir Cyril Astley Clarke. — 2nd ed. / with a chapter on myocardial metabolism by Peter Harris. — Edinburgh : Churchill Livingstone, 1981. — 347p : ill,maps,3ports ; 26cm
Previous ed.: 1977. — Includes bibliographies and index
ISBN 0-443-02081-7 : £26.00 B81-23674

616.9′897 — Nuclear power industries. Accidents. Medical aspects — *Conference proceedings*

Medical Basis for Radiation Accident Preparedness *(Conference : 1979 : Oak Ridge)*. The medical basis for radiation accident preparedness : proceedings of the REAC/TS International conference: The Medical Basis for Radiation Accident Preparedness, October 18-20, 1979, Oak Ridge, Tennessee, U.S.A. / editors Karl F. Hübner and Shirley A. Fry. — New York ; Oxford : Elsevier/North-Holland, c1980. — xxxviii,545p : ill,1map,1port ; 24cm
Includes index
ISBN 0-444-00431-9 : £23.39 B81-07801

616.99′2′0028 — Man. Tumours. Cells in vitro *compared with* **normal cells in vitro**

Vasiliev, J. M.. Neoplastic and normal cells in culture / J.M. Vasiliev, I.M. Gelfand. — Cambridge : Cambridge University Press, 1981. — xiii,372p : ill ; 24cm. — (Developmental and cell biology series)
Bibliography: p272-346. — Includes index
ISBN 0-521-23149-3 : £36.00
Also classified at 611′.0181′028 B81-37136

616.99′20758 — Man. Tumours. Diagnosis. Electron microscopy

Henderson, Douglas W.. Ultrastructural appearances of tumours. — Edinburgh : Churchill Livingstone, Feb.1982. — [400]p
ISBN 0-443-02435-9 : £40.00 : CIP entry
B81-35923

616.99′2079 — Man. Tumours. Immunology — *Conference proceedings*

Neoplasm immunity : experimental and clinical : proceedings of a Chicago Symposium, Chicago, Illinois, U.S.A., September 13-15, 1978 / editor Ray G. Crispen ; sponsored by University of Illinois at the Medical Center and Illinois Cancer Council. — New York ; Oxford : Elsevier/North-Holland, c1980. — x,572p : ill ; 25cm. — (Developments in cancer research ; v.3)
Includes index
ISBN 0-444-00433-5 : £24.45 B81-06468

616.99′20795 — Man. Tumours. Cells. Natural cell-mediated immunity

Natural cell-mediated immunity against tumors / edited by Ronald B. Herberman. — New York ; London : Academic Press, 1980. — xxi,1321p : ill ; 24cm
Includes bibliographies and index
ISBN 0-12-341350-8 : £36.40 B81-03043

616.99′271059 — Man. Bones & cartilage. Tumours. Surgery

Marcove, Ralph C.. The surgery of tumors of bone and cartilage / Ralph C. Marcove. — New York ; London : Grune & Stratton, c1981. — xi,201p : ill ; 24cm
Bibliography: p186-193. — Includes index
ISBN 0-8089-1342-5 : £16.60 B81-38699

616.99′27107582 — Man. Bones. Tumours. Diagnosis. Applications of cytology

Sanerkin, N. G.. Cytology of bone tumours : a colour atlas with text / N.G. Sanerkin and G.M. Jeffree. — Bristol : John Wright, 1980. — xii,168p : ill(some col.) ; 24cm
Includes bibliographies and index
ISBN 0-7236-0505-x : £32.50 : CIP rev.
B80-10097

616.99′281 — Man. Brain. Tumours

Brain tumours : scientific basis, clinical investigation and current therapy / editors D.G.T. Thomas, D.I. Graham. — London : Butterworths, 1980. — xiv,382p : ill ; 24cm
Includes bibliographies and index
ISBN 0-407-00157-3 : £28.00 : CIP rev.
B80-10637

616.99′284′00222 — Man. Eyes. Tumours — *Illustrations*

Bedford, Michael A.. A colour atlas of ocular tumors / Michael A. Bedford. — London : Wolfe Medical, 1979. — 78p : col.ill ; 27cm. — (Wolfe medical atlases)
Includes index
ISBN 0-7234-0730-4 : £12.00 B81-15325

616.99′286 — Man. Nose & paranasal sinuses. Tumours

Friedmann, Imrich. Pathology of granulomas and neoplasms of the nose and paranasal sinuses. — Edinburgh : Churchill Livingstone, Dec.1981. — [312]p
ISBN 0-443-01410-8 : £25.00 : CIP entry
B81-31629

616.99′4 — Man. Cancer

Israël, Lucien. Conquering cancer / Lucien Israël ; translated from the French by Joan Pinkham. — Harmondsworth : Penguin, 1980. — 269p ; 19cm. — (Pelican books)
Translation of: Le cancer aujourd′hui. — Originally published: New York : Random House, 1978. — Includes index
ISBN 0-14-022276-6 (pbk) : £2.25 B81-07062

616.99′4 — Man. Cancer *continuation*
Oncology supplement : scientific foundations of oncology / edited by Sir Thomas Symington and R.L. Carter. — London : Heinemann Medical, 1980. — x,173p : ill,maps ; 28cm
Includes bibliographies and index
ISBN 0-433-05149-3 (pbk) : £16.00 B81-02453

Richards, B. A.. The topic of cancer. — Oxford : Pergamon, Jan.1982. — [150]p
ISBN 0-08-025937-5 : £6.50 : CIP entry B81-34469

616.99′4 — Man. Cancer — *Conference proceedings*

Conference on Cancer Research in the People's Republic of China and the United States of America *(1st : 1980 : Columbia University)*. Cancer research in the People's Republic of China and the United States of America : epidemiology, causation and new approaches to therapy : [proceedings of the Conference on Cancer Research in the People's Republic of China and the United States of America, March 18-29, 1980] / edited by Paul A. Marks. — New York ; London : Grune & Stratton, c1981. — xiii,273p : ill,maps ; 24cm
Added t.p. in Chinese. — Includes index
ISBN 0-8089-1363-8 : £13.80 B81-18022

Free radicals, lipid peroxidation and cancer. — London : Academic Press, Feb.1982. — [450]p
Conference papers
ISBN 0-12-649180-1 : CIP entry B81-40234

International Symposium on Cancer *(1980 : New York)*. Cancer : achievements, challenges, and prospects for the 1980s / [proceedings of the 1980 International Symposium on Cancer] ; [presented by Memorial Sloan-Kettering Cancer Center] ; [cosponsored by the National Cancer Institute and the American Cancer Society September 14-18, 1980] ; edited by Joseph H. Burchenal, Herbert F. Oettgen. — New York ; London : Grune & Stratton, c1981. — 2v. : ill ; 24cm
Includes bibliographies and index
ISBN 0-8089-1351-4 : Unpriced
ISBN 0-8089-1357-3 (v.2) : £19.40 B81-16624

616.99′4 — Man. Cancer. Diagnosis. Markers — *Conference proceedings*

Markers for diagnosis and monitoring of human cancer. — London : Academic Press, Dec.1981. — [250]p. — (Proceedings of the Serono symposia, ISSN 0308-5503 ; v.46)
Conference papers
ISBN 0-12-181520-x : CIP entry B81-34012

616.99′4 — Man. Cancer — *For children*

Haines, Gail Kay. Cancer / by Gail Kay Haines. — New York ; London : Watts, 1980. — 64p : ill ; 23cm. — (A First book)
Bibliography: p61. — Includes index
ISBN 0-531-04159-x : £2.99 B81-03209

616.99′4 — Man. Cancer. Metastasis — *Conference proceedings*

International Conference on Clinical and Experimental Aspects of Metastasis *(1980 : London)*. Metastasis : clinical and experimental aspects : proceedings of the EORTC Metastasis Group International Conference on Clinical and Experimental Aspects of Metastasis, London, April 21-23, 1980 / edited by K. Hellmann, P. Hilgard, S. Eccles. — The Hague ; London : Nijhoff, 1980. — xxxiv,456p : ill ; 25cm. — (Developments in oncology ; v.4)
Includes bibliographies and index
ISBN 90-247-2424-4 : Unpriced B81-03469

Tumor progression : proceedings of a Chicago symposium, Chicago, Illinois, U.S.A., October 3-5, 1979 / editor Ray G. Crispen ; sponsored by University of Illinois at the Medical Center and Illinois Cancer Council. — New York ; Oxford : Elsevier/North-Holland, c1980. — 388p : ill ; 25cm. — (Developments in cancer research, ISSN 0163-6146 ; v.2)
Includes index
ISBN 0-444-00432-7 : £19.96 B81-12635

616.99′4 — Man. Malignant tumours
Hancock, Barry W.. Lecture notes on clinical oncology / Barry W. Hancock, J. David Bradshaw. — Oxford : Blackwell Scientific, 1981. — vii,215p : ill ; 22cm
Bibliography: p208. - Includes index
ISBN 0-632-00674-9 (pbk) : £5.50 B81-11747

616.99′4 — Man. Melanoma
Ariel, Irving M.. Malignant melanoma / Irving M. Ariel. — New York : Appleton-Century-Crofts ; London : Prentice-Hall, c1981. — xvii,536p : ill ; 25cm
Includes bibliographies and index
ISBN 0-8385-6114-4 : £34.00 B81-36601

616.99′4′0024613 — Man. Cancer — *For nursing*
Marino, Lisa Begg. Cancer nursing / Lisa Begg Marino with 27 contributors. — St. Louis ; London : Mosby, 1981. — xx,635p : ill,maps,forms ; 25cm
Includes bibliographies and index
ISBN 0-8016-3107-6 : £17.50 B81-18972

616.99′4′005 — Man. Cancer — *Serials*
Advances in cancer research. — Vol.33 (1980). — London ; New York : Academic Press, c1980. — vii,325p
ISBN 0-12-006633-5 : Unpriced
ISSN 0065-230x B81-20712

The Year book of cancer. — 1980. — Chicago ; London : Year Book Medical Publishers, c1980. — 500p
ISBN 0-8151-1788-4 : £28.50
ISSN 0084-3679 B81-18800

616.99′4′005 — Man. Malignant tumours — *Serials*
Recent advances in clinical oncology. — No.1. — Edinburgh : Churchill Livingstone, Nov.1981. — [358]p
ISBN 0-443-02230-5 (pbk) : £19.50 : CIP entry
ISSN 0261-7013 B81-30896

616.99′40194 — Man. Cancer. Pathogens: Viruses — *Conference proceedings*
International Congress of Viral Oncology *(1st : 1979 : Naples)*. The role of viruses in human cancer : proceedings of the First International Congress of Viral Oncology of the T. and L. de Beaumont Bonelli Foundation for Cancer Research held in Naples, Italy, September 21-23, 1979 / editors G. Giraldo and E. Beth. — New York ; Oxford : Elsevier/North-Holland, c1980. — 292p : ill ; 24cm
Includes index
ISBN 0-444-00440-8 : £16.98 B81-11144

616.99′4025 — Man. Cancer. Complications & sequelae. Emergency treatment
Oncologic emergencies / edited by John W. Yarbro, Richard S. Bornstein. — New York ; London : Grune & Stratton, c1981. — xiii,430p : ill ; 24cm. — (Clinical oncology monographs)
Includes index
ISBN 0-8089-1317-4 : £16.60 B81-18186

616.99′405 — Laboratory animals: Mammals. Cancer. Prevention. Use of drugs
Inhibition of tumor induction and development / edited by Morris S. Zedeck and Martin Lipkin. — New York ; London : Plenum, c1981. — xiv,233p : ill ; 23cm
Includes bibliographies and index
ISBN 0-306-40687-x : Unpriced B81-40507

616.99′406 — Cancer patients. Blood plasma. Exchange
Immune complexes and plasma exchanges in cancer patients / edited by B. Serrou and C. Rosenfeld. — Amsterdam ; Oxford : Elsevier/North Holland Biomedical, 1981. — xvi,344p : ill ; 25cm. — (Human cancer immunology ; v.1)
Includes bibliographies and index
ISBN 0-444-80237-1 : £34.88
Also classified at 616.99′4079 B81-21390

616.99′406 — Man. Cancer. Therapy
Blyskowski, Anton H.. The discovery of cancer enigma / Anton H. Blyskowski. — London (35 Woodcock Hill, Kenton, Middx) : Scientific Press, c1981. — 190p : ill ; 22cm
Bibliography: p183-190
ISBN 0-9507552-0-6 (pbk) : £6.00 B81-29712

Cancer treatment research / edited by Joseph Aisner and Paul Chang. — The Hague ; London : Nijhoff, 1980. — xvi,271p : ill ; 25cm. — (Developments in oncology ; v.2)
ISBN 90-247-2358-2 : Unpriced B81-00931

616.99′4061 — Doxorubicin

Arcamone, Federico. Doxorubicin : anticancer antibiotics / Federico Arcamone. — New York ; London : Academic Press, 1981. — xiii,369p : ill ; 24cm. — (Medicinal chemistry ; v.17)
Includes index
ISBN 0-12-059280-0 : Unpriced B81-37952

616.99′4061 — Man. Cancer. Adjuvant therapy — *Conference proceedings*

International Conference on the Adjuvant Therapy of Cancer *(2nd : 1979 : Tucson)*. Adjuvant therapy of cancer II / [proceedings of the Second International Conference on the Adjuvant Therapy of Cancer, Tucson, Arizona March 28-31, 1979] ; edited by Stephen E. Jones, Sydney E. Salmon. — New York ; London : Grune & Stratton, c1979. — xx,674p : ill ; 24cm
Includes index
ISBN 0-8089-1213-5 : £19.60 B81-39557

616.99′4061 — Man. Cancer. Drug therapy

Calman, Kenneth C.. Basic principles of cancer chemotherapy / Kenneth C. Calman, John F. Smyth, Martin H.N. Tattersall. — London : Macmillan, 1980. — viii,160p : ill ; 25cm
Includes index
ISBN 0-333-21972-4 (cased) : £15.00 : CIP rev.
ISBN 0-333-30479-9 (pbk) : Unpriced B80-36121

Cancer and chemotherapy / edited by Stanley T. Crooke, Archie W. Prestayko, editorial assistant Nancy Alder. — New York ; London : Academic Press
Vol.2: Introduction to clinical oncology. — 1981. — xv,380p : ill(some col.) ; 24cm
Includes bibliographies and index
ISBN 0-12-197802-8 : £28.20 B81-40769

Cancer and chemotherapy / edited by Stanley T. Crooke, Archie W. Prestayko, editorial assistant Nancy Alder. — New York ; London : Academic Press
Vol.3: Antineoplastic agents. — 1981. — xv,398p : ill ; 24cm
Includes bibliographies and index
ISBN 0-12-197803-6 : £29.20 B81-38919

Carter, Stephen K.. Chemotherapy of cancer / Stephen K. Carter, Marie T. Bakowski, Kurt Hellman. — 2nd ed. — New York ; London : Wiley, c1981. — 379p : ill ; 22cm. — (A Wiley medical publication)
Previous ed.: 1977. — Includes index
ISBN 0-471-08045-4 (pbk) : £9.00 B81-16947

Safer cancer chemotherapy / edited by L.A. Price, Bridget T. Hill, M.W. Ghilchik. — London : Baillière Tindall, c1981. — xii,124p : ill ; 23cm
Conference papers. — Includes index
ISBN 0-7020-0880-x : £9.50 : CIP rev. B81-14421

616.99′4061 — Man. Cancer. Drug therapy. Bestatin

Small molecular immunomodifiers of microbial origin. — Oxford : Pergamon, Aug.1981. — [300]p
Originally published: Baltimore : University Park Press, 1980
ISBN 0-08-027993-7 : £21.00 : CIP entry B81-15929

616.99′4061 — Man. Cancer. Drug therapy — *Conference proceedings*

San Francisco Cancer Symposium *(15th : 1980)*. Pharmaceutical aspects of cancer care / editor Jerome M. Vaeth. — Basel ; London : Karger, 1981. — 183p : ill ; 25cm. — (Frontiers of radiation therapy and oncology ; v.15)
At head of title: 15th Annual San Francisco Cancer Symposium, San Francisco, Calif., March 15-16, 1980. — Includes bibliographies
ISBN 3-8055-1512-x : £32.50 B81-21148

616.99'4061 — Man. Cancer. Drug therapy. Drugs

Cancer chemotherapeutic agents : handbook of clinical data / Mike R. Sather ... [et al.]. — The Hague ; London : Nijhoff Medical, 1979, c1978. — v,199p : ill ; 21cm
Originally published: Boston : G.K. Hall, c1978. — Includes bibliographies
ISBN 90-247-2170-9 (spiral) : Unpriced B81-15713

See-Lasley, Kay. Manual of oncology therapeutics / Kay See-Lasley, Robert J. Ignoffo. — St. Louis ; London : Mosby, 1981. — xviii,457p : ill ; 24cm
Includes index
ISBN 0-8016-4448-8 : £15.25 B81-30120

616.99'4061 — Man. Cancer. Drug therapy. Drugs. Action — *Conference proceedings*

Molecular actions and targets for cancer chemotherapeutic agents / edited by Alan C. Sartorelli, John S. Lazo, Joseph R. Bertino. — New York ; London : Academic Press, 1981. — xxvi,598p : ill ; 24cm. — (Bristol-Myers cancer symposia ; v.2)
Conference papers. — Includes index
ISBN 0-12-619280-4 : £29.80 B81-38702

616.99'4061 — Man. Cancer. Drug therapy. Drugs. Structure & chemical properties

Anticancer agents based on natural product models / edited by John M. Cassady, John D. Douros. — New York ; London : Academic Press, 1980. — xiv,500p : ill ; 24cm. — (Medicinal chemistry ; v.16)
Includes bibliographies and index
ISBN 0-12-163150-8 : Unpriced B81-27286

616.99'4061 — Man. Cancer. Drug therapy. Nitrosoureas — *Conference proceedings*

International Symposium on Nitrosoureas in Cancer Treatment *(1981 : Montpellier)*. Nitrosoureas in cancer treatment : proceedings of the International Symposium on Nitrosoureas in Cancer Treatment held in Montpellier (France), 26-27 January 1981 / sponsored by the Institut National de la Santé et de la Recherche Médicale, the National Cancer Institute and the Centre National de la Recherche Scientifique, under the auspices of the French-American agreement ; editors B. Serrou, P.S. Schein, J.L. Imbach. — Amsterdam ; Oxford : Elsevier/North-Holland Biomedical, 1981. — xv,310p : ill ; 25cm. — (INSERM symposium ; no.19)
Includes index
ISBN 0-444-80343-2 : Unpriced B81-29739

Nitrosources : current status and new development / edited by Archie W. Prestayko ... [et al.] ; assisted by Nancy A. Alder. — New York ; London : Academic Press, 1981. — xix,416p : ill ; 24cm
ISBN 0-12-565060-4 : £19.80 B81-38703

616.99'4061 — Man. Cancer. Drug therapy. Vindesine — *Conference proceedings*

International Vinca Alkaloid Symposium-Vindesine *(1980 : Frankfurt)*. Proceedings of the International Vinca Alkaloid Symposium-Vindesine : Frankfurt a.M., November 1980 : joint event of Arbeitsgemeinschaft Internistische Onkologie der Deutschen Krebsgesellschaft e. V. (AIO) and Eli Lilly GmbH, Deutschland / volume editors W. Brade, G.A. Nagel, S. Seeber. — Basel ; London : Karger, 1981. — xii,458p : ill ; 23cm. — (Beiträge zur Onkologie = Contributions to oncology ; v.6)
Includes summaries in German. — Includes index
ISBN 3-8055-2501-x (pbk) : £25.50 B81-38742

616.99'4061 — Man. Cancer. Therapy. Use of progestogens — *Conference proceedings*

Progestogens in the management of hormone responsive carcinomas : proceedings of an international symposium held at the Royal College of Physicians, London, U.K. 15 July 1980 / edited by R.W. Taylor. — Oxford (52 New Inn Hall St., Oxford OX1 2BS) : Medicine Publishing Foundation, c1980. — 73p : ill ; 24cm. — (The Medicine Publishing Foundation symposium series, ISSN 0260-0242 ; no.2)
ISBN 0-906817-08-0 : Unpriced B81-26092

616.99'4061 — Man. Malignant tumours. Drug therapy. Pharmacokinetic aspects

Emanuel, N. M.. Kinetics of experimental tumour processes. — Oxford : Pergamon, Feb.1982. — [350]p
Translation of: Kinetika eksperimental'nykh opukhlevylch protsessov
ISBN 0-08-024909-4 : £35.00 : CIP entry
Also classified at 616.99'407 B81-35906

616.99'4061 — Streptozotocin

Streptozotocin : fundamentals and therapy / edited by M.K. Agarwal. — Amsterdam ; Oxford : Elsevier/North-Holland Biomedical, 1981. — viii,309p : ill ; 25cm
Includes index
ISBN 0-444-80302-5 : £37.35 B81-22448

616.99'4'06105 — Man. Cancer. Drug therapy — *Serials*

Cancer chemotherapy. — 1980. — Amsterdam ; Oxford (256 Banbury Rd, Oxford OX2 7DH) : Excerpta Medica, 1980. — xiv,486p
ISBN 90-219-3054-4 : Unpriced B81-02985

616.99'40642 — Man. Cancer. Radiotherapy

Fowler, J. F.. Nuclear particles in cancer treatment / J.F. Fowler. — Bristol : Hilger in collaboration with the Hospital Physicists' Association, c1981. — xi,178p : ill ; 22cm. — (Medical physics handbooks, ISSN 0143-0203 ; 8)
Bibliography: p168-173. — Includes index
ISBN 0-85274-521-4 : £11.95 B81-09559

616.99'40642 — Man. Cancer. Radiotherapy. Use of drugs

Radiation-drug interactions in the treatment of cancer / edited by Gerald H. Sokol, Roger P. Maickel. — Chichester : Wiley, c1980. — xvi,235p : ill ; 27cm. — (Wiley series in diagnostic and therapeutic radiology)
Includes index
ISBN 0-471-04697-3 : £16.00 B81-02744

616.99'407 — Man. Cancer. Cells

The **Transformed** cell / edited by Ivan L. Cameron, Thomas B. Pool. — New York ; London : Academic Press, 1981. — xiv,435p : ill ; 24cm. — (Cell biology)
Includes bibliography and index
ISBN 0-12-157160-2 : £45.40 B81-37706

616.99'407 — Man. Malignant tumours. Growth. Kinetics

Emanuel, N. M.. Kinetics of experimental tumour processes. — Oxford : Pergamon, Feb.1982. — [350]p
Translation of: Kinetika eksperimental'nykh opukhlevylch protsessov
ISBN 0-08-024909-4 : £35.00 : CIP entry
Primary classification 616.99'4061 B81-35906

616.99'4071 — Man. Cancer. Pathogenesis — *Conference proceedings*

Jerusalem Symposium on Quantum Chemistry and Biochemistry *(13th : 1980)*. Carcinogenesis : fundamental mechanisms and environmental effects : proceedings of the thirteenth Jerusalem Symposium on Quantum Chemistry and Biochemistry held in Jerusalem, Israel, April 28-May 2, 1980 / edited by Bernard Pullman, Paul O.P. Ts'o and Harry Gelboin. — Dordrecht ; London : Reidel, c1980. — viii,592p : ill ; 25cm. — (Jerusalem symposia on quantum chemistry and biochemistry ; v.13)
Includes bibliographies and index
ISBN 90-277-1171-2 : Unpriced B81-03420

616.99'4071 — Man. Cancer. Pathogens: Chemicals

Sax, N. Irving. Cancer causing chemicals / N. Irving Sax assisted by Elizabeth K. Weisburger ... [et al.]. — New York ; London : Van Nostrand Reinhold, c1981. — ix,466p,[2]p of plates : ill(some col.) ; 29cm
Text on lining papers
ISBN 0-442-21919-9 : £29.95 B81-28468

Veljkovi'c, Veljko. A theoretical approach to the preselection of carcinogens and chemical carcinogenesis / Veljko Veljkovi'c. — New York ; London : Gordon and Breach Science, c1980. — ix,114p : ill ; 24cm
Translation from the Serbo-Croat. — Includes index
ISBN 0-677-05490-4 : Unpriced B81-10660

616.99'4071 — Man. Cancer. Pathogens: Chemicals — *Serials*

IARC monographs on the evaluation of the carcinogenic risk of chemicals to humans. — Vol.24. — Lyon : IARC ; [London] : [H.M.S.O.] [[distributor]], 1980. — 337p
ISBN 92-8321-224-x : £12.00 B81-29448

616.99'4071 — Man. Industrial diseases: Cancer — *Conference proceedings*

Occupational cancer and carcinogenesis / editors H. Vainio, M. Sorsa, K. Hemminki. — Washington ; London : Hemisphere, c1981. — vi,422p : ill ; 27cm
Conference papers. — Pages also numbered 921-1334. — Includes bibliographies and index
ISBN 0-89116-193-7 : £13.95 B81-18626

616.99'4075 — Man. Cells. Carcinogenic effects of chemicals. Short term testing. Evaluation — *Conference proceedings*

Workshop on the Predictive Value of In Vitro Short-Term Screening Tests in the Evaluation of Carcinogenicity *(1980 : Dalen)*. The predictive value of short-term screening tests in carcinogenicity evaluation / Workshop on the Predictive Value of In Vitro Short-Term Screening Tests in the Evaluation of Carcinogenicity held in Dalen, The Netherlands on April 1980 ; organized under the auspices of the Scientific Council of the Netherlands Cancer Society (Koningin Wilhelmina Fonds) ; editors G.M. Williams ... [et al.]. — Amsterdam ; Oxford : Elsevier/North-Holland Biomedical, 1980. — vi,349p : ill ; 25cm. — (Applied methods in oncology ; v.3)
Includes index
ISBN 0-444-80281-9 : £21.74 B81-04531

616.99'407543 — Man. Cancer. Diagnosis. Ultrasonography

Ultrasound in cancer / edited by Barry B. Goldberg. — New York ; Edinburgh : Churchill Livingstone, 1981. — x,223p : ill ; 25cm. — (Clinics in diagnostic ultrasound ; v.6)
Includes index
ISBN 0-443-08144-1 : £12.95 B81-18755

616.99'407572 — Man. Cancer. Diagnosis. Computerised axial tomography — *Conference proceedings*

Computerised axial tomography in oncology / edited by Janet E. Husband and Pauline A. Hobday. — Edinburgh : Churchill Livingstone, 1981. — 200p : ill ; 24cm
Conference papers. — Includes bibliographies and index
ISBN 0-443-02196-1 : £20.00 : CIP rev. B81-06049

616.99'4079 — Cancer patients. Immune complexes

Immune complexes and plasma exchanges in cancer patients / edited by B. Serrou and C. Rosenfeld. — Amsterdam ; Oxford : Elsevier/North Holland Biomedical, 1981. — xvi,344p : ill ; 25cm. — (Human cancer immunology ; v.1)
Includes bibliographies and index
ISBN 0-444-80237-1 : £34.88
Primary classification 616.99'406 B81-21390

616.99'4079 — Man. Malignant tumours. Immunological aspects

Woodruff, Michael F. A.. The interaction of cancer and host : its therapeutic significance / Michael F.A. Woodruff. — New York ; London : Grune & Stratton, c1980. — xviii,467p ; 27cm
Bibliography: p289-419. - Includes index
ISBN 0-8089-1265-8 : £26.20 B81-15018

616.99'40792 — Man. Cancer. Antigens. Serology — *Conference proceedings*

Serologic analysis of human cancer antigens / edited by Steven A. Rosenberg. — New York ; London : Academic Press, 1980. — xv,712p : ill ; 24cm
Conference papers. — Includes bibliographies and index
ISBN 0-12-597160-5 : £25.20 B81-08377

616.99'419 — Man. Blood. Granulocytic leukaemia

Chronic granulocytic leukaemia. — Eastbourne : Praeger, Nov.1981. — [264]p
ISBN 0-03-060053-7 : £14.50 : CIP entry B81-30901

616.99′419′0012 — Man. Blood. Leukaemia. Lymphoid cells. Classification. Use of cell surface markers — *Conference proceedings*

Leukemia Marker Conference *(1981 : Vienna).* Leukemia markers : proceedings of the Leukemia Marker Conference held in Vienna, February 15-18, 1981 / edited by W. Knapp. — London : Academic Press, 1981. — xv,574p : ill ; 24cm
Includes index
ISBN 0-12-416750-0 : £20.00 : CIP rev.
Also classified at 616.4′2 B81-11933

616.99′419′075 — Man. Blood. Leukaemia. Diagnosis. Laboratory techniques

The Leukemic cell / edited by D. Catovsky. — Edinburgh : Churchill Livingstone, 1981. — x,281p,[2]p of plates : ill(some col.) ; 24cm. — (Methods in hematology ; v.2)
Includes index
ISBN 0-443-01911-8 : Unpriced : CIP rev.
B80-18765

616.99′4190757 — Man. Blood. Leukaemia. Diagnosis. Radiology

Roentgenology of the lymphomas and leukemias / editor Benjamin Felson. — New York ; London : Grune & Stratton, c1980. — x,133p : ill ; 29cm
Includes bibliographies and index
ISBN 0-8089-1333-6 : £13.80
Primary classification 616.99′4460757
B81-20676

616.99′424 — Man. Lungs. Cancer

Lung cancer. — The Hague ; London : Hijhoff. — (Cancer treatment and research ; v.1)
Includes index
1. — 1981. — xii,310p : ill ; 25cm
ISBN 90-247-2394-9 : Unpriced B81-13650

Small cell lung cancer / edited by F. Anthony Greco, Robert K. Oldham, Paul A. Bunn, Jr. — New York ; London : Grune & Stratton, c1981. — xi,463p : ill ; 24cm. — (Clinical oncology monographs)
Includes index
ISBN 0-8089-1345-x : £26.20 B81-39561

616.99′424 — Man. Lungs. Cancer — *Conference proceedings*

World Conference on Lung Cancer *(2nd : 1980 : Copenhagen).* Abstracts / II World Conference on Lung Cancer, Copenhagen, Denmark, June 9-13, 1980 ; editors Heine H. Hansen and Per Dombernowsky. — Amsterdam ; Oxford : Excerpta Medica, 1980. — 283p ; 19cm
Includes index
ISBN 90-219-1243-0 (pbk) : Unpriced
B81-01727

616.99′42406′077 — Man. Lungs. Cancer. Therapy — *Programmed instructins*

Bronchogenic carcinoma / Omar M. Salazar ... [et al.]. — New York ; Oxford : Pergamon, c1981. — 379p in various pagings : ill ; 28cm. — (Oncologic, ISSN 0272-5495 ; v.13)
Includes bibliographies and index
ISBN 0-08-027464-1 (pbk) : Unpriced
B81-37275

616.99′43 — Man. Digestive system. Cancer — *Conference proceedings*

Diagnosis and treatment of upper gastrointestinal tumours : proceedings of an international congress, Mainz, September 9-11, 1980 / editors M. Friedman, M. Ogawa, D. Kisner ; associate editors D. Bokelmann, G. Nagel, H.W. Schreiber. — Amsterdam ; Oxford : Excerpta Medica, 1981. — xvii,538p : ill,maps ; 25cm. — (International congress series ; no.542)
Includes index
ISBN 90-219-9500-x : £37.35
ISBN 0-444-90189-2 (Elsevier/North-Holland)
B81-22291

616.99′4′33 — Man. Gastrointestinal tract. Cancer — *Conference proceedings*

Progress and perspectives in the treatment of gastrointestinal tumors. — Oxford : Pergamon, Oct.1981. — [128]p
Conference papers
ISBN 0-08-027979-1 : £20.50 : CIP entry
B81-26784

616.99′433 — Man. Stomach. Cancer — *Conference proceedings*

International Symposium on Gastric Cancer *(1980 : Birmingham).* Gastric cancer : proceedings of an International Symposium on Gastric Cancer, Birmingham, 22-23 September 1980 / editors: J.W.L. Fielding ... [et al.]. — Oxford : Pergamon, 1981. — ix,247p : ill,maps ; 26cm. — (Advances in the biosciences ; v.32)
Includes bibliographies and index
ISBN 0-08-026398-4 : Unpriced : CIP rev.
B81-10513

616.99′4347 — Man. Colon & rectum. Cancer — *Conference proceedings*

Colorectal cancer / edited by K. Welvaart, L.H. Blungart, J. Kreuning. — The Hague ; London : Leiden University Press, 1980. — xii,290p : ill ; 25cm. — (Boerhaave series for postgraduate medical education ; v.18)
Conference papers. — Includes index
ISBN 90-602-1465-x : Unpriced B81-03237

616.99′4′347 — Man. Colon. Cancer. Pathogenesis — *Conference proceedings*

Falk Symposium *(31st ; 1981 : Titisee).* Colonic carcinogenesis. — Lancaster : MTP Press, Feb.1982. — [350]p
ISBN 0-85200-443-5 : £25.00 : CIP entry
B81-36974

616.99′4347 — Man. Large intestine. Cancer

Large bowel cancer / edited by Jerome J. DeCosse. — Edinburgh : Churchill Livingstone, 1981. — ix,225p : ill ; 25cm. — (Clinical surgery international ; v.1)
Includes bibliographies and index
ISBN 0-443-02126-0 : £9.95 B81-32988

616.99′436 — Man. Liver. Cancer. Pathogenesis

Liver carcinogenesis / editors Károly Lapis, Jan Vincents Johannessen. — Washington ; London : Hemisphere, c1979. — v,143p : ill ; 27cm
Includes bibliographies and index
ISBN 0-07-036368-4 : £15.05 B81-05470

616.99′446 — Man. Malignant lymphomas

Hodgkin′s and non-Hodgkin′s lymphomas / edited by Charles A. Coltman, Jr., Harvey M. Golomb. — New York ; London : Grune & Stratton, c1980. — vi,268p : ill ; 29cm. — (Seminars in oncology reprint)
Includes index
ISBN 0-8089-1354-9 : £16.60 B81-15022

Taylor, Clive R.. Hodgkin′s disease and the lymphomas / Clive R. Taylor. — Westmount, Quebec : Eden ; Edinburgh : Churchill Livingstone. — (Annual research reviews. Medicine, ISSN 0703-1654)
Vol.4 / with chapters by Robert Astarita ... [et al.]. — 1980. — 377p : ill ; 22cm
Bibliography: p264-370. - Includes index
ISBN 0-443-02255-0 : Unpriced B81-16173

616.99′446′0012 — Man. Malignant lymphomas. Classification

Malignant lymphoproliferative diseases : proceedings of a Boerhaave course / organized by the Faculty of Medicine, University of Leiden and co-sponsored by University of Southern California, School of Medicine, Los Angeles ; edited by J.G. Van Den Tweel in collaboration with C.R. Taylor, F.T. Bosman. — The Hague ; London : Leiden University Press, 1980. — xii,507p : ill ; 25cm. — (Boerhaave series for postgraduate medical education ; v.17)
Includes bibliographies and index
ISBN 90-602-1451-x : Unpriced B81-06836

616.99′4460757 — Man. Malignant lymphomas. Diagnosis. Radiography

Roentgenology of the lymphomas and leukemias / editor Benjamin Felson. — New York ; London : Grune & Stratton, c1980. — x,133p : ill ; 29cm
Includes bibliographies and index
ISBN 0-8089-1333-6 : £13.80
Also classified at 616.99′4190757 B81-20676

616.99′447 — Man. Pituitary gland. Adenomas — *Programmed instructions*

Sheline, Glenn E.. Pituitary adenomas / Glenn E. Sheline. — New York ; Oxford : Pergamon, c1981. — xvi,SG1-SG25,197,PT1-PT18p : ill ; 28cm. — (Oncologic, multidisciplinary decisions in oncology, ISSN 0272-5495 ; v.12)
Bibliography: p187-193. — Includes index
ISBN 0-08-027463-3 (pbk) : Unpriced
B81-25595

616.99′449 — Women. Breasts. Cancer

Smith, Trevor, *1949-*. Breast cancer / Trevor Smith. — London : Duckworth, 1981. — 112p ; 22cm. — (Paperduck)
Bibliography: p99-108. — Includes index
ISBN 0-7156-1571-8 (pbk) : £4.95 : CIP rev.
B81-17501

616.99′449 — Women. Breasts. Cancer — *For patients*

Baum, Michael. Breast cancer : the facts / Michael Baum with a chapter by Sylvia Denton. — Oxford : Oxford University Press, 1981. — ix,111p,[8]p of plates : ill ; 23cm. — (Oxford medical publications)
Includes index
ISBN 0-19-261265-4 : £4.95 : CIP rev.
B81-25797

616.99′449′005 — Women. Breasts. Cancer — *Serials*

Breast cancer. — 4. — New York ; London : Plenum Medical, c1981. — xii,234p
ISBN 0-306-40667-5 : Unpriced
ISSN 0161-0112 B81-31885

616.99′449′007 — Women. Breasts. Cancer. Information sources — *Lists*

Breast cancer : a handbook of information sources / compiled by Robert Gann & Rosemary Lancaster. — Southampton (South Academic Block, Southampton General Hospital, Southampton S09 4XY) : Wessex Regional Library & Information Service, 1981. — 32p ; 26cm. — (Communication / Wessex Regional Library and Information Service)
Bibliography: p24-32
£1.50 (pbk) B81-15684

616.99′449027 — Laboratory animals: Mice. Mammary glands. Cancer

Mammary tumors in the mouse / edited by J. Hilgers and M. Sluyser. — Amsterdam ; Oxford : Elsevier/North-Holland Biomedical, 1981. — xvi,691p : ill,ports ; 25cm
Includes bibliographies and index
ISBN 0-444-80315-7 : Unpriced B81-39200

616.99′449042 — Women. Breasts. Cancer. Genetic factors

Genetics and breast cancer / edited by Henry T. Lynch. — New York ; London : Van Nostrand Reinhold, c1981. — xii,253p : ill ; 24cm
Includes index
ISBN 0-442-24919-5 : £20.00 B81-36075

616.99′44906 — Women. Breasts. Cancer. Therapy

Breast cancer management : the experience of the Combined Breast Clinic, St. Georges Hospital - The Royal Marsden Hospital / edited by R.C. Coombes ... [et al.]. — London : Academic Press, 1981. — xii,317p : ill ; 24cm
Includes bibliographies and index
ISBN 0-12-790899-4 : £18.00 : CIP rev.
B81-12331

616.99′449061 — Women. Breasts. Cancer. Drug therapy. Aminoglutethimide

A Comprehensive guide to the therapeutic use of aminoglutethimide / editors Richard J. Santen, I. Graig Henderson. — Basel ; London : Karger, c1981. — 160p,[2]p of plates : ill(some col.) ; 23cm. — (Pharmanual ; 2)
Includes bibliographies
ISBN 3-8055-2871-x (pbk) : £11.50 B81-39025

616.99′449061 — Women. Breasts. Cancer. Endocrine therapy

Hormonal management of endocrine-related cancer / edited by Basil A. Stoll. — London : Lloyd-Luke, 1981. — xii,244p,[1]leaf of plates : ill(some col.) ; 26cm
Includes bibliographies and index
ISBN 0-85324-148-1 : Unpriced B81-39133

616.99′44907 — Women. Breasts. Cancer. Cells — *Conference proceedings*

Cell biology of breast cancer / edited by Charles McGrath, Michael J. Bennan and Marvin A. Rich. — New York ; London : Academic Press, 1980. — xv,516p : ill ; 24cm
Conference papers. — Includes bibliographies
ISBN 0-12-483940-1 : Unpriced B81-29789

616.99′449071 — Women. Breasts. Cancer. Role of steroid hormone receptors — *Conference proceedings*

International Study Group for Steroid Hormones. *Meeting (9th : 1979 : Rome).* Endocrinological cancer, ovarian function and disease : proceedings of the IX Meeting of the International Study Group for Steroid Hormones, Rome December 5-7, 1979 / editors H. Adlercreutz ... [et al.]. — Amsterdam ; Oxford : Excerpta Medica, 1981. — xii,400p : ill ; 25cm. — (Research on steroids ; v.9) (International congress series ; no.515)
Includes bibliographies and index
ISBN 90-219-0444-6 : £29.90
Also classified at 616.99′463 ; 618.1′1
B81-15663

616.99′46 — Man. Germ cells. Tumours — *Conference proceedings*

Germ cell tumours. — London : Taylor & Francis, Oct.1981. — [427]p
Conference papers
ISBN 0-85066-223-0 : CIP entry B81-30257

616.99′462 — Man. Bladder. Cancer — *Conference proceedings*

Bladder cancer : principles of combination therapy / [edited by] R.T.D. Oliver, W.F. Hendry, H.J.G. Bloom. — London : Butterworths, 1981. — xix,26p : ill ; 24cm
Conference papers. — Includes bibliographies and index
ISBN 0-407-00187-5 : Unpriced B81-11593

616.99′463 — Men. Prostate gland. Cancer. Role of steroid hormone receptors — *Conference proceedings*

International Study Group for Steroid Hormones. *Meeting (9th : 1979 : Rome).* Endocrinological cancer, ovarian function and disease : proceedings of the IX Meeting of the International Study Group for Steroid Hormones, Rome December 5-7, 1979 / editors H. Adlercreutz ... [et al.]. — Amsterdam ; Oxford : Excerpta Medica, 1981. — xii,400p : ill ; 25cm. — (Research on steroids ; v.9) (International congress series ; no.515)
Includes bibliographies and index
ISBN 90-219-0444-6 : £29.90
Primary classification 616.99′449071
B81-15663

616.99′4′63 — Men. Testes. Cancer

The **Management** of testicular tumours. — London : Edward Arnold, Nov.1981. — [300] p. — (The Management of malignant disease, ISSN 0144-8692 ; 3)
ISBN 0-7131-4326-6 : £20.00 : CIP entry
B81-30579

616.99′465 — Women. Reproductive system. Cancer

DiSaia, Philip J.. Clinical gynecologic oncology / Philip J. DiSaia, William T. Creasman. — St. Louis ; London : Mosby, 1981. — ix,478p : ill ; 26cm
Includes bibliographies and index
ISBN 0-8016-1314-0 : £23.50 B81-09769

Morrow, C. Paul. Synopsis of gynecologic oncology. — 2nd ed. / C. Paul Morrow, Duane E. Townsend. — New York ; Chichester : Wiley, c1981. — xiii,488p : ill ; 27cm
Previous ed.: by Philip J. DiSaia, C. Paul Morrow, Duane E. Townsend. 1975. — Includes bibliographies and index
ISBN 0-471-06504-8 : £20.00 B81-23424

616.99′4′736 — Women. Pelvis. Cancer

Gynecologic oncology. — Edinburgh : Churchill Livingstone, July 1981
Vol.1. — [1300]p
ISBN 0-443-01977-0 : £80.00 : CIP entry
B81-15847

616.99′481 — Man. Brain. Cancer. Metastasis — *Conference proceedings*

Brain metastasis / edited by Leonard Weiss, Harvey A. Gilbert, Jerome B. Posner. — The Hague ; London : Nijhoff, c1980. — xxxi,438p : ill ; 26cm. — (Metastasis ; v.2)
Includes bibliographies and index
ISBN 90-247-2217-9 : Unpriced B81-04733

616.99′484 — Man. Eyes. Uveas. Melanoma — *Conference proceedings*

Symposium on Uveal Melanomas *(1979 : Utrecht).* Symposium on Uveal Melanomas : on the occasion of the Snellen Medal presentation to Dr. W.A. Manschot / edited by A. Hamburg. — The Hague ; London : Junk, 1980. — 121p : ill ; 24cm. — (Documenta ophthalmologica. Proceedings series ; v.24)
"Reprinted from Documenta ophthalmologica, v.50, no.1 (1980)". — Includes bibliographies
ISBN 90-619-3722-1 : Unpriced B81-04421

616.99′491 — Man. Head. Cancer

Cancer of the head and neck / edited by James Y. Suen and Eugene N. Myers. — New York ; Edinburgh : Churchill Livingstone, 1981. — 905p : ill ; 26cm
Includes bibliographies and index
ISBN 0-443-08045-3 : £45.00
Also classified at 616.99′493 B81-18918

616.99′493 — Man. Neck. Cancer

Cancer of the head and neck / edited by James Y. Suen and Eugene N. Myers. — New York ; Edinburgh : Churchill Livingstone, 1981. — 905p : ill ; 26cm
Includes bibliographies and index
ISBN 0-443-08045-3 : £45.00
Primary classification 616.99′491 B81-18918

616.99′49507544 — Man. Abdomen. Cancer. Diagnosis. Ultrasonography

Brascho, Donn J.. Abdominal ultrasound in the cancer patient / Donn J. Brascho, Thomas H. Shawker. — New York ; Chichester : Wiley, c1980. — xv,414p : ill ; 27cm. — (Wiley series in diagnostic and therapeutic radiology)
Includes index
ISBN 0-471-01742-6 : £21.00 B81-08386

616.9′95′00941 — Great Britain. Man. Tuberculosis

Citron, K. M.. Tuberculosis today / K.M. Citron, R.H. Raynes & J.R.H. Berrie. — London : H.M.S.O., 1981. — iii,39p : ill ; 22cm. — (Topics of our time ; 3)
At head of title: Department of Health & Social Security. — Bibliography: p39
ISBN 0-11-320744-1 (pbk) : £3.30 B81-10032

617 — MEDICINE. SURGERY

617

Frontiers in general surgery. — Lancaster : MTP Press, July 1981. — [350]p
ISBN 0-85200-249-1 : £17.95 : CIP entry
Primary classification 617 B81-21603

617 — Medicine. Surgery

Basic surgery / edited by John A. McCredie ; illustrated by Carol Donner. — New York : Macmillan ; London : Baillière Tindall, c1977. — x,660p,[8]p of plates : ill(some col.) ; 26cm
Includes bibliographies and index
ISBN 0-7020-0628-9 (pbk) : £12.50 B81-06658

Clinical science for surgeons / edited by William Burnett. — London : Butterworth, 1981. — xiv,849p : ill,ports ; 26cm
Commissioned by the Royal Australian College of Surgeons. — Includes bibliographies and index
ISBN 0-407-00181-6 : £37.50 B81-10800

Frontiers in general surgery. — Lancaster : MTP Press, July 1981. — [350]p
ISBN 0-85200-249-1 : £17.95 : CIP entry
Also classified at 617 B81-21603

Illingworth, *Sir* **Charles.** Surgical treatment / Sir Charles Illingworth. — Tunbridge Wells : Pitman Medical, 1980. — 336p : ill ; 23cm
Includes index
ISBN 0-272-79593-3 (pbk) : £12.95 : CIP rev.
B80-24525

Liechty, Richard D.. Synopsis of surgery / Richard D. Leichty, Robert T. Soper. — 4th ed. — St Louis ; London : Mosby, 1980. — xii,715p : ill ; 24cm
Previous ed.: 1976. — Bibliography: p664-677. - Includes index
ISBN 0-8016-3012-6 (pbk) : £19.00 B81-00932

The **Management** of difficult surgical problems / edited by Thomas A. Miller and Stanley J. Dudrick. — [London] : Edward Arnold, 1981. — viii,304p : ill ; 24cm
Includes bibliographies
ISBN 0-7131-4387-8 : £16.00 : CIP rev.
B81-02118

Principles of surgery / editor-in-chief Seymour I. Schwartz, associate editors ... [others]. — 3rd ed. — New York ; London : McGraw-Hill PreTest self-assessment and review / edited by Seymour I. Schwartz. — c1981. — xii,253p : ill ; 28cm. — (PreTest series)
Bibliography: p251-253
ISBN 0-07-051649-9 (pbk) : £17.50 B81-23443

Selzer, Richard. Mortal lessons : notes on the art of surgery / Richard Selzer. — London : Chatto & Windus, 1981. — 216p ; 23cm
ISBN 0-7011-2558-6 : £8.50 : CIP rev.
B81-03699

Surgery / edited by James O. Robinson and Ashley Brown. — London : Heinemann Medical, 1980. — 604p : ill ; 26cm
Includes bibliographies and index
ISBN 0-433-28104-9 : £27.50 B81-03058

Surgery. — London : Butterworths, Aug.1981. — (Butterworths international medical reviews, ISSN 0260-0188)
1: Trauma. — [320]p
ISBN 0-407-02316-x : £13.50 : CIP entry
B81-19125

Taylor, Selwyn. A short textbook of surgery. — 5th ed. — London : Hodder & Stoughton Educational, Nov.1981. — [656]p
Previous ed.: 1977
ISBN 0-340-27140-x (pbk) : £7.95 : CIP entry
B81-28763

Thomas, J. Meirion. Aids to postgraduate surgery. — 2nd ed. — Edinburgh : Churchill Livingstone, Jan.1982. — [192]p
Previous ed.: 1976
ISBN 0-443-02514-2 (pbk) : £4.95 : CIP entry
B81-34513

617′.0014 — Medicine. Surgery. Terminology — *Lists*

Tessier, Claudia J.. The surgical word book / Claudia J. Tessier. — Philadelphia ; London : Saunders, 1981. — xi,507p ; 19cm
ISBN 0-7216-8805-5 (pbk) : £12.25 B81-38765

617′.005 — Medicine. Surgery — *Serials*

Advances in surgery. — Vol.14 (1980). — Chicago ; London : Year Book Medical Publishers, c1980. — xii,341p
ISBN 0-8151-4918-2 : Unpriced
ISSN 0065-3411 B81-25498

Current surgical practice. — Vol.3. — London : Edward Arnold, Dec.1981. — [320]p
ISBN 0-7131-4397-5 (pbk) : £20.00 : CIP entry
ISSN 0141-3368 B81-31632

The **Year** book of surgery. — 1980. — Chicago ; London : Year Book Medical Publishers, c1980. — 509p
ISBN 0-8151-7619-8 : Unpriced B81-20404

617′.0076 — Medicine. Surgery — *Questions & answers*

Schwartz, Principles of surgery : PreTest self-assessment and review / edited by Seymour I. Schwartz. — New York ; London : McGraw-Hill. — (PreTest series)
CME examination. — c1981. — viii,26p : ill,1form ; 28cm + 1sheet(28cm)
Unpriced (pbk) B81-26987

617'.0076 — Medicine. Surgery — *Questions & answers* *continuation*
Surgery : PreTest self-assessment and review / edited by Wain L. White. — New York ; London : McGraw-Hill, c1978. — ix,239p : ill ; 22cm. — (PreTest series)
Originally published: Wallingford, Conn. : PreTest Service, 1978. — Bibliography: p235-239
ISBN 0-07-051605-7 (pbk) : £6.95 B81-19469

617'.01 — Medicine. Surgery. Sequelae: Sepsis — *Conference proceedings*
Controversies in surgical sepsis / edited by Stephen Karran. — Eastbourne : Praeger, 1980. — xiv,352p,[1] leaf of plates : ill(some col.) ; 24cm. — (Surgical science series ; v.1) (Praeger special studies)
Includes bibliographies and index
ISBN 0-03-910287-4 : £17.50 : CIP rev. B80-17738

617'.026 — Medicine. Surgery. Emergency treatment
Critical surgical illness / edited by James D. Hardy. — 2nd ed. — Philadelphia ; London : Saunders, 1980. — xiii,702p : ill ; 27cm
Previous ed.: 1971. — Includes bibliographies and index
ISBN 0-7216-4511-9 : £24.25 B81-01858

617'.05 — Medicine. Microsurgery — *Manuals*
Acland, Robert D.. Microsurgery practice manual / Robert D. Acland. — St. Louis ; London : Mosby, 1980. — ix,106p : ill ; 26cm
Includes index
ISBN 0-8016-0076-6 (spiral) : £11.25 B81-08198

617'.07 — Medicine. Surgery. Pathology
Ackerman, Lauren V.. Ackerman's Surgical pathology. — 6th ed. / Juan Rosai. — St. Louis ; London : Mosby, 1981. — 2v.(xii,1702p) : ill ; 27cm
Previous ed.: in 1 vol. 1974. — Includes bibliographies and index
ISBN 0-8016-0045-6 : £85.00 B81-33000

617'.07572 — Man. Diagnosis. Radiography — *For surgery*
Surgical radiology : a complement in radiology and imaging to the Sabiston-Davis-Christopher text of surgery / edited by J. George Teplick, Marvin E. Haskin. — Philadelphia ; London : Saunders
Vol.2. — 1981. — xix,1090-2017,xxip : ill ; 27cm
Includes bibliographies and index
ISBN 0-7216-8782-2 : £40.00 B81-31764

Surgical radiology : a complement in radiology and imaging to the Sabiston Davis-Christopher textbook of surgery / edited by J. George Teplick, Marvin E. Haskin. — Philadelphia ; London : Saunders
ISBN 0-7216-8781-4 : £40.00 B81-08156

617'.092'2 — England. Medicine. Surgery. Organisations: Royal College of Surgeons of England. Fellows, *1965-1973* — *Biographies*
Ross, *Sir* **James Paterson**. Lives of the Fellows of the Royal College of Surgeons of England 1965-1973 : Cecil Wakeley memorial / by Sir James Paterson Ross and W.R. LeFanu ; with an appreciation of Sir Cecil Wakeley by T.C. Hunt. — London : Pitman Medical, 1981. — 405p ; 24cm
ISBN 0-272-79610-7 : £25.00 B81-10837

617'.092'4 — Medicine. Surgery. Sava, George — *Biographies*
Sava, George. A surgeon & his knife / George Sava. — Bognor Regis : New Horizon, c1979. — 179p ; 21cm
ISBN 0-86116-059-2 : £3.95 B81-02639

617'.092'6 — Medicine. Surgery. Decision making — *Case studies*
Sigel, Bernard. Clinical simulations in surgery / Bernard Sigel ; edited by Phillip M. Forman. — New York : Appleton-Century-Crofts ; London : Prentice-Hall, c1981. — xv,160p + Abdick, latent image developer ; 28cm
Bibliography: pxi
ISBN 0-8385-1174-0 (pbk) : £25.05 B81-13663

617'.0944'36 — France. Paris. Medicine. Surgery, *1700-1800*
Gelfand, Toby. Professionalizing modern medicine : Paris surgeons and medical science institutions in the 18th century / Toby Gelfand. — Westport, Conn. ; London : Greenwood Press, 1980. — viii,271p : ill,1facsim,2ports ; 25cm. — (Contributions in medical history, ISSN 0147-1058 ; no.6)
Bibliography: p259-260. - Includes index
ISBN 0-313-21488-3 : £19.50 B81-23647

617.1 — MAN. WOUNDS AND INJURIES

617'.1 — Dancers. Injuries
Arnheim, Daniel D.. Dance injuries : their prevention and care. — 2nd ed. / Daniel D. Arnheim. — St. Louis ; London : Mosby, 1980. — ix,240p : ill,ports ; 23cm
Previous ed.: / by David D. Arnheim with Joan Schlaich, 1975. — Bibliography: p227-228. - Includes index
ISBN 0-8016-0311-0 (pbk) : £8.50 B81-08191

617'.1 — Man. Injuries. Emergency treatment
Huckstep, R. L.. A simple guide to trauma. — 3rd ed. — Edinburgh : Churchill Livingstone, Jan.1982. — [408]p
Previous ed.: 1978
ISBN 0-443-02495-2 (pbk) : £4.95 : CIP entry B81-34512

617'.1'0088054 — Children. Injuries. Surgery
The **Injured** child : surgical management / edited by Judson G. Randolph ... [et al.]. — Chicago ; London : Year Book Medical Publishers, c1979. — xiv,420p : ill ; 24cm
Includes bibliographies and index
ISBN 0-8151-7051-3 : £33.25 B81-07888

617'.1027 — Athletes. Injuries. Prevention — *For teaching*
Klafs, Carl E.. Modern principles of athletic training : the science of sports injury prevention and management / Carl E. Klafs, Daniel D. Arnheim. — 5th ed. — St. Louis ; London : Mosby, 1981. — xiv,576p,4p of plates : ill(some col.),forms ; 25cm
Previous ed.: 1977. — Includes bibliographies and index
ISBN 0-8016-2682-x : £15.50 B81-25044

617'.1027 — Sports & games. Injuries
Muckle, David Sutherland. Injuries in sport. — 2nd ed. — Bristol : J. Wright, Jan.1982. — [176]p
Previous ed.: 1978
ISBN 0-7236-0620-x : CIP entry B81-34660

617'.1027 — Sportsmen & sportswomen. Injuries
Sports fitness and sports injuries / edited by Thomas Reilly ; with a foreword by Dick Jeeps. — London : Faber, 1981. — 293p : ill ; 26cm
Includes bibliographies and index
ISBN 0-571-11628-0 (cased) : £15.00
ISBN 0-571-11629-9 (pbk) : £9.95 B81-10601

617'.1027'05 — Sports & games. Medical aspects — *Serials*
The year book of sports medicine. — 1979-. — Chicago ; [London] : Year Book Medical Publishers, 1979-. — v. : ill ; 24cm
Unpriced B81-11218

The **Year** book of sports medicine. — 1980. — Chicago ; London : Year Book Medical Publishers, c1980. — 369p
ISBN 0-8151-0175-9 : £28.50 B81-18799

617'.1'05 — Man. Injuries caused by accidents. Surgery — *Serials*
Topical reviews in accident surgery. — Vol.2. — Bristol : Wright, Feb.1982. — [240]p
ISBN 0-7236-0614-5 : £15.00 : CIP entry B81-35846

617'.11 — Man. Burns
Care of the burned-injured patient : multidisciplinary involvement / edited by Mary M. Wagner. — London : Croom Helm, c1981. — ix,310p : ill,forms ; 25cm
Bibliography: p289-299. — Incluces index
ISBN 0-7099-2719-3 : £11.95 B81-18836

617'.110592 — Man. Burns. Reconstructive surgery. Techniques
Salisbury, Roger E.. Atlas of reconstructive burn surgery / Roger E. Salisbury, A. Griswold Bevin with a contribution by Freddi S. Salisbury ; illustrations by Harold A. Rydberg. — Philadelphia ; London : Saunders, 1981. — viii,267p : ill(some col.) ; 32cm
Includes index
ISBN 0-7216-7903-x : £32.75 B81-27097

617'.1106 — Man. Burns. Therapy
Cason, J. S.. Treatment of burns / J.S. Cason. — London : Chapman and Hall, 1981. — ix,339p : ill,forms ; 25cm
Includes bibliographies and index
ISBN 0-412-15990-2 : £15.00 B81-19840

617'.11'0954 — India *(Republic).* **Man. Burns**
Jackson, Douglas M.. The burn scene in India and Sri Lanka : report on a Commonwealth Foundation lecture tour, January-February 1980 / by D. MacG. Jackson. — London (Marlborough House, Pall Mall, S.W.1) : Commonwealth Foundation, 1980. — 62p : 1map ; 25cm. — (Occasional paper / Commonwealth Foundation, ISSN 0069-7087 ; no.48)
Cover title
Unpriced (pbk) B81-08048

617'.14 — Man. Wounds. Healing
Irvin, Thomas T.. Wound healing : principles and practice / Thomas T. Irvin. — London : Chapman and Hall, 1981. — 221p,2p of plates : ill(some col.) ; 24cm
Includes index
ISBN 0-412-15980-5 : Unpriced : CIP rev. B81-14412

617'.145 — Man. High velocity gunshot wounds. Surgery
Owen-Smith, M. S.. High velocity missile wounds / M.S. Owen-Smith ; with a foreword by Lord Smith of Marlow. — London : Edward Arnold, 1981. — x,182p : ill ; 24cm
Bibliography: p180. - Includes index
ISBN 0-7131-4371-1 : £12.75 B81-05480

617'.15 — Man. Bones. Fractures. Diagnosis. Radiography. Use of x-rays
Grech, Paul. Casualty radiology : a practical guide for radiological diagnosis / Paul Grech. — London : Chapman and Hall, 1981. — 242p : ill ; 26cm
Includes bibliographies and index
ISBN 0-412-22740-1 : £15.00 : CIP rev. B80-36106

617'.15 — Man. Bones. Fractures. Healing
Sevitt, Simon. Bone repair and fracture healing in man / Simon Sevitt. — Edinburgh : Churchill Livingstone, 1981. — 315p : ill ; 26cm. — (Current problems in orthopaedics)
Includes bibliographies and index
ISBN 0-443-01806-5 : £35.00 : CIP rev. B80-25726

617'.15 — Man. Bones. Fractures. Therapy
DePalma, Anthony F.. DePalma's The management of fractures and dislocations : an atlas. — 3rd ed. / edited by John F. Connolly ; illustrations by Steven McCoy, Barbara B. Finnerson [i.e. Finneson] and William Osburn. — Philadelphia ; London : Saunders, 1981. — 2v.(2153,xxxip) : ill ; 27cm
Previous ed.: Philadelphia : Saunders, 1970. — Includes index
ISBN 0-7216-2666-1 : £36.25
ISBN 0-7216-2702-10-7216-2703-x (vol.1) (vol.2)
Also classified at 617'.1606 B81-37463

McRae, Ronald. Practical fracture treatment. — Edinburgh : Churchill Livingstone, July 1981. — [265]p
ISBN 0-443-01694-1 (pbk) : £4.50 : CIP entry B81-16349

617'.15'6 — Man. Maxillofacial region. Bones. Fractures — *For dentistry*
Killey, H. C.. Killey's fractures of the middle third of the facial skeleton. — 4th ed. — Bristol : J. Wright, Oct.1981. — [104]p. — (A Dental practitioner handbook)
Previous ed.: 1977
ISBN 0-7236-0625-0 (pbk) : £4.50 : CIP entry B81-24660

617′.1606 — Man. Joints. Dislocations. Therapy
DePalma, Anthony F.. DePalma's The management of fractures and dislocations : an atlas. — 3rd ed. / edited by John F. Connolly ; illustrations by Steven McCoy, Barbara B. Finnerson [i.e. Finneson] and William Osburn. — Philadelphia ; London : Saunders, 1981. — 2v.(2153,xxxip) : ill ; 27cm
Previous ed.: Philadelphia : Saunders, 1970. — Includes index
ISBN 0-7216-2666-1 : £36.25
ISBN 0-7216-2702-10-7216-2703-x (vol.1) (vol.2)
Primary classification 617′.15 B81-37463

617′.21 — Man. Trauma
Trauma and after. — London : Pitman Medical, July 1981. — [128]p. — (Ciba Foundation occasional volume)
ISBN 0-272-79623-9 : £4.95 : CIP entry B81-13427

Trimble, Michael R.. Post-traumatic neurosis. — Chichester : Wiley, Nov.1981. — [100]p
ISBN 0-471-09975-9 : £10.00 : CIP entry
Also classified at 616.8′5 B81-30520

617′.21 — Man. Trauma. Therapy
Trauma care / edited by William Odling-Smee and Alan Crockard. — London : Academic Press, 1981. — xii,657p : ill ; 26cm
Includes bibliographies and index
ISBN 0-12-793186-4 : £24.20 : CIP rev. B80-20744

617.3 — MEDICINE. ORTHOPAEDICS

617′.3 — Man. Deformities
Smith, David W. (David Weyhe). Recognizable patterns of human deformation : identification and management of mechanical effects on morphogenesis / by David W. Smith. — Philadelphia ; London : Saunders, 1981. — xii,151p : ill ; 27cm. — (Major problems in clinical pediatrics ; v.21)
Includes index
ISBN 0-7216-8401-7 : £13.25 B81-26953

617′.3 — Medicine. Orthopaedics
Adams, John Crawford. Outline of orthopaedics / by John Crawford Adams. — 9th ed. — Edinburgh : Churchill Livingstone, 1981. — vii,486p : ill ; 23cm
Previous ed.: 1976. — Bibliography: p451-474. - Includes index
ISBN 0-443-02247-x (cased) : Unpriced : CIP rev.
ISBN 0-443-02248-8 (pbk) : £7.50 B80-31693

Browne, Patrick S. H.. Basic facts in orthopaedics / Patrick S.H. Browne. — Oxford : Blackwell Scientific, 1981. — 277p : ill ; 22cm
Bibliography: p266. — Includes index
ISBN 0-632-00718-4 (pbk) : £7.50 B81-24040

Current orthopaedic management / edited by William J. Kane. — New York ; Edinburgh : Churchill Livingstone, 1981. — 352p : ill ; 27cm
Includes bibliographies and index
ISBN 0-443-08152-2 : £18.00 B81-27111

Goldstein, Louis A.. Atlas of orthopaedic surgery / Louis A. Goldstein, Robert C. Dickerson. — 2nd ed. — St. Louis ; London : Mosby, 1981. — xviii,646p : ill ; 29cm
Previous ed.: 1974. — Includes bibliographies and index
ISBN 0-8016-1884-3 : £75.00 B81-30119

Guide to orthopaedics. — Edinburgh : Churchill Livingstone
Includes bibliographies and index
1: Trauma / K.L.G. Mills. — 1981. — 296p : ill ; 25cm
ISBN 0-443-02018-3 (pbk) : Unpriced : CIP rev. B80-05950

Hughes, Sean. New bones : [inaugural lecture] delivered on Tuesday 17th February 1981 / S.P.F. Hughes. — [Edinburgh] : University of Edinburgh, [1981]. — 12p ; 23cm. — (Inaugural lecture / University of Edinburgh ; no.68)
Unpriced (pbk) B81-35078

Mercier, Lonnie R.. Practical orthopedics / Lonnie R. Mercier with Fred J. Pettid. — Chicago ; London : Yearbook Medical Publishers, c1980. — xiii,299p : ill ; 26cm
Includes bibliographies and index
ISBN 0-8151-5863-7 : £10.50 B81-19963

Monk, C. J. E.. Orthopaedics for undergraduates / by C.J.E. Monk. — 2nd ed. — Oxford : Oxford University Press, 1981. — viii,237p : ill ; 22cm. — (Oxford medical publications)
Previous ed.: 1975. — Includes bibliographies and index
ISBN 0-19-261312-x (pbk) : £6.95 B81-26820

617′.3 — Medicine. Orthopaedics. Applications of biomechanics
Clinical biomechanics : a case history approach / edited by Jonathan Black and John H. Dumbleton ; with 28 contributors. — New York ; Edinburgh : Churchill Livingstone, 1981. — xiv,418p : ill ; 26cm
Includes bibliographies and index
ISBN 0-443-08022-4 : £25.00 B81-22182

617′.3 — Medicine. Orthopaedics — *Manuals*
Manual of orthopedics / [edited by] Nancy E. Hilt, Shirley B. Cogburn. — St. Louis ; London : Mosby, 1980. — xvii,846p : ill,forms ; 29cm
Includes bibliographies and index
ISBN 0-8016-2198-4 : Unpriced B81-08154

617′.3 — Medicine. Orthopaedics. Microsurgery — *Conference proceedings*
Symposium on microsurgery : practical use in orthopaedics : Durham, North Carolina September 1977, May 1979 / American Academy of Orthopaedic Surgeons. — St. Louis ; London : Mosby, 1979. — xi,387p : ill ; 26cm
Includes bibliographies and index
ISBN 0-8016-0066-9 : £41.75 B81-08214

617′.30028 — Medicine. Orthopaedics. Applications of engineering
Orthopaedic mechanics. — London : Academic Press, May 1981
Vol.2. — [300]p
ISBN 0-12-281602-1 : CIP entry B81-06065

Orthopaedic mechanics. — London : Academic Press, May 1981
Vol.3. — [250]p
ISBN 0-12-281603-x : CIP entry B81-06064

617′.3′005 — Medicine. Orthopaedics — *Serials*
Current practice in orthopaedic surgery. — Vol.8 (1979). — St. Louis ; London ; Mosby, 1979. — xii,146p
ISBN 0-8016-0089-8 : Unpriced B81-12404

[Instructional course lectures *(American Academy of Orthopaedic Surgeons)*]. Instructional course lectures / the American Academy of Orthopaedic Surgeons. — Vol.28 (1980). — St. Louis, Mo. ; London : C.V. Mosby, 1979-. — 341p
ISBN 0-8016-0032-4 : Unpriced B81-12401

[Instructional course lectures *(American Academy of Orthopaedic Surgeons)*]. Instructional course lectures / the American Academy of Orthopaedic Surgeons. — Vol.29 (1980). — St. Louis ; London : C.V. Mosby, 1980. — ix,156p
ISBN 0-8016-0047-2 : Unpriced B81-18804

The **Year** book of orthopedics. — 1980. — London : Year Book Medical, c1980. — 512p
ISBN 0-8151-1879-1 : Unpriced
ISSN 0084-3938 B81-09709

617′.3′00880542 — Newborn babies. Orthopaedics
Hensinger, Robert N.. Neonatal orthopaedics / Robert N. Hensinger, Eric T. Jones. — New York ; London : Grune & Stratton ; London : Academic Press [distributor], c1981. — xiii,319p : ill ; 24cm. — (Monographs in neonatalogy)
Includes index
ISBN 0-8089-1355-7 : £26.20 B81-40778

617′.375 — Man. Spine. Disorders
Grieve, Gregory P.. Common vertebral joint problems. — Edinburgh : Churchill Livingstone, Aug.1981. — [576]p
ISBN 0-443-02106-6 : £29.50 : CIP entry B81-16409

617′.375 — Man. Spine. Surgery
Manual of spinal surgery. — London : Butterworths, Sept.1981. — [160]p
ISBN 0-407-00159-x : £18.50 : CIP entry B81-21625

617.4 — MEDICINE. SURGICAL OPERATIONS BY SYSTEM

617′.41 — Man. Cardiovascular system, Surgery. Artificial circulation
Techniques in extracorporeal circulation. — 2nd ed. — London : Butterworths, May 1981. — [720]p
Previous ed.: 1979
ISBN 0-407-00173-5 : £40.00 : CIP entry B81-07930

617′.4101 — Man. Cardiovascular system. Surgery. Complications — *Conference proceedings*
Complications in vascular surgery / Victor M. Bernhard, Jonathan B. Towne. — New York ; London : Grune & Stratton, c1980. — xxi,657p : ill ; 24cm
Conference papers. — Includes bibliographies and index
ISBN 0-8089-1283-6 : £27.80 B81-02432

617′.412 — Man. Heart. Surgery
Towards safer cardiac surgery : based upon the proceedings of an international symposium held at the University of York 8-10th April 1980 / edited by D.B. Longmore. — Lancaster : MTP, 1981. — xi,672p,[4]p of plates : ill(some col.) ; 25cm
Includes index
ISBN 0-85200-353-6 : £24.95 : CIP rev. B80-13419

617′.412′00681 — Great Britain. Man. Heart. Surgery. Cost-effectiveness — *Conference proceedings*
British Heart Foundation. *Symposium (1980 : Newcastle-upon-Tyne)*. Can we justify the costs of cardiac surgery and pacemaking? : proceedings of the British Heart Foundation Symposium : 13 June 1980, Postgraduate Centre, Freeman Hospital, Newcastle-upon-Tyne / [executive editor Harold Godfrey]. — Henlow (Henlow Trading Estate, Henlow, Beds.) : Tillots Laboratories, c1980. — 112p : ill ; 21cm
Includes bibliographies
ISBN 0-907465-01-3 (pbk) : £2.50 B81-14096

617′.412028 — Man. Heat. Surgery. Postoperative intensive care
Braimbridge, M. V.. Postoperative cardiac intensive care. — 3rd ed. / M.V. Braimbridge with contributions from M. Jones ... [et al.] ; with a foreword by John W. Kirklin. — Oxford : Blackwell Scientific, 1981. — vii,232p : ill ; 24cm
Previous ed.: 1972. — Includes bibliographies and index
ISBN 0-632-00233-6 : £10.00 : CIP rev. B81-13482

617′.4120645 — Man. Heart. Cardiac pacemakers
Fundamentals of cardiac pacing / edited by Hilbert J.Th. Thalen and Claude C. Meere. — The Hague ; London : Nijhoff, 1979. — 261p : ill,ports ; 25cm. — (Developments in cardiovascular medicine ; v.3)
Conference papers. — Includes index
ISBN 90-247-2245-4 : Unpriced B81-02806

617′.413 — Man. Arteries. Surgery
Femoro-distal bypass. — Tunbridge Wells : Pitman Medical, June 1981. — [296]p
ISBN 0-272-79632-8 : £20.00 : CIP entry B81-13781

617′.413 — Man. Arteries. Surgery. Techniques
Bell, P. R. F.. Operative arterial surgery. — Bristol : J. Wright, Oct.1981. — [168]p
ISBN 0-7236-0610-2 : £13.50 : CIP entry B81-24639

617′.413 — Man. Arteries. Surgery. Techniques *continuation*

Operative techniques in vascular surgery / edited by John J. Bergan and James S.T. Yao. — New York ; London : Grune & Stratton, c1980. — xvii,310p : ill ; 29cm
ISBN 0-8089-1334-4 : £30.40 B81-15021

617′.413 — Man. Blood vessels. Implantation of surgical appliances

Vascular access surgery / edited by Samuel E. Wilson, Milton L. Owens. — Chicago ; London : Year Book Medical, c1980. — xiv,360p : ill,1port ; 24cm
Includes index
ISBN 0-8151-9324-6 : £34.00 B81-04554

617′.414 — Man. Veins. Surgery

Kester, Ralph. A practice of vascular surgery. — London : Pitman Medical, Jan.1982. — [384]p
ISBN 0-272-79640-9 : £25.00 : CIP entry
B81-34154

617′.43 — Man. Obesity. Surgery

Mason, Edward E.. Surgical treatment of obesity / by Edward E. Mason. — Philadelphia ; London : Saunders, 1981. — xii,493p : ill,2forms ; 24cm. — (Major problems in clinical surgery ; v.26)
Includes bibliographies and index
ISBN 0-7216-6141-6 : £21.50 B81-26951

617′.43 — Man. Obesity. Surgery — *Conference proceedings*

Surgical management of obesity / edited by J.D. Maxwell, J-C. Gazet, T.R.E. Pilkington. — London : Academic Press, 1980. — xiii,355p : ill ; 24cm
Conference papers. — Includes index
ISBN 0-12-792818-9 : £15.00 : CIP rev.
B80-10639

617′.44 — Man. Bone marrow. Transplantation — *Conference proceedings*

ICN-UCLA Symposia on Biology of Bone Marrow Transplantation *(1980 : Keystone).* Biology of bone marrow transplantation / [proceedings of the 1980 ICN-UCLA Symposia on Biology of Bone Marrow Transplantation held in Keystone, Colorado, February 17-21, 1980] ; edited by Robert Peter Gale, C. Fred Fox ; managing editor Frances J. Stusser. — New York ; London : Academic Press, 1980. — xx,566p : ill ; 24cm. — (ICN-UCLA Symposia on Molecular and Cellular Biology ; v.17)
Includes index
ISBN 0-12-273960-4 : £25.80 B81-14031

617′.46043 — Children. Reproductive system. Congenital abnormalities. Surgery — *Conference proceedings*

Symposium on Pediatric Urology *(2nd : 1979 : Freiburg i. Br.).* Malformations of the external genitalia : 2nd Syposium on Pediatric Urology, Freiburg i. Br., October 6, 1979 / volume editors M. Westenfelder and R.H. Whitaker. — Basel ; London : Karger, c1981. — 108p : ill ; 23cm. — (Monographs in pediatrics ; v.12)
Includes bibliographies and index
ISBN 3-8055-1509-x (pbk) : £16.00 B81-26226

617′.461 — Man. Artificial kidneys — *Conference proceedings*

International Symposium on Hemoperfusion : Kidney and Liver Supports and Detoxification *(1979 : Haifa).* Hemoperfusion : kidney and liver support and detoxification / [proceedings of the International Symposium on Hemoperfusion : Kidney and Liver Supports and Detoxification held in Haifa, Israel, August 25-26, 1979] ; [sponsored by the National Institute of Arthritis, Metabolism, and Digestive Diseases et al.]. — Washington ; London : Hemisphere
Part 1 / edited by S. Sideman and T.M.S. Chang. — c1980. — vi,473p : ill ; 25cm
Bibliography: p409-467. - Includes index
ISBN 0-89116-152-x : £23.75
Also classified at 617′.556 B81-10205

617′.461 — Man. Kidneys. Caculi. Surgery. Use of ultrasonic waves — *German texts*

Berührungsfreie Nierensteinzertrümmerung durch extrakorporal erzeugte, fokussierte Stoßwellen : Herrn Professor Dr. E. Schmiedt zum 60. Geburtstag am 20.11.1980 gewidmet / Ch. Chaussy ... [et al.], Urologische Klinik und Poliklinik ... [et al.] ; Bandherausgeber Ch. Chaussy und G. Staehler. — Basel ; London : Karger, 1980. — 93p : ill(some col) ; 23cm. — (Beiträge zur Urologie ; Bd.2)
Bibliography: p89-93
ISBN 3-8055-1901-x (pbk) : £14.85 B81-21122

617′.461059 — Man. Kidneys. Haemodialysis & transplantation

Replacement of renal function by dialysis / edited by William Drukker, Frank M. Parsons, John F. Maher. — The Hague ; London : Nijhoff, 1979. — xx,744p : ill,ports ; 26cm
Originally published: 1978. — Includes index
ISBN 90-247-2042-7 (cased) : Unpriced
ISBN 90-247-2227-6 (pbk) : Unpriced
B81-22424

617′.461059 — Man. Kidneys. Haemodialysis — *For nursing*

Gutch, C. F.. Review of hemodialysis for nurses and dialysis personnel / C.F. Gutch, Martha H. Stoner. — 3rd ed. — St. Louis ; London : Mosby, 1980. — xv,241p : ill ; 22cm. — (Mosby′s comprehensive review series)
Previous ed.: 1975. — Bibliography: p212-213. - Includes index
ISBN 0-8016-1994-7 (pbk) : £12.00 B81-08170

617′.461059 — Man. Kidneys. Pentoneal dialysis — *Conference proceedings*

Peritoneal dialysis / editors Robert C. Atkins, Napier M. Thomson, Peter C. Farrell. — Edinburgh : Churchill Livingstone, 1981. — 451p : ill ; 24cm
Includes bibliographies and index
ISBN 0-443-02394-8 : £25.00 : CIP rev.
B81-06046

617′.461059 — Man. Kidneys. Peritoneal dialysis

Peritoneal dialysis / edited by Karl D. Nolph. — The Hague ; Lonodn : Nijhoff, 1981. — xviii,393p : ill ; 25cm. — (Developments in nephrology ; v.2)
Includes index
ISBN 90-247-2477-5 : Unpriced B81-29287

617′.461059′019 — Man. Kidneys. Haemodialysis & transplantation. Psychological aspects

Psychonephrology. — New York ; London : Plenum
1: Psychological factors in hemodialysis and transplantation / edited by Norman B. Levy. — c1981. — xviii,287p : ill ; 24cm
Conference papers. — Includes index
ISBN 0-306-40586-5 : Unpriced B81-26028

617′.461059′05 — Man. Kidneys. Haemodialysis & transplantation — *Conference proceedings* — *Serials*

Proceedings of the European Dialysis and Transplant Association. — Vol.17. — London : Pitman Medical, 1980. — xix,771p
ISBN 0-272-79602-6 : Unpriced B81-15279

Proceedings of the European Dialysis and Transplant Association. — Vol.18. — London : Pitman, Dec.1981. — [816]p
ISBN 0-272-79666-2 (pbk) : £35.00 : CIP entry
ISSN 0308-9401 B81-33871

617′.4610592 — Man. Kidneys. Transplantation

Renal transplantation : theory and practice / edited by Jean Hamburger ... [et al.]. — 2nd ed. — Baltimore ; London : Williams & Wilkins, c1981. — xxiii,384p : ill ; 24cm
Previous ed.: Baltimore : Williams and Wilkins, 1972
ISBN 0-683-03872-9 : £45.00 B81-28497

617′.461′0941 — Great Britain. Man. Kidneys. Donations. Attitudes of public

Lewis, Barbara R.. New dimensions of kidney donorship / Barbara R. Lewis. — Manchester (P.O. Box 88 Manchester M60 1QD) : Department of Management Sciences University of Manchester Institute of Science and Technology, 1981. — 30p : 1ill,forms ; 31cm. — (Occasional paper / Department of Management Sciences, University of Manchester Institute of Science and Technology ; no.8106)
Bibliography: p25
Unpriced (pbk) B81-30913

617′.463 — Men. Foreskin. Circumcision — *Jewish viewpoints*

Pavey, Roger V.. The kindest cut of all / Roger V. Pavey. — Bognor Regis : New Horizon, c1981. — 215p ; 21cm
ISBN 0-86116-121-1 : £4.75 B81-21823

617′.463 — Men. Reproductive system. Surgery

Surgery of the male reproductive tract / edited by L.I. Lipshultz, J.N. Corriere, Jr. and E.S.E. Hafez. — The Hague ; London : Nijhoff, 1980. — viii,266p : ill ; 28cm. — (Clinics in andrology ; v.2)
Includes bibliographies and index
ISBN 90-247-2315-9 : Unpriced B81-06985

617′.471 — Man. Skeletal system. Therapy. External fixators

Advances in external fixation / Renner M. Johnston, editor ; selected papers and discussions from the Continuing Education Course on External Fixation, presented by the Department of Orthopedics and the Office of Postgraduate Medical Education, University of Colorado Health Sciences Center. — Miami : Symposia Spcialists ; Chicago ; London : Distributed by Year Book Medical Publishers, c1980. — x,181p : ill ; 24cm
Includes bibliographies and index
ISBN 0-8151-4909-3 : Unpriced B81-29477

617′.472 — Man. Joints. Rheumatoid arthritis. Surgery

Gschwend, Norbert. Surgical treatment of rheumatoid arthritis / Norbert Gschwend ; with a contribution by Albert Böni ; translated by Gottfried Stiasny. — Philadelphia ; London : Saunders, 1980. — x,310p : ill(some col.) ; 25cm
Translation of: Die operative Behandlung der chronischen Polyarthritis. 2. Aufl. — Bibliography: p283-303. — Includes index
ISBN 0-7216-4332-9 : £40.50 B81-26962

Surgery in rheumatoid arthritis : an up-to-date account / volume editor I. Goldie ; contributors B. Althoff ... [et al.]. — Basel ; London : Karger, 1981. — 213p : ill ; 25cm. — (Reconstruction surgery and traumatology ; v.18)
Includes bibliographies and index
ISBN 3-8055-1445-x : £27.50 B81-21143

617′.48 — Man. Nervous system. Surgery

Current surgical management of neurologic disease / edited by Charles B. Wilson and Julian T. Hoff. — New York ; Edinburgh : Churchill Livingstone, 1980. — xii,355p : ill ; 25cm
Includes bibliographies and index
ISBN 0-443-08042-9 : £22.00 B81-02787

Nerve repair and regeneration : its clinical and experimental basis / edited by Don L. Jewett, H. Relton McCarroll, Jr.. — St Louis ; London : Mosby, 1980. — xiv,371p : ill ; 27cm
Includes bibliographies and index
ISBN 0-8016-2507-6 : £41.75 B81-12541

617′.48′005 — Man. Nervous system. Surgery — *Conference proceedings* — *Serials*

Clinical neurosurgery : proceedings of the Congress of Neurological Surgeons. — Vol.27 (1979). — Baltimore ; London : Williams & Wilkins, 1980. — xxxiv,648p
ISBN 0-683-02022-6 : £53.00
ISSN 0069-4827 B81-20725

617′.48′005 — Man. Nervous system. Surgery — *Serials*

Topical reviews in neurosurgery. — Vol.1. — Bristol : Wright, Feb.1982. — [208]p
ISBN 0-7236-0576-9 : £14.00 : CIP entry
B81-37599

617.5 — REGIONAL MEDICINE AND SURGERY

617'.51 — Man. Ears, nose & throat. Diseases

Cody, D. Thane R.. Diseases of the ears, nose and throat : a guide to diagnosis and management / D. Thane R. Cody, Eugene B. Kern, Bruce W. Pearson. — Chicago ; London : Year Book Medical, c1981. — xiii,512p : ill ; 24cm
Includes bibliographies and index
ISBN 0-8151-1798-1 : £30.50 B81-14158

Farb, Stanley N.. The ear, nose, and throat book : a doctor's guide to better health / Stanley N. Farb. — New York : Appleton-Century-Crofts ; London : Prentice-Hall, c1980. — 158p : ill ; 21cm
Includes index
ISBN 0-8385-2021-9 (cased) : £8.40
ISBN 0-8385-2020-0 (pbk) : £3.85 B81-00933

Foxen, E. H. Miles. Lecture notes on diseases of the ear, nose and throat / E.H. Miles Foxen. — 5th ed. — Oxford : Blackwell Scientific, 1980. — xi,207p : ill ; 22cm
Previous ed.: 1976. — Includes index
ISBN 0-632-00652-8 (pbk) : £4.75 B81-12567

Ludman, Harold. ABC of ear nose and throat / Harold Ludman. — London : British Medical Association, c 1981. — 51p : ill ; 30cm
'Articles published in the British medical journal'
ISBN 0-7279-0078-1 (pbk) : Unpriced B81-29877

617'.51 — Man. Head. Injuries. Sequelae — *Study regions: Tyne and Wear (Metropolitan County). Newcastle upon Tyne*

Cartlidge, N. E. F.. Head injury. — Eastbourne : Saunders, Nov.1981. — [256]p
ISBN 0-7216-2443-x : £17.50 : CIP entry B81-30391

617'.51043 — Man. Head. Congenital abnormalities — *Conference proceedings*

Symposium on diagnosis and treatment of craniofacial anomalies : proceedings of the Symposium of the Educational Foundation of the American Society of Plastic and Reconstructive Surgeons held at New York University Medical Center, New York, May 3-5, 1976 / editors John Marquis Converse, Joseph G. MaCarthy, Donald Wood-Smith. — St. Louis ; London : Mosby, 1979. — xviii,534p : ill ; 29cm
Includes bibliographies and index
ISBN 0-8016-1030-3 : £59.50 B81-10033

617'.51059 — Man. Head & neck. Reconstruction surgery

Reconstruction of the head and neck / edited by Malcolm A. Lesavoy. — Baltimore ; London : Williams & Wilkins, c1981. — xiv,333p : ill ; 26cm
Includes index
ISBN 0-683-04949-6 : £51.50 B81-20760

617'.5106 — Man. Head. Injuries. Therapy

Craniocerebral trauma / editors H. Krayenbühl, P.E. Maspes, W.H. Sweet ; list of contributors R. Braakman ... [et al.]. — Basel ; London : Karger, 1981. — xiv,400p : ill ; 25cm. — (Progress in neurological surgery ; v.10)
Includes bibliographies and index
ISBN 3-8055-0134-x : £74.50 B81-28314

617'.51072 — Man. Head. Pain

Heyck, Hartwig. Headache and facial pain : differential diagnosis, pathogenesis, treatment / by Hartwig Heyck ; translated by Navin Dalal. — Chicago ; London : Year Book Medical, 1981. — v,274p : ill ; 19cm. — (Thieme flexibook)
Translation of: Der Kopfschmerz. 4., neubearb. Aufl. — Includes bibliographies and index
ISBN 0-8151-4411-3 (pbk) B81-31147

617'.510757'05 — Man. Head. Radiology — *Serials*

Radiology of the skull and brain. — Vol.5. — St Louis ; London : C.V. Mosby, 1981. — 533p in various pagings
ISBN 0-8016-3662-0 : £62.75 B81-26599

617'.5140757 — Man. Skull. Diagnosis. Radiography

Shapiro, Robert. Radiology of the normal skull / Robert Shapiro. — Chicago ; London : Year Book Medical, c1981. — xi,366p : ill ; 27cm
Includes bibliographies and index
ISBN 0-8151-7631-7 : £70.00 B81-18964

617'.52 — Man. Maxillofacial region. Diseases

Topazian, Richard G.. Management of infections of the oral and maxillofacial regions / Richard G. Topazian, Morton H. Goldberg. — Philadelphia ; London : Saunders, 1981. — xii,465p : ill ; 27cm
Includes bibliographies and index
ISBN 0-7216-8879-9 : £28.75 B81-34827

617'.52044 — Man. Face. Injuries. Surgery

The **Primary** care of facial injuries / edited by Elvin G. Zook. — London : Edward Arnold, 1981, c1980. — xiii,170p : ill ; 22cm
Originally published: Littleton : PSG Publishing, c1980. — Includes bibliographies and index
ISBN 0-7131-4391-6 : £13.50 B81-25989

617'.52059 — Man. Maxillofacial region. Preprosthetic surgery

Starshak, Thomas J.. Preprosthetic oral and maxillofacial surgery / Thomas J. Starshak, Bruce Sanders. — St. Louis ; London : Mosby, 1980. — xiv,351p : ill ; 27cm
Includes bibliographies and index
ISBN 0-8016-4757-6 : Unpriced B81-08666

617'.52059 — Man. Maxillofacial region. Surgery

Oral and maxillofacial surgery / [edited by] Daniel M. Laskin. — St. Louis ; London : Mosby, 1980
Includes bibliographies and index
Vol.1: The biomedical and clinical basis for surgical practice. — St. Louis ; London : Mosby, 1980. — xiii,736p : ill(some col.),forms ; 265cm
Includes bibliographies and index
ISBN 0-8016-2822-9 : £59.25 B81-08137

617'.520592 — Man. Face. Cosmetic surgery

Pirruccello, Frank W.. Plastic and reconstructive surgery of the face : cosmetic surgery / Frank W. Pirruccello ; with illustrations by Ruth Mark. — Baltimore ; London : Williams & Wilkins, c1981. — xiii,88p : ill ; 29cm
Bibliography: p85-88
ISBN 0-683-06891-1 : £31.25 B81-24339

617'.522 — Man. Mouth. Surgery

Moore, J. R.. Principles of oral surgery. — 3rd ed. — Manchester : Manchester University Press, Dec.1981. — [264]p
Previous ed.: 1976
ISBN 0-7190-0801-8 (pbk) : £6.50 : CIP entry B81-33880

617'.522 — Man. Temporomandibular region. Diseases

Ogus, Hugh D.. Common disorders of the temporomandibular joint / Hugh D. Ogus and Paul A. Toller ; with a foreword by Daniel M. Laskin. — Bristol : John Wright, 1981. — xi,105p : ill ; 22cm. — (A Dental practitioner handbook ; no.26)
Bibliography: p97-100. — Includes index
ISBN 0-7236-0574-2 (pbk) : Unpriced B81-15761

617'.522'0076 — Man. Oral region. Diseases — *Questions & answers — For dentistry*

Wood, Norman K.. Review of diagnosis, oral medicine, radiology, and treatment planning / Norman K. Wood. — St. Louis ; London : Mosby, 1979. — xii,265p : ill ; 26cm
ISBN 0-8016-5614-1 (pbk) : £12.00 B81-08028

617'.522059 — Man. Dentofacial region. Deformities. Surgery

Epker, Bruce N.. Dentofacial deformities : surgical-orthodontic correction / Bruce N. Epker, Larry M. Wolford. — St. Louis ; London : Mosby, 1980. — x,477p : ill ; 29cm
Bibliography: p471-477
ISBN 0-8016-1606-9 : £47.50 B81-19043

617'.52207 — Man. Oral region. Pathology — *For dentistry*

Cawson, R. A.. Aids to oral pathology and diagnosis / R.A. Cawson. — Edinburgh : Churchill Livingstone, 1981. — 126p ; 22cm. — (Churchill Livingstone dental books)
Includes index
ISBN 0-443-01871-5 (pbk) : £3.50 B81-23688

617'.5225 — Man. Cleft palate

Advances in the management of cleft palate / edited by M. Edwards, A.C.H. Watson ; foreword by D.R. Millard Jr. — Edinburgh : Churchill Livingstone, 1980. — xii,298p : ill ; 25cm
Includes index
ISBN 0-443-01601-1 : £12.00 : CIP rev. B80-07399

617'.539 — Man. Thyroid & parathyroid glands. Surgery

Surgery of the thyroid and parathyroid glands. — 2nd ed. / edited by Cornelius E. Sedgwick and Blake Cady in collaboration with Eugene P. Clerkin ... [et al.]. — Philadelphia ; London : Saunders, 1980. — x,241p : ill ; 25cm. — (Major problems in clinical surgery ; v.15)
Previous ed.: published as Surgery of the thyroid gland / by Cornelius E. Sedgwick. 1974. — Includes bibliographies and index
ISBN 0-7216-8054-2 : £12.50 B81-03901

617'.54 — Man. Thorax. Diseases

Disabling chest disease : prevention and care : a report of the Royal College of Physicians by the College Committee on Thoracic Medicine. — [London] : [Royal College of Physicians of London], 1981. — 20p : ill ; 28cm
Originally published: Journal of the Royal College of Physicians of London, v.15, no.2, April 1981
Unpriced (pbk) B81-18317

Thoracic medicine / edited by Peter Emerson. — London : Butterworths, 1981. — xx,1015p,[61]p of plates : ill(some col.) ; 26cm
Includes bibliographies and index
ISBN 0-407-00210-3 : Unpriced B81-28218

617'.54 — Man. Thorax. Surgery. - *Conference proceedings*

The **Present** state of thoracic surgery. — Tunbridge Wells : Pitman Medical, Apr.1981. — [232]p
Conference papers
ISBN 0-272-79592-5 (pbk) : £15.00 : CIP entry B81-07614

617'.54044 — Man. Thorax. Injuries — *Conference proceedings*

Oesophageal and other thoracic problems. — Bristol : Wright, Feb.1982. — [192]p
Conference papers
ISBN 0-7236-0640-4 (pbk) : £13.50 : CIP entry B81-40264

617'.54059'0222 — Man. Thorax. Surgery — *Illustrations*

. Atlas of thoracic surgery / edited by Boris V. Patrovsky ; translated from the Russian by Ludmila Aksenova ; with a foreword to the Enlish language edition by Michael E. DeBakey. — St. Louis ; London : Mosby, 1980. — 2v.(xi,761p) : ill(some col.) ; 30cm
Translation of: Atlas grudnoĭ khirurgii
ISBN 0-8016-3832-1 : Unpriced B81-08155

617'.54062 — Man. Thorax. Physiotherapy

Gaskell, D. V.. The Brompton Hospital guide to chest physiotherapy / D.V. Gaskell and B.A. Webber. — 4th ed. / revised by B.A. Webber. — Oxford : Blackwell Scientific, 1980. — ix,120p : ill ; 22cm
Previous ed.: 1977. — Bibliography: p115. — Includes index
ISBN 0-632-00576-9 (pbk) : £5.50 : CIP rev. B80-29790

617'.548 — Man. Oesophagus. Diseases - *Conference proceedings*

Medical and surgical problems of the esophagus. — London : Academic Press, July 1981. — [430]p. — (Proceedings of the Serono symposia, ISSN 0308-5503 ; no.43)
Conference papers
ISBN 0-12-671450-9 : CIP entry B81-16846

617'.55059'0926 — Man. Abdomen. Surgery — *Case studies*
Schein, Clarence J.. Introduction to abdominal surgery : fifty clinical studies / Clarence J. Schein. — Hagerstown ; London : Harper & Row, c1981. — xiv,521p : ill ; 24cm
Includes bibliographies and index
ISBN 0-06-142381-5 : £19.50 B81-23687

617'.550757 — Man. Abdomen. Diagnosis. Radiography
Abdomen / edited by Abass Alavi, Peter H. Arger. — New York ; London : Grune & Stratton, c1980. — xi,448p : ill ; 26cm. — (Multiple imaging procedures ; v.3)
Includes bibliographies and index
ISBN 0-8089-1306-9 : £25.00 B81-14024

617'.553 — Man. Gastrointestinal tract. Surgical stomata
Stoma care. — Beaconsfield (20 Chiltern Hills Rd., Beaconsfield, Bucks. HP9 1PL) : Beaconsfield, July 1981. — 1v.
ISBN 0-906584-04-3 : £9.50 : CIP entry
Also classified at 617'.919 B81-13874

617'.556 — Man. Artificial livers
Lopukhin œh IU. M.. Hemosorption / Y.M. Lopukhin, M.N. Molodenkov ; translated from the Russian by Nicholas Bobrov and Ludmila Aksenova. — St. Louis ; London : Mosby, 1980. — xi,309p : ill ; 26cm
Translation of: Gemosorpt͡siia. — Bibliography: p285-299. - Includes index
ISBN 0-8016-3029-0 : £28.00 B81-08143

617'.556 — Man. Artificial livers — *Conference proceedings*
International Symposium on Hemoperfusion : Kidney and Liver Supports and Detoxification *(1979 : Haifa)*. Hemoperfusion : kidney and liver support and detoxification / [proceedings of the International Symposium on Hemoperfusion : Kidney and Liver Supports and Detoxification held in Haifa, Israel, August 25-26, 1979] ; [sponsored by the National Institute of Arthritis, Metabolism, and Digestive Diseases et al.]. — Washington ; London : Hemisphere
Part 1 / edited by S. Sideman and T.M.S. Chang. — c1980. — vi,473p : ill ; 25cm
Bibliography: p409-467. - Includes index
ISBN 0-89116-152-x : £23.75
Primary classification 617'.461 B81-10205

617'.556 — Man. Biliary tract. Surgery
Kune, Gabriel A.. The practice of biliary surgery / Gabriel A. Kune, Avni Sali. — 2nd ed. — Oxford : Blackwell Scientific, 1980. — xvi,462p : ill ; 25cm
Previous ed.: Boston, Mass. : Little Brown, 1972. — Includes bibliographies and index
ISBN 0-632-00589-0 : £32.50 : CIP rev. B80-13859

617'.556 — Man. Foetal liver cells. Transplantation — *Conference proceedings*
International Symposium on Fetal Liver Transplantation *(1st : 1979 : Pesaro)*. Fetal liver transplantation : current concepts and future directions : proceedings of the First International Symposium on Fetal Liver Transplantation, Pesaro, Italy, September 1979 / editors Guido Lucarelli, Theodor M. Fliedner, Robert Peter Gale. — Amsterdam ; Oxford : Excerpta Medica, 1980. — vii,325p : ill ; 25cm. — (International congress series ; 514)
Includes bibliographies and index
ISBN 90-219-0462-4 : £25.30 B81-04966

617'.556059 — Man. Biliary tract. Surgery
Hepatic, biliary & pancreatic surgery / edited by John S. Najarian and John P. Delaney. — Miami : Symposia Specialists ; Chicago ; London : Distributed by Year Book Medical, c1980. — 739,xxp : ill ; 24cm
Conference papers. — Includes index
ISBN 0-8151-6331-2 : £66.00
Also classified at 617'.557 B81-08110

Surgery of the gall bladder and bile ducts / editors Lord Smith of Marlow, Dame Sheila Sherlock. — 2nd ed. — London : Butterworths, 1981. — xii,495p : ill ; 24cm
Previous ed.: 1964. — Includes bibliographies and index
ISBN 0-407-00118-2 : Unpriced : CIP rev. B81-04288

617'.557 — Man. Pancreas. Surgery
Hepatic, biliary & pancreatic surgery / edited by John S. Najarian and John P. Delaney. — Miami : Symposia Specialists ; Chicago ; London : Distributed by Year Book Medical, c1980. — 739,xxp : ill ; 24cm
Conference papers. — Includes index
ISBN 0-8151-6331-2 : £66.00
Primary classification 617'.556059 B81-08110

617'.557'0592 — Man. Pancreas. Transplantation
Transplantation of the pancreas / edited by Jules Traeger and Jean-Michel Dubernard. — New York ; London : Grune & Stratton, c1981. — x,237p : ill ; 26cm. — (A Transplantation proceedings reprint)
Includes index
ISBN 0-8089-1396-4 : £19.40 B81-35744

617'.57072 — Man. Arms & shoulders. Pain
Pain in shoulder and arm : an integrated view / edited by J.M. Greep ... [et al.]. — The Hague ; London : Nijhoff, 1979. — ix,305p : ill ; 25cm. — (Developments in surgery ; v.1)
Conference papers. — Includes index
ISBN 90-247-2146-6 : Unpriced B81-03967

617'.572 — Man. Shoulders. Disorders
Kessel, Lipmann. Clinical disorders of the shoulder. — Edinburgh : Churchill Livingstone, July 1981. — [192]p
ISBN 0-443-01904-5 : £14.00 : CIP entry B81-20506

617'.574 — Man. Wrists. Acute injuries. Treatment
Weeks, Paul M.. Acute bone and joint injuries of the hand and wrist : a clinical guide to management / Paul M. Weeks with contributions by Louis A. Gilula ... [et al.] ; illustrations by Vicki Friedman. — St. Louis ; London : Mosby, 1981. — viii,299p : ill ; 27cm
Bibliography: p283-290. — Includes index
ISBN 0-8016-5373-8 : £27.75
Primary classification 617'.575 B81-18973

617'.575 — Man. Hands. Acute injuries. Treatment
Weeks, Paul M.. Acute bone and joint injuries of the hand and wrist : a clinical guide to management / Paul M. Weeks with contributions by Louis A. Gilula ... [et al.] ; illustrations by Vicki Friedman. — St. Louis ; London : Mosby, 1981. — viii,299p : ill ; 27cm
Bibliography: p283-290. — Includes index
ISBN 0-8016-5373-8 : £27.75
Also classified at 617'.574 B81-18973

617'.575 — Patients with hand injuries. Rehabilitation
Wynn Parry, C. B.. Rehabilitation of the hand. — 4th ed. / by C.W. Wynn Parry, assisted by Maureen Salter and Doris Millar with a contribution from Ian Fletcher. — London : Butterworth, 1981. — xv,409p : ill,forms ; 26cm
Previous ed.: 1973. — Includes bibliographies and index
ISBN 0-407-38502-9 : Unpriced B81-17656

617'.575044 — Man. Hands. Injuries. Surgery
Beasley, Robert W.. Hand injuries / Robert W. Beasley. — Philadelphia ; London : Saunders, 1981. — x,384p : ill ; 27cm
Bibliography: p369-372. — Includes index
ISBN 0-7216-1607-0 : £36.50 B81-34828

617'.575059 — Man. Hands. Rheumatoid arthritis. Surgery
Backhouse, Kenneth M.. A colour atlas of rheumatoid hand surgery / Kenneth M. Backhouse, Stewart H. Harrison, Ralph T. Hutchings. — London : Wolfe, c1981. — 216p : ill(some col.),forms ; 32cm. — (Wolfe medical atlases)
Bibliography: p211-212. — Includes index
ISBN 0-7234-0766-5 : £35.00 B81-29683

617'.575059 — Man. Hands. Surgery
The **Practice** of hand surgery / edited by D.W. Lamb and K. Kuczynski. — Oxford : Blackwell Scientific, 1981. — xvi,565p : ill ; 25cm
Includes bibliographies and index
ISBN 0-632-00295-6 : £45.00 B81-28242

617'.575059 — Patients with hand injuries. Rehabilitation. Use of splints
Fess, Elaine Ewing. Hand splinting : principles and methods / Elaine Ewing Fess, Karan S. Gettle, James W. Strickland ; drawings by Craig Gosling and Carol Stahl. — St. Louis ; London : Mosby, 1981. — xvii,317p : ill(some col.),1port ; 26cm
Bibliography: p304-309. - Includes index
ISBN 0-8016-1569-0 : £20.50 B81-14988

617'.58059 — Man. Limbs. Amputation & prostheses
American Academy of Orthopaedic Surgeons. Atlas of limb prosthetics : surgical and prosthetic principles / American Academy of Orthopaedic Surgeons. — St. Louis ; London : Mosby, 1981. — xiii,668p : ill ; 29cm
Includes bibliographies and index
ISBN 0-8016-0058-8 : £59.00 B81-19046

617'.58059 — Man. Limbs. Joints. Arthroplasty — *Conference proceedings*
Revision arthroplasty : proceedings of a symposium held at Sheffield University, 22nd-24th March 1979 / edited by R.A. Elson, A.D.S. Caldwell. — 2nd ed. — Oxford (52 New Inn Hall St., Oxford, OX1 2BS) : Medical Education Services, 1981. — 100p,[2]p of plates : ill(some col.) ; 24cm
Previous ed.: 1979. — Includes bibliographies
ISBN 0-906817-12-9 (pbk) : £5.00 B81-33253

617'.580592 — Man. Joints. Prostheses. Engineering aspects
Introduction to the biomechanics of joints and joint replacement / edited by D. Dowson and V. Wright. — London : Mechanical Engineering Publications, 1981. — x,254p : ill ; 31cm
Includes bibliographies and index
ISBN 0-85298-384-0 : Unpriced B81-23702

617'.580592 — Man. Joints. Prostheses. Lubrication & wear
Dumbleton, John H.. Tribology of natural and artificial joints / John H. Dumbleton. — Amsterdam ; Oxford : Elsevier Scientific, 1981. — xv,460p : ill ; 25cm. — (Tribology series ; 3)
Includes index
ISBN 0-444-41898-9 : £29.63 : CIP rev. B80-10641

617'.581 — Man. Hips. Disorders — *Conference proceedings*
The **Hip** : proceedings of the Seventh open scientific meeting of The Hip Society, 1979. — St. Louis ; London : Mosby, 1979. — xii,334p : ill ; 26cm
Includes bibliographies and index
ISBN 0-8016-0033-2 : £31.25 B81-10034

617'.582059 — Athletes. Knees. Surgery — *Conference proceedings*
Symposium on the athlete's knee : surgical repair and reconstruction, Hilton Head, South Carolina, June, 1978 / American Academy of Orthopaedic Surgeons. — St. Louis ; London : Mosby, 1980. — x,218p : ill(some col.) ; 26cm
Includes bibliographies and index
ISBN 0-8016-0077-4 : £31.25 B81-09762

617'.582059 — Man. Knees. Joints. Arthroscopic surgery
Dandy, David J.. Arthroscopic surgery of the knee / David J. Dandy ; foreword by R.W. Jackson. — Edinburgh : Churchill Livingstone, 1981. — 122p : ill(some col.) ; 29cm. — (Current problems in orthopaedics)
Includes bibliographies and index
ISBN 0-443-02047-7 : £28.00 B81-29371

617'.584 — Man. Arteries. Reconstruction surgery — *Conference proceedings*
Arterial reconstruction of the lower limb : proceedings of an international symposium held in Leuven, Belgium, 7th June 1980 / [sponsored by Meadox Medicals Inc.] ; host R. Suy ; moderator J.J. Cranley ; editors R. Suy, H.L. Shaw. — Oxford (52 New Inn Hall St., Oxford OX1 2BS) : Medical Education Services, c1980. — 99p : ill ; 24cm
Cover title: International symposium on arterial reconstruction of the lower limb
ISBN 0-906817-06-4 (pbk) : £3.50 B81-04896

617'.584059 — Man. Lower legs. Surgery

Rütt, A.. Surgery of the lower leg and foot / A. Rütt ; translated by G. Stiasny. — English ed. — Philadelphia ; London : Saunders, 1980. — ix,358p : ill(some col.) ; 30cm. — (Atlas of orthopaedic operations ; v.2)
Translated from German. — Previous ed.: published as Unterschenkel und Fuss. Stuttgart : Thieme, 1973. — Bibliography: p341-353. — Includes index
ISBN 0-7216-4446-5 : £69.50 B81-11822

617'.585 — Chiropody. Homeopathic techniques

Khan, M. Taufiq. An introduction of biochemic system of medicine for chiropodists / by M. Taufiq Khan. — Edgware (134 Montrose Ave., Edgware, Middx) : M.T. Khan on behalf of Institute of Molecular Medicine, 1980. — 24p : ill ; 21cm
Bibliography: p23
£1.00 (pbk) B81-12501

617'.585 — Man. Feet. Diseases

Common foot disorders : diagnosis and management : a general clinical guide / edited by Donald Neale. — Edinburgh : Churchill Livingstone, 1981. — xii,252p : ill,2forms ; 25cm
Includes bibliographies and index
ISBN 0-443-01938-x (pbk) : £10.95 B81-37099

617'.585'002541 — Great Britain. Chiropodists — *Directories — Serials*

[The Chiropodists register]. . — 1980. — London ([York House, Westminster Bridge Rd, SE1 7UA]) : Printed and published under the authority of the Chiropodists Board, [1980]. — 173p
Unpriced B81-09701

617'.58506 — Man. Feet. Therapy — *For running*

Weisenfeld, Murray F.. The runners' repair manual : a complete program for diagnosing and treating your foot, leg and back problems / by Murray F. Weisenfeld with Barbara Burr. — London : W.H. Allen, 1981. — xvi,193p : ill ; 23
Originally published: New York : St. Martin's Press, 1980. — Includes index
ISBN 0-491-02934-9 : £6.95 B81-27075

617.6 — DENTISTRY

617.6 — Dentistry

A **Companion** to dental studies. — Oxford : Blackwell Scientific, Aug.1981
Vol.1
Book 2: Dental anatomy and embryology. — [416]p
ISBN 0-632-00799-0 : £12.00 : CIP entry B81-24649

617.6 — Dentistry. Surgery

Hampson, E. L.. Hampson's textbook of operative dentistry / E.L. Hampson. — 4th ed. — London : Heinemann Medical, 1980. — 234p : ill ; 26cm
Previous ed.: 1973. — Includes bibliographies and index
ISBN 0-433-13202-7 : £13.75 B81-00130

617.6'0023'42 — England. Dentistry — *Career guides — For graduates*

Careers in dentistry. — London (7, Marylebone Rd., NW1 5HH) : Council for Postraduate Medical Education in England and Wales, 1980. — 48p ; 21cm
Cover title
£2.00 (pbk) B81-40405

617.6'0025'41 — Great Britain. Dentists — *Directories — Serials*

General Dental Council. The dentists register / the General Dental Council. — 1981. — London (37 Wimpole St., W1M 8DQ) : The Council, [1981]. — 44,429p
£12.50 B81-29059

617.6'005 — Dentistry — *Serials*

Current therapy in dentistry. — Vol.7. — St. Louis ; London : C.V. Mosby, 1980. — xiv,552p
ISBN 0-8016-1189-x : £35.75 B81-12405

The **Year** book of dentistry. — 1980. — Chicago ; London : Year Book Medical Publishers, c1980. — 386p
ISBN 0-8151-4100-9 : Unpriced
ISSN 0084-3717 B81-04894

617.6'007'1141 — Great Britain. Dentists. Professional education. Curriculum — *Proposals*

General Dental Council. Recommendations concerning the dental curriculum May 1980. — London (37 Wimpole St., W1M 8DQ) : General Dental Council, [1980]. — 12p ; 21cm
Unpriced (pbk) B81-11756

617.6'007'1141 — Great Britain. Universities. Curriculum subjects: Dentistry. Postgraduate courses — *Lists*

Summary of postgraduate degrees, diplomas and courses in dentistry / Councils for Postgraduate Medical Education National Advice Centre. — [London] ([7 Marylebone Rd., NW1 5HH]) : published by the Council for Postgraduate Medical Education in England and Wales on behalf of the three Councils of the United Kingdom, 1980. — 22p ; 30cm
£2.00 (unbound) B81-34252

617.6'0072 — Dentistry. Research. Methodology

Darby, Michele Leonardi. Research methods for oral health professionals : an introduction / Michele Leonardi Darby, Denise M. Bowen. — St. Louis ; London : Mosby, 1980. — xiii,193p : ill,facsims,forms ; 26cm
Includes bibliographies and index
ISBN 0-8016-1207-1 (pbk) : £10.50 B81-08162

617.6'0076 — Dentistry — *Questions & answers — For dental assistants*

Review of dental assisting / edited by Betty A. Ladley, Shirley A. Wilson. — St. Louis ; London : Mosby, 1980. — xi,256p : ill ; 26cm
Includes bibliographies
ISBN 0-8016-2806-7 (pbk) : £8.25 B81-08725

617.6'0076 — Dentistry — *Questions & answers — For dental hygiene*

Comprehensive review for dental hygienists / edited by Shailer Peterson. — 4th ed. — St. Louis ; London : Mosby, 1980. — x,348p : ill,forms ; 26cm
Previous ed.: 1975. — Includes bibliographies and index
ISBN 0-8016-3802-x (pbk) : Unpriced B81-19529

617.6'0092'4 — Sri Lanka. Dentistry. De Silva, Ivan — *Biographies*

De Silva, Ivan. Bygone days / Ivan de Silva. — Ilfracombe : Stockwell, 1981. — 92p : 1ill ; 19cm
ISBN 0-7223-1505-8 : £4.00 B81-39970

617.6'01 — Dental hygiene

Comprehensive dental hygiene care / Irene R. Woodall ... [et al.]. — St. Louis ; London : Mosby, 1980. — xviii,506p : ill,forms ; 27cm
Bibliography: p477-489. — Includes index
ISBN 0-8016-5624-9 : £14.75 B81-05822

617.6'01 — Dental patients. Behaviour modification — *For preventive dentistry*

Weinstein, Philip. Changing human behavior : strategies for preventive dentistry / Philip Weinstein, Tracy Getz. — St. Louis ; London : Mosby, 1980. — xvii,134p : ill,forms ; 24cm
Bibliography: p128-131. - Includes index
ISBN 0-8016-5405-x (pbk) : £7.50 B81-09599

617.6'01 — Dentistry. Disinfection & sterilisation

Calmes, Robert. Disinfection and sterilization in dental practice / Robert Calmes, Jr., Thomas Lillich. — New York ; London : McGraw-Hill, c1978. — xiii,96p : ill ; 26cm
ISBN 0-07-009661-9 (pbk) : £4.85 B81-08263

617.6'01 — Man. Dental health

Cowell, Colin R.. Promoting dental health. — London : King Edward's Hospital Fund for London, Oct.1981. — [144]p
ISBN 0-900889-83-7 : £7.50 : CIP entry B81-28803

617.6'01 — Man. Dental health. Improvement — *Manuals*

Forrest, John. The good teeth guide / John Forrest. — London : Granada, 1981. — 192p : ill,2facsims ; 21cm
Includes index
ISBN 0-246-11143-7 : £3.95 B81-10071

617.6'01 — Preventive dentistry

Forrest, John. Preventive dentistry / John O. Forrest. — 2nd ed. — Bristol : John Wright, 1981. — ix,128p : ill ; 22cm. — (A Dental practitioner handbook ; no.22)
Previous ed.: 1976. — Includes bibliographies and index
ISBN 0-7236-0553-x (pbk) : Unpriced B81-15762

Your mouth is your business : the dentists' guide to better health / Hyman J.V. Goldberg ... [et al.]. — New York : Appleton-Century-Crofts ; London : Prentice-Hall, c1980. — xix,215p : ill ; 21cm
Includes index
ISBN 0-8385-9943-5 (cased) : £8.40
ISBN 0-8385-9942-7 (pbk) : £3.85 B81-19785

617.6'01 — United States. Preventive dentistry. Role of nutrition

Nizel, Abraham E.. Nutrition in preventive dentistry : science and practice / Abraham E. Nizel. — 2nd ed. — Philadelphia ; London : Saunders, 1981. — xi,611p : ill,forms ; 26cm
Previous ed.: 1972. — Includes index
ISBN 0-7216-6810-0 : £14.00 B81-01708

617.6'01'07 — Children. Dental health education. Teaching. Techniques

Whole healthy or diseased disabled teeth?. — London (78 New Oxford St., WC1A 1AH) : Health Education Council. — (Monograph series / Health Education Council ; no.4)
Phase 1: Results of pilot studies and controlled feasibility trials / authors, Michael Craft, Ray Croucher, Julie Dickinson. — 1981. — 165p : ill,forms ; 30cm
Unpriced (spiral) B81-18822

617.6'023 — United States. Dentistry. Teams

Dental teamwork strategies : interpersonal and organizational approaches / July C. Morton ... [et al.]. — St. Louis ; London : Mosby, 1980. — xiii,181p : ill,forms ; 25cm
Includes bibliographies and index
ISBN 0-8016-0979-8 (pbk) : Unpriced B81-08163

617.6'0233 — United States. Dental assistants. Duties

Anderson, Pauline C.. The dental assistant / Pauline C. Anderson. — New York ; London : Van Nostrand Reinhold, c1981. — vi,282p : ill (some col.) ; 27cm
Previous ed.: Albany, N.Y. : Delmar Publishers, 1974. — Includes index
ISBN 0-442-21873-7 : £11.20 B81-29556

617.6'059 — Dentistry. Surgery

Baum, Lloyd. Textbook of operative dentistry / Lloyd Baum, Ralph W. Phillips, Melvin R. Lund. — Philadelphia ; London : Saunders, 1981. — viii,580p : ill ; 27cm
Includes index
ISBN 0-7216-1601-1 : £21.00 B81-27103

617.6'059 — Man. Teeth. Transplantation

Clinical transplantation in dental specialities / edited by Peter J. Robinson, Louis H. Guernsey. — St. Louis ; London : Mosby, 1980. — xiii,299p : ill ; 27cm
Includes bibliographies and index
ISBN 0-8016-4142-x : Unpriced B81-08215

617.6'06 — Dentistry. Therapy. Planning

Barsh, Laurence I.. Dental treatment planning : for the adult patient / Laurence I. Barsh. — Philadelphia ; London : Saunders, 1981. — xiii,338p : ill,forms ; 27cm
Includes index
ISBN 0-7216-1533-3 : £19.00 B81-27099

617.6'0757 — Dentistry. Diagnosis. Radiographs. Interpretation — *Manuals*

Beeching, Brian W.. Interpreting dental radiographs / Brian W. Beeching. — London (33 Alfred Place WC1E 7DP) : Update Books, 1981. — 150p,[1]leaf of plates : ill(some col.) ; 29cm
Includes index
ISBN 0-906141-20-6 : £12.00 : CIP rev. B80-17740

617.6'07'57 — Dentistry. Diagnosis. Radiography

Mason, Rita A.. A guide to dental radiography. — 2nd ed. — Bristol : Wright, Oct.1981. — [176]p. — (A Dental practitioner handbook ; no.27)
Previous ed.: 1977
ISBN 0-7236-0623-4 (pbk) : £7.75 : CIP entry B81-28185

617.6'0757 — Man. Teeth. Diagnosis. Radiography

Frommer, Herbert H.. Radiology in dental practice / Herbert H. Frommer. — St. Louis ; London : Mosby, 1981. — xiv,303p : ill ; 26cm
Includes index
ISBN 0-8016-1709-x : £23.25 B81-40362

617.6'0757'076 — Man. Teeth. Diagnosis. Radiography — *Questions & answers*

Kasle, Myron J.. Basic principles of oral radiography / Myron J. Kasle, Robert P. Langlais. — Philadelphia ; London : Saunders, 1981. — xvi,242p : ill ; 26cm. — (Exercises in dental radiology ; v.4)
Bibliography: p232. — Includes index
ISBN 0-7216-5291-3 (pbk) : £10.95 B81-26949

617.6'0880814 — Chronically sick persons. Dentistry

Little, James W.. Dental management of the medically compromised patient / James W. Little, Donald A. Falace. — St. Louis ; London : Mosby, 1980. — ix,255p : ill,forms ; 26cm
Includes bibliographies and index
£10.75 (pbk) B81-03847

617.6'32 — Man. Periodontal diseases

MacPhee, Torquil. Essentials of periodontology and periodontics / Torquil MacPhee, and Geoffrey Cowley. — 3rd ed. — Oxford : Blackwell Scientific, 1981. — xi,328p : ill ; 26cm
Previous ed.: 1975. — Includes index
ISBN 0-632-00533-5 : £18.00 B81-10407

Pawlak, Elizabeth A.. Essentials of periodontics / Elizabeth A. Pawlak, Philip M. Hoag ; original drawings by Christo M. Popoff. — 2nd ed. — St. Louis ; London : Mosby, 1980. — x,174p : ill,forms ; 24cm
Previous ed.: 1976. — Includes bibliographies and index
ISBN 0-8016-3764-3 (spiral) : £10.00 B81-00934

617.6'3206 — Man. Periodontal diseases. Therapy

Goldman, Henry M.. Periodontal therapy / Henry M. Goldman, D. Walter Cohen. — 6th ed. — St. Louis ; London : Mosby, 1980. — xiii,1217p,2leaves of plates : ill(some col.),forms ; 27cm
Previous ed.: 1973. — Includes bibliographies and index
ISBN 0-8016-1875-4 : Unpriced B81-08690

617.6'342 — Dentistry. Endodontics

Bence, Richard. Handbook of clinical endodontics / Richard Bence ; with the editorial assistance of Franklin S. Weine ; illustrations by A.A. Zakaria. — 2nd ed. — St. Louis ; London : Mosby, 1980. — xviii,262p : ill ; 28cm
Previous ed.: 1976. — Includes index
ISBN 0-8016-0587-3 (spiral) : £12.75 B81-06512

Pathways of the pulp / edited by Stephen Cohen, Richard C. Burns ; principal illustrator Richard C. Burns. — 2nd ed. — St Louis ; London : Mosby, 1980. — xiv,749p : ill(some col.),forms ; 29cm
Previous ed.: 1976. — Includes bibliographies and index
ISBN 0-8016-1009-5 : Unpriced B81-12545

617.6'43 — Cosmetic dentistry

Denholtz, Melvin. The dental facelift / Melvin Denholtz, Elaine Denholtz. — New York ; London : Van Nostrand Reinhold, c1981. — xiii,187p,[8]p of plates : ill(some col.),ports ; 24cm
Includes index
ISBN 0-442-22021-9 : £11.20 B81-01593

617.6'43 — Man. Teeth. Occlusion

Thomson, Hamish. Occlusion in clinical practice / Hamish Thomson. — Bristol : John Wright, 1981. — v,188p : ill ; 22cm. — (A Dental practitioner handbook ; no.30)
Includes bibliographies and index
ISBN 0-7236-0579-3 (pbk) : Unpriced : CIP rev. B81-14787

617.6'43'0028 — Man. Orthodontic appliances: Begg appliances

Fletcher, G. G. T.. The Begg appliance and technique. — Bristol : J. Wright, Oct.1981. — [204]p
ISBN 0-7236-0570-x : £19.00 : CIP entry B81-24667

617.6'43'0028 — Man. Removable orthodontic appliances. Design & construction

Houston, W. J. B.. Orthodontic treatment with removable appliances / W.J.B. Houston and K.G. Isaacson. — 2nd ed. — Bristol : John Wright, 1980. — vii,189p : ill ; 22cm. — (A Dental practitioner handbook ; no.25)
Previous ed.: 1977. — Includes bibliographies and index
ISBN 0-7236-0566-1 (pbk) : £5.00 : CIP rev. B80-24527

617.6'43'075 — Dentistry. Orthodontics. Diagnosis

Houston, W. J. B.. Orthodontic diagnosis. — 3rd ed. — Bristol : J. Wright, Feb.1982. — [112]p. — (A Dental practitioner handbook ; no.4)
Previous ed.: 1975
ISBN 0-7236-0637-4 (pbk) : £4.00 : CIP entry B81-35845

617.6'45 — Children. Anterior teeth. Trauma. Therapy

The **Management** of traumatized anterior teeth of children / foreword by James Lorraine Trainer. — 2nd ed. / edited by John Anthony Hargreaves, John W. Craig. Howard. L. Needleman. — Edinburgh : Churchill Livingstone, 1981. — viii,189p : ill ; 22cm
Previous ed.: 1970. — Includes bibliographies and index
ISBN 0-443-01716-6 (pbk) : £12.00 B81-22181

617.6'45 — Children. Dentistry

Davis, John M.. An atlas of pedodontics / John M. Davis, David B. Law, Thompson M. Lewis ; photography by Clifford L. Freehe ; illustrations by Virginia E. Brooks. — 2nd ed. — Philadelphia ; London : Saunders, 1981. — xv,504p : ill(some col.) ; 27cm
Previous ed.: / by David B. Law, Thompson M. Lewis, John M. Davis. 1969. — Includes index
ISBN 0-7216-2977-6 : £20.75 B81-12654

Pediatric dental medicine / edited by Donald J. Forrester, Mark L. Wagner, James Fleming. — Philadelphia : Lea & Febiger ; London : Kimpton, 1981. — xv,692p : ill ; 27cm
Includes bibliographies and index
ISBN 0-8121-0663-6 : £22.25 B81-20850

617.6'45 — Children. Dentistry — *Manuals*

Andlaw, R. J.. A manual of paedodontics. — Edinburgh : Churchill Livingstone, Dec.1981. — [200]p
ISBN 0-443-01752-2 (pbk) : £6.50 : CIP entry B81-31361

Handbook of clinical pedodontics / Kenneth D. Snawder ; principal illustrator Michael B. Rulnick. — St Louis ; London : Mosby, 1980. — xvi,296p : ill,forms ; 26cm
Bibliography: p295-296
ISBN 0-8016-2951-9 (spiral) : £14.00 B81-08095

617.6'7 — Man. Teeth. Caries

Dental caries : aetiology, pathology and prevention / L.M. Silverstone ... [et al.]. — London : Macmillan, 1981. — 315p,[1]leaf of plates : ill(some col.) ; 25cm
Includes bibliographies and index
ISBN 0-333-21178-2 (cased) : Unpriced
ISBN 0-333-21179-0 (pbk) : Unpriced B81-25996

617.6'7071 — Man. Teeth. Caries. Role of saliva — *Conference proceedings*

Saliva and dental caries (a special supplement to Microbiology Abstracts) : proceedings of a workshop on saliva and dental caries, June 5-7, 1978, School of Dental Medicine, Health Sciences Center, State University of New York at Stony Brook, Stony Brook, New York / edited by Israel Kleinberg, Solon A. Ellison, Irwin D. Mandel ; presented and sponsored by National Caries Program, National Institute of Dental Research, National Institutes of Health in collaboration with the State University of New York at Stony Brook. — New York ; London : Information Retrieval, 1979. — viii,575p : ill ; 23cm
Includes bibliographies
Unpriced (pbk) B81-33569

617.6'75 — Man. Teeth. Cavities. Resin based fillings

Deubert, L. W.. Tooth-coloured filling materials in clinical practice. — 2nd ed. — Bristol : Wright, Jan.1982. — [144]p. — (A Dental practitioner handbook ; no.16)
Previous ed.: 1972
ISBN 0-7236-0628-5 (pbk) : £7.00 : CIP entry B81-37548

617.6'9'028 — Prosthetic dentistry. Laboratory techniques

Martinelli, Nicholas. Dental laboratory technology. — 3rd ed. / Nicholas Martinelli, S. Charles Spinella. — St. Louis ; London : Mosby, 1981. — viii,502p : ill,facsims,forms ; 27cm
Previous ed.: 1975. — Includes bibliographies and index
ISBN 0-8016-3137-8 : £26.00 B81-14989

617.6'92 — Man. Fixed dentures. Bridges

Roberts, D. H.. Fixed bridge prostheses / D.H. Roberts. — 2nd ed. / with sections by Ian Davies, B.J. Parkins and W.M. Tay. — Bristol : John Wright, 1980. — xl,289p : ill ; 24cm
Previous ed.: 1973. — Includes bibliographies and index
ISBN 0-7236-0545-9 : £14.50 : CIP rev. B80-17741

617.6'92 — Man. Fixed dentures. Implantation. Techniques

Babbush, Charles A.. Surgical atlas of dental implant techniques / Charles A. Babbush. — Philadelphia : London : Saunders, 1980. — xiv,326p : ill(some col.) ; 27cm
Bibliography: p261-316. — Includes index
ISBN 0-7216-1474-4 : £28.00 B81-02305

617.6'92 — Man. Full dentures

Anderson, John N.. Immediate and replacement dentures / John N. Anderson and Roy Storer. — 3rd ed. — Oxford : Blackwell Scientific, 1981. — xi,351p : ill ; 24cm
Previous ed.: 1973. — Bibliography: p335-346. — Includes index
ISBN 0-632-00507-6 (pbk) : £12.00 B81-36481

Boucher, Carl O.. Boucher's prosthodontic treatment for edentulous patients. — George A. Zarb. — St. Louis ; London : Mosby, 1980. — x,630p : ill,1port ; 27cm
Previous ed.: published as Prosthodontic treatment for edentulous patients. 1975. — Bibliography: p569-607. - Includes index
ISBN 0-8016-0725-6 : Unpriced B81-08142

617.6'92 — Man. Overdentures

Brewer, Allen A.. Overdentures / Allen A. Brewer, Robert M. Morrow. — 2nd ed. — St. Louis ; London : Mosby, 1980. — xvii,426p : ill ; 26cm
Includes bibliographies and index
ISBN 0-8016-0785-x : £37.50 B81-24246

617.6'92 — Man. Partial dentures

McCracken, William Lionel. McCracken's Removable partial prosthodontics. — 6th ed. / [by] Davis Henderson, Victor L. Steffel. — St. Louis ; London : Mosby, 1981. — xv,477p : ill,1port ; 27cm
Previous ed.: 1977. — Bibliography: p438-455. — Includes index
ISBN 0-8016-2146-1 : £26.00 B81-33043

Miller, Ernest L.. Removable partial prosthodontics. — 2nd ed. / Ernest L. Miller, Joseph E. Grasso. — Baltimore ; London : Williams & Wilkins, c1981. — xvi,420p : ill,forms ; 26cm
Previous ed.: 1972. — Bibliography: p373-386. - Includes index
ISBN 0-683-05990-4 : £36.75 B81-21915

617.6'92'028 — Man. Dentures. Construction — *Manuals*

Dental laboratory procedures. — St. Louis ; London : Mosby
Vol.1: Complete dentures / [edited by] Robert M. Morrow, Kenneth D. Rudd, Harold F. Eissmann. — 1980. — xiii,541p : ill ; 29cm
Includes bibliographies and index
ISBN 0-8016-3513-6 : £25.75 B81-12001

Dental laboratory procedures / [edited by] Robert M. Morrow, Kenneth D. Rudd, Harold F. Eissmann. — St. Louis ; London : Mosby
Vol.3: Removable partial dentures. — 1981. — xii,675p : ill ; 29cm
Includes bibliographies and index
ISBN 0-8016-3516-0 : £36.50 B81-40356

Dental Laboratory procedures / [edited by] Robert M. Morrow, Kenneth D. Rudd, Harold F. Eissmann. — St. Louis ; London : Mosby, 1980
Fixed partial dentures. — xiv,367p : ill ; 29cm
Includes bibliographies and index
ISBN 0-8016-3517-9 : Unpriced B81-08151

617.6'95 — Dental materials

Combe, E. C.. Notes on dental materials / E.C. Combe ; foreword by A.A. Grant. — 4th ed. — Edinburgh : Churchill Livingstone, 1981. — 333p : ill ; 22cm
Previous ed.: 1977. — Includes bibliographies and index
ISBN 0-443-02054-x (pbk) : £7.25 B81-40145

617.6'95 — Prosthetic dental materials

Restorative dental materials / edited by Robert G. Craig. — 6th ed. — St. Louis ; London : Mosby, 1980. — xiii,478p : ill ; 26cm
Previous ed.: 1975. — Includes bibliographies and index
ISBN 0-8016-3866-6 (pbk) : £17.00 B81-02970

617.7 — OPHTHALMOLOGY

617.7 — Man. Eyes. Diseases

Chawla, Hector Bryson. Essential ophthalmology / Hector Bryson Chawla. — Edinburgh : Churchill Livingstone, 1981. — viii,171p : ill ; 22cm. — (Churchill Livingstone medical text)
Includes index
ISBN 0-443-02171-6 (pbk) : £4.95 : CIP rev. B81-14979

Current genetic, clinical and morphologic problems / volume editor W. Straub. — Basel ; London : Karger, 1981. — 215p : ill ; 25cm. — (Developments in ophthalmology ; v.3)
Four papers in German, 3 in English. — Includes bibliographies
ISBN 3-8055-2000-x : £41.75 B81-38746

Sachsenweger, Rudolf. Illustrated handbook of ophthalmology / Rudolf Sachsenweger ; translated from the German by Elizabeth Julius ; translation editor J.C. Dean Hart. — Bristol : Wright, 1980. — 164p : ill(some col.) ; 20cm
Translation of: Kompendium und Atlas der Augenheilkunde. — Includes index
ISBN 0-7236-0494-0 : Unpriced : CIP rev. B78-21244

617.7 — Ophthalmology

Bankes, James L. Kennerley. Clinical ophthalmology. — Edinburgh : Churchill Livingstone, Feb.1982. — [132]p
ISBN 0-443-02157-0 : £10.00 : CIP entry B81-35716

Glasspool, Michael G.. Ophthalmology. — Lancaster : MTP Press, Sept.1981. — [128]p
ISBN 0-85200-434-6 : £14.95 : CIP entry B81-28266

New directions in ophthalmic research. — London : Yale University Press, Oct.1981. — [344]p
ISBN 0-300-02749-4 : £21.00 : CIP entry B81-31941

Trevor-Roper, Patrick D.. Ophthalmology. — London : Grant McIntyre [May 1981]. — [120] p. — (Pocket consultants)
ISBN 0-86216-031-6 (pbk) : £4.95 : CIP rev. : CIP entry B81-07917

Trevor-Roper, Patrick D.. Ophthalmology / Patrick D. Trevor-Roper. — London : Grant McIntyre, 1981. — 108p : ill(some col.) ; 19cm. — (Pocket consultant)
Cover title. — Includes index
ISBN 0-86286-000-8 (pbk) : £4.50 B81-26945

617.7'0024613 — Man. Eyes. Diseases — *For nursing*

Darling, Vera H.. Ophthalmic nursing / Vera H. Darling and Margaret R. Thorpe. — 2nd ed. — London : Baillière Tindall, 1981. — viii,188p,2p of plates : ill(some col.) ; 20cm. — (Nurses' aids series. Special interest texts)
Previous ed.: 1975. — Includes index
ISBN 0-7020-0829-x (pbk) : £4.95 B81-11638

617.7'005 — Ophthalmology — *Serials*

Advances in ophthalmology. — Vol.42. — Basel ; London : Karger, 1981. — vii,161p
ISBN 3-8055-1025-x : £25.75
ISSN 0065-3004 B81-11873

Ophthalmic & physiological optics : the journal of the British College of Ophthalmic Opticians (Optometrists). — Vol.1, no.1 (1981)-. — Oxford : Pergamon, 1981-. — v. : ill ; 25cm
Three issues yearly. — Continues: British journal of physiological optics
ISSN 0275-5408 = Ophthalmic & physiological optics : Unpriced B81-29111

The year book of ophthalmology. — 1980. — Chicago ; London ([Barnards Inn, EC1]) : Year Book Medical Publishers, c1980. — 374p
ISBN 0-8151-4778-3 : Unpriced
ISSN 0084-392x B81-09117

617.7'06 — Man. Eyes. Therapy

Current ocular therapy / [edited by] Frederick T. Fraunfelder, F. Hampton Roy ; associate editor S. Martha Meyer. — Philadelphia ; London : Saunders, 1980. — xlvi,647p ; 28cm
Includes bibliographies and index
ISBN 0-7216-3860-0 : £24.25 B81-00935

617.7'061 — Man. Eyes. Effects of drugs

Davies, P. H. O'Connor. The actions and uses of ophthalmic drugs : a textbook for students and practitioners / P.H. O'Connor Davies. — 2nd ed. — London : Butterworths, 1981. — xi,.386p,[8]p of plates : ill(some col.) ; 25cm
Previous ed.: 1972. — Includes bibliographies and index
ISBN 0-407-93272-0 : Unpriced : CIP rev. B81-09507

617.7'0913 — Tropical regions. Man. Eyes. Diseases

Rodger, F. C.. Eye disease in the tropics : a practical textbook for developing countries / F.C. Rodger ; foreword by A.W. Woodruff. — Edinburgh : Churchill Livingstone, 1981. — 127p : ill ; 25cm. — (Medicine in the tropics series)
Bibliography: p121-122. — Includes index
ISBN 0-443-02020-5 (pbk) : £6.00 B81-37097

617.7'09676'2 — Developing countries. Man. Eyes. Diseases — *Study regions: Kenya*

Bisley, Geoffrey G.. A handbook of ophthalmology for developing countries / Geoffrey G. Bisley ; with a foreword by J.C. Likimani. — 2nd ed. — Oxford : Oxford University Press, 1980. — 157p,16p of plates : ill(some col.) ; 22cm. — (Oxford medical publications)
Previous ed.: 1973. — Includes index
ISBN 0-19-261244-1 (pbk) : £4.50 : CIP rev. B80-00214

617.7'1 — Man. Eyes. Diseases. Nutritional factors

McLaren, Donald S.. Nutritional ophthalmology / Donald S. McLaren. — 2nd ed. — London : Academic Press, 1980. — xv,438p : ill ; 24cm. — (Nutrition : basic and applied science)
Previous ed.: published as Malnutrition and the eye. 1963. — Bibliography: p341-407. — Includes index
ISBN 0-12-484240-2 : £32.00 : CIP rev. B80-09715

617.7'1 — Man. Eyes. Microsurgery

Girard, Louis J.. Advanced techniques in ophthalmic microsurgery / Louis J. Girard. — St. Louis ; London : Mosby
Vol.2: Corneal surgery. — 1981. — xii,291p,[13]p of plates : ill(some col.) ; 29cm
Pair of stereoscopic spectacles in envelope attached to back cover. — Includes bibliographies and index
ISBN 0-8016-1835-5 : £65.50 B81-09835

World Convention of Microsurgery *(1979 : Singapore).* Ocular microsurgery / World Convention of Microsurgery, Singapore, December 2-9 1979 ; volume editors A.S.M. Lim, L.C.Y. Khoo, and L.B.C. Ang. — Basel ; London : Karger, 1981. — 95p : ill ; 25cm. — (Developments in ophthalmology ; v.1)
Includes bibliographies
ISBN 3-8055-1106-x : £13.20 B81-21250

617.7'1545 — Man. Eyes. Diagnosis. Perimetry

Enoch, Jay M.. Quantitative layer-by-layer perimetry : an extended analysis / Jay M. Enoch, C.R. Fitzgerald, E.C. Campos ; with a foreword by Hans Goldmann. — New York ; London : Grune & Stratton, 1981. — xii,232p : ill ; 24cm. — (Current ophthalmology monographs)
Includes index
ISBN 0-8089-1282-8 : £16.60 B81-18021

617.7'1545 — Man. Eyes. Diagnosis. Perimetry — *Conference proceedings*

International Visual Field Symposium *(4th : 1980 : Bristol).* Fourth International Visual Field Symposium, Bristol, April 13-16, 1980 / edited by E.L. Greve and G. Verriest. — The Hague ; London : Junk, 1981. — x,406p : ill(some col.) ; 24cm. — (Documenta ophthalmologica. Proceedings series ; v.26)
Includes bibliographies and index
ISBN 90-619-3165-7 : Unpriced B81-14656

617.7'1547 — Man. Eyes. Electrodiagnosis

Galloway, N. R.. Ophthalmic electrodiagnosis / N.R. Galloway. — 2nd ed. — London : Lloyd-Luke, 1981. — x,180p : ill ; 24cm. — (Major problems in ophthalmology ; v.1)
Previous ed.: Philadelphia : Saunders, 1975. — Includes bibliographies and index
ISBN 0-85324-152-x : Unpriced B81-19394

617.7'19 — Man. Eyes. Corneas. Diseases

Superficial keratitis / edited by P.C. Maudgal and L. Missotten. — The Hague ; London : Junk, 1981. — 192p : ill ; 25cm. — (Monographs in ophthalmology ; 1)
"Reprinted from Bull. Soc. belge Ophtal. 187-I, 1980" — t.p. verso. — Includes bibliographies
ISBN 90-619-3801-5 : Unpriced B81-26170

617.7′19 — Man. Eyes. Corneas. Diseases — *Conference proceedings*

European Society of Ophthalmology. *Congress (6th : 1980 : Brighton).* The cornea in health and disease : VIth Congress of the European Society of Ophthalmology [held at Brighton, on April 21-25, 1980] / edited by P.D. Trevor-Roper. — London : The Royal Society of Medicine, 1981. — xxxii,1156p : ill ; 25cm. — (Royal Society of Medicine series) (International congress and symposium series / Royal Society of Medicine, ISSN 0142-2367 ; no.40)
Includes papers in French and German. — Includes bibliographies
ISBN 0-12-794647-0 (pbk) : Unpriced : CIP rev.
ISBN 0-12-349050-2 B81-25696

Symposium on medical and surgical diseases of the cornea / [contributors] José I. Barraquer ... [et al.]. — St. Louis ; London : Mosby, 1980. — xiv,641p : ill,ports ; 26cm. — (Transactions of the New Orleans Academy of Ophthalmology)
Includes bibliographies and index
ISBN 0-8016-3666-3 : Unpriced B81-08219

617.7′19 — Man. Eyes. Corneas. Effects of measles

Dekkers, N. W. H. M.. The cornea in measles / N.W.H.M. Dekkers. — The Hague ; London : Junk, c1981. — 121p : ill(some col.),1map ; 25cm. — (Monographs in ophthalmology ; 3)
English text, summaries in English Dutch and French. — Bibliography: p84-97
ISBN 90-619-3803-1 B81-29294

617.7′19′00926 — Man. Eyes. Corneas. Diseases — *Case studies*

Donaldson, David D.. Cornea and sclera / David D. Donaldson. — 2nd ed. — St. Louis ; London : Mosby, 1980. — xiii,506p : ill ; 29cm + 16 stereographic reels (Viewmaster)(112 double fr. : col.). — (Atlas of external diseases of the eye ; v.3)
Previous ed.: 1971. — Reels in pockets. — Includes bibliographies and index
ISBN 0-8016-1434-1 : Unpriced B81-10734

617.7′2 — Man. Eyes. Pars planitis & toxoplasmosis

Schlaegel, T. F.. Ocular toxoplasmosis and pars planitis / by T.F. Schlaegel, Jr. — New York ; London : Grune & Stratton, c1978. — xv,378p : ill,ports ; 24cm. — (Current ophthalmology monographs)
Includes index
ISBN 0-8089-1078-7 : £27.60 B81-15213

617.7′3 — Man. Eyes. Retinas. Diseases. Complications of diabetes

L′Esperance, Francis A.. Diabetic retinopathy : clinical evaluation and management / Francis A. L′Esperance, Jr., William A. James Jr. — St. Louis ; London : Mosby, 1981. — xv,294p : ill(some col.) ; 27cm
Includes bibliographies and index
ISBN 0-8016-2948-9 : £35.25
Also classified at 616.4′62 B81-15001

617.7′3 — Man. Eyes. Retinas. Subretinal space. Diseases — *Conference proceedings*

Conference on Subretinal Space *(1979 : Jerusalem).* Proceedings of the Conference on Subretinal Space, Jerusalem, October 14-19, 1979 / edited by H. Zauberman. — The Hague ; London : Junk, 1981. — x,306p : ill ; 24cm. — (Documenta ophthalmologica. Proceedings series ; v.25)
Includes bibliographies
ISBN 90-619-3721-3 : Unpriced B81-20968

617.7′41 — Man. Eyes. Glaucoma

Leyhecker, Wolfgang. All about glaucoma. — London : Faber, Oct.1981. — [80]p
Translation and revision of: Alles über grünen Star
ISBN 0-571-11764-3 (cased) : £4.95 : CIP entry
ISBN 0-571-11765-1 (pbk) : £1.95 B81-24657

617.7′41061 — Man. Eyes. Glaucoma. Drug therapy. Adrenaline & guanethidine — *Case studies*

Hoyng, F. J.. Pharmacological denervation and glaucoma : a clinical trial report with guanethidine and adrenaline in one eye drop / F.J. Hoyng. — The Hague ; London : Junk, c1981. — ix,150p : ill ; 25cm. — (Monographs in ophthalmology ; 2)
Includes bibliographies
ISBN 90-619-3802-3 : Unpriced B81-20834

617.7′42 — Man. Eyes. Cataracts. Pathology

Mechanisms of cataract formation in the human lens / edited by George Duncan. — London : Academic Press, 1981. — ix,262p,[1]leaf of plates : illi(some col.) ; 24cm
Includes bibliographies and index
ISBN 0-12-223750-1 : £20.00 B81-23549

617.7′42 — Man. Eyes. Cataracts. Surgery — *Conference proceedings*

Cataract Surgical Congress *(6th : 1978 : Houston).* Current concepts in cataract surgery : selected proceedings of the Sixth Biennial Cataract Surgical Congress / editors Jared M. Emery, Adrienne C. Jacobson. — St. Louis ; London : Mosby, 1980. — xxi,466p : ill,1port ; 27cm
Includes index
ISBN 0-8016-1527-5 : £51.00 B81-14997

Symposium on cataracts / [contributors] Nicholas G. Douvas ... [et al.]. — St. Louis ; London : Mosby, 1980. — xiv,436p : ill,ports ; 26cm. — (Transactions of the New Orleans Academy of Ophthalmology)
Includes bibliographies and index
ISBN 0-8016-3674-4 : Unpriced B81-08220

617.7′42 — Man. Eyes. Lenses. Disorders. Related to metabolic disorders of red blood cells — *Conference proceedings*

International Symposium on Red Blood Cell and Lens Metabolism *(2nd : 1979 : University of Texas Medical Branch).* Red blood cell and lens metabolism : proceedings of the Second International Symposium on Red Blood Cell and Lens Metabolism, University of Texas Medical Branch, Galveston, Texas, U.S.A., October 27-29, 1979 / editor : Satish K. Srivastava. — New York ; Oxford : Elsevier/North-Holland, c1980. — xiv,508p : ill ; 25cm. — (Developments in biochemistry, ISSN 0165-1714 ; v.9)
Includes index
ISBN 0-444-00388-6 : £24.19
Primary classification 616.1′51 B81-03987

617.7′42059 — Man. Eyes. Cataracts. Surgery

Jaffe, Norman S.. Cataract surgery and its complications / Norman S. Jaffe. — 3rd ed. — St. Louis ; London : Mosby, 1981. — x,611p : ill ; 27cm
Previous ed.: 1976. — Includes index
ISBN 0-8016-2404-5 : £55.00 B81-09772

617.7′46 — Man. Eyes. Vitreous bodies. Diseases — *Conference proceedings*

Club Jules Gonin. *Meeting (12th : 1980 : Crans-Montana).* Current concepts in diagnosis and treatment of vitreoretinal diseases / 12th Meeting of the Club Jules Gonin, Crans-Montana, March 17-21, 1980 ; volume editors G. Blankenship ... [et al.]. — Basel ; London : Karger, 1981. — xxvi,406p : ill,ports ; 24cm. — (Developments in ophthalmology ; v.2)
Includes bibliographies
ISBN 3-8055-1672-x : £78.60 B81-38743

617.7′46059 — Man. Eyes. Vitreous bodies. Surgery

Michels, Ronald G.. Vitreous surgery / Ronald G. Michels ; Timothy C. Hengst and Gary P. Lees, medical illustrators. — St. Louis ; London : Mosby, 1987. — ix,462p : ill ; 29cm
Includes index
ISBN 0-8016-3494-6 : £51.50 B81-15005

617.7′523 — Contact lenses

Contact lenses : a textbook for practitioner and student / edited by Janet Stone and Anthony J. Phillips. — 2nd ed. — London : Butterworths
Previous ed.: London : Barrie and Jenkins, 1972
Vol.2: Soft and advanced lens fitting techniques and post-fitting care. — 1981. — xiiip,p377-692,19p,[12]p of plates : ill(some col.) ; 26cm
Includes bibliographies and index
ISBN 0-407-93271-2 : Unpriced : CIP rev. B80-13861

617.7′523 — Contact lenses. Design - *Tables*

Musset, Anthony. Contact lens design tables. — London : Butterworths, Sept.1981. — [176]p
ISBN 0-407-00219-7 (pbk) : £9.50 : CIP entry B81-20588

617.7′55 — Man. Eyes. Refraction disorders

Michaels, David D.. Visual optics and refraction : a clinical approach / David D. Michaels. — 2nd ed. — St. Louis ; London : Mosby, 1980. — ix,743p : ill ; 26cm
Previous ed.: 1975. — Includes bibliographies and index
ISBN 0-8016-3414-8 : £47.00 B81-30782

617.7′62 — Man. Eyes. Nerves. Diseases

Ashworth, Bryan. Clinical neuro-ophthalmology / Bryan Ashworth and Ian Isherwood ; with fundus illustrations by Emanuel S. Rosen. — 2nd ed. — Oxford : Blackwell Scientific, 1981. — 298p : ill ; 24cm
Previous ed.: 1973. — Includes index
ISBN 0-632-00593-9 : £32.50 B81-16262

617.7′62 — Man. Eyes. Strabismus

Burian, Hermann M.. Burian-von Noorden′s binocular vision and ocular motility : theory and management of strabismus. — 2nd ed. / Gunter K. von Noorden. — St. Louis ; London : Mosby, 1980. — xviii,502p : ill ; 27cm
Previous ed.: published as Binocular vision and ocular motility / Hermann M. Burian, Gunter K. von Noorden. 1974. — Includes bibliographies and index
ISBN 0-8016-0898-8 : Unpriced B81-08217

617.7′62 — Neuro-ophthalmology. Computerised tomography scanners

Moseley, I. F.. Computerized tomography in neuro-ophthalmology. — London : Chapman and Hall, Sept.1981. — [400]p
ISBN 0-412-21840-2 : £25.00 : CIP entry B81-23908

617.7′62 — Orthoptics

Cashell, G. T. Willoughby. Handbook of orthoptic principles / G.T. Willoughby Cashell, Isobel M. Durran assisted by A.V. MacLellan ; foreword by T. Keith Lyle. — 4th ed. — Edinburgh : Churchill Livingstone, 1980. — 168p : ill ; 22cm
Previous ed.: 1974. — Includes index
ISBN 0-443-02200-3 (pbk) : £5.50 : CIP rev. B80-25731

617.7′62 — Orthoptics — *Conference proceedings*

International Orthoptic Congress *(4th : 1979 : Berne).* Orthoptics, research and practice : transactions of the Fourth International Orthoptics Congress, Berne, Switzerland September 3-9, 1979 / edited by Joyce Mein and Sally Moore. — London : Kimpton, 1981. — xii,291p : ill ; 26cm
Includes bibliographies and index
ISBN 0-85313-806-0 : £25.00 B81-24901

617.7′62′002541 — Great Britain. Orthoptists — *Directories — Serials*

Orthoptists Board. The Orthoptists register. — 1980. — London (184 Kennington Park Rd, SE11 4BU) : The Board, [1980?]. — 40p
ISSN 0474-7526 : Unpriced B81-24142

617.7′62′005 — Neuro-ophthalmology — *Conference proceedings — Serials*

Neuro-ophthalmology. — Vol.10. — St. Louis ; London : C.V. Mosby, 1980. — xi,242p
ISBN 0-8016-1876-2 : £35.75 B81-18796

617.7′71059 — Man. Eyes. Eyelids. Ptosis. Surgery

Beard, Crowell. Ptosis / Crowell Beard ; Joan Esperson Weddell, medical illustrator. — 3rd ed. — St. Louis ; London : Mosby, 1981. — ix,276p : ill,facsims ; 26cm
Previous ed.: 1976. — Includes index
ISBN 0-8016-0532-6 : £35.25 B81-24287

617.7′8 — Man. Eyes. Orbits. Diseases

Krohel, Gregory B.. Orbital disease : a practical approach / Gregory B. Krohel, William B. Stewart, Richard M. Chavis. — New York ; London : Grune & Stratton, c1981. — xv,160p : ill ; 24cm
Bibliography: p145-149. — Includes index
ISBN 0-8089-1343-3 : £13.00 B81-39585

617.8 — OTOLOGY AND AUDIOLOGY

617.8 — Audiology

Martin, Frederick N.. Introduction to audiology / Frederick N. Martin. — 2nd ed. — Englewood Cliffs ; London : Prentice-Hall, c1981. — xiv,458p : ill,forms ; 25cm
Previous ed.: 1975. — Includes bibliographies and index
ISBN 0-13-478131-7 : £12.95 B81-17208

617.8 — Man. Auditory processing disorders

Auditory processing and language : clinical and research perspectives / edited by Philip J. Levinson, Christine Sloan. — New York ; London : Grune & Stratton, c1980. — xvii,226p : ill ; 24cm
Includes index
ISBN 0-8089-1305-0 : £11.00 B81-13934

617.8 — Man. Hearing disorders

Medical audiology : disorders of hearing / Frederick N. Martin, editor. — Englewood Cliffs ; London : Prentice-Hall, c1981. — xii,482p : ill ; 24cm
Includes bibliographies and index
ISBN 0-13-572677-8 : £20.80 B81-14680

617.8 — Man. Hearing disorders — *Conference proceedings*

British Society of Audiology. *Conference (3rd : 1979 : University of Manchester)*. Disorders of auditory function III / [proceedings of the British Society of Audiology third conference, held at the University of Manchester, from 18-20 July, 1979] ; edited by Ian G. Taylor and Andreas Markides. — London : Published for the British Society of Audiology by Academic Press, 1980. — xiv,339p : ill ; 24cm
Includes bibliographies and index
ISBN 0-12-684780-0 : £16.40 : CIP rev. B80-23354

617.8 — Man. Hearing disorders — *For audiology*

Audiology and audiological medicine. — Oxford : Oxford University Press, Aug.1981. — 2v. [(800p.)]. — (Oxford medical publications)
ISBN 0-19-261154-2 : £50.00 : CIP entry B81-18080

617.8′052 — Great Britain. Foundries. Personnel. Hearing. Protection

Champion, A.. Hearing protectors for steelfounders : fettling shop personnel / prepared by A. Champion at the request of SCRATA Health, Safety and Environmental Committee. — Rev. and updated. — Sheffield : Steel Castings Research and Trade Association, 1980. — 33p : ill,1form ; 21cm
Previous ed.: 1980
£5.00 (pbk) B81-06522

617.8′059 — Ears. Surgery — *Illustrations*

Saunders, William H. (William Howerton). Atlas of ear surgery. — 3rd ed. / William H. Saunders, Michael M. Paparella, Andrew W. Miglets ; line drawings by Beverly A. Etter and Nancy Sally. — St. Louis ; London : Mosby, 1980. — x,435p : ill ; 29cm
Previous ed.: / by William H. Saunders, Michael M. Paparella. 1971. — Bibliography: p15-16. - Includes index
ISBN 0-8016-4318-x : £41.75 B81-08153

617.8′059 — Man. Ears. Surgery

Shambaugh, George E.. Surgery of the ear. — 3rd ed. / George E. Shambaugh, Michael E. Glasscock, III. — Philadelphia ; London : Saunders, 1980. — ix,749p : ill(some col.),ports ; 27cm
Previous ed.: / by George E. Shambaugh. 1967. — Includes index
ISBN 0-7216-8142-5 : £40.00 B81-03652

617.8′09 — Medicine. Otology, *to 1979*

Kerr, A. G.. They have ears but they hear not : an inaugural lecture delivered before the Queen′s University of Belfast on 13 February 1980 / A.G. Kerr. — [Belfast] : Queen′s University of Belfast, c1980. — 33p : ill,1plan,ports ; 21cm. — (New lecture series / Queen′s University of Belfast ; no.124)
ISBN 0-85389-188-5 (pbk) : £0.40 B81-05766

617.8′4 — Man. Ears. Tinnitus — *Conference proceedings*

Tinnitus. — London : Pitman, Oct.1981. — [320] p. — (CIBA Foundation symposium ; 85)
Conference proceedings
ISBN 0-272-79639-5 : £22.50 : CIP entry B81-25761

617.8′4 — Man. Middle ear. Chronic otitis media

Smyth, Gordon D. L.. Chronic ear disease / Gordon D.L. Smyth. — New York ; Edinburgh : Churchill Livingstone, 1980. — 225p : ill ; 24cm. — (Monographs in clinical otolaryngology ; v.2)
Includes bibliographies and index
ISBN 0-443-08071-2 : Unpriced B81-12159

617.8′8 — Man. Ears. Otosclerosis

Beales, Philip H.. Otosclerosis / Philip H. Beales. — Bristol : John Wright, 1981. — xiv,200p : ill ; 23cm
Includes bibliographies and index
ISBN 0-7236-0598-x : Unpriced : CIP rev. B81-04312

617.8′9 — Hearing aids

Hearing aid assessment and use in audiographic habilitation / edited by William R. Hodgson, Paul H. Skinner. — Baltimore ; London : Williams & Wilkins, c1981. — xii,303p : ill ; 26cm
Previous ed.: 1977. — Bibliography: p283-294. — Includes index
ISBN 0-683-04092-8 : £33.50 B81-26633

617.8′9 — Man. Hearing. Measurement. Acoustic-reflex stimulation

Hearing assessment with the acoustic reflex / edited by Gerald R. Popelka. — New York ; London : Grune & Stratton, c1981. — vii,168p : ill ; 24cm
Bibliography: p161-168
ISBN 0-8089-1361-1 : £11.60 B81-39584

617.8′9 — United States. Hearing aids. Dispensing — *Manuals*

Loavenbruck, Angela M.. Hearing aid dispensing for audiologists : a guide for clinical service / Angela M. Loavenbruck, Jane Reger Madell. — New York ; London : Grune & Stratton, c1981. — xi,203p : ill,forms ; 24cm
Includes bibliographies and index
ISBN 0-8089-1323-9 : £9.40 B81-18016

617.9 — MEDICINE. SURGICAL TECHNIQUES AND SPECIALITIES

617′.9 — Medicine. Surgery. Techniques

Mowschenson, Peter M.. Aids to undergraduate surgery / Peter M. Mowschenson. — Edinburgh : Churchill Livingstone, c1978 (1981 [printing]). — 144p ; 22cm
Bibliography: p136. — Includes index
ISBN 0-443-02510-x (pbk) : £1.00 B81-38012

Operative surgery : fundamental international techniques / under the general editorship of Charles Rob and Rodney Smith ; associate editor Hugh Dudley. — 3rd ed. — London : Butterworths
Head and neck / edited by J.S.P. Wilson. — c1981. — 2v.(992p) : ill ; 29cm
Previous ed.: 1969. — Includes bibliographies and index
ISBN 0-407-00624-9 : Unpriced : CIP rev.
ISBN 0-407-00622-2 (v.1) : Unpriced
ISBN 0-407-00623-0 (v.2) : Unpriced B81-21646

[Operative surgery. *Selections*]. Atlas of general surgery / Rob and Smith ; compiled by Hugh Dudley. — London : Butterworth, c1981. — 751p : ill ; 29cm
ISBN 0-407-00206-5 : Unpriced : CIP rev. B80-18776

Stillman, Richard M.. Surgical resident′s manual / Richard M. Stillman, Philip N. Sawyer [et al.] ; illustrated by Lynn B. McDowell. — New York : Appleton-Century-Crofts ; London : Prentice-Hall, c1980. — xii,241p : ill,forms ; 21cm
Includes index
ISBN 0-8385-8732-1 (spiral) : £8.15 B81-00936

617′.91 — Medicine. Surgery. Operations — *For patients*

Delvin, David. A patient′s guide to operations / David Delvin. — Harmondsworth : Penguin, 1981. — 329p : ill ; 19cm : 1form. — (Penguin handbooks)
ISBN 0-14-046374-7 (pbk) : £1.95 B81-21034

617′.91 — Medicine. Surgery. Operations — *Manuals*

Brigden, Raymond J.. Operating theatre technique : a textbook for nurses, technicians, operating department assistants, medical students, house surgeons and others associated with the operating theatre / Raymond J. Brigden. — 4th ed. — Edinburgh : Churchill Livingstone, 1980. — xii,811p : ill(some col.) ; 25cm
Previous ed.: 1974. — Includes bibliographies and index
ISBN 0-443-01999-1 : £35.00 : CIP rev. B80-02466

Operative surgery and management / edited by G. Keen. — Bristol : J. Wright, 1981. — xii,860p : ill ; 31cm
Includes index
ISBN 0-7236-0548-3 : £25.00 : CIP rev. B81-10423

617′.91′0028 — Medicine. Surgery. Operations. Techniques — *Manuals*

Contemporary operative surgery / edited by Adrian Marston with Geoffrey V.P. Chamberlain and John P. Blandy. — London : Northwood, 1979. — ix,237p : ill(some col.) ; 31cm. — (A British journal of hospital medicine book)
Includes index
ISBN 0-7198-2566-0 : £12.50 B81-03753

617′.9101 — Man. Infection during surgery. Prevention. Cefuroxime — *Conference proceedings*

Cefuroxime update / edited by Clive Wood and Yvonne Rue. — London : Royal Society of London, 1981. — viii,191p : ill ; 25cm. — (International congress and symposium series / Royal Society of Medicine ; no.38)
Conference papers. — Includes bibliographies
ISBN 0-12-794908-9 (pbk) : Unpriced B81-24248

617′.9101 — Man. Infection during surgery. Prevention. Use of cefuroxime — *Conference proceedings* — *Abstracts*

Cefuroxime update : Stratford-upon-Avon, 30/31 October 1980 : abstracts / edited by Clive Wood and Yvonne Rue. — London : Royal Society of Medicine, [1980]. — 16p ; 25cm. — (Royal Society of Medicine international congress and symposium series ; no.38)
Conference papers
Unpriced (pbk) B81-07320

617'.91'0222 — Medicine. Surgery. Operations — *Illustrations*

Grewe, Horst-Eberhard. Atlas of surgical operations / Horst-Eberhard Grewe and Karl Kremer ; translated by Volker M. Rötzscher and Anthony Zammit ; illustrations by Peter Haller. — Philadelphia ; London : Saunders
Translation of: Chirurgische Operationen
ISBN 0-7216-4273-x : £78.00 B81-26957

617'.91'0321 — Medicine. Surgery. Operations — *Encyclopaedias — For patients*

Stanway, Andrew. A dictionary of operations / Andrew Stanway. — London : Granada, 1981. — 436p ; 21cm. — (A Paladin book)
Includes index
ISBN 0-246-11644-7 (cased) : Unpriced
ISBN 0-586-08368-5 (pbk) : £2.50 B81-27052

617'.9178 — Surgical equipment. Use. Techniques — *Manuals*

Anderson, Robert M.. Technique in the use of surgical tools / Robert M. Anderson, Richard F. Romfh ; foreword by Stephen L. Wangensteen. — New York : Appleton-Century-Crofts ; London : Prentice-Hall, c1980. — x,187p : ill ; 24cm
Includes index
ISBN 0-8385-8843-3 (cased) : £10.75
ISBN 0-8385-8841-7 (pbk) : £8.95 B81-04053

617'.919 — Hospitals. Postoperative patients. Recovery. Effects of provision of preoperative sensory information — *For nursing*

Preoperative sensory preparation to promote recovery / CURN Project ; principal investigator Jo Anne Horsley. — New York ; London : Grune & Stratton, c1981. — xvii,105p : forms ; 23cm. — (Using research to improve nursing practice)
Bibliography: p99-100. — Includes index
ISBN 0-8089-1327-1 (spiral) : Unpriced B81-37754

617'.919 — Hospitals. Postoperative surgical patients. Recovery. Effects of preoperative teaching by nurses

Structured preoperative teaching / CURN Project ; principal investigator Jo Anne Horsley. — New York ; London : Grune & Stratton, c1981. — xvii,167p : ill,forms ; 23cm. — (Using research to improve nursing practice)
Includes bibliographies and index
ISBN 0-8089-1311-5 (spiral) : £5.40 B81-18024

617'.919 — Man. Surgery. Intensive preoperative & postoperative care

Intensive care of the surgical patient / edited by Marshall D. Goldin. — 2nd ed. — Chicago ; London : Year Book Medical, 1981. — xxvi,672p : ill ; 24cm
Previous ed.: Chicago : Year Book Medical, 1971. — Includes bibliographies and index
ISBN 0-8151-3732-x : Unpriced B81-33102

617'.919 — Man. Surgery. Postoperative care

Stoma care. — Beaconsfield (20 Chiltern Hills Rd., Beaconsfield, Bucks. HP9 1PL) : Beaconsfield, July 1981. — 1v.
ISBN 0-906584-04-3 : £9.50 : CIP entry
Primary classification 617'.553 B81-13874

617'.919 — Man. Surgery. Preoperative & postoperative care — *Practical information*

Gray, F. J.. Principles of surgery. — Edinburgh : Churchill Livingstone, Nov.1981. — [192]p
ISBN 0-443-02166-x (pbk) : £4.50 : CIP entry B81-30380

McEntyre, Robert L.. Practical guide to the care of the surgical patient / Robert L. McEntyre. — St. Louis ; London : Mosby, 1980. — vii,268p ; 15cm
Text on inside cover. — Bibliography: p250. — Includes index
ISBN 0-8016-3056-8 (spiral) : Unpriced B81-08563

617'.919 — Man. Surgery. Preoperative care of respiratory system

Margand, Peter M. S.. Preoperative pulmonary preparation : a clinical guide / Peter M.S. Margand, Charlie G. Brooks, Jr. James W. Hunter, II. — Baltimore ; London ([145A Croydon Rd., Beckenham, BR3 3RB]) : Williams & Wilkins, c1981. — xii,135p : ill,forms ; 23cm
Includes bibliographies and index
ISBN 0-683-05587-9 (pbk) : Unpriced B81-22428

617'.919 — Man. Surgery. Therapy. Nutrition

Nutrition and the surgical patient. — Edinburgh : Churchill Livingstone, Nov.1981. — [190]p. — (Clinical surgery international ; v.2)
ISBN 0-443-02249-6 : £9.00 : CIP entry B81-30427

617'.95 — Man. Immunosuppression

Biological relevance of immune suppression : as induced by genetic, therapeutic and environmental factors : second in a series of technology assessment workshops sponsored by Litton Bionetics Inc. / edited by Jack H. Dean, Martin Padarathsingh. — New York ; London : Van Nostrand Reinhold, c1981. — xiii,358p : ill ; 24cm
Includes bibliographies and index
ISBN 0-442-24429-0 : £20.65 B81-29524

Clinical immunosuppression / edited by John R. Salaman and Derek Sampson. — New York ; London : Grune & Stratton, c1980. — ix,183p : ill ; 26cm
Includes index
ISBN 0-8089-1335-2 : £16.00 B81-18018

617'.95 — Man. Organs & tissues. Transplantation

Tissue transplantation. — Edinburgh : Churchill Livingstone, Feb.1982. — [200]p. — (Clinical surgery international ; v.3)
ISBN 0-443-02460-x : £10.00 : CIP entry B81-36210

617'.95 — Man. Organs. Transplantation

Organ transplants. — Bristol : Wright, Feb.1982. — [630]p
ISBN 0-7236-7008-0 : £27.75 : CIP entry B81-35842

617'.95 — Medicine. Applications of plastics — *Conference proceedings*

Plastics in medicine and surgery (PIMS III), 21 and 22 June 1979 / conference sponsored by the PRI Meetings Committee in association with Twente University of Technology (THT), Dr G.J. van Hoytema Stichting. — London (11 Hobart Place, SW1W 0HL) : Plastics and Rubber Institute, [1979]. — 252p in various pagings : ill,maps ; 21cm
Unpriced (pbk) B81-37979

617'.95 — Medicine. Plastic surgery. Techniques

Operative plastic and reconstructive surgery / edited by John N. Barron, Magdy N. Saad ; foreword by Lord Smith of Marlow. — Edinburgh : Churchill Livingstone, 1980. — 3v.(various pagings) : ill ; 29cm
Includes bibliographies and index
ISBN 0-443-01600-3 : £80.00 : CIP rev. B80-12386

617'.95 — Medicine. Reconstruction surgery

Reconstructive procedures in surgery. — Oxford : Blackwell Scientific, Dec.1981. — [500]p
ISBN 0-632-00602-1 : £19.50 : CIP entry B81-33864

617'.95'0019 — Medicine. Plastic surgery. Psychological aspects

Goin, John M.. Changing the body : psychological effects of plastic surgery / John M. Goin, Marcia Kraft Goin. — Baltimore ; London : Williams & Wilkins, c1981. — xvii,225p : ill ; 26cm
Includes index
ISBN 0-683-03630-0 : £36.00 B81-20757

617'.95'005 — Man. Organs & tissues. Transplantation — *Conference proceedings — Serials*

Transplantation today / [Transplantation Society]. — Vol.6. — New York ; London : Grune & Stratton, c1981. — xxx,1305p
ISBN 0-8089-1398-0 : £37.80 B81-35453

617'.95'005 — Medicine. Plastic surgery — *Serials*

Recent advances in plastic surgery. — No.2. — Edinburgh : Churchill Livingstone, 1981. — viii,266p
ISBN 0-443-01943-6 : Unpriced : CIP rev.
ISSN 0309-2674 B80-31705

617'.95'0088042 — Women. Plastic surgery

Grazer, Frederick M.. Body image : a surgical perspective / Frederick M. Grazer, Jerome R. Klingbeil ; drawings by Denis Dykes Sperling. — St. Louis ; London : Mosby, 1980. — xiii,422p : ill(some col.) ; 31cm
Bibliography: p382-412. -Includes index
ISBN 0-8016-1965-3 : Unpriced B81-08674

617'.95'00924 — Medicine. Cosmetic surgery. Willi, Charles H. — *Biographies*

Ludovici, L. J.. Cosmetic scalpel : the life of Charles Willi, beauty-surgeon / L.J. Ludovici. — Bradford-on-Avon : Moonraker, 1981. — 140p ; 23cm
ISBN 0-239-00210-5 : £6.95 B81-26079

617'.95'00924 — Medicine. Plastic surgery — *Personal observations*

Sava, George. The transforming knife / George Sava. — London : Kimber, 1981. — 160p ; 23cm
ISBN 0-7183-0178-1 : £5.50 B81-26141

617'.95'00924 — Plastic surgery. Morgan, Elizabeth, *1947- — Biographies*

Morgan, Elizabeth, *1947-*. The making of a woman surgeon / Elizabeth Morgan. — [London] : W.H. Allen, 1981, c1980. — 368p ; 18cm. — (A Star book)
Originally published: New York : Putnam, 1980
ISBN 0-352-30891-5 (pbk) : £1.60 B81-35604

617'.96 — Genetically disordered patients. Anaesthesia. Complications

Inherited disease and anaesthesia / edited by F.R. Ellis. — Amsterdam ; Oxford : Excerpta Medica, 1981. — xii,463p : ill ; 25cm. — (Monographs in anaesthesiology ; v.9)
Includes bibliographies and index
ISBN 0-444-80266-5 : Unpriced B81-32847

617'.96 — Medicine. Anaesthesia

Ostlere, Gordon. Anaesthetics for medical students / Gordon Ostlere, Roger Bryce-Smith ; with a foreword by C. Langton Hewer. — 9th ed. — Edinburgh : Churchill Livingstone, 1980. — 144p ; 19cm
Previous ed.: 1976. — Includes index
ISBN 0-443-01863-4 (pbk) : £3.75 : CIP rev. B80-25736

617'.96 — Medicine. Anaesthesia — *Manuals*

Stark, David C. C.. Practical points in anesthesiology / by David C.C. Stark with the assistance of R. Bryan Roberts. — 2nd ed. — London : Kimpton, 1980. — 364p : ill ; 21cm
Previous ed.: New York : Medical Examination Pub. Co., 1974. — Includes index
ISBN 0-87488-700-3 (pbk) : £7.50 B81-07507

617'.96 — Medicine. Anaesthesia. Techniques

Thornton, J. A.. Techniques of anaesthesia : with management of the patient and intensive care. — 2nd ed. / J.A. Thornton and C.J. Levy with special chapters and sections by R.E. Atkinson ... [et al.]. — London : Chapman and Hall, 1981. — x,574p : ill,forms ; 24cm
Previous ed.: 1974. — Bibliography: p544-556. - Includes index
ISBN 0-412-15970-8 : £16.50 : CIP rev. B80-36127

617'.96 — Medicine. Anaesthesiology — *Conference proceedings*

World Congress of Anaesthesiologists *(7th : 1980 : Hamburg).* 7th World Congress of Anaesthesiologists : Hamburg, F.R.G., September 14-21, 1980 : under the patronage of the President of the Federal Republic of Germany : abstracts / editors E. Rügheimer, J. Wawersik, M. Zindler. — Amsterdam ; Oxford : Excerpta Medica, 1980. — xvi,589p ; 24cm. — (International congress series ; no.533)
Includes index
ISBN 90-219-1240-6 (pbk) : £31.51 B81-39028

617′.96 — Medicine. Anaesthesiology — *Conference proceedings continuation*

World Congress of Anaesthesiologists *(7th : 1980 : Hamburg).* Anaesthesiology : proceedings of the 7th World Congress of Anaesthesiologists, Hamburg, September 14-21, 1980 / editors E. Rügheimer, M. Zindler. — Amsterdam ; Oxford : Excerpta Medica, 1981. — xxxv,1068p : ill ; 25cm. — (International congress series ; no.538)
Bibliography: pxxxv. - Includes index
ISBN 90-219-0468-3 : £67.05
ISBN 0-444-90186-8 (Elsevier/North-Holland)
B81-22294

617′.96′024613 — Medicine. Anaesthesia — *For nursing*

Wachstein, Jennifer. Anaesthesia and recovery room techniques. — 3rd ed. / Jennifer Wachstein, Jean A.H. Smith ; with a foreword by O.P. Dinnick. — London : Baillière Tindall, 1981. — viii,165p : ill(some col.),forms ; 20cm. — (Nurses′ aids series)
Previous ed.: 1976. — Ill on inside front cover. — Includes bibliographies and index
ISBN 0-7020-0867-2 (pbk) : £4.75 : CIP rev.
B81-16938

Wallace, C. J.. Anaesthetic nursing / C.J. Wallace. — London : Pitman Medical, 1981. — 278p : ill ; 23cm
Includes index
ISBN 0-272-79542-9 : Unpriced : CIP rev.
B78-38462

617′.96′0289 — Anaesthetic equipment. Safety aspects

Wyant, Gordon M.. Mechanical misadventures in anaesthesia / Gordon M. Wyant. — Toronto ; London : University of Toronto Press, c1978. — xvii,174p,[1]leaf of plates : ill(some col.) ; 24cm
Bibliography: p141-168. — Includes index
ISBN 0-8020-5423-4 : £10.50 B81-25469

617′.96′05 — Medicine. Anaesthesiology — *Serials*

Monographs in anaesthesiology. — 8. — Amsterdam ; Oxford (256 Banbury Rd, Oxford) : Excerpta Medica, 1981. — 336p
ISBN 0-444-80213-4 : £38.12 B81-30720

617′.96′088054 — Children. Anaesthesia

Davenport, Harold T.. Paediatric anaesthesia / Harold T. Davenport. — 3rd ed. — London : Heinemann Medical, 1980. — x,273p : ill ; 23cm
Previous ed.: 1973. — Includes bibliographies and index
ISBN 0-433-07152-4 : £12.00 B81-03438

Rees, G. Jackson. Paediatric anaesthesia : trends in current practice / G. Jackson Rees, T. Cecil Gray. — London : Butterworths, 1981. — xi,194p : ill ; 24cm
Includes bibliographies and index
ISBN 0-407-00114-x : Unpriced : CIP rev.
B81-12345

Smith, Robert M. (Robert Moors). Anesthesia for infants and children / Robert M. Smith. — 4th ed. — St Louis ; London : Mosby, 1980. — xii,702p : ill(some col.),forms ; 27cm
Previous ed.: St Austell : Kingston, 1968. — Ill on lining papers. — Includes bibliographies and index
ISBN 0-8016-4699-5 : £41.75 B81-16659

617′.96′0926 — Medicine. Anaesthesia — *Case studies — Conference proceedings*

Clinical anesthesia : case selections from the University of California, San Francisco / [edited by] Philip L. Wilkinson, Jay Ham, Ronald D. Miller. — St. Louis ; London : Mosby, 1980. — xii,324p : ill ; 27cm
Proceedings of clinical conferences. — Includes bibliographies and index
ISBN 0-8016-3423-7 : Unpriced B81-08663

617′.96′0941 — Great Britain. Medicine. Anaesthesia — *Serials*

Handbook of British anaesthesia. — 1980/81. — London : Macmillan, c1980. — 92p
ISSN 0260-2873 : £5.95 B81-09686

617′.962 — Medicine. Closed anaesthesia

Lowe, Harry J.. The quantitative practice of anesthesia : use of closed circuit / Harry J. Lowe, Edward A. Ernst. — Baltimore ; London : Williams & Wilkins, c1981. — xv,234p : ill,1port ; 26cm
Includes index
ISBN 0-683-05200-4 : £42.00 B81-20755

617′.964 — Medicine. Spinal analgesia

Greene, Nicholas M.. Physiology of spinal anesthesia / Nicholas M. Greene ; with a foreword by John Gillies. — 3rd ed. — Baltimore ; London : Williams & Wilkins, c1981. — xii,278p : ill ; 24cm
Previous ed.: 1969. — Includes bibliographies and index
ISBN 0-683-03554-1 : £38.50 B81-24344

617′.96748 — Man. Nervous system. Anaesthesia

Anesthesia and neurosurgery / [edited by] James E. Cottrell, Herman Turndorf. — St. Louis ; London : Mosby, 1980. — xiii,433p : ill ; 27cm
Includes bibliographies and index
ISBN 0-8016-1036-2 : £39.00 B81-08034

A **Basis** and practice of neuroanesthesia / edited by Emeric Gordon. — 2nd completely rev. ed. — Amsterdam ; Oxford : Excerpta Medica, 1981. — xv,354p : ill ; 25cm. — (Monographs in anaesthesiology ; v.2)
Previous ed.: 1975. — Includes bibliographies and index
ISBN 0-444-80252-5 : £35.50 B81-36756

617′.967′54 — Man. Thorax. Surgery. Anaesthesia

Gothard, J. W. W.. Anaesthesia for thoracic surgery. — Oxford : Blackwell Scientific, Feb.1982. — [216]p
ISBN 0-632-00578-5 : £16.00 : CIP entry
B81-36969

617′.9676 — Dentistry. Anaesthesia & analgesia — *Conference proceedings*

International Dental Congress on Modern Pain Control *(2nd : 1979 : London).* S.A.A.D. digest : papers presented at Second International Dental Congress on Modern Pain Control, July 1979, London. — London (53 Wimpole St., W1M 7DF) : Society for the Advancement of Anaesthesia in Dentistry, [1980?]. — 225p : ill ; 25cm
ISBN 0-902976-02-8 (pbk) : Unpriced
B81-29225

617′.9676 — Dentistry. Anaesthesia & analgesia. Techniques

Kaufman, L.. General anaesthesia, local analgesia and sedation in dentistry. — Oxford : Blackwell Scientific, Nov.1981. — [192]p
ISBN 0-632-00847-4 (pbk) : £9.50 : CIP entry
B81-30902

617′.9676 — Dentistry. Local anaesthesia

Howe, Geoffrey L.. Local anaesthesia in dentistry / Geoffrey L. Howe and F. Ivor H. Whitehead. — 2nd ed. — Bristol : John Wright, 1981. — viii,94p : ill ; 22cm. — (A Dental practitioner handbook ; no.14)
Previous ed.: 1972. — Includes index
ISBN 0-7236-0599-8 (pbk) : Unpriced
B81-27579

Jastak, J. Theodore. Regional anesthesia of the oral cavity / J. Theodore Jastak, John A. Yagiela. — St. Louis ; London : Mosby, 1981. — xi,212p : ill ; 29cm
Includes bibliographies and index
ISBN 0-8016-2434-7 : £14.75 B81-32997

Malamed, Stanley F.. Handbook of local anesthesia / Stanley F. Malamed ; original drawings by Susan B. Clifford. — St. Louis ; London : Mosby, 1980. — xi,249p : ill,forms ; 28cm
Includes bibliographies and index
ISBN 0-8016-3072-x (spiral) : Unpriced
B81-08157

617′.96798 — Children. Congenital abnormalities. Anaesthesia

Anesthetic implications of congenital anomalies in children / [edited by] Linda C. Stehling, Howard L. Zauder ; foreword by Josef Warkany. — New York : Appleton-Century-Crofts ; London : Prentice-Hall, c1980. — xiv,202p : ill ; 24cm
Includes index
ISBN 0-8385-0102-8 : £12.05 B81-03222

617′.96798 — Newborn babies. Anaesthesia

Hatch, David J.. Neonatal anaesthesia / David J. Hatch and Edward Sumner. — London : Edward Arnold, 1981. — xii,207p : ill ; 24cm. — (Current topics in anaesthesia, ISSN 0144-8684 ; 5)
Includes bibliographies and index
ISBN 0-7131-4370-3 : £14.95 B81-09614

617′.9682 — Childbirth. Labour. Epidural analgesia — *Conference proceedings*

Epidural analgesia in obstetrics : a second symposium, University of Warwick, Coventry / [organised by] Obstetric Anaesthetists Association ; Andrew Doughty (editor). — London : Lloyd-Luke, 1980. — xvi,208p : ill,1 port ; 22cm
Includes bibliographies and index
ISBN 0-85324-146-5 (pbk) : £7.50 B81-06300

617′.98′00222 — Children. Surgery — *Illustrations*

Spitz, Lewis. A colour atlas of paediatric surgical diagnosis / Lewis Spitz, G.M. Steiner, R.B. Zachary. — London : Wolfe Medical Publications, 1981. — 240p : ill(some col.) ; 27cm
Includes index
ISBN 0-7234-0763-0 : Unpriced B81-33579

618 — GYNAECOLOGY AND OBSTETRICS

618 — Girls, to 16 years. Medical aspects

Huffman, John W.. The gynecology of childhood and adolescence / John W. Huffman, Sir C. John Dewhurst, Vincent J. Capraro. — 2nd ed. — Philadelphia ; London : Saunders, 1981. — viii,588p : ill ; 27cm
Previous ed.: 1968. — Includes bibliographies and index
ISBN 0-7216-4816-9 : £40.00 B81-34830

618 — Gynaecology & obstetrics

Dilts, P. V.. Core studies in obstetrics and gynecology / P.V. Dilts Jr., J.W. Greene Jr., J.W. Roddick Jr. — 3rd ed. — Baltimore ; London : Williams & Wilkins, c1981. — xvii,242p : ill ; 23cm : 2forms
Previous ed.: 1977. — Includes index
ISBN 0-683-02572-4 (pbk) : £19.00 B81-20762

Gynecology and obstetrics : the health care of women / Seymour L. Romney ... [et al.]. — 2nd ed. — New York ; London : McGraw-Hill, c1981. — xiv,1310p : ill ; 26cm
Previous ed.: 1975. — Includes bibliographies and index
ISBN 0-07-053582-5 : £33.50 B81-08115

Hull, M. G. R.. Undergraduate obstetrics and gynaecology / M.G.R. Hull, Gillian Turner, D.N. Joyce ; edited by G. Dixon. — Bristol : Wright, 1980. — vii,270p : ill ; 22cm
Includes bibliographies and index
ISBN 0-7236-0564-5 (pbk) : £5.00 : CIP rev.
B80-18777

Integrated obstetrics and gynaecology for postgraduates. — 3rd ed. — Oxford : Blackwell Scientific, Nov.1981. — [900]p
Previous ed.: 1976
ISBN 0-632-00684-6 : £45.00 : CIP entry
B81-30328

Neeson, Jean D.. The practitioner′s handbook of ambulatory ob/gyn / Jean D. Neeson, Connie R. Stockdale. — New York ; Chichester : Wiley, c1981. — xii,394p : ill ; 24cm. — (A Wiley medical publication)
Text on lining papers. — Includes bibliographies and index
ISBN 0-471-05670-7 : £13.25 B81-33229

618 — Gynaecology & obstetrics
continuation

Page, Ernest W.. Human reproduction : essentials of reproductive and perinatal medicine / Ernest W. Page, Claude A. Villee, Dorothy B. Villee. — 3rd ed. — Philadelphia ; London : Saunders, 1981. — xvii,526p : ill ; 25cm
Previous ed.: 1976. — Includes bibliographies and index
ISBN 0-7216-7053-9 : Unpriced
Primary classification 612'.6 B81-33221

618 — Gynaecology & obstetrics. Drug therapy. Antibiotics

Gibbs, Ronald S.. Antibiotic therapy in obstetrics and gynecology / Ronald S. Gibbs, Allan J. Weinstein. — New York ; Chichester : Wiley, c1981. — x,215p : ill ; 23cm
Bibliography: p195-203. — Includes index
ISBN 0-471-06003-8 (pbk) : £9.10 B81-16952

618 — Gynaecology & obstetrics — *Early works*

Medieval woman's guide to health : the first English gynecological handbook / middle English text, with introduction and modern English translation by Beryl Rowland. — London : Croom Helm, 1981. — xvii,192p : ill ; 24cm
Parallel middle English text and English translation. — Text on lining papers. — Includes bibliography and index
ISBN 0-7099-2216-7 : £10.95 B81-37485

618 — Gynaecology & obstetrics. Emergency treatment — *Manuals*

Heller, Luz. Emergencies in gynecology and obstetrics / Luz Heller ; translated by Hans E. Kaiser. — Chicago ; London : Year Book Medical Publishers, 1981. — 178p : ill ; 19cm. — (Thieme flexibook)
Translation of: Notfälle in Gynäkologie und Geburtshilfe. 2nd ed. — Includes index
ISBN 0-8151-4225-0 (pbk) : £6.00 B81-30927

618 — Gynaecology & obstetrics — *For house physicians*

Anderson, Mary M. (Mary Margaret). A handbook of obstetrics and gynaecology for the house officer / Mary M. Anderson. — London : Faber, 1981. — 173p ; 20cm
Includes index
ISBN 0-571-11649-3 (pbk) : £3.95 : CIP rev. B81-00937

618'.05 — Gynaecology & obstetrics — *Serials*

Journal of obstetrics and gynaecology : the journal of the Institute of Obstetrics and Gynaecology. — Vol.1, no.1 (Aug.1980)-. — Bristol : John Wright, 1980. — v. : ill ; 25cm
Quarterly
ISSN 0144-3615 = Journal of obstetrics and gynaecology : £17.50 per year B81-08361

618'.05 — Gynaecology & obstetrics - *Serials*

Progress in obstetrics and gynaecology. — Vol.1. — Edinburgh : Churchill Livingstone, May 1981. — [324]p
ISBN 0-443-02178-3 (pbk) : £12.00 : CIP entry B81-07583

618'.05 — Gynaecology & obstetrics — *Serials*

Progress in obstetrics and gynaecology. — Vol.1-. — Edinburgh : Churchill Livingstone, 1981-. — v. : ill,facsims ; 24cm
Annual
ISSN 0261-0140 = Progress in obstetrics and gynaecology : £14.00 B81-34025

618'.076 — Gynaecology & obstetrics — *Questions & answers*

Obstetrics and gynecology : PreTest self-assessment and review / edited by Alan H. DeCherney. — New York ; London : McGraw-Hill, c1978. — ix,210p : ill ; 22cm. — (PreTest series)
Originally published: Wallingford, Conn. : PreTest Service, 1978. — Bibliography: p207-210
ISBN 0-07-051602-2 (pbk) : £6.95 B81-19470

618.1 — GYNAECOLOGY

618.1 — Gynaecology — *For women*

Saunders, Peter, *1937-*. Womanwise : every woman's guide to gynaecology / Peter Saunders. — London : Hale, [1981]. — 205p : ill ; 23cm
Originally published: London : Pan, 1980. — Includes index
ISBN 0-7091-9286-x : £6.95 B81-34733

618.1 — Women. Reproductive system. Disorders

Rhodes, Philip. Women only : a gynaecological guide / by Philip Rhodes. — London : British Medical Association, [1981?]. — 31p : ill ; 19cm. — (A Family doctor booklet)
£0.50 (unbound) B81-39049

618.1 — Women. Reproductive system. Disorders — *For women*

Saunders, Peter, *1937-*. Womanwise : every woman's guide to gynaecology / Peter Saunders. — London : Pan, 1981. — 205p : ill ; 18cm
Includes index
ISBN 0-330-26374-9 (pbk) : £1.75 B81-26240

618.1'0022'2 — Women. Reproductive system. Disorders — *Illustrations*

Tindall, V. R.. A colour atlas of clinical gynaecology / V.R. Tindall. — [London] : Wolfe Medical, 1981. — 131p : col.ill ; 27cm. — (Wolfe medical atlases)
Includes index
ISBN 0-7234-0761-4 : Unpriced B81-18468

618.1'0024613 — Gynaecology — *For nursing*

Gynaecology in nursing practice / edited by M.A. Shorthouse and M.G. Brush. — London : Baillière Tindall, 1981. — x,246p : ill ; 21cm
Includes bibliographies and index
ISBN 0-7020-0841-9 (pbk) : £7.50 : CIP rev. B81-13502

618.1'007 — Patients. Health education. Special subjects: Women. Reproductive system. Diseases — *For nursing*

Women's health care : a guide for patient education / edited by E. Dorsey Smith. — New York : Appleton-Century-Crofts ; London : Prentice-Hall, c1981. — xv,187p : ill ; 24cm. — (Appleton patient education series)
Includes bibliographies and index
ISBN 0-8385-9825-0 (pbk) : £8.05 B81-36603

618.1'00973 — United States. Gynaecology — *For women*

Derbyshire, Caroline. The new woman's guide to health and medicine / Caroline Derbyshire ; foreword by John P. Bunker. — New York : Appleton-Century-Crofts ; London : Prentice-Hall, c1980. — xvi,320p : ill ; 21cm
Bibliography: p299-311. — Includes index
ISBN 0-8385-6759-2 (cased) : £8.40
ISBN 0-8385-6758-4 (pbk) : : £3.85 B81-02309

618.1'059 — Women. Reproductive system. Surgery. Complications

Complications in obstetric and gynecologic surgery : prevention, diagnosis, and treatment / edited by George Schaefer, Edward A. Graber. — Hagerstown ; London : Harper & Row, c1981. — xvii,492p : ill ; 26cm
Includes bibliographies and index
ISBN 0-06-142330-0 : £26.00 B81-25977

618.1'059 — Women. Reproductive system. Surgery. Techniques

Lees, David H.. A colour atlas of gynaecological surgery / David H. Lees, Albert Singer. — London : Wolfe Medical
Vol.5: Infertility surgery / with a contribution by Robert M.L. Winston. — c1981. — 200p : ill(some col.) ; 31cm
Bibliography: p191-195. — Includes index
ISBN 0-7234-0727-4 : Unpriced B81-39178

618.1'06 — Women. Reproductive system. Therapy

Gynaecological therapeutics / edited by D.F. Hawkins. — London : Baillière Tindall, 1981. — viii,287p : ill ; 25cm
Includes bibliographies and index
ISBN 0-7020-0797-8 : £14.50 B81-21875

618.1'0757 — Women. Reproductive system. Diagnosis. Radiography

Whitehouse, G. H.. Gynaecological radiology / G.H. Whitehouse. — Oxford : Blackwell Scientific, 1981. — 240p : ill ; 24cm
Includes bibliographies and index
ISBN 0-632-00726-5 : £24.00 B81-24038

618.1'1 — Women. Ovaries. Disorders — *Conference proceedings*

International Study Group for Steroid Hormones. *Meeting (9th : 1979 : Rome)*. Endocrinological cancer, ovarian function and disease : proceedings of the IX Meeting of the International Study Group for Steroid Hormones, Rome December 5-7, 1979 / editors H. Adlercreutz ... [et al.]. — Amsterdam ; Oxford : Excerpta Medica, 1981. — xii,400p : ill ; 25cm. — (Research on steroids ; v.9) (International congress series ; no.515)
Includes bibliographies and index
ISBN 90-219-0444-6 : £29.90
Primary classification 616.99'449071 B81-15663

618.1'407545 — Medicine. Colposcopy

Atlas of colposcopy. — Completely rev. 5th ed. / by G. Mestwerdt ... [et al.], edited by Emanuel A. Friedman / translated by E. Judith Friedman and Emanuel A. Friedman. — Philadelphia ; London : Saunders, 1981. — 176p : ill(some col.),1port ; 29cm
Translation of: Atlas der Kolposkopie. 5 Aufl.. — Bibliography: p163-167. — Includes index
ISBN 0-7216-6268-4 : £42.00 B81-37462

618.1'5059 — Women. Vagina. Surgery

Surgery of the vulva and vagina : a practical guide / Edward H. Copenhaver ... [et al.]. — Philadelphia ; London : Saunders, 1981. — xii,110p ; 27cm
Bibliography: p105-106. - Includes index
ISBN 0-7216-2718-8 : £17.50
Also classified at 618.1'6059 B81-16464

618.1'6059 — Women. Vulva. Surgery

Surgery of the vulva and vagina : a practical guide / Edward H. Copenhaver ... [et al.]. — Philadelphia ; London : Saunders, 1981. — xii,110p ; 27cm
Bibliography: p105-106. - Includes index
ISBN 0-7216-2718-8 : £17.50
Primary classification 618.1'5059 B81-16464

618.1'72 — Women. Menstrual problems

Birke, Lynda. Why suffer? : periods and their problems. — 2nd ed. — London : Virago, Jan.1982. — [80]p
Previous ed.: 1979
ISBN 0-86068-284-6 (pbk) : £1.95 : CIP entry B81-33761

618.1'72 — Women. Premenstrual syndrome — *Conference proceedings*

The **Premenstrual** syndrome : proceedings of a workshop held during the Sixth International Congress of Psychosomatic obstetrics and Gynecology / edited by Pieter A. van Keep and Wulf H. Utian ... assisted by Pamela Freebody. — Lancaster : MTP, 1981. — 121p : ill ; 23cm
Includes bibliographies and index
ISBN 0-85200-387-0 : £8.95 B81-23988

618.1'78059 — Test tube babies

In vitro fertilization and embryo transfer. — Lancaster : MTP Press, Jan.1982. — [410]p
ISBN 0-85200-438-9 : £29.00 : CIP entry B81-38819

618.1'9 — Women. Breasts. Diseases — *Conference proceedings*

Symposium on Mammary Pathology *(1st : 1979 : Paris)*. New frontiers in mammary pathology / [proceedings of the First Symposium on Mammary Pathology organised by the International Society Against Breast Cancer, and held December 3-7, 1979 in Paris, France] ; edited by K.H. Hollmann, J de Brux and J.M. Verley. — New York ; London : Plenum, c1981. — viii,319p : ill ; 26cm
Includes bibliographies and index
ISBN 0-306-40655-1 : Unpriced B81-37500

618.1′90757 — Women. Breasts. Diagnosis. Radiography — *Illustrations*

Nathan, Ted. An atlas of normal and abnormal mammograms. — Oxford : Oxford University Press, Dec.1981. — [140]p. — (Oxford medical publications)
ISBN 0-19-261346-4 : £30.00 : CIP entry
B81-32044

618.1′907582 — Women. Breasts. Diagnosis. Needle aspiration. Aspirates: Cells — *Illustrations*

Grubb, Chandra. Colour atlas of breast cytopathology / Chandra Grubb ; foreword by John H. Wyllie. — Aylesbury : HM & M, c1981. — 55p : chiefly col.ill ; 28cm
Includes index
ISBN 0-85602-088-5 : Unpriced B81-27708

618.2 — OBSTETRICS

618.2 — Obstetrics

Amiel, Gerald J. Essential obstetric practice / Gerald J. Amiel. — Lancaster : MTP, 1981. — x,260p : ill ; 24cm
Includes index
ISBN 0-85200-361-7 (pbk) : £5.75 B81-33074

Bender, S. Practical student obstetrics / by S. Bender and V.R. Tindall ; illustrated by Audrey Besterman. — London : Heinemann Medical, 1980. — vi,435p : ill ; 18cm
Text on inside covers. — Includes index
ISBN 0-433-02403-8 (pbk) : £12.50 B81-00938

Fergusson, I. L. C. Records and curiosities in obstetrics and gynaecology. — London : Baillière Tindall, Nov.1981. — [176]p
ISBN 0-7020-0896-6 : £5.00 : CIP entry
B81-30165

Gebbie, Donald A. M. Reproductive anthropology. — Chichester : Wiley, Nov.1981. — [416]p
ISBN 0-471-27985-4 : £19.50 : CIP entry
B81-31204

Huang, C. L.-H. Companion to obstetrics. — Lancaster : MTP Press, Jan.1982. — [260]p
ISBN 0-85200-379-x : £8.95 : CIP entry
B81-34579

Obstetrical practice / edited by Silvio Aladjem ; illustrated by Edwin V. Hord. — St. Louis ; London : Mosby, 1980. — xiv,877p,1leaf of plates : ill(some col.) ; 26cm
Includes bibliographies and index
ISBN 0-8016-0114-2 : £29.00 B81-02633

Obstetrics / by ten teachers. — 13th ed. / under the direction of Stanley G. Clayton ; edited by Stanley G. Clayton, T.L.T. Lewis, G. Pinker. — London : Edward Arnold, c1980. — x,541p : ill ; 25cm
Previous ed.: 1972. — Includes index
ISBN 0-7131-4365-7 : £13.50 : CIP rev.
B80-18778

Obstetrics illustrated / Matthew M. Garrey ... [et al.]. — 3rd ed.. — Edinburgh : Churchill Livingstone, 1981. — 544p : ill(some col.) ; 25cm
Previous ed.: 1974. — Includes index
ISBN 0-443-02513-4 (pbk) : £4.35 B81-33743

Principles and practice of obstetrics & perinatology / edited by Leslie Iffy, Harold A. Kaminetzky. — New York ; London : Wiley, c1981. — 2v.(xxviii,1830,40p,4p of plates) : ill (some col.),2ports ; 25cm. — (A Wiley medical publication)
Includes index
ISBN 0-471-05040-7 : £85.00
Also classified at 618.3′2 B81-29271

Stirrat, G. M. Obstetrics. — London (39 Great Russell St., WC1B 3PH) : Grant McIntyre, Apr.1981. — [250]p. — (Pocket consultants)
ISBN 0-86216-011-1 (pbk) : £5.95 : CIP entry
B81-08858

Stirrat, Gordon M. Obstetrics / G.M. Stirrat. — London : Grant MacIntyre, 1981. — 282p : ill ; 19cm. — (Pocket consultant)
Cover title. — Includes index
ISBN 0-86286-002-4 (pbk) : £5.95 B81-31662

Williams, J. Whitridge. Williams Obstetrics. — 16th ed. / Jack A. Pritchard, Paul C. MacDonald. — New York : Appleton-Century-Crofts ; London : Prentice-Hall, c1980. — xvi,1179p,[8]p of plates : ill(some col.),1form ; 27cm
Previous ed.: 1976. — Includes bibliographies and index
ISBN 0-8385-9731-9 : £31.55 B81-02709

618.2 — Obstetrics — *For midwifery*

Myles, Margaret F. Textbook for midwives : with modern concepts of obstetric and neonatal care / Margaret F. Myles. — 9th ed. — Edinburgh : Churchill Livingstone, 1981. — xvii,890p : ill[some col] ; 24cm
Previous ed.: 1975. — Includes index
ISBN 0-443-02011-6 (cased) : Unpriced : CIP rev.
ISBN 0-443-02010-8 (pbk) : £12.00 B80-11474

618.2 — Women. Pregnancy & childbirth

Kitzinger, Sheila. Pregnancy and childbirth / Sheila Kitzinger ; photography by Camilla Jessel. — London : Joseph, 1980. — 351p : ill (some col.) ; 25cm
Bibliography: p336. — Includes index
ISBN 0-7181-1918-5 : £8.95 B81-00939

618.2 — Women. Uterus. Cervix. Effects of pregnancy

The **Cervix** in pregnancy and labour : clinical and biochemical investigations / edited by David A. Ellwood and Anne B.M. Anderson ; foreword by Mostyn P. Embrey. — Edinburgh : Churchill Livingstone, 1981. — 201p : ill ; 24cm
Conference papers. — Includes bibliographies and index
ISBN 0-443-02304-2 : £16.00 : CIP rev.
B81-04269

618.2′001′9 — Women. Pregnancy & childbirth. Psychological aspects

Whelan, Elizabeth M. The pregnancy experience : the psychology of expectant parenthood / Elizabeth M. Whelan. — New York ; London : Norton, c1978. — 202p ; 22cm
Bibliography: p189-193. — Includes index
ISBN 0-393-01179-8 : £6.75 B81-02510

618.2′001′9 — Women. Pregnancy, childbirth & parenthood. Psychological aspects

Grossman, Frances Kaplan. Pregnancy, birth and parenthood / Frances Kaplan Grossman, Lois S. Eichler, Susan A. Winickoff ; with Margery Kistin Anzalone, Mariam H. Gofseyeff, Susan P. Sargent. — San Francisco ; London : Jossey-Bass, 1980. — xviii,306p ; 24cm. — (The Jossey-Bass social and behavioral science series)
Bibliography: p278-296. - Includes index
ISBN 0-87589-465-8 : £12.75 B81-06489

Pregnancy, childbirth and parenthood / Paul Ahmed, editor. — New York ; Oxford : Elsevier, c1981. — xxx,414p : ill,1map ; 24cm. — (Coping with medical issues)
Includes bibliographies and index
ISBN 0-444-00558-7 : £20.97 B81-36762

618.2′001′9 — Women. Pregnancy. Psychological aspects

Pregnancy : a psychological and social study / edited by S. Wolkind and E. Zajicek. — London : Academic Press, 1981. — x,228p ; 24cm
Includes bibliographies and index
ISBN 0-12-762080-x : £10.40 : CIP rev.
B81-12332

618.2′00240431 — Women. Pregnancy & childbirth — *For fathers*

Forbes, Ruth. Father-to-be / by Ruth Forbes. — London : British Medical Association, [1981]. — 31p : ill ; 19cm. — (A Family doctor booklet)
£0.40 (unbound) B81-17743

618.2′00240431 — Women. Pregnancy & childbirth — *For mothers*

Kitzinger, Sheila. Sheila Kitzinger′s birth book : a journal of your thoughts and feelings about childbirth / with photographs by Suzanne Arms. — [London] : Fontana Paperbacks, 1980. — [152]p : ill ; 24cm
ISBN 0-00-636293-1 (pbk) : £2.95 B81-11056

618.2′00240431 — Women. Pregnancy & childbirth — *Manuals* — *For parents*

Brady, Margaret Y. Having a baby easily : a guide to natural birth / by Margaret Y. Brady. — Completely rev. and reset. — Wellingborough : Thorsons, 1981. — 143p : ill ; 22cm
Previous ed.: London : Health for all, 1969. — Bibliography: p137. — Includes index
ISBN 0-7225-0668-6 (pbk) : £2.95
Also classified at 649′.122 B81-24170

618.2′0024613 — Obstetrics — *For nursing*

Anderson, Barbara Gallatin. Obstetrics for the nurse. — 3rd ed. / Barbara G. Anderson, Pamela J. Shapiro. — New York ; London : Van Nostrand Reinhold, c1981. — 272p : ill (some col.) ; 27cm
Previous ed.: Albany, N.Y. : Delmar Publishers, 1972. — Bibliography: p260-262. — Includes index
ISBN 0-442-21840-0 : £10.45 B81-29522

Jensen, Margaret Duncan. Handbook of maternity care : a guide for nursing practice / Margaret Duncan Jensen, Irene M. Bobak. — St. Louis ; London : Mosby, 1980. — xi,286p : ill,forms ; 28cm
Includes index
ISBN 0-8016-2490-8 (spiral) : Unpriced
B81-08537

618.2′007 — Patients. Health education. Special subjects. Women. Pregnancy & childbirth — *For nursing*

Maternity care : a guide for patient education / edited by E. Dorsey Smith. — New York : Appleton-Century-Crofts ; London : Prentice-Hall, c1981. — xv,208p : ill ; 24cm. — (Appleton patient education series)
Includes bibliographies and index
ISBN 0-8385-6170-5 (pbk) : £8.10 B81-36604

618.2′00913 — Tropical regions. Obstetrics — *For midwifery*

Ojo, O. A. A textbook for midwives in the tropics. — 2nd ed. — London : Edward Arnold, Feb.1982. — [450]p
Previous ed.: 1976
ISBN 0-7131-4413-0 (pbk) : £5.00 : CIP entry
B81-36393

618.2′00973 — United States. Adolescent girls. Pregnancy, childbirth & parenthood

Teenage parents and their offspring / edited by Keith G. Scott, Tiffany Field, Euan G. Robertson. — New York ; London : Grune & Stratton, 1981. — xv,328p : ill ; 24cm
Includes index
ISBN 0-8089-1314-x : £13.80 B81-18181

618.2′2 — Obstetrics. Diagnosis. Ultrasonography

Recent advances in perinatal pathology and physiology / edited by D.N. White. — Letchworth : Research Studies Press, c1980. — xiv,245p : ill ; 29cm. — (Ultrasound in biomedicine research series ; 4)
Includes bibliographies and index
ISBN 0-471-27925-0 (pbk) : £19.00 B81-10101

618.2′4 — Antenatal medicine. Diagnosis — *Serials*

Prenatal diagnosis. — Vol.1, no.1 (Jan.1981)-. — Chichester : Wiley, 1981-. — v. : ill ; 25cm
Quarterly
£35.00 per year B81-17487

618.2′4 — Nottinghamshire. Antenatal classes

Perkins, Elizabeth R. Parentcraft : a comparative study of teaching method / Elizabeth R. Perkins. — [Nottingham] : University of Nottingham, 1979. — 28leaves ; 30cm. — (Occasional paper / Leverhulme Health Education Project ; no.16)
Unpriced (pbk) B81-22731

618.2′4 — Pregnant women. Antenatal education

Perkins, Elizabeth R. Education for childbirth and parenthood / Elizabeth R. Perkins. — London : Croom Helm, c1980. — 180p ; 23cm
Bibliography: p170-177. — Includes index
ISBN 0-7099-0273-5 : £10.95 : CIP rev.
B80-17745

618.2'4 — Pregnant women. Medical care
Perkins, Elizabeth R.. Having a baby : an educational experience? / Elizabeth R. Perkins. — [Nottingham] : University of Nottingham, 1978. — 39,7leaves ; 30cm. — (Occasional paper / Leverhulme Health Education Project ; no.6)
"This paper is based on research initiated by Dr. Suzanne Packer, to which Miss Sally Snell, B.Sc., made a major contribution"
Unpriced (pbk) B81-22820

618.2'4'094252 — Nottinghamshire. Pregnant women. Antenatal education
Perkins, Elizabeth R.. Antenatal classes in Nottinghamshire : the pattern of official provision / Elizabeth R. Perkins. — [Nottingham] : University of Nottingham, 1978. — 12,[28]leaves : forms ; 30cm. — (Occasional paper / Leverhulme Health Education Project ; no.9)
Unpriced (pbk) B81-22819

618.3 — Pregnant women. Interactions with foetuses. Immunological aspects
Cauchi, Maurice N.. Obstetric and perinatal immunology. — London : Edward Arnold, Oct.1981. — [128]p. — (Current topics in immunology, ISSN 0305-8204 ; 16)
ISBN 0-7131-4384-3 : £12.00 : CIP entry
B81-27930

618.3'07 — Pregnant women. Diseases. Physiological aspects
Clinical physiology in obstetrics / edited by Frank Hytten and Geoffrey Chamberlain ; foreword by Sir John Dewhurst. — 3rd ed. — Oxford : Blackwell Scientific, 1980. — xi,506p : ill ; 24cm
Includes index
ISBN 0-632-00654-4 : £28.00 : CIP rev.
B80-18751

618.3'2 — Man. Embryos & foetuses. Death — *Conference proceedings*
New York State Health Department Birth Defects Symposium *(10th : 1979 : Albany, New York)*. Human embryonic and fetal death : proceedings of the tenth Annual New York State Health Department Birth Defects Symposium / edited by Ian H. Porter, Ernest B. Hook. — New York ; London : Academic Press, c1980. — xvi,371p : ill ; 24cm. — (Birth Defects Institute symposia)
Includes index
ISBN 0-12-562860-9 : £15.20 B81-17711

618.3'2 — Man. Foetuses & newborn babies. Diseases
Babson, S. Gorham. Diagnosis and management of the fetus and neonate at risk : a guide for team care. — 4th ed / S. Gorham Babson, Martin L. Pernoll, Gerda I. Benda with the assistance of Katherine Simpson. — St. Louis ; London : Mosby, c1980. — xiii,345p : ill,forms ; 27cm
Previous ed.: published as Management of high-risk pregnancy and intensive care of the neonate. 1975. — Text on lining papers. — Includes bibliographies and index
ISBN 0-8016-0415-x : £22.50 B81-32642

618.3'2 — Man. Foetuses & newborn babies. Patholgy
Fetal and neonatal pathology : perspectives for the general pathologist. — Eastbourne : Praeger, Feb.1982. — [272]p
ISBN 0-03-061714-6 : £15.00 : CIP entry
B81-39235

618.3'2 — Man. Foetuses. Developmental disorders — *Conference proceedings*
Fetal growth retardation / edited by F. André van Assche and William B. Robertson ; foreword by Marcel Renaer. — Edinburgh : Churchill Livingstone, 1981. — 265p : ill ; 24cm
Conference papers. — Includes bibliographies and index
ISBN 0-443-02356-5 : £20.00 : CIP rev.
B81-18111

618.3'2 — Perinatal medicine
Obstetric anesthesia and perinatology / [edited by] Ermelando V. Cosmi. — New York : Appleton-Century-Crofts ; London Prentice-Hall, c1981. — xiii,769p : ill ; 24cm
Includes index
ISBN 0-8385-7196-4 : £31.90 B81-37689

Principles and practice of obstetrics & perinatology / edited by Leslie Iffy, Harold A. Kaminetzky. — New York ; London : Wiley, c1981. — 2v.(xxviii,1830,40p,4p of plates) : ill (some col.),2ports ; 25cm. — (A Wiley medical publication)
Includes index
ISBN 0-471-05040-7 : £85.00
Primary classification 618.2 B81-29271

618.3'2 — Perinatal medicine. Applications of biochemistry — *Conference proceedings*
Samuel Z. Levine Conference *(1979 : Paris)*. Physiological and biochemical basis for perinatal medicine : the Samuel Z. Levine Conference 1st International Meeting, Paris Dec. 10-13, 1979 / (organised by Alexandre Minkowski) ; editors M. Monset-Couchard, A. Minkowski. — Basel ; London : Karger, c1981. — xi,368p : ill ; 25cm
English text, English and French forewords. — Includes bibliographies
ISBN 3-8055-1283-x : £39.00 B81-26327

618.3'2 — Perinatal medicine — *Conference proceedings*
Asia Oceania Congress of Perinatology *(1st : 1979 : Singapore)*. Problems in perinatology : proceedings of First Asia Oceania Congress of Perinatology Singapore, November 25-28 1979 / jointly organised by Obstetrical and Gynaecological Society of Singapore and Singapore Paediatric Society ; edited by Sultan M.M. Karim, K.L. Tan. — Lancaster : MTP, [1980]. — xi,612p ; 24cm
Includes index
ISBN 0-85200-574-1 : £19.85 B81-03413

Changing patterns of child bearing and child rearing. — London : Academic Press, Feb.1982. — [170]p
Conference papers
ISBN 0-12-171660-0 : CIP entry
Also classified at 649'.1 B81-35915

618.3'2 — Pregnant women. Perinatal diseases
Clinical perinatology. — 2nd ed. / edited by Silvio Aladjem, Audrey K. Brown, Claude Sureau. — St Louis ; London : Mosby, 1980. — xxix,637p,2 leaves of plates : ill(some col.),forms,1port ; 26cm
Previous ed.: 1974. — Includes bibliographies and index
ISBN 0-8016-0103-7 : £41.75
Also classified at 618.92'01 B81-13254

Perinatal diseases / by 14 authors ; edited by Richard L. Naeye, John M. Kissane and Nathan Kaufman. — Baltimore ; London ([266 Fulham Rd., SW10 9EL]) : Williams & Wilkins, c1981. — xl,425p : ill ; 26cm. — (International Academy of Pathology monograph ; no.22)
Includes bibliographies and index
ISBN 0-683-06301-4 : £44.00 B81-29173

618.3'2 — Pregnant women. Perinatal diseases — *Conference proceedings*
Perinatal infections. — Amsterdam ; Oxford : Excerpta Medica, 1980. — xi,292p : ill ; 25cm. — (Ciba Foundation symposium. New series ; 77)
Conference papers. — Includes bibliographies and index
ISBN 90-219-4083-3 : £22.12 B81-02986

618.3'2'005 — Perinatal medicine — *Serials*
Advances in perinatal medicine. — Vol.1-. — New York ; London ([88 Middlesex St., E1 7EX]) : Plenum Medical Book Co., 1981-. — v. : ill ; 24cm
Unpriced B81-23149

618.3'2075 — Man. Foetuses. Diagnosis — *Conference proceedings*
International Symposium on Recent Advances in Prenatal Diagnosis *(1st : 1980 : Bologna)*. Recent advances in prenatal diagnosis : proceedings of the first International Symposium on Recent Advances in Prenatal Diagnosis, Bologna, 15th-16th September 1980 / edited by C. Orlandi, P.E. Polani, L. Bovicelli. — Chichester : Wiley, 1981. — xviii,326p : ill,1map ; 24cm
Includes bibliographies and index
ISBN 0-471-09987-2 : £1975 : CIP rev.
B81-13894

618.3'2075 — Man. Foetuses. Diagnosis. Laboratory techniques
Laboratory investigation of fetal disease / edited by A.J. Barson ; with a foreword by J.A. Davis. — Bristol : Wright, 1981. — xiii,504p : ill ; 25cm
Includes bibliographies and index
ISBN 0-7236-0563-7 : Unpriced : CIP rev.
B80-22028

618.3'20756 — Man. Foetuses & newborn babies. Blood. Gases. Monitoring
Clinical perinatal biochemical monitoring / [edited by] Niels H. Lauersen, Howard M. Hochberg. — Baltimore ; London : Williams & Wilkins, c1981. — xvi,296p : ill ; 26cm
Bibliography: p269-294. — Includes index
ISBN 0-683-04901-1 : £36.00 B81-24342

618.3'20795 — Man. Foetuses & newborn babies. Immune reactions — *Conference proceedings*
Immunological aspects of infection in the fetus and newborn / editors H.P. Lambert, C.B.S. Wood. — London : Academic Press, 1981. — xii,249p : ill ; 24cm. — ([The Beecham colloquia])
Conference papers. — Includes bibliographies and index
ISBN 0-12-434660-x : Unpriced B81-29816

618.3'261 — Pregnant women. Blood. Coagulation disorders
Graeff, H.. Coagulation disorders in obstetrics : pathobiochemistry, pathophysiology, diagnosis, treatment / by H. Graeff and W. Kuhn in co-operation with U. Bleyl with contributions by H. Burchardi, R. Hafter and R. von Hugo ; translated by A. Davies ; forewords by E.A. Friedman, F.K. Beller and J. Zander. — Philadelphia ; London : Saunders, 1980. — xviii,162p : ill ; 25cm. — (Major problems in obstetrics and gynecology ; v.13)
Translation of: Gerinnungsstörungen in der Geburtshilfe. — Bibliography: p135-157. — Includes index
ISBN 0-7216-4192-x : £17.00 B81-02074

618.3'261 — Pregnant women. Toxemia — *Conference proceedings*
International Meeting on EPH Gestosis *(12th : 1980 : Dubrovnik)*. Current status of EPH gestosis : proceedings of the Twelfth International Meeting on EPH Gestosis, Dubrovnik, Yugoslavia, May 18-25, 1980 / edited by Asim Kurjak, Ernst T. Rippmann, Vojin Šulović. — Amsterdam ; Oxford : Excerpta Medica, 1981. — xiv,524p : ill ; 25cm. — (International congress series ; no.534)
Includes index
ISBN 90-219-0455-1 : £35.65 B81-15046

618.3'92 — Women. Miscarriages
Pizer, Hank. Coping with a miscarriage. — London : Jill Norman, July 1981. — [192]p
Originally published: New York : Dial, 1980
ISBN 0-906908-54-x (cased) : £6.50 : CIP entry
ISBN 0-906908-55-8 (pbk) : £3.50 B81-13503

618.3'97 — Childbirth. Premature labour
Preterm labor / edited by M.G. Elder, Charles H. Hendricks. — London : Butterworths, 1981. — 329p : ill ; 25cm. — (Butterworths international medical reviews, ISSN 0144-9478. Obstetrics and gynecology ; 1)
Includes bibliographies and index
ISBN 0-407-02300-3 : Unpriced B81-26166

618.4 — Childbirth. Home confinement
Kitzinger, Sheila. Birth at home / Sheila Kitzinger ; with photographs by Suzanne Arms. — Rev. ed. — Oxford : Oxford University Press, 1980. — 156p,[4]p of plates : ill ; 20cm
Previous ed.: 1979. — Bibliography: p149-152. — Includes index
ISBN 0-19-286020-8 (pbk) : £1.95 : CIP rev.
B80-25739

618.4 — Childbirth. Labour
O'Driscoll, Kieran. Active management of labour / Kieran O'Driscoll, Declan Meagher. — London : Saunders, 1980. — vi,192p : ill(some col.) ; 24cm. — (Clinics in obstetrics and gynaecology. Supplement ; 1)
Includes index
ISBN 0-7216-6916-6 : £6.95 : CIP rev.
B80-23358

618.4 — Childbirth. Role of fathers — *Case studies*

Perkins, Elizabeth R.. Men on the labour ward / Elizabeth R. Perkins. — [Nottingham] : University of Nottingham, 1980. — ii,25leaves ; 30cm. — (Occasional paper / Leverhulme Health Education Project ; no.22)
Unpriced (pbk) B81-22735

618.4'0880621 — Great Britain. Royal families. Childbirth, *ca 1665-1860*

Dewhurst, Jack. Royal confinements / Jack Dewhurst. — London : Weidenfeld and Nicolson, c1980. — 205p : ill,1geneal.table ; 23cm
Bibliography: p195-198. - Includes index
ISBN 0-297-77847-1 : £9.95 B81-08278

618.4'092'4 — Childbirth. Theories of Leboyer, Frederick

Berezin, Nancy. The gentle birth book : a practical guide to Leboyer family-centred delivery / Nancy Berezin. — London : Murray, 1981. — 159p : ill ; 24cm
Bibliography: p156-157
ISBN 0-7195-3829-7 (pbk) : £4.95 : CIP rev. B81-14967

618.4'5 — Natural childbirth

Bradley, Robert A.. Husband-coached childbirth / by Robert A. Bradley. — 3rd ed. — London : Harper & Row, c1981. — xiii,238p : ill ; 22cm
Previous ed.: 1974. — Includes index
ISBN 0-06-014850-0 : £6.95 B81-38254

618.92 — PAEDIATRICS

618.92 — Adopted children & fostered children. Medical aspects

Medical practice in adoption and fostering : an introduction / edited by Marie Oxtoby. — London (11 Southwark St., SE1 1RQ) : British Agencies for Adoption and Fostering, 1981. — 47p ; 21cm. — (Practice series / British Agencies for Adoption and Fostering, ISSN 0260-0803 ; no.4)
Cover title. — Bibliography: p45-47
ISBN 0-903534-34-7 (pbk) : £1.50 B81-29598

618.92 — Babies, to 1 year. Diseases — *For general practice*

Jenkins, Graham Curtis. The first year of life / Graham Curtis Jenkins, Richard C.F. Newton. — Edinburgh : Churchill Livingstone, 1981. — 278p : ill,forms ; 22cm. — (The Library of general practice ; vol.2)
Forms on inside covers. — Includes bibliographies and index
ISBN 0-443-01717-4 (pbk) : £8.50 : CIP rev. B80-31715

618.92 — Children. Developmental disorders. Therapy

The **Practical** management of the developmentally disabled child / [edited by] Albert P. Scheiner, Israel F. Abroms. — St. Louis ; London : Mosby, 1980. — xiv,461p,[1] leaf of plates : ill(some col.),forms ; 26cm
Includes index
ISBN 0-8016-0061-8 : £28.50 B81-02968

618.92 — Children. Diseases

Hughes, James G.. Synopsis of pediatrics / James G. Hughes with the collaboration of thirty-five faculty members of the University of Tennessee Center for the Health Science and three guest contributors. — 5th ed. — St. Louis ; London : Mosby, 1980. — xi,915p : ill ; 24cm
Previous ed.: 1975. — Includes bibliographies and index
ISBN 0-8016-2309-x (pbk) : Unpriced B81-12598

Hull, David. Essential paediatrics / David Hull, Derek I. Johnston ; illustrated by Geoffrey Lyth. — Edinburgh : Churchill Livingstone, 1981. — ix,305p : ill(some col.),1col.map ; 24cm
Includes bibliographies and index
ISBN 0-443-02202-x (cased) : Unpriced : CIP rev.
ISBN 0-443-01953-3 (pbk) : £10.00 B80-03677

Jolly, Hugh. Diseases of children / Hugh Jolly. — 4th ed. — Oxford : Blackwell Scientific, 1981. — ix,689p,[2]leaves of plates : ill(some col.) ; 26cm
Previous ed.: 1976. — Includes bibliographies and index
ISBN 0-632-00707-9 : £16.00 B81-16261

Russo, Raymond M.. Practical points in pediatrics. — 3rd ed / Raymond M. Russo, Vymutt J. Gururaj. — Bern : Huber ; London : Kimpton, 1981. — 438p : ill,facsims ; 22cm
Previous ed.: / by John E. Allen, Vymutt J. Gururaj, Raymond M. Russo. London : Kimpton, 1977. — Includes index
ISBN 0-87488-727-5 (cased) : Unpriced B81-16124

Survey of clinical pediatrics. — 7th ed / [edited by] Edward Wasserman, Donald S. Gromisch. — New York ; London : McGraw-Hill, c1981. — xiv,527p : ill ; 25cm
Previous ed.: 1974. — Includes index
ISBN 0-07-068431-6 : £24.25 B81-12773

Zander, Luke. Children's illnesses / Luke Zander ; illustrated by the Hayward Art Group. — Feltham : Hamlyn Paperbacks, 1981. — 48p : ill ; 17cm. — (Pocket health guides)
ISBN 0-600-20316-6 (pbk) : £0.85 B81-40889

618.92 — Children. Diseases — *For primary health workers*

Primary health care of the young / [compiled by] Jane A. Fox. — New York ; London : McGraw-Hill, c1981. — xxi,1001p : ill ; 27cm
Includes bibliographies and index
ISBN 0-07-021741-6 : £25.95 B81-10234

618.92 — Children. Diseases. Psychosocial aspects

Behavioral pediatrics : psychosocial aspects of child health care / [edited by] Stanford B. Friedman, Robert A. Hoekelman. — New York ; London : McGraw-Hill, c1980. — xiii,434p : ill ; 25cm
Includes bibliographies and index
ISBN 0-07-022426-9 : £13.75 B81-10239

618.92 — Children. Growth. Disorders

Tanner, J. M.. Atlas of children's growth. — London : Academic Press, Aug.1981. — [200]p
ISBN 0-12-683340-0 : CIP entry B81-18126

618.92 — Children, to 3 years. Developmental disorders. Diagnosis — *Manuals*

Knobloch, Hilda. Manual of developmental diagnosis : the administration and interpretation of the revised Gesell and Amatruda developmental and neurologic examination / Hilda Knobloch in collaboration with Frances Stevens with assistance from Anthony F. Malone. — Hagerstown ; London : Harper & Row, c1980. — xiii,286p : ill ; 22cm
Bibliography: p273. — Includes index
ISBN 0-06-141437-9 (pbk) : £11.00 B81-06563

618.92

Meadow, Roy. Lecture notes on paediatrics. — 4th ed. — Oxford : Blackwell Scientific, Sept.1981. — [320]p
Previous ed.: 1978
ISBN 0-632-00824-5 : £5.25 : CIP entry
Primary classification 618.92 B81-21596

618.92 — Paediatrics

Controversies in child health and pediatric practice / David H. Smith, Robert A. Hoekelman [editors]. — New York ; London : McGraw-Hill, c1981. — ix,463p : ill ; 25cm
Includes index
ISBN 0-07-058510-5 : £24.25 B81-09937

Habel, Alex. Aids to paediatrics. — Edinburgh : Churchill Livingstone, Dec.1981. — [160]p
ISBN 0-443-02205-4 (pbk) : £4.00 : CIP entry B81-31624

Hughes, Walter T.. Pediatric procedures. — 2nd ed. / Walter T. Hughes, E. Stephen Buescher. — Philadelphia ; London : Saunders, 1980. — x,367p : ill,2plans,1form ; 26cm
Previous ed.: / by Walter T. Hughes. 1964. — Includes bibliographies and index
ISBN 0-7216-4826-6 : £14.25 B81-01765

Meadow, Roy. Lecture notes on paediatrics. — 4th ed. — Oxford : Blackwell Scientific, Sept.1981. — [320]p
Previous ed.: 1978
ISBN 0-632-00824-5 : £5.25 : CIP entry
Also classified at 618.92 B81-21596

618.92 — Paediatrics. Advisory services. Use of telephones

Brown, Jeffrey L.. Telephone medicine : a practical guide to pediatric telephone advice / Jeffrey L. Brown. — St. Louis ; London : Mosby 1980. — xi,154p : 1form
Includes index
ISBN 0-8016-0856-2 (23cmspiral) : £9.25 B81-05817

618.92 — Paediatrics — *Manuals*

Nutbeam, Helen M.. A handbook for examinations in paediatrics. — Oxford : Blackwell Scientific, July 1981. — [144]p
ISBN 0-632-00703-6 : £4.80 : CIP entry B81-22690

618.92'000240431 — Children. Diseases — *For parents*

Delvin, David. Common childhood illnesses and how to cope with them / David Delvin. — [London] : Corgi, 1981. — 191p ; 18cm
ISBN 0-552-11637-8 (pbk) : £1.25 B81-17169

618.92'00024613 — Paediatrics — *For nursing*

Sacharin, Rosa M.. Principles of paediatric nursing / Rosa M. Sacharin ; foreword by Olive Hulme. — Edinburgh : Churchill Livingstone, 1980. — 452p : ill ; 25cm
Bibliography: p441-443. - Includes index
ISBN 0-443-01635-6 (pbk) : Unpriced : CIP rev. B79-12969

618.92'00024613 — Paediatrics - *For nursing*

Speirs, A. L.. Paediatrics for nurses. — London : Pitman Medical, Apr.1981. — [256]p ; pbk
ISBN 0-272-79613-1 : £5.95 : CIP entry B81-04343

618.92'0005 — Paediatrics — *Serials*

Advances in pediatrics. — Vol.27 (1980). — London : Year Book Medical, c1980. — 446p
ISBN 0-8151-0499-5 : £35.00
ISSN 0065-3101 B81-09705

Recent advances in paediatrics. — No.6. — Edinburgh : Churchill Livingstone, 1981. — viii,264p
ISBN 0-443-02208-9 : Unpriced
ISSN 0309-0140 B81-20412

The **Year** book of pediatrics. — 1981. — Chicago ; London : Year Book Medical Publishers, 1981. — 480p
ISBN 0-8151-6564-1 : Unpriced
ISSN 0084-3954 B81-25000

618.92'00076 — Paediatrics — *Questions & answers*

Hoekelman, principles of pediatrics : preTest self-assessment and review / edited by Robert A. Hoekelman. — New York ; London : McGraw-Hill, c1981. — xi,230p : ill ; 28cm. — (PreTest series)
Bibliography: p225-230
ISBN 0-07-051648-0 (pbk) : £17.50 B81-12781

Hull, David. Essential paediatric MCQs. — Edinburgh : Churchill Livingstone, Jan.1982. — [192]p
ISBN 0-443-02235-6 (pbk) : £4.00 : CIP entry B81-34638

Krugman, Richard D.. Review of pediatrics / Richard D. Krugman. — Philadelphia ; London : Saunders, 1980. — x,123p : ill ; 27cm
ISBN 0-7216-5549-1 (pbk) : £5.95 B81-02479

Pediatrics : pretest self-assessment and review / edited by Richard P. Lipman. — New York ; London : McGraw-Hill, Health Professions Division, c1978. — ix,243p : ill ; 22cm. — (Pre Test series)
Bibliography: p237-243
ISBN 0-07-051603-0 (pbk) : £6.95 B81-26928

618.92'00088041 — Boys. Medical aspects

Pediatric andrology / edited by S.J. Kogan and E.S.E. Hafez. — The Hague ; London : Nijhoff, 1981. — x,218p : ill ; 28cm. — (Clinics in andrology ; v.7)
Includes bibliographies and index
ISBN 90-247-2407-4 : Unpriced B81-17115

618.92'000913 — Tropical regions. Paediatrics

Paediatrics in the tropics : current review / edited by R.G. Hendrickse. — Oxford : Oxford University Press, 1981. — xii,375p : ill,maps ; 24cm. — (Oxford medical publications)
Includes bibliographies and index
ISBN 0-19-261291-3 : £20.00 : CIP rev.
B81-00940

618.92'00092'2 — United States. Paediatrics. Organisations: American Academy of Pediatrics. Members — *Biographies* — *Serials*

American Academy of Pediatrics. Biographical directory of the American Academy of Pediatrics / compiled for the Academy by Jacques Cattell Press. — 1st ed. (1980)-. — New York ; London : R.R. Bowker Co., 1980-. — v. ; 28cm
Irregular
Unpriced B81-13218

618.92'0024 — Babies, to 1 year. Diagnosis by parents

Spencer, N. J.. Aspects of illness-related decision making by parents of small children / N.J. Spencer. — [Nottingham] : University of Nottingham, 1978. — 14,ii,[22]leaves : 1ill ; 30cm. — (Occasional paper / Leverhulme Health Education Project ; no.10)
Unpriced (pbk) B81-22826

618.92'0061 — Children. Drug therapy

Pincus, Catzel. The paediatric prescriber. — 5th ed. — Oxford : Blackwell Scientific, May 1981. — [320]p
Previous ed.: 1974
ISBN 0-632-00586-6 (pbk) : £4.50 : CIP entry
B81-09985

618.92'0072 — Children. Diseases. Symptoms

Illingworth, Ronald S.. Common symptoms of disease in children. — 7th ed. — Oxford : Blackwell Scientific, Jan.1982. — [384]p
Previous ed.: 1979
ISBN 0-632-00814-8 : £9.50 : CIP entry
B81-39226

618.92'0075'024613 — Medicine. Children. Diagnosis — *For nursing*

Droske, Susan Colvert. Pediatric diagnostic procedures : with guidelines for preparing children for clinical tests / Susan Colvert Droske, Sally A. Francis. — New York ; Chichester : Wiley, c1981. — xxi,293p : ill,forms ; 22cm. — (A Wiley medical publication)
Includes bibliographies and index
ISBN 0-471-04928-x (pbk) : £7.65 B81-24892

618.92'00754 — Children. Diagnosis. Physical examination — *Manuals*

Barness, Lewis A.. Manual of pediatric physical diagnosis / Lewis A. Barness. — 5th ed. — Chicago ; London : Year Book Medical, 1981. — xii,296p : ill ; 20cm
Previous ed.: Chicago : Year Book Medical, 1972. — Includes index
ISBN 0-8151-0493-6 (pbk) : £11.25 B81-19958

Gundy, John H.. Assessment of the child in primary health care / John H. Gundy. — New York ; London : McGraw-Hill, c1981. — xiii,193p : ill,forms ; 23cm
Bibliography: p177. - Includes index
ISBN 0-07-025197-5 (pbk) : £5.50 B81-17102

618.92'01 — High risk newborn babies. Emergency transfer — *For medical personnel*

Ferrara, Angelo. Emergency transfer of the high-risk neonate : a working manual for medical, nursing and administrative personnel / Angelo Ferrara, Anantham Harin. — St. Louis ; London : Mosby, 1980. — viii,355p : ill,plans,forms ; 24cm
Includes index
ISBN 0-8016-1565-8 (pbk) : Unpriced
B81-08559

618.92'01 — Newborn babies. Diseases

Clinical perinatology. — 2nd ed. / edited by Silvio Aladjem, Audrey K. Brown, Claude Sureau. — St Louis ; London : Mosby, 1980. — xxix,637p,2 leaves of plates : ill(some col.),forms,1port ; 26cm
Previous ed.: 1974. — Includes bibliographies and index
ISBN 0-8016-0103-7 : £41.75
Primary classification 618.3'2 B81-13254

Philip, Alistair G. S.. Neonatology : a practical guide / by Alistair G.S. Philip. — 2nd ed. — London : Kimpton, 1980. — [11],563p : ill,1form ; 22cm
Previous ed.: 1977. — Bibliography: p[6-7]. — Includes index
£8.50 (pbk) B81-07508

618.92'01 — Newborn babies. Intensive care

Korones, Sheldon B.. High-risk newborn infants : the basis for intensive nursing care / Sheldon B. Korones ; with editorial assistance of, and a chapter by Jean Lancaster. — 3rd ed. — St. Louis ; London : Mosby, 1981. — xi,399p : ill ; 25cm
Previous ed.: 1976. — Includes bibliographies and index
ISBN 0-8016-2738-9 : £13.00 B81-28917

Roberton, N. R. C.. Physiological basis of neonatal intensive care. — London : Edward Arnold, Apr.1981. — [192]p
ISBN 0-7131-4372-x (pbk) : £12.00 : CIP entry
B81-00131

618.92'0977 — Children. Eyes. Diseases

Helveston, Eugene M.. Pediatric ophthalmology practice / Eugene M. Helveston, Forrest D. Ellis. — St. Louis ; London : Mosby, 1980. — xii,303p : ill,1form ; 29cm
Bibliography: p289-291. - Includes index
ISBN 0-8016-2129-1 : Unpriced B81-08676

618.92'0977 — Children. Eyes. Diseases - *Conference proceedings*

International Society for Paediatric Ophthalmology. *Meeting (2nd : 1979 : Verona).* Paediatric ophthalmology. — Chichester : Wiley, Aug.1981. — [600]p. — (A Wiley medical publication)
Conference papers
ISBN 0-471-10040-4 : £40.00 : CIP entry
B81-16868

618.92'0978 — Babies. Hearing disorders — *Conference proceedings*

Winnipeg Conference on Early Management of Hearing Loss *(1980).* Early management of hearing loss : proceedings of the Winnipeg Conference on Early Managment of Hearing Loss, Winnipeg, Manitoba, April 26-29, 1980 / edited by George T. Mencher, Sanford E. Gerber. — New York ; London : Grune & Stratton, c1981. — xviii,468p : ill,forms ; 24cm
Includes bibliographies and index
ISBN 0-8089-1346-8 : £11.00 B81-18182

618.92'0978 — Children. Hearing disorders

Bess, Fred H.. Audiology, education, and the hearing impaired child / Fred H. Bess, Freeman E. McConnell. — St. Louis ; London : Mosby, 1981. — xiv,321p : ill,1facsim,forms ; 25cm
Includes bibliographies and index
ISBN 0-8016-0671-3 : £12.00 B81-31153

618.92'0978075 — Children. Hearing disorders. Diagnosis — *For parents*

Testing the hearing of young children / Michael Nolan ... [et al.]. — London (45 Hereford Rd., W2 5AH) : National Deaf Children's Society, c1981. — 16p : ill ; 21cm
£0.20 (pbk) B81-37772

618.92'09789 — Children's hearing aids — *For parents*

Hearing aids / Kim McArthur ... [et al.]. — London (45 Hereford Rd., W2 5AH) : National Deaf Children's Society, c1981. — 28p : ill ; 21cm
£0.30 (pbk) B81-37774

618.921'2 — Children. Heart. Diseases

Jordan, S. C.. Heart disease in paediatrics. — 2nd ed. — London : Butterworths, June 1981. — [352]p. — (Postgraduate paediatrics series)
Previous ed.: 1972
ISBN 0-407-19941-1 : £21.00 : CIP entry
B81-09508

618.92'12 — Children. Heart. Diseases — *Polyglot texts*

Neuere Aspekte der Kinderkardiologie II / Herausgeber des Bandes F. Stocker, J.W. Weber und F. Wyler. — Basel ; London : Karger, 1980. — 125p : ill,ports ; 23cm. — (Pädiatrische Fortbildungskurse für die Praxis = Cours de perfectionnement en pédiatrie pour le praticien ; Bd.51)
Text in English, French and German. — Includes bibliographies
ISBN 3-8055-0926-x (pbk) : Unpriced
B81-09615

618.92'12043 — Newborn babies. Heart. Congenital diseases

Rowe, Richard D.. The neonate with congenital heart disease. — 2nd ed. / by Richard D. Rowe, Robert M. Freedom, Ali Mehrizi ; with echocardiographic contributions by Kenneth R. Bloom. — Philadelphia ; London : Saunders, 1981. — xii,716p : ill ; 24cm. — (Major problems in clinical pediatrics ; v.5)
Previous ed.: 1968. — Includes bibliographies and index
ISBN 0-7216-7775-4 : £24.25 B81-27253

618.92'1'205 — Children. Heart. Diseases — *Serials*

Paediatric cardiology. — Vol.4. — Edinburgh : Churchill Livingstone, Nov.1981. — [576]p
ISBN 0-443-02139-2 : £32.00 : CIP entry
ISSN 0261-7021 B81-30895

618.92'12075 — Babies. Heart. Diagnosis

Moller, James H.. Heart disease in infancy / James H. Moller, William A. Neal. — New York : Appleton-Century-Crofts ; London : Prentice-Hall, c1981. — x,502p : ill ; 25cm
Includes index
ISBN 0-8385-3671-9 : £23.75 B81-09296

618.92'12075 — Children. Heart. Diseases. Diagnosis

Zuberbuhler, J. R.. Clinical diagnosis in pediatric cardiology / J.R. Zuberbuhler ; foreword by Richard D. Rowe. — Edinburgh : Churchill Livingstone, 1981. — 183p : ill ; 25cm. — (Modern pediatric cardiology)
Includes bibliographies and index
ISBN 0-443-01889-8 : £18.00 B81-22180

618.92'1207543 — Children. Heart. Diagnosis. Cross-sectional echocardiography

Pediatric echocardiography - cross sectional, M-code and Doppler / editor Nils-Rune Lundström. — Amsterdam ; Oxford : Elsevier/North-Holland Biomedical, 1980. — viii,355p : ill ; 25cm
Includes index
ISBN 0-444-80262-2 : £25.69 B81-04080

618.92'1207543 — Children. Heart. Diagnosis. Echocardiography

Goldberg, Stanley J.. Pediatric and adolescent echocardiography : a handbook / Stanley J. Goldberg, Hugh D. Allen, David J. Sahn. — 2nd ed. — Chicago ; London : Year Book Medical Publishers, 1980. — xix,495p : ill,1form ; 24cm
Previous ed.: 1975. — Includes index
ISBN 0-8151-3720-6 : £33.75 B81-07148

618.92'1207547 — Children. Heart. Diagnosis. Electrocardiograms. Interpretation

Park, Myung K.. How to read pediatric ECG'S / Myung K. Park, Warren G. Guntheroth. — Chicago ; London : Year Book Medical, c1981. — xi,165p : ill ; 26cm
Includes index
ISBN 0-8151-6654-0 (pbk) : £16.50 B81-18969

618.92'12807 — Children. Heart. Arrhythmia. Electrophysiology

Pediatric cardiac dysrhythmias / edited by Paul C. Gillette, Arthur Garson, Jr. — New York ; London : Grune & Stratton, c1981. — xvi,474p : ill ; 27cm. — (Clinical cardiology monographs)
Includes index
ISBN 0-8089-1332-8 : £25.00 B81-35745

618.92′128′07547 — Children. Heart. Dysrhythmia. Diagnosis. Electrocardiograms. Interpretation

Garson, Arthur. A guide to cardiac dysrhythmias in children / Arthur Garson, Jr., Paul C. Gillette, Dan G. McNamara. — New York ; London : Grune & Stratton, c1980. — viii,198p : ill ; 18x26cm. — (Clinical cardiology monographs)
Text on lining paper. — Two cards in pocket
ISBN 0-8089-1261-5 : £11.00 B81-04779

618.92′13 — Children. Blood vessels. Diseases. Complications of diabetes — *Conference proceedings*

Diabetic angiopathy in children : International Workshop, Berlin 1979 / volume editor Bruno Weber. — Basel ; London : Karger ; Chichester : Wiley [distributor], 1981. — xvi,378p : ill ; 25cm. — (Pediatric and adolescent endocrinology ; v.9)
Includes bibliographies
ISBN 3-8055-1574-x : £49.50
Primary classification 618.92′462 B81-21782

618.92′132 — Young persons. Blood. Hypertension — *Conference proceedings*

Hahnemann International Symposium on Hypertension *(6th : 1980 : Philadelphia)*. Hypertension in the young and the old : the Sixth Hahnemann International Symposium on Hypertension / editors Gaddo Onesti, Kwan Eun Kim. — New York ; London : Grune & Stratton, c1981. — xviii,356p : ill,1map ; 27cm
Includes index
ISBN 0-8089-1319-0 : £22.20
Also classified at 618.97′6132 B81-35743

618.92′15 — Children. Blood. Diseases

Hematology of infancy and childhood / edited by David G. Nathan, Frank A. Oski. — 2nd ed. — Philadelphia ; London : Saunders, 1981. — 2v.(xiii,1574p) : ill ; 27cm
Previous ed.: 1974. — Includes index
ISBN 0-7216-6678-7 : Unpriced
ISBN 0-7216-6676-0 (v.1) : £34.00
ISBN 0-7216-6677-9 (v.2) : £34.00 B81-27100

Lanzkowsky, Philip. Pediatric hematology-oncology : a treatise for the clinician / Philip Lanzkowsky. — New York ; London : McGraw-Hill, c1980. — xii,432p : ill ; 25cm
Includes index
ISBN 0-07-036340-4 : £18.75
Also classified at 618.92′994 B81-00941

618.92′2′00428 — Newborn babies. Respiratory system. Diseases. Intensive care

Newborn respiratory care / edited by Marvin D. Lough, Thomas J. Williams, John E. Rawson. — Chicago ; London : Year Book Medical Publishers, c1979. — xvi,333p Rb ill ; 24cm
Includes bibliographies and index
ISBN 0-8151-5635-9 : £17.00 B81-06250

618.92′238 — Children. Bronchi. Asthma

Asthma in children : natural history, assessment, treatment and recent advance / edited by Jan A. Kuzemko ; with contributions from H. Amos ... [et al.]. — 2nd ed. — Tunbridge Wells : Pitman Medical, 1980. — 168p : ill ; 23cm
Previous ed.: 1976. — Includes index
ISBN 0-272-79563-1 : £7.95 : CIP rev. B80-03678

618.92′238 — Children. Bronchi. Asthma — *For children*

Snell, Nigel. Jane has asthma / Nigel Snell. — London : Hamilton, 1981. — [25]p : col.ill ; 16x17cm
ISBN 0-241-10642-7 : £2.50 : CIP rev. B81-25760

Wilson, Pearl M.. Mummy why can′t I breathe / Pearl M. Wilson ; photographs by James Barbone. — London : Angus & Robertson, 1981, c1978. — [27]p : col.ill ; 22cm
Originally published: West Melbourne : Nelson, 1978
ISBN 0-207-95966-8 : £3.95 B81-23060

618.92′24 — Newborn babies. Lungs. Diseases

Avery, Mary Ellen. The lung and its disorders in the newborn infant. — 4th ed. / by Mary Ellen Avery, Barry D. Fletcher and Roberta G. Williams. — Philadelphia ; London : Saunders, 1981. — xv,367p : ill ; 27cm. — (Major problems in clinical pediatrics ; v.1)
Previous ed.: 1974. — Includes bibliographies and index
ISBN 0-7216-1462-0 : £26.00 B81-34789

618.92′24 — Newborn babies. Lungs. Therapy

Neonatal pulmonary care / edited by Donald W. Thibeault and George A. Gregory ; with critical comments by Victor Chernick, Nicholas Nelson, Leo Stern. — Menlo Park, Calif. ; London : Addison-Wesley, c1979. — xv,479p : ill ; 24cm
Bibliography: p420-466. — Includes index
ISBN 0-201-02481-0 : £24.20 B81-08112

618.92′3950654 — Great Britain. Children. Rickets. Prevention & treatment. Vitamin D

Great Britain. *Working Party on Fortification of Food with Vitamin D*. Rickets and osteomalacia / report of the Working Party on Fortification of Food with Vitamin D. Committee on Medical Aspects of Food Policy. — London : H.M.S.O., 1980. — xii,66p : ill ; 25cm. — (Report on health and social subjects ; 19)
At head of title: Department of Health and Social Security. — Bibliography: p54-66
ISBN 0-11-320747-6 (pbk) : £3.90
Also classified at 616.3′950654 B81-10030

618.92′3995 — Children. Phenylketonuria. Treatment

Clayton, Barbara E.. Benefits arising from studies of an inherited metabolic disorder : an inaugural lecture delivered at the University, 5 February, 1980 / by Barbara E. Clayton ; under the chairmanship of L.C.B. Gower. — [Southampton] : University of Southampton, 1980. — 12p : 2ill ; 21cm
Bibliography: p12
ISBN 0-85432-214-0 (pbk) : £0.50 B81-23557

618.92′4 — Children. Endocrine system. Diseases

Clinical paediatric endocrinology. — Oxford : Blackwell Scientific, May 1981. — [608]p
ISBN 0-632-00698-6 : £35.00 : CIP entry B81-08799

Frasier, S. Douglas. Pediatric endocrinology / S. Douglas Frasier. — New York ; London : Grune & Stratton, c1980. — viii,375p : ill ; 24cm
Includes bibliographies and index
ISBN 0-8089-1272-0 : £16.60 B81-19717

Pediatric endocrinology / edited by Jean-Claude Job, Michel Pierson ; American edition translated and adapted by Raphael Goldstein ; foreword by Melvin M. Grumbach. — New York ; Chichester : Wiley, 1981. — xi,739p : ill ; 27cm
Translation of: Endocrinologie pédiatrique et croissance. — Includes bibliographies and index
ISBN 0-471-05257-4 : £63.00 B81-29304

618.92′462 — Children. Diabetes

Craig, Oman. Childhood diabetes and its management / Oman Craig. — 2nd ed. — London : Butterworths, 1981. — xi,316p : ill ; 23cm. — (Postgraduate paediatrics series)
Previous ed.: 1977. — Includes bibliographies and index
ISBN 0-407-00209-x : Unpriced B81-16045

Farquhar, J. W.. The diabetic child / J.W. Farquhar. — 3rd ed. — Edinburgh : Churchill Livingstone, 1981. — 133p : ill ; 19cm. — (A Churchill Livingstone patiet handbook)
Previous ed.: published as Notes for the guidance of parents of diabetic children. 1975. — Includes index
ISBN 0-443-02193-7 (pbk) : £1.30 B81-29370

618.92′462 — Children. Diabetes. Complications: Diseases of blood vessels — *Conference proceedings*

Diabetic angiopathy in children : International Workshop, Berlin 1979 / volume editor Bruno Weber. — Basel ; London : Karger ; Chichester : Wiley [distributor], 1981. — xvi,378p : ill ; 25cm. — (Pediatric and adolescent endocrinology ; v.9)
Includes bibliographies
ISBN 3-8055-1574-x : £49.50
Also classified at 618.92′13 B81-21782

618.92′46206 — Children. Diabetes. Therapy

Management of juvenile diabetes mellitus / [edited by] Howard S. Traisman. — 3rd ed. — St. Louis ; London : Mosby, 1980. — xii,348p,[1]p of plates : ill(some col.),facsims,forms ; 26cm
Previous ed.: 1971. — Includes index
ISBN 0-8016-5020-8 : £33.75 B81-08144

618.92′5 — Children. Skin. Diseases

Hurwitz, Sidney. Clinical pediatric dermatology / Sidney Hurwitz. — Philadelphia ; London : Saunders, 1981. — x,481p : col.ill ; 27cm
Includes index
ISBN 0-7216-4872-x : £49.75 B81-29302

618.92′6 — Children. Urogenital system. Diseases

Belman, A. Barry. Genitourinary problems in pediatrics / by A. Barry Belman, George W. Kaplan. — Philadelphia ; London : Saunders, 1981. — xii,337p : ill ; 27cm. — (Major problems in clinical pediatrics ; v.23)
Includes bibliographies and index
ISBN 0-7216-1678-x : £32.25 B81-38876

Paediatric urology. — 2nd ed. — London : Butterworths, Jan.1982. — [564]p
Previous ed.: 1968
ISBN 0-407-35152-3 : £38.50 : CIP entry B81-34665

618.92′63 — Children. Enuresis. Prevention — *Manuals* — *For parents*

Meadow, Roy. Help for bed wetting / Roy Meadow. — Edinburgh : Churchill Livingstone, 1980. — 43p : ill ; 19cm. — (A Churchill Livingstone patient handbook)
ISBN 0-443-02236-4 (pbk) : £0.95 B81-09378

618.92′68 — Boys. Cryptorchidism

The **Undescended** testis / [edited by] Eric W. Fonkalsrud, Wolfgang Mengel. — Chicago ; London : Yearbook Medical, c1981. — xvi,279p : ill ; 24cm
Includes index
ISBN 0-8151-3257-3 : £28.50 B81-19048

618.92′694 — Children. Intersexuality

The **Intersex** child / volume editor Nathalie Josso. — Basel ; London : Karger, c1981. — viii,273p : ill ; 25cm. — (Pediatric and adolescent endocrinology ; v.8)
Includes bibliographies and index
ISBN 3-8055-0909-x : £42.90 B81-30691

618.92′723 — Children. Rheumatic diseases

Ansell, Barbara M.. Rheumatic disorders in childhood / Barbara M. Ansell. — London : Butterworths, 1980. — vi,299p,[7]p of plates : ill(some col.) ; 23cm. — (Postgraduate paediatrics series)
Includes bibliographies and index
ISBN 0-407-00186-7 : £25.00 : CIP rev. B80-12912

618.92′7′3043 — Children. Spine. Spina bifida

James, C. C. M.. Spina bifida occulta. — London : Academic Press, Aug.1981. — [200]p
ISBN 0-12-792162-1 : CIP entry B81-15805

618.92′74 — Children. Muscles. Floppy infant syndrome

Dubowitz, Victor. The floppy infant / by Victor Dubowitz. — 2nd ed. — s.l. : Spastics International Medical Publications ; London : Heinemann Medical [distributor], 1980. — vii,158p : ill ; 25cm. — (Clinics in developmental medicine ; no.76)
Previous ed.: 1969. — Bibliography: p147-154. - Includes index
ISBN 0-433-07902-9 : £4.00 B81-06946

618.92'8 — Newborn babies. Nervous system. Disorders

Volpe, Joseph J.. Nerology of the newborn / by Joseph J. Volpe. — Philadelphia ; London : Saunders, 1981. — xv,648p : ill ; 27cm. — (Major problems in clinical pediatrics ; v.22)
Includes index
ISBN 0-7216-9077-7 : £35.75 B81-29700

618.92'85206 — Neurotic children. Psychotherapy — *Case studies — Personal observations — Collections*

Frédéric, Hélène. Martin / Hélène Frédéric and Martine Malinsky with the assistance of Michelle de Wilde ; translated by John McGreal and Susan Lipshitz. — London : Routledge & Kegan Paul, 1981. — xviii,102p ; 21cm
Translation of: Martin : un enfant battait sa mère
ISBN 0-7100-0814-7 : £7.50 : CIP rev.
B81-04311

618.92'853'00240431 — Children. Epilepsy — *For parents*

McMullin, G. P.. Children who have fits / G.P. McMullin. — London : Duckworth, 1981. — 64p ; 22cm. — (Paperduck)
Bibliography: p63. — Includes index
ISBN 0-7156-1551-3 (pbk) : £3.95 : CIP rev.
B81-10465

618.92'855 — Children. Communication disorders

Hassibi, Mahin. Disordered thinking and communication in children / Mahin Hassibi and Harry Breuer, Jr.. — New York ; London : Plenum, c1980. — vi,207p ; 24cm
Bibliography: p195-204. - Includes index
ISBN 0-306-40490-7 : Unpriced
Primary classification 618.92'89 B81-05098

618.92'855 — Children. Communication disorders. Assessment & therapy. Techniques

Weiss, Curtis E.. Communicative disorders : prevention and early intervention / Curtis E. Weiss, Herold S. Lillywhite. — 2nd ed. — St. Louis ; London : Mosby, 1981. — xi,267p : ill ; 24cm
Previous ed.: 1976. — Bibliography: p214-217. — Includes index
ISBN 0-8016-5389-4 (pbk) : £9.50 B81-33001

618.92'855 — Great Britain. Learning disordered children. Medical aspects — *Case studies*

Quin, Vera. Reading and spelling difficulties : a medical approach / Vera Quin and Alan MacAuslan. — London : Hodder and Stoughton, 1981. — 146p : ill ; 22cm
Bibliography: p134-138. — Includes index
ISBN 0-340-25755-5 (pbk) : £2.95 : CIP rev.
B81-13487

618.92'855'0019 — Children. Speech disorders. Psycholinguistic aspects

Grunwell, Pamela. The nature of phonological disability in children / Pamela Grunwell. — London : Academic Press, 1981. — ix,243p ; 24cm. — (Applied language studies)
Bibliography: p225-237. — Includes index
ISBN 0-12-305250-5 : £12.80 : CIP rev.
B81-06033

618.92'8553 — Children. Reading disorders — *Case studies*

Spache, George D.. Case studies in reading disability / George D. Spache, Ken McIlroy, Paul C. Berg. — Boston, Mass. ; London : Allyn and Bacon, c1981. — xii,234p : ill ; 25cm
Bibliography: p227-234
ISBN 0-205-07258-5 : Unpriced B81-11296

618.92'8582 — Young persons. Personality disorders: Self-destructive behaviour

Self-destructive behavior in children and adolescents / edited by Carl F. Wells, Irving R. Stuart. — New York ; London : Van Nostrand Reinhold, c1981. — xiv,348p : ill ; 24cm
Includes bibliographies and index
ISBN 0-442-24741-9 : £16.95 B81-37785

618.92'8588'05 — Children. Mental handicaps. Prevention — *Conference proceedings*

Prevention of mental handicap : proceedings of the one-day conference held at Ridge Hill Mental Handicap Unit, Stourbridge, West Midlands on Friday, 14th September, 1979 / organised by the Midlands Division of the British Institute of Mental Handicap ; Chairman J.W. Parsons. — Kidderminster (Wolverhampton Rd, Kidderminster, Worcs. DY10 3PP) : British Institute of Mental Handicap, 1980. — 63p : ill ; 21cm
Includes bibliographies
ISBN 0-906054-29-x (pbk) : £3.75 B81-02320

618.92'8589 — Children. Hyperactivity

Schrag, Peter. The myth of the hyperactive child and other means of child control / Peter Schrag and Diane Divoky. — Harmondsworth : Penguin, 1981, 1975. — 280p ; 20cm
Originally published: New York : Pantheon Books, 1975. — Includes index
ISBN 0-14-022179-4 (pbk) : £2.95 B81-16978

618.92'858906 — Children. Hyperactivity. Therapy — *Case studies*

Intervention with hyperactive children : a case study approach / [edited by] Marvin J. Fine. — Lancaster : MTP Press, c1980. — 247p : ill ; 25cm
Includes bibliographies and index
ISBN 0-85200-536-9 : £11.50 B81-03082

618.92'89 — Children. Behavioural disorders

Behavioral problems in childhood : a primary care approach / edited by Stewart Gabel. — New York ; London : Grune & Stratton, c1981. — xxii,447p : ill ; 26cm
Includes index
ISBN 0-8089-1336-0 : £26.20 B81-40806

618.92'89 — Children. Cognitive disorders

Hassibi, Mahin. Disordered thinking and communication in children / Mahin Hassibi and Harry Breuer, Jr.. — New York ; London : Plenum, c1980. — vi,207p ; 24cm
Bibliography: p195-204. - Includes index
ISBN 0-306-40490-7 : Unpriced
Also classified at 618.92'855 B81-05098

618.92'89 — Children. Psychiatry

Steinberg, Derek. Using child psychiatry. — London : Hodder & Stoughton Oct.1981. — [224]p
ISBN 0-340-26835-2 : £1.25 : CIP entry
B81-28077

618.92'89 — Maladjusted children. Psychiatry

Three further clinical faces of childhood / edited by E. James Anthony and Doris C. Gilpin. — Lancaster : MTP, c1981. — 322p : ill ; 24cm
Includes bibliographies and index
ISBN 0-85200-558-x : £14.75 B81-34363

618.92'89'005 — Children. Mental disorders — *Serials*

Yearbook of the International Association for Child and Adolescent Psychiatry and Allied Professions : the child and his family. — Vol.6, Preventive child psychiatry in an age of transitions. — New York ; Chichester : Wiley, c1980. — xv,645p
ISBN 0-471-08403-4 : £17.50 B81-10257

618.92'89025 — Children. Mental disorders. Emergency treatment

Khan, Aman U.. Psychiatric emergencies in pediatrics / Aman U. Khan. — Chicago ; London : Year Book Medical Publishers, c1979. — xi,253p : ill ; 24cm
Includes bibliographies and index
ISBN 0-8151-5029-6 : £18.00 B81-06247

618.92'89071 — Children. Behavioural disorders. Environmental factors

The **Ecosystem** of the "sick" child : implications for classification and intervention for disturbed and mentally retarded children / edited by Suzanne Salzinger, John Antrobus, Joseph Glick. — New York ; London : Academic Press, 1980. — xvii,308p : ill,1form ; 24cm
Includes bibliographies and index
ISBN 0-12-617250-1 : £14.00 B81-19333

618.92'8914 — Children. Psychoses. Psychotherapy

Tustin, Frances. Autistic states in children / Frances Tustin. — London : Routledge & Kegan Paul, 1981. — xi,276p,[8]p of plates : ill ; 23cm
Bibliography: p256-263. — Includes index
ISBN 0-7100-0763-9 : £12.50 B81-36314

618.92'89142 — Children. Behaviour therapy

Ross, Alan O.. Child behaviour therapy : principles, procedures, and empirical basis / Alan O. Ross. — New York ; Chichester : Wiley, c1981. — xvii,425p : ill ; 24cm
Bibliography: p383-409. — Includes index
ISBN 0-471-02981-5 : £12.25 B81-09784

618.9'289142 — Deviant children. Behaviour therapy

Herbert, Martin. Behavioural treatment of problem children : a practice manual / Martin Herbert. — London : Academic Press, 1981. — x,226p : ill ; 26cm
Bibliography: p215-221. — Includes index
ISBN 0-12-791971-6 (cased) : £9.80
ISBN 0-12-791973-2 (pbk) : Unpriced
B81-20863

618.92'8'916 — Mentally handicapped children. Behaviour therapy — *Manuals*

Foxen, Tom. Training staff in behavioural methods. — Manchester : Manchester University Press
Instructor's handbook. — Sept.1981. — 1v.
ISBN 0-7190-0845-x (pbk) : £10.00 : CIP entry
B81-28190

Foxen, Tom. Training staff in behavioural methods. — Manchester : Manchester University Press
Trainee workbook. — Sept.1981. — 1v.
ISBN 0-7190-0830-1 (pbk) : £4.50 : CIP entry
B81-28191

618.92'89165 — Maladjusted children. Play therapy — *Case studies*

Axline, Virginia M.. Dibs : in search of self : personality development in play therapy / Virginia M. Axline. — Harmondsworth : Penguin, 1981, c1964. — 197p ; 18cm
Originally published: Boston, Mass.: Houghton, Mifflin, 1964 ; London : Gollancz, 1966
ISBN 0-14-021344-9 (pbk) : £1.50 B81-29158

618.92'9 — Children. Communicable diseases

Feign, Ralph D.. Textbook of pediatric infectious diseases / Ralph D. Feign, James D. Cherry. — Philadelphia ; London : Saunders, 1981. — 2v.(xxvi,1858p) : ill ; 28cm
Includes bibliographies and index
ISBN 0-7216-3596-2 : Unpriced
ISBN 0-7216-3586-5 (v.1) : £38.75
ISBN 0-7216-3594-6 (v.2) : £25.75 B81-27104

Illingworth, Ronald S.. Infections and immunisation in childhood. — Edinburgh : Churchill Livingstone, July 1981. — [88]p. — (Patient handbook)
ISBN 0-443-02238-0 (pbk) : £1.20 : CIP entry
B81-19159

Krugman, Saul. Infectious diseases of children. — 7th ed. / Saul Krugman, Samuel L. Katz. — St. Louis ; London : Mosby, 1981. — xi,607p,11p of plates : ill(some col.) ; 27cm
Previous ed.: 1977. — Includes bibliographies and index
ISBN 0-8016-2796-6 : £31.50 B81-09766

Kuz'micheva, A. T.. Infectious diseases in children / A.T. Kuzmicheva. I.V. Sharlai. — Moscow : Mir ; [London] : distributed by Central Books, 1980. — 422p,[8]p of plates : ill (some col.) ; 23cm
Translation and revision of: Detskie infektsionnye bolezni. — Includes index
ISBN 0-7147-1602-2 : £5.95 B81-23521

618.92'994 — Children. Cancer

Lanzkowsky, Philip. Pediatric hematology-oncology : a treatise for the clinician / Philip Lanzkowsky. — New York ; London : McGraw-Hill, c1980. — xii,432p : ill ; 25cm
Includes index
ISBN 0-07-036340-4 : £18.75
Primary classification 618.92'15 B81-00941

618.92′994 — Children. Cancer *continuation*

Pediatric oncology : with a special section on rare primitive neuroectodermal tumors / edited by G. Bennett Humphrey ... [et al.]. — The Hague ; London : Nijhoff. — (Cancer treatment and research ; v.2)
1. — 1981. — xiii,298p : ill ; 25cm
Includes index
ISBN 90-247-2408-2 : Unpriced B81-15267

618.92′995 — Children. Tuberculosis

Miller, F. J. W.. Tuberculosis in children. — Edinburgh : Churchill Livingstone, Sept.1981. — [344]p. — (Medicine in the tropics)
ISBN 0-443-01574-0 (pbk) : £7.50 : CIP entry B81-22688

618.97 — GERIATRICS

618.97 — Geriatrics

Adams, George F.. Essentials of geriatric medicine. — 2nd ed. — Oxford : Oxford University Press, Sept.1981. — [132]p. — (Oxford medical publications)
Previous ed.: 1977
ISBN 0-19-261352-9 (pbk) : £4.95 : CIP entry B81-21638

The **Core** of geriatric medicine : a guide for students and practitioners / edited by Leslie S. Libow, Frederick T. Sherman. — St. Louis ; London : Mosby, 1981. — xix,354p : ill ; 25cm
Includes index
ISBN 0-8016-3096-7 : £17.25 B81-18970

Eldercare : a practical guide to clinical geriatrics / editors Mary O'Hara-Devereaux, Len Hughes Andrus, Cynthia D. Scott ; technical editor Mary I. Gary. — New York ; London : Grune & Stratton, c1981. — xv,368p : ill,forms ; 29cm
Includes bibliographies and index
ISBN 0-8089-1285-2 : £12.40 B81-33741

The **Geriatric** imperative : an introduction to gerontology and clinical geriatrics / edited Anne R. Somers, Dorothy R. Fabian. — New York : Appleton-Century-Crofts ; London : Prentice-Hall, c1981. — xx,356p : ill ; 23cm
Includes index
ISBN 0-8385-3130-x (pbk) : £11.55 B81-36652

Geriatrics for everyday practice : a concise compendium / editors J. Andrews, H.P. von Hahn. — Basel ; London : Karger, 1981. — viii,220p : ill ; 23cm
Includes bibliographies and index
ISBN 3-8055-1803-x (pbk) : £9.90 B81-38093

Hodgkinson, H. M.. An outline of geriatrics. — London : Academic Press, Apr.1981. — [160]p. — (Monographs for students of medicine)
Previous ed.: 1975
ISBN 0-12-351460-6 (pbk) : £4.80 : CIP entry B81-06625

Hodkinson, H. M.. An outline of geriatrics / H.M. Hodkinson. — 2nd ed. — London : Academic Press, 1981. — xiii,166p : ill ; 23cm
Previous ed.: 1975. — Bibliography: p159-160. — Includes index
ISBN 0-12-792035-8 (pbk) : £4.80 B81-33159

Wilcock, G. K.. Geriatrics / G.K. Wilcock and A.M. Middleton. — London : Grant McIntyre, 1980. — 172p ; 19cm. — (Pocket consultant)
Cover title. — Bibliography: p161. — Includes index
ISBN 0-86216-035-9 (pbk) : £4.95 : CIP rev. B80-19794

618.97 — Geriatrics — *Conference proceedings*

Geriatrics for the practitioner : proceedings of a seminar held in Amsterdam, July 8-11, 1981 / editors A.N.J. Reinders Folmer, J. Schouten. — Amsterdam ; Oxford : Excerpta Medica, 1981. — 225p : ill ; 25cm. — (International congress series ; no.554)
Includes bibliographies and index
ISBN 90-219-0498-5 : Unpriced B81-35560

618.97 — Old persons. Diseases

Martin, Anthony, *1938-*. Problems in geriatric medicine / Anthony Martin. — Lancaster : MTP, 1981. — 195p : ill ; 24cm. — (Problems in practice series)
Includes index
ISBN 0-85200-319-6 : £7.95 B81-38031

618.97 — Old persons. Medical aspects

Brocklehurst, John Charles. Geriatric medicine for students. — 2nd ed. — Edinburgh : Churchill Livingstone, Oct.1981. — [320]p
Previous ed.: 1976
ISBN 0-443-02491-x (pbk) : £4.95 : CIP entry B81-28049

618.97′0024613 — Geriatrics — *For nursing*

Care of the aging. — Edinburgh : Churchill Livingstone, Oct.1981. — [256]p. — (Recent advances in nursing, ISSN 0144-6592 ; 2)
ISBN 0-443-02187-2 : £7.00 : CIP entry B81-25299

618.97′0024613 — Old persons. Medical aspects — *For nursing*

Nursing and the aged / edited by Irene Mortenson Burnside. — 2nd ed. — New York ; London : McGraw-Hill, c1981. — xxi,710p : ill ; 25cm
Previous ed.: 1976. — Includes bibliographies and index
ISBN 0-07-009211-7 : £14.50 B81-10127

618.97′005 — Geriatrics - *Serials*

Advanced geriatric medicine. — 1. — London : Pitman Medical, Sept.1981. — [176]p
ISBN 0-272-79629-8 : £10.00 : CIP entry B81-20569

618.97′005 — Geriatrics — *Serials*

Recent advances in geriatric medicine. — No.2. — Edinburgh : Churchill Livingstone, Jan.1982. — [280]p
ISBN 0-443-02320-4 (pbk) : £14.00 : CIP entry
ISSN 0144-0519 B81-34505

618.97′025 — Old persons. Acute diseases. Emergency treatment

Acute geriatric medicine / edited by Davis Coakley. — London : Croom Helm, c1981. — 290p : ill ; 23cm
Includes bibliographies and index
ISBN 0-7099-0150-x : £14.95 B81-10409

618.97′6132 — Old persons. Blood. Hypertension — *Conference proceedings*

Hahnemann International Symposium on Hypertension *(6th : 1980 : Philadelphia)*. Hypertension in the young and the old : the Sixth Hahnemann International Symposium on Hypertension / editors Gaddo Onesti, Kwan Eun Kim. — New York ; London : Grune & Stratton, c1981. — xviii,356p : ill,1map ; 27cm
Includes index
ISBN 0-8089-1319-0 : £22.20
Primary classification 618.92′132 B81-35743

618.97′65 — Old persons. Skin. Diseases

Korting, G. W.. Geriatric dermatology / by G.W. Korting ; translated by William Curth and Helen Ollendorff Curth. — Philadelphia ; London : Saunders, 1980. — ix,194p : col.ill ; 26cm
Translation of: Die Haut im Alter und ihre Krankheiten. — Bibliography: p161-186. — Includes index
ISBN 0-7216-5495-9 : £25.00 B81-26965

618.97′6855 — Old persons. Communication disorders

Aging : communication processes and disorders / editors Daniel S. Beasley, G. Albyn Davis. — New York ; London : Grune & Stratton, c1981. — 375p : ill ; 17cm
Includes bibliographies and index
ISBN 0-8089-1281-x : £16.60 B81-18184

Language and communication in the elderly : clinical, therapeutic, and experimental issues / edited by Loraine K. Obler, Martin L. Albert. — Lexington : Lexington Books ; [Farnborough, Hants.] : Gower [distributor], 1981, c1980. — xii,220p : ill ; 24cm. — (The Boston University series in gerontology)
Includes bibliographies and index
ISBN 0-669-03868-7 : £15.00 B81-22946

618.97′689 — Geriatrics. Psychiatry

Verwoerdt, Adrian. Clinical geropsychiatry / Adrian Verwoerdt. — 2nd ed. — Baltimore ; London : Williams & Wilkins, c1981. — xxx,371p ; 24cm
Previous ed.: 1976. — Includes index
ISBN 0-683-08592-1 : £44.50 B81-10656

618.97′689 — Old persons. Behavioural disorders. Diagnosis & treatment — *Case studies*

Hussain, Richard A.. Geriatric psychology : a behavioral perspective / Richard A. Hussain. — New York ; London : Van Nostrand Reinhold, c1981. — xii,244p : ill,1form ; 24cm
Bibliography: p225-239. — Includes index
ISBN 0-442-21916-4 : £16.95 B81-36076

618.97′689 — Old persons. Mental disorders

Lodge, Brian. What's happening to grandad? : a mental change in the elderly / Brian Lodge. — [London] : MIND, 1980. — 18p ; 30cm
£0.75 (pbk) B81-29341

618.97′68914 — Old persons. Psychotherapy

Brink, T. L.. Geriatric psychotherapy / T.L. Brink. — New York ; London : Human Sciences Press, 1979. — 318p ; 22cm
Bibliography: p288-308. — Includes index
ISBN 0-87705-346-4 : £10.75 B81-39457

618.97′68918 — Old persons. Mental disorders. Drug therapy. Psychotropic drugs

Ban, Thomas A.. Psycho pharmacology for the aged / Thomas A. Ban. — Basel ; London : Karger, 1980. — ix,215p ; 23cm
Bibliography: p147-208
ISBN 3-8055-1204-x (pbk) : Unpriced B81-10108

618.97′68983 — Old persons. Brain. Alzheimer's disease

Organic mental impairment in the elderly : implications for research, education and the provision of services : a report of the Royal College of Physicians / by the College Committee on Geriatrics. — [London] : [Royal College of Physicians of London], [1981]. — 29p ; 28cm
Originally published: in the Journal of the Royal College of Physicians of London, Vol.15 No.3 July 1981
Unpriced (unbound) B81-30660

618.97′68983 — Old persons. Senile dementia

Wolanin, Mary Opal. Confusion : prevention and care / Mary Opal Wolanin, Linda Ree Fraelich Phillips. — St. Louis ; London : Mosby, 1981. — xv,415p : ill,forms ; 25cm
Includes bibliographies and index
ISBN 0-8016-5629-x : £13.50 B81-14998

618.9′89′024362 — Children. Psychiatry — *For welfare workers*

Lask, Judith. Child psychiatry and social work. — London : Tavistock, Sept.1981. — [224]p. — (Tavistock library of social work practice ; SSP219)
ISBN 0-422-77080-9 (cased) : £9.50 : CIP entry
ISBN 0-422-77090-6 (pbk) : £4.50 B81-21556

619 — EXPERIMENTAL MEDICINE

619 — Experimental medicine — *Festschriften*

Advances in experimental medicine : a centenary tribute to Claude Bernard / editors H. Parvez and S. Parvez. — Amsterdam ; Oxford ([256 Banbury Rd., Oxford OX2 7DE]) : Elsevier/North-Holland Biomedical, 1980. — xviii,643p : ill,1port ; 25cm
Includes index
ISBN 0-444-80259-2 : £36.40 B81-01547

619 — Great Britain. Vivisection — *Serials*

Statistics of experiments on living animals, Great Britain / Home Office. — 1980. — London : H.M.S.O., 1981. — 35p. — (Cmnd. ; 8301)
ISBN 0-10-183010-6 : £3.50 B81-35966

619′.0942 — England. Medicine. Research. Laboratory animals — *Practical information*

Handbook for the animal licence holder / edited by H.V. Wyatt. — London : Institute of Biology, 1980. — iv,44p ; 21cm
Includes bibliographies and index
ISBN 0-900490-13-6 (pbk) : Unpriced B81-12047

620 — ENGINEERING

620 — Engineering. Decision making

Decision models for industrial systems engineers and managers. — Oxford : Pergamon, June 1981. — [476]p
ISBN 0-08-027612-1 : £29.00 : CIP entry B81-17535

620 — Engineering science

Rutherford, Stuart H.. Meaningful engineering science : is your theory really practical? / Stuart H. Rutherford. — London : Mechanical Engineering Publications, c1980. — xi,210p : ill ; 21cm
Includes index
ISBN 0-85298-449-9 (pbk) : Unpriced B81-00132

620 — Engineering science — *For schools*

McCorkindale, H. K.. Engineering science / H.K. McCorkindale. — Edinburgh : McDougall, c1980. — 180p : ill ; 20x25cm
Includes index
ISBN 0-7157-1984-x (pbk) : £3.50 B81-03648

620 — Engineering science — *For technicians*

Lowe, T. T.. Engineering science : level 2 / T.T. Lowe. — Walton-on-Thames : Nelson, 1981. — 130p : ill ; 22cm. — (Nelson TEC books)
Includes index
ISBN 0-17-741121-x (pbk) : £2.95 B81-22421

Titherington, D.. Engineering science : a third level course. — London : McGraw Hill, Feb.1982. — [232]p
ISBN 0-07-084646-4 : £3.95 : CIP entry B81-39249

620 — Great Britain. Engineering. Inventions. Development

Glegg, Gordon L.. The development of design. — Cambridge : Cambridge University Press, 1981. — 80p : ill ; 23cm
Includes index
ISBN 0-521-23794-7 : £7.50 B81-19753

620′.00068 — Great Britain. Engineering industries: GKN. Management. Policies, ***1977-1981 — Trade union viewpoints***

GKN : a case of British industry at risk / a report from TASS. — Richmond (Onslow Hall, Little Green, Richmond, Surrey, TW9 1QN) : AUEW-TASS, [1981]. — 8p ; 21cm
Unpriced (unbound) B81-35527

620′.001′515353 — Engineering. Mathematics. Boundary element methods — *Conference proceedings*

International Seminar on Recent Advances in Boundary Element Methods *(2nd : 1980 : University of Southampton)*. New developments in boundary element methods : proceedings of the second International Seminar on Recent Advances in Boundary Element Methods, held at the University of Southampton, March 1980 / edited by C.A. Brebbia ; sponsored by the International Society for Computational Methods in Engineering. — London : Butterworths, 1980. — 392p : ill ; 24cm
ISBN 0-408-01127-0 : Unpriced B81-37468

620′.00212 — Engineering — *Technical data*

Exacta engineering : reference tables and data. — Birkenhead (c/o 10 Westwood Court, Birkenhead, Merseyside L43 6XF) : Exacta, [1981]. — [20]p : 2ill ; 9x17cm
Cover title. — Originally published: Birkenhead : Picturettes, 1973
Unpriced (pbk) B81-10713

620′.00218 — Engineering. Standards. Preparation

A Guide to the preparation of engineering specifications / The Engineering Equipment Users Association ; [editor Peter Watts]. — London : Design Council, 1980. — 30p : ill ; 21cm
Cover title. — Text, ill on inside covers
ISBN 0-85072-116-4 (pbk) : £3.50 : CIP rev. B80-19255

620′.00228 — Model industrial plants. Construction — *Manuals*

Lamit, Louis Gary. Industrial model building / Louis Gary Lamit and Engineering Model Associates, Inc.. — Englewood Cliffs ; London : Prentice-Hall, c1981. — xv,380p : ill,plans ; 29cm
Includes index
ISBN 0-13-461566-2 : £19.45 B81-22358

620′.0023′41 — Great Britain. Engineering — *Career guides*

Moss, Stephen. Careers in engineering / Stephen Moss and Alexa Stace. — London : Kogan Page, 1981. — 118p : ill ; 19cm
ISBN 0-85038-353-6 (cased) : £5.95 : CIP rev.
ISBN 0-85038-354-4 (pbk) : £2.50 B80-25747

620′.0028 — Industrial equipment — *Serials*

Process equipment news : new products for busy managers. — Vol.1, no.1 (Feb.1980)-. — Swanley (Warwick House, Swanley, Kent BR8 8JF) : Hulton Technical Press, 1980-. — v. : ill ; 30cm
Monthly
ISSN 0261-7412 = Process equipment news : £12.00 per year B81-32887

620′.0028 — Industry. Applications of microprocessors

Microprocessors in industry. — Manchester : NCC Publications, July 1981. — [180]p
ISBN 0-85012-322-4 (pbk) : CIP entry B81-18045

620′.0028′54 — Engineering. Applications of computer systems — *Conference proceedings*

International Symposium on Computing Methods in Applied Sciences and Engineering *(4th : 1979 : Versailles)*. Computing methods in applied sciences and engineering : proceedings of the Fourth International Symposium on Computing Methods in Applied Sciences and Engineering, Versailles, France, December 10-14, 1979 / organised by Institut de recherche d′informatique et d′automatique (IRIA) ; sponsored by AFCET, GAMNI, IFIP TC-7 ; scientific secretaries J.F. Bourgat, A. Marrocco ; secretary Th. Bricheteau ; edited by R. Glowinski, J.L. Lions. — Amsterdam ; Oxford : North-Holland, 1980. — ix,724p : ill ; 23cm
Includes 4 chapters in French. — Includes bibliographies
ISBN 0-444-86008-8 : £29.98 B81-01647

620′.0029′44281 — Yorkshire. Engineering components — *Buyers′ guides — Serials*

Engineering Industries Association. *Yorkshire & Humberside Region*. Yorkshire & Humberside Region buyers guide / Engineering Industries Association. — 1978-. — Bradford (7 Tong La., Bradford, BD4 3RR) : Northern Advertising Agency (Bradford) Ltd. on behalf of The Association, 1978-. — v. : ill ; 22cm
Annual. — Description based on: 1980/81 issue
ISSN 0260-552x = Yorkshire & Humberside Region buyers guide : Unpriced B81-14365

620′.0042 — Engineering. Design. Research — *Conference proceedings*

Engineering research and design — bridging the gap. — London : Mechanical Engineering Publications, Sept.1981. — [84]p
Conference papers
ISBN 0-85298-475-8 (pbk) : £13.00 : CIP entry B81-27820

620′.0042 — Engineers. Professional education. Curriculum subjects: Engineering. Design — *Conference proceedings*

Education of tomorrow′s engineering designers. — London : Mechanical Engineering Publications, Sept.1981. — [120]p
Conference proceedings
ISBN 0-85298-482-0 (pbk) : £19.00 : CIP entry B81-28172

620′.0042′0724 — Engineering. Design. Use of models

David, F. W.. Experimental modelling in engineering. — London : Butterworths, Oct.1981. — [200]p
ISBN 0-408-01139-4 (pbk) : £10.00 : CIP entry B81-25306

620′.00425 — Engineering components. Design

Shoup, Terry E.. Introduction to engineering design : with graphics and design projects / Terry E. Shoup, Leroy S. Fletcher, Edward V. Mochel. — Englewood Cliffs ; London : Prentice-Hall, c1981. — xiv,391p : ill,facsims ; 24cm
Includes bibliographies and index
ISBN 0-13-482364-8 (pbk) : £12.55 B81-34949

620′.00425 — Engineering. Design

Faupel, Joseph H.. Engineering design : a synthesis of stress analysis and materials engineering. — 2nd ed. / Joseph H. Faupel, Franklin E. Fisher. — New York ; Chichester : Wiley, c1981. — xiv,1056p : ill ; 24cm
Previous ed.: 1964. — Includes index
ISBN 0-471-03381-2 : £21.50 B81-21263

Hawkes, Barry. Engineering design for technicians : full coverage of TEC Engineering Design III / Barry Hawkes, Ray Abinett. — London : Pitman, 1981. — viii,152p : ill ; 25cm
Includes index
ISBN 0-273-01675 x (pbk) : Unpriced B81-40390

Hubka, Vladimir. Principles of engineering design. — London : Butterworths, June 1981. — [96]p
Translation of: Allgemeienes Vorgehensmodell des Konstruierens
ISBN 0-408-01105-x : £6.00 : CIP entry B81-12892

620′.00425 — Engineering. Design - *For technicians*

Oldham, D.. Engineering design - TEC level III. — Cheltenham : Thornes, Aug.1981. — [224]p
ISBN 0-85950-303-8 (pbk) : £3.95 : CIP entry B81-16900

620′.00425′015114 — Engineering. Design. Mathematics. Approximation

Furman, T. T.. Approximate methods in engineering design / T.T. Furman. — London : Academic Press, 1981. — viii,388p,folded leaf : ill ; 24cm. — (Mathematics in science and engineering ; v.155)
Includes bibliographies and index
ISBN 0-12-269960-2 : Unpriced : CIP rev. B80-20756

620′.00425′02854 — Engineering. Design. Applications of computer systems — *Conference proceedings*

European Conference on Computer Aided Design in Medium Sized and Small Industries *(1st : 1980 : Paris)*. CAD in medium sized and small industries : proceedings of the First European Conference on Computer Aided Design in Medium Sized and Small Industries MICAD 80, Paris, 23-26 September 1980 / edited by Jean Mermet. — Amsterdam ; Oxford : North-Holland, c1981. — x,664p : ill ; 23cm
ISBN 0-444-86145-9 : £33.65 B81-18485

620′.00425′05 — Engineering. Design — *Serials*

[Eureka *(Beckenham)***]**. Eureka : innovative engineering design. — Vol.1, no.1 (Dec. 1980)-. — Beckenham (1 Copers Cope Rd, Beckenham, Kent BR32 1NB) : Findlay Publications, 1980-. — v. : ill ; 26cm
Monthly
£21.00 per year B81-24136

620′.0044 — Engineering equipment. Automatic testing — *Conference proceedings*

Automatic Testing & Test and Measurement ′81 *(Conference : Wiesbaden)*. Automatic Testing & Test and Measurement ′81 : Konferenzunterlagen = conference proceedings : Rhein-Main-Halle, Wiesbaden 23, 24, 25, 26, März 1981. — [Buckingham] : [Network], [c1981]. — 4v. : ill ; 30cm
Parallel German text and English translation and summary. — Cover title
ISBN 0-904999-81-5 (pbk) : Unpriced
ISBN 0-904999-82-3 (v.2) : £30.00
ISBN 0-904999-83-1 (v.3) : £30.00
ISBN 0-904999-84-x (v.4) : £30.00 B81-33006

620'.0044 — Engineering equipment. Automatic testing — *Conference proceedings*
continuation

Automatic Testing 77 *(Conference : Brighton).* Automatic Testing 77 : conference proceedings : Metropole Convention Centre, Brighton, England, 28-30 November 1977. — Newport Pagnell : Network, c1977
Cover title
Session no.1: Component testing. — 45leaves : ill ; 30cm
£9.00 (pbk) B81-28944

Automatic Testing 77 *(Conference : Brighton).* Automatic Testing 77 : conference proceedings : Metropole Convention Centre, Brighton, England, 28-30 November 1977. — Newport Pagnell : Network, 1977
Cover title
Session no.2: How ATE can save money and manpower. — 74p : ill ; 30cm
£9.00 (pbk) B81-28945

Automatic Testing 77 *(Conference : Brighton).* Automatic Testing 77 : conference proceedings : Metropole Convention Centre, Brighton, England, 28-30 November 1977. — Newport Pagnell : Network, 1977
Cover title
Session no.3: ATE for equipment production and maintenance. — 176p : ill ; 30cm
£12.00 (pbk) B81-28946

Automatic Testing 77 *(Conference : Brighton).* Automatic Testing 77 : conference proceedings : Metropole Convention Centre, Brighton, England, 28-30 November 1977. — Newport Pagnell : Network, 1977
Cover title
Session no.4: Testing of complex systems. — 108p : ill ; 30cm
£9.00 (pbk) B81-28947

620'.0044 — Engineering. Measurement & control

Haslam, J. A.. Engineering instrumentation and control. — London : Edward Arnold, Oct.1981. — [308]p
ISBN 0-7131-3431-3 (pbk) : £5.50 : CIP entry B81-27979

620'.0044 — Engineering. Measurement — *For technicians*

Davey, D. J.. Technician instrumentation and control 4 / D.J. Davey, E.R. Robinson. — London : Cassell, 1981. — 209p : ill ; 22cm. — (Cassell's TEC series)
Includes index
ISBN 0-304-30795-5 (pbk) : Unpriced
Also classified at 629.8 B81-40564

620'.0044 — Measuring instruments

Instrumentation / [the Instrumentation Course Team]. — 2d ed. — Milton Keynes : Open University Press. — (Technology : a second level course)
At head of title: The Open University
Mathematics for instrumentation / prepared by the Course Team. — 1980. — 92p : ill ; 30cm. — (T291M)
Previous ed.: 1974
Unpriced (pbk) B81-14719

620'.0044'02462 — Engineering. Measurement & control *For technicians*

Adams, L. F.. Engineering Instrumentation and Control IV. — London : Hodder and Stoughton, July 1981. — [256]p. — (The Higher technician series)
ISBN 0-340-26147-1 (pbk) : £4.75 : CIP entry B81-13489

620'.00452 — Reliability engineering

Dhillon, B. S.. Engineering reliability : new techniques and applications / B.S. Dhillon, Chanan Singh. — New York ; Chichester : Wiley, c1981. — xix,339p : ill ; 24cm. — (Wiley series in systems engineering and analysis)
Includes bibliographies and index
ISBN 0-471-05014-8 : £23.00 B81-23343

O'Connor, Patrick D. T.. Practical reliability engineering / Patrick D.T. O'Connor. — London : Heyden, c1981. — xvii,299p : ill ; 25cm
Includes bibliographies and index
ISBN 0-85501-496-2 : Unpriced B81-24266

620'.00452'05 — Reliability engineering — *Serials*

Reliability engineering : an international journal. — Vol.1, no.1 (July/Sept.1980)-. — London : Applied Science, 1980-. — v. : ill ; 24cm
Quarterly
ISSN 0143-8174 = Reliability engineering : £37.50 per year B81-02000

620'.00452'0724 — Engineering equipment. Reliability. Mathematical models

Henley, Ernest J.. Reliability engineering and risk assessment / Ernest J. Henley, Hironitsu Kumamoto. — Englewood Cliffs ; London : Prentice-Hill, c1981. — xxiv,568p : ill ; 24cm
Includes index
ISBN 0-13-772251-6 : £25.35 B81-09295

620'.0046 — Engineering equipment. Faults. Diagnosis — *Manuals*

Systematic fault diagnosis. — London : Godwin, Feb.1982. — [162]p
ISBN 0-7114-5739-5 : £20.00 : CIP entry B81-40237

620'.005 — Engineering — *Serials*

Journal of engineering and applied sciences / College of Engineering, King Abdulaziz University. — Vol.1, no.1 (1981)-. — Oxford : Pergamon, 1981-. — v. : ill ; 26cm
Quarterly
ISSN 0191-9535 = Journal of engineering and applied sciences : Unpriced B81-33702

Kempe's engineers year book. — 86th ed (1981). — London (30, Calderwood St., SE18 6QH) : Morgan-Grampian, c1980. — 2v
ISSN 0075-5400 : Unpriced B81-09040

620'.0068 — Engineering industries. Management

Cleland, David I.. Engineering management / David I. Cleland, Dundar F. Kocaoglu. — New York ; London : McGraw-Hill, 1981. — x,469p : ill ; 25cm. — (McGraw-Hill series in industrial engineering and management science)
Includes bibliographies and index
ISBN 0-07-011316-5 : £15.25 B81-36477

620'.0068'4 — Engineering industries. Project management

Thompson, Peter, *1930-*. Organization and economics of construction / Peter Thompson. — London : McGraw-Hall, 1981. — xiii,146p : ill,forms ; 28cm. — (University series in civil engineering)
Includes index
ISBN 0-07-084122-5 (pbk) : £7.95 B81-18240

620'.0068'4 — Great Britain. Engineering. Projects. Management. Role of information services

Bitz, A. S.. An approach to the potential importance of information in engineering / A.S. Bitz and B.S. Owen. — Newcastle-upon-Tyne : Department of Mechanical Engineering, Newcastle-upon-Tyne University, 1981. — 111p : forms ; 30cm. — (BL R & D report ; 5603)
Cover title
Unpriced (pbk) B81-16327

620'.007'1141 — Great Britain. Engineering industries. Personnel. Training

Moon, J.. 16 Years on : a perspective on industrial training from the viewpoint of the EITBV / by J. Moon. — Sheffield : Association of Colleges for Further and Higher Education, [1981]. — 21p ; 21cm
Paper presented at the Association of Colleges for Further and Higher Education Annual General Meeting, 26-27 Feb. 1981, the Institution of Electrical Engineers, London
£0.75 (pbk) B81-17809

620'.007'1141835 — Dublin. Universities: Trinity College *(Dublin). School of Engineering.* **Graduates —** *Directories*

Trinity College. A record of graduates, 1841-1981 / the School of Engineering, Trinity College Dublin. — 5th ed. — [Dublin] ([Trinity College, Dublin 2]) : [School of Engineering, Trinity College, Dublin], [1981]. — 157p ; 21cm
Previous ed.: 197-?
Unpriced (pbk) B81-18632

620'.007'11422 — London & Home Counties. Higher education institutions. Curriculum subjects: Engineering. Courses — *Serials*

Engineering education in the region. — 1980/81. — London : London and Home Counties Regional Advisory Council for Technological Education, [1980?]. — 52p
ISBN 0-85394-076-2 : £0.90 B81-06143

620'.007'11481 — Norway. Higher education institutions. Curriculum subjects: Engineering

Sim, A. C.. Engineering education in Norway / by A.C. Sim. — Dagenham (North East London Polytechnic, Longbridge Rd., Dagenham, Essex RM8 2AS) : Centre for Research in Engineering Education, 1980. — 14p : 1ill ; 21cm. — (CREE repo ; 1)
Unpriced (pbk) B81-09422

620'.0072041 — Great Britain. *Science Research Council. Engineering Processes Committee — Serials*

Great Britain. *Science Research Council. Engineering Processes Committee.* Report of the committee for the year ... / Science Research Council, Engineering Processes Committee. — 1979/80-. — Swindon : The Council, [1981]-. — v. ; 30cm
Annual. — Cover title: Great Britain. Science Research Council. Engineering Processes Committee. Annual report. — Merger of: Great Britain. Science Research Council. Chemical Engineering and Technology Committee. Report of the committee for the year ... ; and, Great Britain. Science Research Council. Manufacturing Technology Committee. Report of the committee for the year ..
ISSN 0261-5843 = Report of the committee - Science Research Council. Engineering Processes Committee B81-35808

620'.0072042582 — Engineering. Research organisations: Warren Spring Laboratory — *Serials*

Warren Spring Laboratory. Annual report / Warren Spring Laboratory. — 1980. — Stevenage : The Laboratory, 1980. — [6]p
Unpriced B81-29413

620'.00724 — Engineering. Applications of mathematical models

. Case studies in mathematical modelling. — London (4 Graham Lodge, Graham Rd, NW4 3DG) : Pentech Press, June 1981. — [240]p
ISBN 0-7273-0311-2 : £16.00 : CIP entry B81-14785

620'.0092'2 — Engineering — *Biographies*

Carvill, James. Famous names in engineering / James Carvill. — London : Butterworths, 1981. — 93p : ill,ports ; 25cm
Bibliography: p83-93
ISBN 0-408-00539-4 (cased) : Unpriced
ISBN 0-408-00540-8 (pbk) : Unpriced B81-32995

620'.00944 — France. Engineering. Innovation

Aigrain, Pierre. Innovative engineering in France : strengths and weaknesses / Pierre Aigrain. — London (2 Little Smith St., SW1P 3DL) : Fellowship of Engineering, [1979]. — 26p ; 21cm. — (Third distinction lecture / Fellowship of Engineering)
Unpriced (pbk) B81-31384

620'00962 — Egypt. Engineering. Policies of government

Moore, Clement Henry. Images of development : Egyptian engineers in search of industry / Clement Henry Moore. — Cambridge, Mass. ; London : MIT, c1980. — x,252p : ill ; 24cm
Includes index
ISBN 0-262-13161-7 : £15.50 B81-09349

620.1 — ENGINEERING MECHANICS AND MATERIALS

620.1 — Applied mechanics

Mechanics today / edited by S. Nemat-Nasser. — Oxford : Published by Pergamon on behalf of the American Academy of Mechanics. — (Pergamon mechanics today series)
Vol.6. — 1981. — xxii,204p : ill ; 26cm
Includes index
ISBN 0-08-024749-0 : £21.00 B81-25420

620.1 — Applied mechanics *continuation*

Shelley, Joseph F.. Engineering mechanics : statics and dynamics / Joseph F. Shelley. — New York ; London : McGraw-Hill, c1980. — xvi,939p : ill(some col.) ; 25cm
Ill, text on lining papers. — Includes index
ISBN 0-07-056555-4 : £20.25 B81-23451

620.1 — Applied mechanics — *Conference proceedings*

International Congress of Theoretical and Applied Mechanics *(15th : 1980 : University of Toronto)*. Theoretical and applied mechanics : proceedings of the XVth International Congress of Theoretical and Applied Mechanics, University of Toronto, Canada, August 17-23, 1980 / edited by F.P.J. Rimrott and B. Tabarrok. — Amsterdam ; Oxford : North-Holland, 1980. — xxxi,457p : ill,ports ; 27cm
Includes bibliographies and index
ISBN 0-444-85411-8 : £30.53
Primary classification 531 B81-23606

620.1 — Applied mechanics — *For technicians*

Ayling, D. S.. Mechanical science 3 checkbook. — London : Butterworths, Nov.1981. — [128] p. — (Butterworth's checkbook series)
ISBN 0-408-00665-x (cased) : £6.95 : CIP entry
ISBN 0-408-00649-8 (pbk) : £3.50 B81-30517

Rix, Max A.. Mechanical science : level III / Max A. Rix. — Colophoa ; London : Van Nostrand Reinhold, 1980. — ix,118p : ill ; 25cm. — (Technical education courses)
Includes index
ISBN 0-442-30390-4 (cased) : £9.00
ISBN 0-442-30391-2 (pbk) : £4.25 B81-08718

620.101'51'7 — Applied mechanics. Mathematics. Numerical methods

Naylor, D. J.. Finite elements in geotechnical engineering. — Swansea (91 West Cross Lane, West Cross, Swansea, W. Glam.) : Pineridge, Apr.1981. — [220]p
ISBN 0-906674-11-5 : £12.00 : CIP entry B81-10461

620.1'03 — Applied statics

Morrow, H. W.. Statics and strength of materials / H.W. Morrow. — Englewood Cliffs ; London : Prentice-Hall, c1981. — xiv,514p : ill ; 25cm
Includes index
ISBN 0-13-844720-9 : £14.25
Also classified at 620.1'12 B81-22721

Peterson, Aldor C.. Applied engineering mechanics : statics / Aldor C. Peterson. — 2nd ed. — Boston, Mass. ; London : Allyn and Bacon, c1981. — xi,285p : ill ; 25cm
Previous ed.: publised as Applied mechanics for engineers and technicians : statics. 1967. — Includes index
ISBN 0-205-07131-7 (corrected) : Unpriced B81-29949

620.1'05 — Solids. Applied mechanics

Engineering mechanics : solids / [Engineering Mechanics: Solids Course Team]. — Milton Keynes : Open University Press. — (Technology : a second level course)
At head of title: The Open University
Block 2: Statics. — 1980. — 87p : ill ; 30cm. — (T232 ; 3 and 4)
Contents: Unit 3: Newton's laws - Unit 4: Free body diagrams
ISBN 0-335-17001-3 (pbk) : Unpriced B81-14718

Engineering mechanics : solids / [Engineering Mechanics: Solids Course Team]. — Milton Keynes : Open University Press. — (Technology : a second level course)
At head of title: The Open University
Block 6: Structures. — 1980. — 72p : ill ; 30cm. — (T232 ; 10/11)
Contents: Unit 10: Stress analysis - Unit 11: Structural components
ISBN 0-335-17005-6 (pbk) : Unpriced B81-14717

Engineering mechanics : solids / [Engineering Mechanics: Solids Course Team]. — Milton Keynes : Open University Press. — (Technology : a second level course)
At head of title: The Open University
Block 7: Work, energy, power. — 1980. — 8,70p : ill ; 30cm. — (T232 ; 12/13)
Contents: Units 12/13: Work, energy, power
ISBN 0-335-17006-4 (pbk) : Unpriced B81-14716

620.1'06 — Applied hydromechanics

Simon, Andrew L.. Practical hydraulics / Andrew L. Simon. — 2nd ed. — New York ; Chichester : Wiley, c1981. — xi,403p : ill ; 25cm
Previous ed.: 1976. — Bibliography: p397-399. - Includes index
ISBN 0-471-05381-3 : Unpriced B81-08516

620.1'06 — Fluid power

McCloy, D.. Control of fluid power : analysis and design / D. McCloy and H.R. Martin. — 2nd (rev.) ed. — Chichester : Horwood, 1980. — 505p : ill ; 24cm. — (Ellis Horwood series in engineering science)
Previous ed.: Harlow : Longman, 1973. — Includes index
ISBN 0-85312-135-4 : £26.00 : CIP rev. B80-17750

620.1'06 — Fluid power equipment. Variable speed drives — *Conference proceedings*

Developments in variable speed drives for fluid machinery : conference sponsored by the Power Industries Division of the Institution of Mechanical Engineers and the Institution of Electrical Engineers, 9 June 1981, Institution Headquarters, 1 Birdcage Walk, Westminster, London. — London : Published by Mechanical Engineering Publications for the Institution of Mechanical Engineers, 1981. — 65p : ill ; 30cm. — (I Mech E conference publications ; 1981-5)
ISBN 0-85298-474-x (pbk) : Unpriced B81-28884

620.1'06'0288 — Fluid flow machinery. Maintenance & repair — *Conference proceedings*

Fluid Handling Conference *(2nd : 1980 : Harrogate)*. Interflow '80 : the Fluid Handling Conference Harrogate February 6, 7 & 8, 1980 : the 2n Fluid Handling Conference was held in Harrogate on February 6, 7 & 8, 1980 and organised in conjunction with the Institution of Chemical Engineers and the Institution of Plant Engineers. — Croydon (Trenton House, Imperial Way, Croydon CR0 4RR) : Trenton Exhibitions Ltd, 1980. — A80,B42p : ill ; 30cm
£15.00 (spiral) B81-06098

620.1'06'05 — Fluid handling equipment — *Serials*

[**Fluids handling** *(London : 1981)*]. Fluids handling. — Vol.1, no.1 (Feb./Mar.1981)-. — London : Turret Press, 1981-. — v. : ill ; 30cm
Six issues yearly
ISSN 0261-5878 = Fluids handling (London. 1981) : £18.50 per year B81-34026

620.1'064 — Industries. Use of rheometry

Rheometry : industrial applications / edited by Kenneth Walters. — Chichester : Research Studies Press, c1980 300 viii,418p : ill, 24cm. — [426]p. — (Materials science research studies series)
ISBN 0-471-27878-5 : £25.00 : CIP rev. B80-27122

620.1'1 — Materials

Ashby, Michael F.. Engineering materials : an introduction to their properties and applications / by Michael F. Ashby and David R.H. Jones. — Oxford : Pergamon, 1980. — x,278p : ill ; 26cm. — (International series on materials science and technology ; v.34) (Pergamon international library)
Text on inside covers. — Includes index
ISBN 0-08-026139-6 (cased) : £15.00 : CIP rev.
ISBN 0-08-026138-8 (pbk) : £4.75 B80-08793

620.1'1 — Materials — *For civil engineering*

Derucher, Kenneth N.. Materials for civil and highway engineers / Kenneth N. Derucher, Conrad P. Heins. — Englewood Cliffs ; London : Prentice-Hall, c1981. — xi,464p : ill,forms ; 24cm
Includes bibliographies and index
ISBN 0-13-560490-7 : £16.85 B81-14676

620.1'1 — Materials — *For craftwork — For schools*

Pettit, T.. Appreciation of materials and design / T. Pettit. — London : Edward Arnold, 1981. — 200p : ill,maps ; 25cm. — (Craft education)
ISBN 0-7131-0356-6 (pbk) : £5.95 B79-21792

620.1'1 — Materials science — *For technicians*

Bolton, W.. Materials technology for technicians 2. — London : Butterworths, Nov.1981. — [96]p
ISBN 0-408-01117-3 : £4.95 : CIP entry B81-30516

Bolton, W.. Materials technololgy for technicians 3. — London : Butterworths, Feb.1982. — [100]p
ISBN 0-408-01116-5 : £4.95 : CIP entry B81-36951

Bolton, W. (William), *1933-*. Materials technology 4 / W. Bolton. — Sevenoaks : Butterworths, 1981. — 117p : ill ; 25cm. — (Butterworths technician series)
Bibliography: p117
ISBN 0-408-00584-x (pbk) : Unpriced : CIP rev. B81-23914

620.1'1 — Materials. Surfaces. Pretreatment

Surface pretreatments of plastics and metals. — London : Applied Science, Dec.1981. — [256]p
ISBN 0-85334-992-4 : £22.00 : CIP entry B81-31516

620.1'1'02854 — Materials science. Applications of digital computer systems — *Conference proceedings*

Computers in materials technology : proceedings of the international conference held at the Institute of Technology Linköping University, Sweden, June 4-5, 1980 / edited by T. Ericsson. — Oxford : Pergamon, 1981. — x,224p : ill ; 24cm
Includes index
ISBN 0-08-027570-2 : £14.50 : CIP rev. B81-16867

620.1'1'05 — Materials science — *Serials*

Progress in materials science. — Vol.25. — Oxford : Pergamon, Dec.1981. — [420]p
ISBN 0-08-029096-5 : £48.00 : CIP entry B81-33853

Res mechanica letters : rapid communications in structural mechanics and materials science. — Vol.1, no.1 (Jan.1981)-. — Barking : Applied Science, 1981-. — v. : ill ; 24cm
Monthly
ISSN 0144-7831 = Res mechanica letters : Unpriced
Also classified at 624.1'71'05 B81-20061

620.1'1'072041 — Great Britain. *Science Research Council. Materials Committee — Serials*

Great Britain. *Science Research Council. Materials Committee*. Report for the year / Science Research Council, Engineering Board, Materials Committee. — 1979-1980 -. — Swindon : Materials Committee Secretariat, Science and Engineering Research Council, [1981]-. — v. ; 30cm
Annual. — Cover title: Annual report (Great Britain. Science Research Council. Materials Committee). — Continues: Great Britain. Science Research Council. Materials Science and Technology Committee. Annual report
Unpriced B81-39546

620.1'12 — Bulk materials. Sampling

Smith, R.. The sampling of bulk materials / R. Smith, G.V. James. — London : Royal Society of Chemistry, 1981. — viii,191p : ill ; 23cm. — (Analytical sciences monographs, ISSN 0583-8894 ; v.8)
Includes index
ISBN 0-85186-810-x : Unpriced : CIP rev. B80-33694

620.1'12 — Materials. Chemical analysis. Electron spin resonance spectraoscopy & nuclear magnetic resonance spectroscopy — *Conference proceedings*

Materials Research Society. *Meeting (1980 : Boston, Mass.)*. Nuclear and electron resonance spectroscopies applied to materials science : proceedings of the Materials Research Society Annual Meeting, November 1980, Copley Plaza Hotel, Boston, Massachusetts, U.S.A. / editors E.N. Kaufmann and G.K. Shenoy. — New York ; Oxford : North Holland, c1981. — xii,558p : ill ; 24cm. — (Materials Research Society symposia proceedings, ISSN 0272-9172 ; v.3)
Includes index
ISBN 0-444-00597-8 : Unpriced B81-29005

620.1'12 — Materials. Defects — *Conference proceedings*

Institute of Metallurgical Technicians. *Conference (6th : 1980 : Bradford College)*. Towards a better product — the role of the technician : the papers ... presented at the 6th Annual Conference and Exhibition of the Institute of Metallurgical Technicians held at Bradford College 22-24 July 1980. — London (c/o Publications Department, Northway House, Whetstone, N20 9LW) : Institution of Metallurgists, [1980?]. — iii,69p : ill,forms ; 30cm. — (Conference papers / Institute of Metallurgical Technicians ; no.1MT/3)
Publisher's no.: 1307-80-MT
ISBN 0-901462-12-8 (pbk) : Unpriced B81-23290

620.1'12 — Materials. Failure

Collins, J. A.. Failure of materials in mechanical design : analysis, prediction, prevention / J.A. Collins. — New York ; Chichester : Wiley, c1981. — xv,629p : ill ; 24cm. — (A Wiley-Interscience publication)
Includes index
ISBN 0-471-05024-5 : £25.00 B81-23985

620.1'12 — Materials. Mechanics

Ugural, A. C.. Advanced strength and applied elasticity / A.C. Ugural, S.K. Fenster. — SI version. — London : Edward Arnold, 1981. — xvi,423p : ill ; 22cm
Previous ed.: New York : London : American Elsevier, 1975. — Includes index
ISBN 0-7131-3436-4 : £18.00 B81-25990

620.1'12 — Materials. Mechanics — *Conference proceedings*

International Symposium on the Mechanical Behaviour of Structured Media *(1981 : Ottawa)*. Mechanics of structured media : proceedings of the International Symposium on the Mechanical Behaviour of Structured Media, Ottawa, May 18-21, 1981 / organized by the Department of Civil Engineering, Carleton Unversity, Ottawa, Ontario, Canada ; A.P.S. Selvadurai editor. — Amsterdam ; Oxford : Elsevier, 1981. — 2v : ill ; 25cm
Includes index
ISBN 0-444-41982-9 : Unpriced : CIP rev.
ISBN 0-444-41979-9 (part A.) : Unpriced
ISBN 0-444-41983-7 (part B.) : Unpriced B81-12914

620.1'12 — Materials. Processing. Applications of electron beams & lasers — *Conference proceedings*

Materials Research Society. *Meeting (1980 : Boston, Mass.)*. Laser and electron-beam solid interactions and materials processing : proceedings of the Materials Research Society Annual Meeting, November 1980, Copley Plaza Hotel, Boston, Massachusetts, U.S.A. / editors J.F. Gibbons, L.D. Hess and T.W. Sigmon. — New York ; Oxford : North-Holland, c1981. — xiii,629p : ill ; 24cm. — (Materials Research Society symposia proceedings, ISSN 0272-9172 ; v.1)
Includes index
ISBN 0-444-00595-1 : Unpriced B81-26890

620.1'12 — Materials. Strength

Alexander, J. M. (John Malcolm). Strength of materials / John M. Alexander. — Chichester (Market Cross House, Cooper St., Chichester, W. Sussex PO13 1EB) : Ellis Horwood. — (Ellis Horwood series in engineering science)
Vol.1: Fundamentals. — 1981. — 267p : ill ; 24cm
Bibliography: p260-261. - Includes index
ISBN 0-85312-260-1 : £20.00 B81-16325

Morrow, H. W.. Statics and strength of materials / H.W. Morrow. — Englewood Cliffs ; London : Prentice-Hall, c1981. — xiv,514p : ill ; 25cm
Includes index
ISBN 0-13-844720-9 : £14.25
Primary classification 620.1'03 B81-22721

Peterson, Aldor C.. Applied engineering mechanics: strength of materials / Aldor C. Peterson. — 2nd ed. — Boston [Mass.] ; London : Allyn and Bacon, c1982. — xiii,385p : ill ; 25cm
Previous ed.: published as Applied mechanics : strength of materials. 1969. — Includes index
ISBN 0-205-07222-4 (cased) : Unpriced
ISBN 0-205-07338-7 (International ed.) : £17.95 B81-28984

Willems, Nicholas. Strength of materials / Nicholas Willems, John T. Easley, Stanley T. Rolfe. — New York ; London : McGraw-Hill, c1981. — xviii,508p : ill ; 25cm
Text, ill on lining papers. — Includes index
ISBN 0-07-070297-7 : £18.85 B81-23722

620.1'12 — Materials. Surface. Roughness

Rough surfaces. — London : Longman, Sept.1981. — [272]p
ISBN 0-582-46816-7 : £45.00 : CIP entry B81-25877

620.1'121 — Materials. Thermal stresses. Effects of nonisothermal conditions — *Conference proceedings*

International Conference on Thermal Stresses in Materials and Structures in Severe Thermal Environments *(1980 : Virginia Polytechnic Institute and State University)*. Thermal stresses in severe environments / [proceedings of the International Conference on Thermal Stresses in Materials and Structures in Severe Thermal Environments, held at Virginia Polytechnic Institute and State University, Blackburg, Virginia, March 19-21, 1980] ; edited by D.P.H. Hasselman and R.A. Heller. — New York ; London : Plenum, c1980. — x,737p : ill ; 26cm
Includes index
ISBN 0-306-40544-x : Unpriced B81-06218

620.1'1217 — High temperature corrosion — *Conference proceedings*

Environmental degradation of high temperature materials : ... papers ... presented at the Spring Residential Conference held at the Palace Hotel, Douglas, Isle of Man from 21 March to 3 April 1980 / organised by the Younger Metallurgists Committee of the Institution of Metallurgists, co-sponsored by the Institution of Corrosion Science and Technology. — London (c/o Publications Department, Northway House, Whetstone, N20 9LW) : Institution of Metallurgists, [1980?]. — 2v : ill. — (Spring residential conference / Institution of Metallurgists. Series 3 ; no. 13)
Publisher's no.
Unpriced (pbk) B81-23291

620.1'1217 — Materials. Effects of high temperatures — *Conference proceedings*

Corrosion and mechanical stress at high temperatures / [papers presented in May, 1980 at a two-day meeting on 'Interaction between corrosion and mechanical stress at high temperatures' in Petten, The Netherlands, organised by the Commission of the European Communities, Joint Research Centre, Petten Establishment, in co-operation with the European Federation of Corrosion's Working Group on Corrosion by Hot Gases and Combustion Products, and Nederlands Corrosie Centrum ; edited by V. Guttmann and M. Merz. — London : Applied Science, c1981. — xii,472p : ill ; 23cm
Conference papers
ISBN 0-85334-956-8 : £24.00 : CIP rev. B81-12800

620.1'1223 — Biodegradation

Microbial biodeterioration. — London : Academic Press, Dec.1981. — [450]p. — (Economic microbiology ; v.6)
ISBN 0-12-596556-7 : CIP entry B81-31346

620.1'1223 — Corrosion

West, John M.. Basic corrosion and oxidation / John M. West. — Chichester : Horwood, 1980. — 247p : ill ; 24cm
Includes index
ISBN 0-85312-196-6 : £19.50 : CIP rev. B80-19258

620.1'1223 — Corrosion inhibitors

Rozenfeld, I. L.. Corrosion inhibitors. — London : McGraw-Hill, June 1981. — [352]p
ISBN 0-07-054170-1 : £22.36 : CIP entry B81-12880

620.1'123 — Materials. Elasticity & plasticity. Analysis. Applications of variational methods

Washizu, Kyuichiro. Variational methods in elasticity and plasticity. — 3rd ed. — Oxford : Pergamon, Feb.1982. — [540]p
Previous ed.: 1974
ISBN 0-08-026723-8 : £42.00 : CIP entry B81-35952

620.1'123 — Materials. Fatigue & fracture — *Conference proceedings*

Colloquium on Fracture *(3rd : 1980 : London)*. Fracture and fatigue : elasto-plasticity, thin sheet and micromechanisms problems : proceedings of the Third Colloquium on Fracture, London, 8-10 September 1980 : ECF 3 / edited by J.C. Radon. — Oxford : Pergamon, 1980. — ix,488p : ill ; 26cm. — (International series on the strength and fracture of materials and structures)
Includes bibliographies
ISBN 0-08-026161-2 : £25.00 : CIP rev. B80-13867

Fatigue '81 *(Conference : University of Warwick)*. Materials, experimentation and design in fatigue : proceedings of Fatigue '81 / Society of Environmental Engineers, Fatigue Group conference 24-27 March 1981, Warwick University, England ; edited by F. Sherratt and J.B. Sturgeon. — [Guildford] : Westbury House, c1981. — ix,485p : ill ; 25cm
ISBN 0-86103-042-7 : Unpriced B81-17889

620.1'123 — Materials. Fretting fatigue. Measurement

Fretting fatigue / edited by R.B. Waterhouse. — London : Applied Science, c1981. — x,244p : ill ; 23cm
Includes index
ISBN 0-85334-932-0 : £20.00 B81-23601

620.1'123'0287 — Materials. Stresses & strains. Measurement — *Conference proceedings*

Product Liability and Reliability *(Conference : 1980 : University of Aston in Birmingham)*. Proceedings of the British Society for Strain Measurement and Institution of Production Engineers International Conference "Product Liability and Reliability" held at University of Aston in Birmingham 1-5 September, 1980. — Newcastle upon Tyne (281 Heaton Rd, Newcastle upon Tyne NE6 5QB) : The Society
Vol.1. — 1980. — 396p in various pagings : ill ; 29cm
ISBN 0-9506351-5-4 : Unpriced
Also classified at 342.63'82 B81-38156

620.1'1233 — Materials. Creep

Kraus, Harry. Creep analysis / Harry Kraus. — New York ; Chichester : Wiley, c1980. — xvii,250p : ill ; 24cm
Includes index
ISBN 0-471-06255-3 : £15.00 B81-05606

620.1'1233 — Materials. High temperature creep — *Conference proceedings*

Creep and fracture of engineering materials and structures. — Swansea (91 West Cross Lane, West Cross, Swansea, West Glamorgan) : Pineridge Press, Apr.1981. — [800]p
ISBN 0-906674-10-7 : £38.00 : CIP entry
Also classified at 620.1'126 B81-02674

620.1'1233 — Metals. Plastic deformation

Johnson, W.. Plane strain slip line fields for metal deformation processes. — Oxford : Pergamon, Sept.1981. — [270]p
ISBN 0-08-025452-7 : £16.50 : CIP entry B81-21530

620.1'1233 — Solid materials. Dislocations — *Conference proceedings*
Dislocation modelling of physical systems : proceedings of the international conference, Gainesville, Florida, USA, June 22-27, 1980 / edited by M.F. Ashby ... [et al.]. — Oxford : Pergamon, c1981. — ix,587p : ill ; 25cm. — (An Acta-Scripta Metallurgica conference)
Includes index
ISBN 0-08-026724-6 : £31.00 B81-39860

620.1'126 — Materials. Fatigue & fracture
Cavities and cracks in creep and fatigue. — London : Applied Science, Sept.1981. — [304]p
ISBN 0-85334-965-7 : £24.00 : CIP entry B81-20546

620.1'126 — Materials. Fracture. Mechanics — *Conference proceedings*
Fracture mechanics in design and service : a Royal Society discussion / organized by Sir Hugh Ford ... [ed al.] held on 5 and 6 December 1979. — London : The Society, 1981. — 239p,[3]leaves of plates : ill ; 31cm
Includes bibliographies
ISBN 0-85403-152-9 : £23.00 B81-11467

620.1'126 — Materials. High temperature fracture — *Conference proceedings*
Creep and fracture of engineering materials and structures. — Swansea (91 West Cross Lane, West Cross, Swansea, West Glamorgan) : Pineridge Press, Apr.1981. — [800]p
ISBN 0-906674-10-7 : £38.00 : CIP entry
Primary classification 620.1'1233 B81-02674

620.1'126 — Solid materials. Fracture — *Conference proceedings*
International Conference on Fracture *(5th : 1981 : Cannes)*. Advances in fracture research. — Oxford : Pergamon, Oct.1981. — [3000]p. — (International series on the strength and fracture of materials and structures)
ISBN 0-08-025428-4 : £200.00 : CIP entry B81-27988

620.1'127'05 — Non-destructive testing — *Serials*
International advances in nondestructive testing. — Vol.7. — New York ; London : Gordon and Breach, c1981. — 431p
ISBN 0-677-15700-2 : Unpriced
ISSN 0140-072x B81-31011

Research techniques in nondestructive testing. — Vol.5. — London : Academic Press, Feb.1982. — [400
ISBN 0-12-639055-x : CIP entry
ISSN 0277-7045 B81-35911

620.1'1274 — Materials. Non-destructive testing. Applications of ultrasonic spectroscopy
Fitting, Dale W.. Ultrasonic spectral analysis for nondestructive evaluation / Dale W. Fitting and Laszlo Adler. — New York ; London : Plenum, c1981. — ix,354p : ill,1form ; 26cm
Bibliography: p163-328. — Includes index
ISBN 0-306-40484-2 : Unpriced B81-33673

620.1'1274 — Materials. Testing. Use of ultrasonic waves
Ultrasonic testing. — Chichester : Wiley, Sept.1981. — [640]p
ISBN 0-471-27938-2 : £28.00 : CIP entry B81-22548

620.1'1294 — Acoustic emission
Williams, R. V.. Acoustic emission / R.V. Williams. — Bristol : Hilger, c1980. — xiii,118p : ill ; 22cm
Includes bibliographies and index
ISBN 0-85274-359-9 : £11.95 : CIP rev. B80-12389

620.1'1295 — Materials. Optical bistability — *Conference proceedings*
International Conference on Optical Bistability *(1980 : Asheville, N.C.)*. Optical bistability / [invited papers presented at the International Conference on Optical Bistability, held June 3-5, 1980, in Asheville, North Carolina] ; edited by Charles M. Bowden and Mikael Ciftan and Hermann R. Robl. — New York ; London : Plenum, c1981. — xi,614p : ill ; 26cm
Includes index
ISBN 0-306-40722-1 : Unpriced B81-33670

620.1'1299 — Materials. Electron microscopy
Heimendahl, Manfred von. Electron microscopy of materials : an introduction / Manfred von Heimendahl ; translated by Ursula E. Wolff. — New York ; London : Academic Press, 1980. — xi,228p : ill ; 24cm. — (Materials science and technology)
Translation of: Einführung in die Elektronenmikroskopie. — Includes index
ISBN 0-12-725150-2 : £11.20 B81-16638

620.1'18 — Fibrous composite materials
Fibre composite hybrid materials / edited by N.L. Hancox. — London : Applied Science, c1981. — x,290p : ill ; 23cm
Includes index
ISBN 0-85334-928-2 : £22.80 B81-16776

620.1'18 — Loadbearing fibrous composite materials
Piggott, Michael R.. Load-bearing fibre composites / by Michael R. Piggott. — Oxford : Pergamon, 1980. — ix,277p : ill ; 25cm. — (International series on the strength and fracture of materials and structures) (Pergamon international library)
Includes bibliographies and index
ISBN 0-08-024230-8 (cased) : Unpriced : CIP rev.
ISBN 0-08-024231-6 (pbk) : £6.25 B79-36351

620.1'18'05 — Composite materials - *Serials*
Developments in composite materials. — London : Applied Science, July 1981. — (Developments series)
2: Stress analysis. — [200]p
ISBN 0-85334-966-5 : £16.00 : CIP entry B81-13748

620.1'1892 — Composite materials. Dynamic properties
Hull, Derek. An introduction to composite materials. — Cambridge : Cambridge University Press, Nov.1981. — [246]p. — (Cambridge solid state science series)
ISBN 0-521-23991-5 (cased) : £22.50 : CIP entry
ISBN 0-521-28392-2 (pbk) : £7.95 B81-33621

620.1'2 — Timber
Dinwoodie, J. M.. Timber : its nature and behaviour / J.M. Dinwoodie. — New York ; London : Van Nostrand Reinhold, 1981. — x,190p : ill ; 25cm
Originally published: in Concrete, timber and metals / J.M. Illston, J.M. Dinwoodie, A.A. Smith. — Bibliography: p181-186. — Includes index
ISBN 0-442-30445-5 (cased) : £11.50
ISBN 0-442-30446-3 (pbk) : £5.50 B81-28409

The **International** book of wood / [editor Martyn Bramwell ; art editor Janette Place]. — [London] : Emblem, [1979, c1976] ([1980 printing]). — 276p : ill(some col.),col.maps,plan ; 30cm
Originally published: London : Mitchell Beazley, 1976. — Includes index
ISBN 0-85533-081-3 (cased) : Unpriced
ISBN 0-85533-182-8 (pbk) : £7.95 B81-13984

620.1'2'0688 — Great Britain. Timber. Sale — *Manuals — For land agency*
Eade, C. A.. Sale of timber / by C.A. Eade. — [London] : Royal Institution of Chartered Surveyors, c1976. — 3p ; 21cm. — (Practice leaflet / Royal Institution of Chartered Surveyors. Land Agency and Agriculture Division, ISSN 0305-4713 ; no.17)
Unpriced (unbound) B81-35680

620.1'36'4 — Concrete. Stress analysis
Concrete strength and strains. — Oxford : Elsevier Scientific, Oct.1981. — [550]p. — (Developments in civil engineering ; 3)
Translation and revision of: Rezistențele si Deformațiile Betonului
ISBN 0-444-99733-4 : CIP entry B81-25291

620.1'4 — Materials: Ceramics. Mechanical properties
Davidge, R. W.. Mechanical behaviour of ceramics / R.W. Davidge. — Cambridge : Cambridge University Press, c1979 (1980 [printing]). — viii,165p : ill ; 22cm. — (Cambridge solid state science series)
Bibliography: p157-162. — Includes index
ISBN 0-521-29309-x (pbk) : £4.50 B81-25189

620.1'4 — Materials: Ceramics. Surfaces. Structure & properties — *Conference proceedings*
University Conference on Ceramics *(17th : 1980 : University of California, Berkeley)*. Surfaces and interfaces in ceramic and ceramic-metal systems / [proceedings of the 17th University Conference on Ceramics, which was also the 7th LBL/MMRD International Materials Symposium, held at the University of California at Berkeley from July 28 to August 1, 1980] ; edited by Joseph Pask and Anthony Evans. — New York ; London : Plenum, c1981. — xiii,754p : ill ; 26cm. — (Materials science research ; vol.14)
Includes index
ISBN 0-306-40726-4 : Unpriced B81-35255

620.1'6 — Materials: High temperature alloys — *Conference proceedings*
Behaviour of high temperature alloys in aggressive environments : proceedings of the Petten international conference / edited by I. Kirman ... [et al.] ; conference organized by the: Bond voor Materialenkennis, the Hague, the Netherlands, Commission of the European Communities, Joint Research Centre, Petten Establishment, the Netherlands, the Metals Society, London, United Kingdom and held at the JRC Petten Establishment, Petten (NH), The Netherlands, on 15-18 October, 1979. — London : Metals Society for the Commission of the European Communities Directorate-General Scientific and Technical Information and Information Management, c1980. — xxii,1068p : ill ; 26cm
Includes bibliographies
ISBN 0-904357-30-9 : Unpriced B81-37692

620.1'623 — High temperature alloys. Creep & fatigue
Creep and fatigue in high temperature alloys : proceedings of a course held at the Joint Research Centre of the Commission of the European Communities, Petten Establishment, The Netherlands / and organised by the CEC High Temperature Materials Information Centre, Petten, The Netherlands ; edited by J. Bressers. — London : Applied Science, c1981. — xii,190p : ill ; 23cm
Includes index
ISBN 0-85334-947-9 : £21.00 : CIP rev. B81-06629

620.1'623 — Metals. Anodic protection
Riggs, Olen L.. Anodic protection : theory and practice in the prevention of corrosion / Olen L. Riggs, Jr. and Carl E. Locke ; consulting editor Norman E. Hamner. — New York ; London : Plenum, c1981. — xiii,284p : ill ; 24cm
Includes index
ISBN 0-306-40597-0 : Unpriced B81-24213

620.1'623 — Metals. Corrosion
Evans, Ulick R.. An introduction to metallic corrosion / Ulick R. Evans. — 3rd ed. — London : Edward Arnold, 1981. — 302p : ill ; 23cm
Previous ed.: 1963. — Text on inside cover. — Includes index
ISBN 0-7131-2758-9 (pbk) : £9.95 : CIP rev. B79-25227

620.1'63 — Metals. Damage — *Illustrations*
Engel, Lothar. An atlas of metal damage : surface examination by scanning electron microscope / Lothar Engel, Hermann Klingele ; translated by Stewart Murray. — Munich ; London : Wolfe Science in association with Hanser, 1981. — 271p : ill ; 27cm
Adaptation of: Rasterelektronenmikroskopische Untersuchungen von Metallschäden / Lothar Engel, Hermann Klingele. — Includes index
ISBN 0-7234-0750-9 : £16.00 B81-11417

620.1'63 — Metals. Fatigue
Klesnil, Mirko. Fatigue of metallic materials / Mirko Klesnil and Petr Lukáš. — Amsterdam ; Oxford : Elsevier Scientific, c1980. — 239p : ill ; 25cm. — (Materials science monographs ; 7)
Translation of: Únava kovových materiálů při mechanickém namáhání. — Includes index
ISBN 0-444-99762-8 : £26.09 : CIP rev. B80-18783

620.1′63 — Metals. High energy rate deformation. Role of shock waves — *Conference proceedings*
Shock waves and high-strain-rate phenomena in metals : concepts and applications / edited by Marc A. Meyers and Lawrence E. Murr. — New York ; London : Plenum, c1981. — xiii,1101p : ill ; 26cm
Conference papers. — Includes index
ISBN 0-306-40633-0 : Unpriced B81-27065

620.1′66 — Metals. Ductile fracture — *Conference proceedings*
IUTAM Symposium on Three-Dimensional Constitutive Relations and Ductile Fracture *(1980 : Dourdan)*. Three-dimensional constitutive relations and ductile fracture : proceedings of the IUTAM Symposium on Three-Dimensional Constitutive Relations and Ductile Fracture, Dourdan, France, 2-5 June, 1980 / sponsored by International Union of Theoretical and Applied Mechanics (I.U.T.A.M.) ... [et al.] ; edited by S. Nemat-Nasser. — Amsterdam ; Oxford : North-Holland, c1981. — xv,439p : ill ; 23cm
Includes bibliographies
ISBN 0-444-86108-4 : £38.99 B81-39271

620.1′692 — Metals. Mechanical properties
Le May, Iain. Principles of mechanical metallurgy / Iain Le May. — London : Edward Arnold, 1981. — xiv,416p : ill ; 24cm
Includes index
ISBN 0-7131-3448-8 : £18.50 B81-40559

620.1′7 — Materials: Steel
Elliott, D.. An introduction to steel selection. — Oxford : Oxford University Press, Aug.1981. — (Engineering design guides ; 43)
Part 2: Stainless steels. — [40]p
ISBN 0-19-859179-9 (pbk) : £6.95 : CIP entry B81-16383

620.1′92 — Materials: Polymers
Hall, Christopher. Polymer materials : an introduction for technologists and scientists / Christopher Hall. — London : Macmillan, 1981. — vii,198p : ill ; 24cm
Includes bibliographies and index
ISBN 0-333-28907-2 (cased) : £14.00
ISBN 0-333-28908-0 (pbk) : £6.50p B81-10535

620.1′92 — Materials: Polymers. Structure & mechanical properties
Mechanics of cellular polymers. — London : Applied Science, Oct.1981. — [408]p
ISBN 0-85334-982-7 : £34.00 : CIP entry B81-25719

620.1′920423 — Materials: Polymers. Damage — *Illustrations*
An Atlas of polymer damage : surface examination by scanning electron microscope / Lothar Engel ... [et al.] ; translated by M.S. Welling. — Munich ; London : Wolfe Science in association with Hanser, 1981. — 256p : ill ; 27cm
Translation of: Rasterelektronenmikroskopische Untersuchungen von Kunststoffschaden. — Includes index
ISBN 0-7234-0751-7 : £15.00 B81-11418

620.1′9204232 — Materials: Polymers. Viscoelasticity
Ferry, John D.. Viscoelastic properties of polymers / John D. Ferry. — 3rd ed. — New York ; Chichester : Wiley, c1980. — xxiv,641p : ill ; 24cm
Previous ed.: 1970. — Includes index
ISBN 0-471-04894-1 : £25.70 B81-03065

620.1′9233 — Plastics. Fatigue
Hertzberg, Richard W.. Fatigue of engineering plastics / Richard W. Hertzberg, John A. Manson. — New York ; London : Academic Press, 1980. — xv,295p : ill ; 24cm
Includes index
ISBN 0-12-343550-1 : £20.00 B81-05207

620.1′93 — Materials: Carbon fibres
Delmonte, John. Technology of carbon and graphite fiber composites / John Delmonte. — New York ; London : Van Nostrand Reinhold, c1981. — xii,452p : ill ; 24cm
Includes index
ISBN 0-442-22072-3 : £24.00 B81-21177

620.2 — ENGINEERING. SOUND AND RELATED VIBRATIONS

620.2′1 — Acoustic engineering
Reynolds, Douglas D.. Engineering principles of acoustics : noise and vibration control / Douglas D. Reynolds. — Boston, Mass. ; London : Allyn and Bacon, c1981. — 641p : ill ; 25cm. — (Allyn and Bacon series in mechanical engineering and applied mechanics)
Bibliography: p632-633. - Includes index
ISBN 0-205-07271-2 (corrected cased) : £13.25
ISBN 0-205-07283-6 (pbk) : £8.95 B81-11765

620.2′3′0941 — Great Britain. Noise. Control measures
Mulholland, K. A.. Noise assessment and control / K.A. Mulholland and K. Attenborough. — London : Construction Press, 1981. — viii,139p : ill ; 24cm
Includes index
ISBN 0-86095-882-5 (pbk) : £7.95 B81-32862

620.2′5 — Underwater acoustics — *Conference proceedings*
Underwater acoustics and signal processing : proceedings of the NATO Advanced Study Institute held at Kollekolle, Copenhagen, Denmark, August 18-29, 1980 / edited by Leif Bjorno. — Dordrecht ; London : Reidel published in cooperation with NATO Scientific Affairs Division, c1981. — xv,736p : ill ; 25cm. — (NATO advanced study institutes series. Series C, Mathematical and physical sciences ; v.66)
Includes index
ISBN 90-277-1255-7 : Unpriced
Also classified at 621.38′043 B81-26220

620.3 — ENGINEERING. MECHANICAL VIBRATION

620.3 — Mechanical vibration. Engineering aspects
Bishop, R. E. D.. The mechanics of vibration / by R.E.D. Bishop and D.C. Johnson. — Reissued with minor revisions. — Cambridge : Cambridge University Press, 1979. — xiv,592p : ill ; 27cm
Originally published: 1960. — Includes index
ISBN 0-521-04258-5 : £50.00 B81-25191

Steidel, Robert F.. An introduction to mechanical vibrations / Robert F. Steidel Jr. — 2nd ed., rev. print. — New York ; Chichester : Wiley, [1980], c1979. — xvi,400p : ill ; 24cm
Previous ed.: 1971. — Includes index
ISBN 0-471-08483-2 : £14.45 B81-07220

620.4 — ENGINEERING TECHNOLOGIES

620′.4162 — Marine structures. Construction materials: Concrete
Allen, R. T. L.. Concrete in maritime works / R.T.L. Allen. — 2nd ed. — Slough : Cement and Concrete Association, 1981. — 14p : ill ; 30cm. — (Publication / Cement and Concrete Association ; 46.501)
Previous ed.: 1972
ISBN 0-7210-1235-3 (pbk) : Unpriced B81-34271

620′.4162 — Marine structures. Corrosion resistant materials
Waterman, N. A.. Guide to the selection of materials for marine applications / N.A. Waterman and A.M. Pye. — [Stoke Poges] ([Stoke Poges, Slough, Berks. SL2 4QD]) : Fulmer Research Institute, c1980. — 1v.(loose leaf) : ill ; 30cm
Unpriced B81-17621

620′.4162′07 — Offshore engineering. Information sources — *Conference proceedings*
National offshore information conference papers / edited by Arnold Myers. — Edinburgh (Heriot-Watt University, Riccarton, Edinburgh, EH14 4AS) : Institute of Offshore Engineering, 1980. — 110p ; 30cm
ISBN 0-904046-09-5 (spiral) : £7.50 B81-10894

620′.4162′0711421 — London. Universities: University of London. Curriculum subjects: Offshore engineering. Courses — *Directories*
Directory of London University activities related to offshore development / prepared by the Interdisciplinary Special Committee on Offshore Development. — [Updated version]. — [London] ([c/o H.G. Chubb, Room 36, Senate House, Malet St., WC1E 7HU]) : [The Committee], 1980. — [48]p ; 30cm
Previous ed.: 1973. — Includes index
Unpriced (unbound)
Also classified at 620′.4162′0720421 B81-21892

620′.4162′0720421 — Offshore engineering. Research projects by University of London — *Directories*
Directory of London University activities related to offshore development / prepared by the Interdisciplinary Special Committee on Offshore Development. — [Updated version]. — [London] ([c/o H.G. Chubb, Room 36, Senate House, Malet St., WC1E 7HU]) : [The Committee], 1980. — [48]p ; 30cm
Previous ed.: 1973. — Includes index
Unpriced (unbound)
Primary classification 620′.4162′0711421 B81-21892

620′.416336′05 — North Sea. Offshore engineering — *Serials*
[Newsletter *(Project MASS)*]. Newsletter / Project MASS. — No.1 (Jan.1979)-. — [Glasgow] ([11.05 Livingstone Tower, University of Strathclyde, Glasgow G1 1XH]) : [The Project], [1979]-. — v. ; 30cm
Irregular
ISSN 0260-7832 = Newsletter - Project MASS : Unpriced B81-11867

620′.41732 — Street furniture. Construction — *For landscape design*
Cartwright, Richard M.. The design of urban space / Richard M. Cartwright. — London : Architectural Press, 1980. — ix,163p : ill(some col.),plans(some col.) ; 31cm
Bibliography: p159. - Includes index
ISBN 0-85139-693-3 (cased) : £16.95 : CIP rev.
ISBN 0-85139-694-1 (pbk) : £9.95 B80-23370

620′.43 — Industrial processes: Granulation
Sherrington, P. J.. Granulation / P.J. Sherrington, R. Oliver. — London : Heyden, c1981. — xii,182p : ill ; 26cm. — (Monographs in powder science and technology)
Includes index
ISBN 0-85501-177-7 : Unpriced B81-10606

620′.43 — Materials: Powders — *Conference proceedings*
Powder Europa *(Conference : 1980 : Wiesbaden)*. Powder Europa : 22-24 January 1980 Rhein-Main-Halle Wiesbaden : proceedings of the technical sessions / programme organised by Powder Advisory Centre ; sponsored by International Powder Institute. — [London] ([P.O. Box 78, NW11 0PG]) : [International Powder Institute], [c1980]. — 2v. : ill ; 30cm
Text in English and German. — Cover title. — Includes bibliographies
Unpriced (pbk) B81-38366

620′.43 — Materials: Powders — *Serials*
Journal of powder & bulk solids technology. — Vol.1, no.1 (Summer 1977)-. — London (c/o PO Box 78, NW11 0PG) : International Powder Institute, 1977-. — v. : ill ; 28cm
Quarterly. — Description based on: Vol.4, no.1 (Jan.1980)
ISSN 0147-698x = Journal of powder & bulk solids technology : £30.00 per year B81-10562

620′.43 — Particle technology — *Conference proceedings*
Powtech Conference *(1981 : Birmingham)*. Particle technology / [proceedings of the 1981 Powtech Conference] ; organised by the Institution of Chemical Engineers in conjunction with the Powtech 81 exhibition at the National Exhibition Centre, Birmingham, from 10-13 March 1981. — Rugby : The Institution, c1981. — 1v.(various pagings) : ill ; 22cm. — (The Institution of Chemical Engineers symposium series ; no.63) (EFCE publication series ; no.16)
Also available in pbk: Unpriced (2v.). — EFCE event no.: 241
ISBN 0-85295-133-7 : Unpriced B81-19022

620′.43 — Powders. Isostatic pressing — *Conference proceedings*

International Conference on Isostatic Pressing *(1st : 1978 : Loughborough University of Technology).* Papers presented at 1st International Conference on Isostatic Pressing : 19th-21st September, 1978. — [Loughborough] ([Loughborough, Leics.]) : Loughborough University of Technology
Vol.2. — [1981?]. — 246p in various pagings ; 30cm
Unpriced (unbound) B81-37800

620.7 — SYSTEMS ENGINEERING

620.7 — Systems engineering

Blanchard, Benjamin S.. Systems engineering and analysis / Benjamin S. Blanchard, Wolter J. Fabrycky. — Englewood Cliffs ; London : Pentice-Hall, c1981. — xii,703p : ill ; 24cm. — (Prentice-Hall international series in industrial and systems engineering)
Includes bibliographies and index
ISBN 0-13-881631-x : £18.85 B81-16673

620.7 — Systems engineering — *Conference proceedings*

International Conference on Systems Engineering *(1980 : Coventry Lanchester Polytechnic).* Proceedings of International Conference on Systems Engineering held at Coventry Lanchester Polytechnic, Priory Steet, Coventry CV1 5FB, England, 9-11 September 1980. — Coventry (Priory Street, Coventry CV1 5FB) : Coventry Lanchester Polytechnic, c1980. — viii,649p : ill ; 30cm + Supplement([72]leaves : ill ; 30cm)
ISBN 0-901606-20-0 (pbk) : £25.00 B81-10784

620.7′068 — Systems engineering. Management - *Conference proceedings*

Industrial systems engineering and management in developing countries. — Oxford : Pergamon, June 1981. — [928]p
Conference papers
ISBN 0-08-027611-3 : £56.00 : CIP entry B81-18073

620.8 — ENVIRONMENT ENGINEERING

620.8′2 — Anthropometry — *For design*

Croney, John. Anthropometry for designers / John Croney. — New ed. — London : Batsford Academic and Educational, 1980. — 144p : ill ; 26cm
Previous ed.: published as Anthropometrics for designers. 1971. — Bibliography: p138-142. — Includes index
ISBN 0-7134-1567-3 : £12.50 B81-01555

620.8′2 — Ergonomics

Huchingson, R. Dale. New horizons for human factors in design / R. Dale Huchingson. — New York ; London : McGraw-Hill, c1981. — xiii,562p : ill ; 25cm. — (McGraw-Hill series in industrial engineering and management science)
Includes bibliographies and index
ISBN 0-07-030815-2 : £18.25 B81-19671

Woodson, Wesley E.. Human factors design handbook : information and guidelines for the design of systems, facilities, equipment, and products for human use / Wesley E. Woodson. — New York ; London : McGraw-Hill, c1981. — 1047p : ill,maps,plans ; 29cm
Bibliography: p1015-1018. — Includes index
ISBN 0-07-071765-6 : £57.50 B81-32368

620.8′2 — Industries. Ergonomics

Oborne, David J.. Ergonomics at work. — Chichester : Wiley, Feb.1982. — [304]p
ISBN 0-471-10030-7 : £12.50 : CIP entry B81-35730

620.8′2′0722 — Ergonomics — *Case studies*

Design for work and use. — London : Taylor & Francis, Apr.1981. — [150]p. — (Case studies in ergonomics practice ; v.2)
ISBN 0-85066-208-7 : £10.00 : CIP entry

620.8′6 — Natural disasters. Control measures — *Conference proceedings*

Engineering for protection from natural disasters : proceedings of the International Conference held in Bangkok, 7-9 January 1980 / edited by Pisidhi Karasudhi, A.S. Balasubramaniam and Worsak Kanok-Nukulchai ; [sponsored by the Asian Institute of Technology ... et al.]. — Chichester : Wiley, c1980. — xi,937p : ill,maps,plan ; 25cm
Includes index
ISBN 0-471-27895-5 : Unpriced : CIP rev. B80-22046

621 — MECHANICAL ENGINEERING

621 — Mechanical engineering

Smith, Ken, *1924-*. Mechanical and engineering principles / Ken Smith. — London : Pitman
Vol.1: Statics and dynamics. — 1981. — xii,172p : ill ; 25cm
Includes index
ISBN 0-273-01601-6 (pbk) : £4.50 B81-21841

621 — Mechanical engineering — *Conference proceedings*

Current advances in mechanical design and production : proceedings of the 1st International Conference, Cairo University, Egypt, 27-29 December 1979 / edited by G.S.A. Shawki and co-edited by S.M. Metwalli. — Oxford : Pergamon, 1981. — x,496p : ill ; 26cm
Includes bibliographies and index
ISBN 0-08-027294-0 : £31.00
ISBN 0-08-027306-8 (pbk) : £10.50 : conference participants only B81-11446

621 — Mechanical engineering — *For technicians*

Jones, G. D.. Engineering & mechanical science Level 3 / G.D. Jones. — Walton-on-Thames : Nelson, 1981. — 202p : ill ; 25cm. — (Nelson TEC books)
Includes index
ISBN 0-17-741124-4 (pbk) : £3.95 B81-29119

621′.0212 — Mechanical engineering — *Technical data — Serials*

Mechanical world year book. — 1979-80. — Watford : Model & Allied Publications, c1979. — 512p
ISBN 0-85242-680-1 : £4.50 B81-00133

621.042 — Energy industries. Sites. Decision making

Keeney, Ralph L.. Siting energy facilities / Ralph L. Keeney. — New York ; London : Academic Press, 1980. — xviii,413p : ill ; 24cm
Bibliography: p391-399. — Includes index
ISBN 0-12-403080-7 : £20.60 B81-15124

621.042 — Energy sources — *Conference proceedings*

International Conference on Future Energy Concepts *(3rd : 1981 : London).* Third International Conference on Future Energy Concepts 27-30 January 1981 / organised by the Science, Education and Technology and Power Divisions of the Institution of Electrical Engineers in association with the AIM, Belgium ... [et al.], venue, the Institution of Electrical Engineers, London. — London : IEE, c1981. — xii,360p : ill ; 30cm. — (IEE conference publication, ISSN 0537-9908 ; no.192)
ISBN 0-85296-229-0 (pbk) : Unpriced B81-13224

621.042 — Energy sources — *For schools*

Energy resources / Schools Council Modular Courses in Technology. — Edinburgh : Oliver & Boyd in association with the National Centre for School Technology, 1980
Teacher's guide / Michael Gibson ... [et al.]. — 47p : ill ; 24cm
ISBN 0-05-003381-6 (pbk) : £2.50
ISBN 0-05-003380-8 (set) : £5.20 B81-10227

Energy resources / Schools Council Modular Courses in Technology. — Edinburgh : Oliver & Boyd in association with the National Centre for School Technology, 1980
Workbook. — 35p : ill ; 27cm
ISBN 0-05-003382-4 (unbound) : £2.70
ISBN 0-05-003380-8 (set) : £5.20 B81-10226

621.042 — Energy. Storage & transport

Energy storage and transportation : prospects for new technologies : lectures of a course held at the Joint Research Centre, Ispra, Italy, October 22-26, 1979 / edited by G. Beghi. — Dordrecht ; London : Reidel, c1981. — x,497p : ill ; 24cm
At head of title: Commission of the European Communities. — Includes index
ISBN 90-277-1166-6 : Unpriced B81-14060

621.042 — Energy. Storage — *Conference proceedings*

Energy storage : a vital element in mankind's quest for survival and progress : translations of the First International Assembly held at Dubrovnik, Yugoslavia, 27 May-1 June 1979 / editor Joseph Silverman ; a conference jointly sponsored by the National Academy of Sciences [USA] and the Council of Academies of Science (Yugoslavia). — Oxford : Pergamon, 1980. — xvii,579p : ill,maps ; 26cm
Includes index
ISBN 0-08-025471-3 : £42.00 : CIP rev. B80-12920

621.042 — European Community countries. Energy. Conservation — *Conference proceedings*

New ways to save energy : proceedings of the international seminar held in Brussels, 23-25 October 1979 / edited by A.S. Strub and H. Ehringer. — Dordrecht ; London : Reidel, c1980. — xvi,1252p : ill,ports ; 24cm
Includes papers in Dutch, French and German. — At head of title: Commission of the European Communities. — Includes index
ISBN 90-277-1078-3 : Unpriced B81-04620

621.042′028 — Energy engineering equipment — *For children*

Ackins, Ralph. Energy machines / Ralph Ackins. — Oxford : Blackwell Raintree, c1981. — 32p : ill(some col.) ; 27cm
Originally published: Milwaukee : Raintree Children, c1980. — Includes index
ISBN 0-86256-022-5 : £2.95 B81-17610

621.042′03′21 — Energy engineering — *Encyclopaedias*

Gilpin, Alan. Dictionary of energy technology. — London : Butterworths, Dec.1981. — [448]p
ISBN 0-408-01108-4 : £15.00 : CIP entry B81-31732

621.042′072 — Energy sources. Research organisations — *Directories*

World energy directory. — London : Longman, July 1981. — [630]p
ISBN 0-582-90011-5 : £70.00 : CIP entry B81-15936

621′.0941 — Great Britain. Mechanical engineering — *Serials*

Mechanical engineering technology : journal of the Institution of Technician Engineers in Mechanical Engineering. — Vol.1, no.1(Apr. 1981)-. — London (8 Old Queen St., Westminster SW1H 9HP) : The Institution, 1981-. — v. : ill ; 30cm
Quarterly
ISSN 0261-7188 = Mechanical engineering technology : £10.00 per year B81-32398

621.1 — STEAM ENGINEERING

621.1′09 — Steam engines. Applications, *to 1980*

Bloom, Alan. 250 years of steam / Alan Bloom. — Tadworth : World's Work, c1981. — 195p : ill(some col.),1map,ports ; 27cm
Bibliography: p192. — Includes index
ISBN 0-437-01400-2 : £10.00 B81-27028

621.1′09 — Steam engines, *to ca 1950*

Van Riemsdijk, John. The pictorial history of steam power / J.T. Van Riemsdijk and Kenneth Brown. — London : Octopus, 1980. — 192p : ill(some col),ports ; 33cm
Col.ill on lining papers. — Includes index
ISBN 0-7064-0976-0 : £5.95 B81-04454

621.1'092'4 — Steam engineering. Watt, James — *Biographies*

Dickinson, H. W.. James Watt and the steam engine : the memorial volume prepared for the committee of the Watt centenary commemoration at Birmingham 1919 / by H.W. Dickinson & Rhys Jenkins. — Ashbourne : Moorland, 1981. — xxiii,415p : ill,1map,1coat of arms,facsims,plans,ports,1geneal.table ; 26cm
Facsim. of: ed. originally published: Oxford : Clarendon Press, 1927. — Includes index
ISBN 0-903485-92-3 : £17.50 : CIP rev. B81-10490

621.1'6'0941 — Great Britain. Industrial antiquities: Stationary steam engines — *Visitors' guides*

Hayes, G.. A guide to stationary steam engines / G. Hayes. — Ashbourne : Moorland, c1981. — 160p : ill ; 22cm
Includes index
ISBN 0-86190-026-x (cased) : Unpriced
ISBN 0-86190-020-0 (pbk) : £4.95 B81-38226

621.1'8 — Boilers. Operation — *Manuals*

Boiler operator's handbook / prepared by National Industrial Fuel Efficiency Service Ltd. — Rev. ed. — London : Graham & Trotman, 1981. — viii,151p : ill ; 20cm
Previous ed.: London : National Industrial Fuel Efficiency Service, 1969
ISBN 0-86010-244-0 (cased) : £6.00
ISBN 0-86010-251-3 (pbk) : Unpriced B81-19678

621.1'8 — Flash steam. Recycling — *Manuals*

Flash steam and vapour recovery / Department of Energy. — London (Thames House South, Millbank, SW1P 4QJ) : Department of Energy, [1980]. — 12p : ill(some col.) ; 21cm. — (Fuel efficiency booklet ; 6)
Cover title
Unpriced (pbk) B81-04808

621.1'8 — Industry. Steam power. Generation & use — *Conference proceedings*

The **Generation** and utilization of steam in industry : symposium sponsored by the Power Industries Division of the Institution of Mechanical Engineers, London 14 May 1981. — London : Published by Mechanical Engineering Publications for the Institution of Mechanical Engineers, 1981. — 47p : ill ; 30cm. — (I Mech E conference publications ; 1981-4)
ISBN 0-85298-480-4 (pbk) : Unpriced B81-28888

621.1'84 — Boilers. Feed water. Supply. Use of steam condensates — *Manuals*

How to make the best use of condensate / Department of Energy. — London (Thames House South, Millbank, SW1P 4QJ) : Department of Energy, [1980]. — 16p : ill (some col.) ; 21cm. — (Fuel efficiency booklet ; 9)
Cover title
Unpriced (pbk) B81-01981

621.1'84 — Steam boilers. Efficiency & safety

Boiler efficiency and safety : a guide for managers, engineers and operators responsible for small steam boilers / edited by W.S. Robertson ; contributors H.M. Ashton ... [et al.]. — London : Macmillan [for] Esso, 1981. — 140p : ill,forms ; 24cm
Includes index
ISBN 0-333-27016-9 : £8.95 B81-10534

621.2 — HYDRAULIC POWER

621.2'028'7 — Hydraulic power equipment. Fluids. Testing — *Conference proceedings*

Performance testing of hydraulic fluids : papers presented at the international symposium organized by the Institute of Petroleum, October 1978, London, England / edited by R. Tourret and E.P. Wright. — London : Published by Heyden on behalf of the Institute of Petroleum, London, c1979. — xx,563p : ill ; 24cm
Includes index
ISBN 0-85501-317-6 : £30.00 B81-39552

621.2'028'8 — Hydraulic systems. Maintenance & repair — *Algorithms*

Skinner, S.. Logical troubleshooting in hydraulic systems / compiled by S. Skinner. — Havant, Hants. (P.O. Box 4, New Lane, Havant, Hants. PO9 2NB) : Sperry Vickers, 1981. — 44p : ill ; 30cm
Unpriced (pbk) B81-10352

621.2'0422'0724 — Water power. Experiments — *Manuals — For children*

Catherall, Ed. Water power / Ed Catherall. — Hove : Wayland, 1981. — 32p : col.ill ; 24cm. — (Young scientist)
ISBN 0-85340-870-x : £2.95 B81-40624

621.2'0941 — Great Britain. Hydraulic power supply engineering, *to 1976*

Pugh, B.. The hydraulic age : public power supplies before electricity / by E. Pugh. — London : Mechanical Engineering Publications, 1980. — viii,176p : 1ill,maps,plans ; 22cm
Bibliography: p172-174. - Includes index
ISBN 0-85298-447-2 : £11.95 B81-04610

621.2'1 — England. Midlands. Watermills — *Serials*

Wind and water mills : the occasional journal of the Midland Wind and Water Mills Group. — No.1 (Summer 1980)-. — Smethwick ([c/o John Bedington, 188 Merivale Rd, Smethwick, West Midlands, B66 4EA]) : The Group, 1980-. — v. : ill ; 21cm
Annual
ISSN 0260-504x = Wind and water mills : £0.75 (free to Group members)
Also classified at 621.4'5 B81-04144

621.2'1 — Kent. East Malling & Wateringbury. Watermills, *to 1980*

Fuller, M. J.. The watermills of the East Malling and Wateringbury streams / by M.J. Fuller. — Maidstone (45 Scott St., Maidstone, Kent) : Christine Swift, 1980. — xi,96p : ill,maps,plans ; 26cm
Ill on lining papers. - Limited ed. of 1000 copies. — Includes index
£8.50 B81-18926

621.3 — ELECTRICAL, ELECTRONIC, ELECTROMAGNETIC ENGINEERING

621.3 — Electrical engineering

Baitch, T.. Electrical technology / T. Baitch. — Rev. ed. — Brisbane ; Chichester : Wiley, 1981. — xxiv,527p : ill ; 25cm
Previous ed.: / published in 2 pts. 1972. — Includes index
ISBN 0-471-33382-4 (pbk) : £13.50 B81-40153

Basic electricity. — Oxford : Technical Press, May 1981
Part 3. — [144]p
ISBN 0-291-39632-1 (pbk) : £3.95 : CIP entry B81-14781

Bell, E. C.. Basic electrical engineering and instrumentation for engineers / E.C. Bell, R.W. Whitehead. — 2nd ed. — London : Granada, 1981. — 542p : ill ; 24cm
Previous ed.: London : Crosby Lockwood Staples, 1977. — Includes index
ISBN 0-246-11477-0 (pbk) : £8.95 B81-28977

Fitzgerald, A. E.. Basic electrical engineering : circuits, electronics, machines, controls / A.E. Fitzgerald, David E. Higginbotham, Arvin Grabel. — 5th ed. — New York ; London : McGraw-Hill, c1981. — xiv,937p : ill ; 25cm. — (McGraw-Hill series in electrical engineering. networks and systems)
Previous ed.: 1975. — Includes index
ISBN 0-07-021154-x : £19.50 B81-29828

Müller-Schwartz, Wolfgang. Basic electrical theory and practice / Wolfgang Müller-Schwartz ; translated by E.B. Babler and P.E.O. Babler. — Berlin : Siemens Aktiengesellschaft ; London : Heyden, c1981. — 320p : ill(some col.) ; 22cm
Translation of: Grundlagen der Elektrotechnik. — Includes index
ISBN 0-85501-259-5 : Unpriced B81-27730

Simpson, A.. Light current electrical applications / A. Simpson. — London : Macmillan. — vii,89p : ill ; 21x24cm. — (Macmillan technician series)
ISBN 0-333-23679-3 (pbk) : £4.95 B81-21663

Whitfield, J. F.. Electrical craft principles / J.F. Whitfield. — Stevenage : Peregrinus. — (Crafts studies)
Vol.2. — 2nd ed. — c1981. — xviii,250p : ill ; 30cm
Previous ed.: 1974. — Includes index
ISBN 0-906048-43-5 (pbk) : Unpriced B81-12150

Wildi, Theodore. Electrical power technology / Theodore Wildi with the collaboration of Perry R. McNeill. — New York ; Chichester : Wiley, c1981. — xvi,686p : ill ; 25cm
Bibliography: p667-672. — Includes index
ISBN 0-471-07764-x : £12.15 B81-24887

621.3 — Electrical engineering — *For installation of electric equipment*

Donnelly, E. L.. Electrical installation : theory and practice / E.L. Donnelly. — 3rd ed. — London : Harrap, 1980. — x,228p : ill,1plan ; 22cm
Previous ed.: 1972. — Includes index
ISBN 0-245-53627-2 (pbk) : £3.75 B81-07240

Paddock, J. O.. Related science for electrical installations / J.O. Paddock, R.A.W. Galvin. — London : Hodder and Stoughton, 1980. — vi,330p : ill ; 22cm
Includes index
ISBN 0-340-20882-1 (pbk) : £4.25 : CIP rev. B80-07403

621.3 — Electrical engineering — *For technicians*

Bird, J. O.. Electrical science 3 checkbook. — London : Butterworths, Nov.1981. — [156]p. — (Butterworth's checkbook series)
ISBN 0-408-00657-9 (cased) : £6.95 : CIP entry
ISBN 0-408-00626-9 (vpbk) : £3.50 B81-32030

Hamilton, Roger, *1928-*. Electrical principles for technicians / Roger Hamilton. — Oxford : Oxford University Press, 1980. — viii,231p : ill ; 24cm. — (Electrical and telecommunications technicians series)
Includes index
ISBN 0-19-859360-0 (cased) : £12.50 : CIP rev.
ISBN 0-19-859361-9 (pbk) : £6.95 B80-18357

621.3 — Electrical engineering - *For technicians*

Knight, S. A.. Electronics 2 checkbook. — London : Butterworths, Aug.1981. — [112]p
ISBN 0-408-00639-0 (cased) : £3.75 : CIP entry
ISBN 0-408-00615-3 (pbk) : £3.25 B81-16924

621.3 — Electrical engineering — *For technicians*

Lovelace, T. A.. Electrical principles 3 / T.A. Lovelace. — Walton-on-Thames : Nelson, 1981. — xiv,305p : ill ; 22cm
Includes index
ISBN 0-17-741116-3 (pbk) : £6.50 : CIP rev. B80-01683

Tyler, D. W.. Electrical and electronic applications 2. — London : Butterworths, Oct.1981. — [160]p
ISBN 0-408-00661-7 (cased) : £6.95 : CIP entry B81-25286

621.3 — Electrical engineering — *Manuals*

American electricians' handbook .... — 10th ed. / Wilford I. Summers, editor. — New York ; London : McGraw-Hill, c1981. — 1650p in various pagings : ill ; 24cm
Previous ed.: / John H. Watt, editor. — Includes index
ISBN 0-07-013931-8 : £25.95 B81-23720

Court, M.. Laboratory manual for electrical technology / M. Court. — 2nd ed. — Brisbane ; Chichester : Wiley, 1981. — viii,276p : ill ; 25cm
Previous ed.: published as Laboratory manual for a first course in electrical technology. 1974
ISBN 0-471-33381-6 (pbk) : £8.25 B81-40211

621.3 — Electrical engineering — *Manuals continuation*

Newnes electrical pocket book / edited by E.A. Reeves. — 18th ed. — London : Newnes Technical Books, 1981. — 472p : ill ; 17cm
Previous ed.: 1975. — Includes index
ISBN 0-408-00407-x (pbk) : Unpriced : CIP rev. B81-23920

621.3 — Static electricity. Safety aspects

Electrostatic hazards / [a report prefaced by Arthur Conway from papers delivered at a seminar in 1980 organized by the Scientific and Technical Studies Division of Oyez International Business Communications Ltd.] ; [based on the contributions of P.E. Secker ... et al.]. — London : Oyez, c1980. — viii,47leaves : ill ; 30cm. — (Oyez intelligence reports)
ISBN 0-85120-442-2 (spiral) : Unpriced B81-28531

621.3 — United States. Electrical engineering. Estimating — *Manuals*

Cubit, Harry T.. Electrical construction cost estimating / Harry T. Cubit. — New York ; London : McGraw-Hill, c1981. — ix,297p ; 29cm
Includes index
ISBN 0-07-014885-6 : £22.50 B81-17043

621.3'01'51 — Electrical engineering. Mathematics

Singer, Bertrand B.. Basic mathematics for electricity and electronics / Bertrand B. Singer. — 4th ed. — New York ; London : Gregg Division, McGraw-Hill, c1978. — x,678p : ill (some col.) ; 25cm
Previous ed.: 1972. — Bibliography: p660. — Includes index. — Text on lining papers
ISBN 0-07-057472-3 : £13.25 B81-09917

621.3'01'51 — Electrical engineering. Mathematics — *Questions & answers*

Beiser, Arthur. Schaum's outline of theory and problems of basic mathematics for electricity and electronics / by Arthur Beiser. — New York ; London : McGraw-Hill, 1981. — 170p : ill ; 28cm. — (Schaum's outline series) (Schaum's vocational and technical series)
Includes index
ISBN 0-07-004378-7 (pbk) : £3.50 B81-17105

621.3'03'21 — Electrical engineering — *Encyclopaedias*

Jackson, K. G.. Dictionary of electrical engineering. — 2nd ed. / K.C. Jackson and R. Feinberg. — London : Butterworths, 1981. — 350p : ill ; 22cm
Previous ed.: published London : Newnes, 1965
ISBN 0-408-00450-9 : £8.50 : CIP rev. B80-13426

621.3'072041 — Great Britain. Electrical engineering. Research organisations: Electrical Research Association — *Serials*

ERA Technology news. — 1980, no.1-. — Leatherhead (Cleeve Rd, Leatherhead, Surrey KT22 7SA) : ERA Technology Ltd., 1980-. — v. : ill,ports ; 30cm
Eight issues yearly. — Continues: ERA news. — Description based on: 1981, no.1
ISSN 0144-476x = ERA technology news : Unpriced B81-34037

621.3'076 — Electrical engineering — *Questions & answers — For technicians*

Bird, J. O.. Electrical and electronic principles 2 checkbook / J.O. Bird, A.J.C. May. — London : Butterworths, 1981. — viii,156p : ill ; 20cm. — (Butterworths technical and scientific checkbooks. Level 2)
Includes index
ISBN 0-408-00635-8 (cased) : Unpriced
ISBN 0-408-00600-5 (pbk) : Unpriced B81-27277

Bird, J. O.. Electrical principles 3 checkbook / J.O. Bird, A.J.C. May. — London : Butterworths, 1981. — vi,144p : ill ; 20cm. — (Butterworths technical and scientific checkbooks)
Includes index
ISBN 0-408-00636-6 (cased) : Unpriced : CIP rev.
ISBN 0-408-00601-3 (pbk) : Unpriced B81-03360

621.3'092'4 — Electrical engineering. Edison, Thomas A. — *Biographies*

Wachhorst, Wyn. Thomas Alva Edison : an American myth / Wyn Wachhorst. — Cambridge, Mass. ; London : MIT, c1981. — ix,328p : ill,ports ; 23cm
Bibliography: p275-317. — Includes index
ISBN 0-262-23108-5 : £10.50 B81-39758

621.31 — Electricity supply

Laithwaite, E. R.. Electric energy : its generation, transmission and use / E.R. Laithwaite, L.L. Freris. — London : McGraw-Hill, c1980. — xv,365p : ill ; 23cm. — (McGraw-Hill electrical engineering series)
Includes index
ISBN 0-07-084109-8 (pbk) : £9.95 : CIP rev. B80-04827

621.31 — Electricity supply systems. Planning & automatic control. Applications of computer systems — *Conference proceedings*

Power Systems Computation Conference *(7th : 1981 : Lausanne)*. Proceedings of the Seventh Power Systems Computation Conference : Lausanne 12-17 July 1981. — Guildford, Surrey : Westbury House, c1981. — xix,1225p : ill ; 25cm
Includes index
ISBN 0-86103-025-7 : Unpriced B81-28964

621.31 — United States. Residences. Electricity supply — *Amateurs' manuals*

Cullen, Jim. How to be your own power company / Jim Cullen with J.O. Bugental ; drawings by Gary Verrall ; technical consultant Clyde G. Davis. — New York ; London : Van Nostrand Reinhold, c1980. — 142p : ill,maps ; 29cm
Revision of: The wilderness home powersystem and how to do it. Laytonville : J. Cullen, 1978. — Includes index
ISBN 0-442-24340-5 (cased) : £12.70
ISBN 0-442-24345-6 (pbk) : £8.20 B81-05688

621.31'21 — Electricity. Generation

Vardi, Joseph. Electric energy generation : economics, reliability and rates / Joseph Vardi and Benjamin Avi-Itzhak. — Cambridge, Mass. ; London : MIT, c1981. — xii,176p : ill ; 24cm
Bibliography: p171-174. — Includes index
ISBN 0-262-22024-5 : £15.50 B81-30037

621.31'042 — Electric components — *Buyers' guides — Serials*

The **Product** finder : Swift-Sasco buyers guide. — 1981-. — [London] : Lane Advertising ; Crawley (P.O. Box 2000, Gatwick Rd., Crawley, Sussex RH10 2RU) : [Distributed by] Swift-Sasco, 1981-. — v. : ill ; 30cm
Annual. — Continues: Sasco catalogue
ISSN 0261-4073 = Product finder : £3.00
Also classified at 621.3815'1'0294 B81-31058

621.31'042 — Electric equipment

Miller, Gary M.. Modern electricity/electronics / Gary M. Miller. — Englewood Cliffs : Prentice-Hall, c1981. — xiii,414p : ill ; 25cm
Includes index
ISBN 0-13-593160-6 : £12.95 B81-22698

621.31'042 — Electric equipment — *For technicians*

Bishop, G. D.. Electrical and electronic systems and practice I / G.D. Bishop. — London : Macmillan, 1981. — xiv,101p : ill,facsim ; 21x24cm. — (Macmillan technical series)
ISBN 0-333-30454-3 (pbk) : £4.95 B81-13631

621.31'042 — Electric equipment. Installation

Neidle, Michael. Basic electrical installation principles / Michael Neidle. — London : McGraw-Hill, c1980. — xiv,105p ; 25cm
Includes index
ISBN 0-07-084639-1 (pbk) : £3.25 : CIP rev. B80-18786

621.31'042 — Electric machinery

Nasar, S. A.. Schaum's outline of theory and problems of electric machines and electromechanics / by Syed A. Nasar. — New York ; London : McGraw-Hill, c1981. — 185p : ill ; 28cm. — (Schaum's outline series)
Includes index
ISBN 0-07-045886-3 (pbk) : £4.95 B81-32119

621.31'042 — Electricity supply systems. Installation

Atabekov, V.. Electric power system installation practice / V. Atabekov ; translated from the Russian by O. Volodina. — Moscow : Mir ; [London] : distributed by Central Books, 1979, c1980. — 357p : ill ; 23cm
Translation and revision of: Montazh ėlektricheskikh seteĭ i silovogo ėlektrooborudovaniia. — Includes index
ISBN 0-7147-1608-1 : £3.95 B81-23516

621.31'042 — Rotating electric machinery

McPherson, George. An introduction to electrical machines and transformers / George McPherson. — New York ; Chichester : Wiley, c1981. — xvi,557p : ill ; 24cm
Bibliography: p529-530. — Includes index
ISBN 0-471-05586-7 : £14.30
Also classified at 621.31'4 B81-23330

621.31'042'0943 — West Germany. Electric equipment. Standards — *For British businessmen*

Electrical equipment for the Federal Republic of Germany : requirements and approval procedures applicable to domestic, commercial and industrial equipment. — Hemel Hempstead (Maylands Ave., Hemel Hempstead, Herts. HP2 4SQ) : Technical Help to Exporters, c1981. — vii,96p ; 30cm. — (Technical guide)
ISBN 0-905877-12-8 (pbk) : Unpriced B81-26985

621.31'068'4 — England. Electricity supply industries. Corporate planning, *1981-1988* — *Proposals*

Medium term development plan 1981-88 : the electricity supply industry in England and Wales. — London : Electricity Council, 1981. — 63p : ill ; 30cm
Cover title. — Text on inside cover
Unpriced (spiral) B81-37796

621.31'0941 — Great Britain. Electricity supply — *Statistics — Serials*

Handbook of electricity supply statistics / [Electricity Council]. — 1980 ed.. — [London] : [The Council], [1980]. — viii,141p
ISBN 0-85188-081-9 : Unpriced
ISSN 0440-1905 B81-08350

621.31'21'05 — Electricity. Generation — *Serials*

Power industry research. — Vol.1, no.1 (Jan.1981)-. — London : Academic Press, c1981-. — v. : ill ; 25cm
Quarterly
ISSN 0272-4952 = Power industry research : £48.50 per year B81-36536

621.31'2132 — Electricity supply. Generation. Large-scale fossil-fuelled steam turbogenerators. Use — *Comparative studies*

DeYoung, John H.. Public policy and diffusion of technology : an international comparison of large fossil-fueled generating units / by John H. DeYoung, Jr and John E. Tilton. — University Park ; London : Pennsylvania State University Press, c1978. — viii,102p : ill,1map ; 23cm. — (The Pennsylvania State University studies ; no.43)
Bibliography: p100-102
ISBN 0-271-00547-5 (pbk) : £2.40 B81-07828

621.31'2132 — Great Britain. Power stations. Heat. Utilisation in district heating — *Proposals*

CHP feasibility programme, interim report, shortlisting of cities, for lead city selection / for the Department of Energy. — Epsom (Woodcote Grove, Ashley Road, Epsom, Surrey KT18 5BW) : W.S. Atkins & Partners, 1980. — 96leaves : ill ; 30cm
Unpriced (spiral) B81-40344

621.31'2134 — Great Britain. Wave power

Ross, David, *1925-*. Energy from the waves : the first-ever book on a revolution in technology / by David Ross. — 2nd ed. revised and enlarged. — Oxford : Pergamon, 1981. — xix,148p : ill ; 22cm. — (Pergamon international library)
Previous ed.: 1979. — Bibliography: p142-143. — Includes index
ISBN 0-08-026715-7 (cased) : Unpriced
ISBN 0-08-026716-5 (pbk) : £3.50 B81-25376

621.31′2134 — Tidal power & wave power — *Conference proceedings*

International Symposium on Wave & Tidal Energy *(2nd : 1981 : Cambridge)*. Papers presented at the Second International Symposium on Wave & Tidal Energy held at Cambridge, England, September 23-25, 1981. — Cranfield : BHRA Fluid Engineering, Sept.1981. — [410]p
ISBN 0-906085-43-8 (pbk) : £35.00 : CIP entry B81-27970

621.31′2134 — Wave power — *Conference proceedings*

Power of sea waves : based on the proceedings of a conference on Power from Sea Waves, organised by the Institute of Mathematics and its Applications and held at the University of Edinburgh from June 26-28, 1979 / edited by B. Count. — London : Academic Press, 1980. — xv,449p : ill,maps ; 24cm. — (The Institute of Mathematics and its Applications)
Includes bibliographies
ISBN 0-12-193550-7 : £23.60 : CIP rev. B80-13870

621.31′24′05 — Direct power generation — *Conference proceedings — Serials*

Power sources. — 8. — London : Academic Press, Dec.1981. — [700]p
ISBN 0-12-689155-9 : CIP entry B81-31350

621.31′242 — Batteries — *Conference proceedings*

NATO Symposium on Materials for Advanced Batteries *(1979 : Aussios)*. Materials for advanced batteries / [proceedings of a NATO Symposium on Materials for Advanced Batteries, sponsored by the NATO Special Conference Panel on Materials Science, and held in Aussois, France, September 9-14 1979] ; edited by D.W. Murphy and J. Broadhead and B.C.H. Steele. — New York ; London : Published in coordination with NATO Scientific Affairs Division by Plenum, c1980. — ix,373p : ill ; 26cm. — (NATO conference series. VI, Materials science ; vol.2)
Includes index
ISBN 0-306-40564-4 : Unpriced B81-13378

621.31′242 — Electrochemical cells

Bagotskiĭ, V. S.. Chemical power sources / V.S. Bagotzky and A.M. Skundin ; translated from the Russian by O. Glebov and V. Kisin. — London : Academic Press, 1980. — xix,387p : ill ; 24cm
Bibliography: pxvii-xix. — Includes index
ISBN 0-12-072650-5 : £26.80 : CIP rev. B80-23376

621.31′244 — Electronic equipment. Use of solar cells. Projects — *Amateurs′ manuals*

Bishop, Owen. Electronic projects using solar cells. — London : Babani, Sept.1981. — [128]p
ISBN 0-85934-057-0 (pbk) : £1.95 : CIP entry B81-22542

621.31′244 — Solar energy. Photovoltaic conversion *— Conference proceedings*

Medium-size photovoltaic power plants : proceedings of an EEC/DOE workshop hosted by the Commissariat à l′Energie Solaire and held in Sophia-Antipolis, France, 23-24 October, 1980 / edited by Henry L. Durand, Paul D. Maycock, Wolfgang Palz. — Dordrecht ; London : Reidel, c1981. — viii,155p : ill ; 24cm
At head of title: Commission of the European Communities. — Includes index
ISBN 90-277-1279-4 : Unpriced B81-24904

Third E.C. photovoltaic solar energy conference : proceedings of the International Conference, held at Cannes, France, 27-31 October 1980 / edited by W. Palz. — Dordrecht ; London : Reidel, c1981. — xliv,1132p : ill,ports ; 24cm
At head of title: Commission of the European Communities. — Includes index
ISBN 90-277-1230-1 : Unpriced B81-15251

621.31′33 — Synchronous machinery

Walker, J. H. (Jack Holmes). [Large A.C. machines]. Large synchronous machines : design, manufacture and operation / by J.H. Walker. — Oxford : Clarendon Press, 1981. — xv,258p,xixp of plates : ill,1form ; 25cm. — (Monographs in electrical and electronic engineering) (Oxford science publications)
Originally published: Bhopal : BHEL, 1979. — Includes index
ISBN 0-19-859364-3 : £25.00 B81-36513

621.31′37 — Electric equipment: Switching power converters

Wood, Peter, *1932-*. Switching power converters / Peter Wood. — New York ; London : Van Nostrand Reinhold, c1981. — xiv,446p : ill ; 24cm
Includes index
ISBN 0-442-24333-2 : £19.90 B81-26427

621.31′4 — Control circuits. Voltage transformers *— Standards*

CAMA. *Motor Control Gear Division*. Standard for control circuit voltage transformers / CAMA Motor Control Gear Division. — [London] ([8 Leicester St., WC2H 7BN]) : [The Control and Automation Manufacturers′ Association], [1980]. — 8 leaves ; 31cm
Cover title
£1.50 (pbk) B81-04488

621.31′4 — Power transformers

McPherson, George. An introduction to electrical machines and transformers / George McPherson. — New York ; Chichester : Wiley, c1981. — xvi,557p : ill ; 24cm
Bibliography: p529-530. — Includes index
ISBN 0-471-05586-7 : £14.30
Primary classification 621.31′042 B81-23330

621.31′4′0288 — Power transformers. Maintenance & repair

Khudi͡akov, Z.. Repair of power transformers / Z. Khudyakov ; translated from the Russian by S. Kittell. — Moscow : Mir, 1980 ; [London] : Distributed by Central Books. — 333p : ill ; 21cm
Translation of: Remont transformatorov. — Bibliography: p327. — Includes index
ISBN 0-7147-1595-6 : £3.95 B81-23481

621.31′7 — Electric equipment. Fuses — *Conference proceedings*

International conference on electric fuses and their applications : Wednesday 7, Thursday 8 and Friday 9 April 1976 : conference papers / Liverpool Polytechnic, Faculty of Engineering, Department of Electrical and Control Engineering. — [Liverpool] : The Department, [1976?]. — 435p in various pagings : ill ; 30cm
Cover title
ISBN 0-905436-05-9 (pbk) : £25.00 B81-24917

621.31′7 — Electricity supply systems. Protection

Power system protection / edited by the Electricity Council. — [2nd ed.]. — Stevenage : Peregrinus
Previous ed.: London : Macdonald & Co., 1969
2: Systems and models. — c1981. — xvii,326p : ill ; 24cm
Includes index
ISBN 0-906048-53-2 : Unpriced : CIP rev. B81-16916

621.319 — Electricity distribution equipment — *Conference proceedings*

International Conference on Electricity Distribution *(1981 : Brighton)*. International Conference on Electricity Distribution : 1-5 June 1981 : venue Brighton Centre, Brighton, Sussex. — London : Institute of Electrical Engineers. — (IEE conference publications = IEE actes du congrés, ISSN 0537-9989 ; no.197)
Pt.1: Full texts of contributions included in the programme. — English version. — c1981. — xii,371p : ill ; 30cm
ISBN 0-85296-239-8 (pbk) : Unpriced B81-29228

621.319 — Electricity supply. Transmission & distribution

Weeks, Walter L.. Transmission and distribution of electrical energy / Walter L. Weeks. — New York ; London : Harper & Row, c1981. — 302p : ill ; 25cm
Includes index
ISBN 0-06-046982-x : Unpriced B81-40671

621.319 — Electricity transmission systems. Protective equipment

Power system protection / edited by the Electricity Council. — [New ed.]. — Stevenage : Peregrinus
Previous ed.: London : Macdonald, 1969
1: Principles and components. — c1981. — xviii,525p : ill ; 24cm
Includes index
ISBN 0-906048-47-8 : Unpriced B81-23102

Power system protection. — 2nd ed. — Stevenage : Peregrinus
Previous ed.: London : Macdonald & Co., 1969
Vol.3: Application. — Nov.1981. — [496]p
ISBN 0-906048-54-0 : £22.00 : CIP entry B81-30289

621.319′1 — Electricity supply systems. Automatic control. Applications of computer systems — *Conference proceedings*

Automatic control in power generation, distribution and protection : proceedings of the IFAC Symposium, Pretoria, Republic of South Africa, 15-19 September 1980 / edited by J.F. Herbst. — Oxford : Published for the International Federation of Automatic Control by Pergamon, 1981, c1980. — cxxv,568p : ill ; 31cm. — (IFAC proceedings series)
Includes bibliographies
ISBN 0-08-026709-2 : £46.00 B81-27720

621.319′2 — Electric equipment. Circuits

Bell, David A.. Fundamentals of electric circuits / David A. Bell. — 2nd ed. — London : Prentice-Hall, c1981. — xvi,720p : ill ; 24cm
Previous ed.: Reston : Reston Publishing, 1978. — Includes index
ISBN 0-8359-2127-1 (pbk) : £7.95 B81-27023

Jackson, Herbert W.. Introduction to electric circuits / Herbert W. Jackson. — 5th ed. — Englewood Cliffs ; London : Prentice Hall, c1981. — xviii,717p : ill(some col.) ; 25cm
Previous ed.: c1976. — Includes index
ISBN 0-13-481432-0 : £14.25 B81-16539

Lancaster, Gordon. DC and AC circuits / Gordon Lancaster. — 2nd ed. — Oxford : Clarendon, 1980. — 325p : ill ; 23cm. — (Oxford physics series)
Previous ed.: 1973. — Includes index
ISBN 0-19-851848-x : £20.00 : CIP rev.
ISBN 0-19-851849-8 (pbk) : £9.95 B80-09722

Yorke, R.. Electric circuit theory / by R. Yorke. — Oxford : Pergamon, 1981. — xvii,331p : ill ; 22cm. — (Applied electricity and electronics) (Pergamon international library)
Bibliography: p314-315. — Includes index
ISBN 0-08-026133-7 (cased) : Unpriced : CIP rev.
ISBN 0-08-026132-9 (pbk) : £6.50 B81-03369

621.319′2 — Electric equipment. Circuits. Analysis

Johnson, D. E.. Introductory electric circuit analysis / David E. Johnson and Johnny R. Johnson. — Englewood Cliffs ; London : Prentice Hall, c1981. — xiv,621p : ill ; 25cm
Includes index
ISBN 0-13-500835-2 : £13.65 B81-16541

Taber, Margaret R.. Electric circuit analysis / Margaret R. Taber, Eugene M. Silgalis. — Dallas ; London : Houghton Mifflin, c1980. — xiv,610p : ill ; 24cm
Includes index
ISBN 0-395-26706-4 : Unpriced B81-37841

621.319′2 — Electric equipment. Linear circuits. Analysis

Bobrow, Leonard S.. Elementary linear circuit analysis / Leonard S. Bobrow. — New York ; London : Holt, Rinehart and Winston, c1981. — xi,718p : ill ; 25cm. — (HRW series in electrical and computer engineering)
Includes index
ISBN 0-03-055696-1 : £15.95 B81-16465

Gabel, Robert A.. Signals and linear systems / Robert A. Gabel, Richard A. Roberts. — 2nd ed. — New York ; Chichester : Wiley, c1980. — xiv,492p : ill ; 24cm
Previous ed.: 1973. — Bibliography: p471-472. — Includes index
ISBN 0-471-04958-1 : £16.95 B81-06539

621.319'2'0151 — Electric equipment. Circuits. Mathematics

Papoulis, Athanasios. Circuits and systems : a modern approach / Athanasios Papoulis. — New York ; London : Holt, Rinehart and Winston, 25cm. — viii,435p : ill ; 25cm. — (HRW series in electrical and computer engineering)
Includes index
ISBN 0-03-056097-7 : £16.95 B81-05720

621.319'24 — Buildings. Electric equipment. Installation — *Rules*

Institution of Electrical Engineers. Regulations for electrical installations : IEE wiring regulations / [Institution of Electrical Engineers]. — 15th ed. — Hitchin : The Institution, c1981. — vii,216p : ill,forms ; 30cm
Previous ed.: published as 'Regulations for the electrical equipment of buildings'. 1966. — Includes index
ISBN 0-85296-235-5 (pbk) : Unpriced B81-37715

621.319'24 — Buildings. Electric wiring systems

Johnson, Robert C. (Robert Carl), *1916-1970*. Electrical wiring : design and construction. — Rev. ed. / Robert C. Johnson and Robert Cox. — Englewood Cliffs ; London : Prentice-Hall, c1981. — xii,348p : ill ; 24cm
Previous ed.: 1971. — Includes index
ISBN 0-13-247650-9 : £12.95 B81-14679

621.319'24 — Buildings. Electric wiring systems. Installation

Steward, W. E.. Modern wiring practice. — 9th ed. — London : Newnes Technical Books, Jan.1982. — [304]p
Previous ed.: London : Newnes-Butterworths, 1976
ISBN 0-408-00518-1 (pbk) : £10.00 : CIP entry B81-34128

621.319'24 — Buildings. Electric wiring systems. Installation — *Manuals*

Foley, Joseph H.. Electrical wiring fundamentals / developed and produced by Volt Information Sciences, Inc. ; written by Joseph H. Foley. — New York ; London : Gregg Division, McGraw-Hill, c1981. — viii,288p : ill,plans ; 29cm. — (Contemporary construction series)
Includes index
ISBN 0-07-067561-9 : £7.65 B81-36330

621.319'24 — Electric equipment: Plugs & sockets — *For British exporters*

Electrical plugs : an international survey / Technical Help to Exporters, British Standards Institution. — 3rd (rev.) ed. — Hemel Hempstead (Maylands Ave., Hemel Hempstead, Herts. HP2 4SQ) : Technical Help to Exporters, British Standards Institution, 1980. — 35p : ill ; 21x30cm
Previous ed.: 1977
ISBN 0-903886-42-1 (pbk) : Unpriced B81-16268

621.319'24 — Great Britain. Buildings. Electric wiring systems. Installation - *Questions & answers*

Lewis, M. L.. Multiple choice questions in electrical installation work. — 2nd ed. — London : Hutchinson Educational, Sept.1981. — [64]p
Previous ed.: 1977
ISBN 0-09-146401-3 (pbk) : £3.25 : CIP entry B81-20562

621.319'24 — Great Britain. Churches. Electric wiring systems. Installation — *Manuals*

Lighting and wiring of churches. — Rev. ed. — London (Dean's Yard, SW1P 3NZ) : CIO Publishing, 1981. — 41p : ill ; 21cm
Previous ed.: 1972
ISBN 0-7151-7538-6 (pbk) : £1.60 B81-34805

621.319'24 — Residences. Electric wiring systems — *Amateurs' manuals*

Burdett, Geoffrey. The David & Charles manual of home electrics / Geoffrey Burdett. — Newton Abbot : David & Charles, c1981. — 208p : ill ; 26cm
Includes index
ISBN 0-7153-8112-1 : £8.95 : CIP rev. B81-17497

Home electrics : a practical guide to understanding safe installation and maintenance / edited by Julian Worthington. — London : Orbis, 1981. — 128p : ill(some col.) ; 30cm
Includes index
ISBN 0-85613-348-5 : £3.95 B81-34091

621.319'24 — United States. Electric wiring systems. Installation. Safety measures. Standards. National Fire Protection Association. National electric code — *Commentaries*

Garland, J. D.. National electrical code reference book / J.D. Garland. — 3rd ed. — Englewood Cliffs ; London : Prentice-Hall, c1981. — xiv,608p : ill ; 24cm
Based on the 1981 code. — Previous ed.: 1979. — Text on lining paper. — Includes index
ISBN 0-13-609321-3 : £16.45 B81-39410

McGraw-Hill's national electrical code handbook. — 17th ed. / J.F. McPartland, editor ; John M. McPartland, Guy I. McPartland, assistant editors. — New York ; London : McGraw-Hill, c1981. — xvi,1133,28p : ill ; 24cm
'Based on the current 1981 National Electrical Code'. — Previous ed.: published as NFPA handbook of the national electrical code. 197-. — Includes index. — Includes the text of the code
ISBN 0-07-045693-3 : £17.50 B81-39411

621.319'24 — United States. Residences. Electric wiring systems — *Manuals*

Mullin, Ray C.. Electrical wiring residential : code, theory, plans, specifications, installation methods : based on 1981 National electrical code / Ray C. Mullin. — 7th ed. — New York ; London : Van Nostrand Reinhold, c1981. — vii,280p : ill,plans ; 29cm
Previous ed.: 1978. — Plans on 5 sheets (45x56cm folded to 24x17cm). — Includes index
ISBN 0-442-26311-2 : £12.70 B81-37029

621.319'34 — Insulated electric cables. Current rating — *Standards*

ERA Technology. Current rating standards for distribution cables / ERA Technology. — Leatherhead : [ERA Technology]. — (ERA ; 69-30)
Pt. 3: Sustained current ratings for PVC insulated cables to BS6346, 1969 (ac 50 Hz and dc). — c1981. — 113p : ill,1col.map ; 21cm
ISBN 0-7008-0232-0 (spiral) : £13.00 (£10.00 to members of ERA) B81-38871

621.319'37 — High voltage electric equipment. Vacuum gaps

Latham, R. V.. High voltage vacuum insulation : the physical basis / R.V. Latham. — London : Academic Press, 1981. — xiii,245p : ill ; 24cm
Includes index
ISBN 0-12-437180-9 : £15.80 B81-29815

621.319'37 — High voltage electric equipment. Vacuum gaps & sulphur hexafluoride insulators

Maller, V. N.. Advances in high voltage insulation and arc interruption in SF6 and vacuum / by V.N. Maller and M.S. Naidu. — Oxford : Pergamon, 1981. — ix,282p : ill ; 26cm
Includes index
ISBN 0-08-024726-1 : £14.50 B81-38280

621.32'2 — Battery operated emergency lighting equipment — *Standards*

Industry standard for the construction and performance of battery-operated emergency lighting equipment. — London (8 Leicester St., WC2H 7BN) : BEAMA Ltd, 1978. — 62p : ill ; 30cm
£5.00 (pbk) B81-07692

621.32'2 — Domestic lighting — *Questions & answers*

Lyons, Stanley L.. Domestic lighting. — London : Newnes Technical Books, Jan.1982. — [128]p. — (Questions & answers)
ISBN 0-408-00554-8 (pbk) : £1.95 : CIP entry B81-34129

621.32'2 — Great Britain. Industrial buildings. Electric lighting

Lyons, Stanley L.. Handbook of industrial lighting. — London : Butterworth, Sept.1981. — [320]p
ISBN 0-408-00525-4 : £18.00 : CIP entry B81-27984

621.32'2 — Lighting. Human factors

Boyce, P. R.. Human factors in lighting / P. R. Boyce. — London : Applied Science, c1981. — xiii,421p : ill ; 23cm
Includes index
ISBN 0-85334-912-6 : £26.00 : CIP rev. B80-33708

621.32'2 — Lighting — *Serials*

Developments in lighting. — 2. — London : Applied Science, Dec.1981. — [228]p. — (The Developments series)
ISBN 0-85334-985-1 : £18.00 : CIP entry B81-31514

621.32'2'05 — Electric lighting equipment. Design — *Serials*

Light and design international. — No.1 (Oct.1980)-. — London (410 St. John St., EC1V 4NJ) : Puma, 1980-. — v. : ill,ports ; 29cm
Monthly
ISSN 0260-5716 = Light and design international : £10.00 per year B81-04499

621.32'2'0942219 — Surrey. Godalming. Electric lighting, *1881*

Haveron, Francis. 'The brilliant ray' or 'How the electric light was brought to Godalming in 1881' / by Francis Haveron. — [Godalming] ([c/o Francis Haveron, 5 Hill Court, Ballfield Rd, Godalming, Surrey]) : Godalming Electricity Centenary Celebrations Committee, c1981. — 36p : ill,1map,facsims,ports ; 21cm
Text on inside covers. — Bibliography: on inside cover
Unpriced (pbk) B81-37422

621.32'4'09 — Gas lighting, *to 1980*

Gledhill, David. Gas lighting / David Gledhill. — Aylesbury : Shire, 1981. — 32p : ill,facsims ; 21cm. — (Shire album ; 65)
ISBN 0-85263-539-7 (pbk) : £0.95 B81-17543

621.32'73 — Fluorescent lamps. Phosphors

Butler, Keith H.. Fluorescent lamp phospors : technology and theory / Keith H. Butler. — University Park ; London : Pennsylvania State University Press, c1980. — xv,351p : ill ; 26cm
Includes index
ISBN 0-271-00219-0 : £23.70 B81-02282

621.34 — Electric equipment. Ferromagnetic oxide cores

DeMaw, M. F. Doug. Ferromagnetic-core design and application handbook / M.F."Doug" DeMaw. — Englewood Cliffs ; London : Prentice-Hall, c1981. — x,256p : ill ; 24cm
Includes bibliographies and index
ISBN 0-13-314088-1 : £12.95 B81-17302

621.34 — Superconductive energy storage coils. Energy transfer. Use of thyristor circuits

Kustom, Robert L.. Thyristor networks for the transfer of energy between superconducting coils / Robert L. Kustom. — Madison ; London : University of Wisconsin Press, 1980. — xx,116p : ill ; 24cm
Includes index
ISBN 0-299-08050-1 : £11.85 B81-04923

621.36'05 — Applied optics — *Serials*

Applied optics and optical engineering. — Vol.8. — New York ; London : Academic Press, 1980. — xvii,407p
ISBN 0-12-408608-x : £29.40 B81-16744

621.36'05 — Engineering. Applications of optics — *Serials*

Optics and lasers in engineering : [an international journal]. — Vol.1, no.1 (July/Sept.1980)-. — London : Applied Science, 1980-. — v. : ill ; 24cm
Quarterly
ISSN 0143-8166 = Optics and lasers in engineering : £37.50 per year B81-01992

621.36'2 — Submillimetre waves. Applications — *Conference proceedings*

Submillimetre waves and their applications : proceedings of the third international conference, Guildford, U.K., 29 March-1 April, 1978 / organised by the Institute of Physics in association with the Royal Society ... [et al.] ; guest editor, G.W. Chantry. — Oxford : Pergamon, 1979. — xip,p375-933 : ill(some col.) ; 28cm
Includes index
ISBN 0-08-023817-3 : £15.25 : CIP rev. B79-19181

621.36'6 — Lasers

Verdeyen, Joseph T.. Laser electronics / Joseph T. Verdeyen. — Englewood Cliffs ; London : Prentice-Hall, c1981. — xvi,444p : ill ; 24cm. — (Solid state physical electronics series)
Includes index
ISBN 0-13-523738-6 : £23.05 B81-29540

621.36'6'05 — Lasers — *Serials*

Laser applications. — Vol.4. — New York ; London : Academic Press, 1980. — xi,199p
ISBN 0-12-431904-1 : Unpriced B81-30759

621.36'61 — Heterostructure lasers

Casey, H. C.. Heterostructure lasers / H.C. Casey, Jr., M.B. Panish. — New York ; London : Academic Press. — (Quantum electronics, principles and applications)
Pt.B: Materials and operating characteristics. — 1978. — xiii,330p : ill ; 24cm
Includes index
ISBN 0-12-163102-8 : £23.60 B81-15011

621.36'61 — Semiconductor lasers

Fabian, M. E.. Semiconductor laser diodes : a users handbook / by M.E. Fabian. — Ayr : Electrochemical Publications, 1981. — v,136p : ill ; 24cm
Includes index
ISBN 0-901150-10-x : Unpriced B81-38074

621.36'63 — Helium-mercury direct nuclear pumped lasers

Akerman, M. Alfred. Demonstration of the first visible wavelength direct nuclear pumped laser / M. Alfred Akerman. — New York ; London : Garland, 1979. — vi,75p : ill ; 24cm. — (Outstanding dissertations on energy)
ISBN 0-8240-3984-x : Unpriced B81-40410

621.36'7 — Acoustic imaging

Greguss, Pál. Ultrasonic imaging : seeing by sound : the principles and widespread applications of image formation by sonic, ultrasonic and other mechanical waves / Pál Greguss. — London : Focal, 1980. — 224p : ill ; 25cm
Includes index
ISBN 0-240-51039-9 : £11.95 : CIP rev. B79-36849

621.36'7 — Surface-relief images

Gale, M. T.. Surface-relief images for color reproduction / M.T. Gale and K. Knop. — London : Focal, 1980. — 142p : ill ; 25cm. — (Progress reports in imaging science and technology ; 2)
ISBN 0-240-51068-2 (pbk) : £9.95 B81-07819

621.36'73 — Radiographic photography

Chesney, D. Noreen. Radiographic imaging. — 4th ed. — Oxford : Blackwell Scientific, Dec.1981. — [576]p
Previous ed. published as: Radiographic photography. 1971
ISBN 0-632-00562-9 : £13.00 : CIP entry B81-31645

621.36'73'09 — Radiography, *to 1979*

Mould, R. F.. A history of X-rays and radium with a chapter on radiation units: 1895-1937 / by Richard F. Mould. — Sutton : IPC Building & Contract Journals, c1980. — 100p : ill,facsims,ports ; 30cm
Bibliography: p62-69. - Includes index
ISBN 0-617-00355-6 (pbk) : £12.75
Primary classification 616.07'57'09 B81-04855

621.36'75'02854 — Holography. Applications of digital computer systems

I͡Aroslavskiĭ, L. P.. Methods of digital holography / L.P. Yaroslavskii and N.S. Merzlyakov ; translated from Russian by Dave Parsons. — New York ; London : Consultants Bureau, c1980. — xi,171p : ill ; 24cm
Translation of: Metody t͡sifrovoĭ golografii
ISBN 0-306-10963-8 : Unpriced B81-08592

621.36'78 — Natural resources. Remote sensing

Terrain analysis and remote sensing / edited by John R.G. Townshend. — London : Allen & Unwin, 1981. — xiii,232p,[2]p of plates : ill (some col.),maps,1form ; 26cm
Includes bibliographies and index
ISBN 0-04-551036-9 (cased) : Unpriced
ISBN 0-04-551037-7 (pbk) : Unpriced B81-34514

621.36'78 — Remote sensing. Applications of aerial photography

Curran, Paul J.. Remote sensing : the role of small format light aircraft photography / Paul J. Curran. — Reading (Whiteknights, Reading) : Department of Geography, University of Reading, 1981. — 39p : ill,2maps ; 22cm. — (Geographical papers ; no.75)
Bibliography: p37-39
ISBN 0-7049-0663-5 (pbk) : Unpriced B81-37948

621.36'78 — Remote sensing equipment — *Conference proceedings*

Les **Équipements** de photogrammétrie analytique et de télédétection : symposium international — Paris 12-14 septembre 1978 / publié sous la direction de Maurice Baussard et André Fontanel = Equipment for analytic photogrammetry and remote sensing / [sponsored by] Société française de photogrammétrie et de télédétection, International Society of Photogrammetry (ISP) Commission II. — Paris : Éditions Technip ; London : distributed by Graham & Trotman, 1979. — xvi,525p : ill ; 24cm
English, French and German text
ISBN 2-7108-0372-0 (pbk) : £35.00 B81-34089

621.36'78'024526 — Remote sensing — *For land surveying*

Bullard, R. K.. First steps in remote sensing / R.K. Bullard and P.J. Lakin. — London (c/o A.S. Walker, Forest Rd., E17 4JB) : Department of Land Surveying, North East London Polytechnic, 1981. — xi,61p : ill ; 30cm. — (Working papers / North East London Polytechnic. Department of Land Surveying, ISSN 0260-9142 ; no.3)
Bibliography: p59-61
ISBN 0-907382-02-9 (pbk) : Unpriced B81-35344

621.36'92 — Fibre optics. Applications

Handbook of fiber optics : theory and applications / edited by Helmut F. Wolf. — London : Granada, 1981, c1979. — xii,545p : ill ; 24cm
Originally published: New York : Garland, 1979. — Includes index
ISBN 0-246-11535-1 : £25.00 B81-10070

621.37'45 — Great Britain. Prepayment electricity meters — *Proposals*

Pre-payment meters, repeater meters and token meters / Electricity Consumers' Council. — London (119 Marylebone Rd., NW1 5PY) : The Council, 1980. — 11p ; 30cm. — (Discussion paper / Electricity Consumers' Council ; 3)
Unpriced (pbk) B81-34747

621.38 — ELECTRONIC AND COMMUNICATIONS ENGINEERING

621.38 — Broadcasting. Engineering aspects — *Conference proceedings*

International broadcasting convention : venue, Metropole Conference and Exhibition Centre, Brighton, UK, 20-23 September 1980 / sponsors, Electronic Engineering Association ... [et al.]. — London : Institution of Electrical Engineers, c1980. — 28,xx,354p : ill ; 30cm. — (Conference publication, ISSN 0537-9989 ; no.191)
ISBN 0-85296-222-3 (pbk) : £21.25 B81-07237

621.38 — Communication systems

Pierce, John R.. Introduction to communication science and systems / John R. Pierce and Edward C. Posner. — New York ; London : Plenum, c1980. — xvi,390p : ill ; 24cm. — (Applications of communications theory)
Includes index
ISBN 0-306-40492-3 : Unpriced B81-04424

621.38 — Communications equipment — *For children*

Howard, Sam. Communications machines / Sam Howard. — Oxford : Blackwell Raintree, c1981. — 32p : ill(some col.) ; 27cm
Originally published: Milwaukee : Raintree Children, c1980. — Includes index
ISBN 0-86256-021-7 : £2.95 B81-17605

621.38 — Telecommunication equipment — *Conference proceedings*

Intelec 81 *(Conference : London).* Third International Telecommunications Energy Conference : 19-21 May 1981 : venue Royal Lancaster Hotel, London / Intelec 81 ; organised by the Electronics and Power Divisions of the Institution of Electrical Engineers in association with the Chartered Institution of Building Services ... [et al.]. — [London] : [Institution of Electrical Engineers], c[1981]. — x,356p : ill ; 30cm. — (IEE conference publications, ISSN 0537-9989 ; no.196)
ISBN 0-85296-236-3 (pbk) : Unpriced B81-29234

621.38 — Telecommunication systems. Networks. Analysis

Cravis, Howard. Communications network analysis / Howard Cravis. — Lexington, Mass. : Lexington Books ; [Aldershot] : Gower [distributor], 1981. — xiii,144p : ill ; 24cm. — (Arthur D. Little books)
Includes index
ISBN 0-669-00443-x : £13.50 B81-39696

621.38'028 — Fibre-optic data transmission equipment

Optoelectronics/fiber-optics applications manual / prepared by the Applications Engineering Staff of the Hewlett-Packard Optoelectronics Division ; Stan Gage ... [et al.]. — 2nd ed. — New York ; London : McGraw-Hill, c1981. — 364p in various pagings : ill ; 29cm
Previous ed.: published as Optoelectronics applications manual. 1977. — Includes index
ISBN 0-07-028606-x : £18.95
Primary classification 621.3815'22 B81-39131

621.38'028 — Telecommunication equipment. Transmission equipment — *For technicians*

Danielson, G. L.. Transmission systems for technicians 2 / G.L. Danielson, R.S. Walker. — Sevenoaks : Butterworths, 1981. — 69p ; 25cm. — (Butterworths TEC technician series)
ISBN 0-408-00562-9 (pbk) : Unpriced : CIP rev. B81-03143

621.38'028 — Telecommunication systems. Use of plastics — *Conference proceedings*

Plastics in Telecommunications II *(Conference : 1978 : Institution of Electrical Engineers).* Plastics in Telecommunications II : international conference, 18, 19 and 20 September 1978, Institution of Electrical Engineers, London WC2R 0BL. — London : Plastics and Rubber Institute, [1978?]. — 377p in various pagings : ill ; 21cm
Cover title
£18.00 (£15.30 to members of the Plastics and Rubber Institute) (pbk) B81-37342

621.38'028'3 — Adaptive-array sensor systems

Hudson, J. E.. Adaptive array principles. — Stevenage : Peregrinus, Sept.1981. — [288]p. — (IEE Electromagnetic waves series)
ISBN 0-906048-55-9 : £24.00 : CIP entry B81-20521

Monzingo, Robert A.. Introduction to adaptive arrays / Robert A. Monzingo, Thomas W. Miller. — New York ; Chichester : Wiley, c1980. — xii,543p : ill ; 25cm
Includes index
ISBN 0-471-05744-4 : £19.25 B81-04131

621.38'028'3 — Subsurface antenna systems
King, Ronold W. P.. Antennas in matter : fundamentals, theory, and applications / Ronold W.P. King, Glenn S. Smith with Margaret Owens, Tai Tsun Wu. — Cambridge, Mass. ; London : MIT, c1981. — xvi,868p : ill ; 24cm
Bibliography: p834-839. — Includes index
ISBN 0-262-11074-1 : £46.50 B81-21062

621.38'028'3 — Telecommunication equipment. Antennas
Elliott, Robert S.. Antenna theory and design / Robert S. Elliott. — Englewood Cliffs ; London : Prentice-Hall, c1981. — xiii,594p : ill ; 25cm
Text on lining papers. — Includes bibliographies and index
ISBN 0-13-038356-2 : Unpriced B81-36497

Stutzman, Warren L.. Antenna theory and design / Warren L. Stutzman, Gary A. Thiele. — New York ; Chichester : Wiley, c1981. — x,598p : ill ; 24cm
Includes index
ISBN 0-471-04458-x : £17.00 B81-23984

621.38'028'30151 — Telecommunication equipment. Antennas. Mathematics
Modern topics in electromagnetics and antennas / H. Bach ... [et al.] ; based on lectures delivered at the 1976 Summer Institute at the Technical University, Eindhoven, directors E.J. Maanders and R. Mittra. — Stevenage : Peregrinus, c1977. — 441p in various pagings : ill ; 31cm. — (PPL conference publication ; 13)
ISBN 0-901223-13-1 : Unpriced B81-40118

621.38'03'21 — Telecommunication systems — *Encyclopaedias*
Aries, S. J.. Dictionary of telecommunications / S.J. Aries. — London : Butterworths, 1981. — 329p : ill ; 22cm
ISBN 0-408-00328-6 : Unpriced B81-24945

621.38'0412 — Electroacoustics
Merhaut, Josef. Theory of electroacoustics / Josef Merhaut ; translation by Richard Gerber. — New York ; London : McGraw-Hill, c1981. — xi,317p : ill ; 24cm
Translation of: Teoreticke zaklady elektroakustiky. — Bibliography: p313. — Includes index
ISBN 0-07-041478-5 : £19.25 : CIP rev.
B80-18361

621.38'0413 — Digital communication systems. Error-correcting codes
Clark, George C.. Error-correction coding for digital communications / George C. Clark, Jr. and J. Bibb Cain. — New York ; London : Plenum, c1981. — xii,422p : ill ; 24cm. — (Applications of communications theory)
Includes index
ISBN 0-306-40615-2 : Unpriced B81-36868

621.38'0413 — Digital microwave communication systems
Feher, Kamilo. Digital communications : microwave applications / Kamilo Feher. — Englewood Cliffs ; London : Prentice-Hall, c1981. — xviii,269p : ill ; 25cm
Includes index
ISBN 0-13-214080-2 : £18.20 B81-17176

621.38'0414 — Digital image processing — *Conference proceedings*
Real-time/parallel computing : image analysis / [based on proceedings of part of the Japan-United States Seminar on Research Towards Real-Time Parallel Image Analysis and Recognition, held in Tokyo, Japan, Ocotber 31, 1978-November 4, 19878] ; edited by Morio Onoe, Kendall Preston Jr. and Azriel Rosenfeld. — New York ; London : Plenum, c1981. — xviii,397p ; 26cm
Includes bibliographies and index
ISBN 0-306-40639-x : Unpriced B81-17886

621.38'0414 — Image transmission. Techniques
Image transmission techniques / edited by William K. Pratt. — New York ; London : Academic Press, 1979. — xv,281p : ill ; 24cm. — (Advances in electronics and electron physics. Supplements ; 12)
Includes bibliographies and index
ISBN 0-12-014572-3 : £20.00 B81-27149

621.38'0414 — Optical communication systems — *Conference proceedings*

European Conference on Optical Communication *(6th : 1980 : York)*. Sixth European Conference on Optical Communication, University of York, United Kingdom, 16-19 September 1980 / organised by the Electronics Division of the Institution of Electrical Engineers in association with the Institution of Electronic and Radio Engineers, Institute of Physics, Institute of Mathematics and its Applications with the support of the Convention of National Societies of Electrical Engineers Western Europe (EUREL). — London : Institution of Electrical Engineers, c1980. — xxiv,466p : ill,maps ; 30cm. — (IEE conference publication, ISSN 0537-9989 ; no.190)
ISBN 0-85296-223-1 (pbk) : £26.00 (£18.25 to members of the Institution) B81-04061

621.38'0414 — Telecommunication systems. Applications of fibre optics

Optical fibre communication / technical staff of CSELT. — New York ; London : McGraw-Hill, 1981. — xxxv,883p : ill,ports ; 24cm
Includes index
ISBN 0-07-014882-1 : £29.95 B81-19480

Personick, Stewart D.. Optical fiber transmission systems / Stewart D. Personick. — New York ; London : Plenum, c1981. — xi,179p : ill ; 24cm. — (Applications of communications theory)
Includes index
ISBN 0-306-40580-6 : Unpriced B81-26029

621.38'0414'0321 — Optical communication systems — *Encyclopaedias*

Weik, Martin H.. Fiber optics and lightwave communications standard dictionary / Martin H. Weik. — New York ; London : Van Nostrand Reinhold, c1981. — x,284p : ill ; 24cm
Bibliography: p279-284
ISBN 0-442-25658-2 : £13.90 B81-08710

621.38'0422 — Communications satellites: OTS *(Satellite)*. **Testing** — *Conference proceedings*

International conference on results of tests and experiments with the European OTS Satellite, 8-10 April 1981 : venue the Institution of Electrical Engineers, Savoy Place, London WC2 / organised by the Electronics Divison of the Institution of Electrical Engineers in association with the Institute of Physics, Institution of Electronic and Radio Engineers. — London : Institution of Electrical Engineers, c1981. — viii,139p : ill ; 30cm. — (Conference publication / Institution of Electrical Engineers, ISSN 0537-9989 ; no.199)
ISBN 0-85296-244-4 (pbk) : Unpriced
B81-40833

621.38'043 — Digital communication systems. Signals. Stochastic processing & burst processing

Mars, P.. Stochastic and deterministic averaging processors / P. Mars and W.J. Poppelbaum. — Stevenage : Peregrinus on behalf of the Institution of Electrical Engineers, c1981. — ix,157p : ill ; 24cm. — (IEE digital electronics and computing series ; 1)
Includes index
ISBN 0-906048-44-3 : Unpriced B81-12146

621.38'043 — Signals. Processing — *Conference proceedings*

European Signal Processing Conference *(1st : 1980 : Lausanne)*. Signal processing : theories and applications ; proceedings of EUSIPCO-80, first European Signal Processing Conference, Lausanne, Switzerland, September 16-18, 1980 / edited by M. Kunt and F. De Coulon. — Amsterdam ; Oxford : North-Holland, 1980. — xiii,797p : ill(some col.) ; 27cm
Includes index
ISBN 0-444-86050-9 : £29.64 B81-08109

Underwater acoustics and signal processing : proceedings of the NATO Advanced Study Institute held at Kollekolle, Copenhagen, Denmark, August 18-29, 1980 / edited by Leif Bjorno. — Dordrecht ; London : Reidel published in cooperation with NATO Scientific Affairs Division, c1981. — xv,736p : ill ; 25cm. — (NATO advanced study institutes series. Series C, Mathematical and physical sciences ; v.66)
Includes index
ISBN 90-277-1255-7 : Unpriced
Primary classification 620.2'5 B81-26220

621.38'043 — Telecommunication systems. Digital signals — *Conference proceedings*
International Conference on Telecommunication Transmission *(2nd : 1981 : Institution of Electrical Engineers)*. Second International Conference on Telecommunication Transmission : into the digital era : 17-20 March 1981 / organised by the Electrinics Division of the Institution of Electrical Engineers in association with the Convention of National Societies of Electrical Engineers of Western Europe (EUREL) ... [et al.]. — London : Institution of Electrical Engineers, c1981. — ix,241p : ill,maps ; 30cm. — (IEE conference publication, ISSN 0537-9989 ; no.193)
ISBN 0-85296-232-0 (pbk) : Unpriced
B81-19577

621.38'043 — Telecommunication systems. Digital signals. Processing — *Conference proceedings*
Digital processing of signals in communications : Loughborough, 7th-10th April, 1981. — London (99 Gower St., WC1E 6AZ) : Institution of Electronic and Radio Engineers, c1981. — 535p : ill ; 30cm. — (Proceedings / Institution of Electronic and Radio Engineers ; no.49)
Conference papers. — Includes index
ISBN 0-903748-44-4 (pbk) : Unpriced
B81-23293

621.38'043 — Telecommunication systems. Signals
Connor, F. R.. Signals. — 2nd ed. — London : Edward Arnold, Jan.1982. — [196]p. — (Introductory topics in electronics and telecommunications)
Previous ed.: 1972
ISBN 0-7131-3458-5 (pbk) : £3.95 : CIP entry
B81-35888

Welch, Samuel. Signalling in telecommunications networks / Samuel Welch. — Stevenage : Peter Peregrinus on behalf of the Institution of Electrical Engineers, c1979 (1981 [printing]). — xiii,386p : ill ; 22cm. — (IEE telecommunications series ; 6)
Includes index
ISBN 0-906048-04-4 (cased) : Unpriced
ISBN 0-906048-46-x (pbk) : Unpriced
B81-15431

621.38'043 — Telecommunication systems. Signals. Modulation
Connor, F. R.. Modulation. — 2nd ed. — London : Edward Arnold, Jan.1982. — [196]p
Previous ed.: 1973
ISBN 0-7131-3457-7 (pbk) : £3.95 : CIP entry
B81-33904

621.38'044 — Audiovisual equipment. Use — *Manuals*
A Users guide to simple visual aids and presentations. — London (2 Basil St., SW32 1AG) : ISBA, 1981. — 15p : ill ; 21cm
Bibliography: p15
£1.50 (unbound) B81-18662

621.38'044'0321 — Audiovisual equipment — *Encyclopaedias*
Roberts, R. S.. Dictionary of audio, radio and video / R.S. Roberts. — London : Butterworths, 1981. — 248p : ill ; 22cm
ISBN 0-408-00339-1 : Unpriced B81-19353

621.38'044'068 — Scandinavia. Household audiovisual equipment industries. Management — *Case studies*
McLellan, Ron. Business policy case studies of two hi-fi companies / Ron McLellan. — London (Duncan House, High St., E15 2JB) : Anglian Regional Management Centre, c1981. — 77p : ill ; 30cm. — (The Anglian Regional Management Centre case study series)
Unpriced (pbk) B81-26531

621.381 — ELECTRONIC ENGINEERING

621.381 — Buildings. Electronic security equipment. Construction — *Amateurs' manuals*

Bishop, O. N.. Electronic projects for home security / Owen Bishop. — London : Newnes Technical, 1981. — 92p : ill(some col.) ; 22cm. — (Newnes constructors projects)
ISBN 0-408-00535-1 (pbk) : Unpriced
B81-29826

621.381 — Electronic engineering

Lurch, E. Norman. Fundamentals of electronics / E. Norman Lurch. — 3rd ed. — New York ; Chichester : Wiley, c1981. — xiv,601p : ill ; 24cm
Previous ed.: 1971. — Text on lining papers. — Includes index
ISBN 0-471-03494-0 : Unpriced B81-08518

621.381 — Electronic equipment

Bishop, Owen. Beginner's guide to electronics. — 4th ed. — Sevenoaks : Newnes Technical Books, Sept.1981. — [240]p
Previous ed.: / by Terence Leighton Squires. 1974
ISBN 0-408-00413-4 (pbk) : £3.50 : CIP entry
B81-23921

Electronics pocket book. — 4th ed. / edited by E.A. Parr. — London : Newnes Technical Books, 1981. — 350p : ill ; 19cm
Previous ed.: 1976. — Includes index
ISBN 0-408-00481-9 (pbk) : Unpriced
B81-19454

Horowitz, Paul. The art of electronics / Paul Horowitz, Winfield Hill. — Cambridge : Cambridge University Press, 1980. — xviii,716p : ill ; 26cm
Bibliography: p705-708. — Includes index
ISBN 0-521-23151-5 (cased) : £35.00
ISBN 0-521-29837-7 (pbk) : £12.50 B81-30775

Introductory electronics / [the Introductory Electronics Course Team]. — Milton Keynes : Open University Press. — (Technology : a second level course)
At head of title: The Open University
Unit 1: Systems and circuits ; Unit 2: Signals and amplifiers / prepared by the Course Team. — 1980. — 34,47p : ill ; 30cm. — (T283 ; 1 & 2)
ISBN 0-335-08431-1 (pbk) : Unpriced
B81-14707

Introductory electronics / [the Introductory Electronics Course Team]. — Milton Keynes : Open University Press. — (Technology : a second level course)
At head of title: The Open University
Unit 3: Phasor analysis ; Unit 4: Signals and bandwidth / prepared by the Course Team. — 1980. — 52,48p ; 30cm. — (T283 ; 3 & 4)
ISBN 0-335-08432-x (pbk) : Unpriced
B81-14708

Introductory electronics / [the Introductory Electronics Course Team]. — Milton Keynes : Open University Press. — (Technology : a second level course)
At head of title: The Open University
Unit 5: Equivalent circuits ; Unit 6: Feedback / prepared by the Course Team. — 1980. — 45,48p ; 30cm. — (T283 ; 5 & 6)
ISBN 0-335-08433-8 (pbk) : Unpriced
B81-14709

Introductory electronics / [the Introductory Electronics Course Team]. — Milton Keynes : Open University Press. — (Technology : a second level course)
At head of title: The Open University
Unit 7: Diode and transistor circuits ; Unit 8: Electromagnetic transducers / prepared by the Coures Team. — 1980. — 44,34p : ill ; 30cm. — (T283 ; 7 & 8)
ISBN 0-335-08434-6 (pbk) : Unpriced
B81-14710

Introductory electronics / [the Introductory Electronics Course Team]. — Milton Keynes : Open University Press. — (Technology : a second level course)
At head of title: The Open University
Unit 9: A power amplifier / prepared by the Course Team. — 1980. — 44p : ill ; 30cm. — (T283 ; 9)
ISBN 0-335-08435-4 (pbk) : Unpriced
B81-14711

Introductory electronics / [the Introductory Electronics Course Team]. — Milton Keynes : Open University Press. — (Technology : a second level course)
At head of title: The Open University
Unit 10: Combinational logic ; Unit 11: Sequential logic / prepared by the Course Team. — 1980. — 52,40p : ill ; 30cm. — (T283 ; 10 & 11)
ISBN 0-335-08436-2 (pbk) : Unpriced
B81-14712

Introductory electronics / [the Introductory Electronics Course Team]. — Milton Keynes : Open University Press. — (Technology : a second level course)
At head of title: The Open University
Units 13/14: An instrumentation system / prepared by the Course Team. — 1980. — 64p : ill ; 30cm. — (T283 ; 13/14)
ISBN 0-335-08438-9 (pbk) : Unpriced
B81-14713

Introductory electronics / [the Introductory Electronics Course Team]. — Milton Keynes : Open University Press. — (Technology : a second level course)
At head of title: The Open University
Units 15/16: Digital components and systems / prepared by the Course Team. — 1980. — 64p : ill(some col.) ; 30cm. — (T283 ; 15/16)
ISBN 0-335-08439-7 (pbk) : Unpriced
B81-13182

Laurie, Peter. Electronics explained : a handbook for the layman / by Peter Laurie. — London : Faber, 1980. — 132p : ill
Includes index
ISBN 0-571-11514-4 (cased) : £10.95 : CIP rev.
ISBN 0-571-11593-4 (pbk) : £6.50 B80-12394

Seymour, J.. Electronic devices and components / J. Seymour. — London : Pitman, 1981. — 504p : ill ; 23cm. — (A Pitman international text)
Includes index
ISBN 0-273-01199-5 (pbk) : £8.95 B81-29509

Sinclair, Ian R.. Introducing amateur electronics / Ian R. Sinclair. — 2nd ed. — London (17 Hendon Lane, Finchley, N3) : Keith Dickson, 1981. — 82p : ill ; 22cm
Previous ed.: Kings Langley : Fountain, 1975. — Includes index
ISBN 0-907266-00-2 (pbk) : £3.50 B81-29570

Smith, Ralph J.. Electronics : circuits and devices / Ralph J. Smith. — 2nd ed.. — New York ; Chichester : Wiley, c1980. — xiii,494p : ill (some col.) ; 24cm
Previous ed.: 1973. — Text on lining papers. — Includes index
ISBN 0-471-05344-9 : £14.50 B81-21701

Wilson, F. A.. Elements of electronics / by F.A. Wilson. — London : Babani. — (BP ; 89)
Bk.5: Communication. — 1981. — 248p : ill ; 19cm
ISBN 0-85934-064-3 (pbk) : £2.95 : CIP rev.
B81-15862

621.381 — Electronic equipment. Cooling

Steinberg, Dave S.. Cooling techniques for electronic equipment / Dave S. Steinberg. — New York ; Chichester : Wiley, c1980. — xxi,370p : ill ; 24cm
Includes index
ISBN 0-471-04403-2 : £14.75 B81-03447

621.381 — Electronic equipment — *For schools*

Barker, B. G.. Foundation electronics / B.G. Barker. — Walton-on-Thames : Nelson, 1981. — 154p : ill ; 25cm
Includes index
ISBN 0-17-448121-7 (pbk) : £2.95 B81-13987

621.381 — Electronic equipment - *For technicians*

Cooper, A. L.. Electronics for TEC level II. — Cheltenham : Thornes, Aug.1981. — [250]p
ISBN 0-85950-300-3 (pbk) : £3.95 : CIP entry
B81-16899

621.381 — Electronic equipment — *For technicians*

Ekeland, Norval R.. Basic electronics for engineering technology / Norval R. Ekeland. — Englewood Cliffs ; London : Prentice-Hall, c1981. — xiv,686p : ill ; 24cm
Includes index
ISBN 0-13-060467-4 : £12.95 B81-17283

Kelly, C.. Electronics Level 2/Level 3 / C. Kelly. — Walton-on-Thames : Nelson, 1981. — viii,133p : ill(some col.) ; 25cm. — (Nelson TEC books)
Includes index. — Publisher's no.: NCN 5845-45-0
ISBN 0-17-741123-6 (pbk) : £3.95 B81-29120

Knight, S. A.. Electronics 3 checkbook. — Sevenoaks : Butterworths, Dec.1981. — [128]p
ISBN 0-408-00669-2 (cased) : £6.95 : CIP entry
ISBN 0-408-00623-4 (pbk) : £3.95 B81-31425

621.381 — Electronic equipment — *Manuals*

Zbar, Paul B.. Industrial electronics : a text-lab manual / Paul B. Zbar. — 3rd ed. — New York ; London : Gregg, c1981. — x,278p : ill ; 28cm
Previous ed.: New York : McGraw Hill, 1972
ISBN 0-07-072793-7 (pbk) : £9.25 B81-36278

621.381 — Household electronic equipment. Projects — *Amateurs' manuals*

Flind, Andy. More electronic projects in the home / Andy Flind. — Sevenoaks : Newnes Technical, 1981. — 85p : ill ; 22cm. — (Newnes constructor's projects)
ISBN 0-408-00501-7 (pbk) : Unpriced : CIP rev. B81-17527

621.381 — Industrial electronic equipment

Fundamentals of industrial electronics / V. Gerasimov ... [et al.] ; translated from Russian by Boris V. Kuznetsov. — Moscow : Mir, 1980 ; [London] : Distributed by Central Books. — 335p : ill ; 23cm
Translation of: Osnovy promyshlennoi ėlektroniki. — Includes index
ISBN 0-7147-1606-5 : £3.95 B81-23486

621.381'01'51 — Electronic engineering. Mathematics

Deem, Bill. Electronics math / Bill Deem. — Englewood Cliffs ; London : Prentice-Hall, c1981. — xiv,575p : ill ; 25cm
Includes index
ISBN 0-13-252304-3 : £12.95 B81-20021

621.381'0212 — Electronic equipment — *Technical data*

Metzger, Daniel L.. Electronic components, instruments and troubleshooting / Daniel L. Metzger. — Englewood Cliffs ; London : Prentice-Hall, c1981. — xv,512p : ill ; 25cm
Includes index
ISBN 0-13-250266-6 : £18.80 B81-17218

621.381'022'1 — Electronics. Schematic drawings

Lenk, John D.. Understanding electronic schematics / John D. Lenk. — Englewood Cliffs ; London : Prentice-Hall, c1981. — ix,294p : ill ; 24cm
Includes index
ISBN 0-13-935908-7 : £12.95 B81-23109

621.381'028 — Electronic engineering. Laboratory techniques — *Questions & answers*

Horowitz, Paul. Laboratory manual for The art of electronics / Paul Horowitz, Ian Robinson. — Cambridge : Cambridge University Press, 1981. — 140p in various pagings : ill ; 26cm
ISBN 0-521-24265-7 (cased) : £12.00
ISBN 0-521-28510-0 (pbk) : £4.95 B81-34526

621.381'029'4 — Electronic equipment — *Buyers' guides — Serials*
What's new in electronics. — 1980-. — London (30 Calderwood St., SE18 6QH) : Morgan-Grampian, 1980-. — v. : ill ; 30cm
Six issues yearly. — Description based on: May 1981
ISSN 0262-2254 = What's new in electronics : £12.00 per year B81-39532

621.381'03'21 — Electronic equipment — *Encyclopaedias*
Amos, S. W.. Dictionary of electronics / S.W. Amos. — London : Butterworths, 1981. — 329p : ill ; 22cm
ISBN 0-408-00331-6 : £15.00 : CIP rev. B80-36134

621.381'042 — Electronic & mircowave equipment. Design. Applications by digital computer systems — *Conference proceedings*
Computer-aided-design of electronic and microwave circuits and systems, University of Hull, July 12-14, 1977 : an international conference / sponsored by the University of Hull and the Institute of Electrical and Electronics Engineers, Inc., United Kingdom and Republic of Ireland Section in co-operation with the Circuits and Systems Society. — [New York] : The Institute ; [Hull] : [University of Hull] [distributor], [1980]. — vi,191p : ill ; 30cm
£9.50 (pbk) B81-04766

621.381'042 — Electronic equipment. Reliability - *Manuals*
Electronic reliability data. — Hitchin (Station House, Nightingale Rd, Hitchin, Herts.) : INSPEC, June 1981. — [300]p
ISBN 0-85296-240-1 : £125.00 : CIP entry B81-16352

621.381'042 — Electronic systems. Design
Handbook of electronic systems design / Charles A. Harper, editor-in-chief. — New York ; London : McGraw-Hill, c1980. — 663p in various pagings : ill,maps ; 24cm
Includes index
ISBN 0-07-026683-2 : £19.95 B81-27557

621.381'05 — Electronic equipment — *Serials*
National electronics review. — Vol.16 (1980-1). — London (Abell House, John Lslip St., SW1P 4LN) : National Electronics Council, [1981]. — 64p
ISSN 0305-2257 : £3.00 B81-32660

621.381'07'1241 — Great Britain. Secondary schools. Curriculum subjects: Electronic equipment — *For teaching*
Williams, Michael, *1938 May 30-*. Electronics / prepared by Michael Williams, additional material Jenny Campbell, Peter Slingsby. — Hatfield (College La., Hatfield, Hertfordshire, AL10 9AA) : Association for Science Education, c1979. — 36p,[43]p : ill ; 30cm. — (Topic brief / LAMP Project ; no.15)
ISBN 0-902786-54-7 (pbk) : £1.40 B81-06380

621.381'076 — Electronic engineering — *Questions & answers*
Hafer, Charles R.. Electronics engineering for professional engineers' examinations / Charles R. Hafer. — New York ; London : McGraw-Hill, c1980. — xv,309p : ill ; 22cm
Bibliography: p297-298. - Includes index
ISBN 0-07-025430-3 : £11.70 B81-05100

621.381'1 — Complex electronic control systems. Purchase, installation & maintenance. Contracts — *For customers*
A **Guide** to the procurement of complex electronic control and supervisory systems. — London (8 Leicester St., WC2H 7BN) : The Control and Automation Manufacturers Association, c1974. — 35p ; 21cm
English text with foreword in French, German, Italian, Spanish
Unpriced (pbk) B81-06208

621.381'1 — Electronic control systems
Fröhr, F.. Introduction to electronic control engineering. — London : Heyden, Jan.1982. — [330]p
Translation of: Einführung in die elektronische Regelungstechnik
ISBN 0-85501-290-0 (pbk) : CIP entry B81-34776

621.381'3 — Microwave equipment — *Conference proceedings*
European Microwave Conference *(7th : 1977 : Copenhagen)*. Microwave 77 : 7th European Microwave Conference, Monday 5 to Thursday 8 September 1977, Bella Center Copenhagen, Denmark : conference proceedings / supported by Dansk Ingeniøforening in cooperation with the convention of National Societies of Electrical Engineering of Western Europe ... [et al.]. — Sevenoaks (36 High St., Sevenoaks, Kent TN13 1JG) : Microwave Exhibitions and Publishers Ltd, [1977]. — xiii,717p : ill ; 30cm
Unpriced (pbk) B81-15227

European Microwave Conference *(8th : 1978 : Paris)*. Conference proceedings : 8th European Microwave Conference 78, Monday 4 to Friday 8 September 1978, Hotel Meridien, Paris, France / supported by Société des éléctriciens des éléctroniciens et radioéléctriciens Groupement des industries élétriques, in co-operation with EUREL - the Convention of National Societies of Electrical Engineering of Western Europe ... [et al.]. — Sevenoaks (36 High St., Sevenoaks, Kent TN13 1JG) : Microwave Exhibitions and Publishers, [1979]. — 835p : ill,1port ; 30cm
Unpriced (pbk) B81-15230

European Microwave Conference *(9th : 1979 : Brighton)*. Conference proceedings : 9th European Microwave Conference 79, Monday 17 to Thursday 20 September 1979, The Brighton Centre, Brighton, England / supported by Institution of Electrical Engineers, Institution of Electronic and Radio Engineers, in co-operation with EUREL - The Convention of National Societies of Electrical Engineering of Western Europe ... [et al.]. — Sevenoaks (36 High St., Sevenoaks, Kent TN13 1JG) : Microwave Exhibitions and Publishers, [1980]. — 736p : ill,ports ; 30cm
Unpriced (pbk) B81-15228

European Microwave Conference *(10th : 1980 : Warsaw)*. Conference proceedings : 10th European Microwave Conference 80, Monday 8 to Friday 12 September 1980, The Palace of Culture and Science, Warszawa, Poland / supported by Association of Polish Electrical Engineers, in cooperation with Polish Academy of Science ... [et al.]. — Sevenoaks (36 High St., Sevenoaks, Kent TN13 1JG) : Microwave Exhibitions and Publishers, [1981]. — 774p : ill,ports ; 30cm
Unpriced (pbk) B81-15229

621.381'325 — Electronic equipment. Semiconductor microwave amplifiers. Design
Ha, Tri T.. Solid-state microwave amplifier design / Tri T. Ha. — New York ; Chichester : Wiley, c1981. — xiv,326p : ill ; 24cm
Includes index
ISBN 0-471-08971-0 : £26.25 B81-33154

621.381'33 — Microwave equipment: Antennas
James, J. R.. Microstrip antenna : theory and design. — Stevenage : Peregrinus, Sept.1981. — [336]p. — (IEE electromagnetic waves series ; 12)
ISBN 0-906048-57-5 : £24.00 : CIP entry B81-20495

621.381'33 — Microwave equipment: Antennas — *Conference proceedings*
Advanced antenna technology / edited by P.J.B. Clarricoats. — [Sevenoaks] : Microwave Exhibitions & Publishers, c1981. — 454p : ill ; 30cm. — (MEPL reprint series)
Conference papers. — Includes index
Unpriced (pbk) B81-30100

621.381'33 — Microwave equipment: Flat dipole antennas
Dubost, G.. Flat radiating dipoles and applications to arrays. — Chichester : Wiley, Aug.1981. — [118]p. — (Electronics & electrical engineering research studies : research studies on antennas series ; 1)
ISBN 0-471-10050-1 : £10.00 : CIP entry B81-19206

621.3815 — Digital electronic equipment
Joynson, R. H.. An introduction to digital electronics and logic / R.H. Joynson. — London : Edward Arnold, 1981. — x,182p : ill ; 22cm
Includes index
ISBN 0-7131-3440-2 (pbk) : £4.25 : CIP rev. B81-27929

Lenk, John D.. Handbook of digital electronics / John D. Lenk. — Englewood Cliffs ; London : Prentice-Hall, c1981. — xii,384p : ill ; 24cm
Includes index
ISBN 0-13-377184-9 : £14.25 B81-23115

Sinclair, Ian R.. Beginner's guide to digital electronics / Ian R. Sinclair. — Sevenoaks : Newnes Technical, 1980. — 146p : ill ; 19cm
Includes index
ISBN 0-408-00449-5 (pbk) : Unpriced : CIP rev. B80-08797

621.3815 — Digital electronic equipment. Design. Applications of microcomputer systems
Peatman, John B.. Digital hardware design / John B. Peatman. — International student ed. — Auckland ; London : Mcgraw-Hill, c1980. — xi,438p : ill ; 21cm
Includes index
ISBN 0-07-066470-6 (pbk) : £6.95 B81-29759

621.3815 — Digital electronic equipment. Experiments
Leach, Donald P.. Experiments in digital principles / Donald P. Leach. — 2nd ed. — New York ; London : McGraw-Hill, c1981. — 188p : ill,forms ; 28cm
Previous ed.: 1976
ISBN 0-07-036916-x (pbk) : £8.50 B81-39418

621.3815 — Digital electronic equipment — *For technicians*
Bird, J. O.. Digital techniques 2 checkbook. — London : Butterworths, Jan.1982. — [64]p. — (Butterworths checkbook series)
ISBN 0-408-00674-9 (pbk) : £3.75 : CIP entry B81-34408

621.3815 — Discrete electronic components
Mazda, F. F.. Discrete electronic components. — Cambridge : Cambridge University Press, Nov.1981. — [178]p
ISBN 0-521-23470-0 : £18.00 : CIP entry B81-30898

621.3815'1 — Electronic components — *Manuals*
Ginsberg, Gerald L.. A user's guide to selecting electronic components / Gerald L. Ginsberg. — New York ; Chichester : Wiley, c1981. — xii,249p : ill ; 29cm. — (A Wiley-Interscience publication)
Includes index
ISBN 0-471-08308-9 : £17.00 B81-23980

621.3815'1'0294 — Electronic components — *Buyers' guides — Serials*
The **Product** finder : Swift-Sasco buyers guide. — 1981-. — [London] : Lane Advertising ; Crawley (P.O. Box 2000, Gatwick Rd., Crawley, Sussex RH10 2RU) : [Distributed by] Swift-Sasco, 1981-. — v. : ill ; 30cm
Annual. — Continues: Sasco catalogue
ISSN 0261-4073 = Product finder : £3.00
Primary classification 621.31'042 B81-31058

621.3815'2 — Applied solid state physics
Applied solid state science : advances in materials and device research / editor Raymond Wolfe. — New York ; London : Academic Press
Suppl. 2: Silicon integrated circuits / edited by Dawon Kahng
Pt. A. — 1981. — x,416p : ill ; 24cm
Includes index
ISBN 0-12-002954-5 : £28.60 B81-29769

621.3815'2 — High frequency semiconductor devices
Kovács, Ferenc. High-frequency application of semiconductor devices / Ferenc Kovács ; [translated by T. Sárkány]. — Amsterdam : Oxford : Elsevier, c1981. — 391p : ill ; 25cm. — (Studies in electrical and electronic engineering ; 5)
Translation of: Félvezetök nagyfrekvenciás alkalmazása. — Includes index
ISBN 0-444-99756-3 : £31.56 : CIP rev. B80-18791

621.3815'2 — Metal oxide semiconductor devices. Design
McCarthy, Oliver J.. MOS device and circuit design. — Chichester : Wiley, Feb.1982. — [288]p
ISBN 0-471-10026-9 : £17.60 : CIP entry
B81-36237

621.3815'2 — Metal oxide semiconductor devices. Instabilities
Davis, J. R.. Instabilities in MOS devices / J.R. Davis. — New York ; London : Gordon and Breach, c1981. — xv,175p : ill ; 24cm. — (Electrocomponent science monographs ; v.1)
Includes index
ISBN 0-677-05590-0 : Unpriced B81-27150

621.3815'2 — Power semiconductor devices
Lander, Cyril W.. Power electronics / Cyril W. Lander. — London : McGraw-Hill, c1981. — x,386p : ill ; 23cm
Bibliography: p377-381. - Includes index
ISBN 0-07-084123-3 (pbk) : £7.95 B81-27310

621.3815'2 — Semiconductor devices
Device physics / volume editor Cyril Hilsum. — Amsterdam ; New York : North-Holland, c1981. — xv,970p : ill ; 25cm. — (Handbook on semiconductors ; v.4)
Includes bibliographies and index
ISBN 0-444-85347-2 : £71.70 B81-16602

Nashelsky, Louis. Devices : discrete and integrated / Louis Nashelsky, Robert Boylestad. — Englewood Cliffs ; London : Prentice-Hall, c1981. — xii,428p : ill ; 25cm
Includes index
ISBN 0-13-208165-2 : £12.30 B81-17181

621.3815'2 — Semiconductor devices — *Conference proceedings*
European Solid State Device Research Conference *(10th : 1980 : York)*. Solid state devices 1980 : nine invited papers presented at the tenth European Solid State Device Research Conference (ESSDERC) and the fifth Symposium on Solid State Device Technology held at the University of York, 15-18 September 1980 / [sponsored by the European Physical Society ... [et al.]] ; edited by J.E. Carroll. — Bristol : Institute of Physics, c1981. — vi,225p : ill ; 25cm. — (Conference series / Institute of Physics, ISSN 0305-2346 ; no.57)
Includes bibliographies
ISBN 0-85498-148-9 : £25.00 B81-16583

621.3815'2 — Semiconductor devices. Durability & efficiency
Reliability and degradation. — Chichester : Wiley, Jan.1982. — [424]p. — (The Wiley series in solid state devices and circuits)
ISBN 0-471-28028-3 : £19.20 : CIP entry
B81-33800

621.3815'2 — Semiconductor devices. Power supply devices
Hnatek, Eugene R.. Design of solid-state power supplies / Eugene R. Hnatek. — 2nd ed. — New York ; London : Van Nostrand Reinhold, c1981. — xii,621p : ill ; 24cm
Previous ed.: 1971. — Includes index
ISBN 0-442-23429-5 : £20.65 B81-00943

621.3815'2'0287 — Semiconductor devices. Measurement & testing
Grin, G. I.. Semiconductor devices measurements and tests / G. Grin ; translated from the Russian by Alexander Repyev. — Moscow : Mir, 1981 ; [London] : Distributed by Central Books. — 208p : ill ; 21cm
Translation of: Izmerenie parametrov i ispytanie poluprovodnikovykh priborov. — Bibliography: p208. — Includes index
ISBN 0-7147-1589-1 : £2.95 B81-23482

621.3815'22 — Semiconductor devices: Light-emitting diodes
Optoelectronics/fiber-optics applications manual / prepared by the Applications Engineering Staff of the Hewlett-Packard Optoelectronics Division ; Stan Gage ... [et al.]. — 2nd ed. — New York ; London : McGraw-Hill, c1981. — 364p in various pagings : ill ; 29cm
Previous ed.: published as Optoelectrontics applications manual. 1977. — Includes index
ISBN 0-07-028606-x : £18.95
Also classified at 621.38'028 B81-39131

621.3815'28 — Bipolar & field effect power transistors
Blicher, Adolph. Field-effect and bipolar power transistor physics / Adolph Blicher. — New York ; London : Academic Press, 1981. — xxiii,312p : ill ; 24cm
Includes index
ISBN 0-12-105850-6 : £27.20 B81-40775

621.3815'28 — Transistor equipment. Servicing — *Manuals*
King, Gordon J.. Servicing radio, hi-fi and TV equipment. — 3rd ed. — Sevenoaks : Newnes, Nov.1981. — [192]p
Previous ed.: published as: Rapid servicing of transistor equipment. London : Newnes-Butterworths, 1973
ISBN 0-408-01126-2 (pbk) : £5.90 : CIP entry
B81-31267

621.3815'28 — Transistors
Sinclair, Ian R.. Transistors. — 4th ed. / Ian R. Sinclair. — London : Newnes Technical, 1980. — 104p : ill ; 17cm. — (Questions & answers)
Previous ed.: published as 'Questions and answers on transistors' / by Clement Brown. 1969. — Includes index
ISBN 0-408-00485-1 (pbk) : £1.75 : CIP rev.
B80-23382

621.3815'28'0212 — Transistors. Equivalents — *Technical data*
Michaels, Adrian. International transistor equivalents guide / by Adrian Michaels. — London : Babani, 1981. — 299p ; 18cm
ISBN 0-85934-060-0 (pbk) : £2.95 B81-16189

621.3815'284 — Electronic equipment. Circuits. Field effect transistors
Designing with field-effect transistors / Siliconix Inc. ; editor in chief Arthur D. Evans. — New York ; London : McGraw-Hill, c1981. — ix,293p : ill ; 24cm
Includes bibliographies and index
ISBN 0-07-057449-9 : £17.15 B81-36474

621.3815'284 — Electronic equipment. Vertical metal oxide semiconductor field effect transistors. Projects — *Amateurs' manuals*
Penfold, R. A.. VMOS projects / by R.A. Penfold. — London : Babani, 1981. — 97p : ill ; 18cm
ISBN 0-85934-058-9 (pbk) : £1.95 B81-16188

621.3815'3 — Digital circuits
Malvino, Albert Paul. Digital principles and applications / Albert Paul Malvino, Donald P. Leach. — 3rd ed. — New York ; London : McGraw-Hill, 1981. — vi,490p : ill ; 24cm
Previous ed.: 1975. — Includes index
ISBN 0-07-039875-5 : £12.68 B81-17721

621.3815'3 — Digital circuits. Logic design. Projects
McCurdy, Lyle B.. Digital logic design and applications : an experimental approach / Lyle B. McCurdy, Albert L. McHenry. — Englewood Cliffs ; London : Prentice-Hall, c1981. — xii,122p : ill ; 29cm(pbk)
Includes bibliographies
ISBN 0-13-212381-9 : £9.70 B81-39911

621.3815'3 — Electronic equipment. Circuits
Buckley, P. M.. Basic electronic circuits / P.M. Buckley, A.H. Hoskyns ; answers prepared by Andrew Shewan. — London : Spon, 1980. — xv,138p : ill ; 25cm
Includes index
ISBN 0-419-11420-3 (pbk) : £4.95 : CIP rev.
B79-36357

Dennis, W. H.. Electronic components and systems. — London : Butterworths, Jan.1982. — [256]p
ISBN 0-408-01111-4 : £12.50 : CIP entry
B81-34420

Sinclair, Ian R.. Practical electronics handbook / Ian R. Sinclair. — London : Butterworth, 1980. — 186p : ill ; 22cm. — (Newnes technical books)
Bibliography: p182-183. — Includes index
ISBN 0-408-00447-9 (pbk) : £3.00 : CIP rev.
B80-08798

621.3815'3 — Electronic equipment. Circuits. Design. Optimisation. Applications of computer systems
Brayton, Robert K.. Sensitivity and optimization / Robert K. Brayton, Robert Spence. — Amsterdam ; Oxford : Elsevier Scientific, 1980. — xii,368p : ill ; 25cm. — (CAD of electronic circuits ; vo.2)
Includes bibliographies and index
ISBN 0-444-41929-2 : £25.29 B81-06515

621.3815'3 — Electronic equipment. Circuits — *For schools*
Coull, James. Electronics : a practical guide to simple circuits / James Coull. — Edinburgh : Holmes McDougall, c1980. — 74p : ill ; 19x25cm
ISBN 0-7157-1985-8 (pbk) : £1.95 B81-00944

621.3815'3'0212 — Electronic equipment. Circuits — *Technical data*
Markus, John. Modern electronic circuits reference manual : over 3,630 modern electronic circuits, each complete with values of all parts and performance details, organized in 103 logical chapters for quick reference and convenient browsing / John Markus. — New York ; London : McGraw-Hill, c1980. — xv,1238p : ill ; 29cm
Includes index
ISBN 0-07-040446-1 : £31.50 B81-39459

621.3815'30422 — Electronic equipment. Transistor circuits. Design
Amos, S. W.. Principles of transistor circuits. — 6th ed. — Sevenoaks : Butterworths, Oct.1981. — [350]p
Previous ed.: 1975
ISBN 0-408-01106-8 (cased) : £10.50 : CIP entry
ISBN 0-408-00599-8 (pbk) : £6.95 B81-25287

621.3815'30423 — Electronic equipment. Light-emitting diode circuits. Construction — *Amateurs' manuals*
Soar, R. N.. 50 simple L.E.D. circuits / by R.N. Soar. — London : Babani. — (BP ; 87)
Bk.2. — 1981. — 57p : ill ; 18cm
ISBN 0-85934-062-7 (pbk) : £1.35 : CIP rev.
B81-13757

621.3815'3'05 — Electronic equipment. Circuits — *Serials*
[Electronics digest *(London)***]**. Electronics digest. — Vol., no.1 (Summer 1980)-. — London : 145 Charing Cross Rd, W2H 3EE : Modmags, 1980-. — v. : ill ; 29cm
Quarterly
ISSN 0260-891x : £1.50 per issue B81-09077

621.3815'324 — Active filters. Design. Applications of minicomputer systems & pocket programmable electronic calculators
Moschytz, G. S.. Active filter design handbook : for use with programmable pocket calculators and minicomputers / G.S. Moschytz and P. Horn. — Chichester : Wiley, c1981. — viii,316p : ill ; 26cm
Bibliography: p177-179. — Includes index
ISBN 0-471-27850-5 : £16.00 : CIP rev.
B81-00134

621.3815'324 — Electric filters. Design
Williams, Arthur B.. Electronic filter design handbook / Arthur B. Williams. — New York ; London : McGraw-Hill, c1981. — xiv,541p in various pagings : ill ; 24cm
Includes bibliographies and index
ISBN 0-07-070430-9 : £27.95 B81-19486

621.3815'34 — Electronic counters
Oberman, R. M. M.. Counting and counters / R.M.M. Oberman. — London : Macmillan, 1981. — ixii,171p : ill ; 25cm
Includes index
ISBN 0-333-30512-4 : £15.00 B81-10536

621.3815'34 — Electronic equipment. High speed pulse circuits
Früngel, Frank B. A.. High speed pulse technology / by Frank B.A. Früngel. — New York ; London : Academic Press
Translation of: Impulstechnik
Vol.4: Sparks and laser pulses. — 1980. — xiii,488p : ill,plans ; 24cm
Includes index
ISBN 0-12-269004-4 : £31.80 B81-14558

621.3815'35 — Electronic equipment. Operational amplifiers

Dostál, Jiří. Operational amplifiers / Jiří Dostál ; [translated from the Czech by Karel Kieslich]. — Amsterdam ; Oxford : Elsevier Scientific, 1981. — 488p : ill ; 25cm. — (Srudies in electrical and electronic engineering ; vol.4)
Translation of: Operační zesilovače. — Includes index
ISBN 0-444-99760-1 : Unpriced : CIP rev. B80-18794

Hughes, Fredrick W.. Op amp handbook / Fredrick W. Hughes. — Englewood Cliffs ; London : Prentice-Hall, c1981. — x,294p : ill ; 25cm
Includes index
ISBN 0-13-637298-8 : £14.25 B81-25058

Irvine, Robert G.. Operational amplifier characteristics and applications / Robert G. Irvine. — Englewood Cliffs ; London : Prentice-Hall, c1981. — xv,462p : ill,1port ; 25cm
Includes index
ISBN 0-13-637751-3 : £16.20 B81-25510

621.3815'36 — Frequency synthesis. Phase-lock techniques

Egan, William F.. Frequency synthesis by phase lock / William F. Egan. — New York ; Chichester : Wiley, c1981. — xix,279p : ill ; 24cm
Bibliography: p269-274. - Includes index
ISBN 0-471-08202-3 : £16.00 B81-11298

621.3815'363 — Frequency synthesisers. Design

Manassewitsch, Vadim. Frequency synthesizers : theory and design / Vadim Manassewitsch. — 2nd ed. — New York ; London : Wiley, c1980. — xiii,582p : ill ; 24cm
Previous ed.: 1976. — Includes index
ISBN 0-471-07917-0 : £19.25 B81-03207

621.3815'37 — Telecommunication equipment. Computer-controlled switching systems. Programming — *Conference proceedings*

International Conference on Software Engineering for Telecommunication Switching Systems *(4th : 1981 : University of Warwick)*. Fourth International Conference on Software Engineering for Telecommunication Switching Systems : 20-24 July 1981 / organised by the Institution of Electrical Engineers in association with the British Computer Society (BCS), Institute of Mathematics and its Applications (IMA), Institution of Electronic and Radio Engineers. — London : Institution of Electrical Engineers, c1981. — vi,220p : ill ; 30cm. — (Conference publication / Institution of Electrical Engineers, ISSN 0537-9989 ; no.198)
ISBN 0-85296-242-8 (pbk) : Unpriced B81-36918

621.3815'37 — Telecommunication equipment. Switching systems

Hills, M. T.. Telecommunications switching principles / M.T. Hills. — London : Allen & Unwin, 1981. — xiii,327p : ill ; 24cm. — (Telecommunication systems design, ISSN V.2)
Includes index
ISBN 0-04-621029-6 (pbk) : Unpriced : CIP rev. B81-06041

Pearce, J. Gordon. Telecommunications switching / J. Gordon Pearce. — New York ; London : Plenum, 1981. — ix,338p : ill,1map ; 24cm. — (Applications of communications theory)
Includes index
ISBN 0-306-40584-9 : Unpriced B81-27114

621.3815'48 — Cathode ray oscilloscopes

Hickman, Ian. Oscilloscopes : how to use them, how they work / Ian Hickman. — London : Newnes Technical Books, 1981. — 122p : ill (some col.) ; 22cm
Includes index
ISBN 0-408-00472-x (pbk) : Unpriced B81-19350

621.3815'48 — Electronic electricity measuring instruments
Lenk, John D.. Handbook of electrical meters : theory and application / John D. Lenk. — Rev. and enl.. — Englewood Cliffs ; London : Prentice-Hall, c1981. — xii,228p : ill ; 24cm
Previous ed.: 1970. — Includes index
ISBN 0-13-377333-7 : £12.30 B81-12526

621.3815'48 — Electronic measuring instruments
De Sa, A.. Principles of electronic instrumentation / A. de Sa. — London : Edward Arnold, 1981. — vii,280p : ill ; 25cm
Includes bibliographies and index
ISBN 0-7131-2799-6 (pbk) : £9.50 : CIP rev. B80-13872

621.3815'48 — Electronic measuring instruments. Construction — *Amateurs' manuals*
Rayer, F. G.. Electronic timer projects. — London : Babani, Nov.1981. — [96]p. — (BP93)
ISBN 0-85934-068-6 (pbk) : £1.95 : CIP entry B81-30406

621.3815'48 — Electronic testing equipment. Construction — *Amateurs' manuals*
Ainslie, Alan C.. Electronic test equipment projects / Alan C. Ainslie. — London : Newnes Technical, 1981. — 88p : ill(some col.) ; 22cm. — (Newnes constructors projects)
ISBN 0-408-00528-9 (pbk) : Unpriced B81-29824

621.3815'48 — Electronic testing equipment — *Manuals*
Electronic test equipment. — St Albans : Granada, Nov.1981. — [320]p
ISBN 0-246-11478-9 : £20.00 : CIP entry B81-30392

621.3815'48'024658 — Electronic equipment. Automatic testing — *For management*
Automatic testing could help in your business : — a guide to managers. — London : Electronic Engineering Association, [1981?]. — 8p : ill ; 21cm
Unpriced (pbk) B81-36807

621.381'7 — Microelectronic engineering. Use of high resolution lithography
Electron-beam technology in microelectronic fabrication / edited by George R. Brewer. — New York ; London : Academic Press, 1980. — xi,362p : ill ; 24cm
Includes bibliographies and index
ISBN 0-12-133550-x : £20.60 B81-01531

621.381'71 — Materials: Amorphous & polycrystalline semiconductor films
Polycrystalline and amorphous thin films and devices / edited by Lawrence L. Kazmerski. — New York ; London : Academic Press, 1980. — xv,304p : ill ; 24cm. — (Materials science and technology)
Bibliography: p293-295. - Includes index
ISBN 0-12-403880-8 : £21.00 B81-05574

621.381'71 — Microelectronic devices
Burkitt, Alan. The silicon civilisation / by Alan Burkitt and Elaine Williams. — London : W.H. Allen, 1980. — 266p ; 23cm
Bibliography: p257-258. — Includes index
ISBN 0-491-02730-3 : £6.95 B81-27545

621.381'71'05 — Microelectronic devices — *Serials*
. Polymicros / Bristol Polytechnic. — No.1 (Nov.1980)-. — Bristol (c/o Peter Taylor, Department of Economics and Social Science, Bristol Polytechnic, Coldharbour Lane, Frenchay, Bristol) : The Polytechnic, 1980-. — v. ; 30cm
ISSN 0260-9436 = Polymicros : Unpriced B81-13692

621.381'71'076 — Microelectronic devices — *Questions & answers — For technicians*
Vears, R. E.. Microelectronic systems 1 checkbook / R.E. Vears. — London : Butterworths, 1981. — viii,81p : ill ; 20cm. — (Butterworths technical and scientific checkbooks. Level 1)
Includes index
ISBN 0-408-00638-2 (cased) : Unpriced
ISBN 0-408-00552-1 (pbk) : Unpriced B81-27276

621.381'73 — Digital integrated circuits — *Amateurs' manuals*
Rayer, F. G.. Digital IC projects / by F.G. Rayer. — London : Babani, 1981. — 91p : ill ; 18cm
ISBN 0-85934-059-7 (pbk) : £1.95 B81-16187

621.381'73 — Digital integrated circuits. Design
Hope, G. S.. Integrated devices in digital circuit design / G.S. Hope. — New York ; Chichester : Wiley, c1981. — xx,368p : ill ; 24cm
Includes index
ISBN 0-471-07920-0 : £17.10 B81-17241

621.381'73 — Electronic equipment. Integrated circuits
Jowett, Charles E.. Materials and processes in electronics. — London : Hutchinson, Sept.1981. — [320]p
ISBN 0-09-145100-0 : £20.00 : CIP entry B81-20174

621.381'73 — Electronic equipment. Integrated circuits. Analysis & design

Chirlian, Paul M.. Analysis and design of integrated circuits. — London : Harper & Row
Vol.1: Semi conductor devices. — Jan.1982. — 1v.
ISBN 0-06-318213-0 (pbk) : £5.95 : CIP entry B81-35880

Chirlian, Paul M.. Analysis and design of integrated circuits. — London : Harper & Row
Vol.2: Digital electronics. — Jan.1982. — 1v.
ISBN 0-06-318214-9 (pbk) : £5.95 : CIP entry B81-35879

Chirlian, Paul M.. Analysis and design of integrated circuits. — London : Harper & Row
Vol.3: Analogue electronics. — Jan.1982. — 1v.
ISBN 0-06-318215-7 (pbk) : £8.95 : CIP entry B81-35878

Chirlian, Paul M.. Analysis and design of integrated electronic circuits / Paul M. Chirlian. — New York ; London : Harper & Row, c1981. — xvi,1072p : ill,facsims ; 25cm
Includes bibliographies and index
ISBN 0-06-041266-6 : £15.75 B81-05857

621.381'73 — Electronic equipment. Integrated circuits. Design & applications

Stout, David F.. Handbook of microcircuit design and application / David F. Stout ; edited by Milton Kaufman. — New York ; London : MacGraw-Hill, c1980. — xii,447p in various pagings : ill ; 24cm
Includes index
ISBN 0-07-061796-1 : £18.20 B81-05549

621.381'73 — Electronic equipment. Integrated circuits. Projects — *Amateurs' manuals*

Heiserman, David L.. Beginner's handbook of IC projects / David L. Heiserman. — Englewood Cliffs ; London : Prentice-Hall, c1981. — xiv,216p : ill ; 24cm. — (A reward book)
ISBN 0-13-074229-5 (cased) : Unpriced
ISBN 0-13-074286-4 (pbk) : Unpriced B81-36599

Rayer, F. G.. IC projects for beginners. — London : Babani, Feb.1982. — [96]p
ISBN 0-85934-072-4 (pbk) : £1.95 : CIP entry B81-38317

621.381'73 — Electronic equipment. Large scale integrated circuits

Large scale integration. — Chichester : Wiley, Nov.1981. — [352]p. — (The Wiley series in solid state devices and circuits)
ISBN 0-471-27988-9 : £16.25 : CIP entry B81-31073

621.381'73 — Electronic equipment. Large scale integrated circuits — *Conference proceedings*
VLSI 81 *(Conference : University of Edinburgh).* VLSI 81 : very large scale integration / [proceedings of the first International Conference on Very Large Scale Integration held at the University of Edinburgh from 18-21 August 1981, organised by the University of Edinburgh Departments of Computer Science and Electrical Engineering and the Wolfson Microelectronics Institute, with the assistance of CEP Consultants Ltd ...]. — London : Academic Press, 1981. — xiii,363p : ill ; 24cm
Includes bibliographies
ISBN 0-12-296860-3 : £15.00 B81-39784

621.381'73 — Electronic equipment. Large scale integrated circuits. Fine line lithography
Fine line lithography / edited by Roger Newman. — Amsterdam ; Oxford : North-Holland, 1980. — vii,481p : ill ; 23cm. — (Materials processing - theory and practices ; v.1)
Includes bibliographies and index
ISBN 0-444-85351-0 : £40.68 B81-03006

621.381'73 — Electronic equipment. Linear integrated circuits
Young, Thomas, *1934-*. Linear integrated circuits / Thomas Young. — New York ; Chichester : Wiley, c1981. — xi,495p : ill ; 25cm. — (Electronic technology series)
Includes index
ISBN 0-471-97941-4 : £12.25 B81-23386

621.381'73 — Electronic equipment. Linear integrated circuits. Experiments
Tischler, Morris. Experiments in amplifiers, filters, oscillators, and generators / Morris Tischler. — New York ; London : McGraw-Hill, c1981. — vi,170p : ill ; 28cm. — (Linear integrated circuit applications)
Bibliography: p170
ISBN 0-07-064780-1 (pbk) : £4.95 B81-25916

Tischler, Morris. Experiments in general and biomedical instrumentation / Morris Tischer. — New York ; London : McGraw-Hill, c1981. — vi,201p : ill ; 28cm. — (Linear integrated circuit applications series)
Adaptation of: Linear integrated circuit applications. s.l., s.n. 1977. — Bibliography: p201
ISBN 0-07-064781-x (pbk) : £7.75 B81-39261

621.381'73 — Electronic equipment. Thick film hybrid integrated circuits
Pitt, Keith E. G.. An introduction to thick film component technology / Keith E. G. Pitt. — Luton (Mackintosh House, Napier Rd, Luton LU1 1RG) : Mackintosh Publications, 1981. — xi,124p,[16]p of plates : ill ; 21cm
Bibliography: p105-110. — Includes index
ISBN 0-904705-37-4 (pbk) : £10.50 B81-26616

621.381'73042 — Digital complementary metal oxide semiconductor integrated circuits
Hnatek, Eugene R.. User's guidebook to digital CMOS integrated circuits / Eugene R. Hnatek. — New York ; London : McGraw-Hill, c1981. — ix,339p : ill ; 24cm
Includes index
ISBN 0-07-029067-9 : £17.50 B81-29724

621.381'73'5 — Electronic equipment: Integrated circuits. Operational amplifiers. Projects
Parr, E. A.. How to use op-amps. — London : Babani, Oct.1981. — [160]p
ISBN 0-85934-063-5 (pbk) : £2.25 : CIP entry B81-27967

621.381'735 — Electronic equipment: Linear integrated circuits. Operational amplifiers
Shepherd, I. E.. Operational amplifiers. — London : Longman, Oct.1981. — [304]p
ISBN 0-582-46089-1 : £25.00 : CIP entry B81-30466

621.381'74 — Electronic equipment. Printed circuit boards. Design & manufacture — *Manuals*
Leonida, Giovanni. Handbook of printed circuit design, manufacture, components & assembly / by Giovanni Leonida. — Ayr (29 Barns St, Ayr) : Electrochemical Publications, 1981. — xvii,569p : ill ; 24cm
Translation and revision from the Italian. — Includes index
ISBN 0-901150-09-6 : Unpriced B81-26311

621.381'74 — Electronic equipment. Printed circuits. Boards. Design
Scarlett, J. A.. Printed circuit boards for microelectronics / by J.A. Scarlett. — 2nd ed. — Ayr (29 Barns St., Ayr KA7 1XB) : Electrochemical Publications, 1980. — xvii,284p : ill ; 24cm
Previous ed.: New York ; London : Van Nostrand Reinhold, 1970. — Includes index
£31.00 B81-04901

621.3819'52 — IBM computing centres. Design
Høie, Tore A.. Central systems architecture : planning and controlling complex IBM computing centres / Tore A. Høie. — Amsterdam ; Oxford : North-Holland, c1981. — x,596pxxxixp : ill ; 23cm
Includes index
ISBN 0-444-86163-7 : £30.65 B81-22444

621.3819'58 — Digital computers
Bartee, Thomas C.. Digital computer fundamentals / Thomas C. Bartee. — 5th ed. — New York ; London : McGraw-Hill, c1981. — xii,637p : ill,forms ; 25cm
Previous ed.: 1977. — Includes index
ISBN 0-07-003894-5 (cased) : £16.05
ISBN 0-07-066172-3 (pbk) : £5.95 B81-10065

Oleksy, Jerome E.. Microprocessor and digital computer technology / Jerome E. Oleksy, George B. Rutkowski. — Englewood Cliffs ; London : Prentice-Hall, c1981. — xii, 419p : ill ; 25cm
Includes index
ISBN 0-13-581116-3 : Unpriced
Also classified at 621.3819'5835 B81-32616

Tomek, Ivan. Introduction to computer organization / Ivan Tomek. — London : Pitman, 1981. — xii,456p : ill ; 24cm. — (Digital system design series)
Originally published: Rockville, Md. : Computer Science Press, 1981. — Bibliography: p445-448. — Includes index
ISBN 0-273-01710-1 : Unpriced
ISBN 0-914894-08-0 (U.S.) B81-40391

621.3819'58 — Great Britain. Electronic point of sale systems — *Technical data*
Guide to retail data capture systems. — Brighton (5 East St., Brighton BN1 1HP) : Retail Management Development Programme, 1980 (1981 [printing]). — 264p : ill ; 30cm
Bibliography: p260-264
Unpriced (spiral) B81-08135

621.3819'58 — Microcomputers & microprocessors
Givone, Donald D.. Microprocessors / microcomputers : an introduction / Donald D. Givone, Robert P. Roesser. — Tokyo ; London : McGraw-Hill Kogakusha, c1980. — xii,420p : ill ; 21cm. — (McGraw-Hill series in electical engineering)
Bibliography: p408-409. - Includes index
ISBN 0-07-066298-3 (pbk) : £7.50 B81-10381

621.3819'582 — Digital computers. Arithmetic units
Spaniol, Otto. Computer arithmetic : logic and design / Otto Spaniol. — Chichester : Wiley, c1981. — 280p : ill ; 24cm. — (Wiley series in computing)
Translation from the German. — Bibliography: p266-278. - Includes index
ISBN 0-471-27926-9 : £13.50 B81-16333

621.3819'582 — Digital computers. Arithmetic units. Design
Gosling, John B.. Design of arithmetic units for digital computers / John B. Gosling. — London : Macmillan, 1980. — x,139p : ill ; 24cm. — (Macmillan computer science series)
Bibliography: p130-134. - Includes index
ISBN 0-333-26397-9 (cased) : £14.00 B81-04414

621.3819'582 — Digital computers. Design
Iliffe, J. K.. Advanced computer design. — London : Prentice-Hall, Jan.1982. — [400]p
ISBN 0-13-011254-2 : £15.00 : CIP entry B81-34419

621.3819'582 — Digital computers. Design. Applications of switching theory
Hill, Fredrick J.. Introduction to switching theory and logical design / Frederick [i.e. Fredrick] J. Hill, Gerald R. Peterson. — 3rd ed. — New York ; Chichester : Wiley, c1981. — xv,617p : ill ; 24cm
Previous ed.: 1974. — Includes index
ISBN 0-471-04273-0 : £16.30 B81-30804

621.3819'582 — Digital computers. Logic design
Wiatrowski, Claude A.. Logic circuits and microcomputer systems / Claude A. Wiatrowski, Charles H. House. — New York ; London : McGraw-Hill, c1980. — xiv,413p : ill ; 25cm. — (McGraw-Hill series in electrical engineering)
Includes index
ISBN 0-07-070090-7 : £17.95 B81-19472

621.3819'582 — Digital computers. Logic design & testing
Roth, J. Paul. Computer logic, testing and verification / J. Paul Roth. — London : Pitman Rc 1980. — xx,176p : ill ; 24cm. — (Digital system design series)
Includes bibliographies and index
ISBN 0-273-08475-5 : £15.50 B81-04511

621.3819'583 — Digital computers. Firmware & restructurable hardware
IFIP Working Conference on Firmware, Microprogramming and Restructurable Hardware *(1980 : Linz).* Firmware, microprogramming and restructurable hardware : proceedings of the IFIP Working Conference on Firmware, Microprogramming and Restructurable Hardware, Linz, Austria, April 28-May 1, 1980 / sponsored by IFIP Technical Committee 2: Programming ... [et al.] in co-operation with ACM SIGMICRO, IEEE TCMICRO ; program committee: F. Anceau ... [et al.] ; edited by Gerhard Chroust and Jörg R. Mühlbacher. — Amsterdam ; Oxford : North-Holland, 1980. — vii,310p : ill ; 23cm
Includes biliographies and index
ISBN 0-444-86056-8 : £17.05 B81-04788

621.3819'5832 — Digital computers. Peripheral equipment
Wilkinson, Barry, *1947-*. Computer peripherals / Barry Wilkinson and David Horrocks. — London : Hodder and Stoughton, 1980. — viii,310p : ill ; 24cm
Includes bibliographies and index
ISBN 0-340-23649-3 (cased) : £12.95 : CIP rev.
ISBN 0-340-32652-3 (pbk) : £6.75 B80-09270

621.3819'5833 — Digital computers. Direct access storage devices — *Technical data*
Computer hardware record : large random access storage systems. — [London] : National Computing Centre, c1980. — 1v.(loose-leaf) ; 23cm
Unpriced B81-16964

621.3819'5835 — Digital computers. Logic circuits
Hutchison, David, *1949-*. Fundamentals of computer logic / David Hutchinson. — Chichester : Ellis Horwood ; New York ; Chichester : Halsted Press, 1981. — 214p : ill ; 24cm. — (Ellis Horwood series in computers and their applications, ISSN ISSN 0271-6135)
Bibliography: p187-192. - Includes index
ISBN 0-85312-258-x : £17.50 B81-23113

621.3819'5835 — Great Britain. Manufactured goods. Microprocessors
Northcott, Jim. Microprocessors in manufactured products / Jim Northcott with John Marti, Anthony Zeilinger ; foreword by Sir Charles Carter. — London : Policy Studies Institute, 1980. — x,48p ; 21cm. — (Reports / Policy Studies Institute ; no.590)
ISBN 0-85374-185-9 (pbk) : £3.25 B81-07163

621.3819'58'35 — Industrial equipment. Microprocessors. Software. Design
Foulger, R. J.. Programming embedded microprocessors. — Manchester : NCC Publications, Feb.1982. — [230]p
ISBN 0-85012-344-5 (pbk) : £15.00 : CIP entry B81-37594

621.3819'5835 — Industrial equipment. Use of microprocessors

The Engineering of microprocessor systems : guidelines on system development / Electrical Research Association. — Oxford : Pergamon, 1979. — xii175p : ill ; 31cm. — (Pergamon international library)
ISBN 0-08-025435-7 (cased) : £7.75 : CIP rev.
ISBN 0-08-025434-9 (pbk) : £2.95 B79-28759

621.3819'5835 — Microcomputers. Circuits. Construction — *Amateurs' manuals*

Parr, E. A.. Practical computer experiments / by E.A. Parr. — London : Bernard Babani, 1980. — 91p : ill ; 18cm
ISBN 0-900162-98-8 (pbk) : £1.75 : CIP rev. B80-17761

621.3819'5835 — Microcomputers. Circuits. Construction. Projects — *Study examples: Motorola 6800 — Amateurs' manuals*

Clements, Alan. Building your own microcomputer. — London : Prentice-Hall, Feb.1982. — [600]p
ISBN 0-13-086223-1 : £17.95 : CIP entry B81-35790

621.3819'5835 — Microprocessors

Cahill, S. J.. Digital and microprocessor engineering. — Chichester : Ellis Horwood, Dec.1981. — [544]p. — (Ellis Horwood series in electrical and electronic engineering)
ISBN 0-85312-351-9 : £30.00 : CIP entry B81-35877

Heffer, D. E.. Basic principles and practice of microprocessors / D.E. Heffer, G.A. King and D. Keith. — London : Edward Arnold, 1981. — vii,200p : ill ; 25cm
Includes index
ISBN 0-7131-3426-7 (pbk) : £5.95 : CIP rev. B80-32775

Oleksy, Jerome E.. Microprocessor and digital computer technology / Jerome E. Oleksy, George B. Rutkowski. — Englewood Cliffs ; London : Prentice-Hall, c1981. — xii, 419p : ill ; 25cm
Includes index
ISBN 0-13-581116-3 : Unpriced
Primary classification 621.3819'58 B81-32616

Simmonds, W. H.. Microprocessors and their applications : with glossary of terms / W.H. Simmonds. — Chislehurst : Sira, 1978. — M-1—M-24,G-1—G-24p : ill ; 30cm
Unpriced (pbk) B81-32976

Wood, Alec. Microprocessors. — Sevenoaks : Newnes Technical Books, Oct.1981. — [144]p
ISBN 0-408-00580-7 (pbk) : £2.25 : CIP entry B81-25285

621.3819'5835 — Microprocessors. Applications — *For management*

Crabb, John H.. Microprocessors and management / by John H. Crabb. — London : Institute of Cost and Management Accountants, 1981. — 96p : ill ; 21cm
ISBN 0-901308-59-5 (pbk) : Unpriced B81-26898

621.3819'5835 — Microprocessors — *For technicians*

Sinclair, Ian. Microelectronic systems level 1. — Eastbourne : Holt, Rinehart and Winston, Jan.1982. — [112]p
ISBN 0-03-910313-7 (pbk) : £2.50 : CIP entry B81-35899

621.3819'5835 — Microprocessors. Maintenance & repair

Coffron, James W.. Practical troubleshooting techniques for microprocessor systems / James W. Coffron. — Englewood Cliffs ; London : Prentice-Hall, c1981. — lx,246p : ill ; 25cm
Includes index
ISBN 0-13-694273-3 : £13.95 B81-36596

621.3819'598 — Digital computers. Pattern recognition. Use of context

Fu, K. S.. Statistical pattern classification using contextual information / K.-S. Fu and T.S. Yu. — Chichester : Research Studies Press, c1980. — x,191p : ill ; 24cm. — (Electronic & electrical engineering research studies. Pattern recognition & image processing series ; 1)
ISBN 0-471-27859-9 : Unpriced : CIP rev. B80-35112

621.3819'598 — Image processing by digital computer systems

Structured computer vision : machine perception through hierarchical computation structures / edited by S. Tanimoto and A. Klinger. — New York ; London : Academic Press, 1980. — xi,234p : ill ; 24cm
Bibliography: p223-234
ISBN 0-12-683280-3 : £11.80 B81-33162

621.3819'598 — Image processing by digital computer systems - *Conference proceedings*

Languages and architecture for image processing. — London : Academic Press, July 1981. — [300]p
Conference papers
ISBN 0-12-223320-4 : CIP entry B81-14873

621.384 — RADIO AND RADAR

621.3841 — Radio equipment. Electromagnetic compatibility

Electromagnetic compatibility in radio engineering. — Oxford : Elsevier Scientific, Dec.1981. — [320]p. — (Studies in electrical and electronic engineering ; v.6)
ISBN 0-444-99722-9 : £40.00 : CIP entry B81-31613

621.3841 — Radio equipment. Electromagnetic compatibility — *Conference proceedings*

Proceedings of the conference on electromagnetic compatibility : University of Southampton, 16th-18th September 1980 / organized by the Institution of Electronic and Radio Engineers in association with the Institution of Electrical Engineers ... [et al.]. — London (99 Gower St., WC1E 6AZ) : IERE, c1980. — viii,396p : ill ; 30cm. — (IERE conference proceedings ; no.47)
Includes bibliographies and index
ISBN 0-903748-42-8 (pbk) : £28.00 B81-11339

621.3841 — Radio equipment — *For technicians*

Danielson, G. L.. Radio systems for technicians 2 / G.L. Danielson, R.S. Walker. — [London] : Butterworths, c1981. — 75p : ill ; 25cm. — (Butterworths TEC technician series)
ISBN 0-408-00561-0 (pbk) : Unpriced : CIP rev. B81-00135

Danielson, G. L.. Radio systems for technicians 3. — London : Butterworths, Feb.1982. — [112]p
ISBN 0-408-00588-2 (pbk) : £5.95 : CIP entry B81-36376

621.3841'068 — Radio engineering. Management aspects

Ross, John F.. Handbook for radio engineering managers / J.F. Ross. — London : Butterworths, 1980. — 947p : ill ; 24cm
Includes bibliographies and index
ISBN 0-408-00424-x : £35.00 B81-00945

621.3841'09417 — Ireland *(Republic).* **Radio engineering**

Radio science in Ireland / [editor B.K.P. Scaife]. — Dublin ([19, Dawson St., Dublin 2]) : Royal Irish Academy, 1981. — 16p ; 21cm
Cover title. — Text on inside covers. — Bibliography: p14-16
ISBN 0-901714-19-4 (pbk) : £0.50 B81-36798

621.3841'1 — Radio waves. Diffraction by antennas

Clarke, R. H. (Richard Henry). Diffraction theory and antennas / R.H. Clarke and John Brown. — Chichester : Horwood, 1980. — 292p : ill ; 24cm. — (Ellis Horwood series in electrical and electronic engineering)
Bibliography: p277-279. — Includes index
ISBN 0-85312-182-6 : £25.00 : CIP rev. B80-08799

621.3841'1 — Radio waves. Diffraction by aperture antennas

Jull, Edward V.. Aperture antennas and diffraction theory. — Stevenage : Peregrinus, July 1981. — [192]p. — (Electromagnetic wave series ; 10)
ISBN 0-906048-52-4 : £21.50 : CIP entry B81-13899

621.3841'1 — Radio waves. Long-distance reception — *Amateurs' manuals*

Penfold, R. A.. An introduction to radio dx-ing. — London : Babani, Sept.1981. — [128]p
ISBN 0-85934-066-x (pbk) : £1.95 : CIP entry B81-22539

621.3841'1 — Radio waves. Propagation — *Conference proceedings*

International Conference on Antennas and Propagation *(2nd : 1981 : University of York).* Second International Conference on Antennas Propagation : 13-16 April 1981 / organized by the Electronics Division of the Institution of Electrical Engineers in association with the Institute of Electrical and Electronics Engineers / Inc. (Antennas and Propagation Society) ... [et al.]. — [London] : [The Institution], [c1981]. — 2v. : ill ; 30cm. — (IEE Conference publications, ISSN 0527-9989 ; no.195)
Includes bibliographies
ISBN 0-85296-234-7 (pbk) : Unpriced
Primary classification 621.3841'35 B81-22904

621.3841'3 — Amateur radio equipment. Construction — *Manuals*

Hawker, Pat. Amateur radio techniques / Pat Hawker. — 7th ed. / diagrams drawn by Derek Cole. — London : Radio Society of Great Britain, 1980. — 368p ; 25cm
Previous ed.: 1978. — Includes index
ISBN 0-900612-51-7 (pbk) : £6.80 B81-00946

621.3841'3 — Synthetic materials - *For electronics - Conference proceedings*

Synthetic materials for electronics. — Oxford : Elsevier Scientific, Apr.1981. — [320]p. — (Materials science monographs ; 8)
Conference papers
ISBN 0-444-99741-5 : £45.00 : CIP entry B81-05159

621.3841'34'0212 — Radio equipment. Semiconductor devices — *Technical data*

Semiconductor data book : characteristics of approx. 10,000 transistors, FETs, UJTs, diodes, rectifiers, optical semiconductors, triacs and SCRs. — 11th ed / compiled by A.M. Ball. — London : Newnes Technical, 1981. — 175p ; 28cm
Previous ed.: published as Radio valve and semiconductor data. 1975
ISBN 0-408-00479-7 (pbk) : Unpriced : CIP rev. B81-20641

621.3841'35 — Radio equipment: Antennas — *Conference proceedings*

International Conference on Antennas and Propagation *(2nd : 1981 : University of York).* Second International Conference on Antennas Propagation : 13-16 April 1981 / organized by the Electronics Division of the Institution of Electrical Engineers in association with the Institute of Electrical and Electronics Engineers / Inc. (Antennas and Propagation Society) ... [et al.]. — [London] : [The Institution], [c1981]. — 2v. : ill ; 30cm. — (IEE Conference publications, ISSN 0527-9989 ; no.195)
Includes bibliographies
ISBN 0-85296-234-7 (pbk) : Unpriced
Also classified at 621.3841'1 B81-22904

621.3841'36 — Radio equipment: Receivers — *Conference proceedings*

Clerk Maxwell Commemorative Conference on Radio Receivers and Associated Systems *(1981 : University of Leeds).* Clerk Maxwell Commemorative Conference on Radio Receivers and Associated Systems, University of Leeds, 7-9 July 1981. — [London] : [Institution of Electronic and Radio Engineers], [c1981]. — 487p : ill ; 30cm. — (Proceedings / Institution of Electronic and Radio Engineers ; no.50)
ISBN 0-903748-45-2 (pbk) : Unpriced B81-36714

621.3841'36'09 — Radio equipment: Receivers, *to 1930 — Collectors' guides*

Constable, Anthony. Early wireless / Anthony Constable. — Tunbridge Wells : Midas, 1980. — 160p : ill,facsims ; 24cm. — (The Midas collectors' library)
Includes index
ISBN 0-85936-125-x : £8.50 B81-04475

621.3841'366 — Radio equipment: Crystal receivers. Projects *— Amateurs' manuals*

Wilson, F. A.. Electronics simplified : crystal set construction. — London : Babani, Oct.1981. — [96]p
ISBN 0-85934-067-8 (pbk) : £1.50 : CIP entry B81-27413

621.3841'51 — Amateur radio equipment

Stokes, Gordon. Amateur radio / by Gordon Stokes and Peter Bubb. — Guildford : Lutterworth, 1981. — 192p,8p of plates : ill ; 23cm. — (Practical handbook series)
Bibliography: p185. — Includes index
ISBN 0-7188-2477-6 : £8.95 B81-26830

621.3841'51 — Shortwave radio links

Wiesner, Lothar. Telegraph and data transmision over shortwave radio links. — 2nd ed. — London : Heyden, Apr.1981. — [200]p
Translation of: Fernschreib- und Datenübertragung über Kurzwelle. — Previous ed.: 1977
ISBN 0-85501-291-9 (pbk) : CIP entry B81-07464

621.3841'52 — Frequency modulation amateur radio equipment: Repeaters *— Lists — Serials*

The **International** VHF-FM guide. — 1981. — Maidenhead (41 Castle Drive, Maidenhead, Berks. SL6 6DB) : J. Baldwin & K. Partridge, c1981. — 112 in various pagings
ISBN 0-9506523-1-8 : £1.50 B81-27129

621.3841'66 — Amateur radio stations *— Manuals*

Hawker, Pat. A guide to amateur radio / Pat Hawker, G3VA. — 18th ed. — London : Radio Society of Great Britain, 1980. — 140p : ill ; 25cm
Previous ed.: London : Newnes-Butterworths, 1979. — Includes index
ISBN 0-900612-53-3 : Unpriced B81-02804

621.3841'66'02541 — Great Britain. Amateur radio stations *— Directories — Serials*

RSGB amateur radio call book. — 1981 ed.. — London : Radio Society of Great Britain, c1980. — 173p
ISBN 0-900612-52-5 : Unpriced B81-04847

621.3841'7 — Radio waves. Detectors, *to 1916*

Phillips, Vivian J.. Early radio wave detectors / Vivian J. Phillips. — Stevenage : Peregrinus in association with the Science Museum, c1980. — xv,223p : ill,1facsim,ports ; 23cm. — (History of technology series ; 2)
Bibliography: p217. — Includes index
ISBN 0-906048-24-9 : £16.00 : CIP rev. B80-17762

621.3841'85 — Shortwave radio equipment: Receivers. Construction *— Amateurs' manuals*

Rayer, F. G.. Projects in amateur radio : and short wave listening / F.G. Rayer. — London : Newnes Technical, 1981. — 90p : ill(some col.) ; 22cm. — (Newnes constructors projects)
ISBN 0-408-00502-5 (pbk) : Unpriced B81-29825

621.3845'4'0288 — Citizens' Band radio equipment. Accessories. Construction *— Amateurs' manuals*

Penfold, R. A.. C.B. projects. — London : Babani, Nov.1981. — [96]p
ISBN 0-85934-071-6 (pbk) : £1.95 : CIP entry B81-30885

621.3845'4'0288 — Citizens' Band radio equipment. Repair *— Amateurs' manuals*

Schultz, Lawrence E.. How to repair CB radios / Lawrence E. Schultz. — New York ; London : McGraw-Hill, c1980. — vii,184p : ill ; 21cm. — (Electro skills series)
Includes index
ISBN 0-07-055638-5 (pbk) : £7.45 B81-03624

621.3845'4'0321 — Great Britain. Citizens' Band radio communication. Jargon *— Dictionaries*

Moore, Chas. CB language : the complete dictionary of trucker talk / by Chas Moore (Mr. Blue Sky). — London : Star, 1981. — 122p ; 18cm
ISBN 0-352-30998-9 (pbk) : £1.35 B81-23583

Moore, Chas. CB language : the complete dictionary of trucker talk / Chas Moore. — London : W.H. Allen, 1981. — 122p ; 19cm
ISBN 0-491-02726-5 : £3.95 B81-30820

621.3845'4'0941 — Great Britain. Citizens' Band radio

Ainslie, Alan C.. UK CB handbook. — London : Newnes Technical Books, Jan.1982. — [200]p
ISBN 0-408-01177-7 (pbk) : £4.95 : CIP entry B81-34576

Big Hal's CB handbook. — London (124 Cornwall Rd., S.E.1) : Grant Jarvis, Sept.1981. — [80]p
ISBN 0-907741-00-2 (pbk) : £0.95 : CIP entry B81-27880

621.3845'4'0941 — Great Britain. Citizens' band radio

Nichols, Richard. CB Radio : a handbook / Richard Nichols. — [London] : Star, 1981. — 137p : ill,1map ; 18cm
ISBN 0-352-30882-6 (pbk) : £1.25 B81-17817

621.3845'4'0941 — Great Britain. Citizens' Band radio

Nichols, Richard. CB Radio : a handbook / Richard Nichols. — London : W.H. Allen, 1981. — 137p : ill,1map ; 19cm
ISBN 0-491-02716-8 : £3.95 B81-30818

621.3845'4'0941 — Great Britain. Citizens' Band radio communication *— Manuals*

Christos, George. CB for the serious user. — Amersham (Olympic House, 63 Woodside Rd, Amersham, Bucks. HP6 6AA) : Woodside Books, Dec.1981. — [160]p
ISBN 0-9507884-0-6 (pbk) : £2.99 : CIP entry B81-38296

621.3845'4'0941 — Great Britain. Citizens' Band radio communication *— Serials*

CB : citizens band. — Vol.1, no.1 (Dec. 1980)-. — London (145, Charing Cross Rd., WC2H 0EE) : Modmags, 1980-. — v. ; 29cm
Monthly
ISSN 0261-0361 = CB. Citizens band : £0.50 B81-13100

621.3845'4'0973 — United States. Citizens' Band radio communication

The **Big** dummy's guide to C.B. radio. — 2nd ed. — Summertown, Tenn. : Book Publishing Co. ; London (335 City Rd, E.C.1) : Distributed by Kona Publications, 1977. — 125p : ill
Previous ed.: 1976. — Includes index
ISBN 0-913990-04-3 (pbk) : Unpriced B81-19791

621.3845'4'0973 — United States. Citizens' Band radio communication *— Manuals*

Bradley, William J.. Citizens band radio digest / by William J. Bradley. — Northfield : DBI Books ; London : Arms and Armour [distributor], c1976. — 192p : ill ; 28cm
ISBN 0-695-80677-7 (pbk) : £3.00 B81-15703

621.3846 — Alaska. Long-distance telephone equipment: High frequency radio equipment

Schnurr, L.. Inter-exchange radio trunking using HF circuits : State of Alaska contract X20131, Institute project B7/79 / L. Schnurr. — Chelmsford ([Victoria Rd.], Chelmsford, Essex CM1 1LL) : Chelmer Institute of Higher Education, 1980. — 69p : ill ; 30cm
Cover title. — Alternate pages blank
ISBN 0-907262-02-3 (pbk) : Unpriced B81-25072

621.385 — TELEPHONY

621.385'092'4 — Telephony. Bell, Alexander Graham

Parton, Chris G.. Sound as a bell / Chris Parton. — Hamilton (Almada St., Hamilton, ML3 0JB, Lanarkshire) : Bell College of Technology, 1981. — 11p ; 30cm. — (Occasional papers / Bell College. Library)
ISBN 0-906249-03-1 (unbound) : £1.50 B81-26130

621.388 — TELEVISION

621.388 — Digital television equipment

Stafford, R. H.. Digital television : bandwidth reduction and communication aspects / R.H. Stafford. — New York ; Chichester : Wiley, c1980. — xiv,387p : ill ; 24cm
Bibliography: p325-371. - Includes index
ISBN 0-471-07857-3 : £18.70 B81-10543

621.388 — Personal video equipment

Newnes book of video / editor K.G. Jackson. — London : Newnes Technical, 1980. — 128p : ill,ports ; 25cm
Includes bibliographies and index
ISBN 0-408-00475-4 (pbk) : £5.95 : CIP rev. B80-12918

621.388 — Video equipment *— Amateurs' manuals*

Money, S. A.. Video equipment. — Sevenoaks : Newnes, Sept.1981. — [112]p. — (Questions and answers)
ISBN 0-408-00553-x (pbk) : £1.95 : CIP entry B81-23922

621.388 — Video equipment *— Buyers' guides — Serials*

Video review. — Dec.1980-. — Sutton : IPC Business Press, 1980-. — v. : ill,ports ; 30cm
Monthly
ISSN 0261-3263 = Video review : £10.00 per year
Also classified at 028.1'37 B81-25475

Video today. — Oct.1980-. — London : Modmags ; London : Argus Press Sales & Distribution [distributor], 1980-. — v. : ill (some col.),ports ; 29cm
Monthly
ISSN 0144-6010 = Video today : £10.00 per year
Also classified at 028.1'37 B81-25476

621.388 — Video equipment *— Manuals*

White, Gordon. Video explained. — Sevenoaks : Newnes, Dec.1981. — [288]p
ISBN 0-408-00506-8 : £9.95 : CIP entry B81-31735

621.388 — Video equipment *— Serials*

[**ACE international** *(English edition)*]. ACE international : the business magazine of the hi-fi/video industry in Europe. — [English ed.]. — Vol.1 (June 1977)-. — Fribourg ; London (189 Fore St., Angel Place, N18 2TU) : Ace international, 1977-. — v. : ill(some col.),ports ; 28cm
Nine issues yearly. — Also published in German, French and Italian editions. — Description based on: Vol.4, no.9
ISSN 0148-8856 = ACE international. English edition : Unpriced
Also classified at 621.389'3 B81-32238

621.388'00212 — Television equipment *— Technical data — Serials*

International video yearbook. — 1981-. — Poole : Blandford Press, 1981-. — v. : ill ; 23cm
Continues: Video yearbook
ISSN 0261-1910 = International video yearbook : £19.50 B81-16809

621.388'00973 — United States. Television

Television today : a close-up view : readings from TV guide / edited by Barry Cole. — Oxford : Oxford University Press, 1981. — xi,480p ; 21cm
Includes index
ISBN 0-19-502798-1 (cased) : Unpriced
ISBN 0-19-502799-x (pbk) : £4.25 B81-29452

621.388′07′10411 — Scotland. Schools. Curriculum subjects: Television

Scottish Council for Educational Technology. *Subcommittee on Educational Broadcasting.* Television studies in Scottish schools / Scottish Council for Educational Technology, Subcommittee on Educational Broadcasting ; edited by J.F. Murray. — Glasgow (74 Victoria Crescent Rd., Glasgow G12 9JN) : The Council, 1980. — iii,54p : ill ; 30cm. — (SCET occasional working paper ; no.6)
ISBN 0-86011-022-2 (pbk) : £2.00 B81-04848

621.389 — PUBLIC ADDRESS SYSTEMS, SOUND RECORDING, ETC

621.389′2 — Buildings. Burglar alarms

Barnard, Robert L. Intrusion detection systems : principles of operation and application / Robert L. Barnard. — Boston, [Mass.] ; London : Butterworth, c1981. — 339p : ill,plans ; 24cm
Bibliography: p321-325. — Includes index
ISBN 0-409-95026-2 : Unpriced B81-33232

621.389′3 — High-fidelity sound recording & reproduction equipment — *Buyers′ guides*

World hi-fi guide / [consultant Jonathan Kettle]. — London : Phoebus Publishing, 1981. — 64p : ill(some col.) ; 31cm
ISBN 0-7112-0093-9 : £3.95 B81-36889

621.389′3 — High-fidelity sound recording & reproduction equipment — *Serials*

[ACE international *(English edition)*]. ACE international : the business magazine of the hi-fi/video industry in Europe. — [English ed.]. — Vol.1 (June 1977)-. — Fribourg ; London (189 Fore St., Angel Place, N18 2TU) : Ace international, 1977-. — v. : ill(some col.),ports ; 28cm
Nine issues yearly. — Also published in German, French and Italian editions. — Description based on: Vol.4, no.9
ISSN 0148-8856 = ACE international. English edition : Unpriced
Primary classification 621.388 B81-32238

Hifi year book and home entertainment. — 1981-. — Sutton : IPC Electrical-Electronic Press, 1981-. — v. : ill ; 30cm
Continues: Hifi yearbook
ISSN 0260-7875 = Hifi year book and home entertainment : £3.00 B81-06688

621.389′32 — Sound recording — *Manuals*

Eargle, John. Sound recording / John Eargle. — 2nd ed. — New York ; London : Van Nostrand Reinhold, c1980. — xi,355p : ill ; 24cm
Previous ed.: 1976. — Includes bibliographies and index
ISBN 0-442-22557-1 : £16.45 B81-00136

621.389′32 — Sound recording. Techniques — *Manuals*

Tombs, David. Sound recording : from microphone to master tape / David Tombs. — Newton Abbot : David & Charles, c1980. — 222p : ill ; 23cm
Includes index
ISBN 0-7153-7954-2 : Unpriced : CIP rev. B80-18797

621.389′32 — Tape-slide presentations. Making — *Manuals*

Lewell, John. Multivision : the planning, preparation and projection of audio-visual presentations / by John Lewell. — London : Focal, c1980. — 251p,[8]p of plates : ill(some col.),1form ; 24cm
ISBN 0-240-51026-7 : £10.95 : CIP rev.
ISBN 0-8038-4728-9 (U.S.) B79-23909

621.389′33 — Juke boxes, *1937-1948* — *Illustrations*

Lynch, Vincent. Jukeboxes : the golden age / text by Vincent Lynch and Bill Henkin ; photographs by Kazuhiro Tsuruta ; preface by David Rubinson. — London : Thames and Hudson, 1981. — 110p : col.ill ; 21cm
ISBN 0-500-27241-7 (pbk) : £4.50 B81-38692

621.389′33 — Record players — *Collectors′ guides*

Proudfoot, Christopher. Collecting phonographs and gramophones / Christopher Proudfoot. — London : Studio Vista, 1980. — 119p : ill(some col.) ; 26cm. — (Christie′s South Kensington collectors series)
Bibliography: p118-119
ISBN 0-289-70883-4 : £6.95 B81-03631

621.389′332 — High-fidelity sound reproduction equipment. Construction — *Amateur′s manuals*

Rayer, F. G. Audio projects / by F.G. Rayer. — London : Babani, 1981. — 90p : ill ; 19cm. — (BP ; 90)
ISBN 0-85934-065-1 (pbk) : £1.95 : CIP rev. B81-15861

621.389′332′0294 — High-fidelity sound reproduction equipment — *Buyers′ guides* — *Serials*

World hi-fi guide. — 1981-. — London ([Holywell House, Worship St., EC2A 2EN]) : [Macdonald & Co.], 1980-. — v. : ill ; 30cm
ISSN 0261-5770 = World hi-fi guide : £1.50 B81-33323

621.39 — ELECTRICAL ENGINEERING. SPECIAL BRANCHES

621.39 — Electronic equipment. Filamentary A15 superconductors — *Conference proceedings*

Topical Conference on A15 Superconductors *(1980 : Brookhaven National Laboratory).* Filamentary A15 superconductors / edited by Masaki Suenaga and Alan F. Clark ; [proceedings of the Topical Conference on A15 Superconductors, sponsored by the ICMC, held at Brookhaven National Laboratory, Upton, New York, May 1980. — New York ; London : Plenum, c1980. — xv,368p : ill ; 26cm. — (Cryogenic materials series)
Includes index
ISBN 0-306-40622-5 : Unpriced B81-08455

621.4 — HEAT ENGINEERING AND PRIME MOVERS

621.4 — Alternative energy sources

Larsen, Egon. New sources of energy and power / Egon Larsen ; illustrations by George Foster. — Rev. ed. — London : Muller, 1980. — 136p : ill,maps,plans,ports ; 24cm
Previous ed.: 1976. — Bibliography: p129-130. - Includes index
ISBN 0-584-10371-9 : £6.95 : CIP rev. B80-07408

621.4 — Alternative energy sources — *Serials*

Alternative times : (the A.T.) : a rundown of alternative energy news and views — plus items on nuclear power — reviews — dates — information — and more. — No.2 (Apr.1981)-. — London (35 Wedmore St., N19 4RU) : R.Stevens, 1981-. — v. ; 30cm
Continues: The A.T.
ISSN 0261-6033 = Alternative times : £3.00 per year B81-33295

The A.T. : alternative times. — No.1 (Mar.1981). — London (The Shed, 35 Wedmore St., N19 4RU) : R. Stevens, 1981. — v. ; 30cm
Continued by: Alternative times. — Only one issue published
£0.15 per issue B81-33294

621.4 — Energy sources — *For children*

Dudley, Nigel. Energy / written by Nigel Dudley ; illustrated by Pat Borer. — Loughborough : Ladybird, c1981. — 50p : col.ill ; 18cm. — (Conservation)
Text, ill on lining papers. — Includes index
ISBN 0-7214-0636-x : £0.50 B81-28978

621.4 — Energy. Storage - *Conference proceedings*

International Conference on Energy Storage *(1981 : Brighton).* Proceedings of the International Conference on Energy Storage, Brighton, April 1981. — Bedford : BHRA Fluid Engineering, May 1981. — [700]p
ISBN 0-906085-50-0 (pbk) : £40.00 : CIP entry B81-08880

621.4 — Perpetual motion machines — *Proposals*

Plunkett, Olliver. Masses of energy / by Olliver Plunkett. — London (Poste Restante, 10 Parkway, N.W.1) : O. Plunkett, 1981. — 1sheet : 1ill ; 30x21cm
Unpriced B81-36687

621.4′0028′8 — Industrial energy supply equipment. Maintenance — *Manuals*

Elonka, Stephen Michael. Standard plant operators′ manual / Stephen Michael Elonka. — 3rd ed. — New York ; London : McGraw-Hill, c1980. — 541p : ill,1form,ports ; 25cm
Previous ed.: 1975. — Includes index
ISBN 0-07-019298-7 : £12.90 B81-00947

621.4′009 — Engines, *to 1979*

Day, John, *1918-*. Engines : the search for power / John Day. — London : Hamlyn, 1980. — 256p : ill(some col.) ; 31cm
Includes index
ISBN 0-600-33167-9 : £14.95 B81-04058

621.402 — Heat. Storage & regeneration

Schmidt, Frank W. Thermal energy storage and regeneration / Frank W. Schmidt, A. John Willmott. — Washington ; London : Hemisphere Publishing Corporation, c1981. — xvi,352p : ill ; 25cm. — (Series in thermal and fluids engineering)
Includes index
ISBN 0-07-055346-7 : £24.95 B81-23448

621.402 — Industrial processes. Wast heat. Recovery

Reay, David A. Heat recovery systems : a directory of equipment and techniques / D.A. Reay. — London : Spon, 1979. — xiv,590p : ill ; 26cm
Includes bibliographies and index
ISBN 0-419-11400-9 : £22.50 B81-04074

621.402 — Waste heat. Recovery. Techniques — *Serials*

Journal of heat recovery systems. — Vol.1, no.1 (1981)-. — Oxford : Pergamon, 1981-. — v. : ill ; 28cm
Quarterly
ISSN 0198-7593 = Journal of heat recovery systems : Unpriced B81-0904

621.402′028′7 — Heat engineering. Measurement

Preobrazhenskiĭ, V. P. Measurements and instrumentation in heat engineering / V.P. Preobrazhensky ; translated from the Russian by Boris Kuznetsov. — Moscow : Mir, 1980 ; [London] : Distributed by Central Books. — 2v. : ill ; 23cm
Translation of: Teplotekhnicheskie izmerenii͡a i pribory. — Includes index
ISBN 0-7147-1604-9 : £9.95 B81-2348

621.402′2′0911 — Cold regions. Materials. Heat transfer — *For construction industries*

Lunardini, Virgil J. Heat transfer in cold climates / Virgil J. Lunardini. — New York ; London : Van Nostrand Reinhold, c1981. — xiv,731p : ill,charts, maps ; 24cm
Includes bibliographies and index
ISBN 0-442-26250-7 : £33.60 B81-3681

621.402′3 — Furnaces. Combustion. Mathematical models

Khalil, Essam Eldin. Modelling of furnace and combustor flows. — Tunbridge Wells : Abacus Press, Jan.1982. — [300]p. — (Energy and engineering science series)
ISBN 0-85626-303-6 : £17.50 : CIP entry B81-3377

621.402′5 — Furnaces

Glinkov, M. A. A general theory of furnaces / M.A. Glinkov, G.M. Glinkov ; translated from the Russian by V. Afanasyev. — Moscow : Mir, 1981 ; [London] : Distributed by Central Books. — 286p : ill ; 21cm
Translation of: Obshchai͡a teorii͡a pecheĭ. — Bibliography: p280-281. — Includes index
ISBN 0-7147-1590-5 : £3.95 B81-2348

621.402'5 — Heat pipes

Ivanovskiĭ, M. N.. The physical properties of heat pipes. — Oxford : Clarendon Press, Sept.1981. — [250]p. — (Oxford studies in physics)
Translation of: Fizicheskie osnovy teplovykh trub
ISBN 0-19-851466-2 : £25.00 : CIP entry B81-22610

621.402'5 — Heat pipes — *Conference proceedings*

International Heat Pipe Conference *(4th : 1981 : London)*. Advances in heat pipe technology. — Oxford : Pergamon, Dec.1981. — [745]p
ISBN 0-08-027284-3 : £42.00 : CIP entry B81-31357

621.402'5 — Heat pumps

McMullan, J. T.. Heat pumps. — Bristol : Hilger, Sept.1981. — [180]p
ISBN 0-85274-419-6 : £15.00 : CIP entry B81-20547

621.43 — INTERNAL COMBUSTION ENGINES

621.43 — Internal combustion engines

Nunney, M. J.. Engine technology 1 / M.J. Nunney. — London : Butterworth, 1981. — 120p : ill ; 25cm. — (Butterworths technician series)
ISBN 0-408-00511-4 (pbk) : Unpriced : CIP rev. B81-00137

621.43 — Internal combustion engines. Gases. Flow

Benson, Rowland S.. The thermodynamics and gas dynamics of internal combustion engines. — Oxford : Clarendon Press
Vol.1. — Jan.1982. — [500]p
ISBN 0-19-856210-1 : £40.00 : CIP entry B81-34382

621.43'3 — Gas turbines

Harman, Richard T. C.. Gas turbine engineering : applications, cycles and characteristics / Richard T.C. Harman. — London : Macmillan, 1981. — xvii,270p : ill ; 25cm
Includes index
ISBN 0-333-24680-2 (cased) : £18.00
ISBN 0-333-30476-4 (pbk) : £8.95 B81-15035

621.43'3 — Gas turbines. Aerothermodynamics

Whittle, *Sir* Frank. Gas turbine aero-thermodynamics : with special reference to aircraft propulsion / Sir Frank Whittle. — Oxford : Pergamon, 1981. — xii,261p,[1]leaf of plates : ill,1port ; 26cm. — (Pergamon international library)
ISBN 0-08-026719-x (cased) : Unpriced
ISBN 0-08-026718-1 (pbk) : £7.50 B81-27807

621.43'3 — Gas turbines. Materials

Developments in gas turbine materials. — London : Applied Science, May 1981. — (Developments series)
1. — [208]p
ISBN 0-85334-952-5 : £14.00 : CIP entry B81-10501

621.43'52 — Turbojets, *to 1945*

Constant, Edward W.. The origins of the turbojet revolution / Edward W. Constant II. — Baltimore ; London : Johns Hopkins University Press, c1980. — xiv,311p : ill ; 24cm. — (Johns Hopkins studies in the history of technology. New series ; no.5)
Includes index
ISBN 0-8018-2222-x : £13.50 B81-11815

621.43'6'094 — European diesel engines — *Technical data — Serials*

Diesel engines for the world. — 1980/81 ed. — Maidstone (Earl House, Earl St., Maidstone, Kent ME14 1PE) : Whitehall Press, c1980. — 151p
ISSN 0141-1381 : Unpriced B81-29969

621.44 — GEOTHERMAL ENGINEERING

621.44 — Energy sources: Geothermal energy — *Conference proceedings*

International Seminar on the Results of EC Geothermal Energy Research *(2nd : 1980 : Strasbourg)*. Advances in European geothermal research : proceedings of the Second International Seminar on the Results of EC Geothermal Energy Research, 4-6 March 1980 / edited by A.S. Strub and P. Ungemach. — Dordrecht ; London : Reidel, c1980. — xvi,1086p : ill,ports ; 24cm
At head of title: Commission of European Communities
ISBN 90-277-1138-0 : Unpriced B81-39184

621.45 — WIND POWER

621.4'5 — England. Midlands. Windmills — *Serials*

Wind and water mills : the occasional journal of the Midland Wind and Water Mills Group. — No.1 (Summer 1980)-. — Smethwick ([c/o John Bedington, 188 Merivale Rd, Smethwick, West Midlands, B66 4EA]) : The Group, 1980-. — v. : ill ; 21cm
Annual
ISSN 0260-504x = Wind and water mills : £0.75 (free to Group members)
Primary classification 621.2'1 B81-04144

621.4'5 — England. Windmills

Vince, John. Discovering windmills / John Vince ; line drawings by the author. — [New] ed. — Aylesbury : Shire, 1981. — 64p : ill ; 18cm. — (Discovering series ; no.13)
Previous ed.: 1977. — Bibliography: p63. — Includes index
ISBN 0-85263-567-2 (pbk) : £1.25 B81-40741

621.4'5 — Leicestershire. Windmills

Moon, Nigel. The windmills of Leicestershire and Rutland / Nigel Moon. — Melton Mowbray (Wymondham, Melton Mowbray, Leics.) : Sycamore, 1981. — 214p : ill ; 29cm
Limited ed. of 500 numbered copies. — Bibliography: p211
ISBN 0-905837-09-6 : £24.00 B81-31668

621.4'5 — Wiltshire. Windmills, *to 1979*

Watts, Martin. Wiltshire windmills / Martin Watts. — Trowbridge (Bythesea Rd., Trowbridge, Wilts.) : Wiltshire Library & Museum Service, 1980. — 48p : ill,1map ; 21cm
Map on inside cover. — Bibliography: p43
ISBN 0-86080-067-9 (pbk) : £1.75 B81-04432

621.4'5 — Wind power

Hunt, V. Daniel. Windpower : a handbook on wind energy conversion systems / V. Daniel Hunt. — New York ; London : Van Nostrand Reinhold, c1981. — xvii,610p : ill,maps ; 26cm
Bibliography: p508-520. — Includes index
ISBN 0-442-27389-4 : £29.65 B81-21174

621.4'5 — Wind power — *For children*

Catherall, Ed. Wind power / Ed Catherall ; [illustrated by Ted Draper]. — Hove : Wayland, 1981. — 32p : col.ill ; 24cm. — (Young scientist)
ISBN 0-85340-820-3 : £2.95 B81-24337

621.45 — Wind power systems — *Conference proceedings*

BWEA Wind Energy Conference *(3rd : 1981 : Cranfield)*. Proceedings of the Third BWEA Wind Energy Conference. — Cranfield : BHRA Fluid Engineering, July 1981. — [220]p
ISBN 0-906085-56-x (pbk) : £25.00 : CIP entry B81-22587

621.4'5 — Wind power systems — *Conference proceedings*

International Symposium on Wind Energy Systems *(3rd : 1980 : Lyngby)*. Papers presented at the Third International Symposium on Wind Energy Systems held in Lyngby, Copenhagen, Denmark, August 26th-29th, 1980 / organised and sponsored by BHRA Fluid Engineering, the Technical University of Denmark ; [editors H.S. Stephens, C.A. Stapleton]. — Cranfield : BHRA Fluid Engineering, c1980. — vii,579p : ill,maps ; 30cm
ISBN 0-906085-47-0 (pbk) : £35.00 : CIP rev. B80-12922

621.46 — ELECTRIC MOTORS, ION MOTORS, PLASMA MOTORS

621.46'2 — Direct current electric motors. Variable speed drives. Control devices: Thyristor circuits

Sen, P. C.. Thyristor DC drives / P.C. Sen. — New York ; Chichester : Wiley, c1981. — xix,307p : ill ; 24cm
Includes index
ISBN 0-471-06070-4 : £24.00 B81-23427

621.46'2 — Electric motors

Hindmarsh, J.. Worked examples in electrical machines and drives. — Oxford : Pergamon, Aug.1981. — [150]p. — (Applied electricity and electronics) (Pergamon international library)
ISBN 0-08-026131-0 (cased) : £8.50 : CIP entry
ISBN 0-08-026130-2 (pbk) : £5.00 B81-16396

621.46'2 — Low noise electric motors

Yang, S. J.. Low-noise electrical motors / S.J. Yang. — Oxford : Clarendon Press, 1981. — x,101p : ill ; 24cm. — (Monographs in electrical and electronic engineering) (Oxford science publications)
Includes bibliographies and index
ISBN 0-19-859332-5 : £12.50 : CIP rev. B81-08907

621.47 — SOLAR ENERGY ENGINEERING

621.47 — Solar energy

Rapp, Donald. Solar energy / Donald Rapp. — Englewood Cliffs ; London : Prentice-Hall, c1981. — xi,516p : ill ; 24cm
Includes index
ISBN 0-13-822213-4 : £20.80 B81-16647

Solar energy handbook / Jan F. Kreider, editor-in-chief and Frank Kreith. — New York ; London : McGraw Hill, c1981. — 1,120p in various pagings : ill,ports ; 24cm. — (McGraw-Hill series in modern structures)
Includes bibliographies and index
ISBN 0-07-035474-x : £25.50 B81-24257

621.47 — Solar energy collectors. Solar selective surfaces

Agnihotri, O. P.. Solar selective surfaces / O.P. Agnihotri, B.K. Gupta. — New York ; Chichester : Wiley, c1981. — xx,215p : ill ; 24cm. — (Alternate energy)
Includes index
ISBN 0-471-06035-6 : £21.75 B81-23717

621.47 — Solar energy — *Conference proceedings*

Conference on Solar Energy *(1980 : London)*. Solar energy in the 80s : proceedings of the Conference on Solar Energy held in London, 14-15 January 1980 / organised by Heliotechnic Associates International, London ; edited by Costis Stambolis. — Oxford : Pergamon, 1981. — x,235p : ill,plans ; 26cm
Includes index
ISBN 0-08-026123-x : £26.00 B81-08213

Recent developments in solar energy : proceedings of a symposium organised by the Institute of Mathematics and its Applications held in Dublin on February 17th, 1977. — Southend-on-Sea (Maitland House, Warrior Sq., Southend-on-Sea, Essex SS1 2JY) : The Institute, c1977. — v,73p : ill ; 20cm. — (Symposium proceedings series / Institute of Mathematics and its Applications ; no.15)
Includes bibliographies
Unpriced (spiral) B81-13275

621.47 — Solar energy — *For children*

Catherall, Ed. Solar power / Ed Catherall ; [illustrated by Ted Draper]. — Hove : Wayland, 1981. — 32p : col.ill ; 24cm. — (Young scientist)
ISBN 0-85340-819-x : £2.95 B81-24334

621.47 — Solar energy — *For engineering*

Duffie, John A.. Solar engineering of thermal processes / John A. Duffie, William A. Beckman. — New York ; Chichester : Wiley, c1980. — xvii,762p : ill ; 25cm
Includes bibliographies and index
ISBN 0-471-05066-0 : £13.90 B81-04138

621.47'028 — Solar energy equipment

O'Connor, Daniel J.. 101 patented solar energy uses / Daniel J. O'Connor. — New York ; London : Van Nostrand Reinhold, c1981. — 110p : chiefly ill,plans ; 28cm
Includes index
ISBN 0-442-24432-0 (pbk) : £6.70 B81-11421

621.47'028 — Solar energy equipment. Materials

Solar materials science / edited by Lawrence E. Murr. — New York ; London : Academic Press, 1980. — xii,788p : ill ; 24cm
Includes bibliographies and index
ISBN 0-12-511160-6 : £19.60 B81-05849

621.47'09 — Solar energy. Applications, *to 1979*

Butti, Ken. A golden thread : 2500 years of solar architecture and technology / by Ken Butti and John Perlin. — London : Boyars, 1981, c1980. — xi,289p : ill,facsims,maps,plans,ports ; 24cm
Originally published: Palo Alto : Cheshire Books ; New York, London : Van Nostrand Reinhold, 1980. — Includes index
ISBN 0-7145-2730-0 (pbk) : £5.95 : CIP rev. B81-03706

621.47'1 — Solar energy. Storage — *Conference proceedings*

Thermal storage of solar energy : proceedings of an international TNO-symposium held in Amsterdam, The Netherlands, 5-6 November 1980 : co-sponsored by Commission of the European Communities, Dutch Section of the International Solar Energy Society, The Royal Institution of Engineers in The Netherlands / C. den Ouden (editor). — The Hague ; London : Nijhoff, c1981. — 371p : ill ; 25cm
At head of title: Netherlands Organization for Applied Scientific Research. — Includes index
ISBN 90-247-2492-9 : Unpriced B81-23255

621.48 — NUCLEAR ENGINEERING

621.48 — Nuclear engineering

Knief, Ronald Allen. Nuclear energy technology : theory and practice of commercial nuclear power / Ronald Allen Knief. — Washington [D.C.] ; London : Hemisphere Publishing ; New York ; London : McGraw-Hill, c1981. — xv,605p : ill,1map ; 25cm. — (McGraw-Hill series in nuclear engineering)
Ill on lining papers. — Bibliography: p571-587. — Includes index
ISBN 0-07-035086-8 : £20.95 B81-32305

621.48 — Nuclear power

Bennet, Donald J.. The elements of nuclear power / D.J. Bennet. — 2nd ed. — London : Longman, 1981. — xxi,232p : ill ; 24cm
Previous ed.: 1972. — Bibliography: p226. — Includes index
ISBN 0-582-30504-7 (pbk) : £7.95 B81-27109

Greenhalgh, Geoffrey. The necessity for nuclear power / Geoffrey Greenhalgh. — London : Graham & Trotman, 1980. — xiv,250p : ill ; 25cm
ISBN 0-86010-201-7 (cased) : £16.00
ISBN 0-86010-249-1 (pbk) : £6.50 B81-12966

Murray, Raymond L.. Nuclear energy : an introduction to the concepts, systems, and applications of nuclear processes / Raymond L. Murray. — 2nd ed. (in SI/metric units). — Oxford : Pergamon, 1980. — xix,317p : ill ; 24cm. — (Pergamon international library) (Pergamon unified engineering series ; v.22)
Previous ed.: 1975. — Includes index
ISBN 0-08-024751-2 (cased) : £15.00 : CIP rev.
ISBN 0-08-024750-4 (pbk) : £6.50 B80-06459

621.48 — Nuclear power — *Conference proceedings*

Uranium and nuclear energy: 1980 : proceedings of the Fifth International Symposium held by the Uranium Institute, London, 2-4 September 1980. — Guildford (PO Box 63, Bury St., Guildford GU2 5BH) : Westbury House in cooperation with the Uranium Institute, c1981. — xvi,359p : ill,1map ; 24cm
ISBN 0-86103-041-9 : Unpriced B81-14695

621.48 — Nuclear power — *For children*

Hawkes, Nigel. Nuclear / Nigel Hawkes. — London : Watts, 1981. — 38p : col.ill,1col.map,1col.plan,ports ; 30cm. — (Energy)
Ill on lining papers. — Includes index
ISBN 0-85166-870-4 : £3.99 B81-13685

621.48 — Nuclear power industries. Accidents — *Conference proceedings*

Planning for rare events : nuclear accident preparedness and management. — Oxford : Pergamon, Dec.1981. — [280]p. — (IIASA proceedings series ; v.14)
Conference papers
ISBN 0-08-028703-4 : £27.50 : CIP entry B81-32041

621.48 — Nuclear power — *S.C.R.A.M. viewpoints*

Nuclear power : anyone interested? : a simple illustrated guide to Scotland's possible energy options / [editorial team : Ian Baird ... et al.]. — Aberdeen (163 King St., Aberdeen) : Aberdeen People's Press, 1980. — 32p : ill,1map ; 22cm
Text on inside covers. — Bibliography: on inside cover
ISBN 0-906074-11-8 (pbk) : £0.75 B81 33108

621.48 — Nuclear power — *Third World First & Students Against Nuclear Energy viewpoints*

Nuclear links : the chain-reaction of energy arms and underdevelopment / edited by Adi Cooper ... [et al.]. — London (9 Poland St., W.C.1) : Students Against Nuclear Energy, [1981]. — 33p : ill ; 30cm
Bibliography: p33
£0.50 (pbk) B81-18992

621.48'01'54 — Nuclear power. Chemical aspects

Benedict, Manson. Nuclear chemical engineering. — 2nd ed. / Manson Benedict, Thomas H. Pigford, Hans Wolfgang Levi. — New York ; London : McGraw-Hill, c1981. — xv,1008p : ill ; 25cm. — (McGraw-Hill series in nuclear engineering)
Previous ed.: 1957. — Includes index
ISBN 0-07-004531-3 : £24.25 B81-29827

621.48'05 — Nuclear power — *Serials*

Atomic energy news : bulletin of the Institution of Nuclear Engineers. — Apr.1980-. — London (1 Penerley Rd, SE6 2LQ) : The Institution, 1980-. — v. : ill ; 30cm
Monthly
ISSN 0260-3020 = Atomic energy news : [Unpriced] B81-07006

Progress in nuclear energy. — Vol.7. — Oxford : Pergamon, Nov.1981. — [234]p
ISBN 0-08-029090-6 : £40.00 : CIP entry B81-32015

621.48'06 — Nuclear power. Organisations — *Directories*

The Nuclear power issue : a guide to who's doing what in the U.S. and abroad / edited by Kimberly J. Mueller. — Claremont : California Institute of Public Affairs ; London : Prior [[distributor]], c1981. — 106p : ill ; 28cm. — (Who's doing what series ; 8)
Includes index
ISBN 0-912102-44-6 (pbk) : £9.50 B81-22134

621.48'072041 — Great Britain. Nuclear engineering. Research organisations: United Kingdom Atomic Energy Authority — *Serials*

United Kingdom Atomic Energy AuthorityReport and accounts of the United Kingdom Atomic Energy Authority for the year ended 31 March ... — 1980. — London : 11 Charles II St., SW1Y 4QP : The Authority, [1980]. — 76p
ISBN 0-7058-0812-2 : £2.00 B81-01759

621.48'0941 — Great Britain. Nuclear power

Bacon, Hilary. Power corrupts : the arguments against nuclear power / Hilary Bacon and John Valentine. — London : Pluto, 1981. — 95p ; 20cm
ISBN 0-86104-345-6 (pbk) : £1.50 B81-27490

Bunyard, Peter. Nuclear Britain / Peter Bunyard. — London : New English Library, 1981. — 207p ; 18cm
Bibliography: p207
ISBN 0-450-05108-0 (pbk) : £1.50 B81-29637

621.48'0941 — Great Britain. Nuclear power — *Fabian viewpoints*

Cook, Robin F.. No nukes! / Robin Cook. — London : Fabian Society, 1981. — 24p : ill ; 22cm. — (Fabian tract, ISSN 0307-7535 ; 475)
Text on inside covers. — Includes bibliographies
ISBN 0-7163-0475-9 (pbk) : £0.75 B81-33010

621.48'0941 — Great Britain. Nuclear power. First report from the Select Committee on Energy, session 1980-81 — *Critical studies*

Great Britain. *Department of Energy*. Nuclear power : the Government's response to the Select Committee on Energy's report on the Nuclear power programme, session 1980-81, H.C. 114-1. — London : H.M.S.O., [1981]. — 22p ; 25cm. — (Cmnd. ; 8317)
At head of title: Department of Energy
ISBN 0-10-183170-6 (unbound) : £2.30 B81-35385

621.48'0941 — Great Britain. Nuclear power. Proposals — *Inquiry reports*

First report from the Select Committee on Energy, session 1980-81 : the government's statement on the new nuclear power programme. — London : H.M.S.O., 1981
Vol.1: Report and minutes of proceedings. — 124p ; 25cm. — (HC ; 114-I)
ISBN 0-10-276181-7 (pbk) : £5.30 B81-14319

First report from the Select Committee on Energy, session 1980-81 : the government's statement on the new nuclear power programme. — London : H.M.S.O., 1981
Vol.2: Minutes of evidence (Part 1). — xii,641p,[1]folded leaf ; 25cm. — (HC : 114-II)
ISBN 0-10-275681-3 (pbk) : £14.70 B81-14320

First report from the Select Committee on Energy, session 1980-81 : the government's statement on the new nuclear power programme. — London : H.M.S.O., 1981
Vol.3: Minutes of evidence (Part 2) ; Appendices (Part 1). — ixp,p644-1031 : ill,maps ; 25cm. — (HC ; 114-iii)
ISBN 0-10-275381-4 (pbk) : £9.90 B81-14321

First report from the Select Committee on Energy, session 1980-81 : the government's statement on the new nuclear power programme. — London : H.M.S.O., 1981
Vol.4: Appendices (Part 2). — xiiip,p1032-1342 : ill ; 25cm. — (HC ; 114-iv)
ISBN 0-10-275481-0 (pbk) : £8.70 B81-14322

621.48'0941 — Great Britain. Nuclear power — *Socialist Workers Party viewpoints*

Simons, Mike. Worker's power, not nuclear power : a Socialist Workers' Party pamphlet / by Mike Simons. — [London] ([265 Seven Sisters Rd, N4 2DE]) : [Socialists Unlimited], [1980]. — 47p : ill,2maps ; 21cm
Cover title. — Bibliography: p47
ISBN 0-905998-08-1 (pbk) : £0.50 B81-1627

621.48'0947 — Soviet Union. Nuclear engineering

Petros'īants, A. M.. Problems of nuclear science and technology : the Soviet Union as a world nuclear power / by A.M. Petrosy'ants ; translated from the Russian by W.E. Jones. — 4th ed., (rev. and enl.) (1st English ed.). — Oxford : Pergamon, 1981. — xv,417p : ill ; 26cm
Translation of: Problemy atomnoi nauki i tekhniki. 4th ed., (rev. and enl.)
ISBN 0-08-025462-4 : £23.00 : CIP rev. B80-2714

621.48'3 — Nuclear reactors

Glasstone, Samuel. Nuclear reactor engineering / Samuel Glasstone, and Alexander Sesonske ; prepared under the auspices of the Technical Information Center, U.S. Department of Energy. — 3rd ed. — New York ; London : Van Nostrand Reinhold, c1981. — xv,805p : ill ; 24cm
Previous ed.: 1967. — Includes bibliographies and index
ISBN 0-442-20057-9 : £29.65 B81-1718

621.48'3 — Nuclear reactors. Use of water. Chemical aspects — *Conference proceedings*

Water chemistry of nuclear reactor systems 2 : proceedings of an international conference organized by the British Nuclear Energy Society and co-sponsored by the Royal Society of Chemistry, Bournemouth, 14-17 October, 1980. — London ([1 Great George St., SW1P 3AA]) : British Nuclear Energy Society, 1981. — 426p : ill ; 30cm
ISBN 0-7277-0126-6 (pbk) : £40.00 B81-30815

621.48'32 — Nuclear reactors. Design. Thermal factors

Winterton, R. H. S.. Thermal design of nuclear reactors / R.H.S. Winterton. — Oxford : Pergamon, 1981. — x,192p : ill ; 26cm. — (Pergamon international library)
Includes index
ISBN 0-08-024215-4 (cased) : Unpriced
ISBN 0-08-024214-6 (pbk) : £7.50 B81-27804

621.48'323 — Nuclear reactors. Radiation shields. Design. Applications of digital computer systems

Wood, J.. Computational methods in reactor shielding. — Oxford : Pergamon, Dec.1981. — [450]p. — (Pergamon international library)
ISBN 0-08-028685-2 (cased) : £25.00 : CIP entry
ISBN 0-08-028686-0 (pbk) : £9.50 B81-33856

621.48'332 — Nuclear power stations. Construction materials

Roberts, J. T. Adrian. Structural materials in nuclear power systems / J.T. Adrian Roberts. — New York ; London : Plenum, c1981. — xiii,485p : ill ; 24cm. — (Modern perspectives in energy)
Includes index
ISBN 0-306-40669-1 : Unpriced B81-31775

621.48'335 — Irradiated nuclear fuels. Testing — *Conference proceedings*

Post-irradiation examination : proceedings of the conference held in Grange-over-Sands on 13-16 May 1980. — London (c/o Telford, 1 Great George St., SW1P 3AA) : British Nuclear Energy Society, 1981. — 366p : ill ; 30cm
ISBN 0-7277-0111-8 (pbk) : £36.00 B81-17767

621.48'35 — Cumbria. Sellafield. Nuclear reactors: British Nuclear Fuels Limited *Windscale and Calder Works.* **Safety measures**

Great Britain. *Health and Safety Executive.* Windscale : management of safety. — London : Health & Safety Executive, Apr.1981. — [40]p
ISBN 0-7176-0076-9 (pbk) : CIP entry B81-10515

621.48'35 — Great Britain. Nuclear reactors. Inspection — *Conference proceedings*

Symposium on Inspection of UK Reactors *(1980 : Newport, Glos.).* Proceedings of Symposium on Inspection of UK Reactors : 30th September 1980, Newport, Glos. / [organized by] BNES Western Branch. — [London] : [Telford for the British Nuclear Energy Society], [1981]. — 415p in various pagings : ill ; 32cm
ISBN 0-7277-0137-1 : £25.00 B81-35406

621.48'35 — Nuclear reactors. Steel pressure vessels. Fracture toughness. Non-destructive testing — *Conference proceedings*

International Seminar on Non-Destructive Examination in Relation to Structural Integrity *(1st : 1979 : West Berlin).* Non-destructive examination in relation to structural integrity : proceedings of the 1st International Seminar on 'Non-destructive Examination in Relation to Structural Integrity' held at the International Congress Center Berlin, Berlin (West), Germany, 22nd August 1979, in conjunction with the 5th International Conference on Structural Mechanics in Reactor Technology / organizational support, Bundesanstalt für Materialprüfung (BAM), Berlin, ICC Department of Organization and Operation ; Seminar Technical Co-ordinator and Chairman, R.W. Nichols ; edited by R.W. Nichols. — London : Applied Science, c1980. — xviii,294p : ill ; 23cm
Includes index
ISBN 0-85334-908-8 : £24.00 : CIP rev. B80-17764

621.48'37'0289 — Radioactive materials. Handling — *Manuals*

Stewart, Donald C.. Handling radioactivity : a practical approach for scientists and engineers / Donald C. Stewart. — New York ; Chichester : Wiley, c1981. — xiv,282p : ill ; 24cm
Includes index
ISBN 0-471-04557-8 : £20.00 B81-17089

621.48'38 — Nuclear waste materials. Disposal

Lindblom, Ulf. Nuclear waste disposal. — Oxford : Pergamon, June 1981. — [80]p
ISBN 0-08-027608-3 (cased) : £7.50 : CIP entry
ISBN 0-08-027595-8 (pbk) : £3.95 B81-16853

621.48'38 — Radioactive waste materials. Disposal

Dlouhý, Zdeněk. Disposal of radioactive wastes. — Oxford : Elsevier Scientific, Dec.1981. — [300]p. — (Studies in environmental science ; 15)
ISBN 0-444-99724-5 : £35.00 : CIP entry B81-31615

621.48'38'0155 — Radioactive waste materials. Disposal within rock. Geological aspects — *Conference proceedings*

Predictive geology. — Oxford : Pergamon, Dec.1981. — [222]p. — (Computers & geology)
Conference papers
ISBN 0-08-026246-5 : £17.50 : CIP entry B81-32042

621.48'4 — Fusion reactors. Plasmas

Plasma physics and nuclear fusion research / edited by Richard D. Gill. — London : Academic Press, 1981. — xx,688p : ill ; 26cm
Includes bibliographies and index
ISBN 0-12-283860-2 : £27.60 B81-30643

621.48'4'07204 — Europe. Nuclear fusion technology. Research organisations: Joint European Torus, *1965-1980*

Willson, Denis. A European experiment. — Bristol : Hilger, Oct.1981. — [175]p
ISBN 0-85274-543-5 (cased) : £10.00 : CIP entry
ISBN 0-85274-549-4 (pbk) : £5.00 B81-27377

621.5 — PNEUMATIC, VACUUM, LOW TEMPERATURE TECHNOLOGY

621.5 — Pneumatic engineering

Paterson, E. B.. Practical pneumatics : an introduction to low cost automation / E.B. Paterson. — Auckland ; London : McGraw-Hill, c1979. — 143p : ill ; 31cm
Includes index
£11.95 (corrected) B81-29947

621.5'1 — Compressors

Cherkasskiĭ, V. M.. Pumps, fans, compressors / V.M. Cherkassky ; translated from the Russian by B.A. Nikolaev. — Moscow : Mir ; [London] : Distributed by Central Books, 1980. — 388p : ill ; 23cm
Translation of: Nasosy, ventilíatory, kompressory. — Includes index
ISBN 0-7147-1594-8 : £4.50
Also classified at 621.6 B81-23594

621.5'5 — Vacuum technology

O'Hanlon, John F.. A user's guide to vacuum technology / John F. O'Hanlon. — New York ; Chichester : Wiley, c1980. — xiii,402p : ill ; 24cm
Includes index
ISBN 0-471-01624-1 : £13.35 B81-00948

621.5'6 — Industries. Ammonia absorption refrigeration

Bogart, Marcel. Ammonia absorption refrigeration in industrial processes / Marcel Bogart. — Houston ; London : Gulf Publishing, c1981. — x,475p,[3]leaves of plates (2folded) : ill ; 24cm
Includes index
ISBN 0-87201-027-9 : £37.50 B81-32884

621.5'6 — Refrigeration

Dossat, Roy J.. Principles of refrigeration / Roy J. Dossat. — 2nd ed., SI version. — New York ; Chichester : Wiley, c1981. — 612p : ill ; 24cm
Previous ed.: 1961. — Includes index
ISBN 0-471-06219-7 : £14.70 B81-09757

Trott, A. R.. Refrigeration and air-conditioning / A.R. Trott. — London : McGraw-Hill, c1981. — 310p : ill ; 24cm
Includes index
ISBN 0-07-084543-3 : £12.95
Also classified at 697.9 B81-25146

621.5'7 — Developing countries. Medical equipment: Vaccine storage refrigerators. Maintenance & use — *Manuals*

Elford, Jonathan. How to look after a refrigerator / author Jonathan Elford ; language consultant Sam McCarter ; illustration and design Richard Inglis Associates ; production editor Denise Ayres. — London (85 Marylebone High St., W1M 3DE) : AHRTAG, c1980. — 58p : ill,1form ; 27cm
ISBN 0-907320-00-7 (pbk) : Unpriced B81-04952

621.5'7'0288 — Refrigeration equipment. Servicing - *For apprentices*

Reed, G. H.. Refrigeration. — 2nd ed. — London : Applied Science, July 1981. — [248]p
Previous ed.: 1972
ISBN 0-85334-964-9 : £12.00 : CIP entry B81-13735

621.5'7'0288 — Refrigeration equipment. Servicing — *Manuals*

Meredith, F. H.. Refrigeration technician's pocket book / F.H. Meredith. — London : Butterworths, 1981. — 133p : ill ; 19cm
Includes index
ISBN 0-408-00545-9 (pbk) : Unpriced B81-27141

621.5'9'05 — Crogenic engineering — *Conference proceedings — Serials*

Advances in cryogenic engineering. — Vol.25. — New York ; London : Plenum Press, c1980. — xvi,852
ISBN 0-306-40504-0 : Unpriced B81-09288

621.5'9'05 — Cryogenic engineering — *Conference proceedings — Serials*

Advances in cryogenic engineering. — Vol.26. — New York ; London : Plenum Press, c1980. — xiv,703p
ISBN 0-306-40531-8 : Unpriced
ISSN 0065-2482 B81-20721

621.6 — ENGINEERING. FANS, BLOWERS, PUMPS

621.6 — Fans & pumps

Cherkasskiĭ, V. M.. Pumps, fans, compressors / V.M. Cherkassky ; translated from the Russian by B.A. Nikolaev. — Moscow : Mir ; [London] : Distributed by Central Books, 1980. — 388p : ill ; 23cm
Translation of: Nasosy, ventilíatory, kompressory. — Includes index
ISBN 0-7147-1594-8 : £4.50
Primary classification 621.5'1 B81-23594

621.6 — Pumps - *Conference proceedings*

British Pump Manufacturers' Association. *Technical Conference (7th : 19871 : York).* Pumps - the developing needs. — Cranfield : B.H.R.A. Fluid Engineering, Apr.1981. — 1v.
ISBN 0-906085-52-7 (pbk) : £24.00 : CIP entry B81-04336

621.8 — MACHINERY, FASTENINGS, ETC

621.8 — Large machinery — *For children*

Kiley, Denise. Biggest machines / Denise Kiley. — Oxford : Blackwell Raintree, c1981. — 31p : ill(some col.) ; 27cm
Originally published: Milwaukee : Raintree Children, c1980. — Includes index
ISBN 0-86256-020-9 : £2.95 B81-17609

621.8 — Machinery

Shigley, Joseph Edward. Theory of machines and mechanisms / Joseph Edward Shigley, John Joseph Uicker, Jr. — Auckland ; London : McGraw-Hill, c1980. — xiv,577p ; 21cm. — (McGraw-Hill series in mechanical engineering)
Text on inside covers. — Includes index
ISBN 0-07-056884-7 (cased) : Unpriced
ISBN 0-07-066560-5 (pbk) : £6.95 B81-29590

621.8 — Power transmission systems — *Serials*

Modern power systems : incorporating Energy international. — Vol.1, no.1 (Jan. 1981)-. — Crawley (17 the Broadway, Crawley, Sussex RH10 1AG) : Miller Freeman, 1981-. — v. : ill ; 30cm
Monthly. — Continues: Energy international
ISSN 0260-7840 = Modern power systems : Unpriced B81-20291

621.8 — Turbomachinery

Balje, O. E.. Turbomachines : a guide to design, selection and theory / O.E. Balje. — Chichester : Wiley, c1981. — x,513p : ill ; 24cm
Includes index
ISBN 0-471-06036-4 : £33.45 B81-28308

621.8'072041 — Great Britain. ***Science Research Council. Machines and Power Committee*** **—** ***Serials***

Great Britain. *Science Research Council. Machines and Power Committee*. Report for the year ... / Science Research Council, Engineering Board, Machines and Power Committee. — 1979-80-. — Swindon : The Committee, [1980]-. — v. ; 30cm
Annual. — Cover title: Annual report (Great Britain. Science Research Council. Machines and Power Committee). — Continues: Great Britain. Science Research Council. Aeronautical and Mechanical Engineering Committee. Annual report ; and, in part, Great Britain. Science Research Council. Electrical and Systems Engineering Committee. Annual report
ISSN 0262-0928 = Report for the year - Science Research Council. Engineering Board. Machines and Power Committee : Unpriced B81-38993

621.8'11 — Turbomachinery. Heat transfer & fluid flow

Morris, W. David. Heat transfer and fluid flow in rotating coolant channels. — Chichester : Wiley, Jan.1982. — [244]p. — (Mechanical engineering research studies ; 2)
ISBN 0-471-10121-4 : £13.00 : CIP entry B81-34476

621.8'15 — Machinery. Design

Burr, Arthur H.. Mechanical analysis and design / Arthur H. Burr. — New York ; Oxford : Elsevier, c1981. — xxvi,640p : ill ; 28cm
Includes index
ISBN 0-444-00324-x : Unpriced B81-32384

Hall, Allen S.. Schaum's outline of theory and problems of machine design / Allen S. Hall, Jr., Alfred R. Holowenko, Herman G. Laughlin. — SI(metric) ed. adapted and converted to SI units by P.C. Hills and M.D. Bennett. — New York ; London : McGraw-Hill, c1980. — 3544p : ill ; 28cm. — (Schaum's outline series)
Previous ed.: 1961. — Includes index
ISBN 0-07-084352-x (pbk) : £5.25 B81-10344

621.8'15 — Machinery. Design. Probabilistic methods

Haugen, Edward B.. Probabilistic mechanical design / Edward B. Haugen. — New York ; Chichester : Wiley, c1980. — xxii,626p : ill ; 24cm
Includes index
ISBN 0-471-05847-5 : £19.80 B81-05194

621.8'15'02854 — Great Britain. Mechanical engineering. Design. Applications of digital computer systems. Management — *Conference proceedings*

Managing computer aided design : conference sponsored by the Process Industries Division of the Institution of Mechanical Engineers, 19 November 1980, Institution Headquarters, 1 Birdcage Walk, Westminster, London. — London : Mechanical Engineering for the Institution, 1980. — 47p : ill,plans ; 30cm. — (I Mech E conference publications ; 1980-8)
ISBN 0-85298-470-7 (pbk) : Unpriced B81-11047

621.8'22 — Gas bearings - *Conference proceedings*

International Gas Bearing Symposium *(8th : 1981 : Leicester Polytechnic)*. Papers presented at the 8th International Gas Bearing Symposium. — Cranfield : BHRA Fluid Engineering, Apr.1981. — [325]p
ISBN 0-906085-54-3 : £20.00 : CIP entry B81-07936

621.8'24'0212 — Engineering components: Mechanical springs - *Technical data - For design*

Brown, A. A. D.. Mechanical springs. — Oxford : Oxford University Press, Apr.1981. — [56]p. — (Engineering design guides ; 42)
ISBN 0-19-859181-0 (pbk) : £6.95 : CIP entry B81-05122

621.8'24'06041 — Great Britain. Engineering components: Springs. Organisations: Spring Research and Manufacturers' Association — *Directories — Serials*

Spring Research & Manufacturers' Association. Membership directory / the Spring Research & Manufacturers' Association. — 1980-1981-. — Sheffield (Henry St., Sheffield S3 7EQ) : The Association, 1980-. — v. ; 21cm
Annual
ISSN 0261-667x = Membership directory — Spring Research & Manufacturers' Association : Unpriced B81-32424

621.8'6 — Materials handling equipment

Harris, Frank, *1944-*. Construction plant : excavating and materials handling, equipment and methods / Frank Harris. — London : Granada, 1981. — vi,230p : ill ; 24cm
Bibliography: p223-224. — Includes index
ISBN 0-246-11237-9 (cased) : £15.00
ISBN 0-246-11557-2 (pbk) : Unpriced
Primary classification 629.2'25 B81-24513

621.8'6'05 — Materials handling equipment — *Buyers' guides — Serials*

MHBG : materials handling buyers' guide. — 12th ed. (1981). — London (886, High Road, Finchley, N12 9SB) : Turret Press, c1980. — 291p
ISSN 0142-114x : Unpriced B81-08750

621.8'6'09417 — Ireland *(Republic)*. **Materials handling equipment** — *Serials*

Materials handling yearbook. — 1981-. — Blackrock (22, Brookfield Ave., Blackrock, County Dublin) : Jemma Publications for the Irish Institute of Materials Handling, 1981-. — v. : ill ; 30cm
Cover title: Materials handling year book
Unpriced B81-13323

621.8'63 — Great Britain. Fork-lift trucks. Safety measures — *Proposals*

Royal Society for the Prevention of Accidents. Certification of industrial power truck operators : a report of the committee set up to consider a national scheme. — Birmingham : National Occupation of the Health and Safety Committee of the Royal Society for the Prevention of Accidents, c1981. — 45p : ill,forms ; 30cm
£5.00 (spiral) B81-14046

621.8'64 — England. Cathedrals. Lifting equipment: Windlasses

Backinsell, William G. C.. Medieval windlasses at Salisbury, Peterborough, & Tewkesbury / William G.C. Backinsell. — Salisbury (22 Minster St., Salisbury, Wilts. SP1 1TQ) : South Wilts Industrial Archaeology Society, 1980. — [8]p : ill ; 30cm. — (Historical monograph / South Wiltshire Industrial Archaeology Society ; 7)
ISBN 0-906195-06-3 (unbound) : £0.40 B81-15758

621.8'672 — Pipelines. Design

Stephenson. Pipeline design for water engineers. — 2nd ed. — Oxford : Elsevier Scientific, July 1981. — [226]p. — (Developments in water science)
Previous ed.: 1976
ISBN 0-444-41991-8 : CIP entry B81-13839

621.8'672 — Pipes. Water hammer

Sharp, B. B.. Water hammer : problems and solutions / B.B. Sharp. — London : Edward Arnold, 1981. — vii,144p : ill ; 24cm
Bibliography: p139-142. — Includes index
ISBN 0-7131-3427-5 : £11.75 B81-29149

621.8'672 — Piping systems

Kentish, D. N. W.. Industrial pipework. — London : McGraw-Hill, Oct.1981. — [352]p
ISBN 0-07-084557-3 : £35.00 : CIP entry B81-27345

621.8'672 — Slurry pipelines. Wear by slurry

Wear in slurry pipelines / editor Lavinia Gittins. — Cranfield : BHRA Fluid Engineering, c1980. — v,173p : ill ; 30cm. — (BHRA information series ; no.1)
Includes bibliographies
ISBN 0-906085-45-4 (pbk) : £15.00 B81-06161

621.8'672 — Solids. Hydraulic transport in pipes — *Conference proceedings*

International Conference on the Hydraulic Transport of Solids in Pipes *(6th : 1979 : Canterbury)*. Hydrotransport 6 : papers presented at the sixth International Conference on the Hydraulic Transport of Solids in Pipes : held at Canterbury, U.K. September 26th-28th 1979 / organised and sponsored by BHRA Fluid Engineering ; [editors H.S. Stephens, L. Gittins]. — Beford : BHRA Fluid Engineering, c1979. — 2v.(xix,563p) : ill,2plans ; 30cm
Includes index
ISBN 0-906085-21-7 (pbk) : Unpriced : CIP rev
ISBN 0-906085-22-5 (Vol.1) : Unpriced
ISBN 0-906085-23-3 (Vol.2) : Unpriced B79-27530

International Conference on the Hydraulic Transport of Solids in Pipes *(7th : 1980 : Sendai)*. Hydrotransport 7 : Sendai, Japan, 4-6 November 1980 : papers presented at the seventh International Conference on the Hydraulic Transport of Solids in Pipes / organised and sponsored by BHRA Fluid Engineering and Slurry Transport Society of Japan ; [editors H.S. Stephens, L. Gittins]. — Bedford : BHRA Fluid Engineering, c1980. — vi,444 : ill,maps ; 30cm
ISBN 0-906085-46-2 (pbk) : Unpriced : CIP rev B80-27161

621.8'6720212 — Piping systems — *Technical data*

Kentish, D. N. W.. Pipework design data. — London : McGraw-Hill, Oct.1981. — [272]p
ISBN 0-07-084558-1 : £30.00 : CIP entry B81-27346

621.8'672'0221 — Piping systems. Technical drawings. Draftsmanship

Hartman, William. Pipe drafting / William Hartman, Fred Williams. — New York ; London : McGraw-Hill, c1981. — viii,191p : ill ; 28cm
Includes index
ISBN 0-07-026945-9 (pbk) : £7.75 B81-39417

Lamit, Louis Gary. Piping systems : drafting and design / Louis Gary Lamit. — Englewood Cliffs ; London : Prentice-Hall, c1981. — xii,612p : ill,plans ; 29cm
Includes index
ISBN 0-13-676445-2 : £19.45 B81-19939

621.8'7'0289 — Construction equipment: Lifting equipment. Safety aspects — *Manuals*

Dickie, D. E.. [Rigging manual]. Lifting tackle manual / compiled by D.E. Dickie ; United Kingdom editor Douglas Short. — Rev. ed. — London : Butterworths, 1981, c1975. — x,188p : ill ; 26cm
Previous ed.: Toronto : Construction Safety Association of Ontario, 1975
ISBN 0-408-00446-0 : £18.00 : CIP rev. B80-36140

621.8'73 — Lifting equipment: Cranes — *For children*

Dixon, Annabelle. Cranes. — London : A & C Black, Jan.1982. — [32]p. — (Science explorers)
ISBN 0-7136-2161-3 : £2.50 : CIP entry
B81-33849

621.8'73'0212 — Lifting equipment: Cranes — *Technical data — Serials*

Cranes today handbook. — 1976. — Edgware ([290A Hale La., Edgware, Middx HA8 8NP]) : MW Publishers, c1976. — 256p
ISSN 0260-745x : £3.00 B81-35991

Cranes today handbook. — 1977. — Edgware (290A Hale La., Edgware, Middx HA8 8NP) : MW Publishers, c1977. — 304p
ISSN 0260-745x : £4.00 B81-35992

Cranes today handbook. — 1978. — Edgware (290A Hale La., Edgware, Middx HA8 8NP) : MW Publishers, c1978. — 312p
ISSN 0260-745x : Unpriced B81-35993

Cranes today handbook. — 1980. — Edgware (290A Hale La., Edgware, Middx HA8 8NP) : MW Publishers, c1980. — 448p
ISSN 0260-745x : Unpriced B81-35994

Cranes today handbook. — 1981. — Edgware (290A Hale La., Edgware, Middlesex, HA8 8NP) : MW Publishers, [1981]. — 512p
ISBN 0-9507429-0-2 : Unpriced
ISSN 0260-745x B81-31588

621.8'73'0289 — Construction equipment: Lifting equipment: Cranes. Safety aspects — *Manuals*

Dickie, D. E.. Crane handbook / compiled by D.E. Dickie. — Rev. ed. / United Kingdom editor Douglas Short. — London : Butterworths, 1981, c1975. — 312p : ill ; 26cm
Previous ed.: Toronto : Construction Safety Association of Ontario, 1975
ISBN 0-408-00445-2 : Unpriced : CIP rev.
B80-23389

621.8'8 — Engineering components: Fastenings — *Buyers' guides*

Fastenings locator '80 / editor C. Robbie Robinson. — 5th ed. — London (Morgan-Grampian Hse., Calderwood St., SE18 6QH) : Morgan-Grampian (Publishers), [1980]. — 114p : ill ; 29cm
Previous ed.: 1977
£6.00 (pbk) B81-13026

621.8'85 — Engineering components: Elastomeric seals. Physical properties

Engineering properties of seal elastomers : a basic guide / [BRMA]. — London (90 Tottenham Court Rd., WIP 0BR) : BRMA, [1981?]. — 24p : ill(some col.) ; 30cm
Cover title
Unpriced (pbk) B81-29454

621.8'85 — Engineering components: Fluid seals — *Conference proceedings*

International Conference on Fluid Sealing *(8th : 1978 : University of Durham)*. Papers presented at the eighth International Conference on Fluid Sealing : held at the University of Durham, England, September 11-13, 1978 / conference sponsored and organised by BHRA Fluid Engineering. — Cranfield : BHRA Fluid Engineering, c1978. — 2v.(512p in various pagings] : ill ; 30cm
Includes index
ISBN 0-900983-93-0 (pbk) : Unpriced : CIP rev.
ISBN 0-900983-94-9 (v.1)
ISBN 0-900983-95-7 (v.2) B78-29655

International Conference on Fluid Sealing *(9th : 1981 : Noordwijkerhout)*. Papers presented at the ninth International Conference on Fluid Sealing : held at the Leeuwenhorst Congres Center, Noordwijkerhout, Netherlands, April 1-3, 1981 / conference sponsored and organised by BHRA Fluid Engineering. — Cranfield : BHRA Fluid Engineering, [1981?]. — vi,466p : ill ; 30cm
ISBN 0-906085-51-9 (pbk) : Unpriced : CIP rev. B81-04337

621.8'85 — Engineering components: Seals

Warring, R. H.. Seals and sealing handbook / by R. H. Warring. — Morden : Trade & Technical Press, c1981. — xxi,458,viiip : ill ; 24cm
Includes index
ISBN 0-85461-082-0 : Unpriced B81-30661

621.8'9 — Cams & gears. Effectiveness of lubricants. Evaluation - *Conference proceedings*

Performance and testing of gear oils and transmission fluids. — London : Heyden, June 1981. — [451]p
Conference papers
ISBN 0-85501-326-5 : £40.00 : CIP entry
B81-14417

621.8'9 — Friction & wear

Kragel'skiĭ, I. V.. Friction and wear. — Oxford : Pergamon, May 1981. — [450]p
Translation of: Osnovy raschetov na trenie i iznos
ISBN 0-08-025461-6 : £31.00 : CIP entry
B81-05169

621.8'9 — Friction & wear. Effects of heat — *Conference proceedings*

Leeds-Lyon Symposium on Tribology *(6th : 1979 : Lyon)*. Thermal effects in tribology : proceedings of the 6th Leeds-Lyon Symposium on Tribology held in the Institut national des sciences appliquées de Lyon, France September 18-21 1979 / edited by D. Dowson ... [et al.]. — London : Mechanical Engineering Publications for the Institute of Tribology, Leeds University and the Institut national des sciences appliquées Lyon, 1980. — viii,340p : ill ; 30cm
Includes index
ISBN 0-85298-467-7 (pbk) : £40.00 B81-01616

621.8'9 — Lubricants: Continuum fluid films

Fluid film lubrication / William A. Gross ... [et al.] ; prepared under the auspices of Technical Information Center, U.S. Department of Energy. — New York ; Chichester : Wiley, 1980. — x,774p : ill ; 24cm
Extension and revision of: Gas film lubrication / by W.A. Gross. 1962. — Includes index
ISBN 0-471-08357-7 : £18.75 B81-04419

621.8'9 — Lubrication

Cameron, A.. Basic lubrication theory. — 3rd ed. / A. Cameron ; with additional material by C.M.Mc. Ettles. — Chichester : Ellis Horwood, 1981. — 256p : ill ; 24cm. — (Ellis Horwood series in engineering science)
Previous ed.: 1976. — Bibliography: p252-253. — Includes index
ISBN 0-85312-177-x (cased) : £12.50 : CIP rev.
ISBN 0-85312-362-4 (pbk) : Unpriced
B80-06462

Lansdown, A. R.. Lubrication. — Oxford : Pergamon, Feb.1982. — [200]p. — (Materials engineering practice)
ISBN 0-08-026728-9 (cased) : £12.50 : CIP entry
ISBN 0-08-026727-0 (pbk) : £4.90 B81-35934

621.8'9 — Materials: Polymers. Friction & wear

Bartenev, G. M.. Friction and wear of polymers. — Oxford : Elsevier Scientific, June 1981. — 1v.. — (Tribology series ; v.6)
ISBN 0-444-42000-2 : CIP entry B81-18074

Friction and wear in polymer-based materials. — Oxford : Pergamon, May 1981. — [400]p
Translation of: Trenie i iznos materialov na osnove polimerov
ISBN 0-08-025444-6 : £32.00 : CIP entry
B81-07600

621.8'9 — Tribology

Buckley, Donald H.. Surface effects in adhesion, friction, wear, and lubrication / Donald H. Buckley. — Amsterdam ; Oxford : Elsevier, 1981. — ix,631p : ill ; 25cm. — (Tribology series ; v.5)
Includes index
ISBN 0-444-41966-7 : Unpriced : CIP rev.
Also classified at 621.8'9 B81-07451

Buckley, Donald H.. Surface effects in adhesion, friction, wear, and lubrication / Donald H. Buckley. — Amsterdam ; Oxford : Elsevier, 1981. — ix,631p : ill ; 25cm. — (Tribology series ; v.5)
Includes index
ISBN 0-444-41966-7 : Unpriced : CIP rev.
Primary classification 621.8'9 B81-07451

Tribology : friction, lubrication and wear / edited by A.Z. Szeri. — Washington ; London : Hemisphere, c1980. — xii,548p : ill ; 25cm
Includes index
ISBN 0-07-062663-4 : £24.00 B81-05984

621.8'9 — Tribology — *Conference proceedings*

Leeds-Lyon Symposium on Tribology *(7th : 1980 : University of Leeds)*. Friction and traction : proceedings of the 7th Leeds-Lyon Symposium on Tribology held in the Institute of Tribology, Department of Mechanical Engineering, University of Leeds, England, 9-12 September 1980 / edited by D. Dowson ... [et al.]. — Guildford : Westbury House for the Institute of Tribology, Leeds University and the Institut National des Sciences Appliquées, Lyon, c1981. — viii,368p : ill ; 31cm
Includes index
ISBN 0-86103-053-2 : Unpriced B81-38224

621.8'9 — Tribology - *Manuals*

Friction, wear and lubrication. — Oxford : Pergamon, Sept.1981. — 3v.
Translation of: Trenie, iznashivanie i smazka
ISBN 0-08-027591-5 : £60.00 : CIP entry
B81-20115

621.9 — WORKSHOP TOOLS

621.9 — Woodworking equipment — *Manuals*

Wearing, Robert. Woodwork : aids and devices / Robert Wearing ; [illustrations by Gay Galsworthy]. — London : Evans, 1981. — 208p : ill ; 22cm
ISBN 0-237-44995-1 : £6.95 B81-38253

621.9 — Woodworking machines

Stokes, Gordon. Machines for better woodwork / Gordon Stokes. — London : Evans, 1980. — 143p : ill ; 22cm
ISBN 0-237-44931-5 : £6.95 : CIP rev.
B80-12925

621.9'0028'8 — Small tools. Sharpening — *Amateurs' manuals*

Walton, Harry. Home and workshop guide to sharpening / by Harry Walton. — New York ; London : Barnes & Noble, 1974, c1967. — 160p : ill ; 21cm. — (Everyday handbooks ; no.418) (A Popular Science skill book)
Originally published: New York : Popular Science, 1967. — Includes index
ISBN 0-06-463418-3 (pbk) : £1.95 B81-07264

621.9'005 — Workshop equipment — *Serials*

Workshop equipment news. — No.1 (Dec.1980)-. — Ilford (28 Hampton Rd, Ilford, Essex IG1 1PS) : Wordsworth Trade Press, 1980-. — v. : ill ; 28cm
Quarterly
ISSN 0260-6887 = Workshop equipment news : £3.00 for six issues B81-10260

621.9'02 — Machine tools

Pollack, Herman W.. Manufacturing and machine tool operations / Herman W. Pollack. — 2nd ed. — Englewood Cliffs ; London : Prentice-Hall, c1979. — xviii,637p : ill ; 24cm
Previous ed.: 1968. — Includes index
ISBN 0-13-555771-2 : £14.25 B81-25171

621.9'02 — Machine tools. Design — *Conference proceedings*

International Machine Tool Design and Research Conference *(21st : 1980 : Swansea)*. Proceedings of the Twenty-First International Machine Tool Design and Research Conference : held in Swansea 8th-12th September, 1980 / edited by J.M. Alexander. — Swansea : Department of Mechanical Engineering, University College of Swansea in association with Macmillan, 1981. — 631p : ill ; 30cm
Includes index
ISBN 0-333-30847-6 : £46.00 B81-38636

621.9′02 — Metal-cutting machine tools. Stability. Determination. Mathematics

Lazarev, G. S.. Stability of the metal cutting process / Grigory Lazarev. — Boston Spa : British Library Lending Division, c1981. — 170p : ill ; 30cm
Translation of: Ustoĭchivost′ protšessa rezaniīa metallov
ISBN 0-85350-180-7 (pbk) : Unpriced B81-37368

621.9′02 — Woodworking machines. Automatic stacking units

Stephenson, R.. Outfeed and stacking units for woodworking machinery / by R. Stephenson. — Stevenage : Furniture Industry Research Association, [1980]. — 50p : ill ; 30cm
£16.00 (£8.00 to members of the Association) (spiral) B81-06486

621.9′02′02341 — Great Britain. Machine tools industries — *Career guides* — *For graduates*

Careers for graduates in the machine tool industry. — 1977-. — London (62 Bayswater Rd, W2 3PH) : Machine Tool Trades Association, 1976-. — v. ; 21cm
Annual. — Description based on: 1979
ISSN 0142-5226 = Careers for graduates in the machine tool industry : Unpriced B81-04811

621.9′023′02854 — Machine tools. Numerical control. Applications of digital computer systems — *Conference proceedings*

MANUFACONT ′80 *(Conference : Budapest)*. Control problems and devices in manufacturing technology 1980 : proceedings of the 3rd IFAC/IFIP Symposium, Budapest, Hungary, 22-25 October 1980 (MANUFACONT ′80) / edited by T.M.R. Ellis. — Oxford : Published for The International Federation of Automotive Control by Pergamon, 1981. — x,375p : ill,plans ; 31cm. — (IFAC proceedings series)
Includes index
ISBN 0-08-026720-3 : £29.00 : CIP rev. B81-13892

621.9′08′0901 — Palaeolithic flint tools

Timms, Peter. Flint implements of the Old Stone Age / Peter Timms. — 2nd ed. — Aylesbury : Shire, 1980. — 56p : ill,maps ; 21cm. — (Shire archaeology ; 2)
Previous ed.: 1974. — Bibliography: p22. — Includes index
ISBN 0-85263-517-6 (pbk) : £1.50 B81-07221

621.9′08′09361 — Great Britain. Neolithic stone tools

Pitts, Michael W.. Later stone implements / Michael W. Pitts. — Princes Risborough : Shire Publications, 1980. — 56p : ill,maps ; 21cm. — (Shire archaeology series ; 14)
Bibliography: p52-54. - Includes index
ISBN 0-85263-518-4 (pbk) : £1.50 B81-07738

621.9′08′0937 — Ancient Roman iron hand tools, *B.C.27-A.D.500* — *German texts*

Gaitzsch, Wolfgang. Eiserne römische Werkzeuge : Studien zur römischen Werkzeugkunde in Italien und den nördlichen Provinzen des Imperium Romanum / Wolfgang Gaitzsch. — Oxford : B.A.R., 1980. — 2v.(410p,74p of plates) : ill ; 30cm. — (BAR. International series ; 78)
Bibliography: p386-392. — Includes index
ISBN 0-86054-089-8 (pbk) : £15.00 B81-16544

621.9′2 — Grinding wheels

Crawshaw, Margaret. Abrasive wheels. — London : Health and Safety Executive, May 1981. — [15]p
ISBN 0-7176-0075-0 (pbk) : £1.00 : CIP entry B81-12374

621.9′2′0289 — Great Britain. Portable grinding machines. Safety measures

Great Britain. *Health and Safety Executive*. Portable grinding machines. — London : Health and Safety Executive, Oct.1981. — [40] p. — (HS(G)18)
ISBN 0-11-883444-4 (pbk) : CIP entry B81-24631

621.9′23 — Derbyshire. Hathersage region. Grindstones. Manufacture, *to 1950*

Tomlinson, Tom D.. Querns, millstones and grindstones : made in Hathersage & district / by Tom D. Tomlinson. — Hathersage ([The Vicarage, Hathersage, Sheffield S30 1AB]) : Hathersage Parochial Church Council, 1981. — 20p : ill ; 22cm
£0.50 (pbk) B81-18654

621.9′3 — Cutting machines: Guillotines. Safety measures

Guillotines and shears. — London : Health & Safety Executive, July 1981. — [36]p. — (HS (G))
ISBN 0-11-883434-7 (pbk) : CIP entry B81-13835

621.9′3 — Southern England. Bronze Age socketed axes. Manufacture

Needham, Stuart. The Bulford-Helsbury manufacturing tradition : the production of Stogursey socketed axes during the later Bronze Age in southern Britain / Stuart Needham. — London : British Museum, 1981. — 72p : ill,1map ; 30cm. — (Occasional paper / British Museum, ISSN 0142-4815 ; no.13)
Bibliography: p67-72
ISBN 0-86159-012-0 (pbk) : Unpriced B81-29232

621.9′84 — Drop forged dies. Design

Thomas, A. (Alwyne). Die design / by A. Thomas. — Sheffield (Shepherd St., Sheffield S3 7BA) : Drop Forging Research Association, [1980]. — 83p : ill ; 30cm. — (DFRA forging handbook)
£25.00 (pbk) B81-26632

622 — MINING

622′.01′5195 — Mining. Statistical mathematics

Journel, A. G.. Mining geostatistics / A.G. Journel and Ch. J. Huijbregts. — London : Academic Press, 1978 (1981 [printing]). — x,600p : ill ; 23cm
Bibliography: p581-590. — Includes index
ISBN 0-12-391056-0 (pbk) : Unpriced B81-34706

622′.028 — Mining industries. Automatic control systems. Applications of computer systems — *Conference proceedings*

Automation in mining, mineral and metal processing : proceedings of the 3rd IFAC Symposium, Montreal, Canada 18-20 August 1980 / editors J. O′Shea and M. Polis. — Oxford : Published for the International Federation of Automatic Control by Pergamon, 1981 c1980. — xv,662p : ill ; 31cm. — (IFAC proceedings series)
Includes bibliographies
ISBN 0-08-026164-7 : £63.00 : CIP rev.
Primary classification 669′.028 B80-27302

622′.07204238 — Somerset. Mines. Historiology. Organisations: Somerset Mines Research Group — *Serials*

Somerset Mines Research Group. — Dec.1980-. — [Highbridge] ([c/o A. Bowman, Bowood, Edith Mead La., Highbridge, Somerset TA9 4HD]) : Somerset Mines Research Group, 1980-. — v. ; 30cm
Two issues yearly
ISSN 0261-2143 = Somerset Mines Research Group (Newsletter) : Free to Group members B81-25039

622′.0936 — Europe. Prehistoric mining

Shepherd, R.. Prehistoric mining and allied industries / R. Shepherd. — London : Academic Press, 1980. — xii,272p : ill,maps ; 24cm. — (Studies in archaeological science)
Bibliography: p257-265. - Includes index
ISBN 0-12-639480-6 : £16.00 : CIP rev. B80-31784

622′.13 — Mineral deposits. Prospecting. Applications of geochemistry

Govett, G. J. S.. Rock geochemistry in mineral exploration. — Oxford : Elsevier Scientific, Jan.1982. — [355]p. — (Handbook of exploration geochemistry ; v.3)
ISBN 0-444-42021-5 : CIP entry B81-34491

622′.13′015195 — Mineral deposits. Estimation. Applications of statistical mathematics

Henley, Stephen. Nonparametric geostatistics. — London : Applied Science, Sept.1981. — [160]p
ISBN 0-85334-977-0 : £13.00 : CIP entry B81-20160

622′.15 — Mineral deposits. Prospecting. Applications of geophysics

Developments in geophysical exploration methods / edited by A.A. Fitch. — London : Applied Science. — (The Developments series)
2. — c1981. — ix,234p : ill ; 23cm
Includes index
ISBN 0-85334-930-4 : £18.00 B81-17008

Griffiths, D. H.. Applied geophysics for geologists and engineers : the elements of geophysical prospecting / by D.H. Griffiths and R.F. King. — 2nd ed. — Oxford : Pergamon, 1981. — xii,230p[2]folded leaves of plates : ill,maps ; 21cm. — (Pergamon international library)
Previous ed.: published as Applied geophysics for engineers and geologists. 1965. — Bibliography: p203-207. — Includes index
ISBN 0-08-022071-1 (cased) : £12.50
ISBN 0-08-022072-x (pbk) : £5.95 B81-16112

622′.153 — Mineral deposits. Prospecting. Magnetotelluric sounding methods

Kaufman, Alexander A.. The magnetotelluric sounding method / Alexander A. Kaufman and George V. Keller. — Amsterdam ; Oxford : Elsevier Scientific, 1981. — xiv,595p : ill,charts,maps ; 25cm. — (Methods in geochemistry and geophysics ; 15)
Bibliography: p585-591. - Includes index
ISBN 0-444-41863-6 : £57.17 B81-21388

622′.159 — Mineral deposits. Prospecting. Applications of reflection of artificially generated seismic waves

Waters, Kenneth H.. Reflection seismology : a tool for energy resource exploration / Kenneth H. Waters. — 2nd ed. — New York ; Chichester : Wiley, c1981. — xvi,453p,[4]leaves of plates(2folded) : ill(some col.) ; 26cm
Previous ed.: 1978. — Includes bibliographies and index
ISBN 0-471-08224-4 : £31.50 B81-33228

622′.1828 — Natural gas deposits & petroleum deposits. Prospecting. Applications of reflection of artifically generated seismic waves. Data. Deconvolution

McQuillin, R.. An introduction to seismic interpretation / R. McQuillin, M. Bacon, W. Barclay. — London : Graham & Trotman, 1979 (1980 [printing]). — 199p : ill(some col.),maps ; 30cm
Includes bibliographies and index
ISBN 0-86010-111-8 : £19.00 B81-13171

622′.1841′09931 — New Zealand. Gold. Prospecting — *Amateurs′ manuals*

Fairservice, Sandy. Gold in your bottle : fossicking for fun in New Zealand / by Sandy and Judy Fairservice. — Christchurch [N.Z.] ; London : Whitcoulls, 1981. — 63p : ill,maps, 2forms ; 21cm
Bibliography: p63
ISBN 0-7233-0655-9 (pbk) : Unpriced B81-34931

622′.1843′099447 — New South Wales. Woodlawn. Copper deposits. Prospecting. Applications of geophysics

Geophysical case study of the Woodlawn orebody New South Wales, Australia : the first publication of methods and techniques tested over a base metal orebody of the type which yields the highest rate of return on mining investment with modest capital requirements / editor Robert J. Whiteley. — Oxford : Pergamon, 1981. — xix,588p,[1]p of plates : ill,maps ; 26cm + 24 folded sheets in pocket (ill)
In slip case. — Includes bibliographies and index
ISBN 0-08-023996-x : £41.50 : CIP rev. B80-0880

622'.19 — Underwater treasure hunting
Williams, Mark. Deep sea treasure / Mark Williams. — London : Heinemann, 1981. — 179p : ill(some col.),maps,ports(some col.) ; 24cm
Includes index
ISBN 0-434-86660-1 : £9.95 B81-32357

622'.19'0941 — Great Britain. Treasure hunting — *Manuals*
Johnson, Kate. The complete book of treasure hunting / Kate Johnson ; photographs by Roger Johnson. — London : Granada, 1981, c1980. — 192p : ill,1map ; 18cm. — (A Mayflower book)
Originally published: London : Barker, 1980. — Includes index
ISBN 0-583-13420-3 (pbk) : £1.50 B81-31387

622'.23 — Drilling. Drilling fluids
Chilingarian, George V.. Drilling and drilling fluids / by G.V. Chilingarian and P. Vorabutr with contributions from Danial Acosta ... [et al.]. — Amsterdam ; Oxford : Elsevier Scientific, 1981. — xx,767p : ill ; 25cm. — (Developments in petroleum science ; 11)
Includes bibliographies and index
ISBN 0-444-41867-9 : £52.83 : CIP rev.
B80-19796

622'.334'072041 — Great Britain. Coal. Mining. Research projects by Mining Research and Development Establishment — *Serials*
Mining Research and Development Establishment
[Projects *(Mining Research and Development Establishment)*]. Projects / Mining Research and Development Establishment. — 1979-80. — Burton-on-Trent (Ashley Road, Stanhope Bretby, Staffs. DE15 0QD) : National Coal Board Mining Research and Development Establishment, [1980]. — 49p
ISSN 0140-4393 : Unpriced B81-08694

622'.334'0924 — Staffordshire. Silverdale. Coal. Mining, *1917-1925 — Personal observations*
Brown, Harold, *1906-*. Most splendid of men : life in a mining community 1917-25 / Harold Brown. — Poole : Blandford, 1981. — 186p,[8]p of plates : ill,2ports ; 23cm
Includes index
ISBN 0-7137-1107-8 : £4.95 B81-10191

622'.334'0942997 — Gwent. Blaenavon. Coal mines: Big Pit, *to 1980*
Thomas, W. Gerwyn. Big Pit, Blaenafon / written by W. Gerwyn Thomas = Big Pit, Blaenafon / Ysgrifennwyd y llyfryn hwn gan W. Gerwyn Thomas ; cy fieithiad Cymraeg gan W. Morgan Rogers. — Cardiff : National Museum of Wales, 1981. — 47p : ill,maps,1port ; 16x23cm
Parallel English text and Welsh translation. — Ill and text on inside cover
ISBN 0-7200-0233-8 (pbk) : Unpriced
B81-31688

622'.338 — Deep waters. Offshore natural gas deposits & petroleum deposits. Exploration wells. Floating drilling
Sheffield, Riley. Floating drilling : equipment and its use / Riley Sheffield. — Houston ; London : Gulf Publishing, 1980. — ix,257p : ill,forms ; 24cm. — (Practical drilling technology ; v.2)
Includes index
ISBN 0-87201-289-1 : £11.75 B81-02933

622'.338'03 — Natural gas & petroleum deposits. Extraction — *Polyglot dictionaries*
Elsevier's oil and gas field dictionary in six languages : English-American, French, Spanish, Italian, Dutch and German / compiled by L.Y. Chaballe, L. Masuy and J.-P. Vandenberghe with an Arabic supplement by Shawky Salem. — Amsterdam ; Oxford : Elsevier Scientific, 1980. — 672p ; 25cm
ISBN 0-444-41833-4 : £55.00 : CIP rev.
B80-18369

622'.3382 — Petroleum deposits. Enhanced recovery
Latil, Marcel. Enhanced oil recovery / Marcel Latil with the assistance of Charles Bardon, Jacques Burger, Pierre Sourieau ; translation from the French by Paul Ellis. — Paris : Technip ; London : distributed by Graham & Trotman, 1980. — xiv,236p : ill ; 24cm
At head of title: Institut français du pétrole. — Includes index
ISBN 2-7108-0381-x (pbk) : £23.00 B81-19623

622'.3382 — Petroleum deposits. Fractured reservoirs. Engineering aspects
Reiss, Louis H.. The reservoir engineering aspects of fractured formations / Louis H. Reiss ; translated from the French by Max Creusot. — Paris : Technip ; London : Marketed and distributed by Graham & Trotman, 1980. — xii,108p : ill ; 24cm. — (Institut français du pétrole publications)
At head of title: Institut français du pétrole. — Bibliography: p99-102. — Includes index
ISBN 2-7108-0374-7 (pbk) : £13.00 B81-34458

622'.3382 — Petroleum deposits. Reservoirs. Exploitation. Engineering aspects — *Conference proceedings*
Reservoir engineering : its role in hydro-carbon resources development. — Kuwait : Organization of Arab Petroleum Exporting Countries ; London : Distributed by Graham & Trotman, 1979. — 326p : ill ; 24cm
Conference papers
£11.00 (pbk) B81-34074

622'.3382 — Petroleum deposits. Reservoirs. Fractures. Engineering aspects
Van Golf-Racht, T. D.. Fundamentals of fractured reservoir engineering. — Oxford : Elsevier Scientific, Jan.1982. — [720]p. — (Developments in petroleum science ; 12)
ISBN 0-444-42046-0 : CIP entry B81-37526

622'.3382'01576 — Petroleum deposits. Extraction. Applications of microbiology
Moses, V.. Bacteria and the enhancement of oil recovery. — London : Applied Science Publishers, Jan.1982. — [188]p
ISBN 0-85334-995-9 : £15.00 : CIP entry
B81-33785

622'.3382'028 — Petroleum drilling equipment. Internal combustion engines — *Technical data*
Lynch, Philip F.. The powertrain / Philip F. Lynch. — Houston ; London : Gulf, c1980. — ix,165p : ill ; 28cm. — (A Primer in drilling & production equipment ; v.1)
Includes index
ISBN 0-87201-198-4 (pbk) : Unpriced
B81-26862

622'.3382'0289 — Petroleum deposits. Extraction. Accidents: Blowouts. Prevention & control
Blowout prevention and well control / Chambre syndicale de la recherche et de la production du pétrole et du gaz naturel, Comité des techniciens, Commission exploitation sous-commission forage ; translation from the French by Paul W. Ellis. — London : Graham & Trotman, 1981. — xvi,164p,[2]folded leaves of plates : ill,forms ; 24cm
ISBN 0-86010-337-4 (pbk) : £17.00 B81-34078

622'.3382'0683 — North Sea. Offshore petroleum industries. Roughnecks & roustabouts. Recruitment, selection & retention
Livy, Bryan. Oil rig workers in the North Sea : their selection and retention / by Bryan Livy and James Vant. — London (Gresham College, Basinghall St., EC2V 5AH) : City University Business School, 1980. — 20leaves : ill ; 30cm. — (Working paper series / City University Business School, ISSN 0140-1041 ; no.18)
Unpriced (pbk) B81-04986

622'.34'094687 — Spain. Huelva *(Province)*. **Metals mines. Industrial antiquities. Excavation of remains**
Rothenburg, Beno. Ancient mining and metallurgy in South-west Spain. — London (c/o Institute of Archaeology, University of London, Gordon Sq., WC1H 0PW) : Institute for Archaeo-Metallurgical Studies, Dec.1981. — 1v.. — (Metals in history)
ISBN 0-906183-01-4 : £18.00 : CIP entry
B81-38836

622'.367 — South Yorkshire *(Metropolitan County)*. **Wadsley. Ganister. Mining,** *to 1950*
Castle, J.. Candles, corves and clogs / by J. Castle. — 35p,[4]p of plates : 1ill,1map ; 21cm
Unpriced (pbk) B81-29367

622'.6 — Coal mines. Ropes. Maintenance — *Manuals*
Ropeman's handbook. — 3rd ed. — London : National Coal Board in collaboration with the Health and Safety Executive and the Federation of Wire Rope Manufacturers, 1980. — 176p : ill ; 21cm
Previous ed.: 1966. — Includes index
Unpriced (pbk) B81-09838

622'.67 — Mines. Electric winding equipment
Chatterjee, P. K.. Winding engine calculations for the mining engineer. — 2nd ed. — London : Spon, Feb.1982. — [192]p
Previous ed.: / by Alexander Bernard Price. London : General Electric Co., 1955
ISBN 0-419-12650-3 : £15.00 : CIP entry
B81-35729

622'.7 — Minerals. Processing
Wills, B. A.. Mineral processing technology : an introduction to the practical aspects of ore treatment and mineral recovery (in SI/metric units) / by B.A. Wills. — 2nd ed. — Oxford : Pergamon, 1981. — xi,525p : ill ; 22cm. — (Pergamon international library) (International series on materials science and technology ; v.29)
Previous ed.: 1979. — Includes index
ISBN 0-08-027322-x (cased) : Unpriced
ISBN 0-08-027323-8 (pbk) : £8.25 B81-40091

622'.7 — Minerals. Processing — *Conference proceedings*
International Mineral Processing Congress *(13th : 1979 : Warsaw)*. Mineral processing : Thirteenth International Mineral Processing Congress, Warsaw, June 4-9, 1979, proceedings / editor J. Laskowski ; consulting editors R. Bortel, F. Łętowski, J. Szczypa. — Amsterdam ; Oxford : Elsevier Scientific, 1981. — 2v.(xvii,2115p) : ill ; 24cm. — (Developments in mineral processing ; 2)
English text, English, French, German and Russian abstracts
ISBN 0-444-99775-x : £125.00 : CIP rev.
B80-08259

622'.752'0724 — Ores. Flotation. Mathematical models
Mineral and coal flotation circuits : their simulation and control / A.J. Lynch ... [et al.]. — Amsterdam ; Oxford : Elsevier Scientific, 1981. — xiv,291p : ill ; 25cm. — (Developments in mineral processing ; 3)
Bibliography: p270-283. - Includes index
ISBN 0-444-41919-5 : £24.53 B81-11142

623 — MILITARY ENGINEERING

623 — Armour
Ballistic materials and penetration mechanics / edited by Roy C. Laible. — Amsterdam ; Oxford : Elsevier Scientific, 1980. — ix,297p : ill ; 25cm. — (Methods and phenomena : v.5)
Includes index
ISBN 0-444-41928-4 : £29.23 B81-05750

623'.043 — Military microwave equipment — *Conference proceedings*
Military microwaves : conference proceedings Wednesday 25th to Friday 27th October 1978, the Wembley Conference Centre, London, England / supported by the Institution of Electrical Engineers and Institution of Electronic and Radio Engineers. — Sevenoaks (36 High St., Sevenoaks, Kent TN13 1JG) : Microwave Exhibitions and Publishers, [1978?]. — 476p : ill ; 30cm
£18.00 (pbk) B81-14634

Military microwaves '80 : conference proceedings Wednesday 22nd to Friday 27th October 1980, the Cunard International Hotel London, England / supported by EUREL - the Convention of National Societies of Electrical Engineers of Western Europe, the Institution of Electrical Engineers in co-operation with Microwave Theory and Techniques Society of the IEEE. — Sevenoaks (36 High St., Sevenoaks, Kent TN 14G) : Microwave Exhibitions and Publishers, [1980?]. — 706p : ill ; 30cm
£30.00 (pbk) B81-14635

623'.043'05 — Military electronic equipment — *Serials*

Miltronics. — Vol.1, no.1 (Sept.1980)-. — Eton (50, High St., Eton, Berks.) : Eton Publ. Co., 1980-. — v. : ill,ports ; 30cm
Six issues yearly
ISSN 0144-5243 = Miltronics : £18.00 per year B81-05031

623'.05 — Military equipment — *For Latin American military forces — Serials*

Defense Latin America. — Vol.1, no.1 (Mar. 1977)-. — Winchester (Granville House, St. Peter St., Winchester, Hants.) : Kingswood Publications, 1977-. — v. : ill ; 33cm
Six issues yearly. — Description based on: Vol.5, no.2 (Apr. / May 1981)
ISSN 0261-233x = Defense Latin America : Unpriced B81-31591

623'.05 — Military equipment — *Serials*

Military enthusiast. — No.1-. — Cologne : Eshel ; West Drayton (Tavistock Rd, West Drayton UB7 7QE, Middlesex) : COMAG [Distributor], [1980?]-. — v. : ill ; 27cm
Monthly. — Description based on: No.5
£7.50 per year B81-29407

623'.09 — Military equipment, *B.C.3000-A.D.1700*

Saxtorph, Niels M.. Warriors and weapons 3000 B.C. to A.D. 1700 : in colour / by Niels M. Saxtorph ; illustrated by Stig Bramsen ; [translated into English by Bob and Inge Gosney]. — London : Blandford, 1972 (1975 [printing]). — 260p : ill(some col.),maps ; 19cm
Translation of: Krigsfolk gennem tiden. — Bibliography: p253-254. - Includes index
ISBN 0-7137-0735-6 : £3.95 B81-11585

623'.094 — Europe. Military equipment, *700-1500*

Funcken, Liliane. The age of chivalry / Liliane and Fred Funchen. — London : Ward Lock. — (Arms and uniforms)
Translation of: Le costume, l'armure et les armes au temps de la chevalerie
Pt.2: Castles, forts and artillery, 8th to 15th century .... — 1981. — 109p : col.ill ; 25cm
Ill on lining papers. — Includes index
ISBN 0-7063-5936-4 : £7.95 : CIP rev.
Primary classification 355.1'4'094 B81-03701

Funcken, Liliane. The age of chivalry. — London : Ward Lock
Part 3: The Renaissance. — Feb.1982. — [112]p
ISBN 0-7063-5937-2 : £6.95 : CIP entry
Primary classification 355.1'4'094 B81-37566

623'.0941 — Great Britain. *Army*. Military equipment

Gudgin, Peter. British army equipment : combat vehicles and weapons of the modern British army / Peter Gudgin. — London : Arms & Armour Press, c1981. — 80p : ill ; 26cm
Includes index
ISBN 0-85368-267-4 (cased) : £6.95
ISBN 0-85368-267-4 (pbk) : £3.95 B81-20282

623'.1'0903 — Fortifications, *1300- — Serials*

Fort : the Fortress Study Group newsletter. — 1 (Spring 1976)-. — [Liverpool] ([c/o Dr Q Hughes, The Liverpool School of Architecture, University of Liverpool, PO Box 147, Liverpool L69 3BX]) : The Group, 1976-. — v. : ill ; 30cm
Two issues yearly (1976-1978), annual (1979-). — Supplement: Fort. Supplement. — Continued in part by: Casemate
ISSN 0261-586x = Fort : Unpriced B81-31592

Fort / Fortress Study Group. — 7(1979). — Liverpool (School of Architecture, University of Liverpool, [Liverpool] L69 3BX) : The Group, 1979. — 80p
ISSN 0261-586x : Unpriced B81-31581

Fort / Fortress Study Group. — 8 (1980). — [Liverpool] ([c/o Dr. Q. Hughes, The Liverpool School of Architecture, University of Liverpool, PO Box 147, Liverpool L69 3BX]) : The Group, 1980. — 106p
ISSN 0261-586x : Unpriced B81-31589

Fort. Supplement / Fortress Study Group. — [No.1]-. — Liverpool (c/o Dr. Q. Hughes, The Liverpool School of Architecture, University of Liverpool, PO Box 147, Liverpool L69 3BX) : The Group, 1980-. — v. : ill ; 30cm
Supplement to: Fort
ISSN 0261-5851 = Fort. Supplement : Unpriced B81-31593

623'.1'0961 — North Africa. Byzantine fortifications, *500-800*

Pringle, Denys. The defence of Byzantine Africa from Justinian to the Arab Conquest : an account of the military history and archaeology of the African provinces in the sixth and seventh centuries / Denys Pringle. — Oxford : B.A.R., 1981. — 2v.(xxi,699p) : ill,maps,plans ; 30cm. — (BAR. International series ; 99)
Bibliography: p449-514. — Index
ISBN 0-86054-119-3 (pbk) : £28.00 B81-36615

623'.12'093951 — Europe. Lower Danube River region. Ancient Roman fortifications

Scorpan, C.. Limes Scythiae : topographical and statigraphical research on the late Roman fortifications on the Lower Danube / C. Scorpan. — Oxford : B.A.R., 1980. — [10],219p,[17]p of plates : ill,maps,plans ; 30cm. — (BAR. International series ; 88)
Bibliography: p[7]-[10]
ISBN 0-86054-102-9 (pbk) : £9.00 B81-36590

623'.1944 — France. Fortifications: Maginot Line, *to 1980*

Kemp, Anthony. The Maginot Line : myth and reality / Anthony Kemp. — London : Warne, 1981. — 120p : ill,2maps,plans ; 23cm
Ill on lining papers. — Bibliography: p117-118. — Includes index
ISBN 0-7232-2712-8 : £7.95 B81-13186

623'.3'072041 — Research & development by Great Britain. *Ministry of Defence, 1980*

Research and development in MOD 1980 / [prepared by Ministry of Defence Public Relations and Central Office of Information]. — [London] : H.M.S.O., [1980?]. — 46p : ill ; 30cm
Cover title. — Text on inside covers
Unpriced (spiral) B81-37359

623'.38 — Nuclear shelters. Construction — *Manuals*

Croft, Colin G. Your nuclear shelter : how to build and equip it / Colin G. Croft. — London (5 Huxley Parade, Great Cambridge Rd, N.18) : Croft & Lewis, [1980]. — 132p,[8]p of plates : ill(some col.),plans ; 21cm
Includes index
£4.00 (pbk) B81-03260

623'.38 — Residences. Nuclear shelters. Construction — *Manuals*

Domestic nuclear shelters : advice on domestic shelters providing protection against nuclear explosions : a Home Office guide. — [London] : HMSO, c1981. — 15p : ill(some col.) ; 21cm
Cover title. — Text on inside covers
ISBN 0-11-340737-8 (pbk) : £0.50 B81-09876

Domestic nuclear shelters : technical guidance : a Home Office guide. — [London] : HMSO, c1981. — ii,128p : ill,plans ; 30cm
Cover title
ISBN 0-11-340738-6 (pbk) : £5.50 B81-09877

623.4 — Weapon systems

Lee, R. G.. Introduction to battlefield weapons systems and technology. — Oxford : Pergamon, Sept.1981. — [198]p
ISBN 0-08-027043-3 (cased) : £16.50 : CIP entry
ISBN 0-08-027044-1 (pbk) : £6.75 B81-20477

623.4 — Weapon systems. International political aspects

Howe, Russell Warren. Weapons : the international game of arms, money and diplomacy / Russell Warren Howe. — [London] : Abacus, 1981, c1980. — xlii,798p ; 20cm
Originally published: Garden City, N.Y. : Doubleday, 1980. — Includes index
ISBN 0-349-11750-0 (pbk) : £3.95 B81-39875

623'.4'0321 — Weapons, *to 1979 — Encyclopaedias*

Weapons : an international encyclopedia from 5000 BC to 2000 AD / the Diagram Group. — London : Macmillan, 1980. — 320p : ill (some col.) ; 29cm
Ill on lining papers. — Bibliography: p310-311. — Includes index
ISBN 0-333-29511-0 : £9.95 : CIP rev. B80-1980[illegible]

623.4'05 — Armies. Infantry. Military equipment: Weapons — *Serials*

Brassey's infantry weapons of the world. — 2nd ed. (1979). — London : Brassey's, 1979. — 480p
ISBN 0-904609-10-3 : £25.00
ISBN 0-8448-1368-0 (Crane Russak) B81-0356[illegible]

623.4'05 — Military equipment: Weapons — *Serials*

World armaments and disarmament : SIPRI yearbook. — 1981. — London : Taylor & Francis, 1981. — xxvii,518p
ISBN 0-85066-215-x : £19.50 : CIP rev.
ISSN 0347-2205
Also classified at 623.4'05 B81-1239[illegible]

623.4'05 — Military equipment: Weapons - *Serials*

World armaments and disarmament : SIPRI yearbook. — 1981. — London : Taylor & Francis, 1981. — xxvii,518p
ISBN 0-85066-215-x : £19.50 : CIP rev.
ISSN 0347-2205
Primary classification 623.4'05 B81-1239[illegible]

623.4'094 — European armies. Military equipment: Weapons, *1701-1714*

Kemp, Anthony. Weapons and equipment of the Marlborough wars / line illustrations by John Mollo. — Poole : Blandford Press, 1980. — 172p : ill,facsims,1port ; 26cm
Bibliography: p160-162. - Includes index
ISBN 0-7137-1013-6 : £9.95 : CIP rev. B80-1837[illegible]

623.4'0947 — Union of Soviet Socialist Republics. *Armiia*. Military equipment: Weapons

Isby, David C.. Weapons and tactics of the Soviet Army / David C. Isby. — London : Jane's, 1981. — 384p : ill ; 26cm
Includes index
ISBN 0-7106-0089-5 : £15.00 B81-3326[illegible]

623.4'1'0212 — Artillery - *Technical data*

Brassey's artillery of the world. — 2nd ed., fully rev. and updated. — Oxford : Brassey's, Aug.1981. — [270]p
Previous ed.: 1977
ISBN 0-08-027035-2 : £25.00 : CIP entry B81-1639[illegible]

623.4'4'0904 — Military equipment: Firearms, *1900-1977 — Encyclopaedias*

Hogg, Ian V.. Military small arms : of the 20th century : a comprehensive illustrated encyclopedia of the world's small calibre firearms / Ian V. Hogg and John Weeks. — 4th ed. fully rev. and updated. — London : Arms & Armour, 1981. — 288p : ill ; 28cm
Previous ed.: 1977. — Includes index
ISBN 0-85368-456-1 : £14.95 : CIP rev. B81-1286

623.4'41 — Great Britain. Prehistoric flint arrowheads. Archaeological investigation

Green, H. Stephen. The flint arrowheads of the British Isles : a detailed study of material from England and Wales with comparanda from Scotland and Ireland / H. Stephen Green. — Oxford : B.A.R., 1980. — 2v(xxiv,469p) : ill,maps ; 30cm. — (BAR. British series, ISSN 0143-3032 ; 75)
Includes bibliographies
ISBN 0-86054-077-4 (pbk) : £15.00 B81-1655[illegible]

623.4'41 — Western European swords, *1050-1550*

Oakeshott, Ewart. The sword in the age of chivalry / R. Ewart Oakeshott ; with drawings by the author. — Rev. ed. — London : Arms and Armour, 1981. — 156p,[48]p of plates : ill ; 26cm
Previous ed.: London : Lutterworth, 1964. — Bibliography: p148-149. — Includes index
ISBN 0-85368-277-1 : £14.95 B81-2206[illegible]

23.4′42 — Military equipment: Rifles & sub-machine guns, *ca 1900-1980*

Myatt, Frederick. An illustrated guide to rifles and sub-machine guns / Frederick Myatt. — London : Salamander, c1981. — 160p : ill (some col.) ; 23cm
Bibliography: p159
ISBN 0-86101-077-9 : £3.95 B81-17612

23.4′43 — Military equipment: Pistols & revolvers, *to 1945*

Ezell, Edward C.. Handguns of the world. — London : Arms & Armour Press, Nov.1981. — [768]p
ISBN 0-85368-504-5 : £18.50 : CIP entry B81-30426

23.4′5115′09 — Military equipment: Underwater mines, *1776-1972*

Griffiths, Maurice. The hidden menace / by Maurice Griffiths. — Greenwich : Conway Maritime Press, 1981. — 159p : ill ; 23cm
Includes index
ISBN 0-85177-186-6 : £5.50 B81-04658

23.4′5119′0922 — New Mexico. Los Alamos. Nuclear bombs. Research & development, *1943-45 — Personal observations — Collections*

Reminiscences of Los Alamos 1943-1945 / edited by Lawrence Badash, Joseph O. Hirschfelder and Herbert P. Broida. — Dordrecht ; London : Reidel, c1980. — xxi,188p ; 23cm. — (Studies in the history of modern science ; v.5)
Includes index
ISBN 90-277-1097-x (cased) : Unpriced
ISBN 90-277-1098-8 (pbk) : Unpriced B81-03809

23.4′5119′0941 — Great Britain. Nuclear weapons. Development, *to 1979*

Menaul, Stewart. Countdown : Britain′s strategic nuclear forces / Stewart Menaul. — London : Hale, 1980. — 188p,[24]p of plates : ill,ports ; 23cm
Includes index
ISBN 0-7091-8592-8 : £8.25 B81-01908

23.4′55 — Firearms. Ammunition — *Identification manuals*

Hogg, Ian V.. The cartridge guide. — London : Arms and Armour, Jan.1982. — [160]p
ISBN 0-85368-468-5 : £8.95 : CIP entry B81-33779

23.4′55′0904 — Military equipment: Firearms. Ammunition, *1945-1980*

Labbett, P.. Military small arms ammunition of the world, 1945-1980 / P. Labbett ; drawings and packages chapter by P.J.F. Mead. — London : Arms and Armour, 1980. — 128p : ill,facsims ; 26cm
ISBN 0-85368-294-1 : £8.95 : CIP rev. B80-13430

23′.633 — Armoured trains, *1880-1945*

Balfour, G.. The armoured train : its development and usage / G. Balfour. — London : Batsford, 1981. — 168p : ill,13maps,1plan,ports ; 26cm
Bibliography: p165-166. — Includes index
ISBN 0-7134-2547-4 : £9.95 B81-06815

23.74′09′04 — Military vehicles, *1914-1945 — Illustrations — For modelling*

Modell magazin war album : rare naval, military, and aviation photographs for modellers and enthusiasts, from the files of Modell magazin of Germany. — Watford : Model and Allied Publications, 1978
Parallel German text and English translation
[5]. — 96p : ill(some col.) ; 20cm
Spine title: War album 5
ISBN 0-85242-667-4 (pbk) : £3.25 B81-36138

23.74′6 — Military aeroplanes — *Identification manuals*

Taylor, Michael J. H.. Major combat aircraft / compiled by Michael J.H. Taylor and Kenneth Munson ; edited by John W.R. Taylor. — New ed. — London : Jane′s, 1981. — 264p : ill ; 12x19cm. — (Jane′s pocket book)
Previous ed.: i.e. New ed., London : Macdonald and Jane′s, 1978. — Includes index
ISBN 0-7106-0121-2 : £5.95 B81-39354

623.74′6′0212 — Air forces — *Technical data*

Air forces of the world / compiled by David C. Mondey and Kenneth Munson ; and edited by John W.R. Taylor. — London : Jane′s, 1981. — 256p : ill ; 12x19cm. — (Jane′s pocket book)
ISBN 0-7106-0012-7 : £4.95 B81-19506

623.74′6′0212 — Military aircraft — *Technical data*

The **Hamlyn** concise guide to military aircraft of the world / editor Chris Chant. — London : Hamlyn, 1981. — 224p : ill(some col.) ; 25cm
Includes index
ISBN 0-600-34971-3 : £7.95
ISBN 0-600-34966-7 (pbk) : £4.95 B81-31986

623.74′6′0222 — Military aircraft — *Illustrations*

Seo, Hiroshi. Military aircraft of the world / Hiroshi Seo. — London : Jane′s, 1981. — 93p : chiefly col.ill ; 20x27cm
ISBN 0-7106-0104-2 : £4.95 B81-28457

623.74′6′0321 — Military aircraft — *Encyclopaedias*

The **Encyclopedia** of world air power / consultant editor Bill Gunston. — London : Hamlyn-Aerospace, 1981, c1980. — 384p : ill (some col.),col.maps ; 30cm
Includes index
ISBN 0-600-34989-6 (pbk) : £7.95 B81-37330

623.74′6′09 — Military aircraft, *to 1980 — For children*

Gunston, Bill. Warplanes / by Bill Gunston ; illustrated by Ron Jobson. — London : Granada, 1981. — 64p : col.ill ; 19cm. — (Granada guides)
Includes index
ISBN 0-246-11565-3 : £1.95 B81-39309

Kershaw, Andrew. Guide to combat aircraft / Andrew Kershaw ; illustrated by Ron Jobson and Jim Dugdale ; edited by Bill Bruce. — London : Watts, 1981, c1980. — 24p : chiefly col.ill ; 23cm. — (Explorer guides)
Bibliography: p24 — Includes index
ISBN 0-85166-935-2 : £2.99 B81-26017

623.74′6′09 — Naval aircraft, *to 1979 — Illustrations*

Watts, Anthony J.. [A source book of aircraft carriers and their aircraft]. A source book of naval aircraft and aircraft carriers / Anthony J. Watts. — London : Ward Lock, c1980. — 128p : ill ; 12x17cm. — (Source books)
Originally published: 1977. — Includes index
ISBN 0-7063-6052-4 : £2.95
Also classified at 623.8′255′09 B81-03926

623.74′6′09044 — Military aeroplanes, *1939-1945 — Illustrations*

Gunston, Bill. Aircraft of World War 2 / Bill Gunston. — London : Octopus, 1980. — 207p : ill(some col.) ; 29cm
Ill on lining papers
ISBN 0-7064-1287-7 : £4.95 B81-05867

623.74′6′09046 — Military aircraft, *1960-1980 — Illustrations*

Aircraft illustrated book of military aircraft / [compiled by Allan Burney]. — London : Ian Allan, 1981. — [32]p : all col.ill ; 24cm
ISBN 0-7110-0955-4 (pbk) : £0.95 B81-24857

623.74′6′091713 — Western bloc military forces. Military aeroplanes — *Illustrations*

Trim, Michael. Combat aircraft : the warplanes of the West Roles - armament - performance, 31 aircraft illustrated in colour / [painted by Michael Trim ; text by Arthur Reed]. — [London] : Fontana, 1979. — 1folded sheet ([12]p) : col.ill ; 25cm. — (Domino ; 16)
ISBN 0-00-685456-7 : £0.85 B81-20255

623.74′6′091717 — Warsaw Pact air forces. Military aircraft

Sweetman, Bill. The Hamlyn concise guide to Soviet military aircraft / Bill Sweetman. — London : Hamlyn, 1981. — 207p : ill(some col.) ; 25cm
Includes index
ISBN 0-600-34947-0 (cased) : £7.95
ISBN 0-600-34968-3 (pbk) : £4.95 B81-29123

623.74′6′091821 — North Atlantic Treaty Organization air forces. Military aircraft — *Illustrations*

Horseman, Martin. NATO air power album / Martin Horseman & Denis J. Calvert. — London : Ian Allan, 1980. — 111p : ill,3maps ; 25cm
Maps on lining papers
ISBN 0-7110-1061-7 : £5.95 B81-02756

623.74′6′0941 — Great Britain. Preserved military aeroplanes, *1939-1945*

Bowyer, Chaz. Surviving World War II aircraft / Chaz Bowyer. — London : Batsford, 1981. — 64p : col.ill ; 20cm
ISBN 0-7134-3431-7 (pbk) : £1.95 B81-33067

623.74′6′0941 — Great Britain. *Royal Air Force.* **Military aeroplanes,** *1940*

Green, William, *19---*. Aircraft of the Battle of Britain / William Green. — London : Jane′s Publishing, 1980. — 64p : ill ; 18x22cm
Originally published: London : Macdonald & Co. ; London : Pan Books, 1969
ISBN 0-7106-0060-7 (pbk) : £1.95
Also classified at 623.74′6′0943 B81-09221

623.74′6′0943 — German military forces. Military aircraft, *1910-1980 — Encyclopaedias*

Philpott, Bryan. The encyclopedia of German military aircraft. — London : Arms and Armour Press, Sept.1981. — [192]p
ISBN 0-85368-427-8 : £7.95 : CIP entry B81-23820

623.74′6′0943 — Germany. *Luftwaffe.* **Military aeroplanes,** *1939-1945 — Illustrations*

Feist, Uwe. Luftwaffe in World War II / by Uwe Feist and René J. Francillon. — Fallbrook : Aero ; [London] : Arms & Armour [distributor]
Pt.3 / Uwe Feist. — c1980. — 100p : ill(some col.),ports ; 27cm. — (Aero pictorials ; 6)
ISBN 0-8168-0320-x (pbk) : £3.95 B81-23377

623.74′6′0943 — Germany. *Luftwaffe.* **Military aeroplanes,** *1940*

Green, William, *19---*. Aircraft of the Battle of Britain / William Green. — London : Jane′s Publishing, 1980. — 64p : ill ; 18x22cm
Originally published: London : Macdonald & Co. ; London : Pan Books, 1969
ISBN 0-7106-0060-7 (pbk) : £1.95
Primary classification 623.74′6′0941 B81-09221

623.74′6′0968 — South Africa. *South African Air Force.* **Aeroplanes,** *to 1980*

Potgieter, Herman. Aircraft : of the South African Air Force / pictures Herman Potgieter ; text Willem Steenkamp. — London : Jane′s, 1981. — 180p : col.ill ; 29cm
Originally published: Cape Town : Struik, 1980. — Ill. on lining papers. — Includes index
ISBN 0-7106-0117-4 : £9.95 B81-30097

623.74′6′0973 — American military forces. Military aircraft, *1939-1945*

Munson, Kenneth George. American aircraft of World War II. — Poole : Blandford, Apr.1981. — [159]p. — (Pocket encyclopaedia of world aircraft in colour)
ISBN 0-7137-0944-8 : £2.95 : CIP entry B81-00949

623.74′6′0973 — United States. *Air Force.* **Military aircraft,** *1970-1979 — Illustrations*

Peacock, Lindsay T.. U.S. Air Force in the 1970s. — London : Arms and Armour Press, Jan.1982. — [68]p. — (Warbirds illustrated series ; 3)
ISBN 0-85368-438-3 : £3.50 : CIP entry B81-33782

623.74′6′0973 — United States. *Navy.* **Military aircraft,** *1970-1979 — Illustrations*

Peacock, Lindsay T.. U.S. Navy combat aircraft in the 1970s. — London : Arms and Armour Press, Jan.1982. — [68]p. — (Warbirds illustrated series ; 4)
ISBN 0-85368-458-8 : £3.50 : CIP entry B81-33781

623.74′62′0212 — Military training aeroplanes — *Technical data*

Military transport and training aircraft / compiled by Michael J.H. Taylor and Kenneth Munson ; edited by John W.R. Taylor. — [2nd ed]. — London : Jane′s, 1981. — 272p : ill ; 12x19cm. — (Jane′s pocket book ; 5)
Previous ed.: 1979. — Includes index
ISBN 0-7106-0094-1 : £4.95
Also classified at 623.74′65′0212 B81-19514

623.74′63 — Avro Lancaster aeroplanes, *to 1980* — *Illustrations*

Lancaster photo album / compiled and edited by Neville Franklin. — Cambridge : Stephens, 1981. — 96p : chiefly ill ; 24cm
ISBN 0-85059-477-4 (pbk) : £3.95 B81-19775

623.74′63 — Boeing B-52 aeroplanes

Ethell, Jeffrey. B-52 Stratofortress / Jeff Ethell & Joe Christy. — London : Ian Allan, 1981. — 128p : ill(some col.),ports ; 25cm. — (Modern combat aircraft ; 8)
Bibliography: p127
ISBN 0-7110-1070-6 : £6.95 B81-29738

623.74′63 — Boeing B-52 aeroplanes, *to 1980*

Boyne, Walter J.. Boeing B-52 : a documentary history / Walter Boyne. — London : Jane′s, 1981. — 160p : ill,map,ports ; 28cm
Includes index
ISBN 0-7106-0122-0 : £8.95 B81-39449

623.74′63 — Boeing B17 aeroplanes, *to 1980*

Kinsey, Bert. B-17 Flying Fortress in detail and scale. — London : Arms and Armour Press, Oct.1981. — [72]p. — (Detail and scale series ; 2)
ISBN 0-85368-500-2 : £3.95 : CIP entry
B81-25735

623.74′63 — Buccaneer aeroplanes, *to 1980*

Allward, Maurice. Buccaneer / Maurice Allward. — London : Ian Allan, 1981. — 127p : ill (some col.),ports ; 25cm. — (Modern combat aircraft ; 7)
ISBN 0-7110-1076-5 : £6.95 B81-11051

623.74′63 — De Havilland Mosquito aeroplanes, *to 1979*

Birtles, Philip. Mosquito : a pictorial history of the DH98 / Philip Birtles. — London : Jane′s, 1980. — 192p : ill,ports ; 27cm
Bibliography: p192
ISBN 0-7106-0065-8 : £8.95 B81-03335

Bowyer, Michael J. F.. Mosquito / Michael J.F. Bowyer and Bryan Philpott. — Cambridge : Stephens, 1980. — 120p : ill ; 25cm. — (Classic aircraft ; no.7)
Ill on lining papers. — Bibliography: p117
ISBN 0-85059-432-4 : £7.50 : CIP rev.
Also classified at 623.74′63 B80-17766

623.74′63 — Heinkel He 111 aeroplanes, *to 1945*

Nowarra, Heinz J.. Heinkel He 111 : a documentary history / Heinz Nowarra. — London : Jane′s, 1980. — 256p : ill ; 25cm
Translation of: Die He 111. — Bibliography: p248. - Includes index
ISBN 0-7106-0046-1 : £8.95 B81-06766

623.74′63 — Model De Havilland Mosquito aeroplanes. Making — *Manuals*

Bowyer, Michael J. F.. Mosquito / Michael J.F. Bowyer and Bryan Philpott. — Cambridge : Stephens, 1980. — 120p : ill ; 25cm. — (Classic aircraft ; no.7)
Ill on lining papers. — Bibliography: p117
ISBN 0-85059-432-4 : £7.50 : CIP rev.
Primary classification 623.74′63 B80-17766

623.74′63 — Republic Aircraft F-105 Thunderchief aeroplanes, *to 1980*

Scutts, Jerry. F-105 Thunderchief / J.C. Scutts. — London : Ian Allan, 1981. — 112p : ill (some col.),maps ; 25cm. — (Modern combat aircraft ; 10)
ISBN 0-7110-1096-x : £6.95 B81-31859

623.74′63′09044 — Bomber aeroplanes, *1939-1945*

Gunston, Bill. An illustrated guide to bombers of World War II / Bill Gunston. — London : Salamander, 1980. — 160p : ill(some col.) ; 23cm
Col.ill on lining papers
ISBN 0-86101-069-8 : £2.95 B81-04467

623.74′63′0941 — Great Britain. *Royal Air Force.* **Bomber aeroplanes,** *1939-1945*

Green, William, *1927-*. RAF bombers / William Green and Gordon Swanborough. — London : Jane′s. — (WW2 aircraft fact files)
Pt.2. — 1981. — 76p : ill(some col.) ; 27cm
Cover title
ISBN 0-7106-0118-2 (pbk) : £4.95 B81-39448

623.74′63′0941 — Great Britain. *Royal Air Force.* **V-bomber aeroplanes,** *to 1980*

Jackson, Robert, *1941-*. V-bombers / Robert Jackson. — London : Ian Allan, 1981. — 112p : ill(some col.) ; 25cm. — (Modern combat aircraft ; 11)
ISBN 0-7110-1100-1 : £6.95 B81-36739

623.74′63′0973 — United States. *Air Force.* **Bomber aeroplanes,** *1928-1980*

Jones, Lloyd S.. U.S. bombers 1928 to 1980s / by Lloyd S. Jones. — 3rd ed. — Fallbrook : Aero ; [London] : Arms & Armour [distributor], 1980. — 271p : ill ; 29cm
Previous ed.: 1974. — Ill on lining papers
ISBN 0-8168-9128-1 : £8.95 B81-23379

623.74′64 — Allied fighter aeroplanes, *1939-1945*

Gunston, Bill. An illustrated guide to allied fighters of World War II / Bill Gunston. — London : Salamander, c1981. — 160p : ill (some col.) ; 23cm
ISBN 0-86101-081-7 : £3.95 B81-17614

623.74′64 — British Aerospace Harrier aeroplanes

Mason, Francis K.. Harrier. — Cambridge : Patrick Stephens, Oct.1981. — [216]p
ISBN 0-85059-501-0 : £10.95 : CIP entry
B81-27992

623.74′64 — Focke-Wulf FW 190 aeroplanes, *1937-1945*

Grinsell, Robert. Focke-Wulf FW190 / text by Robert Grinsell ; illustrations by Rikyu Watanabe. — London : Jane′s, 1980. — 48p : ill(some col.),2ports ; 34cm
Ill on lining papers
ISBN 0-7106-0032-1 : £4.95 B81-05660

623.74′64 — Hawker Hunter aeroplanes, *to 1980*

Mason, Francis K.. Hawker Hunter : biography of a thoroughbred / Francis K. Mason ; foreword by Bill Bedford. — Cambridge : Stephens, 1981. — 216p : ill ; 25cm
Ill on lining papers. — Includes index
ISBN 0-85059-476-6 : £10.95 B81-19674

623.74′64 — Lockheed F-104 Starfighter aeroplanes, *to 1975*

Reed, Arthur. F-104 Starfighter / Arthur Reed. — London : Ian Allan, 1981. — 112p : ill (some col.),facsims,ports ; 25cm. — (Modern combat aircraft ; 9)
ISBN 0-7110-1089-7 : £6.95 B81-24860

623.74′64 — McDonnell Douglas Phantom II aeroplanes, *to 1980*

Kinsey, Bert. F-4 Phantom II (USAF) in detail and scale. — London : Arms and Armour Press. — (Detail and scale series ; 1)
Part 1. — Oct.1981. — [72]p
ISBN 0-85368-501-0 (pbk) : £3.95 : CIP entry
B81-25736

623.74′64 — Messerschmitt Bf 109 aeroplanes, *to 1967*

Grinsell, Robert. Messerschmitt Bf 109 / text by Robert Grinsell ; illustrations by Rikyu Watanabe. — London : Jane′s, 1980. — 48p : ill(some col.),ports ; 34cm
Ill on lining papers
ISBN 0-7106-0034-8 : £4.95 B81-19874

623.74′64 — Messerschmitt Me 262 aeroplanes, *to 1945*

Boyne, Walter J.. Messerschmitt Me 262 : arrow to the future / by Walter J. Boyne. — London : Jane′s, 1981, c1980. — viii,188p : ill(some col.),ports ; 27cm
Originally published: Washington : Smithsonia Institution Press, 1980. — Ill on lining papers. — Bibliography: p187
ISBN 0-7106-0080-1 : £7.95 B81-1085

623.74′64 — Mustang P-51 aeroplanes, *1940-1945*

Ethell, Jeffrey. Mustang : a documentary history of the P-51 / by Jeffrey Ethell. — London : Jane′s, 1981. — 176p : ill,ports ; 29cm
Bibliography: p174. — Includes index
ISBN 0-7106-0070-4 : £8.95 B81-2344

Grinsell, Robert. P51 Mustang / text by Robert Grinsell ; illustrations by Rikyu Watanabe. — London : Jane′s, 1980. — 48p : ill(some col.) ; 34cm
Ill on lining papers
ISBN 0-7106-0033-x : £4.95 B81-0566

623.74′64 — Supermarine Spitfire aeroplanes, *to 1968*

Sweetman, Bill. Spitfire / text by Bill Sweetman illustrations by Rikyu Watanabe. — London : Jane′s, 1980. — 48p : ill(some col.) ; 34cm
Originally published: New York : Crown, 1980
ISBN 0-7106-0035-6 : £4.95 B81-1029

623.74′64 — Supermarine Spitfire XVI aeroplanes: Spitfire TB752, *to 1979*

Deal, Lewis E.. The Manston Spitfire : TB752 / [compiled and written by Lewis E. Deal]. — Rochester : North Kent Books, 1981. — 66p[4]p of plates : ill(some col.),facsims,ports
ISBN 0-9505733-5-3 (pbk) : £1.50 B81-3311

623.74′64′09 — Fighter aeroplanes, *to 1980*

The **Illustrated** encyclopedia of fighters / editor-in-chief Bill Gunston. — [London] : Macdonald, [c1981]. — 255p : ill(some col.) ; 31cm
Includes index
ISBN 0-356-07569-9 : £8.95 B81-3853

623.74′64′09044 — Fighter aeroplanes, *1939-1945* — *Illustrations*

Trim, Michael. Fighter planes of World War II : 37 famous aircraft illustrated in colour, German, British, Italian, Russian, Japanese, American / [written and painted by Michael Trim]. — [London] : Fontana, 1980. — 1folde sheet([12]p) : col.ill ; 25cm. — (Domino ; 23)
ISBN 0-00-685464-8 : £0.95 B81-2026

623.74′64′09045 — Fighter aeroplanes, *1950-1959*

Gunston, Bill. Fighters of the 50s. — Cambridge : Stephens, Sept.1981. — [192]p
ISBN 0-85059-463-4 : £10.95 : CIP entry
B81-2012

623.74′64′0924 — Europe. Republic Aircraft F-84F aeroplanes. Flying under adverse weather conditions — *Personal observations*

Bach, Richard. Stranger to the ground / Richard Bach. — London : Granada, 1981, c1972. — 175p : 1map ; 18cm. — (A Panther book)
Originally published: London : Cassell, 1964
ISBN 0-586-05312-3 (pbk) : £1.25 B81-3138

623.74′64′0941 — Great Britain. *Royal Air Force.* **Fighter aeroplanes,** *1939-1945*

Green, William, *1927-*. RAF fighters / William Green and Gordon Swanborough. — London : Jane′s. — (WW2 aircraft fact files)
Pt.3. — 1981. — 60p : ill(some col.) ; 27cm
Cover title
ISBN 0-7106-0119-0 (pbk) : £4.95 B81-3944

623.74′65′0212 — Military transport aeroplanes — *Technical data*

Military transport and training aircraft / compiled by Michael J.H. Taylor and Kenneth Munson ; edited by John W.R. Taylor. — [2nd ed]. — London : Jane′s, 1981. — 272p : ill ; 12x19cm. — (Jane′s pocket book ; 5)
Previous ed.: 1979. — Includes index
ISBN 0-7106-0094-1 : £4.95
Primary classification 623.74′62′0212 B81-1951

623.74′7 — Military lorries — *Technical data*

Modern military trucks / [compiled by] Christopher F. Foss. — London : Jane's, 1981. — 267p : ill ; 12x19cm. — (Jane's pocket book)
ISBN 0-7106-0091-7 : £4.95 B81-17816

623.74′7 — Military vehicles: Bedford QL lorries

Conniford, Mike. Bedford QL / researched by Mike Conniford. — Reading (12 Westdene Cres., Caversham, Reading RG4 7HD) : Inkpen Art Productions, c1981. — 17p : ill ; 30cm. — (Military vehicle pamphlet ; no.5)
Cover title. — Text on inside cover
ISBN 0-907403-04-2 (pbk) : £1.25 B81-13976

623.74′7 — Military vehicles: Canadian military pattern 8cwt lorries

Conniford, Mike. CMP (Canadian Military Pattern) 8 cwts / researched by Mike Conniford. — Reading (12 Westdene Cres., Caversham, Reading) : Inkpen, c1981. — 17p : ill ; 30cm. — (Military vehicle pamphlet ; 8)
Cover title. — Text on inside cover
ISBN 0-907403-08-5 (pbk) : £1.25 B81-36916

623.74′7′0228 — Model military land vehicles. Construction — *Manuals*

Fairhurst, Peter. Making model wartime vehicles / written and illustrated by Peter Fairhurst. — [London] : Carousel, 1980. — 112p : ill ; 20cm
ISBN 0-552-54175-3 (pbk) : £0.75 B81-08465

623.74′72 — Military vehicles: British four-wheeled 30 cwt lorries

Conniford, Mike. British 4-wheeled 30-cwts / researched by Mike Conniford. — Reading (12 Westdene Cres., Caversham, Reading RG4 7HD) : Inkpen Art Productions, c1981. — 17p : ill ; 30cm. — (Military vehicle pamphlet ; 7)
Cover title
ISBN 0-907403-06-9 (pbk) : £1.25 B81-27057

623.74′722′0973 — United States. *Army*. Jeep military vehicles, *1939-1945 — Illustrations*

The **Jeep** / compiled for the Olyslager Organisation by Bart H. Vanderveen. — Rev. ed. — London : Warne, 1981. — 64p : ill,ports ; 19x26cm. — (Olyslager auto library)
Previous ed.: 1971. — Bibliography: p64. - Includes index
ISBN 0-7232-2778-0 : £11.50 B81-20969

623.74′75′0212 — Armoured combat vehicles — *Technical data*

Modern tanks and armoured fighting vehicles / [compiled by] Christopher F. Foss. — 3rd ed. — London : Jane's, 1981. — 288p : ill ; 12x19cm. — (Jane's pocket book)
Previous ed.: Published as Jane's pocket book of modern tanks and armoured fighting vehicles. 1977. — Includes index
ISBN 0-7106-0092-5 : £4.95 B81-19511

623.74′75′05 — Armoured combat vehicles — *Serials*

Aero-armor series. — Vol.12. — Fallbrook, Calif. : Aero Pulishers ; [London] : Arms & Armour Press, c1980. — 52p
ISBN 0-8168-2044-9 : £2.50 B81-24695

Aero-armor series. — Vol.13. — Fallbrook, Calif. : Aero Publishers ; [London] : Arms & Armour Press, c1980. — 52p
ISBN 0-8168-2046-5 : £2.50 B81-24694

623.74′75′0973 — United States. *Army*. Armoured combat vehicles

Zaloga, Steven J.. Modern American armour. — London : Arms and Armour Press, Jan.1982. — [88]p
ISBN 0-85368-248-8 : £6.95 : CIP entry B81-33780

623.74′75′0973 — United States. *Army*. Armoured combat vehicles, *1935-1945 — Illustrations*

. American armour / [compiled by] Simon Forty. — London : Ian Allan, 1981. — 96p : chiefly ill ; 24cm. — (1939-1945 portfolio)
ISBN 0-7110-1052-8 (pbk) : £3.95 B81-07216

623.74′752 — Armoured combat vehicles: Centurion tanks

Dunstan, Simon. Centurion / Simon Dunstan. — London : Ian Allan, 1980. — 124p : ill(some col.) ; 24cm. — (Modern combat vehicles)
Ill on lining papers
ISBN 0-7110-1063-3 : £7.95 B81-03218

623.74′752′09 — Armoured combat vehicles: Tanks, *to 1950*

Macksey, Kenneth. The tank pioneers / Kenneth Macksey. — London : Janes's, 1981. — vi,228p,[16]p of plates : ill,maps,ports ; 25cm
Bibliography: p221-222. - Includes index
ISBN 0-7106-0090-9 : £9.50 B81-15991

623.74′752′09 — Armoured combat vehicles: Tanks, *to 1980 — For children*

Anson, Clive. Tanks / by Clive Anson ; illustrated by Ross Wardle and Doug Post. — London : Granada, 1981. — 64p : col.ill ; 19cm. — (Granada guides)
Includes index
ISBN 0-246-11628-5 : £1.95 B81-39305

Kershaw, Andrew. Guide to tanks / Andrew Kershaw ; illustrated Doug Post, Ross Wardle and Pete Robinson. — London : Watts, 1981, c1980. — 24p : chiefly col.ill ; 23cm. — (Explorer guides)
Bibliography: p24. — Includes index
ISBN 0-85166-934-4 : £2.99 B81-26018

623.74′752′09044 — Armoured combat vehicles: Tanks, *1939-1945*

Ellis, Chris. Tanks of World War 2 / Chris Ellis. — London : Octopus, 1981. — 207p : col.ill ; 29cm
Ill on lining papers
ISBN 0-7064-1288-5 : £6.95 B81-18196

An **Illustrated** guide to World War II tanks and fighting vehicles / [edited by Christopher F. Foss]. — London : Salamander, c[1981]. — 160p : ill(some col.) ; 23cm
ISBN 0-86101-083-3 : £3.95 B81-17611

623.8 — SHIPS, SHIPBUILDING AND SEAMANSHIP

623.8′03′21 — English language. Nautical terms — *Dictionaries*

Blackburn, Graham. The illustrated dictionary of nautical terms. — Newton Abbot : David & Charles, Jan.1982. — [368]p
ISBN 0-7153-8296-9 : £9.95 : CIP entry B81-38302

623.8′1 — Ships. Design, *1670 — Early works*

Deane, *Sir* Anthony. Deane's Doctrine of naval architecture, 1670 / edited and introducted by Brian Lavery. — London : Conway Maritime, 1981. — 128p : ill,facsims,plans,1port ; 31cm
ISBN 0-85177-180-7 : £20.00 B81-25948

623.8′171 — Ports. Ships. Hydrodynamics

. Ship behaviour in ports and their approaches. — London : National Ports Council
Pt.3: The prediction of squat for vessels in shallow waters. — 1981. — 9,[10]leaves ; 30cm
ISBN 0-86073-054-9 (spiral) : £10.00 B81-13628

623.8′2 — Boats & ships — *For children*

Fenner, Sal. Sea machines / Sal Fenner. — Oxford : Blackwell Raintree, c1981. — 31p : col.ill ; 27cm
Originally published: Milwaukee : Raintree Children, c1980. — Includes index
ISBN 0-86256-025-x : £2.75 B81-17607

623.8′2 — Boats. Metal components. Corrosion

Warren, Nigel. Metal corrosion in boats / Nigel Warren. — London : Stanford Maritime, 1980. — 224p,xvi p of plates : ill ; 23cm
Bibliography: p217-218. - Includes index
ISBN 0-540-07397-0 : £7.95 : CIP rev. B80-10111

623.8′2 — Boats. Purchase — *Manuals*

Robinson, Bill, *1918-*. The right boat for you / Bill Robinson. — London : Hale, 1981. — 174p,[24]p of plates : ill,plans ; 21cm
Originally published: New York : Holt, Rinehart and Winston, 1974. — Includes index
ISBN 0-7091-8727-0 : £6.50 B81-07732

623.8′2 — Ships. Chemicals

Chemicals in ships / edited by L. Kenworthy. — London : Marine Management for the Institute of Marine Engineers, c1978. — xiii,25p : ill ; 22cm
Includes bibliographies and index
ISBN 0-900976-72-1 : Unpriced B81-37619

623.8′2 — Ships — *Identification manuals*

Dodman, Frank E.. The Observer's book of ships / Frank E. Dodman. — New ed. — London : Warne, 1981, c1973. — 192p,[8]p of plates : ill (some col.) ; 15cm. — (The Observer's series ; 15)
Includes index
ISBN 0-7232-1622-3 : £1.95 B81-21186

623.8′2′00321 — Ships, *to 1978 — Encyclopaedias*

Encyclopedia of ships and seafaring / editor Peter Kemp. — London : Stanford Maritime, 1980. — 256p : ill(some col.),charts(some col.),col.maps,plans,ports(some col.) ; 28cm
Includes index
ISBN 0-540-07194-3 : £9.95 : CIP rev. B79-17643

623.8′2′009 — Ships, *to 1979*

The **Ship**. — London : H.M.S.O.
At head of title: National Maritime Museum
The century before steam : the development of the sailing ship, 1700-1820 / Alan McGowan. — 1980. — 60p : ill(some col.) ; 21x22cm
Ill on lining papers. — Bibliography: p58. — Includes index
ISBN 0-11-290314-2 : £2.95 B81-19884

The **Ship**. — London : H.M.S.O.
At head of title: National Maritime Museum
Channel packets and ocean liners, 1850-1970 / John M. Maber. — 1980. — 60p : ill ; 21x22cm
Ill on lining papers. — Bibliography: p58. — Includes index
ISBN 0-11-290316-9 : £2.95 B81-19886

The **Ship**. — London : H.M.S.O.
At head of title: National Maritime Museum
The life and death of the merchant sailing ship, 1815-1965 / Basil Greenhill. — 1980. — 60p : ill ; 21x22cm
Ill on lining papers. — Includes index
ISBN 0-11-290317-7 : £2.95 B81-19885

623.8′2′00941 — Great Britain. Ships. Construction, *to 1947*

Abell, *Sir* Westcott. The shipwright's trade / by Sir Westcott Abell. — London : Conway Maritime Press, 1981. — xiii,218p,xix p of plates : 1ill ; 23cm
Originally published: Cambridge : Cambridge University Press, 1948. — Includes index
ISBN 0-85177-237-4 : £9.50 B81-07989

623.8′201 — Model ships. Construction

Mansir, Richard. A guide to ship modelling. — London : Arms & Armour Press, Sept.1981. — [320]p
ISBN 0-85368-505-3 : £18.50 : CIP entry B81-28206

623.8′201 — Plank-on-frame model boats. Making — *Manuals*

Underhill, Harold A.. Plank-on-frame models : and scale masting and rigging by Harold A. Underhill. — Glasgow : Brown, Son and Ferguson
Vol.1: Scale Hull construction / with plans and sketches by the author. — 1958 (1981 [printing]). — ix,157p,[24]p of plates : ill,plans ; 24cm
Includes index
ISBN 0-85174-186-x : £10.00 B81-21812

623.8′201 — Radio controlled model boats. Radio controls

Rayer, F. G.. Radio control for beginners / by F.G. Rayer. — London : Bernard Babani, 1980. — 92p : ill ; 18cm
ISBN 0-900162-99-6 (pbk) : £1.75 : CIP rev.
B80-22034

623.8′2012 — Model schooners, *1763-1775.* **Construction** — *Manuals*

Hahn, Harold M.. The colonial schooner 1763-1775 / Harold M. Hahn. — Greenwich : Conway Maritime, 1981. — 176p : ill,maps,1facsim,ports ; 29cm
ISBN 0-85177-215-3 : £12.50 B81-21400

623.8′202 — Small boats. Construction — *Manuals*

Nicolson, Ian. Building small boats. — London : Allen & Unwin, Jan.1982. — [304]p
ISBN 0-04-623014-9 : £12.95 : CIP entry
B81-33910

623.8′202 — Small boats. Hulls. Fitting out — *Amateurs′ manuals*

Toghill, Jeff. The Boat owner′s fitting out manual / Jeff Toghill. — Revised ed. — London : Stanford Maritime, 1980. — 223p : ill ; 26cm
Previous ed.: Terry Hills, N.S.W. : Reed, 1979. — Includes index
ISBN 0-540-07398-9 : £10.95 : CIP rev.
B80-12928

623.8′202 — Small boats. Purchase — *Manuals*

Jarman, Colin. Buying a boat / Colin Jarman. — Newton Abbot : David & Charles, c1980. — 191p : ill,plans ; 23cm
Includes index
ISBN 0-7153-7960-7 : £6.50 : CIP rev.
B80-23392

623.8′202′0288 — Small boats. Maintenance & repair — *Amateurs′ manuals*

Mosenthal, Basil. Ready for sea : a guide to systematic boat maintenance power and sail / Basil Mosenthal and Dick Hewitt. — London : Adlard Coles : Granada, 1981. — 128p : ill ; 24cm
Bibliography: p127. - Includes index
ISBN 0-229-11647-7 (pbk) : £2.95 B81-12138

623.8′203′09 — Sailing vessels, *to 1980* — *Illustrations*

Hawkins, Clifford W.. Argosy of sail : a photographic history of sail / Clifford W. Hawkins. — Auckland ; London : Collins, 1980. — 184p : chiefly ill,ports ; 29cm
Includes index
ISBN 0-00-216964-9 : £10.95 B81-01579

623.8′207 — Danish wooden boats, *1870-1930*

Nielsen, Christian. Wooden boat designs : classic Danish boats measured and described / by Christian Nielsen ; translated by Erik J. Friis. — London : Stanford Maritime, 1980. — xii,161p : ill,1map ; 29cm
Translation of: Danske bådtyper
ISBN 0-540-07396-2 : £7.95 : CIP rev.
B80-09276

623.8′207 — Wooden boats. Maintenance & repair — *Amateurs′ manuals*

Scarlett, J. A.. Wooden boats : restoration & maintenence manual / John Scarlett. — Newton Abbot : David & Charles, c1981. — 223p : ill ; 26cm
Includes index
ISBN 0-7153-8077-x : £10.95 B81-23441

623.8′208 — Boats. Improvement — *Amateurs′ manuals*

Damour, Jacques. 101 tips and hints for your boat / by Jacques Damour ; translated by Jeremy Howard-Williams. — London : Granada, 1981. — 189p : ill ; 24cm
Translation from the French
ISBN 0-229-11652-3 : £4.95 B81-15316

623.8′208 — Boats. Maintenance & repair — *Amateurs′ manuals*

Lane, Carl D.. The boatman′s manual : a complete manual of boat handling, operation, maintenance and seamanship / by Carl D. Lane ; drawings by the author. — 4th rev. and enl. ed. — New York ; London : W.W. Norton, c1979. — xii,705p : ill(some col.),1map,1facsim ; 19cm
Previous ed.: i.e. Completely rev. ed., published as The new boatman′s manual. London : Coles, 1967. — Text, ill on lining papers. — Includes index
ISBN 0-393-03190-x : £11.50
Primary classification 797.1 B81-02451

623.8′21 — Humberside. Brigg. Prehistoric wooden boats. Archaeological investigation

The **Brigg** ′raft′ and her prehistoric environment / edited by Sean McGrail. — Oxford : B.A.R., 1981. — ixx,288p : ill,maps,plans ; 30cm. — (Archaeological series / National Maritime Museum ; no.6) (BAR. British series ; 89)
Includes bibliographies and index
ISBN 0-86054-131-2 (pbk) : £13.00 B81-36630

623.8′22 — Scotland. Shetland. Sixareens, *to ca 1900*

Sandison, Charles. The Sixareen and her racing descendants / by Charles Sandison. — Lerwick (Prince Alfred St., Lerwick, Shetland ZE1 0EP) : Shetland Times, 1981. — viii,53p : ill,map ; 22cm
Originally published: Lerwick : Manson, 1954
ISBN 0-900662-30-1 (pbk) : Unpriced
B81-16220

623.8′22 — Sloops: Spray *(Ship)*

Slack, Kenneth E.. In the wake of the spray. — Havant : Kenneth Mason, Nov.1981. — [275]p
Originally published: New Brunswick : Rutgers University Press, 1966
ISBN 0-85937-274-x : £9.95 : CIP entry
B81-30282

623.8′22 — Yachts

Motor boat and yachting manual. — 19th ed. — London : Stanford, Jan.1982. — [288]p
Previous ed.: 1973
ISBN 0-540-07400-4 : £8.95 : CIP entry
Primary classification 623.8′231 B81-35032

623.8′22′0916336 — England. Solent. Sailing vessels, *1880-1980* — *Illustrations*

Beken of Cowes *(Firm)*. A hundred years of sail / Beken of Cowes. — London : Collins, 1981. — [194]p(some folded) : chiefly ill,1port ; 37cm
ISBN 0-00-216811-1 : £30.00 B81-37611

623.8′223 — Great Britain. Mirror sailing dinghies. Organisations: Mirror Class Association — *Serials*

Mirror Class Association. Year book / Mirror Class Association. — 1981. — [Rugby] ([9 North St., Rugby, Warwickshire CV21 2AB]) : [The Association], [1981?]. — 52p
Unpriced B81-36554

623.8′223 — Norfolk sailing dinghies, *to 1979*

Buckerfield, Paul. A real boat : the Norfolk dinghy story / by Paul Buckerfield. — Norwich ([5 Western Ave., Thorpe St. Andrew, Norwich NR7 0HA]) : The Norfolk 14-foot One-Design Dinghy Class, 1980. — v,78p : ill,ports ; 21cm
ISBN 0-9507098-0-8 (pbk) : £3.50 B81-06935

623.8′223 — Sailing catamarans

Andrews, Jim. Catamarans for cruising / Jim Andrews ; diagrams by the author. — 2nd ed.. — London : Hollis & Carter, 1981. — 223p,[4]p of plates : ill ; 21cm
Previous ed.: 1974. — Includes index
ISBN 0-370-10339-4 (cased) : Unpriced
ISBN 0-370-30382-2 (pbk) : £4.50 B81-11510

623.8′224 — Sailing ships: Sigyn *(Ship), to 1979*

Pipping, Knut. The Museum ship ′Sigyn′ of Wårdö / by Knut Pipping. — Greenwich : Trustees of the National Maritime Museum, [1980]. — ii,23p : ill ; 21cm. — (Occasional lecture / National Maritime Museum, ISSN 0141-1268 ; no.2)
ISBN 0-905555-47-3 : Unpriced B81-24920

623.8′224′09034 — Merchant sailing ships, *1850-1920*

The **Medley** of mast and sail : a camera record : 525 photographic illustrations ... — Brighton ([P.O. Box 430, Brighton, Sussex]) : Teredo II / with an introduction by Alex. A. Hurst. — 1981. — xxi,473p : ill(some col.),1map,ports ; 25cm
Ill on lining papers. — Includes index
£17.00 (corrected) B81-4078

623.8′231 — Motorboats

Motor boat and yachting manual. — 19th ed. — London : Stanford, Jan.1982. — [288]p
Previous ed.: 1973
ISBN 0-540-07400-4 : £8.95 : CIP entry
Also classified at 623.8′22 B81-3503

623.8′2314 — Hydrofoil boats — *Serials*

Jane′s surface skimmers. — 14th ed. (1981)-. — London : Jane′s, 1981. — 380p
£29.50
Primary classification 629.3′05 B81-2008

623.8′2314 — Luxury yachts, *1840-1914*

Drummond, Maldwin. Salt-water palaces / Maldwin Drummond ; introduction by the Ea Mountbatten of Burma. — London : Debrett, c1979. — 140p : ill,1map,1coat of arms,1facsim,plans,ports ; 27cm
Ill on lining papers. — Includes index
ISBN 0-905649-27-3 : £8.95 B81-2667

623.8′234′0916336 — English Channel. Ferry services. Passenger steamships, *to 1980*

Greenway, Ambrose. A century of cross-Channel passenger ferries / Ambrose Greenway. — London : Ian Allan, 1981. — 124p : ill ; 25cm
Ill on lining papers. — Includes index
ISBN 0-7110-1069-2 : £7.95 B81-3280

623.8′24 — Merchant ships, *ca 1930-1979*

Ransome-Wallis, P.. Merchant ship panorama / P. Ransome-Wallis. — London : Ian Allan, 1980. — 160p : ill ; 30cm
Bibliography: p158. — Includes index
ISBN 0-7110-1057-9 : £10.95 B81-0311

623.8′24 — Merchant ships — *Identification manuals*

Talbot-Booth′s merchant ships. — Sandwich (Dept. T.B-S, Pillory Gate Wharf, Sandwich, Kent) : Marinart, 1979
Vol.3 / edited by R.A. Streater and D.G. Greenman ; consultant editor E.C. Talbot-Booth ; illustrated by D.G. Greenman, F.R. Langridge ; additional illustrations by E.C. Talbot-Booth ; production/research by P.I. Streater ... [et al.]. — 523p : ill ; 31cm
Includes index
ISBN 0-85038-139-8 : £20.00 B81-3314

623.8′24′0682 — Merchant ships. Maintenance. Management

Thomas, B. E. M.. Management of shipboard maintenance / B.E.M. Thomas. — London : Stanford, 1980. — 143p : ill,forms ; 25cm
Spine title: Shipboard maintenance. — Bibliography: p141. — Includes index
ISBN 0-540-07354-7 : £5.95 : CIP rev.
B80-1782

623.8′24′0973 — United States. *Maritime Commission.* **Merchant ships,** *to 1952*

Sawyer, L. A.. From America to United States : in four parts : the history of the merchant shi types built in the United States of America under the long-range programme of the Maritime Commission / L.A. Sawyer and W.H. Mitchell. — Kendal : World Ship Societ
Part 1. — 1979. — 120p : ill ; 25cm
Includes index
ISBN 0-905617-08-8 (pbk) : Unpriced
B81-4033

623.8′2432 — Atlantic Ocean. Passenger paddle steamers, *1818-1865*

Spratt, H. Philip. Transatlantic paddle steamers by H. Philip Spratt. — 2nd ed. — Glasgow : Brown, Son & Ferguson, 1980. — 92p,vi fold leaves,ixp of plates : ill ; 22cm
Previous ed.: 1951. — Bibliography: p80-82. — Includes index
ISBN 0-85174-158-4 : £7.00 B81-0527

623.8'2432 — Avon. Bristol. Steam liners: Great Britain *(Ship)*. Restoration. Projects: S.S. Great Britain Project
Ball, Adrian. S.S. Great Britain / Adrian Ball & Diana Wright. — Newton Abbot : David & Charles, c1981. — 96p : ill(some col.),1map,facsims(some col.),ports ; 22x30cm
ISBN 0-7153-8096-6 : £7.95 : CIP rev. B81-06076

623.8'2432 — Steam liners: Great Eastern *(Ship)*
Emmerson, George S.. The greatest iron ship S.S. Great Eastern / George S. Emmerson. — Newton Abbot : David & Charles, [1981]. — 182p : ill,ports ; 24cm
Bibliography: p176. - Includes index
ISBN 0-7153-8054-0 : £8.95 B81-14611

623.8'2436 — Scotland. Strathclyde Region. Firth of Clyde. Passenger steamships, *1812-1979*
Davies, Kenneth, *1927-*. The Clyde passenger steamers / Kenneth Davies. — Ayr : Kyle, 1980. — 280p,[33]p of plates : ill,1map ; 23cm
Bibliography: p271-273. - Includes index
ISBN 0-906955-05-x : Unpriced B81-10406

623.8'245 — Great Britain. Cargo ships: Steam coasters, *to ca 1950*
Waine, Charles V.. Steam coasters and short sea traders / Charles V. Waine ; illustrated by the author. — 2nd ed. — Albrighton (Mount Pleasant, Beamish La., Albrighton) : Waine Research, 1980. — 157p : ill(some col.),1map,plans ; 31cm
Previous ed.: 1976. — Ill on lining papers. — Includes index
ISBN 0-905184-04-1 : £11.95 B81-20799

623.8'245 — Liquefied natural gas. Freight transport. Shipping. Technological development, *to 1978*
Ffooks, Roger. Natural gas by sea : the development of a new technology / Roger Ffooks. — London : Gentry, 1979. — 234p,[6]p of plates : ill(some col.),maps,facsims,ports ; 25cm
Includes index
ISBN 0-85614-054-6 : £18.50 B81-18890

623.8'245 — Ships: Tankers — *Manuals — For deck officers*
Baptist, C.. Tanker handbook for deck officers / by C. Baptist. — 6th ed. — Glasgow : Brown, Son & Ferguson, 1980. — ix,298p,[18] leaves of plates (16 fold.) : ill(some col.),plans ; 22cm
Previous ed.: 1975. — Includes index
ISBN 0-85174-386-2 : £19.00 B81-10945

623.8'25 — Great Britain. *Royal Navy*. Steam boats, *to 1979*
Stapleton, N. B. J.. Steam picket boats : and other small steam craft of the Royal Navy / by N.B.J. Stapleton ; with a foreword by H.R.H. The Prince Philip, Duke of Edinburgh. — Lavenham : Terence Dalton, 1980. — xiii,106p : ill,facsims, 2ports ; 23cm
Bibliography: p101. - Includes index
ISBN 0-900963-63-8 : £6.95 B81-03087

623.8'25 — Small warships — *Conference proceedings*
Symposium on Small Fast Warships and Security Vessels *(1978 : London)*. Proceedings of the Symposium on Small Fast Warships and Security Vessels : held at the London Tara Hotel, Kensington, London, March 7-9, 1978. — London ([10 Upper Belgrave St., SW1X 8BQ]) : Royal Institute of Naval Architects, 1978. — 257p : ill ; 30cm
Unpriced (pbk) B81-25389

623.8'25 — Warships — *Identification manuals*
Lyon, Hugh. Fighting ships. — London (Elsley Court, 20 Great Titchfield St., W1P 7AD) : Kingfisher, Oct.1981. — [128]p. — (Kingfisher guides)
ISBN 0-86272-006-0 : £2.50 : CIP entry B81-27448

623.8'25'09 — Warships, *to 1980 — For children*
Kershaw, Andrew. Guide to fighting ships / Andrew Kershaw ; illustrated by Cliff and Wendy Meadway ; edited by Bill Bruce. — London : Watts, 1981, c1980. — 24p : chiefly col.ill,1map ; 23cm. — (Explorer guides)
Bibliography: p24. — Includes index
ISBN 0-85166-936-0 : £2.99 B81-26016

623.8'25'0904 — Warships, *1939-1979 — Encyclopaedias*
Fighting ships of the world : an illustrated encyclopedia of modern sea power / consultant editor Antony Preston. — London : Hamlyn in association with Phoebus, 1980. — 352p : ill (some col.) ; 31cm
This material first appeared in Weapons and warfare, 1977-1980. — Includes index
ISBN 0-600-34970-5 : £9.95 B81-24065

623.8'25'09044 — Warships, *1939-1945*
Butler, James G.. Fighting ships in perspective / James G. Butler. — London : Ian Allan, 1981. — 105p : ill,plans ; 30cm
Ill on lining papers. — Bibliography: p102. — Includes index
ISBN 0-7110-1028-5 : £8.95 B81-32805

623.8'25'0941 — Great Britain. *Royal Navy*. Warships — *Technical data*
Moore, John E.. Warships of the Royal Navy / John E. Moore. — New ed. — London : Jane's, 1981. — 120p : ill ; 27cm
Previous ed.: 1979. — Includes index
ISBN 0-7106-0105-0 : £8.95 B81-19503

623.8'25'0973 — United States. *Navy*. Warships
Polmar, Norman. The ships and aircraft of the U.S. fleet. — 12th ed. / by Norman Polmar. — London : Arms and Armour, c1981. — 421p : ill ; 25cm
Previous ed.: London : Brassey's, 1978
ISBN 0-85368-397-2 : £12.50 B81-36511

623.8'252 — Battleships. Armaments, *1860-1945*
Hodges, Peter. The big gun : battleship main armament 1860-1945 / by Peter Hodges ; drawings by the author. — Greenwich : Conway Maritime, 1981. — 144p : ill ; 26cm
ISBN 0-85177-144-0 : £9.50 B81-07395

623.8'252'09034 — Battleships, *1858-1945 — Illustrations*
Wright, Paul. Famous battleships : from the Gloire to the Yamato, 16 great warships illustrated in colour / [... painted by Paul Wright]. — [London] : Fontana, 1979. — 1folded sheet([12]p) : col.ill ; 25cm. — (Domino ; 14)
ISBN 0-00-685454-0 : £0.85 B81-20256

623.8'252'09044 — Allied navies. Battleships, *1939-1945*
Garzke, William H.. British, Soviet, French and Dutch battleships of World War II / by William H. Garzke, Jr., Robert O. Dulin, Jr. ; line drawings by Thomas G. Webb. — London : Jane's, c1980. — xi,391p,[14]p of plates : ill,plans ; 29cm
Bibliography: p377-385. - Includes index
ISBN 0-7106-0078-x : £16.00 B81-16161

623.8'252'0941 — Great Britain. *Royal Navy*. Battle cruisers: Hood *(Ship)*, *1918-1941*
Northcott, Maurice P.. Hood / Maurice Northcott. — London : Arms and Armour, 1981. — 60p(some folded) : ill,plans ; 26cm. — (Man o' war ; 6)
Cover title. — Originally published: London : Bivouac Books, 1975. — Text, ill on inside covers
ISBN 0-85368-145-7 (pbk) : Unpriced B81-41009

623.8'252'0941 — Great Britain. *Royal Navy*. Queen Elizabeth class battleships, *1912-1945*
Raven, Alan. Queen Elizabeth class battleships / Alan Raven, John Roberts. — London (3 New Plaistow Rd., E15 3JA) : Battle of Britain Prints International, 1978. — 52p : ill(some col.) ; 26cm. — (Ensign ; 4)
Originally published: London : Bivouac, 1975
ISBN 0-85368-194-5 (pbk) : £3.50 B81-38204

623.8'252'0973 — United States. *Navy*. Battleships, *1886-1923*
Reilly, John C.. [American predreadnought battleships]. American battleships 1886-1923 : predreadnought design and construction / by John C. Reilly, Jr and Robert L. Scheina. — London : Arms and Armour, c1980. — 259p,[5]fold. p of plates : ill,plans ; 29cm
Originally published: Annapolis, Md : Naval Institute Press, 1980. — Bibliography: p215-235. — Includes index
ISBN 0-85368-446-4 : £14.95 B81-12647

623.8'253'09 — Warships: Cruisers, *to 1980*
Ireland, Bernard. Cruisers / Bernard Ireland. — London : Hamlyn, c1981. — 172p : ill(some col.) ; 31cm
Ill on lining papers. — Includes index
ISBN 0-600-32127-4 : £7.95 B81-22058

623.8'253'0934 — Warships: Cruisers, *1880-1980*
Preston, Antony. Cruisers / Antony Preston. — London : Arms and Armour, 1980. — 191p : ill(some col.),maps(some col.) ; 31cm
Includes index
ISBN 0-85368-105-8 : £6.95 : CIP rev. B80-17618

623.8'254'0941 — Great Britain. *Royal Navy*. Hunt class destroyers, *1938-1945*
Raven, Alan. Hunt class escort destroyers / Alan Raven and John Roberts. — London : Arms & Armour, c1980. — 56p : ill(some col.) ; 26cm. — (Man o' war ; 4)
Cover title. — Ill. on inside covers
ISBN 0-85368-363-8 (pbk) : £3.50 B81-34857

623.8'255'09 — Aircraft carriers, *to 1980*
Friedman, Norman, *1946-*. Carrier air power / Norman Friedman ; drawings by John Roberts. — Greenwich : Conway Maritime, 1981. — 192p : ill ; 31cm
ISBN 0-85177-216-1 : £12.50 B81-25947

623.8'255'09 — Aircraft carriers, *to 1980 — Illustrations*
Watts, Anthony J.. [A source book of aircraft carriers and their aircraft]. A source book of naval aircraft and aircraft carriers / Anthony J. Watts. — London : Ward Lock, c1980. — 128p : ill ; 12x17cm. — (Source books)
Originally published: 1977. — Includes index
ISBN 0-7063-6052-4 : £2.95
Primary classification 623.74'6'09 B81-03926

623.8'257'0904 — Submarines, *1955-1980 — Illustrations*
Brittain, Tom. Submarines : a guide to the world's undersea navies, 23 types of modern submarines described and illustrated in colour / [painted by Tom Brittain and Paul Wright]. — [London] : Fontana, 1979. — 1folded sheet ([12]p) : col.ill ; 25cm. — (Domino ; 19)
ISBN 0-00-685469-9 : £0.85 B81-20261

623.8'2572'0943 — Germany *(Federal Republic)*. *Bundesmarine*. Submarines, *to 1980*
Rössler, Eberhard. The U-boat : the evolution and technical history of German submarines / by Eberhard Rössler ; translated by Harold Erenberg. — London : Arms and Armour Press, 1981. — 384p : ill,map,plans ; 26cm
Translation of: Geschichte des deutschen Ubootbaus. — Bibliography: p375-376. — Includes index
ISBN 0-85368-115-5 : £27.50 : CIP rev. B81-10499

623.8'26 — Great Britain. *Royal Navy*. Fleet tugs: Sark *(Ship)*
'Bufflehead'. The hunting of the Sark / 'Bufflehead' writes a cautionary tale of naval research. — Orwell (41 High Street, Orwell, Cambs.) : Ellisons' Editions, c1981. — 14p : ill,1port ; 22cm
Unpriced (pbk) B81-17013

623.8'28 — Great Britain. Steam lifeboats, *1889-1928*
Farr, Grahame. The steam life-boats : with notes on earlier projects, and overseas steam life-boats / Grahame Farr. — Portishead (98 Combe Ave., Portishead, Bristol BS20 9JX) : G. Farr, 1981. — 24p : ill,1map,plans ; 21cm. — (Papers on life-boat history ; no.5)
ISBN 0-905033-06-x (pbk) : £0.75 B81-15685

623.8'28 — Lifeboat services. Technological innovation — *Serials*
Life-boat international / Royal National Life-boat Institution. — 1980. — Poole (West Quay Rd., Poole, Dorset BH15 1HZ) : RNLI, [1981]. — iv,33p
ISSN 0308-7441 : £1.00 B81-25019

623.8′28 — Scotland. Shetland. Fishing boats, *to 1979*

Nicolson, James R.. Shetland's fishing vessels / by J.R. Nicolson. — Lerwick : Shetland Times, 1981. — [44]p : ill ; 22cm
ISBN 0-900662-31-x (pbk) : Unpriced B81-16488

623.8′432 — Ships. Steel hulls. Construction. Welding

Phillip, L. D.. Shipyard welding processes for hull construction / by L.D. Phillips. — London ([10 Upper Belgrave St., SW1X 8BQ]) : Royal Institution of Naval Architects, c1980. — 34p,[6]p of plates : ill ; 30cm. — (Maritime technology monograph ; no.7)
Unpriced (pbk) B81-37946

623.8′44 — Clinker built wooden boats. Hulls. Construction

McKee, Eric. Clenched lap or clinker : an appreciation of a boatbuilding technique / Eric McKee. — Greenwich : National Maritime Museum, 1972 (1980 [printing]). — 30p,[2]p leaves of plates : ill ; 30cm
£1.25 (pbk) B81-09181

623.8′501 — Marine engineering equipment: Pumps

Crawford, J.. Marine and offshore pumping and piping systems / J. Crawford. — London : Butterworth, 1981. — 380p : ill ; 24cm. — (Marine engineering series)
Includes index
ISBN 0-408-00548-3 : Unpriced
Also classified at 623.8′501 B81-39806

623.8′501 — Marine piping systems

Crawford, J.. Marine and offshore pumping and piping systems / J. Crawford. — London : Butterworth, 1981. — 380p : ill ; 24cm. — (Marine engineering series)
Includes index
ISBN 0-408-00548-3 : Unpriced
Primary classification 623.8′501 B81-39806

623.8′503 — Ships. Electric equipment

Watson, G. O.. Marine electrical practice / G.O. Watson. — 5th ed. / specialist contributors G.A. Bowie ... [et al.]. — London : Butterworths, 1981. — viii,444p : ill ; 25cm. — (Marine engineering series)
Previous ed.: 1971. — Includes index
ISBN 0-408-00498-3 : Unpriced B81-35281

623.8′503′0288 — Boats. Electric equipment. Maintenance & repair — *Amateurs′ manuals*

Watney, John, *1919-*. Boat electrics / John Watney. — Newton Abbot : David & Charles, c1981. — 159p : ill ; 22cm
Includes index
ISBN 0-7153-7957-7 : £7.50 B81-08705

623.8′5641 — Small boats. Radio equipment. Use — *Manuals*

Wilkes, Kenneth. Radio and radar in sail and power boats / Kenneth Wilkes ; illustrated by Bill Streets ; photographs by Guy Gurney. — Lymington : Nautical, 1980. — 119p : ill(some col.),1chart,1map ; 19cm
Includes index
ISBN 0-245-53191-2 : £4.95
Also classified at 623.89′33 B81-06792

623.8′6 — Yachts. Cabins. Construction — *Amateurs′ manuals*

Saunders, Mike, *1940-*. Yacht joinery and fitting : practical guidance on the planning and building of cabin accommodation in sailing and power craft / Mike Saunders ; illustrated by Mike Saunders and Richard F. Reeves. — London : Hollis & Carter, 1981. — 191p,[1] fold.leaf of plates : ill(some col.) ; 25cm
Includes index
ISBN 0-370-30253-2 : £9.95 : CIP rev.
B80-23394

623.8′62 — Yachts. Self steering gears. Construction — *Amateurs′ manuals*

Belcher, Bill. Yacht wind-vane steering. — Newton Abbot : David & Charles, Nov.1981. — [192]p
ISBN 0-7153-8176-8 : £9.95 : CIP entry
B81-30576

623.8′7′076 — Marine engineering — *Questions & answers — For engineer cadets of merchant ships*

Engineer cadet training scheme : phase II, sea service guided study programme / Merchant Navy Training Board. — London (30/32 St. Mary Axe, EC3A 8ET) : The Board, c1980. — 40p : ill,forms ; 30cm
Unpriced (pbk) B81-09512

623.8′722 — Ships. Steam engines

McBirnie, S. C.. Marine steam engines and turbines. — 4th ed. / S.C. McBirnie. — London : Butterworths, 1980. — 709p : ill ; 24cm. — (Marine engineering series)
Previous ed.: / by W.J. Fox and S.C. McBirnie, London : Newnes-Butterworths, 1970. — Includes index
ISBN 0-408-00387-1 : £15.00 : CIP rev.
B79-31241

623.8′7234′0288 — Boats. Petrol engines. Maintenance & repair — *Amateurs′ manuals*

Goring, Loris. The care and repair of marine petrol engines / Loris Goring. — London : Adlard Coles : Granada, 1981. — 133p : ill ; 22cm
Includes index
ISBN 0-229-11641-8 : £7.50 B81-24341

623.8′7236 — Ships. Diesel engines

Burghardt, M. David. Marine diesels / M. David Burghardt, George D. Kingsley. — Englewood Cliffs ; London : Prentice-Hall, c1981. — x,178p : ill,plans ; 25cm
Includes index
ISBN 0-13-556985-0 : £10.35 B81-12673

623.8′7236 — Ships. Low-speed diesel engines

Woodward, John B.. Low speed marine diesel / John B. Woodward. — New York ; Chichester : Wiley, 1981. — xii,271p : ill,plans ; 24cm. — (Ocean engineering)
Includes index
ISBN 0-471-06335-5 : £27.50 B81-24221

623.8′73 — Ships. Boilers

. Marine steam boilers. — 4th ed. / James H. Allen and Roy M. Leach. — London : Butterworths, 1980. — 591p : ill ; 24cm. — (Marine engineering series)
Previous ed.: / by J.H. Milton. London : Newnes-Butterworths, 1970. — Includes index
ISBN 0-408-00416-9 : £15.00 : CIP rev.
B79-25234

623.8′74 — Ships. Fuel. Consumption *related to* **speed** — *Conference proceedings*

Speakers′ papers on ship's speed and consumption from the seminar held in Athens, May 18/19, 1981. — [London] : Lloyd's of London Press, [1981]. — 138leaves in various foliations : ill,1facsim ; 31cm
ISBN 0-907432-05-0 : Unpriced B81-37625

623.8′74 — Ships. Fuel supply systems — *Conference proceedings*

Speakers′ papers on fuel supply from the seminar on ship's speed and consumption held in Athens, May 18/19, 1981. — [London] : Lloyd's of London Press, [1981]. — 154leaves in various foliations : ill ; 31cm
ISBN 0-907432-10-7 : Unpriced B81-37624

623.88 — Seamanship

Danton, Graham. The theory and practice of seamanship / by Graham Danton. — 8th ed. — London : Routledge & Kegan Paul, 1980, c1978. — xv,522p,24p of plates : ill ; 24cm
Previous ed.: 1978. — Includes index
ISBN 0-7100-0502-4 : £12.50 B81-05543

623.88 — Seamanship — *Manuals*

Forsberg, Gerald. Brown's pocket-book for seamen / compiled by Gerald Forsberg. — [Glasgow] : Brown, Son & Ferguson, 1981. — vi,184p : ill(some col.),2charts ; 13x18cm
Includes index
ISBN 0-85174-391-9 : £10.00 B81-33383

Mort, S. W.. Bluewater seamanship / by S.W. Mort. — Glasgow : Brown, Son & Ferguson, 1981. — 93p : ill,2charts,2plans,1port ; 24cm
ISBN 0-85174-403-6 : Unpriced B81-32477

623.88 — Seamanship — *Stories, anecdotes*

The **Bunkside** companion. — London : Stanley Paul, Oct.1981. — 1v.
ISBN 0-09-146250-9 : £6.95 : CIP entry
B81-26802

623.88′03′21 — Seamanship — *Encyclopaedias*

Noel, John V.. The VNR dictionary of ships & the sea / John V. Noel. — New York ; London : Van Nostrand Reinhold, c1981. — vi,393p : col ill ; 24cm
Ill on lining papers
ISBN 0-442-25631-0 : £14.95 B81-02190

623.88′0941 — Great Britain. Coastal waters. Seamanship — *Practical information*

Stanfords pocket guide 1981 : including Dover, Portsmouth, Harwich, Devonport high water tables, tidal differences for over 150 harbours, weather forecasts, coastguard facilities, radio beacons, conversion tables / [compiled by D. Goatcher]. — London : Stanford Maritime, c1980. — 32p : ill,maps ; 21cm
Cover title
ISBN 0-540-07230-3 (pbk) : £0.95 B81-15568

623.88′22 — Small sailing boats. Sailing. Seamanship — *Manuals*

Davison, Tim. The Laser book / Tim Davison ; photographs by Tim Hore. — London (13 Fernhurst Rd, S.W.6) : Fernhurst Books, 1979. — 64p : ill ; 25cm
ISBN 0-906754-00-3 (pbk) : £3.95 B81-05632

623.88′223 — Sailing boats. Sailing. Seamanship — *Manuals*

Davies, John, *1913-*. The sailing handbook / John Davies. — London : Hamlyn, 1981. — 224p : ill(some col.),col.charts ; 19cm
Includes index
ISBN 0-600-36469-0 : £3.50 B81-25539

623.88′223 — Sailing. Seamanship — *Manuals*

Mitchell, Alastair. The R.Y.A./N.S.S.A. National Proficiency & Coaching Schemes / [Alastair Mitchell, Bob Bond]. — 2nd ed. — [Edinburgh] ([8 Frederick St., Edinburgh, EH2 2HB]) : R.Y.A. Scottish Council, 1979. — 1v.(loose leaf) : ill,maps ; 26cm
Previous ed.: 1975
£10.85 B81-23339

623.88′223 — Seamanship — *For yachting — Manuals*

Riley, R. J. F.. Stanford's sailing companion. — 4th ed. / R.J.F. Riley. — London : Stanford, 1980. — 255p : ill,charts,maps,facsims ; 30cm
Previous ed.: / by F.S. Campbell & R.J.F. Riley. 1976. — Includes index
ISBN 0-540-07181-1 : £7.95 : CIP rev.
B80-22083

623.88′223 — Single-handed voyages by sailing vessels — *Manuals*

Mulville, Frank. Single-handed cruising and sailing / Frank Mulville. — London : Nautical, 1981. — 184p : ill ; 22cm
Includes index
ISBN 0-333-31806-4 : £7.95 B81-21792

623.88′24′0941 — Great Britain. Merchant shipping. Personnel. Competence. Examinations — *Statistics — Serials*

Examinations for Certificates of Competency in the Merchant Navy : statistics / Department of Trade, Marine Division. — 1978. — London (Branch 2B, Sunley House, 90 High Holborn, WC1) : The Department, 1979. — 11p
Unpriced B81-07376

623.88′8 — Shipping. Safety measures

Ships operational safety manual / Polytech International. — [Luton] ([1 Cardigan St., Luton LU2 1RP]) : [Polytech International], [c1979]. — 1v.(loose-leaf) : ill,forms ; 31cm
Cover title
ISBN 0-906314-09-7 : Unpriced B81-10865

623.88′8 — Yachts. Sailing. Emergencies — *Manuals*

Hollander, Neil. The yachtsman's emergency handbook : the complete survival manual / Neil Hollander & Harald Mertes. — London : Angus & Robertson, 1980. — 254p : ill(some col.) ; 24cm
Includes index
ISBN 0-207-95815-7 : £8.95 B81-01585

623.88'81 — Freight transport. Shipping. Ships. Cargoes. Stowage

Thomas, R. E. (Robert Ellis). Stowage : the properties and stowage of cargoes / by R.E. Thomas. — Rev. ed. / revised by O.O. Thomas. — Glasgow : Brown, Son & Ferguson, 1971, c1981 (1981 [printing]). — x,564p,[23]p of plates : ill(some col.),plans ; 22cm
Previous ed.: i.e. 6th. 1968. — Includes index
ISBN 0-85174-000-6 : £21.00 B81-35512

623.88'82 — Knots — *Manuals*

Davies, E. T. (Edward Thomas). An introduction to knots / by E.T. Davies. — Glasgow : Brown, Son & Ferguson, 1981. — 70p : ill (some col.) ; 18cm
Includes index
ISBN 0-85174-406-0 (pbk) : £3.00 B81-38963

Fry, Eric C.. The Shell book of knots and decorative ropework (combined). — Newton Abbot : David & Charles, Sept.1981. — [176]p
Originally published: as The Shell book of knots and ropework, 1977 ; and as The Shell book of practical and decorative ropework, 1979
ISBN 0-7153-8197-0 : £7.95 : CIP entry
Also classified at 746.4 B81-22507

623.88'82 — Knots - *Manuals*

Russell, John. Knots. — London : Ward Lock, May 1981. — [96]p. — (Concorde)
ISBN 0-7063-6010-9 (pbk) : £2.95 : CIP entry
B81-07469

623.88'82 — Sailing ships. Rigging. Wire ropes. Splicing — *Manuals*

Skirving, R. Scot. Wire splicing / by R. Scot Skirving ; drawings by J. Hazelton ; and photographs by E.A. Bradford. — 2nd ed. — Glasgow : Brown, Son & Ferguson, 1980. — vii,49p : ill ; 19cm
Previous ed.: 1932
ISBN 0-85174-154-1 (pbk) : £2.50 B81-26009

623.88'84 — Great Britain. Coastal waters. Ships. Routes. Planning. Safety aspects — *Manuals*

Great Britain. *Department of Trade.* A guide to the planning and conduct of sea passages / Department of Trade. — London : H.M.S.O., 1980. — [30]p,[5]folded leaves of plates : col.ill,charts ; 30cm
ISBN 0-11-512923-5 (pbk) : £4.25 B81-04856

623.88'84 — Ships. Collisions. Prevention — *Manuals*

Brown, H. H.. Brown's rule of the road manual : the rule of the road at sea. — 17th ed. / rev. by H.H. Brown. — Glasgow : Brown, Son & Ferguson, 1981. — 165p,[1]folded leaf of plates : ill(some col.) ; 19cm
Previous ed.: 1976
ISBN 0-85174-405-2 : £5.50 B81-21359

623.89 — Distances between ports — *Tables*

Caney, R. W.. Reed's marine distance tables / compiled for the publishers by R.W. Caney and J.E. Reynolds. — 4th ed. — London : Reed, 1978. — 202p,[1]leaf of plates : 1col.map ; 22cm
Previous ed.: 1976. — Includes index
ISBN 0-900335-51-3 (pbk) : £6.25 B81-16133

623.89 — Seamanship. Celestial navigation — *Manuals — For yachting*

Blewitt, Mary. Celestial navigation for yachtsmen / Mary Blewitt. — 8th ed. — London : Stanford Maritime, 1981. — 68p : ill,2forms ; 23cm
Previous ed.: 1978. — Includes index
ISBN 0-540-07276-1 : £2.50 : CIP rev.
ISBN 0-540-07403-9 B80-23225

Coutts, Craig. Blue water yacht navigation / Craig Coutts. — London : Cassell, 1979. — 132p : ill,charts,maps ; 25cm
Maps on lining papers. — Includes index
ISBN 0-304-30451-4 : £5.95 B81-02183

623.89 — Seamanship. Celestial navigation — *Questions & answers — For yachting*

Watkins, Gordon. Exercises in astro-navigation. — London : Stanford Maritime, Oct.1981. — [160]p
ISBN 0-540-07190-0 (pbk) : £3.95 : CIP entry
B81-25724

623.89 — Seamanship. Celestial navigation. Sight reductions — *Questions & answers — For yachting*

Wilkes, Kenneth. Exercises for the ocean yacht navigator / Kenneth Wilkes. — 2nd ed. — Lymington : Nautical, 1980. — 188p : ill ; 21cm
Previous ed.: 1976
ISBN 0-245-53618-3 : £4.95 B81-03729

623.89 — Seamanship. Navigation — *Manuals*

Frost, A.. Practical navigation for second mates : including chartwork to cover the practical navigation and chartwork papers for D.O.T. certificates Class V, Class IV and Class III / by A. Frost. — 5th ed. — Glasgow : Brown, Son & Ferguson, 1981. — ix,281p : ill,charts ; 22cm
Previous ed.: 1977. — Includes index
ISBN 0-85174-397-8 : £10.00 B81-28425

Moody, Alton B.. Navigation afloat : a manual for the seaman : Alton B. Moody / foreword by M.W. Richey. — London : Hollis & Carter, 1980. — 751p : ill,1map ; 23cm
Bibliography: p653-678. - Includes index
ISBN 0-370-30087-4 : £15.00 : CIP rev.
B80-05421

623.89 — Shipping. Navigational aids: Charts — *Manuals*

Moore, D. A.. Marine chartwork. — 2nd ed. — London : Stanford Maritime, Nov.1981. — [118]p
Previous ed.: 1967
ISBN 0-540-07269-9 (pbk) : £2.95 : CIP entry
B81-30181

623.89'0247971 — Seamanship. Navigation — *For yachting*

Blewitt, Mary. Navigation for yachtsmen / Mary Blewitt. — 3rd ed., rev. — London : Stanford, 1979. — 101p : ill,charts ; 22cm
Previous ed.: 1973. — Includes index
ISBN 0-540-07274-5 : £2.95 : CIP rev.
B79-32602

Derrick, David. Navigation for offshore and ocean sailors. — Newton Abbot : David & Charles, Nov.1981. — [160]p
ISBN 0-7153-8086-9 : £7.95 : CIP entry
B81-30389

Howell, F. S.. Navigation primer for yachtsmen / F.S. Howell. — Huntingdon, Cambs : Imray, Laurie, Norie & Wilson, 1980. — xi,229p : ill (some col.),charts,maps,facsims ; 21cm
Bibliography: p185. - Includes index
ISBN 0-85288-071-5 (pbk) : Unpriced
B81-19786

Navigation. — Newton Abbot : David & Charles, Sept.1981. — [160]p
ISBN 0-7153-8246-2 (cased) : £6.95 : CIP entry
ISBN 0-7153-8258-6 (pbk) B81-21536

Wilkes, Kenneth. Practical yacht navigator / Kenneth Wilkes. — 3rd ed. — London : Nautical, 1979 (1981 [printing]). — 208p : ill,charts ; 21cm
Previous ed.: 1974. — Includes index
ISBN 0-333-31837-4 : £7.95 B81-21786

623.89'05 — Seamanship. Navigation — *Practical information — Serials*

Brown's nautical almanac daily tide tables for .... — 104th year (1981). — Glasgow : Brown, Son & Ferguson, [1980]. — 1010p in various pagings
ISSN 0068-290x : Unpriced B81-08266

623.89'05 — Seamanship. Navigation — *Serials*

Great Britain. *Hydrographic Department.* Annual summary of Admiralty notices to marines / Hydrographic Department. — 1981. — [Taunton] : The Department, [1981]. — 221p
Unpriced B81-15285

623.89'076 — Seamanship. Navigation — *Questions & answers — For yachting*

Anderson, Bill. Navigation exercises for yachtsmen. — 2nd ed. — London : Stanford Maritime, Oct.1981. — [75]p
Previous ed.: 1974
ISBN 0-540-07275-3 (pbk) : £3.50 : CIP entry
B81-25725

623.89'089994 — Polynesian seamanship. Navigation

Lewis, David, *1917-.* The voyaging stars secrets of the Pacific Island navigators / David Lewis. — [London] : Fontana, 1980, c1978. — 208,[8]p of plates : ill,charts,maps,ports ; 20cm
Originally published: Sydney ; London : Collins, 1978. — Bibliography: p202-203. - Includes index
ISBN 0-00-636046-7 (pbk) : £1.75 B81-12003

623.89'2 — Great Britain. Merchant ships. Navigation equipment. Surveying — *Manuals*

Great Britain. *Department of Trade.* Survey of merchant shipping navigational equipment installations : instructions for the guidance of surveyors / Department of Trade. — London : H.M.S.O., 1980. — iv,26p : 2ill ; 30cm
ISBN 0-11-512979-0 (pbk) : £2.50 B81-07816

623.89'22 — Ships. Pilotage — *Manuals*

Armstong, Malcolm C.. Practical ship-handling / by Malcolm C. Armstrong. — Glasgow : Brown, Son & Ferguson. — viii,110p : ill ; 22cm
Includes index
ISBN 0-85174-387-0 : £7.50 B81-15415

623.89'29 — Coastal waters. Seamanship. Navigation — *Manuals*

Fraser, Bruce, *19---.* Weekend navigator / Bruce Fraser. — London : Adlard Coles : Granada, 1981. — ix,308p : ill,charts(some col.),facsims ; 26cm
Charts on lining papers. — Includes index
ISBN 0-229-98661-7 : £9.95 B81-39462

623.89'29'077 — Coastal waters. Seamanship. Navigation — *Programmed instructions*

Smith, Gerry. Coastal navigation : a programmed learning course / Gerry Smith. — 2nd ed. — London : Adlard Coles, 1981. — vii,182p : ill,charts(some col.),maps,facsims ; 26cm
Previous ed.: London : Elek, 1977. — Chart (folded sheet) as insert. — Includes index
ISBN 0-229-11655-8 : £6.95 B81-12494

623.89'2916451 — Bering Sea & Bering Strait — *Pilots' guides*

Bering Sea and Strait pilot : north-west and north coasts of Alaska from Cape Douglas to the Alaska-Canada boundary, the Aleutian Islands, and the north-east coast of Siberia from Mys Lopatka peninsula to vicinity of Mys Yakan, with off-lying islands. — 5th ed. — [Taunton] ([Hydrographic Dept., Ministry of Defence, Taunton, Somerset]) : Hydrographer of the Navy, 1980. — xviii,373p : ill,charts(some col.),maps(some col.) ; 31cm. — (NP ; 23)
Previous ed.: 1966. — Includes index
Unpriced B81-20995

623.89'291824 — Gulf of Aden — *Pilots' guides*

Red Sea and Gulf of Aden Pilot : Suez Canal, Gulf of Suez and Gulf of 'Aqaba, Red Sea, Gulf of Aden, south-east coast of Arabia from Ras Baghashwa to Ras al Junaiz, coast of Africa from Ras Asir to Ras Binnah, Socotra and adjacent islands. — 12th ed. — [Taunton] ([Ministry of Defence (Navy), Taunton, Somerset, TA1 2DN]) : Hydrographer of the Navy, 1980. — xvi,284p : ill,charts(some col.) ; 31cm. — (N.P.64)
Previous ed.: 1967. — Includes index
Unpriced
Primary classification 623.89'291824
B81-22227

623.89'291824 — Red Sea — *Pilots' guides*

Red Sea and Gulf of Aden Pilot : Suez Canal, Gulf of Suez and Gulf of 'Aqaba, Red Sea, Gulf of Aden, south-east coast of Arabia from Ras Baghashwa to Ras al Junaiz, coast of Africa from Ras Asir to Ras Binnah, Socotra and adjacent islands. — 12th ed. — [Taunton] ([Ministry of Defence (Navy), Taunton, Somerset, TA1 2DN]) : Hydrographer of the Navy, 1980. — xvi,284p : ill,charts(some col.) ; 31cm. — (N.P.64)
Previous ed.: 1967. — Includes index
Unpriced
Also classified at 623.89'291824 B81-22227

623.89'294 — Western Europe. Harbours — *Pilots' guides — For cruising*

Cruising Association handbook. — 6th ed. — London (Ivory House, St. Katharine Dock, E1 9AT) : The Association, 1981. — xviii,509p : charts ; 26cm
Previous ed.: 1971. — 'Cruising Association handbook Spring 1981 corrections' (8p ; 22cm.) in pocket. — Bibliography: p499-500. — Includes index
ISBN 0-9503742-1-0 : Unpriced : CIP rev.
B81-08930

623.89'2941'0247971 — Great Britain. Coastal waters. Seamanship. Navigation — *Practical information — For yachting — Serials*

The **Macmillan** & Silk Cut nautical almanac. — 1981-. — London : Macmillan, 1980-. — v. : ill ; 28cm
Annual
ISSN 0260-2709 = Macmillan & Silk Cut nautical almanac : £8.95 B81-01997

623.89'29411 — Scotland. Coastal waters. Pilots' guides: Lindsay, Alexander. Rutter of the Scottish Seas — *Critical studies*

Taylor, A. B.. Alexander Lindsay : a rutter of the Scottish Seas circa 1540 / abridged version of a manuscript by the late A.B. Taylor ... ; edited by I.H. Adams and G. Fortune. — Greenwich : National Maritime Museum, 1980. — iv,64p : ill,maps,facsims ; 30cm. — (Maritime monographs and reports, ISSN 0307-8590 ; no.44-1980)
ISBN 0-905555-31-7 (pbk) : Unpriced
B81-26930

623.89'29411 — Western Scotland. Coastal waters — *Pilots' guides*

Brackenbury, Mark. Scottish West Coast pilot : the mainland and Inner Hebrides from Troon to Ullapool and the Summer Isles / Mark Brackenbury ; charts drawn by Alan Wakeman. — London : Stanford Maritime, [1981]. — 143p : ill,charts,2maps ; 24cm
Includes index
ISBN 0-540-07195-1 : £9.95 : CIP rev.
B81-05147

623.89'29422 — England. Solent. Navigation — *Manuals — For yachting*

Coles, K. Adlard. Creeks & harbours of the Solent : Needles to Chichester / K. Arnold Coles. — 9th ed / rev. by David Sylvester-Bradley. — [Lymington] : Nautical, 1981. — 142p : ill,maps(some col.) ; 26cm
Previous ed.: 1972. — Maps on lining papers. — Includes index
ISBN 0-333-31808-0 : £12.00 B81-21768

623.89'29422 — Southern England. Coastal regions — *Illustrations — For navigation*

Oldale, Adrienne. Navigating Britain's coastline : Portland to Dover / Adrienne & Peter Oldale. — Newton Abbot : David & Charles, c1981. — 88p : ill,chiefly col.charts ; 20x30cm
English text, English, French and German introductions
ISBN 0-7153-7934-8 : £6.95 B81-19709

623.89'29422 — Southern England. Coastal waters — *Pilots' guides*

Brandon, Robin. South England pilot. — [14th ed.] / Robin Brandon. — St. Ives, Cambs. : Imray, Laurie, Norie and Wilson
Previous ed.: published in 1 vol. as The pilot's guide to the English channel / W. Eric Wilson. 1968
Vol.4: Start Point to Land's End. — 1979. — 152p : ill(some col.),col.charts,col.maps ; 30x40cm
ISBN 0-85288-067-7 (pbk) : £17.50 B81-39487

Brandon, Robin. South England pilot. — [14th ed.] / Robin Brandon. — St. Ives, Cambs. : Imray, Laurie, Norie and Wilson
Previous ed.: published in 1 vol. as The pilot's guide to the English Channel / W. Eric Wilson. 1968
Vol.5: The Scilly Isles. — 1980. — 37p : ill (some col.),col.maps ; 30x40cm
ISBN 0-85288-069-3 (pbk) : Unpriced
B81-39486

623.89'294275 — Merseyside *(Metropolitan County)*. Mersey River. Navigability — *Serials*

Report on the state of the navigation of the River Mersey ... to the Secretary of State for Transport. — 1976. — [London] : H.M.S.O., [1977?]. — 13p
Unpriced B81-08229

623.89'294359 — West Germany. Lower Saxony. Coastal waters — *Pilots' guides*

Brackenbury, Mark. Frisian pilot : Den Helder to Brunsbüttel and the Kiel Canal / Mark Brackenbury ; charts designed by the author and drawn by E.H. Wilson. — London : Stanford Maritime, 1979. — 151p : ill,charts,maps ; 24cm
Dibliography: p145. Includes index
ISBN 0-540-07185-4 : Unpriced : CIP rev.
Primary classification 623.89'294921
B79-17647

623.89'29441'0247971 — North-western France. Coastal waters — *Pilots' guides — For yachting*

Jefferson, David. Brittany and Channel Islands cruising guide : Cherbourg to St Nazaire : including the Channel Islands and Brittany canals / David Jefferson ; harbour plans drawn by Stan Townsend. — London : Stanford Maritime, 1981. — 208p : ill,charts,1map ; 24cm
Includes index
ISBN 0-540-07186-2 : £10.95 : CIP rev.
B81-03156

623.89'2946 — South-eastern Spain. Coastal waters. Navigation — *For yachting*

Brandon, Robin. East Spain pilot / Robin Brandon. — 2nd ed. — St. Ives, Cambs. : Imray Laurie Norie and Wilson
Ch.VII: Islas Baleares : the complete yachtsman's guide to Ibiza, Formentera, Mallorca and Menorca. — [1980]. — 164p,[3] folded leaves of plates : ill,charts(some col.),maps(some col.) ; 30cm
Cover title. — Previous ed.: 1977
ISBN 0-85288-070-7 (pbk) : Unpriced
B81-39034

623.89'294921 — Northern Netherlands. Coastal waters — *Pilots' guides*

Brackenbury, Mark. Frisian pilot : Den Helder to Brunsbüttel and the Kiel Canal / Mark Brackenbury ; charts designed by the author and drawn by E.H. Wilson. — London : Stanford Maritime, 1979. — 151p : ill,charts,maps ; 24cm
Bibliography: p145. — Includes index
ISBN 0-540-07185-4 : Unpriced : CIP rev.
Also classified at 623.89'294359 B79-17647

623.89'3 — Boats. Electric navigation equipment & electronic navigation equipment

French, John, *1936-*. Electrics and electronics for small craft / John French. — 2nd ed. — London : Adlard Coles : Granada, 1981. — 254p : ill,1facsim ; 26cm
Previous ed.: published as Electrical and electronic equipment for yachts. 1973. — Includes index
ISBN 0-229-11612-4 : £15.00 B81-24343

623.89'32 — Shipping. Navigational aids: Radio signals — *Lists — Serials*

Admiralty list of radio signals. Volume 2, Radiobeacons, radio direction-finding stations, radar beacons. — 1981. — Taunton (Hydrographic Department, Ministry of Defence, Taunton, Somerset TA1 2DN) : Hydrographer of the Navy, c1981. — 338p
£5.90 B81-24988

Admiralty list of radio signals. Volume 3, Radio weather services. — Taunton (Hydrographic Department, Ministry of Defence, Taunton, Somerset TA1 2DN) : Hydrographer of the Navy, c1980. — 409p
£6.90 B81-02821

Admiralty list of radio signals diagrams relating to weather reporting and forecast areas. — 1980. — Taunton (Hydrographic Department, Ministry of Defence, Taunton, Somerset TA1 2DN) : Hydrographer of the Navy, c1980. — [20p]
£1.50 B81-10312

623.89'33 — Ships. Automatic radar plotting aids. Use — *Manuals*

Jones, K. D.. Automatic radar plotting aids manual : a mariners guide to the use of ARPA / by K.D. Jones and A.G. Bole. — Liverpool (Byron St., Liverpool, L3 3AF) : Department of Maritime Studies, Liverpool Polytechnic, c1981. — ix,148p : ill,charts ; 31cm
Unpriced (spiral) B81-13597

623.89'33 — Small boats. Radar equipment. Use — *Manuals*

Wilkes, Kenneth. Radio and radar in sail and power boats / Kenneth Wilkes ; illustrated by Bill Streets ; photographs by Guy Gurney. — Lymington : Nautical, 1980. — 119p : ill(some col.),1chart,1map ; 19cm
Includes index
ISBN 0-245-53191-2 : £4.95
Primary classification 623.8'5641 B81-06792

623.89'4 — Seamanship. Signalling — *Manuals*

. Brown's signalling : how to learn the international code of visual and sound signals : based on information contained in the 1965 [i.e.1969] International Code of signals. — 9th ed. / revised by A.R. Palmer. — Glasgow : Brown, Son & Ferguson, 1979. — 229p,[5]p of plates : ill(some col.) ; 18cm
Previous ed.: i.e. Rev. ed.: 1974. — International regulations for preventing collisions at sea (booklet: 31p) as insert
ISBN 0-85174-350-1 : £4.00 B81-27032

623.89'42'09411 — Scotland. Lighthouses, *to 1980*

Munro, R. W.. Scottish lighthouses / R.W. Munro. — Stornoway : Thule, 1979. — 307p : ill,maps,facsims,1plan,ports ; 23cm
Ill on lining papers. — Bibliography: p279-287. - Includes index
ISBN 0-906191-32-7 : £9.95 B81-17118

623.89'42'0942258 — East Sussex. Beachy Head. Lighthouses, *to 1974*

Armstrong, Robert, *1940-*. The Beachy Head light / by Robert Armstrong. — [Eastbourne] ([20 Pevensey Rd, Eastbourne, E. Sussex]) : [Sound Forum], [1979]. — [34]p : 1ill ; 19cm
£0.35 (unbound)
Primary classification 283'.092'4 B81-06212

623.89'45'05 — Shipping. Navigational aids: Lights — *Lists — Serials*

Admiralty list of lights and fog signals. Volume D, Eastern side of Atlantic Ocean from Goulet de Brest southward, including off-lying islands : corrected to ... 17th May ... — 1980. — [Taunton] ([Hydrographic Department, Ministry of Defence, Taunton, Somerset TA1 2DN]) : Hydrographer of the Navy, c1980. — 288p
£3.50 B81-00138

Admiralty list of lights and fog signals. Volume M, Arctic Ocean, coast of USSR from Norwegian border to Bering Strait : corrected to ANM weekly edition no.18/81 dated 9th May 1981. — 1981. — Taunton (Hydrographic Department, Ministry of Defence, Taunton, Somerset TA1 2DN) : Hydrographer of the Navy, c1981. — 165p
£3.25 B81-34028

Admiralty list of lights and fog signals. volume F, Arabian Sea, Bay of Bengal and Pacific Ocean north of the Equator. — 1980. — Taunton (Hydrographic Department, Ministry of Defence, Taunton, Somerset) : Hydrographer of the Navy, c1980. — 845p
£8.50

Admiralty list of lights and fog signals. Volume H. Northern and Eastern coasts of Canada, including River Saint Lawrence and Saint Lawrence Seaway : corrected to ANM weekly edition no.46 dated 22nd November 1980. — 1981. — [Taunton] ([Hydrographic Department, Ministry of Defence, Taunton Somerset]) : Hydrographer of the Navy, c1981. — 336p
£4.00 B81-15159

623.89'45'05 — Shipping. Navigational aids: Lights — *Lists — Serials* *continuation*

Admiralty list of lights and fog signals. Volume J, Western side of North Atlantic Ocean from Maine to Cabo Orange, including Gulf of Mexico and Caribbean Sea : corrected to ANM weekly edition no.26/79 dated 31st December 1980. — 1981. — [Taunton] ([Hydrographic Department, Ministry of Defence, Taunton, Somerset TA1 2DN]) : Hydrographer of the Navy, c1981. — 639p
£6.00 B81-13405

624 — CIVIL ENGINEERING

624 — Civil engineering. Quantity surveying

Hughes, Geoffrey Arthur. Civil engineering quantities. — Hornby : Construction Press, July 1981. — [220]p
ISBN 0-86095-878-7 : £12.50 : CIP entry B81-14440

624 — Construction

Construction technology / S.S. Ataev ... [et al.] ; edited by S.S. Ataev ; translated from the Russian by I.V. Savin. — Moscow : Mir ; [London] : distributed by Central Books, 1980. — 461p : ill,plans ; 23cm
Translation and revision of: Tekhnologiīa stroitel'nogo proizvodstva. 2nd ed. — Includes index
ISBN 0-7147-1592-1 : £5.95 B81-23520

624 — Construction. Estimating — *Manuals*

Geddes, Spence. Estimating for building and civil engineering works / Spence Geddes. — 7th ed. / edited by G. Chrystal-Smith. — London : Butterworths, 1981. — 402p : ill ; 26cm
Previous ed.: London : Newnes-Butterworths, 1976. — Includes index
ISBN 0-408-00515-7 : Unpriced B81-26108

624 — Construction. Estimating. Measurement

Gardner, M.. Measurement, level 2. — London : Longman, Sept.1981. — [250]p. — (Longman technician series : construction and civil engineering)
ISBN 0-582-41584-5 (pbk) : £5.95 : CIP entry B81-30292

624 — Construction. Sites. Levelling & surveying

Clancy, John. Site surveying and levelling / John Clancy. — London : Edward Arnold, 1981. — xii,244p : ill ; 22cm
Includes index
ISBN 0-7131-3439-9 (pbk) : £4.75 : CIP rev. B81-22518

Pettet, John. Site surveying and levelling, second level / John Pettet. — London : Hutchinson, 1981. — 128p : ill,plans ; 24cm. — (Hutchinson TEC texts)
Includes index
ISBN 0-09-143621-4 (pbk) : £4.95 B81-32515

624 — Construction. Sites. Setting out. Accuracy. Testing

Ryan, Nicholas M.. Accuracy of setting out in construction work / Nicholas M. Ryan. — Dublin (St. Martin's House, Waterloo Rd., Dublin 4) : An Foras Forbartha, 1981. — iv,18p : ill ; 30cm
ISBN 0-906120-45-4 (spiral) : £1.50 B81-38040

624 — England. Civil engineering. Contracts. Site administration — *Manuals*

Elsby, W. L.. The engineer and construction control / W.L. Elsby. — London : Telford, 1981. — 88p : ill ; 22cm
ISBN 0-7277-0117-7 (pbk) : £4.50 B81-14667

624 — Great Britain. Civil engineering. Contracts: Institution of Civil Engineers. Conditions of contract and forms of tender, agreement and bond for use in connection with works of civil engineering construction. 5th edition — *Commentaries*

Furmston, M. P.. Contractors' guide to the I.C.E. conditions of contract, 5th edition / by Michael Furmston. — Sutton : IPC Building & Contract Journals Ltd, c1980. — 16p : ill ; 30cm
£2.05 (pbk) B81-37972

624 — Great Britain. Construction. Subcontracting. Contracts: National Federation of Building Trades Employers. Standard (Non-Nominated) Form of Sub-Contract — *Commentaries*

Powell-Smith, Vincent. Contractors' guide to the standard (non-nominated) form of building sub-contract / by Vincent Powell-Smith. — Sutton : IPC Building & Contract Journals Ltd, c1980. — 27p : ill ; 30cm
£2.95 (pbk) B81-37973

624 — Great Britain. Small scale construction. Tendering & contracting. Procedure — *For surveying*

Tendering and contract procedures for small and medium sized projects : a review and alternative approach / [prepared by a working party of the Building Surveying Division, Royal Institution of Chartered Surveyors]. — London : Royal Institution of Chartered Surveyors, c1981. — 15p ; 30cm
Cover title
ISBN 0-85406-132-0 (pbk) : Unpriced B81-35678

624 — Structures

Francis, A. J. (Arthur James). Introducing structures : a textbook for students of civil and structural engineering, building and architecture / A.J. Francis. — Oxford : Pergamon, 1980. — vii,293p : ill ; 22cm. — (Pergamon international library)
Bibliography: p284-285. - Includes index
ISBN 0-08-022701-5 (cased) : £14.00 : CIP rev.
ISBN 0-08-022702-3 (pbk) : £4.95 B80-02479

624 — Structures built by Brunel, Isambard Kingdom

Beckett, Derrick. Brunel's Britain / Derrick Beckett. — Newton Abbot : David & Charles, [1980]. — 222p : ill,maps,plans,ports ; 24cm
Bibliography: p217-218. — Includes index
ISBN 0-7153-7973-9 : £8.50 : CIP rev. B80-18805

624 — Structures — *For schools*

Structures / Alan Blundell ... [et al.]. — Edinburgh : Oliver & Boyd in association with the National Centre for School Technology, 1981. — 94p : ill ; 24cm. — (Schools Council modular courses in technology)
ISBN 0-05-003389-1 (pbk) : £2.30
ISBN 0-05-003390-5 (Teacher's guide) : £2.00
ISBN 0-05-003391-3 (Workbook) : £2.50 B81-32953

624'.0212 — Civil engineering — *Technical data*

Parmley, Robert O.. Field engineer's manual / Robert O. Parmley. — New York ; London : McGraw-Hill, c1981. — xxvii,611p : ill,charts ; 15cm
Includes index
ISBN 0-07-048513-5 : £17.50 B81-27524

624'.028 — Construction equipment — *Technical data*

Construction plant & equipment. International annual. — 1980/81. — London (Morgan Grampian House, 30 Calderwood St., Woolwich, SE18 6QH) : Morgan Grampian (Construction Press), [1980?]. — 485p
ISSN 0143-5876 : Unpriced B81-00139

624'.028 — Great Britain. Construction equipment — *Serials — For local government*

PSLG : public service & local government. — Vo.7, no.3 (Mar.1977)-. — London (Addison Bridge Places, Kensington, W14) : BWS Pub., 1977-. — v. : ill ; 30cm
Monthly. — Continues: Public service and local government appointments. — Description based on: Vol.9, no.9 (Sept.1979)
ISSN 0144-4212 = PSLG. Public service & local government : £8.50 per year B81-05972

624'.028'5404 — Construction. Applications of microcomputer systems — *Conference proceedings*

Small computer systems and their applications in construction : proceedings of the conference held in London on 19 February 1980. — London : Institution of Civil Engineers, 1980. — 129p : ill ; 22cm
ISBN 0-7277-0106-1 : £11.00 B81-10086

624'.028'7 — Great Britain. Construction. Measurement — *French texts*

[Principles of measurement (international) for works of construction. *French*]Principes de metre (internationaux) pour travaux de construction / [Royal Institution of Chartered Surveyors]. — London : The Institution, 1979. — 20p ; 30cm
£6.00 (pbk) B81-37274

624'.03'21 — Civil engineering — *Encyclopaedias*

Scott, John S.. [The Penguin dictionary of civil engineering]. Dictionary of civil engineering / John S. Scott ; illustrated by Clifford Bayliss. — 3rd ed. — London : Granada, 1981. — 308p : ill ; 23cm
Originally published: Harmondsworth : Penguin, 1980
ISBN 0-246-11574-2 : £8.95 B81-24444

624'.068 — Civil engineering industries. Management

Marsh, P. D. V.. Contracting for engineering and construction projects. — 2nd ed. — Farnborough, Hants. : Gower, July 1981. — [230]p
Previous ed.: 1969
ISBN 0-566-02232-x : £12.50 : CIP entry B81-14815

624'.068 — Construction industries. Management

Forster, G.. Construction site studies. — London : Longman, Sept.1981. — [320]p. — (Longman technician series : construction and civil engineering)
ISBN 0-582-41567-5 (pbk) : £8.95 : CIP entry B81-30293

624'.068 — Construction industries. Management — *Forms*

Fisk, Edward R.. Construction engineer's form book / Edward Fisk. — New York ; Chichester : Wiley, c1981. — 1v.(loose-leaf) : ill,forms ; 30cm
ISBN 0-471-06307-x (unbound) : £34.95 B81-30103

624'.068 — Developing countries. Construction industries. Small firms. Management

Miles, Derek. The small building contractor and the client : how to run your business successfully / by Derek Miles. — London : Intermediate Technology, 1980. — 270p : ill ; 22cm
ISBN 0-903031-67-1 (pbk) : £6.95 B81-27760

624'.068 — United States. Construction industries. Management

Barrie, Donald S.. Directions in managing construction : a critical look at present and future industry practices, problems, and policies / Donald S. Barrie. — New York ; Chichester : Wiley, c1981. — xvii,468p : ill ; 24cm. — (Construction management and engineering)
Includes index
ISBN 0-471-04642-6 : £33.00 B81-33013

Royer, King. The construction manager in the 80's / King Royer. — Englewood Cliffs ; London : Prentice-Hall, c1981. — xvi,431p : ill,facsims,forms,1port ; 29cm
Supersedes: The construction manager. 1974. — Bibliography: p298-321. — Includes index
ISBN 0-13-168690-9 : £20.80 B81-19654

624'.068'1 — Construction industries. Financial management — *Conference proceedings*

Construction projects : their financial policy and control. — London : Construction Press, Feb.1982. — [160]p
Conference papers
ISBN 0-86095-876-0 : £18.50 : CIP entry B81-36371

624'.068'1 — United States. Construction. Costs. Control

Ahuja, Hira N.. Successful construction cost control / Hira N. Ahuja. — New York ; Chichester : Wiley, c1980. — xvii,388p : ill ; 24cm. — (Construction management and engineering)
Bibliography: p381-383. — Includes index
ISBN 0-471-05378-3 : £18.25 B81-02417

624'.068'1 — United States. Construction. Costs. Control *continuation*

Ward, Sol A.. Cost control in design and construction / Sol A. Ward and Thorndike Litchfield. — New York ; London : McGraw-Hill, c1980. — vii,231p : ill ; 24cm
Bibliography: p223-224. - Includes index
ISBN 0-07-068139-2 : £12.50 B81-06472

624'.068'3 — Construction industries. Project personnel management

Anderson, S. D.. Project manpower management : management processes in construction practice / S.D. Anderson, R.W. Woodhead. — New York ; Chichester : Wiley, c1981. — xi,264p : ill ; 29cm
Includes index
ISBN 0-471-95979-0 : £24.30 B81-24050

624'.068'4 — Civil engineering industries. Project management

Peters, Glen. Project management and construction control / Glen Peters. — London : Construction, 1981. — xi,130p : ill ; 24cm
Bibliography: p127-128. — Includes index
ISBN 0-86095-892-2 (pbk) : £7.95 B81-29369

624'.068'4 — Construction industries. Project management

Programmes in construction : a guide to good practice. — Ascot : Chartered Institute of Building, [1981]. — 80p : ill,1plan,forms ; 30cm
Bibliography: p78-80
ISBN 0-906600-14-6 (pbk) : Unpriced : CIP rev. B80-22217

624'.068'8 — Great Britain. Construction industries. Marketing

Bell, R. (Richard). Marketing and larger construction firm / by R. Bell. — Ascot : Chartered Institute of Building, 1981. — 30p ; 30cm. — (Occasional paper / Chartered Institute of Building, ISSN 0306-6878 ; no.22)
ISBN 0-906600-25-1 (pbk) : Unpriced B81-32494

624'.07'11422 — London & Home Counties. Construction industries. Personnel. Professional education. Courses — *Directories* — *Serials*

[Education for the construction industry in the region *(London and Home Counties Regional Advisory Council for Technological Education)*]. Education for the construction industry in the region / London and Home Counties Regional Advisory Council for Technological Education. — 1981/83. — London : The Council, 1981. — 42p
ISBN 0-85394-086-x : £0.75 B81-36307

624'.076 — Great Britain. Civil engineering. Organisations: Institution of Civil Engineers. Corporate members. Academic requirements — *Regulations*

The route to corporate membership / the Institution of Civil Engineers. — [London] : [Telford], 1981. — 42p ; 21cm. — (ICE ; 43)
Includes index
£2.50 (pbk) B81-29636

624'.076 — Great Britain. Civil engineers. Professional education. Institution of Civil Engineers examinations. Essays. Techniques

The ICE essays / a guide to preparation and writing ; B. Madge ... [et al.] ; cartoons by Field. — London : Telford, 1981. — 57p : ill ; 21cm
ISBN 0-7277-0119-3 (pbk) : £2.50 B81-10082

624'.09'01 — Construction, *to ca 1500* — *For children*

Fagg, Christopher. How they built long ago / [author] Christopher Fagg ; [editor] Adrian Sington. — London : Hutchinson, 1981. — 75p : ill(some col.) ; 33cm
Text on lining papers. — Includes index
ISBN 0-09-144440-3 : £5.50 : CIP rev. B81-26799

624'.0911 — Permafrost regions. Civil engineering

Permafrost : engineering design and construction / Associate Committee on Geotechnical Research, National Research Council of Canada ; edited by G.H. Johnston. — New York ; Chichester : Wiley, c1981. — xxxii,540p : ill,maps ; 26cm
Bibliography: p483-529. — Includes index
ISBN 0-471-79918-1 : £22.00 B81-29296

624'.09172'4 — Developing countries. Civil engineering. Applications of appropriate technology — *Conference proceedings*

Appropriate technology in civil engineering : proceedings of the conference held by the Institution of Civil Engineers, 14-16 April, 1980. — London : Telford for the Institution of Civil Engineers, c1981. — 223p : ill,maps,plans ; 31cm
Includes bibliographies
ISBN 0-7277-0100-2 : £24.00 B81-32858

624'.092'2 — Civil engineering, *1780-1880* — *Biographies*

Craven, John. Breakthrough / John Craven and Molly Cox. — London : British Broadcasting Corporation, 1981. — 104p : ill,1facsim,ports ; 23cm
ISBN 0-563-17936-8 : £4.50 B81-17951

624'.092'4 — Civil engineering. Narutowicz, Gabrjel — *Biographies* — *Polish texts*

Piłsudski, Józef. Wspomnienia o gabrjelu narutowiczu / Józef Piłsudski. — Londyn [i.e. London] : Orbis Books, 1980. — 61p ; 20cm
ISBN 0-901149-15-2 (pbk) : Unpriced B81-19509

624'.092'4 — United States. Civil engineering. Design. Latrobe, Benjamin Henry — *Illustrations*

Latrobe, Benjamin Henry. The engineering drawings of Benjamin Henry Latrobe / edited with an introductory essay by Darwin H. Stapleton. — New Haven ; London : Published for the Maryland Historical Society by Yale University Press, 1980. — xx,256p,10p of plates : ill(some col.),maps,facsims,plans ; 29cm. — (The Papers of Benjamin Henry Latrobe. Series 2. The architectural and engineering drawings)
Bibliography: p248-252. — Includes index
ISBN 0-300-02227-1 : £39.40 : CIP rev. B80-20779

624'.0941 — Great Britain. Civil engineering — *For technicians*

Jones, D. M.. Technician construction technology 3 : civil engineering / D.M. Jones. — London : Cassell, 1981. — 169p : ill,plans ; 24cm. — (Cassell's TEC series)
Bibliography: p169
ISBN 0-304-30551-0 (pbk) : £5.50 B81-32383

624'.09427 — Northern England. Civil engineering structures — *Visitors' guides*

Barbey, M. F.. Civil engineering heritage : Northern England / M.F. Barbey. — London : Telford, 1981. — ix,178p : ill,maps ; 23cm
Bibliography: p167-168. — Includes index
ISBN 0-7277-0098-7 : £9.75 B81-13996

624.1 — STRUCTURAL ENGINEERING

624.1 — Space structures — *Conference proceedings*

International Conference on Space Structures *(2nd : 1975 : University of Surrey)*. 2nd International Conference on Space Structures / organised by Department of Civil Engineering University of Surrey, Guildford, England September, 1975 ; [W.J. Supple, ed.]. — [Guildford] (Guildford, Surrey GU2 5XH) : The Department, c1975. — x,931p : ill,plans ; 28cm
Includes bibliographies
Unpriced (pbk) B81-04169

624.1'00411 — Scotland. Structural engineering, *1931-1981* — *Conference proceedings*

Structural engineering in Scotland, 1931-1981. — London (4 Graham Lodge, Graham Rd., NW4 3DG) : Pentech Press, Oct.1981. — [176]p
Conference papers
ISBN 0-7273-1902-7 : £15.00 : CIP entry B81-28088

624.1'01 — Structures. Aesthetic aspects — *For municipal engineering*

Oxenham, J. R.. Aesthetics in municipal engineering / by J.R. Oxenham. — 2nd ed. — London : Institution of Municipal Engineers, 1979. — 11p : ill ; 21cm. — (Protection of the environment ; monograph no.12)
Previous ed.: 1972
£0.75 (pbk) B81-06521

624.1'01'515353 — Structural engineering. Mathematics. Finite element methods

Cook, Robert D.. Concepts and applications of finite element analysis / Robert D. Cook. — 2nd ed. — New York ; Chichester : Wiley, c1981. — xix,537p : ill ; 24cm
Previous ed.: 1974. — Text, ill on lining papers. — Includes index
ISBN 0-471-03050-3 : £22.35 B81-39801

624.1'042'0285404 — Great Britain. Quantity surveying. Applications of microcomputer systems

Chartered quantity surveyors and the micro-computer. — London : Royal Institution of Chartered Surveyors, 1981. — 100p : ill ; 30cm
Cover title. — Study carried out by the Construction Industry Computing Association based on work by David Scoins, Simon Bensasson and Robert Davidson
ISBN 0-85406-131-2 (pbk) : Unpriced B81-35675

624.1'042'0941 — Great Britain. Quantity surveying — *Serials*

QS weekly. — Issue no.1 (Jan.1977)-. — London (4 Addison Bridge Place, Kensington W14 9BR) : BWS, 1977-. — v. : ill,ports ; 42cm
Description based on: Issue no.2 (3rd Feb.1977)
ISSN 0261-6734 = QS weekly : £7.50 per year B81-32248

624.1'06041 — Great Britain. Structural engineering. Organisations: Institution of Structural Engineers — *Directories* — *Serials*

Institution of Structural Engineers[Year book and directory of members *(Institution of Structural Engineers)*]. Year book and directory of members / Institute of Structural Engineers. — 1981. — London (11 Upper Belgrave Street, W1X 8BH) : John Morris Publicity, [1980]. — 236p in various pagings
£8.00 (£4.00 to members) B81-12408

624.1'0724 — Structural engineering. Mathematical models

Carmichael, D. G.. Structural modelling and optimization : a general methodology for engineering and control / D.G. Carmichael. — Chichester : Ellis Horwood, 1981. — 306p : ill ; 24cm. — (Ellis Horwood series in engineering science)
Bibliography: p275-303. — Includes index
ISBN 0-85312-283-0 : £21.50
ISBN 0-85312-300-4 (pbk) : Unpriced
ISBN 0-470-27114-0 (Halsted Press) B81-33222

624.1'5 — Construction. Sites. Dewatering

Powers, J. Patrick. Construction dewatering : a guide to theory and practice / J. Patrick Powers. — New York ; Chichester : Wiley, c1981. — xxii,484p : ill ; 24cm. — (Wiley series of practical construction guides)
Includes index
ISBN 0-471-69591-2 : £24.80 B81-23715

624.1'5 — Structures. Foundations. Analysis

Scott, Ronald F.. Foundation analysis / Ronald F. Scott. — Englewood Cliffs ; London : Prentice-Hall, c1981. — xii,545p : ill ; 24cm. — (Civil engineering and engineering mechanics series)
Includes index
ISBN 0-13-329169-3 : £19.45 B81-17305

624.1'5 — Structures. Foundations. Design

Ambrose, James. Simplified design of building foundations / James Ambrose. — New York : Chichester : Wiley, c1981. — x,338p : ill,plans ; 22cm
Text on lining papers. — Includes index
ISBN 0-471-06267-7 : £15.75 B81-34919

Smith, G. N.. Elements of foundation design / G.N. Smith, E.L. Pole. — London : Granada, 1980. — xi,222p : ill ; 23cm
Includes bibliographies and index
ISBN 0-246-11429-0 (cased) : £10.75
ISBN 0-246-11215-8 (pbk) : £6.95 B81-10072

624.1′5′0321 — Structures. Foundations — *Encyclopaedias*

Barker, John A. (John Arthur). Dictionary of soil mechanics and foundation engineering / John A. Barker. — London : Construction Press, 1981. — 210p ; 24cm
ISBN 0-86095-885-x (pbk) : £12.50 : CIP rev.
B81-06588

624.1′513 — Engineering. Applications of soil freezing — *Conference proceedings*

International Symposium on Ground Freezing *(2nd : 1980 : Trondheim).* Ground freezing, 1980. — Oxford : Elsevier Scientific, Dec.1981. — [350]p. — (Developments in geotechnical engineering ; v.28)
ISBN 0-444-42010-x : CIP entry B81-38297

624.1′513 — Oceans. Bed. Soils. Testing — *For offshire engineering — Conference proceedings*

Offshore site investigation : proceedings of a conference held in March 1979, in London / sponsored by the Society for Underwater Technology, the Geological Society of London, the Instsitution of Civil Engineers ; organised by the Seabed Sampling & Site Investigation Committee of the Society for Underwater Technology ; edited by D.A. Ardus. — London : Graham & Trotman, 1980. — 291p : ill,maps,facsims,plans ; 31cm
ISBN 0-86010-160-6 : £25.00 B81-07518

624.1′513 — Soils & rocks. Properties — *For engineering*

Bell, F. G.. Engineering properties of soils and rocks / F.G. Bell. — London : Butterworths, 1981. — 149p : ill,plans,1form ; 24cm
Includes index
ISBN 0-408-00537-8 (pbk) : £4.95 : CIP rev.
B80-36154

624.1′513 — Soils. Testing. Laboratory techniques — *For civil engineering*

Head, K. H.. Manual of soil laboratory testing. — London (4 Graham Lodge, Graham Rd, NW4 3DG) : Pentech Press, Sept.1981
Vol.2: Permeability, quick shear strength and compressibility tests. — [350]p
ISBN 0-7273-1305-3 : £15.00 : CIP entry
B81-23824

624.1′513 — Structural engineering. Grouting

Bowen, Robert. Grouting in engineering practice / Robert Bowen. — 2nd ed. — London : Applied Science Publishers, 1981. — ix,285p : ill,maps ; 23cm
Previous ed.: 1975. — Includes index
ISBN 0-85334-943-6 : £19.00 B81-23700

624.1′5132 — Rocks. Mechanics

Goodman, Richard E.. Introduction to rock mechanics / Richard E. Goodman. — New York ; Chichester : Wiley, c1980. — xii,478p,[1]folded leaf of plates : ill ; 24cm
Includes bibliographies and index
ISBN 0-471-04129-7 : £13.70 B81-08210

624.1′5136 — Soils. Geotechnical properties — *For civil engineering*

Holtz, Robert D.. An introduction to geotechnical engineering / Robert D. Holtz, William D. Kovacs. — Englewood Cliffs ; London : Prentice-Hall, c1981. — xiv,733p : ill ; 24cm. — (Prentice—Hall civil engineering and engineering mechanics series)
Bibliography: p701-717. — Includes index
ISBN 0-13-484394-0 : £20.25 B81-28219

624.1′5136 — Soils. Mechanics

Atkinson, J. H.. Foundations and slopes : an introduction to applications of critical state soil mechanics / J.H. Atkinson. — London : McGraw-Hill, 1981. — xvii,382p : ill ; 23cm. — (University series in civil engineering)
Includes bibliographies and index
ISBN 0-07-084118-7 (pbk) : £9.95 B81-27765

624.1′5136 — Soils. Shear. Testing

Chandler, M. P.. An open-sided field direct shear box with applications in geomorphology / by M.P. Chandler, D.C. Parker and M.J. Selby. — Norwich : Published for the British Geomorphological Research Group by Geo Abstracts, c1981. — 44p : ill,1form ; 21cm. — (Technical bulletin / British Geomorphological Research Group, ISSN 0306-3380 ; no.27)
Text on inside cover. — Bibliography: p36-40
ISBN 0-86094-068-3 (pbk) : Unpriced
B81-35339

624.1′5136 — Structures. Foundations. Soils. Mechanics

Liu, Cheng. Soils and foundations / Cheng Liu and Jack B. Evett. — Englewood Cliffs : Prentice-Hall, c1981. — xii,319p : ill ; 24cm
Includes index
ISBN 0-13-822239-8 : £12.95 B81-22708

624.1′5136′01515353 — Soils. Mechanics. Applications of finite element methods. Applications of computer systems

Smith, I. M.. Programming the finite element method. — Chichester : Wiley, Jan.1982. — [352]p
ISBN 0-471-28003-8 (cased) : £20.00 : CIP entry
ISBN 0-471-10098-6 (pbk) : £9.00 B81-34580

624.1′5136′076 — Soils. Mechanics — *Questions & answers*

Capper, P. Leonard. Problems in engineering soils / P. Leonard Capper, W. Fisher Cassie, James D. Geddes. — 3rd ed. — London : Spon, 1980. — xv,287p : ill ; 22cm
Previous ed.: 1971. — Includes index
ISBN 0-419-11840-3 (pbk) : £5.75 : CIP rev.
B80-04840

624.1′52 — Blasting

Hemphill, Gary B.. Blasting operations / Gary B. Hemphill. — New York ; London : McGraw-Hill, c1981. — xiv,258p : ill,2facsims ; 25cm
Includes index
ISBN 0-07-028093-2 : £16.00 B81-02596

624.1′52 — Civil engineering. Earthwork

Horner, P. C.. Earthworks / P.C. Horner. — London : Telford, 1981. — 52p : ill ; 15x21cm. — (ICE works construction guides)
Bibliography: p50-52
ISBN 0-7277-0091-x (pbk) : £2.50 B81-10081

624.1′54 — Great Britain. Structures. Foundations. Steel piles — *Technical data*

Cornfield, G. M.. Steel bearing piles / by G.M. Cornfield. — Rev. ed. / revised by British Steel Corporation BSC Sections and Tubes Division. — Croydon : Constrado, c1980. — 44p,[8]p of plates : ill ; 30cm
ISBN 0-86200-022-x (pbk) : £3.00 B81-23306

624.1′54 — Structures. Foundations. Piles. Design & construction — *Conference proceedings*

Recent developments in the design and construction of piles : proceedings of the conference held at the Institution of Electrical Engineers, 21-22 March, 1979. — London : Institution of Civil Engineers, 1980. — 408p : ill ; 31cm
ISBN 0-7277-0082-0 : £24.00 B81-10765

624.1′54 — Structures. Foundations. Piles. Driving

Dawson, W. A. (William Alec). Pile driving / W.A. Dawson. — London : Telford, 1981. — 27p : ill ; 15x21cm. — (ICE works construction guides)
ISBN 0-7277-0093-6 (pbk) : £2.00 B81-10083

624.1′54 — Structures. Foundations. Precast concrete piles

Broms, Bengt B.. Precast piling practice / Bengt B. Broms. — London : Telford, 1981. — 126p : ill ; 30cm
Bibliography: p125-126
ISBN 0-7277-0121-5 (pbk) : £6.00 B81-30814

624.1′62 — Embankments

Peter, Pavol[**Kanálové a ochranné hrádze.** *English*]. Canal and river levées. — Oxford : Elsevier Scientific, Dec.1981. — [450]p. — (Developments in geotechnical engineering ; 29)
Translation of: Kanálové a ochranné hrádze
ISBN 0-444-99726-1 : £40.00 : CIP entry
B81-31618

624.1′7 — Structures. Theories

Lowe, P. G.. Basic principles of plate theory. — Glasgow : Surrey University Press, Jan.1982. — [190]p
ISBN 0-903384-26-4 (cased) : £17.00 : CIP entry
ISBN 0-903384-25-6 (pbk) : £8.50 B81-33757

Thompson, J. M. T.. Instabilities and catastrophes in science and engineering. — Chichester : Wiley, Jan.1982. — [240]p
ISBN 0-471-09973-2 : £13.50 : CIP entry
B81-34648

624.1′71 — Buildings. Steel frames. Design. Applications of plasticity theory

Horne, M. R.. Plastic design of low-rise frames. — London : Granada, May 1981. — [232]p
ISBN 0-246-11199-2 : £25.00 : CIP entry
B81-04248

624.1′71 — Civil engineering. Structural analysis

Young, B. W.. Energy methods of structural analysis : theory, worked examples and problems / B.W. Young. — London : Macmillan, 1981. — viii,163p : ill ; 24cm
Includes index
ISBN 0-333-27776-7 (pbk) : £4.95 B81-27882

624.1′71 — Structural components. Statics & strength

Cerny, Ladislaw. Elementary statics and strength of materials / Ladislaw Cerny. — New York ; London : McGraw-Hill, c1981. — xv,317p : ill ; 24cm
Text on lining papers. — Includes index
ISBN 0-07-010339-9 : £15.25 B81-36282

Halperin, Don A.. Statics and strength of materials / Don A. Halperin ; consultants D. Dorsey Moss, H. William Succop, Jr. — 2nd ed. — New York ; Chichester : Wiley, c1981. — x,287p : ill ; 25cm
Previous ed.: 1976. — Includes index
ISBN 0-471-05651-0 : Unpriced B81-08520

624.1′71 — Structures. Analysis

Fraser, Donald J.. Conceptual designs and preliminary analysis of structures / Donald J. Fraser. — Marshfield, Mass. ; London : Pitman, c1981. — xi,297p : ill ; 25cm
Bibliography: p292-293. — Includes index
ISBN 0-273-01645-8 : Unpriced B81-40112

Shaeffer, R. E.. Building structures : elementary analysis and design / R.E. Shaeffer ; with full page illustrations by Pat Pinnell. — Englewood Cliffs ; London : Prentice-Hall, c1980. — xiv,336p : ill,maps,plans ; 29cm
Bibliography: p289-290. — Includes index
ISBN 0-13-086561-3 : £18.85
Also classified at 624.1′771 B81-02777

624.1′71 — Structures. Analysis. Plastic methods

Moy, Stuart S. J.. Plastic methods for steel and concrete structures / Stuart S.J. Moy. — London : Macmillan, 1981. — xiii,221p : ill ; 25cm
Includes index
ISBN 0-333-27563-2 (cased) : Unpriced
ISBN 0-333-27564-0 (pbk) : Unpriced
B81-29727

624.1′71 — Structures. Continuous media. Mechanics

Valid, Roger. Mechanics of continuous media and analysis of structures / Roger Valid ; foreword by Paul Germain ; [translated by Tradunion]. — Amsterdam ; Oxford : North-Holland, c1981. — xiii,357p : ill ; 23cm. — (North-Holland series in applied mathematics and mechanics ; v.26)
Translation of: La méchanique des milieux continus et le calcul des structures. — Includes index
ISBN 0-444-86150-5 : £26.71 B81-23638

624.1′71 — Structures. Dynamics

Lenczner, David. Movements in buildings / by David Lenczner. — 2nd ed. — Oxford : Pergamon, 1981. — ix,110p : ill ; 22cm. — (Pergamon international library)
Previous ed.: 1973. — Bibliography: p107-108. - Includes index
ISBN 0-08-024755-5 (cased) : £7.50
ISBN 0-08-024756-3 (pbk) : £5.00 B81-19105

Major, Alexander. Dynamics in civil engineering : analysis and design / Alexander Major. — Rev. and enl. ed. — Budapest : Akadémiai Kiadó ; London : Collet′s, c1980. — 4v : ill ; 25cm
Translation from the German. — Previous ed.: published in 1 vol. as Vibration analysis and design of foundations for machines and turbines. London : Collet′s, 1962. — Bibliography: p215-274 (Vol.4). - Includes index
ISBN 0-569-00234-6 : £60.00 B81-10376

624.1′71 — Structures. Mechanics

Cowan, Henry J.. Architectural structures : an introduction to structural mechanics / Henry J. Cowan. — 1st metric ed.. — London : Pitman, 1980. — xvi,320p : ill ; 25cm. — (A Pitman international text)
Previous ed.: i.e. 2nd ed. New York: Elsevier, c1976. — Includes bibliographies and index
ISBN 0-273-01054-9 (cased) : Unpriced
ISBN 0-273-01076-x (pbk) : £8.25 B81-36500

Oden, J. T.. Mechanics of elastic structures. — 2nd ed., J.T. Oden and E.A. Ripperger. — Washington ; London : Hemisphere, c1981. — xv,460p : ill ; 24cm
Previous ed.: 1967. — Bibliography: p445-449. — Includes index
ISBN 0-07-047507-5 : £24.25 B81-40048

624.1′71 — Structures. Safety & reliability - *Conference proceedings*

Structural safety and reliability. — Oxford : Elsevier Scientific, June 1981. — [1000]p
Conference papers
ISBN 0-444-41994-2 : CIP entry B81-15818

624.1′71 — Structures. Vibration. Formulae

Blevins, Robert D.. Formulas for natural frequency and mode shape / Robert D. Blevins. — New York ; London : Van Nostrand Reinhold, c1979. — xi,492p : ill ; 26cm
Includes index
ISBN 0-442-20710-7 : £24.40 B81-11183

624.1′71′015129434 — Structures. Analysis. Applications of matrices

Bhatt, P.. Problems in structural analysis by matrix methods. — Lancaster : Construction Press, Apr.1981. — [480]p
ISBN 0-86095-881-7 : £9.95 : CIP entry B81-06589

624.1′71′02854 — Structures. Analysis. Applications of digital computer systems

Gutkowski, Richard M.. Structures : fundamental theory and behavior / Richard M. Gutkowski. — New York ; London : Van Nostrand Reinhold, c1981. — xii,511p : ill,2charts ; 26cm
Includes index
ISBN 0-442-22983-6 : £25.90 B81-10182

624.1′71028′54 — Structures. Analysis. Applications of digital computer systems

Ross, C. T. F.. Computer analysis of skeletal structures. — London : Spon, Nov.1981. — [100]p
ISBN 0-419-11970-1 : £12.50 : CIP entry B81-31268

624.1′71′05 — Structures. Mechanics — *Serials*

Res mechanica letters : rapid communications in structural mechanics and materials science. — Vol.1, no.1 (Jan.1981)-. — Barking : Applied Science, 1981-. — v. : ill ; 24cm
Monthly
ISSN 0144-7831 = Res mechanica letters : Unpriced
Primary classification 620.1′1′05 B81-20061

624.1′71′076 — Structures. Analysis — *Questions & answers*

Logie. Structures : basic theory with worked examples / Logie. — Walton-on-Thames : Nelson, 1981. — xi,182p : ill ; 25cm
Includes index. — Publisher′s no.: NCN 420-5891-0
ISBN 0-17-771171-x (pbk) : £4.95 : CIP rev. B81-07926

624.1′75 — Structures. Wind loads — *Conference proceedings*

Wind engineering : proceedings of the fifth international conference, Fort Collins, Colorado, USA, July 1979 / edited by J.E. Cermak. — Oxford : Pergamon, 1980. — 2v.(xxv,1444p) : ill,ports ; 26cm
Includes index
ISBN 0-08-024745-8 : £1.00 : CIP rev. B80-13436

624.1′76 — Structures. Fatigue & fracture

Developments in fracture mechanics. — London : Applied Science Publishers, Sept.1981. — (The Developments series)
2. — [328]p
ISBN 0-85334-973-8 : £25.00 : CIP entry B81-20162

Parker, A. P.. The mechanics of fracture and fatigue : an introduction / A.P. Parker. — London : Spon, 1981. — x,167p : ill ; 25cm
Includes index
ISBN 0-419-11460-2 (cased) : Unpriced : CIP rev.
ISBN 0-419-11470-x (pbk) : Unpriced B81-16348

624.1′76 — Structures. Wind loads. Effects — *For design*

Scruton, C.. An introduction to wind effects on structures / C. Scruton. — [Oxford] : Published for the Design Council, the British Standards Institution and the Council of Engineering Institutions by Oxford University Press, c1981. — 79p : ill ; 30cm. — (Engineering design guides ; 40)
Cover title. — Bibliography: p75-78. — Includes index
ISBN 0-19-859178-0 (pbk) : £12.50 B81-26167

624.1′762 — Structures. Effects of ground movements — *Conference proceedings*

Ground movements and structures : proceedings of the 2nd international conference held at The University of Wales Institute of Science and Technology, Cardiff, April 1980 / edited by James D. Geddes ; sponsored by The Department of Civil Engineering and Building Technology, The University of Wales Institute of Science and Technology, and The Institution of Structural Engineers. — London : Pentech, 1981. — xi,964p : ill,maps,plans ; 25cm
Includes bibliographies
ISBN 0-7273-0701-0 : Unpriced : CIP rev. B81-03178

624.1′77 — Construction. Use of membranes

Rankilor, P. R.. Membranes in ground engineering / P.R. Rankilor. — Chichester : Wiley, c1981. — ix,377 : ill,1map ; 26cm
Bibliography: p368-370. — Includes index
ISBN 0-471-27808-4 : £19.50 : CIP rev. B80-25783

624.1′771 — Structures. Design

Lin, T. Y.. Structural concepts and systems for architects and engineers / T.Y. Lin, Sidney D. Stotesbury. — New York ; Chichester : Wiley, c1981. — xiii,507p : ill,plans ; 25cm
Bibliography: p505-507. — Includes index
ISBN 0-471-05186-1 : £22.35 B81-34924

Salvadori, Mario. Structural design in architecture / Mario Salvadori, Matthys Levy. — 2nd ed. / with example and problem solutions by Howard H.M. Hwang. — Englewood Cliffs ; London : Prentice-Hall, c1981. — xxii,458p : ill ; 24cm
Previous ed.: 1967. — Includes index
ISBN 0-13-853473-x : £16.20 B81-12522

Shaeffer, R. E.. Building structures : elementary analysis and design / R.E. Shaeffer ; with full page illustrations by Pat Pinnell. — Englewood Cliffs ; London : Prentice-Hall, c1980. — xiv,336p : ill,maps,plans ; 29cm
Bibliography: p289-290. — Includes index
ISBN 0-13-086561-3 : £18.85
Primary classification 624.1′71 B81-02777

624.1′771 — Structures. Design. Optimisation

Kirsch, Uri. Optimum structural design : concepts, methods and applications / Uri Kirsch. — New York ; London : McGraw-Hill, c1981. — xiv,441p : ill ; 25cm
Includes index
ISBN 0-07-034844-8 : £24.25 B81-23958

624.1′771′028542 — Structures. Design. Applications of digital computer systems. Programming

Iyengar, N. G. R.. Programming methods in structural design. — London : Edward Arnold, Dec.1981. — [264]p
Originally published: New Delhi : Affiliated East-West Press, 1980
ISBN 0-7131-3453-4 : £10.00 : CIP entry B81-33873

624.1′773 — Structures. Frames. Dynamics

Henrych, Josef. The dynamics of arches and frames / by Josef Henrych. — Amsterdam ; Oxford : Elsevier Scientific, 1981. — 463p : ill ; 25cm. — (Developments in civil engineering ; 2)
Translation from the Czech. — Bibliography: p457-458. — Includes index
ISBN 0-444-99792-x : Unpriced
Also classified at 624.1′775 B81-32844

624.1′773 — Structures. Space frames - *Manuals*

Analysis, design and construction of double-layer grids. — London : Applied Science, June 1981. — [424]p
ISBN 0-85334-910-x : £43.00 : CIP entry B81-12787

624.1′773 — Structures. Trusses. Configurations — *Technical data*

Melaragno, Michele. Simplified truss design / Michele Melaragno. — New York ; London : Van Nostrand Reinhold, c1981. — xi,404p : ill,facsims,ports ; 27cm
Bibliography: p397-400. — Includes index
ISBN 0-442-25129-7 : £20.65 B81-01894

624.1′774 — Cable-stayed structures & cable-suspended structures. Design & construction

Irvine, H. Max. Cable structures / H. Max Irvine. — Cambridge, Mass. ; London : MIT Press, c1981. — x,259p : ill ; 24cm. — (The MIT Press series in structural mechanics ; 1)
Includes index
ISBN 0-262-09023-6 : £8.75 B81-39639

624.1′774 — Structures. Thin-walled bars

Gjelsvik, Atle. The theory of thin walled bars / Atle Gjelsvik. — New York ; Chichester : Wiley, c1981. — ix,248p : ill ; 24cm
Includes index
ISBN 0-471-08594-4 : £22.00 B81-33015

624.1′775 — Structures. Arches. Dynamics

Henrych, Josef. The dynamics of arches and frames / by Josef Henrych. — Amsterdam ; Oxford : Elsevier Scientific, 1981. — 463p : ill ; 25cm. — (Developments in civil engineering ; 2)
Translation from the Czech. — Bibliography: p457-458. — Includes index
ISBN 0-444-99792-x : Unpriced
Primary classification 624.1′773 B81-32844

624.1′776 — Structures. Plates & shells. Stress analysis

Ugural, A. C.. Stresses in plates and shells / A.C. Ugural. — New York ; London : McGraw-Hill, c1981. — xv,317p : ill ; 25cm
Includes index
ISBN 0-07-065730-0 : £22.95 B81-39819

624.1′7762 — Structures. Thin cylindrical elastic fluid-filled shells. Waves. Propagation

Fuller, C. R.. Characteristics of wave propagation and energy distributions in cylindrical elastic shells filled with fluid / by C.R. Fuller and F.J. Fahy. — [Southampton] ([Highfield, Southampton SO9 5NH]) : Institute of Sound and Vibration Research, University of Southampton, 1981. — 28p,[14]leaves : ill ; 30cm. — (ISVR technical report ; no.116)
Unpriced (spiral) B81-30922

624.1′7762 — Structures. Thin shells. Theories

Mollman, H.. Introduction to the theory of thin shells. — Chichester : Wiley, Feb.1982. — [224]p
ISBN 0-471-28056-9 : £17.00 : CIP entry
B81-36245

624.1′8 — Structures. Composite materials - *Conference proceedings*

International Conference on Composite Structures *(1st : 1981 : Paisley College of Technology)*. Composite structures. — London : Applied Science, Aug.1981. — [744]p
ISBN 0-85334-988-6 : £70.00 : CIP entry
B81-19205

624.1′821 — Concrete foundations. Bolted joints with steel columns. Design & construction

Holding down systems for steel stanchions / [by a joint working party of the Concrete Society and the British Constructional Steelwork Association]. — [London] ([Terminal House, Grosvenor Gardens, SW1W 0AJ]) : Concrete Society, c1980. — 23p : ill ; 30cm
ISBN 0-7210-1222-1 (pbk) : £3.00 B81-23304

624.1′821 — Construction materials: Steel — *Conference proceedings*

Construction: A Challenge For Steel *(Conference : 1980 : Luxembourg)*. Construction: A Challenge For Steel : international conference, Luxembourg 24/26 September 1980 / [organized by] Commission of the European Communities [Directorate General Internal Market and Industrial Affairs]. — English Language ed. — Guildford : Westbury House, c1981. — 426p : ill,plans ; 24cm
ISBN 0-86103-052-4 (pbk) : Unpriced
B81-27167

624.1′821 — Great Britain. External steel structural components. Fire protection — *Technical data*

Law, Margaret, *1928-*. Fire safety of bare external structural steel / Margaret Law and Turlogh O′Brien. — Croydon : Constrado, 1981. — 88p : ill ; 30cm
ISBN 0-86200-026-2 (pbk) : £6.00 B81-34262

624.1′821 — Great Britain. Steel structural components. Fire protection — *Technical data*

Elliott, D. A.. Protection of structural steelwork / D.A. Elliott. — 2nd ed. — Croydon : Constrado, c1981. — 51p : ill ; 30cm
Previous ed.: 1974. — Includes index
ISBN 0-86200-025-4 (pbk) : £3.00 B81-23305

624.1′821 — Steel & concrete composite structures. Design

Composite structures / European Convention for Constructional Steelwork ... ; prepared by the Technical General Secretariat of the ECCS. — London : Construction Press, 1981. — 183p : ill ; 24cm
ISBN 0-86095-872-8 : £17.50 : CIP rev.
B80-22089

Yam, Lloyd C. P.. Design of composite steel-concrete structures / Lloyd C.P. Yam. — [London] : Surrey University Press, 1981. — xv,168p : ill ; 24cm
Includes index
ISBN 0-903384-22-1 : £14.95 : CIP rev.
B80-22087

624.1′821 — Steel structures. Design

Lambert, F. W.. Structural steelwork. — 3rd ed. — London : George Godwin, Aug.1981. — [150]p. — (Godwin study guides)
Previous ed.: London : Macdonald and Evans, 1973
ISBN 0-7114-5712-3 (pbk) : £5.00 : CIP entry
B81-16378

MacGinley, T. J.. Steel structures. — London : Spon, Nov.1981. — [250]p
ISBN 0-419-11710-5 (pbk) : £6.00 : CIP entry
B81-31269

624.1′821 — Structures. Steel composite materials. Joints — *Conference proceedings*

Joints in structural steelwork : the design and performance of semi-rigid and rigid joints in steel and composite structures and their influence on structural behaviour : proceedings of the international conference held at Teesside Polytechnic, Middlesborough, Cleveland, 6-9th April 1981 / organised by Teesside Polytechnic with co-sponsors the Institution of Structural Engineers ... [et al.] ; edited by J.H. Howlett, W.M. Jenkins, R. Stainsby. — London (Estover Rd., Plymouth, Devon PLS 7PZ) : Pentech Press, 1981. — xvi,[809]p : ill ; 24cm
ISBN 0-7273-1001-1 : Unpriced : CIP rev.
B81-07612

624.1′821′094 — Europe. Steel structures. Design — *Standards*

European Convention for Constructional Steelwork. *Technical General Secretariat*. European recommendations for steel construction / European Convention for Constructional Steelwork ... ; prepared by the Technical General Secretariat of the ECCS. — London : Construction Press, 1981. — xi,355p : ill ; 24cm + 1pamphlet(50p : ill ; 24cm)
ISBN 0-86095-870-1 (pbk) : £19.50 : CIP rev.
B80-24573

624.1′83′05 — Construction materials: Masonry — *Serials*

The **International** journal of masonry construction. — Vol.1, no.1 (Mar.1980)-. — London : United Trade Press, 1980-. — v. : ill ; 29cm
Quarterly
ISSN 0143-0602 = International journal of masonry construction : £20.00 per year
B81-00951

624.1′832′0941132 — Scotland. Orkney. Stone structures — *Aerial photographs*

Moberg, Gunnie. Stone built : Orkney photographs / by Gunnie Moberg. — Stromness (Stromness, Orkney) : Stromness Books & Prints, 1979. — [40]p : all ill ; 20x25cm
Unpriced (pbk) B81-07226

624.1′834 — Concrete. Slipforming

Batterham, R. G.. Slipform concrete / R.G. Batterham. — Lancaster : Construction Press, 1980. — 107p : ill ; 24cm
Bibliography: p103. — Includes index
ISBN 0-86095-855-8 : £7.95 : CIP rev.
B80-10113

624.1′834 — Construction materials: Concrete

Mindess, Sidney. Concrete / Sidney Mindess, J. Francis Young. — Englewood Cliffs ; London : Prentice-Hall, c1981. — xvi,671p : ill ; 24cm. — (Civil engineering and engineering mechanics series)
Includes bibliographies and index
ISBN 0-13-167106-5 : £22.10 B81-17175

624.1′834 — Prestressed concrete structural components. Ducts. Grouting — *Manuals*

Budge, C. J.. Preparing and grouting ducts in prestressed concrete members / C.J. Budge. — 2nd ed. — Slough : Cement and Concrete Association, 1981. — 7p : ill(some col.),1map ; 30cm. — (Construction guide, ISSN 0143-6880)
Previous ed.: 1971
ISBN 0-7210-1233-7 (unbound) : Unpriced
B81-24076

624.1′834 — Reinforced concrete structures. Design. Limit-state method

Hughes, B. P. (Barry Peter). Limit state theory for reinforced concrete design : SI units / B.P. Hughes. — 3rd ed. — London : Pitman, 1980. — xxiv,697p : ill,forms ; 24cm
Previous ed.: 1976. — Includes index
ISBN 0-273-01543-5 : £15.00 B81-00952

624.1′834′0924 — Concrete. Use. Advisory services. Wigmore, Victor S. — *Biographies*

Wigmore, Victor S.. Memoirs of a concrete consultant / Victor S. Wigmore. — Bognor Regis : New Horizon, c1979. — 218p ; 21cm
Includes index
ISBN 0-86116-127-0 : £3.95 B81-21806

624.1′8341 — Construction materials: Glass fibre reinforced concrete — *Conference proceedings*

International Congress on Glassfibre Reinforced Cement *(1979 : London)*. The developing success of GRC : proceedings of the International Congress on Glassfibre Reinforced Cement, London, 10-12 October, 1979 / organised by the Glassfibre Reinforced Cement Association (GRCA) in collaboration with Conference Services Limited, London ; editor, Hayden Jeffery. — Gerrards Cross (Farthings End, Dukes Ride, Gerrards Cross, Bucks. SL9 7LD) : The Association, 1980. — 121p : ill,forms ; 30cm
ISBN 0-7210-1213-2 (pbk) : Unpriced
B81-17870

624.1′8341 — Construction materials: Reinforced concrete. Detailing — *Technical data*

Barker, John A. (John Arthur). Reinforced concrete detailing / John A. Barker. — 2nd ed. — London : Oxford University Press, 1981. — xx,304p : ill ; 31cm. — (Oxford science publications)
Previous ed.: 1967. — Includes index
ISBN 0-19-859523-9 : £45.00 : CIP rev.
B81-07457

624.1′8341 — Reinforced & prestressed concrete structures. Design

Oladapo, I. O.. Fundamentals of the design of concrete structures / I.O. Oladapo. — London : Evans, 1981. — ix,213p : ill ; 22cm
Includes index
ISBN 0-237-50177-5 (pbk) : Unpriced
B81-33453

624.1′8341 — Reinforced concrete structural components

Ferguson, Phil M.. Reinforced concrete fundamentals / Phil H. Ferguson. — 4th ed., SI version / SI conversion by Henry J. Cowan. — New York ; Chichester : Wiley, c1981. — x,694p : ill ; 24cm
Previous ed.: 1973. — Includes index
ISBN 0-471-05897-1 : £18.75 B81-23247

624.1′8341 — Reinforced concrete structures. Design

Reynolds, Charles E.. Reinforced concrete designer′s handbook. — 9th ed. / by Charles E. Reynolds and James C. Steadman. — Mount Durand : Toucan, 1981. — xiv,505p : ill ; 31cm. — (A Viewpoint publication)
Previous ed.: 1974. — Includes index
ISBN 0-7210-1198-5 (cased) : Unpriced
ISBN 0-7210-1199-3 (pbk) : Unpriced
B81-26845

624.1′8341 — Structural engineering. Design. Use of prestressed & reinforced microconcrete models — *Conference proceedings*

Reinforced and prestressed microconcrete models / edited by F.K. Garas and G.S.T. Armer. — Lancaster : Construction Press, 1980. — 387p : ill ; 31cm
Conference papers. — Includes index
ISBN 0-86095-880-9 : £21.00 B81-05460

624.1′83412 — Prestressed concrete structural components. Design

Abeles, P. W.. Prestressed concrete designer′s handbook. — 3rd ed. / by P.W. Abeles and B.K. Bardhan-Roy. — Slough : Cement and Concrete Association, 1981. — xxii,556p : ill ; 24cm. — (A Viewpoint publication)
Previous ed.: 1976
ISBN 0-7210-1232-9 (cased) : Unpriced
ISBN 0-7210-1227-2 (pbk) : Unpriced
B81-38475

Lin, T. Y.. Design of prestressed concrete structures. — 3rd ed. / T.Y. Lin, Ned H. Burns. — New York ; Chichester : Wiley, c1981. — 646p : ill ; 24cm
Previous ed.: New York : Wiley, 1963. — Includes index
ISBN 0-471-01898-8 : £24.00 B81-37110

624.1′83412′0218 — Construction. Use of prestressed concrete — *Standards*

Fédération internationale de la précontrainte. *Commission on Prestressing Steels and Systems*. Recommendations for acceptance and application of post-tensioning systems / [FIP Commission on Prestressing Steels and Systems]. — Slough : Published for the Fédération internationale de la précontrainte by the Cement and Concrete Association, 1981. — 30p : ill ; 30cm
Cover title. — Bibliography: p30
ISBN 0-7210-1231-0 (pbk) : Unpriced
B81-24770

624.1′83414 — Precast concrete structural components. Joints

Structural joints in precast concrete : manual / the Institution of Structural Engineers. — London (11 Upper Belgrave St., SW1X 8BH) : The Institution, 1978. — 56p : ill ; 30cm
£9.00 (£6.00 to members of the Institution) (pbk) B81-04762

624.1′8342 — Structural components: Reinforced concrete slabs. Analysis & design

Park, R. (Robert). Reinforced concrete slabs / R. Park, W.L. Gamble. — New York ; Chichester : Wiley, c1980. — xvii,618p : ill ; 24cm
Includes index
ISBN 0-471-65915-0 : £21.40 B81-03788

624.1′836 — Structures. Loadbearing brickwork. Design

Hendry, A. W.. An introduction to load bearing brickwork design / A.W. Hendry, B.P. Sinha and S.R. Davies. — Chichester : Horwood, 1981. — 184p : ill ; 24cm. — (Ellis Horwood series in engineering science)
Text on lining papers. — Includes index
ISBN 0-85312-216-4 (cased) : £15.00 : CIP rev.
ISBN 0-85312-355-1 (student ed) : Unpriced
ISBN 0-470-27227-9 (Wiley) : £15.00
B81-13853

624.1′84 — Structural engineering materials: Loadbearing timber. Physical properties — *For architectural design*

Breyer, Donald E.. Design of wood structures / by Donald E. Breyer with contributions by John A. Ank. — New York ; London : McGraw-Hill, c1980. — xvii,542p : ill,2maps ; 25cm
Includes index
ISBN 0-07-007671-5 : £16.50 B81-03039

624.1′84 — Timber structural components. Design — *Manuals*

Structural timber design and technology. — London : Construction Press, Feb.1982. — [240]p
ISBN 0-86095-889-2 : £19.95 : CIP entry
B81-36348

624.1′9 — Underground structures. Construction

Underground structures and mines construction practices. — Moscow : Mir ; [London] : Distributed by Central Books
Translation of: Tekhnologiía stroitel′stva podzemnykh sooruzheniĭ i shakht
[Pt.1]: Driving horizontal workings and tunnels / N.M. Pokrovsky ; translated from the Russian by I.V. Savin. — 1980. — 421p : ill ; 23cm
Bibliography: p416-417. — Includes index
ISBN 0-7147-1607-3 : £5.50 B81-23484

624.1′9′05 — Underground structures — *Serials*

Advances in tunnelling technology and subsurface use = Développement des travaux en souterrain. — Vol.1, no.1 (1981)-. — Oxford : Pergamon on behalf of the International Tunnelling Association, 1981-. — v. : ill ; 30cm
Three issues yearly. — Text in English and French
ISSN 0275-5416 : Unpriced
Also classified at 624.1′93′05 B81-26585

624.1′9′09 — Underground structures, *to 1980*

Pennick, Nigel. The subterranean kingdom : a survey of man-made structures beneath the earth / by Nigel Pennick ; line illustrations by the author. — Wellingborough : Turnstone, 1981. — 160p : ill,maps,plans ; 22cm
Bibliography: p153-158. — Includes index
ISBN 0-85500-140-2 (pbk) : £4.50 B81-29250

624.1′93 — Tunnels

Megaw, T. M.. Tunnels. — Chichester : Ellis Horwood, Apr.1981. — (Ellis Horwood series in engineering science : Mechanical & civil engineering)
Vol.2. — 1v.
ISBN 0-85312-361-6 : £25.00 : CIP entry
B81-08939

624.1′93 — Tunnels & tunnelling

Megaw, T. M.. Tunnels : planning, design, construction / T.M. Megaw and J.V. Bartlett. — Chichester : Horwood. — (Ellis Horwood series in engineering science)
Vol. 1. — c1981. — 284p : ill,maps ; 24cm
Text on lining papers. — Includes bibliographies and index
ISBN 0-85312-223-7 : £25.00 : CIP rev.
ISBN 0-470-27151-5 (Wiley) : £25.00
B81-08922

624.1′93 — Vehicle tunnels. Aerodynamics & ventilation — *Conference proceedings*

International Symposium on the Aerodynamics and Ventilation of Vehicle Tunnels *(3rd : 1979 : Sheffield)*. Papers presented at the Third International Symposium on the Aerodynamics and Ventilation of Vehicle Tunnels, Sheffield England, March 1979 / BHRA Fluid Engineering ; [edited by H.S. Stephens, P.A. Wood]. — Bedford : BHRA Fluid Engineering, 1979. — 2v.(703p) : ill ; 30cm
ISBN 0-906085-28-4 (pbk) : Unpriced : CIP rev. B79-09596

624.1′93′05 — Tunnelling — *Serials*

Advances in tunnelling technology and subsurface use = Développement des travaux en souterrain. — Vol.1, no.1 (1981)-. — Oxford : Pergamon on behalf of the International Tunnelling Association, 1981-. — v. : ill ; 30cm
Three issues yearly. — Text in English and French
ISSN 0275-5416 : Unpriced
Primary classification 624.1′9′05 B81-26585

624.1′93′09421 — London. Underground tunnels, *to 1980*

Pennick, Nigel. Tunnels under London / by Nigel Pennick. — 2nd ed. — Cambridge (142 Pheasant Rise, Bar Hill, Cambridge CB3 8SD) : Fenris-Wolf, 1981. — 24p : ill,maps ; 30cm
Previous ed.: 1980. — Bibliography: p23-24
Unpriced (pbk) B81-18376

Pennick, Nigel. Tunnels under London / Nigel Pennick. — 3rd ed. — Bar Hill (142 Pheasant Rise, Bar Hill, Cambridge CB3 8SD) : Electric Traction, 1981. — 28p : ill,maps ; 21cm
Previous ed.: Cambridge : Fenris-Wolf, 1981. — Bibliography: p26
Unpriced (pbk) B81-37732

624.2 — BRIDGES

624′.2 — Bridges — *For children*

Dixon, Annabelle. Bridges / Annabelle Dixon. — London : Black, c1981. — 32p : ill,1port ; 23cm. — (Science explorers)
Includes index
ISBN 0-7136-2140-0 : £2.95 : CIP rev.
B81-30456

624′.2 — Scotland. Rural regions. Footbridges. Design & construction

Footbridges in the countryside : design and construction / Reiach Hall Blyth Partnership ; commissioned by the Countryside Commission for Scotland. — [Perth] : [The Commission], 1981. — 101p(15 folded) : ill,forms ; 30cm
Bibliography: p93-97
ISBN 0-902226-52-5 (pbk) : Unpriced
B81-32454

624′.2′094128 — Scotland. Tay River. Bridges

Bridge of the Tay. — [Perth?] : [Perth Civic Trust?], [1980?]. — 16p : ill ; 22cm
Cover title. — Compiled by Primary VII, Caledonian Road School
Unpriced (pbk) B81-09340

624′.4′0941 — Great Britain. Steel box girder bridges. Design. Standards: British Standards Institution. Steel, concrete and composite bridges — *Conference proceedings*

The **Design** of steel bridges / edited by K.C. Rockey and H.R. Evans. — London : Granada, 1981. — 485p : ill ; 24cm
Conference papers
ISBN 0-246-11339-1 : £25.00 B81-10069

624′.4′0942921 — Gwynedd. Menai Strait. Railway bridges: Britannia Bridge, *1845-1970*. **Design & construction**

Pontydd Menai = The Menai bridges. — [Caernarfon] ([County Offices, Caernarfon, Gwynedd]) : Gwynedd Archives Service in association with the Welsh Arts Council, c1980. — [36]p : ill(some col.),facsims,ports ; 22cm + Catalogue([12]p ; 22cm)
Parallel Welsh text and English translation. — Catalogue ([12]p) as insert
ISBN 0-905171-73-x (pbk) : Unpriced
Also classified at 624′.55′0942921 B81-20852

624′.55′094283 — Humberside. Road bridges: Humber Bridge. Construction

Bridging the Humber / compiled by George Wilkinson ; photographs by D. Lee ... [et al.]. — York (15 Coney St., York [Y01 1YT]) : Cerialis, c1981. — [120]p : ill(some col.),1map,(1col.port) ; 30cm
ISBN 0-9501098-6-x (pbk) : £7.50 B81-35321

The **Humber** Bridge : the eighth wonder of the world. — [Grimsby] (384 Cleethorpe Rd., Grimsby, South Humberside) : Aspinall Holdings, c1981 (Grimsby : Graphic Press). — 136p : ill ; 30cm
Published: as a supplement to the Humberside & South Yorkshire Executive
Unpriced (pbk) B81-35322

The **Humberside** connection : how the bridge was built / ... prepared and edited by Basil Reed. — Wallington : Home Publishing, [1981]. — 64p : ill(some col.),1map ; 30cm
Unpriced (pbk) B81-28863

624′.55′0942921 — Gwynedd. Menai Strait. Road bridges: Menai Suspension Bridge. Design & construction

Pontydd Menai = The Menai bridges. — [Caernarfon] ([County Offices, Caernarfon, Gwynedd]) : Gwynedd Archives Service in association with the Welsh Arts Council, c1980. — [36]p : ill(some col.),facsims,ports ; 22cm + Catalogue([12]p ; 22cm)
Parallel Welsh text and English translation. — Catalogue ([12]p) as insert
ISBN 0-905171-73-x (pbk) : Unpriced
Primary classification 624′.4′0942921
B81-20852

624′.6′0941492 — Scotland. Dumfries and Galloway Region. Kirkcudbright. Bridges: Kirkcudbright Bridge, *to 1926*

Collin, T. R.. Bridging the Dee at Kirkcudbright / [T.R. Collin]. — [Kirkcudbright] : [Stewartry Museum], 1981. — 28p : ill,facsims ; 22cm
£1.25 (pbk) B81-34345

624′.86′0942991 — Gwent. Newport. Transporter bridges: Newport Transporter Bridge

James, Leslie, *1944-*. Newport transporter bridge / [Leslie James]. — [Newport, Gwent] ([John Frost Sq., Newport, Gwent NPT 1PA]) : Newport Museum and Art Gallery, 1980. — [3]p : ill ; 21x31cm
Unpriced (unbound) B81-36070

625.1 — RAILWAY ENGINEERING

625.1′0074′02 — Great Britain. Railway museums — *Directories* — *Serials*

Railways restored : Association of Railway Preservation Societies′ official year book. — 1981. — London : I. Allan, 1981. — 96p
ISBN 0-7110-1102-8 : £1.95
Primary classification 385′.025′41 B81-31042

625.1′0092′2 — Great Britain. Railways. Stephenson, George, *1781-1848* **& Stephenson, Robert** — *Biographies*

Robbins, Michael. George & Robert Stephenson / Michael Robbins. — New ed. — London : H.M.S.O., 1981. — viii,69p,[8]p of plates : ill,maps,ports ; 22cm
At head of title: National Railway Museum, York, Science Museum, London. — Previous ed.: London : Oxford University Press, 1966. — Bibliography: p63-64. — Includes index
ISBN 0-11-290342-8 (pbk) : £1.75 B81-29275

625.1′0092′4 — Great Britain. Railway mechanical engineering. Hewison, Christian H. — *Biographies*

Hewison, Christian H.. From shedmaster to the Railway Inspectorate / Christian H. Hewison. — Newton Abbot : David & Charles, c1981. — 176p,[16]p of plates : ill ; 23cm
ISBN 0-7153-8074-5 : £6.95 B81-23083

625.1′00941 — Great Britain. Railway engineering, *1948-1980*

Johnson, John, *1913-*. British Railways engineering 1948-80 / by John Johnson and Robert A. Long ; editor in chief, Roland C. Bond ; foreword by Sir Peter Parker. — London : Mechanical Engineering Publications, 1981. — x,636p : ill ; 26cm
Bibliography: p604-606. - Includes index
ISBN 0-85298-446-4 : £19.00 B81-18363

625.1′00941 — Great Britain. Railway services. Lines — *Technical data*

Oakley, Michael. Diesel enthusiast′s pocket guide : including electrics / Michael Oakley. — Truro : Barton
[1]: Eastern Region south. — [1981]. — [50]p : ill(some col.),maps(some col.) ; 19cm
ISBN 0-85153-402-3 (unbound) : £0.75 B81-30043

Oakley, Michael. Diesel enthusiast′s pocket guide : including electrics / Michael Oakley. — Truro : Barton
[2]: Yorkshire and Lincolnshire. — [1981]. — [50]p : ill(some col.),maps(some col.) ; 19cm
ISBN 0-85153-403-1 (unbound) : £0.75 B81-30044

Oakley, Michael. Diesel enthusiast′s pocket guide : including electrics / Michael Oakley. — Truro : Barton
[3]: Northern England. — [1981]. — [50]p : ill (some col.),maps(some col.) ; 19cm
ISBN 0-85153-404-x (unbound) : £0.75 B81-30045

Oakley, Michael. Diesel enthusiast′s pocket guide : including electrics / Michael Oakley. — Truro : Barton
[4]: L.M. Region south. — [1981]. — [50]p : ill (some col.),maps(some col.) ; 19cm
ISBN 0-85153-405-8 (unbound) : £0.75 B81-30046

625.1′00941 — Great Britain. Railways. Engineering aspects

Cooper, B. K.. British Rail handbook / B.K. Cooper. — London : Ian Allan, 1981. — 172p : ill,1map ; 16cm
ISBN 0-7110-1027-7 : £2.95 B81-29633

625.1′00941 — Great Britain. Railways. Industrial antiquities

Nock, O. S.. Railway archaeology / O.S. Nock. — Cambridge : Stephens, 1981. — 192p : ill,maps,facsims ; 25cm
Includes index
ISBN 0-85059-451-0 : £8.95 : CIP rev. B81-03179

Ransom, P. J. G.. The archaeology of railways / P.J.G. Ransom. — Tadworth : World′s Work, c1981. — 304p : ill(some col.),maps ; 27cm
Bibliography: p298-299. — Includes index
ISBN 0-437-14401-1 : £12.50 B81-40556

625.1′009429′29 — Gwynedd. Narrow gauge railway services: Festiniog Railway. Deviation. Construction, *to 1981*

Hollingsworth, J. B.. Ffestiniog adventure : the Ffestiniog railway′s deviation project / [Brian Hollingsworth]. — Newton Abbot : David & Charles, c1981. — 191p : ill,maps,ports ; 23cm
Includes index
ISBN 0-7153-7956-9 : £6.50 B81-19866

625.1′1′0941 — Great Britain. Railways. Design, *1830-1960*

Haresnape, Brian. Design for steam : 1830-1960 / Brian Haresnape. — London : Ian Allan, 1981. — 176p : ill,facsims ; 30cm
Ill on lining papers
ISBN 0-7110-1081-1 : £9.95 B81-32808

625.1′9 — Miniature railways & model railways

Hollingsworth, J. B.. Model railroads / Brian Hollingsworth. — London : Hamlyn, 1981. — 192p : ill(some col.),plans ; 32cm
Bibliography p190. - Includes index
ISBN 0-600-34944-6 : £5.95 B81-22051

625.1′9 — Model railways

Andress, Michael. PSL model railway guide / Michael Andress. — Cambridge : Stephens
5: Operating your layout. — 1981. — 64p : ill,1map,facsims ; 24cm
ISBN 0-85059-436-7 (pbk) : £2.95 : CIP rev. B81-04386

Andress, Michael. PSL model railway guide / Michael Andress. — Cambridge : Stephens
6: Branch line railways. — 1981. — 64p : ill ; 24cm
ISBN 0-85059-437-5 (pbk) : £2.95 : CIP rev. B81-04387

625.1′9 — Model railways. Baseboards. Making — *Manuals*

Baseboard construction : simple ways to build baseboards for model railways from gauges Z to O, using well proven methods / edited by Chris Ellis. — [Kingston] ([4 Surbiton Hall Close, Kingston, Surrey]) : Model Trains, 1981. — 20p : ill,plans ; 21cm
£1.50 (corrected) B81-29946

625.1′9 — Model railways. Construction

Simmons, Norman. How to go railway modelling. — 4th ed. — London : Cambridge : Stephens, Sept.1981. — [216]p
Previous ed.: 1980
ISBN 0-85059-557-6 : £8.95 : CIP entry B81-21590

625.1′9 — Model steam locomotives — *Serials*

Locomotives large & small : [the quarterly magazine for the steam enthusiast]. — No.1 (Nov. 1979)-. — Shanklin (Cross St., Shanklin, Isle of Wight) : Saunders the Printers (IW), 1979-. — v. : ill ; 28cm
ISSN 0260-2970 = Locomotives large & small : £3.25 per year
Primary classification 625.2′61′0941 B81-02007

625.1′9 — Triang & Triang-Hornby ′oo′ gauge model railway equipment, *1955-1972* — *Illustrations*

Stanford, Tony. A short history of Triang railways : ′00′ guage precision electric and clockwork scale models / by Tony Stanford. — London (7 Cecil Court, W.C.2) : Cranbourn, [1981]. — 33p : chiefly ill,facsims ; 31cm
Cover title
Unpriced (pbk) B81-15113

625.1′9′028 — Model railway equipment. Electronic equipment. Construction — *Manuals*

Penfold, R. A.. Model railway projects. — London : Babani, Nov.1981. — [112]p
ISBN 0-85934-070-8 (pbk) : £1.95 : CIP entry B81-30404

625.1′9′05 — Model railways — *Serials*

PSL′s practical guide to railway modelling. — No.1. — Cambridge : Stephens, Sept.1981. — [96]p
ISBN 0-85059-548-7 : £3.95 : CIP entry B81-20510

625.1′9′0924 — Model railways. Construction, *1950-1975* — *Personal observations*

Hancock, P. D.. Narrow gauge adventure : the story of the Craig & Mertonford & its associated standard gauge lines / P.D. Hancock. — 2nd ed. — Seaton : Peco, 1980. — 127p : ill,maps ; 26cm
Previous ed: 1975. — Includes index
ISBN 0-900586-54-0 : £5.95 B81-01781

625.2′09′047 — Trains, *ca 1970-1980*

Dunn, John, *1938-*. Modern trains / John Dunn. — London : New English Library, 1980. — 155p : col.ill ; 28cm
Col. ill on lining papers. — Includes index
ISBN 0-450-04755-5 : £9.95 B81-02245

625.2′0941 — Great Britain. Railway services: British Rail. Rolling stock — *History*

Haresnape, Brian. British Rail fleet survey / Brian Haresnape. — London : Ian Allan
1: Early prototype and pilot scheme diesel-electrics. — 1981. — 80p : ill ; 29cm
ISBN 0-7110-1121-4 (pbk) : £2.50 B81-32809

625.2′09422′395 — Kent. Shepway *(District)*. **Narrow gauge railway services: Romney, Hythe and Dymchurch Railway. Locomotives & rolling stock**

Smith, R. Lloyd. A miniature guide to the Romney, Hythe and Dymchurch Railway : includes details of all locomotives and rolling stock / R. Lloyd Smith and P. Ross. — [Hounslow] ([200 Great West Rd., Hounslow, Middx]) : Romney, Hythe & Dymchurch Railway Association, 1981. — 33p : ill,1maps ; 21cm
Map on inside cover. — Bibliography: p33
£0.80 (pbk) B81-25596

625.2′09424′13 — Gloucestershire. Forest of Dean *(District)*. **Railway services: Dean Forest Railway. Preserved rolling stock**

Dean Forest Railway Society : guide & stockbook (including Forest railway history). — 3rd ed / compiled by M.J. Harding. — [Gloucester] ([c/o C.H.L. Bathurst, 7 Bullfinch Rd., Heron Park, Gloucester GL4 8LX]) : Dean Forest Railway Society, 1981?. — 47p : ill,1map ; 21cm
Previous ed.: 1980?
ISBN 0-9507099-1-3 (pbk) : £1.00 B81-27763

625.2′3 — North Yorkshire. York. Museums: National Railway Museum. Exhibits: Royal trains, *1832-1952*

Jenkinson, David. Palaces on wheels : Royal carriages at the National Railway Museum / David Jenkinson and Gwen Townend. — London : H.M.S.O., 1981. — 65p : ill(some col.),1facsim,ports ; 21x22cm
Ill on lining papers
ISBN 0-11-290366-5 : £3.95 B81-36322

625.2′3′0941 — Great Britain. Rolling stock: Coaches, *to 1980*

Kichenside, Geoffrey. 150 years of railway carriages / Geoffrey Kichenside. — Newton Abbot : David & Charles, c1981. — 93p : ill ; 25cm. — (Railway history in pictures)
ISBN 0-7153-8196-2 : £6.50 : CIP rev. B81-17498

625.2′4 — Rail freight transport. Engineering aspects — *Conference proceedings*

Rail freight : a contribution to the conservation of energy : conference sponsored by the Railway Division of The Institution of Mechanical Engineers and The Private Wagon Federation, London 5 March 1981. — Bury St Edmunds : Mechanical Engineering [for] The Institution of Mechanical Engineers, 1981. — 72p : ill ; 30cm. — (I Mech E conference publications ; 1981-2)
ISBN 0-85298-472-3 (pbk) : Unpriced B81-18663

625.2′6 — Locomotives. Propulsion systems: Magnetic levitation

Mulhall, B. E.. Magnetic levitation for railways. — Oxford : Clarendon Press, Aug.1981. — [100]p
ISBN 0-19-854802-8 : £12.50 : CIP entry B81-15835

625.2′6′0941 — Great Britain. Preserved locomotives — *Lists — Serials*
Preserved locomotives. — 1981-. — London : Ian Allan, 1981-. — v. : ill ; 15cm. — (abc)
Annual
ISSN 0261-0326 = Preserved locomotives : £0.50 B81-20718

625.2′6′0941 — Great Britain. Railway services: British Rail. Locomotive depots. Locomotives — *Illustrations*
Diesels and electrics on shed / [compiled] by Rex Kennedy. — Oxford : Oxford Publishing Vol.3: Western Region. — 1981. — [104]p : chiefly ill,1map ; 23cm
ISBN 0-86093-042-4 : £5.95 B81-26629

625.2′6′0941 — Great Britain. Railway services: British Rail. Locomotives & multiple units, *1968-1979 — Illustrations*
BR motive power panorama / [compiled by] Peter Dobson & John Chalcraft. — London : Ian Allan, 1981. — 123p : chiefly ill ; 25cm
ISBN 0-7110-1079-x : £5.95 B81-05969

625.2′6′0941 — Great Britain. Railway services: British Rail: Locomotives & multiple units — *Lists — Serials*
British Rail locoshed book. — 1981. — London : I. Allan, 1981. — 79p. — (abc)
ISBN 0-7110-1112-5 : £0.40 B81-30840

625.2′6′0941 — Great Britain. Railway services: British Rail. Locomotives — *Identification manuals*
Locomotives / [compiled by] Colin J. Marsden. — London : Ian Allan, 1981. — 144p : ill ; 19cm. — (Motive power recognition ; 1)
ISBN 0-7110-1109-5 (pbk) : £1.95 B81-32803

625.2′6′0941 — Great Britain. Railway services: British Rail. Named locomotives
Named locomotives of British Rail : diesel and electric / compiled and edited by Michael Oakley. — Truro : Barton, [1980]. — [56]p : chiefly ill ; 21cm
ISBN 0-85153-386-8 (pbk) : £2.95 B81-05565

625.2′6′0941 — Great Britain. Railway services: British Rail. Rolling stock. Locomotives & multiple units — *Lists*
British Railways spotters companion / compiled by the National Railway Enthusiasts Association. — 3rd ed. — Oxford : Oxford Publishing, 1981. — 80p : ill ; 16cm
Previous ed.: 1980
ISBN 0-86093-117-x (pbk) : £0.60 B81-26619

625.2′6′0941 — Great Britain. Railway services: British Rail. Rolling stock. Locomotives & multiple units — *Lists — Serials*
British Rail motive power, combined volume. — 1981. — London : Ian Allan, 1981. — 221p. — (abc)
ISBN 0-7110-1127-3 : £1.75 B81-20719

625.2′61 — Barry Island. Railway scrap yards: Woodham Brothers. Scrap: Steam locomotives — *Illustrations*
Handley, Brian. Graveyard of steam / Brian Handley ; with a foreword by Wynford Vaughan Thomas. — London : Allen & Unwin, 1979. — [80]p : chiefly ill ; 23cm. — (Steam past)
Includes index
ISBN 0-04-385072-3 (corrected) : £3.95 : CIP rev. B78-37765

625.2′61 — Garratt steam locomotives, *to 1980*
Durrant, A. E.. Garratt locomotives of the world. — Newton Abbot : David & Charles, Aug.1981. — [176]p
ISBN 0-7153-7641-1 : £10.00 : CIP entry B81-17492

625.2′61 — North-east England. Steam locomotives. Driving, *1914-1944*
Semmens, P. W. B.. North Eastern engineman : driver Syd Midgley and fifty years of steam / P.W.B. Semmens. — Truro : Barton, c1980. — 119p : ill,2facsims,ports ; 22cm
ISBN 0-85153-391-4 (pbk) : £2.95 B81-06173

625.2′61 — Steam locomotives. Driving — *Manuals*
Hollingsworth, J. B.. How to drive a steam locomotive / Brian Hollingsworth. — Harmondsworth : Penguin, 1981, c1979. — vi,152p : ill ; 25cm
Originally published: London : Astragal Books, 1979. — Bibliography: p150. - Includes index
ISBN 0-14-005529-0 (pbk) : £2.95 B81-21081

625.2′61 — Steam locomotives — *Manuals*
Hilton, John. The steam locomotive and its operation / John Hilton. — Hadlow ([19 Lonewood Way, Hadlow, Tonbridge, Kent TN11 0JB]) : J. Hilton, 1980. — 53p : ill ; 21cm
£1.50 (pbk) B81-06474

625.2′61′060428 — North-east England. Steam locomotives. Preservation. Organisations: North Eastern Locomotive Preservation Group, *to 1979*
North Eastern revival : a story of the North Eastern Locomotive Preservation Group. — 2nd ed. — [Sacriston] ([41 Front St., Daisy Hill, Sacriston, Durham]) : N.E.L.P.G., 1979. — 61p : ill ; 21cm
Previous ed.: 1975. — Text on inside covers
ISBN 0-9504349-1-4 (pbk) : Unpriced B81-20828

625.2′61′09 — Steam locomotives, *to 1979*
Classic steam / general editor Patrick B. Whitehouse. — London : Hamlyn, 1980. — 192p : ill(some col.) ; 32cm. — (A Bison book)
Includes index
ISBN 0-600-34938-1 : £5.95 B81-02916

625.2′61′09 — Steam locomotives, *to 1980*
Greggio, Luciano. The steam locomotive / Luciano Greggio ; translated and adapted by Peter Kalla-Bishop ; artwork by Guido Canestrari. — London : Hamlyn, 1980. — 263p : ill(some col.) ; 30cm
Translation from the Italian. — Bibliography: p261-263. - Includes index
ISBN 0-600-38428-4 : £12.00 B81-03642

625.2′61′0924 — East Anglia. Railway services: British Rail. *Eastern Region.* Great Eastern lines. Steam locomotives. Operation, *1913-1960 — Personal observations*
Hill, Jim. Buckjumpers, Gobblers and Clauds : a lifetime on Great Eastern and LNER footplates / Jim Hill. — Truro : Barton, c1981. — 112p : ill,1port ; 21cm
ISBN 0-85153-396-5 (pbk) : £2.95 B81-29680

625.2′61′0924 — Eastern England. Railway services: London and North Eastern Railway. Great Northern lines. Steam locomotives. Operation, *1920-1930 — Personal observations*
Bonnett, Harold. Smoke and steam! : footplate memories of the G.N. and L.N.E.R. in the 1920s / Harold Bonnett. — Truro : Barton, c1981. — 109p : ill ; 21cm
ISBN 0-85153-395-7 (pbk) : £2.95 B81-29681

625.2′61′0924 — Great Britain. Steam locomotives. Hedley, William — *Biographies*
Brooks, Philip R. B.. William Hedley, locomotive pioneer / by Philip R.B. Brooks. — Newcastle upon Tyne (Sandyford House, Archbold Terrace, Newcastle upon Tyne NE2 1ED) : Tyne and Wear Industrial Monuments Trust, 1980. — 16p : ill,1facsim,1map,1port ; 21cm
Cover title. — Map on inside cover
ISBN 0-906283-07-8 (pbk) : £0.45 B81-04465

625.2′61′0924 — Hereford and Worcester. Railway services: British Rail. *Western Region.* Steam locomotives. Operation, *ca 1950-1960 — Personal observations*
Barfield, Tony. Panniers and Prairies : more memories of a Western Region fireman / Tony Barfield. — Truro : Barton, c1981. — 108p : ill,1map ; 21cm
ISBN 0-85153-394-9 (pbk) : £2.95 B81-29885

625.2′61′0924 — Southern England. Railway services: British Rail. *Southern Region.* Steam locomotives, *1956-1967 — Personal observations*
Aynsley, B. W.. Nothing like steam! : footplate work on Southern Region / B.W. Aynsley. — Truro : Barton, c1980. — 112p : ill,1 port ; 22cm
ISBN 0-85153-393-0 (corrected : pbk) : £2.95 B81-05527

625.2′61′0924 — West Midlands *(Metropolitan County).* Birmingham. Saltley. Railway services: British Rail. *London Midland Region.* Steam locomotives. Firing, *1950-1959 — Personal observations*
Essery, Terry. More firing days at Saltley / Terry Essery. — Truro : Barton, [1980]. — 163p,[7]p of plates : ill,1ports ; 21cm
ISBN 0-85153-376-0 (pbk) : £2.95 B81-06000

625.2′61′0941 — Great Britain. Class S160 steam locomotives, *1939-1980*
Higgins, R. N.. Over here : the story of the United States Army Transportation Corps class S160 locomotives / R.N. Higgins ; foreword by F.J. Bellwood. — Rochdale (176 Drake St., Rochdale, Lancs. OL16 1UP) : Big Jim Publishing, 1980. — 80p : ill(some col.) ; 25cm
ISBN 0-907224-00-8 (pbk) : £2.75 B81-07849

625.2′61′0941 — Great Britain. Preserved steam locomotives — *Illustrations*
Railway world book of steam railways. — London : Ian Allan, 1981. — [32]p : all col.ill ; 24cm
ISBN 0-7110-0954-6 (pbk) : £0.95 B81-24858

625.2′61′0941 — Great Britain. Preserved steam locomotives — *Serials*
Steam. — ′81. — London : Allen & Unwin, 1981. — [236]p
ISBN 0-04-385082-0 : Unpriced : CIP rev.
ISBN 0-04-385083-9 (pbk) B81-15877

Steam. — ′82. — London : Allen and Unwin, Feb.1982. — [250]p
ISBN 0-04-385091-x (pbk) : £4.95 : CIP entry B81-39243

625.2′61′0941 — Great Britain. Railway services: British Rail. Steam locomotives, *1948-1968*
Cockman, F. G.. British Railways′ steam locomotives / F.G. Cockman. — Princes Risborough : Shire, 1980. — 80p : ill ; 21cm. — (History in camera)
Bibliography: p72. - Includes index
ISBN 0-85263-531-1 (pbk) : £2.50 B81-05580

625.2′61′0941 — Great Britain. Railway services: British Rail. Steam locomotives, *1961-1964 — Illustrations*
Blenkinsop, R. J.. Silhouettes of the big four / R.J. Blenkinsop. — Oxford : Oxford Publishing, c1980. — [96]p : chiefly ill ; 30cm
ISBN 0-902888-78-1 : £5.50 B81-01779

625.2′61′0941 — Great Britain. Railway services: British Rail. Steam locomotives, *ca 1950-ca 1965 — Illustrations*
Heiron, George. Steam′s Indian summer / George Heiron and Eric Treacy. — London : Allen & Unwin, 1979. — 126p : chiefly ill ; 23cm. — (Steam past)
Includes index
ISBN 0-04-385070-7 : £4.25 : CIP rev. B78-36781

625.2′61′0941 — Great Britain. Railway services: London and North Eastern Railway. 2-6-0 steam locomotives, *to 1967*
Clay, John F.. The LNER 2-6-0 classes / John F. Clay & J. Cliffe. — London : Ian Allan, 1978. — 80p,[24]p of plates : ill ; 23cm
Bibliography: p80
ISBN 0-7110-0844-2 : £3.50 B81-22082

625.2′61′0941 — Great Britain. Railway services: London and North Eastern Railway. Steam locomotives, *1870-1967 — Illustrations*
Bloom, Alan. Locomotives of the London and North Eastern Railway / written by Alan Bloom ; compiled by David Williams. — [Norwich] : [Jarrold], c1980. — [32]p : ill(some col.),1map,ports ; 25cm. — (Jarrold railway series ; 4)
Text, ill, map and ports on inside covers
ISBN 0-85306-920-4 (pbk) : £1.00 B81-08306

625.2′61′0941 — Great Britain. Railway services: London and North Eastern Railway. Steam locomotives, *1950-1963 — Illustrations*
Keeley, Raymond. Memories of LNER steam / Raymond Keeley. — London : Ian Allan, 1980. — 110p : chiefly ill ; 25cm
ISBN 0-7110-1038-2 : £6.95 B81-03112

625.2'61'0941 — Great Britain. Railway services: London and North Eastern Railway. Steam locomotives. Engineering aspects

Locomotives of the L.N.E.R.. — Rugeley (c/o N.J. Claydon, 'Rannoch' 72 Upper Way, Upper Longdon, Rugeley, Staffs. WS15 1QA) : Railway Correspondance and Travel Society
Part 3B: Tender engines — classes D1 to D12. — 1980. — 108p,[50]p of plates : ill ; 21cm
ISBN 0-901115-46-0 (pbk) : £5.25 B81-18223

625.2'61'0941 — Great Britain. Railway services. Steam locomotives, *1898-1960* — *Illustrations*

Steam in camera 1898-1960 : second series / [compiled by] Patrick Russell ; photographs from the LCGB Ken Nunn Collection. — London : Ian Allan, 1981. — 112p : all ill ; 25cm
ISBN 0-7110-1068-4 : £5.95 B81-10545

625.2'61'0941 — Great Britain. Stanier steam locomotives, *to 1980*

Haresnape, Brian. Stanier locomotives : a pictorial history / by Brian Haresnape. — [New rev. and enl. ed.]. — London : Ian Allan, 1981. — 126p : ill ; 25cm
Previous ed.: 1970
ISBN 0-7110-1098-6 : £6.95 B81-24450

625.2'61'0941 — Great Britain. Steam locomotives, *1922-1968* — *Illustrations*

The **Steam** cameramen / compiled by Brian Morrison for the Railway Photographic Society. — Oxford : Oxford Publishing, c1980. — [240]p : chiefly ill,ports ; 29cm
In a slip case. — Includes index
ISBN 0-86093-115-3 : £25.00 B81-05869

625.2'61'0941 — Great Britain. Steam locomotives, *1962-1968*

Adley, Robert. In search of steam 1962-68 / Robert Adley. — Poole : Blandford, 1981. — 157p : ill(some col.),maps,col.ports ; 27cm
Includes index
ISBN 0-7137-1091-8 : £10.95 : CIP rev. B81-10488

625.2'61'0941 — Great Britain. Steam locomotives — *Serials*

Locomotives large & small : [the quarterly magazine for the steam enthusiast]. — No.1 (Nov. 1979)-. — Shanklin (Cross St., Shanklin, Isle of Wight) : Saunders the Printers (IW), 1979-. — v. : ill ; 28cm
ISSN 0260-2970 = Locomotives large & small : £3.25 per year
Also classified at 625.1'9 B81-02007

625.2'61'0941 — Great Britain. Steam locomotives, *to 1967* — *Illustrations*

Treacy, Eric. Portrait of steam / Eric Treacy. — London : Ian Allan, 1967 (1981 [printing]). — 200p : chiefly ill ; 29cm
ISBN 0-7110-1162-1 : £6.95 B81-36745

625.2'61'0941 — Great Britain. Steam locomotives, *to 1968*

Bloom, Alan. Locomotives of British railways / written by Alan Bloom ; compiled by David Williams. — Norwich : Jarrold, c1980. — [32]p : col.ill,1map,ports ; 25cm. — (Jarrold railway series ; 5)
Text, ports, map on inside covers
ISBN 0-85306-939-5 (pbk) : £1.00 B81-18857

625.2'61'0942 — England. Railway services: Great Western Railway. Castle class steam locomotives, *to 1965*

Holden, Bryan. Portraits of 'Castles' : portraits of every Western Region Castle class locomotives, with footplate comments : photographs from the Kenneth H. Leech collection / Bryan Holden & Kenneth H. Leech ; with additional research & drawings by Richards S. Potts. — Ashbourne : Moorland in association with Barbryn Press, c1981. — 128p : ill,ports ; 26cm
ISBN 0-903485-89-3 : £6.50 : CIP rev. B81-08863

625.2'61'0942 — England. Railway services: Great Western Railway. Steam locomotives, *1950-1962* — *Illustrations*

Spirit of the Great Western / [compiled] by Mike Esau. — Oxford : Oxford Publishing, c1980. — [120]p : chiefly ill ; 29cm
ISBN 0-86093-110-2 : £5.95 B81-14258

625.2'61'0942 — England. Railway services: Great Western Railway. Steam locomotives, *to 1965* — *Illustrations*

100 years of the Great Western : an album portraying the Great Western Railway and British Railway (Western Region) up to the end of steam / [compiled] by D. Nicholas and S.J. Montgomery. — Oxford : Oxford Publishing, c1981. — [106]p : chiefly ill,1facsim ; 28cm
Ill on lining papers
ISBN 0-86093-123-4 : £5.95 B81-26545

625.2'61'09422 — Southern England. Railway services: British Rail. *Southern Region.* Branch lines. Steam locomotives, *1950-1966* — *Illustrations*

Southern branch line steam / [compiled by] Tony Fairclough and Alan Wills. — Truro : Barton 3. — c1980. — 95p : chiefly ill ; 23cm
ISBN 0-85153-383-3 : £5.95 B81-29887

625.2'61'09422 — Southern England. Railway services: British Rail. *Southern Region.* Lord Nelson class steam locomotives, *to ca 1965*

Winkworth, D. W.. Maunsell's Nelsons / D.W. Winkworth. — London : Allen & Unwin, 1980. — 123p : ill ; 23cm. — (Steam past)
Includes index
ISBN 0-04-385079-0 : £6.95 : CIP rev. B80-10564

625.2'61'09422 — Southern England. Railway services: Southern Railway, *1937-1967.* Bulleid Pacific type steam locomotives

Rogers, H. C. B.. Bulleid Pacifics at work / H.C.B. Rogers. — London : Ian Allan, 1980. — 128p : ill,1port ; 30cm
Ill on lining papers. — Includes index
ISBN 0-7110-1074-9 : £9.95 B81-04670

625.2'61'094223 — Kent. Railway services: London, Chatham & Dover Railway. Steam locomotives, *to 1898*

Bradley, D. L.. The locomotive history of the London Chatham and Dover railway / D.L. Bradley. — New rev. ed. — London (95 Chestnut Ave., Forest Gate, E7 0JF) : Railway Correspondence and Travel Society, 1979. — 127p,[60]p of plates : ill,2maps ; 21cm
Previous ed.: 1960
ISBN 0-901115-47-9 (pbk) : £4.50 B81-18486

625.2'61'09423 — South-west England. Railway services: British Rail. Somerset & Dorset Joint line. Steam locomotives, *1950-1959* — *Illustrations*

Peters, Ivo. The Somerset and Dorset in the 'fifties / by Ivo Peters. — Oxford : Oxford Publishing Co.
Pt.2: 1955-1959. — 1981. — [128]p : chiefly.ill,2maps,1port ; 29cm
Ill on lining papers
ISBN 0-86093-103-x : £5.95 B81-31936

625.2'61'09423 — South-west England. Railway services: Somerset & Dorset Joint Railway. 2-8-0 steam locomotives, *to 1980*

Milton, D.. The Somerset and Dorset 2-8-0's / by D. Milton. — 2nd ed. — Washford (The Railway Station, Washford, Somerset) : Somerset & Dorset Railway Museum Trust, 1980. — 28p : ill ; 22cm
Previous ed.: 1971. — Bibliography: p27
ISBN 0-9506790-1-1 (pbk) : Unpriced B81-18650

625.2'61'09426 — East Anglia. Steam locomotives, *ca 1935-1979* — *Illustrations*

Steam in East Anglia / [compiled by] Colin Shewring. — King's Lynn (P.O. Box 21, King's Lynn PE30 2QP) : Becknell, 1980. — 96p : chiefly ill,maps ; 24cm
ISBN 0-907087-01-9 (pbk) : £3.95 B81-02983

625.2'61'094294 — South Wales. Steam locomotives, *to 1965* — *Illustrations*

Hale, Michael. Steam in South Wales / [compiled] by Michael Hale. — Oxford : Oxford Publishing
Vol.1: The valleys. — c1980. — [95]p : chiefly ill(some col.),maps ; 28cm
ISBN 0-86093-112-9 : £5.95 B81-32153

625.2'61'0942975 — Mid Glamorgan. Merthyr Tydfil. Tramroads: Merthyr Tramroad. Steam locomotives: Penydarren Locomotive

Owen-Jones, Stuart. The Penydarren locomotive / written by Stuart Owen-Jones. — Cardiff : Amgueddfa Genedlaethol Cymru, 1981. — 32p : ill,1map,1facsim ; 21cm
ISBN 0-7200-0239-7 (pbk) : £0.95 B81-31680

625.2'61'09561 — Turkey. Steam locomotives, *to 1980*

Talbot, E.. Steam in Turkey : an enthusiasts' guide to the steam locomotives of Turkey / by E. Talbot. — Harrow : Continental Railway Circle, 1981. — 124p : ill,3maps ; 24cm
Bibliography: p121
ISBN 0-9503469-6-9 (pbk) : £3.90 B81-39551

625.2'61'096 — Africa. Steam locomotives, *to 1980*

Durrant, A. E.. Steam in Africa / A.E. Durrant, A.A. Jorgensen, C.P. Lewis. — London : Hamlyn, [c1981]. — 207p : ill(some col.),maps ; 31cm
Bibliography: p205. — Includes index
ISBN 0-600-34946-2 : £10.00 B81-25456

625.2'61'0968 — South Africa. Steam locomotives

Siviter, Roger. Focus on South African steam / Roger Siviter. — Newton Abbot : David & Charles, c1981. — 89p : chiefly ill,maps ; 25cm
ISBN 0-7153-8087-7 : £5.95 : CIP rev. B81-11950

625.2'61'09931 — New Zealand. Steam locomotives, *1952-1971*

Cooke, John, *19---*. New Zealand steam finale / John Cooke & John Vogel. — Auckland ; London : Collins, 1979. — 159p : ill(some col.) ; 29cm
Ill on lining papers. — Bibliography: p159
ISBN 0-00-216951-7 : £7.95 B81-02222

625.2'63'0212 — Electric locomotives — *Technical data*

Harris, Ken. World electric locomotives / compiled and edited by Ken Harris. — London : Jane's, 1981. — 160p : ill ; 27cm
Includes index
ISBN 0-7106-0101-8 : £8.75 B81-19507

625.2'63'0941 — Great Britain. Railway services: British Rail. Electric locomotives — *Lists* — *Serials*

British Rail locomotives. — 1981-. — London : Ian Allan, 1981-. — v. : ill ; 15cm. — (abc)
Annual. — Continues: British Rail diesel locomotives. — Continues in part: British Rail electric locomotives & multiple units
ISSN 0261-3034 = British Rail locomotives : £0.50
Also classified at 625.2'66'0941 B81-20720

625.2'63'0941 — Great Britain. Railway services: British Rail. Electric locomotives. Liveries, *to 1979*

Dyer, Malcom. A history of British Railways diesel and electric locomotive liveries. — Rev. ed. / compiled by Malcolm Dyer, [edited by Michael Oakley], [photos supplied by John C. Baker ... et al.]. — Potters Bar (7 Robert Close, Potters Bar, Herts.) : Diesel & Electric Group, c1980. — 22p : ill(some col.) ; 29cm
Previous ed.: 1979
Unpriced (unbound)
Also classified at 625.2'66'0941 B81-18597

625.2'63'0941 — Great Britain. Railway services: British Rail. Electric locomotives. Numbering, *to 1979*

Oakley, Michael. A history of British Railways diesel & electric locomotive numberings / [written and edited by Michael Oakley] ; [numberings compiled by Malcolm Tarrey]. — Potters Bar (7 Robert Close, Potters Bar, Herts.) : Diesel & Electric Group, c1980. — 15p : ill ; 30cm
£0.60 (unbound)
Also classified at 625.2'66'0941 B81-18594

625.2′63′0941 — Great Britain. Railway services: British Rail. Rolling stock: Electric multiple units — *Lists — Serials*

British Rail multiple-units. — 1981-. — London : Ian Allan, 1981-. — v. : ill ; 15cm. — (abc)
Annual. — Continues : British Rail diesel multiple-units. — Continues in part: British Rail electric locomotives & multiple-units
ISSN 0261-2844 = British Rail multiple-units : £0.50
Also classified at 625.2′66′0941 B81-20717

625.2′63′09422 — Southern England. Railway services: British Rail. *Southern Region.* **Rolling stock: Multiple units,** *to 1979*

Beecroft, G. D.. Southern Region multiple-unit trains / G.D. Beecroft. — 2nd ed. — Purley (6a Purley Parade, High St., Purley, Surrey, CR2 2AB) : Southern Electric Group, 19891. — 71p : ill ; 21cm
Cover title. — Previous ed.: 1979
ISBN 0-9502376-9-8 (pbk) : £1.90 B81-18302

625.2′66′0941 — Great Britain. Railway services: British Rail. Diesel locomotives — *Illustrations*

Diesels nationwide. — Oxford : Oxford Publishing Co.
Vol.3 / compiled by David H. Allen. — 1981. — [128]p : chiefly.ill,maps ; 19cm
ISBN 0-86093-113-7 : £5.95 B81-22147

625.2′66′0941 — Great Britain. Railway services: British Rail. Diesel locomotives — *Lists — Serials*

British Rail locomotives. — 1981-. — London : Ian Allan, 1981-. — v. : ill ; 15cm. — (abc)
Annual. — Continues: British Rail diesel locomotives. — Continues in part: British Rail electric locomotives & multiple units
ISSN 0261-3034 = British Rail locomotives : £0.50
Primary classification 625.2′63′0941 B81-20720

625.2′66′0941 — Great Britain. Railway services: British Rail. Diesel locomotives. Liveries, *to 1979*

Dyer, Malcom. A history of British Railways diesel and electric locomotive liveries. — Rev. ed. / compiled by Malcolm Dyer, [edited by Michael Oakley], [photos supplied by John C. Baker ... et al.]. — Potters Bar (7 Robert Close, Potters Bar, Herts.) : Diesel & Electric Group, c1980. — 22p : ill(some col.) ; 29cm
Previous ed.: 1979
Unpriced (unbound)
Primary classification 625.2′63′0941 B81-18597

625.2′66′0941 — Great Britain. Railway services: British Rail. Diesel locomotives. Numbering, *to 1979*

Oakley, Michael. A history of British Railways diesel & electric locomotive numberings / [written and edited by Michael Oakley] ; [numberings compiled by Malcolm Tarrey]. — Potters Bar (7 Robert Close, Potters Bar, Herts.) : Diesel & Electric Group, c1980. — 15p : ill ; 30cm
£0.60 (unbound)
Primary classification 625.2′63′0941 B81-18594

625.2′66′0941 — Great Britain. Railway services: British Rail. Diesel locomotives, *to 1979 — Illustrations*

Railway world book of modern railways. — London : Ian Allen, 1981. — [32]p : all col.ill ; 24cm
ISBN 0-7110-0953-8 (pbk) : £0.95 B81-24856

625.2′66′0941 — Great Britain. Railway services. British Rail. Diesel shunting locomotives, *to 1980 — Illustrations*

The Diesel shunter : a practical record / [compiled] by Colin J. Marsden. — Oxford : Oxford Publishing, 1981. — [128]p : chiefly ill ; 28cm
ISBN 0-86093-108-0 : £5.95 B81-26620

625.2′66′0941 — Great Britain. Railway services: British Rail. Rolling stock: Diesel multiple units — *Lists — Serials*

British Rail multiple-units. — 1981-. — London : Ian Allan, 1981-. — v. : ill ; 15cm. — (abc)
Annual. — Continues : British Rail diesel multiple-units. — Continues in part: British Rail electric locomotives & multiple-units
ISSN 0261-2844 = British Rail multiple-units : £0.50
Primary classification 625.2′63′0941 B81-20717

625.2′66′09422 — England. Thames Valley. Railway services: British Rail. *Western Region.* **Diesel locomotives,** *1963-1980 — Illustrations*

Jones, K. G.. Diesels west of Paddington / K.G. Jones. — London : Ian Allen, 1981. — 93p : ill,maps ; 24cm
ISBN 0-7110-1082-x : £5.95 B81-18361

625.2′66′09426 — East Anglia. Diesel locomotives, *1957-1970 — Illustrations*

Allen, Ian Cameron. Diesels in East Anglia / by Ian Cameron Allen. — Oxford : Oxford Publishing, c1980. — [80]p : chiefly ill ; 28cm
ISBN 0-86093-105-6 : £4.95 B81-01964

625.2′662 — Advanced Passenger Train, *to 1980*

British Rail. Advanced Passenger Train / compiled by Geoffrey Body in conjunction with the staff of the General Manager, BR (LMR), Euston. — Weston-super-Mare (21 Southside, Weston-super-Mare, BS23 2QU) : Avon-Anglia Publications and Services in association with British Rail, London Midland and Scottish Regions, c1981. — 48p : ill,plans ; 20cm
ISBN 0-905466-37-3 (pbk) : £1.95 B81-23558

625.2′662′0941 — Brush diesel locomotives, *1940-1978 — Illustrations 692 0104043*

Toms, George. Brush diesel locomotives 1940-78 / George Toms. — Sheffield : Turntable, 1978. — 112p : ill(some col.) ; 30cm
ISBN 0-902844-48-2 : Unpriced B81-05044

625.2′662′0941 — Great Britain. Railway services: British Rail. Class 37 diesel-electric locomotives — *Illustrations*

British Rail class 37′s : a picture study. — Gloucester (2 Hill View, Fox-Elms, Gloucester) : Peter Watts, 1979. — [20]p : chiefly ill ; 15x21cm. — (Diesel picture library)
ISBN 0-906025-12-5 (pbk) : £0.80 B81-15313

Morrison, Brian. The power of the 37s / by Brian Morrison. — Oxford : Oxford Publishing Co., c1980. — [128]p : chiefly.ill(some col.) ; 28cm
Ill on lining papers
ISBN 0-86093-093-9 : £5.95 B81-31938

625.2′662′0941 — Great Britain. Railway services: British Rail. Class 40 diesel-electric locomotives, *to 1980 — Ilustrations*

Class 40s at work / [compiled by] John Vaughan. — London : Ian Allan, 1981. — 128p : ill ; 30cm
Ill on lining papers. — Includes index
ISBN 0-7110-1120-6 : £7.95 B81-31991

625.2′662′0941 — Great Britain. Railway services. British Rail. Deltic class diesel-electric locomotives

Webb, Brian. The Deltic locomotives of British Rail. — Newton Abbot : David & Charles, Jan.1982. — [96]p
ISBN 0-7153-8110-5 : £6.95 : CIP entry B81-33822

625.2′662′0941 — Great Britain. Railway services: British Rail. English Electric diesel-electric locomotives, *to 1981*

English electric traction album / [compiled by] John Glover. — London : Ian Allan, 1981. — 110p : col.ill ; 25cm
ISBN 0-7110-1059-5 : £5.95 B81-10533

625.2′662′0942 — England. Railway services: British Rail. *Western Region.* **Western Class diesel-electric locomotives,** *to 1977 — Illustrations*

Profile of the Westerns / [compiled] by D. Nicholas & S. Montgomery. — Oxford : Oxford Publishing, c1980. — [79]p : chiefly ill ; 28cm. — (Profile series)
ISBN 0-86093-116-1 : £5.50 B81-32152

625.2′664′0941 — Great Britain. Hymek class diesel-hydraulic locomotives: D7017 & D7018

Crane, John M.. Preserved class 35s : Hymeks D7017, D7018 / [compiled by John M. Crane]. — Potters Bar (7 Robert Close, Potters Bar, Herts) : Diesel & Electric Group, [1980]. — 13p : ill ; 21cm
Unpriced (unbound) B81-18588

625.2′664′0941 — Great Britain. Railway services: British Rail. Class 14 diesel hydraulic locomotives, *to 1980*

Hembry, P. J.. Class 14 : the cinderellas of the diesel-hydraulic era / written by P.J. Hembry. — Potters Bar (7 Robert Close, Potters Bar, Herts.) : Diesel & Electric Group, c1980. — 24p : ill ; 29cm
£0.75 (unbound) B81-18593

625′.66′07402516 — Derbyshire. Crich. Museums: Tramway Museum — *Visitors′ guides*

Tramway Museum. *Society.* The Tramway Museum. — Matlock : The Tramway Museum Society, c1979. — [16]p : ill(some col.) ; 25cm
Cover title. — Text on inside covers
ISBN 0-9501045-7-4 (pbk) : Unpriced B81-16150

625′.66′094 — Europe. Steam trams, *to ca 1950*

Baddeley, Geoffrey E.. The continental steam tram / by Geoffrey E. Baddeley. — London : Light Rail Transit Association in association with the Tramway and Light Railway Society, 1980. — 280p : ill,maps,1plan ; 22cm
Bibliography: p276-278
ISBN 0-900433-78-7 (pbk) : Unpriced B81-13329

625′.66′09421 — West London. Trams, *to 1937 — Illustrations*

Trams in west London : a pictorial souvenir / [compiled by] D.W. Willoughby, E.R. Oakley. — Hartley : D.W. Willoughby and E.R. Oakley ; Hartley (27 Dickens Close, Hartley, Dartford, Kent DA3 8DP) : Nemo Productions [distributor], 1978. — 44p,[1]folded leaf of plates : ill,1map ; 22cm
ISBN 0-903479-10-9 (pbk) : £0.95 B81-10840

625′.66′09427623 — Lancashire. Blackburn *(District).* **Tram services. Trams,** *to 1949*

Fergusson, R. P.. The first in the kingdom : 1881-1981 : a history of buses & trams in Blackburn & Darwen / by R.P. Fergusson, G. Holden, C. Reilly. — [Blackburn] ([48 Delph Approach, Blackburn BB1 2BH]) : [Darwen Transport Group], [1981]. — 54p : ill ; 22cm
Cover title
£1.50 (pbk)
Primary classification 629.2′2233′09427623 B81-23559

625′.66′0942819 — West Yorkshire *(Metropolitan County).* **Leeds. Trams,** *to 1954 — Illustrations*

Wiseman, R. J. S.. Leeds / R.J.S. Wiseman. — Huddersfield : Advertiser Press, 1980. — 48p : ill ; 22cm. — (British tramways in pictures ; 4)
£2.45 (pbk) B81-29703

625.7 — ROAD CONSTRUCTION

625.7′25′09417 — Ireland *(Republic).* **Roads. Geometric aspects. Design. Standards** — *Proposals*

O Cinneide, D.. Geometric design guidelines : (classification, alignment, cross-section) = Treoirlinte deartha geoméadracha : (rangú, ailíniú, trasghearradh) / D. O. Cinneide, P. McGuinness, J. Devlin. — Rev. [ed.]. — Dublin (The National Institute for Physical Planning and Construction Research, St. Martin′s House, Waterloo Rd., Dublin 4) : An Foras Forbartha, 1980. — iv,57p : ill ; 30cm. — (RT ; 180)
Previous ed.: 1977
ISBN 0-900115-95-5 (spiral) : £2.00 B81-25953

625.7′94 — England. Southern West Midlands. Signposts & waymarks

Drinkwater, P.. Ways and waymarks in the four-shires / by P. Drinkwater. — Shipston-on-Stour (56 Church St., Shipston-on-Stour, Warwickshire) : P. Drinkwater, 1980. — xii,93p : ill,1map,1geneal.table ; 23cm
Includes index
Unpriced (pbk) B81-17765

625.7'94 — Turkey. Ancient Roman milestones
French, David, *1933-*. Roman roads and milestones of Asia Minor = Roma cağinda Kücük Asya'daki yollar ve mil taşlari / David French. — Oxford : B.A.R.. — (BAR. International series ; 105) (Monograph / British Institute of Archaeology at Ankara ; no.3)
Fasc.1: The Pilgrim's Road = Fasikül 1: Haci Yolu. — 1981. — 129,65p,[10]p of plates(some folded) : col.maps ; 30cm
English and Turkish text. — Bibliography: p8-12
ISBN 0-86054-123-1 (pbk) : £10.00
Primary classification 388.1'0939'2 B81-36609

625.8 — Roads. Pavements. Strength. Measurement. Use of Dynaflect
Jermyn, T. M.. Pavement strength evaluation using Dynaflect / T.M. Jermyn. — Áth Cliath [j.e Dublin] (Teach Mháirtín, Bóthar Waterloo, Ath Cliath 4) : An Foras Forbartha Teoranta, 1980. — 22p : ill ; 30cm
Cover title
Unpriced (pbk) B81-23216

625.8'2 — Ireland *(Republic)*. Roads. Materials: Gravel. Physical properties
Davitt, S.. The physical characteristics of granular materials from 17 sources used in road construction in Ireland second report = Saintréithe fisiciúla ábhar gránaithe ó 17 fhoinsí in Éirinn An Dara Tuarascáil / S. Davitt. — Dublin (St Martin's House, Waterloo Rd., Dublin 4) : An Foras Forbartha, 1979. — 142p : ill,1map ; 30cm
Bibliography: p7
ISBN 0-906120-29-2 (spiral) : £2.00
B81-23215

625.8'4 — Roads. Surfaces. Precast concrete paving blocks
Lilley, A. A.. Concrete block paring for lightly trafficked roads and paved areas / by A.A. Lilley and A.J. Clark. — 2nd ed. — Slough : Cement and Concrete Association, 1980. — 16p : ill ; 30cm
Previous ed.: 1978. — Text on inside covers
ISBN 0-7210-1218-3 (pbk) : Unpriced
B81-08972

625.8'4 — Roads. Surfaces. Precast concrete paving blocks — *Standards*
Cement and Concrete Association. Specification for precast concrete paving blocks / Cement and Concrete Association, County Surveyors' Society, Interpave. — Slough (Wexham Springs, Slough SL3 6PL) : Cement and Concrete Association ; [Lewes] : County Surveyors' Society ; [Liecester] : Interpave, 1980. — 7p : ill ; 30cm
Cover title
ISBN 0-7210-1214-0 (pbk) : £0.50 B81-03651

627 — HYDRAULIC ENGINEERING

627 — Hydraulic engineering
Hwang, Ned H. C.. Fundamentals of hydraulic engineering systems / Ned H.C. Hwang. — Englewood Cliffs ; London : Prentice-Hall, c1981. — xvi,367p : ill,1map ; 24cm. — (Prentice-Hall series in environmental sciences)
Includes index
ISBN 0-13-340000-x : £18.80 B81-25470

Simon, Andrew L.. Basic hydraulics / Andrew L. Simon. — New York ; Chichester : Wiley, c1981. — xi,226p : ill ; 24cm
Bibliography: p221-223. — Includes index
ISBN 0-471-07965-0 : £9.30 B81-09785

627'.003 — Hydraulic engineering — *Polyglot dictionaries*
Troskolanski, Adam Tadeusz. Dictionary of hydraulic machinery. — Oxford : Elsevier Scientific, Dec.1981. — [800]p
ISBN 0-444-99728-8 : £70.00 : CIP entry
B81-31616

627'.0228 — Hydraulic engineering. Use of models
Novák, Pavel. Models in hydraulic engineering : physical principles and design applications / P. Novák and J. Cábelka. — Boston [Mass.] ; London : Pitman, c1981. — xix,459p : ill,maps,plans ; 24cm. — ([Monographs and surveys in water resources engineering] ; 4)
Revised translation of: Modelový výzkum. — Includes bibliographies and index
ISBN 0-273-08436-4 : Unpriced B81-40383

627'.0724 — Hydraulic systems. Models
Sharp, J. J.. Hydraulic modelling / J.J. Sharp. — London : Butterworths, 1981. — 242p : ill ; 25cm
Includes index
ISBN 0-408-00482-7 : Unpriced : CIP rev.
B81-00140

627'.125 — Rivers. Flow. Calculation. Mathematical models — *For engineering*
Cunge, J. A.. Practical aspects of computational river hydraulics / J.A. Cunge, F.M. Holly, Jr, A. Verwey. — Boston [Mass.] ; London : Pitman, c1980. — xvi,420p : ill,maps ; 24cm. — ([Monographs and surveys in water resources engineering] ; 3)
Bibliography: p407-415. — Includes index
ISBN 0-273-08442-9 : £30.00 B81-03197

627'.13'0941 — Great Britain. Canals. Construction, *to 1827*
Burton, Anthony. The canal builders / Anthony Burton. — 2nd ed. — Newton Abbot : David & Charles, c1981. — 230p,[16]p of plates : ill,map,2facsims,ports ; 23cm
Previous ed.: London : Eyre Methuen, 1972. — Bibliography: p223-225. — Includes index
ISBN 0-7153-8120-2 : £8.50 : CIP rev.
B81-09482

627'.13'0941 — Great Britain. Canals. Structures
Harris, Robert, *1946 Mar.5-*. Canals and their architecture / Robert Harris. — London : Godfrey Cave, 1980. — 222p,[4]p of plates : ill (some col.),facsims,maps,ports ; 25cm. — (Excursions into architecture)
Previous ed.: London : H. Evelyn, 1969. — Bibliography: p217-218. — Includes index
ISBN 0-906223-20-2 (cased) : £12.50
ISBN 0-906223-21-0 (pbk) : £6.95 B81-00953

627'.2 — Harbours. Design & construction
Bruun, Per. Port engineering. — 3rd ed. / Per Bruun with contributions by E.G. Frankel ... [et al.]. — Houston ; London : Gulf Publishing, c1981. — xi,787p : ill,maps,ports ; 26cm
Previous ed.: c1976. — Includes index
ISBN 0-87201-739-7 : £56.50 B81-32879

627'.31'09421 — London. Docks, *to 1980*. Civil engineering aspects
Greeves, Ivan S.. London docks 1800-1980 : a civil engineering history / Ivan S. Greeves. — London : Telford, 1980. — xii,155p : ill,maps,plans ; 25cm
Ill on lining papers. — Bibliography: p140-141. - Includes index
ISBN 0-7277-0114-2 : £12.50 B81-10088

627'.5 — Derelict land. Reclamation. Ecological aspects
Bradshaw, A. D.. The restoration of land : the ecology and reclamation of derelict and degraded land / by A.D. Bradshaw and M.J. Chadwick. — Oxford : Blackwell Scientific, 1980. — xi,317p : ill,maps ; 25cm. — (Studies in ecology ; v.6)
Includes bibliographies and index
ISBN 0-632-09180-0 : £13.50 : CIP rev.
B79-28774

627'.5 — Polluted land. Reclamation — *Conference proceedings*
Reclamation of contaminated land : proceedings of a Society of Chemical Industry conference held at the Congress Theatre, Eastbourne, England, 22-25 October 1979. — London : The Society, 1980. — 598p in various pagings : ill,maps ; 30cm
Includes bibliographies and index
ISBN 0-901001-68-6 (pbk) : Unpriced
B81-21699

627'.7 — Underwater engineering — *Conference proceedings*
Underwater technology : offshore petroleum : proceedings of the international conference, Bergen, Norway, April 14-16, 1980 / edited by L. Atteraas ... [et al.]. — Oxford : Pergamon, 1980. — ix,417p : maps ; 26cm
Includes bibliographies and index
ISBN 0-08-026141-8 : £27.50 : CIP rev.
B80-12930

627'.72 — Underwater engineering. Diving - *Manuals*
Subsea manned engineering. — London : Baillière Tindall, Aug.1981. — [500]p
ISBN 0-7020-0749-8 : £25.00 : CIP entry
B81-16936

627'.72'09 — Underwater diving, *to 1980*
Vallintine, Reg. Divers and diving / Reg Vallintine. — Poole : Blandford, 1981. — 169p : ill(some col.),ports ; 20cm
Bibliography: p165-166. — Includes index
ISBN 0-7137-0855-7 (cased) : £4.95 : CIP rev.
ISBN 0-7137-1128-0 (pbk) : £2.95 B81-00954

627'.98 — North Sea. Offshore structures. Maintenance & repair
Duffy, Daphne E.. PRIMO 81 : platform repair inspection maintenance offshore North Sea 1981 : a guide to the background, market and technology related to the inspection, maintenance and repair of offshore structures / compiled by Daphne E. Duffy. — London : Heyden on behalf of the Institute of Petroleum, c1981. — ix,122p : ill ; 30cm
Includes bibliographies
ISBN 0-85501-661-2 (pbk) : Unpriced
B81-32975

627'.98 — Offshore drilling rigs. Effects of ocean waves
Sarpkaya, Turgut. Mechanics of wave forces on offshore structures / Turgut Sarpkaya, Michael Isaacson. — New York ; London : Van Nostrand Reinhold, c1981. — xiv,651p,[1]leaf of plates : ill(some col.) ; 24cm
Includes bibliographies and index
ISBN 0-442-25402-4 : £28.15 B81-29518

627'.98 — Offshore steel structures. Fracture — *Conference proceedings*
European Offshore Steels Research Seminar *(1978 : Cambridge)*. European Offshore Steels Research Seminar, Cambridge, UK, 27-29 November 1978 : proceedings / sponsored by UK Department of Energy, Commission of the European Communities. — Cambridge : Published on behalf of the UK Department of Energy by the Welding Institute, c1980. — 593p in various pagings : ill ; 30cm
ISBN 0-85300-140-5 (pbk) : Unpriced
B81-04473

627'.98 — Offshore structures — *Conference proceedings*
International Conference on The Behaviour of Off-shore Structures *(2nd : 1979 : Imperial College)*. Proceedings of the Second International Conference on the Behaviour of Off-shore Structures : held at Imperial College, London, England, August 28th-31st, 1979 / [editors, H.S. Stephens, S.M. Knight]. — Cranfield : BMRA Fluid Engineering, c1979. — 3v. : ill,maps ; 30cm
Cover title: BOSS 79. — Includes index
ISBN 0-906085-34-9 (pbk) : Unpriced : CIP rev.
ISBN 0-906085-35-7 (v.1)
ISBN 0-906085-36-5 (v.2)
ISBN 0-906085-37-3 (v.3) B79-20181

627'.98 — Offshore structures. Design & construction — *Conference proceedings*
International Symposium on Integrity of Offshore Structures *(3rd : 1981 : University of Glasgow)*. Integrity of offshore structures. — London : Applied Science, Oct.1981. — [624]p
ISBN 0-85334-989-4 : £20.00 : CIP entry
B81-25721

627'.98 — Offshore structures. Design. Use of models — *Conference proceedings*
Offshore structures : the use of physical models in their design / edited by G.S.T. Armer and F.K. Garas. — Lancaster : Construction Press, 1981. — 360p : ill ; 31cm
Conference papers. — Includes index
ISBN 0-86095-874-4 : £22.50 B81-05414

628 — SANITARY ENGINEERING

628 — Great Britain. Water industries. Energy. Conservation — *Conference proceedings*
Symposium on Energy Use and Conservation in the Water Industry *(1980 : London)*. Symposium on Energy Use and Conservation in the Water Industry : proceedings of Symposium held in London, England, on 3rd and 4th December 1980. — London (6, Sackville St., W1X 1DD) : Institution of Water Engineers and Scientists, [1980]. — 159p in various pagings : ill,1map ; 21cm
Unpriced (pbk) B81-32811

628 — Sanitary engineering — *Conference proceedings*
Cairo International Regional Seminar on Sanitary Engineering *(1979)*. Proceedings of the Cairo International Regional Seminar on Sanitary Engineering, 5-10 May 1979. — Watford : Building Research Establishment, c1980. — vii,172p : ill,1map,plans ; 30cm
Includes bibliographies
Unpriced (pbk) B81-21050

628'.03'21 — Sanitary engineering — *Encyclopaedias*
Scott, John S.. Dictionary of waste and water treatment / John S. Scott, Paul G. Smith. — London : Butterworths, 1981. — 359p : ill ; 22cm
ISBN 0-408-00495-9 : Unpriced B81-39807

628'.06'041 — Great Britain. Sanitary engineering. Organisations: Institution of Public Health Engineers — *Directories* — *Serials*
Institution of Public Health Engineers. Year book and list of members / the Institution of Public Health Engineers. — 1978. — London (86 Edgware Rd., W2 2HP) : Professional Publications, [1978?]. — 512p
Unpriced B81-06695

Institution of Public Health Engineers. Year book, list of members and buyers' guide / the Institution of Public Health Engineers. — 1981. — London (86 Edgware Rd, W2 2YW) : Sterling Publications, [1981]. — 544p
Unpriced B81-36295

628.1 — WATER SUPPLY

628.1 — Developing countries. Drinking water supply. Programmes — *Directories*
The **International** Drinking Water Supply and Sanitation Decade directory. — [London] : Published by World Water magazine in collaboration with the World Health Organisation ; [London] : Thomas Telford [distributor], c1981. — 407p : ill,maps ; 30cm
ISBN 0-7277-0129-0 : £40.00
Also classified at 628.4'45'07201724
B81-36890

628.1 — United States. Hospitals. Water supply systems
Miller, C. Eugene. Water technology for hospital engineers / C. Eugene Miller. — New York ; London : Garland STPM, c1978. — ix,248p : ill ; 24cm. — (Garland library for hospital engineers)
Includes index
ISBN 0-8240-7008-9 : £35.00 B81-14160

628.1 — Waste water — *Festschriften*
Water science and technology. — Oxford : Pergamon, Dec.1981. — [500]p
ISBN 0-08-029095-7 (pbk) : £25.00 : CIP entry
B81-33855

628.1 — Water supply engineering — *For agricultural industries*
Waterhouse, James. Water engineering for agriculture. — London : Batsford Academic and Educational, Nov.1981. — [368]p
ISBN 0-7134-1409-x : £17.95 : CIP entry
B81-30358

628.1'07'2 — Water supply. Research
Water research topics. — Chichester : Ellis Horwood, June 1981
Vol.1. — [192]p
ISBN 0-85312-349-7 : £19.50 : CIP entry
B81-12898

628.1'074'02446 — Hereford and Worcester. Hereford. Museums: Herefordshire Waterworks Museum — *Visitors' guides*
The **Broomy** Hill engines, Hereford. — Hereford (c/o 87 Ledbury Rd., Hereford) : Herefordshire Waterworks Museum Trust, [1981]. — 1folded sheet : ill ; 21cm + Poster (folded sheet ; 44x31cm)
Unpriced B81-26612

628.1'0941 — Great Britain. Water supply engineering, *1820-1900*
Binnie, G. M.. Early Victorian water engineers / G.M. Binnie. — London : Telford, 1981. — ix,310p : ill,maps,facsim,ports ; 25cm
Ill on lining papers. — Includes index
ISBN 0-7277-0128-2 : £9.50 B81-30013

628.1'09412'8 — Scotland. Tayside Region. Perth. Water supply, *to 1979*
Waterways of Perth. — [Perth?] : [Perth Civic Trust?], [1980?]. — 24p : ill,1map ; 22cm
Cover title. — Compiled by Primary VII, Caledonian Road School
Unpriced (pbk) B81-09343

628.1'096 — Africa. Water supply & waste water — *Conference proceedings*
WEDC Conference *(6th : 1980 : Zaria)*. Water and waste engineering in Africa : 6th WEDCV conference 24 28 March 1980 at Ahmadu Bello University, Zaria, Nigeria : proceedings / edited by John Pickford and Susan Ball. — Loughborough (Loughborough, Leics. LE11 3TU) : Department of Civil Engineering, University of Technology, 1981. — 203p : ill,maps ; 30cm
ISBN 0-906055-11-3 (pbk) : £15.00 B81-21431

628.1'0973 — United States. Natural resources: Water. Engineering aspects
Hammer, Mark J.. Hydrology and quality of water resources / Mark J. Hammer, Kenneth A. MacKichan. — New York ; Chichester : Wiley, c1981. — ix,486p : ill,maps ; 25cm
Includes index
ISBN 0-471-02681-6 : Unpriced B81-10042

628.1'1 — Waste water. Contaminants: Viruses — *Conference proceedings*
International Symposium on Viruses and Wastewater Treatment *(1980 : University of Surrey)*. Viruses and wastewater treatment : proceedings of the International Symposium on Viruses and Wastewater Treatment, held at the University of Surrey, Guildford, 15-17 September 1980 / editors M. Goddard and M. Butler. — Oxford : Pergamon, 1981. — ix,306p : ill ; 26cm
Includes bibliographies and index
ISBN 0-08-026401-8 : £25.00 : CIP rev.
B81-05151

628.1'3 — Concrete liquid containers. Design
Anchor, R. D.. Design of liquid-retaining concrete structures / R.D. Anchor. — [Guildford] : Surrey University Press, 1981. — xv,153p : ill ; 24cm
Includes index
ISBN 0-903384-24-8 : £14.25 B81-17860

628.1'61 — Great Britain. Natural resources: Water. Quality. Effects of mining industries — *Conference proceedings*
Scientific Section symposium on mining and water pollution : Nottingham, England 3rd June 1981. — [London] ([6 Sackville St., Piccadilly, W1X 1DD]) : Institution of Water Engineers and Scientists, Scientific Section, [1981]. — 64p in various pagings : 2ill,1map ; 21cm
Conference papers. — Cover title: Mining and Water pollution. — At head of title: Institution of Water Engineers and Scientist
Unpriced (pbk) B81-33103

628.1'61 — Natural resources: Water. Chemical analysis. Multielement methods
A **Survey** of multielement and related methods of analysis for waters, sediments and other materials of interest to the water industry (1980) : methods for the examination of waters and associated materials. — London : H.M.S.O., 1981. — 46p : ill ; 30cm
Prepared by the Standing Committee of Analysts. — Bibliography: p37-42. — Includes index
ISBN 0-11-751529-9 (pbk) : £3.20 B81-40399

628.1'61 — Natural resources: Water. Quality. Ecological aspects
Water quality in catchment ecosystems / edited by A.M. Gower. — Chichester : Wiley, c1980. — xii,335p : 1ill ; 24cm. — (The Institution of Environmental Sciences series)
Bibliography: p305-326. — Includes index
ISBN 0-471-27692-8 : £18.00 : CIP rev.
B80-11487

628.1'61 — Ponds. Water. Quality. Management — *For fisheries*
Boyd, Claude E.. Water quality management for pond fish culture. — Oxford : Elsevier Scientific, Jan.1982. — [500]p. — (Developments in aquaculture and fisheries science ; 9)
ISBN 0-444-42054-1 : CIP entry B81-39217

628.1'61 — Water. Contaminants: Chromium. Quantitative analysis. Laboratory techniques
National Water Council. *Standing Committee of Analysts*. Chromium in raw and potable waters and sewage effluents 1980 : two methods, both tentative : methods for examination of water and associated materials. — London : H.M.S.O., c1981. — 21p ; 30cm
Written by the Standing Committee of Analysts
ISBN 0-11-751528-0 (pbk) : £2.20 B81-36467

628.1'61'028 — Natural resources: Water. Chemical analysis. Laboratory techniques
Methods of analysis. — Leeds (West Riding House, 67 Albion St., Leeds LS1 5AA) : Yorkshire Water Authority, 1981. — [408]p : ill ; 30cm
ISBN 0-905057-11-2 (spiral) : Unpriced
B81-33085

628.1'62 — Water. Purification
Handbook of water purification. — London : McGraw-Hill, Oct.1981. — [768]p
ISBN 0-07-084555-7 : £45.00 : CIP entry
B81-28826

Hudson, Herbert E.. Water clarification processes : practical design and evaluation / Herbert E. Hudson Jr.. — New York ; London : Van Nostrand Reinhold, c1981. — xiv,353p : ill,plans ; 24cm. — (Van Nostrand Reinhold environmental engineering series)
Includes index
ISBN 0-442-24490-8 : £19.90 B81-29519

628.1'62'0941 — Great Britain. Water supply. Treatment — *Serials*
Standing Technical Committee on Water Treatment. Biennial report / Standing Technical Committee on Water Treatment. — 1st (1976-78)-. — London (Queen Anne's Gate, SW1H 9BT) : National Water Council, 1979-. — v. : ill ; 30cm. — (Standing Technical Committee report / Department of the Environment, National Water Council)
ISSN 0260-6119 = Biennial report - Standing Technical Committee on Water Treatment : £2.00 B81-04769

628.1'62'0941 — Great Britain. Water. Treatment — *Conference proceedings*
Symposium on the water treatment scene - the next decade : proceedings of symposium held in London, England, on 5th and 6th December 1979 / The Institution of Water Engineers and Scientists. — London : The Institution, [1980?]. — 191p in various pagings : ill,1map ; 31cm
Unpriced (pbk) B81-38711

628.1'662 — Natural resources: Water. Disinfectants: Chlorine. Chemical analysis. Laboratory techniques
National Water Council. *Standing Committee of Analysts*. Chemical disinfecting agents in water and effluents, and chlorine demand 1980 : methods for the examination of waters and associated materials / [Standing Committee of Analysts]. — London : H.M.S.O., [1980]. — 44p ; 30cm
ISBN 0-11-751493-4 (pbk) : £3.20 B81-13276

628.1'67 — Water. Desalination
Principles of desalination. — 2nd ed. / edited by K.S. Spiegler, A.D.K. Laird. — New York ; London : Academic Press
Previous ed.: published in 1 vol. 1966. — Includes bibliographies and index
Part A. — 1980. — xiii,357,vip : ill ; 24cm
ISBN 0-12-656701-8 : £26.40 B81-15126

628.1′68 — Great Britain. Fresh waters. Pollution. Biological aspects
Mason, C. F.. Biology of freshwater pollution. — London : Longman, Oct.1981. — [224]p
ISBN 0-582-45596-0 (pbk) : £5.50 : CIP entry
B81-28112

628.1′68 — United States. Natural resources: Water. Organic pollutants. Chemical analysis. Mass spectrometry. Spectra — *Technical data*
Middleditch, Brian S.. Mass spectrometry of priority pollutants / Brian S. Middleditch, Stephen R. Missler and Harry B. Hines. — New York ; London : Plenum, c1981. — xii,308p : ill ; 24cm
Includes index
ISBN 0-306-40505-9 : Unpriced B81-17970

628.1′68′05 — Water. Pollution. Scientific & technical aspects — *Serials*
Water pollution research journal of Canada. — New ser., Vol.15, no.1-. — New York ; Oxford : Pergamon Press, 1980-. — v. : ill,map ; 26cm
Quarterly. — Continues: Water pollution research in Canada
£13.63 per year B81-02034

628.1′68′0724 — Water. Pollution. Experiments — *For schools*
Williams, D. I. (David Ivor). Experiments on water pollution / D.I. Williams and D. Anglesea. — Hove : Wayland, 1978. — 63p : ill ; 27cm. — (Experiments in pollution and conservation)
Bibliography: p62. - Includes index
ISBN 0-85340-565-4 : £3.75 B81-17645

628.1′6846 — Water. Pollution by runoff of farmyard manure — *Conference proceedings*
Nitrogen losses and surface run-off from landspreading of manures : proceedings of a workshop in the EEC programme of coordination of research on effluents from livestock, held at The Agricultural Institute, Johnstown Castle Research Centre, Wexford, Ireland, May 20-22, 1980 / sponsored by the Commission of the European Communities, Directorate-General for Agriculture and Directorate-General for Research, Science and Education ; edited by J.C. Brogan. — The Hague ; London : Nijhoff/Junk for the Commission of the European Communities, 1981. — xiv,471p : ill,maps ; 25cm. — (Developments in plant and soil sciences ; v.2)
Includes bibliographies
ISBN 90-247-2471-6 : Unpriced
Primary classification 631.8′61 B81-15261

628.1′688′41 — Great Britain. Natural resources: Water. Pollution. Control measures
Robertson, Lawrence. Pollution of sea and rivers / by Lawrence Robertson. — 2nd ed. — London : Institution of Municipal Engineers, 1979. — 11p : ill ; 21cm. — (Protection of the environment ; monograph no.14)
Previous ed.: 1972
£0.75 (pbk) B81-03860

628.1′688′422 — London. Thames River region. Pollution. Control measures, *to 1980*
Wood, Leslie B.. The restoration of the tidal Thames. — Bristol : Hilger, Jan.1982. — [250]p
ISBN 0-85274-447-1 : £22.00 : CIP entry
B81-33792

628.2 — DRAINAGE, SEWERAGE

628′.212 — Urban regions. Storm drainage systems. Design
Stephenson, David, *1943-*. Stormwater hydrology and drainage / D. Stephenson. — Amsterdam ; Oxford : Elsevier Scientific, 1981. — ix,276p : ill ; 25cm. — (Developments on water science ; 14)
Includes bibliographies and index
ISBN 0-444-41998-5 : £24.61 : CIP rev.
B81-16864

628′.24 — Surface drainage systems. Design
Bartlett, Ronald E.. Surface water sewerage / Ronald E. Bartlett. — 2nd ed. — London : Applied Science, 1981. — viii,147p : ill,2maps ; 23cm
Previous ed.: 1976. — Bibliography: p136-138. — Includes index
ISBN 0-85334-925-8 : £12.00 : CIP rev.
B80-22093

628.3 — SEWAGE TREATMENT AND DISPOSAL

628.3 — Sewage sludge — *Conference proceedings*
Characterization, treatment and use of sewage sludge : proceedings of the Second European Symposium held in Vienna, October 21-23, 1980 / edited by P. L′Hermite and H. Ott. — Dordrecht ; London : Reidel, c1981. — xvii,803p : ill ; 24cm
Text in English, French, German. — At head of title: Commission of the European Communities. — Includes bibliographies and index
ISBN 90-277-1294-8 : Unpriced B81-27897

628.3 — Waste water. Recycling
Dean, R. B.. Water reuse. — London : Academic Press, Dec.1981. — [300]p
ISBN 0-12-208080-7 : CIP entry B81-31335

628.3 — Waste water. Treatment
Schroeder, Edward D.. Water and wastewater treatment / Edward D. Schroeder. — Tokyo ; London : McGraw-Hill Kogakusha, c1977. — xi,370p : ill ; 21cm. — (McGraw-Hill series in water resources and environmental engineering)
Includes index
ISBN 0-07-085677-x (pbk) : £5.25 B81-12105

628.3′01′51 — Sewage. Treatment & disposal. Calculations
Wilson, F. K.. Design calculations in wastewater treatment / F. Wilson. — London : Spon, 1981. — xv,221p : ill ; 25cm
Bibliography: p214-215. — Includes index
ISBN 0-419-11690-7 (cased) : Unpriced : CIP rev.
ISBN 0-419-11700-8 (pbk) : Unpriced
B81-13495

628.3′51 — Waste materials. Biological treatment — *Conference proceedings*
Energetics and technology of biological elimination of wastes : proceedings of the international colloquium, held in Rome, October 17-19, 1979 / edited by G. Milazzo. — Amsterdam ; Oxford : Elsevier Scientific, 1981. — viii,252p : ill ; 25cm. — (Studies in environmental science ; 9)
Includes five papers in French
ISBN 0-444-41900-4 : Unpriced : CIP rev.
B80-10654

628.3′51 — Waste water. Biological treatment
Winkler, M. A. Biological treatment of waste-water / M.A. Winkler. — Chichester : Horwood, 1981. — 301p : ill ; 24cm
Text on lining papers. — Includes bibliographies and index
ISBN 0-85312-204-0 : £25.50 : CIP rev.
ISBN 0-470-27185-1 (Wiley) : £25.50
B81-08923

628.3′51 — Waste water. Treatment. Use of biological fluidised beds
Biological fluidised bed treatment of water and wastewater / editors P.F. Cooper and B. Atkinson. — Chichester (Market Cross House, Cooper St., Chichester, W. Sussex P319 1EB) : Published for the Water Research Centre Stevenage Laboratory by Ellis Horwood, 1981. — 411p : ill ; 24cm
Conference papers. — Includes index
ISBN 0-85312-262-8 : £32.50 B81-16331

628.3′54 — Sewage. Treatment. Activated sludge process
Bulking of activated sludge : prevention or cure?. — Chichester : Ellis Horwood, Dec.1981. — [260]p
ISBN 0-85312-350-0 : £22.50 : CIP entry
B81-36983

628.3′54 — Waste materials. Anaerobic digestion — *Conference proceedings*
International Symposium on Anaerobic Digestion *(1st : 1979 : Cardiff)*. Anaerobic digestion : proceedings of the First International Symposium on Anaerobic Digestion held at University College, Cardiff, Wales, September 1979 / edited by D.A. Stafford, B.I. Wheatley and D.E. Hughes. — London : Applied Science, 1980. — xii,528p : ill ; 23cm
Includes bibliographies and index
ISBN 0-85334-904-5 : £38.00 : CIP rev.
B80-17774

628.3′8 — Scotland. Agricultural land. Sewage sludge. Disposal
Disposal of sewage sludge on agricultural land. — Edinburgh (West Mains Rd., Edinburgh EH9 3JG) : East of Scotland College of Agriculture, 1981. — 13p ; 21cm. — (Publication / The Scottish Agricultural Colleges, ISSN 0308-5708 ; no.76)
Unpriced (unbound) B81-19435

628.4 — PUBLIC CLEANSING AND SANITATION

628.4′4 — Solid waste materials. Management
Tchobanoglous, George. Solid wastes : engineering principles and management issues / George Tchobanoglous, Hilary Theisen, Rolf Eliassen. — Tokyo ; London : McGraw-Hill Kogakusha, c1977. — xv,621p : ill,plans ; 21cm. — (McGraw-Hill series in water resources and environmental engineering)
Includes bibliographies and index
ISBN 0-07-085791-1 (pbk) : £5.25 B81-12107

Wilson, David C.. Waste management. — Oxford : Clarendon Press, July 1981. — [350]p
ISBN 0-19-859001-6 : £36.00 : CIP entry
B81-14909

628.4′4 — Waste materials. Management — *Conference proceedings*
Waste treatment and utilization 2. — Oxford : Pergamon, Dec.1981. — [587]p
Conference papers
ISBN 0-08-024012-7 : £47.50 : CIP entry
B81-34222

628.4′4′094 — European Community countries. Waste materials. Management
European Conference on Waste Management *(1980 : Wembley)*. Waste Management / Europäische Konferenz für Abfallbehandlung=European Conference on Waste Management=Conférence Européenne sur la Gestion des Déchets, Wembley, England, June 17-19, 1980 ; edited by Jeremy Woolfe. — Dordrecht ; London : Reidel, c1981. — ix,277p ; 24cm
At head of title: Kommission der Europäischen Gemeinschaften, Commission of the European Communities, Commission des Communautés Européenes
ISBN 90-277-1338-3 (corrected) : Unpriced
ISBN 90-277-1338-3 B81-35757

628.4′42′0942 — England. Solid waste materials. Collection — *Statistics* — *Serials*
Waste collection statistics. Actuals / CIPFA Statistical Information Service. — 1978-79-. — London : Chartered Institute of Public Finance and Accountancy, 1980-. — v. ; 30cm
Annual. — Continues: Refuse collection statistics
ISSN 0260-7603 = Waste collection statistics. Actuals (corrected) : £4.50 B81-06901

628.4′45 — Waste materials. Disposal
Skitt, John. Waste disposal management and practice / John Skitt. — London : Knight, 1979. — 216p : ill,forms ; 29cm
Includes index
ISBN 0-85314-293-9 : £27.50 : CIP rev.
B79-11842

628.4′45′07201724 — Developing countries. Waste materials. Disposal. Projects — *Directories*
The International Drinking Water Supply and Sanitation Decade directory. — [London] : Published by World Water magazine in collaboration with the World Health Organisation ; [London] : Thomas Telford [distributor], c1981. — 407p : ill,maps ; 30cm
ISBN 0-7277-0129-0 : £40.00
Primary classification 628.1 B81-36890

628.4′45′0942 — England. Solid waste materials. Disposal by local authorities — *Statistics* — *Serials*
Waste disposal statistics. Actuals / CIPFA Statistical Information Service. — 1979-80-. — London : Chartered Institute of Public Finance and Accountancy, 1981-. — v. ; 30cm
Annual. — Continues in part: Waste disposal statistics
ISSN 0140-0150 = Waste disposal statistics. Actuals : £5.00 B81-26380

628.4′45′0942 — England. Solid waste materials. Disposal by local authorities — *Statistics — Serials* *continuation*

Waste disposal statistics. Estimates / CIPFA Statistical Information Service. — 1980-81-. — London : Chartered Institute of Public Finance and Accountancy, 1980-. — v. ; 30cm
Annual. — Continues: Waste disposal statistics based on estimates
ISSN 0140-0142 = Waste disposal statistics. Estimates (corrected) : £5.00 B81-08228

628.4′45′094259 — Buckinghamshire. Waste materials. Disposal. Planning — *Proposals*

Waste disposal plan : draft for consultation / Buckinghamshire County Council. — Aylesbury (County Hall, Aylesbury, Bucks.) : County Engineers Department, 1980. — 131p : ill,maps,forms ; 30cm
Unpriced (pbk) B81-12589

628.4′45′094261 — Norfolk. Waste materials. Disposal — *Proposals*

Corsie, I.. Waste disposal plan / I. Corsie, County Surveyor, J.M. Shaw, County Planning Officer. — [Norwich] ([County Hall, Martineau Lane, Norwich NR1 2DH]) : Norfolk County Council, 1981. — 74p : ill,maps ; 30cm
At head of title: Norfolk County Council
Unpriced (spiral) B81-30104

628.5 — POLLUTION AND INDUSTRIAL SANITATION ENGINEERING

628.5 — Environment. Pollution. Control. Use of microorganisms

Dart, R. K.. Microbiological aspects of pollution control / R.K. Dart and R.J. Stretton. — 2nd ed. — Amsterdam ; Oxford : Elsevier Scientific, 1980. — lx,265p : ill ; 24cm. — (Fundamental aspects of pollution control and environmental science ; 6)
Previous ed.: 1977. — Includes index
ISBN 0-444-41918-7 : £23.55 : CIP rev. B80-19277

628.5′05 — Environment. Pollution. Control measures — *Serials*

Advances in environmental science and technology. — Vol.11. — New York ; Chichester : Wiley, c1981. — xvii,491p
ISBN 0-471-05984-6 : £26.40
ISSN 0065-2563 B81-25029

628.5′3 — Atmosphere. Pollution. Control measures

Air pollution control / edited by Werner Strauss. — New York ; Chichester : Wiley. — (Environmental science and technology)
Part IV / edited by Gordon M. Bragg and Werner Strauss. — c1981. — xi,356p : ill,maps,1port ; 24cm
Includes index
ISBN 0-471-07957-x : £27.30 B81-33367

628.5′32 — Atmosphere. Pollution by chemicals from energy industries. Control measures

Reducing pollution from selected energy transformation sources : a study accomplished for the Commission of the European Communities, Environment and Consumer Protection Service / Chem Systems International Ltd. — London : Graham & Trotman for the Commission of the European Communities, 1976 (1977 [printing]). — xi,230p : ill ; 23cm
ISBN 0-86010-036-7 : £9.50 B81-08244

628.5′32 — Great Britain. Workplaces. Air. Pollutants: Dangerous gases. Detection & measurement

Detection and measurement of hazardous gases / edited by C.F. Cullis and J.G. Firth. — London : Heinemann, 1981. — 226p : ill ; 24cm
Includes index
ISBN 0-435-71030-3 : £25.00 : CIP rev. B81-13474

628.5′32 — Industrial chemicals: Dangerous heavier than air gases. Risks. Analysis. Mathematical models — *Conference proceedings*

Heavy gas and risk assessment : proceedings of a symposium on heavy gas, September 3-4, 1979, Frankfurt/Main / edited by Sylvius Hartwig. — Dordrecht ; London : Reidel, c1980. — viii,306p : ill ; 25cm
Includes contributions in German. — Includes index
ISBN 90-277-1108-9 : Unpriced B81-04483

628.5′32 — Industries. Dust. Control — *Conference proceedings*

Dust control : a symposium / sponsored by the Institution of Chemical Engineers North Western Branch and the Institute of Materials Handling Bulk Solids Panel in association with the University of Salford, 21-22 March 1978. — [Manchester] ([Dept. of Chemical Engineering, UMIST, Manchester M60 1QD]) : [The Institution], [1981?]. — 180p in various pagings : ill ; 30cm
£12.00 (£10.00 to members) (spiral) B81-38157

628.5′32 — Workplaces. Air. Pollutants: Ozone

Hughes, Donald, *1931—*. The toxicity of ozone / by D. Hughes. — London (3 St Andrews Hill, EC4V 5BY) : Science Reviews, c1979. — viii,38p ; 21cm. — (Occupational hygiene monograph, ISSN 0141-7568 ; no.3)
Bibliography: p27-38
ISBN 0-905927-30-3 (pbk) : £2.75 : CIP rev. B80-00231

628.5′4 — Industrial effluents. Treatment

Industrial effluent treatment. — London : Applied Science Publishers
Includes index
Vol.1: Water and solid wastes / edited by J.K. Walters and A. Wint. — 1981. — x,351p : ill ; 23cm
ISBN 0-85334-891-x : £22.00 : CIP rev. B80-09740

Industrial effluent treatment. — London : Applied Science
Vol.2: Air and noise / edited by J.K. Walters and A. Wint. — c1981. — ix,308p : ill,plans ; 23cm
Includes index
ISBN 0-85334-939-8 : £22.00 B81-28246

628.5′4 — Industrial waste materials. Tips. Stability. Prediction. Applications of centrifugal testing of models

Malîushitskiĭ, ÎU. N.. The centrifugal model testing of waste-heap embankments / Yu. N. Malushitsky ; edited by A.N. Schofield ; translated by David R. Crane. — Cambridge : Cambridge University Press, 1981. — xi,206p : ill,1form ; 24cm
Translation of: Ustoĭchivost′ naspeĭ-otvalov. — Bibliography: p200-201. — Includes index
ISBN 0-521-22423-3 : £30.00 B81-18190

628.5′4 — Industrial waste materials. Treatment & disposal — *Conference proceedings*

Turkish-German Environmental Engineering Symposium *(3rd : 1979 : Istanbul)*. Treatment and disposal of liquid and solid industrial wastes : proceedings of the Third Turkish-German Environmental Engineering Symposium, Istanbul, July 1979 / edited by Kriton Curi. — Oxford : Pergamon, 1980. — ix,515p : ill,maps ; 26cm
Includes bibliographies and index
ISBN 0-08-023999-4 : £33.50 : CIP rev. B80-23404

628.5′4′0973 — United States. Environment. Pollution by industries. Control measures

Sell, Nancy J.. Industrial pollution control : issues and techniques / Nancy J. Sell. — New York ; London : Van Nostrand Reinhold, c1981. — xviii,359p : ill ; 24cm. — (Van Nostrand Reinhold environmental engineering series)
Includes index
ISBN 0-442-20398-5 : £14.95 B81-06383

628.5′46 — Biochemical industries. Effluents. Treatment & disposal — *Conference proceedings*

Effluent treatment in the biochemical industries : Process biochemistry′s third international conference : conference papers, 6/7 November 1979 : the complete set of papers given at last year′s conference at Mount Royal Hotel, London, England. — Watford (177 Hagden La., Watford WD1 8LW) : Wheatland Journals Ltd., c1980. — [149]p : ill ; 30cm
"The Conference organised by The Conference Division, Wheatland Journals Ltd.". — Cover title. — Includes bibliographies
Unpriced (pbk) B81-37790

628.7 — RURAL SANITARY ENGINEERING

628′.746 — Great Britain. Agricultural industries. Waste materials: Plastics. Recycling

Bevis, M. J.. Plastics waste resources in the agricultural, horticultural and produce distribution industries / by M.J. Bevis & A.J. Ham. — London : British Plastics Federation, c1981. — 35p,[3]leaves of plates : ill ; 30cm. — (Publication / British Plastics Federation ; no.276/1)
£7.50 (£5.00 to members) (spiral) B81-24067

628′.7462 — Waste materials: Pesticides. Disposal

Pesticide wastes : a technical memorandum on arisings and disposal including a code of practice / Department of the Environment. — London : H.M.S.O., 1980. — 50p : 1ill ; 21cm. — (Waste management paper ; no.21)
Bibliography: p48-49
ISBN 0-11-751484-5 (pbk) : £3.50 B81-06121

628′.7466 — Livestock. Waste materials: Slurry. Constituents: Phosphorus compounds. Environmental aspects — *Conference proceedings*

Phosphorus in sewage sludge and animal waste slurries : proceedings of the EEC Seminar organized jointly by the CEC and the Institute for Soil Fertility, Haren (Gr.) and held in Groningen, Netherlands on June 12 and 13, 1980 / sponsored by the Commission of the European Communities, Directorate-General for Agriculture and Directorate-General for Research, Science and Education ; edited by T.W.G. Hucker and G. Catroux. — Dordrecht ; London : Reidel, c1981. — vii,443p : ill ; 24cm
Includes bibliographies and index
ISBN 90-277-0317-5 : Unpriced B81-26070

628.92 — FIRE FIGHTING TECHNOLOGY

628.9′2 — Fire prevention & fire fighting — *For schools*

Science : general. — London : Macmillan Education for the Home Office, 1981. — 1portfolio : ill(some col.) ; 30cm. — (11 to 16+ project fire)
A Home Office/Schools Council project
ISBN 0-333-31773-4 : £10.95 B81-38632

628.9′2 — Great Britain. Business firms. Fire protection & fire fighting — *Manuals*

Lyons, W. A.. Action against fire / by W.A. Lyons. — London (Unit 5, Seager Buildings, Brookmill Road, London SE8) : Alan Osborne, c1981. — 112p : ill ; 21cm
Bibliography: p111-112
ISBN 0-904657-18-3 (pbk) : £3.95 B81-39173

628.9′2 — Great Britain. Residences. Fire prevention & fire fighting — *For schools*

Home economics : disco disaster. — London : Macmillan Education for the Home Office, 1981. — 1portfolio : ill(some col.) ; 30cm. — (11 to 16+ project fire)
A Home Office/Schools Council project
ISBN 0-333-31774-2 : £9.95 B81-38633

628.9′22 — Hydrocarbon processing plants. Fire protection — *Manuals*

Fire protection manual : for hydrocarbon processing plants / edited by Charles H. Vervalin. — Houston ; London : Gulf
Vol.2. — c1981. — vii,429p : ill ; 29cm
Includes index
ISBN 0-87201-288-3 : £40.75
ISBN 0-87201-286-7 (v.1) : Unpriced B81-32955

628.9′22 — Industries. Fire protection — *Manuals*
Planning fire safety in industry. — Rev. 1980 ed., Fire Protection Association, Industrial Fire Protection Association. — London (Aldermary House, Queen St., EC4N 1TJ) : [Fire Protection Association], [1980]. — 59p ; 21cm
Cover title. — Previous ed.: / Fire Protection Association. — Includes bibliographies
Unpriced (pbk) B81-14556

628.9′25 — Fire fighting equipment
Mahoney, Gene. Introduction to fire apparatus and equipment / Gene Mahoney. — Boston, Mass. ; London : Allyn and Bacon, c1981. — 386p : ill,1form ; 24cm
Includes index
ISBN 0-205-07160-0 (pbk) : Unpriced B81-18238

628.9′25 — Great Britain. Fire engines, *to 1980*
Whitehead, Trevor. Fire engines / Trevor Whitehead. — Princes Risborough : Shire, 1981. — 32p : 1facsim ; 21cm. — (Shire album ; 68)
Bibliography: p32
ISBN 0-85263-555-9 (pbk) : £0.95 B81-40858

628.9′25 — Great Britain. Fire fighting vehicles
Creighton, John. Fire engines of the United Kingdom / John Creighton. — Hornchurch : Ian Henry, 1981. — 57p : ill ; 24cm. — (64 transport series ; 4)
Includes index
ISBN 0-86025-853-x : £3.95 B81-39809

628.9′25′09421 — London. Fire fighting, *1939-1945*
Wallington, Neil. Firemen at war : the work of London′s fire-fighters in the Second World War / Neil Wallington. — Newton Abbot : David & Charles, c1981. — 222p : ill ; 23cm
Bibliography: p215. — Includes index
ISBN 0-7153-7964-x : £6.95 B81-29559

628.9′252 — Fire fighting. Water supply
Cozad, F. Dale. Water supply for fire protection / F. Dale Cozad. — Englwood Cliffs ; London : Prentice-Hall, c1981. — xiv,299p : ill ; 24cm
Bibliography: p295-296. — Includes index
ISBN 0-13-945964-2 : £12.30 B81-16677

628.95 — PUBLIC LIGHTING

628.9′5 — Roads. Lighting
Bommel, W. J. M. van. Road lighting / W.J.M. van Bommel, J.B. de Boer. — London : Macmillan, 1980. — 328p,[8]p of plates : ill (some col.) ; 25cm. — (Philips technical library)
Bibliography: p287-297. - Includes index
ISBN 0-333-30679-1 : £30.00 B81-05263

628.96 — SANITARY ENGINEERING. PEST CONTROL

628.9′6 — Pests. Biological control
Samways, Michael J.. Biological control of pests and weeds / Michael J. Samways. — London : Edward Arnold, 1981. — iv,57p : ill ; 22cm. — (The Institute of Biology studies in biology, ISSN 0537-9024 ; no.132)
Bibliography: p56-57. — Includes index
ISBN 0-7131-2822-4 (pbk) : £1.95 : CIP rev. B81-12874

628.9′657 — Pests: Insects. Control. Use of semiochemicals — *Conference proceedings*
Management of insect pests with semiochemicals : concepts and practice / [proceedings of an international colloquium ... held March 23-28 1980, in Gainesville, Florida] ; edited by Everett R. Mitchell. — New York ; London : Plenum, c1981. — xiv,514p : ill ; 26cm
Includes bibliographies and index
ISBN 0-306-40630-6 : Unpriced B81-23353

Semiochemicals : their role in pest control / edited by Donald A. Nordlund, Richard L. Jones, W. Joe Lewis. — New York ; Chichester : Wiley, c1981. — xlx,306p : ill ; 24cm
Includes bibliographies and index
ISBN 0-471-05803-3 : £25.20 B81-33011

629 — TRANSPORT ENGINEERING, AUTOMATIC CONTROL SYSTEMS, ETC

629.04 — Automatic vehicle locating systems
Skomal, Edward N.. Automatic vehicle locating systems / Edward N. Skomal. — New York ; London : Van Nostrand Reinhold, c1981. — viii,323p : ill,2maps ; 24cm
Bibliography: p319-320. — Includes index
ISBN 0-442-24495-9 : £24.25 B81-36079

629.04′09173′2 — Urban regions. Public transport. Engineering aspects
Vuchic, Vukan R.. Urban public transportation : system and technology / Vucan R. Vuchic. — Englewood Cliffs ; London : Prentice-Hall, c1981. — xiv,673p : ill,plans ; 25cm
Includes bibliographies and index
ISBN 0-13-939496-6 : £27.25 B81-33751

629.04′5 — Man. Navigation. Role of magnetism
Baker, R. Robin. Human navigation : and the sixth sense / R. Robin Baker. — London : Hodder and Stoughton, 1981. — vi,138p : ill,maps ; 24cm. — (Biological science texts)
Bibliography: p129-133. - Includes index
ISBN 0-340-26082-3 (cased) : £8.95
ISBN 0-340-26081-5 (pbk) : Unpriced B81-17962

629.04′6 — Fast vehicles — *For children*
Stevens, Chris, *19---*. Fastest machines / Chris Stevens. — Oxford : Blackwell Raintree, c1981. — 31p : ill(some col.) ; 27cm
Originally published: Milwaukee : Raintree Children, c1980. — Includes index
ISBN 0-86256-023-3 : £2.95 B81-17606

629.04′6 — Great Britain. Vehicles. Fuels. Conservation — *Proposals*
Advisory Council on Energy Conservation. *Transport Working Group.* Review of the UK transport energy outlook : and policy recommendations. — London : H.M.S.O., 1981. — v,38p ; 25cm. — (Energy paper ; no.147) (Paper / Advisory Council on Energy Conservation ; 11)
Prepared by the Transport Working Group of the Advisory Council on Energy Conservatoin. — At head of title: Department of Energy
ISBN 0-11-410920-6 (pbk) : £4.00 B81-40970

629.04′6 — Vehicles. Construction materials: Composite fibrous materials — *Conference proceedings*
Conference on Fibrous Composites in Structural Design *(4th : 1978 : San Diego)*. Fibrous composites in structural design / [proceedings of the Fourth Conference on Fibrous Composites in Structural Design held in San Diego, California, November 14-17, 1978] ; edited by Edward M. Lenoe, Donald W. Oplinger and John J. Burke. — New York ; London : Published in cooperation with the Metals and Ceramics Information Center at Battelle Columbus Laboratories [by] Plenum, c1980. — xiii,873p : ill ; 28cm
Includes index
ISBN 0-306-40354-4 : Unpriced B81-09915

629.04′6′0153 — Physics — *Study examples: Physics of vehicles — For schools*
Ponchaud, R. D.. Getting around / R.D. Ponchaud. — Slough : University Tutorial Press, 1980. — 133p : ill ; 23cm
ISBN 0-7231-0799-8 (pbk) : £1.60 B81-06501

629.04′6′0221 — Vehicles. Technical drawings. Draftsmanship, *1600-1979*
Baynes, Ken. The art of the engineer / Ken Baynes and Francis Pugh. — Guildford : Lutterworth, 1981. — 240p : ill(some col.),facsims,plans(some col.),ports ; 35cm
Includes index
ISBN 0-7188-2506-3 : £28.00 B81-23729

629.04′6′0228 — Model vehicles — *Serials*
[Model mechanics *(Hemel Hempstead)***]**. Model mechanics. — Vol.1, no.1 (Feb.1979) - Vol. 2, no.2 (Mar.1980). — Hemel Hempstead : Model & Allied Publications, 1979-1980. — ill ; 30cm
Monthly. — Continued by: Model maker (Hemel Hempstead : 1980)
ISSN 0143-6589 = Model mechanics (Hemel Hempstead) : £7.50 per year B81-02809

629.04′6′0883632 — Police vehicles — *Technical data*
Ingleton, Roy D.. Police vehicles of the world / Roy D. Ingleton. — London : Ian Allan, 1981. — 156p : ill ; 23cm
Includes index
ISBN 0-7110-1015-3 : £7.95 B81-32927

629.1 — AEROSPACE ENGINEERING

629.1 — Aerospace engineering. Materials
Nica, Alexandru. Mechanics of aerospace materials. — Oxford : Elsevier Scientific, Oct.1981. — [330]p. — (Materials science monographs ; 9)
ISBN 0-444-99729-6 : £32.00 : CIP entry B81-25318

629.1′03′21 — Aeronautics & astronautics — *Encyclopaedias*
Aviation-space dictionary. — 6th ed. / editor Ernest J. Gentle ; co-editor Lawrence W. Reithmaier. — Fallbrook : Aero ; [London] : Arms & Armour [distributor], 1980. — 272p : ill ; 28cm
Previous ed.: 1974
ISBN 0-8168-3002-9 : £10.50 B81-23378

629.1′05 — Aerospace engineering — *Serials*
Progress in aerospace sciences. — Vol.19. — Oxford : Pergamon, Dec.1981. — [320]p
ISBN 0-08-029098-1 : £61.00 : CIP entry B81-33854

629.1′1 — Atmosphere. Aerospace vehicles. Flight. Trajectories. Optimisation
Vinh, Nguyen X.. Optimal trajectories in atmospheric flight / Nguyen X. Vinh. — Amsterdam ; Oxford : Elsevier Scientific, 1981. — xviii,402p : ill ; 25cm. — (Studies in astronautics ; v.2)
Includes index
ISBN 0-444-41961-6 : £35.44 B81-22292

629.13 — AERONAUTICS

629.13 — Aeronautics
Van Sickle, Neil D.. Van Sickle′s modern airmanship. — 5th ed. / edited by John F. Welch. — New York ; London : Van Nostrand Reinhold, c1981. — ix,878p : ill,charts,facsims,forms ; 24cm
Previous ed.: 1971. — Includes index
ISBN 0-442-25793-7 : £18.70 B81-21246

629.13′0025′411 — Scotland. Aviation — *Directories*
Scotland scanned : a guide to aviation in Scotland. — 4th ed / edited by Paul R. Wiggins and Alan J. Reid. — Edinburgh (Flat 21, 104 Dalry Rd., Edinburgh EH11 2DW) : Central Scotland Aviation Group, 1979. — 148p : ill,maps ; 21cm
Previous ed.: 1977
ISBN 0-9503891-3-7 (pbk) : Unpriced B81-26067

629.13′003′21 — Aviation — *Encyclopaedias*
Jane′s encyclopedia of aviation / compiled and edited by Michael J.H. Taylor ; foreword by John W.R. Taylor ; contributors Bill Gunston ... [et al.]. — London : Jane′s, 1980. — 5v.(ix,1078p) : ill(some col.),ports ; 27cm
In slip case. — Includes index
ISBN 0-7106-0710-5 : £45.00 B81-11741

629.13′009 — Aeronautics, *to 1980 — For children*
Maynard, Christopher. Aircraft / by Chris Maynard and John Paton. — London : Kingfisher, 1981. — 93p : ill(some col.) ; 19cm. — (A Kingfisher factbook)
Includes index
ISBN 0-86272-014-1 : £2.50 : CIP rev. B81-14406

629.13′0092′4 — Aeronautical engineering. Wallis, ***Sir* Barnes** — *Biographies*
Morpurgo, J. E.. Barnes Wallis : a biography / by J.E. Morpurgo. — Updated ed. — London : Ian Allan, 1981. — xvi,400p,[16]p of plates : ill,ports ; 23cm
Previous ed.: Harlow : Longman, 1972. — Includes index
ISBN 0-7110-1119-2 : £11.95 B81-19386

629.13'0092'4 — Aviation. De Havilland, *Sir* Geoffrey — *Biographies*

De Havilland, *Sir* Geoffrey. Sky fever : the autobiography of Sir Geoffrey de Havilland. — Shrewsbury : Airlife, c1979. — 239p,[8]p of plates : ill,ports ; 23cm
Includes index
ISBN 0-906393-02-7 : £6.95 B81-12118

629.13'009422'145 — Surrey. Weybridge. Brooklands. Aircraft. Flying, *1908-1950*

Johnson, Howard. Wings over Brooklands. — Weybridge (The Oil Mills, Weybridge, Surrey) : Whittet Books, Oct.1981. — [160]p
ISBN 0-905483-20-0 (cased) : £8.95 : CIP entry
ISBN 0-905483-21-9 (pbk) : £4.95
Primary classification 338.4'76291'3009422145
B81-27990

629.13'00973 — United States. Aeronautics — *Practical information*

Foster, Timothy R. V.. The aviator's catalog : a source book of aeronautica / Timothy R.V. Foster. — New York ; London : Van Nostrand Reinhold, c1981. — 255p : ill,maps,ports ; 28cm
Includes index
ISBN 0-442-21201-1 (cased) : Unpriced
ISBN 0-442-22465-6 (pbk) : £12.70 B81-08712

629.13'074'022725 — Hampshire. Farnborough. Air displays: Farnborough Air Display, *1948-1979* — *Personal observations*

Baxter, Raymond. Raymond Baxter's Farnborough commentary / foreword by John Cunningham. — Cambridge : Stephens, 1980. — 112p : chiefly ill,ports ; 25cm
ISBN 0-85059-434-0 : £6.95 : CIP rev.
B80-17777

629.13'074'094 — Western Europe. Air displays — *Lists* — *Serials*

Airshows. — 1980. — Leicester : Midland Counties Publications, c1981. — 43p
ISBN 0-904597-35-0 : £3.45 B81-35957

629.13'09 — Aircraft. Flying, *to 1980*

Brown, Douglas, *19---*. Flyers / Douglas Brown. — London : Hamlyn, 1981. — 93p : ill(some col.),col.maps,1plan,ports ; 28cm. — (History eye-witness)
Ill on lining papers. — Includes index
ISBN 0-600-30494-9 : £2.95 B81-24160

629.13'09 — Aviation. Mysteries, *to 1954*

McKee, Alexander. Into the blue : great mysteries of aviation / by Alexander McKee. — London : Souvenir, 1981. — 296p,[16]p of plates : ill,facsims,1plan,ports ; 23cm
ISBN 0-285-62476-8 : £8.95 B81-25180

629.13'09'041 — Aeroplanes. Flights, *1903-1908*

Gibbs-Smith, C. H.. The world's first aeroplane flights, (1903-1908) : and earlier attempts to fly / by Charles H. Gibbs-Smith. — 5th impression with amendments. — London : H.M.S.O., 1977. — 32p : ill ; 22cm. — (A Science Museum booklet)
Previous ed.: 1965. — Text on inside cover
ISBN 0-11-290033-x (pbk) : £0.60 B81-39815

629.13'0911 — Arctic Ocean. Flights by semi-rigid airships, *1928:* **Italia** *(Airship)*

McKee, Alexander. Ice crash / Alexander McKee. — London : Granada, 1981, c1979. — 400p,[8]p of plates : ill,maps,ports ; 18cm. — (A Panther book)
Originally published: London : Souvenir, 1979. — Bibliography: p391-393. — Includes index
ISBN 0-586-05191-0 (pbk) : £1.95 B81-38168

629.13'092'2 — Great Britain. Aviation. Involvement of royal families, *to 1980*

Cooksley, Peter G.. Flight royal : the Queen's Flight & royal flying in five reigns / Peter G. Cooksley. — Cambridge : Stephens, 1981. — 112p : ill,ports ; 25cm
Ill on lining papers. — Bibliography: p110. — Includes index
ISBN 0-85059-490-1 : £6.95
Also classified at 358.4'4'0941 B81-32843

629.13'092'4 — Aeroplanes. Flying. Batten, Jean — *Biographies*

Batten, Jean. Alone in the sky / by Jean Batten ; drawings by L.R. Williams. — Shrewsbury : Airlife, 1979. — 190p,[12]p of plates : ill,ports ; 22cm
Based on: My life / by Jean Batten. London : Harrap, 1938
ISBN 0-906393-01-9 : £6.95 B81-39360

629.13'092'4 — Aeroplanes. Flying. Doolittle, Jimmy — *Biographies*

Glines, Carroll V.. Jimmy Doolittle : master of the calculated risk / Carroll V. Glines. — New York ; London : Van Nostrand Reinhold, 1980. — 202p : ill,ports ; 23cm
Originally published: New York : Macmillan, 1972. — Includes index
ISBN 0-442-23102-4 (pbk) : £3.70 B81-05599

629.13'092'4 — Aeroplanes. Flying. Johnson, Amy — *Biographies* — *For children*

Snell, Gordon. Amy Johnson : queen of the air / by Gordon Snell. — London : Hodder and Stoughton, 1980. — 128p : ill,maps,ports ; 25cm. — (Twentieth century people)
Includes index
ISBN 0-340-25203-0 : £4.95 : CIP rev.
B80-13440

629.13'092'4 — Great Britain. Aeroplanes. Flying. Penrose, Harald — *Biographies*

Penrose, Harald. Cloud Cuckooland / Harald Penrose ; illustrated by David Gibbings. — Shrewsbury : Airlife, 1981. — 155p : ill ; 23cm
ISBN 0-906393-07-8 : £6.95 B81-14685

629.13'092'4 — United States. Biplanes. Flights — *Personal observations*

Bach, Richard. Biplane / Richard Bach ; prelude by Ray Bradbury ; photographs by Paul E. Hansen and the author. — London : Granada, 1981, c1966. — 153p,[8]p of plates : ill ; 18cm. — (A Panther Book)
Originally published: New York : Harper & Row, 1966
ISBN 0-586-05311-5 (pbk) : £1.25 B81-32917

629.13'0941'6 — Northern Ireland. Aviation, *to 1980*

Corlett, John. Aviation in Ulster. — Belfast : Blackstaff Press, Nov.1981. — [128]p
ISBN 0-85640-252-4 (pbk) : £6.95 : CIP entry
B81-32016

629.13'09422'58 — East Sussex. Eastbourne. Aviation, *1911-1921*

Armstrong, Robert, *1940-*. Wings over Eastbourne / by Robert Armstrong. — [Eastbourne] ([20 Pevensey Rd, Eastbourne, E. Sussex]) : [Sound Forum], c1980. — [51]p : 1port ; 19cm
£0.45 (unbound) B81-04143

629.132 — Flight — *For children*

Bauer, Ernst W.. Flight / Ernst W. Bauer ; [translated by Brenda Groth]. — St. Albans : Hart-Davis, 1981. — 47p : ill(some col.) ; 26cm
Translated from the German
ISBN 0-247-13152-0 : £3.25 B81-24522

629.132'07'1241 — Great Britain. Secondary schools. Curriculum subjects: Flight — *For teaching*

Bavage, Trevor. Flight / prepared by Trevor Bavage. — Hatfield (College La., Hatfield, Hertfordshire, AL10 9AA) : Association for Science Education, c1978. — 23p,[29]leaves : ill ; 30cm. — (Topic brief / LAMP Project ; no.120)
ISBN 0-902786-42-3 (pbk) : £0.80 B81-06126

629.132'3'071041 — Great Britain. Schools. Students, 5-14 years. Curriculum subjects: Aircraft. Aerodynamics — *For teaching*

Slack, Derek. Flying starts here / Derek Slack. — Basingstoke (Houndmills, Basingstoke RG21 2XS) : Globe Education [for] West Sussex County Council, 1981. — 36p : ill,forms ; 30cm. — (Science horizons. Level 2b)
Bibliography: p10. — List of films: p10
ISBN 0-333-28541-7 (pbk) : £3.95 B81-31308

629.132'52 — Aeroplanes. Flying. Emergencies — *Case studies* — *For pilots*

Cass, Martin. The pilot in command / Martin Cass. — Shrewsbury : Airlife, 1980. — 213p : ill,1chart ; 23cm
ISBN 0-906393-05-1 : £7.50 B81-39165

629.132'52 — Aeroplanes. Flying — *Manuals*

Birch, N. H.. Flight briefing for pilots / N.H. Birch, A.E. Bramson. — London : Pitman
The IMC rating manual / illustrated by A.E. Bramson. — 1981. — vii,375p,[10]p of plates(2 folded) : ill,charts,forms ; 20cm
Includes index
ISBN 0-273-01732-2 : Unpriced B81-27153

629.132'52 — Great Britain. Civil aviation. Radiotelephony. Procedure — *Manuals*

Durber, Raymond. R T procedures for pilots : or 'who's that down there saying, "who's that up there?"?' : an introduction to correct radiotelphony procedure / by Raymond Durber. — Shrewsbury : Airlife, c1979. — 71p : ill ; 19cm
ISBN 0-906393-03-5 : Unpriced B81-39164

629.132'5217 — Light aircraft. Flying. Use of navigation instruments — *Manuals*

Hoy, David. Instrument flying : the intrument rating / David Hoy ; illustrated by L.R. Williams. — Shrewsbury : Airlife, c1981. — 128p : ill(some col.),col.charts,1form ; 23cm
ISBN 0-906393-06-x : Unpriced B81-39163

629.132'5217'0973 — United States. Light aircraft. Flying — *For private pilots*

Ramsey, Dan. Budget flying : how to earn your private pilot license and enjoy flying economically / by Dan Ramsey. — New York ; London : McGraw-Hill, c1981. — xii,194p : ill ; 24cm. — (McGraw Hill series in aviation)
Includes index
ISBN 0-07-051202-7 : £13.75 B81-23449

629.133 — Aircraft — *For children*

Girard, Pat. Flying machines / Pat Girard. — Oxford : Blackwell Raintree, c1981. — 32p : ill (some col.) ; 27cm
Originally published: Milwaukee : Raintree Children, c1980. — Includes index
ISBN 0-86256-024-1 : £2.95 B81-17608

629.133'0212 — Aircraft — *Technical data*

Green, William, *19---*. The observer's book of aircraft / compiled by William Green ; with silhouettes by Dennis Punnett. — 1981 ed. 30th ed. — London : Warne, 1981. — 256p : ill ; 15cm. — (The Observer's pocket series ; 11)
Previous ed.: 1980. — Includes index
ISBN 0-7232-1618-5 : £1.80 B81-15749

629.133'03'21 — Aircraft, *to 1978* — *Encyclopaedias*

The **Illustrated** encyclopaedia of aircraft / edited by David Mondey. — London : Hamlyn, 1979, c1978. — 320p : ill(some col.) ; 30cm
Includes index
ISBN 0-600-30378-0 : £6.95 B81-02252

629.133'09 — Aircraft, *to 1979*

Macknight, Nigel. The colour encyclopedia of aircraft / by Nigel and Nicola Macknight ; foreword by Sheila Scott. — London : Octopus, 1980. — 224p : ill(some col.),1facsim,ports (some col.) ; 31cm
Ill on lining papers
ISBN 0-7064-1303-2 : £5.95 B81-04669

629.133'09 — Aircraft, *to 1980* — *For children*

Maynard, Christopher. Aircraft / by Chris Maynard and John Paton. — London : Pan, 1981. — 93p : ill(some col.),ports ; 18cm. — (A Piccolo factbook)
Text on inside cover. — Includes index
ISBN 0-330-26416-8 (pbk) : £1.25 B81-38775

629.133'0941 — Great Britain. Preserved aircraft — *Lists*

Riley, Gordon, *1950-*. Vintage aircraft directory / by Gordon Riley. — 5th ed. — [Reading] : G. Riley ; London (3 New Plaistow Rd., E15 3JA) : Distributed by Battle of Britain Prints, c1979. — 72p : ill ; 18cm
Previous ed.: 1976
ISBN 0-900913-16-9 (pbk) : £1.25 B81-05101

629.133'1 — Radio controlled model aircraft — *Manuals*

Vale, Adrian. Radio controlled model aircraft : a complete guide for beginners / Adrian Vale ; with cartoons by 'Raf'. — Old Woking : Gresham Books, 1979. — x,181p : ill,1plan,1port ; 21cm
Bibliography: p180-181
ISBN 0-905418-04-2 (pbk) : £4.25 B81-06187

629.133'134 — Indoor model aeroplanes. Construction & flying — *Manuals*

Williams, Ron. Building and flying indoor model airplanes / written and illustrated by Ron Williams. — London : John Murray, 1981. — 271p : ill,plans,ports ; 28cm
Originally published: New York : Simon and Schuster, 1981. — Includes index
ISBN 0-7195-3855-6 (pbk) : £6.95 B81-37457

629.133'134 — Radio controlled model aeroplanes. Construction & flying — *Manuals*

Whitehead, Gordon, *1944-*. Radio control scale aircraft : models for everyday flying / by Gordon Whitehead. — Guildford ([P.O. Box 81], Guildford, Surrey, [GU2 3RL]) : RM Books, 1980. — 308p : ill,1port ; 21cm
£6.95 (pbk) B81-05301

629.133'1352 — Radio controlled model helicopters

Snitjer, Wil. Radio control helicopters for the practical model flyer / by Wil Snitjer ; translated from the original Dutch by the author ; edited and revised by Maurice Tait ; line illustrations by H. Sluyter. — Guildford ([P.O. Box 81, Guildford, Surrey GU1 3RL]) : R.M. Books, 1981. — 117p : ill ; 21cm
Unpriced (pbk) B81-15041

629.133'3 — Man-powered flight, *to 1979*

Grosser, Morton. Gossamer Odyssey : the triumph of human-powered flight / Morton Grosser ; with a foreword by HRH Prince Charles. — London : Joseph, 1981. — xxi,298p,[32]p of plates : ill(some col.),plans,ports(some col.) ; 24cm
Bibliography: p280-284. — Includes index
ISBN 0-7181-2033-7 : £8.50 B81-34422

629.133'34 — Aeroplanes — *For children*

Sheahan, Denis. Aeroplanes. — London : A & C Black, Jan.1982. — [32]p. — (Science explorers)
ISBN 0-7136-2149-4 : £2.50 : CIP entry B81-33848

629.133'34 — Airlines. Aeroplanes

McAllister, Chris. Planes and airports / Chris McAllister. — London : Batsford, 1981. — 64p : ill(some col.),1col.map ; 20cm
Includes index
ISBN 0-7134-3911-4 (pbk) : £1.95
Also classified at 387.7'36 B81-33066

629.133'34 — De Havilland aeroplanes, *1919-1939 — Readings from contemporary sources*

De Havilland : the golden years 1919-1939 / edited and compiled by Richard Riding. — Sutton (Quadrant House, The Quadrant, Sutton, Surrey SM2 5AS) : I.P.C. Transport, c1981. — 223,4p of plates : ill(some col.),facsims,plans,2ports ; 30cm. — (A Flight international special)
Ill on inside covers. — Facsimile reprints
ISBN 0-617-00332-7 (pbk) : £4.25 B81-10020

629.133'34 — Preserved aeroplanes

Mulelly, Ian S.. Airworthy! : flying vintage aircaft / Ian S. Mulelly, Hugh R. Smallwood. — Poole : Blandford, 1981. — 128p : ill(some col.),ports ; 26cm
Includes index
ISBN 0-7137-0966-9 : £8.95 : CIP rev. B81-08943

629.133'34'0222 — Airlines. Aeroplanes — *Illustrations*

Young, John, *1930-*. Airliners : a colour guide to modern airliners, 38 aircraft types illustrated, identification — performance / [painted by John Young and Michael Trim ... ; text by Brian Calvert]. — [London] : Fontana, 1979. — 1folded sheet([12]p) : col.ill ; 25cm. — (Domino ; 12)
ISBN 0-00-685455-9 : £0.85 B81-20742

629.133'34'0222 — Civil aeroplanes — *Illustrations*

Seo, Hiroshi. Civil aircraft of the world / Hiroshi Seo. — London : Jane's, 1981. — 95p : chiefly col.ill ; 20x27cm
ISBN 0-7106-0102-6 : £4.95 B81-28458

629.133'340422 — Second-hand light aircraft — *Buyers' guides*

The **Aviation** consumer used aircraft guide / Richard B. Weeghman editor. — New York ; London : McGraw-Hill, c1981. — vii,227p : ill,1port ; 29cm. — (McGraw-Hill series in aviation)
Includes index
ISBN 0-07-002543-6 : £13.50 B81-29565

629.133'340423'0212 — Commercial aeroplanes — *Technical data*

Commercial transport aircraft / compiled by Michael J.H. Taylor and Kenneth Munson ; edited by John W.R. Taylor. — [2nd ed]. — London : Jane's, 1981. — 262p : ill ; 12x19cm. — (Jane's pocket book ; 3)
Previous ed.: 1973. — Includes index
ISBN 0-7106-0093-3 : £4.95 B81-19504

629.133'340423'0321 — Commercial aircraft — *Encyclopaedias*

The **Illustrated** encyclopedia of commercial aircraft / Editor-in-chief Bill Gunston. — [Leicester] : Windward, [c1980]. — 326p : ill (some col.),plans ; 31cm
Includes index
ISBN 0-7112-0060-2 : £8.95 B81-00955

629.133'34'09 — Civil aircraft, *1950-1980 — Illustrations*

Aircraft illustrated book of civil aircraft / [compiled by Allan Burney]. — London : Ian Allan, 1981. — 30p : all col.ill ; 24cm
ISBN 0-7110-0956-2 (pbk) : £0.95 B81-24859

629.133'34'0904 — Aeroplanes, *1900-1945*

Jerram, Michael F.. Antiques of the air / Michael F. Jerram. — London : New English Library, 1980. — 192p : ill(some col.),1port ; 29cm
Includes index
ISBN 0-450-04813-6 : £9.95 B81-03103

629.133'34'0971 — Canada. Aircraft, *1909-1980*

Molson, K. M.. Canadian aircraft since 1909. — London : Putnam, Nov.1981. — [600]p
ISBN 0-370-30095-5 : £20.00 : CIP entry B81-30345

629.133'343 — Biplanes, *to 1940*

Bowyer, Chaz. The age of the biplane / Chaz Bowyer. — London : Hamlyn, 1981. — 192p : ill(some col.),ports ; 31cm. — (A Bison book)
Bibliography: p191. — Includes index
ISBN 0-600-34945-4 : £6.95 B81-32389

629.133'343 — Commercial propeller-driven aeroplanes, *to 1977*

The **Illustrated** encyclopedia of propeller airliners / Editor-in-chief Bill Gunston. — [London] : Windward, [c1980]. — 256p : ill(some col.) ; 31cm
ISBN 0-7112-0062-9 : £7.95 B81-01756

629.133'343 — Handley Page Dart Herald aeroplanes, *to 1979*

Cowell, G.. Handley Page Herald / G. Cowell. — London : Jane's, 1980. — 154p : ill,1facsim ; 22cm. — (An Airline Publications book)
ISBN 0-7106-0045-3 : £7.95 B81-05409

629.133'343 — Sopwith aeroplanes, *1912-1920*

King, H. F.. Sopwith aircraft 1912-1920 / H. F. King. — London : Putnam, 1981, c1980. — 323p : ill ; 23cm
Includes index
ISBN 0-370-30050-5 : £13.00 B81-11515

629.133'347'09 — Seaplanes, *to ca 1950*

Allward, Maurice. An illustrated history of seaplanes & flying boats / Maurice Allward. — Ashbourne : Moorland, c1981. — 160p : ill ; 22cm
Includes index
ISBN 0-86190-011-1 : £6.95 B81-23117

629.133'347'0916336 — England. Solent. Seaplanes, *1910-1980*

Sea planes and flying boats of the Solent / edited by Adrian B. Rance with contributions by J.A. Bagley ... [et al.]. — Southampton : Southampton University Industrial Archaeology Group in association with Southampton City Museums, 1981. — 64p : ill,maps,facsims ; 30cm
Ill on inside covers
ISBN 0-905280-03-2 (pbk) : £1.80 B81-33594

629.133'349 — Boeing 747 aeroplanes, *to 1980*

Lucas, Jim. Boeing 747 : the first 10 years in service / Jim Lucas. — London : Jane's, 1981. — 160p : ill ; 22cm
ISBN 0-7106-0088-7 : £8.95 B81-17732

629.133'349 — Concorde aeroplanes. Great Britain. *Parliament. House of Commons. Industry and Trade Committee.* **'Concorde'** *— Critical studies*

Great Britain. *Department of Industry*. Concorde : the Government's reply to the Second Report from Industry and Trade Committee for the session 1980-81 (HC 265) / Department of Industry. — London : H.M.S.O., [1981]. — 9p ; 25cm. — (Cmnd. ; 8308)
ISBN 0-10-183080-7 (unbound) : £1.40 B81-35008

629.133'349 — Concorde aeroplanes. Operation, *to 1981 — Personal observations*

Calvert, Brian. Flying Concorde / Brian Calvert. — [London] : Fontana, 1981. — 253p,[16]p of plates : ill(some col.) ; 20cm
Includes index
ISBN 0-00-636290-7 (pbk) : £3.95 B81-25928

629.133'349 — Concorde aeroplanes, *to 1980*

Calvert, Brian. Flying Concorde / Brian Calvert. — Shrewsbury : Airlife, 1981. — 253p, [12]p of plates : ill,maps,plans ; 20cm
Includes index
ISBN 0-906393-14-0 : £7.95 B81-39361

629.133'349 — Sud-Aviation Caravelle aeroplanes, *to 1980*

Avrane, A.. Sud Est Caravelle / A. Avrane, M. Gilliand, J. Guillem. — London : Jane's, 1981. — 223p : ill ; 22cm
ISBN 0-7106-0044-5 : £8.95 B81-22083

629.133'352 — Crop spraying helicopters — *Conference proceedings*

Agricultural Aviation Group all-day symposium jointly with Rotorcraft Section : Wednesday 14th February 1979 : presented at The Royal Aeronautical Society. — London (4 Hamilton Place, W1V 0BQ) : [The Society], [1979]. — 132p in various pagings : ill ; 30cm
Includes bibliographies
Unpriced (pbk)
Primary classification 632'.94 B81-37730

629.133'352 — Helicopters

Brown, Eric, *1919-*. The helicopter in civil operations / Eric Brown. — London : Granada, 1981. — 177p : ill,1map ; 24cm
Includes index
ISBN 0-246-11221-2 : £8.95 B81-24460

629.133'352'01 — Helicopters. Theories

Johnson, Wayne. Helicopter theory / Wayne Johnson. — Princeton ; Guildford : Princeton University Press, c1980. — xxii,1089p : ill ; 25cm
Bibliography: p961-1084. - Includes index
ISBN 0-691-07971-4 (corrected) : £52.90 B81-03948

629.134'1 — Aeroplanes. Design. Safety aspects

Thurston, David B.. Design for safety / David B. Thurston. — New York ; London : McGraw-Hill, c1980. — x,196p : ill ; 25cm. — (McGraw-Hill series in aviation)
Includes index
ISBN 0-07-064554-x : £8.95 B81-01729

629.134'31 — Airframes

Cutler, John. Understanding aircraft structures. — St. Albans : Granada, Oct.1981. — [176]p
ISBN 0-246-11310-3 : £9.75 : CIP entry B81-25784

629.134′353 — Aeroplanes. Gas turbines

Kerrebrock, Jack L.. Aircraft engines and gas turbines / Jack L. Kerrebrock. — Cambridge, Mass. ; London : MIT Press, c1977. — x,285p : ill ; 24cm
Includes index
ISBN 0-262-11064-4 : £17.50 B81-02407

629.134′52 — Aeronautics. Research. Cryogenic wind tunnels — *Conference proceedings*

International Symposium on Cryogenic Wind Tunnels *(1st : 1979 : University of Southampton)*. First International Symposium on Cryogenic Wind Tunnels : proceedings of the Symposium held in the Department of Aeronautics and Astronautics at the University of Southampton, England, April 1979. — [Southampton] : [The Department], [1979?]. — 330p in various pagings : ill ; 30cm
Cover title
Unpriced (pbk) B81-39547

629.134′53′0924 — Percival Mew aeroplanes. Test flights, *1937-1939* — *Personal observations*

Henshaw, Alex. [The flight of the Mew Gull]. The flight of the Mewgull / Alex Henshaw. — London : Hamlyn Paperbacks, 1981, c1980. — 310p,[8]p of plates : ill,maps,ports ; 18cm
Originally published: London : J. Murray, 1980. — Includes index
ISBN 0-600-20425-1 (pbk) : £1.75 B81-31962

629.134′53′0924 — Supermarine Spitfire aeroplanes. Test flights, *1939-1946* — *Personal observations*

Henshaw, Alex. Sigh for a Merlin : testing the Spitfire / Alex Henshaw. — London : Hamlyn Paperbacks, 1980, c1979. — xiv,210p,[8]p of plates : ill,1map,1plan,ports ; 18cm
Originally published: London : Murray, 1979. — Includes index
ISBN 0-600-20151-1 (pkbk) : £1.50 B81-03012

629.135 — Aeroplanes. Radio equipment

Powell, J.. Aircraft radio systems / J. Powell. — London : Pitman, c1981. — viii,255p : ill ; 26cm
Includes index
ISBN 0-273-08444-5 : Unpriced B81-38447

629.135 — Aircraft. Instruments

Pallett, E. H. J.. Aircraft instruments : principles and applications / E.H.J. Pallett ; with a foreword by Sir Vernon Brown. — 2nd ed. — London : Pitman, 1981. — xvii,414p : ill ; 26cm
Previous ed.: 1972. — Includes index
ISBN 0-273-01539-7 : Unpriced B81-38406

629.135′1 — Aircraft. Navigational aids: Very high frequency omni directional radio range

Bramson, A. E.. Flying the V.O.R. / by Alan Bramson and Neville Birch ; illustrated by Alan Bramson. — Shrewsbury : Airlife, [1981?]. — vi,42p : col.ill,charts ; 20cm
ISBN 0-906393-00-0 : Unpriced B81-39167

629.135′2 — Aeroplanes. Speed & altitude. Measurement

Gracey, William. Measurement of aircraft speed and altitude / William Gracey. — New York ; Chichester : Wiley, c1981. — xiv,262p : ill ; 29cm
Includes index
ISBN 0-471-08511-1 : £21.00 B81-33425

629.135′4 — Aircraft. Electrical systems

Bent, Ralph D.. Aircraft electricity and electronics / Ralph D. Bent, James L. McKinley. — 3rd ed. — New York ; London : Gregg, c1981. — vii,359p : ill ; 28cm. — (Aviation technology series)
Previous ed.: published as Electricity and electronics for aerospace vehicles / by James L. McKinley and Ralph D. Bent for Northrop Institute of Technology. New York : McGraw-Hill, 1971. — Includes index
ISBN 0-07-004793-6 (pbk) : £10.15 B81-36277

629.136′6 — Great Britain. Air traffic control systems. Very high frequency radio frequency wavebands — *Lists*

Davies, Ken, *19---*. UK VHF airband guide : (guide to air traffic control frequencies in the UK) / Ken Davies. — 2nd ed. — Hounslow (Noble Corner, Great West Rd., Hounslow, Middx., TW5 0PA) : Airline Publication and Sales, c1981. — 31p : charts,1maps ; 21cm
Cover title. — Previous ed.: 1979
ISBN 0-905117-82-4 (pbk) : £1.50 B81-34893

629.136′6′0941 — Great Britain. Air traffic. Control

Field, Arnold. The control of air traffic / [by Arnold Field]. — [Eton] ([50 High St., Eton, Berks]) : [Eton]
Vol.1. — c1980. — 95p : ill(some col.),1col.map ; 31cm
Includes index
ISBN 0-907159-01-x : £12.95 B81-17144

629.2 — MOTOR VEHICLES

629.2 — Motor vehicle engineering — *For technicians*

Kett, P. W.. Motor vehicle science. — London : Chapman and Hall, Sept.1981
Part 1. — [220]p
ISBN 0-412-23590-0 (cased) : £9.50 : CIP entry
ISBN 0-412-22100-4 (pbk) : £4.50 B81-23909

Kett, P. W.. Motor vehicle science. — London : Chapman & Hall
Part 2. — Dec.1981. — [300]p
ISBN 0-412-23600-1 (cased) : £10.00 : CIP entry
ISBN 0-412-23610-9 (pbk) : £5.00 B81-31711

Nunney, M. J.. Vehicle technology 2. — London : Butterworths, Dec.1981. — [120]p
ISBN 0-408-00594-7 (pbk) : £5.75 : CIP entry B81-31423

629.2 — Motor vehicles

Hillier, V. A. W.. Fundamentals of motor vehicle technology / V.A.W. Hillier, F. Pittuck. — 3rd ed. — London : Hutchinson, 1981. — 471p : ill ; 24cm
Previous ed.: 1972. — Includes index
ISBN 0-09-143161-1 (pbk) : £5.95 B81-24158

629.2′0212 — Motor vehicles — *Technical data* — *Serials*

Technical service data. — 1979 ed. — Chertsey : Palgrave Pub., 1979. — 260p
£4.30 B81-00141

Technical service data. — 1980 ed. — Chertsey : Palgrave Pub., 1980. — 268p
£5.40 B81-00142

629.2′022′2 — Motor vehicles — *Illustrations* — *For children*

Purnell's big picture book of cars and trucks. — Maidenhead : Purnell, 1981. — [48]p : all col.ill ; 27cm
ISBN 0-361-05071-2 : £2.75 B81-22270

629.2′068 — Great Britain. Motor vehicle industries. Management

Hartley, John R.. Management of vehicle production / John Hartley. — London : Butterworth, 1981. — 147p : ill,1map,plans ; 24cm
Includes index
ISBN 0-408-00396-0 : Unpriced : CIP rev. B80-04878

629.2′076 — Motor vehicles — *Questions & answers*

Hirst, J.. Motor vehicle craft studies part 1 / editor R. Brooks ; authors J. Hirst, J. Whipp. — 2nd ed. — London : Macmillan, 1981. — 266p : ill ; 30cm. — (Macmillan motor vehicle craft studies series)
Previous ed.: 1971
ISBN 0-333-32383-1 : £5.95 B81-40515

629.2′092′4 — England. Motor vehicles, *1900-1978* — *Personal observations*

Griffin, J. B.. History of past and present motor vehicle transport over 58 years / J.B. Griffin. — Bognor Regis : New Horizon, c1980. — 102p,[6]p of plates : ill,2facsims ; 21cm
ISBN 0-86116-723-6 : £4.59 B81-21827

629.2′092′4 — Great Britain. Motor vehicle engineering. Platt, Maurice — *Biographies*

Platt, Maurice. An addiction to automobiles : the occupational autobiography of an engineer and journalist / Maurice Platt ; with line drawings by Gary Kemp. — London : Warne, 1980. — vii,198p,[16]p of plates : ill,ports ; 24cm
Includes index
ISBN 0-7232-2713-6 : £12.50 B81-01761

629.22 — MOTOR VEHICLES. SPECIAL TYPES

629.2′2 — Heavy road vehicles

Leeming, David J.. Heavy vehicle technology. — 2nd ed. — London : Hutchinson, Apr.1981. — [256]p
Previous ed.: 1976
ISBN 0-09-144691-0 (pbk) : £4.95 : CIP entry B81-02085

629.2′2122 — Model cars

Model cars / general editor Vic Smeed. — London : Hamlyn, 1980. — 192p : ill(some col.),ports(some col.) ; 32cm. — (A Bison book)
Includes index
ISBN 0-600-34943-8 : £5.95 B81-02917

629.2′2122 — Model cars. Construction — *Manuals*

Scarborough, Gerald. How to go car modelling. — Cambridge : Stephens, Oct.1981. — [152]p
ISBN 0-85059-454-5 : £8.95 : CIP entry B81-30193

629.2′214 — Scale model commercial vehicles. Construction — *Manuals*

Scarborough, Gerald. Making model trucks : and other commercial vehicles / Gerald Scarborough. — Cambridge : Stephens, 1980. — 112p : ill ; 25cm
Ill on lining papers. — Bibliography: p109-110
ISBN 0-85059-438-3 : £7.50 : CIP rev. B80-17781

629.2′218 — Radio controlled model racing cars

Laidlaw-Dickson, D. J.. Radio controlled model racing cars / D.J. Laidlaw-Dickson. — Watford : Model & Allied Publications, 1979. — 136p : ill ; 21cm
ISBN 0-85242-675-5 (pbk) : £3.75 B81-29870

629.2′218 — Radio controlled model racing cars — *Serials*

[Model cars *(1981)*]. Model cars. — Vol.1, no.1 (Spring 1981)-. — Hemel Hempstead : Model & Allied Publications, 1981-. — v. : ill ; 26cm
Quarterly
£0.90 per issue B81-38191

629.2′218 — Scalextric model racing car equipment, *to 1980*

Gillham, Roger. Scalextric / [Roger Gillham]. — Yeovil : Haynes, 1981. — 134p : ill,1port ; 28cm. — (A Foulis book)
ISBN 0-85429-286-1 : Unpriced B81-36794

629.2′2192 — Model Allchin Royal Chester traction engines. Construction — *Manuals*

Hughes, W. J.. Building the Allchin : Modelling Royal Chester a 1 1/2 in. scale general purpose traction engine / by W.J. Hughes. — Watford : Model & Allied, 1979. — 256p : ill ; 25cm
ISBN 0-85242-635-6 (pbk) : £6.95 B81-37747

629.2′222 — Aston Martin & Lagonda cars, *to 1978*

Harvey, Chris. Aston Martin and Lagonda / Chris Harvey. — Oxford : Oxford Illustrated, c1979. — 245p,[16]p of plates : ill(some col.),ports ; 26cm
Includes index
ISBN 0-902280-68-6 : £17.95 B81-18699

629.2′222 — Aston Martin V8 cars, *to 1980*
McComb, F. Wilson. Aston Martin V8s : DBS V8, V8, Vantage, Volante, Lagonda, Bulldog / F. Wilson McComb. — London : Osprey, 1981. — 135p : ill(some col.),ports ; 22cm. — (Osprey autohistory)
Includes index
ISBN 0-85045-399-2 : £5.95 : CIP rev.
B81-02668

629.2′222 — Austin-Healey cars — *Serials*
The **Austin** Healey year book. — 1978-. — Cobham (Holmerise, Seven Hills Rd, Cobham, Surrey) : Magpie, c1978-. — v. : ill ; 30cm
ISSN 0260-664x = Austin Healey year book : Unpriced B81-04168

629.2′222 — British Leyland cars, *to 1979*
Daniels, Jeff. British Leyland : the truth about the cars / Jeff Daniels. — London : Osprey, 1980. — 192p : ill ; 26cm
Includes index
ISBN 0-85045-392-5 : £7.95 B81-12471

629.2′222 — Bugatti cars, *to 1947*
Borgeson, Griff. Bugatti by Borgeson. — London : Osprey, Aug.1981. — [224]p
ISBN 0-85045-414-x : £9.95 : CIP entry
B81-18094

629.2′222 — Cars
AA book of the car. — 3rd ed., Repr. with amendments. — London : Published by Drive Publications Limited for the Automobile Association, 1980, c1976. — 408p : ill(some col.),1col.map ; 27cm
Previous ed.: 1970. — Includes index
ISBN 0-340-25312-6 : £9.95 B81-00956

629.2′222 — Cars — *For children*
Clark, James, *1924-*. Cars / by James Clark ; illustrated by John Bailey/Bercker Studios Ltd and John Dyess. — Oxford : Blackwell Raintree, c1981. — 48p : col.ill ; 24cm. — (A Look inside)
Includes index
ISBN 0-86256-030-6 : £2.95 B81-17348

629.2′222 — Cars. Road tests — *Collections — Serials*
Motor. Road test annual. — 1980. — Sutton (Surrey House, 1, Throwley Way, Sutton, Surrey) : IPC Specialist and Professional Press, [1980?]. — 247p
ISBN 0-617-00275-4 : £4.50
ISSN 0307-7020 B81-01552

629.2′222 — Cars. Sale — *Amateurs′ manuals*
Grahame, Johnathan S. G.. Selling your car privately : full of valuable advice and tips : a must for every motorist / [written by Johnathan S.G. Grahame]. — [S.l.] : [J.S.G. Grahame], [c1979]. — 7leaves ; 21cm
Cover title
£0.75 (pbk) B81-11415

629.2′222 — Citroën SM cars, *to 1980*
Daniels, Jeff. Citroën SM : 2.7 litre V6 Maserati engine / Jeff Daniels. — London : Osprey, 1981. — 135p : ill(some col.) ; 22cm. — (Osprey autohistory)
Includes index
ISBN 0-85045-381-x : £5.95 : CIP rev.
B81-02666

629.2′222 — Customised cars
Filby, Peter. The fun car explosion / Peter Filby. — Cobham : Bookshop, [1979?]. — 139p : ill,ports ; 28cm. — (British specialist cars series ; v.3)
ISBN 0-906189-01-2 (pbk) : Unpriced
B81-40369

629.2′222 — De Tomaso cars, *to 1980*
Wyss, Wallce A.. De Tomaso automobiles. — London : Osprey, Oct.1981. — [224]p
ISBN 0-85045-440-9 : £10.95 : CIP entry
B81-30264

629.2′222 — De Tomaso Pantera cars, *1970-1980*
Norbye, Jan P.. De Tomaso Pantera : 351 V8 Pantera, L, GTS, Gr3, GT4 / Jan P. Norbye. — London : Osprey, 1980. — 135p : ill(some col.),ports ; 22cm. — (Osprey auto History)
Includes index
ISBN 0-85045-382-8 : £5.95 B81-00957

629.2′222 — Ferrari 275 GTB & 275 GTS cars, *to 1980*
Webb, Ian. Ferrari 275 GTB & GTS. — London : Osprey, Oct.1981. — [136]p. — (Autohistory)
ISBN 0-85045-402-6 : £5.95 : CIP entry
B81-27962

629.2′222 — Ferrari cars, *to 1979*
Prunet, Antoine. The road cars / by Antoine Prunet ; [translated by Gerald Roush]. — Cambridge : Stephens, 1980. — 446p : ill(some col.),ports ; 26cm. — (The Ferrari legend)
Translation of: Les Ferrari de route et de rêve
ISBN 0-85059-433-2 : £19.95 B81-29551

629.2′222 — Ford Capri cars, *to 1980*
Walton, Jeremy. Capri / Jeremy Walton. — [Yeovil] : Foulis, 1981. — 285p : ill,ports ; 26cm. — (A Foulis motoring book)
Includes index
ISBN 0-85429-279-9 : Unpriced
Also classified at 796.7′2 B81-31774

629.2′222 — Ford Escort RS cars *to 1980*
Robson, Graham. Ford Escort RS. — London : Osprey, Oct.1981. — [136]p. — (Autohistory)
ISBN 0-85045-401-8 : £5.95 : CIP entry
B81-27963

629.2′222 — Jaguar cars — *Illustrations — Serials*
The **Jaguar** driver′s year book. — 1978. — Cobham (Holmerise, Seven Hills Rd., Cobham, Surrey) : Magpie Pub., c1979. — 120p
ISBN 0-906234-02-6 : £6.00
ISSN 0141-4941 B81-12736

The **Jaguar** driver′s year book. — 1979-80. — Cobham (′Holmerise′ Seven Hills Rd., Cobham, Surrey) : Magpie, c1980. — 119p
ISBN 0-906234-04-2 : Unpriced
ISSN 0141-4941 B81-00958

629.2′222 — Jaguar E-type cars
Skilleter, Paul. The Jaguar E-type : a collector′s guide / by Paul Skilleter. — London : Motor Racing Publications, 1979 (1981 [printing]). — 128p : ill ; 19x24cm
ISBN 0-900549-46-7 : £7.95 B81-17079

629.2′222 — Jowett Jupiter cars, *& 1953*
Nankivell, Edmund. The Jowett Jupiter : the car that leaped to fame / Edward Nankivell. — London : Batsford, 1981. — 144p : ill,ports ; 26cm
Includes index
ISBN 0-7134-3835-5 : £9.95 B81-33065

629.2′222 — Lamborghini cars, *to 1980*
Crump, Richard. Lamborghini. — London : Osprey, Sept.1981. — [208]p
ISBN 0-85045-408-5 : £12.95 : CIP entry
B81-20508

629.2′222 — Lamborghini Countach cars, *to 1980*
Marchet, Jean-François. Lamborghini Countach : LP500, LP400, Countach & S, V12 mid-engine / Jean-François Marchet & Peter Coltrin. — London : Osprey, 1981. — 135p : ill(some col.),facsims,ports ; 22cm. — (Osprey autohistory)
Includes index
ISBN 0-85045-390-9 : £5.95 : CIP rev.
B81-02667

629.2′222 — Lancia cars, *to 1980*
Lancia / compiled from the archives of Autocar by Peter Garnier. — London : Hamlyn, 1981. — 288p : ill(some col.) ; 30cm
ISBN 0-600-34934-9 : £10.00 B81-25540

629.2′222 — Lotus Seven cars, *to 1980*
Ortenburger, Dennis. The legend of the Lotus Seven. — London : Osprey, Nov.1981. — [224]p
ISBN 0-85045-411-5 : £11.95 : CIP entry
B81-38842

629.2′222 — Mercedes-Benz V8 cars, *1963-1979*
McComb, F. Wilson. Mercedes-Benz V8s : limousines, saloons, sedans 1963 to date / F. Wilson McComb. — London : Osprey, 1980. — 135p : ill(some col.),ports ; 22cm. — (Osprey autoHistory)
Includes index
ISBN 0-85045-383-6 : £5.95 B81-00959

629.2′222 — MG sports cars, *1955-1978*
Robson, Graham. The MGA, MGB and MGC : a collector′s guide / by Graham Robson. — London : Motor Racing Publications, c1978. — 136p : ill,ports ; 19x24cm
ISBN 0-900549-43-2 : £6.95 B81-09164

629.2′222 — Morris Minor 1000 cars, *to 1980*
Skilleter, Paul. Morris Minor. — London : Osprey Publishing, May 1981. — [224]p
ISBN 0-85045-344-5 : £9.95 : CIP entry
B81-12818

629.2′222 — Porsche 911 cars, *to 1979*
Frère, Paul. Porsche 911 story / Paul Frère ; foreword by Ferry Porsche. — 2nd ed. — Cambridge : Stephens, 1980. — 209p : ill(some col.) ; 25cm
Previous ed.: 1976. — Includes index
ISBN 0-85059-482-0 : £10.95 B81-29720

Harvey, Chris. Porsche 911 / Chris Harvey. — Oxford : Oxford Illustrated, c1980. — 225p,[16]p of plates : ill(some col.),ports(some col.) ; 26cm
Includes index
ISBN 0-902280-78-3 : £17.95 : CIP rev.
B80-33765

629.2′222 — Porsche 911 cars, *to 1980*
Cotton, Michael. Porsche 911 turbo. — London : Osprey, Oct.1981. — [136]p. — (Autohistory)
ISBN 0-85045-400-x : £5.95 : CIP entry
B81-27961

629.2′222 — Porsche 924, 928 & 944 cars, *to 1980*
Sloniger, Jerry. Porsche 924, 928, 944. — London : Osprey, Oct.1981. — [200]p
ISBN 0-85045-415-8 : £9.95 : CIP entry
B81-28820

629.2′222 — Rolls-Royce Silver Cloud cars, *to 1979*
Robson, Graham. Rolls-Royce Silver Cloud : Phantom V, VI and Bentley S series, Continental / Graham Robson. — London : Osprey, 1980. — 135p : ill(some col.) ; 22cm. — (Osprey autoHistory)
Includes index
ISBN 0-85045-380-1 : £5.95 B81-00960

629.2′222 — Saab cars, *to 1979*
Chatterton, Mark. Saab : the innovator / Mark Chatterton. — Newton Abbot : David & Charles, 1980. — 160p : ill(some col.),ports ; 24cm
Col. ill. on lining papers
ISBN 0-7153-7945-3 : £8.95 : CIP rev.
B80-12935

629.2′222 — Second-hand cars. Purchase — *Amateurs′ manuals*
Goffey, Chris. How to buy a good used car / by Chris Goffey. — London : Foulsham, c1981. — 96p,[16]p of plates : ill ; 18cm
Includes index
ISBN 0-572-01136-9 (pbk) : £1.50 B81-29609

Grahame, Johnathan S. G.. The complete approach to buying a used car : full of valuable advice and tips / [written by Johnathan S.G. Grahame]. — [S.l.] : [J.S.G. Grahame], [c1979]. — 6leaves ; 21cm
Cover title
£0.75 (pbk) B81-11414

629.2′222 — Sports cars, *1945-1980*
Dymock, Eric. Postwar sports cars : the modern classics / Eric Dymock. — London : Ebury, 1981. — 188p : ill(some col.) ; 29cm
Ill on lining papers. — Includes index
ISBN 0-85223-219-5 : £9.95 B81-40917

629.2′222 — Sports cars, *to 1980*
Nye, Doug. Sports cars / Doug Nye. — London : Ward Lock, 1980. — 93p : ill(some col.) ; 25cm. — ([Classic car guides])
Includes index
ISBN 0-7063-6037-0 : £3.95 : CIP rev.
B80-10120

Posthumus, Cyril. Sports cars / Cyril Posthumus and David Hodges ; artwork by Malcolm Ward. — London : Hamlyn, c1981. — 207p : ill(some col.) ; 29cm. — (Automobile library)
ISBN 0-600-32133-9 : £8.95 B81-40753

629.2'222 — Sunbeam Tiger sports cars, *to 1978*
Taylor, Mike, *1948-*. Tiger : the making of a sports car / Mike Taylor. — London : Gentry, 1979. — 224p,[8]p of plates : ill(some col.),facsims,ports ; 25cm
Includes index
ISBN 0-85614-052-x : £9.95 B81-18895

629.2'222 — Triumph cars, *to 1978*
Langworth, Richard M.. Triumph cars : the complete 75-year history / Richard Langworth and Graham Robson. — London : Motor Racing, 1979. — 312p : ill,facsims,ports ; 26cm
Includes index
ISBN 0-900549-44-0 : £14.95 B81-01619

629.2'222 — Triumph sports cars, *to 1980 — Readings from contemporary source*
Triumph sports / compiled by Peter Garnier from the archives of Autocar. — London : Hamlyn. — 160p : ill(some col.),facsims,ports ; 31cm
ISBN 0-600-32149-5 : £7.95 B81-32385

629.2'222'015 — Great Britain. Secondary schools. Curriculum subjects: Cars. Scientific aspects — *For teaching*
Mills, Dave. Science & the motor car / prepared by Dave Mills, Lyn Meredith. — Hatfield (College La., Hatfield, Hertfordshire, AL10 9AA) : Association for Science Education, c1978. — 19p,[25]leaves : ill ; 30cm. — (Topic brief / LAMP Project ; no.12)
ISBN 0-902786-47-4 (pbk) : £0.80 B81-06381

629.2'222'0207 — Cars — *Humour*
Angrave, Bruce. Angrave's amazing autos / Bruce Angrave. — London : Warne, 1980. — [63]p : ill ; 22cm ; pbk
ISBN 0-7232-2711-x : £2.50 B81-01566

629.2'222'0212 — Cars — *Technical data*
Blunsden, John. The observer's book of automobiles. — 24th ed. / compiled by John Blunsden. — London : Warne, 1981. — 192p : ill ; 15cm. — (The Observer's pocket series ; 21)
Previous ed.: 1980
ISBN 0-7232-1617-7 : £1.80 B81-15748

Stobbs, W. Michael. The best cars. — London : Pelham Books, Nov.1981. — [286]p
ISBN 0-7207-1376-5 : £9.50 : CIP entry B81-30394

629.2'222'0212 — Cars — *Technical data — For maintenance & repair*
Seale, J. N.. Car service data : covering 1200 British, European, Japanese and Australian cars and light vans from 1966. — 4th ed. / compiled by J.N. Seale. — London : Hamlyn, 1981. — 304p ; 19cm
Previous ed.: 1978
ISBN 0-600-34962-4 : £5.95 B81-22075

629.2'222'09 — Cars, *1945-1979*
Twite, Mike. Classic cars since 1945 / Michael Twite ; photography Jasper Spencer-Smith. — Poole : Blandford Press, 1981. — 160p : ill (some col.) ; 26cm
Includes index
ISBN 0-7137-1065-9 : £8.95 B81-26287

629.2'222'09 — Cars, *to 1979 — For children*
Cars. — [London] : Sparrow, 1980. — [24]p : ill (some col.) ; 29cm. — (Discoverers)
Adaptation of: The Superbook of cars. — Bibliography: p24
ISBN 0-09-923580-3 (pbk) : £0.70 B81-07984

629.2'222'09 — Cars, *to 1980*
Flower, Raymond. 100 years of motoring : an RAC social history of the car / Raymond Flower, Michael Wynn Jones ; foreword by Prince Michael of Kent ; preface by Jeffrey D. Rose. — Croydon : Published by the Royal Automobile Club in association with McGraw-Hill, 1981. — 224p : ill(some col.),facsims,ports ; 27cm
Includes index
ISBN 0-86211-018-1 : £13.95 B81-38225

Ward, Ian. Motoring for the millions. — Poole : Blandford Press, Sept.1981. — [160]p
ISBN 0-7137-1071-3 : £6.95 : CIP entry B81-22535

629.2'222'09 — Cars, *to 1980 — Illustrations — For children*
Cars. — Maidenhead : Purnell, 1981. — [28]p : chiefly col.ill ; 27cm. — (All in colour picture books)
ISBN 0-361-05068-2 : £1.25 B81-19309

629.2'222'09041 — Cars, *to 1918*
Sedgwick, Michael. Veteran cars / Michael Sedgwick. — London : Ward Lock, 1980. — 93p : ill(some col.) ; 25cm. — ([Classic car guides])
Includes index
ISBN 0-7063-6035-4 : £3.95 : CIP rev. B80-10123

629.2'222'09041 — Cars, *to 1930*
Davis, Pedr. Veteran & vintage cars / text & photography by Pedr Davis. — Newton Abbot : David & Charles, c1981. — 208p : ill(some col.) ; 26x32cm
ISBN 0-7153-8134-2 : £10.50 B81-25352

629.2'222'09042 — Cars, *1919-1930*
Sedgwick, Michael. Vintage cars / Michael Sedgwick. — London : Ward Lock, 1980. — 93p : ill(some col.) ; 25cm. — ([Classic car guides])
Includes index
ISBN 0-7063-6036-2 : £3.95 : CIP rev. B80-10124

629.2'222'0941 — British cars, *1920-1930*
Spicer, S. J. L.. The motor cars we owned : Austin, Ford, Morris, Vauxhall, 1920-1930 / S.J.L. Spicer. — Hornchurch : Ian Henry, 1981. — 33p : ill ; 16x22cm
ISBN 0-86025-848-3 : £2.95 B81-12282

629.2'222'0941 — British cars, *1945-1967*
Wood, Jonathan. The enthusiast's guide to British postwar classic cars / Jonathan Wood. — London : Osprey, 1980. — 272p : ill,ports ; 26cm
Bibliography: p269-270. — Includes index
ISBN 0-85045-377-1 (corrected) : £9.95 : CIP rev. B80-23407

629.2'222'0941 — British cars, *1960-1964 — Illustrations*
British cars of the early sixties 1960-1964 / compiled for the Olyslager Organisation by David J. Voller. — London : Warne, 1981. — 64p : ill ; 19x26cm. — (Olyslager auto library)
Includes index
ISBN 0-7232-2764-0 : £4.95 B81-20979

629.2'222'0941 — British cars — *Technical data — Serials*
Brief British passenger car data / the Associated Octel Company Limited. — 1981. — London (20 Berkeley Sq., W1X 6DT) : The Company, [1981]. — 42,xiip
Unpriced B81-29060

629.2'222'0941 — Great Britain. Cars — *For business firms — Serials*
Company car. — No.1-. — London (64, West Smithfield, EC1A 9EE) : FF Publishing, 1980-. — ill ; 30cm
Quarterly. — Description based on: No.3
ISSN 0261-0426 = Company car : £1.00 B81-15080

629.2'222'0943 — German cars — *Technical data — German texts — Serials*
Technische Daten deutscher Personenkraftwagen / AK Chemie. — 1981. — Biebesheim : AK Chemie ; London (20 Berkeley Sq., W1X 6DT) : Associated Octel Company, [1981]. — 61p in various pagings
Unpriced B81-32196

629.2'222'0944 — French cars — *Technical data — French texts — Serials*
Caractéristiques techniques des voitures particulières françaises / Octel S.A.. — 1981. — Paris : Octel S.A. ; London (20 Berkeley Sq., W1X 6DT) : Associated Octel Company [distributor], [1981]. — 38,xiip
Unpriced B81-29061

629.2'222'0945 — Italian cars — *Technical data — Italian texts — Serials*
Dati technici delle autovetture italiane / Società italiana additivi per carburanti. — 1981. — Milano : S.I.A.C. ; London (20 Berkeley Sq., W1X 6DT) : Associated Octel Company, [1981]. — 52p in various pagings
Unpriced B81-32197

629.2'222'0973 — United States. Cars, *1920-1940*
Wise, David Burgess. Classic American automobiles / by David Burgess Wise ; special photography by Nicky Wright. — London : Ebury, 1980. — 189p : ill(some col.),facsims,ports ; 32cm
Col. ill on lining papers. — Includes index
ISBN 0-85223-187-3 : £8.50 B81-02265

629.2'2233 — Buses, *to 1980*
Bruce, J. Graeme. A source book of buses. — London : Ward Lock, Oct.1981. — [128]p
ISBN 0-7063-6054-0 : £2.95 : CIP entry B81-28066

629.2'2233 — Dennis buses & motor coaches, *to 1979 — Illustrations*
Hannay, R. N.. Dennis buses in camera / R.N. Hannay. — London : Ian Allan, 1980. — 112p : ill ; 24cm
ISBN 0-7110-1044-7 : £5.95 B81-06158

629.2'2233 — London. Routemaster buses, *to 1981 — Illustrations*
Routemaster roundabout : a silver jubilee of service 1956-1981 / [compiled by] J.H. Blake and R.J. Williamson. — London (36 Cheddington Rd., N18 1LS) : Regent Transport, [1981]. — 64p : all col.ill ; 30cm
ISBN 0-906473-03-9 (pbk) : £3.50 B81-40838

629.2'2233'0941 — Great Britain. Bus services. Buses, *1904-1979*
Booth, Gavin. The classic buses / Gavin Booth. — London : Ian Allen, 1980. — 121p : ill,facsims ; 30cm
Ill on lining papers
ISBN 0-7110-1037-4 : £6.95 B81-02965

629.2'2233'0941 — Great Britain. Buses, *1930-1940*
Kye, David, *1929-*. The British bus scene in the 1930's / David Kaye. — London : Ian Allan, 1981. — 112p : ill,facsims,1port ; 25cm
ISBN 0-7110-1137-0 : £5.95 B81-36740

629.2'2233'0941 — Great Britain. Buses, *to 1975 — Illustrations*
Fenton, Mike, *1946-*. Omnibus gallery / Mike Fenton. — Cambridge : Stephens, 1981. — 88p : chiefly ill ; 25cm
ISBN 0-85059-503-7 : £4.95 : CIP rev. B81-07911

629.2'2233'09411 — Scotland. Bus services: W. Alexander & Sons (Northern) Ltd, W. Alexander & Sons (Midland) Ltd & W. Alexander & Sons (Fife) Ltd. Buses, *to 1981 — Technical data*
W. Alexander & Sons Limited. — [London] ([52 Old Park Ridings, N21 2ES]) : P.S.V. Circle. — (Fleet history ; PM8)
Part 3: (1938 to 1961) : incorporating David Lawson Limited, Kirkintilloch and the Pitlochry Motor Company Limited. — [1981]. — 92p,[4]p of plates : ill ; 30cm
Unpriced (pbk) B81-39914

629.2'2233'09421 — London. Bus services: London Transport. Buses, *to 1979 — Illustrations*
London's city buses / [compiled by] John A. Gray. — London : Ian Allan, 1979. — 128p : chiefly ill ; 25cm
ISBN 0-7110-0932-5 : £5.50 B81-22437

629.2'2233'09421 — London. Buses — *Serials*
London buses. — 1980 ed. — Shepperton : Ian Allan, 1980. — 80p
ISBN 0-7110-1049-8 : £1.95 B81-00143

629.2'2233'09422 — England. Home Counties. Bus services: London Country Bus Services. Routemaster buses, *to 1980*
Clark, Richard, *1948-*. In shades of green : the story of the Country Routemasters / Richard Clark. — London (36 Cheddington Rd., N18 1LS) : Regent Transport, c1980. — 47p : ill ; 30cm
ISBN 0-906473-02-0 (pbk) : £2.95 B81-07121

629.2′2233′09422 — Englnad. Home Counties. Bus services: London County Bus Services. Buses & a motor coaches

Chapman, Mark, *1956-*. London Country buses and Green Line coaches / Mark Chapman. — 1979/80 ed. / incorporating fleet list at 1st July 1979 compiled by David Stewart. — Stanmore : Capital Transport, 1979. — 64p : ill ; 21cm
Previous ed.: 1978
ISBN 0-904711-17-x (pbk) : £1.50 B81-40370

629.2′2233′09422 — South-east England. Buses, *1945-1980 — Illustrations*

Buses in camera, South-East / [compiled by] John Parke. — London : Ian Allan, 1981. — 112p : ill ; 25cm
ISBN 0-7110-0878-7 : £5.95 B81-32804

629.2′2233′0942496 — West Midlands *(Metropolitan County)*. Birmingham. Bus services. Birmingham City Transport. Buses, *to 1969*

Keeley, Malcolm. Birmingham city transport : a history of its buses and trolleybuses / by Malcolm Keeley, Monty Russell, Paul Gray on behalf of the 1685 Group and the Birmingham & Midland Motor Omnibus Trust. — Glossop : Transport Publishing, c1977. — 190p : ill,1map ; 21x30cm
Map attached to inside back cover
ISBN 0-903839-18-0 : £8.60 B81-18386

629.2′2233′0942527 — Nottinghamshire. Nottingham. Bus services. Nottingham City Transport. Buses, *to 1978*

Groves, F. P.. Nottingham City Transport / by F.P. Groves. — Glossop : Transport Publishing, c1978. — 95p : ill(some col.),col.facsims,maps ; 21x30cm
Text, ill on lining papers
ISBN 0-903839-25-3 : £6.75 B81-33122

629.2′2233′0942751 — Merseyside *(Metropolitan County)*. Birkenhead. Buses, *to 1970*

Fifty years of Birkenhead buses / [compiled] by Tom Turner. — [Glossop] : [Transport Publishing Company for Wallasey Tramcar Preservation Group], c1978. — 48p : ill ; 30cm
ISBN 0-903839-30-x (pbk) : £2.00 B81-36082

629.2′2233′09427623 — Lancashire. Blackburn *(District)*. Bus services. Buses, *to 1981*

Fergusson, R. P.. The first in the kingdom : 1881-1981 : a history of buses & trams in Blackburn & Darwen / by R.P. Fergusson, G. Holden, C. Reilly. — [Blackburn] ([48 Delph Approach, Blackburn BB1 2BH]) : [Darwen Transport Group], [1981]. — 54p : ill ; 22cm
Cover title
£1.50 (pbk)
Also classified at 625′.66′09427623 B81-23559

629.2′24 — Commercial vehicles. Preservation

Jenkinson, Keith. Preserving commercial vehicles. — Cambridge : Stephens, Feb.1982. — [128]p
ISBN 0-85059-502-9 : £9.95 : CIP entry B81-35838

629.2′24 — Foden lorries, *to 1980 — Illustrations*

Foden / [compiled by] E.L. Cornwell. — London : Ian Allan, 1981. — 95p : chiefly ill ; 25cm. — (Trucks in camera)
ISBN 0-7110-1097-8 : £4.95 B81-24855

629.2′24 — Heavy road vehicles. Design & construction

Nunes, Joseph. Diesel-heavy duty truck application and performance factors / Joseph Nunes. — Englewood Cliffs ; London : Prentice-Hall, c1981. — xii,179p : ill ; 24cm
Includes index
ISBN 0-13-211102-0 (pbk) : £8.40 B81-14697

629.2′24 — Lorries — *For children*

Crews, Donald. Truck / Donald Crews. — London : Bodley Head, 1981, c1980. — [32]p : all col.ill ; 21x26cm
Originally published: New York : Greenwillow, 1980
ISBN 0-370-30396-2 : £3.50 B81-16110

629.2′24 — Motor vans, *to 1979*

Martinez, Alberto. Vans. — London : Osprey, Nov.1981. — [192]p
Translation of: Les vans
ISBN 0-85045-441-7 : £8.95 : CIP entry B81-30580

629.2′24 — Off-road trucks

Ingram, Arthur. Off-highway and construction trucks / Arthur Ingram and Colin Peck. — Poole : Blandford, 1980. — 160p : ill(some col.) ; 26cm
Includes index
ISBN 0-7137-0960-x : £6.95 : CIP rev.
Also classified at 629.2′25 B80-18381

629.2′24′0294 — Commercial vehicles — *Buyers′ guides — Serials*

Commercial vehicle & PSV buyer′s guide. — 5-. — London : Kogan Page, 1981-. — v. : ill,maps ; 28cm
Annual. — Continues: Commercial vehicle buyer′s guide
ISSN 0261-0450 = Commercial vehicle & PSV buyer′s guide : £8.25 B81-31003

629.2′24′09 — Lorries — *History*

Kennett, Pat. World trucks / Pat Kennett. — Cambridge : Stephens
No.11: International. — 1981. — 88p : ill,facsims,1port ; 25cm
Ill on lining papers
ISBN 0-85059-449-9 : Unpriced : CIP rev. B81-07910

Kennett, Pat. World trucks / Pat Kennett. — Cambridge : Stephens
No.12: Berliet. — 1981. — 88p : ill,facsims,ports ; 25cm
Ill on lining papers
ISBN 0-85059-450-2 : Unpriced B81-24470

629.2′24′0941 — Great Britain. Commercial vehicles. Use, *1904-1978 — Case studies*

Bampton, Daphne. Rare and interesting commercial vehicles / by Daphne Bampton. — Melksham : Venton, c1979. — 172p,32p of plates : ill ; 23cm
Includes index
ISBN 0-85993-027-0 : £8.95 B81-01961

629.2′24′0973 — United States. Lorries

Martinez, Alberto. The long haul : trucking in America / Alberto Martinez, Jean-Loup Nory. — London : Hamlyn, s1980. — 175p : ill(some col.),ports(some col.) ; 31cm
Translation of: Les camions Americains
ISBN 0-600-34955-1 : £7.95 B81-14263

629.2′25 — Construction motor vehicles

Ingram, Arthur. Off-highway and construction trucks / Arthur Ingram and Colin Peck. — Poole : Blandford, 1980. — 160p : ill(some col.) ; 26cm
Includes index
ISBN 0-7137-0960-x : £6.95 : CIP rev.
Primary classification 629.2′24 B80-18381

629.2′25 — Earth-moving machinery

Harris, Frank, *1944-*. Construction plant : excavating and materials handling, equipment and methods / Frank Harris. — London : Granada, 1981. — vi,230p : ill ; 24cm
Bibliography: p223-224. — Includes index
ISBN 0-246-11237-9 (cased) : £15.00
ISBN 0-246-11557-2 (pbk) : Unpriced
Also classified at 621.8′6 B81-24513

629.2′272 — Bicycles

Ayres, Martin. Cycles & cycling / Martin Ayres. — London : Newnes Technical Books, 1981. — 81p : ill ; 17cm. — (Questions & answers)
Includes index
ISBN 0-408-00484-3 (pbk) : Unpriced B81-19453

629.2′272 — Bicycles — *For children*

Dixon, Annabelle. Bicycles / Annabelle Dixon. — London : Black, c1981. — 32p : ill,1port ; 23cm. — (Science explorers)
Includes index
ISBN 0-7136-2138-9 : £2.95 : CIP rev. B81-26723

Hossent, Harry. The Beaver book of bikes / Harry Hossent ; illustrated by Peter Gregory ; cartoons by Maggie Ling. — London (Banda House, Cambridge Grove, W6 0LE) : Beaver, 1980. — 127p : ill ; 18cm
ISBN 0-600-20198-8 (pbk) : £0.95 B81-10025

629.2′272 — Bicycles — *Manuals*

Knottley, Peter. You and your bicycle. — London : Ward Lock, Sept.1981. — [96]p
ISBN 0-7063-5960-7 (cased) : £3.95 : CIP entry
ISBN 0-7063-5961-5 (pbk) : £2.50 B81-25873

629.2′272 — Moulton bicycles, *to 1979*

Hadland, Tony. The Moulton bicycle / by Tony Hadland. — [Reading] ([2 Allwrights Cottages, Gallowstree Common, Reading, RG4 9DA]) : [T. Hadland], c1980. — 72p : ill ; 21cm
ISBN 0-9507431-0-0 (pbk) : Unpriced B81-10548

629.2′272′05 — Bicycles — *Serials*

Bicycle times. — No.1 (May 1980)-. — Newcastle upon Tyne (1 Warwick Ave., Whickham, Newcastle upon Tyne) : Kelthorn, 1980-. — v. : ill,ports ; 42cm
Monthly
ISSN 0260-6097 = Bicycle times : £5.00 per year B81-04819

Bicycle trade times. — No.1 (May 1980)-. — Newcastle upon Tyne (1 Warwick Ave., Whickham, Newcastle upon Tyne) : Kelthorn, 1980-. — v. : ill,ports ; 42cm
Monthly
ISSN 0260-6003 = Bicycle trade times : Unpriced B81-04820

629.2′275 — AMC motorcycles, *1947-1979 — Illustrations*

The First AMC racing scene. — Leatherhead (P.O. Box 20, Leatherhead, Surrey) : Bruce Main-Smith, c1980. — 64p : chiefly ill,ports ; 21cm
Ill on inside covers
Unpriced (pbk) B81-36802

629.2′275 — Ariel motorcycles, *1931-1980 — Illustrations*

The First classic Ariel scene. — Leatherhead (P.O. Box 20, Leatherhead, Surrey) : Bruce Main-Smith, c1981. — 64p : chiefly ill,ports ; 21cm
Ill on inside covers
Unpriced (pbk) B81-36803

629.2′275 — Douglas motorcycles, *to 1957*

Clew, Jeff. The Douglas motorcycle : 'The best twin' / Jeff Clew. — Rev. & enl. ed. — Yeovil : Foulis, c1981. — 250p : ill,facsims,ports ; 25cm. — (A Foulis motorcycling book)
Previous ed.: published as The best twin. Norwich : Goose, 1974. — Includes index
ISBN 0-85429-299-3 : £7.95 B81-31123

629.2′275 — Heavyweight motorcycles, *1905-1980*

Winfield, Mike. The superbikes / Mike Winfield and Laurie Caddell. — London : Orbis Publishing, 1981. — 160p : col.ill ; 29cm
ISBN 0-85613-280-2 : £5.95 B81-34242

629.2′275 — Lightweight motorcycles, *to 1980*

Woollett, Mick. Lightweight bikes / Mick Woollett. — London : Batsford, 1981. — 64p : ill(some col.),ports ; 20cm
Includes index
ISBN 0-7134-3913-0 (pbk) : £1.95 B81-33064

629.2′275 — Matchless motorcycles, *to 1969*

Hartley, Peter, *1933-*. Matchless : once the largest British motorcycle manufacturer / Peter Hartley. — London : Osprey, 1981. — 208p : ill,ports ; 24cm
Includes index
ISBN 0-85045-404-2 : £9.95 : CIP rev. B81-02669

629.2′275 — Motorcycles

Caddell, Laurie. Powerbikes / Laurie Caddell. — Poole : Blandford, 1981. — 160p : ill(some col.) ; 26cm
Includes index
ISBN 0-7137-1021-7 : £8.95 B81-24218

629.2'275 — Motorcycles — *For children*
Aspel, Geoff. Motor cycles / by Geoff Aspel ; illustrated by Jim Dugdale and Cliff Meadway. — London : Granada, 1981. — 64p : col.ill ; 19cm. — (Granada guides)
Includes index
ISBN 0-246-11629-3 : £1.95 B81-39303

Lorin, Philippe. All about motorbikes / Philippe Lorin, Jean Retailleau ; translated by Anthea Bell. — St. Albans : Hart-Davis Educational, 1981. — 52p : ill(some col.),1map,ports ; 27cm
Translated from the French. — Ill on lining papers
ISBN 0-247-13085-0 : £3.45 B81-24466

629.2'275 — Motorcycles — *Manuals*
Dyson, John. The motorcycling book / John Dyson ; illustrated by Lionel Willis. — Harmondsworth : Puffin, 1981, c1977. — 178p : ill ; 20cm. — (Puffin plus)
Originally published: Harmondsworth : Penguin, 1977. — Includes index
ISBN 0-14-031426-1 (pbk) : £1.10 B81-25198

Willoughby, Vic. Back to basics / Vic Willoughby. — Yeovil : Haynes, 1981. — 120p : ill,1port ; 24cm. — (A Foulis motorcycling book)
ISBN 0-85429-288-8 (pbk) : £1.95 B81-24211

629.2'275 — Norton twin cylinder motorcycles, *to 1979*
Bacon, Roy. Norton twins : the postwar 500, 600, 750, 850 & lightweight twins. — London : Osprey, Sept.1981. — [208]p
ISBN 0-85045-423-9 : £7.95 : CIP entry
B81-20466

629.2'275 — Trail motorcycles — *Buyers' guides*
Melling, Frank. Enduro motorcycles. — London : Osprey, Nov.1981. — [144]p
ISBN 0-85045-406-9 (pbk) : £5.95 : CIP entry
B81-30615

629.2'275 — Triumph motorcycles, *to 1960*
Davies, Ivor, *1913-*. It's a Triumph / Ivor Davies. — Yeovil : Haynes, 1980. — 237p : ill,facsims,ports ; 26cm. — (A Foulis motorcycling book)
ISBN 0-85429-182-2 : £8.50 B81-01832

629.2'275 — Triumph motorcycles, *to 1980*
Bacon, Roy H.. Triumph twins and triples / Roy Bacon. — London : Osprey, 1981. — 192p : ill,ports ; 22cm. — (Osprey collector's library)
ISBN 0-85045-403-4 : £7.95 : CIP rev.
B81-12872

629.2'275 — Triumph motorcycles, *to 1981*
Louis, Harry. The story of Triumph motor cycles / Harry Louis and Bob Currie. — 3rd ed. — [Cambridge] : Stephens, 1981. — 144p : ill,ports ; 25cm
Previous ed.: 1978. — Includes index
ISBN 0-85059-480-4 : £7.95 B81-33217

629.2'275'0294 — Motorcycles — *Buyers' guides — Serials*
Daily mail Motorcycle Show review. — [1981]. — London : Harmondsworth Publications for Associated Newpapers Group, c1981. — 64p
ISSN 0140-4954 : £0.75 B81-24698

629.2'275'09 — Motorcycles, *to 1960*
Crowley, T. E.. Discovering old motorcycles / T.E. Crowley. — [New] ed. — Aylesbury : Shire, 1981. — 55p : ill,1facsim,ports ; 18cm. — (Discovering series ; no.160)
Previous ed.: 1977. — Bibliography: p52-53. — Includes index
ISBN 0-85263-557-5 (pbk) : £0.95 B81-40743

629.2'28 — Lotus racing cars, *to 1978*
Nye, Doug. Theme Lotus / Doug Nye. — London : Motor Racing Publications, 1978. — 200p : ill,ports ; 26cm
ISBN 0-900549-40-8 : £9.95 B81-17080

629.2'28 — Porsche racing cars, *1970-1979*
Frère, Paul. Porsche racing cars of the 70s / Paul Frère. — Cambridge : Stephens, 1980. — 164p : ill(some col.),ports ; 25cm
Includes index
ISBN 0-85059-442-1 : £8.95 B81-32724

629.2'28 — Racing cars — *For children*
Rutland, Jonathan. The young engineer book of supercars / [written by Jonathan Rutland] ; [illustrators Malcolm English et al., special photography by Peter Mackertich]. — London : Usborne, 1978. — 32p : chiefly ill(some col.) ; 28cm
Bibliography: p32. - Includes index
ISBN 0-86020-181-3 (pbk) : Unpriced
B81-19744

629.2'28'09 — Racing cars, *to 1979*
Nye, Doug. Racing cars / Doug Nye. — London : Ward Lock, 1980. — 93p : ill(some col.) ; 25cm. — ([Classic car guides])
Includes index
ISBN 0-7063-6038-9 : £3.95 : CIP rev.
B80-10126

629.2'292 — Steam road wagons, *to ca 1960*
Whitehead, R. A.. A kaleidoscope of steam wagons / by R.A. Whitehead. — London (17 Air St., W.1) : Marshall Harris & Baldwin, 1979. — [96]p : ill,facsims,1port ; 31cm
Facsims on lining papers. — Includes index
ISBN 0-906116-10-4 : £5.95 B81-09258

629.2'292'0941 — Great Britain. Preserved traction engines — *Illustrations*
Finch, Barry J.. Traction engines in colour / Barry J. Finch. — London : Ian Allan, 1980. — 111p : ill(some col.) ; 19x25cm
ISBN 0-7110-1032-3 : £10.95 B81-03111

629.2'292'0941 — Great Britain. Traction engines, *to 1960 — Illustrations*
Beaumont, Anthony. Steam at work : road and farm engines / Anthony Beaumont. — Newton Abbot : David & Charles, c1981. — 95p : ill ; 26cm
Includes index
ISBN 0-7153-8121-0 : £6.50 : CIP rev.
B81-14426

629.2'293 — Battery operated cars
Hamilton, William, *1934-*. Electric automobiles : energy, environmental, and economic prospects for the future / Willam Hamilton. — Bogotá ; London : McGraw-Hill, c1980. — xxi,425p : ill ; 29cm
Includes index
ISBN 0-07-025735-3 : £16.50 B81-10841

629.2'293 — Battery operated road vehicles
Christian, Jeffrey M.. World guide to battery-powered road transportation : comparative technical and performance specifications / compiled by Jeffrey M. Christian. — New York ; London : McGraw-Hill, c1980. — 392p : ill ; 29cm
Includes index
ISBN 0-07-010790-4 : £34.50 B81-38877

629.23 — MOTOR VEHICLES. CONSTRUCTION

629.2'31 — Cars. Avant garde designs, *1933-1979*
Piccard, Jean-Rodolphe. Dream cars / Jean-Rodolphe Piccard ; [translated from the French by Ian Norris]. — London : Orbis, 1981. — 201p : ill(some col.),ports ; 32cm
ISBN 0-85613-382-5 : Unpriced B81-28913

629.2'31 — Motor vehicles. Durability — *Conference proceedings*
Impact of vehicle design on whole life costing : conference sponsored by the Automobile Division of the Institution of Mechanical Engineers and co-sponsored by the Institute of Automotive Engineer Assessors, Institution Headquarters 21-23 October 1980. — London : Mechanical Engineering for the Institution of Mechanical Engineers, 1980. — 142p : ill ; 30cm. — (I Mech E conference publications ; 1980-7)
Includes bibliographies
ISBN 0-85298-468-5 (pbk) : Unpriced
B81-11049

629.2'31 — Road vehicles. Stress analysis — *For design*
Fenton, John, *1931-*. Vehicle body layout and analysis / by John Fenton. — London : Mechanical Engineering Publications, 1980. — xvii,184p : ill ; 24cm
ISBN 0-85298-445-6 : £19.50 B81-04482

629.24/7 — MOTOR VEHICLES. PARTS

629.2'43 — Cars. Suspension
Campbell, Colin, *1913-*. Automobile suspensions / Colin Campbell. — London : Chapman and Hall, 1981. — x,213p : ill ; 22cm
Includes index
ISBN 0-412-16420-5 (cased) : £8.50 : CIP rev.
B80-36166

629.2'5 — Cars. Engines
Crouse, William H.. Automotive fuel, lubricating, and cooling systems. — 6th ed. / William H. Crouse, Donald L. Anglin. — New York ; London : Gregg Division/McGraw-Hill, c1981. — ix,325p : ill ; 28cm
Previous ed.: 1976. — Includes index
ISBN 0-07-014862-7 (pbk) : £12.50 B81-24284

Ellinger, Herbert E.. Automotive engines : theory and servicing / Herbert E. Ellinger. — [Updated and expanded]. — Englewood Cliffs ; London : Prentice-Hall, 1981. — xi,430p : ill ; 29cm
Previous ed.: 1974. — Includes index
ISBN 0-13-054999-1 : £11.00 B81-21368

629.2'504 — Cars. Petrol engines. Tuning — *Amateurs' manuals*
Campbell, Colin. Tuning for economy. — London : Chapman and Hall, Dec.1981. — [100]p
ISBN 0-412-23480-7 (cased) : £8.00 : CIP entry
ISBN 0-412-23490-4 (pbk) : £4.00 B81-31710

629.2'504 — Cars. Stratified charge engines — *Conference proceedings*
Stratified charge automotive engines : conference sponsored by the Automobile Division of the Institution of Mechanical Engineers, 25-26 November 1980, Institution Headquarters, 1 Birdcage Walk, Westminster, London. — London : Mechanical Engineering for the Institution, 1980. — 116p : ill ; 30cm. — (I Mech E conference publications ; 1980-9)
ISBN 0-85298-469-3 (pbk) : Unpriced
B81-11050

629.2'504 — Motor vehicles. Petrol engines. Tuning — *Amateurs' manuals*
Gayler, Bob. Piper tuning manual / Bob Gayler. — Sparkford : Foulis, 1981. — 44p : ill ; 27cm
ISBN 0-85429-292-6 (pbk) : £2.95 B81-26265

629.2'504 — Vehicles. Four-stroke petrol engines. Tuning — *Amateurs' manuals*
Bell, A. Graham. Performance tuning in theory and practice : four strokes / A. Graham Bell. — Yeovil : Haynes, 1981. — 252p : ill ; 24cm. — (A Foulis book)
Includes index
ISBN 0-85429-275-6 : Unpriced B81-17138

629.2'504 — Vehicles. Two-stroke engines. Tuning - *Amateurs' manuals*
Bacon, Roy. Two-stroke tuning. — Isleworth : Transport Bookman Publications, May 1981. — 1v.
ISBN 0-85184-039-6 (pbk) : £4.25 : CIP entry
B81-13840

629.2'52 — Cars. Petrol engines. Fibre reinforced plastics intake manifolds. Design & manufacture
Rowbotham, E. M.. Achieving the impossible : plastic intake manifold / E.M. Rowbotham, G.D. Suthurst. — London : British Plastics Federation, 1980. — 23p : ill ; 30cm
Paper no.33 of Markets for the 80's : The Reinforced Plastics Congress 1980
Unpriced (unbound) B81-25233

629.2'538 — Motor vehicles. Petrol. Quality — *Statistics — Serials*
World-wide survey of motor gasoline quality. — May 1981. — [Ellesmere Port] ([Ellesmere Port, South Wirral L65 4HF]) : Associated Octel Co. Ltd., 1981. — 102p
Unpriced B81-29047

629.2'54 — Cars. Electric equipment
Crouse, William H.. Automotive electronics and electrical equipment / William H. Crouse. — 9th ed. — New York ; London : Gregg Division, c1981. — viii,360p : ill ; 28cm
Previous ed.: published as Automotive electrical equipment. 1977. — Includes index
ISBN 0-07-014831-7 (pbk) : £12.50 B81-20797

629.2′54′0288 — Motor vehicles. Electric equipment. Maintenance & repair — *Manuals*

Weathers, Tom. Fundamentals of electricity and automotive electrical systems / Tom Weathers, Jr., Claud C. Hunter. — Englewood Cliffs ; London : Prentice-Hall, c1981. — viii,216p : ill ; 28cm
Includes index
ISBN 0-13-337030-5 (pbk) : £11.00 B81-25458

629.2′54′076 — Cars. Electrical systems — *Questions & answers*

Coker, A. J.. Automobile electrical systems / A.J. Coker. — 4th ed / rev. by Bob Krafft. — London : Newnes Technical, 1981. — 153p : ill ; 17cm. — (Questions & answers)
Previous ed.: published as Questions and answers on automobile electrical systems. 1973. — Includes index
ISBN 0-408-00598-x (pbk) : Unpriced : CIP rev. B81-12852

629.2′6 — Cars. Bodywork. Design, *to 1981*

Oliver, George A.. Cars and coachbuilding : one hundred years of road vehicle development / George Oliver. — London : Sotheby Parke Bernet published in association with the Institute of British Carriage and Automobile Manufacturers, 1981. — 256p,[16]p of plates : ill(some col.) ; 28cm
Bibliography: p251. — Includes index
ISBN 0-85667-105-3 : Unpriced B81-28938

629.2′6 — Cars. Custom-built bodywork, *1928-1931* — *Readings from contemporary sources*

The **golden** age of the luxury car : an anthology of articles & photographs from Autobody 1927-1931 / edited by George Hildebrand. — New York : Dover Publications ; London : Constable, c1980. — viii,152p : ill,ports ; 29cm
Includes index
ISBN 0-486-23984-5 (pbk) : £3.60 B81-22262

629.2′6 — Cars. Glass reinforced plastic bodywork

Wood, Richard, *1915-*. Car bodywork in glass reinforced plastics / Richard Wood. — London : Pentech, 1980. — 212p : ill ; 23cm
Bibliography: p208. — Includes index
ISBN 0-7273-0304-x : £8.95 : CIP rev. B80-13442

629.2′6 — Motor vehicles. Bodywork — *For technicians*

Fairbrother, J.. Fundamentals of vehicle bodywork / J. Fairbrother. — London : Hutchinson, 1981. — 157p : ill ; 25cm
Includes index
ISBN 0-09-144390-3 (cased) : £12.00 : CIP rev.
ISBN 0-09-144391-1 (pbk) : £5.95 B81-02354

629.2′6′0288 — Cars. Bodywork. Maintenance & repair — *Manuals*

Deroche, A. G.. The principles of auto body repairing and repainting. — 3rd ed / A.G. Deroche and N.N. Hildebrand. — Englewood Cliffs ; London : Prentice-Hall, c1981. — xviii,663p : ill ; 25cm
Previous ed.: / by A. Tait, A.G. Deroche, N.N. Hildebrand. 1976. — Includes index
ISBN 0-13-705665-6 : £12.30 B81-17296

629.2′6′0288 — Great Britain. Motor vehicles. Refinishing — *Serials*

Automotive & commercial refinisher. — Sept.1980-. — High Wycombe (PO Box 46, Burke House, 21 High St., High Wycombe HP11 2BZ) : Burke House Periodicals, 1980-. — v. : ill ; 30cm
Monthly
ISSN 0144-3496 = Automotive & commercial refinisher : Unpriced B81-04875

629.2′7 — Cars. Electronic equipment. Projects — *Amateurs′ manuals*

Penfold, R. A.. Electronic projects for cars and boats. — London : Babani, Oct.1981. — [96]p. — (BP94)
ISBN 0-85934-069-4 (pbk) : £1.95 : CIP entry B81-30192

629.28 — MOTOR VEHICLES. OPERATION AND MAINTENANCE

629.28′32 — Cars. Driving — *Manuals*

Hardwicke, T. H.. Teach yourself to drive / by T.H. Hardwicke. — London (31 The Pines, Chase Rd., Oakwood N14 4EX) : T.H. Hardwicke, c1981. — 56leaves : ill ; 36cm
Includes index
Unpriced (pbk) B81-37105

Jones, H.. RAC learner driver′s guide / H. Jones. — Plymouth : Published by Continua Productions in association with the Royal Automobile Club, 1979 (1980 [printing]). — viii,117p : ill ; 19cm
Includes index
ISBN 0-7227-0108-x (pbk) : £1.25 B81-27736

Sullivan, Norman. The complete learner driver : a reference book for all drivers, driving instructors and — particularly — learning drivers / Norman Sullivan. — London (83 Pall Mall [SW1Y 5HS]) : Royal Automobile Club, 1980. — viii,389p : ill ; 22cm
Includes index
ISBN 0-902628-87-9 (pbk) : £4.50 B81-01622

Topper, A. Tom. Very advanced driving / by A. Tom Topper. — Fully revised and re-set. — Kingswood : Elliot Right Way, 1981. — 191p : ill ; 18cm. — (Paperfronts)
Previous ed.: 1970. — Includes index
ISBN 0-7160-0665-0 (pbk) : £0.75 B81-24319

629.28′44 — Great Britain. Heavy commercial vehicles. Driving tests

Soye, David P.. A guide to the heavy goods vehicle driving test and licences / David P. Soye. — 3rd ed. — London : Kogan Page, 1981. — 95p : ill,forms ; 22cm
Previous ed.: 1978
ISBN 0-85038-458-3 (cased) : £5.95
ISBN 0-85038-459-1 (pbk) : £3.25 B81-19542

629.28′722 — Audi 100 cars. Maintenance & repair — *Amateurs′ manuals*

Audi 100, Avant, 5000 1976-80 autobook : Audi 100 Avant L 1977-80, Audi 100 Avant GL-5S 1978-80, Audi 100 Avant CD-5E 1977-80, Audi 100 LS, GLS 1976-78, Audi 100 GL-5E 1977-80, Audi 100 L5S 1978-80, Audi 100 GL-5S 1978-80, Audi 100 CD-5E 1978-80, Audi 5000 1978-80 / by the Autobooks team of writers and illustrators. — Brighton : Autobooks, [1980]. — 208p : ill ; 25cm. — (The Autobook series of workshop manuals)
Includes index
ISBN 0-85147-954-5 : £4.95 B81-20871

629.28′722 — Austin mini Metro cars. Maintenance & repair — *Amateurs′ manuals*

Legg, A. K.. Austin Metro owners workshop manual : models covered Austin mini Metro Standard, L and HLE. 998cc, Austin mini Metro 1.3S and 1.3HLS. 1275cc / A.K. Legg. — Yeovil : Haynes, c1981. — 174p : ill ; 28cm
Includes index
ISBN 0-85696-718-1 : Unpriced B81-31394

Metro 1.0, 1.3, 1980-81 autobook : Austin Metro 1.0, L, HLE 1981-81, Austin Metro 1.35, HLS 1980-81 / by the Autobooks team of writers and illustrators. — Wakefield : Autobooks, 1981. — 144p : ill ; 25cm. — (The Autobook series of workshop manuals ; 986)
Includes index
ISBN 0-85146-177-8 : £5.95 B81-36869

629.28′722 — BMW 2000 & 2002 cars. Maintenance & repair — *Amateurs′ manuals*

BMW 2000/2002 : BMW 2000/2002 1966/76 : BMW 2000 1966-73, BMW 2000 CA 1966-70, BMW 2000 CS 1966-70, BMW 2000 TI 1966-69, BMW 2000 TI Lux 1966-70, BMW 2002 1968-76, BMW 2002 Tii 1971-76 / by the Autbooks team of writers and illustrators. — Wakefield : Autobooks, 1981. — 183p ; 25cm. — (Autobooks special workshop manual ; 601)
Includes index
ISBN 0-85146-150-6 : £5.95 B81-34088

629.28′722 — British Leyland Mini cars. Maintenance & repair — *Amateurs′ manuals*

Mini : owners maintenance and repair guide : all 848, 970, 997, 998, 1071, 1098 and 1275cc manual and automatic models, 1959-80 / by the Autobooks team of technical writers and illustrators. — 2nd ed., fully rev.. — Brighton : Autobooks, [1980]. — 196p : ill(some col.) ; 25cm
Previous ed.:1979. — Includes index
ISBN 0-85146-044-5 : £4.95 B81-20874

629.28′722 — British Leyland Princess cars. Maintenance & repair — *Amateurs′ manuals*

Princess 18/22 : Leyland Princess 1800, HL 1975-78, 2200 HL, HLS 1975-78, Austin 1800 HL 1975, 2200 HL 1975, Morris 1800 HL 1975, 2200 HL 1975, Wolseley 2200 1975. — 3rd ed. / UNIPART. — [Brighton] : [Autobooks, by arrangement with Unipart], [1980]. — 176p : ill ; 26cm
Previous ed.: published as Princess 18-22 1975-77 autobook / by Kenneth Ball and the Autobooks team of technical writers. — Includes index
ISBN 0-85146-938-8 : £4.95 B81-20866

629.28′722 — Cars. Maintenance & repair — *Amateurs′ manuals*

Bott, John, *19---*. Car care / John Bott. — London : Warne, 1981. — 63p : ill ; 22cm. — (An Observer′s guide. Home and garden)
ISBN 0-7232-2480-3 (pbk) : £1.95 B81-21258

RAC motorists′ easy guide to car care and repair. — London : Royal Automobile Club
1: How a car works. — 1980. — 48p : ill ; 21cm
Includes index
ISBN 0-902628-78-x (pbk) : £1.00 B81-38712

Ward, Ian, *1949-*. Car maintenance made easy / Ian Ward. — London : Orbis, c1980. — 64p : ill(some col.) ; 29cm
Includes index
ISBN 0-85613-043-5 : £2.95 B81-09794

629.28′722 — Cars. Maintenance & repair — *Manuals*

Remling, John. Basics / John Remling. — New York ; Chichester : Wiley, c1981. — 501p in various pagings : ill,forms ; 28cm. — (Wiley automotive series)
Includes index
ISBN 0-471-04762-7 (pbk) : £8.00 B81-09660

629.28′722 — Cars. Repair — *Manuals*

Grouse, William H.. Automotive technician′s handbook / William H. Crouse and Donald L. Anglin. — New York ; London : McGraw-Hill, c1979. — vii,664p : ill ; 29cm
Includes index
ISBN 0-07-014751-5 : £15.95 B81-27562

629.28′722 — Citroën 2CV cars, Citroën Ami cars & Citroën Dyane cars. Maintenance & repair — *Amateurs′ manuals*

Coomber, Ian. Citroën 2-cylinder owners workshop manual : models covered Citroën 2cv, Ami (except Super) and Dyane / I.M. Coomber. — Yeovil : Haynes, c1981. — 182p : ill(some col.) ; 28cm. — (Owners workshop manual)
Includes index
ISBN 0-85696-196-5 : £5.95 B81-10595

629.28′722 — Colt 1400 GLX cars. Maintenance & repair — *Amateurs′ manuals*

Strasman, Peter G.. Colt 1400 GLX owners workshop manual : models covered : all models of the Colt 1400 GLX hatchback / Peter G. Strasman. — Yeovil : Haynes, c1981. — 244p : ill(some col.) ; 28cm
Includes index
ISBN 0-85696-600-2 : £5.95 B81-29358

629.28′722 — Daimler Sovereign cars. Maintenance & repair — *Amateurs′ manuals*

Jaguar XJ6, Daimler Sovereign : Jaguar XJ6 2.8 litre 1968-73, XJ6 3.4 litre, XJ 3.4 1975-78, XJ6 4.2 litre, XJ 4.2 1968-78, Daimler Sovereign 2.8 litre 1969-73, Sovereign 3.4 litre 1975-77, Sovereign 4.2 litre 1969-78. — 7th ed. / UNIPART. — [Brighton] : [Autobooks, by arrangement with Unipart], [1979]. — 192p : ill ; 26cm
Previous ed.: published as Jaguar XJ6, Daimler Sovereign 1968-78 autobook / by Kenneth Ball and the Autobooks team of technical writers. — Includes index
ISBN 0-85146-915-9 : £4.95
Also classified at 629.28′722 B81-20868

629.28′722 — Fiat Strada cars. Maintenance & repair — *Amateurs′ manuals*

Strasman, Peter G.. Fiat Strada : all UK models, 1979 to 1980 65L, 65CL and 75CL / by Peter G. Strasman. — Yeovil : Haynes, c1981. — 109p : ill ; 24cm. — (Owner′s handbook / servicing guide)
ISBN 0-85696-652-5 (pbk) : £2.75 B81-16442

Strasman, Peter G.. Fiat Strada owners workshop manual : models covered UK, Strada 65L and 65CL models with 1301cc engine, Strada 75CL models with 1498cc engine, USA, Strada Standard and Custom models with 91-44 cu in (1498cc) engine / Peter G. Strasman. — Yeovil : Haynes, c1981. — 201p : ill ; 28cm. — (Owners workshop manual)
Includes index
ISBN 0-85696-479-4 : £5.95 B81-10596

629.28′722 — Ford Capri 1300 & 1600 OHV cars. Maintenance & repair — *Amateurs′ manuals*

Ball, Kenneth. Ford Capri 1300 OHV, 1600 OHV 1968-79 autobook : Ford Capri 1300 OHV series 1 1968-74, Ford Capri 1300 GT OHV series 1 1968-71, Ford Capri 1600 OHV series 1 1968-72, Ford Capri 1600 GT OHV series 1 1968-72, Ford Capri 1300 OHV series 2 1974-1979 / by Kenneth Ball and the Autobooks team of technical writers. — [9th ed. fully rev.]. — Brighton : Autobooks, [1979]. — 176p : ill ; 26cm. — (The Autobook series of workshop manuals)
Previous ed.: 1978. — Includes index
ISBN 0-85147-973-1 : Unpriced B81-16621

629.28′722 — Ford Capri 2000 & 3000 cars. Maintenance & repair — *Amateurs′ manuals*

Ford Capri V4, V6 1969-80 autobook : Ford Capri 2000 V4, Series 1 1969-74, Ford Capri 3000 V6, Series 1 1969-74, Ford Capri 3000 V6, Series 2 1974-78, Ford Capri 3000 V6, Series 3 1978-80. — [8th ed., fully rev.] / by the Autobooks team of writers and illustrators. — Brighton : Autobooks, [1980]. — 168p : ill ; 25cm. — (The Autobook series of workshop manuals)
Previous ed.: published as Ford Capri 2000 V4, 3000 V6, 1969/79 autobook / by Kenneth Ball and the Autobooks team of technical writers. — Includes index
ISBN 0-85146-148-4 : £4.95 B81-20873

629.28′722 — Ford Cortina Mk 4 cars. Maintenance & repair — *Amateurs′ manuals*

. Ford Cortina Mk.4 1976-79 autobook : Ford Cortina Mk.4 1.3, L 1976-79 Ford Cortina Mk.4 1.6, GL, Ghia 1976-79 Ford Cortina Mk.4 2.0 GL, S, Ghia 1976-79, Ford Cortina Mk.4 2.3, GL, S, 1977-79. — [4th ed., fully rev.], by the Autobooks team of writers and illustrators. — Wakefield : Autobooks, [1980] ([1981 printing]). — 184p : ill ; 25cm. — (The Autobook series of workshop manuals)
Previous ed.: 1979. — Includes index
ISBN 0-85146-124-7 : Unpriced B81-32559

629.28′722 — Ford Cortina Mk3 cars. Maintenance & repair — *Amateurs′ manuals*

Haynes, J. H.. Ford Cortina III owners workshop manual / by J.H. Haynes, P.G. Strasman and B.L. Chalmers-Hunt. — Yeovil : Haynes, c1979. — 240p : ill(some col.) ; 28cm
Includes index
ISBN 0-900550-70-8 : £5.95 B81-29745

629.28′722 — Ford Escort cars. Maintenance & repair — *Amateurs′ manuals*

Ford Escort 1975-80 autobook : Ford Escort Popular 1.1, 1.3 1975-80, Ford Escort Popular Plus 1.1, 1.3 1975-80, Ford Escort 1.1, L 1975-80, Ford Escort 1.3, L, GL 1975-80, Ford Escort Sport 1.3, 1.6 1975-80, Ford Escort Ghia 1.3, 1.6 1975-80, Ford Escort Van 30, 45 1975-80 / by the Autobooks team of writers and illustrators. — [6th ed., fully rev.]. — Brighton : Autobooks, [1980]. — 138p : ill ; 25cm. — (The Autobook series of workshop manuals)
Previous ed.: published as Ford Escort 1975-79 autobook. — Includes index
ISBN 0-85146-173-5 : £4.95 B81-20872

629.28′722 — Ford Mustang V8 cars. Maintenance & repair — *Amateurs′ manuals*

Haynes, J. H.. Ford Mustang owners workshop manual / by J.H. Haynes, Bruce Gilmour and Marcus S. Daniels. — Yeovil : Haynes, c1979. — 288p : ill ; 29cm
Includes index
ISBN 0-85696-357-7 : £5.95 B81-40584

629.28′722 — Ford New Escort cars. Maintenance & repair — *Amateurs′ manuals*

Ford new Escort (front wheel drive) : 1980-81 autobook : Ford Escort 1.1, L 1980-81, Ford Escort 1.3, L, Ghia 1980-81, Ford Escort 1.6L, GL, Ghia, XR3 1980-81 / by the Autobooks team of writers and illustrators. — Wakefield : Autobooks, 1981. — 184p : ill ; 25cm. — (Autobooks owners workshop manual ; 984)
Includes index
ISBN 0-85146-176-x : Unpriced B81-38022

629.28′722 — Hillman Hunter cars. Maintenance & repair — *Amateurs′ manuals*

Ball, Kenneth. Chrysler Hillman Hunter 1966-79 autobook : Chrysler Hunter, Super 1977-79, Hillman Hunter, Super, GL, GLS, GT 1966-77, Hillman GT 1969-70, Humber Sceptre 1967-76, Singer Vogue 1966-70, Sunbeam Rapier, H120 1967-76, Sunbeam Alpine, GT 1969-75, Sunbeam Arrow 1969-72 / by Kenneth Ball and the Autobooks team of technical writers. — [7th ed., fully rev.]. — Brighton : Autobooks, [1978]. — 160p : ill ; 25cm. — (The Autobook series of workshop manuals)
Previous ed.: published as Hillman Hunter 1966-1977 autobook. 1977. — Includes index
ISBN 0-85147-987-1 : Unpriced B81-16146

629.28′722 — Honda Civic cars. Maintenance & repair — *Amateurs′ manuals*

Ball, Kenneth. Civic 1973-77 autobook : Honda Civic 1200 1973-77, Honda Civic 1500 1975-77, Honda Civic 1975-77 / Kenneth Ball and John Plummer. — [2nd ed., fully rev.]. — Brighton : Autobooks, [1978]. — 176p : ill ; 26cm. — (Autobooks owners workshop manual ; 844)
Previous ed.: published as Civic 1973-6 autobook. — Includes index
ISBN 0-85147-756-9 : Unpriced B81-37671

629.28′722 — Jaguar XJ6 cars. Maintenance & repair — *Amateurs′ manuals*

Jaguar XJ6, Daimler Sovereign : Jaguar XJ6 2.8 litre 1968-73, XJ6 3.4 litre, XJ 3.4 1975-78, XJ6 4.2 litre, XJ 4.2 1968-78, Daimler Sovereign 2.8 litre 1969-73, Sovereign 3.4 litre 1975-77, Sovereign 4.2 litre 1969-78. — 7th ed. / UNIPART. — [Brighton] : [Autobooks, by arrangement with Unipart], [1979]. — 192p : ill ; 26cm
Previous ed.: published as Jaguar XJ6, Daimler Sovereign 1968-78 autobook / by Kenneth Ball and the Autobooks team of technical writers. — Includes index
ISBN 0-85146-915-9 : £4.95
Primary classification 629.28′722 B81-20868

629.28′722 — Lancia Beta cars, *1973-1980.* **Maintenance & repair** — *Amateurs′ manuals*

Methuen, P. M.. Lancia Beta owners workshop manual : models covered, UK : Lancia Beta Saloon, Coupe, HPE and Spider, series A and B models with 1297cc, 1301cc, 1438cc, 1585cc, 1592cc, 1756cc and 1995cc engines, USA : Lancia Beta Sedan, Coupe and HPE models with 107cu in (1.8 liter) and 122cu in (2 liter) engines, covers most features of Zagato models / P.M. Methuen. — Yeovil : Haynes, c1981. — 283p : ill(some col.) ; 28cm
Includes index
ISBN 0-85696-533-2 : £5.95 B81-29359

629.28′722 — Lotus Elan cars. Maintenance & repair — *Amateurs′ manuals*

Lotus Elan : Elan Plus 2 1962/74 : Lotus Elan 1600 1962-64, Lotus Elan Series 2 Convertible ... 1964-66, Lotus Elan Series 3 FH Coupé ... 1965-68, Lotus Elan Series 4 FH Coupé 1968-73, Lotus Elan Plus 2 FH Coupé ... 1967-69, Lotus Elan Plus 2S FH Coupé ... 1969-74 / by the Autobooks team of writers and illustrators. — Wakefield : Autobooks, 1981. — 160p,[9]p of plates : ill ; 25cm. — (Autobooks special workshop manual ; 600)
Includes index
ISBN 0-85147-894-8 : £5.95 B81-34087

629.28′722 — Mercedes-Benz 220/8 cars. Maintenance & repair — *Amateurs′ manuals*

Ball, Kenneth. Mercedes-Benz 220/8 1968-72 autobook : Mercedes-Benz 220/8 1968-72 / by Kenneth Ball and the Autobooks team of technical writers. — [2nd ed., fully rev.]. — Brighton : Autobooks, [1978]. — 176p : ill ; 26cm. — (The Autobook series of workshop manuals)
Previous ed.: 1972. — Includes index
ISBN 0-85147-990-1 : Unpriced B81-16623

629.28′722 — Mercedes-Benz 220B cars. Maintenance & repair — *Amateurs′ manuals*

Ball, Kenneth. Mercedes-Benz 22OB 1959-65 autobook : Mercedes-Benz 220B 1959-65, Mercedes-Benz 220SB 1959-65, Mercedes-Benz 220SEB 1959-65, Mercedes-Benz 220SEBC 1961-65 / by Kenneth Ball. — [2nd ed. fully rev.]. — Brighton : Autobooks, [1979]. — 186p : ill ; 26cm
Previous ed.: 1971. — Includes index
ISBN 0-85147-942-1 : £5.95 B81-16216

629.28′722 — MGB cars. Maintenance & repair — *Amateurs′ manuals*

MGB 1969-80 autobook : MG MGB Mk2 1969-71, MG MGB GT Mk2 1969-71, MG MGB Mk3 1971-80, MG MGB GT Mk3 1971-80 / by the Autobooks team of writers and illustrators. — [11th ed., fully rev.]. — Brighton : Autobooks, [1980]. — 192p : ill ; 25cm. — (The Autobook series of workshop manuals)
Previous ed.: 1979. — Includes index
ISBN 0-85146-172-7 : £4.95 B81-20867

629.28′722 — Peugeot 305 cars. Maintenance & repair — *Amateurs′ manuals*

Hawes, R. G. O.. Peugeot 305 owners workshop manual / R.G.O. Hawes. — Yeovil : Haynes, c1981. — 194p : ill(some col.) ; 28cm. — (Owners workshop manual)
Includes index
ISBN 0-85696-538-3 : £5.95 B81-10597

629.28′722 — Peugeot 504 diesel cars. Maintenance & repair — *Amateurs′ manuals*

Mead, John S.. Peugeot 504 owners workshop manual / John S. Mead. — Yeovil : Haynes, c1981. — 201p : ill ; 28cm. — (Owners workshop manual ; 663)
Includes index
ISBN 0-85696-663-0 : £5.95 B81-24530

629.28′722 — Porsche 924 cars. Maintenance & repair — *Amateurs′ manuals*

Lipton, Charles. Porsche 924 owners workshop manual : models covered : Porsche 924, Porsche 924 Turbo / Charles Lipton. — Newbury Park, Calif. ; Yeovil : Haynes, c1981. — 289p : ill(some col.) ; 28cm
Includes index
ISBN 0-85696-397-6 : Unpriced B81-17140

629.28′722 — Reliant Scimitar cars. Maintenance & repair — *Amateurs′ manuals*

Reliant Scimitar : Reliant Scimitar 2.5 GT 1968-70, Reliant Scimitar 3.0 GT 1968-70, Reliant Scimitar 3.0 GTE 1968-79 / by the Autobooks team of writers and illustrators. — Wakefield : Autobooks, 1981. — 184p,[7]p of plates : ill ; 25cm. — (Autobooks special workshop manual)
Includes index
ISBN 0-85146-151-4 : Unpriced B81-38024

629.28′722 — Renault 5 cars. Maintenance & repair — *Amateurs′ manuals*

Renault 5 1972-80 autobook : Renault 5 1977-80, Renault 5L 1972-77, Renault 5TL 1972-80, Renault 5TS 1975-80, Renault 5GTL 1976-80, Renault 5 1300 automatic 1979-80. — [6th ed., fully rev.] / by the Autobooks team of writers and illustrators. — Brighton : Autobooks, [1980]. — 162p : ill ; 25cm. — (The Autobook series of workshop manuals)
Previous ed.: published as Renault 5 1972-78 autobook / by Kenneth Ball and the Autobooks team of technical writers. — Includes index
ISBN 0-85146-114-x : £4.95 B81-20870

629.28′722 — Renault 8, 10 & 1100 cars. Maintenance & repair — *Amateurs′ manuals*

Ball, Kenneth. Renault 8, 1962-71 autobook / by Kenneth Ball and the Autobook Team of Technical Writers. — [5th ed., fully rev.]. — Brighton : Autobooks, [1976]. — 170p : ill ; 26cm. — (Autobook Owners Workshop Manual ; 715)
Previous ed.: 1972. — Includes index
ISBN 0-85147-657-0 : Unpriced B81-37670

629.28′722 — Renault 30 cars. Maintenance & repair — *Amateurs′ manuals*

Renault 30 1975-80 autobook : Renault 30TS 1975-80, Renault 30TX 1979-80 / by the Autobooks team of writers and illustrators. — 2nd ed. — Wakefield : Autobooks, 1981. — 144p : ill ; 25cm
Previous ed.: published as Renault 30 1975-1977 autobook / by Kenneth Ball and the Autobooks team of technical writers. 1978. — Includes index
ISBN 0-85146-149-2 : £4.95 B81-23229

629.28′722 — Simca 1100 & 1204 cars. Maintenance & repair — *Amateurs′ manuals*

Haynes, J. H.. Simca 1100 & 1204 owners workshop manual / by J.H. Haynes and P.G. Strasman. — Yeovil : Haynes, c1979. — 248p : ill ; 29cm
Includes index
ISBN 0-85696-507-3 : £5.95 B81-40583

629.28′722 — Skoda Estelle cars. Maintenance & repair — *Amateurs′ manuals*

Coomber, Ian. Skoda Estelle owners workshop manual : models covered, all Skoda Estelle models: 105S, 105L, 120L, 120LE, 120LS, 120GLS, 120LSE ; 1046cc and 1174cc / I.M. Coomber. — Yeovil : Haynes, c1981. — 157p : ill(some col.) ; 28cm. — (Owners workshop manual ; 604)
Includes index
ISBN 0-85696-604-5 : £5.95 B81-24959

629.28′722 — Talbot Alpine cars. Maintenance & repair — *Amateurs′ manuals*

Talbot Alpine 1975-80 autobook : Talbot Alpine GL, S, GLS 1975-80, Talbot Alpine LS, SX 1980. — [3rd ed., fully rev.] / by the Autobooks team of writers and illustrators. — Wakefield : Autobooks, [1980]. — 184p : ill ; 25cm. — (The Autobook series of workshop manuals)
Previous ed.: Published as Chrysler Alpine 1975-77 autobook / by Kenneth Ball and the Autobooks team of technical writers. 1978. — Includes index
ISBN 0-85146-144-1 : £4.95 B81-13646

629.28′722 — Vauxhall Victor FE cars & Vauxhall VX cars. Maintenance & repair — *Amateurs′ manuals*

Haynes, J. H.. Vauxhall Victor & VX4/90 FE series owners workshop manual / by J.H. Haynes and B.L. Chalmers-Hunt. — Yeovil : Haynes, c1979. — 263p : ill ; 29cm
Includes index
ISBN 0-85696-541-3 : £5.95 B81-40585

629.28′722 — Volkswagen Golf 1100 & 1300 cars. Maintenance & repair — *Amateurs′ manuals*

Golf 1100, 1300 1974-80 autobook : Volkswagen Golf N 1100 1974-80, Volkswagen Golf L 1100 1974-80, Volkswagen Golf LS 1300 1979-80, Volkswagen Golf GLS 1300 1979-80 / by the Autobooks team of writers and illustrators. — [4th ed., fully rev.]. — Brighton : Autobooks, [1980]. — 144p : ill ; 25cm. — (The Autobook series of workshop manuals)
Previous ed.: published as Golf N, L, 1100 1974-79 autobook. — Includes index
ISBN 0-85146-145-x : £4.95 B81-20865

629.28′722 — Volvo 260 cars. Maintenance & repair — *Amateurs′ manuals*

Volvo 260 series 1975-80 autobook : Volvo 264 DL, GL, GLE 1975-80, Volvo 265 DL, GL, GLE 1976-80. — [2nd ed., fully rev.] / by the Autobooks team of writers and illustrators. — Wakefield : Autobooks, [1980]. — 146p : ill ; 25cm. — (The Autobook series of workshop manuals)
Previous ed.: published as Volvo 260 series 1975-78 autobook / by Kenneth Ball and the Autobooks team of technical writers. 1978. — Includes index
ISBN 0-85146-147-6 : £4.95 B81-20869

629.28′722′05 — Old British cars. Maintenance & repair — *Amateurs′ manuals — Serials*

Practical classics : [the do-it-yourself magazine for the older-car owner and enthusiast]. — Vol.1, no.1 (Apr.1980)-. — Beckenham (5 Rectory Rd, Beckenham, Kent) : PPG Pub., 1980-. — v. : ill ; 29cm
Monthly. — Description based on: Vol.1, no.2 (June 1980)
ISSN 0260-2911 = Practical classics : £8.00 per year B81-04644

629.28′74 — Great Britain. Commercial vehicles. Maintenance & repair. Data. Recording — *Standards*

Vehicle maintenance reporting standards : handbook / Institute of Road Transport Engineers. — London (1 Cromwell Place, SW7 2JF) : Published by the Institute of Road Transport Engineers by kind permission of the American Trucking Association, 1981. — 1v.(loose-leaf) : ill,forms ; 32cm
Unpriced B81-24294

629.28′772 — Bicycles. Maintenance & repair — *Amateurs′ manuals*

Guide to bicycle repair and maintenance. — New York ; London : McGraw-Hill, c1981. — 101p : ill ; 28cm. — (McGraw-Hill paperbacks home improvement series)
ISBN 0-07-045965-7 (pbk) : £2.95 B81-34705

629.28′772 — Honda PA50 Camino mopeds. Maintenance & repair — *Amateurs′ manuals*

Rogers, Chris. Honda PA 50 Camino owners workshop manual / by Chris Rogers. — Yeovil : Haynes, c1981. — 94p : ill(some col.) ; 27cm
Routine maintenance guide (fold. sheet) as insert. — Includes index
Unpriced (corrected : pbk) B81-18419

629.28′775 — Honda CB650 four cylinder motorcycles. Maintenance & repair — *Amateurs′ manuals*

Meek, Martyn. Honda CB650 fours owners workshop manual : models covered CB650Z 626cc introduced UK 1978, USA 1979, CB650A 626cc introduced USA 1979, CB650 CA 626cc introduced USA 1979 / by Martyn Meek. — Yeovil : Haynes, c1981. — 160p : ill (some col.) ; 27cm + 1 Routine maintenance guide(1 Sheet : ill ; 54x41cm). — (Owners workshop manual)
Includes index
ISBN 0-85696-665-7 (pbk) : £3.95 B81-19776

629.28′775 — Honda CB750 & CB900 four cylinder motorcycles. Maintenance & repair — *Amateurs′ manuals*

Shoemark, Pete. Honda 750 & 900 dohc Fours : owners workshop manual / by Pete Shoemark. — Yeovil : Haynes, c1980. — 156p : ill(some col.) ; 27cm
Routine maintenance guide (folded sheet) as insert. — Includes index
ISBN 0-85696-535-9 (pbk) : Unpriced B81-08071

629.28′775 — Honda XL80, XR80, XL100, XL125, XL185, XR185 & XR200 motorcycles. Maintenance & repair — *Amateurs′ manuals*

Rogers, Chris. Honda XL/XR 80-200 owners workshop manual : models covered XL80S. 80cc, XR80. 80cc, XL100S. 99cc, XL125S. 124cc, XL185S. 180cc, XR185. 180cc, XR200. 195cc / by Chris Rogers. — Yeovil : Haynes, c1981. — 178p : ill (some col.) ; 27cm + 1 sheet (54x41cm folded to 27x21cm)
Includes index
ISBN 0-85696-566-9 (pbk) : Unpriced B81-31392

629.28′775 — Motorcycles. Maintenance & repair — *Amateurs′ manuals*

Motorcycle workshop / consultant editor David Buxton ; [book editors Yvonne Deutch, Randal Gray] ; [designer Val Heneghan]. — London : Collins, 1981. — 217p : ill(some col.) ; 30cm
Includes index
ISBN 0-00-411860-x : £7.95 B81-38896

Thorpe, John, *1928-*. Be your own motor cycle mechanic / John Thorpe ; with a foreword by Charles Deane. — London : Orbis, 1980. — 192p : col.ill ; 22cm
Includes index
ISBN 0-85613-035-4 : £4.95 B81-00961

629.28′775 — Motorcycles. Spraying & customising — *Amateurs′ manuals*

Revere, Paul. Do your own motor-bike spraying & customizing / by Paul Revere. — London : Foulsham, c1981. — 96p,[4]p of plates : ill (some col.) ; 23cm
Includes index
ISBN 0-572-01130-x : £4.95 B81-32547

629.28′775 — Suzuki GS850 motorcycles. Maintenance & repair — *Amateurs′ manuals*

Meek, Martyn. Suzuki GS850 fours owners workshop manual : models covered : GS850 GN843cc introduced UK 1979, USA 1978, GS850 GT843cc introduced UK and USA 1979, GS850 GLT843cc introduced USA only 1979 / by Martyn Meek. — Yeovil : Haynes, c1980. — 160p : ill(some col.) ; 27cm + Routine maintenance guide(folded sheet : col.ill ; 41x54cm. folded to 21x27cm). — (Owners workshop manual)
Includes index
ISBN 0-85696-536-7 (pbk) : Unpriced B81-11579

629.28′775 — Yamaha XS1100 motorcycles. Maintenance & repair — *Amateurs′ manuals*

Shoemark, Pete. Yamaha XS1100 Fours owners workshop manual : models covered XS1100E. 1101cc, XS1100F and SF. 1101cc, XS1100G. 1101cc, XS1100SG. 1101cc / by Pete Shoemark. — Yeovil : Haynes, c1981. — 190p : ill (some col.) ; 27cm + 1 sheet (54x41cm folded to 27x21cm)
Includes index
ISBN 0-85696-483-2 (pbk) : Unpriced B81-31393

629.3 — HOVERCRAFT

629.3′05 — Hovercraft — *Serials*

Jane′s surface skimmers. — 14th ed. (1981)-. — London : Jane′s, 1981. — 380p
£29.50
Also classified at 623.8′2314 B81-20082

629.4 — ASTRONAUTICS

629.4 — Astronautics — *For children*

Deutsch, Keith. Space travel : in fact and fiction / by Keith Deutsch. — New York ; London : Watts, 1980. — 86p : ill,ports ; 27cm. — (Fact and fiction series)
Bibliography: p81-83. - Includes index
ISBN 0-531-04156-5 : £2.99 B81-02248

629.4 — Instantaneous interstellar space flight. Use of black holes & iron stars

Berry, Adrian. The iron sun / Adrian Berry. — [London] : Coronet, 1979, c1977. — 176p : ill ; 18cm
Originally published: London : Cape, 1977. — Bibliography: p161-165. — Includes index
ISBN 0-340-23231-5 (pbk) : £0.95 B81-36884

629.4′1 — Space flight

Ince, Martin. Space / Martin Ince. — London : Sphere, 1981. — 215p,[8]p of plates : ill ; 18cm
ISBN 0-7221-4910-7 (pbk) : £1.50 B81-09346

629.4′1′09 — Space flight, *to 1980 — For children*

Cowley, Stewart. Space flight / by Stewart Cowley. — London : Kingfisher, 1981. — 91p : ill(some col.),ports(some col.) ; 19cm. — (A Kingfisher factbook)
Includes index
ISBN 0-86272-012-5 : £2.50 : CIP rev. B81-14404

629.4'1'09 — Space flight, *to 1981* **—** *For children*

Cowley, Stewart. Space flight / by Stewart Cowley. — London : Pan, 1981. — 91p : ill (some col.),charts,ports ; 18cm. — (A Piccolo factbook)
Text on inside cover. — Includes index
ISBN 0-330-26359-5 (pbk) : £1.25 B81-38770

629.44 — Space shuttles — *For children*

Furniss, Tim. The story of the space shuttle. — 2nd ed. — London : Hodder and Stoughton Children's Books, Feb.1982. — [128p]p
Previous ed.: 1979
ISBN 0-340-27967-2 : £5.95 : CIP entry B81-36369

629.44'5 — Outer space. Manned space flight. Skylab

Astronauts' requirements : ways to the stars! / edited by Brian Blair-Giles. — Surbiton (40 Claremont Rd., Surbiton, Surrey KT6 4RF) : B. Blair-Giles, c1981. — 77p in various pagings : ill,music,forms ; 30cm
£7.00 (unbound) B81-19584

629.45'009 — Manned space flight, *to 1980*

Furniss, Tim. Man in space / Tim Furniss. — London : Batsford Academic and Educational, 1981. — 72p : ill,ports ; 26cm. — (Today's world)
Bibliography: p70. — Includes index
ISBN 0-7134-3582-8 : £5.50 B81-10021

629.45'0092'2 — American astronauts, *to 1965*

Wolfe, Tom. The right stuff / Tom Wolfe. — Toronto ; London : Bantam, 1981, c1979. — 368p ; 18cm
Originally published: New York : Farrar, Straus and Giroux ; London : Cape, 1979
ISBN 0-553-17734-6 (pbk) : £1.50 B81-17103

629.45'0092'4 — Astronautics. Collins, Michael, *1930- — Biographies — For children*

Collins, Michael, *1930-*. Flying to the Moon : and other strange places / Michael Collins ; illustrated with photographs and line drawings. — [London] : Piccolo, 1981, c1976. — 139p,[12]p of plates : ill,maps ; 18cm
Originally published: New York : Farrar, Straus and Giroux, 1976 ; London : Robson, 1979
ISBN 0-330-26212-2 (pbk) : £1.25 B81-26325

629.47'022'2 — Space vehicles — *Illustrations*

Trim, Michael. Spacecraft : a colour guide to manned spaceflight, rockets - dockings - space stations - moon-landings - space shuttles - robot explorers / [... painted by Michael Trim]. — [London] : Fontana, 1979. — 1folded sheet ([12]p) : col.ill ; 25cm. — (Domino ; 20)
ISBN 0-00-685459-1 : £0.85 B81-20263

629.47'09 — Space vehicles, *to 1980* **—** *For children*

Ridpath, Ian. Spacecraft / by Ian Ridpath ; illustrated by Ross Wardle. — London : Granada, 1981. — 64p : col.ill ; 19cm. — (Granada guides)
Includes index
ISBN 0-246-11626-9 : £1.95 B81-39308

629.8 — AUTOMATIC CONTROL SYSTEMS

629.8 — Automatic control systems

Bretschi, Jürgen. Automatic inspection systems for industry. — Kempston (35 High St., Kempston, Bedford MK42 7BT) : IFS Publications, Dec.1981. — [230]p
Translation of: Intelligente Messsysteme zur Automatisierung technischer Prozesse
ISBN 0-903608-20-0 (pbk) : £23.00 : CIP entry B81-32055

629.8 — Automatic control systems — *For technicians*

Davey, D. J.. Technician instrumentation and control 4 / D.J. Davey, E.R. Robinson. — London : Cassell, 1981. — 209p : ill ; 22cm. — (Cassell's TEC series)
Includes index
ISBN 0-304-30795-5 (pbk) : Unpriced
Primary classification 620'.0044 B81-40564

629.8 — Control systems

Control engineering / [the Control Engineering Course Team]. — Milton Keynes : Open University Press. — (Technology : a third level course)
At head of title: The Open University
Unit 16: File / prepared by the Course Team. — 1978. — 46p : ill,1port ; 30cm. — (T391 : unit 16)
Bibliography: p41
ISBN 0-335-06339-x (pbk) : Unpriced B81-29130

629.8 — Control systems — *Conference proceedings*

International Conference on Control and its Applications *(1981 : University of Warwick)*.
International Conference on Control and its Applications : 23-25 March 1981 / organised by the Computing and Control Division of the Institution of Electrical Engineers in association with the Institute of Electrical and Electronics Engineers (Control Systems Society and the United Kingdom and Republic of Ireland Section) ... [et al.]. — London : Institution of Electrical Engineers, c1981. — xii,387p : ill ; 30cm. — (Conference publication, ISSN 0537-9989 ; no.194)
ISBN 0-85296-231-2 (pbk) : Unpriced B81-19578

629.8 — Decentralised control systems

Singh, Madan G.. Decentralised control / Madan G. Singh. — Amsterdam ; Oxford : North-Holland, c1981. — xv,335p : ill ; 23cm. — (North-Holland systems and control series ; v.1)
Includes index
ISBN 0-444-86198-x : £23.62 B81-39270

629.8 — Pressure-sensing switches. Design — *Manuals*

Lyons, Jerry L.. The designer's handbook of pressure-sensing devices / Jerry L. Lyons. — New York ; London : Van Nostrand Reinhold, c1980. — xi,289p : ill,forms ; 26cm
Includes index
ISBN 0-442-24964-0 : £20.65 B81-03102

629.8'042 — Automatic control systems. Hydraulic equipment — *Conference proceedings*

Pneumatic and hydraulic components and instruments in automatic control : proceedings of the IFAC Symposium, Warsaw, Poland 20-23 May 1980 / edited by H.J. Leskiewicz and M. Zaremba. — Oxford : Published for the International Federation of Automatic Control by Pergamon, 1981. — x,280p : ill ; 31cm
Includes bibliographies
ISBN 0-08-027317-3 : £31.00
Also classified at 629.8'045 B81-16111

629.8'045 — Automatic control systems. Compressed air equipment — *Conference proceedings*

Pneumatic and hydraulic components and instruments in automatic control : proceedings of the IFAC Symposium, Warsaw, Poland 20-23 May 1980 / edited by H.J. Leskiewicz and M. Zaremba. — Oxford : Published for the International Federation of Automatic Control by Pergamon, 1981. — x,280p : ill ; 31cm
Includes bibliographies
ISBN 0-08-027317-3 : £31.00
Primary classification 629.8'042 B81-16111

629.8'05 — Automatic control systems — *Serials*

Control and dynamic systems. — Vol.16 (1980). — New York ; London : Academic Press, c1980. — x,371p
ISBN 0-12-012716-4 : Unpriced
ISSN 0090-5267 B81-03525

Control and dynamic systems. — Vol.17 (1981). — New York ; London : Academic Press, c1981. — xviii,424p
ISBN 0-12-012717-2 : £18.20
ISSN 0090-5267 B81-35099

629.8'0724 — Automatic control systems. Mathematical models

Elloy, Jean-Pierre. Classical and modern control with worked examples / by Jean-Pierre Elloy and Jean-Marie Piasco ; translated from the original French by Barbara Beeby. — Oxford : Pergamon, 1981. — xi,195p : ill ; 24cm. — (International series on systems and control ; vol.2)
Includes index
ISBN 0-08-026745-9 (cased) : Unpriced : CIP rev.
ISBN 0-08-026746-7 (pbk) : £6.95 B81-09491

629.8'3 — Digital control systems

Katz, Paul. Digital control using microprocessors. — Hemel Hempstead : Prentice-Hall, June 1981. — [300]p
ISBN 0-13-212191-3 : £14.95 : CIP entry B81-14384

Kuo, Benjamin C.. Digital control systems / Benjamin C. Kuo. — New York ; London : Holt, Rinehart and Winston, c1980. — xiv,730p : ill ; 25cm. — (HRW series in electrical and computer engineering)
Includes index
ISBN 0-03-057568-0 : £14.95 B81-00962

629.8'312 — Automatic control. Applications of nonlinear programming — *Conference proceedings*

Control applications of nonlinear programming : proceedings of the IFAC Workshop, Denver, Colorado, USA 21 June 1979 / edited by H.E. Rauch. — Oxford : Published for the International Federation of Automatic Control by Pergamon, 1980. — vii,125p : ill ; 31cm. — (IFAC proceedings series)
Includes bibliographies and index
ISBN 0-08-024491-2 : £12.50 : CIP rev. B80-12939

629.8'312 — Automatic control systems. Mathematical models. System identification — *Conference proceedings*

Bubnicki, Zdzisław. Identification of control plants / by Zdzisław Bubnicki. — Amsterdam ; Oxford : Elsevier Scientific, 1980. — xl,312p : ill ; 25cm. — (Studies in automation and control ; 3)
Translation of: Identyfikacja procesów sterowania. — Bibliography: p300-308. — Includes index
ISBN 0-444-99767-9 : £28.34 : CIP rev. B80-07844

IFAC Symposium on Identification and System Parameter Estimation *(5th : 1979 : Darmstadt)*.
System identification : tutorials presented at the 5th IFAC Symposium on Identification and System Parameter Estimation, F.R. Germany, September 1979 / edited by R. Isermann. — Oxford : Published for the International Federation of Automatic Control by Pergamon. — (IFAC proceedings series)
Originally published: in Automatica, v.16, no.5 1980
[Vol.1]. — 1981. — v,505-587p : ill ; 29cm
Includes bibliographies
ISBN 0-08-027583-4 (pbk) : £5.00 B81-27724

629.8'312 — Control systems. Design. Applications of computer systems — *Conference proceedings*

Computer aided design of control systems : proceedings of the IFAC symposium, Zürich, Switzerland, 29-31 August 1979 / edited by M.A. Cuenod. — Oxford : Published for the International Federation of Automatic Control by Pergamon, 1980. — xiii,688p : ill ; 31cm
Includes index
ISBN 0-08-024488-2 : £63.00 : CIP rev. B80-03205

629.8'312 — Control systems. Design. Mathematical models

Towill, Denis R.. Coefficient plane models for control system analysis and design / Denis R. Towill. — Chichester : Research Studies, c1981. — xv,271p : ill ; 24cm. — (Mechanical engineering research studies ; 1)
Bibliography: p253-265. — Includes index
ISBN 0-471-27955-2 : £16.00 B81-17237

629.8′312 — Control systems. Mathematics

Systems modelling and optimisation. — Stevenage : Peregrinus, Oct.1981. — [224]p. — (IEE control engineering series ; 16)
ISBN 0-906048-63-x (pbk) : £13.00 : CIP entry B81-27474

629.8′312 — Control systems. Optimisation. Applications of vector-valued functions

Salukvadze, M. E.. Vector-valued optimization problems in control theory / M.E. Salukvadze ; translated by John L. Casti. — New York ; London : Academic Press, 1979. — x,217p ; 24cm. — (Mathematics in science and engineering ; v.148)
Translation of: Zadachi vektornoi optimizatsii v teorii upravleniia. — Bibliography: p208-219
ISBN 0-12-616750-8 : Unpriced B81-11503

629.8′312 — Control systems. Vibration. Analysis

Beards, C. F.. Vibration analysis and control system dynamics / C.F. Beards. — Chichester : Horwood, 1981. — 169p : ill ; 24cm. — (Ellis Horwood series in engineering science)
Includes index
ISBN 0-85312-242-3 (cased) : £16.50 : CIP rev.
ISBN 0-85312-294-6 (Student ed) : Unpriced
ISBN 0-470-27255-4 (Wiley) : £16.50 B81-20515

629.8′312 — Control theory

Owens, D. H.. Multivariable and optimal systems. — London : Academic Press, Dec.1981. — [300]p
ISBN 0-12-531720-4 : CIP entry B81-31345

629.8′312 — Control theory — *Conference proceedings*

Third IMA conference on control theory. — London : Academic Press, Jan.1982. — [950]p
Conference papers
ISBN 0-12-473960-1 : CIP entry B81-34409

629.8′312 — Feedback systems. Dynamics

Mees, A. I.. Dynamics of feedback systems / A.I. Mees. — Chichester : Wiley, c1981. — x,214p : ill ; 24cm
Bibliography: p198-206. - Includes index
ISBN 0-471-27822-x : £12.95 B81-16332

629.8′312 — Multivariable systems

Patel, Rajnikant V.. Multivariable system theory and design. — Oxford : Pergamon, Dec.1981. — [385]p. — (International series on systems and control ; v.4) (Pergamon international library)
ISBN 0-08-027297-5 (cased) : £20.00 : CIP entry
ISBN 0-08-027298-3 (pbk) : £9.50 B81-32038

629.8′312 — Optimal control theory

Leitmann, George. The calculus of variations and optimal control : an introduction / George Leitmann. — New York ; London : Plenum, c1981. — xvi,311p : ill ; 24cm. — (Mathematical concepts and methods in science and engineering ; v.24)
Bibliography: p305-307. — Includes index
ISBN 0-306-40707-8 : Unpriced
Primary classification 515′.64 B81-32646

Pallu de la Barrière, R.. Optimal control theory : a course in automatic control theory / R. Pallu de La Barrière ; translated by Scripta Technica ; edited by Bernard R. Gelbaum. — New York : Dover ; London : Constable, 1980, c1967. — xii,412p : ill ; 24cm
Translation of : Cours d′automatique théorique. — Originally published: London : Saunders, 1967. — Bibliography: p405-408. - Includes index
ISBN 0-486-63925-8 (pbk) : £4.40 B81-05551

Ryan, E. P.. Optimal relay and saturating control system synthesis. — Stevenage : Peregrinus, Sept.1981. — [352]p. — (IEE control engineering series ; 14)
ISBN 0-906048-56-7 : £32.00 : CIP entry B81-20496

629.8′312′03 — Control theory — *Polyglot dictionaries*

Multilingual glossary of automatic control technology. — Oxford : Pergamon, Aug.1981. — [230]p
ISBN 0-08-027607-5 : £16.50 : CIP entry B81-21593

629.8′32 — Linear control systems. Analysis & design

D′Azzo, John J.. Linear control system analysis and design : conventional and modern / John J. D′Azzo, Constantine H. Houpis. — 2nd ed. — New York ; London : McGraw-Hill, c1981. — xvi,751p : ill ; 24cm. — (McGraw-Hill series in electrical engineering)
Previous ed.: 1975. — Includes index
ISBN 0-07-016183-6 : £20.95 B81-39116

629.8′32 — Linear systems. Automatic control

Sage, Andrew P.. Linear systems control / Andrew P. Sage. — London : Pitman, 1981, c1978. — vi,546p : ill ; 24cm
Originally published: Champaign, Ill. : Matrix, 1978. — Includes index
ISBN 0-273-01648-2 : £14.95 B81-36324

629.8′32′015157 — Linear control systems. Functional analysis

Leigh, J. R.. Functional analysis and linear control theory / J.R. Leigh. — London : Academic Press, 1980. — ix,160p : ill ; 24cm. — (Mathematics in science and engineering ; v.156)
Bibliography: p147-155. — Includes index
ISBN 0-12-441880-5 : Unpriced : CIP rev. B80-29887

629.8′36 — Adaptive control systems

Self-tuning and adaptive control. — Stevenage : Peregrinus, Oct.1981. — [352]p. — (IEE control engineering series ; 15)
ISBN 0-906048-62-1 (pbk) : £13.50 : CIP entry B81-27475

629.8′92 — Industrial robots

Engelberger, Joseph F.. Robotics in practice : management and applications of industrial robots / Joseph F. Engelberger ; with a foreword by Isaac Asimov. — London : Kogan Page in association with Avebury, 1980. — xvii,291p,xip of plates : ill(some col),forms ; 24cm
Bibliography: p279-283. — Includes index
ISBN 0-85038-392-7 : £18.50 : CIP rev. B80-19809

629.8′92 — Robots

Henson, Hilary. Robots. — London (Elsley Court, 20 Great Titchfield St., W1P 7AD) : Kingfisher, Sept.1981. — [80]p
ISBN 0-86272-003-6 : £3.95 : CIP entry B81-20165

629.8′92 — Robots — *For children*

Kleiner, Art. Robots / by Art Kleiner ; illustrated by Jerry Scott. — Oxford : Blackwell Raintree, c1981. — 48p : col.ill ; 24cm. — (A Look inside)
Includes index
ISBN 0-86256-033-0 : £2.95 B81-17349

Lambert, Mark, *1946-*. Robots / Mark Lambert. — London : Macdonald, 1981. — 32p : col.ill ; 29cm. — (Eye openers!)
Bibliography: p31. - Includes index
ISBN 0-356-07094-8 : £2.50 B81-20277

630 — AGRICULTURE

630 — Great Britain. City farms — *Directories*

Where to find city farms in Britain / [written by city farm groups] ; [produced and edited by the City Farm Advisory Service]. — London (c/o Inter Action Trust, 15 Wilkin St., N.W.5) : City Farm Advisory Service, [1980?]. — 68p : ill,map,plans ; 21cm
Includes index
£1.00 (pbk) B81-29753

630′.0941 — Great Britain. Agriculture — *For children*

Crabtree, Vicky. Farming today. — London : Muller, Nov.1981. — [128]p
ISBN 0-584-10412-x : £5.95 : CIP entry B81-32002

630′.2′03411 — Scotland. Agriculture — *Career guides — Serials*

Opportunities in agriculture / the Scottish Agricultural Colleges. — 1981. — Edinburgh (West Mains Rd, Edinburgh EH9 3JG) : East of Scotland College of Agriculture, 1981. — 21p. — (Publication / the Scottish Agricultural Colleges, ISSN 0308-5708 ; no.79)
Unpriced B81-30834

630′.3′21 — Agriculture — *Encyclopaedias*

Dalal-Clayton, D. B.. Black′s agricultural dictionary / D.B. Dalal-Clayton. — London : Black, 1981. — xii,499p : ill ; 23cm
ISBN 0-7136-2130-3 : £12.00 : CIP rev. B81-14399

630′.5 — Agriculture — *Serials*

Advances in agronomy. — Vol.33. — New York ; London : Academic Press, 1980. — xii,374p
ISBN 0-12-000733-9 : Unpriced
ISSN 0065-2113 B81-20707

Advances in applied biology. — Vol.6. — London : Academic Press, Dec.1981. — [320]p
ISBN 0-12-040906-2 : CIP entry
ISSN 0309-1791 B81-31331

International agricultural development. — Nov./Dec.1980-. — Gowborough (Thorpe House, Goft Rd, Gowborough, East Sussex TN6 1DL) : Pharos Pub. Services, 1980-. — v. : ill(some col.),ports ; 30cm
Ten issues yearly. — Continues: Third world agriculture
ISSN 0261-4413 = International agricultural development : £27.00 per year B81-32702

630′.68 — Agricultural industries. Farms. Management

Buckett, Maurice. An introduction to farm organisation and management / by Maurice Buckett. — Oxford : Pergamon, 1981. — x,313p : ill ; 26cm. — (Pergamon international library)
Includes index
ISBN 0-08-024433-5 (cased) : Unpriced
ISBN 0-08-024432-7 (pbk) : £8.50 B81-33449

630′.68 — Developing countries. Agricultural industries. Management. British organisations: Agricultural Administration Network - *Serials*

[Newsletter *(Agricultural Administration Network)*]. Newsletter / Agricultural Administration Network. — No.1 (Nov.1979)-. — London : Overseas Development Institute, 1979-. — v. ; 21cm
Three issues yearly. — Description based on: No.4 (Nov.1980)
ISSN 0260-7883 = Newsletter - Agricultural Administration Network : Unpriced B81-06903

630′.68 — Great Britain. Agricultural industries. Farms. Management. Applications of digital computer systems

Farm planning by computer / Ministry of Agriculture, Fisheries and Food. — 2nd ed. — London : H.M.S.O., 1979 (1980 [printing]). — 139p : ill,forms ; 25cm. — (Reference book ; 419)
Previous ed.: 1971. — Table on 1 folded sheet in pocket
ISBN 0-11-240314-x (pbk) : £5.75 B81-23437

630′.68 — Great Britain. Agricultural industries. Farms. Management. Applications of digital computer systems — *Conference proceedings*

Effective use of computing for farm accounting. — Aldershot : Gower, Dec.1981. — [80]p
Conference papers
ISBN 0-566-03028-4 : £16.50 : CIP entry B81-35874

630′.68 — United States. Agricultural industries. Farms. Management — *Manuals*

Harsh, Steven B.. Managing the farm business / Stephen B. Harsh, Larry J. Connor, Gerald D. Schwab. — Englewood Cliffs ; London : Prentice-Hall, c1981. — xv,384p : ill,1map ; 25cm
Includes bibliographies and index
ISBN 0-13-550376-0 : £13.25 B81-36174

630′.68 — United States. Agricultural industries. Farms. Management — *Manuals*
continuation

Kay, Ronald D.. Farm management : planning, control, and implementation / Ronald D. Kay. — New York ; London : McGraw-Hill, c1981. — xiii,370p : ill,forms ; 25cm
Includes bibliographies and index
ISBN 0-07-033462-5 : £14.50 B81-17635

630′.68 — United States. Agricultural industries. Management

Downey, W. David. Agribusiness management / W. David Downey, John K. Trocke. — New York ; London : McGraw-Hill, c1981. — x,459p : ill ; 25cm
Includes index
ISBN 0-07-017645-0 : £12.55 B81-23963

630′.68′8 — Great Britain. Agricultural products. Marketing

Barker, J. W. (John William), *1953-*. Agricultural marketing / J.W. Barker. — Oxford : Oxford University Press, 1981. — vi,226p : ill ; 23cm. — (Oxford science publications)
Bibliography: p219-221. — Includes index
ISBN 0-19-859468-2 (cased) : £12.50 : CIP rev.
ISBN 0-19-859469-0 (pbk) : £5.95 B81-15945

630′.7 — Agriculture. Information sources

Information sources in agriculture and food science / editor G.P. Lilley. — London : Butterworths, 1981. — xiv,603p : 1ill ; 23cm. — (Butterworths guides to information sources)
Includes index
ISBN 0-408-10612-3 : Unpriced
Also classified at 641.1′07 B81-34995

630′.7′1142 — England. Further education institutions & higher education institutions. Curriculum subjects: Agriculture. Courses — *Directories*

Courses in agriculture and allied subjects in England and Wales / edited by J.G. Cooke. — York (Askham Bryan College, York YO2 3PR) : Agricultural Education Association, c1981. — 70p ; 30cm
ISBN 0-901409-02-2 (spiral) : £2.00
B81-32644

630′.7′114283 — North Humberside. Agricultural industries. Personnel. Professional education

Stevenson, Ann. Agricultural education and training in North Humberside : a survey of experience and attitudes / Ann Stevenson and David Symes. — [Hull] : Department of Geography, University of Hull, 1979. — iii,144p : ill,maps ; 30cm. — (Miscellaneous series / Department of Geography, University of Hull ; no.23)
ISBN 0-85958-108-x (spiral) : Unpriced
Also classified at 331.25′92 B81-02311

630′.72 — Agriculture. Research — *Serials*

Rothamsted Experimental Station. Report for ... / Rothamsted Experimental Station. — 1980. — Harpenden (Harpenden, Herts AL5 2JQ) : Lawes Agricultural Trust, 1981. — 2v.
£8.00 B81-31558

630′.7204 — European Community countries. Agriculture. Research projects — *Directories* — *Serials*

AGREP : permanent inventory of agricultural research projects in the European Communities / Commission of the European Communities. Vol.1, Main list, research projects. — 1980. — The Hague ; London : Nijhoff, 1980. — x,841p
ISBN 90-247-2466-x : Unpriced B81-25035

AGREP : permanent inventory of agricultural research projects in the European Communities / Commission of the European Communities. Vol.2, Indexes. — 1980. — The Hague ; London : Nijhoff, 1980. — ix,231p
ISBN 90-247-2467-8 : Unpriced B81-25034

630′.72041 — Great Britain. Agriculture. Research organisations: Agricultural Research Council — *Serials*

Agricultural Research Council. Report of the Agricultural Research Council for the year .... — 1979/80. — London : H.M.S.O., 1980. — v,125p
ISBN 0-10-200381-5 : £8.80 B81-09119

630′.7204134 — Agriculture. Research organisations: Edinburgh Centre of Rural Economy — *Serials*

Edinburgh Centre of Rural Economy. Annual report, April ... to March ... / Edinburgh Centre of Rural Economy. — 1979-80-. — Penicuik (Bush House, Milton Bridge, Penicuik, Midlothian EH26 0PJ) : The Centre, 1980. — 30p
Unpriced B81-09710

630′.720416 — Northern Ireland. Agriculture. Research organisations: Northern Ireland Agricultural Trust — *Serials*

Northern Ireland Agricultural Trust. Annual report of the Northern Ireland Agricultural Trust for the year ended 31 March ... — 13th (1980). — Belfast : H.M.S.O., 1981. — 28p
ISBN 0-337-05257-3 : £2.20 B81-35112

630′.720416 — Northern Ireland. Agriculture. Research projects by Agricultural Research Institute of Northern Ireland — *Serials*

Agricultural Research Institute of Northern Ireland. Annual report / Agricultural Research Institute of Northern Ireland. — 53rd (1979-1980). — Hillsborough (Hillsborough, Co. Down) : The Institute, [1980]. — 45p
Unpriced B81-13413

630′.72042 — England. Agriculture. Research organisations: Agricultural Development and Advisory Service — *Serials*

Agricultural Development and Advisory Service. Annual report / ADAS. — 1980. — London : H.M.S.O., 1981. — [iv],107p
ISBN 0-11-241179-7 : £4.50
ISSN 0142-0895 B81-33469

630′.72042613 — Norfolk. Terrington St Clement. Agricultural industries. Experimental farms: Terrington Experimental Husbandry Farm — *Serials*

Terrington Experimental Husbandry Farm. Annual review / Terrington Experimental Husbandry Farm. — 21st(1981). — [Terrington St Clement] ([Terrington St Clement, Kings Lynn, Norfolk PE34 4PW]) : The Farm, [1981]. — i,40p
Unpriced B81-32405

630′.72042657 — Cambridgeshire. Boxworth. Agricultural industries. Experimental farms: Boxworth Experimental Husbandry Farm — *Serials*

Boxworth Experimental Husbandry Farm. Annual review / Boxworth Experimental Husbandry Farm. — 1981. — Boxworth (Boxworth, Cambridge CB3 8NN) : The Farm, [1981]. — vi,46p
Unpriced B81-31586

630′.76 — Agriculture — *Questions & answers* — *For West African students*

Akinsanmi, Oluyemi. Objective tests : O-level agricultural science / O. Akinsanmi, M. Lyth,. — Harlow : Longman, 1980. — vii,55p : ill ; 22cm. — (Study for success)
ISBN 0-582-60688-8 (pbk) : £0.80 B81-37406

630′.76 — England. Agricultural industries. Personnel. Proficiency. Testing, *1938-1980*

Sheppy, Phillip C.. Proficiency testing for agriculture and horticulture in England and Wales / Phillip C. Sheppy. — [Kenilworth] ([YFC Centre, National Agricultural Centre, Kenilworth, Warwickshire CV8 2LG]) : [National Proficiency Tests Council for Agriculture and Horticulture], 1980. — 58p : ill ; 30cm
£2.50 (pbk) B81-12531

630.9 — AGRICULTURE. HISTORICAL AND GEOGRAPHICAL TREATMENT

630′.9 — Agriculture, *to 1980*

Heiser, Charles B.. Seed to civilization : the story of food / Charles B. Heiser, Jr. — 2nd ed. — Oxford : W.H. Freeman, c1981. — xii,254p : ill,maps ; 24cm
Previous ed.: 1973. — Bibliography: p239-245. — Includes index
ISBN 0-7167-1264-4 (cased) : £13.40
ISBN 0-7167-1265-2 (pbk) : £6.20 B81-36484

630′.913 — Tropical regions. Agriculture

Compendium for agricultural developments in the tropics and subtropics. — Oxford : Elsevier, June 1981
Chapter 1: Climate. — [850]p
ISBN 0-444-41952-7 : CIP entry B81-11912

630′.915′4 — Arid regions. Agriculture

Settling the desert / edited by L. Berkofsky, D. Faiman, J. Gale. — Sede Boqer : Jacob Blaustein Institute for Desert Research ; London : Gordon and Breach Science, c1981. — xvi,274p : ill,maps ; 24cm
Includes index
ISBN 0-677-16280-4 : Unpriced
Also classified at 333.73 ; 307.7′2′09154
B81-35182

630′.915′4 — Arid regions. Food. Production

Advances in food-producing systems for arid and semarid lands / [proceedings of a symposium on advances in food-producing systems for arid and semiarid lands in Kuwait, February, 1980] ; sponsored by Kuwait Foundation for the Advancement of Sciences ; edited by Jamal T. Manassah, Ernest J. Briskey. — New York ; London : Academic Press, 1981. — 2v.(xvi,1274p) : ill ; 25cm
Includes bibliographies
ISBN 0-12-467301-5 (cased) : Unpriced
ISBN 0-12-467302-3 (pt.2) : £30.80
ISBN 0-12-467321-x (pt.1:pbk) : Unpriced
ISBN 0-12-467322-8 (pt.2:pbk) : Unpriced
B81-39783

630′.9182′1 — Caribbean region. Agriculture — *For Caribbean students*

Ramharacksingh, R.. Caribbean primary agriculture / R. Ramharacksingh ; illustrated by G.J. Galsworthy. — London : Cassell
Bk.3. — 1981. — 95p : ill(some col.) ; 25cm
ISBN 0-304-30788-2 (pbk) : Unpriced
B81-40571

Ramharacksingh, R.. Caribbean primary agriculture / R. Ramharacksingh ; illustrated by G.J. Galsworthy. — London : Cassell
Workbook 3. — 1981. — 64p : ill ; 25cm
ISBN 0-304-30789-0 (pbk) : Unpriced
B81-40562

630′.9182′1 — Caribbean region. Agriculture — *For Caribbean students* — *For schools*

Ramharacksingh, R.. Caribbean primary agriculture / R. Ramharacksingh ; illustrated by G.J. Galsworthy. — London : Cassell
Book 1. — 1981. — 63p : ill(some col.) ; 25cm
ISBN 0-304-30766-1 (pbk) : Unpriced
B81-26285

Ramharacksingh, R.. Caribbean primary agriculture / R. Ramharacksingh ; illustrated by G.J. Galsworthy. — London : Cassell
Book 2. — 1981. — 80p : ill(some col.) ; 25cm
ISBN 0-304-30764-5 (pbk) : Unpriced
B81-26284

630′.92′4 — England. Agriculture. Cherrington, John — *Biographies*

Cherrington, John. On the smell of an oily rag : my 50 years in farming / John Cherrington. — London : Northwood, 1979 (1980 printing). — v,178p : ill,ports ; 22cm. — (A Big farm management book)
ISBN 0-7198-2528-8 : £5.95 B81-02924

630′.92′4 — New Zealand. Agriculture. McLeod, David — *Biographies*

McLeod, David. Down from the tussock ranges / David McLeod. — Christchurch [N.Z.] ; London : Whitcoulls, 1980. — 254p ; 22cm
ISBN 0-7233-0640-0 : Unpriced B81-03754

630′.92′4 — New Zealand. Otaki Gorge. Agriculture — *Personal observations*

Marriott, Les. Life in the Gorge / Les Marriott ; illustrated by Jean Oates. — Christchurch, N.Z. ; London : Whitcoulls, 1981. — 148p : ill ; 22cm
ISBN 0-7233-0654-0 : Unpriced B81-34943

630′.92′4 — North Yorkshire. North York Moors. Agriculture — *Personal observations*

Fussey, Joyce. Cows in the corn / Joyce Fussey. — London : Magnum, 1981, c1978. — 144p : 1map ; 18cm
Originally published: London : Elek, 1978
ISBN 0-417-05100-x (pbk) : £1.25 B81-08480

630′.92′4 — Saskatchewan. Agriculture — *Personal observations* — *Welsh texts*

Davies, Evan, *1882?-1958*. [Beyond the Old Bone Trail. Welsh]. Arswyd yr unigeddau / gan Evan Davies ac Aled Vaughan ; [troswyd o′r Saesneg gan Phebe Puw]. — Llandysul : Gwasg Gomer, 1980. — 167p : 1 map,1 port ; 19cm
Translation of: Beyond the Old Bone Trail
ISBN 0-85088-992-8 (pbk) : £2.25 B81-03918

630′.92′4 — Welsh Marches. Agriculture — *Personal observations*

Holgate, John, *1924-*. A sheep′s eye view / John Holgate. — London : Pan in association with Peter Davies, 1981, c1979. — 202p ; 18cm
Originally published: London : P. Davies, 1979
ISBN 0-330-26408-7 (pbk) : £1.25 B81-39005

630′.92′6 — Great Britain. Farmers - *Case studies - For children*

Haddrell, Allan. A day with a farmer / Allan & Christine Haddrell. — Hove : Wayland, 1980. — 55p : ill,ports ; 24cm. — (A Day in the life)
Bibliography: p55
ISBN 0-85340-781-9 : £3.25 B81-05090

630′.9361 — Great Britain. Prehistoric agriculture — *Conference proceedings*

Farming practice in British prehistory / edited by Roger Mercer. — Edinburgh : Edinburgh University Press, c1981. — xxvi,245p : ill ; 24cm
Conference papers. — Ill on inside covers. — Includes bibliographies and index
ISBN 0-85224-414-2 (pbk) : £9.50 B81-39174

630′.941 — Great Britain. Agriculture - *Serials*

Agriculture. — 1978-79. — London : Health & Safety Executive, July 1981. — [30]p
ISBN 0-11-883436-3 (pbk) : CIP entry
B81-14937

630′.941 — Great Britain. Agriculture — *Serials*

British farmer and stockbreeder. Year book and farm diary. — 1981. — London (Surrey House, 1 Throwley Way, Sutton SM1 4QQ) : British Farmer and Stockbreeder, c1980. — 276p
ISBN 0-617-00214-2 : £5.00 B81-09228

630′.942 — England. Agriculture, *1735-1910* — *For schools*

Sturgess, Roy. The rural revolution in an English village. — Cambridge : Cambridge University Press, Nov.1981. — [45]p. — (Cambridge introduction to the history of mankind)
ISBN 0-521-22800-x (pbk) : £1.95 : CIP entry
B81-33617

630′.942 — England. Agriculture — *Questions & answers*

Practical proficiency tests for agriculture / National Proficiency Tests Council for Agriculture and Horticulture. — Kenilworth (YFC Centre, National Agricultural Centre, Kenilworth, Warwickshire CV8 2LG) : The Council, [1980]. — 1v.(loose-leaf) ; 22cm
£6.50 B81-12533

630′.9425′79 — Oxfordshire. Brightwell-cum-Sotwell. Agriculture, *ca 1900*

Everex, Tom. Farming memories / by Tom Everex. — [Wallingford] ([Middle Farm, Church La., Brightwell-cum-Sotwell, Wallingford OX10 0SD]) : [K. Owen], c1981. — 8p : 1map ; 22cm
Unpriced (pbk) B81-35504

630′.946 — Spain. Agriculture, *ca 1200* — *Early works*

Ibn al ʻAwwām, Yaḥya ibn Muḥammad. [Kitab al felaha. English. Selections]. A Moorish calendar : from the Book of Agriculture of Ibn al Awam / translated by Philip Lord ; edited & illustrated by Peter Lord ; with a foreword by Sir John Glubb. — Wantage : Black Swan, 1979, c1978. — viii,54p : ill ; 21cm
Translation of: Selections from Kitab al felaha. — Includes index
ISBN 0-905475-05-4 : Unpriced B81-11100

630′.966 — West Africa. Agriculture

Aduayi, E. A.. General agriculture and soils / E.A. Aduayi and E.E. Ekong. — London : Cassell, 1981. — 102p : ill ; 25cm. — (Cassell′s tropical agriculture series ; book 1)
Includes index
ISBN 0-304-30207-4 (pbk) : £2.95 B81-20894

630′.987′47 — Venezuela. Parmana region. Prehistoric agriculture

Roosevelt, Anna Curtenius. Parmana : prehistoric maize and manioc subsistance along the Amazon and Orinoco / Anna Curtenius Roosevelt. — New York ; London : Academic Press, c1980. — xv,320p : ill,maps ; 25cm. — (Studies in archaeology)
Bibliography: p273-314. — Includes index
ISBN 0-12-595350-x : £16.60 B81-21839

631 — CROPS, AGRICULTURAL EQUIPMENT AND OPERATIONS

631 — Crops

Hartmann, Hudson T.. Plant science : growth, development and utilization of cultivated plants / Hudson T. Hartmann, William J. Flocker, Anton M. Kofranek. — Englewood Cliffs ; London : Prentice-Hall, c1981. — xii,676p : ill,maps ; 29cm
Includes bibliographies and index
ISBN 0-13-681056-x : £17.50 B81-21369

Langer, R. H. M.. Agricultural plants. — Cambridge : Cambridge University Press, Nov.1981. — [328]p
ISBN 0-521-22450-0 (cased) : £20.00 : CIP entry
ISBN 0-521-29506-8 (pbk) : £7.95 B81-33619

631 — Plants. Use by man — *For schools*

Gosden, Sheila. Plans & man / Sheila Gosden. — Glasgow : Blackie, 1981. — 32p : ill,1map ; 17x25cm. — (Modular science)
ISBN 0-216-91079-x (pbk) : £1.40 B81-39188

631.2 — FARM BUILDINGS AND STRUCTURES

631.2′07204 — Western Europe. Agricultural industries. Farms. Buildings. Research — *Lists* — *Serials*

Farm building research and development index / the Scottish Farm Buildings Investigation Unit. — 1980. — Aberdeen (Craibstone, Bucksburn, Aberdeen AB2 9TR) : The Unit, 1980. — 28p
ISBN 0-902433-20-2 : £1.00 B81-15163

631.2′09412′1 — Scotland. Grampian Region. Agricultural industries. Farms. Buildings, *to 1979*

Walker, Bruce. Farm buildings in the Grampian Region : an historical exploration : a report / by Bruce Walker to the Countryside Commission for Scotland. — [Aberdeen] ([Department of Leisure, Recreation & Tourism, Woodhill House, Ashgrove Road West, Aberdeen AB9 2LU]) : Grampian Regional Council, 1979. — 72p : ill,maps,plans ; 30cm
Map on inside cover
£2.00 (spiral) B81-04868

631.2′0942 — England. Agricultural industries. Farms. Buildings

Darley, Gillian. The National Trust book of the farm / Gillian Darley ; with photographs by Pamela Toler. — London : National Trust, c1981. — 256p : ill(some col.),2maps,plans ; 29cm
Bibliography: p250-252. — Includes index
ISBN 0-297-78006-9 : £11.50 B81-37409

631.2′2′094278 — Cumbria. Stone barns

Davis, N.. Barns and barn conversion in Cumbria / by N. Davis. — [Uxbridge] ([Brunel University, Uxbridge, Middx UB8 9PH]) : [Department of Building Technology], [1979?]. — vi,163p : ill,maps,plans ; 30cm
Bibliography: p162-163
£5.00 (pbk) B81-18005

631.2′7 — Hedging — *Manuals*

Hart, Edward. Hedge laying and fencing. — Wellingborough : Thorsons, Nov.1981. — [128]p
ISBN 0-7225-0701-1 (cased) : £6.95 : CIP entry
ISBN 0-7225-0700-3 (pbk) : £2.95 B81-30487

631.3 — AGRICULTURAL MACHINERY AND IMPLEMENTS

631.3 — Agricultural machinery

Culpin, Claude. Farm machinery / Claude Culpin. — 10th ed. — London : Granada, 1981. — 450p : ill ; 24cm
Previous ed.: London : Crosby Lockwood Staples, 1976. — Includes bibliographies and index
ISBN 0-246-11539-4 (cased) : £17.50 : CIP rev.
ISBN 0-246-11585-8 (pbk) : Unpriced
B81-13907

631.3 — British horse-drawn agricultural machinery

Smith, D. J. (Donald John). Discovering horse-drawn farm machinery / D.J. Smith. — Princes Risborough : Shire, 1979. — 96p : ill ; 18cm
Bibliography: p94. — Includes index
ISBN 0-85263-464-1 (pbk) : £0.85 B81-37982

631.3′09361 — Great Britain. Agricultural equipment, *to ca 400*

Rees, Sian E.. Ancient agricultural implements / Sian E. Rees. — Princes Risborough : Shire, 1981. — 72p ; 21cm. — (Shire archaeology series ; 15)
Bibliography: p31. — Includes index
ISBN 0-85263-535-4 (pbk) : £1.95 B81-40853

631.3′0941 — Great Britain. Agricultural equipment & machinery, *1500-1900*

Fussell, G. E.. The farmer′s tools : the history of British farm implements, tools and machinery AD 1500-1900 / by G.E. Fussell. — London : Orbis Publishing, 1981. — 246p,111p of plates : ill,1facsim ; 24cm
Originally published: London : Melrose, 1952. — Bibliography: p225-230. — Includes index
ISBN 0-85613-359-0 : £15.00 B81-26669

631.3′12 — Agricultural equipment: Ploughs

Ploughs and ploughing : tractors and traction. — Edinburgh (West Mains Rd, Edinburgh EH9 3JG) : East of Scotland College of Agriculture, 1981. — 38p : ill ; 21cm. — (Publication / The Scottish Colleges of Agriculture, ISSN 0308-5708 ; no.80)
Cover title. — Bibliography: p36-37
Unpriced (pbk) B81-38570

631.3′71 — Agriculture. Applications of solar energy — *Conference proceedings*

International Seminar on Energy Conservation and the Use of Solar and Other Renewable Energies in Agriculture, Horticulture and Fishculture *(1980 : Polytechnic of Central London)*. Energy conservation and use of renewable energies in the bio-industries : proceedings of the International Seminar on Energy Conservation and the Use of Solar and Other Renewable Energies in Agriculture, Horticulture and Fishculture, held at the Polytechnic of Central London, 15-19 September 1980 / editor F. Vogt. — Oxford : Pergamon, 1981. — xi,574p : ill,maps ; 26cm
ISBN 0-08-026866-8 : £42.00 B81-18929

631.4 — AGRICULTURE. SOILS

631.4 — Soil science

Gerrard, John. Soils and landforms. — London : Allen & Unwin, Oct.1981. — [256]p
ISBN 0-04-551048-2 (cased) : £15.00 : CIP entry
ISBN 0-04-551049-0 (pbk) : £7.95
Primary classification 551.4 B81-26737

631.4 — Soil science — *For geography*

Fenwick, I. M.. Soils process & response. — London : Duckworth, Nov.1981. — [208]p
ISBN 0-7156-1394-4 : £18.00 : CIP entry B81-30262

631.4 — Soils. Conservation

Troeh, Frederick R.. Soil and water conservation : for productivity and environmental protection / Frederick R. Troeh, J. Arthur Hobbs, Roy L. Donahue ; editorial assistance Miriam R. Troeh. — Englewood Cliffs ; London : Prentice-Hall, c1980. — xv,718p : ill,maps ; 24cm
Includes bibliographies and index
ISBN 0-13-822155-3 : £16.20
Also classified at 333.91'16 B81-04426

631.4 — Soils. Conservation — *Conference proceedings*

Conservation 80 *(Conference : Silsoe)*. Soil conservation : problems and prospects / edited by R.P.C. Morgan ; [proceedings of Conservation 80, the International Conference on Soil Conservation, held at the National College of Agricultural Engineering, Silsoe, Bedford, UK, 21st-25th July 1980]. — Chichester : Wiley, c1981. — xvi,576p : ill,maps ; 24cm
Includes bibliographies and index
ISBN 0-471-27882-3 : £22.00 B81-17240

631.4 — Soils. Properties

Principles and applications of soil geography. — London : Longman, Nov.1981. — [320]p
ISBN 0-582-30014-2 (pbk) : £6.95 : CIP entry B81-30185

Soils and agriculture / edited by P.B. Tinker. — Oxford : Published for the Society of Chemical Industry by Blackwell Scientific, 1980. — viii,151p : ill ; 24cm. — (Critical reports on applied chemistry ; v.2)
Includes bibliographies and index
ISBN 0-632-00722-2 (pbk) : £8.00 : CIP rev. B80-25821

631.4'072042 — England. Agricultural land. Soils. Research by Agricultural Science Service — *Serials*

Agricultural Science Service. Crop nutrition and soil science : Agricultural Science Service research and development reports. — 1979-. — London : H.M.S.O., 1981-. — v. ; 21cm. — (Reference book / Ministry of Agriculture, Fisheries and Food)
Annual. — Continues in part: Pest Infestation Control Laboratory. Pest Infestation Control Laboratory report; and, also in part, Regional Agricultural Science Service. Annual report
ISSN 0261-717x = Crop nutrition and soil science : £3.50
Also classified at 631.5 B81-32409

631.4'1 — Herbicides. Interactions with soils

Interactions between herbicides and the soil / edited by R.J. Hance. — London : Published for the European Weed Research Society [by] Academic Press, 1980. — xii,349p : ill ; 24cm
Includes summary in French and German. — Includes bibliographies and index
ISBN 0-12-323840-4 : £20.60 : CIP rev. B80-27205

631.4'1 — Soils. Chemical properties

The **Chemistry** of soil processes / edited by D.J. Greenland and M.H.B. Hayes. — Chichester : Wiley, c1981. — xiii,714p : ill ; 24cm
Includes bibliographies and index
ISBN 0-471-27693-6 : £36.00 : CIP rev. B80-22110

631.4'1 — Soils. Chemical reactions. Environmental aspects

Environmental control of soil chemical processes / edited by W.I. Kelso. — Swansea (c/o P.S. Wright, Soil Survey of England and Wales, University College of Swansea, Singleton Park, Swansea SA2 8PP) : Welsh Soil Discussion Group, 1977. — 117p : ill,maps ; 21cm. — (Report / Welsh Soils Discussion Group ; no.18)
Conference papers
Unpriced (pbk) B81-33356

631.4'1 — Soils. Chemical reactions. Thermodynamics

Sposito, Garrison. The thermodynamics of soil solutions / Garrison Sposito. — Oxford : Clarendon Press, 1981. — xii,223p : ill ; 24cm. — (Oxford science publications)
Includes bibliographies and index
ISBN 0-19-857568-8 : £24.00 : CIP rev. B81-02360

631.4'16 — Clay & soils. Constituents: Minerals. Chemical analysis. Spectroscopy. Techniques — *Conference proceedings*

Advanced chemical methods for soil and clay minerals research : proceedings of the NATO Advanced Study Institute, held at the University of Illinois, July 23-August 4, 1979 / edited by J.W. Stucki and W.L. Banwart. — Dordrecht ; London : Reidel in cooperation with NATO Scientific Affairs Division, c1980. — x,476p : ill ; 25cm. — (NATO advanced study institutes series. Series C, Mathematical and physical sciences ; v.63)
Includes bibliographies and index
ISBN 90-277-1158-5 : Unpriced B81-07065

631.4'17 — Arid regions. Agriculture. Role of nitrogen in soils

Soil water and nitrogen : in Mediterranean-type environments / edited by John Monteith and Colin Webb. — The Hague ; London : Nijhoff, 1981. — xviii,338p : ill,maps ; 25cm. — (Developments in plant and soil sciences ; v.1)
'Selected reviews reprinted from Plant and Soil Vol.58 (1981)'. — Includes bibliographies and index
ISBN 90-247-2406-6 : Unpriced
Primary classification 631.4'32'09154 B81-25961

631.4'3 — Soil physics. Applications

Hillel, Daniel. Applications of soil physics / Daniel Hillel. — New York ; London : Academic Press, 1980. — xiv,385p : ill ; 24cm
Bibliography: p357-376. — Includes index
ISBN 0-12-348580-0 : £25.20 B81-05712

631.4'3 — Soils & sediments. Analysis. Use of scanning electron microscopy

Smart, Peter. Electron microscopy of soils & sediments. — Oxford : Clarendon Press, June 1981. — [250]p
ISBN 0-19-854515-0 : £20.00 : CIP entry B81-15841

631.4'3 — Soils. Physics

Hillel, Daniel. Fundamentals of soil physics / Daniel Hillel. — New York ; London : Academic Press, 1980. — xvii,413p : ill ; 24cm
Bibliography: p387-405. — Includes index
ISBN 0-12-348560-6 : £19.60 B81-00144

631.4'32'09154 — Arid regions. Agriculture. Role of water in soils

Soil water and nitrogen : in Mediterranean-type environments / edited by John Monteith and Colin Webb. — The Hague ; London : Nijhoff, 1981. — xviii,338p : ill,maps ; 25cm. — (Developments in plant and soil sciences ; v.1)
'Selected reviews reprinted from Plant and Soil Vol.58 (1981)'. — Includes bibliographies and index
ISBN 90-247-2406-6 : Unpriced
Also classified at 631.4'17 B81-25961

631.4'5 — Soils. Erosion

Soil erosion : a publication of the British Geomorphological Research Group / edited by M.J. Kirkby and R.P.C. Morgan. — Chichester : Wiley, c1980. — xiii,312p : ill,maps ; 24cm. — (Landscape systems)
Includes bibliographies and index
ISBN 0-471-27802-5 : £22.50 B81-06936

Zachar, Dušan. Soil erosion. — Oxford : Elsevier Scientific, Dec.1981. — [400]p. — (Developments in soil science ; 10)
Translation of: Erózia pôdy
ISBN 0-444-99725-3 : £35.00 : CIP entry B81-31614

631.4'5 — Soils. Erosion. Assessment — *Conference proceedings*

Workshop on Assessment of Erosion in USA and Europe *(1978 : State University, Ghent)*. Assessment of erosion / [based on the proceedings of the Workshop on Assessment of Erosion in USA and Europe, held at the Faculty of Agricultural Sciences, State University Ghent, Belgium from 27 February to 3 March 1978.] ; edited by M. de Boodt, D. Gabriels. — Chichester : Wiley, c1980. — xviii,563p,[2]pof plates : ill(some col),maps ; 26cm
Includes bibliographies and index
ISBN 0-471-27899-8 : £27.50 B81-09655

631.4'7 — Soils. Surveying

Dent, David. Soil survey and land evaluation. — London : Allen & Unwin, Oct.1981. — [304]p
ISBN 0-04-631013-4 (cased) : £15.00 : CIP entry
ISBN 0-04-631014-2 (pbk) : £7.95 B81-26738

631.4'7 — Soils. Surveying - *For engineering*

Brink, A. B. A.. Soil survey for engineering. — Oxford : Oxford University Press, Aug.1981. — [340]p. — (Monographs on soil survey)
ISBN 0-19-854537-1 : £24.00 : CIP entry B81-15920

631.4'7'05 — Soils. Surveys — *Serials*

Soil survey and land evaluation. — Vol.1, no.1 (Jan.1981)-. — Norwich (34 Duke St., Norwich NR3 3AP) : Geo Books, 1981-. — v. ; 25cm
Quarterly
ISSN 0260-9088 = Soil survey and land evaluation : £3.50 per year B81-17480

631.4'94248 — Warwickshire. Soils

Soils in Warwickshire. — Harpenden : Soil Survey. — (Soil survey record ; no.66)
4: Sheet SP 26/39 (Nuneaton) / W.A.D. Whitfield and G.R. Beard. — 1980. — x,186p,[5]p of plates : ill,maps ; 21cm + 2maps(2folded leaves ; 68x87cm)
Bibliography: p158-161. - Includes index
£8.00 with maps (£2.00 without maps) (pbk) B81-09429

631.4'942846 — North Yorkshire. North York Moors. Soils

Carroll, D. M. (Douglas Michael). Soils of the North York Moors / D.M. Carroll and V.C. Bendelow. — Harpenden : Soil Survey of England and Wales, 1981. — viii,132p,[7]p of plates : ill,maps(some col.) ; 21cm + 2folded sheets(maps). — (Special survey / Soil Survey ; no.13)
Also available without maps. — Bibliography: p124-126. — Includes index
£8.00 (pbk) (Without maps) : £4.00 B81-37805

631.4'9931 — New Zealand. Soils

Gibbs, H. S.. New Zealand soils : an introduction / H.S. Gibbs. — Wellington, N.Z. ; Oxford : Oxford University Press, c1980. — 115p : ill (some col.),col.maps ; 25cm
Includes bibliographies
ISBN 0-19-558057-5 (pbk) : £8.50 B81-18300

631.4'998 — Arctic. Soils. Surveying

Linell, Kenneth A.. Soil and permafrost surveys in the Arctic / Kenneth A. Linell and John C.F. Tedrow. — Oxford : Clarendon Press, 1981. — viii,279p : ill,charts,maps ; 23cm. — (Monographs on soil survey) (Oxford science publications)
Bibliography: p255-263. — Includes index
ISBN 0-19-857557-2 : £25.00 : CIP rev. B81-02554

631.5 — AGRICULTURE. CULTIVATION AND HARVESTING

631.5 — Crops. Growth. Effects of photosynthesis

Techniques in bioproductivity and photosynthesis. — Oxford : Pergamon, June 1981. — [160]p. — (Pergamon international library)
ISBN 0-08-027382-3 (cased) : £15.00 : CIP entry (pbk) : £8.00 B81-09489

631.5 — Crops. Nutrition. Manganese — *Serials*

Manganese in agriculture : a quarterly bulletin of abstracts. — Vol.1, no.1 (Oct.1980)-. — Tring (M.B. House, Wigginton, Tring, Hertfordshire HP23 6ED) : Micronutrient Bureau, 1980-. — v. ; 30cm
ISSN 0261-5010 = Manganese in agriculture : Unpriced
Also classified at 636.089'23924 B81-29099

631.5 — Crops. Nutrition. Molybdenum — *Serials*

Molybdenum in agriculture : a quarterly bulletin of abstracts. — Vol.1, no.1 (Oct.1980)-. — Tring (M.B. House, Wigginton, Tring, Hertfordshire HP23 6ED) : Micronutrient Bureau, 1980-. — v. ; 30cm
ISSN 0261-5045 = Molybdenum in agriculture : Unpriced
Also classified at 636.089'23924 B81-29100

631.5 — Crops. Nutrition. Trace elements — *Serials*

Micronutrient news. — Vol.1, no.1 (Oct.1980)-. — Tring (M.B. House, Wigginton, Tring, Hertfordshire HP23 6ED) : Micronutrient Bureau, 1980-. — v. : ill,ports ; 30cm
Quarterly
ISSN 0261-5002 = Micronutrient news : Unpriced
Also classified at 636.089'23924 B81-29098

631.5 — Crops. Productivity. Biological factors

Spedding, C. R. W.. Biological efficiency in agriculture. — London : Academic Press, May 1981. — [350]p
ISBN 0-12-656560-0 : CIP entry B81-06044

631.5 — England. Crops. Nutrition. Research by Agricultural Science Service — *Serials*

Agricultural Science Service. Crop nutrition and soil science : Agricultural Science Service research and development reports. — 1979-. — London : H.M.S.O., 1981-. — v. ; 21cm. — (Reference book / Ministry of Agriculture, Fisheries and Food)
Annual. — Continues in part: Pest Infestation Control Laboratory. Pest Infestation Control Laboratory report; and, also in part, Regional Agricultural Science Service. Annual report
ISSN 0261-717x = Crop nutrition and soil science : £3.50
Primary classification 631.4'072042 B81-32409

631.5'0913 — Tropical crops. Cultivation

Williams, C. N.. Tree and field crops of the wetter regions of the Tropics / C.N. Williams, W.Y. Chew, J.H. Rajaratnam. — London : Longman, 1980, c1979. — ix,262p : ill,maps ; 22cm. — (Intermediate tropical agriculture series)
Bibliography: p249. - Includes index
ISBN 0-582-60319-6 (pbk) : £3.50 : CIP rev. B79-35929

631.5'21'05 — Crops. Seeds. Quality — *Serials*

Seed quality / NIAB. — 1979. — Cambridge (Huntingdon Rd., Cambridge CB3 0LE) : National Institute of Agricultural Botany, 1979. — 15p. — (Technical leaflet / National Institute of Agricultural Botany ; no.1)
£0.15 B81-09697

631.5'3 — Crops. Breeding for disease & pest resistance

Russell, G. E.. Plant breeding for pest and disease resistance / G.E. Russell. — London : Butterworths, 1978 (1981 [printing]). — 485p : ill ; 24cm. — (Studies in the agricultural and food sciences)
Includes bibliographies and index
ISBN 0-408-10781-2 (pbk) : Unpriced B81-27035

631.5'3 — Crops. Genetic engineering — *Conference proceedings*

The **Manipulation** of genetic systems in plant breeding : a Royal Society discussion : held on 29 and 30 October 1980 / organized by H. Rees ... [et al.]. — London : The Royal Society, 1981. — 209p,1leaf of plates : ill ; 31cm
Originally published: in Philosophical transactions of the Royal Society of London. — Includes bibliographies
ISBN 0-85403-165-0 : £20.30 B81-36280

631.5'3 — Crops. Planting times. Astrological aspects — *Calendars* — *Serials*

Working with the stars. — 1981. — East Grinstead (Peredur, East Grinstead, Sussex) : Lanthorn Press, c1981. — 44p
ISBN 0-906155-14-2 : Unpriced B81-13203

631.5'3 — Plants. Breeding. Genetic aspects

Welsh, James R.. Fundamentals of plant genetics and breeding / James R. Welsh. — New York ; Chichester : Wiley, c1981. — xiv,290p : ill,facsims ; 24cm
Includes bibliographies and index
ISBN 0-471-02862-2 : Unpriced B81-10039

631.5'3 — Plants. Propagation — *Manuals*

Guyton, Anita. The pocket book of propagation. — London : Evans Bros, May 1981. — [128]p
ISBN 0-237-45556-0 : £1.75 : CIP entry B81-04240

Wright, Robert C. M.. The complete book of plant propagation : a practical guide to the various methods of propagating trees, shrubs, herbaceous plants, fruits and vegetables / Robert C.M. Wright and Alan Titchmarsh. — London : Ward Lock, 1981. — 180p : ill(some col.) ; 26cm
Includes index
ISBN 0-7063-5994-1 : £7.95 B81-14154

631.5'4 — Crops. Growth. Regulation. Use of chemicals

Luckwill, Leonard C.. Growth regulators in crop production / Leonard C. Luckwill. — London : Edward Arnold, 1981. — 59p : ill ; 22cm. — (The Institute of Biology's studies in biology ; no.129)
Bibliography: p60
ISBN 0-7131-2816-x : £1.95 : CIP rev. B80-33780

631.5'4 — Crops. Growth. Regulation. Use of chemicals — *Serials*

[News bulletin *(British Plant Growth Regulator Group)***]**. News bulletin / British Plant Growth Regulator Group. — Vol.1, no.1 (May 1977)-. — [Ashford] ([c/o Dr. G. Goldwin, Dept. of Horticulture, Wye College, Nr. Ashford, Kent]) : The Group, 1977-. — v. ; 26cm
Three issues yearly. — Description based on: Vol.3, no.3 (Apr.1980)
ISSN 0144-7602 = News bulletin — British Plant Growth Regulator Group : £12.00 per year (free to Group members) B81-06784

631.5'4 — Crops. Productivity. Physiological aspects — *Conference proceedings*

Physiological processes limiting plant productivity / [edited by] C.B. Johnson. — London : Butterworths, 1981. — 395p : ill ; 24cm
Conference papers. — Includes bibliographies and index
ISBN 0-408-10649-2 : Unpriced : CIP rev. B81-02571

631.5'58 — Crops. Yields. Increases — *Conference proceedings*

Opportunities for increasing crop yields : taken from proceedings of a meeting held at the University of Reading, 17-21 September 1979 to celebrate the 75th anniversary of the Association of Applied Biology [i.e. Biologists] / edited by R.G. Hurd, P.V. Biscoe, and C. Dennis. — Boston [Mass.] ; London : Pitman, c1980. — xi,410p : ill ; 25cm. — (The Pitman international series in applied biology)
Includes bibliographies and index
ISBN 0-273-08481-x : £24.00 B81-02283

631.5'8 — Crops. Organic cultivation

Biological husbandry. — London : Butterworths, Sept.1981. — [280]p
Conference papers
ISBN 0-408-10726-x : £25.00 : CIP entry B81-23905

631.5'83 — Heated greenhouses. Crops. Growth. Effects of energy conservation

Hurd, R. G.. Fuel saving in greenhouses : the biological aspects / R.G. Hurd and G.F. Sheard. — London : Grower, 1981. — viii,55p : ill ; 21cm. — (Grower guide ; no.20)
Bibliography: p52-55. — Includes index
ISBN 0-901361-50-x (pbk) : £3.50 B81-11395

631.5'84'072041 — Great Britain. Crops. Organic cultivation. Research requirements — *Conference proceedings*

Elm Farm Research Centre Colloquium *(1980)*. The research needs of biological agriculture in Great Britain : a report on the discussions of the Elm Farm Research Centre Colloquium November 1980. — Hamstead Marshall (Hamstead Marshall, Near Newbury, Berks. RG15 0HR) : Elm Farm Research Centre, 1981. — 74p : ill,facsim ; 30cm. — (Report / Elm Farm Research Centre ; no.1)
Unpriced (unbound) B81-34915

631.6 — AGRICULTURE. LAND RECLAMATION AND DRAINAGE

631.6'1 — Trees & shrubs. Clearance

Intermediate Technology Development Group. *Agriculture Panel*. Land clearance : alternative techniques for removing trees and bushes / compiled by the Agriculture Panel of the Intermediate Technology Development Group. — London : Intermediate Technology, c1981. — iv,65p : ill ; 26cm
ISBN 0-903031-77-9 (pbk) : £1.95 B81-27759

631.6'2'0341 — Agricultural land. Drainage — *French & English dictionaries*

Kennedy, M. N.. A handbook of irrigation and drainage terms, English-French = Irrigation et drainage fran cais-anglais / compiled by M.N. Kennedy. — Bishop's Waltham (Hazel Holt, Bishop's Waltham, Hants., SO3 1GA) : J.W.A. Newhouse, c1981. — 44p ; 21cm
ISBN 0-9502591-3-6 (pbk) : Unpriced
Primary classification 631.7'03'41 B81-34982

631.7 — AGRICULTURE. IRRIGATION

631.7 — Agricultural land. Irrigation — *Conference proceedings*

U.K. Irrigation Association. *Inaugural Conference (1980 : National College of Agricultural Engineering)*. Irrigation : the way ahead : proceedings of the Inaugural Conference of the U.K. Irrigation Association Ltd / editor M.K.V. Carr ; sponsored by Barclays Bank Ltd. and held at the National College of Agricultural Engineering, October 15, 1980. — [S.l.] : U.K. Irrigation Association in co-operation with the National College of Agricultural Engineering, 1981. — v,83p : ill,1chart,1map,ports ; 30cm. — (U.K. Irrigation Association publication ; no.1) (National College of Agricultural Engineering occasional paper ; no.10)
Unpriced (pbk) B81-26840

631.7'03'41 — Irrigation — *French & English dictionaries*

Kennedy, M. N.. A handbook of irrigation and drainage terms, English-French = Irrigation et drainage fran cais-anglais / compiled by M.N. Kennedy. — Bishop's Waltham (Hazel Holt, Bishop's Waltham, Hants., SO3 1GA) : J.W.A. Newhouse, c1981. — 44p ; 21cm
ISBN 0-9502591-3-6 (pbk) : Unpriced
Also classified at 631.6'2'0341 B81-34982

631.7'072 — Agricultural land. Irrigation. Management. Applications of operations research

ORAGWA International Conference *(1979 : Jerusalem)*. Operations research in agriculture and water resources : proceedings of the ORAGWA International Conference held in Jerusalem, November 25-29, 1979 / edited by Dan Yaron and Charles S. Tapiero. — Amsterdam ; Oxford : North-Holland, 1980. — xviii,586p : ill,1map,plans,forms ; 23cm
Includes bibliographies and index
ISBN 0-444-86044-4 : £29.23 B81-05797

631.7'0955'52 — Iran. Zagros Mountains. Irrigation

Lister, H.. Irrigation in the Zagros Mountains, Iran / H. Lister. — [Newcastle-upon-Tyne] : University of Newcastle-upon-Tyne, 1978. — 78p : ill,maps ; 24cm. — (Research series / University of Newcastle upon Tyne Department of Geography ; n.12)
Bibliography: p68-70
£1.50 (pbk) B81-06100

631.8 — AGRICULTURE. FERTILISERS

631.8 — Fertilisers & soil conditioners. Use

Follett, Roy H.. Fertilizers and soil amendments / Roy H. Follett, Larry S. Murphy, Roy L. Donahue. — Englewood Cliffs ; London : Prentice-Hall, c1981. — xv,557p : ill ; 25cm
Includes bibliographies and index
ISBN 0-13-314336-8 : £16.20 B81-25457

631.8′1941′0212 — Great Britain. Fertilisers — *Statistics — Serials*

Fertiliser statistics / the Fertiliser Manufacturers Association. — 1980. — London (93 Albert Embankment, SE1 7TU) : The Association, [1981?]. — [7]p
Unpriced B81-31026

631.8′61 — Farmyard manure. Nitrogen. Losses during use — *Conference proceedings*

Nitrogen losses and surface run-off from landspreading of manures : proceedings of a workshop in the EEC programme of coordination of research on effluents from livestock, held at The Agricultural Institute, Johnstown Castle Research Centre, Wexford, Ireland, May 20-22, 1980 / sponsored by the Commission of the European Communities, Directorate-General for Agriculture and Directorate-General for Research, Science and Education ; edited by J.C. Brogan. — The Hague ; London : Nijhoff/Junk for the Commission of the European Communities, 1981. — xiv,471p : ill,maps ; 25cm. — (Developments in plant and soil sciences ; v.2)
Includes bibliographies
ISBN 90-247-2471-6 : Unpriced
Also classified at 628.1′6846 B81-15261

631.8′61 — Soils. Liquid farmyard manure. Nitrogen compounds. Chemical reactions. Kinetics. Mathematical models — *Conference proceedings*

Modelling nitrogen from farm wastes : models and systems for studying the transformation and fate of nitrogen from animal effluents applied to soils / [proceedings of a seminar in the EEC Programme of Coordination of Research on Animal Effluents, organised by H. Laudelout, and held at the Université Catholique de Louvain-la-Neuve, Belgium, October 10-11, 1978] ; edited by J.K.R. Gasser. — London : Applied Science Publishers, c1979. — vii,195p : ill ; 23cm
Includes bibliographies
ISBN 0-85334-869-3 : £11.30 : CIP rev.
B79-31248

632 — AGRICULTURE. PLANT INJURIES, DISEASES, PESTS

632 — Crops. Contaminants: Fluorides

Robinson, J. B. D.. Fluorine : its occurrence, analysis, effects on plants, diagnosis and control / J.B.D. Robinson. — Slough : Commonwealth Agricultural Bureaux, 1977, c1978. — 36p ; 25cm. — (Special publication / Commonwealth Bureau of Soils ; no.6)
Bibliography: p24-30
ISBN 0-85198-431-2 (pbk) : £2.50 B81-05654

632′.072042 — England. Crops. Diseases & pests. Research by Agricultural Science Service — *Serials*

Agricultural Science Service. Crop pests and diseases : Agricultural Science Service research and development reports. — 1979-. — London : H.M.S.O., 1981-. — v. ; 21cm. — (Reference book / Ministry of Agriculture, Fisheries and Food)
Annual. — Continues in part: Pest Infestation Control Laboratory. Pest Infestation Control Laboratory report; and, also in part, Regional Agricultural Science Service. Annual report
ISSN 0261-6963 = Crop pests and diseases : £4.50 B81-32408

632′.0913 — Tropical regions. Crops. Diseases & pests

Hill, D. S.. Pests and diseases of tropical crops. — London : Longman, June 1981. — (Intermediate tropical agriculture series)
Vol.1: Principles and methods of control. — [192]p
ISBN 0-582-60614-4 (pbk) : £3.00 : CIP entry
B81-10438

632.3 — AGRICULTURE. PLANT DISEASES

632′.3 — Plants. Diseases. Control — *Conference proceedings*

Plant disease control : resistance and susceptibility / edited by Richard C. Staples, Gary H. Toenniessen. — New York ; Chichester : Wiley, c1981. — xix,339p : ill ; 24cm. — (Environmental science and technology, ISSN 0194-0287)
Includes bibliographies and index
ISBN 0-471-08196-5 : £19.60 B81-23711

632.4 — AGRICULTURE. FUNGUS DISEASES

632′.4 — Crops. Fungal wilt diseases

Fungal wilt diseases of plants / edited by Marshall E. Mace, Alois A. Bell, Carl H. Beckman. — New York ; London : Academic Press, 1981. — xi,640p : ill ; 24cm
Includes bibliographies and index
ISBN 0-12-464450-3 : £32.60 B81-33163

632′.4′0913 — Tropical crops. Pathogens: Fungi

Holliday, Paul. Fungus diseases of tropical crops / Paul Holliday. — Cambridge : Cambridge University Press, 1980. — xv,607p ; 26cm
Includes bibliographies and index
ISBN 0-521-22529-9 : £55.00 B81-01649

632′.4′52 — Crops. Downy mildews

The **Downy** mildews. — London : Academic Press, Oct.1981. — [580]p
ISBN 0-12-656860-x : CIP entry B81-27353

632.5 — AGRICULTURE. HARMFUL PLANTS

632′.58 — Crops. Weeds. Control measures — *Conference proceedings*

British Crop Protection Conference — Weeds *(1980 : Brighton)*. Proceedings of the 1980 British Crop Protection Conference — Weeds : (15th British Weed Control Conference) 17th to 20th November 1980, Hotel Metropole, Brighton, England ... organised by the British Crop Protection Council. — Malvern : [The Council], [1981]. — 3v.(997p) : ill ; 21cm
Includes bibliographies
ISBN 0-901436-63-1 : Unpriced
ISBN 0-901436-64-x (v.2)
ISBN 0-901436-65-8 (v.3) B81-40823

632′.58 — Scotland. Crops. Weeds: Wild oats. Control

Wild-oat control in arable farming. — Edinburgh (West Mains Rd., Edinburgh EH9 3JG) : East of Scotland College of Agriculture, 1981. — 10p ; 21cm. — (Publication / The Scottish Agricultural Colleges, ISSN 0308-5708 ; no.75)
Unpriced (unbound) B81-16792

632′.58′09 — Crops. Weeds. Distribution

A **Geographical** atlas of world weeds / LeRoy Holm ... [et al.]. — New York ; Chichester : Wiley, c1979. — xlix,391p ; 26cm
Introduction in ten languages
ISBN 0-471-04393-1 : £28.70 B81-33226

632.6 — AGRICULTURE. ANIMAL PESTS

632′.6′072042 — England. Stored crops. Pests. Research by Agricultural Science Service — *Serials*

Agricultural Science Service. Storage pests : Agricultural Science Service research and development reports. — 1979-. — London : H.M.S.O., 1981-. — v. ; 21cm. — (Reference book / Ministry of Agriculture, Fisheries and Food)
Annual. — Continues in part: Pest Infestation Control Laboratory. Pest Infestation Control Laboratory report ; and, also in part, Regional Agricultural Science Service. Annual report
ISSN 0261-6971 = Storage pests : £2.95
B81-32407

632′.68′072042 — England. Crops. Pests: Birds. Research by Agricultural Science Service — *Serials*

Agricultural Science Service. Mammal and bird pests : Agricultural Science Service research and development reports. — 1979-. — London : H.M.S.O., 1981. — v. ; 21cm. — (Reference book / Ministry of Agriculture, Fisheries and Food)
Annual. — Continues in part: Pest Infestation Control Laboratory. Pest Infestation Control Laboratory report ; and, also in part, Regional Agricultural Science Service. Annual report
ISSN 0261-7161 = Mammal and bird pests : £2.95
Primary classification 632′.69′0072042
B81-35458

632′.69′0072042 — England. Crops. Pests: Mammals. Research by Agricultural Science Service — *Serials*

Agricultural Science Service. Mammal and bird pests : Agricultural Science Service research and development reports. — 1979-. — London : H.M.S.O., 1981. — v. ; 21cm. — (Reference book / Ministry of Agriculture, Fisheries and Food)
Annual. — Continues in part: Pest Infestation Control Laboratory. Pest Infestation Control Laboratory report ; and, also in part, Regional Agricultural Science Service. Annual report
ISSN 0261-7161 = Mammal and bird pests : £2.95
Also classified at 632′.68′072042 B81-35458

632′.6974428 — Feral cats. Control measures — *Conference proceedings*

The **Ecology** and control of feral cats : proceedings of a symposium held at Royal Holloway College, University of London 23rd and 24th September 1980. — Potters Bar : Universities Federation for Animal Welfare, c1981. — 99p : ill,1map ; 21cm
Bibliography: p99
£2.50 (pbk) B81-19722

632.7 — AGRICULTURE. INSECT PESTS

632′.7 — Great Britain. Stored food. Pests: Insects — *Field guides*

Common insect pests of stored food products : a guide to identification. — 6th ed. / edited by Paul Freeman. — London : Trustees of the British Museum (Natural History), 1980. — 69p : ill ; 21cm. — (British Museum (Natural History) eononomic series ; no.15) (Economic series / British Museum (Natural History) ; no.15)
Previous ed.: 1972. — Includes index
ISBN 0-565-00830-7 (pbk) : Unpriced : CIP rev. B80-20797

632′.771 — Scotland. Crops. Pests: Leatherjackets. Control measures

Leather jackets and their control. — Edinburgh (West Mains Rd., Edinburgh EH9 3JG) : East of Scotland College of Agriculture, 1981. — 7p : col.ill ; 21cm. — (Publication / The Scottish Agricultural Colleges, ISSN 0308-5708 ; no.77)
Unpriced (unbound) B81-31316

632.8 — AGRICULTURE. VIRAL AND RICKETTSIAL DISEASES

632′.8′072043 — Crops. Virus diseases. Research in West German institutions

Torrance, L.. Virus diseases of plants : report of a visit to West Germany 9-29 November 1980 / L. Torrance. — [London] ([Great Westminster House, Horseferry Rd., SW1P 2AE]), [1981?]. — 16p : ill ; 30cm
Cover title. — At head of title: Ministry of Agriculture, Fisheries and Food
Unpriced (pbk) B81-36270

632.9 — AGRICULTURE. PEST CONTROL

632′.9 — Crops. Pests. Control

Flint, Mary Louise. Introduction to integrated pest management / Mary Louise Flint and Robert van den Bosch. — New York ; London : Plenum, 1981. — xv,240p : ill,map ; 24cm
Bibliography: p22.-236. — Includes index
ISBN 0-306-40682-9 : Unpriced B81-29874

632′.94 — Chemicals. Application from aircraft — *Conference proceedings*
Agricultural Aviation Group all-day symposium jointly with Rotorcraft Section : Wednesday 14th February 1979 : presented at The Royal Aeronautical Society. — London (4 Hamilton Place, W1V 0BQ) : [The Society], [1979]. — 132p in various pagings : ill ; 30cm
Includes bibliographies
Unpriced (pbk)
Also classified at 629.133′352 B81-37730

632′.95 — Crops. Pesticides. Physical processes
Hartley, G. S.. Physical principles of pesticide behaviour : the dynamics of applied pesticides in the local environment in relation to biological response / G.S. Hartley, I.J. Graham-Bryce. — London : Academic Press
Vol.2. — 1980. — xviip,p519-1024 : ill ; 24cm
Bibliography: p975-1007. - Includes index
ISBN 0-12-328402-3 : £31.00 : CIP rev.
B80-09746

632′.95 — Pesticides. Use. Safety measures — *Conference proceedings*
Education and safe handling in pesticide application. — Oxford : Elsevier Scientific, Nov.1981. — 1v.. — (Studies in environmental science ; 18)
Conference papers
ISBN 0-444-42041-x : CIP entry B81-34009

632′.95′0289 — Great Britain. Agriculture. Use of pesticides. Safety measures
Poisonous chemicals on the farm / Health and Safety Executive. — 2nd ed. — London : HMSO, 1980. — iii,38p : ill ; 21cm. — (Health and safety series booklet. HS(G) ; 2)
Previous ed.: 1978
ISBN 0-11-883414-2 (pbk) : £2.50 B81-08190

632′.95042 — Pesticides: Organochlorines. Toxic effects
Mercier, M.. Criteria (dose/effect relationships) for organochlorine pesticides : reports of a working group of experts prepared for the Commission of the European Communities, Directorate-General for Employment and Social Affairs, Health and Safety Directorate / rapporteur M. Mercier. — Oxford : Published for the Commission of the European Communities by Pergamon, 1981. — xv,381p : ill ; 23cm
Bibliography: p373-381
ISBN 0-08-023441-0 (pbk) : £25.00 : CIP rev.
B81-12371

632′.95042 — Pesticides. Residues. Chemical analysis
Analysis of pesticide residues / edited by H. Anson Moye. — New York ; Chichester : Wiley, c1981. — viii,467p : ill ; 24cm. — (Chemical analysis ; v.58)
Includes index
ISBN 0-471-05461-5 : £25.75 B81-17377

632′.95′072042 — England. Crops. Pesticides. Research by Agricultural Science Service — *Serials*
Agricultural Science Service. Pesticide science : Agricultural Science Service research and development reports. — 1979-. — London : H.M.S.O., 1981-. — v. ; 21cm. — (Reference book / Ministry of Agriculture, Fisheries and Food)
Annual. — Continues in part: Pest Infestation Control Laboratory. Pest Infestation Control Laboratory report; and, also in part, Regional Agricultural Science Service. Annual report
ISSN 0261-7196 = Pesticide science (London) : £3.50 B81-32406

632′.95′0941 — Great Britain. Crops. Pesticides approved under Agricultural Chemicals Approval Scheme — *Lists* **—** *Serials*
List of approved products and their uses for farmers and growers / Agricultural Chemicals Approved Scheme. — 1981. — London : H.M.S.O., 1981. — 331p
£4.50 B81-15083

632′.954 — Herbicides. Action
Ashton, Floyd M.. Mode of action of herbicides / Floyd M. Ashton, Alden S. Crafts. — 2nd ed. — New York ; Chichester : Wiley, c1981. — x,525p : ill ; 24cm
Previous ed.: 1973. — Includes bibliographies and index
ISBN 0-471-04847-x : £28.50 B81-28304

632′.954 — Herbicides: Methylchlorophenoxyacetic acid, 2,4— dichlorophenoxyacetic acid & 2,4,5— trichlorophenoxyacetic acid, *to 1979*
Kirby, Celia. The hormone weedkillers : a short history of their discovery and development / Celia Kirby. — Croydon : BCPC Publications, c1980. — 55p ; 22cm
Bibliography: p55
ISBN 0-901436-62-3 (pbk) : £2.50 B81-04932

632′.96 — Plants. Diseases & pests. Biological control
Microbial control of pests and plant diseases 1970-80 / edited by H.D. Burges. — London : Academic Press, 1981. — 949p : ill ; 24cm
Includes bibliographies and index
ISBN 0-12-143360-9 : £41.40 B81-36864

633 — AGRICULTURE. FIELD CROPS

633′.087′0724 — Field crops. Varieties. Field experiments — *Serials*
Varieties in trials / National Institute of Agricultural Botany. — 1981. — Cambridge (Huntingdon Rd, Cambridge) : NIAB, [1981]. — 50p
£1.00 B81-30805

633.1 — AGRICULTURE. CEREAL CROPS

633.1 — Cereals. Chemical analysis. Near infrared spectroscopy — *Conference proceedings*
NIR ′80 : proceedings of a symposium on near infra-red (NIR) analysis held at FMBRA, Chorleywood on 21st October 1980 / edited by C.R.H. Parsons. — Rickmansworth (Chorleywood, Rickmansworth, Herts. WD3 5SH) : Flour Milling and Baking Research Association, c1981. — 52p : ill ; 21cm
Bibliography: p51-52
ISBN 0-907503-00-4 (pbk) : £5.00 (£2.00 to members) B81-27894

633.1′046 — Cereals. Drying & storage
McLean, K. A.. Drying and storing combinable crops / by K.A. McLean. — Ipswich : Farming Press, 1980. — 281p : ill ; 23cm
Includes index
ISBN 0-85236-108-4 : £8.25 B81-04688

633.1′0468 — Cereals. Controlled atmosphere storage — *Conference proceedings*
Controlled atmosphere storage of grains : an international symposium held from 12 to 15 May 1980 at Castelgandolfo (Rome) Italy / edited by J. Shejbal. — Amsterdam ; Oxford : Elsevier Scientific, 1980. — viii,608p : ill ; 25cm. — (Developments in agricultural engineering ; 1)
Includes index
ISBN 0-444-41939-x : £45.56 : CIP rev.
B80-31852

633.1′047′0942 — England. Cereals. Varieties — *Lists* **—** *Serials*
Classified list of cereal varieties, England & Wales / National Institute of Agricultural Botany. — 1981/82. — Cambridge (Huntingdon Rd, Cambridge CB3 0LE) : NIAB, [1981]. — 14p
ISSN 0306-9257 : £1.00 B81-30874

633.1′0493 — Cereals. Diseases. Control measures
Strategies for the control of cereal disease / edited for the Federation of British Plant Pathologists by J.F. Jenkyn and R.T. Plumb. — Oxford : Blackwell Scientific, 1981. — ix,219p : ill ; 26cm
Includes bibliographies and index
ISBN 0-632-00716-8 : £13.00 B81-18497

633.1′0494 — Cereals. Take-all disease. Control measures
Biology and control of take-all. — London : Academic Press, Apr.1981. — [500]p
ISBN 0-12-065320-6 : CIP entry B81-06621

633.1′0941 — Great Britain. Cereals. Cultivation
Soper, M. H. R.. British cereals : wheat, barley and oats / M.H.R. Soper. — London : Association of Agriculture, 1979. — 37p,[4]p of plates : ill ; 21cm. — (Modern agriculture series)
Unpriced (pbk) B81-32610

633.1′13 — Wheat. Breeding
Wheat science - today and tomorrow / edited by L.T. Evans and W.J. Peacock. — Cambridge : Cambridge University Press, 1981. — x,290p : ill,port ; 24cm
Based on papers presented at a Symposium in honour of Sir Otto Frankel. — List of works by O.H. Frankel : p285-290. — Includes bibliographies
ISBN 0-521-23793-9 : £18.50 : CIP rev.
B81-06894

633.1′17 — Winter wheat — *Conference proceedings*
Crop Conference *(1980 : Cambridge)*. Winter wheat : Crop Conference, Cambridge, 17-18 December 1980 / chairman for 17 December J.H. Cossins, chairman for 18 December J.D. Ivins. — Cambridge : National Institute of Agricultural Botany, [1981]. — 107p : ill,maps ; 24cm
Proceedings of the 16th NIAB Crop Conference, 1980. — Includes bibliographies
£2.50 (pbk) B81-29601

633.1′71 — Crops: Pearl millet
Rachie, Kenneth O.. Pearl millet / Kenneth O. Rachie and J.V. Majmudar [i.e. Majumdar]. — University Park ; London : Pensylvania State University Press, c1980. — 307p : ill ; 27cm
ISBN 0-271-00234-4 : £17.75 B81-25648

633.1′8 — Rice. Production
De Datta, Surajit K.. Principles and practices of rice production / Surajit K. De Datta. — New York ; Chichester : Wiley, c1981. — xix,618p : ill ; 24cm
Includes bibliographies and index
ISBN 0-471-08074-8 : £26.80 B81-30023

633.2/3 — AGRICULTURE. FORAGE CROPS

633.2 — Hay. Production — *For children*
Patterson, Geoffrey. The story of hay. — London : Deutsch, July 1981. — [32]p
ISBN 0-233-97356-7 : £4.50 : CIP entry
B81-14813

633.2′02 — Great Britain. Agricultural land: Swards. Constituents & productivity. Changes — *Conference proceedings*
Changes in sward composition and productivity : proceedings of a symposium / organised by the British Grassland Society 20-22 September 1978 held at the University of York ; organising committee A.H. Charles ... [et al.] ; editors A.H. Charles, R.J. Haggar. — Maidenhead : The Society, 1979. — vi,253p : ill ; 24cm. — (Occasional symposium / British Grassland Society, ISSN 0572-7022 ; no.10)
Includes bibliographies
ISBN 0-905944-01-1 (pbk) : £10.00 (£7.00 to members of the Society) B81-14506

633.2′02 — Great Britain. Grassland. Native plants. Seeds. Production
Wells, Terry. Creating attractive grasslands using native plant species / Terry Wells, Shirley Bell and Alan Frost. — [Shewsbury] : Nature Conservancy Council, [c1981]. — 35p : ill(some col.) ; 30cm
Bibliography: p31
ISBN 0-86139-114-4 (pbk) : Unpriced
B81-38714

633.2′02 — Ireland *(Republic)*. **Pastures. Metabolisable energy —** *Case studies*
Grainger, J. H. (John Harrison). Utilised metabolisable energy per hectare : report of a visit to Eire, 11-13 May 1981 / J.H. Grainger. — [Pinner] : ADAS, [1981]. — 9p ; 30cm
Unpriced (unbound) B81-40829

633.2′02 — Scotland. Crops: Grasses. Varieties — *Lists* **—** *Serials*
Classification of grass and clover varieties for Scotland / the Scottish Agricultural Colleges. — 1981-82. — Edinburgh (West Mains Rd., Edinburgh EH9 3JG) : Crop Production, Advisory and Development Department, East of Scotland College of Agriculture, 1981. — 16p. — (Publication / the Scottish Agricultural Colleges, ISSN 0308-5708 ; no.78)
ISSN 0308-5716 : Unpriced
Also classified at 633.3′27′09411 B81-31043

633.2′02′0913 — Tropical regions. Environment. Adaptation of grass crops
Humphreys, L. R.. Environmental adaptation of tropical pasture plants / L.R. Humphreys. — London : Macmillan, 1981. — ix,261p : ill,3maps ; 24cm
Bibliography: p221-252. — Includes index
ISBN 0-333-26820-2 : £28.00 : CIP rev.
Also classified at 633.3′0913 B80-11062

633.2′02′0941 — Great Britain. Crops: Grasses. Production & use
Grass : its production and utilization / edited by W. Holmes. — Oxford : Published for the British Grassland Society by Blackwell Scientific, 1980. — xiv,295p : ill,1map ; 22cm
Bibliography: p271-287. — Includes index
ISBN 0-632-00618-8 (pbk) : £8.50 : CIP rev.
B80-24590

633.2′087′0942 — England. Herbage. Varieties — *Lists — Serials*
Classified list of herbage varieties, England & Wales : National Institute of Agricultural Botany. — 1980/81. — Cambridge (Huntingdon Rd, Cambridge CB3 0LE) : The Institute, [1980]. — 18p
£1.00 B81-12397

633.2′557′0942 — England. Forage crops: Maize. Varieties — *Lists — Serials*
Recommended varieties of forage maize / NIAB. — 1981. — Cambridge (Huntingdon Rd, Cambridge CB3 0LE) : National Institute of Agricultural Botany, [1981]. — 6p. — (Farmers leaflet / National Institute of Agricultural Botany ; no.7)
£0.20 B81-30856

633.3 — Crops: Legumes
Duke, James A.. Handbook of legumes of world economic importance / James A. Duke. — New York ; London : Plenum, 1981. — xi,345p : ill ; 28cm
Bibliography: p341-345
ISBN 0-306-40406-0 : Unpriced B81-15220

633.3′04976 — Crops: Legumes. Pests: Bruchids. Ecological aspects — *Conference proceedings*
The **Ecology** of bruchids attacking legumes (pulses) : proceedings of the international symposium held at Tours (France), April 16-19, 1980 / edited by V. Labeyrie. — The Hague ; London : Junk, 1981. — xiv,233p : ill,maps,ports ; 25cm. — (Series entomologica ; v.19)
Includes bibliographies
ISBN 90-619-3883-x : Unpriced B81-28319

633.3′0913 — Tropical regions. Environment. Adaptation of legume crops
Humphreys, L. R.. Environmental adaptation of tropical pasture plants / L.R. Humphreys. — London : Macmillan, 1981. — ix,261p : ill,3maps ; 24cm
Bibliography: p221-252. — Includes index
ISBN 0-333-26820-2 : £28.00 : CIP rev.
Primary classification 633.2′02′0913 B80-11062

633.3′27′09411 — Scotland. Crops: Clover. Varieties — *Lists — Serials*
Classification of grass and clover varieties for Scotland / the Scottish Agricultural Colleges. — 1981-82. — Edinburgh (West Mains Rd., Edinburgh EH9 3JG) : Crop Production, Advisory and Development Department, East of Scotland College of Agriculture, 1981. — 16p. — (Publication / the Scottish Agricultural Colleges, ISSN 0308-5708 ; no.78)
ISSN 0308-5716 : Unpriced
Primary classification 633.2′02 B81-31043

633.3′4 — Crops: Soya beans
Botsford, Jenny. Soya / Jenny Botsford. — Hove : Wayland, 1980. — 70p : ill,1map ; 20x22cm. — (World resources)
Includes index
ISBN 0-85340-676-6 : £3.75 B81-05377

633.3′9 — Great Britain. Forage crops: Kale, rape & radishes. Varieties — *Lists — Serials*
Recommended varieties of green fodder crops / NIAB. — 1980. — Cambridge (Huntingdon Rd, Cambridge CB3 3LE) : National Institute of Agricultural Botany, [1980?]. — 11p. — (Farmers leaflet / National Institute of Agricultural Botany ; no.2)
£0.30 B81-13204

633.3′9 — Scotland. Feedingstuffs: Kale. Production
Kale. — Edinburgh (West Mains Rd., Edinburgh, EH9 3JG) : East of Scotland College of Agriculture, 1981. — 9p ; 21cm. — (Publication / The Scottish Agricultural Colleges, ISSN 0308-5708 ; no.74)
Unpriced (unbound) B81-16786

633.4 — AGRICULTURE. ROOT AND TUBER CROPS

633′.4 — Great Britain. Root crops. Violet root rot
Violet root rot of carrots and other root crops. — Rev. / [revised by N.J. Bradshaw] ; [edited by J.S.W. Dickens]. — Pinner (Tolcarne Drive, Pinner, Middx HA5 2DT) : Ministry of Agriculture, Fisheries and Food (Publications), 1980. — 1folded sheet([6]p) : ill(some col.) ; 21cm. — (Leaflet ; 346)
Originally published: 197-?
Unpriced B81-17865

633′.491′072041 — Potatoes. Production. Research in British institutions — *Directories — Serials*
Survey of potato research in the United Kingdom . — 1980. — London (50, Hans Crescent, SW1X 0NB) : Potato Marketing Board, [1980]. — 80p
ISSN 0141-1861 : Unpriced B81-04648

633′.491′09411 — Scotland. Seed potatoes. Production
Scottish seed potato production : recommended procedures. — Aberdeen (581 King St., Aberdeen AB9 1UD) : North of Scotland College of Agriculture, 1981. — 27p ; 22cm. — (Publication / The Scottish Agricultural Colleges, ISSN 0308-5708 ; no.71)
Unpriced (unbound) B81-16791

633′.4917′09411 — Scotland. Potatoes. Varieties — *Lists — Serials*
Potato varieties / the Scottish Agricultural Colleges. — 1981. — Edinburgh (West Mains Road, Edinburgh EH9 3JG) : East of Scotland College of Agriculture, 1980. — 15p. — (Publication / The Scottish Agricultural Colleges, ISSN 0308-5708 ; no.72)
Unpriced B81-11222

633′.4917′0942 — England. Potatoes. Varieties — *Lists — Serials*
Classified list of potato varieties, England & Wales / National Institute of Agricultural Botany. — 1981/82. — Cambridge (Huntingdon Rd, Cambridge CB3 0LE) : NIAB, [1981]. — 11p
ISSN 0140-0401 : £1.00 B81-30873

Recommended varieties of potatoes / NIAB. — 1981/82. — Cambridge (Huntingdon Rd, Cambridge CB3 0LE) : National Institute of Agricultural Botany, [1981]. — 12p. — (Farmers leaflet / National Institute of Agricultural Botany ; no.3)
£0.20 B81-30855

633′.49193 — Potatoes. Diseases
Potato diseases. — Cambridge (Huntingdon Rd., Cambridge CB3 0LE) : National Institute of Agricultural Botany, [1981?]. — 40p : col.ill ; 22cm
Cover title. — Text on inside cover
Unpriced (pbk) B81-40654

633.5 — AGRICULTURE. FIBRE CROPS

633.5′197′091811 — Eastern hemisphere. Cotton. Pests: Insects — *Field guides*
Imperial Chemical Industries. *Plant Protection Division.* Cotton pest identification manual / [ICI Plant Protection Division]. — Fernhurst (Fernhurst, Haslemere, Surrey) : The Division [Old World]. — [1981?]. — 35p : col.ill ; 15x21cm
Cover title
Unpriced (spiral) B81-18902

633.5′197′097 — America. Cotton. Pests: Insects — *Field guides*
Imperial Chemical Industries. *Plant Protection Division.* Cotton pest identification manual / [ICI Plant Protection Division]. — Fernhurst (Fernhurst, Haslemere, Surrey) : The Division American continent. — [1981?]. — 40p : col.ill ; 15x21cm
Cover title
Unpriced (spiral) B81-18903

633.6 — AGRICULTURE. SUGAR AND STARCH PLANTS

633.6′8 — Sago. Production — *Conference proceedings*
International Sago Symposium *(2nd : 1979 : Kuala Lumpur).* Sago : the equatorial swamp as a natural resource : proceedings of the Second International Sago Symposium held in Kuala Lumpur, Malaysia, September 15-17, 1979 / edited by W.R. Stanton and M. Flach. — The Hague ; London : Nijhoff, 1980. — 244p : ill,facsims,maps,ports ; 25cm. — (World crops ; v.1)
Includes bibliographies and index
ISBN 90-247-2470-8 : Unpriced B81-26169

633.7 — AGRICULTURE. ALKALOIDAL CROPS

633.7′1 — Tobacco. Production
Akehurst, B. C.. Tobacco / B.C. Akehurst. — 2nd ed. — London : Longman, 1981. — xiii,764p : ill ; 23cm. — (Tropical agriculture series)
Previous ed.: 1968. — Bibliography: p687-736. — Includes index
ISBN 0-582-46817-5 : £45.00 B81-23689

633.8 — AGRICULTURE. PLANTS FOR PERFUMES, FLAVOURINGS, MEDICINAL PURPOSES, ETC

633.8′2 — Great Britain. Hops. Marketing — *Serials*
English hops : journal of the Hops Marketing Board. — Jan. 1981-. — Paddock Wood ([Hop Pocket La., Paddock Wood, Tonbridge, Kent]) : The Board, 1981-. — v. : ill ; 30cm
Six issues yearly
ISSN 0261-2674 = English hops : Unpriced
B81-20324

633.8′53 — Crops: Oilseed rape. Nutrition
Holmes, M. R. J. Nutrition of the oilseed rape crop. — London : Applied Science, c1980. — x,158p : ill ; 23cm
Bibliography: p143-154. — Includes index
ISBN 0-85334-900-2 : £10.00 : CIP rev.
B80-11946

633.8′53 — Great Britain. Crops: Oilseed rape. Varieties — *Lists — Serials*
Varieties of oilseed rape / NIAB. — 1981. — Cambridge (Huntingdon Rd, Cambridge CB3 0LE) : National Institute of Agricultural Botany, [1981]. — 8p. — (Farmers leaflet / National Institute of Agricultural Botany ; no.9)
£0.20 B81-30854

634 — FRUIT. CULTIVATION

634 — Crops: Fruit. Biochemistry — *Conference proceedings*
Recent advances in the biochemistry of fruit and vegetables. — London : Academic Press, Dec.1981. — [250]p. — (Annual proceedings of the Phytochemical Society of Europe, ISSN 0309-9393 ; 18)
Conference papers
ISBN 0-12-268420-6 : CIP entry
Also classified at 635 B81-33868

634 — Fruit. Cultivation
Johns, Leslie. The complete book of fruit / Leslie Johns & Violet Stevenson ; illustrated by Marianne Yamaguchi. — London : Angus & Robertson, 1979. — 309p,[32]p of plates : ill (some col.) ; 27cm
Ill on lining papers. — Bibliography: p298-301. - Includes index
ISBN 0-207-14337-4 : £10.00
Also classified at 641.6′4 B81-00963

634 — Fruit — *For children*
Squire, David. Fruit / David Squire. — Hove : Wayland, 1981. — 72p : ill ; 20x22cm. — (World resources)
Bibliography: p71. - Includes index
ISBN 0-85340-804-1 : £3.75 B81-12980

634 — Fruit. Showing — *Manuals*
Whitehead, George E.. Growing for showing / George E. Whitehead ; with drawings by Anne Shingleton. — London : Faber, 1978 (1981 [printing]). — 176p : ill ; 20cm
Includes index
ISBN 0-571-11706-6 (pbk) : £2.50
Primary classification 635 B81-13039

634 — Gardens. Fruit. Cultivation
Spiller, Mary. Growing fruit / Mary Spiller ; drawings by Andrew Ingham. — London : Allen Lane, 1980. — 319p : ill ; 23cm
Bibliography: p315. — Includes index
ISBN 0-7139-1300-2 : £7.50 B81-00145

Stevenson, Violet. Grow and cook / Violet Stevenson. — [London] : Coronet, 1979, c1976. — 175p : ill ; 18cm
Originally published: Newton Abbot : David and Charles, 1976. — Includes index
ISBN 0-340-23233-1 (pbk) : £0.85
Primary classification 635 B81-13261

634 — Gardens. Fruit. Cultivation — *Manuals*
Wilson, Jim, *1926-*. Your fruit and vegetables / [author Jim Wilson]. — Nottingham : Floraprint, 1979. — 64p : ill(some col.) ; 30cm. — (A Floraprint colour guide)
Cover title. — Includes index
ISBN 0-903001-31-4 (pbk) : £1.40
Also classified at 635 B81-28240

634 — Post-harvest fruit. Physiology. Effects of environment
Postharvest : an introduction to the physiology and handling of fruit and vegetables / R.H.H. Wills ... [et al.]. — London : Granada, 1981. — 161p : ill ; 23cm
Includes bibliographies and index
ISBN 0-246-11556-4 : Unpriced
Also classified at 635 B81-30666

634'.0468 — Stored fruit. Quality — *Conference proceedings*
Long Ashton Symposium *(7th : 1979)*. Quality in stored and processed vegetables and fruit : proceedings of a symposium held at Long Ashton Research Station University of Bristol, 8-12 April 1979 / edited by P.W. Goodenough and R.K. Atkin. — New York ; London : Academic Press, 1981. — xi,398p : ill ; 24cm
At head of title: Seventh Long Ashton Symposium 1979. — Includes bibliographies and index
ISBN 0-12-289740-4 : £25.80 : CIP rev.
Primary classification 664'.807 B81-08796

634'.047'0941 — Great Britain. Fruit. Varieties. Trials — *Serials*
[Annual review *(National Fruit Trials (Experimental station))*]. Annual review / National Fruit Trials. — 1979-. — Faversham (Brogdale Farm, Faversham, Kent ME13 8XZ) : The Trials [1980-]. — v. ; 21cm
Continues: Annual report (National Fruit Trials (Experimental station))
ISSN 0260-4973 = Annual review - National Fruit Trials : Unpriced B81-00964

634'.11'0688 — Great Britain. Apples. Marketing — *Serials*
Top fruit times : we speak for English. — No.1 (July 1980)-. — Tunbridge Wells (Union House, The Pantiles, Tunbridge Wells, Kent) : Apple and Pear Development Council, 1980-. — v. : ill ; 42cm
Quarterly
ISSN 0260-4906 = Top fruit times : Unpriced
Also classified at 634'.13'0688 B81-03282

634'.13'0688 — Great Britain. Pears. Marketing — *Serials*
Top fruit times : we speak for English. — No.1 (July 1980)-. — Tunbridge Wells (Union House, The Pantiles, Tunbridge Wells, Kent) : Apple and Pear Development Council, 1980-. — v. : ill ; 42cm
Quarterly
ISSN 0260-4906 = Top fruit times : Unpriced
Primary classification 634'.11'0688 B81-03282

634'.653 — Avocados
Doeser, Linda. The little green avocado book. — Loughton : Piatkus, Oct.1981. — [64]p
ISBN 0-86188-122-2 (cased) : £15.00 : CIP entry
ISBN 0-86188-125-7 (pbk) : £1.25 B81-27472

634'.65331 — Avocados. Cultivation from pips — *Manuals*
Perper, Hazel. The avocado pip grower's handbook / Hazel Perper ; illustrated by Timothy Perper. — Rev. ed. — Harmondsworth : Penguin, 1981. — 62p : ill ; 20cm. — (Penguin handbooks)
Previous ed.: New York : Walker, 1965
ISBN 0-14-046422-0 (pbk) : £1.25 B81-16973

634'.8 — Grapes — *For children*
Langley, Andrew. Grapes / Andrew Langley. — Hove : Wayland, 1981. — 71p : ill ; 20x22cm. — (World resources)
Bibliography: p70. — Includes index
ISBN 0-85340-810-6 : £3.75 B81-17060

634.9 — FORESTRY

634.9 — Arboriculture — *Conference proceedings*
Research for practical arboriculture : proceedings of a seminar held in February 1980 at the Lancashire College of Agriculture at Preston and arranged by the Forestry Commission and the Arboricultural Association. — Edinburgh : The Commission, c1981. — 132p : ill ; 21cm. — (Occasional paper / Forestry Commission ; no.10)
Includes bibliographies
ISBN 0-85538-091-8 (pbk) : £2.00 B81-39943

634.9 — Arboriculture — *Serials*
The **International** tree crops journal : the journal of agroforestry. — Vol.1, no.1 (1980)-. — Berkhamstead (P.O. Box 97, Berkhamstead, Herts HP4 2PX) : A B Academic Publishers, 1980-. — v. : ill ; 21cm
Quarterly
ISSN 0143-5698 = International tree crops journal : £25.00 per year B81-20293

634.9'072041 — Forestry. Research in British institutions — *Serials*
[Report on forest research *(London)*]. Report on forest research for the year ended March ... / [Forestry Commission]. — 1980. — London : H.M.S.O., 1980. — vii,86p
ISBN 0-11-710119-2 : £4.90
ISSN 0436-4120 B81-03307

634.9'0913 — Tropical regions. Tree plantations
Evans, Julian. Plantation forestry in the tropics. — Oxford : Clarendon, Feb.1982. — [350]p
ISBN 0-19-859464-x : £20.00 : CIP entry B81-36229

634.9'092'4 — Forestry. Baker, Richard St Barbe — *Biographies*
Baker, Richard St Barbe. My life my trees / Richard St Barbe Baker. — Forres : Findhorn, 1979, c1970. — xv,167,[4]p of plates : ill,ports ; 21cm
Originally published: London: Lutterworth, 1970
ISBN 0-905249-40-2 (pbk) : £2.25 B81-22235

634.9'0941 — Great Britain. Forestry
James, N. D. G.. The forester's companion. — 3rd ed. — Oxford : Blackwell, Oct.1981. — [400]p
ISBN 0-631-12796-8 (cased) : £15.00 : CIP entry
ISBN 0-631-12797-6 (pbk) : £5.95 B81-28014

634.9'0942 — England. Forestry, *to 1975*
James, N. D. G.. A history of English forestry / N.D.G. James. — Oxford : Blackwell, 1981. — xii,339p : ill,maps,1facsim ; 26cm
Bibliography: p314-331. — Includes index
ISBN 0-631-12495-0 : £19.50 : CIP rev. B81-02372

634.9'0973 — United States. Forestry
Regional silviculture of the United States / edited by John W. Barrett. — 2nd ed. — New York ; Chichester : Wiley, c1980. — xii,551p : ill,maps ; 24cm
Previous ed.: New York : Ronald Press, 1962. — Includes bibliographies and index
ISBN 0-471-05645-6 : £16.85 B81-12942

634.9'5 — Great Britain. Urban regions. Trees. Planting & care — *Manuals*
Trees in towns : maintenance and management / editors Brian Clouston, Kathy Stansfield ; contributors Giles Biddle ... [et al.]. — London : Architectural, 1981. — 168p,[32]p of plates : ill,plans ; 23cm
Includes index
ISBN 0-85139-658-5 : £13.95
Also classified at 715'.2'0941 B81-22191

634.9'56 — Trees. Vegetative propagation — *Conference proceedings*
Vegetative propagation of trees in the 1980s : extended summary of a meeting at Merrist Wood Agricultural College, Worplesdon, near Guildford, Surrey, England, February 19-20, 1981 / edited by K.A. Longman. — [Aberystwyth] ([c/o D.G. Jones, Dept. of Agricultural Botany, University College of Wales, Aberystwyth, Dyfed SY23 3DD]) : Published by the Association of Applied Biologists in conjunction with the Department of Forestry, University of Oxford, 1981. — 22p ; 30cm. — (CFI occasional papers ; no.15)
Unpriced (pbk) B81-14612

634.9'56'0684 — Afforestation. Project mangement — *Manuals*
Fraser, A. I.. A manual on the management of plantation forests / by A. I. Fraser. — Penicuik (21 Biggar Rd, Silverburn, Penicuik, Midlothian, EH26 9LQ) : International Forest Science Consultancy, [1980]. — 127p : ill,forms ; 30cm
Bibliography: p127
£5.50 (spiral) B81-03577

634.9'6 — Trees. Diseases & pests
Manion, Paul D.. Tree disease concepts / Paul D. Manion. — Englewood Cliffs ; London : Prentice-Hall, c1981. — xv,399p : ill ; 24cm
Includes bibliographies and index
ISBN 0-13-930701-x : £15.35 B81-37179

634.9'728643 — Great Britain. Elm trees. Dutch elm disease. Control — *Manuals*
Duchars, A.. Dutch Elm disease / A. Duchars. — [Chelmsford] ([County Hall, Chelmsford CM1 1LX]) : [Essex County Council], [1981?]. — 8p : ill ; 21cm
Cover title. — Text on inside cover
£0.10 (pbk) B81-24769

634.9'7286768 — Elm trees. Pests: Large elm bark beetles. Effects of chemicals
Studies on chemically mediated behaviour in the large elm bark beetle, Scolytus scolytus (F.) (Coleoptera: Scolytidae) : field trials, 1979 / Margaret M. Blight ... [et al.]. — Farnham (Alice Holt Lodge, Wrecclesham, Farnham, Surrey GU10 4LH) : Forestry Commission Research Station, c1980. — 34p : ill ; 21cm. — (Research and development paper / Forestry Commission ; no.129)
Bibliography: p32-33
ISBN 0-85538-087-x (pbk) : £1.50 B81-05491

634.9'75'0681 — Great Britain. Timber trees: Conifers. Capital investment. Analysis. Management aspects
Busby, R. J. N.. Investment appraisal in forestry : with particular reference to conifers in Britain / R.J.N. Busby and A.J. Grayson. — London : H.M.S.O., 1981. — vi,90p : ill ; 21cm. — (Forestry Commission booklet ; 47)
Bibliography: p36-37
ISBN 0-11-710190-7 (pbk) : £3.75 B81-23662

634.9'7516781 — Scotland. Lodgepole pine trees. Pests: Pine beauty moths. Insecticides: Fenitrothion. Aerial spraying. Effects. Monitoring
Aerial application of insecticide against pine beauty moth / edited by A.V. Holden and D. Bevan. — Edinburgh : : Forestry Commission, c1981. — 112p : ill ; 30cm. — (Occasional paper / Forestry Commission ; no.11)
Cover title
ISBN 0-85538-093-4 (pbk) : £2.50 B81-39944

634.9′99′09411 — Scotland. Upland regions. Agricultural industries. Farms. Afforestation — *Case studies*

Mutch, W. E. S.. The interaction of forestry and farming : 13 case studies from the hills and uplands / W.E.S. Mutch, A.R. Hutchison. — [Edinburgh] : Department of Forestry and Natural Resources, University of Edinburgh, 1980. — 113p : ill ; 30cm. — (Economics and management series ; no.2)
Bibliography: p107
£2.50 (pbk) B81-14288

635 — GARDENING

635 — Crops: Vegetables. Biochemistry — *Conference proceedings*

Recent advances in the biochemistry of fruit and vegetables. — London : Academic Press, Dec.1981. — [250]p. — (Annual proceedings of the Phytochemical Society of Europe, ISSN 0309-9393 ; 18)
Conference papers
ISBN 0-12-268420-6 : CIP entry
Primary classification 634 B81-33868

635 — Gardening

Bonar, Ann. Book of basic gardening / Ann Bonar. — Poole : Blandford, [1981]. — 95p : col.ill,1form,1port ; 15cm. — ('How to')
Includes index
ISBN 0-7137-1051-9 (pbk) : £1.95 B81-08470

Gammidge, Ian. Gardeners Mirror : a complete month-by-month guide to the gardening year / [written by Ian Gammidge]. — London : Mirror, 1981. — 26p : ill(some col.) ; 36cm
ISBN 0-85939-249-x (unbound) : £0.50 B81-19416

Loads, Fred. Fred Loads′ gardening tips of a lifetime. — London : Hamlyn, 1980. — 175p : ill,1port ; 25cm
Includes index
ISBN 0-600-38795-x : £5.00 B81-02523

Mather, Jim. Jim Mather solves your garden problems. — London : Foulsham, c1981. — 128p,[4]p of plates : ill(some col.) ; 23cm
Includes index
ISBN 0-572-01120-2 : £3.95 B81-16710

Reader′s digest new illustrated guide to gardening : how to plant and care for flowers, shrubs, fruit and vegetables / [edited and designed by The Reader′s Digest Association Limited]. — London : Reader′s Digest, 1981, c1979. — 416p : ill(some col.) ; 22x24cm
Cover title. — Originally published: 1979. — Based on the Reader′s digest illustrated guide to gardening. — Text on lining papers. — Includes index
£10.95 B81-37170

Whiten, Geoff. Enjoy gardening with the Whitens / Geoff and Faith Whiten. — Nottingham : Floraprint, 1979. — 128p : ill(some col.),plans (some col.),ports ; 30cm
Includes index
ISBN 0-903001-38-1 (pbk) : £1.99 B81-28241

635 — Gardening — *For children*

Pavord, Anna. Growing things. — London : Macmillan Children′s Books, Feb.1982. — [32] p. — (Help yourself)
ISBN 0-333-30858-1 : £2.50 : CIP entry B81-35784

635 — Gardens. Evergreen plants

Beckett, Kenneth. The complete book of evergreens / Kenneth A. Beckett ; line drawings by Rosemary Wise. — London : Ward Lock, 1981. — 160p : ill(some col.) ; 26cm
Includes index
ISBN 0-7063-5989-5 : £7.95 B81-39960

635 — Gardens. Plants

Bloom, Adrian. Adrian Bloom′s guide to garden plants. — Norwich : Jarrold. — (A Jarrold garden series)
Bk.7: Alpines. — c1981. — [32]p : col,1port ; 20cm
Text, port on inside covers
ISBN 0-85306-935-2 (pbk) : Unpriced B81-31130

Hibbert, Alan. Plants in action : a scientific background to gardening / Alan Hibbert and Judy Brooks. — London : British Broadcasting Corporation, 1981. — 168p : ill(some col.),ports ; 31cm
Includes index
ISBN 0-563-16446-8 : £9.50 B81-17952

635 — Gardens. Vegetables. Cultivation

Bonar, Ann. Book of vegetable gardening / Ann Bonar. — Poole : Blandford, [1981]. — 95p : ill(some col.),2forms,1port ; 15cm. — ('How to')
Includes index
ISBN 0-7137-1046-2 (pbk) : £1.95 B81-08471

Salter, P. J.. Know & grow vegetables. — Oxford : Oxford University Press
Vol.2. — Jan.1982. — [224]p
ISBN 0-19-217727-3 (cased) : £5.95 : CIP entry
ISBN 0-19-286017-8 (pbk) : £2.95 B81-34376

Stevenson, Violet. Grow and cook / Violet Stevenson. — [London] : Coronet, 1979, c1976. — 175p : ill ; 18cm
Originally published: Newton Abbot : David and Charles, 1976. — Includes index
ISBN 0-340-23233-1 (pbk) : £0.85
Also classified at 634 ; 641.6′5 ; 641.6′4 B81-13261

635 — Gardens. Vegetables. Cultivation — *Manuals*

Carr, David, *1930-*. Vegetables / David Carr. — London : Ebury, 1981. — 63p : ill(some col.) ; 26cm. — (A Green fingers guide)
ISBN 0-85223-193-8 : £2.50 B81-16473

Hamilton, Geoff. Gardeners′ world vegetable book / Geoff Hamilton. — London : BBC, 1981. — 71p : ill ; 21cm
Includes index
ISBN 0-563-17962-7 (pbk) : £1.50 B81-37145

Wilson, Jim, *1926-*. Your fruit and vegetables / [author Jim Wilson]. — Nottingham : Floraprint, 1979. — 64p : ill(some col.) ; 30cm. — (A Floraprint colour guide)
Cover title. — Includes index
ISBN 0-903001-31-4 (pbk) : £1.40
Primary classification 634 B81-28240

635 — Great Britain. Gardens. Self-sufficiency — *Manuals*

Seymour, John, *1914-*. [The self-sufficient gardener]. The complete food garden / John Seymour. — [London] : Fontana, 1980, c1978. — 256p : ill(some col.),charts ; 28cm
Originally published: London : Faber, 1978. — Includes index
ISBN 0-00-635652-4 (pbk) : £6.50 B81-00965

635 — Horticultural industries. Nursery stock. Cultivation

Dick, Lila. An introduction to modern nursery stock production. — London : Muller, May 1981. — [192]p
ISBN 0-584-10410-3 (cased) : £6.95 : CIP entry
ISBN 0-584-10411-1 (pbk) : £3.50 B81-12825

635 — Indoor plants: Vegetables. Cultivation — *Manuals*

Spoczynska, Joy O. I.. Self-sufficiency in a flat / Joy O.I. Spoczynska ; illustrated by Melchior Spoczynski. — London : Sphere, 1981, c1980. — 136p : ill ; 18cm
Originally published: London : Wildwood House, 1980
ISBN 0-7221-8089-6 (pbk) : £1.25
Also classified at 641.4 B81-35524

635 — Plants. Nurseries — *Manuals*

Stanley, John, *19---*. The modern nurseryman / John Stanley and Alan Toogood. — London : Faber, 1981. — 412p,[8]p of plates : ill,2plans ; 23cm
Bibliography: p400-401. — Includes index
ISBN 0-571-11544-6 (cased) : £15.00 : CIP rev.
ISBN 0-571-11547-0 (pbk) : £7.50 B80-23416

635 — Post-harvest vegetables. Physiology. Effects of environment

Postharvest : an introduction to the physiology and handling of fruit and vegetables / R.H.H. Wills ... [et al.]. — London : Granada, 1981. — 161p : ill ; 23cm
Includes bibliographies and index
ISBN 0-246-11556-4 : Unpriced
Primary classification 634 B81-3066

635 — Scotland. Fife Region. Cupar. Country houses: Dalgairn House. Gardens. Plants useful to man. Cultivation — *Personal observations*

Banks, Roger. Living in a wild garden / Roger Banks. — Tadworth : World′s Work, c1980. — 128p : ill(some col.) ; 26cm
Bibliography: p126. - Includes index
ISBN 0-437-01200-x : £7.95 B81-0701

635 — Small gardens. Cultivation

Pearson, Robert. Gardening in a small space / Robert Pearson. — London : Royal Horticultural Society, 1980. — 48p : ill ; 22cm. — (Wisley handbook ; 38)
ISBN 0-906603-07-2 (pbk) : £0.95 B81-3666

635 — Vegetables & flowers. Showing — *Manuals*

Whitehead, George E.. Growing for showing / George E. Whitehead ; with drawings by Anne Shingleton. — London : Faber, 1978 (1981 [printing]). — 176p : ill ; 20cm
Includes index
ISBN 0-571-11706-6 (pbk) : £2.50
Also classified at 634 B81-1303

635′.0207 — Gardening — *Humour*

Parker, Cliff. How to avoid your garden / Cliff Parker ; illustrated by Barry Robson. — London : New English Library, 1981. — 144 : ill ; 20cm
ISBN 0-450-05065-3 (pbk) : £1.25 B81-1178

635′.0240816 — Gardening — *For physically handicapped persons*

Hadfield, Kate. Gardening for the handicapped : and the disenchanted / Kate Hadfield. — Harwood (21 Ruins La., Harwood, Bolton BL2 3JQ) : Tell Tale, 1981. — 23p ; 21cm
Includes index
ISBN 0-906692-13-x (pbk) : £0.40 B81-1434

635′.028 — Great Britain. Gardening tools, *to 1935*

Sanecki, Kay N.. Old garden tools / Kay N. Sanecki. — Aylesbury : Shire, 1979. — 32p : ill,facsims ; 21cm. — (Shire album ; 41)
Text, facsim. on inside covers
ISBN 0-85263-470-6 (pbk) : £0.85 B81-3783

635′.03′21 — Gardening — *Encyclopaedias*

Everett, Thomas H.. The New York Botanical Garden illustrated encyclopedia of horticulture / Thomas H. Everett. — New York ; London : Garland
Vol.1: A-Be. — c1980. — xx,355p,[16]p of plates : ill(some col.) ; 31cm
Ill on lining paper
Unpriced B81-2902

Everett, Thomas H.. The New York Botanical Garden illustrated encyclopedia of horticulture / Thomas H. Everett. — New York ; London : Garland
Vol.2: Be-Cha. — c1981. — p357-704,[16]p of plates : ill(some col.) ; 31cm
Ill on lining paper
ISBN 0-8240-7232-4 : Unpriced B81-2688

Everett, Thomas H.. The New York Botanical Garden illustrated encyclopedia of horticulture / Thomas H. Everett. — New York ; London : Garland
Vol.3: Cha-Di. — c1981. — p705-1058,[16]p of plates : ill(some col.) ; 31cm
Ill on lining paper
ISBN 0-8240-7233-2 : Unpriced B81-2688

Everett, Thomas H.. The New York Botanical Garden illustrated encyclopedia of horticulture / Thomas H. Everett. — New York ; London : Garland
Vol.4: Di-Fu. — c1981. — xxp,p1059-1422,[16]p of plates : ill(some col.) ; 32cm
ISBN 0-8240-7234-0 : Unpriced B81-2688

635′.03′21 — Gardening — *Encyclopaedias*
continuation

Everett, Thomas H.. The New York botanical garden illustrated encyclopedia of horticulture / Thomas H. Everett. — New York ; London : Garland
Ill on lining papers
Vol.5: G-Id. — c1981. — xx,p1423-1772[16p] of plates : ill(some col.) ; 32cm
ISBN 0-8240-7235-9 : Unpriced B81-33198

635′.043 — Gardens. Plants. Propagation

Prockter, Noël J.. Simple propagation : propagation by seed, division, layering, cuttings, budding and grafting / Noël J. Prockter. — New and rev. ed. — London : Faber, 1981, c1976. — 246p : ill ; 20cm
Previous ed.: 1963. — Includes index
ISBN 0-571-11707-4 (pbk) : £2.75 : CIP rev.
B81-00966

635′.043 — Gardens. Plants. Propagation — *Manuals*

Browne, Janet. Growing from cuttings and other means / Janet Browne. — London : Ward Lock, 1981. — 116p : ill(some col.) ; 20cm. — (Concorde gardening books)
Includes index
ISBN 0-7063-5993-3 : £2.95 B81-39863

Carr, David, *1930-*. Propagation / David Carr. — London : Ebury, 1981. — 63p : ill(some col.) ; 26cm. — (A Green fingers guide)
ISBN 0-85223-194-6 : £2.50 B81-16475

635′.0434 — Plants. Nurseries. Plants. Propagation. Stooling techniques

McMillan Browse, P. D. A.. Stooling nursery stock / P.D.A. McMillan Browse. — London : Grower Books, 1980. — 18p : 1ill ; 21cm. — (Grower guide ; no.19)
ISBN 0-901361-48-8 (pbk) : £1.00 B81-09357

635′.0441 — Ireland *(Republic)*. Hardy nursery stock. Grafting

Lamb, J. G. D.. An introduction to the grafting of hardy nursery stock / J.G.D. Lamb and F. Nutty. — Dublin (19 Sandymount Ave., Dublin 4) : An Foras Taluntais, 1981. — 21p : ill ; 21cm. — (Handbook series / An Foras Taluntais ; no.18)
ISBN 0-905442-52-0 (pbk) : Unpriced
B81-30052

635′.0468 — Stored vegetables. Quality — *Conference proceedings*

Long Ashton Symposium *(7th : 1979)*. Quality in stored and processed vegetables and fruit : proceedings of a symposium held at Long Ashton Research Station University of Bristol, 8-12 April 1979 / edited by P.W. Goodenough and R.K. Atkin. — New York ; London : Academic Press, 1981. — xi,398p : ill ; 24cm
At head of title: Seventh Long Ashton Symposium 1979. — Includes bibliographies and index
ISBN 0-12-289740-4 : £25.80 : CIP rev.
Primary classification 664′.807 B81-08796

635′.0483 — Gardening in greenhouses

Phillips, Sue. Greenhouse gardening / Sue Phillips ; line drawings by Robert Micklewright. — Feltham : Hamlyn Paperbacks, 1981. — 175p : ill ; 18cm
Includes index
ISBN 0-600-20283-6 (pbk) : £1.25 B81-08979

635′.0483 — Greenhouses

Hart, Colin. Greenhouses / Colin Hart ; illustrations by Vanessa Pancheri. — London : Hodder and Stoughton, 1981. — 214p : ill ; 20cm. — (Teach yourself books)
Includes index
ISBN 0-340-25110-7 (pbk) : £1.95 B81-12213

635′.0483 — Greenhouses. Vegetables. Commercial cultivation — *Manuals*

Walls, Ian. Modern greenhouse methods : vegetables. — London : Muller, Nov.1981. — [160]p
ISBN 0-584-10388-3 : £9.95 : CIP entry
B81-30533

635′.0484 — Gardens. Organic cultivation

Boland, Maureen. Old wives′ lore for gardeners / Maureen and Bridget Boland. — London : Macdonald Futura, 1981. — 126p : ill ; 18cm
Includes index. — Contents: Old wives′ lore for gardeners / Maureen & Bridget Boland. Originally published: London : Bodley Head, 1976 - Gardener′s magic & other old wives′ lore / Bridget Boland. Originally published London : Bodley Head, 1977
ISBN 0-7088-1845-5 (pbk) : £1.00 B81-17433

635′.0484 — Gardens. Organic cultivation — *Manuals*

Hills, Lawrence D.. Fertility gardening / Lawrence D. Hills. — London (25 Lloyd Baker St., WC1X 9AT) : Cameron & Tayleur in association with David & Charles, 1981, c1980. — 223p : ill ; 23cm
ISBN 0-7153-8188-1 : £6.50 B81-19833

Maintaining your garden fertility / drawings by Dominic Poelsma. — Stowmarket (Walnut Tree Manor, Haughley, Stowmarket, Suffolk IP14 3RS) : Soil Association, c1980. — 15p : ill ; 21cm
ISBN 0-905200-23-3 (pbk) : Unpriced
B81-38595

635′.049 — Crops: Vegetables. Diseases & pests

Dixon, G. R.. Vegetable crop diseases / G.R. Dixon. — London : Macmillan, 1981. — xiv,404p : ill ; 24cm
Includes bibliographies and index
ISBN 0-333-23574-6 : £35.00 B81-39954

635′.049 — Great Britain. Gardens. Plants. Diseases & pests

Buczacki, Stefan T.. Collins guide to the pests, diseases and disorders of garden plants / Stefan T. Buczacki and Keith M. Harris ; illustrated by Brian Hargreaves. — London : Collins, 1981. — 512p,24leaves of plates : col.ill ; 23cm
Bibliography: p493-495. — Includes index
ISBN 0-00-219103-2 : £15.00 B81-31773

635′.04958 — Great Britain. Gardens. Weeds. Control measures — *Manuals*

Chancellor, Richard J.. Garden weeds : and their control / Richard J. Chancellor ; with illustrations by Hilary Broad. — London : Inkata, 1980. — 93p : ill(some col.) ; 30cm
Bibliography: p90. - Includes index
ISBN 0-909605-21-1 : Unpriced B81-09383

635′.04958′0941 — Great Britain. Gardens. Weeds. Control measures — *Manuals*

Ailes, Valerie. The need to weed / devised and written by Valerie Ailes ; illustrated by Daphne Gander ; (front cover by Andrew Miller). — Wheathampstead (Wheathampstead, St. Albans, Herts. AL4 8QU) : Murphy Chemical Ltd., c1981. — 159p : ill(some col.) ; 20cm
Includes index
ISBN 0-9507435-0-x : £2.50 B81-22079

635′.04995′0941 — Great Britain. Gardens. Pesticides — *Lists*

Directory of garden chemicals / British Agrochemicals Association Ltd. — 6th ed. — London (93 Albert Embankment, SE1 7TU) : The Association, 1981. — 44p ; 22cm
Previous ed.: 1980
£1.00 (pbk) B81-16054

635′.04995′0941 — Great Britain. Horticultural industries. Hardy nursery stock. Pesticides

Greaves, D. A.. Hardy nursery stock : 1971, 1976 / D.A. Greaves and J.M.A. Sly, J.R. Cutler. — [Pinner] ([Tolcarne Drive, Pinner, Middlesex HA5 2DT]) : ADAS, 1979. — iii,126p : facsims,forms ; 30cm. — (Pesticide usage survey report ; 14) (Reference book ; 514)
£4.50 (pbk) B81-08192

635′.05 — Gardening — *Serials*

[Gardening world *(Brentwood)*]. Gardening world : for pleasure and profit. — Vol.1, no.1 (Aug. 1980). — Brentwood (Sovereign House, Brentwood, Essex CM14 4SE) : Sovereign Publications, 1980-. — v. : ill ; 29cm
Monthly
ISSN 0144-3828 = Gardening world (Brentwood) : £0.55 per issue B81-00146

635′.05 — Gardens. Plants. Serials: ′Garden′, *The* — *Indexes — Serials*

Index to the Journal and Proceedings of the Royal Horticultural Society and list of awards. Supplement for .... — 1966-1975. — London : The Society, 1980. — 267p
ISBN 0-906603-12-9 : Unpriced B81-29974

635′.07204127 — Scotland. Tayside Region. Dundee. Horticulture. Research organisations: Scottish Horticultural Research Institute — *Serials*

Scottish Horticultural Research Institute. Annual report for the year / the Scottish Horticultural Research Institute. — 1979. — Dundee (Invergowrie, Dundee DD2 5DA) : The Institute, 1980. — 141p
Unpriced B81-13202

635′.072042376 — Cornwall. Camborne. Horticulture. Research organisations: Rosewarne Experimental Horticulture Station — *Serials*

Rosewarne Experimental Horticulture Station. Annual review : incorporating results of experiments and development work at Rosewarne and Isles of Scilly Stations / Rosewarne Experimental Horticulture Station. — 1979-. — Camborne (Camborne, Cornwall TR14 OAB) : The Station, [1979?]-. — v. ; 21cm
Continues: Rosewarne Experimental Horticulture Station. Annual report. — Description based on: 1980 issue
ISSN 0262-2866 = Annual review - Rosewarne Experimental Horticulture Station : Unpriced
B81-39734

635′.072042489 — Great Britain. Vegetables. Research organisations: National Vegetable Research Station — *Serials*

National Vegetable Research Station. Annual report / National Vegetable Research Station. — 31st(1980). — Wellesbourne (Wellesbourne, Warwick CV35 9EF) : The Station, 1981. — 196p
ISSN 0510-002x : £3.00 B81-32429

635′.0720427662 — Lancashire. Kirkham. Horticulture. Research organisations: Fairfield Experimental Horticulture Station — *Serials*

[Summary annual review for ... *(Fairfield Experimental Horticulture Station)*]. Summary annual review for ... / Fairfield Experimental Horticulture Station. — 1979-. — Kirkham (Greenhalgh, Kirkham, Lancs., PR4 3HH) : The Station, 1980-. — v. : ill ; 21cm
Continues: Annual report (Fairfield Experimental Horticulture Station)
ISSN 0260-8081 = Summary annual review for ... - Fairfield Experimental Horticulture Station : Unpriced B81-09187

635′.072042845 — Horticulture. Research organisations: Stockbridge House Experimental Horticulture Station — *Serials*

[Annual review *(Stockbridge House Experimental Horticulture Station)*]. Annual review / Stockbridge House Experimental Horticulture Station. — 1979-. — Selby (Cawood, Selby, Yorkshire Y08 0TZ) : The Station, 1980-. — v. : ill ; 21cm
Continues: Annual report (Stockbridge House Experimental Horticulture Station)
ISSN 0261-1481 = Annual review - Stockbridge House Experimental Horticulture Station : Unpriced B81-16738

635′.088054 — Gardening. Activities for children

Ross, Alison. Gardening with children / Alison Ross ; with line drawings by Juliet Renny. — London : Faber, 1980. — 176p : ill ; 22cm
Bibliography: p161-163. — Includes index
ISBN 0-571-11564-0 : £5.25 : CIP rev.
B80-18822

635′.092′2 — Great Britain. Gardening, *to 1979* — *Biographies*

Hadfield, Miles. British gardeners : a biographical dictionary / Miles Hadfield, Robert Harling, Leonie Highton. — London : Zwemmer in association with Conde Nast, 1980. — 320p : ill(some col.),facsims,plans,ports ; 31cm
Ill on lining papers. — Includes index
ISBN 0-302-00541-2 : £20.00 B81-02849

635'.092'4 — England. Horticulture. Willmott, Ellen — *Biographies*

Le Lièvre, Audrey. Miss Willmott of Warley Place : her life and her gardens / Audrey le Lièvre. — London : Faber : 1980. — 240p,[8]p of plates : ill,1maps,ports ; 23cm
Includes index
ISBN 0-571-11622-1 : £9.50 : CIP rev. B80-12406

635'.092'4 — Great Britain. Horticulture. Research & development, *1922-1965* — *Personal observations*

Lawrence, William J. C.. Catch the tide : adventures in horticultural research / William J.C. Lawrence. — London : Grower, 1980. — 117p : ill,ports ; 21cm
ISBN 0-901361-46-1 (pbk) : £3.00 B81-11132

635'.0941 — Great Britain. Gardening

Scott-James, Anne. Down to earth / Anne Scott-James ; with drawings by Osbert Lancaster. — Rev. ed. — London : Joseph, 1981. — xiv,191p,[16]p of plates : ill ; 23cm
Previous ed.: 1971. — Includes index
ISBN 0-7181-2022-1 : £7.95 B81-23685

635'.0941 — Great Britain. Gardening — *Early works*

Jekyll, Gertrude. Wood and garden. — Woodbridge : Antique Collectors' Club, Dec.1981. — [286]p
Originally published: London : Longman, 1899
ISBN 0-907462-11-1 : £12.50 : CIP entry B81-36999

635'.09411 — Scotland. Gardening — *Manuals*

Robertson, Sid. The germination game / Sid Robertson & Jameson Clark ; with a foreword by Alan Gemmell ; illustrated by Rod McLeod. — Glasgow : Molendinar, 1980. — 104p : ill,2ports ; 24cm
Includes index
ISBN 0-904002-31-4 (pbk) : £3.95 B81-28227

635'.0942 — England. Horticulture — *Questions & answers*

Practical proficiency tests for horticulture / National Proficiency Tests Council for Agriculture and Horticulture. — Kenilworth (YFC Centre, National Agricultural Centre, Kenilworth, Warwickshire CV8 2LG) : The Council, [1980]. — 1v.(loose-leaf) ; 22cm
£6.50 B81-12532

635'.0973 — United States. Gardens. Vegetables. Cultivation — *Manuals*

Knott, James Edward. Knott's handbook for vegetable growers. — 2nd ed. / Oscar A. Lorenz, Donald N. Maynard. — New York ; Chichester : Wiley, c1980. — ix,390p : ill ; 22cm
Previous ed.: published as Handbook for vegetable growers. 1957. — Includes index
ISBN 0-471-05322-8 (spiral) : £9.00 B81-04456

635'.0973 — United States. Non-indigenous plants. Introduction, *to 1977*

Haughton, Claire Shaver. Green immigrants : the plants that transformed America / Claire Shaver Haughton ; drawings by Russell Peterson. — New York ; London : Harcourt Brace Jovanovich, c1978. — xii,450p : ill ; 24cm
Includes index
ISBN 0-15-137034-6 : £8.50 B81-29631

635'.23'0966 — West Africa. Food crops: Yams - *Conference proceedings*

Yams = Ignames. — Oxford : Clarendon Press, Aug.1981. — 1v.
Conference papers
ISBN 0-19-854557-6 : £15.00 : CIP entry B81-16356

635'.5 — Gardens. Salad vegetables. Cultivation — *Manuals*

Johns, Patrick A.. Success with home grown salads / Patrick A. Johns. — London : Grower, 1981. — 34p : ill ; 21cm. — (Grower garden guide ; no.4)
ISBN 0-901361-59-3 (pbk) : £0.95 B81-33080

635'.5283 — Great Britain. Greenhouses. Lettuces. Cultivation

Lettuce under glass. — Rev. and repr. — London : Grower, c1981. — 105p : ill ; 21cm. — (Grower guide ; no.21)
Previous ed.: published as Glasshouse lettuce / by J.G. Large. 1972
£3.50 (pbk) B81-30800

635'.63'094 — Europe. Cucumbers. Cultivation — *Manuals*

Cucumbers. — London : Grower, 1980. — 72p : ill ; 21cm. — (Grower guide : no.15)
ISBN 0-901361-43-7 (pbk) : £3.50 B81-02313

635'.642 — Gardens. Tomatoes. Cultivation

Success with home-grown tomatoes. — London : Grower, 1981. — 25p : ill ; 21cm. — (Grower garden guide ; no.2)
ISBN 0-901361-51-8 (pbk) : £0.90 B81-27717

635'.642 — Tomatoes. Cultivation — *Manuals*

Jones, Clay. Growing tomatoes : with a note on cucumbers, peppers and aubergines / Clay Jones ; illustrated by Andrew Farmer. — Harmondsworth : Penguin, 1981. — 116p : ill ; 20cm. — (Penguin handbook)
ISBN 0-14-046388-7 (pbk) : £1.50 B81-17032

635'.642'0942 — England, Guernsey & Netherlands. Tomatoes. Cultivation — *Comparative studies*

Dempster, J. H.. Tomato management : England, Holland and Guernsey compared / J.H. Dempster. — London : Grower, 1980. — ix,84p : ill ; 21cm. — (Grower guide ; no.16)
ISBN 0-901361-44-5 (pbk) : £3.50 B81-06573

635'.651 — Crops: Broad beans — *Conference proceedings*

Vicia faba : feeding value, processing and viruses : proceedings of a seminar in the EEC Programme of Coordination of Research on the Improvement of the Production of Plant Proteins, held at Cambridge England, June 27-29, 1979 / sponsored by the Commission of the European Communities, Directorate-General for Agriculture, Coordination of Agricultural Research ; edited by D.A. Bond. — The Hague ; London : Nijhoff for the Commission of the European Communities, 1980. — x,422p : ill ; 25cm. — (World crops : production, utilization, and description ; v.3)
ISBN 90-247-2362-0 : Unpriced B81-03769

Vicia faba : physiology and breeding : proceedings of a seminar in the EEC Programme of Coordination of Research on the Improvement of the Production of Plant Proteins, organized by the Centrum voor Agrobiologisch Onderzoek (Centre for Agrobiological Research), Wageningen, The Netherlands, held in Wageningen, June 24-26, 1980 / sponsored by the Commission of the European Communities, Directorate-General for Agriculture, Coordination of Agricultural Research ; editedby R. Thompson. — The Hague ; London : Nijhoff for the Commission of the European Communities, c1981. — ix,358p : ill ; 25cm. — (World crops)
Includes bibliographies
ISBN 90-247-2496-1 : Unpriced B81-23224

635'.7 — Gardens. Herbs. Cultivation — *For children*

Hemphill, Elizabeth. Your first book of herb gardening / Elizabeth Hemphill ; illustrated by David Mitchelhill. — London : Angus & Robertson, 1980. — 45p : ill(some col.) ; 25cm
Includes index
ISBN 0-207-14353-6 : £3.50 B81-00147

Verey, Rosemary. The herb growing book / written by Rosemary Verey ; feature illustrations by Barbara Firth ; activity illustrations by Elizabeth Wood. — London : Methuen, 1980. — 41p : col.ill ; 28cm
Includes index
ISBN 0-416-89140-3 : £2.95 : CIP rev. B80-18393

635'.7 — Gardens. Herbs. Cultivation — *Manuals*

Carruthers, Barbara. The herb grower's guide / Barbara Carruthers ; illustrated by Charlotte Cox. — London : Warne, 1981. — 64p : ill ; 22cm. — (An Observer's guide)
Bibliography: p64
ISBN 0-7232-2482-x (pbk) : £1.95 B81-16460

635.9 — GARDENING. FLOWERS AND ORNAMENTAL PLANTS

635.9 — Gardens. Ornamental plants

The **Macdonald** encyclopedia of plants & flowers / edited by Frances Perry. — London : Macdonald, 1976 (1981 [printing]). — [544]p : ill(some col.) ; 19cm
Translation of: Il tutto verde. — Originally published: as 'The good gardener's guide to indoor and outdoor plants and flowers'. 1976. — Includes index
ISBN 0-354-04458-3 (pbk) : £3.95
Also classified at 635.9'65 B81-13260

635.9'022'2 — Gardens. Flowering plants — *Illustrations*

Angel, Marie. Cottage flowers / Marie Angel. — London : Pelham, 1980. — 46p : col.ill ; 28cm
ISBN 0-7207-1259-9 : £4.95
Primary classification 820.8'036 B81-03115

Penn, Irving. Flowers / photographs by Irving Penn. — London : Cape, 1980. — 94p : all col.ill ; 27cm
ISBN 0-224-01894-9 : £20.00 B81-02778

635.9'092'4 — England. Gardens. Flowering plants. Cultivation — *Personal observations*

Fish, Margery. A flower for every day / Margery Fish ; with a foreword by C.D. Brickell. — London : Faber, 1981. — 208p,[16]p of plates : ill ; 23cm
Originally published: London : Studio Vista, 1965. — Includes index
ISBN 0-571-11776-7 : £5.95 B81-17777

635.9'0941 — Great Britain. Gardens. Ornamental flowering plants — *For children*

Stanton, Harry. Garden flowers / written and photographed by Harry Stanton. — Loughborough : Ladybird, c1981. — 49p : col.ill ; 18cm. — (Nature series)
Ill. text on lining papers. — Includes index
ISBN 0-7214-0667-x : £0.50 B81-26634

635.9'0942 — England. Gardens. Flowering plants — *Illustrations*

Sanders, Rosanne. Portrait of a country garden / Rosanne Sanders. — London : Aurum, c1980. — [93]p : col.ill ; 31cm
ISBN 0-906053-16-1 : £7.95
Primary classification 821'.008'036 B81-03134

635.9'153 — Ornamental plants. Propagation — *Manuals*

Mossman, Keith. Plants for free : how to start your own plants / Keith Mossman ; illustrated by Vana Haggerty. — Harmondsworth : Penguin, 1981. — 200p : ill ; 20cm. — (Penguin handbooks)
Includes index
ISBN 0-14-046387-9 (pbk) : £1.75 B81-17031

635.9'31 — Gardens. Annual & biennial flowering plants

Gould, Ralph. Annuals and biennials / Ralph Gould. — London : Royal Horticultural Society, 1979. — 39p : ill ; 21cm. — (Wisley handbook ; 35)
ISBN 0-900629-98-3 (pbk) : £0.95 B81-36662

635.9'31'0222 — Gardens. Annual & biennial flowering plants — *Illustrations*

Blamey, Philip. Annuals & biennials : the quickest way to a garden of colour, 82 summer flowers from seed and how to grow them / [... painted and written by Philip and Marjorie Blamey]. — [London] : Fontana, 1979. — 1 folded sheet([12]p) : col.ill ; 25cm. — (Domino ; 15)
ISBN 0-00-685462-1 : £0.85 B81-20254

635.9'32 — Gardens. Hardy perennial plants

Toogood, Alan R.. Making the most of hardy perennials / by Alan Toogood. — Nottingham : Floraprint, 1980. — 96p : col.ill ; 27cm
Includes index
ISBN 0-903001-45-4 : £4.95 B81-00967

635.9′32′0321 — Gardens. Hardy perennial plants — *Encyclopaedias*
Beckett, Kenneth. Growing hardy perennials / Kenneth A. Beckett. — London : Croom Helm, c1981. — x,182,[8]p of plates : ill(some col.) ; 24cm
Includes index
ISBN 0-7099-0621-8 : £6.95 : CIP rev. B81-12312

635.9′33111 — Gardens. Clematis
Fisk, Jim. Clematis / Jim Fisk. — London : Royal Horticultural Society, 1979, c1978. — 32p : ill ; 21cm. — (Wisley handbook ; 21)
Text on inside cover. — Bibliography: p32
ISBN 0-900629-71-1 (pbk) : £0.85 B81-01833

635.9′33111 — Gardens. Delphiniums
Edwards, Colin. Delphiniums / Colin Edwards. — London : Dent, 1981. — 192p,[24]p of plates : ill(some col.),ports ; 24cm
Includes index
ISBN 0-460-04423-0 : £9.95 B81-11490

635.9′33135 — Cultivated violets
Coombs, Roy E.. Violets : the history and cultivation of scented violets / Roy E. Coombs. — London : Croom Helm, c1981. — 142p : ill ; 23cm
Bibliography: p128-136. — Includes index
ISBN 0-7099-0704-4 : £6.95 B81-25153

635.9′33166 — Gardens. Camellias
Trehane, David. Camellias / David Trehane. — London : Royal Horticultural Society, 1980. — 40p : ill(some col.) ; 22cm. — (Wisley handbook ; 37)
ISBN 0-906603-06-4 (pbk) : £0.95 B81-36661

635.9′33216 — Gardens. Geraniums & pelargoniums. Cultivation
Shellard, Alan. Geraniums for home and garden / Alan Shellard. — Newton Abbot : David & Charles, 1981. — 232p : ill(some col.) ; 23cm
Includes index
ISBN 0-7153-8124-5 : £8.95 : CIP rev. B81-17495

635.9′33216 — Great Britain. Gardens. Geraniums & pelargoniums — *Serials*
The **Year** book of the British Pelargonium and Geranium Society. — 1981. — Farnham (c/o Mrs M. O. Salmon, 1 Mayfield Close, Badshot Lea, Farnham, Surrey GU9 9NJ) : The Society, c1981. — 47p
£0.60 B81-29040

635.9′33322 — Gardens. Sweet peas — *Serials*
The **sweet** pea annual. — 1981. — Cirencester (c/o L.H.O. Williams, Acacia Cottage, Down Ampney, Cirencester, Glos. GL7 5QW) : The Society, c1981. — vii,152p
£3.00 B81-24156

635.9′33372 — Gardens. Roses. Cultivation
Hessayon, D. G.. The rose expert / D.G. Hessayon. — Waltham Cross (Britannica House, Waltham Cross, Herts.) : PBI Publications, c1981. — 128p : col.ill ; 24cm
Includes index
ISBN 0-903505-14-2 (pbk) : £1.95 B81-36275

635.9′33372 — Gardens. Roses. Cultivation — *Manuals*
Carr, David, *1930-*. Roses / David Carr. — London : Ebury, 1981. — 63p : ill(some col.) ; 26cm. — (A Green fingers guide)
ISBN 0-85223-192-x : £2.50 B81-16474

Harkness, Jack. How to grow roses / by Jack Harkness ; drawings by Betty Harkness. — St. Albans (Bone Hill, Chiswell Green La., St. Albans, Herts.) : Royal National Rose Society, 1980. — 93p : ill ; 21cm
Unpriced (pbk) B81-25412

635.9′33372 — Gardens. Shrub roses
Thomas, Graham Stuart. Shrub roses of today / written and illustrated by Graham Stuart Thomas ; with a key to the major groups of cultivated roses by Gordon D. Rowley. — Rev. ed. — London : Dent, 1980. — 241p,[20] leaves of plates : ill(some col.) ; 23cm
Previous ed.: i.e. Rev. ed., 1974. — Bibliogrpahy: p221-223. — Includes index
ISBN 0-460-04533-4 : £10.95 B81-00968

635.9′33372′06041 — Great Britain. Gardens. Roses. Organisations: Royal National Rose Society — *Serials*
The **Rose** annual / the Royal National Rose Society. — 1981. — St Albans (Bone Hill, Chiswell Green La., St Albans, Hertfordshire) : The Society, c1981. — 256p
Private circulation B81-25487

635.9′3344 — Gardens. Fuchsias
Saunders, Eileen. Wagtails book of fuchsias / Elieen Saunders. — Godalming (1 Park Ave., Peper Harow Park, Godalming, Surrey) : E.R.M. Saunders
Vol.4. — c1976. — 112p : ill(some col.),col.maps,ports ; 31cm
Unpriced B81-31475

635.9′3344 — Great Britain. Gardens. Fuchsias. Organisations: British Fuchsia Society — *Serials*
The **Fuchsia** annual / the British Fuchsia Society. — 1981. — [Brookwood] ([c/o R. Ewart, The Bungalow, Brookwood Military Cemetery, Brookwood, Woking, Surrey]) : The Society, c1981. — 103p
Unpriced B81-23502

635.9′3355 — Gardens. Chrysanthemums — *Serials*
The **Chrysanthemum** year book / National Chrysanthemum Society. — 1981. — London (65 St Margaret′s Ave., Whetstone N20 9HT) : The Society, [1981]. — 118p
Unpriced B81-35127

635.9′3355 — Gardens. Dahlias. Cultivation
Damp, Philip. Growing dahlias / Philip Damp. — London : Croom Helm, c1981. — 139p,[8]p of plates : ill(some col.) ; 24cm
Includes index
ISBN 0-7099-0800-8 : £5.95 : CIP rev. B81-14890

635.9′3355 — Great Britain. Gardens. Dahlias. Organisations: National Dahlia Society — *Serials*
National Dahlia Society. January bulletin / National Dahlia Society. — 1981. — Leamington Spa (c/o P. Damp, 26 Burns Rd, Lillington, Leamington Spa, Warwickshire) : The Society, 1981. — 68p
Cover title: N.D.S. January bulletin
Free to Society members only B81-12398

635.9′3362 — Gardens. Azaleas & rhododendrons
Kessell, Mervyn S.. Rhododendrons and azaleas. — Poole : Blandford Press, Oct.1981. — [192]p
ISBN 0-7137-1076-4 : £8.95 : CIP entry B81-30310

635.9′33672 — Great Britain. Gardens. Primulas. Organisations: National Auricula and Primula Society. *Southern Section* — *Serials*
. Year book / National Auricula & Primula Society (Southern Section). — 1980. — [Carshalton Beeches] (67 Warnham Court Rd., Carshalton Beeches, Surrey) : [The Society], [1980]. — 72p
ISSN 0305-1110 : Unpriced B81-06687

635.9′33672 — Northern England. Gardens. Primulas. Organisations: National Auricula and Primula Society. *Northern Section* — *Serials*
National Auricula and Primula Society. *Northern Section*. Year book / The National Auricula and Primula Society (Northern Section). — 1980. — Cheadle (c/o D.G. Hadfield, 146 Queens Rd., Cheadle Hume, Cheadle, Cheshire SK8 5HY) : The Society, [1980]. — 60p
£1.50 B81-04541

635.9′3375 — Gardens. Gentians. Cultivation
Bartlett, Mary. Gentians / Mary Bartlett. — New rev. ed., with line drawings by Rosemary Smith, J.S. Pringle and N. Cruttwell. — Sherborne : Alphabooks, 1981. — 144p : ill (some col.) ; 25cm
Previous ed.: Poole : Blandford, 1975. — Bibliography: p142. - Includes index
ISBN 0-906670-18-7 : £9.50 B81-17129

635.9′3381 — Pot plants: African violets. Cultivation
Rector, Carolyn K.. How to grow African violets / by Carolyn K. Rector ; illustrated by Robert Blanchard. — 2nd ed. — Poole : Blandford, 1969, c1971 (1981 [printing]). — 95p : ill ; 19cm
Previous ed.: San Francisco : Lane, 1951 ; Poole : Blandford, 1956. — Includes index
ISBN 0-7137-1254-6 (pbk) : £1.95 B81-34947

635.9′3415 — Cultivated orchids
Bechtel, Helmut. The manual of cultivated orchid species / Helmut Bechtel, Phillip Cribb, Edmund Launert. — Poole : Blandford, 1981. — 444p : ill(some col.) ; 28cm
Translation of: Orchideenatlas. — Bibliography: p425-427. - Includes index
ISBN 0-7137-1097-7 : £35.00 : CIP rev. B81-02121

635.9′3415 — Orchids. Cultivation
Black, Peter McKenzie. The complete book of orchid growing / Peter McKenzie Black ; with a contribution by Wolfgang Rysy. — London : Ward Lock, c1980. — 160p : ill(some col.) ; 26cm
Includes index
ISBN 0-7063-5512-1 : £9.95 B81-14153

635.9′3424 — Gardens. Irises
Cassidy, G. E.. Growing irises. — London : Croom Helm, Jan.1982. — [152]p
ISBN 0-7099-0706-0 : £8.50 : CIP entry B81-34311

635.9′3424′05 — Gardens. Irises — *Serials*
The **Iris** year book / The British Iris Society. — 1980. — [Richmond] ([c/o G.E. Cassidy, 67 Bushwood Rd, Kew, Richmond, Surrey TW9 3BG]) : The Society, c1980. — 101p
ISBN 0-901483-22-2 : Unpriced B81-20424

635.9′34324 — Cultivated tulips
Lodewijk, Tom. The book of tulips / Tom Lodewijk ; edited by Ruth Buchan ; [translation from the Dutch Stephen T. Moskey]. — London : Cassel [i.e. Cassell], 1979. — 128p : ill(some col.),facsims,maps,ports ; 30cm
Translation of: Het boek van de tulp. — Bibliography: p127
ISBN 0-304-30526-x : £6.95 B81-02850

635.9′34324′05 — Gardens. Lilies — *Serials*
Lilies ... and other liliaceae. — 1978-9. — London : Royal Horticultural Society, c1978/9. — 120p
ISBN 0-906603-05-6 : £1.50
ISSN 0075-949x B81-04625

635.9′393 — Algae. Production & use — *Conference proceedings*
International Symposium on the Production and Use of Micro-Algae Biomass *(1978 : Akko)*.
Algae biomass : production and use / [includes papers written or revised and updated to 1980 of lectures presented at the International Symposium on the Production and Use of Mico-Algae Biomass, Akko, Israel, September 17-22, 1978, sponsored by the National Council for Research and Development, Israel and the Gesellschaft für Strahlen- und Umweltforschung (GSF), Munich, Germany] ; editors Gedaliah Shelef, Carl J. Soeder ; technical editorial assistence by Miriam Bababan. — Amsterdam ; Oxford : Elsevier/North-Holland, 1980. — xvii,852p : ill,1map ; 25cm
Includes bibliographies and index
ISBN 0-444-80242-8 : £59.65 B81-18487

635.9′42′0321 — Gardens. Flowering plants. Cultivation from seeds — *Encyclopaedias*
Garden flowers from seed : an illustrated dictionary / edited by Richard Gorer. — Exeter : Webb & Bower, 1981 : ill. — 208p : ill(some col.) ; 25cm
ISBN 0-906671-32-9 : £8.95 : CIP rev. B81-31066

635.9'44 — Gardens. Flowering bulbs, flowering corms, flowering rhizomes & flowering tubers. Varieties — *Illustrations*

Blamey, Philip. Bulbs : bulbs, corms and tubers for house and garden seasons - heights - cultivation, over 120 varieties illustrated in colour / [... painted and written by Philip and Marjorie Blamey]. — [London] : Fontana, 1979. — 1folded sheet([12]p) : col.ill ; 25cm. — (Domino ; 22)
ISBN 0-00-685452-4 : £0.85 B81-20253

635.9'44'0222 — Gardens. Flowering bulbs — *Illustrations*

Budden, H.. Bulbous flowers : a colonial nurseryman's cataloque / by H. Budden. — Wellington [N.Z.] ; Oxford : Oxford University Press, c1979. — 108p : col.ill,1port ; 18cm
Facsim of: edition published Wellington, N.Z. : s.n., 188-
ISBN 0-19-558055-9 : £5.95 B81-04609

635.9'5 — United States. Gardens. Prairie plants. Cultivation — *Manuals*

Smith, J. Robert. The prairie garden : 70 native plants you can grow in town or country / J. Robert Smith with Beatrice S. Smith. — Wisconsin ; London : University of Wisconsin Press, 1980. — viii,219p : ill(some col.),1map ; 22cm
Bibliography: p212-214. — Includes index
ISBN 0-299-08300-4 (cased) : £13.50
ISBN 0-299-08304-7 (pbk) : Unpriced
B81-22352

635.9'51'794 — California. Gardens. Californian wild flowering plants. Cultivation — *Manuals*

Schmidt, Marjorie G.. Growing California native plants / Marjorie G. Schmidt ; drawings by Beth D. Merrick. — Berkeley ; London : University of California Press, c1980. — ix,366p,8p of plates : ill(some col.) ; 22cm. — (California natural history guides ; 45)
Bibliography: p333-337. — Includes index
ISBN 0-520-03761-8 : £9.50 B81-01599

635.9'54 — Great Britain. Gardens. Shade-tolerant plants

Paterson, Allen. Plants for shade / Allen Paterson. — London : Dent, 1981. — x,214p,[8]p of plates : col.ill ; 24cm
Bibliography: p206. — Includes index
ISBN 0-460-04419-2 : £7.95 B81-24525

635.9'55 — Gardens. Succulents. Cultivation — *For children*

Tarsky, Sue. The prickly plant book / written by Sue Tarsky ; feature illustrations by Grahame Corbett ; activity illustrations by Will Giles. — London : Methuen/Walker, 1980. — 41p : col.ill ; 28cm. — (How does your garden grow?)
Includes index
ISBN 0-416-89130-6 : Unpriced : CIP rev.
B80-13445

635.9'55 — Gardens with alkaline soils. Plants. Cultivation

Evison, J. R. B.. Gardening on lime and chalk / J.R.B. Evison ; [photographs by Pat Bridley]. — London : Royal Horticultural Society, 1981. — 48p : ill,1map ; 21cm. — (Wisley handbook ; 39)
ISBN 0-906603-13-7 (pbk) : £1.15 B81-31494

635.9'55 — Great Britain. Gardens. Plants flourishing in dry conditions

Chatto, Beth. The dry garden / Beth Chatto. — London : Dent, 1978 (1980 [printing]). — 189p,[16]p of plates : ill ; 24cm
Bibliography: p177. — Includes index
ISBN 0-460-02222-9 (pbk) : £3.50 B81-21855

635.9'55 — Peat gardens. Plants. Cultivation

Evans, Alfred. The peat garden / by Alfred Evans ; [drawings by Jill Sleigh ; photographs by Pat Brindley, Alfred Evans, J. Downward]. — London : Royal Horticultural Society, 1981. — 39p : ill ; 21cm. — (Wisley handbook ; 41)
ISBN 0-906603-15-3 (pbk) : £1.15 B81-31486

635.9'55 — Succulents. Cultivation

Bloom, Adrian. Adrian Bloom's guide to cacti & succulents / text by Ken March. — Norwich : Jarrold Colour Publications, c1981. — [32]p : col.ill ; 19cm. — (A Jarrold garden series ; bk.8)
Unpriced (pbk) B81-32615

635.9'642 — Greenkeeping — *Serials*

The **Greenkeeper's** year book and who's who : [the official handbook of the British Golf Greenkeepers Association]. — 1980-. — London (17 Farringdon St., EC4) : Ellison Publications, [1980]-. — v. : ill ; 21cm
Annual. — Cover title: The Greenkeeper's yearbook
ISSN 0261-2011 = Greenkeeper's year book and who's who : £6.50 (Free to Association members) B81-20084

635.9'647 — Gardens. Lawns. Cultivation — *Manuals*

Carr, David, *1930-*. Lawns / David Carr. — London : Ebury, 1981. — 63p : ill(some col.) ; 26cm. — (A Green fingers guide)
ISBN 0-85223-191-1 : £2.50 B81-16476

635.9'65 — Flowering indoor plants. Cultivation — *Manuals*

Kramer, Jack, *1927-*. An illustrated guide to flowering houseplants : how to enjoy year-round colour in your home featuring 150 plants / Jack Kramer. — London : Salamander, c1981. — 160p : ill(some col.) ; 23cm
Includes index
ISBN 0-86101-078-7 : £2.95 B81-17613

635.9'65 — Indoor gardening — *Manuals*

Manaker, George H.. Interior plantscapes : installation, maintenance, and management / George H. Manaker. — Englewood Cliffs ; London : Prentice-Hall, c1981. — x,283p : ill,1facsim ; 24cm
Includes bibliographies and index
ISBN 0-13-469312-4 : £12.95 B81-25459

635.9'65 — Indoor plants

Gundrey, Elizabeth. Plants and flowers in the home / [authors Elizabeth Gundry i.e. Gundrey, Cynthia Wickham] ; [illustrator Sue Richards]. — London : Marshall Cavendish, 1974 (1979 printing). — 79p : ill(some col.) ; 29cm
ISBN 0-85685-755-6 (pbk) : £1.25 B81-19566

Herwig, Rob. A pocket guide to houseplants : 300 houseplants in colour / Rob Herwig. — Guildford : Lutterworth, 1981. — 128p : col.ill ; 20cm
Translation from the Dutch. — Includes index
ISBN 0-7188-2514-4 (pbk) : £2.50 B81-24210

The **Macdonald** encyclopedia of plants & flowers / edited by Frances Perry. — London : Macdonald, 1976 (1981 [printing]). — [544]p : ill(some col.) ; 19cm
Translation of: Il tutto verde. — Originally published: as 'The good gardener's guide to indoor and outdoor plants and flowers'. 1976. — Includes index
ISBN 0-354-04458-3 (pbk) : £3.95
Primary classification 635.9 B81-13260

635.9'65 — Indoor plants. Cultivation

Huxley, Alyson. Huxley's house of plants / Alyson and Anthony Huxley. — Poole : Blandford, 1980. — 144p : col.ill ; 27cm
Originally published: London : Paddington Press, 1978. — Includes index
ISBN 0-7137-1124-8 : £6.95 B81-00969

635.9'65 — Indoor plants. Cultivation — *Manuals*

Day, Valerie. Success with plants in the home / Valerie Day. — London : Grower, 1981. — 43p : ill ; 21cm. — (Grower garden guide ; no.3)
Bibliography: p43
ISBN 0-901361-58-5 (pbk) : £0.95 B81-33079

Minot, Victor. Indoor plants : keeping them alive and well / by Victor Minot. — London : Foulsham, c1981. — 120p : ill(some col.) ; 23cm
Originally published: Slough : Foulsham for W.H. Smith and Son, 1979. — Includes index
ISBN 0-572-01013-3 : £3.95 B81-16717

635.9'65 — Indoor plants. Diseases. Control — *Manuals*

Bonar, Ann. What's wrong with my plant? : a guide to the care and cure of ailing houseplants / Chuck Crandall adapted by Ann Bonar ; illustrated by Andrew Farmer. — Harmondsworth : Penguin, 1981. — 111p : ill ; 20cm. — (Penguin handbooks)
Previous ed.: San Francisco : Chronicle Books, 1976 ; London : Muller, 1978. — Includes index
ISBN 0-14-046436-0 (pbk) : £1.50 B81-16972

635.9'65 — Indoor plants. Hydroculture

Loewer, H. Peter. Growing plants in water : the indoor gardener's guide to simple hydroculture / H. Peter Loewer ; illustrated by the author. — Rev. and expanded ed. — Harmondsworth : Penguin, c1981. — 108p : ill ; 20cm
Previous ed.: published as The indoor water gardener's how-to handbook. New York : Walker, 1973. — Includes index
ISBN 0-14-046406-9 (pbk) : £1.50 B81-16974

635.9'65 — Window boxes. Plants. Cultivation

Guyton, Anita. The pocket book of plants for patios, balconies and window-sills / Anita Guyton. — London : Evans, 1981. — 128p : ill ; 17cm
ISBN 0-237-45500-5 (pbk) : £1.75 : CIP rev.
Also classified at 635.9'671 B80-18396

635.9'65'0222 — Indoor plants — *Illustrations*

Wilkinson, John, *1934-*. House plants : foliage plants for home and office, over 100 illustrated in colour, potting — watering — feeding — care / [... painted by John Wilkinson ; text by Anthony Huxley]. — [London] : Fontana, 1979. — 1folded sheet([12]p) : col.ill ; 25cm. — (Domino ; 11)
ISBN 0-00-685451-6 : £0.85 B81-20746

635.9'65'0321 — Indoor plants — *Encyclopaedias*

Proudley, Brian. Indoor plants : a popular guide / Brian & Valerie Proudley. — Poole : Blandford, 1981. — 176p : col.ill ; 21cm
Includes index
ISBN 0-7137-1003-9 : £5.95 : CIP rev.
B81-02120

635.9'66 — Cut flowers. New varieties. Production

New cut flower crops. — London : Grower, 1980. — xi,80p : ill ; 21cm. — (Grower guide ; no.18)
ISBN 0-901361-47-x (pbk) : £3.50 B81-11396

635.9'66 — Plants: Flowering bulbs. Cut flowers. Production — *Manuals*

Cut flowers from bulbs. — London : Grower, 1981. — 81p : ill ; 21cm. — (Grower guide ; no.22)
ISBN 0-901361-57-7 (pbk) : £3.75 B81-29289

635.9'671 — Balconies & patios. Plants. Cultivation

Guyton, Anita. The pocket book of plants for patios, balconies and window-sills / Anita Guyton. — London : Evans, 1981. — 128p : ill ; 17cm
ISBN 0-237-45500-5 (pbk) : £1.75 : CIP rev.
Primary classification 635.9'65 B80-18396

635.9'672 — Gardens. Rock plants: Alpine plants

Ingwersen, Will. Alpine garden plants / Will Ingwersen ; photographs by Robin Fletcher. — Poole : Blandford, 1981. — 153p : col.ill ; 20cm
Bibliography: p150. - Includes index
ISBN 0-7137-0968-5 : £4.95 B81-15211

635.9'672 — Gardens. Rock plants: Alpine plants. Cultivation

Foster, Raymond. Rock garden and alpine plants. — Newton Abbot : David & Charles, Nov.1981. — [288]p
ISBN 0-7153-8203-9 : £12.50 : CIP entry
B81-31808

Heath, Royton E.. The Collingridge guide to collectors' alpines : their cultivation in frames and alpine houses / Royton E. Heath. — 2nd ed. — Richmond upon Thames : Collingridge, 1981. — 543p,[56]p of plates : ill(some col.) ; 24cm
Previous ed.: published as Collectors' alpines. 1964. — Bibliography: p536. - Includes index
ISBN 0-600-36784-3 : £20.00 B81-22052

635.9′672 — Rock gardens — *Amateurs' manuals*
Schacht, Wilhelm. Rock gardens / Wilhelm Schacht ; edited and with an introduction by Jim Archibald ; [translation by Babel Translations]. — New York : Universe ; Sherborne : Alphabooks, 1981. — 192p : ill (some col.,) ; 23cm
Translation of: Der Steingarten. 5.Ausg. — Previous ed.: published as Rock gardens and their plants. Poole : Blandford, 1963. — Bibliography: p187-188. - Includes index
ISBN 0-906670-19-5 : £7.95 B81-21871

635.9′674 — Tropical aquariums. Water plants
De Thabrew, W. Vivian. Popular tropical aquarium plants / W. Vivian De Thabrew. — Cheltenham : Thornhill, 1981. — 200p : ill ; 22cm
Bibliography: p197. — Includes index
ISBN 0-904110-56-7 : £8.00 B81-36573

635.9′674 — Water gardens
Perry, Frances. The water garden / Frances Perry. — London : Ward Lock, 1981. — 176p : ill(some col.) ; 25cm
Includes index
ISBN 0-7063-5965-8 : £7.95 B81-39959

635.9′674 — Water gardens — *Manuals*
Heritage, Bill. Ponds and water gardens / Bill Heritage. — Poole : Blandford, 1981. — 168p : ill(some col.) ; 20cm
Includes index
ISBN 0-7137-1015-2 (cased) : £4.95
ISBN 0-7137-1141-8 (pbk) : £2.95 B81-15399

635.9′74 — Commercial nurseries. Climbing plants. Propagation — *Manuals*
McMillan Browse, P. D. A. The commercial production of climbing plants / P.D.A. McMillan Browse. — London : Grower, 1981. — x,97p : ill ; 30cm
Bibliography: p42
ISBN 0-901361-49-6 (pbk) : £7.00 B81-11133

635.9′75 — Crops: Foliage plants. Production
Foliage plant production / Jasper N. Joiner, editor. — Englewood Cliffs ; London : Prentice-Hall, c1981. — xix,614p : ill ; 24cm
Includes bibliographies and index
ISBN 0-13-322867-3 : £16.20 B81-17212

635.9′76 — Gardens. Flowering shrubs
Hunt, Peter, *1917-*. Garden shrubs / Peter Hunt ; illustrated by Design Bureau. — London : Hamlyn, 1969 (1980 printing). — 159p : col.ill ; 19cm
Includes index
ISBN 0-600-35379-6 : £2.50 B81-02198

635.9′76 — Gardens. Shrubs — *Lists*
Hellyer, Arthur George Lee. Garden shrubs. — London : Dent, May 1981. — 1v.
ISBN 0-460-04474-5 : £9.95 : CIP entry B81-04203

635.9′76′0321 — Gardens. Shrubs — *Encyclopaedias*
The **Hillier** colour dictionary of trees and shrubs. — Newton Abbot : David & Charles, c1980. — 324p : col.ill ; 22cm
ISBN 0-7153-8192-x : £9.95 : CIP rev.
Also classified at 635.9′77′0321 B81-04245

Hillier's manual of trees & shrubs. — 5th ed. — Newton Abbot : David & Charles, Nov.1981. — [600]p
Previous ed.: 1977
ISBN 0-7153-8302-7 : £9.50 : CIP entry
Primary classification 635.9′77′0321 B81-31236

635.9′76′0941 — Great Britain. Gardens. Ornamental shrubs. Selection & cultivation
Hellyer, A. G. L.. The Collingridge book of ornamental garden shrubs : the enthusiast's guide to shrub selection, cultivation and propagation / Arthur Hellyer ; with watercolour drawings by Cynthia Newsome-Taylor ; and line drawings by G.R. Kingbourn. — 2nd ed. — Richmond upon Thames : Collingridge, 1981. — 144p : ill(some col.) ; 31cm
Previous ed.: / published as Shrubs in colour. 1965. — Includes index
ISBN 0-600-36787-8 : £8.50 B81-22059

Smith, Geoffrey, *1928-*. Shrubs & small trees / Geoffrey Smith ; flower drawings by Leslie Greenwood and practical drawings by Ian Garrard. — Rev. ed. — London : Hamlyn, 1981. — 175p : ill(some col.) ; 27cm
Previous ed.: published as Shrubs and small trees for your garden. 1973. — Includes index
ISBN 0-600-30517-1 : £6.95
Also classified at 635.9′77′0941 B81-37167

635.9′77 — Gardens. Trees
Mitchell, Alan. The gardener's book of trees. — London : Dent, Sept.1981. — [256]p
ISBN 0-460-04403-6 : £12.95 : CIP entry B81-20146

635.9′77 — Small gardens. Trees
Knight, F. P.. Trees for small gardens / F.P. Knight. — London : Royal Horticultural Society, 1980, c1979. — 40p : ill ; 21cm. — (Wisley handbook ; 36)
Bibliography: p40
ISBN 0-900629-99-1 (pbk) : £1.15 B81-36663

635.9′77′0321 — Gardens. Trees — *Encyclopaedias*
The **Hillier** colour dictionary of trees and shrubs. — Newton Abbot : David & Charles, c1980. — 324p : col.ill ; 22cm
ISBN 0-7153-8192-x : £9.95 : CIP rev.
Primary classification 635.9′76′0321 B81-04245

Hillier's manual of trees & shrubs. — 5th ed. — Newton Abbot : David & Charles, Nov.1981. — [600]p
Previous ed.: 1977
ISBN 0-7153-8302-7 : £9.50 : CIP entry
Also classified at 635.9′76′0321 B81-31236

635.9′77′0941 — Great Britain. Gardens. Trees. Selection & cultivation
Smith, Geoffrey, *1928-*. Shrubs & small trees / Geoffrey Smith ; flower drawings by Leslie Greenwood and practical drawings by Ian Garrard. — Rev. ed. — London : Hamlyn, 1981. — 175p : ill(some col.) ; 27cm
Previous ed.: published as Shrubs and small trees for your garden. 1973. — Includes index
ISBN 0-600-30517-1 : £6.95
Primary classification 635.9′76′0941 B81-37167

635.9′772 — Bonsai. Cultivation
Roger, A. S.. Bonsai / by A.S. Roger ; [drawings by W.H. Brown ; photographs by A.S. Roger, Harry Smith Collection/Seiyokan Bonsai, and Michael Warren]. — London : Royal Horticultural Society, 1981. — 32p : ill ; 21cm. — (Wisley handbook ; 40)
Bibliography: p32
ISBN 0-906603-14-5 (pbk) : £0.85 B81-31485

635.9′823 — Greenhouses. Flowering plants. Commercial cultivation — *Manuals*
Walls, Ian. Modern greenhouse methods : flowers and plants. — London : Muller, Nov.1981. — [224]p
ISBN 0-584-10386-7 : £10.50 : CIP entry B81-32003

635.9′823 — Ornamental plants. Nurseries. Horticultural greenhouses. Management — *Manuals*
Boodley, James W.. The commercial greenhouse handbook / James W. Boodley. — New York ; London : Van Nostrand Reinhold, 1981. — vi,568p : ill ; 24cm
Also available in pbk: £12.30. — Includes index
ISBN 0-442-23146-6 : £18.70 B81-21234

636 — LIVESTOCK, PETS

636 — Animals. Use by man
Henderson, W. M.. Man's use of animals / W.M. Henderson. — Cardiff : University of Wales Press, 1981. — 32p : ill ; 21cm
ISBN 0-7083-0803-1 (pbk) : Unpriced : CIP rev. B81-10463

636 — Livestock. Behaviour
Craig, James V.. Domestic animal behavior : causes and implications for animal care and management / James V. Craig. — Englewood Cliffs ; London : Prentice-Hall, c1981. — xvii,364p : ill,maps ; 24cm
Includes bibliographies and index
ISBN 0-13-218339-0 : £12.95 B81-18316

636 — Livestock — *For children*
My favourite book of farm animals. — London : Dean, 1980, c1978. — [16]p : col.ill ; 29cm
ISBN 0-603-00219-6 : £0.75 B81-38078

Shapiro, Larry. Our animal friends / [written by Larry Shapiro] ; [designed and illustrated by Carroll Andrus ; paper engineering by Tor Lokvig]. — [Swindon] : Child's Play, c1979. — [10]p : chiefly col.ill ; 18cm. — (A Kaleidoscope book ; bk.1)
Cover title. — Originally published: Los Angeles : Intervisual Communications, 1979. — Text, ill on lining papers
ISBN 0-85953-096-5 : Unpriced B81-32883

636′.0022′2 — Livestock — *Illustrations — For children*
My first book of the farm. — London : Dean, [1980]. — [8]p : all col.ill ; 15cm. — (A Dean board book)
ISBN 0-603-00237-4 (pbk) : £0.25 B81-06336

636′.0072042 — England. Livestock. Research by Agricultural Science Service — *Serials*
Agricultural Science Service. Animal science : Agricultural Science Service research and development reports. — 1979-. — London : H.M.S.O., 1981-. — v. ; 21cm. — (Reference book / Ministry of Agriculture, Fisheries and Food)
Annual. — Continues in part: Pest Infestation Control Laboratory. Pest Infestation Control Laboratory report; and, also in part, Regional Agricultural Science Service. Annual report
ISSN 0261-698x = Animal science : £3.50 B81-32410

636′.009 — Livestock, *to 1980*
Clutton-Brock, Juliet. Domesticated animals : from early times / Juliet Clutton-Brock. — London : Heinemann in association with British Museum (Natural History), 1981. — 208p : ill(some col.),maps ; 26cm
Ill on lining papers. — Bibliography: p200-205. — Includes index
ISBN 0-434-13950-5 : £9.95 B81-35372

636′.00966 — West Africa. Livestock — *For schools*
Ositelu, G. S.. Animal science / G.S. Ositelu. — London : Cassell, 1981. — 105p : ill ; 25cm. — (Cassell's tropical agriculture series ; Bk.3)
Bibliography: p95. — Includes index
ISBN 0-304-30209-0 (pbk) : £2.95 B81-27771

636′.01′0942763 — Lancashire. Helmshore. Agricultural industries. Experimental livestock farms: Great House Experimental Husbandry Farm — *Serials*
Great House Experimental Husbandry Farm. Annual review / Great House Experimental Husbandry Farm. — 1980. — Helmshore (Helmshore, Rossendale, Lancs., BB4 4AJ) : The Farm, 1981. — i,52p
Unpriced B81-10573

Great House Experimental Husbandry Farm. Annual review / Great House Experimental Husbandry Farm. — 1981. — Rossendale (Helmshore, Rossendale, Lancs. BB4 4AJ) : The Farm, 1981. — i,53p
Unpriced B81-29108

636.08′2′0942565 — Zoos. Animals in danger of extinction. Breeding — *Study examples: Whipsnade Zoo*
Huxley, Elspeth. Whipsnade : captive breeding for survival / Elspeth Huxley. — London : Collins, 1981. — 159p,[20]p of plates : ill(some col.),1map,ports ; 23cm
Bibliography: p153-154. — Includes index
ISBN 0-00-216341-1 : £8.95 B81-18991

636.08′21 — Livestock. Breeding. Genetic aspects
Maciejowski, Janusz. Genetics and animal breeding. — Oxford : Elsevier Scientific. — (Developments in animal veterinary sciences ; 10)
Part B: Stock improvement methods. — Oct.1981. — [230]p
ISBN 0-444-99732-6 : £35.00 : CIP entry B81-25290

636.08′21 — Livestock. Rare breeds — *Serials*
Livestock heritage. — Vol.1, no.1 (1981)-. — London (1 Shepherd's Hill, N6 5AH) : Published for the Rare Breeds Survival Trust by Lined Up PR, 1981-. — v. : ill,ports ; 30cm
ISSN 0261-5037 = Livestock heritage : £1.25 per issue B81-29076

636.08′21′05 — Livestock: Small mammals. Breeding. Genetic aspects — *Serials*
Small Mammal Genetics Circle. — Vol.1, pt.1 (Jan.1981)-. — [Coventry] ([c/o Mr M. Stokes, 3 Allied Close, Holbrooks, Coventry]) : The Circle, 1981-. — v. ; 30cm
Quarterly. — Description based on: Vol.1, pt.2 (Apr.1981)
ISSN 0261-5509 = Small Mammal Genetics Circle (Newsletter) : Unpriced B81-30827

636.08′3 — Great Britain. Agricultural industries: Smallholdings. Livestock. Management
Isaac, Peter, *1932-*. Taking stock / Peter Isaac. — London : Jill Norman, 1981. — 168p : ill,plans ; 22cm
ISBN 0-906908-42-6 (pbk) : £3.95 B81-19543

636.08′3 — Great Britain. Livestock. Management. Welfare aspects — *Serials*
[**Newsletter** *(Farm Animal Welfare Co-ordinating Executive)*]. Newsletter / Farm Animal Welfare Co-ordinating Executive. — Autumn 1979-. — Cheltenham (c/o Miss D. Hayman, Dolphin House, Charlton Park Gate, Cheltenham) : The Executive, 1979-. — v. ; 21cm
Annual
ISSN 0144-6169 = Newsletter — Farm Animal Welfare Co-ordinating Executive : Free B81-06523

636.08′3 — Livestock. Care & management — *Manuals*
The **Complete** book of raising livestock and poultry : a smallholder's guide / edited by Katie Thear and Alistair Fraser ; photography Brian Hale. — [London] : Martin Dunitz, 1981, c1980. — 224p,[16]p of plates : ill(some col.),plans ; 29cm
Includes index
ISBN 0-906348-11-0 : £8.95 B81-00970

636.08′3′02341 — Great Britain. Animals. Care — *Career guides*
Rosier, Iris. Working with animals / Iris Rosier and Lucky Shepherd. — London : Watts, c1980. — 64p : ill ; 26cm. — (Choosing a career)
Includes bibliographies and index
ISBN 0-85166-851-8 : £3.95 B81-00971

636.08′3′0924 — Cumbria. Lake District. Animals. Care, *ca 1930-1978* — *Personal observations*
Ratcliffe, Jane. Fly high, run free / Jane Ratcliffe ; with a foreword by Virginia McKenna. — Harmondsworth : Penguin, 1981, c1979. — 189p,[8]p of plates : ill ; 18cm
Originally published: London : Chatto & Windus, 1979. — Bibliography: p183-184. — Includes index
ISBN 0-14-005570-3 (pbk) : £1.50 B81-37252

636.08′3′0924 — Livestock. Training. Woodhouse, Barbara — *Biographies*
Woodhouse, Barbara. Talking to animals / Barbara Woodhouse. — Harmondsworth : Penguin, 1981, c1980. — 217p,[16]p of plates : ill,ports ; 18cm
Originally published: London : Faber, 1954
ISBN 0-14-005752-8 (pbk) : £1.50 B81-27650

636.08′31 — Great Britain. Agricultural industries. Farms. Animal housing. Environmental aspects — *Conference proceedings*
Environmental aspects of housing for animal production. — London : Butterworths, Sept.1981. — [528]p
Conference papers
ISBN 0-408-10688-3 : £45.00 : CIP entry B81-23916

636.08′32′0924 — Great Britain. Welfare work with animals — *Personal observations*
May, Paula. Animals in my life / by Paula May. — [London] (42 Dowdeswell Close, SW15 [5RP]) : P. May, c1979. — 92p ; 21cm
£3.00 (pbk) B81-06102

636.08′4 — Livestock. Grazing
Grazing animals / edited by F.H.W. Morley. — Amsterdam ; Oxford : Elsevier Scientific, 1981. — xv,411p : ill,maps ; 30cm. — (World animal science. Subseries B, Disciplinary approach ; B1)
Includes bibliographies and index
ISBN 0-444-41835-0 : Unpriced : CIP rev. B80-10662

636.08′52 — Livestock. Nutrition
McDonald, P.. Animal nutrition. — 3rd ed. — London : Longman, July 1981. — [448]p
Previous ed.: Edinburgh : Oliver and Boyd, 1973
ISBN 0-582-44399-7 : £9.95 : CIP entry B81-15943

636.08′52 — Livestock. Nutrition — *Conference proceedings*
Recent advances in animal nutrition - 1980 / [edited by] William Haresign. — London : Butterworths, 1981. — 236p : ill ; 25cm. — (Studies in the agricultural and food sciences)
Conference papers. — Includes bibliographies and index
ISBN 0-408-71013-6 : £17.00 B81-05987

636.08′52′05 — Livestock. Nutrition — *Serials*
Recent advances in animal nutrition. — 1981. — London : Butterworths, Dec.1981. — [192]p. — (Studies in the agricultural and food sciences)
ISBN 0-408-71014-4 : £17.00 : CIP entry B81-31718

636.08′552 — Silage. Biochemistry
McDonald, Peter, *1926-*. The biochemistry of silage / Peter McDonald. — Chichester : Wiley, c1981. — 226p : ill ; 24cm
Includes index
ISBN 0-471-27965-x : £16.00 : CIP rev. B81-28043

636.08′85 — Laboratory animals. Care — *For laboratory technicians*
Inglis, J. K.. Introduction to laboratory animal science and technology / J.K. Inglis. — Oxford : Pergamon, 1980. — xi,323p : ill ; 26cm. — (Pergamon international library)
Bibliography: p299-303. — Includes index
ISBN 0-08-023772-x (cased) : £20.00 : CIP rev.
ISBN 0-08-023771-1 (pbk) : £9.95 B80-08832

636.08′85 — Laboratory animals. Genetics. Applications of probabilities
Green, Earl L.. Genetics and probability in animal breeding experiments : a primer and reference book on probability, segregation, assortment, linkage and mating systems for biomedical scientists who breed and use genetically defined laboratory animals for research / Earl L. Green. — London : Macmillan, 1981. — xv,271p : ill,1plan,forms ; 25cm
Bibliography: p258-260. - Includes index
ISBN 0-333-27243-9 : £20.00 B81-13403

636.08′85′02944 — European Community countries. Laboratory animals — *Buyers' guides* — *Serials*
Laboratory animals buyers guide. — 1981-82. — Basildon (33 Furrowfelde, Kingswood, Basildon, Essex SS16 5HA) : Laboratory Animals Ltd., [1981?]. — 53p
ISSN 0309-7382 : Unpriced B81-31059

636.08′87 — Pets. Care
Speer, John. Vet / John Speer. — London : ITV Books, 1981. — 125p : ill ; 20cm
ISBN 0-900727-83-7 (pbk) : Unpriced B81-18469

636.08′87 — Pets. Care - *For children*
Animals all round. — London : Ward Lock, June 1981. — [48]p
ISBN 0-7063-6082-6 : £2.95 : CIP entry B81-12890

636.08′87 — Pets. Care — *For children*
Pope, Joyce. The young pet owner's handbook / Joyce Pope. — Maidenhead : Purnell, 1981. — 125p : ill(some col.) ; 20cm
Includes index
ISBN 0-361-05052-6 : £2.99 B81-39276

636.08′87 — Pets. Health. Role of diet
Clark, Linda. Linda Clark's health & nutrition book for pets / by Linda Clark. — Wellingborough : Thorsons, 1981. — 128p : ill ; 22cm
Originally published: San Francisco : Strawberry Hill Press, 197-. — Bibliography: p125. — Includes index
ISBN 0-7225-0665-1 (pbk) : Unpriced B81-08719

636.08′87 — Pets. Psychic powers
Wylder, Joseph Edward. Psychic pets : the secret life of animals / Joseph Edward Wylder. — London : New English Library, 1981, c1978. — 127p,[8]p of plates : ill ; 18cm
Originally published: New York : Stonehill, 1978 ; London : Dent, 1980. — Bibliography: p120-121. — Includes index
ISBN 0-450-05101-3 (pbk) : £1.25 B81-22844

636.08′87 — Pets: Small animals. Care — *For children*
Stonefield, Marilyn. Hamsters, gerbils, rabbits, mice & guinea pigs / by Marilyn Stonefield ; illustrated by Jim Robins. — London : Macdonald, 1981. — 64p : ill(some col.) ; 21cm
Bibliography: p62. — Includes index
ISBN 0-356-06380-1 (cased) : £2.95
ISBN 0-356-06340-2 (pbk) : £1.25 B81-38577

636.08′87′014 — Pets. Names
Room, Adrian. Pet names / Adrian Room. — Bognor Regis : New Horizon, c1979. — 91p ; 22cm
ISBN 0-86116-078-9 : £2.50 B81-21804

636.08′87′0321 — Pets. Care — *Encyclopaedias*
Prince, Alison. The good pets guide / written and illustrated by Alison Prince. — London : Armada, 1981. — 189p : ill ; 20cm. — (An Armada original)
ISBN 0-00-691772-0 (pbk) : £1.00 B81-32643

636.08′87′05 — Pets — *Serials*
[**News** *(PDSA Club)*]. News / PDSA Club : the magazine for all friends of animals. — [No.1]-. — Dorking (PDSA House, South St., Dorking, Surrey, RH4 2LB) : People's Dispensary for Sick Animals, 1980-. — ill,ports ; 42cm
Six issues yearly
ISSN 0260-4795 = News — PDSA Club : £2.00 per year (free to club members) B81-02810

636.089 — VETERINARY MEDICINE

636.089 — Livestock: Small animals. Veterinary care — *Manuals*
Kirk, Robert W.. Handbook of veterinary procedures and emergency treatment / Robert W. Kirk, Stephen I. Bistner. — 3rd ed. — Philadelphia ; London : Saunders, 1981. — xiii,1008p : ill ; 19cm
Previous ed.: 1976. — Text on lining papers. — Includes bibliographies and index
ISBN 0-7216-5475-4 : £17.50 B81-31146

636.089 — Reptiles. Diseases
Diseases of the Reptilia. — London : Academic Press
Vol.2. — Oct.1981. — [250]p
ISBN 0-12-187902-x : CIP entry B81-26788

636.089′05 — Veterinary medicine — *Serials*
The **veterinary** annual. — 21st issue. — Bristol : Scientechnica, c1981. — 302p
ISBN 0-85608-031-4 : Unpriced B81-15553

The **Veterinary** annual. — 22nd issue. — Bristol : Wright, Jan.1982. — [400]p
ISBN 0-85608-035-7 : £15.00 : CIP entry
ISSN 0083-5870 B81-35030

636.089′092′4 — Great Britain. Veterinary medicine. McFadyean, John — *Biographies*
Pattison, Iain H.. John McFadyean. — London : J.A. Allen, Nov.1981. — [240]p
ISBN 0-85131-352-3 : £9.50 : CIP entry B81-30467

636.089′092′4 — Great Britain. Veterinary medicine — *Personal observations*
Bowring, Mary. Animals round the clock / Mary Bowring. — London : W.H. Allen, 1981. — 188p ; 23cm
ISBN 0-491-02924-1 : £6.95 B81-28970

636.089′092′4 — Great Britain. Veterinary medicine. Straiton, Eddie — *Biographies*
Straiton, Eddie. A vet at large / Eddie Straiton. — London : Arrow, 1981. — 217p ; 18cm
ISBN 0-09-926690-3 (pbk) : £1.25 B81-35173

636.089′092′4 — Veterinary medicine. Herriot, James — *Biographies*
Herriot, James. The Lord God made them all / James Herriot ; drawings by Larry. — London : Joseph, c1981. — 347p : ill ; 23cm
ISBN 0-7181-2026-4 : £6.95 B81-25616

636.089′092′4 — Zoos. Veterinary medicine — *Personal observations*
Taylor, David, *1934-*. Doctor in the zoo : the making of a zoo vet / David Taylor ; with line drawings by Frankie Coventry. — London : Unwin Paperbacks, 1980. — 250p : ill ; 18cm
Originally published: London : Allen and Unwin, 1978
ISBN 0-04-925016-7 (pbk) : £1.25 : CIP rev. B79-35399

636.089′1 — Livestock: Meat animals. Anatomy
Macgregor, Roderick. The structure of the meat animals : a guide to their anatomy and physiology / by the late Roderick Macgregor ; illustrated by A.P Burton. — 3rd ed. / revised by Frank Gerrard. — Oxford : Technical Press, 1980. — v,266p : ill ; 22cm
Previous ed.: 1965. — Includes index
ISBN 0-291-39625-9 (pbk) : £5.50 B81-10192

636.089′239 — Livestock. Energy metabolism — *Conference proceedings*
Symposium on Energy Metabolism *(8th : 1979 : Cambridge)*. Energy metabolism : proceedings of the Eighth Symposium on Energy Metabolism held at Churchill College, Cambridge, September, 1979 / [edited by] Laurence E. Mount. — London : Butterworths, 1980. — xix,484p : ill ; 24cm. — (Studies in the agricultural and food sciences) (EAAP publication ; no.26)
Includes index
ISBN 0-408-10641-7 : £29.50 : CIP rev. B80-11509

636.089′23924 — Livestock. Nutrition. Manganese — *Serials*
Manganese in agriculture : a quarterly bulletin of abstracts. — Vol.1, no.1 (Oct.1980)-. — Tring (M.B. House, Wigginton, Tring, Hertfordshire HP23 6ED) : Micronutrient Bureau, 1980-. — v. ; 30cm
ISSN 0261-5010 = Manganese in agriculture : Unpriced
Primary classification 631.5 B81-29099

636.089′23924 — Livestock. Nutrition. Molybdenum — *Serials*
Molybdenum in agriculture : a quarterly bulletin of abstracts. — Vol.1, no.1 (Oct.1980)-. — Tring (M.B. House, Wigginton, Tring, Hertfordshire HP23 6ED) : Micronutrient Bureau, 1980-. — v. ; 30cm
ISSN 0261-5045 = Molybdenum in agriculture : Unpriced
Primary classification 631.5 B81-29100

636.089′23924 — Livestock. Nutrition. Trace elements — *Serials*
Micronutrient news. — Vol.1, no.1 (Oct.1980)-. — Tring (M.B. House, Wigginton, Tring, Hertfordshire HP23 6ED) : Micronutrient Bureau, 1980-. — v. : ill,ports ; 30cm
Quarterly
ISSN 0261-5002 = Micronutrient news : Unpriced
Primary classification 631.5 B81-29098

636.089′2398 — Livestock. Proteins. Metabolism — *Conference proceedings*
Protein deposition in animals / P.J. Buttery, D.B. Lindsay. — London : Butterworths, 1980. — 305p : ill ; 24cm
Conference papers. — Includes bibliographies and index
ISBN 0-408-10676-x : £16.00 : CIP rev. B80-18398

636.089′262 — Female livestock. Reproductive system. Physiology
Hunter, R. H. F.. Physiology and technology of reproduction in female domestic animals / R.H.F. Hunter. — London : Academic Press, 1980. — xiii,393p,1leaf of plates : ill(some col.) ; 24cm
Includes bibliographies and index
ISBN 0-12-361950-5 : £25.00 : CIP rev. B80-20808

636.089′51141 — Great Britain. Veterinary medicine. Proprietary drugs — *Lists* — *Serials*
ABPI compendium of data sheets for veterinary products. — 1980-81. — London (162 Regent St., WIR 6DD) : Datapharm, c1980. — vii,497p
ISBN 0-907102-01-8 : Unpriced
ISSN 0307-1332 B81-03667

636.089′59 — Veterinary medicine. Toxicology
Clarke, Myra L.. Veterinary toxicology. — 2nd ed. / Myra L. Clarke, D.. Harvey, D.J. Humphreys. — London : Baillière Tindall, 1981. — 328p ; 26cm
Previous ed.: / by E.G.C. Clarke and Myra L. Clarke. 1975. — Bibliography: p304. — Includes index
£16.00 B81-40668

Clarke, Myra L.. Veterinary toxicology. — 2nd ed. — London : Baillière Tindall, July 1981. — [336]p
Previous ed.: 1975
ISBN 0-7020-0862-1 : £14.50 : CIP entry B81-13459

Veterinary toxicology / edited by Michal Bartík, Alois Piskač. — Amsterdam ; Oxford : Elsevier Scientific, 1981. — 346p,[16]p of plates : ill (some col.) ; 25cm. — (Developments in animal and veterinary sciences ; 7)
Bibliography: p327-336. - Includes index
£27.22 (corrected) B81-23195

636.089′59′511 — Michigan. Livestock. Toxic effects of contamination of feedingstuffs by polybrominated biphenyls, ***1973-1974***
Egginton, Joyce. [The poisoning of Michigan]. Bitter harvest / Joyce Egginton. — London : Secker & Warburg, 1980. — 351p : 1map ; 24cm
Originally published: New York : Norton, 1980. — Includes index
ISBN 0-436-14150-7 : £9.95 B81-06346

636.089′6 — Livestock. Diseases
Thornton, Horace. Thornton's meat hygiene. — 7th ed. / J.F. Gracey. — London : Baillière Tindall, 1981. — viii,436p,4p of plates : ill (some col.) ; 26cm
Previous ed.: published as Textbook of meat hygiene / Horace Thornton and J.F. Gracey. 1974. — Includes index
ISBN 0-7020-0831-1 : £18.00
Primary classification 363.1′929 B81-22407

636.089′6′005 — Livestock. Diseases — *Serials*
Advances in veterinary science and comparative medicine. — vol.24 (1980). — New York ; London : Academic Press, c1980. — 325p
ISBN 0-12-039224-0 : Unpriced B81-10271

Veterinary clinics of North America. Large animal practice. — Vol.1, no.1 (May 1979)-. — Philadelphia ; London : Saunders, 1979-. — v. : ill ; 24cm
Two issues yearly. — Continues in part: Veterinary clinics of North America
ISSN 0196-9846 : £13.50 B81-21338

636.089′6′00941 — Great Britain. Livestock. Diseases — *Serials*
Return of proceedings under the Diseases of Animals Act, 1950 / Ministry of Agriculture, Fisheries and Food, Department of Agriculture and Fisheries for Scotland, Welsh Office, Agriculture Department. — 1980. — London : H.M.S.O., 1981. — 13p
ISBN 0-11-240873-7 : £1.90 B81-28387

636.089′607 — Livestock. Diseases. Biochemical aspects
Clinical biochemistry of domestic animals. — 3rd ed., edited by Jiro J. Kaneko, contributors Jack C. Bartley ... [et al.]. — New York ; London : Academic Press, 1980. — xiii,832p : ill ; 25cm
Previous ed.: 197-. — Includes bibliographies and index
ISBN 0-12-396350-8 : £33.60 B81-16619

636.089′607 — Livestock: Small animals. Pathology
Kelly, D. F.. Notes on pathology for small animal clinicians. — Bristol : Wright, Feb.1982. — [112]p. — (A Veterinary practitioner handbook)
ISBN 0-85608-037-3 (pbk) : £7.50 : CIP entry B81-37597

636.089′6′072041 — Great Britain. Livestock. Diseases. Research organisations: Institute for Research on Animal Diseases — *Serials*
Institute for Research on Animal Diseases. Report / Institute for Research on Animal Diseases. — 1979/80. — Compton (Near Newbury Compton, Berkshire) : The Institute, 1981. — 154p
ISBN 0-7084-0181-3 : Unpriced B81-31604

636.089′69 — Livestock. Communicable diseases
Hagan, William Arthur. Hagan and Bruner's infectious diseases of domestic animals : with reference to etiology, pathogenicity, immunity, epidemiology, diagnosis and biologic therapy. — 7th ed. / James Howard Gillespie, John Francis Timpney. — Ithaca ; London : Comstock, 1981. — 854p : ill,1map,1port ; 28cm
Previous ed. published as: Hagan's infectious diseases of domestic animals. Ithaca ; London : Cornell University Press, 1973. — Includes bibliographies and index
ISBN 0-8014-1333-8 : £20.00 B81-27261

636.089′6925 — Livestock. Rift Valley fever — *Conference proceedings*
Rift Valley fever : proceedings of a workshop on Rift Valley fever, Herzlia, Israel, March 18-21, 1980 / volume editors T.A. Swartz, M.A. Klingberg, N. Goldblum ; associate editor C.M. Papier. — Basel ; London : Karger, c1981. — xii,196p : ill,maps ; 23cm. — (Contributions to epidemiology and biostatistics ; v.3)
Includes bibliographies and index
ISBN 3-8055-1770-x (pbk) : £22.00
Primary classification 616.9′25 B81-36175

636.089′69′25 — Livestock. Virus diseases
Virus diseases of food animals. — London : Academic Press
Vol.1. — Nov.1981. — [300]p
ISBN 0-12-282201-3 : CIP entry B81-28792

Virus diseases of food animals. — London : Academic Press
Vol.2. — Dec.1981. — [300]p
ISBN 0-12-282202-1 : CIP entry B81-31339

636.089′7 — Veterinary medicine. Surgery
Fundamental techniques in veterinary surgery / Charles D. Knecht ... [et al.]. — Philadelphia ; London : Saunders, 1981. — xiii,305p : ill ; 27cm
Previous ed.: 1975. — Includes bibliographies and index
ISBN 0-7216-5463-0 : £16.00 B81-27102

636.089′77 — Livestock: Vertebrates. Eyes. Diseases
Slatter, Douglas H.. Fundamentals of veterinary ophthalmology / Douglas H. Slatter. — Philadelphia ; London : Saunders, 1981. — xiii,821p : ill(some col.) ; 27cm
Text on lining paper. — Includes index
ISBN 0-7216-8357-6 : £53.25 B81-37461

636.1 — LIVESTOCK. HORSES

636.1 — Livestock: Horses
Bradley, Melvin. Horses : a practical and scientific approach / Melvin Bradley. — New York ; London : McGraw-Hill, 1981. — x,580p : ill ; 25cm
Includes index
ISBN 0-07-007065-2 : £16.25 B81-19539

636.1 — Livestock: Horses *continuation*

Evans, J. Warren. Horses : a guide to selection, care and enjoyment / J. Warren Evans. — Oxford : W.H. Freeman, c1981. — xvi,683p : ill ; 25cm
Bibliography: p649-672. — Includes index
ISBN 0-7167-1253-9 : £12.80 B81-37381

Henschel, Georgie. Illustrated guide to horses and ponies / by Georgie Henschel. — London : Kingfisher, 1980. — 196p : ill(some col.),ports(some col.) ; 27cm
Bibliography: p191. — Includes index
ISBN 0-7063-6004-4 : £6.95 B81-02627

Macgregor-Morris, Pamela. [All about horses]. The horse : the comprehensive guide to breeds, riding and management / Pamela Macgregor-Morris & E. Hartley Edwards ; with a foreword by Anne [i.e. Ann] Moore. — London : Orbis Publishing, 1974 (1980 printing). — 143p : col.ill,col.ports ; 30cm
Ill on lining papers. — Includes index
£4.50 B81-03619

636.1 — Livestock: Horses, 3-4 years. Training — *Amateurs' manuals*

Knox-Thompson, Elaine. The young horse / Elaine Knox-Thompson and Suzanne Dickens. — Auckland ; London : Collins, 1979. — 91p,[6]p of plates : ill(some col.),port ; 26cm
Bibliography: p91
ISBN 0-00-195081-9 : £5.95 B81-02272

636.1 — Livestock: Horses. Breeding, training & care

Sutcliffe, Anne. Breeding & training a horse or pony / Anne Sutcliffe. — Newton Abbot : David & Charles, c1981. — 165p : ill,2forms ; 23cm
Includes index
ISBN 0-7153-7953-4 : £5.95 B81-20808

636.1 — Livestock: Horses — *For children*

Dell, Catherine. The wonder book of horses / [Catherine Dell]. — London : Ward Lock, 1981. — 37p : col.ill ; 27cm
Includes index
ISBN 0-7063-6130-x : £2.50 B81-39961

Edwards, Elwyn Hartley. Know your horses / written by Elwyn Hartley Edwards ; illustrated by David Nockels. — London : Methuen/Walker, 1980. — 42p : ill(some col.) ; 27cm. — (Animal friends)
Col. ill on lining papers
ISBN 0-416-89060-1 : £2.95 : CIP rev. B80-19286

Fry, Fiona Somerset. Horses / Fiona Somerset Fry. — London : A. & C. Black, 1981. — 64p : ill ; 26cm
Includes index
ISBN 0-7136-2114-1 : £3.95 : CIP rev. B81-08819

Goffe, Toni. Wonder why book of XYZ of horses / written and illustrated by Toni Goffe. — Ealing : Transworld, 1981. — [32]p : col.ill ; 28cm
Cover title. — Text on inside cover
ISBN 0-552-57053-2 (pbk) : £0.95 B81-21402

Horses. — [London] : Sparrow, 1980. — [24]p : ill(some col.) ; 29cm. — (Discoverers)
Adaptation of: The Superbook of horses. — Bibliography: p24
ISBN 0-09-923570-6 (pbk) : £0.70 B81-14525

Isenbart, Hans-Heinrich. Horses and riding / [translated from the original German text of Hans-Heinrich Isenbart by Brenda F. Groth]. — St. Albans : Hart-Davis, 1981. — 37p : col.ill ; 15x16cm. — (Questions answered)
ISBN 0-247-13092-3 : £1.50 B81-39470

Richardson, Julie. Horses and ponies / by Julie Richardson : illustrated by Libby King. — London : Granada, 1981. — 64p : col.ill ; 19cm. — (Granada guides)
Includes index
ISBN 0-246-11564-5 : £1.95 B81-39302

636.1 — Spain. Coto Doñana. Livestock: Andalusian horses: Stallions — *Illustrations*

Vavra, Robert. Stallion of a dream / Robert Vavra ; with an introduction by Peter Ustinov. — London : Collins, 1981, c1980. — [64]p : chiefly col.ill ; 27cm
ISBN 0-00-216885-5 : £6.95 B81-33437

636.1′0022′2 — Livestock: Horses. Breeds — *Illustrations*

Nockels, David. Horses : a colour guide to the world's principal horse and pony breeds, origins — uses — sizes / [painted by David Nockels ; text by Elwyn Hartley Edwards]. — [London] : Fontana, 1979. — 1folded sheet ([12]p) : col.ill ; 25cm. — (Domino ; 21)
ISBN 0-00-685448-6 : £0.85 B81-20259

636.1′0022′2 — Livestock: Horses — *Illustrations — For children*

Horses and ponies. — Maidenhead : Purnell, 1979, 1981 [printing]. — [28]p : chiefly col.ill ; 27cm. — (All in colour picture books)
ISBN 0-361-04545-x : £1.25 B81-23423

Roberts, Peter, *19—*. Purnell's big picture book of horses and ponies / [photographs by Peter Roberts]. — Maidenhead : Purnell, 1981. — [48]p : all col.ill ; 27cm
ISBN 0-361-05072-0 : £2.75 B81-22269

636.1′0023 — Occupations involving horses — *Career guides*

Russell, Valerie. A guide to careers with horses / Valerie Russell. — London : Pelham, 1980. — 128p ; 21cm. — (Pelham horsemaster series)
Includes index
ISBN 0-7207-1280-7 : £5.50 B81-00972

636.1′005 — Livestock: Horses — *For children — Serials*

Princess Tina pony book. — 1981. — London : IPC Magazines, c1980. — 75p
ISBN 0-85037-564-9 : £2.00 B81-06861

Riding annual. — 1981. — London : IPC Magazines, c1980. — 79p
ISBN 0-85037-570-3 : £2.40 B81-06862

636.1′005 — Livestock: Horses — *Serials*

Equi : a bi-monthly magazine devoted to promoting the ultimate wellbeing and continuance of all members of the equine race. — No.1 (Nov./Dec.1980)-. — Warrington (9 Rostherne Ave., Lowton St. Lukes, Warrington, Cheshire WA3 2QD) : Equi Publication, 1980-. — v. : ill ; 30cm
ISSN 0260-8103 = Equi : £8.00 per year B81-09209

636.1′00941 — Great Britain. Livestock: Horses — *Practical information*

Norback, Craig T.. The horseman's catalog / Craig Norback and Peter Norback ; consulting editor Albert E. Hart, Jr. — New York ; London : McGraw-Hill, c1979. — vii,520p : ill,1form ; 29cm
ISBN 0-07-047135-5 : £10.50 B81-14589

636.1′082 — Livestock: Horses. Breeding — *Manuals*

Rossdale, Peter. Horse breeding / Peter Rossdale. — Newton Abbot : David & Charles, c1981. — 320p : ill ; 24cm
Includes index
ISBN 0-7153-7987-9 : £15.00 : CIP rev. B81-00149

636.1′083 — Livestock: Horses. Care — *Manuals*

Bullock, John. Care of the horse / John Bullock. — Richmond upon Thames : Country Life Books ; London : Distributed by Hamlyn, 1980. — 111p : ill(some col.) ; 25cm
Includes index
ISBN 0-600-32216-5 : £5.95 B81-15132

Horse sense. — London : Dent, 1980. — 126p : col.ill ; 20cm. — (A QED book)
Includes index
ISBN 0-460-04515-6 : £2.95 B81-24526

Knox-Thompson, Elaine. Guide to riding and horse care / Elaine Knox-Thompson, Suzanne Dickens. — Rev. and repr. — London : Orbis Publishing, 1980 (1981 [printing]). — 158p : ill ; 27cm
Previous ed.: Auckland : Paul Hamlyn, 1977. — Ill on lining papers. — Includes index
ISBN 0-85613-319-1 : £5.95
Primary classification 798.2′3 B81-23539

636.1′084 — Livestock: Horses. Feeding

Cunha, Tony J.. Horse feeding and nutrition / Tony J. Cunha. — New York ; London : Academic Press, 1980. — xvi,292p : ill ; 24cm. — (Animal feeding and nutrition)
Includes index
ISBN 0-12-196560-0 : £17.20 B81-15128

636.1′0852 — Horses. Nutrition — *For horse breeding*

Leighton Hardman, A. C.. Equine nutrition / A.C. Leighton Hardman. — London : Pelham, 1980. — 112p : ill ; 21cm. — (Pelham horsemaster series)
Includes index
ISBN 0-7207-1244-0 : £5.95 B81-00150

636.1′12′09438 — Poland. Arab horses — *Illustrations*

A **Photographic** history of the Polish Arabian / [compiled] by Gladys Brown Edwards. — Rockville, Md. : Arab Ink ; Northleach (PO Box 1, Northleach, Cheltenham, Glos.) : A. Heriot [distributor], 1978. — 136p : all ill ; 29cm
ISBN 0-906382-01-7 (pbk) : Unpriced B81-12940

636.1′2 — Racehorses. Racing. Races. Winners, *1960-1980*. **Pedigrees** - *Collections*

Pickering, Martin. Pedigrees of leading winners, 1960-1980. — London : J.A. Allen, July 1981. — [200]p
ISBN 0-85131-372-8 : £25.00 : CIP entry B81-19217

636.1′2′09046 — Race horses, *1961-1979*

Magee, Michael. Champions / Michael Magee ; with photographs by Pat Bayes. — London : Sidgwick & Jackson, 1980. — 191p : ill(some col.),ports ; 30cm
Originally published: Don Mills : Nelson, 1980
ISBN 0-283-98723-5 : £12.50 B81-03097

636.1′2′0924 — Great Britain. Racehorses. Training. Murless, *Sir Noel* — *Biographies*

Fitzgeorge-Parker, Tim. The guv'nor : a biography of Sir Noel Murless / Tim Fitzgeorge-Parker. — London : Collins, 1980. — 248p,[24]p of plates : ill,ports ; 24cm
Includes index
ISBN 0-00-216296-2 : £8.95 B81-01580

636.1′2′094 — Europe. Racehorses — *Serials*

The European racehorse : incorporating The British racehorse. — Vol.1, no.1 (Spring issue 1981)-. — London (c/o Turf Newspapers, 55 Curzon St., W1) : European Racing and Breeding Publications, 1981-. — v. : ill ; 21cm
Five issues yearly. — Continues: The British racehorse
ISSN 0260-7468 = European racehorse : £18.00 per year B81-33946

636.1′2′0941 — Great Britain. Racehorses in training — *Lists — Serials*

Sporting chronicle horses in training. — 1981. — Manchester (Thomson House, Manchester M60 4BJ) : Sporting Chronicle Publications, [1981?]. — 640p
Cover title: Horses in training
£6.00 B81-23148

636.1′32 — Thoroughbred horses. Breeding. Genetic aspects

Robertson, J. B.. The principles of heredity applied to the racehorse. — London : J.A. Allen, July 1981. — [43]p
ISBN 0-85131-374-4 : £5.00 : CIP entry B81-25699

636.1'32'0341 — Thoroughbred horses — *French & English dictionaries*
Kearney, Mary Louise. A glossary of French bloodstock terminology. — London : J. A. Allen, June 1981. — [48]p
ISBN 0-85131-354-x (pbk) : £2.50 : CIP entry
B81-13553

636.1'4 — Harness horses. Training — *Manuals*
Walrond, Sallie. Breaking a horse to harness. — London : Pelham, Nov.1981. — [96]p
ISBN 0-7207-1369-2 : £6.50 : CIP entry
B81-30363

636.1'5 — Irish Draught horses — *Serials*
Irish draught horse yearbook. — 1978-. — Dunlaoire (Northumberland Chambers, Northumberland Ave., Dunlaoire, County Dublin) : Agricultural Publications, 1978-. — v. : ill ; 30cm
Unpriced B81-32888

636.1'5 — Shire horses — *Serials*
Horse & driving : [heavy horses, driving and dressage]. — 3rd year, no.2 (Summer 1979)-. — Bradford : Watmoughs, 1979-. — v. : ill ; 30cm
Quarterly (Summer 1979/Summer 1980), Six issues yearly (Sept./Oct.1980-). — Continues: Heavy horse & driving. — Description based on: 4th year, no.3 (Sept./Oct.1980)
ISSN 0142-7008 = Horse & driving : £13.50 per year
Also classified at 798.2'3 ; 798'.6'05
B81-00973

636.1'5'0941 — British carthorses
Hart, Edward. Heavy horses / Edward Hart. — London : Batsford, 1981. — 64p : ill(some col.),ports(some col.) ; 20cm
Bibliography: p61-62. — Includes index
ISBN 0-7134-3805-3 (pbk) : £1.95 B81-34861

636.1'5'0941 — British carthorses. Use — *Manuals*
Rayner, Nick. The heavy horse manual / Nick Rayner and Keith Chivers ; photographs by Barry Rickman. — Newton Abbot : David & Charles, c1981. — 208p : ill,ports ; 25cm
Bibliography: p202. — Includes index
ISBN 0-7153-8057-5 : £10-95 : CIP rev.
B81-14955

636.1'6 — Great Britain. Livestock: Ponies. Judging
Taylor, Alison, *19---*. Hints to young judges / by Alison Taylor. — [London] : National Pony Society, c1978. — 5p ; 22cm
Unpriced (unbound) B81-07159

636.1'6 — Great Britain. Livestock: Welsh cobs & Welsh ponies — *Serials*
The **Welsh** Pony and Cob Society journal. — 1980. — Aberystwyth (6, Chalybeate St., Aberystwyth, Dyfed) : The Society, 1980. — 348p
Unpriced B81-00151

The **Welsh** Pony and Cob Society journal. — 1981. — Aberystwyth (3 Chalybeate St., Aberystwyth, Dyfed) : The Society, [1981?]. — 344p
Unpriced B81-15284

636.1'6 — Great Britain. Livestock: Welsh cobs & Welsh ponies. Welsh cobs & ponies, *to 1979*
Davies, Wynne. Welsh ponies and cobs / Wynne Davies. — London : J.A. Allen, 1980. — xi,506p : ill,facsims,ports ; 24cm
Includes index
ISBN 0-85131-361-2 : £12.95 B81-04573

636.1'6 — Livestock: New Forest ponies — *Lists — Serials*
. The New Forest pony stud book. — Vol.22. — [Ringwood] ([c/o Beacon Corner, Burley, Ringwood, Hants]) : New Forest Pony Breeding and Cattle Society, [1980]. — 158p
Unpriced B81-24110

636.1'6 — Livestock: Ponies. Care — *Manuals*
Hearne, Tina. Care for your pony / text by Tina Hearne ; illustrations by Terry Riley and Mike Woodhatch/David Lewis Artists. — Glasgow : Collins, 1981. — 32p : col.ill ; 23cm
Includes index
ISBN 0-00-410203-7 (pbk) : £1.25 B81-39454

Webber, Toni. Caring for your pony / Toni Webber ; illustrated by Vanessa Pancheri. — Sevenoaks : Hodder and Stoughton 1980. — 151p : ill ; 20cm. — (Teach yourself books)
Includes index
ISBN 0-340-25109-3 (pbk) : £1.75 CIP rev.
B81-03141

636.1'6 — Livestock: Ponies - *For children*
Henschel, Georgie. All about your pony. — London : Ward Lock, June 1981. — [104]p. — (Horseman's handbooks)
ISBN 0-7063-6122-9 (pbk) : £2.95 : CIP entry
B81-12313

636.1'6 — Livestock: Ponies. Training & care — *Manuals*
Akrill, Caroline. Showing the ridden pony : a guide to the selection, training and production of ridden and working ponies under saddle / by Caroline Akrill ; illustrations by Elaine Roberts. — London : J.A. Allen, 1981. — 138p,[12]p of plates : ill,ports ; 22cm
Bibliography: p134. — Includes index
ISBN 0-85131-359-0 : £6.95 : CIP rev.
B81-12847

636.1'6'05 — Livestock: Ponies — *Serials*
National Pony Society. The National Pony Society review. — 1981. — Alton (c/o Brigadier J.D. Lofts, 7 Cross & Pillory La., Alton, Hants.) : The Society, [1981]. — 126p
Unpriced B81-21944

636.1'8 — Cornwall. Pets: Donkeys — *Personal observations*
Tangye, Derek. A donkey in the meadow / Derek Tangye. — London : Sphere, 1980, c1965. — 157p : ill ; 18cm
Originally published: London : Joseph, 1965
ISBN 0-7221-8376-3 (pbk) : £1.10 B81-00152

Tangye, Derek. A donkey in the meadow / Derek Tangye. — Large print ed. — Bath : Chivers, 1981, c1965. — 187p ; 23cm. — (A New Portway large print book)
Originally published: London : Joseph, 1965
ISBN 0-85119-110-x : Unpriced B81-15221

636.1'8 — Pets: Donkeys. Breeding & care
Morris, Dorothy. Keeping a donkey / Dorothy Morris. — Princes Risborough : Shire, 1979. — 80p : ill ; 21cm
Includes index
ISBN 0-85263-435-8 (pbk) : £1.75 B81-07308

636.2 — LIVESTOCK. RUMINANTS, CATTLE

636.2'0092'4 — United States. Livestock: Cattle. Production. Ranches. Bratt, John — *Biographies*
Bratt, John. Trails of yesterday / by John Bratt ; introduction by Nellie Snyder Yost. — Lincoln, [Neb.] ; London : University of Nebraska Press, 1980, c1949. — xix,302p,[27]p of plates : ill,ports ; 21cm
ISBN 0-8032-1157-0 (cased) : £10.50
ISBN 0-8032-6055-5 (pbk) : £3.30 B81-05103

636.2'07'0222 — Livestock: Calves — *Illustrations — For children*
Miller, Jane, *1925-*. A calf is born / Jane Miller. — London : Dent, 1981. — [41]p : ill ; 25cm
Ill on lining papers
ISBN 0-460-06986-1 : £3.50 : CIP rev.
B80-12408

636.2'08245 — Livestock: Cattle. Artificial insemination
Herman, Harry A.. Improving cattle by the millions : NAAB and the development and worldwide application of artificial insemination / Harry A. Herman. — Columbia ; London : University of Missouri Press, 1981. — viii,377p : ill,1map,ports ; 25cm
Includes index
ISBN 0-8262-0320-5 : £16.80 B81-38216

636.2'084 — Livestock: Ruminants. Feeding & nutrition
Recent developments in ruminant nutrition / editors W. Haresign, D.J.A. Cole. — London : Butterworths, 1981. — ix,367p : ill ; 24cm
Includes bibliographies and index
ISBN 0-408-10804-5 (pbk) : Unpriced : CIP rev. B81-21647

636.2'08'5 — Livestock: Ruminants. Feeding systems
Wilson, P. N.. Improved feeding of cattle and sheep. — St. Albans : Granada, Jan.1982. — [256]p
ISBN 0-246-11210-7 (pbk) : £9.95 : CIP entry
B81-34152

636.2'0855 — Livestock: Ruminants. Feedingstuffs. Constituents: Proteins. Sources — *Conference proceedings*
Protein and energy supply for high production of milk and meat. — Oxford : Pergamon for the United Nations, Jan.1982. — [190]p
Conference papers
ISBN 0-08-028909-6 : £15.00 : CIP entry
B81-38300

636.2'089'094 — European Community countries. Livestock: Calves. Veterinary aspects — *Conference proceedings*
Calving problems and early viability of the calf : a seminar in the EEC Programme of Coordination of Research on Beef Production held at Freising, Federal Republic of Germany, May 4-6, 1977 / sponsored by the Commission of the European Communities, Directorate-General for Agriculture, Coordination of Agricultural Research ; edited by B. Hoffmann, I.L. Mason, J. Schmidt. — The Hague ; London : Nijhoff for the Commission of the European Communities, 1979. — x,593p : ill ; 24cm. — (Current topics in veterinary medicine and animal science ; v.4)
Includes bibliographies
ISBN 90-247-2195-4 : Unpriced B81-16203

636.2'0892397 — Livestock: Ruminants. Lipids. Metabolism
Lipid metabolism in ruminant animals / editor William W. Christie. — Oxford : Pergamon, 1981. — vii,452p : ill ; 28cm
Includes bibliographies and index
ISBN 0-08-023789-4 : £29.00 B81-27806

636.2'0894552'00941 — Great Britain. Livestock: Cattle. Parasites: Worms. Control by management of pastures
Grazing plans for the control of stomach and intestinal worms in sheep and in cattle / ADAS, Ministry of Agriculture, Fisheries and Food. — Pinner (Tolcarne Drive, Pinner, Middx HA5 2DT) : The Ministry, 1980. — 17p : ill ; 21cm. — (Booklet ; 2154)
Unpriced (pbk)
Also classified at 636.3'0894552'00941
B81-17748

636.2'0895532 — Livestock: Cattle. Veterinary care. Homeopathy
MacLeod, G.. The treatment of cattle by homoeopathy / by G. MacLeod ; index by Maurice Prior. — Saffron Walden : Health Science Press, c1981. — 148p ; 23cm
Includes index
ISBN 0-85032-196-4 : £8.50 B81-29711

636.2'0896'00913 — Tropical region. Livestock: Cattle. Diseases
Diseases of cattle in the tropics : economic and zoonotic relevance / edited by Miodrag Ristic and Ian McIntyre. — The Hague ; London : Nijhoff, 1981. — xii,662p : ill,1maps ; 25cm. — (Current topics in veterinary medicine and animal science ; v.6)
Includes bibliographies and index
ISBN 90-247-2429-5 : Unpriced B81-40127

636.2'0896079 — Livestock: Ruminants. Immunology — *Conference proceedings*
The **Ruminant** immune system / edited by John E. Butler ; associate editors J. Robert Duncan, Klaus Nielson. — New York ; London : Plenum, c1981. — xxiv,891p : ill ; 26cm. — (Advances in experimental medicine and biology ; V.137)
Conference papers. — Includes index
ISBN 0-306-40641-1 : Unpriced B81-37501

636.2'089'758 — Livestock: Cattle. Lameness
Greenough, Paul R.. Lameness in cattle. — 2nd ed. — Bristol : J. Wright, Sept.1981. — [496]p
Previous ed.: / Paul R. Greenough, Finlay J. MacCallum, A. David Weaver. Edinburgh : Oliver & Boyd, 1972
ISBN 0-85608-030-6 : £25.00 : CIP entry
B81-21550

636.2'13 — Livestock: Beef cattle. Feeding & nutrition

Perry, Tilden Wayne. Beef cattle feeding and nutrition / Tilden Wayne Perry. — New York ; London : Academic Press, 1980. — xv,383p : ill ; 24cm. — (Animal feeding and nutrition)
Includes bibliographies and index
ISBN 0-12-552050-6 : £19.60 B81-07361

636.2'13 — New Zealand. Livestock: Beef cattle. Breeding — *Conference proceedings*

World Congress on Sheep and Beef Cattle Breeding *(1980 : Massey University and Lincoln College, N.Z.)*. Report on World Congress on Sheep and Beef Cattle Breeding, New Zealand 28 October-17 November 1980 / B.R. Nuttall. — Trawsgoed (RLHAO, ADAS Centre, Trawsgoed) : ADAS, 1981. — 70p : ill,1map ; 30cm
Unpriced (unbound)
Also classified at 636.3'082'09931 B81-38571

636.2'13 — Texas. Livestock: Cattle. Production. Ranches, *to 1880*

Jordan, Terry G.. Trails to Texas : Southern roots of Western cattle ranching / Terry G. Jordan. — Lincoln [Neb.] ; London : University of Nebraska Press, c1981. — xv,220p : ill,maps,1port ; 23cm
Bibliography: p191-214. — Includes index
ISBN 0-8032-2554-7 : £10.40 B81-29377

636.2'13'0973 — United States. Livestock: Beef cattle. Production

Lasley, John F.. Beef cattle production / John F. Lasley. — Englewood Cliffs ; London : Prentice-Hall, c1981. — xii,468p : ill,maps,forms ; 24cm
Includes index
ISBN 0-13-072629-x : £12.95 B81-12720

636.2'14 — Eastern England. Livestock: Dairy cattle. Yields — *Statistics* — *Serials*

[Report for the year ended September ... *(National Milk Records)*. Areas 3, Eastern area, East Midland area, South Eastern area edition]. Report for the year ended September ... / National Milk Records. Areas 3, Eastern area East Midland area, South Eastern area edition. — 1980. — Thames Ditton : Milk Marketing Board, [1981?]. — 140p
Unpriced B81-23498

636.2'14 — England. West Midlands. Livestock: Dairy cattle. Yields — *Statistics* — *Serials*

[Report for the year ended September ... *(National Milk Records)*. Areas 2, North Midland area, West Midland area, North Wales area, South Wales area edition]. Report for the year ended September ... / National Milk Records. Areas 2, North Midland area, West Midland area, North Wales area, South Wales area edition. — 1980. — Thames Ditton : Milk Marketing Board, [1981?]. — 188p
Unpriced
Also classified at 636.2'14 B81-23501

636.2'14 — Northern England. Livestock: Dairy cattle. Yields — *Statistics* — *Serials*

[Report for the year ended September ... *(National Milk Records)*. Areas 1 Far Northern area, Mid Northern area edition]. Report for the year ended September ... / National Milk Records. Areas 1, Far Northern area, Mid Northern area edition. — 1980. — Thames Ditton : Milk Marketing Board, [1981?]. — 100p
Unpriced B81-23499

636.2'14 — Southern England. Livestock: Dairy cattle. Yields — *Statistics* — *Serials*

[Report for the year ended September ... *(National Milk Records)*. Areas 4, Southern area, Mid Western area, Far Western area edition]. Report for the year ended September ... / National Milk Records. Areas 4, Southern area, Mid Western area, Far Western area edition. — 1980. — Thames Ditton : Milk Marketing Board, [1981?]. — 192p
Unpriced B81-23500

636.2'14 — Wales. Livestock: Dairy cattle. Yields — *Statistics* — *Serials*

[Report for the year ended September ... *(National Milk Records)*. Areas 2, North Midland area, West Midland area, North Wales area, South Wales area edition]. Report for the year ended September ... / National Milk Records. Areas 2, North Midland area, West Midland area, North Wales area, South Wales area edition. — 1980. — Thames Ditton : Milk Marketing Board, [1981?]. — 188p
Unpriced
Primary classification 636.2'14 B81-23501

636.2'142 — Devon. Dairy farming. Robertson, James, *1945-* — *Biographies*

Robertson, James, *1945-*. Any fool can be a dairy farmer / James Robertson ; drawings by Charles Gore. — Ispwich : Farming Press, 1980. — 171p : ill,1plan ; 23cm
ISBN 0-85236-110-6 : £6.50 B81-04096

636.2'142 — Great Britain. Livestock: Dairy cattle: Cows. Herds. Yields — *Statistics* — *Serials*

Other dairy breeds with improved contemporary comparisons. — 1981. — [Thames Ditton] : Milk Marketing Board, [1981?]. — 109p in various pagings
ISSN 0260-1982 : Unpriced B81-36559

636.2'142 — Livestock: Dairy cattle. Diseases

Ahmed, Ehsanullah. Diseases of dairy animals / by Ehsanullah Ahmed. — 2nd ed. — Hyderabad : Seven Seas ; Luton : Apex Books Concern, 1981. — 78p ; 17cm
Previous ed.: 1971. — Includes index
ISBN 0-904812-42-1 (pbk) : £1.60 : CIP rev. B81-11935

636.2'2 — Livestock: Old Gloucester cattle, *to 1979*

Stout, Adam. The Old Gloucester : the story of a cattle breed / Adam Stout. — Gloucester : Alan Sutton, 1980. — 96p : ill,maps,ports ; 23cm
Bibliography: p86-91. - Includes index
ISBN 0-904387-42-9 : £4.95 : CIP rev. B80-12409

636.2'23 — Great Britain. Livestock: Aberdeen-Angus cattle. Herds — *Lists* — *Serials*

Aberdeen-Angus Cattle Society The **Aberdeen-Angus** herd book. — Vol.105. — Perth (6 King's Place, Perth) : The Aberdeen-Angus Cattle Society, 1981. — 278p
Unpriced B81-32667

The **Aberdeen-Angus** herd book. — Vol.103. — Perth (6, King's Place, Perth) : The Aberdeen-Angus Cattle Society, 1979. — 282p
Unpriced B81-21931

636.2'23 — Great Britain. Livestock: Galloway cattle. Herds — *Lists* — *Serials*

The **Galloway** herd book. — Vol.98 (1979-1980). — Castle Douglas (131, King St., Castle Douglas, Kirkcudbright DG7 1LZ) : Galloway Cattle Society of Great Britain and Ireland, [1981?]. — 64p
Unpriced B81-15087

636.2'23 — Ireland *(Republic)*. **Livestock: Irish-Angus cattle. Herds** — *Lists* — *Serials*

Irish angus herd book. — Vol.11 (1978). — Dublin (Agriculture House, Kildare St., Dublin 2) : Irish Angus Cattle Society, [1978?]. — 43p
Unpriced B81-13199

Irish angus herd book. — Vol.12 (1979). — Dublin (Agriculture House, Kildare St., Dublin 2) : Irish Angus Cattle Society, [1979?]. — 38p
Unpriced B81-13198

636.2'24 — Great Britain. Livestock: Jersey cattle. Organisations: Jersey Cattle Society of the United Kingdom — *Serials*

Jersey Cattle Society of the United Kingdom. Herd book & directory of members / the Jersey Cattle Society of the United Kingdom. — Vol.90 (1978)-. — Reading (154 Castle Hill, Reading, Berkshire RG1 7RP) : The Society, 1978-. — v. ; 30cm
Annual. — Continues: Jersey herd book & directory (Jersey Cattle Society of the United Kingdom). — Description based on: Vol.91 (1979)
ISSN 0261-0574 = Herd book & directory of members — Jersey Cattle Society of the United Kingdom : £15.00 B81-15149

636.2'24 — Guernsey. Livestock: Guernsey cattle. Herds — *Lists* — *Serials*

Royal Guernsey Agricultural and Horticultural Society. The herd book of the Bailiwick of Guernsey / the Royal Guernsey Agricultural and Horticultural Society. — Vol.89 (1980). — Guernsey (2 Cornet St., Guernsey) : The Society, [1981]. — 81p
Unpriced B81-34051

636.2'34 — Great Britain. Livestock: Friesian cattle & Holstein cattle: Cows. Herds. Yields — *Statistics* — *Serials*

British Friesian/Holstein bulls with improved contemporary comparisons. — 1981. — [Thames Ditton] : Milk Marketing Board, [1981?]. — iv,215p
ISSN 0260-1990 : Unpriced B81-36560

636.2'94 — Scotland. Livestock: Red deer. Management

Red deer management : a practical book for the management of wild red deer in Scotland. — Inverness : Red Deer Commission, 1981. — 100p : ill(some col.) ; 21cm
Bibliography: p100
ISBN 0-11-491692-6 (pbk) : £5.00 B81-37389

636.3 — LIVESTOCK. SHEEP AND GOATS

636.3 — Livestock: Sheep. Production

Sheep and goat production. — Oxford : Elsevier Scientific, Feb.1982. — [350]p. — (World animal science. C ; 1)
ISBN 0-444-41989-6 : CIP entry
Also classified at 636.3'9 B81-35707

Speedy, Andrew W.. Sheep production : science into practice / Andrew W. Speedy. — London : Longman, 1980. — 195p : ill,1map,plans,forms ; 14x22cm. — (Longman handbooks in agriculture)
Bibliography: p190. - Includes index
ISBN 0-582-45582-0 (pbk) : £6.95 : CIP rev. B80-04274

636.3'00941 — Great Britain. Livestock: Sheep. Production — *Manuals*

Wilde, R. M.. Grasslambs : an intensive system of lamb production from temporary grassland / R.M. Wilde, N.E. Young and J.E. Newton. — Maidenhead (Hurley, Maidenheath, Berks SL6 5LR) : Grassland Research Institute, 1980. — 36p : ill ; 21cm. — (Farmer's booklet, ISSN 0308-0285 ; no.2)
Unpriced (pbk) B81-05778

636.3'082'09931 — New Zealand. Livestock: Sheep. Breeding — *Conference proceedings*

World Congress on Sheep and Beef Cattle Breeding *(1980 : Massey University and Lincoln College, N.Z.)*. Report on World Congress on Sheep and Beef Cattle Breeding, New Zealand 28 October-17 November 1980 / B.R. Nuttall. — Trawsgoed (RLHAO, ADAS Centre, Trawsgoed) : ADAS, 1981. — 70p : ill,1map ; 30cm
Unpriced (unbound)
Primary classification 636.2'13 B81-38571

636.3'0894552'00941 — Great Britain. Livestock: Sheep. Parasites: Worms. Control by management of pastures

Grazing plans for the control of stomach and intestinal worms in sheep and in cattle / ADAS, Ministry of Agriculture, Fisheries and Food. — Pinner (Tolcarne Drive, Pinner, Middx HA5 2DT) : The Ministry, 1980. — 17p : ill ; 21cm. — (Booklet ; 2154)
Unpriced (pbk)
Primary classification 636.2'0894552'00941 B81-17748

636.3'2 — Livestock: Dorset Down sheep. Flocks — *Lists — Serials*

Dorset Down Sheep Breeders' Association. The Dorset Down Flock book. — Vol.73 (1981). — Bath (c/o A.S.R. Austin, Brierley House, Summer La., Combe Down, Bath) : The Association, [1981]. — 43p
£2.00 (free to Association members) B81-25030

636.3'2 — Livestock: Dorset Horn sheep. Flocks — *Lists — Serials*

Dorset Horn Sheep Breeders' Association. The flock book of Dorset Horn sheep (incorporating the Poll Dorset Horn sheep). — Vol.90. — Dorchester (The Secretary, 3 High West St., Dorchester, Dorset) : Dorset Horn Sheep Breeders' Association, [1981]. — 160p
£3.00 (free to members) B81-33314

Dorset Horn Sheep Breeders' Association. The flock book of Dorset Horn sheep (incorporating the Poll Dorset Horn Sheep). — Vol.89. — Dorchester (c/o J.M. Gill, 3 High West St., Dorchester, Dorset) : The Association, [1981]. — 124p
ISSN 0305-2400 : £3.00 (free to Association members) B81-36300

636.3'2 — Livestock: Jacob sheep. Flocks — *Lists — Serials*

Jacob Sheep Society. Flock book / Jacob Sheep Society. — Vol.4. — Ringwood (c/o Mrs J. Earll, 242 Ringwood Rd, St. Leonards, Ringwood, Hants. BH24 2SB) : The Society, [1981]. — 108p in various pagings
£3.00 B81-31894

636.3'2 — Livestock: Suffolk sheep. Flocks — *Lists — Serials*

Suffolk Sheep Society. The Suffolk sheep flock book. — Vol.95. — Ipswich (Suffolk Showground, Bucklesham Rd, Ipswich) : Suffolk Sheep Society, 1981. — 483p
Cover title: Flock book (Suffolk Sheep Society)
Unpriced B81-36532

636.3'9 — Livestock: Goats. Production

Goat production. — London : Academic Press, Aug.1981. — [550]p
ISBN 0-12-273980-9 : CIP entry B81-18087

Sheep and goat production. — Oxford : Elsevier Scientific, Feb.1982. — [350]p. — (World animal science. C ; 1)
ISBN 0-444-41989-6 : CIP entry
Primary classification 636.3 B81-35707

636.3'9'005 — Livestock: Goats — *Serials*

[Year book *(British Goat Society)*]. Year book / British Boat Society. — 1980. — Bury St. Edmunds (The Secretary, Rousham, Bury St. Edmunds, Suffolk IP30 9LJ) : The Society, 1980. — 174p
£3.50 B81-15552

636.3'9083 — Livestock: Goats. Care & management — *Manuals*

Mackenzie, David, *b.1916*. Goat husbandry / by David Mackenzie. — 4th ed. / revised and edited by Jean Laing. — London : Faber, 1980. — 375p : ill,1map,2plans ; 23cm
Previous ed.: 1970. — Bibliography: p363-364. - Includes index
ISBN 0-571-18024-8 (cased) : £7.50 : CIP rev.
ISBN 0-571-11322-2 (pbk) : £3.95 B80-27231

Salmon, Jill. The goatkeeper's guide / Jill Salmon. — 2nd ed. — Newton Abbot : David & Charles, 1981. — 168p,[8]p of plates : ill ; 23cm
Includes index
ISBN 0-7153-8055-9 : £5.95 : CIP rev. B81-03364

636.4 — LIVESTOCK. PIGS

636.4 — Livestock: Pigs. Production — *Manuals*

Whittemore, Colin T.. Pig production : the scientific and practical principles / Colin T. Whittemore. — London : Longman, 1980. — vii,145p : ill ; 14x22cm. — (Longman handbooks in agriculture)
Includes index
ISBN 0-582-45590-1 (pbk) : £5.50 B81-00974

636.4'007204195 — Livestock: Pigs. Research by Institute of Agricultural Research

Riley, J. E.. Report on a visit to the Institute of Agricultural Research, Moore Park, County Fermoy, Eire, March, 1981 / J.E. Riley. — [Pinner] : ADAS, [1981]?. — 6p : ill ; 30cm
At head of title: Ministry of Agriculture, Fisheries and Food
Unpriced (unbound) B81-39000

636.4'00913 — Tropical regions. Livestock: Pigs. Production

Eusebio, J. A.. Pig production in the tropics / J.A. Eusebio. — Harlow : Longman, 1980. — x,115p : ill ; 22cm. — (Intermediate tropical agriculture series)
Includes bibliographies and index
ISBN 0-582-60617-9 (pbk) : £2.50 B81-24478

636.4'009423 — South-west England. Livestock: Pigs. Production — *Serials*

Pig production in South West England. — 1979-80. — Exeter : University of Exeter, Agricultural Economics Unit, 1981. — 36p. — (Agricultural enterprise studies in England and Wales. Economic report, ISSN 0306-8900 ; no.75)
£1.50 B81-24993

636.4'083 — Livestock: Pigs. Care & management — *Amateurs' manuals*

Mitchelmore, Peter. The Pigkeeper's guide / Peter Mitchelmore. — Newton Abbot : David & Charles, c1981. — 128p : ill,plans ; 23cm
ISBN 0-7153-7995-x : £4.95 B81-15061

636.4'0855 — Livestock: Pigs. Feedingstuffs. Additives: Copper — *Conference proceedings*

Copper in animal wastes and sewage sludge : proceedings of the EEC Workshop organised by the Institut national de la recherche agronomique (INRA), Station d'agronomie, Bordeaux, France, and held at Bordeaux, October 8-10, 1980 / sponsored by the Commission of the European Communities Directorate-General for Agriculture and Directorate-General for Research, Science and Education ; edited by P. L'Hermite and J. Dehandt. — Dordrecht ; London : Reidel, c1981. — xiv,378p : ill,1map ; 24cm
Includes bibliographies
ISBN 90-277-1293-x : Unpriced
Also classified at 363.7'384 B81-28462

636.4'089'094 — European Community countries. Livestock: Pigs. Veterinary aspects — *Conference proceedings*

The **Welfare** of pigs : a seminar in the EEC Programme of Coordination of Research on Animal Welfare held in Brussels, November 25-26, 1980 / sponsored by the Commission of the European Communities, Directorate-General for Agriculture, Coordination of Agricultural Research ; edited by W. Sybesma. — The Hague ; London : Nijhoff for the Commission of the European Communities, 1981. — ix,334p : ill ; 25cm. — (Current topics in veterinary medicine and animal science ; v.11)
ISBN 90-247-2521-6 : Unpriced B81-36870

636.4'08923 — Livestock: Pigs. Digestive system

Current concepts of digestion and absorption in pigs : proceedings of a seminar held at the National Institute for Research in Dairying on 19-20 July 1979 / editors A.G. Low and I.G. Partridge. — Reading ([Shinfield, Reading, RG9 IAT]) : National Institute for Research in Dairying, 1980. — 222p : ill,ports ; 21cm. — (Technical bulletin / National Institute for Research in Dairying ; 3)
Inlcudes bibliographies and index
ISBN 0-7084-0167-8 (pbk) : £6.00 B81-06322

636.4'08926 — Livestock: Pigs. Reproduction

Hughes, P. E.. Reproduction in the pig / P.E. Hughes, M.A. Varley. — London : Butterworth, 1980. — x,241p : ill ; 24cm
Includes bibliographies and index
ISBN 0-408-70946-4 (cased) : £14.00 : CIP rev.
ISBN 0-408-70921-9 (pbk) : £8.95 B80-11511

636.4'0894575 — Great Britain. Livestock: Pigs. Aujeszky's disease. Eradication — *Proposals*

Aujeszky's disease : briefing on a self-funded scheme for eradication. — [London] : National Farmers' Union, [1981?]. — 8p ; 21cm
Cover title
Unpriced (pbk) B81-25209

636.4'0896'0072044 — Livestock: Pigs. Diseases. Research in French institutions

Wells, G. A. H.. Institutes in France concerned with research into diseases of pigs : report of a study tour undertaken in France, 28-31 October 1980 / G.A.H. Wells. — [London] ([Great Westminster House, Horseferry Rd, SW1P 2AE]) : ADAS, [1981]. — 29p : 1map ; 30cm. — (ADAS study tour programme / Ministry of Agriculture, Fisheries and Food ; 1980-81)
Cover title. — Bibliography: p23-28
Unpriced (pbk) B81-36289

636.4'13'0943 — West Germany. Pigs for slaughter. Care — *Inquiry reports*

Christie, A. N.. Welfare of pigs to slaughter : report of a study tour undertaken in Holland and West Germany, September 1980 / A.N. Christie. — [London] ([Great Westminster House, Horseferry Rd., SW1P 2AE]) : ADAS, [1981]. — 52p : ill ; 30cm. — (ADAS study tour programme / Ministry of Agriculture, Fisheries and Food ; 1980-81)
Cover title
Unpriced (pbk)
Also classified at 636.4'13'09492 B81-36272

636.4'13'09492 — Netherlands. Pigs for slaughter. Care — *Inquiry reports*

Christie, A. N.. Welfare of pigs to slaughter : report of a study tour undertaken in Holland and West Germany, September 1980 / A.N. Christie. — [London] ([Great Westminster House, Horseferry Rd., SW1P 2AE]) : ADAS, [1981]. — 52p : ill ; 30cm. — (ADAS study tour programme / Ministry of Agriculture, Fisheries and Food ; 1980-81)
Cover title
Unpriced (pbk)
Primary classification 636.4'13'0943 B81-36272

636.5 — LIVESTOCK. POULTRY

636.5 — Poultry. Intensive production — *Serials*

World poultry industry. — May 1980-. — Sutton (1 Throwley Way, Sutton, Surrey SM1 4QQ) : Agricultural Press, 1980-. — v. : ill,ports ; 30cm
Continues : Poultry industry
ISSN 0260-387x = World poultry industry : £7.00 per year B81-02006

636.5'08'3 — Poultry. Care & management — *Amateurs' manuals*

Laud, Peter. Keeping your own poultry. — Wellingborough : Thorsons, Feb.1982. — [128]p
ISBN 0-7225-0711-9 (cased) : £6.95 : CIP entry
ISBN 0-7225-0712-7 (pbk) : £2.95 B81-35847

636.5'0896'0072042654 — Poultry. Diseases. Research organisations: Houghton Poultry Research Station — *Serials*

Houghton Poultry Research Station. Report of the Houghton Poultry Research Station. — 1975-76. — Hougton (Houghton, Huntingdon, Cambs.) : The Research Station, [1977?]. — 96p
ISSN 0307-4927 : Unpriced B81-29415

Houghton Poultry Research Station. Report of the Houghton Poultry Research Station. — 1977-78. — Houghton (Houghton, Huntingdon, Cambs.) : The Research Station, [1979?]. — 103p
ISSN 0307-4927 : Unpriced B81-29416

636.5′96 — Pets: Doves. Care

Gos, Michael W.. Doves / Michael W. Gos. — Neptune, N.J. ; Reigate : T.F.H., c1981. — 93p : ill(some col.) ; 21cm
Ill on lining papers
ISBN 0-87666-828-7 : £1.25 B81-40762

636.5′96 — Pets: Pigeons

Wheeler, Harry G.. Exhibition and flying pigeons / by Harry G. Wheeler ; with drawings by Lexi Hiscocks and more than 85 black and white photographs, many by the photographer Karl Stauber. — Hindhead : Spur, c1978. — viii,327p,8leaves of plates : ill(some col.) ; 25cm. — (Exhibition and family pets series)
Includes index
ISBN 0-904558-27-4 : Unpriced B81-09278

636.6 — LIVESTOCK. BIRDS(OTHER THAN POULTRY)

636.6 — Birds in captivity. Feeding & nutrition

Lint, Kenton C.. Diets for birds in captivity / Kenton C. Lint & Alice Marie Lint. — Poole : Blandford, 1981. — x,222p ; 23cm
Bibliography: p203-206. — Includes index
ISBN 0-7137-1087-x : £19.95 : CIP rev.
B81-00975

636.6 — Pets: Birds. Diseases

Raethel, Heinz-Sigurd. Bird diseases / Heinz-Sigurd Raethel ; translated by Christa Ahrens. — Neptune, N.J. ; Reigate : T.F.H., c1981. — 93p : ill(some col.) ; 21cm
Translation of: Krankheiten der Vogel. — Ill on lining papers
ISBN 0-87666-897-x : £1.25 B81-40756

636.6′8 — Ornamental wildfowl. Care & breeding

Johnson, A. A.. Ornamental waterfowl : a guide to their care and breeding / by A.A. Johnson and W.H. Payn ; text drawings by Robert Gillmor. — 4th ed. — Hindhead : Spur Publications, 1979. — 104p,16p of plates : ill (some col.) ; 23cm
Previous ed.: 1974. — Includes index
ISBN 0-904558-71-1 : £5.00 B81-10053

636.6′86 — Aviary birds — *Manuals*

Vriends, Matthew M.. Starting an aviary / Matthew M. Vriends. — Neptune : T.F.H. Publications ; Reigate : T.F.H. (Great Britain) [distributor], c1981. — 253p : ill(some col.) ; 21cm
Ill on lining papers. — Includes index
ISBN 0-87666-898-8 : £4.95 B81-29498

636.6′86 — Cage birds & aviary birds: Soft-billed birds

Vriends, Matthew M.. Encyclopedia of softbilled birds / Matthew M. Vriends. — Reigate : T.F.H., c1980. — 221p : ill(some col.) ; 21cm
Ill on lining papers. — Includes index
ISBN 0-87666-891-0 : Unpriced B81-31111

636.6′86′0222 — Cage birds & aviary birds. Care — *Illustrations*

Heinzel, Hermann. Cage birds : a colour guide for cage and aviary, over 100 birds illustrated and described — feeding — breeding — daily care / [... painted and written by Hermann Heinzel]. — [London] : Fontana, 1979. — 1folded sheet([12]p) : col.ill ; 25cm. — (Domino ; 9)
ISBN 0-00-685449-4 : £0.85 B81-20741

636.6′862 — Pets: Canaries. Care

Speicher, Klaus. Singing canaries / Klaus Speicher. — Neptune, N.J. ; Reigate : T.F.H., c1981. — 93p : ill(some col.) ; 21cm
Translation of: Kamersanger im Federkleid. — Ill on lining papers
ISBN 0-87666-875-9 : £1.25 B81-40755

636.6′862 — Pets: Canaries — *Manuals*

Vriends, Matthew M.. Handbook of canaries / Matthew M. Vriends. — Neptune : T.F.H. ; Reigate : T.F.H. (Great Britain) [distributor], c1980. — 351p : ill(some col.),1plan ; 22cm
Bibliography: p347-348. — Includes index
ISBN 0-87666-876-7 : £4.95 B81-00976

636.6′862 — Pets: Society finches. Breeding

Roberts, Mervin F.. Breeding society finches / by Mervin F. Roberts. — Hong Kong : T.F.H. Publications ; Reigate : Distributed by T.F.H. (Great Britain), c1979. — 93p : ill(some col.) ; 21cm
Ill on lining papers. — Bibliography: p92-93
ISBN 0-87666-991-7 : £1.00 B81-08178

636.6′862 — Pets: Waxbills. Care

Gos, Michael W.. Waxbills / Michael W. Gos. — Neptune, N.J. ; Reigate : T.F.H., c1981. — 92p : ill(some col.) ; 21cm
Ill on lining papers
ISBN 0-87666-839-2 : £1.25 B81-40761

636.6′862 — Pets: Zebra finches. Care

Roberts, Mervin F.. Zebra finches / Mervin F. Roberts. — Neptune, N.J. ; Reigate : T.F.H., c1981. — 93p : ill(some col.) ; 21cm
Ill on lining papers
ISBN 0-87666-882-1 : £1.25 B81-40760

636.6′864 — Pets: Budgerigars

Radtke, Georg A.. Budgerigars / Georg A. Radtke. — Hong Kong : T.F.H. Publications ; Reigate : Distributed by T.F.H. (Great Britain), 1979. — 93p : ill(some col.) ; 21cm
Translation of: Wellensittiche - mein Hobby. Verb. Aufl.. — Ill on lining papers
ISBN 0-87666-984-4 : £1.00 B81-08176

636.6′864 — Pets: Budgerigars. Care

Rogers, Cyril H.. Budgerigars / Cyril Rogers. — Edinburgh : Bartholomew, 1976. — 93p : col.ill,1col.map ; 19cm
Includes index
ISBN 0-7028-1051-7 (pbk) : £1.25 B81-09604

636.6′865 — Pets: African grey parrots. Care

Paradise, Paul R.. African grey parrots / Paul R. Paradise. — Neptune, N.J. ; Reigate : T.F.H., c1979. — 93p : ill(some col.) ; 21cm
Ill on inside covers
ISBN 0-87666-977-1 : £1.00 B81-09439

636.6′865 — Pets: African grey parrots. Training — *Manuals*

Teitler, Risa. Training African grey parrots / by Risa Teitler. — Hong Kong : T.F.H. Publications ; Reigate : Distributed by T.F.H. (Great Britain), c1979. — 93p : ill(some col.),ports(some col.) ; 21cm
Port on lining papers. — Bibliography: p93
ISBN 0-87666-994-1 : £1.00 B81-18454

636.6′865 — Pets: Conures

Silva, Tony. Conures / Tony Silva and Barbara Kotlar. — Neptune ; Reigate : T.F.H., c1980. — 91p : ill(some col.),col.ports ; 21cm
Ill on lining papers
ISBN 0-87666-893-7 : £1.00 B81-10685

636.6′865 — Pets: Lories. Care

Gos, Michael W.. Lories / Michael W. Gos. — Neptune, N.J. ; Reigate : T.F.H., c1981. — 93p : ill(some col.),1port ; 21cm
Ill on lining papers
ISBN 0-87666-832-5 : £1.25 B81-40757

636.6′865 — Pets: Parakeets. Care — *Manuals*

Vriends, Matthew M.. Dwarf parrots / Mathew M. Vriends and Petra Bleher. — Hong Kong : T.F.H. Publications ; Reigate : Distributed by T.F.H. (Great Britain), c1979. — 91p : ill(some col.) ; 21cm
Col Ill on lining papers
ISBN 0-87666-996-8 : £1.00 B81-18455

636.6′865 — Pets: Parrots. Care

De Grahl, Wolfgang. Parrots. — London : Ward Lock, Apr.1981. — [160]p
Translation of the German
ISBN 0-7063-6080-x : £7.95 : CIP entry
B81-07485

636.7 — LIVESTOCK. DOGS

636.7 — Livestock: Dogs

Swedrup, Ivan. The pocket encyclopaedia of dogs / Ivan Swedrup ; illustrations by Studio Frank, Erik O. Stövling. — Poole : Blandford, 1975 (1981 [printing]). — 248p : ill(some col.) ; 18cm. — (Blandford colour series)
Translated from the Swedish. — Bibliography: p243-244. — Includes index
ISBN 0-7137-1173-6 (pbk) : £2.95 B81-2280

636.7 — Livestock: Dogs — *For children*

Laurey, Harriet. The life of a dog. — London : Hutchinson, Sept.1981. — [32]p. — (Animal lives)
ISBN 0-09-145420-4 : £2.95 : CIP entry
B81-2255

636.7 — Pets: Dogs

. The dog : the breeds, the care and the training / with a foreword by Barbara Woodhouse. — London : Orbis Publishing, 1976 (1980 [printing]). — 239p : col.ill ; 30cm
Ill on lining papers. — Includes index
ISBN 0-85613-033-8 : £4.50 B81-0361

Palmer, Joan. A dog of your own / Joan Palmer ; consultant Bruce Sessions ; illustrated by John Francis and John Green. — London : Salamander, c1980. — 240p : ill(some col.) ; 32cm
Col. ill on lining papers. — Includes index
ISBN 0-86101-061-2 : £8.95 B81-0263

636.7 — Pets: Dogs — *For children*

My favourite book of dogs. — London : Dean, 1980, c1978. — [16]p : col.ill ; 29cm
ISBN 0-603-00218-8 : £0.75 B81-3848

636.7′00141 — Pets: Dogs. Communication with man — *Personal observations*

Rowdon, Maurice. The talking dogs / Maurice Rowdon. — London : Sphere, 1980, c1978. — 235p,[8]p of plates : ill ; 18cm
Originally published: London : Macmillan, 1978. — Bibliography: p230-231. — Includes index
ISBN 0-7221-7511-6 (pbk) : £1.50 B81-0340

636.7′00207′19 — Pets: Dogs — *Humour*

Graham, Richard, *1925-*. The good dog's guide to better living. — London : Jay Landesman, Oct.1981. — [64]p
ISBN 0-905150-37-6 : £3.50 : CIP entry
B81-3019

636.7′003′21 — Livestock: Dogs — *Encyclopaedias*

Encyclopedia of the dog / general editor Richard Marples ; American consultant John Mandeville. — London : Octopus, 1981. — 192p : col.ill ; 31cm
Includes index
ISBN 0-7064-1247-8 : £7.95 B81-3483

Palmer, Joan. An illustrated guide to dogs : a practical guide designed to help you choose the most suitable dog for you and your home / Joan Palmer. — London : Salamander, c1981. — 240p : ill(some col.) ; 23cm
Ill on lining papers. — Includes index
ISBN 0-86101-094-9 : £3.95 B81-3482

636.7′006′041 — Great Britain. Livestock: Dogs. Organisations: Kennel Club — *Serials*

Kennel Club. The Kennel Club year book. — 1980/81. — London (1 Clarges St., Picadilly, W1Y 8AB) : The Club, 1980. — 348p
Unpriced B81-0902

636.7′006′0411 — Scotland. Livestock: Dogs. Organisations: Scottish Kennel Club, *to 1880*

Leiper, Sally M.. A kennel club for Scotland. — Aberdeen : Aberdeen University Press, May 1981. — [72]p
ISBN 0-08-025752-6 (cased) : £5.25 : CIP entry
ISBN 0-08-025753-4 (pbk) : £3.75 B81-0604

636.7′009 — Livestock: Dogs, *to 1980*

Dog tales : an anthology / collected by Jean and Frank Jackson. — Manchester (5 James Leigh St., Manchester M60 15X) : Marples, [1981?]. — 207p : ill ; 21cm
ISBN 0-903034-09-3 (pbk) : £4.25 B81-1367

636.7'0092'4 — Pets: Dogs — *Personal observations*
Hollingworth, Patricia J.. Maggie, the dog of my life / Patricia J. Hollingworth ; illustrated by Norma Ingram. — Ilfracombe : Stockwell, 1981. — 48p : ill ; 18cm
ISBN 0-7223-1445-0 (pbk) : £1.98 B81-16771

636.7'00941 — Great Britain. Livestock: Dogs — *Serials*
Dog world annual. — 1981. — Ashford : Dog World, [1980]. — cxx,320p
£3.75 B81-09702

636.7'00941 — Great Britain. Livestock: Dogs, *to 1901*
Ritchie, Carson I. A.. The British dog : its history from earliest times / Carson I.A. Ritchie. — London : Hale, 1981. — 208p,[32]p of plates : ill ; 24cm
Bibliography: p196-197. — Includes index
ISBN 0-7091-8589-8 : £9.95 B81-12187

636.7'01'0924 — England. Pets: Dogs. Boarding establishments — *Personal observations*
Cooper, Diana, *1919-*. Up to scratch / Diana Cooper. — London : Joseph, 1981. — 223p ; 23cm
ISBN 0-7181-1973-8 : £6.95 B81-18704

636.7'07 — Pets: Puppies
Forbush, Gabrielle E.. Puppies / by Gabrielle E. Forbush. — Hong Kong : T.F.H. Publications ; Reigate : Distributed by T.F.H. (Great Britain), c1979. — 93p : ill(some col.) ; 21cm
ISBN 0-87666-674-8 : £1.00 B81-23369

636.7'082 — Livestock: Dogs. Breeding
Cavill, David. All about mating, whelping and weaning / David Cavill. — London : Pelham, 1981. — 142p : ill ; 26cm
Bibliography: p139. — Includes index
ISBN 0-7207-1323-4 : £6.95 : CIP rev.
B81-11914

Frankling, Eleanor. Practical dog breeding and genetics / Eleanor Frankling. — 7th ed., rev. / revised by Trevor Turner. — London : Popular Dogs, 1981. — 191p : ill ; 23cm
Previous ed.: revised by Joan Woodyatt 1978. — Bibliography: p186. — Includes index
ISBN 0-09-144010-6 : £5.95 B81-02597

636.7'0824 — Livestock: Dogs. Reproduction. Veterinary aspects
Joshua, Joan O.. Reproductive clinical problems in the dog. — Bristol : Wright, Feb.1982. — [176]p. — (A Veterinary practitioner handbook)
ISBN 0-85608-036-5 : £9.00 : CIP entry
B81-37598

636.7'083 — Livestock: Dogs. Care
Allcock, James. A dog of your own / James Allcock ; illustrated by Mike Morris. — Rev. ed. — London : Sheldon, 1981. — viii,104p : ill ; 22cm
Previous ed.: 1979. — Includes index
ISBN 0-85969-164-0 (pbk) : £1.95 B81-29744

636.7'083 — Livestock: Dogs. Training — *Manuals*
Loeb, Jo. Super-training your dog / Jo and Paul Loeb. — Englewood Cliffs ; London : Prentice-Hall, c1981. — 234p ; 24cm
Includes index
ISBN 0-13-876730-0 : £6.95 B81-28420

Watson, Miller. Basic dog training / by Miller Watson. — Hong Kong : T.F.H. Publications ; Reigate : Distributed by T.F.H. (Great Britain), c1979. — 93p : ill(some col.) ; 21cm
Ill on lining papers
ISBN 0-87666-673-x : £1.00 B81-23368

636.7'08'3 — Pets: Dogs. Care
Holmes, John. Looking after your dog. — London : Ward Lock, Sept.1981. — [128]p
ISBN 0-7063-6144-x : £4.95 : CIP entry
B81-23839

636.7'083 — Pets: Dogs. Training — *Manuals*
Stranger, Joyce. How to own a sensible dog / Joyce Stranger ; illustrated with photographs by Sean Hagerty. — London : Corgi, 1981. — 171p : ill ; 18cm
ISBN 0-552-11803-6 (pbk) : £1.25 B81-39661

White, Kay. How to have a well-mannered dog / Kay White and J.M. Evans ; pictures by Harold White. — Kingswood : Elliot Right Way, c1981. — 160p : ill ; 18cm. — (Paperfronts)
Includes index
ISBN 0-7160-0667-7 (pbk) : £0.75 B81-24321

636.7'0852 — Livestock: Dogs. Nutrition — *Conference proceedings*
International Symposium on the Nutrition of the Dog and Cat *(1978 : Hanover)*. Nutrition of the dog and cat : proceedings of the International Symposium on the Nutrition of the Dog and Cat arranged by the Institute of Animal Nutrition in conjunction with the 200-year Anniversary of the Veterinary School, Hanover, Federal Republic of Germany, 26 June 1978 / editor R.S. Anderson. — Oxford : Pergamon, 1980. — ix,204p : ill ; 26cm
Includes bibligraphies and index
ISBN 0-08-025526-4 : £12.00 : CIP rev.
Also classified at 636.8'0852 B80-18402

636.7'0886 — Guide dogs. Training — *Personal observations*
Godwin, Fay. Tess : the story of a guide dog / photographs by Fay Godwin ; text by Peter Purves. — London : Gollancz, 1981. — 128p : col.ill,col.maps ; 27cm
ISBN 0-575-02959-5 : £4.95 B81-17856

636.7'089 — Livestock: Dogs. Veterinary aspects
Coffey, David J.. A veterinary surgeon's guide to dogs / David Coffey. — Tadworth : World's Work, c1980. — 191p : ill ; 22cm
Includes index
ISBN 0-437-02500-4 : £4.95 B81-00977

636.7'0896 — Livestock: Dogs. Diseases
TV Vet. The TV Vet dog book : recognition and treatment of common dog ailments / by the TV Vet. — 3rd (revised) ed. — Ipswich : Farming Press, 1980, c1974. — 208p : ill ; 25cm
Previous ed.: 1978. — Includes index
ISBN 0-85236-105-x : Unpriced B81-14337

636.7'08961207547 — Livestock: Dogs. Heart. Electrocardiography
Tilley, Lawrence P.. Essentials of canine and feline electrocardiography / Lawrence P. Tilley ; with 1188 illustrations by Loretta Tilley. — St. Louis ; London : Mosby, 1979. — xi,337p : ill ; 27x29cm
Bibliography: p327-333. — Includes index
ISBN 0-8016-4963-3 : £21.75
Also classified at 636.8'08961207547
B81-15417

636.7'1 — Pets: Dogs. Breeds
Boorer, Wendy. Dogs. — London (Elsley Court, 20 Great Titchfield St., W1P 7AD) : Kingfisher, Oct.1981. — [128]p. — (Kingfisher guides)
ISBN 0-86272-005-2 : £2.50 : CIP entry
B81-27446

636.7'2 — Bichon frises. Care
Weil, Martin. Bichon frise / Martin Weil. — Neptune, N.J. ; Reigate : T.F.H., c1981. — 125p : ill(some col.) ; 21cm
Ill on lining papers
ISBN 0-87666-739-6 : £1.25 B81-40763

636.7'2 — Great Britain. Tibetan terriers. Organisations: Tibetan Terrier Association — *Serials*
[Year book *(Tibetan Terrier Association)***]**. Year book / the Tibetan Terrier Association. — No.8. — [Welwyn] ([c/o Mr and Mrs M. Cain, Lynbrook Kennels, Gwynfa Close, Welwyn, Hertfordshire AL6 OPR]) : The Association, 1981. — 64p
£1.25 B81-24096

636.7'3 — Alsatian dogs. Care — *Encyclopaedias*
Pickup, Madeleine. The German shepherd dog (Alsatian) owner's encyclopaedia / Madeleine Pickup. — 2nd ed. — London : Pelham, 1981. — 107p,[8]p of plates : ill ; 23cm
Previous ed.: published as The Alsatian owner's encyclopaedia. 1964
ISBN 0-7207-1300-5 : £5.50 B81-08488

636.7'3 — Alsatian dogs. Relationships with man — *Case studies*
Richardson, Anthony, *b.1899*. One man and his dog / by Anthony Richardson. — London : Harrap, 1960 (1980 [printing]). — 251p,15p of plates : ill,ports ; 23cm
ISBN 0-245-52292-1 : £6.95
Also classified at 304.2 B81-09777

636.7'3 — Dobermanns
Curnow, Fred. The Dobermann / Fred Curnow and Jean Faulks. — 5th ed., rev. — London : Popular Dogs, 1980. — 209p,[16] of plates : ill ; 23cm. — (Popular Dogs' breed series)
Previous ed.: 1979. — Bibliography: p202. - Includes index
ISBN 0-09-143140-9 : £7.50 B81-00978

636.7'3 — Great Britain. Sheepdogs
Halsall, Eric. Sheepdogs : my faithful friends / Eric Halsall ; foreword by Phil Drabble. — Cambridge : Stevens, 1980. — 224p : ill,ports ; 25cm
Bibliography: p222. — Includes index
ISBN 0-85059-431-6 : £8.95 : CIP rev.
B80-10671

636.7'3 — Old English sheepdogs
Davis, Ann. The old English sheepdog / Ann Davis. — Fifth ed., rev. — London : Popular Dogs, 1981. — 178p : ill ; 23cm. — (Popular Dogs' breed series)
Previous ed.: 1978. — Bibliography: p171. — Includes index
ISBN 0-09-144340-7 : £7.50 B81-15574

Woods, Sylvia. Old English sheepdogs / Sylvia Woods & Ray Owen. — London : Faber, 1981. — 240p,[12]p of plates : ill,ports ; 21cm
Includes index
ISBN 0-571-11620-5 : £7.95 B81-08739

636.7'3 — Pets: Alsatian dogs: Sabre — *Personal observations*
Sparks, H. J.. Sabre : the story of a dog / H.J. Sparks. — Bognor Regis : New Horizon, c1978. — 86p : ill ; 22cm
ISBN 0-86116-048-7 : £3.50 B81-21708

636.7'3 — Pets: Rottweilers. Care
Klem, Joan R.. Rottweilers / Joan R. Klem and Susan C. Rademacher. — Neptune, N.J. ; Reigate : T.F.H., c1981. — 125p : ill(some col.) ; 21cm
Ill on lining papers
ISBN 0-87666-726-4 : £1.25 B81-40758

636.7'52 — Golden retrievers
Tudor, Joan. The golden retriever / Joan Tudor. — 8th ed. — London : Popular Dogs, 1981. — 251p,[16]p of plates : ill,ports ; 23cm. — (Popular dogs' breed series)
Previous ed.: 1980. — Bibliography: p241. — Includes index
ISBN 0-09-144980-4 : £7.50 : CIP rev.
B81-12325

636.7'52 — Gun dogs for rough shooting. Training — *Manuals*
Moxon, P. R. A.. Training the roughshooter's dog / P.R.A. Moxon. — London : Popular Dogs, 1977 (1981 [printing]). — 157p,[16]p of plates : ill ; 23cm
Includes index
ISBN 0-09-144000-9 : £6.95 B81-00979

636.7'52 — Gun dogs. Training — *Manuals*
Moxon, P. R. A.. Gundogs : training and field trials / P.R.A. Moxon. — 13th ed. rev. — London : Popular Dogs, 1981. — 256p,[24]p of plates : ill,1port ; 23cm
Previous rev. ed.: 1978. — Includes index
ISBN 0-09-145440-9 : £7.50 : CIP rev.
B81-04246

636.7'52 — Irish setters
Roberts, Janice. The Irish setter / Janice Roberts. — 2nd ed. rev.. — London : Popular Dogs, 1981. — 196p,[16]p of plates : ill,1port ; 23cm. — (Popular Dogs' breed series)
Previous ed.: 1978. — Bibliography: p187-188. — Includes index
ISBN 0-09-145510-3 : £7.50 : CIP rev.
B81-17520

636.7'52 — Labradors

Howe, Lorna Katherine Curzon, *Countess*. The labrador retriever / Lorna, Countess Howe and Geoffrey Waring. — 7th ed. — London : Popular Dogs, 1981. — 219p,[16]p of plates : ill ; 23cm. — (Popular dogs breed series)
Previous ed.: 1978. — Includes index
ISBN 0-09-144730-5 : £7.50 : CIP rev. B81-03675

McCarty, Diane. Labrador retrievers / by Diane McCarty. — Neptune, N.J. ; Reigate : T.F.H., c1979. — 125p : ill(some col.) ; 21cm
Ill on lining papers
ISBN 0-87666-689-6 : £1.25 B81-40765

636.7'52 — Labradors: Puppies. Development — *For children*

Jessel, Camilla. The puppy book / Camilla Jessel. — London : Methuen, 1980. — [32]p : col.ill ; 26cm
ISBN 0-416-87430-4 : £2.95 : CIP rev. B79-23337

636.7'52 — Wales. Labradors. Organisations: Labrador Retriever Club of Wales — *Serials*

[Year book *(Labrador Retriever Club of Wales)*]. Year book / Labrador Retriever Club of Wales. — 1980-1981-. — Llantrisant (c/o M. Williams, 6 Dan-y-Felin, Llantrisant, Pontyclun, Mid Glam. CF7 8EH) : The Club, 1981-. — v. : ill,ports ; 21cm
Annual. — Cover-title: Year book of the Labrador Retriever Club of Wales
ISSN 0260-5627 = Year book — Labrador Retriever Club of Wales : Unpriced B81-34050

636.7'53 — Bloodhounds

Lowe, Brian. Hunting the clean boot : the working bloodhound / Brian Lowe ; foreword by Phil Drabble. — Poole : Blandford Press, 1981. — x,236p : ill,maps,1facsim,ports ; 23cm. — (Adventure sports series)
Ill on lining papers. — Includes index
ISBN 0-7137-0950-2 : £8.95 : CIP rev. B81-00980

636.7'53 — Foxhounds

Moore, Daphne. Foxhounds / Daphne Moore. — London : Batsford, 1981. — 173p,[32]p of plates : ill ; 24cm
Includes index
ISBN 0-7134-2389-7 : £12.50 B81-29482

636.7'53 — Foxhounds - *Early works*

Beckford, Peter. Thoughts on hunting. — London : J.A. Allen, June 1981. — [244]p
ISBN 0-85131-367-1 : £6.75 : CIP entry B81-12797

636.7'53 — Great Britain. Greyhounds — *Encyclopaedias*

Regan, Ivy M.. The greyhound owner's encyclopaedia / Ivy M. Regan. — 2nd ed. — London : Pelham, 1981. — 139p : ill,ports ; 23cm
Previous ed.: 1975
ISBN 0-7207-1348-x : £5.95 B81-21163

636.7'53 — Ireland *(Republic)*. Greyhounds — *Lists — Serials*

The **Irish** greyhound stud book / the Irish Coursing Club. — Vol.58 (Jan.-Dec.79). — Clonmel ([Davis Rd., Clonmel, Co. Tipperary, Irish Republic]) : Sporting Press, 1979. — lxlvi,874p
Unpriced B81-14532

636.7'55 — Edinburgh. Skye terriers: Greyfriars Bobby

Macgregor, Forbes. The story of Greyfriars Bobby / by Forbes Macgregor. — Edinburgh (34 George IV Bridge, Edinburgh) : Ampersand, c1980. — 51p : ill ; 22cm
£1.00 (pbk) B81-04649

636.7'55 — Edinburgh. Skye terriers: Greyfriars Bobby — *Stories, anecdotes*

Macgregor, Forbes. Authenticated facts relating to Greyfriars Bobby / collected and arranged by Forbes Macgregor. — [Edinburgh] : [F. Macgregor], [1980?]. — [18]leaves ; 22cm
Cover title
£0.75 (pbk) B81-32351

636.7'55 — Jack Russell terriers

Tottenham, Katherine. The Jack Russell terrier. — Newton Abbot : David & Charles, Jan.1982. — [160]p
ISBN 0-7153-8156-3 : £8.50 : CIP entry B81-33821

636.7'55 — Miniature schnauzers. Care

Pisano, Berverly. Miniature schnauzers / by Beverly Pisano and Gloria Lewis. — Neptune, N.J. ; Reigate : T.F.H., c1979. — 125p : ill (some col.) ; 21cm
Ill on lining papers
ISBN 0-87666-690-x : £1.25 B81-40764

636.7'55 — Staffordshire bull terriers

Morley, W. M.. The Staffordshire bull terrier. — Newton Abbot : David & Charles, Jan.1982. — [176]p
ISBN 0-7153-8232-2 : £6.95 : CIP entry B81-33817

636.7'55 — West Highland white terriers

Dennis, D. Mary. The West Highland white terrier. — 6th ed. — London : Hutchinson, July 1981. — [192]p
Previous ed.: 1978
ISBN 0-09-145450-6 : £7.50 : CIP entry B81-13497

636.7'6 — Pomeranian dogs

Pomeranians / edited by Beverly Pisano. — Neptune ; Reigate : T.F.H., c1980. — 125p : ill (some col.) ; 21cm
Ill on lining papers
ISBN 0-87666-707-8 : £1.00 B81-10686

636.7'6 — Shih tzus

Dadds, Audrey. The shih tzu / Audrey Dadds ; foreword by C.R. Duke. — 3rd ed., rev.. — London : Popular Dogs, 1981. — 210p,[16]p of plates : ill,ports ; 23cm. — (Popular Dogs' breed series)
Previous ed.: 1978. — Bibliography: p203-204. — Includes index
ISBN 0-09-143130-1 : £7.50 B81-03190

636.7'6 — Yorkshire terriers

Huxham, Mona. All about the Yorkshire Terrier / Mona Huxham. — 2nd ed. — London : Pelham, 1981. — 240p : ill,ports ; 26cm
Includes index
ISBN 0-7207-1318-8 : £6.95 : CIP rev. B81-17504

636.7'7 — Livestock: Dogs. Breeds — *Illustrations*

Nockels, David. Dogs : a colour guide to 94 dog breeds, working dogs — guards — hounds — companions — origins — characters — sizes / [painted by David Nockels ; text by Wendy Boorer]. — [London] : Fontana, 1979. — 1folded sheet([12]p) : col.ill ; 25cm. — (Domino ; 6)
ISBN 0-00-685446-x : £0.85 B81-20749

636.7'7 — Pets: Puppies — *Illustrations — For children*

Kittens and puppies. — Maidenhead : Purnell, 1979 (1981 [printing]). — [28]p : chiefly col.ill ; 27cm. — (All in colour picture books)
ISBN 0-361-04547-6 : £1.25
Primary classification 636.8'7 B81-23422

636.8 — PETS. CATS

636.8 — Pets: Cats

Bürger, Manfred. The big book of cats / photographs: Erich Tylinek ; text: Manfred Burger ; line drawings by Michael Lissman ; [translated by Alisa Jaffa]. — Newton Abbot : David & Charles, 1980, c1979. — 250,[5]p : ill (some col.) ; 28cm
Translation of: Das grosse Katzenbuch. — Bibliography: p[3]. — Includes index
ISBN 0-7153-7836-8 : £8.50 B81-02630

Johnson, Norman H.. The complete kitten and cat book / Norman H. Johnson with Saul Galin. — Rev. ed. — London : Hale, 1981, c1980. — 288p,[16]p of plates : ill ; 25cm
Previous ed.: New York : Harper and Row, 1979. — Includes index
ISBN 0-7091-8357-7 : £8.25 B81-17131

Loxton, Howard. Cats / [author Howard Loxton ; [designed and edited by Keith Lye] ; [illustrated by David Nockels ... et al.]. — London : Kingfisher, 1981. — 125p : ill(some col.) ; 20cm. — (Kingfisher guides)
Includes index
ISBN 0-7063-6101-6 : £2.50 : CIP rev. B81-0316

Metcalf, Christine. Cats / Christine Metcalf ; illustrated by Peter Warner. — London : Hamlyn, 1969 (1980 printing). — 159p : ill (some col.) ; 19cm
Bibliography: p158. - Includes index
ISBN 0-600-35378-8 : £2.50 B81-1301

Pond, Grace. [All about cats]. The cat : the breeds, the care and the training / Grace Pond ; with a foreword by Beverley Nichols. — London : Orbis Publishing, 1974 (1980 [printing]). — 144p : col.ill ; 30cm
Ill on lining papers. — Includes index
ISBN 0-85613-032-x : £4.50 B81-0386

Pond, Grace. The observer's book of cats : describing all recognized varieties / Grace Pond. — 3rd cd. completly rev. / photographs by Anne Cumbers. — London : Warne, 1979. — 181p,16p of plates : ill(some col.) ; 15cm. — (The Observer's pocket series)
Previous ed.: i.e. 2nd rev. ed. 1975. — Includes index
ISBN 0-7232-1594-4 : £1.95 B81-3178

636.8 — Pets: Cats. Behaviour — *Stories, anecdote*

Millard, Adele. Cats : in fact and legend / Adele Millard ; illustrations by Gavin Rowe. — London : Piccolo, 1981, c1976. — 109p : ill ; 18cm
Originally published: New York : Sterling ; London : Ward Lock, 1976
ISBN 0-330-25737-4 (pbk) : £0.90 B81-0353

636.8 — Pets: Cats — *For children*

My favourite book of cats. — London : Dean, 1980, c1978. — [16]p : col.ill ; 29cm
ISBN 0-603-00217-x : £0.75 B81-3848

636.8'005 — Pets: Cats — *Serials*

[Cats *(Idle : 1981)*]. Cats. — No.1 (Apr.1981)-. — [Idle, W. Yorkshire] : [Watmoughs], 1981-. — v. : maps,port ; 30cm
Monthly
ISSN 0260-3837 = Cats (Idle. 1981) : £23.00 per year B81-3405

636.8'009173'2 — Urban regions. Pets: Cats — *Illustrations*

Webb, John, *1935-*. Town cats / John Webb. — London : Joseph, 1980. — 128p : chiefly ill ; 26cm
ISBN 0-7181-1968-1 : £4.95 B81-0191

636.8'0092'4 — Cornwall. Pets: Cats — *Personal observations*

Tangye, Derek. A cat affair / Derek Tangye. — Large print ed. — Bath : Chivers, 1981, c1974. — 243p ; 23cm. — (New portway)
Originally published: London : Joseph, 1974
ISBN 0-85119-103-7 B81-1296

Tangye, Derek. Lama / Derek Tangye. — Large print ed. — Bath : Chivers, 1980, c1966. — 197p ; 23cm
Originally published: London : Joseph, 1966
ISBN 0-85997-478-2 : £5.50 : CIP rev. B80-1780

636.8'0097 — Pets: Cats. North American breeds — *Encyclopaedias*

Wilson, Meredith. Encyclopedia of American cat breeds / by Meredith Wilson. — Neptune, N.J ; Reigate : T.F.H., c1978. — 352p : ill(some col.) ; 22cm
Includes index
ISBN 0-87666-855-4 : £6.95 B81-0594

636.8'083 — Pets: Cats. Care

Cutts, Paddy. Pedigree cats & kittens : how to choose and care for them / Paddy Cutts and Christina Payne. — London : Batsford, 1981. — 64p : ill(some col.) ; 20cm. — (A Batsford paperback)
Includes index
ISBN 0-7134-3915-7 (pbk) : £1.95 B81-3316

636.8′083 — Pets: Cats. Care *continuation*
Pond, Grace. Cats / Grace Pond & Angela Sayer. — Edinburgh : Bartholomew, 1976. — 94p : col.ill,1col.map ; 19cm
Includes index
ISBN 0-7028-1061-4 (pbk) : £1.25 B81-09603

636.8′08′3 — Pets: Cats. Care
Tottenham, Katharine. Looking after your cat. — London : Ward Lock, Sept.1981. — [128]p
ISBN 0-7063-6143-1 : £4.95 : CIP entry
B81-16939

636.8′083 — Pets: Cats. Care — *For children*
Laurey, Harriet. The life of a cat. — London : Hutchinson, June 1981. — [32]p. — (Animal lives)
ISBN 0-09-145010-1 : £2.95 : CIP entry
B81-12328

636.8′084 — Pets: Cats. Feeding
Graham, Richard, *1925-*. Cuisine for cats / by Richard Graham ; illustrations by Don Grant. — London : Jay Landesman, c1980. — 63p : ill ; 19cm
ISBN 0-905150-18-x : £3.50 : CIP rev.
B80-22159

636.8′0852 — Pets: Cats. Nutrition — *Conference proceedings*
International Symposium on the Nutrition of the Dog and Cat *(1978 : Hanover)*. Nutrition of the dog and cat : proceedings of the International Symposium on the Nutrition of the Dog and Cat arranged by the Institute of Animal Nutrition in conjunction with the 200-year Anniversary of the Veterinary School, Hanover, Federal Republic of Germany, 26 June 1978 / editor R.S. Anderson. — Oxford : Pergamon, 1980. — ix,204p : ill ; 26cm
Includes bibliographies and index
ISBN 0-08-025526-4 : £12.00 : CIP rev.
Primary classification 636.7′0852 B80-18402

636.8′0896 — Pets: Cats. Diseases
TV Vet. [Cats, their health and care]. Illustrated textbook of cat diseases : owner′s guide to cat ailments and conditions / by the TV Vet. — Neptune : T.F.H. Publications ; Reigate : T.F.H. (Great Britain) [distributor], [c1980]. — 188p : ill(some col.) ; 21cm
Originally published: Ipswich : Farming Press, 1977. — Ill on lining papers. — Includes index
ISBN 0-87666-865-1 : £4.50 B81-32929

West, Geoffrey P.. All about your cat′s health / Geoffrey West. — London : Pelham, 1980. — 160p : ill ; 26cm
Includes index
ISBN 0-7207-1277-7 : £6.95 B81-08092

636.8′08961207547 — Pets: Cats. Heart. Electrocardiography
Tilley, Lawrence P.. Essentials of canine and feline electrocardiography / Lawrence P. Tilley ; with 1188 illustrations by Loretta Tilley. — St. Louis ; London : Mosby, 1979. — xi,337p : ill ; 27x29cm
Bibliography: p327-333. — Includes index
ISBN 0-8016-4963-3 : £21.75
Primary classification 636.7′08961207547
B81-15417

636.8′089699419 — Pets: Cats. Blood. Leukaemia — *Conference proceedings*
International Feline Leukemia Virus Meeting *(3rd : 1980 : St. Thomas, Virgin Islands)*. Feline leukemia virus : proceedings of the Third International Feline Leukemia Virus Meeting, St. Thomas, United States Virgin Island, May 5-9, 1980 / edited : William D. Hardy, Jr., Myron Essex, Alexander J. McClelland. — New York ; Oxford : Elsevier/North Holland, c1980. — xvii,552p : ill ; 25cm. — (Developments in cancer research ; v.4)
Includes index
ISBN 0-444-00569-2 : £35.18 B81-16600

636.8′2 — Shorthaired cats
Lauder, Phyllis. The British, European and American shorthair cat / Phyllis Lauder. — London : Batsford, 1981. — 160p,[24]p of plates : ill ; 23cm
Includes index
ISBN 0-7134-3885-1 : £7.95 B81-37935

636.8′7 — Pets: Cats. Breeds — *Illustrations*
Ovenden, Denys. Cats : a colour guide to the pedigree cat breeds of the world / [painted by Denys Ovenden ; text by Howard Loxton]. — [London] : Fontana, 1979. — 1folded sheet ([12]p) : col.ill ; 25cm. — (Domino ; 7)
ISBN 0-00-685447-8 : £0.85 B81-20738

636.8′7 — Pets: Cats — *Illustrations*
Baldauski, Karen. The cat coloring book / Karen Baldauski ; introduction and captions by Laura S. Hair. — New York : Dover Publications ; London : Constable, c1980. — [48]p : ill(some col.) ; 28cm. — (Dover pictorial archive series)
Ill on inside covers
ISBN 0-486-24011-8 (pbk) : £1.50 B81-09856

636.8′7 — Pets: Kittens — *Illustrations* — *For children*
Kittens and puppies. — Maidenhead : Purnell, 1979 (1981 [printing]). — [28]p : chiefly col.ill ; 27cm. — (All in colour picture books)
ISBN 0-361-04547-6 : £1.25
Also classified at 636.7′7 B81-23422

636.9 — LIVESTOCK. RABBITS, GUINEA PIGS, ETC

636′.9322 — Great Britain. Livestock: Rabbits. Organisations: British Rabbit Council — *Serials*
British Rabbit Council[Year book *(British Rabbit Council)***]Year** book / British Rabbit Council. — 1980. — Newark (Purefoy House, 7 Kirkgate, Newark, Notts.) : The Council, [1980]. — 84p
Free to members B81-08748

636′.9322 — Great Britain. Livestock: Rabbits — *Serials*
[Rabbits *(Idle)***]**. Rabbits : [incorporating Fur & feather] : [official journal of the British Rabbit Council]. — No.1 (Thursday 12 Mar.1981)-. — [Idle, W. Yorkshire] : Watmoughs, 1981-. — v. : ill,ports ; 30cm
Fortnightly. — Continues: Fur and feather
ISSN 0260-6771 = Rabbits (Idle) : £17.00 per year B81-32188

636′.9322 — Pets: Rabbits. Care — *For children*
Laurey, Harriet. The life of a rabbit. — London : Hutchinson, June 1981. — [32]p. — (Animal lives)
ISBN 0-09-145020-9 : £2.95 : CIP entry
B81-12323

636.9′3233 — Laboratory animals: Rats. Electrocardiography - *Conference proceedings*
The **rat** electrocardiogram in acute and chronic pharmacology and toxicology. — Oxford : Pergamon, July 1981. — [208]p
Conference papers
ISBN 0-08-026867-6 : £23.00 : CIP entry
B81-14430

636′.93233 — Pets: Gerbils & hamsters. Care
Smith, K. W.. Hamsters & gerbils / K.W. Smith. — Edinburgh : Bartholomew, 1976. — 64p : col.ill,1form ; 19cm
Includes index
ISBN 0-7028-1082-7 (pbk) : £1.25 B81-09602

636′.93233 — Pets: Gerbils. Care
Paradise, Paul R.. Gerbils / Paul R. Paradise. — Neptune ; Reigate : T.F.H., c1980. — 93p : ill (some col.) ; 21cm
Ill on lining papers
ISBN 0-87666-757-4 : £1.00 B81-19837

636′.93234 — Pets: Guinea pigs. Care — *Manuals*
Hearne, Tina. Care for your guinea pig / text by Tina Hearne ; illustrations by Terry Riley and Mike Woodhatch/David Lewis Artists. — Glasgow : Collins, 1981. — 32p : col.ill ; 23cm
Includes index
ISBN 0-00-107206-4 (pbk) : £1.25 B81-39453

636′.974442 — Pets: Foxes. Cubs — *Correspondence, diaries, etc*
Wright, Barbara, *1928-*. Lucky : the story of a fox cub / Barbara Wright. — London : Barker, c1980. — 92p : ill ; 19x22cm
ISBN 0-213-16779-4 : £4.50 B81-01736

636′.974442 — Zoos. Canidae. Care — *Conference proceedings*
Association of British Wild Animal Keepers. *Symposium (5th : 1980 : London)*. Management of canids and mustelids : proceedings of Symposium 5 of the Association of British Wild Animal Keepers / [edited by Jon Barzdo]. — Dunstable (c/o G. Lucas, 5 Chequers Cottages, Whipsnade, Dunstable, Beds. LU6 2LJ) : The Association, c1981. — 59p : ill ; 21cm
Includes index
Unpriced (pbk)
Also classified at 636′.974447 B81-38952

636′.974447 — Livestock: Ferrets. Care — *Manuals*
Wellstead, Graham. The ferret and ferreting guide / Graham Wellstead. — Newton Abbot : David & Charles, 1981. — 157p : ill,1port ; 23cm
Bibliography: p151-152. — Includes index
ISBN 0-7153-8013-3 : £6.50 : CIP rev.
Also classified at 799.2′3 B81-17493

636′.974447 — Pets: Ferrets. Breeding & care
Winsted, Wendy. Ferrets / Wendy Winsted. — Neptune, N.J. ; Reigate : T.F.H., c1981. — 93p : ill(some col.) ; 21cm
Ill on lining papers
ISBN 0-87666-930-5 : £1.25 B81-40759

636′.974447 — Zoos. Mustelidae. Care — *Conference proceedings*
Association of British Wild Animal Keepers. *Symposium (5th : 1980 : London)*. Management of canids and mustelids : proceedings of Symposium 5 of the Association of British Wild Animal Keepers / [edited by Jon Barzdo]. — Dunstable (c/o G. Lucas, 5 Chequers Cottages, Whipsnade, Dunstable, Beds. LU6 2LJ) : The Association, c1981. — 59p : ill ; 21cm
Includes index
Unpriced (pbk)
Primary classification 636′.974442 B81-38952

636.9′772 — Bonsai. Cultivation — *Amateurs′ manuals*
Adams, Peter D.. The art of Bonsai. — London : Ward Lock, Sept.1981. — [176]p
ISBN 0-7063-5860-0 : £6.95 : CIP entry
B81-23836

637 — DAIRY PRODUCTS

637 — Dairy products — *For children*
Langley, Andrew. Dairy produce / Andrew Langley. — Hove : Wayland, 1981. — 71p : ill,1port ; 20x22cm. — (World resources)
Bibliography: p71. - Includes index
ISBN 0-85340-805-x : £3.75 B81-12979

637′.01′576 — Dairy products. Manufacture. Microbiological aspects
Dairy microbiology. — Barking : Applied Science Publishers, July 1981
Vol.1: The microbiology of milk. — [272]p
ISBN 0-85334-948-7 : £23.00 : CIP entry
B81-13733

637′.01′576 — Dairy products. Microbiological aspects
Dairy microbiology. — London : Applied Science, Aug.1981
Vol.2: The microbiology of milk products. — [336]p
ISBN 0-85334-961-4 : £24.00 : CIP entry
B81-17511

637′.1 — Milk
The **Miracle** of your morning milk. — London (National Dairy Centre, John Princes St., W1M 0AP) : National Dairy Council, 1980. — 13p : col.ill ; 21cm
Unpriced (unbound) B81-21070

637′.124 — Livestock: Cattle: Cows. Machine milking
Machine milking / editors C.C. Thiel and F.H. Dodd. — Repr. with minor revision. — Reading ([Shinfield, Reading, RG9 2AT]) : National Institute for Research in Dairying, 1979. — 391p : ill ; 21cm. — (Technical bulletin / National Institute for Research in Dairying ; 1)
Previous ed.: 1977. — Includes index
ISBN 0-7084-0116-3 (pbk) : £7.00 B81-06331

637′.125 — Milking machines

Lowe, F. R.. Milking machines : a comprehensive guide for farmers, herdsmen and students / by F.R. Lowe. — Oxford : Pergamon, 1981. — ix,181p : ill ; 26cm. — (Pergamon international library)
Includes index
ISBN 0-08-024381-9 (cased) : Unpriced B81-38270

637′.146 — Yoghurt

Facts about yogurt / from the National Dairy Council. — London (John Princes St., W1M OAP) : The Council, [1981?]. — 15p : col.ill ; 21cm
ISBN 0-902748-28-9 (unbound) : Unpriced B81-25981

637′.23 — Butter. Making — *Manuals*

Clarke, V.. Butter & cheese making / V. Clarke & M. Sheppard ; edited and with a foreword by K.D. Maddever ; line drawings by Peter Haillay. — Rev. ed. — Sherborne (Sherborne, Dorset) : Alphabooks, 1980. — 96p : ill ; 21x22cm
Previous ed.: published as Cheese and butter. London : Hart-Davis, 1956
ISBN 0-906670-00-4 (cased) : £5.95
ISBN 0-906670-14-4 (pbk) : £2.95
Also classified at 637′.23 B81-03569

637′.23 — Cheeses. Making — *Manuals*

Clarke, V.. Butter & cheese making / V. Clarke & M. Sheppard ; edited and with a foreword by K.D. Maddever ; line drawings by Peter Haillay. — Rev. ed. — Sherborne (Sherborne, Dorset) : Alphabooks, 1980. — 96p : ill ; 21x22cm
Previous ed.: published as Cheese and butter. London : Hart-Davis, 1956
ISBN 0-906670-00-4 (cased) : £5.95
ISBN 0-906670-14-4 (pbk) : £2.95
Primary classification 637′.23 B81-03569

637′.3 — Cheeses. Manufacture

Davis, J. G.. Cheese / by J.G. Davis. — Edinburgh : Churchill Livingstone
Vol.4: Annotated bibliography with subject index / compiled with the assistance of Doris Knight. — 1975. — v,306p ; 26cm
ISBN 0-443-01114-1 : £12.00 B81-19499

Scott, R.. Cheesemaking practice / R. Scott. — London : Applied Science, c1981. — xix,475p : ill,1plan ; 23cm
Bibliography: p462-466. — Includes index
ISBN 0-85334-927-4 : £24.50 B81-28247

637′.352 — Soft cheeses. Making — *Manuals*

Pinder, Polly. Soft cheeses / [text and drawings by Polly Pinder]. — London : Search, 1978. — 32p : ill(some col.) ; 17cm. — (Home-made ; 8)
ISBN 0-85532-423-6 (pbk) : £0.70 B81-04708

638 — INSECT CULTURE

638′.1 — Bee-keeping — *Manuals*

Meyer, Owen. The beekeeper′s handbook. — Wellingborough : Thorsons, Sept.1981. — [256]p
ISBN 0-7225-0669-4 (cased) : £4.95 : CIP entry B81-21513

638′.1′0913 — Tropical regions. Bee-keeping — *Conference proceedings*

Conference on Apiculture in Tropical Climates *(1st : 1976 : London)*. Apiculture in tropical climates. — London : International Bee Research Association, Nov.1981. — [208]p
Originally published: 1976
ISBN 0-86098-100-2 (pbk) : £17.50 : CIP entry B81-32004

638′.145 — Queen honey-bees. Rearing — *Manuals*

Snelgrove, L. E.. Queen rearing / by L.E. Snelgrove. — 4th ed. — Weston-super-Mare (Pleasant View, Bleadon Hill, Weston-super-Mare, Avon BS24 9JT) : Snelgrove & Smith, 1981. — 344p : ill,1port ; 22cm
Bibliography: p329-337. — Includes index
ISBN 0-9507426-1-9 (pbk) : Unpriced B81-32854

638′.146 — Bees. Swarming. Prevention & control. Techniques

Snelgrove, L. E.. Swarming : its control and prevention / by L.E. Snelgrove. — 3rd ed. — Weston-super-Mare (Pleasant View, Bleadon Hill, Weston-super-Mare, Avon BS24 9JT) : Snelgrove & Smith, 1981. — 110p : ill ; 22cm
Includes index
ISBN 0-9507425-0-3 (pbk) : £3.50 B81-25149

638′.15 — Honey-bees. Diseases

Bailey, L.. Honey bee pathology. — London : Academic Press, Dec.1981. — [150]p
ISBN 0-12-073480-x : CIP entry B81-31332

638′.5725 — Praying mantises. Rearing — *Amateurs′ manuals*

Heath, George L.. Rearing and studying the praying mantids / by George L. Heath. — Weybridge (c/o A.E.S. Registrar, 8 Heather Close, New Haw, Weybridge, Surrey KT15 3PF) : Amateur Entomologists Society, 1980. — 15p : ill ; 22cm. — (AES leaflet ; no.36)
Cover title
Unpriced (pbk) B81-13153

638′.5726 — Laboratory animals: Locusts

Barrass, Robert. The locust : a laboratory guide / Robert Barrass. — 3rd ed. — London : Heinemann Educational, 1980. — vi,74p : ill,2maps ; 22cm
Previous ed.: Winchester : Shurlock, 1974. — Bibliography: p70-71. - Includes index
ISBN 0-435-60100-8 (pbk) : £2.50 : CIP rev. B80-20664

638′.5769 — Pets: Ladybirds. Care — *For children*

Goldsmith, John, *1947-*. It′s easy to have a ladybird to stay / John Goldsmith ; illustrations by Judith Allan ; advisory editor Caroline O′Hagan. — London : Chatto & Windus, 1981. — [24]p : col.ill ; 17cm
ISBN 0-7011-2577-2 : £1.95 B81-30673

638′.5796 — Pets: Ants. Care — *For children*

Goldsmith, John, *1947-*. It′s easy to have ants to stay / by John Goldsmith ; illustrations by Judith Allan ; advisory editor Caroline O′Hagan. — London : Chatto and Windus, 1981. — [24]p : col.ill ; 17cm
ISBN 0-7011-2579-9 : £1.95 B81-30669

639.1 — HUNTING AND TRAPPING

639′.11′0924 — Mozambique. Big game. Commercial hunting — *Personal observations*

Manners, Harry. Kambaku! / Harry Manners. — London : Muller, 1981, c1980. — 209p,[12]p of plates : ill,2col.maps ; 22cm
Originally published: Johannesburg : Ernest Stanton, 1980. — Maps on lining papers
ISBN 0-584-97072-2 : £5.95 B81-34942

639.2 — FISHING, WHALING, SEALING

639′.2 — Fisheries. Management

Fisheries management / edited by Robert T. Lackey and Larry A. Nielsen. — Oxford : Blackwell Scientific, 1980. — x,422p : ill,maps,1port ; 25cm
Includes bibliographies and index
ISBN 0-632-00615-3 : £25.00 : CIP rev. B80-13886

639′.2 — Fishery management

Everhart, W. Harry. Principles of fishery science. — 2nd ed. / W. Harry Everhart, William D. Youngs. — Ithaca ; London : Comstock, 1981. — 349p : ill ; 22cm
Previous ed.: 1975. — Includes bibliographies and index
ISBN 0-8014-1334-6 : £10.00 B81-10957

639′.2′072 — Fisheries. Management. Operations research — *Conference proceedings*

NATO Symposium on Allied Operations Research in Fishing *(1979 : Marine Technology Centre, Trondheim)*. Allied operations research in fishing / [proceedings of a NATO Symposium on Allied Operations Research in Fishing, held August 14-17, 1979, at The Marine Technology Centre, Trondheim, Norway] ; edited by K. Brian Haley. — New York ; London : Published in cooperation with NATO Scientific Affairs Division by Plenum, c1981. — xvi,490p : ill,maps ; 26cm. — (NATO conference series. II, Systems science ; v.10)
Includes index
ISBN 0-306-40634-9 : Unpriced B81-34709

639′.2′0740291292 — Scotland. Fife Region. Anstruther. Museums: Scottish Fisheries Museum — *Visitors′ guides*

The **Scottish** Fisheries Museum. — Derby : Pilgrim Press, c1981. — 16p : ill(some col.),maps ; 20cm
Ill on inside covers. — Bibliography: p16
ISBN 0-900594-57-8 (pbk) : £0.35 B81-23389

639′.2′0973 — United States. Fishermen. Working life

Meltzer, Michael. The world of the small commercial fishermen : their lives and their boats / Michael Meltzer. — New York : Dover Publications ; London : Constable, 1980. — 89p : ill,maps,plans ; 28cm
Bibliography: p89
ISBN 0-486-23945-4 (pbk) : £3.00 B81-22264

639′.2′09811 — Brazil. Amazon River Basin. Fishing by South American Indians

Smith, Nigel J. H.. Man, fishes, and the Amazon / Nigel J.H. Smith. — New York ; Guildford : Columbia University Press, 1981. — x,180p : ill,1map ; 24cm
Bibliography: p159-171. — Includes index
ISBN 0-231-05156-5 : £13.95 B81-26276

639′.22 — Oceans. Fisheries. Resources. Exploitation. Management

Connell, J. J.. Trends in fish utilization. — Farnham : Fishing News Books, Jan.1982. — [116]p
ISBN 0-85238-120-4 (pbk) : £6.00 : CIP entry B81-35894

639′.22 — Oceans. Fisheries. Resources. Management

Laevastu, Taivo. Fisheries oceanography and ecology. — Farnham : Fishing News Books, Nov.1981. — [224]p
ISBN 0-85238-117-4 : £19.50 : CIP entry B81-30623

Study of the sea. — Farnham : Fishing News Books, July 1981. — [272]p
ISBN 0-85238-112-3 : £25.00 : CIP entry
Primary classification 551.46 B81-16893

639′.22′028 — Sea fishing equipment: Nets. Materials

Klust, Gerhard. Netting materials for fishing gear. — 2nd ed. — Farnham : Fishing News Books, Feb.1982. — [192]p. — (FAO fishing manuals)
Previous ed.: 1973
ISBN 0-85238-118-2 (pbk) : CIP entry B81-38826

639′.22′028 — Sea fishing equipment: Seine nets

Thomson, David B.. Seine fishing : bottom fishing with rope warps and wing trawls / David B. Thomson. — Rev. [ed.]. — Farnham : Fishing News Books, c1981. — xvi,208p : ill,chart,map,plans ; 26cm
Previous ed.: published as: The seine net. 1969. — Bibliography: p199-201. — Includes index
ISBN 0-85238-113-1 : £14.50 : CIP rev. B81-08915

639′.22′0916336 — North Sea. Sea fishing — *For children*

Milton, Barry. Fishing boat / Barry Milton ; photographs by Chris Fairclough. — London : Black, c1980. — 25p : col.ill,1col.map,col.ports ; 22cm. — (BEANS. People at work)
ISBN 0-7136-2077-3 : £2.50 : CIP rev. B80-13888

639'.22'0941135 — Scotland. Shetland. Sea fishing — *Practical information — Serials*
Harry's Shetland fishing almanac. — 1981. — Lerwick (Prince Alfred St., Lerwick) : The Shetland Times, 1981. — 64p
ISBN 0-900662-29-8 : Unpriced B81-14545

639'.22'09966 — Palau Islands. Coastal waters. Fishing
Johannes, R. E.. Words of the lagoon : fishing and marine lore in the Palau district of Micronesia / R.E. Johannes. — Berkeley ; London : University of California Press, c1981. — xiv,245p,[8]p of plates : ill,1chart,1map,ports ; 27cm
Bibliography: p207-223. — Includes index
ISBN 0-520-03929-7 : £15.00 B81-36570

639'.2758 — Tuna. Fishing. Rod-and-line techniques — *Manuals*
Ben-Yami, M. Tuna fishing with pole and line / edited by M. Ben-Yami. — Farnham : Published by arrangement with the Food and Agriculture Organization of the United Nations by Fishing News Books, c1980. — xii,150p : ill,1map,plans ; 23cm. — (FAO fishing manuals)
Bibliography: p148-149
ISBN 0-85238-111-5 (pbk) : £6.50 : CIP rev. B80-13889

639'.28'05 — Whaling — *Serials*
International Whaling Commission. Report of the International Whaling Commission. — 31st (1979-1980). — Cambridge (The Red House, Station Rd, Histon, Cambridge CB4 4NP) : The Commission, 1981. — ix,846p
Unpriced B81-32215

639'.29'09714 — Canada. Gulf of St Lawrence. Mammals: Seals. Commercial hunting, *to 1979*
Chantraine, Pol. The living ice : the story of the seals and the men who hunt them in the Gulf of St. Lawrence / Pol Chantraine ; translated by David Lobdell. — Toronto : McClelland and Stewart ; Edinburgh : MacDonald [distributor], c1980. — 238p : ill,maps ; 24cm
Trnslation of: La grande mouvée
ISBN 0-7710-1960-2 : £6.95 B81-37718

639.3 — FISH CULTURE, FISH AS PETS

639.3'4 — Aquariums
Hunnam, Peter. The living aquarium. — London : Ward Lock, Oct.1981. — [240]p
ISBN 0-7063-6127-x : £15.00 : CIP entry B81-28040

639.3'4 — Aquariums — *Amateurs' manuals*
Mills, Dick. Illustrated guide to aquarium fishes / Dick Mills. — London : Kingfisher, 1981. — 197p : ill(some col.) ; 27cm
Bibliography: p193. — Includes index
ISBN 0-7063-6102-4 : Unpriced : CIP rev. B81-03703

639.3'4 — Laboratory animals: Fish. Care. Use of aquariums
Aquarium systems. — London : Academic Press, Aug.1981. — [420]p
ISBN 0-12-333380-6 : CIP entry B81-18130

639.3'4 — Tropical aquariums. Fish. Care — *Manuals*
Axelrod, Herbert R.. Tropical fish / by Herbert R. Axelrod. — Hong Kong : T.F.H. Publications ; Reigate : Distributed by T.F.H. (Great Britain), c1980. — 90p : ill(some col.) ; 21cm
Ill on lining papers
ISBN 0-87666-510-5 : £1.00 B81-18456

639.3'4'03 — Aquariums. Fish — *Encyclopaedias*
The aquarium lexicon. — Poole : Blandford, Sept.1981. — [600]p
Translation of: Lexicon der Aquaristik und Ichthyologie
ISBN 0-7137-1146-9 : CIP entry B81-22677

639.3'4'0321 — Aquariums. Fish — *Encyclopaedias*
Frank, Stanislav. The illustrated encyclopedia of aquarium fish / by Stanislav Frank. — London : Octopus, 1980. — 351p : ill(some col.) ; 24cm
Translation from the Czech. — Bibliography: p345. — Includes index
ISBN 0-7064-0862-4 : £4.95 B81-18191

639.3'42 — Marine aquariums. Fish. Care — *Manuals*
Axelrod, Herbert R.. Marine fish / by Herbert R. Axelrod and Warren E. Burgess. — Hong Kong : T.F.H. Publications ; Reigate : Distributed by T.F.H. (Great Britain), c1979. — 93p : ill(some col.) ; 21cm
Ill on lining papers
ISBN 0-87666-513-x : £1.00 B81-18457

639.3'44 — Tropical freshwater aquariums. Fish. Care
Harrison, C. J. (Clifford John). Tropical fish / C.J. Harrison. — Edinburgh : Bartholomew, 1976. — 95p : col.ill ; 19cm
Includes index
ISBN 0-7028-1091-6 (pbk) : £1.25 B81-09598

639.3'44 — Tropical freshwater aquariums. Fish — *Illustrations*
Nicholls, James. Aquarium fishes : a colour guide to over 200 fishes for the freshwater aquarium, choice — feeding — breeding — care / [painted by James Nicholls ; text by Gwynne Vevers]. — [London] : Fontana, 1979. — 1folded sheet([12]p) : col.ill ; 25cm. — (Domino ; 10)
ISBN 0-00-685450-8 : £0.85 B81-20739

639.3'752 — Aquariums. Goldfish. Breeding & care
Goldfish / edited by Paul R. Paradise. — Neptune, N.J. ; Reigate, T.F.H., c1979. — 93p : ill(some col.) ; 21cm
Ill on inside covers
£1.00 B81-09446

639.3'752 — Pets: Goldfish. Care
Hervey, George F.. The goldfish / by George F. Hervey and Jack Hems ; illustrated with line drawings by A. Fraser-Brunner. — Rev ed.. — London : Faber, 1968 (1981 [printing]). — 271p : ill,1map ; 20cm
Previous ed.: London : Batchworth, 1948. — Bibliography: p257-264. - Includes index
ISBN 0-571-11611-6 (pbk) : £3.25 B81-10608

639.3'755 — Salmon farming
Salmon ranching / edited by J.E. Thorpe. — London : Academic Press, 1980. — x,441p : ill,maps ; 24cm
Includes bibliographies and index
ISBN 0-12-690660-2 : £32.40 : CIP rev. B80-18828

639.3'758 — Aquariums. Discus fish. Care
Silva, Tony. Discus / Tony Silva and Barbara Kotlar. — Reigate : T.F.H., c1980. — 93p : ill (some col.) ; 21cm
Col.ill on lining papers
ISBN 0-87666-535-0 : £1.00 B81-00982

639.3'758 — Grey mullet. Aquaculture
Aquaculture of grey mullets / edited by O.H. Oren. — Cambridge : Cambridge University Press, 1981. — xxi,507p : ill,maps ; 24cm. — (International Biological Programme ; 26)
English text, English, French, Russian and Spanish lists of contents. — Includes bibliographies and index
ISBN 0-521-22926-x : £55.00 : CIP rev. B81-19193

639.4/7 — CULTURE OF INVERTEBRATES

639'.4811 — Great Britain. Scallops. Fishing. Underwater diving
Hardy, David, *1946-*. Scallops and the diver-fisherman / David Hardy. — Farnham : Fishing News Books, c1981. — x,134p : ill ; 23cm
Bibliography: p126. — Includes index
ISBN 0-85238-114-x : £8.50 : CIP rev. B81-12792

639'.5 — Pets: Wood-lice. Care — *For children*
Goldsmith, John, *1947-*. It's easy to have wood-lice to stay / text by John Goldsmith ; illustrations by Judith Allan ; advisory editor Caroline O'Hagan. — London : Chatto & Windus, 1981. — [24]p : col.ill ; 17cm
ISBN 0-7011-2578-0 : £1.95 B81-30672

639.9 — WILDLIFE CONSERVATION

639.9 — Developing countries. Arid regions. Rangeland ecosystems. Conservation. Role of traditional techniques of livestock management — *Study examples: Turan Biosphere Reserve*
Nyerges, A. Endre. The ecology of domesticated animals under traditional management in Iran : preliminary results from the Turan Biosphere Reserve / by A. Endre Nyerges. — London : Overseas Development Institute, Agricultural Administration Unit, 1979. — 44p : ill,maps ; 21cm. — (Pastoral network paper ; 9d)
Bibliography: p43-44
Unpriced (unbound) B81-18023

639.9 — Great Britain. Marine organisms. Conservation
Nature conservation in the Marine environment report of the NCC/NERC Joint Working Party on Marine Wildlife Conservation. — London : Nature Conservancy Council, [c1979]. — 65p : ill ; 30cm
ISBN 0-86139-083-0 (pbk) : £2.50 B81-38708

639.9 — Great Britain. Organisms. Habitats. Conservation
King, Angela. Paradise lost? : the destruction of Britain's wild life habitats : a Friends of the Earth book / by Angela King and Czech Conroy ; foreword by David Bellamy. — London (9 Poland St., W1V 3DG) : Friends of the Earth, [c1980]. — 32p : ill(some col.),1port ; 21cm
Cover title
ISBN 0-905966-24-4 (pbk) : £0.95 B81-11482

639.9 — Nature conservation. Sites. Surveys
The **IBP** survey of conservation sites an experimental study / edited by A.R. Clapham. — Cambridge : Cambridge University Press, 1980. — xx,344p : ill,2col.maps,facsims,forms ; 24cm. — (International Biological Programme ; 24)
English text, French, Spanish and Russian contents pages. — Bibliography: p331-336. — Includes index
ISBN 0-521-22697-x : £25.00 B81-07210

639.9 — Organisms. Conservation. Genetic aspects
Frankel, O. H.. Conservation and evolution / O.H. Frankel and Michael E. Soulé. — Cambridge : Cambridge University Press, 1981. — viii,327p : ill,maps ; 24cm
Bibliography: p278-309. — Includes index
ISBN 0-521-23275-9 (cased) : £25.00
ISBN 0-521-29889-x (pbk) : £7.95 B81-15333

639.9 — Wildlife. Conservation — *For children*
Burton, Robert, *1941-*. Wildlife in danger / Robert Burton. — London : Macmillan Children's, 1981. — 49p : col.ill,2col.maps ; 36cm. — (The Macmillan colour library)
Includes index
ISBN 0-333-30791-7 : £3.95 B81-21784

639.9'05 — Animals. Protection — *Serials*
Animals international. — Vol.1, no.1 (Jan.-Mar.1981)-. — London (c/o 106 Jermyn St, SW1Y 6EE) : World Society for the Protection of Animals, 1981-. — ill,ports ; 30cm
Quarterly. — Merger of: Animalia ; and ISPA news. — Also published in French and German editions
Unpriced B81-27130

639.9'06'01 — Nature conservation. International organisations, *ca 1880-1980*
Boardman, Robert. International organization and the conservation of nature / Robert Boardman. — London : Macmillan, 1981. — 215p ; 23cm
Bibliography: p185-187. — Includes index
ISBN 0-333-26265-4 : £15.00 B81-21868

639.9'06'01 — Wildlife. Conservation. Organisations: World Wildlife Fund — *Serials*
Pandamonium. — [Autumn?] 1980-. — [Godalming] ([11 Ockford Rd, Godalming, Surrey]) : World Wildlife Fund, 1980-. — v. : ill,ports ; 30cm
Quarterly. — Description based on: Summer 1981
ISSN 0261-7439 = Pandamonium : Free to members of WWF Support Groups only
B81-32796

639.9'092'2 — Wildlife. Conservation — *Biographies — For children*

Craven, John, *1940-*. John Craven's wildlife report / John Craven. — London : Hamilton, 1981. — 128p : ill,maps,ports ; 24cm
Includes index
ISBN 0-241-10645-1 (cased) : £5.50 : CIP rev.
ISBN 0-241-10701-6 (pbk) : £3.50 B81-25700

639.9'092'4 — Australia, New Zealand & Malaysia. Animals. Conservation — *Personal observations*

Durrell, Gerald. Two in the bush / Gerald Durrell ; illustrated by B.L. Driscoll. — Large print ed. — Leicester : Ulverscroft, 1980, c1966. — 360p : ill ; 23cm. — (Ulverscroft large print series)
Originally published: London : Collins, 1966
ISBN 0-7089-0516-1 : £4.25 : CIP rev.
B80-17698

639.9'0941 — Great Britain. Nature conservation

Mabey, Richard. The common ground : a place for nature in Britain's future? / Richard Mabey. — London : Arrow in association with the Nature Conservancy Council, 1981, c1980. — 266p,[8]p of plates : ill,1map ; 20cm
Originally published: London : Hutchinson, 1980
ISBN 0-09-926450-1 (pbk) : £1.95 B81-40723

Nature conservation : an introduction / Nature Conservancy Council. — London (19 Belgrave Sq., SW1X 8PY) : The Council, c1978. — 1folded sheet([6]p) : col.ill ; 21cm
Bibliography: p6
ISBN 0-901204-57-9 : Unpriced B81-11185

639.9'0941 — Great Britain. Organisms. Introduction. Conservation aspects

Wildlife introductions to Great Britain : the introduction, re-introduction and restocking of species in Great Britain : some policy implications for nature conservation : report / by the Working Group on Introductions of the UK Committee for International Nature Conservation. — London : Published by the Nature Conservancy Council on behalf of the UK Committee for International Nature Conservation, 1979. — 32p : ill ; 30cm
Includes bibliographies
ISBN 0-86139-090-3 (pbk) : £1.20 B81-38709

639.9'0941 — Great Britain. Urban regions. Organisms. Conservation

Cole, Lyndis. Wildlife in the city : a study of practical conservation projects / compiled by Lyndis Cole. — [London] : [Nature Conservancy Council], Administrations & Operations Divisions, [1980]. — 28p ; 30cm
ISBN 0-86139-110-1 (spiral) : Unpriced
B81-38713

639.9'0941 — Great Britain. Wildlife. Conservation. Effects of agricultural chemicals — *For teaching*

Palmer, Margaret, *1935-*. Agricultural chemicals and wildlife / compiled for the Nature Conservancy Council by Margaret Palmer. — Huntingdon (PO Box 6, Godwin House, George St., Huntingdon, Cambs. PE18 6BU) : Nature Conservancy Council, 1980. — 48leaves : ill ; 30cm. — (Nature conservation & agriculture ; project 2)
ISBN 0-86139-108-x (pbk) : £1.50 B81-12694

639.9'0941 — Great Britain. Wildlife. Conservation — *Serials*

Natural world : the magazine of the Royal Society for Nature Conservation. — No.1 (Spring 1981)-. — London (4 Bloomsbury Sq., WC1A 2RL) : Illustrated Newspapers on behalf of the Society, 1981-. — v. : ill,ports ; 28cm
Three issue yearly. — Continues: Conservation review
ISSN 0261-7358 = Natural world : Free to members of Conservation Trusts B81-32793

639.9'09411'1 — North-West Scotland. Nature conservation

Nature Conservancy Council. *North West Scotland Region*. Nature Conservancy Council, North West (Scotland) Region. — Inverness (Fraser Darling House, 9 Culduthel Rd., Inverness I42 4AG) : Nature Conservancy Council, North West Scotland Region, c1980. — 1folded sheet([6]p) : ill,1map ; 21cm
ISBN 0-86139-097-0 : Unpriced B81-30928

639.9'09416 — Northern Ireland. Agricultural land. Nature conservation — *Conference proceedings*

Nature conservation and agriculture : a conference organised by The New University of Ulster Institute of Coninuing Education in association with the Ulster Trust for Nature Conservation. — [Londonderry] : [The Institute], 1980. — [51]p : ill ; 26cm
Unpriced (pbk) B81-21762

639.9'09423'5 — Devon. Nature conservation — *Serials*

Nature in Devon : the journal of the Devon Trust for Nature Conservation. — 1-. — Exeter (75 Queen St., Exeter, Devon) : The Trust, 1980-. — v. : ill,maps ; 24cm
Annual. — Continues: Journal of the Devon Trust for Nature Conservation (1978)
ISSN 0143-9634 = Nature in Devon : Unpriced B81-35089

639.9'09426'54 — Cambridgeshire. Holme. Nature reserves: Holme Fen National Nature Reserve

Nature Conservancy Council. Holme Fen National Nature Reserve / Nature Conservancy Council. — Huntingdon [Cambs] (P.O. Box 6, Godwin House, George St., Huntingdon, Cambs. PE18 6BU) : Nature Conservancy Council, East Midlands Region, c1978. — 1folded sheet(([4]p)) : 1ill,1map ; 21cm
ISBN 0-86139-032-6 : Unpriced B81-04749

639.9'09428'8 — Northumberland. National parks: Northumberland National Park. Nature conservation — *For environment planning*

Nature conservation in the Northumberland National Park. — Newcastle upon Tyne ([c/o] National Park Officer, Bede House, All Saints Centre, Newcastle upon Tyne) : [Northumberland National Park and Countryside Committee], 1975. — i,54p,[5]p of plates : maps ; 30cm. — (Working paper / Northumberland National Park ; 2)
Bibliography: p28
Unpriced (spiral) B81-29620

639.9'09429'29 — Gwynedd. Harlech. Nature reserves: Morfa Harlech National Nature Reserve

Nature Conservancy Council. Morfa Harlech National Nature Reserve / Nature Conservancy Council. — Bangor (Ffordd Penrhos, Bangor, Gwynedd LL57 2LQ) : Nature Conservancy Council, North Wales Region, c1978. — 1folded sheet(([4]p)) : 1 ill,1map ; 21cm
ISBN 0-86139-034-2 : Unpriced B81-04750

639.9'0994 — Australia. Wildlife. Conservation

Frith, H. J.. Wildlife conservation / H.J. Frith. — Rev. ed. — London : Angus & Robertson, 1979. — xiv,416p,viii,60p of plates : ill(some col.),maps(some col.) ; 25cm. — ([Australian natural science library])
Previous ed.: 1973. — Map on lining papers. — Bibliography: p381-399. - Includes index
ISBN 0-207-13649-1 : £10.00 B81-19380

639.9'2 — Gardens. Wildlife. Habitats. Creation — *Manuals*

Wilson, Ron. The back garden wildlife sanctuary book / Ron Wilson ; with new line drawings by Ann Roper and John Heritage. — Harmondsworth : Penguin, 1981, c1979. — 152p : ill ; 25cm. — (Penguin handbooks)
Originally published: London : Astragal Books, 1979. — Includes bibliographies and index
ISBN 0-14-046915-x (pbk) : £2.95 B81-21082

639.9'5092'4 — England. Gamekeeping. Mursell, Norman - *Biographies*

Mursell, Norman. Come dawn, come dusk. — London : Allen & Unwin, July 1981. — [168]p
ISBN 0-04-799014-7 : £8.95 : CIP entry
B81-13771

639.9'5'096 — Africa. Game wardens — *For children*

Kinloch, Bruce, *19---*. Game wardens in Africa / Bruce Kinloch ; [translated by Brenda F. Groth]. — St. Albans : Hart-Davis, c1981. — 32p : col.ill ; 26cm. — (Natural science series)
Translation from the German. — Includes index
ISBN 0-247-13155-5 : £2.95 B81-39607

639.9'5'0967825 — Tanzania. Game reserves: Selous Game Reserve

Robins, Eric. Secret Eden : Africa's enchanted wilderness / Eric Robins ; photographs by Marion Kaplan. — London : Elm Tree Books, 1980. — 128p : ill(some col.),2maps,ports ; 28cm
Bibliography: p127
ISBN 0-241-10423-8 : £8.95 : CIP rev.
B80-18830

639.9'7829'41 — Great Britain. Birds. Conservation — *Personal observations*

Robinson, Peter. Bird detective. — London : Hamilton, Feb.1982. — [192]p
ISBN 0-241-10709-1 : £7.95 : CIP entry
B81-36388

639.9'782941 — Great Britain. Gardens. Birds. Care

The birds in your garden. — Sandy (The Lodge, Sandy, Beds. SG19 2DL) : Royal Society for the Protection of Birds, c1980. — 31p : col.ill ; 21cm
Unpriced (unbound) B81-27601

639.9'782942961 — Dyfed. Llandyssul. Bird sanctuaries: New Quay Bird Hospital

Bryant, Alan. A second chance : the story of the New Quay Bird Hospital / by Alan Bryant ; drawings by Steven Jaremko. — London : Dent, 1981. — 199p,[8]p of plates : ill ; 23cm
Includes index
ISBN 0-460-04480-x : £7.95 : CIP rev.
B81-28030

639'.97841'0941 — Great Britain. Wildfowl reserves

McCullagh, Sheila. Where wild geese fly / Sheila McCullagh ; with drawings by Peter Scott. — St. Albans : Hart-Davis, 1981. — 47p : ill(some col.),3maps ; 25cm
Text and ill on inside covers. — Includes index
ISBN 0-247-13190-3 (pbk) : £1.95 B81-39310

639.9'79 — Great Britain. Mammals. Rabies. Control measures

Gibbs, Roy. Rabies : you and your pets / Roy Gibbs. — Melksham : Venton, c1981. — 150p,[24]p of plates : ill,maps,facsims ; 23cm. — (White horse library)
Bibliography: p143-147. — Includes index
ISBN 0-85475-137-8 : £8.75 B81-40111

639.9'795 — Whales. Conservation

Allen, K. Radway. Conservation and management of whales / K. Radway Allen. — Seattle : Washington Sea Grant ; London : Butterworths, 1980. — ix,107p : ill ; 24cm
Bibliography: p101-103. - Includes index
ISBN 0-408-10725-1 : £10.00
Also classified at 599.5 B81-03738

639.9'79725 — England. Donkeys. Protection. Svendsen, Elisabeth D. — *Biographies*

Svendsen, Elisabeth D.. Down among the donkeys / Elisabeth Svendsen. — London : Pan, 1981. — 190p,[8]p of plates : ill,ports ; 18cm
ISBN 0-330-26316-1 (pbk) : £1.25 B81-19698

Svendsen, Elisabeth D.. Down among the donkeys / Elisabeth Svendsen. — London : Hale, 1981. — 189p,[16]p of plates : ill,ports ; 23cm
ISBN 0-7091-9309-2 : £6.95 B81-24553

639.9'797357 — Great Britain. *Red Deer Commission — Serials*

Great Britain. *Red Deer Commission*. Annual report for ... / the Red Deer Commission. — 1980. — Edinburgh : H.M.S.O., 1981. — 19p
ISBN 0-11-491739-6 : £1.90 B81-31031

639.9'7974447 — Great Britain. Otters. Conservation

Havins, Peter J. Neville. The otter in Britain / Peter J. Neville Havins. — London : Hale, 1981. — 192p,[16]p of plates : ill ; 23cm
Bibliography: p183-184. - Includes index
ISBN 0-7091-8580-4 : £7.50 B81-18390

639.9'7974447 — Great Britain. Otters. Conservation *continuation*

Jenkins, D. (David), *1926-*. Conserving otters / D. Jenkins. — Cambridge : Natural Environment Research Council, Institute of Terrestrial Ecology, 1980. — 14p : ill,2maps ; 21cm
ISBN 0-904282-44-9 (pbk) : £1.00 B81-07304

639.9'79748'06041132 — Scotland. Orkney. Mammals: Seals. Hunting. Prevention. Organisations: Selkie

Flint, Sue. Let the seals live! / Sue Flint ; foreword by Sir Frank Fraser Darling. — [Stornoway] : Thule, 1979. — 170p : ill,maps,ports ; 22cm
Bibliography: p170
ISBN 0-906191-35-1 (cased) : £5.95 B81-17083

639.9'9 — Rare plants. Conservation — *Conference proceedings*

The **Biological** aspects of rare plant conservation / [proceedings of an international conference held at King's College, Cambridge, England 14-19 July 1980 ; convened by G.Ll. Lucas ... [et al.] and sponsored by the Linnean Society of London and the Botanical Society of the British Isles] ; edited by Hugh Synge. — Chichester : Wiley, c1981. — xxviii,558p : ill,maps,forms ; 24cm
Includes bibliographies and index
ISBN 0-471-28004-6 : £30.00 : CIP rev.
B81-28128

640 — HOUSEHOLD MANAGEMENT

640 — Australia. Households. Self-sufficiency — *Manuals*

Boddy, Michael. Surviving in the eighties / Michael Boddy and Richard Beckett ; illustrated by Janet Dawson Boddy. — Sydney ; London : Allen & Unwin, 1980. — 196p : ill,plans ; 28cm
Bibliography: p194. — Includes index
ISBN 0-86861-106-9 (cased) : £15.95
ISBN 0-86861-114-x (pbk) : £7.50 B81-08375

640 — Families. Resources. Management

Deacon, Ruth E.. Family resource management : principles and applications / Ruth E. Deacon, Francile M. Firebaugh. — Boston, [Mass.] ; London : Allyn and Bacon, c1981. — vii,257p : ill ; 25cm
Bibliography: p231-242. — Includes index
ISBN 0-205-06994-0 : £11.95 B81-01681

640 — Great Britain. Households. Self-sufficiency — *Manuals*

Humphreys, John. Living off the land / by John Humphreys ; photographs: Dave Parfitt. — London (Burghley Hall, 809 High Rd., E.11) : Percival Marshall, c1979. — 95p : ill ; 21cm. — (A 'Shooting times and country magazine' production)
ISBN 0-85242-677-1 (pbk) : £2.95 B81-37742

640 — Great Britain. Rural regions. Households. Self-sufficiency — *Manuals*

Gordon, Sally. The good life / Sally Gordon. — London : Dent, 1981. — 222p : ill(some col.) ; 28cm
Includes index
ISBN 0-460-04516-4 : £9.95 B81-39416

640 — Hertfordshire. Welwyn region. Self-sufficiency - *Personal observations*

Wigens, Anthony. The clandestine farm / Anthony Wigens. — London : Granada, 1981, c1980. — 142p : ill,1map ; 20cm. — (A Paladin book)
Ill on inside back cover. — Bibliography: p139-142
ISBN 0-586-08305-7 (pbk) : £1.50 B81-18904

640 — Home economics — *For Caribbean students*

Gill, Veda. Caribbean home economics / Veda Gill and Elisabeth Hildyard. — London : Macmillan Caribbean
Bk.2. — 1981. — v,153p : ill ; 25cm
Includes index
ISBN 0-333-30432-2 (pbk) : £2.10 B81-40518

McLean, Barbara. Concise home economics for the Caribbean examinations / Barbara McLean. — [London] : Collins, 1981. — 90p : ill ; 23cm
Includes index
ISBN 0-00-329414-5 (pbk) : £1.25 B81-34241

640 — Home economics — *For schools*

Moses, Howell. About the home / Howell Moses & Ann Salway. — St. Albans : Hart-Davis Educational, 1981. — 96p : ill,1facsim ; 25cm. — (New learning for living ; 2)
Text on inside cover. — Includes index
ISBN 0-247-12980-1 (pbk) : £2.15 B81-18200

640 — Home economics - *For schools*

Nuffield home economics. — London : Hutchinson Educational, June 1981
The basic course. — [192]p
ISBN 0-09-145601-0 (pbk) : £2.95 : CIP entry
B81-12326

Nuffield home economics. — London : Hutchinson Educational, July 1981
Masters for worksheets and OHP's for the basic course. — [64]p
ISBN 0-09-145581-2 : £15.00 : CIP entry
B81-13499

Nuffield home economics. — London : Hutchinson Educational, June 1981
Teachers' guide to the basic course. — [320]p
ISBN 0-09-145591-x (pbk) : £8.00 : CIP entry
B81-12327

640 — Home economics — *For schools*

Ruth, Beryl. Home economics / Beryl Ruth ; illustrated by Quentin Blake ; diagrams by Cyril Deakins. — 4th ed. — London : Heinemann Educational, 1981. — 177p : ill,plans ; 20cm
Previous ed.: 1974. — Includes index
ISBN 0-435-42264-2 (pbk) : £2.25 B81-23372

640 — Household management — *Manuals*

Beeton, *Mrs.*. Mrs Beeton's cookery and household management. — [New ed.]. — London : Ward Lock, 1980. — 1606p,[60]p of plates : ill(some col.),plans ; 26cm
Previous ed.: published as Cookery and household management, 1960. — Includes index
ISBN 0-7063-5743-4 : £14.95
Also classified at 641.5 B81-12033

640 — Household management - *Manuals*

Chandler, Barbara. How to cope at home. — London : Ward Lock, June 1981. — [160]p
ISBN 0-7063-5918-6 : £6.95 : CIP entry
B81-12842

640 — Household management — *Manuals*

The **Dairy** book of home management / [general editor Neil Tennant]. — New ed. — [London] : Published by Macdonald Educational on behalf of the Dairy Industry, 1980. — 384p : ill(some col.),facsims ; 24cm
Previous ed.: London : Wolfe, 1969. — Includes index
ISBN 0-356-07296-7 : £1.95 B81-02449

Good Housekeeping home hints / by Good Housekeeping Institute ; [text Cassandra Kent] ; [cartoons Robert Broomfield]. — London : Ebury Press, 1981. — 128p : ill ; 23cm
Includes index
ISBN 0-85223-205-5 (cased) : £5.95
ISBN 0-85223-190-3 (pbk) : £2.95 B81-18707

Madden, Deirdre. Home and community / Deirdre Madden. — Dublin : Gill and Macmillan, 1981. — 348p : ill ; 27cm
Includes index
ISBN 0-7171-0997-6 (pbk) : £5.40
Also classified at 941.085'8 B81-21406

Penny, Jean. Gran's old fashioned remedies, wrinkles and recipes / Jean Penny. — Bognor Regis : New Horizon, c1980. — 55p ; 21cm
ISBN 0-86116-219-6 : £3.25 B81-21810

640 — Household management — *Practical information*

Clark, Muriel. Home management : a fresh approach / Muriel Clark and Pauline Swaine. — London : Cassell, 1981. — 282p : ill ; 22cm
Bibliography: p272. — Includes index
ISBN 0-304-30603-7 (pbk) : £5.95 : CIP rev.
B81-14455

What our grandmothers knew / Reader's Digest. — London : Reader's Digest Association, c1979 (1981 [printing]). — 32p ; 19cm
Unpriced (pbk) B81-22937

640 — Self-sufficiency

Allaby, Michael. The politics of self-sufficiency / Michael Allaby and Peter Bunyard. — Oxford : Oxford University Press, 1980. — vii,242p ; 21cm
Bibliography: p233-235. - Includes index
ISBN 0-19-217695-1 (cased) : £7.95 : CIP rev.
B80-03722

Pedler, Kit. The quest for Gaia : a book of changes / Kit Pedler. — London : Granada, 1981, c1979. — 222p : ill ; 20cm. — (A Paladin book)
Originally published: London : Souvenir, 1979
ISBN 0-586-08365-0 (pbk) : £2.50 B81-07142

640'.43'088042 — Women. Time. Allocation — *Manuals*

Mackenzie, R. Alec. About time! : a woman's guide to time management / Alec Mackenzie and Kay Cronkite Waldo. — New York ; London : McGraw-Hill, 1981. — xii,242p : ill,forms ; 21cm
Includes index
ISBN 0-07-044651-2 (pbk) : £4.50 B81-26929

640'.46'0924 — Domestic service. Harrison, Rosina — *Biographies*

Harrison, Rosina. Rose : my life in service / Rosina Harrison. — Large print ed. — Leicester : Ulverscroft, 1981, c1975. — 432p ; 23cm
Originally published: London : Cassell, 1975
ISBN 0-7089-0685-0 : £5.00 : CIP rev.
B81-25691

640'.46'0942 — England. Country houses. Domestic service, *1800-1900*

Hartcup, Adeline. Below stairs in the great country houses / Adeline Hartcup. — London : Sidgwick & Jackson, 1980. — 214p : ill,1facsim,ports ; 24cm
Bibliography: p207-209. — Includes index
ISBN 0-283-98695-6 : £8.95 B81-00983

640'.46'0942 — England. Domestic service, *1837-1950*

Huggett, Frank E.. Life below stairs : domestic servants in England from Victorian times / Frank E. Huggett. — London : Book Club Associates, 1977. — 186p : ill,facsims,ports ; 26cm
Includes index
Unpriced B81-39122

640'.7'041 — Great Britain. Home economics teachers. Professional education

Moon, Mary. Teaching home economics / Mary Moon. — London : Batsford Academic and Educational, 1981. — 202p : ill ; 23cm
Includes bibliographies and index
ISBN 0-7134-1833-8 : £6.95 B81-27214

640'.71 — Education. Curriculum subjects: Home economics. Teaching

Chamberlain, Valerie M.. Creative home economics instruction / Valerie M. Chamberlain, Joan M. Kelly. — 2nd ed. — New York ; London : Webster Division, c1981. — 256p : ill,forms ; 23cm
Previous ed.: 1975. — Includes index
ISBN 0-07-010424-7 (pbk) : £8.25 B81-10232

640'.7'101724 — Developing countries. Educational institutions. Curriculum subjects: Home economics. Teaching

Olaitan, Samson O.. Introduction to the teaching of home economics / Samson O. Olaitan and Obiora N. Agusiobo. — Chichester : Wiley, c1981. — xiv,327p : ill,plans,form ; 24cm. — (Education in Africa)
Includes bibliographies and index
ISBN 0-471-27807-6 (cased) : £16.50
ISBN 0-471-27806-8 (pbk) : Unpriced
B81-23433

640'.7'12 — Secondary schools. Curriculum subjects: Home economics. Academic achievement of students. Assessment — *For teaching*

Black, H. D.. Diagnostic assessment in home economics : a teacher's handbook / by H.D. Black and W.B. Dockrell with G. Leckenby. — [Edinburgh] ([16 Moray Place, Edinburgh EH3 6DR]) : Scotland Council for Research in Education, c1981. — x,76p : ill,forms ; 22cm
ISBN 0-901116-27-0 (pbk) : £2.20 B81-32299

640'.7'124271 — Cheshire. Secondary schools. Curriculum subjects: Home economics

Hall, B. D.. Home economics in secondary education : report for the Director of Education / Bryan D. Hall. — Chester ([Research Library, County Hall, Chester CH1 1SF]) : Central Policy and Research Unit, Cheshire County Council, [1980]. — 54,5p : ill,forms ; 30cm
ISBN 0-904073-09-2 (pbk) : £5.00 B81-15471

640'.73'0941 — Great Britain. Consumer goods & consumer services — *Manuals* — *For consumers*

Delbridge, Rosemary. Buy right : the Money-go-round guide to consumer affairs / Rosemary Delbridge, Mary McAnally ; illustrated by Jim Friell. — London : Pan, 1981. — 144p : ill,2facsims ; 18cm. — (Pan information)
Includes index
ISBN 0-330-26181-9 (pbk) : £1.25 B81-05450

640'.76 — Home economics - *Questions & answers* - *For schools*

Creese, Angela. 1050 questions and answers in home economics. — 2nd ed. — London : Bell & Hyman, July 1981. — [183]p
Previous ed.: London : Mills & Boon, 1970
ISBN 0-7135-2061-2 (pbk) : £1.95 : CIP entry B81-15909

640'.941 — Great Britain. Home economics — *For women's institutes*

Home economics handbook. — London : WI Books, c1981. — v,55p ; 21cm
Includes index
ISBN 0-900556-66-8 (pbk) : Unpriced : CIP rev. B81-14423

640'.941 — Great Britain. Household management, *1800-1900* — *Practical information* — *Readings from contemporary sources*

Drury, Elizabeth. The butler's pantry book / Elizabeth Drury. — London : Black, 1981. — 192p : ill,facsims ; 23cm
Bibliography: p181-183. — Includes index
ISBN 0-7136-2144-3 : £6.95 : CIP rev.
Also classified at 641.5941 B81-22526

640'.941 — Great Britain. Household management — *Manuals* — *Early works*

Grandmother's lore : a collection of household hints from past and present / [compiled by] Simone Sekers. — London : Hodder and Stoughton, 1980. — 192p ; 21cm
Bibliography: p191-192
ISBN 0-340-25303-7 : £4.95 : CIP rev. B80-19818

640'.941 — Great Britain. Household management, *to 1979*

Yarwood, Doreen. The British kitchen : housewifery since Roman times / Doreen Yarwood. — London : Batsford, 1981. — 190p : ill ; 26cm
Bibliography: p183-184. - Includes index
ISBN 0-7134-1430-8 : £9.95 B81-15966

640'.944'361 — France. Paris. Household management, *1392-1394* — *Early works* — *French texts*

Le Menagier de Paris / edited by Georgine E. Brereton and Janet M. Ferrier ; with a foreword by Beryl Smalley. — Oxford : Clarendon, 1981. — lxv,374p ; 22cm
French text, English introduction, and notes. — Bibliography: p339-343. — Includes index
ISBN 0-19-815748-7 : £35.00 B81-36854

641 — FOOD AND DRINK, NUTRITION

641'.01'3 — Gastronomy — *Early works*

Brillat-Savarin, Jean-Anthelme. The philosopher in the kitchen / Jean-Anthelme Brillat-Savarin ; translated by Anne Drayton. — Harmondsworth : Penguin, c1970 (1981 [printing]). — 379p ; 20cm. — (Penguin handbooks)
Translation of: La physiologie du goût
ISBN 0-14-046157-4 (pbk) : £2.95 B81-21032

641'.01'30922 — Western Europe. Gastronomy — *Personal observations* — *Collections*

Cradock, Fanny. Time to remember : a cook for all seasons / Fanny and Johnnie Cradock. — Exeter : Webb & Bower, 1981. — 160p : ill (some col.),ports ; 26cm
ISBN 0-906671-33-7 : £7.95 : CIP rev. B81-19201

641'.074'02256 — East Sussex. Brighton. Museums: Brighton Museum. Exhibits: Items associated with food & drinks — *Catalogues*

Eat drink and be merry : an exhibition about food and drink in England [held at] Brighton Museum, May 2-August 2 1981 / sponsored by the Brighton Festival Society. — [Brighton] ([The Royal Pavilion, Brighton BN1 1UE]) : [The Royal Pavilion, Art Gallery and Museums], [1981]. — 140p,[16]p of plates : ill,ports ; 21cm
Unpriced (pbk) B81-25259

641'.0944 — France. Food & drinks — *Visitors' guides*

Binns, Richard. French leave, 1981 / Richard Binns. — Amersham (Amersham Rd., Amersham, Bucks. HP6 5PE) : Chiltern House, 1980. — 160p : ill,maps(some col.) ; 20cm
Includes index
ISBN 0-9507224-0-5 : £3.95 B81-05773

641.1 — Food. Chemical constituents & properties

Gaman, P. M.. The science of food : an introduction to food science, nutrition and microbiology / by P.M. Gaman and K.B. Sherrington. — 2nd ed. — Oxford : Pergamon, 1981. — xii,245p : ill ; 26cm. — (Pergamon international library)
Previous ed.: 1977. — Bibliography: p235. - Includes index
ISBN 0-08-025896-4 (cased) : £12.50 : CIP rev.
ISBN 0-08-025895-6 (pbk) : £5.50 B80-09293

Hawthorn, John, *1921-*. Foundation of food science / John Hawthorn. — Oxford : W.H. Freeman, c1981. — xi,195p : ill ; 25cm
Includes index
ISBN 0-7167-1295-4 : £10.00
ISBN 0-7167-1296-2 (pbk) : £4.95 B81-37385

641.1 — Food science

Pyke, Magnus. Food science and technology. — 4th ed. — London : John Murray, July 1981. — [320]p
Previous ed.: 1970
ISBN 0-7195-3850-5 (pbk) : £7.50 : CIP entry
Also classified at 664 B81-14897

641.1'0212 — Proprietary food. Nutritional values — *Tables*

The Food value counter / [compiled by] Bridgid Herridge. — London : New English Library, 1981. — 159 ; 19cm
ISBN 0-450-05068-8 (pbk) : £1.25 B81-26095

641.1'024642 — Food science — *For catering*

Robins, G. V.. Food science in catering / G.V. Robins. — London : Heinemann, 1980. — xix,234p : ill ; 25cm
Bibliography: p222. - Includes index
ISBN 0-434-91733-8 (pbk) : £8.50 B81-03971

641.1'042 — Food. Calorific values - *Lists*

Fielding, Jean. Calorie controlled meals. — Havant : Mason, Aug.1981. — [32]p
Originally published: 1974
ISBN 0-85937-103-4 (pbk) : £0.20 : CIP entry B81-18048

641.1'042 — Proprietary food. Calorific values — *Tables*

Sherman, Alexandra. Pocket calorie guide to branded foods / by Alexandra Sherman. — London : Arlington, 1979 (1981 [printing]). — 217p ; 13cm. — (Arlington pocket books)
ISBN 0-85140-307-7 (pbk) : £0.95 B81-37981

641.1'05 — Food science — *Serials*

Home food adviser : an occasional publication of the Home Food Science Section, Ministry of Agriculture, Fisheries and Food. — No.1-. — Bristol (Long Ashton Research Station, Bristol BS18) : The Section, 1977. — v. : ill ; 21cm
Irregular. — Description based on: No.3
£0.80
Also classified at 664'.005 B81-0579

641.1'07 — Food science. Information sources

Information sources in agriculture and food science / editor G.P. Lilley. — London : Butterworths, 1981. — xiv,603p : 1ill ; 23cm. — (Butterworths guides to information sources
Includes index
ISBN 0-408-10612-3 : Unpriced
Primary classification 630'.7 B81-3499

641.1'2'05 — Food. Proteins — *Serials*

Developments in food proteins. — 1. — London Applied Science, Nov.1981. — [352]p. — (The Developments series)
ISBN 0-85334-987-8 : £30.00 : CIP entry B81-3042

641.1'3 — Food. Carbohydrates

Developments in food carbohydrate. — London : Applied Science Publishers
3: Disaccharides. — Jan.1982. — [232]p
ISBN 0-85334-996-7 : £21.00 : CIP entry B81-3378

641.2'1'05 — Alcoholic drinks — *Serials*

Wining & dining : incorporating Wine & dine : eating out and entertaining in. — Vol.1, no.1 (Dec.1980)-. — London (16 Ennismore Ave., W4 1SF) : HS Publishing, 1980-. — v. : ill ; 30cm
Monthly. — Continues: Wine & dine
ISSN 0261-3956 = Wining & dining : £9.50 per year
Primary classification 641.3'005 B81-2791

641.2'2 — Fortified wines: Port

Robertson, George. Port. — London : Faber, Jan.1982. — [188]p
Originally published: 1978
ISBN 0-571-11766-x (pbk) : £3.50 : CIP entry B81-3380

641.2'2 — Wines

Paterson, John, *1931-*. Choosing your wine / John Paterson. — Rev. and enl. ed. — London : Hamlyn, c1981. — 128p : ill(some col.),maps ; 23cm
Previous ed.: published as The Hamlyn pocket dictionary of wines. 1980. — Includes index
ISBN 0-600-33217-9 : £3.50 B81-3732

Price, Pamela Vandyke. The taste of wine / Pamela Vandyke Price. — 2nd ed., 3rd impression. — London : Macdonald, 1981, c1976. — 192p : ill(some col.) ; 28cm : col.maps
Previous ed.: 1975. — Bibliography: p191. — Includes index
ISBN 0-356-08344-6 (cased) : Unpriced
ISBN 0-354-04804-x (pbk) : £5.95 B81-3320

641.2'2 — Wines — *For wines trades*

Hogg, Anthony. Off the shelf / written by Anthony Hogg. — 4th ed. — Harlow (Gilbey House, Harlow, Essex) : Gilbey Vintners, 1980. — 184p : ill(some col.),col.maps,facsims,ports ; 20cm
Previous ed.: 1977. — Bibliography: p174-176. — Includes index
ISBN 0-9502679-1-0 (pbk) : Unpriced B81-1252

641.2'2'014 — Wines. Names. Pronunciation — *Encyclopaedias*

Jones, Robert, *1946-*. The imbibers guide to wine pronunciation / Robert Jones. — Bicester (Lairg House, Chapel St., Bicester, Oxon OX6 7BD) : Imbibers Ltd., 1980. — 78p ; 15cm
ISBN 0-9507055-0-0 (pbk) : £1.25 B81-1759

641.2'2'0294 — Wines — *Buyers' guides*

Bone, Arthur. Book of choosing & enjoying wine / Arthur Bone. — Poole : Blandford, [1981]. — 95p : col.ill,col.maps,facsims,1port ; 15cm. — ('How to')
Includes index
ISBN 0-7137-1049-7 (pbk) : £1.95 B81-1953

641.2′2′0321 — Wines — *Encyclopaedias*

Paterson, John, *1931-*. The Hamlyn pocket dictionary of wines / John Paterson. — London : Hamlyn, 1980. — 256p ; 15cm
ISBN 0-600-39498-0 (pbk) : £1.25 B81-00984

641.2′2′05 — Wines — *Buyers′ guides — Serials*

Which? wine guide. — 1981-. — London : Consumers′ Association, 1980-. — v. : ill ; 21cm
Annual
ISSN 0260-7379 = Which? wine guide : £4.95
Also classified at 380.1′456632′002541
B81-07194

641.2′2′09436 — Austria. Wines

Hallgarten, S. F.. The wines and wine gardens of Austria / by S.F. & F.L. Hallgarten. — Watford : Argus Books, 1979. — xii,339p,[16]p of plates : col.ill,maps,coat of arms ; 22cm
Ill on lining papers. — Bibliography: p318-321. — Includes index
ISBN 0-85242-643-7 : £6.95 B81-37744

641.2′52 — Scotch whiskies, *to 1974*

Lockhart, *Sir* Robert Bruce. Scotch. — 5th ed. — London : Putnam, Sept.1981. — [184]p
Originally published: 1974
ISBN 0-370-30910-3 : £4.95 : CIP entry
B81-21648

641.2′6 — Health food drinks

Young, Mala. Drinks & snacks / [Mala Young] ; [illustrated by Susan Neale]. — Newton Abbot : David & Charles, c1981. — 48p : ill ; 21cm. — (Health food cooking)
ISBN 0-7153-8041-9 (pbk) : £1.50
Also classified at 641.5′637 B81-12727

641.3 — Food

Still, Jean. Food selection & preparation / Jean Still. — New York : Macmillan ; London : Collier Macmillan, c1981. — xii,435p : ill ; 25cm
Bibliography: p409-410. — Includes index
ISBN 0-02-417510-2 : £11.95 B81-36116

641.3 — France. Food. Purchase — *Practical information — For British tourists — Serials*

The Do it yourself French holiday. — 1981-. — Oxford (36 Church Meadow, Milton-under-Wychwood, Oxford OX7 6JG) : Ashgarth Enterprises, 1980-. — v. : ill ; 21cm
Annual
ISSN 0261-3972 = Do it yourself French holiday : £1.99
Also classified at 641.5944′05 B81-28705

641.3 — Western world. Food. Purchase — *Practical information — For British tourists*

Wright, Carol. The holiday cook : recipes and shopping away from home / Carol Wright. — Newton Abbot : David & Charles, c1981. — 160p ; 23cm
Includes index
ISBN 0-7153-8017-6 : £4.95
Primary classification 641.5 B81-08702

641.3′003′21 — Food — *Encyclopaedias*

Crabbe, David. The world food book : an A-Z, atlas and statistical source book / David Crabbe and Simon Lawson. — London : Kogan Page, 1981. — 240p : ill,maps ; 29cm
Bibliography: p240
ISBN 0-85038-255-6 : £14.50 B81-36172

641.3′005 — Food — *Serials*

Advances in food research. — Vol.26. — New York ; London : Academic Press, 1980. — vii,316p
ISBN 0-12-016426-4 : Unpriced
ISSN 0065-2628 B81-20710

Wining & dining : incorporating Wine & dine : eating out and entertaining in. — Vol.1, no.1 (Dec.1980)-. — London (16 Ennismore Ave., W4 1SF) : HS Publishing, 1980-. — v. : ill ; 30cm
Monthly. — Continues: Wine & dine
ISSN 0261-3956 = Wining & dining : £9.50 per year
Also classified at 641.2′1′05 B81-27912

641.3′0068′7 — Great Britain. Food. Physical distribution

Tanburn, Jennifer. Food distribution : its impact on marketing in the ′80s / by Jennifer Tanburn. — London (301 Market Towers, New Covent Garden Market, 1 Nine Elms La., SW8 5NQ) : Central Council for Agricultural and Horticultural Co-operation, 1981. — vii,60p : ill ; 30cm
Includes index
£20.00 (spiral) B81-25944

641.3′0068′8 — England. National Federation of Women′s Institutes cooperative food markets. Organisation — *Manuals*

The WI market handbook. — 4th revision. — London : National Federation of Women′s Institutes, 1978. — 37,[11]p ; 21cm
Previous ed.: 1972. — Includes index
ISBN 0-900556-55-2 (pbk) : Unpriced
B81-10861

641.3′009 — Food, *to 1980 — Conference proceedings*

International Conference on Ethnological Food Research *(3rd : 1977 : Cardiff)*. Food in perspective : proceedings of the Third International Conference on Ethnological Food Research, Cardiff, Wales, 1977 / edited by Alexander Fenton and Trefor M. Owen. — Edinburgh : Donald, c1981. — xii,425p : ill,maps ; 24cm
Includes bibliographies
ISBN 0-85976-044-8 : £20.00 B81-19313

641.3′0094 — Food: European dishes — *Encyclopaedias*

Major, Sally. Eating out : a guide to European dishes / Sally Major. — Newton Abbot : David & Charles, c1981. — 87p : ill ; 21cm
ISBN 0-7153-8056-7 : £1.95 : CIP rev.
B81-08916

641.3′00944 — Food: French dishes — *Encyclopaedias*

Nelson, Dawn. French / Dawn and Douglas Nelson. — London : Proteus, 1980. — 161p : ill ; 19cm. — (Diners′ dictionary)
ISBN 0-906071-32-1 : £2.95 B81-13994

641.3′00944 — France. Food — *For schools*

White, Fred, *1910-*. French food and customs / Fred White ; adapted from Simone Wyn Griffith′s A table!. — London : Hodder and Stoughton, 1981. — 46p : ill ; 25cm
ISBN 0-340-25898-5 (pbk) : £1.25 : CIP rev.
B81-06069

641.3′00944′7 — Food: South-west French dishes

Brown, Michael, *1931-*. Food and wine of south-west France : Bordeaux to the Pays Basque : a gastronomic guide / Michael and Sybil Brown. — London : Batsford, 1980. — 240p,[8]p of plates : col.ill,maps ; 26cm
Bibliography: p232-234. — Includes index
ISBN 0-7134-1847-8 : £12.50 B81-00985

641.3′02 — Health food

Bowen, Carol. A to Z of health foods / Carol Bowen. — London : Hamlyn Paperbacks, 1981, c1979. — 175p : ill ; 18cm. — (Hamlyn kitchen library)
Originally published: Feltham : Hamlyn, 1979. — Includes index
ISBN 0-600-20298-4 (pbk) : £1.50
Also classified at 641.5′637 B81-29241

Hewitt, James. Foods for health : a guide to natural nutrition / James Hewitt ; illustrated by Heather Sherratt. — Sevenoaks : Teach Yourself Books, 1981. — 200p : ill ; 20cm. — (Teach yourself books)
Bibliography: p195-197. — Includes index
ISBN 0-340-26749-6 (pbk) : £1.95 : CIP rev.
B81-18144

641.30′2 — Spirulina. Nutritional aspects

Hanssen, Maurice. Spirulina. — Wellingborough : Thorsons, Nov.1981. — [64]p
ISBN 0-7225-0742-9 (pbk) : £0.75 : CIP entry
B81-34210

641.3′02′0941 — Great Britain. Health food

The Health food guide / edited by Michael Balfour. — [Enl. ed.] / foreword by Len Deighton. — London : Pan, 1981. — 424p ; 20cm
Previous ed.: London : Garnstone Press, 1972
ISBN 0-330-25988-1 (pbk) : £1.95 B81-23561

641.3′31 — Great Britain. Bread & flour. Nutritional values — *Inquiry reports*

Panel on Bread, Flour and other Cereal Products. Nutritional aspects of bread and flour / report of the Panel on Bread, Flour and other Cereal Products, Committee on Medical Aspects of Food Policy. — London : H.M.S.O., 1981. — x,64p : ill ; 25cm. — (Report on health and social subjects ; 23)
At head of title: Department of Health and Social Security. — Bibliography: p55-64
ISBN 0-11-320757-3 (pbk) : £3.90 B81-27552

641.3′372 — Tea

Woodward, Nancy Hyden. Teas of the world / Nancy Hyden Woodward. — New York : Collier ; London : Collier Macmillan, c1980. — 184p : ill,ports ; 26cm
ISBN 0-02-082870-5 (pbk) : £3.95 B81-19594

641.3′37′2 — Tea

Wright, Carol. The pocket book of tea and coffee. — London : Evans, Oct.1981. — [128]p
ISBN 0-237-45586-2 (pbk) : £1.75 : CIP entry
Also classified at 641.3′37′3 B81-25781

641.3′373 — Coffee

Roden, Claudia. Coffee / Claudia Roden. — Harmondsworth : Penguin, 1981, c1977. — 136p : ill ; 20cm. — (Penguin handbooks)
Originally published: London : Faber, 1977. — Includes index
ISBN 0-14-046489-1 (pbk) : £1.75 B81-21003

641.3′37′3 — Coffee

Wright, Carol. The pocket book of tea and coffee. — London : Evans, Oct.1981. — [128]p
ISBN 0-237-45586-2 (pbk) : £1.75 : CIP entry
Primary classification 641.3′37′2 B81-25781

641.3′38 — Food & drinks. Flavourings. Nutritional aspects — *Conference proceedings*

Nutritive sweeteners. — London : Applied Science, Jan.1982. — [272]p
Conference papers
ISBN 0-85334-997-5 : £28.00 : CIP entry
B81-34787

641.3′382 — Cider vinegar

Charmine, Susan E.. About cider vinegar : the natural key to health and vitality / by Susan E. Charmine. — Wellingborough : Thorsons, 1980. — 64p ; 18cm
Includes index
ISBN 0-7225-0658-9 (pbk) : £0.75 B81-08256

641.3′383 — Spices

Hayes, Elizabeth S.. [Spices and herbs around the world]. Spices and herbs : lore & cookery / Elizabeth S. Hayes ; illustrations by J.M. Yeatts. — New York : Dover ; London : Constable, 1980, c1961. — 266p : ill ; 22cm
Originally published: Garden City, N.Y. : Doubleday, 1961. — Bibliography: p257-259. — Includes index
ISBN 0-486-24026-6 (pbk) : £1.95
Primary classification 641.3′57 B81-05389

Kybal, Jan. Herbs and spices / by Jan Kybal ; illustrated by Jiřina Kaplická ; [translated by Olga Kuthanová]. — London : Hamlyn, c1980. — 224p : ill(some col.),1map ; 22cm. — (A Hamlyn colour guide)
Translation from the Czech. — Includes index
ISBN 0-600-34613-7 : £2.95
Primary classification 641.3′57 B81-22053

Spices. — London : Longman, Apr.1981. — (Tropical agriculture series)
Vol.1. — [560]p
ISBN 0-582-46811-6 : £33.00 : CIP entry
B81-03827

Spices. — London : Longman, Apr.1981. — (Tropical agriculture series)
Vol.2. — [416]p
ISBN 0-582-46342-4 : £25.00 : CIP entry
B81-03826

641.3′383′0222 — Spices — *Illustrations*

Blamey, Philip. Herbs & spices : cook′s guide to 60 herbs and spices illustrated in colour - identification - cultivation - uses / [... painted and written by Philip and Marjorie Blamey]. — [London] : Fontana, 1979. — 1folded sheet ([12]p) : col.ill ; 25cm. — (Domino ; 13)
ISBN 0-00-685453-2 : £0.85
Also classified at 641.3′57′0222 B81-20264

641.3′57 — Herbs

Encyclopedia of herbs / [editor Renny Harrop] ; [designer Caroline Austin] ; [illustrated by Caroline Austin]. — London : Marshall Cavendish, 1977 (1979 printing). — 143p : col.ill ; 29cm
ISBN 0-85685-746-7 (pbk) : £1.99 B81-19568

Genders, Roy. The complete book of herbs and herb growing / Roy Genders. — London : Ward Lock, 1980. — 176p : ill(some col.) ; 26cm
Includes index
ISBN 0-7063-5780-9 : £6.95 : CIP rev. B80-04287

Hayes, Elizabeth S.. [Spices and herbs around the world]. Spices and herbs : lore & cookery / Elizabeth S. Hayes ; illustrations by J.M. Yeatts. — New York : Dover ; London : Constable, 1980, c1961. — 266p : ill ; 22cm
Originally published: Garden City, N.Y. : Doubleday, 1961. — Bibliography: p257-259. — Includes index
ISBN 0-486-24026-6 (pbk) : £1.95
Also classified at 641.3′383 B81-05389

Kybal, Jan. Herbs and spices / by Jan Kybal ; illustrated by Jiřina Kaplická ; [translated by Olga Kuthanová]. — London : Hamlyn, c1980. — 224p : ill(some col.),1map ; 22cm. — (A Hamlyn colour guide)
Translation from the Czech. — Includes index
ISBN 0-600-34613-7 : £2.95
Also classified at 641.3′383 B81-22053

Macleod, Dawn. Popular herbs : their history, growth and use / Dawn Macleod. — 2nd ed. — [London] : Duckworth, 1981. — xii,191p,[11]p of plates : ill ; 22cm
Previous ed.: published as A book of herbs. 1968. — Bibliography: p189-190
ISBN 0-7156-1526-2 (pbk) : Unpriced B81-30090

641.3′5′7 — Herbs

Rutherford, Meg. A pattern of herbs. — London : Allen & Unwin, May 1981. — [152]p
Originally published: 1975
ISBN 0-04-635011-x (pbk) : £2.95 : CIP entry B81-04348

641.3′57 — Herbs — *Field guides*

Sloover, Jacques de. Wild herbs. — Newton Abbot : David & Charles, Sept.1981. — [224]p
Translation of: Guide des herbes sauvages
ISBN 0-7153-8221-7 : £6.95 : CIP entry B81-21509

641.3′57 — Herbs. Use — *Manuals*

Ceres. Herbal teas, tisanes and lotions / by Ceres ; line illustrations by Juliet Renny and Alison Ross, colour photography by Paul Turner. — Wellingborough : Thorsons, 1981. — 128p,[8]p of plates : ill(some col.) ; 22cm
ISBN 0-7225-0677-5 (pbk) : £3.50 : CIP rev. B81-11927

Fenton, Joy. Herbs for health and happiness / Joy Fenton. — Ilfracombe : Stockwell, 1981. — 68p : ill ; 19cm
ISBN 0-7223-1442-6 (pbk) : £1.95 B81-25504

Law, Donald. The concise herbal encyclopedia. — Edinburgh : Bartholomew, Jan.1982. — [256]p
Originally published: 1973
ISBN 0-7028-8091-4 (pbk) : £4.95 : CIP entry B81-38290

641.3′57′0222 — Culinary herbs — *Illustrations*

Blamey, Philip. Herbs & spices : cook′s guide to 60 herbs and spices illustrated in colour - identification - cultivation - uses / [... painted and written by Philip and Marjorie Blamey]. — [London] : Fontana, 1979. — 1folded sheet ([12]p) : col.ill ; 25cm. — (Domino ; 13)
ISBN 0-00-685453-2 : £0.85
Primary classification 641.3′383′0222 B81-20264

641.3′6 — Meat

All about meat. — London (5 St. John′s Sq., Smithfield, EC1M 4DE) : Meat Promotion Executive of the Meat and Livestock Commission, [1981]. — 17p : ill(some col.) ; 21cm
Cover title. — Text on inside cover
Unpriced (pbk) B81-37397

641.3′73′0942 — English cheeses

Harper, Gerald. The Gerald Harper good cheese guide. — [London] ([National Dairy Centre, John Princes St., W1M 0AP]) : English Country Cheese Council, [1981?]. — 30p : col.ill,1col.map ; 21cm
Cover title
Unpriced (pbk) B81-27491

641.3′8 — Honey

Mellor, Isha. Honey / Isha Mellor ; illustrated by Rodney Shackell. — London : W.H. Allen, 1980. — 80p : ill ; 21cm
ISBN 0-491-02723-0 : £2.95 B81-00155

641.3′9′091822 — Mediterranean region. Seafood

Davidson, Alan, *1924-*. Mediterranean seafood : a handbook giving the names in seven languages of 150 species of fish, with 50 crustaceans, molluscs and other marine creatures, and an essay on fish cookery with over 200 recipes from the Mediterranean and Black Sea countries / Alan Davidson. — 2nd ed. — Harmondsworth : Penguin, 1981. — 429p : ill,1map ; 20cm
Previous ed.: 1972. — Bibliography: p397-402. — Includes index
ISBN 0-14-046174-4 (pbk) : £4.95 B81-40082

641.4 — Food. Preservation

Developments in food preservation. — London : Applied Science. — (The Developments series)
1. — Oct.1981. — [320]p
ISBN 0-85334-979-7 : £28.00 : CIP entry B81-25842

641.4 — Food. Preservation — *Amateurs′ manuals*

Good Housekeeping complete book of home preserving / Good Housekeeping Institute. — London : Ebury, 1981. — 192p : ill(some col.) ; 25cm
Includes index
ISBN 0-85223-198-9 : £8.50 B81-40157

Spoczynska, Joy O. I.. Self-sufficiency in a flat / Joy O.I. Spoczynska ; illustrated by Melchior Spoczynski. — London : Sphere, 1981, c1980. — 136p : ill ; 18cm
Originally published: London : Wildwood House, 1980
ISBN 0-7221-8089-6 (pbk) : £1.25
Primary classification 635 B81-35524

Westland, Pamela. Food for keeps : everything you need to know about preserving / Pamela Westland. — London : Granada, 1981. — 224p ; 18cm. — (A Mayflower book)
Includes index
ISBN 0-583-13334-7 (pbk) : £1.95 B81-37121

641.4′53 — Food. Deep freezing — *Amateurs′ manuals*

Major, Sally. Pocket A to Z guide to freezing food / by Sally Major. — London : Arlington, 1981. — 151p ; 13cm
ISBN 0-85140-530-4 (pbk) : £0.85 B81-15065

641.5 — COOKERY

641.5 — Cookery — *For children*

Picton, Margaret. Understanding cookery / Margaret Picton. — 3rd ed. — London : Blackie, 1980. — 189p : col.ill ; 22cm
Previous ed.: i.e. Revised metric ed. 1975
ISBN 0-216-91050-1 (pbk) : £3.50 B81-02729

641.5 — Cookery — *Manuals*

Haselgrove, N. M.. The how and why of cookery / by N.M. Haselgrove and K.A. Scallon. — 4th ed. / extensively revised ... by Jennifer Kelly. — London : Granada, 1981. — 168p : ill ; 25cm
Previous ed.: St. Albans : Hart-Davis, MacGibbon, 1976. — Includes index
ISBN 0-246-11497-5 : £5.95 B81-21686

Leith, Prudence. The cook′s handbook / Prue Leith. — Leicester : Windward, c1981. — 224p : ill ; 27cm
Bibliography: p223. - Includes index
ISBN 0-7112-0058-0 : £6.95 B81-11644

Waldegrave, Caroline. Basic cooking skills / Caroline Waldegrave ; with an introduction by Prue Leith. — Cambridge : Published for J Sainsbury Limited by Woodhead-Faulkner, c1981. — 40p : ill ; 20cm. — (Sainsbury′s food guides ; no.9)
Cover title
£0.30 (pbk) B81-35753

641.5 — Cookery — *Manuals* — *For schools*

Creese, Angela. Revision notes for 'O' Level and CSE cookery. — 3rd ed. — London : Bell & Hyman, Oct.1981. — [96]p. — (Allman revision notes)
Previous ed.: 1974
ISBN 0-7135-2207-0 (pbk) : £1.50 : CIP entry B81-30464

Forsyth, Anne. Beginning cookery. — London : Bell & Hyman, Nov.1981. — [80]p
ISBN 0-7135-1275-x (pbk) : £2.95 : CIP entry B81-30387

Haselgrove, N. M.. The how and why of cookery : an O-level cookery course / by N.M. Haselgrove and K.A. Scallon. — 4th ed. / extensively rev. by Jennifer Kelly. — St. Albans : Hart-Davis Educational, 1981. — 168p : ill,plans ; 25cm
Previous ed.: 1976. — Includes index
ISBN 0-247-13096-6 (pbk) : £2.85 B81-24462

641.5 — Food: Dishes for families with babies — *Recipes*

Yates, Annette. The babyfood and family cookbook / Annette Yates ; edited by Mary Norwak. — London : Foulsham, c1980. — 95p : ill ; 22cm
Includes index
ISBN 0-572-01036-2 (pbk) : £1.95 B81-07011

641.5 — Food: Dishes prepared using limited cooking facilities — *Recipes*

Whitehorn, Katharine. [Kitchen in the corner]. Cooking in a bedsitter / Katharine Whitehorn. — Harmondsworth : Penguin, 1963, c1961 (1981 [printing]). — 192p ; 19cm. — (Penguin handbooks)
Originally published: London : MacGibbon & Kee, 1961. — Includes index
ISBN 0-14-046086-1 (pbk) : £1.35 B81-16989

641.5 — Food — *Recipes*

The **Art** of cooking. — London : Marshall Cavendish, 1979. — 296p : col.ill ; 30cm
Ill on lining papers. — Includes index
ISBN 0-85685-477-8 : £7.95 B81-17576

Barker, Alex. Woman′s own cookbook : a new complete guide to family cooking / by Alex Barker. — London : Hamlyn, c1981. — 256p : ill(some col.) ; 27cm
Includes index
ISBN 0-600-39295-3 : £5.95 B81-29124

Beeton, *Mrs.*. Mrs Beeton′s cookery and household management. — [New ed.]. — London : Ward Lock, 1980. — 1606p,[60]p of plates : ill(some col.),plans ; 26cm
Previous ed.: published as Cookery and household management, 1960. — Includes index
ISBN 0-7063-5743-4 : £14.95
Primary classification 640 B81-12033

641.5 — Food — *Recipes* *continuation*

Blackwood, Caroline. Darling, you shouldn't have gone to so much trouble / Caroline Blackwood and Anna Haycraft ; drawings by Zé. — London : Cape, 1980. — 224p : ill ; 23cm
Includes index
ISBN 0-224-01834-5 : £6.50 : CIP rev. B80-20815

The **Campus** cookbook : over 90 simple, tasty recipes / edited by David J. Lock and Hilary J. Lotinga. — Bath : Bath University Press, 1980. — 72p : ill ; 21cm
Includes index
ISBN 0-86197-024-1 : Unpriced B81-00156

Ceserani, Victor. Practical cookery / Victor Ceserani, Ronald Kinton. — 5th ed. — London : Edward Arnold, 1981. — v,415p : ill ; 23cm
Previous ed.: 1974. — Includes index
ISBN 0-7131-0509-7 : £4.95 B81-18482

Chatto, James. The seducer's cookbook. — Newton Abbot : David & Charles, Oct.1981. — [64]p
ISBN 0-7153-8201-2 (pbk) : £3.95 : CIP entry B81-28126

Child, Julia. From Julia Child's kitchen / Julia Child ; photographs and drawings by Paul Child ; additional technical photographs by Albie Walton. — Harmondsworth : Penguin, 1981, c1978. — xiii,640p : ill ; 20cm. — (Penguin handbooks)
Previous ed.: New York : Knopf, 1975. — Includes index
ISBN 0-14-046371-2 (pbk) : £3.95 B81-21041

Christian, Glynn. The LBC radio cookbook. — London : Jill Norman and Hobhouse, Nov.1981. — [80]p
ISBN 0-906908-77-9 (pbk) : £1.95 : CIP entry B81-33634

Coles, Angela. The reluctant cook / Angela Coles. — Weybridge : Whittet, 1980. — 192p : ill ; 25cm
Includes index
ISBN 0-905483-18-9 : £5.95 : CIP rev. B80-22169

Conil, Jean. Variations on a recipe : how to create your own original dishes / by Jean Conil and Hugh Williams. — Loughton ([17 Brook Rd., Loughton, Essex IG10 1BW]) : Piatkus, 1980. — 128p : ill ; 23cm
ISBN 0-86188-060-9 (corrected) : £4.95 : CIP rev. B80-13890

Conil, Jean. Variations on a recipe : how to create your own original dishes / Jean Conil and Hugh Williams. — London : New English Library, 1981, c1980. — 128p : ill ; 20cm. — (New English Library books for cooks)
Originally published: Loughton : Piatkus, 1980
ISBN 0-450-05059-9 (pbk) : £1.25 B81-17196

Cooking for today. — London : IPC Magazines, c1980. — 192p : ill ; 18cm
At head of cover title: Woman's weekly. — Includes index
£0.50 (pbk) B81-17294

Cox, Nicola. Good food from Farthinghoe / Nicola Cox ; with line illustrations by David Green. — London : Gollancz in association with Peter Crawley, 1981. — 256p : ill ; 26cm
Includes index
ISBN 0-575-02979-x : £8.50 B81-27256

Davenport, Philippa. Davenport's dishes. — London : Jill Norman, July 1981. — [160]p
ISBN 0-906908-47-7 (cased) : £6.50 : CIP entry
ISBN 0-906908-48-5 (pbk) : £3.50 B81-15898

Davies, Louise. Easy cooking for three or more / Louise Davies ; illustrated by Tony Odell. — Harmondsworth : Penguin, 1975 (1981 [printing]). — 234p : ill ; 20cm. — (Penguin handbooks)
Includes index
ISBN 0-14-046219-8 (pbk) : £1.50 B81-21007

Deghy, Guy. The new gourmet : a cookbook for the eighties / Guy Deghy ; illustrations by Norman Mansbridge. — London : Dent, 1980. — 207p : ill ; 23
Includes index
ISBN 0-460-04399-4 (pbk) : £5.95 : CIP rev. B80-18834

Dimbleby, Josceline. A taste of dreams / Josceline Dimbleby ; illustrations by Peggy Chapman. — London : Sphere, [1980]. — 143p : ill ; 25cm
Originally published: / with illustrations by Nicholas Dimbleby. London : Hodder and Stoughton, 1976. — Includes index
ISBN 0-7221-2988-2 (pbk) : £2.95 B81-00157

Elliot, Rose. Your very good health / Rose Elliot. — [London] : Fontana, 1981. — xvi,207p ; 20cm
Includes index
ISBN 0-00-636205-2 (pbk) : £1.95 B81-34918

Fulton, Margaret. Cooking for pleasure : over 550 delicious recipes / Margaret Fulton. — [London] : Octopus, 1981. — 350p : ill(some col.) ; 30cm
Ill on lining papers. — Includes index
ISBN 0-7064-1402-0 : £5.95 B81-24950

The **Good** housekeeping step-by-step cookbook / [editor-in-chief Gill Edden]. — London : Ebury, 1980. — 512p,[16]p of plates : ill (some col.) ; 29cm
Includes index
ISBN 0-85223-159-8 : £14.95 B81-00986

Hambro, Nathalie. Particular delights. — London : Jill Norman, Oct.1981. — [144]p
ISBN 0-906908-34-5 : £6.95 : CIP entry B81-27460

Hanbury Tenison, Marika. The Sunday telegraph cookbook / Marika Hanbury Tenison ; illustrated by Ursula Sieger ; photographs by Bob Croxford. — London : Granada, 1980. — vii,279p,[30]p of plates : ill(some col.) ; 26cm
Includes index
ISBN 0-246-11127-5 : £9.95 B81-00987

Hillman, Libby. [Lessons in gourmet cooking]. Libby Hillman's gourmet cookbook : 434 easy-to-prepare recipes / by Libby Hillman. — New York : Dover ; London : Constable, 1980, c1971. — 356p : ill ; 22cm. — (Dover cookbooks)
Originally published: New York : Hearthside Press, 1963. — Includes index
ISBN 0-486-23994-2 (pbk) : £2.50 B81-07294

Howe, Robin. International cooking / Robin Howe. — London (36 Park St., W1Y 4DE) : Park Lane Press, 1980. — 192p : col.ill ; 19cm
Ill on lining papers. — Includes index
£3.75 B81-00158

Hume, Rosemary. Penguin cordon bleu cookery / Rosemary Hume and Muriel Downes ; illustrated by Juliet Renny. — Harmondsworth : Penguin, 1963 (1981 [printing]). — 508p : ill ; 20cm
Includes index
ISBN 0-14-046097-7 (pbk) : £1.95 B81-27660

Hume, Rosemary. [Penguin Cordon Bleu cookery]. Cordon Bleu cookery / Rosemary Hume & Muriel Downes. — London : Macdonald Phoebus, c1981. — 284p : col.ill ; 30cm
Originally published: Harmondsworth : Penguin, 1963. — Includes index
ISBN 0-356-07564-8 (pbk) : £4.95 B81-37812

Kerr, Graham. The new seasoning / Graham Kerr. — 2nd ed. — Tring : Lion, 1981, c1976. — 238p : ill ; 18cm
Previous ed.: New York : Simon and Schuster, 1976 ; Berkhamsted : Lion, 1977. — Includes index
ISBN 0-85648-362-1 (pbk) : £1.50 B81-17015

Leith, Prudence. Leith's cookery course / Prudence Leith and Caroline Waldegrave. — London : Deutsch, 1980, c1979. — 787p,[32]p of plates : ill(some col.) ; 24cm
Originally published: in 3 vols. London : Fontana, 1979-1980. — Includes index
ISBN 0-233-97153-x : £12.50 B81-00988

Lincoln Cathedral cookery book. — [Lincoln] : The Cathedral, 1980. — vi,198p : ill ; 22cm
Includes index
ISBN 0-9502690-2-6 (spiral) : Unpriced B81-10639

Nilson, Bee. The Penguin cookery book / Bee Nilson. — 3rd ed. — London : Allen Lane, 1980, c1972. — 479p,[16]p of plates : ill(some col.) ; 23cm
Previous ed.: 1972. — Includes index
ISBN 0-7139-1378-9 : £7.50 B81-08459

The **Opera** House cookbook / compiled by Robin Hambro ; with a foreword by Sir Geraint Evans ; illustrated by Simon Gooch. — London : Weidenfeld and Nicolson, c1980. — 223p : ill,ports ; 24cm
Includes index
ISBN 0-297-77806-4 : £7.95 B81-00160

O'Sullivan, Richard. Man about the kitchen / by Richard O'Sullivan ; with cartoons by Larry. — London (Elm House, Elm St., WC1X 0BP) : Circle, [1980?]. — 95p : ill,ports ; 22cm
Includes index
ISBN 0-907120-01-6 : £4.95 B81-00161

Parkes, Antoinette. The country weekend cookbook. — London : Collins, Oct.1981. — [230]p
ISBN 0-00-216318-7 : £9.95 : CIP entry B81-24586

Patten, Marguerite. Cooking in pictures / Marguerite Patten ; [illustrations by Gabrielle Stoddart]. — London : Mirror Books, 1981. — 215p : ill ; 18cm
ISBN 0-85939-250-3 (pbk) : £1.25 B81-05983

Patten, Marguerite. Dear diary / Marguerite Patten. — London : Mirror, 1980. — 287p : ill ; 18cm
Includes index
ISBN 0-85939-229-5 (pbk) : £1.75 B81-00989

Pomeroy, Elizabeth. [St Michael better cooking step-by-step]. Cooking step-by-step / Elizabeth Pomeroy. — London : Octopus, 1981 c1978. — 157p : col.ill ; 28cm
Originally published: London : Sundial, 1978. — Includes index
ISBN 0-7064-1587-6 (pbk) : £1.99 B81-34833

Ray, Elizabeth. Good housekeeping country cooking / Elizabeth Ray. — London : Ebury, 1979. — 320p,[16]p of plates : ill(some col.),maps ; 25cm
Text, maps on lining papers. — Includes index
ISBN 0-85223-145-8 : £7.95 B81-09520

Royal College of Art cook book / [compiled and edited at the Royal College of Art by Joan Catlin and Joy Law]. — London : RCA, 1980. — [156]p : ill ; 21cm
ISBN 0-902490-50-8 (spiral) : Unpriced B81-07884

A **second** helping from the Oxfordshire kitchen / [compiled by Gwyn Owen from contributions by members of CPRE Oxfordshire] ; [illustrated by Peggy de Buriatte]. — [London] ([4 Hobart Place, SW1W 0HY]) : [Council for the Protection of Rural England], [1981?]. — 44p : ill ; 21cm
Text and ill on inside covers
Unpriced (pbk) B81-34979

Smith, Beverley Sutherland. A taste of class / Beverley Sutherland Smith ; photographer Ray Joyce. — Sydney ; London : Summit, [1980]. — 159p : col.ill ; 29cm
Includes index
ISBN 0-7271-0503-5 : £4.95 B81-00159

641.5 — Food — *Recipes* *continuation*

Smith, Delia. Delia Smith's cookery course. — London : British Broadcasting Corporation
Pt.3. — 1981. — viiip,p490-720 : ill(some col.) ; 23cm
Bibliography: p707-708. - Includes index
ISBN 0-563-16456-5 (pbk) : £4.25 B81-15474

Smith, Mari. Simple kitchen skills and recipes. — London : Edward Arnold, Jan.1982. — [64]p
ISBN 0-7131-0566-6 (pbk) : £1.75(non-net) : CIP entry B81-33886

Smith, Michael, *1929-*. Cooking with Michael Smith. — London : Dent, 1981. — 214p,[16]p of plates : ill(same col.) ; 26cm
Includes index
ISBN 0-460-04461-3 : £9.95 : CIP rev. B81-05149

Taylor, Sally. Andy & Flo's cookery book / compiled by Sally Taylor ; cartoons by Reg Smythe. — London : Mirror, 1980. — 158p : ill ; 18cm
ISBN 0-85939-131-0 (pbk) : £0.85 B81-07182

Tyn-y-Rhos cook book. — [Oswestry] ([Tyn-y-Rhos Hall, Weston Rhyn, Oswestry, Salop]) : [M. Thompson-Butler-Lloyd], [1981?]. — [32]p ; 21cm
Cover title
Unpriced (pbk) B81-33552

Webber, Kathie. Cooking with unusual foods / Kathie Webber ; line drawings by Oriol Bath-David Lewis Associates. — London : Sidgwick & Jackson, 1981. — 185p : ill ; 24cm
Text, ill on lining papers. — Includes index
ISBN 0-283-98719-7 : £6.95 B81-12293

West, Elizabeth. Kitchen in the hills. — London : Faber, Oct.1981. — [192]p
ISBN 0-571-11709-0 : £5.95 : CIP entry B81-28029

What's cooking in the N.L.S. / compiled by Jean Grainge, Rhona Paterson. — [Musselburgh] ([11, Eskside East, Musselburgh, Midlothian]) : Derek Grainge, c1981. — 36p ; 22cm
ISBN 0-9507581-0-8 (pbk) : £0.80 B81-38395

Wolfenden, Joan. Recipes to relish : good cooking & entertaining at home / by Joan Wolfenden. — London : Pelham, 1981, c1979. — 175p : col.ill ; 24cm
Originally published: Bonchurch, I.O.W. : Peacock Vane, 1979. — Text, ill on lining papers. — Includes index
ISBN 0-7207-1303-x : £7.50 B81-11806

Wright, Carol. The holiday cook : recipes and shopping away from home / Carol Wright. — Newton Abbot : David & Charles, c1981. — 160p ; 23cm
Includes index
ISBN 0-7153-8017-6 : £4.95
Also classified at 641.3 B81-08702

641.5 — Food — *Recipes — Early works*

Martha Washington's Booke of Cookery ; and Booke of sweetmeats : being a family manuscript, curiously copied by an unknown hand sometime in the seventeenth century, which was in her keeping from 1749 ... : transcribed by Karen Hess with historical notes and copious annotations. — New York ; Guildford : Columbia University Press, 1981. — ix,518p : facsims ; 24cm
Bibliography: p469-489. — Includes index
ISBN 0-231-04930-7 : £12.35 B81-24012

641.5 — Food. Recipes — *Facsimiles*

Bradley, Richard, *1688-1732*. The country housewife and lady's director / by Richard Bradley ; furnished with an introduction, a list of recipe contributors, a glossary, notes, and bibliography by Caroline Davidson. — London : 45 Lamond Rd., SW10 0HU : Prospect Books, 1980. — 1v.(various pagings) : ill,2col maps,1facsim,1port ; 22cm
Facsim of: ed. published London : s.n., 1736. — Maps on lining papers. — Includes index
ISBN 0-907325-01-7 : £18.00 B81-09553

641.5 — Food — *Recipes — For children*

Feasts : for special or greedy days / written and produced by McPhee Gribble Publishers ; illustrated by David Lancashire. — Harmondsworth : Puffin, 1976, c1979 (1979 [printing]). — [32]p : ill(some col.) ; 20cm. — (Practical puffins ; 16)
ISBN 0-14-049165-1 (pbk) : £0.80 B81-01741

First steps in cooking. — London : Ward Lock, June 1981. — [48]p
ISBN 0-7063-6081-8 : £2.95 : CIP entry B81-12879

Neat eats / recipes supplied and tested by the Good Housekeeping Institute ; illustrated by Colin Mier. — London : Ebury Press, 1981. — 61p : col.ill ; 30cm
Includes index
ISBN 0-85223-157-1 : £3.95 B81-39651

641.5 — Food — *Recipes — For schools*

King, Aileen. Better cookery. — London : Bell & Hyman, Sept.1981. — [512]p
ISBN 0-7135-2053-1 (cascd) : £4.95 : CIP entry
ISBN 0-7135-2055-8 (pbk) : £3.90 B81-28205

641.5'028 — Cookery. Techniques — *Manuals — For physically handicapped persons*

Ellis, Audrey. Cooking made easy for disabled people / Audrey Ellis ; foreword by Anne Davies. — Cambridge : Published for J. Sainsbury Limited by Woodhead-Faulkner, 1981. — 32p : ill ; 21cm. — (Sainsbury's food guides ; no.8)
Cover title. — Text on inside cover. — Bibliography: p32
£0.30 (pbk) B81-37268

641.5'03'21 — Cookery — *Encyclopaedias*

Stobart, Tom. The cook's encyclopaedia : ingredients and processes / Tom Stobart. — London : Batsford, 1980. — 463p ; 26cm
ISBN 0-7134-0910-x : £12.50 B81-00162

641.5'076 — Cookery — *Questions & answers*

Ceserani, Victor. Questions on practical cookery / Victor Ceserani, Ronald Kinton. — 2nd ed. — London : Edward Arnold, 1981. — 96p : ill ; 22cm
Previous ed.: 1976
ISBN 0-7131-0563-1 (pbk) : £1.95 B81-21767

641.5'09'03 — Food, *1650-1900 — Recipes*

Grigson, Jane. Food with the famous / Jane Grigson. — Harmondsworth : Penguin, 1981, c1979. — 256p : 1ill,ports ; 20cm. — (Penguin handbooks)
Originally published: London : Joseph, 1979. — Includes index
ISBN 0-14-046444-1 (pbk) : £2.50 B81-21040

641.5'0941 — Great Britain. Rural regions. Restaurants. Food — *Recipes*

Kent, Elizabeth. Country cuisine : cooking with country chefs / Elizabeth Kent ; wines chosen by Jancis Robinson ; special illustrations by Jane Jamieson. — London : Sidgwick & Jackson, 1980. — 415p : ill,map ; 24cm
Bibliography: p406. — Includes index
ISBN 0-283-98636-0 : £9.95 B81-01930

641.5'3 — Suppers — *Recipes*

[Complete cookery. *Selections*]. Easy supper dishes. — Maidenhead : Purnell, 1981. — 47p : ill ; 26cm. — (Purnell jiffy cook series)
Originally published: as part of Complete cookery. — Includes index
ISBN 0-361-05019-4 (pbk) : £0.99 B81-14672

641.5'52 — Food: Inexpensive dishes: Dishes prepared using Magimix Food processors — *Recipes*

Patten, Marguerite. The A-Z of economy with Magimix : 68 recipes written for food processors / by Marguerite Patten. — Isleworth (25 Lower Sq., Isleworth, Middx) : 1CTC, [1981?]. — 36p ; 15x22cm
Cover title
Unpriced (spiral) B81-37674

641.5'52 — Food: Inexpensive dishes: Dishes prepared using Robot-chef food processors — *Recipes*

Patten, Marguerite. The A-Z of economy with Robot-Chef : 68 recipes written for food processors / by Marguerite Patten. — Isleworth (25 Lower Sq., Isleworth, Middx) : 1CTC, [1981?. — 36p ; 15x22cm
Cover title
Unpriced (spiral) B81-3767

641.5'52 — Food: Inexpensive dishes — *Recipes*

Duff, Gail. Cooking on a shoestring / Gail Duff. — London : Pan in association with Macmillan, 1981, c1979. — 314p ; 20cm
Originally published: London : Macmillan, 1979. — Includes index
ISBN 0-330-26238-6 (pbk) : £1.95 B81-0299

Goode, Shirley. More for your money / Shirley Goode and Erica Griffiths ; illustrations by M.J. Mott. — Harmondsworth : Penguin, 1981. — vi,237p : ill ; 20cm. — (Penguin handbooks)
Includes index
ISBN 0-14-046426-3 (pbk) : £1.95 B81-2101

Innes, Jocasta. The pauper's cookbook / Jocasta Innes. — Repr. with revisions. — Harmondsworth : Penguin, 1981, c1971. — 238p ; 20cm. — (Penguin handbooks)
Includes index
ISBN 0-14-046164-7 (pbk) B81-2103

McMillan, Norma. Budget family cooking / [recipes Norma McMillan]. — London : Marshall Cavendish, [1981]. — 96p : ill(some col.) ; 22cm. — (Supercook's Kitchen)
Includes index
ISBN 0-85685-724-6 (pbk) : £0.99 B81-1757

Nilsen, Angela. Just like mother used to make : food from the '30s and '40s / compiled by Angela Nilsen and June Weatherall ; designed by Ian Escott ; photographs by Studio Lorenzini ; hand-colouring by Michael Barton. — London (Elm House, Elm St., WC1X 0BP) : Circle, 1980. — 128p : ill(some col.),facsims,ports ; 26cm
Includes index
ISBN 0-907120-02-4 : £6.95 B81-0016

Rivers, Patrick. Diet for a small island / by Patrick and Shirley Rivers. — Wellingborough : Turnstone, 1981. — 255p : ill,maps ; 22cm
Bibliography: p251-252. — Includes index
ISBN 0-85500-137-2 (pbk) : £4.50 : CIP rev.
Also classified at 641.5'637 B81-1917

641.5'55 — Food: Time-saving dishes — *Recipes*

Bracken, Peg. The I still hate to cook book / Pe Bracken ; illustrated by Hilary Knight. — [London] : Corgi, 1980, c1966. — 156p : ill ; 18cm
Originally published: London : Arlington, 1967 — Includes index
ISBN 0-552-11544-4 (pbk) : £1.35 B81-0702

Fast food / edited by Alison Kerr. — London : Octopus, 1981. — 77p : col.ill ; 27cm
Ill on lining papers. — Includes index
ISBN 0-7064-1510-8 : £1.99 B81-3483

Stone, Su. Entertaining without hassle / Su Stone. — Ilfracombe : Stockwell, 1981. — 77p : ill ; 19cm
Includes index
ISBN 0-7223-1491-4 : £4.00 B81-3997

Westland, Pamela. The 60-minute cookbook / by Pamela Westland. — London : Faber, 1980. — 191p,[8]p of plates : ill(some col.) ; 26cm
Includes index
ISBN 0-571-11554-3 (cased) : £7.95 : CIP rev.
ISBN 0-571-11555-1 (pbk) : £2.50 B80-1781

641.5'61 — Food: Dishes for one person — *Recipes*

Beaulieu, Mirelle. Cooking for myself / Mirelle Beaulieu. — South Yarmouth, Mass. : John Curley ; [Skipton] : Distributed by Magna Print, 1979, c1979. — 223p ; 23cm
Translation of: Je cuisine pour moi. — Published in large print. — Includes index
ISBN 0-89340-191-9 : £5.25 B81-4022

641.5′61 — Food: Dishes for one person — *Recipes* *continuation*

Brostoff, Deanna. Food for one : eating and cooking on your own / Deanna Brostoff. — Cambridge : Published for J. Sainsbury Limited by Woodhead-Faulkner, 1979 (1980 [printing]). — 32p : ill ; 22cm. — (Sainsbury′s food guides ; no.1)
Cover title. — Text on inside cover
£0.30 (pbk) B81-37261

641.5′61 — Food: Dishes for two persons — *Recipes*

Cooking for two / [edited by Yvonne Deutch]. — London : Marshall Cavendish, 1978 (1979 printing). — 144p : col.ill ; 29cm
ISBN 0-85685-747-5 (pbk) : £1.90 B81-17579

641.5′622 — Babies. Food: Dishes using natural food — *Recipes*

Castle, Sue. The complete guide to preparing baby foods / Sue Castle. — Rev. ed. — [London] : Magnum, 1980, c1973. — 255p ; 20cm
Previous ed.: Garden City, N.Y. : Doubleday, 1973. — Includes index
ISBN 0-417-04580-8 (pbk) : £1.75 B81-07280

641.5′622 — Babies. Food — *Recipes*

McLean, Paula. Good food for babies and toddlers / Paula McLean. — London : Angus & Robertson, c1979. — 71p : ill ; 20cm
Bibliography: p68. — Includes index
ISBN 0-207-13833-8 (pbk) : £1.95 B81-31658

641.5′622 — Children. Food — *Recipes*

Berry, Mary, *1935-*. Food for children / Mary Berry. — Cambridge : Published for J. Sainsbury Limited by Woodhead-Faulkner, 1980 (1981 [printing]). — 32p : ill ; 21cm. — (Sainsbury′s food guides ; no.6)
Cover title. — Text on inside cover
£0.30 (pbk) B81-37266

641.5′622 — Children. Health food dishes — *Recipes*

Young, Mala. Children′s meals / [Mala Young] ; [illustrated by Susan Neale]. — Newton Abbot : David & Charles, c1981. — 48p : ill ; 21cm. — (Health food cooking)
ISBN 0-7153-8037-0 (pbk) : £1.50 B81-12730

641.5′622 — Food — *Recipes* — *For playgroups*

Fun and food for playgroups / illustrated by Stephen Grizzell. — 4th ed. — [Birmingham] ([PPA West Midlands Regional Office, 6 Princes Chambers, Corporation St., Birmingham B2 4RN]) : West Midlands Pre-School Playgroup Association, 1980. — 33p : ill ; 16x22cm
Previous ed.: 1979. — Bibliography: p33
ISBN 0-901755-21-4 (pbk) : Unpriced B81-07331

641.5′63 — Food for special diets — *Recipes*

Leslie, Jill. Modified diets : coping with special needs in the family / Jill Leslie for the British Nutrition Foundation. — Cambridge : Published for J. Sainsbury Limited by Woodhead-Faulkner, c1980. — 32p : ill ; 22cm. — (Sainsbury′s food guides ; no.5)
Cover title. — Text on inside cover. — Bibliography: p32
£0.30 (pbk) B81-37267

641.5′63 — Food: Low cholesterol dishes — *Recipes*

Ringrose, Helen. Healthy heart cookbook / Helen Ringrose. — Sydney ; London : Summit, 1978. — 207p : ill ; 29cm
Includes index
ISBN 0-7271-0351-2 : Unpriced B81-00990

641.5′63 — Food: Macrobiotic dishes — *Recipes*

Esko, Edward. Macrobiotic cooking for everyone / Edward & Wendy Esko. — Tokyo : Japan Publications ; Hemel Hempstead : International Book Distributors [distributor], 1980. — 272p : ill ; 26cm
Bibliography: p271-272
ISBN 0-87040-469-5 (pbk) : £9.30 B81-28470

641.5′63 — Slimmers. Food: Main courses — *Recipes*

Hughes, Joyce. Slimming magazine′s main meal cookbook / Joyce Hughes and Audrey Eyton. — London : Arrow, 1980. — 188p : ill ; 18cm. — (Slimming magazine handbooks ; no.3)
Includes index
ISBN 0-09-924430-6 (pbk) : £1.00 B81-02890

641.5′63 — Slimmers. Food: Convenience food dishes — *Recipes*

Hughes, Joyce. Slimming magazine′s quick food diet book / Joyce Hughes and Audrey Eyton. — London : Arrow, 1980. — 137p : ill ; 18cm. — (Slimming magazine handbooks ; no.4)
Includes index
ISBN 0-09-924440-3 (pbk) : £1.00 B81-02891

641.5′631 — Migraine sufferers. Food — *Recipes*

Hills, Hilda Cherry. Good food to fight migraine / by Hilda Cherry Hills. — London (225 Putney Bridge Rd., London SW15 2PY) : Roberts Publications, 1979. — 173p : ill ; 21cm
Cover title. — Includes index
ISBN 0-906185-09-2 (pbk) : Unpriced B81-09252

Wentworth, Josie A.. The migraine guide & cookbook / Josie A. Wentworth ; introduction by Katharina Dalton. — London : Sidgwick & Jackson, 1981. — 237p : ill,forms ; 23cm
Bibliography: p228-231. - Includes index
ISBN 0-283-98741-3 : £6.95
Also classified at 616.8′57071 B81-17649

641.5′631 — Sick persons. Food — *Recipes*

Nilson, Bee. Cooking for special diets / Bee Nilson. — 3rd ed. — Harmondsworth : Penguin, c1981. — 479p : ill ; 20cm. — (Penguin handbooks)
Previous ed.: 1971. — Includes index
ISBN 0-14-046095-0 (pbk) : £3.95 B81-25443

641.5′6314 — Diabetics. Food — *Recipes*

Family cookbook / the American Diabetes Association, the American Dietetic Association ; illustrated by Lauren Rosen. — Englewood Cliffs ; London : Prentice-Hall, c1980. — xvi,391p : ill ; 25cm
Includes index
ISBN 0-13-024901-7 : Unpriced B81-16669

Taylor, Elisabeth Russell. The diabetic cookbook / Elisabeth Russell Taylor. — London : Hamlyn, 1981. — 128p : ill(some col.) ; 23cm
Includes index
ISBN 0-600-32249-1 : £3.50 B81-38556

641.5′635 — Food: Dishes prepared using microwave ovens: Low calorie dishes — *Recipes*

Microwave cooking. — Minneapolis : Litton Microwave Cooking Products ; New York ; London : Van Nostrand Reinhold
Vol.6: On a diet / [Litton Microwave Cooking Center]. — 1980. — 160p : col.ill ; 29cm
Includes index
ISBN 0-442-24526-2 : £8.20 B81-21387

641.5′635 — Slimmers. Food: Dishes prepared using Magimix food processors — *Recipes*

Hanbury Tenison, Marika. Slimming with Magimix : 64 recipes written for food processors / by Marika Hanbury Tenison. — Isleworth (25 Lower Sq., Isleworth, Middx) : 1CTC, 1980 (1981 [printing]). — 47p ; 15x22cm
Cover title
ISBN 0-9506518-4-2 (spiral) : Unpriced B81-37682

641.5′635 — Slimmers. Food — *Recipes*

[Complete cookery. *Selections*]. Cooking for slimmers. — Maidenhead : Purnell, 1981. — 47p : ill ; 26cm. — (Purnell jiffy cook series)
Originally published: as part of Complete cookery. — Includes index
ISBN 0-361-05018-6 (pbk) : £0.99 B81-14671

Nidetch, Jean. Weight Watchers programme cookbook / by Jean Nidetch. — London : New English Library, c1980. — 368p,[8]p of plates ; col.ill ; 24cm
Originally published: Great Neck, N.Y. : Hearthside, 1976. — Includes index
ISBN 0-450-04831-4 : £5.95 B81-03445

Norman, Cecilia. The sociable slimmer′s cookbook / Cecilia Norman ; illustrated by Kate Simunek photographs by Roger Tuff. — London : Hutchinson, 1981. — 236p,[8]p of plates : ill(some col.) ; 23cm
Includes index
ISBN 0-09-143110-7 : £6.95 B81-08433

Pappas, Lou Seibert. Gourmet cooking : the slim way / Lou Seibert Pappas ; [drawings by Robert Rose]. — London : Evans, 1980, c1977. — 193p : ill ; 22cm
Originally published: Reading, Mass. ; London : Addison-Wesley, 1977. — Includes index
ISBN 0-237-44960-9 : £6.75 B81-00991

Slim & trim cookbook / consultant nutritionist Jenny Salmon. — London : Hamlyn, c1981. — 144p : ill(some col.) ; 25cm
Includes index
ISBN 0-600-32229-7 : £4.50 B81-22054

641.5′636 — Vegetarians. Food — *Recipes*

Dutton, Dave. The vegetarian cookbook / Dave Dutton. — Feltham : Hamlyn Paperbacks, 1981. — 208p : ill ; 18cm
Includes index
ISBN 0-600-20197-x (pbk) : £1.50 B81-32352

Elliot, Rose. Vegetarian dishes of the world / Rose Elliot. — London : Collins, 1981. — 352p ; 27cm
Includes index
ISBN 0-00-411231-8 : £8.95 B81-40579

Scott, David, *1944-*. Grains! Beans! Nuts! / David Scott ; illustrated by Steve Hardstaff. — London : Rider, 1980. — 264p : ill ; 24cm
Bibliography: p255-256. — Includes index
ISBN 0-09-141681-7 (pbk) : £5.95 : CIP rev. B80-07868

641.5′636′0956 — Vegetarians. Food: Middle Eastern dishes — *Recipes*

Scott, David, *1944-*. Middle Eastern vegetarian cookery / David Scott ; illustrated by Steve Hardstaff. — London : Rider, 1981. — 176p : ill ; 24cm
Bibliography: p170. — Includes index
ISBN 0-09-145341-0 (pbk) : £4.95 : CIP rev. B81-12321

641.5′637 — Food: Dishes using natural foods — *Recipes*

Bateman, Michael. The Sunday times guide to the world′s best food / Michael Bateman, Caroline Conran, Oliver Gillie ; illustrations by Susan J. Curtis ; photography by Christine Hanscomb. — London : Hutchinson, 1981. — 246p,[8]p of plates : ill(some col.) ; 28cm
Includes index
ISBN 0-09-143890-x : £9.95 B81-21416

Black, Maggie. Eating naturally : recipes for food with fibre / Maggie Black and Pat Howard. — London : Faber, 1980. — 148p ; 23cm
Bibliography: p145. - Includes index
ISBN 0-571-11602-7 (cased) : £6.95 : CIP rev.
ISBN 0-571-11603-5 (pbk) : £3.25 B80-18835

Gordon, Karen Elizabeth. The garden of eternal swallows : a natural foods cookbook / Karen Elizabeth Gordon. — Boulder : Shambhala ; London : Routledge & Kegan Paul [distributor], c1980. — 163p : ill ; 23cm
ISBN 0-394-73948-5 (pbk) : £4.95 B81-25450

Handslip, Carole. The Sainsbury book of wholefood cooking / Carole Handslip. — London (59 Grosvenor St., W.1) : Published exclusively for J. Sainsbury Limited by Cathay Books, 1981. — 91p : col.ill ; 22cm
Text and ill on lining papers. — Includes index
ISBN 0-86178-067-1 : £0.99 B81-19347

Liddell, Caroline. The wholefoods cookbook / Caroline Liddell ; illustrated by Sharon Finmark. — [London] : Coronet, 1980. — 240 : ill ; 18cm
Includes index
ISBN 0-340-25454-8 (pbk) : £1.50 : CIP rev. B80-10139

641.5′637 — Food: Dishes using natural foods — *Recipes* *continuation*

Quick, Vivien. The real food cookbook : wholefood recipes for healthy nutrition / by Vivien Quick and Clifford Quick. — 2nd ed., (rev., enl.). — Wellingborough : Thorsons, 1981. — 160p : ill ; 22cm
Previous ed.: published as Everywoman′s wholefood cook book. 1974. — Includes index
ISBN 0-7225-0687-2 (pbk) : £2.95 B81-08825

641.5′637 — Health food dishes — *Recipes*

Bowen, Carol. A to Z of health foods / Carol Bowen. — London : Hamlyn Paperbacks, 1981, c1979. — 175p : ill ; 18cm. — (Hamlyn kitchen library)
Originally published: Feltham : Hamlyn, 1979. — Includes index
ISBN 0-600-20298-4 (pbk) : £1.50
Primary classification 641.3′02 B81-29241

Rivers, Patrick. Diet for a small island / by Patrick and Shirley Rivers. — Wellingborough : Turnstone, 1981. — 255p : ill,maps ; 22cm
Bibliography: p251-252. — Includes index
ISBN 0-85500-137-2 (pbk) : £4.50 : CIP rev.
Primary classification 641.5′52 B81-19178

Young, Mala. Main dishes / [Mala Young] ; [illustrated by Susan Neale]. — Newton Abbot : David & Charles, c1981. — 48p : ill ; 21cm. — (Health food cooking)
ISBN 0-7153-8038-9 (pbk) : £1.50 B81-12726

641.5′637 — Health food snacks — *Recipes*

Young, Mala. Drinks & snacks / [Mala Young] ; [illustrated by Susan Neale]. — Newton Abbot : David & Charles, c1981. — 48p : ill ; 21cm. — (Health food cooking)
ISBN 0-7153-8041-9 (pbk) : £1.50
Primary classification 641.2′6 B81-12727

641.5′638 — Food: Low fat dishes — *Recipes*

Green, Henrietta. Fine-flavoured food : a new approach to low-fat cookery / Henrietta Green ; illustrated by Wendy Brammell. — London : New English Library, 1981, c1978. — 156p : ill ; 20cm. — (New English Library books for cooks)
Originally published: London : Faber, 1978. — Includes index
ISBN 0-450-05105-6 (pbk) : £1.25 B81-26151

641.5′638 — Slimmers. Food: Low fat dishes — *Recipes*

Slimming magazine′s complete dieting revolution. — London : Deutsch, 1981. — 216p,[8]p of plates : ill(some col.) ; 24cm
Ill on lining papers. — Includes index
ISBN 0-233-97372-9 : £6.95 : CIP rev.
B81-20120

641.5′64 — Food: Spring dishes — *Recipes*

A **Little** book of Easter recipes : a gallimaufry of Easter fare. — Diss (Blo′ Norton Hall, Diss, Norfolk IP22 2JD) : M.G. Scott, 1981. — 14p ; 17cm
Cover title
ISBN 0-907396-02-x (pbk) : £0.75 B81-17648

641.5′64 — Food: St Valentine′s Day dishes — *Recipes*

Scott, Shirley. A little book of Valentine recipes : a gallimaufry of fare for lovers. — Diss (Blo′ Norton Hall, Near Diss, Norfolk IP22 2JD) : M.G. Scott, c1981. — 14p : 1ill ; 19cm
Cover title. — Authors: Shirley & Michael Scott
ISBN 0-907396-01-1 (pbk) : £0.75 B81-11717

641.5′64 — Food: Summer dishes — *Recipes*

Burros, Marian. The summertime cookbook : elegant but easy dining, indoors and out / by Marian Burros and Lois Levine ; illustrations by Rosalie Petrash Schmidt. — New York : Collier Books ; London : Collier Macmillan, 1980, c1972. — 224p : ill ; 21cm
Includes index
ISBN 0-02-011190-8 (pbk) : £2.95 B81-15624

641.5′66 — Food: Christmas dishes: Dishes prepared using Magimix food processors — *Recipes*

Boxer, Arabella. Christmas with Magimix : recipes written for food processors / by Arabella Boxer. — Sunbury : ICTC, 1981. — 34p : ill ; 15x22cm
Cover title
ISBN 0-9506518-8-5 (spiral) : Unpriced
B81-40408

641.5′66 — Food: Christmas dishes — *Recipes*

Holder, Judith. Christmas fare. — Exeter : Webb & Bower, Nov.1981. — [64]p
ISBN 0-906671-34-5 : £3.95 : CIP entry
Primary classification 769.5 B81-30976

Poole, Shona Crawford. Cooking for Christmas & other feasts : a unique collection of recipes from all over the world / Shona Crawford Poole. — Feltham : Hamlyn, 1980. — xv,208p : ill ; 20cm
Bibliography: p199-200. — Includes index
ISBN 0-600-20003-5 (pbk) : £1.25 B81-00164

Thomson, George L.. Christmas recipes / written out in manuscript form and illustrated by George L. Thomson. — Edinburgh : Canongate, 1980. — 89p : col.ill ; 31cm
Includes index
ISBN 0-86241-005-3 : £4.95 B81-14219

641.5′676 — Food: Kosher dishes: Dishes prepared using Magimix food processors — *Recipes*

Rose, Evelyn. Jewish cookery with Magimix : 36 recipes written for food processors / by Evelyn Rose. — Isleworth (25 Lower Sq., Isleworth, Middx) : 1CTC, [1981?]. — 29p ; 15x22cm
Cover title
Unpriced (spiral) B81-37678

641.5′676 — Jews. Food — *Recipes*

Jackson, Judy. The home book of Jewish cookery / Judy Jackson. — London : Faber, 1981. — 169p ; 21cm
Includes index
ISBN 0-571-11697-3 (cased) : £7.95 : CIP rev.
ISBN 0-571-11737-6 (pbk) : Unpriced
B81-00165

641.5′68 — Dishes for buffets. Decoration — *Manuals*

Emery, William. Culinary design and decoration / William Emery ; illustrations by Joyce Tuhill. — London : Northwood Books, 1980. — 135p,[16]p of plates : ill(some col.) ; 26cm
Includes index
ISBN 0-7198-2754-x : £8.95 B81-21916

641.5′68 — Food: Dishes for buffets — *Recipes*

Mengelatte, PierreBuffets and receptions / [edited and compiled by] Pierre Mengelatte, Walter Bickel, Albin Abelanet ; editor Michael Small ; assistant editor Mabel Quin. — 3rd ed. — London : Virtue, 1980. — xv,1221p : ill (some col.) ; 27cm
Translated from the French. — Previous ed.: 1979. — Includes index
ISBN 0-900778-11-3 : £31.00 : CIP rev.
B80-08285

641.5′68 — Food: Dishes for dinner parties & dishes for supper parties — *Recipes*

McMillan, Norma. Cooking for friends / [recipes Norma McMillan]. — London : Marshall Cavendish, [1981]. — 96p : ill(some col.) ; 22cm. — (Supercook′s kitchen)
Includes index
ISBN 0-85685-728-9 (pbk) : £0.99 B81-17575

641.5′68 — Food: Dishes for seasonal festivals — *Recipes*

Paston-Williams, Sara. The National Trust book of Christmas and festive day recipes. — Newton Abbot : David & Charles, Sept.1981. — [96]p
ISBN 0-7153-8100-8 : £4.50 : CIP entry
B81-22503

641.5′68 — Food: Dishes for special occasions — *Recipes*

Macqueen, Sheila. Sheila Macqueen′s flowers and food for special occasions / with recipes by Diana Baldwin. — London : Ward Lock, 1980. — 96p : col.ill ; 26cm. — (A Hyperion book)
Includes index
ISBN 0-7063-5942-9 : £6.95
Also classified at 745.92′6 B81-0843

641.5′68 — Food: Party dishes — *Recipes*

Green, Maureen. Giving a party : how to survive while your guests enjoy themselves / Maureen Green ; with illustrations by Jo Nesbitt. — London : Astragal, 1980. — 246p : ill ; 26cm
Bibliography: p235-236. — Includes index
ISBN 0-906525-18-7 : £8.95 B81-0016

Logan, Michael. Tomorrow′s dinner cooked tonight : 72 complete menus for easy entertaining / Michael Logan & Lisl Popper ; with a foreword by Mapie, Comtesse de Toulouse-Lautrec ; illustrated by Ginger Tilley. — London : P. Davies, 1971 (1979 printing). — xvi,72[i.e.144]p : ill ; 26cm
Text on lining papers. — Includes index
ISBN 0-432-11720-2 : £4.95 B81-2341

Rose, Evelyn. The entertaining cookbook / Evelyn Rose. — London : Robson, 1980. — 358p,[8]p of plates : ill(some col.) ; 25cm
Includes index
ISBN 0-86051-093-x : £8.95 : CIP rev.
B80-1781

641.5′7 — Cookery — *Manuals* **—** *For chefs*

Martland, Richard E.. Basic cookery : fundamental recipes and variations / Richard E. Martland, Derek A. Welsby. — London : Heinemann, 1980. — xvii,411p : ill ; 24cm
Includes index
ISBN 0-434-92232-3 (pbk) : £4.95 B81-0261

641.5′78 — Outdoor cookery - *Manuals*

Roden, Claudia. Picnic. — London : 90 Great Russell St., WC1B 3PY : J.U. Norman, Apr.1981. — [352]p
ISBN 0-906908-11-6 : CIP entry B81-0430

641.5′8 — Food: Dishes prepared using woks — *Recipes*

Lo, Kenneth. The Wok cookbook / Kenneth Lo. — London : Granada, 1981. — 157p : ill ; 18cm. — (A Mayflower book)
Includes index
ISBN 0-583-12929-3 (pbk) : £1.25 B81-1894

641.5′87 — Food: Dishes prepared using pressure cookers — *Recipes*

Doeser, Linda. Supercook′s cooking under pressure / [text prepared and edited by Linda Doeser]. — London : Marshall Cavendish, 1977 (1979 printing). — 82p : col.ill ; 29cm
ISBN 0-85685-753-x (pbk) : £1.25 B81-1957

641.5′882 — Food: Dishes prepared using microwave ovens — *Recipes*

Microwave cooking : adapting conventional recipes / Litton Microwave Cooking Products. — Minnetonka : Publication Arts ; New York ; London : Van Nostrand Reinhold, c1979. — 159p : col.ill ; 29cm
Includes index
ISBN 0-442-24845-8 : £8.20 B81-1118

641.5′882 — Microwave ovens — *Manuals*

Harris, Jan. First steps in microwave cooking / by Jan Harris ; editor: Angus Waycott. — Southampton (69 Lyon St., Southampton [SD2 0LW]) : Inklon, 1981. — 28p ; 16x22cm
Includes index
ISBN 0-9507618-0-x (pbk) : £1.75 B81-3287

641.5′884 — Food: Dishes prepared using crock-pots — *Recipes*

Hughes, Joyce. The cook-pot & casserole book / Joyce Hughes. — London : Ward Lock, 1981. — 139p : ill(some col.) ; 26cm
At head of title: Kenwood. — Includes index
ISBN 0-7063-5784-1 : £4.95
Primary classification 641.8′21 B81-3989

641.5'884 — Food: Dishes prepared using crock-pots — *Recipes* *continuation*
Lomask, Martha. Low, slow, delicious : recipes for casseroles and electric slow-cooking pots / Martha Lomask. — London : Faber, 1980. — 160p,[8]p of plates : col.ill ; 26cm
Includes index
ISBN 0-571-11384-2 : £7.95 : CIP rev.
Primary classification 641.8'21 B80-25866

641.5'89 — Food: Dishes cooked in one utensil — *Recipes*
Westland, Pamela. One-pot cooking / Pamela Westland. — London : Elm Tree, 1978. — xii,160p,[8]p of plates : col.ill ; 24cm
Includes index
ISBN 0-241-89599-5 : £5.95 : CIP rev. B78-11105

641.5'89 — Food: Dishes prepared using blenders, dishes prepared using food mixers & dishes prepared using food processors — *Recipes*
Patten, Marguerite. Marguerite Patten's multi-mixer cookbook. — Glasgow : Collins, 1981. — 96p : ill(some col.) ; 28cm
Includes index
ISBN 0-00-411212-1 (pbk) : Unpriced B81-39772

Ridgway, Judy. Mixer, blender and processor cookery / Judy Ridgway ; illustrated by Vanessa Pancheri. — Sevenoaks : Hodder, 1981. — 202p : ill ; 20cm. — (Teach yourself books)
Includes index
ISBN 0-340-26748-8 (pbk) : £1.95 B81-19108

641.5'89 — Food: Dishes prepared using food processors — *Recipes*
Allison, Sonia. Sonia Allison's food processor cookbook / written with Patricia Hudson. — Loughton (Loughton, Essex) : Piatkus, 1980. — xii,209p,[8]p of plates : col.ill ; 23cm
Includes index
ISBN 0-86188-064-1 : £5.95 : CIP rev. B80-22173

641.5'89 — Food: Dishes prepared using Magimix food processors — *Recipes*
Hanbury Tenison, Marika. The Magimix and food processor cookery / Marika Hanbury Tenison ; illustrated by Val Biro. — Isleworth (25 Lower Sq., Isleworth, Middx) : 1CTC, 1981, c1978. — 224p : ill ; 24cm
Originally published: London : Hutchinson, 1978. — Text on lining papers. — Includes index
ISBN 0-9506518-1-8 : £4.95 B81-37672

. Magimix recipe book. — Rev. [ed.]. — Sunbury-on-Thames (25 Hanworth Rd., Sunbury-on-Thames, TW16 5DA) : 1CTC, 1981, c1977. — 66p : (col.ill) ; 20cm
Previous ed.: 1977
Unpriced (spiral) B81-37673

641.5'89 — Food: Irish dishes: Dishes prepared using Magimix food processors — *Recipes*
Connery, Clare. Irish cookery with Magimix : recipes written for food processors / by Clare Connery. — Sunbury (25 Hanworth Rd., Sunbury, Middx) : ICTC, 1981. — 34p ; 15x22cm
Cover title
ISBN 0-907642-00-4 (spiral) : Unpriced B81-37675

641.59'1822 — Food: Mediterranean dishes — *Recipes*
Boxer, Arabella. Mediterranean cookbook / Arabella Boxer ; photographs by Tessa Traeger. — London : Dent, 1981. — 256p,[8]p of plates : col.ill ; 25cm
Includes index
ISBN 0-460-04442-7 : £9.95 : CIP rev. B81-22630

Wolfert, Paula. Mediterranean cooking / Paula Wolfert ; illustrations by Agnetta Neroth. — London : Pan, 1980. — 256p : ill ; 20cm
Originally published: New York : Quadrangle / New York Times Book Co., 1977. — Includes index
ISBN 0-330-26177-0 (pbk) : £1.95 B81-00167

641.593/9 — COOKERY AND RECIPES OF SPECIAL COUNTRIES

641.5937 — Food. Ancient Roman dishes — *Recipes*
Roman cook book / [illustrations by Gill and Ronald Embleton]. — Newcastle upon Tyne : Frank Graham, [1981?]. — 32p : ill ; 22cm
ISBN 0-85983-127-2 (pbk) : £0.70 B81-33451

641.5941 — Food: British dishes, *1700-1900* — *Recipes*
Drury, Elizabeth. The butler's pantry book / Elizabeth Drury. — London : Black, 1981. — 192p : ill,facsims ; 23cm
Bibliography: p181-183. — Includes index
ISBN 0-7136-2144-3 : £6.95 : CIP rev.
Primary classification 640'.941 B81-22526

641.5941 — Food: British dishes, *1939-1945* — *Recipes*
Minns, Raynes. Bombers and mash : the domestic front 1939-45 / Raynes Minns. — London : Virago, 1980. — 236p : ill,facsims ; 25cm
Bibliography: p201-202. - Includes index
ISBN 0-86068-041-x (pbk) : £4.95
Primary classification 941.084'088042 B81-03349

641.5941 — Food: British dishes — *Recipes*
Duff, Gail. Food from the country / Gail & Mick Duff. — London : Macmillan, 1981. — 182p : ill(some col.),1port ; 25cm
Includes index
ISBN 0-333-27821-6 : £8.95 B81-25609

641.5941 — Food: Dishes associated with fiction in English by Dickens, Charles, *1812-1870* — *Recipes*
Marshall, Brenda. Mr Pickwick's plentiful portions : the Charles Dickens' cookbook for today / Brenda Marshall. — London : Muller, 1980. — 176p : ill ; 27cm
Includes index
ISBN 0-584-95538-3 : £6.50 B81-04654

641.59411 — Food: Scottish dishes — *Recipes*
Gow, Rosalie. Modern ways with traditional Scottish recipes / Rosalie Gow. — Edinburgh : Ramsay Head, 1980. — 112p ; 22cm
Includes index
ISBN 0-902859-68-4 : £4.95 B81-20056

Pattullo, Dione. The best of Scottish cooking : in colour / Dione Pattullo. — Edinburgh : Johnston & Bacon, 1979. — 96p,[16]p of plates : ill(some col.) ; 18cm
Includes index
ISBN 0-7179-4255-4 (pbk) : £1.75 B81-12663

641.5942 — Food: English dishes, *1584-1813* — *Recipes*
Simmons, Rosemary. Rare receipts / drawn by Rosemary Simmons ; described by Gillian Goodwin. — London (29 Chalcot Sq., NW1) : Gelofer Press, c1981. — [16]p : ill ; 22cm. — (The Good housewife)
ISBN 0-9506529-2-x (pbk) : £1.05 B81-29604

641.5942 — Food. English dishes, *ca 1390* - *Recipes*
Knight, Katherine. Fit for a king. — London : Evans Bros, Aug.1981. — [160]p
ISBN 0-237-45548-x : £7.25 : CIP entry B81-16886

641.5942 — Food: English dishes — *Recipes*
Berriedale-Johnson, Michelle. Olde Englishe recipes / Michelle Berriedale-Johnson. — Loughton : Piatkus, 1981. — 176p : ill ; 23cm
Includes index
ISBN 0-86188-091-9 : £5.95 : CIP rev. B81-09476

Grigson, Jane. English food : an anthology / chosen by Jane Grigson ; with illustrations by Gillian Zeiner. — Harmondsworth : Penguin, 1977, c1974 (1981 [printing]). — 322p : ill ; 20cm. — (Penguin handbooks)
Originally published: London : Macmillan, 1974. — Bibliography: p311-312. — Includes index
ISBN 0-14-046243-0 (pbk) : £2.50 B81-21114

Sutherland, Douglas, *1919-*. The colonel's cookbook / Douglas Sutherland with Diana Sutherland and Wendy Hartman. — London : Muller, 1980. — 141p : ill ; 21cm
Includes index
ISBN 0-584-10373-5 : £5.75 : CIP rev. B80-18836

641.5942 — Food: English regional dishes — *Recipes*
Ayrton, Elisabeth. English provincial cooking / Elisabeth Ayrton ; [photographs Tony Copeland]. — London : Mitchell Beazley, c1980. — 224p : col.ill,maps(some col.) ; 27cm
Bibliography: p217-218. — Includes index
ISBN 0-85533-217-4 : £8.95 B81-25268

641.59423'3 — Food: Dorset dishes — *Recipes*
Easlea, Kate. Dorset dishes / by Kate Easlea. — Southampton : Cave, 1979. — 32p ; 16x21cm
Includes index
ISBN 0-86146-004-9 (pbk) : £0.50 B81-40926

641.59425'1 — Food: Derbyshire dishes — *Recipes*
Derbyshire cookery : recipes / collected by Janet Arthur. — Clapham, N. Yorkshire : Dalesman, 1976 (1980 [printing]). — 62p : ill ; 22cm
ISBN 0-85206-336-9 (pbk) : £1.10 B81-03599

641.59428'8 — Food: Northumberland dishes — *Recipes*
Slack, Margaret. Northumbrian fare / by Margaret Slack ; illustrations by Valary Gustard. — Newcastle upon Tyne : Frank Graham, c1981. — 64p : ill ; 22cm
Includes index
ISBN 0-85983-122-1 (pbk) : £1.20 B81-21285

641.59429 — Food: Welsh dishes — *Recipes*
Freeman, Bobby. First catch your peacock : a book of Welsh food / Bobby Freeman. — [Cardiff] ([85 Wyndham Cres., Cardiff CF1 9EG]) : Image Imprint, 1980. — 243p,[16]p of plates : ill(some col.) ; 22cm
Bibliography: p224-225. — Includes index
ISBN 0-9507254-0-4 : Unpriced B81-11404

641.5944 — England. Food: French dishes — *Recipes*
Rubenstein, Helge. Good Housekeeping French cookery / Helge Rubenstein. — London : Ebury, 1981. — 144p : col.ill ; 28cm
Includes index
ISBN 0-85223-197-0 : £8.95 B81-40916

641.5944 — Food: French dishes — *Recipes*
Ancelet, Danielle. Cuisine of France / Danielle Ancelet ; preface by Roland Magne ; with 300 recipes illustrated in color ; [translated from the French by Adèle Dejey]. — London : W.H. Allen, 1981. — [191]p : col.ill ; 28cm
Includes index
ISBN 0-491-02865-2 : £6.95 B81-26675

Bjorklund, Gertrude. Menus plaisirs. — London : Burke, May 1981. — 1v
ISBN 0-222-00803-2 : £6.50 : CIP entry B81-04334

The **Elle** cookbook / introduction by Jane Grigson ; translated by R.F. Fullick ; photographs by A. Bouillaud, Ph. Leroy and Y. Jannes. — London : Michael Joseph, 1981. — 191p : col.ill ; 32cm
Includes index
ISBN 0-7181-1926-6 : £10.00 B81-39770

Ellwood, Caroline, *1947-*. The Sainsbury book of French cooking / Caroline Ellwood. — London (59 Grosvenor St., W.1) : Published exclusively for J. Sainsbury by Cathay, 1981. — 92p : col.ill,1col.map ; 22cm
Includes index
ISBN 0-86178-065-5 : £0.99 B81-07408

Olney, Richard. Simple French food. — London : Jill Norman & Hubhouse, Oct.1981. — [336]p
Originally published: New York : Atheneum, 1975
ISBN 0-906908-22-1 : £7.95 : CIP entry B81-28120

641.5944 — Food: French dishes — *Recipes* *continuation*

Pellaprat, Henri-Paul. Modern French culinary art. — Revised ed. — Coulsdon : Virtue and Co., July 1981. — [1037]p
ISBN 0-900778-07-5 : £30.00 : CIP entry
B81-17524

Willan, Anne. The Observer French cookery school / by Anne Willan ; with an anthology of French cooking and kitchen terms compiled by Jane Grigson. — London : Macdonald Futura, 1980. — 305p : col.ill ; 27cm
Bibliography: p296. - Includes index
ISBN 0-354-04523-7 : £12.95 B81-05992

641.5944 — Food: French regional dishes — *Recipes*

David, Elizabeth, *1913-*. French provincial cooking / Elizabeth David. — Rev. ed., repr. with revisions. — Harmondsworth : Penguin in association with Michael Joseph, 1970 (1981 [printing]). — 584p : ill ; 20cm
Originally published: 1967. — Bibliography: p535-550. — Includes index
ISBN 0-14-046099-3 (pbk) : £2.95 B81-33607

641.5'944 — Food. French regional dishes — *Recipes*

Willan, Anne. French regional cooking. — London : Hutchinson, Oct.1981. — [304]p
ISBN 0-09-146210-x : £12.95 : CIP entry
B81-26765

641.5944'05 — Food: French dishes — *Recipes — For British tourists — Serials*

The **Do** it yourself French holiday. — 1981-. — Oxford (36 Church Meadow, Milton-under-Wychwood, Oxford OX7 6JG) : Ashgarth Enterprises, 1980-. — v. : ill ; 21cm
Annual
ISSN 0261-3972 = Do it yourself French holiday : £1.99
Primary classification 641.3 B81-28705

641.5945 — Food: Italian dishes — *Recipes*

David, Elizabeth, *1913-*. Italian food / Elizabeth David ; drawings by Renato Guttuso. — Rev. ed., repr. with revisions. — Harmondsworth : Penguin, 1977 (1981 [printing]). — 268p : ill ; 20cm
Originally published: 1963. — Includes index
ISBN 0-14-046098-5 (pbk) : £2.25 B81-35513

Reynolds, Mary. The Sainsbury book of Italian cooking / Mary Reynolds. — London (59 Grosvenor St., W.1) : Published exclusively for J. Sainsbury Limited by Cathay, 1981. — 92p : col.ill,1col.map ; 22cm
Includes index
ISBN 0-86178-066-3 : £0.99 B81-07407

641.5947 — Food: Russian dishes — *Recipes*

Nicolaieff, Nina. The Russian cookbook / Nina Nicolaieff and Nancy Phelan. — London : Macmillan, 1981. — 176p ; 20cm. — (Papermac)
Includes index
ISBN 0-333-31922-2 (pbk) : £2.95 B81-24092

641.595 — Food: Asian dishes — *Recipes*

De Mustchine, Bruce. Bruce de Mustchine's Asian cookbook / illustrated by Tony Richards. — London : New English Library, 1981. — 206p : ill ; 20cm + 1card(col.ill ; 12x19cm). — (New English Library books for cooks)
Includes index
ISBN 0-450-05137-4 (pbk) : £1.25 B81-22841

Passmore, Jacki. All Asian cookbook : Japan, China, Korea, India, Malaysia, Singapore, Indonesia, Laos, Thailand, Burma, Cambodia, Vietnam, Philippines, Sri Lanka / Jacki Passmore. — London : Spring, 1979, c1978. — 224p : col.ill ; 29cm
Originally published: Dee Why West : Ure Smith, 1978. — Includes index
ISBN 0-600-30445-0 : £4.95 B81-01902

641.595 — Food: Oriental dishes — *Recipes*

Dimbleby, Josceline. Curries and oriental cookery / Josceline Dimbleby. — 2nd (rev.) impression. — Cambridge : Published for J. Sainsbury Limited by Woodhead-Faulkner, 1981. — 96p : ill(some col.),1port ; 18cm. — (A Sainsbury's cookbook)
Originally published: 1980
£0.75 (pbk) B81-37262

641.5951 — Food: Chinese regional dishes — *Recipes*

Lo, Kenneth. Chinese provincial cooking / Kenneth Lo. — London : Sphere, 1981, c1979. — 282p : 1map ; 20cm
Originally published: London : Elm Tree, 1979. — Includes index
ISBN 0-7221-5583-2 (pbk) : £1.75 B81-20774

Lo, Kenneth. Regional Chinese cookbook / Kenneth Lo. — London : Hamlyn, c1981. 176p : ill(some col.),maps ; 27cm
Includes index
ISBN 0-600-32238-6 : £5.95 B81-32354

641.5954 — Food: Indian dishes — *Recipes*

Hosain, Attia. Indian cooking / Attia Hosain & Sita Pasricha. — Rev. ed. — Feltham : Hamlyn, 1981, c1962. — 210p : ill ; 18cm
Previous ed.: 1969. — Includes index
ISBN 0-600-32036-7 (pbk) : £1.50 B81-10179

Pandya, Michael. Complete Indian cookbook / Michael Pandya. — London : Hamlyn, c1980. — 176p : col.ill ; 27cm
Includes index
ISBN 0-600-34918-7 : £5.95 B81-00992

Wickramasinghe, Priya. Spicy and delicious. — London : Coronet, July 1981. — [192]p
Originally published: London : Dent, 1979
ISBN 0-340-26676-7 (pbk) : £1.25 : CIP entry
Also classified at 641.59549'3 B81-14953

641.5954 — Food: Indian regional dishes — *Recipes*

Taneja, Meera. Indian regional cookery / Meera Taneja. — London : Mills & Boon, 1980. — 207p,[16]p of plates : col.ill,1map ; 26cm
Includes index
ISBN 0-263-06433-6 : £7.95 B81-06657

641.59549'3 — Food: Sri Lanka dishes — *Recipes*

Wickramasinghe, Priya. Spicy and delicious. — London : Coronet, July 1981. — [192]p
Originally published: London : Dent, 1979
ISBN 0-340-26676-7 (pbk) : £1.25 : CIP entry
Primary classification 641.5954 B81-14953

641.59593 — Food: Thai dishes — *Recipes*

Brennan, Jennifer. Thai cooking. — London : Jill Norman & Hobhouse, Oct.1981. — [224]p
Revision of: The original Thai cookbook. New York : Marek, 1981
ISBN 0-906908-63-9 : £7.95 : CIP entry
B81-28006

641.59598 — Food: Indonesian dishes — *Recipes*

Owen, Sri. [The home book of Indonesian cookery]. Indonesian food and cookery / by Sri Owen. — London (45 Lamont Rd, SW10 0HU) : Prospect, 1980. — 255p : ill,1 map ; 22cm
Previous ed.: London : Faber, 1976. — Map on inside back cover. — Bibliography: p249-250. — Includes index
ISBN 0-907325-00-9 (pbk) : £4.95 B81-06363

641.596 — Food: African dishes — *Recipes*

Olaore, Ola. African cooking / by Ola Olaore. — London : Foulsham, c1980. — 96p,[8]p of plates : ill(some col.) ; 23cm
Includes index
ISBN 0-572-01131-8 (pbk) : £3.50 B81-00993

641.5973 — Food: American dishes — *Recipes*

Farmer, Fannie. The Fannie Farmer cookbook. — 12th ed. / rev. by Marion Cunningham with Jeri Laber ; illustrated by Lauren Jarrett. — London : Norman, 1981. — xiv,811p : ill ; 24cm
Previous ed.: Boston, Mass. : Little, Brown, 1965. — Text on lining papers. — Includes index
ISBN 0-906908-18-3 : £12.00 : CIP rev.
B81-08898

Lomask, Martha. The all-American cookbook : America's favourate dishes for non-American cooks / Martha Lomask. — Loughton : Piatkus, 1981. — 256p : ill(some col.),maps ; 26cm
Map on lining papers. — Includes index
ISBN 0-86188-121-4 : £8.95 : CIP rev.
B81-27473

641.6 — COOKERY AND RECIPES BASED ON SPECIAL MATERIALS

641.6 — Food: Dishes using seed sprouts — *Recipes*

Sellmann, Per. The complete sprouting book : a guide to growing and using sprouted seeds / by Per and Gita Sellmann ; translated from the Swedish by Kit Zweigbergk and Palden Jenkins. — Wellingborough : Turnstone, 1981. — 128p : ill ; 22cm
Translation of: Allt om groddar. — Bibliography: p125-126. - Includes index
ISBN 0-85500-105-4 (pbk) : £2.75 : CIP rev.
B81-17835

641.6'1 — Preserved food — *Recipes*

Norwak, Mary. The complete book of home preserving / Mary Norwak. — London : New English Library, 1981, c1979. — 236p : ill ; 20cm. — (New English Library books for cooks)
Originally published: London : Ward Lock, 1978. — Includes index
ISBN 0-450-05116-1 (pbk) : £1.25 B81-37750

641.6'16 — Chutneys & pickles — *Recipes*

Lambert, Heather. The Sainsbury book of preserves & pickles / Heather Lambert. — London : Published for J. Sainsbury by Cathay, 1981. — 93p : col.ill ; 22cm
Index and ill on lining papers
ISBN 0-86178-069-8 : £0.99
Also classified at 641.8'52 B81-22081

641.6'2 — Food: Dishes using alcoholic drinks — *Recipes*

Allison, Sonia. Spirited cooking. — Newton Abbot : David & Charles, Oct.1981. — [96]p
ISBN 0-7153-8015-x : £7.50 : CIP entry
B81-30332

641.6'374 — Food: Dishes using chocolate — *Recipes*

Chocolate cooking / edited by Judy Ridgway. — London : Octopus, 1981. — 77p : ill(some col.) ; 28cm
Ill on lining papers. — Includes index
ISBN 0-7064-1476-4 : £1.99 B81-18195

641.6'383 — Food: Dishes using spices — *Recipes*

David, Elizabeth, *1913-*. Spices, salt and aromatics in the English kitchen / Elizabeth David. — Repr. with revisions. — Harmondsworth : Penguin, 1975, c1970 (1981 [printing]). — 277p ; 20cm. — (Penguin handbooks)
Bibliography: p249-253. — Includes index
ISBN 0-14-046163-9 (pbk) : £1.95
Primary classification 641.6'57 B81-13980

641.6'383 — Health food dishes using spices — *Recipes*

Young, Mala. Using herbs & spices / [Mala Young] ; [illustrated by Susan Neale]. — Newton Abbot : David & Charles, c1981. — 48p : ill ; 21cm. — (Health food cooking)
ISBN 0-7153-8040-0 (pbk) : £1.50
Also classified at 641.6'57 B81-12731

641.6'383 — Slimmers. Food: Dishes using spices — *Recipes*

Peplow, Elizabeth. Stay slim with herbs and spices / Elizabeth Peplow ; illustrated by Yvonne Skargon. — London : Darton, Longman & Todd, 1981. — vii,120p : ill ; 22cm
Bibliography: p112. — Includes index
ISBN 0-232-51464-x (pbk) : £2.95 : CIP rev.
Primary classification 641.6'57 B81-02361

641.6'384 — Food: Curried dishes — *Recipes*

Beedell, Suzanne. The curry cook book / Suzanne Beedell. — London : Sphere, 1979. — 174p ; 18cm
Includes index
ISBN 0-7221-1532-6 (pbk) : £0.95 B81-11315

641.6′4 — Food: Dishes using fruit — *Recipes*

Ashmore, Gwyneth. The pocket book of fruit & nut cooking / Gwyneth Ashmore. — London : Evans, 1981. — 128p : ill ; 17cm
Includes index
ISBN 0-237-45547-1 (pbk) : £1.75 : CIP rev. B80-18405

Dinnage, Paul. The book of fruit and fruit cookery / Paul Dinnage ; illustrations by Meg Rutherford. — London : Sidgwick and Jackson, 1981. — 277p : ill ; 24cm
Includes index
ISBN 0-283-98553-4 : £8.95 B81-26617

Dixon, Pamela. New ways with fresh fruit and vegetables / Pamela Dixon. — London : Faber, 1973 (1981 printing). — 224p ; 20cm
Includes index
ISBN 0-571-11698-1 (pbk) : £2.25 : CIP rev.
Also classified at 641.6′5 B81-23762

Johns, Leslie. The complete book of fruit / Leslie Johns & Violet Stevenson ; illustrated by Marianne Yamaguchi. — London : Angus & Robertson, 1979. — 309p,[32]p of plates : ill (some col.) ; 27cm
Ill on lining papers. — Bibliography: p298-301. - Includes index
ISBN 0-207-14337-4 : £10.00
Primary classification 634 B81-00963

Stevenson, Violet. Grow and cook / Violet Stevenson. — [London] : Coronet, 1979, c1976. — 175p : ill ; 18cm
Originally published: Newton Abbot : David and Charles, 1976. — Includes index
ISBN 0-340-23233-1 (pbk) : £0.85
Primary classification 635 B81-13261

641.6′4 — Food: Fruit dishes: Dishes prepared using microwave ovens — *Recipes*

Collins, Val. The microwave fruit and vegetable cookbook. — Newton Abbot : David & Charles, Oct.1981. — [120]p
ISBN 0-7153-8199-7 : £5.95 : CIP entry
Also classified at 641.6′5 B81-27948

Microwave cooking / [Litton Microwave Cooking Center]. — Minneapolis : Litton Microwave Cooking Products ; New York ; London : Van Nostrand Reinhold, c1981
Microwave oven power level setting guide (folded sheet) as insert. — Includes index
[Vol.7]: Fruits & vegetables. — 160p : col.ill ; 29cm
ISBN 0-442-25649-3 (corrected) : £8.20
Also classified at 641.6′5 B81-30795

641.6446 — Food: Dishes using carob beans — *Recipes*

Whiteside, Lorraine. The carob cookbook. — Wellingborough : Thorsons, Nov.1981. — [96]p
ISBN 0-7225-0726-7 (pbk) : £0.95 : CIP entry B81-30586

641.6′5 — Food: Vegetable dishes: Dishes prepared using microwave ovens — *Recipes*

Collins, Val. The microwave fruit and vegetable cookbook. — Newton Abbot : David & Charles, Oct.1981. — [120]p
ISBN 0-7153-8199-7 : £5.95 : CIP entry
Primary classification 641.6′4 B81-27948

Microwave cooking / [Litton Microwave Cooking Center]. — Minneapolis : Litton Microwave Cooking Products ; New York ; London : Van Nostrand Reinhold, c1981
Microwave oven power level setting guide (folded sheet) as insert. — Includes index
[Vol.7]: Fruits & vegetables. — 160p : col.ill ; 29cm
ISBN 0-442-25649-3 (corrected) : £8.20
Primary classification 641.6′4 B81-30795

641.6′5 — Food: Vegetable dishes — *Recipes*

Cross, Rena. A feast of vegetables / by Rena Cross ; edited by Mary Norwak. — London : Foulsham, c1980. — 96p : ill ; 22cm. — (From a country kitchen)
Includes index
ISBN 0-572-00902-x (pbk) : £1.95 B81-00994

Dixon, Pamela. New ways with fresh fruit and vegetables / Pamela Dixon. — London : Faber, 1973 (1981 printing). — 224p ; 20cm
Includes index
ISBN 0-571-11698-1 (pbk) : £2.25 : CIP rev.
Primary classification 641.6′4 B81-23762

Grigson, Jane. Jane Grigson's vegetable book : with a new introduction, glossary and table of equivalent weights and measures for the American edition / illustrated by Yvonne Skargon. — Harmondsworth : Penguin, 1980, c1979 (1981 [printing]). — 618p : ill ; 20cm. — (Penguin handbooks)
Originally published: London : Joseph, 1978. — Includes index
ISBN 0-14-046352-6 (pbk) : £3.50 B81-21112

Norwak, Mary. Buying and cooking vegetables / Mary Norwak. — Cambridge : Published for J. Sainsbury Limited by Woodhead-Faulkner, 1980 (1980 [printing]). — 40p : ill ; 21cm. — (Sainsbury's food guides ; no.4)
Cover title. — Text on inside cover
£0.30 (pbk) B81-37263

Stevenson, Violet. Grow and cook / Violet Stevenson. — [London] : Coronet, 1979, c1976. — 175p : ill ; 18cm
Originally published: Newton Abbot : David and Charles, 1976. — Includes index
ISBN 0-340-23233-1 (pbk) : £0.85
Primary classification 635 B81-13261

641.6′5 — Health food vegetable dishes — *Recipes*

Young, Mala. Vegetables & salads / [Mala Young] ; [illustrated by Susan Neale]. — Newton Abbot : David & Charles, c1981. — 48p : ill ; 21cm. — (Health food cooking)
ISBN 0-7153-8036-2 (pbk) : £1.50
Also classified at 641.8′3 B81-12728

641.6′5′07 — Hotel industries & catering industries. Personnel. Training. Curriculum subjects: Vegetable cookery — *Manuals*

Training in vegetable cookery. — [Wembley] : HCITB, [1981?]. — 1portfolio ; 28x32cm
Unpriced B81-33178

641.6′521 — Food: Dishes using potatoes — *Recipes*

Robyns, Gwen. The potato cookbook / Gwen Robyns. — London : Pan, 1980. — 140p : ill ; 20cm
Originally published: Owings Mills : Stemmer House, c1976. — Includes index
ISBN 0-330-26176-2 (pbk) : £1.50 B81-00168

641.6′521 — Food: Potato dishes — *Recipes*

Weikersheim, *Princess*. Appealing potatoes / Princess Weikersheim ; illustrated by Martin Williams. — London : Hutchinson, 1981. — 96p : ill ; 23cm
Includes index
ISBN 0-09-143220-0 : £4.95 : CIP rev. B80-23429

641.6′565 — Food: Dishes using beans — *Recipes*

Eno, David. The little brown bean book / text & illustrations David Eno ; calligraphy Jenny Ivermee. — Winchester (P.O. Box 23, Winchester, Hants. SO23 9TP) : Jumper, 1978 (1979 [printing]). — 31p : ill ; 15cm
ISBN 0-903981-10-6 (pbk) : Unpriced B81-13363

Mallos, Tess. The bean cookbook / Tess Mallos. — Leicester : Windward, c1980. — 128p : ill (some col.) 29cm
Includes index
ISBN 0-7112-0088-2 : £4.95 B81-39058

641.6′565 — Food: Dishes using pulses — *Recipes*

Dixon, Pamela. Pulse cookery : wholesome recipes with peas, beans and lentils : includes sweet dishes / by Pamela Dixon ; illustrated by Clive Birch. — Wellingborough : Thorsons, 1980. — 128p : ill ; 22cm. — (A Thorsons wholefood cookbook)
Includes index
ISBN 0-7225-0647-3 (cased) : £5.95 : CIP rev.
ISBN 0-7225-0621-x (pbk) : £2.95 B80-17820

Westland, Pamela. Bean feast / Pamela Westland. — London : Granada, 1981. — 189p ; 18cm. — (A Mayflower book)
Includes index
ISBN 0-583-13167-0 (pbk) : £1.50 B81-02491

641.6′5655 — Food: Dishes using soya beans — *Recipes*

Forster, Dorothy. Cooking with Tvp. — Wellingborough : Thorsons, Nov.1981. — [96]p
ISBN 0-7225-0720-8 (pbk) : £0.95 : CIP entry B81-30585

641.6′57 — Food: Dishes using herbs — *Recipes*

David, Elizabeth, *1913-*. Spices, salt and aromatics in the English kitchen / Elizabeth David. — Repr. with revisions. — Harmondsworth : Penguin, 1975, c1970 (1981 [printing]). — 277p ; 20cm. — (Penguin handbooks)
Bibliography: p249-253. — Includes index
ISBN 0-14-046163-9 (pbk) : £1.95
Also classified at 641.6′383 B81-13980

641.6′57 — Health food dishes using herbs — *Recipes*

Young, Mala. Using herbs & spices / [Mala Young] ; [illustrated by Susan Neale]. — Newton Abbot : David & Charles, c1981. — 48p : ill ; 21cm. — (Health food cooking)
ISBN 0-7153-8040-0 (pbk) : £1.50
Primary classification 641.6′383 B81-12731

641.6′57 — Slimmers. Food: Dishes using herbs — *Recipes*

Peplow, Elizabeth. Stay slim with herbs and spices / Elizabeth Peplow ; illustrated by Yvonne Skargon. — London : Darton, Longman & Todd, 1981. — vii,120p : ill ; 22cm
Bibliography: p112. — Includes index
ISBN 0-232-51464-x (pbk) : £2.95 : CIP rev.
Also classified at 641.6′383 B81-02361

641.6′6 — Food: Meat dishes — *Recipes*

Allison, Sonia. The Bisto book of meat cookery / Sonia Allison. — Newton Abbot : David & Charles, c1980. — 128p : ill(some col.) ; 28cm
Includes index
ISBN 0-7153-7893-7 : £4.95 : CIP rev. B80-13457

Make it with meat : recipes with British meat / [photography Melvin Grey]. — London (5 St. John's Sq., Smithfield, EC1M 4DE) : Meat Promotion Executive of the Meat and Livestock Commission, [1981]. — [16]p : col.ill ; 21cm
Unpriced (unbound) B81-37396

Reynolds, Mary. Buying and cooking meat / Mary Reynolds. — Cambridge : Published for J. Sainsbury Limited by Woodhead-Faulkner, 1979 (1980 [printing]). — 40p : ill(some col.) ; 22cm. — (Sainsbury's food guides ; no.3)
Cover title. — Text on inside cover
£0.30 (pbk) B81-37265

641.6′6 — Food: Offal dishes — *Recipes*

Special offal. — London (5 St. John's Sq., Smithfield, EC2M 4DE) : Meat Promotion Executive of the Meat and Livestock Commission, [1981]. — [16]p : col.ill ; 21cm
Unpriced (unbound) B81-37395

641.6′6 — Pâtés & terrines — *Recipes*

Doorn, Joyce van. Making your own pâté : make your own chicken liver pâté, jugged hare pâté, salmon mousse, mushroom pâté, sausagemeat bread, steak-and-kidney pie, fish pâté, or vegetable pâté / Joyce van Doorn ; [translated by Andy and Nicolette Colborne] ; [illustrations by Jane Greenwood]. — Dorchester : Prism, 1980. — 118p : ill ; 21cm
Translation from the Dutch. — Includes index
ISBN 0-907061-01-x (cased) : £5.95
ISBN 0-907061-02-8 (pbk) : £2.95 B81-07643

641.6'63 — Food: Lamb dishes — *Recipes*

The **Great** British lamb guide : all you need to know to make the most of your British lamb. — London (5 St. John's Sq., Smithfield, EC1M 4DE) : Applied Creativity on behalf of the Meat Promotion Executive of the Meat and Livestock Commission, c1980. — 34p : col.ill ; 21cm
Cover title. — Text on inside covers
Unpriced (pbk) B81-37398

641.6'64'0944 — Food: French pork dishes — *Recipes*

Grigson, Jane. Charcuterie & French pork cookery / Jane Grigson ; illustrated by M.J. Mott. — Harmondsworth : Penguin, 1970, c1967 (1981 [printing]). — 347p : ill ; 20cm. — (Penguin handbooks)
Originally published: London : Michael Joseph, 1967. — Includes index
ISBN 0-14-046158-2 : £2.95 B81-25442

641.6'65 — Food: Poultry dishes — *Recipes*

Pomeroy, Elizabeth. The Hamlyn chicken cookbook / Elizabeth Pomeroy. — Rev. and updated ed. — London : Hamlyn, 1981. — 127p : ill(some col.) ; 23cm
Previous ed.: published as Chicken cookbook. 1973. — Includes index
ISBN 0-600-32233-5 : £3.50 B81-24161

641.6'73 — Cheesecakes — *Recipes*

Black, Maggie. Cheesecakes / Maggie Black. — London : Ward Lock, 1980. — 96p : col.ill ; 27cm
Includes index
ISBN 0-7063-5853-8 : £3.95 : CIP rev. B80-04296

641.6'73 — Food: Cheese dishes — *Recipes*

Berry, Mary, *1935-*. Cooking with cheese / Mary Berry ; illustrations by Laura Potter. — London : Batsford, 1980. — 120p : ill ; 26cm
Includes index
ISBN 0-7134-1925-3 : £6.95 B81-00995

Todd, Jane. Egg and cheese cookbook / Jane Todd. — London : Hamlyn, 1981. — 128p : ill (some col.) ; 23cm
Includes index
ISBN 0-600-32217-3 : £3.50
Primary classification 641.6'75 B81-24062

641.6'75 — Food: Egg dishes — *Recipes*

Todd, Jane. Egg and cheese cookbook / Jane Todd. — London : Hamlyn, 1981. — 128p : ill (some col.) ; 23cm
Includes index
ISBN 0-600-32217-3 : £3.50
Also classified at 641.6'73 B81-24062

641.6'754 — Omelets — *Recipes*

Crêpes, soufflés & omelets / edited by Rhona Newman. — London : Octopus, 1981. — 77p : ill(some col.) ; 28cm
Ill on lining papers. — Includes index
ISBN 0-7064-1477-2 : £1.99
Primary classification 641.8 B81-18194

641.6'8 — Food: Dishes using honey — *Recipes*

Francis, Claude. The book of honey / Claude Francis & Fernande Gontier ; illustrated by Stephen Zinkus. — London : Hale, 1981, c1979. — 175p : ill ; 24cm
Originally published: Brookline, Mass : Autumn Press, 1979. — Includes index
ISBN 0-7091-8647-9 : £6.95 B81-17136

Wittich, Boris. A taste of honey / Boris Wittich ; line drawings and design Peter Haillay ; [translation by Sara Moncur]. — Sherborne : Alphabooks, 1981. — 92p : ill ; 21cm
Translation of: Rund um den Honig
ISBN 0-906670-16-0 (cased) : £5.95
ISBN 0-906670-17-9 (pbk) : Unpriced B81-29529

641.6'9 — Food: Seafood dishes — *Recipes*

Ridgway, Judy. The seafood kitchen / Judy Ridgway. — London : Ward Lock, 1981. — 165p : ill (some col.) ; 26cm
Includes index
ISBN 0-7063-5992-5 : £7.95 : CIP rev. B80-19822

641.6'9'091631 — Food: North Atlantic seafood dishes — *Recipes*

Davidson, Alan, *1924-*. North Atlantic seafood / Alan Davidson. — Harmondsworth : Penguin, 1980, c1979. — 512p : ill,4maps,1coat of arms,1port ; 20cm. — (Penguin handbooks)
Originally published: London : Macmillan, 1979. — Bibliography: p477-493. — Includes index
ISBN 0-14-046298-8 (pbk) : £5.95 B81-00170

641.6'91 — Food: Game dishes — *Recipes*

Game cookery : preparation, freezing, cooking and recipes of game. — Brinscall (School La., Brinscall, Chorley, Lancs.) : Countryside Publications, [1980]. — 120p : ill ; 22cm
Cover title: The complete guide to game cookery
ISBN 0-86157-002-2 (cased) : £3.50
ISBN 0-86157-035-9 (pbk) : £1.90 B81-04185

641.6'92 — Food: Fish dishes: Dishes prepared using Magimix food processors — *Recipes*

Hanbury Tenison, Marika. Fish cookery with Magimix : recipes written for food processors / by Marika Hanbury Tenison. — Sunbury (Hanworth Rd., Sunbury, Middx) : 1CTC, 1981. — 31p ; 15x22cm
Cover title
ISBN 0-9506518-7-7 (spiral) : Unpriced B81-37680

641.6'92 — Food: Fish dishes — *Recipes*

Hanbury Tenison, Marika. New fish cookery / Marika Hanbury Tenison. — London : Granada, 1979 (1980 [printing]). — 256p ; 18cm. — (A Mayflower book)
Includes index
ISBN 0-583-12861-0 (pbk) : £1.25 B81-02062

Smith, Michael, *1927-*. A fine kettle of fish / Michael Smith. — London : BBC, 1981. — 46p ; 18cm
ISBN 0-563-17933-3 (pbk) : £1.00 B81-19346

641.7 — COOKERY. SPECIAL PROCESSES AND TECHNIQUES

641.7'1 — Baking — *Recipes*

Home baking made easy. — London : Marshall Cavendish, 1979. — 184p : col.ill ; 30cm
Includes index
ISBN 0-85685-704-1 : £5.95 B81-19573

641.7'1 — Health food dishes. Baking — *Recipes*

Young, Mala. Baking / [Mala Young] ; [illustrated by Susan Neale]. — Newton Abbot : David & Charles, c1981. — 48p : ill ; 21cm. — (Health food cooking)
ISBN 0-7153-8039-7 (pbk) : £1.50 B81-12729

641.7'6 — Food: Barbecue dishes — *Recipes*

Wenham, Lynette. The barbecue cookbook / Lynette Wenham. — Wellington [N.Z.] ; London (11 Southampton Row, WC1B 5HA) : A.H. & A.W. Reed, 1978. — 175p : ill ; 22cm
Includes index
ISBN 0-589-01065-4 (spiral) : £2.95 B81-15319

641.7'9 — Food. Non-cooked dishes — *Recipes*

Bowen, Carol. No need to cook book / Carol Bowen. — London : Hamlyn, 1981. — 128p : ill(some col.) ; 23cm
Includes index
ISBN 0-600-32241-6 : £3.50 B81-24163

641.8 — COOKERY. COMPOSITE DISHES

641.8 — Crepes — *Recipes*

Crêpes, soufflés & omelets / edited by Rhona Newman. — London : Octopus, 1981. — 77p : ill(some col.) ; 28cm
Ill on lining papers. — Includes index
ISBN 0-7064-1477-2 : £1.99
Also classified at 641.8'2 ; 641.6'754 B81-18194

641.8 — Flans — *Recipes*

Quiches & flans / edited by Deirdre Sadlier. — London : Octopus, 1981. — 77p : col.ill ; 28cm
Ill on lining papers. — Includes index
ISBN 0-7064-1511-6 : £1.99 B81-20274

641.8 — Food: Dishes using batter — *Recipes*

Norman, Cecilia. [The crêpe and pancake cookbook]. Pancakes and pizzas / Cecilia Norman. — London : Granada, 1980, c1979. — 159p ; 18cm. — (A Mayflower book)
Originally published: London : Barrie and Jenkins, 1979. — Includes index
ISBN 0-583-13219-7 (pbk) : £0.95 B81-00171

641.8'12 — Food: Starters — *Recipes*

Conil, Jean. Variations on a starter / by Jean Conil and Hugh Williams. — Loughton (Loughton, Essex) : Piatkus, 1980. — 139p : ill ; 23cm
Includes index
ISBN 0-86188-062-5 : £4.95 : CIP rev. B80-22178

Conil, Jean. Variations on a starter / Jean Conil and Hugh Williams. — London : New English Library, 1981, c1980. — 139p : ill ; 20cm. — (New English Library books for cooks)
Originally published: Loughton : Piatkus, 1980. — Includes index
ISBN 0-450-05060-2 (pbk) : £1.25 B81-17195

Hanbury Tenison, Marika. Soups and starters / Marika Hanbury Tenison. — [New ed.]. — London : Granada, 1980. — 238p ; 23cm
Previous ed.: published as Soups and hors d'oeuvres. Harmondsworth : Penguin, 1969. — Includes index
ISBN 0-246-11302-2 : £5.95
Primary classification 641.8'13 B81-00172

Jackson, Andrew. The pocket book of simple starters / Andrew and Anne Jackson. — London : Evans, 1980. — 128p : ill ; 17cm
Includes index
ISBN 0-237-44993-5 (pbk) : £1.75 : CIP rev. B80-05988

641.8'12 — Hors d'oeuvres — *Recipes*

[Complete cookery. *Selections*]. Soups and starters. — Maidenhead : Purnell, 1981. — 47p : ill ; 26cm. — (Purnell jiffy cook series)
Originally published: as part of Complete cookery. — Includes index
ISBN 0-361-05017-8 (pbk) : £0.99
Primary classification 641.8'13 B81-14673

641.8'12 — Starters: Dishes using natural foods — *Recipes*

Greer, Rita. Superb soups and starters. — Wellingborough : Thorsons, Sept.1981. — [128]p
ISBN 0-7225-0691-0 (pbk) : £2.95 : CIP entry
Primary classification 641.8'13 B81-22561

641.8'13 — Soups: Dishes using natural foods — *Recipes*

Greer, Rita. Superb soups and starters. — Wellingborough : Thorsons, Sept.1981. — [128]p
ISBN 0-7225-0691-0 (pbk) : £2.95 : CIP entry
Also classified at 641.8'12 B81-22561

641.8'13 — Soups — *Recipes*

[Complete cookery. *Selections*]. Soups and starters. — Maidenhead : Purnell, 1981. — 47p : ill ; 26cm. — (Purnell jiffy cook series)
Originally published: as part of Complete cookery. — Includes index
ISBN 0-361-05017-8 (pbk) : £0.99
Also classified at 641.8'12 B81-14673

Eno, David. The little brown soup book / text & illustrations David Eno ; calligraphy Jenny Irvermee. — Winchester (P.O. Box 23, Winchester, Hants. SO23 9TP) : Juniper, 1979. — 30p : ill ; 15cm
ISBN 0-903981-13-0 (pbk) : Unpriced B81-08005

Hanbury Tenison, Marika. Soups and starters / Marika Hanbury Tenison. — [New ed.]. — London : Granada, 1980. — 238p ; 23cm
Previous ed.: published as Soups and hors d'oeuvres. Harmondsworth : Penguin, 1969. — Includes index
ISBN 0-246-11302-2 : £5.95
Also classified at 641.8'12 B81-00172

641.8′15 — Bread — *Recipes*

Cakes, pastries and breads : 500 recipes / edited by Norma MacMillan. — London : Octopus, 1981. — 228p : ill ; 22cm
Includes index
ISBN 0-7064-1514-0 : £1.99
Primary classification 641.8′653 B81-34834

Holloway, Malcolm. Book of bread & breadmaking / Malcolm Holloway. — Poole : Blandford, [1981]. — 95p : ill(some col.),1port ; 15cm. — ('How to')
Includes index
ISBN 0-7137-1048-9 (pbk) : £1.95 B81-08469

McCay, Clive M.. The Cornell bread book : 54 recipes for nutritious loaves, rolls & coffee cakes / Clive M. McCay & Jeanette B. McCay. — Rev. and enlarged version. — New York : Dover ; London : Constable, 1980. — 27p : ill ; 28cm
Previous ed.: published as You can make Cornell bread. Englewood, Fl., 1973
ISBN 0-486-23995-0 (pbk) : £1.40 B81-39194

McMillan, Norma. Cakes, breads, biscuits / [recipes Norma McMillan]. — London : Marshall Cavendish, [1981]. — 96p : ill(some col.) ; 22cm. — (Supercook's kitchen)
Includes index
ISBN 0-85685-725-4 (pbk) : £0.99
Primary classification 641.8′653 B81-17574

Roberts, Ada Lou. The new book of favorite breads from Rose Lane Farm / by Ada Lou Roberts ; drawings by Edward J. Roberts. — Rev. and enl.. — New York : Dover ; London : Constable, 1981, c1970. — 192p : ill ; 21cm
Originally published: New York : Hearthside Press, 1970. — Includes index
ISBN 0-486-24091-6 (pbk) : £2.05 B81-39071

641.8′15′09429 — Wales. Bread — *Recipes*

Freeman, Bobby. A book of Welsh bread : recipes for the old, traditional wholegrain wheat, barley and rye breads of Wales, adapted for baking today / by Bobby Freeman. — Cardiff (85 Wyndham Crescent, Cardiff CF1 9EG) : Image Imprint, c1981. — [48]p : ill ; 15cm
ISBN 0-9507254-2-0 (pbk) : Unpriced B81-29036

641.8′2 — Main courses — *Recipes*

Berry, Mary, *1935-*. Mary Berry's main course. — London : Batsford, 1981. — 120p,[4]p of plates : ill(some col.) ; 25cm
Includes index
ISBN 0-7134-0920-7 (cased) : Unpriced
ISBN 0-7134-0901-5 (pbk) : £4.95 B81-27210

Bowen, Carol. Hamlyn all colour book of main dishes / Carol Bowen. — London : Hamlyn, c1981. — 124p : ill(some col.) ; 31cm
Includes index
ISBN 0-600-32248-3 : £3.99 B81-40754

Conil, Jean. Variations on a main course : how to create your own original dishes / by Jean Conil and Hugh Williams. — Loughton (17 Brook Rd., Loughton, Essex IG10 1BW) : Piatkus, 1981. — 144p : ill ; 23cm
Includes index
ISBN 0-86188-074-9 : £4.95 B81-09255

641.8′2 — Soufflés — *Recipes*

Crêpes, soufflés & omelets / edited by Rhona Newman. — London : Octopus, 1981. — 77p : ill(some col.) ; 28cm
Ill on lining papers. — Includes index
ISBN 0-7064-1477-2 : £1.99
Primary classification 641.8 B81-18194

641.8′21 — Food: Casserole dishes — *Recipes*

Hughes, Joyce. The cook-pot & casserole book / Joyce Hughes. — London : Ward Lock, 1981. — 139p : ill(some col.) ; 26cm
At head of title: Kenwood. — Includes index
ISBN 0-7063-5784-1 : £4.95
Also classified at 641.5′884 B81-39898

Lomask, Martha. Low, slow, delicious : recipes for casseroles and electric slow-cooking pots / Martha Lomask. — London : Faber, 1980. — 160p,[8]p of plates : col.ill ; 26cm
Includes index
ISBN 0-571-11384-2 : £7.95 : CIP rev.
Also classified at 641.5′884 B80-25866

McMillan, Norma. Casserole cooking / [recipes Norma McMillan]. — London : Marshall Cavendish, [1981]. — 96p : ill(some col.) ; 22cm. — (Supercook's kitchen)
Includes index
ISBN 0-85685-727-0 (pbk) B81-17578

641.8′22 — Food: Pasta dishes — *Recipes*

Hurst, Bernice. The perfect pasta / Bernice Hurst ; illustrations by Ronald Hurst. — Goring-on-Thames : Elvendon, 1981. — 32p : ill ; 16cm
ISBN 0-906552-06-0 (pbk) : £0.50 B81-28727

Lousada, Patrica. Pasta Italian style / Patricia Lousada. — Cambridge : Woodhead-Faulkner for J. Sainsbury Ltd., 1981. — 96p : ill(some col.) ; 19cm. — (A Sainsbury cookbook)
£0.75 (pbk) B81-38902

641.8′24 — Pizzas — *Recipes*

The **Pizza** cookbook / edited by Norma MacMillan. — London : Octopus, 1981. — 77p : ill(some col.) ; 27cm
Includes index
ISBN 0-7064-1512-4 : £1.99 B81-19510

641.8′3 — Food: Salad dishes — *Recipes*

Eno, David. The little brown salad book / text & illustrations David Eno ; calligraphy Jenny Irvermee. — Winchester (P.O. Box 23, Winchester, Hants. SO23 9TP) : Juniper, 1979. — 30p : ill ; 15cm
ISBN 0-903981-14-9 (pbk) : Unpriced B81-08006

Hurst, Bernice. The perfect salad / Bernice Hurst ; illustrated by Ronald Hurst. — Goring-on-Thames (33 Elvendon Rd., Goring-on-Thames, Reading, Berks.) : Elvendon, 1979. — 32p : ill ; 15cm
ISBN 0-906552-03-6 (pbk) : £0.50 B81-12628

641.8′3 — Health food salad dishes — *Recipes*

Young, Mala. Vegetables & salads / [Mala Young] ; [illustrated by Susan Neale]. — Newton Abbot : David & Charles, c1981. — 48p : ill ; 21cm. — (Health food cooking)
ISBN 0-7153-8036-2 (pbk) : £1.50
Primary classification 641.6′5 B81-12728

641.8′3′09 — Food: Salad dishes, *to ca 1700* — *Recipes*

Simmons, Rosemary. The good housewife sallets and salmagundis / drawn by Rosemary Simmons ; described by Gillian Goodwin. — London (29 Chalcot Sq., N.W.1) : Gelofer, c1980. — [32]p : ill ; 22cm
ISBN 0-9506529-1-1 (pbk) : Unpriced B81-11716

641.8′4 — Sandwiches — *Recipes*

Bowen, Carol. The giant sandwich book / Carol Bowen. — Feltham : Hamlyn Paperbacks, 1981. — 191p : ill ; 18cm. — (Hamlyn kitchen library)
Includes index
ISBN 0-600-20317-4 (pbk) : £1.25 B81-26083

641.8′52 — Preserves. Making — *Amateurs' manuals*

Avery, Jane. Making your own preserves / Jane and Rob Avery ; [illustrated by Trevor Aldous]. — Dorchester : Prism, c1981. — 112p : ill ; 20x21cm
Includes index
ISBN 0-907061-17-6 (cased) : Unpriced
ISBN 0-907061-18-4 (pbk) : Unpriced B81-38115

Ridgway, Judy. Home preserving / Judy Ridgway ; illustrated by Vanessa Pancheri. — London : Teach Yourself, 1980. — 184p : ill ; 20cm
Includes index
ISBN 0-340-24794-0 (pbk) : £1.75 : CIP rev. B80-10143

641.8′52 — Preserves — *Recipes*

Lambert, Heather. The Sainsbury book of preserves & pickles / Heather Lambert. — London : Published for J. Sainsbury by Cathay, 1981. — 93p : col.ill ; 22cm
Index and ill on lining papers
ISBN 0-86178-069-8 : £0.99
Primary classification 641.6′16 B81-22081

641.8′52 — Preserves using honey — *Recipes*

Geiskopf, Susan. The sunshine larder : using honey to preserve the natural goodness of summer's bounty. — Wellingborough : Thorsons, Sept.1981. — [160]p
ISBN 0-7225-0696-1 (pbk) : £3.50 : CIP entry B81-22560

641.8′53 — Confectionery: Sweets — *Recipes* — *For children*

Leggatt, Jenny. Sweets for presents / by Jenny Leggatt ; illustrated by Maureen Galvani. — Over : Dinosaur, c1981. — [24]p : col.ill ; 16x19cm. — (Dinosaur's action books)
ISBN 0-85122-270-6 (cased) : £1.85 : CIP rev.
ISBN 0-85122-212-9 (pbk) : £0.70 B80-17821

641.8′6 — Desserts — *Recipes*

500 puddings and desserts recipes / edited by Norma MacMillan. — London : Octopus, 1981. — 228p : ill ; 22cm
Includes index
ISBN 0-7064-1513-2 : £1.99 B81-28250

Berry, Mary, *1935-*. Glorious puds / Mary Berry. — London : New English Library, 1981. — 168p ; 20cm
Originally published: London : Dent, 1980. — Includes index
ISBN 0-450-05203-6 (pbk) : £1.25 B81-40627

[Complete cookery. *Selections*]. Puddings and desserts. — Maidenhead : Purnell, 1981. — 47p : ill ; 26cm. — (Purnell jiffy cook series)
Originally published: as part of Complete cookery. — Includes index
ISBN 0-361-05020-8 (pbk) : £0.99 B81-14670

Conil, Jean. Variations on a dessert : how to create your own original dishes / by Jean Conil and Hugh Williams. — Loughton : Piatkus, 1981. — 144p : ill ; 23cm. — (A Julian Friedmann book)
Includes index
ISBN 0-86188-079-x : £4.95 : CIP rev. B81-04280

Conil, Jean. Variations on a dessert. — London : New English Library, Feb.1982. — [144]p
Originally published: Loughton : Piatkus, 1981
ISBN 0-450-05205-2 (pbk) : £1.25 : CIP entry B81-36206

McMillan, Norma. Favourite desserts / [recipes, Norma McMillan]. — London : Marshall Cavendish, [1981?]. — 96p : ill(some col.) ; 22cm. — (Supercook's kitchen)
Includes index
ISBN 0-85685-726-2 (pbk) : £0.99 B81-19574

Woman's realm book of cakes & desserts. — London : Hamlyn, c1981. — 156p : col.ill ; 26cm
Ill on lining papers. — Includes index
ISBN 0-600-32230-0 : £3.99
Primary classification 641.8′653 B81-29125

641.8′6 — Health food confectionery — *Recipes*

Hunt, Janet, *1942-*. The wholefood sweets book / by Janet Hunt ; illustrated by Clive Birch. — Wellingborough : Thorsons, 1981. — 128p : ill ; 22cm. — (A Thorsons wholefood cookbook)
Includes index
ISBN 0-7225-0654-6 (cased) : Unpriced
ISBN 0-7225-0653-8 (pbk) : £2.95 B81-14771

641.8′65 — Pastries: Dishes prepared using Magimix food processors — *Recipes*

Barber, Lucille. Pastry making with Magimix : 72 recipes written for food processors / by Lucille Barber. — Isleworth (25 Lower Sq., Isleworth, Middx) : 1CTC, [1981]. — 45p ; 15x22cm
Cover title
Unpriced (spiral) B81-37681

641.8′65 — Pastries — *Recipes*

Fred′s pastry book / [recipes compiled by Bridget Jones] ; [photography by Paul Williams] ; [edited by Carol Bowen] ; [illustrations by David Mostyn]. — London : Hamlyn, c1981. — 128p : ill(some col.) ; 23cm
Includes index
ISBN 0-600-32245-9 : £3.50 B81-37326

641.8′652 — Pies — *Recipes*

Hurst, Bernice. The perfect pie / Bernice Hurst ; illustrations by Ronald Hurst. — Goring-on-Thames : Elvendon, 1981. — 32p : ill ; 16cm
ISBN 0-906552-05-2 (pbk) : £0.50 B81-28726

641.8′653 — Cakes: Dishes prepared using Magimix food processors — *Recipes*

Berry, Mary, *1935-*. Cake making with Magimix : recipes written for food processors / by Mary Berry. — Sunbury (25 Hanworth Rd., Sunbury, Middx) : ICTC, 1978. — 32p ; 15x22cm
Cover title
ISBN 0-9506518-2-6 (spiral) : Unpriced
B81-37676

641.8′653 — Cakes: Dishes prepared using Robot-chef food processors — *Recipes*

Berry, Mary, *1935-*. Cake making with Robot-Chef : 32 recipes written for food processors / by Mary Berry. — Isleworth (25 Lower Sq., Isleworth, Middx) : 1CTC, [1978?]. — 32p ; 15x22cm
Cover title
Unpriced (spiral) B81-37677

641.8′653 — Cakes — *Recipes*

Berry, Mary. Fast cakes / by Mary Berry. — Loughton : Piatkus, c1981. — 207,[12]p of plates : col.ill ; 26cm
Includes index
ISBN 0-86188-059-5 : £6.95 : CIP rev.
B81-07620

Cakes, pastries and breads : 500 recipes / edited by Norma MacMillan. — London : Octopus, 1981. — 228p : ill ; 22cm
Includes index
ISBN 0-7064-1514-0 : £1.99
Also classified at 641.8′15 B81-34834

Good housekeeping complete book of cakes and pastries / by Good Housekeeping Institute. — London : Ebury in collaboration with Tate & Lyle Refineries, 1981. — 184p : ill(some col.) ; 26cm
Includes index
ISBN 0-85223-189-x : £6.95 B81-19552

Holt, Geraldene. Geraldene Holt′s cake stall. — London : Hodder and Stoughton, 1980. — 240p ; 23cm
ISBN 0-340-25409-2 : £6.95 : CIP rev.
B80-10684

McMillan, Norma. Cakes, breads, biscuits / [recipes Norma McMillan]. — London : Marshall Cavendish, [1981]. — 96p : ill(some col.) ; 22cm. — (Supercook′s kitchen)
Includes index
ISBN 0-85685-725-4 (pbk) : £0.99
Also classified at 641.8′654 ; 641.8′15
B81-17574

Spencer, Jill. Hamlyn all colour book of cakes and cake decorating / Jill Spencer. — London : Hamlyn, 1980. — 125p : col.ill ; 30cm
Ill on lining papers. — Includes index
ISBN 0-600-32225-4 : £3.99 B81-00169

Woman′s realm book of cakes & desserts. — London : Hamlyn, c1981. — 156p : col.ill ; 26cm
Ill on lining papers. — Includes index
ISBN 0-600-32230-0 : £3.99
Also classified at 641.8′6 B81-29125

641.8′654 — Biscuits — *Recipes*

Allison, Sonia. Sonia Allison′s biscuit book. — Loughton : Piatkins, Nov.1981. — [96]p
ISBN 0-86188-126-5 : £3.50 : CIP entry
B81-30377

McMillan, Norma. Cakes, breads, biscuits / [recipes Norma McMillan]. — London : Marshall Cavendish, [1981]. — 96p : ill(some col.) ; 22cm. — (Supercook′s kitchen)
Includes index
ISBN 0-85685-725-4 (pbk) : £0.99
Primary classification 641.8′653 B81-17574

641.87 — PREPARATION OF BEVERAGES

641.8′72 — Wines. Making — *Amateurs′ manuals*

Ekins, R.. Worldwide winemaking recipes : by R. Ekins. — [Andover] : [Amateur Winemaker], 1978. — 115p : ill ; 18cm
Bibliography: p115
ISBN 0-900841-53-2 (pbk) : £0.75 B81-05920

Leverett, Brian. Instant winemaking / by Brian Leverett. — Andover : Amateur Winemaker, [1980]. — 75p ; 18cm
Includes index
£1.00 (pbk) B81-01872

Mitchell, J. R. (John Richard), *1934*. Improving your finished wine / by John Mitchell. — [Andover] : ′Amateur Winemaker′, 1978. — 109p,[2] leaves of plates : ill(some col.) ; 18cm
Bibliography: p109. - Includes index
ISBN 0-900841-50-8 (pbk) : £1.20 B81-01773

Parrack, Anne. Commonsense winemaking / by Anne Parrack. — Andover : Amateur Winemakers, 1978. — 206p : ill ; 18cm
Bibliography: p133.— Includes index
ISBN 0-900841-52-4 (pbk) : £1.25 B81-02079

Turner, Ben. Andy & Flo′s book of beer & wine making / by Ben Turner. — London : Mirror, 1980. — 140p : ill ; 18cm
Ill on inside cover. — Includes index
ISBN 0-85939-227-9 (pbk) : £0.85
Also classified at 641.8′73 B81-07021

641.8′73 — Brewing — *Amateurs′ manuals*

Leverett, Brian. Home beermaking / Brian Leverett. — Dorchester : Prism, 1980. — 106p : ill ; 21cm
Includes index
ISBN 0-907061-07-9 (cased) : £5.95
ISBN 0-907061-08-7 (pbk) : £2.95 B81-01626

Newsom, W. G.. The happy brewer : - the principles and practice of home brewing / by W.G. Newsom. — [Andover] : ′Amateur Winemaker′, 1978. — 109p : ill ; 18cm
Includes index
ISBN 0-900841-49-4 (pbk) : £1.00 B81-01777

Turner, Ben. Andy & Flo′s book of beer & wine making / by Ben Turner. — London : Mirror, 1980. — 140p : ill ; 18cm
Ill on inside cover. — Includes index
ISBN 0-85939-227-9 (pbk) : £0.85
Primary classification 641.8′72 B81-07021

Turner, Ben. Home brewed beer & cider / by Ben Turner. — Wakefield : EP Publishing, 1981. — 96p : ill(some col.) ; 24cm
ISBN 0-7158-0638-6 (cased) : Unpriced
ISBN 0-7158-0736-6 (pbk) : £2.50
Also classified at 641.8′73 B81-33667

Whitehouse, Albert. Home brewing : an illustrated guide / Albert Whitehouse. — Newton Abbot : David & Charles, c1981. — 48p : ill ; 26cm
Bibliography: p46. - Includes index
ISBN 0-7153-7985-2 : £3.95 B81-20811

641.8′73 — Cider. Making — *Amateurs′ manuals*

Turner, Ben. Home brewed beer & cider / by Ben Turner. — Wakefield : EP Publishing, 1981. — 96p : ill(some col.) ; 24cm
ISBN 0-7158-0638-6 (cased) : Unpriced
ISBN 0-7158-0736-6 (pbk) : £2.50
Primary classification 641.8′73 B81-33667

641.8′74 — Alcoholic drinks — *For bartenders*

International guide to drinks / compiled by the United Kingdom Bartenders′ Guild. — 8th ed. — London : Hutchinson, 1981. — 240p,[16]p of plates : ill(some col.),1map ; 22cm
Previous ed.: 1978. — Bibliography: p228. — Includes index
ISBN 0-09-145921-4 (pbk) : £3.95 B81-32511

641.8′74 — Cocktails — *Recipes*

Walter, Michael, *19---*. The Cinzano cocktail book : the complete guide to home cocktails / by Michael Walker. — London : Queen Anne, 1980. — 96p : ill(some col.) ; 29cm
Includes index
ISBN 0-362-00514-1 : £4.95 B81-02240

641.8′74 — Liqueurs. Making — *Amateurs′ manuals*

Doorn, Joyce van. Making your own liqueurs : recipes for making fruits in alcohol, ratafias, liqueurs from herbs and flowers, bitters, elixirs, and love-potions / Joyce van Doorn. — Dorchester : Prism, 1980, c1977. — 117p : ill ; 21cm
Translation from the Dutch. — Includes index
ISBN 0-907061-03-6 (cased) : £5.95
ISBN 0-907061-04-4 (pbk) : £2.95 B81-07644

641.8′74 — Man. Hangovers

Freud, Clement. Hangovers / Clement Freud ; illustrated by Bill Tidy. — London : Sheldon, 1981. — 80p : ill ; 21cm
Text and ill on lining papers
ISBN 0 85969-355-4 : £3.95 B81-40328

642 — FOOD AND MEAL SERVICE

642′.3 — Camping. Catering — *For Girl Guides*

Robertson, Elizabeth, *1926-*. Catering : for camps & holidays / Elizabeth Robertson. — London : Girl Guides Association, 1981. — 39p : ill ; 21cm
Bibliography: p39
£0.50 (pbk) B81-22743

642′.4 — Catering — *Conference proceedings*

International Symposium on Catering Systems Design *(2nd : 1979 : Harrogate)*. Advances in catering technology : proceedings of the Second International Symposium on Catering Systems Design / organised by the Catering Research Unit, University of Leeds, and held in Harrogate, England, 10-13 September 1979 ; conference organiser John F. Armstrong ; edited by G. Glew. — London : Applied Science, c1980. — xii,492p : ill,2plans ; 23cm
Includes index
ISBN 0-85334-844-8 : £40.00 : CIP rev.
B80-09763

642′.6 — Catering. Waitering — *Manuals*

Task cards, food service. — Wembley (Ramsey House, Central Sq., Wembley, Middx HA9 7AP) : Hotel and Catering Industry Training Board, [1981]. — 15leaves : ill ; 30cm
Cover title
Unpriced (spiral) B81-33182

642′.6′07 — Waiters & waitresses. Training — *Manuals*

Training in food service. — [Wembley] : HCITB, [1981?]. — [128]p ; 27x30cm + 2pamphlets ([4];[8];21cm)
Cover title
Unpriced (spiral) B81-33176

643 — THE HOME AND ITS EQUIPMENT

643 — Residences — *Illustrations* — *For children*

Testa, Fulvio. An ideal home. — London : Abelard-Schuman, Oct.1981. — [32]p
ISBN 0-200-72768-0 : £4.95 : CIP entry
B81-26757

643′.022′2 — Household objects — *Illustrations* — *For children*

Daniels, Meg. Indoors. — London : Blackie, Feb.1982. — [12]p. — (Blackie concertina books)
ISBN 0-216-91129-x : £0.95 : CIP entry
B81-36033

643′.028′9 — Residences. Safety measures - *Amateurs′ manuals*

Creese, Angela. Safety for your family. — 2nd ed. — London : Bell & Hyman, Aug.1981. — [281]p
Previous ed.: London : Mills & Boon, 1968
ISBN 0-7135-2070-1 (pbk) : CIP entry
Also classified at 616.02′52′024649 B81-16361

643′.16 — Houses. Security measures

Hughes, Denis. The security survey. — Aldershot : Gower, Feb.1982. — [160]p
ISBN 0-566-02291-5 : £12.50 : CIP entry
B81-36213

643′.2 — United States. Mobile homes — *Amateurs′ manuals*

Practical guide to mobile homes. — New York ; London : Van Nostrand Reinhold, c1980. — 144p : ill(some col.),plans ; 29cm
ISBN 0-442-25638-8 : £9.70 B81-25559

643′.3 — Residences. Kitchens. Management

Chandler, Barbara. The gas kitchen companion / Barbara Chandler and Annette Yates ; illustrated by Ken Astrop. — London : Ward Lock in co-operation with British Gas, 1980. — 96p : col.ill ; 24x26cm
Includes index
ISBN 0-7063-6053-2 : £3.95 B81-00997

643′.53 — Great Britain. Residences. Nurseries, *1837-1901*

Miall, Antony. The Victorian nursery book / by Antony and Peter Miall. — London : Dent, 1980. — 192p,[16]p of plates : ill(some col.),music,facsims ; 25cm
ISBN 0-460-04460-5 : £9.50 : CIP rev.
B80-17823

643′.604 — Household equipment for physically handicapped children. Making — *Amateurs′ manuals*

Caston, Don. Easy to make aids for your handicapped child / Don Caston. — London : Souvenir, 1981. — vii,134p : ill ; 22cm. — (Human horizons series) (A Condor book)
ISBN 0-285-64950-7 (cased) : £6.95
ISBN 0-285-64955-8 (pbk) : £4.95 B81-25179

643′.604 — Physically handicapped persons. Household equipment. Making — *Amateurs′ manuals*

Grainger, Stuart E.. Making aids for disabled living / Stuart E. Grainger. — London : Batsford, 1981. — 87p : ill ; 26cm
ISBN 0-7134-3934-3 : £5.95 B81-37932

643′.6′071041 — Great Britain. Schools. Students, 5-14 years. Curriculum subjects: Household equipment — *For teaching*

Induni, Anne. Materials in the home / Anne Induni. — Basingstoke (Houndmills, Basingstoke RG21 2XS) : Globe Education [for] West Sussex County Council, 1981. — 33p : ill,forms ; 30cm. — (Science horizons. Level 1)
Bibliography: p11
ISBN 0-333-31300-3 (pbk) : £3.95 B81-31306

43′.7 — Houses. Improvement — *Amateurs′ manuals*

The **Knack**. — London : Marshall Cavendish, Feb.1982. — 24v.
ISBN 0-85685-999-0 : CIP entry B81-37580

43′.7 — Houses. Renovation — *Amateurs′ manuals*

Taylor, Alan, *1901-*. The pocket book of home renovation / Alan Taylor. — London : Evans, c1980. — 112p : ill ; 17cm
Includes index
ISBN 0-237-45501-3 (pbk) : £1.75 : CIP rev.
B80-18407

43′.7 — Residences. Decorating — *Amateurs′ manuals*

King, Harold, *1927-*. Book of home decorating / Harold and Elizabeth King. — Poole : Blandford, [1981]. — 95p : col.ill ; 15cm. — ('How to')
Includes index
ISBN 0-7137-1050-0 (pbk) : £1.95 B81-08472

Mix and match home decoration / [Ethne Clarke ... et al.]. — London : Hamlyn, 1981. — 64p : ill(some col.) ; 25cm
Includes index
ISBN 0-600-30518-x (pbk) : £1.50 B81-36665

Todman, James. Decorating your home / by James Todman ; drawings by N. Mackenzie. — London : Chancerel, c1979. — 93p : ill(some col.),plans,1port ; 21cm. — (Action books)
ISBN 0-905703-19-7 : £1.95 B81-21232

643′.7 — Residences. Interiors. Decorating — *Amateurs′ manuals*

The **Complete** book of decorating / edited by Corinne Benicka. — London : Hamlyn in association with Phoebus, 1980. — 255p : ill (some col.),plans ; 31cm
'This material first appeared in Das grosse praktische Einrichtungsbuch′ — title page verso. — Includes index
ISBN 0-600-30502-3 : £8.95
Primary classification 747 B81-02423

643′.7 — Residences. Maintenance & repair — *Amateurs′ manuals*

The **Encyclopedia** of home maintenance / edited by Julian Worthington. — London : Orbis, 1981. — 192p : ill(some col.) ; 29cm
Includes index
ISBN 0-85613-320-5 (cased) : Unpriced
ISBN 0-85613-340-x (pbk) : £3.95 B81-39965

The **Hamlyn** guide to home maintenance. — London : Hamlyn, 1979, c1977. — 528p : ill (some col.) ; 26cm
Includes index. — Contents: Home repair and maintenance / Tony Wilkins — Home building work / Bill Goodson — Home plumbing / Ernest Hall — Home electrics / Geoffrey Burdett — Home decorating / Tony Wilkins
ISBN 0-600-36393-7 : £5.95 B81-01831

James, Trevor, *1949-*. Repairing houses : a step-by-step guide / Trevor James. — London : Sphere, 1981. — [297]p : ill ; 30cm
ISBN 0-7221-5050-4 (pbk) : £5.95 B81-23351

Keegan, Patrick. The reluctant handyman. — Weybridge : Whittet Books, Oct.1981. — [192]p
ISBN 0-7112-0204-4 : £5.95 : CIP entry
B81-28067

Reader′s digest concise repair manual. — 1st ed, Repr. with amendments. — London : Reader′s Digest, 1980, c1977. — 264p : ill(some col.) ; 28cm
Includes index
£6.95 B81-13022

Wilkins, Tony. Do-it-yourself : a basic manual / Tony Wilkins ; illustrations by Bill Thacker. — [London] : Teach Yourself Books, 1980. — 152p : ill ; 18cm. — (Teach yourself books)
Includes index
ISBN 0-340-25737-7 (pbk) : £1.25 B81-00998

643′.7′0941 — Great Britain. Residences. Maintenance, repair & improvement — *Serials*

Popular DIY : for practical home repairs & improvements. — Vol.1, no.1 (Dec.1980)-. — Brentwood (Sovereign House, Brentwood, Essex CM14 4SE) : Sovereign Publications for Popular DIY Ltd, 1980-. — v. : ill ; 28cm
Monthly
£9.60 per year B81-05445

643′.7′0973 — United States. Houses. Renovation — *Amateurs′ manuals*

Rooney, William F.. Practical guide to home restoration / by William F. Rooney. — New York ; London : Van Nostrand Reinhold, c1980. — 143p : ill(some col.),facsims ; 29cm
ISBN 0-442-25400-8 : £9.70 B81-04411

643′.7′0973 — United States. Residences. Maintenance & repair — *Amateurs′ manuals*

Home emergency repair book / by Xyzyx Information Corporation. — New York ; London : McGraw-Hill, c1978. — 191p : ill ; 28cm
Originally published: in 2 vols. H.E.L.P., home emergency ladies pal ; and, More H.E.L.P. for home care. 1972
ISBN 0-07-072229-3 (pbk) : £5.95
Primary classification 363.1′3′0973 B81-16444

Seaquist, Edgar O.. Diagnosing and repairing house structure problems / Edgar O. Seaquist, Jr. — New York ; London : McGraw-Hill, c1980. — x,255p : ill ; 25cm
Ill on lining papers. — Includes index
ISBN 0-07-056013-7 : £8.95 B81-00999

644 — HOUSEHOLD UTILITIES

644 — Buildings. Air conditioning, heating & ventilation equipment. Cost effectiveness. Promotion. Use of control systems

Controls and energy savings / Department of Energy. — London (Room 1312, Thames House South, Millbank SW1P 4QJ) : Department of Energy, [1980]. — 10p : ill ; 21cm. — (Fuel efficiency booklet ; 10)
Cover title
Unpriced (pbk) B81-06284

644 — Energy resources. Conservation by households

Alves, Ronald. Living with energy / text by Ronald Alves ; photographs by Charles Milligan ; preface by Ralph Nader. — London : Macmillan, 1978. — 128p : ill(some col.) ; 25cm
Bibliography: p127-128
ISBN 0-333-23732-3 (pbk) : £4.95 B81-17831

644 — Great Britain. Residences. Energy. Conservation — *Amateurs′ manuals*

Hammond, Garry. Save it : the energy consumer′s handbook / Garry Hammond and Carol Russell ; consultant Kevin Newport. — London : Pan, 1980, c1979. — 160p : ill ; 18cm. — (Pan information)
Bibliography: p152. — Includes index
ISBN 0-330-26207-6 (pbk) : £1.25 B81-01000

644 — Great Britain. Residences. Energy. Consumption & conservation — *Serials*

Heatline / the bulletin of the Energy Advice Unit. — Vol.1, no.1 (June 1980)-. — Newcastle upon Tyne (81 Jesmond Rd, Newcastle upon Tyne NE2 1NH) : The Unit, 1980-. — v. : ill ; 30cm
ISSN 0144-7572 = Heatline : £5.00 per year
B81-02338

644 — United States. Energy. Conservation — *Amateurs′ manuals*

Norback, Peter. The consumer′s energy handbook / Peter Norback, Craig Norback. — New York ; London : Van Nostrand Reinhold, c1981. — 362p : ill,plans ; 29cm
Bibliography: p353-355. — Includes index
ISBN 0-442-26066-0 : £14.95 B81-25361

644′.1 — Great Britain. Residences. Heating. Costs. Reduction

Clayton, Michael, *1924-*. Cutting the cost of energy : a practical guide for the householder / Michael Clayton. — Newton Abbot : David & Charles, c1981. — 127p : ill ; 22cm
Includes index
ISBN 0-7153-7927-5 : £4.95 B81-08698

644′.1′0151 — England. Secondary schools. Curriculum subjects: Applications of digital computer systems in calculations about heating of residences — *For teaching*

Home heating / Schools Council, Computers in the Curriculum ; edited by R.D. Masterton and R.E.J. Lewis ; from the original work by R.D. Masterton and P.W. Smith. — [London] : [Schools Council Publications] : Distributed by Edward Arnold, [1979]. — vii,50p : ill,1map ; 30cm
ISBN 0-7131-0225-x (unbound) : £9.20
B81-12291

645 — HOUSEHOLD FURNISHINGS

645 — Embroidered household furnishing. Making — *Manuals*
Lemon, Jane. Embroidered boxes & other construction techniques / Jane Lemon ; with photographs by Valerie Harding and Rob Matheson. — London : Faber, 1980. — 189p,[8]p of plates : ill(some col.) ; 26cm
Bibliography: p189
ISBN 0-571-11606-x : £10.50 : CIP rev. B80-18840

645'.4 — Upholstering — *Amateurs' manuals*
Ward, Kitty. Upholstery. — London : Paul, Sept.1981. — 1v.
ISBN 0-09-145681-9 (pbk) : £5.50 : CIP entry B81-22615

646 — CLOTHING, SEWING, ETC

646.2'044 — Sewing machines — *Amateurs' manuals*
Thompson, Angela, *1927-*. The complete book of the sewing machine / Angela Thompson. — London : Hamlyn, c1980. — 198p : ill(some col.) ; 28cm
Includes index
ISBN 0-600-30503-1 : £6.95 B81-02753

646.2'1 — Soft furnishings. Making — *Manuals*
Encyclopedia of home sewing / [edited by Yvonne Deutch] ; [designed by Linda Cole]. — London : Marshall Cavendish, 1977 (1979 printing). — 243p : ill(some col.) ; 29cm
Includes index
ISBN 0-85685-750-5 : £2.99 B81-19572

646.2'13 — Soft furnishings: Loose covers. Making — *Manuals*
Davies, Mary. Tailored loose covers. — London : Paul, Oct.1981. — 1v.
ISBN 0-09-145660-6 (cased) : £6.95 : CIP entry
ISBN 0-09-145661-4 (pbk) : £4.95 B81-26770

646'.3 — Clothing — *For children*
Burton, Terry. My clothes : a picture story book for pre-school children / [illustrated by Terry Burton]. — London : Macdonald Educational [for] Marks & Spencer, c1980. — [8]p : chiefly col.ill ; 18x19cm
Cover title. — Text, ill on inside covers
ISBN 0-356-07395-5 : £0.40 B81-04950

646'.3 — Fur clothing, *to 1980*
Ewing, Elizabeth. Fur in dress / Elizabeth Ewing. — London : Batsford, 1981. — 168p,4p of plates : ill(some col.),facsims,ports(some col.) ; 26cm
Bibliography: p163-164. — Includes index
ISBN 0-7134-1741-2 : £15.00 B81-27211

646'.31'029441 — Great Britain. Physically handicapped persons' clothing — *Buyers' guides*
Clothing and dressing for adults / compiler and editor E. R. Wilshere. — [5th ed.]. — Oxford (Nuffield Orthopaedic Centre, Oxford OX3 7LD) : Oxford Area Health Authority (Teaching), c1981. — 44p : ill ; 30cm. — (Equipment for the disabled)
Previous ed.: 1976. — Includes index
£3.00 (pbk) B81-27541

646'.34 — Women's clothing — *For overweight women*
Goday, Dale. Dressing thin : how to look ten, twenty, up to thirty-five pounds thinner without losing an ounce! / by Dale Goday with Molly Cochran. — London : Omnibus, 1980. — 127p : ill ; 21cm
ISBN 0-86001-733-8 (pbk) : Unpriced B81-39086

646'.34 — Women's clothing. Selection — *Manuals*
Perceval, Sara. Star image. — London : Unwin Paperbacks, Oct.1981. — [160]p
ISBN 0-04-391005-x (pbk) : £2.25 : CIP entry B81-28153

646.4 — Clothing. Making — *Manuals*
Creative dressing : the unique collection of top designer looks that you can make yourself / [compiled by] Kaori O'Connor. — London : Routledge & Kegan Paul, 1980. — 192p : ill (some col.) ; 28cm
ISBN 0-7100-0680-2 : £8.95 : CIP rev.
Also classified at 746.9'2 B80-20818

Creative dressing : the unique collection of top designer looks that you can make yourself / [compiled by] Kaori O'Connor. — Harmondsworth : Penguin, 1981, c1980. — 192p : ill(some col.),ports(some col.) ; 27cm
Originally published: London : Routledge & Kegan Paul. 1980
ISBN 0-14-046437-9 (pbk) : £4.95
Also classified at 746.9'2 B81-40480

646.4 — Clothing. Repair — *Amateurs' manuals*
Goldsworthy, Maureen. Mend it! : a complete guide to clothes repair / Maureen Goldsworthy. — London : Mills & Boon, 1979. — 127p : ill ; 25cm
ISBN 0-263-06404-2 (pbk) : £3.25 B81-01874

646.4 — Old persons' clothing. Crocheting & knitting — *Patterns*
Hollingworth, Shelagh. Knitting & crochet for the physically handicapped & elderly / Shelagh Hollingworth ; photographs by Brian Hollingworth ; line drawings by Shelagh and Giles Hollingworth. — London : Batsford, 1981. — 120p : ill ; 26cm
Includes index
ISBN 0-7134-3340-x : £7.95
Also classified at 646.4'01 B81-19639

646.4'01 — Physically handicapped persons' clothing. Crocheting & knitting — *Patterns*
Hollingworth, Shelagh. Knitting & crochet for the physically handicapped & elderly / Shelagh Hollingworth ; photographs by Brian Hollingworth ; line drawings by Shelagh and Giles Hollingworth. — London : Batsford, 1981. — 120p : ill ; 26cm
Includes index
ISBN 0-7134-3340-x : £7.95
Primary classification 646.4 B81-19639

646.4'06 — Clothing for children, to 5 years. Making — *Manuals*
The **Complete** book of babycrafts : how to make beautiful clothes and toys for your child / consultant editor, Eleanor Van Zandt ; house editor, Mary Lambert. — London : Ebury, 1981. — 184p : col.ill ; 30cm
ISBN 0-85223-214-4 : £7.95
Also classified at 745.592 B81-40918

646.4'06 — Clothing for children, to 11 years. Making — *Patterns*
Cardy, Lynn. Kid's clothes. — London : Bell & Hyman, Oct.1981. — [128]p
ISBN 0-7135-1295-4 (cased) : £7.95 : CIP entry
ISBN 0-7135-1296-2 (pbk) : £4.95 B81-24654

646.4'07 — Clothing. Crocheting — *Patterns*
Hubert, Margaret. Weekend crochet projects / Margaret Hubert. — New York ; London : Van Nostrand Reinhold, 1981. — 96p,[4]p of plates : ill(some col.) ; 29cm
Includes index
ISBN 0-442-23850-9 : £11.20 B81-32719

646.4'2'04 — Women's underwear. Making — *Manuals*
Lingerie. — Newton Abbot : David and Charles, Oct.1981. — [152]p
ISBN 0-7153-8174-1 : £9.50 : CIP entry B81-27949

646.4'3'04 — Dressmaking — *For schools*
Goldsworthy, Maureen. Knowing your sewing. — London : Bell & Hyman, July 1981. — [64]p
Originally published: London : Mills & Boon, 1978
ISBN 0-7135-2002-7 (pbk) : £3.00 : CIP entry B81-21501

646.4'304 — Skirts & women's coats. Making — *Manuals*
Heath, Samuel. Coat and skirt making : skirts, trousers, jackets, coats / Samuel Heath. — 6th ed. — London : Granada, 1981. — 132p : ill ; 29cm
Previous ed.: published as Ladies coat and skirt making. London : Crosby Lockwood, 1971. — Includes index
ISBN 0-246-11500-9 : £7.95 : CIP rev. B81-08904

646.4'3204 — Dressmaking — *Manuals*
Cock, Valerie I.. Dressmaking simplified / Valerie I. Cock. — 3rd ed. — London : Granada, 1981. — 239p : ill ; 23cm
Previous ed.: London : Crosby Lockwood Staples, 1976
ISBN 0-246-11501-7 : £4.95 B81-24452

Cock, Valerie I.. Dressmaking simplified / Valerie I. Cock. — 3rd ed. — [St. Albans] : Hart-Davis Educational, 1981. — 239p : ill ; 22cm
Previous ed.: London : Crosby Lockwood Staples, 1976
ISBN 0-247-13150-4 (pbk) : £2.85 B81-24451

Giles, Rosalie P.. Dressmaking with special fabrics / Rosalie P. Giles. — London : Mills & Boon, 1976 (1977 [printing]). — 112p : ill ; 21cm
Includes index
ISBN 0-263-06406-9 (pbk) : £3.50 B81-35283

Sew simple : a step by step guide to dressmaking / English Sewing Ltd. — London : Hutchinson, 1980. — 233p : ill ; 24x25cm
ISBN 0-09-143610-9 (cased) : £8.95 : CIP rev.
ISBN 0-09-143611-7 (pbk) : £4.95 B80-12418

Watts, Gwyneth. Modern dress making : a textbook for students / Gwyneth Watts. — London : Hutchinson, 1981. — 119p : ill ; 25cm
Includes index
ISBN 0-09-143630-3 (cased) : £9.95
ISBN 0-09-143631-1 (pbk) : £5.50 B81-15575

646.4'3204 — Dressmaking. Patterns. Cutting
Shoben, Martin. Pattern cutting and making up : the professional approach / Martin Shoben & Janet Ward. — London : Batsford Academic and Educational
3: Collars, pockets and other style variations. — 1980. — 160p : col.ill ; 26cm
Includes index
ISBN 0-7134-3561-5 (cased) : £16.50
ISBN 0-7134-3562-6 (pbk) : £9.95 B81-12693

646.4'3204 — Dressmaking. Patterns. Cutting — *Manuals*
Melliar, Margaret. Pattern cutting / Margaret Melliar. — New ed. — London : Batsford Academic and Educational, 1981. — 112p : ill ; 25cm
Previous ed.: London : Batsford, 1968. — Bibliography: p112
ISBN 0-7134-3939-4 (pbk) : £6.50 B81-37850

646.4'3204 — Dressmaking. Patterns. Design — *Manuals*
Aldrich, Winifred. Metric pattern cutting. — London : Bell & Hyman, Feb.1982. — [144]p
Originally published: London : Mills and Boon, 1979
ISBN 0-7135-2007-8 : £5.95 : CIP entry B81-40238

Bray, Natalie. Dress pattern designing : the basic principles of cut and fit / Natalie Bray. — 4th ed., (Metric). — London : Granada, 1981, c1974. — viii,132p : ill ; 28cm
Originally published: London : Crosby Lockwood Staples, 1974. — Includes index
ISBN 0-246-11716-8 (pbk) : £5.95 B81-39614

Campbell, Hilary. Designing patterns : a fresh approach to pattern cutting / Hilary Campbell. — Cheltenham : Thornes, 1980. — 123p : chiefly col.ill ; 32cm
ISBN 0-85950-404-2 (pbk) : £5.95 : CIP rev. B80-02830

Lee, Pamela. Pattern designing and adaptation for beginners / Pamela Lee and Rozanne Hawksley ; illustrated by Rozanne Hawksley. — London : Granada, 1981. — 229p : ill ; 29cm
Bibliography: p228-229
ISBN 0-246-11235-2 : £8.95 : CIP rev. B81-13898

646.4′37 — Patchwork skirts. Designs — *Patterns*
Pfeiffer, Nancy. Easy-to-make patchwork skirts : step-by-step instructions and full size templates for 12 skirts & 2 aprons / Nancy Pfeiffer. — New York : Dover ; London : Constable, 1980. — 25p,24 leaves of plates : ill ; 28cm. — (Dover needlework series)
ISBN 0-486-23888-1 (pbk) : £2.95 B81-23274

646.4′7 — Embroidered ceremonial clothing. Making — *Manuals*
Dean, Beryl. Embroidery in religion and ceremonial / Beryl Dean. — London : Batsford, 1981. — 288p,[8]p of plates : ill(some col.) ; 26cm
Bibliography: p282. — Includes index
ISBN 0-7134-3325-6 : £25.00
Also classified at 746.44 B81-37844

646.4′7 — Theatre. Costumes. Making — *Manuals*
Emery, Joy Spanabel. Stage costume techniques / Joy Spanabel Emery ; drawings by Jerry R. Emery. — Englewood Cliffs ; London : Prentice-Hall, c1981. — xix,362p : ill ; 25cm
Includes bibliographies and index
ISBN 0-13-840330-9 : £12.95 B81-22725

646.4′7 — Wedding dresses, *1260-1900*. Sewing - *Patterns*
Bullen, Nicholas. Making classic wedding dresses. — London : Bell & Hyman, July 1981. — [80]p
ISBN 0-7135-1283-0 (pbk) : £5.95 : CIP entry B81-18107

646.5′04 — Women′s hats. Making — *Manuals*
Couldridge, Alan. The hat book / written and illustrated by Alan Couldridge ; general editor Charlotte Parry-Crooke ; knitting section : Celia Dowell ; photography : David Bradfield. — London : Batsford, 1980. — 127p : ill(some col.) ; 30cm
Includes index
ISBN 0-7134-2385-4 : £6.95 B81-01606

646.7 — MANAGEMENT OF PERSONAL AND FAMILY LIVING, GROOMING

646.7′042 — Adolescent girls. Cleanliness & personal appearance — *Manuals*
Saunders, Rubie. [Good grooming for girls]. Top to toe : good grooming for girls / Rubie Saunders ; illustrated by Carolyn Bentley. — [London] : Piccolo, 1981, c1977. — 64p : ill ; 18cm
Originally published: New York ; London : Watts, 1977. — Includes index
ISBN 0-330-25999-7 (pbk) : £0.80 B81-05219

646.7′2 — Natural beauty care products. Making & use — *Manuals*
Horrocks, Lorna. Natural beauty : taking care of your body, face and hair with natural ingredients / Lorna Horrocks ; with colour illustrations by Marianne Yamaguchi. — London : Angus & Robertson, c1980. — 205p : ill(some col.) ; 26cm
Includes index
ISBN 0-207-14420-6 : £6.95 B81-22789

646.7′2 — Women. Beauty care. Use of natural food
Kendall, Suzy. Natural appeal / Suzy Kendall & Pat Wellington. — London : Dent, 1980. — 136p : ill,ports ; 22cm
Includes index
ISBN 0-460-04525-3 (pbk) : £3.95 : CIP rev. B80-25871

646.7′2 — Women. Beauty care. Use of natural products — *Manuals*
Guyton, Anita. The book of natural beauty / Anita Guyton ; illustrations by Kate Simunek. — London : Stanley Paul, 1981. — 128p : ill ; 24cm
Includes index
ISBN 0-09-145621-5 (pbk) : £4.95 : CIP rev. B81-20143

646.7′2 — Women. Beauty care. Use of plants — *Manuals*
Budd, Mavis. So beautiful : my grandmother′s natural beauty creams, lotions and remedies / Mavis Budd. — Guildford : Lutterworth, 1981. — 64p : ill ; 21cm
ISBN 0-7188-2511-x : £2.95 B81-24216

646.7′2 — Women. Teeth. Beauty care — *Manuals*
Knox, Norma. A dazzling smile / [text by Norma Knox, Joy Langridge, Mundy Ellis] ; [illustrations by Roberta Colegate-Stone et al.]. — [Kettering] ([Newtown St., Woodford, Kettering, Northants NN14 4HW]) : Kingfisher, c1980. — 28p : ill(some col.) ; 21cm. — (The New y o u beauty programme)
Cover title. — Text on inside covers
Unpriced (pbk)
Also classified at 646.7′26′088042 B81-19770

646.7′2′088042 — Women. Beauty care — *Manuals*
Baker, Oleda. How to renovate yourself from head to toe. — London : Severn House, Sept.1981. — [224]p
ISBN 0-7278-2015-x : £7.95 : CIP entry B81-21516

Beauty workshop / [editor Brenda Marshall]. — London : Marshall Cavendish, c1979. — 80p : ill(some col.) ; 28cm
Originally published: 1978. — Includes index
ISBN 0-85685-351-8 (pbk) B81-12964

Collins, Joan. The Joan Collins beauty book. — London : Macmillan, 1980. — 180p : ill(some col.),ports ; 26cm
Includes index
ISBN 0-333-28385-6 : £6.95 : CIP rev. B80-20819

The **Face** and body book / general editor Miriam Stoppard. — [London] : Windward, c1980. — 256p : ill(some col.),ports ; 28cm
Includes index
ISBN 0-7112-0072-6 : £9.95 B81-00173

Gallant, Ann. Principles and techniques for the beauty specialist / Ann Gallant. — 2nd ed. Cheltenham : Thornes, c1980. — 384p : ill ; 25cm
Previous ed.: 1975. — Includes index
ISBN 0-85950-444-1 (cased) : £12.00 : CIP rev.
ISBN 0-85950-449-2 (pbk) : £7.50 B80-10147

Hagman, Ann. The aestheticienne : simple theory and practice / Ann Hagman in association with W.E. Arnould-Taylor. — Cheltenham : Thornes, 1981. — ix,181p : ill ; 24cm
Includes index
ISBN 0-85950-308-9 (pbk) : £4.75 : CIP rev. B81-12801

Lord, Shirley. You are beautiful and how to prove it / Shirley Lord. — Rev. and enl. ed. — London : Unwin Paperbacks, 1980, c1978. — 258p : ill,map ; 20cm
Previous ed.: published as The easy way to good looks. New York : Crowell, c1976. — Includes index
ISBN 0-04-613041-1 (pbk) : £3.50 : CIP rev. B80-23431

Palmer, Catherine. Beauty for free : a compendium of beauty secrets from hearsay, history and hedgerow / Catherine Palmer. — London : Cape, 1981. — 128p : ill,ports ; 20cm
Bibliography: p124. — Includes index
ISBN 0-224-01798-5 : £5.95 B81-16796

646.7′2′0922 — Women. Beauty care — *Personal observations — Collections — Interviews*
Furstenberg, Ira, *Fürstin*. Young at any age : thirty-three of the world′s most elegant women reveal how they stay beautiful / Princess Ira Furstenberg. — London : Weidenfeld & Nicolson, c1981. — 186p : ports ; 24cm
ISBN 0-297-77921-4 : £7.95 B81-26469

646.7′24 — Man. Hair. Care
Kingsley, Philip. The complete hair book / Philip Kingsley ; drawings by Ron Jones. — London : Magnum, 1980, c1979. — 240p : ill ; 20cm
Originally published: New York : Grosset & Dunlap, 1979. — Includes index
ISBN 0-417-05760-1 (pbk) : £1.95 B81-05544

646.7′24′088042 — Women. Hair. Beauty care — *Manuals*
Clark, Felicity. Vogue guide to hair care / Felicity Clark. — Harmondsworth : Penguin, 1981. — 96p,[8]p of plates : ill(some col.) ; 20cm. — (Penguin handbooks)
Includes index
ISBN 0-14-046485-9 (pbk) : £1.95 B81-37208

646.7′242 — Hairdressing services
Jeremiah, Rosemary M.. How you can make money in the hairdressing business. — Cheltenham : Thomas, Jan.1982. — [112]p
ISBN 0-85950-330-5 (pbk) : £2.95 : CIP entry B81-34786

646.7′242′015 — Hairdressing. Scientific aspects
Openshaw, Florence. Advanced hairdressing science. — London : Longman, Sept.1981. — [240]p
ISBN 0-582-41583-7 (pbk) : £5.95 : CIP entry B81-25729

646.7′242′015 — Hairdressing. Scientific aspects — *Questions & answers*
Hampson, J.. Objective tests in hairdressing science. — London : Longman, Sept.1981. — [96]p. — (Longman objective tests)
ISBN 0-582-41238-2 (pbk) : £1.95 : CIP entry B81-28203

646.7′26 — Women. Eyelids. Cosmetics. Use — *Manuals*
Eye magic : the new you beauty programme / [text by Sarah Collins et al.] ; [illustrations by Roberta Colegate-Stone et al.]. — [Kettering] ([Newtown St., Woodford, Kettering, Northants. NN14 4HW]) : Kingfisher, c1981. — 28p : ill(some col.) ; 21cm
Cover title
Unpriced (pbk) B81-26065

646.7′26 — Women. Face. Cosmetics. Use — *Manuals*
Daly, Barbara. Daly beauty / Barbara Daly. — London : Macdonald, 1980. — 64p : col.ill,1col.port ; 27cm
ISBN 0-356-07179-0 (pbk) : £1.75 B81-04835

646.7′26 — Women. Face. Cosmetics. Use. Techniques
Price, Joan, *19---*. Making faces / Joan Price & Pat Booth. — London : Joseph, 1980. — 191p : ill(some col.),ports ; 26cm
Includes index
ISBN 0-7181-1878-2 : £9.50 B81-01609

Shen, Peter. Peter Shen′s makeup for success / by Peter Shen with Joyce Wilson. — London : Angus & Robertson, 1981, c1980. — 160p : ill ; 26cm
ISBN 0-207-95981-1 (pbk) : £4.95 B81-12568

646.7′26′088042 — Women. Face. Cosmetics. Use — *Manuals*
Clark, Felicity. Vogue guide to make-up / Felicity Clark. — Harmondsworth : Penguin, 1981. — 90p,[16]p of plates : ill(some col.) ; 20cm. — (Penguin handbooks)
Includes index
ISBN 0-14-046443-3 (pbk) : £1.95 B81-37212

Jones, Kathleen, *1936-*. Making faces / [text by Kathleen Jones et al.] ; [illustrations by Roberta Colegate-Stone et al.]. — [Kettering] ([Newtown St., Woodford, Kettering, Northants NN14 4HW]) : Kingfisher, c1980. — 28p : ill(some col.) ; 21cm. — (The New y o u beauty programme)
Cover title. — Text on inside covers
Unpriced (pbk) B81-19772

646.7′26′088042 — Women. Hands & feet. Beauty care — *Manuals*
Roberts, Pat. Expressive hands / [text by Pat Roberts et al.] ; [illustrations by Roberta Colegate-Stone]. — [Kettering] ([Newtown St., Woodford, Kettering, Northants NN14 4HW]) : Kingfisher, c1981. — 28p : ill(some col.) ; 21cm. — (The New y o u beauty programme)
Cover title. — Text on inside covers
Unpriced (pbk) B81-19769

646.7′26′088042 — Women. Lips. Cosmetics. Use — *Manuals*

Knox, Norma. A dazzling smile / [text by Norma Knox, Joy Langridge, Mundy Ellis] ; [illustrations by Roberta Colegate-Stone et al.]. — [Kettering] ([Newtown St., Woodford, Kettering, Northants NN14 4HW]) : Kingfisher, c1980. — 28p : ill(some col.) ; 21cm. — (The New y o u beauty programme)
Cover title. — Text on inside covers
Unpriced (pbk)
Primary classification 646.7′2 B81-19770

646.7′26′088042 — Women. Skin. Beauty care — *Manuals*

Clark, Felicity. Vogue guide to skin care / Felicity Clark. — Harmondsworth : Penguin, 1981. — 94p,[8]p of plates : ill(some col.) ; 20cm. — (Penguin handbooks)
Includes index
ISBN 0-14-046484-0 (pbk) : £1.95 B81-37211

Knox, Norma. A glowing complexion / [text by Norma Knox, Joy Leslie Gibson, Mundy Ellis] ; [illustrations by Valerie Hill et al.]. — [Kettering] ([Newtown St., Woodford, Kettering, Northants NN14 4HW]) : Kingfisher, c1981. — 27p : ill(some col.) ; 21cm. — (The New y o u beauty programme)
Cover title. — Text on inside covers
Unpriced (pbk) B81-19773

646.7′9 — Great Britain. Retirement. Planning — *Manuals*

Francis, Gladys M.. Active and independent / by Gladys Francis. — London (36 Eccleston Sq., SW1V 1PF) : B. Edsall, c1980. — 48p : ill ; 21cm
ISBN 0-902623-28-1 (pbk) : Unpriced
B81-18590

647 — INSTITUTIONAL MANAGEMENT

647 — England. Country houses of historical importance. Financial management

Butler, John, *1932-*. The economics of historic country houses / John Butler. — London : Policy Studies Institute, 1981. — viii,138p ; 21cm
ISBN 0-85374-186-7 (pbk) : £4.95 B81-09962

647′.2′0924 — Great Britain. Night clubs. Twemlow, C. — *Biographies*

Twemlow, C.. The tuxedo warrior / by C. Twemlow. — Manchester (Croxley House, Lloyd St., Manchester) : City Major, 1980. — 94p,[4]p of plates : ports ; 19cm
ISBN 0-9507213-0-1 (pbk) : £1.00 B81-06536

647′.6 — Great Britain. Hotel industries. Receptionists. Duties — *Questions & answers*

Bull, Jean. Questions in hotel reception. — Cheltenham : Thornes, Jan.1982. — [160]p
ISBN 0-85950-310-0 (pbk) : £2.50 : CIP entry
B81-33772

647′.9 — Residential institutions. Household management — *Manuals*

Branson, Joan C.. Hotel, hostel and hospital housekeeping. — 4th ed. — London : E. Arnold, Feb.1982. — [208]p
Previous ed.: 1976
ISBN 0-7131-0581-x (pbk) : £4.50 : CIP entry
B81-35835

647.94 — HOTELS, INNS, VACATION ACCOMMODATION, ETC

647′.94 — Exhibition centres & conference centres

Lawson, Fred. Conference, convention and exhibition facilities : a handbook of planning, design and management / Fred Lawson. — London : Architectural Press, 1981. — xi,268p : ill,plan ; 31cm
Bibliography: p364. — Includes index
ISBN 0-85139-101-x : £35.00 B81-32880

647′.94 — Great Britain. Hotel industries. Energy. Conservation

Energy conservation : a guide to the hotel and catering industry on how to ′save it′. — [Wembley] : Hotel and Catering Industry Training Board, c1979. — 12p : col.ill ; 21cm
Unpriced (pbk)
Also classified at 647′.95 B81-33195

647′.94 — Great Britain. Marketing by independent hotels — *Manuals*

Marketing for independent hoteliers. — Wembley : Hotel and Catering Industry Training Board, [1981?]. — 48p : ill,1map,forms ; 30cm
Cover title
Unpriced (pbk) B81-33190

647′.94 — Hotels. Planning

Doswell, Roger. Marketing and planning hotels and tourism projects / Roger Doswell and Paul R. Gamble. — London : Hutchinson, 1981, c1979. — viii,216p : ill,1form ; 24cm
Originally published: London : Barrie & Jenkins, 1979. — Includes index
ISBN 0-09-146271-1 (pbk) : £5.95 B81-39180

647′.94 — Youth hostels — *Directories* — *Serials*

International youth hostel handbook. Vol.1, Europe and Mediterranean countries. — 1980. — [Welwyn Garden City] ([Midland Bank Chambers, Howardsgate, Welwyn Garden City, Herts.]) : International Youth Hostel Federation, c1980. — 192p
Unpriced B81-03862

International youth hostel handbook. Vol.1, Europe and Mediterranean countries. — 1981. — Welwyn Garden City (Midland Bank Chambers, Howardsgate, Welwyn Garden City, Herts.) : International Youth Hostel Federation, c1981. — 191p
Unpriced B81-11876

International youth hostel handbook. Vol.2, Africa, America, Asia, Australasia. — 1981. — Welwyn Garden City (Midland Bank Chambers, Howardsgate, Welwyn Garden City, Herts.) : International Youth Hostel Federation, c1981. — 128p
Unpriced B81-11877

647′.94′0285404 — Hotel industries. Applications of microcomputer systems

A **Report** on some training and operational implications of microcomputers in the hotel and catering industry / prepared by the Department of Hotel, Catering & Tourism Management, University of Surrey for the Hotel and Catering Industry Training Board. — Wembley : Hotel and Catering Industry Training Board, 1980. — 117,21p : ill ; 30cm. — (Research report / Hotel and Catering Industry Training Board)
Unpriced (pbk)
Also classified at 647′.95′0285404 B81-33194

647′.94′068 — Great Britain. Hotel industries. Small firms. Management — *Manuals*

Hotel & catering industry small business training aid : employing people in small hotel and catering businesses. — [Wembley] : HCITB, [1979]. — 1v.(loose-leaf) : ill ; 33cm
2 portfolios in pockets
Unpriced
Also classified at 647′.95′068 B81-33179

Hotel & catering industry small business training aid : employing people in small hotel and catering businesses. — [Updated]. — [Wembley] : HCITB, [1980], c1979. — 1v.(loose-leaf) : ill ; 33cm
Previous ed.: [1979]. — 2 portfolios in pockets
Unpriced
Also classified at 647′.95′068 B81-33180

647′.94′068 — Great Britain. Hotels. Purchase — *Manuals*

Quest, Miles. How to buy your own hotel / Miles Quest. — London : Northwood, 1979. — 221p : ill,facsims,ports ; 22cm
Includes bibliographies and index
ISBN 0-7198-2764-7 : £4.95 B81-08252

647′.94′07 — Great Britain. Hotel industries. Personnel. Induction training. Way to Work schemes

Quest, Miles. The way to work : new schemes to prepare young people for jobs in the hotel and catering industry / by Miles Quest. — Wembley (Ramsey House, Central Sq., Wembley, Middx HA9 7AP) : Hotel and Catering Industry Training Board, [1981?]. — 19p : ill,ports ; 30cm
Cover title
Unpriced (pbk)
Also classified at 647′.95′07 B81-33550

647′.94′07 — Great Britain. Hotel industries. Personnel. Training — *Proposals*

Hotel and Catering Industry Training Board. Five year plan 1979-85 / Hotel and Catering Industry Training Board. — [Wembley] ([Ramsey House, Central Sq., Wembley, Middx HA9 7AP]) : [H.C.I.T.B.], [1979?]. — 34p : col.ill ; 21x30cm
Cover title
Unpriced (pbk)
Also classified at 647′.95′07 B81-33188

647′.94′071143 — West Germany. Hotel industries. Professional education

Continental craft training study : German report. — [Wembley] : HCITB, [1979?]. — 48p : ill (some col.),1col.map ; 31cm
Cover title
Unpriced (pbk)
Also classified at 647′.95′071143 B81-33171

647′.94′071144 — France. Hotel industries. Professional education

Continental craft training study : French report. — [Wembley] : Hotel and Catering Industry Training Board, 1979. — 32p : col.ill ; 31cm
Cover title. — Text on inside cover
Unpriced (pbk)
Also classified at 647′.95′071144 B81-33172

647′.941708 — Ireland *(Republic)*. **Camping & caravanning. Sites** — *Directories* — *Serials*

Caravan & camping parks / Irish Tourist Board. — 1980. — Dublin (Baggot Street Bridge, Dublin 2) : The Board, [1980?]. — 43p
£0.25 B81-05077

647′.94408′05 — Europe. Camping & caravanning. Sites — *Directories* — *Serials*

Guide to British and continental camping and caravanning sites / RAC. — 6th rev. ed. — London (83 Pall Mall, SW1) : Royal Automobile Club, 1981. — xxiv,400p
Cover title: RAC guide to British and continental camping and caravanning sites. — Spine title: British and continental camping and caravanning sites
ISBN 0-902628-35-6 : £6.00
ISSN 0146-3470 B81-16837

647′.94408′05 — Western Europe. Camping & caravanning. Sites — *Directories* — *Serials*

Alan Rogers′ selected sites for caravanning and camping in Europe. — 1981. — Brighton : Deneway Guides and Travel, c1980. — 208p
ISBN 0-901586-20-x : £1.45
ISSN 0065-5686 B81-09070

647′.9441 — Great Britain. Bed & breakfast accommodation — *Directories* — *Serials*

David Murdoch′s bed and breakfast stops. — 1981. — Paisley : Farm Holiday Guides, c1981. — 112p
£0.60 B81-13416

647′.9441 — Great Britain. Conference centres — *Directories* — *Serials*

The **Conference** blue book : your guaranteed guide to conference venues in the British Isles. — 1978/79-. — London (Spectrum House, 183 Askew Rd, W12 9AX) : Spectrex (London), 1978-. — v. : ill,plans ; 30cm
Annual. — Published on behalf of: Spectrum Communications Ltd. — Description based on: 1980/81 issue
ISSN 0260-2431 = Conference blue book : £12.50 B81-08321

647′.9441 — Great Britain. Residential conference centres & exhibition centres — *Directories* — *Serials*

Conferences meetings & exhibitions welcome. — 1980-. — Kingston upon Thames (31 Castle St., Kingston upon Thames, Surrey KT1 1ST) : Lewis Publications, c1980. — v. : ill ; 21cm
Annual
ISSN 0260-776x = Conferences meetings & exhibitions welcome : Unpriced B81-09154

647′.9441 — Great Britain. Self-catering vacation accommodation — *Directories* — *Serials*

Furnished holidays in Britain. — 1981. — Paisley : Farm Holiday Publications, c1981. — 224p
£0.70 B81-13418

647'.9441'00240816 — Great Britain. Vacation accommodation — *Directories — For physically handicapped persons*

Holidays for the physically handicapped. — 1981. — London : Royal Association for Disability and Rehabilitation, [1980?]. — 632p
ISSN 0300-4295 : £0.50 B81-06706

647'.9441'005 — Great Britain. Vacation accommodation — *Directories — Serials*

Britain, BTA's commended country hotels, guest houses and restaurants. — 1981. — London : British Tourist Authority, 1981. — 116p
ISBN 0-7095-0578-7 : Unpriced
Also classified at 647'.9541'05 B81-09698

Guide to Britain's best holidays. — 1981. — Paisley : Farm Holiday Guides, c1981. — 160p
£0.70 B81-13420

647'.9441'005 — Great Britain. Vacation accommodation — *Directories — Serials — For families*

Family holiday guide. — 1981. — Kingston upon Thames (31, Castle St., Kingston upon Thames, Surrey KT1 1ST) : Lewis Publications, c1980. — 223p
ISSN 0071-3740 : £0.75 B81-15170

647'.944101 — Great Britain. Hotels — *Directories*

United Kingdom group owners / [Data Research Group]. — [1980]. — Great Missenden : The Group, 1980. — 120p
ISBN 0-86099-284-5 : Unpriced B81-03084

647'.944101'05 — Great Britain. Hotels — *Directories — Serials*

BHRCA official guide to hotels and restaurants in Great Britain, Ireland and overseas. — 53rd ed. (1981). — London : British Hotels, Restaurants and Caterers Association, [1981?]. — 608p in various pagings
Cover title: British hotels & restaurants
ISBN 0-900202-12-2 : £3.80
Also classified at 647'.9541'05 B81-16833

Britain, hotels & restaurants. — [1981]. — London : British Tourist Authority, c1981. — 426p
ISBN 0-7095-0579-5 : Unpriced
Also classified at 647'.9541'05 B81-13318

Great Britain and Ireland / Michelin. — 1981. — London : Michelin Tyre Co., c1981. — 601p
ISBN 2-06-006501-1 : £4.75
Also classified at 647'.9541'05 B81-15282

United Kingdom group owners / [Data Research Group]. — [1981]. — Great Missenden : The Group, 1981. — 237p
ISBN 0-86099-314-0 : Unpriced B81-29063

United Kingdom hotels with 10 or more bedrooms / [Data Research Group]. — [1981]. — Great Missenden : The Group, 1981. — 479p
ISBN 0-86099-302-7 : £31.00 B81-37238

647'.944108'05 — Great Britain. Camping & caravanning. Sites — *Directories — Serials*

Caravan and campsites in Britain. — '81. — London : Charles Letts, 1981. — 194p. — (Letts Guide)
ISBN 0-85097-333-3 : £1.75
ISSN 0142-6249 B81-09069

David Murdoch's guide to caravans and camping holidays. — 1981. — Paisley : Farm Holiday Guides, c1981. — 104p
£0.60 B81-13422

Good camps guide. — 1981. — Brighton : Deneway Guides and Travel, c1980. — 95p
ISBN 0-901586-21-8 : £1.00
ISSN 0142-5978 B81-09068

647'.944108'05 — Great Britain. Caravanning. Sites — *Directories — Serials*

Caravan & chalet sites. — 1981. — Teddington (38 Hampton Rd, Teddington, Middlesex TW11 0JE) : Haymarket Publishing in conjunction with the National Federation of Site Operators, c1981. — 202p
Spine title: The Sites handbook of the NFSO
£1.00 B81-23131

Caravan Club. Sites directory and handbook / the Caravan Club. — 1981/82. — [East Grinstead] ([East Grinstead House, West Sussex RH19 1UA]) : The Club, [1981]. — 304p
Sites map with each issue
Free to club members only B81-24150

647'.94411 — Scotland. Self-catering vacation accommodation — *Directories — Serials*

Scotland self catering accommodation. — 1981. — Edinburgh : Scottish Tourist Board, [1980]. — xiv,242p
£0.75 B81-04906

647'.94411 — Scotland. Vacation accommodation — *Directories — For young persons*

Small group holiday guide. — Bridge of Weir (Quarrier's Homes, Bridge of Weir, Renfrewshire PA11 3SA) : I.T. Resource Centre, [1980]. — 48p : ill ; 30cm + suppl.1(4 leaves; 30cm). — (ITKIT ; 1)
£0.90 (pbk)
Also classified at 647'.94427 B81-37610

647'.94411 — Scotland. Vacation accommodation: Farmhouses — *Directories — Serials*

Farm holiday guide & country holiday houses. Scotland. — 34th year (1981). — Paisley : Farm Holiday Guides, c1981. — 128p
£0.80 B81-13417

647'.94411'005 — Scotland. Bed & breakfast accommodation — *Directories — Serials*

Scotland, where to stay. Bed and breakfast : Bed and breakfast places, farmhouses and university accommodation = Où se loger en Ecosse. Chambres et petit déjeuner, gîtes ruraux et résidences universitaires = Wo übernachtet man in Schottland. Privatpensionen, Bauernhöfe und Unterbringung in den Universitäten. — 1980-. — Edinburgh : Scottish Tourist Board, 1979-. — v. : ill ; 21cm
Annual. — Text in English, introduction also in French and German. — Continues: Where to stay in Scotland. Bed and breakfast. — Description based on: 1981 issue
ISSN 0260-7905 = Scotland, where to stay. Bed and breakfast : £0.75 B81-06909

647'.94411'005 — Scotland. Vacation accommodation — *Directories — Serials*

Scotland, where to stay. Hotels and guest houses : hotels, guest houses and university accommodation = Où se loger en Ecosse. hôtels, pensions de famille et résidences universitaires = Wo übernachtet man in Schottland. Hotels, Gasthäuser und Unterbringung in den Universitäten. — 1980-. — Edinburgh : Scottish Tourist Board, 1979-. — v. : ill ; 21cm
Annual. — Text in English, introduction also in French and German. — Continues: Where to stay in Scotland. Hotels, guest houses and university accommodation. — Description based on: 1981 issue
ISSN 0260-7913 = Scotland, where to stay. Hotels and guest houses : £1.00 B81-06674

Scotland's best holidays. — 1981. — Paisley : Farm Holiday Guides, c1981. — 108p
£0.60 B81-13421

647'.9441108'05 — Scotland. Camping & caravanning. Sites — *Directories — Serials*

Scotland camping & caravan sites. — 1981. — Edinburgh : Scottish Tourist Board, [1981?]. — xii,68p
ISBN 0-85419-172-0 : £0.70 B81-15165

647'.944114'005 — Scotland. Western Isles. Vacation accomodation — *Directories — Serials*

Where to stay in the Western Isles / Western Isles Tourist Organisation. — 1978. — [Stornoway] ([Tourist Information Centre, South Beach Quay, Stornoway, Isle of Lewis]) : The Organisation, [1978?]. — 10p
£0.10 B81-09083

647'.944121'005 — Scotland. Grampian Region. Vacation accommodation — *Directories — Serials*

Grampian region : register of accommodation. — 1979. — Aberdeen (Woodhill House, Ashgrove Road West, Aberdeen AB9 2LU) : Department of Leisure, Recreation & Tourism, Grampian Regional Council, [1979?]. — 56p
ISSN 0144-6797 : Unpriced B81-12737

[Grampian Region *(Register of accommodation)*]. Grampian region : register of accommodation. — 1981. — Aberdeen (Woodhill House, Ashgrove Rd West, Aberdeen AB9 2LU) : Department of Leisure, Recreation and Tourism, Grampian Regional Council, [1980]. — 68p
ISSN 0144-5332 : Unpriced B81-09099

647'.944121'05 — Scotland. Grampian Region. Vacation accommodation — *Directories — Serials*

Grampian region : register of accommodation. — 1976-. — Aberdeen (Woodhill House, Ashgrove Rd West, Aberdeen AB9 2LU) : Department of Leisure, Recreation & Tourism, Grampian Regional Council, 1976-. — v. : ill,maps ; 30cm
Annual. — Subtitle varies. — Description based on: 1978
ISSN 0144-6797 = Grampian region : Unpriced B81-02035

647'.94417 — Ireland *(Republic).* **Vacation accommodation: Farmhouses** — *Directories — Serials*

Farm holidays in Ireland. — 1981. — Dublin (7 Clare St., Dublin 2) : Libra House in association with Failte Tuaithe, Irish Farm Holidays Association, [1981?]. — 124p
ISBN 0-904169-13-8 : Unpriced B81-20435

647'.9441701'05 — Ireland *(Republic).* **Hotels: Country houses** — *Directories — Serials*

Irish country houses and restaurants. — 1976-. — [Dublin] ([c/o Baggot St. Bridge, Dublin 2]) : The Irish Country Houses and Restaurants Association assisted by Bord Fáilte, 1976-. — v. : ill ; 21cm
Annual. — Description based on: 1979 issue
Unpriced
Also classified at 647'.95417'05 B81-09196

647'.9441707'05 — Ireland *(Republic).* **Youth hostels** — *Directories — Serials*

Irish Youth Hostel Association. Leabhrán / An Óige. — 42nd ed. (1980). — Baile Átha Cliath [Dublin] (39 Cearnog Moinseó, D., Baile Atha Cliath 1) : An Óige, 1980. — 117p
Cover title: Irish Youth Hostel Association handbook
Unpriced B81-20413

Irish Youth Hostel Association. Leabhrán / An Óige. — 43rd ed. (1981). — Baile Átha Cliath [Dublin] (39 Cearnóg Moinseó, D., Baile Átha Cliath 1) : An Óige, 1981. — 125p
Cover title: Irish Youth Hostel Association handbook
Unpriced B81-20417

647'.9442 — England. Vacation accommodation: Farmhouses — *Directories — Serials*

Farm holiday guide & country holiday houses. England. — 34th year (1981). — Paisley : Farm Holiday Guides, c1981. — 552p
£1.00 B81-13419

647'.9442'005 — England. Vacation accommodation — *Directories — Serials*

England's best holidays. — 1981. — Paisley : Farm Holiday Guides, c1981. — 144p
£0.60 B81-13415

647'.944201 — England. Hotels — *Visitors' guides*

Slater, John, *1941-*. Just off for the weekend : Slater's hotel guide / John Slater. — London : Pan, 1981. — xv,315p : 1ill,maps ; 20cm
ISBN 0-330-26045-6 (pbk) : £2.50 B81-09717

647'.944201 — England. Inns, *to 1980*

Burke, John, *1922-*. The English inn / John Burke. — London : Batsford, 1981. — 192p,[4]p of plates : ill(some col.) ; 26cm
Bibliography: p189. — Includes index
ISBN 0-7134-2127-4 : £9.95 B81-37957

647′.9442′05 — England. Short-stay out-of-season vacation accommodation — *Directories* — *Serials*

Let′s go / English Tourist Board. — 1980/81. — London (4 Grosvenor Gardens, SW1W 0DU) : The Board, c1980. — 239p
Unpriced B81-04035

647′.944207′025 — England. Youth hostels — *Directories* — *Serials*

Youth Hostels Association (England and Wales). Handbook / Youth Hostels Association (England and Wales). — 1981. — St. Albans : The Association, [1980?]. — 127p
ISSN 0512-9559 : £0.20 B81-06672

647′.9442101′025 — London. Hotels — *Directories* — *Serials*

Britain. London hotels & restaurants including budget accommodation / [British Tourist Authority]. — 1981. — [London] : The Authority in co-operation with the English Tourist Board and the London Tourist Board, [1980?]. — vi,138p
ISBN 0-7095-0618-x : £0.95 B81-06943

647′.9442106′05 — London. Hostels — *Directories* — *Serials*

Hostels in London / London Council for the Welfare of Women and Girls and YWCA Accommodation and Advisory Service. — 1979/80-. — London (16 Great Russell St., WC1B 3LR) : The Service, [1979]-. — v. ; 21cm
Annual. — Continues: Staying in London. — Description based on: 1980/81 issue
ISSN 0261-2895 = Hostels in London : £1.00 B81-26391

647′.944213201 — London. Westminster *(London Borough).* **Hotels: Ritz Hotel,** *to 1979*

Montgomery-Massingberd, Hugh. The London Ritz : a social and architectural history / Hugh Montgomery-Massingberd & David Watkin ; photographs by Keith Collie. — London : Aurum, c1980. — 189p : ill(some col.),facsims,1plan,ports ; 31cm
Includes index
ISBN 0-906053-01-3 : £14.95 B81-06555

647′.9442301 — South-west England. Hotels — *Visitors′ guides*

Pubbing eating & sleeping in the S.W. : the guide to value for money / editor R.L. Elliott. — Tavistock (Merchant′s House, Barley Market St., Tavistock, Devon) : Heritage in association with New English Library, c1981. — 175p : ill,2maps ; 18cm
Previous ed.: 1980
ISBN 0-903975-18-1 (pbk) : £0.90
Also classified at 647′.95423 B81-17827

647′.9442317 — Wiltshire. Pewsey. Permanent caravans. Sites: Homelands — *Personal observations*

Glazzard, Cicely. Home sweet home / Cicely Glazzard. — Bognor Regis : New Horizon, c1979. — 37p,[8]p of plates : ill ; 21cm
ISBN 0-86116-179-3 : £1.95 B81-21866

647′.944235′005 — Devon. Vacation accommodation — *Directories* — *Serials*

Devon′s country accommodation. — 1981. — Exeter (County Hall, Exeter, Devon) : Devon Tourism Office, [1981?]. — 52p
ISBN 0-86114-289-6 : Unpriced B81-15168

647′.94423508′05 — Devon. Camping & caravanning. Sites — *Directories* — *Serials*

Devon′s touring caravan & camp sites. — 1981. — Exeter (County Hall, Exeter, Devon) : Devon Tourism Office, [1981?]. — 32p
ISBN 0-86114-290-x : £0.20
ISSN 0144-7874 B81-15169

647′.94423′59501 — Devon. Torquay. Hotels: Imperial *(Hotel), to 1981*

Denes, Gabor. The Imperial, Torquay. — Newton Abbot : David & Charles, Jan.1982. — [160]p
ISBN 0-7153-8051-6 : £7.50 : CIP entry B81-33824

647′.9442511′005 — England. Peak District. National parks: Peak District National Park. Vacation accommodation — *Directories* — *Serials*

Accommodation and catering, Peak National Park / [prepared by the Information Section of the Peak National Park Office]. — 1979. — [Bakewell] ([Aldern House, Bakewell]) : Information Section of the Peak National Park Office, [1979?]. — 16p
£0.08 B81-06912

647′.9442591 — Buckinghamshire. Olney. Inns, *1600-1980*

Knight, Elizabeth. The old inns of Olney / by Elizabeth Knight. — Buckingham : Barracuda Books, 1981. — 104p : ill,maps,facsims ; 24cm
Maps on lining papers. — Bibliography: p100. — Includes index
ISBN 0-86023-159-3 : £8.95 B81-37631

647′.94427 — Northern England. Vacation accommodation — *Directories* — *For young persons*

Small group holiday guide. — Bridge of Weir (Quarrier′s Homes, Bridge of Weir, Renfrewshire PA11 3SA) : I.T. Resource Centre, [1980]. — 48p : ill ; 30cm + suppl.1(4 leaves; 30cm). — (ITKIT ; 1)
£0.90 (pbk)
Primary classification 647′.94411 B81-37610

647′.94429′005 — Wales. Vacation accommodation — *Directories* — *Serials*

Holidays in Wales. — 1981. — Paisley : Farm Holiday Guides, c1981. — 138p
£0.60 B81-13414

647′.944408′05 — France. Camping & caravanning. Sites — *Directories* — *Serials*

Campsites in France. — 1981. — London : Letts, 1981. — 198p
ISBN 0-85097-338-4 : £2.50 B81-16234

647′.94709′068 — North America. Camping. Sites. Management

Wilkinson, Robert E.. Camps : their planning and management / Robert E. Wilkinson. — St. Louis ; London : Mosby, 1981. — x,291p : ill,plans,forms ; 25cm
Includes bibliographies and index
ISBN 0-8016-5550-1 : £11.25 B81-24240

647.95 — CATERING INSTITUTIONS, RESTAURANTS, PUBLIC HOUSES, ETC

647′.95 — Catering establishments. Kitchens. Management

Fuller, John, *1916-*. Professional kitchen management / John Fuller. — New ed. — London : Batsford, 1981. — 410p : ill,forms ; 23cm
Previous ed.: i.e. 3rd ed. published as Chef′s manual of kitchen management. 1977. — Includes index
ISBN 0-7134-2714-0 (cased) : Unpriced
ISBN 0-7134-2715-9 (pbk) : £9.95 B81-36705

647′.95 — Great Britain. Catering industries. Energy. Conservation

Energy conservation : a guide to the hotel and catering industry on how to ′save it′. — [Wembley] : Hotel and Catering Industry Training Board, c1979. — 12p : col.ill ; 21cm
Unpriced (pbk)
Primary classification 647′.94 B81-33195

647′.95 — Hotel industries & catering industries. Personnel. Training. Curriculum subjects: Counter service of food & drinks — *Manuals*

Training in counter service. — 2nd ed. — Wembley : Hotel and Catering Industry Training Board, 1981. — [79]p ; 27x29cm
Unpriced (spiral) B81-33175

647′.95 — Restaurants — *For children*

Lenga, Rosalind. Let′s go to a restaurant / Rosalind Lenga ; general editor Henry Pluckrose. — London : Watts, c1980. — 32p : col.ill ; 22cm. — (Let′s go series)
ISBN 0-85166-890-9 : £2.95 B81-01948

647′.95 — Wine waiters & wine waitresses. Training — *Manuals*

Training in wine service. — [Wembley] : HCITB, [1981?]. — 1portfolio : ill,2maps ; 28x32cm
Unpriced B81-33177

647′.95′0285404 — Catering industries. Applications of microcomputer systems

A **Report** on some training and operational implications of microcomputers in the hotel and catering industry / prepared by the Department of Hotel, Catering & Tourism Management, University of Surrey for the Hotel and Catering Industry Training Board. — Wembley : Hotel and Catering Industry Training Board, 1980. — 117,21p : ill ; 30cm. — (Research report / Hotel and Catering Industry Training Board)
Unpriced (pbk)
Primary classification 647′.94′0285404 B81-33194

647′.95′06041 — Great Britain. Industrial catering. Organisations: Industrial Catering Association — *Regulations*

Industrial Catering Association. Rules and standing orders / The Industrial Catering Association. — [Richmond] ([1 Victoria Parade, by 331 Sandycombs Rd, Richmond, Surrey, TW9 3NB]) : The Association], 1980. — 36p ; 12cm
Cover title
Unpriced (pbk) B81-10857

647′.95′06041 — Great Britain. Industrial catering. Organisations: Industrial Catering Association — *Serials*

ICA communicator : the bi-monthly journal of the Industrial Catering Association. — Issue 33 (June 1981)-. — Eastbourne : John Offord (Publications) Ltd., 1981-. — v. : ports ; 30cm
Continues: Bulletin (Industrial Catering Association)
ISSN 0261-3905 = ICA communicator : £3.00 per year B81-33296

647′.95′068 — Catering industries. Management — *Manuals*

Steel, James. Control in catering / James Steel. — 3rd ed. — London : Barrie & Jenkins, 1979. — 198p : ill ; 23cm
Previous ed.: 1977. — Includes index
ISBN 0-214-20659-9 : £6.95 B81-24169

647′.95′068 — Great Britain. Catering establishments. Management. Research projects — *Lists* — *Serials*

HCIMA research register. — 1979-1980. — London (191 Trinity Rd., SW17 7HN) : Hotel, Catering and Institutional Management Association, 1979-1980. — v. ; 22cm
Continued by: HCIMA research register for the hotel, catering and tourism industry. — Description based on: 1980 update
ISSN 0261-2062 : £20.00 for 1980 update B81-20077

HCIMA research register for the hotel, catering and tourism industry. — 1979-. — London (191 Trinity Rd, SW17 7HN) : Hotel, Catering and Institutional Management Association, [1981]-. — v. ; 23cm
Annual. — Continues: HCIMA research register. — First two issues repeat chronological designation of last two issues of preceding title
ISSN 0261-2968 = HCIMA research register for the hotel, catering and tourism industry : Unpriced B81-32236

647′.95′068 — Great Britain. Catering industries. Small firms. Management — *Manuals*

Hotel & catering industry small business training aid : employing people in small hotel and catering businesses. — [Wembley] : HCITB, [1979]. — 1v.(loose-leaf) : ill ; 33cm
2 portfolios in pockets
Unpriced
Primary classification 647′.94′068 B81-33179

Hotel & catering industry small business training aid : employing people in small hotel and catering businesses. — [Updated]. — [Wembley] : HCITB, [1980], c1979. — 1v.(loose-leaf) : ill ; 33cm
Previous ed.: [1979]. — 2 portfolios in pockets
Unpriced
Primary classification 647′.94′068 B81-33180

647'.95'0681 — Catering industries. Costs. Control

Hughes, Janet. Costing and calculations for catering / Janet Hughes and Brian Ireland. — Cheltenham : Thornes, 1981. — vi,170p : ill,forms ; 24cm
ISBN 0-85950-493-x (pbk) : £2.75 : CIP rev.
Primary classification 510'.24642 B81-03356

647'.95'0681 — Catering industries. Costs. Control — *Manuals*

Kotas, Richard. Food and beverage control / Richard Kotas and Bernard Davis. — 3rd ed. — Glasgow : International Textbook Co., 1981. — viii,179p : ill,forms ; 22cm
Previous ed: published as Food cost control. 1976. — Includes index
ISBN 0-7002-0277-3 (pbk) : Unpriced
B81-01001

647'.95'0687 — Purchasing by catering industries

Stefanelli, John M.. Purchasing : selection and procurement for the hospitality industry / John M. Stefanelli. — New York ; Chichester : Wiley, c1981. — viii,502p : ill,forms ; 25cm. — (Wiley service management series)
Includes index
ISBN 0-471-04538-1 (corrected) : £10.50
ISBN 0-471-04583-1 B81-20203

647'.95'0688 — Great Britain. Hotel & catering industries. Customer relations

Another satisfied customer if you use these training cards in customer relations. — [Wembley] ([P.O. Box 18, Wembley, HA9 7AP]) : Hotel & Catering Industry Training Board, [1981?]. — 1portfolio : ill ; 24cm + 1booklet(33p : ill ; 21cm)
Unpriced B81-34702

647'.95'07 — Bartenders. Training — *Manuals*

Training in bar service. — [Wembley] : HCITB, [1981?]. — [124]p ; 27x30cm + 1pamphlet([8] p;21cm)
Cover title
Unpriced (spiral) B81-33174

647'.95'07 — Great Britain. Catering industries. Personnel. Induction training. Way to Work schemes

Quest, Miles. The way to work : new schemes to prepare young people for jobs in the hotel and catering industry / by Miles Quest. — Wembley (Ramsey House, Central Sq., Wembley, Middx HA9 7AP) : Hotel and Catering Industry Training Board, [1981?]. — 19p : ill,ports ; 30cm
Cover title
Unpriced (pbk)
Primary classification 647'.94'07 B81-33550

647'.95'07 — Great Britain. Catering industries. Personnel. Training — *Proposals*

Hotel and Catering Industry Training Board. Five year plan 1979-85 / Hotel and Catering Industry Training Board. — [Wembley] ([Ramsey House, Central Sq., Wembley, Middx HA9 7AP]) : [H.C.I.T.B.], [1979?]. — 34p : col.ill ; 21x30cm
Cover title
Unpriced (pbk)
Primary classification 647'.94'07 B81-33188

647'.95'071141 — Great Britain. Further education institutions. Curriculum subjects: Catering. Students

Ellis, Paul, *1948-*. Craft 1, the craft student / Paul Ellis. — [Wembley] ([Ramsey House, Central Sq., Wembley, Middx HA9 7AP]) : [Hotel and Catering Industry Training Board], 1979. — 38p,[15]p : ill,forms ; 30cm
Unpriced (spiral) B81-33187

647'.95'071143 — West Germany. Catering industries. Professional education

Continental craft training study : German report. — [Wembley] : HCITB, [1979?]. — 48p : ill (some col.),1col.map ; 31cm
Cover title
Unpriced (pbk)
Primary classification 647'.94'071143
B81-33171

647'.95'071144 — France. Catering industries. Professional education

Continental craft training study : French report. — [Wembley] : Hotel and Catering Industry Training Board, 1979. — 32p : col.ill ; 31cm
Cover title. — Text on inside cover
Unpriced (pbk)
Primary classification 647'.94'071144
B81-33172

647'.954 — Europe. Coffee houses — *Illustrations*

Hamm, Manfred. Coffee houses of Europe / introduction [i.e. text] by George Mikes ; photographs by Manfred Hamm ; edited by Jürgen Boettcher. — London : Thames and Hudson, c1980. — 136p : chiefly col.ill ; 28cm
Translation of: Europäische Kaffeehäuser
ISBN 0-500-54063-2 : £15.00 B81-03107

647'.954 — Western Europe. Relais Routiers — *Directories — French texts*

Guide des Relais Routiers. — 1980. — London : Routiers, 1980. — 506p
£3.75 B81-00174

647'.9541'05 — Great Britain. Public houses & restaurants — *Directories — Serials*

The Best of British pubs and other places to eat and drink. — 3nd ed. rev. ('81). — London : Letts, 1981. — 216p
ISBN 0-85097-328-7 : £2.50 B81-13194

647'.9541'05 — Great Britain. Public houses selling unpressurised beers — *Directories — Serials*

Good beer guide / Campaign for Real Ale. — 1981. — St. Albans (34 Alma Rd, St. Albans, Herts. AL1 3BW) : CAMRA in association with Arrow Books, c1981. — 237,36p
ISBN 0-09-925260-0 : £3.50 B81-12419

647'.9541'05 — Great Britain. Relais Routiers — *Directories — Serials*

Guide to British relais routiers. — 3rd ed. — [London] : Collins, c1981. — 121p
ISBN 0-00-447401-5 : £1.95 B81-29072

647'.9541'05 — Great Britain. Restaurants — *Directories — Serials*

BHRCA official guide to hotels and restaurants in Great Britain, Ireland and overseas. — 53rd ed. (1981). — London : British Hotels, Restaurants and Caterers Association, [1981?]. — 608p in various pagings
Cover title: British hotels & restaurants
ISBN 0-900202-12-2 : £3.80
Primary classification 647'.944101'05
B81-16833

Britain, BTA's commended country hotels, guest houses and restaurants. — 1981. — London : British Tourist Authority, 1981. — 116p
ISBN 0-7095-0578-7 : Unpriced
Primary classification 647'.9441'005 B81-09698

Britain, hotels & restaurants. — [1981]. — London : British Tourist Authority, c1981. — 426p
ISBN 0-7095-0579-5 : Unpriced
Primary classification 647'.944101'05
B81-13318

Great Britain and Ireland / Michelin. — 1981. — London : Michelin Tyre Co., c1981. — 601p
ISBN 2-06-006501-1 : £4.75
Primary classification 647'.944101'05
B81-15282

Just a bite. — 1981. — London : Egon Ronay in association with Penguin Books, 1981. — 428p
ISBN 0-14-005379-4 : £2.25 B81-24682

647'.9541'068 — Great Britain. Teashops. Management — *Manuals*

Graham, Winifred, *1896-*. How to run a tearoom / Winifred Graham. — Loughton : Piatkus, 1981. — 192p ; 21cm
Includes index
ISBN 0-86188-082-x : £5.50 B81-22200

647'.954121 — Scotland. Grampian Region. Restaurants — *Directories*

Eating out in Grampian Region. — Aberdeen : Department of Leisure, Recreation and Tourism, Regional Council, [1981]. — [40]p : 1map ; 21x10cm
Cover title
Unpriced (pbk) B81-11715

Eating out in Grampian region. — Aberdeen : Department of Leisure, Recreation and Tourism, Grampian Regional Council, [1981?]. — [44]p : ill,1map ; 21x10cm
Cover title
Unpriced (pbk) B81-32991

647'.95417'05 — Ireland *(Republic)*. Restaurants — *Directories — Serials*

Irish country houses and restaurants. — 1976-. — [Dublin] ([c/o Baggot St. Bridge, Dublin 2]) : The Irish Country Houses and Restaurants Association assisted by Bord Fáilte, 1976-. — v. : ill ; 21cm
Annual. — Description based on: 1979 issue
Unpriced
Primary classification 647'.9441701'05
B81-09196

647'.95421 — London. Public houses selling unpressurised beers — *Visitors' guides*

Protz, Roger. Capital ale / Roger Protz ; illustrations by Martin Tomlinson. — London : Arrow, 1981. — 192p : ill,1map ; 18cm
Includes index
ISBN 0-09-925590-1 (pbk) : £1.95 B81-23071

647'.95421'05 — London. Public houses — *Directories — Serials*

Publicans, public houses & licensed restaurants. — 1981. — Southend-on-Sea (Directory House, Southend-on-Sea, Essex) : London & Provincial Directories, [1981]. — [86]p
Unpriced B81-32694

647'.95421'05 — London. Restaurants — *Serials*

Dine out. — Vol.1, no.1 (Autumn 1980)-. — London (314 Dukes Mews, N10 2QF) : D. and R. Madison, 1980-. — v. : ill,ports ; 30cm
Three issues yearly
ISSN 0144-655x = Dine out : £0.60 per issue
B81-09210

647'.9542133 — London. Hammersmith and Fulham *(London Borough)*. Public houses: Golden Lion *(Public house : Hammersmith and Fulham), to 1979*

Murray, John J. (John James). The quest of the Golden Lion / by John J. Murray. — London ([56 Palewell Park, London SW14 8JH]) : Fulham and Hammersmith Historical Society, 1981. — vii,79p : ill,2maps ; 21cm
Includes index
£3.50 (pbk) B81-20779

647'.95422 — South-east England. Public houses — *Visitors' guides*

Gerard-Pearse, Peter. The drinkers' guide to walking : London and the South East / [researched, walked, photographed, compiled and written by Peter Gerard-Pearse and Nigel Matheson]. — New York ; London : Proteus, 1981. — 158p : ill,maps ; 23cm
ISBN 0-906071-74-7 (cased) : £5.50
ISBN 0-906071-73-9 (pbk) : £3.50
Also classified at 914.22'04858 B81-34927

647'.954223 — Kent. Public houses selling unpressurised beers — *Directories*

Guide to real ale in Kent. — [Rochester] ([41 Clive Rd, Rochester, Kent]) : CAMRA in Kent, [1980]. — 80p,[1]folded leaf of plates : maps ; 21cm
Text on inside cover
Unpriced (pbk) B81-26271

647'.95422395 — Kent. Folkestone. Public houses, *to 1979*

Bishop, C. H.. Old Folkestone pubs : old inns, taverns and hotels of the ancient borough of Folkestone / by C.H. Bishop. — [Maidstone] ([Springfield, Maidstone, Kent ME14 2LH]) : Kent County Council, County Library, [1980?]. — iii,107p : ill ; 21cm
Text on inside back cover
ISBN 0-905155-30-0 (pbk) : £0.90 B81-09541

647′.9542275 — Hampshire. New Forest. Public houses
Boel, Geoff. Picturesque pubs of the New Forest / by Geoff Boel. — Southampton : G.F. Wilson, 1981. — 25p : ill ; 19x24cm
ISBN 0-900810-29-7 (pbk) : Unpriced B81-22802

647′.95423 — South-west England. Public houses & restaurants — *Visitors′ guides*
Matheson, Nigel. The drinker′s guide to walking : the South West / [researched, walked, photographed, compiled and written by Nigel Matheson and Peter Gerard-Pearse]. — New York ; London : Proteus, 1981. — 159p : ill,maps ; 23cm
ISBN 0-906071-76-3 (cased) : £6.50
ISBN 0-906071-75-5 (pbk) : £3.50
Also classified at 914.23′04858 B81-34932

Pubbing eating & sleeping in the S.W. : the guide to value for money / editor R.L. Elliott. — Tavistock (Merchant′s House, Barley Market St., Tavistock, Devon) : Heritage in association with New English Library, c1981. — 175p : ill,2maps ; 18cm
Previous ed.: 1980
ISBN 0-903975-18-1 (pbk) : £0.90
Primary classification 647′.9442301 B81-17827

647′.9542313 — Wiltshire. Swindon region. Public houses selling unpressurised beers — *Directories*
Real ale around Swindon / Campaign for Real Ale, Swindon & N. Wilts Branch. — [Swindon] ([Old Estate House, Foxhill, Swindon SN4 0DR]) : [The Branch], [c1981]. — [68]p : ill,maps ; 15cm
Cover title. — Text on inside cover
£0.20 (pbk) B81-27037

647′.9542716 — Cheshire. Macclesfield. Public houses, *to 1980*
Wreglesworth, Paul. The pubs and breweries of Macclesfield / Paul Wreglesworth, Neil Richardson, Alan Gall. — Macclesfield (81 Thornton Ave., Macclesfield, Cheshire SK11 7XL) : P. Wreglesworth, N. Richardson, A. Gall. — 40p : ill,facsims,ports ; 30cm
ISBN 0-907511-00-7 (pbk) : £1.50
Primary classification 338.4′76633′0942716 B81-16733

647′.9542733 — Greater Manchester *(Metropolitan County).* **Blackley. Public houses,** *to 1980*
Hall, Roger, *1943-*. The pubs of Blackley / by Roger Hall. — [Blackley] ([c/o R. Hall, 123 Hill La., Blackley Manchester M9 2PW]) : N. Richardson, [1980]. — 20p : ill,maps,coats of arms,facsims,1plan ; 30cm
Cover title. — Text, ill on inside cover
£1.00 (pbk) B81-05790

647′.954284 — North Yorkshire. Public houses selling unpressurised beers — *Directories*
North Yorkshire ale / editor Michael Mackintosh ; assistant editor David Gamstan. — 4th ed. — York (Beech Cottage, Elvington, York, YO4 5AA) : CAMRA (North Yorkshire Ale), 1981. — 96p : ill,maps ; 23cm
Previous ed.: 1980
ISBN 0-9506987-1-7 (pbk) : £1.30 B81-34926

647′.954299 — Gwent. Public houses selling unpressurised beers — *Directories*
Real ale in Gwent / Campaign for Real Ale. — Newport, Gwent (51 Somerset Rd., Newport, Gwent NPT 7GA) : CAMRA, Newport and Gwent Branch, c1980. — 31p : maps ; 21cm
Cover title
£0.60 (pbk) B81-00175

648 — HOUSEKEEPING

648 — Stains. Removal — *Amateurs′ manuals*
Grunfeld, Nina. Spot check : how to cope with household stains / Nina Grunfeld and Michael Thomas. — Kingswood : World′s Work, 1981, c1980. — 33p : col.ill ; 23cm
Cover title. — Includes index
ISBN 0-437-06520-0 (pbk) : £1.00 B81-10379

648′.1 — Laundering - *For schools*
Ling, E. M.. Modern household science. — 4th ed. — London : Bell & Hyman, July 1981. — [258]p
Previous ed.: London : Mills & Boon, 1979
ISBN 0-7135-2073-6 (pbk) : £2.95 : CIP entry
Primary classification 677 B81-15910

648′.5′028 — Household materials. Cleaning. Techniques — *Manuals*
Phillips, Barty. [Wonder worker′s complete book of cleaning]. The complete book of cleaning / Barty Phillips. — Feltham : Hamlyn Paperbacks, 1981, c1980. — 255p : ill ; 18cm
Originally published: London : Sidgwick and Jackson, 1980. — Includes index
ISBN 0-600-20351-4 (pbk) : £1.50 B81-08978

648′.9 — Residences. Removal — *For children*
Snell, Nigel. Sally moves house / Nigel Snell. — London : Hamilton, 1981. — [25]p : col.ill ; 16x17cm
ISBN 0-241-10639-7 : £2.50 : CIP rev. B81-25757

649.1 — HOME CARE OF CHILDREN

649′.1 — Children. Home care — *Conference proceedings*
Changing patterns of child bearing and child rearing. — London : Academic Press, Feb.1982. — [170]p
Conference papers
ISBN 0-12-171660-0 : CIP entry
Primary classification 618.3′2 B81-35915

649′.1 — Children. Home care — *Manuals* — *For parents*
Jolly, Hugh. Book of child care / Hugh Jolly. — 3rd ed. — London : Allen & Unwin, 1981. — 612p : ill ; 24cm
Previous ed.: i.e. Rev. ed., 1978. — Includes index
ISBN 0-04-649010-8 : Unpriced : CIP rev. B81-00176

649′.1 — Children, to 7 years. Home care — *For nursery nursing*
Brain, Jean. Child care and health : for nursery nurses / Jean Brain and Molly D. Martin. — Amersham : Hulton, 1980. — viii,311p : ill ; 24cm
Includes bibliographies
ISBN 0-7175-0824-2 (pbk) : £4.90 B81-06384

649′.1′019 — Children. Home care. Psychological aspects — *Manuals* — *For parents*
Shure, Myrna B.. Problem-solving techniques in childbearing / Myrna B. Schure, George Spivak. — San Francisco ; London : Jossey-Bass, 1978. — xix,261p ; 24cm. — (The Jossey-Bass social and behavioral science series)
Bibliography: p243-254. — Includes index
ISBN 0-87589-366-x : £11.20 B81-15103

649′.1′024613 — Children. Home care — *For nursery nursing*
Geraghty, Patricia. Caring for children. — London : Bailliere Tindall, Oct.1981. — [304]p
ISBN 0-7020-0887-7 (pbk) : £8.50 : CIP entry B81-28818

649′.1′0248 — Children. Home care — *Manuals* — *For babysitters*
Doeser, Linda. Everything you always wanted your babysitter to know / Linda Doeser. — Loughton : Piatkus, 1981. — 91p : ill ; 21cm
ISBN 0-86188-109-5 : £1.95 : CIP rev. B81-14442

649′.1′07 — Parents. Education. Curriculum subjects: Home care of children
Handbook of parent education / edited by Marvin J. Fine. — New York ; London : Academic Press, 1980. — xv,341p : ill ; 24cm. — (Educational psychology)
Includes bibliographies and index
ISBN 0-12-256480-4 : £10.40 B81-22158

649′.1′0715 — United States. Parents. Education. Curriculum subjects: Home care of children. Teaching methods
Harman, David. Learning to be parents : principles, programs and methods / David Harman, Orville G. Brim, Jr. — Beverly Hills ; London : Sage, c1980. — 272p ; 23cm
Includes bibliographies and index
ISBN 0-8039-1272-2 : £9.35 B81-16183

649′.122 — Babies. Home care
You and your baby / authors David Brown ... [et al.] ; executive editor Evelyn Brown. — [London] : British Medical Association. — (A family doctor publication)
Part 1: Pregnancy and birth. — c1981. — 94p : ill(some col.) ; 20cm
Previous ed.: 1979
Unpriced (pbk) B81-33128

649′.122 — Babies. Home care. Fallacies — *For parents*
Behrstock, Barry B.. The parent′s when-not-to-worry book / Barry B. Behrstock with Richard Trubo. — New York ; London : Harper & Row, c1981. — x,262p ; 22cm
Bibliography: p246-254. — Includes index
ISBN 0-06-337017-4 : £6.95 B81-28455

649′.122 — Babies. Home care — *Manuals*
Stainer, J. W.. You and your baby / J.W. Staines, Margery J. Mitchell. — Melbourne ; Oxford : Oxford University Press, 1978. — 103p : ill ; 25cm
Bibliography: p105. — Includes index
ISBN 0-19-550565-4 (pbk) : £5.00 B81-39264

649′.122 — Babies. Home care — *Manuals* — *For parents*
Brady, Margaret Y.. Having a baby easily : a guide to natural birth / by Margaret Y. Brady. — Completely rev. and reset. — Wellingborough : Thorsons, 1981. — 143p : ill ; 22cm
Previous ed.: London : Health for all, 1969. — Bibliography: p137. — Includes index
ISBN 0-7225-0668-6 (pbk) : £2.95
Primary classification 618.2′00240431 B81-24170

Garner, Lesley. The basic baby book / Lesley Garner. — London (178 Wardour St., W.1) : Magread, 1980. — 127p : ill ; 18cm. — (A Moat Hall book)
ISBN 0-427-00434-9 (pbk) : £1.00 B81-01002

Rakowitz, Elly. Living with your new baby / Elly Rakowitz and Gloria S. Rubin ; foreword by Elisabeth Bing. — Feltham : Hamlyn Paperbacks, 1981, c1978. — 288p ; 18cm
Originally published: New York : F. Watts, 1978 ; London : Souvenir Press, 1980. — Bibliography: p279-282. - Includes index
ISBN 0-600-20458-8 (pbk) : £1.50 B81-22283

649′.122 — Children, to 5 years. Home care — *Manuals*
Leach, Penelope. Baby and child / Penelope Leach ; photography by Camilla Jessel. — Harmondsworth : Penguin, 1979, c1977 (1981 [printing]). — 509p : ill(some col.) ; 21cm. — (Penguin handbooks)
Originally published: London : Joseph, 1977
ISBN 0-14-046393-3 (pbk) : £5.95 B81-40083

649′.122 — Children, to 5 years. Home care — *Manuals* — *For parents*
Rayner, Claire. Baby and young child care : a practical guide for parents of children aged 0-5 years / Claire Rayner. — Maidenhead : Purnell, 1981. — 224p : ill(some col.) ; 27cm
Includes index
ISBN 0-361-04924-2 : £7.95 B81-16707

649′.122′0222 — Babies, to 1 year. Home care — *Manuals* — *Illustrations*
Trimmer, Eric. The first year / Eric Trimmer ; edited by Ruth Thomson ; illustrated by Stephanie Manchipp. — [Plymouth] ([Torr La., Plymouth PL3 5UA]) : Farley Health Products, c1979. — 93p : ill(some col.),1form,1port ; 21cm
Ill on lining papers
ISBN 0-905703-43-x : £1.95 B81-21238

649.12′3 — Children, to 5 years. Development — *For child care*
Hicks, Patricia. Introduction to child development. — Harlow : Longman, Sept.1981. — [160]p. — (Longman early childhood education ; no.6)
ISBN 0-582-36149-4 (pbk) : £3.75 : CIP entry B81-25692

649′.15 — Handicapped children. Home care — *For parents*

Purser, Ann. You and your handicapped child / by Ann Purser. — London : Allen & Unwin, 1981. — 149p ; 23cm
Bibliography: p148-149
ISBN 0-04-649012-4 : Unpriced : CIP rev.
B81-02546

649′.3 — Babies. Breast feeding

Kitzinger, Sheila. The experience of breastfeeding / Sheila Kitzinger. — London : Croom Helm in association with Penguin, c1979. — 255p : ill ; 23cm
Originally published: Harmondsworth : Penguin, 1979. — Includes index
ISBN 0-7099-0162-3 : £8.95 : CIP rev.
B79-35409

Stables, Jenny. A mother's guide to breastfeeding / Jenny Stables. — London : Star, 1981. — 109p,[4]p of plates : ill ; 18cm
Bibliography: p108-109
ISBN 0-352-30696-3 (pbk) : £1.25 B81-14146

649′.3 — Babies. Breast feeding — *Conference proceedings*

International Symposium on Breast Feeding *(1980 : Tel-Aviv)*. Human milk : its biological and social value : selected papers from the International Symposium on Breast Feeding, Tel-Aviv, February 24-28, 1980 / edited by S. Freier and A.I. Eidelman. — Amsterdam ; Oxford : Excerpta Medica, 1980. — xi,341p : ill ; 25cm. — (International congress series ; 518)
Includes bibliographies and index
ISBN 90-219-0463-2 : £26.32 B81-04079

649′.3 — Babies. Breast feeding — *Manuals — For health visitors*

Helsing, Elisabet. Breast-feeding in practice : a manual for health workers. — Oxford : Oxford University Press, Jan.1982. — [200]p. — (Oxford medical publications)
ISBN 0-19-261298-0 (pbk) : £3.95 : CIP entry
B81-33825

649′.5 — Activities for children — *For parents*

Johnson, June. 555 ways to amuse a child : crafts, hobbies and creative ideas for the child from six to twelve / June Johnson ; drawings by Beryl Bennett. — U.K. ed. abridged and adapted. — Kingswood : Elliot Right Way, c1981. — 173p : ill ; 18cm. — (Paperfronts)
Previous ed.: published as 838 ways to amuse a child. New York : Gramercy, 1960. — Includes index
ISBN 0-7160-0668-5 (pbk) : £0.75 B81-24320

649′.5 — Children, 1-3 years. Play — *Manuals — For parents*

Marzollo, Jean. Supertot : a parent's guide to toddlers / by Jean Marzollo ; illustrated by Irene Trivas. — London : Allen & Unwin, 1980. — 167p : ill,1form ; 15x23cm
Originally published: New York : Harper & Row, 1977. — Bibliography: p164. — Includes index
ISBN 0-04-649006-x : £5.50 : CIP rev.
B79-36384

649′.5 — Children, *8-13 years.* **Play**

Roberts, Alasdair. Out to play : the middle years of childhood / by Alasdair Roberts. — [Aberdeen] : Aberdeen University Press, 1980. — xvii,173p ; 22cm
Bibliography: p159-165. - Includes index
ISBN 0-08-025719-4 (cased) : Unpriced : CIP rev.
ISBN 0-08-025718-6 (pbk) : Unpriced
B80-06490

649′.5′0222 — Children. Play — *Illustrations — For children*

Wik, Lars. Playtime / [photographs by Lars Wik]. — London : Methuen, 1978 (1979 [printing]). — [16]p all col.ill ; 17x18cm. — (Look and see books)
ISBN 0-416-87980-2 (spiral) : £0.85
B81-06303

649′.5′05 — Activities for children — *Serials — For parents*

Learning together : the magazine poster-pack for parents and children. — 1-4. — London : Evans Brothers, 1980-1980. — 4v. : ill ; 31cm
Six issues yearly. — Only four issues published. — Description based on: 2
ISSN 0143-7801 = Learning together : £4.50 per year B81-36557

649′.64 — Children. Behaviour modification — *Manuals*

Westmacott, E. V. S.. Behaviour can change / E.V.S. Westmacott and R.J. Cameron. — Basingstoke : Globe Education, 1981. — 150p : ill ; 22cm
Bibliography: p145
ISBN 0-333-29608-7 (pbk) : Unpriced
B81-36689

649′.64 — Children. Behaviour modification — *Manuals — For parents*

Schaefer, Charles E.. How to help children with common problems / Charles E. Schaefer, Howard L. Millman. — New York ; London : Van Nostrand Reinhold, c1981. — xiv,431p ; 24cm
Includes bibliographies and index
ISBN 0-442-24506-8 : £11.95 B81-06089

649′.64 — Children, to 5 years. Behaviour modification

Powell, Marcene Lee. Assessment and management of developmental changes and problems in children / Marcene Lee Powell ; chapter 9 contributed by Peggy L. Pipes ; original photographs by Janis K. Smith ; original drawings by Mary K. Shrader ; original cover by Greg Owen. — 2nd ed. — St. Louis ; London : Mosby, 1981. — x,344p : ill ; 26cm
Previous ed.: published as Assessment and management of developmental changes in children. 1976. — Includes bibliographies and index
ISBN 0-8016-1520-8 (pbk) : £9.25
Primary classification 155.4′22 B81-25462

649′.64 — New Zealand. Children. Corporal punishment

Ritchie, Jane. Spare the rod. — London : Allen & Unwin, Dec.1981. — [155]p
ISBN 0-86861-107-7 : £10.00 : CIP entry
B81-31639

649′.65 — Children. Sex education — *For parents*

Parents children & sex : a new sex education guide for parents / editor John Robson. — North Strathfield : Family Life Movement of Australia ; Elesham, 1979. — 50p : ill ; 14x21cm. — (A Family life guide book)
ISBN 0-909922-88-8 (pbk) : £0.85 B81-10355

649′.65 — Sex education - *For parents*

Pickering, Lucienne. Parents listen. — London : Geoffrey Chapman, Sept.1981. — [80]p
ISBN 0-225-66311-2 (pbk) : £1.95 : CIP entry
B81-20121

649.8 — HOME NURSING

649′.8 — Maladjusted persons. Home care

Neuman, Frederic. Caring : home treatment for the emotionally disturbed. — Wellingborough : Turnstone Press, Feb.1982. — [208]p
Originally published: New York : Dial Press, 1980
ISBN 0-85500-168-2 (pbk) : £3.95 : CIP entry
B81-35854

650 — BUSINESS PRACTICES

650 — Business practices

Hathaway, S.. An introduction to business : the world of work / S. Hathaway, C. Thomas. — London : Holt, Rinehart and Winston, c1980. — 294p : ill,1map,forms ; 22cm. — (Holt business texts)
Includes index
ISBN 0-03-910274-2 (pbk) : Unpriced : CIP rev. B80-13893

Taylor, Alan, *1919-*. The world of work : a textbook for the Business Education Council general award courses / Alan Taylor, Don Davison ; illustrated by Janet Payne. — Stockport : Polytech, 1979. — 230p : ill,facsims,forms ; 22cm. — (Business Education Council general award courses)
Includes index
ISBN 0-85505-030-6 (pbk) : £3.00 B81-37966

650′.03′21 — Business practices — *Encyclopaedias*

Giordano, Albert G.. Concise dictionary of business terminology / Albert G. Giordano. — Englewood Cliffs ; London : Prentice-Hall, c1981. — 225p ; 21cm. — (A Spectrum book)
ISBN 0-13-166553-7 (cased) : Unpriced
ISBN 0-13-166546-4 (pbk) : £3.85 B81-22757

650.1 — Business enterprise. Success — *Manuals*

Farnsworth, Terry. Managing for success : the Farnsworth formulas / Terry Farnsworth ; illustrated by Ray Jelliffe. — New York ; London : McGraw-Hill, c1981. — 170p : ill ; 24cm
ISBN 0-07-084547-6 : £5.95 : CIP rev.
B81-08878

Sherman, Harold M.. Extra success potential : the art of out-thinking and out-sensing others in business and everday life / Harold Sherman and Al Pollard. — Englewood Cliffs ; London : Prentice-Hall, c1981. — 195p ; 22cm
ISBN 0-13-298117-3 (cased) : Unpriced
ISBN 0-13-298109-2 (pbk) : £4.15 B81-34951

650.1′0207 — Business enterprise. Success — *Humour*

Masters, Roderick. The Roderick Masters book of money-making schemes, or, How to become enormously wealthy with virtually no effort. — London : Routledge & Kegan Paul, 1981. — 110p : ill ; 24cm
Includes index
ISBN 0-7100-0973-9 : £5.50 : CIP rev.
B81-28812

650.1′024042 — Business enterprise. Success — *Manuals — For women*

Nelson, Rachel. Success without tears : a woman's guide to the top / Rachel Nelson. — London : Star, 1980, c1979. — 168p ; 18cm
Originally published: London : Weidenfeld and Nicolson, 1979. — Includes index
ISBN 0-352-30653-x (pbk) : £1.25 B81-00177

650.1′4 — Job hunting. Interviews — *Manuals*

Fletcher, Clive. Facing the interview : a guide to self-preparation and presentation / Clive Fletcher. — London (40 Museum Street, London WC1A 1LU) : Unwin Paperbacks, 1981. — ix,101p ; 18cm
ISBN 0-04-380023-8 (pbk) : £1.75 B81-11128

George, David. How to prepare for interviews : a practical guide / David George. — London : Harrap, 1981. — 31p : forms ; 18cm
ISBN 0-245-53712-0 (pbk) : £1.25 B81-19682

650.1′4 — Job hunting — *Manuals*

Getting a new job / [edited by Edith Rudinger]. — London : Consumers' Association, c1981. — 176p : ill ; 20cm
Includes index
ISBN 0-85202-191-7 (pbk) : Unpriced
ISBN 0-340-25908-6 (Hodder & Stoughton)
B81-33666

650.1′4 — Job hunting — *Manuals — For executives*

Golzen, Godfrey. Changing your job / Godfrey Golzen & Philip Plumbley. — 4th (rev.) ed. — London : Kogan Page, 1981. — 203p : ill ; 23cm
Previous ed.: 1978
ISBN 0-85038-408-7 (cased) : £8.25
ISBN 0-85038-409-5 (pbk) : £4.25 B81-28899

650.1′4 — Occupations. Application forms. Filling — *Manuals — Serials*

Filling the gaps. — 1-. — Liverpool (Waterloo Buildings, Cases St., Liverpool L1 1HP) : Impact Foundation, 1976-. — v. ; 30cm
Irregular. — Description based on: 3
£0.10 B81-13101

650.1'4 — Personnel. Selection. Interviewing — *Manuals — For interviewees*

Bostwick, Burdette E.. 111 proven techniques and strategies for getting the job interview / Burdette E. Bostwick. — New York ; Chichester : Wiley, c1981. — x,285p : ill ; 24cm
Includes index
ISBN 0-471-07762-3 : £8.00 B81-23718

650'.76 — Business practices — *Questions & answers*

Clough, D.. Cross modular assignments for BEC higher / Danny Clough, William Green and Anthony Amrit Nasta. — London : Heinemann Educational
Students' book. — 1981. — 94p : ill,1map,1plan ; 30cm
ISBN 0-435-45070-0 (pbk) : £1.95 B81-40374

651 — OFFICE PRACTICES

651 — Great Britain. Office practices. Automation

Office automation survey. — Slough (Clove House, The Broadway, Farnham Common, Slough, Berkshire SL2 3PQ) : Urwick Nexos Ltd., 1981. — 10[i.e.58]leaves : 1ill ; 30cm
Unpriced (pbk) B81-28299

651 — Office practices

Denyer, J. C.. Office management / J.C. Denyer. — 5th ed. / revised by Josephine Shaw. — Plymouth : Macdonald and Evans, 1980. — x,646p : ill,forms ; 22cm
Previous ed.: 1974. — Bibliography: p624-626. - Includes index
ISBN 0-7121-1525-0 (pbk) : £4.95 B81-01003

Shaw, Josephine. Office practice. — 2nd ed. — Sevenoaks : Hodder & Stoughton, Oct.1981. — [224]p. — (Teach yourself books)
Previous ed.: 1972
ISBN 0-340-26832-8 (pbk) : £1.95 : CIP entry B81-26731

Watcham, Maurice. Watcham's office practice. — London : McGraw-Hill
Book 1. Handbook and solutions / Margaret Rees-Boughton assisted by Elizabeth Taylor. — 3rd ed. — c1980. — ix,143p : ill,1plan,forms ; 25cm
Previous ed.: 1975
ISBN 0-07-084632-4 (pbk) : £4.95 : CIP rev. B80-23436

651 — Office practices. Automation. Management

Birchall, David. Tomorrow's office today : managing technological change / D.W. Birchall and V.J. Hammond. — London : Business Books, 1981. — ix,202p : ill,forms ; 24cm
Bibliography: p189-190. — Includes index
ISBN 0-09-144920-0 : Unpriced : CIP rev. B81-02551

Pritchard, J. A. T.. Planning office automation. — Manchester : NCC Publications, Jan.1982. — [200]p
ISBN 0-85012-331-3 (pbk) : CIP entry B81-34578

651 — Office practices. Automation. Testing. Techniques

Managing office automation : pilot schemes and equipment trials / Urwick Nexos. — Slough : Urwick Nexos Limited, [1981?]. — ii,36leaves : ill ; 30cm. — (Managing office automation) (Urwick Nexos report series ; 2)
Bibliography: leaf 36
ISBN 0-907535-02-x (pbk) : Unpriced B81-33095

651 — Office practices — *Manuals*

Feldman, Sally. The complete desk book / Sally Feldman. — London : Hamlyn, 1981. — 208p : forms ; 25cm
Bibliography: p156-160. — Includes index
ISBN 0-600-33208-x (cased) : £4.95
ISBN 0-600-38455-1 (pbk) : £2.95 B81-22768

651 — Offices — *For management*

The **Director's** guide to better offices / edited by Richard Barber ; editorial consultant H. Beric Wright ; design Brian Cronk, Ron Starbuck ; illustrations Keith Howard. — London : Director Publications for the Institute of Directors, [1981?]. — 104p : ill,plans,ports ; 30cm
Unpriced (pbk) B81-38383

651'.076 — Office practices — *Questions & answers*

Harrison, John, *1931-*. World of work : an office practice workbook / John Harrison. — London : Pitman Business Education, 1981. — 63p : ill,forms ; 30cm
ISBN 0-273-01495-1 (unbound) : £1.25 B81-21979

Holden, Thelma B.. Questions about the office / T.B. Holden. — London : Edward Arnold, c1981. — vi,73p : ill ; 22cm : forms
ISBN 0-7131-0589-5 (pbk) : £1.95 : CIP rev. B81-28033

Objective tests in office practice / edited by Glenys M. Lardi ; items written by V. Carley ... [et al.]. — London : Longman, 1980. — 55p ; 20cm. — (Longman objective tests series)
ISBN 0-582-41574-8 (pbk) : £1.50 : CIP rev. B80-39656

Rennie, Margaret. Exercises in elementary office practice / Margaret Rennie. — 4th ed. — London : Heinemann Educational, 1981. — 58p : ill,forms ; 25cm
Previous ed.: 1978
ISBN 0-435-45538-9 (pbk) : £1.50 B81-03439

651'.076 — Office practices — *Questions & answers — For schools*

Greig, R. A.. Multiple choice questions on office practice and secretarial duties. — London : Edward Arnold, Jan.1982. — [96]p
ISBN 0-7131-0629-8 (pbk) : £2.50 : CIP entry B81-33900

651'.07'8 — Business firms. Office practices. Teaching aids

Leduchowicz, T.. A guide to developing office training packages and kits / prepared by T. Leduchowicz. — [Slough] : Thamesman, c1981. — 56p ; 21cm
Bibliography: p35
ISBN 0-906537-02-9 (pbk) : Unpriced B81-20880

651'.2 — Offices. Effects of automation — *Forecasts*

The **Office** of the future. — Farnborough, Hants. : Gower
No.1: Planning for the office of the future. — Nov.1981. — [160]p
ISBN 0-566-03404-2 (pbk) : £4.95 : CIP entry B81-30532

651.3 — United States. Schools. Offices. Management — *Manuals*

Sweeney, R. Carol. Handbook for educational secretaries and office personnel / R. Carol Sweeney, Emery Stoops. — Boston, Mass. ; London : Allyn and Bacon, c1981. — vii,206p : ill ; 25cm
Bibliography: p197-200. — Includes index
ISBN 0-205-07292-5 : £14.95 B81-16425

651.3'7 — Business firms. Office practices: Clerical procedures. Management

Stankard, Martin F.. Successful management of large clerical operations : a guide to improving service transaction systems / Martin F. Stankard. — New York ; London : McGraw-HIll, c1981. — xvii,268p : ill ; 24cm
Bibliography: p257-260. - Includes index
ISBN 0-07-060831-8 : £12.50 B81-09933

651.3'7 — Office practices: Clerical procedures

Binnie, Jennifer. Basic clerical assignments / Jennifer Binnie and Katharine Glennon. — London : Edward Arnold, 1981. — 68p : ill,maps,facsims,1plan,forms
ISBN 0-7131-0552-6 : £2.50 : CIP rev. B81-02662

651.3'7 — Office practices: Clerical procedures — *Manuals*

Brealey, Ronald. Clerical duties activity course and workbook / Ronald Brealey. — London : Longman, 1980. — 212p : ill,forms ; 25cm
Includes index
ISBN 0-582-41197-1 (pbk) : £3.95 : CIP rev. B79-19379

651.3'74 — Office practices: Clerical procedures

Foster, Thelma. Office skills. — Cheltenham : Thornes, Sept.1981. — [250]p
ISBN 0-85950-459-x (pbk) : £3.50 : CIP entry B81-22502

651.3'741 — Medical secretaryship — *Manuals*

Drury, Michael. The medical secretary's and receptionist's handbook / Michael Drury. — 4th ed. — London : Baillière Tindall, c1981. — vi,295p : ill,forms ; 24cm
Previous ed.: 1975. — Includes index
ISBN 0-7020-0858-3 (pbk) : £5.75 B81-38073

651.3'741 — Secretaries. Duties — *Manuals*

Medlyn, Myrtle. Secretarial services / Myrtle Medlyn, Wendy Unwin. — Amersham : Hulton, 1980. — 176p : ill,forms. — (Hulton BEC books)
ISBN 0-7175-0840-4 (pbk) : £2.40 B81-05581

651.3'741 — Secretaryship — *Manuals*

Leafe, Margaret. Secretarial duties : revision notes and exercises / Margaret Leafe. — London : Edward Arnold, 1981. — 92p : ill ; 22cm
ISBN 0-7131-0553-4 (pbk) : £2.25 : CIP rev. B81-16380

651.3'741 — United States. Dental services. Practices. Secretaryship

Douglas, Mary Ann. Secretarial dental assistant / Mary Ann Douglas ; Claire Williamson technical consultant ; Angela R. Emmi series editor. — New York ; London : Van Nostrand Reinhold, c1981. — v,313p : ill,forms ; 27cm
Includes index
ISBN 0-442-21860-5 : £11.20 B81-29521

651.3'741'076 — Secretaries. Duties — *Questions & answers*

Eaton, Vera. Talking shop : a secretarial assignments book / Vera Eaton. — London : Pitman, 1981. — 92p : ill,forms ; 30cm + Teaching notes(26p: ill,forms ; 30cm)
ISBN 0-273-01598-2 (pbk) : £3.25
ISBN 0-273-01599-0 (Teaching notes) : £2.50 B81-21971

651.3'741'0973 — United States. Secretaries. Duties — *Manuals*

Church, Olive D.. Instructor's manual to accompany Office systems and careers : a resource for administrative assistants / Olive D. Church and Anne E. Schatz. — Boston [Mass.] ; London : Allyn and Bacon, c1981. — 301p : ill,forms ; 24cm
ISBN 0-205-07135-x (pbk) : £1.00 B81-26395

Church, Olive D.. Office systems and careers : a resource for administrative assistants / Olive D. Church and Anne E. Schatz. — Boston ; London : Allyn and Bacon, c1981. — 672p : ill,2plans,forms ; 25cm
Includes bibliographies
ISBN 0-205-07134-1 : £18.95 B81-19032

651.3'741'0973 — United States. Secretaries. Duties — *Questions & answers*

Church, Olive D.. Office Dynamics Company, an office services and temporary help agency practice set : six in-baskets for the upward bound secretary in training with career exploration / Olive Church. — Boston ; London : Allyn and Bacon, c1981. — 233p : ill,1map,facsims,plan,forms ; 28cm
ISBN 0-205-07136-8 (pbk) : £6.95 B81-16215

651.3'743 — Business firms. Receptionists — *Manuals*

Atkins, Hazel. The receptionist / Hazel Atkins. — London : Edward Arnold, 1981. — 108p : ill ; 25cm : forms
Includes index
ISBN 0-7131-0580-1 (pbk) : £3.25 : CIP rev. B81-16360

651.5 — Accounting. Records management
Grimsley, Bob. Management accounting systems and records. — 2nd ed. — Aldershot : Gower, Oct.1981. — [125]p
Previous ed.: 1972
ISBN 0-566-02339-3 : £12.50 : CIP entry B81-24619

651.5 — Great Britain. Hotel industries & catering industries. Personnel records
Kelly, T. K.. A study of personnel records and manpower planning : report of the findings of a survey of firms in the hotel and catering industry / T.K. Kelly. — [Wembley] : [Hotel and Catering Industry Training Board], 1971 (1976 [printing]). — 72,1-42p : ill,col.forms ; 30cm
Unpriced (spiral) B81-33173

651.5 — Office practices. Paperwork. Management — *Manuals*
Knox, Frank M.. Managing paperwork : a key to productivity / Frank M. Knox. — Farnborough, Hants. : Gower, c1980. — x,249p : ill,forms ; 24cm
Includes index
ISBN 0-566-02262-1 : £15.00 B81-11607

651.5 — Production management. Records management
Tooley, Desmond F.. Production control systems & records. — 2nd ed. — Farnborough, Hants : Gower, May 1981. — [160]p
Previous ed.: 1972
ISBN 0-566-02253-2 : £12.50 : CIP entry B81-04258

651.5'042 — England. Primary schools. Students. Personal records. Records management
Clift, Philip. Record keeping in primary schools. — London : Macmillan, July 1981. — [256]p. — (Schools Council research studies)
ISBN 0-333-30945-6 (pbk) : £5.95 : CIP entry B81-13810

651.5'04261 — United States. Psychiatric medical records. Records management. Problem Oriented Medical Records
Ryback, Ralph S.. The problem oriented record in psychiatry and mental health care. — Rev. ed. / Ralph S. Ryback, Richard Longabaugh, D. Robert Fowler. — New York ; London : Grune & Stratton, c1981. — xiii,270p : ill,forms ; 28cm
Previous ed.: 1974. — Bibliography: p253-264. — Includes index
ISBN 0-8089-1308-5 (pbk) : £18.20 B81-35420

651.5'3 — Office practices. Filing — *Manuals*
Stewart, Jeffrey R.. Progressive filing. — 9th ed. / Jeffrey R. Stewart, Jr., Judith A. Scharle, Gilbert Kahn. — New York ; London : Gregg Division/McGraw-Hill, c1980. — vii,136p : ill (some col.),forms ; 25cm
Previous ed.: / by Gilbert Kahn, Theodore Yerian, Jeffrey R. Stewart, Jr. 1969. — Includes index
ISBN 0-07-061445-8 : £5.40 B81-01004

651.5'9 — Great Britain. Companies. Superannuation schemes. Records management. Applications of digital computer systems
Barker, R.. Using computers for pension schemes' record keeping and benefit statements / R. Barker and A.S. Fishman. — Aldershot : Gower, [1981?]. — 57p : ill ; 22cm
ISBN 0-566-03411-5 (pbk) : Unpriced : CIP rev. B81-14425

651.5'9 — Industries. Productivity. Effects of automation of records management
Kalthoff, Robert J.. Productivity and records automation / Robert J. Kalthoff, Leonard S. Lee. — Englewood Cliffs ; London : Prentice-Hall, c1981. — xiv,386p : ill,1form ; 25cm
Includes bibliographies and index
ISBN 0-13-725234-x : £17.45
ISBN 0-13-725184-x (Limited ed.) : Unpriced B81-37175

651.5'9 — United States. Personal records. Data banks — *Lists*
Norback, Craig T.. The computer invasion / Craig T. Norback. — New York ; London : Van Nostrand Reinhold, c1981. — xiv,288p ; 29cm
ISBN 0-442-26121-7 : £16.10 B81-31985

651.7 — Business practices. Communication
Buffton, J. M.. Making contact / J.M. Buffton, R.A. Ingham. — London : Holt, Rinehart and Winston. — (Holt business texts)
2: People and communication. — c1981. — 195p : ill ; 22cm
Includes index
ISBN 0-03-910300-5 (pbk) : £2.95 B81-23051

651.7 — Business practices. Communication — *Manuals*
Saunders, Peter, *1923-*. People and communication / Peter Saunders ; illustrated by Janet Payne. — Stockport : Polytech, 1979. — 104p : ill,maps,forms ; 22cm. — (A Business Education Council course. General level)
Includes index
ISBN 0-85505-028-4 (pbk) : Unpriced B81-09348

651.7 — Electronic mail
Welch, W. J.. Electronic mail systems. — Manchester : NCC Publications, Nov.1981. — [105]p. — (Office technology in the 80s)
ISBN 0-85012-350-x (pbk) : £4.00 : CIP entry B81-39238

651.7'3 — Business firms. Telephones. Use — *Manuals*
Estill, Louise. Be confident about using the telephone / by Louise Estill. — Gerrards Cross (15 Kingsway, Gerrards Cross, Bucks. SL9 8NS) : Louise Estill Teaching Aids
Pt.1: A basic course in how to be a courteous and efficient telephone user : with progressive exercises. — c1980. — 17p + Notes for teachers(4p ; 21cm) ; 21cm
ISBN 0-907732-00-3 (unbound) : £1.00 B81-36263

Estill, Louise. Be confident about using the telephone / by Louise Estill. — Gerrards Cross (15 Kingsway, Gerrards Cross, Bucks. SL9 8NS) : Louise Estill Teaching Aids
Pt.2: Advice and exercises on eight important types of call. — c1980. — 24p : forms ; 21cm
ISBN 0-907732-01-1 (unbound) : £1.00 B81-36264

651.7'4 — Business practices. Written communication — *Manuals*
Parsons, C. J.. Written communication for business students : a guide to succesful examination technique / C.J. Parsons, S.J. Hughes. — 3rd ed. — London : Edward Arnold, 1981. — 202p : ill,facsims,forms ; 22cm
Previous ed.: 1975
ISBN 0-7131-0512-7 (pbk) : Unpriced : CIP rev. B80-33833

Saville, Jenny. The business letter writer / Jenny and Tim Saville. — London : Ward Lock, 1981. — 175p ; 19cm
ISBN 0-7063-6115-6 (pbk) : £1.95 : CIP rev. B81-12888

651.7'4 — Dictation — *Manuals — For businessmen*
Schrag, Adele F.. How to dictate : a guide for organizing, planning, and dictating correspondence / Adele F. Schrag. — New York ; London : Gregg, c1981. — 84p : ill ; 23cm
ISBN 0-07-055601-6 (pbk) : £4.25 B81-26256

651.7'4 — English language. Business English — *Questions & answers*
Smith, Leila R.. English for careers : business, professional, and technical / Leila R. Smith. — 2nd ed. — New York ; Chichester : Wiley, c1981. — xiv,410p : ill,facsims ; 28cm
Previous ed.: New York : Wiley, 1977. — Includes index
ISBN 0-471-07718-6 (pbk) : £7.80 B81-13083

651.7'5 — Business correspondence in English — *For non-English speaking students*
Love, Charles. Commercial correspondence : for students of English as a second language / Charles Love, Joseph Tinervia. — 2nd ed. — New York ; London : McGraw-Hill, c1980. — 197p : ill ; 28cm
Previous ed.: 197-?
ISBN 0-07-038785-0 (corrected : pbk) : £3.50 B81-10235

651.7'5 — Business correspondence — *Manuals — For secretaries*
Kinsey, T. L.. Business letters : for secretarial students / T.L. Kinsey. — Amersham : Hulton, 1980. — 128p : ill,facsims ; 24cm
ISBN 0-7175-0830-7 (pbk) : £2.10 B81-03337

651.7'5 — Legal business correspondence — *Forms & precedents — For company directors & company secretaries*
Mitchell, Ewan. The director's and company secretary's handbook of draft legal letters / Ewan Mitchell ; illustrations by Tobi. — 2nd ed. — London : Business Books, 1979. — xxxii,596p : ill,forms ; 23cm
Previous ed.: 1974. — Includes index
ISBN 0-220-67001-3 : £15.00 B81-16346

651.8 — Business practices. Applications of data processing systems. Management aspects
Keen, Jeffrey S.. Managing systems development / Jeffrey S. Keen. — Chichester : Wiley, c1981. — xiii,343p : ill,forms ; 24cm. — (Wiley series in information processing)
Includes index
ISBN 0-471-27839-4 : £9.75 B81-16334

651.8 — Great Britain. Publishing industries. Word processing systems. Use
Oakeshott, Priscilla. The current use of word processors by British publishers / Priscilla Oakeshott and Jack Meadows. — Leicester : Primary Communication Research Centre, University of Leicester, c1981. — ii,31p ; 22cm. — (BL (R & D) report ; no.5598) (Occasional papers / Primary Communications Research Centre University of Leicester, ISSN 0144-6460)
ISBN 0-906083-15-x (pbk) : £2.00 B81-16330

651.8 — Great Britain. Solicitorship. Practices. Applications of word processing systems
Chalton, S. N. L.. Computers and word processors in a solicitor's office / [S.N.L. Chalton]. — [Guildford] ([Braboeuf Manor, St Catherines, Guildford GU3 1HA]) : College of Law, 1981. — v,43p ; 22cm
£2.50 (pbk)
Also classified at 651.8'4 B81-12278

651.8 — Offices. Word processing systems
Bergerud, Marly. Word/information processing concepts : careers, technology, and applications / Marly Bergerud, Jean Gonzalez. — New York ; Chichester : Wiley, c1981. — xi,383p : ill,forms ; 29cm
Includes index
ISBN 0-471-08499-9 : £9.50 B81-23313

Morgan, Tom. Word processing : the challenge of new technology : six articles / by Tom Morgan ; reprinted from Local government chronicle. — London (Publications Division, 11 Bury St., EC3A 5AP) : Brown, Knight & Truscott (Holdings), [1981?]. — 30p : ill ; 21cm
ISBN 0-904677-12-5 (pbk) : £2.00 B81-26273

651.8 — United States. Offices. Word processing systems
Bergerud, Marly. Word processing : concepts and careers / Marly Bergerud and Jean Gonzalez. — 2nd ed. — New York ; Chichester : Wiley, c1981. — xvii,237p : ill,forms ; 28cm. — (Wiley word processing series)
Previous ed.: 1978. — Includes index
ISBN 0-471-06010-0 (pbk) : £7.75 B81-24942

651.8 — Word processing systems
Morgan, Richard, *1938-*. Word processing / Richard Morgan, Brian Wood. — London : Oyez, c1981. — viii,152p,[4]p of plates : ill ; 23cm
Includes index
ISBN 0-85120-563-1 : Unpriced B81-28528

Simons, G. L.. Introducing word processing. — Oxford : NCC Publications, Sept.1981. — [200]p
ISBN 0-85012-320-8 (pbk) : £8.50 : CIP entry B81-28133

651.8 — Word processing systems — *For businessmen*

Townsend, Kevin. Choosing and using a word processor. — Aldershot : Gower, Dec.1981. — [230]p
ISBN 0-566-03408-5 (pbk) : £9.50 : CIP entry B81-35875

651.8 — Word processing systems — *For Irish businessmen* — *Serials*

The **Irish** word processing guide. — 1981-. — Dublin (P.O. Box 5, 51 Sandycove Rd, Dun Laoghaire, Dublin) : Hamilton Press for Office Automation Consultants, 1981-. — v. : ill,ports ; 30cm
Annual
Unpriced B81-24703

651.8 — Word processing systems — *Programmed instructions*

Layman, N. Kathryn. Word processors : a programmed training guide with business applications / N. Kathryn Layman, Adrienne Giacobbe Renner. — Englewood Cliffs ; London : Prentice-Hall, c1981. — xii,353p : ill ; 22cm
Includes index
ISBN 0-13-963520-3 (spiral) : £13.95 B81-28423

651.8 — Word processing systems — *Serials*

Word processing now : a Business systems & equipment publication. — July 1978-. — London (76 Oxford St., W1) : Maclean-Hunter, 1978-. — v. : ill,ports ; 29cm
Quarterly. — Supplement to: Business systems & equipment (London : 1972). — Description based on: 1981 issue
ISSN 0144-2066 = Word processing now : Unpriced B81-38996

651.8'4 — Business firms. Computer systems. Installation — *Manuals* — *For management*

Guidelines for computer managers / [National Computing Centre]. — Manchester : NCC Publications, 1981. — 265p ; 22cm
Includes bibliographies
ISBN 0-85012-248-1 : £15.00 : CIP rev. B80-06987

651.8'4 — Electronic office equipment

Yeomans, J. M.. A product guide to office automation / J.M. Yeomans. — Slough (Clove House, The Broadway, Farnham Common, Slough, Berks. SL2 3PG) : Urwick Nexos Limited, c1981. — ii,20p : 1ill ; 30cm
Text on back cover
ISBN 0-907535-00-3 (pbk) : Unpriced B81-19287

651.8'4 — Great Britain. Business firms. Digital computer systems — *Buyers' guides* — *Serials*

Computing marketplace. — Aldershot : Gower, Jan.1982. — [500]p
ISBN 0-566-03401-8 : £19.50 : CIP entry B81-37541

651.8'4 — Great Britain. Solicitorship. Practices. Applications of digital computer systems

Chalton, S. N. L.. Computers and word processors in a solicitor's office / [S.N.L. Chalton]. — [Guildford] ([Braboeuf Manor, St Catherines, Guildford GU3 1HA]) : College of Law, 1981. — v,43p ; 22cm
£2.50 (pbk)
Primary classification 651.8 B81-12278

Ruoff, Theodore B. F.. The solicitor and his silicon chip : a simple and practical guide to the introduction of the computer into a solicitor's practice / Theodore Ruoff. — London : Oyez, c1981. — ix,117p ; 22cm
Includes index
ISBN 0-85120-569-0 (pbk) : Unpriced B81-28526

651.8'42 — Business practices. Applications of digital computer systems. Programming

Brown, Gary DeWard. Beyond COBOL : survival in business applications programming / Gary D. Brown. — New York ; Chichester : Wiley, c1981. — vii,200p : ill,forms ; 24cm
Includes index
ISBN 0-471-09030-1 : £12.25 B81-37115

651.8'443 — Great Britain. Government departments. Office equipment. Computer systems. Visual display terminals. Use. Ergonomic factors — *Inquiry reports*

Report of the CCTA/PSA Working Party examining the requirements for accommodating visual display systems in government offices. — [London] : Central Computer and Telecommunications Agency, 1981. — 44p : ill ; 30cm
ISBN 0-7115-0035-5 (pbk) : Unpriced B81-40167

651'.9334'091724 — Developing countries. Cooperatives. Office practices

Launder, John. Office management for co-operatives : a self-teaching text / by John Launder and the Co-operatives Panel, Intermediate Technology Development Group. — London : Intermediate Technology, c 1980. — 103p : ill ; 21cm
ISBN 0-903031-73-6 (pbk) : £2.95 B81-27762

651'.936211'0942 — England. Hospitals. Office practices — *For medical secretaries*

Collin, Marion. Hospital office practice / Marion Collin. — London : Baillière Tindall, 1981. — vii,133p : ill,forms ; 24cm
Bibliography: p128. — Includes index
ISBN 0-7020-0873-7 (pbk) : £4.50 : CIP rev. B81-13494

652.3 — TYPING

652.3 — Typing. Layout — *Manuals*

Alexander, Vonnie. Specimen layouts for typists : a reference book for students, word processing operators, office workers, non-professionals / by Vonnie Alexander. — Christchurch [N.Z.] ; London : Whitcoulls, 1981. — 202p : ill,facsims,forms ; 30cm
Bibliography: p125-126. — Includes index
ISBN 0-7233-0668-0 (pbk) : Unpriced B81-38077

652.3 — Typing — *Manuals*

Rowe, Brenda. Type it yourself / Brenda Rowe. — Harmondsworth : Penguin, 1981. — 128p : ill ; 21cm
Originally published: London : Pitman, 1975. — Bibliography: p123
ISBN 0-14-046457-3 (pbk) : £1.95 B81-27655

Trevethin, Hazel. Typing skill & speed / Hazel Trevethin. — London : Macmillan, 1981. — vi,58p ; 14x21cm
ISBN 0-333-30505-1 (spiral) : Unpriced B81-34195

652.3'0076 — Typing — *Questions & answers*

Hayhurst, Phyllis. Longman typing project / Phyllis Hayhurst. — London : Longman, 1981. — 90p : ill ; 19x25cm
Includes index
ISBN 0-582-41578-0 (pbk) : £2.50 B81-22183

Hindmarsh, Sara. Supplementary typewriting exercises / Sara Hindmarsh. — London : Edward Arnold, 1981
1: Business letters. — 59p ; 28cm
ISBN 0-7131-0533-x (pbk) : £2.25 : CIP rev. B81-02384

Hindmarsh, Sara. Supplementary typewriting exercises / Sara Hindmarsh. — London : Edward Arnold, 1981
2: Column work and tabulation. — 59p ; 28cm
ISBN 0-7131-0534-8 (pbk) : £2.25 : CIP rev. B81-06896

Hindmarsh, Sara. Supplementary typewriting exercises / Sara Hindmarsh. — London : Edward Arnold, 1981
3: Memos and invoices. — 61p : forms ; 28cm
ISBN 0-7131-0535-6 (pbk) : £2.25 : CIP rev. B81-06897

Quint, Marie. Progressive typewriting assignments / Marie Quint, Anne Edwards. — London : Longman, 1981. — 242p ; 20x26cm. — (Longman secretarial studies series)
ISBN 0-582-41119-x (pbk) : £3.95 : CIP rev. B80-35207

Sharp, Doreen. Typewriting : in three languages / Doreen Sharp = Dactylographie : en trois langues / Huguette Sallès = Maschineschreiben : in drei Sprachen / Annelore Schliz. — London : McGraw-Hill, c1981. — ix,183p ; 30cm
English, French and German text
ISBN 0-07-084641-3 (spiral) : £5.95 B81-37723

652.3'0076 — Typing — *Questions & answers* — *For schools*

Gow, Marion. Type it simply / Marion Gow. — London : Edward Arnold, 1980. — 108p : ill,forms ; 21x30cm
Notebook format
ISBN 0-7131-0481-3 (pbk) : £3.25 : CIP rev. B80-13896

652.3'0076 — Typing — *Questions & answers* — *For West African students*

Ezenekwe, Adolphus S.. Typing practice : for WAEC SC examinations / Adolphus S. Ezenekwe. — London : Macmillan, 1981. — iv, 124p ; 21x30cm
ISBN 0-333-30509-4 (pbk) : £1.60 B81-38801

652.3'0077 — Typing — *Manuals* — *Programmed instructions*

Lewis, June R.. A programmed typewriting course / June R. Lewis. — Plymouth : Macdonald & Evans, 1981. — 2v. : ill,facsims,forms ; 19x25cm
ISBN 0-7121-1693-1 (spiral) : £3.75 B81-36139

652.3'024 — Typing — *Manuals* — *For slow learning students*

Heller, Jack. Typing : for individual achievement / Jack Heller. — New York ; London : Gregg, c1981. — iv,92leaves : ill ; 22x29cm
Previous ed.: S.L. : J. Heller, 1979
ISBN 0-07-027921-7 : £9.75 B81-31120

652.4 — OFFICE PRACTICES. DUPLICATING

652'.4 — Office practices. Reprography

Stewart, Jeffrey R.. Office reprographics / Jeffrey R. Stewart, Jr., Judith A. Scharle. — New York ; London : McGraw-Hill, c1979. — 152,[100]p : ill,forms,plans ; 28cm
ISBN 0-07-061298-6 (pbk) : £4.30 B81-03090

653 — SHORTHAND

653'.18 — Shorthand. Dictation — *Questions & answers* — *For medical shorthand typists*

Davis, Phyllis E.. Medical dictation and transcription / Phyllis E. Davis, Nancy V. Hershelman. — 2nd ed. — New York ; Chichester : Wiley, c1981. — ix,468p ; 17x25cm. — (A Wiley medical publication)
Previous ed.: 1967
ISBN 0-471-06023-2 (spiral) : £8.35 B81-24897

653'.18 — Shorthand — *For medical secretaries*

Davis, Phyllis E.. Medical shorthand / Phyllis E. Davis, Nancy V. Hershelman. — 2nd ed. — New York ; Chichester : Wiley, c1981. — vi,323p ; 17x25cm. — (A Wiley medical publication)
Previous ed.: 1967
ISBN 0-471-06024-0 : £8.35 B81-24943

653'.42 — New Era shorthand — *Questions & answers*

Quint, Marie. Progressive shorthand passages. — London : Longman. — (Longman secretarial studies series)
Book 1: Speed development 0-80 wpm. — Dec.1981. — [40]p
ISBN 0-582-41589-6 (pbk) : £1.95 : CIP entry B81-32593

Quint, Marie. Progressive shorthand passages. — London : Longman. — (Longman secretarial studies series)
Book 3: Speed development 80-120wpm. — Dec.1981. — [48]p
ISBN 0-582-41590-x (pbk) : £1.95 : CIP entry B81-32594

653'.4242'07 — Pitman shorthand. Teaching

Canning, B. W.. Teaching Pitman's shorthand / B.W. Canning. — London : Pitman,, c1981. — 185p : ill ; 22cm
Bibliography: p181-182. - Includes index
ISBN 0-273-01540-0 (pbk) : £7.95 B81-07282

653'.4270423 — Gregg shorthand — *Manuals — For teaching*

Gregg, John Robert. Instructor's handbook for Gregg speed building, series 90 : John Robert Gregg, Louis A. Leslie, coauthor, Charles E. Zoubek, coauthor / Kay Mendenhall, instructor ; shorthand written by Jerome P. Edelman. — New York ; London : McGraw-Hill, c1979. — lx,94p ; 28cm
ISBN 0-07-024480-4 (pbk) : £3.25 B81-26655

653'.428 — Teeline. Dictation — *Questions & answers*

Hill, I. C.. Teeline dictation and drill book / I.C. Hill and G.S. Hill. — London : Heinemann Educational, 1980. — 121p ; 25cm
ISBN 0-435-45343-2 (pbk) : £2.95 : CIP rev. B80-13897

653'.428 — Teeline. Teaching — *Manuals*

Hill, I. C.. Teeline word list. — London : Heinemann Educational, Oct.1981. — [176]p
ISBN 0-435-45344-0 (pbk) : £2.95 : CIP entry B81-25861

657 — ACCOUNTING

657 — Accounting

Bishop, K. R.. Numeracy and accounting / K.R. Bishop and B.H. Molloy. — London : Cassell, 1980. — x,230p : ill,forms ; 22cm. — (Cassell's BEC series. National level)
ISBN 0-304-30333-x (pbk) : £2.95 B81-01005

Cashin, James A.. Schaum's outline of theory and problems of accounting 1 / by James A. Cashin and Joel J. Lerner. — 2nd ed. — New York ; London : McGraw-Hill, c1980. — 278p : ill,forms ; 28cm. — (Schaum's outline series)
Previous ed.: 1973. — Includes index
ISBN 0-07-010251-1 (pbk) : £3.50 B81-19684

Castle, E. F.. Principles of accounts / E.F. Castle, N.P. Owens. — 6th ed. — Plymouth : Macdonald and Evans, c1981. — viii,440p ; 18cm. — (The M & E handbook series)
Previous ed.: 1978. — Includes index
ISBN 0-7121-1692-3 (pbk) : £3.25 B81-20764

Forbes numbers game : that's a lot of GAAP and other accounting controversies from the editors of Forbes / edited and with an introduction by Lawrence Minard and David A. Wilson. — Englewood Cliffs ; London : Prentice-Hall, c1980. — xvi,175p ; 23cm
Anthology of 34 Forbes The Numbers game articles. — Includes index
ISBN 0-13-325100-4 (pbk) : £4.50 B81-17210

Francis, D. Pitt. Numeracy and accounting / D. Pitt Francis. — London : Holt, Rinehart and Winston, c1981. — viii,342p : ill ; 22cm. — (Holt business text)
Includes index
ISBN 0-03-910301-3 (pbk) : £3.95 : CIP rev. B81-01006

Glautier, M. W. E.. Basic accounting practice / M.W.E. Glautier, B. Underdown and A.C. Clark. — 2nd ed. — London : Pitman, 1980. — xv,426p : ill,forms ; 25cm. — (A Pitman international text)
Previous ed.: 1978. — Includes index
ISBN 0-273-01597-4 (Pbk) : £6.95 B81-00178

Jopson, H.. Jopson's accounts : for school and college exams / H. Jopson. — London : Pitman Education, 1981. — iv,284p : ill ; 23cm
Includes index
ISBN 0-273-01491-9 (pbk) : Unpriced B81-11017

Langley, F. P.. Workbook in accounting. — 3rd ed. — London : Butterworths, Oct.1981. — [280]p
Previous ed.: 1975
ISBN 0-408-10823-1 (pbk) : £7.50 : CIP entry B81-30460

Lee, G. A.. Modern financial accounting / G.A. Lee. — 3rd ed. — Walton-on-Thames : Nelson, 1981. — ix,543p ; 26cm. — (Nelson series in accounting and finance)
Previous ed.: 1975. — Includes index
ISBN 0-17-761057-3 (cased) : Unpriced
ISBN 0-17-771058-6 (pbk) : £7.95 B81-18460

Meigs, Walter B.. Accounting : the basis for business decisions. — 5th ed. / Walter B. Meigs, Robert F. Meigs. — New York ; London : McGraw-Hill, c1981. — xxii,1090p : ill,forms ; 25cm
Previous ed.: 1977. — Text on lining papers. — Includes index
ISBN 0-07-041551-x : £14.65 B81-12052

Riggs, Henry E.. Accounting : a survey / Henry E. Riggs. — New York ; London : McGraw-Hill, 1981. — xvii,552p : ill ; 24cm
Includes index
ISBN 0-07-052851-9 : £13.25 B81-19540

Wood, Frank. Accounting 2 : a textbook for the Business Education Council national award courses / Frank Wood and Joe Townsley. — Stockport : Polytech, 1980. — 310p : ill ; 22cm. — (Business Education Council national award courses)
Includes index
ISBN 0-85505-041-1 (pbk) : £4.80 B81-22909

657 — Accounting. Decision making

Libby, Robert. Accounting and human information processing : theory and applications / Robert Libby. — Englewood Cliffs ; London : Prentice-Hall, c1981. — xiii,203p : ill ; 24cm. — (Prentice-Hall contemporary topics in accounting series)
Bibliography: p185-198. — Includes index
ISBN 0-13-001818-x (cased) : Unpriced
ISBN 0-13-001800-7 (pbk) : £6.70 B81-40168

657 — Accounting — *Manuals*

Briston, Richard J.. Introduction to accountancy and finance / R.J. Briston ; contributors R.J. Briston ... [et al.]. — London : Macmillan in association with the Institute of Cost and Management Accountants, 1981. — xiv,663p : ill ; 25cm
Includes bibliographies and index
ISBN 0-333-24669-1 (cased) : £20.00
ISBN 0-333-30101-3 (pbk) : Unpriced B81-21795

Meigs, Walter B.. Modern advanced accounting / Walter B. Meigs, A.N. Mosich, E. John Larsen. — 2nd ed., International student ed. — Tokyo ; London : McGraw-Hill Kogakusha, c1979. — xix,744p : ill,forms ; 21cm
Previous ed.: 1975. — Includes index
ISBN 0-07-066403-x (pbk) : £7.50 B81-10123

657 — Accounting. Quantitative methods

Quantitative and accounting methods : a textbook for the Business Education Council national award courses / contributing authors Frank Wood ... [et al.]. — Stockport : Polytech, 1980. — 394p : ill ; 22cm. — (Business Education Council national award courses)
Includes index
ISBN 0-85505-042-x (pbk) : £4.80 B81-22915

657'.01'51 — Accounting. Mathematics

Numeracy and accounting : a text for the Business Education Council National award courses / contributing authors Ron Jones ... [et al.]. — Stockport : Polytech, 1979. — 349p : ill ; 22cm. — (Business Education Council national award courses)
Includes index
ISBN 0-85505-033-0 (pbk) : £4.20 B81-22907

657'.0218 — Accounting. Standards. Political aspects

Solomons, David. The political implications of accounting and accounting standard setting : being the third Arthur Young lecture delivered within the University of Glasgow on 22nd October, 1980 / by David Solomons. — [Glasgow] : University of Glasgow Press, 1980. — 26leaves ; 30cm. — (Arthur Young lecture ; no.3)
Bibliography: p24-26
ISBN 0-85261-165-x (spiral) : Unpriced B81-35081

657'.0218 — Accounting — *Standards — Serials*

International accounting standards : the full texts of all International Accounting Standards extant at 1 March ... — 1981-. — London : Institute of Chartered Accountants in England and Wales, 1981-. — v. ; 21cm
Annual
ISSN 0261-3913 = International accounting standards : £4.50 B81-29664

657'.023'411 — Scotland. Accountancy — *Career guides*

Institute of Chartered Accountants of Scotland. The C.A. student guide / Institute of Chartered Accountants of Scotland. — [Edinburgh] ([27 Queen St., Edinburgh EH2 1LA) : [The Institute], 1981. — 56p ; 21cm
Includes index
Unpriced (pbk) B81-37739

657'.023417 — Ireland *(Republic)*. **Accountancy** — *Career guides*

Chartered accountant 81. — [Dublin] ([7 Fitzwilliam Place, Dublin 2]) : Institute of Chartered Accountants in Ireland, 1981. — 65p : ill(some col.),forms,col.ports ; 21cm
Includes index
£0.20 (pbk) B81-17753

657'.02'4658 — Accounting - *For business studies*

Claret, Jake. Accounting 2. — London : McGraw-Hill, June 1981. — [256]p. — (Business education courses)
ISBN 0-07-084621-9 (pbk) : £4.50 : CIP entry B81-14461

657'.024658 — Accounting — *For business studies*

Francis, D. Pitt. Accounting concepts and methods : accounting 2 / D. Pitt Francis. — London : Holt, Rinehart and Winston, c1981. — 100p ; 30cm. — (Holt business texts)
ISBN 0-03-910310-2 (pbk) : £1.95 B81-23100

Francis, D. Pitt. Accounting concepts and methods. — Eastbourne : Holt-Saunders, Jan.1982. — [105]p
ISBN 0-03-910342-0 (pbk) : £4.00 : CIP entry B81-33926

Turner, D. E.. Accounting and numeric methods for business students. — London : Edward Arnold, Sept.1981. — [304]p
ISBN 0-7131-0590-9 (pbk) : £3.50 : CIP entry B81-22517

Wilkinson, Gill. Numeracy and accounting / Gill Wilkinson ; advisory editor Patricia Callender. — Amersham : Hulton Educational, 1981. — 252p : ill ; 24cm. — (Hulton BEC books)
Includes index
ISBN 0-7175-0841-2 (pbk) : £3.80 B81-13666

657'.025'41 — Great Britain. Accountancy — *Directories — Serials — For graduates*

Directory of firms with training opportunities for graduates of universities in Great Britain and holders of CNAA degrees / The Institute of Chartered Accountants in England and Wales. — 1980. — London : The Institute, [1979]. — 56p
Unpriced B81-20028

Directory of firms with training opportunities for graduates of universities in Great Britain and holders of CNAA degrees / The Institute of Chartered Accountants in England and Wales. — 1981. — London : The Institute, [1980?]. — 60p
Unpriced B81-20029

657'.025'41 — Great Britain. Accountancy — *Directories — Serials — For school leavers*

Directory of firms with training opportunities for non-graduates / Institute of Chartered Accountants in England and Wales. — 1980/81. — London : The Institute, [1980]. — 51p
Unpriced B81-20408

657′.028′54 — Accounting. Information systems. Applications of digital computer systems

Moscove, Stephen A.. Accounting information systems : concepts and practice for effective decision making / Stephen A. Moscove, Mark G. Simkin. — New York ; Chichester : Wiley, c1981. — xx,616p : ill,forms ; 25cm. — (Wiley series in accounting and information systems)
Includes index
ISBN 0-471-03369-3 : Unpriced B81-08519

657′.028′5404 — Accounting. Applications of small digital computer systems

Hayes, Rick Stephan. Simplified accounting for the computer industry / Rick Stephan Hayes, C. Richard Baker. — New York ; Chichester : Wiley, c1981. — vii,191p : ill,forms ; 29cm. — (Small business management series, ISSN 0217-6054) (A Ronald Press publication)
Includes index
ISBN 0-471-05703-7 : £15.50 B81-23981

657′.03′21 — Accounting — *Encyclopaedias*

Estes, Ralph. Dictionary of accounting / Ralph Estes. — Cambridge, Mass. ; London : MIT Press, c1981. — 161p : ill ; 21cm
ISBN 0-262-05024-2 (cased) : £9.30
ISBN 0-262-55009-1 (pbk) : Unpriced
B81-28351

Houghton, Diane. Accounting terms and book-keeping procedures explained / Diane Houghton, Ralph G. Wallace. — Farnborough, Hants. : Gower, c1980. — x,268p ; 22cm
ISBN 0-566-00393-7 (pbk) : £6.95 : CIP rev.
B80-25880

Houghton, Diane. Students′ accounting vocabulary / Diane Houghton, Ralph G. Wallace. — Farnborough, Hants. : Gower, c1980. — x,268p ; 22cm
ISBN 0-566-00330-9 (pbk) : £4.95 : CIP rev.
B80-25881

Robinson, David F.. Key definitions in finance and accounting / David Robinson. — London : Muller, 1980. — 125p : ill ; 21cm. — (A language of its own)
ISBN 0-584-10546-0 (cased) : £5.95 : CIP rev.
ISBN 0-584-10556-8 (pbk) : £3.95
Primary classification 332′.03′21 B80-27258

657′.06′041 — Great Britain. Accountancy. Organisations: Institute of Cost and Management Accountants — *Directories — Serials*

Institute of Cost and Management Accountants. List of members ... , as at 1st July ... / the Institute of Cost and Management Accountants. — 1980-1981. — [London] ([63 Portland Place, W1 4AB]) : The Institute, [1980]. — xvii,651p
ISSN 0306-6711 : Unpriced B81-00179

657′.06′042 — England. Accountancy. Organisations: Institute of Chartered Accountants in England and Wales — *Directories — Serials*

Institute of Chartered Accountants in England and Wales. List of members and firms / the Institute of Chartered Accountants in England and Wales. — 1980/81. — London : The Institute, [1980]. — lx,1060p
ISBN 0-85291-273-0 : £13.00 B81-10578

657′.07′1141 — Great Britain. Higher education institutions. Curriculum subjects: Accountancy. Degree courses — *Directories — Serials*

Degree studies and the accountancy profession / Accounting Education Consultative Board. — 1980 ed. — London (c/o P.M.C. Vincent, 11 Copthall Ave., EC2P 2BJ) : The Board, [1980?]. — 27p
Continues:
Unpriced B81-13087

657′.0724 — Accounting. Mathematical models

Mepham, Michael J.. Accounting models / Michael J. Mepham. — Stockport : Polytech, 1980. — 624p : ill ; 23cm
Includes bibliographies and index
ISBN 0-85505-040-3 (pbk) : £8.80 B81-22908

657′.076 — Accounting — *Questions & answers — For West African students*

Okolo, M. N.. Key to book-keeping and accounts / M.N. Okolo. — London : Longman, 1980. — 204p ; 25cm. — (Longman commercial studies)
ISBN 0-582-65029-1 (pbk) : £2.00 B81-12732

657′.076 — Accounts — *Questions & answers — For Nigerian students*

Baston, Andrew. Key to elements of accounts : for elementary and intermediate stage students / by Andrew Baston. — Nigerian ed. / prepared by S.A. Alle. — London : Cassell, 1980. — 229p ; 22cm
ISBN 0-304-30254-6 (pbk) : £4.00 B81-27770

657′.092′4 — Great Britain. Accountancy. Smallpeice, *Sir* Basil — *Biographies*

Smallpeice, *Sir* Basil. Of comets and queens / Sir Basil Smallpeice. — Shrewsbury : Airlife, 1981, c1980. — 274p,18p of plates : ill,ports ; 23cm
Includes index
ISBN 0-906393-10-8 : £10.95 B81-22193

657′.094 — Western Europe. Accounting

Oldham, K. Michael. Accounting systems and practice in Europe. — 2nd ed. — Farnborough : Gower, Aug.1981. — [200]p
Previous ed.: 1975
ISBN 0-566-02147-1 : £15.00 : CIP entry
B81-16368

657′.0941 — Great Britain. Accounting. Standards. Formulation — *Proposals*

Accounting Standards Committee. Setting accounting standards : report and recommendations by the Accounting Standards Committee. — [London] : [Institute of Chartered Accountants in England & Wales], c1981. — 56p ; 21cm
ISBN 0-85291-300-1 (pbk) : Unpriced
B81-23365

657′.0941 — Great Britain. Accounting — *Standards — Serials*

Accounting Standards Committee. Accounting standards / [Accounting Standards Committee] ; prepared by members of the staff of the Technical Directorate, The Institute of Chartered Accountants in England and Wales. — 1981. — London : The Institute, c1981. — 372p
ISBN 0-85291-298-6 : Unpriced B81-32902

657′.0941 — Great Britain. Business firms. Accounting — *For banking*

Leslie, James. Business accounting ′A′ : study guide / James Leslie. — Edinburgh (20 Rutland Square, Edinburgh) : Institute of Bankers in Scotland, 1978. — 161p ; 30cm
£3.00 (pbk) B81-07686

Scott, I. W. S.. Business accounting ′B′ : study guide / by I.W.S. Scott. — [Edinburgh] ([20 Rutland Square, Edinburgh]) : Institute of Bankers in Scotland, [1979?]. — 95p ; 30cm
£2.75 (pbk) B81-07687

657′.0942 — England. Accountancy — *Manuals — Serials*

Institute of Chartered Accountants in England and Wales. Digest of Technical releases as at 1 March ... / the Institute of Chartered Accountants in England and Wales. — 1981. — [London] : The Institute, [1981]. — 59p
Also issued as part of: Institute of Chartered Accountants in England and Wales. Members′ handbook. Vol.4, Temporary reference material
Unpriced B81-26587

657′.0942 — England. Accounting. Standards. Institute of Chartered Accountants in England and Wales. Statements of standard accounting practice — *Critical studies*

Couldery, Frederick A. J.. Accounting standards study book / by Fredk. A.J. Couldery. — 3rd ed. — London : Gee, 1981. — 100p ; 25cm. — (A Gee′s study book)
Previous ed.: 1979
ISBN 0-85258-207-2 (pbk) : £3.75 B81-18271

Harvey, Mike. Current cost accounting : an introduction to SSAP 16 / Mike Harvey, Fred Keer. — London : Certified Accountants Educational Trust, c1981. — xii,132p : ill ; 21cm
Bibliography: p97
ISBN 0-900094-40-0 (pbk) : Unpriced
B81-25255

657′.0943 — West Germany. Accountancy

Services provided by Wirtschaftsprüfer in the Federal Republic of Germany. — London : Printed and published on behalf of the Anglo-German Liaison Committee by The Institute of Chartered Accountants in England and Wales, 1981. — [16]p ; 30cm
Unpriced (spiral) B81-38931

657′.0973 — United States. Accounting

Accountant′s handbook. — 6th ed. / edited by Lee J. Seidler, D.R. Carmichael. — New York ; Chichester : Wiley, c1981. — 2v.(2004p in various pagings) : ill,forms ; 25cm. — (The Wiley/Ronald series in professional accounting and business)
Previous ed.: / edited by Rufus Wixon, Walter G. Kell, Norton M. Bedford. New York : Ronald Press, 1970. — Text on lining papers. — Includes bibliographies and index
ISBN 0-471-05505-0 : £47.65 B81-24885

657′.2 — Book-keeping

Clarke, Ken. An Introduction to book-keeping : book-keeping and accounts / Ken Clarke, Fred Crook. — London : Holt, Rinehart and Winston, c1981. — 282p : ill,forms ; 22cm. — (Holt business texts)
Includes index
ISBN 0-03-910305-6 (pbk) : £3.95 : CIP rev.
B81-10436

Wood, Frank. Book-keeping and accounts / Frank Wood. — London : Longman, 1981. — 310p : ill ; 22cm
Includes index
ISBN 0-582-41177-7 (pbk) : £2.95 : CIP rev.
B81-08845

657′.2 — Book-keeping — *Manuals*

Chronicler. Fred learns book-keeping / The Chronicler. — [London] ([8 John St., WC1N 2HY]) : Continua Productions, 1978. — 144p : ill,forms ; 19cm
Text on lining papers. — Includes index
ISBN 0-7227-0106-3 (pbk) : £1.95 B81-37643

657′.2 — Book-keeping - *Manuals*

Kellock, John. A manual of basic bookkeeping. — London : Bell & Hyman, July 1981. — [160]p
ISBN 0-7135-1285-7 (pbk) : £2.50 : CIP entry
B81-15911

657′.2 — Great Britain. Small firms. Book-keeping — *Manuals*

Whitehead, Geoffrey. Simplified book-keeping for small businesses / Geoffrey Whitehead. — Holmforth (P.O. Box 1, Holmforth, Huddersfield HD7 2RP) : Vyner, c1978. — 176p : ill,forms ; 22cm
Includes index
ISBN 0-906628-00-8 (pbk) : £2.00 B81-05686

657′.3 — Companies. Financial statements

Developments in financial reporting / edited by Thomas A. Lee. — Oxford : Philip Allan, 1981. — xii,292p : ill,1facsim ; 23cm
Includes bibliographies
ISBN 0-86003-512-3 (cased) : £16.00 : CIP rev.
ISBN 0-86003-612-x (pbk) : £7.95 B81-13548

657′.3 — Great Britain. Companies. Accounts. Added value statements

Gray, Sidney. Value added reporting : uses and measurement : a research study / Sidney Gray, Keith Maunders. — London : Association of Certified Accountants, c1980. — 71p ; 30cm
Bibliography: p64-71
ISBN 0-900094-39-7 (pbk) : Unpriced
B81-40884

657'.3 — Price-level accounting

Chambers, R. J.. Price variation and inflation accounting / R.J. Chambers. — Sydney ; London : McGraw-Hill, c1980. — 174p : ill ; 24cm
Bibliography: p145-147. - Includes index
ISBN 0-07-093560-2 (pbk) : £10.25 B81-10368

Kirkman, P. R. A.. Accounting under inflationary conditions / Patrick R.A. Kirkman. — 2nd ed. — London : Allen & Unwin, 1978. — xiii,300p : 1ill ; 23cm
Previous ed.: 1974. — Includes index
ISBN 0-04-332067-8 (cased) : £10.50 : CIP rev.
ISBN 0-04-332068-6 (pbk) : £5.50 B78-30760

657'.3'0941 — Great Britain. Companies. Published accounts — *Serials*

Survey of published accounts. — 1979. — London : Institute of Chartered Accountants in England and Wales, 1980. — 300p
ISBN 0-85291-248-x : Unpriced B81-08788

657'.3'0973 — United States. Companies. Financial statements

Beaver, William H.. Financial reporting : an accounting revolution / William H. Beaver. — Englewood Cliffs ; London : Prentice-Hall, c1981. — xx,213p : ill ; 24cm. — (Prentice-Hall contemporary topics in accounting series)
Includes bibliographies and index
ISBN 0-13-316141-2 (cased) : Unpriced
ISBN 0-13-316133-1 (pbk) : £6.45 B81-17177

657'.32'0973 — United States. Companies. Financial statements. Presentation — *Manuals*

Main Hurdman & Cranstoun guide to preparing financial reports / editors Morton B. Solomon, Kenneth J. Dirkes, John R. Deming. — New York ; Chichester : Wiley, c1981. — 290p ; 28cm + supplement([16]p : 25cm)
Includes index
ISBN 0-471-09104-9 (pbk) : £47.65 B81-24896

Newman, Benjamin. Forms manual for the CPA : for audit, review, and compilation of financial statements / Benjamin Newman. — New York ; Chichester : Wiley, c1980. — xxi,574p : ill,forms ; 24cm
Includes index
ISBN 0-471-05762-2 : Unpriced B81-19960

657'.33 — Companies. Financial statements. Use by investors

Benston, George J.. Investors' use of financial accounting statement numbers : a review of evidence from stock market research : being the second Arthur Young Lecture delivered within the University of Glasgow on 23rd October, 1979 / by George J. Benston. — [Glasgow] : University of Glasgow Press, 1981. — 56leaves ; 30cm. — (Arthur Young lecture ; no.2)
Bibliography: p46-56
ISBN 0-85261-166-8 (spiral) : Unpriced B81-35082

657'.33'024332 — Balance sheets. Interpretation — *For banking*

Hutchinson, H. H.. Interpretation of balance sheets / H.H. Hutchinson. — 4th ed., rev. — London : Institute of Bankers, 1977. — 44p ; 21cm
Previous ed.: 1972
£1.50 (pbk) B81-11673

657'.42 — Cost accounting

Cashin, James A.. Cost accounting / James A. Cashin, Ralph S. Polimeni. — New York ; London : McGraw-Hill, c1981. — xvii,854p : ill ; 25cm
Includes index
ISBN 0-07-010213-9 : £15.75 B81-10238

McEntegart, R. C.. Costing and budgetary control / R.C. McEntegart. — Stockport : Polytech, 1980. — 362p : ill ; 22cm
Includes index
ISBN 0-85505-043-8 (pbk) : £4.80 B81-22914

Mearns, I. J.. Fundamentals of cost accounting. — London : Longman, June 1981. — [160]p. — (Longman professional education series)
ISBN 0-582-41575-6 (pbk) : £2.95 : CIP entry B81-13826

Roche, A.. Accounting control systems. — London : Longman, June 1981. — [185]p. — (Longman professional education series)
ISBN 0-582-40002-3 (pbk) : £2.95 : CIP entry B81-13824

657'.42 — Cost accounting — *Manuals*

Lucey, T.. Costing : an instructional manual / T. Lucey. — Winchester : D.P. Publications, 1981. — v,453p : ill ; 22cm
Includes index
ISBN 0-905435-18-4 (pbk) : £3.95 : CIP rev. B81-13580

Shah, Pravin P.. Cost control and information systems : a complete guide to effective design and implementation / Pravin P. Shah. — New York ; London : McGraw-Hill, c1981. — xv,575p : ill,forms ; 24cm
Bibliography: p552-555. — Includes index
ISBN 0-07-056369-1 (corrected) : £17.50 B81-27521

657'.45 — Auditing

Current auditing developments / compiled and edited by Emile Woolf. — 2nd ed. — London : Gee, 1980. — 106p ; 25cm. — (A Gee's study book)
Previous ed.: 1978
ISBN 0-85258-202-1 (pbk) : £3.75 B81-32376

Howard, Leslie R.. Principles of auditing / Leslie R. Howard. — 20th ed. — Plymouth : Macdonald & Evans, 1981. — xv,408p : ill,forms ; 24cm
Previous ed.: published as Taylor & Perry's principles of auditing. 1976. — Includes index
ISBN 0-7121-2029-7 (pbk) : £7.50 B81-39554

Manual of auditing. — 3rd ed. / Coopers & Lybrand. — London : Gee, 1981. — xxxv,760p : ill,forms ; 26cm
Previous ed.: / by Vivian R.V. Cooper. 1969. — Includes index
ISBN 0-85258-208-0 : £20.00 B81-36084

Millichamp, A. H.. Auditing : an instrumental manual for accounting students / A.H. Millichamp. — 2nd ed. — Winchester : D.P. Publications, 1981. — ix,447p ; 22cm
Previous ed.: 1978. — Includes index
ISBN 0-905435-06-0 (pbk) : £3.75 B81-40110

Pratt, M. J. (Michael John). Auditing. — London : Longman, Sept.1981. — [384]p
ISBN 0-582-29527-0 (pbk) : £9.50 : CIP entry B81-25879

Santocki, J.. Auditing : a conceptual and systems approach / J. Santocki. — Stockport : Polytech, 1979. — vi,396p : ill ; 22cm
Includes index
ISBN 0-85505-038-1 (pbk) : £5.00 B81-22913

Woolf, Emile. Auditing today. — 2nd ed. — London : Prentice-Hall, Feb.1982. — [592]p
Previous ed.: 1979
ISBN 0-13-052159-0 (pbk) : £9.95 : CIP entry B81-35791

657'.45 — Auditing. Analytical review

Westwick, C. A.. Do the figures make sense? : a practical guide to analytical review / C.A. Westwick ; with a foreword by J.B. Holden. — London : Institute of Chartered Accountants in England and Wales, 1981. — x,78p : ill ; 21cm
Bibliography: p74-76. — Includes index
ISBN 0-85291-295-1 (pbk) : Unpriced B81-29015

657'.45 — Great Britain. Companies. Audit committees

Chambers, A. D.. 1978 survey of audit committees in the United Kingdom : a summary of findings / by A.D. Chambers and A.J. Snook. — London : City University Business School, 1979. — 59 leaves ; 30cm. — (Working paper series / City University Business School, ISSN 0140-1041 ; no.10)
Unpriced (pbk) B81-01007

657'.45 — Great Britain. Nationalised industries. Value for money auditing

Hatch, John, *1949-*. Value for money audits : new thinking on the nationalised audits / John Hatch and John Redwood. — London (8 Wilfred St., S.W.1) : Centre for Policy Studies, 1981. — iii,27p ; 21cm
Cover title
ISBN 0-905880-37-4 (pbk) : £1.60 B81-26825

657'.45 — Organisations. Published accounts. Auditing

Mills, Adam. Annual audit and annual accounts / Adam Mills. — London : Muller, 1980. — 154p ; 21cm. — ([Money matters])
Includes index
ISBN 0-584-10573-8 : £5.95 : CIP rev. B80-24616

657'.45 — United States. Companies. Audit committees. Role

Braiotta, Louis. The audit director's guide : how to serve effectively on the corporate audit committee / Louis Braiotta, Jr. ; foreword by John C. Biegler. — New York ; Chichester : Wiley, c1981. — xvi,303p : ill ; 24cm
Includes bibliographies and index
ISBN 0-471-05866-1 : £13.25 B81-09750

657'.45'0151952 — Auditing. Statistical mathematics. Sampling

Guy, Dan M. An introduction to statistical sampling in auditing / Dan M. Guy. — New York ; Chichester : Wiley, c1981. — xvi,229p : ill ; 25cm. — (Wiley series in accounting and information systems)
Bibliography: p213-214. - Includes index
ISBN 0-471-04232-3 : Unpriced B81-08522

657'.45'0218 — Auditing — *Standards*

Institute of Chartered Accountants in England and Wales. [Members' handbook. Part 3]. Auditing and reporting 1981 : a reprint of Part II of the Member's handbook containing Auditing standards and guidelines and other statements on auditing / Institute of Chartered Accountants in England and Wales. — London : [The Institute], c1981. — 237p ; 21cm
ISBN 0-85291-278-1 (pbk) : Unpriced B81-36090

657'.45'0218 — Great Britain. Auditing. Standards

Woolf, Emile. The official auditing standards : 1980 / [... prepared for the Trust by Emile Woolf]. — London : Certified Accountants Educational Trust, c1981. — 33p ; 21cm. — (Auditing) (Workbook ; no.U16)
Unpriced (pbk) B81-41029

657'.45'02854 — Auditing. Applications of digital computer systems

Sardinas, Joseph L.. EDP auditing : a primer / Joseph L. Sardinas, Jr., John G. Burch, Jr., Richard J. Asebrook. — New York ; Chichester : Wiley, c1981. — ix,209p : ill ; 24cm
Includes index
ISBN 0-471-12305-6 (pbk) : £6.30 B81-18678

Thomas, A. J.. Audit of computer systems / A.J. Thomas, I.J. Douglas. — Manchester : NCC Publications, 1981. — 203p : ill ; 21cm
Bibliography: p195-196. — Includes index
ISBN 0-85012-299-6 (pbk) : £9.50 B81-38062

657'.452 — Great Britain. Companies. Published accounts. Audit reports

Shaw, J. C.. The audit report : what it says and what it means / J.C. Shaw. — London : Published for the Institute of Chartered Accountants of Scotland by Gee, 1980. — v,76p ; 21cm
ISBN 0-85258-203-x (pbk) : £3.75 B81-06277

657'.453 — Computerised accounts. Auditing

Jancura, Elise G.. Establishing controls and auditing the computerized accounting system / Elise G. Jancura, Robert Boos. — New York ; London : Van Nostrand Reinhold, c1981. — vii,288p : ill,1plan,forms ; 26cm
Includes index
ISBN 0-442-80507-1 : £14.95 B81-05989

657'.458 — Companies. Internal auditing

Chambers, A.. Internal auditing. — London : Pitman, Oct.1981. — [360]p
ISBN 0-273-01632-6 : £11.95 : CIP entry B81-30256

657'.458 — Organisations. Internal auditing — *Manuals*

Bigg, Walter William. Bigg & Davies' internal auditing. — 5th ed. / R. S. Waldron. — London : HFL, 1980. — v,329p : ill ; 22cm
Previous ed.: / by E. H. Woolf, 1973. — Includes index
ISBN 0-372-30042-1 (pbk) : £6.95 : CIP rev. B80-06988

657'.46'0973 — United States. Companies. Taxation. Accounting

Miles, Catherine E.. Business and personal taxes 1981 / Catherine E. Miles, Joseph E. Lane Jr. — [New ed.]. — Boston [Mass.] ; London : Allyn and Bacon, c1981. — x,421p : facsims ; 25cm
Previous ed.: i.e. 4th revision, published as Business and personal taxes. 1977. — Text on lining papers. — Includes index
ISBN 0-205-07163-5 : £11.95 B81-01008

657'.48 — Financial accounting

Guter, A.. Financial accounting / A. Guter and M. Guter. — 2nd ed. — Sevenoaks : Teach Yourself Books, 1981. — x,346p ; 18cm. — (Business and management studies)
Previous ed.: 1978. — Includes index
ISBN 0-340-26566-3 (pbk) : £2.95 B81-09773

Horngren, Charles T.. Introduction to financial accounting / Charles T. Horngren. — Englewood Cliffs ; London : Prentice-Hall, c1981. — xviii,745p : ill,forms ; 24cm. — (Prentice-Hall series in accounting)
Includes index
ISBN 0-13-483743-6 : £13.65 B81-17220

Lewis, Richard, *1941- Sept.30-*. Advanced financial accounting / Richard Lewis, David Pendrill, Davis S. Simon. — London : Pitman, 1981. — xii,564p : ill ; 23cm
Includes bibliographies and index
ISBN 0-273-01640-7 (pbk) : £8.95 B81-22312

Samuels, John. Advanced financial accounting. — London : McGraw-Hill, Sept.1981. — [352]p
ISBN 0-07-084571-9 (pbk) : £9.95 : CIP entry
Also classified at 657'.48 B81-21602

657'.48 — Financial accounting — *Comparative studies*

Comparative international accounting / edited by Christopher Nobes, Robert Parker ; foreword by Edward Stamp. — Oxford : Philip Allan, 1981. — xvi,379p ; 24cm
Includes bibliographies and index
ISBN 0-86003-515-8 : £13.95 B81-26895

657'.48 — Financial accounting — *Manuals*

Jennings, A. R. (Alan Robert). Financial accounting : an instructional manual for professional level accountancy students / A.R. Jennings. — Winchester : D.P. Publications
Includes index
Manual 1. — 1981. — vii,578p ; 22cm
ISBN 0-905435-19-2 (pbk) : £5.75 : CIP rev. B81-13566

657'.48 — Great Britain. Business firms. Price-level accounting — *Manuals*

CCA-the easy way : a step-by-step operating manual intended primarily for the use of small and medium-sized businesses. — [London] ([c/o Institute of Chartered Accountants in England and Wales, P.O. Box 433, Moorgate Place, EC2P 2BJ]) : Accounting Standards Committee, 1980. — v,145p : 2ill,forms ; 30cm
ISBN 0-85291-277-3 (pbk) : Unpriced B81-11087

657'.48 — Price-level accounting

Beaufrère, Paul. Current cost accounting on trial / Paul Beaufrère. — London (Bow Bells House, Bread St., EC4M 9EL) : W. Greenwell
1: A case study. — 1981. — 15,xileaves ; 31cm
£15.00 (pbk) B81-40840

657'.48

Samuels, John. Advanced financial accounting. — London : McGraw-Hill, Sept.1981. — [352]p
ISBN 0-07-084571-9 (pbk) : £9.95 : CIP entry
Primary classification 657'.48 B81-21602

657'.48 — United States. Companies. Insolvency. Accounting

Newton, Grant W.. Bankruptcy and insolvency accounting : practice and procedure / Grant W. Newton. — 2nd ed. — New York ; Chichester : Wiley, c1981. — xii,676p : forms ; 24cm. — (The Wiley/Ronald series in professional accounting and business)
Previous ed.: New York : Ronald Press, c1975. — Bibliography: p641-650. — Includes index
ISBN 0-471-07992-8 : £30.00 B81-38023

657'.73 — Great Britain. Companies. Assets. Valuation — *Manuals*

Bowie, N. W.. Asset valuations / by N.W. Bowie. — Reading (Whiteknights, Reading RG6 2AW) : Centre for Advanced Land Use Studies. College of Estate Management, 1981. — 14p ; 25cm. — (Property valuation handbook ; D1)
Cover title
ISBN 0-902132-57-1 (pbk) : Unpriced B81-30911

Royal Institution of Chartered Surveyors. *Assets Valuation Standards Committee.* Guidance notes on the valuation of assets / prepared by the Assets Valuation Standards Committee. — 2nd ed. — London : Royal Institution of Chartered Accountants, 1981. — 308,12p ; 32cm
Previous ed.: 1976
£24.00 (£20.00 to members) B81-35681

657'.832 — England. Charities. Published accounts

Bird, Peter, *1934-*. Financial reporting by charities : report of a research study supported by the Research Sub-Committee of the Institute of Chartered Accountants in England & Wales / Peter Bird and Peter Morgan-Jones. — [London] : Institute of Chartered Accountants in England and Wales, 1981. — 263p ; 24cm
Bibliography: p243-244. — Includes index
ISBN 0-85291-289-7 (pbk) : Unpriced B81-14639

657'.833 — England. Housing associations. Accounts. Auditing — *Manuals*

Gray, Desmond J.. Housing association accounts and their audit : a practice manual / Desmond J. Gray, John H. Lawton, Peter A. Smith. — London : Institute of Chartered Accountants in England and Wales, 1980. — xvi,221p : forms ; 24cm. — (Industry accounting and auditing guides)
Includes index
ISBN 0-85291-260-9 (pbk) : Unpriced B81-07899

657'.833 — United States. Real property. Accounting — *Manuals*

Wiley, Robert J.. Real estate accounting and mathematics handbook / Robert J. Wiley. — New York ; Chichester : Wiley, c1980. — xxiv,310p : ill,forms ; 24cm. — (Real estate for professional practitioners, ISSN 0190-1087)
Includes index
ISBN 0-471-04812-7 : £14.50 B81-06979

657'.834 — England. Magistrates' courts. Accounting — *Inquiry reports*

Great Britain. *Parliament. House of Commons. Committee of Public Accounts.* Sixth report from the Committee of Public Accounts : together with the proceedings of the Committee and minutes of evidence, session 1980-81 : Home Office : accounting arrangements for magistrates' courts' transactions. — London : H.M.S.O., [1981]. — xi,5p ; 25cm. — ([HC] ; 226)
ISBN 0-10-222681-4 (pbk) : £2.30 B81-35384

657'.837'00941 — Great Britain. Hotel industries & catering industries. Accounting

Kotas, Richard. Accounting in the hotel and catering industry / Richard Kotas. — 4th ed. — London : International Textbook Co.,, 1981. — 344p : ill ; 25cm
Previous ed.: 1972. — Includes index
ISBN 0-7002-0279-x (pbk) : £8.50 : CIP rev. B81-12389

657'.9042'0941 — Great Britain. Small firms. Accounting — *Manuals*

Millington, I. E.. Direct accounting for the self-employed and small businesses : book-keeping eliminated by new flow charted method of accounts office procedures / I.E. Millington. — Stockport (11 Grebe Walk, Offerton, Stockport, Cheshire) : Direct Accounting, c1981. — [53]leaves : ill,forms ; 30cm
Unpriced (unbound) B81-26441

657'.95 — Companies. Accounts

Reid, Walter. The meaning of company accounts. — 3rd ed. — Farnborough, Hants. : Gower, Sept.1981. — [362]p
Previous ed.: 1974
ISBN 0-566-02284-2 (cased) : £15.00 : CIP entry
ISBN 0-566-02285-0 (pbk) : £9.50 B81-28192

657'.96 — Great Britain. Companies. Groups. Accounts

Robertson, A. T. (Alan T). Group accounts / A.T. Robertson and W.J. Jarvis. — London : Gee, 1980. — 182p : ill ; 22cm
Includes index
ISBN 0 85258-190-4 (pbk) : £4.95 B81-05531

657'.98 — Great Britain. Clubs. Accounting — *For treasurers*

Peters, M. A.. The club treasurer's handbook : an essential guide to club accounting and administration / M.A. Peters. — Bristol (P.O. Box 260, 15 Pembroke Road, Bristol BS99 7DX) : Rose/Jordan, c1980. — vii,127p : ill ; 21cm
Includes index
ISBN 0-907313-00-0 (pbk) : £7.00 B81-09542

658 — MANAGEMENT

658 — Business firms. Management

Deverell, C. S.. Business administration and management / by C.S. Deverell. — 4th ed. — London : Gee, 1980. — 422p : ill ; 22cm
Previous ed.: 1973. — Bibliography: p415-418. - Includes index
ISBN 0-85258-188-2 (pbk) : £5.95 B81-19789

Kilgannon, Pete. Administration in business / Peter Kilgannon, Christine Davies. — London : McGraw-Hill, c1980. — xxi,342p : ill,facsims,forms ; 25cm. — (McGraw-Hill business education courses)
Includes index
ISBN 0-07-084603-0 (pbk) : £4.95 : CIP rev. B80-11076

Milner, Don. The management of work : administration in business / Don Milner, Mike Taylor. — London : Holt, Rinehart and Winston, c1981. — viii,312p : ill ; 22cm. — (Holt business texts)
Includes index
ISBN 0-03-910307-2 (pbk) : £3.95 : CIP rev. B81-12377

Williamson, R. J.. Business organization / R.J. Williamson. — London : Published on behalf of the Institute of Marketing and the CAM Foundation [by] Heinemann, 1981. — xi,273p : ill ; 24cm
Bibliography: p261-267. — Includes index
ISBN 0-434-92262-5 (pbk) : £7.95 B81-26057

658 — Management

Burke, Ronald S.. Introduction to management practice / Ronald S. Burke, Lester R. Bittel. — New York ; London : McGraw-Hill, c1981. — xi,580p : ill(some col.),forms ; 25cm
Includes index
ISBN 0-07-009042-4 : £13.75 B81-17040

Coventry, William F.. Management made simple / William F. Coventry. — 7th ed. / revised by John L. Barker. — London : Heinemann, 1981 — xvi,288p : ill ; 22cm. — (Made simple books)
Previous ed.: i.e. rev. ed. London : W.H. Allen 1978. — Includes bibliographies and index
ISBN 0-434-98453-1 (pbk) : £2.95 B81-23212

658 — Management *continuation*

Management handbook : operating guidelines, techniques and practice / Paul Mali, editor in chief. — New York ; Chichester : Wiley, c1981. — xxviii,1522p : ill,facsims,forms ; 25cm. — (A Ronald Press publication)
Text on lining papers. — Includes bibliographies and index
ISBN 0-471-05263-9 : £31.70 B81-24940

Stewart, Rosemary. The reality of organizations / Rosemary Stewart. — London : Pan in association with Macmillan, 1972, c1970 (1979 printing). — 189p : ill ; 18cm. — (Management series)
Originally published: London : Macmillan, 1970. — Bibliography: p183-184. — Includes index
ISBN 0-330-23249-5 (pbk) : £1.25 B81-39936

658 — Management — *Conference proceedings*

CIOS World Management Congress *(18th : 1978 : New Delhi)*. Management and the world of tomorrow : key issues for management in economic growth, technological change and human welfare : the proceedings of the 18th CIOS World Management Congress. — Farnborough, Hants. : Gower, c1981. — xii,437p : ill ; 25cm
ISBN 0-566-02239-7 : £15.00 B81-11619

658 — North Africa. Business opportunities — *For British businessmen*

Harrison, Roger, *1947-*. North Africa : business opportunities in the 1980s : Algeria, Libya, Morocco, Tunisia / [compiled] : Metra Consulting / [report prepared by Roger Harrison]. — [London] : Metra Consulting, c1981. — xiii,361p : maps ; 30cm
Text on inside cover
ISBN 0-902231-29-4 (spiral) : Unpriced B81-34671

658'.001 — Administration. Theories

Dunsire, Andrew. Administration. — Oxford : Robertson, Apr.1981. — [262]p
Originally published: 1973
ISBN 0-85520-020-0 (pbk) : £4.95 : CIP entry B81-09979

658'.001'5192 — Management. Applications of stochastic control theory

Applied stochastic control in econometrics and management science / edited by Alain Bensoussan, Paul Kleindorfer, Charles S. Tapiero. — Amsterdam ; Oxford : North-Holland, 1980. — xv,304p : ill ; 23cm. — (Contributors to economic analysis ; 130)
Includes bibliographies
ISBN 0-444-85408-8 : £21.73
Primary classification 330'.01'5192 B81-05826

658'.0024613 — Management — *For nursing*

Management for nurses : a multidisciplinary approach. — 2nd ed. / edited by Marie Streng Berger ... [et al.]. — St Louis ; London : Mosby, 1980. — ix,296p : ill,forms ; 24cm
Previous ed.: / edited by Sandra Stone. 1976. — Includes bibliographies and index
ISBN 0-8016-4815-7 (pbk) : £7.75 B81-01009

Marriner, Ann. Guide to nursing management / Ann Marriner. — St. Louis ; London : Mosby, 1980. — xiv,242p : ill ; 24cm
Includes bibliographies and index
ISBN 0-8016-3121-1 (pbk) : Unpriced B81-08169

658'.002462 — Management — *For engineering*

Amos, John M.. Management for engineers / John M. Amos, Bernard R. Sarchet. — Englewood Cliffs ; London : Prentice-Hall, c1981. — xiii,370p : ill,forms,ports ; 25cm. — (Prentice-Hall international series in industrial and systems engineering)
Includes bibliographies and index
ISBN 0-13-549402-8 : Unpriced B81-33360

Wortman, Leon A.. Effective management for engineers and scientists / Leon A. Wortman. — New York ; Chichester : Wiley, c1981. — xv,275p : ill ; 24cm
Includes index
ISBN 0-471-05523-9 : £9.50 B81-09786

658'.003'21 — Management — *Encyclopaedias*

Johannsen, Hano. International dictionary of management / Hano Johannsen, G. Terry Page. — 2nd rev. ed. — London : Macmillan, 1980. — 376p : ill,2maps ; 22cm
Previous ed.: London : Kogan Page, 1975
ISBN 0-333-30592-2 (pbk) : £6.95 B81-05391

Johannsen, Hano. International dictionary of management / Hano Johannsen, G. Terry Page. — 2nd rev. ed. — London : Kogan Page, 1980. — 376p : ill,maps ; 23cm
Previous ed.: 1975
ISBN 0-85038-332-3 : £12.00 B81-01010

658'.005 — Business firms. Management — *Serials*

In business : the brief for managing your own business. — Issue no.1 (Mar.30, 1981)-. — New Malden : Croner, 1981-. — v. : col.maps ; 30cm
Twenty two issues yearly
ISSN 0260-6909 = In business : Unpriced B81-29075

658'.007 — Management. Information sources

Dare, Gillian A.. The manager's guide to getting the answers / Gillian A. Dare and K.G.B. Bakewell ; illustrations by Kevin Hughes. — London : Library Association, 1980. — 69p : ill ; 21cm
Bibliography: p48-57. - Includes index
ISBN 0-85365-843-9 (pbk) : Unpriced : CIP rev. B80-31922

658'.007 — Management. Information sources — *Lists*

Thompson, Marilyn Taylor. Management information : where to find it / Marilyn Taylor Thompson. — Metuchen ; London : Scarecrow, 1981. — vii,272p ; 23cm
Includes index
ISBN 0-8108-1424-2 : £12.00 B81-37031

658'.007'041 — Great Britain. Business studies — *Serials*

COMLON. — [No.1] (Autumn 1979)-. — London (10 East Rd, N.1) : Metcalfe Cooper, 1979-. — v. : ill ; 30cm
Quarterly. — Journal of: London Chamber of Commerce and Industry. Commercial Education Scheme
ISSN 0260-8944 = COMLON : £2.70 per year B81-09049

658'.007'11 — Business schools — *Directories*

Coulson-Thomas, Colin. The BGA guide to business schools : for prospective students and employers / compiled by Colin Coulson-Thomas. — 5th ed. — Plymouth : Published for the Business Graduates Association Ltd [by] Macdonald and Evans, 1981. — x,118p ; 22cm
Previous ed.: 1979
ISBN 0-7121-0290-6 (pbk) : £4.95 B81-23103

658'.007'1141 — Great Britain. Business schools *compared with* **business schools in France**

Whitley, Richard. Masters of business?. — London : Tavistock, Dec.1981. — [220]p. — (Tavistock studies in sociology)
ISBN 0-422-76500-7 : £10.50 : CIP entry
Also classified at 658'.007'1144 B81-31703

658'.007'1141 — Great Britain. Business schools. Curriculum subjects: Management — *Forecasts*

Developing managers for the 1980s / edited by Cary L. Cooper. — London : Macmillan, 1981. — xxxvii,149p : ill ; 23cm
Includes index
ISBN 0-333-25510-0 : £15.00 : CIP rev.
Also classified at 658'.007'1173 B81-15090

658'.007'1141 — Great Britain. Business studies graduates. Organisations: Business Graduates Association — *Directories* — *Serials*

Business Graduates Association. The Business Graduates Association address book. — 1981. — London (87 Jermyn St, SW1Y 6JD) : The Association, 1981. — 275p
ISBN 0-906285-08-9 : Unpriced
ISSN 0308-0455 B81-15554

658'.007'1141 — Great Britain. Higher education institutions. Curriculum subjects: Management — *Conference proceedings*

Advances in management education / edited by John Beck and Charles Cox. — Chichester : Wiley, c1980. — x,360p : ill ; 24cm
Conference papers. — Includes bibliographies and index
ISBN 0-471-27775-4 : £15.90 : CIP rev. B80-25887

658'.007'11411 — Scotland. Further education institutions. Curriculum subjects: Business studies. Organisations: Scottish Business Education Council. Courses — *Serials*

Scottish Business Education Council. Business education guide / Scottish Business Education Council. — 1978/79-. — Edinburgh (22 Great King St., Edinburgh EH3 6QH) : The Council, 1978-. — v. ; 30cm
Annual. — Description based on: 1981/82 issue
ISSN 0144-0101 = Business education guide - Scottish Business Education Council : Unpriced B81-32213

658'.007'1142 — England. Educational institutions. Curriculum subjects: Management

Johnson, Ron. Training for management / by Ron Johnson ; summer meeting Thursday and Friday, 11 and 12 June 1981, Scarborough. — Sheffield : The Association of Colleges for Further and Higher Education, [1981]. — 9p ; 21cm
£0.75 (unbound) B81-31211

658'.007'1142 — England. Housing associations. Personnel. Professiona education. Curriculum subjects: Management

Management and supervisory skills / Housing Training Project. — London ([City University, St John St., EC1V 4PB]) : Housing Research Group, c1980. — 50p ; 21cm. — (Guide to housing training ; no.6)
Cover title. — Bibliography: p48
ISBN 0-907255-05-1 (pbk) : Unpriced
Primary classification 658'.007'1142 B81-06325

658'.007'1142 — England. Local authorities. Housing departments. Personnel. Professional education. Curriculum subjects: Management

Management and supervisory skills / Housing Training Project. — London ([City University, St John St., EC1V 4PB]) : Housing Research Group, c1980. — 50p ; 21cm. — (Guide to housing training ; no.6)
Cover title. — Bibliography: p48
ISBN 0-907255-05-1 (pbk) : Unpriced
Also classified at 658'.007'1142 B81-06325

658'.007'1142132 — London. Westminster *(London Borough)*. **Business schools. Ex-students. Organisations: London Business School.** *Association* — *Directories* — *Serials*

London Business School. *Association*. Address book / London Business School Association. — 1981. — London (9 Courtleigh Gardens, NW11 9JX) : A.P. Books for the Association, 1981. — xvi,[368]p
ISBN 0-906285-09-7 : Unpriced
ISSN 0308-0471 B81-35961

658'.007'11422 — England. Thames Valley. Higher education institutions. Curriculum subjects: Management — *Serials*

Thamesman : the journal of the Thames Valley Regional Management Centre. — No.1-. — [Slough] ([Wellington St., Slough SL1 1YG]) : The Centre, 1978-. — v. : ill ; 30cm
Irregular. — No.7 described as special issue. — Description based on: No.6 (Mar.1980)
Free B81-06527

658'.007'11422 — London & Home Counties. Management. Courses — *Directories* — *Serials*

[Bulletin of special courses *(London and Home Counties Regional Advisory Council for Technological Education)*]. Bulletin of special courses / London and Home Counties Regional Advisory Council for Technological Education. — 1981/82. — London : The Council, 1981. — [33]p
ISBN 0-85394-088-6 : £1.25
Primary classification 380.1'07'11422 B81-36306

658'.007'1144 — France. Business schools *compared with* **business schools in Great Britain**
Whitley, Richard. Masters of business?. — London : Tavistock, Dec.1981. — [220]p. — (Tavistock studies in sociology)
ISBN 0-422-76500-7 : £10.50 : CIP entry
Primary classification 658'.007'1141 B81-31703

658'.007'114437 — France. Fontainebleau. International business schools. Ex-students. Organisations: INSEAD International Alumni Association — *Directories — Serials*
INSEAD International Alumni Association. Address book / INSEAD International Alumni Association. — 1981. — London (9 Courtleigh Gardens, NW11 9JX) : A.P. Books, 1981. — 360p
ISBN 0-906285-07-0 : Unpriced
ISSN 0304-4270 B81-16743

658'.007'1173 — United States. Business schools. Curriculum subjects: Management — *Forecasts*
Developing managers for the 1980s / edited by Cary L. Cooper. — London : Macmillan, 1981. — xxxvii,149p : ill ; 23cm
Includes index
ISBN 0-333-25510-0 : £15.00 : CIP rev.
Primary classification 658'.007'1141 B81-15090

658'.00722 — Great Britain. Industries. Management — *Case studies*
Tyes, S.. Case studies in industrial management / S. Tyes. — London (Duncan House, High St., E15 2JB) : Anglian Regional Management Centre, c1981. — 129p : ill,maps,facsims ; 30cm. — (The Anglian Regional Management Centre case study series)
Unpriced (pbk) B81-26534

658'.00722 — United States. Business firms. Management — *Case studies — For schools*
Poe, Roy W.. Getting involved with business / Roy W. Poe, Herbert G. Hicks, Olive D. Church. — New York ; London : McGraw-Hill, 1981. — x,566p : ill,forms ; 24cm
Includes index
ISBN 0-07-050335-4 : £9.95
Also classified at 332.024'00973 B81-17037

658'.0076 — Business firms. Management — *Questions & answers*
Green, W.. Cross-modular assignment workbook : for BEC national level and related courses / W. Green, D. Clough and A.A. Nasta. — London : Holt Rinehart and Winston, 1981. — 50p : ill,1map,1plan ; 30cm. — (Holt business texts)
ISBN 0-03-910323-4 (pbk) : £1.75 : CIP rev. B81-13842

658'.0076 — Management — *Questions & answers*
Volkell, Randolph Z.. GMAT graduate management admission test : a test preparation guide / Randolph Z. Volkell. — New York ; Chichester : Wiley, c1981. — xiv,241p : ill ; 28cm. — (Wiley self-teaching guides)
ISBN 0-471-05286-8 (pbk) : £5.30 B81-23252

658'.009172'4 — Developing countries. Management
Management practice in developing countries / edited by Julius O. Onah. — London : Cassell, 1981. — x,352p : 1ill,3forms ; 22cm
ISBN 0-304-30608-8 (pbk) : Unpriced B81-08531

658'.0092'4 — Industries. Management. Theories of Taylor, Frederick W.
Merkle, Judith A.. Management and ideology : the legacy of the international scientific management movement / Judith A. Merkle. — Berkeley ; London : University of California Press, c1980. — ix,325p ; 23cm
Bibliography: p299-313. - Includes index
ISBN 0-520-03737-5 : £11.50 B81-05114

658'.00941 — Great Britain. Business firms. Management — *For workers' cooperatives*
Naughton, Tony. Work-aid : business management for co-operatives and community enterprises / Tony Naughton. — Edenbridge (Commonwork Trust, Bore Place, Bough Beech, Edenbridge, Kent TN8 7AR) : Commonwork Publications, 1981. — 107p : ill ; 21cm
Includes index
ISBN 0-9507442-0-4 (pbk) : £2.95 : CIP rev. B81-07488

658'.00941 — Great Britain. Companies. Management — *Manuals*
Company administration handbook. — 4th ed. — Farnborough, Hants. : Gower, 1980. — xxiii,802p : ill,plans,forms ; 24cm
Previous ed.: 1977. — Supplement (7p) as insert. — Includes bibliographies and index
ISBN 0-566-02154-4 : £24.00 : CIP rev. B80-06492

658'.00941 — Great Britain. Industries & trades. Management — *For accounting*
Allen, Brian L.. General management : an introduction for accountants / Brian L. Allen. — London : Institute of Chartered Accountants in England and Wales, 1981. — x,63p ; 21cm. — (The accountant in industry and commerce)
Bibliography: p63
ISBN 0-85291-296-x (pbk) : Unpriced B81-29013

658'.00941 — Great Britain. Industries. Management. Implications of industrial relations
Storey, John, *19---*. The challenge to management control / John Storey. — London : Business Books, 1981, c1980. — 192p : ill ; 22cm
Originally published: London : Kogan Page, 1980. — Bibliography: p181-188. — Includes index
ISBN 0-09-145941-9 (pbk) : £4.95 B81-28672

658'.00941 — Great Britain. Management — *Serials*
The **British** journal of administrative management. — Vol.31, no.1 (Apr.1981)-. — Beckenham (205 High St., Beckenham, Kent BR3 1BA) : Institute of Administrative Management, 1981-. — v. : ill ; 21cm
Monthly. — Continues: Administrative management (London)
ISSN 0260-9096 = British Journal of administrative management : £17.50 per year (free to Institute members) B81-29097

658'.00952 — Japan. Business firms. Management
Sasaki, Naoto. Management and industrial structure in Japan / by Naoto Sasaki. — Oxford : Pergamon, 1981. — ix,141p : ill ; 22cm. — (Pergamon international library)
Includes index
ISBN 0-08-024056-9 (cased) : Unpriced (pbk) : £4.95 B81-29670

658'.00973 — United States. Industries. Management — *Manuals*
Pacifico, Carl R.. Practical industrial management : insights for managers / Carl R. Pacifico, Daniel B. Witwer. — New York ; Chichester : Wiley, c1981. — x,375p : ill ; 24cm
Includes index
ISBN 0-471-08190-6 : £11.75 B81-11307

658'.022 — Great Britain. Home-based employment — *Manuals*
Franklin, Olga. A practical guide to making money at home / Olga Franklin. — New ed. — London : MacDonald, 1981. — xii,129p ; 23cm
Previous ed.: 1977. — Includes index
ISBN 0-354-04680-2 (cased) : £6.95
ISBN 0-354-04681-0 (pbk) : Unpriced B81-38463

658'.022'0941 — Great Britain. Small firms. Management — *Manuals*
The **Guardian** guide to running a small business / edited by Clive Woodcock. — London : Kogan Page, 1980. — 208p : ill,facsims ; 22cm
Bibliography: p203. — Includes index
ISBN 0-85038-373-0 (cased) : £6.00
ISBN 0-85038-382-x (pbk) : £3.50 B81-02876

Perry, William, *1913-*. Going solo : a guide to running your own business / by William Perry and Derek Jones. — Rev. ed. — London : British Broadcasting Corporation, 1981. — 64p : ill ; 24cm
Previous ed.: 1975
ISBN 0-563-16488-3 (pbk) : £1.95 B81-40079

Rabey, Gordon P.. Manager : outlining for busy managers the key points of effective management / by Gordon P. Rabey. — Lichfield (22 Bore St., Lichfield, Staffs. WS13 6LP) : Institute of Supervisory Management, c1979. — iv,100p : ill ; 21cm. — (The supervisors do-it-yourself series ; 2)
Includes index
£2.00 (pbk) B81-11819

658'.022'0941 — Great Britain. Small firms. Organisation & management — *Manuals*
Mogano, M.. How to start and run your own business / M. Mogano. — London : Graham & Trotman, 1980. — 126p : ill ; 23cm
ISBN 0-86010-233-5 (cased) : £5.00
ISBN 0-86010-232-7 (pbk) : £2.95 B81-04125

658'.022'0941 — Great Britain. Small firms. Organisation — *Manuals*
Edwards, Richard, *1946-*. Running your own business / Richard Edwards. — Rev. reprint. — London : Oyez, 1980, c1979. — 96p ; 20cm. — (Owl books)
Bibliography: p88-91. — Includes index
ISBN 0-7063-5518-0 (cased) : Unpriced
ISBN 0-7063-5697-7 (pbk) : £2.50 B81-13033

The **Guardian** guide to running a small business / edited by Clive Woodcock. — 2nd ed. — London : Kogan Page, 1981. — 240p ; 23cm
Previous ed.: 1980. — Bibliography p233. — Includes index
ISBN 0-85038-476-1 (cased) : Unpriced : CIP rev.
ISBN 0-85038-477-x (pbk) : £4.25 B81-21577

Macneill, Charles, *1919-*. Make money with your own business in 30 days / by Charles Macneill. — Stanford le Hope (38 Fairview Ave., Stanford le Hope, Essex) : C. Macneill, c1980. — [105]p : forms ; 21cm
Unpriced (pbk) B81-12765

658'.022'0973 — United States. Small firms. Management
Hogsett, Robert N.. Profit planning for small business / Robert N. Hogsett. — New York ; London : Van Nostrand Reinhold, c1981. — xiv,231p : ill ; 24cm
Includes index
ISBN 0-442-24907-1 : £16.95 B81-37778

Pickle, Hal B.. Small business management / Hal B. Pickle, Royce L. Abrahamson. — 2nd ed. — New York ; Chichester : Wiley, c1981. — xiv,546p : ill,forms ; 24cm. — (The Wiley series in management, ISSN 0271-6046)
Previous ed.: 1976. — Includes index
ISBN 0-471-06218-9 : £11.90 B81-13160

658'.022'0973 — United States. Small firms. Management — *Manuals*
Justis, Robert T.. Managing your small business / Robert T. Justis. — Englewood Cliffs ; London : Prentice-Hall, c1981. — xii,464p : ill,plans,forms,ports ; 25cm
Bibliography: p451-452. — Includes index
ISBN 0-13-551010-4 : Unpriced B81-36496

658'.022'0973 — United States. Small firms. Manuals
Albert, Kenneth J.. Straight talk about small business : what other books don't tell you about the pitfalls and profits of starting and managing your own business / Kenneth J. Albert. — New York ; London : McGraw-Hill, c1981. — xiii,242p ; 21cm
Includes index
ISBN 0-07-000949-x : £11.50 B81-10372

658'.022'0994 — Australia. Small firms. Management — *Manuals*
English, John W.. How to organise and operate a small business in Australia / John W. English. — Sydney ; London : Allen & Unwin, 1981. — ix,205p : ill,forms ; 23cm
Includes index
ISBN 0-86861-282-0 (cased) : £12.00
ISBN 0-86861-290-1 (pbk) : Unpriced B81-26684

58'.041 — Great Britain. Self-employment — *Case studies*
Pettit, Rosemary. Occupation, self employed. — London : Wildwood House, Sept.1981. — [208]p
Originally published: 1977
ISBN 0-7045-0432-4 (pbk) : £4.50 : CIP entry
B81-25126

58'.041 — Great Britain. Spare-time business enterprise — *Manuals*
Knightley, M.. The spare-time-business ideas book / M. Knightley and G. Foster. — London : Malcolm Stewart Books, 1977 (1980 [printing]). — 81p ; 25cm. — (Kingfisher business guides)
ISBN 0-904132-33-1 (pbk) : £3.90 B81-11984

58'.041 — Self-employment — *For school leavers*
Whitehead, Geoffrey. Working for yourself is also a career! / by Geoffrey Whitehead. — Huddersfield (P.O. Box No.1, Homfirth, Huddersfield HD7 2RP) : Vyner, 1979. — [24]p : ill,1map ; 30cm. — (The Simplex careers series ; C.1)
Text on inside covers
ISBN 0-906628-01-6 (pbk) : £0.80 B81-29000

58'.041 — Self-employment — *Manuals*
Golzen, Godfrey. Working for yourself : the Daily Telegraph guide to self-employment / Godfrey Golzen. — 4th ed. — London : Kogan Page, 1981. — 285p : ill,facsims ; 23cm
Previous ed.: 1980. — Bibliography: p262-263. — Includes index
ISBN 0-85038-455-9 (cased) : Unpriced : CIP rev. (pbk) : £4.25 B81-15848

58'.049 — Business firms. International disputes. Settlement
Duckworth, David S.. Troubleshooting : international business problems / by David S. Duckworth and Ian S. Blackshaw. — London : Oyez, 1980. 120p : ill ; 23cm
Bibliography: p117. - Includes index
ISBN 0-85120-476-7 : £9.75 B81-04841

58'.049 — Multinational companies. Management
Vernon, Raymond. Manager in the international economy. — 4th ed. / Raymond Vernon, Louis T. Wells, Jr. — Englewood Cliffs ; London : Prentice-Hall, c1981. — x,434p : ill ; 24cm
Previous ed.: 1976. — Includes index
ISBN 0-13-549550-4 : £9.05 B81-16644

58'.05 — Data processing services. Management
Schaeffer, Howard. Data center operations : a guide to effective planning, processing and performance / Howard Schaeffer. — Englewood Cliffs ; London : Prentice-Hall, c1981. — xxi,474p : ill,forms ; 29cm
Bibliography: p467-470. — Includes index
ISBN 0-13-196360-0 : £19.20 B81-17216

58'.05 — Management. Applications of data processing systems
Anderson, R. G.. Data processing : and management information systems / R.G. Anderson. — Plymouth : Macdonald and Evans, 1979. — xiii,466p : ill,forms ; 18cm. — (The M & E handbook series)
Previous ed.: 1978. — Includes index
ISBN 0-7121-0417-8 (pbk) : £2.75 B81-11082

58'.054 — Business firms. Applications of digital computer systems
Sardinas, Joseph L.. Computing today : an introduction to business data processing / Joseph L. Sardinas, Jr. — Englewood Cliffs ; London : Prentice-Hall, c1981. — xv,490p ; 23cm
Includes bibliographies and index
ISBN 0-13-165092-0 (pbk) : £11.85 B81-34955

58'.054 — Business firms. Applications of digital computer systems. Applications of digital computer systems in business firms. Management aspects — *Serials*
Business computing : the magazine for decision makers. — Issue 1 (July/Aug.1980)-. — London (4 Valentine Place, S.E.1) : Computer Age Ltd, 1980-. — v. : ill,ports ; 30cm
Monthly
ISSN 0260-5724 = Business computing : £9.00 per year B81-03278

658'.054 — Business firms. Applications of microcomputer systems. Management aspects
Edwards, C.. Developing microcomputer-based business systems. — London : Prentice-Hall, Feb.1982. — [240]p
ISBN 0-13-204560-5 (cased) : £9.95 : CIP entry
ISBN 0-13-204552-4 (pbk) : £5.95 B81-38306

658'.054 — Companies. Digital computer systems. Management
Strauss, Melvin J.. Computer capacity : a production control approach / by Melvin J. Strauss. — New York ; London : Van Nostrand Reinhold, c1981. — xii,265p : ill ; 26cm
Includes index
ISBN 0-442-26243-4 : £21.20 B81-37783

658'.054 — Industries. Management. Applications of computer systems — *Conference proceedings*
Computers : applications in industry and management : proceedings of the international seminar held at the University of Patras, Greece 29 July-17 August, 1979 / edited by Constantine L. Gaudas and Girish C. Pande. — Amsterdam ; Oxford : North-Holland, 1980. — xi,450. : ill,plans,forms ; 23cm
Includes bibliographies and index
ISBN 0-444-86053-3 : £19.88 B81-08277

658'.054 — Management. Applications of digital computer systems
Fuori, William M.. Introduction to the computer : the tool of business / William M. Fuori. — London : Prentice-Hall, c1981. — xvii,621p : ill(some col.),facsims(some col.),forms(some col.) ; 24cm
Previous ed.: 1976. — Includes index
ISBN 0-13-480210-1 (pbk) : £6.95 B81-22697

658'.054'0683 — Business firms. Data processing services. Personnel. Motivation — *For management*
Couger, J. Daniel. Motivating and managing computer personnel / J. Daniel Couger, Robert A. Zawacki. — New York ; Chichester : Wiley, c1980. — xv,213p : ill ; 24cm. — (Business data processing)
Text on lining papers. — Includes index
ISBN 0-471-08485-9 : Unpriced B81-08444

658.1 — COMPANY ORGANISATION AND FINANCE

658.1 — Great Britain. Manufacturing industries. British business firms. Organisation structure *compared with* **organisation structure of American manufacturing firms in Great Britain**
Jamieson, Ian. Capitalism and culture : a comparative analysis of British and American manufacturing organisations / Ian Jamieson. — Farnborough, Hants. : Gower, c1980. — xiii,240p : forms ; 23cm
Bibliography: p219-233. — Includes index
ISBN 0-566-00356-2 : £12.50 : CIP rev.
B80-12420

658.1'0973 — United States. Companies. Organisation structure
Edwards, Richard C.. Contested terrain : the transformation of the workplace in the twentieth century / Richard Edwards. — London : Heinemann, c1979. — ix,261p ; 21cm
Originally published: New York : Basic Books, 1979. — Bibliography: p244-252. — Includes index
ISBN 0-435-82271-3 (pbk) : £4.50 : CIP rev.
B80-13903

658.1'0994 — Australia. Companies. Organisation structure
Byrt, W. J.. The Australian company : studies in strategy and structure / W.J. Byrt. — London : Croom Helm, c1981. — 170p ; 22cm
Includes index
ISBN 0-7099-0615-3 (pbk) : £14.00 : CIP rev.
B81-12876

658.1'1 — Business firms. Organisation
Ellis, Raymond, *1947-*. The business organisation and its environment / by Raymond Ellis. — London : Gee, 1979. — xi,171p : ill ; 22cm. — (Gee BEC series of study books)
Bibliography: p165. — Includes index
ISBN 0-85258-167-x (pbk) : £2.65 B81-09810

658.1'1'0941 — Great Britain. Business firms. Organisation. Techniques
Starting a healthy business. — London : Hamlyn, c1980. — 207p : ill,2maps,forms ; 22cm. — (Managing your business guides)
Includes bibliographies and index
ISBN 0-600-35365-6 : £5.00 B81-05455

658.1'144'0941 — Great Britain. Private companies. Organisation
How to form a private company. — 29th ed. / edited by Alec Just. — Bristol : Jordan, 1980. — 72p : 1facsim,1port ; 21cm
Previous ed.: 1972. — Includes index
ISBN 0-85308-058-5 (pbk) : £3.00 B81-09162

658.1'149'0968 — South Africa. Subsidiaries of British companies. Establishment — *Practical information*
The **Setting** up of subsidiary companies in South Africa and Namibia (South West Africa) / Department of Trade. — London ([1 Victoria St., SW1H 0ET]) : The Department, 1980. — 11p ; 21cm
Previous ed.: 1976. — Bibliography: p1
Unpriced (pbk)
Also classified at 658.1'149'09688 B81-06286

658.1'149'09688 — Namibia. Subsidiaries of British companies. Establishment — *Practical information*
The **Setting** up of subsidiary companies in South Africa and Namibia (South West Africa) / Department of Trade. — London ([1 Victoria St., SW1H 0ET]) : The Department, 1980.— 11p ; 21cm
Previous ed.: 1976. — Bibliography: p1
Unpriced (pbk)
Primary classification 658.1'149'0968
B81-06286

658.1'5 — Business firms. Financial management
Morine, John. Riding the recession. — London : Business Books, Oct.1981. — [184]p
ISBN 0-09-145870-6 (cased) : £12.00 : CIP entry
ISBN 0-09-145871-4 (pbk) : £4.95 B81-27371

Moss, Scott. An economic theory of business strategy. — Oxford : Robertson, July 1981. — [250]p
ISBN 0-85520-386-2 (cased) : £12.95 : CIP entry
ISBN 0-85520-394-3 (pbk) : £4.50 B81-13751

658.1'5 — Companies. Financial management
Rockley, L. E.. Finance for the non-accountant / by L.E. Rockley. — 3rd ed. — London : Business Books, 1979. — xii,337p : ill ; 24cm
Previous ed.: 1976. — Includes index
ISBN 0-220-67021-8 : £10.50
ISBN 0-220-67022-6 (pbk) : Unpriced
B81-15584

Samuels, J. M.. Management of company finance / J.M. Samuels and F.F. Wilkes. — Walton-on-Thames : Nelson
Students manual. — 1981. — 183p : ill ; 28cm
ISBN 0-17-771092-6 (pbk) : £5.95 B81-40724

Wright, M. G.. Financial management / M.G. Wright. — 2nd ed. — London : McGraw-Hill, c1980. — xiv,246p : ill ; 23cm
Previous ed.: 1970. — Includes index
ISBN 0-07-084542-5 (pbk) : £7.95 : CIP rev.
B80-12421

658.1'5 — Financial management
Christy, George A.. Finance : environment and decisions / George A. Christy, Peyton Foster Roden. — 3rd ed. — New York ; London : Harper & Row, c1981. — xiv,445p : ill ; 24cm
Previous ed.: 1976. — Includes index
ISBN 0-06-041302-6 : Unpriced B81-26200

Neave, Edwin H.. Financial management : theory and strategies / Edwin H. Neave, John C. Wiginton. — Englewood Cliffs ; London : Prentice-Hall, c1981. — xvi,394p : ill ; 25cm
Includes bibliographies and index
ISBN 0-13-316109-9 : £13.60 B81-17279

658.1'5 — Financial management *continuation*

Watts, B. K. R.. Business and financial management / B.K.R. Watts. — 4th ed. — Plymouth : Macdonald and Evans, 1981. — xiii,340p : ill ; 18cm. — (The M & E handbook series)
Previous ed.: 1978. — Includes index
ISBN 0-7121-0289-2 (pbk) : £2.75 B81-03558

658.1'5 — Great Britain. Private companies. Valuation — *Manuals*

Andrews, Michael, *1947-*. Valuing private companies / Michael Andrews and John Carrell. — Woking (P.O. Box 3, Woking, Surrey) : Templegate Press, 1981. — iii,95p : 2 ports ; 21cm
Includes index
ISBN 0-903583-08-9 (pbk) : Unpriced B81-17678

658.1'5'024657 — Financial management — *For accounting*

Brockington, Raymond. Financial management : an instructional manual for business and accountancy students / Raymond Brockington. — 2nd ed. — Winchester : D.P. Publications, 1981. — v,294p ; 22cm
Previous ed.: 1978. — Includes index
ISBN 0-905435-16-8 (pbk) : Unpriced B81-16489

658.1'5'0724 — Companies. Financial management. Mathematical models

Financial modelling in corporate management. — Chichester : Wiley, Jan.1982. — [448]p
ISBN 0-471-10021-8 : £17.50 : CIP entry B81-34490

658.1'5'09417 — Ireland *(Republic).* **Business firms. Financial management**

MacCormac, M. J.. Financial management / M.J. MacCormac and J. J. Teeling. — 3rd ed. — Dublin : Gill and Macmillan, 1980. — 200p : ill ; 22cm
Previous ed: 1976. — Includes bibliographies
ISBN 0-7171-1068-0 (pbk) : £5.40 B81-08279

658.1'5'0973 — United States. Business firms. Financial management

Brealey, Richard. Principles of corporate finance / Richard Brealey, Stewart Myers. — New York ; London : McGraw-Hill, c1981. — xxii,794p : ill ; 25cm. — (McGraw-Hill series in finance)
Text on inside covers. — Includes bibliographies and index
ISBN 0-07-007380-5 : £13.75 B81-10206

658.1'5'0973 — United States. Business firms. Financial management. Techniques

O'Connor, Dennis J.. Managerial finance : theory and techniques / Dennis J. O'Connor, Alberto T. Bueso. — Englewood Cliffs ; London : Prentice-Hall, c1981. — xiv,546p : ill ; 24cm
Includes bibliographies and index
ISBN 0-13-550269-1 : £13.65 B81-25993

658.1'51 — Business firms. Financial analysis

Ford, John Kingston. A framework for financial analysis / John Kingston Ford. — Englewood Cliffs ; London : Prentice-Hall, c1981. — xi,190p : ill ; 23cm
Includes bibliographies and index
ISBN 0-13-330241-5 (pbk) : £6.45 B81-26104

658.1'51 — Business firms. Financial management. Decision making — *Manuals*

Lumby, Stephen. Investment appraisal : and related decisions / Stephen Lumby. — Walton-on-Thames : Nelson, 1981. — viii,261p : ill ; 22cm. — (Nelson series in accounting and finance)
Includes bibliographies and index
ISBN 0-17-761055-7 (cased) : Unpriced
ISBN 0-17-771060-8 (pbk) : £4.75 B81-14627

658.1'51 — Business firms. Financial management. Decision making. Multiple criteria methods

Spronk, Jaap. Interactive multiple goal programming : applications to financial planning / Jaap Spronk. — Boston, Mass. ; London : Nijhoff, c1981. — xii,259p : ill ; 24cm. — (International series in management science/operations research)
Includes bibliographies and index
ISBN 0-89838-064-2 : Unpriced B81-26966

658.1'51 — Financial management. Decision making. Theories

Haley, Charles W.. The theory of financial decisions / Charles W. Haley, Lawrence D. Schall. — 2nd ed. — International student ed. — Auckland ; London : McGraw Hill, c1979. — xvi,508p : ill ; 21cm. — (McGraw-Hill series in finance)
Previous ed.: 1973. — Bibliography: p484-497. — Includes index
ISBN 0-07-066317-3 (pbk) : £9.95 B81-29758

658.1'51 — Great Britain. Business firms. Financial management. Ratios — *Case studies*

Dun & Bradstreet management ratios : comparative indicators of business performance / compiled by Dun & Bradstreet Ltd. — London : Publications Division, Dun & Bradstreet, [1980]. — 1v.(loose-leaf) ; 32cm
Unpriced B81-11188

658.1'51'0724 — Great Britain. Business firms. Financial analysis. Econometric models

Taffler, Richard J.. The assessment of financial viability and the measurement of company performance / by R.J. Taffler. — London (Basinghall St., EC2V 5AH) : Gresham College, c1981. — 26leaves,[8]leaves of plates : ill ; 30cm. — (Working paper series / City University Business School, ISSN 0140-1041 ; no.27)
Bibliography: leaves 24-26
Unpriced (pbk) B81-36905

658.1'511 — Great Britain. Price-level accounting. Management aspects

Finnett, D. W.. Current cost accounting and management decisions / by D.W. Finnett and C.R. Horsley. — London : Institute of Cost and Management Accountants, 1979. — iv,75p : ill ; 21cm. — (Management accounting in inflation series)
ISBN 0-901308-54-4 (pbk) : Unpriced B81-26901

658.1'511 — Management accounting

Bull, R. J.. Accounting in business / R.J. Bull. — 4th ed. — London : Butterworths, 1980. — 506p : ill ; 24cm
Previous ed.: 1976. — Includes bibliography and index
ISBN 0-408-10669-7 (cased) : £12.95 : CIP rev.
(pbk) : £7.95 B80-10688

Horngren, Charles T.. Introduction to management accounting / Charles T. Horngren. — 5th ed. — London : Prentice-Hall, 1981. — xvi,638p : ill ; 24cm. — (Prentice-Hall series in accounting)
Previous ed.: 1978. — Bibliography: p605-606. — Includes index
ISBN 0-13-487264-9 (pbk) : £7.50 B81-24905

Willson, James D.. Controllership : the work of the managerial accountant. — 3rd ed. / James D. Willson and John B. Campbell. — New York ; Chichester : Wiley, c1981. — ix,889p[1] folded leaf of plates : ill,facsims,forms ; 24cm
Previous ed.: / by J. Brooks Heckert and James D. Willson. New York : Ronald Press, 1963. — Includes index
ISBN 0-471-05711-8 : £38.50 B81-33738

658.1'511 — Management accounting — *For business studies*

Schattke, Rudolph W.. Managerial accounting : concepts and uses / Rudolph W. Schattke, Howard G. Jenson. — 2nd ed.. — Boston [Mass.] ; London : Allyn and Bacon, c1981. — xiv,585p : ill + Instructor's manual(245p : ill ; 28cm) ; 25cm
Previous ed.: Boston, Mass. : Allyn and Bacon, 1974. — Text on lining papers. — Includes index
ISBN 0-205-07319-0 : Unpriced B81-26208

658.1'511'077 — Management accounting — *Programmed instructions*

Madden, Donald L.. Management accounting : a self-teaching guide / Donald L. Madden ; instructional editing by Karen M. Hess. — New York ; Chichester : Wiley, c1980. — x,326p : ill ; 26cm. — (Wiley self-teaching guides)
Includes index
ISBN 0-471-03135-6 (pbk) : £5.95 B81-06236

658.1'511'0941 — Great Britain. Management accounting — *Conference proceedings*

Managing for profit. — London : McGraw-Hill, Jan.1982. — [160]p
Conference papers
ISBN 0-07-084575-1 : £10.50 : CIP entry B81-3883

658.1'511'0941 — Great Britain. Management accounting — *For banking*

Walker, T. M.. Management accounting and business finance : study guide / by T.M. Walker. — 2nd ed. — [Edinburgh] ([20 Rutland Square, Edinburgh]) : Institute of Bankers in Scotland, [1979?]. — 149p ; 21cm
Previous ed.: 1974. — Includes index
£2.25 (pbk)
Primary classification 338.6'041'0941
B81-0769

658.1'511'0941 — Great Britain. Management accounting — *Study examples: Hardy Heating Co. Ltd*

Ray, Graham. Hardy Developments Ltd.. — Farnborough : Gower Publishing, Oct.1981. — [300]p
ISBN 0-566-02251-6 (cased) : £12.50 : CIP entry
ISBN 0-566-02252-4 (pbk) : £6.50 B81-2582

658.1'512 — Great Britain. Companies. Financial statements. Disclosure, *1900-1940*

Edwards, J. R. (John Richard). Company legislation and changing patterns of disclosure in British company accounts 1900-1940 / J.R. Edwards. — London : Institute of Chartered Accountants in England and Wales, 1981. — ii,77p : facsims ; 25cm
ISBN 0-85291-306-0 (pbk) : Unpriced
B81-3671

658.1'52 — Capital investment by business firms. Decision making

Levy, Haim. Capital investment and financial decisions. — 2nd ed. — London : Prentice-Hall, Jan.1982. — [624]p
Previous ed.: 1978
ISBN 0-13-113589-9 : £12.95 : CIP entry
B81-3397

658.1'52 — Capital investment by business firms. Decision making — *Conference proceedings*

Risk, capital costs, and project financing decisions / edited by Frans G.J. Derkinderen, Roy L. Crum. — Boston, Mass. ; London : Nijhoff ; London : Distributors Kluwer Academic, c1981. — xiv,274p : ill ; 24cm. — (Nijenrode studies in business ; v.6)
Conference papers. — Includes bibliographies
ISBN 0-89838-046-4 : Unpriced B81-0927

658.1'52 — Capital investment by business firms. Risks. Evaluation

Hull, J. C.. The evaluation of risk in business investment / by J.C. Hull. — Oxford : Pergamon, 1980. — xiv,177p : ill ; 21cm. — (Pergamon international library)
Includes bibliographies
ISBN 0-08-024075-5 (cased) : £12.00 : CIP rev
ISBN 0-08-024074-7 (pbk) : £6.00 B80-0699

658.1'5224 — Finance. Borrowing. Procedure — *Manuals*

Wood, Oliver G.. How to borrow money / Oliver G. Wood, Jr. and William C. Barksdale, Jr. — New York ; London : Van Nostrand Reinhold, c1981. — ix,145p ; 24cm
Includes index
ISBN 0-442-25204-8 : £11.85 B81-3130

658.1'5242 — Great Britain. Industrial equipment. Leasing

Hubbard, Graham. Finance leasing : a guide for lessees in the UK / by Graham Hubbard. — London (63 Portland Place, W1N 4AB) : Institute of Cost and Management Accountants, 1980. — 139p : forms ; 21cm
Includes index
ISBN 0-901308-56-0 (pbk) : £4.95 B81-0101

658.1'5242 — United States. Industrial equipment. Leasing. Management

Baker, C. Richard. Lease financing : a practical guide / C. Richard Baker, Rick Stephan Hayes. — New York ; Chichester : Wiley, c1981. — v,200p ; 24cm
Bibliography: p191-194. — Includes index
ISBN 0-471-06040-2 : £14.00 B81-3337

58.1′53 — Great Britain. Business firms. Executives. Tax avoidance — *Manuals*

Rook, Alan. The complete executive′s tax handbook : how to reduce tax on remuneration and fringe benefits : with supplementary comment for the technical reader / Alan Rook and John Carrell with Stanton Marcus. — Woking : Financial Techniques, 1979. — vii,213p : ill ; 21cm + supplement to Jan.1981 (8p ; 21cm)
Includes index
ISBN 0-903583-07-0 : £9.00 B81-37147

58.1′53 — Great Britain. Partnerships. Tax avoidance — *Manuals*

Eastaway, Nigel. Tax and financial planning for professional partnerships / Nigel Eastaway and Brian Gilligan. — London : Butterworths, 1981. — xiv,273p : ill ; 22cm. — (Butterworths tax management series)
Includes index
ISBN 0-406-19004-6 (pbk) : Unpriced B81-36509

58.1′54 — Capital investment. Budgeting

Capital budgeting under conditions of uncertainty / edited by Roy L. Crum, Frans G.J. Derkinderen. — Boston, Mass. ; London : Nijhoff, c1981. — xii,238p : ill ; 24cm. — (Nijenrode studies in business ; v.5)
Includes bibliographies
ISBN 0-89838-045-6 : Unpriced B81-06505

58.1′54 — Financial management. Budgeting

Handbook of budgeting / [edited by] H.W. Allen Sweeny, Robert Rachlin. — New York ; Chichester : Wiley, 1981. — xii, 778p : ill,forms ; 24cm. — (Systems and controls for financial management series, ISSN 0190-1117)
Text on lining paper. — Includes index
ISBN 0-471-05621-9 : £28.00 B81-30792

Madsen, Vagn. Human factors in budgeting : judgement and evaluation / Vagn Madsen, Thomas Polesie. — London : Pitman, 1981. — 133p : ill ; 24cm
Bibliography: p126-128. — Includes index
ISBN 0-273-01672-5 : Unpriced B81-38371

58.1′54 — Great Britain. Capital investment. Budgeting — *For banking*

Fisher, J.. Financial analysis and capital budgeting decisions / by J. Fisher. — Edinburgh (20 Rutland Sq., Edinburgh) : Institute of Bankers in Scotland, [1980]. — 134p ; 30cm
£3.00 (spiral) B81-06145

58.1′55 — Business firms. Profits. Planning. Applications of breakeven analysis

Tucker, Spencer A.. Profit planning decisions with the break-even system / Spencer A. Tucker. — Farnborough, Hants. : Gower, c1980. — xix,213p : ill ; 28cm
Includes index
ISBN 0-566-02255-9 : £15.00 B81-04528

58.1′552 — Financial management. Costing — *Conference proceedings*

Cutting the costs of financial services. — Aldershot : Gower, Sept.1981. — [130]p
Conference papers
ISBN 0-566-03027-6 (pbk) : £19.50 : CIP entry B81-31241

58.1′552 — Financial management. Marginal costing. Techniques

Rickwood, C. P.. Marginal costing / by C.P. Rickwood and A.G. Piper. — London : Institute of Cost and Management Accountants, 1980. — 78p : ill ; 21cm
ISBN 0-901308-58-7 (pbk) : Unpriced B81-26900

58.1′552 — Industries. Costs. Control — *Manuals* — *For management*

Tagliaferri, Louis E.. Creative cost improvement for managers / Louis E. Tagliaferri. — New York ; Chichester : Wiley, c1981. — viii,199p : ill,2forms ; 26cm. — (Wiley self-teaching guides)
Bibliography: p179-180. — Includes index
ISBN 0-471-08708-4 (pbk) : £6.75 B81-33423

658.1′553 — Industries. Maintenance services. Costs. Reduction — *Conference proceedings*

Minimizing the cost of maintenance : proceedings of the conference organized by the Metals Society and held at the Café Royal, London on 15 and 16 May 1980. — London : Metals Society, 1980. — 129p : ill ; 30cm
Includes index
ISBN 0-904357-33-3 (pbk) : £25.00 (£20.00 to members of the Society) B81-04951

658.1′554 — Business firms. Profits. Improvement

Fenton, John, *1938-*. How to double your profits within the year : an action plan for your business / John Fenton. — London : Pan in association with Heinemann, 1981. — 208p : ill,forms ; 18cm. — (Pan business/management)
ISBN 0-330-26321-8 (pbk) : £1.50 B81-19696

658.1′554 — Business firms. Profits. Improvement. Techniques

Fenton, John, *1938-*. How to double your profits within the year / John Fenton. — London : Heinemann, 1981. — 178p : ill,forms ; 26cm
Bibliography: p171
ISBN 0-434-90565-8 : £9.95 B81-23236

658.1′554 — Industrial buildings. Heating systems. Hot pipes. Thermal insulation. Cost-effectiveness

The **Economic** thickness of insulation for hot pipes / Department of Energy. — London (Room 1312, Thames House South, Millbank, SW1P 4QJ) : Department of Energy, 1980. — 40p : ill ; 21cm. — (Fuel efficiency booklet ; 8)
Cover title
Unpriced (pbk) B81-20050

658.1′554 — Projects. Evaluation. Cost-benefit analysis

Pearce, D. W.. The social appraisal of projects : a text in cost-benefit analysis / D.W. Pearce, C.A. Nash. — London : Macmillan, 1981. — xiv,225p : ill ; 25cm
Bibliography: p215-221. - Includes index
ISBN 0-333-19303-2 (cased) : £18.00
ISBN 0-333-19304-0 (pbk) : Unpriced B81-21794

658.1′592 — Small firms. Financial management

Kitzing, Donald. Credit and collections for small business / Donald Kitzing. — New York ; London : McGraw-Hill, c1981. — 174p : ill,forms ; 21cm
Includes index
ISBN 0-07-034915-0 : £11.95 B81-37621

658.1′592′0941 — Great Britain. Small firms. Financial management — *Manuals*

Tolley′s survival kit for small businesses : financial management in a changing economic climate / Touche Ross & Co.. — Croydon : Tolley, c1981. — 43p : ill(some col.) ; 30cm. — (A Benn Group publication)
ISBN 0-85459-040-4 (pbk) : £2.95 B81-33112

658.1′599 — Multinational companies. Financial management

Giannotti, John B.. Treasury management : a practitioner′s handbook / John B. Giannotti, Richard W. Smith. — New York : Chichester : Wiley, c1981. — xix,508p : ill,forms ; 25cm
Includes index
ISBN 0-471-08062-4 : £27.65 B81-34921

Kettell, Brian. The finance of international business / Brian Kettell. — London : Graham & Trotman, 1979. — xviii,275p : ill,facsims ; 24cm
Bibliography: p261-267. — Includes index
ISBN 0-86010-151-7 : £15.00 B81-01718

Wood, Douglas. International business finance / Douglas Wood, James Byrne. — London : Macmillan, 1981. — vii,297p : ill ; 23cm
Includes bibliographies and index
ISBN 0-333-21215-0 : £20.00 : CIP rev. B80-10690

Zenoff, David B.. Management principles for finance in the multinational / by David B. Zenoff. — London : Euromoney, c1980. — 208p : ill ; 30cm
Bibliography: p201-205. — Includes index
ISBN 0-903121-17-4 (pbk) : Unpriced B81-12962

658.1′599 — Multinational companies. Financial management. Implications of variation in foreign exchange rates

Currency risk and the corporation / edited by Boris Antl. — London : Euromoney, [1980?]. — 193p ; 30cm
Bibliography: p191—192
ISBN 0-903121-14-x (pbk) : Unpriced B81-19766

658.1′599′0941 — British companies. Overseas activities. Financial management

Finney, Malcolm J.. UK companies operating overseas : tax and financial strategies : a specially commissioned report / by Malcolm J. Finney and Martin J. Packman. — London : Oyez, c1981. — 71leaves,[1]folded leaf of plates : ill ; 30cm. — (Oyez intelligence reports)
ISBN 0-85120-532-1 (spiral) : Unpriced B81-28532

658.1′6 — Great Britain. Companies. Purchase by managers — *Conference proceedings*

Management buyouts : corporate trend for the 80′s? : proceedings of a national conference, 19 March 1981, University of Nottingham / edited by R.V. Arnfield ... [et al.]. — Nottingham : Industrial & Business Liaison Office University of Nottingham, c1981. — 129p ; 30cm
£12.00 (spiral) B81-36266

658.1′6 — United States. Business firms. Acquisition. Management aspects

Bing, Gordon. Corporate acquisitions / Gordon Bing. — Houston ; London : Gulf Publishing, c1980. — xi,248p ; 24cm
Includes index
ISBN 0-87201-009-0 : £8.25 B81-10768

658.1′6 — United States. Business firms. Sale & purchase — *Manuals*

Douglas, F. Gordon. How to profitably sell or buy a company or business / F. Gordon Douglas. — New York ; London : Van Nostrand Reinhold, 1981. — ix,286p : ill,forms ; 24cm
Includes index
ISBN 0-442-23336-1 : £16.90 B81-29520

658.1′8 — Multinational companies. Organisation structure

The **Management** of headquarters-subsidiary relationships in multinational corporations. — Farnborough, Hants. : Gower, Sept.1981. — [352]p
ISBN 0-566-00484-4 : £15.00 : CIP entry B81-21535

658.2 — PLANT MANAGEMENT

658.2′02 — Buildings. Maintenance. Management aspects

Lee, Reginald. Building maintenance management / Reginald Lee. — 2nd ed. — London : Granada, 1981. — viii,360p : ill ; 22cm
Previous ed.: London : Crosby Lockwood Staples, 1976. — Includes index
ISBN 0-246-11608-0 (pbk) : £10.75 : CIP rev. B81-13838

658.2′02 — Terotechnology — *Conference proceedings*

International Congress on Terotechnology *(1st : 1979 : London)*. First International Congress on Terotechnology : 1-3 May 1979, Café Royal, Regent Street, London W1, England / sponsored by the National Terotechnology Centre ; organised by Conference Communication. — [Great Britain] : [s.n.]
Papers. — [1979]?. — [144]p : ill,forms ; 30cm
Cover title
Unpriced (spiral) B81-37787

International Congress on Terotechnology *(1st : 1979 : London)*. First International Congress on Terotechnology : 1-3 May 1979, Café Royal, Regent Street, London W1, England / sponsored by the National Terotechnology Centre ; organised by Conference Communication. — [Great Britain] : [s.n.]
Supplementary vol. — [1979]?. — [17]p ; 30cm
Cover title
Unpriced (spiral) B81-37786

658.2′4 — Great Britain. Workplaces. Interiors. Electric lighting. Cost effectiveness

Energy management and good lighting practices / Department of Energy. — London (Thames House South, Millbank, SW1P 4QJ) : Information Division, Department of Energy, [1980]. — 12p : ill ; 21cm. — (Fuel efficiency booklet ; 12)
Cover title
Unpriced (pbk) B81-06285

658.2′6 — Great Britain. Companies. Energy. Conservation

Energy audits 2 / Department of Energy. — London (Room 1312, Thames House South, Millbank, SW1P 4QJ) : Department of Energy, [1980]. — 17p : ill ; 21cm. — (Fuel efficiency booklet ; 11)
Cover title
Unpriced (pbk) B81-01982

658.2′6 — Great Britain. Industries. Energy. Conservation. Management — *Manuals*

Payne, Gordon A.. The energy managers' handbook / Gordon A. Payne. — 2nd ed. — Guildford : Westbury House, 1980. — xii,156p : ill ; 22cm
Previous ed.: 1977. — Bibliography: p146-152. — Includes index
ISBN 0-86103-032-x (cased) : Unpriced : CIP rev.
ISBN 0-86103-033-8 (pbk) : Unpriced
B80-31932

658.2′6 — Great Britain. Industries. Fuels. Conservation

Fuel economy handbook / written and c ompiled by National Industrial Fuel Efficiency Service Ltd. — 2nd ed. / edited by W. Short. — London : Graham & Trotman, 1979 (1981 [printing]). — x,317p : ill ; 23cm
Previous ed.: 1974
ISBN 0-86010-130-4 : £12.50 B81-36198

658.2′6 — Industries. Energy. Conservation. Management

Murphy, W. R.. Energy management. — London : Butterworths, Dec.1981. — [290]p
ISBN 0-408-00508-4 : £17.00 : CIP entry
B81-31734

O'Callaghan, Paul W.. Design and management for energy conservation. — Oxford : Pergamon, Dec.1981. — [250]p
ISBN 0-08-027287-8 : £15.00 : CIP entry
B81-31743

658.3 — PERSONNEL MANAGEMENT

658.3 — Business firms. Personnel management

Fisher, Martin. Controlling labour costs / Martin Fisher. — London : Kogan Page, 1981. — 200p : ill ; 23cm
Includes index
ISBN 0-85038-425-7 : £10.50 : CIP rev.
B80-29974

658.3 — Personnel management

Armstrong, Pat. People in organisations / Pat Armstrong & Chris Dawson. — Huntingdon (45 Park Rd., Buckden, Huntingdon, Cambs.) : ELM Publications, 1981. — vi,404p : ill ; 21cm + tutor's pack(24p; 32cm)
Bibliography: p364-365. — Includes index
ISBN 0-9505828-2-4 (pbk) : £5.90 B81-37632

Bennett, Roger. Managing personnel and performance : an alternative approach / Roger Bennett. — London : Business Books, 1981. — xxii,250p : ill ; 24cm
Bibliography: p239-247. — Includes index
ISBN 0-09-144550-7 (cased) : Unpriced : CIP rev.
ISBN 0-09-144551-5 (pbk) : £5.50 B81-01012

DuBrin, Andrew J.. Personnel and human resource management / Andrew J. DuBrin. — New York ; London : Van Nostrand, c1981. — x,566p : ill(some col.),forms ; 24cm
Includes bibliographies and index
ISBN 0-442-25407-5 : £14.20 B81-03489

Graham, H. T.. Human resources management / H.T. Graham. — 3rd ed. — Plymouth : Macdonald and Evans, 1980. — x,278p : ill,1form ; 19cm. — (The M & E handbook series)
Previous ed.: 1978. — Bibliography: p267. — Includes index
ISBN 0-7121-0817-3 (pbk) : £2.50 B81-00180

Honey, Peter. Solving people-problems / Peter Honey. — London : McGraw-Hill, c1980. — x,137p : ill ; 24cm
Includes index
ISBN 0-07-084544-1 : £7.95 B81-10233

Humphrey, Peter. How to be your own personnel manager. — London : Institute of Personnel Management, June 1981. — [160]p
ISBN 0-85292-273-6 (pbk) : £1.95 : CIP entry
B81-12894

Karlins, Marvin. The human use of human resources / Marvin Karlins. — New York ; London : McGraw-Hill, c1981. — xiii,173p ; 24cm. — (McGraw-Hill series in management)
Bibliography: p161-166. — Includes index
ISBN 0-07-033298-3 (cased) : £8.50 B81-31322

Managing human resources / edited by A.G. Cowling and C.J.B. Mailer. — London : Edward Arnold, 1981. — vii,248p : ill,1form ; 22cm
Includes index
ISBN 0-7131-0569-0 (pbk) : £6.95 : CIP rev.
B81-14957

Pigors, Paul. Personnel administration : a point of view and a method / Paul Pigors, Charles A. Myers. — 9th ed. — Auckland ; London : McGraw-Hill, c1981. — xv,588p : ill,forms ; 24cm
Previous ed.: 1977. — Includes bibliographies and indexes
ISBN 0-07-066478-1 (pbk) : £6.95 B81-31329

Sayles, Leonard R.. Managing human resources / Leonard R. Sayles, George Strauss. — 2nd ed. — Englewood Cliffs ; London : Prentice-Hall, c1981. — xiii,510p : ill,forms ; 25cm
Previous ed.: 1977. — Includes index
ISBN 0-13-550418-x : £12.95 B81-14107

Thomason, George F.. A textbook of personnel management. — 4th ed. — London : Institute of Personnel Management, Sept.1981. — [640] p. — (Management in perspective)
Previous ed.: 1978
ISBN 0-85292-301-5 : £10.95 : CIP entry
B81-20531

658.3 — Personnel management. Applications of behavioural sciences

Lupton, Tom. Industrial behaviour and personnel management / Tom Lupton. — London : Institute of Personnel Management, 1964 (1978 [printing]). — 88p : ill ; 19cm
ISBN 0-85292-164-0 (pbk) : £2.50 B81-11589

658.3 — Personnel management. Applications of economics

Bridge, John. Economics in personnel management / John Bridge. — London : Institute of Personnel Management, 1981. — viii,264p : ill ; 22cm
Bibliography: p247-256. — Includes index
ISBN 0-85292-260-4 (pbk) : £8.95 B81-22062

658.3 — Personnel management — *Manuals*

Bell, John, *1947-*. An employee management handbook : a practical guide on managing people and employment law / John Bell. — Watford : Engineering Industry Training Board, 1981. — xv,367p : ill,forms ; 24cm
Bibliography: p341-356. — Includes index
ISBN 0-85083-517-8 : £9.95 : CIP rev.
B81-15933

Hunsaker, Phillip L.. The art of managing people / Phillip L. Hunsaker, Anthony J. Alessandra. — Englewood Cliffs ; London : Prentice-Hall, c1980. — xiii,270p : ill ; 24cm. — (A Spectrum book)
Includes bibliographies and index
ISBN 0-13-047472-x (cased) : £10.35 (pbk) : £5.15 B81-12644

Lorentzen, John F.. The manager's personnel problem solver : a handbook of creative solutions to human relations problems in your organization / John F. Lorentzen. — Englewood Cliffs ; London : Prentice-Hall, c1980. — xvi,266p : forms ; 24cm. — (A Spectrum book)
Includes index
ISBN 0-13-549915-1 (cased) : £10.35
ISBN 0-13-549907-0 (pbk) : £4.50 B81-0174

658.3′001′9 — Personnel management. Applications of transactional analysis — *Manuals*

Clements, Ron. A guide to transactional analysis a handbook for managers and trainers / by Ron Clements. — Woking (c/o Ron Clements, 29 Paxton Gardens, Woodham La., Woking GU21 5TS, Surrey) : Insight Training, c1980. — 58p : ill ; 22cm
Bibliography: p56-58
Unpriced (pbk) B81-0986

Wagner, Abe. The transactional manager : how to solve people problems with transactional analysis / Abe Wagner. — Englewood Cliffs ; London : Prentice-Hall, c1981. — xi,196p : ill 24cm. — (A Spectrum book)
Bibliography: p191. — Includes index
ISBN 0-13-928192-4 (cased) : Unpriced
ISBN 0-13-928184-3 (pbk) : £3.85 B81-2546

658.3′0028′54 — Personnel management. Applications of digital computer systems

Ive, Tony. Personnel computer systems. — London : McGraw-Hill, Nov.1981. — [216]p
ISBN 0-07-084572-7 : £9.95 : CIP entry
B81-2877

Wilke, Edgar. The computer in personnel work / Edgar Wille, Valerie Hammond. — London : Institute of Personnel Management, 1981. — 239p : forms ; 18cm. — (Management paperbacks)
Includes index
ISBN 0-85292-274-4 (pbk) : £5.55 B81-1399

658.3′00722 — Great Britain. Personnel management — *Case studies*

Personnel file / edited by Keith Corby, Shelagh Robinson. — London : Institute of Personnel Management, 1981. — 134p : 1ill ; 29cm
ISBN 0-85292-281-7 (pbk) : £5.60 B81-2133

658.3′00941 — Great Britain. Business firms. Personnel management

Employees, health and safety. — London : Hamlyn, c1980. — 207p : ill,1map,1facsim,forms ; 22cm. — (Managing your business guides)
Includes index
ISBN 0-600-35367-2 : £5.00
Primary classification 363.1′1′0941 B81-0545

658.3′00941 — Great Britain. Personnel management — *Serials*

Personnel and training databook. — 1982. — London : Kogan Page, Nov.1981. — [360]p
ISBN 0-85038-493-1 : £13.95 : CIP entry
B81-3363

Personnel and training management yearbook and directory. — 1981. — London : Kogan Page 1980. — 358p
ISBN 0-85038-329-3 : £12.95
ISSN 0306-6673 B81-0187

Personnel executive : the independent viewpoint. — 1st issue (July 1981)-. — London (109 Waterloo Rd, SE1 8UL) : Business Publications, 1981-. — v. : ill,ports ; 30cm
Monthly
ISSN 0261-9776 = Personnel executive : £20.00 per year B81-3653

658.3′00973 — United States. Personnel management

Mondy, R. Wayne. Instructor's manual to accompany Personnel : the management of human resources / R. Wayne Mondy, Robert M. Noe, III in collaboration with Harry N. Mills, Jr. — Boston [Mass.] ; London : Allyn and Bacon, c1981. — ix,340p,[40]p ; 28cm
Unpriced (pbk) B81-1889

58.3′00973 — United States. Personnel management *continuation*

Mondy, R. Wayne. Personnel : the management of human resources / R. Wayne Mondy, Robert M. Noe in collaboration with Harry N. Mills, Jr.. — Boston, Mass. ; London : Allyn and Bacon, c1981. — xxiv,599p : ill,forms,ports ; 25cm
Bibliography: p559-578. — Includes index
ISBN 0-205-07217-8 (cased) : Unpriced
ISBN 0-205-07729-3 (International ed.) : £8.95
B81-11291

Werther, William B.. Personnel management and human resources / William B. Werther, Jr., Keith Davis. — New York ; London : McGraw-Hill, c1981. — xx,508p : ill,facsims,forms ; 24cm
Includes index
ISBN 0-07-069436-2 : £12.75 B81-24560

58.3′01 — Personnel turnover. Management aspects

Rothwell, Sheila. Labour turnover : its costs, causes and control / Sheila Rothwell. — Farnborough : Gower for the Henley Centre for Employment Policy Studies, c1980. — xiii,95p : ill ; 30cm
Bibliography: p73
ISBN 0-566-03019-5 (pbk) : £25.00 B81-07520

58.3′02 — Great Britain. Buildings. Planned maintenance — *Manuals*

Planning building maintenance : a guide for practitioners / prepared by the Building Division of the Royal Institution of Chartered Surveyors. — London : Royal Institution of Chartered Surveyors, c1980. — [16]p : ill ; 30cm. — (Practice note / Building Surveyors Division of the Royal Institution of Chartered Surveyors, ISSN 0143-3342 ; n.4)
Cover title. — Ill on inside cover
Unpriced (pbk) B81-11558

8.3′02 — Management. Supervision

Eckles, Robert W.. Supervisory management / Robert W. Eckles, Ronald L. Carmichael, Bernard R. Sarchet. — 2nd ed. — New York ; Chichester : Wiley, c1981. — xiv,524p : ill,forms ; 25cm. — (Wiley series in management)
Previous ed.: 1975. — Includes index
ISBN 0-471-05947-1 : £14.50 B81-17243

Evans, David, *1947-*. Supervisory management : principles and practice / David Evans. — London : Holt, Rinehart and Winston, c1981. — xii,580p ; 25cm. — (Holt business texts)
Includes index
ISBN 0-03-910309-9 (pbk) : £6.50 : CIP rev.
B81-03811

8.3′02 — Management. Supervision — *Manuals*

Halloran, Jack. Supervision : the art of management / Jack Halloran. — Englewood Cliffs ; London : Prentice-Hall, c1981. — xi,531p : ill,forms ; 25cm
Includes bibliographies and index
ISBN 0-13-876276-7 : £11.65 B81-16523

Hancox, David. The supervisor′s pocket guide / by David Hancox. — London : Industrial Society, 1981. — iv,32p ; 20cm
Text on inside cover
ISBN 0-85290-206-9 (pbk) : £1.50 B81-29365

Weiss, W. H.. Supervisor′s standard reference handbook / W.H. Weiss. — Englewood Cliffs ; London : Prentice-Hill, c1980. — 256p ; 26cm
Includes index
ISBN 0-13-877142-1 : £12.20 B81-02945

8.3′02 — Personnel management. Supervision

Bittel, Lester R.. Essentials of supervisory management / Lester R. Bittel. — New York ; London : Gregg Division, McGraw-Hill, c1981. — viii,280p : ill ; 26cm
Includes index
ISBN 0-07-005571-8 (spiral) : £8.95
B81-10365

658.3′02′0941 — Great Britain. Industries. Management. Supervision — *Manuals*

Corfield, Tony. The supervisor and the organised worker / Tony Corfield. — Lichfield (22 Bore St., Lichfield, Staffordshire WS13 6LP) : Institute of Supervisory Management, [1981?]. — vii,193p : ill ; 21cm. — (The Supervisors ′self-development′ series ; 4)
£3.00 (pbk) B81-34347

658.3′042 — United States. Old personnel. Employment. Management aspects

Jacobson, Beverly. Young programs for older workers : case studies in progressive personnel policies / Beverly Jacobson. — New York ; London : Van Nostrand Reinhold, c1980. — xvii,123p ; 24cm. — (Van Nostrand Reinhold/Work in America Institute series)
Includes index
ISBN 0-442-25405-9 : £12.70 B81-03941

658.3′044 — Great Britain. Industries. Skilled personnel. Management aspects

Skilled manpower and training policies : a management view / report of the BIM Labour Market Panel. — London : British Institute of Management, [c1981]. — v,42p : ill ; 30cm
ISBN 0-85946-117-3 (pbk) : Unpriced
B81-33143

658.3′045 — Great Britain. Business firms. Skilled personnel. Organisation — *Case studies*

Miller, W. H.. Building a skilled workforce : a case study of employment and training practices in an oil platform construction yard / by W.H. Miller. — Edinburgh (2-3 Queen St., Edinburgh) : MSC Office for Scotland, 1981. — 45p ; 30cm
Unpriced (pbk) B81-39284

658.3′06 — Job design

Savall, Henri. Work and people : an economic evaluation of job-enrichment / by Henri Savall ; translated from the French by M.A. Woodhall. — Oxford : Clarendon, 1981. xxi,216p : ill ; 24cm
Translation of: Enrichir le travail humain dans les entreprises et les organisations. 2e éd. — Bibliography: p191-216. - Includes index
ISBN 0-19-874093-x : £15.00 B81-17774

658.3′06 — Job evaluation

Elizur, Dov. Job evaluation : a systematic approach / Dov Elizur. — Farnborough, Hants. : Gower, c1980. — xi,165p : ill,forms ; 23cm
Bibliography: p160-165
ISBN 0-566-02120-x : £10.50 : CIP rev.
B80-17828

658.31 — Personnel. Interviewing — *Questions & answers*

Hackett, Penny. Interview skills training. — 2nd ed. — London : Institute of Personnel Management, Aug.1981. — [350]p. — (Management reports)
Previous ed.: 1978
ISBN 0-85292-299-x (spiral) : £25.00 : CIP entry B81-25118

658.3′11 — Personnel. Recruitment & selection — *Manuals*

Hackett, Penny. The Daily telegraph recruitment handbook. — 2nd ed. — London : Kogan Page, Nov.1981. — [244]p
Previous ed.: 1979
ISBN 0-85038-488-5 : £12.50 : CIP entry
B81-34961

Hackett, Penny. The Daily telegraph recruitment handbook. — 2nd ed. — London : New Opportunity Press, Dec.1981. — [224]p
Previous ed.: London : Kogan Page, 1979
ISBN 0-903578-95-6 : £8.50 : CIP entry
B81-40251

Plumbley, Philip. The person for the job : the complete guide to successful recruitment and selection / Philip Plumbley and Roger Williams. — 2nd, extensively rev. ed. — London : Kogan Page, 1981. — 160p ; 23cm
Previous ed.: London : British Broadcasting Corporation, 1972. — Bibliography: p158-160
ISBN 0-85038-448-6 : £7.95 : CIP rev.
B81-20599

658.3′1124′071142 — England. Housing associations. Personnel. Professional education. Curriculum subjects: Interviewing

Improving housing interviews / Housing Training Project. — London ([City University, St John St., EC1V 4PB]) : Housing Research Group, c1980. — 70p : forms ; 21cm. — (Guide to housing training ; no.3)
Cover title. — Bibliography: p68-70
ISBN 0-907255-02-7 (pbk) : Unpriced
Primary classification 658.3′1124′071142
B81-10830

658.3′1124′071142 — England. Local authorities. Housing departments. Personnel. Professional education. Curriculum subjects: Interviewing

Improving housing interviews / Housing Training Project. — London ([City University, St John St., EC1V 4PB]) : Housing Research Group, c1980. — 70p : forms ; 21cm. — (Guide to housing training ; no.3)
Cover title. — Bibliography: p68-70
ISBN 0-907255-02-7 (pbk) : Unpriced
Also classified at 658.3′1124′071142
B81-10830

658.3′122 — Great Britain. Women personnel. Maternity schemes. Management

Guide to maternity arrangements. — London (140 Gt. Portland St., W1) : Incomes Data Services, 1981. — 90p : forms ; 25cm
Bibliography: p87-88. — Includes index
Unpriced (pbk) B81-38124

658.3′124 — Organisations. Personnel. Training — *Manuals*

Robinson, Kenneth R.. A handbook of training management. — London : Kogan Page, Dec.1981. — [256]p
ISBN 0-85038-527-x : £13.50 : CIP entry
B81-38851

658.3′124′0321 — Personnel. Training — *Encyclopaedias*

Glossary of training terms. — 3rd ed. / Training Services, Manpower Services Commission. — London : H.M.S.O., 1981. — 93p ; 21cm
Previous ed.: by Department of Employment. 1971
ISBN 0-11-888511-1 (pbk) : £4.50 B81-37798

658.3′1244 — United States. Personnel. Training. Curriculum subjects: Industrial health & industrial safety

ReVelle, Jack B.. Safety training methods / Jack B. Re Velle. — New York ; Chichester : Wiley, c1980. — xii,248p : ill ; 24cm
Includes index
ISBN 0-471-07761-5 : Unpriced B81-08445

658.3′125 — Organisations. Personnel. Control. Role of performance appraisal

Stewart, Valerie. Managing the poor performer. — Farnborough : Gower, Nov.1981. — [250]p
ISBN 0-566-02248-6 : £12.50 : CIP entry
B81-32017

658.3′125 — Personnel. Performance. Appraisal — *Manuals*

Olson, Richard Fischer. Performance appraisal : a guide to greater productivity / Richard Fischer Olsen. — New York ; Chichester : Wiley, c1981. — xi,191p : ill ; 26cm
Bibliography: p185-186. — Includes index
ISBN 0-471-09134-0 (pbk) : £5.95 B81-37112

658.3′134 — Great Britain. Personnel. Redundancy. Personal adjustment — *Manuals*

Kemp, Fred. Coping with redundancy. — London : Kogan Page, Nov.1981. — [250]p
ISBN 0-85038-526-1 : £7.95 : CIP entry
B81-33639

Kemp, Fred. Focus on redundancy / Fred Kemp, Bernard Buttle & Derek Kemp. — London : Kogan Page, 1980. — 260p : ill ; 22cm
Bibliography: p255-256. — Includes index
ISBN 0-85038-374-9 (cased) : £6.95 : CIP rev.
ISBN 0-85038-375-7 (pbk) : £3.95 B80-24071

658.3′134 — Great Britain. Professional personnel. Redundancy — *Practical information*

Redundancy : guidance for professional people. — London : Royal Society of Chemistry, c1981. — 17p ; 21cm
Bibliography: p15
£1.00 (free to members) (pbk) B81-23166

658.3′134′0973 — United States. Companies. Personnel. Redundancy. Policies of companies

Cross, Michael. U.S. corporate personnel reduction policies. — Aldershot : Gower, Dec.1981. — [142]p
ISBN 0-566-00501-8 : £11.50 : CIP entry
B81-31609

658.3′14 — Industries. Management. Effectiveness. Improvement — *Conference proceedings*

Toward managerial effectiveness : applied research perspectives on the managerial task / edited by John Machin, Rosemary Stewart, Colin Hales. — Farnborough, Hants. : Gower, c1981. — ix,160p : ill,1form ; 23cm
Conference papers. — Includes bibliographies
ISBN 0-566-00470-4 : Unpriced : CIP rev.
B81-06077

658.3′14 — Industries. Productivity. Improvement. Applications of psychology

Psychology and industrial productivity : a reader / edited by Michael M. Gruneberg and David J. Oborne. — London : Macmillan, 1981. — xvi,340p : ill ; 30cm
Includes bibliographies and index
ISBN 0-333-27074-6 : £25.00 B81-40514

658.3′14 — Personnel. Absenteeism. Management aspects

Taylor, P. J. (Peter John), *1940-*. Absenteeism : causes and control. — 3rd rev. ed. — London : Industrial Society, 1978 (1980 [printing]). — 33p ; 21cm. — (Notes for managers ; no.15)
Author: P.J. Taylor. — Previous ed.: 1973. — Text on cover
ISBN 0-85290-169-0 (pbk) : Unpriced
B81-29927

658.3′1422 — Ireland *(Republic)*. Arts graduates. Employment. Job satisfaction

Scholefield, Derek Arthur. Arts graduates : five years on : career development and personal satisfaction / report prepared by Derek Arthur Scholefield. — Dublin (21 Fitzwilliam Sq., Dublin 2) : Higher Education Authority, 1980. — 22p : 1form ; 24cm
ISBN 0-904556-12-3 (pbk) : £0.50
Primary classification 331.11′423 B81-19620

658.3′1422 — Job satisfaction

Hankin, Barclay. Managing job satisfaction. — London (23 Queens Gate, S.W.7) : Hillbex Press, Dec.1981. — [100]p
ISBN 0-9507838-0-3 (pbk) : £3.00 : CIP entry
B81-35020

658.3′1423 — Job enrichment

Myers, M. Scott. Every employee a manager / M. Scott Myers. — 2nd ed. — New York ; London : McGraw-Hill, c1981. — xii,285p : ill ; 21cm
Previous ed.: 1970. — Includes index
ISBN 0-07-044269-x : £11.95 B81-27526

658.3′1423 — Job redesign

Autonomy and control at the workplace. — London : Croom Helm, Dec.1981. — [240]p
ISBN 0-7099-0410-x : £13.95 : CIP entry
B81-31441

658.3′145 — Business firms. Personnel. Interpersonal relationships. Communication - *Case studies - For business studies*

Jones, A. T.. The Aztec file. — Cheltenham : Thornes, Aug.1981. — [80]p
ISBN 0-85950-499-9 (pbk) : £2.50 : CIP entry
B81-16904

658.3′15 — Great Britain. Companies. Personnel. Disclosure of company information: Disclosure by employers

Communication with people at work. — London : Confederation of British Industry, 1977. — 32 : ill ; 21cm
Text on inside cover
£1.00 (pbk) B81-12658

658.3′15 — Great Britain. Personnel. Disclosure of financial information: Disclosure by employers. Non-book materials

Hussey, Roger. You see what I mean? : audio-visual reporting to employees / [Roger Hussey]. — [London] ([3] London Wall Buildings, EC2M 5PH]) : Touche Ross, c1980. — 27p : col.ill,ports(some col.) ; 30cm
Cover title
Unpriced (pbk) B81-10719

658.3′15′0722 — Great Britain. Industrial relations. Management aspects — *Case studies*

Tyes, S.. Case studies in industrial relations / S. Tyes. — London (Duncan House, High St., E15 2JB) : Anglian Regional Management Centre, c1981. — 55p : ill ; 30cm. — (The Anglian Regional Management Centre case study series)
Unpriced (pbk) B81-26535

658.3′15′0941 — Great Britain. Industrial relations. Management

Managerial roles in industrial relations : towards a definitive survey of research and formulation of models / edited by Michael Poole and Roger Mansfield. — Farnborough, Hants. : Gower, c1980. — xii,162p ; 23cm
Bibliography: p142-153. - Includes index
ISBN 0-566-00377-5 : £9.50 : CIP rev.
B80-08852

658.3′152 — Industries. Management. Participation of personnel

The Political economy of co-operation and participation : a third sector / edited by Alasdair Clayre. — Oxford : Oxford University Press, 1980. — viii,212p ; 23cm
Includes bibliographies and index
ISBN 0-19-877137-1 (cased) : £10.00 : CIP rev.
ISBN 0-19-877138-x (pbk) : unpriced
B80-11080

658.3′152′094 — Western Europe. Companies. Management. Participation of personnel, *to 1980*

Thimm, Alfred. The false promise of codetermination : the changing nature of European workers′ participation / Alfred L. Thimm. — Lexington, Mass. : Lexington Books, c1980 ; [Aldershot] : Gower [distributor], 1981. — xiv,301p : ill ; 24cm
Includes index
ISBN 0-669-04108-4 : £16.50 B81-33136

658.3′152′0941 — Great Britain. Industries. Management. Participation of personnel

Bate, Paul. Exploring participation / Paul Bate and Lain Mangham. — Chichester : Wiley, c1981. — xii,290p : ill ; 24cm
Bibliography: p275-283. — Includes index
ISBN 0-471-27921-8 : £11.95 : CIP rev.
B81-19176

658.3′152′0941 — Great Britain. Industries. Management. Participation of personnel — *Case studies*

Marchington, Mick. Responses to participation at work : a study of the attitudes and behaviour of employees, shop stewards and managers in a manufacturing company / Mick Marchington. — Farnborough, Hants. : Gower, c1980. — xii,213p : 1form ; 23cm
Bibliography: p205-213
ISBN 0-566-02148-x : £10.50 : CIP rev.
B80-05483

658.3′152′0941 — Great Britain. Organisations. Management. Participation of personnel

Practical participation and involvement. — London : Institute of Personnel Management. — 209p : ill ; 29cm
Bibliography: p205-209
ISBN 0-85292-288-4 (pbk) : Unpriced
B81-23977

658.3′152′09411 — Scotland. Industries & trades. Management. Participation of personnel

Cressey, P.. Employee participation in Scottish industry and commerce : a survey of attitudes and practices / P. Cressey, J. McInnes with the direction of J.E.T. Eldridge. — [Glasgow] : Centre for Research in Industrial Democracy and Participation, University of Glasgow, 1980. — 101,v p : ill,1map ; 30cm
£2.00 (pbk) B81-04905

658.3′152′0973 — United States. Companies. Management. Participation of personnel

Witte, John F.. Democracy, authority, and alienation in work : workers′ participation in an American corporation / John F. Witte. — Chicago ; London : University of Chicago Press, 1980. — xii,216p : ill ; 24cm
Bibliography: p207-211. - Includes index
ISBN 0-226-90420-2 : £15.00 B81-1367

658.3′152′0973 — United States. Industries. Management. Control by personnel, *to 1978*

Montgomery, David. Workers′ control in America : studies in the history of work, technology, and labor struggles / David Montgomery. — Cambridge : Cambridge University Press, 1979 (1980 [printing]). — x,189p ; 23cm
Bibliography: p181-189
ISBN 0-521-28006-0 (pbk) : £3.95 B81-0354

658.3′152′0985 — Industries. Management. Participation of personnel — *Study regions: Per*

Stephens, Evelyne Huber. The politics of workers′ participation : the Peruvian approach in comparative perspective / Evelyne Huber Stephens. — New York ; Academic Press, c1980. — xvi,293p : 1ill ; 24cm. — (Studies in social discontinuity)
Bibliography: p269-275. — Includes index
ISBN 0-12-666250-9 : £16.00 B81-0309

658.3′153 — Multinational companies. Industrial relations. Management. Decision making. Role o trade unions — *Inquiry reports*

Brooks, Dennis. Industrial relations and employment in multinational companies : a survey of trade union views / by Dennis Brooks with W.R. Hawes and N. Banerji. — [London] : Department of Employment, Socia Science Branch, 1980. — v,55p ; 30cm
Unpriced (pbk) B81-222

658.3′2′0941 — Great Britain. Industries. Personnel. Remuneration. Management aspects

Handbook of salary and wage systems. — 2nd e — Farnborough : Gower, Oct.1981. — [430]p
Previous ed.: 1975
ISBN 0-566-02261-3 : £17.50 : CIP entry
B81-2582

658.3′2′0941 — Great Britain. Personnel. Remuneration. Management aspects

Armstrong, Michael, *1928-*. A handbook of sala administration / Michael Armstrong & Helen Murlis. — London : Kogan Page, 1980. — 246p : ill,2facsim,forms ; 23cm
Includes index
ISBN 0-85038-369-2 : £12.50 B81-069

658.3′225 — Great Britain. Profit sharing — *Manuals — For management*

Guide to profit sharing / [Incomes Data Service Ltd]. — London (140 Great Portland St., W. : IDS, 1981. — 91p ; 25cm
Includes index
£5.00 (pbk) B81-323

658.3′225 — Salesmen. Incentive schemes. Design

Barry, John W.. Effective sales incentive compensation / John W. Barry, Porter Henry — New York ; London : McGraw-Hill, c198 — viii,213p : ill,forms ; 21cm
Includes index
ISBN 0-07-003860-0 : £12.50 B81-100

658.3′254 — Great Britain. Company cars. Provision. Management aspects

Donkin, Norman. Company car policy guide / b Norman Donkin and Tony Vernon-Harcourt. — Saffron Walden (Debden Green, Saffron Walden, Essex CB11 3LX) : Monks, 1981. — 38p,[7]p ; 30cm
£21.00 (spiral) B81-271

658.3′82 — Industrial health & industrial safety. Management aspects

Chissick, Seymour S.Occupational health and safety management / edited by S.S. Chissick, R. Derricott. — Chichester : Wiley, c1981. — xv,705p : ill(some col.),forms,ports ; 24cm. — (Properties of materials safety and environmental factors)
Includes bibliographies and index
ISBN 0-471-27646-4 : £35.00 : CIP rev.
B80-037

658.3'82'0941 — Great Britain. Industrial health. Management aspects

Coates, T.. The manager's responsibility for health / T. Coates. — London : Industrial Society, 1979, c1978. — 33p ; 21cm. — (Notes for managers ; no.30)
Bibliography: p29
ISBN 0-85290-174-7 (pbk) : £1.25 B81-07896

658.3'822 — Great Britain. Personnel. Alcoholism. Treatment. Policies

Great Britain. *Health and Safety Executive*. The problem drinker at work. — London : HMSO, May 1981. — [15]p
ISBN 0-11-883428-2 (pbk) : £1.50 : CIP entry B81-13864

658.3'822 — Personnel. Alcoholism. Social aspects

Alcohol problems in employment / edited by Brian D. Hore and Martin A. Plant. — London : Croom Helm in association with the Alcohol Education Centre, c1981. — 208p : ill ; 23cm
Bibliography: p196-205. - Includes index
ISBN 0-7099-1202-1 : £14.95 B81-06937

658.3'822 — Scotland. Personnel. Alcoholism

Alcohol & employment : (a problem and an opportunity) : report of the Working Party on Alcohol in Employment appointed by the Professional/General Services Committee and the Scottish Council on Alcoholism. — [Edinburgh] ([49 York Place, Edinburgh EH1 3JD]) : The Council, 1981. — 64p : 1map ; 22cm
Cover title. — Bibliography: p33
Unpriced (pbk) B81-18764

658.3'822 — United States. Industries. Personnel. Alcoholism

Brisolara, Ashton. The alcoholic employee : a handbook of useful guidelines / by Ashton Brisolara. — New York ; London : Human Sciences Press, c1979. — 168p : ill ; 21cm. — (Drug abuse and alcoholism series)
Includes index
ISBN 0-87705-327-8 : £16.25 B81-39451

658.3'822'097 — North America. Personnel: Alcoholics & drug addicts. Treatment

Shain, Martin. Employee-assistance programs : philosophy, theory, and practice / Martin Shain, Judith Groeneveld. — [Lexington, Mass.] : Lexington Books ; [Farnborough, Hants.] : Gower [distributor], 1980. — xvi,236p ; 24cm
Bibliography: p221-227. - Includes index
ISBN 0-669-02737-5 : £15.00 B81-08582

658.4 — EXECUTIVE MANAGEMENT

658.4 — Business firms. Management. Techniques

Glueck, William F.. Business policy and strategic management / William F. Glueck. — 3rd ed. — New York ; London : McGraw-Hill, 1980. — xvii,891p : ill,ports ; 25cm. — (McGraw-Hill series in management)
Previous ed.: published as Business policy. 1976. — Ill on lining papers. — Includes index
ISBN 0-07-023519-8 : £11.95 B81-01679

Kuntz, Walter N.. Modern corporate management : new approaches to financial control, operations, customer developments, and equity sources / Walter N. Kuntz. — Englewood Cliffs ; London : Prentice-Hall, c1978. — 226p : ill,forms,1port ; 29cm
Includes index
ISBN 0-13-589754-8 : £21.40 B81-25167

658.4 — Executive management. Techniques — *Manuals*

Arnold, John D.. Shooting the executive rapids : the first crucial year of a new assignment / John D. Arnold. — New York ; London : McGraw-Hill, c1981. — xv,268p : ill ; 24cm
Includes index
ISBN 0-07-002312-3 : £12.95 B81-23447

658.4 — Management. Leadership — *Manuals*

Siu, R. G. H.. The master manager / R.G.H. Siu. — New York ; Chichester : Wiley, c1980. — x,341p : ill ; 24cm
Includes index
ISBN 0-471-07961-8 : £9.50 B81-00182

658.4 — Management. Techniques

Belasco, James A.. Management today / James A. Belasco, David R. Hampton, Karl F. Price. — 2nd ed. — New York ; Chichester : Wiley, c1981. — xii,460p : ill,forms ; 24cm. — (Wiley series in management, ISSN 0271-6046)
Previous ed.: 1975. — Includes index
ISBN 0-471-08579-0 (pbk) : £10.95 B81-24938

Drucker, Peter F.. Managing in turbulent times / Peter F. Drucker. — London : Pan in association with Heinemann, 1981, c1980. — 237p ; 18cm
Originally published: London : Heinemann, 1980. — Includes index
ISBN 0-330-26347-1 (pbk) : £1.95 B81-22897

Eldin, Hamed Kamal. Management science applications : computing and systems analysis / Hamed Kamal Eldin with Hooshang M. Beheshti. — New York ; Oxford : North Holland, c1981. — xv,316p : ill ; 24cm
Includes bibliographies and index
ISBN 0-444-00422-x : £16.77 B81-36759

Hampton, David R.. Contemporary management / David R. Hampton. — 2nd ed. — New York ; London : McGraw-Hill, c1981. — xx,570p : ill(some col.),ports ; 24cm. — (McGraw Hill series in management)
Previous ed.: 1977. — Includes index
ISBN 0-07-025935-6 : £13.95 B81-23450

Management skills / edited by W.T. Singleton. — Lancaster : MTP, 1981. — xvi,303p : ill,ports ; 24cm. — (The Study of real skills ; v.3)
Includes bibliographies and index
ISBN 0-85200-091-x : £14.95 B81-33076

Massie, Joseph L.. Managing : a contemporary introduction / Joseph L. Massie, John Douglas. — 3rd ed. — Englewood Cliffs ; London : Prentice-Hall, c1981. — xiv,545p : col.ill ; 24cm
Previous ed.: 1977. — Includes index
ISBN 0-13-550327-2 : £11.65 B81-12518

Pascarella, Perry. Industry week's guide to tomorrow's executive : humanagement in the future corporation / Perry Pascarella ; foreword by Stanley J. Modic. — New York ; London : Van Nostrand Reinhold, c1981. — xiii,199p ; 24cm
Bibliography: p191-196. — Includes index
ISBN 0-442-23122-9 : £12.70 B81-05706

Patten, Frederick. Who's the manager? / by Frederick Patten. — [Enfield] ([35 Old Park View, Enfield, EN2 7EG]) : [F. Patten Associates], [c1981]. — 142p : ill,forms ; 21cm. — (Achieving manager series ; 1)
Bibliography: p142
£2.75 (pbk) B81-21662

658.4 — Management. Techniques — *Manuals*

Contemporary readings in organizational behavior. — 3rd ed. / [compiled by] Fred Luthans, Kenneth R. Thompson. — New York ; London : McGraw-Hill, c1981. — xviii,501p : ill ; 24cm. — (McGraw-Hill series in management)
Previous ed.: compiled by Fred Luthans. 1977. — Includes bibliographies
ISBN 0-07-039148-3 (pbk) : £9.25 B81-19673

Heller, Robert, *1932-*. The business of winning / by Robert Heller. — London : Sidgwick & Jackson, 1980 (1981 [printing]). — 227p ; 22cm
Includes index
ISBN 0-283-98787-1 (pbk) : £2.95 B81-23178

Luthans, Fred. Organizational behavior / Fred Luthans. — 3rd ed. — New York ; London : McGraw-Hill, c1981. — xxii,666,I1-I14p : ill ; 25cm. — (McGraw-Hill series in management)
Previous ed.: 1977. — Includes index
ISBN 0-07-039144-0 : £13.95 B81-27186

Luthans, Fred. Organizational behavior / Fred Luthans. — 3rd ed., International student ed.. — Auckland ; London : McGraw-Hill, 1981. — xxii,666p : ill ; cm
Previous ed.: 1977. — Includes index
ISBN 0-07-066396-3 (pbk) : £7.50 B81-30645

Mitton, Daryl G.. Managerial clout : take action, get results, influence people & events / Daryl G. Mitton & Betty Lilligren-Mitton. — Englewood Cliffs ; London : Prentice-Hall, c1980. — viii,232p : ill ; 24cm. — (A Spectrum book)
Includes index
ISBN 0-13-549816-3 (cased) : £10.45
ISBN 0-13-549808-2 (pbk) : £5.15 B81-00181

658.4 — Organisations. Management

Chung, Kae H.. Organizational behavior : developing managerial skills / Kae H. Chung, Leon C. Megginson. — New York ; London : Harper & Row, c1981. — xv,560p : ill ; 25cm
Includes index
ISBN 0-06-041299-2 : £12.25 B81-23671

Foy, Nancy. The yin and yang of organizations : a scintillating guide to the best in current management thinking / by Nancy Foy. — London (39 Great Russell St., WC1B 3PH) : Grant McIntyre, 1981, c1980. — 277p : ill ; 23cm
Originally published: New York : Morrow, 1980. — Bibliography: p264-268. - Includes index
ISBN 0-86216-038-3 : £7.95 B81-10189

Hicks, Herbert G.. Management. — 4th ed. / Herbert G. Hicks, C. Ray Gullett. — New York ; London : McGraw-Hill, c1981. — xx,668p : col.ill ; 25cm. — (McGraw-Hill series in management)
Previous ed.: published as The management of organizations. 1977. — Includes bibliographies and index
ISBN 0-07-028773-2 : £13.95
ISBN 0-07-066328-9 (International student ed.) : £6.95 B81-23957

658.4 — Organisations. Management *expounded by* man. Nervous system

Beer, Stafford. Brain of the firm : the managerial cybernetics of organization : companion volume to the heart of enterprise / Stafford Beer. — 2nd ed. — Chichester : Wiley, c1981. — xiii,417p : ill ; 24cm
Previous ed.: London : Allen Lane, 1972. — Bibliography: p405-410. - Includes index
ISBN 0-471-27687-1 : £11.50 B81-10605

658.4'001'9 — Organisations. Management — *Psychoanalytical perspectives*

Kets de Vries, Manfred F. R.. Organizational paradoxes : clinical approachs to management / Manfred F.R. Kets de Vries. — London : Tavistock, 1980. — x,214p : ill ; 22cm
Includes index
ISBN 0-422-77270-4 (cased) : £6.50 : CIP rev.
ISBN 0-422-77280-1 (pbk) : £3.25 B80-11530

658.4'00207 — Management. Theories — *Humour*

Martin, Thomas L.. Malice in blunderland / by Thomas L. Martin, Jr.. — New York ; London : McGraw-Hill, c1973 (1980 [printing]). — 143p ; 21cm
Includes index
ISBN 0-07-040634-0 (pbk) : £4.50 B81-39818

658.4'002462 — Management. Techniques — *For engineering*

Management and the technical professional / edited by Charles H. Vervalin. — Houston ; London : Gulf, c1981. — viii,261p : ill,forms ; 28cm
Includes bibliographies
ISBN 0-87201-480-0 (pbk) : Unpriced B81-26627

658.4'0092'4 — United States. Industries. Management. Taylor, Frederick W. — *Biographies*

Nelson, Daniel. Frederick W. Taylor and the rise of scientific management / Daniel Nelson. — Madison ; London : University of Wisconsin Press, 1980. — xii,259p : 1port ; 24cm
Bibliography: p245-246. — Includes index
ISBN 0-299-08160-5 : £11.70 B81-02409

658.4'00973 — United States. Management. Techniques
Musselman, Vernon A.. Introduction to modern business : issues and environment / Vernon A. Musselman, Eugene H. Hughes. — 8th ed. / in collaboration with John H. Jackson. — Englewood Cliffs ; London : Prentice-Hall, c1981. — xiv,638p : col.ill,forms,ports ; 26cm
Previous ed.: 1977. — Bibliography: p610-613. — Includes index
ISBN 0-13-488072-2 : £12.30 B81-17180

658.4'01 — Business firms. Planning
Shaw, W. C.. How to do a company plan and put it into action. — London : Business Books, Oct.1981. — [224]p
ISBN 0-09-145980-x : £12.50 : CIP entry B81-27370

658.4'012 — Corporate planning
Ackoff, Russell L.. Creating the corporate future : plan or be planned for / Russell L. Ackoff. — New York ; Chichester : Wiley, c1981. — xi,297p : ill ; 24cm
Bibliography: p287-290. — Includes index
ISBN 0-471-09009-3 : £10.50 B81-23249

Chandler, John. Techniques of scenario planning. — Maidenhead : McGraw-Hill, Oct.1981. — [192]p
ISBN 0-07-084570-0 : £13.95 : CIP entry B81-27378

Hussey, D. E.. Corporate planning. — 2nd ed. — Oxford : Pergamon, July 1981. — [468]p
Previous ed.: 1974
ISBN 0-08-024073-9 (cased) : £19.50 : CIP entry
ISBN 0-08-025839-5 (pbk) : £9.50 B81-13451

The **Realities** of planning. — Oxford : Pergamon, Sept.1981. — [224]p
ISBN 0-08-022226-9 : £15.00 : CIP entry B81-23745

Reinharth, Leon. The practice of planning : strategic, administrative and operational / Leon Reinharth, H. Jack Shapiro, Ernest A. Kallman. — New York ; London : Van Nostrand Reinhold, c1981. — xiv,385p : ill ; 24cm
Includes bibliographies and index
ISBN 0-442-21917-2 : £14.95 B81-17189

658.4'012 — Corporate planning. Applications of dynamical systems theory
Lyneis, James M.. Corporate planning and policy design : a system dynamics approach / James M. Lyneis. — Cambridge, Mass. ; London : MIT Press, c1980. — xv,519p : ill ; 24cm. — (MIT Press/Wright-Allen series in system dynamics)
Includes bibliographies and index
ISBN 0-262-12083-6 : £18.60 B81-30773

658.4'012 — Multinational companies. Management. Long-range planning
Channon, Derek F.. Process factors in multinational strategic planning / D.F. Channon. — Manchester (Booth Street West, Manchester M15 6PB) : Centre for Business Research in association with Manchester Business School, University of Manchester, c1980. — 93p : ill ; 30cm. — (Research report / Centre for Business Research, ISSN 0306-5227)
Unpriced (spiral) B81-14291

658.4'012 — Organisations. Long-range planning
Levin, Richard I.. The executive's illustrated primer of long-range planning / Dick Levin with lots of help from Ginger Travis and John Branch. — Englewood Cliffs ; London : Prentice-Hall, c1981. — ix,214p : ill ; 24cm
Includes index
ISBN 0-13-294140-6 : £7.75 B81-16515

658.4'012 — Organisations. Management. Long-range planning
Tourangeau, Kevin W.. Strategy management : how to plan, execute, and control strategic plans for your business / Kevin W. Tourangeau. — New York ; London : McGraw-Hill, c1981. — viii,243p : ill,forms ; 24cm
Includes index
ISBN 0-07-065043-8 : £13.95 B81-10068

658.4'012'0722 — Northern Europe. Business firms. Management. Policies. Formulation — *Case studies*
McLellan, Ron. Business policy formulation : text & process studies / Ron McLellan, Graham Kelly. — London (Duncan House, High St., E15 2JB) : Anglian Regional Management Centre, c1981. — 53p : ill ; 30cm. — (The Anglian Regional Management Centre case study series)
Bibliography: p52-53
Unpriced (pbk) B81-26532

658.4'012'0722 — Scandinavia. Business firms. Management. Policies. Formulation — *Case studies*
McLellan, Ron. Business policy case studies in Scandinavian companies / Ron McLellan. — London (Duncan House, High St., E15 2JB) : Anglian Regional Management Centre, c1981. — 65p : ill ; 30cm. — (The Anglian Regional Management Centre case study series)
Unpriced (pbk) B81-26533

658.4'012'0973 — United States. Business firms. Management. Policies. Formulation. Decision making — *Case studies*
Glueck, William F.. Business policy and strategic management / William F. Glueck. — 3rd ed. — Tokyo ; London : McGraw-Hill Kogakusha, c1980. — xvii,891p : ill,maps,ports ; 24cm. — (McGraw-Hill series in management)
Previous ed.: published as Business policy. 1976. — Includes index
ISBN 0-07-066299-1 (pbk) : £5.95 B81-05260

658.4'013 — Management. Control systems
Stout, Russell. Management or control? : the organizational challenge / Russell Stout, Jr. — Bloomington ; London : Indiana University Press, c1980. — xi,211p ; 22cm
Bibliography: p189-202. — Includes index
ISBN 0-253-12082-9 : £7.80 B81-01013

658.4'02 — Business firms. Development. Role of teams
Woodcock, Mike. Organisation development through teambuilding. — Farnborough, Hants. : Gower, Oct.1981. — [150]p
ISBN 0-566-02320-2 : £12.50 : CIP entry B81-28048

658.4'02 — Management. Teams
Belbin, R. M.. Management teams : why they succeed or fail / R. Meredith Belbin ; with a foreword by Anthony Jay. — London : Heinemann, 1981. — xii,179p : ill ; 23cm
Bibliography: p171-172. — Includes index
ISBN 0-434-90126-1 : £7.95 B81-37486

658.4'02 — United States. Industries. Management. Bureaucracy, *1860-1920* — *Marxist viewpoints*
Clawson, Dan. Bureaucracy and the labor process : the transformation of U.S. industry 1860-1920 / Dan Clawson. — New York ; London : Monthly Review Press, c1980. — 284p ; 21cm
Bibliography: p269-278. - Includes index
ISBN 0-85345-542-2 (cased) : £8.95
ISBN 0-85345-543-0 (pbk) : Unpriced B81-07026

658.4'03 — Business firms. Management. Decision making
Heller, Frank A.. Competence and power in managerial decision-making : a study of senior levels of organization in eight countries / Frank A. Heller, Bernhard Wilpert in collaboration with Peter Docherty ... [et al.]. — Chichester : Wiley, c1981. — xiv,242p : ill,forms ; 24cm
Bibliography: p220-231. - Includes index
ISBN 0-471-27837-8 : £13.60 B81-09753

658.4'03 — Business firms. Management. Decision making. Quantitative methods
Gallagher, Charles A.. Quantitative methods for business decisions / Charles A. Gallagher, Hugh J. Watson. — Auckland ; London : McGraw-Hill, c1980. — xvi,604p : ill ; 24cm
Includes bibliographies and index
ISBN 0-07-022751-9 (cased) : Unpriced
ISBN 0-07-066292-4 (pbk) : £7.95 B81-29591

Trueman, Richard E.. Quantitative methods for decision making in business / Richard E. Trueman. — Chicago ; London : Dryden, c1981. — 733p : ill ; 25cm
Bibliography: p731-733. - Includes index
ISBN 0-03-051356-1 : £13.95 B81-2309

658.4'03 — Companies. Management auditing
Sayle, Allan J.. Management audits : the assessment of quality management systems / Allan J. Sayle. — London : McGraw-Hill, c1981. — x,186p : ill,forms ; 24cm
Includes index
ISBN 0-07-084556-5 : £11.50 : CIP rev. B81-0264

658.4'03 — Large scale projects. Planning. Decision making
Schulman, Paul R.. Large-scale policy making / Paul R. Schulman. — New York ; Oxford : Elsevier, c1980. — xvi,146p : ill ; 24cm
Includes index
ISBN 0-444-99075-5 : £8.20 B81-0617

658.4'03 — Large scale projects. Planning. Decision making. Political aspects
Hall, Peter. Great planning disasters / Peter Hall. — Harmondsworth : Penguin, 1981, c1980. — x,308p : ill ; 21cm
Originally published: London : Weidenfeld & Nicolson, 1979. — Bibliography: p287-297. — Includes index
ISBN 0-14-081323-3 (pbk) : £4.50 B81-3791

658.4'03 — Management. Creative thought
Rawlinson, J. G.. Creative thinking and brainstorming / J. Geoffrey Rawlinson. — Farnborough : Gower, c1981. — xiv,129p : ill 22cm
Includes index
ISBN 0-566-02247-8 : £10.50 : CIP rev. B80-2998

Rawlinson, J. G.. Introduction to creative thinking and brainstorming / J.G. Rawlinson. — Rev. and updated ed. — London : British Institute of Management, c1981. — 55p : ill ; 21cm
Previous ed: published as Creative thinking & brainstorming. 1970. — Bibliography: p53-55
ISBN 0-85946-114-9 (pbk) : Unpriced B81-2924

658.4'03 — Management. Decision making
Prescott, Bryan D.. Effective decision-making : a self-development programme / Bryan D. Prescott. — Farnborough, Hants. : Gower, c1980. — ix,90p : ill ; 22cm
ISBN 0-566-02211-7 (pbk) : £7.50 B80-1015

Shirley, Robert C.. Strategy and policy formation : a multifunctional orientation / Robert C. Shirley, Michael H. Peters, Adel I. El-Ansary. — 2nd ed.. — New York ; Chichester : Wiley, c1981. — xvi,286p : ill ; 24cm. — (Wiley serie in management)
Previous ed.: 1976. — Includes index
ISBN 0-471-06510-2 (pbk) : £6.50 B81-0965

658.4'03 — Management. Problem solving
De Bono, Edward. Edward De Bono's atlas of management thinking. — London : Temple Smith, Sept.1981. — [224]p
ISBN 0-85117-213-x : £9.95 : CIP entry B81-2668

658.4'03 — Policies. Formulation. Problem solving
Mason, Richard O.. Challenging strategic planning assumptions : theory, cases and techniques / Richard O. Mason and Ian I. Mitroff. — New York ; Chichester : Wiley, c1981. — xii,324p : ill ; 24cm
Bibliography: p303-315. — Includes index
ISBN 0-471-08219-8 : £19.00 B81-3315

658.4'03 — Risks. Assessment
Dealing with risk : the planning, management and acceptability of technological risk / editor Richard F. Griffiths. — Manchester : Manchester University Press, c1981. — xxii,144p : ill,maps ; 23cm
Includes bibliographies and index
ISBN 0-7190-0819-0 : £1.50 B81-2076

658.4'03 — Risks. Management — *Manuals*
Bannister, J. E.. Practical risk management / by J.E. Bannister and P.A. Bawcutt. — London : Witherby, 1981. — xii,240p : ill ; 23cm
Includes index
ISBN 0-900886-22-6 : £12.50 B81-16491

658.4'03 — United States. Industries. Risks. Management
Williams, C. Arthur. Risk management and insurance / C. Arthur Williams, Jr., Richard M. Heins. — 4th ed. — New York ; London : McGraw-Hill, c1981. — xiii,721p : ill ; 25cm
Previous ed.: c1976. — Includes bibliographies and index
ISBN 0-07-070564-x : £15.75 B81-09939

658.4'03'019 — Management. Decision making. Psychological aspects — *For business studies*
Worrall, Norman. People and decisions / Norman Worrall. — London : Longman, 1980. — viii,254p : ill ; 24cm. — (Understanding business)
Includes index
ISBN 0-582-35540-0 (pbk) : £4.50 B81-05216

658.4'03'028 — Business firms. Management. Decision making. Techniques
Baker, Alan J.. Business decision making / Alan J. Baker. — London : Croom Helm, c1981. — 266p : ill ; 23cm
Bibliography: p252-258. - Includes index
ISBN 0-85664-871-x (cased) : £12.95
ISBN 0-85664-872-8 (pbk) : £6.95 B81-17847

658.4'03'02854 — Management. Decision making. Applications of digital computer systems
Bonczek, Robert H.. Foundations of decision support systems / Robert H. Bonczek, Clyde W. Holsapple, Andrew B. Whinston. — New York ; London : Academic Press, 1981. — xvii,393p : ill ; 24cm. — (Operations research and industrial engineering)
Includes bibliographies and index
ISBN 0-12-113050-9 : £19.60 B81-38868

658.4'03'0285424 — Business firms. Problem solving. Applications of digital computer systems. Programming languages: Fortran language — *Programmed instructions*
Honess, C. Brian. Structured business problem solving with FORTRAN / C. Brian Honess. — Boston [Mass.] ; London : Allyn and Bacon, c1981. — viii,244p : ill ; 28cm
Includes index
ISBN 0-205-07332-8 (pbk) : £1.00 B81-26202

658.4'03'0285424 — Business firms. Problem solving. Applications of digital computer systems. Programming languages: Fortran language — *Questions & answers*
Honess, C. Brian. Instructor's manual to accompany Structured business problem solving with FORTRAN / C. Brian Honess. — Boston [Mass.] ; London : Allyn and Bacon, c1981. — 85p : ill ; 24cm
ISBN 0-205-07333-6 (pbk) : Unpriced B81-26402

658.4'03'05 — Policies. Decision making — *Serials*
Policy studies review annual. — Vol.1 (1977)-. — Beverly Hills ; London : Sage, 1977-. — v. : ill ; 24cm
Description based on: Vol.4 (1980)
ISSN 0163-108x = Policy studies review annual : £22.00 B81-15546

Policy studies review annual. — Vol.2 (1978). — Beverly Hills ; London : Sage, c1978. — 751p
ISBN 0-8039-1100-9 : £22.00
ISSN 0163-108x B81-21950

658.4'03'072 — Organisations. Management. Decision making. Use of research
Rothman, Jack. Using research in organizations : a guide to successful application / Jack Rothman ; foreword by Ronald G. Havelock. — Beverly Hills ; London : Sage in cooperation with the National Institute of Social Work, London, and the Center for Research on Utilization of Scientific Knowledge, Institute of Social Research, University of Michigan, c1980. — 229p : ill,1form ; 22cm. — (Sage library of social research ; v.101)
Includes bibliographies and index
ISBN 0-8039-1442-3 (cased) : £11.25 B81-07014

658.4'03'0722 — United States. Industries. Management. Decision making — *Case studies*
Brewerton, F. J.. Instructor's resource manual to accompany Management decisions and organizational policy / Kenneth W. Olm ... [et al.], third edition / prepared by F.J. Brewerton. — Boston [Mass.] ; London : Allyn and Bacon, c1981. — ix,277p ; 24cm
Includes bibliographies
ISBN 0-205-07216-x (pbk) : £1.00 B81-26403

Management decisions and organizational policy. — 3rd ed., Kenneth W. Olm ... [et al.]. — Boston, Mass. ; London : Allyn and Bacon, c1981. — x,489p : ill ; 25cm
Previous ed.: / by Francis J. Bridges, Kenneth W. Olm and J. Allison Barnhill. 1977
ISBN 0-205-07215-1 (corrected) : Unpriced
ISBN 0-205-07217-8 B81-33388

658.4'03'076 — Management. Problem solving — *Questions & answers*
Farthing, Joni. Business mazes / Joni Farthing. — St. Albans : Hart-Davis Educational, 1981. — 80p ; 22cm
ISBN 0-247-13148-2 (pbk) : Unpriced B81-39475

658.4'032 — Management. Systems analysis
FitzGerald, Jerry. Fundamentals of systems analysis. — 2nd ed., Jerry FitzGerald, Ardra F. FitzGerald, Warren D. Stallings, Jr. — New York ; Chichester : Wiley, c1981. — xvii,593p : ill,forms ; 25cm
Previous ed.: / John M. FitzGerald, Ardra F. FitzGerald. 1973. — Bibliography: p489-491. - Includes index
ISBN 0-471-04968-9 : Unpriced B81-08521

Lanford, H. W.. System management : planning and control / H.W. Lanford. — Port Washington ; London : National University Publications : Kennikat, 1981. — xi,191p : ill ; 22cm
Bibliography: p184-187. — Includes index
ISBN 0-8046-9223-8 : £12.75 B81-25550

658.4'032 — Work study
Barnes, Ralph M.. Motion and time study : design and measurement of work / Ralph M. Barnes. — 7th ed. — New York ; Chichester : Wiley, c1980. — xi,689p : ill,forms ; 24cm
Previous ed.: 1968. — Bibliography: p661-677. — Includes index
ISBN 0-471-05905-6 : £12.00 B81-01014

658.4'032'0722 — Management. Systems analysis — *Case studies*
Krone, Robert M.. Systems analysis and policy sciences : theory and practice / Robert M. Krone. — New York ; Chichester : Wiley, c1980. — xxvii,216p : ill,1map ; 24cm
Includes bibliographies and index
ISBN 0-471-05864-5 : £11.75 B81-08336

658.4'033 — Management. Applications of optimal control theory
Sethi, Suresh P.. Optimal control theory : applications to management science / Suresh P. Sethi, Gerald P. Thompson. — Boston, Mass. ; London : Nijhoff, c1981. — xiv,481p : ill ; 24cm. — (International series in management science/operations research)
Bibliography: p451-464. — Includes index
ISBN 0-89838-061-8 : Unpriced B81-27089

658.4'033 — Management. Decision making. Mathematics. Fuzzy sets
Negoita, C. V.. Fuzzy systems / C.V. Negoita. — Tunbridge Wells : Abacus, 1981. — viii,111p : ill ; 24cm. — (Cybernetics and systems series ; 2)
Includes index
ISBN 0-85626-164-5 : Unpriced : CIP rev. B80-03237

658.4'033 — Management. Mathematical models
Cook, Thomas M.. Introduction to management science / Thomas M. Cook, Robert A. Russell. — 2nd ed. — Englewood Cliffs ; London : Prentice-Hall, c1981. — xviii,763p : ill,maps ; 25cm
Previous ed.: 1977. — Includes index
ISBN 0-13-486092-6 : Unpriced B81-33361

Dannenbring, David G.. Management science : an introduction / David G. Dannenbring, Martin K. Starr. — New York ; London : McGraw-Hall, c1981. — xviii,763p : ill,2ports ; 25cm. — (McGraw-Hill series in quantitative methods for management)
Text on inside covers. — Includes index
ISBN 0-07-015352-3 : £16.50 B81-26927

658.4'034 — Management. Applications of stochastic systems
Grassmann, Winfried K.. Stochastic systems for management / Winfried K. Grassmann. — London : Edward Arnold, c1981. — xii,358p : ill ; 24cm
Includes bibliographies and index
ISBN 0-7131-3437-2 : £15.00 B81-34994

658.4'034 — Management. Operations research
Wilkes, F. M.. Elements of operational research / F.M. Wilkes. — London : McGraw-Hill, c1980. — xv,343p : ill ; 24cm
Bibliography: p337. - Includes index
ISBN 0-07-084546-8 (cased) : £12.50 : CIP rev.
ISBN 0-07-084540-9 (pbk) : £7.95 B80-18842

658.4'034 — Organisation & methods
Anderson, R. G.. Organisation and methods / R.G. Anderson. — 2nd ed. — Plymouth : Macdonald and Evans, 1980. — xii,370p : ill,forms ; 19cm. — (The M & E handbook series)
Previous ed.: 1973. — Includes index
ISBN 0-7121-1536-6 (pbk) : £3.50 B81-00183

658.4'034'0724 — Management. Operations research. Mathematical models
Buffa, Elwood S.. Management science/operations research : model formulation and solution methods / Elwood S. Buffa, James S. Dyer. — 2nd ed. — New York ; Chichester : Wiley, c1981. — xi,718p : ill(some col.) ; 24cm
Previous ed.: 1977. — Includes bibliographies and index
ISBN 0-471-05851-3 : £19.45 B81-21085

Dunn, Robert A.. Management science : a practical approach to decision making / Robert A. Dunn, Kenneth D. Ramsing. — New York : Macmillan ; London : Collier Macmillan, c1981. — x,527 : ill ; 27cm
Includes index
ISBN 0-02-330510-x : £13.50 B81-21446

Krajewski, Lee J.. Management science : quantitative methods in context / Lee J. Krajewski, Howard E. Thompson. — New York ; Chichester : Wiley, c1981. — xx,544p : ill,1map ; 25cm. — (The Wiley series in management)
Includes index
ISBN 0-471-06109-3 : £12.25 B81-10541

658.4'0353 — Management. Simulation games
Elgood, Chris. Handbook of management games. — 2nd ed. — Farnborough : Gower, Oct.1981. — [220]p
Previous ed.: Epping : Gower, 1976
ISBN 0-566-02229-x : £12.50 : CIP entry B81-28847

658.4'0383 — Systems design. Security aspects
Squires, T.. Security in systems design. — Manchester : NCC Publications, Apr.1981. — [54]p
ISBN 0-85012-304-6 (pbk) : CIP entry B81-12393

658.4'0388 — Europe & United States. Management. Information systems: Machine-readable files
Davis, B.. Data base in perspective / Brian Davis. — Manchester : NCC Publications, 1980. — 110p ; 22cm
ISBN 0-85012-219-8 (pbk) : £10.00 B81-01015

658.4'0388 — Management. Information systems
Bentley, Trevor J.. Making information systems work / Trevor J. Bentley. — London : Macmillan, 1981. — x,229p : ill,forms ; 23cm
Includes index
ISBN 0-333-24134-7 : £20.00 : CIP rev. B79-29543

658.4'0388 — Management. Information systems *continuation*

Duffy, Neil M.. Information management : an executive approach / Neil M. Duffy, Michael G. Assad. — Cape Town ; Oxford : Oxford University Press, 1980. — x,243p : ill ; 23cm
Bibliography: p233-236. — Includes index
ISBN 0-19-570190-9 : £15.95 B81-25978

658.4'0388 — United States. Business firms. Management. Information systems: Machine-readable files. Management

Weldon, Jay-Louise. Data base administration / Jay-Louise Weldon. — New York ; London : Plenum, c1981. — xii,250p : ill ; 24cm. — (Applications of modern technology in business)
Includes index
ISBN 0-306-40595-4 : Unpriced B81-24235

658.4'0388'02854 — Management. Information systems: Digital computer systems. Implementation

Lucas, Henry C.. Implementation : the key to successful information systems / Henry C. Lucas, Jr. — New York ; Guildford : Columbia University Press, 1981. — x,208p : ill ; 24cm
Bibliography: p201-205. — Includes index
ISBN 0-231-04434-8 : £18.60 B81-27031

658.4'0388'0722 — Management. Information systems — *Case studies*

Lucas, Henry C.. A casebook for management information systems / Henry C. Lucas, Jr., Cyrus F. Gibson. — 2nd ed. — New York ; London : McGraw-Hill, c1981. — x,460p : ill ; 24cm. — (McGraw-Hill series in management information systems)
Previous ed.: 1976
ISBN 0-07-038939-x (pbk) : £9.50 B81-36283

658.4'04 — Project management

Harrison, F. L.. Advanced project management / F.L. Harrison. — Aldershot : Gower, c1981. — xiii,317p : ill ; 23cm
Bibliography: p313-314. — Includes index
ISBN 0-566-02249-4 : £12.50 : CIP rev. B81-19195

Spinner, M.. Elements of project management : plan, schedule and control / M. Spinner. — Englewood Cliffs ; London : Prentice-Hall, c1981. — xi,212p : ill,forms ; 25cm
Includes bibliographies and index
ISBN 0-13-269852-8 : Unpriced B81-36492

658.4'04 — Project management. Influence of uncertainty

Fung, W. K. H.. A general framework for the evaluation of capital projects under uncertainty / W.K.H. Fung. — Manchester (P.O. Box 88, Manchester M60 1QD) : Department of Management Sciences, University of Manchester Institute of Science and Technology, 1981. — 20p ; 31cm. — (Occasional paper / Department of Management Sciences, University of Manchester Institute of Science and Technology ; no.8103)
Bibliography: p19-20
Unpriced (pbk) B81-18009

658.4'04 — Project management. Problem solving

King, L. Thomas. Problem solving in a project environment : a consulting process / L. Thomas King. — New York ; Chichester : Wiley, c1981. — xi,204p : ill,forms ; 24cm
Bibliography: p165-167. - Includes index
ISBN 0-471-08115-9 : £10.70 B81-16337

658.4'06 — Multinational companies. Organisation development

Heenan, David A.. Multinational organization development / David A. Heenan, Howard V. Perlmutter. — Reading, Mass. ; London : Addison-Wesley, c1979. — xiv,194p : ill,forms ; 21cm. — (Organization development)
Bibliography: p191-194
ISBN 0-201-02953-7 (pbk) : £4.50 B81-07364

658.4'06 — Organisation development. Applications of systems theory

Systems theory for organization development / edited by Thomas G. Cummings. — Chichester : Wiley, c1980. — xvii,362p : ill ; 24cm. — (Wiley series on individuals, groups and organizations)
Includes bibliographies and index
ISBN 0-471-27691-x : £16.50 : CIP rev. B80-25898

658.4'06 — Organisation development. Role of careers planning of personnel

Schein, Edgar H.. Career dynamics : matching individual and organizational needs / Edgar H. Schein. — Reading, Mass. ; London : Addison-Wesley, c1978. — xii,276p : ill ; 21cm. — (Organization development)
Bibliography: p270-276
ISBN 0-201-06834-6 (pbk) : £3.95 B81-07827

658.4'06 — Organisation development. Role of management of teams

Patten, Thomas H.. Organizational development through teambuilding / Thomas H. Patten, Jr. — New York ; Chichester : Wiley, c1981. — xvi,295p : ill,forms ; 24cm
Bibliography: p270-290. - Includes index
ISBN 0-471-66945-8 : £14.50 B81-24051

658.4'06 — Organisational change. Techniques. Management aspects

Techniques of organizational change / Stephen R. Michael ... [et al.]. — New York ; London : McGraw-Hill, c1981. — x,363p : ill,forms ; 24cm
Includes bibliographies and index
ISBN 0-07-041775-x : £14.95 B81-32386

658.4'063'0941 — Great Britain. Industries. Innovation. Management

Boyle, Denis. The challenge of change : developing business leaders for the 1980s / Denis Boyle and Bill Braddick. — Aldershot : Gower in association with Ashridge Management College, 1981. — xvi,45p : ill,ports ; 22cm
ISBN 0-566-02283-4 (pbk) : Unpriced : CIP rev. B81-04257

658.4'07124 — Management skills. Development — *Conference proceedings*

Perspectives on managerial effectiveness : a review based on papers of a research symposium in January 1979 / organised in association with the Training Services Division of the Manpower Services Commission ; editors Morris Brodie and Roger Bennett. — Slough (Wellington St., Slough SL1 1YG) : Thames Valley Regional Management Centre, c1979. — 140p : 1ill ; 22cm
Includes bibliographies and index
ISBN 0-906537-01-0 (pbk) : £3.50 B81-20978

658.4'07'124 — Managers. Training

New approaches to management development. — Farnborough, Hants. : Gower, Dec.1981. — [150]p
ISBN 0-566-02290-7 : £12.50 : CIP entry B81-31820

658.4'07124 — Managers. Training. Exercises

A **Handbook** of management training exercises / edited by John Adair ... [et al.]. — London : British Association for Industrial and Commercial Education
Vol.2 / edited by John Adair and David Després. — 1980. — 1v.(loose-leaf) : ill ; 32cm
ISBN 0-85171-078-6 : Unpriced B81-19288

658.4'07124 — Managers. Training. Self-development

Management self-development : concepts and practices / edited by Tom Boydell and Mike Pedler. — Farnborough : Gower, c1981. — xv,254p : ill ; 23cm
Includes bibliographies
ISBN 0-566-02194-3 : £12.50 B81-37915

658.4'071243 — Great Britain. Business schools. Curriculum subjects: Mid-career training of managers

Mant, Alistair. The dynamics of management education : observations on the mid-career development process / Alistair Mant. — Aldershot : Gower, c1981. — xiv,89p : ill ; 23cm
ISBN 0-566-02282-6 : Unpriced : CIP rev. B81-14971

658.4'071244 — Great Britain. Managers. Industrial training. Curriculum subjects: Industrial relations

Brewster, Chris. Industrial relations training for managers / Chris Brewster and Stephen Connock. — London : Kogan Page, 1980. — 237p : ill,forms ; 23cm
Bibliography: p228-231. - Includes index
ISBN 0-85038-397-8 : £12.95 : CIP rev. B80-36211

658.4'071245 — Great Britain. Buildings. Maintenance. Managers. Training

Educating for more effective maintenance management : how this can be good value for money : proceedings of the Institute of Building Seminar held in London on 1 and 2 May 1980. — Ascot (Englemere, Kings Ride, Ascot, Berks. SL5 8BJ) : The Institute, 1980. — 38p : 1form ; 30cm
ISBN 0-906600-33-2 (pbk) : Unpriced : CIP rev. B80-22208

658.4'07125 — Potential managers. Assessment — *Manuals*

Stewart, Andrew, *1942-*. Tomorrow's managers today : the identification and development of management potential / Andrew Stewart, Valerie Stewart. — 2nd ed. — London : Institute of Personnel Management, 1981. — 269p : ill,forms ; 22cm
Previous ed.: published as Tomorrow's men today. 1976. — Bibliography: p255-261. — Includes index
ISBN 0-85292-300-7 (pbk) : £8.55 : CIP rev. B81-08879

658.4'07134'0941 — Great Britain. Managers. Redundancy — *Practical information*

Tideswell, M.. Guidelines for the redundant manager / M. Tideswell. — [London] : British Institute of Management Foundation, Research and Publications Division, 1980. — 96p ; 30cm. — (Managers guides ; no.2)
Bibliography: p93-96
ISBN 0-85946-111-4 (spiral) : £4.80 B81-05269

658.4'07'14205 — Managers. Motivation. Incentives - *Serials*

Rewarding top management. — [No.1]-. — Farnborough, Hants. : Gower, July 1981. — [152]p
ISBN 0-566-02326-1 : £10.00 : CIP entry B81-13832

658.4'08 — Companies. Social responsibility — *For management*

Clutterbuck, David. How to be a good corporate citizen : a manager's guide to making social responsibility work — and pay / David Clutterbuck. — London : McGraw-Hill, c1981. — 294p ; 24cm
Bibliography: p288-289. — Includes index
ISBN 0-07-084560-3 : £12.95 : CIP rev. B81-13435

658.4'08 — Multinational companies. Social responsibility — *Correspondence, diaries, etc.*

O'Mahony, Patrick J.. Multinationals and human rights / Patrick J. O'Mahony. — Great Wakering : Mayhew-McCrimmon, 1980. — 318p : facsims ; 21cm
ISBN 0-85597-302-1 (pbk) : £3.50 B81-04614

658.4'08'0973 — United States. Business firms. Social responsibility

Corporations and their critics : issues and answers to the problems of corporate social responsibility / edited by Thornton Bradshaw and David Vogel. — New York ; London : McGraw-Hill, c1981. — xxvii,285p : ill ; 21cm
Includes index
ISBN 0-07-007075-x : £12.50 B81-10202

658.4'08'0973 — United States. Business firms. Social responsibility *continuation*

Private enterprise and public purpose : an understanding of the role of business in a changing social system / S. Prakash Sethi and Carl L. Swanson, editors. — New York ; Chichester : Wiley, c1981. — xvii,461p : ill ; 24cm. — (Wiley series in management)
ISBN 0-471-07697-x (pbk) : £9.05 B81-24939

658.4'09 — United States. Business firms. Executives. Personal power. Achievement. Use of manipulative behaviour

Jones, William M.. Survival : a manual on manipulating / William M. Jones. — Englewood Cliffs ; London : Prentice-Hall, 1981, c1979. — 261p ; 21cm. — (A Reward book)
Originally published: 1979. — Includes index
ISBN 0-13-879098-1 (pbk) : £2.75 B81-28424

658.4'092 — Management. Leadership

Tramel, Mary E.. Executive leadership : how to get it & make it work / Mary E. Tramel, Helen Reynolds. — Englewood Cliffs ; London : Prentice-Hall, c1981. — iv,268p : ill,forms ; 24cm. — (A Spectrum book)
ISBN 0-13-294132-5 (cased) : Unpriced
ISBN 0-13-294124-4 (pbk) : £4.85 B81-37181

658.4'093 — Management. Time factors

Reynolds, Helen. Executive time management. — Farnborough, Hants. : Gower, July 1981. — [174]p
ISBN 0-566-02297-4 : £9.50 : CIP entry B81-14883

658.4'093 — Organisations. Managers. Time. Allocation — *Manuals*

Rutherford, Robert D.. Just in time : immediate help for the time-pressured / Robert D. Rutherford. — New York ; Chichester : Wiley, c1981. — xv,201p ; 22cm
ISBN 0-471-08434-4 : £8.25 B81-27045

658.4'2 — Executives

Levinson, Harry. Executive. — [Rev. ed.] / Harry Levinson with the assistance of Cynthia Lang. — Cambridge, Mass. ; London : Harvard University Press, 1981. — viii,370p ; 25cm
Previous ed.: published as The exceptional executive. 1968. — Includes index
ISBN 0-674-27395-8 : £11.10 B81-38139

658.4'2'02541 — Great Britain. Companies. Directors — *Directories* — *Serials*

The Directory of directors. — 1981. — East Grinstead : Thomas Skinner Directories, c1981. — vii,1475p
ISBN 0-611-00649-9 : Unpriced B81-16753

658.4'2'088042 — Great Britain. Women managers, *1968-1979*

Fogarty, Michael P.. Women in top jobs 1968-1979 / Michael P. Fogarty, Isobel Allen and Patricia Walters. — London : Heinemann Educational, 1981. — vi,273p ; 23cm
At head of title: Policy Studies Institute. — Includes index
ISBN 0-435-83806-7 : £14.00 : CIP rev.
Primary classification 331.4'81 B81-27935

658.4'2'0941 — Great Britain. Business firms. Managers

The British manager in profile / Roger Mansfield ... [et al.]. — London : Research and Publications Division, BIM Foundation, c1981. — 44p : forms ; 30cm. — (Management survey report ; no.51)
Bibliography: p38-39
ISBN 0-85946-116-5 (pbk) : Unpriced B81-37821

658.4'2'0941 — Great Britain. Companies. Directors. Duties

Parker, Hugh. Letters to a new chairman / Hugh Parker. — [London] : Director Publications, 1979. — 40p : ill,1port ; 21cm
£2.00 (pbk) B81-38382

658.4'2'0941 — Great Britain. Companies. Managers

Managers in focus. — Aldershot : Gower, Jan.1982. — [194]p
ISBN 0-566-00468-2 : £12.50 : CIP entry B81-34280

658.4'22 — Companies. Boards of directors. Role

Mills, Geoffrey, *1910-*. On the board / Geoffrey Mills. — Aldershot : Gower in association with the Institute of Directors, c1981. — vii,232p : ill ; 23cm
Includes index
ISBN 0-566-02260-5 : £12.50 : CIP rev. B81-16367

Mueller, Robert Kirk. The incompleat board : the unfolding of corporate governance / Robert Kirk Mueller. — Lexington, Mass. : Lexington Books ; [Aldershot] : Gower [distributor], 1981. — xviii,283p : ill ; 24cm. — (Arthur D. Little books)
Includes index
ISBN 0-669-04339-7 : £16.50 B81-38469

658.4'22 — Great Britain. Companies. Boards of directors. Professional conduct

Guidelines for directors : incorporating Standard boardroom practice / prepared by a special committee of the Institute of Directors under the Chairmanship of Sir Charles Hardie ; with a foreword : Lord Pritchard. — Repr. with revisions. — London : Institute of Directors, 1980. — 77p ; 22cm
Previous ed.: 1980. — Includes index
£3.90 (pbk) B81-38379

658.4'22 — Great Britain. Nationalised industries. Boards of directors. Representation of consumers

Jones, Trefor T.. The representation of the consumer interest in the management of nationalised industries : the case for and against board members / Trefor T. Jones. — Manchester (P.O. Box 88, Manchester M60 1QD) : Department of Management Sciences, University of Manchester Institute of Science & Technology, 1980. — 25p ; 31cm. — (Occasional paper / University of Manchester Institute of Science and Technology Department of Management Sciences ; no.8010)
Unpriced (pbk) B81-11507

658.4'5 — Management. Communication

Zand, Dale E.. Information, organization, and power : effective management in the knowledge society / Dale E. Zand. — New York ; London : McGraw-Hill, c1981. — xiv,209p : ill ; 21cm
Includes index
ISBN 0-07-072743-0 : £9.75 B81-19468

658.4'5 — Management. Communication — *Manuals*

Bergin, Francis J.. Practical communication / Francis J. Bergin. — 2nd ed. — London : Pitman, 1981. — vi,170p : ill ; 22cm
Previous ed.: 1976. — Bibliography: p167. — Includes index
ISBN 0-273-01629-6 (pbk) : Unpriced B81-38443

Capps, Randall. Communication for the business and professional speaker / Randall Capps, Carley H. Dodd, Larry James Winn. — New York : Macmillan ; London : Collier Macmillan, c1981. — ix,300p : ill ; 26cm
Includes bibliographies and index
ISBN 0-02-319250-x (pbk) : £7.95 B81-33393

658.4'5 — Organisations. Communication

Hunt, Gary T.. Communication skills in the organization / Gary T. Hunt. — Englewood Cliffs ; London : Prentice-Hall, c1980. — xvi,345p : ill ; 24cm
Bibliography: p334-340. - Includes index
ISBN 0-13-153296-0 : £9.05 B81-13111

658.4'5 — Organisations. Management. Communication

Koehler, Jerry W.. Organizational communication : behavioral perspectives / Jerry W. Koehler, Karl W.E. Anatol, Ronald L. Applbaum. — 2nd ed. — New York ; London : Holt, Rinehart and Winston, 1981. — viii,360p : ill ; 25cm
Previous ed.: 1976. — Bibliography: p349-356. - Includes index
ISBN 0-03-049376-5 : £9.25 B81-05753

Machin, John L. J.. The expectation approach : improving managerial communication and performance / John L.J. Machin. — London : McGraw-Hill, c1980. — xv,304p : ill ; 24cm
Bibliography: p298-300
ISBN 0-07-084539-5 : Unpriced : CIP rev. B80-19311

658.4'5'05 — Organisations. Communication — *Serials*

Organizational communication : abstracts, analysis, and review. — 1976-1977 ; Vol.5-. — Beverly Hills ; London : Published in cooperation with American Business Communication Association [and] International Communications Association [by] Sage, [197-]-. — v. ; 22cm
Annual. — Continues: Organizational communication abstracts. — Vols. for 1916-1977 published by: American Business Communication Association. — Description based on: Vol.5
ISSN 0149-1644 = Organizational communication : Unpriced B81-08363

Organizational communication. — Vol.6. — Beverly Hills ; London : Published in cooperation with the American Business Communication Association [and] International Communication Association [by] Sage, c1981. — 357p
ISBN 0-8039-1606-x : £11.95
ISSN 0149-1644 B81-35124

658.4'52 — Management. Oral communication

Timm, Paul R.. Functional business presentations : getting across / Paul R. Timm. — Englewood Cliffs : Prentice-Hall, c1981. — xiii,206p : ill,forms ; 23cm
Includes index
ISBN 0-13-331470-7 (pbk) : £7.10 B81-22702

658.4'53 — Management. Written communication — *Manuals*

De Leeuw, Eric. Written communications in industry : a handbook for managers and administrators / Eric de Leeuw. — Luton (Industrial Management House, Cardiff Rd., Luton, Beds., LU2 1RQ) : Institution of Industrial Managers, 1981. — 47p : ill ; 21cm
ISBN 0-9507612-0-6 (pbk) : £1.70 B81-28968

658.4'53'071142 — England. Housing associations. Personnel. Professional education. Curriculum subjects: Written communication

Letter and report writing / Housing Training Project. — London ([City University, St John St., EC1V 4PB]) : Housing Research Group, c1980. — 60p : ill ; 21cm. — (Guide to housing training ; no.4)
Cover title. — Bibliography: p59-60
ISBN 0-907255-03-5 (pbk) : Unpriced
Primary classification 658.4'53'071142 B81-06328

658.4'53'071142 — England. Local authorities. Housing departments. Personnel. Professional education. Curriculum subjects: Written communication

Letter and report writing / Housing Training Project. — London ([City University, St John St., EC1V 4PB]) : Housing Research Group, c1980. — 60p : ill ; 21cm. — (Guide to housing training ; no.4)
Cover title. — Bibliography: p59-60
ISBN 0-907255-03-5 (pbk) : Unpriced
Also classified at 658.4'53'071142 B81-06328

658.4'563 — Meetings. Organisation — *Manuals*

Locke, Michael, *1943-*. How to run committees and meetings : a guidebook to practical politics / Michael Locke. — London : Macmillan, 1980. — x,190p ; 23cm
Bibliography: p182-184. - Includes index
ISBN 0-333-27053-3 (cased) : £10.00 : CIP rev.
ISBN 0-333-29035-6 (pbk) : £2.95 B80-20852

Seekings, David. How to organize effective conferences and meetings / David Seekings. — London : Kogan Page, 1981. — 208p : ill ; 24cm
Includes index
ISBN 0-85038-368-4 : £12.00 B81-16139

658.4'6 — Business firms. Evaluation. Techniques - *For consultants*

Reeves, Tom Kynaston. Surveys at work. — London : McGraw-Hill, Sept.1981. — [288]p
ISBN 0-07-084563-8 : £15.95 : CIP entry B81-20549

658.4'6 — Business firms. Evaluation. Techniques — *For consultants*

Reeves, Tom Kynaston. Surveys at work. — London : McGraw-Hill, Sept.1981
Student project manual. — [288]p
ISBN 0-07-084568-9 (pbk) : £7.95 : CIP entry B81-21572

658.4'6'06041 — Great Britain. Management consultants. Organisations: Institute of Management Consultants — *Serials*

Institute of Management Consultants. Yearbook / Institute of Management Consultants. — 1981-. — London (86 Edgware Rd, W2 2YW) : Sterling Professional Publications, 1981-. — v. : ill ; 21cm
Annual. — Spine title: IMC yearbook. — Continues: Institute of Management Consultants. List of members
ISSN 0260-373x = Yearbook - Institute of Management Consultants (corrected) : Unpriced B81-20069

658.4'7 — Companies. Security measures

Russell, A. Lewis. Corporate and industrial security / A. Lewis Russell. — Houston ; London : Gulf Publishing, c1980. — ix,275p : ill,forms ; 24cm
Includes index
ISBN 0-87201-796-6 : £8.75 B81-02977

658.4'7'06041 — Great Britain. Industries. Security. Organisations: International Professional Security Association — *Directories — Serials*

International Professional Security Association. Directory of corporate, associate and group members of the Association and fellows, members and graduates of the Institution / International Professional Security Association incorporating Institute of Industrial Security directory of members. — 1978-. — [London] : Batiste, 1978-. — v. ; 21cm
Continues: Industrial Police and Security Association Directory of corporate, associate and group members of the Association and fellows, members and graduates of the Institution
ISSN 0260-8340 = Directory of corporate, associate and group members of the Association and fellows, members and graduates of the Institution - International Professional Security Association incorporating Institute of Industrial Security : Unpriced B81-09206

658.4'7'0973 — Industries & trades. Security measures

Finneran, Eugene D.. Security supervision : a handbook for supervisors and managers / Eugene D. Finneran. — Boston [Mass.] ; London : Butterworth, c1981. — xii,280p : ill,forms ; 24cm
Includes index
ISBN 0-409-95025-4 : Unpriced B81-33030

Green, Gion. Introduction to security. — 3rd ed / Gion Green. — Boston, [Mass.] ; London : Butterworth, c1981. — xx,395p : ill,forms,plans ; 25cm
Previous ed.: Los Angeles : Security World Pub. Co., 1978. — Bibliography: p377-380. — Includes index
ISBN 0-409-95036-x : Unpriced B81-33231

658.4'73 — Companies. Fraud by personnel. Prevention — *Serials*

Fraud report : a monthly confidential intelligence service aimed at the prevention of corporate crime. — Issue no.1 (Mar.1981)-. — Morden (Eagle Chambers, 6 Rose Hill Court, St. Helier Ave., Morden, Surrey SM4 6JT) : Corporate Security Information Services, 1981-. — v. ; 30cm
ISSN 0261-5339 = Fraud report : £95.00 per year B81-33949

658.4'73'05 — Security measures — *Serials*

Security report. — Vol.1, no.1 (Dec.1980)-. — Lausanne : Elsevier Sequoia ; Oxford (Mayfield House, 256 Banbury Rd, Oxford OX2 7DH) : Elsevier International Bulletins, 1980-. — v. : ill ; 30cm
Monthly
£75.00 per year B81-05679

658.4'78 — Computer systems. Risks. Management

Perry, William E.. Computer control and security : a guide for managers and systems analysts / William E. Perry. — New York ; Chichester : Wiley, c1981. — xiii,207p : ill,1form ; 24cm
Includes index
ISBN 0-471-05235-3 : £14.50 B81-24054

658.4'78 — Computer systems. Security measures

Squires, Tony. Computer security - the personnel aspect / Tony Squires. — Manchester : NCC Publications, 1980. — 149p ; 21cm
Bibliography: p149
ISBN 0-85012-246-5 (pbk) : £12.50 : CIP rev. B80-22221

658.4'78 — Computer systems. Security measures. Management aspects

Talbot, J. R.. Management guide to computer security / J.R. Talbot ; edited by D.M. Powell. — Farnborough : Gower, c1981. — xi,180p ; 23cm
Includes index
ISBN 0-566-02190-0 : £12.50 B81-36290

658.5 — PRODUCTION MANAGEMENT

658.5 — Great Britain. Manufacturing industries. Production maragers. Job content — *Sources of data: Newspapers. Advertisments*

Hill, T. J. (Terence Joseph). The production manager's task and contribution / T.J. Hill, H. Boothroyd and E.P. Sharman. — Coventry (Coventry CV4 7AL) : Centre for Industrial Economic and Business Research, University of Warwick. — 43p : 1ill ; 31cm. — (Discussion paper. General series / Centre for Industrial Economic and Business Research, University of Warwick ; no.94)
Unpriced (pbk) B81-40059

658.5 — Manufacturing industries. Management

Smith, Martin R.. Manufacturing controls : how the manufacturing manager can improve profitability / Martin R. Smith. — New York ; London : Van Nostrand Reinhold, c1981. — lx,173p : ill,forms ; 24cm
Includes index
ISBN 0-442-21942-3 : £16.95 B81-37026

658.5 — Production management

Buffa, Elwood S.. Elements of production/operations management / Elwood S. Buffa. — New York ; Chichester : Wiley, c1981. — vii,250p : ill ; 24cm
A shortened version of the author's Modern production/operations management, 6th ed. — Includes bibliographies and index
ISBN 0-471-08532-4 (pbk) : £7.75 B81-24937

Dervitsiotis, Kostas N.. Operations management / Kostas N. Dervitsiotis. — New York ; London : McGraw-Hill, c1981. — xiii,771p : ill ; 25cm. — (McGraw-Hill series in industrial engineering and management science)
Includes bibliographies and index
ISBN 0-07-016537-8 : £15.75 B81-10125

Management and production readings / edited by Ray Wild. — Harmondsworth : Penguin, 1981, c1980. — 376p : ill ; 20cm. — (Penguin education) (Penguin modern management readings)
ISBN 0-14-080393-9 (pbk) : £3.95 B81-21006

Riggs, James L.. Production systems : planning analysis and control / James L. Riggs. — 3rd ed. — New York ; Chichester : Wiley, c1981. — xv,649p : ill ; 25cm. — (The Wiley series in management)
Previous ed.: 1976. — Includes bibliographies and index
ISBN 0-471-05946-3 : £15.70 B81-16944

658.5 — Production management — *Manuals*

Tersine, Richard J.. Production/operations management : concepts, structure and analysis / Richard J. Tersine. — New York ; Oxford : North-Holland, 1980. — 680p : ill ; 26cm
Includes bibliographies and index
ISBN 0-444-00326-6 : £8.89 B81-08111

Wild, Ray. Essentials of production and operations management : a workbook of notes and assignments / Ray Wild. — London : Holt, Rinehart and Winston, c1981. — 80p : ill ; 30cm. — (Holt business texts)
ISBN 0-03-910302-1 (pbk) : Unpriced B81-25216

658.5 — Production management. Quantitative methods

Bestwick, P. F.. Quantitative production management. — London : Pitman, Feb.1982. — [512]p
ISBN 0-273-01614-8 : £14.95 : CIP entry B81-35778

658.5 — Production management. Quantitative methods — *Questions & answers*

Bestwick, P. F.. Solutions manual to Quantitative production management. — London : Pitman, Feb.1982. — [192]p
ISBN 0-273-01613-x (pbk) : £9.95 : CIP entry B81-35779

658.5'00941 — Great Britain. Production management

Operations management in practice / edited by C.D. Lewis. — Oxford : Philip Allan, 1981. — x,454p ; 23cm
Includes bibliographies and index
ISBN 0-86003-511-5 (cased) : £18.00
ISBN 0-86003-611-1 (pbk) : £8.95 B81-24916

658.5'036 — Production management. Decision making

Schroeder, Roger G.. Operations management : decision making in the operations function / Roger G. Schroeder. — New York ; London : McGraw-Hill, c1981. — xv,680p : col.ill,1facsim,1plan ; 25cm. — (McGraw-Hill series in management)
Text, ill. on lining papers. — Includes bibliographies and index
ISBN 0-07-055612-1 : £13.95 B81-24254

658.5'036 — Production management. Planning. Applications of information systems

Verzijl, J. J.. Planning and information systems for job allocation / J.J. Verzijl. — London : Macmillan, 1981. — vii,117p : ill ; 23cm
Includes index
ISBN 0-333-29545-5 : Unpriced B81-33668

658.5'036 — Production management. Systems analysis — *Conference proceedings*

IFIP-TC5 International Workshop on Automation of Production Planning and Control *(1980 : Trondheim)*. Production management systems : proceedings of the IFIP TC-5 International Workshop on Automation of Production Planning and Control, Trondheim, Norway, 3-5 September 1980 / edited by P. Falster and A. Rolstadås ; sponsors International Federation for Information Processing (IFIP), Production Engineering Laboratory, SINTEF—NTH. — Amsterdam ; Oxford : North-Holland, c1981. — viii,221p : ill ; 23cm
Includes bibliographies and index
ISBN 0-444-86176-9 : Unpriced B81-25532

658.5'3 — Production management. Scheduling

French, Simon. Sequencing and scheduling. — Chichester : Ellis Horwood, June 1981. — [192]p. — (Ellis Horwood series in mathematics and its applications)
ISBN 0-85312-299-7 : £18.50 : CIP entry B81-13862

658.5'421 — Methods time measurement. Core data

Evans, Peter, *1950-*. MTM core data : manual for MTM-2 analysts / Peter Evans. — Warrington (P.O. 20, Warrington, Cheshire, WA2 7ET) : Methods-Time Measurement Association, c1981. — 66leaves in various foliations : ill ; 30cm
Unpriced (pbk) B81-19404

658.5'421 — Time study
Jay, Tony A.. Time study / Tony A. Jay. — Poole : Blandford, 1981. — 207p : ill,forms ; 23cm. — (Blandford management series)
Includes index
ISBN 0-7137-1085-3 (cased) : £6.95 : CIP rev.
ISBN 0-7137-1126-4 (pbk) : £3.95 B81-08942

658.5'6 — United States. Products. Safety aspects
Kolb, John. Product safety and liability : a desk reference / John Kolb and Steven S. Ross. — New York ; London : McGraw-Hill, c1980. — xvi,688p : ill,forms ; 24cm
Bibliography: p631-640. — Includes index
ISBN 0-07-035380-8 : £17.95 B81-08108

658.5'6'02854 — Production control systems using digital computer systems. Design
Bertrand, J. W. M.. Production control and information systems for component-manufacturing shops / J.W.M. Bertrand and J.C. Wortmann. — Amsterdam ; Oxford : Elsevier Scientific, 1981. — xv,404p : ill ; 25cm. — (Studies in production and engineering economics ; 1)
Bibliography: p395-399. — Includes index
ISBN 0-444-41964-0 : £28.85 B81-19277

658.5'62 — Industries. Quality control. Role of personnel
Morland, Julia, *1958-*. Quality circles / by Julia Morland. — London : Industrial Society, 1981. — 28p : ill,forms ; 21cm
ISBN 0-85290-207-7 (pbk) : £2.00 B81-25557

658.5'62 — Quality control
Besterfield, Dale H.. Quality control / Dale H. Besterfield. — Englewood Cliffs ; London : Prentice-Hall, c1979. — ix,309p : ill,1form ; 25cm
Includes index
ISBN 0-13-745232-2 : £12.95 B81-02603

658.5'62'015195 — Quality control. Statistical mathematics — *For schools*
Cutting it fine / [Schools Council Project on Statistical Education]. — Slough : Published for the Schools Council by Foulsham Educational, c1981. — 16p : ill,1map ; 21cm + teachers' notes(19p : ill ; 21cm). — (Statistics in your world. [Level 3])
ISBN 0-572-01082-6 (pbk) : Unpriced
ISBN 0-572-01109-1 (teachers' notes) : Unpriced B81-16723

658.5'68 — Sampling inspection. Theories
Hald, A.. Statistical theory of sampling inspection by attributes / A. Hald. — London : Academic Press, 1981. — xiv,515p : ill ; 24cm. — (Probability and mathematical statistics)
Bibliography: p495-507. — Includes index
ISBN 0-12-318350-2 : £35.00 B81-26321

658.5'7 — Great Britain. Management. In-house research by companies — *Case studies*
Williams, Allan P. O.. The structure and function of in-house personnel research units and conditions enhancing their effectiveness / by Allan P.O. Williams and Rosalie Silverstone. — [London] : [City University Business School], c1981. — 48leaves ; 30cm. — (Working paper series / City University Business School, ISSN 0140-1041 ; no.25)
Bibliography: leaf 48
Unpriced (pbk) B81-37617

658.5'7 — Research & development by industries. Management
Management of research and innovation / edited by Burton V. Dean, Joel L. Goldhar. — Amsterdam ; Oxford : North-Holland, c1980. — x,300p : ill ; 24cm. — (TIMS studies in the management sciences ; v.15)
Includes bibliographies and index
ISBN 0-444-86009-6 (pbk) : Unpriced B81-13252

658.5'75 — New products. Development
Cafarelli, Eugene J.. Developing new products and repositioning mature brands : a risk-reduction system that produces investment alternatives / Eugene J. Cafarelli. — New York ; Chichester : Wiley, c1980. — xii,253p,[1]folded leaf of plates : ill ; 24cm. — (Ronald series on marketing management)
Bibliography: p249. — Includes index
ISBN 0-471-04634-5 : Unpriced B81-08724

658.5'75 — New products. Management
Corporate strategy and product innovation / edited by Robert R. Rothberg. — 2nd ed. — New York : Free Press ; London : Collier Macmillan, c1981. — xiv,529p : ill ; 25cm
Previous ed.: 1976. — Bibliography: p510-515. — Includes index
ISBN 0-02-927520-2 : £10.95 B81-29325

658.5'75'0973 — United States. New products. Design & marketing
Urban, Glen L.. Design and marketing of new products / Glen L. Urban, John R. Hauser. — Englewood Cliffs ; London : Prentice-Hall, c1980. — xx,618p : ill,facsims,forms ; 24cm. — (Prentice-Hall international series in management)
Bibliography: p583-608. - Includes index
ISBN 0-13-201269-3 : £15.60 B81-04425

658.5'752'0722 — Great Britain. Industrial design. Management aspects — *Case studies*
Leslie, Peter J.. Employing a designer : a management guide to the selection, employment and payment of staff and consultant industrial designers / [Peter J. Leslie]. — London : Design Council, 1980. — 46p : ill,forms ; 30cm
ISBN 0-85072-111-3 (pbk) : £5.00 B81-10382

658.7 — MATERIALS MANAGEMENT

658.7 — Materials management
Blanchard, Benjamin S.. Logistics engineering and management / Benjamin S. Blanchard. — 2nd ed. — Englewood Cliffs ; London : Prentice-Hall, c1981. — xiii,436p : ill ; 24cm. — (Prentice-Hall international series in industrial and systems engineering)
Previous ed.: 1974. — Bibliography: p426-430. — Includes index
ISBN 0-13-540088-0 : £16.35 B81-22715

658.7 — Materials management — *Manuals*
Bailey, Peter. Materials management handbook. — Farnborough, Hants. : Gower, Nov.1981. — [340]p
ISBN 0-566-02272-9 : £15.00 : CIP entry B81-30960

658.7'2 — Purchasing by companies. Planning — *For management*
Parsons, W. J.. Improving purchasing performance. — Farnborough : Gower, Sept.1981. — [180]p
ISBN 0-566-02271-0 : £12.50 : CIP entry B81-21561

658.7'2 — Purchasing by industries. Price management
Farrington, Brian. Industrial purchase price management / Brian Farrington. — Farnborough, Hants. : Gower in association with the Institute of Purchasing and Supply, c1980. — xiv,187p : ill ; 23cm
Includes index
ISBN 0-566-02186-2 : £15.00 : CIP rev. B80-11533

658.7'2 — Purchasing by organisations
Heinritz, Stuart F.. Purchasing : principles and applications / Stuart F. Heinritz, Paul V. Farrell. — 6th ed. — Englewood Cliffs ; London : Prentice-Hall, c1981. — vii,487p : ill,2forms ; 24cm
Previous ed.: 1971. — Bibliography: p473-475. — Includes index
ISBN 0-13-742163-x : £12.95 B81-25061

658.7'2 — Stock control. Purchasing
Baily, Peter. Purchasing principles and management. — 4th ed. — London : Pitman, Oct.1981. — [352]p
Previous ed. published as: Purchasing principles and techniques. 1977
ISBN 0-273-01719-5 (pbk) : £8.25 : CIP entry B81-30155

Zenz, Gary Joseph. Purchasing and the management of materials. — 5th ed. / Gary J. Zenz. — New York ; Chichester : Wiley, c1981. — xiii,514p : ill ; 24cm
Previous ed.: published as Purchasing management / by J.H. Westing, I.V. Fine and G.J. Zenz. 1976. — Includes index
ISBN 0-471-06091-7 : £15.00 B81-11306

658.7'2'094 — Europe. Purchasing
International marketing and purchasing of industrial goods. — Chichester : Wiley, Feb.1982. — [432]p
ISBN 0-471-27987-0 : £17.50 : CIP entry
Primary classification 658.8'094 B81-36235

658.7'2'0941 — Great Britain. Purchasing by manufacturing industries
Farrington, Brian. The purchasing function / Brian Farrington and Michael Woodmansey. — London : Research and Publications Division, BIM Foundation, c1980. — iv,23p : 1ill ; 30cm. — (Management survey report ; no.50)
Bibliography: p23
ISBN 0-85946-113-0 (pbk) : £7.50 B81-08292

658.7'85 — Materials. Storage. Management
Compton, H. K.. Storehouse and stockyard management / H.K. Compton. — 2nd ed. — Plymouth : Macdonald & Evans, 1981. — xiv,530p : ill,forms ; 23cm
Previous ed.: London : Business Books, 1970. — Bibliography: p514-518. — Includes index
ISBN 0-7121-1965-5 : £18.00 B81-39549

658.7'87 — Great Britain. Retail trades. Goods. Bar marking codes. Location — *Manuals*
Guideline on the location of bar code symbols / Article Number Association (UK) Limited. — London (6 Catherine St., WC2B 5JJ) : The Association, 1980. — 14leaves,[11]leaves of plates : ill ; 30cm
Unpriced (spiral) B81-37975

658.7'87 — Great Britain. Retail trades. Goods. Marking codes — *Manuals*
Article Number Association (UK). Retail article numbering and symbol marking operating manual / Article Number Association (UK) Limited. — Rev. ed. — London (6 Catherine St., WC2B 5JJ) : The Association, 1980. — 71,[18]leaves : ill ; 30cm
Previous ed. i.e. 2nd ed.: 1979
Unpriced (spiral) B81-37974

658.7'87 — Stock control — *Conference proceedings*
The **Economics** and management of inventories. — Oxford : Elsevier Scientific, Nov.1981. — [1000]p. — (Studies in production and engineering economics)
Conference papers
ISBN 0-444-99718-0 : £70.00 : CIP entry B81-30411

658.7'87 — Stock control — *Manuals*
Morrison, Alex. Storage and control of stock for industry and public undertakings / Alex Morrison. — 3rd ed. — London : Pitman, 1981. — xv,311p,24p of plates : ill ; 22cm
Previous ed.: 1967. — Includes index
ISBN 0-273-00731-9 (pbk) : Unpriced B81-38875

658.7'87 — United States. Stock control systems. Management — *Conference proceedings*
Multi-level production/inventory control systems : theory and practice / edited by Leroy B. Schwarz. — Amsterdam ; Oxford : North-Holland, c1981. — x,398p : ill ; 25cm. — (TIMS studies in the management sciences ; v.16)
Bibliography: p379-390
ISBN 0-444-86096-7 : Unpriced B81-32851

658.7'87'0724 — Stock control. Operations research. Mathematical models
Lewis, C. D.. Scientific inventory control / C.D. Lewis. — 2nd ed. — London : Butterworths, 1981. — ix,209p : ill ; 23cm
Previous ed.: 1970. — Includes bibliographies and index
ISBN 0-408-00595-5 : Unpriced : CIP rev. B81-25097

658.7'88'0941 — Great Britain. Goods. Physical distribution — *Questions & answers* — *For business studies*
Robertshaw, R. H.. Elements of distribution / R.H. Robertshaw and J.R. Willans ; illustrated by Janet Payne. — Stockport : Polytech, 1979. — 120p : ill,forms ; 22cm. — (A Business Education Council Course. General level)
Includes index
ISBN 0-85505-029-2 (pbk) : £3.00 B81-38008

658.7′88′0942 — England. Consumer goods. Physical distribution — *For accounting*

Newton, Keith. Distribution : an introduction for accountants / Keith Newton. — [London] : Institute of Chartered Accountants in England and Wales, 1981. — vii,84p : ill ; 21cm. — (The Accountant in industry and commerce)
Bibliography: p80-81
ISBN 0-85291-291-9 (pbk) : Unpriced B81-18666

658.7′88′0971 — Canada. Goods. Physical distribution. Management

Distribution management handbook / [Don Firth et al.]. — Toronto ; London : McGraw-Hill Ryerson, c1980. — 342p : ill ; 24cm
Includes index
ISBN 0-07-077975-9 : £20.95 B81-10367

658.8 — MARKETING

658.8 — Industrial marketing

Hutt, Michael D.. Industrial marketing management / Michael D. Hutt, Thomas W. Speh. — Chicago ; London : Dryden, c1981. — 463p : ill ; 25cm
Includes index
ISBN 0-03-052656-6 : £12.95 B81-22866

658.8 — Marketing

Baker, Michael J.. Marketing : an introductory text / Michael J. Baker. — 3rd ed. — London : Macmillan, 1979. — xxiv,488p : ill ; 23cm
Previous ed.: 1974. — Bibliography: p475-480. — Includes index
ISBN 0-333-23639-4 (cased) : £12.00 : CIP rev.
ISBN 0-333-23640-8 (pbk) : £5.95 B79-20224

Davidson, J. H.. Offensive marketing : or how to make your competitors followers / J.H. Davidson. — [Rev. and updated]. — Harmondsworth : Penguin, 1975 (1979 printing). — xvi,330p : ill ; 18cm. — (Pelican library of business and management)
Previous ed.: London : Cassell, 1972. — Includes index
ISBN 0-14-021871-8 (pbk) : £1.95 B81-22167

Davis, Kenneth R.. Marketing management / Kenneth R. Davis. — 4th ed. — New York ; Chichester : Wiley, c1981. — xix,778p : ill,2maps,forms ; 25cm. — (Wiley series in marketing)
Previous ed.: New York : Ronald Press, 1972. — Includes index
ISBN 0-471-05948-x : £13.30 B81-09756

Effective marketing management / Martin Christopher... [et al.]. — [Cranfield] : Cranfield Management Resource ; [Aldershot] : Gower, c1980. — 192p : ill ; 31cm
ISBN 0-566-02237-0 : Unpriced : CIP rev. B80-24637

Frain, John. Introduction to marketing / John Frain. — Plymouth : Macdonald & Evans, 1981. — viii,238p : ill ; 22cm. — (The M & E BECbook series)
Bibliography: p231-233. — Includes index
ISBN 0-7121-0959-5 (pbk) : £4.95 B81-32972

Holtje, Herbert F.. Schaum′s outline of theory and problems of marketing / by Herbert F. Holtje. — New York ; London : McGraw-Hill, c1981. — 149p : ill ; 28cm. — (Schaum′s outline series)
Includes index
ISBN 0-07-029661-8 (pbk) : £3.50 B81-06804

Mandell, Maurice I.. Marketing. — 2nd ed / Maurice I. Mandell, Larry J. Rosenberg. — Englewood Cliffs ; London : Prentice-Hall, c1981. — xviii,653p : ill(some col.) ; 25cm
Previous ed.: / by Larry J. Rosenberg. 1977. — Includes index
ISBN 0-13-556225-2 : £14.70 B81-33149

Marketing classics : a selection of influential articles / [compiled by] Ben M. Enis, Keith K. Cox. — 4th ed. — Boston [Mass.] ; London : Allyn and Bacon, c1981. — xv,533p : ill ; 24cm
Previous ed.: 1977. — Includes bibliographies and index
ISBN 0-205-07325-5 (pbk) : Unpriced B81-26397

Oliver, Gordon. Marketing today / Gordon Oliver. — Englewood Cliffs ; London : Prentice-Hall, 1980. — xii,339p : ill ; 23cm
Includes index
ISBN 0-13-558288-1 (pbk) : £7.95 : CIP rev. B80-18416

Stanton, William J.. Fundamentals of marketing / William J. Stanton. — 6th ed. — New York ; London : McGraw-Hill, c1981. — xvii,604p : ill(some col.),1col.map,1port ; 25cm. — (McGraw-Hill series in marketing)
Previous ed.: 1978. — Includes index
ISBN 0-07-060891-1 : £16.75 B81-12054

Tinniswood, Peter. Marketing decisions / Peter Tinniswood. — Harlow : Longman, 1981. — 183p : ill ; 24cm. — (Understanding business)
Includes index
ISBN 0-582-35543-5 (pbk) : £3.95 B81-39671

Wilson, M. T.. The management of marketing / Mike Wilson. — Farnborough, Hants. : Gower, c1980. — xvii,141p : ill ; 31cm
Bibliography: p137-138. — Includes index
ISBN 0-566-02191-9 : £15.00 : CIP rev. B80-25892

658.8 — Marketing. Decision making — *Case studies*

Kerin, Roger A.. Strategic marketing problems : cases and comments / Roger A. Kerin, Robert A. Peterson. — 2nd ed. — Boston [Mass.] ; London : Allyn and Bacon, c1981. — xiii,577p : ill + Instructor′s manual(328p : ill ; 24cm : pbk) : maps,facsims ; 25cm
Previous ed.: 1978
ISBN 0-205-07329-8 : Unpriced
ISBN 0-205-07330-1 (Instructor′s manual) : Unpriced B81-26837

658.8 — Marketing — *For business studies*

Cannon, Tom. Basic marketing : a workbook of notes and assignments / T. Cannon. — London : Holt, Rinehart and Winston, c1981. — 58p : ill ; 30cm. — (Holt business texts)
ISBN 0-03-910311-0 (pbk) : £1.50 B81-23098

658.8 — Marketing — *Manuals*

Marketing handbook. — 2nd ed. / edited by Michael Rines. — Aldershot : Gower in association with Marketing magazine, c1981. — xvii,372p : ill ; 24cm
Previous ed.: / by John Stapleton. 1974. — Includes index
ISBN 0-566-02200-1 : £15.00 B81-37914

Udell, Jon G.. Marketing in an age of change : an introduction / Jon G. Udell, Gene R. Laczniak. — New York ; Chichester : Wiley, c1981. — xix,577p : ill(some col.),1map,facsims ; 24cm. — (Wiley series in marketing)
Includes bibliographies and index
ISBN 0-471-08169-8 : £10.25 B81-11302

658.8 — Marketing. Planning

Stapleton, John. How to prepare a marketing plan. — 3rd ed. — Farnborough, Hants. : Gower Press, Dec.1981. — [250]p
Previous ed.: 1974
ISBN 0-566-02288-5 : £15.00 : CIP entry B81-31610

658.8 — Marketing. Role of persuasion

Schwerin, Horace S.. Persuasion in marketing : the dynamics of marketing′s great untapped resource / Horace S. Schwerin and Henry H. Newell ; foreword by Mary Wells Lawrence. — New York ; Chichester : Wiley, c1981. — xiii,259p : ill ; 24cm
Includes index
ISBN 0-471-04554-3 : £14.50 B81-18997

658.8 — United States. Government. Marketing of goods & services by business firms — *Manuals*

Cohen, William A.. How to sell to the government : a step-by-step guide to success / William A. Cohen ; foreword by Paul L. Smith. — New York ; Chichester : Wiley, c1981. — xii,434p : ill,facsims,forms ; 24cm
Includes index
ISBN 0-471-08103-5 : £9.50 B81-23244

658.8′0023 — Marketing — *Career guides*

Taylor, Felicity. Careers in marketing / Felicity Taylor. — London : Kogan Page, 1980. — 117p : ill,1form ; 19cm
Spine title: Marketing and allied professions
ISBN 0-85038-365-x (cased) : £4.95 : CIP rev.
ISBN 0-85038-366-8 (pbk) : £1.95 B80-11086

658.8′0023′41 — Great Britain. Marketing — *Career guides*

A **Career** in marketing, advertising and public relations / edited by Norman A. Hart and Gilbert W. Lamb ; foreword by Lord Robens of Woldingham. — London : Heinemann on behalf of the CAM Foundation and the Institute of Marketing, c1981. — xxiii,164p : ill ; 22cm
Bibliography: p155. - Includes index
ISBN 0-434-90711-1 (pbk) : £4.95
Also classified at 659.2′023′41 B81-23387

658.8′003′21 — Marketing — *Encyclopaedias*

Hart, Norman A.. Glossary of marketing / Norman A. Hart, John Stapleton. — 2nd ed. — London : Heinemann ... on behalf of the Institute of Marketing and the CAM Foundation, c1981. — 206p ; 19cm
Previous ed.: 1977
ISBN 0-434-91861-x (pbk) : £4.50 B81-35368

658.8′007′04 — Europe. Industrial marketing. Information sources — *Serials*

Published data on European industrial markets / Industrial Aids Limited. — [1981 ed.]. — London (14 Buckingham Palace Rd, SW1W 0QP) : Industrial Aids Limited, c1981. — 270p
Unpriced B81-36530

658.8′00722 — Marketing — *Case studies*

Corey, E. Raymond. Problems in marketing. — 6th ed., E. Raymond Corey, Christopher H. Lovelock, Scott Ward. — New York ; London : McGraw-Hill, 1981. — xviii,810p : ill,facsims ; 25cm. — (McGraw Hill series in marketing)
Previous ed.: by Steven H. Star ... [et al.], 1977
ISBN 0-07-013141-4 : £15.95 B81-30646

Proudman, A. J.. The marketing casebook : cases for analysis and planning / A.J. Proudman. — London : Associated Business Press, 1980. — xxii,284p : ill ; 23cm
Bibliography: p283-284
ISBN 0-85227-241-3 : £12.50 B81-09946

658.8′00722 — Marketing — *Case studies* — *For business studies*

Strategy and marketing. — Oxford : Philip Allan, Jan.1982. — [384]p
ISBN 0-86003-516-6 (cased) : £25.00 : CIP entry
ISBN 0-86003-615-4 (pbk) : £12.50 B81-38822

Strategy and marketing. — Oxford : Philip Allan, Jan.1982
Instructor′s manual. — [432]p
ISBN 0-86003-616-2 (pbk) : £8.50 : CIP entry B81-38823

658.8′00722 — United States. Marketing — *Case studies*

Talarzyk, W. Wayne. Cases for analysis in marketing / W. Wayne Talarzyk. — 2nd ed. — Chicago ; London : Dryden Press, c1981. — x,378p : ill,facsims,forms ; 24cm
Previous ed.: 1977
ISBN 0-03-058179-6 (pbk) : £4.95 B81-23093

658.8′0076 — Marketing — *Questions & answers*

Enis, Ben M.. Instructor′s manual to accompany Marketing classics : a selection of influential articles, fourth edition / Bem [i.e. Ben] M. Enis and Keith K. Cox in collaboration with George H. Lucas and John C. Sanders. — Boston [Mass.] ; London : Allyn and Bacon, c1981. — 71p ; 22cm
Includes bibliographies
ISBN 0-205-07326-3 (pbk) : £1.00 B81-26400

658.8'0094 — European Community countries. Marketing by business firms — *Comparative studies*

International marketing and purchasing executives in five European countries / edited by Peter W. Turnbull and Malcolm T. Cunningham in association with I.D. Ford and Elling Homse. — London : Macmillan, 1981. — xv,133p : ill ; 23cm
Includes index
ISBN 0-333-28989-7 : £20.00 B81-23260

658.8'00941 — Great Britain. Marketing by business firms — *Manuals*

Selling, importing and exporting. — London : Hamlyn, c1980. — 208p : ill,1form ; 22cm. — (Managing your business guides)
Includes bibliographies and index
ISBN 0-600-35366-4 : £5.00 B81-05113

658.8'00941 — Great Britain. Marketing — *Practical information — Serials*

[Monthly review *(Mintel Inmformation Services)*]. Monthly review / Mintel Information Services. — No.1 (Dec.1979)-. — London (20 Buckingham St., Strand WC2N 6EE) : The Services, 1979-. — v. ; 30cm
Description based on: No.13 (Dec.1980)
ISSN 0260-9444 = Monthly review — Mintel Information Services : £35.00 per year B81-13691

658.8'00956 — Middle East. Marketing

Vassiliou, G.. Marketing in the Middle East / G. Vassiliou. — London : Graham & Trotman, 1980. — vi,158p : ill ; 24cm
ISBN 0-86010-198-3 (pbk) : £25.00 B81-04550

658.8'094 — Europe. Marketing

International marketing and purchasing of industrial goods. — Chichester : Wiley, Feb.1982. — [432]p
ISBN 0-471-27987-0 : £17.50 : CIP entry
Also classified at 658.7'2'094 B81-36235

658.8'09'9141 — Great Britain. Tourist industries. Marketing — *Forecasts — Serials*

Tourism ... : Statements of marketing intent. — [197-]-. — [London] : British Tourist Authority, [197-]-. — v. : ill ; 30cm
Annual. — Description based on: 1980/81 issue
ISSN 0144-8099 = Tourism : Unpriced B81-20034

658.81 — SALES MANAGEMENT

658.8'1 — Sales management

Still, Richard R.. Sales management : decisions, strategies, and cases. — 4th ed. / Richard R. Still, Edward W. Cundiff, Norman A.P. Govoni. — Englewood Cliffs ; London : Prentice-Hall, c1981. — xx,699p : ill,forms ; 25cm
Previous ed.: 1976. — Includes index
ISBN 0-13-788059-6 : £14.25 B81-25994

658.8'1 — Sales management — *Manuals*

Beer, Michael, *1926-*. The many arts of sales management / Michael Beer. — London : McGraw-Hill, 1981, c1980. — viii,196p : ill ; 24cm
Originally published: Radnor, Pa. : Chilton, 1980. — Includes index
ISBN 0-07-084562-x : £9.95 : CIP rev. B81-14380

Dunn, Albert H.. Managing hour sales team / Albert H. Dunn & Eugene M. Johnson. — Englewood Cliffs ; London : Prentice-Hall, c1980. — x,256p : ill,forms ; 24cm. — (A Spectrum book)
Includes bibliographies and index
ISBN 0-13-550905-x (cased) : 9.05
ISBN 0-13-550897-5 (pbk) : £4.50 B81-02445

Fenton, John, *1938-*. The A-Z of sales management / John Fenton. — London : Pan in association with Heinemann, 1981, c1979. — 168p : ill,forms ; 18cm. — (Pan business/sales)
Originally published: London : Heinemann, 1979
ISBN 0-330-26323-4 (pbk) : £1.75 B81-19693

Sweeney, Neil R.. Managing a sales team : techniques for field sale managers. — London : Kogan Page, Dec.1981. — [272]p
ISBN 0-85038-539-3 : £10.95 : CIP entry B81-40246

658.8'12 — Companies. Customer services. Management aspects

Christopher, Martin. Customer service and distribution strategy / Martin Christopher, Philip Schary, Tage Skjott-Larsen. — London : Associated Business Press, 1979. — viii,191p : ill ; 23cm
Includes bibliographies and index
ISBN 0-85227-216-2 : £10.50 B81-07120

658.8'18 — Marketing. Forecasting

Bolt, Gordon J.. Market and sales forecasting : a total approach / Gordon J. Bolt. — 2nd ed. — London : Kogan Page, 1981. — 347p : ill,forms ; 23cm
Previous ed.: 1971. — Includes index
ISBN 0-85038-308-0 : £12.50 : CIP rev. B80-11087

658.82 — SALES PROMOTION

658.8'2 — Great Britain. Goods. Full-line forcing & tie-in sale - *Inquiry reports*

Great Britain. *Monopolies and Mergers Commission.* Full-line forcing and tie-in sales : a report on the practice of requiring any person to whom goods or services are supplied to acquire other goods or services as a condition of that supply / Monopolies and Mergers Commission. — London : H.M.S.O., [1981]. — v,55p ; 25cm. — (HC ; 212)
ISBN 0-10-221281-3 (pbk) : £3.90 B81-19013

658.8'2 — Sales promotion

Managing sales promotion / edited by Julia Piper. — Farnborough, Hants. : Gower in association with Marketing magazine, c1980. — xvi,280p : ill,facsims ; 23cm
Bibliography: p273. — Includes index
ISBN 0-566-02206-0 : £15.00 : CIP rev. B80-25903

658.8'2'02541 — Great Britain. Sales promotion services — *Directories — Serials*

Incentive marketing and sales promotion annual review and buyers' guide. — 1981-82. — Croydon : Maclaren, 1981. — 220p
ISSN 0143-5884 : £1.20 B81-36558

658.83 — MARKET RESEARCH AND ANALYSIS

658.8'3 — Market research — *For management*

Crimp, Margaret. The marketing research process / Margaret Crimp. — Englewood Cliffs ; London : Prentice-Hall, c1981. — xiii,256p : ill ; 23cm
Bibliography: p234-235. — Includes index
ISBN 0-13-557710-1 (pbk) : £6.95 : CIP rev. B81-22483

Myers, John G.. Marketing research and knowledge development : an assessment for marketing management / John G. Myers, William F. Massy, Stephen A. Greyser. — Englewood Cliffs ; London : Prentice-Hall, c1980. — xiv,306p ; 24cm
Includes index
ISBN 0-13-557686-5 : £12.30 B81-04878

658.8'3 — Marketing. Research

Chisnall, Peter M.. Marketing research : analysis and measurement / Peter M. Chisnall. — 2nd ed. — London : McGraw-Hill, c1981. — xi,391p : ill ; 23cm
Previous ed.: 1973. — Includes index
ISBN 0-07-084559-x (cased) : Unpriced : CIP rev.
ISBN 0-07-084124-1 (pbk) : £8.50 B81-13436

658.8'3'025 — Market research organisations — *Directories — Serials*

The **International** research directory of market research organisations / the Market Research Society [and] British Overseas Trade Board. — 5th ed. (1980)-. — London (15, Belgrave Sq., SW1X 8PF) : The Society, 1980-. — 565p in various pagings
ISBN 0-906117-01-1 : Unpriced B81-04897

658.8'342 — Consumer behaviour

Woods, Walter A.. Consumer behavior : adapting and experiencing / Walter A. Woods. — New York ; Oxford : North Holland, c1981. — xvi,485p : ill ; 24cm
Bibliography: p443-460. - Includes index
ISBN 0-444-00430-0 : £13.21 B81-11297

658.8'35 — South-east Asia. Consumer goods. Marketing. Forecasts — *Conference proceedings*

Marketing trends in the Asia Pacific region. — Aldershot : Gower, Feb.1982. — [224]p
Conference papers
ISBN 0-566-02361-x : £75.00 : CIP entry B81-36215

658.84 — MARKETING. CHANNELS OF DISTRIBUTION

658.8'4'0941 — Great Britian. Distributive trades. Management

Watson, Peter, *1947-*. The organization and economics of distribution / Peter Watson, John Williamson. — London : McGraw-Hill, c1981. — xii,192p : ill ; 25cm. — (McGraw-Hill business education courses)
Includes index
ISBN 0-07-084248-5 (pbk) : £3.95 : CIP rev. B81-13437

658.8'48 — Great Britain. Exports to Arab countries. Marketing — *For British businessmen — Conference proceedings*

Advertising and marketing in Arabia / [proceedings of a one-day conference held on 18 February 1981 by the Arab-British Chamber of Commerce]. — London (26A Albermarle St., W1A 4BL) : The Chamber of Commerce, 1981. — 40p ; 30cm. — (An Arab-British Chamber of Commerce publication) (Focus reports / Arab-British Chamber of Commerce)
Unpriced (pbk) B81-18814

658.8'48 — Great Britain. Importing — *Manuals*

Lambourne, G.. Importing for beginners / Gerald G. Lambourne. — 3rd ed. — London : Malcolm Stewart Books, 1980. — 62p ; 25cm. — (Kingfisher business guides)
Previous ed.: 1979. — Bibliography: p57-58. - Includes index
ISBN 0-904132-53-6 (pbk) : £3.50 B81-11990

658.8'48 — United States. Exports to China. Marketing — *For American businessmen*

Massimino, Sal T.. How to sell to the People's Republic of China / Sal T. Massimino. — London : Oyez, c1980. — xi,153p : ill,2maps,1form ; 24cm
Includes index
ISBN 0-85120-526-7 (corrected) : Unpriced B81-30934

658.8'48'0722 — Great Britain. Exports. Marketing — *Case studies*

Smith, A. Andy. Case studies in export dynamics / A. Smith & T.K. Reeves. — London (Duncan House, High St., E15 2JB) : Anglian Regional Management Centre, c1981. — 92p ; 30cm. — (The Anglian Regional Management Centre case study series)
Unpriced (pbk) B81-26536

658.8'48'0941 — Great Britain. Exporting — *Manuals*

Lambourne, G.. Exporting for beginners / G. Lambourne. — London : Malcolm Stewart Books, 1977 (1980 [printing]). — 76p ; 25cm. — (Kingfisher business guides)
Bibliography: p72. - Includes index
ISBN 0-904132-32-3 (pbk) : £3.90 B81-11991

Lambourne, G.. Exporting for beginners / Gerald G. Lambourne. — 2nd ed. — London (P.O. Box 265, N3 2QF) : Malcolm Stewart, 1981. — 80p : ill,2forms ; 25cm. — (Kingfisher business guides)
Previous ed.: 1977. — Bibliography: p75-76. — Includes index
ISBN 0-904132-56-0 (pbk) : £4.50 B81-40380

658.85 — SALESMANSHIP

658.8'5 — Salesmanship

Marks, Ronald B.. Instructor's manual to accompany Personal selling : an interactive approach / Ronald B. Marks. — Boston, Mass. ; London : Allyn and Bacon, c1981. — xxv,230p : ill ; 24cm
ISBN 0-205-07328-x (pbk) : £1.00 B81-16299

Marks, Ronald B.. Personal selling : an interactive approach / Ronald B. Marks. — Boston [Mass.] ; London : Allyn and Bacon, c1981. — viii,534p : ill,maps,facsims,forms ; 25cm
Includes index
ISBN 0-205-07327-1 : Unpriced B81-26206

658.8'5 — Salesmanship — *Manuals*

Anderson, B. Robert. Professional selling / B. Robert Anderson. — 2nd ed. — Englewood Cliffs ; London : Prentice-Hall, c1981. — x,389p : ill ; 24cm
Previous ed.: 1977. — Bibliography: p384-385. — Includes index
ISBN 0-13-725960-3 : £10.75 B81-16645

Blake, Robert R.. The Grid for sales excellence : new insights into a proven system of effective sales / Robert R. Blake, Jane Srygley Mouton. — 2nd ed. — New York ; London : McGraw-Hill, c1980. — viii,238p : ill,1form ; 24cm
Previous ed.: 1970. — Includes index
ISBN 0-07-005680-3 : £9.55 B81-01016

Brownstone, David M.. Sell your way to success / David M. Brownstone. — New York ; Chichester : Wiley, c1979. — x,212p ; 22cm
Bibliography: p203-204. — Includes index
ISBN 0-471-09257-6 (cased) : £8.00
ISBN 0-471-09242-8 (pbk) : Unpriced B81-23349

Nordstrom, Richard D.. Introduction to selling : an experiential approach to skill development / Richard D. Nordstrom. — New York : Macmillan ; London : Collier Macmillan, c1981. — xiii,315p : ill,forms ; 26cm
Includes bibliographies and index
ISBN 0-02-388200-x (pbk) : £6.95 B81-36171

658.8'5 — Salesmen. Stress. Control

Stern, Frances Meritt. Stress-less selling : a guide to success for men & women in sales / Frances Meritt Stern, Ron Zemke. — Englewood Cliffs ; London : Prentice Hall, c1981. — xvii,302p : ill ; 24cm. — (A Spectrum book)
Bibliography: p291-295. — Includes index
ISBN 0-13-852749-0 (cased) : Unpriced
ISBN 0-13-852731-8 (pbk) : Unpriced B81-18312

658.8'5'019 — Salesmanship. Applications of transactional analysis — *Manuals*

Villere, Maurice F.. Successful personal selling through TA / Maurice F. Villere, Claude P. Duet. — Englewood Cliffs ; London : Prentice-Hall, c1980. — xi,271p : ill,1form ; 24cm. — (A Spectrum book)
Bibliography: p262-264. - Includes index
ISBN 0-13-864579-5 (cased) : £8.40
ISBN 0-13-864561-2 : £4.50 B81-06749

658.8'5'0922 — United States. Salesmanship — *Personal observations — Collections*

How I made the sale that did the most for me : fifty great sales stories told by fifty great salespeople / edited by J. Mel Hickerson. — New York ; Chichester : Wiley, c1981. — xxi,372p : ill,facsims,ports ; 24cm
ISBN 0-471-07769-0 : £7.50 B81-23325

658.8'5'0973 — United States. Salesmanship — *Manuals*

Grikscheit, Gary M.. Handbook of selling : psychological, managerial and marketing bases / Gary M. Grikscheit, Harold C. Cash, W.J.E. Crissy. — New York ; Chichester : Wiley, c1981. — xxi,671p : ill ; 24cm. — (Ronald series on marketing management)
Bibliography: p484-495. — Includes index
ISBN 0-471-04482-2 : £22.00 B81-30019

658.87 — RETAILING

658.8'7 — Retailing - *Manuals*

Foster, Ann. The retail handbook. — London : McGraw-Hill, Sept.1981. — [192]p
ISBN 0-07-084565-4 (pbk) : £5.95 : CIP entry B81-20548

658.8'7'002341 — Great Britain. Retailing — *Career guides*

Douglas, Carol. Working in retailing / Carol Douglas. — London : Batsford Academic and Educational, 1980. — 96p,[8]p of plates : ill ; 23cm
Includes index
ISBN 0-7134-2361-7 : £5.75 B81-01017

658.8'7'00941 — Great Britain. Retailing — *Statistics*

. The Retail management data book. — [Brighton] ([5 East St., Brighton N1 1HP]) : Retail Management Development Programme, 1980. — 1v(loose-leaf) : ill ; 33cm
Unpriced B81-08136

The Retail management data book / [Retail Management Development Programme Limited]. — 2nd ed. — Brighton (5 East St., Brighton BN1 1HP) : RMOP, [1981]. — 2v.(Loose-leaf) : ill ; 33cm
Previous ed.: 1980
Unpriced B81-21756

658.8'702'0687 — Great Britain. Multiple shops. Stock control. Purchasing

Douglas, R. A.. A study of supplier selection by multiple retailers and cash and carries / R.A. Douglas and P.J. McGoldrick. — Manchester : Dept. of Management Sciences, University of Manchester Institute of Science and Technology, 1981. — 36p : forms ; 31cm. — (Occasional paper / Department of Management Sciences, University of Manchester Institute of Science and Technology ; no.8109)
Unpriced (pbk)
Also classified at 658.8'705'0687 B81-40831

658.8'705'0687 — Great Britain. Cash and carry depots. Stock control. Purchasing

Douglas, R. A.. A study of supplier selection by multiple retailers and cash and carries / R.A. Douglas and P.J. McGoldrick. — Manchester : Dept. of Management Sciences, University of Manchester Institute of Science and Technology, 1981. — 36p : forms ; 31cm. — (Occasional paper / Department of Management Sciences, University of Manchester Institute of Science and Technology ; no.8109)
Unpriced (pbk)
Primary classification 658.8'702'0687 B81-40831

658.8'708'0941 — Great Britain. Franchising

Gunz, Sally. Franchising / by Sally Gunz, T. Regan, Derek F. Channon. — Manchester (Booth Street West, Manchester M15 6PB) : Centre for Business Research in association with Manchester Business School, University of Manchester, [1980]. — 117p ; 30cm. — (Research report / Centre for Business Research, ISSN 0306-5227)
Unpriced (spiral) B81-14290

Mendelsohn, Martin. The guide to franchising. — 3rd ed. — Oxford : Pergamon, Jan.1982. — [240]p
ISBN 0-08-025845-x : £15.00 : CIP entry B81-34468

658.8'708'0973 — United States. Franchising

Friedlander, Mark P.. Handbook of successful franchising / Mark P. Friedlander, Jr., Gene Gurney. — New York ; London : Van Nostrand Reinhold, c1981. — x,458p : 1ill ; 29cm
ISBN 0-442-22986-0 : £16.95 B81-35252

658.8'72'0973 — United States. Mail-order firms. Organisation — *Manuals*

Simon, Julian L.. How to start and operate a mail-order business / Julian L. Simon. — 3rd ed. / with contributions by Paul Bringe [et al.]. — New York ; London : McGraw-Hill, c1981. — xvii,536p : ill,facsims,forms ; 25cm
Previous ed.: 1976. — Bibliography: p505-510. - Includes index
ISBN 0-07-057417-0 : £11.95 B81-06166

658.88 — CREDIT MANAGEMENT

658.8'8'05 — Credit management — *Serials*

D & B creditnews. — Vol.1, no.1 (Feb. 1981)-. — London : Dun & Bradstreet, 1981-. — v. : ill,ports ; 30cm
Monthly. — Continues: Credit reporter
ISSN 0261-8982 = D & B creditnews : £75.00 per year B81-38187

658.8'8'0941 — Great Britain. Credit management

Goddard, Scott. Credit management : a survey of credit control and debt collection policies and practice / Scott Goddard and Steve Jay. — Poole : Research and Publications Division, BIM Foundation, c1981. — iv,50p ; 30cm. — (Management survey report ; no.52)
Bibliography: p50
ISBN 0-85946-115-7 (pbk) : Unpriced B81-33330

659.1 — ADVERTISING

659.1 — Advertising

Fulop, Christina. Advertising, competition and consumer behaviour. — Eastbourne : Holt, Rinehart and Winston, Oct.1981. — [192]p
ISBN 0-03-910295-5 : £12.50 : CIP entry B81-31206

Johnson, J. Douglas. Advertising today / J. Douglas Johnson ; [illustrator Judith McCarty]. — Chicago ; Henley-on-Thames : Science Research Associates, c1978. — x,395p,[16]p of plates : ill(some col.),maps,facsims ; 31cm
Includes index
ISBN 0-574-19355-3 (pbk) : £10.70 B81-09325

Mandell, Maurice I.. Advertising / Maurice I. Mandell. — 3rd ed. — Englewood Cliffs ; London : Prentice-Hall, c1980. — xiv,752p,[4]p of plates : ill(some col.),facsims ; 24cm
Previous ed.: 1974. — Bibliography: p738-744. — Includes index
ISBN 0-13-014449-5 : £17.20 B81-40128

659.1 — Advertising — *Manuals*

White, Roderick. Advertising : what it is and how to do it / Roderick White. — London : McGraw-Hill in association with the Advertising Association, c1980. — xi,230p,[16]p of plates : ill,1map,facsims,forms ; 24cm
Bibliography: p219-220. - Includes index
ISBN 0-07-084538-7 : £6.50 : CIP rev. B80-18417

659.1 — Advertising. Positioning

Ries, Al. Positioning : the battle for your mind / by Al Ries and Jack Trout. — New York ; London : McGraw-Hill, c1981. — xii,246p ; 21cm
Includes index
ISBN 0-07-065263-5 : £6.95 B81-03959

659.1 — Public service advertising

Public communication campaigns / edited by Ronald E. Rice, William J. Paisley. — Beverley Hills ; London : Sage, c1981. — 328p ; 22cm
Bibliography: p293-313. — Includes index
ISBN 0-8039-1578-0 : £18.75 B81-38962

659.1'028 — Advertising. Techniques

Wademan, Victor. Money-making advertising : a guide to advertising that sells / Victor Wademan. — New York ; Chichester : Wiley, c1981. — xiii,142p : ill,facsims ; 24cm
Includes index
ISBN 0-471-06276-6 : £9.75 B81-18995

659.1'042'0973 — United States. Society. Role of advertising

Packard, Vance. The hidden persuaders / Vance Packard. — Reprinted with introduction and epilogue. — Harmondsworth : Penguin, 1981. — 248p ; 18cm
Originally published: New York : McKay ; London : Longmans, Green, 1957. — Includes index
ISBN 0-14-020585-3 (pbk) : £1.50 B81-27653

659.1'0722 — Advertising — *Case studies*

Greyser, Stephen A.. Cases in advertising and communications management / Stephen A. Greyser. — 2nd ed. — Englewood Cliffs ; London : Prentice-Hall, c1981. — xviii,644p : ill,facsims,forms ; 24cm
Previous ed.: 1972. — Includes index
ISBN 0-13-118513-6 : £15.35 B81-26908

659.1'0941 — Great Britain. Advertising, *to 1979*

Nevett, T. R.. Advertising in Britain. — London : Scolar Press, May 1981. — [288]p
ISBN 0-85967-598-x (cased) : £15.00 : CIP entry
ISBN 0-85967-632-3 (pbk) : £6.95 B81-08808

659.1'0973 — United States. Advertising

Bolen, William H.. Advertising / William H. Bolen. — New York ; Chichester : Wiley, c1981. — xviii,504p,[8]p of plates : ill(some col.),1map,facsims ; 25cm. — (Wiley series in marketing)
Ill on lining papers. — Includes index
ISBN 0-471-03486-x : £12.00 B81-16948

659.1'0973 — United States. Advertising by companies — *Manuals*

Garbett, Thomas F.. Corporate advertising : the what, the why, and the how / Thomas F. Garbett. — New York ; London : McGraw-Hill, c1981. — xi,252p : ill,facsims ; 25cm
Includes index
ISBN 0-07-022787-x : Unpriced B81-26656

659.1'11 — Great Britain. Advertising. Effectiveness — *Case studies*

Advertising works : papers from the IPA Advertising Effectiveness Awards, Institute of Practitioners in Advertising, 1980 / edited and introduced by Simon Broadbent. — London : Holt, Rinehart and Winston, 1981. — xvi,207p : ill,facsims ; 25cm
Includes index
ISBN 0-03-910322-6 : £10.00 : CIP rev. B81-07421

659.1'125 — In-house advertising agencies

Holtje, Herbert F.. How to be your own advertising agency / Bert Holtje ; illustrated by Roger Engelke. — New York ; London : McGraw-Hill, c1981. — viii,215p : ill ; 24cm. — (A James Peter Book)
Bibliography: p206-209. — Includes index
ISBN 0-07-029665-0 : £12.95 B81-39259

659.1'125'094 — Western Europe. Advertising agencies — *Statistics* — *Serials*

Campaign Europe annual agency survey. — July 1979-. — London (Haymarket Pub., 22 Lancaster Gate, W2 3LY) : Campaign Europe, 1979-. — v. : ill ; 29cm
Supplement to: Campaigneurope. — Description based on: 1980 issue
Unpriced B81-04869

659.13 — Advertising media

Davis, Martyn P.. The effective use of advertising media : a practical guide / by Martyn P. Davis. — London : Published in association with the Institute of Marketing and the CAM Foundation [by] Business Books, 1981. — xxiv,322p ; 24cm
Includes index
ISBN 0-09-142970-6 (cased) : Unpriced : CIP rev.
ISBN 0-09-142971-4 (pbk) : £5.95 B80-23468

659.13 — Pictorial advertising — *Illustrations* — *Serials*

Modern publicity. — Vol.49 (1980). — London : Studio Vista, 1980. — 191p
ISBN 0-289-70898-2 : £19.50 B81-02781

659.13'025 — Advertising media — *Directories* — *Serials*

Overseas media guide / Overseas Press and Media Association. — 14th ed. (1980). — London (122 Shaftesbury Ave., W1V 8HA) : The Association, [1980]. — 208p
£5.00 B81-00184

659.13'14 — Cars. Pictorial advertising — *Illustrations* — *Serials*

Advertisement parade annual. M, Cars and associated products. — 1981. — Rustington (82a, The Street, Rustington, West Sussex BN16 3NR) : Visual Publications, [1981?]. — 132p
ISBN 0-903887-77-0 : Unpriced B81-09124

659.13'14 — Clothing. Pictorial advertising — *Illustrations* — *Serials*

Advertisement parade annual. C, Fashion and footwear. — 1981. — Rustington (82a, The Street, Rustington, West Sussex BN16 3NR) : Visual Publications, [1981?]. — 132p
ISBN 0-903887-75-4 : Unpriced B81-09125

659.13'14 — Cosmetics, perfumes & toiletries. Pictorial advertising — *Illustrations* — *Serials*

Advertisement parade annual. D, Beauty and hygiene. — 1981. — Rustington (82a, The Street, Rustington, West Sussex BN16 3NR) : Visual Publications, [1981?]. — 132p
ISBN 0-903887-76-2 : Unpriced B81-09123

659.13'14 — Food & drinks. Pictorial advertising — *Illustrations* — *Serials*

Advertisement parade annual. B, Food and drink. — 1981. — Rustington (82a, The Street, Rustington, West Sussex BN16 3NR) : Visual Publications, [1981?]. — 132p
ISBN 0-903887-74-6 : Unpriced B81-09122

659.13'14 — Household equipment. Pictorial advertising — *Illustrations* — *Serials*

Advertisement parade annual. A, Household appliances and articles. — 1981. — Rustington (82a, The Street, Rustington, West Sussex BN16 3NR) : Visual Publications, [1981?]. — 132p
ISBN 0-903887-73-8 : Unpriced B81-09121

659.13'42 — Outdoor advertising posters — *Illustrations*

Henderson, Sally. Billboard art / Sally Henderson & Robert Landau ; edited by Michelle Feldman ; with an introduction by David Hockney. — London : Angus & Robertson, 1981, c1980. — 112p : ill(some col.),ports(some col.) ; 21x28cm
Bibliography: p4
ISBN 0-207-95973-0 (pbk) : £4.95 B81-17731

659.13'42'0942561 — Bedfordshire. North Bedfordshire *(District).* **Outdoor advertising. Regulation** — *Proposals*

North Bedfordshire. *Borough Council.* Advertisements : a guide to design / NBBC. — [Bedford] ([37 Goldington Rd., Bedford MK40 3LQ]) : [North Bedfordshire Borough Council], [1977]. — 2,[10]leaves : ill ; 30cm
Cover title
Unpriced (pbk) B81-26358

659.14'0941 — Great Britain. Broadcast advertising — *Codes of conduct*

Independent Broadcasting Authority. The IBA code of advertising standards and practice. — London (70 Brompton Rd., SW3 1EY) : IBA, 1981. — 20p ; 23cm
Includes index
Unpriced (pbk) B81-40885

659.14'3'0973 — United States. Television advertising

Busch, H. Ted. The making of a television commercial / H. Ted Busch & Terry Landeck. — New York : Macmillan ; London : Collier Macmillan, c1980. — xi,175p : ill ; 21cm
ISBN 0-02-518830-5 : £6.25 B81-38656

659.1'5 — Libraries. Displays — *Manuals*

Franklin, Linda Campbell. Library display ideas / Linda Campbell Franklin. — Jefferson, N.C. : McFarland ; Folkestone : Distributed by Bailey Bros. & Swinfen, 1980. — xiv,230p : ill ; 24cm
Includes index
ISBN 0-89950-008-0 (cased) : Unpriced
ISBN 0-89950-009-9 (pbk) : £6.35 B81-38762

659.1'52 — Fashion. Modelling — *Career guides*

Household, Nicki. Working as a model / Nicki Household. — London : Batsford Academic and Educational, 1981. — 104p : ill ; 23cm
Includes index
ISBN 0-7134-2339-0 : £5.75 B81-29483

659.1'52'025 — Trade exhibitions — *Directories* — *Serials*

The Exhibitor's handbook. — 1981/82. — London : Kogan Page, 1981. — x,365p
ISBN 0-85038-453-2 : £12.95 : CIP rev.
ISSN 0260-1508 B81-14464

659.1'9072 — Newspapers with British imprints. Supplements. Advertising by advertising agencies

Incorporated Society of British Advertisers. Press supplements and the advertiser / [The Incorporated Society of British Advertisers]. — 2nd ed. — London (2 Basil St., SW13 1AG) : ISBA, 1977. — 8p ; 21cm
Cover title. — Previous ed.: 1973
Unpriced (pbk) B81-18664

659.1'96633'0941 — Great Britain. Breweriana — *Collectors' guides*

Wilson, Keith, *1947-*. An introduction to breweriana : a study of British brewery advertising relics / by Keith Wilson. — Northampton (101 Fullingdale Rd., Northampton NN3 2PZ) : Brewtique, c1981. — 80p : ill ; 22cm
ISBN 0-9507495-0-8 (pbk) : £1.95 B81-35308

659.2 — PUBLIC RELATIONS

659.2 — Business firms. Public relations

Coulson-Thomas, Colin. Public relations. — London : Business Books, Sept.1981. — [256]p
ISBN 0-09-142960-9 : £15.00 : CIP entry B81-17516

659.2 — Business firms. Public relations — *Manuals*

Bland, Michael. Be your own PR man : a public relations guide for the small businessman / Michael Bland. — London : Kogan Page, 1981. — 176p : ill ; 23cm
ISBN 0-85038-394-3 : £9.95 B81-16140

659.2 — Public relations

Reilly, Robert T.. Public relations in action / Robert T. Reilly. — Englewood Cliffs : Prentice-Hall, c1981. — xii,468p : ill,facsims,ports ; 25cm
Includes bibliographies and index
ISBN 0-13-738526-9 : £12.30 B81-22704

659.2'023'41 — Great Britain. Public relations — *Career guides*

A Career in marketing, advertising and public relations / edited by Norman A. Hart and Gilbert W. Lamb ; foreword by Lord Robens of Woldingham. — London : Heinemann on behalf of the CAM Foundation and the Institute of Marketing, c1981. — xxiii,164p : ill ; 22cm
Bibliography: p155. - Includes index
ISBN 0-434-90711-1 (pbk) : £4.95
Primary classification 658.8'0023'41 B81-23387

659.2'0722 — United States. Public relations — *Case studies*

Center, Allen H.. Public relations practices : case studies. — 2nd ed. / Allen H. Center, Frank E. Walsh. — Englewood Cliffs ; London : Prentice-Hall, c1981. — xiv,363p : ill,1map,facsims,ports ; 24cm
Previous ed.: / by Allen H. Center 1975. — Includes bibliographies and index
ISBN 0-13-738716-4 (pbk) : £9.05 B81-25168

659.2'93805 — Transport services. Public relations

Wragg, David W.. Publicity and customer relations in transport management. — Aldershot : Gower, Nov.1981. — [120]p
ISBN 0-566-00442-9 (pbk) : £8.50 : CIP entry B81-30561

659.2'99141 — Great Britain. Tourism. Promotion — *Proposals*

British Tourist Authority. Strategic plan : 1981 to 1985 / British Tourist Authority. — London : British Tourist Authority, 1981. — 23p ; 30cm
Cover title
ISBN 0-7095-0900-6 (pbk) : £1.50 B81-37363

659.2′991423 — South-west England. Tourism. Promotion — *Proposals*

West Country Tourist Board. A strategy for tourism in the West Country / West Country Tourist Board, English Tourist Board. — [Exeter] ([Trinity Court, Southernhay East, Exeter EX1 1QS]) : [West Country Tourist Board], 1980. — 27,A37p,1folded leaf of plates : 1col.map ; 30cm
Cover title
£2.50 (spiral) B81-10736

660 — CHEMICAL TECHNOLOGY

660 — Chemical technology — *Case studies — For schools*

Harrison, W.. Industrial chemistry. — London : Edward Arnold, Jan.1982. — 1v.
ISBN 0-7131-0588-7 (pbk) : CIP entry B81-34581

660 — Chemical technology. Environmental aspects

Chemical engineering and the environment / edited by A.A. Teja. — Oxford : Published for the Society of Chemical Industry by Blackwell Scientific, 1981. — ix,100p : ill ; 24cm. — (Critical reports on applied chemistry ; v.3)
Bibliography: p95-96. — Includes index
ISBN 0-632-00693-5 (pbk) : £8.00 B81-20019

660′.03′21 — Chemical technology — *Encyclopaedias*

Encyclopedia of chemical technology / editorial board Herman F. Mark ... [et al.]. — 3rd ed. — New York ; Chichester : Wiley
At head of title: Kirk-Othmer. — Previous ed.: / Raymond Eller Kirk and Donald Frederick Othmer. New York ; London : Interscience, 1963-73
Vol.7: Copper alloys to distillation / executive editor, Martin Grayson, associate editor David Eckroth. — c1979. — xxvi,891p : ill ; 27cm
ISBN 0-471-02043-5 : £60.00 B81-26172

Encyclopedia of chemical technology. — 3rd ed. / [executive editor Martin Grayson] ; [associate editor David Eckroth]. — New York ; Chichester : Wiley
Previous ed.: / by Kirk and Othmer. New York : London : Interscience, 1963-72
Vol.11: Fluorine compounds, organic to gold and gold compounds. — c1980. — xxvi,995p : ill ; 27cm
At head of title Kirk - Othmer
ISBN 0-471-02064-8 : £60.00 B81-10762

Encyclopedia of chemical technology. — 3rd ed. / [executive editor Martin Grayson] ; [associate editor David Eckroth]. — New York ; Chichester : Wiley
Previous ed.: / by Kirk and Othmer. New York : London : Interscience, 1963-72
Vol.12: Gravity concentration to hydrogen energy. — 1980. — xxvi,1037p : ill ; 27cm
At head of title: Kirk - Othmer
ISBN 0-471-02065-6 : £60.00 B81-10763

Encyclopedia of chemical technology / editorial board Herman F. Mark ... [et al.]. — 3rd ed. — New York ; Chichester : Wiley
Previous ed.: / by Raymond Eller Kirk and Donald Frederick Othmer. 1963-1972
Vol.13: Hydrogen-ion activity to laminated materials, glass / executive editor Martin Grayson ; associate editor David Eckroth. — c1981. — xxvi,993p : ill ; 27cm
At head of title: Kirk-Othmer
ISBN 0-471-02066-4 : £60.00 B81-29488

Encyclopedia of chemical technology / editorial board Herman F. Mark ... [et al.]. — 3rd ed. — New York ; Chichester : Wiley
Previous ed.: / by Raymond Eller Kirk and Donald Frederick Othmer. 1963-1972
Vol.14: Laminated wood-based composites to mass transfer / executive editor Martin Grayson ; associate editor David Eckroth. — c1981. — xxvi,981p : ill ; 27cm
At head of title: Kirk-Othmer
ISBN 0-471-02067-2 : £60.00 B81-24976

Encyclopedia of chemical technology. — 3rd ed. — New York ; Chichester : Wiley
At head of title: Kirk-Othmer. — Previous ed.: / by Kirk and Othmer, New York : London : Interscience, 1963-72
Index : volumes 9 to 12 : enamels to hydrogen energy. — c1981. — 254p ; 26cm
ISBN 0-471-02066-4 (pbk) : Unpriced B81-24927

660.2 — CHEMICAL ENGINEERING

660.2 — Chemical engineering

Danckwerts, P. V.. Insights into chemical engineering : (selected papers of P.V. Danckwerts) / by P.V. Danckwerts. — Oxford : Pergamon, 1981. — xviii,307p : ill ; 26cm
Includes index
ISBN 0-08-026250-3 : £27.00 : CIP rev. B81-13434

660.2 — Industrial processes. Chemical analysis. Sampling

Cornish, D. C.. Sampling systems for process analysers / D.C. Cornish, G. Jepson, M.J. Smurthwaite. — London : Butterworths, 1981. — xiv,453p : ill ; 26cm
Includes bibliographies and index
ISBN 0-408-00261-1 : Unpriced : CIP rev. B80-00809

660.2 — Two-phase flow. Bubble processes. Applications

Azbel, David. Two-phase flows in chemical engineering / David Azbel with editorial assistance by Philip Kemp-Pritchard. — Cambridge : Cambridge University Press, 1981. — xx,311p : ill ; 24cm
Includes index
ISBN 0-521-23772-6 : £45.00 B81-39908

660.2′025′41 — Great Britain. Chemical engineering. Consultants — *Directories — Serials*

Institution of Chemical Engineers. List of consultants / the Institution of Chemical Engineers. — 1981/82. — Rugby : The Institution, c1981. — [103]p in various pagings
Unpriced B81-32800

660.2′0724 — Chemical engineering. Simulations: Flowcharts. Construction. Applications of digital computer systems. SIMUL system

Steady-state flow-sheeting of chemical plants / edited by P. Benedek ; [translated by M. Preisich]. — Amsterdam ; Oxford : Elsevier Scientific, 1980. — 409p : ill ; 25cm. — (Chemical engineering monographs ; v.12)
Translation from the Hungarian. — Includes index
ISBN 0-444-99765-2 : £29.25 : CIP : rev. B80-18846

660.2′8 — Chemical engineering plants — *Conference proceedings*

Future developments in process plant technology : conference sponsored by the Process Industries Division of the Institution of Mechanical Engineers in conjunction with the Process Plant Association : 24-25 February 1981, Institution Headquarters, 1 Birdcage Walk, Westminster, London. — London : Published by Mechanical Engineering Publications for the Institution of Mechanical Engineers, 1981. — 164p : ill,plans ; 30cm. — (I Mech E conference publications ; 1981-1)
ISBN 0-85298-471-5 (pbk) : Unpriced B81-23682

660.2′8 — Chemical engineering. Process analysis

Resnick, William. Process analysis and design for chemical engineers / William Resnick. — New York ; London : McGraw-Hill, c1981. — xix,363p : ill ; 24cm. — (McGraw-Hill chemical engineering series)
Bibliography: p352-355. - Includes index
ISBN 0-07-051887-4 : £18.00
Also classified at 660.2′83 B81-13660

660.2′8 — Great Britain. Chemical engineering plants. Design & construction. Lump sum contracts. Standard conditions

Model form of conditions of contract for process plants : suitable for lump-sum contracts in the United Kingdom. — Rev. [ed.]. — Rugby : Institution of Chemical Engineers, 1981. — iv,57p : 2forms ; 29cm
Previous ed.: 1968. — Includes index
ISBN 0-85295-132-9 (pbk) : Unpriced B81-29512

660.2′8′0068 — Great Britain. Chemical engineering plant equipment industries. Resources. Management

Better uses of resources in the manufacture of process plant / Process Plant EDC. — London (Millbank Tower, Millbank, London SW1P 4QX) : National Economic Development Office, 1980. — iv,10p ; 21cm
ISBN 0-7292-0424-3 (pbk) : Unpriced B81-14633

660.2′804 — Chemical engineering. Design. Safety aspects — *Conference proceedings*

Design for safety : a symposium organised by the Midland Branch of the Institution of Chemical Engineers at Aston University, September 12-14, 1977. — Birmingham (IHD Dept., University of Aston in Birmingham, Birmingham B4 7ET) : Midlands Branch, Institution of Chemical Engineers, c1980. — [197]p : ill,plans ; 30cm
Unpriced (pbk) B81-10943

660.2′804 — Chemical engineering plants. Design. Implications of explosions — *Conference proceedings*

Design and siting of buildings to resist explosions and fire. — [London] : Oyez, [1981]. — iv,50leaves : ill ; 30cm. — (Oyez intelligence reports)
Conference papers. — Edited by Arthur Conway
ISBN 0-85120-552-6 (spiral) : £55.00 B81-14480

660.2′804 — Chemical plants. Dust extraction systems

A **user** guide to dust and fume control / produced by the Engineering Committee Working Party on Dust and Fume Control. — Rugby : Institution of Chemical Engineers, c1981. — iii,130p : ill ; 21cm
Bibliography: p125-128
ISBN 0-85295-125-6 (pbk) : Unpriced B81-33680

660.2′804 — Chemical plants. Pressure piping systems. Inspection. Safety measures — *Standards*

Institute of Petroleum. Pressure piping systems inspection safety code / Institute of Petroleum. — London : Heyden on behalf of the Institute, 1978, c1979 (1979 [printing]). — viii,21p : 1form ; 31cm. — (Institute of Petroleum model code of safe practice in the petroleum industry ; pt.13)
ISBN 0-85501-323-0 : Unpriced B81-27719

660.2′804 — Great Britain. Chemical engineering plants. Air. Pollutants: Toxic materials. Control measures

A **Guide** to the evaluation and control of toxic substances in the work environment / prepared by the Occupational Hygiene Sub-Committee of the Chemical Industry Safety and Health Council of the Chemical Industries Association. — London (93 Albert Embankment, SE1 7TU) : Health Committee of the Chemical Industry Safety and Health Council of the Chemical Industries Association, c1980. — 48p ; 30cm
Unpriced (pbk) B81-11855

660.2′8′0681 — Chemical engineering plants. Project management. Costs. Control — *Manuals*

Kharbanda, O. P.. Project cost control in action / O.P. Kharbanda, E.A. Stallworthy, L.F. Williams. — Farnborough, Hants. : Gower, c1980. — xxii,273p : ill,forms ; 23cm
Bibliography: p239-248. — Includes index
ISBN 0-566-02164-1 : £15.00 : CIP rev. B80-06493

660.2′8′0941 — Great Britain. Chemical engineering plants. Reliability — *Conference proceedings*

Reliable production in the process industries : EFCE event no. 244 / organised by the Scottish Branch of the Institution of Chemical Engineers in Edinburgh, 29-30 April 1981 ; editor of the proceedings C.D. Grant. — Rugby : Institution of Chemical Engineers, c1981. — 224p : ill,forms ; 21cm. — (Institution of Chemical Engineers symposium series, ISSN 0307-0492 ; no.66) (EFCE publication series ; no.19)
Conference papers
ISBN 0-85295-137-x (pbk) : Unpriced B81-27515

660.2′81 — Chemical engineering. Automation — *Conference proceedings*

Instrumentation and automation in the paper, rubber, plastics and polymerisation industries : proceedings of the 4th IFAC Conference Ghent, Belgium, 3-5 June 1980 / edited by A. Van Cauwenberghe. — Oxford : Published for the International Federation of Automatic Control by Pergamon, 1981. — xxix,665p : ill ; 31cm
Includes bibliographies
ISBN 0-08-024487-4 : £50.00 B81-25341

660.2′81 — Chemical engineering. Design — *Conference proceedings*

Current design thinking : a symposium organised by the Midlands Branch of the Institution of Chemical Engineers at Aston University, September 12-14, 1979. — Birmingham (IHD Dept., University of Aston in Birmingham, Birmingham B4 3ET) : Midlands Branch, Institution of Chemical Engineers, c1980. — [339]p : ill,plans,forms ; 30cm
Unpriced (pbk) B81-10942

660.2′81 — Chemical engineering. Process control. Applications of digital computer systems

Ray, W. Harmon. Advanced process control / W. Harmon Ray. — New York ; London : McGraw-Hill, c1981. — xii,376p : ill ; 25cm. — (McGraw-Hill chemical engineering series)
Includes index
ISBN 0-07-051250-7 : £22.10 B81-01019

660.2′81 — Chemical engineering. Process control. Applications of digital computer systems — *Conference proceedings*

Making computer control work in the process industries : December 17/18th, 1980 / editors A. Browes, J. Carroll, J. Hancock. — Manchester (c/o B. Atkinson, Dept. of Chemical Engineering, UMIST, P.O. Box 88, Sackville St., Manchester M60 8QD) : Institution of Chemical Engineers, North Western Branch, c1980. — 128p in various pagings : ill ; 30cm. — (Symposium papers 1980 / Institution of Chemical Engineers. North Western Branch ; no.5)
At head of title: Institution of Chemical Engineers, North Western Branch
ISBN 0-906636-08-6 (pbk) : £12.00 (£10.00 to members of the Institution) B81-28280

660.2′82 — Chemical engineering equipment. Materials — *Technical data*

Evans, Lee S.. Chemical and process plant : a guide to the selection of engineering materials / Lee S. Evans. — 2nd ed. — London : Hutchinson, 1980. — 190p ; 25cm
Previous ed.: published as Selecting engineering materials for chemical and process plant. London : Business Books, 1974. — Includes index
ISBN 0-09-142790-8 : £12.50 : CIP rev. B80-13909

660.2′83 — Chemical engineering equipment: Electrostatic precipitators

Böhm, Jaroslav. Electrostatic precipitators. — Oxford : Elsevier Scientific, Dec.1981. — [370] p. — (Chemical engineering monographs ; v.14)
Translation of: Elektrické odlučovače
ISBN 0-444-99764-4 : £35.00 : CIP entry B81-31612

660.2′83 — Chemical engineering equipment: Pumps — *Conference proceedings*

Pumps and pumping / edited by P.L. Marshall. — Manchester (c/o B. Atkinson, Department of Chemical Engineering, UMIST, P.O. Box 88, Sackville St., Manchester M9 3DA) : Institute of Chemical Engineers, North Western Branch, 1980. — 75p in various pagings : ill ; 30cm. — (Symposium papers 1980 / North Western Branch. Institution of Chemical Engineers ; No.3)
Conference papers
ISBN 0-906636-06-x (pbk) : Unpriced B81-15680

660.2′83 — Chemical engineering equipment: Reactors. Design

Rose, L. M.. Chemical reactor design in practice. — Oxford : Elsevier Scientific, Sept.1981. — [400]p. — (Chemical engineering monographs ; v.13)
ISBN 0-444-42018-5 : CIP entry B81-28196

660.2′83 — Chemical engineering plants. Design

Resnick, William. Process analysis and design for chemical engineers / William Resnick. — New York ; London : McGraw-Hill, c1981. — xix,363p : ill ; 24cm. — (McGraw-Hill chemical engineering series)
Bibliography: p352-355. - Includes index
ISBN 0-07-051887-4 : £18.00
Primary classification 660.2′8 B81-13660

660.2′83 — Chemical engineering plants. Polymer components

Butt, L. T.. Use of polymers in chemical plant construction / L.T. Butt and D.C. Wright. — London : Applied Science, c1980. — viii,156p : ill ; 23cm
Includes index
ISBN 0-85334-914-2 : £14.00 : CIP rev. B80-18418

660.2′842 — Chemical engineering. Separation

Henley, Ernest J.. Equilibrium-stage separation operations in chemical engineering / Ernest J. Henley and J.D. Seader. — New York ; Chichester : Wiley, c1981. — xxvi,742p : ill ; 24cm
Includes index
ISBN 0-471-37108-4 : £20.90 B81-23319

660.2′842 — Chemical engineering. Separation. Use of membranes — *Conference proceedings*

Membrane Processes / [papers of a symposium held in Manchester] November 12th 1980 ; edited by M.G. Metcalfe. — Manchester (c/o B. Atkinson, Department of Chemical Engineering, UMIST, P.O. Box 88, Manchester M60 8QD) : Institution of Chemical Engineers, North Western Branch, 1980. — 84p in various pagings : ill ; 30cm. — (North Western Branch papers / Institution of Chemical Engineers ; no.4)
ISBN 0-906636-07-8 (pbk) : £6.00(£5.00 to members of the Institution) B81-18011

660.2′842 — Solid materials. Separation from liquid materials

Solid-liquid separation. — 2nd ed. — London : Butterworths, Nov.1981. — [480]p. — (Butterworths monographs in chemistry and chemical engineering)
Previous ed.: 1977
ISBN 0-408-70943-x : £30.00 : CIP entry B81-31182

660.2′842 — Solid materials. Separation from liquid materials — *Conference proceedings*

Proceedings of the symposium solids/liquids separation practice : Department of Chemical Engineering, University of Leeds, England, 27-29 March 1979 / [organised by the] Yorkshire Branch of the Institution of Chemical Engineers. — [Leeds?] ([c/o Dr. P.E. Preece, Secretary, Department of Chemical Engineering, University of Leeds]) : [The Branch], [1979?]. — vi,263p : ill ; pbk
Cover title
Unpriced B81-26286

660.2′842′05 — Chemical engineering. Separation — *Serials*

Journal of separation process technology. — Vol.1, no.1 (Summer 1979)-. — London (P.O. Box 78, NW11 0PG) : Childwall University Press, 1979-. — v. : ill ; 28cm
Quarterly
ISSN 0260-6275 = Journal of separation process technology : £25.00 per year B81-09044

660.2′842′05 — Chemical engineering. Separation - *Serials*

Progress in filtration and separation. — Vol.2. — Oxford : Elsevier Scientific, July 1981. — [350]p
ISBN 0-444-42006-1 : CIP entry
Primary classification 660.2′8424′05 B81-19137

660.2′8423 — Solids. Pneumatic transport

Klinzing, George E.. Gas-solid transport / George E. Klinzing. — New York ; London : McGraw-Hill, c1981. — xvi,175p : ill ; 25cm. — (McGraw-Hill chemical engineering series)
Includes bibliographies and index
ISBN 0-07-035047-7 : £19.95 B81-36281

660.2′8424′05 — Filtration - *Serials*

Progress in filtration and separation. — Vol.2. — Oxford : Elsevier Scientific, July 1981. — [350]p
ISBN 0-444-42006-1 : CIP entry
Also classified at 660.2′842′05 B81-19137

660.2′84245 — Filter cake. Formation. Restriction. Use of shear-stress filtration

Rushton, A.. Shear effects in cake formation mechanisms / by A. Rushton, M. Hosseini & Alan Rushton. — [Leeds] : [University of Leeds, Department of Chemical Engineering], [1981]. — [10]p : ill ; 30cm
Unpriced (unbound) B81-26438

660.2′84245 — Ultrafiltration — *Conference proceedings*

Symposium on Ultrafiltration Membranes and Applications *(1979 : Washington, D.C.)*.
Ultrafiltration membranes and applications / [proceedings of the Symposium on Ultrafiltration Membranes and Applications, sponsored by the American Chemical Society, and held in Washington, D.C., September 9-14, 1979] ; edited by Anthony R. Cooper. — New York ; London : Plenum, c1980. — xiv,707p : ill ; 26cm. — (Polymer science and technology ; v.13)
Includes index
ISBN 0-306-40548-2 : Unpriced B81-13377

660.2′84245′028 — Horizontal belt filters. Development, *to 1980*

Bond, A. P.. The development of large horizontal belt filters / by A.P. Bond, K. Blendulf and M. Harvey. — [S.l.] : [Delkor Technik (Pty) Ltd.], [1981?]. — [19] leaves : ill ; 30cm
Unpriced (unbound) B81-31407

660.2′8426 — Evaporating ovens. Safety measures

Evaporating and other ovens. — London : Health & Safety Executive, July 1981. — [56]p. — (HS(G))
ISBN 0-11-883433-9 (pbk) : CIP entry B81-13505

660.2′8426 — Solids. Thermal drying

Drying ′80 / edited by Arun S. Mujumdar. — Washington ; London : Hemisphere ; London : McGraw-Hill [distributor]
Vol.1: Developments in drying. — c1980. — ix,518p : ill ; 29cm
Includes index
ISBN 0-89116-200-3 : £30.25
ISBN 0-89116-188-0 (set) : Unpriced B81-10061

Drying ′80 / edited by Arun S. Mujumdar. — Washington ; London : Hemisphere ; London : McGraw-Hill [distributor]
Vol.2: Proceedings of the Second International Symposium. — c1980. — ix,532p : ill ; 29cm
Conference papers. — Includes index
ISBN 0-89116-201-1 : £28.25
ISBN 0-89116-188-0 (set) : Unpriced B81-10062

660.2′8426 — Spray drying

Masters, K.. Spray drying handbook / K. Masters. — 3rd ed. — London : Godwin, 1979. — xv,687p : ill ; 23cm
Previous ed.: published as Spray drying. 1976. — Bibliography: p668-679. — Includes index
ISBN 0-7114-4924-4 : £30.00 : CIP rev. B79-30202

660.2′8426′05 — Solids. Drying — *Serials*

Advances in drying. — Vol.1-. — Washington ; London ([c/o Halsted Press, Baffins La., Chichester, Sussex]) : Hemisphere, 1980-. — v. ; 25cm
Irregular
ISSN 0272-4790 = Advances in drying : £26.75 B81-10240

660.2′84292 — Fluid mixing equipment

Sweeney, E. T.. An introduction and literature guide to mixing / E.T. Sweeney. — Bedford (Cranfield, Bedford MK43 0AJ) : BHRA Fluid Engineering, c1978. — 54p : ill ; 30cm. — (BHRA Fluid Engineering series ; v.5)
ISBN 0-900983-77-9 (pbk) : £6.50 B78-00349

660.2′84292 — Fluids. Mixing — *Conference proceedings*

Fluid mixing : a symposium / organised by the Yorkshire Branch and Fluid Mixing Processes Group of the Institution of Chemical Egnineers. — Rugby : The Institution, c1981. — 185p in various pagings : ill ; 21cm. — (The Institution of Chemical Engineers symposium series ; no.64)
ISBN 0-85295-135-3 (pbk) : Unpriced B81-27152

660.2′84292 — Fluids. Mixing. Terminology — *Standards*

Institution of Chemical Engineers. *Fluid Mixing Group*. Recommended standard terminology and nomenclature for mixing / [Institution of Chemical Engineers, Fluid Mixing Group] ; prepared by J.C. Middleton, M.F. Edwards, I. Stewart. — Rugby : The Institution of Chemical Engineers, c1980. — iii,19p : ill ; 21cm
ISBN 0-85295-138-8 (pbk) : £3.00 B81-06111

660.2′84292 — Materials. Mixtures. Experiments. Statistical analysis

Cornell, John A.. Experiments with mixtures : designs, models, and the analysis of mixture data / John A. Cornell. — New York ; Chichester : Wiley, c1981. — xvii,305p : ill ; 24cm. — (Wiley series in probability and mathematical statistics)
Bibliography: p297-301. — Includes index
ISBN 0-471-07916-2 : £19.40 B81-23248

660.2′84292 — Particulate solids. Mixing — *Conference proceedings*

Mixing of particulate solids : 2nd European symposium / [proceedings of part of the 1981 Powtech Conference] ; organised by the Institution of Chemical Engineers in conjunction with the Powtech 81 exhibition at the National Exhibition Centre, Birmingham, from 10-13 March 1981. — Rugby : The Institution, c1981. — 261p in various pagings : ill ; 22cm. — (The Institution of Chemical Engineers symposium series ; no.65) (EFCE publication series ; no.15)
Also availiable in pbk : Unpriced. — EFCE event no.: 241
ISBN 0-85295-134-5 : Unpriced B81-19016

660.2′844′9 — Industrial fermentation — *Conference proceedings*

Mixed culture fermentation. — London : Academic Press, Nov.1981. — [250]p. — (Special publications of the Society for General Microbiology ; 5)
Conference papers
ISBN 0-12-147480-1 : CIP entry B81-28784

660.2′8449 — Industrial fermentation. Microbiological aspects — *Conference proceedings*

Trends in the biology of fermentations for fuels and chemicals : [proceedings of a symposium on trends in the biology of fermentations for fuels and chemicals, held December 7-11, 1980, at Brookhaven National Laboratory, Upton, New York] / edited by Alexander Hollaender and Robert Rabson ... [et al.]. — New York ; London : Plenum, c1981. — xii,591p : ill ; 26cm. — (Basic life sciences, ISSN 0090-5542 ; v.18)
Includes index
ISBN 0-306-40752-3 : Unpriced B81-36185

660.2′94515′0681 — Great Britain. Aerosols. Cost-effectiveness

Cost-effectiveness of aerosol products / British Aerosol Manufacturers′ Association. — London (93 Albert Embankment SE1 7TU) : The Association, [1981]. — 29p ; 30cm
Unpriced (pbk) B81-18237

660.2′993 — Chemical engineering. Explosive exothermic chemical reactions — *Conference proceedings*

Runaway reactions : unstable products and combustible powders : a symposium organised by the North Western Branch of the Institution of Chemical Engineers. — Rugby (George E. Davis Building, 165 Railway Terrace, Rugby, Warwickshire CV21 3HQ) : Institution of Chemical Engineers, c1981. — 303p in various pagings : ill ; 22cm. — (Institution of Chemical Engineers symposium series ; no.68)
ISBN 0-85295-136-1 : Unpriced B81-19437

660.2′9′93 — Industrial chemicals: Polymer dispersions — *Conference proceedings*

The **Effect** of polymers on dispersion properties. — London : Academic Press, Feb.1982. — [400]p
Conference papers
ISBN 0-12-682620-x : CIP entry B81-40233

660.2′994 — Chemical engineering. Chemical reactions. Kinetics

Mohilla, Rezsö. Chemical process dynamics. — Oxford : Elsevier Scientific, Dec.1981. — [300]p. — (Fundamental studies in engineering ; 4)
Translation of: Vegyipari folyamatok dinamikája
ISBN 0-444-99730-x : £35.00 : CIP entry B81-33863

Smith, J. M. (Joe Mauk). Chemical engineering kinetics / J.M. Smith. — 3rd ed. — New York ; London : McGraw-Hill, c1981. — xix,676p : ill ; 25cm. — (McGraw-Hill chemical engineering series)
Previous ed.: 1970. — Text on lining papers. — Includes index
ISBN 0-07-058710-8 : £20.75 B81-09938

660.2′994′0724 — Chemical engineering. Chemical reactions. Kinetics. Mathematical models — *Conference proceedings*

Dynamics and modelling of reactive systems : proceedings of an advance seminar conducted by the Mathematics Research Center The University of Wisconsin-Madison October 22-24, 1979 / edited by Warren E. Stewart, W. Harmon Ray, Charles C. Conley. — New York ; London : Academic Press, 1980. — xi,413p : ill ; 24cm. — (Publication ... of the Mathematics Research Center, the University of Wisconsin-Madison ; no.44)
Includes bibliographies and index
ISBN 0-12-669550-4 : £9.80 B81-07218

660.2′995 — Chemical engineering. Catalysis

Catalysis and chemical processes / editors R. Pearce, W.R. Patterson. — [London] : Leonard Hill, 1981. — xix,348p : ill ; 24cm
Includes index
ISBN 0-249-44160-8 : £25.00 : CIP rev. B81-18040

660.2′995 — Industrial chemicals: Catalysts. Design

Trimm, David L.. Design of industrial catalysts / David L. Trimm. — Amsterdam ; Oxford : Elsevier Scientific, 1980. — xi,314p : ill ; 26cm. — (Chemical engineering monographs ; v.11)
Includes index
ISBN 0-444-41906-3 : £26.76 : CIP rev. B80-11972

660.2′995 — Industrial chemicals: Heterogenous catalysts. Deactivation — *Conference proceedings*

Catalyst deactivation : proceedings of the international symposium, Antwerp, October 13-15, 1980 / edited by B. Delmon and G.F. Froment. — Amsterdam ; Oxford : Elsevier Scientific, 1980. — ix,602p : ill ; 25cm. — (Studies in surface science and catalysis ; 6)
Conferance papers. — Includes index
ISBN 0-444-41920-9 : £40.51 : CIP rev. B80-18705

660.6 — INDUSTRIAL BIOLOGY

660′.6 — Industrial biology

Marstrand, Pauline K.. Patterns of change in biotechnology / by Pauline K. Marstrand. — Brighton (Mantell Building, Falmer, Brighton, Sussex. BN1 9RF) : Science Policy Research Unit, University of Sussex, c1981. — 83p ; 30cm. — (SPRU occasional paper series ; no.15)
Bibliography: p67-83
ISBN 0-903622-16-5 (spiral) : Unpriced B81-36468

Smith, John E.. Biotechnology. — London (Edward Arnold), Dec.1981. — [64]p. — (The Institute of Biology′s studies in biology, ISSN 0537-9024 ; no.136)
ISBN 0-7131-2835-6 (pbk) : £2.25 : CIP entry B81-31557

660′.6 — Industrial biology — *Conference proceedings*

From genetic experimentation to biotechnology — the critical transition. — Chichester : Wiley, Feb.1982. — [300]p
Conference papers
ISBN 0-471-10148-6 : £20.00 : CIP entry B81-37596

660′.6′0941 — Great Britain. Industrial biology

Great Britain. *Department of Industry*. Biotechnology / presented to Parliament by the Secetary of State for Industry by command of Her Majesty March 1981. — London : H.M.S.O., 1981. — 11p ; 25cm. — (Cmnd. ; 8177)
ISBN 0-10-181770-3 (unbound) : £1.40 B81-18910

660′.62 — Industrial microbiology

Smith, George. Smith′s introduction to industrial mycology. — 7th ed. — London : Edward Arnold, Nov.1981. — [384]p
Previous ed.: 1969
ISBN 0-7131-2811-9 : £30.00 : CIP entry B81-30605

660′.62′05 — Industrial microbiology — *Serials*

Progress in industrial microbiology. — Vol.16 — Oxford : Elsevier Scientific, Nov.1981. — [375]p
ISBN 0-444-42037-1 : CIP entry B81-32019

661 — INDUSTRIAL CHEMICALS

661′.0029′44 — Europe. Industrial chemicals — *Buyers′ guides* — *Serials*

European chemical buyers′ guide. — 1981/2. — Sutton : IPC Industrial Press, c1981. — 724p in various pagings
ISBN 0-617-00431-5 : £30.00 B81-35806

661′.2 — Nitric, phosphoric & sulphuric acids. Manufacture — *Conference proceedings*

International Conference on Fertilizers *(3rd : 1979 : London)*. Fertilizer acids : Nitric acid. Phosphoric acid. Sulphuric acid : proceedings of the British Sulphur Corporation′s Third International Conference on Fertilizers, London, 12-14 November 1979 / editor A.I. More. — London : Parnell House, 25 Wilton Road, London SW1V 1NH : British Sulphur Corporation, 1980. — 724p in various pagings : ill ; 22cm
£150.00 B81-10844

661′.25 — Phosphoric acids. Manufacture. OXY hemihydrate process

Caesar, M. B.. The OXY hemihydrate phosphioric acid process : paper read before the Fertiliser Society of London on 16th October 1980 / by M.B. Caesar, H.C. Smith and L.E. Mercando. — London (93 Albert Embankment, SE1 7TU) : Fertiliser Society, [1980]. — 19p : ill ; 21cm. — (Proceedings / Fertiliser Society ; no.192)
Unpriced (pbk) B81-08272

661′.34 — Ammonia. Industrial synthesis

Strelzoff, Samuel. Technology and manufacture of ammonia / Samuel Strelzoff. — New York ; Chichester : Wiley, c1981. — xxii,283p : ill ; 24cm
Includes index
ISBN 0-471-02722-7 : £40.20 B81-28305

661′.34 — Industrial chemicals: Ammonia. Small scale production. PARC process

Van Weenen, W. F.. New concept ammonia process with higher efficiency : paper read before the Fertiliser Society of London on 16th October 1980 / by W.F. van Weenen and J. Tielrooy. — [London] (93 Albert Embankment, SE1 7TU) : Fertiliser Society, [1980]. — 24p : ill ; 21cm. — (Proceedings / Fertiliser Society ; no.191)
Unpriced (pbk) B81-06999

661′.8 — Industrial chemicals: Enzymes — *Serials*

Topics in enzyme and fermentation biotechnology . — 6. — Chichester : Ellis Horwood, Nov.1981. — [256]p
ISBN 0-85312-372-1 : £19.50 : CIP entry
ISSN 0140-0835 B81-32012

661'.804'028 — Petrochemicals plants. Fluid flow machinery — *Conference proceedings*

Fluid machinery for the oil petrochemical and related industries : European congress sponsored by The Power Industries Division of the Institution of Mechanical Engineers and The Division of Mechanical Engineering and Naval Architecture of The Royal Dutch Institution of Engineers, The Hague, 24-26 March 1981. — Bury St Edmunds : Mechanical Engineering for The Institution of Mechanical Engineers, 1981. — 178p : ill,1map ; 30cm. — (I Mech E conference publications ; 1981-3)
ISBN 0-85298-484-7 (pbk) : Unpriced B81-18661

662.1 — FIREWORKS

662'.1 — Industrial pyrotechnics

Barbour, Richard T.. Pyrotechnics in industry / Richard T. Barbour. — New York ; London : McGraw-Hill, c1981. — viii,190p : ill ; 25cm
Includes index
ISBN 0-07-003653-5 : £16.50 B81-36473

662.2 — EXPLOSIVES

662'.2'0212 — Explosives — *Technical data*

LASL explosive property data / editors Terry R. Gibbs, Alphonse Popolato ; contributors John F. Baytos ... [et al.]. — Berkeley ; London : University of California Press, c1980. — x,471p : ill ; 26cm. — (Los Alamos series on dynamic material properties)
ISBN 0-520-04012-0 : £22.50 B81-27787

662'.2'0216 — Great Britain. Authorised explosives — *Lists* — *Serials*

List of authorised explosives / Health and Safety Executive. — Jan.1981. — London : H.M.S.O., 1981. — 30p
ISBN 0-11-883421-5 : £1.75 B81-14544

662.6 — FUELS

662'.6 — Biomass fuels. Production — *Conference proceedings*

International Conference on Biomass *(1980 : Brighton)*. Energy from biomass : 1st E.C. Conference : proceedings of the International Conference on Biomass held at Brighton, England, 4-7 November 1980 / edited by W. Palz, P. Chartier and D.O. Hall. — London : Applied Science, c1981. — xxiii,982p : ill,maps,ports ; 23cm
At head of cover title: Commission of the European Communities. — Includes index
ISBN 0-85334-970-3 : £39.00 : CIP rev. B81-20543

Symposium on Biotechnology in Energy Production and Conservation *(2nd : 1979 : Gatlinburg)*. Second symposium on biotechnology in energy production and conservation : proceedings of the Second Symposium on Biotechnology in Energy Production and Conservation held in Gatlinburg, Tennessee October 3-5, 1979 / sponsored by the Department of Energy and the Oak Ridge National Laboratory ; editor Charles D. Scott. — New York ; Chichester : Wiley, c1980. — vi,353p : ill,maps ; 23cm. — (Biotechnology and bioengineering symposium, ISSN 0572-6565 ; no.10)
Includes index
ISBN 0-471-09015-8 (pbk) : £19.00 B81-09617

662'.6 — Biomass fuels. Production — *Serials*

Progress in biomass conversion. — Vol.2. — New York ; London : Academic Press, 1980. — x,216p
ISBN 0-12-535902-0 : £11.00
ISSN 0192-6551 B81-33722

662'.6 — Biomass fuels. Production. Use of short rotation forestry

Production of energy from short rotation forestry / edited by N. Neenan and G. Lyons. — Dublin (19 Sandymount Ave., Dublin 4) : An Foras Talúntais, 1980. — v,128p : ill,maps,plans ; 22cm
ISBN 0-905442-48-2 (pbk) : Unpriced B81-17676

662'.6 — Energy resources: Biomass

White, L. P.. Biomass as fuel. — London : Academic Press, Dec.1981. — [250]p
ISBN 0-12-746980-x : CIP entry B81-31351

662'.6 — Energy sources: Biomass

Bungay, Henry R.. Energy, the biomass options / Henry R. Bungay. — New York ; Chichester : Wiley, c1981. — ix,347p : ill ; 24cm. — (Alternate energy)
Bibliography: p325-339. — Includes index
ISBN 0-471-04386-9 : £18.70 B81-23315

662'.6 — Europe. Energy sources: Biomass

Energy from biomass in Europe / edited by W. Palz and P. Chartier. — London : Applied Science, c1980. — xiv,234p : maps ; 23cm
Includes bibliographies
ISBN 0-85334-934-7 : £15.00 : CIP rev. B80-22232

662'.6 — Fuels

Francis, Wilfrid. Fuels and fuel technology : a summarized manual. — 2nd (SI) ed. / by Wilfrid Francis and Martin C. Peters. — Oxford : Pergamon, 1980. — xv,716p : ill,1map ; 26cm
Previous ed.: in 2 vols. / by Wilfrid Francis, 1965
ISBN 0-08-025249-4 (cased) : £42.50 : CIP rev.
ISBN 0-08-025250-8 (pbk) : £14.95 B80-06498

662'.6 — Fuels. Production. Use of waste materials

Porteous, Andrew. Refuse derived fuels / Andrew Porteous. — London : Applied Science, c1981. — xii,137p : ill,1plan ; 23cm. — (Energy from wastes series)
Includes bibliographies and index
ISBN 0-85334-937-1 : £12.00 B81-23603

662.6'2 — Coal. Liquefaction. Thermal processing

Whitehurst, D. Duayne. Coal liquefaction : the chemistry and technology of thermal processes / D. Duayne Whitehurst, Thomas O. Mitchell, Malvina Farcasiu with the association of Nancy H. Lin. — New York ; London : Academic Press, 1980. — xv,378p : ill ; 24cm
Includes index
ISBN 0-12-747080-8 : £11.00 B81-04675

662.6'2 — Coal. Processing. Environmental aspects — *Conference proceedings*

Environmental effects of utilising more coal : the proceedings of a conference organised by the Council for Environmental Science and Engineering, Royal Geographical Society, London, 11th and 12th December 1979 / edited by F.A. Robinson. — London : Burlington House, W1V OBN : Royal Society of Chemistry, c1980. — vii,203p : ill,charts,maps ; 21cm. — (Special publication / Royal Society of Chemistry ; no.37)
ISBN 0-85186-805-3 (pbk) : Unpriced B80-22233

662.6'2 — Coal technology

Chemistry of coal utilization. — New York ; Chichester : Wiley
2nd supplementary vol. / prepared under the guidance of the Committee on Chemistry of Coal Utilization ; edited by Martin A. Elliott. — c1981. — xxi,2374p : ill,maps ; 26cm
Includes index
ISBN 0-471-07726-7 : £102.00 B81-24219

662.6'2 — Coal technology — *Conference proceedings*

Coal chem — 2000 / a symposium organised by the Sheffield and District Centre (Yorkshire Branch) of the Institution of Chemical Engineers. — Rugby : Institution of Chemical Engineers, c1980. — 321p in various pagings : ill,maps ; 22cm. — (Institution of Chemical Engineers symposium series ; no.62)
ISBN 0-85295-124-8 : £15.00 B81-31507

New coal chemistry : a Royal Society discussion held on 21 and 22 May 1980 / organised by A. Spinks, J.M. Thomas and J. Gibson. — London : The Society, 1981. — 215p,[6]p of plates : ill ; 21cm
First published: in 'Philosophical Transactions of the Royal Society of London', series A. vol. 300 (no.1453), p.1-215 - title page verso
ISBN 0-85403-159-6 : £25.50 B81-18989

662'.66 — Synthetic fuels. Production

Benn, F. R.. Production and utilisation of synthetic fuels : an energy economics study / F.R. Benn, J.O. Edewor and C.A. McAuliffe. — London : Applied Science Publishers, c1981. — xv,251p : ill ; 23cm
Includes index
ISBN 0-85334-940-1 : £20.00 B81-23701

662'.669 — Fuels: Alcohols — *Conference proceedings*

Proceedings of workshop on power alcohol : 23rd January 1981 : held at Mortimer Hill, Mortimer, Reading. — Marlborough : British Anaerobic and Biomass Association, [1981?]. — 47leaves in various foliations : ill ; 30cm
Unpriced (spiral) B81-40846

662'.74 — Portable steel charcoal kilns. Construction — *Manuals*

Whitehead, W. D. J.. The construction of a transportable charcoal kiln / W.D.J. Whitehead. — [London] : Tropical Products Institute, 1980. — 19p,[1]folded leaf of plates : ill ; 30cm. — (Rural technology guide, ISSN 0141-898x ; 13)
ISBN 0-85954-127-4 (pbk) : £1.30 B81-13945

663 — BEVERAGE MANUFACTURES

663 — Drinks. Bottling — *Serials*

The Bottler's year book. — 1980. — Purley : B.Y.B. Limited, [1980?]. — 375p in various pagings
£5.00 B81-15545

663 — Energy & materials. Consumption by drinks containers manufacturing industries

Boustead, I.. Energy and packaging. — Chichester : Ellis Horwood, Oct.1981. — [430]p
ISBN 0-85312-206-7 : £45.00 : CIP entry B81-28021

663'.3 — Brewing & malting

Malting and brewing science. — 2nd ed. — London : Chapman and Hall
Previous ed.: 1971
Part 1: Malt and sweet wort. — Oct.1981. — [300]p
ISBN 0-412-16580-5 : £15.00 : CIP entry B81-27938

663'.3 — Brewing — *Conference proceedings*

European Brewery Convention. *Congress (18th : 1981 : Copenhagen)*. European Brewery Convention. — Eynsham (1 Abbey St., Eynsham, Oxford OX8 1JJ) : IRL Press, Oct.1981. — [800]p
Conference papers
ISBN 0-904147-30-4 : £36.00 : CIP entry B81-31093

663'.3'015 — Brewing. Scientific aspects

Brewing science / edited by J.R.A. Pollock. — London : Academic Press. — (Food science and technology)
Vol.2. — 1981. — xxi,666p : ill ; 24cm
Includes bibliographies and index
ISBN 0-12-561002-5 : £41.00 : CIP rev. B80-23484

663'.52'09415 — Irish whiskies. Distilling, *to 1978*

Magee, Malachy. 1000 years of Irish whiskey / Malachy Magee. — Dublin : O'Brien, 1980. — 144p : ill,facsims,1port ; 26cm
Ill on lining papers. — Includes index
ISBN 0-905140-71-0 : £8.80 B81-01020

663'.6 — Soft drinks. Production - *Serials*

Developments in soft drinks technology. — London : Applied Science, July 1981. — (Developments series)
2. — [288]p
ISBN 0-85334-962-2 : £23.00 : CIP entry B81-13734

664 — FOOD MANUFACTURES

664 — Food. Autoxidation — *Conference proceedings*

Workshop on Autoxidation Processes *(1979 : Natick)*. Autoxidation in food and biological systems / [proceedings of the Workshop on Autoxidation Processes, held at the U.S. Army Natick Research and Development Command, Natick, Massachusetts, October 29-31, 1979] ; edited by Michael G. Simic and Marcus Karel. — New York ; London : Plenum, c1980. — xii,659p : ill ; 26cm
Includes bibliographies and index
ISBN 0-306-40561-x : Unpriced B81-07413

664 — Food technology

Pyke, Magnus. Food science and technology. — 4th ed. — London : John Murray, July 1981. — [320]p
Previous ed.: 1970
ISBN 0-7195-3850-5 (pbk) : £7.50 : CIP entry
Primary classification 641.1 B81-14897

664'.001'5 — Great Britain. Secondary schools. Curriculum subjects: Food. Scientific aspects — *For teaching*

Wiltsher, Ruth. Science & food / prepared by Ruth Wiltsher. — Hatfield (College La., Hatfield, Hertfordshire, AL10 9AA) : Association for Science Education, c1978. — 19p,[17]leaves : ill ; 30cm. — (Topic brief / LAMP Project ; no.11)
ISBN 0-902786-46-6 (pbk) : £0.70 B81-06379

664'.005 — Food technology — *Serials*

Home food adviser : an occasional publication of the Home Food Science Section, Ministry of Agriculture, Fisheries and Food. — No.1-. — Bristol (Long Ashton Research Station, Bristol, BS18) : The Section, 1977. — v. : ill ; 21cm
Irregular. — Description based on: No.3
£0.80
Primary classification 641.1'05 B81-05791

664'.02 — Food. Preservation & processing. Effects of water

Water activity : influences on food quality : a treatise on the influence of bound and free water on the quality and stability of foods and other natural products / edited by Louis B. Rockland, George F. Stewart. — New York ; London : Academic Press, 1981. — xviii,921p : ill ; 24cm
Includes bibliographies and index
ISBN 0-12-591350-8 : £33.60 B81-35402

664'.02 — Food. Processing: Maillard reactions

Maillard reactions in food. — Oxford : Pergamon, June 1981. — [500]p. — (Progress in food and nutrition science ; v.5)
ISBN 0-08-025496-9 : £65.00 : CIP entry B81-19210

664'.02852'06041 — Great Britain. Food. Cold storage. Organisations: National Cold Storage Federation — *Serials*

National Cold Storage Federation. Year book of the National Cold Storage Federation. — 1981. — London : Tavistock House (North), Tavistock Sq., WC1H 9HZ : [The Federation], [1980?]. — 165p
£5.00 B81-06917

664'.06 — Food. Additives

Taylor, R. J. (Reginald James). Food additives / R.J. Taylor. — Chichester : Wiley, c1980. — xv,126p ; 24cm. — (The Institution of Environment Sciences series)
Includes index
ISBN 0-471-27684-7 (cased) : £10.50 : CIP rev.
ISBN 0-471-27683-9 (pbk) : £4.75 B80-04306

664'.06 — Food. Processing. Use of enzymes — *Conference proceedings*

Enzymes and food processing / [an industry-university cooperation symposium organised under the auspices of the National College of Food Technology, University of Reading, 31 March-2 April, 1980] ; edited by G.G. Birch, N. Blakebrough and K.J. Parker. — London : Applied Science, c1981. — xii,296p : ill ; 23cm
Includes index
ISBN 0-85334-935-5 : £22.00 B81-16777

664'.06 — Natural colouring agents — *Conference proceedings*

Natural colours for food and other uses / [an international symposium organised and sponsored by Roche Products Limited at the Europa Hotel, London on 25th October 1979] ; edited by J.N. Counsell. — London : Applied Science, c1981. — x,167p : ill ; 23cm
Includes bibliographies and index
ISBN 0-85334-933-9 : £13.00 B81-16778

664'.07 — Food & drinks. Undesirable flavours. Analysis & control — *Conference proceedings*

The **Analysis** and control of less desirable flavors in foods and beverages / edited by George Charalambous. — New York ; London : Academic Press, 1980. — x,358p : ill ; 24cm
Conference papers. — Includes index
ISBN 0-12-169065-2 : £15.80 B81-14755

664'.07 — Food. Chemical analysis

Egan, H.. Pearson's chemical analysis of food. — 8th ed. — Edinburgh : Churchill Livingstone, Aug.1981. — [864]p
Previous ed. published as: Chemical analysis of foods
ISBN 0-443-02149-x : £20.00 : CIP entry B81-16408

664'.07 — Food. Constituents: Trace metals. Chemical analysis. Atomic absorption spectroscopy. Samples. Preparation

Blake, C. J.. Sample preparation methods for the analysis of metals in food by atomic absorption spectrometry : a literature review / C.J. Blake. — Leatherhead (Randalls Rd., Leatherhead, Surrey) : British Food Manufacturing Industries Research Association, 1980. — 53p ; 30cm. — (Scientific & technical surveys / Leatherhead Food R.A., ISSN 0144-2074 ; no.122)
English text, English, French and German summaries. — Bibliography: p35-53
Unpriced (pbk) B81-16312

664'.07 — Food. Contaminants: Agricultural chemicals. Chemical analysis — *Manuals*

Analytical methods for pesticides and plant growth regulators / edited by Gunter Zweig. — New York ; London : Academic Press
Vol.11: Updated general techniques and additional pesticides / edited by Gunter Zweig and Joseph Sherma. — 1980. — xiii,408p : ill ; 24cm
Includes bibliographies and index
ISBN 0-12-784311-6 : Unpriced B81-17006

664'.07 — Food. Quantitative analysis. Nuclear magnetic resonance spectroscopy

Coveney, L. V.. The application of nuclear magnetic resonance spectroscopy to the rapid analysis of food / L.V. Coveney. — Leatherhead (Randalls Rd., Leatherhead, Surrey) : British Food Manufacturing Industries Research Association, 1980. — 22p : ill ; 30cm. — (Scientific and technical surveys / Food R.A., ISSN 0144-2074 ; no.123)
English text, English, French and German summaries. — Bibliography: p18-22
Unpriced (pbk) B81-16316

664'.07 — Food. Volatile constituents. Qualitative analysis. Glass capillary gas chromatography

Jennings, Walter, *1922-*. Qualitative analysis of flavor and fragrance volatiles by glass capillary gas chromatography / Walter Jennings, Takayuki Shibamoto. — New York ; London : Academic Press, 1980. — vii,472p : ill ; 25cm
Includes index
ISBN 0-12-384250-6 : £25.00 B81-15019

664'.07 — Great Britain. Processed food. Quality. Assessment. Role of Campden Food Preservation Research Association

Sensory evaluation of product quality : services, techniques and facilities at Campden Research Station, Division of Agriculture and Quality. — Chipping Campden (Chipping Campden, Glos., GL55 6LD) : Campden Food Preservation Research Association, [1981?]. — [20]p,[3]p of plates : ill ; 30cm
Unpriced (pbk) B81-29336

664'.096 — Food industries. Waste materials. Disposal & recovery — *Conference proceedings*

Food industry wastes. — London : Applied Science Publishers, Nov.1981. — [256]p
Conference papers
ISBN 0-85334-957-6 : £20.00 : CIP entry B81-30419

664'.122 — Cane sugar. Processing

Baikow, V. E.. Manufacture and refining of raw cane sugar. — 2nd completely revised ed. — Oxford : Elsevier Scientific, Oct.1981. — [300] p. — (Sugar series ; 2)
Previous ed.: 1967
ISBN 0-444-41896-2 : CIP entry B81-32090

Delden, Edward. Standard fabrication practices for cane sugar mills / Edward Delden. — Amsterdam ; Oxford : Elsevier Scientific, 1981. — xxii,253p : ill ; 25cm. — (Sugar series ; 1)
Bibliography: pxi. - Includes index
ISBN 0-444-41958-6 : £23.85 B81-23642

664'.122'8 — Sugar refining industries. By-products

Paturau, J. Maurice. By-products of the cane sugar industry. — 2nd ed. — Oxford : Elsevier Scientific, Nov.1981. — [378]p. — (Sugar series ; 3)
ISBN 0-444-42034-7 : CIP entry B81-32025

664'.153'0687 — Great Britain. Confectionery. Physical distribution. Management — *Case studies*

Smith, K. J. G.. Distribution in the confectionery industry / K.J.G. Smith. — Newcastle upon Tyne : University of Newcastle upon Tyne, Transport Operations Research Group, 1979. — 118p : ill,maps ; 30cm. — (Research report / Transport Operations Research Group ; no.31)
Bibliography: p116-118
Unpriced (pbk) B81-13335

664'.62 — Babies. Artificial food. Composition — *Inquiry reports*

Great Britain. *Working Party on the Composition of Foods for Infants and Young Children*. Artificial feeds for the young infant / report of the Working Party on the Composition of Foods for Infants and Young Children, Committee on Medical Aspects of Food Policy. — London : H.M.S.O., 1980. — viii,104p ; 25cm. — (Report on health and social subjects ; no.18)
Cover title. — Bibliography: p84-104
ISBN 0-11-320734-4 (pbk) : £4.50 B81-12460

664'.62'0941 — Great Britain. Babies, to 3 years. Artificial food. Standards — *Proposals*

Great Britain. *Food Standards Committee*. Food Standards Committee report on infant formulae : (artificial feeds for the young infant). — London : H.M.S.O., 1981. — 33p ; 25cm. — (FSC/REP/73)
At head of title: Ministry of Agriculture, Fisheries and Food
ISBN 0-11-241226-2 (pbk) : £2.50 B81-24788

664'.7203 — Cereals. Grinding. Technical aspects — *Manuals*

Stoate, David. The miller's manual / compiled by David Stoate. — [Chew Stoke] ([Church Gate House, Chew Stoke, Bristol BS18 8TU]) : [D. Stoate], c1981. — 399p : ill ; 22cm
£15.00 (spiral) B81-28975

664'.7207 — Scotland. Oatmeal milling watermills, *1700-1900*

Gauldie, Enid. The Scottish country miller 1700-1900 : a history of water-powered meal milling in Scotland / Enid Gauldie. — Edinburgh : Donald, c1981. — ix,254p : ill ; 24cm
Bibliography: p234-242. — Includes index
ISBN 0-85976-067-7 : £15.00 B81-27722

664'.725 — Rice. Grinding. Techniques

Flynn, G.. An industrial profile of rice milling / G. Flynn and P.A. Clarke. — London : Tropical Products Institute, Overseas Development Administration, 1980. — iv,6p : ill ; 30cm. — (Report of the Tropical Products Institute. G, ISSN 0144-9982 ; 148)
English text, French and Spanish summaries
ISBN 0-85954-132-0 (pbk) : £0.70 B81-13222

664'.752 — Commercial baking

Hanneman, L. J.. Bakery : bread & fermented goods / L.J. Hanneman. — London : Heinemann, 1980. — xi,208p : ill ; 24cm
Includes index
ISBN 0-434-90708-1 : £8.50 B81-10282

664'.7523 — Bread. Manufacture. Techniques

Flynn, G.. An industrial profile of breadmaking / G. Flynn and A.W. James. — London : Tropical Products Institute, Overseas Development Administration, 1980. — iv,12p : ill ; 30cm. — (Report of the Tropical Products Institute. G, ISSN 0144-9982 ; 147)
English text, French and Spanish summaries
ISBN 0-85954-131-2 (pbk) : £0.90 B81-13223

664'.804711 — Quick-frozen raspberries — *Standards*

Campden Food Preservation Research Association. Specifications for raw materials and final product for quick frozen raspberries / Campden Food Preservation Research Association ; prepared in collaboration with participating members of the British Frozen Food Federation and the Processed Vegetable Growers Association. — Chipping Campden (Chipping Campden, Glos. GL55 6LD) : The Research Association, 1980. — 2,6 leaves ; 30cm
Cover title
Unpriced (pbk) B81-13238

664'.80475 — Quick-frozen strawberries — *Standards*

Campden Food Preservation Research Association. Specifications for raw materials and final product for quick frozen strawberries / Campden Food Preservation Research Association ; prepared in collaboration with participating members of the British Frozen Food Federation and the Processed Vegetable Growers Association. — Chipping Campden (Chipping Campden, Glos. GL55 6LD) : The Research Association, 1979. — 3,7 leaves : ill ; 30cm
Cover title
Unpriced (pbk) B81-13240

664'.80513 — Quick-frozen sliced carrots — *Standards*

Campden Food Preservation Research Association. Specifications for raw materials and final product for sliced carrots (rings) / Campden Food Preservation Research Association ; prepared in collaboration with participating members of the British Frozen Food Federation and the Processed Vegetable Growers Association. — Chipping Campden (Chipping Campden, Glos. GL55 6LD) : The Research Association, 1979. — 3,9 leaves ; 26cm
Cover title
Unpriced (pbk) B81-13236

664'.80521 — Quick-frozen potato chips — *Standards*

Campden Food Preservation Research Association. Specifications for raw materials and final product for potato chips / Campden Food Preservation Research Association ; prepared in collaboration with participating members of the British Frozen Food Federation and the Processed Vegetable Growers Association. — Chipping Campden (Chipping Campden, Glos. GL55 6LD) : The Research Association, 1979. — 4,12 leaves ; 26cm
Cover title
Unpriced (pbk) B81-13235

664'.80535 — Quick-frozen broccoli spears — *Standards*

Campden Food Preservation Research Association. Specifications for raw materials and final product for quick frozen broccoli spears / Campden Food Preservation Research Association ; prepared in collaboration with participating members of the British Frozen Food Federation and the Processed Vegetable Growers Association. — Chipping Campden (Chipping Campden, Glos. GL55 6LD) : The Research Association, 1980. — 4,9 leaves : ill ; 30cm
Cover title
Unpriced (pbk) B81-13234

664'.80553 — Quick-frozen cut celery — *Standards*

Campden Food Preservation Research Association. Specifications for raw materials and final product for quick frozen cut celery / Campden Food Preservation Research Association ; prepared in collaboration with participating members of the British Frozen Food Federation and the Processed Vegetable Growers Association. — Chipping Campden (Chipping Campden, Glos. GL55 6LD) : The Research Association, 1980. — 3,5 leaves ; 30cm
Cover title
Unpriced (pbk) B81-13237

664'.805651 — Quick-frozen broad beans — *Standards*

Campden Food Preservation Research Association. Specifications for raw materials and final product for quick frozen broad beans / Campden Food Preservation Research Association ; prepared in collaboration with participating members of the British Frozen Food Federation and the Processed Vegetable Growers Association. — Rev. [ed.]. — Chipping Campden (Chipping Campden, Glos. GL55 6LD) : The Research Association, 1979. — 4,8 leaves ; 26cm
Cover title. — Previous ed.: 1979
Unpriced (pbk) B81-13233

664'.805652 — Quick-frozen sliced green beans — *Standards*

Campden Food Preservation Research Association. Specifications for raw materials and final product for quick frozen cut green beans / Campden Food Preservation Research Association ; prepared in collaboration with participating members of the British Frozen Food Federation and the Processed Vegetable Growers Association. — Chipping Campden (Chipping Campden, Glos. GL55 6LD) : The Research Association, 1980. — 3,6 leaves ; 30cm
Cover title .
Unpriced (pbk) B81-13239

664'.805652 — Quick-frozen whole green beans — *Standards*

Campden Food Preservation Research Association. Specifications for raw materials and final product for quick frozen whole green beans / Campden Food Preservation Research Association ; prepared in collaboration with participating members of the British Frozen Food Federation and the Processed Vegetable Growers Association. — Chipping Campden (Chipping Campden, Glos. GL55 6LD) : The Research Association, 1980. — 3,6 leaves ; 30cm
Cover title
Unpriced (pbk) B81-13241

664'.807 — Processed fruit & processed vegetables. Quality — *Conference proceedings*

Long Ashton Symposium *(7th : 1979).* Quality in stored and processed vegetables and fruit : proceedings of a symposium held at Long Ashton Research Station University of Bristol, 8-12 April 1979 / edited by P.W. Goodenough and R.K. Atkin. — New York ; London : Academic Press, 1981. — xi,398p : ill ; 24cm
At head of title: Seventh Long Ashton Symposium 1979. — Includes bibliographies and index
ISBN 0-12-289740-4 : £25.80 : CIP rev.
Also classified at 634'.0468 ; 635'.0468 B81-08796

664'.9'0028 — Great Britain. Meat processing equipment — *Buyers' guides — Serials*

Buyer's guide to the meat industry : the comprehensive guide to meat machinery. — 1980-. — [London] : [Northwood], [1980]-. — v. : ill ; 30cm
Annual. — Supplement to: Meat. — Continues: Meat supplier. — Description based on: 1981 issue
ISSN 0260-8871 = Buyer's guide to the meat industry : £5.00 B81-10567

664'.9'005 — Meat & meat products. Processing — *Serials*

Developments in meat science. — 2. — London : Applied Science, Nov.1981. — [304]p. — (The Developments series)
ISBN 0-85334-986-x : £26.00 : CIP entry B81-30417

664'.9'0941 — Great Britain. Meat & meat products. Quality control

Meat and meat products. — Barking : Applied Science Publishers, May 1981. — [224]p
ISBN 0-85334-951-7 : £19.00 : CIP entry B81-04250

664'.94'0952 — Japan. Fish. Processing

Suzuki, Taneko. Fish and krill protein : processing technology / Taneka Suzuki. — London : Applied Science, c1981. — xiv,260p : ill ; 23cm
Includes index
ISBN 0-85334-954-1 : £19.50 : CIP rev. B81-06030

665 — INDUSTRIAL OILS, FATS, WAXES, GASES

665 — Industrial chemicals: Fats & oils

Fats and oils : chemistry and technology / edited by R.J. Hamilton and A. Bhati. — London : Applied Science, 1980. — xii,255p : ill ; 23cm
Conference papers. — Includes index
ISBN 0-85334-915-0 : £24.00 : CIP rev. B80-18422

665.3 — VEGETABLE FATS AND OILS

665'.3 — Vegetable oils — *For children*

Watson, Tom. Vegetable oils / Tom & Jenny Watson. — Hove : Wayland, 1981. — 72p : ill,1map,ports ; 20x22cm. — (World resources)
Includes index
ISBN 0-85340-811-4 : £3.75 B81-17055

665.5 — PETROLEUM

665.5'028'9 — Great Britain. Petroleum refining industries. Safety measures — *Standards*

Institute of Petroleum. Refining safety code. — 3rd ed. — London : Heyden, Oct.1981. — [200]p
Previous ed.: 1965
ISBN 0-85501-663-9 : £20.00 : CIP entry B81-25738

665.5'3 — Petroleum refining industries. Energy. Conservation

Energy conservation in refining and petrochemistry. — Paris : Technip ; London : Marketed and distributed by Graham & Trotman, 1979. — vi,177p : ill ; 24cm. — (Institut français du pétrole publications)
ISBN 2-7108-0349-6 (pbk) : £13.00 B81-34459

665.5'38 — Paraffin products

Paraffin products. — Oxford : Elsevier Scientific, Jan.1982. — [320]p. — (Developments in petroleum science ; 14)
Translation of: Köolaj paraffinok
ISBN 0-444-99712-1 : £50.00 : CIP entry B81-34492

665.5'38'0218 — Petroleum & petroleum products — *Standards — Serials*

IP standards for petroleum and its products. Part 1, Methods for analysis and testing. — 1979. — London : Heyden and Son on behalf of the Institute of Petroleum, c1979. — 2v.
ISBN 0-85501-330-3 : Unpriced B81-09715

IP standards for petroleum and its products. Part 1, Methods for analysis and testing. — 1981. — London : Heyden and Son on behalf of the Institute of Petroleum, c1981. — 2v.
Unpriced B81-32222

665.5'42 — Plastics petroleum storage containers — *Standards*

Great Britain. *Health and Safety Commission.* Petroleum-spirit (plastic containers) : draft regulations : consultative document / Health and Safety Commission. — London : H.M.S.O., 1981. — 14p : ill ; 30cm
ISBN 0-11-883426-6 (unbound) : £1.50 B81-18217

665.5'44 — Offshore petroleum pipelines — *Conference proceedings*

Offshore oil and gas pipeline technology / [a report prepared by A.C. Palmer]. — London : Oyez, 1981. — 136leaves : ill ; 30cm
Conference papers
ISBN 0-85120-564-x (spiral) : Unpriced
Also classified at 665.7'44 B81-18635

665.7/8 — INDUSTRIAL GASES

665.7′4 — Gas supply — *For children*

Cook, Brian. Gas / Brian Cook. — London : Watts, 1981. — 38p : ill(some col.),col.maps,1col.port ; 30cm. — (Energy)
Text and ill on lining papers. — Includes index
ISBN 0-85166-918-2 : £3.99 B81-34685

665.7′42 — Prestressed concrete liquefied gases storage structures. Design

Bruggeling, A. S. G.. Prestressed concrete for the storage of liquefied gases / A.S.G. Bruggeling ; [translated by C.V. Amerongen]. — [Slough] : Viewpoint, 1981. — 111p : ill ; 30cm
Translated from the Dutch
ISBN 0-7210-1187-x (pbk) : Unpriced B81-19444

665.7′44 — Offshore natural gas pipelines — *Conference proceedings*

Offshore oil and gas pipeline technology / [a report prepared by A.C. Palmer]. — London : Oyez, 1981. — 136leaves : ill ; 30cm
Conference papers
ISBN 0-85120-564-x (spiral) : Unpriced
Primary classification 665.5′44 B81-18635

665.7′7 — Fuels: Methane. Production. Use of agricultural waste materials & household waste materials

Hobson, P. N.. Methane production from agricultural and domestic wastes / P.N. Hobson, S. Bousfield, R. Summers. — London : Applied Science, c1981. — xi,269p : ill ; 23cm. — (Energy from wastes series)
Includes bibliographies and index
ISBN 0-85334-924-x : £20.00 B81-23602

665.7′73 — Liquefied petroleum gas

Williams, A. F.. Liquefied petroleum gases. — 2nd ed., rev. and extended. — Chichester : Ellis Horwood, Oct.1981. — [560]p
Previous ed.: 1974
ISBN 0-85312-360-8 : £39.50 : CIP entry B81-28171

665.8 — Compressed gases

Handbook of compressed gases / Compressed Gas Association. — 2nd ed. — New York ; London : Van Nostrand Reinhold, c1981. — xii,507p : ill ; 27cm
Previous ed.: 1966. — Includes index
ISBN 0-442-25419-9 : £33.40 B81-26039

665.8′1 — Fuels: Hydrogen

McAuliffe, C. A.. Hydrogen and energy / by Charles A. McAuliffe. — London : Macmillan, 1980. — x,109p : ill,1map ; 25cm. — (Energy alternatives series)
Includes index
ISBN 0-333-18432-7 : £12.00 : CIP rev. B80-11090

Williams, L. O.. Hydrogen power : an introduction to hydrogen energy and its applications / L.O. Williams. — Oxford : Pergamon, 1980. — ix,158p : ill ; 26cm. — (Pergamon international library)
Includes bibliographies and index
ISBN 0-08-024783-0 (cased) : Unpriced : CIP rev.
ISBN 0-08-025422-5 (pbk) : £4.50 B80-12972

665.8′1 — Fuels: Hydrogen — *Conference proceedings*

Hydrogen as an energy vector : proceedings of the international seminar, held in Brussels, 12-14 February 1980 / edited by A.A. [i.e. A.S.] Strub and G. Imarisio. — Dordrecht ; London : Reidel, c1980. — xii,703p : ill,ports ; 24cm
Includes papers in German and French. — At head of title: Commission of the European Communities. — Includes index
ISBN 90-277-1124-0 : Unpriced B81-03519

665.8′1 — Fuels: Hydrogen. Storage. Use of metal hydrides — *Conference proceedings*

Miami International Symposium on Metal-Hydrogen Systems *(1981)*. Metal-hydrogen systems. — Oxford : Pergamon, Jan.1982. — [1750]p
ISBN 0-08-027311-4 : £75.00 : CIP entry B81-37532

666 — CERAMICS AND RELATED TECHNOLOGIES

666 — Ceramics — *Conference proceedings*

Special ceramics 7 / [... papers ... presented at a meeting of the Basic Science Section held at Bedford College, London, on 15th-18th December, 1980] ; edited by Derek Taylor and Paul Popper. — Stoke-on-Trent : British Ceramic Society, 1981. — xi,265p : ill ; 21cm. — (Proceedings of the British Ceramic Society ; no.31)
Includes index
Unpriced (pbk) B81-31491

666′.0212 — Ceramics — *Technical data*

Conrad, John W.. Contemporary ceramic formulas / John W. Conrad. — New York : Macmillan ; London : Collier Macmillan, c1980. — xiv,261p,[28]p of plates : ill(some col.) ; 22cm
Bibliography: p258-261
ISBN 0-02-527640-9 : £6.95 B81-38651

666′.028′9 — Ceramics. Manufacture. Safety measures

Institute of Ceramics. Health & safety in ceramics : (a guide for educational workshops & studios) / Institute of Ceramics. — Stoke-on-Trent (Federation House, Station Rd., Stoke-on-Trent ST4 2RY) : The Institute, 1980. — 35p : ill ; 22cm
Cover title
ISBN 0-907034-00-4 (pbk) : £2.00 : CIP rev. B80-11895

666′.1 — Glass

Rawson, Harold. Properties and applications of glass / Harold Rawson. — Amsterdam ; Oxford : Elsevier Scientific, 1980. — xii,318p : ill ; 25cm. — (Glass science and technology ; 3)
Bibliography: p292-306. - Includes index
ISBN 0-444-41922-5 : £22.37 : CIP rev. B80-22238

666′.1 — Glass. Defects

Clark-Monks, C.. Stones and cord in glass / by C. Clark-Monks and J.M. Parker. — Sheffield : Society of Glass Technology, 1980. — vii,200p : ill ; 21cm
Includes index
Unpriced (pbk) B81-10944

666′.1 — Glass — *For children*

Fox, Julian. Glass / Julian Fox. — Hove : Wayland, 1980. — 72p : ill ; 20x22cm. — (World resources)
Includes index
ISBN 0-85340-789-4 : £3.75 B81-05546

666′.1 — Ireland. Glass industries, *1745-1835*

Warren, Phelps. Irish glass. — 2nd ed. — London : Faber, Sept.1981. — [260]p. — (Faber monographs on glass)
Previous ed.: 1970
ISBN 0-571-18028-0 : £25.00 : CIP entry B81-21467

666′.6 — China. Chekiang. Yüeh pottery kilns. Excavation of remains

Yüeh ware kiln-sites in Chekiang. — [London] ([South Kensington, S.W.7]) : Victoria & Albert Museum in association with the Oriental Ceramic Society, c1976. — 78p in various pagings, viiip of plates : ill ; 29cm. — (Chinese translations ; no.6)
Translated from the Chinese. — Originally published: in K′ao-ku Hsüeh Pao, 1959 No.3, p107-119 ; in K′ao-ku T′ung-Hsün, 1958, No.8, p44-47 ; in Wên wu, 1965 No.11, p21-34. — Contents: Yü-Yao Hsien by Chin Tsu-ming — Huang-Yen Hsien by staff of the Chekiang Bureau of Antiquities - Wên Chou by staff of the Chekiang Bureau of Antiquities
Unpriced (pbk) B81-20753

666′737′0942579 — Oxfordshire. Shiplake. Bricks. Manufacture, *1869-1935*

Brickmaking in Shiplake 1869-1935 / compiled by members of Shiplake Women′s Institute. — Shiplake (Burnbank, Shiplake, Oxon.) : E.M.B. Young, 1980. — [8]p : ill,1map,1facsim ; 21cm
Unpriced (pbk) B81-09571

666′.8 — Concrete

Ramachandran, V. S.. Concrete science. — London : Heyden, Nov.1981. — [400]p
ISBN 0-85501-703-1 : CIP entry B81-30625

666′.89 — Concrete. Crushed rock aggregates. Properties

Teychenné, D. C.. The use of crushed rock aggregates in concrete / D.C. Teychenné. — Watford : Building Research Establishment, 1978. — 74p : ill ; 30cm
£2.40 (pbk) B81-14332

666′.893 — Concrete — *Conference proceedings*

Concrete International *(Conference : 1980 : London)*. Discussion / CI80 (Concrete International 1980) ; The Concrete Society. — Lancaster : Construction, 1981. — 248p : ill ; 31cm
ISBN 0-86095-860-4 : Unpriced B81-16200

666′.94 — Great Britain. Cement industries. Energy. Conservation — *Proposals*

Malkin, L. S.. The cement industry : energy consumption and conservation in the cement industry : a report / prepared for the Department of Energy by L.S. Malkin. — [London] : Published in consultation with the Cement Makers′ Federation and the Central Electricity Generating Board by the Department of Energy and Department of Industry, 1980. — vi,54p : ill,1map ; 30cm. — (Energy audit series ; no.11)
Unpriced (pbk) B81-13923

666′.94 — Wood wool cement slabs. Labour intensive techniques

Flynn, G.. An industrial profile of wood wool/cement slab manufacture / G. Flynn and A.J. Hawkes. — London : Tropical Products Institute, 1980. — iv,6p[1]folded leaf of plates : 1plan ; 30cm. — (Tropical Products Institute, ISSN 0144-9982 ; G146)
ISBN 0-85954-119-3 (pbk) : £0.65 B81-06129

666′.94′091724 — Developing countries. Cement. Small scale manufacture

Spence, R. J. S.. Small-scale production of cementitious materials / R.J.S. Spence. — London : Intermediate Technology, c1980. — 49p : ill ; 21cm
ISBN 0-903031-74-4 (pbk) : £1.95 B81-27758

667 — CLEANING, DYEING, INKS, COATINGS

667 — Colour technology

Billmeyer, Fred W.. Principles of color technology. — 2nd ed. / Fred W. Billmeyer, Jr., Max Saltzman. — New York ; Chichester : Wiley, c1981. — xv,240p[8]p of plates : ill (some col.) ; 29cm
Previous ed.: New York ; London : Interscience, 1966. — Bibliography: p197-230. — Includes index
ISBN 0-471-03052-x : £20.00 B81-28303

667′.29 — Naturally occurring pigments — *For artists*

Thomas, Anne Wall. Colors from the earth : the artists′ guide to collecting, preparing, and using them / Anne Wall Thomas. — New York ; London : Van Nostrand Reinhold, c1980. — 96p,[4]p of plates : ill(some col.),2maps ; 24cm
Bibliography: p90-93. - Includes index
ISBN 0-442-25786-4 : £10.45 B81-06128

667′.29 — Pigments. Dispersion

Dispersion of powders in liquids. — 3rd ed. — London : Applied Science, Nov.1981. — [532]p
Previous ed.: 1973
ISBN 0-85334-990-8 : £32.00 : CIP entry B81-30423

667′.3 — Fabrics. Foam dyeing — *Conference proceedings*

Foam processing for dyeing and finishing. — Manchester : Shirley Institute, Sept.1981. — [80]p. — (Shirley Institute publication, ISSN 0306-5154 ; S.42)
Conference papers
ISBN 0-903669-38-2 (pbk) : £16.00 : CIP entry B81-28802

667′.6 — Paints. Chemical properties

Turner, G. P. A.. Introduction to paint chemistry : and principles of paint technology / G.P.A. Turner. — 2nd ed. — London : Chapman and Hall, 1980. — 229p : ill ; 22cm
Previous ed.: 1967. — Bibliography: p218-219. — Includes index
ISBN 0-412-16180-x (cased) : £15.00
ISBN 0-412-16190-7 (pbk) : £6.95 B81-06805

667′.6′05 — Paints. Manufacture — *Serials*

Paint & resin. — Vol.51, no.2 (Mar./Apr.1981)-. — Rickmansworth (Penn House, Penn Place, Rickmanworth, Herts. WD3 1SN) : Wheatland Journals, 1981-. — v. : ill ; 29cm
Six issues yearly. — Continues: Paint manufacture
ISSN 0261-5746 = Paint & resin : £19.35 per year
Also classified at 668′.37′05 B81-32192

667′.63 — Waterborne paints

Martens, Charles R.. Waterborne coatings : emulsion and water-soluble paints / Charles R. Martens. — New York ; London : Van Nostrand Reinhold, c1981. — x,316p : ill ; 24cm
Includes index
ISBN 0-442-25137-8 : £16.90 B81-04615

667′.9 — Coatings — *Conference proceedings*

Developments in coating and laminating : papers presented at a Shirley Institute Conference on 27 March 1981. — Manchester : Shirley Institute, c1981. — 98p : ill ; 30cm. — (Shirley Institute publication, ISSN 0306-5154 ; S.41)
ISBN 0-903669-37-4 (pbk) : £16.00 (£12.00 to members of the Shirley Institute) B81-33009

667′.9 — Coatings. Thickness. Measurement

Thickness testing of electroplated and related coatings / Institute of Metal Finishing, Industrial and Technical Committee ; edited by S.W. Baier. — Redhill : Portcullis Press
Vol.2. — 1981. — 82p : ill ; 23cm
ISBN 0-86108-092-0 (pbk) : Unpriced B81-40314

667′.9 — Finishing — *Serials*

Finishing handbook and directory. — 1981. — London (127 Stanstead Rd., SE23 1JE) : Sawell Publications, [1981]. — 539p
£20.25 B81-31041

668.1 — SURFACE ACTIVE AGENTS

668′.1′094 — Europe. Surface-active agents — *Lists*

Surfactants Europa : a directory of surface active agents available in Europe. — London : George Godwin
Vol.1. — Jan.1982. — [390]p
ISBN 0-7114-5736-0 (pbk) : £30.00 : CIP entry B81-35901

668′.14 — Detergents. Qualitative analysis. Cost-effectiveness — *Laboratory manuals*

Milwidsky, B. M.. Detergent analysis. — London : Godwin, Jan.1982. — [290]p
ISBN 0-7114-5735-2 : £20.00 : CIP entry B81-35031

668.3 — ADHESIVES AND RELATED PRODUCTS

668′.3 — Adhesives - *Serials*

Developments in adhesives. — London : Applied Science, May 1981. — (The developments series)
2. — [284]p
ISBN 0-85334-958-4 : £24.00 : CIP entry B81-06628

668′.37′05 — Resins. Manufacture — *Serials*

Paint & resin. — Vol.51, no.2 (Mar./Apr.1981)-. — Rickmansworth (Penn House, Penn Place, Rickmanworth, Herts. WD3 1SN) : Wheatland Journals, 1981-. — v. : ill ; 29cm
Six issues yearly. — Continues: Paint manufacture
ISSN 0261-5746 = Paint & resin : £19.35 per year
Primary classification 667′.6′05 B81-32192

668′.374 — Epoxy resins — *Serials*

Epoxy resins and plastics. — Prepublication issue (Dec.1980); no.1 (Jan.1981)-. — [Braintree] : R.H. Chandler Ltd., c1980-. — v. ; 30cm
Monthly
ISSN 0260-8677 = Epoxy resins and plastics : £35.00 per issue B81-09204

668.4 — PLASTICS

668.4 — Plastics

DuBois, J. Harry. Plastics / J. Harry DuBois, Frederick W. John. — 6th ed. — New York ; London : Van Nostrand Reinhold, c1981. — xiii,461p : ill,forms ; 24cm
Previous ed.: 1974. — Includes index
ISBN 0-442-26263-9 : £24.00 B81-08713

Grandilli, Peter A.. Technician's handbook of plastics / Peter A. Grandilli. — New York ; London : Van Nostrand Reinhold, c1981. — vii,246p : ill ; 24cm
Includes index
ISBN 0-442-23870-3 : £14.95 B81-25383

668.4 — Plastics — *For children*

Vale, Corwyn. Plastics / Corwyn Vale. — Hove : Wayland, 1981. — 72p : ill ; 20x22cm. — (World resources)
Bibliography: p70. - Includes index
ISBN 0-85340-818-1 : £3.75 B81-27176

668.4 — Plastics. Manufacture

Plastics pneumatic conveying and bulk storage. — London : Applied Science, Oct.1981. — [320]p
ISBN 0-85334-983-5 : £27.00 : CIP entry B81-25720

668.4 — Plastics. Manufacture & applications

Crawford, R. J.. Plastics engineering. — Oxford : Pergamon, Sept.1981. — [360]p. — (Progress in polymer science ; v.7)
ISBN 0-08-026262-7 (cased) : £31.25 : CIP entry
ISBN 0-08-026263-5 (pbk) : £10.50 B81-21555

668.4′05 — Plastics. Processing — *Serials*

Plastics and rubber processing and applications : an international journal. — Vol.1, no.1 (Mar.1981)-. — London : Applied Science on behalf of the Plastics and Rubber Institute, 1981-. — v. : ill ; 30cm
Quarterly. — Merger of: Plastics and rubber. Materials and applications ; and, Plastics and rubber. Processing
ISSN 0144-6045 = Plastics and rubber processing and applications : Unpriced
Also classified at 678′.2′05 B81-25040

668.4′1 — Great Britain. Plastics. Processing. Applications of industrial robots & microelectronic devices

Microelectronics & robotics — opportunities for application in plastics processing. — London : British Plastics Federation, [1981?]. — 8p ; 30cm
£1.50 (free to members) (spiral) B81-24389

668.4′1 — Plastics. Processing. Applications of ionising radiation — *Conference proceedings*

Radiation processing for plastics and rubber : international conference : 15 to 17 June 1981 : Bedford Hotel, Brighton, Sussex. — London (11 Hobart Place, SW1W 0HL) : The Plastic and Rubber Institute, 1981. — 278p in various pagings : ill ; 22cm
Cover title
Unpriced (pbk)
Also classified at 678′.2′028 B81-26346

668.4′1 — Polymers. Stabilisation

Developments in polymer stabilisation / edited by Gerald Scott. — London : Applied Science. — (The Development series)
4. — c1981. — x,290p : ill ; 23cm
Includes index
ISBN 0-85334-920-7 : £24.50 : CIP rev. B80-33875

668.4′12 — Plastics. Moulds & dies. Design — *Manuals*

Sors, László. Plastic molds and dies / László Sors, László Bardócz, István Radnóti ; [translated by Endre Darabant]. — New York ; London : Van Nostrand Reinhold, c1981. — 495p,[3]fold p of plates : ill ; 25cm
Translation of: Müanyagalakitó szerszámok. — Includes index
ISBN 0-442-27889-6 : £25.90 B81-25380

668.4′197 — Plastics materials. Inflammability — *Conference proceedings*

Plastics, rubbers and fire : proceedings of a RAPPA seminar held at Shawbury on 7th November 1979. — Shrewsbury (Shawbury, Shrewsbury, Shrops. SY4 4NR) : Rubber and Plastics Research Association of Great Britain, c1979. — 66p : ill ; 30cm
Unpriced (spiral)
Also classified at 678′.4 B81-10675

668.4′197 — Plastics. Testing — *Standards*

Handbook of plastics test methods. — 2nd ed. — London : Godwin, Sept.1981. — [430]p
Previous ed.: / by G.C. Ives, J.A. Mead and M.M. Riley. London : Iliffe, 1971
ISBN 0-7114-5618-6 : £28.50 : CIP entry B81-23852

668.4′22 — Thermosetting plastics. Applications

Thermosetting plastics. — London : Godwin, Sept.1981. — [216]p
ISBN 0-7114-5617-8 : £16.00 : CIP entry B81-20464

668.4′225 — Flexible polyurethane foam materials

Woods, George. Flexible polyurethane foams. — London : Applied Science, Oct.1981. — [368]p
ISBN 0-85334-981-9 : £29.00 : CIP entry B81-25718

668.4′23 — Thermoplastics. Injection moulding

Whelan, A.. Injection moulding materials. — London : Applied Science Publishers, Jan.1982. — [384]p
ISBN 0-85334-993-2 : £30.00 : CIP entry B81-33786

668.4′23 — Thermoplastics. Injection moulding - *Serials*

Developments in injection moulding. — London : Applied Science, Sept.1981. — (The Developments series)
2: Improving efficiency. — [320]p
ISBN 0-85334-968-1 : £28.00 : CIP entry B81-20544

668.4′23′028 — Blow moulding — *Conference proceedings*

Advances in Blow Moulding II *(Conference : 1981 : London).* Conference, Advances in Blow Moulding II, 20 & 21 May 1981, the Rainbow Suite, 99 Kensington High Street, London W8. — London : Plastics and Rubber Institute, c1981. — 135p in various pagings : ill ; 21cm
Unpriced (pbk) B81-26372

668.4′234 — Polyolefine stabilizers — *Lists*

World index of polyolefine stabilizers. — London : Kogan Page, July 1981. — [250]p
ISBN 0-85038-462-1 : £55.00 : CIP entry B81-20648

668.4′236 — Polyvinyl acetate. Emulsion polymerisation - *Conference proceedings*

Emulsion polymerization of vinyl acetate. — London : Applied Science, Sept.1981. — [288]p
Conference papers
ISBN 0-85334-971-1 : £26.00 : CIP entry B81-20542

668.4′236 — Polyvinyl chloride — *Conference proceedings*

PVC processing : international conference, 6 and 7 April 1978, Royal Holloway College, Egham Hill, Surrey. — London (11 Hobart Place, SW1W 0HL) : Plastic and Rubber Institute, [1978]. — 1v.(various pagings) : ill,2plans ; 21cm
Conference papers
Unpriced (pbk) B81-37060

668.4′237 — Polyvinyl chloride. Manufacture

Manufacture and processing of pvc. — London : Applied Science, Sept.1981. — [300]p
ISBN 0-85334-972-x : £24.00 : CIP entry B81-20541

668.4′9 — Great Britain. Plastics components. In-house manufacture

Karas, G. Christopher. The in-house moulder : his skills and attitudes : report of a study undertaken on behalf of the Polymer Engineering Directorate / G. Christopher Karas. — London : Science Research Council, 1980. — 26p ; 30cm
ISBN 0-901660-43-4 (spiral) : Unpriced B81-14330

668.4′9 — Plastics products. Design & manufacture

Brown, R. L. E.. Design and manufacturers of plastic parts / R.L.E. Brown. — New York ; Chichester : Wiley, c1980. — xii,204p : ill ; 29cm
Includes index
ISBN 0-471-05324-4 : £17.65 B81-08379

668.4′94 — Glass fibre reinforced plastics

A **Guide** to high performance plastics composites. — London : British Plastics Federation, Reinforced Plastics Group, c1980. — 48p : ill ; 30cm. — (A British Plastics Federation publication ; no.252/1)
£12.50 (£8.00 to members) (pbk) B81-24071

668.4′94 — Reinforced plastics — *Conference proceedings*

Reinforced Plastics Congress *(12th : 1980 : Brighton)*. Markets for the 80′s : the 12th Reinforced Plastics Congress 1980 / The British Plastics Federation Reinforced Plastics Group. — London : The Federation, 1980. — 242p : ill ; 30cm
£25.00 (pbk) B81-25232

668.4′94′05 — Reinforced plastics — *Serials*

Developments in reinforced plastics. — 1-. — London : Applied Science, 1980-. — v. : ill ; 23cm. — (Developments series)
Irregular
ISSN 0260-9185 = Developments in reinforced plastics : £26.00 B81-09246

668.5 — PERFUMES AND COSMETICS

668′.54 — Perfumes. Manufacture

Wells, F. V.. Perfumery technology : art, science, industry / F.V. Wells and Marcel Billot. — 2nd ed. / revised and enlarged by F.V. Wells. — Chichester (Market Cross House, Cooper St., Chichester, West Sussex PO19 1EB) : Ellis Horwood, 1981. — xi,449p : ill ; 24cm
Previous ed.: 1975. — Includes index
ISBN 0-85312-301-2 : £35.00 B81-26057

668.6 — AGRICULTURAL CHEMICALS

668′.62 — Fertilisers. Chemical analysis & testing

Lance, G. E. N.. A review of recent developments in methods for the sampling, physical testing and chemical analysis of fertilisers : papers read before the Fertiliser Society of London on 11th December 1980 / by G.E.N. Lance & A.C. Docherty. — [London] (93 Albert Embankment, SE1 7TU) : Fertiliser Society, [1980]. — 55p : ill ; 21cm. — (Proceedings / Fertiliser Society ; no.194)
Cover title
£5.00 (pbk) B81-08271

668′.62 — Fertilisers. Manufacture. Chemcial analysis. Applications of computer systems — *Case studies*

Scheer, J. C.. The development and use of a computer controlled analytical system : paper read before the Fertiliser Society of London on 11th December 1980 / by J.C. Scheer and T.J. Brans. — London (93 Albert Embankment, SE1 7TU) : Fertiliser Society, [1980]. — 47p : ill ; 21cm. — (Proceedings / Fertiliser Society ; no.195)
£5.00 (pbk) B81-06998

668′.65 — Controlled release pesticides — *Conference proceedings*

Controlled release of bioactive materials : based on the Symposium at the 6th International Meeting of the Controlled Release Society in New Orleans, Louisiana, August 1979 / edited by Richard Baker. — New York ; London : Academic Press, 1980. — xiii,473p : ill ; 24cm
Includes index
ISBN 0-12-074450-3 : £19.40
Primary classification 615′.1 B81-05968

International Symposium on Controlled Release of Bioactive Materials *(7th : 1980 : Ft. Lauderdale)*. Controlled release of pesticides and pharmaceuticals / [proceedings of the Seventh International Symposium on Controlled Release of Bioactive Materials, held July 27-30, 1980, in Ft. Lauderdale, Florida] ; edited by Danny H. Lewis. — New York ; London : Plenum, c1981. — ix,340p : ill ; 26cm
Includes index
ISBN 0-306-40743-4 : Unpriced
Primary classification 615′.1 B81-34690

668.7′2 — Toys — *For children*

Burton, Terry. My toys : a picture story book for pre-school children / [illustrated by Terry Burton]. — London : Macdonald Educational [for] Marks & Spencer, c1980. — [8]p : chiefly col.ill ; 18x19cm
Cover title. — Text, ill on inside covers
ISBN 0-356-07394-7 : £0.40 B81-02952

668.9 — INDUSTRIAL POLYMERS

668.9 — Polymers. Blends — *Conference proceedings*

Joint Italian-Polish Seminar on Multicomponent Polymeric Systems *(1st : 1979 : Capri)*. Polymer blends : processing, morphology and properties : [proceedings of the First Joint Italian-Polish Seminar on Multicomponent Polymeric Systems, held in Capri, Italy, October 16-21, 1979.] / edited by Ezio Martuscelli, Rosario Palumbo and Marian Kryszewski. — New York ; London : Plenum, c1980. — xii,510p : ill ; 26cm
Includes index
ISBN 0-306-40578-4 : Unpriced B81-26661

668.9 — Polymers. Degradation & stabilisation — *Serials*

Developments in polymer degradation. — 3. — London : Applied Science, c1981. — x,321p. — (Developments series)
ISBN 0-85334-942-8 : £30.00
ISSN 0260-4310 B81-24103

668.9 — Polymers. Stabilisation - *Serials*

Developments in polymer stabilisation. — London : Applied Science, Sept.1981. — (The Developments series)
5. — [240]p
ISBN 0-85334-967-3 : £22.00 : CIP entry B81-20545

668.9′072041 — Great Britain. *Science Research Council. Polymer Engineering Directorate — Serials*

Great Britain. *Science Research Council. Polymer Engineering Directorate*. Report for the year ended 31 December ... / Polymer Engineering Directorate, Science Research Council. — 1980. — London (3 Charing Cross Rd, WC2H 0HW) : The Directorate, [1981]. — 20p in various pagings
Unpriced B81-32395

669 — METALLURGY

669 — Metallurgy — *For non-destructive testing*

Basic metallurgy for non-destructive testing / editor J.L. Taylor. — 2nd ed. — Northampton (1 Spencer Parade, Northampton, NN1 5AA) : British Institute of Non-Destructive Testing, 1979 (1981 [printng]). — iii,80p : ill ; 30cm
″ ... based on a series of articles of the same title first published in the British journal of non-destructive testing". — Previous ed.: 1974. — Includes index
Unpriced (pbk) B81-19339

669 — Metals — *For children*

Kerrod, Robin. Metals / Robin Kerrod. — London : Macdonald Educational, 1981. — 48p : ill(some col.),1col.map ; 29cm. — (Visual science)
Includes index
ISBN 0-356-07111-1 : £3.50 B81-21156

669 — Metals — *For schools*

Bavage, Trevor. Metals / Trevor Bavage. — Glasgow : Blackie, 1981. — 32p : ill ; 17x25cm. — (Modular science)
ISBN 0-216-90582-6 (pbk) : £1.40 B81-10728

669 — Metals. Production — *Conference proceedings*

Papers presented at recent advances in hardmetal production : 17-19 September 1979 / sponsored by Dept. of Materials Engineering & Design Loughborough University of Technology and Metal Powder Report. — [Loughborough] ([Loughborough, Leics.]) : [Loughborough University of Technology], [c1979]. — 2v. : ill,2maps ; 30cm
Unpriced (pbk) B81-37758

669 — Minor metals. Marketing — *Conference proceedings*

Seminar on Marketing Minor Metals *(1981 : Amsterdam)*. Proceedings of Metal bulletin′s Seminar on Marketing Minor Metals, Amsterdam - May 20, 1981. — London : Metal Bulletin PLC, c1981. — 68p ; 30cm
ISBN 0-900542-56-x (pbk) : £12.00 B81-40142

669 — Nonferrous metals. Extractive metallurgy

Gill, C. B.. Nonferrous extractive metallurgy / C.B. Gill. — New York ; Chichester : Wiley, c1980. — xi,346p : ill ; 29cm
Includes bibliographies and index
ISBN 0-471-05980-3 : £21.25 B81-04500

669 — Nonferrous metals. Production

Topics in non-ferrous extractive metallurgy / edited by A.R. Burkin. — Oxford : Published for the Society of Chemical Industry by Blackwell Scientific, 1980. — x,134p : ill ; 24cm. — (Critical reports on applied chemistry ; v.1)
Includes index
ISBN 0-632-00648-x (pbk) : £8.00 : CIP rev. B80-05997

669′.00212 — Metals — *Technical data*

Ross, Robert B.. Metallic materials specification handbook / Robert B. Ross. — 3rd ed. — London : Spon, 1980. — xii,793p ; 26cm
Previous ed.: 1972. — Includes index
ISBN 0-419-11360-6 : £37.50 : CIP rev. B79-31882

669′.009′01 — Prehistoric metallurgy. Archaeological investigation — *Serials*

IAMS newsletter / Institute for Archaeo-Metallurgical Studies. — No.1 (1980)-. — London (Institute of Archaeology, University of London, 31 Gordon Sq., WC1H 0PY) : The Institute, 1980-. — v. : ill ; 30cm
Irregular. — Description based on: No.2 (1981)
ISSN 0261-068x = IAMS newsletter : Unpriced B81-17479

669′.00939′2 — Turkey. Prehistoric metallurgy

De Jesus, Prentiss S.. The development of prehistoric mining and metallurgy in Anatolia / Prentiss S. de Jesus. — Oxford : B.A.R., 1980. — 2v.(495p) : ill,maps ; 30cm. — (BAR. International series, ISSN 0143-3067 ; 74)
Bibliography: p164-189. — Includes index
ISBN 0-86054-082-0 (pbk) : £17.50 B81-16543

669′.028 — Metals industries. Automatic control systems. Applications of computer systems — *Conference proceedings*

Automation in mining, mineral and metal processing : proceedings of the 3rd IFAC Symposium, Montreal, Canada 18-20 August 1980 / editors J. O′Shea and M. Polis. — Oxford : Published for the International Federation of Automatic Control by Pergamon, 1981 c1980. — xv,662p : ill ; 31cm. — (IFAC proceedings series)
Includes bibliographies
ISBN 0-08-026164-7 : £63.00 : CIP rev.
Also classified at 622′.028 B80-27302

669′.028′2 — Iron. Smelting. Use of electric furnaces — *Conference proceedings*

Electric melting and holding furnaces in ironfoundries, March 25th-27th 1980, University of Warwick. — [Birmingham] ([Alvechurch, Birmingham B48 7QB]) : [British Cast Iron Research Association], c1980. — 443p in various pagings : ill ; 31cm
ISBN 0-901000-23-x : Unpriced B81-37734

669′.028′2 — Metallurgical furnaces

Krivandin, V. A.. Metallurgical furnaces / V.A. Krivandin, B.L. Markov ; translated from the Russian by V.V. Afanasyev. — Moscow : Mir ; [London] : Distributed by Central Books, 1980. — 509p : ill ; 23cm
Translation of: Metallurgicheskie pechi. — Bibliography: p488-490. — Includes index
ISBN 0-7147-1593-x : £5.95 B81-23592

669.1 — METALLURGY OF FERROUS METALS

669′.1 — Iron. Prehistoric metallurgy

The **Coming** of the age of iron / edited by Theodore A. Wertime and James D. Muhly ; contributors James A. Charles ... [et al.]. — New Haven ; London : Yale University Press, 1980. — xix,555p : ill,maps ; 25cm
Includes index
ISBN 0-300-02425-8 : £17.30 B81-09389

669′.141′094281 — England. Iron. Production, 1100-1500 — *Study regions: Yorkshire*

Moorhouse, Stephen. Medieval iron production / [text by Stephen Moorhouse] ; [drawings by Caroline Moorhouse]. — Wakefield (c/o David Michelmore, Horbury Hall, Church St., Horbury, Wakefield, W. Yorks.) : Bolton Percy Gatehouse Preservation Trust, 1980. — 8p : ill ; 22cm. — (Bolton Percy Gatehouse occasional publications ; no.1)
Cover title. — Bibliography: p7-8
£0.30 (pbk) B81-05075

669′.142 — Steel

Honeycombe, R. W. K.. Steels : microstructure and properties / R.W.K. Honeycombe. — London : Edward Arnold, 1981. — xi,224p : ill ; 23cm. — (Metallurgy and materials science)
Includes index
ISBN 0-7131-2793-7 (pbk) : £8.50 : CIP rev. B80-11974

669′.142 — Steel. Production

Moore, C.. Modern steelmaking methods / [by C. Moore, R.I. Marshall]. — London (c/o Publications Department, Northway House, Whetstone, N20 9LW) : Institution of Metallurgists, 1980?. — 121p : ill ; 21cm. — (Monograph / Institution of Metallurgists ; no. 6)
ISBN 0-901462-06-3 (pbk) : Unpriced B81-23292

669.2/7 — METALLURGY OF NONFERROUS METALS

669′.22′09 — Gold, *to 1980*

Buranelli, Vincent. Gold : an illustrated history / Vincent Buranelli. — Leicester : Windward, 1981, c1979. — 224p : ill(some col.),maps,facsims,ports(some col.) ; 29cm
Originally published: New York : December, 1979. — Includes index
ISBN 0-7112-0203-6 : £12.95 B81-15660

Kettell, Brian. Gold. — London : Graham & Trotman, Sept.1981. — [250]p
ISBN 0-86010-257-2 : £9.75 : CIP entry B81-28145

669′.3 — Great Britain. Copper industries. Energy. Conservation — *Proposals*

The **Copper** industry : energy consumption and conservation in the copper industry. — [London] : Issued jointly by the Department of Energy and the Department of Industry, 1981. — 56p : ill ; 30cm. — (Energy audit series ; no.12)
Prepared by the BNF Metals Technology Centre
Unpriced (pbk) B81-29926

669′.56 — Cadmium — *Conference proceedings*

International Cadmium Conference *(1st : 1977 : San Francisco)*. Edited proceedings / First International Cadmium Conference, San Francisco 31 January-2 February 1977 ; [organized by] Cadmium Association, Cadmium Council, International Lead Zinc Research Association. — London : Metal Bulletin for the organizers, 1978. — 265p : ill,maps ; 30cm
£32.25 (pbk) B81-05300

International Cadmium Conference *(1st : 1977 : San Francisco)*. Edited proceedings / First International Cadmium Conference, San Francisco 31 January-2 February 1977 ; [organizers] Cadmium Association, London, Cadmium Council, New York, International Lead Zinc Research Organization, New York. — London : Published by Metal Bulletin for the organizers, 1978. — 265p : ill,maps ; 30cm
Unpriced (pbk) B81-14483

International Cadmium Conference *(2nd : 1979 : Cannes)*. Edited proceedings : second International Cadmium Conference, Cannes, 6-8 February 1979. — Worcester Park : Published by the Metal Bulletin for the Organizers Cadmium Association, Cadmium Council, International Lead Zinc Research Organization, 1980. — 239p : ill,maps ; 30cm
Text on inside cover. — Includes bibliographies and index
Unpriced (pbk) B81-15661

669′.72 — Light metal alloys. Metallurgy

Polmear, I. J.. Light alloys : metallurgy of the light metals / I.J. Polmear. — London : Edward Arnold, 1981. — x,214p : ill ; 23cm. — (Metallurgy and materials science)
Includes bibliographies and index
ISBN 0-7131-2819-4 (pbk) : £8.95 B81-38433

669′.722 — Aluminium — *For children*

Keevil, David J.. Aluminium / David J. Keevil. — Hove : Wayland, 1980. — 72p : ill ; 20x23cm. — (World resources)
Includes index
ISBN 0-85340-794-0 : £3.75 B81-05283

669.9 — PHYSICAL AND CHEMICAL METALLURGY

669′.9 — Alloys. Structure & physical properties — *Technical data*

Smith, William F.. Structure and properties of engineering alloys / William F. Smith. — New York ; London : McGraw-Hill, c1981. — 512p : ill ; 25cm. — (McGraw-Hill series in materials science and engineering)
Text on lining papers. — Includes index
ISBN 0-07-058560-1 : £20.75 B81-09935

669′.9 — Chemical metallurgy

Moore, J. J.. Chemical metallurgy / J.J. Moore ; co-authors E.A. Boyce ... [et al.]. — London : Butterworths, 1981. — xix,380p : ill ; 24cm
Includes bibliographies and index
ISBN 0-408-00567-x (cased) : Unpriced
ISBN 0-408-00430-4 (pbk) : Unpriced B81-19455

669′.94 — High temperature alloys. Phase stability

Phase stability in high temperature alloys : proceedings of a course held at the Joint Research Centre of the Commission of the European Communities, Petten Establishment, The Netherlands / and organised by the CEC High Temperature Materials Information Centre, Petten, The Netherland ; edited by V. Guttmann. — London : Applied Science, c1981. — vii,154p : ill ; 23cm
Includes index
ISBN 0-85334-946-0 : £19.00 : CIP rev. B81-12798

669′.94 — Metals. Phase transitions

Porter, David A.. Phase transformation in metals and alloys / David A. Porter, Kenneth E. Easterling. — New York ; London : Van Nostrand Reinhold, c1981. — xii,446p : ill ; 25cm
Includes bibliographies and index
ISBN 0-442-30439-0 (cased) : £18.00
ISBN 0-442-30439-0 (pbk) : £8.95 B81-37777

669′.95 — Metals. Structure

Barrett, Charles S.. Structure of metals : crystallographic methods, principles and data. — 3rd rev ed. / C.S. Barrett, T.B. Massalski. — Oxford : Pergamon, 1980. — xv,654p : ill ; 23cm. — (International series on materials science and technology ; v.35) (Pergamon international library)
Previous ed.: i.e. 3rd ed. New York : McGraw-Hill, 1966. — Includes index
ISBN 0-08-026171-x (cased) : £27.00 : CIP rev.
ISBN 0-08-026172-8 (pbk) : £9.00 B80-13465

669′.95′05 — Metallography — *Conference proceedings — Serials*

Microstructural science. — Vol.8, Proceedings of the twelfth Annual Technical Meeting of the International Metallographic Society. — New York ; Oxford : Elsevier, c1980. — 400p
ISBN 0-444-00561-7 : £25.09 B81-11231

669′.96142 — Steel. Physical metallurgy

Leslie, William C.. The physical metallurgy of steels / William C. Leslie. — Washington ; London : Hemisphere, c1981. — xii,396p : ill ; 25cm. — (McGraw-Hill series in materials science and engineering)
Includes index
ISBN 0-07-037780-4 : £24.25 B81-32132

669′.96142 — Steel. Production. Chemical analysis — *Conference proceedings*

Chemists′ Conference *(32nd : 1979 : Scarborough)*. Proceedings of the Thirty-second Chemists′ Conference : Royal Hotel, Scarborough, May 15-17, 1979. — London : Research and Development Department, British Steel Corporation, 1980. — 120p : ill ; 30cm
(pbk) B81-28722

669′.9673′0212 — Ferro-alloying metals. Physical properties — *Technical data*

Properties of selected ferrous alloying elements / edited by Y.S. Touloukian, C.Y. Ho. — New York ; London : McGraw-Hill, c1981. — xvi,269p : ill ; 29cm. — (McGraw-Hill/CINDAS data series on material properties ; v.III—1)
ISBN 0-07-065034-9 : £23.50 B81-32338

670 — MANUFACTURES

670 — Manufacture

Harris, P. J. (Patrick John). Manufacturing technology 3 / P.J. Harris. — London : Butterworth, 1981. — 105p : ill ; 25cm. — (Butterworths technician series)
ISBN 0-408-00493-2 (pbk) : Unpriced B81-19390

Kazanas, H. C.. Basic manufacturing processes / H.C. Kazanas, Glenn E. Baker, Thomas Gregor. — New York ; London : Gregg Division/McGraw-Hill, c1981. — 378p : ill ; 28cm
Bibliography: p374-375. — Includes index
ISBN 0-07-033465-x (pbk) : £12.25 B81-10118

670′.29′441 — Great Britain. Kitemarked products — *Buyers′ guides — Serials*

British Standards Institution. BSI buyers guide. — 1981/82. — [Hemel Hempstead] ([Maylands Ave., Hemel Hempstead, Herts. HP2 4SQ]) : [Certification and Assessment Department, British Standards Institution], [1981]. — 128p
Unpriced B81-21951

670.42 — Production engineering — *For technicians*

Black, Bruce J.. Manufacturing technology for level-3 technicians / Bruce J. Black. — London : Edward Arnold, 1981. — vi,250p : ill ; 22cm
Includes index
ISBN 0-7131-3430-5 (pbk) : £4.95 B81-31295

Haslehurst, M.. Manufacturing technology / M. Haslehurst. — 3rd ed. — London : Hodder and Stoughton, 1981. — vi,394p : ill ; 22cm. — (Higher technician series)
Previous ed.: 1972. — Includes index
ISBN 0-340-26980-4 (pbk) : £3.75 : CIP rev. B81-16392

670.42 — Production engineering — *For technicians* *continuation*

Pritchard, R. T.. Technician manufacturing technology II / R.T. Pritchard. — London : Hodder and Stoughton, 1981. — viii,198p : ill ; 22cm
Includes index
ISBN 0-340-22099-6 (pbk) : £3.45 : CIP rev. B81-13488

670.42′3 — Materials. Grinding & polishing

Burkart, Walter. Grinding and polishing : theory and practice / [W. Burkart and K. Schmotz]. — Redhill : Portcullis, 1981. — xvi,345p : ill ; 24cm
Translation of: Handbuch für das Schleifen und Polieren. 4 Aufl. — Includes index
ISBN 0-86108-079-3 : Unpriced B81-39444

670.42′3 — Workshop practice — *For technicians*

Courtney, J. V.. Workshop processes and materials : level I / J.V. Courtney. — New York ; London : Van Nostrand Reinhold, c1980. — xv,217p : ill ; 26cm. — (Technical education courses)
Includes index
ISBN 0-442-30326-2 (cased) : £10.50
ISBN 0-442-30327-0 (pbk) : Unpriced B81-08717

670.42′7 — Process control. Applications of digital computer systems — *Conference proceedings*

Digital computer applications to process control : proceedings of the 6th IFAC-IFIP Conference Düsseldorf, F.R. Germany 14-17 October 1980 / edited by R. Isermann and H. Kaltenecker. — Oxford : Published for the International Federation of Automatic Control by Pergamon, 1981 c1980. — xiv,581p : ill ; 31cm. — (IFAC proceedings series)
Includes bibliographies
ISBN 0-08-026749-1 : £43.00 : CIP rev. B81-02084

670.42′7′05 — Factories. Automated assembly lines — *Serials*

Assembly automation. — Vol.1, no.1 (Nov. 1980)-. — Bedford (35 High St., Kempston, Bedford MK42 7BT) : IFS Publications, 1980-. — ill ; 30cm
Quarterly
£34.00 per year B81-13090

670′.68 — Great Britain. Manufacturing industries. Women managers

Women in management. — London : Industrial Society, 1980. — 27p : ill ; 25cm
£3.00 (pbk) B81-07573

670′.68′4 — United States. Declining manufacturing industries. Management, ***1950-1979*** — *Comparative studies*

Harrigan, Kathryn Rudie. Strategies for declining business / Kathryn Rudie Harrigan. — Lexington : Lexington Books, c1980 ; [Farnborough, Hants.] : Gower [distributor], 1981. — xiii,424p : ill ; 24cm
Bibliography: p407-418. — Includes index
ISBN 0-669-03641-2 : £18.50 B81-05503

671 — METAL MANUFACTURES

671 — Metals. Fabrication & welding - *For technicians*

Flood, C. R.. Welding and metal fabrication. — London : Butterworths, Aug.1981. — 1v.
ISBN 0-408-00448-7 (pbk) : CIP entry B81-16923

671 — Metals. Industrial processes — *Conference proceedings*

Sagamore Army Materials Research Conference *(25th : 1978).* Advances in metal processing / [proceedings of the twenty-fifth Sagamore Army Materials Research Conference, held July 17-21, 1978, Sagamore Hotel, at Bolton Landing, Lake George, New York] ; edited by John J. Burke, Robert Mehrabian and Volker Weiss. — New York ; London : Plenum, c1981. — x,388p : ill ; 25cm. — (Sagamore army materials research conference proceedings)
Includes bibliographies and index
ISBN 0-306-40651-9 : Unpriced B81-39995

671.2 — Foundry work

Fundamentals of foundry technololgy / edited by P.D. Webster. — Redhill, Portcullis, 1980. — x,496p : ill ; 25cm
Includes index
ISBN 0-86108-078-5 : Unpriced B81-13331

671.2 — Foundry work. Processes & techniques — *For schools*

Bolan, John. Casting and moulding. — London : Heinemann Educational, Oct.1981. — [112]p
ISBN 0-435-75090-9 (pbk) : £5.95 : CIP entry B81-27957

671.2′53 — Pressure die casting

Upton, B.. Pressure diecasting. — Oxford : Pergamon. — (Materials engineering practice)
Part 1: Metals, machines, furnaces. — Feb.1982. — [160]p
ISBN 0-08-027621-0 (cased) : £12.50 : CIP entry
ISBN 0-08-027622-9 (pbk) : £4.95 B81-35935

671.2′53 — Pressure die casting. Safety measures

Safety in pressure die casting. — 6th ed. — London (34 Berkeley Sq., W1X 6AJ) : Zinc Alloy Die Casters Association, 1980. — 12p : ill,plans ; 30cm
Cover title. — Previous ed.: 1972
Unpriced (pbk) B81-14129

671.3 — Metal engineering components. Orientation

Hamer, H. E. den. Interordering : a new method of component orientation / H.E. den Hamer. — Amsterdam ; Oxford : Elsevier Scientific, 1980. — ix,159p : ill ; 25cm. — (Studies in mechanical enginering ; v.2)
Includes index
ISBN 0-444-41933-0 : £22.64 B81-11141

671.3′6 — Metals. Heat treatment — *Conference proceedings*

Heat treatment ′79 : proceedings of an international conference organized by the Heat Treatment Committee of the Metals Society, in association with the Heat Treating Division of the American Society for Metals, and held at the Metropole Hotel, Birmingham, 22-24 May 1979. — London : Metals Society, 1980. — 237p : ill ; 31cm
Includes index. — Publishers no.: Book 261
ISBN 0-904357-25-2 : £30.00 (£24.00 to members) B81-00185

671.3′7 — Powder metallurgy

Bal′shin, M. ÎU.. General principles of powder metallurgy / M.Yu. Balshin, S.S. Kiparisov ; translated from the Russian by I.V. Savin. — Moscow : Mir, 1980 ; [London] : Distributed by Central Books. — 248p : ill ; 21cm
Translation of: Osnovy poroshkovoĭ metallurgii. — Includes index
ISBN 0-7147-1603-0 : £2.95 B81-23488

671.3′7 — Superalloys. Powder metallurgy — *Conference proceedings*

Papers presented at powder metallurgy superalloys : aerospace materials for the 1980′s : a metal powder report conference : Mövenpick-Holiday Inn, Zürich 18-20 November 1980. — [Shrewsbury] ([18 Talbot Chambers, Market St., Shrewsbury, SY1 1LG]) : [MPR Publishing Services], c1980. — 2v. : ill ; 30cm
Unpriced (pbk) B81-37759

671.5′2 — Automated welding — *Conference proceedings*

Developments in mechanised, automated and robotic welding : an international conference : London — 18-20 November 1980 / Conference technical director G.R. Salter ; Chairmen J.F. McWaters ... [et al.]. — Cambridge : Welding Institute, c1981. — 326p in various pagings : ill,1form ; 30cm
ISBN 0-85300-149-9 (pbk) : Unpriced B81-31661

671.5′2 — Metals. Welding

Gardner, J.. Welding engineering science and metallurgy / J. Gardner. — 2nd ed. — London : Price, 1980. — 110p : ill ; 22cm
Previous ed.: 1972. — Includes index
ISBN 0-85380-140-1 (pbk) : £1.80 B81-05524

671.5′2 — Metals. Welding — *Conference proceedings*

Weld pool chemistry and metallurgy : an international conference, London, 15-17 April 1980 / conference technical director, N. Bailey. — Cambridge : Welding Institute
Vol.2: Discussion. — c1981. — p359-389 : ill ; 30cm
ISBN 0-85300-148-0 (pbk) : Unpriced B81-16304

671.5′20422 — Welded structures. Residual stresses

Residual stresses and their effect. — Cambridge : Welding Institute, c1981. — 55p : ill ; 30cm
Bibliography: p48-55
ISBN 0-85300-141-3 (pbk) : £11.10 B81-18502

671.5′212 — Arc welding

Leake, Kenneth. Electric arc welding. — 3rd ed. — Sevenoaks : Newnes Technical Books, Aug.1981. — [128]p. — (Questions & answers)
Previous ed.: published as Questions and answers on electric arc welding
ISBN 0-408-01128-9 (pbk) : £1.95 : CIP entry B81-16926

671.5′212 — Arc welding — *Conference proceedings*

Arc physics and weld pool behaviour : an international conference, London 8-10 May 1979 / conference technical director W. Lucas ; chairman P.T. Houldcraft ... [et al.]. — Cambridge : Welding Institute
Vol.2: Discussion. — c1981. — 401-458p : ill ; 30cm
ISBN 0-85300-147-2 (pbk) : Unpriced (available only with V.1) B81-13933

671.8′23 — Coil-coated metal strips. Production & use — *Conference proceedings*

Production and use of coil-coated strip : proceedings of the international conference organized by the Metals Society in association with the Institute of Sheet Metal Engineering and the Birmingham Metallurgical Association and held in the Metropole Hotel, Birmingham, from 30 September to 2 October 1980. — London : Metals Society, c1981. — vi,177p : ill ; 30cm
Includes bibliographies and index. — Publisher′s no.: Bk.274
ISBN 0-904357-37-6 (pbk) : Unpriced B81-31220

671.8′42′028 — Wire manufacturing machinery — *Buyers′ guides — Serials*

Wire industry machinery guide. — 26th ed. (1981). — Oxted : Magnum Publications, [1981]. — 264p
Unpriced B81-33462

672 — FERROUS METALS MANUFACTURES

672 — Iron & steel industries. Energy. Conservation — *Conference proceedings*

Energy-conscious iron- and steelmaking : proceedings of an international conference on energy-conscious iron- and steelmaking organized jointly by The Metals Society, London, and the Verein 'Eisenhütte Österreich', Leoben, and held at the Montanuniversität, Leoben, Austria on 21-24 April, 1980. — London : Metals Society, c1981. — vii,175p : ill ; 31cm
Includes bibliographies and index
ISBN 0-904357-32-5 : Unpriced B81-39650

672.5′20423 — Welded ferritic steel. Defects. Detection by ultrasonic waves. Methods

Size measurement and characterisation of weld defects by ultrasonic testing : a collaborative project carried out on behalf of the Mechanical Engineering and Machine Tools Requirements Board, Department of Industry. — Cambridge : The Welding Institute, c1979. — (Report series / Welding Institute)
Pt.1: Non-planar defects in ferritic steels. — 83p : ill(some col.) ; 30cm
ISBN 0-85300-130-8 (pbk) : Unpriced B81-11821

672.8'23 — Tin plate — ***Conference proceedings***
International Tinplate Conference *(2nd : 1980 : London).* Second International Tinplate Conference : London, October 6th-10th, 1980. — Greenford : International Tin Research Institute, [1981]. — 528p : ill,ports ; 25cm. — (I.T.R.I. publication ; no.600)
Unpriced B81-31124

673 — NONFERROUS METALS MANUFACTURES

673'.52253 — Zinc alloy die castings - *Technical data - For design*
Chivers, A. R. L.. Zinc diecasting. — Oxford : Oxford University Press, Apr.1981. — [36]p. — (Engineering design guides ; 41)
ISBN 0-19-859180-2 (pbk) : £5.95 : CIP entry
B81-05121

673'.722732 — Aluminium & aluminium alloys. Anodising
Henley, V. F.. Anodic oxidation of aluminium and its alloys. — Oxford : Pergamon, Feb.1982. — [150]p. — (Materials engineering practice)
ISBN 0-08-026726-2 (cased) : £12.50 : CIP entry
ISBN 0-08-026725-4 (pbk) : £4.95 B81-35933

674 — TIMBER MANUFACTURES

674 — Timber. Use — ***Manuals***
Hardie, A. D. K.. An elementary manual of timber utilisation / by A.D.K. Hardie. — Penicuik (21 Biggar Rd., Silverburn, Penicuik, Midlothian, EH26 9LQ) : International Forest Science Consultancy, 1980. — ii,98p : ill,1form ; 30cm
Bibliography: p91-92. — Includes index
£5.00 (spiral) B81-04876

674'.12 — Timber. Microstructure — ***Illustrations***
Butterfield, B. G.. Three-dimensional structure of wood : an ultrastructural approach. — 2nd ed. / B.G. Butterfield and B.A. Meylan. — London : Chapman and Hall, 1980. — 103p : ill ; 31cm
Previous ed.: / by B.A. Meylan and B.G. Butterfield. 1972. — Bibliography: p94-99. - Includes index
ISBN 0-412-16320-9 : £19.50 : CIP rev.
B80-23523

674'.134 — Wood. Chemical properties
Sjöström, Eero. Wood chemistry : fundamentals and applications / Eero Sjöström. — New York ; London : Academic Press, 1981. — xi,223p : ill ; 24cm
Translation of: Puukemia. — Includes bibliographies and index
ISBN 0-12-647480-x : £14.60 B81-38867

674'.88 — Wooden kitchen utensils. Making — ***Manuals***
Studley, Vance. The woodworker's book of wooden kitchen utensils / Vance Studley. — New York ; London : Van Nostrand Reinhold, c1981. — 128p : ill ; 29cm
Bibliography: p125. — Includes index
ISBN 0-442-24726-5 : £13.55 B81-31776

675 — LEATHER AND FUR PROCESSING

675 — Leather — ***For children***
Gibbs, Richard. Leather / Richard Gibbs. — Hove : Wayland, 1981. — 72p : ill,1map ; 20x22cm. — (World resources)
Bibliography: p70. — Includes index
ISBN 0-85340-817-3 : £3.75 B81-27175

676 — PULP AND PAPER TECHNOLOGY

676 — Paper, paperboard & pulp. Manufacture. Use of chemicals — ***Conference proceedings***
Innovation in the Paper Industry for the Corporate Executive *(Conference : 1980 : Venice)*. Proceedings of the Conference 'Innovation in the Paper Industry for the Corporate Executive' : Venice, May 1980 / sponsored by Paper magazine ; edited by Eric Haylock and Jack Elliott. — London (25 New Street Sq., EC4A 3JA) : 'Paper', c1980. — 123p : ill ; 30cm
ISBN 0-510-49990-2 (spiral) : Unpriced
B81-34604

676 — Pulp & paper. Manufacture
Pulp and paper : chemistry and chemical technology. — New York ; Chichester : Wiley
Vol.2. — 3rd ed. / James P. Casey, editor. — c1980. — xxii,p821-1446 : ill ; 24cm
Previous ed.: New York ; London, 1960. — Includes index
ISBN 0-471-03176-3 : £26.75 B81-31227

. Pulp and paper : chemistry and chemical technology. — New York ; Chichester : Wiley
Vol.3. — 3rd ed. / James P. Casey, editor. — c1981. — xxxii,p1447-2011 : ill ; 24cm
Previous ed.: New York ; London : Interscience, 1961. — Includes index
ISBN 0-471-03177-1 : £38.50 B81-33227

676'.2 — Paper — ***For children***
Fobbester, Jim. Paper / Jim Fobbester. — Hove : Wayland, 1980. — 72p : ill ; 20x22cm. — (World resources)
Bibliography: p70. — Includes index
ISBN 0-85340-795-9 : £3.75 B81-02762

676'.2 — Paper. Manufacture
Handbook of paper science. — Oxford : Elsevier Scientific
Vol.2: The structure and physical properties of paper. — Nov.1981. — [250]p
ISBN 0-444-41974-8 : CIP entry B81-30373

676'.23 — Paper. Webs. Formation & consolidation — ***Conference proceedings***
EUCEPA-79 *(Conference : London).* Web formation & consolidation : conference papers = Formation et consolidation de la feuille : communications = Blattbildung und Konsolidierung : Vortrage / EUCEPA-79, 18th International Conference London, 21-24 May 1979. — [London] ([3 Plough Place E.C.4]) : [British Paper and Board Industry Federation], [1979?]. — 2v. : ill ; 21cm
Includes papers in French and German. — Cover title
Unpriced (pbk) B81-15604

676'.27 — Paper. Manufacture. Measurement & control
McGill, Robert J.. Measurement and control in papermaking / by the late Robert J. McGill. — Bristol : Hilger, c1980. — xi,424p : ill,1port ; 29cm
Bibliography: p412-418
ISBN 0-85274-162-6 : £45.00 : CIP rev.
B80-12978

677 — TEXTILE MANUFACTURES

677 — High performance textile products — ***Serials***
High performance textiles. — Vol.1, no.1 (July 1980)-. — Lausanne ; Oxford (Mayfield House, 256 Banbury Road, Oxford OX2 7DH) : Published by Elsevier Sequoia in conjunction with the Shirley Institute, 1980. — v. ; 30cm. — (Elsevier international bulletins)
Monthly
ISSN 0144-5871 = High performance textiles : £75.00 per year B81-03578

677 — Textile industries. Energy. Conservation — ***Conference proceedings***
Shirley International Seminar *(12th : 1980 : Shirley Institute).* Profitable energy saving in the textile industry : papers presented at the 12th Shirley International Seminar 16-18 September 1980. — Manchester : Shirley Institute, c1980. — iv,246p : ill ; 30cm. — (Shirley Institute publication, ISSN 0306-5154 ; S.40)
ISBN 0-903669-36-6 (pbk) : £16.00 (£12 to members of Shirley Institute) B81-06227

677 — Textiles
Joseph, Marjory L.. Introductory textile science / Marjory L. Joseph. — 4th ed. — New York ; London : Holt, Rinehart and Winston, c1981. — x,406p,[8]p of plates : ill(some col.) ; 25cm
Previous ed.: 1977. — Bibliography: p374-378. — Includes index
ISBN 0-03-056884-6 : £12.50 B81-22998

677 — Textiles - *For schools*
Ling, E. M.. Modern household science. — 4th ed. — London : Bell & Hyman, July 1981. — [258]p
Previous ed.: London : Mills & Boon, 1979
ISBN 0-7135-2073-6 (pbk) : £2.95 : CIP entry
Also classified at 648'.1 B81-15910

677 — Textiles. Terminology
Burnham, Dorothy K.. Warp and weft. — London : Routledge & Kegan Paul, Sept.1981. — [210]p
Originally published: Toronto : Royal Ontario Museum, 1980
ISBN 0-7100-0955-0 : £12.50 : CIP entry
B81-21478

677'.0068'4 — Textile industries. Technological change. Management — ***Conference proceedings***
Textile Institute. *Conference (64th : 1980 : Asheville).* Managing technological change : papers presented at the 64th Annual Conference October 12-15 1980 Asheville NC USA / the Textile Institute. — Manchester (10 Blackfriars St., Manchester M3 5DR) : The Institute, c1980. — 379p in various pagings : ill ; 28cm
ISBN 0-900739-42-8 (pbk) : Unpriced
B81-14212

677'.007'1241 — Great Britain. Secondary schools. Curriculum subjects: Textile fibres & fabrics — ***For teaching***
Sears, John. Fibres & fabrics / prepared by John Sears, Kaye Wakefield, additional material by Trevor Bavage ... [et al.]. — Hatfield (College La., Hatfield, Hertfordshire,AL10 9AA) : Association for Science Education, c1978. — 14p[22]leaves : ill ; 30cm. — (Topic brief / LAMP Project ; no.14)
ISBN 0-902786-51-2 (pbk) : £0.80 B81-11101

677'.0076 — Textiles - *Questions & answers - For schools*
Hartley, Kathleen. Topics and questions in textiles. — London : Heinemann Educational, June 1981
Pupil's book. — [80]p
ISBN 0-435-42834-9 (pbk) : £2.50 : CIP entry
B81-12342

Hartley, Kathleen. Topics and questions in textiles. — London : Heinemann Educational, June 1981
Teacher's book. — [64]p
ISBN 0-435-42833-0 (pbk) : £3.95 : CIP entry
B81-12355

677'.009 — Textiles. Design & manufacture, *to 1980*
Ponting, Kenneth G.. Discovering textile history and design / K.G. Ponting. — Aylesbury : Shire, 1981. — 72p : ill ; 18cm. — (Discovering series ; no.261)
Bibliography: p70-71. — Includes index
ISBN 0-85263-551-6 (pbk) : £1.50 B81-40748

677'.025854 — Shuttleless looms
Vincent, J. J.. Shuttleless looms / J.J. Vincent. — Manchester (10 Blackfriars St., Manchester M3 5DR) : Published in Association with the Worshipful Company of Weavers to commemorate their 850th anniversary [by] the Textile Institute, 1980. — xvi,142p : ill ; 23cm
Includes index
ISBN 0-904095-32-0 : £11.30 B81-04024

677'.02822 — Ireland. Dyeing, spinning & weaving. Traditional techniques, *to 1978*
Irish spinning, dyeing and weaving : an anthology, from original documents / collected by Lillias Mitchell. — Dundalk : Dundalgan, 1978. — 80p,[16]p of plates : ill ; 23cm
ISBN 0-85221-101-5 : £4.50 B81-10628

677'.028245'068 — Home-based machine knitting industries. Organisation — ***Manuals***
Lorant, Tessa. Earning and saving with a knitting machine / Tessa Lorant. — 2nd ed. — [Wells] ([The Old Vicarage, Godney, Wells, Somerset, BA5 1RX]) : Thorn, 1981. — 46p : ill ; 22cm. — (Profitable knitting series)
Cover title. — Previous ed.: 1980
ISBN 0-906374-11-1 (pbk) : Unpriced
B81-28891

677'.02854 — Shuttleless weaving machines
Talavášek, Oldřich. Shuttleless weaving machines / by Oldřich Talavášek and Vladimír Svatý. — Amsterdam ; Oxford : Elsevier Scientific, 1981. — 622p : ill ; 24cm. — (Textile science and technology ; 3)
Translation of: Bezčlunkové stavy. — Includes index
ISBN 0-444-99758-x : £41.51 : CIP rev.
B80-17843

677′.02862 — Great Britain. Knitting yarns — *Buyers′ guides — Serials*

Buyers′ guide to knitting yarns, home sewing aids, haberdashery and craft materials. — 1981 ed. — London (6 Ludgate Sq., EC4M 7AS) : Knitting & Haberdashery Review, [1981?]. — ii,68p
Cover title: Knitting & haberdashery buyers′ guide
Unpriced
Primary classification 687′.8′029441 B81-20415

677′.02864 — Fabrics

Ladbury, Ann. Fabrics / Ann Ladbury. — London : Methuen Paperbacks, 1981, c1979. — 292p : ill ; 20cm. — (Magnum books)
Originally published: London : Sidgwick & Jackson, 1979. — Includes index
ISBN 0-417-06040-8 (pbk) : £2.50 B81-19617

677′.02864 — Great Britain. Art galleries & museums. Exhibits: Fabrics manufactured by Warner & Sons, *1850-1980 — Catalogues*

Bury, Hester. A choice of design 1850-1980 : fabrics by Warner & Sons Ltd.. — London (7 Noel St., W.1.) : Warner & Sons, Sept.1981. — [116]p
ISBN 0-9506587-1-5 (pbk) : £5.50 : CIP entry
B81-28403

677′.02864 — Needle-punched fabrics. Manufacture

Purdy, A. T.. Needle-punching / A.T. Purdy. — Manchester (10 Blackfriars St., Manchester, M3 5DR) : Textile Institute, 1980. — 63p : ill ; 21cm. — (Monograph series / The Textile Institute ; no.3)
Includes index
ISBN 0-900739-32-0 (pbk) : Unpriced
B81-07269

677′.02864 — Woven fabrics. Geometrical aspects

Cloth geometry. — Manchester (10 Blackfriars St., Manchester M3 kDR) : Textile Institute, c1978. — ill ; 23cm. — (A classic textile reprint)
Facsimile reprints from: Journal of the textile industry, 1937, v.28, no.3. — Contents: The geometry of cloth structure / by F.T. Peirce - The application of differential geometry to the study of the deformation of cloth under stress / by J.R. Womersley
ISBN 0-900739-28-2 (pbk) : £3.30 B81-21757

677′.029 — Great Britain. Textile industries. Waste materials: Plastics. Recycling

Bevis, M. J.. Plastics waste resources from textile and related industries (carpets, plastics coating and synthetic fabrics) / by M.J. Bevis & J.W. Bromley. — London : British Plastics Federation, c1980. — 31p : ill,1form ; 30cm. — (Publication / British Plastics Federation ; no.277/1)
£7.50 (£5.00 to members) (spiral) B81-24068

677′.0724 — Textiles. Experiments — *For schools*

Gohl, E. P. G.. Investigations in textile science / E.P.G. Gohl and L.D. Vilensky. — [British ed.]. — Glasgow : Blackie, 1980. — 78p : ill,facsims,forms ; 25cm
Previous ed.: i.e. Australian ed., published as Investigating textiles. Melbourne : Longman Cheshire, 1977. — Bibliography: p77
ISBN 0-216-90853-1 (pbk) : £1.95 B81-04995

677′.3164 — Worsted wool fabrics. Manufacture. Techniques

Brearley, Alan. The worsted industry : an account of the worsted industry and its processes from fibre to fabric. — 2nd ed. / by Alan Brearley and John A. Iredale. — Leeds : Wira, 1980. — viii,198p : ill ; 21cm
Previous ed.: published as Worsted / by Alan Brearley ; London : Pitman, 1964. — Bibliography: p152-153. - Includes index
ISBN 0-900820-14-4 (pbk) : £5.50 B81-07243

677′.616 — Upholstery fabrics

Symonds, W. E.. A concise guide to upholstery fabrics / by W.E. Symonds. — Stevenage : Furniture Industry Research Association, 1981. — 49p : ill ; 30cm
£15.00 (£7.00 to members of FIRA) (spiral)
B81-21898

677.7 — CORDAGE, TRIMMINGS AND RELATED PRODUCTS

677′.71 — Great Britain. Nets. Making, *to 1950*

Sanctuary, Anthony. Rope, twine and net making / Anthony Sanctuary. — Aylesbury : Shire, 1980. — 32p : ill ; 21cm. — (Shire album ; 51)
ISBN 0-85263-502-8 (pbk) : £0.75 B81-07307

678 — ELASTOMERS AND ELASTOMER PRODUCTS

678 — Elastomers & rubber

Developments in rubber technology. — London : Applied Science. — (The Developments series)
2: Synthetic rubbers / edited by A. Whelan and K.S. Lee. — c1981. — x,275p : ill ; 23cm
Includes index
ISBN 0-85334-949-5 : £22.00 : CIP rev.
B81-01021

678 — Elastomers. Accelerated curing. Use of organic compounds

Blokh, G. A.. Organic accelerators and curing systems for elastomers / G.A. Blokh ; translated by R.J. Moseley. — Shrewsbury : Rubber and Plastics Research Association of Great Britain, 1981. — xiii,324p : ill ; 21cm. — (International polymer science and technology monograph ; 3)
Translation of the Russian. — Bibliography: p323-324
ISBN 0-902348-22-1 (pbk) : Unpriced
B81-35284

678 — Elastomers. Reinforcement. Use of textiles

Textile reinforcement of elastomers. — London : Applied Science Publishers, Feb.1982. — [272]p
ISBN 0-85334-998-3 : £24.00 : CIP entry
B81-35856

678.2/4 — RUBBER TECHNOLOGY

678′.2 — Rubber — *Conference proceedings*

Rubbercon ′81 *(Conference : Harrogate)*.
Rubbercon ′81 : the International Rubber Conference, Harrogate, England, 8-12 June 1981. — London (11, Hobart Place, SW1W 0HL) : Plastics and Rubber Institute, [c1981]. — 2v. : ill ; 21cm
ISBN 0-903107-32-5 (pbk) : Unpriced
B81-29756

678′.2′028 — Rubber. Processing. Applications of ionising radiation — *Conference proceedings*

Radiation processing for plastics and rubber : international conference : 15 to 17 June 1981 : Bedford Hotel, Brighton, Sussex. — London (11 Hobart Place, SW1W 0HL) : The Plastic and Rubber Institute, 1981. — 278p in various pagings : ill ; 22cm
Cover title
Unpriced (pbk)
Primary classification 668.4′1 B81-26346

678′.2′05 — Rubber. Processing — *Serials*

Plastics and rubber processing and applications : an international journal. — Vol.1, no.1 (Mar.1981)-. — London : Applied Science on behalf of the Plastics and Rubber Institute, 1981-. — v. : ill ; 30cm
Quarterly. — Merger of: Plastics and rubber. Materials and applications ; and, Plastics and rubber. Processing
ISSN 0144-6045 = Plastics and rubber processing and applications : Unpriced
Primary classification 668.4′05 B81-25040

678′.2′05 — Rubber — *Serials*

Progress of rubber technology. — Vol.44 (1981). — London : Applied Science, Nov.1981. — [148]p
ISBN 0-85334-984-3 : £18.00 : CIP entry
B81-30418

678′.4 — Rubber. Inflammability — *Conference proceedings*

Plastics, rubbers and fire : proceedings of a RAPPA seminar held at Shawbury on 7th November 1979. — Shrewsbury (Shawbury, Shrewsbury, Shrops. SY4 4NR) : Rubber and Plastics Research Association of Great Britain, c1979. — 66p : ill ; 30cm
Unpriced (spiral)
Primary classification 668.4′197 B81-10675

678.6 — NATURAL ELASTOMERS

678′.63′0212 — Natural rubber products — *Technical data — Serials*

Natural rubber formulary / Malaysian Rubber Producers′ Research Association. — 1980. — Brickendonbury (Tun Abdul Razak Laboratory, Brickendonbury, Hertford SG13 8NL) : The Association, [1980?]. — vi,130p
Unpriced B81-07311

678.7 — SYNTHETIC ELASTOMERS

678′.71 — Synthetic latexes. Applications

Polymer latices and their applications. — London : Applied Science Publishers, Sept.1981. — [244]p
ISBN 0-85334-975-4 : £19.00 : CIP entry
B81-20163

678′.72 — Synthetic rubber. Applications — *Conference proceedings*

Synthetic rubbers for high temperature and engineering applications : Friday 10 April 1981 : the Kensington Close Hotel, Wrights Lane, London W8. — London (11 Hobart Place, SW1W 0HL) : The Plastics and Rubber Institute, 1981. — 98p : ill ; 30cm
Conference papers. — Cover title
Unpriced (pbk) B81-26349

679 — MANUFACTURES. IVORY, FEATHER, FIBRE, BRISTLE, TOBACCO AND OTHER PRODUCTS

679′.7 — Pipe tobacco. British blends — *Lists*

McGahey, Martin. The tobacco index / compiled by Martin McGahey. — 2nd ed. — Exeter (c/o M. McGahey, 245 High St., Exeter) : Association of Independent Tobacco Specialists, c1980. — 18p : ill ; 22cm
Cover title. — Previous ed.: 1979. — Text on inside covers. — Includes index
ISSN 0144-7688 (pbk) : £0.25 B81-05487

679′.7 — Snuff — *Lists*

The A.I.T.S. snuff index. — [No.1]-. — [Exeter] ([c/o M. McGahey, 245 High St., Exeter]) : Association of Independent Tobacco Specialists in association with the Society of Snuff Grinders, Blenders and Purveyors, [1981?]. — v. ; 21cm
Annual. — Cover title
ISSN 0261-2380 = A.I.T.S. snuff index : £0.35
B81-15472

680 — CRAFTS

680 — Craft work — *For schools*

Caborn, Colin. Integrated craft and design / Colin Caborn and Ian Mould. — London : Harrap, 1981. — 299p : ill,plans ; 25cm
Includes index
ISBN 0-245-53633-7 (pbk) : £4.95
Also classified at 745.4 B81-19677

680′.24054 — Crafts — *For children*

Daitz, Myrna. Crafty ideas. — London : Severn House, Oct.1981. — [128]p
ISBN 0-7278-2009-5 : £6.95 : CIP entry
B81-24678

680′.6′041 — Great Britain. Crafts. Organisations *— Directories — Serials*

The **Craftsman′s** directory. — 1981-. — Godalming (Brook House, Mint St., Godalming, Surrey GU7 1HE) : S. & J. Lance, 1981-. — v. ; 19cm
Annual
ISSN 0261-2135 = Craftsman′s directory : £3.00 B81-25038

680′.68 — Great Britain. Art and craft shops. Management — *Manuals*

Lewis, Ralph. Making and managing an art & craft shop / Ralph Lewis. — Newton Abbot : David and Charles, c1981. — 159p ; 22cm
Includes index
ISBN 0-7153-8065-6 : £6.50 B81-13389

680′.7′12 — Secondary schools. Curriculum subjects: Crafts. Academic achievement of students. Assessment — *For teaching*

Black, H. D.. Diagnostic assessment in technical education : a teacher′s handbook / by H.D. Black and W.B. Dockrell. — [Edinburgh] ([16 Moray Place, Edinburgh EH3 6DR]) : Scottish Council for Research in Education, c1980. — x,75p : ill,forms ; 22cm
ISBN 0-901116-25-4 (pbk) : £2.20 B81-32300

680′.9411 — Scotland. Crafts

Scottish crafts now / [Crafts Consultative Committee]. — Edinburgh (102 Telford Rd., Edinburgh EH4 2NP) : Scottish Development Agency Small Business Division, c1980. — 80p : ill(some col.),ports(some col.) ; 30cm
ISBN 0-905574-02-8 (pbk) : £3.95 B81-19935

680′.9428′1 — Yorkshire. Rural crafts

Williams, Ann, *1938-*. Country crafts in Yorkshire / by Ann Williams. — Clapham, N. Yorkshire : Dalesman, 1980. — 72p : ill,ports ; 22cm
Bibliography: p72
ISBN 0-85206-612-0 (pbk) : £1.75 B81-08241

680′.9669 — Nigeria. Crafts — *For teaching*

Oyelọla, P.. Nigerian crafts / P. Oyelọla. — London : Macmillan, 1981. — xi,83p : ill ; 25cm
ISBN 0-333-28607-3 (pbk) : £1.35 B81-39087

680′.9716 — Nova Scotia. Rural crafts

Barss, Peter. Older ways : traditional Nova Scotian craftsmen / Peter Barss ; craft notes by Joleen Gordon. — Toronto ; London : Van Nostrand Reinhold, c1980. — 138p : ill,1map,ports ; 25cm
Bibliography: p137-138
ISBN 0-442-29628-2 : £12.70 B81-21407

680′.973 — United States. Crafts, *1655-1855* — *Illustrations*

Copeland, Peter F.. Early American trades : coloring book / Peter F. Copeland. — New York : Dover ; London : Constable, 1980. — [48]p : chiefly ill(some col.) ; 28cm. — (Dover coloring book)
Ill on inside covers
ISBN 0-486-23846-6 (pbk) : £1.50 B81-05338

681.1 — MANUFACTURES. ANALOGUE AND DIGITAL INSTRUMENTS

681.1′1′05 — Clocks & watches — *Serials*

[Timecraft *(Ashford)*]. Timecraft : clocks & watches : official journal of the Watch & Clock Book Society. — Vol.1, no.1 (Jan.1981)-. — Ashford (PO Box 22, Ashford, Kent) : Brant Wright Associates, 1981-. — v. : ill ; 30cm
Monthly
ISSN 0260-5988 = Timecraft (Ashford) : £12.00 per year B81-10561

681.1′1′0922 — North-east England. Clockmakers & watchmakers, *to 1900*

Bates, Keith. The clockmakers of Northumberland and Durham / by Keith Bates. — Morpeth (Rothbury, Morpeth, Northd. NE65 7YB) : Pendulum, c1980. — 303p,[3]p leaves of plates : ill(some col.),facsims,1plan,geneal.tables ; 31cm
Ill on lining papers. — Bibliography: p298-299. - Includes index
ISBN 0-9506935-0-2 : Unpriced B81-19778

681.1′13 — British long case clocks, *to ca 1845*

Edwardes, Ernest L.. The grandfather clock : an historical and descriptive treatise on the English long case clock with notes on some Scottish, Welsh and Irish examples / by Ernest L. Edwardes. — 4th ed. — Altrincham : Sherratt, 1980. — xvi,215p,8,151p of plates : ill ; 26cm
Previous ed.: 1971. — Includes index
ISBN 0-85427-054-x : £15.00 B81-32815

681.1′13 — British white dial long case clocks, *to 1870*

Loomes, Brian. White dial clocks : the complete guide / Brian Loomes. — [2nd ed.]. — Newton Abbot : David & Charles, c1981. — 268p : ill ; 24cm
Previous ed.: published as The white dial clock. 1974. — Includes index
ISBN 0-7153-8073-7 : £12.50 B81-19712

681.1′13 — Long case clocks — *Collectors′ guides*

Robinson, Tom. The longcase clock. — Woodbridge : Antique Collectors′ Club, Dec.1981. — [350]p
ISBN 0-907462-07-3 : £29.50 : CIP entry B81-34965

681.1′13 — Long case clocks, *to ca 1925* — *Collectors′ guides* — *Serials*

Timepiece : price guide to longcase clocks. — Vol.1, no.1 (Sept.1980) ; 1981-. — Ashford (PO Box 22, Ashford, Kent) : Brant Wright Associates, 1980. — v. : ill ; 30cm
Quarterly
£0.85 per issue B81-05682

681.1′13 — Scottish long case clocks, *1780-1870*

Hudson, Felix. Scottish longcase clocks 1780-1870 / by Felix Hudson. — [Ticehurst] ([New House, High St., Ticehurst, Wadhurst, Sussex TN5 7AL]) : Antiquarian Horology, [1981?]. — 77p in various pagings : ill ; 25cm. — (Monograph / Antiquarian Horological Society ; no.22)
Cover title. — Reprinted from Antiquarian horology
Unpriced (pbk) B81-29177

681.1′13′0922 — Northern England. Clockmakers, *to 1900* — *Lists*

Reid, C. Leo. North Country clockmakers : of the the 17th, 18th and 19th centuries / C. Leo Reid. — Morpeth (Rothbury, Morpeth, Northd. NE65 7IB) : Pendulum, 1981, c1925. — 140p,[7]p of plates : ill(some col.) ; 22cm
Facsim of: 1st ed. Newcastle-upon-Tyne : Andrew Reid, 1925
ISBN 0-9506935-1-0 : £12.00 B81-34978

681.1′13′0922 — Warwickshire. Leamington Spa & Warwick. Clockmakers, *to 1850*

Seaby, Wilfred A.. Clockmakers of Warwick and Leamington (to 1850) / Wilfred A. Seaby. — Warwick (Market Place, Warwick) : Warwickshire Museum, 1981. — 64p : ill ; 21cm. — (Warwickshire master craftsmen)
Bibliography: p64
ISBN 0-9505942-7-x (pbk) : Unpriced B81-14586

681.1′13′0942 — English bracket & mantel clocks, *ca 1600-ca 1900* — *Collectors′ guides*

Nicholls, Andrew. English bracket and mantel clocks. — Poole : Blandford, Sept.1981. — [160]p
ISBN 0-7137-1009-8 : £4.95 : CIP entry B81-22533

681.1′14′09033 — England. Kemp, Robert, *19---*. **Private collections: Pocket watches,** *ca 1700-1930*

Kemp, Robert, *1908 May 12-*. The Englishman′s watch / by Robert Kemp. — Altrincham : Sherratt, 1979. — 148p,[65]p of plates : ill,2ports ; 26cm
Bibliography: p142-144. — Includes index
ISBN 0-85427-052-3 : £12.00 B81-10773

681.2 — MANUFACTURES. MEASURING INSTRUMENTS

681′.2 — Weighing equipment, *to ca 1920*

Graham, J. T. (John Thomas). Scales and balances : a guide to collecting / J.T. Graham. — Aylesbury : Shire, 1981. — 32p : ill ; 21cm. — (Shire album ; 55)
Bibliography: p32
ISBN 0-85263-547-8 (pbk) : £0.95 B81-17542

681.4 — MANUFACTURES. OPTICAL EQUIPMENT

681′.4 — Multilayer filters. Design. Applications of computer systems

Liddell, Heather M.. Computer-aided techniques for the design of multilayer filters / Heather M. Liddell ; consultatnt editor H.G. Jerrard ; foreword by H.A. Macleod. — Bristol : Hilger, c1981. — 194p : ill ; 26cm
Bibliography: p183-187. — Includes index
ISBN 0-85274-233-9 : £20.00 B81-08096

681′.4 — Optical instruments. Manufacture & testing

De Vany, Arthur S.. Master optical techniques / Arthur S. De Vany. — New York ; Chichester : Wiley, c1981. — viii,600p : ill ; 24cm. — (Wiley series in pure and applied optics)
Text on lining paper. — Includes bibliographies and index
ISBN 0-471-07720-8 : £38.50 B81-37114

681′.41 — Camera obscuras, *to 1980*

Hammond, John H.. The camera obscura : a chronicle / John H. Hammond. — Bristol : Hilger, 1981. — xi,182p : ill ; 26cm
Bibliography: p165-178. — Includes index
ISBN 0-85274-451-x : £13.50 : CIP rev. B81-27398

681′.418 — Electronic photographic equipment. Projects — *Amateurs′ manuals*

Penfold, R. A.. Electronic projects in photography / R.A. Penfold and J.W. Penfold. — London : Newnes Technical, 1981. — 87p : ill(some col.) ; 22cm. — (Newnes constructors projects)
ISBN 0-408-00500-9 (pbk) : Unpriced : CIP rev. B81-14911

681.6/7 — MANUFACTURES. PRINTING, DUPLICATING AND OTHER SPECIAL-PURPOSE MACHINERY

681′.75 — Scientific instruments

Jones, Barry E.. Instrument science and technology. — Bristol : Hilger
Vol.1. — Jan.1982. — [145]p
ISBN 0-85274-438-2 : £7.00 : CIP entry B81-34775

681′.75′0740291443 — Scotland. Strathclyde Region. Glasgow. Universities: University of Strathclyde. Stock: Scientific instruments — *Catalogues*

University of Strathclyde. Catalogue of the collection of historical scientific instruments in the University of Strathclyde. — [Glasgow] ([Richmond St., Glasgow G1 1XQ]) : Collins Exhibition Hall, University of Strathclyde, 1980. — 141p ; 21cm
Includes index
£2.00 (pbk) B81-35532

681′.754 — High performance liquid chromatography equipment. Maintenance & repair — *Manuals*

Runser, Dennis J.. Maintaining and troubleshooting HPLC systems : a user′s guide / Dennis J. Runser. — New York ; Chichester : Wiley, c1981. — xiii,163p : ill ; 24cm
Includes index
ISBN 0-471-06479-3 : £17.00 B81-23426

681′.76041 — Pressure vessels. Design

Bednar, Henry H.. Pressure vessel design handbook / Henry H. Bednar. — New York ; London : Van Nostrand Reinhold, c1981. — ix,321p : ill,maps ; 24cm
Includes index
ISBN 0-442-25416-4 : £22.55 B81-37781

681′.761 — Dental equipment & dental materials. Manufacture. Laboratory techniques

Blakeslee, Richard W.. Dental technology : theory and practice / Richard W. Blakeslee, Robert P. Renner, Alexander Shiu. — St. Louis ; London : Mosby, 1980. — xiii,365p : ill,1form ; 27cm
Includes bibliographies and index
ISBN 0-8016-0695-0 : £17.75 B81-02969

681′.761 — Electronic medical equipment. Design

Design of microcomputer-based medical instrumentation / Willis J. Tompkins and John G. Webster, eds. — Englewood Cliffs ; London : Prentice Hall, c1981. — xiii,495p : ill ; 25cm
Includes bibliographies and index
ISBN 0-13-201244-8 : £18.15 B81-16536

681′.763 — Great Britain. Agricultural machinery. Materials: Polymers

The **Use** of polymers in agricultural machinery : a study of present polymer applications and recommendations on how agricultural machinery manufacturers can be assisted in making correct and wider use of polymers in the future : a report / for the Polymer Engineering Directorate of the Science Research Council by the National College of Agricultural Engineering, Cranfield Institute of Technology. — Bedford (Silsoe, Bedford MK45 4DT) : [The College], 1980. — 82p ; 30cm
Unpriced (pbk) B81-35671

681′.766 — Hydrocyclones — *Conference proceedings*

Papers presented at an international conference on hydrocyclones : held at Churchill College, Cambridge, U.K. October 1980 / organised ... by BHRA Fluid Engineering ; [edited by G. Priestley, H.S. Stephens]. — Bedford (Cranfield, Bedford MK43 0AJ) : BHRA Fluid Engineering, 1980. — 248p : ill ; 29cm
Cover title: Hydrocyclones. — Includes bibliographies
ISBN 0-906085-48-9 (pbk) : £27.00 B81-03135

681′.766 — Pressure vessels — *Conference proceedings*

International Conference on Pressure Vessel Technology *(4th : 1980 : London)*. Pressure vessel technology / conference organized by the Institution of Mechanical Engineers, the American Society of Mechanical Engineers and the Japan High Pressure Technology Institute. — London : Published by Mechanical Engineering Publications for the Institution of Mechanical Engineers, 1980
Cover title
Vol.3: Additional papers and written discussions. — 118p : ill ; 30 cm
ISBN 0-85298-458-8 (pbk) : Unpriced
B81-28357

681′.7664 — Great Britain. Soft drinks pressure dispensing systems — *Standards*

National Association of Soft Drinks Manufacturers. Code of practice for the dispense of soft drinks by pressure systems / National Association of Soft Drinks Manufacturers Limited. — Twickenham (2 Holly Rd., Twickenham, Middx. TW1 4EF) : NASDM, 1980. — 48p : ill(some col.) ; 21cm
Unpriced (pbk) B81-22959

681′.7677 — Domestic knitting machines — *Buyers′ guides*

Lorant, Tessa. Choosing and buying a knitting machine / Tessa Lorant. — Wells (The Old Vicarage, Godney, Wells, Somerset BE5 1RX) : Thorn, 1980. — 48p : ill ; 22cm. — (Profitable knitting series)
Cover title. — Bibliography: p47
ISBN 0-906374-13-8 (pbk) : £1.25 B81-03231

681.8 — MANUFACTURES. MUSICAL INSTRUMENTS

681′.81621′0216 — Pianos. Serial numbers. Dates

The **Musician′s** piano atlas / edited by S.K. Taylor. — Macclesfield (Sunderland House, Sunderland St., Macclesfield, Cheshire) : Omicron Publishing, 1981. — 216p : ill ; 21cm
ISBN 0-907507-00-x (pbk) : £8.90 B81-26078

681′.82 — London. Kensington and Chelsea *(London Borough)*. **Museums: Victoria and Albert Museum. Stock: Musical boxes,** *to ca 1900*

Victoria and Albert Museum. Musical-boxes at the Victoria & Albert Museum : an introduction / Carole Patey. — London : H.M.S.O., 1980. — 36p : ill(some col.),music,facsims ; 15x21cm
Also available accompanied by a sound cassette, £4.50. — Bibliography: p36
ISBN 0-11-290350-9 (pbk) : £1.25 B81-08259

682 — BLACKSMITHING

682′.1′02541 — Great Britain. Farriers — *Directories — Serials*

Farriers Registration Council. Register of persons engaged in farriery and the shoeing of horses / Farriers Registration Council. — 1980-. — London (4 Royal College St., NW1 0TU) : The Council, 1980-. — v. ; 30cm
Irregular
ISSN 0260-325x = Register of persons engaged in farriery and the shoeing of horses : £5.50
B81-02033

682′.4 — Blacksmithing. Ironworking — *Manuals*

McRaven, Charles. Country blacksmithing / by Charles McRaven ; photographs by Linda Moore McRaven and the author ; drawings by Chandis Ingenthron and the author. — London : Harper & Row, c1981. — 191p : ill,ports ; 22x23cm
Includes index
ISBN 0-06-014870-5 : £7.95
ISBN 0-06-090870-x (pbk) : Unpriced
B81-38255

683.4 — FIREARMS

683.4 — Air guns & gas guns

Walter, John. The airgun book / John Walter. — London : Arms and Armour, c1981. — 146p : ill ; 26cm
ISBN 0-85368-257-7 : £8.50 B81-23253

Wesley, L.. Air-guns and air-pistols / L. Wesley. — New ed. / revised by G.V. Cardew. — London : Cassell, 1979. — xvi,208p,28p of plates : ill ; 21cm
Previous ed.: 1971. — Includes index
ISBN 0-304-30375-5 : £7.50 B81-04926

683.4 — British firearms. Accessories, *1760-1860*

Neal, W. Keith. British gunmakers : their trade cards, cases & equipment 1760-1860 / W. Keith Neal & D.H.L. Back. — Warminster : Compton Press, c1980 300 166p : ill (facsims), 26cm
Include index
ISBN 0-900193-58-1 : £19.95
Also classified at 769.5 B81-08286

683.4′0029′473 — United States. Firearms, *1900-1978 — Buyers′ guides*

Lewis, Jack. The Gun digest book of modern gun values / by Jack Lewis ; edited by Harold A. Murtz. — 3rd ed. — Northfield : DBI ; London : Arms and Armour [distributor], c1981. — 383p : ill ; 28cm
Previous ed.: 1978
ISBN 0-910676-19-4 (pbk) : £5.50 B81-24326

683.4′005 — Firearms — *Serials*

Gun digest. — 1981 ed.. — London : Arms and Armour Press, c1980. — 448p
ISBN 0-910676-09-7 : £5.50 B81-09235

Guns illustrated. — 13th ed. (1981). — London : Arms and Armour Press, c1980. — 288p
ISBN 0-910676-12-7 : £4.50 B81-09236

683.4′0075 — Firearms. Collecting

Gun collector′s digest / edited by Joseph J. Schroeder. — Northfield : DBI Books ; London : Arms and Armour [distributor], c1977
Vol.2. — 287p : ill ; 28cm
ISBN 0-695-80684-x (pbk) : £4.00 B81-15699

683.4′009 — Firearms, *to 1980*

Wilkinson, Frederick. A source book of small arms. — London : Ward Lock, May 1981. — [128]p
ISBN 0-7063-6055-9 : £3.95 : CIP entry
B81-07468

683.4′00973 — United States. Firearms. Use, *to ca 1860*

Russell, Carl P.. Guns on the early frontiers : a history of firearms from Colonial times through the years of the western fur trade / by Carl P. Russell. — Lincoln [Neb.] ; London : University of Nebraska Press, 1980, c1957. — xv,395p : ill,maps ; 21cm
Originally published: Berkeley : University of California Press, 1957. — Bibliography: p357-381. — Includes index
ISBN 0-8032-3857-6 (cased) : Unpriced
ISBN 0-8032-8903-0 (pbk) : £4.20 B81-14104

683.4′26 — Black powder shotguns

Black powder gun digest / edited by Jack Lewis with Dan Cotterman ... [et al.]. — 2nd ed. — Northfield : DBI Books ; London : Arms and Armour [distributor], c1977. — 288p : ill,facsims,ports ; 28cm
Previous ed.: 1972?
ISBN 0-695-80714-5 (pbk) : £4.00 B81-15706

Fadala, Sam. The black powder handgun / by Sam Fadala. — Northfield, Ill. : DBI ; London : Arms & Armour [distributor], c1981. — 288p : ill,ports ; 28cm
ISBN 0-910676-22-4 (pbk) : £4.50 B81-23380

683.4′26′0941 — British shotguns, *to 1980*

Hastings, Macdonald. The shotgun / Macdonald Hastings. — Newton Abbot : David & Charles, c1981. — 240p : ill(some col.),1facsim,ports (some col.) ; 25cm
Includes index
ISBN 0-7153-8062-1 : £12.50 : CIP rev.
B81-19182

683.4′3 — Pistols. Cartridges. Loading — *Amateurs′ manuals*

Nonte, George C.. Handloading for handgunners / by George C. Nonte, Jr.. — Northfield : DBI Books ; London : Arms and Armour [distributor], c1978. — 288p : ill ; 28cm
ISBN 0-695-81199-1 (pbk) : £4.00 B81-15705

683.4′3′05 — Pistols — *Serials*

Handgunner. — No.1 (July/Aug.1980)-. — Colchester (7 Dentons Terrace, Wivenhoe, Colchester, Essex) : Handgunner Ltd., 1980-. — v. : ill ; 30cm
Six issues yearly
£6.00 per year B81-09073

683.4′3′09 — Pistols, *1300-1800*

Müller, Heinrich. Guns, pistols, revolvers : hand-firearms from the 14th to the 19th centuries / Heinrich Müller ; photographs by Gerd Platow ; [translated from the German by M.O.A. Stanton] ; [revised by Claude Blair]. — London : Orbis, 1981, c1980. — 224p : ill(some col.) ; 28cm
Bibliography: p215-217. — Includes index
ISBN 0-85613-365-5 : £12.50 B81-38117

683.4′3′09 — Pistols, *to 1979 — Encyclopaedias*

Myatt, Frederick. The illustrated encyclopedia of pistols & revolvers : an illustrated history of hand guns from the sixteenth century to the present day / Frederick Myatt. — London : Salamander, 1980. — 208p : col.ill,facsims,ports ; 32cm
Col. ill on lining papers. — Bibliography: p208. — Includes index
ISBN 0-86101-063-9 : £8.95 B81-03128

683′.43′0904 — Pistols, *1870-1977 — Encyclopaedias*

Myatt, Frederick. An illustrated guide to pistols and revolvers / Frederick Myatt. — London : Salamander, c1981. — 159p : ill(some col.),ports ; 23cm
Ill on lining papers. — Bibliography: p159
ISBN 0-86101-097-3 : £3.95 B81-34790

683.4′3′0973 — United States. Pistols

Pistol & revolver digest / edited by Dean A. Grennell & Jack Lewis. — 2nd ed. — Northfield : DBI Books ; London : Arms and Armour [distributor], c1979. — 288p : ill ; 28cm
Previous ed.: 1976?
ISBN 0-695-81274-2 (pbk) : £4.00 B81-15704

683.8 — MANUFACTURES. HOUSEHOLD EQUIPMENT

683′.83′0289 — Great Britain. Household electric equipment. Safety aspects — *For schools*

Science : electricity. — London : Macmillan Education for the Home Office, 1981. — 1portfolio : ill(some col.) ; 30cm. — (11 to 16+ project fire)
A Home Office/Schools Council project
ISBN 0-333-31772-6 : £9.95 B81-38635

684 — WOODWORKING, METALWORKING, FURNITURE MAKING, FURNISHINGS

684′.08 — Wood turning — *Amateurs′ manuals*

Underwood, Frank. Beginner′s guide to woodturning. — London : Newnes Technical Books, Sept.1981. — [192]p
ISBN 0-408-00507-6 (pbk) : £3.25 : CIP entry B81-30274

684′.08 — Woodworking

Love, George. The theory and practice of woodwork / George Love. — Harlow : Longman, 1981. — iv,156p : ill ; 25cm
Previous ed.: 1969. — Bibliography: p152. — Includes index
ISBN 0-582-33125-0 (pbk) : £2.75 B81-27235

Scott, E. F. (Ernest Frederick). The Mitchell Beazley illustrated encyclopaedia of working in wood : tools, methods, materials, classic constructions / Ernest Scott. — London : Mitchell Beazley, c1980. — 272p : ill(some col.),1col.map ; 29cm
Includes index
ISBN 0-85533-290-5 : £12.50 B81-03347

684′.08 — Woodworking — *Amateurs′ manuals*

Basic carpentry. — London : Marshall Cavendish, 1977 (1979 printing). — 64p : ill (some col.) ; 29cm
ISBN 0-85685-754-8 (pbk) : £1.25 B81-17580

Dean, A. Grennell. Home workshop digest : 'How to make the things you need and want' / by Dean A. Grennell. — Northfield, Ill. : DBI Books ; London : Arms and Armour distributors, c1981. — 256p : ill,facsims,ports ; 28cm
Port. on inside cover
ISBN 0-910676-14-3 (pbk) : £4.00 B81-24529

Making things easy. — London (Conti-Products Division, 18 Long La., EC1A 9NT) : Aaronson, c1977. — 56p : col.ill ; 30cm
Cover title. — Ill, text on inside covers
£0.95 (pbk) B81-18770

684′08 — Woodworking — *Amateurs′ manuals*

Wood. — London : Marshall Cavendish, 1978. — 135p : col.ill ; 26cm
Ill on lining papers. — Includes index
ISBN 0-85685-314-3 : £4.95 B81-01824

684′.08 — Woodworking — *For schools*

Hepton, Barry. Woodwork / Barry Hepton and Roger Way. — [Harlow] : [Longman], c1981. — 1(portfolio). — (Longman craft cards)
Contents: Booklets ([4]p; ill; 30cm), 48 cards (ill; 30x21cm)
ISBN 0-582-22296-6 : Unpriced B81-13665

Wilkins, Frank. Woodwork : for student, apprentice and handyman / Frank Wilkins. — 3rd ed. — Christchurch [N.Z.] ; London : Whitcoulls, 1981. — 373p : ill,1form ; 25cm
Previous ed.: 1973. — Bibliography: p368. — Includes index
ISBN 0-7233-0644-3 : Unpriced B81-34928

Willacy, David M.. Woodwork for you / David M. Willacy. — London : Hutchinson, 1981. — 192p : ill,maps ; 30cm
ISBN 0-09-145521-9 (pbk) : Unpriced B81-36346

684′.08 — Woodworking — *Manuals*

Lewis, Gaspar J.. Cabinetmaking, patternmaking, and millwork / Gaspar J. Lewis. — New York ; London : Van Nostrand Reinhold, c1981. — viii,438p : ill ; 24cm
Includes index
ISBN 0-442-24785-0 : £14.20 B81-26036

684′.08 — Woodworking. Projects — *Amateurs′ manuals*

Russell, Robert B.. Attractive and easy-to-build wood projects : plans and step-by-step instructions for furniture and household objects / Robert B. Russell ; photographs by Roger Turner. — New York : Dover ; London : Constable, 1980. — 72p : ill ; 29cm
ISBN 0-486-23965-9 (pbk) : £1.75 B81-18583

684′.08 — Woodworking. Projects — *For schools*

Punter, Ian. Projects and designs in woodwork / Ian Punter. — London : Batsford Academic and Educational, 1981. — 95p : ill ; 26cm
Includes index
ISBN 0-7134-3549-6 (cased) : £5.50
ISBN 0-7134-3550-x (pbk) : Unpriced B81-10024

684′.08′024372 — Woodworking — *Manuals* — *For teaching*

Hughes, Gwyn. Woodcraft / Gwyn Hughes. — London : Batsford Academic and Educational, 1981. — 72p : ill ; 26cm. — (Teaching today)
Bibliography: p70. — Includes index
ISBN 0-7134-3960-2 : £5.50 B81-37849

684′.084 — Woodworking. Lamination. Techniques

Castle, Wendell. The Wendell Castle book of wood lamination / Wendell Castle, David Edman ; photography by George Kamper. — New York ; London : Van Nostrand Reinhold, 1980. — 160p : ill ; 29cm
Includes index
ISBN 0-442-21478-2 : £14.20 B81-03101

684′.09 — Metalworking — *For African students*

Edwards, R.. Metalwork projects : for African schools and colleges / R. Edwards. — London : Cassell, 1981. — 99p : ill ; 22x27cm
ISBN 0-304-30372-0 (pbk) : £3.50 B81-29396

684′.09 — Metalworking — *For schools*

Feirer, John L.. General metals / John L. Feirer. — 5th ed. — New York ; London : Webster Division, c1981. — v,474p : ill(some col.) ; 25cm. — (McGraw-Hill publications in industrial education)
Previous ed.: 1974. — Includes index
ISBN 0-07-020380-6 : £11.95 B81-19488

684′.09′071242 — England. Secondary schools. Curriculum subjects: Metalwork. Projects — *For teaching*

Evans, Harry T.. Jobs for the boys : more metalwork ideas for teachers and students / by Harry T. Evans. — Oxford : Technical Press, 1981. — 139p : ill,plans ; 21cm
ISBN 0-291-39502-3 (pbk) : Unpriced : CIP rev. B81-14394

Punter, Ian. Projects and designs in metalwork / Ian Punter. — London : Batsford Academic and Educational, 1981. — 95p : ill ; 26cm
Includes index
ISBN 0-7134-3510-0 : £4.95 B81-37847

684.1′0029′441 — Great Britain. Furniture. Materials & components — *Buyers′ guides*

Shipman, J. M.. FIRA directory of furniture trade services and spare capacity / compiled by J.M. Shipman. — Stevenage : FIRA, [1981?]. — [78]leaves ; 30cm
£50.00 (£20.00 to members of FIRA) (pbk) B81-18951

684.1′0068′2 — Great Britain. Furniture. Manufacture. Factories. Layout. Planning

Stephenson, R.. Factory planning for efficient production / by R. Stephenson. — Stevenage : Furniture Industry Research Association, [1981?]. — 45p : ill ; 30cm
£15.00 (£7.00 to members) (spiral) B81-38068

684.1′04 — Great Britain. Furniture. Materials: Wood chipboards. Standards

Furniture Industry Research Association. Specification of chipboard for furniture performance levels and test methods / Furniture Industry Research Association. — Stevange : The Association, 1981. — 91p : ill ; 30cm. — (FIRA handbook ; no.2)
£25.00 (£10.00 to FIRA members) (spiral) B81-16668

684.1′04 — Wooden mission furniture. Making — *Amateurs′ manuals*

Mission furniture : how to make it / Popular Mechanics Company. — New York : Dover ; London : Constable, 1980. — 342p : ill,plans ; 21cm
Edited by Henry Haven Windsor. — Originally published: in 3v. Chicago : Popular Mechanics Company, 1909-1912. — Includes index
ISBN 0-486-23966-7 (pbk) : £3.15 B81-06559

684.1′04′0924 — Cabinet-making — *Personal observations*

Krenov, James. James Krenov, worker in wood. — New York ; London : Van Nostrand Reinhold, c1981. — 128p : chiefly ill(some col.) ; 32cm
Includes index
ISBN 0-442-26336-8 : £15.00 B81-36811

684.1′042 — Wooden furniture. Making — *Manuals*

Buckley, Larry. Easy-to-make slotted furniture : 12 contemporary designs / Larry Buckley. — New York : Dover ; London : Constable, 1980. — 44p : ill ; 28cm
ISBN 0-486-23983-7 (pbk) : £1.35 B81-23280

Leggatt, Alex. Carpentry for the home / Alex & Sandra Leggatt. — London : Batsford, 1981. — 167p : ill ; 26cm
Includes index
£7.95 B81-13138

The **Woodwork** book / introduced by John Makepeace ; [editor, Piers Dudgeon] ; [illustrators Rob Shone et al.]. — London : Ward Lock, 1980. — 192p : ill(some col.),ports (some col.) ; 30cm
Originally published: London : Pan, 1980. — Includes index
ISBN 0-7063-6074-5 : £8.95 B81-02963

684.1′0443 — Antique furniture. Refinishing — *Manuals*

Bennett, Michael, *1937-*. Refinishing antique furniture / Michael Bennett. — [Leicester] : Dryad, 1980. — 71p,[4]p of plates : ill(some col.) ; 22cm
Includes index
ISBN 0-85219-139-1 : Unpriced B81-20958

684.1′2 — Furniture. Upholstery. Machine sewing

Walsh, C. J.. Machine developments in upholstery sewing / by C.J. Walsh. — Stevenage : Furniture Industry Research Association, [1981?]. — 126p : ill ; 30cm
£40.00 (£25.00 to members of FIRA) (spiral) B81-27540

684.1′2 — Unholstering. Techniques — *Manuals*

McDonald, Robert J.. Modern upholstering techniques / Robert J. McDonald. — London : Batsford, 1981. — 144p,[4]p of plates : ill(some col.) ; 26cm
Includes index
ISBN 0-7134-2197-5 : £7.95 B81-15962

684.1′3 — Chairs. Expanded plastics frames

Tyler, A. C.. Expanded plastics chair frames / by A.C. Tyler. — Stevenage : Furniture Industry Research Association, 1981. — 68p : ill ; 30cm
£15.00 (£7.00 to members of FIRA) (spiral) B81-27538

684.1′6 — Residences. Cupboards. Making — *Manuals*

Siegele, H. H.. Cabinets and built-ins / H.H. Siegele. — New York : Sterling ; London : Oak Tree, 1980, c1961. — 100p : plans ; 21cm. — (Home craftsman series)
Originally published: Chicago : Drake, 1961. — Includes index
£2.95 (pbk) B81-03255

684.1′6 — Wooden storage furniture. Making — *Amateurs′ manuals*

Jones, Peter, *1934-*. Shelves, closets & cabinets : from A-frames to Z-outs / by Peter Jones ; illustrated by Mary Kornblum, Gary Tong and Minas Chepikian. — New York ; London : Service Communications : Van Nostrand Reinhold, 1981, c1977. — 304p : ill(some col.) ; 28cm
Includes index
ISBN 0-442-26424-0 (pbk) : £8.95 B81-29523

685 — LEATHER, FUR AND RELATED PRODUCTS

685′.3102′0941 — Great Britain. Shoes. Design

Oldham, Stuart. Design and design management in the UK footwear industry. — London : Design Council, Jan.1982. — [48]p
ISBN 0-85072-127-x (pbk) : £5.00 : CIP entry B81-40243

685′.53 — Camping equipment: Trailer tents — *Serials*

Trailer world : the trailer campers magazine. — Apr.1981-. — Sidcup (104 Station Rd., Sidcup, Kent DA15 7DE) : Stone Industrial Publications, 1981-. — v. : ill ; 30cm
Monthly. — Description based on: May 1981 issue
ISSN 0261-4065 = Trailer world : £0.60 per issue B81-31056

686 — PRINTING AND RELATED ACTIVITIES

686 — Developing countries. School texts. Production

Richaudeau, François. The design and production of textbooks : a practical guide / François Richaudeau ; translated by Christine Martinoni. — Farnborough, Hants. : Gower, 1980. — xii,225p : ill(some col.),facsims ; 23cm
Translation of: Conception et production des manuels scolaires. — Five copies of Questionnaire analysis grid (sheet : [2]p.) as inserts. — Bibliography: p197-200
ISBN 0-566-00290-6 : £15.60 : CIP rev. B80-11537

686.2 — PRINTING

686.2 — Great Britain. Organisations. Printing departments. Effects of technological development

Dutson, Harry. Inplant printing : today and tomorrow / based on a research project undertaken for Urwick Nexos by Harry Dutson & Michael Dyson. — [Slough] ([Clove House, The Broadway, Farnham Common, Slough, Berkshire SL2 3PQ]) : [Urwick Nexos Ltd], [1980?]. — 36p : ill ; 30cm
Cover title
Unpriced (pbk) B81-12666

686.2 — Printing. Estimating

Estimating for printers. — 11th ed. (rev.). — London : British Printing Industries Federation, 1980. — 200p,[2]p of plates (folded sheet) : ill,forms ; 22cm
Previous ed.: i.e. 10th ed. (rev.), 1979. — Bibliography: p189-192. — Includes index
£12.00 B81-10636

686.2′05 — Printing — *Serials*

Penrose : international review of the graphic arts. — Vol.73 (1981). — London : Northwood Publications, c1980. — 300p
ISBN 0-7198-2639-x : £17.50
ISSN 0141-8645 B81-32212

686.2′09429′98 — Gwent. Chepstow. Printers, *1806-1980*

Waters, Ivor. Chepstow printers and newspapers / Ivor Waters ; illustrations by Mercedes Waters. — Chepstow (41 Hardwick Ave., Chepstow, Gwent NP6 5DS) : Moss Rose, c1981. — 86p : ill,1map,facsims ; 23cm
Originally published in shortened form: Chepstow : Chepstow Society, 1970. — Bibliography: p79. — Includes index
ISBN 0-906134-12-9 : £8.50 B81-23546

686.2′0945 — Italy. Printing, *ca 1450-ca 1700*

Rhodes, Dennis E.. Studies in early Italian printing. — London (35 Palace Court, W2 4LS) : Pindar Press, Oct.1981. — [384]p. — (Studies in the history of printing ; 1)
ISBN 0-907132-02-2 : £25.00 : CIP entry B81-27993

686.2′17′09 — Latin alphabet. Typefaces, *1960*

Morison, Stanley. Selected essays on the history of letter-forms in manuscript and print / Stanley Morison ; edited by David McKitterick. — Cambridge : Cambridge University Press, 1981. — 2v.(xxii,416p, 126p of plates) : ill,facsims ; 31cm
In slip case. — Includes index
ISBN 0-521-22338-5 : £120.00
ISBN 0-521-22456-x (v.1)
ISBN 0-521-22457-8 (v.2) B81-17900

686.2′2 — Printing. Graphics

Silver, Gerald A.. Graphic layout and design / Gerald A. Silver. — New York ; London : Van Nostrand Reinhold, c1981. — vi,312p : ill (some col.) ; 20x24cm
Includes index
ISBN 0-442-26774-6 : £10.45 B81-26433

686.2′2 — Typography

Swann, Cal. Techniques of typography / by Cal Swann. — Reprinted with corrections. — London : Lund Humphries, 1980, c1969. — 96p : ill,3facsims ; 20x21cm
ISBN 0-85331-442-x (pbk) : £4.95 B81-00186

686.2′2′05 — Typography. Serials: Fleuron, *The,* **′Signature′ & ′Typography′** — *Critical studies*

Shipcott, Grant. Typographical periodicals between the wars : a critique of The Fleuron, Signature and Typography / Grant Shipcott. — Oxford (Headington, Oxford OX3 0BP) : Oxford Polytechnic Press, 1980. — xiv,111p : ill,facsims ; 27cm
Bibliography: p107-108. - Includes index
ISBN 0-902692-19-4 (cased) : £15.00 : CIP rev.
ISBN 0-902692-20-8 (pbk) : £8.95 B80-04311

686.2′2′09 — Typography, *to 1979*

McLean, Ruari. The Thames and Hudson manual of typography / Ruari McLean. — London : Thames and Hudson, c1980. — 216p : ill,facsims ; 25cm. — (The Thames and Hudson manuals)
Half title: Typography. — Bibliography: p210-214. — Includes index
ISBN 0-500-67022-6 : £8.95 B81-01022

686.2′2544 — Printing. Composition. Applications of word processing systems

Van Uchelen, Rod. Word processing : a guide to typography, taste, and in-house graphics / Rod van Uchelen. — New York ; London : Van Nostrand Reinhold, 1980. — 128p : ill,ports ; 24cm
Includes index
ISBN 0-442-28647-3 (cased) : £11.20
ISBN 0-442-28646-5 (pbk) : £5.95 B81-11436

686.2′25 — Phototypesetting. Design

Haley, Allan. Phototypography : a guide to in-house typesetting & design / Allan Haley. — London : Hale, 1981, c1980. — 143p : ill ; 29cm
Originally published: New York : Scribner, 1980. — Includes index
ISBN 0-7091-9243-6 : £8.95 B81-31293

686.2′2544 — Printing. Composition. Applications of digital computer systems

Rice, Stanley. CRT typesetting handbook / Stanley Rice. — New York ; London : Van Nostrand Reinhold, c1981. — vi,409p : ill ; 29cm
ISBN 0-442-23889-4 : £26.25 B81-21408

686.2′315 — Offset lithographic printing equipment. Operation — *Manuals*

Porter, A. S.. A manual for lithographic press operation / A.S. Porter. — London : 15a The Broadway, Wimbledon, SW19 2PS : Litho Training Services, 1979. — viii,303p : ill ; 22cm
Originally published: 1977. — Bibliography: pvi. - Includes index
ISBN 0-906091-01-2 (cased) : £10.95 B81-08487

686.2′315′09 — Lithography, *to 1980* — *Chichewan texts*

Jaffu, Symon. History of lithography = Mbiri ya lithography. — [Plymouth] ([Tavistock Pl., Plymouth PL4 8AT]) : [Plymouth College of Art and Design], [1981]. — [24]p : ill,ports ; 15x21cm
Translation from English into Chewa. — Author: Symon Jaffu
Unpriced (pbk) B81-25451

686.3 — BOOKBINDING

686.3 — Bookbinding

Diehl, Edith. Bookbinding : its background and technique / by Edith Diehl. — New York : Dover ; London : Constable, 1980. — 684p in various pagings,92p of plates : ill ; 21cm
Originally published: in 2 vols. New York : Rinehart, 1946. — Bibliography: p203-219. — Includes index
ISBN 0-486-24020-7 (pbk) : £7.20 B81-23237

686.3 — General serials in English: Penny magazine. Binding

Binding the penny magazine 1833. — [Birmingham] : Morenardo, 1980. — [12]p : ill ; 18cm
£2.20 (pbk) B81-34817

686.3′02 — Hand bookbinding — *Manuals*

Akers, Robert C.. Single section bookbinding / Robert C. Akers. — Leicester : Dryad, c1980. — 15p : col.ill ; 15x21cm. — (Dryad leaflet ; 530)
ISBN 0-85219-135-9 (pbk) : Unpriced B81-20889

Ashman, John. Bookbinding : a beginner′s manual / John Ashman ; illustrated by Tig Sutton. — London : A. & C. Black, 1981. — 103p : ill ; 26cm
Includes index
ISBN 0-7136-2113-3 : £7.95 : CIP rev. B81-01023

686.4 — PHOTOCOPYING

686.4′024658 — Reprography — *For management*

Hanson, Richard E.. The manager′s guide to copying and duplicating / Richard E. Hanson. — New York ; London : McGraw-Hill, c1980. — xii,225p : ill,facsims,forms ; 24cm
Includes index
ISBN 0-07-026080-x : £8.95 B81-10341

686.4′068 — Organisations. Reprographic departments. Management

Crix, F. C.. Reprographic management handbook / F.C. Crix. — 2nd ed. — London : Published in conjunction with the London Institute of Reprographic Technology [by] Business Books, c1979. — xiii,332p : ill,1facsim,plans,forms ; 24cm
Previous ed.: 1975. — Bibliography: p323-324. - Includes index
ISBN 0-220-67010-2 : £12.50 B81-16345

686.4′3 — Micrography

Kish, Joseph L.. Micrographics : a user′s manual / Joseph L. Kish, Jr. — New York ; Chichester : Wiley, c1980. — ix,196p : ill,forms ; 24cm
Includes index
ISBN 0-471-05524-7 : £11.25 B81-0473

686.4′4 — Kirlian photography

Gennaro, L.. Kirlian photography : research and prospects / L. Gennaro, F. Guzzon, P. Marsigli. — London : East West Publications, 1980. — 104p,[48]p of plates : ill(some col.),col.ports ; 23cm
Translation of: La foto Kirlian. — Bibliography: p103-104
ISBN 0-85692-045-2 : £5.95 B81-0102

687 — MANUFACTURES. CLOTHING

687′.068 — Great Britain. Knitting & sewing industries. Home-based small firms. Organisation — *Manuals*

Brady, Christine. Sewing and knitting from home / Christopher Brady. — London : Pelham, 1981. — 110p ; 21cm. — (Business from home) Bibliography: p106. — Includes index
ISBN 0-7207-1295-5 : £4.95 B81-1531

687′.8′029441 — Great Britain. Haberdashery — *Buyers′ guides* — *Serials*

Buyers′ guide to knitting yarns, home sewing aids, haberdashery and craft materials. — 1981 ed. — London (6 Ludgate Sq., EC4M 7AS) : Knitting & Haberdashery Review, [1981?]. — ii,68p
Cover title: Knitting & haberdashery buyers′ guide
Unpriced
Also classified at 677′.02862 B81-2041

688.4 — MANUFACTURES. SMOKERS′ SUPPLIES

688′.4 — Tobacco smoking accessories, *to 1950*

Scott, Amoret. Smoking antiques / Amoret and Christopher Scott. — Aylesbury : Shire, 1981. — 32p : ill ; 21cm. — (Shire album ; 66)
Text based on the authors′ Discovering smoking antiques. 1970
ISBN 0-85263-540-0 (pbk) : £0.95 B81-1755

688'.42 — Clay tobacco pipes. Archaeological investigation

The **Archaeology** of the clay tobacco pipe / edited by Peter Davey. — Oxford : B.A.R.. — v,391p : ill,maps,facsims ; 30cm. — (BAR. British series, ISSN 0143-3032 ; 78)
Includes bibliographies
ISBN 0-86054-088-x (pbk) : £11.00 B81-16557

688'.42 — Clay tobacco pipes, *to ca 1940*

The **Archaeology** of the clay tobacco pipe / edited by Peter Davey. — Oxford : B.A.R.. — (BAR. International series ; 92)
4: Europe 1. — 1980. — 318p : ill,maps,facsims,1plan,1port ; 30cm
Text in English, German and Dutch. — Includes bibliographies
ISBN 0-86054-106-1 (pbk) : £12.00 B81-36607

The **Archaeology** of the clay tobacco pipe / edited by Peter Davey. — Oxford : B.A.R.. — (BAR. International series ; 106(ii))
5: Europe 2
Pt.2. — 1981. — p111-468 : ill,1map,facsims ; 30cm
Dutch text and English translation. — Bibliography: p364-367
ISBN 0-86054-124-x (pbk) : £16.00 B81-36608

688.6 — MANUFACTURES. CARRIAGES, WAGONS, CARTS, WHEELBARROWS

688.6 — Agricultural vehicles: English wagons. Construction, *to ca 1950*

Jenkins, J. Geraint. The English farm wagon : origins and structure / J. Geraint Jenkins. — 3rd ed. — Newton Abbot : David & Charles, c1981. — xvi,248p : ill,1map ; 23cm
Previous ed.: 1972. — Bibliography: pxvi. — Includes index
ISBN 0-7153-8119-9 : £8.95 B81-25355

688.6 — England. Gypsy caravans

Jones, E. Alan. Gypsy caravans : their history and restoration / by E. Alan Jones. — Malton (Signs-Malton Joiners Shop, Mount Rd., Malton, Yorkshire) : Signs-Malton, c1981. — [32]p : ill,ports ; 21cm
ISBN 0-9507399-0-1 (pbk) : Unpriced B81-34847

688.6 — Horse-drawn caravans, *to 1980*

Smith, D. J. (Donald John). Discovering horse-drawn caravans / D.J. Smith. — Aylesbury : Shire, 1981. — 63p : ill,plans ; 18cm. — (Discovering series ; no.258)
Bibliography: p62. — Includes index
ISBN 0-85263-565-6 (pbk) : £1.25 B81-40747

688.6 — Horse-drawn carriages. Restoration — *Manuals*

Isles, George. The restoration of carriages / George Isles. — London : J.A. Allen, 1981. — 190p : ill ; 24cm
Bibliography: p183-186. — Includes index
ISBN 0-85131-366-3 : £15.00 : CIP rev. B81-14870

688.6 — Horse-drawn carriages, *to 1979*

Walrond, Sallie. Looking at carriages / Sallie Walrond. — London : Pelham, 1980. — 240p,[8]p of plates : ill(some col.) ; 26cm
Includes index
ISBN 0-7207-1282-3 : £14.00 B81-03116

688.6 — Horse-drawn vehicles — *Collectors' guides*

Smith, D. J. (Donald John). Collecting & restoring horse-drawn vehicles / Donald J. Smith. — Cambridge : Stephens, 1981. — 192p : ill ; 24cm
Bibliography: p181-183
ISBN 0-85059-429-4 : £8.95 B81-15276

688.6 — Lincolnshire. Corby Glen. Wheelwrighting, *1864-1883 — Correspondence, diaries, etc.*

Bird, George, *fl.1862-1883*. The diaries of George Bird / edited by John A. Liddie. — Nottingham : Dept. of Adult Education, University of Nottingham, [1980]. — iv,382p ; 30cm. — (Record series / Centre for Local History University of Nottingham ; 3)
Unpriced (pbk) B81-10109

688.6 — Perambulators, *to 1980*

Hampshire, Jack. Prams, mailcarts and bassinets : a definitive history of the child's carriage / Jack Hampshire. — Tunbridge Wells : Midas, 1980. — 240p : ill,facsims,ports ; 29cm. — (A Midas collectors' library definitive history)
Includes index
ISBN 0-85936-121-7 : £19.50 B81-02267

688.7 — MANUFACTURES. RECREATIONAL EQUIPMENT

688.7'2 — Lines Bros. Minic toys, *to 1970*

Richardson, Sue. Minic : Lines Bros. tinplate vehicles / by Sue Richardson. — Windsor (15 Bell lane, Eton Wick, Windsor) : Mikansue, 1981. — 146p : ill,facsims ; 25cm
ISBN 0-904338-01-0 (pbk) : £5.95 B81-37051

688.7'2 — Meccano Dinky toys, *1934-1964 — Collectors' guides*

Gibson, Cecil. A history of British dinky toys : model car and vehicle issues 1934-1964 / by Cecil Gibson. — Windsor (15 Bell La., Eton Wick, Windsor, Berks. SL4 6LQ) : Mikansue and Modellers' World, 1973 (1980 [printing]). — 152p : ill,facsims ; 22cm
Originally published: Hemel Hempstead : Model Aeronautical Press, 1966
ISBN 0-904338-00-2 (pbk) : Unpriced B81-07075

688.7'2 — Toys — *Illustrations — For children*

Daniels, Meg. Toys. — London : Blackie, Feb.1982. — [12]p. — (Blackie concertina books)
ISBN 0-216-91127-3 : £0.95 : CIP entry B81-36032

688.7'2'09 — Toys, *to ca 1935*

King, Constance Eileen. Antique toys and dolls / Constance E. King. — London : Studio Vista/Christie's, 1979. — 256p : ill(some col.),facsims ; 29cm
Bibliography: p250-251. - Includes index
ISBN 0-289-70834-6 : £19.95 B81-02237

688.7'2'0904 — Metal toys, *1900-1950 — Collectors' guides*

Gardiner, Gordon. The price guide to metal toys / Gordon Gardiner and Alistair Morris. — Woodbridge : Antique Collector's Club, c1980. — 214p : ill(some col.),facsims ; 29cm
ISBN 0-902028-92-8 : £14.50 B81-38397

688.7'2'094321 — East German toys: Seiffen region toys, *1850 — Catalogues — Facsimiles*

The **Toy** sample book of Waldkirchen / [English version by Ruth Michaelis-Jena and Patrick Murray]. — New ed. / with notes by Manfred Bachmann. — London (16 Cecil Court W.C.2) : Peter Stockham at Images, 1978. — 31p,[50] leaves of plates : ill(some col.) ; 29x44cm
Translation of: Das waldkirchner Spielzeugmusterbuch. — Previous ed.: S.l. : s.n. 1977. — Limited ed. of 110 copies. — In slip case. — Bibliography: p30-31
£55.00 B81-34688

688.7'2'0973074014 — New England. Barenholtz, Bernard. Private collections: American toys, *1830-1900*

Barenholtz, Bernard. American antique toys 1830-1900 / Bernard Berenholtz, Inez McClintock ; photographs by Bill Holland. — London ([11 New Fetter La., EC4P 4EE]) : New Cavendish Books, 1980. — 282p : ill(some col.),facsims ; 28x30cm
Bibliography: p282. - Includes index
ISBN 0-904568-31-8 : £19.50 B81-06747

688.7'23'0942 — English dolls' houses, *1700-1900*

Greene, Vivien. English dolls' houses : of the eighteenth and nineteenth centuries / by Vivien Greene. — Revised (with corrections). — London : Bell & Hyman, 1979. — 224p,1leaf of plates : ill,1facsim ; 29cm
Previous ed.: London : Batsford, 1955. — Includes index
ISBN 0-7135-1101-x : £19.00 B81-03980

688.7'4 — Board & table games equipment, *to 1950*

Bell, R. C.. Board and table games antiques / R.C. Bell. — Aylesbury : Shire, 1981. — 32p : ill ; 21cm. — (Shire album ; 60)
Bibliography: p32
ISBN 0-85263-538-9 (pbk) : £0.95 B81-17553

688.7'6 — Recreation facilities. Artificial playing surfaces

Tipp, G.. Polymeric surfaces for sport and recreation. — London : Applied Science, Oct.1981. — [440]p
ISBN 0-85334-980-0 : £32.00 : CIP entry B81-25717

688.7'912 — Angling equipment. Making — *Manuals*

Rickards, Barrie. Fishing tackle : making, maintenance and improvement / Barrie Rickards and Ken Whitehead with contributions from Les Beecroft. — London : Black, 1981. — x,253p : ill ; 24cm
Bibliography: p249-250. — Includes index
ISBN 0-7136-2054-4 : £8.95 B81-22072

688.7'912 — Angling. Rods. Making — *Manuals*

Lewers, Dick. How to build a fishing rod / David Lewers. — Newton Abbot : David & Charles, 1981, c1980. — 79p : ill ; 17x25cm
Includes index
ISBN 0-7153-8190-3 : £4.95 B81-29731

688.7'912 — Fly fishing. Flies. Tying — *Manuals*

Collyer, David J.. Fly-dressing II / David J. Collyer ; line drawings by Susan and Sharon Collyer. — Newton Abbot : David & Charles, 1981. — 248p : ill(some col.) ; 23cm
ISBN 0-7153-8145-8 : £12.50 B81-36855

Rice, Freddie. Fly-tying illustrated : wet and dry patterns / Freddie Rice. — London : Batsford, 1981. — 176p,[8]p of plates : ill(some col.) ; 24cm
Bibliography: p171-172. — Includes index
ISBN 0-7134-2363-3 : £9.95 B81-27209

688.7'912 — Fly fishing. Flies. Tying. Techniques — *Amateurs' manuals*

Wakeford, Jacqueline. Flytying techniques : a full colour guide / Jacqueline Wakeford ; camera sequences by David Hawker. — London : Benn, 1980. — 150p : ill(some col.) ; 29cm
Bibliography: p145. — Includes index
ISBN 0-510-22528-4 : £9.95 : CIP rev. B80-02507

688.8 — PACKAGING TECHNOLOGY

688.8 — Consumer goods. Packages. Design — *For marketing*

Handbook of package design research / edited by Walter Stern. — New York ; Chichester : Wiley, c1981. — xiii,576p ; 26cm
Includes index
ISBN 0-471-05901-3 : £28.00 B81-33017

688.8 — Consumer goods. Packaging

Roth, Lászlo. Package design : an introduction to the art of packaging / Laszlo Roth. — Englewood Cliffs ; London : Prentice-Hall, c1981. — xii,212p : ill ; 28cm. — (A Spectrum book)
Includes bibliographies and index
ISBN 0-13-647842-5 (cased) : Unpriced
ISBN 0-13-647834-4 (pbk) : £9.05 B81-25507

688.8 — Freight containers. Securing

Cole, Anthony R.. The securing of ISO containers : theory and practice : an ICHCA survey / by Anthony R. Cole. — London : International Cargo Handling Co-ordination Association, c1981. — x,95p : ill,plans,forms ; 30cm
ISBN 0-906297-19-2 (pbk) : £35.00 (£25.00 to members; free to corporate members) B81-22929

688.8'05 — Freight transport. Packaging — *Serials*

Transit packaging : a monthly report published by Elsevier Sequoia in conjunction with Pira. — Vol.1, no.1 (Nov.1980)-. — Lausanne : Elsevier Sequoia ; Oxford (Mayfield House, 256 Banbury Rd, Oxford OX2 7DH) : Elsevier International Bulletins, 1980-. — v. : ill ; 30cm
ISSN 0260-3675 = Transit packaging : £75.00 per year B81-05592

690 — BUILDINGS. CONSTRUCTION

690 — Buildings. Construction

Fincham, John, *1947-*. Construction science and materials 2 / John Fincham, David Watkins. — [London] : Butterworths, c1981. — 160p : ill ; 25cm. — (Butterworths TEC technician series)
ISBN 0-408-00488-6 (pbk) : Unpriced B81-28322

Huntington, Whitney Clark. Building construction materials and types of construction / Whitney Clark Huntington (deceased), Robert E. Mickadeit. — 5th ed. / chapter 10 written by William Cavanaugh. — New York ; Chichester : Wiley, c1981. — viii,471p : ill ; 28cm
Previous ed.: 1975. — Bibliography: p437-446. - Includes index
ISBN 0-471-05354-6 : Unpriced B81-08577

King, Harold, *1927-*. Building techniques / H. King and D. Nield. — 3rd ed. / revised by J.C. Sanson. — London : Chapman and Hall. — (Science paperbacks ; 24)
Previous ed.: London : Spon, 1967. — Includes index
Vol.2: Services. — 1980. — xiv,141p : ill ; 22cm
ISBN 0-412-21780-5 (pbk) : £4.50 B81-08576

Roberts, K. (Keith), *19---*. Construction technology / K. Roberts. — Walton-on-Thames : Nelson. — (Nelson TEC Books)
Level 3. — 1981. — 213p : ill ; 25cm
ISBN 0-17-741120-1 (pbk) : £4.75 B81-26305

Seeley, Ivor H.. Building technology / Ivor H. Seeley. — 2nd ed. — London : Macmillan, 1980. — viii,207p : ill,plans ; 27cm
Previous ed.: 1974. — Includes index
ISBN 0-333-30717-8 (cased) : £14.00
ISBN 0-333-30718-6 (pbk) : £6.50 B81-02049

690 — Buildings. Construction — *For architectural design*

AJ handbook of building structure / edited by Allan Hodgkinson. — 2nd ed. — London : Architectural Press, 1980. — 390p : ill,ports ; 31cm
Previous ed.: 1974. — Includes index
ISBN 0-85139-273-3 (cased) : £20.00
ISBN 0-85139-272-5 B81-06083

690 — Buildings. Construction — *For technicians*

Chudley, R.. Construction technology 2 checkbook. — London : Butterworths, Dec.1981. — [128]p
ISBN 0-408-00671-4 (cased) : £6.50 : CIP entry
ISBN 0-408-00803-x (pbk) : £3.25 B81-31426

Fullerton, R. L.. Construction technology Level 2. — Freeland : Technical Press
Vol.1. — Nov.1981. — [144]p
ISBN 0-291-39653-4 (pbk) : £4.45 : CIP entry B81-32029

Fullerton, R. L.. Construction technology Level 2. — Freeland : Technical Press
Vol.2. — Nov.1981. — [144]p
ISBN 0-291-39654-2 (pbk) : £4.45 : CIP entry B81-32028

690 — Buildings. Construction - *For technicians*

Hall, F.. Building services and equipment 5 checkbook. — London : Butterworths, Aug.1981. — [112]p
ISBN 0-408-00651-x (cased) : £3.75 : CIP entry
ISBN 0-408-00614-5 (pbk) : £3.25 B81-16925

690 — Buildings. Construction — *Manuals*

Limon, Alec C.. Beginner's guide to building construction / Alec Limon. — London : Newnes Technical, 1980. — 150p : ill,1plan ; 19cm
Includes index
ISBN 0-408-00399-5 (pbk) : £3.50 : CIP rev. B80-08858

690 — Great Britain. Buildings. Construction. Sites. Building materials. Control

Johnston, John E.. Site control of materials : handling, storage and protection / John E. Johnston. — London : Butterworths, 1981. — 140p : ill,1plan,forms ; 25cm
Includes index
ISBN 0-408-00377-4 : Unpriced : CIP rev. B81-16922

Materials control and waste in building : a plan for action / prepared by the Site Management Practice Committee of the Chartered Institute of Building. — Ascot (Englemere, Kings Ride, Ascot, Berks. SL5 8BJ) : The Institute, 1980. — 23p ; 30cm
Bibliography: p22-23
ISBN 0-906600-31-6 (pbk) : Unpriced : CIP rev. B80-19325

690′.022′1 — Buildings. Technical drawings. Draftsmanship. Use of reprography

Stitt, Fred A.. Systems drafting : creative reprographics for architects and engineers / Fred A. Stitt. — New York ; London : McGraw-Hill, c1980. — ix,245p : ill,plans ; 29cm
Includes index
ISBN 0-07-061550-0 : £14.95 B81-05384

690′.028 — Building equipment: Scaffolding. Use

Wilshere, C. J.. Access scaffolding / C.J. Wilshere. — London : Telford, 1981. — 34p : ill ; 15x21cm. — (ICE works construction guides)
ISBN 0-7277-0090-1 (pbk) : £2.00 B81-10080

690′.028′7 — United States. Building industries. Metrication

Hornung, William J.. Metric architectural construction drafting and design fundamentals / William J. Hornung. — Englewood Cliffs ; London : Prentice-Hall, c1981. — xii,196p : ill,plans,1port ; 29cm
Text on lining papers. — Includes index
ISBN 0-13-579367-x : £11.00 B81-22357

690′.03′41 — Buildings. Construction — *French & English dictionaries*

Butterworth, B.. Dictionary of building terms. — Lancaster : Construction Press, June 1981. — [120]p
ISBN 0-86095-886-8 : £8.95 : CIP entry B81-13578

690′.05 — Buildings. Construction — *Serials*

Construction papers / the Chartered Institute of Building. — Vol.1, no.1 (1980)-. — Ascot (Englemere, Kings Ride, Ascot, Berkshire SL5 8BJ) : The Institute, 1980-. — v. : ill ; 24cm
Three issues yearly
ISSN 0144-8587 = Construction papers : £12.00 per year B81-09687

690′.068 — Building industries. Management

Oxley, R.. Management techniques applied to the construction industry / R. Oxley and J. Poskitt. — 3rd ed. — London : Granada, 1980. — vi,298p : ill,map,plans,forms ; 24cm
Previous ed.: London : Lockwood, 1971. — Bibliography: p293-294. — Includes index
ISBN 0-246-11341-3 (cased) : £12.00
ISBN 0-246-11434-7 (pbk) : £6.95 B81-08243

690′.068 — Great Britain. Building industries. Management

Calvert, R. E.. Introduction to building management / R.E. Calvert. — 4th ed. — London : Butterworths, 1981. — 443p : ill,forms ; 23cm
Previous ed.: 1970. — Includes bibliographies and index
ISBN 0-408-01102-5 (cased) : Unpriced
ISBN 0-408-00520-3 (pbk) : Unpriced B81-27140

690′.068′1 — Buildings. Design. Life cycle costing

Dell'Isola, Alphonse J.. Life cycle costing for design professionals / Alphonse J. Dell'Isola, Stephen J. Kirk. — New York ; London : McGraw-Hill, c1981. — x,224p : ill,plans,forms ; 29cm
Bibliography: p219-220. — Includes index
ISBN 0-07-016280-8 : £17.50 B81-29566

690′.068′4 — Great Britain. Building industries. Project management. Training

Education for project management in building : a report by a working party of the Chartered Institute of Building. — Ascot : Chartered Institute of Building, [1981]. — 17p : ill ; 30cm
ISBN 0-906600-39-1 (pbk) : Unpriced B81-2936

690′.076 — Buildings. Construction — *Questions & answers — For technicians*

Chudley, R.. Construction technology 1 checkbook / R. Chudley. — London : Butterworths, 1981. — vi,112p : ill ; 20cm. — (Butterworths technical and scientific checkbooks. Level 1)
Includes index
ISBN 0-408-00642-0 (cased) : Unpriced : CIP rev.
ISBN 0-408-00602-1 (pbk) : Unpriced B81-0018

690′.15 — Houses. Slated roofs & tiled roofs. Lead sheet flashings

Lead sheet flashings : for slate and tile roofing. — London (34 Berkeley) : Lead Development Association, 1981. — 20p : ill(some col.) ; 30cm
Unpriced (unbound) B81-2760

690′.1823′0218 — Windows — *Standards*

Windows / Method of Building [Branch]. — Croydon (Sales Office, Block C, Whitgift Centre, Wellesley Rd., Croydon, Surrey) : [The Branch]
Programme 3: Archital Luxfer Ltd, Solent range product data : this forms part III of Agreement CR10602/W3/12 operative from 1 July 1981 to 30 June 1984. — 1981. — 40p : ill ; 30cm. — (Method of building ; 08-022)
ISBN 0-86177-066-8 (pbk) : £2.00 B81-3505

Windows / [Method of Building Branch]. — Croydon (Sales Office, Block C, Whitgift Centre, Wellesley Rd., Croydon, Surrey) : [The Branch]
Programme 3: Beta Aluminium Products Ltd, Weatherbeater range, cost data : Agreement CR10602/W3/13 operative from 1 July 1981 to 30 June 1984. — 1981. — 35p : 1map ; 30cm. — (Method of building ; 08-068)
Unpriced (pbk) B81-3506

Windows / [Method of Building Branch]. — Croydon (Sales Office, Block C, Whitgift Centre, Wellesley Rd., Croydon, Surrey) : [The Branch]
Programme 3: Crittall Windows Ltd, luminair ranges 50 and 35 product data : this forms part III of Agreement CR10602/W3/15 operative from 1 July 1981 to 30 June 1984. — 1981. — 75p : ill ; 30cm. — (Method of building ; 08-024)
ISBN 0-86177-068-4 (pbk) : £3.60 B81-3505

Windows / [Method of Building Branch]. — Croydon (Sales Office, Block C, Whitgift Centre, Wellesley Rd., Croydon, Surrey) : [The Branch]
Programme 3: Crittall Windows Ltd, SMW MOD 100 range, product data : this forms part III of Agreement CR10602/W3/15 operative from 1 July 1981 to 30 June 1984. — 1981. — 32p : ill ; 30cm. — (Method of building ; 08-026)
ISBN 0-86177-070-6 (pbk) : £1.60 B81-3505

Windows / [Method of Building Branch]. — Croydon (Sales Office, Block C, Whitgift Centre, Wellesley Rd., Croydon, Surrey) : [The Branch]
Programme 3: East & Son Ltd Silux range product data : this forms part III of Agreement CR10602/W3/16 operative from 1 July 1981 to 30 June 1984. — 1981. — 39p : ill ; 30cm. — (Method of building ; 08-029)
ISBN 0-86177-073-0 (pbk) : £2.00 B81-3505

Windows / [Method of Building Branch]. — Croydon (Sales Office, Block C, Whitgift Centre, Wellesley Rd., Croydon, Surrey) : [The Branch]
Programme 3: Mckechnie Engineering (Reading) Ltd, Ideal 990 range product data : this forms part III of Agreement CR10602/W3/17 operative from 1 July 1981 to 30 June 1984. — 1981. — 32p : ill ; 30cm. — (Method of building ; 08-027)
ISBN 0-86177-071-4 (pbk) : £1.60 B81-3505

90'.1823'0218 — Windows — *Standards* *continuation*

Windows / [Method of Building Branch]. — Croydon (Sales Office, Block C, Whitgift Centre, Wellesley Rd, Croydon, Surrey) : [The Branch]. — (Method of building ; 08-028)
Programme 3: Rea Metal Windows Ltd, W20 series range product data : this forms part 3 of Agreement CR 10602/W3/23 operative from 1 July 1981 to 30 June 1984. — 1981. — 36p : ill ; 30cm
ISBN 0-86177-072-2 (corrected : pbk) : £1.80
B81-38679

Windows / [Method of Building Branch]. — Croydon (Sales Office, Block C, Whitgift Centre, Wellesley Rd., Croydon, Surrey) : [The Branch]
Programme 3: Turner-Fain Ltd, Gladiator range product data : this forms part III of Agreement CR10602/W3/27 operative from 1 July 1981 to 30 June 1984. — 1981. — 44p : ill ; 30cm. — (Method of building ; 08-025)
ISBN 0-86177-069-2 (pbk) : £2.20 B81-35056

90'.24 — Buildings. Maintenance & conversion — *For technicians*

Chudley, R.. The maintenance and adaptation of buildings / R. Chudley ; illustrated by the author. — London : Longman, 1981. — 167p : ill,plans,1form ; 22cm. — (Longman technician series. Construction and civil engineering)
Bibliography: p163. — Includes index
ISBN 0-582-41573-x (pbk) : £3.95 B81-27107

90'.24 — Buildings. Maintenance — *Manuals*

Building maintenance and preservation : a guide for design and management / edited by Edward D. Mills. — London : Butterworths in association with the Building Centre Trust, 1980. — 203p : ill ; 31cm
Bibliography: p193-199. — Includes index
ISBN 0-408-00470-3 : Unpriced : CIP rev.
B80-08301

90'.24 — England. Housing associations. Personnel. Professional education. Curriculum subjects: Reporting requirements for repairs to residences

Repairs reporting / Housing Training Project. — London ([City University, St John St., EC1V 4PB]) : Housing Research Group, c1980. — 44p : ill ; 21cm. — (Guide to housing training ; no.5)
Cover title. — Bibliography: p40-41
ISBN 0-907255-04-3 (pbk) : Unpriced
Primary classification 690'.24 B81-06327

90'.24 — England. Local authorities. Housing departments. Personnel. Professional education. Curriculum subjects: Reporting requirements for repair to residences

Repairs reporting / Housing Training Project. — London ([City University, St John St., EC1V 4PB]) : Housing Research Group, c1980. — 44p : ill ; 21cm. — (Guide to housing training ; no.5)
Cover title. — Bibliography: p40-41
ISBN 0-907255-04-3 (pbk) : Unpriced
Also classified at 690'.24 B81-06327

90'.24 — Great Britain. Buildings. Defects. Causes

Ransom, W. H.. Building failures. — London : Spon, Aug.1981. — [120]p
ISBN 0-419-11750-4 (cased) : £12.00 : CIP entry
ISBN 0-419-11760-1 (pbk) : £6.00 B81-18154

90'.24 — Great Britain. Buildings. Maintenance. Standard costs — *Lists* — *Serials*

BMCIS building maintenance price book. — 1980-. — Kingston upon Thames (85 Clarence St, Kingston upon Thames, Surrey KT1 1RB) : Building Maintenance Cost Information Service, 1980-. — v. ; 21cm
Annual
ISSN 0261-2933 = BMCIS building maintenance price book : £4.50 B81-27132

690'.24 — Great Britain. Buildings of historical importance. Conversion

Working Party on Alternative Uses of Historic Buildings. Britain's historic buildings : a policy for their future use / [Working Party on Alternative Uses of Historic Buildings]. — London : BTA on behalf of the Working Party, [1980?]. — 94p : ill ; 30cm
Bibliography: p93
ISBN 0-7095-0670-8 (pbk) : Unpriced
B81-12648

690'.24 — Scotland. Buildings of historical importance. Conversion

New uses for older buildings in Scotland : a manual of practical encouragement : a report / prepared by the Scottish Civic Trust for the Scottish Development Department. — Edinburgh : H.M.S.O., 1981. — 164p : ill,plans ; 30cm
Bibliography: p156-158. — Includes index
ISBN 0-11-491694-2 (pbk) : £12.00 B81-23653

690'.24'0941 — Great Britain. Buildings. Maintenance — *For local authorities* — *Serials*

[Members' reference book *(Society of Chief Architects of Local Authorities)*]. Members' reference book / Society of Chief Architects of Local Authorities. — 1979/80-. — London (86 Edgeware Rd, W2 2YW) : Sterling Publications, 1979. — v. : ill,ports ; 21cm
Annual. — Continues: Year book (Society of Chief Architects of Local Authorities). — Description based on: 1980/81
ISSN 0261-1627 = Members' reference book — Society of Chief Architects of Local Authorities (corrected) : Unpriced
Also classified at 721'.0941 B81-20416

690'.5'21 — Shops. Fitting — *Manuals*

Mun, David. Shops : a manual of planning and design. — London : Architectural Press, Nov.1981. — [192]p
ISBN 0-85139-610-0 : £18.95 : CIP entry
B81-30414

690'.54'0684 — Great Britain. Industrial buildings. Project management — *Manuals* — *For clients*

Chartered Institute of Building. Building for industry and commerce : clients guide. — Ascot (Englemere, Kings Ride, Ascot, Berks. SL5 8BJ) : Chartered Institute of Building, [1980]. — 29p : ill ; 30cm
ISBN 0-906600-24-3 (pbk) : £5.00 B81-06347

690'.571'0288 — Catering establishments. Buildings. Maintenance

Gladwell, D. C.. Practical maintenance and equipment : for hoteliers, licensees and caterers / D.C. Gladwell. — 2nd ed. — London : Hutchinson, 1981, c1974. — xii,223p : ill ; 22cm. — (Catering and hotel management books)
Previous ed.: London : Barrie and Rockliff, 1968. — Bibliography: p210. — Includes index
ISBN 0-09-145121-3 (pbk) : £5.95 B81-17077

690'.65 — Great Britain. Churches. Repair — *Manuals*

A Guide to church inspection and repair. — London : CIO, 1980. — 30p ; 21cm
Bibliography: p27-30
ISBN 0-7151-7536-x (pbk) : £1.40 B81-05818

690'.8 — Residences. Defects. Causes

Structural failure in residential buildings. — London : Granada
Translation of: Schwachstellen. 2 durchges. Aufl. Wiesbaden: Bauverlag, 1977-
Vol.4: Internal walls, ceilings and floors / Erich Schild ... [et al.] ; illustrations by Volker Schnapauff ; [translated from the German by TST Translations]. — 1981. — 154p : ill ; 31cm
Includes bibliographies and index
ISBN 0-246-11479-7 : Unpriced B81-24471

690'.8 — Scotland. Residences. Rehabilitation by housing associations

Clark, David, *1946-*. Turning slums into homes — the way forward : SFHA research report / David Clark. — [Scotland] : [S.n.], [1981]. — 34leaves : ill,1map ; 30cm
Cover title
Unpriced (pbk) B81-27147

690'.8'0973 — United States. Residences. Construction

Reiner, Laurence E.. Methods and materials of residential construction / Laurence E. Reiner. — Englewood Cliffs ; London : Prentice-Hall, c1981. — xiii,301p : ill ; 29cm
Includes index
ISBN 0-13-578864-1 : £17.45 B81-36173

690'.83 — Great Britain. Occupied local authority housing. Improvement & maintenance

Phased improvement with tenants in residence : a study of the repair amd improvement of older houses / by Shankland Cox Partnership for the Department of the Environment. — [London] ([2 Marsham St., SW1P 3EB]) : The Department, 1981. — 119p : ill,1facsim,plans ; 30cm
£2.50 (pbk) B81-37515

690'.83 — Houses. Construction

[Housing Association maintenance training. *Part 1*]. House construction : a practical guide for non-technical people / compiled by the National Building Agency. — Lancaster : Construction Press, 1981. — 146p : ill,plans ; 21cm
Bibliography: p133-134. — Includes index
ISBN 0-86095-895-7 (pbk) : Unpriced
ISBN 0-86095-895-7 B81-38418

690'.83 — Houses. Construction — *For children*

Barton, Byron. Building a house / by Byron Barton. — London : Macrae, 1981. — [32]p : chiefly ill(some col.) ; 21x26cm
ISBN 0-86203-051-x : £4.95 : CIP rev.
B81-16914

690'.83 — Scotland. Local authority housing. Exteriors — *Technical data*

Common details external works. — Edinburgh (53 Melville St., Edinburgh EH3 7HL) : Scottish Local Authorities Special Housing Group, [1980]. — 1v.(loose-leaf) : ill ; 31cm
Unpriced B81-10863

690'.83 — Scotland. Strathclyde Region. Strathkelvin *(District)*. **Houses. Extension. Design**

A Guide to house extensions / [Strathkelvin District Council]. — [Bishopbriggs] ([14 Springfield Rd., Bishopbriggs]) : [The Council], [1980?]. — [10]p : ill ; 21x31cm
Cover title
Unpriced (pbk) B81-11852

690'.8'9 — Agricultural industries. Farms. Buildings. Design & siting. Environmental aspects — *For architects*

Weller, John. Agricultural buildings. — Edinburgh (6 Castle St., Edinburgh EH2 3AT) : Capital Planning Information, Sept.1981. — 1v.. — (SSRC planning reviews ; no.2)
ISBN 0-906011-12-4 (pbk) : £3.00 : CIP entry
B81-26686

690'.892 — Forage bunker silos — *Standards*

Bunker silo construction / ADAS, Ministry of Agriculture, Fisheries and Food. — Pinner (Tolcarne Drive, Pinner, Middx HA5 2DT) : The Ministry, 1980. — 13p : ill,plans ; 21cm. — (Leaflet ; 761)
Unpriced (unbound) B81-17746

691 — BUILDING MATERIALS

691 — Building materials — *Conference proceedings*

European Conference on Building Materials *(1980)*. Building materials : proceedings of the 1980 European conference / [based on the 1980 European Conference on Building Materials] ; [sponsored by Alena Enterprises of Canada] ; edited by V.M. Bhatnagar. — Lancaster : Construction Press, 1981. — 155p : ill ; 31cm
Includes index
ISBN 0-86095-866-3 : £15.00 B81-10220

691 — Building materials. Thermal properties

CIBS guide. — 4th ed. — London : Chartered Institution of Building Services
Forms part of the Building services manual. — Previous ed.: 1965
A3: Thermal properties of building structures, 1980. — c1980. — 46p : ill ; 30cm
Unpriced (pbk) B81-31502

691 — Great Britain. Building product industries & trades. Products — *Technical data* — *Serials*

Barbour compendium. [Building products]. — 1976-. — Lancaster : Construction Press by agreement with Barbour Index Ltd., 1976-. — v. : ill ; 30cm
Annual. — Description based on: 1980 issue
ISSN 0260-9169 = Barbour compendium. Building products : £26.00 B81-11869

Barbour compendium. [Building products]. — 1981. — Lancaster : Construction Press by agreement with Barbour Index Ltd., 1981. — 872p
ISBN 0-86095-842-6 : £26.00
ISSN 0260-9169 B81-20296

691′.076 — Building materials — *Questions & answers* — *For technicians*

Pritchard, M. D. W.. Building science and materials 2 checkbook / M.D.W. Pritchard. — London : Butterworths, 1981. — viii,110p : ill ; 20cm. — (Butterworths technical and scientific checkbooks. Level 2)
Includes index
ISBN 0-408-00640-4 (cased) : Unpriced
ISBN 0-408-00607-2 (pbk) : Unpriced
B81-27273

691′.1 — Building materials: Timber

Kubler, Hans. Wood as building and hobby material : how to use lumber, wood-base panels and roundwood wisely in construction, for furniture and as fuel / Hans Kubler. — New York ; Chichester ; Wiley, c1980. — xii,256p ; 24cm
Bibliography: p231-234. - Includes index
ISBN 0-471-05390-2 : £10.70 B81-04413

691′.3 — Building materials: Precast concrete

Levitt, M.. Precast concrete. — London : Applied Science, Jan.1982. — [244]p
ISBN 0-85334-994-0 : £19.00 : CIP entry
B81-34573

691′.6′05 — Building materials: Glass. Use — *Serials*

Glass and glazing news. — Jan.1980-. — London (6 Mount Row, W1Y 6DY) : Glass and Glazing Federation, 1980-. — v. : ill ; 30cm
Six to eight issues yearly. — Description based on: Sept.1980
ISSN 0260-6321 = Glass and glazing news : Unpriced B81-06531

691′.9 — Developing countries. Residences. Building materials: Mud — *Proposals*

Agarwal, Anil. Mud, mud : the potential of earth-based materials for Third World housing / by Anil Agarwal. — London (10 Percy St., W1P 0DR) : Earthscan, c1981. — 99p : ill ; 21cm
ISBN 0-905347-18-8 (pbk) : £2.50 B81-38457

691′.92 — Building materials: Plastics. Use — *Conference proceedings*

ICP/RILEM/IBK International Symposium *(1981 : Prague)*. Plastics in material and structural engineering. — Oxford : Elsevier Scientific, Jan.1982. — [900]p. — (Developments in civil engineering ; 5)
ISBN 0-444-99710-5 : £50.00 : CIP entry
B81-34493

Plastics in building : a series of papers. — London : British Plastics Federation, [1980]. — 69p : ill ; 30cm
Conference papers
£10.00 (£5.00 to members) (spiral) B81-24069

692 — BUILDINGS. PLANS, SPECIFICATIONS, ESTIMATING, CONTRACTS

692 — Buildings. Construction. Pre-contract practices

Pre-contract practice : for architects and quantity surveyors / The Aqua Group. — 6th ed. — London : Granada, 1980. — 101p : ill,forms ; 23cm
Previous ed.: London : Crosby Lockwood Staples, 1974. — Includes index
ISBN 0-246-11338-3 (pbk) : £4.95 : CIP rev.
B80-18428

692 — Great Britain. Building surveyors. Duties. Standard conditions

Conditions of engagement for building surveying services / prepared by the Building Surveyors Division of the Royal Institution of Chartered Surveyors. — London : Royal Institution of Chartered Surveyors, c1981. — 22p ; 22cm + 1pamphlet(4p ; 20cm)
Pamphlet in pocket
ISBN 0-85406-135-5 (pbk) : Unpriced
B81-35683

692 — Great Britain. Residences. Surveying — *Manuals*

Structural surveys of residential property : a practice note / prepared by the Building Surveyors Division, Royal Institution of Chartered Surveyors. — London : Royal Institution of Chartered Surveyors, c1981. — 24p ; 21cm
ISBN 0-85406-134-7 (pbk) : Unpriced
B81-35676

692′.02472 — Buildings. Construction. Auxiliary practices — *For architecture*

Willis, Arthur J.. The architect in practice / Arthur J. Willis and W.N.B. George ; in collaboration with Christopher J. Willis and H.P. Scher. — 6th ed. — London : Granada, 1981. — xvi,251p : forms ; 24cm
Previous ed: London : Crosby Lockwood Staples, 1974. — Bibliography: p239-244. - Includes index
ISBN 0-246-11554-8 (pbk) : £9.95 : CIP rev.
B81-13905

692′.1 — Buildings. Construction. Technical drawings. Interpretation

Wallach, Paul I.. Reading construction drawings / Paul I. Wallach, Donald E. Hepler. — New York ; London : McGraw-Hill, 1981. — vi,313p : ill,plans,forms ; 29cm
Ill on lining papers. — Includes index
ISBN 0-07-067940-1 : £13.95 B81-19533

692′.2 — Architectural drawings. Detailing — *Illustrations*

Ramsey, Charles G.. Architectural graphic standards / Ramsey/Sleeper. — 7th ed. / Robert T. Packard, editor. — New York ; Chichester : Wiley, c1981. — 785p : ill,maps,plans ; 30cm
At head of title: The American Institute of Architects. — Previous ed.: 1970. — Includes index
ISBN 0-471-04683-3 : £47.00 B81-23324

692.2′275 — Royal Enfield motorcycles, *to 1970*

Hartley, Peter. The story of Royal Enfield motor cycles. — Cambridge : Patrick Stephens, Oct.1981. — [128]p
ISBN 0-85059-467-7 : £8.95 : CIP entry
B81-27991

692′.3 — Building specifications. Preparation — *Manuals*

Bowyer, Jack. Practical specification writing : for architects and surveyors / Jack Bowyer. — London : Hutchinson, 1981. — 167p ; 25cm
Includes index
ISBN 0-09-144400-4 (cased) : £12.00 : CIP rev.
ISBN 0-09-144401-2 (pbk) : Unpriced
B81-00188

Rosen, Harold J.. Construction specifications writing : principles and procedures / Harold J. Rosen. — 2nd ed. — New York ; Chichester : Wiley, c1981. — xi,235p : forms ; 29cm. — (Wiley series of practical construction guides)
Previous ed.: 1974. — Includes index
ISBN 0-471-08328-3 : £17.50 B81-35616

692′.3 — Great Britain. Buildings. Construction. Standard method of measurement

Saunt, Trevor J.. Revision notes on building measurement / Trevor J. Saunt. — London : Butterworths, 1981. — 102p : ill,plans ; 25cm. — (Revision notes for building students)
ISBN 0-408-00277-8 (corrected : pbk) : Unpriced B81-30705

692′.3 — Great Britain. Houses. Construction. Standards. Guarantees: National House Building Council scheme

Tapping, A. P. de B.. Guarantees for new homes : a guide to the National House-Building Council Scheme. — 2nd ed. / by A.P. de B Tapping and R. Rolfe. — London : Oyez, 1981. — xii,374p ; 22cm
Previous ed.: / by D.P. Marten and P.M. Luff, 1974. — Includes index
ISBN 0-85120-543-7 (pbk) : Unpriced
B81-2165

692′.5 — Buildings. Construction. Estimating

Wainwright, W. Howard. Practical builders' estimating / W. Howard Wainwright and A.A.B. Wood. — 4th ed. — London : Hutchinson, 1981. — 188p ; 24cm
Previous ed.: 1977
ISBN 0-09-144931-6 (pbk) : £5.50 : CIP rev.
B81-0208

692′.5 — Buildings. Construction. Estimating — *Manuals*

The **Practice** of estimating / compiled and editec by P.A. Harlow. — Ascot : Chartered Institut of Building, c1981. — 165p : ill ; 30cm
Includes index
ISBN 0-906600-41-3 (pbk) : Unpriced : CIP rev. B81-1440

692′.5 — Great Britain. Buildings. Construction. Bills of quantities

Skinner, D. W. H.. The contractor's use of bills of quantities / by D.W.H. Skinner. — Ascot : Chartered Institute of Building, 1981. — 32p : ill ; 30cm. — (Occasional paper / Chartered Institute of Building, ISSN 0306-6878 ; no.24)
ISBN 0-906600-35-9 (pbk) : Unpriced : CIP rev. B81-0742

692′.5 — Great Britain. Buildings. Construction. Standard costs — *For estimating* — *Lists* — *Serials*

Hutchins' priced schedules. — 37th ed. (1981). - Bexhill-on-Sea : Hutchins Priced Schedules, [1981]. — xviii,244p
Unpriced B81-2413

Laxton's building price book. — 153rd ed. (1981). — East Grinstead : Kelly's Directories c1980. — xxxi,759p
ISBN 0-610-00536-7 : Unpriced
ISSN 0305-6589 B81-0175

692′.5 — Great Britain. Buildings. Construction. Standard costs — *Lists*

Schedule of rates for building works 1980 / [Directorate of Quantity Surveying Services], Department of the Environment, Property Services Agency. — 4th ed. — London : H.M.S.O., 1981. — 569p ; 31cm
Previous ed.: 1979. — Includes index
ISBN 0-11-671066-7 : £50.00 B81-3769

692′.5 — Great Britain. Buildings. Construction. Standard costs — *Lists* — *Serials*

BCIS quarterly review of building prices. — Issue No.1-. — Kingston upon Thames (85 Clarence St, Kingston upon Thames, Surrey KT1 1RB) : Building Cost Information Servic of the Royal Institution of Chartered Surveyors, 1981-. — v. ; 30cm
ISSN 0260-6216 = BCIS quarterly review of building prices : £60.00 per year B81-2713

Spon's architects' and builders' price book. — 107th ed. (1982). — London : Spon, Nov.1981 — [560]p
ISBN 0-419-12460-8 : £12.00 : CIP entry
ISSN 0306-3046 B81-311

Spon's architects' and builders' price book / edited by Davis, Belfield and Everest. — 106t ed. (1981). — London : Spon, 1980
1981 : 106th ed. — xviii,572p
ISBN 0-419-12090-4 : £10.50 : CIP rev.
ISSN 0306-3046 B80-259

692′.5 — Scotland. Agricultural industries. Farms. Buildings. Construction. Standard costs — *Lists — Serials*

Farm building cost guide. — 1981. — Aberdeen (Craibstone, Bucksburn, Aberdeen AB2 9TR) : Scottish Farm Buildings Investigation Unit, c1981. — 63p
ISBN 0-902433-21-0 : £3.00
ISSN 0309-4146 B81-25016

692′.8 — Great Britain. Buildings. Construction. Contracts. Standard conditions: Joint Contracts Tribunal. Standard form of building contract. 1980 — *Algorithms*

Jones, Glyn P.. A new appoach to the 1980 standard form of building contract / Glyn P. Jones. — Lancaster : Construction, 1980. — 244p : ill ; 22x30cm
ISBN 0-86095-819-1 : £27.50 B81-10807

692′.8 — Scotland. Local authority housing. Exteriors. Contracts. Standard conditions — *Texts*

Standard preambles external works. — Edinburgh (53 Melville St., Edinburgh EH3 7HL) : Scottish Local Authorities Special Housing Group, [1980]. — 1v.(loose-leaf) ; 31cm
Unpriced B81-10862

692′.8′0941 — Great Britain. Buildings. Construction. Contracts. Administration — *Manuals*

Contract administration : for architects and quantity surveyors / The Aqua Group. — 5th ed. with supplement on the JCT 1980 form. — London : Granada, 1981. — 121p : ill,forms ; 24cm
Previous ed.: 1979. — Includes index
ISBN 0-246-11555-6 (pbk) : £6.95 : CIP rev. B81-00189

692′.8′0941 — Great Britain. Buildings. Construction. Contracts — *For quantity surveying*

Ramus, J. W.. Contract practice for quantity surveyors / J.W. Ramus. — London : Heinemann, 1981. — vii,214p : ill,facsism,forms ; 22cm
Includes index
ISBN 0-434-91675-7 (pbk) : £7.50 B81-10779

692′.8′0942 — England. Buildings. Construction. Contracts

Colley, E. J.. Faculty of Building presents The art of coarse contract : presented to The London Branch (September 1980) / by E. J. Colley. — Borehamwood (10 Manor Way, Borehamwood, Herts. WD6 1QQ) : Faculty of Building, [1980 or 1981]. — 1folded sheet ; 30x63cm folded to 30x21cm
Unpriced (unbound) B81-33254

693 — BUILDINGS. CONSTRUCTION IN SPECIAL MATERIALS AND FOR SPECIAL PURPOSES

693′.1 — England. Pennines. Dry stone walls

Raistrick, Arthur. The Pennine walls / by Arthur Raistrick. — Clapham [N. Yorkshire] : Dalesman, 1981. — 40p : ill,maps ; 19cm
Originally published: 1946
ISBN 0-85206-637-6 (pbk) : £0.75 B81-37156

693′.21 — Brickwork — *Manuals*

Tempest, P. J.. Initial skills in bricklaying : a practical guide / P.J. Tempest ; photographs Chris Locke ; illustration Susan Burton ; prepared for vocational and non-vocational courses in colleges, training centres, workshops, and for self-teaching. — Oxford : Pergamon, 1981. — x,97p : ill ; 26cm. — (Pergamon international library)
Bibliography: p97
ISBN 0-08-025424-1 (cased) : Unpriced : CIP rev.
ISBN 0-08-025423-3 (pbk) : £3.95 B81-05144

693′.21 — Buildings. Structural components: Brickwork

Hendry, A. W.. Structural brickwork / Arnold W. Hendry. — London : Macmillan, 1981. — x,209p : ill,plans ; 25cm
Includes index
ISBN 0-333-25748-0 : £15.00 B81-23018

693′.4 — Great Britain. Agricultural industries. Farms. Buildings. Concrete block walls. Construction

Barnes, Maurice M.. Concrete block walls / Maurice M. Barnes. — Slough : Cement and Concrete Association, 1981. — [8]p : ill ; 30cm. — (Farm note, ISSN 0307-0352 ; 11)
ISBN 0-7210-1229-9 (unbound) : Unpriced B81-27518

693′.4 — Panel double skin brick/block walls — *Technical data — For design*

Wilby, C. B.. Design graphs for brick/block double skin panel walls / C. Wilby. — London : Applied Science Publishers, c1981. — xi,132p : chiefly ill ; 23cm
Includes index
ISBN 0-85334-945-2 : £12.00 : CIP rev. B81-03835

693′.5 — Agricultural industries. Farms. Buildings. Concrete foundations. Construction — *Manuals*

Barnes, Maurice M.. Concrete foundations for farm buildings / Maurice M. Barnes. — 2nd ed. — Slough : Cement and Concrete Association, 1981. — 1folded sheet : ill,1map ; 30cm. — (Farm note, ISSN 0307-0352 ; 9)
Previous ed.: 1980
ISBN 0-7210-1230-2 (unbound) : Unpriced B81-24077

693′.54′0941 — Great Britain. Reinforced concrete building components. Design. Detailing — *Manuals*

Whittle, Robin. Reinforcement detailing manual / Robin Whittle. — Slough : Cement and Concrete Association, 1981. — x,118p : ill ; 30cm. — (A Viewpoint publication)
ISBN 0-7210-1223-x (spiral) : Unpriced B81-38477

693′.71 — Buildings. Steel frames. Plastic design

Morris, L. J.. Plastic design / by L.J. Morris and A.L. Randall. — Repr. with minor amendments and additions. — Croydon (12 Addiscombe Rd, Croydon CR9 5JH) : Constructional Steel Research & Development Organisation, 1979, c1975. — 60p : ill ; 30cm + Supplement(55p:ill;30cm)
Supplement incorporates charts from publications nos.23 and 29. — Bibliography: p52
Unpriced (pbk) B81-28533

693′.71 — Roofs. Steel diaphragm deckings. Design — *Standards*

Bryan, E. R.. Steel diaphragm roof decks : a design guide with tables for engineers and architects / E.R. Bryan and J.M. Davies. — London : Granada, 1981. — 92p : ill ; 28cm
Includes index
ISBN 0-246-11506-8 (pbk) : Unpriced : CIP rev. B81-15817

693.8′2 — Buildings. Fire-resistant materials. Design

Malhotra, H. L.. Design of fire-resisting structures. — Glasgow : Surrey University Press, Feb.1982. — [210]p
ISBN 0-903384-28-0 : £16.50 : CIP entry B81-36040

693.8′3′0212 — Buildings. Insulation — *Technical data — Serials*

The **Insulation** handbook. — 1981. — Watford (177 Hagden La., Watford WD1 8LW) : Comprint, [1980]. — 352p
£8.00 B81-10274

693.8′32 — Buildings. Heat. Conservation — *For architecture*

Weller, J. W.. Thermal energy conservation : building and services design / by J.W. Weller and A. Youle. — London : Applied Science, c1981. — viii,269p : ill ; 23cm
Includes index
ISBN 0-85334-938-x : £21.00 : CIP rev. B81-02672

693.8′32 — Great Britain. Commercial buildings & industrial buildings. Building components: Profiled steel claddings. Thermal insulation — *Standards*

Hill, H. S.. Thermal insulation of profiled steel cladding / H.S. Hill. — Croydon : Constrado, c1981. — 12p : ill ; 30cm
ISBN 0-86200-024-6 (pbk) : £1.50 B81-23308

693.8′32 — Great Britain. Residences. Thermal insulation — *Proposals*

Domestic insulation / Electricity Consumers′ Council. — London (119 Marylebone Rd., NW1 5PY) : The Council, 1979. — 15p : ill ; 30cm. — (Discussion paper / Electricity Consumers′ Council ; 2)
Unpriced (pbk) B81-34746

693.8′5 — Buildings. Damage by roots of trees

Cutler, D. F.. Tree roots and buildings / D.F. Cutler, I.B.K. Richardson. — London : Construction Press, 1981. — 94p : ill,1map ; 21cm
Bibliography: p91-92. — Includes index
ISBN 0-86095-898-1 (pbk) : £4.50 B81-27110

693.8′52 — Earthquake resistant buildings. Design & construction

Green, Norman B.. Earthquake resistant building design and construction / Norman B. Green. — 2nd ed. — New York ; London : Van Nostrand Reinhold, c1981. — xi,197p : ill,plans ; 24cm
Previous ed.: 1978. — Includes index
ISBN 0-442-28799-2 : £14.20 B81-26041

693.8′52 — United States. Buildings. Earthquake resistant equipment. Design

McGavin, Gary L.. Earthquake protection of essential building equipment : design, engineering, installation / Gary L. McGavin. — New York ; Chichester : Wiley, c1981. — xiv,464p : ill ; 24cm
Bibliography: p345-348. — Includes index
ISBN 0-471-06270-7 : £24.50 B81-33018

693′.97 — Buildings. Industrialised construction

Sullivan, Barry James. Industrialization in the building industry / Barry James Sullivan ; foreword by Moshe Safdie ; introduction by R. Buckminster Fuller. — New York ; London : Van Nostrand Reinhold, c1980. — xviii,253p : ill,plans ; 22x29cm
Includes index
ISBN 0-442-27941-8 : £19.90 B81-03636

694 — CARPENTRY, JOINERY

694 — Carpentry & joinery

Brett, Peter. Carpentry and joinery for building craft students / Peter Brett. — London : Hutchinson
Includes index
1. — 1981. — 144p : ill ; 25cm
ISBN 0-09-143510-2 (cased) : £9.95
ISBN 0-09-143511-0 (pbk) : £4.95 B81-28670

Brett, Peter. Carpentry and joinery for building craft students 2 / Peter Brett. — London : Hutchinson, 1981. — 189p : ill ; 25cm
Includes index
ISBN 0-09-144190-0 (cased) : Unpriced : CIP rev.
ISBN 0-09-144191-9 (pbk) : £5.95 B81-00190

694 — Carpentry & joinery — *For children*

Fyson, Nance Lui. Carpenter / Nance Lui Fyson ; photographs by Sally Greehill. — London : Black, c1980. — 25p : col.ill,col.ports ; 22cm. — (BEANS. People at work)
ISBN 0-7136-2038-2 : £2.50 : CIP rev. B80-13915

694 — Carpentry & joinery — *Manuals*

Austin, C. K.. Site carpentry / C.K. Austin. — London ([10 Elm St.] London WC1X 0BP) : Northwood, 1979 (1980 [printing]). — 140p : ill ; 31cm. — (A ′Building trades journal′ book)
Includes index
ISBN 0-7198-2730-2 : Unpriced B81-08175

Baker, Glenn E.. Carpentry fundamentals / Glenn Baker, Rex Miller. — New York ; London : Gregg, c1981. — x,517p : ill(some col.),1map,plans ; 29cm. — (Contemporary construction series)
Includes index
ISBN 0-07-003361-7 : £11.75 B81-27563

694 — Residences. Carpentry & joinery — *Amateurs' manuals*

Clayton, Michael, *1924-*. Home carpentry / Michael Clayton with Bernard Houghton. — Newton Abbot : David & Charles, c1981. — 48p : ill ; 21cm. — (Penny pinchers)
Cover title
ISBN 0-7153-8029-x (pbk) : £1.50 B81-20991

694 — Residences. Carpentry & joinery — *Manuals*

Badzinski, Stanley. Carpentry in residential construction / Stanley Badzinski, Jr. — 2nd ed. — Englewood Cliffs ; London : Prentice-Hall, c1981. — xii,335p : ill ; 25cm
Previous ed.: 1972. — Bibliography: p325-326. — Includes index
ISBN 0-13-115238-6 : £11.00 B81-19826

694 — Timber framed houses. Construction — *Standards*

. Structural recommendations for timber frame housing / Timber Research and Development Association. — Lancaster : Construction Press, 1980. — 103p : ill,plans ; 31cm
Bibliography: p101-103
ISBN 0-86095-890-6 : £15.00 B81-09260

694'.2 — Carpentry — *Amateurs' manuals*

Hayward, Charles. Carpentry. — 2nd ed. — London : Hodder and Stoughton, Sept.1981. — [224]p. — (Teach yourself books)
Originally published: 1960
ISBN 0-340-27112-4 (pbk) : £1.25 : CIP entry B81-22482

694'.2'0942 — England. Buildings. Construction. Carpentry, *449-1890*

Hewett, C. A.. English historic carpentry / by Cecil A. Hewett. — London : Phillimore, 1980. — xiv,338p,[8]p of plates : ill,plans ; 26cm
Bibliography: pxiii-xiv. — Includes index
ISBN 0-85033-354-7 : £20.00 B81-19306

696 — PLUMBING, PIPE FITTING, HOT WATER SUPPLY

696 — Buildings. Energy. Conservation

Meckler, Milton. Energy conservation in buildings and industrial plants / Milton Meckler. — New York ; London : McGraw-Hill, c1981. — x,270p : ill,maps,forms ; 24cm
Includes index
ISBN 0-07-041195-6 : £15.75 B81-16211

696 — Buildings. Energy. Conservation — *Conference proceedings*

Experience of energy conservation in buildings. — Lancaster : Construction Press, June 1981. — [160]p
Conference papers
ISBN 0-86095-875-2 : £17.50 : CIP entry B81-13521

International Council for Building Research Studies and Documentation. *Symposium (1976 : British Building Research Establishment)*. Engergy conservation in the built environment : proceedings of the 1976 symposium of the International Council for Building Research Studies and Documentation (CIB) held at the British Building Research Establishment / editor Roger G. Courtney. — Lancaster : Construction Press, 1976. — 603p : ill,plans ; 31cm
Includes 4 papers and summaries in French. — Added t.p. in French. — Includes index
ISBN 0-904406-28-8 : £24.50 B81-05200

696 — Buildings. Engineering services

Billington, Neville S.. Building services engineering. — Oxford : Pergamon, Aug.1981. — [500]p. — (International series on building environmental engineering ; v.1)
ISBN 0-08-026741-6 (cased) : £33.00 : CIP entry
ISBN 0-08-026742-4 (pbk) : £10.00 B81-20619

696 — Buildings. Engineering services — *For technicians*

Tyler, H. A.. Environmental science : level IV / H.A. Tyler. — New York ; London : Van Nostrand Reinhold, 1980. — xiv,208p : ill ; 26cm. — (Higher technical education courses)
Includes index
ISBN 0-442-30344-0 (cased) : £11.50
ISBN 0-442-30345-9 (pbk) : Unpriced B81-08716

696 — Buildings. Engineering services — *Illustrations*

Mueller, Jerome F.. Standard mechanical and electrical details / Jerome F. Mueller. — New York ; London : McGraw-Hill, c1981. — vii,339p : chiefly ill,forms ; 29cm
Includes index
ISBN 0-07-043960-5 : £14.70 B81-02228

696 — Buildings. Engineering services — *Questions & answers — For technicians*

Hall, F.. Building services and equipment 4 checkbook / F. Hall. — London : Butterworths, 1981. — vi,138p : ill ; 20cm. — (Butterworths technical and scientific checkbooks. Level 4)
Includes index
ISBN 0-408-00641-2 (cased) : Unpriced : CIP rev.
ISBN 0-408-00613-7 (pbk) : Unpriced B81-03144

696 — Buildings. Piping systems. Maintenance & repair

Shuldener, Henry L.. Water and piping problems in large and small buildings : a troubleshooter's guide / Henry L. Shuldener, James B. Fullman. — New York ; Chichester : Wiley, c1981. — xiv,207p : ill ; 24cm
Includes index
ISBN 0-471-08082-9 : £15.75 B81-23346

696 — Buildings. Use of solar energy — *Conference proceedings*

SOLAR/80 *(Conference : Caracas)*. Solar cooling and dehumidifying : proceedings of the First International Conference, SOLAR/80, Caracas, Venezuela, 3-6 August 1980 / edited by A.R. Martinez. — Oxford : Pergamon, 1981. — xiii,267p : ill,maps ; 26cm
Text in English and Spanish. — Includes index
ISBN 0-08-027571-0 : £16.50 : CIP rev. B81-15902

696 — Eastern United States. Buildings. Engineering services. Installation. Standard costs *— Lists — Serials*

[The Berger building & design cost file. Volume II, Mechanical and electrical trades *(Eastern edition)***]**. The Berger building & design cost file. Volume II, Mechanical and electrical trades : unit prices. — Eastern ed. — 1981-. — New York ; London : Van Nostrand Reinhold, c1981-. — v. : ill,plans ; 28 cm
Annual. — Continues in part: Berger building cost file (Eastern edition) ; and , The Berger design cost file
£18.70 B81-29981

696 — United States. Buildings. Engineering services — *Manuals*

Handbook of mechanical and electrical systems for buildings / H.E. Bovay, Jr., editor in chief. — New York ; London : McGraw-Hill, c1981. — 843p in various pagings : ill ; 24cm
Includes index
ISBN 0-07-006718-x : £39.95 B81-23726

696 — United States. Energy-efficient buildings. Design — *Case studies*

Energy-efficient buildings / edited by Walter F. Wagner, Jr.. — New York ; London : McGraw-Hill, c1980. — ix,182p : ill,charts,maps,plans ; 31cm. — (An Architectural record book)
Includes index
ISBN 0-07-002344-1 : £18.15 B81-04472

696'.1 — Buildings. Plumbing — *Manuals*

Thiesse, James L.. Plumbing fundamentals / James L. Thiesse. — New York ; London : Gregg Division, McGraw-Hill, c1981. — vii,182p : ill,plans ; 29cm. — (Contemporary construction series)
Includes index
ISBN 0-07-064191-9 : £9.25 B81-24186

696'.1 — Residences. Plumbing — *Amateurs' manuals*

Hall, Ernest. The David & Charles manual of home plumbing. — Newton Abbot : David & Charles, Feb.1982. — [224]p
ISBN 0-7153-8146-6 : £8.95 : CIP entry B81-35825

Hall, Ernest. Plumbing in the house / Ernest Hall. — London : Hodder and Stoughton, 1981. — 254p : ill ; 18cm. — (Teach yourself books)
Includes index
ISBN 0-340-25959-0 (pbk) : £1.95 B81-12214

696'.1 — Sanitary appliances — *Standards*

Sanitary appliances / [Method of Building Branch]. — Croydon (Sales Office, Block C, Whitgift Centre, Wellesley Rd., Croydon, Surrey) : [The Branch]
UMB Group Ltd product data
Amendment No.1: Agreement no. S437817 operative from 1 April 1978 - 30 March 1981, now extended to 30 September 1982 : supersedes TPE08-411, April 1978. — 1981. — 32p : ill ; 30cm. — (Method of building ; 08-411)
ISBN 0-86177-075-7 (pbk) : £1.70 B81-35053

696'.1'113 — Buildings. Plumbing. Design. Implications of cold climate

Design of water and wastewater services for cold climate communities. — Oxford : Pergamon, Sept.1981. — [190]p
ISBN 0-08-029079-5 : £20.00 : CIP entry B81-28486

696'.12'0941 — Great Britain. Buildings. Water supply systems

Hall, F.. Heating technology / F. Hall. — New York ; London : Van Nostrand Reinhold, 1981. — xiv,183p : ill ; 26cm. — (Advanced craft) (VNR crafts series)
Includes index
ISBN 0-442-30399-8 (cased) : £10.50
ISBN 0-442-30400-5 (pbk) : £5.25
Also classified at 697'.00941 B81-17152

Hall, F.. Plumbing : cold water supplies, drainage and sanitation / F. Hall. — New York ; London : Van Nostrand Reinhold, 1981. — xiii,159p : ill ; 26cm. — (Advanced craft) (VNR craft series)
Includes index
ISBN 0-442-30392-0 (cased) : £10.00
ISBN 0-442-30393-9 (pbk) : £4.95
Also classified at 696'.13'0941 B81-17151

696'.13'0941 — Great Britain. Buildings. Drainage systems

Hall, F.. Plumbing : cold water supplies, drainage and sanitation / F. Hall. — New York ; London : Van Nostrand Reinhold, 1981. — xiii,159p : ill ; 26cm. — (Advanced craft) (VNR craft series)
Includes index
ISBN 0-442-30392-0 (cased) : £10.00
ISBN 0-442-30393-9 (pbk) : £4.95
Primary classification 696'.12'0941 B81-17151

696'.182 — Developing countries. Rural regions. Lavatories. Design & construction. Health aspects

Pacey, Arnold. Rural sanitation : planning and appraisal : an OXFAM document / with research by Catherine Goyder. — London : Intermediate Technology, c1980. — 68p : ill,plans ; 21cm
Bibliography: p67-68
ISBN 0-903031-72-8 (pbk) : £1.60 B81-27761

696'.6 — Great Britain. Residences. Solar energy hot water supply systems. Installation — *Amateurs' manuals*

Heating water by the sun : a layman's guide to the use of flat plate solar collectors for domestic water heating and for heating swimming pools / edited by W.B. Gillett and M.G. Hutchins. — London : International Solar Energy Society, UK Section, c1981. — 21p : ill,maps ; 30cm
Bibliography: p17
ISBN 0-904963-25-x (pbk) : £3.00 B81-38007

696′.6′0941 — Great Britain. Buildings. Hot water supply systems

Hall, F.. Plumbing : hot water supply and heating systems / F. Hall. — New York ; London : Van Nostrand Reinhold, c1981. — xiii,143p : ill ; 26cm. — (Advanced craft) (VNR crafts series)
Includes index
ISBN 0-442-30394-7 (cased) : £10.00 (pbk) : £4.95
Primary classification 697′.00941 B81-17150

697 — BUILDINGS. HEATING, VENTILATING, AIR-CONDITIONING

697 — Buildings. Air conditioning & heating equipment. Control systems

Letherman, K. M.. Automatic controls for heating and air conditioning. — Oxford : Pergamon, May 1981. — [220]p. — (International series on heating, ventilation and refrigeration ; v.15)
ISBN 0-08-023222-1 : £12.50 : CIP entry
B81-07616

697 — Buildings. Air conditioning, heating & ventilation equipment

Hall, F.. Heating, ventilating and air conditioning / F. Hall. — Lancaster : Construction Press, 1980. — 141p : ill ; 23x29cm
Bibliography: p137. - Includes index
ISBN 0-86095-884-1 : £9.95 : CIP rev.
B80-17852

Porges, John. Handbook of heating, ventilating and air conditioning. — 8th ed. — London : Butterworth, Sept.1981. — [250]p
Previous ed.: 1976
ISBN 0-408-00519-x : £12.50 : CIP entry
B81-28202

697 — Buildings. Heat transfer

Pratt, A. W.. Heat transmission in buildings. — Chichester : Wiley, Sept.1981. — [304]p
ISBN 0-471-27971-4 : £17.50 : CIP entry
B81-23753

697 — Buildings. Heating systems — *For design*

McLaughlin, Ronald K.. Heating services design / Ronald K. McLaughlin, R. Craig McLean, W. John Bonthron. — London : Butterworths, 1981. — 445p : ill ; 25cm
Includes index
ISBN 0-408-00380-4 : £20.00 : CIP rev.
B80-12984

697 — Buildings. Heating, ventilation & air conditioning. Control systems

Fisk, D. J.. Thermal control of buildings / D.J. Fisk. — London : Applied Science, c1981. — xvii,246p : ill ; 23cm
Includes bibliographies and index
ISBN 0-85334-950-9 : £21.00 : CIP rev.
B81-06068

Schneider, Raymond K.. HVAC control systems / Raymond K. Schneider. — New York ; Chichester : Wiley, c1981. — x,358p : ill ; 25cm
Includes index
ISBN 0-471-05180-2 : £11.55 B81-23395

697 — Great Britain. Heating & air conditioning equipment. Installation. Standard costs — *Serials*

Spon′s mechanical and electrical services price book. — 13th ed. (1982). — London : Spon, Nov.1981. — [500]p
ISBN 0-419-12470-5 : £8.25 : CIP entry
ISSN 0305-4543 B81-31166

697′.00941 — Great Britain. Buildings. Heating systems

Hall, F.. Heating technology / F. Hall. — New York ; London : Van Nostrand Reinhold, 1981. — xiv,183p : ill ; 26cm. — (Advanced craft) (VNR crafts series)
Includes index
ISBN 0-442-30399-8 (cased) : £10.50
ISBN 0-442-30400-5 (pbk) : £5.25
Primary classification 696′.12′0941 B81-17152

Hall, F.. Plumbing : hot water supply and heating systems / F. Hall. — New York ; London : Van Nostrand Reinhold, c1981. — xiii,143p : ill ; 26cm. — (Advanced craft) (VNR crafts series)
Includes index
ISBN 0-442-30394-7 (cased) : £10.00 (pbk) : £4.95
Also classified at 696′.6′0941 B81-17150

697′.03 — Great Britain. Commercial buildings. Central heating systems. Efficiency. Determination. Use of degree days

Degree days / Department of Energy. — London (Thames House South, Millbank, SW1P 4QJ) : Department of Energy, [1980]. — 18p : ill,1map ; 21cm. — (Fuel efficiency booklet ; 7)
Cover title
Unpriced (pbk) B81-04944

697′.03 — Residences. Central heating systems. Installation — *Amateurs′ manuals*

Crabtree, Trevor. Do your own central heating installation / Trevor Crabtree ; edited by Ron Grace. — London : Foulsham, c1980. — 144p : ill,plans ; 23cm
ISBN 0-572-01054-0 : £4.50 B81-01025

697′.042 — Household solid fuel heating appliances. Installation — *Manuals*

A Guide to the safe installation of solid fuel central heating. — Dublin (Ballymun Rd., Dublin 9) : Institute for Industrial Research and Standards, [1980?]. — 24p : ill ; 21cm
£0.75 (pbk) B81-01026

697′.07′0941 — Great Britain. Residences. Heating equipment — *Serials*

Domestic heating + plumbing, bathrooms, kitchens : incorporating Domestic heating news and Plumbing news & domestic heating review. — 1976-. — London (30 Old Burlington St., W1X 2AE) : Troup Publications, 1976-. — v. : ill ; 29cm
Monthly. — Continues: Domestic heating news. — Description based on: June 1981
ISSN 0308-8561 = Domestic heating + plumbing, bathrooms, kitchens (corrected) : £15.00 per year B81-39725

697′.22 — Woodburning stoves — *Buyers′ guides*

McGuigan, Dermot. Burning wood / Dermot McGuigan. — Dorchester : Prism, 1979. — 91p : ill ; 22cm
ISBN 0-904727-78-5 (cased) : £3.95
ISBN 0-904727-79-3 (pbk) : Unpriced
B81-40651

697′.54 — Energy resources. Conservation. Role of district heating systems

Diamant, R. M. E.. District heating and cooling for energy conservation / R.M.E. Diamant and David Kut. — London : Architectural Press, 1981. — x,464p : ill ; 25cm
Includes bibliographies and index
ISBN 0-85139-154-0 : £30.00 : CIP rev.
B81-12796

697′.54′0941 — Great Britain. District heating — *Socialist Environment and Resources Association viewpoints*

Community heating projects / Socialist Environment and Resources Association. — London (9 Poland St., W1V 3DG) : SERA, 1980. — 24p ; 22cm
Cover title. — Text on inside covers. — Bibliography: on inside back cover
£0.30 (pbk) B81-33557

697′.78 — Buildings. Solar energy heating systems

Schubert, Richard C.. Fundamentals of solar heating / Richard C. Schubert, L.D. Ryan. — Englewood Cliffs ; London : Prentice-Hall, c1981. — xiii,321p : ill,maps ; 24cm
Includes index
ISBN 0-13-344457-0 : £15.55 B81-17285

697′.78 — Buildings. Solar energy heating systems. Design

Tully, Gordon. Solar heating systems : analysis and design with the sun-pulse method / Gordon Tully. — New York ; London : McGraw-Hill, c1981. — x,222p : ill ; 24cm. — (An Energy learning systems book)
Bibliography: p206-209. — Includes index
ISBN 0-07-065441-7 : £16.95 B81-23990

697′.78′028 — Residences. Solar energy hot water heating systems. Plastics components

Plastics in solar heating : a series of papers. — London : British Plastics Federation, [1980]. — 121p in various pagings : ill,1map,1form ; 30cm
Conference papers
£10.00 (£5.00 to members) (spiral) B81-24066

697′.78′0722 — Great Britain. Buildings. Solar energy heating systems — *Case studies*

Oppenheim, David. Small solar buildings : in cool northern climates / David Oppenheim. — London : Architectural Press, 1981. — 139p : ill,maps,plans ; 21x30cm
Bibliography: p114-117. - Includes index
ISBN 0-85139-596-1 (pbk) : £12.95 B81-18232

697′.78′0722 — Western Europe. Residences. Solar energy heating systems — *Case studies*

Houghton-Evans, W.. Solar houses in Europe : how they have worked / edited by W. Palz and T.C. Steemers ; compiled and wiriten by W. Houghton-Evans, D. Turrent, C. Whittaker. — Oxford : Published for the Commission of the European Communities by Pergamon, 1981. — vii,303p : ill,maps ; 26cm. — (Pergamon international library)
ISBN 0-08-026743-2 (cased) : £17.00
ISBN 0-08-026744-0 (pbk) : £8.50 B81-15274

697′.78′094 — European Community countries. Residences. Solar energy heating systems

Jäger, F.. Solar energy applications in houses : performance and economics in Europe / by F. Jäger. — Oxford : Published for The Commission of The European Communities by Pergamon, 1981. — xi,176p : ill,maps ; 26cm
Bibliography: p173-176
ISBN 0-08-027573-7 : £14.50 : CIP rev.
B81-13770

697′.78′094 — Western Europe. Residences. Solar energy heating systems — *Conference proceedings*

Recent developments in solar collector design : conference (C25) at the Royal Institution, London, January 1981. — London (19 Albemarle St., W1X 3HA) : UK Section of the International Solar Energy Society, c1981. — 99p : ill ; 30cm
Cover title. — Includes bibliographies
ISBN 0-904963-23-3 (pbk) : Unpriced
B81-11506

697.9 — Buildings. Air conditioning & ventilation

Croome, Derek J.. Airconditioning and ventilation of buildings / Derek J. Croome and Brian M. Roberts. — 2nd ed. — Oxford : Pergamon. — (International series in heating, ventilation and refrigeration ; v.14)
Previous ed.: in 1v. 1975
Vol.1. — 1981. — xx,575p : ill,forms ; 26cm
Includes bibliographies and index
ISBN 0-08-024779-2 : £25.00 : CIP rev.
B80-00814

Pita, Edward G.. Air conditioning principles and systems : an energy approach / Edward G. Pita. — New York ; Chichester : Wiley, c1981. — xiii,467p : ill,plans,forms ; 25cm
Includes index
ISBN 0-471-04214-5 : £12.60 B81-18996

Trott, A. R.. Refrigeration and air-conditioning / A.R. Trott. — London : McGraw-Hill, c1981. — 310p : ill ; 24cm
Includes index
ISBN 0-07-084543-3 : £12.95
Primary classification 621.5′6 B81-25146

697.9′2′0287 — Buildings. Air. Infiltration. Measurement — *Conference proceedings*

AIC Conference *(1st : 1980 : Windsor)*. Air infiltration instrumentation and measuring techniques : 1st AIC Conference (held at Cumberland Lodge, Windsor Great Park, Berkshire, U.K. 6-8 October 1980) : proceedings. — Bracknell (Old Bracknell Lane, Bracknell, Berks. RG12 4AH) : Air Infiltration Centre, c1981. — xii,371p : ill,ports ; 30cm
′This report is part of the work of the IEA Energy Conservation in Buildings & Community Systems Programme′
£35.00 (pbk) B81-26275

697.9′3 — Air conditioning equipment. Design & installation — *Standards*
Unit air conditioning : including heat pumps : guide to good practice (revised) incorporating essential information for customers / [prepared by the Refrigeration and Unit Air Conditioning Group of the Heating and Ventilating Contractors′ Association and the British Refrigeration and Air Conditioning Association, in collaboration with the Chartered Institution of Building Services]. — London : Heating and Ventilating Contractors′ Association, 1980. — 19p : ill ; 30cm
Cover title. — Text on inside covers
Unpriced (pbk) B81-37085

697.9′3551 — Hospitals. Air. Contamination. Prevention. Use of protective air enclosures
White, P. A. F.. Protective air enclosures in health buildings / P.A.F. White. — London : Macmillan, 1981. — viii,182p : ill,plans ; 25cm
Includes index
ISBN 0-333-27678-7 : £15.00 B81-21789

698 — BUILDINGS. DECORATING, GLAZING, ETC

698 — Buildings. Decorating
Hurst, A. E.. Painting and decorating. — 9th ed. / A.E. Hurst and J.H. Goodier ; collaborator on paint technology sections W.M. Morgans. — London : Griffin, 1980. — xv,600p,[6]p of plates : ill(some col.) ; 24cm
Previous ed.: 1963. — Bibliography: p562-565. — Includes index
ISBN 0-85264-243-1 : £28.00 B81-19545

698 — Buildings. Decorating — *Manuals*
Painting and decorating : an information manual / Padim technical authors, A. Fulcher ... [et al.]. — 2nd ed. — London : Granada, 1981. — ix,226p : ill ; 22cm
Previous ed.: London : Crosby Lockwood Staples, 1975. — Includes index
ISBN 0-246-11613-7 (pbk) : £6.95 : CIP rev. B81-15816

698′.1 — Residences. Decorating. Painting — *Amateurs′ manuals*
Innes, Jocasta. Paint magic : the home decorator′s guide to painted finishes / Jocasta Innes. — [London] : Windward, c1981. — 239p : ill(some col.) ; 29cm
Bibliography: p239.. — Includes index
ISBN 0-7112-0201-x : £12.95 B81-17914

698′.5 — Buildings. Double glazing — *Manuals*
Specialize in making & fitting glass/plastic panelled double glazing units. — Sunderland (6 Norfolk St., Sunderland SR1 1EA) : Willowbrook Publications, c1980. — 66p : ill ; 30cm
Cover title
Unpriced (pbk) B81-23297

698′.9 — Contract carpeting — *Technical data* — *Serials*
Contract carpeting and smooth floorcoverings : the comprehensive reference book for specifiers, architects, interior designers and contractors. — 1981-. — London : Benn Publications in association with Cabinet maker & retail furnisher, 1981-. — v. : ill ; 30cm
Annual. — Continues: Contract carpeting
ISSN 0260-9479 = Contract carpeting and smooth floorcoverings : £12.00 B81-14355

698′.9 — Residences. Floor coverings. Choice & installation — *Amateurs′ manuals*
Wade, Carlson. Floor decorating / Carlson Wade. — South Brunswick [New York] : Barnes ; London : Yoseloff, c1979. — 182p,[4]p of plates : ill(some col.) ; 29cm
Includes index
ISBN 0-498-01810-5 : Unpriced B81-35325

700 — ARTS

700 — Arts
Baudelaire, Charles. Baudelaire : selected writings on art and artists / translated with an introduction by P.E. Charvet. — Cambridge : Cambridge University Press, 1981, c1972. — 460p ; 20cm
Translated from the French. — Originally published: Harmondsworth : Penguin, 1972
ISBN 0-521-28287-x (pbk) : £8.95 : CIP rev. B81-19127

Clark, Kenneth, *1903-*. Moments of vision. — London : Murray, Sept.1981. — [224]p
ISBN 0-7195-3860-2 : £9.50 : CIP entry B81-21521

700 — Arts - *Critical studies*
Temenos. — Dulverton : Watkins, Apr.1981. — [272]p
ISBN 0-7224-0188-4 (pbk) : £5.00 : CIP entry B81-07941

700 — English arts, *1603-1642*. Special subjects: Great Britain. Stuart dynasty — *Critical studies*
Parry, Graham. The culture of the Stuart Court, 1603-42. — Manchester : Manchester University Press, Apr.1981. — 1v.
ISBN 0-7190-0825-5 : £16.50 : CIP entry
Also classified at 700′.79 B81-02124

700 — European arts, *1150-1606*. Special themes: Antichrist — *Critical studies*
Emmerson, Richard Kenneth. Antichrist in the Middle Ages : a study of medieval apocalypticism, art, and literature / Richard Kenneth Emmerson. — Manchester : Manchester University Press, c1981. — x,366p,[8]p of plates : ill ; 23cm
Originally published: Seattle : University of Washington Press, 1981. — Bibliography: p312-338. — Includes index
ISBN 0-7190-0829-8 : £22.50 B81-33664

700 — European arts, *1800-1920*. Special subjects: Femmes fatales — *Critical studies*
Bade, Patrick. Femme fatale : images of evil and fascinating women / Patrick Bade. — London : Ash & Grant, 1979. — 128p : ill(some col.),ports(some col.) ; 31cm
Includes index
ISBN 0-904069-20-6 : £5.95 : CIP rev. B78-35420

700 — European arts, *ca 395-1500*. Special subjects: Non-European primitive peoples & imaginary peoples — *Critical studies*
Friedman, John Block. The monstrous races in medieval art and thought / John Block Friedman. — Cambridge [Mass.] ; London : Harvard University Press, 1981. — xiii,268p : ill,facsims ; 24cm
Includes index
ISBN 0-674-58652-2 : £14.00 B81-40034

700 — European arts, *ca 1500-1957*. Special themes: Grotesque — *Critical studies*
Kayser, Wolfgang. The grotesque : in art and literature / Wolfgang Kayser ; translated by Ulrich Weisstein. — New York ; Guildford : Columbia University Press, 1981, c1963. — 224p,[27]p of plates : ill ; 21cm
Translation of: Das Groteske. — Originally published: Bloomington : University of Indiana Press, 1963. — Includes index
ISBN 0-231-05336-3 (cased) : £16.25
ISBN 0-231-05337-1 (pbk) : £5.75 B81-39719

700 — French arts, *1789-1880*. Special subjects: France. Republicanism — *Critical studies*
Agulhon, Maurice. Marianne into battle : Republican imagery and symbolism in France 1789-1880 / Maurice Agulhon ; translated by Janet Lloyd. — Cambridge : Cambridge University Press, 1981. — viii,235p : ill,ports ; 24cm
Translation of: Marianne au combat. — Bibliography: p228-235
ISBN 0-521-23577-4 (cased) : £18.50 : CIP rev.
ISBN 0-521-28224-1 (pbk) : £6.95 B81-08947

700 — Visual arts
Fry, Roger. Vision and design / Roger Fry ; edited by J.B. Bullen. — London : Oxford University Press, 1981. — xxv,243p,[8]p of plates : ill,2ports ; 20cm. — (Oxford paperbacks)
Originally published: London : Chatto & Windus, 1920. — Bibliography: p237. — Includes index
ISBN 0-19-281317-x (pbk) : £4.50 : CIP rev. B81-10491

700′.1 — Arts. Aesthetics
Margolis, Joseph. Art and philosophy / by Joseph Margolis. — Brighton : Harvester, 1980. — vi,350p ; 24cm
Originally published: Nyborg, Denmark : F. Lokkes ; Atlantic Highlands, N.J. : Humanities Press, 1976. — Bibliography: p307-333. — Includes index
ISBN 0-85527-837-4 : £24.00 : CIP rev. B80-10162

700′.1 — Arts. Appreciation
Sporre, Dennis J.. Perceiving the arts : an introduction to the humanities / Dennis J. Sporre. — Englewood Cliffs ; London : Prentice-Hall, c1981. — ix,214p : ill,music,plans ; 24cm
Originally published: Dubuque : Kendall-Hunt, 1978. — Includes index
ISBN 0-13-657031-3 (pbk) : £6.95 B81-33129

700′.1 — Arts. Criticism
Radford, Colin. The nature of criticism / Colin Radford and Sally Minogue. — Brighton : Harvester, 1981. — x,180p ; 23cm
Includes index
ISBN 0-7108-0082-7 : £18.95 : CIP rev. B81-03167

700′.1 — Arts. Realism — *Marxist viewpoints*
Lovell, Terry. Pictures of reality : aesthetics, politics, pleasure / Terry Lovell. — London : BFI, 1980. — 111p ; 22cm
Bibliography: p100-111
ISBN 0-85170-102-7 (cased) : £5.90
ISBN 0-85170-103-5 (pbk) : £2.95 B81-07126

700′.1 — Arts. Theories
Taylor, Roger, *1940-*. Beyond art : what art is and might become if freed from cultural elitism / Roger Taylor. — Brighton : Harvester, 1981. — 183p ; 23cm
Includes index
£16.95 B81-19516

700′.1′08 — Western arts. Influence of Christianity
Robertson, Alec. Contrasts : the arts and religion / Alec Robertson. — Rev. ed. — Worcester : Stanbrook Abbey Press, 1980. — xvii,166p : col.ill ; 20cm
Previous ed.: London : S.C.M. Press, 1947. — Limited ed. of 350 copies. - In slip case. — Includes index
Unpriced B81-18780

700′.1′9 — Arts. Aesthetics. Psychological aspects
Advances in intrinsic motivation and aesthetics / edited by Hy I. Day. — New York ; London : Plenum, c1981. — xii,503p : ill ; 24cm
Includes bibliographies and index
ISBN 0-306-40606-3 : Unpriced
Primary classification 153.8 B81-32645

Psychology and the arts. — Brighton : Harvester Press, Oct.1981. — [336]p
ISBN 0-85527-958-3 : CIP entry B81-30335

700′.1′9 — Arts. Perception
Caws, Mary Ann. The eye in the text : essays on perception, mannerist to modern / Mary Ann Caws. — Princeton ; Guildford : Princeton University Press, c1981. — 204p,[32]p of plates : ill,facsims ; 25cm
Includes index
ISBN 0-691-06453-9 (cased) : £14.20
ISBN 0-691-01377-2 (pbk) : £5.00 B81-40886

700′.25′41 — Great Britain. Arts centres — *Directories* — *Serials*
Directory of arts centres. — 2-. — Eastbourne : J. Offord Publications in association with the Arts Council of Great Britain, 1981-. — v. : ill ; 21cm
Annual. — Continues: A Directory of arts centres in England, Scotland and Wales
ISSN 0144-7459 = Directory of arts centres : £6.50 B81-38186

700′.5 — Arts — *Critical studies* — *Serials*
Temenos. — 2. — Dulverton : Watkins, Jan.1982. — [284]p
ISBN 0-7224-0197-3 (pbk) : £5.00 : CIP entry B81-39236

700′.5 — Arts — *Serials*

CTO : call to order. — 1st issue -. — Southampton (149 Kathleen Rd, Sholing, Southampton, Hampshire SO2 8LP) : [s.n.], c1980-. — v. : ill ; 30cm
Irregular
ISSN 0260-5821 = CTO. Call to order : £0.50 per issue B81-12738

Moz-art : Birmingham's quarterly arts magazine. — No.1 (July-Sept.)-. — Birmingham (73 Birchwood Cres., Birmingham 12) : [s.n.], [1980]-. — v. : ill ; 27cm
Description based on: No.2 (Oct.-Jan.)
ISSN 0261-1341 = Moz-art : £0.20 per issue B81-15070

Slade magazine : murals — poems, drawings, photography, other articles —. — [No.1]. — London (University College London, Gower St., WC1) : Slade School of Art, [1977]-. — v. : ill ; 30cm
Annual. — Description based on: [No.3]
ISSN 0144-6428 = Slade magazine : Free B81-03590

ZG. — No.1 (80)-. — London (23 Montrell Rd, SW2) : Gallery Press, [1980]-. — v. : ill,ports ; 30cm
Irregular
£0.65 B81-25491

700′.6′042574 — Oxfordshire. Oxford. Arts. Organisations: Oxford Area Arts Council — *Serials*

[Newsletter *(Oxford Area Arts Council)*]. Newsletter / Oxford Area Arts Council. — [1976?]-. — Oxford (Old Fire Station Arts Centre) : The Council, [1976?]-. — v. : ill,plans ; 30cm
Two issues yearly. — Continued by: Tuition, entertainment, news, views
£0.10 B81-08769

Tuition, entertainment, news, views / Oxford Area Arts Council. — Autumn 1980-. — Oxford (40 George St., Oxford OX1 2AQ) : The Council, 1980-. — v. : ill ; 21cm
Three issues yearly. — Continues: Newsletter (Oxford Area Arts Council)
ISSN 0260-8383 = Tuition, entertainment, news, views : £10.00 B81-08768

700′.7′0429 — Wales. Education. Curriculum subjects: Arts

Webster, Roger. Y celfyddydau ac addysg yng Nghymru = The arts and education in Wales / Roger Webster. — [Bangor, Gwynedd] ([10 Wellfield House, Bangor, Gwynedd]) : Cymdeithas Gelfyddydau Gogledd Cymru, 1979. — [16]p ; 22cm. — (Darlith Ben Bowen Thomas = Ben Bowen Thomas lecture ; 1978)
Parallel Welsh and English text
ISBN 0-901833-89-4 (pbk) : Unpriced B81-04030

700′.7′1073 — United States. Educational institutions. Curriculum subjects: Arts — *Proposals*

Arts and the schools / Jerome J. Hausman, editor ; assisted by Joyce Wright ... [et al.]. — New York ; London : McGraw-Hill, c1980. — xvii,332p : ill ; 24cm. — ([A study of schooling in the United States])
Bibliography: p291-323. — Includes index
ISBN 0-07-027225-5 : £8.95 B81-01027

700′.7′15 — Great Britain. Adult education. Organisations: Workers' Educational Association. Curriculum subjects: Arts — *Serials*

WEA arts newsletter : the arts and working people. — No.1 (Spring 1981)-. — London : Workers' Educational Association, 1981-. — v. : ill ; 26cm
ISSN 0261-5754 = WEA arts newsletter : £0.30 per issue B81-33240

700′.79 — Commonwealth countries. Arts councils. Role — *Conference proceedings*

The **Arts** Council phenomenon : a conference report. — [London] ([98 Portland Place, W1N 4ET]) : [Calouste Gulbenkian Foundation United Kingdom and Commonwealth Branch], [1981]. — 64p ; 30cm
Cover title
£1.50 (pbk) B81-22382

700′.79 — English arts. Patronage by Stuart dynasty, *1603-1642*

Parry, Graham. The culture of the Stuart Court, 1603-42. — Manchester : Manchester University Press, Apr.1981. — 1v.
ISBN 0-7190-0825-5 : £16.50 : CIP entry
Primary classification 700 B81-02124

700′.79 — Great Britain. Arts. Patronage. Organisations: Arts Council of Great Britain — *Serials*

Arts Council of Great Britain. Annual report and accounts : progress and renewal / Arts Council of Great Britain. — 35th (1979/80). — London : The Council, [1980]. — 139p
ISSN 0066-8133 : £1.20 B81-00191

700′.79 — Ireland *(Republic)*. Arts. Patronage. Organisation: Arts Council *(Ireland)* — *Serials*

Arts Council *(Ireland)*. Annual report / the Arts Council. — 1978. — [Dublin] ([70, Merrion Sq., Dublin 2]) : The Council, [1980]. — 47p
Unpriced B81-06730

700′.7′9429 — Wales. Eisteddfodau: Eisteddfod Genedlaethol Frenhinol Cymru, *1858-1868* — *Welsh texts*

Edwards, Hywel Teifi. Gŵyl Gwalia : yr Eisteddfod Genedlaethol yn oes aur Victoria 1858-1868 / Hywel Teifi Edwards. — Llandysul : Gwasg Gomer, 1980. — xi,453p,[27]p of plates : ill,1facsim,ports ; 22cm
ISBN 0-85088-593-0 : £9.50 B81-01946

700′.9 — Arts, *to 1970* — *Chronologies*

Paxton, John. Calendar of creative man / John Paxton and Sheila Fairfield ; with a foreword by Dame Veronica Wedgwood. — London : Macmillan, 1980, c1979. — xxviii,497p,[16]p of plates : ill(some col.),ports(some col.) ; 29cm
ISBN 0-333-18157-3 : £17.50 : CIP rev. B79-23371

700′.9 — Arts, *to 1979*

Kingston, Jeremy. Arts and artists / Jeremy Kingston. — London : Aldus, 1980. — 336p : ill(some col.),music,ports(some col.) ; 30cm
Ill. on lining papers. — Includes index
ISBN 0-490-00460-1 : £10.95 B81-08381

700′.9′034 — Romanticism

Morse, David, *19---*. Perspectives on romanticism : a transformational analysis / David Morse. — London : Macmillan, 1981. — xiii,310p ; 23cm
Includes index
ISBN 0-333-28296-5 : £15.00 B81-40575

700′.92′2 — Artists, *1752-1977* — *Biographies*

Matson, Katinka. Short lives : portraits of writers, painters, poets, actors, musicians and performers in pursuit of death / Katinka Matson. — London : Pan, 1981, c1980. — xiii,362p : ill,ports ; 20cm. — (Picador)
Originally published: New York : Morrow, 1980. — Includes bibliographies
ISBN 0-330-26219-x (pbk) : £2.50 B81-09895

700′.92′2 — English arts. Bloomsbury Group, *to 1920* — *Biographies*

Edel, Leon. Bloomsbury : a house of lions / Leon Edel. — Harmondsworth : Penguin, 1981, c1979. — 288p ; 20cm
Originally published: London : Hogarth Press, 1979. — Bibliography: p275-278. — Includes index
ISBN 0-14-005624-6 (pbk) : £2.50 B81-37417

700′.92′4 — American arts. Warhol, Andy, *1960-1969* — *Biographies*

Warhol, Andy. Popism : the Warhol ′60s / Andy Warhol and Pat Hackett. — London : Hutchinson, 1981, c1980. — 310p,[16]p of plates : ill,2facsims,ports ; 24cm
Originally published: New York : Harcourt Brace Jovanovich, 1980. — Includes index
ISBN 0-09-144580-9 : £7.95 B81-06014

700′.94 — European arts, *1800-1900* — *Critical studies*

Peckham, Morse. Beyond the tragic vision : the quest for identity in the nineteenth century / by Morse Peckham. — Cambridge : Cambridge University Press, 1981, c1962. — 380p ; 23cm
Originally published: New York : Braziller, 1962. — Includes index
ISBN 0-521-28153-9 (pbk) : £6.25 : CIP rev. B81-07431

700′.94 — European arts. Dadaism — *Critical studies*

New studies in Dada : essays and documents / edited by Richard Sheppard. — Driffield (16 Howl La., Hutton, Driffield YO25 9QA) : Hutton Press, 1981. — 196p : facsims ; 23cm
English, French and German text. — Bibliography: p188 — Includes index
ISBN 0-907033-05-9 : Unpriced B81-37606

700′.941 — Great Britain. Arts — *Critical studies — Serials*

Beyond the white gates. — 1. — London (7 Arkwright Rd, NW3) : Mat Coward, 1980-. — v. : ill,ports ; 30cm
Irregular
£0.40 B81-27924

700′.942 — English arts. Influence of biblical typology, *1837-1900*

Landow, George P.. Victorian types, Victorian shadows : Biblical typology in Victorian literature, art and thought / George P. Landow. — Boston [Mass.] ; London : Routledge & Kegan Paul, 1980. — xiii,266p,8p of plates : ill ; 22cm
Includes index
ISBN 0-7100-0598-9 : £13.50 : CIP rev. B80-35273

700′.942 — English arts. Political aspects — *Conference proceedings*

Art & Politics : proceedings of a conference on art and politics held on 15th and 16th April, 1977 / edited by Brandon Taylor. — Winchester (Park Ave., Winchester SO23 8DL) : Winchester School of Arts Press, 1980. — 120p : ill,1port ; 23cm
ISBN 0-9506783-1-7 (pbk) : Unpriced B81-01028

700′.9421 — London. Arts, *1939-1945*

Hewison, Robert. Under siege : literary life in London 1939-1945 / Robert Hewison. — London : Quartet, 1979, c1977. — x,219p,[8]p of plates : ill,ports ; 20cm
Originally published: London : Weidenfeld and Nicolson, 1977. — Includes index
ISBN 0-7043-3283-3 (pbk) : £2.95 B81-23106

700′.9424 — England. West Midlands. Arts — *Serials*

Arts report. — No.1 (Apr.1981)-. — [Birmingham] ([Arts Shop, City Arcade, Birmingham B2 4TX]) : West Midlands Arts, 1981-. — v. : ill,ports ; 41cm
Monthly. — Continues: News sheet (West Midlands Arts)
ISSN 0260-8723 = Arts report : Unpriced B81-38515

700′.9429 — Wales. Arts

Cledwyn of Penrhos, Cledwyn Hughes, *Baron*. Celfydydd a′r Cymro cyffredin = Art and the average Welshman / Yr Arglwydd/Lord Cledwyn o Benrhos. — [Bangor, Gwynedd] ([10 Wellfield House, Bangor, Gwynedd]) : Cymdeithas Gelfyddydau Gogledd Cymru, 1980. — [16]p ; 22cm. — (Darlith Ben Bowen Thomas = Ben Bowen Thomas lecture ; 1979)
Parallel Welsh and English text
ISBN 0-901833-96-7 (pbk) : Unpriced B81-03909

700′.947′0740153 — Washington, D.C.. Museums: Hirshhorn Museum and Sculpture Garden. Exhibits: Russian avant garde arts, *1910-1930* — *Catalogues*

The **Avant-garde** in Russia, 1910-1930 : new perspectives / organized and edited by Stephanie Barron adn Maurice Tuchman. — Los Angeles : Los Angeles County Museum of Art ; Cambridge, Mass. ; London : Distributed by MIT, c1980. — 288p : ill,facsims,ports ; 29cm
Published to accompany an exhibition at the Los Angeles County Museum of Art and the Hirshhorn Museum and Sculpture Garden, Smithsonian Institution, Washington, D.C., 1980-1981. — Bibliography: p286
ISBN 0-262-20040-6 : £9.30
Primary classification 700′.947′074019494 B81-09645

700'.947'074019494 — California. Los Angeles. Museums: Los Angeles County Museum of Art. Exhibits: Russian avant garde arts, *1910-1930* — *Catalogues*

The **Avant-garde** in Russia, 1910-1930 : new perspectives / organized and edited by Stephanie Barron adn Maurice Tuchman. — Los Angeles : Los Angeles County Museum of Art ; Cambridge, Mass. ; London : Distributed by MIT, c1980. — 288p : ill,facsims,ports ; 29cm
Published to accompany an exhibition at the Los Angeles County Museum of Art and the Hirshhorn Museum and Sculpture Garden, Smithsonian Institution, Washington, D.C., 1980-1981. — Bibliography: p286
ISBN 0-262-20040-6 : £9.30
Also classified at 700'.947'0740153 B81-09645

700'.952 — Japanese arts. Aesthetics

Izutsu, Toshihiko. The theory of beauty in the classical aesthetics of Japan / by Toshihiko and Toyo Izutsu. — The Hague ; London : Nijhoff, 1981. — x,167p ; 25cm. — (Philosophy and world community)
At head of title: International Institute of Philosophy
ISBN 90-247-2381-7 : Unpriced B81-17128

700'.96 — African arts. Social aspects

Brain, Robert. Art and society in Africa / Robert Brain. — London : Longman, 1980. — 304p : ill ; 22cm
Bibliography: p285-290. — Includes index
ISBN 0-582-64578-6 (cased) : Unpriced
ISBN 0-582-64579-4 (pbk) : £7.95 B81-26139

701 — VISUAL ARTS. PHILOSOPHY AND THEORY

701'.03 — Visual arts. Social aspects

Cork, Richard. The social role of art : essays in criticism for a newspaper public / Richard Cork. — London : Fraser, 1979. — 104p ; 23cm
ISBN 0-86092-042-9 : £6.95 : CIP rev. B79-30211

Wilson, Frank Avray. Art as revelation : the role of art in human existence / Frank Avray Wilson. — Fontwell : Centaur, 1981. — 294p : ill ; 21cm
Includes index
ISBN 0-900000-96-1 : £8.75 : CIP rev. B81-27399

701'.1'7 — Visual arts. Aesthetics

Anand, Mulk Raj. Seven little-known birds of the inner eye / Mulk Raj Anand. — Rutland, Vt : Tuttle, 1978 ; London : Prentice-Hall [distributor]. — 157p,[1]leaf of plates : ill ; 23cm
Bibliography: p151-152. — Includes index
ISBN 0-8048-0936-4 : £10.55 B81-25170

702 — VISUAL ARTS. MISCELLANY

702'.3'41 — Great Britain. Visual arts — *Career guides*

Ball, Linda, *1950-*. Careers in art and design / Linda Ball. — London : Kogan Page, 1981. — 160p ; 19cm
ISBN 0-85038-349-8 (corrected : cased) : Unpriced
ISBN 0-85038-384-4
ISBN 0-85038-352-8 (pbk) : £2.95 B81-18565

702'.8 — Visual arts. Materials & techniques — *Manuals*

The **Artist's** manual : equipment, materials, techniques / consultant editors Stan Smith, H.F. Ten Holt ; foreword by Paul Hogarth. — London : Macdonald, 1980. — 320p : ill(some col.),facsims ; 26cm
Includes index
ISBN 0-356-06799-8 : £9.95 B81-05074

702'.8 — Visual arts. Techniques — *Manuals*

Sparkes, Roy. A handbook of art techniques / Roy Sparkes. — London : Batsford Academic and Educational, 1981. — 96p,16p of plates : ill ; 23cm
Bibliography: p93-96
ISBN 0-7134-3386-8 : £4.95 B81-24324

Step-by-step artist's techniques / edited by Victoria Funk. — Oxford : Phaidon, 1980. — 126p : ill(some col.) ; 18x23cm. — (A QED book)
Includes index
ISBN 0-7148-2121-7 : £3.95 B81-03456

702'.8'12 — Collages. Techniques — *Manuals*

Allen, Janet, *1937-*. The Observer book of collage : in association with Copydex / Janet Allen. — London (31 Foubert's Place W1V 1HE) : Bergstrom & Boyle Books Ltd., c1980. — 79p : ill(some col.) ; 21cm
ISBN 0-903767-35-x (cased) : £5.95 B81-06437

Vanderbilt, Gloria, *1924-*. Gloria Vanderbilt book of collage / Gloria Vanderbilt with Alfred Allan Lewis. — New York ; London : Van Nostrand Reinhold, c1981. — 111p : ill ; 28cm
Includes index
ISBN 0-442-25403-2 (pbk) : £8.15 B81-35253

704 — VISUAL ARTS. SPECIAL ASPECTS

704'.03969883'074013 — United States. Art galleries. Exhibits: Surinam Maroon visual arts — *Catalogues*

Price, Sally. Afro-American arts of the Suriname rain forest / Sally and Richard Price. — Berkeley ; London : University of California Press, c1980. — 237p : ill(some col.),col.maps,ports ; 28cm
To accompany an exhibition held at the Frederick S. Wright Gallery UCLA and at various other locations. — Bibliography: p225-228. — Includes index
ISBN 0-520-04412-6 (pbk) : £9.75 B81-27264

704.9'42 — British portraits. Special subjects: Keats, John, *1795-1821* & persons associated with Keats, John, *1795-1821* — *Illustrations*

Richardson, Joanna. Keats and his circle : an album of portraits / collected and presented by Joanna Richardson. — London : Cassell, 1980. — vi,127p : ill,chiefly ports ; 26cm
Includes index
ISBN 0-304-30711-4 : £8.95 B81-10301

704.9'42'07402132 — Great Britain. *National Portrait Gallery*. Exhibits: Portraits, *ca 1220-ca 1960* — *Illustrations*

Great Britain. *National Portrait Gallery*. National Portrait Gallery in colour / edited by Richard Ormond ; with an introduction by John Hayes. — London : Studio Vista in association with the Gallery, 1979. — 128p : ill,chiefly ports(some col.) ; 31cm
Includes index
ISBN 0-289-70872-9 (cased) : £6.95
ISBN 0-289-70879-6 (pbk) : £4995 B81-01746

704.9'421'094 — European visual arts, *1850-1910*. Special subjects: Nudes — *Sociological perspectives*

Pearsall, Ronald. Tell me, pretty maiden : the Victorian and Edwardian nude / Ronald Pearsall. — Exeter : Webb & Bower, 1981. — 176p : ill(some col.) ; 26cm
Includes index
ISBN 0-906671-24-8 : £8.95 B81-24563

704.9'423 — London. Camden *(London Borough)*. Museums: British Museum. Exhibits: Ancient Roman portraits. Special subjects: Augustus, *Emperor of Rome — Catalogues*

Walker, Susan. Augustus : handlist of the exhibition and supplementary studies / Susan Walker and Andrew Burnett. — London : British Museum, 1981. — vii,64p : ill ; 30cm. — (Occasional paper / British Museum, ISSN 0142-4815 ; no.16)
Bibliography: pv-vi
ISBN 0-86159-015-5 (pbk) : Unpriced B81-22906

704.9'424 — Visual arts. Special subjects: Mona Lisa — *Illustrations*

Mona Lisas / compiled by Mary Rose Storey ; introduction by David Bourdon. — London : Constable, 1980. — 96p : ill(some col.) ; 23cm
Includes index
ISBN 0-09-463890-x (pbk) : £3.50 B81-05870

704.9'424 — Women. Beauty *expounded by* **Western visual arts,** *ca 1970*

Feminine beauty / [compiled by] Kenneth Clark. — London : Weidenfeld & Nicolson, 1980. — 199p : chiefly ill(some col.),ports(some col.) ; 29cm
Includes index
ISBN 0-297-77677-0 : £10.00 B81-06567

704.9'432'09 — Visual arts, *to ca 1950*. **Special subjects: Animals —** *Critical studies — Irish texts*

An tAinmhí : Ó Lascaux go Picasso. — Baile Átha Cliath [i.e. Dublin] : Oifig in tSoláthair, c1980. — [34]p : col.ill ; 30cm
At head of title: Músaem Náisiúnta na Staire Aiceanta (Páras). — Ill on lining papers
£1.10 B81-23651

704.9'434'07402527 — Nottinghamshire. Nottingham. Museums: Nottinghamshire Castle Museum. Exhibits: Visual arts. Special subjects: Plants — *Catalogues*

Garden of Flora : nature and the artist, past, present and future : an exhibition / created by Dorothie Field as a homage to Carolus Von Linnaeus. — Nottingham ([Castle Gate] Nottingham [NG1 6EL]) : Castle Museum & Art Gallery, 1981. — [16]p : 1facsim ; 15x21cm
Unpriced (pbk) B81-38650

704.9'48'0904 — Religious visual arts, *1900-1980* — *Illustrations*

Lealman, Brenda. The image of life / Brenda Lealman and Edward Robinson. — [Oxford] ([Religious Experience Research Unit, Manchester College, Oxford]) : Christian Education Movement, c1980. — 60p : ill ; 21cm. — (Exploration into experience)
ISBN 0-905022-61-0 (pbk) : £1.50 B81-01970

704.9'482 — Christian funerary visual arts. Influence of pagan imagery, *200-400*

Murray, *Sister* **Charles**, *1939-*. Rebirth and afterlife : a study of the transmutation of some pagan imagery in early Christian funerary art / Sister Charles Murray. — Oxford : B.A.R., 1981. — 183p,39p of plates : ill ; 30cm
ISBN 0-86054-118-5 (corrected : pbk) : £10.00 B81-38680

704.9'482 — Icons, *to 700*

Grabar, André. Christian iconography : a study of its origins / André Grabar. — London : Routledge & Kegan Paul, 1969, c1968 (1980 [printing). — l,174p,[202]p of plates : ill,ports ; 26cm. — (The A.W. Mellon lectures in the fine arts)
Originally published: Princeton : Princeton University Press, 1968. — Bibliography: p149-158. — Includes index
ISBN 0-7100-0605-5 (pbk) : £7.50 B81-23079

704.9'491235'0938 — Ancient Greek visual arts. Special themes: Freedom — *Critical studies*

Haynes, D. E. L.. Greek art and the idea of freedom / Denys Haynes. — London : Thames and Hudson, c1981. — 108p : ill ; 22cm. — (The 1977 Brown & Haley lectures)
Bibliography: p104-105. - Includes index
ISBN 0-500-23331-4 : £6.95 B81-09848

704.9'49338 — West Yorkshire *(Metropolitan County)*. Bradford. Art galleries: Bradford Art Galleries and Museums. Exhibits: English visual arts. Special subjects: Industries — *Catalogues*

Six artists in industry. — [Bradford] : [Bradford Art Galleries and Museums], [1981]. — [40]p : ill,ports ; 32cm
Published to accompany an exhibition held at Bradford, 1981
Unpriced (pbk) B81-37154

704.9′497928 — Norfolk. Norwich. Art galleries: Sainsbury Centre for Visual Arts. Exhibits: Visual arts associated with Ballets Russes in England — *Catalogues*

The **Diaghilev** Ballet in England / an exhibition organized by David Chadd and John Gage ; Sainsbury Centre for Visual Arts, University of East Anglia, Norwich, 11 October-20 November 1979, The Fine Art Society, New Bond Street, London, 3 December 1979-11 January 1980. — [Norwich] ([University of East Anglia, Norwich NR4 7TJ]) : [The Centre], [1979]. — 64p,xvip of plates : ill(some col.),music ; 21cm
At head of title: 45th Norfolk and Norwich Triennial Festival of Music and the Arts, October 1979. — Bibliography: p63-64
Unpriced (pbk) B81-39491

704.9′499047 — Visual arts, *to 1980.* **Special subjects: Wars** — *Critical studies*

Keegan, John. The nature of war / John Keegan & Joseph Darracott. — London : Cape, 1981. — xi,276p : ill(some col.),ports ; 32cm. — (A Jonathan-James book)
ISBN 0-224-01926-0 : £15.00 B81-18461

706 — VISUAL ARTS. ORGANISATIONS AND MANAGEMENT

706 — Visual arts. Organisations — *Directories* — *Serials*

International directory of arts. Volume I. Museums, universities, associations, restorers, names. — 15 ed. (1981/82). — Frankfurt : Art Adres-Verlag Müller ; London : George Prior [distributor], [1980]. — 802p
ISBN 3-921529-02-6 : Unpriced B81-21930

International directory of arts. Volume II. Antique dealers, numismatics, art galleries, auctioneers, publishers, periodicals, booksellers, artists, collectors. — 15 ed. (1981/82). — Frankfurt : Art Adres-Verlag Müller ; London : George Prior [distributor], [1980]. — 948p
ISBN 3-921529-02-6 : Unpriced B81-27127

706′.042527 — Nottingham. Visual arts. Organisations: Nottingham Society of Artists, *to 1979*

Nottingham Society of Artists. For the very joy of art : the first hundred years of the Nottingham Society of Artists / by Marjorie Macmillan. — [Nottingham] ([12 Nicker Hill, Normanton-on-the-Wolds, Nottingham NG12 5GD]) : The Society, 1980. — 108p : ill,facsims,ports ; 22cm
Ill on lining papers. — Includes index
£3.00 B81-07229

707 — VISUAL ARTS. STUDY AND TEACHING

707′.041 — Great Britain. Art studios

The **Artists** studio handbook / edited by Liz Lydiate. — Sunderland : Artic Producers, c1981. — 31p : ill,2ports ; 30cm
Includes index
ISBN 0-907730-00-0 (pbk) : £2.00 B81-40278

707′.1 — Schools. Curriculum subjects: Visual arts. Projects

Schuman, Jo Miles. Art from many hands : multicultural art projects for home and school / Jo Miles Schuman. — Englewood Cliffs : Prentice-Hall, c1981. — 251p,[16]p of plates : ill ; 24cm. — (A Spectrum book)
Bibliography: p238-251. — Includes index
ISBN 0-13-047217-4 (cased) : Unprice
ISBN 0-13-047209-3 (pbk) : £7.10 B81-22706

707′.11422 — London & Home Counties. Further education institutions. Curriculum subjects: Visual arts. Courses — *Directories* — *Serials*

Art & design education in the region / London and Home Counties Regional Advisory Council for Technological Education. — 1981/83. — [London] : [The Council], [1980]. — 21p
ISBN 0-85394-081-9 : £0.50 B81-15146

707′.11425895 — Hertfordshire. Bushey. Art schools: Herkomer Art School, *1901-1918*

Longman, Grant. The Herkomer Art School and subsequent developments 1901-1918 / [Grant Longman]. — Bushey (48 Duncan Way, Bushey, Herts.) : E.G. Longman, 1981. — 16p : ill,1plan,ports ; 30cm. — (Bushey reference paper ; no.2)
£1.80 (pbk) B81-20365

707′.1142753 — Merseyside *(Metropolitan County).* **Liverpool. Art galleries: Walker Art Gallery. Exhibits: Items associated with City of Liverpool School of Architecture and Applied Art** — *Catalogues*

The **Art** sheds 1894-1905 : an exhibition to celebrate the centenary of the University of Liverpool 1981 / Walker Art Gallery, Liverpool. — [Liverpool] ([Municipal Buildings, Dale St., Liverpool L69 2DH]) : Merseyside County Council, [1981]. — [72]p : ill,ports ; 24cm
Exhibition catalogue
ISBN 0-901534-73-0 (pbk) : Unpriced
B81-23616

707′.124264 — Suffolk. Schools. Students, 8-14 years. Curriculum subjects: Visual arts. Teaching

Art in the middle years of schooling 8-14. — [Ipswich] ([Grimwade St., Ipswich IP4 1LJ]) : Suffolk County Council Education Committee, [1981?]. — 92p : ill ; 30cm
Cover title. — Bibliography: p89-92
ISBN 0-86055-071-0 (pbk) : Unpriced
B81-24421

707′.2 — Visual arts. Historiology

Pointon, Marcia. History of art : a student′s handbook / Marcia Pointon. — London : Allen & Unwin, 1980. — x,83p : ill ; 21cm
Includes index
ISBN 0-04-701010-x (cased) : £7.95 : CIP rev.
ISBN 0-04-701011-8 (pbk) : £3.50 B80-19328

707′.4′02132 — London. Westminster *(London Borough).* **Restaurants: Restaurant Boulestin. Exhibits: Visual arts. Visual artists associated with Restaurant Boulestin** — *Catalogues*

Hooker, Denise. A salute to Marcel Boulestin and Jean-Emile Laboureur : an exhibition of artists associated with the Restaurant Boulestin at the Restaurant Boulestin, 25 Southampton Street, London WC2, May 20-June 5, at the Parkin Gallery, 11 Motcomb Street, London SW1, June 10-July 3. — London (11 Motcomb St., S.W.1) : Michael Parkin Fine Art, 1981. — 40p,[12]p of plates : ill(some col.),ports ; 25cm
Text by Denise Hooker
Unpriced (pbk) B81-31495

707′.5′0924 — Europe. Art objects. Plunder by Hitler, Adolf, *1938-1945*

De Jaeger, Charles. The Linz file. — Exeter : Webb and Bower, Aug. 1981. — [224]p
ISBN 0-906671-30-2 : £8.95 : CIP entry
B81-19202

708 — VISUAL ARTS. GALLERIES, MUSEUMS, PRIVATE COLLECTIONS

708′.0025′41 — Great Britain. Art galleries - *Directories - Serials*

Libraries, museums and art galleries year book. — 1978-1979. — Cambridge : James Clarke, May 1981. — [272]p
ISBN 0-227-67835-4 : £23.00 : CIP entry
ISSN 0075-899x
Primary classification 027′.0025′41 B81-14963

708.147′1′09 — New York *(City).* **Art galleries: Metropolitan Museum of Art,** *to 1980*

Hibbard, Howard. The Metropolitan Museum of Art New York / Howard Hibbard. — London : Faber, 1980. — 592p : ill(some col.),maps,facsims(some col.),ports(some col.) ; 28cm
Bibliography: p598. - Includes index
ISBN 0-571-11623-x : £25.00 : CIP rev.
B80-18862

708.2 — Great Britain. Elizabeth II, *Queen of Great Britain.* **Private collections: Visual arts** — *Critical studies*

Plumb, J. H.. Royal heritage : the reign of Elizabeth II. — London : British Broadcasting Corporation, 1981. — 184p : ill(some col.),ports(some col.) ; 26cm
″Published in association with the television series written by Huw Wheldon and J.H. Plumb″. — Includes index
ISBN 0-563-17862-0 : £10.50 B81-17946

708.2 — Great Britain. Royal families, *973-1976.* **Private collections: Visual arts** — *Critical studies*

Plumb, J. H.. Royal heritage : the story of Britain′s royal builders and collectors / by J.H. Plumb ; published in association with the television series written by Huw Wheldon and J.H. Plumb. — London : British Broadcasting Corporation, 1977 (1981 [printing]). — 360p : ill(some col.),facsims,ports(some col.) ; 30cm
Includes index
ISBN 0-563-17974-0 (pbk) : £8.50
Primary classification 941′.009′92 B81-27707

708.2′132 — London. Westminster *(London Borough).* **Art galleries: P. and D. Colnaghi and Co.. Exhibits: Art objects** — *Catalogues*

Objects for a Wunderkammer : 10 June to 31 July 1981 / selected and edited by Alvar González-Palacios ; assisted by Luigi D′Urso. — London (14 Old Bond St., W1) : P & D Colnaghi, [1981]. — xx,331p : ill(some col.) ; 26cm
Published to accompany an exhibition at P. & D. Colnaghi, 1981. — Bibliography: p20
Unpriced (pbk) B81-29195

708.2′132 — London. Westminster *(London Borough).* **Government buildings: Palace of Westminster. House of Lords. Stock: Visual arts** — *Catalogues*

Great Britain. *Parliament. House of Lords.* Works of art in the House of Lords / edited by Maurice Bond. — London : HMSO, 1980. — 108p : ill(some col.),1coat of arms,facsims,1plan,ports(some col.) ; 20x22cm
Ill on inside covers. — Includes index
ISBN 0-11-700897-4 (pbk) : £3.95 B81-05019

708.2′132′005 — London. Westminster *(London Borough).* **Art galleries: Royal Academy** — *Serials*

Royal Academy. Royal Academy (year book). — 1981. — Henley-on-Thames : A. Ellis, Oct.1981. — [192]p
ISBN 0-85628-108-5 : £10.00 : CIP entry
B81-28046

708.2′132′0922 — London. Westminster *(London Borough).* **Art galleries: Wallace Collection. Founders** — *Biographies*

Hughes, Peter, *1941-*. The founders of the Wallace collection / by Peter Hughes. — London (Manchester Sq., W1M 6BN) : Trustees of the Wallace Collection, 1981. — 60p,ivp of plates : ill(some col.),facsims,ports (some col.) ; 18cm
Bibliography: p60
Unpriced (pbk) B81-21744

708.2′132′0924 — London. Westminster *(London Borough).* **Art galleries: Royal Academy of Arts. Casson,** *Sir* **Hugh** — *Correspondence, diaries, etc.*

Casson, *Sir* **Hugh.** Diary / Hugh Casson. — London : Macmillan, 1981. — 174p : ill(some col.) ; 25cm
ISBN 0-333-31112-4 : £8.75 B81-24031

708.2′134 — London. Kensington and Chelsea *(London Borough).* **Museums: Victoria and Albert Museum,** *1974-1978*

Victoria and Albert Museum. Review of the years 1974-1978 / Victoria & Albert Museum ; [edited by A.P. Burton]. — London : H.M.S.O., 1981. — 180p,[8]p of plates : ill,1port ; 25cm
Bibliography: p143-168
ISBN 0-11-290359-2 (pbk) : £6.75 B81-38961

708.2′753 — Merseyside *(Metropolitan County).* **Liverpool. Art galleries: University of Liverpool.** *Art Gallery.* **Stock** — *Catalogues*

University of Liverpool. *Art Gallery.* An introduction to the art collections of the University of Liverpool. — Liverpool (3 Abercromby Square, Liverpool, L69 3BX) : Art Gallery, 1981. — 15p ; 30cm + 1handlist (19p; 30cm)
Cover title
Unpriced (pbk) B81-26884

708.2′911′025 — Scotland. Art galleries — *Directories*

Read, Neil. Guide to art galleries in Scotland / compiled by Neil Read and Tom Wilson. — Edinburgh : Harris, 1981. — 53p : ill ; 20cm
ISBN 0-904505-72-3 (pbk) : £1.95 B81-37341

708.2′9134 — Edinburgh. Art galleries: National Gallery of Scotland — *Catalogues*

National Gallery of Scotland. Illustrations / National Gallery of Scotland. — Edinburgh ([The Mound, Edinburgh EH2 2EL]) : Trustees of the National Galleries of Scotland, 1980. — 158p : all ill,ports ; 30cm
ISBN 0-903148-09-9 (pbk) : Unpriced B81-10096

708.2′9134′05 — Edinburgh. Art galleries: National Galleries of Scotland — *Serials*

National Galleries of Scotland. News / the National Galleries of Scotland. — Jan./Feb.1981-. — [Edinburgh] ([17 Ainslee Place, Edinburgh EH3 6AU]) : [Trustees of the National Galleries of Scotland], 1981-. — v. : ill
Six issues yearly. — Continues: National Galleries of Scotland. Bulletin
ISSN 0261-3220 = News — National Galleries of Scotland : Unpriced B81-25004

708.7′312 — Russia *(RSFSR).* **Moscow. Museums. Exhibits: Visual arts**

Moscow / edited by Valeri S. Turchin ; [translated from the German by Barbara Beedham]. — Montclair : Allanheld and Schram ; London : Prior, c1981. — 207p : ill (some col.),ports(some col.) ; 35cm. — (Great centers of art)
Ill on lining papers
ISBN 0-86043-502-4 : £18.50 B81-18273

709 — VISUAL ARTS. HISTORICAL AND GEOGRAPHICAL TREATMENT

709 — Visual arts — *Critical studies*

Berger, John. About looking / John Berger. — London : Writers and Readers, 1980. — 198p : ill ; 22cm
ISBN 0-906495-25-3 (cased) : £5.95
ISBN 0-906495-30-x (pbk) : £2.95 B81-22080

Lynton, Norbert. Looking at art. — London (Elsley Court, 20 Great Titchfield St, W1P 7AD) : Kingfisher, Oct.1981. — [180]p
ISBN 0-86272-004-4 : £6.95 : CIP entry B81-27447

709 — Visual arts, *to 1980* — *Critical studies*

Elsen, Albert E.. Purpose of art : an introduction to the history and appreciation of art / Albert E. Elsen. — 4th ed. — New York ; London : Holt, Rinehart and Winston, c1981. — x,453p : ill(some col.),facsims,plans,ports ; 26cm
Previous ed.: 1972. — Bibliography p433-439. — Includes index
ISBN 0-03-049766-3 (pbk) : £12.50 B81-22857

709′.01 — Ancient visual arts

Art in the ancient world. — London : Faber, June 1981. — [608]p
Translation from the French
ISBN 0-571-11743-0 : £20.00 : CIP entry B81-12897

709′.01 — Visual arts, *to ca 900*

Larousse encyclopedia of prehistoric and ancient art : art and mankind / general editor René Huyghe [text prepared by Emily Evershed ... [et al.] from the French original L′art et l′homme]. — 2nd ed. — London : Hamlyn, 1970, c1962 (1981 [printing]). — 415p,[32]p of plates : ill(some col.),maps,ports ; 30cm
Translation of: L′art et l′homme008r19811970. — Previous ed.: i.e. rev. ed. 1966. — Includes index
ISBN 0-600-02377-x (pbk) : £6.95 B81-32353

709′.01′1094 — Western Europe. Megalithic visual arts

Twohig, Elizabeth Shee. The Megalithic art of Western Europe / Elizabeth Shee Twohig. — Oxford : Clarendon, 1981. — xi,259p,[272]p of plates : ill(some col.),maps ; 29cm
Bibliography: p240-251. — Includes index
ISBN 0-19-813193-3 : £50.00 : CIP rev. B80-08861

709′.01′10972 — Maya visual arts

Stierlin, Henri. The art of the Maya : from the Olmecs to the Toltec-Maya / Henri Stierlin ; [translated by Peter Graham]. — London : Macmillan, 1981. — 211p : col.ill,maps,plans ; 32cm
Translation from the French. — Bibliography: p205-206. — Includes index
ISBN 0-333-27703-1 : £25.00 B81-38798

709′.01′109798 — Southern Alaskan visual arts: Eskimo visual arts & Aleut visual arts

Ray, Dorothy Jean. Aleut and Eskimo art : tradition and innovation in South Alaska / Dorothy Jean Ray. — London : C. Hurst, c1981. — 251p : ill,1map,ports ; 29cm
Originally published: Seattle : University of Washington Press, 1980. — Bibliography: p225-237. — Includes index
ISBN 0-905838-62-9 : £19.50 B81-26024

709′.02 — European visual arts, *980-1420.* **Social aspects**

Duby, Georges. The age of the cathedrals : art and society 980-1420 / Georges Duby ; translated by Eleanor Levieux and Barbara Thompson. — London : Croom Helm, 1981. — v,312p,[31]p of plates : ill ; 24cm
Translation of: Le temps des cathédrales, a revised edition of the work first published in French in 3 vols.. — Includes index
ISBN 0-7099-0807-5 : £14.95 B81-33445

709′.02 — European visual arts, *ca 1050-ca 1450* — *Critical studies*

Shaver-Crandell, Anne. The Middle Ages. — Cambridge : Cambridge University Press, Dec.1981. — [122]p. — (Cambridge introduction to the history of art ; 2)
ISBN 0-521-23209-0 (cased) : £7.25 : CIP entry
ISBN 0-521-29870-9 (pbk) : £3.95 B81-32530

709′.02 — Visual arts, *ca 40-ca 1500*

Larousse encyclopedia of Byzantine and medieval art / general editor René Huyghe ; [text prepared by Emily Evershed ... et al. from the French original]. — Rev. [ed.]. — London : Hamlyn, 1968 (1981 [printing]). — ill(some col.),maps,plans ; 29cm. — (Art and mankind)
Translation of: one vol. of L′art et l′homme. — Previous ed.: 1963. — Includes index
ISBN 0-600-02378-8 (pbk) : £6.95 B81-30945

709′.02′4 — European visual arts, *1400-1600* — *Critical studies*

Letts, Rosa Maria. The Renaissance / Rosa Maria Letts. — Cambridge : Cambridge University Press, 1981. — 106p : ill(some col.),1facsim,1plan,ports(some col.) ; 25cm. — (Cambridge introduction to the history of art ; [3])
Bibliography: p102. — Includes index
ISBN 0-521-23394-1 : £6.95
ISBN 0-521-29957-8 (pbk) : £3.50 B81-17071

709.02′4 — London. Camden *(London Borough).* **Museums: British Museum. Exhibits: Western European art objects,** *1400-1600.* **Collections: Waddesdon Bequest**

Tait, Hugh. The Waddesdon Bequest. — London : British Museum Publications, Sept.1981. — [128]p
ISBN 0-7141-1357-3 (pbk) : £4.95 : CIP entry B81-23830

709′.03 — European visual arts, *ca 1400-ca 1800*

Larousse encyclopedia of renaissance and baroque art / general editor René Huyghe ; [text prepared by Emily Evershed ... et al. from the French original]. — London : Hamlyn, 1964 (1981 [printing]). — 444p : ill(some col.),maps,ports (some col.) ; 29cm. — (Art and mankind)
Translation of: one vol. of L′art et l′homme. — Previous ed.: 1964. — Includes index
ISBN 0-600-02373-7 (pbk) : £6.95 B81-27205

709′.03 — Scotland. National Trust properties. Art objects, *1500-1980*

Treasures in trust / edited by A.A. Tait. — Edinburgh : Produced in association with the National Trust for Scotland [by] H.M.S.O., 1981. — 103p : ill(some col.),1plan,ports(some col.) ; 25cm
Includes bibliographies
ISBN 0-11-491745-0 (pbk) : Unpriced
Primary classification 720′.9411 B81-36659

709′.03′2 — European visual arts, *1600-1700* — *Critical studies*

Mainstone, Madeleine. The seventeenth century / Madeleine & Rowland Mainstone. — Cambridge : Cambridge University Press, 1981. — 96p : ill(some col.),ports(some col.) ; 25cm. — (Cambridge introduction to the history of art ; [4])
Bibliography: p92. — Includes index
ISBN 0-521-22162-5 : £6.95
ISBN 0-521-29376-6 (pbk) : £3.50 B81-17070

709′.03′307402132 — London. Westminster *(London Borough).* **Art galleries: Heim Gallery (London). Exhibits: European visual arts,** *1700-1800* — *Catalogues*

Art as decoration : summer exhibition 17 June-28 August 1981. — London (59 Jermyn St., SW1Y 6LX) : Heim Gallery (London), [1981]. — [33],36p : ill ; 25cm. — (Heim exhibition catalogues ; no.34)
Unpriced B81-31477

709′.03′4 — Visual arts, *1770-1948* — *Critical studies*

Canaday, John. Mainstreams of modern art / John Canaday. — 2nd ed. — New York ; London : Holt, Rinehart and Winston, c1981. — xii,484p : ill(some col.),ports(some col.) ; 26cm
Previous ed.: London : Thames & Hudson, 1959. — Includes index
ISBN 0-03-057638-5 (pbk) : £10.95 B81-22964

709′.04 — Jewish visual arts, *1900-1980* — *Critical studies*

Kampf, Avram. Jewish experience in the art of the twentieth century. — Oxford : Phaidon, Oct.1981. — [224]p
ISBN 0-7148-2154-3 : £15.00 : CIP entry B81-27945

709′.04 — Visual arts, *1800-1980*

Larousse encyclopedia of modern art : from 1800 to the present day / general editor René Huyghe ; [text prepared by Emily Evershed ... et al. from the French original]. — Updated ed. — London : Hamlyn, 1980, c1965. — 416p,[2]p of plates : ill(some col.),ports (some col.) ; 29cm. — (Art and mankind)
Translation of: L′art et l′homme. — Previous ed.: 1965. — Includes index
ISBN 0-600-02380-x (pbk) : £6.95 B81-38554

709′.04 — Visual arts, *1880-1979* — *Critical studies*

Hughes, Robert, *1938-.* The shock of the new : art and the century of change / Robert Hughes. — London : British Broadcasting Corporation, 1980. — 423p : ill(some col.),ports(some col.) ; 29cm
Bibliography: p410-414. - Includes index
ISBN 0-563-17780-2 : £15.50 B81-02249

709′.04 — Visual arts, *1900-1980* — *Critical studies*

Lambert, Rosemary. The twentieth century / Rosemary Lambert. — Cambridge : Cambridge University Press, 1981. — 90p : ill(some col.),plans ; 25cm. — (Cambridge introduction to the history of art ; [7])
Bibliography: p88. — Includes index
ISBN 0-521-22715-1 : £6.95
ISBN 0-521-29622-6 (pbk) : £3.50 B81-17072

709'.04 — Visual arts, *1900-1980* — *Encyclopaedias*

The **Oxford** companion to twentieth-century art. — Oxford : Oxford University Press, Oct.1981. — [600]p
ISBN 0-19-866119-3 : £17.50 : CIP entry B81-26761

709'.04 — Visual arts, *1900-1980*. Influence of primitive visual arts

Wentinck, Charles. Modern and primitive art / Charles Wentinck ; [translated by Hilary Davies]. — Oxford : Phaidon, 1979, c1978. — 30p,[79]p of plates : col.ill ; 27cm. — (Phaidon 20th-century art)
Translation of: Moderne und primitive Kunst. — Originally published: New York : Dutton, c1978
ISBN 0-7148-1957-3 : £6.95 B81-29689

709'.04 — Visual arts. Psycho-realism — *Critical studies*

Sylvester, David C.. Psycho-realism : the meaning and significance of a modern art movement / by David C. Sylvester. — London (Blackheath, S.E.3) : New Art Studio, 1981. — [16]p ; 26cm
£0.25 (unbound) B81-28248

709'.04'012 — Art deco — *Critical studies*

Arwas, Victor. Art Deco / Victor Arwas. — London : Academy Editions, 1980. — 315p : ill (some col.),1plan ; 32cm
Ill on lining papers. — Bibliography: p306-309. — Includes index
ISBN 0-85670-586-1 : £25.00 B81-02803

709'.04'063 — Surrealism

Pound, Ezra. The coward surrealists / castigated by Ezra Pound. — [Great Britain] : [s.n.], [1981]. — [4]p ; 26cm
Cover title. — Limited ed. of 100 copies
Unpriced (pbk) B81-26148

709'.04'07402132 — London. Westminster *(London borough)*. Arts galleries: Tate Gallery. Exhibits: Foreign visual arts, *1900-1978* — *Catalogues*

Tate Gallery. Catalogue of the Tate Gallery's collection of modern art : other than works by British artists / [compiled by] Ronald Alley. — London : Tate Gallery in association with Sotheby Parke Bernet, 1981. — xx,799p : ill,ports ; 26cm
Includes index
ISBN 0-85667-102-9 : Unpriced B81-38646

709'.04'607402789 — Cumbria. Brampton. Museums: LYC Museum and Art Gallery. Exhibits: Visual arts, *1960-1980* — *Catalogues*

81 March 7 : Bill Fitzgibbons, Dave King, Shirley Neil, D. & B. Wright, Meg Zair, Rose Frain. — Brampton (Banks, Brampton, Cumbria CA8 2JH) : LYC Museum & Art Gallery, c1981. — [58]p : ill,ports ; 15cm
Cover title
Unpriced (pbk) B81-16960

709'.2'2 — Cumbria. Brampton. Museums: LYC Museum and Art Gallery. Exhibits: English visual arts. Jennings, Chris; Johnstone, David & Liddell, Peter — *Catalogues*

Jennings, Chris. Stones & mirrors / by Chris Jennings. High Down dreams / by David Johnstone. Lost in art / by Peter Liddell. — [Brampton] ([Banks, Brampton, Cumbria CA8 2JH]) : LYC Museum & Art Gallery, [1980]?. — [30]p : ill ; 14cm
Unpriced (pbk) B81-12696

709'.2'2 — Cumbrian visual artists — *Biographies*

Hall, Marshall, *1931-*. The artists of Cumbria : an illustrated dictionary of Cumberland, Westmoreland, North Lancashire and North Yorkshire painters, sculptors, draughtsmen and engravers born between 1615 and 1900 / by Marshall Hall. — Newcastle upon Tyne (26, Jesmond Road, Newcastle upon Tyne, NE2 4QP) : Marshall Hall, 1979. — 102p,2plates : ill,1map,ports ; 29cm. — (Artists of the regions series ; v.2)
Ports. on lining papers. — Bibliography: p99-100
ISBN 0-903858-01-0 : Unpriced B81-37474

709'.2'2 — English visual arts. Brotherhood of Ruralists — *Critical studies*

Usherwood, Nicholas. The Brotherhood of Ruralists : Ann Arnold, Graham Arnold, Peter Blake, Jann Haworth, David Inshaw, Annie Ovenden, Graham Ovenden / Nicholas Usherwood. — London : Lund Humphries in association with the London Borough of Camden, 1981. — 84p : ill(some col.),ports (some col.) ; 24cm
ISBN 0-85331-446-2 (pbk) : £5.95 B81-25983

709'.2'2 — Visual arts — *Biographies* — *Serials*

Dictionary of contemporary artists. — 1981-. — Oxford : Clio Press, c1981. — v. ; 25cm
Annual
£20.00 B81-33713

709'.2'2 — Visual arts. Women artists — *Feminist viewpoints*

Parker, Rozsika. Old mistresses : women, art and ideology. — London : Routledge & Kegan Paul, Nov.1981. — [250]p
ISBN 0-7100-0879-1 (cased) : £10.50 : CIP entry
ISBN 0-7100-0911-9 (pbk) : £5.95 B81-30600

709'.2'2 — Western visual arts. Women artists, *ca 1400-1975* — *Biographies*

Fine, Elsa Honig. Women & art : a history of women painters and sculptors from the Renaissance to the 20th century / Elsa Honig Fine. — Montclair, [N.J.] : Allanheld & Schram ; London : Prior, 1978 (1981 [printing]). — xiii,240p,4p of plates : ill(some col.),ports ; 26cm
Bibliography: p225-230. — Includes index
ISBN 0-86043-198-3 (pbk) : £8.50 B81-35315

709'.2'4 — Belgium. Ostend. Museums: Stedelijk Van Abbemuseum. Exhibits: German visual arts. Rainer, Arnulf — *Catalogues*

Rainer, Arnulf. Arnulf Rainer. — Eindhoven : [Stedelijk Van Abbemuseum] ; London : [Whitechapel Art Gallery], 1980. — [126]p : chiefly ill(some col.) ; 28cm
Published to accompany an exhibition at the Stedelijk Van Abbemuseum, Eindhoven and the Whitechapel Art Gallery, London, 1980. — English, German and Dutch text. — Sheet of text as insert
£7.50 (pbk)
Primary classification 709'.2'4 B81-06101

709'.2'4 — Berkshire. Bracknell. Arts centres: South Hill Park Arts Centre. Exhibits: English visual arts. Dean, Graham — *Catalogues*

Graham Dean : paintings, drawings, photographs and films : [catalogue of an] exhibition organised by South Hill Park Arts Centre [held at] South Hill Park Arts Centre, Bracknell, 27 June to 26 July 1981 ... [et al.]. — [Bracknell] ([Bracknell, Berkshire]) : [The Centre], c1981. — [16]p : ill ; 30cm
ISBN 0-9507205-2-6 (pbk) : Unpriced B81-37733

709'.2'4 — Cardiff. Museums: National Museums of Wales. Exhibits: English visual arts. Underwood, Leon — *Catalogues*

Underwood, Leon. Leon Underwood : Mexico & after : sculpture, paintings, drawing and prints 1928-36 : Amgueddfa Genedlaethol Cymru, Caerdydd, National Museum of Wales, Cardiff, 6 August-16 September 1979. — [Cardiff] : [National Museum of Wales], [1979]. — [16]p : ill ; 24cm
Text by A. D. Fraser Jenkins. — Bibliography. p[16]
£0.50 (pbk) B81-28885

709'.2'4 — Danish visual arts. Jorn, Asger, *1965-1973* — *Critical studies*

Atkins, Guy. Asger Jorn : the final years 1965-1973 : a study of Asger Jorn's artistic development from 1965 to 1973 and a catalogue of his oil paintings from that period / Guy Atkins with the help of Troels Andersen. — London : Lund Humphries, 1980. — 241p : ill(some col.),facsims,ports ; 31cm
Includes index
ISBN 0-85331-438-1 : £45.00 B81-16270

709'.2'4 — English experimental visual arts. Boyle, Mark — *Critical studies*

Locher, J. L.. Mark Boyle's journey to the surface of the earth / J.L. Locher. — Stuttgart ; London : Mayer, 1978. — 270p : ill(some col.),maps(some col.),ports(some col.) ; 24cm
Unpriced (pbk) B81-09952

709'.2'4 — English visual arts. Morris, William, *1834-1896* — *Critical studies*

William Morris and Kelmscott. — London : Design Council, Nov.1981. — [156]p
ISBN 0-85072-121-0 (pbk) : £7.00 : CIP entry B81-30612

709'.2'4 — German experimental visual arts. Beuys, Joseph — *Critical studies*

Tisdall, Caroline. Joseph Beuys. — [London] ([9 Dering St., New Bond St., W.1]) : [Anthony d'Offay], c1980. — 1sheet([6]p) ; 29cm
Author: Caroline Tisdall
Unpriced B81-22808

709'.2'4 — Great Britain. Art galleries. Exhibits: English visual arts. Loker, John — *Catalogues*

Loker, John. John Loker : ten years work. — Bristol (16 Narrow Quay Bristol BS1) : Arnolfini Gallery, c1981. — 20p : ill(some col.) ; 21cm
Published on the occasion of a touring exhibition, 1981. — Bibliography: p19
ISBN 0-9503885-7-2 (pbk) : Unpriced B81-09574

709'.2'4 — Great Britain. Arts. Patronage. Organisations: Arts Council of Great Britain. Exhibits: Swiss visual arts. Giacometti, Alberto - *Catalogues*

Giacometti, Alberto. Giacometti : sculptures, paintings, drawings : [catalogue of] an Arts Council exhibition [at] Manchester, Whitworth Art Gallery, University of Manchester, 10 January to 21 February 1981, Bristol, City of Bristol Museum and Art Gallery, 28 February to 28 March 1981, London, Serpentine Gallery, 10 April to 17 May 1981. — London : Arts Council of Great Britain, c1980. — 80p : ill,ports ; 21cm
ISBN 0-7287-0265-7 (pbk) : Unpriced B81-18724

709'.2'4 — Italian visual arts. Leonardo, *da Vinci* — *Critical studies*

Brizio, Anna Maria. Leonardo the artist / Anna Maria Brizio, Maria Vittoria Brugnoli, André Chastel. — London : Hutchinson, 1981, c1980. — 192p : ill(some col.),facsims(some col.),ports (some col.) ; 22cm
Includes index
ISBN 0-09-142641-3 : £4.95 B81-32443

Kemp, Martin, *1942-*. Leonardo da Vinci : the marvellous works of nature and man / Martin Kemp. — London : Dent, 1981. — 384p : ill,ports ; 26cm
Includes index
ISBN 0-460-04354-4 : £14.95 B81-33420

709'.2'4 — Italian visual arts. Leonardo, *da Vinci* — *Critical studies* — *For children*

Raboff, Ernest. Leonardo da Vinci / by Ernest Raboff. — London : Ernest Benn, 1980. — [32]p : ill(some col.) ; 29cm. — (Art for children)
ISBN 0-510-00102-5 : £3.95 B81-14475

709'.2'4 — Italian visual arts. Michelangelo — *Critical studies*

Summers, David, *1941-*. Michelangelo and the language of art / by David Summers. — Princeton ; Guildford : Princeton University Press, c1981. — xvii,626p,[32]p of plates : ill,plans ; 26cm
Bibliography: p586-607. — Includes index
ISBN 0-691-03957-7 (cased) : £26.50
ISBN 0-691-10097-7 (pbk) : £9.20 B81-18563

709'.2'4 — Kent. Canterbury. Universities: University of Kent at Canterbury. *Library*. Exhibits: English visual arts. Jones, David, *1895-1974* — *Catalogues*

David Jones : poet and artist. — [Canterbury, Kent] : Kent University Library, 1980. — 19p,[4]p of plates : ill ; 21cm
Unpriced (pbk) B81-32333

709′.2′4 — London. Tower Hamlets *(London Borough).* Art galleries: Whitechapel Art Gallery. Exhibits: German visual arts. Rainer, Arnulf — *Catalogues*

Rainer, Arnulf. Arnulf Rainer. — Eindhoven : [Stedelijk Van Abbemuseum] ; London : [Whitechapel Art Gallery], 1980. — [126]p : chiefly ill(some col.) ; 28cm
Published to accompany an exhibition at the Stedelijk Van Abbemuseum, Eindhoven and the Whitechapel Art Gallery, London, 1980. — English, German and Dutch text. — Sheet of text as insert
£7.50 (pbk)
Also classified at 709′.2′4 B81-06101

709′.2′4 — London. Westminster *(London Borough).* Art galleries: Institute of Contemporary Arts. Exhibits: American visual arts. Masi, Denis — *Catalogues*

Masi, Denis. Denis Masi. — London ([12 Carlton House Terrace, S.W.1]) : Institute of Contemporary Arts, 1979. — 32p : chiefly ill ; 30cm
Published to accompany an exhibition held at the ICA, 1979. — Limited ed. of 500 copies. — Bibliography: p30-31
ISBN 0-905263-01-4 (pbk) : Unpriced B81-16802

709′.2′4 — London. Westminster *(London Borough).* Art galleries: Institute of Contemporary Arts. Exhibits: American visual arts. Stuart, Michelle — *Catalogues*

Stuart, Michelle. Paperwork / Michelle Stuart ; [text Sarah Kent]. — London ([12 Carlton House Terrace, S.W.1]) : Institute of Contemporary Arts, c1979. — [32]p : ill,1port ; 25cm
Published to accompany an exhibition held at the ICA, 1979. — Bibliography: p[31]-[32]
Unpriced (pbk) B81-16806

709′.2′4 — London. Westminster *(London Borough).* Art galleries: Institute of Contemporary Arts. Exhibits: German visual arts. Naber, Bernd — *Catalogues*

Kent, Sarah, *1941-*. Bernd Naber : paintings as objects / [text Sarah Kent] ; [photographs Norbert Radler]. — London ([12 Carlton House Terrace, S.W.1]) : Institute of Contemporary Arts, c1979. — [16]p : ill(some col.),ports ; 23cm
Published to accompany an exhibition held at the ICA, 1979
Unpriced (pbk) B81-16804

709′.2′4 — London. Westminster *(London Borough).* Art galleries: Institute of Contemporary Arts. Exhibits: Israeli visual arts. Toren, Amikam — *Catalogues*

Toren, Amikam. Replacing : by Amikam Token [i.e. Toren] / Placing Amikam Token [i.e. Toren] : an introductory essay by Sarah Kent. — London (12 Carlton House Terrace, S.W.1) : Institute of Contemporary Arts, [1979]. — [52]p : ill ; 26cm
Published to accompany an exhibition at the ICA, 1979
Unpriced (pbk) B81-20677

709′.2′4 — London. Westminster *(London Borough).* Art galleries: Institute of Contemporary Arts. Exhibits: Yugoslav visual arts. Dimitrijević, Braco — *Catalogues*

Kent, Sarah, *1941-*. Braco Dimitrijević / [text Sarah Kent]. — London (Nash House, The Mall, S.W.1) : Institute of Contemporary Arts, c1979. — [36]p : ill ; 26cm
Published to accompany an exhibition at the ICA, 1979. — Bibliography: p[35]-[36]
Unpriced (pbk) B81-16805

709′.2′4 — London. Westminster *(London Borough).* Art galleries: Serpentine Gallery. Exhibits: American visual arts. Westermann, H. C. — *Catalogues*

Westermann, H. C.. H.C. Westermann / published by Ernest Benn Limited in cooperation with the Arts Council of Great Britain on the occasion of an exhibition at the Serpentine Gallery, London, 5 December 1980 to 8 February 1981 ; [edited by Susan Benn and Paul Langridge]. — London : Benn, 1980. — [56]p : chiefly ill(some col.),ports ; 20cm
Ill on inside covers
ISBN 0-510-00115-7 (pbk) : Unpriced B81-08031

709′.2′4 — London. Westminster *(London Borough).* Art galleries: Serpentine Gallery. Exhibits: English visual arts. Smith, Sam, *1908-* — *Catalogues*

Smith, Sam, *1908-*. Sam Smith / published by Ernest Benn Limited in cooperation with the Arts Council of Great Britain on the occasion of an exhibition at the Serpentine Gallery, London, 5 December 1980 to 8 February 1981 ; [edited by Susan Benn and Paul Langridge]. — London : Benn, 1980. — [56]p : chiefly ill (some col.),2ports ; 20cm
Ill on inside covers
ISBN 0-510-00114-9 (pbk) : Unpriced B81-08030

709′.2′4 — London. Westminster *(London Borough).* Art galleries: Tate Gallery. Exhibits: American experimental visual arts. Rauschenberg, Robert — *Catalogues*

Rauschenberg, Robert. Robert Rauschenberg. — London : Tate Gallery Publications Department, [1981]. — [24]p : ill(some col.),1port ; 30cm
To accompany an exhibition held at the Tate Gallery
£2.00 (pbk) B81-23296

709′.2′4 — London. Westminster *(London Borough).* Cultural institutions: Goethe Institute *(London).* Exhibits: German visual arts. Vakily, Helmut — *Catalogues*

Vakily, Helmut. Helmut Vakily manual multiples : editions of original drawings / [written by Jürgen Morschel] ; [translated by Robert Goldsmith. — London (50 Princes Gate (Exhibition Rd.) SW7 [South Kensington]) : Goethe Institute London, 1981. — [8]p : ill,1port ; 21cm
Bibliography: p7
Unpriced (unbound) B81-38005

709′.2′4 — Scotland. Fife Region. St Andrews. Art galleries: Balcarres Gallery. Exhibits: Scottish visual arts. Paolozzi, Eduardo — *Catalogues*

Paolozzi, Eduardo. The development of the idea / Eduardo Paolozzi ; [exhibition compiled by The Glasgow League of Artists]. — [St Andrews] ([University of St Andrews, 93 North St., St Andrews, Fife]) : [Crawford Centre for the Arts], [1980]. — [18]p : ill(some col.) ; 21cm
Published to accompany an exhibition at the Crawford Centre for the Arts, University of St Andrews, 1979. — Cover title
Unpriced (pbk) B81-10396

709′.2′4 — Scotland. Strathclyde Region. Glasgow. Art galleries: Glasgow Print Studio Gallery. Exhibits: Scottish visual arts. Cosgrove, Jimmy — *Catalogues*

Cosgrove, Jimmy. Recent work / Jimmy Cosgrove. — [Glasgow] ([128 Ingram St., Glasgow G1 1EJ]) : Glasgow Print Studio Gallery, c1980. — 16]p : ill ; 19cm + leaflet ([4]p : 1port ; 18cm)
Unpriced (pbk) B81-11857

709′.2′4 — Scotland. Strathclyde Region. Glasgow. Art galleries: Third Eye Centre. Exhibits: Scottish visual arts. McLean, Bruce — *Catalogues*

McLean, Bruce. Bruce McLean. — Glasgow (350 Sauchiehall St., Glasgow G2 3JD) : Third Eye Centre, 1980. — 36p : ill,1port ; 21x23cm
Published to accompany the exhibition New Works and Performance/Actions Positions held at the Scottish Arts Council Fruit Market Gallery, Edinburgh, Third Eye Centre, Glasgow and Arnolfini, Bristol, 1979. — Limited ed. of 750 copies
ISBN 0-906474-11-6 (pbk) : Unpriced B81-16803

709′.2′4 — Visual arts. Criticism. Berenson, Bernard — *Biographies*

Secrest, Meryle. Being Bernard Berenson : a biography / Meryle Secrest. — Harmondsworth : Penguin, 1980, c1979. — xxii,473p : ill,ports ; 20cm
Originally published: New York : Hart, Rinehart and Winston, ; 1979 London : Weidenfeld and Nicolson, 1980. — Includes index
ISBN 0-14-005697-1 (pbk) : £3.95 B81-16976

709′.2′4 — Visual arts. Criticism. Holanda, Francisco de — *Critical studies*

Bury, J. B. (John Bernard). Two notes on Francisco De Holanda / by J.B. Bury. — London : Warburg Institute, University of London, 1981. — 45p ; 25cm. — (Warburg Institute surveys, ISSN 0083-7202 ; 7)
Bibliography: p30-45
ISBN 0-85481-058-7 (pbk) : Unpriced B81-16196

709′.2′4 — West Midlands *(Metropolitan County).* Birmingham. Art galleries: Birmingham Museums & Art Gallery. Exhibits: English visual arts. Epstein, Jacob — *Catalogues*

Epstein, Jacob, *1880-1959*. Rebel angel : sculpture and watercolours by Sir Jacob Epstein 1880-1959 : Birmingham Museums & Art Gallery 16 October-30 November 1980 / [written by Evelyn Silber]. — Birmingham (Chamberlain Sq., Birmingham B3 3DH) : Publications Unit, City Museum and Art Gallery, c1980. — 35p : ill,ports ; 20x21cm
ISBN 0-7093-0058-1 (pbk) : £1.60 B81-10954

709′.2′4 — West Midlands *(Metropolitan County).* Birmingham. Art galleries: Birmingham Museums & Art Gallery. Exhibits: English visual arts. Southall, Joseph — *Catalogues*

Breeze, George. Joseph Southall 1861-1944 : artist-craftsman. — Birmingham (Publication Unit, Birmingham Museums & Art Gallery, Birmingham B3 3DH) : Birmingham Museums & Art Gallery, 1980. — 112p,[4]p of plates : ill (some col.),ports ; 30cm
Catalogue of an exhibition held at the City Museum & Art Gallery, Birmingham, 8 August-30 September and at The Fine Art Society, London, 14 October-7 November 1980. — Catalogue by George Breeze
ISBN 0-7093-0057-3 (pbk) : £4.50 B81-10722

709′.37 — Ancient Roman visual arts — *Critical studies*

A **Handbook** of Roman art. — Oxford : Phaidon, Oct.1982. — [320]p
ISBN 0-7148-2214-0 (pbk) : £10.00 : CIP entry B81-24659

Woodford, Susan. The art of Greece and Rome. — Cambridge : Cambridge University Press, Dec.1981. — [122]p. — (Cambridge introduction to the history of art)
ISBN 0-521-23222-8 (cased) : £7.25 : CIP entry
ISBN 0-521-29873-3 (pbk) : £3.95
Primary classification 709′.38 B81-32531

709′.37 — Ancient Roman visual arts, *to ca 400* **—** *Critical studies*

Strong, Donald E.. Roman art / Donald Strong ; prepared for press by J.M.C. Toynbee. — Reprinted in integrated format, with additions to the bibliography. — Harmondsworth : Penguin, 1980, c1976. — 357p : ill,maps,ports ; 21cm. — (The Pelican history of art)
Bibliography: p329-337. — Includes index
ISBN 0-14-056139-0 (pbk) : £10.00 B81-01926

709′.38 — Ancient Greek visual arts — *Critical studies*

Robertson, Martin. A shorter history of Greek art / Martin Robertson. — Cambridge : Cambridge University Press, 1981. — xi,239p : ill,1plan ; 29cm
Bibliography: p217-218. — Includes index
ISBN 0-521-23629-0 (cased) : £28.00 : CIP rev.
ISBN 0-521-28084-2 (pbk) : £9.95 B81-19119

Woodford, Susan. The art of Greece and Rome. — Cambridge : Cambridge University Press, Dec.1981. — [122]p. — (Cambridge introduction to the history of art)
ISBN 0-521-23222-8 (cased) : £7.25 : CIP entry
ISBN 0-521-29873-3 (pbk) : £3.95
Also classified at 709′.37 B81-32531

709′.38′8 — Mycenaean visual arts, *B.C.3000-B.C.1550*

Higgins, R. A.. Minoan and Mycenaean art / Reynold Higgins. — Rev. ed. — London : Thames and Hudson, 1981. — 216p : ill(some col.),1map,plans ; 22cm. — ([The World of art library])
Previous ed.: 1967. — Bibliography: p195-196. — Includes index
ISBN 0-500-18184-5 : £5.95
Also classified at 709′.39′18 B81-16955

709′.39′18 — Minoan visual arts, *B.C.3000-B.C.1550*
Higgins, R. A.. Minoan and Mycenaean art / Reynold Higgins. — Rev. ed. — London : Thames and Hudson, 1981. — 216p : ill(some col.),1map,plans ; 22cm. — ([The World of art library])
Previous ed.: 1967. — Bibliography: p195-196. — Includes index
ISBN 0-500-18184-5 : £5.95
Primary classification 709′.38′8 B81-16955

709′.4 — European visual arts, *1408-1819.* **Influence of allegory of Calumny of Apelles**
Cast, David. The Calumny of Apelles : a study in the humanist tradition / David Cast. — New Haven ; London : Yale University Press, 1981. — xv,243p : ill ; 22cm. — (Yale publications in the history of art ; 28)
Bibliography: p233-238. — Includes index
ISBN 0-300-02575-0 : £20.00 B81-32487

709′.4 — European visual arts, *to ca 1790 — Early works*
Reynolds, *Sir* **Joshua**. Discourse on art. — London : Yale University Press, Sept.1981. — [384]p
Originally published: 1975
ISBN 0-300-02775-3 : £5.95 : CIP entry B81-30244

709′.4′07402574 — Oxfordshire. Oxford. Museums: Ashmolean Museum. Exhibits: European visual arts, *1500-1900 — Catalogues.*
The **Most** beautiful statues : the taste for antique sculpture 1500-1900 : an exhibition held at the Ashmolean Museum from 26 March to 10 May 1981 / compiled by Francis Haskell and Nicholas Penny. — Oxford : Ashmolean Museum, 1981. — xiv,82p : ill ; 24cm
Bibliography: p65-66. - Includes index
ISBN 0-900090-83-9 (pbk) : Unpriced B81-18276

709′.4′074094923 — Netherlands. Amsterdam. Reynst, Jan & Reynst, Gerard. Private collections: European visual arts, *to ca 1650*
Logan, Anne-Marie S.. The ′Cabinet′ of the brothers Gerard and Jan Reynst / Anne-Marie S. Logan. — Amsterdam ; Oxford : North-Holland, 1979. — 293p,[2]folded p of plates : ill,facsims,ports,geneal.tables ; 26cm. — (Koninklijke Nederlandse Akademie Van Wetenschappen Verhandelingen afdeling letterkunde. Nieuwe reeks ; d.99)
Ill on lining papers. — Bibliography: p269-272. - Includes index
ISBN 0-7204-8342-5 : Unpriced B81-15495

709′.41 — British visual arts. Artists, *ca 1900-1930 - Directories*
Dolman, Bernard. Dictionary of contemporary British artists. — Woodbridge : Antique Collectors′ Club, May 1981. — 1v.
Originally published: 1929
ISBN 0-902028-99-5 : £19.50 : CIP entry B81-12358

709′.41 — Great Britain. Art objects — *Encyclopaedias*
Treasures of Britain and treasures of Ireland / [edited by Drive Publications Limited for the Automobile Association]. — 4th ed. — London : Drive Publications for the Automobile Association, c1980. — 680p : col.ill,col.maps,col.facsims,col.ports ; 29cm
Previous ed.: 1976. — Col.ill on lining papers
£8.95
Primary classification 914.1′04858′0321 B81-09879

709′.41′07402165 — London. Lambeth *(London Borough).* **Art galleries: Hayward Gallery. Exhibits: British visual arts —** *Catalogues — Serials*
Hayward annual. — 1980. — London : Arts Council of Great Britain, c1980. — 62p
ISBN 0-7287-0248-7 : Unpriced B81-08789

709′.41′07402789 — Cumbria. Brampton. Museums: LYC Museum and Art Gallery. Exhibits: British visual arts, *1964-1981 — Catalogues*
Innes, Moira. 81 February 7 / Moira Innes, Rachel Gibson, Sandra Riley. — Brampton (Banks, Brampton, Cumbria CA8 2JH) : LYC Museum & Art Gallery, c1981. — [38]p : chiefly ill ; 14cm
Cover title
£0.35 (pbk) B81-09761

709′.42 — English visual arts, *1900-1939.* **Modernism —** *Critical studies*
Harrison, Charles, *1942-*. English art and modernism 1900-1939 / Charles Harrison. — London : Allen Lane, 1981. — 416p : ill,ports ; 24cm
Bibliography: p395-400. — Includes index
ISBN 0-7139-0792-4 : £20.00 B81-12045

709′.42 — London. Westminster *(London Borough).* **Art galleries: Julian Hartnoll** *(Gallery).* **Exhibits: Items associated with Aesthetic Movement**
Aspects of the aesthetic movement : including books, ceramics, furniture, glass, textiles : an exhibition organised by Dan Klein Ltd, held at Julian Hartnoll, 5 December to 22 December 1978. — [London] ([10 Canonbury Place, N.1.]) : [Dan Klein], [1978]. — 48p : ill(some col.) ; 21cm
Catalogue compiled by Paul Atterbury
Unpriced (pbk) B81-19777

709′.42′07402132 — London. Westminster *(London Borough).* **Art galleries: Serpentine Gallery. Exhibits: English visual arts —** *Catalogues*
Summer shows 1981 / Serpentine Gallery. — London : Arts Council of Great Britain, [1981]. — [64]p : ill,ports ; 15x22cm
ISBN 0-7287-0290-8 (pbk) : Unpriced B81-39128

709′.42′07402789 — Cumbria. Carlisle *(District).* **Brampton. Art galleries: LYC Museum and Art Gallery. Exhibits: English visual arts —** *Catalogues*
81 June : Joel Fisher, Paul Martin, Bill Woodrow, Valerie Kirk, Martin Prekop : 87 / LYC Museum & Art Gallery. — Brampton (Banks, Brampton, Cumbria CA8 2JH) : LYC Museum & Art Gallery, c1981. — [41]p : ill,ports ; 14cm
£0.35 (pbk) B81-25552

709′.42′07402789 — Cumbria. Carlisle *(District).* **Brampton. Art galleries: LYC Museum and Art Gallery. Exhibits: English visual arts,** *1930-1980 — Catalogues*
81 August 1 / Winifred Nicholson ... [et al.]. — Brampton (Banks, Brampton, Cumbria CA8 2JH) : LYC Museum & Art Gallery, c1981. — [52]p : ill,ports ; 14cm
ISBN 0-9504571-1-6 (unbound) : £0.35 B81-32983

81 July 4 / Tony Knipe ... [et al.]. — Brampton (Banks, Brampton, Cumbria CA8 2JH) : LYC Museum & Art Gallery, c1981. — [46]p : ill,ports ; 14cm
ISBN 0-9504571-1-6 (unbound) : £0.35 B81-32982

709′.42′07402789 — Cumbria. Carlisle *(District).* **Brampton. Art galleries: LYC Museum and Gallery. Exhibits: English visual arts,** *1970-1980 — Catalogues*
81 April 4 / David Doods [i.e. Dodds] ... [et al.]. — Brampton (Banks, Brampton, Cumbria CA8 2JH) : LYC Museum & Art Gallery, c1981. — [10]p,[23]p of plates : chiefly ill,ports ; 14cm
Cover title
£0.35 (pbk) B81-17937

81 September 5 / Gordon Senior ... [et al.]. — Brampton (Banks, Brampton, Cumbria CA8 2JH) : LYC Museum & Art Gallery, c1981. — [42]p : chiefly ill,ports ; 14cm
Cover title
ISBN 0-9504571-1-6 (pbk) : £0.25 B81-37070

709′.42′07407453 — Soviet Union. Leningrad. Museums: Ermitazh. Stock: English visual arts, *1500-1900 — Catalogues*
The **Hermitage** : English art sixteenth to nineteenth century : paintings, sculpture, prints and drawings, minor arts / [compiled and introduced by Larissa Dukelskaya] ; [translated from the Russian by Philip Taylor ... et al.]. — Leningrad : Aurora Art Publishers ; London : Collets′, c1979. — 314p,[4]p folded p of plates : chiefly ill(some col.),ports(some col.) ; 30cm
Bibliography: p296-301
ISBN 0-569-08426-1 : Unpriced B81-27258

709′.43′07402132 — London. Westminster *(London Borough).* **Cultural institutions: Goethe Institute** *(London).* **Exhibits: German visual arts from Autoren Galerie 1 —** *Catalogues*
Autoren Galerie 1 München : concept, artwork, documentation / [edited & designed by Helmut Vakily] ; [photography by Heidrun Löhr et al.]. — London (50 Princes Gate (Exhibition Rd.) SW7 South Kensington) : Goethe Institute London, 1981. — 36p : ill(some col.),ports ; 21x22cm
English text, English and German introduction
Unpriced (pbk) B81-38006

709′.431′55 — German visual arts. Berlin Secession, *ca 1900-ca 1930*
Paret, Peter. The Berlin Secession : modernism and its enemies in imperial Germany / Peter Paret. — Cambridge, Mass. ; London : Belknap, 1980. — 269p,[2]leaves of plates : ill (some col.),2facsims ; 24cm
Bibliography: p253-262. — Includes index
ISBN 0-674-06773-8 : £10.50 B81-06571

709′.436′13 — Viennese visual arts, *1898-1918*
Vergo, Peter. Art in Vienna 1898-1918. — Oxford : Phaidon, Sept.1981. — [256]p
Originally published: 1975
ISBN 0-7148-2222-1 : £11.95 : CIP entry B81-21483

709′.44 — French visual arts, *1500-1700*
Blunt, Anthony. Art and architecture in France 1500 to 1700 / Anthony Blunt. — 4th ed. — Harmondsworth : Penguin, 1980, c1981. — 476p : ill,maps,plans,ports ; 22cm. — (The Pelican history of art)
Previous ed.: 1973. — Bibliography: p447-453. — Includes index
£17.95 (cased)
ISBN 0-14-056004-1
Also classified at 720′.944 B81-30952

709′.44 — French visual arts, *1830-1872.* **Criticism. Gautier, Théophile —** *Critical studies*
Snell, Robert. Théophile Gautier. — Oxford : Oxford University Press, Nov.1981. — [240]p
ISBN 0-19-815768-1 : £20.00 : CIP entry B81-28859

709′.45 — Italian visual arts, *to 1800 — Illustrations*
Denvir, Bernard. Art treasures of Italy / Bernard Denvir. — London : Orbis Publishing, 1980. — 320p : chiefly col.ill,col.ports ; 35cm
Includes index
ISBN 0-85613-306-x : £12.50 B81-01029

709′.45′31 — Italy. Venice. Visual arts, *to ca 1800 — Visitors′ guides — Early works*
Ruskin, John. The stones of Venice / John Ruskin ; edited and introduced by Jan Morris. — London : Faber, 1981. — 239p : ill(some col),facsims(some col),port ; 29cm
Includes index
ISBN 0-571-11815-1 : £12.50 : CIP rev. B81-21464

709′.47 — Russian visual arts, *to 1976*
An **Introduction** to Russian art and architecture / edited by Robert Auty and Dimitri Obolensky with the editorial assistance of Anthony Kingsford ; with chapters by Robin Milner-Gulland & John Bowlt. — Cambridge : Cambridge University Press, 1980 (1981 [printing]). — xiii,194p : ill,plans,ports ; 23cm. — (Companion to Russian studies ; 3)
Bibliography: p173-181. — Includes index
ISBN 0-521-28384-1 (pbk) : £7.50 : CIP rev. B81-13803

709′.48 — Viking visual arts, *ca 800- ca 1150*
Wilson, David M.. Viking art / by David M. Wilson and Ole Klindt-Jensen. — 2nd ed. — London : Allen and Unwin, 1980. — 173p,ixxxp of plates : ill ; 26cm
Previous ed.: 1966. — Bibliography: p162-166. — Includes index
ISBN 0-04-709018-9 : £10.00 B81-05702

709′.51 — Chinese visual arts, *to 1912*

Jenyns, Soame. Chinese art : gold, silver, later bronzes, cloisonné, Cantonese enamel, lacquer, furniture, wood / by R. Soame Jenyns & William Watson. — 2nd ed. / Preface and revisions by William Watson. — Oxford : Phaidon, 1980. — 277p : ill(some col) ; 28cm
Translation of: Arts de la Chine. — Previous ed.: London : Oldbourne, 1963
ISBN 0-7148-2135-7 : £14.95 B81-13288

709′.54 — Indian visual arts — *Critical studies*

The **arts** of India. — Oxford : Phaidon, Oct.1981. — [208]p
ISBN 0-7148-2150-0 : £25.00 : CIP entry B81-30469

709′.56 — Middle Eastern visual arts. Influence of classical culture, *to ca 1200*

Weitzmann, Kurt. Classical heritage in Byzantine and Near Eastern art / Kurt Weitzmann. — London : Variomum Reprints, 1981. — 326p in various pagings : ill,1port ; 30cm. — (Collected studies series ; CS140)
Includes 2 papers in German. — Includes index
ISBN 0-86078-087-2 : £67.50 B81-40851

709′.561 — Turkish visual arts, *to 1979*

The **Art** and architecture of Turkey / edited by Ekrem Akurgal ; photographs by Leo Hilber. — Oxford : Oxford University Press, 1980. — 268p : ill(some col.),2maps,plans ; 31cm
Maps on lining papers. — Bibliography: p249-258 - Includes index
ISBN 0-19-211451-4 : £35.00 : CIP rev. B80-19330

709′.73 — United States. Visual arts. Attitudes of society, *ca 1825-1970*

Lynes, Russell. The tastemakers : the shaping of American popular taste / Russell Lynes ; with a new afterword. — New York : Dover ; London : Constable, 1980. — xii,372p : ill,facsims,ports ; 23cm
Originally published: New York : Harper, 1954. — Bibliography: p353-356. - Includes index
ISBN 0-486-23993-4 (pbk) : £3.50 B81-18492

709′.791 — Hopi visual arts

Hopi kachina : spirit of life : dedicated to the Hopi tricentennial, 1680-1980 / edited by Dorothy K. Washburn. — [San Francisco] : California Academy of Sciences ; Seattle ; London : Distributed by The University of Washington Press, c1980. — 158p : ill(some col.) ; 28cm
Published ... in association with the exhibition "Hopi Kachina : spirit of life". — Bibliography : p156-158
ISBN 0-295-95751-4 (pbk) : £8.95 B81-28995

709′.94 — Australian kitsch, *to 1979*

Humphries, Barry. Barry Humphries′ treasury of Australian kitsch. — London : Macmillan, 1980. — 96p : chiefly ill(some col.),facsims (some col.),ports(some col.) ; 27cm
ISBN 0-333-29955-8 : £5.95 B81-03969

709′.94 — Australian visual arts, *to 1979* — *Festschriften*

Australian art and architecture : essays presented to Bernard Smith / edited by Anthony Bradley & Terry Smith. — Melbourne ; Oxford : Oxford University Press, 1980. — viii,257p : ill,ports ; 29cm
Includes index
ISBN 0-19-550588-3 : £35.00 B81-26819

711 — ENVIRONMENT PLANNING

711 — Environment planning. Applications of ecology

Edington, John M.. Ecology and environmental planning / John M. Edington and M. Ann Edington. — London : Chapman and Hall, 1977 (1981 [printing]). — 246p : ill,maps ; 24cm. — (Science paperbacks ; 1977)
Bibliography: p227-238. — Includes index
ISBN 0-412-23680-x : Unpriced : CIP rev. B81-13861

711 — Environment planning. Role of chartered surveyors

The **Chartered** surveyor in planning and development. — London : Royal Institution of Chartered Surveyors, c1981. — 10p : ill ; 21cm
Text on inside cover
£3.00 (£2.50 to members) (pbk) B81-40969

711 — Great Britain. Environment planning. Applications of quantity surveying

Ferry, Douglas J.. A study of quantity surveying in planning / D.J.O. Ferry. — [London] : Royal Institution of Chartered Surveyors, 1979. — 27,[9]p ; 30cm
Study commissioned by the Quantity Surveyors Research and Development Committee of the RICS
Unpriced (pbk) B81-35674

711 — Great Britain. Environment planning. Use of soil surveys

Selman, Paul. The application of soil survey and land capability classification in planning / Paul Selman. — [Glasgow] ([Bourdon Building, 177 Renfrew St., Glasgow, G3 4HU]) : [Glasgow School of Art Department of Planning], [1981]. — [28]leaves,[1]leaf of plates : ill ; 30cm. — (Planning monograph / Glasgow School of Art. Planning Department ; no.1)
Cover title. — Bibliography: leaves 25-26
£1.20 (spiral) B81-10388

711′.028′54 — Environment planning. Applications of digital computer systems — *Serials*

Computers, environment and urban systems : an international journal. — Vol.5, no.1/2 (1980)-. — New York ; Oxford : Pergamon, 1980. — v. ; 28cm
Quarterly. — Continues: Urban systems
ISSN 0198-9715 = Computers, environment and urban systems : Unpriced B81-26377

711′.0720417 — Ireland *(Republic).* **Environment planning. Organisations: National Institute for Physical Planning and Construction Research. Research projects** — *Serials*

National Institute for Physical Planning and Construction Research. Review : including accounts for year to 31 December ... / the National Institute for Physical Planning and Construction Research. — 1977-. — Dublin (St. Martin′s House, Waterloo Rd, Dublin 4) : The Institute, 1977-. — v. ; 30cm
Annual. — Continues: National Institute for Physical Planning and Construction Research. Review of work programmes
Unpriced B81-14371

National Institute for Physical Planning and Construction Research. Review / the National Institute for Physical Planning and Construction Research. — 1978. — Dublin (St. Martin′s House, Waterloo Rd, Dublin 4) : The Institute, [1979?]. — 52p
Unpriced B81-14372

National Institute for Physical Planning and Construction Research. Review of work programmes / An Foras Forbartha. — 1975/76. — [Dublin] ([St. Martin′s House, Waterloo Rd, Dublin 4]) : [The Institute], 1976. — v. ; 30cm
Continues: National Institute for Physical Planning and Construction Research. Forbairt. — Continued by: National Institute for Physical Planning and Construction Research Review. — Only 1 issue published under this title
Unpriced B81-14370

711′.09′034 — Environment planning, *1800-1980*

Planning and the environment in the modern world. — London : Mansell. — (Studies in history, planning and the environment)
vol.3: Planning for conservation / edited by Roger Kain. — 1981. — xii,292p : ill,maps ; 25cm
Includes index
ISBN 0-7201-0904-3 : £15.75 : CIP rev. B80-23553

711′.092′2 — Great Britain. Environment planning, *1870-1980* - *Biographies*

Pioneers in British planning. — London : Architectural Press, May 1981. — [240]p
ISBN 0-85139-563-5 (pbk) : £8.95 : CIP entry B81-12369

711′.0941 — Great Britain. Environment planning — *Conference proceedings*

Funding the future : the report of a conference studying new initiatives in architecture, planning and construction / arranged and edited by Charles McKean. — [London] ([66 Portland Place, W1N 4AF]) : ERA Publications Board, Eastern Region RIBA, 1977. — 24p : ill ; 16x21cm
Text on inside covers
Unpriced (pbk) B81-37049

711′.0941 — Great Britain. Environment planning — *For engineering*

Hobbs, F. D.. Planning for engineers and surveyors / F.D. Hobbs and J.F. Doling. — Oxford : Pergamon, 1981. — xii,219p : ill ; 26cm. — (Pergamon international library)
Includes bibliographies and index
ISBN 0-08-025459-4 (cased) : £13.00
ISBN 0-08-025458-6 (pbk) : £6.50 B81-09297

711′.0941 — Great Britain. Environment planning. Implementation

Implementation - views from an ivory tower : papers from a staff seminar held at Oxford Polytechnic, November 1978 / edited by Chris Minay. — [Oxford] ([Gypsy La., Headington, Oxford, OX3 OBP]) : Oxford Polytechnic, Department of Town Planning, 1979. — iv,57p : ill ; 30cm. — (Working paper / Oxford Polytechic Department of Town Planning ; no.43)
Includes bibliographies
Unpriced (pbk) B81-04637

711′.0941 — Great Britain. Environmental planning. Policies of government, *1979-1980* — *Labour Party (Great Britain) viewpoints*

Land environment and planning : the Tory record to December 1980. — London : Labour Party, 1981. — 55p ; 30cm. — (Information paper / Labour Party Research Department ; no.17)
At head of title: The Labour Party
£0.60 (unbound) B81-28275

711′.09411 — Scotland. Environment planning. Participation of community councils

Masterson, Michael P.. Participation in planning : the role of Scottish community councils : a report for the Scottish Development Department / by Michael P. Masterson. — [Edinburgh] ([New St Andrew′s House, St James Centre, Edinburgh EH1 3SZ]) : [The Department], 1980. — 106columns ; 21x30cm
Cover title. — Bibliography: Columns 88-90
Unpriced (spiral) B81-29525

711′.09411 — Scotland. Green belts. Environment planning — *Conference proceedings*

Planning control in the green belt and urban fringe : a note of proceedings of a series of mid career courses held in October 1979. — Glasgow : The Planning Exchange, 1980. — 39leaves ; 30cm. — (Forum report / Planning Exchange ; 21)
Unpriced (pbk) B81-34613

711′.0942 — England. Environment planning. Participation of public. Advisory services: Town and Country Planning Association. *Planning Aid Service*

Curtis, B.. Planning aid : an analysis based on the Planning Aid Service of the Town and Country Planning Association / B. Curtis and D. Edwards. — Reading : School of Planning Studies, University of Reading, 1980. — x,142p ; 30cm. — (Occasional papers / School of Planning Studies, University of Reading ; OP1)
Bibliography: p139-142
ISBN 0-7049-0750-x (pbk) : £3.00 B81-01603

711′.0942 — England. Environment planning — *Statistics* — *Serials*

Planning and development statistics. Estimates / CIPFA Statistical Information Service. — 1980-81. — London : Chartered Institute of Public Finance and Accountancy, 1980. — 40p
ISSN 0144-901x (corrected) : £10.00 B81-20032

711'.0942 — England. Green belts. Environment planning

Gault, *Iain*. Green belt policies in development plans / Iain Gault. — [Oxford] ([Gypsy La., Headington, Oxford OX3 0BP]) : [Oxford Polytechnic, Department of Town Planning], 1981. — 140p : col.maps ; 30cm. — (Working paper / Oxford Polytechnic Department of Town Planning ; no.41)
£4.00 (pbk) B81-13924

711'.12 — Scotland. Lothian Region. Structure plans. Examination in public

Gray, John G.. Road end : or some comments on the highway's section of the examination in public into the Lothian Region structure plan / John G. Gray. — [Edinburgh] ([1 Albyn Place, Edinburgh EH2 4NG]) : [Edina], [1980]. — 44p ; 21cm
Cover title
£0.50 (pbk) B81-11845

711'.3'018 — Scotland. Strathclyde Region. Structure planning. Methodology

Hayton, Keith. An appraisal of forecasting methodology and integration in the Strathclyde structure plan / Keith Hayton. — [Glasgow] ([177] Renfrew St., Glasgow G3 6RQ]) : Department of Planning, Glasgow School of Art, 1979. — 24leaves : ill ; 30cm. — (Occasional papers / Glasgow School of Art : Department of Planning ; 3)
Cover title
£1.20 (spiral) B81-12703

Hayton, Keith. An appraisal of the plan generation methodology of the Strathclyde structure plan / Keith Hayton. — [Glasgow] ([177 Renfrew St., Glasgow G3 6RQ]) : Department of Planning, Glasgow School of Art, 1979. — 17leaves ; 30cm. — (Occasional papers / Glasgow School of Art : Department of Planning ; 2)
Cover title
£1.20 (spiral) B81-12704

711'.3'0941 — Great Britain. Rural regions. Environment planning, *1920-1939*

Sheail, John. Rural conservation in inter-war Britain / John Sheail. — Oxford : Clarendon Press, 1981. — xiv,263p : ill,maps ; 25cm. — (Oxford research studies in geography)
Includes index
ISBN 0-19-823236-5 : £16.50 B81-17164

711'.3'0941 — Great Britain. Rural regions. Environment planning, *1948-1978*

Blacksell, Mark. The countryside : planning and change / Mark Blacksell, Andrew W. Gilg. — London : Allen & Unwin, 1981. — 262p : ill,maps ; 24cm. — (The Resource management series ; 2)
Bibliography: p239-249. — Includes index
ISBN 0-04-711008-2 : Unpriced
ISBN 0-04-711009-0 (pbk) : Unpriced
B81-26860

711'.3'0941 — Great Britain. Rural regions. Environment planning — *Serials*

Countryside planning yearbook. — Vol.1, 1980-. — Norwich : Geo Books, 1980-. — v. ; 24cm
ISSN 0143-8190 = Countryside planning yearbook : Unpriced B81-09105

Countryside planning yearbook. — Vol.2 (1981). — Norwich : Geo Books, 1981. — 225p
ISBN 0-86094-079-9 : Unpriced
ISBN 0-86094-080-2 (pbk)
ISSN 0143-8190 B81-36556

711'.3'0941223 — Scotland. Highland Region. Moray *(District)*. **Speyside. Environment planning** — *Proposals*

Speyside local plan. — Elgin ([District Headquarters, Elgin, Morayshire IV30 1BX]) : Department of Physical Planning & Development, Moray District Council, 1980. — 40 leaves : maps(some col.) ; 30cm
Unpriced (spiral) B81-19793

711'.3'0941232 — Scotland. Grampian Region. Gordon *(District)*. **Environment planning. Participation of public**

Gordon. *District Council*. Gordon District public participation local plan. — [Inverurie] ([Gordon House, Blackhall Rd., Inverurie AB5 9WA]) : [Director of Planning, Gordon District Council], 1981. — 17,[25]p,[9]p of plates : ill(some col.),maps(some col.),facsims ; 30cm
Unpriced (spiral) B81-34668

711'.3'0941232 — Scotland. Grampian Region. Gordon *(District)*. **Environment planning** — *Proposals*

Gordon. *District Council*. Gordon District local plan. — Inverurie (Gordon House, Blackhall Rd., Inverurie AB5 9WA) : Director of Planning, Gordon District Council, 1981. — 107,[53]leaves of plates(some folded) : ill(some col.),col.maps ; 30cm + 1proposals map (66x104cm folded to 17x26cm)
Proposals map in pocket
Unpriced (spiral) B81-34676

711'.3'094124 — Scotland. Grampian Region. Kincardine and Deeside *(District)*. **Environment planning** — *Proposals*

Kincardine suburban area draft local plan. — Stonehaven (Carlton House, Arduthie Rd., Stonehaven AB3 2DP) : Kincardine and Deeside District Council, [1981]. — 125p : ill,maps(some col.) ; 30cm
Four draft proposals maps and key on folded leaves in pockets
£2.00 (spiral) B81-31660

711'.3'094131 — Scotland. Central Region. Rural regions. Structure planning — *Proposals*

Central Region western rural area structure plan : report of initial consultations. — [Stirling] ([Viewforth, Stirling FK8 2ET]) : Central Regional Council, Department of Planning, 1980. — 38p : 1map ; 30cm
Cover title
Unpriced (pbk) B81-12705

711'.3'0941318 — Scotland. Central Region. Falkirk *(District)*. **Structure planning** — *Proposals*

Central Region. *Regional Council*. Structure plan for Falkirk District : issues & choices report / Central Regional Council. — [Stirling] ([Viewforth, Stirling FK8 2ET]) : Central Regional Council, Department of Planning, 1980. — 171p in various pagings : ill,maps ; 30cm
Cover title
Unpriced (pbk) B81-12715

Structure plan : Falkirk District structure plan : issues & choices summary. — [Stirling] ([Viewforth, Stirling FK8 2ET]) : Central Regional Council, [1980]. — 39p : ill,maps ; 30cm
Cover title
Unpriced (pbk) B81-12714

711'.3'094141 — Scotland. Strathclyde Region. Structure planning — *Proposals*

Strathclyde structure plan 1981, consultative draft / [Strathclyde Regional Council]. — [Glasgow] ([Stathclyde House, India St., Glasgow]) : Strathclyde Regional Council, [1981]. — 141p : maps(some col.) ; 30cm
2 folded sheets (maps) as inserts
Unpriced (pbk) B81-29137

711'.3'0941446 — Scotland. Strathclyde Region. Monklands *(District)*. **Environment planning** — *Proposals*

Monklands. *District Council*. Monklands District local plan 1980 : draft written statement / [prepared by] A.I. Cowe. — [Coatbridge] (['Redholme', Laird St., Coatbridge, Strathclyde]) : [Monklands District Council], 1980. — 163p ; 30cm
Unpriced (spiral) B81-35352

711'.3'0941449 — Scotland. Strathclyde Region. Northern Motherwell *(District)*. **Environment planning** — *Proposals*

Motherwell. *District Council*. Northern area local plan : draft written statement / Motherwell District Council. — Motherwell (P.O. Box 14, Civic Centre, Motherwell ML1 1TW) : The Council, 1981. — [101]p,[4]folded leaves of plates : col.maps ; 30cm
Map (1 folded sheet) in pocket
Unpriced (spiral) B81-26566

711'.3'0941629 — Magherafelt *(District)*. **Environment planning. Magherafelt Area Plan**

Magherafelt area plan : statement by Department of the Environment for Northern Ireland. — Belfast : H.M.S.O., 1981. — 10p ; 25cm
ISBN 0-337-08167-0 (unbound) : £1.20
B81-22303

711'.3'09422165 — Surrey. Mole Valley *(District)*. **Environment planning**

Planning in Mole Valley. — London (Publicity House, Streatham Hill, SW2 4TR) : Pyramid, [1980]. — 28p : ill,1map ; 21cm
Unpriced (pbk) B81-09903

711'.3'094225 — East Sussex. Environment planning — *Proposals*

East Sussex. *County Council*. County structure plan 1980 : incorporating the County structure plan 1978 and the first alteration to the plan 1980 as approved by the Secretary of State for the Environment / East Sussex County Council. — Lewes (Southover House, Southover Rd., Lewes, East Sussex, BN7 1YA) : East Sussex County Council, Planning Department, [1980]. — xxiv,118p,[4]folded leaves of plates : ill(some col.),col.maps,facsims ; 31cm
ISBN 0-86147-001-x (pbk) : £5.00 B81-20230

711'.3'094225 — East Sussex. Structure planning — *Proposals*

County structure plan 1981 review : consultative draft. — Lewes (Southover House, Southover Rd., Lewes, E. Sussex BN7 1YA) : East Sussex County Council, Planning Department, 1981. — 26p : 1ill ; 30cm
ISBN 0-86147-006-0 (pbk) : £2.00 B81-37832

East Sussex. *County Council*. Alteration to the county structure plan 1980 : policies and proposals / East Sussex County Council. — Lewes (Southover House, Southover Rd., Lewes, E. Sussex BN7 1YA) : East Sussex County Council, Planning Department, 1981. — iv,31p ; 30cm. — (Publication / East Sussex County Council Planning Department ; no.P/250)
ISBN 0-86147-003-6 (pbk) : £1.50 B81-27846

711'.3'094226 — West Sussex. Structure planning — *Serials*

West Sussex structure plan annual monitoring report / West Sussex County Council. — 1980. — Chichester (c/o County Planning Officer, County Hall, Chichester) : County Planning Dept, 1980. — 77,ca68p
ISBN 0-900800-36-4 : £2.00 B81-24973

711'.3'094233 — Dorset. Structure planning. Participation of public

Draft structure plan report on public consultation : Dorset structure plan (excluding South East Dorset) / [Dorset County Council]. — Dorchester (Dorset Structure Plan Team [County Planning Department, County Hall, Dorchester DT1 1XJ]) : Dorset County Council, 1981. — 192p : maps,1form ; 30cm. — (DSP ; 20)
ISBN 0-85216-280-4 (pbk) : £2.00 B81-18608

711'.3'094233 — Dorset. Structure planning — *Proposals*

Dorset structure plan (excluding South East) : DSP.18 draft written statement for public consultation / [Dorset County Council]. — Dorchester, Dorset ([County Planning Department, County Hall, Dorchester, Dorset DT1 1XJ]) : Structure Plan Team, Dorset County Council, 1980. — lx,204p : maps(some col.) ; 30cm
ISBN 0-85216-273-1 (pbk) : £2.50 B81-37053

711'.3'0942336 — Dorset. Purbeck ***(District).*** **Coastal regions. Environment planning —** ***Proposals***

Purbeck. *District Council*. Purbeck heritage coast : planning and management : joint policy statement / Purbeck District Council, Dorset County Council, West Dorset District Council. — [Dorchester] ([County Library, Colliton Park, Dorchester DT1 1XJ]) : [Dorset County Council, Library Service], [1980]. — 8p,[1] folded leaf of plates : 1map ; 30cm
Cover title
ISBN 0-85216-258-8 (pbk) : £0.25 B81-09861

711'.3'0942561 — Bedfordshire. North Bedfordshire ***(District).*** **Rural regions. Environment planning —** ***Proposals***

North Bedfordshire. *Borough Council*. Rural planning policy for North Bedfordshire / [North Bedfordshire Borough Council]. — [Bedford] ([37 Goldington Rd., Bedford MK40 3LQ]) : [The Council], 1980. — 37p,[1]folded leaf of plates : 1map ; 30cm
Bibliography: p37
Unpriced (pbk) B81-26366

711'.3'094261 — Norfolk. Environment planning — ***Proposals***

Norfolk County Council development plan scheme as approved by the Planning Sub-Committee on 16th January, 1981. — Norwich (Martineau Lane, Norwich NR1 2DH) : Norfolk County Council, [1981]. — 23p : 1ill ; 30cm
£1.00 (unbound) B81-26996

711'.3'094261 — Norfolk. Structure planning

Norfolk structure plan : fourth monitoring report : the county strategy / Norfolk County Council Planning and Transportation Committee. — Norwich ([c/o] County Planning Officer, County Hall, Martineau La., Norwich, NR1 2DH) : Norfolk County Council, 1981. — iv,85p : ill,2maps ; 30cm
£1.00 (spiral) B81-19562

711'.3'09426712 — Essex. Uttlesford ***(District).*** **Rural regions. Environment planning —** ***Proposals***

Uttlesford. *District Council*. Rural areas district plan / Uttlesford District Council. — [Great Dunmow] ([Council Offices, High St., Great Dunmow, Essex CM6 1AN]) : [The Council]
Cover title
Part 2: Written statement of village policies Felsted. — [1981?]. — 11p,[4]folded leaves of plates : maps ; 30cm
£0.50 (pbk) B81-20232

Uttlesford. *District Council*. Rural areas district plan / Uttlesford District Council. — [Great Dunmow] ([Council Offices, High St., Great Dunmow, Essex CM6 1AN]) : [The Council]
Cover title
Part 2: Written statement of village policies Thaxted. — [1981?]. — 13p,[1]folded leaf of plates : 1map ; 30cm
£0.50 (pbk) B81-20231

711'.3'09426715 — Essex. Braintree ***(District).*** **Environment planning —** ***Proposals***

District plan for Braintree and surrounding villages : draft plan for public consultation / Braintree District Council. — Braintree District Council. — [174]p : maps ; 30cm
Four maps [4 folded sheets] in pockets
£2.00 (pbk) B81-29891

711'.3'094275 — Merseyside ***(Metropolitan County).*** **Structure planning —** ***Proposals***

Merseyside. *County Council*. Merseyside structure plan : written statement / Merseyside County Council. — [Liverpool] ([P.O. Box 95, Metropolitan House, Old Hall St., Liverpool L69 3EL]) : [The Council], 1980. — vii,175p : ill(some col.),col.maps ; 31cm
Col. map (1 folded sheet) in pocket. — Includes index
Unpriced (spiral) B81-18595

711'.3'094278 — Cumbria. Environment planning

Cumbria planning handbook. — [London] : [Burrow], [1981]. — 44p : ill,1map ; 22cm
Unpriced (pbk) B81-24085

711'.4 — Environment planning by local authorities — ***Conference proceedings***

Local government and environmental planning and control. — Aldershot : Gower, Jan.1982. — [298]p
Conference papers
ISBN 0-566-00440-2 : £15.00 : CIP entry B81-34282

711'.4 — Town planning

Bracken, Ian. Urban planning methods. — London : Methuen, Oct.1981. — [400]p
ISBN 0-416-74860-0 (cased) : £12.00 : CIP entry
ISBN 0-416-74870-8 (pbk) : £6.00 B81-25297

Posokhin, Mikhail. Towns for people / Mikhail Posokhin ; [translated from the Russian by Natalie Ward and Christopher English]. — Moscow : Progress Publishers ; [London] : Central Books [distributor], c1980. — 219p : ill,maps,facsims,plans ; 27cm
Translation of: Gorod dlīā cheloveka. — Bibliography: p219
ISBN 0-7147-1626-x : £4.95 B81-32941

The **Urban** landscape : historical development and management. — London : Academic Press, Feb.1982. — [160]p. — (Special publication / Institute of British Geographers, ISSN 0073-9006 ; 13)
ISBN 0-12-747020-4 : CIP entry B81-35913

711'.4 — Town planning - ***Conference proceedings***

Traffic, transportation and urban planning. — London : Godwin, Apr.1981. — (International forum series)
Conference papers
Vol.1. — [256]p
ISBN 0-7114-5713-1 (pbk) : £12.00 : CIP entry B81-05156

Traffic, transportation and urban planning. — London : Godwin, Apr.1981. — (International forum series)
Conference papers
Vol.2. — [256]p
ISBN 0-7114-5714-x (pbk) : £12.00 : CIP entry B81-05157

711'.4 — Urban regions. Environment planning

Lynch, Kevin. A theory of good city form / Kevin Lynch. — Cambridge, Mass. ; London : MIT, c1981. — 514p : ill,maps,plans ; 24cm
Bibliography: p459-483. — Includes index
ISBN 0-262-12085-2 : £15.50 B81-30029

711'.4'01 — Town planning. Theories

McConnell, Shean. Theories for planning : an introduction / Shean McConnell. — London : Heinemann, 1981. — xvi,208p : ill,maps ; 22cm
Includes index
ISBN 0-434-91236-0 (pbk) : £7.95 B81-39655

711'.4'02854 — England. Town planning. Applications of digital computer systems — ***Conference proceedings***

The **Use** of computers in town planning : papers given at a one day seminar held on 15th October 1980 / Town & Country Planning Association & Polytechnic of the South Bank Town Planning Department ; editor Ian Twinn. — London (Wandsworth Rd., SW8 2J2) : Department of Town Planning, Polytechnic of the South Bank, 1980. — 49 leaves : forms ; 30cm. — (Planning conference paper ; 13)
£2.00 (pbk) B81-11828

711'.4'071141 — Great Britain. Higher education institutions. Curriculum subjects: Town planning — ***Serials***

[Span ***(Bristol)*****]**. Span / the Student Planners Association. — No.1-. — Bristol (26 Logan Rd., Bishopston, Bristol BS7 8DT) : The Association, [1980?]-. — v. ; 30cm
ISSN 0261-4081 = Span (Bristol) : Unpriced B81-31054

711'.4'0722 — London. Inner areas. Redevelopment — ***Case studies***

Urban renaissance in London : exercises in regenerating the inner city. — London : Greater London Council, [1980]. — 36p : ill,1map ; 30cm
ISBN 0-7168-1139-1 (pbk) : Unpriced B81-34891

711'.4'09034 — Town planning, ***1800-1914***

The **Rise** of modern urban planning 1800-1914 / edited by Anthony Sutcliffe. — London : Mansell, 1980. — xi,235p : ill,maps,plans ; 25cm. — (Studies in history, planning and the environment)
Conference papers. — Includes index
ISBN 0-7201-0902-7 : £13.25 : CIP rev. B80-10700

711'.4'091812 — Western world. Town planning, ***1780-1914 — Comparative studies***

Sutcliffe, Antony. Towards the planned city : Germany, Britain, the United States and France 1780-1914 / Anthony Sutcliffe. — Oxford : Basil Blackwell, 1981. — x,230p : ill,facsims ; 25cm. — (Comparative studies in social and economic history ; 3)
Bibliography: p210-222. — Includes index
ISBN 0-631-11001-1 (cased) : £15.00
ISBN 0-631-12599-x (pbk) : £6.50 B81-24271

711'.4'0922 — Great Britain. Town planning — ***Biographies***

Pioneers in British planning / edited by Gordon E. Cherry. — London : Architectural Press, 1981. — viii,232p, xxxiip of plates : ill,maps,plans,ports ; 24cm
Includes index
ISBN 0-85139-566-x (pbk) : £8.95 B81-26347

711'.4'094 — Western Europe. Urban regions. Environment planning. Geographical aspects

Burtenshaw, D.. The city in West Europe / D. Burtenshaw, M. Bateman and G.J. Ashworth. — Chichester : Wiley, c1981. — xx,340p : ill,maps ; 24cm
Bibliography: p310-324. — Includes index
ISBN 0-471-27929-3 : £15.50 B81-37107

711'.4'0941 — Great Britain. Town planning, ***1860-1920***

British town planning : the formative years / edited by Anthony Sutcliffe. — Leicester : Leicester University Press, 1981. — xi,211p : ill,maps,plans,ports ; 24cm. — (Themes in urban history)
Bibliography: p201-203. — Includes index
ISBN 0-7185-1174-3 : £14.00 : CIP rev. B81-15831

711'.4'09411 — Scotland. Environment planning. Local plans — ***Conference proceedings***

Discussion Forum on local plans : report of two Discussion Forums held in Dundee on 28 September 1979 and in Glasgow on 11 December 1979. — Glasgow : The Planning Exchange, 1980. — 21leaves : 1 form ; 30cm. — (Forum report / Planning Exchange ; 20)
Unpriced (pbk) B81-34614

Local plan progress review. — Glasgow (186 Bath St., Glasgow G2 4HG) : The Planning Exchange, 1981. — 50p ; 30cm. — (Forum report / Planning Exchange ; 25)
Unpriced (pbk) B81-29599

711'.4'0941235 — Scotland. Grampian Region. Aberdeen. Central areas. Environment planning — ***Proposals***

Central District local plan : report of survey. — Aberdeen (St Nicholas House, Aberdeen) : Department of Planning and Building Control, City of Aberdeen District Council, 1980. — 92p : ill,maps(some col.) ; 30cm
Unpriced (spiral) B81-19796

711'.4'094124 — Scotland. Grampian Region. Kincardine and Deeside ***(District).*** **Environment planning. Local plans**

Kincardine suburban area local plan survey report . — [Stonehaven] ([Carlton House, Arduthie Rd, Stonehaven, Deeside]) : Kincardine & Deeside District Council, Department of Planning, [1980]. — 85p(7 fold) : plans ; 30cm
Unpriced (spiral) B81-19881

711'.4'094126 — Scotland. Tayside Region. Montrose. Environment planning — ***Proposals***

Angus. *District Council*. Montrose local plan : written statement / [Angus District Council]. — [Forfar] ([County Buildings, Forfar DD8 3LG]) : The Council, 1980. — 116p : maps (some col.) ; 30cm + 1map(83x60cm folded to 30x21cm)
£2.00 (spiral) B81-09370

711'.4'0941292 — Scotland. Fife Region. Newburgh. Environment planning — *Proposals*

North East Fife. *District Council.* Newburgh local plan. — [Cupar] ([County Buildings, St. Catherine St., Cupar, Fife]) : North East Fife District Council Department of Physical Planning, 1980. — 30leaves,[1]folded leaf of plates : ill,coats of arms,plans ; 30cm
£2.00 (spiral) B81-20227

North East Fife. *District Council.* Newburgh local plan draft. — [Cupar] ([County Buildings, St. Catherine St., Cupar, Fife]) : North East Fife District Council Department of Physical Planning, [1979]. — 30leaves,[1]folded leaf of plates : ill,coats of arms,plans ; 30cm
Cover title
£2.00 (spiral) B81-20226

711'.4'0941318 — Scotland. Central Region. Falkirk *(District)*. Denny. Environment planning — *Proposals*

Denny and district local plan / Falkirk District Council, Department of Planning. — Falkirk (Municipal Buildings, Falkirk [FK1 5RS]) : [The Department], 1979-1980. — 4v. : maps ; 30cm
ISBN 0-906586-00-3 (pbk) : Unpriced
B81-32343

711'.4'094133 — Scotland. Lothian Region. Broxburn region. Environment planning — *Proposals*

Broxburn area local plan : policy options report / West Lothian District Council. — [Edinburgh] ([District Headquarters, South Bridge St., Bathgate, Edinburgh EH48 1TS]) : [The Council], 1980. — 28p,[3]folded leaves of plates : maps ; 30cm
Cover title
Unpriced (pbk) B81-09444

711'.4'094134 — Edinburgh. Newbridge & Kirkliston. Environmental planning — *Proposals*

Newbridge and Kirkliston local plan : draft policies and proposals. — [Edinburgh] ([City Chambers, High St., Edinburgh EH1 1YJ]) : City of Edinburgh District Council, Planning Department, 1980. — 6leaves,[2]leaves of plates : 2maps ; 30cm
Unpriced (pbk) B81-12708

711'.4'094134 — Edinburgh. Queensferry. Environment planning — *Proposals*

Queensferry local plan : draft policies and proposals. — [Edinburgh] ([City Chambers, High St., Edinburgh EH1 1YJ]) : City of Edinburgh District Council, Planning Department, 1980. — 9p,2leaves of plates : ill,maps ; 30cm
Unpriced (pbk) B81-12712

711'.4'094135 — Scotland. Lothian Region. Dalkeith. Environment planning — *Proposals*

Dalkeith local plan / prepared by the Midlothian District Council. Department of Planning and Building Control. — [Roslin] : [The Council]
2: Policies and proposals. — [1980]. — 38p : ill,1col.maps,1col.plan ; 21cm
Folded sheet (text, plan) in pocket
Unpriced (pbk) B81-32367

711'.4'0941385 — Scotland. Borders Region. Galashiels & Tweedbank. Environment planning. Participation of public

Borders Region. *Department of Physical Planning and Development.* Galashiels/Tweedbank local plan : public participation report / Borders Regional Council, Department of Physical Planning and Development. — St. Boswell (Newtown, St. Boswells [Roxburghshire 1D6 OSA]) : The Department, 1980. — 26p ; 30cm
Unpriced (pbk) B81-37605

711'.4'0941385 — Scotland. Borders Region. Galashiels & Tweedbank. Environment planning — *Proposals*

Borders Region. *Department of Physical Planning and Development.* Galashiels/Tweedbank local plan : written statement / Borders Regional Council, Department of Planning and Development. — St. Boswells (Newtown, St. Boswells, [Roxburghshire TD6 OSA]) : The Department, 1980. — 52p,[2]folded leaves of plates : col.maps ; 30cm
Map on folded leaf in pocket
Unpriced (pbk) B81-37604

711'.4'0941392 — Scotland. Borders Region. Kelso. Environment planning — *Proposals*

Kelso issues report / Borders Regional Council, Department of Physical Planning and Development. — St. Boswells (c/o David P. Douglas, Director of Physical Planning and Development, Regional Headquarters, Newtown, St. Boswells, Roxburghshire TD6 0SA) : Borders Regional Council, 1980. — 25p : 1map,plans ; 30cm
Cover title: Kelso local plan
Unpriced (pbk) B81-35261

711'.4'0941432 — Scotland. Strathclyde Region. Duntocher & Hardgate. Environment planning — *Proposals*

Clydebank. *District Council.*
Duntocher/Hardgate local plan / Clydebank District Council. — [Clydebank] ([Rosebery Pl., Clydebank G81 1UA]) : [The Council], 1979. — 40p : 2maps ; 30cm
Unpriced (pbk) B81-11978

Duntocher/Hardgate local plan : draft / Clydebank District Council. — [Clydebank] ([Rosebery Pl., Clydebank G81 1UA]) : [The Council], 1979. — 50 leaves : 2maps ; 30cm
Unpriced (pbk) B81-11979

711'.4'0941432 — Scotland. Strathclyde Region. Duntocher & Hardgate. Environment planning. Publicity & consultation

Duntocher/Hardgate local plan publicity and consultations / Clydebank District Council. — [Clydebank] ([Rosebery Pl., Clydebank G81 1UA]) : [The Council], 1979. — 62p : 1map,facsims ; 30cm
Unpriced (pbk) B81-11980

711'.4'0941436 — Scotland. Strathclyde Region. Bishopbriggs. Environment planning — *Proposals*

Strathkelvin. *District Council.* Strathkelvin District (Bishopbriggs Area) : local plan / [Strathkelvin District Council]. — Kirkintilloch (Council Chambers, Kirkintilloch) : [The Council], 1980. — 40p ; 30cm + 2proposals maps(90x88cm folded to 30x22cm ; 88x60cm folded to 22x30cm)
Unpriced (spiral) B81-12710

711'.4'0941436 — Scotland. Strathclyde Region. Kirkintilloch. Environment planning — *Proposals*

Strathkelvin District (Kirkintilloch area) local plan : initial report (as approved by Strathkelvin District Council) on 24th February 1977. — Bishopbriggs (1A Churchill Way, Bishopbriggs) : Strathkelvin District Council, Planning Department, [1977?]. — 15leaves : 1plan ; 30cm
Cover title
Unpriced (spiral) B81-12587

Strathkelvin District (Kirkintilloch area) local plan : written statement. — Kirkintilloch (P.O. Box 4, Council Chambers, Kirkintilloch, Glasgow G66 1PW) : Strathkelvin District Council, 1980. — 100p ; 31cm + 2maps : col.
Unpriced (spiral) B81-12588

711'.4'0941443 — Scotland. Strathclyde Region. Eastern Glasgow. Environment planning. Participation of public

Nelson, Sarah. Participating in GEAR : public involvement in an area-based urban renewal programme / Sarah Nelson. — [Glasgow] ([16 Richmond St., Glasgow G1 1X9]) : Strathclyde Area Survey, 1980. — 133p : 1map ; 30cm
Bibliography: p125-131
£3.00 (pbk) B81-35669

711'.4'0941443 — Scotland. Strathclyde Region. Glasgow. Baillieston. Environment planning — *Proposals*

Survey report : Baillieston Daldowie local plan / City of Glasgow District Council. — [Glasgow] ([84 Queen St., Glasgow G1 3DP]) : [Director of Planning, Glasgow District Council], [1980]. — 69p,[16]leaves of plates : maps ; 30cm
Cover title
Unpriced (pbk) B81-36909

711'.4'0941443 — Scotland. Strathclyde Region. Glasgow. Calton. Environment planning — *Proposals*

Calton local plan : written statement / City of Glasgow District Council. — Glasgow (84 Queen St., Glasgow, G1 3DP) : Planning Department, 1978. — 84p,[2]leaves of plates : ill,maps ; 30cm
Unpriced (unbound) B81-09643

711'.4'0941443 — Scotland. Strathclyde Region. Glasgow. Carmunnock. Environment planning — *Proposals*

Survey report : Carmunock local plan / City of Glasgow District Council. — [Glasgow] ([84 Queen St., Glasgow G1 3Dp]) : [Director of Planning, Glasgow District Council], [1979]. — 59p,[13]leaves of plates : ill,maps,plans ; 30cm
Unpriced (spiral) B81-40124

711'.4'0941443 — Scotland. Strathclyde Region. Glasgow. Dennistoun. Environment planning — *Proposals*

Glasgow. *District Council.* Dennistoun local plan : written statement / City of Glasgow District Council. — Glasgow (84 Queen St., Glasgow G1 3DP) : City of Glasgow District Council, 1981. — 41p,[6]leaves of plates(2folded) : ill,plans ; 30cm
Cover title
Unpriced (spiral) B81-28298

711'.4'0941443 — Scotland. Strathclyde Region. Glasgow. Govanhill. Environment planning — *Proposals*

Written statement : Govanhill local plan / City of Glasgow District Council. — [Glasgow] ([84 Queen St., Glasgow G1 3DP]) : [Director of Planning, Glasgow District Council], [1981]. — 26p,[2]folded leaves of plates : 1map,1plan ; 30cm
Cover title
Unpriced (spiral) B81-36907

711'.4'0941443 — Scotland. Strathclyde Region. Glasgow. Parkhead. Environment planning — *Proposals*

Parkhead local plan : written statement. — Glasgow (84 Queen St., Glasgow, G1 3DP) : Glasgow District Council Planning Department, 1980. — 71p : ill,maps ; 30cm
Unpriced (unbound) B81-09644

711'.4'0941443 — Scotland. Strathclyde Region. Glasgow. Pollokshields & Dumbreck. Environment planning — *Proposals*

Additional area report : Pollokshields Dumbreck local plan / City of Glasgow District Council. — [Glasgow] ([84 Queen St., Glasgow G1 3DP]) : [Director of Planning, Glasgow District Council], [1980]. — [36]p : maps ; 30cm
Cover title
Unpriced (spiral) B81-36911

Pollokshields/Dumbreck local plan draft written statement / [City of Glasgow District Council]. — Glasgow (84 Queen St., Glasgow G1 3DP) : Director of Planning Glasgow District Council, 1981. — 66p : ill,1maps ; 30cm
Map in pocket
Unpriced (spiral) B81-27866

Survey report : Pollokshields Dumbreck local plan / City of Glasgow District Council. — [Glasgow] ([84 Queen St., Glasgow G1 3DP]) : [Director of Planning, Glasgow District Council], [1979]. — 76p,[12]leaves of plates : maps ; 30cm
Cover title
Unpriced (pbk) B81-36910

711'.4'0941443 — Scotland. Strathclyde Region. Glasgow. Shettleston & Tollcross. Environment planning

Shettleston/Tollcross local plan : survey report. — Glasgow (84 Queen St., Glasgow, G1 3DP) : [City of Glasgow District Council Planning Department], 1978. — 90p,[10]leaves of plates : maps ; 30cm
Cover title
Unpriced (spiral) B81-09641

711'.4'0941443 — Scotland. Strathclyde Region. Glasgow. Shettleston & Tollcross. Environment planning — *Proposals*

Shettleston/Tollcross local plan : written statement. — Glasgow (84 Queen St., Glasgow, G1 3DP) : [City of Glasgow District Council Planning Department], 1979. — 59p : ill,maps ; 30cm
Cover title
Unpriced (spiral) B81-09642

711'.4'0941443 — Scotland. Strathclyde Region. Glasgow. Yorkhill. Environment planning — *Proposals*

Written statement : Yorkhill local plan / City of Glasgow District Council. — [Glasgow] ([84 Queen St., Glasgow G1 3DP]) : [Director of Planning, Glasgow District Council], [1981]. — 33p : ill,maps ; 30cm
Cover title. — Map (40x81cm. folded to 22x19cm.) in pocket
Unpriced (spiral) B81-36906

711'.4'0941449 — Scotland. Strathclyde Region. Wishaw. Environment planning — *Proposals*

Survey report and policy options, Wishaw local plan / Motherwell District Council. — [Motherwell] ([P.O. Box 14, Civic Centre, Motherwell ML1 1TW]) : The Council, 1980. — 43p,[3]p leaves of plates : ill,maps ; 30cm
Unpriced (spiral) B81-11981

711'.4'0941469 — Scotland. Strathclyde Region. Lanark. Environment planning — *Proposals*

Clydesdale. *District Council*. Lanark local plan : written statement, policies & proposals : draft for publicity and consultation purposes / Clydesdale District Council. — [Lanark] ([South Vennel, Lanark ML11 7JT]) : [Clydesdale District Council], [1981]. — 25p : ill,maps ; 30cm + Proposals map(60x84cm folded to 30x22cm)
Cover title
Unpriced (pbk) B81-33600

711'.4'0942 — England. Environment planning. Policies of local authorities — *Case studies*

Approaches to local planning / edited by Colin Fudge. — Bristol (Rodney Lodge, Grange Rd., Clifton, Bristol BS8 4EA) : University of Bristol, School for Advanced Urban Studies, c1978. — 82p ; 30cm. — (Working paper / University of Bristol, School for Advanced Urban Studies, ISSN 0141-464x ; W.P.3)
£1.00 (pbk) B81-09425

711'.4'0942132 — London. Westminster *(London Borough)*. **Covent Garden. Environment planning. Proposals. Role of community action groups,** *ca 1965-ca 1975*

Anson, Brian. I'll fight you for it! : behind the struggle for Covent Garden / Brian Anson. — London : Cape, 1981. — xv,270p,[16]p of plates : ill,facsims,ports ; 23cm
Includes index
ISBN 0-224-01795-0 (cased) : £8.95
ISBN 0-224-01839-6 (pbk) : £4.95 B81-09167

711'.4'0942132 — London. Westminster *(London Borough)*. **Piccadilly Circus. Proposed redevelopment,** *to 1986*

Piccadilly Circus : from controversy to construction. — [London] : Greater London Council, [1980]. — 33p : ill(some col.),col.maps ; 26cm
Cover title
ISBN 0-7168-1145-6 (pbk) : £1.50 B81-34882

711'.4'0942234 — Kent. Canterbury. Environment planning — *Proposals*

Canterbury City District Plan report on choices and strategy / [Canterbury City Council]. — Canterbury (Civic Centre, Canterbury, Kent) : [The Council], 1981. — ii,196p,[14]folded leaves of plates : ill,maps ; 30cm
£2.75 (spiral) B81-38399

711'.4'09422372 — Kent. Offham. Conservation areas: Offham Conservation Area. Environment planning — *Proposals*

Offham conservation study. — [Maidstone] ([c/o Planning Director, Council Offices, The Air Station, West Malling, Maidstone, Kent ME19 6LZ]) : Tonbridge & Malling District Council, 1981. — 44p,[17]p of plates : ill,1map ; 30cm
Unpriced (pbk) B81-25999

711'.4'09422372 — Kent. Plaxtol & Fairlawne. Environment planning. Conservation — *Proposals*

Plaxtol and Fairlawne : conservation study. — [West Malling] ([Council Offices, The Air Station, West Malling, Maidstone, Kent ME19 6LZ]) : Tonbridge and Malling District Council, 1981. — 48p,[19]p of plates : ill,2maps ; 30cm
Cover title
Unpriced (pbk) B81-24422

711'.4'0942332 — Dorset. Shaftesbury. Environment planning — *Proposals*

Dorset. *County Council*. Shaftesbury town plan — 1981 / Dorset County Council, North Dorset District Council. — [Dorchester] : [c/o County Planning Officer, County Hall, Dorchester, DT1 1XJ], [The Councils] (1981). — 15p,[3]folded leaves of plates : 3maps(some col.) ; 30cm
ISBN 0-85216-278-2 (pbk) : £0.75 B81-24327

711'.4'0942356 — Devon. Exeter. Quayside. Environment planning — *Proposals*

Green, R. J.. Exeter Quayside conservation study / [R.J. Green, E. Mather]. — Exeter ([Room G53, County Hall, Exeter EX2 4BQ]) : [Local Government Library], 1981. — 30leaves : ill,maps,plans ; 21x30cm
Cover title
ISBN 0-86114-331-0 (pbk) : Unpriced B81-34631

711'.4'0942496 — West Midlands *(Metropolitan County)*. **Birmingham. Urban renewal**

Safe as houses? : urban renewal — the crisis now / City of Birmingham. — [Birmingham] ([120 Edward St, Birmingham B3 2EZ]) : Urban Renewal Section of Environmental Health Department, [1981]. — 18p : ill,maps(same col.) ; 30x42cm
Cover title
Unpriced (pbk) B81-34441

711'.4'0942497 — West Midlands *(Metropolitan County)*. **Solihull** *(District)*. **Conservation areas**

Richardson, T. R.. Conservation areas in Solihull / by T.R. Richardson. — London : Institution of Municipal Engineers, 1979. — 20p : ill,plans ; 21cm. — (Protection of the environment ; monograph no.30)
£1.00 (pbk) B81-04810

711'.4'0942534 — Lincolnshire. Lincoln. Nettleham Road. Environment planning — *Proposals*

Land north-west of Nettleham Road : developers design guide / City of Lincoln. — Lincoln (Director of Planning & Architecture, City Hall, Beaumont Fee, Lincoln LN1 1DF) : City of Lincoln, 1981. — [10]p : ill,plans ; 30cm
£0.40 (spiral) B81-37418

711'.4'0942534 — Lincolnshire. Lincoln. North eastern periphery. Environment planning — *Proposals*

North Eastern periphery draft district plan, written statement. — [Lincoln] ([City Hall, Beaumont Fee, Lincoln, LN1 1DF]) : [Lincoln City Council, Department of Planning and Architecture], 1981. — 12p,[3]p of plates : maps ; 30cm
Cover title
£1.00 (spiral) B81-35414

711'.4'0942534 — Lincolnshire. Lincoln. Skewbridge region. Environment planning — *Proposals*

Skewbridge district plan : joint brief / [Lincolnshire County Council] and Lincoln City Council. — [Lincoln] ([City Hall, Beaumont Fee, Lincoln LN1 1DF]) : [Lincoln City Council], 1981. — 4,ip : 1map ; 30cm
£0.35 (pbk) B81-09369

711'.4'0942539 — Lincolnshire. Spalding & Pinchbeck. Environment planning — *Proposals*

South Holland. *District Council*. The Spalding and Pinchbeck district plan / South Holland District Council. — Spalding (12 Market Place, Spalding, Lincs.) : South Holland District Planning Office
Housing. — 1981. — 10leaves ; 30cm
Unpriced (spiral) B81-18462

South Holland. *District Council*. The Spalding and Pinchbeck district plan / South Holland District Council. — Spalding (12 Market Place, Spalding, Lincs.) : South Holland District Planning Office
Industry and commerce. — 1981. — 12leaves,[3]leaves of plates : maps ; 30cm
Unpriced (spiral) B81-18463

711'.4'0942561 — Bedfordshire. Bedford. Great Ouse River region. Environment planning — *Proposals*

North Bedfordshire. *Borough Council*. Bedford's riverside : a plan for the River Great Ouse / [North Bedfordshire Borough Council]. — [Bedford] ([37 Goldington Rd., Bedford MK40 3LQ]) : [The Council], 1980. — 14p,xiii leaves,[1]folded leaf of plate ; ill : 2maps ; 30cm
Map on folded leaf in pocket
Unpriced (spiral) B81-26359

711'.4'0942561 — Bedfordshire. Bedford. Town planning, *1945-1974*

Jones, Arthur. For the record — Bedford 1945-74 : land use and financial planning. — Bedford (6 Mill St., Bedford) : Roberts Publishing, Nov.1981. — 1v.
ISBN 0-9507778-0-3 (pbk) : £7.25 : CIP entry B81-33646

711'.4'0942561 — Bedfordshire. Harrold. Environment planning — *Proposals*

North Bedfordshire. *Borough Council*. Harrold village plan / D.S. Edgley, Chief Planner, North Bedfordshire Borough Council. — [Bedford] ([37-45 Goldington Rd., Bedford MK40 3LQ]) : The Council, 1981. — 37,iiip + 1folded sheet(plan; 60x82cm) : ill,2maps,1plan ; 30cm
Folded plan in pocket
Unpriced (pbk) B81-37991

North Bedfordshire. *Borough Council*. Harrold village plan : draft / [North Bedfordshire Borough Council]. — [Bedford] ([37 Goldington Rd., Bedford MK40 3LQ]) : [The Council], 1980. — 30,viiip : 2maps, ; 30cm
Two comments sheets and 1 map on folded leaf in pocket
Unpriced (pbk) B81-26364

711'.4'0942561 — Bedfordshire. Kempston. Environment planning — *Proposals*

North Bedfordshire. *Borough Council*. Kempston district plan : written statement / North Bedfordshire Borough Council. — [Bedford] ([37 Goldington Rd., Bedford MK40 3LQ]) : [The Council], 1981. — 45p ; 30cm + 1map (1leaf: 68x93cm folded to 19x26cm)
Cover title
Unpriced (pbk) B81-26363

North Bedfordshire. *Borough Council*. Kempston district plan / North Bedfordshire Borough Council. — [Bedford] ([37 Goldington Rd., Bedford MK40 3LQ]) : [The Council]
Community involvement
Stage 2. — 1979. — 49,vip ; 30cm
Unpriced (pbk) B81-26362

North Bedfordshire. *Borough Council*. Kempston district plan / North Bedfordshire Borough Council. — [Bedford] ([37 Goldington Rd., Bedford MK40 3LQ]) : [The Council]
Cover title
Community involvement
Stage 3. — 1981. — 14p ; 30cm
Unpriced (pbk) B81-26361

711'.4'0942561 — Bedfordshire. Riseley. Conservation areas: Riseley conservation area. Environment planning — *Proposals*

Riseley and its conservation area / Department of Planning and Development, North Bedfordshire Borough Council. — [Bedford] ([37 Goldington Rd., Bedford MK40 3LQ]) : [The Council], 1980. — 36p,[6]folded leaves of plates : ill,maps,plans ; 30cm
Map on inside cover
Unpriced (pbk) B81-26367

711'.4'0942561 — Bedfordshire. Wilshamstead. Environment planning — *Proposals*

North Bedfordshire. *Borough Council.* Wilshamstead village plan / North Bedfordshire Borough Council. — [Bedford] ([37 Goldington Rd., Bedford MK40 3LQ]) : [The Council], 1980. — 28p : ill,2maps ; 21x30cm
Cover title. — Two maps on 2 folded leaves in pocket
Unpriced (pbk) B81-26369

711'.4'0942561 — Bedfordshire. Wootton. Environment planning — *Proposals*

North Bedfordshire. *Borough Council.* Wootton village plan / [North Bedfordshire Borough Council]. — [Bedford] ([37 Goldington Rd., Bedford MK40 3LQ]) : [The Council], 1980. — 23,xvp,[1]folded leaf of plates : ill,maps ; 30cm
Map on 1 folded leaf in pocket
Unpriced (pbk) B81-26368

711'.4'0942582 — Hertfordshire. Stevenage. Environment planning, *to 1978.* **Political aspects**

Mullan, Bob. Stevenage Ltd : aspects of the planning and politics of Stevenage New Town 1942-78 / Bob Mullan. — London : Routledge & Kegan Paul, 1980. — xviii,420p : 1 map,plans ; 23cm. — (International library of sociology)
Bibliography: p385-412. — Includes index
ISBN 0-7100-0538-5 : £14.95 : CIP rev.
B80-11991

711'.4'0942583 — Hertfordshire. Panshanger. Environmental planning — *Proposals*

Panshanger issue study / [Welwyn Hatfield District Council, East Hertfordshire District Council, Hertfordshire County Council]. — [Hatfield] ([16 St. Albans Road East, Hatfield, Herts.]) : Welwyn Hatfield District Council, 1979. — 32,14leaves : ill,maps ; 30cm
£50.00 (pbk) B81-40291

711'.4'0942586 — Hertfordshire. Mardley Heath & Oaklands. Environment planning — *Proposals*

Mardley Heath and Oaklands : study report for public discussion / [Welwyn Hatfield District Council]. — East Hatfield (A.G. Swanson, Controller of Technical Services, 16 St. Aldates Rd., East Hatfield, Herts.) : The Council, [1981?]. — 54p : 1map,col.plans ; 30cm
Unpriced (spiral) B81-38581

Welwyn Hatfield. *District Council.* Mardley Heath and Oaklands policy statement 1973 / [Welwyn Hatfield District Council]. — East Hatfield (c/o A.G. Swanson, Controller of Technical Services 16 St. Albans Rd., East Hatfield, Herts.) : The Council, [1981?]. — 35p : 2plans ; 30cm
Unpriced (spiral) B81-38580

711'.4'0942613 — Norfolk. Downham Market. Environment planning. Participation of public

Downham Market draft district plan : statement of public participation and consultation. — [King's Lynn] (Borough Planning Officer, 27 Queen St., King's Lynn, Norfolk PE30 1HT) : West Norfolk Borough Council, [1981?]. — 171p : ill,maps,1form ; 30cm
Unpriced (spiral) B81-22749

711'.4'0942654 — Cambridgeshire. Ramsey. Environment planning — *Proposals*

Ramsey district plan. — Huntingdon ([c/o Planning Department, Pathfinder House, St Mary's St., Huntingdon, Cambs. PE18 6TN]) : Huntingdon District Council, 1980. — 49p : maps,plans ; 30cm
£2.00 (pbk) B81-12090

711'.4'0942657 — Cambridgeshire. Landbeach & Waterbeach. Environment planning — *Proposals*

Waterbeach & Landbeach district plan : draft. — Cambridge (c/o Planning Officer, South Cambridgeshire Hall, Hills Rd., Cambridge CB2 1PB) : South Cambridgeshire District Council, 1981. — 18,iiip,[3]folded leaves of plates : maps ; 30cm
Cover title
Unpriced (pbk) B81-24381

711'.4'09426'57 — Cambridgeshire. Milton. Environment planning — *Proposals*

Joint Planning Team of South Cambridgeshire District Council, Cambridge City Council. Milton area draft district plan / Joint Planning Team of South Cambridgeshire District Council, Cambridge City Council, with Cambridgeshire County Council. — [Cambridge] ([South Cambridgeshire Hall, 9 Hills Rd., Cambridge CB2 1PB]) : [South Cambridgeshire District Council Planning and Architects Department], 1981. — 42p,viiip,[2]folded leaves of plates : plans ; 30cm
Map (folded sheet) in pocket
Unpriced (pbk) B81-19585

711'.4'0942657 — Cambridgeshire. Milton. Environment planning — *Proposals*

Joint Planning Team of South Cambridgeshire District Council, Cambridge City Council. Survey and the basis for a plan : Milton area, joint district plan : consultative report / Joint Planning Team of South Cambridgeshire District Council, Cambridge City Council with Cambridgeshire County Council. — [Cambridge] ([South Cambridgeshire Hall, Hills Rd., Cambridge CB2 1PB]) : [The District Council], 1980. — 42p : maps,plans ; 30cm
Cover title
Unpriced (pbk) B81-19100

711'.4'09426715 — Essex. Belchamp Walter. Environment planning — *Proposals*

Belchamp Walter village guideline / prepared by the Planning Department, Braintree District Council. — [Braintree] ([Town Hall, Braintree, Essex CM7 8HB]) : The Council, [1980]. — 10p : 1ill,1col.map ; 21x30cm
Col.map (1folded sheet) in pocket
£0.50 (pbk) B81-23059

711'.4'0942753 — Merseyside *(Metropolitan County).* **Liverpool. Environment planning**

City of Liverpool planning handbook 1981. — Wallington : Home Publishing, [1981]. — 112p : ill(some col.),maps ; 24cm
Unpriced (pbk) B81-26645

711'.4'0942876 — Tyne and Wear *(Metropolitan County).* **Newcastle upon Tyne. Inner areas. Environment planning** — *Proposals*

Newcastle upon Tyne. *City Council.* Newcastle city centre local plan : draft proposals / City of Newcastle upon Tyne. — [Newcastle upon Tyne] ([Civic Centre, Newcastle upon Tyne NE7 8PH]) : [City of Newcastle upon Tyne in association with Tyne & Wear County Council], [1981?]. — 64p : ill,maps(some col.),plans ; 30cm
Cover title. — 'Proposals map' (1folded sheet) as insert
Unpriced (pbk) B81-25902

711'.4'0973 — United States. Cities. Environment planning

Branch, Melville C.. Continuous city planning : integrating municipal management and city planning / Melville C. Branch ; illustrated by the author. — New York ; Chichester : Wiley, c1981. — xiii,181p : ill,plans,forms ; 25cm
Includes bibliographies and index
ISBN 0-471-08943-5 : £14.70 B81-30020

711'.4'0973 — United States. Urban renewal. Role of capital investment by industries

Cities and firms / edited by Herrington J. Bryce. — Lexington, Mass. : Lexington Books ; [Aldershot] : Gower [distributor], 1981, c1980. — xiv,218p : ill ; 24cm
Includes bibliographies and index
ISBN 0-669-04042-8 : £12.50 B81-32985

711'.43'0722 — Western Europe. Planned villages. Environment planning — *Case studies*

Bray, Carl. New villages : case studies / Carl Bray. — [Headington] ([Gypsy Lane, Headington, Oxford OX3 0BP]) : [Oxford Polytechnic, Department of Town Planning]. — (Working paper / Oxford Polytechnic Department of Town Planning ; no.51)
No.1: New Ash Green. — 1981. — xv,40p : 1ill,1map,1plan ; 30cm
Bibliography: p39-40
£1.80 (pbk) B81-28276

Bray, Carl. New villages : case studies / Carl Bray. — [Headington] ([Gypsy Lane, Headington, Oxford OX3 0BP]) : [Oxford Polytechnic, Department of Town Planning]. — (Working paper / Oxford Polytechnic Department of Town Planning ; no.52)
No.2: South Woodham Ferrers. — 1981. — xv,34p : 1ill,1map,plans ; 30cm
Bibliography: p33-34
£1.65 (pbk) B81-28277

Bray, Carl. New villages : case studies / Carl Bray. — [Headington] ([Gypsy Lane, Headington, Oxford OX3 0BP]) : Oxford Polytechnic, Department of Town Planning]. — (Working paper / Oxford Polytechnic Department of Town Planning ; no.53)
No.3: Christiana. — 1981. — xv,37p : 1ill,maps ; 30cm
Bibliography: p36-37
£1.75 (pbk) B81-28278

711'.45 — England. Garden cities. Planning & construction by Pilkington Brothers, *1909-1922*

Penny, Barbara R.. Pilkington Brothers' garden village ventures : the end of the garden city-suburb movement / by Barbara R. Penny. — Liverpool : Department of Civic Design, University of Liverpool, 1976. — 22leaves ; 30cm. — (Working paper / University of Liverpool Department of Civic Design ; WP1)
£0.75 (pbk) B81-06832

711'.5'0941 — Great Britain. Buildings. Rehabilitation

Rehabilitation or new building?. — [London] : [Royal Institution of Chartered Surveyors], [1981]. — 40p : ill ; 30cm
Bibliography: p38-39
£2.40 (£2.00 to members) (pbk) B81-22243

711'.5'0941 — Great Britain. Urban renewal

New approaches to urban renewal : report for the Department of Environment. — London : National Building Agency, 1981. — 24p : ill,1plan ; 30cm
ISBN 0-901502-61-8 (pbk) : £3.00 B81-25399

711'.5'0973 — United States. Urban renewal

Urban revitalization / edited by Donald B. Rosenthal. — Beverly Hills ; London : Sage, c1980. — 308p : 1ill ; 22cm. — (Urban affairs annual reviews ; v.18)
Includes bibliographies
ISBN 0-8039-1190-4 (cased) : £12.50
ISBN 0-8039-1191-2 (pbk) : £6.25 B81-03795

711'.5522 — Norfolk. Norwich. Offices. Development. Planning — *Proposals*

Norwich office policy review. — Norwich (County Hall, Martineau La., Norwich, Norfolk NR1 2DH) : Norfolk County Council, 1981. — 22p ; 30cm
Unpriced (unbound) B81-38173

711'.5522'09411 — Scotland. Shopping centres. Planning — *Conference proceedings*

Shopping content of development plans : a summary of a seminar held at the Planning Exchange in June 1980. — Glasgow (186 Bath St., Glasgow G2 4HG) : Planning Exchange, [1980]. — 18leaves : ill ; 30cm. — (Forum report / Planning Exchange ; 24)
Unpriced (pbk) B81-38623

711'.5522'0941443 — Great Britain. Cities. Central business districts. Redevelopment — *Study regions: Scotland. Strathclyde Region. Glasgow*

Sim, Duncan. Central area redevelopment and its effect on office linkages : the example of Glasgow / Duncan Sim. — [Oxford] ([Gypsy La., Headington, Oxford OX3 OBP]) : Oxford Polytechnic, 1980. — 20p,[11] leaves of plates : maps,1plan ; 30cm. — (Discussion paper in geography / Oxford Polytechnic, ISSN 0309-1910 ; no.11)
Unpriced (pbk) B81-03286

711'.5522'094226 — West Sussex. Shopping centres. Planning — *Proposals*

Shopping : consultation document. — Chichester : West Sussex County Council, 1981. — 10,iiip ; 30cm
Cover title
ISBN 0-86260-017-0 (spiral) : Unpriced
B81-37088

711′.5522′0942525 — Nottinghamshire. Sutton-in-Ashfield. Idlewells. Redevelopment

The **Idlewells** story / by Janice Barnes ... [et al.] ; cover and illustrations by Horace Gilkes ; photographs by Sean Sprague. — Nottingham (24 Lea Rd., Ravenshead, Nottingham NG15 9EG) : Sutton Study Group, 1981. — 86p : ill,plans ; 30cm
Ill on inside cover
£0.95 (pbk) B81-40001

711′.5522′0942539 — Lincolnshire. Spalding. Shopping areas. Environment planning — ***Proposals***

Shopping and Spalding town centre : issues and objectives / South Holland District Council. — Spalding (Planning Department, 12 Market Place, Spalding, Lincs.) : South Holland District Council, 1981. — [32]p : ill,maps,plans ; 30cm
At head of title: Spalding and Pinchbeck District Plan
Unpriced (spiral) B81-37740

711′.5524 — Clwyd. Mineral deposits. Exploitation. Environment planning

Mineral working in Clwyd / Clwyd County Council. — [Mold] ([Shire Hall, Mold, Clwyd CH7 6NG]) : Clwyd County Council
Minerals subject plan : draft for consultation. — 1980. — iii,104p,4 leaves of plates(some folded) : ill,4maps(some col.) ; 29cm
£2.00 (pbk) B81-07537

711′.5524 — Scotland. Large industrial firms. Sites. Planning — ***Conference proceedings***

Site selection for large industry : report of a seminar held from 30 January - 1 February 1979, at the University of Stirling. — Glasgow : The Planning Exchange, [1979?]. — 65leaves ; 30cm. — (Forum report / Planning Exchange ; 16)
Unpriced (pbk) B81-64612

711′.5524′0941432 — Scotland. Strathclyde Region. Clydebank ***(District).*** **Enterprise zones. Environment planning —** ***Proposals***

Clydebank district enterprise zone / [Clydebank District Council]. — [Clydebank] (Clydebank District Council Offices, [Clydebank] G81 1TG) : [The Council], 1981. — 30p in various pagings,[1]folded leaf of plates : ill,1map ; 30cm
Cover title
Unpriced (pbk) B81-29505

711′.558′094131 — Scotland. Central Region. Recreation facilities. Planning — ***Proposals***

Central Region strategy for urban recreation, countryside recreation & tourism (3) : consultation draft / Central Regional Council. — [Stirling] ([Viewforth, Stirling FK8 2ET]) : [The Council], 1979. — iv leaves,65p : maps ; 30cm
Cover title
Unpriced (pbk) B81-12706

711′.558′0973 — United States. Urban regions. Outdoor recreation facilities. Planning

Gold, Seymour M.. Recreation planning and design / Seymour M. Gold. — New York ; London : McGraw-Hill, c1980. — ix,322p : ill,maps,2forms ; 29cm. — (McGraw-Hill series in landscape and landscape architecture)
Bibliography: p307-312. - Includes index
ISBN 0-07-023644-5 : £16.50 B81-03721

711′.58 — Wales. Award-winning housing schemes — ***Serials***

Awards for good design in housing in Wales = Gwobrau cynllunwaith tai da yng Nghymru. — 1978-. — [Cardiff] ([Information Division, Cathays Park, Cardiff CF1 3NQ]) : [Welsh Office], 1978-. — v. : ill ; 21cm
Annual. — Parallel text in English and Welsh. — Prepared by: Welsh Office and the Central Office of Information
ISSN 0260-5651 = Awards for good design in housing in Wales : Unpriced B81-04491

711′.58′094143 — Scotland. Strathclyde Region. Northern Strathclyde Region. Local authority housing. Planning

Pritchard, William, *1953-*. An assessment of district council housing plans : Strathclyde region Dunbarton sub-region / by William pritchard. — Edinburgh (19 Claremont Crescent, Edinburgh EH7 4QD) : Scottish Council of Social Service, 1980. — 40 leaves ; 30cm. — (Housing plans & Scottish housing, ISSN 0143-201x)
£1.00 (pbk) B81-06452

711′.58′0942261 — West Sussex. Gatwick Airport region. Housing. Environment planning — ***Proposals***

Policies for the control of residential development in noise sensitive areas around Gatwick Airport : West Sussex Structure Plan Review, discussion paper no.2 / [West Sussex County Council]. — Chichester (County Hall, Chichester, West Sussex, PO19 1RL) : [The Council], 1981. — [10]p,[1]folded leaf of plates : map ; 30cm
ISBN 0-86260-012-x (spiral) : Unpriced B81-38526

711′.59′0941915 — Ireland ***(Republic).*** **Urban regions. Housing. Redevelopment —** ***Study regions: Waterford (County). Waterford***

Gribbin, Eugene. Urban housing Waterford : a case study of two areas / Eugene Gribbin, Patrick Braniff. — [Dublin] (c/o An Foras Forbartha, St. Martin's House, Waterloo Rd, Dublin 4) : Joint Housing Conference Committee, 1979. — 120p : ill(some col.),maps,plans(some col.) ; 25x34cm
ISBN 0-906120-19-5 (pbk) : £9.00 B81-38035

711′.7 — Transport. Planning

Bayliss, Brian. Planning and control in the transport sector. — Farnborough, Hants. : Gower, Aug.1981. — [214]p
ISBN 0-566-00407-0 : £12.50 : CIP entry B81-16363

711′.7′091732 — Urban regions. Transport. Planning

Black, John, *1948-*. Urban transport planning : theory and practice / John Black. — London : Croom Helm, c1981. — 248p : ill ; 22cm. — (Croom Helm series in geography and environment)
Bibliography: p222-240. - Includes index
ISBN 0-85664-782-9 (cased) : £12.95 : CIP rev.
ISBN 0-7099-0353-7 (pbk) : £6.95 B80-03248

711′.7′0941 — Great Britain. New towns. Transport. Planning, ***to 1980***

Potter, Stephen, *1953-*. Transport planning in the garden cities / by Stephen Potter, New Towns Study Unit, the Open University. — Rewritten and rev. ed. — [Milton Keynes] : [The Unit], 1981. — vi,75p : ill,maps,plans ; 25cm
Previous ed.: published as Transport and new towns. Vol.1 : The historical perspectives. 1976. — Bibliography: p74-75
ISBN 0-335-00279-x (pbk) : Unpriced B81-15277

711′.7′0941 — Great Britain. Transport. Planning

Adams, John, *1938-*. Transport planning : vision and practice / John Adams. — London : Routledge & Kegan Paul, 1981. — xi,272p : ill,maps ; 22cm
Includes index
ISBN 0-7100-0844-9 (pbk) : Unpriced B81-39348

711′.7′094134 — Edinburgh. Transport. Planning — ***Proposals***

Transportation in the Edinburgh area : discussion paper. — [Edinburgh] ([c/o B. Laidlaw, Regional Headquaters, George IV Bridge, Edinburgh]) : Lothian Regional Council, 1979. — 11p,[16]leaves of plates : col.ill,col.maps ; 30cm + Technical appendices(pbk : iii, 42p,[32]leaves of plates(18 folded) : col.ill,col.maps ; 30cm)
Unpriced (pbk) B81-12101

711′.73 — Great Britain. Residential areas. Roads. Layout. Planning — ***Standards***

A **Design** guide for residential areas, highway standards. — [Chelmsford] ([Planning Department, County Hall, Chelmsford CM1 1LF]) : Essex County Council, 1980. — 56p : ill,plans ; 30cm
£3.50 (cased) B81-07056

711′.73′0942176 — London. Newham ***(London Borough).*** **Roads. Planning —** ***Proposals***

Newham. London Borough of Newham transport policy. — London (Director of Engineering & Survey, 25 Nelson St., E6 4EH) : London Borough of Newham, 1980. — vii,57p(2fold.) : ill(some col.),maps ; 31cm
Unpriced (pbk) B81-21901

711′.73′0942586 — Hertfordshire. Hatfield. Motorway A1(M). Environment planning — ***Proposals***

The **Welwyn** Hatfield A1(M) Hatfield Corridor district plan : report of studies and presentation of planning options. — Welwyn Garden City (A.G. Swanson, Controller of Technical Services, 40 Church Rd, Welwyn Garden City) : Welwyn Hatfield District Council, [1981?]. — 69p : ill,1map,plans ; 30cm
Unpriced (pbk) B81-38584

711′.74 — England. Shopping areas. Pedestrianisation

Roberts, John, *1929-*. Pedestrian precincts in Britain / John Roberts. — London (103 Waterloo Rd., SE1 8UL) : Transport & Environment Studies, c1981. — viii,166p : ill,maps,1form ; 21cm
Bibliography: p158-166
ISBN 0-905545-02-8 (pbk) : £9.75 B81-23159

711′.76 — Scotland. Central Lowlands. Canals: Forth and Clyde Canal. Environmental planning

Forth and Clyde Canal local (subject) plan : the main issues. — [Glasgow] ([20 India St., Glasgow, G2 4PF]) : Forth and Clyde Canal Working Party, 1980. — v,13p : ill,1chart ; 20x30cm
Unpriced (pbk) B81-12584

712 — LANDSCAPE DESIGN

712 — Garden features. Construction — ***Amateurs' manuals***

Clayton, Michael, *1924-*. Garden construction / Michael Clayton with Bernard Houghton. — Newton Abbot : David & Charles, c1981. — 48p : ill ; 21cm. — (Penny pinchers)
Cover title
ISBN 0-7153-8031-1 (pbk) : £1.50 B81-20992

712′.6 — Gardens. Planning — ***Amateurs' manuals***

The **Garden** planner / consultant editor Ashley Stephenson. — London : Collins, 1981. — 247p : ill(some col.) ; 31cm
Originally published: London : Fontana, 1981. — Includes index
ISBN 0-00-411662-3 : £9.95 B81-39652

Taylor, Alan, *1901-*. The pocket book of garden construction / Alan Taylor. — London : Evans Brothers, 1981. — 127p : ill ; 17cm
Includes index
ISBN 0-237-45562-5 (pbk) : £1.95 : CIP rev. B81-14844

712′.6 — Small gardens. Planning — ***Amateurs' manuals***

Fletcher, Cyril. Planning the small garden / Cyril Fletcher. — [London] : Collins, 1981. — 128p : ill(some col.),plans,ports(some col.) ; 25cm
Includes index
ISBN 0-00-410412-9 (cased) : £4.95
ISBN 0-00-410405-6 (pbk) : £2.95 B81-09327

712′.6 — Town gardens. Planning — ***Amateurs' manuals***

Bryan, Felicity. The town gardener's companion / Felicity Bryan ; illustrated by Sheilagh Noble. — London : Deutsch, 1981. — x,182p,8p of plates : ill(some col.) ; 24cm
Includes index
ISBN 0-233-97351-6 : £6.95 B81-39662

Llewellyn, Roddy. Roddy Llewellyn's town gardens : a guide to planning and planting / by Roddy Llewellyn ; illustrations by Robin Williams and Roddy Llewellyn. — London : Weidenfeld and Nicolson, 1981. — 192p : ill (some col.),plans ; 26cm
Bibliography: p182-183. — Includes index
ISBN 0-297-77911-7 : £7.95 B81-37408

712′.6 — Woodland gardens. Planning — *Manuals*

Foster, Raymond. The woodland garden : a practical guide / Raymond Foster ; with line illustrations by Rosemary Wise. — London : Ward Lock, 1980. — 160p : ill ; 25cm
Includes index
ISBN 0-7063-5990-9 : £7.95 B81-01030

712′.6′09 — Gardens — *History* — *Serials*

Journal of garden history : an international quarterly. — Vol.1, no.1 (Jan.-Mar. 1981)-. — London (4 John St., WC1N 2ET) : Taylor & Francis, 1981-. — v. : ill ; 25cm
ISSN 0144-5170 = Journal of garden history : £30.00 per year B81-10559

712′.6′0904 — Gardens. Design, *1900-1980*

20th century decorating architecture & gardens : 80 years of ideas & pleasure from House & garden / book edited by Mary Jane Pool ; text edited & chapter introductions by Caroline Seebohm. — London : Weidenfeld & Nicolson, c1980. — 320p : ill(some col.),plans,ports ; 31cm
Includes index
ISBN 0-297-77878-1 : £15.00
Primary classification 747.2′049 B81-04065

712′.6′0917671 — Islamic countries. Gardens, *to 1979*

Lehrman, Jonas. Earthly paradise : garden and courtyard in Islam / Jonas Lehrman. — London : Thames and Hudson, c1980. — 240p : ill(some col.),plans ; 28cm
Bibliography: p233-236. — Includes index
ISBN 0-500-01236-9 : £22.00 B81-02292

712′.6′0924 — Great Britain. Gardens. Landscaping. Lutyens, *Sir* **Edwin**

Weaver, Lawrence. Houses and gardens by E.L. Lutyens / described and criticised by Lawrence Weaver. — Woodbridge : Antique Collectors′ Club, 1981. — xl,344p : ill,plans ; 31cm
Originally published: London : Country Life, 1913. — Ill on lining papers. — Includes index
ISBN 0-902028-98-7 : £19.50 : CIP rev.
Primary classification 728.8′3′0924 B81-12359

712′.6′0941 — Great Britain. Gardens. Planning — *Manuals*

Paterson, Allen. The Hamlyn book of garden ideas / Allen Paterson. — London : Hamlyn, 1979. — 157p : ill(some col.),1chart,col.plans ; 29cm
Col. ill on lining papers. — Bibliography: p152. — Includes index
ISBN 0-600-31449-9 : £5.95 B81-01601

712′.6′0941 — Great Britain. Small gardens. Planning — *Amateurs′ manuals*

Hobhouse, Penelope. The smaller garden : planning & planting / Penelope Hobhouse. — London : Collins, 1981. — 192p : ill(some col.),plans ; 28cm
Bibliography: p190. — Includes index
ISBN 0-00-216644-5 : £8.95 : CIP rev. B81-07601

712′.6′0942 — England. Cottages. Gardens, *to 1980*

Scott-James, Anne. The cottage garden / Anne Scott-James. — London : Allen Lane, 1981. — 159p,[16]p of plates : ill(some col.) ; 24cm
Ill on lining papers. — Includes index
ISBN 0-7139-1263-4 : £9.95 B81-16525

712′.6′0942 — England. Front gardens

Lycett Green, Candida. The front garden / Candida Lycett Green, Christopher Sykes. — London : Elm Tree, 1981. — 64p : col.ill,ports (some col.) ; 22cm
Ill on lining papers
ISBN 0-241-10548-x : £5.95 : CIP rev. B81-07586

712′.6′0942 — England. Gardens, *1066-1500*

McLean, Teresa. Medieval English gardens / Teresa McLean. — London : Collins, 1981. — 298p,[12]p of plates : ill,maps,plans ; 24cm
Bibliography: p273-283. — Includes index
ISBN 0-00-211535-2 (corrected) : £12.50 B81-10669

712′.6′0942 — England. Gardens, *to 1980* — *For children*

Gibberd, Vernon. The garden in England / by Vernon Gibberd ; illustrated by the author. — Cambridge : Published for the National Trust by Dinosaur, c1981. — 32p : col.ill ; 23cm
ISBN 0-85122-218-8 (pbk) : £0.80 : CIP rev. B80-09778

712′.6′0942440924 — Hereford and Worcester. Worcestershire. Farmhouses: Clack′s Farm. Gardens — *Personal observations*

Billitt, Arthur. The story of Clack′s Farm. — London : Ward Lock, Sept.1981. — [176]p
ISBN 0-7063-5995-x (cased) : £6.95 : CIP entry
ISBN 0-7063-6134-2 (pbk) : £3.95 B81-23837

712′.6′0942842 — North Yorkshire. Ripon. Landscape gardens: Studley Royal

Mr. Aislabie′s gardens : three North Yorkshire gardens landscaped during the 18C by John Aislabie (1670-1742) and his son William (1700-1781). — Bradford (40 North View, Wilsden, Bradford, W. Yorkshire) : New Arcadians, 1981. — [26]p : ill,facsims,1port ; 21x30cm + 1catalogue([4]p: 1ill ; 21x30cm)
Published to accompany an exhibition held at Bradford Museums and Art Galleries, Cartwright Hall, 1981
Unpriced (pbk)
Also classified at 712′.6′0942849 B81-26115

712′.6′0942849 — North Yorkshire. Hambleton *(District).* **Landscape gardens: Hackfall & Kirkby Fleetham**

Mr. Aislabie′s gardens : three North Yorkshire gardens landscaped during the 18C by John Aislabie (1670-1742) and his son William (1700-1781). — Bradford (40 North View, Wilsden, Bradford, W. Yorkshire) : New Arcadians, 1981. — [26]p : ill,facsims,1port ; 21x30cm + 1catalogue([4]p: 1ill ; 21x30cm)
Published to accompany an exhibition held at Bradford Museums and Art Galleries, Cartwright Hall, 1981
Unpriced (pbk)
Primary classification 712′.6′0942842 B81-26115

712′.6′0952 — Japan. Gardens. Landscape design

Bring, Mitchell. Japanese gardens : design and meaning / Mitchell Bring, Joss Wayembergh. — New York ; London : McGraw-Hill, c1981. — ix,214p,[8]p of plates : ill(some col.),1map,plans ; 25cm. — (McGraw-Hill series in landscape and landscape architecture)
Bibliography: p212. — Includes index
ISBN 0-07-007825-4 : £13.50 B81-31122

712′.7′0941 — Great Britain. Royal residences. Gardens

Plumptre, George. Royal gardens. — London : Collins, Oct.1981. — [224]p
ISBN 0-00-211871-8 : £9.95 : CIP entry B81-24585

713′.0941 — Great Britain. Roads. Landscape design

Rose, R. W.. The landscaping of roads / by R.W. Rose. — 2nd ed. — London : Institution of Municipal Engineers, 1980. — 15p : ill ; 21cm. — (Protection of the environment ; monograph no.3)
Previous ed.: 1971
£0.75 (pbk) B81-02819

715′.2′0941 — Great Britain. Urban regions. Landscape design. Use of trees

Trees in towns : maintenance and management / editors Brian Clouston, Kathy Stansfield ; contributors Giles Biddle ... [et al.]. — London : Architectural, 1981. — 168p,[32]p of plates : ill,plans ; 23cm
Includes index
ISBN 0-85139-658-5 : £13.95
Primary classification 634.9′5 B81-22191

717 — Cities. Skylines. Aesthetic aspects

Attoe, Wayne. Skylines : understanding and molding urban silhouettes / Wayne Attoe. — Chichester : Wiley, c1981. — xiv,128p : ill,plans ; 20x26cm
Bibliography: p121-123. — Includes index
ISBN 0-471-27940-4 : £14.75 B81-35614

717 — Gardens. Stone structures. Construction — *Amateurs′ manuals*

Hamilton, Geoff. Do your own garden stone work / by Geoff Hammilton. — London : Foulsham, c1981. — 128p,[4]p of plates : ill (some col.) ; 23cm
Includes index
ISBN 0-572-01138-5 : £4.95 B81-32550

717 — Northern Europe. Mazes

Pennick, Nigel. European troytowns / Nigel Pennick. — [Cambridge] ([12 Pheasant Rise, Bar Hill, Cambridge CB3 8SD][Fenris-Wolf]), [1981]. — 6p,[2]p of plates : ill ; 30cm
Bibliography: p5
Unpriced (unbound) B81-11995

719 — NATURAL LANDSCAPES

719 — England. Landscape. Aesthetic aspects. Evaluation by public — *Study regions: Cotswolds*

Preece, R. A.. An evaluation by the general public of scenic quality in the Cotswolds area of outstanding natural beauty : a basis for monitoring future change / R.A. Preece. — [Oxford] ([Gypsy La., Headington, Oxford, OX3 0PB]) : Oxford Polytechnic, [1980]. — 84p : ill,maps ; 30cm. — (Working paper / Oxford Polytechnic Department of Town Planning ; no.48)
Bibliography: p80-84
£2.75 (pbk) B81-06146

719 — Landscape — *Serials*

Landscape research. — Vol.2, no.1 (Autumn 1976)-. — Manchester (c/o Landscape Studies, Department of Town and Country Planning, The University, Manchester M13 9PL) : Landscape Research Group, 1976-. — v. : ill ; 30cm
Three issues yearly. — Continues: Landscape research news. — Description based on: Vol.3, no.3 (Autumn 1978)
ISSN 0142-6397 = Landscape research : £16.00 per year (free to Group members) B81-04490

719′.012 — Wales. Landscape. Classification

Great Britain. *Welsh Office. Planning Services.* A landscape classification of Wales / Planning Services, Welsh Office. — Cardiff (Crown Building, Cathays Park, Cardiff CF1 3NQ) : Planning Services, Welsh Office, [1980]. — iii,106p : ill,maps(some col.) ; 30cm
Fold sheet (map) in pocket. — Bibliography: p104-106
ISBN 0-904251-41-1 (pbk) : £4.95 B81-03660

719′.06′0411 — Scotland. Landscape conservation. Organisations: National Trust for Scotland, *to 1980*

Skinner, Basil C.. A place in trust / Basil Skinner. — Edinburgh (11 Buccleuch Place, Edinburgh 8) : University of Edinburgh Department of Extra-Mural Studies, 1981. — 48p ; 21cm
Bibliography: p48
Unpriced (pbk)
Primary classification 719′.06′042 B81-23164

719′.06′042 — England. Landscape conservation. Organisations: National Trust, *to 1980*

Skinner, Basil C.. A place in trust / Basil Skinner. — Edinburgh (11 Buccleuch Place, Edinburgh 8) : University of Edinburgh Department of Extra-Mural Studies, 1981. — 48p ; 21cm
Bibliography: p48
Unpriced (pbk)
Also classified at 363.6′9′06042 ; 719′.06′0411 ; 363.6′9′060411 B81-23164

719′.06′04259 — Buckinghamshire. Southern Buckinghamshire. Landscape conservation. Organisations: Council for the Protection of Rural England. *Penn Country Branch, to 1980*

Council for the Protection of Rural England. *Penn Country Branch.* The first fifty years : a short history of the Penn Country Branch of the Council for the Protection of Rural England / by Richard Sadler. — [Beaconsfield] ([c/o Mrs. C.A. Pitcher, Seelys Farm, Beaconsfield, Bucks. HP9 2LL]) : Penn Country Branch of the Council for the Protection of Rural England, 1980. — vi,43p : 1map ; 21cm
£1.00 (pbk) B81-13664

719′.07′1041 — Great Britain. Rural regions. Landscape conservation. Personnel. Professional education. Courses — *Directories* — *Serials*

A **Directory** of training opportunities in countryside conservation and recreation / Countryside Commission. — 1978-79-. — Cheltenham (John Dower House, Crescent Place, Cheltenham, Glos. GL50 3RA) : The Commission, [1978?]-. — v. ; 20cm
Issued every two years. — Description based on: 1981-82
ISSN 0260-5449 = Directory of training opportunities in countryside conservation and recreation : Unpriced B81-04903

719′.09 — Landscape — *History* — *Serials*

Landscape history : journal of the Society for Landscape Studies. — Vol.1 (1979)-. — [Middlesborough] ([c/o Mr B.J.D. Harrison, Leeds University Adult Education Centre, 37 Harrow Rd, Middlesborough TS5 5N7]) : The Society, 1979-. — v. : ill ; 30cm
Annual
ISSN 0143-3768 = Landscape history : Free to Society members B81-04641

719′.0941 — Great Britain. Landscapc. Effects of agriculture

Shoard, Marion. The theft of the countryside / by Marion Shoard ; with a foreword by Henry Moore. — London : Temple Smith, 1980 (1981 [printing]). — 269p,[16]p of plates : ill,maps ; 23cm
Includes index
ISBN 0-85117-200-8 (pbk) : £9.00
ISBN 0-85117-201-6 (pbk) B81-37166

719′.0942 — England. Landscape

Muir, Richard, *1943-*. Shell guide to reading the landscape / Richard Muir. — London : Joseph, 1981. — 368p,[32]p of plates : ill(some col.),maps,plans,1port ; 26cm
Bibliography: p356-359. - Includes index
ISBN 0-7181-1971-1 : £10.50 B81-22209

719′.09423′57 — Devon. East Devon *(District)*. **Coastal regions. Heritage coasts: East Devon Heritage Coast. Environment planning** — *Proposals*

East Devon Heritage Coast. — Exeter (Country Hall, Topsham Rd., Exeter EX2 4QH) : Devon County Council, Planning Department, 1980. — 63p : ill,col.maps ; 30cm
ISBN 0-86114-287-x (pbk) : £1.00 B81-10627

719′.09425′6 — Bedfordshire. Landscape — *For environment planning*

Bedfordshire : landscape and wildlife : landscape technical volume. — Bedford ([County Hall, Bedford, MK42 9AP]) : Bedfordshire County Council, Council Planning Department, 1980. — 63p,[28]p,39leaves of plates(some folded) : maps ; 30cm
Unpriced (spiral) B81-12591

719′.09747′3 — New York *(State)*. **Lower Hudson Valley. Landscape. Influence of man**, *1800-1900*

O′Brien, Raymond J.. American sublime : landscape and scenery of the Lower Hudson Valley / Raymond J. O′Brien. — New York ; Guildford : Columbia University Press, 1981. — xii,353p : ill,maps ; 24cm
Bibliography: p333-347. — Includes index
ISBN 0-231-04778-9 : £12.35 B81-27078

719′.32′0942 — England. National parks. Sociopolitical aspects

MacEwen, Ann. National parks. — London : Allen and Unwin, Jan.1982. — [296]p. — (The Resource management series ; 5)
ISBN 0-04-719003-5 (cased) : £15.00 : CIP entry
ISBN 0-04-719004-3 (pbk) : £8.00 B81-33908

719′.32′094288 — Northumberland. National parks: Northumberland National Park. Environment planning — *Proposals*

Northumberland. *National Park and Countryside Committee*. Northumberland National Park Plan / [Northumberland National Park and Countryside Committee]. — [S.l.] : Northumberland National Park and Countryside Committee, 1977. — 99p,[22]p of plates : ill,col.maps,plans ; 30cm
Unpriced (pbk) B81-37364

719′.32′094288 — Northumberland. National parks: Northumberland National Park. Landscape — *For environment planning*

The **landscape** of the Northumberland National Park. — Newcastle upon Tyne ([c/o] National Park Officer, Bede House, All Saints Centre, Newcastle upon Tyne) : [Northumberland National Park and Countryside Committee], 1976. — 30,xviip,[4]p of plates : maps ; 30cm. — (Working paper / Northumberland National Park ; 3)
Bibliography: p30
Unpriced (spiral) B81-29618

719′.33′094295 — Mid Wales. Landscape. Effects of afforestation

Landscape and forestry in mid-Wales : a land-use survey. — [London] : Youth Hostels Association, 1974. — 9p : 1map ; 30cm
Unpriced (unbound) B81-34696

720 — ARCHITECTURE

720 — Architecture

Allsop, Bruce. A modern theory of architecture / Bruce Allsop. — London : Routledge & Kegan Paul, 1977 (1981 [printing]). — 102p : ill,music ; 25cm
ISBN 0-7100-0950-x (pbk) : £3.95 B81-39347

720 — Architecture — *Early works*

North, Roger, *1653-1734*. Of buildings : Roger North′s writings on architecture / edited by Howard Colvin and John Newman. — Oxford : Clarendon Press, 1981. — xxvii,160p,[16]p of plates : ill,plans,1port ; 26cm
Includes index
ISBN 0-19-817325-3 : £17.50 : CIP rev. B80-08867

720 — Architecture. Social aspects

Meaning and behaviour in the built environment / edited by Geoffrey Broadbent, Richard Bunt, Tomas Llorens. — Chichester : Wiley, c1980. — xiii,372p : ill ; 25cm
Includes bibliographies and index
ISBN 0-471-27708-8 : £18.50 : CIP rev. B80-25955

720′.1 — Architecture — *Philosophical perspectives*

Fawcett, Chris. Architectural jottings 1 : bits of existence : conjectures from the AA / Chris Fawcett. — London (c/o Architectural Association, 36 Bedford Sq., W.C.1) : [C. Fawcett], 1981. — [27]leaves : ill ; 30cm
Cover title
Unpriced (pbk) B81-35670

720′.207 — Architecture — *Cartoons*

Hellman, Louis. All Hellman breaks loose / design and production by Louis Hellman and Stuart Moss. — London (165 Brecknock Rd., N19 5AD) : Arcus, 1980. — 144p : all ill ; 22x28cm
ISBN 0-907306-00-4 (pbk) : £4.25 B81-15188

720′.22′2 — Cumbria. Lowther. Country houses: Lowther Castle. Stock: Architectural drawings, *1680-1810* — *Catalogues*

Architectural drawings from Lowther Castle, Westmorland / edited by Howard Colvin, J. Mordaunt Crook, Terry Friedman. — [London] : Society of Architectural Historians of Great Britain, 1980. — 17p,32p of plates : ill,plans ; 25cm. — (Architectural history monographs ; no.2)
Includes index
ISBN 0-9507350-0-0 (pbk) : Unpriced B81-10360

720′.22′2 — Europe. Art galleries. Exhibits: American architectural drawings. Wright, Frank Lloyd — *Catalogues*

Wright, Frank Lloyd. Frank Lloyd Wright : three quarters of a century of drawings / [text by] Alberto Izzo, Camillo Gubitosi ; [translated from the Italian by Stella Cragie]. — London : Academy Editions, 1981. — [199]p : chiefly ill (some col.),plans(some col.) ; 23cm
Catalogue of an exhibition organised by the Institute of Architectural Analysis of the University of Naples, in collaboration with the Frank Lloyd Wright Memorial Foundation, Taliesin, Arizona. — Translation of: Frank Lloyd Wright. — Originally published: Florence : Centro Di ; London : Distributed by Academy Editions, 1977. — Bibliography: [7]p. — Includes index
Unpriced (pbk) B81-31323

720′.22′2 — Fantasy buildings. Architectural features — *Illustrations*

Fantastic architecture : personal and eccentric visions / [compiled by] Michael Schuyt and Joost Elffers ; text by George R. Collins. — Lodnon : Thames and Hudson, 1980. — 247p : chiefly ill(some col.),ports ; 30cm
Includes index
ISBN 0-500-34082-x : £16.00 B81-05659

720′.22′2 — Great Britain. Architecture. Organisations: Architectural Association. Exhibits: Portuguese architectural drawings. Guedes, Amancio — *Catalogues*

Guedes, Amancio. Amancio Guedes. — London ([34 Bedford Sq., WC1B 3ES]) : Architectural Association, c1980. — 48p : ill ; 18cm
Published to accompany an exhibition of works by Amancio Guedes held at the Architectural Association, London, 1980. — Cover title. — Ill. on lining papers
Unpriced (pbk) B81-12753

720′.22′2 — Great Britain. Architecture. Organisations: Architectural Association. Exhibits: Scottish architectural drawings. Mackintosh, Charles Rennie — *Catalogues*

Mackintosh, Charles Rennie. Some designs / by C.R. Mackintosh. — London (34 Bedford Sq., WC1) : Architectural Association, c1981. — 49p : ill,plans ; 18cm
Published to accompany an exhibition at the Architectural Association, London, 1981. — Cover title. — Bibliography: p49
£2.50 (pbk) B81-17943

720′.22′2 — Italian architectural drawings. Botta, Mario — *Illustrations*

Botta, Mario. Mario Botta : architecture and projects in the ′70 / edited by Italo Rota ; texts Emilio Battisti, Kenneth Frampton. — London : Academy Editions, 1981,c1979. — 119p : chiefly ill,plans ; 24cm
Published to accompany exhibitions held in 1979 at the School of Architecture in Syracuse University, New York and at the Milan Triennale in the Design Gallery sector. — Parallel Italian and English text. — Bibliography: p119
Unpriced (pbk) B81-31324

720′.22′2 — London. Westminster *(London Borough)*. **Art galleries: Fischer Fine Art. Exhibits: European architectural drawings,** *1700-1980* — *Catalogues*

British & European architectural drawings 18th-20th century : an anthology : February-March 1981. — London (30 King St., S.W.1) : Fischer Fine Art, [1981]. — [34]p : chiefly ill(some col.),plans ; 26cm
Text on inside covers. — Exhibition catalogue
Unpriced (pbk) B81-17572

720′.22′2 — Nottinghamshire. Nottingham. Universities. Libraries: University of Nottingham. *Manuscripts Department*. **Stock: Archives of Ossington Estate: Architectural drawings,** *1780-1818* — *Catalogues*

University of Nottingham. *Manuscripts Department*. Denison of Ossington architectural plans / University of Nottingham Manuscripts Department. — [Nottingham] : [The Department], [1981?]. — [15]p ; 30cm
£1.00 (pbk) B81-37512

720′.22′2 — Vernacular architecture — *Illustrations* — *For children*

Herbert, Helen. Buildings with character / by Helen Herbert. — Cambridge : Dinosaur, c1980. — [24]p : chiefly ill ; 21x30cm
ISBN 0-85122-215-3 (pbk) : £0.65 : CIP rev. B80-07449

720′.28′4 — Architectural drawings. Techniques — *Manuals*

Weidhaas, Ernest R.. Architectural drafting and design / Ernest R. Weidhaas. — 4th ed.. — Boston [Mass.] ; London : Allyn and Bacon, c1981. — xi,436,[46]p : ill,plans ; 29cm
Previous ed.: 1977. — Includes index
ISBN 0-205-07100-7 : £15.95
Also classified at 721 B81-01877

720′.28′4 — Architectural measured drawings. Techniques — *Manuals*

Chitham, Robert. Measured drawing for architects / Robert Chitham. — London : Architectural, 1980. — viii,119p : ill,plans ; 31cm
Includes index
ISBN 0-85139-391-8 (cased) : £9.50
ISBN 0-85139-392-6 (pbk) : £5.95 B81-03124

720′.28′4 — Architectural working drawings. Arrangement

A **Sample** set of architects′ working drawings : a systematic arrangement. — Rev. — [Watford] : Building Research Establishment, Department of the Environment, 1978, c1976. — 1portfolio : chiefly ill,plans ; 31cm. — (Building Research Establishment package)
Previous ed.: 1976
£6.70 B81-15032

720′.28′8 — Converted buildings & renovated buildings

Cantacuzino, Sherban. Saving old buildings / Sherban Cantacuzino and Susan Brandt. — London : Architectural Press, 1980. — x,230p : ill,maps,plans ; 31cm
ISBN 0-85139-498-1 : £25.00 : CIP rev.
B80-17858

720′.28′8 — England. Buildings of historical importance. Conservation — *Serials*

English heritage monitor / Planning and Research Services, English Tourist Board. — 1978.- — London (4, Grosvenor Gardens, SW1W 0DU) : The Board, 1978. — 49p
ISSN 0260-0420 : £3.00
Also classified at 306′.4 B81-04872

English heritage monitor / Planning and Research Services, English Tourist Board. — 1980. — London (4 Grosvenor Gardens, SW1W 0DU) : The Board, 1980. — 51p
ISSN 0260-0420 : £3.50
Also classified at 306′.4 B81-04871

720′.28′8 — England. Vernacular buildings. Conservation

Bowyer, Jack. Vernacular building conservation / Jack Bowyer ; with illustrations by the author. — London : Architectural Press, 1980. — 184p : ill,maps ; 31cm
Bibliography: p181. - Includes index
ISBN 0-85139-701-8 : £25.00 B81-04804

720′.28′8 — Great Britain. Buildings of historical importance. Conservation & restoration

Handbook of building crafts in conservation : a commentary on Peter Nicholson′s The new practical builder and workman′s companion, 1823 / edited by Jack Bowyer. — London : Hutchinson, 1981. — 375p : ill,plans ; 29cm
Includes index
ISBN 0-09-142210-8 : £40.00 B81-28668

720′.5 — Architecture — *Serials*

[Affiche *(Greenbelt)*]. Affiche : the bi-monthly architectural journal. — June/July 1980-. — Greenbelt [Md.] ; London (10 Barley Mow Passage, Chiswick, W4) : Innovative Informations, 1980-. — v. : ill,maps,ports ; 30cm
£20.00 per year B81-03584

720′.6′04 — Europe. Architecture. Organisations: Taller de Arquitectura, *to 1980*

Hodgkinson, Peter. Taller de Arquitectura / [director] Ricardo Bofill. — London ([34 Bedford Sq., W.C.1]) : Architectural Association, [c1981]. — 48p : ill,1port ; 18cm
Published on the occasion of an exhibition at the Architectural Association, London, 1981. — Cover title. — Authors Peter Hodgkinson and Charles Jencks. — Bibliography: p48
Unpriced (pbk) B81-08655

720′.6′041 — Great Britain. Architectural design. Organisations: Royal Institute of British Architects — *Directories* — *Serials*

Royal Institute of British Architects. RIBA directory of members. — 1979. — London : The Institute, c1978. — 412p in various pagings
Cover title: Members (Royal Institute of British Architects)
ISSN 0305-2427 : £12.00 B81-21934

Royal Institute of British Architects. RIBA directory of practices. — 1981. — London : The Institute, c1981. — 277p in various pagings
Cover title: Practices (Royal Institute of British Architects)
ISSN 0305-2435 : £15.00 B81-24115

720′.6′041 — Great Britain. Architecture. Organisations: Faculty of Architects and Surveyors — *Serials*

Faculty of Architects and Surveyors. Year book and list of members / the Faculty of Architects and Surveyors Limited. — 1981. — London (86, Edgware Rd, W2 2YW) : Sterling Publications, [1981?]. — 224p
Spine title: FAS yearbook/list of members
ISSN 0141-8823 : Unpriced
Primary classification 526.9′06′041 B81-21341

720′.6′041 — Great Britain. Architecture. Organisations: Incorporated Association of Architects and Surveyors — *Directories* — *Sersials*

[Reference book & list of members *(Incorporated Association of Architects & Surveyors)*]. Reference book & list of members / the Incorporated Association of Architects & Surveyors. — 1981. — London (25 Catherine St., WC2B 5JW) : Millbank Publications, [1981]. — 316p
Unpriced
Also classified at 526.9′06′041 B81-32276

720′.6′0429 — Wales. Architectural design. Organisations: Society of Architects in Wales — *Serials*

[Year book *(Society of Architects in Wales)*]. Year book / Society of Architects in Wales. — 1 (1979/80). — Macclesfield ([Charles Roe House, Chestergate, Macclesfield, Cheshire SK11 6DZ]) : McMillan Martin on behalf of RIBA Wales Region, [1980]. — 76p
Unpriced B81-09140

720′.68 — United States. Architectural design. Practices. Management

Coxe, Weld. Managing architectural and engineering practice / Weld Coxe. — New York ; Chichester : Wiley, c1980. — xi,177p : ill,forms ; 24cm
Includes index
ISBN 0-471-08203-1 : £10.00 B81-04507

720.9 — ARCHITECTURE. HISTORICAL AND GEOGRAPHICAL TREATMENT

720′.9 — Architecture, *to 1699*

Ball, Victoria Kloss. Architecture and interior design : a basic history through the seventeenth century / Victoria Kloss Ball. — New York ; Chichester : Wiley, c1980. — xiii,448p,[16]p of plates : ill(some col.),plans ; 29cm
Bibliography: p411-418. - Includes index
ISBN 0-471-05162-4 (cased) : £24.00
ISBN 0-471-08719-x (pbk) : £13.50
Also classified at 747.2 B81-05664

720′.9 — Architecture, *to 1973*

Great architecture of the world / general editor John Julius Norwich. — London : Mitchell Beazley, 1975 (1979 [printing]). — 288p : ill (some col.),maps,plans ; 30cm
Includes index
ISBN 0-85533-067-8 (cased) : Unpriced
ISBN 0-85533-183-6 (pbk) : £6.95 B81-13983

720′.9 — Architecture, *to 1979*

Bagenal, Philip. The illustrated atlas of the world′s great buildings : a history of world architcture from the classical perfection of the Parthenon to the breathtaking grandeur of the skyscraper / Philip Bagenal and Jonathan Meades. — London : Salamander, c1980. — 192p : col.ill,col.maps ; 31cm
Includes index
ISBN 0-86101-059-0 : £7.95 B81-05462

George, William. World architecture / William George. — Poole : Blandford, 1980. — 168p : ill(some col.) ; 20cm
Includes index
ISBN 0-7137-0953-7 (cased) : £3.95 : CIP rev.
ISBN 0-7137-1089-6 (pbk) : £2.95 B80-18434

720′.9 — Western world. Architecture, *to 1979*

Architecture of the western world / edited and with an introduction by Michael Raeburn ; foreword by Sir Hugh Casson ; individual chapters by J.J. Coulton ... [et al.]. — London : Orbis, 1980. — 304p : ill(some col.),maps,plans ; 30cm
Bibliography: p295-296. - Includes index
ISBN 0-85613-059-1 : £16.00 B81-06656

720′.92′2 — Architectural design. Adam, Robert & Adam, James — *Illustrations* — *Facsimiles*

Adam, Robert. The works in architecture of Robert & James Adam / with a new introduction by Henry Hope Reed. — New York : Dover Publications ; London : Constable, 1980. — xii,23p,105p of plates : ill,plans ; 47cm
Facsim of: editions published London, 1778-1882. — Bibliography: pviii
ISBN 0-486-23810-5 : Unpriced B81-12456

720′.92′2 — Ireland. Architects, *1600-1720* — *Biographies*

Loeber, Rolf. A biographical dictionary of architects / Rolf Loeber in Ireland 1600-1720. — London : Murray, 1981. — 127p : 1geneal.table ; 23cm
Includes index
ISBN 0-7195-3832-7 : £15.00 : CIP rev.
B81-25689

720′.92′4 — Architectural design. Burges, William — *Biographies*

Crook, J. Mordaunt. William Burges and the high Victorian dream / J. Mordaunt Crook. — London : John Murray, 1981. — 454p,xi,[156]p of plates : ill(some col.),plans,ports ; 25cm
Bibliography: p417-424. — Includes index
ISBN 0-7195-3822-x : £40.00 B81-27006

720′.924 — Architectural design. Lutyens, *Sir* **Edwin** — *Biographies*

Gradidge, Roderick. Edwin Lutyens. — London : Allen & Unwin, Sept.1981. — [192]p
ISBN 0-04-720023-5 : £12.95 : CIP entry
B81-22567

720′.92′4 — Architectural design. Lutyens, *Sir Edwin* — *Biographies*

Lutyens, Mary. Edwin Lutyens / by his daughter Mary Lutyens. — London : Murray, 1980. — x,294p,[16]p of plates : ill,1facsim,ports ; 23cm
Includes index
ISBN 0-7195-3777-0 : £12.95 B81-01031

720′.92′4 — Architectural design. Moore, Charles, *1925-* — *Critical studies*

Allen, Gerald. Charles Moore / by Gerald Allen. — New York : Whitney Library of Design ; London : Granada, 1981, c1980. — 127p : ill (some col.),plans ; 24cm. — (Monographs on contemporary architecture)
ISBN 0-246-11503-3 : £9.95 B81-10655

720′.92′4 — Architectural design. Pelli, Cesar — *Critical studies*

Pastier, John. Cesar Pelli / by John Pastier. — New York : Whitney Library of Design ; London : Granada, 1981, c1980. — 120p : ill (some col.),plans,1port ; 24cm. — (Monographs in contemporary architecture)
ISBN 0-246-11504-1 : £9.95 B81-10654

720′.92′4 — Architectural design. Poulson, John — *Biographies*

Poulson, John. John Poulson — the price : the autobiography of John Poulson, architect. — London : Joseph, 1981. — 203p,[4]p of plates : 2ill,ports ; 23cm
ISBN 0-7181-2016-7 : £7.95 B81-37688

720′.92′4 — Cardiff. Museums: National Museum of Wales. Exhibits: Architectural design. Burges, William — *Catalogues*

The **Strange** genius of William Burges, ′art-architect′, 1827-1881 : a catalogue to a centenary exhibition organised jointly by the National Museum of Wales, Cardiff, and the Victoria and Albert Museum, London. edited by J. Mordaunt Crook / catalogue entries by Mary Axon and Virginia Glenn. — Cardiff : National Museum of Wales, 1981. — 155p : ill,plans ; 25cm
Bibliography: p154
ISBN 0-7200-0234-6 (pbk) : Unpriced
B81-39931

720'.92'4 — England. Architectural design. Nash, John, *1752-1835 — Biographies*

Summerson, John. The life and work of John Nash architect / John Summerson. — London : Allen & Unwin, 1980. — 217p,48p of plates : ill,maps,plans,ports ; 26cm
Map on lining papers. — Includes index
ISBN 0-04-720021-9 : £20.00 : CIP rev.
B80-18436

720'.92'4 — England. Architectural design. Webb, Philip — *Biographies*

Lethaby, W. R.. Philip Webb and his work / by W.R. Lethaby. — [New ed.]. — London (35 Newton Ave., W3 8AR) : Raven Oak Press, c1979. — viii,323p,11p of plates : ill,plans,port ; 22cm
Previous ed.: London : Oxford University Press, 1935. — Includes index
ISBN 0-906997-00-3 : £12.00 B81-02982

720'.92'4 — Great Britain. Architectural design. Richardson, *Sir Albert* **—** *Biographies*

Houfe, Simon. Sir Albert Richardson : the Professor / Simon Houfe. — Luton : White Crescent Press, c1980. — 240p,16p of plates : ill,facsims,ports ; 23cm
Ill on lining papers. — Includes index
ISBN 0-900804-26-2 : £6.95 B81-05115

720'.92'4 — Italy. Architectural design. Albini, Franco — *Critical studies — Italian texts*

Franco Albini : 1930-1970. — London : Academy, c1981. — 184p : ill(some col.),maps,plans,1port ; 23cm
Exhibition catalogue. — Italian text with English summaries
Unpriced (pbk) B81-38960

720'.92'4 — Italy. Architectural design. Palladio, Andrea — *Critical studies*

Farber, Joseph C.. Palladio's architecture and its influence : a photographic guide / photographs by Joseph C. Farber ; text by Henry Hope Reed. — New York : Dover Publications ; London : Constable, c1980. — xiv,129p : ill ; 30cm
ISBN 0-486-23922-5 (pbk) : £3.90
Primary classification 720'.941 B81-14127

720'.92'4 — Scotland. Architectural design. Lorimer, *Sir Robert* **—** *Critical studies*

Savage, Peter. Lorimer and the Edinburgh craft designers / Peter Savage. — Edinburgh : Harris, 1980. — xx,191p,[103]p of plates : ill,facsims,plans,ports ; 24x25cm
Bibliography: p181. — Includes index
ISBN 0-904505-39-1 : £36.00 B81-04955

720'.92'4 — United States. Architectural design. Latrobe, Benjamin Henry — *Correspondence, diaries, etc.*

Latrobe, Benjamin Henry. The journals of Benjamin Henry Latrobe 1799-1820 : from Philadelphia to New Orleans / Edward C. Carter II, John C. Van Horne and Lee W. Formwalt, editors ; Samuel Wilson, Jr., consulting editor. — New Haven ; London : Published for the Maryland Historical Society by Yale University Press, 1980. — xxxiv,351p,[17]p of plates : ill(some col.),maps,facsims,1col.plan,1col.port ; 29cm. — (The Papers of Benjamin Henry Latrobe. Series 1, Journals ; v.3)
Facsims on lining papers. — Includes index
ISBN 0-300-02383-9 : £41.00 B81-18859

720'.92'4 — United States. Architectural design. Stern, Robert A. M. — *Critical studies*

Stern, Robert A. M.. Robert Stern / introductory essay by Vincent Scully. — London (7 Holland St., W8) : Architectural Design, c1981. — 80p : ill(some col.),plans,1port ; 28cm
Unpriced (pbk) B81-29562

720'.92'4 — United States. Architectural design. Sullivan, Louis H. — *Critical studies*

Menocal, Narciso G.. Architecture as nature : the transcendentalist idea of Louis Sullivan / Narciso G. Menocal. — Madison ; London : University of Wisconsin Press, 1981. — xix,232p : ill,plans ; 24cm
Bibliography: p203-223. — Includes index
ISBN 0-299-08150-8 : £14.60 B81-29782

720'.941 — Great Britain. Architectural design. Palladian style, *1600-1900*

Farber, Joseph C.. Palladio's architecture and its influence : a photographic guide / photographs by Joseph C. Farber ; text by Henry Hope Reed. — New York : Dover Publications ; London : Constable, c1980. — xiv,129p : ill ; 30cm
ISBN 0-486-23922-5 (pbk) : £3.90
Also classified at 720'.973 ; 720'.92'4
B81-14127

720'.941 — Great Britain. Architecture, *1700-1800 — For children*

Gibberd, Vernon. 18th-century buildings / written and illustrated by Vernon Gibberd. — Over : Published for the National Trust by Dinosaur, c1980. — 32p : col.ill ; 21cm. — (Seeker's notebook ; no.1)
ISBN 0-85122-216-1 (pbk) : £0.75 : CIP rev.
B80-09779

720'.941 — Great Britain. Architecture, *1800-1900 — For children*

Gibberd, Vernon. 19th-century buildings / written and illustrated by Vernon Gibberd. — Over : Published for the National Trust by Dinosaur, c1980. — 32p : col.ill ; 21cm. — (Seeker's notebook ; no.2)
ISBN 0-85122-217-x (pbk) : £0.75 : CIP rev.
B80-09780

720'.941 — Great Britain. Architecture, *1900-1910 — Biographies — Encyclopaedias*

Gray, A. Stuart. Edwardian architecture. — London : Duckworth, Oct.1981. — [384]p
ISBN 0-7156-1012-0 : £45.00 : CIP entry
B81-30494

720'.941 — Great Britain. New towns. Buildings. Architectural features

Opher, Philip. Architecture and urban design in six British new towns / Philip Opher, Clinton Bird. — [Headington] : Urban Design, Oxford Polytechnic, c1981. — 148p in various pagings : ill,maps,plans ; 15x21cm
Also available in three vols as Milton Keynes ; Cumbernauld, Irvine, East Kilbride ; Runcorn, Warrington. — Includes bibliography
ISBN 0-907420-01-x (pbk) : £5.95 B81-25225

720'.941 — Great Britain. Vernacular buildings. Architectural features

Brunskill, R. W.. Traditional buildings of Britain : an introduction to vernacular architecture / R.W. Brunskill. — London : Gollancz in association with Peter Crawley, 1981. — 160p : ill,1map ; 26cm
Bibliography: p155-156. — Includes index
ISBN 0-575-02887-4 : £8.95 B81-27257

720'.9411 — Scotland. National Trust properties. Architectural features, *1500-1980*

Treasures in trust / edited by A.A. Tait. — Edinburgh : Produced in association with the National Trust for Scotland [by] H.M.S.O., 1981. — 103p : ill(some col.),1plan,ports(some col.) ; 25cm
Includes bibliographies
ISBN 0-11-491745-0 (pbk) : Unpriced
Also classified at 709'.03 B81-36659

720'.9411 — Scotland. New towns. Buildings. Architectural features

Opher, Philip. Cumbernauld, Irvine, East Kilbride : an illustrated guide / Philip Opher, Clinton Bird. — [Headington] : Urban Design, Oxford Polytechnic, c1980. — 18,18,12p : ill,maps,plans ; 15x21cm. — (British new towns)
Cover title. — Also available in Architecture and urban design in six British new towns. — Includes bibliography
ISBN 0-9504310-9-5 (pbk) : £1.50 B81-25224

720'.9416 — Northern Ireland. Buildings. Architectural features

Evans, David, *1934-*. The diamond as big as a square : an introduction to the towns and buildings of Ulster / by David Evans and Marcus Patton. — [Downpatrick] ([c/o Maybrook House, Raleagh Rd., Crossgar, Downpatrick]) : Ulster Architectural Heritage Society, 1981. — ill,maps,1plan ; 21cm
Bibliography: p39
£1.50 (pbk) B81-37157

720'.9418'35 — Dublin. Buildings. Architectural features

Lalor, Brian. Dublin : ninety drawings / by Brian Lalor. — London : Routledge & Kegan Paul, 1981. — viii,136p : ill,maps ; 28cm
Maps on lining papers
ISBN 0-7100-0809-0 : £8.95 B81-36881

720'.9418'4 — Wicklow *(County)*. **Bray. Buildings of historical importance. Architectural features**

Garner, William, *1944-*. Bray : architectural heritage / William Garner. — Dublin (St Martin's House, Waterloo Rd., Dublin 4) : An Foras Forbartha, c1980. — viii,96p : ill,1map,1plan ; 21cm
Bibliography: p79-80
ISBN 0-906120-39-x (pbk) : £3.00 B81-17805

720'.9418'6 — Offaly *(County)*. **Tullamore. Buildings of historical importance. Architectural features**

Garner, William, *1944-*. Tullamore : architectural heritage / William Garner ; sponsored by the Heritage Trust. — Dublin (St Martin's House, Waterloo Rd., Dublin 4) : An Foras Forbartha, c1980. — viii,78p : ill,1map,plans ; 21cm. — (National heritage inventory)
ISBN 0-906120-40-3 (pbk) : £2.80 B81-38041

720'.9418'82 — Carlow *(County)*. **Carlow. Buildings of historical importance. Architectural features**

Garner, William, *1944-*. Carlow : architectural heritage / William Garner. — Dublin (St. Martin's House, Waterloo Rd., Dublin 4) : Foras Forbartha, c1980. — vii,92p : ill ; 21cm. — (National heritage inventory)
ISBN 0-906120-38-1 (pbk) : £3.00 B81-17920

720'.9419'3 — Clare *(County)*. **Ennis. Buildings of historical importance. Architectural features**

Garner, William, *1944-*. Ennis : architectural heritage / William Garner ; sponsored by the Heritage Trust. — Dublin (St Martin's House, Waterloo Rd., Dublin 4) : An Foras Forbartha, c1981. — viii,80p : ill,1map,plans ; 21cm. — (National heritage inventory)
ISBN 0-906120-41-1 (pbk) : £3.00 B81-38042

720'.942 — Architectural design. Partnerships: Howell Killick Partridge & Amis *(Firm)*. **Buildings. Architectural features**

Howell Killick Partridge & Amis : architecture / introduction by Sherban Cantacuzino. — London : Lund Humphries, 1981. — 128p : ill (some col.),plans ; 25cm
ISBN 0-85331-444-6 (cased) : £12.50
ISBN 0-85331-411-x (pbk) : £9.95 B81-37172

720'.942 — England. Architecture, *to 1979*

Richards, J. M.. The National Trust book of English architecture / J.M. Richards. — London : National Trust, c1981. — 288 p : ill (some col.),plans ; 26cm
Bibliography: p282-283. - Includes index
ISBN 0-297-77901-x : £12.95 B81-22408

West, T. W.. Discovering English architecture / T.W. West. — Aylesbury : Shire, 1979. — 128p : ill ; 18cm. — (Discovering series ; 244)
Based on the author's Architecture in England, revised and updated with new photographs. — Bibliography: p126. — Includes index
ISBN 0-85263-455-2 (pbk) : £1.25 B81-05096

720'.942 — England. Buildings. Reconstruction. Architectural design, *1940-1980*

Esher, Lionel Brett, *Viscount*. A broken wave : the rebuilding of England 1940-1980 / Lionel Esher. — London : Allen Lane, 1981. — 326p : ill ; 25cm
Includes index
ISBN 0-7139-1199-9 : £12.95 B81-40477

720'.9421 — London. Architecture — *Serials*

RIBA London Region. — 1980-. — Macclesfield (Byron House, London Rd, Macclesfield, Cheshire SK11 7QX) : published on behalf of the RIBA London Region by Macmillan Martin, [1980]-. — v. : ill ; 29cm
Annual
Free to London Region members of RIBA
B81-05444

720'.9421 — London. Buildings, *1837-1887*. Architectural features

Stamp, Gavin. Victorian buildings of London 1837-1887 : an illustrated guide / Gavin Stamp and Colin Amery. — London : Architectural Press, 1980. — 175p : ill,maps,plans ; 26cm
Includes index
ISBN 0-85139-500-7 : £12.95 B81-05671

720'.9422'3 — Kent. Vernacular buildings, *1200-1900*. Architectural features

Traditional Kent buildings : studies by students at the School of Architecture, Canterbury College of Art. — No.1-. — [Maidstone] ([c/o The Education Department, Springfield, Maidstone, ME14 2LJ]) : Kent County Council Education Committee, 1980-. — v. : ill ; 30cm
Irregular
ISSN 0260-4116 = Traditional Kent buildings : £1.50 B81-06097

720'.9423'93 — Avon. Blaise Hamlet. Buildings of historical importance. Architectural features

Temple, Nigel. Blaise Hamlet, Henbury, near Bristol / [prepared by Nigel Temple]. — [London] : National Trust, c1975. — [4]p ; 22cm
Unpriced (unbound) B81-33574

Temple, Nigel. Blaise Hamlet, Henbury, near Bristol / [prepared by Nigel Temple]. — [London] : National Trust, c1978. — [4]p ; 22cm
Unpriced (unbound) B81-33575

720'.9424'41 — Hereford and Worcester. Bewdley. Buildings. Architectural features — *Walkers' guides*

Bewdley : a town trail. — [Bewdley] : [Bewdley Civic Society], [1981]. — 4p : ill,1map ; 30cm
Unpriced (unbound) B81-15114

720'.9425'3 — Lincolnshire. Buildings. Architectural features

Lincolnshire buildings : a list of amendments and additions to Pevsner's Lincolnshire History and Archaeology. — [Lincoln] ([North Lincolnshire Area Office, 47 Newland, Lincoln LN1 1XZ]) : The Society, [1980]. — 34p ; 30cm
Unpriced (unbound) B81-26858

720'.9425'91 — Buckinghamshire. Milton Keynes. Buildings. Architectural features

Opher, Philip. Milton Keynes : an illustrated guide / Philip Opher, Clinton Bird. — [Headington] : Urban Design, Oxford Polytechnic, c1981. — 49p : ill,maps,plans ; 15x21cm. — (British new towns)
Cover title. — Also available in Architecture and urban design in six British new towns. — Bibliography: p49
ISBN 0-907420-00-1 (pbk) : £1.75 B81-25223

720'.9426 — East Anglia. Buildings. Architectural features — *Serials*

Recent East Anglian buildings / Eastern Region, Royal Institute of British Architects. — 1979-80 ed. — London (66 Portland Place, W1N 4AD) : ERA Publications Board, [1979?]. — [15]p
Unpriced B81-23143

Recent East Anglian buildings / Eastern Region, Royal Institute of British Architects. — 1980. — London (66 Portland Place, W1N 4AD) : ERA Publications Board, [1980?]. — 30p
Unpriced B81-20430

720'.9426 — East Anglia. Secondary schools. Curriculum subjects: East Anglia. Architecture — *For teaching*

East Anglia's built environment as an educational resource / Eastern Region, Royal Institute of British Architects ; edited by Brian Goodey. — London (66 Portland Place, W1N 4AD) : ERA Publications Board, 1981. — 36p : ill,plans ; 30cm
Includes bibliographies
ISBN 0-907598-00-5 (pbk) : £2.70 B81-24006

720'.9427'18 — Cheshire. Runcorn. Buildings. Architectural features

Opher, Philip. Runcorn, Warrington : an illustrated guide / Philip Opher, Clinton Bird. — [Headington] : Urban Design, Oxford Polytechnic, c1980. — 30,18p : ill,maps,plans ; 15x21cm. — (British new towns)
Cover title. — Also available in Architecture and urban design in six British new towns. — Includes bibliography
ISBN 0-9504310-7-9 (pbk) : £1.50
Also classified at 720'.9427'19 B81-25222

720'.9427'19 — Cheshire. Warrington. Buildings. Architectural features

Opher, Philip. Runcorn, Warrington : an illustrated guide / Philip Opher, Clinton Bird. — [Headington] : Urban Design, Oxford Polytechnic, c1980. — 30,18p : ill,maps,plans ; 15x21cm. — (British new towns)
Cover title. — Also available in Architecture and urban design in six British new towns. — Includes bibliography
ISBN 0-9504310-7-9 (pbk) : £1.50
Primary classification 720'.9427'18 B81-25222

720'.9428'19 — West Yorkshire *(Metropolitan County)*. Leeds. Buildings. Architectural features — *Walkers' guides*

Godward, Brian. Walk about : a guided walk about the centre of Leeds, with an introduction to some of its buildings and places ... / Brian Godward. — Rev. ed. — [Leeds] (23 Clarendon Rd., Leeds LS2 9NZ) : Leeds Civic Trust, 1981. — [28]p : ill,1map ; 30x11cm
Previous ed.: 1973
ISBN 0-905671-02-3 (pbk) : £0.70 B81-22748

720'.9428'27 — South Yorkshire *(Metropolitan County)*. Doncaster. Buildings. Architectural features

Walton, Colin. The changing face of Doncaster / by Colin Walton. — Doncaster (c/o Central Library, Waterdale, Doncaster, DN1 3JE) : Doncaster Metropolitan Borough Council, [1981?]. — 66p : ill,2maps,1plan,1port ; 24cm
Originally published: by the author, 1980
ISBN 0-906976-01-4 (pbk) : £3.40 B81-34351

720'.9428'36 — Humberside. Beverley. Buildings. Architectural features

Hall, Ivan. Historic Beverley / by Ivan & Elisabeth Hall ; documentary research by G.B. Drummond, B.A. English. — 2nd ed. — Beverley ([16] Butcher Row, Beverley [HU17 0AE]) : Beverley Bookshop, 1981. — 107p : ill,map,plans ; 25cm
Previous ed.: York : William Sessions Ltd., 1973. — Includes index
ISBN 0-9505765-1-4 (pbk) : £5.95 B81-12511

720'.944 — France. Architecture, *1500-1700*

Blunt, Anthony. Art and architecture in France 1500 to 1700 / Anthony Blunt. — 4th ed. — Harmondsworth : Penguin, 1980, c1981. — 476p : ill,maps,plans,ports ; 22cm. — (The Pelican history of art)
Previous ed.: 1973. — Bibliography: p447-453. — Includes index
£17.95 (cased)
ISBN 0-14-056004-1
Primary classification 709'.44 B81-30952

720'.945'31 — Italy. Venice. Architecture, *to 1979*

Howard, Deborah. The architectural history of Venice / Deborah Howard. — London : Batsford, 1980. — 263p : ill,maps,plans ; 26cm
Bibliography: p249-255. — Includes index
ISBN 0-7134-1188-0 : £15.00 B81-06797

720'.947'312 — Russia *(RSFSR)*. Moscow. Buildings. Architectural features

Promyslov, V. F.. Moscow : past and present / V. Promyslov ; [translated from the Russian by Doris Bradbury]. — Moscow : Progress Publishers ; [London] : Distributed by Central Books, c1980. — 303p : ill(some col.),1facsim,1plan ; 25cm
Translation of: Zemli͡a Moskva
£4.50 B81-09576

720'.962'16 — Egypt. Cairo. Buildings of historical importance. Architectural features — *Walkers' guides*

Freeman-Grenville, G. S. P.. The beauty of Cairo : a historical guide to the chief Islamic and Coptic monuments / G.S.P. Freeman-Grenville. — London : East-West Publications, c1981. — 127p : ill,maps,plans ; 19cm
Bibliography: p117. — Includes index
ISBN 0-85692-061-4 (pbk) : £2.95 B81-29131

720'.9729 — West Indies. Buildings. Architectural features

Buisseret, David. Historic architecture of the Caribbean / David Buisseret. — London : Heinemann, 1980. — xv,93p : ill,maps,plans ; 26cm
Includes bibliographies and index
ISBN 0-435-98130-7 (cased) : £12.00 : CIP rev.
ISBN 0-435-98131-5 (pbk) : £4.90 B80-11546

720'.973 — United States. Architectural design. Palladian style, *1600-1900*

Farber, Joseph C.. Palladio's architecture and its influence : a photographic guide / photographs by Joseph C. Farber ; text by Henry Hope Reed. — New York : Dover Publications ; London : Constable, c1980. — xiv,129p : ill ; 30cm
ISBN 0-486-23922-5 (pbk) : £3.90
Primary classification 720'.941 B81-14127

720'.973 — United States. Architectural design. Partnerships: Hardy Holzman Pfeiffer Associates. Projects

Sorkin, Michael. Hardy Holzman Pfeiffer / by Michael Sorkin ; photographs by Norman McGrath. — New York : Whitney Library of Design ; London : Granada, 1981. — 120p : ill (some col.),plans ; 24cm. — (Monographs on contemporary architecture)
ISBN 0-246-11594-7 : £10.95 B81-39311

720'.973 — United States. Architecture, *1607-1976*

Whiffen, Marcus. American architecture 1607-1976 / Marcus Whiffen and Frederick Koeper. — London : Routledge 3 Kegan Paul, 1981. — xv,495p : ill,plans ; 26cm
Originally published: Cambridge, Mass. : MIT Press, 1980. — Bibliography: p457-467. — Includes index
ISBN 0-7100-0813-9 : £22.50 : CIP rev.
B81-03830

720'.973 — United States. Architecture, *to 1979 — Encyclopaedias*

Hunt, William Dudley. Encyclopedia of American architecture / William Dudley Hunt, Jr.. — New York ; London : McGraw-Hill, c1980. — x,612p : ill,plans ; 29cm
Includes index
ISBN 0-07-031299-0 : £21.00 B81-05461

720'.9797 — Washington *(State)*. Buildings. Architectural features

Woodbridge, Sally B.. A guide to architecture in Washington State : an environmental perspective / Sally B. Woodbridge and Roger Montgomery ; essay on landscape design by David C. Streatfield. — Seattle ; London : University of Washington Press, c1980. — xv,483p : ill,maps ; 23cm-
Text on lining paper. — Bibliography: p458-460. - Includes index
ISBN 0-295-95761-1 : £15.00 B81-17297

721 — ARCHITECTURAL DESIGN

721 — Architectural design. Environmental aspects

The **design** connection : energy and technology in architecture / edited by Ralph W. Crump, Martin J. Harms. — New York ; London : Van Nostrand Reinhold, c1981. — xv,184p : ill,1chart,plans,1port ; 22x29cm. — (Preston Thomas memorial series in architecture)
Conference papers. — Includes index
ISBN 0-442-23125-3 : £14.95 B81-26425

Environmental physics in construction. — St. Albans : Granada, Feb.1982. — [224]p
Translation and revision of: Bauphysik
ISBN 0-246-11224-7 : £25.00 : CIP entry
B81-35796

721 — Architectural design — *Manuals*

Weidhaas, Ernest R.. Architectural drafting and design / Ernest R. Weidhaas. — 4th ed.. — Boston [Mass.] ; London : Allyn and Bacon, c1981. — xi,436,[46]p : ill,plans ; 29cm
Previous ed.: 1977. — Includes index
ISBN 0-205-07100-7 : £15.95
Primary classification 720'.28'4 B81-01877

721 — Architectural design. Plans. Interpretation

Weidhaas, Ernest R.. Instructor's handbook for Reading architectural plans for residential and commercial construction / Ernest R. Weidhaas. — 2nd ed. — Boston, Mass. ; London : Allyn and Bacon, c1981. — 106p : ill,forms,plans ; 28cm
Previous ed.: 1977
ISBN 0-205-07167-8 (pbk) : Unpriced
B81-28903

Weidhaas, Ernest R.. Reading architectural plans : for residential and commercial construction / Ernest R. Weidhaas. — 2nd ed. — Boston, Mass. ; London : Allyn and Bacon, 1981. — xi,303p,36 folded leaves of plates : ill(some col.),plans,forms ; 28cm
Previous ed.: 1977
ISBN 0-205-07155-4 (spiral) : £12.75
B81-19828

721 — Buildings. Design & construction. Implications of climate

Givoni, B.. Man, climate and architecture. — 2nd ed. — London : Applied Science Publishers, Jan.1982. — [483]p. — (Architectural science series)
Previous ed.: Amsterdam ; Barking : Elsevier, 1969
ISBN 0-85334-108-7 : £15.00 : CIP entry
B81-33787

721 — Great Britain. Architectural design. Effects of conservation of energy resources — *Standards*

CIBS Building Energy Code. — London (222 Balham High., SW12 9BS) : Chartered Institution of Building Services
Pt.2: Calculation of energy demands and targets for the design of new buildings and services
Section (a): Heated and naturally ventilated buildings. — 1981. — 71p : ill,forms ; 30cm
"Building energy demand worksheet" (10 leaves) as insert. — Bibliography: p67
Unpriced (pbk) B81-22417

721 — Prefabricated buildings

Russell, Barry. Building systems, industrialisation and architecture. — Chichester : Wiley, Dec.1981. — [624]p
ISBN 0-471-27952-8 : £25.00 : CIP entry
B81-32592

721 — United States. Architectural design. Environmental aspects

Wells, Malcolm. Gentle architecture / Malcolm Wells. — New York ; London : McGraw-Hill, c1981. — 178p : ill,1map ; 25cm
Bibliography: p169-173. — Includes index
ISBN 0-07-069245-9 : £15.75 B81-23997

721'.01'03 — Architectural design, *1800-1980*. Social aspects

Buildings and society : essays on the social development of the built environment / edited by Anthony D. King. — London : Routledge & Kegan Paul, 1980. — ix,318p : ill,map,plans ; 26cm
Includes bibliographies and index
ISBN 0-7100-0616-0 : £25.00 : CIP rev.
B80-27365

721'.01'9 — Architectural design. Psychological aspects

Lym, Glenn Robert. A psychology of building : how we shape and experience our structured spaces / Glenn Robert Lym. — Englewood Cliffs ; London : Prentice-Hall, c1980. — xix,155p : ill,plans ; 25cm. — (The Patterns of Social behavior series) (A Spectrum book)
Includes index
ISBN 0-13-735225-5 (cased) : £8.40
ISBN 0-13-735217-4 (pbk) : £3.20 B81-05416

721'.021'2 — Architectural design — *Standards*

Rich, Peter. Principles of element design. — 2nd ed. — London : George Godwin, Jan.1982. — [150]p
Previous ed.: 1977
ISBN 0-7114-5627-5 (pbk) : £8.50 : CIP entry
B81-33982

721'.0212 — Architectural design — *Standards*

Time-saver standards for building types / edited by Joseph de Chiara and John Hancock Callender. — 2nd ed. — New York ; London : McGraw-Hill, 1980. — xvii,1277p : ill,plans ; 29cm
Previous ed.: 1973. — Includes index
ISBN 0-07-016265-4 : £34.40 B81-10838

721'.0212 — Architectural design — *Technical data*

Neufert, Ernst. Architects' data / Ernst Neufert. — 2nd (international) English ed. / general editor Vincent Jones ; editorial consultant George Atkinson ; USA editor Wm Dudley Hunt Jr. ; editor John Thackara ; deputy editor Richard Miles. — London : Granada, 1980. — xiv,433p : ill,plans ; 31cm
Previous ed.: / edited and revised by Rudolf Herz from translations from the German. London : Lockwood, 1970. — Bibliography: p413-428. — Includes index
ISBN 0-246-11258-1 : £25.00 B81-03530

721'.028'54 — Architectural design. Applications of computer systems

Reynolds, R. A.. Computer methods for architects / R.A. Reynolds. — London : Butterworth, 1980. — 149p : ill,plans ; 31cm
Bibliography: p141-145. — Includes index
ISBN 0-408-00476-2 : £15.00 : CIP rev.
B80-11547

721'.0441'0942462 — Staffordshire. Newcastle-under-Lyme. Buildings. Architectural features: Building materials: Stone — *Visitors' guides*

Holloway, Sam. A guide to the building stones of Newcastle-under-Lyme, Staffordshire / Sam Holloway and Keith Sims. — Keele ([Keele, Staffs.]) : [Keele University Library], 1981. — 24p : 1map ; 22cm. — (Occasional publication / Keele University Library ; no.17)
Unpriced (pbk) B81-19656

721'.0441'0942542 — Leicestershire. Leicester. Buildings. Architectural features: Building materials: Stone — *Visitors' guides*

Whitaker, J. H. McD.. Building stones of Leicester : a city trail / by J.H.McD. Whitaker. — Leicester (96 New Walk, Leicester LE1 6TD) : Leicestershire Museums, Art Galleries and Records Service, 1981. — 16p : ill ; 15x21cm. — (Leicestershire Museums publication ; no.20)
ISBN 0-85022-071-8 (pbk) : Unpriced
B81-18931

721'.0445 — Architectural design. Use of concrete & expanded polystyrene

Ritter, Paul. Concrete fit for people : a practical introduction to a bio-functional eco-architecture for the third millennium A.D. / Paul Ritter. — Perth, W. Australia : Down to Earth Bookshop Press ; Oxford : Pergamon [distributor], 1980. — 112p : ill(some col.),plans,ports ; 30cm
ISBN 0-08-024671-0 : £14.95 : CIP rev.
B79-34971

721'.0445 — Concrete masonry. Design

Tovey, A. K. Concrete masonry : for the designer / A.K. Tovey. — Slough (Wexham Springs, Slough SL3 6PL) : Cement and Concrete Association, 1981. — 20p : ill(some col.) ; 30cm. — (Cement and Concrete Association publication ; 48.049)
ISBN 0-7210-1225-6 (pbk) : Unpriced
B81-37993

721'.0448 — Cruck buildings. Architectural features

Alcock, N. W.. Cruck construction. — London : Council for British Archaeology, Sept.1981. — [184]p. — (CBA research reports, ISSN 0589-9036 ; no.42)
ISBN 0-906780-11-x (pbk) : £10.00 : CIP entry
B81-26691

721'.0448 — England. Timber-framed buildings. Design & construction, *ca 1250-ca 1700*

Timber Framed Buildings *(1980 : Great Britain)*. Timber framed buildings : a catalogue written by Richard Harris to accompany the touring exhibition Timber Framed Buildings. — [London] : Arts Council of Great Britain, c1980. — 32p : ill ; 15x22cm
Cover title. — Bibliography: p32. — Ill on inside covers
ISBN 0-7287-0256-8 (pbk) : Unpriced
B81-0807

721'.0448 — London. Waltham Forest *(London Borough)*. Timber framed buildings. Architectural features

Batsford, Marjorie. Timber-framed buildings in Waltham Forest / by Marjorie Batsford. — London : Walthamstow Antiquarian Society, 1980. — 22p,[4]p of plates : ill,1map,plans ; 30cm. — (Occasional publication / Walthamstow Antiquarian Society ; no.18)
Includes index
ISBN 0-85480-039-5 (pbk) : £0.50 B81-0612

721'.04497'0941 — British prefabricated buildings, *1800-1900*

Herbert, Gilbert. Pioneers of prefabrication : the British contribution in the nineteenth century / Gilbert Herbert. — Baltimore ; London : The Johns Hopkins University Press, c1978. — xii,228p : ill,1map,plans ; 25cm. — (The Johns Hopkins studies in nineteenth-century architecture)
Bibliography: p213-219. — Includes index
ISBN 0-8018-1852-4 : £12.25 B81-2206

721'.0467 — Architectural design. Implications of conservation of energy resources

Building design for energy economy / The Ove Arup Partnership. — Lancaster : Construction Press, 1980. — 132p : ill ; 31cm
Includes index
ISBN 0-86095-850-7 : £15.00 : CIP rev.
B80-2229

721'.0913 — Hot regions. Buildings. Design & construction — *Manuals*

Building in hot climates : a selection of overseas building notes / prepared by the Overseas Division of the Building Research Establishment, United Kingdom. — London : H.M.S.O., 1980. — iv,520p : ill,plans ; 31cm
Includes bibliographies and index
ISBN 0-11-670759-3 : £35.00 B81-1521

721'.0915'4 — Arid tropical regions. Architectural design

Saini, Balwant Singh. Building in hot dry climates / Balwant Singh Saini. — Chichester Wiley, c1980. — 176p : ill,plans ; 26cm
Based on Building environment / by Balwant Singh Saina. Sydney : Angus and Robertson, 1973. — Includes index
ISBN 0-471-27764-9 : £15.00 : CIP rev.
B80-2229

721'.0941 — Great Britain. Buildings. Design & construction

A **Clients** guide to design & build / Construction Industry Research & Information Association. — London : CIRIA, c1981. — 12p ; 20x21cm
Cover title
ISBN 0-86017-167-1 (corrected : pbk) : £1.50 (£0.80 to members of CIRIA) B81-3312

721'.0941 — Great Britain. Buildings. Design & construction — *For local authorities — Serials*

[Members' reference book *(Society of Chief Architects of Local Authorities)*]. Members' reference book / Society of Chief Architects of Local Authorities. — 1979/80-. — London (86 Edgeware Rd, W2 2YW) : Sterling Publications, 1979. — v. : ill,ports ; 21cm
Annual. — Continues: Year book (Society of Chief Architects of Local Authorities). — Description based on: 1980/81
ISSN 0261-1627 = Members' reference book — Society of Chief Architects of Local Authorities (corrected) : Unpriced
Primary classification 690'.24'0941 B81-2041

21′.45 — England. Fan vaults, *ca 1300-1540*
Leedy, Walter C.. Fan vaulting : a study of form, technology, and meaning / Walter C. Leedy, Jr. — London : Scolar, 1980. — v,234p : ill,plans ; 27cm
Bibliography: p230. - Includes index
ISBN 0-85967-610-2 : £16.00 : CIP rev.
B80-19335

21′.46 — Buildings. Domes — *For children*
MacGregor, Anne. Domes : a project series for young people / Anne and Scott MacGregor. — [Leeds] : Pepper, 1981. — 56p : ill ; 29cm
ISBN 0-560-74512-5 : £3.95 B81-34272

22 — ARCHITECTURE. ANCIENT AND ORIENTAL

22′.44 — India. Islamic architecture, *1340-1690*
Merklinger, E.. Indian Islamic architecture. — Warminster : Aris & Phillips, July 1981. — [168]p
ISBN 0-85668-193-8 : CIP entry B81-13746

22′.7 — Ancient Rome. Architecture, *B.C.27-A.D.337*
Ward-Perkins, J. B.. Roman imperial architecture / J.B. Ward-Perkins. — 2nd (integrated) ed. — Harmondsworth : Penguin, 1981. — 532p : ill,maps,plans ; 22cm. — (The Pelican history of art)
Previous ed.: published as parts 2-4 of Etruscan and Roman architecture / by Axel Boëthius, J.B. Ward-Perkins. 1970. — Bibliography: p498-510. — Includes index
ISBN 0-14-056045-9 (cased) : £20.00
B81-27634

24 — ARCHITECTURE. MODERN PERIOD, 1400-

24 — Western world. Architecture, *1800-1980*
Ball, Victoria Kloss. Architecture and interior design : Europe and America from the Colonial Era to today / Victoria Kloss Ball. — New York ; Chichester : Wiley, c1980. — xvii,442p,[16]p of plates : ill(some col.),plans ; 29cm
Bibliography: p399-409. - Includes index
ISBN 0-471-05161-6 : £24.00
ISBN 0-471-08722-x (pbk) : Unpriced
Also classified at 747.2′04 B81-10607

24.9′1 — Architectural design, *1910-1933 — Illustrations*
Smithson, Alison. The heroic period of modern architecture / Alison and Peter Smithson. — London : Thames and Hudson, 1981. — 80p : ill(some col.),plans(some col.) ; 30cm
Includes index
ISBN 0-500-27229-8 (pbk) : £4.95 B81-38686

24.9′1 — Architectural design, *1970-1980 — Case studies*
Kultermann, Udo. Architecture in the seventies / Udo Kultermann. — London : Architectural Press, 1980. — 149p : ill,maps,plans ; 31cm
ISBN 0-85139-048-x : £15.95 : CIP rev.
B80-22299

24.9′1 — Architectural design. Arts and Crafts movement
Davey, Peter, *1940-*. Arts and crafts architecture : the search for earthly paradise / Peter Davey. — London : Architectural Press, 1980. — 224p : ill,plans ; 26cm
Bibliography: p214-218. - Index
ISBN 0-85139-049-8 : £12.95 B81-03982

24.9′1 — Architecture, *1900-1980*
Banham, Reyner. Design by choice / Reyner Banham ; edited by Penny Sparke. — London : Academy Editions, 1981. — 152p : ill(some col.),1port ; 30cm. — (Ideas in architecture)
Bibliography: p143-147. — Includes index
Unpriced (pbk)
Also classified at 745.4′442 B81-29563

24.9′1 — Buildings. Architectural features, *ca 1970-1980*
Post-modern classicism : the new synthesis / guest-edited by Charles Jencks. — London (42 Leinster Gardens, W2) : Architectural Design Profile, c1980. — 143p : ill(some col.),plans ; 28cm
Unpriced (pbk) B81-07952

725 — ARCHITECTURE. PUBLIC BUILDINGS

725′.0954′56 — India *(Republic).* **Delhi. Public buildings. Architectural features,** *1900-1939*
Irving, Robert Grant. Indian summer : Lutyens, Baker and Imperial Delhi. — London : Yale University Press, Nov.1981. — [352]p
ISBN 0-300-02422-3 : £20.00 : CIP entry
B81-35022

725′.0973 — United States. Public institutions. Buildings. Architectural design
Redstone, Louis G.. Institutional buildings : architecture of the controlled environment / by Louis G. Redstone. — New York ; London : McGraw-Hill, c1980. — ix,181p : ill,plans ; 32cm. — (An Architectural record book)
Includes index
ISBN 0-07-002343-3 : £18.50 B81-15725

725.1 — ARCHITECTURE. GOVERNMENT BUILDINGS

725′.13′0941 — Great Britain. Town halls. Architectural features, *1820-1914*
Cunningham, Colin. Victorian and Edwardian town halls / Colin Cunningham. — London : Routledge & Kegan Paul, 1981. — xv,315p : ill,plans ; 26cm
Includes index
ISBN 0-7100-0723-x : £25.00 : CIP rev.
B81-14935

725′.17′09753 — Washington, D.C.. Official residences: White House. Architectural features, *to 1979*
Ryan, William, *1914-*. The White House : an architectural history / by William Ryan and Desmond Guinness. — New York ; London : McGraw-Hill, c1980. — x,196p,[16]p of plates : ill(some col.),maps,facsims,plans,col.ports ; 28cm
Bibliography: p187-188. — Includes index
ISBN 0-07-054352-6 : £14.95 B81-04740

725′.18 — Fortifications. Architectural features, *1800-1914 — Chronologies*
Hughes, Quentin. A chronology of events in fortification from 1800 to 1914 ; & An illustrated English glossary of terms used in military architecture / by Quentin Hughes. — Liverpool (c/o Quentin Hughes, Liverpool School of Architecture, University of Liverpool PO Box 147, Liverpool L61 3BX) : Fortress Study Group, 1980. — 98p : ill,plans ; 30cm
Unpriced (pbk) B81-27615

725′.18 — Hampshire. Portsmouth. Naval bases: H.M. Naval Base Portsmouth. Architectural features, *1700-1850*
Coad, J. G.. Historic architecture of H.M. Naval Base Portsmouth, 1700-1850 / by Jonathan Coad ; with a foreword by Sir Terence Lewin. — Portsmouth (c/o The Secretary, Society of Friends, Portsmouth Royal Naval Museum, H.M. Naval Base, Portsmouth, Hants PO1 3LR) : Portsmouth Royal Naval Museum Trading Co. in conjunction with the Society for Nautical Research, 1981. — vi,58p,[4]p of plates : ill,col.maps ; 25cm
′Reprinted from the February 1981 issue of the Mariners mirror ...′ — t.p. verso
Unpriced (pbk) B81-24207

725.2 — ARCHITECTURE. COMMERCIAL BUILDINGS

725′.23 — Great Britain. Offices. Buildings. Interiors. Architectural design
The **Structure** and design of tomorrow′s office : a report / prepared by Urwick Nexos Limited in collaboration with Francis Kinsman Associates Limited. — [Slough] ([Clove House, The Broadway, Farnham Common, Slough, Berkshire SL2 3PQ]) : [Urwick Nexos Ltd.], c1980. — iv,38leaves ; 30cm
Unpriced (spiral) B81-12619

725.3 — ARCHITECTURE. TRANSPORTATION AND STORAGE BUILDINGS

725′.33′0941 — Great Britain. Railway services: London, Midland and Scottish Railway, *to 1948.* **Architectural features** — *Illustrations*
Anderson, V. R.. A pictorial record of L.M.S. architecture / by Roy Anderson and Gregory Fox. — Oxford : Oxford Publishing, c1981. — [300]p : chiefly ill,plans ; 29cm
Ill on lining papers. — Includes index
ISBN 0-86093-083-1 : £15.00 B81-15692

725′.33′0942 — England. Railway services: Great Western Railway. Buildings. Architectural features
Leigh, Chris. GWR country stations / Chris Leigh. — London : Ian Allan, 1981. — 128p : ill,plans ; 25cm
Includes index
ISBN 0-7110-1108-7 : £5.95 B81-36738

725.4 — ARCHITECTURE. INDUSTRIAL BUILDINGS

725′.4 — Derbyshire. Hathersage. Mills, *1800-1902*
Tomlinson, Tom D.. The mills of Hathersage 1800 to 1902 / by Tom P. Tomlinson. — [Hathersage] ([The Vicarage, Hathersage, Sheffield S30 1AB]) : [Hathersage Parochial Church Council], [1979]. — [12]p : ill,1map ; 21cm
Cover title. — Text on inside covers
£0.30 (pbk) B81-18658

725′.4 — Disused industrial buildings. Redevelopment & reuse — *For architects*
Recycling industrial buildings. — Edinburgh (6 Castle St., Edinburgh EH2 3AT) : Capital Planning Information, Sept.1981. — [53]p. — (SSRC planning reviews ; no.1)
ISBN 0-906011-11-6 (pbk) : £3.00 : CIP entry
B81-25121

725′.4′0941 — Great Britain. Industrial buildings. Architectural design
Factories : planning and design. — London : Architectural Press, Nov.1981. — [320]p
ISBN 0-85139-302-0 : £29.95 : CIP entry
B81-30415

725.5 — ARCHITECTURE. HEALTH AND WELFARE BUILDINGS

725′.5 — Health centres. Buildings. Design
Cammock, Ruth. Primary health care buildings : briefing and design guide for architects and their clients / Ruth Cammock. — London : Architectural Press, 1981. — 93p,[8]p of plates : ill ; 23cm
Bibliography: p93
ISBN 0-85139-962-2 : £10.50 B81-26030

725′.5 — Health service buildings. Architectural design
Cox, Anthony. Design for health care / Anthony Cox and Philip Groves. — London : Butterworths, 1981. — viii,120p : ill,plans ; 30cm. — (The Butterworths design series for architects and planners)
Bibliography: p118. — Includes index
ISBN 0-408-00389-8 : Unpriced B81-27139

725.7 — ARCHITECTURE. REFRESHMENT AND PARK STRUCTURES

725′.72′0942 — England. Public houses. Architectural design
Davis, Ben. The traditional English pub : a way of drinking / Ben Davis. — London : Architectural Press, 1981. — x,157p,[16]p of plates : ill(some col.) ; 26cm
Bibliography: p147-149. — Includes index
ISBN 0-85139-055-2 : £10.95 B81-11401

725.8 — ARCHITECTURE. RECREATION BUILDINGS

725′.8 — Great Britain. Sports & games buildings. Architectural design — *Manuals*
Handbook of sports and recreational building design / the Sports Council Technical Unit for Sport ; edited by Geraint John and Helen Heard. — London : Architectural Press, 1981
Vol.1: Ice rinks and swimming pools. — ix,155p : ill,plans,ports ; 31cm
Bibliography: p148-149. - Includes index
ISBN 0-85139-586-4 : £29.50 : CIP rev.
ISBN 0-85139-600-3 (set) : £100.00 B80-22301

725'.8 — Great Britain. Sports & games buildings. Architectural design — *Manuals*
continuation

Handbook of sports and recreational building design / the Sports Council Technical Unit for Sport ; edited by Geraint John and Helen Heard. — London : Architectural Press, 1981
Vol.2: Indoor sports. — ix,214p : ill,1map,plans,ports ; 31cm
Bibliography: p207-208. - Includes index
ISBN 0-85139-587-2 : £35.00 : CIP rev.
ISBN 0-85139-600-3 (set) : £100.00 B80-22302

Handbook of sports and recreational building design / the Sports Council Technical Unit for Sport ; edited by Geraint John and Helen Heard. — London : Architectural Press, 1981
Vol.3: Outdoor sports. — ix,176p : ill,1map,plans ; 31cm
Bibliography: p168-170. - Includes index
ISBN 0-85139-598-8 : £29.50 : CIP rev.
ISBN 0-85139-600-3 (set) : £100.00 B81-04393

Handbook of sports and recreational building design / the Sports Council Technical Unit for Sport ; edited by Geraint John and Helen Heard. — London : Architectural Press, 1981
Vol.4: Sports data. — ix,134p : ill,plans,ports ; 31cm
Bibliography: p134
ISBN 0-85139-599-6 : £25.00 : CIP rev.
ISBN 0-85139-600-3 (set) : £100.00 B81-04392

725'.8 — Sports facilities. Design & planning

Perrin, Gerald A.. Design for sport. — London : Butterworths, Dec.1981. — [160]p
ISBN 0-408-00365-0 : £18.00 : CIP entry
B81-31721

725'.822 — Great Britain. Cinemas. Architectural features, *to 1979*

Atwell, David. Cathedrals of the movies : a history of British cinemas and their audiences / David Atwell. — London : Architectural Press, 1980. — xiv,194p : ill,plans,2ports ; 26cm
Bibliography: p189-190. — Includes index
ISBN 0-85139-562-7 : £12.95 B81-04963

725'.882'0924 — Great Britain. Theatres. Architectural design. Matcham, Frank — *Critical studies*

Frank Matcham : theatre architect / edited by Brian Mercer Walker. — Belfast : Blackstaff, c1980. — xii,178p : ill,facsims,plans,1port ; 25cm
Ill on lining papers. — Bibliography: p175. - Includes index
ISBN 0-85640-231-1 : £12.75 : CIP rev.
B80-23557

726 — ARCHITECTURE. RELIGIOUS BUILDINGS

726'.1207 — Italy. Rome. Ancient Roman temples: Pythagorean Temple. Architectural features, *to 1980*

Strong, Ronald J.. The Pythagorean Temple in Rome / Ronald J. Strong. — [Lutton] ([17 Longfield, Lutton, West Devon PL21 9SN]) : [R.J. Strong], 1980. — 22p,[2] leaves of plates : 3ill ; 26cm
Limited ed. of 100 numbered copies
£2.00 (pbk) B81-04763

726'.4 — Italy. Rome. Oratories: Casa dei Filippini. Architectural features

Connors, Joseph. Borromini and the Roman Oratory : style and society / Joseph Connors. — New York : Architectural History Foundation ; London : MIT, c1980. — xiv,375p : ill,facsims,plans ; 27cm
Includes some text in Italian. — Bibliography: p361-368. - Includes index
ISBN 0-262-03071-3 : £27.90 B81-17065

726'.5 — Churches. Architectural features — *For children*

Watkins, Peter, *1934-*. Here's the church / Peter Watkins & Erica Hughes ; illustrated by Gill Tomblin. — London (8 Cork St., W1X 2AA) : Julia MacRae, 1980. — 94p : ill,music ; 24cm
Includes index
ISBN 0-86203-055-2 : £4.95 B81-13132

726'.5'0942 — England. Churches. Anglo-Saxon architectural features

Taylor, H. M. (Harold McCarter). Anglo-Saxon architecture / by H.M. Taylor and Joan Taylor. — Cambridge : Cambridge University Press
Vol.1 ; [Vol.2]. — 1980, c1965. — 2v. : ill,plans ; 23cm
In slip case. — Includes bibliographies
ISBN 0-521-29914-4 (pbk) : £17.50 B81-08149

726'.5'0942 — England. Parish churches. Architectural features, *to 1900*

Child, Mark. English church architecture : a visual guide / Mark Child. — London : Batsford, 1981. — 119p : ill ; 26cm
Includes index
£6.95 B81-13139

Foster, Richard, *1946-*. Discovering English churches : a beginner's guide to the story of the parish church from before the Conquest to the Gothic Revival / Richard Foster. — London : British Broadcasting Corporation, 1981. — 296p : ill(some col.),ports ; 26cm
Includes index
ISBN 0-563-16466-2 : £12.00 B81-25277

726'.5'094233 — Dorset. Parish churches. Architectural features — *History*

Pitfield, F. P.. Dorset parish churches / described and depicted by F.P. Pitfield. — Sherborne : Dorset Publishing, 1981
A-D. — 232p : ill,maps,music,plans ; 31cm
Limited ed. of 595 numbered copies bound in full leather. — Ill on lining papers
ISBN 0-902129-60-0 : £37.50 B81-27757

726'.5'094241 — England. Cotswolds. Parish churches. Architectural features

Verey, David. Cotswold churches. — Gloucester (17a Brunswick Rd, Gloucester GL1 1HG) : Alan Sutton, Sept.1981. — [192]p
ISBN 0-904387-78-x (pbk) : £3.95 : CIP entry
B81-24650

726'.5'094241 — Gloucestershire. Churches. Architectural features

Verey, David. Gloucestershire churches. — Gloucester (17a Brunswick Rd, Gloucester GL1 1HG) : Alan Sutton, May 1981. — [64]p
ISBN 0-904387-80-1 (pbk) : £2.95 : CIP entry
B81-08835

726'.5'0945632 — Italy. Rome. Churches. Architectural features

Beny, Roloff. The churches of Rome / Roloff Beny & Peter Gunn. — London : Weidenfeld and Nicholson, c1981. — 288p : ill(some col.),1map ; 28cm
Bibliography: p284. — Includes index
ISBN 0-297-77903-6 : £15.00 B81-40215

726'.5'0947 — Eastern Europe. Wooden churches. Architectural features

Buxton, David. The wooden churches of Eastern Europe. — Cambridge : Cambridge University Press, Dec.1981. — [384]p
ISBN 0-521-23786-6 : £42.50 : CIP entry
B81-37001

726'.5'09563 — Turkey. Istanbul. Churches. Architectural features — *French texts*

Ebersolt, Jean. Les églises de Constantinople / Jean Ebersolt et Adolphe Thiers ; préface de Gilbert Dagron. — London (66 Lyncroft Gardens, NW6 1JY) : Dorian Press, 1979. — vii,294p,[61]p of plates(6 folded) : ill,plans ; 35cm. — (Byzantine art and architecture ; R1)
Facsim of: edition published Paris : Ministère de l'instruction publique, 1913. — Bibliography: p281-283. - Includes index
ISBN 0-906175-03-8 : £68.00 B81-03768

726'.5'09797 — Washington. Churches, *to 1916.* **Architectural features** — *Illustrations*

Pearson, Arnold. Early churches of Washington State / photographs by Arnold Pearson ; text by Esther Pearson. — Seattle ; London : University of Washington Press, c1980. — ix,182p : ill,1map ; 27cm
Bibliography: p177-179. — Includes index
ISBN 0-295-95713-1 : £13.50 B81-06552

726'.596 — Italy. Florence. Baptisteries: Battistero di San Giovanni. Bronze doors - *Illustrations*

Finn, David, *19---*. The Florence Baptistery doors / photographs David Finn ; introduction Kenneth Clark ; commentaries by George Robinson. — London : Thames and Hudson, c1980. — 328p : chiefly ill(some col.) ; 30cm
Ill on lining papers. — Bibliography: p327. — Includes index
ISBN 0-500-23313-6 : £25.00 B81-0467

726'.597'094238 — Somerset. Parish churches. Towers. Architectural features

Wright, Peter Poyntz. The parish church towers of Somerset : their construction, craftsmanship and chronology 1350-1550 / by Peter Poyntz Wright ; with a foreword by Aehred Watkin. — [Amersham] : Avebury, 1981. — xi,217p : ill,1map,plans ; 31cm
Bibliography: p216. — Includes index
ISBN 0-86127-502-0 : £20.00 : CIP rev.
B81-1591

726'.6'094451 — France. Chartres. Cathedrals: Cathédrale de Chartres. Architectural features

Adams, Henry. Mont-Saint-Michel and Chartres / Henry Adams ; introduction by Lord Briggs. — London : Hamlyn, 1980. — 192p : ill(some col.),1map,1plan,ports,3geneal.tables ; 32cm. — (A Bison book)
Originally published: Washington : Adams, 1904. — Ill on lining papers. — Includes index
ISBN 0-600-34182-8 : £7.95
Also classified at 726'.7 B81-0594

726'.7 — France. Mont-Saint-Michel. Abbeys: Abbaye de Mont-Saint-Michel. Architectural features

Adams, Henry. Mont-Saint-Michel and Chartres / Henry Adams ; introduction by Lord Briggs. — London : Hamlyn, 1980. — 192p : ill(some col.),1map,1plan,ports,3geneal.tables ; 32cm. — (A Bison book)
Originally published: Washington : Adams, 1904. — Ill on lining papers. — Includes index
ISBN 0-600-34182-8 : £7.95
Primary classification 726'.6'094451 B81-0594

726'.7 — Somerset. Glastonbury. Abbeys: Glastonbury Abbey. Architectural features

Bond, Frederick Bligh. An architectural handbook of Glastonbury Abbey : with a historical chronicle of the building / by Frederick Bligh Bond. — London (c/o J. Jackson, 36 College Court, W6 9DZ) : Research into Lost Knowledge Organization ; Wellingborough : Distributed by Thorsons, 1981. — 88p,[17]p of plates : ill,1col.plan ; 22cm
Facsim. of: 2nd ed., originally published: Bristol : Everard, 1910. — Bibliography: p88. — Includes index
ISBN 0-902103-06-7 (pbk) : £3.95 B81-1820

726'.7'094 — Western Europe. Monasteries. Architectural features, *to 1960*

Braunfels, Wolfgang. Monasteries of Western Europe : the architecture of the Orders / Wolfgang Braunfels ; [translated by Alastair Laing]. — London : Thames and Hudson, c1972 (1980 [printing]). — 263p : ill,facsims,plans ; 28cm
Translation of: Abendländische Klosterbaukunst. Includes selections from documentary sources with parallel Latin text and English translation. — Bibliography: p251-254. - Includes index
ISBN 0-500-27201-8 (pbk) : £7.50 B81-0534

727 — ARCHITECTURE. EDUCATIONAL AND RESEARCH BUILDINGS

727'.1'042 — Schools for children confined to wheelchairs. Architectural design

Goldsmith, Brian C.. Design data for wheelchair children : with particular reference to designing special schools for physically handicapped children / Brian C. Goldsmith. — London (346 Kensington High St., W14 8NS) Disabled Living Foundation, 1979. — xiii,120p : ill,plans ; 30cm
Bibliography: p117-118. — Includes index
ISBN 0-901908-37-1 (pbk) : £4.50 B81-1108

727'.3'0942819 — West Yorkshire *(Metropolitan County).* **Leeds. Universities: University of Leeds. Red brick buildings. Architectural features** — *Walkers' guides*

Beresford, Maurice. Walks round red brick / Maurice Beresford. — Leeds : Leeds University Press, 1980. — 108p : ill,maps ; 20x21cm
Unpriced (pbk) B81-27895

727'.6574'0924 — London. Kensington & Chelsea *(London Borough).* **Museums: British Museum** *(Natural History).* **Buildings. Architectural design by Waterhouse, Alfred**

Girouard, Mark. Alfred Waterhouse and the Natural History Museum / Mark Girouard. — [London] : British Museum (Natural History), 1981. — 64p : ill(some col.),plans,ports ; 22x23cm. — (Publication / British Museum (Natural History) ; no.831)
ISBN 0-565-00831-5 (pbk) : Unpriced B81-05656

727'.6574'0924 — London. Kensington and Chelsea *(London Borough).* **Museums: British Museum (Natural History). Buildings. Architectural design by Waterhouse, Alfred**

Girouard, Mark. Alfred Waterhouse and the Natural History Museum / Mark Girouard. — New Haven ; London : Yale University Press in association with the British Museum (Natural History), c1981. — 64p : ill(some col.),plans,ports ; 23x24cm
Ill on lining papers. — Bibliography: p5
ISBN 0-300-02578-5 : £4.95 B81-13256

728 — ARCHITECTURE. RESIDENCES

728 — Bedfordshire. North Bedfordshire *(District).* **Residences. Extensions. Architectural design** — *Standards*

Residential extensions and space about buildings : a guide to design / NBBC. — [Bedford] ([37 Goldington Rd., Bedford MK40 3LQ]) : [North Bedfordshire Borough Council], 1979. — 31p : ill ; 30cm
Cover title
Unpriced (pbk) B81-26365

728 — Earth sheltered residences. Architectural design

Ahrens, Donna. Earth sheltered homes : plans and designs / Underground Space Center, University of Minnesota ; Donna Ahrens, Tom Ellison, Ray Sterling. — New York ; London : Van Nostrand Reinhold, c1981. — 125p : ill (some col.),plans ; 23x29cm
Includes index
ISBN 0-442-28675-9 (pbk) : Unpriced
ISBN 0-442-28676-7 (pbk) : £8.45 B81-39886

728 — Great Britain. Residences. Chimneys & fireplaces

The **Fireplace** book : the comprehensive guide to fireplaces / [editor: H.J.C. Brown]. — Windsor (341 St Leonard's Rd, Windsor, SL4 3DS) : Roshfield Publications, 1980. — iv,140p : ill (some col.) ; 30cm
Cover title
ISBN 0-9507245-0-5 (pbk) : £4.95 B81-03137

728 — Residences. Chimneys

Fry, Neill. Chimney faults and cures / by Neill Fry. — [Billericay] ([67 High St., Billericay, Essex]) : [J.K. Wildman], [1981]. — 20p,[3] folded leaves of plates : ill ; 21cm
Cover title
£1.00 (pbk) B81-18767

728 — Scotland. Lothian Region. West Lothian *(District).* **Residences. Extensions. Architectural design** — *Standards*

Thinking about alterations and extensions / West Lothian District Council Department of Planning. — Linlithgow (Old County Buildings, High St., Linlithgow, W. Lothian EH49 7EX) : West Lothian District Council Department of Physical Planning, [1981?]. — 16p : ill ; 21cm
Cover title
Unpriced (pbk) B81-34900

728'.01'03 — Illinois. Chicago. Residences, *1873-1913.* **Architectural features. Social aspects**
Wright, Gwendolyn. Moralism and the model home : domestic architecture and cultural conflict in Chicago 1873-1913 / Gwendolyn Wright. — Chicago ; London : University of Chicago Press, 1980. — viii,382p : ill,facsims,plans ; 24cm
Bibliography: p349-369. — Includes index
ISBN 0-226-90835-6 : £10.50 B81-02679

728'.028 — Residences. Improvement & extensions — *Amateurs' manuals*
The **Weekend** builder : a practical guide to major home improvements and extensions / edited by Julian Worthington. — London : Orbis, 1981. — 144p : ill(some col.) ; 30cm
Includes index
ISBN 0-85613-337-x : £3.95 B81-34084

728'.043'09411 — Scotland. Residencies for old persons. Architectural design — *Manuals*
Great Britain. *Scottish Development Department.* Housing for the elderly / Scottish Development Department. — Edinburgh : H.M.S.O., 1980. — [63]p : ill,plans ; 30cm. — (Scottish housing handbook ; 5)
ISBN 0-11-491651-9 (pbk) : £4.75 B81-06124

728'.0722 — Australia. Residences. Architectural features — *Case studies*
Knox, Alistair. Alternative housing : building with the head, the heart and the hand / Alistair Knox. — Sutherland, N.S.W. : Albatross ; Tring : Lion, 1980. — 150p : ill (some col.),ports(some col.) ; 25cm
ISBN 0-85648-278-1 (pbk) : £5.95 B81-09942

728'.09'04 — Residences. Architectural design, *1900-1980*
20th century decorating architecture & gardens : 80 years of ideas & pleasure from House & garden / book edited by Mary Jane Pool ; text edited & chapter introductions by Caroline Seebohm. — London : Weidenfeld & Nicolson, c1980. — 320p : ill(some col.),plans,ports ; 31cm
Includes index
ISBN 0-297-77878-1 : £15.00
Primary classification 747.2'049 B81-04065

728'.0914'3 — Hilly regions. Residences. Architectural design
Abbott, Derek. Hill housing : a comparative study / Derek Abbott and Kimball Pollit. — London : Granada, 1980. — xii,308p : ill,maps,plans ; 26cm
Bibliography: p300-302. - Includes index
ISBN 0-246-11203-4 : £19.50 : CIP rev. B80-23558

728'.0915'4 — Arid regions. Residences. Planning & architectural design
Housing in arid lands : design and planning / edited by Gideon Golany. — London : Architectural Press, 1980. — xi,257p : ill,maps, plans ; 31cm
Includes bibliographies and index
ISBN 0-85139-270-9 : £55.00 : CIP rev. B80-19337

728'.09173'4 — Rural regions. Residences. Architectural features
Country living : 32 examples from around the world / edited by Franco Magnani ; translated by Frances Alexander. — London : Studio Vista, 1980. — 96p : chiefly ill(some col.),plans ; 29cm
Translated from the Italian
ISBN 0-289-70962-8 : £4.95 B81-35415

728'.092'4 — United States. Residences. Architectural design. Staub, John F. — *Critical studies*
Barnstone, Howard. The architecture of John F. Staub : Houston and the South / by Howard Barnstone with the assistance of Stephen Fox, Jerome Iowa and David Courtwright ; photography by Rick Gardner and Rob Muir ; foreword by Vincent Scully. — Austin ; London : University of Texas Press, c1979. — xiii,363p,[24]p ofplates : ill(some col.),maps,plans,ports ; 29cm
Ill on lining papers. — Bibliography: p338-346. - Includes index
ISBN 0-292-74012-3 : £21.00
ISBN 0-292-74013-1 (Special ed.) : £60.00 B81-03632

728'.0941 — Great Britain. Residences. Architectural features — *Serials*
Daily Mail book of home plans. — 1981. — Redhill (45 Station Rd, Redhill, Surrey) : Plan Magazines, c1980. — 208p
ISSN 0141-8386 : £2.50 B81-24139

728'.0942 — England. Residences. Architectural features, *to ca 1900*
Cave, Lyndon F.. The smaller English house : its history and development / by Lyndon F. Cave. — London : Hale, 1981. — 240p,[40]p of plates : ill,maps,plans ; 24cm
Bibliography: p233-234. — Includes index
ISBN 0-7091-8866-8 : £9.50 B81-26245

728'.09421 — London. Residences. Architectural design. Greater London Council plans — *Collections*
Preferred dwelling plans / GLC (Department of Architecture and Civic Design]. — 2nd ed. — London : Architechural Press, 1981. — 84p : ill,plans ; 21x30cm
Previous ed.: 1977
ISBN 0-85139-246-6 (pbk) : £5.95 B81-18233

728'.0973 — United States. Award-winning residences. Architectural features, *1956-1980*
25 years of Record houses / edited by Herbert L. Smith Jr.. — New York ; London : McGraw-Hill, c1981. — xii,207p : ill(some col.),plans ; 32cm. — (Architectural record books)
Includes index
ISBN 0-07-002357-3 : £20.95 B81-40045

728'.0973 — United States. Residences. Architectural design, *1850* — *Early works*
Sloan, Samuel. [The model architect]. Sloan's Victorian buildings : illustrations of and floor plans for 56 residences & other structures / Samuel Sloan ; with an introduction by Harold N. Coolridge, Jr. — New York : Dover Publications ; London : Constable, 1980. — 104,102p,[187]p of plates : ill,plans ; 31cm
Facsimile of: 1st ed., originally published in 2 vols. Philadelphia : E.S. Jones & Co., 1852
ISBN 0-486-24009-6 (pbk) : £8.45 B81-30114

728.3 — Houses. Foundations. Design & construction
Barnbrook, G.. House foundations : for the builder and building designer / G. Barnbrook. — Slough (Wexham Springs, Slough SL3 6PL) : Cement and Concrete Association, 1981. — 35p : ill(some col.) ; 30cm. — (Cement and Concrete Association publication ; 45.048)
ISBN 0-7210-1224-8 (pbk) : Unpriced B81-37992

728.3 — Massachusetts. Massachusetts Bay region. Timber framed houses. Architectural features, *1625-1725*
Cummings, Abbott Lowell. The framed houses of Massachusetts Bay, 1625-1725 / Abbott Lowell Cummings. — Cambridge, Mass. ; London : Harvard University Press, c1979. — xiv,261p : ill,maps,1coat of arms,plans ; 27x31cm
Includes index
ISBN 0-674-31680-0 : £28.00 B81-32464

728.3'028'8 — Canada. Houses, *to ca 1940.* **Restoration**
Hutchins, Nigel. Restoring old houses / Nigel Hutchins ; [pen and ink drawings: John Player] ; [diagrams: Graham Thomas]. — New York ; London : Van Nostrand Reinhold, c1980. — 240p : ill(some col.),plans ; 27cm
Bibliography: p230-233. — Includes index
ISBN 0-442-29625-8 : £20.20 B81-08553

728.3'094 — Western Europe. Houses. Architectural features, *ca 1960-ca 1980* — *Illustrations*
Einzig, Richard. Classic modern houses in Europe. — London : Architectural Press, Nov.1981. — [176]p
ISBN 0-85139-479-5 : £20.00 : CIP entry B81-30437

728.3'0941 — Great Britain. Houses. Archaeological investigation
Brunskill, R. W.. Houses. — London : Collins, Sept.1981. — [250]p. — (Collins archaeology)
ISBN 0-00-216243-1 (cased) : £13.50 : CIP entry
ISBN 0-00-216342-x (pbk) : £7.95 B81-20151

728.3′09423′42 — Guernsey. Houses, *1400-1787.* **Architectural features**

McCormack, John, *1939-*. The Guernsey house / by John McCormack ; with illustrations by Carel Toms, George Bramall and Robert Hardwick. — London : Phillimore, 1980. — xii,403p,[25]p of plates : ill(some col.),maps,plans ; 26cm
Ill on lining papers. — Includes index
ISBN 0-85033-380-6 : £15.00 B81-19369

728.3′09423′42 — London. Greenwich *(London Borough).* **Boys′ boarding schools: Royal Hospital School. School life,** *1926-1930 — Personal observations*

Turner, H. D. T.. The Royal Hospital School, Greenwich / by H.D.T. Turner. — London : Phillimore, 1980. — 195p,[24]p of plates : ill,maps,ports ; 23cm
Includes index
ISBN 0-85033-372-5 : £8.95 B81-19870

728.3′1 — United States. Town houses & flats. Architectural design

Apartments, townhouses & condominiums. — 3rd ed. / edited by Mildred F. Schmertz. — New York ; London : McGraw-Hill, 1981. — ix,198p : ill(some col.),plans ; 32cm. — (An Architectural record book)
Previous ed.: / edited by Elisabeth Kendall Thompson. New York : McGraw-Hill, 1975. London : McGraw-Hill, 1976. — Includes index
ISBN 0-07-002356-5 : £23.95 B81-31766

728.3′12′0942337 — Dorset. Poole. Town houses: Scaplen′s Court, *ca 1590-ca 1980.* **Architectural features**

Smith, G. M. (Graham Milton). The history & architecture of Scaplen′s Court, Poole / by G.M. Smith. — Poole (The Guildhall, Market St., Poole BH15 1NP) : Borough of Poole Museums Service, c1980. — 16p : ill,1facsim,plans ; 15x21cm. — (Poole local history publication ; no.3)
Cover title. — Text, ill on covers. — Includes bibliography
ISBN 0-86251-003-1 (pbk) : Unpriced B81-30034

728.3′14′043 — United States. Old persons′ flats. Layout

Howell, Sandra C.. Designing for aging : patterns of use / Sandra C. Howell. — Cambridge, Mass. ; London : MIT Press, c1980. — xii,329p : ill,plans,1form ; 23x29cm
Bibliography: p323-324. - Includes index
ISBN 0-262-08107-5 : £15.50 B81-07410

728.7′2′0973 — United States. Second homes. Architectural design

Lees, Alfred W.. Popular science leisure homes / by Alfred W. Lees with Ernest V. Heyn. — New York ; London : Van Nostrand Reinhold, c1980. — x,342p : ill(some col.),plans(some col.),ports ; 25cm. — (Popular science books)
Bibliography: p341
ISBN 0-442-21263-1 : £14.20 B81-06001

728.8′09794′94 — California. Los Angeles. Large houses. Architectural features *— Illustrations*

Gill, Brendan. The dream come true : great houses Los Angeles / Brendan Gill ; photographs by Derry Moore ; and with the assistance of Chistopher Phillips. — London : Thames and Hudson, 1980. — 216p : ill(some col.),ports ; 29cm
Ill on lining papers. — Includes index
ISBN 0-500-34084-6 : £14.00 B81-02294

728.8′1′094121 — Scotland. Grampian Region. Castles. Architectural features

Graham, Cuthbert. Grampian : the castle country / by Cuthbert Graham. — Aberdeen (Woodhill House, Ashgrove Rd. West, Aberdeen [AB9 2LU]) : Department of Leisure, Recreation and Tourism, Grampian Regional Council, [1981]. — 62p : ill(some col.),2col.maps ; 20x22cm
Bibliography: p61-62
£1.50 (pbk) B81-18639

728.8′1′094167 — Carrickfergus *(District).* **Carrickfergus. Castles: Carrickfergus Castle. Architectural features**

McNeill, T. E.. Carrickfergus Castle : County Antrim / T.E. McNeill. — Belfast : H.M.S.O., 1981. — xiii,88p,20p of plates : ill(some col.),plans ; 27cm. — (Northern Ireland archaeological monographs ; no.1)
At head of title: Department of the Environment for Northern Ireland. — Bibliography: p87-88
ISBN 0-337-08164-6 (pbk) : £5.90 B81-22218

728.8′3′0924 — Great Britain. Country houses. Architectural design. Lutyens, *Sir* **Edwin**

Weaver, Lawrence. Houses and gardens by E.L. Lutyens / described and criticised by Lawrence Weaver. — Woodbridge : Antique Collectors′ Club, 1981. — xl,344p : ill,plans ; 31cm
Originally published: London : Country Life, 1913. — Ill on lining papers. — Includes index
ISBN 0-902028-98-7 : £19.50 : CIP rev.
Also classified at 712′.6′0924 B81-12359

728.8′3′0924 — Great Britain. Country houses designed by Adam, Robert. Architectural features

Beard, Geoffrey. Robert Adam′s country houses. — Edinburgh : Bartholomew, May 1981. — [32]p
ISBN 0-7028-8061-2 : £1.95 : CIP entry B81-07927

728.8′3′0941 — Great Britain. Country houses of historical importance. Architectural features *— Illustrations*

Andreae, Sophie. Silent mansions : more country houses at risk / Sophie Andreae, Marcus Binney, Catherine Griffiths. — London (3 Park Square West, NW1 4LJ) : SAVE Britain′s Heritage, 1981. — [36]p : ill ; 21x30cm
Includes index
ISBN 0-905978-07-2 (pbk) : Unpriced B81-26563

728.8′3′0942 — England. Country houses. Architectural design, *1835-1914*

Franklin, Jill. The gentleman′s country house and its plan 1835-1914 / Jill Franklin. — London : Routledge & Kegan Paul, 1981. — xvi,279p : ill,plans ; 26cm
Includes index
ISBN 0-7100-0622-5 : £15.95 : CIP rev. B80-35301

728′.9 — Greenhouses. Architectural features, *1800-1900*

Koppelkamm, Stefan. Glasshouses and wintergardens of the nineteenth century. — St. Albans : Granada, Oct.1981. — [148]p
Translation of: Gewächshäuser und Wintergärten im 19. Jahrhundert
ISBN 0-246-11630-7 : £15.00 : CIP entry B81-25785

728′.92′09411 — Scotland. Agricultural industries. Farms. Buildings. Architectural features, *1750-1970*

Fenton, Alexander. The rural architecture of Scotland / Alexander Fenton, Bruce Walker. — Edinburgh : Donald, 1981. — xi,242p : ill,1map,plans ; 29cm
Bibliography: p225-234. - Includes index
ISBN 0-85976-020-0 : £15.00 B81-19343

728′.92′0942561 — Bedfordshire. North Bedfordshire *(District).* **Agricultural industries. Farms. Buildings. Architectural design** *— Standards*

Farm buildings : a guide to design / NBBC. — [Bedford] ([37 Goldington Rd., Bedford MK40 3LQ]) : [North Bedfordshire Borough Council], [1977] ([1978] [printing]). — 18p : ill ; 30cm
Cover title. — Bibliography: p18
Unpriced (pbk) B81-26360

729 — ARCHITECTURAL DETAIL AND DECORATION

729 — Buildings. Exterior space. Architectural design

Ashihara, Yoshinobu. Exterior design in architecture / Yoshinobu Ashihara. — Rev. ed. — New York ; London : Van Nostrand Reinhold, 1981. — 143p : ill,plans ; 26cm
Previous ed.: 1970. — Bibliography: p143. — Includes index
ISBN 0-442-21203-8 (pbk) : £8.45 B81-37030

729 — Buildings. Interiors. Environment *— Conference proceedings*

The Environment inside buildings : proceedings of a symposium organised by the Institute of Mathematics and its Applications held in London on 2nd May, 1979. — Southend-on-Sea (Maitland House, Warrior Sq., Southend-on-Sea, Essex SS1 2JY) : The Institute, c1980. — ix,134p : ill ; 20cm. — (Symposium proceedings series / Institute of Mathematics and its Applications ; no.21)
Unpriced (spiral) B81-13268

729 — Urban regions. Structures. Architectural features. Colour

Color in townscape : handbook in six parts for architects, designers and contractors, for city-dwellers and other observant people / [compiled by] Martina Düttmann, Friedrich Schmuck, Johannes Uhl ; translated from German by John William Gabriel. — London : Architectural Press, 1981. — 191p : ill(some col.),facsims ; 27cm
ISBN 0-85139-104-4 : Unpriced B81-18234

729′.09421 — London. Buildings. Architectural features: Decorations *— Illustrations*

The **London** book / foreword by Sir Hugh Casson ; editor Ian Hessenberg. — London (31 Foubert′s Place, W1V 1HE) : Bergstrom + Boyle, c1980. — [185]p : chiefly ill,ports ; 31cm
ISBN 0-903767-15-5 : £9.95 B81-05458

729′.0944 — France. Buildings. Architectural features. Decorations. Rococo style, *to 1750*

Kimball, Fiske. [The creation of the rococo]. The creation of the rococo decorative style / by Fiske Kimball. — New York : Dover ; London : Constable, 1980. — xvii,242p,[104]p of plates : ill,facsims,plans ; 28cm
Originally published: Philadelphia : Philadelphia Museum of Art, 1943. — Includes index
ISBN 0-486-23989-6 (pbk) : £6.30 B81-05663

729′.0973 — United States. Buildings. Interiors. Architectural features

Interior spaces designed by architects. — 2nd ed. / edited by Charles K. Hoyt. — New York ; London : McGraw-Hill, c1981. — 213p : ill (some col.),plans ; 32cm. — (An Architectural record book)
Previous ed.: 1976. — Includes index
ISBN 0-07-002354-9 : £20.95 B81-23444

729′.29 — Buildings. Acoustics *— For architectural design*

Smith, B. J.. Acoustics and noise control. — London : Longman, Nov.1981. — [300]p
ISBN 0-582-41125-4 (pbk) : £7.95 : CIP entry B81-30152

729′7′0941 — Great Britain. Ancient Roman mosaics

Neal, David S.. Roman mosaics in Britain. — Gloucester (17a Brunswick Rd., Gloucester GL1 1HG) : Alan Sutton, June 1981. — [208]p
ISBN 0-904387-64-x (pbk) : £9.95 : CIP entry B81-09466

730 — SCULPTURES AND OTHER PLASTIC ARTS

730 — London. Camden *(London Borough).* **Museums: British Museum. Stock: Ancient Egyptian plastic arts. Special subjects: Animals** *— For children*

Animals in Ancient Egypt : a British Museum Education Service trail. — [London] : [British Museum Publications], 1981. — 16p : ill,1map,1plan ; 30cm
Bibliography: p16
Unpriced (unbound) B81-30802

730′.092′4 — Russian plastic arts. Tatlin, V. E.. Reproductions

Chalk, Martyn. Missing, presumed destroyed : seven reconstructions of lost works by V.E. Tatlin / by Martyn Chalk. — [Kingston upon Hull] ([Queen Victoria Sq., Kingston upon Hull HU1 3RA]) : Ferens Art Gallery, [1981]. — 23p : ill,2facsims,1port ; 24cm
Unpriced (pbk) B81-29822

730'.0942 — English plastic arts, *1618-1806*
Goldsmith, John, *1947-*. Past masters : the lives they led, the works they created / by John Goldsmith. — London : Reader's Digest Association, 1981. — 47p : ill(some col.),ports (some col.) ; 19cm
Unpriced (pbk) B81-22941

730'.0966'83 — Benin plastic arts, *to 1980*
Ben-Amos, Paula. The art of Benin / Paula Ben-Amos. — London : Thames and Hudson, 1980. — 94p : ill(some col.),1map,1facsim,1plan ; 25cm
Bibliography: p94. — Includes index
ISBN 0-500-06009-6 (pbk) : £4.95 B81-04957

730'.09711'307401471 — United States. Museums. Exhibits: Pacific Northwest Coast Indian plastic arts from American Museum of Natural History — *Catalogues*
Objects of bright pride : Northwest Coast Indian art from the American Museum of Natural History / [edited by] Allen Wardwell. — New York : Center for Inter-American Relations ; Seattle ; London : Distributed by University of Washington Press, c1978. — 128p : ill(some col.) ; 28cm
Published to accompany an exhibition held at the Cleveland Museum of Art and others. — Bibliography: p126-127
ISBN 0-295-95664-x (pbk) : Unpriced
ISBN 0-88894-259-1 (Canada) B81-24008

730'.74'02142 — London. Camden *(London Borough).* **Museums: British Museum. Exhibits: Sculptures** — *Illustrations*
Moore, Henry, *1898-*. Henry Moore at the British Museum. — London : British Museum Publications, Oct.1981. — [128]p
ISBN 0-7141-2010-3 : £7.95 : CIP entry B81-30319

730'.92'4 — American sculptures. Umlauf, Charles — *Illustrations*
Umlauf, Charles. The sculpture and drawing of Charles Umlauf / with an essay by Gibson A. Danes. — Austin ; London : University of Texas Press, c1980. — 148p : ill(some col.),ports(some col.) ; 29cm
ISBN 0-292-77561-x : £16.25 B81-32513

730'.92'4 — Berkshire. Bracknell. Art galleries: South Hill Park Arts Centre. Exhibits: English ceramic sculptures. Raby, June — *Catalogues*
Three craftswomen in residence : June Raby ceramicist, Valerie Mead jeweller/silversmith, Justine Douglas jeweller/silversmith. — Bracknell : South Hill Park Arts Centre, [1980]. — [12]p : ill,3ports ; 20x22cm + 3 sheets(20x21cm)
Published to accompany an exhibition at South Hill Park Arts Centre, Bracknell, 1980
Unpriced (pbk)
Primary classification 739.27'092'2 B81-18988

730'.92'4 — Berkshire. Bracknell. Arts centres: South Hill Park Arts Centre. Exhibits: English sculptures. Lewis, Peter, *1939-* — *Catalogues*
Peter Lewis, South Hill Park. — Bracknell (Bracknell, Berks.) : South Hill Park Arts Centre, 1981. — [12]p : ill ; 14cm
Cover title. — Text on inside covers
Unpriced (pbk) B81-40563

730'.92'4 — Dublin. Art galleries: Douglas Hyde Gallery. Exhibits: German sculptures. Kienholz, Edward — *Catalogues*
Scott, David, *1948-*. Edward Kienholz : tableaux 1961-1979. — [Dublin] ([Trinity College, Dublin 2]) : [The Douglas Hyde Gallery], [1981]. — 35p : ill(some col.) ; 24cm
Catalogue of an exhibition held at the Douglas Hyde Gallery, Trinity College, Dublin, 12 January-21 February, 1981. — Catalogue by David Scott
Unpriced (pbk) B81-17919

730'.92'4 — English sculptures. Crampton, Sean — *Illustrations*
Crampton, Sean. Humans, beasts, birds / sculptures, Sean Crampton ; photographs, Clive Hicks ; poems, William Anderson. — Chipping Norton (35 West St., Chipping Norton,) : Kedros, 1981. — v,26p : ill ; 21cm
ISBN 0-907454-01-1 (pbk) : £3.60
Primary classification 821'.914 B81-35016

730'.92'4 — English sculptures. Flaxman, John — *Biographies*
Irwin, David, *1933-*. John Flaxman 1755-1826 : sculptor, illustrator, designer / David Irwin. — London : Studio Vista, 1979. — xviii,249p : ill,ports ; 29cm
Col. ill on lining papers. — Bibliography: p233-239. — Includes index
ISBN 0-289-70885-0 : £22.50 B81-01887

730'.92'4 — English sculptures. Moore, Henry, *1898-* — *Illustrations*
Moore, Henry, *1898-*. Henry Moore. — London : Macmillan, Sept.1981. — [336]p
ISBN 0-333-27804-6 : £30.00 : CIP entry B81-23942

730'.92'4 — English sculptures. Ritchie, Walter — *Illustrations*
Ritchie, Walter. Sculpture in brick and other materials / Walter Ritchie. — [Kenilworth] ([2 Rosemary Hill, Kenilworth, CV5 1BN]) : W. Ritchie, c1978. — 112p : chiefly ill ; 30cm
ISBN 0-9506205-0-5 (pbk) : £6.00 B81-34246

730'.92'4 — French bronze sculptures. Barye, Antoine-Louis — *Catalogues*
Pivar, Stuart. The Barye bronzes / by Stuart Pivar. — [Woodbridge] : Antique Collectors' Club, c1974 (1981 [printing]). — 284p : ill,facsims ; 29cm
Includes index
ISBN 0-902028-30-8 : £22.50 B81-40062

730'.92'4 — French sculptures. Rodin, Auguste — *Reviews* — *Anthologies*
Rodin : in perspective / edited by Ruth Butler. — Englewood Cliffs ; London : Prentice-Hall, c1980. — xii,202p,[10]p of plates : ill,ports ; 23cm. — (The Artist in perspective series) (A Spectrum book)
Includes index
ISBN 0-13-782326-6 (cased) : Unpriced
ISBN 0-13-782318-5 (pbk) : £3.85 B81-06023

730'.92'4 — Great Britain. Art galleries. Exhibits: English sculptures. Abrahams, Ivor — *Catalogues*
Abrahams, Ivor. Ivor Abrahams : sculptures and works on paper / a touring exhibition organised by the Mayor Gallery, 22a Cork Street, London W1 ; Portsmouth, City Museum and Art Gallery March 31st-April 29 1979 ... [et al.]. — London (22a Cork St., W1) : Mayor Gallery, [1979 or 1980]. — [16]p : ill,1port ; 26cm
Text and ill. on inside covers
Unpriced (pbk) B81-37518

730'.92'4 — Great Britain. Arts. Patronage. Organisations: Arts Council of Great Britain. Exhibits: English sculptures. Dobson, Frank — *Catalogues*
True and pure sculpture : Frank Dobson 1886-1963 : a Kettle's Yard exhibition, toured by the Arts Council of Great Britain. — Cambridge (Northampton St., Cambridge CB3 3AQ) : Kettle's Yard, c1981. — [36]p : ill,ports ; 30cm
ISBN 0-907074-10-3 (pbk) : Unpriced B81-34892

730'.92'4 — Great Britain. *National Portrait Gallery.* **Exhibits: English portrait sculptures. Chantrey,,** *Sir* **Francis** — *Catalogues*
Potts, Alex. Sir Francis Chantrey 1781-1841 : sculptor of the great / Alex Potts. — London : National Portrait Gallery, 1980. — 36p : ports ; 24cm
Published to accompany an exhibition held at the National Portrait Gallery, London and the Mappin Art Gallery, Sheffield, 1981. — Bibliography: p11. — Includes index
ISBN 0-904017-37-0 (pbk) : Unpriced B81-16416

730'.92'4 — Italian bronze sculptures. Bugatti, Rembrandt — *Catalogues*
Harvey, Mary, *1936-*. The bronzes of Rembrandt Bugatti (1885-1916) : an illustrated catalogue and biography / by Mary Harvey. — Ascot (Windsor Forest Stud, Mill Ride, Ascot, Berkshire, SL5 8LT) : Palaquin, 1979. — 112p : ill,facsims,ports ; 30cm
Bibliography: p97-101. - Includes index
ISBN 0-906814-00-6 (pbk) : £8.00 B81-06119

730'92'4 — Italian sculptures. Bernini, Gian Lorenzo — *Critical studies*
Wittkower, Rudolf. Gian Lorenzo Bernini. — 3rd ed., enl. — Oxford : Phaidon, Oct.1981. — [290]p
Previous ed.: 1966
ISBN 0-7148-2193-4 : £25.00 : CIP entry B81-27969

730'.92'4 — Italian sculptures. Donatello. Influence of classical sculptures — *Critical studies*
Greenhalgh, Michael. Donatello and his sources. — London : Duckworth, Oct.1981. — [212]p
ISBN 0-7156-1562-9 : £18.00 : CIP entry B81-31176

730'.92'4 — Japanese sculptures. Enkū — *Critical studies*
Tanahashi, Kazuaki. Monk Enku. — London : Wildwood House, Nov.1981. — [192]p
ISBN 0-7045-0382-4 (pbk) : £5.95 : CIP entry B81-30350

730'.92'4 — London. Kensington and Chelsea *(London Borough).* **Art galleries: Taranman. Exhibits: French slate sculptures. Ubac, Raoul** — *Catalogues*
Ubac, Raoul. Ardoises / Raoul Ubac. — London (236 Brompton Rd, SW3 2BB) : Taranman, c1980. — [14]p,15leaves of plates : ill ; 24cm
Catalogue of the exhibition at Taranman, 9 October-8 November, 1980. — Limited ed. of 300 copies, of which the first 20 are numbered
ISBN 0-906499-08-9 (pbk) : Unpriced B81-09584

730'.92'4 — London. Westminster *(London Borough).* **Art galleries: Institute of Contemporary Arts. Exhibits: Romanian sculptures. Neagu, Paul** — *Catalogues*
Neagu, Paul. Paul Neagu : sculpture / [written by Sarah Kent]. — London (Nash House, The Mall, S.W.1) : Institute of Contemporary Arts, c1979. — [48]p : ill ; 26cm
Exhibition catalogue
Unpriced (pbk) B81-16801

730'.92'4 — Washington *(State).* **Tacoma. Art galleries: Tacoma Art Museum. Exhibits: American sculptures. McCracken, Philip** — *Catalogues*
McCracken, Philip. Philip McCracken / introduction by [written by] Colin Graham. — Seattle ; London : Published for the Tacoma Art Gallery by the University of Washington Press, c1980. — 136p : chieflyill(some col.),ports ; 29cm
Published to accompany an exhibition at the Tacoma Art Museum, Tacoma, Washington, 1980. — Bibliography: p136
ISBN 0-295-95771-9 : £9.00 B81-05965

730'.92'4 — West Glamorgan. Swansea. Art galleries: Glynn Vivian Art Gallery and Museum. Exhibits: English sculptures. Mitchell, Denis — *Catalogues*
Mitchell, Denis. Festival exhibition of sculpture by Denis Mitchell : 6 October-3 November 1979. — Swansea (Alexandra Rd., Swansea, SA1 5DZ) : Glynn Vivian Art Gallery and Museum, c1979. — [72]p : chiefly ill,2ports ; 30cm
Bibliography: p11
Unpriced (pbk) B81-39494

730'.9421 — London. Sculptures — *Visitors' guides*
Byron, Arthur. London statues : a guide to London's outdoor statues and sculpture / Arthur Byron. — London : Constable, 1981. — xiv,433p : ill,maps,ports ; 18cm
Bibliography: p424-425. - Includes index
ISBN 0-09-463430-0 : £5.95
Primary classification 731'.76'09421 B81-15178

730'.944 — French sculptures, *1600-1800* — *Critical studies*
Souchal, François. French sculptors of the 17th and 18th centuries : the reign of Louis XIV : illustrated catalogue / François Souchal with the collaboration of Françoise de la Moureyre, Henriette Dumuis ; [translated from the French by Elsie and George Hill]. — Oxford : Cassirer [Vol.2]: G-L. — 1981. — xii,459p : ill,ports,geneal.tables ; 30cm
Geneal.tables on lining papers. — Includes index
ISBN 0-85181-043-8 : £70.00 B81-13045

730'.945 — Italian sculptures, *1400-1500* — *Critical studies*
Pope-Hennessy, John, *1913-*. The study and criticism of Italian sculpture / John Pope-Hennessy. — New York : Metropolitan Museum of Art ; Princeton ; Guildford : Published in association with Princeton University Press, c1980. — 270p : ill,ports ; 26cm
ISBN 0-691-03967-4 : £24.90 B81-17122

730'.966 — West African sculptures
Bamert, Arnold. Africa : tribal art of forest and savanna / Arnold Bamert ; [translated from the German by James Ramsay]. — London : Thames and Hudson, c1980. — xii,332p : col.ill,maps(some col.) ; 33cm
Translation of: Afrika. — Maps on lining papers. — Bibliography: p327-329. - Includes index
ISBN 0-500-23318-7 : £25.00 B81-05197

730'.973 — American sculptures. New realism, *to 1979* — *Critical studies*
Lindey, Christine. Superrealist painting & sculpture / Christine Lindey. — London : Orbis, 1980. — 160p : ill(some col.) ; 27cm
Bibliography: p149-154. — Includes index
ISBN 0-85613-074-5 : £12.50
Primary classification 759.13 B81-02437

730'.973'07402615 — Norfolk. Norwich. Art galleries: Sainsbury Centre for Visual Arts. Exhibits: American sculptures — *Catalogues*
Baskin, Blumenfeld, Fesenmaier, Leonelli. — [Norwich] : [Sainsbury Centre for Visual Arts], [1981]. — [24]p : ill,ports ; 21cm
Exhibition held at the Sainsbury Centre for Visual Arts, Norfolk
Unpriced (pbk) B81-27609

731 — SCULPTURES. MATERIALS, EQUIPMENT, TECHNIQUES, FORMS

731'.2 — Concrete sculptures. Making by children
Leyh, Elizabeth. Concrete sculpture in the community / Elizabeth Leyh ; foreword by Ed Berman ; photographs by Ros Asquith and Alex Levac. — London : Inter-Action Inprint in association with the Institute for Social Enterprise, 1980. — x,88p : ill ; 21cm. — (The Inter-Action community arts series)
ISBN 0-904571-30-0 (cased) : £6.95 : CIP rev.
ISBN 0-904571-31-9 (pbk) : £2995 B80-19848

731.4 — Sculptures. Techniques — *Manuals*
Irving, Donald J.. Sculpture : material and process / Donald J. Irving. — New York ; London : Van Nostrand Reinhold, c1970 (1981 [printing]). — 144p : ill ; 26cm
Bibliography: p140-141. — Includes index
ISBN 0-442-25187-4 (pbk) : £10.15 B81-39887

731.4'62 — Wood carvings. Techniques — *Manuals*
Bridgewater, Alan. The craft of woodcarving / Alan & Gill Bridgewater. — Newton Abbot : David & Charles, c1981. — 159p : ill ; 26cm
Includes index
ISBN 0-7153-8035-4 : £6.95 : CIP rev.
B81-00192

Green, David, *1929-*. Carving in wood : a personal approach to an old craft / David Green. — London : Gollancz in association with Peter Crawley, 1981. — 141p,[8]p of plates : ill(some col.) ; 23cm
Bibliography: p131-134. — Includes index
ISBN 0-575-02964-1 : £7.95 B81-29676

Woods, Maurice. Woodcarving : an introduction / Maurice Woods. — London : Black, 1981. — 92p : ill ; 26cm
Includes index
ISBN 0-7136-2148-6 : £6.95 : CIP rev.
B81-24675

731.4'62 — Wood sculptures. Techniques — *Manuals*
Prince, Arnold. Carving wood and stone : an illustrated manual / Arnold Prince. — Englewood Cliffs ; London : Prentice-Hall, c1981. — xiv,194p : ill ; 25cm. — (A Spectrum book)
Includes index
ISBN 0-13-115311-0 (cased) : Unpriced
ISBN 0-13-115303-x (pbk) : £4.85
Also classified at 731.4'63 B81-28475

731.4'63 — Stone sculptures. Techniques — *Manuals*
Prince, Arnold. Carving wood and stone : an illustrated manual / Arnold Prince. — Englewood Cliffs ; London : Prentice-Hall, c1981. — xiv,194p : ill ; 25cm. — (A Spectrum book)
Includes index
ISBN 0-13-115311-0 (cased) : Unpriced
ISBN 0-13-115303-x (pbk) : £4.85
Primary classification 731.4'62 B81-28475

731'.549'094 — European monumental stone reliefs. Romanesque style, *1000-1200* — *Critical studies*
Hearn, M. F.. Romanesque sculpture : the revival of monumental stone sculpture in the eleventh and twelfth centuries / M.F. Hearn. — Oxford : Phaidon, 1981. — 240p : ill ; 29cm
Bibliography: p225-233. — Includes index
ISBN 0-7148-2168-3 : £22.00 B81-23579

731'.74'07402132 — Great Britain. Science. Organisations: Royal Society. Stock: Portrait busts — *Catalogues*
Royal Society. The Royal Society catalogue of portraits / by Norman H. Robinson ; with biographical notes by Eric G. Forbes. — London : The Society, 1980. — 343p : ports ; 25cm
Includes index
ISBN 0-85403-136-7 : £25.00
Primary classification 757'.074'02132
B81-04113

731'.75'0972 — Mexican carved masks
Cordry, Donald. Mexican masks / by Donald Cordry. — Austin ; London : University of Texas Press, c1980. — xxiv,280p : ill(some col.),2maps,ports(some col.) ; 29cm
Bibliography: p260-266. — Includes index
ISBN 0-292-75050-1 : £23.95 B81-01888

731'.76'0942 — England. Churches. Monuments, *ca 1100-1900*
Kemp, B. R.. English church monuments / Brian Kemp. — London : Batsford, 1980. — 208p : ill ; 26cm
Ill on lining papers. — Bibliography: p193. - Includes index
£17.50 B81-13050

731'.76'09421 — London. Statues — *Visitors' guides*
Byron, Arthur. London statues : a guide to London's outdoor statues and sculpture / Arthur Byron. — London : Constable, 1981. — xiv,433p : ill,maps,ports ; 18cm
Bibliography: p424-425. - Includes index
ISBN 0-09-463430-0 : £5.95
Also classified at 730'.9421 B81-15178

731'.82 — Ships. Figureheads, *to ca 1950*
Costa, Giancarlo. Figureheads : carving on ships from ancient times to twentieth century / Giancarlo Costa. — Lymington : Nautical, 1981. — 175p : ill(some col.) ; 28cm
Bibliography: p174-175
ISBN 0-333-31809-9 : £14.95 B81-22855

731'82 — Wood carvings. Special subjects: Human figures. Techniques — *Manuals*
Tangerman, E. J.. Carving faces and figures in wood / E.J. Tangerman. — New York : Sterling ; London : Oak Tree, c1980. — 128p : ill ; 21cm. — (Home craftsman series)
Includes index
ISBN 0-7061-2707-2 (pbk) : £2.95 B81-01827

731'.823 — North Yorkshire. Sheriff Hutton. Parish churches: St. Helen and the Holy Cross *(Church : Sheriff Hutton)*. Alabaster effigial monuments. Special subjects: Edward, *Prince of Wales, ca.1475-1484*
Routh, Pauline E.. The Sherrif Hutton Alabaster : a re-assessment / by Pauline Routh and Richard Knowles ; photographs by Geoffrey Wheeler. — Wakefield (30 Newland Court, Sandal, Wakefield WF1 5AG) : Rosalba Press, 1981. — 30p : ill,facsims ; 21cm
ISBN 0-907604-00-5 (pbk) : Unpriced
B81-25253

732 — PRIMITIVE, ANCIENT, ORIENTAL SCULPTURES

732'.2'09684 — South Africa. Natal. Drakensberg Mountains. San rock paintings. Symbolism - *Critical studies*
Lewis-Williams, David. Believing and seeing. — London : Academic Press, May 1981. — [300] p. — (Studies in anthropology)
ISBN 0-12-447060-2 : CIP entry B81-0662

732'.23'093614 — Southern Scotland. Prehistoric rock carvings
Morris, Ronald W. B.. The prehistoric rock art of Southern Scotland (except Argyll and Galloway) / Ronald W.B. Morris. — Oxford : B.A.R., 1981. — 187p : ill,maps ; 30cm. — (BAR. British series ; 86)
Bibliography: p180-184
ISBN 0-86054-116-9 (pbk) : £4.50 B81-3663

732'.8 — Egypt. Abydos. Ancient Egyptian temples: Temple of Seti 1. Relief sculptures. Special subjects: Ancient Egyptian religion. Rituals
David, A. Rosalie. A guide to religious ritual at Abydos. — Warminster : Aris & Phillips, Apr.1981. — [224]p. — (Modern Egyptology)
ISBN 0-85668-060-5 : £15.00 : CIP entry
ISBN 0-85668-200-4 (pbk) B81-0883

733 — CLASSICAL SCULPTURES

733 — Classical sculptures, *1500-1900*
Haskell, Francis. Taste and the antique : the lure of classical sculpture 1500-1900 / Francis Haskell and Nicholas Penny. — New Haven ; London : Yale University Press, 1981. — xvi,376p : ill,facsims,ports ; 27cm
Bibliography: p344-365. - Includes index
ISBN 0-300-02641-2 : £20.00 B81-1905

736 — CARVING AND CARVINGS

736'.2'0937 — Great Britain. Ancient Roman engraved gems
Henig, Martin. A corpus of Roman engraved gemstones from British sites / Martin Henig. — 2nd ed. — Oxford : B.A.R., 1978. — 323,lxxvip of plates : ill ; 30cm. — (BAR. British series ; 8)
Previous ed.: 1974. — Bibliography: p3-14
Unpriced (pbk) B81-1631

736'.23 — Diamonds. Lapidary
Watermeyer, Basil. Diamond cutting : a complete guide to diamond processing / Basil Watermeyer. — Cape Town ; London : Purnell, c1980. — 387p : ill(some col.) ; 25cm
ISBN 0-86843-030-7 : £12.75 B81-0172

736'.4'0922 — Warwickshire. Warwick. Woodcarvers, *ca 1800-1914*
Stevens, Ann. The woodcarvers of Warwick / by Ann Stevens. — Warwick (Market Place, Warwick) : Warwickshire Museum, c1980. — 43p,[4]p of plates : ill,facsim,ports ; 21cm. — (Warwickshire master craftsmen)
ISBN 0-9505942-5-3 (pbk) : Unpriced
B81-1252

736'.4'0942296 — Berkshire. Windsor. Castles. Collegiate churches: Windsor Castle. *St. George's Chapel*. Wood carvings — *Illustrations*
Bond, Maurice. Life and faith in the Middle Ages : scenes from wood-carvings in St George's Chapel, Windsor / text by Maurice Bond ; illustrations by John Davey. — [s.l.] : [s.n.], 1980 ([Windsor] : Luff). — [16]p : chiefly ill ; 21cm
Text, ill on inside covers
Unpriced (pbk) B81-3912

736'.5 — Slate. Inscriptions. Lettering
Kindersley, David. Letters slate cut : workshop practice and the making of letters / David Kindersley and Lida Lopes Cardozo. — London : Lund Humphries, 1981. — 36,[60]p of plates : ill ; 28cm
ISBN 0-85331-429-2 (pbk) : £7.95 B81-1712

736'.5'0942886 — Northumberland. Woodhorn. Parish churches: Woodhorn Church. Stone carvings — *Visitors' guides*
Coatsworth, Elizabeth, *1941-*. The carved stones of Woodhorn Church / Elizabeth Coatsworth. — Ashington (Wansbeck) : Wansbeck District Council, 1981. — 39p : ill,plans ; 21cm
Plans on inside covers. — Bibliography: p36-37
ISBN 0-907008-01-1 (pbk) : £1.00 B81-3840

36'.62'0945 — Italian ivory carvings, *ca 1000-1100*
Bergman, Robert P.. The Salerno ivories : ars sacra from medieval Amalfi / Robert P. Bergman. — Cambridge, Mass. ; London : Harvard University Press, 1980. — xv,268p,[112]p of plates : ill,facsims ; 27cm
Bibliography: p149-150. - Includes index
ISBN 0-674-78528-2 : £22.50 B81-21068

36'.62'09798 — Alaskan Eskimo ivory carvings, *to 1979*
Ray, Dorothy Jean. Artists of the tundra and the sea / by Dorothy Jean Ray. — Seattle ; London : University of Washington Press, 1980. — xx,170p : ill,1map ; 21cm
Originally published: Seattle : University of Washington Press ; Nottingham : Hall, 1961. — Bibliography: p163-165. - Includes index
ISBN 0-295-95732-8 (pbk) : £5.40 B81-06465

36'.7'09 — Personal accessories: Fans, *to 1979 — Collectors' guides*
Mayor, Susan. Collecting fans / Susan Mayor. — London : Studio Vista, 1980. — 118p : ill(some col.) ; 26cm. — (Christie's South Kensington collectors series)
Bibliography: p115-118
ISBN 0-289-70881-8 : £6.95 B81-02683

37 — NUMISMATICS

37'.05 — Coins & medals — *Collectors' guides — Serials*
Coin year book / compiled by the staff of Coin monthly. — 15th ed. (1982). — Brentwood : Numismatic Pub. Co. ; Watford : Argus Book [distributor], c1981. — 386p
ISBN 0-901265-17-9 : £5.95
ISSN 0307-6571 B81-35965

37'.074'02142 — London. Camden *(London Borough).* **Museums: British Museum.** *Department of Coins and Medals.* **Stock: Acquisitions** — *Catalogues*
British Museum. *Department of Coins and Medals.* New acquisitions / Department of Coins and Medals ; [edited by N.J.L. Turner]. — London : British Museum. — (Occasional paper / British Museum, ISSN 0142-4815 ; no.25)
No.1 (1976-77). — 1981. — 151p : ill ; 30cm
ISBN 0-86159-025-2 (pbk) : Unpriced B81-19317

37'.3'09429 — Welsh public house tokens — *Lists*
Todd, Neil B.. Tavern tokens in Wales / by Neil B. Todd. — Cardiff : Amgueddfa Genedlaethol Cymru, 1980. — xxv,236p : ill,maps,facsims ; 30cm
Bibliography: px-xv
£8.00 (pbk) B81-25903

7.4'075 — Coins. Collecting — *Manuals — For children*
Hill, C. W. (Cuthbert William). Collecting coins / C.W. Hill. — London : Granada, 1980. — 109p : ill ; 20cm
Bibliography: p105. — Includes index
ISBN 0-246-11324-3 : £3.95 B81-00193

7.4'09 — Coins, *to 1980 — Collectors' guides*
Hobson, Burton. Coin collecting as a hobby / by Burton Hobson. — Enl. and rev. ed. — New York : Sterling ; London : Oak Tree Press, c1980. — 191p : ill ; 21cm
Previous ed.: 1977
£3.95
ISBN 0-7061-2057-4 B81-05227

7.4'0917'4927 — Arabic coins, *to 1979*
Plant, Richard J.. Arabic coins and how to read them / by Richard J. Plant. — 2nd ed.(rev.). — London : Seaby, 1980. — 150p : ill,geneal.tables ; 22cm
English and Arabic text. — Previous ed.: 1973. — Includes index
ISBN 0-900652-52-7 (pbk) : £4.50 : CIP rev.
Also classified at 909'.04927'0024737 B80-04890

7.4'09497 — Yugoslavia. Coins, *to ca 1850.* **Hoards** — *Catalogues*
Mirnik, I. A.. Coin hoards in Yugoslavia / I. A. Mirnik. — Oxford : B.A.R., 1981. — 247p : ill,maps ; 30cm. — (BAR. International series ; 95)
Bibliography: p165-196
ISBN 0-86054-111-8 (pbk) : £10.00 B81-36580

737.4935 — Parthian coins, *B.C.248-A.D.65*
Sellwood, David. An introduction to the coinage of Parthia / by David Sellwood. — 2nd ed. — London : Spink, 1980. — 322p,[10]p of plates : ill ; 23cm
Previous ed.: 1971. — Bibliography: p309-317
£10.00 B81-04809

737.49361 — Great Britain. Celtic coins, *to B.C.54 — Conference proceedings*
Coinage and society in Britain and Gaul : some current problems / edited by Barry Cunliffe. — London : Council for British Archaeology, 1981. — 94p : ill,maps ; 30cm. — (Research report / Council for British Archaeology, ISSN 0589-9036 ; no.38)
Conference papers. — Includes bibliographies and index
ISBN 0-906780-04-7 (pbk) : Unpriced : CIP rev.
Also classified at 737.49364 B81-05155

737.49364 — France. Celtic coins, *to B.C.58 — Conference proceedings*
Coinage and society in Britain and Gaul : some current problems / edited by Barry Cunliffe. — London : Council for British Archaeology, 1981. — 94p : ill,maps ; 30cm. — (Research report / Council for British Archaeology, ISSN 0589-9036 ; no.38)
Conference papers. — Includes bibliographies and index
ISBN 0-906780-04-7 (pbk) : Unpriced : CIP rev.
Primary classification 737.49361 B81-05155

737.4937 — Ancient Roman coins
Sear, David R.. Roman coins : and their values / David R. Sear. — 3rd rev. ed. — London : Seaby, 1981. — 376p,12 leaves of plates : ill,1map ; 23cm
Previous ed.: 1970. — Includes index
ISBN 0-900652-57-8 : £10.00 : CIP rev. B81-01032

737.4937 — Great Britain. Ancient Roman coins
Casey, P. J.. Roman coinage in Britain / P.J. Casey. — Princes Risborough : Shire Publications, 1980. — 64p : ill,maps ; 21cm. — (Shire archaeology series ; 12)
Bibliography: p62. - Includes index
ISBN 0-85263-494-3 (pbk) : £1.50 B81-07740

737.4938'074'02574 — Oxfordshire. Oxford. Museums: Ashmolean Museum. *Department of Antiquities.* **Stock: Ancient Greek gold coins & Ancient Greek silver coins** — *Catalogues*
Sylloge nummorum Graecorum. — London : Published for the British Academy by Oxford University Press
Vol.5: Ashmolean Museum, Oxford
Pt.4: Paeonia-Thessaly (nos.3313-3934). — 1981. — Plates LXIX-LXXXII : ill ; 39cm
Includes index
ISBN 0-19-726001-2 : Unpriced B81-18834

737.4941'0216 — British coins — *Catalogues*
Sylloge of coins of the British Isles. — London : Published for the British Academy by the Oxford University Press and Spink
27: Coins in Lincolnshire collections / by Antony Gunstone. — 1981. — xxxv,171p,[69]p of plates : ill,1port ; 26cm
Bibliography: pxxxii-xxxv. — Includes index
ISBN 0-19-725993-6 : Unpriced B81-38907

737.4941'0216 — British coins — *Catalogues — Serials*
Sylloge of coins of the British Isles. — 28. — London : Oxford University Press for the British Academy, 1981. — xl,118p
ISBN 0-19-726002-0 : £24.00 B81-29658

737.4941'05 — British coins — *History — Serials*
The **British** numismatic journal. — Vol.49 (1979). — [S.l.] (c/o N.J. Mayhew, Heberden Coin Room, Ashmolean Museum, Oxford QX1 2PH) : British Numismatic Society, 1980. — 151p,22p of plates
Unpriced B81-13699

737'.49415'05 — Irish coins, *995- — Collectors' guides — Serials*
Collectors' coins. Ireland. — 6th ed. — Torquay : Rotographic Publications, [1981?]. — 64p
ISBN 0-901170-49-6 : Unpriced B81-25020

737.4942 — English coins, *1760- — Collectors' guides — Serials*
Collectors' coins. England. — 8th ed. (1981). — Torquay : Rotographic Publications, [1980?]. — 81p
ISBN 0-901170-57-7 : £0.90 B81-06718

737.49591 — Burmese coins, *to 1979*
Robinson, M.. The coins and banknotes of Burma / by M. Robinson and L.A. Shaw. — Manchester (c/o Secretary, Lancashire and Cheshire Numismatic Society, Friends Meeting House, 6 Mount St., Manchester 2) : M. Robinson, c1980. — xiii,160p,xivp of plates : ill,1map,facsims(some col.), 1plan ; 23cm
Bibliography: p157-160
ISBN 0-9507053-0-6 (pbk) : £10.50
Also classified at 769.5'59591 B81-05463

737'.6'0939407401468 — Connecticut. New Haven. Museums: Yale Babylonian Collection. Stock: Middle Eastern seals — *Catalogues*
Yale Babylonian Collection. Early Near Eastern seals in the Yale Babylonian Collection / [compiled by] Briggs Buchanan ; introduction and seal inscriptions by William W. Hallo ; Ulla Kasten, editor. — New Haven ; London : Yale University Press, c1981. — xxiv,498p : ill ; 29cm
Bibliography: p495-498. — Includes index
ISBN 0-300-01852-5 : £45.50 B81-34521

738 — CERAMICS

738'.092'2 — Pottery. Manufacture by hand. Wedgwood *(Family), to 1897*
Wedgwood, Barbara. The Wedgwood circle, 1730-1897 : four generations of a family and their friends / Barbara and Hensleigh Wedgwood. — London : Studio Vista, c1980. — xiii,386p,[56]p of plates : ill(some col.),1facsim,ports.(some col.),geneal.table ; 24cm
Geneal.table on lining papers. — Bibliography: p371-374. — Includes index
ISBN 0-289-70892-3 : £9.95 B81-08328

738'.093 — Ancient ceramics — *Conference proceedings*
Scientific studies in ancient ceramics / edited by M.J. Hughes. — London : British Museum, 1981. — 177p : ill,maps ; 30cm. — (Occasional paper / British Museum, ISSN 0142-4815 ; no.19)
Conference papers. — Includes bibliographies
ISBN 0-86159-018-x (pbk) : Unpriced B81-29231

738.1 — CERAMICS. MATERIALS, EQUIPMENT, TECHNIQUES

738.1 — Pottery. Making — *Italian texts — Facsimiles*
Piccolpasso, Cipriano. I tre libri dell'arte del vasaio = The three books of the potter's art / by Cipriano Piccolpasso ; a facsimile of the manuscript in the Victoria and Albert Museum, London ; translated and introduced by Ronald Lightbown and Alan Caiger-Smith. — London : Scolar, 1980. — 2v. : ill(some col.),maps,plans ; 32cm
Italian text with English translation. — In slip case. — Bibliography: pxxix-xl
ISBN 0-85967-452-5 : £95.00 B81-40154

738.1 — Pottery. Making — *Manuals*
Birks, Tony. [Outline guide to pottery]. Basic pottery / Tony Birks ; with drawings by Michael Woods. — [Wellington, N.Z.] : A.H. & A.W. Reed ; Sherbourne : Alphabooks, 1980, c1975. — 100p : ill(some col.) ; 21cm
Originally published: Poole : Blandford, 1975. — Bibliography: p97. — Includes index
ISBN 0-906670-15-2 (cased) : £5.95
ISBN 0-906670-03-9 (pbk) : £2.95 B81-01033

Bunn, Roger. Pottery and ceramics / Roger Bunn. — London : Macmillan, 1979. — 104p : ill ; 23cm. — (Leisure learning series)
Bibliography: p100
ISBN 0-333-27123-8 : £6.95 : CIP rev. B79-25303

738.1 — Pottery. Making — *Manuals*
continuation

Casson, Michael. The craft of the potter / by Michael Casson ; edited by Anna Jackson. — London : British Broadcasting Corporation, 1977 (1980 [printing]). — 128p : ill(some col.),ports ; 31cm
Bibliography: p128
ISBN 0-563-16463-8 : £5.50 B81-05434

738.1'024372 — Pottery. Making — *Manuals — For teaching*

Bates, Shirley. Pottery / Shirley Bates. — London : Batsford Academic and Educational, 1981. — 72p : ill ; 26cm. — (Teaching today)
Bibliography: p70. — Includes index
ISBN 0-7134-3976-9 : £5.50 B81-37848

738.1'03'21 — Pottery. Making — *Encyclopedias*

Fournier, Robert. Illustrated dictionary of pottery form / Robert Fournier ; drawings by Sheila Fournier. — New York ; London : Van Nostrand Reinhold, c1981. — xiii,256p : ill ; 25cm
ISBN 0-442-26112-8 : £15.00 B81-36813

738.2 — PORCELAIN

738.2'0278 — Pottery & porcelain. Makers' marks — *Identification manuals*

Cushion, John P.. Handbook of pottery and porcelain marks / compiled by J.P. Cushion in collaboration with W.B. Honey. — 4th ed. rev. and expanded. — London : Faber, 1980. — 272p : ill,maps ; 26cm
Previous ed.: 1965. — Includes index
ISBN 0-571-04922-2 : £10.50 : CIP rev.
B80-17864

738.2'09 — Pottery & porcelain, *to 1979*

Cooper, Emmanuel. A history of world pottery / Emmanuel Cooper. — 2nd ed. — London : Batsford, 1981. — 216p,[4]p of plates : ill,maps ; 26cm
Previous ed.: published as 'A history of pottery'. London : Longman, 1972. — Bibliography: p209-211. - Includes index
ISBN 0-7134-3394-9 : £9.95 B81-15964

738.2'0942 — English overglaze transfer printed pottery & porcelain, *to ca 1980*

Williams-Wood, Cyril. English transfer-printed pottery and porcelain : a history of over-glaze printing / by Cyril Williams-Wood. — London : Faber, 1981. — 249p,[8]p of plates : ill(some col.) ; 26cm. — (Faber monographs on pottery and porcelain)
Ill on lining papers. — Bibliography: p.240-243. — Includes index
ISBN 0-571-11694-9 : £25.00 : CIP rev.
B81-24681

738.2'095'07402574 — Oxfordshire. Oxford. Museums: Ashmolean Museum. Exhibits: Oriental pottery & porcelain. Collections: Reitlinger Collection — *Catalogues*

Ashmolean Museum. Eastern ceramics : and other works of art from the collection of Gerald Reitlinger : catalogue of the Memorial exhibition. — Oxford : Ashmolean Museum, 1981. — 159p,viiip of plates : ill(some col.),2ports ; 25cm
ISBN 0-85667-115-0 (cased) : Unpriced
ISBN 0-900090-78-2 (pbk) : Unpriced
B81-32441

738.2'0951 — Chinese celadon pottery & porcelain. Lung-Ch'üan style

Chou, Jên. Technical studies on Lung-Ch'ün celadons of successive dynasties / by Chou Jên, Chang Fu-K'ang & Chêng Yung-Fu. — [London] ([South Kensington, S.W.7]) : Victoria & Albert Museum in association with Oriental Ceramic Society, c1977. — 61p : ill ; 29cm. — (Chinese translations ; no.7)
Translation from the Chinese. — Originally published: in K'ao-Ku Hsüeh-Pao, 1973, no.1, p131-156
Unpriced (pbk) B81-18713

738.2'0951 — Chinese porcelain, *ca 1350-ca 1600*

Pope, John Alexander. Chinese porcelains from the Ardebil Shrine / by John Alexander Pope. — 2nd ed. — London : Sotheby Parke Bernet, 1981. — xv,194p,142 leaves of plates : ill,1map,1plan ; 29cm
Previous ed.: Washington : Smithsonian Institution, 1956. — Captions on verso of plates. — Bibliography: p163-172. — Includes index
ISBN 0-85667-097-9 : Unpriced B81-15036

738.2'0951 — Chinese pottery & porcelain, *618-906*

Medley, Margaret. T'ang pottery and porcelain / by Margaret Medley. — London : Faber, 1981. — 151p,[16]p of plates : ill(some col.),1map ; 26cm. — (The Faber monographs on pottery and porcelain)
Bibliography: p145-146. - Includes index
ISBN 0-571-10957-8 : £20.00 B81-10616

738.2'0951 — Chinese pottery & porcelain, *to ca 1440*

Fêng, Hsien-ming. Problems concerning the development of Chinese porcelain, / Fêng Hsien-ming. A study of Mang-K'ou wares and the Fu-Shao technique of Sung and Yüan at Ching-tê-Chên / Lin Hsin-kuo. — [London] ([South Kensington, S.W.7]) : Victoria & Albert Museum in association with the Oriental Ceramic Society, c1978. — 20,22p[3]p of plates : ill ; 29cm. — (Chinese translations ; no.8)
Translation from the Chinese. — Originally published in Wen Wu, 1973, no.7, p20-27, 14 ; K'AO KU, 1974, no.6, p386-393, 405
Unpriced (pbk) B81-18715

738.2'0951'07402142 — London. Camden *(London Borough).* **Museums: British Museum. Exhibits: Chinese porcelain,** *1300-1500.* **Collections: Addis Collection** — *Catalogues*

British Museum. Chinese porcelain from the Addis collection : twenty-two pieces of Chingtehchen porcelain presented to the British Museum / by J.M. Addis ; photographs by Kodansha. — London : Published for the Trustees of the British Museum by British Museum Publications, c1979. — 90p : ill(some col.) ; 30cm
Bibliography: p89. — Includes index
ISBN 0-7141-1410-3 : £25.00 : CIP rev.
B78-07691

738.2'0951'07402142 — London. Camden *(London Borough).* **Museums: British Museum. Exhibits: Chinese pottery & porcelain,** *to 1279 — Catalogues*

Kiln sites of ancient China : an exhibition lent by the Peoples's Rebublic of China / compiled by Penelope Hughes-Stanton and Rose Kerr. — [London] ([31b Torrington Sq., WC1E 7JL]) : Oriental Ceramic Society, [1981]. — x,164p : ill (some col.),2maps ; 30cm
Bibliography: p111-113. — Includes index
ISBN 0-903421-19-4 (pbk) : Unpriced
Also classified at 738.2'0951'07402574
B81-18633

738.2'0951'07402574 — Oxfordshire. Oxford. Museums: Ashmolean Museum. Exhibits: Chinese pottery & porcelain, *to 1279 — Catalogues*

Kiln sites of ancient China : an exhibition lent by the Peoples's Rebublic of China / compiled by Penelope Hughes-Stanton and Rose Kerr. — [London] ([31b Torrington Sq., WC1E 7JL]) : Oriental Ceramic Society, [1981]. — x,164p : ill (some col.),2maps ; 30cm
Bibliography: p111-113. — Includes index
ISBN 0-903421-19-4 (pbk) : Unpriced
Primary classification 738.2'0951'07402142
B81-18633

738.2'3 — Daniel pottery & porcelain, *to 1846*

Berthoud, Michael. H. & R. Daniel 1822-1846 / by Michael Berthoud. — Wingham (The Old Ship, High St., Wingham, Kent) : Micawber, 1980. — 159p,[72]p of plates : ill(some col.),geneal.tables ; 26cm
Includes index
ISBN 0-9507103-0-x : £24.00 B81-06572

738.2'3 — Staffordshire. Stoke-on-Trent. Museums: City Museum and Art Gallery *(Stoke-on-Trent).* **Exhibits: Wedgwood pottery & porcelain** — *Catalogues*

Wedgwood of Etruria & Barlaston : an exhibition to celebrate the 250th anniversary of Josiah Wedgwood FRS 1730-1795, 14 July-27 September 1980 / City Museum and Art Gallery Hanley, Stoke on Trent, Staffs.. — Stoke on Trent : The Museum, c1980. — 139p : ill,2ports ; 20x21cm
ISBN 0-905080-07-6 (pbk) : Unpriced
B81-0676

738.2'3 — Wedgewood pottery & porcelain — *Collectors' guides*

Buten, David. Let's collect Wedgwood ware / with text by David Buten. — Norwich : Jarrold, c1981. — [32]p ; col.ill : 1port ; 19cm. — (Jarrold Let's collect series)
Text and port on inside covers. — Bibliography: p[32]
ISBN 0-85306-907-7 (pbk) : Unpriced
B81-1935

738.2'7 — Bow porcelain

Adams, Elizabeth. Bow porcelain. — London : Faber, Oct.1981. — [240]p
ISBN 0-571-11696-5 : £27.50 : CIP entry
B81-3117

738.2'7 — Goss porcelain — *Collectors' guides*

Pine, Nicholas. Goss china arms, decorations and their values / Nicholas Pine ; [photography Michael Edwards]. — Havant (Goss and Crested China Ltd., West House, Portsdown Hill Rd., Havant, Hants. PO9 3JY) : Milestone, c1979. — 120p : ill,coats of arms ; 24cm
ISBN 0-903852-07-1 (pbk) : £6.75 B81-0451

738.2'7 — Hereford and Worcester porcelain: Worcester porcelain, *1775-1800*

Godden, Geoffrey A.. Caughley and Worcester porcelains 1775-1800 / Geoffrey A. Godden. — Woodbridge : Antique Collectors' Club, c1981. — xxxvii,336p : ill(some col.),maps,facsims ; 26cm
Originally published: London Jenkins, 1969. — Bibliography: p163. — Includes index
ISBN 0-907462-01-4 : £27.50
Also classified at 738.2'7 B81-2142

738.2'7 — Shropshire porcelain: Caughley porcelain, *1775-1800*

Godden, Geoffrey A.. Caughley and Worcester porcelains 1775-1800 / Geoffrey A. Godden. — Woodbridge : Antique Collectors' Club, c1981. — xxxvii,336p : ill(some col.),maps,facsims ; 26cm
Originally published: London Jenkins, 1969. — Bibliography: p163. — Includes index
ISBN 0-907462-01-4 : £27.50
Primary classification 738.2'7 B81-2142

738.2'7 — Shropshire porcelain: Coalport & Coalbrookdale porcelain, *to 1900*

Godden, Geoffrey A.. Coalport and Coalbrookdale porcelains / Geoffrey A. Godden. — Woodbridge : Antique Collectors' Club, c1981. — xxxi,309p : ill(some col.),2maps ; 26cm
Originally published: London : Jenkins, 1970. — Bibliography: p152. — Includes index
ISBN 0-907462-02-2 : £27.50 B81-2142

738.2'7 — Staffordshire. Stoke-on-Trent. Museums: City Museum and Art Gallery *(Stoke-on-Trent).* **Exhibits: New Hall porcelain,** *to 1835 — Catalogues*

Holgate, David. New Hall porcelain : bicentenary exhibition 1781-1981 : 27 April-27 June 1981, Stoke-on-Trent City Museum and Art Gallery, Bethesda St., Hanley / [written by David Holgate] ; [edited by Pat Halfpenny] ; [design Rosie Hurt] ; [photography Pam Rigby]. — Stoke-on-Trent ([Bethesda St.], Hanley, Stoke-on-Trent, [ST1 4HS]) : Stoke-on-Trent City Museum and Art Gallery, 1981. — ill,1facsim ; 21cm
ISBN 0-905080-11-4 (pbk) : Unpriced
B81-375C

738.2'7 — Worcester porcelain, *1751-1793 — Collectors' guides*

Branyan, Lawrence. Worcester blue and white porcelain 1751-1790 : an illustrated encyclopaedia of the patterns / Lawrence Branyan, Neal French and John Sandon. — London : Barrie & Jenkins, 1981. — 367p : ill (some col.) ; 25cm
Bibliography: p364. — Includes index
ISBN 0-09-144060-2 : £48.00 B81-24159

738.3 — POTTERY

738.3'0917'6710740949512 — Greece. Athens. Museums: Mouseion Mpenakē. Exhibits: Islamic pottery, *ca 850-1300 — Catalogues*

Philon, Helen. Early Islamic ceramics : ninth to late twelfth centuries / Helen Philon ; foreword Angelos Delivorias ; preface Ernst J. Grube ; an essay on the inscriptions, Manijeh Bayani-Wolpert ; a technical note, R.E. Jones ; drawings by T. Townsend Walford ; photographs by Vanessa Stamford. — [S.l.] : Islamic Art Publications ; London : Distributed for Sotheby Parke Bernet Publications by Philip Wilson, 1980. — xviii,323p,xxxiip of plates : ill (some col.),map ; 32cm. — (Catalogue of Islamic art ; v.1)
At head of title: Benaki Museum Athens. — Map on lining papers. — Bibliography: p307-316. — Includes index
Unpriced (corrected) B81-17602

738.3'0932'07402659 — Cambridgeshire. Cambridge. Museums: Fitzwilliam Museum. Exhibits: Ancient Egyptian pottery *— Catalogues*

Bourriau, Janine. Umm el-Ga'ab. — Cambridge : Cambridge University Press, Oct.1981. — [144]p
ISBN 0-521-24065-4 (cased) : £20.00 : CIP entry
ISBN 0-521-28415-5 (pbk) : £5.95 B81-32522

738.3'09362'651 — Cambridgeshire. Nene Valley. Ancient Roman pottery

Howe, M. D.. Roman pottery from the Nene Valley : a guide / by M.D. Howe, J.R. Perrin and D.F. Mackreth. — Peterborough : City Museum and Art Gallery, 1981. — 28p : ill ; 30cm. — (Occasional paper / Peterborough City Museum)
Bibliography: p28
£1.00 (pbk) B81-31382

738.3'09362'8104 — North Yorkshire. York. Ancient Roman pottery. Archaeological investigations

Perrin, J. R.. Roman pottery from the Colonia. — London : Council for British Archaeology, Aug.1981. — [68]p. — (The Archaeology of York ; v.16)
ISBN 0-900312-71-8 (pbk) : £6.00 : CIP entry B81-25127

738.3'0939'3 — Eastern Turkish pottery, *B.C.2000-B.C.1 — Catalogues*

Russell, H. F.. Pre-classical pottery of Eastern Anatolia : based on a survey by Charles Burney of sites along the Euphrates and around Lake Van / H.F. Russell. — Oxford : B.A.R., 1980. — vi,176p : ill,maps ; 30cm. — (Monograph / British Institute of Archaeology at Ankara ; no.2) (BAR. International series ; 85)
Bibliography: p160-176
ISBN 0-86054-098-7 (pbk) : £8.50 B81-36584

738.3'09411 — Scottish pottery *— History — Serials*

Scottish pottery historical review. — No.5 (1980)-. — Edinburgh (c/o Mr G.D.R. Cruickshank, Huntly House Museum, 142 Canongate, Edinburgh 8) : Scottish Pottery Society, 1980-. — v. : ill ; 30cm
Annual. — Continues: Archive news (Scottish Pottery Society (Edinburgh Area))
ISSN 0144-1302 = Scottish pottery historical review : Unpriced B81-06705

738.3'09422'76 — Hampshire. Hamwih. Pottery, *700-1000*

Hodges, Richard. The Hamwih pottery : the local and imported wares from 30 years' excavations at Middle Saxon Southampton and their European context. — London : Council for British Archaeology, July 1981. — [112]p. — (Southampton Archaeological Research Committee reports ; 2) (CBA research report ; 37)
ISBN 0-900312-99-8 (pbk) : £12.50 : CIP entry B81-20575

738.3'09423'595 — Devon pottery: Torquay pottery. Collecting *— Serials*

[Newsletter *(Torquay Pottery Collectors' Society)*]. Newsletter / the Torquay Pottery Collectors' Society. — Oct.1976-. — Bedford (c/o Mr. K. Paull, 2 The Lodge, High St., Clapham, Bedford MK41 6AJ) : The Society, 1976-. — v. ; 21cm
Quarterly. — Description based on: Jan.1981 issue
ISSN 0143-5590 = Newsletter - Torquay Pottery Collectors' Society : £0.40 per issue (Free to members) B81-32897

738.3'0952'16 — Netherlands. Groningen. Museums: Groningen Museum voor stad en Lande. Exhibits: Mino pottery *— Catalogues*

Faulkner, R. F. J.. Shino and Oribe Kiln sites : a loan exhibition of Mino shards from Toki City at the Ashmolean Museum, Oxford, February 1981 and the Groninger Museum, Groningen, April 1981 / by R.F.J. Faulkner and O.R. Impey. — [London] ([5 South Villas, NW1 9BS]) : Sawers in association with the Ashmolean Museum, c1981. — 96p,1folded leaf of plates : ill(some col.),maps,1plan ; 26cm
Includes index
ISBN 0-903697-11-4 (pbk) : £9.00
Primary classification 738.3'0952'16 B81-15986

738.3'0952'16 — Oxfordshire. Oxford. Museums: Ashmolean Museum. Exhibits: Mino pottery *— Catalogues*

Faulkner, R. F. J.. Shino and Oribe Kiln sites : a loan exhibition of Mino shards from Toki City at the Ashmolean Museum, Oxford, February 1981 and the Groninger Museum, Groningen, April 1981 / by R.F.J. Faulkner and O.R. Impey. — [London] ([5 South Villas, NW1 9BS]) : Sawers in association with the Ashmolean Museum, c1981. — 96p,1folded leaf of plates : ill(some col.),maps,1plan ; 26cm
Includes index
ISBN 0-903697-11-4 (pbk) : £9.00
Also classified at 738.3'0952'16 B81-15986

738.3'095691 — Syrian pottery, *ca 1100-1400*

Porter, Venetia. Medieval Syrian pottery : (Raqqa ware) / by Venetia Porter. — Oxford : Ashmolean Museum, 1981. — vii,55p : ill,1map ; 23cm
Bibliography: p53
ISBN 0-900090-82-0 (pbk) : Unpriced B81-18277

738.3'0979 — South-western United States. Prehistoric pottery. Designs. Variation

Plog, Stephen. Stylistic variation in prehistoric ceramics : design analysis in the American Southwest / Stephen Plog. — Cambridge : Cambridge University Press, 1980. — viii,160p : ill,maps ; 24cm. — (New studies in archaeology)
Bibliography: p142-155. — Includes index
ISBN 0-521-22581-7 : £12.50 B81-05629

738.3'0985 — Peruvian Moche pottery

Bankes, George. Moche pottery from Peru / George Bankes. — London : Published for the Trustees of the British Museum by British Museum Publications, c1980. — 55p : ill,1map ; 24cm
Bibliography: p55
ISBN 0-7141-1558-4 (pbk) : £2.75 B81-07254

738.3'0985'07402496 — West Midlands *(Metropolitan County).* **Birmingham. Art galleries: City Museum and Art Gallery,** *Birmingham.* **Exhibits: Peruvian pottery,** *to 1532 — Catalogues*

Jones, Jane Peirson. Pots, plants and animals from Peru : an exhibition of pottery representations of plants, animals, birds and men from Ancient Peru : Birmingham City Museums and Art Gallery, January 27th-April 10th 1978 / Jane Peirson Jones. — Birmingham (Chamberlain Sq., Birmingham B3 3DH) : Publications Unit City Museums and Art Gallery, c1978. — [18]p : ill,2maps ; 21cm
Unpriced (pbk) B81-22835

738.3'7 — Blue & white transfer printed pottery, *1780-1880 — Encyclopaedias*

Coysh, A. W.. The dictionary of blue and white printed pottery, 1780-1880. — Woodbridge : Antique Collectors' Club, Nov.1981. — 1v.
ISBN 0-907462-06-5 : £19.50 : CIP entry B81-30621

738.3'7 — Dutch delftware: Delft delftware, *1650-1800*

Fourest, Henry-Pierre. Delftware : faience production at Delft / Henry-Pierre Fourest ; translated by Katherine Watson. — London : Thames and Hudson, 1980. — 201p : ill(some col.) ; 33cm
Translation of: La faïence de Delft. — Bibliography: p195-196. - Includes index
ISBN 0-500-23325-x : £40.00 B81-05412

738.3'7 — Middle East. Halaf pottery. Excavation of remains

Frankel, David. Archaeologists at work : studies on Halaf pottery / David Frankel. — London : British Museum Publications, c1979. — 32p : ill,maps,facsims ; 24cm
Cover title. — Ill on inside covers. — Bibliography: p30
ISBN 0-7141-1101-5 (pbk) : Unpriced B81-08118

738.3'7 — Nottinghamshire. Nottingham. Museums: Nottingham Castle Museum. Exhibits: Nottinghamshire salt-glazed stoneware, *ca 1690-1800*

Wood, Pamela J.. 'Made at Nottm' : an introduction to Nottingham salt-glazed stoneware / [text by Pamela J. Wood]. — [Nottingham] ([City of Nottingham, Arts Department, Nottingham NG1 6EL]) : [Nottingham Castle Museum], c1980. — 28p : ill(some col.),map ; 21cm
Bibliography: p28
Unpriced (pbk) B81-07786

738.3'7 — Staffordshire pottery. Designs, *1780-1976.* **Special subjects: Great Britain & United States** *— Collectors' guides*

Coysh, A. W.. Collecting ceramic landscapes : British and American landscapes on printed pottery / A.W. Coysh and Frank Stefano Jr. — London : Lund Humphries, 1981. — 80p : ill ; 28cm
ISBN 0-85331-445-4 : £10.00 B81-22122

738.3'82'09377 — Apulian pottery: Red figure vases

Trendall, A. D.. The red-figured vases of Apulia. — Oxford : Clarendon Press. — (Oxford monographs on classical archaeology)
Vol.2: Late Apulian. — Nov.1981. — [600]p
ISBN 0-19-813219-0 : £35.00 : CIP entry B81-30970

738.4 — ENAMELS

738.4 — Handicrafts: Enamelling *— Manuals*

Metal and enamel / [edited by Linda Fox]. — London : Marshall Cavendish, 1978. — 135p : col.ill ; 26cm
Ill on lining papers. — Includes index
ISBN 0-85685-265-1 : £4.95
Primary classification 745.56 B81-03655

Patterson, Pam. Introduction to enamelling / Pam Patterson. — Sydney ; London : A.H. & A.W. Reed, 1978. — 61p : ill(some col.) ; 27cm
ISBN 0-589-50050-3 : Unpriced B81-22137

738.4′0944′66 — London. Camden *(London Borough)*. Museums: British Museum. Exhibits: Limoges painted enamels. Collections: Keir Collection — *Catalogues*

Gauthier, Marie-Madeleine. Medieval enamels masterpieces from the Keir Collection. — London : British Museum for the Abbas Establishment, Vaduz, Liechtenstein, Oct.1981. — 1v.
ISBN 0-7141-1358-1 : £8.95 : CIP entry B81-30190

738.5 — MOSAICS

738.5′2 — Italy. Churches. Cosmatesque mosaic floors, *ca 1100-1300*

Glass, Dorothy F.. Studies on Cosmatesque pavements / Dorothy F. Glass. — Oxford : B.A.R., 1980. — xi,246p,[2]folded leaves of plates : ill,plans ; 30cm. — (BAR. International series ; 82)
Bibliography: p235-242. — Includes index
ISBN 0-86054-100-2 (pbk) : £15.00 B81-36586

738.5′2′09362 — England. Ancient Roman mosaics. Geometrical designs

Neal, David S.. Roman mosaics in Britain : an introduction to their schemes and a catalogue of paintings / by David S. Neal. — London (31 Gordon Sq., WC1H 0PP) : Society for the Promotion of Roman Studies, 1981. — 127p,[76]p of plates : ill(some col.) ; 30cm. — (Britannia monograph series ; no.1)
Ill on two microfiche in pockets. — Includes index
Unpriced (pbk) B81-29564

738.6 — ORNAMENTAL BRICKS AND TILES

738.6′05 — Decorative ceramic tiles — *Serials*

Glazed expressions / Tiles & Architectural Ceramics Society. — Summer 1981-. — Telford (c/o Ironbridge Gorge Museum, Ironbridge, Telford TF8 7AW) : The Society, 1981-. — v. : ill ; 30cm
Irregular
ISSN 0261-0329 = Glazed expressions : £0.55 per issue B81-33948

738.6′0941 — British decorative tiles, *1837-1901*

Van Lemmen, Hans. Victorian tiles / Hans Van Lemmen. — Aylesbury : Shire, 1981. — 32p : ill ; 21cm. — (Shire album ; 67)
Bibliography: p32
ISBN 0-85263-548-6 (pbk) : £0.95 B81-17557

738.8 — LIGHTING FIXTURES, STOVES, FIGURINES, ETC

738.8 — Oxfordshire. Oxford. Museums: Museum of the History of Science. Exhibits: Drug jars, *1550-1800 — Catalogues*

Hill, C. R. (Christopher Robin). Drug jars / C.R. Hill and R.E.A. Drey. — Oxford : Museum of the History of Science, 1980. — vi,41p : ill (some col.) ; 24cm. — (Catalogue / (Museum of the History of Science) ; 3)
Bibliography: p38. — Includes index
Unpriced (pbk) B81-29253

738.8′2′09 — Pottery & porcelain figurines, *to ca 1900*

Hughes, Therle. Pottery and porcelain figures / Therle Hughes. — [London] : Country Life, 1981. — 128p : ill(some col.) ; 23cm. — (The Country Life library of antiques)
Includes index
ISBN 0-600-30456-6 : £6.95 B81-22386

739 — ART METALWORK

739 — Corkscrews, *to ca 1930 — Collectors′ guides*

Perry, Evan. Corkscrews and bottle openers / Evan Perry. — Aylesbury : Shire, 1980. — 32p : ill ; 21cm. — (Shire album ; 59)
ISBN 0-85263-534-6 (pbk) : £0.95 B81-07876

739.2 — WORK IN PRECIOUS METALS

739.2′2722 — Italy. Goldsmiths, *1200-1800*

Churchill, Sidney John Alexander. The goldsmiths of Italy : some account of their guilds, statutes, and work / Sidney John Alexander Churchill. — New York ; London : Garland, 1979. — xv,182p,[21]p of plates : ill ; 29cm. — (A Dealers′ and collectors′ bookshelf. Metalwork)
Facsim. of: 1926 ed. / compiled by Cyril G.E. Bunt. London : M. Hopkinson. —
Bibliography: p161-173. — Includes index
ISBN 0-8240-3357-4 : Unpriced B81-41013

739.2′2724 — Great Britain. Goldsmithing. Wickes, George, *1698-1761 — Biographies*

Barr, Elaine. George Wickes 1698-1761 : Royal goldsmith / Elaine Barr. — London : Studio Vista : Christie′s, 1980. — xiii,210p : ill,facsims,geneal.tables,1map,ports ; 26cm
Ill on lining papers. — Bibliography: p206. — Includes index
ISBN 0-289-70877-x : £18.95 B81-03098

739.2′27361 — Great Britain. Bronze age gold artefacts

Taylor, Joan J.. Bronze Age goldwork of the British Isles / Joan J. Taylor. — Cambridge : Cambridge University Press, 1980. — xiv,199p,62p of plates : ill,maps ; 31cm. — (Gulbenkian archaeological series)
Bibliography: p73-74. — Includes index
ISBN 0-521-20802-5 : £45.00 B81-07972

739.2′274971′07402134 — London. Kensington and Chelsea *(London Borough)*. Museums: Victoria and Albert Museum. Exhibits: Yugoslav goldware: Serbian goldware, *1300-1700 — Catalogues*

Masterpieces of Serbian goldsmiths′ work, 13th-18th century : an exhibition organised by the Museum of Applied Art, Belgrade in conjunction with the Victoria and Albert Museum, with the support of the Visiting Arts Unit of the British Council. 1 July-2 August 1981. — London ([South Kensington, SW7 2RL]) : Victoria and Albert Museum, 1981. — 68p : ill ; 20x21cm
Bibliography: p67
ISBN 0-905209-16-8 (pbk) : Unpriced B81-32313

739.2′3′028 — Silversmithing — *Manuals*

Loyen, Frances. The Thames and Hudson manual of silversmithing / Frances Loyen. — London : Thames and Hudson, c1980. — 192p : ill ; 25cm. — (The Thames and Hudson manuals)
Bibliography: p188. — Includes index
ISBN 0-500-67021-8 : £7.95 B81-00194

739.2′34 — Silverware. Making — *Manuals*

Redinger, Ruel O.. Silver : an instructional guide to the silversmith′s art / Ruel O. Redinger. — Englewood Cliffs ; London : Prentice-Hall, c1981. — viii,159p : ill ; 24cm. — (A spectrum book)
Includes index
ISBN 0-13-810218-x (cased) : Unpriced
ISBN 0-13-810200-7 (pbk) : £5.15 B81-16594

739.2′3722 — Scotland. Highland Region. Inverness. Silversmiths, *1663-1919*

MacDougall, Margaret O.. Inverness silversmiths / Margaret O. MacDougall. — Inverness (Castle Wynd, Inverness IV2 3ED) : Inverness Museum and Art Gallery, [1980]. — [12]p ; 21cm. — (Inverness Museum and Art Gallery ; 1)
Unpriced (pbk) B81-11672

739.2′373611′074029134 — Edinburgh. Museums: National Museum of Antiquities of Scotland. Stock: Pictish silver products from St Ninian′s Isle — *Catalogues*

St Ninian′s Isle treasured / [compiled by] Joanna Close-Brooks. — Edinburgh : H.M.S.O., 1981. — [22]p : chiefly ill,maps ; 25cm
Ill. of objects from the National Museum of Antiquities of Scotland. — Bibliography: p3
ISBN 0-11-491738-8 (pbk) : £1.00 B81-34346

739.2′3737′074094 — Europe. Museums. Exhibits: Ancient Roman silver products: Esquiline treasure

Shelton, Kathleen J.. The Esquiline Treasure. — London : British Museum Publications, Apr.1981. — [192]p
ISBN 0-7141-1356-5 : £30.00 : CIP entry B81-02122

739.2′3742 — English silverware, *1500- — Collectors′ guides*

Inglis, Brand. The Arthur Negus guide to British silver / Brand Inglis ; foreword by Arthur Negus ; consultant editor Arthur Negus. — London : Hamlyn, 1980. — 160p : ill(some col.) ; 25cm
Bibliography: p158. - Includes index
ISBN 0-600-33199-7 : £5.50 B81-04793

739.27 — JEWELLERY

739.27 — Jewellery

Harvey, Anne. Jewels / Anne Harvey ; illustrated by Philip Argent. — London : Hutchinson, 1981. — [56]p : ill(some col.),1port ; 18cm. — (The Leprechaun library)
Bibliography: p56
ISBN 0-09-145550-2 : £1.95 : CIP rev. B81-22613

St. Maur, Suzan. The jewellery book / Suzan St. Maur & Norbert Streep. — London : Methuen Paperbacks, 1981. — 198p : ill ; 20cm. — (Magnum books)
ISBN 0-417-04720-7 (pbk) : £1..5 B81-19618

739.27′092′2 — Berkshire. Bracknell. Art galleries: South Hill Park Arts Centre. Exhibits: English silver jewellery. Mead, Valerie & Douglas, Justine — *Catalogues*

Three craftswomen in residence : June Raby ceramicist, Valerie Mead jeweller/silversmith, Justine Douglas jeweller/silversmith. — Bracknell : South Hill Park Arts Centre, [1980]. — [12]p : ill,3ports ; 20x22cm + 3 sheets(20x21cm)
Published to accompany an exhibition at South Hill Park Arts Centre, Bracknell, 1980
Unpriced (pbk)
Also classified at 730′.92′4 B81-18988

739.27′092′4 — English jewellery. Heron, Susanna — *Interviews*

Heron, Susanna. Bodywork plus : Dydd lau 13 Tachwedd-Dydd Sadwrn 6 Rhagfyr 1980 = Thursday 13 November-SSaturday 6 December 1980 / Susan Heron ; [translation : Siân Edwards]. — Caerdydd [i.e. Cardiff] (53 Heol Siarl, Caerdydd) : Cyngor Celfyddydau Cymru, [1980]. — [8]p : ill ; 30cm
Parallel Welsh text and English translation
Unpriced (unbound) B81-07971

739.27′092′4 — London *(City)*. Gold & silver industries & trades. Guilds: Worshipful Company of Goldsmiths. Exhibits: English jewellery. Coates, Kevin — *Catalogues*

Kevin Coates : an exhibition of jewels : presented by the Worshipful Company of Goldsmiths at Goldsmiths′ Hall, Foster Lane, London EC2 ... 6th-17th July [1981] ... — [London] ([Foster La., EC2V 6BN]) : [Worshipful Company of Goldsmiths], 1981 printing. — [12]p : ill(some col.),1port ; 15x21cm
Unpriced (unbound) B81-32312

739.27′094 — European jewellery, *1700-1935*

Becker, Vivienne. Antique and twentieth century jewellery : a guide for collectors / Vivienne Becker. — London : N.A.G., 1980. — 301p,[32]p of plates : ill(some col.) ; 26cm
Bibliography: p291. — Includes index
ISBN 0-7198-0081-1 : £15.00 B81-38400

739.27′094 — European jewellery, *ca 1450-ca 1650*

Hackenbroch, Yvonne. Renaissance jewellery / Yvonne Hackenbroch. — London : Sotheby Park Bernet published in association with the Metropolitan Museum, New York, 1979. — xv,424p,xxxxvp of plates : ill(some col.),facsims,ports ; 34cm
Bibliography: p379-384. — Includes index
ISBN 3-406-05751-9 : Unpriced B81-11566

739.27′8 — Military sweetheart brooches — *Illustrations*

Jarmin, K. W.. Military ″sweetheart″ brooches / by K.W. Jarmin. — [Colchester] ([1 Ash St., Boxford, Colchester, Essex CO6 5HJ]) : K.W. Jarmin, [1981]. — [32]p : chiefly col.ill,1port ; 21cm
ISBN 0-9507543-0-7 (pbk) : £2.00 B81-32549

739.3 — CLOCKS AND WATCHES

739′.37 — Clocks, *to 1950* **-** *Collectors′ guides*

Lloyd, H. Alan. Some outstanding clocks over 700 yesrs, 1250-1950. — Woodbridge : Antique Collectors′ Club, June 1981. — [160]p
Originally published: London : Leonard Hill, 1958
ISBN 0-907462-04-9 : £29.50 : CIP entry B81-12381

739′.37 — Clocks, *to 1963* **—** *Collectors′ guides*

De Carle, Donald. Clocks and their value : illustrated guide to ancient and modern clocks with a unique chart of all known Tompion numbered clocks / Donald de Carle. — 4th ed. — London : N.A.G., 1979. — x,159p : ill ; 22cm
Previous ed.: 1975. — Bibliography: p159
ISBN 0-7198-0180-x : £5.25 B81-16477

739′.3742 — English clocks, *to ca 1850* **—** *Collectors′ guides*

Barker, David, *1939-*. The Arthur Negus guide to English clocks / David Barker ; foreword by Arthur Negus ; consultant editor Arthur Negus. — London : Hamlyn, 1980. — 192p : ill(some col.),facsims ; 25cm
Includes index
ISBN 0-600-33198-9 : £5.50 B81-05106

739.4 — IRONWORK

739′.4 — Cast ironwork — *Collectors′ guides*

Ames, Alex. Collecting cast iron : Alex Ames. — Ashbourne : Moorland, c1980. — 143p : ill ; 25cm
Bibliography: p136-138. - Includes index
ISBN 0-86190-001-4 : £7.95 : CIP rev. B80-12996

739.5 — WORK IN COPPER, BRASS, TIN, ETC

739′.511′0941 — British copperware, *to ca 1900* **—** *Collectors′ guides*

Hornsby, Peter. The Arthur Negus guide to British pewter, copper and brass / Peter Hornsby ; foreword by Arthur Negus ; consultant editor Arthur Negus. — London : Hamlyn, 1981. — 176p : ill(some col.) ; 25cm
Includes index
ISBN 0-600-34217-4 : £5.95
Primary classification 739′.52′0941 B81-40937

739′.512′09361 — Great Britain. Celtic bronze artefacts, *1-700*

Kilbride-Jones, H. E.. Celtic craftsmanship in bronze / H.E. Kilbride-Jones. — London : Croom Helm, c1980. — 266p : ill,maps ; 26cm. — (Croom Helm studies in archaeology)
Includes index
ISBN 0-7099-0387-1 : £15.95 : CIP rev. B80-07455

739′.52 — Horse brasses — *Collectors′ guides*

Brears, Peter C. D.. Horse brasses / Peter C.D. Brears. — London : Country Life Books, 1981. — 127p : ill(some col.),1port ; 23cm. — (The Country Life library of antiques)
Bibliography: p125-126. — Includes index
ISBN 0-600-32131-2 : £6.95 B81-22770

739′.52′0941 — British brassware, *to ca 1900* **—** *Collectors′ guides*

Hornsby, Peter. The Arthur Negus guide to British pewter, copper and brass / Peter Hornsby ; foreword by Arthur Negus ; consultant editor Arthur Negus. — London : Hamlyn, 1981. — 176p : ill(some col.) ; 25cm
Includes index
ISBN 0-600-34217-4 : £5.95
Also classified at 739′.511′0941 ; 739′.533′0941 B81-40937

739′.522′0288 — England. Monumental brasses. Repair

Egan, Brian. The repair of monumental brasses / [Bryan Egan, Martin Stuchfield]. — Newport Pagnell : Enthusiasts, c1981. — 56p ; 26cm
ISBN 0-907700-04-7 (unbound) : Unpriced B81-40455

739′.522′09422 — Southern England. Monumental brasses. Indents

Sadler, A. G.. The indents of lost monumental brasses in Southern England / A.G. Sadler. — Ferring-on-Sea (224, Goring Way, Ferring-on-Sea, Worthing, West Sussex) : A.G. Sadler
Appendix. — 1980. — 316p in various pagings : ill ; 21cm
Unpriced B81-12267

739′.522′0942513 — Derbyshire. Hathersage. Parish churches: St. Michael and All Angels *(Church: Hathersage).* **Monumental brasses**

Lester, G. A.. [Brasses and brass-rubbing in the Peak District. Selections]. The Eyre brasses of Hathersage / G.A. Lester. — [Hathersage] ([The Vicarage, Hathersage, Sheffield S30 1AB]) : [Hathersage Parochial Church Council], [1980]. — [12]p : ill,1geneal.table ; 21cm
Cover title. — Geneal.table on inside cover
£0.40 (pbk) B81-19088

739′.522′094265 — Cambridgeshire. Monumental brasses — *Lists*

Heseltine, P. J.. The figure brasses of Cambridgeshire / P.J. Heseltine. — St. Neots (e 105 Great North Rd., Eaton Socon, St. Neots, Cambs.) : Solo, c1981. — 90p : ill,coats of arms ; 21cm
Bibliography: p15-16
ISBN 0-9507623-0-x (pbk) : Unpriced B81-34985

739′.533 — Pewterware

Brett, Vanessa. Phaidon guide to pewter / Vanessa Brett. — Oxford : Phaidon, c1981. — 256p : ill(some col.),maps ; 23cm
Bibliography: p246-247. — Includes index
ISBN 0-7148-2172-1 : £9.95 : CIP rev. B81-06590

739′.533 — Pewterware — *Collectors′ guides*

Sterner, Gabriele. Pewter : through five hundred years / Gabriele Sterner. — London : Studio Vista, c1979. — 160p : ill(some col.),1col.port ; 20cm. — (Christie′s South Kensington collectors′ guides)
Translation of: Zinn. — Bibliography: (4)p. — Includes index
ISBN 0-289-70870-2 : £4.95 B81-01788

739′.533′0941 — British pewterware, *to ca 1900* **—** *Collectors′ guides*

Hornsby, Peter. The Arthur Negus guide to British pewter, copper and brass / Peter Hornsby ; foreword by Arthur Negus ; consultant editor Arthur Negus. — London : Hamlyn, 1981. — 176p : ill(some col.) ; 25cm
Includes index
ISBN 0-600-34217-4 : £5.95
Primary classification 739′.52′0941 B81-40937

739.7 — ARMS AND ARMOUR

739.7 — London. Tower Hamlets *(London Borough).* **Museums: Tower of London.** *Armouries.* **Exhibits: Armour & weapons associated with animals —** *Visitors′ guides — For children*

Adams, Carol. Animals, arms and armour at the Tower of London / Carol Adams ; illustrated by Diana Fyfe. — Truro (Anchor & Hope Cottage, Cove Hill, Perran-an-Worthal, Truro) : Corbett, 1981. — [16]p : ill ; 21x15cm
ISBN 0-904836-11-8 (pbk) : £0.50 B81-20876

739.7′2 — Edged weapons — *Collectors′ guides*

Southwick, Leslie. The price guide to antique edged weapons. — Woodbridge : Antique Collectors′ Club, Sept.1981. — 1v.
ISBN 0-902028-94-4 : CIP entry B81-25657

739.7′4′09 — Firearms, *1326-1900* **—** *Collectors′ guides*

Durdík, Jan. Firearms / Jan Durdík, Miroslav Mudra, Miroslav Šáda. — London : Hamlyn, 1981. — 247p : ill(some col.) ; 29cm
Translation from the Czech. — Bibliography: p240-242. — Includes index
ISBN 0-600-33632-8 : £7.50 B81-22846

741 — DRAWINGS

741 — Colouring books — *Texts*

Cassin, S.. Pencil fun / S. Cassin & D. Smith ; illustrated by A. Rodger. — Glasgow : Collins. — (First steps) (Collins help your child series)
1. — 1980. — 34p : chiefly ill ; 26cm
ISBN 0-00-197009-7 (pbk) : £0.65 B81-14174

Cassin, S.. Pencil fun / S. Cassin & D. Smith ; illustrated by A. Rodger. — Glasgow : Collins. — (First steps) (Collins help your child series)
2. — 1981. — 34p : chiefly ill ; 26cm
ISBN 0-00-197020-8 (pbk) : £0.65 B81-14175

Striker, Susan. The second anti-colouring book / Susan Striker, Edward Kimmel. — London : Scholastic, 1980, c1979. — 50 leaves(some folded) : ill ; 28cm. — (Hippo books)
Originally published: Eastbourne : Holt, Rinehart & Winston, 1979
ISBN 0-590-70025-1 (pbk) : £1.75 B81-02751

741 — Picture books — *Texts*

Cassinelli, Attilio. The ball of wool / Attilio. — U.K. ed. — London : Good Reading, c1978. — [26]p : all col.ill ; 18x26cm. — (Think and say books)
Cover title. — Previous ed.: Florence : Giunti Marzocco, 1975
ISBN 0-904223-42-6 : Unpriced B81-15363

Cassinelli, Attilio. Buck and champ / Attilio. — U.K. ed. — London : Good Reading, c1978. — [26]p : all col.ill ; 18x26cm. — (Think and say books)
Cover title. — Previous ed.: Florence : Giunti Marzocco, 1975
ISBN 0-904223-38-8 : Unpriced B81-15362

Cassinelli, Attilio. Raindrops / Attilio. — U.K. ed. — London : Good Reading, c1978. — [26]p : all col.ill ; 18x26cm. — (Think and say books)
Cover title. — Previous ed.: Florence : Giunti Marzocco, 1975
ISBN 0-904223-37-x : Unpriced B81-15364

Cassinelli, Attilio. Teddy at bedtime / Attilio. — U.K. ed. — London : Good Reading, c1978. — [26]p : all col.ill ; 18x26cm. — (Think and say books)
Cover title. — Previous ed.: Florence : Giunti Marzocco, 1975
ISBN 0-904223-41-8 : Unpriced B81-15359

Cassinelli, Attilio. Think and think again / Attilio. — U.K. ed. — London : Good Reading, c1978. — [26]p : all col.ill ; 18x26cm. — (Think and say books)
Cover title. — Previous ed.: Florence : Giunti Marzocco, 1975
ISBN 0-904223-40-x : Unpriced B81-15360

Cassinelli, Attilio. Three small birds / Attilio. — U.K. ed. — London : Good Reading, c1978. — [26]p : all col.ill ; 18x26cm. — (Think and say books)
Cover title. — Previous ed.: Florence : Giunti Marzocco, 1975
ISBN 0-904223-39-6 : Unpriced B81-15361

741′.06′042 — English illustrations. Organisations: Association of Illustrators — *Serials*

The **Illustrators** despatch. — Dec./Jan. ([1980/81])-. — London (17 Carlton House Terrace, SW1) : Association of Illustrators, 1980-. — v. : ill ; 29x41cm folded to 29x14cm
Six issues yearly. — Supplement to: Illustrators (London)
ISSN 0260-8324 = Illustrators despatch : Unpriced B81-09202

741′.074′014967 — New Jersey. Princeton. Art galleries: Princeton University. *Art Museum.* **Exhibits: Drawings,** *1500-1979* **—** *Catalogues*

Works on paper : Princeton alumni collections. — Princeton ; Guildford : Art Museum, Princeton University in association with Princeton University Press, c1981. — 261p : chiefly ill,ports ; 25cm
Published to accompany an exhibition held at the Art Museum, Princeton University, 1981
ISBN 0-691-03977-1 : £18.10
Primary classification 750′.74′014967 B81-37155

741'.074'02134 — London. Kensington and Chelsea *(London Borough).* Museums: Victoria and Albert Museum. Exhibits: Western drawings — *Catalogues*
Drawing : technique & purpose : Victoria & Albert Museum, 28 January-26 April, 1981. — [London] : H.M.S.O., [1981]. — 69p : ill ; 21cm
Exhibition catalogue. — Bibliography: p5
Unpriced (pbk) B81-11131

741'.092'4 — English caricatures. Cruikshank, George. Illustrations for books — *Critical studies*
Buchanan-Brown, John. The book illustrations of George Cruikshank / John Buchanan-Brown. — Newton Abbot : David & Charles, c1980. — 256p : ill,facsims,1ports ; 26cm
Includes index
ISBN 0-7153-7862-7 : £12.50 : CIP rev. B80-13478

741'.092'4 — English drawings. Beardsley, Aubrey — *Biographies*
Benkovitz, Miriam J.. Aubrey Beardsley : an account of his life / by Miriam J. Benkovitz. — London : Hamilton, 1981. — 226p : ill,facsims,ports ; 24cm
Includes index
ISBN 0-241-10382-7 : £8.95 : CIP rev. B80-18865

741'.092'4 — English illustrations. Blake, William. Illustrations for Grave, *The* by Blair, Robert, *1699-1746 - Critical studies*
Essick, Robert. Robert Blair's The grave. — London : Scolar Press, Apr.1981. — [120]p
ISBN 0-85967-529-7 : £30.00 : CIP entry B81-04285

741'.092'4 — English illustrations. Greenaway, Kate — *Biographies*
Engen, Rodney K.. Kate Greenaway : a biography / Rodney Engen. — London : Macdonald, 1981. — 240p : ill(some col.),ports,geneal.tables ; 26cm
Geneal.tables on lining papers. — Includes index
ISBN 0-354-04200-9 : £14.95 B81-40845

741'.092'4 — English illustrations. Stothard, Charles. Death — *Correspondence, diaries, etc.*
Hobart, Henry. The death of Charles Stothard : an eyewitness account / with an introduction by Richard Knowles. — Wakefield (Seckar House, Seckar La., Woolley, Wakefield) : Box Tree, [1981?]. — [10]p ; 19cm
Author: Henry Hobart. — Limited ed. of 100 copies
Unpriced (pbk) B81-31406

741'.0924 — English illustrations. Turner, J. M. W.. Illustrations for English literature by Scott, *Sir Walter* **—** *Critical studies*
Finley, Gerald. Landscapes of memory : Turner as illustrator to Scott / Gerald Finley. — London : Scolar, 1980. — 272p : ill,2maps,2ports ; 27cm
Bibliography: p265-267. - Includes index
ISBN 0-85967-562-9 : £30.00 B81-03658

741'.092'4 — French illustrations. Doré, Gustave — *Biographies*
Richardson, Joanna. Gustave Doré : a biography / Joanna Richardson. — London : Cassell, 1980. — 176p : ill,ports ; 25cm
Bibliography: p166-172. - Includes index
ISBN 0-304-30455-7 : £7.95 B81-04557

741'.0945 — Italian drawings, *1400-1500* **—** *Critical studies*
Ames-Lewis, Francis. Drawing in early renaissance Italy. — London : Yale University Press, Sept.1981. — [208]p
ISBN 0-300-02551-3 : £15.00 : CIP entry B81-30243

741.2 — DRAWINGS. MATERIALS, EQUIPMENT, TECHNIQUES

741.2 — Drawing — *Manuals — Illustrations — For children*
Kilroy, Sally. Copycat : drawing book / by Sally Kilroy. — Harmondsworth : Penguin, 1981. — [32]p : ill(some col.) ; 23cm. — (Picture Puffins)
ISBN 0-14-050358-7 (pbk) : £0.95 B81-16979

741.2 — Drawings. Techniques
Malins, Frederick. Drawing ideas of the masters. — Oxford : Phaidon, Oct.1981. — [128]p
ISBN 0-7148-2123-3 : £7.95 : CIP entry B81-30480

741.2 — Drawings. Techniques — *For children*
Layfield, Kathie. Drawing / written and illustrated by Kathie Layfield ; photographs by Tim Clark. — Loughborough : Ladybird, c1980. — 51p : ill(some col.) ; 18cm. — (Learnabout —)
Ill (some col.) on lining papers. — Includes index
ISBN 0-7214-0495-2 : £0.40 B81-03219

741.2 — Drawings. Techniques — *Manuals*
Crabb, Thomas. Painting and drawing : a beginner's guide / Thomas Crabb. — London : Park Lane, 1981. — 80p : col.ill ; 28cm
Bibliography: p79. — Includes index
£0.95 (pbk)
Primary classification 751.4 B81-24926

Edwards, Betty. Drawing on the right side of the brain / Betty Edwards. — London : Souvenir, 1981, c1979. — vii,207p : ill,ports ; 24cm
Originally published: Los Angeles : J.P. Tarcher, c1979. — Bibliography: p203-205. — Includes index
ISBN 0-285-62468-7 : £6.95 B81-07071

Gettings, Fred. Techniques of drawing / Fred Gettings. — London : Orbis, 1981, c1969. — 112p : ill ; 25cm
Originally published: London : Studio Vista, 1969. — Includes index
ISBN 0-85613-383-3 : £5.95 B81-38939

How to draw & paint / [consultant editor Stan Smith]. — London : Ebury, 1981. — 319p : ill (some col.),ports(some col.) ; 31cm. — (A Quarto book)
Includes index
ISBN 0-85223-182-2 : £12.95
Primary classification 751.4 B81-23703

Watson, Ernest W.. The Watson drawing book / Ernest W. Watson and Aldren A. Watson. — New York ; London : Van Nostrand Reinhold, 1980, c1962. — 160p : ill ; 26cm
Originally published: New York : Reinhold, 1962. — Includes index
ISBN 0-442-20054-4 (pbk) : £7.45 B81-25269

741.2 — Sketches. Techniques — *Manuals*
Blake, Vernon. The way to sketch : with special reference to water-colour / Vernon Blake. — 2nd ed. — New York : Dover ; London : Constable, 1981. — vi,120p,[9]leaves of plates : ill(some col.) ; 21cm
Originally published: Oxford : Clarendon Press, 1929. — Ill on inside cover. — Includes index
ISBN 0-486-24119-x (pbk) : £2.05 B81-39069

Schwarz, Hans, *1922-*. Draw sketches / Hans Schwarz. — London : Black, 1981. — 47p : ill ; 28cm
ISBN 0-7136-2189-3 (pbk) : £1.50 B81-38890

Watson, Ernest W.. Ernest W. Watson's sketch diary : with instructive text on brush and pencil techniques. — New York ; London : Van Nostrand Reinhold, c1965 (1981 [printing]). — 64p : ill(some col.) ; 26cm
ISBN 0-442-26420-8 (pbk) : £7.60 B81-39888

741.2'024372 — Drawings. Techniques — *Manuals — For teaching*
Pitfield, Norma. Drawing / Norma Pitfield. — London : Batsford Academic and Educational, 1981. — 72p : ill ; 26cm. — (Teaching today)
Bibliography: p70. — Includes index
ISBN 0-7134-3409-0 : £5.50 B81-37851

741.2'35 — Pastel drawings. Techniques — *Manuals*
Scott, Joan. Using pastels / Joan Scott. — London : Warne, 1981. — 64p : ill(some col.) ; 22cm. — (An Observer's guide)
ISBN 0-7232-2466-8 (pbk) : £2.50 B81-16461

741.2'4 — Pencil drawings. Techniques — *Manuals*
Brobbel, John C. Pencil drawing / John C. Brobbel. — London : Warne, 1981. — 64p : ill ; 22cm. — (An Observer's guide)
ISBN 0-7232-2470-6 (pbk) : £1.95 B81-39120

741.2'6 — Ink drawings. Techniques — *Manuals*
Brobbel, John C. Drawing with ink / J.C. Brobbel. — London : Warne, 1981. — 63p : ill ; 22cm. — (An Observer's guide)
ISBN 0-7232-2468-4 (pbk) : £1.95 B81-39119

Huntly, Moira. Draw in brush & ink / Moira Huntly. — London : Black, 1981. — 48p : ill ; 28cm
ISBN 0-7136-2191-5 (pbk) : £1.50 B81-38892

741.5 — CARTOONS, CARICATURES

741.5'09 — Cartoons, *to 1980* **—** *Critical studies*
Harrison, Randall P.. The cartoon : communication to the quick / Randall P. Harrison. — Beverly Hills ; London : Sage, c1981. — 151p : ill ; 23cm. — (The Sage CommText series ; v.7)
Bibliography: p141-150
ISBN 0-8039-1621-3 (cased) : Unpriced
ISBN 0-8039-1622-1 (pbk) : £4.95 B81-36734

741.5'092'4 — French caricatures. Daumier, Honoré — *Critical studies*
Passeron, Roger. Daumier / Roger Passeron ; [translation by Helga Harrison]. — Oxford : Phaidon, 1981. — 329p : ill(some co.l),facsims,ports ; 29cm
Translation of: Daumier. — Bibliography: p315-317. - Includes index
ISBN 0-7148-2119-5 : £45.00 : CIP rev. B81-06599

741.5'9'09033 — Caricatures, *1744-1980* **—** *Collections*
Masters of caricature : from Hogarth and Gillray to Scarfe and Levine / introduction and commentary by William Feaver ; edited by Ann Gould. — London : Weidenfeld and Nicolson, 1981. — 240p : ill(some col.),facsims (some col.),ports ; cm
Ill on lining papers. — Bibliography: p233. — Includes index
ISBN 0-297-77904-4 : £15.00 B81-34795

741.5'941 — British comics — *Texts*
Buddy. — No.1 (Feb.14 1981)-. — London : D.C. Thomson, 1981. — v. : chiefly ill(some col) ; 30cm
Weekly
ISSN 0261-619x = Buddy : £0.12 B81-32264

The **Super** heroes monthly. — Vol.1, nol.1-. — Stockport (Regent House, Heaton La., Stockport, Cheshire SK4 1DG) : Egmont Pub., 1980-. — v. : chiefly ill ; 28cm
ISSN 0261-3476 = Super heroes monthly : £0.40per issue B81-24107

Walt Disney's Mickey magazine. — No.264 (6th Dec. 1980)-. — London : IPC Magazines, 1980-. — ill ; 29cm
Weekly. — Continues: Walt Disney's Mickey Mouse
ISSN 0261-0906 = Walt Disney's Mickey magazine : £0.20 B81-15439

741.5'9411 — Scottish humorous strip cartoons — *Collections from individual artists*
Hendry, Gordon. Red Indians in the desert / by Gordon Hendry. — Wick (17 Breadalbane Terrace, Wick, Caithness KW1 5AT) : G. Hendry, 1981. — 1portfolio : ill ; 30cm
Cover title. — Limited ed. of 100 numbered copies
£0.30 B81-15421

741.5'9411 — Scottish humorous strip cartoons — *Collections from individual artists — Serials*
Oor Wullie. — [1981]. — Glasgow : D.C. Thomson, c1980. — [92]p
ISBN 0-85116-199-5 : £1.05 B81-01034

741.5'942 — English cartoons: Cartoons for 'Vanity fair' — *Critical studies*
Matthews, Roy T.. In Vanity fair. — London : Scolar Press, Sept.1981. — [300]p
ISBN 0-85967-597-1 : £20.00 : CIP entry B81-22545

741.5'942 — English cartoons. Special subjects: War, ***ca 1750-1960***

Huggett, Frank E.. Cartoonists at war / Frank E. Huggett. — [London] : Windward, c1981. — 192p : ill,ports ; 26cm
Ill on lining papers. — Bibliography: p188. — Includes index
ISBN 0-7112-0221-4 : £8.95 B81-36892

741.5'942 — English comics — ***Texts***

Future tense. — No.1 (5 Nov.1980)- no.12 (21 Jan.1981). — London (205 Kentish Town Rd, NW5) : Marvel Comics Ltd., 1980-1981. — v. : chiefly ill ; 29cm
Weekly. — Merged with: Forces in combat, to become: Future tense and forces in combat
ISSN 0261-1457 = Future tense : £0.14 per issue B81-16813

Marvel action. — 1st issue (Apr.1)-. — London (205 Kentish Town Rd, NW5) : Marvel Comics, 1981-. — v. : chiefly ill ; 29cm
Weekly
ISSN 0261-8206 = Marvel action : £0.15 per issue B81-33711

Marvel team-up. — No.1 (1980)-. — London (205 Kentish Town Rd, NW5) : Marvel Comics Ltd., 1980-. — v. : chiefly ill ; 29cm
Weekly
ISSN 0261-1856 = Marvel team-up : £0.12 per issue B81-16814

[Valour ***(London)*****]**. Valour. — Nov.5 1980-. — London (205 Kentish Town Rd, NW5) : Marvel Comics Ltd., 1980-. — v. : chiefly ill ; 29cm
Weekly
ISSN 0261-149x = Valour (London) : £0.14 per issue B81-16815

741.5'942 — English comics — ***Texts — For children***

Future tense and forces in combat. — No.13 (Jan.28 [1981])-. — London (205 Kentish Town Rd, NW5) : Marvel Comics Ltd., c1980-. — v. : chiefly ill ; 29cm
Weekly. — Merger of: Future tense ; and, Forces in combat
ISSN 0261-7366 = Future tense and forces in combat : £0.14 per issue B81-32689

Teddy Bear's playtime. — No.1 (13th June 1981)-no.20 (24th Oct. 1981). — London : IPC Magazines, 1981-1981. — 20v. : chiefly ill ; 30cm
Weekly. — Merged with: Jack and Jill, to become: Jack and Jill and Teddy Bear's playtime
ISSN 0261-6653 = Teddy Bear's playtime : £0.16 per issue B81-32256

741.5'942 — English humorous cartoons, ***1873-1960.*** **Special subjects: War**

Huggett, Frank E.. Cartoonist at war / Frank E. Huggett. — London : Book Club Associates, 1981. — 192p : ill,ports ; 26cm
Bibliography: p188. — Includes index
Unpriced B81-39123

741.5'942 — English humorous cartoons, ***1970-1979 - Collections***

Man bites man. — London : Hutchinson, Sept.1981. — [224]p
ISBN 0-09-145130-2 : £8.95 : CIP entry B81-20490

741.5'942 — English humorous cartoons — ***Collections***

Daily mirror cartoons. — London : Mirror Books, 1981. — 62p : chiefly ill ; 24cm
ISBN 0-85939-278-3 (pbk) : £0.50 B81-34618

Daily star fun. — London : Express Newspapers
Bk.1 / edited by Gerry Lip. — c1981. — [64]p : chiefly ill ; 27cm
ISBN 0-85079-113-8 (pbk) : Unpriced B81-39366

If the caption fits- : the best of the Punch caption competition / edited by Jonathan Sale. — London : Elm Tree, 1981. — [110]p : ill ; 20cm
ISBN 0-241-10668-0 (pbk) : £2.25 : CIP rev. B81-20124

The **Piccolo** book of cartoons / compiled by Deborah and Ray Manley ; cover illustration by David Bull. — London : Pan, 1977 (1980 printing). — [89]p : chiefly ill ; 18cm. — (Piccolo original)
ISBN 0-330-25128-7 (pbk) : £0.60 B81-10296

. Weekend book of jokes. — London : Published by Harmondsworth Publications Ltd. for Associated Newspapers Group
No.22. — 1981. — [64]p : ill ; 24cm
£0.50 (pbk) B81-26875

741.5'942 — English humorous cartoons — ***Collections from individual artists***

Baxter, Glen. The impending gleam. — London : Cape, Oct.1981. — [96]p
ISBN 0-224-01992-9 : £4.95 : CIP entry B81-28075

Calman, Mel. But it's my turn to leave you — / Mel Calman. — London : Eyre Methuen, 1980. — [128]p : all ill ; 21cm
ISBN 0-413-47580-8 (pbk) : £1.95 B81-00195

Dodd, Maurice. The tale of a tail — or The life and times of Boot the dog / by Maurice Dodd and Dennis Collins. — London : Mirror, 1981. — [128]p : ill ; 20cm
ISBN 0-85939-240-6 (pbk) : £1.00 B81-32162

Emett, Rowland. [The early morning milk train. Selections]. Emett's ministry of transport : selected from The early morning milk train and Alarms and excursions. — Harmondsworth : Penguin, 1981. — [110]p : all ill ; 20cm
ISBN 0-14-005052-3 (pbk) : £2.25 B81-15373

Ffolkes, Michael. Rude as you please / Ffolkes. — London : Unwin Paperbacks, 1981. — 96p : all ill ; 18cm
ISBN 0-04-827045-8 (pbk) : £1.25 : CIP rev. B81-20601

McAllister, Bryan. More little boxes : a selection of Bryan McAllister cartoons from the Guardian / commentary by Michael White. — London : Secker & Warburg, 1980. — 94p : chiefly ill ; 18cm
ISBN 0-436-27459-0 (cased) : £3.95
ISBN 0-436-27460-4 (pbk) : £1.50 B81-03004

Maddocks, Peter. The jokes of Maddocks. — London (34 Greek St., W.1.) : Private Eye Productions, 1981. — [96]p : all.ill ; 12x17cm. — (Private Eye cartoon library ; 10)
ISBN 0-233-97421-0 (pbk) : £1.25 B81-35583

Mulroy. The best of Mulroy : cartoons reproduced from Plastics and Rubber Weekly. — London (11 Hobart Place SW1W 0HL) : The Plastics and Rubber Institute, 1981. — 52p : ill ; 21cm
ISBN 0-903107-31-7 (pbk) : £2.00 B81-26350

Oakey, William. 'Ave you been 'ere long?, or, Tales of an unlucky knight / William Oakey. — Tadworth : World's Work, c1981. — [28]p : ill(some col.) ; 18cm
Ill on lining papers
ISBN 0-437-12010-4 : £1.75 B81-36130

Robinson, W. Heath. Inventions / W. Heath Robinson. — 2nd ed. (abridged). — London : Duckworth, 1978. — [130]p : chiefly ill,1port ; 30cm
Previous ed.: 1973
ISBN 0-7156-1561-0 : £3.95 B81-19583

Roger. Kidstuff / [illustrations] by Roger. — London : ITV Books in association with Joseph, 1980. — [40]p : col.ill ; 22cm
ISBN 0-900727-78-0 : £1.95 B81-08583

Roger. The second kidstuff / by Roger. — London : ITV Books in association with Joseph, 1981. — [38]p : col.ill ; 22cm
ISBN 0-900727-86-1 : £2.50 B81-39431

Searle, Ronald. The square egg / Ronald Searle. — Harmondsworth : Penguin, 1980, c1968. — [94]p : all ill ; 20cm
Originally published: London : Weidenfeld & Nicolson, 1968
ISBN 0-14-005467-7 (pbk) : £0.95 B81-00196

741.5'942 — English humorous cartoons — ***Collections from individual artists — Serials***

Jak. Jak cartoons for the London Evening standard & the Daily express. — Book 12. — London : Express Newspapers, c1980. — [96]p
ISBN 0-85079-098-0 : £0.90
ISSN 0143-3830 B81-24133

741.5'942 — English humorous cartoons. Special subjects: Animals — ***Collections from individual artists***

Searle, Ronald. The king of beasts & other creatures / Ronald Searle. — London : Allen Lane, 1980. — [56]p : chiefly col.ill ; 23x24cm
Col. ill on lining papers
ISBN 0-7139-1336-3 : £5.95 B81-01035

741.5'942 — English humorous cartoons. Special subjects: Christmas — ***Collections from individual artists***

Christmas : a selection of bad taste cartoons from the Silvey-Jex Partnership. — [London] ([7 Soho St., Soho Sq. W1V 3QU]) : Silvey-Jex Partnership, c1981. — [32]p : chiefly ill ; 11x14cm. — (A Silvey-Jex bad taste book)
Text, Ill on inside cover
ISBN 0-907280-08-0 (pbk) : £0.60 B81-39283

741.5'942 — English humorous cartoons. Special subjects: Lavatories — ***Collections from individual artists***

Toilet humour number 2's : a second selection of bad taste cartoons from the Silvey-Jex Partnership. — [London] ([7 Soho St., Soho Sq. W1V 3QU]) : Silvey-Jex Partnership, c1981. — [32]p : chiefly ill ; 11x14cm. — (A Silvey-Jex bad taste book)
Ill on inside cover
ISBN 0-907280-07-2 (pbk) : £0.60 B81-39282

741.5'942 — English humorous cartoons. Special subjects: Livestock: Horses. Riding — ***Collections from individual artists***

Peyton, Mike. To horse / Mike Peyton. — London : Harrap, 1980. — 96p : chiefly ill ; 22cm
ISBN 0-245-53613-2 : £3.50 B81-02180

741.5'942 — English humorous cartoons. Special subjects: Love — ***Collections from individual artists***

Simmonds, Posy. True love. — London : Cape, Oct.1981. — [48]p
ISBN 0-224-01895-7 : £4.95 : CIP entry B81-27338

741.5'942 — English humorous cartoons. Special subjects: Pets: Cats — ***Collections from individual artists***

Miles, John Meredith. Cat naps / John Meredith Miles. — London : Dobson, c1980. — [60]p : col.ill ; 16cm
Ill on lining paper
ISBN 0-234-72270-3 : £1.50 B81-05642

741.5'942 — English humorous cartoons. Special subjects: Poets — ***Collections from individual artists***

Seedy. The muses : an every day tale of poets / by Seedy. — Torpoint (Knillcross House, Hr. Anderton Rd., Millbrook, Torpoint, Cornwall) : Kawabata Press, c1981. — [54]leaves : chiefly ill ; 16cm
ISBN 0-906110-31-9 (pbk) : £0.20 B81-31681

741.5'942 — English humorous cartoons. Special subjects: Self-exposure — ***Collections from individual artists***

Flashers : a selection of bad taste cartoons from the Silvey-Jex Partnership. — [London] ([7 Soho St., Soho Sq. W1V 3QU]) : Silvey-Jex Partnership, c1981. — [32]p : chiefly ill ; 11x14cm. — (A Silvey-Jex bad taste book)
Text, Ill on inside cover
ISBN 0-907280-05-6 (pbk) : £0.60 B81-39280

741.5'942 — English humorous cartoons. Special subjects: Skiing — *Collections from individual artists*

Peterson, Craig. The wacky world of skiing / by Craig Peterson ; cartoons by Jerry Emerson. — Christchurch, [N.Z.] ; London : Whitcoulls, [1981], c1980. — [48]p : chiefly ill ; 16x24cm
Originally published: Washington : Stone Wall Press, 1980
ISBN 0-7233-0659-1 (pbk) : Unpriced B81-35621

741.5'942 — English humorous cartoons. Special subjects: Snowmen — *Collections from individual artists*

Snowmen : a selection of bad taste cartoons from the Silvey-Jex Partnership. — [London] ([7 Soho St., Soho Sq. W1V 3QU]) : Silvey-Jex Partnership, c1981. — [32]p : chiefly ill ; 11x14cm. — (A Silvey-Jex bad taste book)
Ill on inside cover
ISBN 0-907280-06-4 (pbk) : £0.60 B81-39279

741.5'942 — English humorous cartoons. Special subjects: Society. Role of women — *Collections from individual artists*

Youens, Paula. Lone thoughts from a broad. — London : Women's Press, Nov.1981. — [96]p
ISBN 0-7043-3881-5 (pbk) : £2.50 : CIP entry B81-32092

741.5'942 — English humorous cartoons. Special subjects: Vertebrates — *Collections from individual artists*

Wildlife : a selection of bad taste cartoons from the Silvey-Jex Partnership. — [London] ([7 Soho St., Soho Sq. W1V 3QU]) : Silvey-Jex Partnership, c1981. — [32]p : chiefly ill ; 11x14cm. — (A Silvey-Jex bad taste book)
Text, Ill on inside cover
ISBN 0-907280-04-8 (pbk) : £0.60 B81-39281

741.5'942 — English humorous strip cartoons — *Collections from individual artists*

Fred **Basset**, the hound that's almost human!. — No. 31. — London ([Carmelite House, Carmelite St., EC4]) : Harmsworth Publications for Associated Newspapers, [1980]. — [66]p
£0.60 B81-01985

Kettle, Roger. The adventures of Legionnaire Beau Peep / by Roger Kettle & Andrew Christine. — London : Express Newspapers. — (Daily star strip cartoon)
Book no.2. — c1981. — [64]p : ill ; 28cm
ISBN 0-85079-112-x (pbk) : £0.70 B81-32093

Parker, Brant. Crock : you'll pay for this all of you! / Parker, Rechin and Wilder. — London : Coronet, 1981, c1979. — [123]p : chiefly ill ; 18cm
Originally published: New York : Fawcett, 1979?
ISBN 0-340-26463-2 (pbk) : £0.75 B81-17145

Smythe, Reg. This is your life, Andy Capp! / cartoons by Reg Smythe. — London : Mirror, 1981. — [59]p : chiefly ill ; 28cm
ISBN 0-85939-260-0 (pbk) : £0.65 B81-29841

741.5'942 — English humorous strip cartoons — *Collections from individual artists — For children*

Bond, Michael. J.D. Polson and the Dillogate affair / by Michael Bond ; illustrated by Roger Wade Walker. — London : Hodder and Stoughton, c1981. — 41p : chiefly col.ill ; 29cm
ISBN 0-340-27068-3 : £3.95 : CIP rev. B81-18068

741.5'942 — English humorous strip cartoons — *Collections from individual artists — Serials*

The **Gambols** book. — No.29. — London : Express Newspapers, c1980. — [96]p
ISBN 0-85079-093-x : £0.90 B81-20303

741.5'942 — English strip cartoons — *Collections — For children — Serials*

The **Beano** book. — 1981. — London : D. C. Thomson, c1980. — [124]p
£1.40 B81-01987

The **Dandy** book. — 1981. — London : D.C. Thomson, c1980. — [256]p
£1.40 B81-02032

Victor book for boys. — 1981. — London : D.C. Thomson, c1980. — 125p
£1.35 B81-02031

741.5'942 — English strip cartoons — *Collections from individual artists*

Aikiku. Letting you know who Kumiko, Taro, Mary, Peter, Fujiko, Kentaro and the big-headed etcetera etcetera people are / Aikiku ; illustrations by Mizu. — [London] ([28, Russell Rd., W14 8HT]) : Barrett, 1979. — 78p : ill ; 26cm
£1.75 (pbk) B81-18366

Dan Dare : pilot of the future / [illustrations created by Frank Hampson]. — London : Hamlyn, 1981. — 94p : chiefly col.ill ; 28cm
ISBN 0-600-36628-6 (pbk) : £1.99 B81-38529

Fisher, Jayne. Meet the garden gang / by Jayne Fisher ; additional material, based on Jayne Fisher's characters, created by Lynne Bradbury and Graham Marlow. — Loughborough : Ladybird, c1981. — [58]p : chiefly col.ill,1port ; 31cm
Ill on lining papers
ISBN 0-7214-7517-5 : £1.95 B81-28745

741.5'942 — English strip cartoons — *Collections from individual artists — For children*

Pizzey, Stephen. Danger on the red planet ... / [written by Stephen Pizzey] ; [comic strip writer Scott Goodall] ; [comic strip artist Gerry Embleton]. — [London] : Macdonald Educational, c1979. — 31p : ill(some col.) ; 28cm. — (Adventure knowledge)
Text on inside covers. — Includes index
ISBN 0-356-06540-5 (pbk) : Unpriced B81-17123

Reid, Ken, *1919-*. Fudge and the dragon / written and illustrated by Ken Reid. — Manchester : Savoy in association with New English Library, 1981. — 124p,[4]leaves of plates : ill(some col.),ports ; 25cm
Originally published: London : University of London Press, 1948
ISBN 0-86130-007-6 (pbk) : £3.50 B81-06802

Reid, Ken, *1919-*. Fudge in Bubbleville / written and illustrated by Ken Reid. — Manchester : Savoy in association with New English Library, 1981. — 123p,[4]leaves of plates : ill(some col.),1port ; 25cm
Originally published: London : University of London Press, 1949
ISBN 0-86130-010-6 (pbk) : £3.50 B81-06803

Sooty's special. — London : Polystyle, c1980. — [48]p : chiefly ill(some col.) ; 29cm
£0.40 (unbound) B81-12780

741.5'942 — English strip cartoons. Special subjects: War — *Collections — For children — Serials*

Warlord. Book for boys. — 1981. — London : D.C. Thomson, c1980. — 125p
£1.35 B81-08324

741.5'942 — Kent. Canterbury. Universities. Repositories: University of Kent at Canterbury. *Centre for the Study of Cartoons and Caricature.* **Exhibits: English cartoons. Special subjects: Political events,** *1940-1965 — Catalogues*

Beaverbrook's England 1940-1965 : an exhibition of cartoon originals by Michael Cummings, David Low, Vicky and Sidney 'George' Strube / ... organised by the Centre for the Study of Cartoons and Caricature, University of Kent at Canterbury ... — [Canterbury] ([Canterbury, Kent CT2 7NZ]) : [Centre for the Study of Cartoons and Caricature, University of Kent at Canterbury], [c1981]. — 96p : ill ; 30cm
Bibliography: p74-75
Unpriced (pbk) B81-32502

741.5'9438 — Polish cartoons. Special subjects: Poland. Politics, *1980-1981 — Collections from individual artists*

Krauze, Andrzej. Andrzej Krauze's Poland. — London (28 Lanacre Ave., NW9 5FN) : Nina Karsov, Oct.1981. — [96]p
ISBN 0-907652-01-8 (pbk) : £4.50 : CIP entry B81-30636

741.5'944 — French humorous cartoons — *Collections from individual artists — For children — English texts*

Uderzo. Asterix and the great divide / written and illustrated by Uderzo ; translated by Anthea Bell and Derek Hockridge. — London : Hodder and Stoughton, 1981. — 48p : col.ill ; 30cm
Translated from the French
ISBN 0-340-25988-4 : £2.50 B81-11851

741.5'944 — French humorous strip cartoons — *Collections from individual artists — Welsh texts*

Goscinny. Asterix a'r ornest fawr / testun gan Goscinny ; lluniau gan Uderzo ; troswyd o'r Ffrangeg gan Alun Jones. — Caerdydd : Gwasg y Dref Wen, c1980. — 48p : col.ill ; 30cm
Translation of: Le combat des chefs
£2.75 B81-03272

Hergé. Teyrnwialen Ottokar / Herge ; troswyd o'r Ffrangeg gan Roger Boore. — Caerdydd : Gwasg y Dref Wen, c1980. — 62p : col.ill ; 31cm. — (Anturiaethau Tintin)
Translation of: Le Sceptre d'Ottokar. — Ill on lining papers
£2.95 B81-31919

741.5'945 — Italian humorous strip cartoons — *Collections from individual artists — English texts*

Peg, Gianni. Alex : the amazing juggler / illustrations by Gianni Peg ; story by Gianni Peg and Renato Ferraro ; told by John Webster. — London : Benn, 1981. — [32]p : col.ill ; 32cm
Translation from the Italian
ISBN 0-510-00089-4 : £4.75 B81-38681

741.5'9485 — Swedish strip cartoons — *Collections from individual artists — For children — English texts*

Karlstrom, Björn. Captain W.E. John's Biggles and the menace from space / text and illustrations by Björn Karlstrom ; English version by Peter James. — London : Hodder and Stoughton, c1981. — 46p : col.ill ; 29cm
Translation from the Swedish
ISBN 0-340-25373-8 (pbk) : £1.25 B81-25088

Karlstrom, Björn. Captain W.E. John's Biggles and the tiger / text and illustrations by Björn Karlstrom ; English version by Peter James. — London : Hodder and Stoughton, c1981. — 46p : col.ill ; 29cm
Translation from the Swedish
ISBN 0-340-23488-1 (pbk) : £1.25 B81-25087

741.5'971 — Canadian humorous cartoons. Special subjects: Children. Home care — *Collections from individual artists*

Johnston, Lynn. Do they ever grow up? : the terrible twos and beyond : 91 cartoons for parents / by Lynn Johnston. — Henley-on-Thames : Cressrelles, 1980, c1978. — [96]p : chiefly ill ; 17x19cm
Originally published: Wayzata, Minn. : Meadowbrook, 1978
ISBN 0-85956-059-7 (pbk) : £1.00 : CIP rev. B80-06023

741.5'973 — American comics — *Texts*

Bat man pocketbook. — No.1-10. — [Stockport] ([Regent House, Heaton Lane, Stockport]) : Egmont Pub., 1978-1980. — v. : col.ill ; 19cm
Irregular. — Description based on: No.4
ISSN 0260-8510 = Bat man pocketbook : Unpriced B81-11870

Captain America. — 1st issue (Feb.25th)-. — [London] ([205-211 Kentish Town Rd, NW5]) : [Marvel Comics], [1981?]-. — v. : chiefly ill ; 29cm
Weekly
ISSN 0261-6203 = Captain America : £0.14 B81-32265

741.5'973 — American comics — *Texts*
continuation

Conan the Barbarian pocket book. — No.1-. — London (205 Kentish Town Rd, N.W.5) : Marvel Comics, c1980-. — v. : chiefly ill ; 21cm. — (Marvel digest series)
Monthly
ISSN 0260-5791 = Conan the Barbarian pocket book : £0.15 per issue B81-03240

[Frantic *(London)***]**. Frantic : [a monthly marvel]. — No.1 (Mar.1980)-. — London (205 Kentish Town Rd, NW5) : Marvel Comics, 1980-. — v. : chiefly ill ; 28cm
ISSN 0260-1311 = Frantic (London) : £6.00 per year B81-07636

The **Incredible** Hulk pocket book. — No.1-. — London (205 Kentish Town Rd, N.W.5) : Marvel Comics, 1980-. — v. : chiefly ill ; 21cm. — (Marvel digest series)
Monthly
ISSN 0260-6607 = Incredible Hulk pocket book : £0.15 per issue B81-03241

Savage action : [a Marvel monthly]. — Vol.1, no.1 (Nov.1980)-. — London (Jadwin House, 205 Kentish Town Rd, NW5) : Marvel Comics, 1980-. — v. : chiefly ill ; 28cm
ISSN 0260-5775 = Savage action : £0.40 per issue B81-03285

Spider-Man pocket book. — [No.1]-. — London (205 Kentish Town Rd, NW5) : Marvel Comics, [1980]-. — v. : chiefly ill ; 21cm. — (Marvel digest series)
Monthly
ISSN 0260-0501 = Spider-Man pocket book : £0.16 per issue B81-00197

Star heroes pocket book. — [No.1]-. — London (205 Kentish Town Rd, NW5) : Marvel Comics, 1980-. — v. : chiefly ill ; 21cm. — (Marvel digest series)
Monthly
ISSN 0260-051x = Star heroes pocket book : £0.15 per issue B81-14220

The **Titans** pocket book. — No.1-. — [London] ([205 Kentish Town Rd, N.W.5]) : [Marvel Comics], [1980]-. — v. : chiefly ill ; 21cm. — (Marvel digest series)
Monthly
ISSN 0260-5708 = Titans pocket book : £0.15 per issue B81-03239

Young romance pocket book. — No.1-. — [London] ([205 Kentish Town Rd, N.W.5]) : [Marvel Comics], [1980]-. — v. : chiefly ill ; 21cm. — (Marvel digest series)
Monthly
ISSN 0260-5740 = Young romance pocket book : £0.15 per issue B81-03244

741.5'973 — American humorous cartoons — *Collections from individual artists*

Kliban, B.. Whack your porcupine : and other drawings / by B. Kliban. — London : Eyre Methuen, 1981, c1977. — [158]p : all ill. ; 13x21cm
Originally published: New York : Workman, 1977
ISBN 0-413-39120-5 (pbk) : £2.50 B81-17994

741.5'973 — American humorous cartoons. Special subjects: Attitudes of United States to South America, *1860-1970* — *Collections*

Johnson, John J.. Latin America in caricature / John J. Johnson. — Austin ; London : University of Texas Press, c1980. — 330p : ill ; 26cm. — (The Texas Pan American series)
Includes index
ISBN 0-292-74626-1 : £12.00 B81-06984

741.5'973 — American humorous cartoons. Special subjects: Bicycles — *Collections from individual artists*

Gorey, Edward. The broken spoke / Edward Gorey. — London : Benn, 1979, c1976. — [64]p : chiefly ill(some col.) ; 13x19cm
ISBN 0-510-00048-7 : £4.95 B81-16992

741.5'973 — American humorous cartoons. Special subjects: Nastiness — *Collections from individual artists*

Erskine, Jim. Throw a tomato : and 151 other ways to be mean and nasty / by Jim Erskine and George Moran. — London : Muller, 1981. — [92]p : chiefly ill ; 18cm
ISBN 0-584-10764-1 (pbk) : £1.95 : CIP rev. B81-07424

741.5'973 — American humorous strip cartoons — *Collections* — *For children*

Walt Disney's superduck saves the day. — [Stockport] : London Editions, [c1981]. — 254p : ill(some col.) ; 19cm. — (Jumbo book ; no.1)
ISBN 0-86173-038-0 (pbk) : £0.95 B81-40985

Walt Disney's thrills and spills : a superthriller starring Mickey Mouse. — [Stockport] : London Editions, [c1981]. — 254p : ill(some col.) ; 19cm. — (Jumbo book ; no.2)
ISBN 0-86173-039-9 (pbk) : £0.95 B81-40986

741.5'973 — American humorous strip cartoons — *Collections from individual artists*

Hart, Johnny. B.C. the sun comes up the sun goes down. — London : Hodder & Stoughton, Aug.1981. — [128]p. — (Coronet books)
ISBN 0-340-26679-1 (pbk) : £0.85 : CIP entry B81-18121

Hart, Johnny. We've got to stop meeting like this / Johnny Hart, Brant Parker. — London : Coronet, 1981, c1975. — [127]p : chiefly.ill ; 18cm
Originally published: New York : Fawcett, 1975
ISBN 0-340-26664-3 (pbk) : £0.75 : CIP rev. B81-08918

Hart, Johnny. The wizard of Id, Ala ka zot!. — London : Hodder & Stoughton, Nov.1981. — [128]p. — (Coronet books)
ISBN 0-340-26802-6 (pbk) : £0.75 : CIP entry B81-31158

Schulz, Charles M.. [The beagle has landed. Selections]. Jogging is in, Snoopy : selected cartoons from The beagle has landed volume 1 / Charles M. Schulz. — London : Coronet, 1981, c1977. — [128]p : chiefly ill ; 18cm
Originally published: New York : Fawcett, 1980
ISBN 0-340-26667-8 (pbk) : £0.75 : CIP rev. B81-13817

Schulz, Charles M.. Love and kisses, Snoopy. — London : Hodder & Stoughton, Oct.1981. — [128]p. — (Coronet books)
ISBN 0-340-26801-8 (pbk) : £0.75 : CIP entry B81-25756

Schulz, Charles M.. Snoopy treasury. — London : Hodder and Stoughton Children's Books, Nov.1981. — [160]p
ISBN 0-340-25341-x : £4.95 : CIP entry B81-31288

Schulz, Charles M.. [Summers fly, winters walk. Selections]. Think about it tomorrow, Snoopy : selected cartoons from Summers fly, winters walk volume 1 / Charles M. Schulz. — London : Coronet, 1981, c1976. — [124]p : chiefly ill ; 18cm
Originally published: New York : Fawcett, 1976?
ISBN 0-340-26467-5 (pbk) : £0.75 B81-17146

Schulz, Charles M.. [Summers fly, winters walk. Selections]. Stay with it, Snoopy. — London : Hodder & Stoughton, Dec.1981. — [128]p. — (Coronet books)
ISBN 0-340-27265-1 (pbk) : £0.85 : CIP entry B81-31445

741.5'973 — American humorous strip cartoons. Schulz, Charles M.. 'Peanuts' — *Critical studies*

Schulz, Charles M.. Charlie Brown, Snoopy and me : and all the other Peanuts characters / Charles M. Schulz with R. Smith Kiliper. — London : W.H. Allen, 1981. — 126p : ill,ports ; 22cm
Includes index
ISBN 0-491-02645-5 : £3.95 B81-28972

741.5'973 — American strip cartoons — *Collections*

Captain America : summer special. — London (205 Kentish Town Rd, N.W.5) : Marvel Comics, c1979. — 63p : chiefly ill(some col.) ; 28cm
Cover title
£0.45 (pbk) B81-32820

Captain Britain : summer special. — [London] ([205 Kentish Town Rd, N.W.5]) : [Marvel Comics], [c1979]. — 50p : chiefly ill(some col.) ; 28cm
Cover title
£0.45 (pbk) B81-32819

741.5'973 — American strip cartoons — *Collections from individual artists*

Schulz, Charles M.. Let's hear it for dinner, Snoopy : selected cartoons from Don't hassle me with your sighs, Chuck Vol.3 / Charles M. Schulz. — London : Coronet, 1980, c1976. — [128]p : chiefly ill ; 18cm
Originally published: New York : Fawcett Publications, 1975
ISBN 0-340-25865-9 (pbk) : £0.75 : CIP rev. B80-24700

Superman. — London : Hamlyn, 1981. — 111p : ill(some col.) ; 25cm
ISBN 0-600-36663-4 (pbk) : £1.99 B81-38530

741.5'973 — American strip cartoons. Disney, Walt. Characters — *For children*

Disneyland holiday special. — London : IPC Magazines, c1980. — 40p : ill(some col.) ; 28cm
£0.45 (unbound) B81-08394

741.5'982 — Argentinian humorous cartoons. Special subjects: Association football — *Collections from individual artists*

Mordillo, Guillermo. Mordillo's football book. — London : Hutchinson, Oct.1981. — 1v.
ISBN 0-09-146460-9 : £6.95 : CIP entry B81-26798

741.6 — COMMERCIAL ART

741.6 — Great Britain. Insurance companies: Scottish Widows' Fund. Bookmarkers, *1890-1914*

Jonker, Abraham. The bookmarkers of the Scottish Widows' Fund / Abraham Jonker. — Torquay (19 Western Rd., Torquay, Devon TQ1 4RJ) : Neopardy Publications, c1981. — 16p : ill,facsims ; 21cm
ISBN 0-9507611-0-9 (pbk) : £2.00 B81-36475

741.6'0148 — Graphic design. Symbols — *Encyclopaedias*

Thompson, Philip. The dictionary of visual language / Philip Thompson, Peter Davenport. — London : Bergstrom and Boyle, 1980. — vii,258p : ill,facsims ; 24cm
Includes index
ISBN 0-903767-07-4 : £12.95 B81-02980

741.6'028 — Graphic design equipment & materials — *Buyers' guides*

Goodchild, Jon. By design : a graphics sourcebook of materials, equipment and services / by Jon Goodchild & Bill Henkin. — New York ; London : Quick Fox, c1980. — 253p : ill,facsims ; 28cm
Bibliography: p213-238. — Includes index
ISBN 0-8256-3122-x (pbk) : Unpriced B81-40288

741.6'0941 — Great Britain. Commercial arts — *Illustrations* — *Serials*

The **Best** of British illustration : the Association of Illustrators ... annual = Les Meilleures illustrations britanniques : le ... annuelle [sic] de l'Association des illustrateurs = Das Beste der Britischen Illustration : das ... Jahrbuch der Gesellschaft der Illustratoren. — 4th ('80)-. — Oxford : Phaidon in association with Graphics World Ltd., 1979-. — v. : ill ; 32cm
Text in English, French and German. — Cover title: The Best of British Illustrators. — Continues: The Association of Illustrators annual
ISSN 0261-3301 = Best of British illustration : £18.50 B81-31023

741.64 — Greater Manchester *(Metropolitan County).* Manchester. Polytechnics. Libraries: Manchester Polytechnic. *Central Library.* Exhibits: Books published by Penguin Books. Pictorial covers, *1960-1980 — Catalogues*

Green, Evelyne. Penguin books : the pictorial cover 1960-1980 : an exhibition at Manchester Polytechnic Central Library May-June 1981 / Evelyne Green. — Manchester : Manchester Polytechnic Library, 1981. — 40,[28]p ; 18cm
Unpriced (pbk) B81-28446

741.64′09181′2 — Western illustrations: Illustrations for books, *to 1980*

Harthan, John. The history of the illustrated book : the Western tradition / John Harthan. — London : Thames and Hudson, c1981. — 288p : ill(some col.),1coat of arms,music,facsims(some col.) ; 30cm
Bibliography: p283-284. — Includes index
ISBN 0-500-23316-0 : £25.00 B81-36071

741.64′0942 — English illustrations. Illustrations for books by Trollope, Anthony — *Critical studies*

Hall, N. John. Trollope and his illustrators / N. John Hall. — London : Macmillan, 1980. — xiv,175p : ill,ports ; 24cm
Includes index
ISBN 0-333-26297-2 : £20.00 : CIP rev.
B79-26533

741.64′0942 — English illustrations. Illustrations for English literature, *1550-1900 — Critical studies*

Hodnett, Edward. Image & text. — London : Scolar Press, Apr.1981. — [284]p
ISBN 0-85967-603-x : £25.00 : CIP entry
B81-04194

741.64′2′0903 — Children's books, *to ca 1800.* Illustrations — *Illustrations*

Pictures from early childrens books / edited by J. Stevens Cox. — Guernsey : Toucan, 1981. — [16]p : chiefly ill,1facsim ; 16cm
ISBN 0-85694-228-6 (pbk) : £0.40 B81-07181

741.67′2 — Fashion design. Drawings. Techniques — *Manuals*

Turnpenny, John M.. Fashion design & illustration / John M. Turnpenny. — London : Hutchinson, 1981. — 96p : ill ; 30cm
ISBN 0-09-143521-8 (pbk) : £7.50
Primary classification 746.9′2 B81-26902

741.9 — DRAWINGS. COLLECTIONS

741.9′241 — Marine illustrations: Illustrations for books & serials, *ca 1800-ca 1900 — Illustrations*

Marine art clipbook / edited and arranged by Peter H. Spectre and George Putz. — New York ; London : Van Nostrand Reinhold, c1980. — 128p : all ill ; 28cm
ISBN 0-442-25190-4 (pbk) : £6.70 B81-07574

741.94′074′01471 — New York *(City).* Libraries: Pierpont Morgan Library. Stock: European drawings, *1375-1825 — Catalogues*

Denison, Cara D.. European drawings 1375-1825 : catalogue / compiled by Cara D. Denison & Helen B. Mules with the assistance of Jane V. Shoaf. — New York ; Oxford : Pierpont Morgan Library ; New York : Oxford University Press, 1981. — 291p : ill(some col.),ports ; 31cm
Catalogue of an exhibition held at the Pierpont Morgan Library. — Bibliography: p21-24. — Includes index
ISBN 0-19-520258-9 : £35.00 B81-26237

741.94′074′02142 — London. Camden *(London Borough).* Museums: British Museum. Stock: European drawings, *ca 1480-ca 1655 — Illustrations*

British Museum. Old Master Drawings in the British Museum : twelve colour postcards with a commentary. — [London] : British Museum Publications, c1980. — 1portfolio : col.ill,col.ports ; 17cm
Notes by Paul Goldman
ISBN 0-7141-2009-x : Unpriced B81-31772

741.942 — England. Braikenridge, George Weare. Private collections. English drawings. Special subjects: Avon. Brislington, *1820-1830*

Stoddard, Sheena. Mr Braikenridge's Brislington / by Sheena Stoddard. — [Bristol] : City of Bristol Museum and Art Gallery with the assistance of the Friends of Bristol Art Gallery, 1981. — 61p : ill,ports ; 21x30cm
ISBN 0-900199-13-x (pbk) : Unpriced
Primary classification 758′.9942393 B81-22163

741.942 — English drawings. Barton, David — *Illustrations*

Barton, David. Going to waste with interruptions / David Barton. — London (45, Wellmeadow Rd., Hither Green, London SE13 6SY) : D. Barton, c1981. — [112]p : all ill ; 21cm
Limited ed. of 500
ISBN 0-907559-01-8 (pbk) : £3.50 B81-33660

Barton, David. Hiding inside / David Barton. — London (45 Wellmeadow Rd., S.E. 12) : D. Barton, 1980. — [32]p : chiefly ill ; 21cm
Limited ed. of 500 copies
ISBN 0-9505907-8-9 (pbk) : £1.50 B81-05953

Barton, David. Insideout / David Barton. — London (45 Wellmeadow Rd., S.E.13) : D. Barton, c1981. — [32]p : chiefly ill ; 21cm
ISBN 0-9505907-9-7 (pbk) : £1.50 B81-18768

Barton, David. Now you see me / David Barton. — London (45 Wellmeadow Rd., S.E. 13) : D. Barton, c1980. — [32]p : chiefly ill ; 21cm
Limited ed. of 500 copies
ISBN 0-9505907-7-0 (pbk) : £1.50 B81-05952

Barton, David. Sequences four : (notebooks 81 to 109) / David Barton. — London (45 Wellmeadow Rd., Hither Green, SE13 [6SY]) : D. Barton, c1981. — [63]p : chiefly ill ; 21cm
Limited ed. of 500 copies
ISBN 0-907559-00-x (pbk) : £2.50 B81-27177

741.942 — English drawings. Burne-Jones, Edward — *Illustrations*

Burne-Jones, Edward. The little Holland house album / by Edward Burne Jones ; with an introduction and notes by John Christian. — North Berwick (Leuchie, North Berwick, East Lothian) : Dalrymple, 1981. — 39p : ill,music,1port ; 25cm
Limited ed. of 200 numbered copies, 175 for sale
ISBN 0-9507301-0-6 : £38.00 B81-19559

741.942 — English drawings. Chadwick, Hulme — *Illustrations*

Chadwick, Hulme. Selected drawings of Hulme Chadwick / with a foreword by Sir Hugh Casson. — [Sunbury-on-Thames] ([Parkside Studio House, Church St., Sunbury-on-Thames, Middx TW16 6RG]) : [Joy Chadwick], [1981]. — [95]p : chiefly ill,1port ; 22x31cm
Limited ed. of 250 copies. — Ill on lining papers
Unpriced B81-26984

741.942 — English drawings. Clairmonte, Christopher — *Illustrations*

Clairmonte, Christopher. Sketchbook / Christopher Clairmonte. — [London] ([2 Motcomb St., S.W.1]) : [Patrick Seale Gallery], [c1981]. — [87]p : chiefly ill ; 30cm
Cover title. — Limited ed. of 500 copies
Unpriced B81-17871

741.942 — English drawings. Dubsky, Mario — *Illustrations*

Dubsky, Mario. Tom Pilgrim's progress among the consequences of Christianity & other drawings. — London (27 Priory Ave., N8 7RN) : Gay Men's Press, Oct.1981. — [84]p
ISBN 0-907040-09-8 (pbk) : £4.95 : CIP entry
B81-27417

741.942 — English drawings. Furnival, John — *Illustrations*

John Furnival. — Sunderland : Ceolfrith Press, 1971. — 16p : ill(some col.),ports ; 42cm
Published on the occasion of the John Furnival Retrospective Exhibition held at the Laing Art Gallery and Annexe, Nov.12-Dec.11th 1971. — Cover title. — Limited ed. of 600 copies of which fifty copies are numbered and signed by John Furnival. — Sixteen prints, sound disc (331/3rpm, mono. ; 7in.). — Bibliography: p13
£1.50 (pbk) B81-36133

741.942 — English drawings. Lawrence, Louis. Special subjects: Seasons — *Illustrations*

Lawrence, Louis. The seasons / [compiled and illustrated by] Louis Lawrence ; foreword by Roy Strong. — Exeter : Webb & Bower, c1981. — [123]p : ill(some col.),all facsims ; 25cm
Reproduction of a manuscript compiled between 1887 and 1890
ISBN 0-906671-22-1 : £6.95 : CIP rev.
Also classified at 759.2 ; 820.8′033 B81-00198

741.942 — English drawings. Stedman, Karl. Special subjects: Cumbria. Kendal — *Illustrations*

Stedman, Karl. Stedman's Kendal. — [Kendal] (2 Wildman St., Kendal, Cumbria LA9 6EN) : Kendal Studio Pottery, c1980. — 40leaves : all ill,1map ; 20x25cm
ISBN 0-9507318-0-3 : Unpriced B81-07150

741.942 — English drawings. Sutherland, Graham, *1940-1944 — Illustrations*

Sutherland, Graham. Sutherland : the wartime drawings / Roberto Tassi ; translated, edited and with a foreword by Julian Andrews. — London : for Sotheby Parke Bernet by Philip Wilson, 1980. — 171p : chiefly ill(some col.) ; 25cm
Translation from the Italian. — Bibliography: p171. - List of films: p171
ISBN 0-85667-095-2 : £14.95 B81-05542

741.942 — English illustrations. Aldridge, Alan, *19--- — Illustrations*

Aldridge, Alan, *1938-*. Phantasia of dockland, rockland and dodos / Alan Aldridge ; illustrated in collaboration with Harry Willock. — London : Cape, 1981. — [78]p : ill(some col.) ; 29cm
ISBN 0-224-01700-4 : £5.95 : CIP rev.
B81-22490

741.942 — English illustrations. Blake, William, *1757-1827.* Illustrations for Divina commedia of Dante Alighieri — *Illustrations*

Klonsky, Milton. Blake's Dante : the complete illustrations to the Divine comedy / by Milton Klonsky. — London : Sidgwick & Jackson, [1981]. — 172p : ill(some col.) ; 30cm
Originally published: New York : Harmony, 1979. — Bibliography: p167. — Includes index
ISBN 0-283-98736-7 : £15.00 B81-37663

741.942 — English illustratons. Goodall, John S. — *Biographies — Illustrations*

Goodall, John S.. Before the war : 1908-1939 / John Strickland Goodall. — London : Macmillan London, 1981. — [48]p : all col.ill,col.ports ; 15x19cm
Ill on lining papers
ISBN 0-333-30674-0 : £3.50 B81-31847

741.942 — Great Britain. Architecture. Organisations: Architectural Association. Exhibits: English drawings. Herron, Ron — *Catalogues*

Herron, Ron. 20 years of drawings / Ron Herron. — London (34 Bedford Sq. W.C.1) : The Architectural Association, [1980]. — [46]p : ill ; 18cm
Published to accompany an exhibition at the Architectural Association, London, 1980. — Cover title
Unpriced (pbk) B81-08610

741.942 — London. Westminster *(London Borough).* Art galleries: Anthony d'Offay *(Firm).* Exhibits: English drawings. Bevan, Robert — *Catalogues*

Robert Bevan 1865-1925 : drawings and watercolours. — London (9 Dering St., New Bond St., W.1) : Anthony d'Offay, [1981]. — [14]p,[12]p of plates : ill ; 18cm
Catalogue of the exhibition held 25th June to 15th August, 1981
Unpriced (pbk)
Primary classification 759.2 B81-40586

741.942 — London. Westminster *(London Borough).* **Art galleries: Anthony d'Offay** *(Firm).* **Exhibits: English drawings. Roberts, William,** *1895-1980 — Catalogues*

Roberts, William, *1895-1980.* William Roberts 1895-1980 : drawings and watercolours. — London (9 Dering St., New Bond St., W.1.) : Anthony d'Offay, [1981?]. — [12]p,[12]p of plates : ill ; 20cm
Unpriced (pbk)
Also classified at 759.2 B81-22845

741.942 — Staffordshire. Stoke-on-Trent. Museums: City Museum and Art Gallery *(Stoke-on-Trent).* **Exhibits: English drawings. Lanyon, Peter —** *Catalogues*

Lanyon, Peter. Peter Lanyon : drawings and graphic work : City Museum & Art Gallery, Stoke-on-Trent, 4 April-16 May 1981 : Museum of Modern Art, Oxford, 23 May-4July 1981 : City Museum & Art Gallery, Plymouth 11 July-22 August 1981. — Stoke-on-Trent ([Bethesda St., Hanley], Stoke-on-Trent, [ST1 4HS]) : City Museum & Art Gallery, 1981. — [76]p : ill(some col.),1port ; 20x21cm
ISBN 0-905080-09-2 (pbk) : Unpriced
B81-37509

741.9429 — Wales. Arts. Patronage. Organisations: Welsh Arts Council. Exhibits: Welsh drawings. Thompson, M. E. (Mary Elizabeth). Special subjects: North Wales. Quarries — *Catalogues*

Artist yn y chwareli : arddangosfa o ddarluniau gan Miss M.E. Thompson (1896-1981) : bywyd, gwaith a golygfeydd chwareli Gogledd Cymru = An artist in the quarries : an exhibition of drawings by Miss M.E. Thompson (1896-1981) the life, work and landscape of the North Wales quarries. — Cardiff : Welsh Arts Council, 1981. — [32]p : ill ; 20x21cm
A Welsh Arts Council touring exhibition
ISBN 0-905171-86-1 (pbk) : Unpriced
B81-33358

741.9436 — Austrian drawings. Klimt, Gustav; Schiele, Egon & Kokoschka, Oskar — *Illustrations*

Klimt, Schiele, Kokoschka : drawings and watercolours / introduction by Otto Breicha ; documentary notes by Christian Nebehay. — London : Thames and Hudson, 1981. — 174p : ill(some col.),ports ; 23cm
Bibliography: p24-25
ISBN 0-500-27239-5 (pbk) : £6.95
Also classified at 759.36 B81-38685

741.944 — French drawings. Sempé. Special subjects: Music — *Illustrations*

Sempé. The musicians / by Sempé. — London : Macmillan, 1981, c1980. — 99p : ill(some col.) ; 31cm
Translation of: Les musiciens de Sempé. — Originally published: New York : Workman, 1980. — Ill on lining papers
ISBN 0-333-31727-0 : £5.95 B81-22071

741.944 — French drawings. Steinlen, Théophile-Alexandre — *Illustrations*

Steinlen, Théophile-Alexandre. Steinlen's drawings : 121 plates from Gil Blas illustré / Théophile-Alexandre Steinlen. — New York : Dover ; London : Constable, 1980. — 119p : all ill(some col.) ; 31cm
Ill on inside covers
ISBN 0-486-23943-8 (pbk) : £3.75 B81-18582

741.944 — French drawings. Steinlen, Théophile-Alexandre. Special subjects: Cats — *Illustrations*

Steinlen, Théophile-Alexandre. Steinlen cats : drawings / by Théophile-Alexandre Steinlen. — New York : Dover ; London : Constable, 1980. — 44p : all ill ; 29cm
ISBN 0-486-23950-0 (pbk) : £1.10 B81-09945

741.944 — London. Camden *(London Borough).* **Museums: British Museum.** *Department of Prints and Drawings.* **Exhibits: French drawings. Watteau, Antoine —** *Catalogues*

British Museum. Watteau drawings in the British Museum / Paul Hulton. — London : Published for the Trustees of the British Museum by British Museum Publications Ltd, c1980. — 32p,[32]p of plates : ill,1facsim,2ports ; 25cm
ISBN 0-7141-0780-8 (pbk) : £4.50 : CIP rev.
B80-22323

741.944 — London. Westminster *(London Borough).* **Art galleries: Parkin Gallery. Exhibits: French drawings. Laborde, Chas —** *Catalogues*

Hooker, Denise. Chas Laborde : an artist's view of London, Paris, Berlin and New York 1926-1932 : 25th March-17th April, 1981. — London (11 Motcomb St., S.W.1) : Michael Parkin Fine Art, [1981]. — [8]p : ill ; 21cm
Published to accompany an exhibition at the Parkin Gallery. — Text by Denise Hooker
Unpriced (pbk) B81-31504

741.944 — Oxfordshire. Oxford. Museums: Ashmolean Museum. Stock: French drawings. Pissarro, Camille — *Catalogues*

Brettell, Richard. A catalogue of the drawings by Camille Pissaro in the Ashmolean Museum, Oxford / Richard Brettell, Christopher Lloyd. — Oxford : Clarendon Press, 1980. — xii,225p,[215]p of plates : ill,1col.port ; 26cm
Bibliography: p90. — Includes index
ISBN 0-19-817357-1 : £40.00 : CIP rev.
B80-18442

741.944'074'0436 — France. Paris. Art galleries: Musée Marmottan. Exhibits: French drawings, *ca1750-ca1850 — Catalogues*

Art in early XIX century France. — London ([147 New Bond St., W.1.]) : Wildenstein, [1981?]. — 74p : ill(some col.),ports(some col.) ; 30cm
Published in connection with an exhibition held at the Musée Marmottan, Paris
Unpriced (pbk)
Primary classification 759.4'074'0436
B81-33111

741.945 — Italian drawings. Bellini, Jacopo — *Illustrations*

Bellini, Jacopo. Jacopo Bellini : selected drawings / edited by Christiane L. Joost-Gaugier. — New York : Dover ; London : Constable, 1980. — xiv p,49p of plates : chiefly ill ; 29cm
ISBN 0-486-23912-8 (pbk) : £2.20 B81-05847

741.945 — Italian drawings. Leonardo, *da Vinci — Illustrations*

Leonardo, *da Vinci.* Leonardo drawings : 60 works / by Leonardo da Vinci. — New York : Dover ; London : Constable, 1980. — 59p : chiefly ill ; 29cm. — (Dover art library)
ISBN 0-486-23951-9 (pbk) : £1.25 B81-06748

741.945 — London. Westminster *(London Borough).* **Art galleries: Royal Academy of Arts. Exhibits: Italian drawings by Leonardo,** *da Vinci* **from Windsor Castle.** *Royal Library — Catalogues*

Pedretti, Carlo. Leonardo da Vinci nature studies from the Royal Library at Windsor Castle / catalogue by Carlo Pedretti ; introduction by Kenneth Clark. — [London] : Royal Academy of Arts, 1981. — 95p : ill,facsims ; 28cm
In slip case with: Leonardo da Vinci, the Codex Hammer, formerly the Codex Leicester / catalogue by Jane Roberts. — Bibliography: p94-95
ISBN 0-384-32298-0 (pbk) : Unpriced
B81-36100

741.973 — American illustrations. Hopper, Edward — *Illustrations*

Levin, Gail. Edward Hopper as illustrator / Gail Levin. — New York ; London : W.W. Norton in association with the Whitney Museum of American Art, c1979. — xi,54,[219]p : ill(some col),1facsim,ports ; 29cm
ISBN 0-393-01243-3 : £15.95 B81-03977

741.973 — California. Long Beach. Art galleries: California State University, Long Beach. *Art Museum and Galleries.* **Exhibits: American drawings. Dine, Jim. Special subjects: Human figures —** *Catalogues*

Dine, Jim. Jim Dine figure drawings 1975-1979 / [edited by] Constance W. Glenn. — New York ; London : Harper & Row, c1979. — 93p : ill (some col.) ; 31cm
Published to accompany an exhibition organized by the Art Museum and Galleries, California State University, 1979. — Bibliography: p90-92
ISBN 0-06-430102-8 (pbk) : £5.95 B81-07066

743 — DRAWINGS. SPECIAL SUBJECTS

743'.4 — Drawings. Special subjects: Human figures. Techniques — *Manuals*

Goldstein, Nathan. Figure drawing : the structure, anatomy, and expressive design of human form / Nathan Goldstein. — 2nd ed. — Englewood Cliffs ; London : Prentice-Hall, c1981. — xii,323p : ill ; 29cm
Previous ed.: 1976. — Bibliography: p313-314. — Includes index
ISBN 0-13-314518-2 (cased) : Unpriced
ISBN 0-13-314435-6 (pbk) : £12.30 B81-25460

Stephen, Charles. Draw figures in action / Charles Stephen. — London : Pitman, 1981, c1980. — 48p : ill ; 28cm
Originally published: New York : Taplinger, 1980
ISBN 0-273-01569-9 (pbk) : £1.50 B81-36646

743'.4 — Pastel drawings. Special subjects: Human figures. Techniques — *Manuals*

Singer, Joe. How to paint figures in pastel / by Joe Singer. — New York : Watson-Guptill ; London : Pitman House, 1980, c1976. — 167p : ill(some col.),ports ; 28cm
Bibliography: p165. - Includes index
ISBN 0-273-01439-0 (pbk) : £4.95 B81-07383

743'.42 — Pastel portrait drawings. Techniques — *Manuals*

Frost, Dennis. Portraits in pastel / Dennis Frost. — London : Search, 1981. — 32p : ill(some col.),1port ; 21cm. — (Leisure arts ; 11)
Port on inside front cover
ISBN 0-85532-442-2 (pbk) : Unpriced
B81-25423

743'.44 — Drawings. Special subjects: Women: Nudes. Techniques — *Manuals*

Spencer, Roy. Draw the human body / Roy Spencer. — London : Black, 1981. — 48p : ill ; 28cm
ISBN 0-7136-2186-9 (pbk) : £1.50 B81-38889

743'.45 — Drawings. Special subjects: Children. Techniques — *Manuals*

Spencer, Roy. Draw children / Roy Spencer. — London : Black, 1981. — 48p : ill ; 28cm
ISBN 0-7136-2190-7 (pbk) : £1.50 B81-38891

743'.49 — Man. Anatomy — *For life drawing*

Raynes, John. Human anatomy for the artist / John Raynes. — London : Hamlyn, c1979. — 192p : ill ; 31cm
Ill on lining papers. — Includes index
ISBN 0-600-34554-8 : £4.95 B81-01036

743'.6 — Drawings. Special subjects: Livestock. Techniques — *Manuals*

Holden, Jenny. Draw farm animals / Jenny Holden. — London : Pitman, 1981, c1980. — 48p : ill ; 28cm
Originally published: New York : Taplinger, 1980
ISBN 0-273-01570-2 (pbk) : £1.50 B81-36649

743'.69725 — Drawings. Special subjects: Horses. Techniques — *Manuals*

Brown, David, *1926-.* Draw horses / David Brown. — London : Pitmn, 1981, c1980. — 48p ; 28cm
Originally published: New York : Taplinger, 1980
ISBN 0-273-01552-4 (pbk) : £1.50 B81-36648

743'.69725 — Drawings. Special subjects: Livestock: Horses — *Manuals*

Savitt, Sam. [Draw horses with Sam Savitt]. How to draw horses / Sam Savitt. — London : Pelham, 1981. — 95p : ill ; 23x29cm
Originally published: New York : Viking, 1981
ISBN 0-7207-1349-8 : £6.50 B81-34537

743'.6974442 — Drawings. Special subjects: Dogs. Techniques — *Manuals*

Morgan, Jeremy, *19---.* Draw dogs / Jeremy Morgan. — London : Pitman, 1981, c1980. — 48p : ill ; 28cm
Originally published: New York : Taplinger, 1980
ISBN 0-273-01589-3 (pbk) : £1.50 B81-36643

743'.83 — Drawings. Special subjects: Nature. Techniques — *Manuals*

Huntly, Moira. Draw nature / Moira Huntly. — London : Black, 1981. — 48p : ill ; 28cm
ISBN 0-7136-2187-7 (pbk) : £1.50 B81-38893

Leslie, Clare Walker. Nature drawing : a tool for learning / Clare Walker Leslie. — Englewood Cliffs ; London : Prentice Hall, c1980. — xvii,206p : ill ; 28cm. — (The Art & design series) (A Spectrum book)
Includes bibliographies and index
ISBN 0-13-610360-x (cased) : Unpriced
ISBN 0-13-610352-9 (pbk) : £4.95 B81-16534

743'.835 — Still-life drawings. Techniques — *Manuals*

Huntly, Moira. Still life / Moira Huntly. — London : Pitman, 1981, c1980. — 48p : ill ; 28cm
Originally published: New York : Taplinger, 1980
ISBN 0-273-01573-7 (pbk) : £1.50 B81-36647

743'.836 — Drawings. Special subjects: Sky. Techniques — *Manuals*

Battershill, Norman. Painting & drawing skies / Norman Battershill ; with illustrations by the author. — London : Pitman, 1981. — 159p : ill (some col.) ; 29cm
Bibliography: p156. - Includes index
ISBN 0-273-01392-0 : £12.50
Primary classification 751.4 B81-15987

743'.837 — Seascape drawings. Techniques — *Manuals*

Battershill, Norman. Draw seascapes / Norman Battershill. — London : Pitman, 1981, c1980. — 48p : ill ; 28cm
Originally published: New York : Taplinger, 1980
ISBN 0-273-01568-0 (pbk) : £1.50 B81-36645

743'.84 — Drawings. Special subjects: Buildings. Techniques — *Manuals*

Davy, Don. Drawing buildings / Don Davy. — Poole : Blandford, 1981. — 96p : chiefly ill ; 25cm
ISBN 0-7137-1109-4 (pbk) : £2.95 : CIP rev.
B81-23826

743'.85 — Drawings. Special subjects: Patterns. Techniques — *Manuals*

Brockett, Anna. Draw patterns / Anna Brockett. — London : Black, 1981. — 47p : ill ; 28cm
ISBN 0-7136-2188-5 (pbk) : £1.50 B81-38894

743'.9'2409 — Illustrations, *to 1980.* **Special subjects: Women** — *Illustrations*

Barker, Ronnie. Sugar and spice. — London : Hodder & Stoughton, Sept.1981. — [120]p
ISBN 0-340-27000-4 (pbk) : £4.50 : CIP entry
B81-23932

745 — DECORATIVE AND MINOR ARTS

745'.06'043 — German decorative arts. Organisations: Deutscher Werkbund, *to 1933*

The **Werkbund** : studies in the history and ideology of the Deutscher Werkbund 1907-1933 / edited by Lucius Burckhardt ; translated by Pearl Sanders. — London : Design Council, 1980. — 117p : ill,maps,plans ; 25cm
Translation of: Werkbund
ISBN 0-85072-108-3 : £12.50 : CIP rev.
B79-37408

745'.09'034 — Decorative arts. Art nouveau style — *Illustrations*

Treasury of Art Nouveau design & ornament : a pictorial archive of 577 illustrations / selected by Carol Belanger Grafton. — New York : Dover Publications ; London : Constable, c1980. — 137p : col.ill ; 29cm. — (Dover pictorial archive series)
ISBN 0-486-24001-0 (pbk) : £2.50 B81-09857

745'.09'04 — Decorative arts, *1940-1979*

Garner, Philippe. The contemporary decorative arts : from 1940 to the present day / Philippe Garner. — Oxford : Phaidon, c1980. — 224p : ill(some col.),ports(some col.) ; 31cm
Bibliography: p224. — Includes index
ISBN 0-7148-2003-2 : £12.95 B81-01705

745'.092'2 — Great Britain & United States. Decorative arts. Arts and Crafts movement. Women artists, *1870-1914* — *Critical studies*

Callen, Anthea. [Angel in the studio]. Women in the arts and crafts movement 1870-1914 / Anthea Callen. — London : Astragal, 1979 (1980 [printing]). — 232p : ill,facsims,plans,ports ; 30cm
Bibliography: p228-229. - Includes index
ISBN 0-906525-20-9 (pbk) : £5.95 B81-03975

745'.092'4 — England. Art galleries. Exhibits: English decorative arts. Ashbee, C. R. — *Catalogues*

C.R. Ashbee & the Guild of Handicraft : an exhibition / organised by Cheltenham Art Gallery and Museum with financial assistance from the Arts Council of Great Britain. — Cheltenham ([40 Clarence St., Cheltenham, Glos.]) : Cheltenham Art Gallery and Museum, c1981. — 64p : ill,facsims,ports ; 21cm
Published to accompany an exhibition held at the Art Gallery and Museum, Cheltenham, Mappin Art Gallery, Sheffield and Fine Art Society, London, 1981
Unpriced (pbk) B81-13185

745'.092'4 — Gloucestershire. Chipping Campden. Decorative arts. Organisations: Guild of Handicraft. Ashbee, C. R.

MacCarthy, Fiona. The simple life : C.R. Ashbee in the Cotswolds / Fiona MacCarthy. — London : Lund Humphries, 1981. — 204p,[24]p of plates : ill,music,ports ; 24cm
Music, text on lining papers. — Bibliography: p192-197. - Includes index
ISBN 0-85331-435-7 : £7.95 B81-07283

745'.0941 — British decorative arts, *1837-1901*

Palmer, Geoffrey, *1912 Aug.22.* The obsterver's book of Victoriana / Geoffrey Palmer and Noel Lloyd. — London : Warne, c1981. — 192p,[8]p of plates : ill(some col.) ; 15cm
Bibliography: p186-185. — Includes index
ISBN 0-7232-1620-7 : £1.95 B81-39854

745'.0941 — British decorative arts, *1890-1940* — *Serials*

Journal of the Decorative Arts Society 1890-1940 . — No.1-. — [London] ([c/o Ms J.M.V. Collins, 118 Greencroft Gardens NW6 3PJ]) : The Society, 1977-. — v. : ill ; 30cm
Annual. — Description based on: No.4
ISSN 0260-9568 = Journal of the Decorative Arts Society 1890-1940 : Free to Society members B81-24990

745'.0941'07402659 — Cambridgeshire. Cambridge. Museums: Fitzwilliam Museum. Exhibits: British decorative arts. Morris and Company — *Catalogues*

Morris & Company in Cambridge : catalogue / by Duncan Robinson and Stephen Wildman ; exhibition organised by the Fitzwilliam Museum, Cambridge and presented by Ciba-Geigy (UK) Limited, September 30 to November 16, 1980. — Cambridge : Cambridge University Press, 1980. — xiv,113p : ill,facsims ; 29cm
Bibliography: pxiii. - Includes index
ISBN 0-521-23310-0 (cased) : £18.50
ISBN 0-521-29903-9 (pbk) : £6.25 B81-02957

745'.0951 — Chinese decorative arts, *to 1980*

Stalberg, Roberta Helmer. China's crafts : the story of how they're made and what they mean / Roberta Helmer Stalberg, Ruth Nesi ; introduction by Audrey Topping. — London : Allen & Unwin, 1981. — 200p : ill(some col.),2maps ; 23cm
Includes bibliographies and index
ISBN 0-04-745009-6 (pbk) : Unpriced : CIP rev. B81-16889

745'.0951 — Chinese decorative arts, *to ca 1900*

Jenyns, Soame, *1904-1976.* Chinese art : textiles, glass and painting, carvings in ivory and rhinoceros horn, carvings in hardstone, snuff bottles, inkcakes and inkstones / by R. Soame Jenyns with the editorial assistance of William Watson. — 2nd ed. / [with] preface and revisions by William Watson. — Oxford : Phaidon, 1981. — 243p : ill(some col.) ; 28cm
Previous ed.: Fribourg : Office du livre, 1965
ISBN 0-7148-2136-5 : £14.95 B81-18949

745.1 — ANTIQUES

745.1 — Antiques

Colour encyclopedia of antiques. — London : Hamlyn, c1980. — 351p : ill(some col.) ; 24cm
Bibliography: p343-344. — Includes index
ISBN 0-600-34149-6 : £4.95 B81-22391

745.1 — Antiques — *Collectors' guides*

Hughes, G. Bernard. The Country life collector's pocket book / G. Bernard Hughes ; illustrations by Therle Hughes. — Richmond upon Thames : Country Life Books, 1980. — 351p : ill ; 16cm
Originally published: 1963. — Includes index
ISBN 0-600-43055-3 : £3.95 B81-25565

Stone, Anne, *1950-*. The antique collector's handbook : how to recognise collect and enjoy antiques / Anne Stone in association with Antique Collector. — London : Ebury, 1981. — 204p : ill ; 23cm
Includes index
ISBN 0-85223-199-7 : £7.95 B81-40920

745.1 — Antiques. Purchase & sale — *Amateurs' manuals*

Lewis, Mel. How to make money from antiques / Mel Lewis. — Poole : Blandford Press, 1981. — vii,160p : ill,1facsim,1form ; 23cm
Bibliography: p155-157. — Includes index
ISBN 0-7137-1084-5 : £4.95 B81-16660

745.1'028'7 — Antiques. Forgeries & reproductions. Detection — *Manuals*

Mills, John Fitzmaurice. How to detect fake antiques / John Fitzmaurice Mills. — London : Arlington, 1972 ([1980 printing]). — 88p,[28]p of plates : ill,facsims ; 22cm
Includes index
ISBN 0-85140-519-3 (pbk) : £1.95 B81-00199

745.1'028'8 — Antiques. Restoration — *Amateurs' manuals*

An **Introduction** to repairing & restoring : books, clocks, furniture, pottery, porcelain, prints, paintings, frames, silver, pewter, brass. — Newton Abbot : David & Charles, c1981. — 296p : ill ; 23cm
Includes index
ISBN 0-7153-8132-6 : £6.95 B81-25353

Mills, John Fitzmaurice. The care of antiques / John Fitzmaurice Mills ; preface by A.E. Werner ; foreword by Norman Brommelle. — Rev. ed. — London : Arlington, c1980. — x,126p,[27]p of plates : ill ; 22cm
Previous ed.: 1964. — Includes index
ISBN 0-85140-518-5 (pbk) : £1.95 B81-20049

Ridley, Jacqueline. The care and repair of antiques : Jacqueline Ridley / illustrated by David Dowland and Joyce Smith. — Poole : Blandford, 1978 (1980 [printing]). — 192p : ill (some col.) ; 19cm. — (Blandford colour series)
Includes index
ISBN 0-7137-1112-4 (pbk) : £2.95 B81-31671

745.1'075 — Antiques. Collecting — *Encyclopaedias*

Hainworth, Henry. A collector's dictionary / Henry Hainworth. — London : Routledge & Kegan Paul, 1981. — viii,119p : ill ; 21cm
ISBN 0-7100-0745-0 (cased) : £5.95 : CIP rev.
ISBN 0-7100-0511-3 (pbk) : £2.95 B80-17867

745.1'075 — Antiques. Collecting — *Serials*

Everything has a value : everyman's guide to collecting - things to furnish, collect, hang on the wall, put in the safe, display, old and new from £5 to £5,000-. — No.1 (Oct.1980)-. — London (27 Wilfred St., SW1E 6PR) : BAC, 1980-. — v. : ill ; 30cm
Monthly
ISSN 0260-8308 = Everything has a value : £10.00 per year B81-09208

745.1'09 — Antiques, *1400-1979*

The **Encyclopedia** of popular antiques / general editor Michael Carter. — London : Octopus, 1980. — 400p : ill(some col.) ; 30cm
Col. ill on lining papers. — Includes index
ISBN 0-7064-0963-9 : £5.95 B81-02146

745.2 — INDUSTRIAL DESIGN

745.2 — Industrial design

Heskett, John. Industrial design / John Heskett. — London : Thames & Hudson, c1980. — 216p : ill,facsims ; 22cm. — ([The world of art library])
Bibliography: p209-212. — Includes index
ISBN 0-500-18181-0 : £5.95 B81-02461

Jones, J. Christopher. Design methods : seeds of human futures / J. Christopher Jones. — 1980 ed. with a review of new topics. — New York ; Chichester : Wiley, c1981. — xxxii,407p : ill ; 23cm
Previous ed.: 1970. — Bibliography: p397-403. — Includes index
ISBN 0-471-27958-7 (pbk) : £7.50 B81-11403

745.2 — Industrial design — *Conference proceedings*

International Council of Societies of Industrial Design. *Congress and Assembly (11th : 1979 : Mexico City)*. Industrial design and human development : proceedings of the XI Congress and Assembly of the International Council of Societies of Industrial Design, Mexico City, October 14-19, 1979 / editors Pedro Ramírez Vázquez, Alejandro Lazo Margain. — Amsterdam ; Oxford : Excerpta Medica, 1980. — xxxvii,354p : ill ; 25cm. — (International congress series ; no.510)
Includes introductory material in English, Spanish and French. — Includes index
ISBN 90-219-0456-x : £30.36 B81-02886

745.2′028′54 — Industrial design. Applications of interactive computer systems — *Conference proceedings*

Interactive design systems conference : Stratford-upon Avon Hilton, 13-15 April 1977 / [conference organized by the Computer Aided Design Centre, Cambridge, England]. — Guildford : Published by IPC Science and Technology for the Computer Aided Design Centre, 1977. — 291p : ill ; 24cm
ISBN 0-902852-80-9 (pbk) : Unpriced B81-04555

745.2′07′1141 — Great Britain. Higher education institutions. Curriculum subjects: Industrial design. Courses — *Directories*

Design courses in Britain. — 1981-82. — London : Design Council, Oct.1981. — [48]p
ISBN 0-85072-122-9 (pbk) : £2.50 : CIP entry B81-31956

745.2′09′03 — Design. Effects of industrialisation, *ca 1750-1979* — *Conference proceedings*

Design and industry : the effects of industrialisation and technical change on design / [edited by Nicola Hamilton]. — London : Design Council, 1980. — 88p : ill,facsims ; 27cm. — (History of design)
Conference papers
ISBN 0-85072-114-8 (pbk) : £12.50 : CIP rev. B80-23577

745.4 — DESIGN AND DECORATION

745.4 — Design

Potter, Norman. What is a designer : things, places, messages / Norman Potter. — Rev. and extended ed. — Reading (73 Blenheim Gardens, Reading RG1 5QJ) : Hyphen, 1980. — 215p ; 22cm
Previous ed.: New York : Van Nostrand Reinhold ; London : Studio-Vista, 1969. — Bibliography: p173-179. — Includes index
ISBN 0-907259-01-4 : £9.75
ISBN 0-907259-00-6 (pbk) : £4.50 B81-03416

745.4 — Design — *Conference proceedings*

Design Research Society. *Conference (1980 : Portsmouth Management Centre)*. Design, science, method : proceedings of the 1980 Design Research Society Conference / conference organized by the Design Research Society in collaboration with Portsmouth Polytechnic ; edited by Robin Jacques and James A. Powell. — Guildford : Westbury, c1981. — xii,332p : ill ; 24cm
Includes bibliographies
ISBN 0-86103-047-8 (pbk) : Unpriced B81-18818

745.4 — Design — *For schools*

Caborn, Colin. Integrated craft and design / Colin Caborn and Ian Mould. — London : Harrap, 1981. — 299p : ill,plans ; 25cm
Includes index
ISBN 0-245-53633-7 (pbk) : £4.95
Primary classification 680 B81-19677

745.4 — Design. Geometric aspects

Barratt, Krome. Logic and design in art, science & mathematics / Krome Barratt. — London : Godwin, 1980. — ix,325p : ill,1map ; 26cm
Bibliography: p312-318. — Includes index
ISBN 0-7114-4206-1 : £14.95 : CIP rev. B79-35434

745.4 — Design. Patterns. Symmetry

Stevens, Peter S.. Handbook of regular patterns : an introduction to symmetry in two dimensions / Peter S. Stevens. — Cambridge, Mass. ; London : M.I.T., c1980. — 400p : ill ; 23cm
Bibliography: p392-393. — Includes index
ISBN 0-262-19188-1 : £23.25 B81-38135

745.4′024372 — Design — *Illustrations* — *For teaching*

Maier, Manfred. Basic principles of design : the foundation program at the School of Design, Basel, Switzerland / Manfred Maier ; [English version Joseph Finocchiaro, William Longhauser, Janet Longhauser]. — Combined ed. — New York ; London : Van Nostrand Reinhold, 1981, c1977. — 384p : chiefly ill (some col.) ; 31cm
Translation of: Elementare Entwurfs- und Gestaltungsprozesse. — Originally published: in 4 vols. 1977. — Contents: Vol.1 Object drawing ... — Vol.2 Memory drawing ... — Vol.3 Material studies ... — Vol.4 Color 1 ..
ISBN 0-442-21206-2 (pbk) : £29.75 B81-36812

745.4′028 — Design. Techniques — *Manuals*

Luddington, David. Design in technical studies / David Luddington ; illustrations by Anthony Valbonesi and Joyce Emslie ; from material supplied by Nigel Plevin. — Glasgow : Blackie, 1981. — 140p : ill ; 18x25cm
Includes index
ISBN 0-216-90916-3 (pbk) : Unpriced B81-39057

745.4′068′8 — United States. Design services. Marketing — *Manuals*

The McGraw-Hill operation update series in marketing professional design services / editorial advisor Gerre Jones. — New York ; London : McGraw-Hill, 1979. — 8v. : ill,facsims,forms ; 26cm
Includes bibliographies and index. — Contents: Manual 1. Introduction to professional services marketing - Manual 2. Getting organized - Manual 3. How to find and gualify prospects - Manual 4. Promotional tools - Manual 5. Effective communication - Manual 6. Presentation - Master outline and guide - Problems and answers
ISBN 0-07-079284-4 (pbk) : £51.95 the set
ISBN 0-07-044711-x (v.1)
ISBN 0-07-044712-8 (v.2)
ISBN 0-07-044713-6 (v.3) (v.4)
ISBN 0-07-044715-2 (v.5)
ISBN 0-07-044716-0 (v.6)
ISBN 0-07-044717-9 (Problems and answers)
ISBN 0-07-044710-1 (Master outline and guide) B81-10532

745.4′441 — Design, *1837-1979*

Ferebee, Ann. A history of design from the Victorian era to the present : a survey of the modern style in architecture, interior design, industrial design, graphic design, and photography / Ann Ferebee. — New York ; London : Van Nostrand Reinhold, 1980, c1970. — 128p : ill,facsims,ports ; 21cm
Includes index
ISBN 0-442-23115-6 (pbk) : £5.95 B81-04046

745.4′442 — Design, *1890-1939*

History of architecture and design 1890-1939. — Milton Keynes : Open University Press. — (Arts : a third level course)
At head of title: Open University Broadcasting supplement
2: Radio 15-32, television 11-24. — 1976. — 90p : ill,plans ; 30cm. — (A305 ; BSZ)
Unpriced (pbk) B81-39330

745.4′442 — Design, *1900-1980*

Banham, Reyner. Design by choice / Reyner Banham ; edited by Penny Sparke. — London : Academy Editions, 1981. — 152p : ill(some col.),1port ; 30cm. — (Ideas in architecture)
Bibliography: p143-147. — Includes index
Unpriced (pbk)
Primary classification 724.9′1 B81-29563

745.4′4924 — French designs. Benedictus, Edouard — *Illustrations*

Benedictus, Edouard. Benedictus′ art deco designs in color / with an introduction by Charles Rahn Fry. — New York : Dover ; London : Constable, 1980. — 46p : all col.ill ; 31cm
Ill on inside covers
ISBN 0-486-23971-3 (pbk) : £3.80 B81-07532

745.4′4924 — Swiss designs. Gos, François. Special subjects: Alpine flowers — *Illustrations*

Gos, François. Alpine flower designs for artists & craftsmen / color plates by François Gos ; black-and-white plates by Karen Baldauski. — New York : Dover ; London : Constable, 1980. — 44p,xvip of plates : ill(some col.) ; 31cm
ISBN 0-486-23982-9 (pbk) : £2.20 B81-09944

745.4′494 — Celtic decorative arts. Motifs — *For schools*

Bain, George. Celtic art : the methods of construction / by George Bain. — Rev. mini book ed. — Glasgow : Maclellan. — (National art of great antiquity) (An Embryo book)
Book 2: Knotwork panels. — 1980. — [32]p : ill,1port ; 11x17cm
Previous ed.: 1944. — Port on inside cover
£0.95 (pbk) B81-40980

745.4′49485 — Sweden. Design, *1920-1980* - *Conference proceedings*

Svensk Form. — London : Design Centre, Apr.1981. — [48]p
ISBN 0-85072-118-0 (pbk) : £5.00 : CIP entry B81-12382

745.4′4972 — Mayan designs — *Illustrations*

Turner, Wilson G.. Maya design coloring book / Wilson G. Turner. — New York : Dover ; London : Constable, 1980. — 41p : ill ; 28cm. — (Dover coloring book)
ISBN 0-486-24047-9 (pbk) : £1.75 B81-23276

745.5 — HANDICRAFTS

745.5 — Handicrafts — *For schools*

Hampson, B. L.. Make it today Brian Hampson & Sheila Howkins. — Edinburgh : Oliver & Boyd
2. — 1981. — 63p : col.ill ; 26cm
Cover title
ISBN 0-05-003427-8 (pbk) : £1.70 B81-40122

745.5 — Handicrafts — *Manuals*

The **Blandford** book of traditional handicrafts / edited by John Rome. — Poole : Blandford, 1981. — vi,169p,[16]p of plates : ill(some col.) ; 26cm
Includes index
ISBN 0-7137-0951-0 : £8.95 : CIP rev. B80-18443

Practical homemaking crafts / edited by Eve Harlow. — [2nd ed.]. — London : Octopus, 1981. — 157p : col.ill ; 28cm
Originally published: London : Sundial, 1976. — Includes index
ISBN 0-7064-1645-7 (corrected pbk) : £2.50 B81-36115

Home crafts. — London : Marshall Cavendish, 1978 (1979 printing). — 247p : col.ill ; 29cm
ISBN 0-85685-748-3 (pbk) : £2.99 B81-19567

Vermeer, Jackie. The bazaar handbook / Jackie Vermeer and Marian Lariviere Frew ; photography by Duane Davis. — New York ; London : Van Nostrand Reinhold, 1980. — 143p,[4]p of plates : ill(some col.) ; 25cm
Includes index
ISBN 0-442-22652-7 : £11.95 B81-00200

745.5 — Handicrafts — *Manuals* — *For children*

101 things to make / compiled by Janet Slingsby ; illustrated by David Mostyn. — London : Hamlyn, 1981. — 156p : col.ill ; 22cm
ISBN 0-600-36478-x : £2.95 B81-25537

745.5 — Handicrafts — *Manuals — For children continuation*

Baker, Sally. Simple crafts for children. — London : WI Books, Nov.1981. — [24]p
ISBN 0-900556-70-6 (pbk) : £0.65 : CIP entry B81-33629

Brown, Rosalie. Things to make / devised and drawn by Rosalie Brown. — Wendover : Published in conjunction with the Girl Guides Association [by] Goodchild, 1977. — 94p : ill ; 23cm
ISBN 0-903445-40-9 : £2.25 B81-01037

Evans, Hilary. Surprises for presents / by Hilary Evans ; illustrated by the author. — Over : Dinosaur, c1981. — [24]p : col.ill ; 16x19cm. — (Dinosaur's action books)
ISBN 0-85122-272-2 (cased) : £1.85
ISBN 0-85122-255-2 (pbk) : £0.70 B81-19477

Hampson, B. L.. Make it today / Brian Hampson & Sheila Howkins. — Edinburgh : Oliver & Boyd
Cover title
1. — 1981. — 63p : ill(some col.) ; 26cm
ISBN 0-05-003425-1 (pbk) : £1.65
ISBN 0-05-003426-x (Teacher's guide) : £2.50 B81-15248

Hart, Tony. Make it with Hart / Tony Hart. — London : Pan, 1981, c1979. — 47p : ill(some col.) ; 25cm. — (Piccolo books)
Originally published: London : G. Whizzard ; Deutsch, 1979
ISBN 0-330-26328-5 (pbk) : £1.95 B81-15053

Hetzer, Linda. Playtime crafts / by Linda Hetzer ; photographs by Steven Mays. — London : Macdonald Raintree Children's Books, 1980. — 48p : ill(some col.) ; 26cm
Originally published: Milwaukee : Raintree, 1978
ISBN 0-356-06238-4 : £2.95 B81-02609

The **Play** and learn book / [edited with] introduction by Henry Pluckrose. — London : Watts, c1981. — 112p : col.ill,music ; 29cm
Includes index
ISBN 0-85166-728-7 : £5.99 B81-26679

Stoker, Diana S.. Rainbow book of things to do / Diana Stoker, Stephanie Connell ; illustrated by Joan Hickson. — London : Thames/Methuen, 1981. — [92]p : col.ill ; 20cm
ISBN 0-423-00080-2 : £3.95 B81-36577

745.5 — Handicrafts. Special subjects: Bears — *Manuals — For children*

Berenstain, Stan. The bears' activity book / by Stan and Jan Berenstain. — London : Collins, 1981, c1979. — 127p : col.ill ; 28cm
Originally published: New York : Random House, 1979
ISBN 0-00-195047-9 (pbk) : £2.95 B81-15234

745.5 — Handicrafts using natural materials — *Manuals*

De Menezes, Patricia. Crafts from the countryside / Patricia de Menezes. — London : Hamlyn, 1981. — 172p : ill(some col.) ; 26cm
Bibliography p170. - Includes index
ISBN 0-600-32199-1 : £5.95 B81-22045

745.5′0243694 — Handicrafts — *Manuals — For Brownie Guides*

Florentine, Muriel. Creative crafts : from scrap and imagination / by Muriel Florentine. — London (Buckingham Palace Rd., SW1W 0PT) : Girl Guides Association, 1981. — 31p : ill (some col.) ; 21x30cm
£0.80 (pbk) B81-23281

Morton, Brenda. Brownie handwork / by Brenda Morton. — 2nd ed. — Glasgow : Brown, Son & Ferguson in collaboration with the Girl Guides Association, c1980. — x,157p : ill ; 18cm
Previous ed.: 1964
ISBN 0-85174-384-6 (pbk) : £4.00 B81-10196

745.5′028 — Great Britain. Handicrafts materials — *Buyers' guides — Serials*

. Craft buyer's guide : the Education Institute of Design, Craft and Technology guide to craft equipment and materials. — 1981. — London : Kogan Page, c1981. — 128p
ISBN 0-85038-384-6 : £5.95
ISSN 0143-4195 B81-08295

745.5′0880542 — Handicrafts for children, to 5 years — *Manuals*

Farnworth, Warren. First art / Warren Farnworth. — London : Evans, 1973 (1975 [printing]). — 112p : ill ; 17x21cm
ISBN 0-237-44996-x (pbk) : £1.95 B81-36504

745.5′0886238 — Sailors' handicrafts — *Manuals*

Beavis, Bill. Sailors' crafts / by Bill Beavis. — London : Allen & Unwin, 1981. — 122p : ill ; 26cm
ISBN 0-04-797004-9 : Unpriced B81-08479

745.53′1 — Leatherware. Making — *Manuals*

Lingwood, Rex. Leather in three dimensions / Rex Lingwood. — New York ; London : Van Nostrand Reinhold, c1980. — 112p : ill(some col) ; 21x24cm
Bibliography: p109. — Includes index
ISBN 0-442-29732-7 (cased) : £9.70
ISBN 0-442-29733-5 (pbk) : £9.70 B81-06348

745.54 — Activities using paper — *Manuals — For children*

McGlashon, Angela. Fun with paints and paper : 100 different things to do! / Angela McGlashon ; illustrated by Gillian Hurry. — London : Carousel, 1981. — 112p : ill ; 20cm
ISBN 0-552-54190-7 (pbk) : £0.85
Also classified at 750′.28 B81-37346

745.54 — Handicrafts using paper — *Manuals*

Paper / [edited by Linda Doeser]. — London : Marshall Cavendish, 1978. — 135p : col.ill ; 26cm
Ill on lining papers. — Includes index
ISBN 0-85685-313-5 : £4.95 B81-02763

745.54′6 — Handicrafts: Decoupage — *Manuals*

Manning, Hiram. Manning on decoupage / Hiram Manning. — Corr. republication. — New York : Dover ; London : Constable, 1980. — 254p : ill(some col.) ; 23cm
Originally published: New York : Hearthside Press, 1969. — Ill on inside covers. — Includes index
ISBN 0-486-24028-2 (pbk) : £3.50 B81-18490

745.55 — Handicrafts using shells — *Manuals*

Boyle, Eileen. Sea shell art : simple and advanced / Eileen Boyle. — Dublin (4 St Kevin's Terrace, Dublin 8) : Libra House, 1981. — 63p : ill ; 21cm
ISBN 0-904169-15-4 (pbk) : £2.20 B81-34518

Haragan, Christine. Shell designs / Christine Haragan. — Tunbridge Wells : Midas, 1980. — 80p : ill(some col.),1port ; 26cm. — (Midas craft library)
Includes index
ISBN 0-85936-137-3 : £6.50 B81-05192

745.56 — Handicrafts: Metalworking — *Manuals*

Metal and enamel / [edited by Linda Fox]. — London : Marshall Cavendish, 1978. — 135p : col.ill ; 26cm
Ill on lining papers. — Includes index
ISBN 0-85685-265-1 : £4.95
Also classified at 738.4 B81-03655

Streeter, Donald. Professional smithing. — London : Murray, Nov.1981. — [144]p
ISBN 0-7195-3904-8 : £7.50 : CIP entry B81-30269

745.58′4 — Handicrafts using scrap materials — *Manuals*

Hoggett, Chris. Design with scrap / Chris Hoggett. — London : Adam & Charles Black, 1980. — viii,198p : ill ; 22cm
Bibliography: p193-194. — Includes index
ISBN 0-7136-1723-3 : £9.95 : CIP rev. B80-18867

745.592 — Paper flying toys. Construction — *Manuals — For children*

Newnham, Jack. Things to fly : gliders, propellers, hang glider-kite and others / written, illustrated and produced by Jack Newnham. — Harmondsworth : Puffin, 1980. — [32]p : col.ill ; 20cm. — (Practical puffins ; no.19)
ISBN 0-14-049167-8 (pbk) : £0.80 B81-05282

745.592 — Toys for handicapped children. Making — *Manuals*

McConkey, Roy. Let's make toys / Roy McConkey, Dorothy M. Jeffree. — London : Condor, 1981. — 240p : ill,forms ; 23cm. — (Human horizons series)
Bibliography: p231-234
ISBN 0-285-64916-7 : £6.95 B81-16324

745.592 — Toys. Making — *Manuals*

The **Complete** book of babycrafts : how to make beautiful clothes and toys for your child / consultant editor, Eleanor Van Zandt ; house editor, Mary Lambert. — London : Ebury, 1981. — 184p : col.ill ; 30cm
ISBN 0-85223-214-4 : £7.95
Primary classification 646.4′06 B81-40918

Gorge, Alice A.. Creative toymaking : dolls, animals, puppets / Alice A. Gorge. — 2nd ed. — Edinburgh : Floris, 1981. — 58p : ill ; 21cm
Previous ed.: London : Ward Lock, 1970
ISBN 0-903540-43-6 (pbk) : £2.95 : CIP rev. B80-19853

745.592 — Toys. Making — *Manuals — For children*

The **New** gold medal book of things to make and do. — London : Dean, c1980. — 45p : col.ill ; 26cm
ISBN 0-603-00205-6 : £1.25 B81-06495

745.592′21 — Dolls. Making — *Manuals*

Marsten, Barbara. Step-by-step dollmaking / Barbara Marsten ; technical writing by Christine Makowski ; illustrations by Tina Bliss ; photography by René Velez. — New York ; London : Van Nostrand Reinhold, c1981. — 144p,[4]p of plates : ill(some col.) ; 29cm
Includes index
ISBN 0-442-25139-4 : £12.70 B81-29517

745.592′21 — Jumeau dolls — *Collectors' guides*

Whitton, Margaret. The Jumeau doll / Margaret Whitton ; photographs by J. Kent Campbell. — New York : Dover in association with the Margaret Woodbury Strong Museum ; London : Constable, 1980. — 79p : ill(some col.),facsims,1port ; 28cm
Bibliography: p79
ISBN 0-486-23954-3 (pbk) : £3.60 B81-23273

745.592′21 — Rag dolls, *1890-1960 — Collectors' guides*

Rustam, Phillis A.. Cloth dolls / Phillis A. Rustam. — South Brunswick : Barnes ; London : Yoseloff, c1980. — 128p,[8]p of plates : ill(some col.),1port ; 29cm
Bibliography: p125. - Includes index
ISBN 0-498-02284-6 : £6.95 B81-05427

745.592′21 — Soft costume dolls. Making — *Manuals*

Greenhowe, Jean. Making mascot dolls / Jean Greenhowe. — London : Batsford, 1981. — 119p,[4]p of plates : ill(some col.) ; 26cm
Includes index
ISBN 0-7134-2177-0 (corrected) : £6.95 B81-27710

745.592′21 — Soft dolls. Making — *Manuals*

Janitch, Valerie. Dolls for sale / Valerie Janitch ; with photographs by Rob Matheson. — London : Faber, 1980. — 79p,[8]p of plates : ill (some col.) ; 22cm
ISBN 0-571-11535-7 (cased) : £5.95 : CIP rev.
ISBN 0-571-11536-5 (pbk) : £2.95 B80-17868

745.592′21′0228 — Dolls. Restoration — *Manuals*

Westfall, Marty. The handbook of doll repair and restoration / by Marty Westfall. — London : Hale, 1981, c1979. — vi,282p,[8]p of plates : ill(some col.) ; 27cm
Originally published: New York : Crown, 1979. — Includes index
ISBN 0-7091-8857-9 : £8.95 B81-12188

745.592'21'094 — European dolls, ***1800-1930*** **—** ***Collectors' guides***

Cieslik, Jürgen. Dolls : European dolls 1800-1930 / Jürgen and Marianne Cieslik ; [translation, Roberta Bailey]. — London : Studio Vista, c1979. — 160p : ill(some col.),1map,facsims,ports ; 21cm. — (Christie's South Kensington collectors' guides)
Translation from the German. — Bibliography: p154. — Includes index
ISBN 0-289-70869-9 : £4.95 B81-15576

745.592'3'094207402579 — Oxfordshire. Rotherfield Greys. Country houses: Greys Court. Exhibits: English dolls' houses. Interiors. Collections: Carlisle collection

The **Carlisle** collection of miniature rooms. — [London] : National Trust, 1981, c1979. — 10p,[4]p of plates : ill ; 22cm
Originally published: London : National Trust, 1973
Unpriced (pbk) B81-22954

745.592'4 — Soft toys. Making - ***Manuals***

Jaffke, Freya. Making soft toys. — Edinburgh : Floris Books, Sept.1981. — [60]p
Translation of: Spielzeug von Eltern selbstgemacht
ISBN 0-903540-46-0 (pbk) : £2.75 : CIP entry B81-20493

745.592'4 — Teddy bears, ***to 1980***

Waring, Philippa. In praise of teddy bears / Philippa & Peter Waring ; designed by Christopher Scott. — [London] : Pictorial Presentations, 1980. — 128p : ill(some col.),facsims,ports(some col.) ; 28cm
ISBN 0-285-62455-5 : £6.95 B81-01038

745.592'8 — Model buildings, ***1289-ca 1850.*** **Construction —** ***Manuals***

Dalby, Stuart. Making model buildings / Stuart Dalby. — Poole : Blandford, 1980. — 93p : ill ; 26cm
ISBN 0-7137-0976-6 : £4.95 : CIP rev. B80-18445

745.592'8 — Models. Making — ***Manuals***

Jackson, Albert, *1943-*. The modelmaker's handbook / Albert Jackson & David Day. — London : Pelham, 1981. — 352p : ill ; 25cm
Includes index
ISBN 0-7207-1250-5 : £12.50 B81-20000

745.592'8'05 — Models. Making — ***Manuals — Serials***

[Model maker *(Hemel Hempstead)*]. Model maker : incorporating Model mechanics. — Vol.1, issue no.1 (Apr.1980)-v.1, issue no.10 (Jan.1981). — Hemel Hempstead : Model & Allied Publications, 1980-1981. — v. : ill ; 25cm
Monthly. — Continues: Model mechanics (Hemel Hempstead). — Description based on: Vol.1, no.8 (Nov.1980)
£9.60 per year B81-04442

745.592'82 — Military models. Making — ***Manuals***

The **Encyclopedia** of military modelling / general editor Vic Smeed ; consultant editor Alec Gee. — London : Octopus, 1981. — 192p : col.ill ; 31cm
Ill on lining papers. — Includes index
ISBN 0-7064-1241-9 : £7.95 B81-24951

745.592'82 — Model soldiers — ***Encyclopaedias***

Garratt, John G.. The world encyclopaedia of model soldiers / John G. Garratt. — London : Muller, 1981. — xii,209p,[16]p of plates : ill (some col.) ; 29cm
Bibliography: p195-201
ISBN 0-584-10711-0 : £19.50 B81-11574

745.592'82 — W. Britain's model soldiers, ***to 1966 — Collectors' guides***

Ruddle, John. Collectors' guide to Britains' model soldiers / by John Ruddle. — Watford : Model and Allied Publications, c1980. — xxxi,158p,[72]p of plates : ill(some col.) ; 23cm
ISBN 0-85242-568-6 : £6.95 B81-29583

745.594 — Decorative fabric covered boxes. Making — ***Amateurs' manuals***

Greatorex, Clemency. Decorative fabric boxes / Clemency Greatorex. — Leicester : Dryad, 1981. — 15p : col.ill ; 15x22cm. — (Dryad leaflet ; 533)
ISBN 0-85219-141-3 (pbk) : Unpriced B81-20893

745.594 — Greetings cards. Making — ***Manuals***

Mallows, Sue. Greeting cards / Sue Mallows. — Leicester : Dryad, 1981. — 15p : col.ill ; 15x21cm. — (Dryad leaflet ; 534)
ISBN 0-85219-142-1 (pbk) : Unpriced B81-20888

745.6 — LETTERING, ILLUMINATION, HERALDIC DESIGN

745.6'1 — Calligraphy — ***Illustrations***

Modern scribes and lettering artists. — London : Studio Vista, 1980. — 160p : ill,1map,facsims ; 29cm
Includes index
ISBN 0-289-70921-0 : £17.50 B81-34692

745.6'1 — Calligraphy — ***Manuals***

Butterworth, Emma Macalik. The complete book of calligraphy. — Wellingborough : Thorsons, Aug.1981. — [160]p
ISBN 0-7225-0704-6 (pbk) : £3.95 : CIP entry B81-16871

Mahoney, Dorothy. The craft of calligraphy / Dorothy Mahoney. — London : Pelham, 1981. — 128p : ill,facsims ; 25cm
Ill on lining papers. — Includes index
ISBN 0-7207-1365-x : £7.95 : CIP rev. B81-28034

Wong, Frederick. The complete calligrapher / Frederick Wong. — New York : Watson Guptill ; London : Pitman, 1980. — 184p : ill (some col.) ; 29cm
Bibliography: p181. - Includes index
ISBN 0-273-01623-7 : £9.95 B81-06244

745.6'1 — Lettering — ***Manuals***

Gray, Bill. Lettering tips : for artists, graphic designers and calligraphers / Bill Gray. — New York ; London : Van Nostrand Reinhold, 1980. — 128p : ill ; 24cm
Bibliography: p127. — Includes index
ISBN 0-442-26103-9 (pbk) : £5.20 B81-01039

Macdonald, Bryon J.. [The art of lettering with the broad pen]. Calligraphy : the art of lettering with the broad pen / Byron J. Macdonald. — London : Peter Owen, 1981, c1966. — [59]p ; 18x25cm
Originally published: New York : Reinhold, 1966
ISBN 0-7206-0564-4 (pbk) : £4.50 B81-37458

745.6'1'076 — Handwriting — ***Questions & answers — For children***

Murdock, Hy. Learn to write book / by Hy Murdock ; illustrated by Hurlston Design Ltd. — [Loughborough] : Ladybird, 1981. — 31p : col.ill ; 24cm
ISBN 0-7214-0651-3 (pbk) : £0.40 B81-11473

745.6'1'0924 — English lettering. Jones, David, ***1895-1974 - Critical studies***

Gray, Nicolete. The painted inscriptions of David Jones. — London : Gordon Fraser, Apr.1981. — [128]p
ISBN 0-86092-058-5 : £25.00 : CIP entry B81-04289

745.6'197 — Latin alphabet. Copperplate calligraphy — ***Manuals***

Kaufman, Herb. Calligraphy in the copperplate style / Herb Kaufman and Geri Homelsky. — New York : Dover ; London : Constable, 1980. — 31p : ill ; 28cm
ISBN 0-486-24037-1 (pbk) : £1.05 B81-23278

745.6'197 — Latin alphabet. Left-handed calligraphy

Studley, Vance. Left-handed calligraphy / Vance Studley. — New York ; London : Van Nostrand Reinhold, 1979. — 64p : ill ; 21cm
Bibliography: p62. — Includes index
ISBN 0-442-26151-9 (pbk) : £4.45 B81-10856

745.6'197'09 — Latin alphabet. Calligraphy, ***to 1600 — Illustrations***

Baker, Arthur, *19---*. Arthur Baker's historic calligraphic alphabets. — New York : Dover ; London : Constable, 1980. — 89p ; 31cm. — (Dover pictorial archive series)
ISBN 0-486-24054-1 (pbk) : £2.10 B81-23275

745.6'197'09 — Latin alphabet. Calligraphy, ***to 1979***

Whalley, Joyce Irene. The pen's excellencie : calligraphy of Western Europe and America / Joyce Irene Whalley. — Tunbridge Wells : Midas, 1980. — 400p,[8]p of plates : ill(some col.),1map,facsims(some col.),ports ; 29cm
Bibliography: p395-397. - Includes index
ISBN 0-85936-168-3 : £60.00 : CIP rev. B80-07459

745.6'1977 — Italic writing — ***Manuals***

Reynolds, Lloyd J.. Italic calligraphy and handwriting exercises and text / Lloyd J. Reynolds. — London : Peter Owen, 1981, c1969. — [64]p ; 23cm
Originally published: New York : Pentalic Corp., 1969
ISBN 0-7206-0563-6 (pbk) : £3.95 B81-37460

745.6'198 — Manuscripts in Greek. Handwriting, ***400-1600***

Barbour, Ruth. Greek literary hands : A.D. 400-1600 / by Ruth Barbour. — Oxford : Clarendon, 1981. — xxxvi,51p : facsims ; 29cm. — (Oxford palaeographical handbooks)
Text in English and classical Greek. — Bibliography: pxxxi-xxxiv. — Includes index
ISBN 0-19-818229-5 : £13.50 B81-28731

745.6'7 — Illuminated manuscripts. Illuminations, ***to 1500.*** **Special subjects: Birds**

Yapp, Brunsdon. Birds in medieval manuscripts. — London : British Library Reference Division, Oct.1981. — [192]p
ISBN 0-904654-54-0 : £9.50 : CIP entry B81-27939

745.6'7'0902307402132 — London. Westminster ***(London Borough).*** **Museums: Wallace Collection. Exhibits: Illuminated manuscripts,** ***1300-1500.*** **Illuminations —** ***Catalogues***

Wallace Collection. Catalogue of illuminated manuscript cuttings / by J.J.G. Alexander. — London (Manchester Sq., W1M 6BN) : Trustees of the Wallace Collection, 1980. — 58p : ill(some col.) ; 24cm
At head of title: Wallace Collection. — Includes index
Unpriced (pbk) B81-13999

745.6'7'0942 — English illuminated manuscripts. Illuminations, ***1200-1500 — Critical studies***

Marks, Richard. The golden age of English manuscript painting 1200-1500 / Richard Marks and Nigel Morgan. — London : Chatto & Windus, 1981. — 119p : col.ill ; 29cm
Bibliography: p34-37
ISBN 0-7011-2539-x (cased) : £12.50
ISBN 0-7011-2540-3 (pbk) : £6.95 B81-26370

745.6'7'0942 — English illuminated manuscripts: Mirroure of the worlde. ***Selections.*** **Illuminations & illustrations —** ***Illustrations***

[The mirroure of the worlde. *Selections*]. The mirroure of the worlde : MS Bodley 283 (England c.1470-1480) : the physical composition, decoration and illustration / with an introduction by Kathleen L. Scott. — Oxford ([c/o C. Dobson, Loxbeech, Mount St., Battle, E. Sussex]) : Printed for the Roxburghe Club, 1980. — xiii,68p,xxi,[4]leaves of plates : ill,facsims(some col.) ; 38cm
Half leather binding
£300.00 B81-37793

745.6'7'0944 — French illuminated manuscripts: Books of hours. Illuminations — ***Illustrations***

[The Wharncliffe Hours]. The Wharncliffe Hours : a fifteenth-century illuminated prayerbook in the collection of the National Gallery of Victoria, Australia / with an introduction and commentaries by Margaret Manion. — [London] : Thames and Hudson, c1981. — 96p : ill(some col.),facsims(some col.) ; 19cm
In slip case. — Bibliography: p96
£12.00 B81-24208

745.6'7'094934 — Illuminated manuscripts in Latin: Bible. *Latin.* *Stavelot.* **Illuminations** — *Critical studies*

Dynes, Wayne. The illuminations of the Stavelot Bible / Wayne Dynes. — New York ; London : Garland, 1978. — vii,305p,67p of plates : ill,facsims ; 21cm. — (Outstanding dissertations in the fine arts)
Bibliography: p273-305
ISBN 0-8240-3225-x : Unpriced B81-26194

745.6'7'0955 — Iranian illuminated manuscripts: Poetry in Persian. Firdawsī. Shahnama: Demotte Shahnama. Illuminations — *Critical studies*

Garbar, Oleg. Epic images and contemporary history : the illustrations of the great Mongol Shahnama / Oleg Grabar and Sheila Blair. — Chicago ; London : University of Chicago Press, 1980. — xiv,210p : ill(some col.),facsims ; 23cm
Includes index
ISBN 0-226-30585-6 : £16.50 B81-16725

745.6'7471 — Ancient Rome. Land. Surveying. Manuscripts in Latin: Codex Arcerianus A. Illustrations — *Critical studies*

Carder, James Nelson. Art historical problems of a Roman land surveying manuscript : the Codex Arcerianus A, Wolfenbüttel / James Nelson Carder. — New York ; London : Garland, 1978. — iii,267p,[122]p of plates : ill,maps,facsims ; 21cm. — (Outstanding dissertations in the fine arts)
Bibliography: p252-256
ISBN 0-8240-3218-7 : Unpriced B81-26933

745.7 — DECORATIVE COLOURING

745.7 — Decorative arts. Applications of titanium sputtering

Mitchell, Clarissa. Titanium sputtering : a new technique for decorative application on jewellery, porcelain and glass / Clarissa Mitchell. — London : Royal College of Art, c1981. — 8p : ill(some col.) ; 30cm. — (RCA papers, ISSN 0141-1365 ; no.11/1981)
Cover title
ISBN 0-902490-51-6 (pbk) : Unpriced B81-27230

745.7'2 — Decorative paintings. Techniques — *Manuals*

Hauser, Priscilla. [The Priscilla Hauser book of tole and decorative painting]. The book of tole & decorative painting / Priscilla Hauser. — London : Studio Vista, 1979, c1978. — 160p : ill(some col.),1port ; 29cm
Originally published: New York : London : Van Nostrand Reinhold, 1977. — Bibliography: p155. — Includes index
ISBN 0-289-70867-2 : £8.95 B81-00201

745.92 — FLOWER ARRANGEMENT

745.92 — Flower arrangement & handicrafts using flowers — *Manuals*

Clements, Julia. Julia Clements' flower arrangements. — London : Batsford, 1976 (1981 [printing]). — 62p : ill(some col.) ; 20cm
ISBN 0-7134-3246-2 (pbk) : £1.95 B81-32877

Taylor, Jean, *1921-*. Plants & flowers : for lasting decoration / Jean Taylor. — London : Batsford, 1981. — 144p,8p of plates : ill(some col.) ; 26cm
Bibliography: p142. — Includes index
ISBN 0-7134-2131-2 : £7.50 B81-19646

745.92 — Flower arrangement — *Manuals*

Aaronson, Marian. Flowers : in the modern manner / Marian Aaronson. — London : Grower, 1981. — 160p : ill(some col.) ; 26cm
Ill on lining papers
ISBN 0-901361-53-4 (cased) : Unpriced
ISBN 0-901361-54-2 (pbk) : Unpriced B81-31937

Adams, Mary. Natural flower arranging / Mary Adams. — London : Batsford, 1981. — 120p,[8]p of plates : ill(some col.) ; 26cm
Includes index
ISBN 0-7134-2677-2 : £7.95 B81-15958

Clements, Julia. The art of arranging a flower / Julia Clements. — London : Batsford, 1981. — 96p,[16]p of plates : ill(some col.) ; 26cm
Includes index
ISBN 0-7134-2679-9 : £7.95 B81-24308

Hemus, Christine. Flower arranging / Christine Hemus ; [illustrations by Margaret Hemus]. — London : WI Books, 1979. — 19p : ill ; 21cm
Cover title
ISBN 0-900556-57-9 (pbk) : £0.50 B81-37725

745.92 — Handicrafts using preserved plants — *Manuals*

Mierhof, Annette. The dried flower book : growing, picking, drying, arranging / Annette Mierhof ; illustrated by Marijke den Boer-Vlamings ; [translated by Jane Meijlink]. — London : Herbert, 1981. — 96p : ill(some col.) ; 28cm
Translation of: Droogbloemen
ISBN 0-906969-11-5 : £6.95
Primary classification 745.92 B81-29486

745.92 — Plants. Preservation — *Manuals*

Mierhof, Annette. The dried flower book : growing, picking, drying, arranging / Annette Mierhof ; illustrated by Marijke den Boer-Vlamings ; [translated by Jane Meijlink]. — London : Herbert, 1981. — 96p : ill(some col.) ; 28cm
Translation of: Droogbloemen
ISBN 0-906969-11-5 : £6.95
Also classified at 745.92 B81-29486

745.92 — Pot-pourri. Making — *Manuals*

Simmons, Rosemary. The good housewife scents and aromatics / drawn by Rosemary Simmons ; described by Gillian Goodwin. — London : 29 Chalcot Sq., N.W.1 : Gelofer, c1979. — [16]p : ill ; 21cm
ISBN 0-9506529-0-3 (pbk) : Unpriced B81-11720

745.92'252 — Ikebana — *Manuals*

Teshigawara, Kasumi. Ikebana : for all seasons / Kasumi Teshigahara. — Newton Abbot : David & Charles, 1981. — 127p : chiefly ill (some col.) ; 27cm
Translation from the Japanese
ISBN 0-7153-8195-4 : £4.95 B81-33007

745.92'6 — Special occasions. Flower arrangement — *Manuals*

Macqueen, Sheila. Sheila Macqueen's flowers and food for special occasions / with recipes by Diana Baldwin. — London : Ward Lock, 1980. — 96p : col.ill ; 26cm. — (A Hyperion book)
Includes index
ISBN 0-7063-5942-9 : £6.95
Primary classification 641.5'68 B81-08434

746 — TEXTILE HANDICRAFTS

746 — Fabric-based visual arts — *Critical studies*

Constantine, Mildred. The art fabric : mainstream / Mildred Constantine, Jack Lenor Larsen. — New York ; London : Van Nostrand Reinhold, [1981?]. — 272p : chiefly ill(some col.) ; 36cm
Bibliography: p257. — Includes index
ISBN 0-442-21638-6 : £27.50 B81-36810

746 — Textile handicrafts. Colour — *Manuals*

Birren, Faber. The textile colorist / Faber Birren ; with illustrations by Shirley Roffe. — New York ; London : Van Nostrand Reinhold, 1980. — 64p : ill(some col),ports ; 28cm
Bibliography: p61-62. — Includes index
ISBN 0-442-23854-1 (pbk) : £9.70 B81-05490

746'.0463 — Handicrafts using felts — *Manuals*

Feldman, Annette. Fun with felt / Annette Feldman. — New York ; London : Van Nostrand Reinhold, c1980. — 176p,[8]p of plates : ill(some col.) ; 29cm
Includes index
ISBN 0-442-25774-0 : £11.95 B81-03203

746'.074'02 — England. Art galleries. Exhibits: Patterned textiles, *ca 1960-1980* — *Catalogues*

Textiles today : a Kettle's Yard exhibition : woven and embroidered works / selected by Marianne Straub. — Cambridge (Northampton St., Cambridge CB3 OAQ) : Kettle's Yard, c1981. — [27]p : ill(some col.) ; 20x21cm
ISBN 0-907074-08-1 (pbk) : Unpriced B81-13230

746'.0941 — West Midlands *(Metropolitan County).* **Birmingham. Art galleries: Birmingham Museums & Art Gallery. Exhibits: Textiles. Morris and Company** — *Catalogues*

Fairclough, Oliver. Textiles by William Morris and Morris & Co., 1861-1940 / Oliver Fairclough and Emmeline Leary ; introduction by Barbara Morris. — London : Thames and Hudson, 1981. — 118p : ill(some col.) ; 24cm
Published in connection with an exhibition held at Birmingham Museums and Art Gallery, March 13th to May 3rd 1981. — Bibliography: p118. — Includes index
ISBN 0-500-27225-5 (pbk) : £5.50 B81-16212

746'.0952 — Japanese textiles. Designs, *to 1960* — *Illustrations*

Textile designs of Japan / compiled by the Japan Textile Colour Design Centre. — [Rev. ed.]. — London (10 Parkfields, Putney, SW15 6NH) : Serindia, c1980
Previous ed.: Osaka, Japan Textile Colour Design Center, 1959-61
1: Free-style designs. — 66p,184 leaves of plates : chiefly ill(some col.) ; 38cm
ISBN 0-906026-05-9 : £60.00 : CIP rev. B80-08318

Textile designs of Japan / compiled by the Japan Textile Colour Design Centre. — [Rev. ed.]. — London (10 Parkfields, Putney, SW15 6NH) : Serindia, c1980
Previous ed.: Osaka : Japan Textile Colour Design Center, 1959-61
2: Geometric designs. — 62p,175 leaves of plates : chiefly ill(some col.) ; 38cm
ISBN 0-906026-06-7 : £60.00 : CIP rev.
ISBN 0-906026-04-0 (set) : £180.00 B80-17870

Textile designs of Japan / compiled by the Japan Textile Colour Design Centre. — [Rev. ed.]. — London (10 Parkfields, Putney, SW15 6NH) : Serindia, c1980
Previous ed.: Osaka : Japan Textile Colour Design Center, 1959-61
3: Okinawan, Ainu & foreign designs. — 54p,168 leaves of plates : chiefly ill(some col.) ; 38cm
ISBN 0-906026-07-5 : £60.00 : CIP rev.
ISBN 0-906026-04-0 (set) : £180.00 B80-33962

746'.09549'15 — Baluchi textile arts

Konieczny, M. G.. Textiles of Baluchistan / M.G. Konieczny. — London : published for the Trustees of British Museum by British Museum Publications, c1979. — 77p : ill(some col.),1map ; 26cm
ISBN 0-7141-1557-6 (cased) : £6.95 : CIP rev.
ISBN 0-7141-1549-5 (pbk) : £3.95 B79-05233

746'.09598 — Indonesian textiles, *to 1980*

Warming, Wanda. The world of Indonesian textiles. — London (10 Parkfields, SW15 6NH) : Serindia, May 1981. — [200]p
ISBN 0-906026-08-3 : £25.00 : CIP entry B81-08883

746'.096 — African textile arts

Picton, John. African textiles : looms, weaving and design / John Picton and John Mack. — London : Published for the Trustees of the British Museum by British Museum Publications, c1979. — 208p : ill(some col.),maps ; 29cm
Bibliography: p204-205. — Includes index
ISBN 0-7141-1552-5 (cased) : £8.95 : CIP rev.
ISBN 0-7141-1553-3 (pbk) : £5.95 B79-26538

746.1 — HANDICRAFTS. SPINNING, WEAVING, ETC

746.1 — Wool. Dyeing, spinning & weaving — *Amateurs' manuals*

Jackson, Constance. The woolcraft book : spinning, weaving and dyeing / Constance Jackson and Judith Plowman. — Auckland [N.Z.] ; London : Collins, 1980. — 192,[16]p of plates : ill(some col.) ; 26cm
Bibliography: p187-188. - Includes index
ISBN 0-00-216968-1 : £7.95 B81-04913

746.1'2 — Handicrafts: Spinning — *Manuals*

Burrill, Jo. Spinning on the wheel / Jo Burrill. — Leicester : Dryad, 1981. — 15p : col.ill ; 15x21cm. — (Dryad leaflet ; 532)
ISBN 0-85219-140-5 (pbk) : Unpriced B81-20887

746.1′2 — Handicrafts: Spinning — *Manuals continuation*

Ross, Mabel. The essentials of handspinning / by Mabel Ross ; with illustrations by Winifred Mainwaring. — Repr. (rev.). — Malvern (Brookend Ridge, Welland, Malvern, Worcs. WR13 6LN) : M. Ross, 1981. — 40p : ill ; 21cm
Cover title. — Originally published: 1980
ISBN 0-9507292-0-5 (pbk) : £1.80 B81-07769

746.1′2 — Spinning wheels. Construction & restoration — *Manuals*

Kronenberg, Bud. Spinning wheel building and restoration / Bud Kronenberg. — New York ; London : Van Nostrand Reinhold, c1981. — 143p : ill ; 29cm
Bibliography: p140. — Includes index
ISBN 0-442-21915-6 : £14.20 B81-29516

746.1′4 — Hand loom weaving — *Amateurs′ manuals*

Black, Mary E.. The key to weaving : a textbook of hand weaving for the beginning weaver / Mary E. Black. — 2nd rev. ed. — New York : Macmillan ; London : Collier Macmillan, 1980. — xvii,698p : ill ; 25cm
Previous ed.: published as New key to weaving. Milwaukee : Bruce, 1957. — Col. ill on lining papers. — Bibliography: p677-679. - Includes index
ISBN 0-02-511170-1 : £13.95 B81-15622

746.1′4 — Handicrafts: Rigid heddle weaving — *Manuals*

Field, Anne, *19---*. Weaving with the rigid heddle loom / Anne Field. — London : Batsford, 1980. — ix,94p,[8]p of plates : ill(some col.) ; 25cm
Includes bibliographies and index
ISBN 0-7134-3400-7 : £5.50 B81-00202

746.1′4 — Handicrafts: Weaving — *Manuals*

Gilmurray, Susan. Weaving tricks / Susan Gilmurray. — New York ; London : Van Nostrand Reinhold, c1981. — 189p : ill ; 24cm
Bibliography: p181-183. — Includes index
ISBN 0-442-26132-2 : £9.70 B81-21173

746.1′4 — Handicrafts: Weaving - *Manuals*

Murray, Rosemary. The essential handbook of weaving. — London : Bell & Hyman, July 1981. — [160]p
ISBN 0-7135-1282-2 : £8.95 : CIP entry B81-18108

746.1′4 — Handicrafts: Weaving — *Manuals*

Ponting, Ken. Beginner′s guide to weaving. — London : Newnes Technical Books, Feb.1982. — [160]p
ISBN 0-408-00574-2 (pbk) : £3.60 : CIP entry B81-36374

746.1′4041 — Handicrafts: Weaving — *Patterns*

Gourlat, Catherine. Weaving in style / Catherine Gourlat ; photographs by Elizabeth Novick. — London : Mills & Boon, 1980. — 59p : ill(some col.) ; 26cm
Translation of: Pissages pas sages
ISBN 0-263-06456-5 : £5.95 B81-00203

Windeknecht, Margaret. Color-and-weave / Margaret and Thomas Windeknecht. — New York ; London : Van Nostrand Reinhold, c1981. — 192p,[4]p of plates : ill(some col.)
Bibliography: p189. — Includes index
ISBN 0-442-23329-9 : £19.50 B81-31778

746.1′4′09669 — Nigeria. Handicrafts: Weaving

Lamb, Venice. Nigerian weaving / Venice Lamb & Judy Holmes. — Roxford (Roxford, Hertingfordbury, Herts.) : H.A. & V.M. Lamb, 1980. — 276p : ill(some col.),maps,ports(some col.) ; 29cm
Bibliography: p271-273. - Includes index
ISBN 0-907129-00-5 : Unpriced B81-06872

746.1′4′0973 — United States. Handicrafts: Weaving — *Technical data*

Beveridge, June H.. Warp/weft/sett : a reference manual for handweavers / June H. Beveridge ; photography by Steven E. Beveridge. — New York ; London : Van Nostrand Reinhold, 1980. — 191p : chiefly ill ; 29cm
Includes index
ISBN 0-442-26129-2 : £17.20 B81-06471

746.2 — LACE MAKING AND RELATED HANDICRAFTS

746.2′2041 — Lace edgings. Knitting — *Patterns*

Lorant, Tessa. Knitted lace edgings / [Tessa Lorant]. — Wells (The Old Vicarage, Godney, Wells, Somerset BA5 1RX) : Thorn, 1981. — 64p : ill ; 22cm
Text on inside covers
ISBN 0-906374-14-6 (pbk) : Unpriced B81-28889

746.2′22 — Bobbin lace. Making — *Manuals*

Lovesey, Nenia. The basic techniques of bobbin lace / [text by Nenia Lovesey] ; [diagrams by Jan Messent]. — London : Search Press, 1979. — 32p : ill(some col.) ; 17cm. — (Needle crafts ; 8)
Ill on inside front cover
ISBN 0-85532-414-7 (pbk) : Unpriced B81-11600

746.3 — TAPESTRIES

746.39413′4 — Scotland. Arts. Patronage. Organisations: Scottish Arts Council. Exhibits: Dovecot Studios tapestries, *1912-1980 — Catalogues*

Master weavers : tapestry from the Dovecot Studios 1912-1980 : an Edinburgh International Festival Exhibition organized by the Scottish Arts Council, 15th August to 14th September 1980. — Edinburgh : Canongate, 1980. — 144p : ill(some col.),ports ; 21x26cm
ISBN 0-86241-001-0 (cased) : Unpriced B81-06246

746.3944 — French tapestries: Bayeux Tapestry. Military aspects

Jewell, Brian, *1925-*. Conquest & Overlord. — Speldhurst : Midas, June 1981. — 1v.
ISBN 0-85936-247-7 (pbk) : £4.95 : CIP entry
Also classified at 746.44 B81-14462

746.4 — BASKETRY, KNITTING, EMBROIDERY, ETC

746.4 — Needlework — *Manuals*

The **Collins** complete book of needlecraft / Jane Kirkwood .. [et al.]. — London : Collins, 1981. — 352p : ill(some col.) ; 29cm
Originally published: London : Marshall Cavendish, 1978. — Folded sheet in pocket. — Includes index
ISBN 0-00-411676-3 : £8.95 B81-39765

Reader′s digest complete guide to needlework. — London : Reader′s Digest, c1981. — 504p : ill (some col.) ; 22x26cm
Bibliography: p504. — Includes index
£10.95 B81-37169

746.4 — Needlework, *to 1980*

Synge, Lanto. Antique needlework. — Poole : Blandford, Sept.1981. — [224]p
ISBN 0-7137-1007-1 : £12.50 : CIP entry B81-22534

746.4 — Ropework — *Manuals*

Fry, Eric C.. The Shell book of knots and decorative ropework (combined). — Newton Abbot : David & Charles, Sept.1981. — [176]p
Originally published: as The Shell book of knots and ropework, 1977 ; and as The Shell book of practical and decorative ropework, 1979
ISBN 0-7153-8197-0 : £7.95 : CIP entry
Primary classification 623.88′82 B81-22507

746.4′03′21 — Needlework — *Encyclopaedias*

Ryan, Mildred Graves. The complete encyclopaedia of stitchcraft / Mildred Graves Ryan ; illustrated by Marta Cone. — British rev. ed. / edited by Patience Maule Horne. — London : Hale, c1981. — 701p : ill ; 24cm
Previous ed.: Garden City, N.Y. : Doubleday, 1979. — Bibliography: p699-701
ISBN 0-7091-9047-6 : £8.95 B81-22102

746.4′07′1142134 — London. Kensington and Chelsea *(London Borough)*. **Needlework schools: Royal School of Needlework,** *to 1981*

Jackson, Winefride. The Royal School of Needlework : yesterday and to-day / 1872-1948 by Winefride Jackson ; 1948 onwards researched by Winefride Jackson and compiled by Elizabeth Pettifer. — Blaby (29 The Fairway, Blaby, Leicester) : Anderson in association with the Royal School of Needlework, 1981. — 36p : ill(some col.) ; 25cm
ISBN 0-9504777-8-8 (pbk) : £1.80 : CIP rev. B81-13554

746.41 — Braiding — *Manuals*

Lacey, Margery. Braid weaving / Margery Lacey & Hetty M. Wickens. — Leicester : Dryad, 1981. — 15p : col.ill ; 15x21cm. — (Dryad leaflet ; 529)
ISBN 0-85219-133-2 (pbk) : Unpriced B81-20886

746.41 — Great Britain. Handicrafts using straw, *to 1980*

Staniforth, A. R.. Straw and straw craftsmen / Arthur Staniforth. — Princes Risborough : Shire, 1981. — 32p ; 21cm. — (Shire album ; 76)
Bibliography: p32
ISBN 0-85263-575-3 (pbk) : £0.95 B81-40856

746.41′2 — Basketry — *Manuals*

Dunwell, J.. Centre cane baskets : hazards & hints / by J. Dunwell. — East Barnet (41 Jackson Rd, East Barnet EN4 8UT) : J. Dunwell, [1980]. — 20p : ill ; 25cm
Cover title
ISBN 0-9505378-1-0 (pbk) : £1.00 B81-00204

746.41′2′0973 — American baskets, *ca 1970-1975 — Critical studies*

Rossbach, Ed. The new basketry / Ed Rossbach. — New York ; London : Van Nostrand Reinhold, 1976 (1980 [printing]). — 128p : ill,ports ; 28cm
Bibliography: p126. - Includes index
ISBN 0-442-27055-0 (pbk) : £5.95 B81-06084

746.42′22 — Macramé — *Amateurs′ manuals*

Hargreaves, Joyce. New ways with macramé / Joyce Hargreaves ; sketches by Joyce Hargreaves ; photographs and diagrams by Brian Hargreaves. — London : Batsford, 1981. — 120p,[4]p of plates : ill(some col.) ; 26cm
Includes index
ISBN 0-7134-3384-1 : £7.50 B81-27544

746.43′2 — Knitting — *Manuals*

Compton, Rae. Practical knitting / Rae Compton. — London : Hamlyn, c1981. — 256p : ill(some col.) ; 29cm
Includes index
ISBN 0-600-37253-7 : £6.95 B81-37328

Lorant, Tessa. The Batsford book of hand and machine knitting / Tessa Lorant ; photography by Tessa Lorant and Jeremy Warburg. — London : Batsford, 1980. — 144p,[4]p of plates : ill(some col.) ; 26cm
Bibliography: p141. - Includes index
ISBN 0-7134-3316-7 : £8.95 B81-01040

Richards, Ena. Knitting / [text by Ena Richards] ; [drawings by Jan Messent. — London : Search, 1980. — 32p : ill(some col.) ; 17cm. — (Needle crafts ; 11)
Ill on inside cover
ISBN 0-85532-428-7 (pbk) : £0.75 B81-02878

Tilling, Meriel. Knitting & crochet / Meriel Tilling ; diagrams by Maggie Greer. — London : Warne, 1981. — 88p,[8]p of plates : ill(some col.) ; 25cm. — (Warne′s art and craft series)
Includes index
ISBN 0-7232-2716-0 : £5.95
Also classified at 746.43′4 B81-20973

746.43′2 — Machine knitting — *Amateurs′ manuals*

Weaver, Mary. Machine knitting technology & patterns / by Mary Weaver. — [Dartford] ([276 Main Rd., Sutton-at-Hone, Dartford, Kent DA4 9HJ]) : [Weaverknits], [c1979]. — 315p : ill(some col.) ; 30cm
Cover title
Unpriced (spiral) B81-10398

746.43'2'028 — Passap Duomatic knitting machines — *Manuals*

Kinder, Kathleen, *1932 Aug.31-*. The Passap Duomatic, Deco and Forma : patterns and comment for all duomatics / Kathleen Kinder ; photography George Kinder, J.W. Lambert & Sons. — Settle (Dalesknit Centre, Settle, N. Yorkshire BD24 9BX) : K. Kinder, 1981. — 143p : ill ; 30cm
Includes index
ISBN 0-9506668-3-1 (spiral) : £6.25 B81-17632

746.43'2041 — Knitting. Designs - *Patterns*

30's family knitting book. — London : Duckworth, Aug.1981. — [96]p
ISBN 0-7156-1601-3 (pbk) : £3.95 : CIP entry B81-20604

746.43'2041 — Knitting — *Patterns*

Compton, Rae. The Hamlyn knitting guide / Rae Compton. — London : Hamlyn, 1980. — 128p : ill(some col.) ; 23cm
Includes index
ISBN 0-600-30501-5 : £2.99 B81-12645

Morgan, Gwyn. Traditional knitting of the British Isles. — London : Ward Lock, Apr.1981. — [104]p
ISBN 0-7063-5787-6 : £6.95 : CIP entry B81-01041

Vale, Nancy. The great family knitting book / Nancy Vale. — London : Mills & Boon, 1980. — 245p : ill(some col.) ; 24cm
Ill on lining paper
ISBN 0-263-06452-2 : £6.95 B81-00205

746.43'2041'0941 — Knitting. British designs — *Patterns*

Pearson, Michael R. R.. Traditional knitting of the British Isles / Michael R.R. Pearson. — [Newcastle upon Tyne] ([Chapel Studios, Jesmond Gates, Jesmond Rd., Newcastle upon Tyne NE2 2EY]) : Esteem Press
The Fisher Gansey patterns of North East England. — 2nd ed. — [1980]. — 84p : ill,1map,ports ; 20x21cm. — (Leisure series. Knitting ; v.1)
Previous ed.: published as Traditional knitting patterns of the British Isles. 1979
ISBN 0-906658-10-1 (pbk) : £3.50 B81-29394

Pearson, Michael R. R.. Traditional knitting of the British Isles / Michael R.R. Pearson. — [Newcastle upon Tyne] ([Chapel Studios, Jesmond Gates, Jesmond Rd., Newcastle upon Tyne NE2 2EY]) : Esteem Press
The Fisher Ganseys of Scotland and the Scottish fleet. — 1980. — 84p : ill,1map,ports ; 20x21cm. — (Leisure series. Knitting ; v.2)
ISBN 0-906658-05-5 (pbk) : £3.50 B81-29395

746.43'2041'0941135 — Knitting. Scottish designs: Shetland designs — *Patterns*

McGregor, Sheila. The complete book of traditional Fair Isle knitting / Sheila McGregor. — London : Batsford, 1981. — 143p,[4]p of plates : ill(some col.) ; 26cm
Bibliography: p140-141. — Includes index
ISBN 0-7134-1432-4 : £7.95 B81-24302

746.43'2041'0948 — Knitting. Traditional Scandinavian designs — *Patterns*

Starmore, Alice. Scandinavian knitwear. — London : Bell & Hyman, Feb.1982. — [128]p
ISBN 0-7135-1308-x : £8.50 : CIP entry B81-35833

746.43'4 — Crocheting — *Manuals*

Ough, Anne Rabun. New directions in crochet : a diagrammed course to easier crocheting, with more than 200 designs and patterns / Anne Rabun Ough. — Newton Abbot : David & Charles, c1981. — 240p,[8]p of plates : ill(some col.) ; 29cm
Includes index
ISBN 0-7153-8166-0 : £8.95 B81-23087

Stearns, Ann. The Batsford book of crochet / Ann Stearns. — London : Batsford, 1981. — 160p,[8]p of plates : ill(some col.) ; 26cm
Ill on lining papers. — Bibliography: p157. — Includes index
ISBN 0-7134-3312-4 : £9.95 B81-33063

Tilling, Meriel. Knitting & crochet / Meriel Tilling ; diagrams by Maggie Greer. — London : Warne, 1981. — 88p,[8]p of plates : ill(some col.) ; 25cm. — (Warne's art and craft series)
Includes index
ISBN 0-7232-2716-0 : £5.95
Primary classification 746.43'2 B81-20973

Walters, James. Crochet / James Walters and Sylvia Cosh. — London : Octopus, 1980. — 80p : ill(some col.) ; 29cm
Col. ill on lining papers. — Includes index
ISBN 0-7064-1347-4 : £2.95 B81-01042

Wilkes, Margaret H.. Broomstick crochet. — Rev. and enl. ed. — London : WI Books, July 1981. — [24]p
ISBN 0-900556-68-4 (pbk) : £0.65 : CIP entry B81-20651

746.43'4041 — Decorative edgings. Crocheting — *Patterns*

Crocheting edgings / edited by Rita Weiss. — New York : Dover ; London : Constable, 1980. — 45p : ill ; 28cm. — (Dover needlework series)
ISBN 0-486-24031-2 (pbk) : £1.05 B81-23279

746.43'6041 — Decorative edgings. Tatting — *Patterns*

Tatting doilies & edgings / edited by Rita Weiss. — New York : Dover Publications ; London : Constable, c1980. — 47p : ill ; 28cm. — (Dover needlework series)
ISBN 0-486-24051-7 (pbk) : £1.10
Also classified at 746.9'6 B81-09851

746.44 — British embroidery. Samplers, *to ca 1900*

Toller, Jane. British samplers : a concise history / by Jane Toller. — Godalming (8 Meadrow, Godalming, Surrey) : Cultural Exhibitions with Phillimore, 1980. — 63p : ill(some col.),1map ; 22cm
Includes index
ISBN 0-85033-383-0 (pbk) : £2.95 B81-19368

746.44 — Churches. Embroideries — *Manuals*

Dean, Beryl. Embroidery in religion and ceremonial / Beryl Dean. — London : Batsford, 1981. — 288p,[8]p of plates : ill(some col.) ; 26cm
Bibliography: p282. — Includes index
ISBN 0-7134-3325-6 : £25.00
Primary classification 646.4'7 B81-37844

746.44 — Embroidery. Berlin work, *1526-1840*

Edwards, Joan. Berlin work : the first of Joan Edwards' small books on the history of embroidery. — Dorking (P.O. Box 10, Dorking, Surrey RN4 2JB) : Bayford Books, c1980. — [16]p : ill,1port ; 21cm
ISBN 0-907287-01-8 (unbound) : £1.25 B81-32179

746.44 — Embroidery. Blackwork, *1600-1965*

Edwards, Joan. Black work : the second of Joan Edwards' small books on the history of embroidery. — Dorking (P.O. Box 10, Dorking, Surrey RN4 2JB) : Bayford Books, c1980. — [20]p : ill,1map,ports ; 21cm
ISBN 0-907287-00-x (unbound) : £1.25 B81-32178

746.44 — Embroidery. Blackwork — *Manuals*

Pascoe, Margaret. Blackwork / [text by Margaret Pascoe]. — London : Search Press, 1979. — 32p : ill(some col.) ; 17cm. — (Needle crafts ; 7)
ISBN 0-85532-415-5 (pbk) : Unpriced B81-14649

746.44 — Embroidery. Design

Messent, Jan. Embroidery design / [text and drawings by Jan Messent]. — London : Search, 1980. — 32p : ill(some col.) ; 17cm. — (Needle crafts ; 9)
Ill on inside cover
ISBN 0-85532-426-0 (pbk) : £0.75 B81-02927

746.44 — Embroidery. Designs based on natural objects

Messant, Jan. Embroidery & nature / Jan Messant. — Watertown, Mass. : Branford ; London : Batsford, 1980. — 168p,[4]p of plates : chiefly ill(some col.) ; 26cm
Bibliography: p165. — Includes index
ISBN 0-7134-1831-1 : £9.95 B81-01043

746.44 — Embroidery. Samplers, *to 1979*

Fawdry, Marguerite. The book of samplers / Marguerite Fawdry, Deborah Brown. — Guildford : Lutterworth, 1980. — 157p : ill (some col.),ports ; 28cm
Ill on lining papers. — Bibliography: p156. — Includes index
ISBN 0-7188-2483-0 : £9.95 B81-01044

746.44 — Embroidery. Smocking — *Manuals*

Keay, Diana. Smocking / [text by Diana Keay] ; [diagrams by Jan Messent]. — London : Search Press, 1979. — 32p : ill(some col.) ; 17cm. — (Needle crafts ; 5)
Ill on inside front cover
ISBN 0-85532-412-0 (pbk) : Unpriced B81-11602

746.44 — English embroidery: Overlord Embroidery. Military aspects

Jewell, Brian, *1925-*. Conquest & Overlord. — Speldhurst : Midas, June 1981. — 1v.
ISBN 0-85936-247-7 (pbk) : £4.95 : CIP entry
Primary classification 746.3944 B81-14462

746.44 — Peruvian embroidery. Cross-stitch — *Patterns*

Jessen, Ellen. Peruvian designs for cross-stitch / Ellen Jessen. — New York ; London : Van Nostrand Reinhold, 1980. — 64p : ill(some col.) ; 20x26cm
Bibliography: p64
ISBN 0-442-21926-1 (pbk) : £5.20 B81-21170

746.44 — Shisha mirror embroidery — *Manuals*

Simpson, Jean, *1942-*. Shisha mirror embroidery : a contemporary approach / Jean Simpson ; photographs by Don Rasmussen ; illustrations by Gwenn Stutzman. — New York ; London : Van Nostrand Reinhold, 1978 (1981 [printing]). — 104p : ill(some col.) ; 28cm
Includes index
ISBN 0-442-27645-1 (pbk) : £8.45 B81-37782

746.44'028 — Machine embroidery — *Manuals*

Phillpott, Pat. Machine embroidery / [text and drawings by Pat Phillpott]. — London : Search, 1980. — 32p : ill(some col.) ; 17cm. — (Needle crafts ; 12)
Ill on inside cover
ISBN 0-85532-429-5 (pbk) : £0.75 B81-02929

746.44'041 — Danish embroidery. Floral designs — *Patterns*

Bengtsson, Gerda. Danish floral charted designs. — [Rev. and enl. ed.] / Gerda Bengtsson. — New York : Dover Publications ; London : Constable, c1980. — v,25p : chiefly ill ; 28cm
Previous ed.: published as Danish embroidery / Haandarbejdets Fremme. London : Batsford, 1959
ISBN 0-486-23957-8 (pbk) : £0.85 B81-09852

746.44'041 — Embroidery — *Patterns*

Gostelow, Mary. Mary Gostelow's book of embroidery projects / with photographs by Martin Gostelow. — Newton Abbot : David & Charles, c1981. — 149p : ill(some col.),ports (some col.) ; 26cm
Includes index
ISBN 0-7153-7890-2 : £7.95 B81-14747

Zimiles, Martha Rogers. Iron-on transfers : from A treasury of needlework designs / Martha Rogers Zimiles. — Iron-on-transfer ed. — New York ; London : Van Nostrand Reinhold, 1980, c1976. — 14,[41]leaves of plates : ill ; 28cm
Previous ed.: published as A treasury of needlework designs. 1976. — Includes index
ISBN 0-442-23119-9 (pbk) : £7.45 B81-21409

746.44′041 — Hungarian embroidery. Designs — *Patterns*

Szalavary, Anne. Hungarian folk designs : for embroiderers and craftsmen / Anne Szalavary. — New York : Dover Publications ; London : Constable, 1980. — vii,119p : chiefly ill,1map ; 29cm. — (Dover pictorial archive series)
ISBN 0-486-23969-1 (pbk) : £2.20 B81-09853

746.44′041 — Swedish embroidery. Cross-stitch - *Patterns*

Counted cross-stitch patterns and designs. — London : Bell & Hyman, July 1981. — [72]p
Translation of: Korsstygns boken
ISBN 0-7135-1276-8 (pbk) : £4.50 : CIP entry B81-14397

746.44′042 — Embroidery. Stitches — *Manuals*

Messent, Jan. Stitchery / [text and drawings by Jan Messent]. — London : Search Press, 1979. — 32p : ill(some col.) ; 17cm. — (Needle crafts ; 6)
Ill on inside front cover
ISBN 0-85532-413-9 (pbk) : Unpriced B81-11601

746.44′09 — Embroidery, *to 1979*

Clabburn, Pamela. Masterpieces of embroidery / Pamela Clabburn. — Oxford : Phaidon, 1981. — 80p : ill(some col.),1port ; 28cm
ISBN 0-7148-2046-6 (pbk) : £6.95 : CIP rev. B80-08320

746.44′092′4 — British embroidery. Jekyll, Gertrude — *Biographies*

Edwards, Joan. Gertrude Jekyll, embroiderer, gardener and artist. — Dorking (P.O. Box 10, Dorking, Surrey, RH4 2JB) : Bayford Books, Nov.1981. — [24]p. — (Joan Edwards′ small books on the history of embroidery ; 4)
ISBN 0-907287-03-4 (pbk) : £1.40 : CIP entry B81-30477

746.44′0941 — Great Britain. Embroidery, *1900-1950*

Edwards, Joan. Chronicle of embroidery 1900-1950 : the third of Joan Edwards′ small books on the history of embroidery. — Dorking (P.O. Box 10, Dorking, Surrey RH4 2JB) : Bayford Books, c1980. — 20p : ill ; 21cm
Cover title
ISBN 0-907287-02-6 (pbk) : £1.40 B81-28333

746.44′0947 — Soviet folk embroidery

Klimova, Nina T.. Folk embroidery of the USSR / Nina T. Klimova. — New York ; London : Van Nostrand Reinhold, c1981. — 128p,[8]p of plates : ill(some col.) ; 29cm
Includes index
ISBN 0-442-24464-9 : £14.95 B81-26034

746.44′095 — Oriental embroidery

Chung, Young Yang. The art of oriental embroidery : history, aesthetics, and techniques / Young Yang Chung ; drawings by the author ; photographs by Jung Ae Lee ... [et al.]. — London : Bell & Hyman, 1980, c1979. — 183p,[16]p of plates : ill(some col.),ports ; 32cm
Originally published: New York : Scribner 1979. — Bibliography: p175-178. — Includes index
ISBN 0-7135-1205-9 : £11.50 B81-18315

746.44′2 — Canvas embroidery — *Manuals*

Windrum, Sarah. Needlepoint / Sarah Windrum. — London : Octopus, 1980. — 80p : ill(some col.) ; 29cm
Col. ill on lining papers. — Includes index
ISBN 0-7064-1346-6 : £2.95 B81-01045

746.44′2 — Canvas embroidery. Oriental designs — *Patterns*

Brent, Eva. Oriental designs in needlepoint / Eva Brent. — London : Routledge & Kegan Paul, 1981, c1979. — 127p,[8]p of plates : ill(some col.) ; 28cm
Originally published: New York : Simon and Schuster, 1979. — Bibliography: p127
ISBN 0-7100-0714-0 (pbk) : £6.95 B81-27899

746.44′2041 — Canvas embroidery. Designs based on Oriental rugs — *Patterns*

Sorensen, Grethe. Needlepoint designs from Oriental rugs / Grethe Sorensen ; drawings by the author ; photography by Lloyd Rule and Richard Baume. — London : Collins, 1981. — 90p,[16]p of plates : ill(some col.) ; 32cm
Bibliography: p90
ISBN 0-00-411678-x : £8.95 B81-39556

746.44′5 — Appliqué — *Manuals*

Patchwork and appliqué / [edited by Sarah Parr] ; [text compiled by Pamela Tubby]. — London : Marshall Cavendish, 1977 (1979 printing). — 140p : col.ill ; 29cm
Includes index
ISBN 0-85685-752-1 (pbk) : £1.99
Also classified at 746.46 B81-19571

746.44′5 — Appliqué: Mola — *Manuals*

Auld, Rhoda L.. Molas : what they are : how to make them : ideas they suggest for creative appliqué / Rhoda L. Auld ; photographs by Lawrence Auld. — New York ; London : Van Nostrand Reinhold, 1977 (1980 [printing]). — 112p,[8]p of plates : ill(some col.),2maps ; 28cm
Bibliography: p109-110. - Includes index
ISBN 0-442-20050-1 (pbk) : £7.45 B81-02955

746.46 — Patchwork — *Manuals*

Brondolo, Barbara. Small patchwork projects : with step-by-step instructions and full-size templates / Barbara Brondolo. — New York : Dover ; London : Constable, 1981. — 28p,24leaves of plates : ill(some col.) ; 28cm
Ill on inside covers
ISBN 0-486-24030-4 (pbk) : £3.35 B81-40296

Fairfield, Helen. Patchwork / Helen Fairfield. — London : Octopus, 1980. — 80p : ill(some col.) ; 29cm
Col. ill on lining papers. — Includes index
ISBN 0-7064-1344-x : £2.95 B81-01046

Patchwork and appliqué / [edited by Sarah Parr] ; [text compiled by Pamela Tubby]. — London : Marshall Cavendish, 1977 (1979 printing). — 140p : col.ill ; 29cm
Includes index
ISBN 0-85685-752-1 (pbk) : £1.99
Primary classification 746.44′5 B81-19571

746.46 — Quilting — *Manuals*

McNeill, Moyra. Quilting / Moyra McNeill. — London : Octopus, 1980. — 80p : ill(some col.) ; 29cm
Col. ill on lining papers. — Includes index
ISBN 0-7064-1345-8 : £2.95 B81-01047

Svennås, Elsie. Advanced quilting / Elsie Svennås ; translated from the Swedish by Richard and Lena Fleming. — London : Evans, 1980. — 143p : ill(some col.) ; 26cm
Translation of: Applikation-lappteknik quilting
ISBN 0-237-45509-9 : £6.95 : CIP rev. B80-18446

746.46 — Strip patchwork. Seminole techniques — *Manuals*

Dudley, Taimi. Strip patchwork : quick and easy patchwork using the Seminole technique / Taimi Dudley. — New York ; London : Van Nostrand Reinhold, c1980. — 128p,[4]p of plates : ill(some col.) ; 29cm
Bibliography: p124-125. — Includes index
ISBN 0-442-20400-0 : £12.70 B81-07223

746.46′041 — Patchwork. Patterns. Design — *Manuals*

Solvit, Marie-Janine. Magnificent patchwork / Marie-Janine Solvit. — London : Search, 1981. — 140p : col.ill ; 26cm
Translation of: 50 modèles de patchwork. — Bibliography: p140
ISBN 0-85532-447-3 : Unpriced B81-25276

746.46′05 — Quilting — *Serials*

[Newsletter *(Quilters′ Guild)*]. Newsletter / the Quilters′ Guild. — No.1 (Winter 1979)-. — Cambridge (13 Orchard St., Cambridge CB1 1JS) : The Guild, 1979-. — v. : ill ; 21cm
Quarterly
ISSN 0261-7420 = Newsletter - Quilters′ Guild : £1.00 per issue (Free to Guild members) B81-32892

746.46′09 — Quilting, *to 1970*

Colby, Averil. Quilting / Averil Colby. — London : Batsford, 1978, c1972. — 212p : ill ; 25cm
Bibliography: p201-210. — Includes index
ISBN 0-7134-2665-9 (pbk) : £5.95 B81-09791

746.46′0973 — American quilts

Hinson, Dolores A.. Quilting manual / Dolores A. Hinson ; drawings by the author. — Rev. and enl. ed. — New York : Dover ; London : Constable, 1980, c1970. — 192p : ill ; 24cm
Previous ed.: New York : Heathside Press, 1966. — Includes index
ISBN 0-486-23924-1 (pbk) : £1.90 B81-04572

746.5 — BEADWORK

746.5′09 — Beadwork, *to 1929*

Clabburn, Pamela. Beadwork / Pamela Clabburn. — Aylesbury : Shire, 1980. — 32p : ill,1facsim ; 21cm. — (Shire album ; 57)
Bibliography: p32
ISBN 0-85263-529-x (pbk) : £0.95 B81-07861

746.5′09669 — New York *(City)*. **Art galleries: Pace Gallery. Exhibits: Yoruba beadwork —** *Catalogues*

Fagg, William. Yoruba beadwork : art of Nigeria / by William Fagg ; edited and with a foreword by Bryce Holcombe ; descriptive catalogue by John Pemberton. — London : Lund Humphries, 1981, c1980. — 99p : ill (some col.),1map ; 23cm
Published to accompany an exhibition held at the Pace Gallery, New York. — Originally published: New York : Rizzoli in cooperation with Pace Gallery, 1980. — Bibliography: p93-95
ISBN 0-85331-443-8 (pbk) : £6.95 B81-12189

746.6 — TEXTILE HANDICRAFTS. PRINTING AND DYEING

746.6 — Dyeing. Plant dyes — *Amateurs′ manuals*

Goodwin, Jill. A dyer′s manual. — London : Pelham, Feb.1982. — [160]p
ISBN 0-7207-1327-7 : £8.50 : CIP entry B81-35849

746.6 — Fabrics. Dyeing & printing — *Amateurs′ manuals*

Allen, Janet, *1937-*. Colour craft / Janet Allen. — London : Hamlyn, 1980. — 172p : ill(some col.) ; 26cm
Ill on lining papers. — Includes index
ISBN 0-600-32200-9 : £5.95 B81-04914

Johnston, Meda Parker. Design on fabrics / Meda Parker Johnston, Glen Kaufman. — 2nd ed. — New York ; London : Van Nostrand Reinhold, 1981. — 173p,[4]p of plates : ill (some col.) ; 29cm
Previous ed.: New York : Reinhold, 1967. — Bibliography: p169-170. — Includes index
ISBN 0-442-26339-2 (cased) : £11.20
ISBN 0-442-23145-8 (pbk) : Unpriced B81-25362

Robinson, Stuart. Beginner′s guide to fabric dyeing and printing. — London : Newnes Technical Books, Feb.1982. — [192]p
ISBN 0-408-00575-0 (pbk) : £3.60 : CIP entry B81-36375

746.6′64 — Fabrics. Tie-dying

Itō, Toshiko. Tsujigahana : the flower of Japanese textile art. — London (10 Parkfields, SW15 6NH) : Serindia Publications, Sept.1981. — [202]p
Translation of: Tsujigahanazome
ISBN 0-906026-09-1 : £115.00 (£95.00 pre-publication) : CIP entry B81-23897

746.7 — TEXTILE HANDICRAFTS. RUGS AND CARPETS

746.7 — Rag rugs

Wiseman, Ann. [Rag tapestries and wool mosaics]. Rug hooking and rag tapestries / Ann Wiseman. — New York ; London : Van Nostrand Reinhold, 1980, c1969. — 100p : ill (some col.) ; 21cm
Originally published: 1969
ISBN 0-442-20658-5 (pbk) : £5.95 B81-21410

746.7 — Rag rugs. Making — *Manuals*

Pearse, Nora. Rag rugs / [text by Nora Pearse, Charis Mostart, Beryl Greenup] ; [diagrams by Jan Messent]. — London : Search, 1980. — 32p : ill(some col.),17cm ; pbk. — (Needle crafts ; 10)
Ill on inside cover
ISBN 0-85532-427-9 : £0.75 B81-02928

746.7′2 — Hand woven rugs. Making — *Manuals*

Knight, Brian. Rug weaving : technique and design / Brian Knight. — London : Batsford, 1980. — 144p,[4]p of plates : ill(some col.) ; 26cm
Bibliography: p142. — Includes index
ISBN 0-7134-2582-2 : £7.95 B81-00206

Mattera, Joanne. Rugweaving : techniques for two-harness / Joanne Mattera. — London : Batsford, 1980, c1979. — 215p : ill(some col.) ; 29cm
Originally published: New York : Watson-Guptill, 1979. — Bibliography: p202-205. — Includes index
ISBN 0-8230-4615-x : £12.50 B81-00207

746.7′2′095495 — Maldivian woven mats

Forbes, Andrew. Weaving in the Maldive Islands, Indian Ocean : the fine mat industry of Suvadiva Atoll (illustrated by mats held in the collection of the Museum of Mankind) / Andrew Forbes and Fawzia Ali. — London (Great Russell St., WC1B 3DG) : British Museum, 1980. — 35,[24]p : ill,map,ports ; 30cm. — (Occasional paper / British Museum, ISSN 0142-4815 no.9)
ISBN 0-86159-008-2 (pbk) : £1.50 B81-04916

746.7′4 — Rugs. Canvas embroidery. Designs — *Manuals*

Kaestner, Dorothy. Designs for needlepoint and latch hook rugs / Dorothy Kaestner ; photographs by George F. Kaestner. — London : Bell & Hyman in association with Scribners, c1978. — xi,177p,[16]p of plates : chiefly ill (some col.) ; 31cm
Bibliography: p177
ISBN 0-684-14837-4 : £8.50 B81-18458

746.7′5 — Oriental rugs

Jerrehian, Aram K.. [Oriental rug primer]. New oriental rugs / by Aram K. Jerrehian, Jr. — London : Ward Lock, 1981, c1980. — 223p : ill(some col.),maps ; 27cm
Originally published: New York : Facts on File, 1980. — Bibliography: p206-209. — Includes index
ISBN 0-7063-6149-0 : £7.95 B81-39958

746.7′5 — Oriental rugs — *Collectors′ guides*

Bennett, Ian. Oriental rugs. — Woodbridge : Antique Collectors′ Club
Vol.1: Caucasian. — Sept.1981. — 1v.
ISBN 0-902028-58-8 : £27.50 : CIP entry B81-25662

Bosly, Caroline. Rugs to riches : an insider′s guide to oriental rugs / Caroline Bosly. — London : Allen & Unwin, 1981. — 247p,8p of plates : ill(some col.),maps ; 24cm
Bibliography: p243. — Includes index
ISBN 0-04-746014-8 : Unpriced : CIP rev. B81-13773

746.7′51 — Chinese carpets & rugs

Hackmack, Adolf. Chinese carpets and rugs / by Adolf Hackmack ; translation by L. Arnold. — Rutland, Vt. : Tuttle ; London : Prentice-Hall [distributor], 1980. — xiii,48p,[28]leaves of plates : ill(some col.),1map ; 27cm
Translation of: Der chinesische Teppich. — Originally published: Tientsin : La Libraire française, 1924. — Includes index
ISBN 0-8048-1258-6 : £10.50 B81-28471

746.7′58 — Turkoman carpets

Loges, Werner. Turkoman tribal rugs / Werner Loges ; translated by Raoul Tschebull. — London : Allen & Unwin, 1980. — 204p : col.ill,maps ; 28cm
Translations and revision of Turkmenische Teppiche. — Map on lining papers. — Bibliography: p204
ISBN 0-04-746013-x : Unpriced : CIP rev. B80-07005

746.7′58 — West Germany. Franconia. Private collections: Turkoman carpets

Hoffmeister, Peter. Turkoman carpets in Franconia / Peter Hoffmeister ; edited with notes by A.S.B. Crosby = Turkmenische Teppiche in Franken / Peter Hoffmeister ; herausgeben mit Anmerkungen von A.S.B. Crosby. — Edinburgh (PO Box 510, Edinburgh EH10 4TA) : Crosby Press, 1980. — 105p : ill (some col.) ; 34cm
Text in English and German. — Bibliography: p102-103
ISBN 0-903580-45-4 : Unpriced : CIP rev. B79-31914

746.7951 — Chinese carpets

Gans-Ruedin, E.. Chinese carpets. — London : Allen & Unwin, Jan.1982. — [198]p
ISBN 0-04-746015-6 : £30.00 : CIP entry B81-33906

746.9 — TEXTILE HANDICRAFTS. COSTUME, FURNISHINGS, ETC

746.9 — Textile child care equipment. Making — *Manuals*

Argent, Jeanne. Things to make for children / Jeanne Argent. — London : Studio Vista, 1979. — 64p : col.ill ; 29cm. — (Creative sewing)
ISBN 0-289-70829-x : £2.95 B81-07700

746.9′2 — Fashion design. Techniques — *Amateurs′ manuals*

Creative dressing : the unique collection of top designer looks that you can make yourself / [compiled by] Kaori O′Connor. — London : Routledge & Kegan Paul, 1980. — 192p : ill (some col.) ; 28cm
ISBN 0-7100-0680-2 : £8.95 : CIP rev.
Primary classification 646.4 B80-20818

Creative dressing : the unique collection of top designer looks that you can make yourself / [compiled by] Kaori O′Connor. — Harmondsworth : Penguin, 1981, c1980. — 192p : ill(some col.),ports(some col.) ; 27cm
Originally published: London : Routledge & Kegan Paul. 1980
ISBN 0-14-046437-9 (pbk) : £4.95
Primary classification 646.4 B81-40480

746.9′2 — Fashion design. Techniques — *Manuals*

Turnpenny, John M.. Fashion design & illustration / John M. Turnpenny. — London : Hutchinson, 1981. — 96p : ill ; 30cm
ISBN 0-09-143521-8 (pbk) : £7.50
Also classified at 741.67′2 B81-26902

746.9′2 — Fashion — *Serials*

Bailey and Litchfield′s ritz newspaper. — No.1 (1976)-. — London (17 Maiden Lane WC2) : Bailey Litchfield Productions, 1976-. — v. : ill ; 42cm
Monthly. — Description based on: No.42 (June 1980)
ISSN 0144-7416 = Bailey and Litchfield′s ritz newspaper : £0.50 per issue B81-03838

746.9′2 — Great Britain. Women′s clothing. Fashion design, *ca 1900-1980*

Bond, David. The Guinness guide to 20th century fashion. — Enfield : Guinness Superlatives Ltd., Oct.1981. — [224]p
ISBN 0-85112-234-5 : £10.95 : CIP entry B81-25829

746.9′2 — Handspun woollen clothing. Knitting — *Patterns*

Ross, Lynn. Knitting patterns for handspun wool / by Lynn Ross. — Rev. ed. — Isle of Arran (Whiting Bay, Isle of Arran, Scotland) : Silverbirch Workshop, 1979. — 15p : ill ; 21cm
Previous ed.: 1978. — Bibliography: p15
Unpriced (pbk) B81-09630

746.9′2 — Women′s clothing. Knitting — *Patterns*

Sanford, Maxine. Romantic knitwear / Maxine Sanford. — London : Barker, c1980. — 62p : ill ; 24cm
ISBN 0-213-16751-4 (cased) : £4.25
ISBN 0-213-16757-3 (pbk) : £2.50 B81-04045

746.9′2′0922 — Fashion designers, *1780-1980* — *Biographies*

Carter, Ernestine. Magic names of fashion / Ernestine Carter. — London : Weidenfeld and Nicolson, 1980. — vii,226p : ill ; 25cm
Bibliography: p214-218. — Includes index
ISBN 0-297-77804-8 : £8.95 B81-01932

746.9′6 — Doilies. Tatting — *Patterns*

Tatting doilies & edgings / edited by Rita Weiss. — New York : Dover Publications ; London : Constable, c1980. — 47p : ill ; 28cm. — (Dover needlework series)
ISBN 0-486-24051-7 (pbk) : £1.10
Primary classification 746.43′6041 B81-09851

747 — INTERIOR DESIGN

747 — Residences. Interior design

Douglas, Peter. The Ideal home book of interiors. — Poole : Blandford Press, Sept.1981. — [120]p
ISBN 0-7137-1093-4 : £10.00 : CIP entry B81-23851

747 — Residences. Interior design — *Amateurs′ manuals*

The **Complete** book of decorating / edited by Corinne Benicka. — London : Hamlyn in association with Phoebus, 1980. — 255p : ill (some col.),plans ; 31cm
′This material first appeared in Das grosse praktische Einrichtungsbuch′ — title page verso. — Includes index
ISBN 0-600-30502-3 : £8.95
Also classified at 643′.7 B81-02423

Pressman, Andy. Integrated space systems : vocabulary for room language / by Andy Pressman and Peter Pressman. — New York ; London : Van Nostrand Reinhold, c1980. — 116p : ill,1facsim ; 22x28cm
Bibliography: p105. - Includes index
ISBN 0-442-23162-8 : £12.70
ISBN 0-442-23167-9 (pbk) : £7.45 B81-12601

747 — Residences. Interior design — *For schools*

Merrett, Joy. Furnishing, decoration and design / Joy Merrett. — Glasgow : Blackie, 1981. — 36p : ill ; 22cm. — (Home economics topic books)
Cover title
ISBN 0-216-90871-x (pbk) : Unpriced B81-08497

747 — Residences. Interior design. Use of plants

Muller-Idzerda, A. C.. Room for plants. — Newton Abbot : David & Charles, Oct.1981. — [144]p
Translation of: Groener wonen
ISBN 0-7153-8175-x : £6.95 : CIP entry B81-28051

747′.05 — Interior design — *Serials*

Decorative art and modern interiors. — Vol.69. — London : Studio Vista, c1980. — xii,188p
ISBN 0-289-70939-3 : £19.95
ISSN 0418-4858 B81-33933

747′.09181′2 — Western world. Residences. Interior design, *1924-1979* — *Interviews*

Brown, Erica. Interior views / Erica Brown ; introduction by Paul Goldberger. — London : Thames and Hudson, 1980. — 173p : col.ill,ports ; 29cm
ISBN 0-500-34085-4 : £11.95 B81-01697

747.2 — Interior design, *to 1699*

Ball, Victoria Kloss. Architecture and interior design : a basic history through the seventeenth century / Victoria Kloss Ball. — New York ; Chichester : Wiley, c1980. — xiii,448p,[16]p of plates : ill(some col.),plans ; 29cm
Bibliography: p411-418. - Includes index
ISBN 0-471-05162-4 (cased) : £24.00
ISBN 0-471-08719-x (pbk) : £13.50
Primary classification 720′.9 B81-05664

747.2'04 — Western world. Interior design, *1800-1980*
Ball, Victoria Kloss. Architecture and interior design : Europe and America from the Colonial Era to today / Victoria Kloss Ball. — New York ; Chichester : Wiley, c1980. — xvii,442p,[16]p of plates : ill(some col.),plans ; 29cm
Bibliography: p399-409. - Includes index
ISBN 0-471-05161-6 : £24.00
ISBN 0-471-08722-x (pbk) : Unpriced
Primary classification 724 B81-10607

747.2'049 — Dictionaries. Interior design, *1900-1980*
20th century decorating architecture & gardens : 80 years of ideas & pleasure from House & garden / book edited by Mary Jane Pool ; text edited & chapter introductions by Caroline Seebohm. — London : Weidenfeld & Nicolson, c1980. — 320p : ill(some col.),plans,ports ; 31cm
Includes index
ISBN 0-297-77878-1 : £15.00
Also classified at 728'.09'04 ; 712'.6'0904
B81-04065

747.2'0491 — Houses designed by Lutyens, *Sir* Edwin : Captain Day's house. Interior design — *Illustrations*
Lutyens, *Sir* Edwin. Lutyens and the sea captain. — London : Scolar Press, Nov.1981. — [40]p
ISBN 0-85967-646-3 : £5.95 (£4.95 until 31/12/81) : CIP entry B81-32011

747.22 — England. Residences. Interior design, *1819-1901*
Lasdun, Susan. Victorians at home / Susan Lasdun ; with an introduction by Mark Girouard. — London : Weidenfeld & Nicolson, c1981. — 160p : ill(some col.),ports ; 21cm
Ill on lining papers. — Includes index
ISBN 0-297-77942-7 : £9.95 B81-39950

747.22 — Great Britain. Residences. Interior design, *1500-1850*
Ayres, James. The Shell book of the home in Britain : decoration, design and construction of vernacular interiors, 1500-1850 / James Ayres. — London : Faber, 1981. — 253p,[8]p of plates : ill,1map ; 24cm
Bibliography: p225-230. - Includes index
ISBN 0-571-11625-6 : £8.95 B81-10598

747'.8521'0973 — United States. Shops. Interior design
The **Interiors** book of shops & restaurants / by the editors of Interiors magazine ; with commentaries by Pilar Viladas. — New York : Whitney Library of Design ; London : Architectural Press, 1981. — 144p : ill(some col.),plans ; 29cm
Includes index
ISBN 0-85139-327-6 : £12.00
Also classified at 747'.8571'0973 B81-32886

747'.8571'0973 — United States. Restaurants. Interior design
The **Interiors** book of shops & restaurants / by the editors of Interiors magazine ; with commentaries by Pilar Viladas. — New York : Whitney Library of Design ; London : Architectural Press, 1981. — 144p : ill(some col.),plans ; 29cm
Includes index
ISBN 0-85139-327-6 : £12.00
Primary classification 747'.8521'0973
B81-32886

747'.88'094 — Western Europe. Residences. Interior decoration, *1600-1700*
Thornton, Peter. Seventeenth century interior decoration in England, France and Holland. — London : Yale University Press, Sept.1981. — [439]p. — (Studies in British art)
Originally published: 1978
ISBN 0-300-02776-1 (pbk) : £9.95 : CIP entry
B81-28157

747'.883'0973 — United States. Houses. Interior design, *1837-1901 — Illustrations — For children*
Lewis, Daniel. The Victorian house coloring book / illustrated by Daniel Lewis ; written and researched by Kristin Helberg. — New York : Dover ; London : Constable, 1980. — 47p : ill (some col.) ; 28cm. — (Dover coloring book) (Dover pictorial archive series)
Ill on inside covers. — Bibliography: p47
ISBN 0-486-23908-x (pbk) : £1.30 B81-07162

747'.9 — Residences. Interior design. Use of photographs — *Amateurs' manuals*
Morrison, Alex. Photofinish / Alex Morrison. — London : Joseph, 1981. — 144p : ill(some col.) ; 29cm
Includes index
ISBN 0-7181-1955-x (pbk) : £6.50 B81-07067

747'.98 — Buildings. Interior design. Use of plants
Scrivens, Stephen. Interior planting in large buildings : a handbook for architects, interior designers, and horticulturists / Stephen Scrivens with contributions from Leo Pemberton ... [et al.]. — London : Architectural Press, 1980. — 129p : ill(some col.),1map,1port ; 31cm
Includes index
ISBN 0-85139-320-9 : £18.95 B81-03123

748 — HANDICRAFTS. GLASS

748.2'028'2 — Handicrafts: Glass-blowing
Littleton, Harvey K.. Glassblowing : a search for form / Harvey K. Littleton. — New York ; London : Van Nostrand Reinhold, 1980, c1971. — 173p : ill(some col.) ; 26cm
Bibliography: p142. — Includes index
ISBN 0-442-24341-3 (pbk) : £8.95 B81-17183

748.29'049 — Glassware, *1890-1930 — Collectors' guides*
Bangert, Albrecht. Glass : art nouveau and art deco / Albrecht Bangert. — London : Studio Vista, c1979. — 160p : ill(some col.),col.map,ports(some col.) ; 20cm. — (Christie's South Kensington collectors guides)
Bibliography: p153-155. — Includes index
ISBN 0-289-70868-0 : £4.95 B81-02864

748.292 — British glassware, *1837-1901*
Manley, Cyril. Decorative Victorian glass. — London : Ward Lock, June 1981. — [128]p
ISBN 0-7063-5966-6 : £17.95 : CIP entry
B81-12841

748.292 — British glassware, *ca 1700-ca 1900 — Collectors' guides*
Brooks, John. The Arthur Negus guide to British glass / John Brooks ; foreword by Arthur Negus ; consultant editor Arthur Negus. — London : Hamlyn, c1981. — 176p : ill(some col.),facsims,2ports ; 25cm
Bibliography: p174. — Includes index
ISBN 0-600-34218-2 : £5.95 B81-40938

748.5'028'2 — Glass. Painting. Techniques
Elskus, Albinas. The art of painting on glass. — London : Routledge & Kegan Paul, July 1981. — [147]p
Originally published: New York : Scribner, 1980
ISBN 0-7100-0906-2 : £10.00 : CIP entry
B81-13722

748.59 — Coloured glassware, *to 1935*
Middlemas, Keith. [Antique glass in color]. Antique coloured glass / Keith Middlemas. — London ([24 Friern Park, N12 9DA]) : Ferndale, 1979, c1971. — 120p : col.ill ; 31cm
Originally published: Garden City, N.Y. : Doubleday ; London : Barrie & Jenkins, 1971
ISBN 0-905746-04-x : £10.50 B81-35518

748.5913 — American stained glass windows. Tiffany, Louis Comfort, *ca 1890-ca 1930 — Critical studies*
Duncan, Alastair. Tiffany windows / Alastair Duncan. — [London] : Thames and Hudson, c1980. — 224p : ill(some col.),1port ; 32cm
Bibliography: p196-199
ISBN 0-500-23321-7 : £20.00 B81-05428

748.592 — England. Churches. Stained glass windows, *ca 760-1979*
Osborne, June. Stained glass in England / June Osborne. — London : Muller, 1981. — 224p : col.ill ; 22cm
Bibliography: p104. - Includes index
ISBN 0-584-97293-8 : £9.95 B81-19756

748.592'23 — Kent. Churches. Lost painted glass
Councer, C. R.. Lost glass from Kent churches : a collection of records from the sixteenth to the twentieth century / by C.R. Councer. — Maidstone (c/o The Museum, St. Faith St., Maidstone, Kent) : Archaeological Society, 1980. — xvi,170p : ill(some col.),coats of arms,geneal.tables ; 23cm. — (Kent records ; v.22)
Includes index
ISBN 0-85033-386-5 : £16.00 B81-19867

748.592'91443 — Scottish stained glass: Strathclyde Region stained glass: Glaswegian stained glass, *1870-1914 — Critical studies*
Donnelly, Michael. Glasgow stained glass : a preliminary study / by Michael Donnelly. — [Glasgow] : Glasgow Museums and Art Galleries, 1981. — 36p : ill(some col.),1port ; 21x22cm
Accompanies an exhibition at the People's Palace Museum, Glasgow, April 1981-April 1982
ISBN 0-902752-12-x (pbk) : Unpriced
B81-25230

748.5994 — Europe. Religious buildings. Stained glass windows. Special subjects: Jesus Christ. Nativity
Halliday, Sonia. The Christmas story in stained glass / photographs by Sonia Halliday and Laura Lushington. — Tring : Lion Publishing, 1980. — [32]p : chiefly col.ill ; 22cm
ISBN 0-85648-291-9 : £1.95 B81-05016

748.5994 — Europe. Stained glass windows. Special subjects: Seasons — *Illustrations*
Halliday, Sonia. The seasons in stained glass / photographs by Sonia Halliday and Laura Lushington. — Tring : Lion Publishing, 1981. — [32]p : chiefly col.ill ; 22cm
ISBN 0-85648-351-6 : £1.95 B81-38203

748.6 — Handicrafts: Glass engraving — *Manuals*
Norman, Barbara, *19---*. Glass engraving / Barbara Norman ; foreword by David Pearce. — Newton Abbot : David & Charles, c1981. — 190p,[48]p of plates : ill ; 25cm
Bibliography: p184. — Includes index
ISBN 0-7153-8027-3 : £8.95 : CIP rev.
B81-03173

748.8'2'094 — European sealed bottles, *1630-1930 — Collectors' guides*
Morgan, Roy. Sealed bottles : their history and evolution (1630-1930) / by Roy Morgan ; researched by Roy Morgan & Gordon Litherland ; editor Andy Payne. — 2nd ed. — Southampton (80 Northam Rd, Southampton) : Southern Collectors Publications, 1980. — 102p : ill,2ports ; 21cm
Previous ed.: Burton-on-Trent : Midlands Antique Bottle Publishing, 1977. — Bibliography: p95. — Includes index
ISBN 0-905438-18-3 (pbk) : £2.95 B81-01048

748.8'2'0941 — British bottles, *1837-1901 — Collectors' guides*
Stockton, John. Victorian bottles : a collector's guide to yesterday's empties / John Stockton. — Newton Abbot : David & Charles, c1981. — 192p : ill,facsims ; 24cm
Bibliography: p189. — Includes index
ISBN 0-7153-8141-5 : 12.50 B81-29728

749 — FURNITURE AND ACCESSORIES

749'.1 — Great Britain. Residences. Interiors. Antique furniture
Shearing, Graham. Antique furniture on a budget : a practical guide to furnishing your home / Graham Shearing. — London : Ebury, 1980. — 160p : ill,1chart ; 25cm
Text on lining paper. — Bibliography: p158. — Includes index
ISBN 0-85223-149-0 : £5.95 B81-01949

749'.1'0288 — Antique furniture. Restoration — *Amateurs' manuals*
Hook, Albert G. [The work of restoration of antique furniture]. Antique furniture : its recognition and restoration / by Albert G. Hook. — [Fontwell] : Centaur, 1981, c1976. — iv,94p : ill ; 21cm
Originally published: Hove : Lockholt, 1976
ISBN 0-900001-15-1 (pbk) : £2.50 B81-38120

749'.1'0288 — Antique furniture. Restoration — *Amateurs' manuals* *continuation*

Smith, Mike, *1938-*. As good as new / Mike Smith. — London : ITV Books in association with Yorkshire Television, 1981. — 109p : ill ; 20cm
ISBN 0-900727-84-5 (pbk) : £1.50 B81-15718

749.2 — Furniture, *to 1918*

World furniture : an illustrated history from earliest times / edited by Helena Hayward. — London : Hamlyn, c1965 (1981 [printing]). — 320p,[28]p of plates : ill(some col.),ports(some col.) ; 34cm
Bibliography: p312. — Includes index
ISBN 0-600-34262-x (pbk) : £6.95 B81-40807

749.2 — Western furniture, *to 1980*

Oates, Phyllis Bennett. The story of Western furniture / Phyllis Bennett Oates ; illustrated by Mary Seymour. — London (65 Belsize La., NW3 5AU) : Herbert Press, 1981. — 253p : ill,maps,plans ; 26cm
Bibliography: p243-244. - Includes index
ISBN 0-906969-09-3 : £8.95 B81-22265

749.2'04 — Furniture, *1830-1980*

Gandy, Charles D.. Contemporary classics : furniture of the masters / Charles D. Gandy, Susan Zimmermann-Stidham. — New York ; London : McGraw-Hill, c1981. — xi,177p : ill,ports ; 25cm
Bibliography: p169-171. — Includes index
ISBN 0-07-022760-8 : £13.95 B81-23673

749.2'049 — Furniture. Designs, *1900-1978*

Garner, Philippe. Twentieth-century furniture / Philippe Garner. — Oxford : Phaidon, 1980. — 224p : ill(some col.),ports ; 31cm
Bibliography: p220. - Includes index
ISBN 0-7148-2133-0 : £14.95 B81-02260

749.213 — American furniture. Phyfe, Duncan — *Critical studies*

McClelland, Nancy. Duncan Phyfe and the English Regency 1795-1830 / by Nancy McClelland ; with a foreword by Edward Knoblock. — New York : Dover ; London : Constable, 1980. — xxix,364p : ill,facsims,ports,geneal.tables ; 24cm
Originally published: New York : W.R. Scott, 1939. — Bibliography: p341-346. - Includes index
ISBN 0-486-23988-8 (pbk) : £4.75 B81-04119

749.2148 — Pennsylvania Dutch furniture

Shea, John G.. The Pennsylvania Dutch and their furniture / John G. Shea. — New York ; London : Van Nostrand Reinhold, c1980. — 226p : ill ; 29cm
Bibliography: p219-222. — Includes index
ISBN 0-442-27546-3 : £14.95 B81-17184

749.22 — English furniture, *1500-1910*

Bly, John. Discovering English furniture / John Bly. — Combined and rev. ed. — Aylesbury : Shire, c1976 (1981 [printing]). — 199p : ill,facsims ; 18cm. — (Discovering series ; no.223)
Previous ed.: published as Discovering English furniture 1500-1720 ; and, Discovering English furniture 1720-1830. 1971. Discovering Victorian and Edwardian furniture. 1973. — Includes index
ISBN 0-85263-359-9 (pbk) : £2.50 B81-21216

Learoyd, Stan. English furniture : construction and decoration 1500-1910 / Stan Learoyd. — London : Evans, 1981. — 128p : ill(some col.) ; 20x26cm
Ill on lining papers. — Includes index
ISBN 0-237-45515-3 : £8.75 : CIP rev.
B81-02362

749.2'2 — English furniture. Russell, Sir Gordon - *Biographies*

Baynes, Ken. Gordon Russell. — London : Design Council, May 1981. — [64]p
ISBN 0-85072-119-9 (pbk) : £5.00 : CIP entry
B81-10003

749.236 — Thonet furniture — *Catalogues — Facsimiles*

Gebrüder Thonet. Thonet Bentwood & other furniture : the 1904 illustrated catalogue : with the 1905-6 and 1907 supplements and price lists in German and English / Thonet ; and with a new introduction by Christopher Wilk. — New York : Dover ; London : Constable, 1980. — 154,[64]p : ill,facsims ; 31cm
German text, English introduction. — Facsim of: ed. published Vienna : Thonet, 1904
ISBN 0-486-24024-x (pbk) : £5.00 B81-15625

749.24'074'02132 — London. Westminster *(London Borough)*. **Art galleries: Wallace Collection. Exhibits: French furniture,** *ca 1640-1820*

De Bellaigue, Geoffrey. Preferences in French furniture / by Geoffrey de Bellaigue. — London (Manchester Sq., W1M 6BN) : Wallace Collection, 1979. — 40p : col.ill,1geneal.table ; 18cm. — (Wallace Collection monographs ; 2)
Unpriced (pbk) B81-32554

749.294 — European furniture, *1830-1910 — Buyers' guides*

Payne, Christopher. The price guide to 19th century European furniture, 1830-1910. — Woodbridge : Antique Collectors' Club, Oct.1981. — [550]p
ISBN 0-902028-91-x : £19.50 : CIP entry
B81-28013

749'.32 — English Windsor chairs, *to 1980*

Sparkes, Ivan G.. English Windsor chairs / Ivan G. Sparkes. — Princes Risborough : Shire, 1981. — 32p ; 21cm. — (Shire album ; 70)
Bibliography: p32
ISBN 0-85263-562-1 (pbk) : £0.95 B81-40859

749'.32'09034 — Chairs. Design, *1850-1960*

A **Century** of chair design / editor Frank Russell ; introduction Philippe Garner ; drawings John Read. — London : Academy Editions, 1980. — 160p : ill(some col.) ; 31cm
Bibliography: p156-157. — Includes index
£15.00 B81-02026

749'.7 — Picture frames. Making — *Amateurs' manuals*

Cope, Anne. Picture framing / John and Jane Cope ; photography by John Warren ; line drawings by Jane Cope. — London : Pan, 1981. — 103p : ill (some col.) ; 25cm. — (Pan craft books)
Includes index
ISBN 0-330-26346-3 (pbk) : £3.50 B81-22901

749'.7 — Pictures. Framing — *Manuals*

Dick, Pamela. Picture framing and mounting. — Rev. and enl. ed. — London : WI Books, Nov.1981. — [12]p
Previous ed.: London : National Federation of Women's Institutes, 1975
ISBN 0-900556-71-4 (pbk) : £0.65 : CIP entry
B81-33628

Wright-Smith, Rosamund. Picture framing / Rosamund Wright-Smith. — London : Orbis Publishing, c1980. — 128p : ill(some col.) ; 30cm
Bibliography: p125. — Includes index
ISBN 0-85613-051-6 : £5.95 B81-00208

750 — PAINTINGS

750'.1 — Paintings. Naturalism — *Quotations — Collections*

Bensusan-Butt, John. On naturalness in art : a lecture based on the sayings of painters and others, with a postscript on aesthetics and index of sources / by John Bensusan-Butt. — Colchester (31b Lexden Rd., Colchester, CO3 3PX) : J. Bensusan-Butt, 1981. — 63p : 1ill ; 22cm
Bibliography: p49-63. - Includes index
ISBN 0-9507464-0-1 (pbk) : £2.00 B81-21660

750'.1'8 — Paintings. Composition. Geometric aspects

Bouleau, Charles. The painter's secret geometry : a study of composition in art / Charles Bouleau ; with a preface by Jacques Villon ; [translated from the French by Jonathan Griffin]. — New York : Hacker Art ; London : Distributed by Art Book, 1980, c1963. — 268p : ill ; 25cm
Translation of: Charpentes, la géométrie secrète des peintres. — Originally published: New York : Harcourt, Brace & World ; London : Thames and Hudson, 1963. — Bibliography: p261-265. — Includes index
ISBN 0-87817-259-9 : £17.50 B81-05073

750'.28 — Activities using paints — *Manuals — For children*

McGlashon, Angela. Fun with paints and paper : 100 different things to do! / Angela McGlashon ; illustrated by Gillian Hurry. — London : Carousel, 1981. — 112p : ill ; 20cm
ISBN 0-552-54190-7 (pbk) : £0.85
Primary classification 745.54 B81-37346

750'.74'014967 — New Jersey. Princeton. Art galleries: Princeton University. *Art Museum.* **Exhibits: Paintings,** *1500-1979 — Catalogues*

Works on paper : Princeton alumni collections. — Princeton ; Guildford : Art Museum, Princeton University in association with Princeton University Press, c1981. — 261p : chiefly ill,ports ; 25cm
Published to accompany an exhibition held at the Art Museum, Princeton University, 1981
ISBN 0-691-03977-1 : £18.10
Also classified at 741'.074'014967 B81-37155

750'.74'02132 — London. Westminster *(London Borough)*. **Art galleries: Tate Gallery** *— Serials*

Tate Gallery. The Tate Gallery. — 1978-80. — London : The Gallery, 1980. — 104p
ISBN 0-905005-67-8 : £2.00 B81-10668

750'.74'02733 — Great Manchester *(Metropolitan County)*. **Manchester. Art galleries: Manchester City Art Gallery. Stock: Paintings,** *to ca 1955 — Catalogues*

Manchester City Art Gallery. Concise catalogue of foreign paintings / Manchester City Art Gallery. — Manchester ([c/o Manchester City Art Gallery, Mosley St., Manchester 2]) : City of Manchester Cultural Services, 1980. — 124p : ill,ports ; 21cm
Includes index
ISBN 0-901673-16-1 (pbk) : Unpriced
B81-07530

750'.74'09492 — Netherlands. Art galleries. Exhibits: Oil paintings, *to 1870 — Lists*

Wright, Christopher, *1945-*. Paintings in Dutch museums : an index of oil paintings in public collections in the Netherlands by artists born before 1870 / compiled by Christopher Wright. — London : Sotheby Parke Bernet, 1980. — xxi,591p : 1map ; 22cm
Bibliography: p569-591
ISBN 0-85667-077-4 : £30.00 B81-03800

751 — PAINTINGS. MATERIALS, EQUIPMENT, TECHNIQUES, FORMS

751.4 — Landscape paintings. Techniques — *Manuals*

Crawshaw, Alwyn. Learn to paint landscapes / Alwyn Crawshaw. — Glasgow : Collins, 1981. — 64p : col.ill,1col.port ; 28cm
ISBN 0-00-411873-1 (pbk) : £3.75 B81-09326

751.4 — Paintings. Composition. Techniques

Malins, Frederick. Understanding paintings : the elements of composition / Frederick Malins. — Oxford : Phaidon, 1980. — 128p : ill(some col.),ports(some col.) ; 30cm
ISBN 0-7148-2114-4 (cased) : £8.95 : CIP rev.
ISBN 0-7148-2116-0 (pbk) : £5.25 B80-13484

751.4 — Paintings. Special subjects: Sky. Techniques — *Manuals*

Battershill, Norman. Painting & drawing skies / Norman Battershill ; with illustrations by the author. — London : Pitman, 1981. — 159p : ill (some col.) ; 29cm
Bibliography: p156. - Includes index
ISBN 0-273-01392-0 : £12.50
Also classified at 743'.836 B81-15987

751.4 — Paintings. Techniques — *Manuals*

Crabb, Thomas. Painting and drawing : a beginner's guide / Thomas Crabb. — London : Park Lane, 1981. — 80p : col.ill ; 28cm
Bibliography: p79. — Includes index
£0.95 (pbk)
Also classified at 741.2 B81-24926

Griffith, Thomas. A practical guide for beginning painters / Thomas Griffith. — Englewood Cliffs ; London : Prentice-Hall, c1981. — xiv,145p,[8]p of plates : ill(some col.),ports ; 29cm. — (The Art and design series) (A Spectrum book)
Bibliography: p137-140. — Includes index
ISBN 0-13-689513-1 (cased) : £12.95
ISBN 0-13-689505-0 (pbk) : £7.95 B81-19655

How to draw & paint / [consultant editor Stan Smith]. — London : Ebury, 1981. — 319p : ill (some col.),ports(some col.) ; 31cm. — (A Quarto book)
Includes index
ISBN 0-85223-182-2 : £12.95
Also classified at 741.2 B81-23703

751.4'09 — Paintings, *to 1979*. Techniques

Techniques of the world's great painters / consultant editor Waldemar Januszczak. — Oxford : Phaidon, c1980. — 192p : ill(some col.),ports ; 31cm. — (A QED book)
Includes index
ISBN 0-7148-2122-5 : £15.00 : CIP rev.
B80-23585

751.42'2 — Watercolour paintings. Detailing. Techniques — *Manuals*

Bolton, Richard. Painting detail in watercolour / Richard Bolton. — London : Search Press, 1981. — 32p : ill(some col.),1port ; 21cm. — (Leisure arts ; 9) (A Pentalic book)
Port on inside cover
ISBN 0-85532-440-6 (pbk) : Unpriced
B81-25243

751.42'2 — Watercolour paintings. Techniques — *Manuals*

Scott, Joan. Beginning watercolour / Joan Scott. — London : Warne, 1981. — 64p : ill(some col.) ; 22cm. — (An Observer's guide)
ISBN 0-7232-2464-1 (pbk) : £2.50 B81-21259

Shackelford, Bud. Experimental watercolor techniques / by Bud Shackelford. — New York : Watson-Guptill ; London : Pitman, 1980. — 144p : ill(some col.) ; 29cm
Bibliography: p143. - Includes index
ISBN 0-273-01622-9 : £12.95 B81-12565

751.42'242 — Miniature watercolour portrait paintings. Techniques — *Manuals — Early works*

Hilliard, Nicholas. A treatise concerning the arte of limning / by Nicholas Hilliard. together with A more compendious discourse concerning ye art of liming / by Edward Norgate ; with a parallel modernized text edited by R.K.R. Thornton and T.G.S. Cain. — Ashington : Mid Northumberland Arts Group in association with Carcanet New Press, 1981. — 139p : ill(some col.),facsims,ports (some col.) ; 23cm
Bibliography: p137-139
ISBN 0-85635-294-2 : £12.00 B81-15729

751.42'2434 — Watercolour paintings. Special subjects: Flowering plants. Techniques — *Manuals*

Coleridge, Sarah Jane. Painting flowers in watercolour / Sarah Jane Coleridge. — London : Search Press, 1981. — 32p : ill(some col.) ; 21cm. — (Leisure arts ; 6) (A Pentalic book)
ISBN 0-85532-405-8 (pbk) : Unpriced
B81-25247

Cooper, Mario. Flower painting in watercolour / Mario Cooper. — Rev. ed. — New York ; London : Van Nostrand Reinhold, 1980. — 144p : ill(some col.) ; 26cm
Previous ed.: 1972. — Includes index
ISBN 0-442-23137-7 (pbk) : £7.45 B81-17182

751.42'2436 — Watercolour landscape paintings. Special subjects: Trees. Techniques

Kautzky, Ted. Painting trees & landscapes in watercolour / Ted Kautzky. — New York ; London : Van Nostrand Reinhold, 1980, c1952. — 96p : ill(some col.) ; 25cm
Originally published: New York : Reinhold ; London : Chapman and Hall, 1952
ISBN 0-442-21918-0 (pbk) : £7.45 B81-21171

751.42'2436 — Watercolour landscape paintings. Techniques — *Manuals*

Burridge, Jan. Painting landscapes in watercolour / Jan Burridge. — London : Search Press, 1981. — 31p : ill(some col.),1port ; 21cm. — (Leisure arts ; 10) (A Pentalic book)
Port on inside cover
ISBN 0-85532-441-4 (pbk) : Unpriced
B81-25248

751.42'2437 — Watercolour seascape paintings. Techniques — *Manuals*

Blake, Wendon. Seascapes in watercolor / by Wendon Blake ; paintings by Claude Croney. — London : Pitman House, 1980. — 80p : ill (some col.) ; 28cm. — (The Artist's painting library)
Originally published: in The watercolor painting book
ISBN 0-273-01363-7 (pbk) : £2.95 B81-19527

Olsen, Herb. Painting the marine scene in watercolor / Herb Olsen. — New York ; London : Van Nostrand Reinhold, 1981, c1967. — 112p : ill(some col.) ; 31cm
Originally published: New York ; London : Reinhold, 1967. — Includes index
ISBN 0-442-26198-5 (pbk) : Unpriced
B81-31780

751.42'6 — Acrylic landscape paintings. Techniques — *Manuals*

Blake, Wendon. Landscapes in acrylic / by Wendon Blake ; paintings by Rudy de Reyna. — London : Pitman House, 1980. — 80p : ill (some col.) ; 28cm. — (The Artist's painting library)
Originally published: in The acrylic painting book
ISBN 0-273-01359-9 (pbk) : £2.95 B81-07385

751.45 — Oil paintings. Techniques — *Manuals*

Handell, Albert. Oil painting workshop / Albert Handell and Leslie Trainor. — New York : Watson-Guptill ; London : Pitman House, 1980. — 144p : ill(some col.) ; 29cm
Bibliography: p141. — Includes index
ISBN 0-273-01621-0 : £12.95 B81-07329

751.45'42 — Oil portrait paintings. Techniques — *Manuals*

Blake, Wendon. Portraits in oil / by Wendon Blake ; paintings by George Passantino. — London : Pitman House, 1980. — 80p : ill (some col.) ; 28cm. — (The Artist's painting library)
Originally published: in The portrait and figure painting book
ISBN 0-273-01361-0 (pbk) : £2.95 B81-07381

751.45'424 — Oil paintings. Special subjects: Women: Nudes. Techniques — *Manuals*

Blake, Wendon. Figures in oil / by Wendon Blake ; paintings by George Passantino. — London : Pitman House, 1980. — 80p ; ill (some col.) ; 28cm. — (The Artist's painting library)
Originally published: in The portrait and figure painting book
ISBN 0-273-01362-9 (pbk) : £2.95 B81-07384

751.45'425 — Oil portrait paintings. Special subjects: Children. Techniques — *Manuals*

Blake, Wendon. Children's portraits in oil / by Wendon Blake ; paintings by George Passantino. — London : Pitman House, 1980. — 80p : ill(some col.) ; 28cm. — (The Artist's painting library)
Originally published: in The portrait and figure painting book
ISBN 0-273-01366-1 (pbk) : £2.95 B81-07380

751.45'436 — Oil landscape paintings. Techniques — *Amateurs' manuals*

Carrington, Joanna. Landscape painting for beginners / Joanna Carrington. — London : Studio Vista, 1979. — 101p : ill(some col.) ; 20cm
Includes index
ISBN 0-289-70904-0 (pbk) : £1.95 B81-40925

751.45'437 — Oil seascape paintings. Techniques — *Manuals*

Blake, Wendon. Seascapes in oil / by Wendon Blake ; paintings by George Cherepov. — London : Pitman House, 1980. — 80p : ill (some col.) ; 28cm. — (The Artist's painting library)
Originally published: in The oil painting book
ISBN 0-273-01365-3 (pbk) : £2.95 B81-07382

751.4'94 — Airbrushing — *Manuals*

Curtis, Seng-gye Tombs. The airbrush book : art, history and technique / Seng-gye Tombs Curtis and Christopher Hunt. — London : Orbis Publishing, 1980. — 160p : ill(some col.),ports ; 29cm
Bibliography: p159. — Includes index
ISBN 0-85613-275-6 : £10.00 B81-05811

751.7'3'09396 — Central Asia. Sogdian wall paintings

Azarpay, Guitty. Sogdian painting : the pictorial epic in oriental art / Guitty Azarpy with contributions by A.M. Belenitskii, B.I. Marshak and Mark J. Dresden. — Berkeley [Calif.] ; London : University of California Press, c1981. — xxii,212p,[32]p of plates : ill (some col.),1map ; 29cm
Includes index
ISBN 0-520-03765-0 : £40.00 B81-39776

751.7'3'09455 — Italian murals: Tuscan murals, *ca 1300-1520*

Borsook, Eve. The mural painters of Tuscany : from Cimabue to Andrea del Sarto / Eve Borsook. — 2nd ed., rev. and enlarged. — Oxford : Clarendon, 1980. — lvii,158p,156p of plates : ill ; 32cm
Previous ed.: London : Phaidon, 1960. — Bibliography: p137-148. - Includes index
ISBN 0-19-817301-6 : £55.00 : CIP rev.
B79-13057

751.7'4 — Hampshire. Southampton. Art galleries: John Hansard Gallery. Exhibits: Panoramic paintings — *Catalogues*

The **Panoramic** image. — Southampton (University of Southampton, Highfield, Southampton SO9 5NH) : John Hansard Gallery, 1981. — 52p : ill ; 21x31cm
Bibliography: p32
ISBN 0-85432-211-6 (pbk) : Unpriced
Also classified at 778.3'6'07402276 B81-27737

751.7'5 — Theatre. Scenery. Painting. Techniques

Polunin, Vladimir. The continental method of scene painting / by Vladimir Polunin ; edited by Cyril W. Beaumont. — London : Dance Books, 1980. — xiii,84p,16 leaves of plates : ill,1plan ; 26cm
Originally published: London : C.W. Beaumont, 1927. — Includes index
ISBN 0-903102-57-9 : £8.95 B81-03229

751.7'7'07402134 — London. Kensington and Chelsea *(London Borough)*. Museums: Victoria and Albert Museum. Stock: Miniature paintings — *Catalogues*

Hall, Garth. Summary catalogue of miniatures in the Victoria and Albert Museum. — Haslemere (Thursley Hall, Haslemere, Surrey GU27 1HA) : Emmett Microform, Sept.1981. — [136]p
ISBN 0-907696-01-5 (pbk) : £3.95 : CIP entry
B81-28701

751.7'7'0917671 — Great Britain. National libraries: British Library. *Department of Oriental Manuscripts and Printed Books*. Stock: Islamic illuminated manuscripts. Miniature paintings. Special subjects: Dragons

Titley, Norah M.. Dragons in Persian, Mughal and Turkish art. — London : British Library Reference Division, Sept.1981. — [36]p
ISBN 0-904654-70-2 (pbk) : £1.95 : CIP entry
B81-25862

751.7′7′09407402132 — London. Westminster *(London Borough).* **Museums: Wallace Collection. Exhibits: European miniature paintings,** *1520-1850*

Wallace Collection. Catalogue of miniatures / by Graham Reynolds. — London (Manchester Sq., W1M 6BN) : Trustees of the Wallace Collection, 1980. — 366p : ill(some col.),ports (some col.) ; 25cm
At head of title: Wallace Collection. — Includes index
Unpriced (pbk) B81-13995

751.7′7′09561 — Great Britain. National libraries: British Library. *Department of Oriental Manuscripts and Printed Books.* **Stock: Turkish illuminated manuscripts. Miniature paintings** — *Catalogues*

Titley, Norah M.. Miniatures from Turkish manuscripts : a catalogue and subject index of paintings in the British Library and British Museum. — London : British Library Reference Division, Dec.1981. — [146]p
ISBN 0-904654-71-0 : £45.00 : CIP entry
Also classified at 751.7′7′09561 B81-34011

751.7′7′09561 — London. Camden *(London Borough).* **Museums: British Museum. Stock: Turkish illuminated manuscripts. Miniature paintings** — *Catalogues*

Titley, Norah M.. Miniatures from Turkish manuscripts : a catalogue and subject index of paintings in the British Library and British Museum. — London : British Library Reference Division, Dec.1981. — [146]p
ISBN 0-904654-71-0 : £45.00 : CIP entry
Primary classification 751.7′7′09561 B81-34011

752 — PAINTINGS. COLOUR

752′.09 — Paintings. Colour. Techniques, *to 1979*

Birren, Faber. History of color in painting / Faber Birren. — New York ; London : Van Nostrand Reinhold, [1980], c1965. — 304p : ill (some col.),facsims,ports ; 32cm
Originally published: New York : Reinhold Pub. Corp., 1965. — Includes index
ISBN 0-442-11118-5 : £18.75 B81-08556

753/758 — PAINTINGS. SPECIAL SUBJECTS

753′.7 — English paintings, *ca 1750-ca 1920.* **Special subjects: Fairies** — *Illustrations*

Fairy paintings / [compiled by] Beatrice Phillpotts. — London : Ash & Grant, 1978. — 16p,40 leaves of plates : ill(some col.),1facsim,ports ; 31cm
ISBN 0-904069-33-8 (cased) : £6.95 : CIP rev.
ISBN 0-904069-32-x (pbk) : £3.95 B78-27509

754′.0943′074017595 — Wisconsin. Milwaukee. Art galleries: Milwaukee Art Center. Exhibits: German genre paintings, *ca 1800-1900.* **Collections: René von Schleinitz Collection** — *Catalogues*

Milwaukee Art Center. The René von Schleinitz Collection of the Milwaukee Art Centre : major schools of German nineteenth-century painting / [compiled by] Rudolf M. Bisanz. — Milwaukee : Milwaukee Art Center ; London : University of Wisconsin Press, 1980. — 293p : ill(some col.) ; 23x30cm
Includes index
ISBN 0-299-07700-4 : £21.00 B81-07685

755′.2 — Russian painted icons: Novgorod painted icons, *1100-1700* — *Illustrations*

Novgorod icons : 12th-17th century / [preface by Dmitry Likhachov] ; [introduction by Vera Laurina and Vasily Pushkariov] ; [preface and introduction translated from the Russian by Kathleen Cook, notes by Elena Larchenko and Diana Miller] ; [designed by Alexander Kokovkin]. — Oxford : Phaidon, 1980. — 346p : chiefly ill(some col.) ; 35cm
Includes index
ISBN 0-7148-2107-1 : £25.00 B81-14053

757 — Great Britain. National theatres: National Theatre. Exhibits: Paintings. Special subjects: Theatre. Actors & actresses: Maugham Collection — *Catalogues*

National Theatre. Guide to the Maugham collection of theatrical paintings / by Raymond Mander and Joe Mitchenson. — [London] : Heinemann [for] the National Theatre, 1980. — 68p : ill(some col.),ports ; 30cm
Published to accompany a permanent exhibition at the National Theatre. — Includes index
ISBN 0-435-18591-8 (pbk) : £3.95 B81-32981

757′.074′02132 — Great Britain. Science. Organisations: Royal Society. Stock: Oil portrait paintings — *Catalogues*

Royal Society. The Royal Society catalogue of portraits / by Norman H. Robinson ; with biographical notes by Eric G. Forbes. — London : The Society, 1980. — 343p : ports ; 25cm
Includes index
ISBN 0-85403-136-7 : £25.00
Also classified at 731′.74′07402132 B81-04113

757′.22′09 — Western paintings, *to 1980.* **Special subjects: Nudes** — *Critical studies*

Lucie-Smith, Edward. The body : images of the nude / Edward Lucie-Smith. — [London] : Thames and Hudson, c1981. — 176p : ill(some col.) ; 32cm
ISBN 0-500-23339-x : £12.95 B81-40580

757′.3 — Europe. Religious buildings. Wall paintings. Special subjects: Becket, Thomas, *Saint, 1100-1400*

Parker, John W.. 'Putte down and auoyded' : wall paintings of St. Thomas Becket / [by John W. Parker]. — 3rd impression with corrections. — [Lincoln] ([6 Minster Yard, Lincoln LN2 1PJ]) : [J.W. Parker], 1974. — 9p : 1ill ; 22cm
Cover title. — '... first written for the Canterbury Cathedral Chronicle, 1970, No.65' — Inside cover
Unpriced (pbk) B81-27041

758 — American paintings, *to 1978.* **Special subjects: Science fiction** — *Illustrations*

Tomorrow and beyond : masterpieces of science fiction art / edited by Ian Summers. — Leicester : Windward, 1978. — 158p : chiefly col.ill ; 31cm
Includes index
ISBN 0-89480-055-8 (pbk) : £4.95 B81-07531

758′.1′090307402659 — Cambridgeshire. Cambridge. Museums: Fitzwilliam Museum. Exhibits: Landscape paintings, *1600-1900* — *Catalogues*

Painting from nature : the tradition of open-air oil sketching from the 17th to 19th centuries : Fitzwilliam Museum, Cambridge 25 November 1980-11 January 1981, Diploma Galleries, Royal Academy of Arts, London 31 January-15 March 1981. — [London] : Arts Council of Great Britain, c1980. — 48p : ill (some col.) ; 25cm
ISBN 0-7287-0263-0 (pbk) : Unpriced B81-18725

758′.1′09492 — Dutch landscape paintings, *1600-1700 - Critical studies*

Stechow, Wolfgang. Dutch landscape painting of the seventeenth century. — 3rd ed. — Oxford : Phaidon, Aug.1981. — [494]p. — (Landmarks in art history)
Previous ed.: 1968
ISBN 0-7148-2185-3 (pbk) : £7.95 : CIP entry B81-16941

758′.2′0941 — British marine paintings, *1900-1980* — *Critical studies*

Brook-Hart, Denys. 20th century British marine painting / Denys Brook-Hart. — Woodbridge : Antique Collector's Club, c1981. — 381p : ill (some col.) ; 28cm
Ill. on lining papers. — Includes index
ISBN 0-902028-90-1 : £25.00 B81-21764

758′7 — London. Greenwich *(London Borough).* **Art galleries: Woodlands Art Gallery. Exhibits. English watercolour paintings. Special subjects: London. Greenwich** *(London Borough), 1750-1950* — *Catalogues*

Woodlands Art Gallery. New pictures for the Art Gallery collection : a catalogue of local pictures in the collection of Woodlands Art Gallery procuced for an exhibition held from 13th December 1980 to 20th January 1981. — London (90 Mycenae Rd., SE3 7SE) : Woodlands Art Gallery, [1980]. — 26p : ill ; 30cm
Unpriced (pbk) B81-08051

758′.9942393 — England. Braikenridge, George Weare. Private collections. English paintings. Special subjects: Avon. Brislington, *1820-1830*

Stoddard, Sheena. Mr Braikenridge's Brislington / by Sheena Stoddard. — [Bristol] : City of Bristol Museum and Art Gallery with the assistance of the Friends of Bristol Art Gallery, 1981. — 61p : ill,ports ; 21x30cm
ISBN 0-900199-13-x (pbk) : Unpriced
Also classified at 741.942 B81-22163

759 — PAINTINGS. HISTORICAL AND GEOGRAPHICAL TREATMENT

759 — Paintings. Painters. Monograms, signatures & symbols, *to 1979* — *Encyclopaedias*

The Shorter dictionary of artists' signatures : including monograms and symbols / [compiled] by Radway Jackson ; introduction by Andrew Festing. — London : Foulsham, c1980. — 224p : ill ; 25cm
Includes index
ISBN 0-572-00898-8 : £9.50 B81-04151

759 — Western paintings. Women painters, *to 1978* — *Critical studies*

Greer, Germaine. The obstacle race : the fortunes of women painters and their work / Germaine Greer. — London : Pan in association with Secker and Warburg, 1981, c1979. — 373p,32p of plates : ill(some col.),ports(some col.) ; 25cm. — (Picador)
Originally published: London : Secker and Warburg, 1979. — Includes index
ISBN 0-330-26320-x (pbk) : £5.95 B81-19706

759.01′13′09364 — France. Dordogne. Grotte du Roc Saint-Cirq. Palaeolithic rock painting — *French texts*

Dams, Lya. L'art pariétal de la Grotte du Roc Saint-Cirq / Lya Dams ; photos Jean Vertut & Marcel Dams. — Oxford : B.A.R., 1980. — 149p,[7]folded leaves of plates : ill,1map ; 30cm. — (BAR. International series ; 79)
French text, English abstract. — Bibliography: p145-147
ISBN 0-86054-092-8 (pbk) : £9.00 B81-36585

759.01′13′094472 — France. Lascaux. Caves. Palaeolithic rock paintings

Bataille, Georges. [Lascaux, or, The birth of art]. Prehistoric painting : Lascaux, or, the birth of art / text by Georges Bataille ; [translated from the French by Austryn Wainhouse]. — Geneva : Skira ; London : Macmillan, 1980. — 149p : col.ill,2maps ; 29cm
Originally published: Lausanne : Skira, 1955. — Includes index
ISBN 0-333-30809-3 : £12.00 B81-07993

759.01′13′096 — Africa. Rock paintings

Ritchie, Carson I. A.. Rock art of Africa / Carson I.A. Ritchie. — South Brunswick : Barnes ; London : Yoseloff, c1979. — 157p,[8]p of plates : ill(some col.) ; 31cm
Includes index
ISBN 0-498-01753-2 : £10.00 B81-37831

759.01′13′096811 — San rock paintings — *Critical studies*

Woodhouse, H. C.. The Bushman art of Southern Africa / H.C. Woodhouse. — London : Macdonald General Books, 1980, c1979. — 124p : ill(some col.),ports(some col.) ; 30cm
Originally published: Cape Town : Purnell, 1979. — Ill on lining papers. — Includes index
ISBN 0-354-04486-9 : £8.95 B81-19747

759.04'6'074 — Art galleries. Exhibits: European paintings, *1600-1700* **—** *Lists*
Wright, Christopher, *1945-*. Italian, French & Spanish paintings of the seventeenth century / [compiled by] Christopher Wright. — [London] : Warne, 1981. — 89p ; 22cm. — (An Observer's guide. Where is it?)
ISBN 0-7232-2423-4 (pbk) : £2.50 B81-21856

759.04'7'074 — Art galleries. Exhibits: European paintings, *1700-1800* **—** *Lists*
Morris, M. A.. European paintings of the eighteenth century / [compiled by] M.A. Morris. — London : Warne, 1981. — 90p ; 22cm. — (An Observer's guide. Where is it?)
ISBN 0-7232-2718-7 (pbk) : £2.50 B81-16458

759.06 — Paintings, *1865-1979* **—** *Critical studies*
Muller, Joseph-Emile. A century of modern painting / Joseph-Emile Muller, Frank Elgar ; [translated by Jane Brenton]. — London : Eyre Methuen, 1980. — 239p : ill(some col.) ; 30cm
Translation of: Cent ans de peinture moderne. — Includes index
ISBN 0-413-48270-7 : £12.50 B81-11518

759.06'074 — Art galleries. Exhibits: Paintings, *1900-1950* **—** *Lists*
Lindey, Christine. Twentieth-century paintings Bonnard to Rothko / [compiled by] Christine Lindey. — London : Warne, 1981. — 87p : ill ; 22cm. — (An Observer's guide. Where is it?)
ISBN 0-7232-2460-9 (pbk) : £2.50 B81-16455

759.06'074'02132 — London. Westminster *(London Borough)*. **Art galleries: Royal Academy of Arts. Exhibitions: Paintings,** *1971-1980* **—** *Illustrations*
A **New** spirit in painting / [catalogue edited by Christos M. Joachimides, Norman Rosenthal, Nicholas Serota]. — London : Royal Academy of Arts, 1981. — 262p : chiefly col.ill ; 28cm
Published to accompany an exhibition at the Royal Academy, London, 1981
ISBN 0-297-77981-8 (pbk) : £6.25 B81-09509

759.13 — American erotic watercolour paintings. Vargas, Alberto — *Illustrations*
Vargas, Alberto. Vargas. — London (30 Craven St., WC2N 5NT) : Plexus, Apr.1981. — [128]p
Originally published: New York : Harmony Books, 1978
ISBN 0-85965-027-8 (cased) : £10.95 : CIP entry
ISBN 0-85965-043-x (pbk) : £5.95 B81-02389

759.13 — American oil paintings. Machetanz, Fred. Special themes: Alaska — *Catalogues*
Machetanz, Sara. The oil paintings of Fred Machetanz / by Sara Machetanz ; with introduction by John A. Diffily. — Leigh-on-Sea : F. Lewis, 1980. — 71p,[49]p of plates : ill(some col.),ports ; 30cm
Limited ed. of 750 copies. — Includes index
ISBN 0-85317-066-5 : £20.00 B81-01771

759.13 — American paintings, *1664-1977* **—** *Critical studies*
American painting : from the colonial period to the present / introduction by John Walker ; text by Jules David Prown and Barbara Rose. — New ed. — Geneva : Skira ; London : Macmillan, 1978, c1977. — 276p : col.ill,col.ports ; 35cm
Previous ed.: published in 2 vols. Lausanne : Skira. 1969. — Bibliography: p255-264. — Includes index
ISBN 0-333-24224-6 : £40.00 B81-10665

759.13 — American paintings, *1850-1882* **—** *Critical studies*
Sheldon, G. W.. Hours with art and artists / G.W. Sheldon. — New York ; London : Garland, 1978. — 13,vii,184p,[12]leaves of plates : ill ; 32cm. — (The Art experience in late nineteenth-century America)
Facsim. of: edition published New York : Appleton, 1882
ISBN 0-8240-2233-5 : Unpriced B81-27280

759.13 — American paintings. Gorky, Arshile — *Critical studies*
Rand, Harry. Arshile Gorky : the implications of symbols / Harry Rand. — Montclair : Allanheld & Schram ; London : Prior, 1981, c1980. — xxi,246p,[4]p of plates : ill(some col.),ports ; 29cm
Bibliography: p225-236. — Includes index
ISBN 0-8390-0209-2 : £22.50 B81-16263

759.13 — American paintings. New realism, *to 1979* **—** *Critical studies*
Lindey, Christine. Superrealist painting & sculpture / Christine Lindey. — London : Orbis, 1980. — 160p : ill(some col.) ; 27cm
Bibliography: p149-154. — Includes index
ISBN 0-85613-074-5 : £12.50
Also classified at 730'.973 B81-02437

759.13 — American watercolour paintings. Cooper, Mario. Techniques
Cooper, Mario. Watercolor by design / Mario Cooper. — New York : Watson-Guptill ; London : Pitman House, 1980. — 144p : ill (some col.) ; 31cm
Bibliography: p142. — Includes index
ISBN 0-273-01625-3 : £12.95 B81-07334

759.13 — American watercolour paintings. Kingman, Dong. Techniques
Kingman, Dong. Dong Kingman's watercolors / by Dong Kingman and Helena Kuo Kingman ; with special photographs by Helena Kuo Kingman. — New York : Watson-Guptill ; London : Pitman House, 1980. — 143p : ill (some col.) ; 31cm
Includes index
ISBN 0-273-01624-5 : £13.95 B81-07333

759.13 — London. Lambeth *(London Borough)*. **Art galleries: Hayward Gallery. Exhibits: American paintings. Hopper, Edward —** *Catalogues*
Edward Hopper 1882-1967 : Hayward Gallery, London 11 February to 29 March 1981 : a selection from the exhibition Edward Hopper - the Art and the Artist held at the Whitney Museum of American Art in New York from 16 September 1980 to 25 January 1981 .... — London : Arts Council of Great Britain, [1981]. — 63p : ill,2ports ; 22cm
Bibliography: p62-63
ISBN 0-7287-0272-x (pbk) : Unpriced B81-18726

759.13'074'017113 — Ohio. Toledo. Art galleries: Toledo Museum of Art. Stock: American painting, *1750-1979* **—** *Catalogues*
Toledo Museum of Art. American paintings / the Toledo Museum of Art ; catalogue by Susan E. Strickler ; edited by William Hutton. — Toledo : The Museum ; London : Distributed by Pennsylvania State University Press, 1979. — 227p : chiefly ill(some col.),ports ; 26cm
ISBN 0-935172-01-7 (pbk) : £8.70 B81-05392

759.2 — Art galleries. Exhibits: English portrait paintings. Sargent, John Singer — *Catalogues*
Lomax, James. John Singer Sargent : and the Edwardian age : an exhibition organised jointly by the Leeds Art Galleries, the National Portrait Gallery, London, and the Detroit Institute of Arts / James Lomax and Richard Ormond. — Leeds : Leeds Art Gallery, c1979. — 112p,[16]p of plates : ill(some col.),ports (some col.) ; 24cm
Includes index
ISBN 0-901981-15-x (pbk) : Unpriced
ISBN 0-904017-27-3 (National Portrait Gallery : cased) : Unpriced
ISBN 0-904017-26-5 (National Portrait Gallery : pbk) : Unpriced B81-06770

759.2 — British paintings, *ca 1700-ca 1850* **—** *Critical studies*
Redgrave, Richard. A century of British painters / Richard and Samuel Redgrave ; [edited by Ruthven Todd]. — 2nd ed. — Oxford : Phaidon, 1981. — viii,612p : ill,ports ; 21cm. — (Landmarks in art history)
Previous ed.: 1947. — Bibliography: p595. — Includes index
ISBN 0-7148-2144-6 (pbk) : £7.50 : CIP rev. B81-07603

759.2 — British paintings. Painters, *1700-1800* **—** *Biographies*
Waterhouse, Ellis. The dictionary of British 18th century painters in oils and crayons / Ellis Waterhouse. — [Woodbridge] : Antique Collectors' Club, c1981. — 443p : ill(some col.),ports(some col.) ; 29cm
Ill on lining papers. — Bibliography: p436-439
ISBN 0-902028-93-6 : £29.50 : CIP rev. B81-08798

759.2 — Cardiff. Museums: National Museum of Wales. Exhibits: English watercolour paintings. Sorrell, Alan. Special subjects: Antiquities in Wales — *Catalogues*
Sorrell, Alan. Alan Sorrell — early Wales re-created. — Cardiff : National Museum of Wales, 1980. — 80p : ill(some col.),1map,plans,1col.port ; 16x23cm
'... published on the occasion of the opening of an exhibition of watercolour reconstructions of Welsh ancient monuments by the late Alan Sorrell ...'. — Also available in Welsh. — Bibliography: p80
ISBN 0-7200-0228-1 (pbk) : £1.50 B81-01914

759.2 — Cardiff. Museums: National Museum of Wales. Exhibits: English watercolour paintings. Sorrell, Alan. Special subjects: Antiquities in Wales — *Catalogues* **—** *Welsh texts*
Sorrell, Alan. Alan Sorrell — ail-greu'r gorffennol / cyfieithwyd i'r Gymraeg gan Cennard Davies. — Caerdydd : Amgueddfa Genedlaethol Cymru, 1980. — 80p : ill(some col.),1map,plans,1col.port ; 16x23cm
Published on the occasion of the opening of an exhibition of watercolour reconstructions of Welsh ancient monuments by the late Alan Sorrell. — Also available in English. — Bibliography: p80
ISBN 0-7200-0229-x (pbk) : £1.50 B81-01915

759.2 — East Sussex. Brighton. Museums: Royal Pavilion, Art Gallery and Museums, Brighton. Exhibits: English watercolour paintings. Alexander, William, *1767-1816*. **Special subjects: China. Social life,** *1792-1794* **—** *Catalogues*
Alexander, William, *1767-1816*. William Alexander : an English artist in imperial China : the Royal Pavilion, Art Gallery and Museums, Brighton, 8 September to 25 October, 1981 : Nottingham University Art Gallery, 23 November to 17 December, 1981. — Brighton (Brighton [BN1 1UE]) : Royal Pavilion, Art Gallery and Museums, 1981. — 80p : ill,1map,ports ; 25cm
Bibliography: p78-79
Unpriced (pbk)
Also classified at 759.2 B81-38674

759.2 — East Sussex. Hailsham. Country houses: Michelham Priory. Exhibits: English watercolour paintings. Petrie, Henry. Special subjects: East & West Sussex. Parish churches. Collections: Sharpe Collection — *Catalogues*
Petrie, Henry. Sussex churches : the Sharpe Collection of watercolours and drawings 1797-1809 / mainly by Henry Petrie. — [Lewes] ([Barbican House, Lewes, Sussex]) : Sussex Archaeological Society, [1980?]. — x,[195]p : ill,1port ; 21cm
Unpriced (pbk) B81-26081

759.2 — England. Art galleries. Exhibits: English watercolour paintings. Reddick, Peter — *Catalogues*
Reddick, Peter. Peter Reddick : cymrodor Gregynog 1979-80 : arddangosfa o dyfrlliwiau ac engrafiadau pren = Peter Reddick : Gregynog fellow 1979-80 : an exhibition of watercolours and wood engravings. — Cardiff (9 Museum Place, Cardiff) : Welsh Arts Council, c1981. — [24]p : ill ; 22cm
A Welsh Arts Council touring exhibition. — Parallel Welsh and English text. — Bibliography: p[24]. — Includes index
ISBN 0-905171-76-4 (pbk) : Unpriced
Also classified at 769.92'4 B81-21161

759.2 — English marine paintings. Wyllie, W. L. — *Critical studies*
Quarm, Roger. W.L. Wyllie. — London : Barrie & Jenkins, Nov.1981. — [144]p
ISBN 0-09-146220-7 : £25.00 : CIP entry B81-28795

759.2 — English paintings. Breckon, Don. Special subjects: Great Britain. Railways — *Illustrations*
Breckon, Don. The railway paintings of Don Breckon. — Newton Abbot : David & Charles, Feb.1982. — [64]p
ISBN 0-7153-8206-3 : £12.50 : CIP entry B81-36396

759.2 — English paintings. Brown, Ford Madox — *Correspondence, diaries, etc.*
Brown, Ford Madox. The diary of Ford Madox Brown. — London : Yale University Press, Oct.1981. — [320]p. — (Studies in British art)
ISBN 0-300-02743-5 : £15.00 : CIP entry B81-32082

759.2 — English paintings. Carrington, Dora — *Critical studies*

Carrington, Noel. Carrington : paintings, drawings and decorations / Noel Carrington ; foreword by Sir John Rothenstein. — Rev. ed. — [London] : Thames and Hudson, 1980. — 95p : ill(some col.),ports(some col.) ; 22cm
Previous ed.: Oxford : Oxford Polytechnic Press, 1978. — Bibliography: p89-92. — Includes index
ISBN 0-500-09143-9 : £7.50 B81-06541

759.2 — English paintings. Compton, Charles, *1828-1884 — Correspondence, diaries, etc.*

Compton, Charles, *1828-1884.* The diary of Charles Compton : artist and civil servant (1828-1884) / edited by Eunice H. Turner ; with a preface by Keith Robinson. — Ilfracombe : Stockwell, 1980. — 132p,[8]p of plates : ill,ports,1geneal.table ; 19cm
ISBN 0-7223-1405-1 : £5.25 B81-04960

759.2 — English paintings. Constable, John, *1776-1837 — Critical studies*

Sunderland, John. Constable / John Sunderland. — Rev. and enl. ed. — Oxford : Phaidon, 1981. — 31p,487leaves : ill(some col.),1port ; 31cm
Previous ed.: 1971. — Leaves printed on both sides. — Bibliography: p28
ISBN 0-7148-2158-6 (cased) : £9.95 : CIP rev. B80-20929

759.2 — English paintings. Cook, Beryl — *Illustrations*

Cook, Beryl. One man show / Beryl Cook. — London : Murray, 1981. — 62p : col.ill ; 26cm
ISBN 0-7195-3881-5 : £5.95 : CIP rev. B81-27461

759.2 — English paintings. Gainsborough, Thomas — *Biographies*

Lindsay, Jack. Thomas Gainborough : his life and art / Jack Lindsay. — London : Granada, 1981. — 244p,[16]p of plates : ill,ports ; 24cm
Bibliography: p226-232. - Includes index
ISBN 0-246-11071-6 : £12.50 B81-21685

759.2 — English paintings. Graham, Rigby — *Illustrations*

Greer, Anne. Rigby Graham / Anne Greer. — Newcastle (Newcastle Bookshop, 1 Side, Newcastle-upon-Tyne 1) : Brian Mills, c1981. — 79p : ill(some col.),1port ; 30cm + 1art print(lithograph,col ; 30cm)
Ltd. ed. of 150 copies. — Bibliography: p79
Unpriced B81-39286

759.2 — English paintings. Herring *(Family)* **—** *Biographies*

Beckett, Oliver. J.F. Herring & Sons : the life and works of J.F. Herring snr and his family / by Oliver Beckett. — London : J.A. Allen, 1981. — 176p,xxivp of plates : ill(some col.),ports,1geneal.table ; 30cm
List of works: p95-179
ISBN 0-85131-335-3 : £25.00 : CIP rev. B80-22335

759.2 — English paintings. Hockney, David — *Critical studies*

Livingstone, Marco. David Hockney / Marco Livingstone. — London : Thames and Hudson, c1981. — 251p : ill(some col.),ports ; 22cm. — ([The world of art library])
Bibliography: p243-244. — Includes index
ISBN 0-500-18185-3 : £7.95 B81-25405

759.2 — English paintings. Hockney, David — *Illustrations*

Hockney, David. Paper pools / David Hockney ; edited by Nikos Stangos. — [London] : Thames and Hudson, c1980. — 100p : chiefly ill(some col.),ports ; 28cm
ISBN 0-500-23311-x : £10.00 B81-00209

759.2 — English paintings. Hogarth, William — *Critical studies*

Bindman, David. Hogarth / David Bindman. — London : Thames and Hudson, c1981. — 216p : ill(some col.),1map,ports(some col.) ; 21cm. — (The World of art library)
Bibliography: p208. — Includes index
ISBN 0-500-20182-x (pbk) : £2.95 B81-30657

759.2 — English paintings. John, Gwen — *Biographies*

Chitty, Susan. Gwen John. — London : Hodder & Stoughton, Sept.1981. — [224]p
ISBN 0-340-24480-1 : £9.95 : CIP entry B81-23953

759.2 — English paintings. Lowry, L. S. — *Personal observations*

Marshall, Tilly. Life with Lowry / Tilly Marshall. — London : Hutchinson, 1980. — 259p,[8]p of plates : ill,ports ; 23cm
ISBN 0-09-144090-4 : £7.95 B81-08129

759.2 — English paintings. North, Marianne — *Biographies*

North, Marianne. A vision of Eden : the life and work of Marianne North / preface by J.P.M. Brenan ; foreword by Anthony Huxley ; biographical note by Brenda E. Moon. — Abridged ed., with additional material / text abridged by Graham Bateman. — Exeter : Published in collaboration with the Royal Botanic Gardens, Kew [by] Webb & Bower, 1980. — 240p : col.ill,2maps,1col.port ; 26cm
Previous ed.: published in 2 vols. as Recollections of a happy life. London : Macmillan, 1892. — Maps on lining papers. — Includes index
ISBN 0-906671-18-3 : £8.95 : CIP rev. B80-19857

759.2 — English paintings. Penrose, Roland — *Biographies*

Penrose, Roland. Scrap book 1900-1981 / Roland Penrose. — London : Thames and Hudson, 1981. — 299p : ill(some col.),facsims,ports ; 28cm
Ill on inside covers. — Includes index
ISBN 0-500-23344-6 : £18.00 B81-38687

759.2 — English paintings. Pre-Raphaelitism — *Critical studies*

Parris, Leslie, *1941-.* The Pre-Raphaelites / by Leslie Parris. — 1st ed. in this format. — London : Tate Gallery, 1980, c1966. — 13,33p of plates : col.ill,3ports ; 21cm. — (Tate Gallery colour book series)
Previous ed.: i.e. Rev. ed., 1973. — Bibliography: p13
ISBN 0-905005-86-4 (pbk) : Unpriced B81-06257

759.2 — English paintings. Pre-Raphaelitism — *Illustrations*

Rose, Andrea. The Pre-Raphaelites. — 2nd ed. — Oxford : Phaidon Press, Aug.1981. — [128]p. — (Phaidon colour library)
Previous ed.: 1977
ISBN 0-7148-2180-2 (cased) : £9.95 : CIP entry
ISBN 0-7148-2166-7 (pbk) : £6.95 B81-16940

759.2 — English paintings. Shayer *(Family)* **—** *Critical studies*

Stewart, Brian. The Shayer family of painters. — London : F. Lewis, Nov.1981. — [160]p
ISBN 0-85317-092-4 : £25.00 : CIP entry B81-30421

759.2 — English paintings. Shepherd, David. Special subjects: Africa. Animals — *Illustrations*

Shepherd, David. Paintings of Africa and India / David Shepherd. — London : Tryon Gallery, c1978. — [75]p : col.ill ; 36x51cm
Limited ed. of 506 signed copies in slip cases, of which 500 are bound in half leather and numbered 1-500, and six are specially bound and lettered A-F
ISBN 0-902189-08-5 : Unpriced
ISBN 0-902189-09-3 (Special ed.) : Unpriced B81-38740

759.2 — English paintings. Sutherland, Graham — *Critical studies*

Hayes, John, *1929-.* The art of Graham Sutherland / John Hayes. — Oxford : Phaidon, 1980. — 190p : ill(some col.),maps,ports(some col.) ; 29cm
Bibliography: p185-187. - Includes index
ISBN 0-7148-2035-0 : £20.00 B81-02966

759.2 — English paintings. Thorburn, Archibald — *Illustrations*

Thorburn, Archibald. Thorburn's landscape. — London : Hamish Hamilton, Oct.1981. — [120]p
ISBN 0-241-10679-6 : £12.50 : CIP entry B81-26754

759.2 — English paintings. Turner, J. M. W., *1796-1819 — Critical studies*

Chamot, Mary. The early works of J.M.W. Turner / by Mary Chamot. — Rev. ed. — London : Tate Gallery, 1972 (1981 [printing]). — 11p,[32]p of plates : col.ill,1port ; 21cm. — (Tate Gallery colour book series)
Previous ed.: 1965. — Bibliography: p11
ISBN 0-905005-91-0 (pbk) : £1.95 B81-21322

759.2 — English paintings. Turner, J. M. W., *1819-1850 — Critical studies*

Butlin, Martin. The later works of J.M.W. Turner / by Martin Butlin. — London : Tate Gallery, 1981, c1965. — 13p,[32]p of plates : col.ill ; 21cm. — (Tate Gallery colour book series)
Bibliography: p13
ISBN 0-905005-96-1 (pbk) : £1.95 B81-21323

759.2 — English paintings. Turner, J. M. W. — *Critical studies*

Gaunt, William. Turner / William Gaunt. — Rev. and enl. ed. / with notes by Robin Hamlyn. — Oxford : Phaidon, 1981. — 31p,48leaves : ill(some col.),ports ; 31cm. — (Phaidon colour library)
Previous ed.: 1971. — Leaves printed on both sides. — Bibliography: p28
ISBN 0-7148-2159-4 (cased) : £9.95 : CIP rev. B80-23589

759.2 — English paintings. Turner, J. M. W.. Works. Exhibition — *Proposals*

The **Case** for a Turner Gallery. — [London] : Turner Society, 1979. — 35p : facsims ; 21cm
Bibliography: p18
ISBN 0-906793-00-9 (pbk) : Unpriced B81-39976

759.2 — English paintings. Waterhouse, J. W. — *Critical studies*

Hobson, Anthony. The art and life of J.W. Waterhouse RA 1849-1917 / Anthony Hobson. — London : Studio Vista, c1980. — x,208p : ill (some col.),ports(some col.) ; 29cm
Bibliography: p201-203. — Includes index
ISBN 0-289-70919-9 : £27.50 B81-28914

759.2 — English paintings. White, Tim. Special subjects: Science fiction. Illustrations for books — *Illustrations*

White, Tim. The science fiction and fantasy world of Tim White. — London : New English Library, 1981. — 143p : chiefly ill(some col.) ; 31cm
ISBN 0-450-04444-0 (corrected) : £9.95 B81-05021

759.2 — English panoramic paintings. Topolski, Feliks. Special subjects: Great Britain. Elizabeth II, *Queen of Great Britain.* **Coronation —** *Illustrations*

Topolski, Feliks. Feliks Topolski's panoramas / with a foreword by H.R.H. The Prince Philip, Duke of Edinburgh ; appreciation, Bernard Denvir ; collage, Feliks Topolski with Peter Ford ; photography, Marcus Harrison. — London : Quartet, 1977. — 56p,[52]p of plates : ill(some col.),2facsims,2ports ; 29cm
ISBN 0-7043-3348-1 (pbk) : £4.95 B81-33653

759.2 — English portrait paintings. Leighton, Sara — *Biographies*

Leighton, Sara. Of savages and kings / by Sara Leighton. — Maidstone : Bachman & Turner, c1980. — 224p,[24]p of plates : ill,ports ; 24cm
ISBN 0-85974-099-4 : £7.95 B81-01049

759.2 — English watercolour paintings, *1600-1800 — Critical studies*

Clarke, Michael, *1952-.* The tempting prospect. — London : British Museum Publications, Sept.1981. — [160]p
ISBN 0-7141-8016-5 : £13.95 : CIP entry B81-22652

759.2 — English watercolour paintings. Bewick, Thomas. Special subjects: Birds — ***Illustrations***
Bewick, Thomas. Thomas Bewick's birds. — London : Gordon Fraser, Oct.1981. — [60]p
ISBN 0-86092-059-3 (pbk) : £3.95 : CIP entry
Also classified at 769.92'4 B81-27439

759.2 — English watercolour paintings. Boyce, George Price — ***Correspondence, diaries, etc.***
Boyce, George Price. The diaries of George Price Boyce / edited by Virginia Surtees. — Norwich (65 Newmarket Rd., Norwich NR2 2HW, Norfolk) : Real World, c1980. — x,127p,9p of plates : ill,ports ; 26cm
Originally published: in the Old Water-colour Society's Club nineteenth annual vol., 1941. — Includes index
ISBN 0-903822-03-2 : Unpriced B81-11789

759.2 — English watercolour paintings. Lawrence, Louis. Special subjects: Seasons — ***Illustrations***
Lawrence, Louis. The seasons / [compiled and illustrated by] Louis Lawrence ; foreword by Roy Strong. — Exeter : Webb & Bower, c1981. — [123]p : ill(some col.),all facsims ; 25cm
Reproduction of a manuscript compiled between 1887 and 1890
ISBN 0-906671-22-1 : £6.95 : CIP rev.
Primary classification 741.942 B81-00198

759.2 — English watercolour paintings. Turner, J.M.W.. Special subjects: England. Rivers & coastal regions — ***Illustrations***
Turner, J. M. W.. Turner's rivers, harbours and coasts / Eric Shanes. — London : Chatto & Windus, 1981. — 160p : chiefly ill(some col.) ; 22x31cm
ISBN 0-7011-2569-1 : £15.00 : CIP rev.
B81-13457

759.2 — English watercolour paintings. White, John, ***fl.1585-1593 — Biographies***
Hull, Howard. An essay on John White : the Elizabethan watercolourist and explorer / Howard Hull. — Shoreham-by-Sea ([c/o H. Hull, 21 Riverbank, Shoreham-by-Sea, Sussex]) : Ixion, c1981. — 14p ; 22cm
Bibliography: p14
Unpriced (pbk) B81-21891

759.2 — London. Westminster ***(London Borough).*** **Art galleries: Anthony d'Offay** ***(Firm).*** **Exhibits: English paintings. Bomberg, David —** ***Catalogues***
David Bomberg 1890-1957 : works from the collection of Lilian Bomberg. — London (9 Dering St., New Bond St. W.1) : Anthony d'Offay, [1981]. — [14]p,[12]p of plates : ill ; 20cm
Catalogue compiled by Anthony d'Offay
Unpriced (pbk) B81-22840

759.2 — London. Westminster ***(London Borough).*** **Art galleries: Anthony d'Offay** ***(Firm).*** **Exhibits: English watercolour paintings. Bevan, Robert —** ***Catalogues***
Robert Bevan 1865-1925 : drawings and watercolours. — London (9 Dering St., New Bond St., W.1) : Anthony d'Offay, [1981]. — [14]p,[12]p of plates : ill ; 18cm
Catalogue of the exhibition held 25th June to 15th August, 1981
Unpriced (pbk)
Also classified at 741.942 B81-40586

759.2 — London. Westminster ***(London Borough).*** **Art galleries: Anthony d'Offay** ***(Firm).*** **Exhibits: English watercolour paintings. Roberts, William,** ***1895-1980 — Catalogues***
Roberts, William, ***1895-1980.*** William Roberts 1895-1980 : drawings and watercolours. — London (9 Dering St., New Bond St., W.1.) : Anthony d'Offay, [1981?]. — [12]p,[12]p of plates : ill ; 20cm
Unpriced (pbk)
Primary classification 741.942 B81-22845

759.2 — London. Westminster ***(London Borough).*** **Art galleries: Marlborough Fine Art (London) Limited. Exhibits: English paintings. Kokoschka, Oskar —** ***Catalogues***
Kokoschka, Oskar. Oskar Kokoschka : (1886-1980) memorial exhibition : 9 May-13 June 1981 Marlborough Gallery Inc ... 26 June-31 July 1981 Marlborough Fine Art (London) Ltd ... — New York : Marlborough Gallery ; London (6 Albemarle St., W1X 3HF) : Marlborough Fine Art (London) Ltd, [1981]. — 88p : ill(some col.),ports(some col.) ; 30cm
Unpriced (pbk) B81-28937

759.2 — London. Westminster ***(London Borough).*** **Art galleries: Marlborough Fine Art (London) Limited. Exhibits: English paintings. Wonnacott, John -** ***Catalogues***
Wonnacott, John. John Wonnacott : first London exhibition, 17 December 1980-31 January 1981. — London (6 Albemarle St., W1X 3HF) : Marlborough Fine Art (London) Ltd, 1981. — 16p : chiefly ill(some col.) ; 30cm
Cat.no.: 376
Unpriced (pbk) B81-13925

759.2 — London. Westminster ***(London Borough).*** **Art galleries: Parkin Gallery. Exhibits: English paintings. Luard, Lowes Dalbiac —** ***Catalogues***
Hooker, Denise. Lowes Dalbiac Luard 1872-1944 : 19 November-6 December 1980. — London (11 Motcomb St., S.W.1) : Michael Parkin Fine Art, [1980]. — [12]p : ill,1port ; 20cm
Published to accompany an exhibition at the Parkin Gallery. — Text by Denise Hooker. — Port. on inside cover
Unpriced (pbk) B81-31503

759.2 — London. Westminster ***(London Borough).*** **Art galleries: Tate Gallery. Exhibits: English paintings. Calcott, Augustus Wall —** ***Catalogues***
Brown, David Blayney. Augustus Wall Callcott / David Blayney Brown. — London : Tate Gallery, 1981. — 94p : ill,2ports ; 25cm
Published to accompany an exhibition held at the Tate Gallery, 1981. — Bibliography: 92-93
ISBN 0-905005-87-2 (pbk) : £4.50 B81-11363

759.2 — London. Westminster ***(London Borough).*** **Art galleries: Tate Gallery. Exhibits: English paintings. Caulfield, Patrick —** ***Catalogues***
Caulfield, Patrick. Patrick Caulfield : paintings 1963-81. — London : Tate Gallery, 1981. — 87p : ill(some col.),1port ; 30cm
Published to accompany an exhibition at the Walker Art Gallery, Liverpool and the Tate Gallery, London, 1981-1982. — Bibliography: p85-87
ISBN 0-905005-23-6 (pbk) : £7.50
Also classified at 759.2 B81-40847

759.2 — London. Westminster ***(London Borough).*** **Art galleries: Tate Gallery. Exhibits: English paintings. Constable, John,** ***1776-1837 — Catalogues***
Tate Gallery. The Tate Gallery Constable collection : a catalogue / by Leslie Parris. — London : Tate Gallery, 1981. — 208p : ill (some col.),1map,ports(some col.),geneal.table ; 22cm
ISBN 0-905005-93-7 : £15.00 B81-37373

759.2 — Merseyside ***(Metropolitan County).*** **Liverpool. Art galleries: Bluecoat Gallery. Exhibits: English paintings. Taborn, David —** ***Catalogues***
Taborn, David. David Taborn. — [Nottingham] : Nottingham University Art Gallery, [1981]. — [19]p : ill(some col.) ; 21cm
Catalogue of the exhibition held at the Nottingham University Art Gallery, and Bluecoat Gallery, Liverpool, 1981
Unpriced (pbk)
Primary classification 759.2 B81-24250

759.2 — Merseyside ***(Metropolitan County).*** **Liverpool. Art galleries: Walker Art Gallery. Exhibits: English paintings. Caulfield, Patrick —** ***Catalogues***
Caulfield, Patrick. Patrick Caulfield : paintings 1963-81. — London : Tate Gallery, 1981. — 87p : ill(some col.),1port ; 30cm
Published to accompany an exhibition at the Walker Art Gallery, Liverpool and the Tate Gallery, London, 1981-1982. — Bibliography: p85-87
ISBN 0-905005-23-6 (pbk) : £7.50
Primary classification 759.2 B81-40847

759.2 — Nottinghamshire. Nottingham. Art galleries: Nottingham University Art Gallery. Exhibits: English paintings. Taborn, David — ***Catalogues***
Taborn, David. David Taborn. — [Nottingham] : Nottingham University Art Gallery, [1981]. — [19]p : ill(some col.) ; 21cm
Catalogue of the exhibition held at the Nottingham University Art Gallery, and Bluecoat Gallery, Liverpool, 1981
Unpriced (pbk)
Also classified at 759.2 B81-24250

759.2 — Nottinghamshire. Nottingham. Art galleries: Nottingham University Art Gallery. Exhibits: English watercolour paintings. Alexander, William, ***1767-1816.*** **Special subjects: China. Social life,** ***1792-1794 — Catalogues***
Alexander, William, ***1767-1816.*** William Alexander : an English artist in imperial China : the Royal Pavilion, Art Gallery and Museums, Brighton, 8 September to 25 October, 1981 : Nottingham University Art Gallery, 23 November to 17 December, 1981. — Brighton (Brighton [BN1 1UE]) : Royal Pavilion, Art Gallery and Museums, 1981. — 80p : ill,1map,ports ; 25cm
Bibliography: p78-79
Unpriced (pbk)
Primary classification 759.2 B81-38674

759.2 — Oxfordshire. Oxford. Museums: Ashmolean Museum. Exhibits: English watercolour paintings. Turner, J. M. W.. Special subjects: Bible — ***Catalogues***
Omer, Mordechai. Turner and the Bible / Mordechai Omer. — Oxford : Ashmolean Museum, 1981. — 48p : ill(some col.) ; 20cm
Published to accompany an exhibition at the Ashmolean Museum, Oxford January-March 1981. — Bibliography: p47-48
ISBN 0-900090-79-0 (pbk) : £3.50
Also classified at 769.92'4 B81-13161

759.2 — Staffordshire. Stoke-on-Trent. Museums: City Museum and Art Gallery ***(Stoke-on-Trent).*** **Exhibits: English watercolour paintings. Haggar, Reginald —** ***Catalogues***
Haggar, Reginald. Reginald Haggar : retrospective exhibition of watercolours 1930-1980 : 12th January-15th February 1980, City Museum and Art Gallery, Bethesda St., Hanley, Stoke-on-Trent : 8th March-5th April 1980 E.M. Flint Art Gallery, Lichfield St., Walsall. — Stoke-on-Trent (Bethesda St., Hanley, Stoke-on-Trent, [ST1 4HS]) : City Museum and Art Gallery, 1980. — [24]p : chiefly ill ; 22cm
£1.50 (pbk)
Also classified at 759.2 B81-37521

759.2 — Suffolk. Sudbury. Museums: Gainsborough's House. Exhibits: English paintings. Gainsborough, Thomas — ***Catalogues***
The **painter's** eye : an exhibition to commemorate the 250th anniversary of the birth of Thomas Gainsborough, R.A.. — [Sudbury] ([D. Coke, Curator, Gainsborough's House, Sudbury, Suffolk]) : [Gainsborough's House Society], 1977. — [16]p : ill,ports ; 30cm
Unpriced (unbound) B81-32715

759.2 — West Midlands ***(Metropolitan County).*** **Walsall. Art galleries: E. M. Flint Art Gallery. Exhibits: English watercolour paintings. Haggar, Reginald —** ***Catalogues***
Haggar, Reginald. Reginald Haggar : retrospective exhibition of watercolours 1930-1980 : 12th January-15th February 1980, City Museum and Art Gallery, Bethesda St., Hanley, Stoke-on-Trent : 8th March-5th April 1980 E.M. Flint Art Gallery, Lichfield St., Walsall. — Stoke-on-Trent (Bethesda St., Hanley, Stoke-on-Trent, [ST1 4HS]) : City Museum and Art Gallery, 1980. — [24]p : chiefly ill ; 22cm
£1.50 (pbk)
Primary classification 759.2 B81-37521

759.2 — West Midlands ***(Metropolitan County).*** **Wolverhampton. Art galleries: Central Art Gallery** ***(Wolverhampton).*** **Exhibits: English paintings. Hunt, William Henry —** ***Catalogues***
William Henry Hunt 1790-1864 / organised by Wolverhampton Art Gallery and Museums with financial assistance from the Arts Council of Great Britain and the Paul Mellon Centre for Studies in British Art, London ; Central Art Gallery, Wolverhampton May 2-30, 1981, Harris Museum and Art Gallery, Preston June 13-July 11, 1981, Hastings Museum and Art Gallery August 15-September 13, 1981. — [Wolverhampton] ([Lichfield St., Wolverhampton, Staffs. WV2 1DU]) : [Wolverhampton Art Gallery], [1981]. — 84p : ill(some col.) ; 21cm
Published to accompany an exhibition at the Central Art Gallery Wolverhampton, Harris Museum and Art Gallery, Preston and Hastings Museum and Art Gallery, 1981
Unpriced (pbk) B81-25385

759.2′074 — Art galleries. Exhibits: British oil paintings, ***1700-1850*** **—** ***Lists***

Gordon, Catherine. British paintings Hogarth to Turner / [compiled by] Catherine Gordon. — London : Warne, 1981. — 90p ; 22cm. — (An Observer's guide. Where is it?)
ISBN 0-7232-2422-6 (pbk) : £2.50 B81-16456

759.2′074′02134 — London. Kensington and Chelsea ***(London Borough).*** **Museums: Victoria and Albert Museum. Stock: British watercolour paintings —** ***Catalogues***

Victoria and Albert Museum. British watercolours in the Victoria and Albert Museum : an illustrated summary catalogue of the national collection / compiled by Lionel Lambourne and Jean Hamilton. — London : Sotheby Parke Bernet in association with the Victoria and Albert Museum, 1980. — xxi,455p,[16]p of plates : ill(some col.),ports (some col.) ; 29cm
Ill on lining papers. — Bibliography: p435. — Includes index
ISBN 0-85667-111-8 : £47.50 B81-07702

759.2′074′02527 — Nottinghamshire. Nottingham. Museums: Nottingham Castle Museum. Stock: English watercolour paintings — ***Critical studies***

Nottingham Castle Museum. English watercolours : in Nottingham Castle / [text David Phillips]. — [Nottingham] ([Arts Department, Nottingham NG1 GEL]) : [Nottingham Castle Museum], c1980. — 12p,[17]p of plates : ill(some col.) ; 21cm
Bibliography: 1p
ISBN 0-905634-02-0 (pbk) : Unpriced B81-29627

759.2′074′02753 — Merseyside ***(Metropolitan County).*** **Liverpool. Art galleries: Walker Art Gallery. Exhibits: British paintings —** ***Catalogues***

John Moores Liverpool exhibition 12 : Walker Art Gallery November 27th 1980 to February 22nd 1981. — [Liverpool] ([William Brown St., Liverpool L3 8EL]) : [Walker Art Gallery], [1980]. — [32]p : chiefly ill(some col.),ports ; 21cm
Unpriced (pbk) B81-08086

759.2′911 — London. Lambeth ***(London Borough).*** **Art galleries: Hayward Gallery. Exhibits: Scottish paintings. Johnstone, William —** ***Catalogues***

Johnstone, William. William Johnstone. — [London] : Arts Council of Great Britain, [1981]. — 64p : ill(some col.) ; 23cm
Published to accompany an exhibition at the Hayward Gallery, London, 11 Feb-29 Mar.1981. — Bibliography: p63
ISBN 0-7287-0266-5 (pbk) : Unpriced B81-18723

759.2′911 — Scotland. Fife Region. St Andrews. Art galleries: Balcarres Gallery. Exhibits: Scottish landscape paintings. Nasmyth, Alexander — ***Catalogues***

Nasmyth, Alexander. Alexander Nasmyth 1758-1840 : Balcarres Gallery, Crawford Centre for the Arts, University of St Andrews, 9 February-11 March 1979. — St Andrews (93 North St., St Andrews, [Fife]) : The Centre, [1979?]. — 19p : ill,ports ; 20cm
Cover title
ISBN 0-906272-01-7 (pbk) : Unpriced B81-10194

759.2′911 — Scottish paintings. Flint, ***Sir*** **William Russell —** ***Biographies***

Lewis, Ralph. Sir William Russell Flint 1880-1969 / Ralph Lewis ; with an introduction by Adrian Bury. — Edinburgh : Skilton, 1980. — 122p : ill(some col.),ports ; 29cm
ISBN 0-284-98568-6 : £12.60 B81-07073

759.2′911 — Scottish paintings. Gillies, W. G. — ***Biographies***

Napier, Philip G.. William Gillies : our neighbour / by Philip G. Napier. — [Endinburgh] (c/o Kall-Kwik Printing, 2 Dundas St., Edinburgh) : P.G. Napier, 1980. — 8p ; 20cm
Cover title
Unpriced (pbk) B81-07635

759.2′911 — Scottish watercolour paintings, ***1878-1980***

Firth, Jack. Scottish watercolour painting / Jack Firth. — Edinburgh : Ramsay Head, 1979. — 96p : ill(some col.) ; 26cm
Includes index
ISBN 0-902859-58-7 : £9.50 B81-02314

759.2′915 — Irish paintings. Barry, James — ***Critical studies***

Pressly, William L.. The life and art of James Barry / William L. Pressly. — New Haven ; London : published for the Paul Mellan Centre for Studies in British Art by Yale University Press, 1981. — xiii,320p : ill(some col.),ports (some col.) ; 27cm. — (Studies in British art)
Bibliography: p303-309. — Includes index
ISBN 0-300-02466-5 : £30.00 B81-34086

759.2′915 — Irish paintings. Horton, W. T.. Interpersonal relationships with Yeats, W. B.

Harper, George Mills. W.B. Yeats and W.T. Horton : the record of an occult friendship / George Mills Harper. — [London] : [Macmillan], [1980]. — x,160p : ill ; 23cm
Includes index
ISBN 0-333-27165-3 : £12.00 : CIP rev.
Primary classification 821′.8 B79-25899

759.2′915 — Irish paintings. Le Brocquy, Louis — ***Critical studies***

Walker, Dorothy. Louis le Brocquy. — Dublin (Knocksedan House, Forrest Great, Swords, Co. Dublin) : Ward River Press, Oct.1981. — [164]p
ISBN 0-907085-13-x : £20.00 : CIP entry B81-30474

759.2′915 — Irish paintings. Orpen, ***Sir*** **William —** ***Biographies***

Arnold, Bruce. Orpen : mirror to an age / Bruce Arnold. — London : Cape, 1981. — 448p,[16]p of plates : ill(some col.),ports(some col.) ; 26cm
Bibliography: p435-437. — Includes index
ISBN 0-224-01581-8 : £16.00 : CIP rev. B80-13487

759.2′915 — Staffordshire. Stoke-on-Trent. Museums: City Museums and Art Gallery ***(Stoke-on-Trent).*** **Exhibits: Irish paintings. Currie, John —** ***Catalogues***

Currie, John. John Currie : paintings and drawings 1905-14 : 22 November-10 January 1980 City Museum and Art Gallery, Bethesda St., Hanley, Stoke-on-Trent. — Stoke-on-Trent (Bethesda St., Hanley, Stoke-on-Trent [ST1 4HS]) : City Museum and Art Gallery, 1980. — [56]p : chiefly ill(some col.),ports ; 15x21cm
Unpriced (pbk) B81-37519

759.2′929 — Cardiff. Art galleries: Oriel ***(Gallery).*** **Exhibits: Welsh paintings,** ***1980-1981.*** **Jones, Glyn,** ***1936-*** **—** ***Catalogues***

Spencer, Charles. Glyn Jones : peintiadau 1980-91 = painting 1980-81 / [Charles Spencer]. — Cardiff : Welsh Arts Council, 1981. — 1sheet ; 21x63cm folded to 21x21cm + catalogue sheet : 2col.ill,1port
Accompanies an exhibition organised by the Welsh Arts Council and held at their Oriel gallery, Cardiff, 12 Feb.-7 March 1981. — Parallel English text and Welsh translation by Siân Edwards
Unpriced B81-13392

759.2′929 — Cardiff. Art galleries: Oriel ***(Gallery).*** **Exhibits: Welsh paintings. Charlton, Evan & Charlton, Felicity —** ***Catalogues***

Charlton, Evan, ***1904-***. Peintiadau diweddar = Recent paintings / Evan & Felicity Charlton. — Cardiff : Welsh Arts Council, 1981. — [8]p (2fold.) : ill(some col.) ; 20x21cm
Published to accompany an exhibition at Oriel, Cardiff, 4-27 June 1981 and Newport Museum and Art Gallery, 5-26 Sept. 1981. — Parallel English text and Welsh translation
ISBN 0-905171-77-2 (unbound) : Unpriced B81-29456

759.2′929 — Wales. Art galleries. Exhibits: Welsh paintings. Holland, Harry — ***Catalogues***

Holland, Harry. Harry Holland / [text by William Packer Welsh translation by Siân Edwards]. — [Cardiff] : [Welsh Arts Council], c1980. — [32]p : ill(some col.),1port ; 23cm
To accompany a Welsh Arts Council touring exhibition, 4 October 1980-24 January 1981. — Parallel English text and Welsh translation
ISBN 0-905171-70-5 (pbk) : Unpriced B81-07336

759.3 — Cornwall. Camelford. Art galleries: North Cornwall Museum and Gallery. Exhibits: German paintings. Halkett, René — ***Catalogues***

Halkett, René. Retrospective exhibition : paintings and drawing 1921-1979 / René Halkett ; supported by South West Arts and the Arts Council. — Camelford (c/o North Cornwall Museum and Gallery, Camelford [Cornwall]) : S. Holden, c1981. — 13p : ill (some col.),1ports ; 22cm
ISBN 0-907580-01-7 (pbk) : Unpriced B81-36466

759.3 — German gouache paintings. Salomon, Charlotte — ***Illustrations***

Salomon, Charlotte. Charlotte : life or theater? : an autobiographical play / by Charlotte Salomon ; introduced by Judith Herzberg ; translated from the German by Leila Vennewitz. — London : Allen Lane in association with Gary Schwartz, 1981. — xvi,784p : ill(some col.),ports ; 28cm
Special ed. of 1,000 copies
ISBN 0-7139-1425-4 : £30.00 B81-39890

759.3 — German paintings. Holbein, Hans, ***ca.1497-1543*** **—** ***Illustrations***

Holbein, Hans, ***ca. 1497-1543***. Holbein : the complete paintings / introduction [and catalogue] by Roy Strong. — London : Granada, 1980. — 96p : chiefly ill(some col.),ports(some col.) ; 20cm. — (The complete paintings)
Translated from the Italian. — Bibliography: p96
ISBN 0-246-11290-5 (cased) : £3.95
ISBN 0-586-05144-9 (pbk) : £1.95 B81-32331

759.3 — German paintings. Modersohn-Becker, Paula — ***Correspondence, diaries, etc.***

Modersohn-Becker, Paula. The letters and journals of Paula Modersohn-Becker / translated and annotated by J. Diane Radycki ; introduction by Alessndra Comini ; epilogue by Adrienne Rich and Lilly Engler. — Metuchen ; London : Scarecrow, 1980. — xvii,344p,[1]leaf of plates : ill,ports ; 23cm
Translation of: Briefe und Tagebuchblätter. — Includes index
ISBN 0-8108-1344-0 : £12.25 B81-06115

759.3 — German paintings. Romanticism, ***1800-1850*** **—** ***Critical studies***

Vaughan, William, ***1943-***. German romantic painting / William Vaughan. — New Haven ; London : Yale University Press, 1980. — 259p : ill(some col.),facsims,ports(some col.) ; 29cm
Bibliography: p247-251. — Includes index
ISBN 0-300-02387-1 : £19.95 B81-01890

759.3 — Great Britain. ***National Portrait Gallery.*** **Exhibits: German portrait paintings. Closterman, John —** ***Catalogues***

Rogers, Malcolm. John Closterman : master of the English Baroque 1660-1711 / [catalogue by Malcolm Rogers]. — London : National Portrait Gallery, 1981. — 20p : ports ; 21cm
Published for the exhibition held at the National Portrait Gallery from 24 July to 4 October 1981
ISBN 0-904017-42-7 (unbound) : Unpriced B81-37951

759.36 — Austrian paintings. Schiele, Egon — ***Critical studies***

Whitford, Frank. Egon Schiele / Frank Whitford. — London : Thames and Hudson, c1981. — 215p : ill(some col.),facsims,ports(some col.) ; 21cm. — (The World of art library)
Bibliography: p205-207. — Includes index
ISBN 0-500-20183-8 (pbk) : £2.95 B81-30654

759.36 — Austrian watercolour paintings. Klimt, Gustav; Schiele, Egon & Kokoschka, Oskar — *Illustrations*

Klimt, Schiele, Kokoschka : drawings and watercolours / introduction by Otto Breicha ; documentary notes by Christian Nebehay. — London : Thames and Hudson, 1981. — 174p : ill(some col.),ports ; 23cm
Bibliography: p24-25
ISBN 0-500-27239-5 (pbk) : £6.95
Primary classification 741.9436 B81-38685

759.37 — Staffordshire. Stoke-on-Trent. Museums: City Museum and Art Gallery *(Stoke-on-Trent).* **Exhibits: Czechoslovak paintings. Borksy, Jiri —** *Catalogues*

Borsky, Jiri. Jiri Borsky : [City Museum & Art Gallery, Hanley, Stoke-on-Trent, 11 Oct-8 Nov.1980]. — Stoke-on-Trent ([Bethesda St.], Hanley, Stoke-on-Trent [ST1 4HS]) : City Museum & Art Gallery, 1980. — [20]p : chiefly ill ; 19x21cm
Cover title
£0.60 (pbk) B81-37522

759.38 — Polish paintings. Hofman, Vlastimil

Dusza, Edward. Malarz zapomnianego pejzażu / Edward Dusza. — London : Oficyna Poetów i Malarzy, 1981. — 31p : ill,1port ; 22cm
Includes summary in English
Unpriced (pbk) B81-31117

759.4 — Cardiff. Museums: National Museum of Wales. Exhibits: French oil paintings. Monet, Claude — *Catalogues*

Monet, Claude. Claude Monet 1840-1926 : an exhibition of paintings from the National Museum of Wales, Cardiff and the Musée Marmottan, Paris : 18 October - 23 November, 1980 / [text by] Peter Cannon-Brookes. — [Cardiff] : National Museum of Wales, c1980. — [45]p : chiefly ill,ports ; 21cm
Bibliography: p[9]
ISBN 0-7200-0231-1 (pbk) : £1.00 B81-05657

759.4 — French abstract paintings. Staël, Nicolas de — *Correspondence, diaries, etc. — French texts*

Staël, Nicolas de. Lettres à Jacques Duborg / Nicolas de Staël. — London (236 Brompton Rd., SW3 2BB) : Taranman, 1981. — [107]p : facsims(some col.) ; 26cm
Limited ed. of 1,000 numbered copies
ISBN 0-906499-11-9 (pbk) : Unpriced B81-34348

759.4 — French paintings, *1700-1800 — Critical studies*

Bryson, Norman. Word and image. — Cambridge : Cambridge University Press, Feb.1982. — [304]p
ISBN 0-521-23776-9 : £27.50 : CIP entry B81-36242

759.4 — French paintings, *1750-1780 — Critical studies*

Fried, Michael. Absorption and theatricality : painting and beholder in the age of Diderot / Michael Fried. — Berkeley ; London : University of California, c1980. — xvii,249p : ill,ports ; 26cm
Includes index
ISBN 0-520-03758-8 : £16.50 B81-11251

759.4 — French paintings, *1845-1862 - Critical studies*

Baudelaire, Charles. Art in Paris, 1845-1862. — Oxford : Phaidon, Aug.1981. — [242]p. — (Landmarks in art history)
These translations originally published: 1965
ISBN 0-7148-2138-1 (pbk) : £5.95 : CIP entry B81-18117

759.4 — French paintings, *ca 1700-ca 1800 — Critical studies*

Goncourt, Edmond de. French eighteenth-century painters : Watteau, Boucher, Chardin, La Tour, Greuze, Fragonard / Edmond and Jules de Goncourt ; [translated with an introduction and edited by Robin Ironside]. — 2nd ed. — Oxford : Phaidon, 1981. — xiii,418p : ill,ports ; 21cm. — (Landmarks in art history)
Translated from the French. — Previous ed.: 1948
ISBN 0-7148-2143-8 (pbk) : £6.50 B81-27699

Goncourt, Edmond de. French eighteenth-century painting. — Oxford : Phaidon, May 1981. — [438]p. — (Landmarks in art history)
Originally published: 1948
ISBN 0-7148-2147-0 (pbk) : £6.95 : CIP entry B81-09987

759.4 — French paintings. Courbet, Gustave. Interpersonal relationships with Proudhon, P.-J.

Rubin, James Henry. Realism and social vision in Courbet & Proudhon / by James Henry Rubin. — Princeton ; Guildford : Princeton University Press, c1980. — xvii,177p,[27]p of plates (1folded) : ill(some col.),facsim,ports ; 25cm. — (Princeton essays on the arts ; 10)
Bibliography: p167-169. - Includes index
ISBN 0-691-03960-7 (cased) : £9.80
ISBN 0-691-00327-9 (pbk) : Unpriced
Also classified at 335'.2 B81-17117

759.4 — French paintings. David, Jacques-Louis — *Biographies*

Brookner, Anita. Jacques-Louis David / Anita Brookner. — London : Chatto & Windus, 1980. — 223p,[103]p of plates : ill(some col.),ports(some col.) ; 26cm
Bibliography: p207-212. - Includes index
ISBN 0-7011-2530-6 : £25.00 : CIP rev. B80-17876

759.4 — French paintings. Delacroix, Eugène — *Critical studies*

Johnson, Lee. The painting of Eugene Delacroix : a critical catalogue : 1816-1831 / Lee Johnson. — Oxford : Clarendon, 1981. — 2v.(xxxix,261,200p,[3]leaves of plates) : ill(some col.),facsims,ports ; 31cm
Includes index
ISBN 0-19-817314-8 : £80-00 (set of 2 vol.): CIP rev. B80-24718

759.4 — French paintings. Gauguin, Paul — *Catalogues*

Gauguin, Paul. Gauguin : the complete paintings / [compiled by] Elda Fezzi. — London : Granada, 1981. — (The Complete paintings)
Translation of: Gauguin
1 / translated by Susan Brill. — 94p : ill(some col.),ports ; 20cm
ISBN 0-246-11288-3 (cased) : £3.95
ISBN 0-586-05142-2 (pbk) : £1.95 B81-12058

Gauguin, Paul. Gauguin : the complete paintings / [compiled by] Elda Fezzi. — London : Granada, 1981. — (The Complete paintings)
Translation of: Gauguin
2 / translated by Jane Carroll. — 96p : ill (some col.),1map,ports ; 20cm
Bibliography: p96
ISBN 0-246-11289-1 (cased) : £3.95
ISBN 0-586-05143-0 (pbk) : £1.95 B81-12059

759.4 — French paintings. Impressionism — *Illustrations*

Ash, Russell. The Impressionists and their art / Russell Ash. — London : Orbis Publishing, c1980. — 192p : chiefly col.ill,col.ports ; 30cm
Bibliography: p46. — Includes index
ISBN 0-85613-292-6 : £7.95 B81-00210

759.4 — French paintings. Kandinsky, Wassily — *Critical studies*

Long, Rose-Carol Washton. Kandinsky : the development of an abstract style / Rose-Carol Washton Long. — Oxford : Clarendon, 1980. — xxvi,201p,[104]p of plates : ill(some col.),facsims,ports ; 26cm
Bibliography: p190-196. — Includes index
ISBN 0-19-817311-3 : £40.00 : CIP rev. B80-18447

759.4 — French paintings. Monet, Claude — *Critical studies*

House, John. Monet. — Rev. and enl. ed. — Oxford : Phaidon, 1981. — 31,[96]p : ill(some col.),ports ; 31cm. — (Phaidon colour library)
Previous ed.: 1977. — Bibliography: p28
ISBN 0-7148-2162-4 (cased) : £9.95 : CIP rev.
ISBN 0-7148-2160-8 (pbk) : £6.95 B81-11925

Levine, Steven Z. Monet and his critics / Steven Z. Levine. — New York ; London : Garland, 1976. — 471p : 1ill ; 22cm. — (Outstanding dissertations in the fine arts)
Bibliography: p441-461. — Includes index
ISBN 0-8240-1995-4 : £47.00 B81-14232

759.4 — French paintings. Nabism, *1888-1896*

Mauner, George L.. The Nabis : their history and their art, 1888-1896 / George L. Mauner. — New York ; London : Garland, 1978. — xiv,326p[157]p of plates : ill,facsims,music ; 21cm. — (Outstanding dissertations in the fine arts)
Bibliography: p316-326
ISBN 0-8240-3240-3 : Unpriced B81-33202

759.4 — French paintings. Pissarro, Camille — *Correspondence, diaries, etc*

Pissarro, Camille. Camille Pissarro : letters to his son Lucien / edited with the assistance of Lucien Pissarro by John Rewald ; [translated from the French manuscript by Lionel Abel]. — 4th ed. — London : Routledge & Kegan Paul, 1980. — 399p,[64]p of plates : ill,facsims,ports ; 25cm
Previous ed.: Mamaroneck : Appel, 1972
ISBN 0-7100-0579-2 : £15.00 B81-05672

759.4 — French paintings. Poussin, Nicolas — *Biographies — French texts — Early works — Facsimiles*

Felibien, André. Felibien's life of Poussin / Claire Pace. — London : Zwemmer, 1981. — 183p : ill,ports ; 26cm
French text with English introduction and notes. — Facsim of: Entretiens sur les vies et sur les ouvrages des plus excellens peintres anciens et modernes. Vol.4. Trevoux : De L'imprimerie De S.A.S., 1725. — Bibliography: p175-177. — Includes index
ISBN 0-302-00542-0 : Unpriced : CIP rev. B80-20930

759.4 — French paintings. Toulouse-Lautrec, Henri de — *Biographies*

Muller, Joseph-Émile. Toulouse-Lautrec / Joseph-Émile Muller ; [translated from the French by Jane Brenton]. — London : Eyre Methuen, 1981. — [39]p,[93]p of plates : ill (some col.),ports(some col.) ; 17cm
Translation of: Toulouse-Lautrec
ISBN 0-413-48220-0 (pbk) : £3.95 B81-30685

759.4 — French paintings. Toulouse-Lautrec, Henri de — *Catalogues*

Toulouse-Lautrec, Henri de. Toulouse-Lautrec : the complete paintings / [compiled by] M.G. Dortu and J.A. Méric. — London : Granada, 1981. — (The Complete paintings)
Translation of: Toulouse-Lautrec
1 / introduction translated by Hilary E. Paddon ; captions translated by Catherine Atthill. — 95p : ill(some col.),ports(some col.) ; 20cm
ISBN 0-246-11292-1 (cased) : £3.95
ISBN 0-586-05137-6 (pbk) : £1.95 B81-12056

Toulouse-Lautrec, Henri de. Toulouse-Lautrec : the complete paintings / [compiled by] M.G. Dortu and J.A. Méric. — London : Granada, 1981. — (The Complete paintings)
Translation of: Toulouse-Lautrec
2 / translated by Catherine Atthill. — 96p : ill (some col.),ports ; 20cm
Bibliography: p96
ISBN 0-246-11294-8 (cased) : £3.95
ISBN 0-586-05138-4 (pbk) : £1.95 B81-12057

759.4 — Germany. West Berlin. Art galleries: Galerie Pels-Leusden. Exhibits: French paintings. Hartung, Hans — *Catalogues*

Hans Hartung : a vision into abstraction 1923-1964 : a 75th birthday tribute / Fischer Fine Art, London, January-February 1981 ; Galerie Pels-Leusden, Berlin April 1981. — London (30 King St., St. James's, S.W.1) : Fischer Fine Art, [1981]. — [24]p : ill(some col.),1port ; 26cm
Exhibition catalogue. — Port on inside cover
Unpriced (pbk)
Primary classification 759.4 B81-15675

759.4 — London. Westminster *(London Borough).* **Art galleries: Fischer Fine Art. Exhibits: French paintings. Hartung, Hans —** *Catalogues*

Hans Hartung : a vision into abstraction 1923-1964 : a 75th birthday tribute / Fischer Fine Art, London, January-February 1981 ; Galerie Pels-Leusden, Berlin April 1981. — London (30 King St., St. James's, S.W.1) : Fischer Fine Art, [1981]. — [24]p : ill(some col.),1port ; 26cm
Exhibition catalogue. — Port on inside cover
Unpriced (pbk)
Also classified at 759.4 B81-15675

759.4′074′0436 — France. Paris. Art galleries: Musée Marmottan. Exhibits: French paintings, *ca1750-ca1850 — Catalogues*
Art in early XIX century France. — London ([147 New Bond St., W.1.]) : Wildenstein, [1981?]. — 74p : ill(some col.),ports(some col.) ; 30cm
Published in connection with an exhibition held at the Musée Marmottan, Paris
Unpriced (pbk)
Also classified at 741.944′074′0436 B81-33111

759.5 — Italian paintings. Canaletto, *1697-1768 — Catalogues*
Canaletto, *1697-1768*. Canaletto : the complete paintings / [compiled by] J.G. Links. — London : Granada, 1981. — 96p : ill(some col.),1port ; 20cm. — (The Complete paintings)
Originally published: in Italian translation as Canaletto. Milan : Rizzoli, 1979. — Bibliography: p96
ISBN 0-246-11296-4 : £3.95
ISBN 0-586-05146-5 (pbk) : Unpriced
B81-12060

759.5 — Italian paintings. Cavallini, Pietro — *Critical studies*
Hetherington, Paul. Pietro Cavallini : a study in the art of late medieval Rome / by Paul Hetherington. — London (78 Redesdale Gardens, Isleworth, Middx, TW7 5JD) : Sagittarius, 1979. — xvii,186p,[98]p of plates : ill ; 25cm
Bibliography: p163-181. - Includes index
ISBN 0-9503163-3-4 : Unpriced B81-13676

759.5 — Italian paintings. Giotto — *Critical studies*
Bellosi, Luciano. Giotto / Luciano Bellosi. — London : Constable, c1981. — 79p : col.ill ; 28cm
£5.95 (pbk) B81-34970

759.5 — Italian paintings. Leonardo, *da Vinci — Critical studies*
Leonardo, *da Vinci*. Leonardo / text by Jack Wasserman. — [New York?] : Doubleday ; Leicester : distributed by Windward, [1981?]. — 179p : chiefly ill(some col.) ; 30cm
Bibliography: p177-178
ISBN 0-7112-0066-1 : Unpriced B81-23310

759.5 — Italian paintings. Modigliani, Amedeo — *Biographies*
Zurcher, Bernard. Modigliani / Bernard Zurcher ; [translated from the French by Jane Brenton. — London : Eyre Methuen, 1981. — 31p,[77]p of plates : ill(some col.),port(some col.) ; 17cm
Translation of: Modigliani
ISBN 0-413-47690-1 (pbk) : £3.95 B81-30684

759.5 — Italian paintings. Reni, Guido — *Biographies — Early works*
Malvasia, Carlo Cesare, *conte*. The life of Guido Reni / Carlo Cesare Malvasia ; translated and with an introduction by Catherine Enggass and Robert Enggass. — University Park ; London : Pennsylvania State University Press, c1980. — 150p,8p of plates : ill,1port ; 24cm
Translation of: Guido Reni
ISBN 0-271-00264-6 : £7.20 B81-26261

759.5 — Italian paintings. Tiziano Vecellio — *Biographies*
Fasolo, Ugo. Titian / Ugo Fasolo ; [translation: Patrick Geagh]. — [London] : Constable, [1981]. — 95p : col.ill,col.maps ; 28cm
Translated from the Italian
ISBN 0-09-464090-4 (pbk) : £5.50 B81-14250

759.5 — Italian paintings. Tiziano Vecellio — *Catalogues*
Tiziano Vecellio. Titian : the complete paintings / [compiled by] Terisio Pignatti. — London : Granada, 1981. — (The Complete paintings) II / translated by Judith Landry. — 95p : chiefly ill(some col.),ports(some col.) ; 20cm
Translation from the Italian. — Bibliography: p96
ISBN 0-246-11298-0 (cased) : £3.95
ISBN 0-586-05148-1 (pbk) : Unpriced
B81-24449

759.5 — Italian paintings. Uccello, Paolo. Hunt in the Forest — *Critical studies*
Paolo Uccello's Hunt in the forest. — Oxford : Ashmolean Museum, 1981. — [28]p : ill(some col.),1facsim,music,ports ; 30cm
ISBN 0-900090-72-3 (pbk) : £2.95 B81-28940

759.5 — Italian paintings. Vivarini, Alvise — *Critical studies*
Steer, John. Alvise Vivarini. — Cambridge : Cambridge University Press, Feb.1982. — [311]p
ISBN 0-521-23363-1 : £49.50 : CIP entry
B81-40271

759.5 — Italian portrait paintings. Sebastiano, *del Piombo — Critical studies*
Hirst, Michael. Sebastiano del Piombo / Michael Hirst. — Oxford : Clarendon Press, 1981. — xvii,175p,[144]p of plates : ill,1facsim,ports ; 29cm. — (Oxford studies in the history of art and architecture)
Bibliography: p160-168. — Includes index
ISBN 0-19-817308-3 : £35.00 B81-38598

759.5′074′014967 — New Jersey. Princeton. Art galleries: Princeton University. *Art Museum.* **Exhibits: Italian paintings. Baroque style,** *ca 1530-ca 1750 — Catalogues*
Italian baroque painting : from New York private collections / John T. Spike. — Princeton ; Guildford : The Art Museum, Princeton University in association with Princeton University Press, c1980. — 127p : ill ; 29cm
Catalogue of the exhibition held at The Art Museum, Princeton University, from 27th April to 7th September 1980. — Bibliography: p121-125
ISBN 0-691-03955-0 (cased) : £16.50
ISBN 0-691-00325-4 (pbkunpriced) B81-06959

759.5′31 — Italian paintings: Venetian paintings, *1700-1800 — Critical studies*
Levey, Michael. Painting in eighteenth-century Venice / Michael Levey. — 2nd ed. — Oxford : Phaidon, 1980. — 256p : ill(some col.),ports (some col.) ; 26cm
Previous ed.: 1959. — Bibliography: p250-251. - Includes index
ISBN 0-7148-2002-4 : £15.00 : CIP rev.
B80-10172

759.5′58 — Italian paintings: Sienese paintings, *to 1490 — Critical studies*
Cole, Bruce. Sienese painting : from its origins to the fifteenth century / Bruce Cole. — New York ; London : Harper & Row, c1980. — xii,243p,5p of plates : ill(some col.) ; 25cm. — (Icon editions)
Bibliography: p225-231. - Includes index
ISBN 0-06-430901-0 : £12.50 B81-04147

759.6 — London. Westminster *(London Borough).* **Spanish cultural institutions: Institute of Spain. Exhibits: Spanish ink paintings. Quintanilla, Manuel** *— Catalogues*
Manuel Quintanilla. — London : 102 Eaton Sq., S.W.1. : Spanish Institute, [1980]. — [19]p : chiefly ill,1facsim ; 21cm
Published to accompany an exhibition held at the Spanish Institute, London, 1980. — Cover title
Unpriced (pbk) B81-08134

759.6 — Spanish paintings. Dali, Salvador — *Biographies*
Maddox, Conroy. Dali / Conroy Maddox. — London : Hamlyn, 1979 (1981 [printing]). — 96p,59plates : ill(some col.),1col.port ; 30cm
Bibliography: p94. — Includes index
ISBN 0-600-34263-8 (pbk) : £2.95 B81-38558

759.6 — Spanish paintings. Goya, Francisco de — *Critical studies*
Salas, Xavier de. Goya / Xavier de Salas ; [translation by G.T. Culverwell]. — London : Studio Vista, 1979, c1978. — 206p : ill(some col.),ports(some col.) ; 34cm
Translation from the Spanish. — Bibliography: p206
ISBN 0-289-70887-7 : £11.95 B81-19733

759.6 — Spanish paintings. Picasso, Pablo, *1881-1907 — Critical studies*
Fabre, Palau. Picasso : life and work of the early years, 1881-1907. — Oxford : Phaidon, Oct.1981. — [560]p
Translation of: Picasso vivo 1881-1907 : infancia y primer juventud de un demiurgo
ISBN 0-7148-2219-1 : £95.00 : CIP entry
B81-24679

759.6 — Spanish paintings. Picasso, Pablo — *Biographies*
Gedo, Mary Mathews. Picasso : art as autobiography / Mary Mathews Gedo. — Chicago ; London : University of Chicago Press, c1980. — xi,304p,[8]p of plates : ill(some col.),ports ; 25cm
Includes index
ISBN 0-226-28482-4 : £12.00 B81-30030

Penrose, Roland. Picasso : his life and work / Roland Penrose. — 3rd ed. — London : Granada, 1981. — xviii,517p,A-D,xxviiip of plates : ill,1map,ports ; 21cm
Previous ed.: Harmondsworth : Penguin, 1971. — Bibliography: p493-499. — Includes index
ISBN 0-246-11532-7 (cased) : £9.95
ISBN 0-586-08380-4 (pbk) : unpriced
B81-18738

Penrose, Roland. Portrait of Picasso / Roland Penrose. — 3rd rev. ed. — [London] : Thames and Hudson, 1981. — 128p : ill,1map,facsims,ports ; 25cm
Previous ed.: London : Lund Humphries, 1971. — Includes index
ISBN 0-500-27226-3 (pbk) : £3.95 B81-25940

759.6 — Spanish paintings. Velázquez, Diego Rodriguez de Silva y — *Catalogues*
Velázquez, Diego Rodriguez de Silva y. Velázquez : the complete paintings / [introduction and catalogue] by Nicola Spinosa ; translated by Catherine Atthill. — London : Granada, 1980. — 95p : chiefly ill(some col.),ports(some col.) ; 20cm. — (The complete paintings)
Translated from the Italian. — Bibliography: p96
ISBN 0-246-11291-3 (cased) : £3.95
ISBN 0-586-05145-7 (pbk) : £1.95 B81-37756

759.7 — Russian paintings. Repin, I. E. — *Biographies*
Parker, Fan. Russia on canvas : Ilya Repin / Fan Parker and Stephen Jan Parker. — University Park ; London : Pennsylvania State University Press, c1980. — xiii,178p,[4]p of plates : ill (some col.),ports ; 27cm
Bibliography: p167-168. — List of works: p155-159. — Includes index
ISBN 0-271-00252-2 : £17.85 B81-26025

759.7 — Scotland. Fife Region. St Andrews. Art galleries: Balcarres Gallery. Exhibits: Russian paintings. Pasternak, Leonid — *Catalogues*
Salmina-Haskell, Larissa. Leonid Pasternak 1862-1945. — [St Andrews] ([St Andrews, Fife]) : Crawford Centre for the Arts, University of St Andrews, [1978]. — 40p : ill ; 20x21cm
Catalogue of an exhibition held at the Crawford Centre for the Arts, University of St Andrews, 28 Jan.-25 Feb. 1978. — Catalogue by Larissa Salmina-Haskell: biographical notes by Jennifer Bradshaw. — Bibliography: p40
ISBN 0-906272-00-9 (pbk) : Unpriced
B81-08076

759.94 — European paintings, *1300-1965 — Critical studies*
Jacobs, Michael, *1952-*. A guide to European painting / Michael Jacobs. — Newton Abbot : David & Charles, c1980. — 272p : col.ill,col.ports ; 33cm
Includes index
ISBN 0-7153-8097-4 : £25.00 : CIP rev.
B80-22341

759.94′074′019493 — California. Pasadena. Art galleries: Norton Simon Museum. Stock: European paintings, *ca 1280-1942 — Catalogues*
Selected paintings at the Norton Simon Museum, Pasadena, California / introduced by Frank Herrmann. — London : Scala/Philip Wilson, 1980. — 143p : chiefly col. ill,col. ports ; 29cm
Includes index
ISBN 0-85667-094-4 (cased) : £7.95
ISBN 0-85667-093-6 (pbk) : Unpriced
B81-36499

759.94'074'02132 — London. Westminster *(London Borough).* **Art galleries: National Gallery. Exhibits: European paintings,** *ca 1450-1977 — Catalogues*

Artist's Eye *(Exhibition) (1981 : National Gallery, London).* The artist's eye : David Hockney looking at pictures in a book at the National Gallery, 1 July-31 August 1981. — London : National Gallery, c1981. — 25p : ill ; 16cm + 8 postcards(col.; 15x11cm)
Postcards in pocket
Unpriced (pbk) B81-31872

759.94'074'0291835 — Dublin. Art galleries: National Gallery of Ireland. Exhibits — *Catalogues*

National Gallery of Ireland. National Gallery of Ireland illustrated summary catalogue of paintings. — Dublin : Gill & Macmillan, Nov.1981. — [392]p
ISBN 0-7171-1144-x (cased) : £25.00 : CIP entry
ISBN 0-7171-1145-8 (pbk) : £10.00 B81-31235

759.9492 — Dutch paintings. Bosch, Hieronymus — *Critical studies*

Snyder, James. Hieronymus Bosch / James Snyder. — London (24 Friern Park, N12) : Ferndale, c1980. — 133p : col.ill ; 30cm. — (The Man and his paintings)
Translated from the French. — Bibliography: p133
ISBN 0-905746-14-7 : £20.00 B81-27535

759.9492 — Dutch paintings, *ca 1400-ca 1650 — Critical studies*

Friedländer, Max J.. From Van Eyck to Bruegel / Max J. Friedländer ; edited and annotated by F. Grossmann ; [translated by Marguerite Kay]. — 4th ed. — Oxford : Phaidon, 1981. — x,409p : ill,ports ; 21cm. — (Landmarks in art history)
Translation of: Von Eyck bis Bruegel. — Previous ed. published: in 2 v. 1969. — Includes index
ISBN 0-7148-2139-x (pbk) : £6.50 : CIP rev.
B81-07602

759.9492 — Dutch paintings, *ca 1400-ca 1700 — Critical studies*

Fromentin, Eugène. The masters of past time : Dutch and Flemish painting from Van Eyck to Rembrandt / Eugène Fromentin ; edited by H. Gerson. — 2nd ed. — Oxford : Phaidon, 1981. — xvi,389p : ill,ports ; 21cm. — (Landmarks in art history)
Translation of: Les Maitres d'autrefois. — Previous ed.: 1948. — Bibliography: p381-383. — Includes index
ISBN 0-7148-2142-x (pbk) : £6.50 : CIP rev.
Also classified at 759.9493 B81-05927

759.9492 — Dutch paintings. Fabritius, Carel — *Critical studies*

Brown, Christopher, *1948-*. Carel Fabritius : complete edition with a catalogue raisonné / Christopher Brown. — Oxford : Phaidon, 1981. — 168p : ill(some col.),maps,facsims,ports ; 29cm
Bibliography: p164-166. — Includes index
ISBN 0-7148-2032-6 : £30.00 B81-29722

759.9492 — Dutch paintings. Gogh, Vincent van — *Biographies*

Elgar, Frank. Van Gogh / Frank Elgar ; [translated from the French by Jane Brenton]. — London : Eyre Methuen, 1981. — [39] p,[93]p of plates : ill(some col.),1facsim,ports (some col.) ; 18cm
Translation of: Van Gogh
ISBN 0-413-48240-5 (pbk) : £3.95 B81-30682

759.9492 — Dutch paintings. Gogh, Vincent van — *Biographies — For children*

Measham, Terry. Van Gogh and his world / Terry Measham. — London : Kingfisher, 1980. — 29p : ill(some col.),1col.map,facsims,ports (some col.) ; 29cm. — (Great masters)
Col.ill on lining papers. — Bibliography: p29. — Includes index
ISBN 0-7063-6031-1 : £2.95 : CIP rev.
B80-17878

759.9492 — Dutch paintings. Gogh, Vincent van — *Critical studies*

Hulsker, Jan. The complete Van Gogh : paintings, drawings, sketches / Jan Hulsker. — Oxford : Phaidon, 1980, c1977. — 198p : ill (some col.),ports(some col.) ; 36cm
Translation of: Van Gogh en zijn weg. — Bibliography: p489-490. - Includes index
ISBN 0-7148-2028-8 : £45.00 B81-03336

Uhde, W.. Van Gogh / W. Uhde with notes by Griselda Pollock. — Rev. and enl. ed. — Oxford : Phaidon, 1981. — 31,[96]p : ill(some col.),ports(some col.) ; 31cm. — (Phaidon colour library)
Previous ed.: 1972. — Bibliography: p28
ISBN 0-7148-2163-2 (cased) : £9.95 : CIP rev.
ISBN 0-7148-2161-6 (pbk) : £6.95 B81-13537

Walker, John A.. Van Gogh studies : five critical essays / John A. Walker. — London (87 Hillfield Ave. N8 7DG) : JAW, 1981. — 72p : ill, ; maps,1facsim,ports ; 30cm
Includes bibliographies
ISBN 0-9507486-0-9 (pbk) : £3.00 B81-40002

759.9492 — Dutch paintings. Gogh, Vincent van — *Critical studies — For children*

Raboff, Ernest. Vincent van Gogh / by Ernest Raboff and Adeline Peter. — London : Ernest Benn, 1980. — [32]p : ill(some col.),ports(some col.) ; 29cm. — (Art for children)
ISBN 0-510-00103-3 : £3.95 B81-14474

759.9492 — Dutch paintings. Vermeer, Jan — *Catalogues*

Vermeer, Jan. Vermeer : the complete paintings / [compiled by] Albert Blankert ; Van Meegeren / Maurizio Villa ; translated by Lucia Wildt. — London : Granada, 1981. — 96p : ill(some col.) ; 20cm. — (The Complete paintings)
Originally published: in Italian translation as Vermeer. Milan : Rizzoli, 1979. — Bibliography: p96
ISBN 0-246-11295-6 : £3.95
ISBN 0-586-05139-2 (pbk) : unpriced
B81-12055

759.9492 — Northern Dutch paintings, *1400-1500 - Critical studies*

Châtelet, Albert. Early Dutch painting. — Oxford : Phaidon, Aug.1981. — [266]p
Translation of: Les primitifs hollandais
ISBN 0-7148-2095-4 : £48.00 : CIP entry
B81-17539

759.9493 — Flemish paintings. Bruegel, Pieter — *Critical studies*

Wied, Alexander. Bruegel / Alexander Wied ; [translation Anthony Lloyd]. — London : Studio Vista, 1980. — 190p : ill(some col.),1port ; 34cm
Translation of the Italian. — Includes index
ISBN 0-289-70974-1 : £12.95 B81-40694

759.9493 — Flemish paintings, *ca 1400-ca 1700 — Critical studies*

Fromentin, Eugène. The masters of past time : Dutch and Flemish painting from Van Eyck to Rembrandt / Eugène Fromentin ; edited by H. Gerson. — 2nd ed. — Oxford : Phaidon, 1981. — xvi,389p : ill,ports ; 21cm. — (Landmarks in art history)
Translation of: Les Maitres d'autrefois. — Previous ed.: 1948. — Bibliography: p381-383. — Includes index
ISBN 0-7148-2142-x (pbk) : £6.50 : CIP rev.
Primary classification 759.9492 B81-05927

759.9494 — Swiss paintings. Giacometti, Alberto — *Personal observations*

Lord, James. A Giacometti portrait / James Lord. — London : Faber, 1981, c1980. — 117p : ill,2ports ; 21cm
Originally published: New York : Farrar Straus Giroux, 1980
ISBN 0-571-11668-x (pbk) : £2.25 B81-09016

759.9494 — Swiss paintings. Klee, Paul — *Critical studies — For children*

Raboff, Ernest. Paul Klee / by Ernest Raboff. — London : Ernest Benn, 1980. — [32]p : ill (some col.) ; 29cm. — (Art for children)
ISBN 0-510-00100-9 : £3.95 B81-14473

759.951 — Chinese watercolour paintings, *1850-1970 — Illustrations*

Hejzlar, Josef. Chinese watercolours / text by josef Hejzlar ; photographs by B. Forman. — London : Cathay, 1980, c1978. — 70p,[96]p of plates : ill(some col.) ; 30cm
Bibliography: p68. — Includes index
ISBN 0-904644-30-8 : £7.95 B81-38937

759.951'0216 — Chinese paintings, *to 1367 — Lists*

Cahill, James, *1926-*. An index of early Chinese painters and paintings : Tang, Sung, and Yüan : incorporating the work of Osvald Sirén and Ellen Johnston Laing / by James Cahill. — Berkeley ; London : University of California Press, c1980. — x,391p ; 26cm
Bibliography : p379-391
ISBN 0-520-03576-3 : £15.00 B81-28994

759.994 — Australian watercolour paintings. Cayley, Neville W.. Special subjects: Parrots — *Illustrations*

Prince, J. H.. Neville Cayley : his Royal Zoological Society of NSW collection of parrots and cockatoos of Australia / J.H. Prince. — Newton Abbot : David & Charles, c1980, c1981. — 80p : ill(some col.),maps ; 37cm
Originally published: Sydney : Reed, 1980. — Ill on lining papers. — Bibliography: p4. — Includes index
ISBN 0-7153-8191-1 : £10.50 B81-36786

760 — GRAPHIC ARTS, PRINTS

760 — Emblem books — *English texts*

Cramer, Daniel. The rosicrucian emblems of Daniel Cramer : the true society of Jesus and the rosy cross : here are forty sacred emblems from Holy Scripture concerning the most precious name and cross of Jesus Christ / by the author Daniel Cramer ; translated by Fiona Tait ; edited by Adam McLean. — Edinburgh (12 Antigua St., Edinburgh) : [A. McLean], c1980. — 65p : ill,1facsim ; 22cm. — (Magnum opus hermetic sourceworks ; no.4)
Translation of: Societas Iesu et roseae crucis vera. — Limited ed. of 250 copies
Unpriced B81-34437

Stolcius, Daniel. The hermetic garden of Daniel Stolcius : composed of flowerlets of philosophy engraved in copper and explained in short verses where weary students of chemistry may find a treasure house and refresh themselves after their laboratory work / translated by Patricia Tahil ; edited with a commentary by Adam McLean. — Edinburgh (12 Antigua St., Edinburgh) : [A. McLean], c1980. — 169p : ill ; 22cm. — (Magnum opus hermetic sourceworks ; no.5)
Translation of: Hortulus hermeticus. — Limited ed. of 250 copies
Unpriced B81-34436

760'.016 — Graphic arts, *to 1977.* **Reproductions** — *Indexes*

Korwin, Yala H.. Index to two-dimensional art works / by Yala H. Korwin. — Metuchen ; London : Scarecrow, 1981. — 2v.(xxvi,1493p) ; 23cm
Contents: v.1. General symbols, abbreviations for books indexed, artist index — v.2. Location symbols, title-subject index
ISBN 0-8108-1381-5 : £48.65 B81-25968

760'.028 — Graphic arts. Techniques. Identification — *Amateurs' manuals*

Matthews, J. W. B.. Identifying pictures : a visual guide to picture making techniques / J.W.B. Matthews. — Bognor Regis : New Horizon, c1981. — 140p : ill ; 21cm
Includes index
ISBN 0-86116-229-3 : £6.95 B81-40120

760'.0442 — French graphic arts, *1800-1899.* **Special subjects: Peasants** — *Critical studies*

Thompson, James, *1947-*. The peasant in French 19th century art : an exhibition organized for the Douglas Hyde Gallery, Trinity College, Dublin, 22 October to 22 November, 1980 / by James Thompson with the assistance of Madeleine Fidell Beaufort and John Horne. — Dublin (Trinity College, Dublin) : The Gallery, [1980]. — viii,192p : ill,2facsims,ports ; 24cm
Includes bibliographies and index
Unpriced (pbk) B81-05027

760'.0442 — Graphic arts, *1963-1980*. Special subjects: Celebrities — *Illustrations*
Fame / [compiled by] Brad Benedict. — London : Elm Tree, 1981, c1980. — 119p : all ports (some col.) ; 25x26cm
Originally published: New York : Harmony, 1980
ISBN 0-241-10537-4 (pbk) : £5.95 B81-05645

760'.04423 — English graphic arts. Special subjects: Theatre. Acting. Doggett, Thomas. Authenticity
Leon, Walter. Thomas Doggett pictur'd : an enquiry into the claims to authenticity of the few supposed representations from life of this famous comedian (born Dublin C.1650, died Eltham 10th September 1721) and such idea of his physical appearance and personality as can be derived therefrom and from contemporary descriptions (including one of his own) / by Walter Leon. — [London] ([18 St. Mary-at-Hill, EC3R 8EE]) : The Company of Watermen & Lightermen of the River Thames, 1980. — 52p : ill,1map,facsims,ports ; 26cm
Unpriced B81-39376

760'.04432 — Graphic arts. Special subjects: Falconiformes — *Illustrations*
Hawks / edited by Lynn Hughes. — London : W.H. Allen, 1981. — 53p : ill(some col.) ; 15cm
ISBN 0-491-02722-2 (corrected) : £2.50
Primary classification 820.8'036 B81-29965

760'.04432 — Graphic arts. Special subjects: Hares — *Illustrations*
Hares / edited by D. Wyn Hughes. — London : W.H. Allen, 1981. — 55p : ill(some col.) ; 18cm
ISBN 0-491-02634-x : £2.50
Primary classification 808.8'036 B81-05705

760'.04432 — Graphic arts. Special subjects: Monkeys, *to 1979* — *Illustrations*
Monkeys / edited by Lynn Hughes. — London : W.H. Allen, 1980. — 53p : col.ill ; 15cm
ISBN 0-491-02692-7 : £2.50
Primary classification 820'.8'036 B81-01549

760'.04432 — Graphic arts. Special subjects: Songbirds, *to 1980* — *Illustrations*
Songbirds / edited by Lynn Hughes. — London : W.H. Allen, c1981. — 53p : col.ill ; 15cm
ISBN 0-491-02791-5 : £2.50
Primary classification 820.8'036 B81-15693

760'.04432 — Graphic arts, *to 1980*. Special subjects: Horses — *Collections*
Horses / edited by Elizabeth Rudd. — London : W.H. Allen, 1981. — 53p : ill(some col.) ; 15cm
ISBN 0-491-02655-2 : £2.50
Primary classification 808.8'036 B81-35739

760'.04436'094207402659 — Cambridgeshire. Cambridge. Museums: Fitzwilliam Museum. Exhibits: English landscape graphic arts, *1750-1850* — *Catalogues*
Beauty, horror and immensity : picturesque landscape in Britain, 1750-1850 / exhibition selected and catalogued by Peter Bicknell. — Cambridge : Cambridge University Press, 1981. — xx,103p,[54]p of plates : ill(some col.) ; 26cm
Published to accompany an exhibition at the Fitzwilliam Museum, Cambridge, 1981. — Bibliography: ppxviii-xx. — Includes index
ISBN 0-521-23880-3 (cased) : £18.50 : CIP rev.
ISBN 0-521-28278-0 (pbk) : £6.95 B81-19121

760'.0445 — Abstract graphic arts. Techniques — *Manuals*
Brooks, Leonard, *1911-*. Painting and understanding abstract art : an approach to contemporary methods / Leonard Brooks. — New York ; London : Van Nostrand Reinhold, 1980, c1964. — 143p : ill(some col.) ; 26cm
Originally published: New York : Reinhold, 1964
ISBN 0-442-24334-0 (pbk) : £7.45 B81-11438

760'.0447 — Graphic arts. Special themes: Dragons — *Illustrations*
Dragons / edited by Elizabeth Rudd. — London : W.H. Allen, 1980. — 55p : ill(some col.) ; 18cm
ISBN 0-491-02604-8 : £2.50
Primary classification 808.8'0375 B81-02747

760'.092'2 — American graphic arts. Curry, John Steuart & Wood, Grant — *Illustrations*
Curry, John Steuart. John Steuart Curry and Grant Wood : a portrait of rural America / Joseph S. Czestochowski. — Columbia ; London : University of Missouri Press with the Cedar Rapids Art Association, 1981. — 224p : chiefly ill(some col.) ; 25cm
Bibliography: p219-221. — Includes index
ISBN 0-8262-0336-1 : £16.90 B81-29544

760'.092'4 — American graphic arts. Audubon, John James. Special subjects: Birds & mammals — *Illustrations*
Audubon, John James. The art of Audubon : the complete birds and mammals / John James Audubon ; with an introduction by Roger Tory Peterson. — London : Macdonald Futura, 1981. — xiii,674p : all col.ill ; 29cm
Includes index
ISBN 0-354-04593-8 : £15.95 B81-05415

760'.092'4 — Dutch graphic arts. Everdingen, Allart van — *Critical studies*
Davies, Alice I.. Allart van Everdingen / Alice I. Davies. — New York ; London : Garland, 1978. — xliii,380p,[209]p of plates : ill,2maps,1port ; 21cm. — (Outstanding dissertations in the fine arts)
Bibliography: p370-380
ISBN 0-8240-3223-3 : Unpriced B81-26932

760'.092'4 — English graphic arts. Aldin, Cecil — *Biographies*
Heron, Roy. Cecil Aldin : the story of a sporting artist / Roy Heron. — Exeter : Webb & Bower, 1981. — 208p : ill(some col.),facsims,ports ; 24cm
Bibliography: p190-197. — List of works: p197-205. — Includes index
ISBN 0-906671-46-9 : £9.95 B81-33270

760'.092'4 — English graphic arts. Bawden, Edward — *Critical studies*
Bliss, Douglas Percy. Edward Bawden / Douglas Percy Bliss. — Godalming (The Raswell, Loxhill, Godalming, Surrey GU8 4BQ) : Pendomer, [1980]. — 197p : ill(some col.),facsims(some col.),ports ; 30cm
Bibliography: p179-197
ISBN 0-906267-02-1 : £17.50
ISBN 0-906267-03-x (De luxe ed.) : Unpriced B81-14213

760'.092'4 — English graphic arts. Bewick, Thomas — *Illustrations*
Bewick, Thomas. The watercolours and drawings of Thomas Bewick and his workshop apprentices / introduced and with editorial notes by Iain Bain. — London : Fraser, 1981. — 2v.(233 ; 230p) : ill(some col.),facsims(some col.),2ports ; 25cm
In slip-case. — Bibliography: p226. — Includes index
ISBN 0-86092-057-7 : Unpriced : CIP rev. B81-16393

760'.092'4 — English graphic arts. Blake, William — *Catalogues*
Butlin, Martin. The paintings and drawings of William Blake / Martin Butlin. — New Haven ; London : Published for the Paul Mellon Centre for Studies in British Art by Yale University Press, 1981. — 2v : ill(some col.),facsims,ports ; 31cm. — (Studies in British art)
Bibliography: p[12]p. — Includes index
ISBN 0-300-02550-5 : Unpriced B81-27011

760'.092'4 — English graphic arts. Graham, Rigby — *Biographies*
Foord, Colleen. Rigby Graham : a monograph / by Colleen Foord. — [Leicester] ([P.O. Box 143, Leicester, LE1 9BN]) : School of Graphics, Leicester Polytechnic, 1981. — [18]p : ill ; 21cm
Unpriced (pbk) B81-32748

760'.092'4 — English graphic arts. Weston, David. Railways — *Illustrations*
Weston, David. Beware of trains / David Weston. — London : Ian Allan, 1981. — 108p : ill (some col.),ports ; 23x29cm
ISBN 0-7110-1060-9 : £15.00 B81-32802

760'.092'4 — Flemish graphic arts. Rubens, Peter Paul. Special subjects: Costume — *Critical studies*
Belkin, Kristin Lohse. The costume book / Kristin Lohse Belkin. — London : Harvey Miller : Heyden, 1978. — 208p,[120]p of plates : ill,coat of arms,facsims,ports ; 27cm. — (Corpus Rubenianum Ludwig Burchard ; pt. 24)
Includes index
ISBN 0-905203-35-6 : Unpriced B81-14665

760'.092'4 — French graphic arts. Le Moyne de Morgues, Jacques — *Critical studies*
Hulton, Paul. The Work of Jacques le Moyne de Morgues : a Huguenot artist in France, Florida and England / foreword, catalogue and introductory studies by Paul Hulton with contributions by D.B. Quinn ... [et al.]. — London : Published for the Trustees of the British Museum by British Museum Publiications in association with the Huguenot Society of London, c1977. — 2v. : ill(some col.),maps,facsims,ports ; 33cm
In slip case. — Bibliography: p221-226. — Includes index. — Contents: v.1 Foreword, catalogue and introductory studies — v.2 Plates
ISBN 0-7141-0737-9 : Unpriced
ISBN 0-7141-0750-6 (v.1)
ISBN 0-7141-0751-4 (v.2) B81-15689

760'.092'4 — Great Britain. Art galleries. Exhibits: English graphic arts. Strang, William, *1859-1921* — *Catalogues*
William Strang RA 1859-1921 : painter-etcher / [exhibition organised by Sheffield City Art Galleries with financial assistance from the Arts Council of Great Britain]. — [Sheffield] ([Graves Art Gallery, Surrey St., Sheffield S1 1XZ]) : The Galleries, [1980]. — 86p : ill(some col.),ports ; 25cm
Published to accompany an exhibition held at the Graves Art Gallery, Sheffield, Glasgow Museums and Art Galleries and the National Portrait Gallery, London, 1980-81. — Includes index
ISBN 0-900660-60-0 (cased) : Unpriced
ISBN 0-900660-61-9 (pbk) : Unpriced B81-16426

760'.092'4 — Ireland. Art galleries. Exhibits: Irish graphic arts. Scott, Patrick, *1921-* — *Catalogues*
Scott, Patrick, *1921-*. Patrick Scott : The Douglas Hyde Gallery, Trinity College, Dublin, Ulster Museum, Belfast, 21st May—28 June 1981, Crawford Municipal Art Gallery, Cork, July—Aug 1981. — [Dublin] : [Trinity College, Dublin], [1981]. — 79p : ill(some col.) ; 25cm
Text by Dorothy Walker
Unpriced (pbk) B81-28222

760'.092'4 — Islamic graphic arts. Tiffou, Edmond — *Biographies*
Tiffou, Edmond. The illuminator / Edmond Tiffou ; translated by Rosalind Mazzawi. — London : Quartet, 1981. — 135p ; 24cm
Translated from a French ms
ISBN 0-7043-2279-x : £6.98 B81-29535

760'.092'4 — Italy. Milan. Art galleries: Galleria A. Jannone. Exhibits: Italian graphic arts. Scolari, Massimo — *Catalogues*
Scolari, Massimo. Massimo Scolari : watercolours and drawing 1965-1980 / edited by Francesco Moschini. — London : Academy Editions, [1980]. — 243p : ill(some col.) ; 24cm
Published to accompany exhibitions of Scolari's watercolours and drawings at the A. Jannone Gallery in Milan and at the A.A.M. Modern Art and Architecture Rome, 1980. — Parallel Italian text and English translation. — Bibliography: p242-243
ISBN 88-7038-025-4 (pbk) : Unpriced
Primary classification 760'.092'4 B81-29547

760'.092'4 — Italy. Rome. Art galleries: Galleria AAM. Exhibits: Italian graphic arts. Scolari, Massimo — *Catalogues*
Scolari, Massimo. Massimo Scolari : watercolours and drawing 1965-1980 / edited by Francesco Moschini. — London : Academy Editions, [1980]. — 243p : ill(some col.) ; 24cm
Published to accompany exhibitions of Scolari's watercolours and drawings at the A. Jannone Gallery in Milan and at the A.A.M. Modern Art and Architecture Rome, 1980. — Parallel Italian text and English translation. — Bibliography: p242-243
ISBN 88-7038-025-4 (pbk) : Unpriced
Also classified at 760'.092'4 B81-29547

760′.092′4 — Japanese graphic arts. Anno, Mitsumasa — *Illustrations*

Anno, Mitsumasa. The unique world of Mitsumasa Anno : selected illustrations 1968-1977 / translated and adapted by Samuel Crowell Morse ; with a foreword by Martin Gardner. — London : Bodley Head, 1980. — 48p : col.ill ; 27cm
Translated from the Japanese
ISBN 0-370-30364-4 : £5.95 : CIP rev.
B80-19858

760′.092′4 — London. Kensington and Chelsea *(London Borough)*. **Art galleries: Taranman. Exhibits: French graphic arts** — *Catalogues*

Asse, Geneviève. Geneviève Asse / preface by Roland Penrose. — London (236 Brompton Rd., SW3 2BB) : Taranman, c1980. — [15] p,8leaves of plates : col.ill ; 24cm
Catalogue of the exhibition at Taranman, 15 January-14 February 1981. — Limited ed. of 300 copies, of which the first 30 are numbered and signed by the artist
ISBN 0-906499-10-0 (pbk) : Unpriced
B81-09583

760′.092′4 — London. Tower Hamlets *(London Borough)*. **Art galleries: Whitechapel Art Gallery. Exhibits: American graphic arts. Marden, Brice** — *Catalogues*

Brice Marden : paintings, drawings and prints 1975-80 / Whitechapel Art Gallery, 8 May-21 June 1981. — London : Whitechapel Art Gallery, 1981. — 64p : ill(some col.) ; 28cm
Published to accompany an exhibition at the Whitechapel Art Gallery, 1981
ISBN 0-85488-052-6 (pbk) : Unpriced
B81-25543

760′.092′4 — London. Westminster *(London Borough)*. **Art galleries: Anthony d′Offay** *(Firm)*. **Exhibits: English graphic arts. Jones, David,** *1895-1974* — *Catalogues*

David Jones : inscriptions. — London (9 Dering St., New Bond St., W.1) : Anthony d′Offay, [1980]. — [18]p,[8]p of plates : ill ; 20cm
Catalogue compiled by Nicolete Gray. — Bibliography: p6
Unpriced (pbk) B81-22843

760′.092′4 — London. Westminster *(London Borough)*. **Art galleries: Tate Gallery. Exhibits: English graphic arts. Jones, David,** *1895-1974* — *Catalogues*

Jones, David, *1895-1974*. David Jones. — London : Tate Gallery, 1981. — 144p : ill (some col.),ports ; 26cm
Published to accompany an exhibition at the Tate Gallery, 1981. — Bibliography: p141-142
ISBN 0-905005-08-2 (cased) : £12.00
ISBN 0-905005-03-1 (pbk) : £7.95 B81-37836

760′.092′4 — London. Westminster *(London Borough)*. **Art galleries: Tate Gallery. Exhibits: Welsh graphic arts. Richards, Ceri** — *Catalogues*

Richards, Ceri. Ceri Richards. — London : Tate Gallery, 1981. — 72p : ill(some col.),ports ; 21cm
Published to accompany an exhibition at the Tate Gallery, 1981. — Bibliography: p70-71
ISBN 0-905005-13-9 (pbk) : £4.95 B81-37837

760′.092′4 — Scotland. Art galleries. Exhibits: Scottish graphic arts. Colquhoun, Robert — *Catalogues*

Colquhoun, Robert. Robert Colquhoun. — [Edinburgh] ([142 Canongate, Edinburgh [H8 8DD]) : City of Edinburgh Museums and Art Galleries, 1981. — 13p : ill,1port ; 30cm
Published to accompany an exhibition at the Glasgow Art Gallery and Aberdeen Art Gallery, 1981. — Text on inside cover
ISBN 0-905072-09-x (pbk) : Unpriced
B81-26851

760′.092′4 — Welsh graphic arts. Davies, W. Mitford — *Biographies* — *Welsh texts*

W. Mitford Davies. — [Caernarfon] ([′Maesincla′, Caernarfon, Gwynedd]) : Gwynedd Library Service, 1980. — [16]p : ill,2ports ; 18x7cm
To accompany an exhibition, held at Oriel Môn, Llangefni in December 1980, organized by Gwynedd Library Service. — Cover title
Unpriced (pbk) B81-12260

760′.0942′07402789 — Cumbria. Carlisle *(District)*. **Brampton. Art galleries: LYC Museum and Art Gallery. Exhibits: English graphic arts,** *1979-1981* — *Catalogues*

81 May 2 / Noel Connor ... [et al.]. — Brampton (Banks, Brampton, Cumbria CA8 2JH) : LYC Museum & Art Gallery, c1981. — [52]p : chiefly ill,3ports ; 14cm
Cover title
Unpriced (pbk) B81-21158

760′.28 — Collagraph prints. Making — *Manuals*

Romano, Clare. The complete collagraph : the art and technique of printmaking from collage plates / by Clare Romano and John Ross ; with a foreword by Andrew Stasik. — New York : Free Press ; London : Collier Macmillan, c1980. — 200p,[16]p of plates : ill (some col.) ; 32cm
Ill on lining papers. — Bibliography: p193-195. — Includes index
ISBN 0-02-926770-6 : £16.95 B81-20848

760′.28 — Prints. Making — *Manuals*

Peterdi, Gabor. Printmaking : methods old and new / Gabor Peterdi. — Rev. and expanded ed. — New York : Macmillan ; London : Collier Macmillan, c1980. — xxxix,384p : ill,ports ; 20cm
Previous ed.: New York : Macmillan, 1971. — Bibliography: p371-372. - Includes index
ISBN 0-02-596060-1 : £14.25 B81-15617

760′.28 — Prints. Making — *Manuals* — *For children*

Herbert, Helen. Printing for presents / by Helen Herbert ; illustrated by the author. — Over : Dinosaur, c1981. — [24]p : ill ; 16x19cm. — (Dinosaur′s action books)
ISBN 0-85122-271-4 (cased) : £1.85 : CIP rev.
ISBN 0-85122-228-5 (pbk) : £0.70 B80-17845

760′.28 — Prints. Making. Techniques

Gilmour, Pat. Artists in print : an introduction to prints and printmaking / Pat Gilmour. — London : British Broadcasting Corporation, 1981. — 144p : ill(some col.),ports(some col.) ; 30cm
Published to accompany the BBC Continuing Education television series Artists in print ...
ISBN 0-563-16449-2 (pbk) : £9.95 B81-15653

760′.28 — Prints. Techniques

Dawson, John. The complete guide to prints and print making techniques and materials. — Oxford : Phaidon, July 1981. — [192]p
ISBN 0-7148-2184-5 : £13.95 : CIP entry
B81-14424

761 — RELIEF PRINTS

761′.2 — Wood engravings — *Manuals*

Mackley, George E.. Wood engraving / by George E. Mackley. — Old Woking : Gresham, 1981. — 124p : ill ; 21cm
Originally published: London : National Magazine Co., 1948. — Bibliography: p123-124
ISBN 0-905418-89-1 (cased) : Unpriced
ISBN 0-905418-84-0 (pbk) : £4.50 B81-16109

764 — CHROMOLITHOGRAPHY AND SERIGRAPHY

764′.8 — Screen prints. Techniques — *Manuals*

Schwalbach, Mathilda V.. Silk-screen printing for artists & craftsmen / Mathilda V. Schwalbach & James A. Schwalbach. — Unabridged and corr. version. — New York : Dover ; London : Constable, 1980, c1970. — 142p,[8]p of plates : ill(some col.) ; 29cm
Previous ed.: published as Screen-process printing for the serigrapher and textile designer. New York : Van Nostrand Reinhold, 1970. — Includes index
ISBN 0-486-24046-0 (pbk) : £4.15 B81-39195

767 — ETCHING AND DRYPOINT

767′.2′0924 — Etchings. Techniques — *Personal observations*

Tanner, Robin. The etcher′s craft / byt Robin Tanner. — [Bristol] ([Queen′s Rd., Bristol BS8 1R2]) : Friends of Bristol Art Gallery, c1980. — 133p : ill ; 27cm
Includes index
ISBN 0-9507242-0-3 : Unpriced B81-23398

769 — PRINTS, BOOK PLATES, POSTCARDS, POSTERS, PAPER MONEY, POSTAGE STAMPS, ETC

769′.42 — England. Rubens, Alfred. Private collections: Prints, *1600-1900*. **Special subjects: Jews**

Rubens, Alfred. A Jewish iconography / by Alfred Rubens. — Rev. ed. — London : Albany House, Petty France, SW1 H9EE : Nonpareil, 1981. — xxxi,277p : ill,ports ; 31cm
Previous ed.: S.l. : Jewish Museum, 1954. — Limited ed. of 650 numbered copies. — In slip case. — Bibliography: pxxx-xxxi. — Includes index
ISBN 0-902068-09-1 : Unpriced B81-22856

769′.436 — British picture postcards, *1900-1980*. **Special subjects: Somerset. Gough′s Cave, Cox′s Cave & Wookey Hole** — *Catalogues*

Irwin, D. J.. A catalogue of the postcards of Gough′s Cave, Cox′s Cave & Wookey Hole, Somerset 1900-1980 / written and compiled by D.J. Irwin. — Crymych (Rhychydwr, Crymych, Dyfed SA41 3RB) : Anne Oldham, 1981. — xx,132p : ill,facsims ; 26cm
Unpriced (pbk) B81-26282

769′.44 — Picture postcards, *to 1914*. **Special subjects: London** — *Illustrations*

Old London postcard album / edited and with an introduction by Charles Skilton. — London : Skilton & Shaw, c1980. — 48p : chiefly ill,ports ; 26cm
ISBN 0-7050-0107-5 : £4.95 B81-03645

769′.4962382 — Dutch prints, *ca 1550-ca 1850*. **Special subjects: Ships** — *Illustrations*

Maritime prints by the Dutch masters / selected, introduced and annotated by Irene de Groot and Robert Vorstman ; with 290 illustrations, including 220 in actual size ; translated from the Dutch by Michael Hoyle. — London : Fraser, 1980. — 284p : ill ; 31cm
Translation from the Dutch. — Bibliography: p277-278. — Includes index
ISBN 0-86092-052-6 : £18.00 : CIP rev.
Primary classification 387.2′09492 B80-13773

769′.4978191 — Wood engravings. Special subjects: Musical instruments — *Illustrations*

Music : a pictorial archive of woodcuts & engravings : 841 copyright-free illustrations for artists & designers / selected by Jim Harter. — New York : Dover ; London : Constable, 1980. — 155p : all ill,music ; 30cm. — (Dover pictorial archive series)
ISBN 0-486-24002-9 (pbk) : £3.90 B81-28931

769′.49941081 — British picture postcards, *1870-1930*. **Special subjects: Great Britain. Social conditions**

Evans, Eric J.. A social history of Britain in postcards 1870-1930 / Eric J. Evans & Jeffrey Richards. — London : Longman, 1980. — 151p : ill,ports ; 21x27cm
Includes bibliographies and index
ISBN 0-582-50292-6 : £8.95 : CIP rev.
B80-13931

769′.49942081′0942 — English engravings. Special subjects: England, *1837-1901* — *Illustrations*

A Victorian view of old England / edited and designed by Paul Wigmore. — London : Collins, 1981. — 128p : ill,1map ; 22x26cm
Includes index
ISBN 0-00-411854-5 : £6.95 B81-38895

769′.49942134 — English prints. Special subjects: London. Kensington and Chelsea *(London Borough)*. **Chelsea,** *ca 1700-ca 1860* — *Critical studies*

Longford, Elizabeth. Images of Chelsea / Elizabeth Longford ; gallery of prints, Harriet O′Keeffe ; catalogue of prints, Jonathan Ditchburn. — Richmond-upon-Thames ([1 Saint Helena Terrace, Richmond, Surrey TW9 1NR]) : Saint Helena Press, 1980. — 270p : ill ; 31cm. — (Images of London ; v.1)
Bibliography: p247-255. — Includes index
ISBN 0-906964-01-6 : £70.00
ISBN 0-906964-00-8 (full leather) : Unpriced
B81-07813

769′.4994237082 — British picture postcards, *1900-1910.* **Special subjects: Cornwall —** *Illustrations*
Views of old Cornwall / picture postcards: Peter Dryden ; text: Sarah Foot. — Bodmin : Bossiney, 1981. — 120p : chiefly ill,1facsim,1port ; 30cm
ISBN 0-906456-54-1 (cased) : Unpriced
ISBN 0-906456-53-3 (pbk) : £2.95 B81-32857

769.5 — American picture postcards, *to 1980 — Collectors′ guides*
Monahan, Valerie. An American postcard collector′s guide / Valerie Monahan. — Poole : Blandford, 1981. — 128p,[32]p of plates : ill (some col.),facsims,ports(some col.) ; 26cm
Bibliography: p124-125. — Includes index
ISBN 0-7137-1113-2 : £8.95 B81-35612

769.5 — British cigarette cards & trade cards, *1945- — Lists — Serials*
The **London** Cigarette Card Company′s trade card and post-1945 cigarette card issues catalogue . — 6th ed. (1981). — Somerton : London Cigarette Card Company, 1981. — x,125p
Unpriced B81-10269

769.5 — British cigarette cards, *1877-1939*
Doggett, F. C.. Cigarette cards and novelties / Frank Doggett. — London : Joseph, 1981. — 96p : ill(some col.),col.coats of arms,facsims (some col.),ports(some col.) ; 30cm
Includes index
ISBN 0-7181-1970-3 : £8.95 B81-07112

769.5 — British cigarette cards, *to 1980 — Collectors′ guides*
The **Complete** catalogue of British cigarette cards. — Exeter : Webb & Bower, Oct.1981. — [224]p
ISBN 0-906671-48-5 : £12.50 : CIP entry B81-27437

769.5 — British postcards, *1894-1939 — Catalogues — Serials*
Picton′s priced catalogue and handbook of pictorial postcards and their postmarks. — 8th ed. (1981). — Chippenham (Citadel Works, Bath Rd, Chippenham, Wilts. SN15 2AB) : BPH Publications, 1980. — 144p
ISBN 0-902633-70-8 : £3.50 B81-03034

769.5 — Christmas cards *to 1900 — Illustrations*
Holder, Judith. Christmas fare. — Exeter : Webb & Bower, Nov.1981. — [64]p
ISBN 0-906671-34-5 : £3.95 : CIP entry
Also classified at 641.5′66 B81-30976

769.5 — Great Britain. Firearms industries. Trade cards, *1760-1860*
Neal, W. Keith. British gunmakers : their trade cards, cases & equipment 1760-1860 / W. Keith Neal & D.H.L. Back. — Warminster : Compton Press, c1980 300 166p : ill (facsims), 26cm
Include index
ISBN 0-900193-58-1 : £19.95
Primary classification 683.4 B81-08286

769.5 — London. Kensington and Chelsea *(London Borough).* **Museums: Victoria and Albert Museum. Stock: English sheet music. Illustrations: Lithographs,** *1837-1900 — Illustrations*
Victorian illustrated music sheets / [compiled by] Catherine Haill. — London : H.M.S.O., 1981. — 32p : chiefly col.ill ; 25cm
At head of title: Victoria & Albert Museum
ISBN 0-11-290355-x (pbk) : £1.95 B81-27542

769.5 — Matchboxes. Salmon & Gluckstein Ltd labels — *Collectors′ guides*
Littler, Eric R.. A striking retailer from Whitechapel / by Eric R. Littler. — [Witham] ([The Vicarage, Church Hill, White Notley, Witham, Essex]) : [E.R. Littler], [1981]. — 26p : ill,facsims ; 30cm
Unpriced (pbk) B81-33245

769.5 — Picture postcards — *Collectors′ guides — Serials*
Stanley Gibbons postcard catalogue. — 1st ed. (1981)-. — London : Stanley Gibbons Publications, 1980-. — v. : ill ; 25cm
Irregular
ISSN 0144-249x = Stanley Gibbons postcard catalogue : £4.95 B81-03595

769.5 — United States. Railway services. Companies. Stock certificates, *1836-1975 — Collectors′ guides*
Hendy, Anne-Marie. American railroad stock certificates / Anne-Marie Hendy. — London : Gibbons, 1980. — viii,168p,[8]p of plates : facsims(some col.) ; 26cm
Bibliography: p7
ISBN 0-85259-296-5 : £9.50 B81-01572

769.5′5942 — English banknotes, *to 1979 — Collectors′ guides*
Duggleby, Vincent. English paper money / Vincent Duggleby. — 2nd ed. — London : Gibbons, 1980. — xii,155p : 2ill,facsims,2ports ; 22cm
Previous ed.: 1975
ISBN 0-85259-246-9 (pbk) : £5.95 B81-04564

769.5′59591 — Burmese banknotes, *to 1979*
Robinson, M.. The coins and banknotes of Burma / by M. Robinson and L.A. Shaw. — Manchester (c/o Secretary, Lancashire and Cheshire Numismatic Society, Friends Meeting House, 6 Mount St., Manchester 2) : M. Robinson, c1980. — xiii,160p,xivp of plates : ill,1map,facsims(some col.), 1plan ; 23cm
Bibliography: p157-160
ISBN 0-9507053-0-6 (pbk) : £10.50
Primary classification 737.49591 B81-05463

769.56′0216 — Postage stamps — *Catalogues*
West, Richard, *1946-*. The whole world stamp catalogue : current stamps and postal items from over 200 countries and where to buy them / researched and written by Richard West ; compiled by Robin Ellis. — London : Pan, 1981. — 160p : col.maps,col.facsims ; 30cm
Includes index
ISBN 0-330-26460-5 (pbk) : £4.95 B81-38105

769.56′0216 — Postage stamps — *Catalogues — Serials*
Stanley Gibbons stamps of the world. — 46th ed. (1981). — London : Gibbons, 1980. — xiv,1810p
ISBN 0-85259-266-3 : Unpriced
ISSN 0081-4210 B81-01951

769.56′06′041 — Postage stamps. Collecting. Organisations: British Philatelic Federation — *Serials*
British Philatelic Federation. Yearbook and philatelic societies directory / the British Philatelic Federation Limited. — 1981. — London (1. Bell Year, WC2A 2JP) : The Federation, [1981?]. — 144p
ISSN 0260-1265 : £2.50 B81-09079

769.56′075 — Postage stamps. Collecting
Watson, James, *1916-*. The Stanley Gibbons book of stamps : and stamp collecting / James Watson ; designed by Philip Clucas ; produced by Ted Smart and David Gibbon. — London : Windward, [1981]. — 221p : ill(some col.),facsims(some col.),ports(some col.) ; 32cm
Includes index
ISBN 0-906558-66-2 : £10.95 B81-38104

769.56′075 — Postage stamps. Collecting — *Manuals*
Harrison, Peter, *19---*. Stamp collecting for profit / Peter & Mary Harrison. — London : Barrie & Jenkins, 1979. — 104p,[8]p of plates : ill,facsims ; 19cm
Bibliography: p103-104
ISBN 0-214-20510-x : £2.95 B81-15990

Mackay, James A.. Stamp collecting / James Mackay. — London (36 Park St., W1Y 4DE) : Park Lane Press, 1980. — 80p : col.ill,col.facsims,col.ports ; 28cm
Bibliography: p74-75. - Includes index
£0.99 (pbk) B81-01864

769.56′075 — Postage stamps. Collecting — *Manuals — For children*
Grant, Neil, *1938-*. Collecting stamps / Neil Grant and Peter Womersley. — London : Granada, 1980. — 127p,[4]p of plates : ill(some col.),facsims,ports ; 20cm
Includes index
ISBN 0-246-11327-8 : £3.95 B81-00211

769.56′2′0924 — Postage stamps. Forgeries. Schröder, Oswald
Lowe, Robson. The Oswald Schröder forgeries / by Robson Lowe. — London (50 Pall Mall, SW1Y 5JZ) : Pall Mall Stamp Co. for Robson Lowe Ltd, [1980?]. — 16p : ill ; 25cm
Cover title. — Text on inside cover. — Includes index
ISBN 0-85397-183-8 (pbk) : £1.50 B81-07726

769.56′3 — Commonwealth postage stamps. Special subjects: Royal weddings, *1947-1981*
The **Royal** wedding and stamps : published by Stanley Gibbons Publications Ltd to commemorate the marriage of HRH The Prince of Wales to the Lady Diana Spencer at St Paul′s Cathedral, London on 29th July 1981 / [written by John Holman]. — London : Gibbons, c1981. — 24p : ill(some col.),ports (some col.),1geneal.table ; 20x21cm
Geneal.table on inside cover
ISBN 0-85259-366-x (pbk) : £1.25 B81-34992

769.56′4 — Great Britain. Railway letter post. Postage stamps, *1957-1980 — Catalogues*
Potter, David, *1932 July 24-*. Great Britain railway letter stamps 1957-1980 : a handbook and catalogue / compiled by David Potter ; edited by Peter Johnson. — [4th ed.]. — Leicester (218 Blue Gates Rd, Leicester LE4 1AE) : Railway Philatelic Group, c1981. — 40p : ill ; 24cm
Previous ed.: published as Great Britain railway letter stamps, 1957-1976
ISBN 0-901667-15-3 : £2.50 B81-21404

769.56′4978′0216 — Postage stamps. Special subjects: Music — *Lists*
Senior, Geoffrey. Music and musicians on postage stamps / [compiled by Geoffrey Senior]. — [Orrell] ([299 Gathurst Rd., Orrell, Greater Manchester WN5 8QE]) : [G. Senior] 2nd supplement. — [1981]. — [40]p ; 26cm
Bibliography: p[39]
£1.00 (unbound) B81-18003

769.56′5′0941 — British first day covers, *1840- — Catalogues — Serials*
Great Britain, including Channel Islands and Isle of Man, first day covers / compiled ... by BB Philatelic Publications Ltd. — 9th ed. (1981). — Evesham (c/o Bredon Hill Stamps, Evesham [Worcs. WR11 6TB]) : BB Philatelic Publications, 1981. — 144p
ISSN 0140-9417 : £1.50 B81-29417

769.56′6′0941 — British specimen postal stationery, *to 1971*
Samuel, Marcus. Specimen stamps and stationery of Great Britain / Marcus Samuel and Alan Huggins. — Saffron Walden (Anso Corner Farm, Hempstead, Saffron Walden, Essex CB10 2NU) : Published for the Great Britain Philatelic Society by G.B. Philatelic Publications Ltd., 1981. — x,254p : ill(some col.),facsims ; 25cm
Includes index
£17.50
Primary classification 769.56941 B81-23031

769.56′7 — Australian postage stamps: Victorian postage stamps. Melbourne cancellations, *1861-1912*
Davies, D. G. (Donald George). The cancellations of Melbourne 1861-1912 / D.G. Davies and G.R. Linfield in collaboration with J.R.W. Purves. — London : Australian States Study Group, Royal Philatelic Society, 1980. — 63p : ill,facsims ; 27cm
Limited ed. of 250 copies
Unpriced (pbk) B81-11671

769.56′7 — British postage stamps. Slogan cancellations, *1917-1918 — Catalogues*
Keneally, R. A.. The first slogan cancellations in Great Britain 1917-1918 : an illustrated reference catalogue and valuations of the war bonds / by R.A. Keneally. — [Carlisle] ([368 Warwick Rd., Carlisle, Cumbria]) : [R.A. Keneally], [1981]. — 33p : facsims ; 30cm
Cover title
Unpriced (pbk) B81-14119

769.56′7 — Commonwealth postage stamps. Numerical cancellations, *ca 1860-ca 1910 — Lists*

Heins, H. H.. Numeral cancellations of the British Empire / compiled by H.H. Heins. — 4th ed. — London (50 Pall Mall S.W.1.) : Robson Lowe, 1979. — 64,20p : ill ; 25cm
Previous ed.: 1967. — Text on inside cover. — Includes: A glossary of abbreviated handstamps / compiled by Kay Horowicz. 3rd ed. 1980
ISBN 0-85397-101-3 (corrected: pbk) : Unpriced
Also classified at 769.56′7 B81-07180

769.56′7 — Postmarks: Abbreviated handstamps, *1459-1951 — Dictionaries*

Heins, H. H.. Numeral cancellations of the British Empire / compiled by H.H. Heins. — 4th ed. — London (50 Pall Mall S.W.1.) : Robson Lowe, 1979. — 64,20p : ill ; 25cm
Previous ed.: 1967. — Text on inside cover. — Includes: A glossary of abbreviated handstamps / compiled by Kay Horowicz. 3rd ed. 1980
ISBN 0-85397-101-3 (corrected: pbk) : Unpriced
Primary classification 769.56′7 B81-07180

769.56′7′091822 — Mediterranean paquebot postmarks, *to 1979*

Drechsel, Edwin. The paquebot marks of Africa, the Mediterranean countries, and their islands / by Edwin Drechsel. — London : Pall Mall Stamp Co. on behalf of Robson Lowe, c1980. — 72p : ill,facsims ; 17x25cm
ISBN 0-85397-185-4 (corrected : pbk) : £7.50
Also classified at 769.56′7′096 B81-17604

769.56′7′0941835 — Dublin postmarks, *1840-1923 — Catalogues*

Kane, William. Catalogue of the postal markings of Dublin, c.1840-1922 / William Kane. — Dublin (P.O. Box 1096, Dublin 1) : M.P. Giffney, c1981. — 28p : ill ; 22cm
Text and ill on inside covers
ISBN 0-9507548-0-3 (pbk) : Unpriced
B81-34699

769.56′7′094228 — Isle of Wight postmarks, *to 1980*

Mackay, James A.. Isle of Wight / by James A. Mackay. — Dumfries (11 Newall Terrace, Dumfries DG1 1LN) : J.A. Mackay, c1981. — 112p,[30]leaves of plates : ill,1map,facsims ; 30cm. — (Islands postal history series ; no.12)
Bibliography: p11-112
£6.90 (pbk) B81-27116

769.56′7′09441 — North-western French island postmarks *— Catalogues*

Newport, O. W.. French islands : a priced catalogue to the postal history of the islands of the North and West coasts of France / by O.W. Newport, J.T. Whitney. — Chippenham : Picton, 1981. — 92p : 1map,facsims ; 22cm
Bibliography: p89-92
ISBN 0-902633-78-3 (corrected : pbk) : £9.95
B81-29132

769.56′7′096 — African paquebot postmarks, *to 1979*

Drechsel, Edwin. The paquebot marks of Africa, the Mediterranean countries, and their islands / by Edwin Drechsel. — London : Pall Mall Stamp Co. on behalf of Robson Lowe, c1980. — 72p : ill,facsims ; 17x25cm
ISBN 0-85397-185-4 (corrected : pbk) : £7.50
Primary classification 769.56′7′091822
B81-17604

769.569171′241 — Commonwealth postage stamps, *1952- — Catalogues — Serials*

The **Commonwealth** catalogue of Queen Elizabeth II stamps. — 1981 ed. — Bristol (7, Richmond Hill Ave., Bristol BS8 1BQ) : Urch, Harris, c1980. — 816p
ISBN 0-901039-11-x : Unpriced
ISSN 0142-7830 B81-01050

769.569171′241′0216 — Commonwealth postage stamps, *1952- — Catalogues — Serials*

John Lister Queen Elizabeth II stamp catalogue. — 1981. — [Dorchester] ([36 Fore St., Evershot, Dorchester, Dorset OT2 0JW]) : Gavin Press, 1980. — 478p
ISBN 0-905868-05-6 : £8.00 B81-09115

The **Urch** Harris Commonwealth catalogue of Queen Elizabeth II postage stamps. — [No.]-. — Bristol (7 Richmond Hill Ave., Bristol BS8 1BQ) : Urch, Harris & Co., 1981-. — v. : ill ; 21cm
Issued every five or six weeks
ISSN 0260-9258 = Urch Harris Commonwealth catalogue of Queen Elizabeth II postage stamps : £1.10 per issue B81-33940

769.569171′241′0216 — Commonwealth postage stamps, *1973-1980.* **Miniature sheets** *— Catalogues*

Commonwealth catalogue of miniature sheets : including post-independence countries / compiled by Minisheets (Regd). — [2nd] updated and rev. ed. / edited by R.J. Marles. — Torquay : Rotographic Publications, 1981. — 72p : ill ; 22cm. — (Collectors′ stamps)
Previous ed.: 1980
ISBN 0-901170-23-2 (pbk) : £1.75 B81-23334

769.569171′241′0216 — Commonwealth postage stamps. Printing flaws *— Catalogues*

Stanley Gibbons catalogue of Commonwealth plate and cylinder varieties 1952-1980 : for use with the Elizabethan specialised stamp catalogue. — London : Gibbons, 1981. — iv,220p : ill ; 23cm
ISBN 0-85259-326-0 (pbk) : £6.50 B81-20997

769.56941 — British newspaper postage stamps, *1860-1870.* **Dies**

Lowe, Robson. Newspaper postage stamps : the De La Rue dies 1860-1870 / by Robson Lowe. — London : Pall Mall Stamp Company for Robson Lowe Ltd, c1980. — 8p : ill ; 25cm
ISBN 0-85397-184-6 (unbound) : £1.25
B81-10401

769.56941 — British penny postage stamps, *1840-1864.* **Plating** *— Tables*

The **Plating** of the penny 1840-1864 : a tabulation of the measured positions of the check letters and other relevant data arranged for easy plate identification
Vol.IV: Die 1, Plates 132 to 175 alphabet II / based on the system devised by Roland Brown ; compiled, written and illustrated by Harold W. Fisher. — Saffron Walden (Anso Corner Farm, Hempstead, Saffron Walden, Essex CM10 2NU) : Published for the Great Britain Philatelic Society by G.B. Philatelic Publications Ltd., 1980. — p465-618 : ill ; 24cm
G.B.P.S. line-engraved plating gauge. — 1 photo.: b & w ; 78x65mm in pocket. — Bibliography: p616
£7.50 (spiral) B81-20030

769.56941 — British specimen postage stamps, *to 1971*

Samuel, Marcus. Specimen stamps and stationery of Great Britain / Marcus Samuel and Alan Huggins. — Saffron Walden (Anso Corner Farm, Hempstead, Saffron Walden, Essex CB10 2NU) : Published for the Great Britain Philatelic Society by G.B. Philatelic Publications Ltd., 1981. — x,254p : ill(some col.),facsims ; 25cm
Includes index
£17.50
Also classified at 769.56′6′0941 B81-23031

769.56941′0216 — British postage stamps, *1840-1958 — Catalogues*

Fine stamps. — London (1 The Adelphi, John Adam St., Strand, London, W.C.2) : W.E. Lea (Philatelists), [1981?]. — 48p : ill,facsims ; 22cm
Cover title
Unpriced (pbk) B81-15744

769.56941′05 — British postage stamps *— Collectors′ guides — Serials*

Collectors stamps of Great Britain : Queen Elizabeth II. — 1981. — Torquay : Rotographic Publications, [1980]. — 100p
Cover title: G.B. stamp varieties
ISBN 0-901170-85-2 : £1.00 B81-05566

769.569423′4 — Channel Islands postage stamps, *to 1969 — Collectors′ guides*

Backman. The postage stamps of the smaller Channel Islands / Backman, Forrester. — Ilford (63 Ravensbourne Gardens, Clayhall, Ilford, Essex IT5 0XH) : Channel Islands Publishing, c1981. — v,106p : ill ; 28cm
Unpriced (pbk) B81-21906

769.569423′4′0216 — Channel Islands postage stamps, *1940- — Catalogues — Serials*

Collect Channel Islands stamps. — 9th ed.. — London : Stanley Gibbons, c1981. — 60p
ISBN 0-85259-316-3 : £1.50
ISSN 0306-5103 B81-22401

769.569427′9′0216 — Manx postage stamps, *1958- — Catalogues — Serials*

Collect Isle of Man stamps. — 5th ed. — London : Stanley Gibbons, c1981. — 40p
ISBN 0-85259-321-x : £1.50
ISSN 0307-7098 B81-22400

769.569436′0216 — Austrian postage stamps *— Catalogues — Serials*

Stanley Gibbons stamp catalogue. Part 2. Austria & Hungary. — 1st ed. 1979-. — London : Stanley Gibbons, 1979-. — v. : ill ; 22cm
Irregular. — Continues in part: Stanley Gibbons foreign stamp catalogue. Europe
ISSN 0142-9760 = Stanley Gibbons stamp catalogue. Part 2. Austria & Hungary : £5.50
Also classified at 769.569439′0216 B81-05401

769.569437′0216 — Czechoslovak postage stamps *— Catalogues — Serials*

Stanley Gibbons stamp catalogue. Part 5. Czechoslovakia & Poland. — 1st ed. 1980-. — London : Stanley Gibbons, 1980-. — v. : ill ; 22cm
Irregular. — Continues in part: Stanley Gibbons foreign stamp catalogue. Europe
ISSN 0142-9795 = Stanley Gibbons stamp catalogue. Part 5. Czechoslovakia & Poland : £8.00
Also classified at 769.569438′0216 B81-05403

769.569438′0216 — Polish postage stamps *— Catalogues — Serials*

Stanley Gibbons stamp catalogue. Part 5. Czechoslovakia & Poland. — 1st ed. 1980-. — London : Stanley Gibbons, 1980-. — v. : ill ; 22cm
Irregular. — Continues in part: Stanley Gibbons foreign stamp catalogue. Europe
ISSN 0142-9795 = Stanley Gibbons stamp catalogue. Part 5. Czechoslovakia & Poland : £8.00
Primary classification 769.569437′0216
B81-05403

769.569438′0216 — Polish postage stamps. Local issues, *1915-1919 — Catalogues*

Hall, A. (Andrew). Poland locals / by A. Hall. — York (5 Bootham, York, YO3 7BN) : J. Barefoot (Investments), c1981. — 123p : ill,maps,facsims ; 30cm. — (European philately ; 6)
Includes index
ISBN 0-906845-07-6 (spiral) : £6.50
B81-35353

769.569439′0216 — Hungarian postage stamps *— Catalogues — Serials*

Stanley Gibbons stamp catalogue. Part 2. Austria & Hungary. — 1st ed. 1979-. — London : Stanley Gibbons, 1979-. — v. : ill ; 22cm
Irregular. — Continues in part: Stanley Gibbons foreign stamp catalogue. Europe
ISSN 0142-9760 = Stanley Gibbons stamp catalogue. Part 2. Austria & Hungary : £5.50
Primary classification 769.569436′0216
B81-05401

769.56945′0216 — Italian postage stamps *— Catalogues — Serials*

Stanley Gibbons stamp catalogue. Part 8. Italy & Switzerland. — 1st ed. 1980-. — London : Stanley Gibbons, 1980-. — v. : ill ; 22cm
Irregular. — Continues in part: Stanley Gibbons foreign stamp catalogue. Europe
ISSN 0142-9825 = Stanley Gibbons stamp catalogue. Part 8. Italy & Switzerland : £6.50
Also classified at 769.569494′0216 B81-05397

769.56946′0216 — Spanish postage stamps *— Catalogues — Serials*

Stanley Gibbons stamp catalogue. Part 9. Portugal & Spain. — 1st ed. 1980-. — London : Stanley Gibbons, 1980-. — v. : ill ; 22cm
Irregular. — Continues in part: Stanley Gibbons foreign stamp catalogue. Europe
ISSN 0142-9833 = Stanley Gibbons stamp catalogue. Part 9. Portugal & Spain : £9.00
Also classified at 769.569469′0216 B81-05398

769.569469′0216 — Portuguese postage stamps — *Catalogues — Serials*

Stanley Gibbons stamp catalogue. Part 9. Portugal & Spain. — 1st ed. 1980-. — London : Stanley Gibbons, 1980-. — v. : ill ; 22cm
Irregular. — Continues in part: Stanley Gibbons foreign stamp catalogue. Europe
ISSN 0142-9833 = Stanley Gibbons stamp catalogue. Part 9. Portugal & Spain : £9.00
Primary classification 769.56946′0216
B81-05398

769.56947′0216 — Soviet postage stamps — *Catalogues — Serials*

Stanley Gibbons stamp catalogue. Part 10, Russia. — 1st ed. (1981)-. — London : Stanley Gibbons, 1981-. — v. : ill ; 22cm
Irregular. — Continues in part: Stanley Gibbons foreign stamp catalogue. Europe
ISSN 0142-9841 = Stanley Gibbons stamp catalogue. Part 10. Russia : £10.50 B81-11225

769.569492′0216 — Benelux postage stamps — *Catalogues — Serials*

Stanley Gibbons stamp catalogue. Part 4. Benelux. — 1st ed. 1979-. — London : Stanley Gibbons, 1979-. — v. : ill ; 22cm
Irregular. — Continues in part: Stanley Gibbons foreign stamp catalogue. Europe
ISSN 0142-9787 = Stanley Gibbons stamp catalogue. Part 4. Benelux : £6.00 B81-05402

769.569494′0216 — Swiss postage stamps — *Catalogues — Serials*

Stanley Gibbons stamp catalogue. Part 8. Italy & Switzerland. — 1st ed. 1980-. — London : Stanley Gibbons, 1980-. — v. : ill ; 22cm
Irregular. — Continues in part: Stanley Gibbons foreign stamp catalogue. Europe
ISSN 0142-9825 = Stanley Gibbons stamp catalogue. Part 8. Italy & Switzerland : £6.50
Primary classification 769.56945′0216
B81-05397

769.56956′0216 — Middle Eastern postage stamps *— Catalogues — Serials*

Stanley Gibbons stamp catalogue. Part 19. Middle East. — 1st ed. 1980-. — London : Stanley Gibbons, 1980-. — v. : ill ; 22cm
Irregular. — Continues in part: Stanley Gibbons foreign stamp catalogue. Overseas
ISSN 0142-9914 = Stanley Gibbons stamp catalogue. Part 19. Middle East : £10.50
B81-05399

769.5695694 — Palestinian postage stamps, *1918-1948 — Catalogues — Serials*

The **Stamps** of Palestine Mandate. — Rev. & enl. 4th ed. (1980-81). — Ilfracombe (41 High St., Ilfracombe, Devon) : M.H. Bale, [1980]. — 131p
Unpriced B81-01051

769.5695694′0216 — Israeli postage stamps — *Catalogues — Serials*

Bale catalogue of Israel postage stamps. — 11th ed. (1981). — Ilfracombe (41 High Street, Ilfracombe EX34 9DA) : Michael H. Bale, [1980]. — 303p
Unpriced B81-08751

769.56958′0216 — Central Asian postage stamps — *Catalogues — Serials*

Stanley Gibbons stamp catalogue. Part 16, Central Asia. — 1st ed. (1981)-. — London : Stanley Gibbons, 1981-. — v. : ill ; 22cm
Irregular. — Continues in part: Stanley Gibbons foreign stamp catalogue. Overseas
ISSN 0142-9884 = Stanley Gibbons stamp catalogue. Part 16. Central Asia : £8.50
B81-11224

769.56959′0216 — South-east Asian postage stamps *— Catalogues — Serials*

Stanley Gibbons stamp catalogue. Part 21, South-East Asia. — 1st ed. (1981)-. — London : Stanley Gibbons, 1981-. — v. : ill ; 22cm
Irregular. — Continues in part: Stanley Gibbons foreign stamp catalogue. Overseas
ISSN 0142-9930 = Stanley Gibbons stamp catalogue. Part 21. South-East Asia : £9.50
B81-35117

769.569593 — Thai postage stamps. Proofs printed by Waterlow & Sons, *1917-1960*

Collins, Peter, *19---*. Thailand : the Waterlow proof sheets 1917-1960 / by Peter Collins. — London (50 Pall Mall SW1Y 5JZ) : Pall Mall Stamp Co. for Robson Lowe, [1981?]. — iii,64p : facsims ; 25cm
ISBN 0-85397-239-7 (pbk) : Unpriced
B81-37666

769.5696′0216 — African postage stamps — *Catalogues — Serials*

Stanley Gibbons stamp catalogue. Part 13, Africa since independence, F-M. — 1st ed. (1981)-. — London : Stanley Gibbons, 1981-. — v. : ill ; 22cm
Irregular. — Continues in part: Stanley Gibbons foreign stamp catalogue. Overseas
ISSN 0261-7137 = Stanley Gibbons stamp catalogue. Part 13. Africa since independence. F-M (corrected) : £8.50 B81-35118

769.569676′0216 — East African postage stamps — *Catalogues*

Minns, John. British East Africa / by John Minns. — London : Royal Philatelic Society, 1981. — viii,134p,[4]p of plates : ill(some col.),facsims(some col.),1port ; 25cm
Limited ed. of 500 numbered copies. — Bibliography: p132. — Includes index
Unpriced B81-34791

769.56971 — Canadian Small Queen postage stamps, *1870-1897 — Collectors' guides*

Hillson, John. The small Queens of Canada / by John Hillson. — London : Pall Mall Stamp Company for Robson Lowe, [1981?]. — 24p : ill ; 25cm
Cover title. — Text on inside cover
ISBN 0-85397-175-7 (pbk) : £3.50 B81-10937

769.5698′0216 — South American postage stamps *— Catalogues — Serials*

Stanley Gibbons stamp catalogue. Part 20. South America. — 1st ed. 1980-. — London : Stanley Gibbons, 1980-. — v. : ill ; 22cm
Irregular. — Continues in part: Stanley Gibbons foreign stamp catalogue. Overseas
ISSN 0142-9922 = Stanley Gibbons stamp catalogue. Part 20. South America : £9.50
B81-05400

769.569881 — Guyana. Registered letter post. Labels & handstamps, *to 1969*

Rego, M. R.. Postal registration in British Guiana / by M.R. Rego. — Harrogate (16 Stray Walk, Harrogate, N. Yorkshire HG2 8HU) : Roses Caribbean Philatelic Society, c1981. — 41p : facsims ; 30cm. — (Roses Caribbean Philatelic handbook ; no.4)
Limited ed. of 200 numbered copies
Unpriced (pbk) B81-19494

769.92′2 — British etchings. Etchers, *1850-1940 — Biographies*

Guichard, Kenneth M.. British etchers 1850-1940 / Kenneth M. Guichard. — 2nd ed. — London (9 Lancashire Court, New Bond St., W.1) : Garton, 1981. — 82p,81p of plates : ill,ports ; 34cm
Previous ed.: 1977. — Bibliography: p7
ISBN 0-906030-09-9 : Unpriced B81-17683

769.92′4 — American etchings. Pennell, Joseph. Special subjects: New York *(City), 1904-1924 — Illustrations*

Pennell, Joseph. Pennell's New York etchings : 90 prints / by Joseph Pennell ; selection & text by Edward Bryant. — New York : Published in cooperation with the Picker Art Gallery of Colgate University by Dover Publications ; London : Constable, 1980. — xv,108p : ill ; 31cm
Bibliography: p107-108
ISBN 0-486-23913-6 (pbk) : £3.60 B81-22263

769.92′4 — American prints. Hassam, Childe — *Illustrations*

Hassam, Childe. 94 prints by Childe Hassam / selected and introduced by Joseph S. Czestochowski. — New York : Dover ; London : Constable, 1980. — xiv,90p : chiefly ill ; 31cm
ISBN 0-486-23981-0 (pbk) : £3.35 B81-05046

769.92′4 — American prints. Hopper, Edward — *Illustrations*

Levin, Gail. Edward Hopper : the complete prints / Gail Levin. — New York ; London : W.W. Norton in association with the Whitney Museum of American Art, c1979. — xi,36,[79]p : ill,ports ; 29cm
Bibliography: p[77]-[78]
ISBN 0-393-01275-1 : £9.95 B81-03981

769.92′4 — Austrian aquatints. Ziegler, Johann. Special subjects: West Germany. Rhine River region, *ca 1790 — Illustrations*

Janscha, L.. Collection de cinquante vues du Rhin les plus intéressantes et les plus pittoresques, depuis Spire jusqu'à Düsseldorf : dessinées sur les lieux d'après nature = Fünfzig malerische nach der Natur gezeichnet / von L. Janscha und von Ziegler gestochen. — Edinburgh : Harris, 1980. — [53]leaves[50] leaves of plates : col.ill ; 59cm + Booklet([8]p : ill(some col.) ; 25cm)
Text in French and German. — Facsim reprint. Originally published: Vienna : Artaria, 1978. — Limited ed. of 775 numbered copies. - Half bound in goatskin blocked in gold. - In box
ISBN 0-86228-000-1 : £950.00 : CIP rev.
Also classified at 914.3′4046 B80-12004

769.92′4 — Czechoslovak engravings. Hollar, Wenceslaus. Special subjects: England, *1637-1677 — Illustrations*

Parry, Graham. Hollar's England : a mid-seventeenth-century view / Graham Parry. — Salisbury : Russell, 1980. — 144p : ill,maps,facsims,ports ; 33cm
Bibliography: p141-142. - Includes index
ISBN 0-85955-014-1 : £15.00 B81-15989

769.92′4 — Czechoslovak prints. Mucha, Alphonse *— Illustrations*

Mucha, Alphonse. Alphonse Mucha : the graphic works. — Rev. ed. / edited by Ann Bridges ; foreword by Jiři Mucha ; contributions by Marina Henderson and Anna Dvořák. — London : Academy, 1980. — 152p : chiefly ill (some col.),col.facsims,1port ; 30cm
Previous ed.: Published as The graphic work of Alphonse Mucha / edited by Jiři Mucha. 1973. — Bibliography: p151-152
ISBN 0-85670-585-3 (cased) : £17.50
ISBN 0-85670-686-8 (pbk) : £9.50 B81-07646

Mucha, Alphonse. The Art Nouveau style book of Alphonse Mucha : all 72 plates from Documents décoratifs in original color / edited by David M.H. Kern. — New York : Dover ; London : Constable, 1980. — [7]p,71p of plates : all ill(some col.) ; 31cm
Translation of: Documents décoratifs. — Ill on inside covers
ISBN 0-486-24044-4 (pbk) : £4.65 B81-18579

769.92′4 — Edinburgh. Art galleries: Printmakers Workshop Gallery. Exhibits: Scottish etching. Reeves, Philip — *Catalogues*

Philip Reeves : retrospective exhibition of etchings. — Edinburgh (29 Market St., Edinburgh [EH1 1DF]) : Printmakers Workshop Gallery, c1980. — [8]p : ill ; 21cm
Published to accompany an exhibition at the Printmakers Workshop Gallery, Edinburgh, 1980. — Cover title. — Text on inside covers
Unpriced (pbk) B81-09808

769.92′4 — England. Art galleries. Exhibits: Dutch prints. Escher, M. C. — *Catalogues*

Escher, M. C.. M.C. Escher : graphics : [Museum and Art Gallery, Manfield 24th Aug.—21st Sept. 1979] : [City Museum and Art Gallery, Stoke-on-Trent 7th Dec.—4th Jan.1980] : [Usher Gallery, Lincoln 11th Jan.—24th Feb.1980]. — Stoke-on-Trent : [Bethesda St., Hanley], Stoke-on-Trent [ST1 4HS] : City Museum and Art Gallery, [1979?]. — [12]p : chiefly ill ; 21cm
Cover title
Unpriced (pbk) B81-37520

769.92'4 — England. Art galleries. Exhibits: English wood engravings. Reddick, Peter — *Catalogues*

Reddick, Peter. Peter Reddick : cymrodor Gregynog 1979-80 : arddangosfa o dyfrlliwiau ac engrafiadau pren = Peter Reddick : Gregynog fellow 1979-80 : an exhibition of watercolours and wood engravings. — Cardiff (9 Museum Place, Cardiff) : Welsh Arts Council, c1981. — [24]p : ill ; 22cm
A Welsh Arts Council touring exhibition. — Parallel Welsh and English text. — Bibliography: p[24]. — Includes index
ISBN 0-905171-76-4 (pbk) : Unpriced
Primary classification 759.2 B81-21161

769.92'4 — English colour prints. Christie, John, *1945-* **—** *Illustrations*

White, Kenneth, *1936-*. Earth dance / Kenneth White ; with a screenprint by John Christie. — Guildford ([22 Sydney Rd., Guildford, Surrey GU1 3LL]) : Circle Press, 1978. — [4]leaves : col.ill ; 31 cm
Parallel English text and French translation. — Limited ed. of 140 copies of which 125 are signed and 15 are marked Artists Proof
Unpriced (pbk)
Primary classification 821'.914 B81-09384

769.92'4 — English engravings. Gill, Eric — *Personal observations*

Potter, Donald. My time with Eric Gill : a memoir / by Donald Potter. — Kenilworth (2 Rosemary Hill, Kenilworth, Warwickshire) : W. Ritchie, c1980. — 30p,[13]p of plates : ill,ports ; 21cm
Limited ed. of 500 copies
ISBN 0-9506205-1-3 : Unpriced B81-34243

769.92'4 — English engravings. Turner, C. (Charles). Special subjects: Poaching — *Illustrations*

Blake, C.. The poacher's progress : in eight plates / from paintings by C. Blake ; engraved by C. Turner. — Edinburgh : Paul Harris, 1981. — 1portfolio : all col.ill,1facsim ; 46x65cm
Originally published: London : C. Turner, 1826. — Limited ed. of 750 numbered copies
ISBN 0-86228-030-3 : £125.00 B81-40877

769.92'4 — English linocuts. Weissenborn, Hellmuth. Special subjects: Animals — *Illustrations*

Weissenborn, Hellmuth. Advanced zoology / Hellmuth Weissenborn. — London (7 Harley Gardens, SW10 9SW) : Acorn Press, c1980. — [36]p : chiefly ill ; 35cm
Limited ed. of 50 numbered copies signed by the artist. - In a slip case
ISBN 0-902015-14-1 : Unpriced B81-11565

769.92'4 — English linocuts. Weissenborn, Hellmuth. Special subjects: Names — *Illustrations*

Abc of names : from antiquity to the present / with linocuts by Hellmuth Weissenborn. — London (7 Harley Gardens, SW10 9SW) : Acorn Press, c1980. — [61]p : col.ill ; 27cm
Limited ed. of 60 numbered copies signed by the artist. - In a slip case
ISBN 0-902015-13-3 : Unpriced B81-11567

769.92'4 — English wood engravings. Bewick, John. Illustrations for books — *Illustrations*

Bewick, John. John Bewick : a selection of wood engravings : being impressions from original wood-blocks. — Newcastle ([209 Osborne Rd, Newcastle upon Tyne NE2 3LH]) : David Esslemont, 1980. — xivp,24leaves : ill ; 25cm
In slip case
ISBN 0-907014-03-8 (cased) : £84.00
ISBN 0-907014-04-6 (cased) : £48.00
ISBN 0-907014-05-4 (pbk) : £35.00 B81-26267

769.92'4 — English wood engravings. Bewick, Thomas. Illustrations for books — *Illustrations*

Bewick, Thomas. Thomas Bewick's fables of Aesop and others : nineteen headpieces / proofed from the original wood-blocks by R. Hunter Middleton ; with an introduction by Iain Bain including four further subjects printed from the wood. — Staplehurst (Great Pagehurst Farm, Staplehurst, Kent) : Florin Press, 1980. — 33p : ill ; 13x18cm
Quarter leather binding. — In slip case. — Limited ed. of 80 copies. — Accompanied by Bewick prints (19 leaves of plates). — Also available without prints in a limited cloth ed.. — Includes index
ISBN 0-906715-03-2 (cased) : £152.00
ISBN 0-906715-04-0 (cloth) : £35.00
B81-26856

769.92'4 — English wood engravings. Bewick, Thomas. Special subjects: Birds — *Illustrations*

Bewick, Thomas. Thomas Bewick's birds. — London : Gordon Fraser, Oct.1981. — [60]p
ISBN 0-86092-059-3 (pbk) : £3.95 : CIP entry
Primary classification 759.2 B81-27439

769.92'4 — English wood engravings. Broadhurst, R. G. — *Illustrations*

Broadhurst, R. G.. Engravings on wood 2 / R.G. Broadhurst. — Birmingham ([9 Crosbie Rd., Harborne, Birmingham B17 9BG]) : [F.E. Pardoe], 1980. — [23]p : chiefly ill ; 19cm
Limited ed. of 120 copies
£3.00 (pbk) B81-10725

769.92'4 — English woodcuts. Nicholson, William. Special subjects: Sports & Londoners — *Illustrations*

Nicholson, William. William Nicholson's An almanac of twelve sports ; and, London types. — Andoversford : Whittington Press, c1980. — 1portfolio : of ill ; 45cm + Prospectus(12p : ill ; 33cm)
Title taken from prospectus. — An almanac of twelve sports originally published with rhymes by Rudyard Kipling: London : Heinemann, 1898. — Limited ed. of 150 sets, of which 12 are hand coloured
Unpriced B81-28427

769.92'4 — French advertising posters. Chéret, Jules — *Catalogues*

Broido, Lucy. The posters of Jules Cheret : 46 full-colour plates & an illustrated catalogue raisonńe / by Lucy Broido. — New York : Dover ; London : Constable, 1980. — xii,60p,46p of plates : ill(some col.),1port ; 31cm
Based on Les affiches illustrées, 1886-1895 / Ernest Maindron. — Bibliography: p55. - Includes index
ISBN 0-486-24010-x (pbk) : £5.20 B81-19004

769.92'4 — French lithographs. Giacommetti, Alberto — *Special subjects: France. Paris — Illustrations*

Giacometti, Alberto. Giacometti's Paris : lithographs from Alberto Giacometti's Paris sans fin published in 1969 by Tériade. — London : Arts Council of Great Britain, [1980?]. — [32]p : ill ; 15cm
Published to accompany an Arts Council exhibition. — Bibliography: p31
ISBN 0-7287-0262-2 (pbk) : £0.90 B81-07756

769.92'4 — French lithographs. Maillol, Aristide. Special subjects: Women: Nudes — *Illustrations*

Maillol, Aristide. Maillol nudes : 35 lithographs / by Aristide Maillol. — New York : Dover ; London : Constable, 1980. — 28p : ill ; 29cm. — (Dover art library)
ISBN 0-486-24000-2 (pbk) : £1.10 B81-10225

769.92'4 — French woodcuts. Kandinsky, Wassily - *Illustrations*

Kandinsky, Wassily. Sounds / Wassily Kandinsky ; translated and with an introduction by Elizabeth R. Napier. — New Haven ; London : Yale University Press, c1981. — vii,136p : ill ; 22cm
Translation of: Klänge. — English and German text
ISBN 0-300-02510-6 (cased) : £21.00 : CIP rev.
ISBN 0-300-02664-1 (pbk) : £8.35
Primary classification 831'.912 B81-17534

769.92'4 — Great Britain. Art galleries. Exhibits: English screen prints. Polley, Ivan. Special subjects: Ships — *Catalogues*

The **Passing** wake : maritime screenprints / by Ivan Polley. — [Edinburgh] ([29 Market St., Edinburgh EH1 1DF]) : Printmakers Workshop [Gallery], [1980]. — [8]p : ill ; 15x21cm
Published to accompany a touring exhibition organised by the Printmakers Workshop. — Bibliography: p8
Unpriced (pbk) B81-09807

769.92'4 — Great Britain. Arts. Patronage. Organisations: Arts Council of Great Britain. Exhibits: Spanish prints. Picasso, Pablo — *Catalogues*

Picasso graphics. — London : Arts Council of Great Britain, 1981. — 55p : ill ; 18cm
Published to accompany an exhibition
ISBN 0-7287-0267-3 (pbk) : Unpriced
B81-18727

769.92'4 — Irish aquatints. Malton, James. Special subjects: Dublin, *ca 1800* **—** *Illustrations*

Malton, James. Dublin views : in colour / James Malton ; with an introduction by Maurice Craig. — Dublin : Dolmen, 1981. — xiv,[57]p : col.ill,1col.coat of arms,2facsims ; 22x29cm
ISBN 0-85105-381-5 (cased) : Unpriced : CIP rev.
ISBN 0-85105-377-7 (pbk) : £8.00 B81-18072

769.92'4 — Japanese prints, *1832-1833.* **Hiroshige. Special subjects: Fish —** *Illustrations*

Hiroshige. A shoal of fishes / Hiroshige. — London : Thames and Hudson, 1980. — [54] leaves : chiefly ill(some col.) ; 27cm
Leaves are concertino folded
ISBN 0-500-01249-0 : £8.50 B81-05915

769.92'4 — London. Westminster *(London Borough).* **Art galleries: Tate Gallery. Exhibits: English prints. Collins, Cecil —** *Catalogues*

Morphet, Richard. The prints of Cecil Collins / by Richard Morphet. — London : Tate Gallery, 1981. — 28p : ill,1port ; 25cm
Bibliography: p28
ISBN 0-905005-18-x (pbk) : Unpriced
B81-37416

769.92'4 — Oxfordshire. Oxford. Museums: Ashmolean Museum. Exhibits: English engravings. Turner, J. M. W.. Special subjects: Bible — *Catalogues*

Omer, Mordechai. Turner and the Bible / Mordechai Omer. — Oxford : Ashmolean Museum, 1981. — 48p : ill(some col.) ; 20cm
Published to accompany an exhibition at the Ashmolean Museum, Oxford January-March 1981. — Bibliography: p47-48
ISBN 0-900090-79-0 (pbk) : £3.50
Primary classification 759.2 B81-13161

769.92'4 — Spanish lithographs. Picasso, Pablo — *Illustrations*

Picasso, Pablo. Picasso lithographs : 61 works / by Pablo Picasso. — New York : Dover ; London : Constable, 1980. — 59p : all ill,ports ; 29cm. — (Dover art library)
ISBN 0-486-23949-7 (pbk) : £1.25 B81-04063

769.92'4 — Spanish prints. Goya, Francisco de — *Critical studies*

Bareau, Juliet Wilson. Goya's prints. — London : British Museum Publications, Oct.1981. — [144]p
ISBN 0-7141-0789-1 (pbk) : £7.95 : CIP entry
B81-30266

769.941 — British steel engravings. Engravers — *Biographies*

Hunnisett, Basil. A dictionary of British steel engravers / by Basil Hunnisett. — Leigh-on-Sea : F. Lewis, 1980. — 148p ; 26cm
Bibliography: p7-8
ISBN 0-85317-067-3 : £18.50 B81-10672

769.942 — English engravings, *1837-1901* **—** *Collectors' guides*

Guise, Hilary. Great Victorian engravings : a collector's guide / Hilary Guise. — London : Astragal Books, 1980. — x,182p : chiefly ill,facsims,ports ; 29cm
Bibliography: p175-177. — Includes index
ISBN 0-906525-10-1 : £15.95 : CIP rev.
B80-22346

769.942 — English prints, *to 1979*
Calloway, Stephen. English prints for the collector / Stephen Calloway. — Guildford : Lutterworth Press, 1980. — 232p : ill(some col.),facsims,ports ; 30cm
Bibliography: p223-228. — Includes index
ISBN 0-7188-2447-4 : £18.00 B81-02632

769.942 — English wood engravings, *1955-1980 — Illustrations*
S.T.E. Lawrence : boxwood blockmaker : wood engravings collected in honour of his eightieth birthday. — Wakefield (Seckar House, Seckar La., Woolley, Wakefield, W. Yorks.) : S. Lawrence, 1980. — [15]p,[37] leaves of plates : all ill ; 28cm
Limited ed. of 250 numbered copies in a slip case
ISBN 0-9507003-0-4 : £26.00 B81-07991

769.942'074'02298 — Berkshire. Bracknell. Arts centres: South Hill Park Arts Centre. Exhibits: English artists' books — *Catalogues*
Book works / [exhibition organised by Jane Rolo and Jennifer Walwin] ; [catalogue designed by Eric Molden and Mahmoud Torkamani]. — Bracknell (Bracknell, [Berks]) : South Hill Park Arts Centre, c1981. — 35p : ill,ports ; 30cm
ISBN 0-9507205-1-8 (pbk) : Unpriced B81-27272

769.9429 — Wales. Arts. Patronage. Organisations: Welsh Arts Council. Exhibits: Welsh prints — *Catalogues*
Y **Broflen** derfynol = The final proof : arddangosfa deithiol wedi'i threfnu gan Cyngor Celfyddydau Cymru mewn cydweithrediad â Felix Rosenstiel's Widow & Son Ltd. = a touring exhibition organised by the Welsh Arts Council in association with Felix Rosenstiel's Widow & Son Ltd. — [Cardiff] : [Welsh Arts Council], c1981. — [30]p : ill,ports ; 21cm
Parallel English text and Welsh translation
ISBN 0-905171-85-3 (pbk) : Unpriced B81-32311

769.952 — Japanese prints, *ca 1660-1860 — Illustrations*
Hillier, J.. Japanese colour prints. — 4th ed. — Oxford : Phaidon, Sept.1981. — [128]p. — (Phaidon colour library)
Previous ed.: 1972
ISBN 0-7148-2167-5 (cased) : £9.95 : CIP entry
ISBN 0-7148-2165-9 (pbk) : £6.95 B81-22654

769.952 — Japanese prints, *to 1979 — Critical studies*
Illing, Richard. The art of Japanese prints / Richard Illing. — London : Octopus, 1980. — 176p : ill(some col.) ; 29cm
Bibliography: p172. — Includes index
ISBN 0-7064-1380-6 : £9.95 B81-01604

770 — PHOTOGRAPHY

770 — Photography
Barthes, Roland. Camera lucida. — London : Cape, Feb.1982. — [128]p
Translation of: La chambre claire
ISBN 0-224-02929-0 : £7.50 : CIP entry B81-40242

Langford, Michael. Advanced photography : a grammar of techniques / Michael J. Langford. — 4th ed. — London : Focal, 1980. — viii,355p,[28]p of plates : ill(some col.) ; 25cm
Previous ed.: 1974. — Includes index
ISBN 0-240-51029-1 (cased) : £9.95 : CIP rev.
ISBN 0-240-51028-3 (pbk) : £7.95 B79-22627

770 — Photography — *For children*
Bostrom, Roald. Cameras / by Roald Bostrom ; illustrated by Tony Baldini and Roald Bostrom. — Oxford : Blackwell Raintree, c1981. — 48p : col.ill ; 24cm. — (A Look inside)
Includes index
ISBN 0-86256-032-2 : £2.95 B81-17351

Decron, Michel. Your first book of photography / Michel Decron and Philippe Lorin ; translated from the French by Christine Hauch. — London : Angus & Robertson, 1980. — 46p : ill(some col.) ; 25cm
Translation of: La photo. — Text on lining papers
ISBN 0-207-95872-6 : £3.50 B81-09282

770'.1'1 — Photography. Composition — *Manuals*
Brück, Axel. Practical composition in photography / Axel Brück. — London : Focal, 1981. — 192p : ill(some col.) ; 25cm. — (Practical photography series)
Includes index
ISBN 0-240-51060-7 : Unpriced B81-19781

Clements, Ben. Photographic composition / Ben Clements and David Rosenfeld. — New York ; London : Van Nostrand Reinhold, 1979, c1974. — xi,260p : ill ; 28cm
Originally published: Englewood Cliffs : Prentice-Hall, 1974. — Includes index
ISBN 0-442-23212-8 (pbk) : £8.20 B81-08614

770'.23'2060417 — Ireland *(Republic).* **Professional photography. Organisations: Irish Professional Photographers Association** — *Serials*
[**Focus** *(Dublin)*]. Focus / Irish Professional Photographers Association. — [No.1]-. — [Dublin] ([c/o P. Hodgins, Photographic Section, Guinness Brewery, Dublin 8]) : The Association, [197-?]-. — v. : ill,ports ; 30cm
Irregular (197-?-1979), six issues yearly (1980-). — Volume numbering introduced with Vol.1, no.1 (June 1980). — Description based on: Jan.1979 issue
Unpriced B81-35091

770'.23'209034 — Professional photography, *to 1900*
Hannavy, John. The Victorian professional photographer / John Hannavy. — Princes Risborough : Shire Publications, 1980. — 32p : ill,facsims,ports ; 21cm. — (Shire album ; 56)
Bibliography: p32
ISBN 0-85263-524-9 (pbk) : £0.85 B81-07736

770'.23'20973 — United States. Photography as a profession
The **Photographer's** business handbook : how to start, finance, and manage a profitable photography business / edited by John Stockwell and Bert Holtje. — New York ; London : McGraw-Hill, c1980. — xi,238p : ill,forms ; 24cm
Includes index
ISBN 0-07-061585-3 : £10.95 B81-04020

770'.28 — Photography — *Amateurs' manuals*
Brück, Axel. Creative camera techniques. — London : Focal Press, Apr.1981. — [180]p
Translation and adaptation of: Fotografische technik und gestaltung
ISBN 0-240-51106-9 : CIP entry B81-00212

Darker, Roger. Make the most of your pictures. — London : Focal Press, Jan.1982. — [168]p
ISBN 0-240-51112-3 (pbk) : £5.00 : CIP entry B81-34404

Eisenstaedt, Alfred. Eisenstaedt's guide to photography / Alfred Eisenstaedt. — Harmondsworth : Penguin, 1981, c1978. — 176p : ill(some col.),ports(some col.) ; 25cm
Originally published: London : Thames and Hudson, 1978
ISBN 0-14-046483-2 (pbk) : £3.95 B81-40481

Grimm, Tom. The basic book of photography / by Tom Grimm ; photographs by Tom and Michele Grimm ; drawings by Ezelda Garcia. — Rev. ed. — New York ; London : New American Library, 1979. — xvi,350p : ill ; 23cm. — (A plume book)
Previous ed.: 1974. — Includes index
ISBN 0-452-25216-4 (pbk) : £4.50 B81-01052

Monk, Barry. Photography / [author Barry Monk]. — London : Ward Lock, 1980. — 125p : ill(some col.),ports ; 20cm. — (A Kingfisher leisure guide)
Includes index
ISBN 0-7063-6027-3 : £2.50 B81-00213

Partridge, Joe. Me and my camera. — London : Ash & Grant, July 1981. — [128]p
ISBN 0-904069-46-x : £4.95 : CIP entry B81-14905

Taking successful pictures / consultant editor Christopher Angeloglou. — London : Collins, 1981. — 96p : ill(some col.) ; 28cm. — (You and your camera photography series)
Includes index
ISBN 0-00-411683-6 (pbk) : £2.95 B81-38161

Wasley, John. [Beginners guide to photography]. The guide to practical photography / John Wasley. — London : Sphere, 1976, c1973 (1980 [printing]). — 202p,[16]p of plates : ill ; 18cm
Originally published: London : Pelham, 1973. — Includes index
ISBN 0-7221-8921-4 (pbk) : £1.40 B81-01053

770'.28 — Photography — *Manuals*
Bailey, David. David Bailey's book of photography. — London : Dent, Oct.1981. — [256]p
ISBN 0-460-04531-8 : £14.95 : CIP entry B81-28825

Kodak handbook for the professional photographer. — Major revision. — [Hemel Hempstead] : Kodak
Previous ed.: 1975
Vol.1: Films and papers — their behaviour, handling, processing and use. — 1981, c1977. — [112]p in various pagings : ill(some col.) ; 30cm
Text on inside covers. — Includes index
ISBN 0-901023-18-3 (pbk) : Unpriced B81-33601

Lichfield, Patrick. Lichfield on photography. — London : Collins, Oct.1981. — [192]p
ISBN 0-00-216469-8 : £9.95 : CIP entry B81-28154

Rhode, Robert B.. Introduction to photography / Robert B. Rhode, Floyd H. McCall. — 4th ed. — New York : Macmillan ; London : Collier Macmillan, c1981. — ix,278p,[8]p of plates : ill (some col.) ; 24cm
Previous ed.: 1976. — Bibliography: p271-274. — Includes index
ISBN 0-02-399630-7 : £9.95 B81-36117

770'.28 — Photography — *Manuals — For backpacking*
Schiffman, Ted. PSL guide to backpacking photography / Ted Schiffman and Susan Lariviere. — Cambridge : Stephens, c1981. — 160p,[8]p of plates : ill(some col.) ; 22cm
Originally published: New York : American Photographic, 1981. — Includes index
ISBN 0-85059-551-7 (cased) : Unpriced
ISBN 0-85059-552-5 (pbk) : £2.95 B81-35259

770'.28'2 — Cameras — *Amateurs' manuals*
Barratt, Mike. Cameras. — London : Newnes Technical Books, Nov.1981. — [120]p. — (Questions & answers)
ISBN 0-408-01138-6 (pbk) : £1.95 : CIP entry B81-31183

Watkins, Derek. Beginner's guide to cameras. — London : Newnes Technical Books, Apr.1981. — [192]p
ISBN 0-408-00510-6 (pbk) : £3.00 : CIP entry B81-00215

770'.28'2 — Photography. Exposure — *Amateurs' manuals*
Gaunt, Leonard. Practical exposure in photography / Leonard Gaunt. — London : Focal Press, 1981. — 192p : ill(some col.) ; 25cm. — (The Practical series)
Includes index
ISBN 0-240-51058-5 : Unpriced B81-26308

770'.28'22 — 35mm cameras — *Manuals*
Freeman, Michael, *1945-*. The 35mm handbook : a complete course from basic techniques to professional applications / Michael Freeman. — London : Windward, c1980. — 320p : ill (some col.),form,col.maps ; 28cm
Bibliography: p320. — Includes index
ISBN 0-7112-0046-7 : £8.95 B81-00214

770′.28′22 — 35mm single lens reflex cameras — *Amateurs′ manuals*

Brown, Dolores. PSL guide to 35mm SLR photography / Dolores Brown. — Cambridge : Stephens, c1981. — 157p,[8]p of plates : ill (some col.) ; 22cm
Includes index
ISBN 0-85059-549-5 (cased) : Unpriced
ISBN 0-85059-550-9 (pbk) : £2.95 B81-33218

770′.28′22 — Automatic 35mm single lens reflex cameras — *Manuals*

Curtin, Denis P.. What are you doing wrong* with your automatic camera : *and how to do it right / Dennis P. Curtin, Barbara London. — Somerville : Curtin & London ; London : Newnes Technical, 1980. — vii,138p : ill(some col.) ; 21cm
Includes index
ISBN 0-408-00542-4 (pbk) : £2.95 B81-23009

Curtin, Denis P.. Your automatic camera / Dennis P. Curtin. — Somerville : Curtin & London ; London : Newnes Technical, 1980. — vii,122p : ill(some col.) ; 21cm
Includes index
ISBN 0-408-00541-6 (pbk) : £2.95 B81-23010

770′.28′22 — Larger format cameras — *Manuals*

Ray, Sidney F.. The Focalguide to large format cameras / Sidney Ray. — London : Focal, c1979. — 190p,[24]p of plates : ill(some col.) ; 19cm
Includes index
ISBN 0-240-51030-5 (pbk) : £3.25 : CIP rev. (U.S.) B79-11121

770′.28′3 — Photography. Processing — *Amateurs′ manuals*

The **Darkroom** book : the comprehensive step-by-step guide to processing your colour or black-and-white photographs / consulting editor Jack Schofield. — London : Spring Books, c1981. — 256p : ill(some col.) ; 29cm
Originally published in You and your camera. — Includes index
ISBN 0-600-35399-0 : £9.95 B81-22060

Foster, Stuart. Film and paper processing. — Sevenoaks : Newnes Technical Books, June 1981. — [160]p
ISBN 0-408-00512-2 (pbk) : £3.00 : CIP entry B81-13561

770′.28′3 — Photography. Processing - *Amateurs′ manuals*

Reynolds, Clyde. Beginner′s guide to processing and printing. — Sevenoaks : Newnes Technical Books, July 1981. — [176]p
ISBN 0-408-00550-5 (pbk) : £3.00 : CIP entry B81-13859

770′.28′3 — Photography. Processing — *Manuals*

Langford, Michael, *1933-*. The darkroom handbook / Michael Langford ; photography consultant Tim Stephens. — London : Ebury, 1981. — 352p : ill(some col.) ; 25cm
Ill on lining papers. — Includes index
ISBN 0-85223-188-1 : £12.95 B81-19550

770′.3 — Photography — *Encyclopaedias*

Harwood, Mary. [Running Press glossary of photography]. The language of photography / Mary Harwood. — [London] : W.H. Allen, 1981, c1978. — [95]p ; 20cm. — (A Start book)
Originally published: Running Press, c1978
ISBN 0-352-30897-4 (pbk) : £1.50 B81-38625

770′.5 — Photography — *Serials*

British journal of photography. Annual. — 1981. — London : H. Greenwood, c1980. — 215,xxviiip
ISBN 0-900414-19-7 : £8.75
ISSN 0068-2217 B81-01054

Hot shoe : [for people in the photographic world]. — No.1-. — [London] ([17, South Molton St., SW1]) : Danpalm, 1979-. — v. : ill ; 38cm
Monthly. — Description based on: No.10
ISSN 0260-5783 = Hot shoe : £0.80 per issue B81-04190

770′.75 — Antique photographs. Collecting — *Serials*

The **photographic** collector. — Vol.1, no.1 (spring 1980)-. — London : Bishopsgate Press, 1980-. — v. : ill,ports ; 28cm
Two issues yearly
ISSN 0260-5155 = Photographic collector : £12.00 per year
Also classified at 771′.075 B81-03574

770′.9 — Photography, *to ca 1940*

Wills, Camfield. History of photography : techniques and equipments / Camfield and Deirdre Wills. — London : Hamlyn, c1980. — 188p : ill(some col.),facsims(some col.),ports (some col.) ; 31cm
Ill on lining papers. — Bibliography: p183-184. — Includes index
ISBN 0-600-32184-3 : £7.95 B81-01602

770′.9 — Photography, *to ca 1970*

Langford, Michael. The story of photography : from its beginnings to the present day / Michael Langford. — London : Focal, 1980. — 163p : ill(some col.),ports ; 25cm
Bibliography: p151-152. - Includes index
ISBN 0-240-51056-9 (cased) : £5.95 : CIP rev.
ISBN 0-240-51044-5 (pbk) : £4.95 B79-34377

770′.9 — Western documentary photography, *to 1979.* **Social aspects**

Freund, Gisèle. Photography & society / by Gisèle Freund. — London : Fraser, 1980. — 231p : ill,facsims,ports ; 21cm
Translation of: Photographie et société. — Includes index
ISBN 0-86092-049-6 : £7.95 : CIP rev. B80-06510

770′.9′04 — Photography, *1900-1978*

Tausk, Petr. Photography in the 20th century / Petr Tausk ; [adapted by the author and translated by Veronica Talbot and J. David Beal]. — London : Focal, 1980. — 344p : ill (some col.),facsims,ports ; 24cm
Translation of: Geschichte der Fotografie im 20. Jahrhundert. — Bibliography: p290-337. - Includes index
ISBN 0-240-51031-3 : £8.95 : CIP rev.
ISBN 0-8038-7199-6 (U.S.) B79-34378

770′.92′2 — Photography, *to 1971 — Personal observations — Collections*

Photography : essays & images : illustrated readings in the history of photography / edited by Beaumont Newhall. — London : Secker & Warburg, 1981, c1980. — 327p : ill,facsims,ports ; 29cm
Includes index
ISBN 0-436-30505-4 (cased) : £17.95
ISBN 0-436-30506-2 (pbk) : £7.95 B81-10764

770′.92′4 — American photography. Adams, Ansel — *Biographies*

Newhall, Nancy. Ansel Adams : the eloquent light : his photographs and the classic biography / by Nancy Newhall. — Rev. ed. — New York : Aperture ; Oxford : Phaidon [distributor], c1980. — 175p : ill,ports ; 36cm
Previous ed.: San Francisco : Sierra Club, 1963
ISBN 0-89381-066-5 : £25.00 B81-19522

770′.92′4 — American photography. Cunningham, Imogen — *Biographies*

Dater, Judy. Imogen Cunningham : a portrait / by Judy Dater in association with The Imogen Cunningham Trust. — London : Gordon Fraser, 1979. — 126p,60p of plates : ill,ports ; 29cm
ISBN 0-86092-041-0 : £12.50 : CIP rev. B79-27772

770′.92′4 — American photography. Engle, Horace — *Critical studies*

Leos, Edward. Other summers : the photographs of Horace Engle / Edward Leos ; foreword by Alan Trachtenberg. — University Park ; London : Pennsylvania State University Press, c1980. — 159p : ill,facsims,ports ; 18x24cm
ISBN 0-271-00236-0 : £11.85 B81-25473

770′.92′4 — English photography. Beken, Keith — *Biographies*

Beken, Keith. The Beken file / by Keith Beken. — Aylesbury : Channel Press, 1980. — 190p : ill(some col.),ports ; 25cm
ISBN 0-906781-02-7 : £8.95 B81-17855

770′.92′4 — English photography. Fincher, Terry — *Biographies*

Fincher, Terry. The Fincher file. — London : Quartet, Sept.1981. — 1v
ISBN 0-7043-2293-5 : CIP entry B81-21494

770′.92′4 — English photography. Talbot, William Henry Fox, *1833-1864*

Buckland, Gail. Fox Talbot and the invention of photography / Gail Buckland. — London : Scolar Press, 1980. — 216p : ill(some col.),facsims,ports ; 28cm
Originally published: Boston, Mass. : Godine, 1980. — Bibliography: p210-212. - Includes index
ISBN 0-85967-599-8 : £20.00 : CIP rev. B80-10182

770′.92′4 — English photography. Wickham, William — *Biographies*

Ward, Kenneth. The world of William Wickham : the biography and photography of a remarkable Victorian / by Kenneth Ward. — Havant : Published by Ian Harrap at the Pallant Press, 1981. — viii,119p : ill,1facsim,ports ; 24cm
ISBN 0-9507141-0-0 : £4.50 B81-09809

770′.92′4 — French photography. Lartigue, J. H. - *Biographies*

Lartigue, J. H.. The autochromes of J.H. Lartigue. — London : Ash and Grant, Sept.1981. — [80]p
Translation of: Les autochromes de J.H. Lartigue
ISBN 0-904069-45-1 : £15.00 : CIP entry B81-20492

770′.92′4 — Scottish photography. Wilson, George Washington — *Critical studies*

Taylor, Roger, *19---*. George Washington Wilson. — Aberdeen : Aberdeen University Press, Nov.1981. — [224]p
ISBN 0-08-025760-7 : £20.00 : CIP entry B81-28790

771 — PHOTOGRAPHY. EQUIPMENT AND MATERIALS

771 — Photographic equipment — *Buyers′ guides*

Holtz, John. In focus / John Holtz. — Poole : Blandford, 1980. — 213p : ill,1facsim ; 24cm. — (A Quarto book)
Originally published: New York : Facts-on-File, 1980. — Includes index
ISBN 0-7137-1105-1 : £5.95 : CIP rev. B80-13932

771 — Photographic equipment — *Manuals*

Holloway, Adrian. The handbook of photographic equipment and techniques / Adrian Holloway. — London : Pan, 1981. — 216p : ill(some col.) ; 24cm
Includes index
ISBN 0-330-26523-7 (pbk) : £5.95 B81-26248

Holloway, Adrian. The handbook of photographic equipment and techniques. — London (9 Henrietta St., W.C.2) : Ash and Grant, June 1981. — [216]p
ISBN 0-904069-44-3 : £7.95 : CIP entry B81-12861

771′.075 — Antique photographic equipment. Collecting — *Serials*

The **photographic** collector. — Vol.1, no.1 (spring 1980)-. — London : Bishopsgate Press, 1980-. — v. : ill,ports ; 28cm
Two issues yearly
ISSN 0260-5155 = Photographic collector : £12.00 per year
Primary classification 770′.75 B81-03574

771.3 — 35mm single lens reflex cameras. Accessories — *Amateurs′ manuals*

Expanding your SLR system / consultant editor David Kilpatrick. — London : Collins, 1981. — 96p : ill(some col.) ; 28cm. — (You and your camera photography series)
Includes index
ISBN 0-00-411685-2 (pbk) : £2.95 B81-38152

771.3′029′4 — Cameras — *Buyers′ guides*

1981 world camera guide / [consultant Nigel Skelsey]. — London : Phoebus Publishing, 1981. — 64p : ill(some col.) ; 31cm
ISBN 0-7112-0094-7 : £3.95 B81-36888

771.3′029′4 — Cameras — *Buyers′ guides* — *Serials*

World camera guide. — 1981-. — London ([Holywell House, Worship St., EC2A 2EN]) : [Macdonald & Co.], 1980-. — v. : ill ; 30cm
ISSN 0261-5762 = World camera guide : £1.50 B81-33324

771.3′09′034 — Cameras, *to 1939*

White, Robert, *1936-*. Discovering old cameras / Robert White. — Aylesbury : Shire, 1981. — 88p : ill ; 18cm. — (Discovering series ; no.260)
Bibliography: p80-82. — Includes index
ISBN 0-85263-542-7 (pbk) : £1.50 B81-40740

771.3′1 — Asahi Pentax cameras — *Manuals*

Keppler, H.. The Asahi Pentax way : the Asahi Pentax photographer′s companion / H. Keppler. — 11th ed. — London : Focal Press, 1979. — xiv,444p : ill(some col.) ; 22cm
Previous ed.: 1978. — Pentax ME, ME Super, MV, MV-1 and MX. Published as supplement (23p : ill ; 20cm) in pocket. — Includes index
ISBN 0-240-51018-6 : £8.95 : CIP rev. B79-00552

771.3′1 — Hasselblad cameras — *Manuals*

Wildi, Ernst. The Hasselblad manual : a comprehensive guide to the system / Ernst Wildi. — London : Focal, 1980. — 301,[64]p of plates : ill(some col.) ; 24cm
Includes index
ISBN 0-240-51042-9 : £14.95 B81-02448

771.3′1 — Minolta XD & XG cameras — *Manuals*

Reynolds, Clyde. Minolta XD, XG : for models XD-5, XD-7, XG-1, XG-2 / Clyde Reynolds. — London : Focal, 1980. — 128p : ill(some col.) ; 21cm. — (Focal camera books)
ISBN 0-240-51035-6 (pbk) : £3.50 : CIP rev. B80-10709

771.3′1 — Nikon cameras & Nikkormat cameras — *Manuals*

Keppler, H.. The Nikon and Nikkormat way / Herbert Keppler. — 2nd ed. — London : Focal, c1980. — 474,xxxii p : ill(some col.) ; 22cm
Previous ed.: 1977. — Includes index
ISBN 0-240-50995-1 : £9.95 : CIP rev. B78-20429

771.3′1 — Nikon EM, FE & FM cameras — *Manuals*

Reynolds, Clyde. Nikon FE FM EM / Clyde Reynolds. — London : Focal, 1980. — 128p : ill(some col.) ; 21cm. — (Focal camera books)
ISBN 0-240-51034-8 (pbk) : £4.95 : CIP rev. B80-10710

771.3′1 — Nikon F3 cameras — *Manuals*

Hayman, Rex. Nikon F3 / Rex Hayman. — London : Focal, 1980. — 128p : ill(some col.) ; 21cm. — (Focal camera books)
ISBN 0-240-51073-9 (pbk) : £4.95 : CIP rev. B80-12456

771.3′1 — Olympus SLR cameras — *Manuals*

London, Barbara. A short course in Olympus photography : a guide to great pictures / Barbara London. — Marblehead, Mass. : Curtin & London ; London : Newnes Technical Books, c1979. — 136p : ill(some col.) ; 26cm
Bibliography: p118. - Includes index
ISBN 0-408-00420-7 (pbk) : Unpriced B81-10378

771.3′52 — Cameras. Lenses

Gaunt, Leonard. Zoom and special lenses / Leonard Gaunt. — London : Focal, 1981. — 128p : ill(some col.) ; 21cm. — (Focal camera books)
Includes index
ISBN 0-240-51069-0 (pbk) : Unpriced B81-26337

Ray, Sidney F.. The photographic lens / Sidney F. Ray. — London : Focal, c1979. — 350p : ill ; 23cm
Bibliography: p332-335. — Includes index
ISBN 0-240-51032-1 : £6.95 : CIP rev. B79-14006

771.3′52 — Cameras. Lenses — *Amateurs′ manuals*

Bancroft, Keith. PSL guide to lenses / Keith Bancroft. — Cambridge : Stephens, c1981. — 157p,[8]p of plates : ill(col.) ; 22cm
Originally published: New York : American Photographic, 1981. — Includes index
ISBN 0-85059-540-1 (cased) : Unpriced
ISBN 0-85059-541-x (pbk) : £2.95 B81-33216

771′.53 — Photographic images. Quality — *Conference proceedings*

Photographic image quality : a symposium held at the University, Oxford, 8th-11th September 1980 / [editor H.H. Adam]. — [London] ([14 South Audley St., W1Y 5DP]) : Science Committee of the Royal Rhotographic Society, 1981. — iv,237p : ill ; 30cm
Cover title
Unpriced (pbk) B81-21698

772 — PHOTOGRAPHY. METALLIC SALTS PROCESSES

772′.4 — Silver halide photography

Carroll, B. H.. Introduction to photographic theory : the silver halide process / B.H. Carroll, G.C. Higgins, T.H. James. — New York ; Chichester : Wiley, c1980. — vi,355p : ill ; 24cm
Includes index
ISBN 0-471-02562-3 : £15.75 B81-08607

774 — HOLOGRAPHY

774 — Holography

Abramson, N.. The making and evaluation of holograms. — London : Academic Press, Nov.1981. — [400]p
ISBN 0-12-042820-2 : CIP entry B81-30187

Solymar, L.. Volume holography and volume gratings. — London : Academic Press, Aug.1981. — [380]p
ISBN 0-12-654580-4 : CIP entry B81-15806

778.3 — PHOTOGRAPHY. SCIENTIFIC AND TECHNOLOGICAL APPLICATIONS, ETC

778.3′5 — Aerial photographs. Pattern recognition

Nagao, Makoto. A structural analysis of complex aerial photographs / Makoto Nagao and Takashi Matsuyama. — New York ; London : Plenum, c1980. — xxiii,199p,[10]p of plates : ill(some col.) ; 26cm. — (Advanced applications in pattern recognition)
Bibliography: p185-190. - Includes index
ISBN 0-306-40571-7 : Unpriced B81-06002

778.3′6′07402276 — Hampshire. Southampton. Art galleries: John Hansard Gallery. Exhibits: Panoramic photography — *Catalogues*

The **Panoramic** image. — Southampton (University of Southampton, Highfield, Southampton SO9 5NH) : John Hansard Gallery, 1981. — 52p : ill ; 21x31cm
Bibliography: p32
ISBN 0-85432-211-6 (pbk) : Unpriced
Primary classification 751.7′4 B81-27737

778.3′7 — High speed photography

Dubovik, A. S.. The photographic recording of high-speed processes / Alexander Dubovik ; translated from the Russian by Arthur Aksenov ; technical editor George H. Lunn. — [Rev. ed.]. — New York ; Chichester : Wiley, c1981. — xxi,553p : ill ; 24cm. — (A Wiley-Interscience publication)
Translation of: Fotograficheskaīa registratsiīa bystroprotekaīushchikh protsessov. Izd. 2-e, perer.. — Previous ed.: Oxford : Pergamon, 1968. — Includes index
ISBN 0-471-04204-8 : £46.50 B81-23983

778.5 — FILM AND TELEVISION PHOTOGRAPHY

778.5′3 — Cinematography — *Manuals*

Daley, Ken. Basic film technique / Ken Daley. — London : Focal, 1980. — 158p : ill,forms ; 22cm. — (Media manuals)
ISBN 0-240-51016-x (pbk) : £3.95 : CIP rev. B80-10711

778.5′3 — Cinematography — *Practical information*

The **Samuelson** manual of cinematography / compiled by Samuelson Film Service. — London (303 Cricklewood Broadway, NW2 6PQ) : Samuelson Film Service, c1981. — 90,110p : ill ; 21cm
Bound tête-bêche with The Samuelson Group of Companies 1981 UK catalogue
ISBN 0-9507513-0-8 (pbk) : £2.00 B81-28904

778.5′3′09 — Cinema films. Cinematography, *to 1978* — *Conference proceedings*

The **Cinematic** apparatus / edited by Teresa de Lauretis and Stephen Heath. — London : Macmillan, 1980. — x,213p,8p of plates : ill ; 23cm
Conference papers. — Includes index
ISBN 0-333-23647-5 : £20.00 : CIP rev. B79-36909

778.5′343 — Cinematography. Lighting

Millerson, Gerald. The technique of lighting for television and motion pictures. — 2nd ed. — London : Focal Press, June 1981. — [372]p. — (Library of communication techniques)
Previous ed.: 1972
ISBN 0-240-51128-x : CIP entry
Primary classification 778.59 B81-13798

778.5′345 — Cinema films. Cinematography. Special effects — *Manuals*

Perisic, Zoran. Special optical effects : in film / Zoran Perisic. — London : Focal, 1980. — 185p : ill ; 24cm
ISBN 0-240-51007-0 : £8.95 : CIP rev. B80-39857

778.5′347 — Cinematography. Animation. Timing

Whitaker, Harold, *1920-*. Timing for animation / Harold Whitaker and John Halas. — London : Focal, 1981. — 142p : ill ; 26cm
ISBN 0-240-50871-8 : £9.95 B81-16482

778.5′349 — Cinematography — *Amateurs′ manuals*

Livingstone, Ches. Filming for pleasure and profit / Ches Livingstone. — London : Macmillan, 1979. — vii,119p : ill ; 23cm. — (Macmillan books for movie makers)
ISBN 0-333-27127-0 (corrected: cased) : £6.95
ISBN 0-333-26804-0 (pbk) : Unpriced B81-35176

778.5′35 — Cinematography. Titling — *Amateurs′ manuals*

Jenkins, Philip, *19---*. The Focalguide to movie titling / Philip Jenkins. — London : Focal, c1980. — 214p,[8]p of plates : ill(some col.) ; 19cm. — (Focal guide)
Includes index
ISBN 0-240-51011-9 (pbk) : £3.25 B81-14230

778.5′38596′0924 — Africa. Vertebrates. Cinematography — *Personal observations*

Plage, Dieter. Wild horizons / Dieter Plage. — London : Collins, 1980. — 216p : ill(some col.),maps,ports ; 25cm
Includes index
ISBN 0-00-216029-3 : £8.95 B81-02273

778.59 — Television programmes. Lighting

Millerson, Gerald. The technique of lighting for television and motion pictures. — 2nd ed. — London : Focal Press, June 1981. — [372]p. — (Library of communication techniques)
Previous ed.: 1972
ISBN 0-240-51128-x : CIP entry
Also classified at 778.5′343 B81-13798

778.59′05 — Television programmes. Cinematography — *Serials*

Zerb : the journal for the Guild of Television Cameramen. — No.7 (Autumn 1978)-. — Hatfield (c/o 2 Burleigh Mead, Hatfield, Herts) : The Guild, 1978-. — v. : ill,ports ; 30cm
Two issues yearly. — Continues: Journal (Guild of Television Cameramen). — Description based on: No.12 (Autumn 1980)
ISSN 0261-1686 = Zerb : £2.50 (free to members) B81-21933

778.59'9 — Videorecording

Buckwalter, Len. The complete home video recorder book / Len Buckwalter. — Toronto ; London : Bantam, 1978. — 377p : ill,1port ; 18cm
ISBN 0-553-12582-6 (pbk) : £1.25 B81-03323

Matthewson, David K.. Beginner's guide to video. — London : Newnes Technical Books, Dec.1981. — [192]p
ISBN 0-408-00577-7 (pbk) : £3.60 : CIP entry B81-31366

Wezel, Ru van. Video handbook / Ru van Wezel ; edited by Gordon J. King. — London : Newnes, 1981. — 403p,[1]leaf of plates : ill (some col.),music,2ports ; 23cm
Translation of: Video handboek. — Includes index
ISBN 0-408-00490-8 : Unpriced B81-38971

778.59'9 — Videorecording — *Manuals — For teaching*

McInnes, James. Video in education and training / James McInnes. — London : Focal, 1980. — 176p : ill ; 24cm
Includes index
ISBN 0-240-51071-2 : £7.95 : CIP rev. B80-36139

778.59'9 — Videotape equipment — *Buyers' guides — Serials*

What video?. — Issue no.1 (Autumn 1980)-. — London (11 ST. Bride St., EC4) : Music and Video Review Ltd., 1980-. — v. : ill ; 30cm
Monthly
£10.00 per year B81-05928

778.59'92 — Videotape recording

Robinson, Joseph F.. Videotape recording : theory and practice / Joseph F. Robinson. — [3rd ed.] / revised by Stephen Lowe. — London : Focal, 1981. — 362p : ill ; 23cm. — (Image and sound technology)
Previous ed.: 1978. — Includes bibliographies and index
ISBN 0-240-51083-6 : Unpriced B81-27138

778.59'92'028 — Videotape recordings. Production — *Amateurs' manuals*

Foss, Hannen. How to make your own video programmes. — London : Hamilton, Feb.1982. — [128]p
ISBN 0-241-10572-2 : £7.95 : CIP entry B81-36382

778.59'92'028 — Videotape recordings. Use. Techniques — *Manuals*

Robinson, Joseph F.. Using videotape / J.F. Robinson, P.H. Beards. — 2nd ed. — London : Focal, 1981. — 171p : ill,facsims ; 22cm. — (Media manuals)
Previous ed.: 1976. — Bibliography: p164
ISBN 0-240-51107-7 (pbk) : £4.95 : CIP rev. B80-24551

778.59'92'05 — Videotape recordings — *Serials*

Popular video : incorporating Music & video. — April 1981-. — London (30 Wellington St., WC2) : M & V Publications, 1981-. — v. : ill,ports ; 30cm
Monthly. — Continues: Music & video
ISSN 0261-4200 = Popular video : £12.00 per year B81-27909

778.6 — COLOUR PHOTOGRAPHY

778.6 — Colour photography — *Amateurs' manuals*

Hattersley, Ralph. Beginner's guide to color photography / Ralph Hattersley. — London : Hale, 1981, c1979. — 223p : ill(some col.) ; 26cm
Originally published: Garden City, N.Y. : Dolphin, 1979
ISBN 0-7091-9151-0 : £8.95 B81-34730

Wakefield, George L.. Colour films. — Sevenoaks : Focal Press, Jan.1982. — [160]p
ISBN 0-240-51109-3 : £5.00 : CIP entry B81-34323

778.6 — Colour photography — *Manuals*

Successful colour photography : the complete guide to seeing and taking better pictures / consultant editor Christopher Angeloglou. — London : Collins, 1981. — 256p : ill(some col.) ; 29cm
'Most of this material first published in You and your camera' - t.p. verso. — Includes index
ISBN 0-00-411682-8 : £10.95 B81-26062

778.6 — Slide photography — *Amateurs' manuals*

Saxby, Graham. The Focalguide to slides : planning, making and showing them / Graham Saxby. — London : Focal, c1979. — 211p : ill (some col.) ; 19cm
Includes index
ISBN 0-240-51004-6 (pbk) : £3.25 : CIP rev. B78-34732

778.7 — PHOTOGRAPHY UNDER SPECIAL CONDITIONS

778.7 — Low light photography — *Amateurs' manuals*

Thorpe, Don O.. PSL guide to available light photography / Don O. Thorpe. — Cambridge : Stephens, c1980. — 160p,[8]p of plates : ill (some col.) ; 22cm. — (PSL guide series)
Includes index
ISBN 0-85059-405-7 (cased) : Unpriced : CIP rev.
ISBN 0-85059-406-5 (pbk) : £2.95 B80-04899

778.7'1 — Outdoor photography — *Manuals*

Freeman, Michael, *1945-*. The manual of outdoor photography / Michael Freeman. — London : Macdonald, 1981. — 224p : ill(some col.) ; 22cm
Includes index
ISBN 0-354-04612-8 : £6.95 B81-24567

778.7'1 — Outdoor photography with automatic 35mm single lens reflex cameras — *Manuals*

London, Barbara. Photographing outdoors with your automatic camera / Barbara London, Richard Boyer. — Somerville : Curtin & London ; London : Newnes Technical, 1981. — vii,137p : ill(some col.) ; 21cm
Includes index
ISBN 0-408-00543-2 (pbk) : £2.95 B81-23012

778.7'2 — Electronic flashlight photography — *Manuals*

Carraher, Ron. Electronic flash photography : a complete guide to the best equipment and creative techniques / Ron Carracher with Colleen Chartier. — Somerville : Curtin & London ; New York ; London : Van Nostrand Reinhold, 1980. — ix,237p : ill(some col.) ; 29cm
Bibliography: p211-212. — Includes index
ISBN 0-442-21463-4 (cased) : £18.70
ISBN 0-442-23135-0 (pbk) : £11.20 B81-05394

778.7'2 — Indoor photography — *Amateurs' manuals*

Freeman, Michael, *1945-*. The manual of indoor photography / Michael Freeman. — London : Macdonald, 1981. — 224p : ill(some col.),1plans,1form ; 22cm
Includes index
ISBN 0-354-04629-2 (corrected) : £6.95 B81-30695

778.7'2 — Indoor photography with automatic 35mm single lens reflex cameras — *Manuals*

London, Barbara. Photographing indoors with your automatic camera / Barbara London, Richard Boyer. — Somerville : Curtin & London ; London : Newnes Technical, 1981. — vii,137p : ill(some col.) ; 21cm
Includes index
ISBN 0-408-00544-0 (pbk) : £2.95 B81-23011

778.7'2 — Photography. Lighting — *Amateurs' manuals*

Creative photographic lighting / consultant editor Christopher Angeloglou. — London : Collins, 1981. — 96p : ill(some col.) ; 28cm. — (You and your camera photography series)
Includes index
ISBN 0-00-411686-0 (pbk) : £2.95 B81-38153

778.7'3 — Underwater photography — *Manuals*

Turner, John. Underwater photography. — London : Focal Press, Jan.1982. — [176]p
ISBN 0-240-51122-0 : £10.00 : CIP entry B81-33928

778.8 — TRICK PHOTOGRAPHY

778.8 — Photography. Special effects — *Amateurs' manuals*

Moser, Lida. PSL guide to special effects / Lida Moser. — Rev. ed.. — Cambridge : Stephens, 1981, c1980. — 141p : ill ; 22cm
Previous ed.: published as Fun in photography. Garden City, N.Y. : Amphoto, 1974. — Includes index
ISBN 0-85059-474-x (cased) : Unpriced
ISBN 0-85059-475-8 (pbk) : 2.95 B81-29721

778.9 — PHOTOGRAPHY OF SPECIAL SUBJECTS

778.9'2 — Portrait photography — *Amateurs' manuals*

How to photograph people / consultant editor John Garrett. — London : Collins, 1981. — 96p : ill(some col.) ; 28cm. — (You and your camera photography series)
Includes index
ISBN 0-00-411684-4 (pbk) : £2.95 B81-38154

Hustler, Tom. How I photograph people / Tom Hustler. — London : Focal, 1979. — 198p,[8]p of plates : ill(some col.),2forms,ports ; 25cm
Includes index
ISBN 0-240-51027-5 : £7.95 : CIP rev.
ISBN 0-8038-3055-6 (U.S.) B79-11124

Wade, John. Portrait photography. — London : Newnes Technical Books, June 1981. — [160]p
ISBN 0-408-00513-0 (Pbk) : £3.00 : CIP entry B81-13540

778.9'25 — Photography. Special subjects: Children — *Manuals*

Hedgecoe, John. Photographing children / [John Hedgecoe]. — London : Mitchell Beazley, c1980. — 160p : chiefly ill(some col.),1port ; 29cm. — (John Hedgecoe's master classes in photography)
Includes index
ISBN 0-85533-222-0 : £11.95 B81-32309

778.9'26 — Photography. Special subjects: Families, *to 1980 — Critical studies*

Hirsch, Julia. Family photographs : content, meaning and effects / Julia Hirsch. — New York ; Oxford : Oxford University Press, 1981. — 139p : ill ; 24cm
Bibliography: p135-139
ISBN 0-19-502889-9 : Unpriced B81-37939

778.9'3 — Photography. Special subjects: Nature — *Manuals*

Izzi, Guglielmo. The complete manual of nature photography / Guglielmo Izzi Francesco Mezzatesta ; translated from the Italian by Adrian Anthony Bertoluzzi. — London : Gollancz, 1981. — 254p : ill(some col.) ; 25cm
Translation of: I Manuali del fotografo la natura. — Includes index
ISBN 0-575-02879-3 : £9.95 B81-38103

778.9'3 — Photography. Special subjects: Organisms

Focus on nature / Oxford Scientific Films, Gerald Thompson ... [et al.] ; foreword by David Attenborough. — London : Faber and Faber, 1981. — 184p : col.ill ; 29cm
Ill on lining papers. — Includes index
ISBN 0-571-11810-0 : £12.50 : CIP rev. B81-21462

778.9'32 — Dutch photography. Special subjects: Elephants — *Collections from individual artists*

Lawick, Hugo van. Encounters with elephants. — London : Collins, Feb.1982. — [128]p
ISBN 0-00-216361-6 : £12.95 : CIP entry B81-35931

778.9′32 — Photography. Special subjects: Birds — ***Manuals***

Richards, Michael W.. The focalguide to bird photography / Michael W. Richards. — London : Focal, 1980. — 158p,[24]p of plates : ill(some col.) ; 19cm
Includes index
ISBN 0-240-51048-8 (pbk) : £3.25 B81-01055

Warham, John. The technique of bird photography. — 4th ed. — London : Focal Press, July 1981. — [328]p
Previous ed.: 1973
ISBN 0-240-51084-4 : CIP entry B81-15822

778.9′36 — Landscape photography — ***Manuals***

Brück, Axel. Practical landscape photography. — London : Focal Press, Nov.1981. — [192]p
ISBN 0-240-51080-1 : £9.95 : CIP entry B81-30444

Kerff, Gerhard. Photographing landscape in colour and black-and-white / Gerhard Kerff ; [translated by Veronica Talbot]. — London : Focal, 1980, c1979. — 140p : ill(some col.) ; 25cm
Translation of: Zauber der Landschaft. — Includes index
ISBN 0-240-51041-0 : £9.95 : CIP rev. B79-31925

Woods, Gerald. Creative techniques in landscape photography / Gerald Woods and John Williams. — London : Batsford, 1980. — 168p,[4]p of plates : ill(some col.),1facsim ; 26cm
Includes index
ISBN 0-7134-2488-5 : £8.95 B81-00216

778.9′4 — Photography. Special subjects: France. Paris — ***Manuals***

Moldvay, Albert. Photographing Paris / Albert Moldvay, Erika Fabian. — Cambridge : Stephens, 1981, c1980. — 128p : col.ill,col.maps ; 24cm. — (PSL travel guide)
Originally published: New York : American Photographic Book Pub. Co., 1980. — Includes index
ISBN 0-85059-522-3 (pbk) : £2.95 B81-14254

778.9′4 — Photography. Special subjects: Italy. Rome — ***Manuals***

Moldvay, Albert. Photographing Rome / Albert Moldvay, Erika Fabian. — Cambridge : Stephens, 1981, c1980. — 128p : col.ill,col.maps ; 24cm. — (PSL travel guide)
Originally published: New York : American Photographic Book Pub. Co., 1980. — Includes index
ISBN 0-85059-517-7 (pbk) : £2.95 B81-14253

778.9′4 — Photography. Special subjects: London — ***Manuals***

Moldvay, Albert. Photographing London / Albert Moldvay, Erika Fabian. — Cambridge : Stephens, 1981, c1980. — 128p : col.ill,col.maps ; 24cm. — (PSL travel guide)
Originally published: New York : American Photographic Book Pub. Co., 1980. — Includes index
ISBN 0-85059-518-5 (pbk) : £2.95 B81-14256

778.9′4 — Photography. Special subjects: Mexico. Acapulco — ***Manuals***

Moldvay, Albert. Photographing Mexico City & Acapulco / Albert Moldvay, Erika Fabian. — Cambridge : Stephens, 1981, c1980. — 128p : col.ill,col.maps ; 24cm. — (PSL travel guide)
Originally published: New York : American Photographic Book Pub. Co., 1980. — Includes index
ISBN 0-85059-520-7 (pbk) : £2.95
Primary classification 778.9′4 B81-14252

778.9′4 — Photography. Special subjects: Mexico. Mexico City — ***Serials***

Moldvay, Albert. Photographing Mexico City & Acapulco / Albert Moldvay, Erika Fabian. — Cambridge : Stephens, 1981, c1980. — 128p : col.ill,col.maps ; 24cm. — (PSL travel guide)
Originally published: New York : American Photographic Book Pub. Co., 1980. — Includes index
ISBN 0-85059-520-7 (pbk) : £2.95
Also classified at 778.9′4 B81-14252

778.9′4 — Photography. Special subjects: Netherlands. Amsterdam — ***Manuals***

Moldvay, Albert. Photographing Amsterdam / Albert Moldvay, Erika Fabian. — Cambridge : Stephens, 1981, c1980. — 128p : col.ill,col.maps ; 24cm. — (PSL travel guide)
Originally published: New York : American Photographic Book Pub. Co., 1980. — Includes index
ISBN 0-85059-519-3 (pbk) : £2.95 B81-14255

778.9′4 — Photography. Special subjects: New York ***(City)*** **—** ***Manuals***

Moldvay, Albert. Photographing New York City / Albert Moldvay, Erika Fabian. — Cambridge : Stephens, 1981, c1980. — 128p : col.ill,col.maps ; 24cm. — (PSL travel guide)
Originally published: New York : American Photographic Book Pub. Co., 1980. — Includes index
ISBN 0-85059-521-5 (pbk) : £2.95 B81-14251

778.9′4 — Photography. Special subjects: Places — ***Manuals***

Day, D. H.. The Focalguide to photographing places / D.H. Day. — London : Focal, c1979. — 160p,[24]p of plates : ill(some col.) ; 19cm
Includes index
ISBN 0-240-50960-9 (pbk) : £3.25 : CIP rev. B79-25854

McKenzie, Peter. The Focal guide to travel photography / Peter McKenzie. — London : Focal, 1981. — 108p,[8]p of plates : ill(some col.) ; 19cm
Includes index
ISBN 0-240-51072-0 (pbk) : £3.25 B81-16091

778.9′93925 — Photography. Special subjects: Weddings — ***Manuals***

Bluffield, Bob. The focalguide to weddings and special occasions / Bob Bluffield. — London : Focal, c1979. — 166p,[16]p of plates : ill(some col) ; 19cm. — (Focalguide)
Includes index
ISBN 0-240-51000-3 : £3.25 : CIP rev. B79-20260

779 — PHOTOGRAPHY. COLLECTIONS

779 — Photography — ***Collections — For creative writing***

Leavitt, Hart Day. Stop, look and write! : effective writing through pictures / by Hart Day Leavitt and David A. Sohn. — Rev. ed. — Toronto ; London : Bantam, 1979. — 232p : ill ; 18cm
Previous ed.: 1964
ISBN 0-553-11887-0 (pbk) : £0.95
Primary classification 808′.042 B81-14289

779′.074′0275 — Merseyside ***(Metropolitan County)*****. Photography. Collections —** ***Lists***

Merseyside directory of photographic sources. — Liverpool : Open Eye, Jan.1982. — [104]p
ISBN 0-9507818-0-0 (pbk) : £3.95 : CIP entry B81-38821

779′.09 — Photography, ***1840-1940 — Collections***

The **Sunday** times book of photography : a century of extraordinary images 1840-1940 / [compiled by] Bruce Bernard ; notes on the photographic processes by Valerie Lloyd. — London : Thames and Hudson, 1980. — 262p : chiefly ill(some col.),ports(some col.) ; 32cm
ISBN 0-500-54065-9 : £14.00 B81-07202

779′.09 — Photography, ***to 1979 — Collections***

First photographs : people, places, and phenomena as captured for the first time by the camera / [compiled by] Gail Buckland. — London : Hale, 1981, c1980. — 272p : ill(some col.),facsims,ports ; 29cm
Originally published: New York : Macmillan ; London : Collier Macmillan, 1980. — Includes index
ISBN 0-7091-8926-5 : Unpriced B81-16709

779′.09′04 — Photography, ***1900- — Collections***

World photography / Ernst Haas ... [et al.] ; editor Bryn Campbell. — London : Hamlyn, c1981. — 320p : ill(some col.),ports ; 35cm
ISBN 0-600-37244-8 : £15.00 B81-34083

779′.092′4 — American photography, ***1900-1950 — Collections from individual artists***

Eisenstaedt, Alfred. Witness to our time / Alfred Eisenstaedt ; foreword by Henry R. Luce. — London : Secker & Warburg, 1980. — 348p : chiefly ill,ports ; 31cm
Includes index
ISBN 0-436-14190-6 (cased) : £12.50
ISBN 0-436-14191-4 (pbk) : £6.95 B81-10521

Ray, Man. Man Ray : the photographic image / edited by Janus ; translator, Murtha Baca. — London : Gordon Fraser, 1980. — 13,179-227p,160p of plates : ill,ports ; 24cm
Translation of: Man Ray
ISBN 0-86092-045-3 (pbk) : £8.95 : CIP rev. B80-17879

Weston, Brett. Brett Weston : photographs from five decades / profile by R.H. Cravens. — Millerton, N.Y. : Aperture ; Oxford : Phaidon [distributor], 1980. — 131p : all ill ; 35cm
Also available in a limited ed. of 400 copies signed by the photographer and accompanied by an original silverprint Reeds, Oregon, 1975. — Bibliography: p128-130
ISBN 0-89381-065-7 : £21.50
ISBN 0-89381-068-1 (Signed ed.) : Unpriced B81-19005

779′.092′4 — Delaware. Newark. Art galleries: Delaware Art Museum. Exhibits: American photography. Sommer, Frederick — ***Catalogues***

Sommer, Frederick. Venus, Jupiter & Mars : the photographs of Frederick Sommer / edited by John Weiss. — London : Travelling Light, c1980. — 69p,24leaves of plates : ill ; 28cm + Exhibition checklist([16]p)
Accompanies an exhibition held at the Delaware Art Museum
ISBN 0-936594-00-4 (pbk) : Unpriced B81-36081

779′.092′4 — English photography, ***1900-1950 — Collections from individual artists***

Beaton, Cecil. Beaton / edited and with text by James Danziger. — London : Secker & Warburg, 1980. — 256p : chiefly ill,ports ; 32cm
Includes index
ISBN 0-436-12400-9 : £14.95 B81-01692

Speller, Reggie. What a picture : photographs of the 30s & 40s / by Reggie ′Scoop′ Speller ; edited by Mary Dunkin. — London : Weidenfeld and Nicolson, 1981. — 128p : chiefly ill,ports ; 27cm
ISBN 0-297-77900-1 (pbk) : £4.95 B81-2988

779′.092′4 — English photography, ***1950- — Collections from individual artists***

Bown, Jane. The gentle eye : 120 photographs / by Jane Bown ; introduction by Patrick O′Donovan. — [London] : The Observer ; London : Thames and Hudson, c1980. — 120p : chiefly ill,ports ; 25cm
Published to accompany an exhibition at the National Portrait Gallery, London, 1980-81. — Includes index
ISBN 0-500-27204-2 (pbk) : £6.95 B81-0186

McCullin, Don. Hearts of darkness / photographs by Don McCullin ; with an introduction by John Le Carré. — London : Secker & Warburg, 1980. — 156p : chiefly ill ; 29cm
Bibliography: p149-156
ISBN 0-436-27480-9 (cased) : £12.50
ISBN 0-436-27481-7 (pbk) : £5.95 B81-1277

779′.092′4 — French photography, ***1900-1950 — Collections from individual artists***

Atget, Eugène. The work of Atget : Old France. — London : Gordon Fraser, Oct.1981. — [180]p
ISBN 0-86092-060-7 : £20.00 : CIP entry B81-2532

Doisneau, Robert. Robert Doisneau : photograph / translation by Vivienne Menkes. — London : Fraser, 1980. — 143p : chiefly ill,ports ; 31cm. — (The Gordon Fraser photographic monographs ; 9)
Translation from the French
ISBN 0-86092-050-x : £20.00 : CIP rev. B80-1788

779′.092′4 — German photography, *1900-1950 — Collections from individual artists*

Metken, Günter. Herbert List : photographs 1930-1970 / Günter Metken ; introduction by Stephen Spender ; [translated from the German by Ingeborg von Zitzewitz]. — [London] : Thames and Hudson, 1981. — 31p,72leaves of plates : chiefly ill,ports ; 28cm
Translation of: Herbert List
ISBN 0-500-54071-3 : £12.50 B81-16965

′79′.092′4 — London. Westminster *(London Borough).* **Art galleries: Photographers′ Gallery. Exhibits: German photography. Schadeberg, Jurgen** — *Catalogues*

Schadeberg, Jurgen. An exhibition of photographs / by Jurgen Schadeberg. — London ([8 Great Newport St., W.C.2]) : Photographers′ Gallery, 1981. — 48p : all ill,1port ; 21cm
Cover title
Unpriced (pbk) B81-29222

′79′.092′4 — Pennsylvania. Philadelphia. Art galleries: Philadelphia Museum of Art. Exhibitions: German photography. Sander, August — *Catalogues*

August Sander : Photographs of an Epoch *(Exhibition : 1980 : United States).* August Sander : Photographs of an Epoch 1904-1959 : man of the twentieth century, Rhineland landscapes, nature studies, architectural and industrial photographs, images of Sardinia : accompanied by excerpts from the writings of August Sander and his contemporaries / [catalogue of an exhibition presented by the Philadelphia Museum of Art, 1980] ; preface by Beaumont Newhall ; historical commentary by Robert Kramer. — New York : Aperture ; Oxford : Phaidon [distributor], c1980. — 125p : ill,ports ; 30cm
Bibliography: p122-124
ISBN 0-89381-058-4 : £13.50
ISBN 0-89381-056-8 (limited ed.) : Unpriced
ISBN 0-89381-064-9 (museum ed.) : Unpriced
B81-19560

79′.092′4 — Texas. Fort Worth. Museums: Amon Carter Museum of Western Art. Exhibits: American photography. Corpron, Carlotta — *Catalogues*

Corpron, Carlotta. Carlotta Corpron : designer with light / text by Martha A. Sandweiss. — Austin ; London : Published for the Amon Carter Museum, Fort Worth, by the University of Texas Press, c1980. — 63p : ill,1port ; 24cm
Bibliography: p60
ISBN 0-292-71064-x (cased) : £9.75
ISBN 0-292-71065-8 (pbk) : £6.45 B81-32518

′9′.094′07402134 — London. Kensington and Chelsea *(London Borough).* **Museums: Victoria and Albert Museum. Exhibits: European photographs,** *to 1979 — Catalogues*

Victoria and Albert Museum. Old and modern masters of photography / Victoria and Albert Museum ; selected and introduced by Mark Haworth-Booth ; foreword by Roy Strong. — London : H.M.S.O., 1981. — 6,59p : all ill,ports ; 32cm
ISBN 0-11-290362-2 (cased) : £11.75
ISBN 0-11-290361-4 (pbk) : £5.75 B81-28505

′9′.0941 — Great Britain. Arts. Patronage. Organisations: Arts Council of Great Britain. Stock: British photography, *1950- — Illustrations*

About 70 photographs / edited by Chris Steele-Perkins ; commentaries by Chris Steele-Perkins and William Messer. — London : Arts Council of Great Britain, c1980. — 147p : ill(some col.),ports ; 26cm
Includes index
ISBN 0-7287-0209-6 (cased) : £9.95 : CIP rev.
ISBN 0-7587-0208-8 (pbk) : £5.95 B80-01309

9′.09428′1907402819 — West Yorkshire *(Metropolitan County).* **Leeds. Art galleries: Leeds Art Galleries. Exhibits: West Yorkshire** *(Metropolitan County)* **photography: Leeds photography,** *1837-1870 — Catalogues*

Budge, Adrian. Early photography in Leeds 1839-1870. — Leeds (Temple Newsam House, Leeds LS15 0AE) : Leeds Art Galleries, 1981. — 48p : ill,facsim,ports ; 30cm
Author: Adrian Budge. — Text and facsims on inside covers. — Includes index
ISBN 0-901981-19-2 (pbk) : £1.50 B81-30083

779′.0952 — Japanese photography, *to 1945 — Collections*

A **Century** of Japanese photography / Japan Photographers Association ; introduction by John W. Dower. — London : Hutchinson, 1981, c1980. — 385p : all.ill(some col.),ports ; 24x31cm
Translation of: Nihon shashin shi, 1840-1945. — Originally published: New York : Random House, 1980. — In a slip case
ISBN 0-09-145500-6 : £25.00 : CIP rev.
B81-20178

779′.09794′07402132 — London. Westminster *(London Borough).* **Art galleries: Photographers′ Gallery. Exhibits: Californian colour photography,** *1978-1980 — Catalogues*

Californian colour : catalogue of an exhibition organised by the Photographers′ Gallery and shown in London July/August 1981. — [London] ([5 Great Newport St., WC2H 7HY]) : [The Gallery], [1981]. — 35p : col.ill ; 24cm
Includes bibliographies
Unpriced (pbk) B81-34275

779′.2′0924 — American portrait photography, *1900-1950 — Collections from individual artists*

Penn, Irving. Worlds in a small room / by Irving Penn as an ambulant studio photographer. — London : Secker & Warburg, 1980, c1974. — 95p : chiefly ill ; 28cm
Originally published: New York : Grossman ; London : Studio Vista, 1974
ISBN 0-436-36633-9 (cased) : £9.95
ISBN 0-436-36634-7 (pbk) : £4.95 B81-05430

779′.2′0924 — American portrait photography, *1941-1980.* **Special subjects: Artists** — *Collections from individual artists*

Newman, Arnold. Artists : portraits from four decades / by Arnold Newman ; foreword by Henry Geldzahler ; introduction by Arnold Newman. — London : Weidenfeld and Nicolson, c1980. — 17,157p : chiefly ports ; 30cm
Includes index
ISBN 0-297-77879-x : £18.00 B81-08620

779′.2′0924 — American portrait photography, *1950- — Collections from individual artists*

Williams, Jonathan. Portrait photographs / Jonathan Williams. — London (233 Camberwell New Rd., SE5) : Coracle, 1979. — 30p : chiefly col.maps ; 22cm
In slip case
ISBN 0-906630-00-2 (pbk) : £9.50
ISBN 0-906630-01-0 (signed ed) B81-11425

779′.2′0924 — American portrait photography, *1950-.* **Special subjects: Celebrities** — *Collections from individual artists*

Warhol, Andy. Andy Warhol′s exposures / photographs by Andy Warhol ; text by Andy Warhol with Bob Colacello. — London : Arrow, 1980, c1979. — 249p : ill,ports ; 29cm
Originally published: New York : Grosset & Dunlap ; London : Hutchinson, 1979. — Includes index
ISBN 0-09-924600-7 (pbk) : £5.95 B81-03305

779′.2′0924 — Canadian portrait photography, *1900-1950.* **Special subjects: Canada. Celebrities** — *Collections from individual artists*

Karsh, Yousuf. Karsh Canadians / Yousuf Karsh. — Toronto ; London : University of Toronto Press, c1978. — 203p : ports ; 32cm
ISBN 0-8020-2317-7 : £20.00 B81-25468

779′.2′0924 — English photography, *1900-1950.* **Special subjects: Upper classes** — *Collections*

Lenare : the art of society photography 1924-1977 / compiled and edited by Nicholas de Ville ; introductory essay by Anthony Haden-Guest. — [London] : Allen Lane, 1981. — 136p : ill,chiefly ports(some col.) ; 33cm
ISBN 0-7139-1418-1 : £15.00 B81-24485

779′.2092′4 — English portrait photography, *1900-1950 — Collections from individual artists*

Vanessa Bell′s family album. — London : Jill Norman, Oct.1981. — [160]p
ISBN 0-906908-36-1 : £8.95 : CIP entry
B81-27436

779′.2′0924 — English portrait photography, *1900-1950.* **Special subjects: Ballet dancers,** *ca 1930-ca 1950 — Collections from individual artists*

Anthony, Gordon. Dancers to remember / the photographic art of Gordon Anthony ; foreword by Dame Margot Fonteyn. — London : Hutchinson, 1980. — 149p : chiefly ports ; 29cm
Bibliography: p149
ISBN 0-09-141690-6 : £12.50 : CIP rev.
B80-09339

779′.2′0924 — Great Britain. *National Portrait Gallery.* **Exhibits: English portrait photography. Parkinson, Norman** — *Catalogues*

Parkinson, Norman. Photographs by Norman Parkinson : fifty years of portraits and fashion / [introduced by] Terence Pepper. — London : Gordon Fraser, 1981. — ill(some col.),chiefly ports ; 27cm
Published in connection with the exhibition held at the National Portrait Gallery from 7th August to 25th October 1981. — Bibliography: p110. — Includes index
ISBN 0-86092-061-5 : £9.95 : CIP rev.
B81-25120

Parkinson, Norman. Photographs by Norman Parkinson : fifty years of portraits and fashion / [introduction by] Terence Pepper. — London : National Portrait Gallery, 1981. — 112p : chiefly ill(some col.),ports(some col.) ; 26cm
Published in connection with the exhibition held at the National Portrait Gallery from 7 August to 25 October, 1981
ISBN 0-904017-41-9 (pbk) : Unpriced
B81-37945

779′.2′0973 — American photography. Special subjects: American cinema films. Acting. Stars, *1950-1960 — Collections*

Film-star portraits of the fifties : 163 glamour photographs / edited with an introduction by John Kobal. — Leicester : Windward, c1980. — xii,163p : chiefly ill,ports ; 29cm
ISBN 0-7112-0200-1 : £5.95 B81-38116

779′.2′0973 — American portrait photography, *1900-1950.* **Special subjects: American cinema films. Acting. Stars,** *1916-1942 — Collections*

Kobal, John. The art of the great Hollywood portrait photographers 1925-1940 / by John Kobal. — London : Allen Lane, 1980. — ix,291p : ports ; 32cm
Bibliography: p287. - Includes index
ISBN 0-7139-1393-2 : £15.00 B81-05426

779′.21 — Photography, *1850-1980.* **Special subjects: Nudes** — *Collections*

Nude : photographs 1850-1980 / edited by Constance Sullivan. — New York ; London : Harper & Row, c1980. — 203p : chiefly ill (some col.),ports ; 34cm
ISBN 0-06-012708-2 : Unpriced B81-27784

779′.24 — Photography, *1950-.* **Special subjects: Women** — *Collections*

Lichfield, Patrick. The most beautiful women in the world. — London : H. Hamilton, Sept.1981. — [160]p
ISBN 0-241-10555-2 : £10.00 : CIP entry
B81-25866

779′.24′0924 — English photography, *1950-.* **Special subjects: Adolescent girls** — *Collections from individual artists*

Hamilton, David, *1933-.* Sisters / by David Hamilton ; text Alain Robbe-Grillet ; [English translation Martha Egan]. — New York ; London : Collins, 1980. — 135p : chiefly ill (some col.) ; 29cm
Translation of: Les demoiselles. — Originally published: New York : Morrow, 1973 ; London : Collins, 1976
ISBN 0-00-216810-3 (pbk) : £6.25 B81-03304

779′.24′0924 — English portrait photography, *1950-.* **Special subjects: Helvin, Marie** — *Collections from individual artists*

Bailey, David, *1938-.* David Bailey′s trouble and strife : photographs / by David Bailey ; preface by J.H. Lartigue ; introduction by Brian Clarke. — [London] : Thames and Hudson, c1980. — 10,[106]p : all ill ; 25cm
ISBN 0-500-54064-0 : £10.00 B81-06558

779′.28 — Erotic photography, *1950- - Collections*

Leidmann, Cheyco. Foxy lady. — London : Plexus, June 1981. — [120]p
ISBN 0-85965-042-1 : £15.95 : CIP entry
B81-09480

779′.36′0924 — English landscape photography, *1950- — Collections from individual artists*

Moore, Raymond. Murmurs at every turn : the photographs of Raymond Moore. — London : Travelling Light, 1981. — 96p : chiefly ill ; 24x25cm
ISBN 0-906333-12-1 (cased) : Unpriced : CIP rev.
ISBN 0-906333-15-6 (pbk) : Unpriced
B81-10002

779′.4′0924 — American photography, *1900-1950.* **Special subjects: Illinois. Chicago,** *1941 — Collections from individual artists*

Feininger, Andreas. Feininger's Chicago, 1941. — New York : Dover ; London : Constable, 1980. — 77p : chiefly ill ; 28cm. — (Dover photography collections)
ISBN 0-486-24007-x (cased) : Unpriced
ISBN 0-486-23991-8 (pbk) : £3.00 B81-23277

779′.4′0924 — American photography, *1950-.* **Special subjects: Massachusetts. Gloucester** *— Collections from individual artists*

Swigart, Lynn. Olson's Gloucester / photographs by Lynn Swigart ; an interview with Lynn Swigart by Sherman Paul ; foreword by George Butterick. — Baton Rouge ; London : Louisiana State University Press, c1980. — xiii,72p : chiefly ill ; 22x25cm
ISBN 0-8071-0765-4 (cased) : £14.95
ISBN 0-8071-0791-3 (pbk) : £6.00 B81-07305

779′.4′0924 — Dutch photography, *1950-.* **Special subjects: Oxfordshire. Oxford** *— Collections from individual artists*

Oorthuys, Cas. [Term in Oxford]. Oxford in focus / Cas Oorthuys ; with an introduction and a new foreword by Alan Bullock. — Oxford : Cassirer, 1963 (1981 [printing]). — 144p : chiefly ill ; 30cm
ISBN 0-85181-100-0 (pbk) : Unpriced
B81-26309

779′.4′0924 — English photography. Special subjects: Ireland *(Republic).* **Ruined country houses** *— Collections from individual artists*

Marsden, Simon. In ruins : the once great houses of Ireland / photographs by Simon Marsden ; edited and with text by Duncan McLaren ; introduction by P.J. Kavanagh. — London : Collins, 1980. — 85p : ill ; 28x30cm
Bibliography: p85
ISBN 0-00-216347-0 : £10.95 B81-07160

779′.4′0924 — Spanish photography, *1950-.* **Special subjects: New York** *(City) — Collections from individual artists*

Hidalgo, Francisco. New York / Francisco Hidalgo. — Schaffhausen : Photographie ; London : Proteus, 1981. — [176]p : chiefly col.ill ; 32cm
ISBN 0-906071-17-8 : £25.00 B81-34263

779′.99427645 — Lancashire. Colne. Public libraries: Colne Library. Stock: Photographs. Special subjects: Lancashire. Pendle *(District) — Catalogues*

Colne Library. Photographic source material for Pendle district in Lancashire : including some materials for Yorkshire & Cumbria : a catalogue / [compiled] by Roy Thistlethwaite. — [Colne] ([Pendle District Libraries, Market St., Colne BB8 0AP]) : [Colne Library], c1981. — [2]p,[38]leaves ; 33cm. — (Colne Library publication ; no.6)
£0.50 (unbound) B81-32754

779′.9974043′0924 — American photography, *1950-.* **Special subjects: New England** *— Collections from individual artists*

Strand, Paul. Time in New England : photographs / by Paul Strand ; text selected and edited by Nancy Newhall ; preface by Paul Metcalf ; afterword by Beaumont Newhall. — Millerton, N.Y. : Aperture ; Oxford : Phaidon [distributor], c1980. — 256p : ill ; 31cm
Originally published: New York : Oxford University Press, 1950. — Also available in a limited ed. of 450 copies numbered and signed by Mrs Paul Strand and Beaumont Newhall, accompanied by an original hand-pulled, dust-grain gravure Iris 1928 signed by Mrs Paul Strand
ISBN 0-89381-060-6 : £21.50
Also classified at 974 B81-19006

779′.9978033′0924 — American photography, *1950-.* **Special subjects: United States. Western states** *— Collections from individual artists*

Adams, Robert, *1937 May 8-.* From the Missouri West : photographs / by Robert Adams. — Millerton, N.Y. : Aperture ; Oxford : Phaidon [distributor], c1980. — [63]p : all ill ; 25x29cm. — (A New images book)
Also available in a limited ed. of 100 copies, accompanied by an original silver print, Bulldozed slash, Tillamook County, Oregon, 1976 numbered and signed by the photographer
ISBN 0-89381-059-2 : £12.50
ISBN 0-89381-063-0 (Limited ed.) : Unpriced
B81-19010

780 — MUSIC

780 — Music

Lovelock, William. The rudiments of music. — London : Bell & Hyman, Nov.1981. — [128]p
Originally published: 1966
ISBN 0-7135-0744-6 (pbk) : £2.95 : CIP entry
B81-34713

Materials and structures of music / William Christ ... [et al.]. — Englewood Cliffs ; London : Prentice-Hall
Previous ed.: 1973. — Includes index
Vol.2. — 3rd ed. — c1981. — ix,438p : ill,music ; 24cm
ISBN 0-13-560433-8 : £11.65 B81-26103

The **Music** forum. — New York ; Guildford : Columbia University Press, 1980
Vol.5 / Felix Salzer, editor ; Carl Schachter, associate editor ; Hedi Siegel editorial assistant. — 402p : ill,music,facsims ; 27cm
Includes index
ISBN 0-231-04720-7 : £15.20 B81-09513

Race, Steve. Dear music lover - / Steve Race. — London : Robson, 1981. — 117p : music,1form ; 23cm
ISBN 0-86051-134-0 : £5.50 : CIP rev.
B81-07621

Shaw, Bernard. Shaw's music : the complete musical criticism ... / edited by Dan H. Laurence. — London : Bodley Head, c1981. — 3v. ; 20cm. — (The Bodley Head Bernard Shaw)
Includes index
ISBN 0-370-30333-4 : Unpriced
ISBN 0-370-30247-8 (v.1) : £15.00
ISBN 0-370-30249-4 (v.2) : £15.00
ISBN 0-370-30248-6 (v.3) : £15.00 B81-26043

780 — Music *— Conference proceedings — German texts*

Musik im Alltag : zehn Kongreßbeiträge / herausgegeben von Reinhold Brinkmann. — Mainz ; London : Schott, c1980. — 166p : ill,music ; 24cm. — (Veröffentlichungen des Instituts für Neue Musik und Musikerziehung Darmstadt, ISSN 0418-3827 ; Bd.21)
Conference papers
ISBN 3-7957-1761-2 (pbk) : £7.50 B81-29012

780 — Music *— Early works*

Hucbald, Guido, and John on music : three medieval treatises / translated by Warren Babb ; edited with introductions by Claude V. Palisca ; index of chants by Alejandro Enrique Planchart. — New Haven ; London : Yale University Press, 1978. — xiv,211p : ill,music,facsim ; 26cm. — (Music theory translation series ; 3)
Translation from the Latin. — Bibliography: pxiii-xiv. - Includes index
ISBN 0-300-02040-6 : £11.05 B81-11556

780 — Music *— For children*

Carter, Leslie. The music people : first music book / conceived, written & illustrated by Leslie Carter ; with educational & pianistic guidance from Angela Carter. — London : Chappell Music, 1980. — 47p : col.ill,music ; 29cm. — (A Music People publication)
ISBN 0-903443-53-8 (pbk) : Unpriced
B81-39563

Headington, Christopher. The performing world of the musician. — London : H. Hamilton, May 1981. — [128]p
ISBN 0-241-10587-0 : £5.95 : CIP entry
B81-12815

McLeish, Kenneth. This is music / Kenneth & Valerie McLeish. — London : Heinemann, 1980. — 78p : ill,ports ; 25cm
Includes index
ISBN 0-434-94995-7 : £4.95 B81-12687

780 — Music *— For schools — Welsh texts*

Richards, Lily. Mwynhau cerddoriaeth / Lily Richards. — 2 argraffiad. — Llandysul : Gwasg Gomer, 1979, c1976. — 111p : ill,music ; 30cm
Previous ed.: 1976
ISBN 0-85088-511-6 (pbk) : £3.00 B81-07534

780 — Music *— Stories, anecdotes*

Borge, Victor. Victor Borge's My favourite comedies in music / by Victor Borge and Robert Sherman. — London : Robson, 1981. — 150p ; 23cm
ISBN 0-86051-151-0 : £5.95 : CIP rev.
B81-15923

Miall, Antony. Musical bumps / Antony Miall ; illustrated by Ken Pyne. — London : Dent, 1981. — 83p : ill ; 23cm
Includes index
ISBN 0-460-04541-5 : £3.50 : CIP rev.
B81-26786

780 — Musical activities *— For children*

Kreusch-Jacob, Dorothée. Music workshop / by Dorothée Kreusch-Jacob ; photographs by Hans Wallner ; translated by Anthea Bell. — [Leeds] : Pepper, 1981. — 45p : ill(some col.),music ; 27cm
Translation of: Aktionsbuch
ISBN 0-560-74516-8 : £4.25 B81-2207

780′.01 — Musicology *— Conference proceedings*

Modern musical scholarship / edited by Edward Olleson. — Stocksfield : Oriel, 1980, c1978. — x,246p,[1]leaf of plates : ill(some col.),music,1port ; 23cm
Conference papers
ISBN 0-85362-180-2 : £16.00
ISBN 0-85362-169-1 B81-0751

780′.07 — England. Music. Patronage, *ca 1550-1630*

Price, David C.. Patrons and musicians of the English Renaissance / David C. Price. — Cambridge : Cambridge University Press, 1981. — xix,250p : 2ill,maps,1port,geneal.tables ; 24cm. — (Cambridge studies in music)
Bibliography: p226-244. - List of music publications: p209-213. - Includes index
ISBN 0-521-22806-9 : £22.50 B81-0982

780'.07 — Italy. Mantua. Music. Patronage, *ca 1500-ca 1600*
Fenlon, Iain. Music and patronage in sixteenth-century Mantua / Iain Fenlon. — Cambridge : Cambridge University Press. — (Cambridge studies in music)
Bibliography: p209-226. - Includes index
Vol.1. — 1980. — xi,233p : ill,1map,2facsims,1plan,1ports,2geneal.tables ; 26cm
ISBN 0-521-22905-7 : £25.00 B81-10190

780'.07 — Society. Influence of music
Small, Christopher, *1927-*. Music, society, education : a radical examination of the prophetic function of music in Western, Eastern and African cultures with its impact on society and its use in education / by Christopher Small. — 2nd rev. ed. — London : Calder, 1980. — 234p ; 21cm. — (A platform book)
Previous ed.: 1977. — Includes index
ISBN 0-7145-3530-3 (cased) : Unpriced
ISBN 0-7145-3614-8 (pbk) : £4.95 B81-11823

780'.07'09 — Western music, *to 1980*. **Social aspects**
Fletcher, Peter, *1936-*. Roll over rock : a study of music in contemporary culture / by Peter Fletcher. — London : Stainer & Bell, c1981. — 175p ; 22cm
Includes index
ISBN 0-85249-576-5 : £6.95 : CIP rev.
B81-10015

780'.08 — Music *related to* **poetry,** *to 1980*
Winn, James Anderson. Unsuspected eloquence. — London : Yale University Press, July 1981. — [384]p
ISBN 0-300-02615-3 : £11.95 : CIP entry
Primary classification 809.1 B81-22673

780'.1 — Music. Aesthetics
Dahlhaus, Carl. Esthetics of music. — Cambridge : Cambridge University Press, Jan.1982. — [116]p
Translation of : Musikästhetik
ISBN 0-521-23508-1 (cased) : £9.95 : CIP entry
ISBN 0-521-28007-9 (pbk) : £3.95 B81-37537

780'.1 — Western music. Aesthetics
Kivy, Peter. The corded shell : reflections on musical expression / by Peter Kivy. — Princeton ; Guildford : Princeton University Press, c1980. — xiv,167p : ill,music ; 25cm. — (The Princeton essays on the arts ; 9)
Bibliography: p159-162. - Includes index
ISBN 0-691-07258-2 (cased) : £8.40
ISBN 0-691-02014-0 (pbk) : £3.35 B81-10169

780'.15 — Music. Appreciation
Harrison, Sidney. How to appreciate music. — London : H. Hamilton, Nov.1981. — [96]p
ISBN 0-241-10681-8 (cased) : £6.95 : CIP entry
ISBN 0-241-10682-6 (pbk) : £3.95 B81-32007

780'.1'5 — Music — *For music appreciation — For schools*
Jenkins, David, *1944-*. Portraits in music / David Jenkins, Mark Visocchi. — London : Oxford University Press
2. — 1981. — 64p : ill,maps,music,ports ; 21x30cm
Text, ill, ports, music on inside covers
ISBN 0-19-321401-6 (pbk) : Unpriced
B81-38716

780'.1'5 — Music — *Formal analyses*
Tovey, Donald Francis. Essays in musical analysis. — London : Oxford University Press
Originally published: in 6 vols. 1935-1944
Concertos and choral works. — Oct.1981. — [448]p
ISBN 0-19-315148-0 (cased) : £9.50 : CIP entry
ISBN 0-19-315149-9 (pbk) : £4.50 B81-25832

Tovey, Donald Francis. Essays in musical analysis. — London : Oxford University Press, Oct.1981
Originally published: in 6 vols. 1935-1944
Symphonies and other orchestral works. — [576]p
ISBN 0-19-315146-4 (cased) : £9.50 : CIP entry
ISBN 0-19-315147-2 (pbk) : £4.50 B81-25783

780'.1'5 — Music — *Formal analyses — For schools*
McCarr, Pat. Music and musicianship leaving certificate. — [Longhope] : [Salesian Publications], [1981?]. — 19p : music ; 32cm
Cover title. — Author: Pat McCarr
Unpriced (pbk) B81-26306

780'.23'41 — Great Britain. Music — *Career guides*
McDonald, Gerald. Training and careers for the professional musician / by Gerald McDonald. — Old Woking : Gresham, 1979. — viii,102p : ill,ports ; 21cm
Bibliography: p99-100. — Includes index
ISBN 0-905418-03-4 (pbk) : £3.95 B81-06955

780'.25'427 — Northern England. Music — *Directories*
Cowell, Margaret. Directory of northern music / compiled by Margaret Cowell. — Ashington (Ashington, Northd.) : Mid Northumberland Arts Group, 1978. — 30cm
Includes index
ISBN 0-904790-05-3 (pbk) : £3.00 (£2.00 to subscribers) B81-06511

780'.3'21 — Music — *Encyclopaedias*
Camilleri, Charles. Camilleri's musical terms / by Charles Camilleri. — Waterloo, Ont. : Waterloo Music Co. ; Aylesbury (The Windmill, Wendover, Aylesbury, Bucks. HP22 6JJ) : Distributed by Roberton Publications, c1980. — 73p ; 21cm
ISBN 0-88909-039-4 (spiral) : £2.50
B81-15051

The **Concise** Oxford dictionaries of music and opera. — [Oxford] : Oxford University Press, [1980]. — 2v.(724 ; 561p) : music ; 21cm. — (Oxford paperbacks)
Slip case title. — In slip case. — Contents: The concise Oxford dictionary of music. 3rd ed. / by Michael Kennedy. Originally published: 1980 - The concise Oxford dictionary of opera / by Harold Rosenthal and John Warrack. 2nd ed., Repr. with corrections. Originally published: 1980
ISBN 0-19-311328-7 : £9.00
ISBN 0-19-311321-x B81-03380

Kennedy, Michael, *1926-*. The concise Oxford dictionary of music. — 3rd ed. / Michael Kennedy ; based on the original publication by Percy Scholes. — London : Oxford University Press, 1980. — 724p : music ; 21cm
Previous ed.: / by Percy A. Scholes ; edited by John Owen Ward. 1973. — Paperback also available in The Concise Oxford dictionaries of music and opera
ISBN 0-19-311315-5 (cased) : £9.50 : CIP rev.
ISBN 0-19-311320-1 (pbk) : £4.50 B80-20938

The **New** Grove dictionary of music and musicians / edited by Stanley Sadie. — London : Macmillan, 1981. — 20v. : ill,music,facsims,ports,geneal.tables ; 26cm
Includes bibliographies and index
ISBN 0-333-23111-2 : £850.00 : CIP rev.
B80-18450

780'.42 — Reggae music, *to 1980 — For schools*
Farmer, Paul, *1950-*. Steelbands & reggae / Paul Farmer. — Harlow : Longman, 1981. — 24p : ill,1map,music,ports ; 23cm. — (Longman music topics)
ISBN 0-582-20097-0 (pbk) : £0.85
Also classified at 785'.06'75 B81-38155

780'.42'05 — Pop music — *Serials*
Contemporary music almanac. — 1980/81-. — New York : Schirmer Books ; London : Collier Macmillan, 1980-. — v. : ill,ports ; 24cm
Annual
ISSN 0196-6200 = Contemporary music almanac : £5.95 B81-23150

Fender musician. — Mar.1981-. — Enfield (Jeffreys Rd, Enfield, Middx EN3 7UF) : CBS-Arbiter, 1981-. — v. : ill,ports ; 42cm
Monthly
ISSN 0261-8222 = Fender musician : £0.25 per issue B81-33704

Smash hits. — Sept.1978-. — Peterborough (117 Park Rd, Peterborough PE1 2TS) : EMAP National Publications, 1978-. — v. : ill(some col.) ; 30cm
Fortnightly
ISSN 0260-3004 = Smash hits : £0.35
B81-04873

780'.42'076 — Pop music — *Questions & answers*
Read, Mike. Mike Read's rock and pop quiz book. — London : Elm Tree in association with Sphere, 1981. — 91p : ill,ports ; 20cm
ISBN 0-7221-7252-4 (pbk) : £1.50 B81-38398

780'.42'09047 — Pop music, *1970-1979*
Jasper, Tony. The 70's : a book of records / Tony Jasper. — London : Macdonald Futura, 1980. — 416p ; 18cm
Bibliography: p102-115
ISBN 0-7088-1944-3 (pbk) : £1.95 B81-05457

780'.42'0922 — Pop music. Stars, *1950-1981*
Elson, Howard. Whatever happened to —? : the great rock and pop nostalgia book / Howard Elson and John Brunton. — London : Proteus, [1981?]. — 159p : ill,ports ; 29cm. — (Proteus rocks)
ISBN 0-906071-46-1 (cased) : Unpriced
ISBN 0-906071-40-2 (pbk) : £4.95 B81-40691

780'.42'0924 — Pop music, *1969-1979 — Personal observations*
Nightingale, Anne. Chase the fade : music, memories & memorabilia / Anne Nightingale. — Poole : Blandford, 1981. — 125p : ill(some col.),facsim(some col.),ports(some col.) ; 26cm
Ill on lining papers. — Includes index
ISBN 0-7137-1167-1 : £5.95 : CIP rev.
B81-02586

780'.42'097292 — Jamaican popular music
Clarke, Sebastian. Jah music : the evolution of the popular Jamaican song / Sebastian Clarke. — London : Heinemann Educational, 1980. — 216p,[12]p of plates : ill,music,ports ; 22cm
Port on inside cover. — List of sound discs: p182-186. — Includes index
ISBN 0-435-82140-7 (pbk) : £4.95 : CIP rev.
B80-07460

780'.42'0973 — American country music, *to 1980*
Dellar, Fred. The best of country music / Fred Dellar and Richard Wootton ; foreword by Don Williams. — London : Octopus, 1980. — 96p : col.ill,ports(some col.) ; 33cm
Col. ill on lining papers. — Includes index
ISBN 0-7064-1204-4 : £3.95 B81-02255

780'.42'0973 — Great Britain. American country music — *Serials*
British Country Music AssociationBritish Country Music Association yearbook. — 1981. — Newton Abbot (P.O. Box 2, Newton Abbot, Devon TQ12 4HT) : The Association, 1981. — 88p
Spine title: B.C.M.A. yearbook
ISSN 0308-4698 : Unpriced B81-27128

780'.5 — Music — *Serials*
Music survey : new series 1949-1952 / edited by Donald Mitchell and Hans Keller. — London : Faber Music in association with Faber, 1981. — 771p in various pagings,[10]leaves of plates : ill,music,facsims,ports ; 23cm
Includes index
ISBN 0-571-10040-6 : £30.00 : CIP rev.
B81-13560

780'.6'041 — Great Britain. Music. Organisations: Incorporated Society of Musicians — *Directories — Serials*
Incorporated Society of Musicians. Handbook & register of members / Incorporated Society of Musicians. — 1979/80. — London (10, Stratford Place, W1N 9AE) : The Society, c1979. — 228p
£8.00 (free to members) B81-05039

780'.6'041 — Great Britain. Music. Organisations: Incorporated Society of Musicians. Members: Performers — *Directories — Serials*
Professional register of artists / The Incorporated Society of Musicians. — 1978/1979. — London (10, Stratford Place, W1N 9AE) : The Society, [1978?]. — 74p
Unpriced B81-05037

780′.6′041 — Great Britain. Music. Organisations: Incorporated Society of Musicians. Members: Performers — *Directories* — *Serials*
continuation

Professional register of artists / The Incorporated Society of Musicians. — 1979/1980. — London (10, Stratford Place, W1N 9AE) : The Society, [1979?]. — 75p
Unpriced B81-05038

780′.6′041 — Music, *to ca 1750.* **British groups** — *Directories*

The **Directory** of British early music groups. — London (62 Princedale Rd., W11 4NL) : Early Music Centre, c1981. — xvi,56p ; 21cm
Cover title. — Text on inside cover. — Includes index
£3.00 (pbk) B81-31481

780′.7 — Education. Curriculum subjects: Music — *Conference proceedings* — *German texts* — *Serials*

Forschung in der Musikerziehung. — 1980. — Mainz ; London : Schott, c1980. — 190p
ISBN 3-7957-2087-7 : £6.60
ISSN 0344-0508 B81-15073

780′.7 — Education. Curriculum subjects: Music — *Serials*

ISME yearbook. — Vol.7 (1980). — Mainz ; London : Schott, c1980. — 184p
Cover title: International music education
ISBN 3-7957-0106-6 : £7.20
ISSN 0172-0597 B81-25479

780′.7 — Great Britain. Music. Organisations: Incorporated Society of Musicians. Members: Private music teachers — *Directories* — *Serials*

Professional register of private teachers of music / The Incorporated Society of Musicians. — 1978/1979. — London (10, Stratford Place, W1N 9AE) : The Society, [1978?]. — 63p
Unpriced B81-05035

Professional register of private teachers of music / The Incorporated Society of Musicians. — 1979/1980. — London (10, Stratford Place, W1N 9AE) : The Society, [1979?]. — 64p
Unpriced B81-05036

780′.72 — Schools. Curriculum subjects: Music. Teaching — *German texts*

Vollmer, Sybille. Die Rezeption des Kreativitätsbegriffs durch die Musikpädagogik / Sibylle Vollmer. — Mainz ; London : Schott, c1980. — 224p ; 21cm. — (Musikpädagogik ; bd.7, ISSN 0172-8202)
Bibliography: p169-224
ISBN 3-7957-1706-x (pbk) : £7.20 B81-34202

780′.7′2941 — Great Britain. Instrumentalists. Professional education

The **Training** of instrumental musicians for performance and teaching / ESTA. — Penrith (37 Frenchfield Gardens, Penrith, Cumbria CA11 8TX) : John Upson, c1981. — 8p : 1ill ; 21cm
Cover title. — Bibliography: p7-8
£0.75 (pbk) B81-25272

780′.7′2941 — Great Britain. Middle schools. Activities: Creative music. Projects

Osborne, Nigel. Creative projects / Nigel Osborne. — London : Chappell Music, c1981. — 32p : ill,maps,music ; 22x28cm. — (Ways with music)
Unpriced (pbk) B81-21967

780′.7′294212 — London *(City).* **Music schools: Guildhall School of Music and Drama,** *to 1980*

Guildhall School of Music and Drama. GSMD : a hundred years' performance / Hugh Barty-King. — London : Published for the Guildhall School of Music and Drama by Stainer & Bell, c1980. — 198p : ill,ports ; 22cm
Includes index
ISBN 0-85249-589-7 : £6.50
Also classified at 792′.07′114212 B81-01950

780′.7′2943 — West Germany. Music schools — *Directories*

Studying music in the Federal Republic of Germany : music, music education, musicology : study guide / edited by Egon Kraus. — Rev. ed. — Mainz ; London : Schott [for] the German Music Council, 1980. — 64p ; 21cm
Previous ed.: i.e. Rev. ed. 1978. — Includes bibliographies and index
ISBN 3-7957-2585-2 (pbk) : £3.60 B81-15208

780′.7′2973 — United States. Middle schools. Musical activities — *For teaching*

Regelski, Thomas A.. Teaching general music : action learning for middle and secondary schools / Thomas A. Regelski. — New York : Schirmer ; London : Collier Macmillan, c1981. — 421p : ill,music,forms ; 25cm
Bibliography: p408-411. — Includes index
ISBN 0-02-872070-9 : £8.95 B81-36163

780′.7′7 — United States. Schools. Curriculum subjects: Music. Teaching methods: Kodály method

Choksy, Lois. The Kodály context : creating an environment for musical learning / Lois Choksy. — Englewood Cliffs ; London : Prentice-Hall, c1981. — xxi,281p : music ; 23cm
ISBN 0-13-516674-8 (cased) : Unpriced
ISBN 0-13-516666-7 (pbk) : £6.45 B81-17219

780′.7′9 — Music festivals, *1980* — *Personal observations*

Levin, Bernard. Conducted tour. — London : Cape, Oct.1981. — [256]p
ISBN 0-224-01896-5 : £7.50 : CIP entry
B81-27343

780′.7′9 — Music. Festivals — *Directories*

International guide to music festivals / edited by Douglas Smith & Nancy Barton ; foreword by Sir Rudolf Bing. — New York : Quick Fox ; London : Book Sales [distributor], c1980. — 246p : ill,ports ; 23cm
Includes index
ISBN 0-8256-3165-3 (pbk) : Unpriced
B81-36158

780′.7′94105 — Great Britain. Music festivals. Organisations: British Federation of Music Festivals — *Serials*

British Federation of Music Festivals. Year book / the British Federation of Music Festivals. — 1981. — Macclesfield (198 Park La., Macclesfield, Cheshire SK11 6UD) : The Federation, [1981]. — 134p
Spine title: Festivals year book
ISSN 0309-8044 : Unpriced B81-23503

780.8 — Music

Wade, Graham. The shape of music. — London : Allison and Busby, Aug.1981. — [128]p
ISBN 0-85031-427-5 (cased) : £6.95 : CIP entry
ISBN 0-85031-428-3 (pbk) : £2.95 B81-16415

780.8′2 — East Germany. Grüssau. Monasteries: Grüssau *(Monastery).* **Musical scores. Disappearance,** *1946*

Lewis, Nigel. Paperchase : the lost music of Grüssau. — London : H. Hamilton, Oct.1981. — [256]p
ISBN 0-241-10235-9 : £9.95 : CIP entry
B81-25703

780.9 — MUSIC. HISTORICAL AND GEOGRAPHICAL TREATMENT

780′.9 — Music. Historiology

Abraham, Gerald. Problems of musical history : the seventh Gwilym James memorial lecture of the University of Southampton : delivered at the University on Friday 22 February 1980 / by Gerald Abraham. — [Southampton] : University of Southampton, 1980. — 20p ; 21cm. — (The Seventh Gwilym James memorial lecture)
ISBN 0-85432-208-6 (pbk) : Unpriced
B81-06276

780′.9 — Music, *to 1971* — *Interviews*

Stravinsky, Igor. Dialogues. — London : Faber, Nov.1981. — [160]p
Originally published as part of: Dialogues and a diary. 1968
ISBN 0-571-10043-0 (pbk) : £3.50 : CIP entry
B81-30966

780′.9 — Music, *to 1980*

Dearling, Robert. The Guinness book of music / Robert and Celia Dearling with Brian Rust. — 2nd ed. — Enfield : Guinness Superlatives, 1981. — 288p : ill(some col.),music,ports(some col.) ; 25cm
Bibliography: p278. - Includes index
ISBN 0-85112-212-4 : £8.95 : CIP rev.
B81-08807

780′.9 — Western music — *Chronologies*

Manson, Adele P.. Calendar of music and musicians / Adele P. Manson. — Metuchen ; London : Scarecrow, 1981. — ix,462p ; 23cm
Bibliography: pviii-ix. — Includes index
ISBN 0-8108-1395-5 : £15.75 B81-29218

780′.9 — Western music, *to 1979* — *For children*

Russell, John, *1914-*. A short history of music / John Russell. — 3rd ed. rev. and enl. — London : Harrap, 1981. — 183p : ill,music,ports ; 24cm
Previous ed.: published as A history of music for young people. 1965. — Includes index
ISBN 0-245-53523-3 (pbk) : £4.50 B81-12295

780′.9 — Western music, *to 1980*

Grout, Donald Jay. A history of western music. — London : Dent, Dec.1981. — [864]p
ISBN 0-460-04546-6 : £12.95 : CIP entry
B81-31723

780′.9 — Western music, *to ca 1850* — *Readings from contemporary sources*

Source readings in music history / selected and annotated by Oliver Strunk. — London : Faber, 1981, c1965
Originally published: in 1 vol. 1952
[1]: Antiquity and the Middle Ages. — xiv,192p : music ; 21cm
Includes index
ISBN 0-571-11650-7 (pbk) : £3.50 B81-10610

Source readings in music history / selected and annotated by Oliver Strunk. — London : Faber, 1981, c1965
Originally published: in 1 vol. 1952
[2]: The Renaissance. — xiv,175p : music ; 21cm
Includes index
ISBN 0-571-11651-5 (pbk) : £3.50 B81-10611

Source readings in music history / selected and annotated by Oliver Strunk. — London : Faber, 1981, c1965
Originally published: in 1 vol. 1952
[3]: The Baroque era. — xiv,218p : music ; 21cm
Includes index
ISBN 0-571-11652-3 (pbk) : £3.50 B81-10612

Source readings in music history / selected and annotated by Oliver Strunk. — London : Faber, 1981, c1965
Originally published: in 1 vol. 1952
[4]The classic era. — xiv,170p : music ; 21cm
Includes index
ISBN 0-571-11653-1 (pbk) : £3.50 B81-10613

Source readings in music history / selected and annotated by Oliver Strunk. — London : Faber, 1981, c1965
Originally published: in 1 vol. 1952
[5]: The Romantic era. — xiv,167p ; 21cm
Includes index
ISBN 0-571-11654-x (pbk) : £3.50 B81-10614

780′.9 — Western music, *to ca 1980*

Kemp, Walter H.. Study companions in music history / Walter H. Kemp. — Ontario : Waterloo Music Company ; Wendover (The Windmill, Wendover, Aylesbury, Bucks.) : Roberton Publications [distributor]
Vol.1: The evolution of musical composition from the Middle Ages to Bach and Handel. — c1979. — xi,241p : ill,music ; 23cm
Bibiliogrpahy: px
£5.00 (pbk) B81-14704

780'.902 — Early music. Musicology
Stevens, Denis. Musicology : a practical guide / Denis Stevens. — London : Macdonald Futura, 1980. — 224p : music,1facsim ; 23cm. — (Yehudi Menuhin music guides)
Includes index
ISBN 0-354-04480-x (cased) : £8.50 (pbk) : £4.95 B81-01740

780'.902'03 — Music, *1000-1643 — Encyclopaedias*
Roche, Jerome. A dictionary of early music. — London : Faber, Sept.1981. — [208]p
ISBN 0-571-10035-x : £6.95 : CIP entry B81-21533

780'.903 — Western music, *1700-1930 — Textual criticism*
Del Mar, Norman. Orchestral variations : confusion and error in the orchestral repertoire / Norman Del Mar. — London (48 Great Marlborough St., W2V 2BN) : Eulenburg, 1981. — xvi,240p : music ; 23cm
ISBN 0-903873-37-0 (pbk) : £7.25 B81-18779

780'.903'1 — European music, *ca 1400-ca 1600 — Conference proceedings*
Music in medieval and early modern Europe : patronage, sources and texts / edited by Iain Fenlon. — Cambridge : Cambridge University Press, 1981. — xiii,409p : ill,facsims,music,1port ; 24cm
Conference papers. — Bibliography: p406-409. — Includes index
ISBN 0-521-23328-3 : £20.00 B81-35632

780'.903'2 — European music, *1580-1750*
Palisca, Claude V.. Baroque music / Claude V. Palisca. — 2nd ed. — Englewood Cliffs ; London : Prentice Hall, c1981. — xiv,300p : ill,music,facsims ; 24cm. — (Prentice-Hall history of music series)
Previous ed.: 1968. — Includes bibliographies and index
ISBN 0-13-055954-7 (cased) : Unpriced
ISBN 0-13-055947-4 (pbk) : £7.80 B81-16532

780'.903'3 — European music, *1770-1800*
Ratner, Leonard G.. Classic music : expression, form, and style / Leonard G. Ratner. — New York ; [London] : Schirmer, c1980. — xvii,475p : music ; 25cm
Bibliography: p444-449. — Includes index
ISBN 0-02-872020-2 : £19.95 B81-20737

780'.903'3 — Western music, *1719-1848 — Readings from contemporary sources*
Music and aesthetics in the eighteenth and early-nineteenth centuries / edited by Peter le Huray and James Day. — Cambridge : Cambridge University Press, 1981. — xvi,597p : ill ; 24cm. — (Cambridge readings in the literature of music)
Bibliography: p571-580. — Includes index
ISBN 0-521-23426-3 : £30-00 : CIP rev. B81-07947

780'.903'4 — European music, *1820-1900 — Critical studies*
Dahlhaus, Carl. Between romanticism and modernism : four studies in the music of the later nineteenth century / Carl Dahlhaus ; translated by Mary Whittall. — Berkeley ; London : University of California Press, c1980. — 129p : music ; 23cm. — (California studies in 19th century music)
Translation of: Zwischen Romantik und Moderne. — Includes index. — Includes: On music and words / by Friedrich Nietzsche ; translated by Walter Kaufmann
ISBN 0-520-03679-4 : £6.00 B81-06261

780'.904 — Avant garde music, *1945-1979*
Griffiths, Paul. Modern music : the avant garde since 1945 / Paul Griffiths. — London : Dent, 1981. — 331p : ill,music ; 24cm
Bibliography: p314-317. — Includes index
ISBN 0-460-04365-x : £15.00 : CIP rev. B80-17882

780'.904 — European music, *1900-1976 — For schools*
Farmer, Paul, *1950-*. Into the modern classics / Paul Farmer. — Harlow : Longman, 1981. — 24p : ill,music,1facsim,ports ; 23cm. — (Longman music topics)
Text on inside covers
ISBN 0-582-20096-2 (pbk) : £0.85 B81-40310

780'.904 — Music, *1900-1979 — Critical studies*
Booker, Mary. Music in the twentieth century : composers and their work / Mary Booker. — Ilfracombe : Stockwell, 1980. — 77p : music ; 19cm
ISBN 0-7223-1397-7 : £3.50 B81-02263

780'.904 — Music, *1908-1969 — Critical studies*
Peyser, Joan. [The new music]. Twentieth-century music : the sense behind the sound / by Joan Peyser. — New York : Schirmer ; London : Collier Macmillan, c1980. — xv,204p : ill,ports ; 21cm
Originally published: New York : Delacorte, 1971. — Bibliography: p193-196. - Includes index
ISBN 0-02-871880-1 (pbk) : £2.50 B81-04097

780'.92'2 — Instrumentalists, *1833-1979 — Illustrations*
The **Great** instrumentalists : in historic photographs : 274 portraits from 1850 to 1950 / edited by James Camner. — New York : Dover ; London : Constable, c1980. — 145p : chiefly ports ; 29cm
Includes index
ISBN 0-486-23907-1 (pbk) : £3.90 B81-05022

780'.92'2 — Music *— Biographies*
International who's who in music and musicians' directory. — 9th ed. / edited by Adrian Gaster. — Cambridge (International Biographical Centre, Cambridge CB2 3QP) : International Who's Who in Music, 1980. — xv,963p ; 24cm
Previous ed.: 1977
ISBN 0-900332-51-4 : Unpriced B81-08074

780'.92'2 — Music. Composers *— Biographies*
The **Dictionary** of composers / edited by Charles Osborne. — London : Book Club Associates, 1977 (1980 [printing]). — 380p : ill,music,facsims,ports ; 24cm
Unpriced B81-39169

An **Illustrated** guide to composers of classical music / [editorial consultant: Peter Gammond]. — London : Salamander, c1980. — 240p : ill (some col.),music,facsims,ports(some col.) ; 23cm
Ports (some col.) on lining papers. — Includes index
ISBN 0-86101-065-5 : £3.95 B81-02439

780'.92'2 — United States. Music. Composers. Organisations: American Society of Composers, Authors and Publishers. Members *— Biographies*
ASCAP biographical dictionary / compiled for the American Society of Composers, Authors and Publishers by Jaques Cattell Press. — 4th ed. — New York ; London : R.R. Bowker, 1980. — xii,589p ; 29cm
Previous eds. privately circulated. — Includes index
ISBN 0-8352-1283-1 : Unpriced B81-15723

780'.92'2 — Western music. Composers, *1685-1976 — Biographies — For children*
Lewis, Brenda Ralph. Famous names in music / Brenda Ralph Lewis. — Hove : Wayland, 1979. — 48p : ports ; 24cm
Bibliography: p46. — Includes index
ISBN 0-85340-623-5 : £2.95 B81-05061

780'.92'2 — Western music. Composers, *1685-ca 1970 — Biographies*
Schonberg, Harold C.. The lives of the great composers / Harold C. Schonberg. — London : Macdonald Futura, 1980, c1970. — 555p : ill ; 20cm
Originally published: New York : Norton, 1970 ; London : Davis-Poynter, 1971. — Bibliography: p533-544. — Includes index
ISBN 0-7088-1928-1 (pbk) : £2.95 B81-02424

780'.92'4 — American music. Cage, John, *1912- — Interviews*
Cage, John, *1912-*. For the birds / John Cage in conversation with Daniel Charles. — Boston [Mass.] ; London : Boyars, 1981. — 239p ; 23cm
Translation of: Pour les oiseaux
ISBN 0-7145-2690-8 : £11.95 : CIP rev. B81-04358

780'.92'4 — American music. Grainger, Percy Aldridge *— Biographies*
Bird, John. Percy Grainger. — London : Faber, Feb.1982. — [360]p
Originally published: London : Elek Books, 1976
ISBN 0-571-11717-1 (pbk) : £6.95 : CIP entry B81-38320

780'.92'4 — American music. Grainger, Percy Aldridge - *Critical studies*
The **Percy** Grainger companion. — London (14 Barlby Rd, W.10) : Thames Publishing, July 1981. — [256]p
ISBN 0-905210-12-3 : £12.50 : CIP entry B81-14786

780'.92'4 — American music. Menotti, Gian Carlo *— Biographies*
Gruen, John. Menotti : a biography / John Gruen. — New York : Macmillan ; London : Collier Macmillan, c1978. — xiii,242p,[24]p of plates : ill,1facsim,ports ; 24cm
Includes index
ISBN 0-02-546320-9 : £9.95 B81-33400

780'.92'4 — Austrian music. Haydn, Joseph *— Biographies*
Landon, H. C. Robbins. Haydn : a documentary study / H.C. Robbins Landon. — [London] : Thames and Hudson, c1981. — 224p : ill(some col.),2maps,facsims,music,ports(some col.),2geneal.tables ; 30cm
Bibliography: p220-221. — Includes index
ISBN 0-500-01252-0 : £18.00 B81-36072

780'.92'4 — Austrian music. Mahler, Gustav *— Biographies*
McCaldin, Denis. Mahler / Denis McCaldin. — Borough Green : Novello, 1981. — 32p ; 19cm. — (Novello short biographies)
Bibliography: p32. — List of works p31
£0.40 (pbk) B81-23207

780'.92'4 — Austrian music. Mozart, Wolfgang Amadeus *— Biographies*
Hildesheimer, Wolfgang. Mozart. — London : Dent, Jan.1982. — [415]p
ISBN 0-460-04347-1 : £15.00 : CIP entry B81-34496

780'.92'4 — Austrian music. Schmidt, Franz *— Biographies*
Tschulik, Norbert. Franz Schmidt : a critical biography / by Norbert Tschulik ; translated by Angela Tolstoshev. — London : Glover & Blair, 1980. — 131p : music ; 23cm
Translated from the German. — List of works: p125-128. — Bibliography: p129-130
ISBN 0-906681-06-5 : £6.50 B81-11495

780'.92'4 — Czechoslovak music. Janáček, Leoš *— Biographies*
Janáček, Leoš. Leoš Janáček. — London : Kahn & Averill, Feb.1982. — [160]p
Translated from the Czech
ISBN 0-900707-68-2 : £5.25 : CIP entry B81-37587

780'.92'4 — Czechoslovakian music. Janáček, Leoš *— Biographies*
Horsbrugh, Ian. Leoš Janáček. — Newton Abbot : David & Charles, Nov.1981. — [232]p
ISBN 0-7153-8060-5 : £10.00 : CIP entry B81-30578

780'.92'4 — England. Visits by Haydn, Joseph
Hogwood, Christopher. Haydn's visits to England / by Christopher Hogwood. — London : Folio Society, 1980. — 116p : ill,music,facsim,ports ; 23cm
Bibliography: p115-116
Unpriced B81-32510

780'.92'4 — English music. Britten, Benjamin *— Biographies*
Blyth, Alan, *1929-*. Remembering Britten / Alan Blyth. — London : Hutchinson, 1981. — 181p,[8]p of plates : music,ports ; 23cm
ISBN 0-09-144950-2 : £7.95 B81-26816

780'.92'4 — English music. Britten, Benjamin — *Biographies continuation*

Headington, Christopher. Britten. — London : Eyre Methuen, July 1981. — [200]p. — (The composer as contemporary)
ISBN 0-413-46510-1 : £7.00 : CIP entry
ISBN 0-413-48280-4 (pbk) : Unpriced B81-15846

Kennedy, Michael, *1926-*. Britten / Michael Kennedy. — London : Dent, 1981. — xi,356p,[12]p of plates : ill,music,ports ; 23cm. — (The Master musicians series)
List of works : 297-330. - List of sound recordings: p331-349. — Includes index
ISBN 0-460-03175-9 : £8.95 B81-16662

780'.92'4 — English music. Davies, Peter Maxwell — *Critical studies*

Griffiths, Paul. Peter Maxwell Davies. — London : Robson, Oct.1981. — [176]p. — (Contemporary composers ; 2)
ISBN 0-86051-138-3 : £6.95 : CIP entry B81-27443

780'.92'4 — English music. Delius, Frederick — *Personal observations*

Fenby, Eric. Delius as I knew him. — New and rev. ed. — London : Faber, Oct.1981. — [288]p
Previous ed.: London : G. Bell, 1936
ISBN 0-571-11836-4 (pbk) : £3.95 : CIP entry B81-27411

780'.92'4 — English music. Dowland, John — *Critical studies*

Poulton, Diana. John Dowland. — New and revised ed. — London : Faber, Sept.1981. — [520]p
Previous ed.: 1972
ISBN 0-571-18022-1 : £15.00 : CIP entry B81-21468

780'.92'4 — English music. Elgar, Edward — *Personal observations*

Menuhin, Yehudi. Sir Edward Elgar : my musical grandfather : an address given to the Elgar Society (London) at the British Institute of Recorded Sound on 19 January 1976 / by Yehudi Menuhin. — London ([c/o The Treasurer, 18 Lyncroft Mansions, Lyncroft Gardens, NW6 UJX]) : Elgar Society (London), 1976. — 9p ; 21cm
£0.50 (unbound) B81-21245

780'.92'4 — English music. Holst, Gustav — *Biographies*

Holst, Imogen. Holst. — 2nd ed. — London : Faber, Oct.1981. — [90]p. — (The Great composers)
Previous ed.: 1974
ISBN 0-571-18032-9 : £4.95 : CIP entry B81-31105

780'.92'4 — English music. Ireland, John, *1879-1962 — Biographies*

Scott-Sutherland, Colin. John Ireland / Colin Scott-Sutherland. — Rickmansworth : Triad Press, 1980. — 28p : ill,music,2ports ; 21cm
Limited ed. of 250 numbered copies
ISBN 0-902070-25-8 (pbk) : £1.95 B81-10771

780'.92'4 — English music. Routh, Francis — *Critical studies*

The **music** of Francis Routh : a short account, to accompany an exhibition at the British Music Information Centre, 10 Stratford Place, London W1, in June 1981. — London (Arlington Park House, W4 4HD) : Redcliffe Edition, c1981. — 7p ; 26cm
Unpriced (unbound) B81-26274

780'.92'4 — English music. Simpson, Robert — *Critical studies — Serials*

[Tonic *(Robert Simpson Society)*]. Tonic : the journal of the Robert Simpson Society. — Vol.1, no.1 (Winter 1980)-. — London (3 Engel Park, NW7 2HE) : The Society, 1980-. — v. ; 22cm
Quarterly
ISSN 0260-7425 = Tonic (Robert Simpson Society) : Unpriced B81-21337

780'.92'4 — English music. Sullivan, *Sir* **Arthur** — *Serials*

[Newsletter *(Sir Arthur Sullivan Society)*]. Newsletter / Sir Arthur Sullivan Society. — No.1 (Mar. 1977)-. — Hull (c/o S. Turnbull, 20 Glencoe St., Anlaby Rd, Hull) : The Society, 1977-. — v ; 21cm
Irregular. — Description based on: No.7 (Jan. 1980)
Unpriced B81-04700

780'.92'4 — English music. Tippett, *Sir* **Michael** — *Critical studies*

Bowen, Meirion. Michael Tippett. — London : Robson, Oct.1981. — [176]p. — (Contemporary composers)
ISBN 0-86051-137-5 : £6.95 : CIP entry B81-27450

780'.92'4 — German music. Bach, Johann Sebastian — *Biographies*

Dowley, Tim. Bach : his life and times / Tim Dowley. — Tunbridge Wells : Midas, 1981. — 144p : ill,music,facsims,ports ; 26cm. — ([Composers])
Bibliography: p128. - List of works: p129-141. - Includes index
ISBN 0-85936-145-4 : £7.50 B81-12600

780'.92'4 — German music. Bach, Johann Sebastian — *Biographies — For children*

Millar, Cynthia. Bach and his world / Cynthia Millar. — London : Kingfisher, 1980. — 29p : ill(some col.),1col.map,music,1facsim,1geneal.table,ports (some col.) ; 29cm. — (Great masters)
Music on lining papers. — Bibliography: p29. - Includes index
ISBN 0-7063-6032-x : £2.95 B81-03646

780'.92'4 — German music. Beethoven, Ludwig van — *Biographies*

Solomon, Maynard. Beethoven / Maynard Solomon. — London : Granada, 1980, c1977. — 559p ; 18cm. — (A Panther book)
Originally published: New York : Schirmer, 1977 ; London : Cassell, 1978. — Bibliography: p511-531. - List of works: p533-542. - Includes index
ISBN 0-586-05189-9 (pbk) : £2.95 B81-02250

780'.92'4 — German music. Brahms, Johannes — *Critical studies*

Dunsby, Jonathan. Structural ambiguity in Brahms : analytical approaches to four works / by Jonathan Dunsby. — [London] : UMI Research Press, c1981. — 120p : music ; 24cm
'A revision of the author's thesis, Leeds University, 1976'. — Bibliography: p115-117. — Includes index
ISBN 0-8357-1159-5 : Unpriced B81-27090

780'.92'4 — German music. Schütz, Heinrich — *Critical studies — Serials*

Schütz-Jahrbuch / im Auftrage der Internationale Heinrich-Schütz-Gesellschaft. — 1 Jahrg. (1979)-. — Kassel ; London ([17 Bucklersbury, Hitchin, Herts.]) : Bärenreiter, 1979-. — v. ; 24cm
Annual
ISSN 0174-2345 = Schütz-Jahrbuch : £11.40 B81-04899

780'.92'4 — German music. Strauss, Richard — *Correspondence, diaries, etc.*

Strauss, Richard. The correspondence between Richard Strauss and Hugo von Hofmannsthal / translated by Hanns Hammelmann and Ewald Osers ; introduction by Edward Sackville-West. — Cambridge : Cambridge University Press, 1980, c1961. — xx,558p : 2facsims,3ports ; 24cm
Translation of: Richard Strauss und Hugo von Hofmannsthal: Briefwechsel. — Originally published: London : Collins, 1961. — Includes index
ISBN 0-521-23476-x (cased) : £29.50 : CIP rev.
ISBN 0-521-29911-x (pbk) : £7.95
Also classified at 831'.912 B80-28594

780'.92'4 — German music. Wagner, Cosima. Marriage to Wagner, Richard

Skelton, Geoffrey. Richard and Cosima Wagner. — London : Gollancz, Feb.1982. — [320]p
ISBN 0-575-03017-8 : £25.00 : CIP entry
Primary classification 782.1'092'4 B81-38324

780'.92'4 — Irish music. O'Riada, Sean — *Critical studies*

Integrating tradition : the achievement of Sean O'Riada. — Dublin : Irish Humanities Centre, Oct.1981. — [170]p
ISBN 0-906462-04-5 : £10.00 : CIP entry B81-28012

780'.92'4 — Music — *Personal observations*

Bush, Alan. In my eighth decade and other essays / by Alan Bush. — London : Kahn & Averill, 1980. — 92p : music ; 22cm
Music on inside covers. — List of works: p81-92
ISBN 0-900707-61-5 (pbk) : £2.95 : CIP rev. B80-22356

Satie, Erik. The writings of Erik Satie / edited and translated by Nigel Wilkins. — London (48 Great Marlborough St., W1V 2BN) : Eulenburg, 1980. — 178p : ill,music,facsims,ports ; 30cm
ISBN 0-903873-57-5 : £9.95 B81-18224

780'.92'4 — Polish music. Lutosławski, Witold — *Critical studies*

Stucky, Steven. Lutosławski and his music / Steven Stucky. — Cambridge : Cambridge University Press, 1981. — ix,252p : music,3ports ; 24cm
Bibliography: p219-237. — Lists of works : p195-212. — List of sound discs : p213-218. — Includes index
ISBN 0-521-22799-2 : £21.50 : CIP rev. B81-10449

780'.92'4 — Polish music. Szymanowski, Karol — *Critical studies*

Samson, Jim. The music of Szymanowski / Jim Samson. — London : Kahn & Averill, 1980. — 220p : music ; 23cm
Music on lining papers. — Bibliography: p215-216. — List of works: p211-213. — Includes index
ISBN 0-900707-58-5 : £8.50 : CIP rev. B80-22357

780'.92'4 — Russian music. Chaĭkovskiĭ, P. I. — *Correspondence, diaries, etc.*

Chaĭkovskiĭ, P. I.. Letters to his family : an autobiography / Piotr Ilyich Tchaikovsky ; translated by Galina von Meck ; with additional annotations by Percy M. Young. — London : Dobson, 1981. — xxv,577p ; 25cm
Translation from the Russian. — Includes index
ISBN 0-234-77250-6 : £17.50 B81-26376

780'.92'4 — Russian music. Shostakovich, Dmitriĭ Dmitrievich — *Biographies*

Shostakovich, Dmitriĭ Dmitrievich. Testimony : the memoirs of Dmitri Shostakovich / as related to and edited by Solomon Volkov ; translated from the Russian by Antonina W. Bouis. — London : Faber, 1981, c1979. — xli,289p[17]p of plates : ill,facsims,ports ; 20cm
Originally published: London : H. Hamilton, 1979. — Includes index
ISBN 0-571-11829-1 (pbk) : £2.95 : CIP rev. B81-21465

Sollertinsky, Dmitri. Pages from the life of Dmitri Shostakovich / by Dmitri & Ludmilla Sollertinsky ; translated by Graham Hobbs & Charles Midgley. — London : Hale, 1981, c1980. — 246p,[8]p of plates : ill,ports ; 23cm
Translation of: Stranitsy zhizni Dmitriia Shostakovicha. — Originally published: New York : Harcourt, Brace, Jovanovich, 1980
ISBN 0-7091-8934-6 : £8.25 B81-18980

780'.92'4 — Welsh music. Thomas, Afan — *Biographies*

David John Afan Thomas .. : côflyfryn y Canmlwyddiant a rhaglen y dathlu = centenary souvenir brochure and programme of events. — [Cwmavon] ([5 Tyr Owen Row, Cwmavon, W. Glam.]) : Afan Thomas Centenary Memorial Fund, 1981. — [32]p : ill,ports ; 22cm
Text in English and Welsh
£0.50 (pbk) B81-23706

780′.92′4 — Welsh music. Thomas, Afan — *Biographies* *continuation*

Wil Ifan. Afan : a Welsh music maker / Wil Ifan. — [Port Talbot] ([18 Cunard Terrace, Cwmafan, Port Talbot]) : Afan Thomas Centenary Memorial Committee, 1980. — 54p : ill,ports ; 22cm
Originally published: Cardiff : Western Mail and Echo, 1944
£1.00 (pbk) B81-23705

780′.92′4 — Welsh music. Williams, Grace — *Critical studies*

Boyd, Malcolm, *1932-*. Grace Williams / Malcolm Boyd. — Cardiff : University of Wales Press on behalf of the Welsh Arts Council, 1980. — 98p : music ; 24cm. — (Composers of Wales ; 4)
Bibliography: p98
ISBN 0-7083-0762-0 (pbk) : Unpriced : CIP rev. B80-22358

780′.941 — Great Britain. Music, *1800-1914*

The **Romantic** age 1800-1914. — London : Athlone Press, Nov.1981. — [560]p. — (The Athlone history of music in Britain ; 5)
ISBN 0-485-13005-x : £45.00 : CIP entry B81-30556

780′.941 — Great Britain. Music — *Gazetteers*

Norris, Gerald. A musical gazetteer of Great Britain & Ireland. — Newton Abbot : David & Charles, Oct.1981. — [352]p
ISBN 0-7153-7845-7 : £11.95 : CIP entry B81-27947

780′.941 — Great Britain. Music — *Serials*

British music yearbook. — 7th ed. (1981). — London : A. & C. Black, 1981. — xv,555p
ISBN 0-7136-2101-x : £9.95 : CIP rev.
ISSN 0306-5928 B80-27414

British music yearbook. — 1982. — London : A. & C. Black, Nov.1981. — [500]p
ISBN 0-7136-2179-6 (pbk) : £12.50 : CIP entry B81-30361

780′.942 — England. Music, *to 1979*

Raynor, Henry. Music in England / Henry Raynor. — London : Hale, 1980. — 256p,[16]p of plates : ill,1facsim,music,ports ; 23cm
Bibliography: p245-248. — Includes index
ISBN 0-7091-8356-9 : £9.50 B81-01906

780′.9427′32 — Greater Manchester *(Metropolitan County)*. **Cadishead & Irlam. Music,** *1850-1980*

Wheaton, Cyril. A heritage of local music / by C. Wheaton. — [Irlam] : Irlam, Cadishead and District Local History Society, 1981. — 7leaves ; 30cm
Unpriced (unbound) B81-40194

780′.943′4 — West Germany. Mid Rhine River region. Music — *Encyclopaedias — German texts*

Musik und Musiker am Mittelrhein : ein biographisches, orts- und landesgeschichtliches Nachschlagewerk / herausgegeben von Hubert Unverricht. — Mainz ; London : Schott. — (Beiträge zur-mittelrheinischein Musikgeschichte ; n.21, ISSN 0522-6937)
Bd.2. — c1981. — 190p : ill,music,facsims,geneal.table,ports ; 21cm
ISBN 3-7957-1321-8 (pbk) : £10.20 B81-34196

780′.945 — Italian music, *1400-1700*

Pirrotta, Nino. Music and theatre from Poliziano to Monteverdi. — Cambridge : Cambridge University Press, Jan.1982. — [400]p. — (Cambridge studies in music)
Translation of: Li due Orfei
ISBN 0-521-23259-7 : £30.00 : CIP entry B81-37553

781 — MUSIC. PRINCIPLES AND TECHNIQUES

781′.22 — Music. Chords

Ashburnham, George. Chord recognition : lesson book / George Ashburnham. — Sutton (22, Effingham Close, Sutton, Surrey SM2 6AG) : Ashburnham School of Music
Pts.4-6. — [1981?]. — leaves 13-24 : ill,music,1port ; 26cm
Cover title. — Includes index
Unpriced (pbk) B81-21123

Ashburnham, George. Chord recognition / by George Ashburnham. — Sutton (22 Effingham Close, Sutton, Surrey SM2 6AG) : Ashburnham School of Music
Unpriced (pbk) B81-12536

781.3 — MUSIC. HARMONY

781.3 — Atonal music. Theories

Rahn, John. Basic atonal theory / John Rahn. — New York ; London : Longman, c1980. — music ; 26cm. — (Longman music series)
Bibliography: p124-132. - Includes index
ISBN 0-582-28117-2 (pbk) : £8.50 B81-13669

781.5 — MUSICAL FORMS

781′.572′09041 — Ragtime music, *1890-1920*

Berlin, Edward A.. Ragtime : a musical and cultural history / Edward A. Berlin. — Berkeley ; London : University of California Press, c1980. — xix,248p : ill,music ; 25cm
Bibliography: p215-237. — Includes index
ISBN 0-520-03671-9 : £9.50 B81-01598

781.6 — MUSIC. COMPOSITION AND PERFORMANCE

781.6′1 — Music. Composition — *Conference proceedings*

Ferienkurse ′80 / herausgegeben von Ernest Thomas. — Mainz ; London : Schott, c1980. — 102p,[4]p of plates : ill,music,ports ; 25cm. — (Darmstädter Beiträge zur newen Musik ; 18)
Conference papers. — Includes articles in English, French and Italian
ISBN 3-7957-1575-x (pbk) : £7.20 B81-29940

781.6′1 — Music. Composition — *Manuals*

Kohs, Ellis B.. Musical composition : projects in ways and means / Ellis B. Kohs. — Metuchen ; London : Scarecrow, 1980. — viii,239p : ill,music ; 29cm
Bibliography: p233-234. — Includes index
ISBN 0-8108-1285-1 : £12.25 B81-08342

781.6′1′09411 — Scotland. Music. Composition — *Serials*

[Newsletter *(Scottish Society of Composers)*]. Newsletter / the Scottish Society of Composers. — No.1 (Dec.1980)-. — Glasgow (c/o Scottish Music Archive, 7 Lilybank Gardens, Glasgow G12 8RZ) : The Society, 1980-. — v. ; 21cm
Quarterly
ISSN 0261-3018 = Newsletter — Scottish Society of Composers : Free to Society members B81-25006

781.6′3 — Music. Interpretation — *For conducting*

Leinsdorf, Erich. The composer′s advocate : a radical orthodoxy for musicians / Erich Leinsdorf. — New Haven ; London : Yale University Press, c1981. — viii,216p : music ; 24cm
Includes index
ISBN 0-300-02427-4 : £6.95 B81-18209

781.6′35 — Music. Conducting

Rudolf, Max. The grammar of conducting : a practical guide to baton techniques and orchestral interpretation / by Max Rudolf. — 2nd ed. — New York ; [London] : Schirmer, c1980. — xviii,471p : ill,music ; 25cm
Previous ed.: 1950. — Includes index
ISBN 0-02-872220-5 : £8.95 B81-20730

781.6′35 — Music. Conducting — *Manuals*

Green, Elizabeth A. H.. The modern conductor : a college text on conducting based on the technical principles of conductor Nicolai Malko as set forth in his The conductor and his baton / Elizabeth A.H. Green. — 3rd ed. — Englewood Cliffs ; London : Prentice-Hall, c1981. — xvii,298p : ill,music ; 24cm
Previous ed.: 1969. — Bibliography: p280-284. — Includes index
ISBN 0-13-590216-9 : £13.25 B81-32503

781.7 — MUSIC OF ETHNIC AND NATIONAL ORIENTATION

781.7 — Music — *Anthropological perspectives*

Musics of many cultures : an introduction / Elizabeth May, editor ; foreword by Mantle Hood. — Berkeley ; London : University of California Press, c1980. — 431p : ill,maps,music,ports ; 27cm
Three sound discs in sleeve attached to inside cover. — Includes bibliographies and index
ISBN 0-520-03393-0 : £30.00 B81-27266

781.7′1 — Music. Origins. Role of behaviour of apes

Williams, Leonard. The dancing chimpanzee : a study of the origin of music in relation to the vocalising and rhythmic action of apes / Leonard Williams. — Rev. ed. — London : Allison & Busby, 1980. — 95p : music ; 23cm
Previous ed.: London : Deutsch, 1967. — Bibliography: p81-83. — Includes index
ISBN 0-85031-341-4 (cased) : £5.95 : CIP rev.
ISBN 0-85032-342-2 (pbk) : £2.50 B80-09342

781.741′025 — Great Britain. Folk music — *Directories — Serials*

The **Folk** directory / the English Folk Dance and Song Society. — 1980. — London : The Society, c1980. — 208p
ISBN 0-85418-127-x : £2.50 (£1.25 to members) B81-00217

781.7411′09 — Scottish music, *to 1980*

Davie, Cedric Thorpe. Scotland′s music / Cedric Thorpe Davie. — Edinburgh : William Blackwood, 1980. — 56p ; 21cm. — (Scottish connection)
Bibliography: p55-56
ISBN 0-85158-136-6 (pbk) : £1.85 B81-07204

781.7′43 — German music, *1800-1826 — Critical studies — Early works*

Weber, Carl Maria von. Writings on music. — Cambridge : Cambridge University Press, Oct.1981. — [395]p
ISBN 0-521-22892-1 : £35.00 : CIP entry B81-25815

781.7437′05 — Czechoslovak music — *Serials*

Czech music : the quarterly journal of the Dvořák Society. — [Vol.1, no.1 (197—)?]-. — London (c/o M. Todd, 15 Quex Rd, NW6 4PP) : The Society, [197-]-. — v ; 21cm
Description based on: Vol.7, no.1 (Jan. 1981)
ISSN 0261-2801 = Czech music : Free to Society members B81-20328

781.75 — Oriental music — *Festschriften*

Music and tradition : essays on Asian and other musics presented to Laurence Picken / edited by D.R. Widdess and R.F. Wolpert. — Cambridge : Cambridge University Press, 1981. — x,244p : ill,music ; 26cm
Includes index
ISBN 0-521-22400-4 : £25.00 B81-05381

781.754 — Indian music, *to 1978 — Critical studies*

Wade, Bonnie C.. Music in India : the classical traditions / Bonnie C. Wade. — Englewood Cliffs ; London : Prentice Hall, c1979. — xix,252p : ill,1map,music,ports ; 24cm. — (Prentice-Hall history of music series)
Bibliography: p212-220. - List of sound discs: p220-233. - List of films: p233-235. - Includes index
ISBN 0-13-607036-1 (cased) : £9.05
ISBN 0-13-607028-0 (pbk) : £6.45 B81-04616

781.766′09 — West African music, *to 1980*

Charters, Samuel. The roots of the blues : an African search / Samuel Charters. — Boston, Mass. ; London : Boyars, 1981. — 151p,[8]p of plates : ill,ports ; 22cm
ISBN 0-7145-2705-x : £7.95 B81-23544

781.773 — American music, *ca 1960-1980 — Scores*

Scores : an anthology of new music / selection and commentary by Roger Johnson. — New York : Schirmer Books ; London : Collier Macmillan, c1981. — xvi,351p : ill,music ; 23x28cm
Bibliography: p347-348. — Includes index
ISBN 0-02-871190-4 (pbk) : £8.95 B81-29324

781.773′088042 — American music. Role of women, *1790-1980*
Ammer, Christine. Unsung : a history of women in American music / Christine Ammer. — Westport, Conn. ; London : Greenwood Press, 1980. — x,317p ; 25cm. — (Contributions in women′s studies, ISSN 0147-104x ; no.14)
Bibliography: p279-288. - Includes index
ISBN 0-313-22007-7 : Unpriced B81-04801

781.91 — MUSICAL INSTRUMENTS

781.91 — Musical instruments
Buchner, Alexander. Colour encyclopedia of musical instruments / by Alexander Buchner ; translated by Simon Pellar. — London : Hamlyn, c1980. — 351p : ill(some col.),music,ports(some col.) ; 24cm
Translation from the Czech. — Bibliography: p346-347. - Includes index
ISBN 0-600-36421-6 : £4.95 B81-22055

781.9′1 — Musical instruments. Making — *Manuals — For children*
McLean, Margaret. Making musical instruments. — London : Macmillan Children′s Books, Feb.1982. — [32]p. — (Help yourself)
ISBN 0-333-30857-3 : £2.50 : CIP entry B81-35785

781.91 — Rock groups. Musical instruments
Rock hardware : the instruments, equipment and technology of rock / edited by Tony Bacon. — Poole : Blandford, 1981. — 224p : ill(some col.),ports(some col.) ; 30cm
List of sound recordings: p205-207. — Includes index
ISBN 0-7137-1190-6 : £10.95 : CIP rev. B81-20589

781.91′025′73 — United States. Musical instruments. Making — *Directories*
Farrell, Susan Caust. Directory of contemporary American musical instrument makers / Susan Caust Farrell. — Columbia ; London : University of Missouri Press, 1981. — xii,216p : ill,1map ; 25cm
ISBN 0-8262-0322-1 : £16.80 B81-38213

781.91′074′029134 — Edinburgh. Museums: Edinburgh University Collection of Historic Musical Instruments. Stock: Folk musical instruments — *Catalogues*
Edinburgh University Collection of Historic Musical Instruments. A check-list of the ethnic musical instruments in the Edinburgh University Collection of Historic Musical Instruments / Keith Pratt. — Edinburgh (Reid School of Music, Teviot Place, Edinburgh EH8 9AG) : The Collection, 1981. — 14p : ill ; 30cm
ISBN 0-907635-00-8 (unbound) : £1.00 B81-27067

781.91′09 — Western musical instruments, *to 1977*
Remnant, Mary. Musical instruments of the West / Mary Remnant. — London : Batsford, 1978 (1981 [printing]). — 240p : ill,facsims,ports ; 24cm
Bibliography: p230-235. — Includes index
ISBN 0-7134-0570-8 (pbk) : £6.95 B81-29297

781.91′09′034 — Musical instruments, *1800-1980*
Montagu, Jeremy. The world of romantic & modern musical instruments / Jeremy Montagu. — Newton Abbot : David & Charles, 1981. — 136p : ill(some col.),ports ; 25cm
Bibliography: p131-132. — Includes index
ISBN 0-7153-7994-1 : £10.50 : CIP rev. B81-14043

782.1 — OPERA

782.1 — Opera
Alexander, Alfred. Operanatomy : an eclectic introduction to the art of the conductor, instrumentalist, composer, producer, and to score reading : analysis of sound, singer, libretto and public, and adjudication of the critic / Alfred Alexander. — 3rd ed., rev. — Old Woking : Gresham, 1979. — 208p : ill,music ; 20cm
Previous ed.: Boston, Mass. : Crescendo, 1974. — Includes index
ISBN 0-905418-40-9 : £3.75 B81-03516

Gattey, Charles Neilson. The elephant that swallowed a nightingale. — London : Hutchinson, Oct.1981. — [160]p
ISBN 0-09-146060-3 : £4.95 : CIP entry B81-27407

782.1 — Opera in Italian, *1816-1926 — Critical studies*
Weaver, William. The golden century of Italian opera : from Rossini to Puccini / William Weaver. — London : Thames and Hudson, 1980. — 256p : ill(some col.),music,facsims,plans,ports ; 28cm
Bibliography: p252. - Includes index
ISBN 0-500-01240-7 : £10.00 B81-02246

782.1′03′21 — Opera — *Encyclopaedias*
Rosenthal, Harold, *1917-*. The concise Oxford dictionary of opera / by Harold Rosenthal and John Warrack. — 2nd ed., reprinted with corrections. — London : Oxford University Press, 1979 (1980 [printing]). — [14],561p : music ; 21cm
Previous ed.: 1964. — Bibliography: p[9]-[10]
ISBN 0-19-311318-x (cased) : £7.50
ISBN 0-19-311321-x (pbk) : £4.50 B81-04178

782.1′06′0421 — London. Amateur operatic societies: Geoids Amateur Operatic Society, *1930-1980*
Baddeley, Geoffrey E.. The Geoids : fifty years of entertainment by the Geoids Amateur Operatic Society / compiled by Geoffrey E. Baddeley. — [Croydon] ([13 Sutton Gardens, Davidson Rd., Croydon, Surrey CR0 6DX]) : G.E. Baddeley, 1980. — 79p : ill,ports ; 22cm
£2.50 (pbk) B81-25992

782.1′07′1 — Opera. Performance — *Stories, anecdotes*
Vickers, Hugh. Even greater operatic disasters. — London : Jill Norman & Hobhouse, Oct.1981. — [80]p
ISBN 0-906908-62-0 : £3.95 : CIP entry B81-27419

782.1′07′942257 — East Sussex. Glynde. Opera. Festivals: Glyndebourne Festival Opera, *to 1980*
Hughes, Spike. Glyndebourne : a history of the festival opera founded in 1934 by Audrey and John Christie / Spike Hughes. — New ed. — Newton Abbot : David & Charles, 1981. — 388p,[16]p of plates : ill,ports ; 26cm
Previous ed.: [London]: Methuen, 1965. — Includes index
ISBN 0-7153-7891-0 : £12.95 : CIP rev. B81-00218

782.1′09 — Opera, *to 1979*
Drummond, John D.. Opera in perspective / John D. Drummond. — London : Dent, 1980. — 383p : ill,2maps,music,1plan ; 24cm
Bibliography: p365-369. - Includes index
ISBN 0-460-04294-7 : £17.50 : CIP rev. B80-01757

Rich, Alan. Opera / Alan Rich. — Poole : Blandford, 1980. — 127p : ill,ports ; 24cm
Includes list of sound recordings
ISBN 0-7137-1104-3 : £4.95 B81-01057

782.1′09 — Opera, *to ca 1700*
Donnington, Robert. The rise of opera. — London : Faber, June 1981. — [367]p
ISBN 0-571-11674-4 : £15.00 : CIP entry B81-12845

782.1′092′2 — Opera. Composers — *Biographies*
Gammond, Peter. An illustrated guide to composers of opera. — London : Salamander, c1980. — 240p : ill(some col.),ports(some col.) ; 23cm
Author: Peter Gammond. — Ill (some col.), ports (some col.) on lining papers. — Includes index
ISBN 0-86101-066-3 : £3.95 B81-01617

782.1′092′4 — England. Opera. Harewood, George Lascelles, *Earl of — Biographies*
Harewood, George Lascelles, *Earl of*. The tongs and the bones : the memoirs of Lord Harewood. — London : Weidenfeld and Nicholson, c1981. — xv,334p,[24]p of plates : ill,1form,ports,2geneal.tables ; 24cm
Text on lining papers. — Includes index
ISBN 0-297-77960-5 : £9.95 B81-40670

782.1′092′4 — Opera in German. Berg, Alban. Lulu *- Critical studies*
Calder, John Mackenzie. The Lulu opera guide. — London : Calder, Apr.1981. — [224]p
ISBN 0-7145-3847-7 (pbk) : £2.00 : CIP entry
Also classified at 782.1′2 B81-05174

782.1′092′4 — Opera in German. Strauss, Richard. Rosenkavalier, *Der — Critical studies*
Strauss, Richard. Der Rosenkavalier / Richard Strauss. — London : Calder, 1981. — 128p : ill,music,ports ; 22cm. — (English National Opera guides ; 8)
Text on inside covers. — Bibliography: p125. — List of sound discs: p126-128. — Includes the libretto by Hugo von Hofmannsthal ; parallel German text and English translation by Alfred Kalisch
ISBN 0-7145-3851-5 (pbk) : £2.00 : CIP rev.
Also classified at 782.1′2 B81-14809

782.1′092′4 — Opera in German. Wagner, Richard *— Biographies*
Westernhagen, Curt von. Wagner : a biography / Curt Von Westernhagen ; translated by Mary Whittall. — Cambridge : Cambridge University Press, 1981. — xxvi,654p,[32]p of plates : ill,map,music,2facsims,ports ; 23cm
Translation of: Wagner. — Originally published: in 2 vols. 1978. — Bibliography: p629-637. — Includes index
ISBN 0-521-28254-3 (pbk) : £7.95 B81-25936

782.1′092′4 — Opera in German. Wagner, Richard *— Critical studies*
Adorno, Theodor W.. In search of Wagner / Theodor Adorno ; translated by Rodney Livingstone. — London : NLB, 1981. — 159p ; 22cm
Translation of: Versuch über Wagner. — Includes index
ISBN 0-86091-037-7 : £7.50 : CIP rev. B81-14042

782.1′092′4 — Opera in German. Wagner, Richard *— Critical studies — Serials*
Wagner news. — Issue no.1 (Sept. 1980)-. — [London] ([c/o Mr P Saul, 6 Sydenham Ave., SE26 6UH]) : [Wagner Society], 1980-. — v. ; 21cm
Eight issues yearly. — Continues in part: Wagner
ISSN 0261-3468 = Wagner news : Free to Society members only B81-24104

782.1′092′4 — Opera in German. Wagner, Richard. Marriage to Wagner, Cosima
Skelton, Geoffrey. Richard and Cosima Wagner. — London : Gollancz, Feb.1982. — [320]p
ISBN 0-575-03017-8 : £25.00 : CIP entry
Also classified at 780′.92′4 B81-38324

782.1′092′4 — Opera in German. Wagner, Richard. Parsifal *— Critical studies*
Beckett, Lucy. Richard Wagner : Parsifal / Lucy Beckett. — Cambridge : Cambridge University Press, 1981. — viii,163p : ill,music ; 23cm. — (Cambridge opera handbooks)
Bibliography: p156-157. — List of sound recordings: p158-160. — Includes index
ISBN 0-521-22825-5 (cased) : £9.95 : CIP rev.
ISBN 0-521-29662-5 (pbk) : £3.95 B81-13796

782.1′092′4 — Opera in German. Wagner, Richard. Ring des Nibelungen *— Critical studies*
Blyth, Alan. Wagner′s Ring : an introduction / Alan Blyth. — London : Hutchinson, 1980. — 146p,[8]p of plates : ill,music ; 22cm
ISBN 0-09-142011-3 (pbk) : £4.95 : CIP rev. B80-13490

782.1′092′4 — Opera in German. Wagner, Richard. Tristan und Isolde *— Critical studies*
Wagner, Richard. Tristan and Isolde / Richard Wagner. — London : Calder, 1981. — 96p : ill,music,ports ; 22cm. — (English National Opera guides ; 6)
Text on inside covers. — Bibliography: p96. — List of sound discs: p94-95. — Includes the libretto by the composer ; parallel German text and English translation by Andrew Porter
ISBN 0-7145-3849-3 (pbk) : £2.00 : CIP rev.
Also classified at 782.1′2 B81-14808

782.1′092′4 — Opera in Italian. Gluck, Christoph Willibald. Orfeo — *Critical studies*

Orfeo / compiled by Patricia Howard. — Cambridge : Cambridge University Press, 1981. — ix,143p : ill,music,ports ; 23cm. — (Cambridge opera handbooks)
Bibliography: p135-136. — List of sound discs: p137-139. — Includes index
ISBN 0-521-22827-1 (cased) : £9.95
ISBN 0-521-29664-1 (pbk) : Unpriced
B81-36129

782.1′092′4 — Opera in Italian. Mozart, Wolfgang Amadeus. Nozze di Figaro - *Critical studies*

Calder, John Mackenzie. The marriage of Figaro. — London : Calder, Apr.1981. — [128]p. — (Royal Opera House guide ; 5)
ISBN 0-7145-3771-3 (pbk) : £2.00 : CIP entry
Also classified at 782.1′2 B81-05172

782.1′092′4 — Opera in Italian. Puccini, Giacomo — *Critical studies*

Osborne, Charles, *1927-*. The complete operas of Puccini : a critical guide / by Charles Osborne. — London : Gollancz, 1981. — 279p,[8]p of plates : ill,music,ports ; 24cm
Bibliography: p273. — Includes index
ISBN 0-575-03013-5 : £10.95 B81-40484

782.1′092′4 — Opera in Italian. Verdi, Giuseppe, *1839-1853* — *Critical studies*

Kimbell, David R. B.. Verdi in the age of Italian Romanticism / David R.B. Kimbell. — Cambridge : Cambridge University Press, 1981. — ix,703p : music ; 24cm
Bibliography: p692-695. - Includes index
ISBN 0-521-23052-7 : £35.00 B81-19754

782.1′092′4 — Opera in Italian. Verdi, Giuseppe, *1839-1859* — *Critical studies*

Baldini, Gabriele. The story of Giuseppe Verdi : Oberto to Un ballo in maschera / Gabriele Baldini ; edited by Fedele d′Amico ; this edition translated and edited by Roger Parker. — Cambridge : Cambridge University Press, 1980. — xx,296p : 1port ; 23cm
Translation of: Abitare la battaglia. — Includes index
ISBN 0-521-22911-1 (cased) : £17.50 : CIP rev.
ISBN 0-521-29712-5 (pbk) : £5.95 B80-26001

782.1′092′4 — Opera in Italian. Verdi, Giuseppe. Otello — *Critical studies*

Verdi, Giuseppe. Otello / Giuseppe Verdi. — London : Calder, 1981. — 80p : ill,music,ports ; 22cm. — (English National Opera guides ; 7)
Text on inside covers. — Bibliography: p80. — List of sound discs: p78-79. — Includes the libretto by Arrigo Boito after Othello by Shakespeare ; parallel Italian text and English translation by Andrew Porter
ISBN 0-7145-3850-7 (pbk) : £2.00 : CIP rev.
Also classified at 782.1′2 B81-14788

782.1′092′4 — Opera in Italian. Verdi, Giuseppe. Traviata, La — *Critical studies*

Verdi, Giuseppe. La Traviata / Giuseppe Verdi. — London : Calder, 1981. — 80p : ill,music,ports ; 22cm. — (English National Opera guides ; 5)
Text on inside covers. — Bibliography: p80. — List of sound discs: p76-79. — Includes the libretto by Francesco Maria Piave after the play La dame aux camélias by Alexandre Dumas fils; parallel Italian text and English translation by Edmund Tracey
ISBN 0-7145-3848-5 (pbk) : £2.00 : CIP rev.
Also classified at 782.1′2 B81-14810

782.1′092′4 — Opera. Singing. Callas, Maria — *Biographies*

Linakis, Steven. Diva : the life and death of Maria Callas / Steven Linakis. — London : Owen, 1981, c1980. — vii,169p,[4]p of plates ; 23cm
Originally published: Englwood Cliffs : Prentice-Hall, 1980. — Includes index
ISBN 0-7206-0578-4 : £7.50 B81-29303

Segalini, Sergio. Callas : portrait of a diva / Sergio Segalini ; translated by Sonia Sabel. — London : Hutchinson, 1981. — 171p : ill,ports ; 21cm
Translation of: Callas, les images d′une voix
ISBN 0-09-143740-7 : £9.95 : CIP rev.
B80-23602

Stassinopoulos, Arianna. Maria : beyond the Callas legend / Arianna Stassinopoulos. — London : Weidenfeld and Nicolson, 1980. — x,329p,[24]p of plates : ill,facsims,ports ; 25cm
Includes index
ISBN 0-297-77544-8 : £8.95 B81-00219

782.1′092′4 — Opera. Singing. Melba, *Dame* **Nellie** — *Biographies*

Melba, *Dame* **Nellie**. Melodies and memories / Nellie Melba ; introduction and notes John Cargher. — London : Hamish Hamilton, 1980. — xv,253p,[16]p of plates : ill,facsims,ports ; 24cm
Originally published: London : Thornton Butterworth, 1925. — Includes index
ISBN 0-241-10410-6 : £8.95 B81-01538

782.1′092′4 — Opera. Singing. Pavarotti, Luciano — *Biographies*

Pavarotti, Luciano. Pavarotti : my own story / with William Wright. — London : Sidgwick & Jackson, 1981. — xviii,314p,[32]p of plates : ill,ports ; 24cm
List of sound discs: p291-305. — Includes index
ISBN 0-283-98763-4 : £8.95 B81-19445

782.1′092′4 — Opera. Singing. Sutherland, Joan — *Biographies*

Adams, Brian. La Stupenda : a biography of Joan Sutherland / Brian Adams. — London : Hutchinson, 1981, c1980. — 329p,[16]p of plates : ill(some col.),ports(some col.) ; 25cm
Bibliography: p317-318. - Includes index
ISBN 0-09-137410-3 : £9.95 B81-04792

782.1′092′4 — United States. Opera. Singing. Tours by Lind, Jenny, *1850-1852*

Ware, W. Porter. P.T. Barnum presents Jenny Lind : the American tour of the Swedish Nightingale / W. Porter Ware and Thaddeus C. Lockard, Jr. — Baton Rouge ; London : Louisiana State University Press, c1980. — xiv,204p,[20]p of plates : ill,music,facsims,ports ; 24cm
Bibliography: p198-200. — Includes index
ISBN 0-8071-0687-9 : £12.00 B81-12664

782.1′092′4 — West Germany. Bayreuth. Opera in German. Wagner, Richard. Festivals: Bayreuther Festspiele, *1876-1914* — *Readings from contemporary sources*

Bayreuth : the early years : an account of the early decades of the Wagner Festival as seen by the celebrated visitors & participants / compiled, edited and introduced by Robert Hartford. — London : Gollancz, 1980. — 284p,[16]p of plates : ill,1facsim,plans,ports ; 24cm
Bibliography: p275-278. - Includes index
ISBN 0-575-02865-3 : £12.50 B81-04524

782.1′09421′32 — London. Westminster *(London Borough)*. **Opera houses: Royal Opera House,** *to 1980*

Drogheda, Charles Garrett Ponsonby Moore, *Earl of*. The Covent Garden album. — London : Routledge & Kegan Paul, Oct.1981. — [192]p
ISBN 0-7100-0880-5 : £15.00 : CIP entry
B81-27983

782.1′09429 — Wales. Opera. Companies: Welsh National Opera — *Serials*

. New / Welsh National Opera. — No.1 (Spring 1978)-. — [Cardiff] ([Johnson Buildings, John St., Cardiff]) : The Opera, 1978-. — v. : ill ; 30cm
Quarterly. — Description based on: No.4 (Winter 1978)
ISSN 0260-8138 = News — Welsh National Opera : £0.12 per issue (free to Friends of the Opera) B81-09138

782.1′0944′36 — France. Paris. Opera houses: Théâtre lyrique, *to 1870*

Walsh, T. J. (Thomas Joseph). Second Empire opera : the Théâtre Lyrique, Paris 1851-1870 / by T.J. Walsh. — London : Calder, 1981. — viii,384p : ill ; 23cm. — (The History of opera)
Bibliography: 367-370. — Includes index
ISBN 0-7145-3659-8 : £15.00 : CIP rev.
B81-06045

782.1′0947′312 — Russia *(RSFSR)*. **Moscow. Opera houses: Bol′shoĭ teatr SSSR,** *to 1978*

Pokrovskiĭ, Boris Aleksandrovich. The Bolshoi : opera and ballet at the greatest theater in Russia / Boris Alexandrovich Pokrovsky and Yuri Nikolayevich Grigorovich ; [translated from the Russian and Italian by Daryl Hislop]. — London : Batsford, 1979. — 238p : col.ill ; 30cm
Originally published: New York : W. Morrow, 1979. — Includes index
ISBN 0-7134-2369-2 : £20.00 B81-12445

782.1′2 — Opera in English. Musgrave, Thea — *Librettos*

Musgrave, Thea. A Christmas carol : opera for Christmas in two acts / libretto and music by Thea Musgrave based on a story by Charles Dickens. — Sevenoaks : Novello, c1981. — 59p ; 19cm
Seven men, 5 women
£1.60 (pbk) B81-34941

782.1′2 — Opera in German. Berg, Alban - *Librettos - German-English parallel texts*

Calder, John Mackenzie. The Lulu opera guide. — London : Calder, Apr.1981. — [224]p
ISBN 0-7145-3847-7 (pbk) : £2.00 : CIP entry
Primary classification 782.1′092′4 B81-05174

782.1′2 — Opera in German. Mozart, Wolfgang Amadeus — *Librettos — German-English parallel texts*

Mozart, Wolfgang Amadeus. [Die Zauberflöte (Libretto). English]. The magic flute / Wolfgang Amadeus Mozart ; libretto by Emanuel Schikaneder ; English translation by Andrew Porter. — London : Faber Music, 1980. — viii,71p ; 23cm
Translation of: Die Zauberflöte
Unpriced (pbk) B81-07633

782.1′2 — Opera in German. Strauss, Richard — *Librettos — German-English parallel texts*

Strauss, Richard. Der Rosenkavalier / Richard Strauss. — London : Calder, 1981. — 128p : ill,music,ports ; 22cm. — (English National Opera guides ; 8)
Text on inside covers. — Bibliography: p125. — List of sound discs: p126-128. — Includes the libretto by Hugo von Hofmannsthal ; parallel German text and English translation by Alfred Kalisch
ISBN 0-7145-3851-5 (pbk) : £2.00 : CIP rev.
Primary classification 782.1′092′4 B81-14809

782.1′2 — Opera in German. Wagner, Richard — *Librettos — German-English parallel texts*

Wagner, Richard. Tristan and Isolde / Richard Wagner. — London : Calder, 1981. — 96p : ill,music,ports ; 22cm. — (English National Opera guides ; 6)
Text on inside covers. — Bibliography: p96. — List of sound discs: p94-95. — Includes the libretto by the composer ; parallel German text and English translation by Andrew Porter
ISBN 0-7145-3849-3 (pbk) : £2.00 : CIP rev.
Primary classification 782.1′092′4 B81-14808

782.1′2 — Opera in Italian. Monteverdi, Claudio — *Librettos — English texts*

Monteverdi, Claudio. Orfeo : opera / by Claudio Monteverdi ; libretto by Alessandro Striggio ; English singing version by Anne Ridler. — Rev. ed. — London : Faber, 1981. — 17p ; 20cm
Translation from the Italian. — Previous ed.: 1975
£0.75 (pbk) B81-17960

782.1′2 — Opera in Italian. Mozart, Wolfgang Amadeus - *Librettos - Italian-English parallel texts*

Calder, John Mackenzie. The marriage of Figaro. — London : Calder, Apr.1981. — [128]p. — (Royal Opera House guide ; 5)
ISBN 0-7145-3771-3 (pbk) : £2.00 : CIP entry
Primary classification 782.1′092′4 B81-05172

782.1′2 — Opera in Italian. Verdi, Giuseppe — *Librettos — Italian-English parallel texts*

Verdi, Giuseppe. Otello / Giuseppe Verdi. — London : Calder, 1981. — 80p : ill,music,ports ; 22cm. — (English National Opera guides ; 7)
Text on inside covers. — Bibliography: p80. — List of sound discs: p78-79. — Includes the libretto by Arrigo Boito after Othello by Shakespeare ; parallel Italian text and English translation by Andrew Porter
ISBN 0-7145-3850-7 (pbk) : £2.00 : CIP rev.
Primary classification 782.1′092′4 B81-14788

Verdi, Giuseppe. La Traviata / Giuseppe Verdi. — London : Calder, 1981. — 80p : ill,music,ports ; 22cm. — (English National Opera guides ; 5)
Text on inside covers. — Bibliography: p80. — List of sound discs: p76-79. — Includes the libretto by Francesco Maria Piave after the play La dame aux camélias by Alexandre Dumas fils; parallel Italian text and English translation by Edmund Tracey
ISBN 0-7145-3848-5 (pbk) : £2.00 : CIP rev.
Primary classification 782.1′092′4 B81-14810

782.1′2 — Opera — *Librettos*

English National Opera guides. — London : John Calder. — (Opera library)
Vol.1: La Cenerentola, Aida, The magic flute, Fidelio / edited by Nicholas John ; with a foreword by Lord Harewood. — 1980. — 422p in various pagings : ill,music,facsims,ports ; 23cm
English, Italian and German text. — Originally published: in 4 vols. 1980. — Includes bibliographies
ISBN 0-7145-3805-1 : £15.00 B81-17159

782.1′3 — Opera — *Plot outlines — For children*

Spence, Keith. Tales from the opera. — London : Methuen/Walker, Sept.1981. — [112]p
ISBN 0-416-05810-8 : £5.95 : CIP entry B81-21628

782.8 — THEATRE MUSIC

782.81 — Musical shows in English, *1866-1979*

Jackson, Arthur. The book of musicals : from Show boat to Evita / by Arthur Jackson ; foreword by Clive Barnes. — Rev. ed. — London : Mitchell Beazley, 1979. — 208p : ill (some col.) ; 29cm
Previous ed.: 1977. — Bibliography: p202-203. — List of films: p198-199. — List of sound recordings: p200-202. — Includes index
ISBN 0-85522-191-7 (pbk) : £2.95 B81-41015

782.81′08996073 — American musical shows featuring coloured artists, *1900-1940*

Sampson, Henry T.. Blacks in blackface : a source book on early black musical shows / by Henry T. Sampson. — Metuchen ; London : Scarecrow, 1980. — x,552p : ill,facsims,ports ; 23cm
Includes index
ISBN 0-8108-1318-1 : £19.25 B81-04141

782.81′092′2 — Musical shows in English. Rodgers, Richard & Hammerstein, Oscar — *Biographies*

Nolan, Frederick. The sound of their music : the story of Rodgers & Hammerstein / Frederick Nolan. — London : Unwin Paperbacks, 1979. — 272p : ill,ports ; 20cm
Originally published: London : Dent, 1978. — Bibliography: p265-266. — Includes index
ISBN 0-04-782003-9 (pbk) : £2.50 : CIP rev. B79-30801

782.81′092′4 — Operettas in French. Offenbach, Jacques — *Biographies*

Faris, Alexander. Jacques Offenbach / Alexander Faris. — London : Faber, 1980. — 275p : ill,music,facsims,ports,1geneal.table ; 24cm
Bibliography: p258-262. - List of works: p236-257. - Includes index
ISBN 0-571-11147-5 : £11.50 : CIP rev. B80-18869

Gammond, Peter. Offenbach : his life and times / Peter Gammond. — Speldhurst : Midas, 1980. — 168p : ill,music,facsims,ports ; 26cm
Bibliography: p160-164. - List of works: p145-159. - Includes index
ISBN 0-85936-231-0 : £8.00 : CIP rev. B80-12460

Harding, James, *1929-*. Jacques Offenbach : a biography / by James Harding. — London : Calder, 1980. — 274p : ill,ports ; 23cm. — (The Opera library)
Bibliography: p263-264. - Includes index
ISBN 0-7145-3835-3 (cased) : £12.95 : CIP rev.
ISBN 0-7145-3841-8 (pbk£5.95) B80-24727

782.81′0973 — Musical plays in English. American writers, *to 1980 — Critical studies*

Bordman, Gerald. American operetta : from H.M.S. Pinafore to Sweeney Todd / Gerald Bordman. — New York ; Oxford : Oxford University Press, 1981. — viii,206p,[16]p of plates : ill,ports ; 22cm
Includes index
ISBN 0-19-502869-4 : Unpriced B81-37964

782.81′2 — Children′s musical plays in English. McCracken, Ethel — *Librettos*

Murdoch, Helen. Jenny and the lucky bags : a musical play for children / book and lyrics by Helen Murdoch ; music by Ethel McCracken. — London : French, c1981. — 46p ; 22cm
Four men, 5 women, supers
ISBN 0-573-05089-9 (pbk) : £2.05 B81-40367

782.81′2 — Children′s musical plays in English. Parr, Andrew — *Librettos*

Parr, Andrew. Dazzle : a new space-tacular musical / book and lyrics by John Gardiner ; music by Andrew Parr. — London (27 John Adam St., WC2N 6HX) : Musicscope, [1981]. — vi,68p : ill ; 21cm
ISBN 0-9507189-0-4 (pbk) : £1.75 B81-37424

782.81′2 — Children′s musical plays in English. Wilson, David Henry — *Librettos*

Wilson, David Henry. Monster man : a play for children / by David Henry Wilson. — Taunton (c/o D.H. Wilson, 3 Beech Close, Hope Corner La., Taunton, Somerset TA2 7NZ) : Hope Corner, 1981. — ii,86p : music ; 21cm
Unpriced (pbk) B81-16052

782.81′2 — Children′s musical plays in English. Wood, David, *1944-* **—** *Librettos*

Wood, David, *1944 Feb.21-*. Cinderella : a family musical / book, music and lyrics by David Wood. — London : French, c1981. — 78p ; 22cm
Nine men, 5 women, supers
ISBN 0-573-16427-4 (pbk) : £2.00 B81-24777

Wood, David, *1944 Feb.21-*. There was an old woman- : a family musical / book, music and lyrics by David Wood. — London : French, c1980. — 49p ; 22cm
Four men, 2 women, children
ISBN 0-573-05051-1 (pbk) : £2.00 B81-04659

782.81′2 — Musical plays in English. American writers. Porter, Cole — *Librettos*

Strachan, Alan. The Mermaid Theatre′s Cole : an entertainment based on the words and music of Cole Porter / devised by Alan Strachan, Benny Green. — New York ; London : Samuel French, [c1981]. — 85p : ill,1port ; 21cm
Five men, 5 women
ISBN 0-573-68135-x (pbk) : £2.45 B81-37644

782.81′2 — Musical plays in English. Burton, Brian J. — *Librettos*

Burton, Brian J.. The murder of Maria Marten, or, The red barn : a melodrama in three acts / by Brian J. Burton ; based on various anonymous Victorian texts ; music and lyrics by Brian J. Burton. — 2nd rev. ed. — Birmingham : Cambridge Jackson, 1980. — 65p,[4]p of plates : ill,music ; 22cm
Five men, 9 women. — Previous ed.: 1967
ISBN 0-85197-051-6 (cased) : £3.95
ISBN 0-85197-052-4 (pbk) : £2.25 B81-15697

782.81′2 — Musical plays in English. Driver, John & Haddow, Jeffrey — *Librettos*

Driver, John. Scrambled / book, music and lyrics by John Driver and Jeffrey Haddow. — New York ; London : French, c1980. — 75p : ill,plans ; 22cm. — (French′s musical library)
Three men, 1 woman
ISBN 0-573-68120-1 (pbk) : £2.10 B81-09654

782.81′2 — Musical plays in English. Gordon, Elaine — *Librettos*

Boobbyer, Juliet. Columba : a play with music / by Juliet Boobbyer, Joanna Sciortino ; music composed by Elaine Gordon with Hawys James, Duncan Morison, Michael O′Callaghan. — Leominster : Fowler Wright, 1981. — 83p : 1map,music ; 26cm
£3.50 (pbk) B81-29964

782.81′2 — Musical plays in English. Hamlisch, Marvin — *Librettos*

Hamlisch, Marvin. They′re playing our song / book by Neil Simon ; music by Marvin Hamlisch ; lyrics by Carole Bayer Sayer. — New York ; London : French, c1980. — 81p ; 21cm
Five men, 4 women
ISBN 0-573-68105-8 (pbk) : £2.10 B81-07765

782.81′2 — Musical plays in English. Hitt, James Alfred — *Librettos*

Hitt, James Alfred. Sherlock Holmes and the curious adventure of the clockwork prince : a Victorian romp / by Clive Haubold ; music by James Alfred Hitt. — New York ; London : French, c1980. — 24p : 1plan ; 19cm
Six men, 4 women, supers
ISBN 0-573-61624-8 (pbk) : £2.10 B81-07764

782.81′2 — Musical plays in English. Jones, Roger, *19---.* **Songs. Words —** *Texts*

Jones, Roger, *19---*. Saints alive! : a musical / by Roger Jones. — Words ed. — Redhill : National Christian Education Council, c1981. — [12]p ; 21cm
ISBN 0-7197-0297-6 (pbk) : £0.25 B81-29168

782.81′2 — Musical plays in English. Kennedy, Jimmy — *Librettos*

Parker, Stewart. Spokesong / by Stewart Parker ; music by Jimmy Kennedy ; lyrics by Stewart Parker. — London : French, c1980. — 96p : music,1plan ; 19cm
Four men, 2 women
ISBN 0-573-61623-x (pbk) : £1.90 B81-09601

782.81′2 — Musical plays in English. McCracken, Ethel — *Librettos*

Murdoch, Helen. A dragon for dinner : a musical play / book and lyrics by Helen Murdoch ; music by Ethel McCracken. — London : French, c1981. — 21p ; 19cm
ISBN 0-573-15203-9 (pbk) : £0.65 B81-33016

782.81′2 — Musical plays in English. McNeff, Stephen — *Librettos*

Causley, Charles. The ballad of Aucassin and Nicolette : a play in three acts / by Charles Causley ; with music by Stephen McNeff ; and illustrations by Yvonne Gilbert. — Harmondsworth : Kestrel Books, 1981. — 118p : ill,music ; 24cm
Based on an early 13th century anonymous French text
ISBN 0-7226-5698-x : £5.50 B81-16468

782.81′2 — Musical plays in English. Menken, Alan — *Librettos*

Ashman, Howard. Kurt Vonnegut′s God bless you, Mr Rosewater / book and lyrics by Howard Ashman ; music by Alan Menken ; additional lyrics by Dennis Green. — New York ; London : French, c1980. — 91p : 1plan ; 22cm. — (French′s musical library)
Ten men, 4 women, supers
ISBN 0-573-68125-2 (pbk) : £2.10 B81-07542

782.81′2 — Musical plays in English. Nield, David — *Librettos*

Nield, David. Tin Pan Ali : musical in two acts / books and lyrics by Jeremy James Taylor ; music by David Nield. — London (10 Rathbone St., W1P 2BJ) : Weinberger, c1981. — 93p ; 21cm
Six men, 7 women, supers
Unpriced (pbk) B81-10681

782.81′2 — Musical plays in English. Rozovsky, Mark & Vetkin, S. — *Librettos*

Rozovsky, Mark. Strider : a play with music / by Mark Rozovsky ; adapted from a story by Leo Tolstoy ; English stage version by Robert Kalfin & Steve Brown ; based on a translation by Tamara Bering Sunguroff ; music originally composed by Mark Rozovsky, S. Vetkin ; original Russian lyrics by Uri Riashentsev ; adaptor, composer of new additional music Norman L. Berman ; new English lyrics by Steve Brown. — New York ; London : French, c1981. — 53p ; 22cm. — (French′s musical library)
Twelve men, 7 women. — Translation from the Russian
ISBN 0-573-68130-9 (pbk) : £2.10 B81-22234

782.81′2 — Musical plays in English. Sell, Colin — *Librettos*

Sell, Colin. Dial ten amazing little boy friends : a musical play / Colin Sell. — London : French, c1980. — 26p ; 19cm
Five men, 5 women
ISBN 0-573-12053-6 (pbk) : £0.60 B81-07743

782.81′2 — Musical plays in English. Wilson, Sandy — *Librettos*

Wilson, Sandy. Divorce me, darling! : a musical play / Sandy Wilson. — London : French, c1981. — 59p : 4plans ; 22cm
Seventeen men, 14 women, supers
ISBN 0-573-08049-6 (pbk) : £2.25 B81-32060

782.81′2 — Operettas in English. Songs. Words — *Texts*

Sage, Angie. The nightmare song / Angie Sage ; from Iolanthe by Gilbert and Sullivan. — London : Angus & Robertson, 1981. — [26]p : col.ill ; 27cm
ISBN 0-207-95884-x : £3.95 B81-12997

782.81′2 — Operettas in French. Offenbach, Jacques — *Librettos* — *English texts*

Offenbach, Jacques. The drum-major′s daughter : comic opera in three acts / by Alfred Duru and Henri Chivot ; music by Jacques Offenbach ; in a new English translation by Geoffrey Wilson ; music adapted and arranged by Max Morris. — Paris : Editions Choudens ; London (1 Montague St., W.C.1) : United Music, c1976. — 102p : 3plans ; 21cm
Twelve men, 9 women, supers. — Translation of: La fille du tambour-major
Unpriced (pbk) B81-11194

782.8′3 — Miracle plays in English, *ca 950-ca 1600.* **Music**

Smoldon, William L.. The music of the medieval church dramas / William L. Smoldon ; edited by Cynthia Bourgeault. — London : Oxford University Press, 1980. — xiv,450p,9p of plates (some folded) : music,facsims ; 25cm
Bibliography: p436-442. — Includes index
ISBN 0-19-316321-7 : £40.00 : CIP rev.
B80-13491

782.95 — BALLET MUSIC

782.9′5′0924 — English ballet music. Sullivan, *Sir* **Arthur. Victoria and Merrie England** - *Critical studies*

Tillett, Selwyn. Victoria and merrie England : a grand national ballet in eight tableaux, the scenario arranged and the ballet invented by Carlo Coppi, music by Arthur Sullivan / a note by Selwyn Tillett. — Saffron Walden (55 Radwinter Rd., Saffron Walden, Essex CB11 3HU) : Sir Arthur Sullivan Society, [1981]. — 26p : 1ill,music,facsims ; 21cm
Facsim. of playbill from the Alhambra Theatre (4p) as insert. — Bibliography: p36
ISBN 0-9507348-0-2 (pbk) : Unpriced
B81-18263

783 — RELIGIOUS MUSIC

783′.092′4 — German religious music. Bach, Johann Sebastian — *Critical studies*

Mellers, Wilfrid. Bach and the Dance of God / Wilfrid Mellers. — London : Faber, 1980. — vii,324p : music ; 24cm
Bibliography: p319-320. — Includes index
ISBN 0-571-11562-4 : £15.00 : CIP rev.
B80-25997

783′.092′4 — German vocal music. Bach, Johann Sebastian. Performance — *Manuals*

Steinitz, Paul. Performing Bach′s vocal music / by Paul Steinitz. — Croydon (Addington Palace, Croydon CR9 5AD) : Addington, 1980. — viii,71p : music ; 22cm
ISBN 0-906851-04-1 (pbk) : £2.95 B81-06978

783.2′1′0924 — Masses in Latin. Byrd, William, *1542 or 3-1623* — *Critical studies*

Kerman, Joseph. The masses and motets of William Byrd / Joseph Kerman. — London : Faber, 1981. — 360p : music ; 24cm. — (The Music of William Byrd ; v.1)
Includes index
ISBN 0-571-11643-4 : £25.00 : CIP rev.
Also classified at 783.4′092′4 B81-24595

783.4 — Church of England. Anthems — *Lists* — *For church year*

Patrick, David. Anthems for SATB : based on the Sunday themes in the Alternative Service book (1980) : a list of recommended music / compiled by David Patrick for the Royal School of Church Music. — [Croydon] : [Royal School of Church Music], [1981]. — 26p ; 30cm
Cover title
£0.60 (pbk) B81-36692

783.4′092′4 — Latin motets. Byrd, William, *1542 or 3-1623* — *Critical studies*

Kerman, Joseph. The masses and motets of William Byrd / Joseph Kerman. — London : Faber, 1981. — 360p : music ; 24cm. — (The Music of William Byrd ; v.1)
Includes index
ISBN 0-571-11643-4 : £25.00 : CIP rev.
Primary classification 783.2′1′0924 B81-24595

783.6′2 — Carols in English. Pagan versions — *Anthologies*

Iles, Norman. The pagan carols restored / by Norman Iles. — [Morecambe] ([381 Marine Rd., Morecambe, Lancashire]) : [N. Iles], c1981
′First published, texts only, 1971′
Vol.1. — 157p ; 21cm
Unpriced (pbk) B81-36136

783.6′2 — Christmas carols in English. Words — *Texts* — *For children*

Wildsmith, Brian. The twelve days of Christmas / illustrated by Brian Wildsmith. — Oxford : Oxford University Press, 1972 (1980 [printing]). — [32]p : chiefly ill(some col.) ; 28cm
ISBN 0-19-272115-1 (pbk) : £1.50 B81-03627

783.6′52 — Christmas carols in English. Words — *Anthologies* — *For children*

Christmas carols. — London : Dean, c1980. — [12]p : col.ill ; 21cm. — (A Dean board book)
Cover title
ISBN 0-603-00235-8 : £0.55 B81-10832

783.6′552 — Christmas carols in English, *1400-1979* — *Collections*

A **Book** of carols : 46 Christmas carols from 1400 to the present day / edited and introduced by Reginald Nettel. — London : Kahn & Averill, 1980. — 120p : ill,music ; 22cm
Ill on lining papers. — Bibliography: p117. - Includes index
ISBN 0-900707-62-3 (pbk) : £2.95 : CIP rev.
B80-22360

783.6′552 — Christmas carols in English — *Collections*

Nine Christmas carols / illuminated by Caroline Garrett Webbe. — [S.l.] : [C.G. Webbe], [1981?]. — [25]p : ill ; 39cm
Limited ed. of 50 copies
Unpriced B81-15513

The **Wexford** carols. — Portlaoise : Dolmen Press, Nov.1981. — [96]p : music
ISBN 0-85105-376-9 (pbk) : £6.00 : CIP entry
B81-33649

783.7 — Gospel songs. Concerts. Organisation - *Manuals*

Thorn, Eric A.. Concert presentations. — Maidstone (PO Box 3, Maidstone, Kent, ME14 1AP) : Third Day Enterprises, July 1981. — [16]p
ISBN 0-9505912-4-6 (pbk) : £0.50 : CIP entry
B81-13467

784 — VOCAL MUSIC

784 — Counter tenors, *to 1980*

Giles, Peter. The counter tenor. — London : Muller, Sept.1981. — [250]p
ISBN 0-584-10474-x : £9.95 : CIP entry
B81-26688

784 — Singing — *For children*

Blackwood, Alan, *1932-*. The performing world of the singer. — London : H. Hamilton, May 1981. — [128]p
ISBN 0-241-10588-9 : £4.95 : CIP entry
B81-12819

784 — Songs in English, *to 1980.* **Origins**

Harrowven, Jean. The origins of rhymes, songs and sayings / Jean Harrowven. — London : Kaye & Ward, 1977 (1980 [printing]). — xi,356p : ill,1port ; 23cm
Bibliography: p333-334. — Includes index
ISBN 0-7182-1267-3 : £6.75
Primary classification 398′.8 B81-04959

784 — Songs in Spanish, *1600-1700.* **Words** — *Anthologies*

Tonos a lo divino ya lo humano / introducción, edición y notas de Rita Goldberg. — London : Tamesis, c1981. — 202p,6pofplates : facsims ; 25cm
Bibliography: p201-202. — Includes index
ISBN 0-7293-0075-7 : Unpriced B81-31762

784′.06′042646 — Suffolk. Aldeburgh. Choirs: Aldeburgh Festival Choir, *to 1980*

Wren, Wilfrid J.. Voices by the sea : the story of the Aldeburgh Festival Choir / by Wilfrid J. Wren ; foreword by Sir Peter Pears. — Lavenham : Dalton, 1981. — x,129p : ill,1map,music,facisms,ports ; 24cm
Map on lining papers. — Includes index
ISBN 0-86138-003-7 : £7.95 B81-27637

784′.09182′1 — Songs in English: Caribbean songs — *Collections*

Mango spice : 44 Caribbean songs / chosen by Yvonne Conolly, Gloria Cameron and Sonia Singham ; with music arranged by Chris Cameron and Vallin Miller ; and with drawings by Maggie Ling. — London : A & C Black, 1981. — [96]p : ill,music ; 21x31cm
Bibliography: [94]p. - Includes index
ISBN 0-7136-2107-9 (spiral) : £4.95
B81-12616

784′.09182′1 — Songs in English: Caribbean songs. Words — *Anthologies*

Mango spice : 44 Caribbean songs : word edition / chosen by Yvonne Conolly, Gloria Cameron and Sonia Singham ; with drawings by Maggie Ling. — London : A & C Black, c1981. — [47]p : ill ; 21cm
Includes index
ISBN 0-7136-2109-5 (pbk) : £1.25(non-net)
B81-12617

784′.092′2 — English choral music. Britten, Benjamin. Collaboration with Auden, W. H., *1936*

Mitchell, Donald. Britten and Auden in the thirties : the year 1936 : the T.S. Eliot Memorial Lectures delivered at the University of Kent at Canterbury in November 1979 / by Donald Mitchell. — London : Faber, 1981. — 176p,[8]p of plates : ill,music,facsims,ports ; 23cm. — (The T.S. Eliot memorial lectures ; 1979)
Includes index
ISBN 0-571-11715-5 : £7.50 B81-11504

784′.092′2 — Singing. King′s Singers, *to 1979*

King′s Singers. The King′s Singers : a self portrait / [written by] Nigel Perrin ... [et al.] ; foreword by Steve Race. — London : Robson, 1980. — 160p : ill,facsims,music,ports ; 26cm
List of sound recordings: p159-160
ISBN 0-86051-109-x : £6.95 : CIP rev.
B80-17885

784′.092′4 — Popular music. Singing. Fields, Gracie — *Biographies*
Fields, Gracie. Sing as we go. — Large print ed. — Bath : Chivers, Oct.1981. — [296]p. — (A New Portway large print book)
Originally published: London : Muller, 1960
ISBN 0-85119-136-3 : £5.40 : CIP entry
B81-25798

784′.092′4 — Popular music. Singing. Hanson, John, *1922-* — *Biographies*
Hanson, John, *1922-*. Me and my red shadow : the autobiography of John Hanson. — London : W.H. Allen, 1980. — 218p,[12]p of plates : ill,ports ; 24cm
Includes index
ISBN 0-491-02359-6 : £6.95 B81-01548

784′.092′4 — Popular music. Singing. O'Hara, Mary — *Biographies*
O'Hara, Mary. The scent of the roses. — Large print ed. — Long Preston : Magna, Sept.1981. — [480]p
ISBN 0-86009-359-x : £4.95 : CIP entry
B81-22501

784′.0924 — Reggae music. Marley, Bob — *Biographies*
Goldman, Vivian. Bob Marley. — London : Hutchinson, July 1981. — [96]p
ISBN 0-09-146481-1 (pbk) : £2.95 : CIP entry
B81-22592

784′.092′4 — Singing. Deller, Alfred — *Biographies*
Hardwick, Michael. Alfred Deller : a singularity of voice / Michael & Mollie Hardwick. — London : Proteus, 1980. — 196p,[8]p of plates : ill,ports ; 24cm
Ill on lining papers. — List of sound recordings; p193-197
ISBN 0-906071-63-1 : £6.95 B81-29786

784′.092′4 — Singing. Trapp, Maria Augusta — *Biographies*
Trapp, Maria Augusta. [The Story of the Trapp family singers]. The sound of music : is based on the story of the Trapp Family singers / by Maria Augusta Trapp. — London : Fontana, 1965, c1953 (1980 [printing]). — 253p ; 18cm
Originally published: Philadelphia : Lippincott, 1949 ; London : Bles, 1953
ISBN 0-00-626468-9 (pbk) : £1.50 B81-39094

784′.092′4 — Songs in English. Campion, Thomas. Now winter nights enlarge — *Critical studies*
Ratcliffe, Stephen. Campion : on song / Stephen Ratcliffe. — Boston, Mass. ; London : Routledge & Kegan Paul, 1981. — xvi,200p : music ; 23cm
ISBN 0-7100-0803-1 : £9.50 : CIP rev.
B81-13723

784′.0942 — Songs in English. Words — *Critical studies*
Booth, Mark W.. The experience of songs. — London : Yale University Press, Sept.1981. — [240]p
ISBN 0-300-02622-6 : £12.25 : CIP entry
B81-30241

784′.0954 — Northern Indian vocal music, *1900-1975*
Meer, Wim van der. Hindustani music in the 20th century / by Wim van der Meer. — The Hague ; London : Nijhoff, 1980. — xii,252p,[8]p of plates : ill,music,ports ; 23cm
Bibliography: p200-205. — List of sound recordings: p205 — 206. — Includes index
ISBN 90-247-2066-4 : Unpriced B81-05380

784.1′005 — Choral music — *Serials*
Chorale. — Vol.1, no.1 (1980)-. — Cookham (12 Bass Mead, Cookham, Berkshire SL6 9DJ) : Chorale Publications, 1980-. — v. : ill ; 30cm
Six issues yearly. — Description based on: Vol.1, no.2 (Oct./Nov.1980)
ISSN 0261-362x = Chorale : £4.90 per year
B81-26588

784.1′006′042937 — Clwyd. Ruthin. Male-voice choirs: Meibion Menlli, *to 1981* — *Welsh texts*
Gwŷr wrth gerdd. — Rhuthun [i.e. Ruthin] (Stryd yr Orsaf, Rhuthun, Clwyd) : Cyngor Gwasanaethau Gwirfoddol Clwyd, c1981. — 167p : ill,ports ; 15x21cm
ISBN 0-906410-02-9 (pbk) : Unpriced
B81-23101

784.3′0092′4 — Lieder & song cycles in German. Schumann, Robert — *Critical studies*
Moore, Gerald, *1899-*. Poet's love : the songs and cycles of Schumann / Gerald Moore. — London : Hamilton, 1981. — xii,247p : music ; 24cm
Includes index
ISBN 0-241-10512-9 (cased) : £15.00
ISBN 0-241-10518-8 (pbk) : £8.95 B81-25906

784.3′0092′4 — Lieder. Brahms, Johannes — *Critical studies*
Bell, A. Craig. The lieder of Brahms / by A. Craig Bell. — Darley ([Darley, Harrogate, N. Yorks.]) : Grian-Aig Press, 1979. — 137p,xxp : music,1port ; 21cm
Includes index
£5.70 (pbk) B81-03259

784.3′0092′4 — Lieder. Singing. Fischer-Dieskau, Dietrich
Whitton, Kenneth S.. Dietrich Fischer-Dieskau. — London : Wolff, Oct.1981. — [320]p
ISBN 0-85496-405-3 : £15.00 : CIP entry
B81-25737

784.3′06 — Ballads in English — *Collections*
Everyman's book of British ballads / edited by Roy Palmer. — London : Dent, 1980. — 256p : ill,music ; 25cm
Includes index
ISBN 0-460-04452-4 : £8.95 : CIP rev.
B80-17886

784.3′061 — Mélodies, *1865-1924* — *Critical studies*
Meister, Barbara. Nineteenth-century French song : Fauré, Chausson, Duparc and Debussy / Barbara Meister. — Bloomington ; London : Indiana University Press, c1980. — xiii,402p ; 24cm
Bibliography: p399. — Includes index
ISBN 0-253-34075-6 : £15.00 B81-02281

784.4′924 — Folk songs in English: American folk songs. Guthrie, Woody — *Biographies*
Klein, Joe. Woody Guthrie : a life / Joe Klein. — London : Faber, 1981. — xv,475p,[32]p of plates : ill,facsims,ports ; 25cm
Includes index
ISBN 0-571-11736-8 : £8.95 B81-11134

784.4′9415′0924 — Irish folk songs. French, Percy — *Biographies*
O'Dowda, Brendan. The world of Percy French. — Belfast : Blackstaff Press, Oct.1981. — [192]p
ISBN 0-85640-255-9 (pbk) : £5.95 : CIP entry
B81-31205

784.4′942 — Folk songs in English — *Collections*
St Clair, Isla. The song and the story / Isla St Clair and David Turnbull. — London : By arrangement with the British Broadcasting Corporation [by] Pelham, 1981. — 90p : ill (some col.),music,ports(some col.) ; 24cm
ISBN 0-7207-1324-2 : £5.95 : CIP rev.
Primary classification 941.07′3′0880623
B81-15859

784.4′9467 — Folk songs in Catalan. Words — *Anthologies* — *English texts*
Catalan songs / chosed and translated by Mercedes Waters and Elvira Heredia ; edited by Ivor Waters. — Chepstow (Ivor Waters, 41 Hardwick Ave., Chepstow, Gwent NP6 5DS) : Moss Rose Press, 1981. — 43p ; 22cm
Parallel Catalan text and English translation. — Limited ed. of 120 copies
ISBN 0-906134-11-0 (pbk) : £1.50 B81-23479

784.4′97671 — Folk songs in English: American folk songs: Ozark folk songs — *Collections*
Ozark folksongs / collected and edited by Vance Randolph. — Revised ed. / introduction by W.K. McNeil. — Columbia [Mo.] ; London : University of Missouri Press
Previous ed. Columbia, Mo. : State Historical Society of Missouri, 1946-50
Vol.1: British ballads and songs. — 1980. — 450p,[5]p of plates : music,ports ; 24cm(pbk)
Bibliography: p441-450
ISBN 0-8262-0297-7 : £6.00 B81-13958

Ozark folksongs / collected and edited by Vance Randolph. — Revised ed. / introduction by W.K. McNeil. — Columbia [Mo.] ; London : University of Missouri Press
Previous ed. Columbia, Mo. : State Historical Society of Missouri, 1946-50
Vol.2: Songs of the South and West. — 1980. — 436p,[6]pof plates : music,ports ; 24cm(pbk)
ISBN 0-8262-0298-5 : £6.00 B81-1395

Ozark folksongs / collected and edited by Vance Randolph. — Revised ed. / introduction by W.K. McNeil. — Columbia [Mo.] ; London : University of Missouri Press
Previous ed. Columbia, Mo. : State Historical Society of Missouri, 1946-50. — Includes index
Vol.4: Religious songs and other items. — 1980. — 455p : music ; 24cm
ISBN 0-8262-0300-0 (pbk) : £6.00 B81-1395

784.5′0028 — Popular songs. Composition — *Manuals*
Attwood, Tony. British songwriter's guide / prepared for R.S. Productions by Tony Attwood. — [Totnes] ([Hamilton House, Nelson Close, Staverton, Totnes, Devon TQ9 6PG]) : [R.S. Productions], [1981]. — [10] leaves ; 30cm
Bibliography: leaf
ISBN 0-906888-06-9 (unbound) : Unpriced
B81-1820

784.5′0028 — Popular songs. Composition — *Serials*
BASCA news : incorporating Songwriters' Guild news. — No.115 (Winter 1979/80)-. — Londo : 148 Charing Cross Rd, WC2H 0LB : British Academy of Songwriters, Composers & Authors, 1979-. — v. : ill ; 23cm
Quarterly. — Official journal of: British Academy of Songwriters, Composers & Authors. — Continues: Songwriters' Guild news. — Description based on: No.117 (Summer 1980)
ISSN 0144-9621 = BASCA news : Free to Academy members only B81-0414

784.5′0075 — Pop music. Items associated with pop music. Collecting — *Serials*
[Record collector *(London : 1980)***]**. Record collector. — No.7 (Mar.1980)-. — London (45 St Mary's Rd, Ealing, W5 5RQ) : Diamond Publishing Group, 1980-. — v. : ill,ports ; 21cm
Monthly. — Continues in part: Beatles book & record collector
ISSN 0261-250x = Record collector (London. 1980) : £0.60 per issue B81-2192

784.5′0092′2 — Pop music. Beatles — *Serials*
[The Beatles book *(1976)***]**. The Beatles book : appreciation society magazine. — No.1 (May 1976)-No.40 (Aug.1979). — London (45 St. Mary's Rd, Ealing, W5 5RQ) : Beat Publications, 1976-1979. — 40v. : ill,ports ; 21cm
Monthly. — Continued by: Record collector (London : 1979)
£0.50 per issue B81-1683

[The Beatles book *(1980)***]**. The Beatles book : appreciation society magazine. — No.47 (Mar.1980)-. — London (45 St. Mary's Rd, Ealing, W5 5RQ) : Beat Publications, 1980-. — v. : ill,ports ; 21cm
Monthly. — Continues in part: Beatles book & record collector
ISSN 0261-1600 = Beatles book (1980) : £8.00 per issue B81-1683

Beatles book & record collector. — No.4 (Dec.1979)-No.6 (Feb.1980). — London (45 St Mary's Rd, Ealing, W5 5RQ) : Beat Publications, 1979-1980. — 3v. : ill,ports ; 21cm
Monthly. — Continues: Record collector (London : 1979). — Continued in part by: The Beatles book (1980)
£0.60 per issue B81-1682

[Record collector *(London : 1979)***]**. Record collector. — No.1 (Sept.1979)-No.3 (Nov.1979) — London (45 St. Mary's Rd, Ealing, W5 5RQ) : Beat Publications, 1979-1979. — 3v. : ill,ports ; 21cm
Weekly. — Continues: The Beatles book (1976). — Continued by: Beatles book & record collector
£0.60 per issue B81-1683

784.5′0092′2 — Pop music. Beatles, *to 1970*

Norman, Philip. Shout! : the true story of the Beatles / Philip Norman. — London : Elm Tree, 1981. — xvi,400p,[32]p of plates : ill,ports ; 24cm
ISBN 0-241-10300-2 (cased) : £8.95
ISBN 0-241-10631-1 (pbk) : £5.95 B81-17018

Stokes, Geoffrey. The Beatles / text by Geoffrey Stokes ; introduction by Leonard Bernstein ; art direction by Bea Feitler. — London : W.H. Allen ; London : Omnibus, 1981, c1980. — 245p,[12]p of plates : ill(some col.),facsims,ports(some col.) ; 31cm. — (A Star book)
Originally published: New York : Times Books, c1980. — Ports on inside covers
ISBN 0-352-30886-9 (pbk) : £5.95
ISBN 0-86001-818-0 (Omnibus) B81-40280

784.5′0092′2 — Pop music. Beatles, *to 1979 — Encyclopaedias*

Friede, Goldie. The Beatles A to Z / by Goldie Friede, Robin Titone, and Sue Weiner. — London : Eyre Methuen, 1981, c1980. — 248p : ill,facsims,ports ; 28cm
Originally published: New York : Methuen, 1980
ISBN 0-413-48380-0 (pbk) : £3.95 B81-32339

784.5′0092′2 — Pop music. Lennon, John & Ono, Yoko — *Interviews*

Lennon, John. The Lennon tapes : John Lennon and Yoko Ono in conversation with Andy Peebles 6 December 1980. — London : British Broadcasting Corporation, 1981. — 95p ; 23cm
ISBN 0-563-17944-9 (pbk) : £1.95 B81-09359

784.5′0092′4 — English pop music. Ant, Adam — *Biographies*

Welch, Chris. Adam & the Ants / Chris Welch. — London : W. H. Allen, 1981. — 128p,[8]p of plates : ill + ports ; 18cm. — (A Star book)
List of sound recordings: p118-128
ISBN 0-352-30963-6 (pbk) B81-39722

784.5′0092′4 — English pop music. John, Elton — *Interviews*

John, Elton. The Elton John tapes : Elton John in conversation with Andy Peebles '21 at 33'. — London : BBC, 1981. — 55p,[16]p of plates : ports ; 23cm
ISBN 0-563-17981-3 (pbk) : £2.00 B81-33450

784.5′0092′4 — Pop music. Lennon, John — *Biographies*

Connolly, Ray. John Lennon 1940-1980 / Ray Connolly. — [London] : Fontana, 1981. — 191,[24]p : ill,ports ; 20cm
List of sound discs: p177-185. — Includes index
ISBN 0-00-636405-5 : £2.50 B81-15138

Doncaster, Patrick. Tribute to John Lennon : his life, his loves, his work and his death / written by Patrick Doncaster. — London : Mirror Books, c1981. — 32p : ill,facsims,ports ; 36cm
Daily mirror special issue
ISBN 0-85939-266-x (unbound) : £0.40 B81-10820

Tyler, Tony. John Lennon : working class hero : the life and death of a legend 1940-1980 / [by Tony Tyler]. — [London] : [IPC Magazines], [1980]. — 37p : ports(some col.) ; 30cm
£0.50 (unbound) B81-12537

784.5′0092′4 — Pop music. Singing. Presley, Elvis, *1970-1977 — Biographies*

Hopkins, Jerry. Elvis : the final years / Jerry Hopkins. — [London] : Star, 1981, c1980. — ix,258p,[12]p of plates : ill,ports ; 18cm
Originally published: London : W.H. Allen, 1980
ISBN 0-352-30859-1 (pbk) : £1.50 B81-17818

784.5′0092′4 — Pop music. Singing. Presley, Elvis — *Biographies*

Wallraf, Rainer. Elvis Presley : an illustrated biography / by Rainer Wallraf and Heinz Plehn ; translation, Judith Waldman. — London : Omnibus Press, c1978. — 117p : ill (some col.),facsims(some col.) ports(some col.) ; 30cm
Translation from the German
ISBN 0-86001-613-7 (pbk) : £3.95 B81-23282

784.5′0092′4 — Pop music. Singing. Richard, Cliff - *Biographies*

Richard, Cliff. Which one's Cliff?. — Sevenoaks : Hodder & Stoughton, Aug.1981. — [256]p. — (Coronet books)
Originally published: London : Hodder & Stoughton, 1977
ISBN 0-340-27159-0 (pbk) : £1.25 : CIP entry B81-15906

784.5′0092′4 — Pop music. Singing. Ross, Diana, *1944- — Biographies*

Brown, Geoff, *1946 Nov.8-*. Diana Ross / Geoff Brown. — London : Sigdwick & Jackson, 1981. — 144p : ill(some col.),ports(some col.) ; 29cm
List of sound discs. — Includes index
ISBN 0-283-98772-3 (cased) : £9.95
ISBN 0-283-98773-1 (pbk) : £6.95 B81-40318

784.5′0092′4 — Pop songs in English. American writers. Dylan, Bob. Words — *Critical studies*

Gray, Michael, *1946-*. The art of Bob Dylan : song & dance man / Michael Gray. — New ed. — London : Hamlyn, 1981. — 236p : 1facsim,ports(some col.) ; 25cm
Previous ed. published as: Song & dance man. London : Hart-Davis, MacGibbon, 1972. — Includes index
ISBN 0-600-34170-4 (cased) : £7.50
ISBN 0-600-34224-7 (pbk) : £4.95 B81-30681

784.5′0092′4 — Popular music. Singing. Doonican, Val — *Biographies*

Doonican, Val. The special years : an autobiography / Val Doonican. — London : Sphere, 1981, c1980. — 181p,[8]p of plates : ill,ports ; 18cm
Originally published: London : Elm Tree, 1980
ISBN 0-7221-3003-1 (pbk) : £1.25 B81-39874

Doonican, Val. The special years : an autobiography / Val Doonican. — Large print ed. — Bath : Chivers, 1981, c1980. — 290p : ill ; 23cm. — (New Portway)
Originally published: London : Elm Tree, 1980
ISBN 0-85119-124-x : Unpriced : CIP rev. B81-13706

784.5′0092′4 — Popular music. Singing. Fields, Gracie — *Biographies*

Burgess, Muriel. Gracie Fields / Muriel Burgess with Tommy Keen. — London : W.H. Allen, 1980 (1981 [printing]). — 125p : ill,facsims,ports ; 20cm. — (A Star book)
ISBN 0-352-30925-3 (pbk) : £1.50 B81-21854

Moules, Joan. Gracie / Joan Moules. — [Emsworth] (2 Lindens Close, Emsworth, Hants) : J. Moules, [1980]. — 55,[10]p : ill,1facsim,ports ; 21cm
Cover title. — Ports on inside covers. — List of sound discs: [10]p
£2.25 (pbk) B81-28335

784.5′0092′4 — Popular music. Singing. Hanson, John, *1922- — Biographies*

Hanson, John, *1922-*. Me and my Red Shadow / John Hanson. — London : W.H. Allen, 1980 (1981 [printing]). — 218p,[8]p of plates : ill,ports ; 18cm. — (A Star book)
Includes index
ISBN 0-352-30879-6 (pbk) : £1.50 B81-21751

784.5′0092′4 — Popular music. Singing. Midler, Bette — *Biographies*

Baker, Robb. Bette Midler / Robb Baker. — Rev. ed. — London : Angus and Robertson, 1980, c1979. — 160p : ill(some col.),ports ; 26cm
Previous ed.: New York : Fawcett, 1979 ; Sevenoaks : Coronet, 1980
ISBN 0-207-95906-4 : £5.95 B81-24322

784.5′0092′4 — Popular music. Singing. O'Hara, Mary, *19--- — Biographies*

O'Hara, Mary, *1935-*. The scent of the roses / Mary O'Hara. — [London] : Fontana, 1981, c1980. — 318p,[8]p of plates : ill,ports ; 18cm
Originally published: London : Joseph, 1980. — Includes index
ISBN 0-00-636326-1 (pbk) : £1.75 B81-40134

784.5′0092′4 — Popular music. Singing. Streisand, Barbra — *Biographies*

Zec, Donald. Barbra : a biography of Barbra Streisand / Donald Zec and Anthony Fowles. — London : New English Library, 1981. — 253p : ill,ports ; 25cm
Ill on lining papers. — List of films: p249. — Includes index
ISBN 0-450-04857-8 : £7.95 B81-34945

784.5′0092′4 — Popular music. Singing. World tours, *1978 — Personal observations*

Midler, Bette. A view from a broad / Bette Midler / photography by Sean Russell. — London : Angus and Robertson, 1980. — 150p : ill(some col.),col.ports ; 26cm
Originally published: New York : Simon and Schuster, 1980
ISBN 0-207-95926-9 : £8.95 B81-05996

784.5′0092′4 — Popular songs in English. American writers. Kern, Jerome. Visits to London, *1905-1910*

Lamb, Andrew. Jerome Kern in Edwardian London / by Andrew Lamb. — Littlehampton (9 Kithurst Close, East Preston, Littlehampton, W. Sussex BN16 2TQ) : [A. Lamb], 1981. — 32leaves ; 30cm
Bibliography: leaf 32
Unpriced (pbk) B81-37830

784.505 — Popular songs in English, *1965-1980*. **Words** — *Anthologies*

Rock voices : the best lyrics of an era / edited by Matt Damsker ; foreword by Paul Gambaccini. — London : Barker, 1981, c1980. — xviii,139p ; 22 cm
Originally published: New York : St. Martin's, 1980
ISBN 0-213-16809-x (pbk) : £3.95 B81-33214

784.5′092′4 — Pop music. Singing. Ronstadt, Linda — *Biographies*

Claire, Vivian. Linda Ronstadt / Vivian Claire. — New York ; London : Flash, c1978. — 72p : ill,ports ; 26cm
List of sound discs: p71-72
ISBN 0-8256-3918-2 (pbk) : £2.95 B81-03342

784.5′092′4 — Popular music. Singing. Piaf, Edith — *Biographies*

Lange, Monique. Piaf. — London : Plexus, Oct.1981. — [240]p
Translation of: Histoire de Piaf
ISBN 0-85965-046-4 (pbk) : £5.95 : CIP entry B81-27468

784.5′2′00924 — American country music. Wynette, Tammy — *Biographies*

Wynette, Tammy. Stand by your man / Tammy Wynette. — London : Arrow, 1981, c1979. — 349p,[16]p of plates : ill,ports ; 18cm
Originally published: New York : Simon and Schuster, 1979 ; London : Hutchinson, 1980. — Includes index
ISBN 0-09-924870-0 (pbk) : £1.75 B81-11440

784.5′2′00973 — American country music — *Encyclopaedias*

Kash, Murray. Murray Kash's book of country / Murray Kash. — [London] : Star, 1981. — 509p ; 18cm
ISBN 0-352-30443-x (pbk) : £2.95 B81-17821

784.5′3′00924 — United States. Blues. King, B. B. — *Biographies*

Sawyer, Charles. [The Arrival of B.B. King]. B.B. King : the authorized biography / Charles Sawyer. — Poole : Blandford, 1981, c1980. — xiv,274p[80]p of plates : ill ; 23cm : ports
Originally published: Garden City : Doubleday, 1980. — List of sound recordings: p235-264. — Includes index
ISBN 0-7137-1231-7 : £5.95 : CIP rev. B81-23829

784.5′4 — Rock music — *Quotations*

The **Book** of rock quotes / compiled by Jonathon Green. — Rev. ed. — London : Omnibus Press, 1978. — 126p : ports ; 26cm
Previous ed.: 1977
ISBN 0-86001-413-4 (pbk) : £2.95 B81-07297

784.5′4′009 — Rock music, *to 1979*

The **Rolling** Stone illustrated history of rock and roll / edited by Jim Miller. — Rev. and updated. — London : Pan, 1981, c1980. — 474p : ill ; 28cm. — (Picador)
Previous ed.: New York : Rolling Stone, 1976. — Includes index
ISBN 0-330-26568-7 (pbk) : £4.95 B81-26371

784.5′4′00922 — Pop music. Blondie — *Biographies*

Schruers, Fred. Blondie / Fred Schruers. — London : Star, 1980. — 134p : ill,ports ; 18cm
Originally published: New York : Tempo, 1980
ISBN 0-352-30778-1 (pbk) : £1.25 B81-01590

784.5′4′00922 — Rock music — *Biographies*

York, William. Who's who in rock : an A-Z of groups, performers, producers, session men, engineers / compiled and edited by William York. — London : Omnibus Press, 1979. — 237p ; 26cm
Originally published: Seattle : Atomic Press, 1978
ISBN 0-86001-608-0 (pbk) : £3.50 B81-34259

784.5′4′00922 — Rock music. Led Zeppelin, *to 1980*

Mylett, Howard. Led Zeppelin / Howard Mylett. — London : Granada, 1976, c1981 (1981 [printing]). — 205p,[16]p of plates : ill,ports ; 18cm. — (A Panther book) (Panther rock series)
ISBN 0-586-04390-x (pbk) : £1.50 B81-34268

784.5′4′00922 — Rock music. Stars — *Illustrations*

Visions of rock / compiled by Mal Burns. — London : Proteus, 1981. — 63p : ill(some col.) ; 28cm
ISBN 0-906071-42-9 (pbk) : £4.95 B81-22103

784.5′4′00942496 — West Midlands *(Metropolitan County).* **Birmingham. Rock music** — *Serials*

Stereotype : a Birmingham fanzine. — No.1-. — [Birmingham] (296 Station Rd, Kings Heath, [Birmingham]) : [s.n.], 1981-. — v. : ill ; 26cm
Quarterly
ISSN 0260-9398 = Stereotype : £0.20 per issue B81-17467

784.5′4′0922 — Rock music. Stars

Herman, Gary. Rock'n'roll Babylon. — London : Plexus, Sept.1981. — [192]p
ISBN 0-85965-040-5 (cased) : £8.95 : CIP entry
ISBN 0-85965-041-3 (pbk) : £4.95 B81-23797

784.5′5′00973 — American soul music — *Serials*

Midnite express. — No.1-. — [Hull] ([c/o R. Dearlove, 10 George St., Hedon, Hull HU2 8JH]) : [s.n.], [1981?]. — v. : ill,ports ; 30cm
ISSN 0261-5053 = Midnite express : £0.50 per issue B81-29101

784.6′24 — Children's songs in English — *Texts*

The **Fox** : went out on a chilly night : an old song / illustrated by Peter Spier. — Harmondsworth : Puffin, 1981. — [48]p : ill (some col.),music ; 18x23cm. — (Picture puffins)
Originally published: Garden City, N.Y. : Doubleday, c1961 ; Tadworth : World's Work, 1962
ISBN 0-14-050304-8 (pbk) : £1.25 B81-22025

784.6′8394268282 — Christmas songs in English, *1837-1900* — *Collections*

A **Victorian** Christmas song book / presented and compiled by Richard Graves. — London : Macmillan, 1980. — 112p : ill(some col.),music ; 29cm
Ill on lining papers
ISBN 0-333-30662-7 : £6.95 B81-04624

784.6′8574192 — Songs in English. Special subjects: Biochemistry. Words — *Texts*

Baum, Harold. The biochemists' songbook. — Oxford : Pergamon, Oct.1981. — [64]p
ISBN 0-08-027370-x (pbk) : £2.50 : CIP entry B81-24598

784.6′8574543 — Songs in English. Special subjects: Seasons. Words — *Anthologies*

Harlequin : 44 songs round the year / chosen by David Gadsby and Beatrice Harrop. — Words ed. / with drawings by David McKee. — London : Black, c1981. — 48p : ill ; 21cm
Includes index
ISBN 0-7136-2157-5 (pbk) : £1.35 B81-38739

784.6′86251′00973 — Folk songs in English: American folk songs. Special subjects: Railways — *Critical studies*

Cohen, Norm. Long steel rail : the railroad in American folksong / Norm Cohen ; music edited by David Cohen. — Urbana ; London : University of Illinois Press, c1981. — xx,710p : ill,music,facsims,ports ; 27cm. — (Music in American life)
Bibliography: p659-689. - List of sound discs: p652-658. - Includes index
ISBN 0-252-00343-8 : £30.00 B81-17368

784.6′86773125 — Waulking songs in Gaelic: Western Isles waulking songs — *Collections*

Hebridean folksongs. — Oxford : Clarendon Press
3: Waulking songs from Vatersay, Barra, Eriskay, South Uist and Benbecula / edited and translated by J.L. Campbell ; tunes transcribed and annotated by Francis Collinson. — 1981. — ix,432p,[2]p of plates : music,4ports ; 23cm
Parallel Gaelic text and English translation. — Added t.p. in Gaelic. — Bibliography: p423-424. — Includes index
ISBN 0-19-815215-9 : £25.00 : CIP rev. B79-22640

784.6′8796358 — Songs in English. Special subjects: Cricket, *to 1980.* **Words** — *Critical studies*

Allen, David Rayvern. A song for cricket / David Rayvern Allen. — London : Pelham, 1981. — 219p : ill(some col.),facsims,music,ports ; 26cm
Includes index
ISBN 0-7207-1287-4 : £10.95 : CIP rev. B81-17503

784.7′19426 — Songs in English. Special subjects: East Anglia. Words — *Anthologies*

New songs of East Anglia : selections from the BBC1 TV series Weekend / with a foreword by Denis Marriott. — Saxmundham (Yoxford, Saxmundham, Suffolk) : Yoxford Publications, 1981. — 35p : 1port ; 21cm
Includes index
ISBN 0-907265-03-0 (pbk) : £1.25 B81-34798

784.9 — MUSIC. VOICE TRAINING AND PERFORMANCE

784.9′3 — Songs. Performance

Moore, Gerald, *1899-*. Singer and accompanist. — London : Hamish Hamilton, Jan.1982. — [256]p
Originally published: London : Methuen, 1953
ISBN 0-241-10741-5 : £9.95 : CIP entry B81-34657

784.9′4 — Bel canto — *Manuals*

Coffin, Berton. Coffin's overtones of bel canto : phonetic basis of artistic singing : with 100 chromatic vowel chart exercises / by Berton Coffin. — Metuchen ; London : Scarecrow, 1980. — xviii,236p : ill,music ; 29cm
Bibliography: p227-232. - Includes index
ISBN 0-8108-1370-x : £15.75 B81-09371

784.9′4 — Music. Sight-singing — *Manuals*

Friedman, Milton M.. A beginner's guide to sightsinging and musical rudiments / Milton M. Friedman. — Englewood Cliffs ; London : Prentice-Hall, c1981. — xiv,274p : ill,chiefly music ; 24cm
Includes index
ISBN 0-13-074088-8 (pbk) : £8.40 B81-17278

784.9′63 — Choral singing. Conducting — *Manuals*

Garretson, Robert L.. Conducting choral music / Robert L. Garretson. — 5th ed. — Boston [Mass.] ; London : Allyn and Bacon, c1981. — xi,417p : ill,music,plans,forms ; 23cm
Previous ed.: 1975. — Includes bibliographies and index
ISBN 0-205-07145-7 : £11.95 B81-03726

785 — MUSIC. INSTRUMENTAL ENSEMBLES

785 — Instrumental pop music — *Serials*

New gandy dancer. — Issue 8 (June 1977)-. — Newcastle Upon Tyne (c/o D. Peckett, 7 Carsair, Fellside Park, Whickham, Newcastle Upon Tyne NE16 5YA) : [s.n.], 1977-. — v. : ill ; 30cm
Irregular. — Continues: Gandy dancer. — Issue 3 published out of sequence, July 1980, under later title. — Issues 1/2 and 4/7 reprinted under later title. — Description based on: Issue 3
ISSN 0260-3330 = New gandy dancer : £1.10 per issue B81-02029

785′.028′4 — Orchestration — *Manuals*

Blatter, Alfred. Instrumentation/orchestration / Alfred Blatter. — New York ; London : Longman, c1981. — xv,423p : ill,music ; 26cm. — (Longman music series)
Includes index
ISBN 0-582-28118-0 : £12.50 B81-29372

785′.06′241 — Great Britain. Symphony orchestras: BBC Symphony Orchestra, *to 1980*

Kenyon, Nicholas. The BBC Symphony Orchestra : the first fifty years 1930-1980 / Nicholas Kenyon. — London : British Broadcasting Corporation, 1981. — xv,543p,[40]p of plates : ill,ports ; 24cm
Includes index
ISBN 0-563-17617-2 : £22.50 B81-2556

785′.06′2411 — Scotland. Chamber orchestras: Scottish Chamber Orchestra — *Serials*

Scottish Chamber Orchestra. Year book / Scottish Chamber Orchestra. — 1979/80-. — [Edinburgh] ([48 Great King St., Edinburgh EH3 6QY]) : [The Orchestra], [1979]-. — v. : ill ; 30cm
Annual
ISSN 0144-722x = Year book - Scottish Chamber Orchestra : £0.50 B81-0444

785′.06′2421 — Chamber music ensembles: String quartets: Amadeus Quartet, *to 1979*

Snowman, Daniel. The Amadeus Quartet : the men and the music / Daniel Snowman. — London : Robson, 1981. — 160p,[20]p of plates : ill,music,facsim,ports ; 24cm
List of sound discs: p137-155. - Includes index
ISBN 0-86051-106-5 : £6.75 B81-2023

785′.06′2421 — England. Chamber orchestras: English Chamber Orchestra, *to 1980*

The **English** Chamber Orchestra : a pictorial review : twentieth anniversary 1980-1981 / [compiled by Anthony Woodhouse]. — [London] ([358 Strand, W.C.2]) : [Bruton Hay], [1980]. — 160p : ill,ports ; 30cm
Ill on inside cover
ISBN 0-9507231-0-x (pbk) : £1.00 B81-3687

785′.06′6 — Orchestras, *to 1980*

Hurd, Michael. The orchestra / Michael Hurd. — Oxford : Phaidon, 1981. — 224p : ill(some col.),music,facsims,ports(some col.) ; 31cm. — (A Quarto book)
Includes index
ISBN 0-7148-2170-5 : £13.95 B81-1794

785′.06′6 — Symphony orchestras. Composition

Del Mar, Norman. Anatomy of the orchestra. — London : Faber, Sept.1981. — [502]p
ISBN 0-571-11552-7 : £25.00 : CIP entry B81-2377

785′.06′67028 — Jazz ensembles. Techniques

Henry, Robert E.. The jazz ensemble : a guide to technique / Robert E. Henry. — Englewood Cliffs ; London : Prentice-Hall, c1981. — x,117p : ill,music ; 29cm. — (A Spectrum book)
Bibliography: p109-117
ISBN 0-13-509992-7 (cased) : Unpriced
ISBN 0-13-509984-6 (pbk) : £5.55 B81-2841

785′.06′7 — Great Britain. Music. Town & village bands, *to 1980*

Weir, Christopher. Village and town bands / Christopher Weir. — Aylesbury : Shire, 1981. — 32p : ill,facsims,ports ; 21cm. — (Shire album ; 61)
Bibliography: p32
ISBN 0-85263-541-9 (pbk) : £0.95 B81-1755

785′.06′71 — Great Britain. Music. Brass bands. Organisations — *Directories* — *Serials*

Directory of British brass bands / the British Federation of Brass Bands. — Vol.3 (1980-81). — [York] ([c/o 47, Hull Rd., York YO1 3JP]) : The Federation, [1980]. — 128p
ISSN 0307-6261 : Unpriced B81-06517

785′.06′71 — Great Britain. Music. Brass bands, *to 1978*

Bainbridge, Cyril. Brass triumphant / Cyril Bainbridge. — London : Muller, 1980. — 171p : ill,ports ; 25cm
List of sound discs: p154-166. - Includes index
ISBN 0-584-10372-7 : £8.95 : CIP rev. B80-24731

Brass bands in the 20th century / edited by Violet & Geoffrey Brand. — Letchworth : Egon, 1979. — 239p : ill,music,facsims,ports ; 25cm
Includes index
ISBN 0-905858-12-3 : £6.95 B81-17913

785′.06′71 — Great Britain. Music. Brass bands, *to 1979*

Brass bands / edited by Peter Gammond and Raymond Horricks. — Cambridge : Stephens, 1980. — 152p : ill,ports ; 25cm. — (Music on record ; 1)
Bibliography: p152
ISBN 0-85059-366-2 : £7.95 B81-29736

785′.06′7108 — Baton twirling — *Serials*

Twirling times / United Twirling Institute. — [No.1]-. — Glasgow (c/o Mrs M. Wilson, 67 Kingswood Drive, Glasgow G44 4RF) : The Institute [1980-]. — v. ; 30cm
Quarterly
ISSN 0260-7549 = Twirling times : £1.00 per year B81-06827

785′.06′75 — Steelband music, *to 1980* — *For schools*

Farmer, Paul, *1950-*. Steelbands & reggae / Paul Farmer. — Harlow : Longman, 1981. — 24p : ill,1map,music,ports ; 23cm. — (Longman music topics)
ISBN 0-582-20097-0 (pbk) : £0.85
Primary classification 780′.42 B81-38155

785′.07′3 — Great Britain. Children's orchestral concerts. Organisation. Mayer, *Sir* **Robert,** *1879-* — *Biographies*

Mayer, *Sir* **Robert,** *1879-*. My first hundred years / by Sir Robert Mayer. — 2nd enl. centenary ed. / introduced by Bernard Levin. — Gerrards Cross : Van Duren, 1979. — xix,104p,[12]p of plates : facsims,ports ; 23cm
Previous ed.: i.e. Centenary ed., 1979. — Includes index
ISBN 0-905715-08-x : £4.50 B81-04898

Mayer, *Sir* **Robert,** *1879-*. My first hundred years / by Sir Robert Mayer. — Centenary ed. — Gerrards Cross : Van Duren, 1979. — 104p,9p of plates : ill,facsims,ports ; 23cm
Includes index
ISBN 0-905715-09-8 : £3.00 : CIP rev. B79-12530

785′.07′3 — London. Concerts: Henry Wood Promenade Concerts — *Proposals*

Simpson, Robert. The Proms and natural justice : a plan for renewal / Robert Simpson ; foreword by Sir Adrian Boult. — London (40 Floral St., WC2) : Toccata, 1981. — vi,66p ; 21cm
Includes index
ISBN 0-907689-00-0 (pbk) : £1.95 B81-34983

785′.07′3 — London. Concerts: Henry Wood Promenade Concerts, *to 1980*

Hall, Barrie. The Proms : and the men who made them / Barrie Hall. — London : Allen & Unwin, 1981. — 232p : ill,ports ; 26cm
Includes index
ISBN 0-04-780024-0 : Unpriced : CIP rev. B81-03671

785′.07′3942178 — London. Concerts: Crystal Palace Saturday Concerts — *Programmes* — *Facsimiles*

Crystal Palace, season 1895-6, programme of Grand Concert : (the second of the fortieth annual series of Saturday concerts), October 19th 1895 ... — [West Wickham] ([4, Harvest Bank Rd., West Wickham, Kent]) : [Vintage Light Music Society], [1981]. — p46-74 : ill,music ; 21cm. — (Collectors′ reprint / Vintage Light Music Society 0307-5524)
Facsim. of ed. published: 1895
Unpriced (pbk) B81-31975

785′.09 — Orchestral music, *to 1979*

Rich, Alan. Classical music : orchestral / by Alan Rich with the assistance of Daniel Schillaci. — Poole : Blandford, 1980. — iv,139p : ports ; 24x12cm. — (The Listener′s guides to music) (A Quarto book)
List of sound discs
ISBN 0-7137-1103-5 : £4.95 B81-01058

785′.092′2 — Music. Conducting — *Biographies*

May, Robin. Behind the baton : a who′s who of conductors / Robin May. — London : Muller, 1981. — 152p : ports ; 25cm
Bibliography: p151-152. - List of sound discs: p144-150
ISBN 0-584-10467-7 (corrected) : £8.95 B81-19096

785′.092′2 — United States. Music. Bands & orchestras. Negro women instrumentalits, *to 1979*

Handy, D. Antoinette. Black women in American bands and orchestras / D. Antoinette Handy. — Metuchen ; London : Scarecrow, 1981. — xii,319p,[56]p of plates : ill,forms,ports ; 23cm
Bibliography: p254-273. - Includes index
ISBN 0-8108-1346-7 : £12.25 B81-17093

785′.092′4 — American popular music. Big bands. Page, Drew — *Biographies*

Page, Drew. Drew′s blues : a sideman′s life with the big bands / Drew Page. — Baton Rouge ; London : Louisiana State University Press, c1980. — 226p,[25]p of plates : ports ; 24cm
Includes index
ISBN 0-8071-0686-0 : £8.95 B81-11993

785′.092′4 — German instrumental music. Stockhausen, Karlheinz — *Critical studies*

Maconie, Robin. The work of Karlheinz Stockhausen / Robin Maconie ; with a foreword by Karlheinz Stockhausen. — London : Marion Boyars, [1981], c1976. — ix,341p : ill,music,facsims ; 24cm
Originally published: London : Oxford University Press, 1976. — Bibliography: p330-333. — Includes index
ISBN 0-7145-2706-8 (pbk) : £9.95 : CIP rev. B81-14860

785′.092′4 — Lancashire. Music. Brass bands. Ratcliffe, Syd — *Biographies*

Chapples, Leslie. From little brass to big brass : a biography of Syd Ratcliffe / compiled by Leslie Chapples. — Burnley (212, Manchester Rd., Burnley, Lancs.) : S. Ratcliffe, c1981. — 88p : ill,2facsims,ports ; 22cm
Unpriced (pbk) B81-39053

785′.092′4 — Music. Conducting. Boult, *Sir* **Adrian** — *Festschriften*

Sir Adrian Boult, Companion of Honour : a tribute / edited by Nigel Simeone and Simon Mundy. — Tunbridge Wells : Midas, 1980. — 96p : ill,facsims,ports ; 24cm. — (Great performers)
Also available in a de-luxe limited ed. of 100 copies. — List of sound discs: p80-96
ISBN 0-85936-212-4 (cased) : £7.50 : CIP rev.
ISBN 0-85936-217-5 (de-luxe ed.) : £25.00
ISBN 0-85936-252-3 (pbk) : Unpriced B80-17887

785′.092′4 — Music. Conducting. Furtwängler, Wilhelm

Pirie, Peter J.. Furtwängler and the art of conducting / Peter Pirie. — London : Duckworth, 1980. — 149p ; 23cm
List of sound discs: p131-144. - Includes index
ISBN 0-7156-1486-x : £9.95 B81-09006

785′.092′4 — Music. Conducting. Previn, André — *Biographies*

Bookspan, Martin. André Previn. — London : Hamish Hamilton, Oct.1981. — [384]p
ISBN 0-241-10676-1 : £8.95 : CIP entry B81-26780

785′.092′4 — Music. Conducting. Stokowski, Leopold — *Biographies*

Chasins, Abram. Leopold Stokowski : a profile / Abram Chasins. — London : Hale, 1981, c1979. — xvii,313p,[16]p of plates : ill,ports ; 23cm
Originally published: New York : Hawthorn Books, 1979. — Bibliography: p276-277. — List of sound discs : p278-296. — Includes index
ISBN 0-7091-8595-2 : £8.95 B81-12186

785′.094 — European court music, *to ca 1900*

Hogwood, Christopher. Music at court / Christopher Hogwood. — London : Gollancz, 1980, c1977. — 127p : ill(some col.),facsims,ports(some col.) ; 25cm
Originally published: London : Folio Society, 1977. — Ill on lining papers
ISBN 0-575-02877-7 : £4.95 B81-00220

785.1′1′0924 — German symphonies. Beethoven, Ludwig van — *Critical studies*

Hopkins, Antony. The nine symphonies of Beethoven / Antony Hopkins. — London : Heinemann, 1981. — vi,290p : music ; 24cm
Bibliography: p286. - Includes index
ISBN 0-435-81427-3 : £12.50 B81-19382

785.42′09 — Jazz, *to 1979*

Jones, Morley. Jazz / Morley Jones. — Poole : Blandford, 1980. — 133p : ports ; 24cm. — (The Listener′s guides) (A Quarto book)
Spine has author statement: Alan Rich. — List of sound discs
ISBN 0-7137-1102-7 : £4.95 B81-01059

785.42′092′2 — Jazz. Musicians, *to 1980* — *Illustrations*

Redfern, David. David Redfern′s jazz album. — London : Eel Pie, 1980. — 159p : ill,ports (some col.) ; 31cm
Includes index
ISBN 0-906008-16-6 : £13.95 B81-13332

785.42′092′4 — Jazz. Basie, Count, *1936-1979* — *Interviews*

Basie, Count. The world of Count Basie / [with] Stanley Dance. — London : Sidgwick & Jackson, 1980. — xxi,399p,[24]p of plates : ill,1facsim,ports ; 24cm
Originally published: New York : Scribner′s Sons, 1980. — Bibliography: p371-374. — List of sound recordings p357-370. — Includes index
ISBN 0-283-98708-1 : £8.95 B81-01541

785.42′092′4 — Jazz. Hammond, John, *1910-* — *Biographies*

Hammond, John, *1910-*. John Hammond on record : an autobiography / with Irving Townsend. — Harmondsworth : Penguin, 1981, c1977. — 432p : ill,ports ; 20cm
Originally published: New York : Ridge Press, 1977. — Includes index
ISBN 0-14-005705-6 (pbk) : £3.50 B81-27649

785.42′092′4 — Jazz. Mingus, Charles — *Biographies*

Mingus, Charles. Beneath the underdog / by Charles Mingus ; edited by Nel King. — Harmondsworth : Penguin, 1975, c1971 ([1980 printing]). — 262p ; 18cm
Originally published: New York : Knopf : London : Weidenfeld & Nicolson, 1971
ISBN 0-14-003880-9 (pbk) : £1.75 B81-16987

785.42′092′4 — Jazz. Trumpet playing. Gillespie, Dizzy — *Biographies*

Gillespie, Dizzy. Dizzy. — London : Quartet, Sept.1981. — [576]p
ISBN 0-7043-3381-3 (pbk) : £6.95 : CIP entry B81-23855

785.42'0973 — United States. Jazz, *1917-1930*

Lyttelton, Humphrey. [Basin Street to Harlem]. The best of jazz : Basin Street to Harlem : jazz masters and masterpieces 1917-1930 / Humphrey Lyttelton. — Harmondsworth : Penguin, 1980, c1978. — 238p,[8]p of plates : ports ; 18cm
Originally published: London : Robson, 1978. — Bibliography: p228. - List of sound discs: p229-230. - Includes index
ISBN 0-14-005195-3 (pbk) : £1.95 B81-01060

785.42'0973 — United States. Jazz, *1930-1940*

Lyttelton, Humphrey. Enter the giants. — London : Robson, Oct.1981. — [228]p. — (The Best of jazz ; 2)
ISBN 0-86051-107-3 : £6.50 : CIP entry B81-27457

785.4'3'095982 — Javanese gamelan music

Lindsay, Jennifer. Javanese gamelan / Jennifer Lindsay. — Kuala Lumpur ; Oxford : Oxford University Press, 1979. — x,59,[1]p,[16]p of plates : ill(some col.),2maps,music,1plan,ports (some col.) ; 22cm. — (Oxford in Asia traditional and contemporary arts)
Bibliography: p[1]. — List of sound discs: p53
ISBN 0-19-580413-9 (pbk) : £4.25 B81-03093

786 — MUSIC. KEYBOARD INSTRUMENTS

786'.09 — Keyboard music, *to 1980*

Unger-Hamilton, Clive. Keyboard instruments / Clive Unger-Hamilton. — Oxford : Phaidon, c1981. — 124p : ill(some col.),music,facsims,ports(some col.) ; 27cm
Includes index
ISBN 0-7148-2177-2 : £7.95 B81-39895

786.1'092'4 — Austrian piano music. Schubert, Franz — *Critical studies*

Porter, Ernest G.. Schubert's piano works / Ernest G. Porter. — London : Dobson, 1980. — viii,173p : music ; 21cm. — (The Student's music library. Historical and critical studies)
Bibliography: p169. — List of works: p161-167. — Includes index
ISBN 0-234-77764-8 : £4.95 B81-06537

786.1'092'4 — French piano music. Fauré, Gabriel, *1845-1924* — *Critical studies*

Long, Marguerite. At the piano with Fauré / Marguerite Long ; translated by Olive Senior-Ellis. — London : Kahn & Averill, 1980. — v,130p : music ; 23cm
Translated from the French. — Facsims on lining papers
ISBN 0-900707-45-3 : £5.25 : CIP rev. B80-22364

786.1'092'4 — Piano playing. Ogdon, John — *Biographies*

Ogdon, Brenda Lucas. Virtuoso : the story of John Ogdon / by Brenda Lucas Ogdon and Michael Kerr. — London : Hamilton, 1981. — x,293,[8]p of plates : ports ; 23cm
Includes index
ISBN 0-241-10375-4 : £9.95 : CIP rev. B81-14848

786.1'092'4 — Polish piano music. Chopin, Frédéric. Performance. Interpretation

Methuen-Campbell, James. Chopin playing : from the composer to the present day / by James Methuen-Campbell. — London : Gollancz, 1981. — 289p,[16]p of plates : ill,ports ; 24cm
Bibliography: p268-272. — Includes index
ISBN 0-575-02884-x : £14.50 B81-11580

786.2'074'02142 — London. Camden *(London Borough)*. **Houses: Fenton House. Exhibits: Keyboard string instruments. Collections: Benton Fletcher Collection** — *Catalogues*

National Trust. A catalogue of early keyboard instuments : the Benton Fletcher collection at Fenton House. — Repr. with further revisions. — [London] : National Trust, 1981, c1957. — 22p ; 22cm
Unpriced (unbound) B81-34544

786.2'1'09 — Pianos, *to 1980*

The **Book** of the piano / edited by Dominic Gill. — Oxford : Phaidon, 1981. — 288p : ill(some col.),1col.map,music(some col.),facsims(some col.),ports(some col.) ; 29cm
Bibliography: p280-281. — List of sound recordings : p281-284. — Includes index
ISBN 0-7148-2036-9 : £19.50 : CIP rev. B81-02123

786.2'23 — Pianos, *1775-1850*

Colt, C. F.. The early piano / C.F. Colt with Antony Miall. — London : Stainer & Bell, 1981. — 160p : ill(some col.),music,facsims,ports ; 22cm
Bibliography: p159
ISBN 0-85249-572-2 : £22.50 B81-12745

786.2'3'0922 — Great Britain. Harpsichord makers

Paul, John, *1920-*. Modern harpsichord makers / John Paul. — London : Gollancz, 1981. — vii,280p : ill,ports ; 26cm
Bibliography: p279-280
ISBN 0-575-02985-4 : £15.50 B81-40485

786.3'041 — Piano playing — *Interviews*

Great pianists speak for themselves / [edited and compiled by] Elyse Mach. — London : Robson, 1981. — xvi,204p : ports ; 24cm
Originally published: New York : Dodd, Mead, 1980. — Includes index
ISBN 0-86051-157-x : £6.95 : CIP rev. B81-22538

786.3'041 — Piano playing. Techniques — *Manuals*

Evans, Roger, *1940-*. How to play piano : a new easy-to-understand way to learn to play the piano / Roger Evans. — London : Elm Tree, 1980. — 104p : ill,music ; 25cm
ISBN 0-241-10399-1 (cased) : Unpriced : CIP rev.
ISBN 0-241-10400-9 (pbk) : £3.50 B80-18870

Grindea, Carola. We make our own music. — 2nd ed. — London : Kahn & Averill, Nov.1981. — [64]p
Previous ed.: 1972
ISBN 0-900707-66-6 (pbk) : £1.50 : CIP entry B81-30222

Last, Joan. Freedom in piano technique : with an appendix for teaching-diploma candidates / Joan Last. — London : Oxford University Press, 1980. — 80p : ill,music ; 20cm
ISBN 0-19-318425-7 (pbk) : £3.95 B81-01796

Palmer, King. The piano. — London : Hodder & Stoughton, Dec.1981. — [144]p. — (Teach yourself books)
ISBN 0-340-26833-6 (pbk) : £2.95 : CIP entry B81-31724

Sheftel, Paul. The keyboard : explorations and discoveries / Paul Sheftel. — New York ; London : Holt, Rinehart and Winston, c1981. — vii,278p : chiefly music ; 28cm
Includes index
ISBN 0-03-043091-7 (corrected : spiral) : £7.95 B81-16277

786.4'154 — Austrian piano sonatas. Schubert, Franz — *Scores* — *Manuscripts* — *Facsimiles*

Schubert, Franz. [Sonatas, piano, D.894, G major]. Piano sonata in G major, op.78 (D.894) : facsimile of the autograph manuscript in the British Library Add. MS 36738 / Franz Schubert ; with an introduction by Howard Ferguson and a note on the paper of the manuscript by Alan Tyson. — London : British Library, 1980. — vii,36p : ill,chiefly music ; 31x38cm. — (British Library music facsimiles ; 2)
Facsim. of: 1st ed., 1827
ISBN 0-904654-38-9 : £25.00 : CIP rev. B80-04359

786.4'254 — German keyboard music. Bach, Johann Sebastian. Wohltemperirte Klavier — *Scores* — *Manuscripts* — *Facsimiles*

Bach, Johann Sebastian. Das wohltemperirte Clavier II : facsimile of the autograph manuscript in the British Library Add. MS 35021 / Johann Sebastian Bach ; with an introduction by Don Franklin and Stephen Daw. — London : British Library, 1980. — vii,22[i.e.44]p : all music ; 40x57cm. — (British Library music facsmiles ; 1)
Facsim. of: 1742(?) manuscript
ISBN 0-904654-37-0 : Unpriced B81-17137

786.5'06'041 — Great Britain. Pipe organ playing. Organisations: Royal College of Organists — *Serials*

Royal College of Organists. Year book / the Royal College of Organists. — 1980-1981. — [London] ([Kensington Gore, SW7 2QS]) : The College, [1980?]. — xiv,41p
Unpriced B81-16238

786.6'2 — Musical instruments: Pipe organs, *to 1979*

Norman, Herbert. The organ today / Herbert Norman and H. John Norman. — [New ed.]. — Newton Abbot : David & Charles, 1980. — ix,212p,[20]p of plates : ill ; 23cm
Previous ed.: London : Barrie & Rockliff, 1966. — Includes index
ISBN 0-7153-8053-2 : £8.95 : CIP rev. B80-23606

786.6'241 — Musical instruments: British pipe organs, *to 1980*

Clutton, Cecil. The British organ. — Rev. and enl. — London : Eyre Methuen, Oct.1981. — [336]p
Previous ed.: London : Batsford, 1963
ISBN 0-413-48630-3 : £20.00 : CIP entry B81-25114

786.7 — Electronic organ playing — *Amateurs' manuals*

Neal, Roy. Play organ professionally : the Roy Neal self-tutor. — Peterborough ([9 Oundle Rd., Chesterton, Peterborough]) : Sceptre Publishers, c1981. — 64p : music ; 31cm
Cover title. — Reference chart ([4]p) as insert
Unpriced (pbk) B81-29895

The **Popular** organist : discover the world of organ playing. — [London] : [Chappell Music]
Bk.1 / by Derek Bellwood ; foreword by Harry Stoneham. — [1980]. — 32p : ill,music ; 28cm
Cover title. — One folded sheet ([4]p.) as insert
Unpriced (pbk) B81-11843

The **Popular** organist : discover the world of organ playing. — London : Chappell Music. — 1980
Bk.2 / by Derek Bellwood. — 40p : ill,music ; 28cm
One folded sheet ([4]p) as insert
Unpriced (pbk) B81-07851

786.9'2 — Musical instruments: Electronic organs

Neal, Roy. The magic of the organ / Roy Neal. — [Peterborough] ([9 Oundle Rd., Chesterton, Peterborough]) : Sceptre Publishers, 1980, c1979. — xiv,154p : ill,music ; 23cm
Originally published: 1979
£5.95 B81-29894

786.9'7 — Piano accordion playing - *Manuals - German texts*

Schneider-Kräupl, Carl. Akkordeonspiel im Flug gelernt : leichte Schule für Gruppen-Einzel-und Selbstunterricht / Carl Schneider-Kräupl. — Mainz ; London : Schott, c1980
Ed 6897
- Bd.1. — 32p : ill,music ; 31cm
Unpriced (pbk) B81-09813

Schneider-Kräupl, Carl. Akkordeonspiel im Flug gelernt : leichte Schule für Gruppen-Einzel-und Selbstunterricht / Carl Schneider-Kräupl. — Mainz ; London : Schott, c1980
Ed 6898
Bd. 2. — 32p : ill,music ; 31cm
Unpriced (pbk) B81-09814

787 — MUSIC. STRING INSTRUMENTS

787′.01′0714 — Bowed string instrument playing

ESTA review 1981 : a selection of articles from ESTA news and views 1976-1980 / edited by Joyce Rathbone ; with a foreword by Yehudi Menuhin. — [England] : European String Teachers′ Association (British Branch) ; Penrith (37 Frenchfield Gardens, Penrith, Cumbria) : J. Upson, c1981. — 128p ; 21cm
Unpriced (pbk) B81-24929

787.1′07′12 — Violin playing

Menuhin, Yehudi. Violin and viola / Yehudi Menuhin and William Primrose ; with a section on the history of the instrument by Denis Stevens. — London : Macdonald Futura, 1980, c1976. — xiii,250p,[13]p of plates : ill,music,ports ; 22cm. — (Yehudi Menuhin music guides)
Originally published: Macdonald and Jane′s, 1976. — Bibliography: p233. - List of sound discs: p235-243. - Includes index
ISBN 0-356-04715-6 (cased) : £8.50
ISBN 0-356-04716-4 (pbk) : £5.50
Also classified at 787.1′09 B81-01859

787.1′07′12 — Violin playing — *Manuals*

Menuhin, Yehudi. Violin. — London : Faber & Faber in association with Faber Music, 1981, c1971. — 144p : ill,music ; 25cm
Originally published: London : Faber Music, 1971
ISBN 0-571-10038-4 (pbk) : £3.95 B81-37920

787.1′07′14 — Violin playing — *For schools*

Wade, Darrell. A tutor for the first year schools′ violin class / by Darrell Wade. — 2nd ed. — Gnosall (16 Anchor Way, Danes Green, Gnosall, Staffs.) : Viking, [1977]. — 40p : ill,chiefly music,1form ; 31cm. — (′Stringing along′)
Cover title. — Previous ed.: 197-?
Unpriced (pbk) B81-10679

787.1′07′14 — Violin playing. Techniques

Auer, Leopold. Violin playing as I teach it / Leopold Auer. — New York : Dover ; London : Constable, 1980. — xii,99p : music ; 22cm
Originally published: New York : Frederick A. Stokes, 1921 ; London : Duckworth, 1960
ISBN 0-486-23917-9 (pbk) : £1.25 B81-01061

Szigeti, Joseph. Szigeti on the violin / Joseph Szigeti ; with a new preface by Spike Hughes. — New York : Dover ; London : Constable, 1979. — xxii,234p : music,1port ; 21cm
Originally published: London : Cassell, 1969. — Includes index
ISBN 0-486-23763-x (pbk) : £2.20 B81-40587

787.1′09 — Violins & violin music, *to ca 1850*

Menuhin, Yehudi. Violin and viola / Yehudi Menuhin and William Primrose ; with a section on the history of the instrument by Denis Stevens. — London : Macdonald Futura, 1980, c1976. — xiii,250p,[13]p of plates : ill,music,ports ; 22cm. — (Yehudi Menuhin music guides)
Originally published: Macdonald and Jane′s, 1976. — Bibliography: p233. - List of sound discs: p235-243. - Includes index
ISBN 0-356-04715-6 (cased) : £8.50
ISBN 0-356-04716-4 (pbk) : £5.50
Primary classification 787.1′07′12 B81-01859

787.1′092′2 — Violin playing, *1630-1979* — *Biographies*

Campbell, Margaret, *19---*. The great violinists / Margaret Campbell. — London : Elek : Granada, 1980. — xxix,366p : ill,ports ; 24cm
Bibliography: p329-331. — List of sound discs: p333-353.— Includes index
ISBN 0-236-40183-1 : £15.00 B81-02280

787.1′092′4 — Violin playing. Pagnanini, Nicolò — *Biographies*

Sugden, John. Niccolo Paganini : supreme violinist or Devil′s fiddler? / John Sugden. — Tunbridge Wells : Midas, 1980. — 168p : ill,1map,facsims,ports ; 26cm
Bibliography: p159-161. — List of sound recordings: p162-164. — Includes index
ISBN 0-85936-202-7 : £7.50 : CIP rev. B80-13937

787.1′2′0924 — Scotland. Highlands. Violins. Making. Grant, Alexander — *Biographies*

Farnell, Graeme. Alexander Grant : Highland fiddle maker / [Graeme Farnell]. — [Inverness] ([Castle Wynd, Inverness IV2 3ED]) : [Inverness Museum and Art Gallery], [1980]. — 6p : 2ill,1facsim,2ports ; 21cm. — (Information sheet / Inverness Museum & Art Gallery ; no.5)
£0.15 (unbound) B81-07318

787.1′542 — German violin sonatas. Beethoven, Ludwig van — *Scores* — *Manuscripts* — *Facsimiles*

Beethoven, Ludwig van. [Sonatas, violin, op.30, no.3, G major]. Violin sonata in G major, op.30, no.3 : facsimile of the autograph manuscript in the British Library Add. MS 37767 / Ludwig van Beethoven ; with an introduction by Alan Tyson. — London : British Library, 1980. — viii,20[i.e.40]p : 1ill,chiefly music ; 28x27cm. — (British Library music facsimiles ; 3)
Facsim. of: 1803 manuscript
ISBN 0-904654-39-7 : £25.00 B81-19846

787′.41′0924 — Double bass playing. Naish, Bronwen — *Biographies*

Naish, Bronwen. Another string to my bow / Bronwen Naish ; illustrated by Nick Baker. — London : Pelham, 1981. — 127p : ill ; 23cm
ISBN 0-7207-1317-x : £6.50 : CIP rev. B81-07470

787′.5′0924 — Wales. Harp playing. Richards, Nansi — *Festschriften* — *Welsh texts*

Nansi / golygwyd gan Marged Jones. — Llandysul : Gwasg Gomer, 1981. — 97p,[9]p of plates : ill,ports ; 22cm
Includes poems by Nansi Richards
ISBN 0-85088-994-4 (pbk) : £1.75 B81-40007

787′.5′09429 — Wales. Harps, *1700-1900* — *Welsh texts*

Rosser, Ann. Teyn a thelynor : hanes y delyn yng Nghymru 1700-1900 / Ann Rosser. — [Ceardydd] : Amgueddfa Werin Cymru, 1981. — xi,140p : maps,facsims,ports(some col.) ; 25cm
Bibliography: p130-134. - Includes index
ISBN 0-85485-048-1 : Unpriced B81-23175

787′.55′09415 — Irish harp music, *1792*

Yeats, Gráinne. Féile na gCruitirí, Béal Feirste 1792 : Gráinne Yeats assesses the music of Carolan and other harper composers which was collected by Edward Bunting at the Belfast Harpers′ Festival 1792. — [Dublin] (26 Merrion Sq., Dublin 2) : Gael Linn, c1980. — 78p : ill,music,facsims,ports ; 22cm
Parallel Irish and English text. — Bibliography: p75
ISBN 0-86233-025-4 (pbk) : Unpriced B81-24895

787.6′1′0712 — Guitar playing — *Manuals*

Cobby, Richard J.. Play guitar : a practical guitar method for 1st and 2nd year students of all ages in class and private tuition / Richard J. Cobby. — Northampton (46, Brookland Rd., Northampton NN1 4SL) : Northampton Guitar Studios
Vol.1. — 4th ed. — 1980, c1976. — 56p : ill,music ; 31cm
Cover title. — Previous ed.: 1978. — Text and music on inside cover
Unpriced (pbk) B81-12961

Dacre, J. B.. Think guitar / by J.B. Dacre. — Andover : A.W. Publications, 1979. — 103p : ill,music ; 21cm
Bibliography: p95. - Includes index
ISBN 0-900841-56-7 (pbk) : £2.00 B81-12626

Stevens, Susan. Help yourself to play the guitar / by Sue Stevens ; illustrated by Rosemary Thornton-Jones. — [London] ([17 Buckingham Palace Road, SW1 0PT]) : Girl Guides Association, 1981. — 32p : ill,music ; 15x21cm
Originally published: / illustrated by Elizabeth Wall. 1975
£0.50 (pbk) B81-08053

788 — MUSIC. WIND INSTRUMENTS

788 — Wind instruments. Construction — *Amateurs′ manuals*

Robinson, Trevor. The amateur wind instrument maker / Trevor Robinson. — Rev. ed. — London : Murray, 1981, c1973. — 116p : ill ; 26cm
Previous ed.: Amherst : University of Massachusetts Press, 1973. — Bibliography: p113-116
ISBN 0-7195-3847-5 (pbk) : £6.50 B81-16167

788′.01′074029134 — Edinburgh. Museums: Edinburgh University Collection of Historic Musical Instruments. Stock: Musical instruments: Brass instruments — *Catalogues*

Edinburgh University Collection of Historic Musical Instruments. A Checklist of the brass musical instruments in the Edinburgh University Collection of Historic Musical Instruments / Arnold Myers. — Edinburgh (Reid School of Music, Teviot Pl., Edinburgh EH8 9AG) : The Collection, 1981. — 21p ; 30cm
Includes index
ISBN 0-907635-01-6 (unbound) : £1.00 B81-25900

788′.05′0712 — Woodwind instrument playing

Saucier, Gene A.. Woodwinds : fundamental performance techniques / Gene A. Saucier. — New York : Schirmer Books ; London : Collier Macmillan, c1981. — xi,241p : ill,music ; 28cm
Includes bibliographies, lists of sound discs and index
ISBN 0-02-872300-7 (spiral) : £9.50 B81-38659

788′.1′0924 — Jazz. Trumpet playing. Davis, Miles - *Biographies*

Carr, Ian. Miles Davis. — London : Quartet, June 1981. — [352]p
ISBN 0-7043-2273-0 : £9.50 : CIP entry B81-14422

788′.51′0712 — Flute playing — *Manuals* — *Early works*

Quantz, Johann Joachim. On playing the flute. — 3rd ed. — London : Faber, Sept.1981. — [400]p
Translation of: Versuch einer Anweisung, die Flöte traversiere zu spielen. Berlin : Voss, 1752. — Previous ed.: 1976
ISBN 0-571-18046-9 (pbk) : £5.95 : CIP entry B81-21470

788′.51′0924 — Flute playing. Galway, James — *Biographies*

Galway, James. James Galway : an autobiography. — Large print ed. — Bath : Chivers, 1980, c1978. — 306p ; 23cm. — (New Portway)
Originally published: London : Chappell : Elm Tree Books, 1978
ISBN 0-85997-480-4 : £5.50 : CIP rev. B80-22365

788′.53′0712 — Recorder playing — *Manuals* — *For schools*

Cox, Heather. Sing, clap and play the recorder : a descant recorder book for beginners / Heather Cox and Garth Rickard. — London : Macmillan Education, 1981. — 2v. : ill,music ; 21x30cm
ISBN 0-333-28043-1 (pbk)
ISBN 0-333-28714-2 (v.2) : £0.95 B81-39092

Pitts, John, *19---*. Recorder : from the beginning / John Pitts. — Leeds : E. J. Arnold
Book 1. — c1980. — 40p : ill,music ; 21x26cm
ISBN 0-560-01243-8 (pbk) : £0.90 B81-21975

Pitts, John, *1938-*. Recorder : from the beginning / John Pitts. — Leeds : E.J. Arnold
Book 2. — c1981. — 48p : ill,music ; 21x26cm
ISBN 0-560-01245-4 (pbk) : £1.20 B81-21976

788′.53′0712 — Recorder playing — *Manuals* — *German texts*

Keetman, Gunild. Elementares Blockflötenspiel : mit Anleitung für Zusammenspiel und Improvisation / Gunild Keetman, Minna Ronnefeld. — Mainz ; London : Schott, c1980. — 2v. : ill,music ; 30cm
Contents: Lehrerband — Schülerarbeitsheft
Unpriced (pbk) B81-09817

788'.53'0712 — Tin whistle playing — *Manuals*

Loane, Brian. How to play the tin whistle / Brian Loane. — [London] : Universal Edition, c1980. — 61p : ill,music,ports ; 18x24cm
Bibliography: p60. — Publisher's no.: YE26930L
ISBN 0-900938-56-0 (pbk) : Unpriced B81-38710

788'.6'06041 — Great Britain. Clarinet & saxophone playing. Organisations: Clarinet and Saxophone Society of Great Britain — *Serials*

Clarinet and saxophone : [official publication of CASS]. — Vol.5, no.3 (July 1980)-. — Wilmington (26 Monks Orchard, Wilmington, Kent) : [Clarinet and Saxophone Society of Great Britain], 1980-. — ill,music ; 25cm
Quarterly. — Continues: CASS news. — Description based on: Vol.5, no.4 (Oct. 1980)
ISSN 0260-390x = Clarinet and saxophone : £0.40 (free to members) B81-02023

788'.66'0712 — Saxophone playing

Harvey, Paul, *1935-*. The saxophonist's bedside book / by Paul Harvey. — London (20 Earlham St., WC2H 9LN) : Fentone Music, c1981. — 29p : ill,music ; 21cm. — (Fentone ; 147)
Cover title
Unpriced (pbk) B81-29714

788'.7'0712 — Oboe playing

Goossens, Leon. Oboe / Leon Goossens and Edwin Roxburgh. — 2nd ed. — London : Macdonald, 1980. — xv,236p,16p of plates : ill,music, facsims,ports ; 22cm. — (Yehudi Menuhin music guides)
Previous ed.: London : Macdonald & Jane's, 1977. — Bibliography: p216-219 - List of sound discs: p221-229. - Includes index
ISBN 0-354-04595-4 (pbk) : £5.50
Primary classification 788'.7'09 B81-08310

788'.7'09 — Oboes & oboe music, *to 1980*

Goossens, Leon. Oboe / Leon Goossens and Edwin Roxburgh. — 2nd ed. — London : Macdonald, 1980. — xv,236p,16p of plates : ill,music, facsims,ports ; 22cm. — (Yehudi Menuhin music guides)
Previous ed.: London : Macdonald & Jane's, 1977. — Bibliography: p216-219 - List of sound discs: p221-229. - Includes index
ISBN 0-354-04595-4 (pbk) : £5.50
Also classified at 788'.7'0712 B81-08310

788'.92 — Northumbrian pipe playing — *Serials*

Northumbrian Pipers' Society magazine. — Vol.1 (1980)-. — Cramlington (c/o R. Butler, 22 Newlyn Drive, Parkside Dale, Cramlington, Northumberland NE23 9RN) : The Society, 1980-. — v. : music,ports ; 21cm
Annual
ISSN 0261-5096 = Northumbrian Pipers' Society magazine : £0.30 B81-30003

788'.92'0922 — Scottish Highland bagpipes. MacCrimmon *(Family)*. **Historicity**

Campsie, Alistair Keith. The MacCrimmon legend : the madness of Angus MacKay / by Alistair Keith Campsie. — Edinburgh : Cannongate, 1980. — 190p ; 23cm
Includes index
ISBN 0-903937-66-2 : £6.95 B81-03956

789.01 — MUSIC. PERCUSSION INSTRUMENTS

789'.1 — Drum playing — *Manuals*

Ryan, Lloyd. The complete drum tutor / Lloyd Ryan. — London : Duckworth, 1981. — 80p : ill,music ; 28cm
ISBN 0-7156-1400-2 (cased) : Unpriced : CIP rev.
ISBN 0-7156-1401-0 (pbk) : £4.95 B80-00846

789'.1'0924 — Pop music. Drum playing. Moon, Keith — *Biographies*

Butler, Dougal. Moon the loon : the rock and roll life of Keith Moon - the most spectacular drummer the world has ever seen / Dougal Butler with Chris Trengrove and Peter Lawrence. — London : Star, 1981. — 231p,[8]p of plates : ill,1facsim,ports ; 18cm
ISBN 0-352-30805-2 (pbk) : £1.50 B81-18649

789'.5'0942563 — Bedfordshire. Ampthill. Parish churches: Ampthill Church. Bells

Pickford, Christipher J.. Ampthill Church bells / by Christopher J. Pickford. — Flitwick (88 Ampthill Rd., Flitwick, Bedford MK45 1BA) : James W. Yates, [1981]. — [10]p : ill,facsims,ports ; 23cm
ISBN 0-9507601-0-2 (pbk) : Unpriced B81-36080

789.9 — ELECTRONIC MUSICAL INSTRUMENTS, MUSIC RECORDING

789.9 — Electronic pop music equipment — *Serials*

Sound international. — No.1 (1978)-. — Croydon (Link House, Dingwall Ave., Croydon CR9 2TA) : Link House Magazines (Croydon), 1978-. — v. : ill,ports ; 30cm
Monthly. — Description based on: No.26, June 1980
ISSN 0144-6037 = Sound international : £9.70 per year B81-04448

789.9'1 — Popular music. Sound discs. Production — *Manuals*

Lambert, Dennis. Producing hit records / by Dennis Lambert with Ronald Zalkind ; foreword by Al Coury. — New York : Schirmer ; London : Collier Macmillan, c1980. — xii,196p : ill,plans,forms,1sample ; 24cm. — (Zadoc music business series)
Accompanied by 1 sound disc (11.34 min. : 33 1/3rpm, stereo : 7in) by Player entitled : Baby come back
ISBN 0-02-871950-6 (cased) : Unpriced
ISBN 0-02-871960-3 (pbk) : £4.95 B81-05086

789.9'9 — Electronic music. Composition. Techniques — *Manuals*

Wells, Thomas H.. The technique of electronic music / Thomas H. Wells. — New York : Schirmer ; London : Collier Macmillan, c1981. — xvi,303p : ill ; 25cm
Originally published: Austin, Tex. : University Stores, 1974. — Includes bibliographies. — List of sound discs: p294-295. — Includes index
ISBN 0-02-872830-0 : £13.95 B81-29338

789.9'9 — Musical instruments: Synthesisers

Graham, Bruce. Music and the synthesiser / by Bruce Graham. — Watford : Argus Books, 1980. — 141p : ill,music ; 21cm
Bibliography: p138-139. — Includes index
ISBN 0-85242-695-x (pbk) : £4.25 B81-22930

789.9'9 — Musical instruments: Synthesisers. Construction — *Amateurs' manuals*

Berry, M. K.. Electronic synthesiser projects / by M.K. Berry. — London : Babani, 1981. — 81p : ill ; 18cm
ISBN 0-85934-056-2 (pbk) : £1.75 : CIP rev. B80-33995

789.9'9'09 — Electronic music, *to 1980*

Mackay, Andy. Electronic music / Andy Mackay. — Oxford : Phaidon, 1981. — 124p : ill(some col.),ports ; 27cm
Includes index
ISBN 0-7148-2176-4 : £7.95 B81-39896

790 — RECREATIONS

790 — Games — *Manuals* — *For children*

Brandreth, Gyles. A game-a-day book / by Gyles Brandreth ; illustrated by Lucy Robinson. — New York : Sterling ; London : Oak Tree, 1980. — 192p : ill ; 21cm
Includes index
ISBN 0-7061-2694-7 : £3.50 B81-00221

790 — United States. Recreation leadership — *Manuals*

Sessoms, H. Douglas. Leadership and group dynamics in recreation services / H. Douglas Sessoms, Jack L. Stevenson. — Boston, Mass. ; London : Allyn and Bacon, c1981. — x,285p : ill,forms ; 25cm
Includes index
ISBN 0-205-07282-8 : Unpriced B81-26216

790'.01 — Leisure & recreation — *Philosophical perspectives*

Shivers, Jay S.. Leisure and recreation concepts : a critical analysis / Jay S. Shivers. — Boston, Mass. ; London : Allyn and Bacon, c1981. — xi,216p ; 24cm
Includes bibliographies and index
ISBN 0-205-06992-4 (pbk) : £5.50 B81-02279

790'.025'41 — Great Britain. Vacation activities — *Directories* — *Serials*

Activity holidays in Britain. — 1981-. — Paisley : Farm Holiday Guides Ltd., 1981-. — v. : ill ; 22cm
Annual
ISSN 0261-5924 = Activity holidays in Britain : £0.60 B81-31565

790'.05 — Leisure activities — *Serials*

Leisure Studies Association quarterly. — Vol.1, no.1 (1980)-. — Edinburgh (c/o J.Long, Tourism and Recreation Unit, University of Edinburgh, [George Sq., Edingburgh EH8 9LJ]) : The Association, 1980-. — v. ; 30cm
Continues: Leisure Studies Association newsletter. — Description based on: Vol.2, no.1 (Jan. 1981)
ISSN 0260-6364 = Leisure Studies Association quarterly : Unpriced B81-20319

790'.06'041 — Great Britain. Recreations. Organisations — *Directories*

. The Recreation management handbook / edited by the Institute of Recreation Management. — 3rd ed. — London : Spon, 1981. — xi,380p ; 25cm
Previous ed.: published as Recreation management yearbook. 1975. — Includes index
ISBN 0-419-11620-6 : £14.75 : CIP rev. B80-17889

790'.068'3 — North America. Recreation services. Leadership & supervision

Kraus, Richard G.. Recreation leadership and supervision : guidelines for professional development. — 2nd ed. / Richard G. Kraus, Gay Carpenter, Barbara J. Bates. — Philadelphia ; London : Saunders College, c1981. — viii,382p : forms ; 25cm. — (Saunders series in recreation)
Previous ed.: 1975. — Bibliography: p354-359. — Includes index
ISBN 0-03-057674-1 : £10.95 B81-25586

790'.06'842166 — London. Wandsworth *(London Borough)*. **Recreation centres. Conversion of Battersea Power Station** — *Proposals*

Binney, Marcus. The colossus of Battersea : a report / by SAVE Britain's Heritage ; [text by Marcus Binney]. — London (3 Park Sq. West, NW1 4LJ) : SAVE Britain's Heritage, c1981. — [32]p : ill(some col.),1map,plans ; 30cm
Cover title. — Text, ill on inside covers
ISBN 0-905978-09-9 (pbk) : Unpriced B81-26625

790'.06'8931 — New Zealand. Outdoor recreation centres: Outdoor Pursuits Centre, *to 1980*

Dingle, Graeme. Seven year adventure. — London : Hodder & Stoughton, Feb.1982. — 1v.
ISBN 0-340-25692-3 : £7.95 : CIP entry B81-35690

790'.06'9 — United States. Recreation services. Management

Rodney, Lynn S.. Administration of recreation, parks and leisure services. — 2nd ed. / Lynn S. Rodney, Robert F. Toalson. — New York ; Chichester : Wiley, 1981. — x,486p : ill,forms ; 24cm
Previous ed.: published as Administration of public recreation. New York : Ronald Press, 1964. — Includes bibliographies and index
ISBN 0-471-05806-8 : Unpriced B81-10041

790'.0941 — Great Britain. Interest vacations — *Practical information*

The **Alternative** holiday catalogue / edited by Harriet Peacock. — London : Pan, 1981. — 233p : ill ; 20cm
ISBN 0-330-26454-0 (pbk) : £1.95 B81-09718

790´.0941 — Great Britain. Public events — *Calendars*

Schofield, Bernard. Events in Britain : a complete guide to annual events in Britain / Bernard Schofield ; with illustrations by the author. — Poole : Blandford, 1981. — 250p : ill,coats of arms,ports ; 25cm
ISBN 0-7137-1230-9 : £8.95 : CIP rev.
B81-23828

790´.09422´162 — Surrey. Guildford ***(District).*** **Leisure facilities** — *Serials*

Guildford. *Public Relations Unit*. Leisure for pleasure : a guide to Guildford Borough Council's leisure and recreational facilities / ... produced by Guildford Borough Council's Public Relations Unit in conjunction with the Leisure and Recreation Department. — [1976]-. — London : Borrow, 1976-. — v. : ill ; 21cm
Irregular. — Description based on: [1981]
ISSN 0261-3522 = Leisure for pleasure : Unpriced
Primary classification 333.78´09422´162
B81-24702

790´.09424 — England. East Midlands. Public events — *Calendars* — *Serials*

[Events ***(Lincoln)*****]**. Events / East Midlands Tourist Board. — 1979-. — Lincoln (Exchequer Gate, Lincoln LN2 1PZ) : The Board, 1979-. — v. ; 30cm
Two issues yearly. — Description based on: 1981 issue
ISSN 0261-0728 = Events (Lincoln) : Unpriced B81-13695

790´.09429 — Wales. Public events — *Serials*

Touch and go = Cael a chael. — 1-. — Llandrindod Wells (The Drama Centre, Tremont Rd, Llandrindod Wells, Powys) : [Touch and Go Network], 1980-. — v. : ill ; 24cm
Description based on: 8 (May [1981])
ISSN 0261-278x = Touch and go : £0.15 per issue B81-39528

790.1 — Activities connected with Christmas — *Collections* — *For children*

Groves, Diana. Christmas is coming / illustrated by Diana Groves. — London : Macdonald Educational, 1981. — [13]leaves : ill(some col.) ; 21x30cm + 1folded sheet(col.ill ; 13x90cm folded to 13x8cm) + sound disc(45rpm,stereo. ; 7in.)
ISBN 0-356-07540-0 (pbk) : Unpriced
B81-38533

790.1 — Activities connected with festivals — *Manuals*

Cordello, Becky Stevens. Celebrations : a unique treasury of holiday ideas featuring appetizing recipes, family games, gala decorations and easy craft activities for over 25 special occasions / Becky Stevens Cordello. — New York : Butterick, c1977. — ix,311p32p of plates : ill(some col.) ; 29cm
Includes index
ISBN 0-88421-034-0 : £9.95 : CIP rev.
B78-27528

790.1 — Activities — *For children*

Macdonald, Maryann. Moving, doing, building, being / Maryann Macdonald ; illustrated by Ross Thomson. — London : Andersen, 1980. — [25]p : col.ill ; 24cm
ISBN 0-905478-79-7 : £2.95 B81-04050

790.1´3 — Games for one player — *Manuals* — *For children*

Brandreth, Gyles. Play it alone! / Gyles Brandreth ; illustrated by David Mostyn. — London : Beaver, 1980. — 127p : ill ; 18cm
ISBN 0-600-33701-4 (pbk) : £0.85 B81-02794

790.1´32 — Collecting — *Manuals*

Lewis, Mel. Collecting for fun and profit / Mel Lewis. — London : Proteus, 1981. — 184p ; 26cm
ISBN 0-906071-69-0 (cased) : £7.50
ISBN 0-906071-23-2 (pbk) : Unpriced
B81-17867

790.1´32´05 — Collecting — *Serials*

[Finders keepers ***(Wellingborough)*****]**. Finders keepers : bi-monthly journal of the great British collectamaniac. — Oct.1980-. — Wellingborough (Old Bottle Emporium, Herriott's La., Wellingborough, Northants.) : Kollectarama, 1980-. — v. : ill ; 30cm
ISSN 0260-5236 = Finders keepers (Wellingborough) : £6.00 per year B81-03276

790.1´34 — Competitions. Winners — *Lists*

Cook, Chris. The Guinness book of winners and champions. — 2nd ed. — Enfield : Guinness Superlatives, Oct.1981. — [256]p
Previous ed.: 1979
ISBN 0-85112-218-3 : £6.95 : CIP entry
B81-28089

790.1´5´0973 — United States. Group recreations. Planning

Kraus, Richard G.. Social recreation : a group dynamics approach / Richard Kraus. — St. Louis ; London : Mosby, 1979. — vii,194p : ill,music,forms ; 23cm
Bibliography: p182-183. — Includes index
ISBN 0-8016-2742-7 (pbk) : £7.75 B81-08080

790.1´922 — Activities for children

Stapleton, Marjorie. Child's play / Marjorie Stapleton. — [London] : Star, 1981, c1980. — 144p : ill ; 18cm
Includes index
ISBN 0-352-30680-7 (pbk) : £1.50 B81-14744

790.1´922 — Activities for children — *For children*

Goldstein-Jackson, Kevin. Activities with everyday objects / Kevin Goldstein-Jackson ; illustrated by Pamela Mara. — London : Granada, 1981, c1980. — 128p : ill ; 18cm
Originally published: London : Souvenir, 1980
ISBN 0-583-30464-8 (pbk) : £0.85 B81-24931

Stoll, Martin. Fun for free / Martin Stoll ; illustrated by Graham Thompson. — London : Armada, 1981. — 128p : ill ; 18cm
Includes index
ISBN 0-00-691866-2 (pbk) : £0.80 B81-12014

Superbook : stories, games, puzzles, tricks, jokes, quizzes, poems, things to make and things to do / [edited and designed by the Reader's Digest Association Limited]. — London : Published by the Reader's Digest Association Limited in conjunction with Mothercare Limited, c1981. — 223p : col.ill ; 31cm
£4.95 B81-34999

790.1´922 — Activities for children — *Illustrations* — *For children*

Ichikawa, Satomi. Let's play / Satomi Ichikawa. — London : Heimemann, 1981. — [32]p : chiefly col.ill ; 23x25cm
ISBN 0-434-94365-7 : £3.95 B81-32358

790.1´922 — Games for children — *Collections* — *For children*

101 games to play / compiled by Elizabeth Cooper ; [illustrations by David Barnett ... et al.]. — London : Hamlyn, 1981. — 157p : col.ill ; 22cm
ISBN 0-600-36479-8 : £2.95 B81-25538

Walt Disney presents Winnie-the-Pooh games to play. — Maidenhead : Purnell, 1981. — [16]p : chiefly col.ill ; 20cm. — (A Hunny pot book)
£0.35 (pbk) B81-09729

790.1´922 — Items of interest to children: Items available by post — *For children*

Gundrey, Elizabeth. 250 more things to send off for / Elizabeth Gundrey ; illustrated by Susie Lacome. — Feltham : Beaver, 1981. — 110p : ill ; 18cm
Includes index
ISBN 0-600-20381-6 (pbk) : £0.90 B81-38434

790.1´922 — Seaside activities for children — *Illustrations* — *For children*

My first book of the seaside. — London : Dean, [1980]. — [8]p : all col.ill ; 15cm. — (A Dean board book)
ISBN 0-603-00238-2 (pbk) : £0.25 B81-06345

790.1´922 — Seasonal activities for children — *For children*

Arthur, Toni. All the year round / Toni Arthur ; illustrated by Lyn Jones. — Harmondsworth : Puffin, 1981. — 160p : ill ; 20cm
Includes index
ISBN 0-14-031320-6 (pbk) : £1.00 B81-37251

790.1´94 — Games for cub scouts — *Collections*

Barclay, V. C.. Cub scout games / collected by V.C. Barclay ; with a foreword by the Founder. — Rev. — Glasgow : Brown, Son & Ferguson, 1978. — xii,95p : ill ; 18cm
Previous ed.: 1971
ISBN 0-85174-326-9 (pbk) : £1.20 B81-00222

790.1´96 — Games for mentally handicapped children

Sternlicht, Manny. Games children play : instructive and creative play activities for the mentally retarded and developmentally disabled child / Manny Sternlicht, Abraham Hurwitz. — New York ; London : Van Nostrand Reinhold, c1981. — ix,117p : ill ; 22cm
Bibliography: p110-112. - Includes index
ISBN 0-442-25857-7 : £9.70 B81-06762

790.2 — Street entertainments, *to 1980*

Cohen, David, ***1945-*****.** The buskers : a history of street entertainment / David Cohen & Ben Greenwood. — Newton Abbot : David & Charles, c1981. — 208p : ill,facsim,ports ; 22cm
Bibliography: p201-204. — Includes index
ISBN 0-7153-8026-5 : £8.50 : CIP rev.
B81-14427

790.2´05 — Performing arts — *Serials*

[P.S ***(London)*****]**. P.S : primary sources. — No.1 (June/July 1979)-. — London (146 Dawes Rd, SW6) : Artstra Information, 1979-. — v. : ill,ports ; 43cm
Irregular. — Subtitle varies. — Description based on: No.5 (Oct./Nov.1980)
ISSN 0260-6445 = P.S. Primary sources : £4.40 per year B81-07792

790.2´09 — Performing arts. Patronage by British royal families, ***ca 1900-1980***

Pertwee, Bill. By royal command. — Newton Abbot : David & Charles, Oct.1981. — [160]p
ISBN 0-7153-8200-4 : £7.50 : CIP entry
B81-24663

790.2´092´2 — Performing arts — *Biographies*

Tynan, Kenneth. Show people : profiles in entertainment / Kenneth Tynan. — London : Weidenfeld and Nicolson, 1980, c1979. — 317p ; 23cm
Originally published: New York : Simon and Schuster, 1979
ISBN 0-297-77842-0 : £8.95 B81-01543

790.2´09411 — Scotland. Performing arts. Touring — *Inquiry reports*

Large- and medium-scale touring in Scotland : a report to the Scottish Arts Council : July 1979. — [Edinburgh] ([19 Charlotte Sq., Edinburgh, EH2 4DF]) : [Scottish Arts Council], [1980]. — 26,[13]p ; 30cm
Unpriced (pbk) B81-11136

790.2´0951 — China. Performing arts, ***1976-1980***

Mackerras, Colin. The performing arts in contemporary China / Colin Mackerras. — London : Routledge & Kegan Paul, 1981. — x,243p,[16]p of plates : ill,ports ; 23cm
Bibliography: p226-228. — Includes index
ISBN 0-7100-0778-7 : £13.50 : CIP rev.
B81-13728

791 — PUBLIC ENTERTAINMENT

791 — Entertainments — *Manuals* — *For children*

Inman, John. Curtain up! / John Inman ; illustrated by Margaret Chamberlain. — London : Heinemann, 1981. — 95p : ill ; 23cm
ISBN 0-434-94380-0 : £4.50 B81-39654

791 — United States. Cowboys. Stunting, ***1880-1980***

Dean, Frank. Cowboy fun / Frank Dean. — New York : Sterling ; London : Oak Tree, c1980. — 128p : ill,ports ; 27cm
Includes index
ISBN 0-7061-2691-2 : £4.95 B81-06964

791'.092'2 — British comedians, *ca 1925-1977*
Midwinter, Eric. Make 'em laugh : famous comedians and their worlds / Eric Midwinter. — London : Allen & Unwin, 1979. — 209p : ill,ports ; 26cm
Includes index
ISBN 0-04-792011-4 : £6.95 : CIP rev.
B78-31603

791'.092'2 — Comedy. Morecambe, Eric & Wise, Ernie — *Biographies*
Morecambe, Eric. There's no answer to that! : an autobiography / by Morecambe & Wise ; with help from Michael Freedland. — London : Barker, c1981. — xii,132p,[16]p of plates : ill ; 24cm
ISBN 0-213-16803-0 : £6.95 B81-34793

791'.092'2 — Great Britain. Entertainments. Grade *(Family)*
Davies, Hunter. The Grades : the first family of British entertainment / Hunter Davies. — London : Weidenfeld and Nicolson, 1981. — xv,268p,[24]p of plates : ill,ports,1geneal.table
Includes index
ISBN 0-297-77953-2 : £8.95 B81-37936

791'.092'4 — Comedy. Allen, Woody — *Biographies*
Palmer, Myles. Woody Allen : an illustrated biography / by Myles Palmer. — London (Bremar House, Sale Place, W2 1PT) : Proteus, 1980. — 142p : ill,ports ; 28cm
List of films: p139-142
ISBN 0-906071-41-0 (cased) : £6.50
ISBN 0-906071-39-9 (pbk) : £3.95 B81-03568

791'.092'4 — Comedy. Burns, George — *Biographies*
Burns, George. The third time around / George Burns. — London : W.H. Allen, c1980. — 219p,[32]p of plates : 1facsim,ports ; 24cm
ISBN 0-491-02932-2 : £6.95 B81-23357

791'.092'4 — Comedy. Chapman, Graham, *1941-* — *Biographies*
Chapman, Graham, *1941-*. A liar's autobiography : volume VII / by Graham Chapman and David Sherlock and also Alex Martin Oh, and David Yallop and also too by Douglas Adams (whose autobiography it isn't) ; with drawings by Jonathan Hills. — London : Eyre Methuen, 1980. — 239p : ill ; 23cm
ISBN 0-413-47570-0 : £5.95 B81-03739

791'.092'4 — Comedy. Hope, Bob — *Biographies*
Thompson, Charles. Bob Hope. — London : Thames Methuen, Sept.1981. — [272]p
ISBN 0-423-00040-3 : £7.50 : CIP entry
B81-22641

791'.092'4 — Entertainments. Grenfell, Joyce — *Biographies*
Grenfell, Joyce. In pleasant places / Joyce Grenfell. — London : Futura, 1980, c1979. — 288p,[8]p of plates : ill,ports ; 18cm
Originally published: London : Macmillan, 1979. — Includes index
ISBN 0-7088-1906-0 (pbk) : £1.50 B81-04893

Joyce / by herself and her friends ; edited by Reggie Grenfell and Richard Garnett. — London : Macmillan, 1980. — 200p,[5]p of plates : ill,ports ; 24cm
Includes index
ISBN 0-333-30673-2 : £7.95 B81-12689

Joyce by herself and her friends / edited by Reggie Grenfell and Richard Garnett. — London : Macdonald Futura, 1981, c1980. — 200p,[4]p of plates : ill,ports ; 18cm
Originally published: London : Macmillan, 1980. — Includes index
ISBN 0-7088-2078-6 (pbk) : £1.25 B81-33208

791'.092'4 — Great Britain. Entertainments. Davis, Clifford — *Biographies*
Davis, Clifford. How I made Lew Grade a millionaire - and other fables : almost an autobiography / Clifford Davis. — London : Mirror Books, 1981. — 208p,[8]p of plates : 1facsim,ports ; 18cm
Includes index
ISBN 0-85939-247-3 (pbk) : £1.95 B81-23167

791'.092'4 — Great Britain. Entertainments. Graham, Marjorie — *Biographies*
Graham, Marjorie. Love, dears! : recorded during 1972 and 1973 / Marjorie Graham. — London : Dobson, 1980. — 96p ; 23cm. — (Ordinary lives ; 4)
ISBN 0-234-72138-3 : £5.95 B81-03728

791'.0941 — British comedy, *1960-1980*
Wilmut, Roger. From fringe to flying circus : celebrating a unique generation of comedy 1960-1980 / Roger Wilmut ; preface by Bamber Gascoigne. — London : Eyre Methuen, 1980. — xxii,264p : ill,facsims,ports ; 26cm
Ill on lining papers. — Includes index
ISBN 0-413-46950-6 : £7.95 : CIP rev.
B80-07928

791'.0941 — Great Britain. Entertainments — *Serials*
Show biz. — No.1 (Mar. 7, 1980)-no.13 (May 30th, 1980). — London (54 Fleet St., EC4Y 1LJ) : Biz Productions, 1980-1980. — 13v. : ill ; 45cm
Weekly
ISSN 0260-3314 = Show biz : £0.25 per issue
B81-04589

791'.09423'38 — Dorset. Bournemouth. Entertainments, *1882-1908*
Barber, Graeme. Bournemouth holiday resort 1882 to 1908 / Graeme Barber. — Bournemouth (The Teachers' Centre, 40 Lowther Rd., Bournemouth [BH8 8NR]) : Bournemouth Local Studies Publications, 1980. — 23p : ill ; 21cm. — (Bournemouth local studies publications ; no.652)
Bibliography: p22-23
ISBN 0-906287-28-6 (pbk) : £0.30 B81-03908

791'.09426'59 — Cambridgeshire. Cambridge. Entertainments — *Calendars* — *Serials*
Cambridge roundabout. — Nov.7th-20th [1980]-Mar.21st-Apr.3rd [1981]. — Cambridge (36 Grantchester Rd, Cambridge) : Cambridge Marketing, 1980-1981. — v. : ill,ports ; 30cm
Fortnightly
£0.30 B81-32260

791.1 — PUBLIC ENTERTAINMENT. TRAVELLING SHOWS

791'.1'0924 — Entertainments: Fairs. Blondini, Michael — *Biographies*
Thomas, Gordon. Bed of nails. — Dublin : O'Brien Press, Sept.1981. — [230]p
ISBN 0-86278-006-3 : £6.30 : CIP entry
B81-22586

791'.1'0924 — Norfolk. Thursford. Fairground equipment powered by steam engines. Preservation. Cushing, George — *Biographies*
Cushing, George. Steam at Thursford. — Newton Abbot : David & Charles, Feb.1982. — [200]p
ISBN 0-7153-8154-7 : £7.95 : CIP entry
B81-35822

791.3 — CIRCUSES

791.3'022'2 — Circuses — *Illustrations* — *For children*
My first book of the circus. — London : Dean, [1980]. — [8]p : all col.ill ; 15cm. — (A Dean board book)
ISBN 0-603-00239-0 (pbk) : £0.25 B81-06337

791.3'3'09 — Clowns, *to 1979*
Hugill, Beryl. Bring on the clowns / Beryl Hugill. — Newton Abbot : David & Charles, c1980. — 224p : ill(some col.),ports(some col.) ; 30cm
Bibliography: p219-220. - Includes index
ISBN 0-7153-7846-5 : £9.50 : CIP rev.
B80-13494

791.3'3'0924 — Circuses. Clowns: Campbell, William — *Biographies*
Campbell, William. Villi the clown. — London : Faber, Sept.1981. — [255]p
ISBN 0-571-11794-5 : £7.50 : CIP entry
B81-23776

791.3'3'0924 — England. Clowns: Grimaldi, Joseph — *Biographies*
Neville, Giles. Incidents in the life of Joseph Grimaldi / by Giles Neville ; paintings by Patricia Neville. — London : Cape, 1980. — 61p : col.ill ; 26cm
ISBN 0-224-01869-8 : £4.95 B81-00223

791.3'3'0924 — England. Clowns: Purvis, Billy — *Biographies* — *Early works*
The Life of Billy Purvis : facsimile of edition of 1875. — Newcastle upon Tyne : Frank Graham, 1981. — 149p : ill ; 19cm
Facsim. of edition published Newcastle-upon-Tyne : T. Arthur, 1875
ISBN 0-85983-176-0 (pbk) : £2.50 B81-14021

791.43 — CINEMA

791.43 — Award-winning cinema films, *1930-1980*
Pickard, Roy. The award movies : a complete guide from A to Z / Roy Pickard. — London : Muller, 1980. — 294p,[48]p of plates : ill,ports ; 25cm
Includes index
ISBN 0-584-10370-0 : £10.95 : CIP rev.
B80-26008

791.43 — Books on cinema films: Books in English — *Critical studies*
Armour, Robert A.. Film : a reference guide / Robert A. Armour. — Westport, Conn. ; London : Greenwood Press, 1980. — xxiv,251p ; 25cm. — (American popular culture, ISSN 0193-6859)
Includes bibliographies and index
ISBN 0-313-22241-x : £19.50
Also classified at 016.79143 B81-23593

791.43 — Cinema films. Authorship. Theories
Theories of authorship : a reader / edited by John Caughie. — London : Routledge & Kegan Paul in association with the British Film Institute, 1981. — ix,316p,[4]p of plates : ill ; 23cm. — (British Film Institute readers film studies)
Bibliography: p302-308. — Includes index
ISBN 0-7100-0649-7 : £11.95
ISBN 0-7100-0650-0 (pbk) : £5.95 B81-18665

791.43 — Cinema films — *Critical studies*
Heath, Stephen. Questions of cinema / Stephen Heath. — London : Macmillan, 1981. — viii,257p : ill ; 22cm. — (Communications and culture)
Includes index
ISBN 0-333-26122-4 (cased) : £12.50
ISBN 0-333-19528-7 (pbk) : Unpriced
B81-38629

791.43 — Cinema films - *For children*
Hill, Gordon. Secrets of film and television. — Sevenoaks : Hodder & Stoughton, May 1981. — [128]p
ISBN 0-340-25496-3 (pbk) : £0.95 : CIP entry
Also classified at 791.45 B81-05158

791.43 — Cinema films. Radicalism. Influence of Brecht, Bertolt
Walsh, Martin. The Brechtian aspect of radical cinema / Martin Walsh ; edited by Keith M. Griffiths. — London : BFI Publishing, 1981. — 136p : ill,ports ; 21cm
Bibliography: p134-136
ISBN 0-85170-112-4 (spiral) : £4.25 : CIP rev.
B81-07940

791.43'01 — Cinema films. Aesthetics
Bordwell, David. Film art : an introduction / David Bordwell, Kristin Thompson. — Reading, Mass. ; London : Addison-Wesley, c1979 (1980 printing). — xi,339p,[2]p of plates : ill(some col.) ; 24cm. — (Addison-Wesley series in speech, drama, and film)
Bibliography: p322-326. — Includes index
ISBN 0-201-00566-2 (pbk) : £6.95 B81-40412

791.43'0232'0924 — American cinema films. Production. Selznick, David O. — *Biographies*
Haver, Ronald. David O. Selznick's Hollywood / written & produced by Ronald Haver. — London : Secker & Warburg, 1980. — ix,425p : ill(some col.),facsims(some col.),ports(some col.) ; 37cm
List of films: p414-417. - Includes index
ISBN 0-436-19128-8 : £35.00 B81-07119

791.43'0233 — Cinema films directed by Bergman, Ingmar - *Critical studies*

Moseley, Philip. Ingmar Bergman. — London : Marion Boyars, June 1981. — [192]p
ISBN 0-7145-2644-4 : £8.95 : CIP entry
B81-09486

791.43'0233'0922 — American cinema films, *1957-1978.* **Directors** — *Critical studies*

Close up : the contemporary director / general editor Jon Tuska ; associate editor Vicki Piekarski ; research editor David Wilson. — Metuchen ; London : Scarecrow, 1981. — v,431p : ill,ports ; 23cm
Includes index
ISBN 0-8108-1366-1 : £15.75 B81-17099

791.43'0233'0922 — American cinema films. Directors, *to 1980*

Gianneth, Louis D.. Masters of the American cinema / Louis Gianneth. — Englewood Cliffs ; London : Prentice-Hill, c1981. — xiv,466p : ill,ports ; 24cm
Includes bibliographies and index
ISBN 0-13-560110-x (cased) : £12.55
ISBN 0-13-560102-9 (pbk) : £9.05 B81-37176

791.43'0233'0924 — American cinema films. Directing. Ford, John, *1895-1973*

Anderson, Lindsay. About John Ford— / Lindsay Anderson. — London : Plexus, c1981. — 256p : ill,ports ; 26cm
List of films:. p248-254 Includes index
ISBN 0-85965-013-8 (cased) : £12.00 : CIP rev.
ISBN 0-85965-014-6 (pbk) : Unpriced
B80-17891

791.43'0233'0924 — American cinema films. Directing. Griffith, David Wark — *Biographies*

Williams, Martin. Griffith : first artist of the movies / Martin Williams. — New York ; Oxford : Oxford University Press, 1980. — xiii,171p : ill,ports ; 22cm
Bibliography: p163-165. - Includes index
ISBN 0-19-502685-3 : £7.95 B81-00224

791.43'0233'0924 — American cinema films. Directing. Huston, John, *1906-* — *Biographies*

Huston, John, *1906-*. An open book / John Huston. — London : Macmillan, 1981, c1980. — 389p : ill,ports ; 24cm
Originally published: New York : Knopf, 1980. — Includes index
ISBN 0-333-31014-4 : £8.95 B81-21787

791.43'0233'0924 — American cinema films. Directing. Polanski, Roman — *Biographies*

Kiernan, Thomas. [The Roman Polanski story]. Repulsion : the life and times of Roman Polanski / Thomas Kiernan. — London : New English Library, 1981, c1980. — 288p,[24]p of plates : ill,ports ; 23cm
Originally published: New York : Grove Press, 1980
ISBN 0-450-04837-3 : £7.95 B81-27113

791.43'0233'0924 — American cinema films. Directing. Wilder, Billy — *Critical studies*

Sinyard, Neil. Journey down Sunset Boulevard : the films of Billy Wilder / Neil Sinyard and Adrian Turner. — Ryde : BCW Publishing, 1979. — xiv,366p : ill ; 23cm
List of films: p354-359. — Includes index
ISBN 0-904159-62-0 : £8.95 B81-04076

791.43'0233'0924 — Austrian cinema films. Directing. Von Sternberg, Josef — *Critical studies*

Sternberg / edited by Peter Baxter. — London : BFI, 1980. — 144p : ill ; 22cm
Bibliography: p143. - List of films: p130-142
ISBN 0-85170-098-5 (cased) : £6.45
ISBN 0-85170-099-3 (pbk) : £3.25 B81-04583

791.43'0233'0924 — British documentary films. Directing. Jennings, Humphrey — *Biographies*

Humphrey Jennings. — London : BFI Publishing, Jan.1982. — [72]p
ISBN 0-85170-118-3 (pbk) : £3.25 : CIP entry
B81-38854

791.43'0233'0924 — Cinema films. Directing. Altman, Robert — *Critical studies*

Karp, Alan. The films of Robert Altman / by Alan Karp. — Metuchen ; London : Scarecrow, 1981. — 171p : ill ; 23cm
Bibliography: p159-165. — Includes index
ISBN 0-8108-1408-0 : £7.00 B81-26912

791.43'0233'0924 — Cinema films. Directing. Borzage, Frank — *Critical studies*

Lamster, Frederick. Souls made great through love and adversity : the film work of Frank Borzage / by Frederick Lamster. — Metuchen ; London : Scarecrow, 1981. — xi,320p : ill ; 23cm
Bibliography: p214-226. — List of films: p195-213. - Includes index
ISBN 0-8108-1404-8 : £8.75 B81-27285

791.43'0233'0924 — Cinema films. Directing. Hawks, Howard — *Critical studies*

Wood, Robin, *1931-*. Howard Hawks / Robin Wood. — Rev. ed. — [London] : BFI Publishing, 1981. — 216p : ill,1port ; 20cm
Previous ed.: London : Warburg, 1968. — List of films: p188-215
ISBN 0-85170-111-6 (pbk) : £3.95 : CIP rev.
B81-28816

791.43'0233'0924 — Danish cinema films. Directing. Dreyer, Carl Theodor — *Critical studies*

Bordwell, David. The films of Carl-Theodor Dreyer / David Bordwell. — Berkeley ; London : University of California Press, 1981. — 251p : ill,ports ; 26cm
Bibliography: p242-248. — List of films: p203-277. — Includes index
ISBN 0-520-03987-4 : £17.50 B81-39754

791.43'0233'0924 — German cinema films. Directing. Lang, Fritz — *Critical studies*

Fritz Lang : the image and the look / edited by Stephen Jenkins. — London : B.F.I. Publishing, 1981. — 173p : ill ; 22cm
ISBN 0-85170-108-6 (cased) : Unpriced : CIP rev.
ISBN 0-85170-109-4 (pbk) : £3.95 B81-07937

791.43'026'0979494 — California. Los Angeles. Hollywood. Cinema films. Costumes. Design, *to 1976*

LaVine, W. Robert. In a glamorous fashion : the fabulous years of Hollywood costume design / W. Robert LaVine ; special assistant and photo consultant Allen Florio. — London : Allen & Unwin, 1981 c1980. — xi,259p : ill,ports ; 28cm
Originally published: New York : Scribner, 1980. — Bibliography: p250-252
ISBN 0-04-391004-1 : £10.95 : CIP rev.
B81-02351

791.43'028 — Cinema films. Stunting

MiKlowitz, Gloria D.. Movie stunts : and the people who do them / Gloria D. MiKlowitz. — New York ; London : Harcourt Brace Jovanovich, c1980. — 64p : ill,ports ; 22cm
Includes index
ISBN 0-15-256038-6 (cased) : Unpriced
ISBN 0-15-256039-4 (pbk) : £1.95 B81-17271

791.43'028'0922 — American cinema films. Acting. Barrymore *(Family)* — *Biographies*

Kotsilibas-Davis, James. The Barrymores : the royal family in Hollywood / by James Kotsilibas-Davis. — London : Arthur Barker, 1981. — 376p : ill,facsims,ports ; 25cm
List of films: p338-366. — Bibliography: p367-368. — Includes index
ISBN 0-213-16805-7 : £9.95 B81-25065

791.43'028'0922 — California. Los Angeles. Hollywood. Cinema films. Acting. Stars, *1915-1979* — *Personal observations* — *Collections*

Close-ups : intimate profiles of movie stars / by their co-stars, directors, screenwriters and friends ; edited by Danny Peary. — Leicester : Windward, c1978. — xvi,606p : ill,ports ; 29cm
Includes index
ISBN 0-7112-0051-3 : £5.95 B81-04909

791.43'028'0922 — California. Los Angeles. Hollywood. Cinema films. Acting. Stars, *1930-1950*

Norman, Barry. The Hollywood greats / Barry Norman. — London : Arrow, 1980, c1979. — 271p,[47]p of plates : ports ; 18cm
Originally published: London : Hodder & Stoughton, 1979. — Includes index
ISBN 0-09-924030-0 (pbk) : £1.95 B81-01973

791.43'028'0922 — California. Los Angeles. Hollywood. Cinema films. Acting. Stars. Social life, *ca 1930-ca 1940*

Finch, Christopher. Gone Hollywood / by Christopher Finch and Linda Rosenkrantz. — London : Weidenfeld and Nicolson, 1980, c1979. — xii,396p : ill,ports ; 24cm
Originally published: Garden City, N.Y. : Doubleday, 1979. — Bibliography: p369-376. — Includes index
ISBN 0-297-77860-9 : £8.95 B81-08246

791.43'028'0922 — Cinema films. Acting. Stars, *1967-1980*

Castell, David. Screen stars of the 70's / David Castell. — Godalming : LSP, c1981. — 141p : ill(some col.) ; 30cm
List of films: p128-136
ISBN 0-85321-082-9 (pbk) : £3.95 B81-26628

791.43'028'0922 — Cinema films. Acting. Stars — *Biographies*

Norman, Barry. The movie greats / Barry Norman. — London : Hodder and Stoughton, 1981. — 319p : ill,ports ; 24cm
Includes index
ISBN 0-340-25972-8 : £7.95 : CIP rev.
B81-10416

791.43'028'0922 — Cinema films: Horror films. Actors — *Biographies*

Pitts, Michael R.. Horror film stars / Michael R. Pitts. — Jefferson, N.C. : McFarland ; Folkestone : distributed by Bailey & Swinfen, 1981. — vii,324p : ill,ports ; 24cm
Bibliography: p303-306. — Includes index
ISBN 0-89950-003-x (cased) : £13.55
ISBN 0-89950-004-8 (pbk) : Unpriced
B81-37035

791.43'028'0924 — America cinema films. Acting. Poitier, Sydney — *Biographies*

Poitier, Sidney. This life / Sidney Poitier. — London : Hodder and Stoughton, 1980. — 374p,[24]p of plates : ports ; 24cm
ISBN 0-340-25654-0 : £7.95 : CIP rev.
B80-12464

Poitier, Sydney. This life. — London : Coronet, Apr.1981. — [448]p
Originally published
ISBN 0-340-26673-2 (pbk) : £1.50 : CIP entry
B81-02651

791.43'028'0924 — American cinema films. Acting. Chaplin, Charles, *1889-1977* — *Biographies*

Chaplin, Charles, *1889-1977*. My early years / Charles Chaplin. — London : Heinemann Educational, 1981, c1964. — 192p,[16]p of plates : ill,facsims,ports ; 20cm
Originally published: in My autobiography. London : Bodley Head, 1964
ISBN 0-435-12252-5 : £1.75 B81-29185

791.43'028'0924 — American cinema films. Acting. Cooper, Gary — *Biographies*

Swindell, Larry. The last hero : a biography of Gary Cooper / Larry Swindell. — London : Robson, 1981. — xiv,343,[32]p of plates : ill,ports ; 23cm
Includes index
ISBN 0-86051-132-4 : £7.50 B81-10519

791.43'028'0924 — American cinema films. Acting. Davis, Bette, *1908-* — *Biographies*

Higham, Charles. Bette. — London : New English Library, Oct.1981. — [256]p
ISBN 0-450-04875-6 : £7.95 : CIP entry
B81-31954

791.43′028′0924 — American cinema films. Acting. Flynn, Errol — *Biographies*

Flynn, Errol. My wicked, wicked ways / Errol Flynn. — London : Pan Books in association with Heinemann, 1961, c1959 (1979 printing). — 379p ; 18cm
Originally published: New York : Putnam′s, 1959 ; London : Heinemann, 1960
ISBN 0-330-23343-2 (pbk) : £1.25 B81-19799

Higham, Charles, *1931-*. Errol Flynn, the untold story / Charles Higham. — London : Granada, 1980 (1981 [printing]). — 416p,[8]p of plates : facsim,ports ; 18cm. — (A Mayflower book)
ISBN 0-583-13440-8 (pbk) : £1.95 B81-24934

791.43′028′0924 — American cinema films. Acting. Garbo, Greta — *Biographies*

Sands, Frederick. The divine Garbo / Frederick Sands and Sven Broman. — London : Sidgwick & Jackson in association with New English Library, 1979 (1981 [printing]). — 160p,16p of plates : ill,ports ; 18cm
Originally published: New York : Grosset & Dunlap 1919. — Includes index
ISBN 0-283-98752-9 (pbk) : £1.75 B81-17202

791.43′028′0924 — American cinema films. Acting. Granger, Stewart — *Biographies*

Granger, Stewart. Sparks fly upward / Stewart Granger. — London : Granada, 1981. — 416p,[24]p of plates : ill,ports ; 24cm
Includes index
ISBN 0-246-11403-7 : £7.95 B81-12136

791.43′028′0924 — American cinema films. Acting. Grant, Cary — *Biographies*

Godfrey, Lionel. Cary Grant : the light touch / Lionel Godfrey. — London : Hale, 1981. — 224p,[24]p of plates : ill,ports ; 23cm
Bibliography: p203-204. — Includes index
ISBN 0-7091-9038-7 : £6.95 B81-26955

791.43′028′0924 — American cinema films. Acting. Keaton, Buster — *Biographies*

Dardis, Tom. Keaton : the man who wouldn′t lie down / Tom Dardis. — Harmondsworth : Penguin, 1980, c1979. — xi,340p : ill,ports ; 20cm
Originally published: New York : Scribner, 1979. — Bibliography: p329-331. — List of films: p285-317. — Includes index
ISBN 0-14-005701-3 (pbk) : £2.50 B81-21116

791.43′028′0924 — American cinema films. Acting. Lovelace, Linda — *Biographies*

Lovelace, Linda. Ordeal / Linda Lovelace with Mike McGrady. — [London] : Star, 1981, c1980. — 206p ; 18cm
Originally published: Seacaucus : Citadel, 1980
ISBN 0-352-30857-5 (corrected : pbk) B81-15068

Lovelace, Linda. Ordeal / by Linda Lovelace with Mike McGrady. — London : W.H. Allen, 1981, c1980. — 206p ; 24cm
Originally published: Seacaucus : Citadel, 1980
ISBN 0-491-02903-9 : £6.95 B81-26444

791.43′028′0924 — American cinema films. Acting. McQueen, Steve — *Biographies*

McCoy, Malachy. Steve McQueen : the unauthorized biography / Malachy McCoy. — [New ed.]. — Sevenoaks : Coronet, 1981, c1980. — 224p,[12]p of plates : ill,ports ; 18cm
Previous ed.: London : Hale, 1974
ISBN 0-340-27059-4 (pbk) : £1.25 B81-21912

791.43′028′0924 — American cinema films. Acting. Peck, Gregory - *Biographies*

Freedland, Michael. Gregory Peck. — London : Hodder and Stoughton, Aug.1981. — [296]p
Originally published: London : W.H. Allen, 1980
ISBN 0-340-26681-3 (pbk) : £1.75 : CIP entry B81-18145

791.43′028′0924 — American cinema films. Acting. Swanson, Gloria — *Biographies*

Swanson, Gloria. Swanson on Swanson / Gloria Swanson. — London : Joseph, 1981, c1980. — vi,535p,[48]p of plates : ill,ports ; 25cm
Originally published: New York : Random House, c1980. — Includes index
ISBN 0-7181-1990-8 : £9.95 B81-15202

791.43′028′0924 — American cinema films. Acting. Winters, Shelley — *Biographies*

Winters, Shelley. Shelley : also known as Shirley / Shelley Winters. — London : Granada, 1981. — 511p : ill,ports ; 24cm
ISBN 0-246-11496-7 : £7.95 B81-15631

791.43′028′0924 — British cinema films. Acting. Sellers, Peter — *Biographies*

Sellers, Michael. P.S. I love you. — London : Collins, Sept.1981. — [256]p
ISBN 0-00-216648-8 : £8.95 : CIP entry B81-20469

791.43′028′0924 — Cinema films. Acting. Bergman, Ingrid — *Biographies*

Bergman, Ingrid. Ingrid Bergman : my story / by Ingrid Bergman and Alan Burgess. — London : Joseph, 1980. — 480p,[64]p of plates : ill,ports ; 24cm
Includes index
ISBN 0-7181-1946-0 : £9.50 B81-01940

791.43′028′0924 — Cinema films. Acting. Dors, Diana — *Biographies*

Dors, Diana. Behind closed Dors / Diana Dors ; associate editer Jack Hobbs. — London : W.H. Allen, 1979. — 208p : ill,ports ; 18cm. — (A Star book)
ISBN 0-352-30335-2 (pbk) : £0.95 : B81-21753

791.43′028′0924 — Cinema films. Acting. Ekland, Britt — *Biographies*

Ekland, Britt. True Britt / Britt Ekland. — London : Sphere, 1980. — 245p,[16]p of plates : ports ; 18cm
List of films: p244-245
ISBN 0-7221-3270-0 (pbk) : £1.50 B81-17874

791.43′028′0924 — Cinema films. Acting. Loren, Sophia — *Biographies*

Levy, Alan. Forever, Sophia : an intimate portrait / by Alan Levy. — London : Hale, 1980, c1979. — xi,227p,[16]p of plates : ill,ports ; 23cm
Originally published: London : Magnum Books, 1979
ISBN 0-7091-8594-4 : £6.50 B81-00225

791.43′028′0924 — Cinema films. Acting. Mason, James, *1909-* — *Biographies*

Mason, James, *1909-*. Before I forget / autobiography and drawings by James Mason. — London : Hamilton, 1981. — x,345p,16p of plates : ill ; 25cm
Includes index
ISBN 0-241-10677-x : £9.95 : CIP rev. B81-20177

791.43′028′0924 — Cinema films. Acting. Sellers, Peter — *Biographies*

Evans, Peter, *1933-*. Peter Sellers : the mask behind the mask / Peter Evans. — Rev. and updated ed. — London : Severn House, 1981, c1980. — 256,[16]p of plates : ill,ports ; 21cm
Previous ed.: London : Frewin, 1969. — List of films: p248-250. — Includes index
ISBN 0-7278-0688-2 : £7.95 B81-14064

Sellers, Michael, *1954-*. P.S. I love you : Peter Sellers 1925-1980 / Michael Sellers with Sarah and Victoria Sellers. — London : Collins, 1981. — 238p,[24]p of plates : ill,facsims,ports ; 23cm
ISBN 0-00-216649-6 : £7.95 B81-39859

Sylvester, Derek. Peter Sellers / Derek Sylvester. — London : Proteus, 1981. — 128p ill(some col.) : ports ; 29cm
List of films: p119-128
ISBN 0-906071-51-8 (cased) : £7.95 B81-37953

791.43′028′0924 — Cinema films. Acting. Todd, Ann — *Biographies*

Todd, Ann. The eighth veil / Ann Todd. — London : Kimber, 1980. — 173p,[24]p of plates : ill,ports ; 24cm
Includes index
ISBN 0-7183-0387-3 : £8.50 B81-01564

791.43′028′0924 — Cinema films. Acting. Topol, Chaim — *Biographies*

Topol, Chaim. Topol / by Topol. — London : Weidenfeld and Nicolson, c1981. — 222p,[12]p of plates : ill,ports ; 25cm
Includes index
ISBN 0-297-77919-2 : £8.50 B81-37931

791.43′05 — Cinema films — *Serials*

Film review. — 1980-81. — London : W.H. Allen, 1980. — 181p
ISBN 0-491-02711-7 : £9.95 B81-02748

[Films *(London)*]. Films. — Vol.1, no.1 (Dec.1980)-. — London (34 Buckingham Palace Rd, SW1) : Thelmill, 1980-. — v. : ill ; 29cm
Monthly. — Cover title: Films on screen and video. — Description based on: Vol.1, no.7 (June 1981)
ISSN 0261-8001 = Films (London) : £14.00 per year B81-33726

John Willis′ screen world. — Vol.31 (1980). — London : Frederick Muller, c1980. — 255p
ISBN 0-584-97068-4 : Unpriced B81-17491

Movie news. — No.1, (Sept. 1980)-. — Isle of Wight (40 Union Street, Isle of Wight, PO33 2LP) : Spartacus Publ., 1980-. — v. : ill ; 30cm
Monthly
ISSN 0260-5090 = Movie news : £9.75 per year B81-02020

791.43′076 — Cinema films — *Questions & answers*

Burt, Rob. The illustrated movie quiz book / written & designed by Rob Burt ; foreword by Barry Norman. — London : Severn House, c1981. — 96p : ill,ports ; 27cm
ISBN 0-7278-2008-7 (pbk) : £2.95 : CIP rev. B81-06600

791.43′09 — Cinema films, *to 1979*

Robertson, Patrick. The Guinness book of film facts and feats / Patrick Robertson ; [editor: Anne Marshall]. — Enfield : Guinness Superlatives, c1980. — 288p : ill(some col.),facsims(some col.),ports ; 25cm
Includes index
ISBN 0-85112-209-4 : £8.95 B81-19764

791.43′09 — Cinema films, *to 1980*

Monaco, James. How to read a film : the art, technology, language, history and theory of film and media / James Monaco ; with diagrams by David Lindroth. — Rev. ed. — New York ; Oxford : Oxford University Press, 1981. — xv,533p : ill,ports ; 24cm
Previous ed.: 1977. — Bibliography: p465-493. — Includes index
ISBN 0-19-502802-3 (cased) : Unpriced
ISBN 0-19-502806-6 (pbk) : £5.95
Also classified at 791.45′09 B81-38069

The **Movie**. — London : Orbis, c1981. — 52v. : ill(some col.),ports(some col.) ; 29cm
£35.20 (pbk) B81-39010

791.43′09′0916 — Cinema films: Horror films, *to 1977*

Butler, Ivan. Horror in the cinema / Ivan Butler. — 3rd ed., rev. — South Brunswick : Barnes ; London : Yoseloff, c1979. — 162p : ill ; 29cm
Previous ed.: London : Zwemmer, 1970. — Includes index
ISBN 0-498-02137-8 : Unpriced B81-21746

791.43′09′093278 — European cinema films: Westerns, *ca 1910-1977*

Frayling, Christopher. Spaghetti westerns : cowboys and Europeans from Karl May to Sergio Leone / Christopher Frayling. — London : Routledge & Kegan Paul, 1981. — xvi,304p : ill,ports ; 25cm. — (Cinema and society)
Bibliography: p289-294. - List of films: p256-266. - Includes index
ISBN 0-7100-0503-2 (cased) : £15.95 : CIP rev.
ISBN 0-7100-0504-0 (pbk) : £8.95 B80-13013

791.43′09′09353 — American cinema films, *to 1976.* **Special themes: Masculinity**
Spoto, Donald. Camerado : Hollywood and the American man / by Donald Spoto. — New York ; London : New American Library, 1978. — xi,238p : ports ; 21cm. — (A Plume book)
Includes index
ISBN 0-452-25186-9 (pbk) : Unpriced
B81-18782

791.43′09′09353 — Cinema films. Special themes: Homosexuality
Russo, Vito. The celluloid closet : homosexuality in the movies / Vito Russo. — Cambridge [Mass.] ; London : Harper & Row, c1981. — xii,276p : ill,facsims ; 25cm
List of films: p247-260. — Includes index
ISBN 0-06-337019-0 (cased) : £7.95
ISBN 0-06-090871-8 (pbk) : Unpriced
B81-35440

791.43′09′09358 — American cinema films: War films, *1945-1970*
Rubin, Steven Ray. Combat films : American realism : 1945-1970 / by Steven Jay Rubin. — Jefferson, N.C. : McFarland ; Folkestone : distributed by Bailey & Swinfen, 1981. — xii,233p : ill,ports ; 24cm
Includes index
ISBN 0-89950-013-7 (cased) : £12.75
ISBN 0-89950-014-5 (pbk) : Unpriced
B81-37037

791.43′092′2 — British cinema films. Korda *(Family) — Personal observations*
Korda, Michael. Charmed lives : a family romance / Michael Korda. — Harmondsworth : Penguin, 1980, c1979. — 498p,[32]p of plates : ill,ports ; 20cm
Originally published: New York : Random House, 1979 ; London : A. Lane, 1980. — Includes index
ISBN 0-14-005402-2 (pbk) : £2.50 B81-07029

791.43′092′2 — Cinema films — *Biographies*
Thomson, David, *1941-*. A biographical dictionary of the cinema / David Thomson. — London : Secker & Warburg, 1980. — v,682p ; 25cm
Previous ed.: 1975
ISBN 0-436-52012-5 (cased) : £15.00
ISBN 0-436-52013-3 (pbk) : £5.95 B81-03541

791.43′092′4 — British cinema films, *to 1914 — Personal observations*
Furniss, Harry. Our lady cinema / Harry Furniss. — New York ; London : Garland, 1978. — 208p : ill ; 19cm. — (The Garland classics of film literature)
Facsim. of edition published Bristol : Arrowsmith, 1914
ISBN 0-8240-2874-0 : Unpriced B81-25529

791.43′0941 — Great Britain. Independent cinema films, *1930-1939*
Traditions of independence : British cinema in the thirties / edited by Don Macpherson in collaboration with Paul Willemen. — London : British Film Institute, 1980. — 226p ; 21cm
Bibliography: p225-226
ISBN 0-85170-093-4 (pbk) : £3.95 B81-01762

791.43′09422 — Southern English cinema films, *to 1921 — Illustrations*
Early film makers of the South Coast. — [Chichester] ([29 Little London, Chichester PO19 1PB]) : [Chichester District Museum], [1981?]. — [15]p : chiefly ill ; 15cm
Published to accompany an exhibition at the Museum. — Cover title. — Bibliography: back inside cover
£0.50 (pbk) B81-37215

791.43′09425′6 — Bedfordshire. Cinemas, *to 1980*
Peck, G. C.. Bedfordshire cinemas / G.C. Peck. — [Bedford] ([County Hall, Bedford, MK42 9AP]) : Bedfordshire County Library, 1981. — [36]p : ill,facsims,1port ; 21x30cm
Cover title
ISBN 0-901051-92-6 (pbk) : Unpriced
B81-40652

791.43′09426 — East Anglia. Cinemas, *to 1979*
Peart, Stephen. The picture house in East Anglia / by Stephen Peart. — Lavenham : Dalton, 1980. — xi,180p : ill,1facsim,ports ; 24cm
Bibliography: p175. — Includes index
ISBN 0-900963-56-5 : £7.95 B81-03228

791.43′0943 — German cinema films, *1933-1945*
Petley, Julian. Capital and culture : German cinema 1933-45 / Julian Petley. — London : British Film Institute, c1979. — 162p ; 21cm
Bibliography: p161-162
ISBN 0-85170-088-8 (pbk) : £2.45 B81-01062

791.43′0943 — German cinema films, *1950-1980 — Critical studies*
Sandford, John. The new German cinema / John Sandford. — London : Wolff, c1980. — 180p : ill,ports ; 24cm
Bibliography: p169-170. — List of films: p176-179. — Includes index
ISBN 0-85496-404-5 : £10.95 : CIP rev.
B80-17892

791.43′0947 — Soviet cinema films, *to 1980*
Vorontsov, IU.. The phenomenon of the Soviet cinema / Yuri Voronstov, Igor Rachuk ; [translated from the Russian by Doris Bradbury]. — Moscow : Progress ; [London] : Distributed by Central Books, c1980. — 422p,[80]p of plates : ill,ports ; 18cm
Translation of: Fenomen sovetskogo kinematografa. — List of films: p392-423
ISBN 0-7147-1613-8 : £3.95 B81-27750

791.43′0973 — American cinema films, *1930-1976*
Medved, Harry. The fifty worst movies of all time : (and how they got that way) / by Harry Medved with Randy Dreyfuss. — London : Angus & Robertson, 1979. — 288p : ill,ports ; 29cm
Originally published: New York : Popular Library, 1978. — Includes index
ISBN 0-207-95891-2 (cased) : £7.95
ISBN 0-207-95892-0 (pbk) : £4.95 B81-03986

791.43′0973 — American cinema films, *1968-1975 — Critical studies*
Monaco, James. American film now : the people, the power, the money, the movies / James Monaco ; with four maps of the film industry by David Lindroth. — New York ; London : New American Library, 1979. — 540p : ill,ports ; 24cm. — (A Plume book)
Bibliography: p459-470. — List of films: p423-458. — Includes index
ISBN 0-452-25212-1 (pbk) : Unpriced
B81-40456

791.43′0973 — American cinema films, *to 1978*
Earley, Steven C.. An introduction to American movies / Steven C. Earley. — New York : New American Library ; London : New English Library, 1978. — xii,337p,[8]p of plates : ill ; 18cm. — (A Mentor book)
Bibliography: p311-315. — Includes index
ISBN 0-451-61638-3 (pbk) : £1.50 B81-01594

791.43′0973 — American silent cinema films, *1912-1920 — Illustrations*
Slide, Anthony. Fifty great American silent films 1912-1920 : a pictorial survey / Anthony Slide & Edward Wagenknecht. — New York : Dover ; London : Constable, 1980. — 139p : ill ; 28cm
ISBN 0-486-23985-3 (pbk) : £4.05 B81-18584

791.43′0973 — American silent cinema films, *to 1936 — Illustrations*
Blum, Daniel. A pictorial history of the silent screen / Daniel Blum. — London : Hamlyn, 1981, c1953. — 334p,[1]p of plates : chiefly ill,facsims,ports ; 30cm
Includes index
ISBN 0-600-34264-6 (pbk) : £6.95 B81-38555

791.43′52 — American film noir cinema films, *1941-1971.* **Characters: Women** — *Feminist viewpoints*
Women in film noir / edited by E. Ann Kaplan. — Rev. ed. — London : BFI Publishing, 1980. — 132p : ill ; 21cm
Previous ed.: 1978
ISBN 0-85170-105-1 (pbk) : £2.75 B81-01570

791.43′53 — Documentary films, *ca 1970-1979 — Interviews*
Rosenthal, Alan, *1936-*. The documentary conscience : a casebook in film making / Alan Rosenthal. — Berkeley ; London : University of California Press, c1980. — x,436p,[16]p of plates : ill,ports ; 24cm
Includes index
ISBN 0-520-03932-7 : £11.75
ISBN 0-520-04022-8 (pbk) : £4.95 B81-01698

791.43′53′0973 — American documentary films, *1931-1942*
Alexander, William, *1938-*. Film on the left : American documentary film from 1931 to 1942 / William Alexander. — Princeton ; Guildford : Princeton University Press, c1981. — xviii,355p,[12]p of plates : ill,ports ; 25cm
Bibliography: p327-340. — Includes index
ISBN 0-691-04678-6 (cased) : £16.00
ISBN 0-691-10111-6 (limited print ed.) : £7.30
B81-26850

791.43′72 — American cinema films: Empire strikes back. Production — *Correspondence, diaries, etc.*
Arnold, Alan. Once upon a galaxy : a journal of the making of The Empire strikes back / Alan Arnold. — London : Sphere, 1980. — vii,277p,[32]p of plates : ill,ports ; 18cm
ISBN 0-7221-5652-9 (pbk) : £1.25 B81-04158

791.43′72 — American cinema films — *Scripts*
42nd Street / edited with an introduction by Rocco Fumento. — Madison ; London : Published for the Wisconsin Center for Film and Theater Research by the University of Wisconsin Press, 1980. — 196p : ill,1facsim ; 23cm. — (Wisconsin/Warner Bros. screenplay series)
Bibliography: p38. — Includes screenplay by Rian James and James Seymour
ISBN 0-299-08100-1 (cased) : £9.00
ISBN 0-299-08104-4 (pbk) : Unpriced
B81-22365

Furthman, Jules. To have and have not / [Screenplay by Jules Furthman and William Faulkner ; based on the novel by Ernest Hemingway] ; edited with an introduction by Bruce F. Kawin. — Madison ; London : Published for the Wisconsin Center for Film and Theater Research by the University of Wisconsin Press, 1980. — 229p : ill ; 23cm. — (Wisconsin/Warner Bros. Screenplay series)
ISBN 0-299-08090-0 (cased) : £8.00 B81-06459

Little Caesar / edited with an introduction by Gerald Peary. — Madison ; London : Published for the Wisconsin Center for Film and Theater Research by University of Wisconsin Press, 1981. — 187p : ill ; 22cm. — (Wisconsin/Warner Bros. screenplay series)
Bibliography: p27-28. — Includes screenplay by Francis Edwards Faragoh from the novel by W.R. Burnett
ISBN 0-299-08450-7 (cased) : Unpriced
ISBN 0-299-08454-x (pbk) : £3.50 B81-38221

Mildred Pierce / edited with an introduction by Albert J. LaValley. — Madison ; London : Published for the Wisconsin Center for Film and Theater Research by the University of Wisconsin Press, 1980. — 259p : ill ; 23cm. — (Wisconsin/Warner Bros. screenplay series)
Includes screenplay by Ranald MacDougall from the novel by James M. Cain
ISBN 0-299-08370-5 (cased) : £9.00
ISBN 0-299-08374-8 (pbk) : Unpriced
B81-22363

Mission to Moscow / edited with an introduction by David Culbert. — Madison ; London : Published for the Wisconsin Center for Film and Theater Research by the University of Wisconsin Press, 1980. — 277p : ill ; 23cm. — (Wisconsin/Warner Bros. screenplay series)
Includes screenplay by Howard Koch
ISBN 0-299-08380-2 (cased) : £9.00
ISBN 0-299-08384-5 (pbk) : Unpriced
B81-22364

The **Public** enemy / edited with an introduction by Henry Cohen. — Madison ; London : Published for the Wisconsin Center for Film and Theater Research by University of Wisconsin Press, 1981. — 187p : ill ; 22cm. — (Wisconsin/Warner Bros. screenplay series)
Bibliography: p34-35. — Includes screenplay by Harvey Thew, based on the novel by Kubec Glasmon and John Bright
ISBN 0-299-08460-4 (cased) : Unpriced
ISBN 0-299-08464-7 (pbk) : £3.50 B81-38222

791.43'72 — American cinema films — *Scripts* *continuation*

Seymour, James. Gold diggers of 1933 / [Screenplay by James Seymour, David Boehm and Ben Markson ; from the stage play by Avery Hopwood] ; edited with an introduction by Arthur Hove. — Madison ; London : Published for the Wisconsin Center for Film and Theater Research by the University of Wisconsin Press, 1980. — 190p : ill ; 23cm. — (Wisconsin/Warner Bros. screenplay series)
ISBN 0-299-08080-3 (cased) : £8.00
ISBN 0-299-08084-6 (pbk) : £2.75 B81-06460

Yankee Doodle Dandy / edited with an introduction by Patrick McGilligan. — Madison ; London : Published for the Wisconsin Center for Film and Theater Research by University of Wisconsin Press, 1981. — 239p : ill,1port ; 22cm. — (Wisconsin/Warner Bros. screenplay series)
Includes screenplay by Robert Buckner and Edmund Joseph, additional material by Julius and Philip Epstein, original story by Robert Buckner
ISBN 0-299-08470-1 (cased) : Unpriced
ISBN 0-299-08474-4 (pbk) : £3.50 B81-38223

791.43'72 — British cinema films - *Scripts*

Palin, Michael. Time bandits. — London : Hutchinson, June 1981. — [160]p
ISBN 0-09-145461-1 : £4.95 : CIP entry
B81-19132

791.43'72 — British cinema films — *Scripts*

Rawlinson, Arthur. Jew Süss / Arthur Rawlinson and Dorothy Farnum. — New York ; London : Garland, 1978. — xviii,174p,[8]leaves of plates : ill ; 19cm. — (The Garland classics of film literature)
Facsimile of: edition published London : Methuen, 1935
ISBN 0-8240-2891-0 : Unpriced B81-25524

791.43'72 — French cinema films: 2 ou 3 chose que je sais d'elle — *Critical studies*

Guzzetti, Alfred. Two or three things I know about her : analysis of a film by Godard / Alfred Guzzetti. — Cambridge, Mass. ; London : Harvard University Press, 1981. — x,366p : ill ; 27cm. — (Harvard film studies)
Includes French text of the filmscript with parallel English translation
ISBN 0-674-91500-3 : £16.50 B81-21067

791.43'75 — British cinema films — *Scripts — Collections*

Shaw, Bernard. The collected screenplays of Bernard Shaw / edited with an introduction by Bernard F. Dukore. — London : Prior, 1980. — xiv,487p,[16]p of plates : ill,ports ; 24cm
ISBN 0-86043-405-2 : £14.95 : CIP rev.
B80-13498

791.43'75 — California. Los Angeles. Hollywood. Cinema films, *1947-1980.* Special subjects: Vietnamese wars — *Critical studies*

Adair, Gilbert. Hollywood's Vietnam : from The green berets to Apocalypse now / Gilbert Adair. — London : Proteus, 1981. — 190p : ill ; 27cm
List of films: p169-190. — Includes index
ISBN 0-906071-86-0 : £7.95 B81-33749

791.43'75 — Cinema films, *1925-1959* — *Reviews*

Grierson, John, *1898-1972.* Grierson on the movies / edited with an introduction by Forsyth Hardy. — London : Faber, 1981. — 200p ; 23cm
Includes index
ISBN 0-571-11665-5 : £7.25 B81-10615

791.43'75 — Cinema films produced by Hammer Film Productions, *to 1976*

The House of horror : the complete story of Hammer Films / [edited by Allen Eyles, Robert Adkinson and Nicholas Fry]. — 2nd ed. — [London] : Lorrimer, 1981. — 144p,[8]p of plates : ill(some col.),ports ; 25cm
Previous ed.: 1973. — List of films: p120-138
ISBN 0-85647-115-1 (pbk) : £2.95 B81-27281

791.43'75 — Cinema films, *to 1975* — *Critical studies*

Allan, Angela. The Sunday times guide to movies on television / Angela and Elkan Allan. — Rev. ed. — London : Hamlyn, 1980. — xii,364p ; 18cm
Previous ed.: London : Times Newspapers, 1973. — Includes index
ISBN 0-600-20033-7 (pbk) : £1.50 B81-04680

Allan, Angela. The Sunday times guide to movies on television / Angela and Elkan Allan. — 1st ed. (rev.). — London : Severn House, 1980. — 364p ; 21cm
Previous ed.: London : Times Newspapers, 1973. — Includes index
ISBN 0-7278-0644-0 : £7.95 B81-04679

791.43'75 — Historical films, *1914-1962* — *Critical studies*

Sorlin, Pierre. The film in history : restaging the past / Pierre Sorlin. — Oxford : Blackwell, 1980. — xii,226p,[8]p of plates : ill ; 22cm
Bibliography: p218-221. — Includes indexes
ISBN 0-631-19510-6 : £9.95 : CIP rev.
B80-08343

791.44 — BROADCASTING

791.44'028'0924 — Great Britain. Radio programmes. Broadcasting. Berryman, Gwen — *Biographies*

Berryman, Gwen. The life and death of Doris Archer. — London : Eyre Methuen, Oct.1981. — [176]p
ISBN 0-413-48640-0 : £6.50 : CIP entry
B81-25307

791.44'092'4 — Great Britain. Radio & television programmes. Broadcasting. Vaughan-Thomas, Wynford — *Biographies*

Vaughan-Thomas, Wynford. Trust to talk / Wynford Vaughan-Thomas. — London : Hutchinson, 1980. — 239p,[8]p plates : ill,ports ; 23cm
ISBN 0-09-143870-5 : £6.95 : CIP rev.
B80-18660

791.44'092'4 — Great Britain. Radio programmes. Broadcasting. Plomley, Roy, *to 1939* — *Biographies*

Plomley, Roy. Days seemed longer : early years of a broadcaster / Roy Plomley. — London : Eyre Methuen, 1980. — 206p,[8]p of plates : ill,ports ; 23cm
Includes index
ISBN 0-413-39730-0 : £6.95 B81-04008

791.44'092'4 — Great Britain. Radio programmes. Broadcasting. Weir, Molly, *1956-1960* — *Biographies*

Weir, Molly. One small footprint / Molly Weir. — Large print ed. — Bath : Chivers, 1981, c1980. — 294p ; 22cm. — (New Portway)
Originally published: London : Hutchinson, 1980
ISBN 0-85119-107-x : Unpriced B81-09248

791.44'5 — Disc jockeys. Techniques — *Manuals*

See, David. How to be a disc jockey / David See. — London : Hamlyn, c1980. — 87p : ill(some col.),ports ; 29cm
Includes index
ISBN 0-600-34642-0 : £2.99 B81-01063

791.44'7 — Great Britain. Radio programmes. Quiz programmes: I'm sorry I haven't a clue — *Scripts*

I'm sorry I haven't a clue. — London : Unwin Paperbacks, Oct.1981. — [128]p
Originally published: London : Robson, 1980
ISBN 0-04-827047-4 (pbk) : £1.95 : CIP entry
B81-24605

791.44'72 — Great Britain. Radio programmes: Any questions — *Personal observations*

Jacobs, David, *1926-*. Any questions. — London : Robson, Oct.1981. — [320]p
ISBN 0-86051-156-1 : £6.95 : CIP entry
B81-27453

791.44'72 — Great Britain. Radio programmes. Comedies: Goon Show, *to 1975*

Wilmut, Roger. The Goon Show companion : a history of goonography / written and compiled by Roger Wilmut ; with a personal memoir by Jimmy Grafton. — London : Robson, 1976 (1981 [printing]). — 160p,[4]p of plates : ill,ports ; 24cm
Includes index
ISBN 0-903895-64-1 : £5.95 B81-40710

791.44'72 — Great Britain. Radio programmes. Drama: Archers, *The, to 1975* — *Personal observations*

Painting, Norman. Forever Ambridge : thirty years of the Archers / Norman Painting. — Rev. ed. — London : Joseph by arrangement with the British Broadcasting Corporation, 1980. — 318p,[16]p of plates : ill,ports,geneal.tables ; 23cm
Previous ed.: 1975. — Geneal.tables on lining papers. — Includes index
ISBN 0-7181-1961-4 : £6.95 B81-00227

791.44'72 — Great Britain. Radio programmes. Drama: Archers, *The, to 1980*

The Archers : the first thirty years / edited by William Smethurst. — London : Eyre Methuen by arrangement with the British Broadcasting Corporation, 1980. — 203p : ill,maps,ports,1geneal.table ; 24cm
Maps on lining papers
ISBN 0-413-47830-0 : £5.95 B81-00228

791.44'72 — Great Britain. Radio programmes. Quiz programmes: My music, *to 1978* — *Personal observations*

Race, Steve. My music : the panel game originated by Edward J. Mason and Tony Shryane / by Steve Race with the contributions of Frank Muir .. [et al.] ; drawings by John Jensen. — Harmondsworth : Penguin, 1980, c1979. — 173p : ill,music ; 19cm
Originally published: London : Robson, 1979. — Includes index
ISBN 0-14-005206-2 (pbk) : £1.25
Also classified at 791.45'72 B81-06641

791.44'72 — Radio programmes: Sports programmes: 'Test Match Special', *to 1980*

Test match special / edited by Peter Baxter. — London : Queen Anne Press, 1981. — 159p : ill,facsims,forms,ports ; 25cm
ISBN 0-362-00547-8 : £6.95 B81-27525

791.45 — Great Britain. Television programmes. Continuity

Morey, John. The space between programmes : television continuity as meta-discourse / John Morey. — London : University of London Institute of Education, [1981]?. — iii,23p ; 21cm. — (Media analysis paper, ISSN 0260-8618 ; 1)
Bibliography: p23
£0.30 (pbk) B81-30111

791.45 — Television programmes — *Critical studies*

Popular television and film : a reader / edited by Tony Bennett ... [et al.] at the Open University — London : BFI in association with Open University Press, 1981. — 353p : ill ; 21cm
Includes bibliographies and index
ISBN 0-85170-115-9 (cased) : £12.00 : CIP rev.
ISBN 0-85170-116-7 (pbk) : £6.25 B81-20189

791.45 — Television programmes - *For children*

Hill, Gordon. Secrets of film and television. — Sevenoaks : Hodder & Stoughton, May 1981. — [128]p
ISBN 0-340-25496-3 (pbk) : £0.95 : CIP entry
Primary classification 791.43 B81-05158

791.45'01'9 — Television programmes. Visual communication. Images. Psychological aspects

Baggaley, Jon. Psychology of the TV image / Jon Baggaley with Margaret Ferguson and Philip Brooks. — Farnborough, Hants. : Gower, c1980. — xv,190p : ill ; 23cm
Bibliography: p174-183. - Includes index
ISBN 0-566-00189-6 : £12.50 : CIP rev.
B80-02527

791.45'0232 — Television programmes. Production — *For children*

Rickard, Graham. A day with a TV producer / Graham Rickard. — Hove : Wayland, 1980. — 55p : ill,ports ; 24cm. — (A Day in the life)
Bibliography: p55
ISBN 0-85340-793-2 : £3.25 B81-04081

791.45'0232 — Television programmes. Production — *Manuals*

Millerson, Gerald. Effective TV production / Gerald Millerson. — London : Focal, 1976 (1980 printing). — 192p : ill,plans ; 22cm. — (Media manuals)
Bibliography: p186
ISBN 0-240-50950-1 (pbk) : Unpriced B81-01064

Watts, Harris. The programme-maker's handbook, or, Goodbye Totter TV. — London (4A Sharpleshall St., NW1 8YL) : Starstream Books, Oct.1981. — [180]p
ISBN 0-9507582-1-3 (cased) : £9.95 : CIP entry
ISBN 0-9507582-0-5 (pbk) : £5.95 B81-31953

791.45'028'0924 — Television programmes. Acting. Timothy, Christopher — *Biographies*

Timothy, Christopher. Vet behind the ears / Christopher Timothy. — London : Severn House, 1981, c1979. — 121p,[4]p of plates : ill,ports ; 21cm
Originally published: London : Pan, 1979
ISBN 0-7278-0698-x : £5.95 : CIP rev. B80-28612

791.45'028'0924 — United States. Television programmes. Drama: All my children. Acting. Warrick, Ruth — *Biographies*

Warrick, Ruth. The confessions of Phoebe Tyler / Ruth Warrick with Don Preston. — Englewood Cliffs ; London : Prentice-Hall, 1980. — x,227p,[32]p of plates : ill,ports ; 24cm
ISBN 0-13-167403-x : £6.45 B81-05091

791.45'09 — Television programmes, *to 1980*

Monaco, James. How to read a film : the art, technology, language, history and theory of film and media / James Monaco ; with diagrams by David Lindroth. — Rev. ed. — New York ; Oxford : Oxford University Press, 1981. — xv,533p : ill,ports ; 24cm
Previous ed.: 1977. — Bibliography: p465-493. — Includes index
ISBN 0-19-502802-3 (cased) : Unpriced
ISBN 0-19-502806-6 (pbk) : £5.95
Primary classification 791.43'09 B81-38069

791.45'092'4 — Great Britain. Television programmes. Broadcasting. Boyle, Katie — *Biographies*

Boyle, Katie. What this Katie did : an autobiography / Katie Boyle. — London : Weidenfeld and Nicolson, 1980. — 197p,[16]p of plates : 1ill,ports ; 24cm
Includes index
ISBN 0-297-77814-5 : £6.95 B81-01065

791.45'092'4 — Great Britain. Television services: News reporting services: Independent Television News. Broadcasting. Bosanquet, Reginald — *Biographies*

Bosanquet, Reginald. Let's get through Wednesday : my 25 years with ITN / Reginald Bosanquet with Wallace Reyburn. — London : New English Library, 1981, c1980. — 189p,[16]p of plates : ill,ports ; 18cm
Originally published: London : Michael Joseph, 1980
ISBN 0-450-05163-3 (pbk) : £1.50 B81-23294

791.45'0941 — Great Britain. Broadcasting services: British Broadcasting Corporation. Television programmes — *Correspondence, diaries, etc.*

Points of view : a collection of letters written to the popular BBC1 television programme / selected, edited and commented on by Barry Took. — London : BBC, 1981. — 95p : facsims ; 21cm
ISBN 0-563-17953-8 (pbk) : £1.50 B81-40321

791.45'3 — West German television films: Arbeiterfilme. Production by Westdeutscher Rundfunk, *1968-1976*

Collins, Richard, *1946-*. WDR and the Arbeiterfilm : Fassbinder, Ziewer and others / Richard Collins, Vincent Porter. — London : BFI Publishing, 1981. — 174p : ill ; 21cm. — (Television monograph ; 12)
Bibliography: p168-170. - List of films: p171-174
ISBN 0-85170-107-8 (pbk) : £3.75 B81-09631

791.45'72 — Children's television programmes: Doctor Who

Lofficier, Jean-Marc. The Doctor Who programme guide / Jean-Marc Lofficier. — London : W.H. Allen
Vol.1. — 1981. — 127p ; 21cm
ISBN 0-491-02804-0 (cased) : £4.50
ISBN 0-426-20139-6 (pbk) : £1.25 B81-22765

Lofficier, Jean-Marc. The Doctor Who programme guide / Jean-Marc Lofficier. — London : W.H. Allen
Vol.2. — 1981. — 111p ; 21cm
List of films: p107-108. — List of sound recordings: p111
ISBN 0-491-02885-7 : £4.50 B81-22766

791.45'72 — Ireland *(Republic)*. **Television programmes: Gay Byrne's Late Late Show,** *to 1980* — *Personal observations*

Collins, Pan. It started on the Late Late Show / Pan Collins. — Dublin (Knocksedan House, Swords, Co. Dublin) : Ward River Press, 1981. — 202p,[4]p of plates : ports ; 18cm
Includes index
ISBN 0-907085-02-4 (pbk) : £2.50 B81-19456

791.45'72 — Israel. Television programmes: News programmes: Kim'at Hatzot

Almost midnight : reforming the late-night news / Itzhak Roeh ... [et al.]. — Beverley Hills ; London : Sage, c1980. — 200p : ill ; 23cm. — (People and communication ; v.11)
Bibliography: p195-197
ISBN 0-8039-1504-7 (cased) : £12.50
ISBN 0-8039-1505-5 (pbk) : £6.25 B81-16982

791.45'72 — Television drama series in English: Coronation Street

Coronation Street / Richard Dyer ... [et al.]. — London : B.F.I. Publishing, 1981. — 101p : ill. — (Television monograph ; 13)
Bibliography: p99-101
ISBN 0-85170-110-8 (pbk) : £3.50 : CIP rev. B81-07934

791.45'72 — Television programmes. Comedies: Monty Python's Flying Circus. Censorship

Hewison, Robert. Monty Python : the case against. — London : Eyre Methuen, Sept.1981. — [96]p
ISBN 0-413-48650-8 (cased) : £8.50 : CIP entry
ISBN 0-413-48660-5 (pbk) : £4.50 B81-23949

791.45'72 — Television programmes. Drama: 'Grange Hill' — *For children* — *Serials*

The Grange Hill magazine. — [No.1]-. — London : IPC Magazines, c1980. — v. : ill,ports ; 30cm
Monthly
ISSN 0260-5287 = Grange Hill magazine : £0.50 per issue B81-05443

791.45'72 — Television programmes. Quiz programmes: My music, *to 1978* — *Personal observations*

Race, Steve. My music : the panel game originated by Edward J. Mason and Tony Shryane / by Steve Race with the contributions of Frank Muir .. [et al.] ; drawings by John Jensen. — Harmondsworth : Penguin, 1980, c1979. — 173p : ill,music ; 19cm
Originally published: London : Robson, 1979. — Includes index
ISBN 0-14-005206-2 (pbk) : £1.25
Primary classification 791.44'72 B81-06641

791.45'75 — Great Britain. Television programmes, *1972-1976* — *Reviews*

James, Clive. Visions before midnight : television criticism from the Observer, 1972-76 / Clive James. — London : Pan, 1981. — 175p ; 20cm. — (Picador)
Originally published: London : Cape, 1977
ISBN 0-330-26464-8 (pbk) : £1.75 B81-38166

791.45'75 — Great Britain. Television programmes, *1976-1979* — *Reviews*

James, Clive. The crystal bucket : television criticism from the Observer 1976-79 / Clive James. — London : Cape, 1981. — 238p ; 23cm
ISBN 0-224-01890-6 : £6.95 B81-09532

791.45'75 — Television drama in English, *to 1981*

Sutton, Shaun. The largest theatre in the world : the Fleming Memorial Lecture / given by Shaun Sutton. — London : BBC, [1981]. — 15p ; 21cm. — (The Fleming memorial lecture)
ISBN 0-563-20007-3 (pbk) : Unpriced B81-26967

791.5 — MINIATURE, TOY, SHADOW THEATRES

791.5'3 — Children's hand puppetry

Ashbrook Puppet Theatre / [illustrated by Kym Dunn]. — [Borrowash] ([Ashbrook Ave., Borrowash, Derbyshire]) : Ockbrook and Borrowash Community Centre Management Committee, c1981. — 22p : ill ; 30cm
Includes plays written by Peggy Dunn
Unpriced (pbk) B81-12259

791.5'3'095982 — Indonesian puppet theatre: Javanese puppet theatre: Wayang kulit

Van Ness, Edward C.. Javanese wayang kulit : an introduction / Edward C. Van Ness, Shita Prawirohardjo. — Kuala Lumpur ; Oxford : Oxford University Press, 1980. — xiii,95p,[20]p of plates : ill(some col.) ; 22cm. — (Oxford in Asia paperbacks) (Oxford in Asia traditional and contemporary arts)
Bibliography: p94-95
ISBN 0-19-580414-7 (pbk) : £7.50 B81-32540

791.5'3'0973 — United States. Puppet theatre: Yale Puppeteers, *1920-1956*

Brown, Forman. Small wonder : the story of the Yale Puppeteers and the Turnabout Theatre / by Forman Brown ; foreword by Ray Bradbury. — Metuchen ; London : Scarecrow, 1980. — xii,269p : ill,1plan,ports ; 23cm
Includes index
ISBN 0-8108-1334-3 : £8.75 B81-08535

792 — THEATRE

792 — England. Theatre. Censorship, *1824-1901*

Stephens, John Russell. The censorship of English drama 1824-1901 / John Russell Stephens. — Cambridge : Cambridge University Press, 1980. — xiv,206p : ill,facsims ; 23cm
Bibliography: p189-193. - Includes index
ISBN 0-521-23021-7 : £17.50 : CIP rev. B80-26013

792 — Theatre

Artaud, Antonin. The theatre and its double : essays / by Antonin Artaud ; translated by Victor Corti. — London : Calder, 1981. — 102p : ill ; 20cm. — (Signature series ; 4)
Translated from the French. — Originally published: London : Calder & Boyars, 1970
ISBN 0-7145-0702-4 (cased) : £4.50
ISBN 0-7145-0703-2 (pbk) : £3.50 B81-11817

Craig, Edward Gordon. On the art of the theatre / by Edward Gordon Craig. — London : Heinemann, 1956 (1980 [printing]). — xxiii,295p,8p of plates : ill,1port ; 21cm
ISBN 0-435-18182-3 (pbk) : £3.50 : CIP rev. B79-10489

Hatlen, Theodore W.. Orientation to the theatre / Theodore W. Hatlen. — 3rd ed. — Englewood Cliffs ; London : Prentice Hall, c1981. — xiii,361p : ill ; 24cm
Previous ed.: New York : Appleton-Century-Crofts, 1972. — Includes bibliographies and index
ISBN 0-13-642108-3 (pbk) : £10.45 B81-33137

792 — Theatre — *For drama schools*

Self, David. The drama & theatre arts course book / David Self. — Basingstoke : Macmillan Education, 1981. — 119p : ill,facsims,plans,ports ; 25cm
Bibliography: p115. — Includes index
ISBN 0-333-27596-9 (pbk) : £2.95 : CIP rev. B80-13500

792′.01′50973 — United States. Theatre. Criticism. American writers, *1850-1900*

Miller, Tice L.. Bohemians and critics : American theatre criticism in the nineteenth century / Tice L. Miller. — Metuchen ; London : Scarecrow, 1981. — x,190p ; 23cm
Bibliography: p177-180. - Includes index
ISBN 0-8108-1377-7 : £8.40 B81-17095

792′.02 — Theatre. Stage management — *Manuals*

Baker, Hendrik. Stage management and theatrecraft : a stage manager's handbook / by Hendrik Baker ; line drawings by Margaret Woodward ; foreword by Basil Dean. — 3rd ed. — London : Miller, 1981. — xv,384p,[45]p of plates : ill,plans ; 19cm
Previous ed.: S.l., s.n., 1971. — Bibliography: p382-384. - Includes index
ISBN 0-85343-556-1 (pbk) : £6.00 B81-16572

792′.022 — England. Spectacular theatre, *1850-1910*

Booth, Michael R.. Victorian spectacular theatre 1850-1910 / Michael R. Booth. — Boston, Mass. ; London : Routledge & Kegan Paul, 1981. — ix,190p,[16]p of plates : ill ; 24cm. — (Theatre production studies)
Bibliography: p172-173. — Includes index
ISBN 0-7100-0739-6 : £12.50 B81-27565

792′.022 — Great Britain. Alternative theatre, *to 1980*

Dreams and deconstructions : alternative theatre in Britain / editor Sandy Craig. — Ambergate : Amber Lane, 1981. — 192p : ill,ports ; 25cm
Bibliography: p187. — Includes index
ISBN 0-906399-19-x (cased) : £7.95
ISBN 0-906399-20-3 (pbk) : Unpriced
B81-29340

792′.022 — London. East End. Penny theatres, *1830-1900*

Sheridan, Paul. Penny theatres of Victorian London / by Paul Sheridan. — London : Dobson, 1981. — xiv,106p : ill ; 23cm
Bibliography: p101. - Includes index
ISBN 0-234-72104-9 : £5.95 B81-17133

792′.022 — United States. Theatre for old persons

Senior adult theatre : the American Theatre Association handbook / edited by Roger Cornish and C. Robert Kase ; contributors Roger Cornish ... [et al.]. — University Park ; London : Pennsylvania State University Press, c1981. — 100p : ill,port ; 22cm
Bibliography: p99-100
ISBN 0-271-00276-x (cased) : £6.30
ISBN 0-271-00275-1 (pbk) : £4.20 B81-38419

792′.0222 — Amateur theatre — *Manuals*

Curry, Jennifer. Amateur theatre / Jennifer Curry ; illustrated by G. Hartfield Illustrators. — London : Teach Yourself Books, 1980. — 223p : ill,plans ; 20cm. — (Teach yourself books)
Bibliography: p213-218. — Includes index
ISBN 0-340-25111-5 (pbk) : £1.95 : CIP rev.
B80-11125

792′.0226 — Children's plays. Production — *For children*

Alfaenger, Peter K.. Make your own theatre / written and illustrated by Peter K. Alfaenger ; translated by Lucilla Watson. — London : Blackie, 1981. — 54p : ill(some col.) ; 27x28cm
Translation of: Le théatre
ISBN 0-216-91085-4 : £5.95 B81-10785

792′.0226 — Schools. Activities: Drama. Production. Techniques

Griffith, Peter, *1951-*. The school play : a complete handbook / Peter Griffith. — London : Batsford Academic and Educational, 1981. — 117p ; 23cm
Bibliography: p105-107. — Includes index
ISBN 0-7134-3541-0 : £5.50 B81-19641

792′.0226′0941 — Great Britain. Theatre in education

Learning through theatre : essays and casebooks on theatre in education / edited by Tony Jackson. — Manchester : Manchester University Press, 1980. — xix,209p : ill ; 24cm
Bibliography: p208-209. - Includes index
ISBN 0-7190-0789-5 (cased) : £11.50 : CIP rev.
ISBN 0-7190-0821-2 (pbk) : £5.50 B80-10190

792′.0233′0722 — Theatre. Directing — *Case studies*

Wills, J. Robert. Directing in the theatre : a casebook / J. Robert Wills. — Metuchen ; London : Scarecrow, 1980. — xi,138p ; 23cm + instructor's manual(vi, 60p : pbk ; 22cm)
ISBN 0-8108-1348-3 (cased) : £6.30
ISBN 0-8108-1345-9 (instructor's manual)
B81-09375

792′.0233′0924 — France. Theatre. Directing. Planchon, Roger

Daoust, Yvette. Roger Planchon : director and playwright / Yvette Daoust. — Cambridge : Cambridge University Press, 1981. — xi,252p : ill,1port ; 24cm
Bibliography: p240-243
ISBN 0-521-23414-x : £18.50
Also classified at 842′.914 B81-24764

792′.0233′0924 — Great Britain. Theatre. Directing. Browne, E. Martin — *Biographies*

Browne, E. Martin. Two in one / E. Martin with Henzie Browne. — Cambridge : Cambridge University Press, 1981. — xi,254p : ill ; 24cm
Includes index
ISBN 0-521-23254-6 : £15.00 : CIP rev.
B81-13532

792′.0233′0924 — Great Britain. Theatre. Directing. Hickman, Charles — *Biographies*

Hickman, Charles. 'Directed by-' / Charles Hickman. — Bognor Regis : New Horizon, c1981. — 114p,[42]p of plates : ill,ports ; 21cm
ISBN 0-86116-734-1 : £7.95 B81-38075

792′.0233′0924 — West Germany. Theatre. Directing. Stein, Peter — *Critical studies*

Patterson, Michael. Peter Stein. — Cambridge : Cambridge University Press, Jan.1982. — [186] p. — (Directors in perspective)
ISBN 0-521-22442-x (cased) : £17.50 : CIP entry
ISBN 0-521-29502-5 (pbk) : £5.50 B81-37550

792′.025 — Theatre. Scenery. Construction — *Manuals*

Gillette, A. S.. Stage scenery : its construction and rigging. — 3rd ed. / A.S. Gillette, J. Michael Gillette. — New York ; London : Harper & Row, c1981. — xv,448p : ill,plans ; 27cm
Previous ed.: 1972. — Bibliography: p440-441. — Includes index
ISBN 0-06-042332-3 : £12.50 B81-28414

792′.025 — Theatre. Stage lighting — *Manuals*

Pilbrow, Richard. Stage lighting / Richard Pilbrow ; foreword by Lord Olivier. — Rev. ed. / with contributions by William Bundy and John B. Read. — London : Studio Vista, 1979. — 176p : ill(some col.),plans ; 26cm
Previous ed.: 1970. — Bibliography: p175. - Includes index
ISBN 0-289-70856-7 : £14.95 B81-01066

792′.025′0924 — Stage design. Craig, Edward Gordon — *Biographies*

Bablet, Denis. The theatre of Edward Gordon Craig / Denis Bablet ; translated by Daphne Woodward. — London : Eyre Methuen, 1981, c1966. — 207p,24p of plates : ill,ports ; 23cm
Translation of Edward Gordon Craig. — Originally published: London : Heinemann, 1966. — Includes index
ISBN 0-413-47870-x (cased) : £9.95
ISBN 0-413-47880-7 (pbk) : Unpriced
B81-19716

Craig, Edward Gordon. Index to the story of my days : some memoirs of Edward Gordon Craig 1872-1907 / with an introduction by Peter Holland. — Cambridge : Cambridge University Press, 1981. — xxx,307p,[30]p of plates : ill,ports ; 23cm
Originally published: London : Hulton, 1957. — Includes index
ISBN 0-521-23609-6 (cased) : £22.50 : CIP rev.
ISBN 0-521-28070-2 (pbk) : £6.95 B81-14943

792′.025′0941 — Great Britain. Theatre. Scenery. Design, *1700-1830*

Rosenfeld, Sybil. Georgian scene painters and scene painting. — Cambridge : Cambridge University Press, Sept.1981. — [205]p
ISBN 0-521-23339-9 : £30.00 : CIP entry
B81-25881

792′.027 — Theatre. Make-up. Techniques — *Manuals*

Corson, Richard. Stage makeup / Richard Corson. — 6th ed. — Englewood Cliffs ; London : Prentice-Hall, c1981. — xvi,420p : ill (some col.),forms ; 29cm
Previous ed.: 1975. — Includes index
ISBN 0-13-840512-3 : £14.90 B81-17222

792′.028 — Acting — *For children*

Swift, Clive. The performing world of the actor. — London : H. Hamilton, May 1981. — [128]p
ISBN 0-241-10585-4 : £4.95 : CIP entry
B81-12822

792′.028 — Acting. Improvisation

Johnstone, Keith. Impro : improvisation and the theatre / Keith Johnstone with an introduction by Irving Wardle. — Corr. ed. — London : Eyre Methuen, 1981. — 208p ; 22cm
Previous ed.: London : Faber, 1979
ISBN 0-413-46430-x (pbk) : £3.95 B81-08532

Polsky, Milton E.. Let's improvise : becoming creative, expressive & spontaneous through drama / Milton E. Polsky. — Englewood Cliffs ; London : Prentice-Hall, c1980. — xvi,316p : ill,music,plans ; 25cm. — (A Spectrum book)
Bibliography: p309-310. - Includes index
ISBN 0-13-532069-0 (cased) : £12.95
ISBN 0-13-532051-8 (pbk) : £5.80 B81-01068

792′.028 — Acting. Preparation — *Manuals*

Stanislavskiĭ, K. S.. An actor prepares / Constantin Stanislavski ; translated by Elizabeth Reynolds Hapgood. — London : Eyre Methuen, 1980, c1936. — 313p ; 20cm. — (An Eyre Methuen dramabook)
Translated from the Russian. — Originally published: New York : Theatre Arts, 1936 ; London : Geoffrey Bles, 1937
ISBN 0-413-46190-4 (pbk) : £3.95 B81-23972

792′.028 — Acting. Techniques

Benedetti, Robert L.. The actor at work / Robert L. Benedetti. — 3rd ed. — Englewood Cliffs ; London : Prentice-Hall, c1981. — xvii,286p : ill ; 24cm. — (Prentice-Hall series in theatre and drama)
Previous ed.: 1976. — Bibliography: p279-281. — Includes index
ISBN 0-13-003673-0 : £9.70 B81-16520

792′.028 — Actors. Superstitions

Huggett, Richard. The curse of Macbeth : and other theatrical superstitions : an investigation / by Richard Huggett. — [Chippenham] : Picton, 1981. — 259p : ill,facsims,ports ; 22cm
Facsims on lining papers. — Includes index
ISBN 0-902633-72-4 : £7.95 B81-22084

792′.028 — Drama. Characters. Acting — *Study examples: Drama in English. Shakespeare, William. Othello. Characters: Othello*

Stanislavskiĭ, K. S.. Creating a role / Constantin Stanislavski ; translated by Elizabeth Reynolds Hapgood ; edited by Hermine I. Popper ; foreword by Robert Lewis. — London : Eyre Methuen, 1981, c1961. — xiv,271p ; 20cm
Translated from the Russian MSS. — Originally published: New York : Theatre Arts, 1961 ; London : Bles, 1963
ISBN 0-413-47760-6 (pbk) : £3.95
Also classified at 792′.028 B81-03919

792′.028 — Drama. Characters. Acting — *Study examples: Drama in Russian. Griboedov, A. S.. Gore ot uma. Characters: Chatski*

Stanislavskiĭ, K. S.. Creating a role / Constantin Stanislavski ; translated by Elizabeth Reynolds Hapgood ; edited by Hermine I. Popper ; foreword by Robert Lewis. — London : Eyre Methuen, 1981, c1961. — xiv,271p ; 20cm
Translated from the Russian MSS. — Originally published: New York : Theatre Arts, 1961 ; London : Bles, 1963
ISBN 0-413-47760-6 (pbk) : £3.95
Primary classification 792′.028 B81-03919

792′.028 — Primary schools. Activities: Drama. Improvisation — *For teaching*

Errington, Eddie. A time and a place / developing improvised drama in the primary school / Eddie Errington. — Driffield (Railway Cottages, Wansford Rd., Driffield, E. Yorks) : Studies in Education, 1980. — 91p : ill ; 18x23cm
Originally published: Richmond, Australia : Primary Education Party, 1979. — Bibliography: p91
ISBN 0-905484-27-4 (pbk) : £3.25 B81-05772

792′.028 — Secondary schools. Activities: Drama. Improvisation — *For teaching*

James, Ronald. A guide to improvisation : a handbook for teachers / by Ronald James & Peter Williams. — Banbury (P.O. Box 44, Banbury, Oxon) : Kemble, c1980. — x,108p ; 22cm
ISBN 0-906835-05-4 (pbk) : £3.00 : CIP rev. B80-10721

792′.028′0207 — Great Britain. Amateur theatre. Acting — *Humour*

Green, Michael. The art of coarse acting, or, How to wreck an amateur dramatic society / Michael Green. — Rev. ed. — London : Arrow, 1980. — 127p,[8]p of plates : ill ; 18cm
Previous ed.: London : Hutchinson, 1964
ISBN 0-09-907530-x (pbk) : £1.25 B81-05226

792′.028′0922 — Great Britain. Actors — *Directories* — *Serials*

Spotlight. Actors. — 1981/82 ed. — London (42 Cranbourn St., WC2H 7AP) : The Spotlight, [1981?]. — 2v.
ISSN 0309-0183 : Unpriced B81-26384

792′.028′0922 — Great Britain. Actresses — *Directories* — *Serials*

Spotlight. Actresses. — 1980/81 ed.. — London (42, Cranbourn St., WC2H 7AP) : Spotlight, [1980?]. — 2v.
ISSN 0308-9827 : Unpriced B81-03570

792′.028′0922 — Great Britain. Child actors — *Directories* — *Serials*

Spotlight. Children (A-Z). — No.2 (1981/82 ed.). — London (42 Cranbourn St., WC2H 7AP) : 'The Spotlight', [1981]. — 346p
ISSN 0142-8926 : Unpriced B81-28378

792′.028′0922 — Great Britain. Theatre. Acting. Wyndham, *Sir Charles & Moore, Mary, 1862-1931* — *Biographies*

Trewin, Wendy. All on stage : Charles Wyndham and the Alberys / Wendy Trewin. — London : Harrap, 1980. — x,244,[16]p of plates : ill,facsims,ports,geneal.tables ; 24cm
Bibliography: p225-230. - Includes index. — Geneal.tables on lining papers
ISBN 0-245-53444-x : £9.95
Also classified at 822′.8 B81-04135

792′.028′0924 — Acting. Bankhead, Tallulah — *Biographies*

Brian, Dennis. Tallulah, darling : a biography of Tallulah Bankhead / Dennis Brian. — London : Sidgwick & Jackson, 1980. — ix,292p,[12]p of plates : ill,ports ; 22cm
Originally published: New York : Pyramid, 1972. — Includes index
ISBN 0-283-98709-x : £6.95 B81-02901

792′.028′0924 — Acting. Fyodorova, Victoria — *Biographies*

Fyodorova, Victoria. The admiral's daughter / Victoria Fyodorova and Haskel Frankel. — Feltham : Hamlyn, 1980, c1979. — 372p,[8]p of plates : ports ; 18cm
Originally published: London : Joseph, 1979. — Includes index
ISBN 0-600-20334-4 (pbk) : £1.50 B81-08284

792′.028′0924 — Acting. Howard, Leslie — *Personal observations*

Howard, Ronald. In search of my father : a portrait of Leslie Howard / Ronald Howard. — London : Kimber, 1981. — 255p,[16]p of plates : ill,ports ; 24cm
List of films: p245-246. - Includes index
ISBN 0-7183-0168-4 : £9.75 B81-29732

792′.028′0924 — Acting. Lawrence, Gertrude — *Biographies*

Morley, Sheridan. Gertude Lawrence / Sheridan Morley. — London : Weidenfeld and Nicolson, c1981. — xii,228p[16]p of plates : ill,ports ; 25cm
Bibliography: p203-205. - List of films: p209. - List of sound discs: p210-216. - Includes index
ISBN 0-297-77882-x : £8.95 B81-05986

792′.028′0924 — Acting. Mills, John, *1908-* — *Biographies*

Mills, John, *1908-*. Up in the clouds, gentlemen please / John Mills. — London : Weidenfeld and Nicolson, 1980. — vii,290p,[24]p of plates : ill,ports ; 24cm
List of films and theatrical productions: p276-280. — Includes index
ISBN 0-297-77841-2 : £8.50 B81-01889

Mills, John, *1908-*. Up in the clouds, gentlemen please / John Mills. — Harmondsworth : Penguin, 1981, c1980. — 427p,[16]p of plates : ill,ports ; 18cm
Originally published: London : Weidenfeld and Nicolson, 1980. — Includes index
ISBN 0-14-005827-3 (pbk) : £1.75 B81-40442

792′.028′0924 — Acting. More, Kenneth — *Biographies*

More, Kenneth. More or less / by Kenneth More. — Bolton-By-Bowland : Magna Print, 1980, c1978. — 547p ; 23cm
Originally published: London : Hodder and Stoughton, 1978. — Published in large print
ISBN 0-86009-218-6 : £6.95 : CIP rev. B79-34383

792′.028′0924 — Acting. West, Mae — *Biographies*

Cashin, Fergus. Mae West : a biography / Fergus Cashin. — London : W.H. Allen, c1981. — 197p,[8]p of plates : ill,ports ; 23cm
List of plays and films: p190. — Includes index
ISBN 0-491-02984-5 : £6.95 B81-27074

792′.028′0924 — Great Britain. Theatre. Acting. Cooke, George Frederick

Wilmeth, Don B.. George Frederick Cooke : Machiavel of the stage / Don B. Wilmeth. — Westport, Conn. ; London : Greenwood Press, 1980. — xv,364p : ill,2facsims,ports ; 25cm. — (Contributions in drama and theatre studies, ISSN 0163-3821 ; no.2)
Bibliography: p345-350. - Includes index
ISBN 0-313-21487-5 : Unpriced B81-04523

792′.028′0924 — Great Britain. Theatre. Acting. Cooke, George Frederick — *Biographies*

Hare, Arnold. George Frederick Cooke : the actor and the man / by Arnold Hare. — London : Society for Theatre Research, c1980. — viii,255p,[8]p of plates : ill,1facsim,ports ; 24cm
Bibliography: p214-218. - Includes index
ISBN 0-85430-031-7 (pbk) : £9.75 B81-04600

792′.028′0924 — Great Britain. Theatre. Acting. Gielgud, *Sir John* — *Biographies*

Gielgud, John. An actor and his time / John Gielgud in collaboration with John Miller and John Powell. — Harmondsworth : Penguin, 1981, c1979. — 228p,[16]pof plates : ports,1geneal.table ; 18cm
Originally published: London : Sidgwick and Jackson, 1979. — Includes index
ISBN 0-14-005636-x (pbk) : £1.50 B81-21015

792′.028′0924 — Great Britain. Theatre. Acting. Langtry, Lillie. Interpersonal relationships with Edward VII, *King of Great Britain*

Brough, James. The prince and the lily / James Brough. — Sevenoaks : Coronet, 1978, c1975. — 332p ; 18cm
Originally published: New York : Coward McCann and Geoghegan ; London : Hodder and Stoughton, 1975. — Includes index
ISBN 0-340-23384-2 (pbk) : £1.10 : CIP rev.
Also classified at 941.082′092′4 B78-23604

792′.028′0924 — Great Britain. Theatre. Acting. Morley, Robert — *Biographies*

Morley, Robert. The best of Robert Morley. — London : Robson, 1981. — 378p ; 24cm
ISBN 0-86051-146-4 : £7.50 : CIP rev. B81-27442

792′.028′0941 — Great Britain. Acting, *1558-1979*

Forbes, Bryan. That despicable race : a history of the British acting tradition / Bryan Forbes. — London : Elm Tree, 1980. — 326p,[8]p of plates : ill(some col.),ports ; 26cm
Bibliography: p311-316. — Includes index
ISBN 0-241-10164-6 : £15.00 B81-01067

792′.03′21 — Theatre — *Encyclopaedias*

Illustrated encyclopaedia of world theatre / introduction by Martin Esslin ; [adapted and amplified under the general editorship of Martin Esslin]. — London : Thames and Hudson, c1977. — 320p : ill,facsims,ports ; 29cm
Based on Friedrichs Theaterlexikon. Hanover : Friedrich, c1969. — Includes bibliographies and index
ISBN 0-500-27207-7 (pbk) : £5.95 B81-17269

792′.07′073 — United States. Education. Curriculum subjects: Drama

Courtney, Richard. The dramatic curriculum / Richard Courtney. — London : Heinemann, 1980. — xiii,124p : ill ; 23cm
Bibliography: p113-121. - Includes index
ISBN 0-435-18181-5 (pbk) : £3.50 B81-16490

792′.07′1041 — Great Britain. Educational institutions. Curriculum subjects: Drama. Teaching — *Serials*

Drama broadsheet / National Association for the Teaching of Drama. — No.1 (Oct.1979)-. — Mitcham (c/o Mrs M. McNeill, 20, Tamworth Park, Mitcham, Surrey CR4 1HY) : The Association, 1979-. — v. : ill ; 30cm
Three issues yearly. — Description based on: No.4 (Autumn 1980)
ISSN 0261-1651 = Drama broadsheet : £0.30 per issue B81-20073

792′.07′1041 — Great Britain. Schools. Activities: Drama. Teaching. Organisations: Educational Drama Association — *Serials*

[Newsletter *(Educational Drama Association)***]**. Newsletter / Educational Drama Association. — [No.1]-. — [Birmingham] ([Mrs A. Tucker, c/o Blakesley Hall School, Yardley Green Rd, Stechford, Birmingham 33]) : The Association, [197-?]-. — v. ; 30cm
Description based on: Feb.1980 issue
ISSN 0260-311x = Newsletter - Educational Drama Association : Unpriced B81-06388

792′.07′1041 — Great Britain. Schools. Curriculum subjects: Drama

Watkins, Brian. Drama and education / Brian Watkins. — London : Batsford, 1981. — 168p ; 23cm
Bibliography: p164-165. — Includes index
ISBN 0-7134-3419-8 : £6.50 B81-36703

792′.07′1042 — England. Schools. Activities: Drama

Allen, John, *1912-*. Drama in schools : its theory and practice / John Allen. — London : Heinemann Educational, 1979 (1981 [printing]). — xii,196p ; 22cm
Bibliography: p184-191. - Includes index
ISBN 0-435-18033-9 (pbk) : £3.95 B81-19318

792′.07′1141 — Great Britain. Higher education institutions. Curriculum subjects: Drama. Courses — *Directories* — *Serials*

Directory of drama courses in higher education / DATEC. — 1980-81. — London (c/o British Theatre Institute, 30 Clareville St., SW7 5AW) : Drama and Theatre Education Council, c1980. — 68p
Unpriced B81-09700

792′.07′114212 — London *(City)*. **Drama schools: Guildhall School of Music and Drama,** *to 1980*

Guildhall School of Music and Drama. GSMD : a hundred years' performance / Hugh Barty-King. — London : Published for the Guildhall School of Music and Drama by Stainer & Bell, c1980. — 198p : ill,ports ; 22cm
Includes index
ISBN 0-85249-589-7 : £6.50
Primary classification 780′.7′294212 B81-01950

792′.07′12 — Great Britain. Secondary schools. Curriculum subjects: Drama. Teaching — *Manuals*

England, Alan. Scripted drama : a practical guide to teaching techniques / Alan England. — Cambridge : Cambridge University Press, 1981. — x,254p ; 23cm
Bibliography: p244-250. — Includes index
ISBN 0-521-23235-x : £17.50 : CIP rev.
ISBN 0-521-28179-2 (pbk) : £5.95 B81-19203

792.09 — THEATRE. HISTORICAL AND GEOGRAPHICAL TREATMENT

792′.09 — Theatre. Attitudes of society, *to 1980*

Barish, Jonas A.. The antitheatrical prejudice / Jonas Barish. — Berkeley ; London : University of California Press, c1981. — x,499p,[8]p of plates : ill,facsims ; 25cm
Includes index
ISBN 0-520-03735-9 : £14.75 B81-34330

792′.09′034 — Theatre, *1835-1967 — Readings from contemporary sources*

The **theory** of the modern stage : an introduction to modern theatre and drama / edited by Eric Bentley. — Repr. with revisions. — Harmondsworth : Penguin, 1976, c1968 (1979 [printing]). — 493p ; 19cm. — (Pelican books)
Includes translations from German, French, Italian. — Bibliography: p485. — Includes index
ISBN 0-14-020947-6 (pbk) : £2.50 B81-13979

792′.09′04 — Theatre, *1873-1979*

Styan, J. L.. Modern drama in theory and practice / J.L. Styan. — Cambridge : Cambridge University Press
Vol.1: Realism and naturalism. — 1981. — xiii,208p : ill,ports ; 23cm
Bibliography: p182-199. - Includes index
ISBN 0-521-22737-2 : £12.50
ISBN 0-521-23068-3 (set) : Unpriced B81-25929

Styan, J. L.. Modern drama in theory and practice / J.L. Styan. — Cambridge : Cambridge University Press
Vol.2: Symbolism, surrealism and the absurd. — 1981. — xi,224p : ill,ports ; 23cm
Bibliography: p199-216. - Includes index
ISBN 0-521-22738-0 : £12.50
ISBN 0-521-23068-3 (set) : Unpriced B81-25930

Styan, J. L.. Modern drama in theory and practice / J.L. Styan. — Cambridge : Cambridge University Press
Vol.3: Expressionism and epic theatre. — 1981. — xii,230p : ill ; 23cm
Bibliography: p210-222. - Includes index
ISBN 0-521-22739-9 : £12.50
ISBN 0-521-23068-3 (set) : Unpriced B81-25931

792′.09′04 — Theatre, *1900-1980*

Wiles, Timothy J.. The theater event : modern theories of performance / Timothy J. Wiles. — Chicago ; London : University of Chicago Press, 1980. — vi,209p ; 24cm
Includes index
ISBN 0-226-89801-6 : £10.50 B81-03196

792′.09′09352042 — United States. Feminist theatre *— Study regions: Minnesota. Minneapolis*

Leavitt, Dinah Luise. Feminist theatre groups / Dinah Luise Leavitt. — Jefferson, N.C. : McFarland : Bailey & Swinfen, 1980. — vi,153p ; 24cm
Bibliography: p124-136. — Includes index
ISBN 0-89950-005-6 : £8.75 B81-37669

792′.09181′2 — Western world. Popular theatre, *ca1800-1977.* **Political aspects** *— Conference proceedings*

Performance and politics in popular drama : aspects of popular entertainment in theatre, film and television 1800-1976 / edited by David Bradby, Louis James, Bernard Sharratt. — Cambridge : Cambridge University Press, 1980 (1981 [printing]). — xii,331p : ill,music,plans ; 23cm
Conference papers. — Bibliography: p319-322. — List of films: p264-269. — Includes index
ISBN 0-521-28524-0 (pbk) : £6.95 : CIP rev. B81-25814

792′.09181′2 — Western world. Popular theatre, *to 1976 — Conference proceedings*

Western popular theatre : the proceedings of a symposium sponsored by the Manchester University Department of Drama / edited by David Mayer and Kenneth Richards. — London : Methuen, 1977 (1980 [printing]). — x,277p : ill ; 22cm
ISBN 0-416-73150-3 (pbk) : £3.95 : CIP rev. B79-37428

792′.092′4 — Great Britain. Theatre, *1880-1914 — Personal observations*

Robertson, W. Graham. Time was : the reminiscences of W. Graham Robertson / with a foreword by Sir John Gielgud. — London : Quartet, 1981. — xvi,343p,[8]p of plates : ill,ports ; 20cm
Originally published: London : Hamish Hamilton, 1931. — Includes index
ISBN 0-7043-3358-9 (pbk) : £4.50 B81-25642

792′.092′4 — New York *(City).* **Theatre,** *1938-1960 — Personal observations*

Hanff, Helene. Underfoot in show business / Helene Hanff. — London : Deutsch, 1980. — 174p ; 21cm
Originally published: New York : Harper & Row, 1962
ISBN 0-233-97277-3 : £5.95 B81-07415

792′.092′4 — Soviet Union. Theatre. Stanislavskiĭ, K. S. *— Biographies*

Stanislavski, K. S.. My life in art / Constantin Stanislavski ; translated by J.J. Robbins. — London : Eyre Methuen, 1980. — 586p ; 20cm. — (An Eyre Methuen dramabook)
Originally published: Boston, Mass. : Little, Brown ; London : Geoffrey Bles, 1924. — Includes index
ISBN 0-413-46200-5 (pbk) : £4.95 B81-23971

792′.092′4 — United States. Theatre. Criticism. Woollcott, Alexander

Burns, Morris U.. The dramatic criticism of Alexander Woollcott / Morris U. Burns. — Metuchen ; London : Scarecrow ; [Folkestone] : [Bailey & Swinfen] [distributor], 1980. — v,286p ; 23cm
Bibliography: p157-182. - Includes index
ISBN 0-8108-1299-1 : £10.50 B81-04518

792′.094 — Europe. Avant garde theatre, *to 1978*

Innes, C. D.. Holy theatre : ritual and the avant garde / Christopher Innes. — Cambridge : Cambridge University Press, 1981. — xi,283p : ill ; 24cm
Includes index
ISBN 0-521-22542-6 : £4.50
Also classified at 792′.0973 B81-25935

792′.0941 — Great Britain. Theatre. Political aspects, *1968-1978*

Itzin, Catherine. Stages in the revolution : political theatre in Britain since 1968 / Catherine Itzin. — London : Eyre Methuen, 1980. — xv,399p ; 21cm
Bibliography: p390-392. - Includes index
ISBN 0-413-39180-9 (cased) : £9.95
ISBN 0-413-46150-5 (pbk) : £4.50
Also classified at 822′.914′09358 B81-03786

792′.0941 — Great Britain. Theatre. Role of women, *ca 1890-ca 1925 — Feminist viewpoints*

Holledge, Julie. Innocent flowers : women in the Edwardian theatre / Julie Holledge. — London : Virago, 1981. — 218p,[8]p of plates : ill,ports ; 21cm
Bibliography: p211-214. — Includes index
ISBN 0-86068-070-3 (cased) : £9.95 : CIP rev.
ISBN 0-86068-071-1 (pbk) : £4.50 B81-04263

792′.09411 — Scotland. Theatre *— Serials*

Scottish theatre news. — Vol.4, no.8 (Mar.1981)-. — Glasgow (346 Sauchiehall St., Glasgow G2 3JD) : Scottish Society of Playwrights, 1981-. — v. : ill,ports ; 21cm
Monthly. — Continues: Newsletter (Scottish Society of Playwrights). — Description based on: Vol.4, no.9 (Apr.1981)
ISSN 0261-4057 = Scottish theatre news (corrected) : £4.00 per year B81-31049

792′.0942 — England. Theatre, *1300-1660*

Wickham, Glynne. Early English stages 1300 to 1600 / Glynne Wickham. — London : Routledge & Kegan Paul, 1981
Vol.3: Plays and their makers to 1576. — xxxvii,357p,[12]p of plates : ill,1facsim ; 25cm
Bibliography: p313-322. — Includes index
ISBN 0-7100-0218-1 : £14.50 : CIP rev. B79-31324

Wickham, Glynne. Early English stages 1300 to 1660 / by Glynne Wickham. — London : Routledge & Kegan Paul
Vol.1: 1300 to 1576. — 2nd ed. — 1980. — xlvi,428p,xxxiiip of plates : ill,plans ; 24cm
Previous ed.: 1959. — Bibliography: p405-413. — Includes index
ISBN 0-7100-0276-9 : £19.50 : CIP rev. B79-35976

792′.0942 — England. Theatre, *1558-1603 — Conference proceedings*

International Conference on Elizabethan Theatre *(7th : 1977 : University of Waterloo).* The Elizabethan Theatre VII : papers given at the Seventh International Conference on Elizabethan Theatre held at the University of Waterloo, Ontario, in July 1977 / edited and with an introduction by G.R. Hibbard. — London : Published in collaboration with the University of Waterloo [by] Macmillan, 1981, c1980. — xii,204p : ill,2maps,ports ; 23cm
Originally published: Ontario : University of Waterloo, 1980. — Includes index
ISBN 0-333-25738-3 : £15.00 B81-22251

792′.0942 — England. Theatre, *1574-1642*

Gurr, Andrew. The Shakespearean stage 1574-1642 / Andrew Gurr. — 2nd ed. — Cambridge : Cambridge University Press, 1980. — xiii,263p : ill,2maps,facsims,2plans,ports ; 23cm
Previous ed.: 1970. — Bibliography: p245-252. — Includes index
ISBN 0-521-23029-2 (cased) : £18.50 : CIP rev.
ISBN 0-521-29772-9 (pbk) : Unpriced B81-03154

792′.0942 — England. Theatre, *1850-1905*

Rowell, George. Theatre in the age of Irving / George Rowell. — Oxford : Blackwell, 1981. — x,189p : ill,1plan,ports ; 26cm. — (Drama and theatre studies)
Bibliography: p175-178. — Includes index
ISBN 0-631-10711-8 : £12.00 : CIP rev. B81-09500

792′.0942 — England. Theatre, *to ca 1975*

The **Revels** history of drama in English. — London : Methuen
Vol.4: 1613-1660. — Nov.1981. — [300]p
ISBN 0-416-13050-x : £25.00 : CIP entry
Primary classification 822′.009 B81-30321

792′.09421 — London. Theatre, *1592-1613*

Nagler, A. M.. Shakespeare′s stage / by A.M. Nagler ; [translated from the German by Ralph Manheim]. — Enlarged ed. — New Haven ; London : Yale University Press, c1981. — xii,137p,[2]p of plates : ill ; 21cm
Previous ed.: 1958. — Bibliography: p132-134. — Includes index
ISBN 0-300-02689-7 (pbk) : £4.85 : CIP rev. B81-23800

792′.09421 — London. Theatre. Performances, *1900-1909 — Chronologies*

Wearing, J. P.. The London stage 1900-1909 : a calendar of plays and players / by J.P. Wearing. — Metuchen ; London : Scarecrow, 1981. — 2v(xvi,1186p) ; 23cm
Includes index
ISBN 0-8108-1403-x : £35.00 B81-22827

792′.09421 — London. Theatres *— Visitors′ guides*

The **London** theatre scene : theatres : hotels, wining, dining, dancing, shopping, sightseeing, transport / edited by Susan Elms ; illustrated by Clive Desmond. — Chislehurst (8 Wykeham Court, Old Perry St., Chislehurst, Kent BR7 6PN) : Cook, c1979. — 175p : ill,maps(some col.),plans ; 18cm
Ill, map on inside covers
ISBN 0-9506503-0-7 (pbk) : £1.50 B81-06351

792'.09421'34 — London. Kensington and Chelsea *(London Borough)*. Theatre. Companies: English Stage Company, *to 1980*

At the Royal Court : 25 years of the English Stage Company / edited by Richard Findlater. — Ambergate : Amber Lane, 1981. — 201p : ill,ports ; 25cm
Ill on lining papers. — Includes index
ISBN 0-906399-22-x : £12.95 : CIP rev.
B81-02673

792'.09424'98 — West Midlands (Metropolitan County). Coventry. Theatre, *to 1642*

Ingram, Reginald K.. The Coventry records. — Manchester : Manchester University Press, June 1981. — [750]p. — (Records of early English drama)
ISBN 0-7190-0837-9 : £40.00 : CIP entry
B81-08876

792'.09426'723 — Essex. Colchester. Theatre, *to 1980*

Butler, Nicholas. Theatre in Colchester / Nicholas Butler. — [Wivenhoe] ([2 Rose La., Wivenhoe, Essex]) : [N. Butler], c1981. — 105p : ill,facsims,plans,ports ; 31cm
ISBN 0-9507376-0-7 : £7.50 B81-29628

792'.0943 — Germany. Theatre, *1900-1933*

Patterson, Michael. The revolution in German theatre 1900-1933 / Michael Patterson. — Boston, Mass. ; London : Routledge & Kegan Paul, 1981. — xiii,232p,[16]p of plates : ill,ports ; 24cm. — (Theatre production series)
Bibliography: p219-220. — Includes index
ISBN 0-7100-0659-4 : £12.50 B81-27564

792'.09438'6 — Poland. Cracow. Theatres. Companies: Teatr Rapsodyczny, *1953-1967 — Polish texts*

Kotlarczyk, Mieczysław. Reduta słowa : kulisy dwu likwidacji Teatru Rapsodycznego Krakowie : (Karty z pamiętnika) / Mieczysław Kotlarczyk. — Londyn (27 Hamilton Rd, Bedford Park, W4 1AL) : Odnowa, 1980. — xv,231p : ports ; 17cm
ISBN 0-903705-36-2 (pbk) : £2.40 B81-21889

792'.0944 — France. Society. Role of theatre. Theories, *1628-1695*

Phillips, Henry. The theatre and its critics in seventeenth-century France / Henry Phillips. — Oxford : Oxford University Press, 1980. — 275p ; 23cm. — (Oxford modern languages and literature monographs)
Bibliograhy: p256-272. - Includes index
ISBN 0-19-815535-2 : £12.00 : CIP rev.
B80-39887

792'.0946'41 — Spain. Madrid. Theatre. Performance, *1931-1936 — Chronologies*

McGaha, Michael D.. The theatre in Madrid during the Second Republic : a checklist / by Michael D. McGaha. — London : Grant & Cutler, 1979. — 105p ; 22cm. — (Research bibliographies & checklists ; 29)
Includes index
ISBN 0-7293-0080-3 (pbk) : £4.80 B81-07292

792'.09669 — Nigeria. Theatre. Companies: Ogunde Theatre, *to 1977*

Clark, Ebun. Hubert Ogunde : the making of Nigerian theatre / Ebun Clark. — Oxford : Oxford University Press, 1979. — xix,170p : ill,ports ; 23cm
Bibliography: p163-166. — Includes index
ISBN 0-19-575446-8 (cased) : £15.00
ISBN 978-15-4024-9 (cased)
ISBN 0-19-575647-9 (pbk) : Unpriced
B81-17778

792'.0972 — Mexico. Theatre. Companies: Poesía en Voz Alta, *to 1963*

Unger, Roni. Poesia en Vox Alta in the theater of Mexico / Roni Unger. — Columbia ; London : University of Missouri Press, 1981. — x,182p : ill ; 23cm
Bibliography: p159-177. — Includes index
ISBN 0-8262-0333-7 : £12.60 B81-38214

792'.0973 — United States. Avant garde theatre, *to 1978*

Innes, C. D.. Holy theatre : ritual and the avant garde / Christopher Innes. — Cambridge : Cambridge University Press, 1981. — xi,283p : ill ; 24cm
Includes index
ISBN 0-521-22542-6 : £4.50
Primary classification 792'.094 B81-25935

792'.0973 — United States. Theatre. Companies: Federal Theatre Project, *to 1939*

The **Federal** Theatre Project : 'free, adult, uncensored' / foreword by John Houseman ; edited by John O'Connor and Lorraine Brown. — London : Eyre Methuen, 1980. — x,228p : ill(some col.),facsims(some col.),ports ; 22x26cm
Includes index
ISBN 0-413-46770-8 (pbk) : £9.95 B81-07875

792.1 — TRAGEDY AND SERIOUS DRAMA

792.1'6 — Miracle plays in English. Production — *For schools*

Leach, Robert, *1942-*. Medieval theatre / Robert Leach & Martyn Briggs. — London : Harrap, 1981. — 40p : ill,1map,music ; 25cm. — (Harrap's theatre workshop)
Bibliography: p40. - List of sound discs: p40
ISBN 0-245-53499-7 (pbk) : £1.95 B81-14623

792.3 — PANTOMIME

792.3'0941 — Great Britain. Pantomime, *to 1980 — For schools*

Leach, Robert, *1942-*. Panto mime / Robert Leach. — London : Harrap, 1980. — 40p : ill,music ; 25cm. — (Harrap's theatre workshop)
Bibliography: p40
ISBN 0-245-53497-0 (pbk) : £9.00 for 5 copies
B81-01883

792.8 — BALLET

792.8 — Ballet

Clarke, Mary, *1923-*. The ballet goer's guide / Mary Clarke & Clement Crisp. — London : Joseph, 1981. — 352p : ill(some col.),ports (some col.) ; 25cm
Includes index
ISBN 0-7181-2013-2 : £9.50 B81-21168

Dell, Catherine. Ballet dancing / by Catherine Dell. — London : Hamlyn, c1979. — 45p : ill (some col.),ports(some col.) ; 33cm
Col. ill on lining papers. — Includes index
ISBN 0-600-31543-6 : £2.50 B81-01072

Guillot, Geneviève. The book of ballet / Geneviève Guillot and Germaine Prudhommeau ; translator Katherine Carson. — Englewood Cliffs ; London : Prentice-Hall, c1976. — vi,418p : ill ; 24cm. — (A Spectrum book)
Translation of: Grammaire de la danse classique. — Includes index
ISBN 0-13-079897-5 (pbk) : £5.80 B81-12604

Harrold, Robert. Ballet / Robert Harrold. — Poole : Blandford, 1980. — 168p : col.ill,ports ; 20cm
Bibliography: p157-159. — Includes index
ISBN 0-7137-1006-3 (cased) : £3.95 : CIP rev.
ISBN 0-7137-1099-3 (pbk) : £2.95 B80-19368

Kerensky, Oleg. Guinness guide to ballet. — Enfield : Guinness Superlatives, Nov.1981. — [224]p
ISBN 0-85112-226-4 : £11.95 : CIP entry
B81-31198

My favourite ballet stories / edited by Beryl Grey. — Guildford : Lutterworth, 1981. — 126p ; 23cm
ISBN 0-7188-2475-x : £5.50 B81-39063

792.8 — Ballet — *For children*

May, Robin. The world of ballet / Robin May. — London : Macmillan, 1981. — 96p : ill (some col.) ; 30cm. — (Macmillan feature books)
Ill on lining papers. — Includes index
ISBN 0-333-30686-4 : £4.95 : CIP rev.
B81-28200

792.8'025'0903 — Ballet. Stage design, *to 1979*

Williams, Peter, *1914-*. Masterpieces of ballet design / Peter Williams. — Oxford : Phaidon, 1981. — 80p : ill(some col.) ; 28cm
ISBN 0-7148-2042-3 (pbk) : £6.95 : CIP rev.
B80-08344

792.8'025'0924 — Soviet Union. Ballet. Companies: Ballets Russes. Stage design. Bakst, Leon — *Critical studies*

Spencer, Charles. Leon Bakst / Charles Spencer. — London : Academy Editions, 1973 (1978 [printing]). — 248p : ill(some col.),ports ; 31cm
Bibliography: p242-246. - Includes index
Unpriced (pbk)
Also classified at 792.8'026'0924 B81-19957

792.8'026 — Ballet. Costume. Design, *to 1980*

Strong, Roy. Designing for the dancer. — London (20 Garrick St., WC2E 8BJ) : Elron, Apr.1981. — [140]p
ISBN 0-904499-11-1 (pbk) : £4.95 : CIP entry
B81-07478

792.8'026'0924 — Russian ballet. Companies: Ballets Russes. Costumes. Design. Bakst, Leon — *Critical studies*

Spencer, Charles. Leon Bakst / Charles Spencer. — London : Academy Editions, 1973 (1978 [printing]). — 248p : ill(some col.),ports ; 31cm
Bibliography: p242-246. - Includes index
Unpriced (pbk)
Primary classification 792.8'025'0924
B81-19957

792.8'092'4 — Ballet. Criticism. Buckle, Richard — *Biographies*

Buckle, Richard. The most upsetting woman / Richard Buckle. — London : Collins, 1981. — 288p,[8]p of plates : ill,facsims,ports ; 23cm. — (Autobiography ; 1)
Includes index
ISBN 0-00-216326-8 : £8.95 : CIP rev.
B81-26712

792.8'0942 — England. Ballet. Companies: Royal Ballet *(Covent Garden)* & Sadler's Wells Royal Ballet, *to 1980*

Bland, Alexander. The Royal Ballet : the first 50 years / Alexander Bland ; with a foreword by Dame Nanette de Valois. — London : Threshold ; London, c1981. — 320p : ill (some col.),ports ; 30cm
Includes index
ISBN 0-901366-11-0 : £17.95 B81-31405

792.8'2 — Ballet. Dancing — *For children*

Davis, Jesse. Purnell's book for young dancers / [Jesse Davis] ; [with a foreword by Dame Alicia Markova]. — Maidenhead : Purnell, 1981. — 59p : ill(some col.),ports ; 27cm
Ill on lining papers
ISBN 0-361-04516-6 : £3.99 B81-26986

792.8'2 — Ballet. Techniques

Robbins, Jane. Classical dance. — Newton Abbot : David & Charles, Feb.1982. — [192]p
ISBN 0-7153-8274-8 : £6.95 : CIP entry
B81-35823

792.8'2'07 — Ballet. Techniques. Teaching

Woolliams, Anne. Ballet studio : an inside view / by Anne Woolliams ; photographs by Andreas Heumann. — Sydney ; London : Ure Smith, 1978. — 144p : ill ; 29cm
Translation of: Ballettsaal. — Originally published: New York : Mereweather Press, 1978. — Ill on lining papers
ISBN 0-7254-0437-x : Unpriced B81-14336

792.8'2'0924 — Ballet. Dancing. Nijinska, Bronislava — *Biographies*

Nijinska, Bronislava. Bronislava Nijinska : early memoirs. — London : Faber & Faber, Jan.1982. — [576]p
ISBN 0-571-11892-5 : £15.00 : CIP entry
B81-33790

792.8′2′0924 — Ballet. Dancing. Pavlova, Anna — *Biographies*
Lazzarini, John. Pavlova : repertoire of a legend / John and Roberta Lazzarini. — New York : Schirmer ; London : Collier Macmillan, c1980. — 224p : ill,1facsim,ports ; 32cm. — (A Dance horizons book)
Bibliography: p214-216. - Includes index
ISBN 0-02-871970-0 : £14.95 B81-15620

792.8′2′0924 — Ballet. Dancing. Pavlova, Anna — *Biographies — For children*
Willson, Robina Beckles. Anna Pavlova : a legend among dancers / by Robina Beckles Willson. — London : Hodder and Stoughton, 1981. — 128p : ill,ports ; 25cm. — (Twentieth century people)
Includes index
ISBN 0-340-25871-3 : £4.95 B81-14746

792.8′2′0924 — Ballet. Dancing. Pavlova, Anna — *Illustrations*
Anna Pavlova : a photographic essay / [compiled by Jasmin Cannon Bell]. — [London] : [H.M.S.O. in collaboration with the Museum of London], [1981]. — 23p : chiefly ill,ports ; 20x21cm
Cover title. — Ill on end papers
ISBN 0-11-290358-4 (pbk) : £1.95 B81-10662

792.8′2′0924 — Ballet. Dancing. Sibley, Antoinette *— Illustrations*
Spatt, Leslie E.. Antoinette Sibley / photographs by Leslie E. Spatt ; text by Mary Clarke ; introduction by Sir Frederick Ashton. — London : Dance Books, 1981. — 128p : chiefly ill,ports ; 32cm
ISBN 0-903102-64-1 : £9.95 B81-35183

792.8′42 — Ballet. Macmillan, Kenneth. Isadora. Creation
Thorpe, Edward. Creating a ballet. — London : Evans, Oct.1981. — [128]p
ISBN 0-237-45554-4 : £7.50 : CIP entry
B81-25730

792.8′45 — Ballet, *1836-1980 — Critical studies*
Brinson, Peter. Ballet and dance : a guide to the repertory / Peter Brinson and Clement Crisp. — Newton Abbot : David & Charles, 1980. — xi,274p,[16]p of plates : ill,ports ; 22cm
Bibliography: p257-259. - Includes index
ISBN 0-7153-8114-8 : £7.95 : CIP rev.
B80-23614

Brinson, Peter. The Pan book of ballet and dance : a guide to the repertory / Peter Brinson and Clement Crisp. — Rev. and expanded ed.. — London : Pan, 1981, c1980. — xi,274p,[16]p of plates : ill ; 20cm
Previous ed.: published as Ballet for all. 1970. — Bibliography: p257-259. - Includes index
ISBN 0-330-26319-6 (pbk) : £2.50 B81-20990

792.8′45 — Ballet. Performance, *1959-1975 — Reviews*
Buckle, Richard. Buckle at the ballet : selected criticism / by Richard Buckle. — London : Dance Books, 1980. — 416p : ill,ports ; 24cm
Includes index
ISBN 0-903102-53-6 : £8.95 B81-01623

792.8′45 — Ballet, *to 1979 — Plot outlines*
Phaidon book of the ballet / editor-in-chief Riccardo Mezzanotte ; editors and picture researchers Francesca Agostini, Ada Jorio ; translated from the Italian by Olive Ordish ; with a preface by Rudolf Nureyev. — Oxford : Phaidon, 1981, c1980. — 323p : ill(some col.),ports ; 28cm
Translation of: Il balletto. — Includes index
ISBN 0-7148-2192-6 : £20.00 B81-23406

792.8′45 — Russian ballet, *1877-1910 — Plot outlines — Collections — For children*
Appleby, William. Nutcracker ; and, Swan lake / by William Appleby and Frederick Fowler ; illustrated by Audrey Walker. — London : Oxford University Press, 1960 (1980 [printing]). — 58p : ill ; 21cm
Contents: Nutcracker ; and, Swan lake. Originally published: 1960. — The sleeping beauty ; and, The firebird / illustrated by Alan Clark. — Originally published: 1964
ISBN 0-19-314924-9 (pbk) : £3.50 B81-06723

792.9 — THEATRE. SPECIFIC PRODUCTIONS

792.9′2 — Drama in English. Shakespeare, William. Coriolanus. Performances by Royal Shakespeare Company in Western Europe, *1979 — Critical studies*
Daniell, David. Coriolanus in Europe / David Daniell. — London : Athlone, 1980. — x,171p : ill,2facsims,ports ; 26cm
ISBN 0-485-11192-6 : £9.95 : CIP rev.
B80-17899

792.9′2 — Drama in German. Brecht, Bertolt. Leben des Galilei. Performance by National Theatre
Hiley, Jim. Theatre at work : the story of the National Theatre′s production of Brecht′s Galileo / Jim Hiley. — London : Routledge & Kegan Paul, 1981. — xi,239p : ill,ports ; 24cm
ISBN 0-7100-0815-5 (cased) : £9.75
ISBN 0-7100-0859-7 (pbk) : £5.95 B81-23707

792.9′5 — Drama in English. Shakespeare, William. Performance, *to 1980*
Berry, Ralph. Changing styles in Shakespeare / Ralph Berry. — London : Allen & Unwin, 1981. — 123p ; 23cm
Includes index
ISBN 0-04-822042-6 : Unpriced : CIP rev.
B81-13449

792.9′5 — Drama in English. Shakespeare, William. Performances in England, *1955-1976 — Critical studies*
David, Richard. Shakespeare in the theatre / Richard David. — Cambridge : Cambridge University Press, 1978 (1981 [printing]). — xv,263p : ill ; 23cm
Includes index
ISBN 0-521-28490-2 (pbk) : £7.95 : CIP rev.
B81-16355

792.9′5 — Drama in English. Shakespeare, William. Productions by Irving, Henry — *Critical studies*
Hughes, Alan, *1939-*. Henry Irving, Shakespearean / Alan Hughes ; with a foreword by John Russell Brown. — Cambridge : Cambridge University Press, 1981. — xvi,304p : ill,1facsim,ports ; 24cm
Includes index
ISBN 0-521-22192-7 : £18.50 B81-10664

792.9′5 — Great Britain. Theatre. Performances, *1945-1979 — Reviews — Anthologies*
Post-war British theatre criticism / [compiled] by John Elsom ; with drawings by Feliks Topolski. — London : Routledge & Kegan Paul, 1980. — 270p : ill ; 23cm
Includes index
ISBN 0-7100-0535-0 (cased) : £8.95 : CIP rev.
ISBN 0-7100-0536-9 (pbk) : £5.95 B80-20956

792.9′5′09421 — London. Theatre. Performances, *1892-1903 — Reviews*
Gielgud, Kate Terry. A Victorian playgoer / Kate Terry Gielgud ; with forewords by John Gielgud, Val Gielgud, Eleanor Gielgud ; edited by Muriel St Clare Byrne. — London : Heinemann, 1980. — xvi,126p,[8]p of plates : ill,ports ; 25cm
Includes index
ISBN 0-435-18320-6 : £9.50 : CIP rev.
B79-25871

792.9′5′09421 — London. Theatre. Performances — *Reviews — Serials*
London theatre record. — Vol.1 issues 1/2 (1-28 Jan.1981)-. — Twickenham (4 Cross Deep Gardens, Twickenham, Middx TW1 4QU) : I. Herbert, 1981-. — v. ; 30cm
Fortnightly
ISSN 0261-5282 = London theatre record : £40.00 per year B81-32255

793 — INDOOR GAMES AND AMUSEMENTS

793 — English pub games
Finn, Timothy. Pub games of England. — 2nd ed. — Cambridge : Oleander, June 1981. — [196]p. — (Oleander games & pastimes ; v.5)
Previous ed.: London : Queen Anne Press, 1975
ISBN 0-900891-66-1 (cased) : £7.50 : CIP entry
ISBN 0-900891-67-x (pbk) : £4.95 B81-14806

793 — Indoor activities — *Manuals*
Brandreth, Gyles. The complete home entertainer / Gyles Brandreth. — London : Hale, 1981. — 240p : ill ; 23cm
ISBN 0-7091-9145-6 : £7.95 B81-31665

793 — Indoor games for two players — *Collections*
Wasley, John. Games for two / John Wasley. — London : Proteus, 1981. — 220p : ill ; 28cm
ISBN 0-906071-26-7 (pbk) : £4.95 B81-25090

793 — Indoor games — *Manuals*
Brandreth, Gyles. Everyman′s indoor games / [compiled by] Gyles Brandreth. — London : Dent, 1981. — 304p : ill ; 24cm
Includes index
ISBN 0-460-04456-7 : £7.95 : CIP rev.
B81-00229

Wiswell, Phil. 'I hate charades' : and 49 other new games / Phil Wiswell. — New York : Sterling ; London : Oak Tree, c1981. — 111p : ill ; 22cm
Includes index
ISBN 0-7061-2803-6 : Unpriced B81-39866

793 — Musical games - *Collections*
Storms, G.. Handbook of music games. — London : Hutchinson Education, Sept.1981. — [152]p
Translation of: Muzikaal Spelenboek
ISBN 0-09-144531-0 (pbk) : £3.95 : CIP entry
B81-20179

793 — Musical games for children — *Collections*
Powell, Harriet. Game-songs with Prof Dogg′s Troupe : learning through fun for the under sevens / Harriet Powell ; foreword by Ed Berman ; drawings by Elizabeth Leyh. — London : Inter-Action Inprint in association with the Institute for Social Enterprise, 1980. — 64p : ill,music ; 21cm + 1 sound cassette. — (The Inter-Action community arts series)
ISBN 0-904571-26-2 (spiral) : £2.95
B81-29760

793.2 — Party games — *Manuals*
Hallett, David. Profit at the party : it′s not magic plus / by David Hallett ; illustrations by Ali Bongo. — Bideford (64 High St., Bideford, Devon) : Supreme Magic, c1981. — 112p : ill,ports ; 26cm
Unpriced B81-40595

793.2′1 — Entertainments: Children′s parties — *Manuals*
Cable-Alexander, Jane. Giving a children′s party / Jane Cable-Alexander ; with photographs by Sandra Lousada and John Cook. — London (39 Park St., W1Y 4DE) : Park Lane, 1980. — 79p : col.ill,music ; 28cm
Includes index
£0.99 (pbk) B81-07004

Morris, Neil. A pocket book of children′s parties / Neil and Ting Morris. — London : Evans Brothers, 1981. — 128p : ill ; 17cm
Includes index
ISBN 0-237-45555-2 (pbk) : £1.95 B81-32498

793.3 — French court dancing, *1690-1725*
Hilton, Wendy. Dance of court & theater : the French noble style 1690-1725 / Wendy Hilton ; edited by Caroline Gaynor ; labanotation by Mireille Backer. — London : Dance Books, 1981. — viii,356p : ill,music,ports ; 29cm
Bibliography: p335-349. — Includes index
ISBN 0-903102-61-7 : £15.00
Also classified at 793.3′2′0944 B81-29707

793.3 — Popular dancing — *Manuals*
Borrows, Frank. The dancers guide for the 1980s / Frank Borrows. — Newbury : National Association of Teachers of Dancing, 1980. — 56p ; 19cm
Bibliography: p55
Unpriced (pbk) B81-04594

793.3′023 — Dancing — *Career guides — For men*
Glasstone, Richard. Male dancing as a career / Richard Glasstone ; photography by Simon Rae-Scott. — London : Kaye & Ward, 1980. — ix,111p : ill,ports ; 22cm
ISBN 0-7182-1253-3 : £4.95 B81-01562

793.3'024796 — Choreography & dancing — *Manuals — For gymnastics*

Honeyman, Jean. Dance training and choreography for gymnasts / Jean Honeyman. — London : Stanley Paul, 1981. — 125p : ill,forms ; 25cm
ISBN 0-09-141800-3 (cased) : £6.95 : CIP rev.
ISBN 0-09-141801-1 (pbk) : £3.95 B80-10192

793.3'09 — Dancing, *to 1979*

Clarke, Mary, *1923-*. The history of dance / Mary Clarke & Clement Crisp. — London : Orbis, 1981. — 256p : ill(some col.) ; 30cm
Bibliography: p248-249. — Includes index
ISBN 0-85613-270-5 : £15.00 B81-15049

Kraus, Richard. History of the dance : in art and education. — 2nd ed. / Richard Kraus, Sarah Alberti Chapman. — Englewood Cliffs ; London : Prentice-Hall, c1981. — x,372p : ill ; 25cm
Previous ed.: 1969. — Includes index
ISBN 0-13-390021-5 : £10.35 B81-19827

793.3'0973 — United States. Dancing, *to 1979*

De Mille, Anges. America dances / Agnes de Mille. — New York : Macmillan ; London : Collier Macmillan, c1980. — xvii,222p,[8]p of plates : ill(some col.),ports(some col.) ; 29cm. — (A Helene Obolensky Enterprises, Inc. book)
Bibliography: p213-214. - Includes index
ISBN 0-02-530730-4 : £13.95 B81-19598

793.3'194 — European dancing — *Manuals*

Imperial Society of Teachers of Dancing. Notes for the professional examinations, grade examinations and dancers' medal tests / Imperial Society of Teachers of Dancing ; compiled by the Committee of the National Dance Branch. — 4th ed. (rev.). — London : the Society, 1979. — 126p : ill ; 22cm
Previous ed.: 1973
£3.00 (pbk) B81-37721

793.3'1941 — British country dancing — *Manuals*

Smedley, Ronald. Let's dance — country style : a handbook of simple, traditional dances / Ronald Smedley and John Tether ; illustrations by Rowland Howls ; technical drawings by John Barber. — Rev. ed. — London : Granada, 1981. — 128p : ill,music ; 20cm
Previous ed.: London : Elek, 1972
ISBN 0-246-11541-6 (pbk) : £2.95 B81-24445

793.3'19411 — Scottish country dancing — *Collections*

Mitchell, John W.. The Whetherly book of Scottish country dances / by John W. Mitchell. — Hove (52, Shirley Drive, Hove, BN3 6UF) : Wallace Mitchell
No.1. — 2nd ed. — [1981]. — 19leaves : ill ; 30cm
Previous ed.: 197-?
Unpriced (unbound) B81-36671

Mitchell, John W.. The Whetherly book of Scottish country dances / by John W. Mitchell. — Hove (52, Shirley Drive, Hove, BN3 6UF) : Wallace Mitchell
No.2. — 2nd ed. — [1981]. — 13leaves : ill ; 30cm
Previous ed.: 1978
Unpriced (unbound) B81-36670

Mitchell, John W.. The Whetherly book of Scottish country dances / by John W. Mitchell. — Hove (52, Shirley Drive, Hove, BN3 6UF) : Wallace Mitchell
No.3. — 2nd ed. — [1981]. — 10leaves ; 30cm
Previous ed.: 1978
Unpriced (unbound) B81-36669

Mitchell, John W.. The Whetherly book of Scottish country dances / John W. Mitchell. — Hove (52, Shirley Drive, Hove, Sussex, BN3 6UF) : Wallace Mitchell
No.10. — [1981]. — 23leaves ; 30cm
Unpriced (unbound) B81-36668

793.3'19411 — Scottish country dancing — *Manuals*

Mitchell, John W.. The Whetherly book of Scottish country dances / by John W. Mitchell. — Hove (52 Shirley Drive, Hove, E. Sussex BW3 6UF) : Wallace Mitchell and Co.
No.9. — [1981?]. — 25leaves ; 30cm
Unpriced (pbk) B81-30653

793.3'19411 — Scottish solo folk dances — *Manuals*

The **Sailors'** hornpipe : Scottish version as danced at Highland Games 1976 ; The Irish jig : Scottish version / prepared by the Technical Committee of the Scottish Official Board of Highland Dancing. — [Edinburgh] ([8 Regent Terrace, Edinburgh 7]) : [Scottish Official Board of Highland Dancing], 1976. — 31p ; 22cm
Cover title
Unpriced (pbk) B81-21961

793.3'1942 — English folk dancing, *to 1980*

Rippon, Hugh. Discovering English folk dance / Hugh Rippon. — 2nd ed. — Aylesbury : Shire, 1981. — 64p : ill ; 18cm. — (Discovering series ; no.206)
Previous ed.: 1975. — Includes index
ISBN 0-85263-543-5 (pbk) : £1.15 B81-17556

793.3'1942 — Morris dancing

Wortley, Russell. Russell Wortley 1912-1980 / [edited by John Jenner and Andrew Richards]. — Cambridge : [Cambridge Morris Men], 1980. — 47p : ill,1map,music,ports ; 30cm
Bibliography: p45-46
Unpriced (pbk) B81-10399

793.3'1954 — Indian dancing

Khokar, Mohan. Traditions of Indian classical dance / Mohan Khokar, text & illustrations. — London : Peter Owen, 1980, c1979. — 168p,[16]p of plates : ill ; 29cm
Includes index
ISBN 0-7206-0574-1 : £10.50 B81-12117

793.3'2 — Body movements. Labananalysis

Bartenieff, Irmgard. Body movement : coping with the environment / by Irmgard Bartenieff ; with Dori Lewis. — New York ; London : Gordon and Breach, 1980. — xiv,289p : ill ; 26cm
Bibliography: p275-286. — Includes index
ISBN 0-677-05500-5 : Unpriced B81-06167

793.3'2 — Dancing. Laban notation

Knust, Albrecht. Dictionary of kinetography Laban (Labanotation) / Albrecht Knust ; translated with the assistance of Diana Baddeley-Lange, Sally Archbutt, Irene Wachtel ; final supervision of text William C. Reynolds ; [illustrations by Annemie Schoenfeldt-Juris]. — Plymouth : Macdonald & Evans, 1979. — 2v. : ill,1port ; 26cm
Translation from the German. - English, German, and French captions. — Originally published: Boston : Plays, 1978. — Includes index
ISBN 0-7121-0416-x : £25.00 B81-08675

793.3'2 — Modern dance. Examinations — *Syllabuses*

Imperial Society of Teachers of Dancing. Modern dance branch : guide to the grade examinations Primary to Grade IV in modern dance and in tap dancing : including the Modern dance set amalgamations and also the Junior Medal tests bronze to gold star / Imperial Society of Teachers of Dancing. — Rev. and enl. ed.. — London : Imperial Society of Teachers of Dancing, 1979. — 78p ; 21cm
Cover title. — Previous ed.: 1971
£2.00 (pbk) B81-09322

793.3'2'071073 — United States. Educational institutions. Cirriculum subjects: Dancing. Teaching

Hays, Joan F.. Modern dance : a biomechanical approach to teaching / Joan F. Hays. — St. Louis ; London : Mosby, 1981. — x,317p : ill ; 24cm
Includes index
ISBN 0-8016-2179-8 (pbk) : £9.25 B81-31151

793.3'2'071242 — England. Secondary schools. Curriculum subjects: Dancing. Teaching

Allcock, Rita. Dance in education / by Rita Allcock and Wendy Bland. — London : Dance Books, 1980. — 179p : ill ; 23cm
ISBN 0-903102-51-x : £4.95 B81-02720

793.3'2'09 — Modern dance, *to 1979*

The **Vision** of modern dance / edited by Jean Morrison Brown. — London : Dance Books, 1980, c1979. — x,196p : ill,ports ; 23cm
Originally published: Princeton : Princeton Book Co., c1979. — Bibliography: p181-194. — Includes index
ISBN 0-903102-54-4 (cased) : £6.00
ISBN 0-903102-55-2 (pbk) : £3.00 B81-01968

793.3'2'0924 — Dancing. Baker, Josephine - *Biographies*

Haney, Lynn. Naked at the feast : a biography of Josephine Baker. — London : Robson, May 1981. — [352]p
ISBN 0-86051-140-5 : £7.50 : CIP entry B81-10006

793.3'2'0924 — Dancing. Churchill, Sarah — *Biographies*

Churchill, Sarah. Keep on dancing : an autobiography / Sarah Churchill ; edited by Paul Medlicott. — London : Weidenfeld and Nicolson, 1981. — x,243p,[16]p of plates : ill,ports ; 24cm
Includes index
ISBN 0-297-77906-0 : £7.95 B81-16305

793.3'2'0944 — France. Theatrical dance, *1690-1725*

Hilton, Wendy. Dance of court & theater : the French noble style 1690-1725 / Wendy Hilton ; edited by Caroline Gaynor ; labanotation by Mireille Backer. — London : Dance Books, 1981. — viii,356p : ill,music,ports ; 29cm
Bibliography: p335-349. — Includes index
ISBN 0-903102-61-7 : £15.00
Primary classification 793.3 B81-29707

793.73 — General knowledge — *Questions & answers*

Ardley, Bridget. 1001 questions and answers. — London (Elsley Court, 20 Great Titchfield St., W1P 7AD) : Kingfisher, Sept.1981. — [160]p
ISBN 0-86272-000-1 : £3.95 : CIP entry B81-20166

Brandling, Redvers. Check up tests in workskills / Redvers Brandling. — London : Macmillan Education, 1981. — 48p : ill,maps ; 26cm
ISBN 0-333-31520-0 (pbk) : Unpriced B81-34695

Hickman, Norman G.. Quintessential quizzes. — London : Unwin Paperbacks, Jan.1982. — [144]p
ISBN 0-04-793050-0 (pbk) : £1.95 : CIP entry B81-33907

Monkhouse, Bob. Celebrity quiz book / Bob Monkhouse. — London : Hamlyn Paperbacks, 1980. — 112p ; 18cm
ISBN 0-600-20111-2 (pbk) : £0.95 B81-02522

793.73 — General knowledge — *Questions & answers — For children*

Holt, Michael. The bumper quiz book / compiled by Michael Holt ; illustrated by Chris Winn. — London : Scholastic, 1981. — 93p : ill ; 18cm. — (A Hippo book)
ISBN 0-590-70029-4 (pbk) : £0.65 B81-14699

793.73 — General knowledge — *Questions & answers — For children — Serials*

Fun-to-know annual. — 1981. — London : IPC Magazines, c1980. — 18p
ISBN 0-85037-623-8 : £1.80 B81-06846

793.73 — Jigsaw puzzles, *to 1980*

Hannas, Linda. The jigsaw book. — London : Hutchinson, Oct.1981. — [96]p
ISBN 0-09-145541-3 (pbk) : £7.95 : CIP entry B81-26766

793.73 — Logical puzzles — *Collections*

Bragdon, Allen. Diabolical diversions. — London : Muller, Apr.1981. — [128]p
Originally published: Garden City : Doubleday, 1980
ISBN 0-584-97070-6 (pbk) : £2.50 : CIP entry
B81-03160

Emmet, E. R.. The Island of Imperfection puzzle book : with other assorted brainteasers / E.R. Emmet. — New York ; London : Barnes & Noble, c1980. — xiv,141p : 21cm
ISBN 0-06-337011-5 (pbk) : £1.95
ISBN 0-06-463512-0 (U.S.) B81-05707

Smullyan, Raymond M.. What is the name of this book? : the riddle of Dracula and other logical puzzles / Raymond Smullyan. — Harmondsworth : Penguin, 1981, c1978. — 255p : ill ; 18cm. — (Pelican books)
Originally published: Englewood Cliffs ; London : Prentice-Hall, 1978
ISBN 0-14-022339-8 (pbk) : £1.95 B81-40439

The **Sunday** times book of brain-teasers. — London : Unwin Paperbacks
Bk.2 / 51 master problems selected, compiled and edited by Victor Bryant and Ronald Postill. — 1981. — [160]p : ill ; 18cm
ISBN 0-04-793046-2 (pbk) : £1.95 : CIP rev.
B81-03672

793.73 — Pictorial puzzles — *Collections — For children*

Walt Disney presents Winnie-the-Pooh friends to find. — Maidenhead : Purnell, 1981. — [16]p : chiefly col.ill ; 20cm. — (A Hunny pot book)
£0.35 (pbk) B81-09730

Walt Disney presents Winnie-the-Pooh hidden pictures. — Maidenhead : Purnell, 1981. — [16]p : chiefly col.ill ; 20cm. — (A Hunny pot book)
£0.35 (pbk) B81-09727

Walt Disney presents Winnie-the-Pooh puzzles. — Maidenhead : Purnell, 1981. — [16]p : chiefly col.ill ; 20cm. — (A Hunny pot book)
£0.35 (pbk) B81-09728

Young, Joyce. The Ladybird book of puzzles / by Joyce and Peter Young ; illustrated by Kathie Layfield. — Loughborough : Ladybird, 1981. — 28p : col.ill ; 24cm
ISBN 0-7214-0650-5 (pbk) : £0.40 B81-20831

793.73 — Pictorial puzzles. Special subjects: Livestock: Ponies — *Collections — For children*

Popescu, Charlotte. Pony puzzles / compiled by Charlotte Popescu ; illustrated by St. Ward. — London : Armada, 1981. — 80p : chiefly ill ; 19cm
ISBN 0-00-691883-2 (pbk) : £0.80 B81-38119

793.73 — Puzzles — *Collections*

Weekend book of mind benders : a selection of tantalising brain teasers from Weekend magazine. — [London] : Harmsworth for Associated Newspapers, c1981. — [64]p : ill,ports ; 24cm
£0.60 (pbk) B81-32813

793.73 — Puzzles — *Collections — For children*

Booth-Jones, Charles. Even more brain ticklers / Charles Booth-Jones ; illustrated by David Mostyn. — London : Beaver, 1980. — 94p : ill ; 18cm
ISBN 0-600-39542-1 (pbk) : £0.75 B81-03329

Dean's funtime puzzlers. — London : Dean
no.1. — c1980. — 64p : ill ; 14cm
ISBN 0-603-00226-9 (pbk) : £0.15 B81-13064

Dean's funtime puzzlers. — London : Dean
no.2. — c1980. — 64p : ill ; 14cm
ISBN 0-603-00227-7 (pbk) : £0.15 B81-13065

Dean's funtime puzzlers. — London : Dean
no.3. — c1980. — 64p : ill ; 14cm
ISBN 0-603-00228-5 (pbk) : £0.15 B81-13066

Dean's funtime puzzlers. — London : Dean
no.4. — c1980. — 64p : ill ; 14cm
ISBN 0-603-00229-3 (pbk) : £0.15 B81-13067

Dean's funtime puzzlers. — London : Dean
no.5. — c1980. — 64p : ill ; 14cm
ISBN 0-603-00230-7 (pbk) : £0.15 B81-13068

Dean's funtime puzzlers. — London : Dean
no.6. — c1980. — 64p : ill ; 14cm
ISBN 0-603-00231-5 (pbk) : £0.15 B81-13069

Flash Gordon versus the beast men. — London : Beaver, 1981. — 80p : chiefly ill ; 18cm. — (Puzzle book ; 5)
ISBN 0-600-20292-5 (pbk) : £0.70 B81-12698

Flash Gordon versus the incredible Kang. — London : Beaver, 1981. — 80p : chiefly ill ; 18cm. — (Puzzle book ; 6)
ISBN 0-600-20293-3 (pbk) : £0.70 B81-12699

Holt, Michael. Figure it out / Michael Holt. — London : Granada. — (A Dragon book)
3 / illustrated by Pat Hickman. — 1981. — [96]p : ill ; 18cm
ISBN 0-583-30302-1 (pbk) : £0.75 B81-11624

Holt, Michael. Figure it out / Michael Holt. — London : Granada. — (A Dragon book)
4 / illustrated by Pat Hickman. — 1981. — [95]p : ill ; 18cm
ISBN 0-583-30304-8 (pbk) : £0.75 B81-11621

Ridout, Ronald. Puzzles galore / Ronald Ridout. — London : Dragon : Granada, 1976 (1979 printing). — [94]p : ill,1map ; 18cm. — (Dragon puzzle books)
ISBN 0-583-30236-x (pbk) : £0.50 B81-22169

Thornton, David, *1935-*. Puzzle it out with Alfie / by David Thornton. — Leeds : D & J Thornton, [1981]. — (The Adventures of Alfie Apple)
No.1. — [23]p : chiefly col. ; 11x15cm
ISBN 0-907339-12-3 (pbk) : £0.50 B81-36110

Weekend book of children's puzzles. — [London] : Harmsworth for Associated Newspapers, c1981. — [64]p : chiefly ill ; 24cm
£0.60 (pbk) B81-32814

Wells, David. Solve it! / David Wells. — London : Granada, 1981. — 91p : ill ; 18cm. — (A Dragon book)
ISBN 0-583-30316-1 (pbk) : £0.60 B81-13054

793.73 — Puzzles: Mazes — *Collections*

Phillips, Dave. Mind-boggling mazes : 40 graphic and 3-D labyrinths / Dave Phillips. — New York : Dover ; London : Constable, 1979. — [61]p : chiefly ill ; 28cm
ISBN 0-486-23798-2 (pbk) : £1.45 B81-11083

793.73 — Puzzles: Mazes - *Collections*

Wood, Les. Mazes and mandalas. — London : Muller, July 1981. — [80]p
ISBN 0-584-10419-7 (pbk) : £3.95 : CIP entry
B81-14458

793.73 — Puzzles. Special subjects: Celebrities — *Collections — For children*

Jamieson, Alan. Who do you know? / Alan Jamieson. — London : Granada, 1981. — 80p : ill,maps ; 18cm. — (A Dragon book)
ISBN 0-583-30459-1 (pbk) : £0.95 B81-31389

793.73 — Puzzles. Special subjects: 'Marvel' comics. Characters — *Collections — For children — Serials*

Superhero fun and games. — No.1 (Mar.1980)-. — London (205 Kentish Town Rd, NW5) : Marvel Comics, [1980]-. — v. : chiefly ill ; 28cm
Monthly
ISSN 0260-0528 = Superhero fun and games : £0.25 per issue B81-07962

793.73 — Puzzles. Special subjects: Names — *Collections — Serials*

The **Name** game magazine. — Vol.1, no.1-. — London : Gadoline House, Godstone Rd, Whyteleafe, Surrey : Moore Harness, 1980-. — v. : ill,ports ; 28cm
Monthly. — Description based on: Vol.1, no.4
£5.50 per year B81-16233

793.73 — Puzzles. Special subjects: Pop music — *Collections — Serials*

Pop puzzles. — Vol.3, no.6-. — Hastings (PO Box 19, Hastings, E. Sussex TN34 1HB) : Dormbourne ; Horsham : Distributed by Wells Gardner, Darton & Co., 1981-. — v. : ill ; 25cm
Monthly. — Continues: Discowords
ISSN 0261-1902 = Pop puzzles : £0.35 per issue B81-16823

793.73 — Puzzles. Special subjects: Transport — *Collections — For children*

Jamieson, Alan. Cars, boats, trains and planes / Alan Jamieson ; illustrated by Philip Page. — Harmondsworth : Puffin, 1981. — 63p : ill,maps ; 20cm. — (An Outdoors puzzle book)
Text on inside back cover
ISBN 0-14-031314-1 (pbk) : £0.80 B81-21008

793.73 — Puzzles. Special subjects: Treasure hunting — *Collections — For children — Serials*

[Treasure trove *(London)*]. Treasure trove. — Vol.1, no.1 [Nov.1980]-v.1, no.3 (Jan.1981). — London (30 Langham St, W1N 5LB) : Byblos Productions, 1980-1981. — 3v. : ill ; 28cm
Monthly
£0.40 per issue B81-17481

793.73 — Scrabble — *Manuals*

Brandreth, Gyles. The complete book of Scrabble / Gyles Brandreth. — London : Hale, 1980. — 168p : ill ; 21cm
ISBN 0-7091-8385-2 : £4.50 B81-0023C

793.73 — Scrabble. Problems — *Collections*

Brandreth, Gyles. The Scrabble puzzle book / Gyles Brandreth. — London : Queen Anne, 1981. — 128p ; 25cm
ISBN 0-362-00570-2 : Unpriced B81-40844

793.73 — Word games: Enneagrams — *Collections*

Graves, Ian D.. Enneagrams : the game of nine letter words / Ian D. Graves. — Cambridge : Oleander, c1981. — 63p : chiefly ill ; 20cm
ISBN 0-900891-78-5 (cased) : £4.20 B81-1648

793.73 — Word puzzles — *Collections*

Doig, Clive. The second book of jigsaw puzzles. — London : Hodder & Stoughton, Oct.1981. — [96]p. — (Knight books)
Originally published: London : British Broadcasting Corporation, 1980
ISBN 0-340-27745-9 (pbk) : £0.85 : CIP entry
B81-2461

Doig, Clive. The third book of jigsaw puzzles. — London : Hodder & Stoughton, Nov.1981. — [96]p. — (Knight books)
ISBN 0-340-27746-7 (pbk) : £0.85 : CIP entry
B81-3012

Richter, Alan. Warne's book of word puzzles : original puzzles for bright minds / Alan Richter. — London : Warne, 1981. — 63p ; 19cm
ISBN 0-7232-2790-x (pbk) : Unpriced
B81-3296

The **Wordfinder** puzzle book. — London : Spher
2. — 1981. — [123]p : ill ; 18cm
ISBN 0-7221-9256-8 (pbk) : £1.00 B81-385

793.73 — Word puzzles — *Collections — For children*

Brandreth, Gyles. The crazy word book / Gyles Brandreth ; illustrated by Jacqui Sinclair. — London : Transworld, 1981. — 110p : ill ; 20cm. — (A Carousel book)
ISBN 0-552-54182-6 (pbk) : £0.75 B81-278

Duncan, Pat, *1921-*. Find a word 3 / Pat Duncan. — London : Beaver, 1981. — 127p ; 18cm
ISBN 0-600-20296-8 (pbk) : £0.75 B81-231

793.73'05 — General knowledge — *Questions & answers — For children — Serials*

The **Look** and learn book of 1001 questions and answers. — 1981. — London : IPC Magazines, c1980. — [76]p
ISBN 0-85037-550-9 : £2.20 B81-124

793.73′05 — Pictorial puzzles — *Collections* — *For children* — *Serials*

Picture puzzles. — No.5. — London (Carmelite House, [Carmelite St.], EC4) : Harmsworth for Associated Newspapers Groups, c1981. — [62]p
£0.45 B81-32890

Walt Disney's puzzle time annual. — 1981. — London : IPC Magazines, c1980. — 79p
ISBN 0-85037-624-6 : £2.40 B81-06864

793.73′05 — Puzzles — *Collections* — *For children* — *Serials*

Fun-to-do annual. — 1981. — London : IPC Magazines, c1980. — 79p
ISBN 0-85037-602-5 : £1.80 B81-06847

Junior puzzler. — No.1 (Winter ed.)-. — London (174 Culford Rd, N1) : J.P.S. Publications, [1980]-. — v. : ill(some col.) ; 28cm
Six issues yearly
ISSN 0261-1163 = Junior puzzler : £0.50 B81-28390

Let's play games. — Vol.1, no.1-. — London (174 Culford Rd, N.1) : Walton Press Sales, 1980-. — v. : ill(some col.) ; 27cm
Six issues yearly
ISSN 0261-1155 = Let's play games : £0.50 B81-28391

793.73′05 — Puzzles — *Collections* — *Serials*

The **Puzzle** paper. — No.1 (Summer 1980)-. — London : Mirror Books, 1980-. — v. : ill ; 36cm
Irregular
ISSN 0261-2615 = Puzzle paper : £0.35 B81-30009

Puzzlers world. — No.1 (1978)-. — London : Model and Allied Publications, 1978-. — v. : ill ; 27cm
Monthly. — Description based on: No.27 (Feb.1981)
ISSN 0261-0256 = Puzzlers world : £7.90 B81-11866

Top puzzles. — No.1 (June/July 1981)-. — Luton (23a George St., Luton, Beds.) : AHC Publications, 1981-. — v. : ill ; 21cm
Continues: Games & puzzles
ISSN 0262-2327 = Top puzzles : £0.60 per issue B81-39515

793.73′2 — Crossword puzzles — *Collections*

The **39th** Pan book of crosswords / edited by Mike Grimshaw. — London : Pan, 1981. — [128]p ; 18cm
ISBN 0-330-26376-5 (pbk) : £0.85 B81-26225

Daily mail book of crossword puzzles. — No.13. — London ([Carmelite House, Carmelite St., EC4]) : Harmsworth Publications for Associated Newspapers Group, [1981?]. — [127]p
£0.60 B81-20715

Daily mirror crossword book. — London : Mirror Books
62. — 1981. — [128]p ; 18cm
ISBN 0-85939-244-9 (pbk) : £0.80 B81-19871

Daily mirror quizword. — London : Mirror Books
Book 14 / compiled by L.C. Browne. — 1981. — [128]p ; 18cm
ISBN 0-85939-258-9 (pbk) : £0.95 B81-27154

Evening news book of crossword puzzles. — [London] ([8 Stratton St., W1X 6AT]) : Harmsworth for Associated Newspapers
No.38. — [1981?]. — [125]p ; 18cm
£0.60 (pbk) B81-16700

Fifth Granada book of crosswords / edited by Patrick Duncan. — London : Granada, 1981. — 100,[22]p : ill ; 18cm. — (A Mayflower book)
ISBN 0-583-13380-0 (pbk) : £0.95 B81-27172

Fourth Granada book of crosswords / edited by Patrick Duncan. — London : Granada, 1981. — 100,[22]p : ill ; 18cm. — (A Mayflower book)
ISBN 0-583-13379-7 (pbk) : £0.95 B81-27174

Guinness book of records crossword / compilers Mary Parker, Ian Parker, W.A. Moyes ; additional research Rosemary Heslop. — Stamford ([Guash Way, Stamford, Lincs., PE9 1XJ]) : Onsworld, c1979. — 66p,[25]leaves, concertina folded ; 18cm
ISBN 0-906806-00-3 (pbk) : £1.95 B81-21378

Henchard, Frank. The eleventh Arrow book of crosswords / compiled by Frank Henchard. — London : Arrow, 1981. — [94]p : ill ; 18cm
ISBN 0-09-923710-5 (pbk) : £0.95 B81-26952

The **Longest** crossword puzzle. — Stamford (Guash Way, Stamford, Lincs., PE9 1XJ) : Onsworld
No.1. — c1980. — [33]leaves, concertina folded ; 20x8cm
ISBN 0-906806-15-1 (pbk) : Unpriced B81-21379

The **Longest** crossword puzzle. — Stamford (Guash Way, Stamford, Lincs., PE9 1XJ) : Onsworld
No.2. — c1980. — [33]leaves, concertina folded ; 20x8cm
ISBN 0-906806-23-2 (pbk) : Unpriced B81-21380

The **Longest** crossword puzzle. — Stamford (Guash Way, Stamford, Lincs., PE9 1XJ) : Onsworld
No.3. — c1980. — [33]leaves, concertina folded ; 20x8cm
ISBN 0-906806-28-3 (pbk) : Unpriced B81-21381

The **Longest** crossword puzzle. — Stamford (Guash Way, Stamford, Lincs., PE9 1XJ) : Onsworld
No.4. — c1980. — [33]leaves, concertina folded ; 20x8cm
ISBN 0-906806-36-4 (pbk) : Unpriced B81-21382

McKay, Tim. Tim McKay's puzzle book. — [London] : [Express Newspapers], [c1981]. — (Express books)
No.2. — 64p : ill,1port ; 21cm
Cover title. — At head of title: Daily Express
ISBN 0-85079-114-6 (pbk) : £0.50 B81-40708

The **Second** Penguin book of Daily Telegraph quick crosswords. — Harmondsworth : Penguin, 1981. — 142p ; 18cm. — (Penguin crossword puzzles)
ISBN 0-14-005872-9 (pbk) : £1.00 B81-33606

Sixth Granada book of crosswords / edited by Patrick Duncan. — London : Granada, 1981. — 100,[22]p : ill ; 18cm. — (A Mayflower book)
ISBN 0-583-13381-9 (pbk) : £0.95 B81-27173

The **Third** Penguin book of Listener crosswords. — Harmondsworth : Penguin, 1980. — 138p : chiefly ill ; 18cm. — (Penguin crossword puzzles)
ISBN 0-14-004822-7 (pbk) : £1.25 B81-11536

Woman's own crosswords. — London : Mirror Books
3. — 1981. — [62]p ; 22cm
ISBN 0-85939-270-8 (pbk) : £0.50 B81-35180

Woman's realm : crossword book. — London : Mirror Books, 1981. — [64]p : ill ; 21cm
ISBN 0-85939-261-9 (pbk) : £0.50 B81-24915

793.73′2 — Crossword puzzles — *Collections* — *For children*

Crossword book. — Loughborough : Ladybird
1 / compiled by Norman Pritchard ; illustrated by Lynn N. Grundy. — 1981. — [30]p : ill (some col.) ; 24cm
ISBN 0-7214-0649-1 (pbk) : £0.40 B81-11470

Daily mirror junior crossword book. — London : Mirror Books
37. — 1981. — [128]p ; 18cm
ISBN 0-85939-245-7 (pbk) : £0.75 B81-19872

Daily mirror junior crossword book. — London : Mirror Books
38. — c1981. — [128]p ; 18cm
ISBN 0-85939-269-4 (pbk) : £0.75 B81-35442

Duncan, Pat, *1921-*. Beaver crossword book / Pat Duncan. — [London] : Beaver, 1979
3. — 102p : ill ; 18cm
ISBN 0-600-32137-1 (pbk) : £0.50 B81-22281

Duncan, Pat, *1921-*. Beaver crossword book / Pat Duncan. — [London] : Beaver
7. — 1981. — 95p ; 18cm
ISBN 0-600-20294-1 (pbk) : £0.75 B81-13148

Duncan, Pat, *1921-*. Beaver crossword book / Pat Duncan. — London : Beaver
8. — 1981. — 95p ; 18cm
ISBN 0-600-20295-x (pbk) : £0.75 B81-31959

Newton, Robert, *1915-*. The first Armada crossword book / compiled by Robert Newton. — London : Armada, 1970 (1980 [printing]). — [127]p ; 18cm
ISBN 0-00-691711-9 (pbk) : £0.75 B81-12012

Newton, Robert, *1915-*. The Seventh Armada crossword book / compiled by Robert Newton. — London : Armada, 1981, c1973. — [128]p ; 19cm
Originally published: London : Collins, 1973
ISBN 0-00-691717-8 (pbk) : £0.80 B81-21182

Newton, Robert, *1915-*. The twelfth Armada crossword book / compiled by Robert Newton. — [London] : Armada, 1977 (1981 [printing]). — [123]p : ill ; 19cm
ISBN 0-00-691721-6 (pbk) : £0.80 B81-29842

Philpott, Roy S.. The clue-cracker's crossword book / compiled by Roy S. Philpott. — Sevenoaks (Mill Rd., Dunton Green, Sevenoaks, Kent) : Knight, 1979. — [96]p ; 18cm
ISBN 0-340-20488-5 (pbk) : £0.50 : CIP rev. B79-17772

793.73′2 — Crossword puzzles. Composition & solution — *Manuals*

Kurzban, Stanley A.. The compleat cruciverbalist, or, How to solve and compose crossword puzzles for fun and profit / Stan Kurzban and Mel Rosen. — New York ; London : Van Nostrand Reinhold, c1981. — xvi,167p : ill ; 24cm
ISBN 0-442-25738-4 : £7.45 B81-06813

793.73′2 — Crossword puzzles. Special subjects: Cinema films — *Collections*

Smith, Ted. Movie addicts' crossword puzzles / compiled by Ted Smith. — London : Warne
Book 1. — c1981. — [94]p ; 19cm
ISBN 0-7232-2493-5 (pbk) : £1.00 B81-09451

Smith, Ted. Movie addicts' crossword puzzles / compiled by Ted Smith. — London : Warne
Book 2. — c1981. — [94]p ; 19cm
ISBN 0-7232-2494-3 (pbk) : £1.00 B81-09451

793.73′2 — Crossword puzzles. Special subjects: Cumbria — *Collections*

Knox, Philip. Cumbrian crosswords : 50 crosswords and answers / compiled by Philip Knox. — Clapham, N. Yorkshire : Dalesman, 1979. — [63]p : ill ; 21cm. — (A 'Dalesman' paperback)
ISBN 0-85206-495-0 (pbk) : £0.90 B81-18466

793.73′2 — Crossword puzzles. Special subjects: Historical events — *Collections* — *For children*

Buckley, Bill. 75 history crosswords / Bill Buckley ; grids and illustrations by Sue Buckley. — London : Edward Arnold, 1981. — 48p : ill ; 25cm
ISBN 0-7131-0503-8 (pbk) : Unpriced B81-11582

793.73′2 — Crossword puzzles. Special subjects: Television programmes — *Collections*

Smith, Ted. TV addicts' crossword puzzles / compiled by Ted Smith. — London : Warne
Book 1. — c1981. — [47]p ; 19cm
ISBN 0-7232-2706-3 (pbk) : £0.75 B81-09452

Smith, Ted. TV addicts' crossword puzzles / compiled by Ted Smith. — London : Warne
Book 2. — c1981. — [45]p ; 19cm
ISBN 0-7232-2707-1 (pbk) : £0.75 B81-09453

793.73′2′05 — Crossword puzzles — *Collections — Serials*

Daily mirror crossword book. — 63. — London : Mirror Books, 1981. — [128]p ; 18cm
ISBN 0-85939-257-0 (pbk) : £0.95 B81-35608

Sunday People crossword book. — 4. — London : Mirror Books, 1981. — [116]p
ISBN 0-85939-252-x : £0.95 B81-25021

793.73′5 — Children's riddles in English — *Texts*

Duncan, Riana. A nutcracker in a tree : a book of riddles / Riana Duncan. — London : Andersen, 1980. — [27]p : ill(some col.) ; 24cm
ISBN 0-905478-83-5 : £3.50 B81-05256

793.73′5 — Riddles in English — *Anthologies — For children*

Cunningham, S. B.. Piccolo book of riddles / S.B. Cunningham ; text illustrations by Karen Heywood. — London : Pan, 1978, c1973 (1980 printing). — 123p : ill ; 18cm. — (Piccolo original)
ISBN 0-330-23642-3 (pbk) : £0.60 B81-03292

793.7′4 — Games using pocket electronic calculators — *Collections — For children*

Hamilton, Ben. Calculator fun and games / Ben Hamilton ; illustrated by Bryan Reading. — London : Armada, 1981. — 123p : ill ; 18cm
ISBN 0-00-691872-7 (pbk) : £0.80 B81-10855

793.7′4 — 'Magic cube'. Solution. Mathematical techniques

Last, Bridget. A simple approach to the magic cube : logical techniques which lead to a solution / Bridget Last. — Stradbroke (Stradbroke, Diss, Norfolk,) : Tarquin Publications, 1980. — 20p : ill ; 21cm
ISBN 0-906212-12-x (pbk) : £0.50 B81-01070

793.7′4 — Mathematical puzzles — *Collections*

Berlekamp, E. R.. Winning ways. — London : Academic Press, Sept.1981. — [800]p
ISBN 0-12-091150-7 : CIP entry B81-21637

Berlekamp, E. R.. Winning ways. — London : Academic Press, Sept.1981
Vol.1. — [400]p
ISBN 0-12-091101-9 (pbk) : CIP entry B81-21635

Berlekamp, E. R.. Winning ways. — London : Academic Press, Sept.1981
Vol.2. — [400]p
ISBN 0-12-091102-7 (pbk) : CIP entry B81-21636

Gardner, Martin. Mathematical circus : more games, paradoxes and other mathematical entertainments from Scientific American... / Martin Gardner. — London : Allen Lane, 1981, c1979. — xiii,272p : ill ; 23cm
Originally published: New York : Knopf, 1979. — Bibliography: p263-272
ISBN 0-7139-1375-4 : £7.95 B81-02705

Kelsey, Kenneth. More number puzzles / Kenneth Kelsey. — London : Frederick Muller, 1981. — 107p ; 22cm
ISBN 0-584-10763-3 (pbk) : £2.25 : CIP rev. B81-12385

Mathematical bafflers / edited by Angela Dunn ; illustrations by Ed Kysar. — New York : Dover ; London : Constable, 1980. — vi,217p : ill ; 22cm
Originally published: New York : McGraw-Hill, 1964
ISBN 0-486-23961-6 (pbk) : £1.90 B81-00231

793.7′4 — Mathematical puzzles — *Collections — For children*

Holt, Michael. Answer me this! / Michael Holt ; illustrated by Rowan Barnes-Murphy. — [London] : Piccolo, 1981. — [93]p : ill ; 18cm
ISBN 0-330-26382-x (pbk) : £0.85 B81-26373

Holt, Michael. Fun with numbers / Michael Holt ; illustrated by Ken Hatherley. — [London] : Piccolo, 1976 (1981 printing). — [123]p : ill ; 18cm
ISBN 0-330-24719-0 (pbk) : £0.85 B81-26374

793.7′4 — Mathematical puzzles — *Collections — For users of pocket programmable electronic calculators*

Snover, Stephen L.. Brain ticklers : puzzles & pastimes for programmable calculators / Stephen L. Snover, Mark Spikell. — Englewood Cliffs : Prentice-Hall, c1981. — xxviii,162p : ill ; 24cm. — (A Spectrum book)
ISBN 0-13-081018-5 (cased) : Unpriced
ISBN 0-13-081000-2 (pbk) : £3.85 B81-22703

793.7′4 — Mathematical puzzles using pocket electronic calculators — *Collections*

Råde, Lennart. Adventures with your pocket calculator / Lennart Råde and Burt A. Kaufman. — Harmondsworth : Penguin, 1980, c1977. — 139p : ill ; 18cm. — (Pelican books)
Originally published: St Louis : CEMREL, 1977. — Bibliography: p136-139
ISBN 0-14-022274-x (pbk) : £0.95 B81-01071

793.7′4 — Number puzzles — *Collections — For children*

Dickinson, Clive. It figures! / Clive Dickinson ; illustrated by Graham Thompson. — London : Hamlyn, 1981. — 95p : ill ; 18cm. — (Beaver books)
ISBN 0-600-20290-9 (pbk) : £0.80 B81-15135

793.7′4 — Rubik's cube. Solution

Taylor, Don, *1945-*. Mastering Rubik's cube / Don Taylor. — Harmondsworth : Penguin, 1981, c1980. — 91p : ill ; 12cm
Originally published: Australia : Book Marketing, 1980
ISBN 0-14-006102-9 (pbk) : £0.95 B81-29605

Wray, C. G.. The cube : how to do it / [C.G. Wray]. — Totternhoe ([The Lawns], Church Green, Totternhoe, Beds. [LU6 1RF]) : [C.G. Wray], c1981]. — 7p : 1ill ; 22cm
Cover title
ISBN 0-9507702-0-5 (pbk) : Unbound B81-34896

793.7′4′05 — Mathematical puzzles — *Collections — Serials*

The **Problem** solver. — Issue 1-. — [Bristol] ([6 Carmarthen Rd, Westbury-on-Trym, Bristol]) : Rain Publications, [1980]-. — v. ; 21cm
Three issues yearly
ISSN 0261-3867 = Problem solver : £0.10 per issue B81-32901

793.8 — Coin tricks — *Manuals*

Supreme Magic present - connoisseurs' coins through / (by arrangement with Harry Stanley's Unique Magic Studio). — Bideford (64 High St., Bideford, Devon) : Supreme Magic, c1981. — 8p : ill ; 25cm
Unpriced (pbk) B81-40602

793.8 — Conjuring — *Amateurs' manuals*

Brooke, Ken. Ken Brooke's magic : the Unique years. — Bideford (64 High St., Bideford, Devon) : Supreme Magic [Co.], c1980. — 222p : ill,facsims,ports ; 26cm
£10.50 B81-06772

793.8 — Conjuring — *Amateurs' manuals — Early works*

Sachs, Edwin. Sleight of hand : a practical manual of legerdemain for amateurs & others / Edwin Sachs. — 2nd enl. ed. — New York : Dover ; London : Constable, 1980. — 408p : ill ; 22cm
Facsim. of: 2nd enl. ed. London : Upcott Gill, 1885. — Includes index
ISBN 0-486-23911-x (pbk) : £3.15 B81-03448

793.8 — Conjuring — *Amateurs' manuals — For children*

Brandreth, Gyles. The big book of magic / Gyles Brandreth ; illustrated by Peter Stevenson. — London : Transworld, 1981. — 142p : ill ; 20cm. — (A Carousel book)
ISBN 0-552-54177-x (pbk) : £0.80 B81-17119

Daniels, Paul. Paul Daniels' magic book. — London : Piccolo, 1980. — 125p : ill ; 18cm
Includes index
ISBN 0-330-26185-1 (pbk) : £0.75 B81-03904

793.8 — Conjuring — *Manuals*

Adair, Ian. Novel notions / Ian Adair. — Bideford (64 High St., Bideford, Devon) : Supreme Magic, c1981. — 48p : ill,ports ; 23cm
Unpriced (pbk) B81-40589

Baker, Roy. Baker's brainwaves / Roy Baker. — Bideford (64 High St., Bideford, Devon) : Supreme Magic, c1981. — 159p : ill,ports ; 23cm
Unpriced B81-40588

De Courcy, Ken. After dinner technique / by Ken de Courcy. — Bideford (64 High St., Bideford, Devon) : Supreme Magic, c1980. — 64p : ill,2ports ; 21cm
Unpriced (pbk) B81-40641

Edwin, *the Magician*. Kids magic my way : a lecture/demonstration / by Edwin the Magician (Edwin Hooper). — Bideford (64 High St., Bideford, Devon) : Supreme Magic, c1981. — 20p : ill,ports ; 23cm
Given at the Magischer Zirkel München Magic Convention 1981
Unpriced (pbk) B81-40599

Gibson, Walter B.. The complete illustrated book of close-up magic : professional techniques fully revealed by a master magician / by Walter B. Gibson. — London : Hale, 1981, c1980. — xviii,426p : ill ; 24cm
Originally published: Garden City, N.Y. : Doubleday, 1980. — Includes index
ISBN 0-7091-8823-4 : £9.95 B81-16705

Lainsbury, Bill. Billy Benbow's best : a selection of routines, tricks, wheezes, dodges, gags and games from 'The Billy Benbo All in One Show' / by Bill Lainsbury ; edited and illustrated by Ken de Courcy. — Bideford (64 High St., Bideford, Devon) : Supreme Magic, c1981. — 28p : ill ; 25cm
Unpriced (pbk) B81-40642

The **Magic** of Frederica / edited by Lewis Ganson ; illustrations by Dennis Patten, Ali Bongo and Hugh Miller ; photographs by G.R. Bartlett, Ken Scholes and Lewis Ganson. — Bideford (64 High St., Bideford, Devon) : Supreme Magic, c1981. — 128p : ill,ports ; 26cm
Unpriced B81-40593

Supreme proudly presents Jack Yates' foreshadowed / (edited and illustrated by Ken de Courcy). — Bideford (64 High St., Bideford, Devon) : Supreme Magic, c1979. — 7p : ill ; 24cm
Unpriced (pbk) B81-40600

Yeager, John. A mixed bag / John Yeager. — Bideford (64 High St., Bideford, Devon) : Supreme Magic, c1981. — 53p : ill,1plan ; 25cm
Unpriced (pbk) B81-40643

793.8 — Conjuring — *Manuals — Early works*

Downs, T. Nelson. The art of magic / T. Nelson Downs ; edited by John Northern Hilliard. — 2nd ed. / with a new introduction by Charles R. Reynolds. — New York : Dover ; London : Constable, c1980. — 348p : ill ; 22cm
Originally published: Buffalo : Downs-Edwards, 1921
ISBN 0-486-24005-3 (pbk) : £2.50 B81-05424

793.8 — Conjuring — *Manuals — Early works continuation*

Hoffmann, *Professor*. [Later magic]. Hoffmann's later magic / by Professor Hoffmann (Angelo John Lewis). — New York : Dover ; London : Constable, 1979. — xviii,554p : ill ; 21cm
Facsim. of: ed. originally published: New York : Dutton, 1904
ISBN 0-486-23757-5 (pbk) : £3.50 B81-40719

793.8 — Conjuring. Mental tricks — *Amateurs' manuals*

Somerville, Neil. Mars / Neil Somerville. — [Reading] ([24 Devonshire Gardens, Tilehurst, Reading, Berks.]) : [N. Somerville], [c1981]. — 16p ; 21cm
Cover title
£3.00 (pbk) B81-25554

793.8 — Conjuring. Mental tricks — *Manuals*

Cameron, Charles W.. Macabre and mental mysteries / Charles W. Cameron. — Bideford (64 High St., Bideford, Devon) : Supreme Magic, c1981. — 63p : ill ; 23cm
Unpriced (pbk) B81-40639

Scalbert, Geoffrey. Scalbert's selected secrets / by Geoffrey Scalbert. — Bideford (64 High St., Bideford, Devon) : Supreme Magic, c1981. — 185p : ill,1port ; 26cm
Unpriced B81-40594

793.8 — Conjuring. Performance — *Manuals*

Dexter, Will. A little magic among friends / written and illustrated by Will Dexter. — Bideford (64 High St., Bideford, Devon) : Supreme Magic, c1981. — 58p : ill ; 24cm
Bibliography: p58
Unpriced (pbk) B81-40601

793.8 — Conjuring. Picking pockets — *Manuals*

Joseph, Eddie. How to pick pockets : a treatise on the fundamental principle, theory and practice of picking pockets, for entertainment purposes only / by Eddie Joseph. — [2nd ed.]. — [Bideford] ([64 High St., Bideford, Devon]) : Supreme Magic, [c1981]. — 38p ; 19cm
Previous ed.: London : Vampire Press, 1946
Unpriced (pbk) B81-40634

793.8 — Conjuring. Use of human body

Fisher, John. Body magic. — London : Hodder & Stoughton, Nov.1981. — [192]p
Originally published: 1979
ISBN 0-340-27109-4 (pbk) : £1.50 : CIP entry B81-30143

793.8 — Oriental conjuring

Ayling, Will. Oriental conjuring and magic / by Will Ayling ; from an index by S.H. Sharpe ; illustrations by L. Edmunds. — Devon ([64 High St., Bideford, Devon]) : Supreme Magic Co. Ltd., c1981. — 384p : ill,ports ; 25cm
Unpriced B81-29339

793.8 — Thumb tie tricks — *Manuals*

Andrews, Max. Sixteen thumb tie gems / by Max Andrews ; illustrations by the author. — 2nd ed. — Bideford (64 High St., Bideford, Devon) : Supreme Magic, 1981, c1980. — 49p : ill ; 19cm
Previous ed.: London : M. Andrews, 1946
Unpriced (pbk) B81-40637

793.8 — Tricks — *Manuals — For children*

Eldin, Peter. The complete practical joker / Peter Eldin ; illustrated by Phil Emms. — London : Sparrow, 1981. — 108p : ill ; 18cm
ISBN 0-09-927090-0 (pbk) : £0.95 B81-36085

Page, Patrick. The jokers' handbook / by Patrick Page ; illustrated by John Cameron. — London : Macdonald, 1981. — 63p : ill(some col.) ; 21cm. — (Whizz kids ; 19)
Bibliography: p62. — Includes index
ISBN 0-356-06379-8 (cased) : £2.95
ISBN 0-356-06339-9 (pbk) : £1.25 B81-38535

793.8 — Tricks using Chinese sticks — *Manuals*

Routines for the chinese sticks. — Bideford (64 High St., Bideford, Devon) : Supreme Magic, c1981. — 8p : ill ; 25cm
Unpriced (pbk) B81-40597

793.8 — Tricks using matchboxes — *Manuals*

The **Jon** Tremaine routine for the 'acrobatic matchbox'. — Bideford (64 High St., Bideford, Devon) : Supreme Magic, c1981. — [4]p : ill ; 26cm
Unpriced (unbound) B81-40598

793.8 — Tricks using objects concealed in the hands — *Manuals*

Ganson, Lewis. Routined manipulation / by Lewis Ganson. — Bideford (64 High St., Bideford, Devon) : Supreme Magic, c1981. — 118,133,254p : ill,ports ; 24cm
Spine title: Complete routined manipulation. — Pt.1 originally published: S.l. : Harry Stanley (Unique Magic Studio), 1958 ; pt.2 originally published: S.l. : Harry Stanley (Unique Magic Studio), 1953 ; pt.3 originally published: S.l. : Harry Stanley (Unique Magic Studio), 1954
Unpriced B81-40590

793.8 — Tricks using shells — *Manuals*

Joseph, Eddie. The Hindu gaming shells / by Eddie Joseph. — Bideford (64 High St., Bideford, Devon) : Supreme Magic, c1981. — 8p : ill ; 25cm
Unpriced (pbk) B81-40591

793.8 — Tricks using thumb tips — *Manuals*

Kenyon, John. Thumbs up! / by John Kenyon ; illustrated by Dennis. — Bideford (64 High St., Bideford, Devon) : Supreme Magic, 1981, c1980. — 43p : ill ; 22cm
Originally published: Birmingham : Goodliffe, 1946
Unpriced (pbk) B81-40635

793.8'092'2 — Conjurors — *Biographies — For children*

Eldin, Peter. Hey presto! / Peter Eldin ; illustrated by Jane Faber. — London : Granada, 1980. — 93p : ill ; 18cm. — (A Dragon book)
ISBN 0-583-30306-4 (pbk) : £0.75 B81-04401

793.8'092'4 — Escapology. Houdini, Harry — *Biographies*

FitzSimons, Raymund. Death and the magician : the mystery of Houdini / Raymund FitzSimons. — Large print ed. — Bath : Chivers, 1981, c1980. — 292p ; 23cm. — (A Lythway biography)
Originally published: London : Hamilton, 1980
ISBN 0-85119-701-9 : £5.25 B81-19763

793'.9 — Board wargaming

Palmer, Nicholas. The best of board wargaming / Nicholas Palmer. — London : Barker, c1980. — ix,194p ; 23cm
ISBN 0-213-16770-0 : £8.50 B81-01682

793'.9 — Fantasy games — *Serials*

Ringwraith's shadow. — No.1-. — Edgware (30 Orchard Drive, Edgware, Middx. HA8 7SD) : S. Goldshaft, 1981-. — v. : ill ; 22cm
Quarterly
ISSN 0261-8826 = Ringwraith's shadow : £0.10 per issue B81-35087

793'.9 — Fantasy role-playing games

Galloway, Bruce. Fantasy wargaming. — Cambridge : Stephens, Nov.1981. — [200]p
ISBN 0-85059-465-0 : £9.95 : CIP entry B81-30581

793'.9 — War games based on battles, *B.C.1288-A.D.1865* — *Manuals*

Grant, Charles, *d.1979*. Wargame tactics / Charles Grant. — London : Cassell, 1979. — x,192p : plans ; 23cm
Bibliography: p187-188. — Includes index
ISBN 0-304-30470-0 : £5.95 B81-01933

793'.9 — War games — *Manuals*

Battlefield command : land combat in the 1980's : (the Combat commander update). — Brooklyn : Enola Games ; Barnet (48 East View, Barnet, Herts., EN5 5TN) : Navwar, [c1980]. — ii,61p : ill ; 28cm
Cover title
Unpriced (pbk) B81-10377

PSL guide to wargaming / compiled and edited by Bruce Quarrie. — Cambridge : Stephens, 1980. — 152p : ill ; 25cm
Ill on lining papers. — Bibliography: p150-151
ISBN 0-85059-413-8 : £5.95 : CIP rev. B80-03275

794 — INDOOR GAMES OF SKILL

794 — Board games — *Manuals*

Bell, R. C.. Discovering old board games / R.C. Bell. — 2nd ed. — Aylesbury : Shire, 1980. — 80p : ill. — (Discovering series ; 182)
Previous ed.: 1973. — Bibliography: p78. — Includes index
ISBN 0-85263-533-8 (pbk) : £1.15 B81-19526

794.1 — CHESS

794.1 — Chess

Karpov, Anatoliĭ. Chess kaleidoscope. — Oxford : Pergamon, Sept.1981. — [176]p. — (Pergamon Russian chess series)
Translation of: Shakhmaty kaleidoscope
ISBN 0-08-026897-8 (cased) : £9.50 : CIP entry
ISBN 0-08-026896-x (pbk) : £5.50 B81-20568

794.1 — Chess. Problems — *Collections*

Larsen, Bent. Bent Larsen's good move guide. — Oxford : Oxford University Press, Oct.1981. — [192]p. — (Oxford chess books)
Translation of: Skak skole
ISBN 0-19-217592-0 (cased) : £7.95 : CIP entry
ISBN 0-19-217593-9 (pbk) : £4.95 B81-25796

794.1'0207 — Chess — *Humour*

Hartston, William R.. Soft pawn / William R. Hartston ; illustrations by Bill Tidy. — London : Hutchinson, 1980. — 94p : ill ; 20cm
Includes index
ISBN 0-09-143421-1 (pbk) : £3.50 B81-06809

794.1'03'21 — Chess — *Encyclopaedias*

The **Penguin** encyclopedia of chess / edited by Harry Golombek. — Rev. and abridged ed. — Harmondsworth : Penguin, 1981. — 578p : ill ; 20cm. — (Penguin handbooks)
Full ed.: published as Golombek's encyclopedia of chess. New York : Crown, 1977 and as Encyclopedia of chess. London : Batsford, 1977. — Bibliography: p526-527. — Includes index
ISBN 0-14-046452-2 (pbk) : £4.95 B81-27640

794.1'06'041 — Great Britain. Chess. Organisations: British Chess Federation — *Serials*

Year book of chess. — 1980-81. — Norwich (4, The Close, Norwich NR1 4DH) : British Chess Federation, [1980?]. — 92p
ISSN 0305-5132 : £2.15 B81-06824

794.1'07'047 — Soviet Union. Chess. Training

Kotov, A. A.. Train like a grandmaster / Alexander Kotov ; translated by Bernard Cafferty. — London : Batsford, 1981. — 124p : ill ; 22cm. — (The Club player's library) (A Batsford chess book)
Translation from the Russian. — Includes index
ISBN 0-7134-3609-3 (pbk) : £4.95 B81-25598

794.1'076 — Chess — *Questions & answers*

Livshitz, A.. Test your chess IQ / by A. Livshitz ; translated and edited by Kenneth P. Neat. — Oxford : Pergamon. — (Pergamon Russian chess series)
Translated from the Russian
Book 1. — 1981. — x,123p : ill ; 25cm
Includes index
ISBN 0-08-023120-9 (cased) : Unpriced : CIP rev.
ISBN 0-08-024118-2 (pbk) : £3.95 B81-25848

794.1'092'2 — Chess. British players, *1976-1980*

Chandler, Murray. The English chess explosion : from Miles to Short / Murray Chandler, Ray Keene with a contribution by Leonard Barden. — London : Batsford, 1981. — 120p : ill ; 22cm. — (Batsford chess books)
Includes index
ISBN 0-7134-4009-0 (pbk) : £4.50 B81-15967

794.1'092'4 — Chess. Botvinnik, M. M. — *Biographies*

Botvinnik, M. M.. Achieving the aim / by M.M. Botvinnik ; translated by Bernard Cafferty. — Oxford : Pergamon, 1981. — vii,226p,[16]p of plates : ill,ports ; 22cm. — (Pergamon Russian chess series)
Translation of: K dostizheniiu tseli
ISBN 0-08-024120-4 : £7.95 : CIP rev. B80-27436

794.1'2 — Chess. Combinations & sacrifices — *Manuals*

Levy, D. N. L.. Play chess combinations and sacrifices / David Levy. — Oxford : Oxford University Press, 1980. — v,186p : ill ; 21cm. — (Oxford chess books)
Includes index
ISBN 0-19-217588-2 (cased) : £8.95 : CIP rev.
ISBN 0-19-217589-0 (pbk) : Unpriced B80-13018

794.1'2 — Chess. Combinations — *Manuals*

Tal, Mikhail. Tal's winning chess combinations : the secrets of winning chess combinations described and explained by the Russian Grandmaster Mikhail Tal / by Mikhail Tal and Victor Khenkin ; translated from the Russian by Hanon W. Russell. — London : Routledge & Kegan Paul, 1980. — 409p : ill ; 23cm
Originally published: New York : Simon & Schuster, 1979
ISBN 0-7100-0630-6 : £9.50 : CIP rev. B80-17903

794.1'2 — Chess — *Manuals*

Barden, Leonard. Play better chess with Leonard Barden / foreword by Viktor Korchnoi. — London : Octopus, 1980. — 153p : chiefly ill,ports ; 29cm
Ill on lining papers. — Includes index
ISBN 0-7064-0967-1 : £4.95 B81-00232

Golombek, Harry. Beginning chess / Harry Golombek. — Harmondsworth : Penguin, 1981. — 224p : ill ; 19cm. — (Penguin handbooks)
Includes index
ISBN 0-14-046412-3 (pbk) : £1.50 B81-27638

Harston, William. Play chess. — London : Hodder & Stoughton. — (Knight books)
2. — Dec.1981. — [96]p
ISBN 0-340-27822-6 (pbk) : £0.95 : CIP entry B81-31372

Livshitz, A.. Test your chess IQ. — Oxford : Pergamon. — (Pergamon Russian chess series)
Book 2. — Nov.1981. — [224]p
ISBN 0-08-026881-1 (cased) : £8.95 : CIP entry
ISBN 0-08-026880-3 (pbk) : £5.95 B81-30971

Povah, Nigel. Chess training / Nigel Povah. — London : Faber, 1981. — 176p : ill ; 21cm
ISBN 0-571-11604-3 (cased) : £6.954
ISBN 0-571-11608-6 (pbk) : £2.95 B81-10603

Suetin, A. S.. Three steps to chess mastery. — Oxford : Pergamon, Jan.1982. — [208]p. — (Pergamon Russian chess series)
Translation of: Laboratoriia shakhmatista and Put' k masterstvu
ISBN 0-08-024139-5 (cased) : £7.95 : CIP entry
ISBN 0-08-024138-7 (pbk) : £4.95 B81-34508

794.1'2 — Chess — *Manuals — For children*

Hansford, Anthony. Let's play chess / Anthony Hansford ; illustrated by John Bolton. — London : Octopus, 1980. — 444p : col.ill,3ports ; 31cm
Ill on lining papers
ISBN 0-7064-1180-3 : £1.99 B81-03556

Hartston, William. Play chess / William Hartston & Jeremy James. — London : British Broadcasting Corporation, 1980. — 96p : ill ; 21cm
ISBN 0-563-17881-7 (cased) : £4.50
ISBN 0-563-17878-7 (pbk) : £1.95 B81-13005

794.1'2 — Chess. Tactics — *Manuals*

Assiac. Opening preparation. — Oxford : Pergamon, Nov.1981. — [210]p. — (Pergamon chess series)
ISBN 0-08-024095-x (cased) : £7.00 : CIP entry
ISBN 0-08-024096-8 (pbk) : £3.95 B81-28844

794.1'22 — Chess. Open games. Openings — *Manuals*

Open games (except Ruy Lopez) / Edmar Mednis ... [et al.]. — Great Neck, N.Y. : R.H.M. Press ; London : Pitman, c1980. — vii,142p : ill ; 21cm. — (Understanding the chess openings)
Cover title: Understanding the open games (except Ruy Lopez) / Andy Soltis ... [et al.]. — Includes index
ISBN 0-273-01668-7 (pbk) : £6.95 B81-20015

794.1'22 — Chess. Openings: Caro-Kahn Defence — *Manuals*

Caro-Kann defense / Raymond Keene ... [et al.]. — Great Neck, N.Y. : R.H.M. Press ; London : Pitman, c1980. — 142p : ill ; 21cm. — (Understanding the chess openings)
Includes index
ISBN 0-273-01670-9 (pbk) : £6.95
ISBN 0-89058-052-9 (U.S.) B81-16652

794.1'22 — Chess. Openings: English Opening — *Manuals*

Watson, John L.. English / John L. Watson. — London : Batsford. — 1980. — (Contemporary chess openings)
3: P-QB4. — [8],319p : ill ; 23cm. — (A Batsford chess book)
Bibliography: p[7]. - Includes index
ISBN 0-7134-2688-8 : £9.95 B81-06812

Watson, John L.. English / John L. Watson. — London : Batsford. — (Contemporary chess openings)
4: Franco, Slav and Flank defences : (1- P-K3, 1- P-KN3, 1- P-KB4, 1- P-QB3, 1- P-QN3, 1- others). — 1981. — x,112p : ill ; 23cm
Bibliography: pix. — Includes index
ISBN 0-7134-2690-x : £7.95 B81-15585

794.1'22 — Chess. Openings: French Defence. Classical Variation — *Manuals*

Heidenfeld, Wolfgang. French classical lines / Wolfgang Heidenfeld, Tim Harding. — London : Batsford, 1979. — 158p : ill ; 22cm. — (Batsford algebraic chess openings) (A Batsford chess book)
Bibliography: p9-10. — Includes index
ISBN 0-7134-1445-6 (pbk) : £6.50 B81-08968

794.1'22 — Chess. Openings: French Defence. Tarrasch Variation — *Manuals*

Keene, Raymond. French Defence : Tarrasch variation / Raymond Keene, Shaun Taulbut. — London : Batsford, 1980. — [x],101p : ill ; 22cm. — (Batsford algebraic chess openings)
Bibliography: pvii. — Includes index
ISBN 0-7134-1898-2 (pbk) : £4.95 B81-10648

Richmond, P. A.. French defence : Tarrasch Variation / P.A. Richmond. — Nottingham : Chess Player, 1980. — 128p : ill ; 21cm
ISBN 0-906042-17-8 (pbk) : Unpriced B81-34356

794.1'22 — Chess. Openings: King's Indian Defence. Variations with 3. P-KN3 — *Manuals*

Geller, Efim. King's Indian Defence : g3 systems / Efim Geller. — London : Batsford, 1980. — 133p : ill ; 22cm. — (Algebraic chess openings) (Batsford chess books)
Includes index
ISBN 0-7134-3605-0 (pbk) : £6.95 B81-06810

794.1'22 — Chess. Openings: Latvian Gambit — *Manuals*

Kapitaniak, T.. Latvian gambit / T. Kapitaniak. — Nottingham : Chess Player, 1980. — 35p : ill ; 21cm
ISBN 0-906042-29-1 (pbk) : Unpriced B81-34361

794.1'22 — Chess. Openings — *Manuals*

Edwards, Raymond. Basic chess openings / by Raymond Edwards. — Rev. ed. — London : Routledge & Kegan Paul, 1981. — viii,104p : ill ; 19cm. — (Routledge chess handbooks ; bk.4)
Previous ed.: 1976. — Bibliography: p102-103. — Includes index
ISBN 0-7100-0853-8 (pbk) : £2.50 : CIP rev. B81-12810

Hartston, William R.. The Penguin book of chess openings / W.R. Hartston. — Harmondsworth : Penguin, 1981. — 252p : ill ; 19cm. — (Penguin handbooks)
ISBN 0-14-046312-7 (pbk) : £1.95 B81-27636

Keene, Raymond. The openings in modern theory and practice / Raymond Keene. — London : Bell & Hyman, 1979. — 144p : ill ; 23cm
Bibliography: p143. — Includes index
ISBN 0-7135-0028-x : £5.95 B81-01069

Kom, Walter. Modern chess openings. — 12th ed. — London : A. & C. Black, Feb.1982. — [412]p
Previous ed.: 1976
ISBN 0-7136-2199-0 (pbk) : £7.95 : CIP entry B81-35831

Samarian, Sergiu. Opening tactics for club players / Sergio [i.e. Sergiu] Samarian ; translated from the French by Elaine Pritchard. — London : Hale, 1980. — 170p : ill ; 23cm
ISBN 0-7091-8128-0 : £7.50 B81-06811

794.1'22 — Chess. Openings: Nimzowitsch Defence — *Manuals*

Harding, T. D.. The Nimzowitsch defence / Tim Harding. — London : Batsford, 1981. — 144p : ill ; 22cm. — (Tournament player's openings) (A Batsford chess book)
Includes index
ISBN 0-7134-3597-6 (pbk) : £5.95 B81-36709

794.1'22 — Chess. Openings: Pirc Defence — *Manuals*

Baker, C. W.. Pirc defence : a second line for white / C.W. Baker. — Nottingham : Chess Player, 1979. — 40p : ill ; 21cm
ISBN 0-906042-22-4 (pbk) : Unpriced B81-34358

Thomas, M.. Pirc defence : a line for white / M. Thomas. — Nottingham : Chess Player, 1980. — 48p : ill ; 21cm
ISBN 0-906042-21-6 (pbk) : Unpriced B81-34359

794.1'22 — Chess. Openings: Pirc — King's Indian Defence. Averbakh System — *Manuals*

Thomas, M.. Averbakh system : Pirc/King's Indian defence / M. Thomas. — Nottingham : Chess Player, 1979. — 88p : ill ; 21cm
ISBN 0-906042-16-x (pbk) : Unpriced B81-34360

794.1'22 — Chess. Openings: Ponziani Opening — *Manuals*

Smith, A.. Ponziani opening / A. Smith, M.A. Ciamarra. — Nottingham : Chess Player, 1980. — 100p : ill ; 21cm
ISBN 0-906042-23-2 (pbk) : Unpriced B81-34362

794.1'22 — Chess. Openings: Queen's Gambit Accepted — *Manuals*

Cafferty, Bernard. A complete defence to 1 d4 : a study of the queen's gambit accepted / by Bernard Cafferty and David Hooper. — Oxford : Pergamon, 1981. — xi,144p : ill ; 26cm. — (Pergamon chess series)
Includes index
ISBN 0-08-024103-4 (cased) : Unpriced : CIP rev.
ISBN 0-08-024102-6 (pbk) : £4.50
Also classified at 794.1'22 B80-23618

794.1′22 — Chess. Openings: Queen′s Gambit Declined. Semi-Slav Defence — *Manuals*
Harding, T. D.. Queen′s gambit declined : semi-slav / T.D. Harding ; edited and revised by A.J. Whiteley. — London : Batsford, 1981. — 168p : ill ; 22cm. — (Batsford algebraic chess openings) (Batsford chess books)
Includes index
ISBN 0-7134-2448-6 (pbk) : £7.50 B81-15054

794.1′22 — Chess. Openings: Ruy Lopez. Exchange Variation — *Manuals*
Thomas, M.. Spanish exchange variation / M. Thomas. — Nottingham : Chess Player, 1980. — 144p : ill ; 21cm
ISBN 0-906042-18-6 (pbk) : Unpriced
B81-40404

794.1′22 — Chess. Openings: Sicilian Defence. 2.P—QB3 variations — *Manuals*
Chandler, Murray. Sicilian: 2c3 : 1e4 c5 2c3 / Murray Chandler. — London : Batsford, 1981. — 110p : ill ; 22cm. — (The Tournament player′s repertoire of openings) (Batsford algebraic chess openings) (A Batsford chess book)
Bibliography: p6. — Includes index
ISBN 0-7134-1933-4 (pbk) : £4.95 B81-33364

794.1′22 — Chess. Openings: Sicilian Defence. Dragon Variation — *Manuals*
Levy, D. N. L.. Sicilian dragon : classical and Levenfish variations / David Levy. — London : Batsford, 1981. — ix,112p : ill ; 22cm. — (Batsford algebraic chess openings) (Batsford chess books)
Bibliography: pix. — Includes index
ISBN 0-7134-2743-4 (pbk) : £4.95 B81-15056

794.1′22 — Chess. Openings: Sicilian Defence. Morra Gambit — *Manuals*
Flesch, János. The Morra Gambit / János Flesch ; translated by John Réti. — London : Batsford, 1981. — x,150p ; 22cm. — (Batsford algebraic chess openings series) (A Batsford chess book)
Translation from the Hungarian. — Includes index
ISBN 0-7134-2188-6 (pbk) : Unpriced
B81-27539

794.1′22 — Chess. Openings: Sicilian Defence. Variations with 2.P-QB3 — *Manuals*
Thomas, M.. Sicilian c3 / M. Thomas. — Nottingham : Chess Player, 1981. — 80p : ill ; 21cm
ISBN 0-906042-40-2 (pbk) : Unpriced
B81-40403

794.1′22 — Chess. Openings: Sokolsky Opening — *Manuals*
Thomas, M.. Sokolsky opening / M. Thomas, A.J. Gillam. — Nottingham : Chess Player, 1981. — 64p : ill ; 21cm
ISBN 0-906042-28-3 (pbk) : Unpriced
B81-34357

794.1′22 — Chess. Queen pawn openings — *Manuals*
Cafferty, Bernard. A complete defence to 1 d4 : a study of the queen′s gambit accepted / by Bernard Cafferty and David Hooper. — Oxford : Pergamon, 1981. — xi,144p : ill ; 26cm. — (Pergamon chess series)
Includes index
ISBN 0-08-024103-4 (cased) : Unpriced : CIP rev.
ISBN 0-08-024102-6 (pbk) : £4.50
Primary classification 794.1′22 B80-23618

794.1′23 — Chess. Middle games — *Manuals*
Keres, Paul. The art of the middle game / Paul Keres and Alexander Kotov ; translated and edited by H. Golombek. — Harmondsworth : Penguin, 1964 (1981 [printing]). — 238p : ill ; 18cm. — (Penguin handbooks)
Translation of: Konsten att vinna i schack. — Includes index
ISBN 0-14-046102-7 (pbk) : £1.75 B81-30947

794.1′24 — Chess. Endgames — *Manuals*
Nunn, John. Tactical chess endings / by John Nunn. — London : Allen & Unwin, 1981. — 204p : ill ; 23cm
Bibliography: p198-199. — Includes index
ISBN 0-04-794013-1 : Unpriced : CIP rev.
B81-26713

Portisch, Lajos. Six hundred endings. — Oxford : Pergamon, Sept.1981. — [328]p. — (Pergamon chess series)
Translation of: 600 vegjatek
ISBN 0-08-024137-9 : £6.95 : CIP entry
B81-22546

794.1′24 — Chess. Endgames. Problems — *Collections*
Speelman, Jon. Analysing the endgame / Jon Speelman. — London : Batsford, 1981. — 142p : ill ; 23cm. — (The Club player′s library) (A Batsford chessbook)
Includes index
ISBN 0-7134-1897-4 (cased) : Unpriced
ISBN 0-7134-1909-1 (pbk) : £4.95 B81-24299

794.1′5 — Chess. Games — *Collections*
Oxford encyclopedia of chess games / edited by David Levy & Kevin O′Connell. — Oxford : Oxford University Press
[Vol.1]. — 1981. — xviii,527p : ill,ports ; 24cm
Includes index
ISBN 0-19-217571-8 : £35.00 : CIP rev.
B81-15836

Wicker, Kevin. 200 modern brilliancies / Kevin Wicker. — London : Batsford, c1981. — viii,133p : ill ; 22cm. — (The Club player′s library) (A Batsford chess book)
ISBN 0-7134-3590-9 (cased) : Unpriced
ISBN 0-7134-3591-7 (pbk) : £4.95 B81-15055

794.1′5′05 — Chess. Games — *Collections* — *Serials*
Knight′s file. — No.1 (Dec.1980)-. — Sowerby Bridge (Freepost, Ripponden, Sowerby Bridge, West Yorkshire HX6 4BR) : Michael Knight, 1980-. — v. : ill ; 21cm
Monthly
ISSN 0260-6828 = Knight′s file : £12.00 per year B81-09042

794.1′52 — Chess. Grandmaster matches. Games, *1971-1979* — *Collections*
Timman, Jan. The art of chess analysis / Jan Timman ; introduction by Lubomir Kavalek. — Great Neck, N.Y. : R.H.M. Press ; London : Pitman, c1980. — 216p : ill ; 21cm
ISBN 0-273-01666-0 (pbk) : £7.95 B81-16655

794.1′57 — Chess. Championships: Chempionat SSSR *(47th : 1979 : Moscow?)*. **Games** — *Collections*
Miles, A. J.. 47th USSR championships 1979 / A.J. Miles. — Nottingham : Chess Player, 1980. — 70p : ill ; 21cm
Includes index
ISBN 0-906042-32-1 (pbk) : Unpriced
B81-38141

794.1′57 — Chess. Championships: European Team Championship *(1980 : Skara)*. **Games** — *Collections*
Miles, A. J.. European team championship : SKARA 80 / A.J. Miles. — Nottingham : Chess Player, 1980. — 87p : ill ; 20cm
Includes index
ISBN 0-906042-33-x (pbk) : Unpriced
B81-35005

794.1′57 — Chess. Championships: World Chess Championship *(1978 : Baguio, Luzon)*
Edmondson, E. B.. Chess scandals : the 1978 World Chess Championship / by E.B. Edmondson ; with annotations by Mikhail Tal based upon his commentary for ′64′. — Oxford : Pergamon, 1981. — x,234p,[16]p of plates : ill,ports ; 26cm. — (Pergamon chess series)
Includes index
ISBN 0-08-024145-x : £7.50 : CIP rev.
B81-04344

794.1′57 — Chess. Tournaments: Clarin Tournament *(2nd : 1979 : Buenos Aires)*. **Games** — *Collections*
Miles, A. J.. Second Clarin tournament : Buenos Aires 1979 / Tony Miles. — Nottingham : Chess Player, 1980. — 56p : ill ; 21cm
Includes index
ISBN 0-906042-31-3 (pbk) : Unpriced
B81-35006

794.1′57 — Chess. Tournaments: Phillips & Drew Kings Chess Tournament *(1980 : London)*. **Games** — *Collections*
Hartston, William R.. London 1980 : Phillips & Drew Kings chess tournament / by W.R. Hartston, S. Reuben. — Oxford : Pergamon, 1981. — ix,222p,[1]leaf of plates : ill,ports ; 22cm. — (Pergamon chess series)
Includes index
ISBN 0-08-024141-7 (cased) : £9.95
ISBN 0-08-024140-9 (pbk) : £5.00 B81-22438

794.1′57 — Chess. Tournaments: Piatigarsky Cup *(1st : 1963 : Los Angeles)*. **Games** — *Collections*
First Piatigorsky Cup ; International Grandmaster Chess Tournament held in Los Angeles, California July, 1963 / edited by Isaac Kashdan ; annotated by Samuel Reshevsky and other tournament participants. — New York : Dover ; London : Constable, 1980, c1965. — xix,204p : ill,ports ; 22cm
Originally published: Los Angeles : Ward Ritchie Press, 1965
ISBN 0-486-24066-5 (pbk) : £2.05 B81-22440

794.1′57 — Television programmes. Special subjects: Chess: Master Game. Games — *Collections*
The **Master** game. — London : British Broadcasting Corporation
Book 2 / Jeremy James and William Hartston. — 1981. — 155p : ill,ports ; 22cm
Includes index
ISBN 0-563-17916-3 (pbk) : £3.95 B81-17949

794.1′59 — Chess. Botvinnik, M. M.. Games — *Collections*
Botvinnik, M. M.. Selected games 1967-1970 / by M.M. Botvinnik ; translated by Kenneth P. Neat. — Oxford : Pergamon, 1981. — vii,312p : ill ; 22cm. — (Pergamon Russian chess series)
Translation of: Ot shakhmatista-k mashine. — Includes index
ISBN 0-08-024124-7 (cased) : Unpriced
ISBN 0-08-024123-9 (pbk) : £5.50 B81-17363

794.1′59 — Chess. Fischer, Bobby. Games — *Collections*
Fischer′s chess games / with an introduction by Raymond Keene. — Oxford : Oxford University Press, 1980. — xxvi,166p : ill ; 24cm
Introduction in English and other languages. — Includes index
ISBN 0-19-217566-1 (pbk) : £12.50 : CIP rev.
B79-27821

794.1′59 — Chess. Games played by Alekh′in, Aleksandr Aleksandrovich — *Collections*
Hort, Vlastimil. Alekhine′s defence. — London : A. & C. Black, Feb.1982. — [256]p
ISBN 0-7136-2205-9 (pbk) : £5.95 : CIP entry
B81-35830

794.1′59 — Chess. Games played by Short, Nigel — *Collections*
Short, David. Nigel Short, chess prodigy. — London : Faber, Oct.1981. — [255]p
ISBN 0-571-11786-4 (cased) : £7.95 : CIP entry
ISBN 0-571-11860-7 (pbk) : £3.95 B81-25325

794.1′59 — Chess. Polugaevskiĭ, Lev. Games — *Collections*
Polugaevskiĭ, Lev. Grandmaster preparation / Lyev Polugayevsky ; translated by Kenneth P. Neat. — Oxford : Pergamon, 1981. — xi,240p : ill ; 26cm. — (Pergamon Russian chess series) (Pergamon international library)
Translation of: Rozhdeniye varianta. — Includes index
ISBN 0-08-024099-2 (cased) : £8.50 : CIP rev.
ISBN 0-08-024098-4 (pbk) : £4.90 B80-11575

794.1′59 — Chess. Tal′, Mikhail. Games, *1956-1976* — *Collections*
Tal′, Mikhail. Study chess with Tal / Mikhail Tal and Alexander Koblenc ; translated from the German by Mike Price ; edited by John Littlewood. — London : Batsford, 1981. — 178p : ill ; 22cm. — (The Club player′s library)
Translation of: Schachtraining mit Exweltmeister Tal. — Includes index
ISBN 0-7134-3606-9 (pbk) : £6.95 B81-37933

794.1′59 — Chess. Tal′, Mikhail. Games, *to 1959* — *Collections*

Thomas, Hilary. Complete games of Mikhail Tal 1936-1959 / Hilary Thomas. — London : Batsford, 1980. — 184p : ill ; 23cm. — (Batsford chess books) ([Grandmaster chess series])
Includes index
ISBN 0-7134-3584-4 (cased) : £8.95
ISBN 0-7134-3585-2 (pbk) : £5.95 B81-06806

794.1′7 — Chess. Playing. Applications of digital computer systems

Harding, T. D.. The chess computer book. — Oxford : Pergamon, Nov.1981. — [150]p. — (Pergamon chess series)
ISBN 0-08-026885-4 (cased) : £10.90 : CIP entry
ISBN 0-08-026884-6 (pbk) : £4.95 B81-28767

Kaplan, Julio. How to get the most from your chess computer / Julio Kaplan ; introduction by Frank Brady. — Great Neck, N.Y. : R.H.M. Press ; London : Pitman, c1980. — 138p : ill ; 21cm
ISBN 0-273-01667-9 (pbk) : £5.95 B81-16656

794.1′8 — Fairy chess. Problems — *Collections*

Dickins, Anthony. Fairy chess problems / Anthony Dickins. — [Kew Gardens] ([6a Royal Parade, Kew Gardens, Surrey]) : [A. Dickins], [c1979]. — 27 leaves : ill,ports ; 30cm
Cover title. — Limited ed. of 125 numbered copies
ISBN 0-901911-17-8 (pbk) : £2.00 B81-03514

794.2 — DRAUGHTS AND SIMILAR GAMES

794.2′2 — Draughts — *Manuals*

Chernev, Irving. The compleat draughts player. — Oxford : Oxford University Press, Apr.1981. — [256]p. — (Oxford chess books)
ISBN 0-19-217587-4 : £6.95 : CIP entry
ISBN 0-19-217586-6 (pbk) : £3.95 B81-02357

794.3 — DARTS

794.3 — Darts

Brown, Derek. The Guinness book of darts. — Enfield : Guinness Superlatives, Sept.1981. — [168]p
ISBN 0-85112-229-9 : £7.50 : CIP entry
B81-20133

794.3 — Darts — *Manuals*

Lowe, John, *19---*. John Lowe on darts / John Lowe. — London : Magnum, 1980. — 96p : ill ; 18cm
ISBN 0-417-06700-3 (pbk) : £0.95 B81-06660

Whitcombe, Dave. How to play darts / Dave Whitcombe. — London : Hamlyn, 1981. — 61p : ill,ports ; 25cm
Ill on lining papers
ISBN 0-600-34658-7 : £2.99 B81-37163

794.3 — Standard darts. Finishes — *Manuals*

Countdown : master dart finishes / Countdown Darts Services. — [East Cowes] ([Binfield Works, East Cowes, Isle of Wight PO32 6NH]) : Countdown Darts Services, 1980. — 24p : ill ; 21x31cm
Cover title. — One sheet as insert
Unpriced (pbk) B81-09238

794.73 — POOL AND SNOOKER

794.7′3 — Pool — *Manuals*

Quinn, Peter. Tackle pool / Peter Quinn ; photographs by Anthony Braithwaite. — London : Stanley Paul, 1981. — 117p,[8]p of plates : ill ; 20cm
ISBN 0-09-143370-3 (cased) : £4.95 : CIP rev.
ISBN 0-09-143371-1 (pbk) : Unpriced
B80-20963

794.7′35 — Snooker

Karnehm, Jack. World snooker / with Jack Karnehm. — London : Pelham, 1981. — 126p : ill(some col.),ports(some col.) ; 30cm
ISBN 0-7207-1328-5 (pbk) : £4.95 B81-18709

794.7′35 — Snooker, *to 1980*

Everton, Clive. Guinness book of snooker. — Enfield : Guinness Superlatives Ltd., Oct.1981. — [166]p
ISBN 0-85112-230-2 : £7.50 : CIP entry
B81-25828

794.7′35 — Snooker. Trick shots — *Manuals*

Reardon, Ray. Ray Reardon′s 50 best trick shots. — Newton Abbot : David & Charles, c1980. — [96]p : ill(some col.) ; 23cm
ISBN 0-7153-7993-3 : £3.95 : CIP rev.
B80-11132

794.7′35′0924 — Snooker. Griffiths, Terry — *Biographies*

Griffiths, Terry. Championship snooker / Terry Griffiths with Clive Everton. — London : Queen Anne Press, 1981. — 135p : ill,ports ; 22cm
ISBN 0-362-00543-5 : £5.95 B81-19645

794.7′35′0924 — Snooker. Higgins, Alex — *Biographies*

Higgins, Alex, *19---*. ″Hurricane″ Higgins′ snooker scrapbook / Alex Higgins with Angela Patmore. — London : Souvenir Press, 1981. — 128p : ill,ports ; 24cm
ISBN 0-285-62486-5 : £6.95
ISBN 0-285-62485-7 (pbk) : £4.95 B81-21829

795 — GAMES OF CHANCE

795.1 — Dice games — *Collections*

Bell, R. C.. Discovering dice and dominoes / R.C. Bell. — Princes Risborough : Shire, 1980. — 48p : ill ; 18cm. — (Discovering series ; no.255)
Bibliography: p47. — Includes index
ISBN 0-85263-532-x (pbk) : £0.95
Also classified at 795.3 B81-04693

795.1 — Dice games — *Manuals*

Tredd, William E.. Dice games : new and old / William E. Tredd. — Cambridge : Oleander, c1981. — 64p : ill ; 21cm
Bibliography: p60-62. - Includes index
ISBN 0-906672-00-7 (cased) : £4.20
ISBN 0-906672-00-7 (pbk) : £1.95 B81-16480

795.3 — Computer bingo

Williams, Richard, *1916-*. Computer bingo / by Richard Williams. — Colwyn Bay (Post Office Box 8, Colwyn Bay, Clwyd) : R. Williams, 1981. — [8]p : ill,1form ; 26cm
Unpriced (pbk) B81-11257

795.3 — Domino games — *Collections*

Bell, R. C.. Discovering dice and dominoes / R.C. Bell. — Princes Risborough : Shire, 1980. — 48p : ill ; 18cm. — (Discovering series ; no.255)
Bibliography: p47. — Includes index
ISBN 0-85263-532-x (pbk) : £0.95
Primary classification 795.1 B81-04693

795.4 — CARD GAMES

795.4 — Card games — *Manuals*

Leeming, Joseph. [Games with playing cards plus tricks and stunts]. Games and fun with playing cards / Joseph Leeming. — New York : Dover ; London : Constable, 1980. — v,184p : ill ; 22cm
Originally published: New York : Watts, 1949. — Includes index
ISBN 0-486-23977-2 (pbk) : £1.75 B81-03315

795.41′2 — Poker — *Manuals*

Parlett, David. Poker and brag / David Parlett. — [Sevenoaks] : Teach Yourself Books, 1980. — viii,209p ; 18cm
Includes index
ISBN 0-340-25115-8 (pbk) : £1.75 B81-03385

795.4′15 — Contract bridge — *Manuals*

Hoffman, Martin. Hoffman on pairs play. — London : Faber, Sept.1981. — [184]p
ISBN 0-571-11750-3 : £6.95 : CIP entry
B81-23778

795.41′5 — Contract bridge — *Manuals*

Reese, Terence. Begin bridge with Reese / Terence Reese. — Harmondsworth : Penguin, 1981, c1977. — 128p ; 19cm. — (A Penguin handbook)
Originally published: New York : Sterling Publishing, 1977 ; London : Bodley Head, 1978. — Includes index
ISBN 0-14-046392-5 (pbk) : £1.50 B81-11748

Reese, Terence. Bridge / Terence Reese. — Sevenoaks : Teach Yourself Books, 1980. — 138p ; 18cm
Includes index
ISBN 0-340-24884-x (pbk) : £1.50 : CIP rev.
B80-36274

795.41′5 — Contract bridge. Pairs games — *Manuals*

Jannersten, Eric. Winning pairs technique / Eric Jannersten and Jan Wohlin ; translated by Hugh Kelsey. — London : Gollancz in association with Peter Crawley, 1980. — 160p : ill ; 22cm. — (Master bridge series)
Translation of: Vinnande Partävlengsteknik
ISBN 0-575-02866-1 (pbk) : £4.95 B81-06180

795.41′5′0321 — Contract bridge — *Encyclopaedias*

Reese, Terence. The bridge player′s alphabetical handbook / Terence Reese and Albert Dormer. — London : Faber, 1981. — 223p ; 22cm
ISBN 0-571-11599-3 : £6.95 B81-10609

795.41′52 — Contract bridge. Acol bidding — *Manuals*

Cohen, Ben. Basic Acol. — 4th ed. — London : Unwin Paperbacks, Oct.1981. — [122]p
Previous ed.: 1979
ISBN 0-04-793049-7 (pbk) : £1.75 : CIP entry
B81-25145

Klinger, Ron. Basic bridge : a guide to good Acol bidding and play / Ron Klinger. — London : Gollancz in association with Peter Crawley, c1978. — 127p ; 26cm. — (Master bridge series)
Originally published: London : Ward Lock, 1978
ISBN 0-575-02637-5 (pbk) : £3.95 B81-09332

795.41′52 — Contract bridge. Acol competitive bidding — *Manuals*

Crowhurst, Eric. Acol in competition / Eric Crowhurst. — London : Pelham, 1980. — 383p ; 23cm
Includes index
ISBN 0-7207-1273-4 : £9.95 B81-02429

795.41′52 — Contract bridge. Bidding. Bids: One no-trump. Responses — *Manuals*

Sowter, Sally. Transfers after one no trump / Sally Sowter. — Nottingham (12 Burton Ave., Carlton, Nottingham NG4 1PT) : Bridge Players Handbooks, 1980. — 32p : ill ; 21cm. — (Bridge conventions)
ISBN 0-906042-11-9 (pbk) : Unpriced
B81-34355

795.41′52 — Contract bridge. Bidding — *Manuals*

Payne, Dick. Bridge : TNT and competitive bidding / Dick Payne & Joe Amsbury. — London : Batsford, 1981. — 175p ; 22cm. — (Batsford bridge series)
Includes index
ISBN 0-7134-2542-3 (cased) : Unpriced
ISBN 0-7134-2543-1 (pbk) : £3.95 B81-36708

795.41′52 — Contract bridge. Bids. Take-out doubles — *Manuals*

Sowter, Tony. The take-out double / Tony Sowter. — Nottingham (12 Burton Ave., Carlton, Nottingham NG4 1PT) : Bridge Players Handbooks, 1980. — 32p : ill ; 21cm. — (Bridge conventions)
ISBN 0-906042-14-3 (pbk) : Unpriced
B81-34354

795.41′52 — Contract bridge. Blackwood slam bidding — *Manuals*

Amsbury, Joe. Control asking : (or Blackwood & all that jazz) / Joe Amsbury. — Nottingham (12 Burton Ave., Carlton, Nottingham NG4 1PT) : Bridge Players Handbooks, 1980. — 32p : ill ; 21cm. — (Bridge conventions)
ISBN 0-906042-25-9 (pbk) : Unpriced
B81-36914

795.41'52 — Contract bridge. Competitive bidding

Flint, Jeremy. Competitive bidding / Jeremy Flint and Richard Sharp. — London : Cassell, 1980. — 202p ; 23cm
ISBN 0-304-30482-4 : £6.25 B81-31216

795.41'52 — Contract bridge. Swiss bidding — *Manuals*

Baker, Bob, *1953 May 21-*. The Swiss convention / Bob Baker. — Nottingham (12 Burton Ave., Carlton, Nottingham NG4 1PT) : Bridge Players Handbooks, 1980. — 31p : ill ; 21cm. — (Bridge conventions)
ISBN 0-906042-12-7 (pbk) : Unpriced B81-34352

795.41'53 — Contract bridge. Bids: No-trumps. Card play

Berthe, Robert. Bridge : step by step card play — no-trumps / Robert Berthe & Norbert Lébely ; foreword by José Le Dentu ; translated by Barry Seabrook. — London : Batsford, 1981. — 167p ; 22cm. — (Batsford bridge series)
Translation of: Perfectionnez votre jeu de la carte pas à pas - le sans-tout
ISBN 0-7134-4153-4 (cased) : Unpriced
ISBN 0-7134-4154-2 (pbk) : £3.95 B81-36706

795.41'53 — Contract bridge. Blocking play & unblocking play — *Manuals*

Reese, Terence. Blocking and unblocking plays in bridge / Terence Reese and Roger Trézel. — London : Gollancz in association with Peter Crawley, 1979, c1976. — 64p : ill ; 20cm. — (Master bridge series)
Originally published: London : Ward Lock, 1976
ISBN 0-575-02749-5 (pbk) : £1.95 B81-10174

795.41'53 — Contract bridge. Card play by defenders — *Manuals*

Kelsey, H. W.. More killing defence at bridge / H.W. Kelsey. — London : Faber, 1972 (1981 printing). — 192p : ill ; 20cm. — (Faber paperback bridge)
ISBN 0-571-11760-0 (pbk) : £2.95 : CIP rev. B81-21460

795.41'53 — Contract bridge. Card play by defenders. Problems — *Collections*

Reese, Terence. Defend with your life / Terence Reese and Eddie Kantar. — London : Faber, 1981. — 160p : ill ; 21cm
ISBN 0-571-11711-2 : £6.25 : CIP rev. B81-12915

795.41'53 — Contract bridge. Card play — *Manuals*

Darvas, Robert. Spotlight on card play. — London : Gollancz, Feb.1982. — [160]p
Translated from the Hungarian. — Originally published: London : Nicholas Kaye, 1960
ISBN 0-575-03078-x (pbk) : £3.95 : CIP entry B81-38322

Fox, G. C. H.. Bridge : the elements of play / G.C.H. Fox. — London : Hale, 1980. — 176p ; 21cm. — (Hale bridge books)
ISBN 0-7091-8320-8 : £4.95 B81-00233

Kelsey, H. W.. Advanced play at bridge / H.W. Kelsey. — London : Faber, 1981, c1968. — 193p ; 20cm
ISBN 0-571-11677-9 (pbk) : £2.25 B81-13070

Kelsey, H. W.. Bridge : the mind of the expert / H.W. Kelsey. — London : Faber, 1981. — 160p : ill ; 21cm
ISBN 0-571-11710-4 : £6.25 : CIP rev. B81-12362

Mollo, Victor. Card play technique, or, The art of being lucky / by Victor Mollo and Nico Gardener. — New ed. — London : Faber, 1971 (1981 printing). — 381p : ill ; 20cm. — (Faber paperback bridge)
Previous ed.: London : Newnes, 1955
ISBN 0-571-11759-7 (pbk) : £3.25 : CIP rev. B81-21459

Reese, Terence. Those extra chances in bridge / Terence Reese and Roger Trézel. — London : Gollancz in association with Peter Crawley, c1978. — 64p : ill ; 20cm. — (Master bridge series)
Originally published: London : Ward Lock, 1978
ISBN 0-575-02634-0 (pbk) : £1.95 B81-10176

Reese, Terence. When to duck when to win in bridge / Terence Reese and Roger Trézel. — London : Gollancz in association with Peter Crawley, 1978. — 64p ; 20cm. — (Master bridge series)
Originally published: London : Ward Lock, 1978
ISBN 0-575-02635-9 (pbk) : £1.95 B81-11524

795.41'53 — Contract bridge. Card play. Problems — *Collections*

Klinger, Ron. Bridge without error / by Ron Klinger. — London : Gollancz in association with Crawley, 1981. — 128p : ill ; 23cm. — (Master bridge series)
ISBN 0-575-02946-3 (pbk) : £3.95 B81-18389

Klinger, Ron. Playing to win at bridge : practical problems for the improving player / Ron Klinger. — London : Gollancz in association with Peter Crawley, c1976 (1979 [printing]). — 125p ; 20cm. — (Master bridge series)
Originally published: London : Ward Lock, 1976
ISBN 0-575-02658-8 (pbk) : £2.50 B81-12646

Roudinesco, Jean-Marc. Play bridge with me : forty problems in card play / by Jean-Marc Roudinesco ; translated and adapted by Hugh Kelsey. — London : Gollancz in association with Peter Crawley, 1980. — 95p ; 22cm. — (Master bridge series)
Translation of: Voulez-vous jouer avec moi au bridge?
ISBN 0-575-02880-7 (pbk) : £3.50 B81-02061

795.41'53 — Contract bridge. Card play — *Stories, anecdotes*

Saunders, P. F.. Bridge with a perfect partner / P.F. Saunders ; foreword by Eric Milnes. — London : Gollancz in association with Peter Crawley, c1976. — 128p ; 20cm. — (Master bridge series)
Originally published: London : Ward Lock, 1976
ISBN 0-575-02746-0 (pbk) : £3.50 B81-05694

795.41'53 — Contract bridge. Deceptive play — *Manuals*

Reese, Terence. Snares and swindles in bridge / Terence Reese and Roger Trézel. — London : Gollancz in association with Peter Crawley, 1979, c1977. — 64p : ill ; 20cm. — (Master bridge series)
Originally published: London : Ward Lock, 1977
ISBN 0-575-02633-2 (pbk) : £1.95 B81-10177

795.41'53 — Contract bridge. Dummy play — *Manuals*

Seabrook, Barry. Bridge : expert dummy-play / Barry Seabrook. — London : Batsford, 1981. — 175p ; 22cm. — (Batsford bridge series)
Includes index
ISBN 0-7134-1827-3 (cased) : Unpriced (pbk) : £3.95 B81-36707

795.41'53 — Contract bridge. Elimination play — *Manuals*

Reese, Terence. Elimination play in bridge / Terence Reese and Roger Trézel. — London : Gollancz in association with Peter Crawley, 1979, c1977. — 77p : ill ; 20cm. — (Master bridge series)
Originally published: London : Ward Lock, 1977
ISBN 0-575-02632-4 (pbk) : £1.95 B81-10178

795.41'53 — Contract bridge. Finessing — *Manuals*

Kelsey, H. W.. Test your finessing / by Hugh Kelsey. — London : Gollancz in association with Peter Crawley, 1981. — 80p ; 20cm. — (Master bridge series)
ISBN 0-575-03004-6 (pbk) : £2.50 B81-33377

795.41'53 — Contract bridge. Safety play — *Manuals*

Reese, Terence. Safety plays in bridge / Terence Reese and Roger Trézel. — London : Gollancz in association with Peter Crawley, c1976. — 63p : ill ; 21cm. — (Master bridge series)
Originally published: London : Ward Lock, 1976
ISBN 0-575-02631-6 : £1.95 B81-10175

795.41'53 — Contract bridge. Trumps. Control — *Manuals*

Kelsey, H. W.. Test your trump control / by Hugh Kelsey. — London : Gollancz in association with Peter Crawley, 1981. — 80p ; 20cm. — (Master bridge series)
ISBN 0-575-03005-4 (pbk) : £2.50 B81-33376

795.41'58 — Contract bridge. Card play. Games — *Collections*

Markus, Rixi. Bridge-table tales / by Rixi Markus. — Newton Abbot : David & Charles, c1980. — 96p : ill ; 22cm
ISBN 0-7153-7947-x : £3.95 : CIP rev. B80-12019

Mollo, Victor. Bridge a la carte. — London : Pelham, Feb.1982. — [144]p
ISBN 0-7207-1385-4 : £8.50 : CIP entry B81-35848

795.41'58 — Contract bridge. Games — *Collections*

Griffiths, J. N. R.. The golden years of bridge / by J.N.R. Griffiths. — London : Gollancz in association with Peter Crawley, 1981. — 127p : ill ; 23cm. — (Master bridge series)
ISBN 0-575-02906-4 (pbk) : £3.95 B81-05807

Mollo, Victor. Bridge in the fourth dimension : further adventures of the Hideous Hog / Victor Mollo. — London : Faber, 1981, c1974. — 160p ; 20cm. — (Faber paperback bridge)
ISBN 0-571-11675-2 (pbk) : £2.25 : CIP rev. B81-04303

795.4'3 — Card games: Patience — *Manuals*

Parlett, David. The Penguin book of patience / David Parlett. — Harmondsworth : Penguin, 1980, c1979. — 367p : ill + 1card(1ill;16cm) ; 18cm. — (Penguin handbooks)
Originally published: London : Allen Lane, 1979. — Bibliography: p357. — Includes index
ISBN 0-14-046346-1 (pbk) : £1.75 B81-07527

795.4'38 — Card tricks — *Manuals*

Ganson, Lewis. Patrick Page's cards to pocket / described by Lewis Ganson. — Bideford (64 High St., Bideford, Devon) : Supreme Magic, c1981. — [4]p ; 25cm
Unpriced (pbk) B81-40605

Hugard, Jean. The royal road to card magic / Jean Hugard and Frederick Braue ; with illustrations by Frank Rigney. — London : Faber, 1949 (1981 printing). — 302p : ill ; 20cm
Includes index
ISBN 0-571-11399-0 (pbk) : £2.95 : CIP rev. B81-21458

The **Interlocked** back-and-front hand card production. — [Bideford] ([64 High St., Bideford, Devon]) : [Supreme Magic], [1981?]. — 6p : ill ; 25cm
Unpriced (unbound) B81-40603

Joseph, Eddie. The invisible influence : the no-touch card act : an illustration of a miraculous psychic phenomenon from India / by Eddie Joseph. — Bideford (64 High St., Bideford, Devon), c1981. — 12p : ill ; 25cm
Unpriced (pbk) B81-40632

Paul Curry's sealed miracles. — Bideford (64 High St., Bideford, Devon) : Supreme Magic, c1978. — 3p ; 23cm
Unpriced (unbound) B81-40604

795.4′38 — Card tricks using card indexes — *Manuals*
Andrews, Max. Sixteen card index gems / by Max Andrews. — [2nd ed.]. — Bideford (64 High St., Bideford, Devon) : Supreme Magic, c1981. — 36p ; 18cm
Previous ed.: London : M. Andrews, 1943
Unpriced (pbk) B81-40636

796 — SPORTS AND GAMES

796 — Mini-sports — *Manuals*
Sleap, Mike. Mini sport / Mike Sleap. — London : Heinemann Educational, 1981. — xiii,210p : ill ; 25cm
Includes bibliographies
ISBN 0-435-86590-0 (pbk) : £8.95 : CIP rev. B79-30268

796 — Outdoor games — *Manuals*
Zigo, Hereward. Summer games for adults and children. — Cambridge : Oleander Press, Feb.1982. — [64]p. — (Oleander games and pastimes series ; v.6)
ISBN 0-906672-05-8 (cased) : £4.20 : CIP entry
ISBN 0-906672-06-6 (pbk) : £1.95 B81-36056

796 — Sports — *For schools*
Hawkey, Roy. Sport science / Roy Hawkey. — London : Hodder and Stoughton, 1981. — vi,138p : ill,ports ; 28cm
Includes index
ISBN 0-340-25127-1 (pbk) : Unpriced : CIP rev. B81-06075

796 — Sports *related to* **work —** *Marxist viewpoints*
Rigauer, Bero. Sport and work / Bero Rigauer ; translated by Allen Guttmann. — New York ; Guilford : Columbia Unviversity Press, 1981. — xxxiv,127p 22cm. — (European perspectives)
Translation of: Sport und Arbeit. — Includes index
ISBN 0-231-05200-6 : £9.75
Also classified at 306′.3 B81-29270

796 — Televised sports
World of Sport sportwatcher′s guide / introduced by Dickie Davies ; edited by Paul Wade. — London : Collins, 1981. — 248p : ill(some col.),ports(some col.) ; 26cm
Spine title: Sportwatcher′s guide
ISBN 0-00-411653-4 (pbk) : £3.95 B81-35324

796′.01 — Athletes. Competitiveness. Improvement. Psychological aspects
Kauss, David R.. Peak performance : mental game plans for maximizing your athletic potential / David R. Kauss. — Englewood Cliffs ; London : Prentice-Hall, c1980. — xiii,300p : ill ; 24cm. — (A Spectrum book)
Includes index
ISBN 0-13-655332-x (cased) : Unpriced
ISBN 0-13-655324-9 (pbk) : £5.15 B81-12608

796′.01 — Sports. Performance. Psychological factors
Walker, Stuart H.. Winning : the psychology of competition / Stuart H. Walker ; illustrations by Thomas C. Price. — New York ; London : Norton, c1980. — xiv,266p : ill ; 25cm
Bibliography: p265-266
ISBN 0-393-03255-8 : £7.25 B81-08793

796′.01 — Sports. Psychosocial aspects
Cratty, Bryant J.. Social psychology in athletics / Bryant J. Cratty. — Englewood Cliffs ; London : Prentice-Hall, c1981. — xiii,303p : ill ; 24cm
Includes bibliographies and index
ISBN 0-13-817650-7 : £11.00 B81-23110

796′.01 — Sports. Skills. Effects of visual perception
Vision and sport / edited by Ian M. Cockerill and William W. MacGillivary. — Cheltenham : Thornes, 1981. — xiii,203p : ill ; 25cm
Includes bibliographies and index
ISBN 0-85950-463-8 : £9.25 B81-29148

796′.019c19 — Sports. Geographical aspects
Bale, John R.. Geographical perspectives on sport. — London : Lepus, Apr.1981. — [192]p
ISBN 0-86019-044-7 (pbk) : £9.50 : CIP entry B81-10500

796′.01′96 — Outdoor activities for handicapped persons
Cotton, Mike. Out of doors with handicapped people / by Mike Cotton. — London : Souvenir, 1981. — 255p,[12]p of plates : ill ; 23cm. — (Human horizons series)
Bibliography: p243-248. — Includes index
ISBN 0-285-64934-5 (cased) : £6.95
ISBN 0-285-64935-3 (pbk) : £4.50 B81-39370

796′.023′41 — Great Britain. Sports — *Career guides*
Barber, Thelma. Working in sport / Thelma Barber. — London : Watts, c1980. — 64p : ill,2ports ; 26cm. — (Choosing a career)
Includes index
ISBN 0-85166-850-x : £3.95 B81-01073

796′.025′41 — Great Britain. Outdoor leisure activities — *Directories — Serials*
The **Outdoor** directory. — [1st ed.]-. — Glasgow (12 York St., Glasgow G2 8LG) : Holmes McDougall, [1980]-. — v. : ill ; 21cm
Annual. — Description based on: [2nd ed.]
ISSN 0143-4640 = Outdoor directory : £1.95 B81-35955

796′.025′41 — Great Britain. Sports facilities — *Directories*
Pelham sports guide. — London : Pelham Books, Jan.1982. — [480]p
ISBN 0-7207-1386-2 (pbk) : £6.95 : CIP entry B81-33843

796′.025′422 — Southern England. Sports facilities — *Directories — Serials*
Sport in the south / Sports Council (Southern Region). — 1981 ed. — Reading (223a Southampton St., Reading RG1 2RB) : Coles & Sons, [1981?]. — 48p
£1.00 B81-14534

796′.05 — Sports — *For children — Serials*
[Scoop *(Annual)*]. Scoop. — 1981. — London : D.C. Thomson, c1980. — 125p
ISBN 0-85116-184-7 : £1.45 B81-03120

Tiger book of sport. — 1981. — London : IPC Magazines, c1980. — 93p
ISBN 0-85037-584-3 : £2.00
ISSN 0140-7120 B81-06863

796′.05 — Sports — *Serials*
The **Sporting** year / compiled by Britain′s leading sports writers and photographers. — 1980. — [S.l.] : I. Margolis, J. Stidolph, c1980. — [56]p
£1.50p B81-05934

796′.06′0411 — Scotland. Sports facilities. Organisations: Scottish Sports Council — *Serials*
Scottish Sports Council. Annual report / the Scottish Sports Council. — 1979-80. — [Edinburgh] ([1 Saint Colme St., Edinburgh EH3 6AA]) : The Council, 1980. — 48p
ISSN 0142-9515 : £2.00 B81-03300

796′.07 — Education. Role of outdoor activities
Ford, Phyllis M.. Principles and practices of outdoor/environmental education / Phyllis M. Ford. — New York ; Chichester : Wiley, c1981. — xii,348p : ill,forms ; 24cm
Includes bibliographies and index
ISBN 0-471-04768-6 : £9.50 B81-23317

796′.07′1242 — England. Boys′ public schools. Activities: Sports & games, *1837-1910*
Mangan, J. A.. Athleticism in the Victorian and Edwardian public school : the emergence and consolidation of the educational ideology / J.A. Mangan. — Cambridge : Cambridge University Press, 1981. — xv,345p : ill,1facsim,port ; 24cm
Bibliography: p309-336. — Includes index
ISBN 0-521-23388-7 : £25.00 : CIP rev. B81-20535

796′.076 — Sports — *Questions & answers*
Quiz sport 1 : questions to test your sporting knowledge. — [Crewe] ([52 Lordsmill Rd., Shavington, Crewe]) : [Preece, Smith, and Thompson], [c1980]. — 27p ; 21cm
Cover title
£0.50 (pbk) B81-39685

Rhys, Chris. Brain of sport : questions and answers from the Radio 2 quiz game / Chris Rhys. — London : British Broadcasting Corporation, 1980. — 80p : ill ; 18cm
ISBN 0-563-17876-0 (pbk) : £1.25 B81-20369

796′.076 — Sports — *Questions & answers — For children*
Eldin, Peter. Sports quiz / Peter Eldin ; illustrated by Tony Graham. — London : Beaver, 1981. — 95p : ill ; 18cm
ISBN 0-600-20284-4 (pbk) : £0.80 B81-26082

796′.08996 — African sportsmen — *Serials*
AfroSport. — Vol.1, no.1 (1978)-. — London (27 St. John′s Square, E.C.1) : PDI Publications, 1978-. — v. : ill ; 30cm
Monthly. — Description based on: Vol.2, no.11 (Aug.1980)
ISSN 0260-454x = AfroSport : £6.00 per year B81-03280

796′.09′047 — Sports, *1979-1980*
Keating, Frank. Bowled over! : a year of sport with Frank Keating. — London : Deutsch, 1980. — 220p ; 23cm
ISBN 0-233-97284-6 : £6.50 : CIP rev. B80-24757

796′.09171′7 — Communist countries. Sports
Freeman, Simon, *1952-*. Sport behind the Iron Curtain / Simon Freeman and Roger Boyes. — London : Proteus, 1980. — 128p : ill(some col.),ports(some col.) ; 30cm. — (Behind the scenes of sport)
ISBN 0-906071-35-6 : £5.95 B81-02485

796′.0941 — Great Britain. Outdoor vacation activities — *Manuals*
Swinglehurst, Edmund. Outdoor and activity holidays in Britain / Edmund Swinglehurst. — London : Thames/Magnum, 1981. — 191p : ill,1facsim ; 20cm. — (A ′Wish you were here′ guide)
ISBN 0-423-00020-9 (pbk) : £1.75 B81-08745

796′.0941 — Great Britain. Sports, *to 1980 — For schools*
Owen, Evan. Sport / Evan Owen. — London : Evans, 1981. — 48p : ill,coats of arms, ports ; 25cm. — (Knowing British history topics)
ISBN 0-237-29259-9 (pbk) : Unpriced B81-12475

796′.09411 — Scotland. Rural regions. Outdoor vacation activities — *For youth hostelling*
Smith, Roger, *1938-*. Outdoor Scotland / Roger Smith. — [Stirling] : Scottish Youth Hostels Association, [1981]. — 144p : ill(some col.),maps(some col.),1port ; 22cm. — (A SYHA golden jubilee publication)
Cover title. — Ill on inside covers
ISBN 0-900651-19-9 (pbk) : £2.00 B81-38257

796′.0947 — Soviet Union. Sports
National folk sports in the USSR / [compiled by Yuri Lukashin] ; [translated from the Russian by James Riordan]. — Moscow : Progress Publishers, c1980 ; [London] : Distributed by Central Books. — 123p,[16]p of plates : ill (some col.) ; 21cm
£2.50 B81-29321

796′.0947 — Soviet Union. Sports, *1861-1976*
Riordan, James. Sport in Soviet society : development of sport and physical education in Russia and the USSR / James Riordan. — Cambridge : Cambridge University Press, 1977 (1980 printing). — ix,435p : ill ; 22cm. — (Soviet and East European studies)
Bibliography: p420-429. - Includes index
ISBN 0-521-28023-0 (pbk) : £6.50 B81-00234

796.2′1′06041 — Great Britain. Roller skating. Organisations: National Skating Association of Great Britain — *Serials*
National Skating Association of Great Britain. Official handbook / National Skating Association of Great Britain. — 1980-81. — London (117 Charterhouse St., EC1M 6AT) : The Association, [1980]. — 157p
£3.00 (free to Association members)
Primary classification 796.91′06′041 B81-26383

796.2'1'09425 — England. East Midlands. Roller skating — *Conference proceedings*

Roller skating : seminar report : the report of seminar held on Tuesday 9th December 1980 at the Leicester Tigers Rugby Football Club / arranged by the Sports Council, East Midland Region, in conjunction with the National Skating Association of Great Britain. — Nottingham (26 Musters Rd., West Bridgford, Nottingham NG2 7PL) : The Council, [1981]. — 35p : 1plan ; 30cm
Bibliography: p30
£1.20 (pbk) B81-23657

796.3 — BALL GAMES

796.31 — Bedfordshire. Ball games: Flat green bowls. Organisations: Beds County Bowling Association — *Serials*

Beds County Bowling Association. Official handbook / Beds County Bowling Association. — 1981. — Bedford (c/o 47 Aspen Ave., Bedford MK41 8DA) : The Association, 1981. — 62p
£0.45 B81-25012

796.31 — England. Ball games: Flat green bowls. Organisations: English Bowling Association — *Serials*

English Bowling Association. Official year book / English Bowling Association. — 1981. — Bournemouth (2 Iddesleigh Rd., Bournemouth BH3 7JR) : [The Association], 1981. — 280p
£1.00 B81-31027

796.31 — Pétanque — *Manuals*

Abney-Hastings, Maurice. The Pernod book of pétanque / by Maurice Abney-Hastings. — London : Allen and Unwin, 1981. — viii,103p,[16]p of plates : ill,ports ; 21cm
Includes index
ISBN 0-04-796058-2 : Unpriced : CIP rev. B81-09496

796.31 — West Sussex. Chichester. Ball games: Flat green bowls. Clubs: Chichester Bowling Club, *to 1981*

Rankin, Stanley J.. The centenary of Chichester Bowling Club 1881 to 1981 : including a history of Priory Park in which the Bowling Green is sited / by Stanley J. Rankin. — [Chichester] ([c/o S.J. Rankin, 44 Belgrave Cres. Chichester, West Sussex PO19 2SB]) : Chichester Duplication Service, [1980]. — 33p : ill,facsims,ports ; 21cm
£1.00 (unbound) B81-27768

796.32 — Netball — *Manuals*

Miles, Anne. Success in netball. — London : Murray, Oct.1981. — [96]p
ISBN 0-7195-3840-8 : £4.50 : CIP entry B81-30316

796.32 — Netball — *Manuals* — *For coaching*

Edwards, Phyl. Netball today / Phyl Edwards and Sue Campbell. — London : Lepus, c1981. — 139p : ill ; 21cm
ISBN 0-86019-049-8 (pbk) : £5.00 B81-16098

Wood, Barbara, *19---*. The fundamentals of netball : for beginner coaches / Barbara Wood. — London : Edward Arnold, 1981. — 55p : ill,forms ; 22cm
ISBN 0-7131-8036-6 (pbk) : £1.95 B81-36873

796.323 — BASKETBALL

796.32'3 — Basketball

Welch, Mel. Basketball / Mel Welch ; colour photographs by All-Sport Limited. — Hove : Wayland, 1981. — 64p : col.ill ; 21cm. — (InterSport)
Includes index
ISBN 0-382-06513-1 : £3.95 B81-24345

796.32'3'077 — Basketball. Coaching — *Manuals*

Tarkanian, Jerry. Winning basketball systems / Jerry Tarkanian, William E. Warren. — Boston ; London : Allyn and Bacon, c1981. — xv,432p : ill ; 24cm
Ill on lining papers. — Includes index
ISBN 0-205-07099-x : £16.95 B81-02045

796.32'32 — Basketball — *Manuals*

Hoy, Len. Tackle basketball / Len Hoy and Cyril A. Carter. — London : Paul, 1980. — 144p : ill,ports ; 20cm
ISBN 0-09-141740-6 (cased) : £4.95 : CIP rev.
ISBN 0-09-141741-4 (pbk) : £2.95 B80-06043

796.32'32 — Basketball — *Manuals* — *For coaching*

Lehane, Jack. Basketball fundamentals : teaching techniques for winning / Jack Lehane. — Boston, Mass. ; London : Allyn and Bacon, c1981. — xiv,242p : ill ; 24cm
Includes index
ISBN 0-205-07119-8 : Unpriced B81-11295

796.33 — FOOTBALL

796.33 — Dublin. Gaelic football. Teams: Dublin Gaelic Football team, *1974-1976*

O'Shea, John. The book of the Dubs / by John O'Shea. — [Dublin] ([Box 286, 276 5th Circular Rd., Dublin 8]) : [Player & Wills (Ireland), [1981?]. — 108p, [8]p of plates : ill,ports ; 19cm
£1.00 (pbk) B81-31398

796.332 — AMERICAN FOOTBALL

796.332'07'7 — American football. Coaching — *Manuals*

Fuoss, Donald E.. Effective football coaching : game-winning techniques for preventing mistakes and errors / Donald E. Fuoss and Rowland "Red" Smith. — Boston, Mass. ; London : Allyn and Bacon, c1981. — xvi,283p : ill ; 25cm
ISBN 0-205-07125-2 : £10.15 B81-04504

796.333 — RUGBY FOOTBALL

796.33'3 — Rugby Union football

Godwin, Terry. Guinness book of rugby facts and feats. — Enfield : Guinness Superlatives, Nov.1981. — [256]p
ISBN 0-85112-214-0 (cased) : £7.95 : CIP entry
ISBN 0-85112-248-5 (pbk) : £5.95 B81-31200

796.33'3'0207 — Rugby Union football — *Humour*

Burton, Mike. Tight heads, loose balls / Mike Burton ; illustrations by Bill Tidy. — London : Queen Anne Press, 1981. — 88p : ill(some col.) ; 26cm
Ill on lining papers
ISBN 0-362-00562-1 : £5.95 B81-39408

796.33'3'0321 — Rugby League football — *Encyclopaedias*

Huxley, John, *1947-*. Encyclopaedia of Rugby League football. — 2nd ed. / compiled by John Huxley and David Howes ; foreword by the Earl of Derby. — London : Hale, 1980. — 159,[12]p of plates : ill,ports ; 23cm
Previous ed.: / compiled by A.N. Gaulton. 1968. — Includes index
ISBN 0-7091-8133-7 : £7.25 B81-04100

796.33'3'05 — Rugby Union football — *Serials*

Rothmans rugby yearbook. — 1980-81. — London : Queen Anne Press, c1980. — 384p
ISBN 0-362-02019-1 : £6.95 B81-00235

796.33'3'060429 — Wales. Rugby Union football. Organisations: Welsh Rugby Union, *to 1980*

Welsh Rugby Union. Fields of praise : the official history of the Welsh Rugby Union 1881-1981 / David Smith and Gareth Williams. — Cardiff : University of Wales Press on behalf of the Welsh Rugby Union, 1980. — xii,505p,[37]p of plates : ill(some col.),coats of arms,ports ; 22cm
Bibliography: p489-495. — Includes index
ISBN 0-7083-0766-3 : £12.95 : CIP rev. B80-17904

796.33'3077 — Middle schools. Curriculum subjects: Rugby Union football. Coaching

French, Ray. Running rugby / Ray French ; foreword by Des Seabrook ; preface by Mike Davis ; line drawings by Ken Tranter. — London : Faber, 1980. — 80p : ill,ports ; 23cm
ISBN 0-571-11597-7 : £4.50 : CIP rev.
ISBN 0-571-11600-0 (pbk) : £1.95 B80-17905

796.33'3'09 — Rugby League football, *to 1980*

Waring, Eddie. Eddie Waring on Rugby League. — London : Muller, Aug.1981. — [128]p
ISBN 0-584-10358-1 : CIP entry B81-18110

796.33'3'0904 — Rugby League football, *to 1980*

Hodgkinson, David. The world of Rugby League. — London : Allen & Unwin, Sept.1981. — [96]p
ISBN 0-04-796059-0 : £4.95 : CIP entry B81-22568

796.33'3'0924 — England. Rugby Union football. Duckham, David — *Biographies*

Duckham, David. Dai for England : the autobiography of David Duckham / foreword by Bill McLaren. — London : Pelham, 1980. — 223p,[16]p of plates : ill,ports ; 23cm
Includes index
ISBN 0-7207-1279-3 : £6.95 B81-01707

796.33'3'0924 — England. Rugby Union football. Uttley, Roger — *Biographies*

Uttley, Roger. Pride in England. — London : Stanley Paul, Nov.1981. — 1v.
ISBN 0-09-146320-3 : £6.95 : CIP entry B81-30263

796.33'3'0924 — Scotland. Rugby Union football. McLauchlan, Ian — *Biographies*

McLauchlan, Ian. Mighty Mouse : an autobiography / Ian McLauchlan with Ian Archer. — London : Stanley Paul, 1980. — 149p,[16]p of plates : ill,ports ; 23cm
ISBN 0-09-143390-8 : £5.95 B81-00236

796.33'3'0924 — Wales. Rugby Union football. Bennett, Phil — *Biographies*

Bennett, Phil. Everywhere for Wales. — London : Paul, Oct.1981. — 1v.
ISBN 0-09-146310-6 : £5.95 : CIP entry B81-26803

796.33'3'0924 — Wales. Rugby Union football. Davies, Gerald, *1945-* — *Biographies*

Davies, Gerald, *1945-*. Gerald Davies : an autobiography. — London : Unwin Paperbacks, 1981, c1979. — xiv,160p : ports ; 18cm
Originally published: London : Allen & Unwin, 1979. — Includes index
ISBN 0-04-796053-1 (pbk) : £1.50 B81-08478

796.33'3'0924 — Wales. Rugby Union football. Williams, J. P. R. — *Biographies*

Williams, J. P. R.. JPR : an autobiography / J.P.R. Williams. — London : Corgi, 1980, c1979. — 256p,[8]p of plates : ill,ports ; 18cm
Originally published: London : Collins, 1979. — Includes index
ISBN 0-552-11410-3 (pbk) : £1.25 B81-05230

796.33'32 — Rugby Union football. Captaining — *Manuals*

Frost, David, *1929-*. Rugby union : captaincy / David Frost with Roger Uttley. — London : Pelham, 1981. — 111p : ill,ports ; 22cm. — (Sporting skills series)
ISBN 0-7207-1301-3 : £5.95 : CIP rev. B81-03175

796.33'32 — Rugby Union football — *Manuals*

Norrie, David. How to play rugby / David Norrie. — London : Hamlyn, 1981. — 61p : ill,1plan,ports ; 25cm
Ill on lining papers
ISBN 0-600-34659-5 : £2.99 B81-37164

796.33'323 — Rugby Union football. Forward play. Techniques — *Manuals*

Edwards, Gareth. Forward skills / Gareth Edwards with Ian Robertson. — London : Paul, 1980. — 64p : ill,ports ; 25cm
ISBN 0-09-142610-3 (cased) : £5.95 : CIP rev.
ISBN 0-09-142611-1 (pbk) : £2.95 B80-24758

McLauchlan, Ian. Rugby union : forward play / Ian McLauchlan and Bill Dickinson. — London : Pelham, 1981. — 120p : ill,ports ; 21cm. — (Sporting skills series)
ISBN 0-7207-1281-5 : £5.95 : CIP rev. B81-02386

796.33'326 — Rugby Union football. Back play. Techniques — *Manuals*
Duckham, David. Rugby union : back play / David Duckham with the assistance of Michael Blair. — London : Pelham, 1981. — 110p : ill,ports ; 21cm
ISBN 0-7207-1316-1 : £5.95 : CIP rev. B81-10452

796.33'362'0941623 — Londonderry *(District)*. **Londonderry. Rugby Union football. Clubs: City of Derry Rugby Football Club,** *to 1981*
City of Derry Rugby Football Club : centenary 1881-1981 : a club history / [edited by David Orr]. — Londonderry (c/o Northland Rd., Londonderry BT48 7JD) : The Club, [1981]. — 108p : ill,ports ; 30cm
Unpriced (pbk) B81-26046

796.33'365'0924 — Wales. Rugby Union football. Teams: Welsh Rugby Union Football Team, *1969-1979 — Personal observations*
Taylor, John, *19---*. Decade of the dragon : a cele-bration of Welsh rugby 1969-1979 / John Taylor. — London : Hodder and Stoughton, 1980. — 248p,[24]p of plates : ill,ports ; 24cm
Includes index
ISBN 0-340-25273-1 : £7.95 : CIP rev. B80-19378

796.33'374 — New Zealand. Rugby Union football. Tours by Springboks, *to 1976*
Barrow, Graeme. All Blacks versus Springboks / Graeme Barrow. — Auckland ; Tadworth : Heinemann, 1981. — 159p,[8]p of plates : 1map,ports ; 23cm
ISBN 0-86863-376-3 : £7.00
Primary classification 796.33'374 B81-37942

796.33'374 — South Africa. Rugby Union football. Tours by All Blacks, *to 1976*
Barrow, Graeme. All Blacks versus Springboks / Graeme Barrow. — Auckland ; Tadworth : Heinemann, 1981. — 159p,[8]p of plates : 1map,ports ; 23cm
ISBN 0-86863-376-3 : £7.00
Also classified at 796.33'374 B81-37942

796.33'374 — South Africa. Rugby Union football. Tours by British Lions, *1980*
James, Carwyn. Injured pride : the Lions in South Africa / Carwyn James and Chris Rea ; edited by Rupert Cherry. — London : Arthur Barker, 1980. — vii,206p,[16]p of plates : ill,1map,ports ; 23cm
ISBN 0-213-16782-4 : £6.50 B81-01075

Thomas, J. B. G.. Wounded Lions : and other 1980 rugby / J.B.G. Thomas. — London : Pelham, c1981. — vii,168p,[16]p of plates : ill,ports ; 23cm
ISBN 0-7207-1309-9 : £7.95 B81-11576

796.33'38 — Seven-a-side Rugby Union football — *Manuals*
Bass, J. C. S. Seven-a-side rugby : including tactics suitable for mini-rugby / J.C.S. Bass. — London : Pelham, 1981. — 143p : ill ; 21cm
Includes index
ISBN 0-7207-1339-0 : £6.50 : CIP rev. B81-14795

796.334 — ASSOCIATION FOOTBALL

796.334 — Association football
Barrett, Norman. The book of football / Norman Barrett. — Maidenhead : Purnell, 1981. — 157p : ill(some col.),ports(some col.) ; 30cm
Ill on lining papers. — Includes index
ISBN 0-361-05078-x : £5.99 B81-33745

McMenemy, Lawrie. Lawrie McMenemy's book of soccer / [Lawrie McMenemy with Norman Barrett] ; [editor: Wendy Hobson] ; [designer Richard Smith] ; [artist: James Ferguson]. — Maidenhead : Purnell, 1981. — 77p : ill(some col.),ports(some col.) ; 29cm
Ill on lining papers. — Includes index
ISBN 0-361-05148-4 : £4.50 B81-37473

Rollin, Jack. Guinness book of soccer facts and feats. — 4th ed. — Enfield : Guinness Superlatives Ltd., Oct.1981. — [256]p
Previous ed.: 1978
ISBN 0-85112-227-2 : £6.95 : CIP entry B81-25827

796.334 — Association football. Finals, *1950-1979*
Miller, David, *1935 Mar.1-*. Cup magic / David Miller. — London : Sidgwick & Jackson, 1981. — 220p ; 18cm
Bibliography: p220
ISBN 0-283-98754-5 (pbk) : £1.50 B81-17191

796.334 — Association football — *For children*
Graham-Cameron, M. G.. Playing football / by M. Graham-Cameron ; illustrated by Colin King. — Cambridge : Dinosaur, c1975. — [24]p : col.ill ; 15x18cm. — (Althea's Dinosaur books)
ISBN 0-85122-090-8 (pbk) : £0.30 B81-26807

796.334 — Association football. Goals
Greaves, Jimmy. Goals! : a unique A to Z collection / Jimmy Greaves ; edited by Norman Giller. — London : Harrap, 1981. — 161p : ill,ports ; 25cm
Ill on lining papers
ISBN 0-245-53787-2 (cased) : £6.95
ISBN 0-245-53796-1 (pbk) : Unpriced B81-40156

796.334'02'022 — Association football — *Rules*
Referees' chart and players' guide to the laws of association football / authorised by the International Football Association Board. — 1980-1981. — London : Pan Books, 1980. — 63p
ISBN 0-330-26266-1 : £0.75
ISSN 0260-2822 B81-01076

796.334'02'024 — Association football match programmes. Collecting — *Manuals*
Shaw, Phil. Collecting football programmes / Phil Shaw. — London : Granada, 1980. — 128p,[8]p of plates : ill(some col.),facsims ; 20cm
ISBN 0-246-11399-5 : £4.50 B81-00237

796.334'05 — Association football — *For children* — *Serials*
Score annual. — 1981. — London : IPC Magazines, c1980. — 91p
ISBN 0-85037-573-8 : £2.00 B81-06858

Shoot! annual. — 1981. — London : IPC Magazines, c1980. — 127p
ISBN 0-85037-580-0 : £2.00 B81-06856

Shoot soccer quiz book. — 1981. — London : IPC Magazines, 1980. — 79p
ISBN 0-85037-581-9 : £2.00 B81-06857

796.334'05 — Association football — *Serials*
BBC match of the day soccer annual. — 1981. — London (35 Marylebone High St., W1M 4AA) : British Broadcasting Corporation, 1980. — 75p
ISBN 0-563-17832-9 : £1.80 B81-12444

796.334'05 — Association football — *Serials* — *For children*
Soccer monthly annual. — 1981. — London : IPC Magazines, [1980?]. — 93p
ISBN 0-85037-613-0 : £2.00 B81-19702

796.334'07 — Association football. Teaching
Gibbon, Alan. Teaching soccer. — London : Bell & Hyman, Oct.1981. — [128]p
ISBN 0-7135-1257-1 (pbk) : £3.95 : CIP entry B81-25833

796.334'076 — Association football — *Questions & answers* — *For children*
Jeffery, Gordon. Football quiz 1981/82 / Gordon Jeffery. — London : Fontana, 1981. — 128p : ill,ports ; 18cm. — (An Armada original)
ISBN 0-00-691945-6 (pbk) : £0.95 B81-38284

Tully, Tom. Beaver football quiz / Tom Tully ; illustrated by Bob Harvey and David Mostyn. — London : Beaver, 1980. — 110p : ill ; 18cm
ISBN 0-600-20177-5 (pbk) : £0.75 B81-02962

796.334'07'7 — Association football. Coaching — *Manuals*
Howe, Don. Super soccer skills / Don Howe ; planned and edited by Norman Barrett ; illustrated by Paul Buckle. — London : Granada, 1981. — 64p : ill ; 20cm. — (A Dragon book)
ISBN 0-583-30486-9 (pbk) : £0.85 B81-37120

Hughes, Charles. The Football Association coaching book of soccer : tactics and skills / Charles Hughes. — London : British Broadcasting Corporation, 1980. — 236p : ill (some col.),ports(some col.) ; 31cm
ISBN 0-563-17808-6 : £8.50
ISBN 0-362-00523-0 (Queen Anne Press) : £8.50 B81-08430

796.334'09 — Association football, *to 1978*
Tyler, Martin. The story of football / [Martin Tyler]. — Updated and rev. ed. — London : Marshall Cavendish, 1978 (1979 printing). — 261p : ill(some col.),facsims,ports(some col.) ; 29cm
Previous ed.: 1976. — Bibliography: p261
ISBN 0-85685-749-1 (pbk) : £2.99 B81-19565

796.334'09 — Association football, *to 1980*
Henderson, Derek. Soccer / Derek Henderson ; foreword by Joe Mercer. — London : Hamlyn, 1980. — 217p : ill,1 facsim, ports ; 29cm
Ill on lining papers. — Bibliography: p217. — Includes index
ISBN 0-600-34653-6 : £4.95 B81-02297

Soccer. — London : Hamlyn, 1981. — 95p : ill (some col.),ports(some col.) ; 25cm. — (Hamlet sports special)
ISBN 0-600-34663-3 (pbk) : £2.25 B81-36667

796.334'09'04 — Association football, *ca 1950-1980*
Wilson, Bob, *1941-*. Bob Wilson's soccer focus. — London : Pelham, 1980. — 192p,[12]p of plates : ill(some col.),ports(some col.) ; 26cm
Includes index
ISBN 0-7207-1283-1 : £6.50 B81-03117

796.334'09'047 — Association football. Matches, *1970-1979*
Moore, Brian, *19---*. The big matches / Brian Moore and Martin Tyler. — London : Queen Anne Press, 1980. — 189p : ill(some col.),facsims,ports(some col.) ; 25cm
Includes index
ISBN 0-362-00501-x : £4.95 B81-11076

796.334'092'2 — Association football — *Biographies* — *For children*
Bebbington, Jim. Famous names in soccer / Jim Bebbington. — Hove : Wayland, 1980. — 48p : ports ; 24cm
Bibliography: p47. - Includes index
ISBN 0-85340-790-8 : £2.95 B81-04006

796.334'092'4 — England. Association football. Banks, Gordon, *1937-* — *Biographies*
Banks, Gordon, *1937-*. Banks of England / Gordon Banks. — London : Macdonald Futura, 1981, c1980. — 164p,[8]p of plates : ill,ports ; 18cm
Originally published: London : A. Barker, 1980. — Includes index
ISBN 0-7088-1967-2 (corrected : pbk) : £1.10 B81-20266

796.334'0924 — England. Association football. Brooking, Trevor — *Biographies*
Brooking, Trevor. Trevor Brooking. — London : Pelham, Oct.1981. — [176]p
ISBN 0-7207-1374-9 : £6.95 : CIP entry B81-28054

796.334'092'4 — England. Association football. Keegan, Kevin, *1951-* — *Biographies* — *For children*
Glanville, Brian. Kevin Keegan / Brian Glanville ; illustrated by Michael Strand. — London : Hamilton, 1981. — 63p : ill,ports ; 22cm. — (Profiles)
ISBN 0-241-10594-3 : £3.25 : CIP rev. B81-0424?

796.334′092′4 — England. Association football. Macdonald, Malcolm, ***1950-*** **—** ***Biographies***

Macdonald, Malcolm, *1950-*. Never afraid to miss / Malcolm Macdonald with Brian Woolnough. — London : Cassell, 1980. — 134p,[8]p of plates : ill,ports ; 23cm
ISBN 0-304-30639-8 : £5.95 B81-22853

796.334′092′4 — England. Association football. Neal, Phil — ***Biographies***

Neal, Phil. Attack from the back / Phil Neal. — London : Barker, c1981. — 151p,[8]p of plates : ports ; 23cm
ISBN 0-213-16783-2 : £5.95 B81-19387

796.334′092′4 — Northern Ireland. Association football. Best, George — ***Biographies***

Best, George. Where do I go from here? / George Best and Graeme Wright. — London : Queen Anne Press, 1981. — 206p,[16]p of plates : ill,ports ; 24cm
ISBN 0-362-00556-7 : £6.95 B81-39407

796.334′0941 — Great Britain. Association football, ***1870-1910***

Hutchinson, John. The football industry. — Glasgow (20 Park Circus, Glasgow G3 6BE) : Richard Drew, Nov.1981. — [96]p
ISBN 0-904002-81-0 (pbk) : £4.95 : CIP entry B81-30894

796.334′0941 — Great Britain. Association football — ***For children — Serials***

Roy of the Rovers annual. — 1981. — London : IPC Magazines, c1980. — 127p
ISBN 0-85037-571-1 : £1.80 B81-06735

Scorcher annual. — 1981. — London : IPC Magazines, c1980. — 95p
ISBN 0-85037-572-x : £1.80 B81-06736

The **Topical** times football book. — 1981. — London : D.C. Thomson, c1980. — 124p
ISBN 0-85116-196-0 : £1.45 B81-02974

796.334′0941 — Great Britain. Association football — ***Serials***

The **Football** Association year book. — 1981-1982. — London : Pelham, Aug.1981. — [192]p
ISBN 0-7207-1352-8 (pbk) : £2.25 : CIP entry B81-23805

Football champions / edited by Ken Johns. — Maidenhead : Purnell Books, 1980. — [60]p : ill(some col.),ports(some col.) ; 27cm
Ill, ports on lining papers
ISBN 0-361-04655-3 : £1.75 B81-03735

796.334′09411 — Scotland. Association football — ***Questions & answers***

The **2nd** Scottish football quizbook / compiled by John Gibson ... [et al.]. — Ayr : Kyle, c1980. — 75p : 1map,ports ; 18cm
ISBN 0-906955-15-7 (pbk) : £0.95 B81-10403

The **Scottish** football quizbook / compiled by John Gibson ... [et al.]. — Ayr : Kyle, c1979. — 71p : 1map ; 15cm
ISBN 0-906955-00-9 (pbk) : £0.95 B81-10402

796.334′09411 — Scotland. Association football — ***Serials***

The **Scottish** football book. — No.26. — London : Stanley Paul, 1980. — 96p
ISBN 0-09-142581-6 : £2.95 : CIP rev. B80-13507

The **Scottish** football book. — No.27. — London : Paul, Sept.1981. — [96]p
ISBN 0-09-146091-3 (pbk) : £3.95 : CIP entry B81-20586

796.334′09428 — North-east England. Association football, ***to 1980***

Rippon, Anton. Great soccer clubs of the North-East. — Ashbourne : Moorland Publishing, Sept.1981. — [128]p
ISBN 0-86190-022-7 : £5.50 : CIP entry B81-28135

796.334′2 — Association football — ***Manuals***

Sexton, Dave. Tackle soccer / David Sexton. — Rev. ed. — London : Stanley Paul, 1981. — 171p : ill,ports ; 19cm
Previous ed.: 1977
ISBN 0-09-145471-9 (pbk) : £3.50 : CIP rev. B81-17519

Yaxley, Mike. Soccer. — London : Batsford Academic and Educational, Feb.1982. — [64]p. — (Competitive sports series)
ISBN 0-7134-3980-7 : £5.95 : CIP entry B81-37576

796.334′2′07 — Association football. Defence. Coaching

Batty, Eric. Coaching modern soccer : defence and other techniques / Eric G. Batty. — London : Faber, 1981. — 128p : ill ; 23cm
ISBN 0-571-11772-4 (cased) : £6.95 : CIP rev.
ISBN 0-571-11773-2 (pbk) : Unpriced B81-24594

796.334′23′07 — Association football. Attack. Coaching

Batty, Eric. Coaching modern soccer - attack / Eric G. Batty. — London : Faber, 1980. — 121p : ill ; 23cm
ISBN 0-571-09840-1 : £5.25 : CIP rev. B80-13019

796.334′26 — Association football. Goalkeeping — ***Manuals***

Wilson, Bob, *1941-*. The art of goalkeeping / Bob Wilson. — 2nd ed. — London : Pelham, 1980. — 176p : ill,ports ; 22cm
Previous ed.: published as Goalkeeping. 1970. — Includes index
ISBN 0-7207-1278-5 : £6.95 : CIP rev. B80-23623

796.334′62′0941 — Great Britain. Association football. Non-league clubs — ***Serials***

The **F.A.** non-league football annual. — 1979-80. — London : Macdonald and Jane's, c1979. — 304p
ISBN 0-354-09085-2 : £0.85
ISSN 0142-6257 B81-29056

796.334′63′09411 — Scotland. Football League football — ***Serials***

Clydesdale Bank Scottish Football League review. — 1980-81-. — Glasgow (19 North Claremont St., Glasgow G3 7NR) : Clive Allan Stuart [for] the Scottish Football League, c1980-. — v. : ill,ports ; 30cm
Annual
ISSN 0260-8804 = Clydesdale Bank Scottish Football League review : £2.00 B81-09039

Scottish Football League. The Scottish Football League handbook. — Season 1980/81. — [Glasgow] ([188 West Regent St., Glasgow G2 4RY]) : [The League], [1980]. — 232p
£2.50 B81-17466

Scottish Football League. The Scottish Football League handbook. — Season 1981/82. — [Glasgow] ([188 West Regent St., Glasgow G2 4RY]) : [The League], [1981]. — 240p
Unpriced B81-35451

796.334′63′0941441 — Scotland. Association football. Clubs: St Mirren Football Club, ***to 1977***

St Mirren F. C. centenary brochure : 1877-1977. — [Paisley] ([St Mirren Pk., Love St., Paisley PA3 2EJ]) : [The Club], [1978]. — 76p : ill,ports ; 24cm
£1.25 (pbk) B81-14062

796.334′63′0941443 — Scotland. Association football. Clubs: Glasgow Celtic Football Club — ***Serials***

Playing for Celtic. — No.13. — London : Paul, Sept.1981. — [96]p
ISBN 0-09-146081-6 (pbk) : £3.95 : CIP entry B81-20584

796.334′63′0941443 — Scotland. Association football. Clubs: Glasgow Celtic Football Club, ***to 1981***

Woods, Pat. Celtic F.C. facts and figures 1888-1981 / compiled by P.Woods. — [Glasgow] ([7, Kinloch St., Glasgow G40 3RN]) : [Celtic Supporters Association], [c1981]. — 88p : ill,ports ; 17cm
Ill on inside covers. — Bibliography: p87-88
£1.00 (pbk) B81-37021

796.334′63′0941443 — Scotland. Association football. Clubs: Rangers Football Club — ***Serials***

Playing for Rangers. — No.12. — London : Stanley Paul, 1980. — 96p
ISBN 0-09-142561-1 : £3.50 : CIP rev. B80-13021

Playing for Rangers. — No.13. — London : Paul, Sept.1981. — [96]p
ISBN 0-09-146071-9 (pbk) : £3.95 : CIP entry B81-20585

796.334′63′0942 — England. Football League football. Clubs, ***1888-1980 — Records of achievement***

Lovett, Norman. The record breakers (1888-1980) / by Norman Lovett. — [Hull] ([33 Boothferry Rd, Hull HU3 6UA]) : [British Programme Collectors' Club]. — (Facts and figures on the Football League Clubs ; no.28)
Vol.1: 1888-1915. — [1981]. — 112p ; 21cm
Cover title
ISBN 0-9504273-7-3 (pbk) : Unpriced B81-23225

Lovett, Norman. The record breakers (1888-1980) : details of over 6,000 Football League and club records / by Norman Lovett. — Hull (33 Boothferry Rd., Hull HU3 6UA) : British Programme Collectors' Club, c1981. — (Facts and figures on the Football League clubs ; no.29)
Vol.2: (1919-1939). — 91p ; 21cm
ISBN 0-9504273-8-1 (pbk) : Unpriced B81-28315

Lovett, Norman. The record breakers (1888-1980) / by Norman Lovett. — [Hull] ([33 Boothferry Rd., Hull HU3 6UA]) : [British Programme Collectors Club]. — (Facts and figures on the Football League clubs ; no.30)
Vol.3: (1946-1959-60). — [c1981]. — 95p : 1port ; 21cm
ISBN 0-9504273-9-x (pbk) : £5.00 B81-31131

Lovett, Norman. The record breakers (1888-1980) / by Norman Lovett. — Hull (33 Boothferry Rd., Hull HU3 6UA) : British Programme Collectors Club. — (Facts and figures on the Football League Clubs ; no.31)
Vol.4: 1960-1980. — c1981. — 95p : plan,1port ; 21cm
ISBN 0-907263-00-3 (pbk) : Unpriced B81-35549

796.334′63′0942143 — England. Association football. Clubs: Arsenal Football Club, ***to 1980***

Rippon, Anton. The story of Arsenal. — Ashbourne : Moorland Publishing, Sept.1981. — [96]p
ISBN 0-86190-023-5 : £4.95 : CIP entry B81-28134

796.334′63′0942176 — England. Association football. Clubs: West Ham United — ***Serials***

West Ham United annual. — 1981-. — Hainault (24 Fowler Rd, Hainault, Ilford, Essex) : Circle Publications, 1980-. — v. : ill,ports ; 20cm
Cover title: West Ham United official annual
ISSN 0261-345x = West Ham United annual : £2.95 B81-24106

796.334′63′0942188 — England. Association football. Clubs: Tottenham Hotspur Football Club, ***to 1979***

Rippon, Anton. The Tottenham Hotspur story / Anton Rippon. — Ashbourne : Moorland Publishing, c1980. — 95p : ill,ports ; 26cm
ISBN 0-903485-97-4 : £4.95 B81-03353

796.334'63'0942191 — England. Association football. Clubs: Crystal Palace Football Club — *Serials*

Crystal Palace official annual. — 1979-80-. — Ilford (24 Fowler Rd, Hainault, Ilford, Essex) : Circle Publications, 1979-. — v. : ill(some col.),ports ; 20cm
ISSN 0261-6882 = Crystal Palace official annual : £2.95 B81-35107

796.334'63'0942496 — England. Association football. Clubs: Aston Villa Football Club, *to 1980*

Rippon, Anton. The story of Aston Villa / Anton Rippon. — Ashbourne : Moorland, c1981. — 96p : ill,ports ; 26cm
ISBN 0-903485-99-0 : £4.95 : CIP rev. B80-24759

796.334'63'0942496 — England. Association football. Clubs: Aston Villa Football Club, *to 1981*

Johnson, Ian. The Aston Villa story / Ian Johnson. — London : Barker, c1981. — x,170p : ill,ports ; 26cm
Ill on lining papers
ISBN 0-213-16794-8 : £5.95 B81-33424

796.334'63'0942527 — England. Association football. Clubs: Nottingham Forest Football Club — *Serials*

Nottingham Forest FC official annual. — 1979-. — Ilford (24 Fowler Rd, Hainault, Ilford, Essex) : Circle Publications, 1978-. — ill,ports ; 20cm
ISSN 0141-3724 = Official annual — Nottingham Forest FC : £2.45 B81-01984

796.334'63'0942542 — England. Association football. Clubs: Leicester City Football Club, *to 1980*

Folliard, Robert. A history of Leicester City Football Club / by Robert Folliard. — Hornchurch : Henry, 1980. — 30p : ill ; 17cm
ISBN 0-86025-700-2 (pbk) : £0.95 B81-06648

796.334'63'0942649 — England. Association football. Clubs: Ipswich Town Football Club — *Serials*

Ipswich Town annual. — 1979. — Hainault (24/26 Fowler Rd, Hainault, Ilford, Essex) : Circle Publications, 1978. — 96p
Cover title: Ipswich town official annual
ISSN 0141-156x : Unpriced B81-15548

Ipswich Town annual. — 1980. — Hainault (24/26 Fowler Rd, Hainault, Ilford, Essex) : Circle Publications, 1979. — 96p
Cover title: Ipswich town offical annual
ISSN 0141-156x : £2.75 B81-15549

Ipswich Town annual. — 1981. — Hainault (24/26 Fowler Rd, Hainault, Ilford, Essex) : Circle Publications, 1980. — 72p
Cover title: Ipswich town official annual
ISSN 0141-156x : £2.95 B81-15550

796.334'63'0942733 — England. Association football. Clubs: Manchester United Football Club — *Serials*

Manchester United F.C. official annual. — 1981. — Hainault (24 Fowler Rd, Hainault, Ilford, Essex) : Circle Publications, c1980. — 96p
ISBN 0-906521-21-1 : £2.95
ISSN 0141-1586 B81-20704

796.334'63'0942753 — England. Association football. Clubs: Everton Football Club — *Serials*

Everton FC official annual. — 1979-. — Ilford (24 Fowler Rd, Hainault, Ilford, Essex) : Circle Publications, 1978-. — ill,ports ; 20cm
ISSN 0141-3732 = Official annual — Everton FC : £2.45 B81-01983

796.334'63'0942753 — England. Association football. Clubs: Liverpool Football Club, *to 1979*

Rippon, Anton. The story of Liverpool FC / Anton Rippon. — Ashbourne : Moorland, c1980. — 96p : ill,ports ; 26cm. — (Moorland sports books)
ISBN 0-903485-98-2 : £4.95 : CIP rev. B80-23624

796.334'63'0942825 — England. Association football. Clubs: Barnsley Football Club, *1953-1959*

Ward, Andrew. Barnsley : a study in football 1953-59 / Andrew Ward & Ian Alister. — Barton-under-Needwood (5 Crowberry La., Barton-under-Needwood, Staffs. DE13 8AF) : Crowberry, 1981. — 139p,[8]p of plates : ill,ports ; 21cm
Includes index
ISBN 0-9507568-0-6 (pbk) : £2.50 B81-27766

796.334'64 — England. Association football. Competitions: F.A. Cup. Finals, *1872-1980 — Readings from contemporary sources*

Tyler, Martin. Cup final extra! / by Martin Tyler. — London : Hamlyn, 1981. — 168p : ill (some col.),facsims,ports ; 31cm
Ill on lining papers
ISBN 0-600-34661-7 : £4.95 B81-22384

796.334'64 — England. Association football. Competitions: F.A. Cup. Finals, *to 1980*

100 F.A. Cups : the history of soccer's greatest club competition. — London : Mirror Books, 1981. — [28]p : ill,ports ; 37cm. — (A Daily mirror soccer special)
At head of title: Soccer Mirror
ISBN 0-85939-253-8 (unbound) : £0.50 B81-24396

Barber, David, *1951-*. We won the cup : a celebration for the 100th F.A. Cup Final / David Barber. — London : Pan in association with the Football Association, 1981. — [203]p : ill ; 20cm
ISBN 0-330-26401-x (pbk) : £1.75 B81-24395

796.334'66 — Association football. English teams, *to 1980*

Rippon, Anton. Eng-Land. — Ashbourne : Moorland Publishing, Oct.1981. — [144]p
ISBN 0-86190-032-4 : £5.95 : CIP entry B81-28010

796.334'66 — England. Association football. Competitions: World Cup *(1966)*. **English teams**

Tyler, Martin. Boys of '66 : the England team that won the World Cup - then and now / Martin Tyler. — London : Hamlyn, 1981. — 160p : ill,ports(some col.) ; 26cm
Includes index
ISBN 0-600-34660-9 : £5.95 B81-40751

796.334'66 — Europe. Association football. Competitions: European Cup, *to 1980*

Motson, John. The European Cup 1955-1980 / John Motson, John Rowlinson. — London : Queen Anne Press, 1980. — 335p : ill,facsims,ports ; 25cm
Bibliography: p328. — Includes index
ISBN 0-362-00512-5 : £10.95 B81-01891

796.336 — AUSTRALIAN FOOTBALL

796.33'6 — Australian Rules football

Sandercock, Leonie. Up where, Cazaly? : the great Australian game / Leonie Sandercock and Ian Turner. — London : Granada, 1981. — x,272p,[24]p of plates : ill,facsims,ports ; 25cm. — (A Paladin book)
Bibliography: p263-264. — Includes index
ISBN 0-246-10996-3 : £7.95 B81-30817

796.34 — RACKET GAMES

796.34 — Real tennis, *to 1980*

Aberdare, Morys George Lyndhurst Bruce, *Baron*. The Willis Faber book of tennis & rackets / Lord Aberdare. — London : Paul, 1980. — 368p,[4]p of plates : ill(some col.),1facsim,plans,ports ; 29cm
Includes index
ISBN 0-09-142710-x : £25.00
Also classified at 796.34'3'09 B81-07149

796.342 — TENNIS

796.342'05 — Lawn tennis — *Serials*

The **Prudential** tennis annual. — 1979. — London (77 Great Peter St., SW1P 2EZ) : Marsh Publications, c1979. — 192p
£1.50 B81-20428

World of tennis : the official yearbook of the International Tennis Federation. — 1981. — London : Queen Anne Press, c1981. — 415p
ISBN 0-362-02033-7 : £8.95
ISSN 0305-6325 B81-30872

796.342'06 — Dublin. Monkstown. Lawn tennis. Clubs: Monkstown Lawn Tennis Club, *to 1978*

Kenna, Caoimhin. A glance back : a brief history of Monkstown Lawn Tennis Club / by Caoimhin Kenna. — [Dublin?] : [Monkstown Lawn Tennis Club], [1979?]. — 28p : ill,facsims,ports ; 30cm
Cover title
£1.00 (pbk) B81-34443

796.342'06'041 — Great Britain. Lawn tennis. Organisations: Lawn Tennis Association — *Serials*

Lawn Tennis Association. The Lawn Tennis Association handbook. — 1981. — London (Barons Court, W14 9EG) : The Association, [1981]. — 451p in various pagings
ISSN 0306-7254 : £4.00 B81-30875

796.342'09 — Lawn tennis, *to 1980*

Jones, Clarence. The Observer's book of tennis / Clarence Jones. — London : Warne, 1981. — 192p : ill,ports ; 15cm. — (The Observer's series ; 81)
Bibliography: p191-192
ISBN 0-7232-1599-5 : £1.80 B81-21187

796.342'09 — Lawn tennis, *to 1980 — For children*

Glanville, Brian. The Puffin book of tennis / Brian Glanville. — Harmondsworth : Puffin, 1981. — 156p,[8]p of plates : ill,ports ; 18cm
Includes index
ISBN 0-14-031339-7 (pbk) : £1.00 B81-25207

796.342'092'2 — Lawn tennis. Borg, Björn. Interpersonal relationships with Borg, Mariana — *Personal observations*

Borg, Mariana. Love match : my life with Björn / Mariana Borg. — London : Sidgwick & Jackson, 1981. — 150p : ports ; 24cm
ISBN 0-283-98796-0 : £6.95 B81-27527

796.342'092'4 — Lawn tennis. Ashe, Arthur — *Biographies*

Ashe, Arthur. Off the court. — London : Eyre Methuen, Feb.1982. — [240]p
ISBN 0-413-49680-5 : £7.50 : CIP entry B81-36381

796.342'092'4 — Lawn tennis. Borg, Björn — *Biographies*

Audette, Larry. Bjorn Borg / Larry Audette. — New York ; London : Quick Fox, c1979. — 106p : ill,ports ; 26cm
ISBN 0-86001-640-4 (pbk) : £2.50 B81-05685

796.342'092'4 — Lawn tennis. Kramer, Jack, *1921- — Biographies*

Kramer, Jack, *1921-*. The game : my 40 years in tennis / by Jack Kramer with Frank Deford. — London : Deutsch, 1981. — 318p,[16]p of plates : ports ; 25cm
Includes index
ISBN 0-233-97307-9 : £8.95 B81-23401

796.342'09421'93 — London. Merton *(London Borough)*. **Lawn tennis. Competitions: Lawn Tennis Championships,** *to 1977*

Robertson, Max. Wimbledon : centre court of the game / Max Robertson. — [New ed.]. — London : British Broadcasting Corporation, c1981. — x,307p : ill,ports ; 26cm
Previous ed.: published as Wimbledon 1877-1977. London : A Barker, 1977
ISBN 0-563-17923-6 : £9.95 B81-25641

796.342'09421'93 — London. Merton *(London Borough)*. **Lawn tennis. Competitions: Lawn Tennis Championships,** *to 1980*

This is Wimbledon : facts and figures about the Championships, Wimbledon / edited by Alan Little. — London : All England Lawn Tennis and Croquet Club, c1981. — 24p : ill,1plan ; 20cm
Text, plan on inside covers
ISBN 0-9507105-1-2 (pbk) : £1.00 B81-34340

796.342'2 — Lawn tennis — *Manuals*

Borg, Björn. My guide to better tennis / Bjorn Borg ; drawings by George Stokes ; edited by Dennis Hart. — London : Express Books, c1981. — 92p : ill,ports ; 22x27cm
ISBN 0-85079-118-9 : £2.50 B81-32859

Horwood, Derek. Play tennis : a practical step-by-step guide with Derek Horwood. — London : British Broadcasting Corporation, 1981. — 96p : ill ; 22cm
Includes index
ISBN 0-563-16455-7 (pbk) : £3.60 B81-24528

King, Billie Jean. Play better tennis : with Billie Jean King and Reginald Brace. — [London] : Octopus, [1981]. — 137p : ill(some col.),ports ; 29cm
Ill on lining papers. — Includes index
ISBN 0-7064-1223-0 : £4.95 B81-24956

796.342'2 — Lawn tennis. Strokes — *Manuals*

Cutler, Merritt. [The tennis book]. Basic tennis illustrated / Merritt Cutler. — New York : Dover ; London : Constable, 1980, c1967. — xii,111p : ill ; 27cm
Originally published: New York : McGraw-Hill, 1967
ISBN 0-486-24006-1 (pbk) : £3.25 B81-33166

796.343 — SQUASH RACKETS

796.34'3 — Squash rackets — *Manuals*

Colburn, Alan. Squash : the ambitious player's guide / Alan Colburn. — London : Faber, 1981. — 110p : ill ; 23cm
ISBN 0-571-11657-4 (cased) : £6.95
ISBN 0-571-11658-2 (pbk) : £2.95 B81-10602

796.34'3'0202 — Squash rackets — *Rules*

Hawkey, Dick. Squash rules for players / Dick Hawkey. — London : Ward Lock, 1981. — 64p : ill ; 19cm. — (A Hyperion book)
ISBN 0-7063-6113-x (pbk) : Unpriced B81-27123

796.34'3'09 — Games: Rackets, *to 1980*

Aberdare, Morys George Lyndhurst Bruce, *Baron*. The Willis Faber book of tennis & rackets / Lord Aberdare. — London : Paul, 1980. — 368p,[4]p of plates : ill(some col.),1facsim,plans,ports ; 29cm
Includes index
ISBN 0-09-142710-x : £25.00
Primary classification 796.34 B81-07149

796.345 — BADMINTON

796.34'5 — Badminton — *Manuals*

Hashman, Judy. Winning badminton / Judy Hashman. — London : Ward Lock, 1981. — 104p : ill,plans ; 25cm. — (A Hyperion book)
ISBN 0-7063-6091-5 (cased) : £6.95 : CIP rev.
ISBN 0-7063-6157-1 (pbk) : Unpriced B81-14419

796.34'5'06042 — England. Badminton. Organisations: Badminton Association of England — *Serials*

Badminton Association of England. The Badminton Association of England's annual handbook. — 1980-81. — Milton Keynes (National Badminton Centre, Bradwell Rd., Loughton Lodge, Milton Keynes MR8 9LA) : The Association, [1980?]. — 124p
£1.50 B81-04701

796.34'5'0924 — Badminton. Gilks, Gillian - *Biographies*

Hunn, David. Gillian Gilks. — London : Ward Lock, June 1981. — [160]p
ISBN 0-7063-6114-8 : £6.95 : CIP entry B81-12889

796.34'5'09417 — Ireland *(Republic)*. **Badminton** — *Serials*

Badminton Ireland : Badminton Union of Ireland official yearbook. — 1977/78-. — Dublin (22 Moore St., Dublin 1) : Sean Graham, 1977-. — v. : ill,ports ; 30cm
Continues: Irish badminton handbook. — Description based on: 1980/81 issue
Unpriced B81-05030

796.346 — TABLE TENNIS

796.34'6 — Table tennis — *Manuals*

Simpson, Peter, *1934 Apr.19-*. How to play table tennis / Peter Simpson ; photography by Don Morley. — London : Hamlyn, 1981. — 60p : ill,ports ; 25cm
Ill on lining papers
ISBN 0-600-38799-2 : £2.99 B81-36666

796.35 — SPORTS USING BALL DRIVEN BY CLUB, MALLET, BAT

796.35 — Ireland *(Republic)*. **Hurling. Ring, Christy** — *Biographies*

Dorgan, Val. Christy Ring : a personal portrait / Val Dorgan. — Dublin : Ward River Press, 1980. — vii,247p,[8]p of plates : ill,ports ; 18cm
ISBN 0-907085-03-2 (pbk) : £3.00 B81-16484

796.352 — GOLF

796.352 — Golf

Alliss, Peter. The Shell book of golf. — Newton Abbot : David & Charles, Oct.1981. — [224]p
ISBN 0-7153-7988-7 : £8.95 : CIP entry B81-30331

796.352 — Golf. Books

Hopkinson, Cecil. Collecting golf books : 1743-1938 / by Cecil Hopkinson ; compiled and arranged by H. R. Grant. — [Droitwich] ([Cutnall Green, Droitwich, Worcs.]) : Grant Books, 1980. — 90p,[8]p of plates : ill,ports ; 25cm
Originally published: London : Constable, 1938. — Limited edition of 250 copies. — Contents: Bibliotheca golfiana / by Joseph F. Murdoch
Unpriced B81-27482

796.352 — Golf — *For children*

Elsey, Neil. Golf / Neil Elsey ; colour photographs by All-Sport Limited. — Hove : Wayland, 1980. — 64p : col.ill,col.ports ; 21cm. — (InterSport)
Includes index
ISBN 0-85340-776-2 : £3.75
ISBN 0-85340-772-x B81-04012

796.352 — Women's golf

Longrigg, Doreen. Ladies on the fairway / Doreen Longrigg. — Speldhurst : Midas Books, 1981. — 91p : ill,1port ; 21cm
ISBN 0-85936-275-2 (pbk) : £3.95 B81-40316

796.352'01'9 — Golf. Psychological aspects

Gallwey, W. Timothy. The inner game of golf. — London : Cape, Oct.1981. — [198]p
ISBN 0-224-02922-3 : £5.95 : CIP entry B81-28074

796.352'02'022 — Golf. Rules

Dobereiner, Peter. Golf rules explained / Peter Dobereiner ; with illustrations by Bert Kitchen. — Rev. ed. — Newton Abbot : David & Charles, 1980. — 156p : ill ; 23cm
Previous ed.: published as Stroke, hole or match? 1976. — Includes index
ISBN 0-7153-8081-8 : £4.95 : CIP rev. B80-23625

Parsons, R. (Rodney). Golfing predicaments : applying the rules — from tee to green : an unofficial guide to the official rules of golf / [compiled by R. Parsons]. — Cheam (Lloyds Bank Chambers, The Broadway, Cheam, Surrey SM3 8BQ) : Entryown Patents, c1981. — 35p ; 21cm
Cover title
Unpriced (pbk) B81-27848

796.352'0207 — Golf — *Humour*

The **Businessman's** book of golf / edited by Cliff Michelmore. — London : Weidenfeld and Nicolson, c1981. — 157p : ill ; 24cm
ISBN 0-297-77851-x : £5.95 B81-36146

796.352'05 — Golf — *Serials*

Golfer's handbook. — 1981. — Glasgow : Munro-Barr Publications, c1981. — xxxii,680p
£12.00 B81-25026

Pelham golf year. — [1st ed.]-. — London : Pelham, 1981-. — v. : ill ; 23cm
Annual
ISSN 0260-9177 = Pelham golf year : £8.00 B81-09247

796.352'06 — Scotland. Lothian Region. North Berwick. Golf. Clubs: North Berwick Golf Club, *to 1963*

Adamson, Alistair Beaton. In the wind's eye : North Berwick Golf Club / Alistair Beaton Adamson. — [Gullane] ([Jasmine Cottage, Templar Place, Gullane, East Lothian]) : A.B. Adamson, 1980. — 92p[4]leaves of plates : ill,maps,facsim,ports ; 24cm
Unpriced B81-14257

796.352'06 — South Yorkshire *(Metropolitan County)*. **Sheffield. Golf. Clubs: Lindrick Golf Club,** *to 1979*

Colver, J. Arthur. A history of Lindrick Golf Club 1891-1979 / by J. Arthur Colver. — Sheffield : Northend, 1980. — 168p,[14]p of plates : ill,plans,ports ; 23cm
Includes index
£7.95 B81-10726

796.352'06'8411005 — Scotland. Golf courses — *Directories* — *Serials*

Scotland, home of golf. — [1981]. — [Edinburgh] : Scottish Tourist Board, [1981?]. — 72p
ISBN 0-85419-175-5 : £0.65 B81-15167

796.352'092'4 — Golf, *1918-1979* — *Personal observations*

Lucas, Laddie. The sport of Prince's : reflections of a golfer / Laddie Lucas. — London : Paul, 1980. — 192p,[12]p of plates : ill,ports ; 25cm
Includes index
ISBN 0-09-143100-x : £7.95 : CIP rev. B80-13942

796.352'092'4 — Golf. Alliss, Peter — *Biographies*

Alliss, Peter. Peter Alliss : an autobiography. — London : Collins, 1981. — 192p : ill,ports ; 25cm
Includes index
ISBN 0-00-216292-x : £7.95 B81-26063

796.352'092'4 — Golf. Jones, Bobby — *Biographies*

Miller, Dick, *1936-*. Triumphant journey : the saga of Bobby Jones and the grand slam of golf / by Dick Miller. — London : Hale, 1981, c1980. — xiv,258p : ill,ports ; 24cm
Includes index
ISBN 0-7091-8768-8 : £7.50 B81-12212

796.352'092'4 — Golf *Personal observations*

Dobereiner, Peter. The best of Dobereiner. — London : Paul, June 1981. — [176]p
ISBN 0-09-145150-7 : £7.95 : CIP entry B81-11958

796.352'3 — Golf — *Manuals*

Hay, Alex. The golf manual / Alex Hay ; foreword by Michael Bonallack. — London : Faber, c1980. — 173p : ill,ports ; 29cm
ISBN 0-571-11642-6 : £7.50 : CIP rev. B80-18871

Jessop, J. C.. Golf / J.C. Jessop. — 5th ed. / revised by Mark Wilson. — Sevenoaks : Hodder and Stoughton, 1981. — 168p : ill ; 20cm. — (Teach yourself books)
Previous ed.: 1972. — Includes index
ISBN 0-340-26747-x (pbk) : £1.95 : CIP rev. B81-13896

Nicklaus, Jack. Play better golf : the swing from A-Z / Jack Nicklaus with Ken Bowden ; illustrated by Jim McQueen. — [London] : Hodder and Stoughton, 1981, c1980. — 200p : ill ; 18cm. — (Coronet books)
Originally published: New York : Pocket Books, 1980
ISBN 0-340-27072-1 (pbk) : £1.10 : CIP rev. B81-14886

Nicklaus, Jack. Total golf techniques / by Jack Nicklaus with Ken Bowden ; illustrated by Jim McQueen. — London : Pan in association with Heinemann, 1981, c1977. — 157p : col.ill ; 28cm
Originally published: London : Heinemann, 1977
ISBN 0-330-26574-1 (pbk) : £3.95 B81-22898

796.354 — CROQUET

796.35'4'0202 — Croquet — *Rules*
Croquet Association. Basic laws of Association Croquet and Golf Croquet / by B.G. Neal. — 2nd ed. — London (The Hurlingham Club, S.W.6) : Croquet Association, 1978. — 16p : ill,plans ; 17cm
Previous ed.: 1975. — Bibliography: piii
Unpriced (pbk) B81-03608

796.35'4'06042 — England. Croquet. Organisations: Croquet Association — *Directories — Serials*
Croquet Association. Directory of the Croquet Association. — 1978-1979. — London (Hurlingham Club, SW6) : The Association, [1978?]. — 46p
£1.25 B81-09031

Croquet Association. Directory of the Croquet Association. — 1980-1981. — London (Hurlingham Club, Ranelagh Gardens, SW6 3PR) : The Association, [1980?]. — 48p
£1.50 B81-09030

796.35'4'09 — Croquet, *to 1981*
Prichard, D. M. C.. The history of croquet / D.M.C. Prichard. — London : Cassell, 1981. — 239p : ill,ports ; 24cm
Bibliography: p233-234. — Includes index
ISBN 0-304-30759-9 : £8.95 B81-34707

796.355 — HOCKEY

796.35'5 — Hockey — *Manuals*
Wein, Horst. The advanced science of hockey / Horst Wein ; translated from the German by Martin Copus ; revised for English readers by John Cadman. — London : Pelham, 1981. — 222p : ill,ports ; 23cm
ISBN 0-7207-1171-1 : £8.50 B81-16471

796.35'5 — Seven-a-side women's hockey & women's indoor hockey — *Rules*
Rules for small-sided games, rules for indoor hockey, information for players and umpires / All England Women's Hockey Association. — London : [A.E.W.H.A.], [1981?]. — 38p : 2ill ; 12cm
Cover title. — Text on inside covers
£0.40 (pbk) B81-40277

796.3'55'0202 — Hockey — *Rules — Serials*
Hockey Rules Board. Rules of the game of hockey with guidance for players and umpires and advice to umpires (with effect from 1st September ...). — 1980. — [London] (c/o Miss L. Hunt, AEWHA, 160 Great Portland St., W1N 5TB) : The Board, c1980. — 95p
£0.50 B81-06729

796.35'5'07 — Hockey. Coaching. Activities
Cadman, John, *1934-*. Games for hockey training / John Cadman. — London : Pelham, 1981. — 158p : ill ; 23cm
ISBN 0-7207-1246-7 : £5.95 B81-21169

796.357 — BASEBALL

796.357'0973 — United States. Baseball, *1950-1960*
Rosenthal, Harold, *19---*. The 10 best years of baseball : an informal history of the fifties / Harold Rosenthal. — New York ; London : Van Nostrand Reinhold, 1981, c1979. — vi,170p,[4]p of plates : ports ; 23cm
Includes index
ISBN 0-442-27063-1 (pbk) : £4.45 B81-26428

796.357'782 — United States. Baseball. Competitions: World Series, *1914-1934 — Programmes*
Souvenir programs of five great World Series : 1914, 1917, 1919, 1926, 1934 / edited by Bert Randolph Sugar. — New York : Dover ; London : Constable, c1980. — 200p : chiefly ill,facsims,ports ; 29cm
ISBN 0-486-23858-x (pbk) : £3.90 B81-24382

796.358 — CRICKET

796.35'8 — Cricket
Cardus, Neville. A fourth innings with Cardus / Neville Cardus. — London : Souvenir, 1981. — 254p ; 23cm
ISBN 0-285-62483-0 : £7.50 B81-18495

The **Penguin** cricketer's companion / edited by Alan Ross. — Rev. and expanded 2nd ed. — Harmondsworth : Penguin, 1981, c1979. — xix,582p ; 20cm
Originally published: London : Eyre Methuen, 1979. — Includes index
ISBN 0-14-005656-4 (pbk) : £2.95 B81-27645

796.35'8 — Cricket — *Stories, anecdotes*
Johnston, Brian, *1912-*. Rain stops play / Brian Johnston ; with cartoons by Bill Tidy ; edited by Lynn Hughes. — London : Unwin Paperbacks, 1981, c1979. — xi,83p : ill ; 18cm
Originally published: London : W.H. Allen, 1979
ISBN 0-04-827029-6 (pbk) : £1.25 B81-19381

Trueman, Fred. You nearly had him that time - and other cricket stories / Fred Trueman and Frank Hardy ; illustrated by David Langdon. — London : Arrow, 1981, c1978. — 128p : ill ; 18cm
Originally published: London : Paul, 1978
ISBN 0-09-925580-4 (pbk) : £1.00 B81-23070

796.35'8'0207 — Cricket — *Humour*
Martin-Jenkins, Christopher. Bedside cricket / Christopher Martin-Jenkins. — London : Dent, 1981. — 88p : ill(some col.) ; 26cm
Ill on lining papers
ISBN 0-460-04545-8 : £5.50 B81-41010

796.35'8'05 — Cricket — *Serials*
Cricket. — '80. — London (Lord's Ground, NW8) : Test & County Cricket Board, [1980?]. — 36p
£0.75 B81-01860

Pelham cricket year. — 3rd ed. — London : Pelham, Nov.1981. — [688]p
Previous ed.: 1980
ISBN 0-7207-1363-3 : £6.95 : CIP entry B81-30584

Playfair cricket annual. — 34th ed. (1981). — London : Queen Anne Press, 1981. — 240p
ISBN 0-362-02030-2 : £1.00
ISSN 0079-2314 B81-26392

Wisden cricketers' almanack. — 1981. — London : Queen Anne Press, [1981]. — 1230p
ISBN 0-362-02031-0 : £7.95
ISBN 0-362-02032-9 (pbk)
ISSN 0142-9213 B81-21942

796.35'8'06842 — England. Cricket grounds
Sampson, Aylwin. Grounds of appeal : the homes of first-class cricket / written and illustrated by Aylwin Sampson ; foreword by H.R.H. The Duke of Edinburgh. — London : Hale, 1981. — xiii,206p : ill,1map ; 17x24cm
Bibliography: p194. — Includes index
ISBN 0-7091-9140-5 : £8.95 B81-34729

796.35'8'076 — Cricket — *Questions & answers*
Culverhouse, Jonathan. Cricket quiz book / [compiled by Jonathan Culverhouse]. — London : Marshall Cavendish, 1979. — 96p : ill(some col.),ports(some col.) ; 28cm
ISBN 0-85685-713-0 (pbk) : £1.99 B81-09385

796.35'8'09 — Cricket, *to 1980 — Records of achievement*
Frindall, Bill. The Wisden book of cricket records / compiled and edited by Bill Frindall. — London : Queen Anne Press, 1981. — 618p ; 24cm
ISBN 0-362-00546-x : £14.00 B81-30677

796.35'8'0904 — Cricket, *1900-1940 — Readings from contemporary sources*
Wisden anthology 1900-1940 / edited by Benny Green. — London : Queen Anne Press, 1980. — vii,1177p : ill,2facsims,ports ; 24cm
Includes index
ISBN 0-362-00513-3 : £20.00 B81-03736

796.35'8'0922 — Cricket — *Biographies*
Sproat, Iain. Debrett's cricketers' who's who / compiled and edited by Iain Sproat ; with an introduction by Colin Cowdrey. — London : Debrett's Peerage, c1980. — 176p : ports ; 22cm
ISBN 0-905649-26-5 : £7.50 B81-35750

796.35'8'0922 — Cricketers, *1945-1980*
Bedser, Alec. Cricket choice / Alec Bedser. — London : Pelham, 1981. — 204p,[16]p of plates : ill,ports ; 23cm
ISBN 0-7207-1341-2 : £6.95 : CIP rev. B81-14797

796.35'8'0924 — Cricket, *1902-1980 — Personal observations*
Travers, Ben. 94 declared : cricket reminiscences / Ben Travers ; foreword by Brian Johnston. — London : Elm Tree, 1981. — xvii,75p,[8]p of plates : ill,ports ; 21cm
ISBN 0-241-10591-9 : £5.95 : CIP rev. B81-07450

796.35'8'0924 — Cricket. Botham, Ian — *Biographies*
Doust, Dudley. Ian Botham : the great all-rounder / Dudley Doust. — [Up-dated]. — London : Granada, 1981. — 272p : ill,ports ; 18cm. — (A Mayflower book)
Previous ed.: London : Cassell, 1980. — Includes index
ISBN 0-583-13452-1 (pbk) : £1.50 B81-1933

796.35'8'0924 — Cricket. D'Oliveira, Basil — *Biographies*
D'Oliveira, Basil. Time to declare : an autobiography / Basil D'Oliveira, with Patrick Murphy. — London : Dent, 1980. — xii,180p,[16]p of plates : 1ill,1facsim,ports ; 23cm
Includes index
ISBN 0-460-04511-3 : £5.95 : CIP rev. B80-2603

796.35'8'0924 — Cricket. Fender, P. G. H. — *Biographies*
Streeton, Richard. P.G.H. Fender : a biography / by Richard Streeton. — London : Faber, 1981. — 194p,[16]p of plates : ill,facsims,ports ; 23cm
Bibliography: p188-190. — Includes index
ISBN 0-571-11635-3 : £5.95 : CIP rev. B81-0107

796.35'8'0924 — Cricket. Fingleton, Jack — *Biographies*
Fingleton, Jack. Batting from memory / Jack Fingleton. — London : Collins, 1981. — 266p,[12]p of plates : ill,ports ; 23cm
Includes index
ISBN 0-00-216359-4 : £8.95 : CIP rev. B81-2015

796.35'8'0924 — Cricket. Grace, W. G. — *Biographies*
Darwin, Bernard. W.G. Grace / Bernard Darwin ; with an introduction by John Arlott. — London : Duckworth : c1978 (1981 [printing]). — 128p : ill,facsims,ports ; 25cm
Bibliography: p125-126. — Includes index
ISBN 0-7156-1540-8 (pbk) : £4.95 B81-2601

Midwinter, Eric. W.G. Grace : his life and times / by Eric Midwinter. — London : Allen & Unwin, 1981. — 175p : ill,1facsim,ports ; 25cm
Bibliography: p169-170. - Includes index
ISBN 0-04-796054-x : Unpriced B81-2097

796.35'8'0924 — Cricket. Hadlee, Richard — *Biographies*
Hadlee, Richard. Hadlee / Richard Hadlee & Dick Brittenden. — [London] : Angus & Robertson, 1981. — xii,195p,[24]p of plates : ports ; 22cm
Ill on lining papers. — Includes index
ISBN 0-207-95982-x : £6.95 B81-2442

796.35'8'0924 — Cricket. Hobbs, *Sir* Jack - *Biographies*
Hobbs, *Sir* Jack. My life story. — London (35 Gloucester Ave., NW1 7AX) : Hambledon Press, July 1981. — [352]p
Originally published: 1935
ISBN 0-907628-00-1 : £6.95 : CIP entry B81-2052

796.35'8'0924 — Cricket. Illingworth, Ray — *Biographies*

Illingworth, Ray. Yorkshire and back : the autobiography of Ray Illingworth / written in association with Don Mosey. — London : Macdonald Futura, 1981, c1980. — 221p,[8]p of plates : ill,ports ; 18cm. — (A Futura book)
Originally published: London : Queen Anne Press, 1980
ISBN 0-7088-2057-3 (pbk) : £1.50 B81-26246

796.35'8'0924 — Cricket. MacLaren, A. C. — *Biographies*

Down, Michael. Archie : a biography of A.C. MacLaren / Michael Down. — London : Allen & Unwin, 1981. — xii,193p,[8]p of plates : ill,facsims,ports ; 23cm
Bibliography: p187-188. - Includes index
ISBN 0-04-796056-6 : Unpriced : CIP rev. B81-06880

796.35'8'0924 — Cricket. Miller, Keith, ***1919-*** **—** *Biographies*

Bose, Mihir. Keith Miller : a cricketing biography / Mihir Bose. — London : Allen & Unwin, 1980, c1979. — 175p,12p of plates : ill,ports ; 22cm
Originally published: Sydney : Allen and Unwin, 1979. — Bibliography: p164-167. — Includes index
ISBN 0-04-920062-3 : £5.50 : CIP rev. B79-35457

796.35'8'0924 — Cricket. Procter, Mike — *Biographies*

Procter, Mike. Mike Procter : and cricket. — London : Pelham, 1981. — 176p,[16]p of plates : ill,ports ; 23cm
Includes index
ISBN 0-7207-1326-9 : £5.95 : CIP rev. B81-04373

796.35'8'0924 — Cricket. Smith, E. J. — *Biographies*

Smith, E. J.. 'Tiger' Smith of Warwickshire and England : the autobiography of E.J. Smith / as told to Patrick Murphy. — Guildford : Lutterworth, 1981. — vii,132p : ill,1facsim,ports ; 23cm
Includes index
ISBN 0-7188-2502-0 : £6.95 B81-18189

796.35'8'0924 — Cricket. Thomson, Jeff — *Biographies*

Thomson, Jeff. Thommo / Jeff Thomson, the world's fastest bowler, tells his own story to David Frith ; foreword by Dennis Lillee. — London : Angus & Robertson, 1980. — 120p,[16]p of plates : ill,ports ; 22cm
Includes index
ISBN 0-207-14034-0 : £4.95 B81-03094

796.35'8'0924 — England. Cricket, ***1980*** **—** *Personal observations*

Craven, Nico. Playing a supporting role / Nico Craven ; with illustrations by Frank Fisher ; and a foreword by Brian Johnston. — [Ponsonby] ([The Coach House, Ponsonby, Seascale, Cumbria, CA20 2BX]) : [N. Craven], c1981. — 156p : ill ; 20cm
£5.95 B81-32543

796.35'82 — Cricket — *Manuals*

Andrew, Keith. Cricket / Keith Andrew, Bob Carter, Les Lenham. — Wakefield : EP, 1978 (1981 [printing]). — 116p : ill ; 21cm. — (EP sport)
ISBN 0-7158-0642-4 (pbk) : £2.95 B81-29743

796.35'826'0922 — Cricket. Batsmen, ***1905-1980***

Dexter, Ted. From Bradman to Boycott : the master batsmen / Ted Dexter. — London : Queen Anne, 1981. — 159p : ports ; 25cm
ISBN 0-354-08560-3 : £7.95 B81-17820

796.35'83 — Cricket. Umpiring — *Manuals*

Constant, David. Cricket : umpiring / David Constant with the assistance of Patrick Murphy. — London : Pelham, 1981. — 120p : ill,facsims ; 22cm. — (Sporting skills series)
ISBN 0-7207-1302-1 : £5.95 B81-18703

796.35'83'0924 — England. Cricket. Umpiring, ***1974-1977*** **—** *Personal observations*

Bird, Dickie. Not out / Dickie Bird. — London : New English Library, 1981, c1978. — x,150p : ill,ports ; 18cm
Originally published: London : A. Barker, 1978
ISBN 0-450-05107-2 (pbk) : £1.25 B81-21364

796.35'862'060422 — South-east England. Club cricket. Organisations: Club Cricket Conference — *Serials*

[Handbook ***(Club Cricket Conference)*****]**.
Handbook / the Club Cricket Conference. — 65th ed. (1981). — New Malden (353 West Barnes La., New Malden, Surrey) : The Conference, [1981]. — 224p
Cover title: Official handbook (Club Cricket Conference)
Unpriced B81-32258

796.35'862'0942191 — London. Croydon ***(London Borough)*****. Cricket. Clubs: Sanderstead Cricket Club,** ***to 1981***

Sanderstead Cricket Club centenary 1881-1981 [editors Mike Corderoy and Robert Jones]. — [Selsdon] ([43 Grenville Ave., Selsdon, Surrey]) : [Sanderstead Cricket Club], [1981?]. — [72]p : ill(some col.),ports (some col.) ; 21cm
Cover title
Unpriced (pbk) B81-26846

796.35'863 — England. County cricket. Competitions: Gillette Cup, ***to 1980*** **—** *Personal observations*

Ross, Gordon, *1917-*. The Gillette Cup 1963 to 1980 / Gordon Ross. — London : Queen Anne Press, 1981. — 189p : ill,ports ; 25cm
ISBN 0-362-00538-9 : £6.95 B81-24402

796.35'863'0922 — South-west England. County cricket, ***1870-1979*** **—** *Biographies*

Foot, David, *1929-*. From Grace to Botham : profiles of 100 West Country cricketers / David Foot. — Bristol (14 Dowry Sq., Bristol 8) : Redcliffe Press, 1980. — 123p,[8]p of plates : ports ; 22cm
ISBN 0-905459-27-x : £4.50 B81-10620

796.35'863'0924 — Gloucestershire. County cricket. Clubs: Gloucestershire County Cricket Club, ***1980*** **—** *Personal observations*

Brain, Brian. Another day, another match : the diary of a county cricketer's season / Brian Brain. — London : Allen & Unwin, 1981. — 115p,[16]p of plates : ill,ports ; 23cm
Includes index
ISBN 0-04-796057-4 : £5.95 : CIP rev. B81-13772

796.35'863'0942 — England. County cricket, ***to 1980***

Martin-Jenkins, Christopher. The Wisden book of county cricket / Christopher Martin-Jenkins ; with statistics edited by Frank Warwick. — London : Queen Anne Press, 1981. — 447p,[16]p of plates : ill,facsims,ports ; 24cm
ISBN 0-362-00545-1 : £11.95 B81-38438

796.35'865 — Cricket. English teams. Captains, ***to 1979***

Gibson, Alan, *1923—*. The cricket captains of England : a survey / Alan Gibson. — London : Cassell, 1979. — 235p,[8]p of plates : ports ; 24cm
Includes index
ISBN 0-304-29779-8 : £7.95 B81-01079

796.35'865 — Cricket. English teams. Test matches with Australian teams, ***to 1980***

Frith, David, *1937-*. England versus Australia : a pictorial history of the test matches since 1877 / David Frith ; forewords by Alan McGilvray, Sir Donald Bradman and Sir Leonard Hutton. — Rev., updated ed. — Guildford : Lutterworth in association with Richard Smart Publishing, 1981. — 320p : ill,facsims,ports ; 30cm
Previous ed.: 1977
ISBN 0-7188-2512-8 : £15.00 B81-18198

796.35'865 — Cricket. Test matches, ***1970-1980***

Willis, Bob. The cricket revolution : test cricket in the 1970s / Bob Willis with Patrick Murphy. — London : Sidgwick & Jackson, 1981. — 194p : ill,ports ; 25cm
Includes index
ISBN 0-283-98759-6 : £7.95 B81-24903

796.35'865 — Cricket. Test matches interrupted by riots, ***1971-1979***

Robinson, Ray, *1905-*. The wildest tests / Ray Robinson. — [2nd rev. and updated ed.]. — London : Cassell, [1980, c1979]. — 221p,[24]p of plates : ill,ports ; 22cm
Previous ed.: London : Pelham, 1972. — Includes index
ISBN 0-304-30548-0 : £5.95 B81-06171

796.35'865 — England. Cricket. Australian teams. Test matches with English teams, ***1902***

Brown, Lionel H.. Victor Trumper and the 1902 Australians / Lionel H. Brown. — London : Secker & Warburg, 1981. — xv,207p,[8]p of plates : ill,ports ; 25cm
Bibliography: p199-200. — Includes index
ISBN 0-436-07107-x : £9.95 : CIP rev. B81-02657

796.35'865 — North America. Cricket. Tours by English cricket teams, ***1859*** **—** *Correspondence, diaries, etc.*

Lillywhite, Fred. The English cricketers' trip to Canada and the United States in 1859 / Fred Lillywhite ; introduction by Robin Marler. — Tadworth : World's Work, c1980. — viii,97p,[23]p of plates : ill,1map ; 22cm
Facsim of: edition published London : F. Lillywhite, 1860
ISBN 0-437-08930-4 : £4.95 B81-03202

796.35'865 — West Indies. Cricket. Tours by English cricket team, ***1981*** **—** *Personal observations*

Boycott, Geoff. In the fast lane : West Indies Tour 1981 / Geoff Boycott. — London : Arthur Barker, c1981. — 223p : ill ; 26cm : 1facsim,ports
Ill on lining papers
ISBN 0-213-16808-1 : £6.95 B81-33205

796.35'865 — West Indies. Cricket. Tours by English cricket team, ***1981*** **—** *Personal observations — Collections*

England v West Indies 1981 : the official England team tour book / edited by Peter Smith. — London : Pelham, 1981. — 192p,[16]p of plates : ill,ports ; 23cm
ISBN 0-7207-1353-6 : £6.95 : CIP rev. B81-17541

796.35'873'0212 — First class cricket, ***1864-1900*****. Matches. Scores —** *Statistics*

First class cricket matches 1864-1866. — Haughton Mills (Haughton Mills, [Retford], Notts) : Association of Cricket Statisticians, [1981?]. — 160p ; 22cm
Unpriced (pbk) B81-37077

First class cricket matches 1867-1869. — Haughton Mills (Haughton Mills, [Retford], Notts) : Association of Cricket Statisticians, [1981?]. — 158p ; 22cm
Unpriced (pbk) B81-37078

First class cricket matches 1870-1872. — Haughton Mills (Haughton Mills, [Retford], Notts) : Association of Cricket Statisticians, [1981?]. — 168p ; 22cm
Unpriced (pbk) B81-37079

First class cricket matches 1873-1874. — Haughton Mills (Haughton Mills, [Retford], Notts) : Association of Cricket Statisticians, [1981?]. — 133p ; 22cm
Unpriced (pbk) B81-37080

First class cricket matches 1875-1876. — Haughton Mills (Haughton Mills, [Retford], Notts) : Association of Cricket Statisticians, [1981?]. — 152p ; 22cm
Unpriced (pbk) B81-37081

First class cricket matches 1877-1878. — Haughton Mills (Haughton Mills, [Retford], Notts) : Association of Cricket Statisticians, [1981?]. — 184p ; 22cm
Unpriced (pbk) B81-37082

First class cricket matches 1879-1880. — Haughton Mills (Haughton Mills, [Retford], Notts) : Association of Cricket Statisticians, [1981?]. — 176p ; 22cm
Unpriced (pbk) B81-37083

796.35'873'0212 — First class cricket, ***1864-1900.*** **Matches. Scores** — *Statistics* *continuation*

First class cricket matches 1881. — Haughton Mills (Haughton Mills, [Retford], Notts) : Association of Cricket Statisticians, [1981?]. — 96p ; 22cm
Unpriced (pbk) B81-37084

796.4 — ATHLETICS

796.4 — Athletics — *For children*

Drut, Guy. Your first book of athletics / Guy Drut and Jacques Piasenta ; translated from the French by Ruby McMillan. — London : Angus & Robertson, 1981 [printing]. — 46p : ill(some col.) ; 25cm
Translation of: L'athletisme. — Text on lining papers
ISBN 0-207-95895-5 : £3.50 B81-09281

796.4'05 — Athletics — *Serials*

Athlete's world : incorporating Athlete's monthly, Marathon runner, R.A.C.E. and Veteris. — Vol.2, no.11 (Nov./Dec.1979)-. — Droitwich (Peterson House, Northbank, Berryhill Industrial Estate, Droitwich, Worcs. WR9 9BL) : Peterson, 1979-. — v. : ill ; 30cm
Monthly. — Continues: R.A.C.E. (Droitwich). — Absorbed: Marathon runner, Apr.1980. — Description based on: Vol.3, no.7 (July/Aug.1980)
ISSN 0260-499x = Athlete's world : £8.00 per year B81-02345

Athletics monthly. — Vol.1, no.1 (Apr.1980)-. — Brighton (33 West St., Brighton, Sussex BN1 2RE) : A.C.M. Webb, 1980-. — v. : ill ; 29cm
Three issues yearly
ISSN 0144-980x = Athletics monthly : £9.50 per year B81-06390

796.4'06'042823 — South Yorkshire *(Metropolitan County).* **Rotherham. Athletics. Clubs: Rotherham Harriers & Athletic Club,** *to 1979*

De Roeck, E. J.. Rotherham Harriers & Athletic Club : the history of the Club 1887-1979 / by E.F. de Roeck. — [Sheffield] ([Manvern, Manvers Rd., Swallownest, Sheffield]) : [E.F. de Roeck], [1981]. — 80p,[17]p of plates : ill,ports ; 21cm
Cover title
£1.50 (pbk) B81-23392

796.4'0941 — Great Britain. Athletics — *Records of achievement* — *Serials*

UK athletics annual / compiled by the National Union of Track Statisticians. — 1981. — [Waltham Cross] ([c/o P. Matthews, 6 Broadfields, Goffs Oak, Waltham Cross, Herts. EN7 5JU]) : NUTS, c1981. — 230p
ISBN 0-904612-08-2 : £3.50 B81-29659

796.4'1 — Gymnastics — *Manuals* — *For children*

Dunn, Walter G.. Olympic gymnastics for boys and girls / Walter G. Dunn. — London : Pelham, 1981. — 190p : ill,1port ; 23cm
ISBN 0-7207-1240-8 : £8.50 B81-23708

796.4'1 — Gymnastics — *Manuals* — *For men*

Arnold, E.. Men's gymnastics / E. Arnold & B. Stocks. — Wakefield : EP, 1979 (1981 [printing]). — 116p : ill ; 21cm. — (EP sport)
ISBN 0-7158-0602-5 : Unpriced
ISBN 0-7158-0668-8 (pbk) : £2.95 B81-32776

796.4'1 — Men. Bodybuilding — *Manuals*

Schwarzenegger, Arnold. Arnold's bodybuilding for men. — London : Pelham, Nov.1981. — [240]p
ISBN 0-7207-1379-x : £6.95 : CIP entry B81-30390

796.4'1 — North-east England. Sports: Weightlifting. Organisations: Yorkshire and North East Counties Amateur Weightlifters Association. Development — *Proposals*

Yorkshire & N.E. Counties Amateur Weight Lifters Assn. : development plan November 1980. — [Leeds] ([Coronet House, Queen St., Leeds LS1 4PW]) : Sports Council, Yorkshire & Humberside, [1980]. — 12p : 1plan ; 30cm
Unpriced (pbk) B81-40038

796.4'1 — Schools. Curriculum subjects: Gymnastics. Teaching — *Manuals*

Long, Bruce. Educational gymnastics. — London : Edward Arnold, Feb.1982. — [128]p
ISBN 0-7131-0623-9 (pbk) : £2.75 : CIP entry B81-37560

Trevor, M. D.. The development of gymnastic skills : a scheme of work for teachers / M.D. Trevor. — Oxford : Blackwell, c1981. — 63p : ill ; 25cm
ISBN 0-631-12577-9 (spiral) : £2.95 B81-17657

796.4'1 — Sport: Bodybuilding. Strand pulling, *to 1980*

Webster, David, *1928-.* Strength lore & strands / by David Webster ; editor Nicola Webster. — Irvine (43 West Rd., Irvine, Ayrshire) : D. Webster, c1978. — 76p,[16]p of plates : ill,facsims,ports ; 22cm
Unpriced (pbk) B81-10385

796.4'1 — Sports: Bodybuilding, *to 1978*

Webster, David, *1928-.* Barbells and beefcake / David Webster. — Irvine (43 West Rd., Irvine, Ayrshire) : [D. Webster], c1979. — 151p : ill,facsims,ports ; 30cm
Unpriced (pbk) B81-12019

796.4'1 — Sports: Weightlifting — *Manuals*

Watson, Bill, *1918-.* Tackle weightlifting / Bill Watson. — Rev. ed. / with foreword by the Bishop of Liverpool. — London : Stanley Paul, 1980. — 110p,[16]p of plates : ill,ports ; 19cm
Previous ed.: 1975
ISBN 0-09-142241-8 (pbk) : £2.95 B81-03523

796.4'1 — Weight training — *Manuals* — *For sports*

Murray, Al. Power training for sport / Al Murray and John Lear. — London : Batsford, 1981. — 120p : ill ; 26cm
Includes index
ISBN 0-7134-1089-2 : £6.95 B81-05981

796.4'1'0924 — Gymnastics. Comaneci, Nadia — *Biographies*

Comaneci, Nadia. Nadia : the autobiography of Nadia Comaneci. — London : Proteus, 1981. — 141p,[24]p of plates : ports(some col.) ; 26cm
ISBN 0-906071-78-x (cased) : £7.95
ISBN 0-906071-56-9 (pbk) : £4.95 B81-40822

796.4'2 — Athletics. Track & field events

McNab, Tom. The complete book of athletics / Tom McNab. — London : Ward Lock, 1980. — 208p : ill(some col.),ports(some col.) ; 26cm
Includes index
ISBN 0-7063-5927-5 : £6.95 : CIP rev. B80-06521

796.4'2 — Athletics. Track & field events — *For children*

Duffy, Tony. Track and field / Tony Duffy ; colour photographs by Tony Duffy, All-Sport Limited. — Hove : Wayland, 1980. — 64p : col.ill,col.ports ; 21cm. — (InterSport)
Includes index
ISBN 0-85340-777-0 : £3.75 B81-01959

796.4'2'015 — Athletics. Track & field events. Scientific aspects

Payne, Howard. The science of track and field athletics / Howard and Rosemary Payne ; foreword by Arthur Gold. — London : Pelham, 1981. — 384p : ill ; 23cm
Includes bibliographies and index
ISBN 0-7207-1288-2 : £12.50 : CIP rev. B81-08813

796.4'2'0321 — Athletics. Track & field events — *Encyclopaedias*

Watman, Mel. Encyclopaedia of track and field events / compiled by Mel Watman. — 5th ed. — New York : St. Martin's Press ; London : Hale, 1981. — 240p,[16]p of plates : ports ; 23cm
Previous ed.: published as Encyclopedia of athletics. 1977. — Includes index
ISBN 0-7091-9242-8 : £8.95 B81-40936

796.4'2'071042 — England. Schools. Curriculum subjects: Athletics. Track & field events. Teaching — *Manuals*

Couling, David, *19---.* Athletics : a handbook for teachers / by David Couling. — London : Hale, 1980. — 167p,[8]p of plates : ill,forms ; 21cm
Bibliography: p160-164. - Includes index
ISBN 0-7091-7543-4 : £5.50 B81-00240

796.4'2'088055 — Great Britain. Junior athletics. Track & field events, *to 1978* — *Records of achievement*

UK junior all time handbook / compiled by the National Union of Track Statisticians. — London : BAAB, 1979. — 128p ; 22cm
ISBN 0-85134-057-1 (pbk) : £1.50 B81-38009

796.4'26 — Athletics. Marathon running

Temple, Cliff. Challenge of the marathon. — London : Stanley Paul, Oct.1981. — 1v.
ISBN 0-09-146431-5 (pbk) : £4.95 : CIP entry B81-30974

796.4'26 — Athletics. Marathon running — *Manuals*

Brasher, Christopher. The marathon. — London : Hodder & Stoughton, Dec.1981. — [128]p
ISBN 0-340-27900-1 (pbk) : £2.95 : CIP entry B81-31437

796.4'26 — Athletics. Running

Fixx, James F.. The complete book of running / James F. Fixx. — Harmondsworth : Penguin, 1981. — xvi,270p : ill ; 20cm. — (Penguin handbooks)
Originally published: New York : Random House, 1977 ; London : Chatto and Windus, 1979. — Bibliography: p253-254. — Includes index
ISBN 0-14-046446-8 (pbk) : £2.50 B81-27656

796.4'26'0924 — Athletics. Middle-distance running. Coe, Sebastian — *Biographies*

Coe, Sebastian. Running free / Sebastian Coe with David Miller. — London : Sidgwick & Jackson, 1981. — 174p,[24]p of plates : ill,ports ; 23cm
Includes index
ISBN 0-283-98684-0 : £6.95 B81-23553

796.4'3 — Athletics. Field events — *Manuals*

Anthony, Don. Field athletics. — London : Batsford, Feb.1982. — [64]p. — (Competitive sports series)
ISBN 0-7134-4281-6 : £5.95 : CIP entry B81-35834

796.4'3 — Athletics. Field events. Techniques

Le Masurier, John. Athletics — field events. — London : Black, Sept.1981. — [96]p. — (Black's picture sports)
ISBN 0-7136-2147-8 : £2.95 : CIP entry B81-22528

796.4'35'0712 — Secondary schools. Curriculum subjects: Athletics. Throwing events. Teaching — *Manuals*

Johnson, Carl. How to teach the throws : a guide for class teachers / Carl Johnson. — [New ed.]. — [London] ([Francis House, Francis St., London SW1P 1DL]) : British Amateur Athletic Board, [1981]. — 32p : ill ; 21cm
Cover title. — Previous ed.: / W.H.C. Paish, C.T. Johnson. 1975
£0.70 (pbk) B81-1574

796.4'35'0924 — Athletics. Shot putting. Capes, Geoff - *Biographies*

Capes, Geoff. Big shot. — London : Paul, Apr.1981. — [160]p
ISBN 0-09-144970-7 : £5.95 : CIP entry B81-0108

796.4'7 — Sports: Acrobatics — *Manuals*

Coulton, Jill. Sports acrobatics / Jill Coulton. — Wakefield : EP Sport, 1981. — 120p : ill ; 21cm
Bibliography: p120
ISBN 0-7158-0770-6 : £4.95
ISBN 0-7158-0771-4 (pbk) : Unpriced B81-3177

796.4′8′09048 — Olympic Games *(22nd : 1980 : Moscow)*

Moskva ′80 = Moscou ′80 = Moscow ′80 = Moskau ′80. — [Moscow] : [Fizkultura i Sport] ; [London] : Central Books [distributor], [1980]. — [312]p : ill(some col.),ports(some col.) ; 30cm
£14.95 B81-22446

796.4′8′0924 — Olympic Games *(22nd: 1980: Moscow) — Personal observations*

Booker, Christopher. The Games war : a Moscow journal / Christopher Booker. — London : Faber, 1981. — 236p : 1map ; 23cm
Includes index
ISBN 0-571-11755-4 (cased) : £5.95
ISBN 0-571-11763-5 (pbk) : Unpriced
B81-22439

796.4′8′0924 — Olympic Games. Coubertin, Pierre de *— Biographies*

MacAloon, John J.. This great symbol : Pierre de Coubertin and the origins of the modern Olympic Games / John J. MacAloon. — Chicago ; London : University of Chicago Press, c1981. — xiv,359p : 1port ; 24cm
Bibliography: p339-348. — Includes index
ISBN 0-226-50000-4 : £15.00 B81-38277

796.5 — OUTDOOR LIFE

796.5 — Orienteering *— Manuals*

Walker, Tony. Discovering orienteering and wayfaring / Tony Walker. — 2nd ed., with additional chapter on wayfaring. — Aylesbury : Shire, 1979. — 48p : ill,maps ; 18cm. — (Discovering series ; no.168)
Previous ed.: 1973. — Bibliography: p47. — Includes index
ISBN 0-85263-468-4 (pbk) : £0.75 B81-40738

796.5′0207 — Orienteering *— Humour*

Vinestock, Gerald. Circular orienteering / by Gerald Vinestock. — Cheltenham (2 Keynsham Bank, London Road, Cheltenham) : G. Vinestock, c1980. — 40p ; 19cm
Unpriced (pbk) B81-39810

796.5′1 — Backpacking *— Manuals*

Marriott, Michael. Start backpacking / Mike Marriott. — London : Stanley Paul, 1981. — 89p : ill,1map ; 24cm
Bibliography: p89
ISBN 0-09-143990-6 (cased) : £5.95
ISBN 0-09-143991-4 (pbk) : £3.95 B81-11560

Robinson, Don. Backpacking / Don Robinson. — Wakefield : EP, 1981. — 119p : ill ; 21cm. — (EP sport)
Bibliography: p117-119
ISBN 0-7158-0601-7 (cased) : £4.95
ISBN 0-7158-0652-1 (pbk) : Unpriced
B81-24044

Ward, Ken, *1926-*. Discovering backpacking / Ken Ward. — Princes Risborough : Shire, 1980. — 48p : ill ; 18cm. — (Discovering series ; no.256)
Bibliography: p47. — Includes index
ISBN 0-85263-466-8 (pbk) : £0.85 B81-02760

96.5′1 — England. West Midlands. Rural regions. Guided walks. Organisation

Jenkinson, Andrew M.. Explore your local countryside : guided walks in the West Midlands : a report / by the project officer, Andrew M. Jenkinson for the Countryside Commission. — Cheltenham (John Dower House, Crescent Place, Cheltenham, Glos., GL50 3RA) : The Commission, c1980. — v,61p : ill,1map,facsims ; 30cm
ISBN 0-86170-021-x (pbk) : £3.40 B81-15613

96.5′1′0289 — Great Britain. Countryside. Recreations: Walking. Safety measures *— For Girl Guides*

Walking safely. — London (17 Buckingham Palace Rd., SW1W OPT) : Girl Guides Association, 1981. — 2v. : 2ill,forms ; 21cm
Includes bibliographies
£0.20 (pbk) B81-40446

796.5′1′06041 — Great Britain. Recreations: Long-distance walking. Organisations: Long Distance Walkers Association *— Serials*

Strider : the journal of the Long Distance Walkers Association. — No.19 (Nov. 1977)-. — Guildford (c/o Mr K. Chesterton, Firle, Chestnut Ave., Guildford, Surrey GU2 4HD) : The Association, 1977-. — v. : ill ; 21cm
Three issues yearly. — Continues: Newsletter (Long Distance Walkers Association). — Description based on: No. 28 (Dec. 1980)
ISSN 0260-812x = Strider : £0.50 per issue (free to Association members) B81-09137

796.5′1′0941 — Great Britain. Backpacking *— Manuals*

Wickers, David. Britain at your feet : a backpacker′s handbook / David Wickers and Art Pedersen ; illustrated by Paul Saunders. — London : Kogan Page, 1980. — 301p : ill ; 21cm
Bibliography: p291-293
ISBN 0-85038-334-x : £5.95 : CIP rev.
B80-01768

Wickers, David. Britain at your feet / David Wickers and Art Pedersen. — London : Hamlyn, 1981, c1980. — 301p : ill,maps ; 20cm
Originally published: London : Kogan Page, 1980. — Bibliography: p291-294
ISBN 0-600-20279-8 (pbk) : £1.75 B81-15137

796.5′1′0941 — Great Britain. Recreations: Long-distance walking *— For adolescents*

Duerden, Frank. Adventure walking for young people / Frank Duerden. — London : Kaye & Ward, 1980. — xv,142p : ill,maps,facsims ; 23cm
ISBN 0-7182-1252-5 : £5.25
ISBN 0-7182-1257-6 (pbk) : £3.95 B81-02262

796.5′1′0941 — Great Britain. Recreations: Walking *— Manuals*

Mattingly, Alan. Tackle rambling / Alan Mattingly. — London : Paul, 1981. — 110p : ill,maps,facsims ; 24cm
ISBN 0-09-144810-7 (cased) : Unpriced : CIP rev.
ISBN 0-09-144811-5 (pbk) : £3.95 B81-13543

796.5′1′0941464 — Scotland. Strathclyde Region. Merrick region. Recreations: Walking *— Personal observations*

McBain, J.. The Merrick and the neighbouring hills : tramps by hill, stream and loch / by J. McBain. — Ayr : Jackson & Sproat, 1980. — 335p,[12]p of plates : ill ; 22cm
Originally published: Ayr : Stephen & Pollock, 1929
£4.50 (pbk)
Primary classification 796.5′1′0941495
B81-10197

796.5′1′0941495 — Scotland. Dumfries and Galloway Region. Merrick Region. Recreations: Walking *— Personal observations*

McBain, J.. The Merrick and the neighbouring hills : tramps by hill, stream and loch / by J. McBain. — Ayr : Jackson & Sproat, 1980. — 335p,[12]p of plates : ill ; 22cm
Originally published: Ayr : Stephen & Pollock, 1929
£4.50 (pbk)
Also classified at 796.5′1′0941464 B81-10197

796.5′1′0942 — England. Recreations: Walking *— Manuals*

Westacott, H. D.. Discovering walking / H.D. Westacott. — Aylesbury : Shire, 1979. — 54p : ill,maps,plans ; 18cm. — (Discovering series ; no.248)
Includes index
ISBN 0-85263-467-6 (pbk) : £0.75 B81-40736

796.5′1′09421 — North London. Recreations: Walking *— Visitors′ guides*

Lundow, Merry. Discovering country walks in North London : Merry Lundow. — 2nd ed. — Aylesbury : Shire, 1981. — 72p : maps ; 18cm. — (Discovering series ; no.240)
Previous ed.: 1978. — Includes index
ISBN 0-85263-574-5 (pbk) : £1.25 B81-40744

796.5′1′09422 — South-east England. Long-distance footpaths: Vanguard Way. Recreations: Walking *— Visitors′ guides*

The **Vanguard** way : (from the suburbs to the sea) : East Croydon to Seaford - 100kms. — South Croydon (c/o 109 Selsdon Park Rd., South Croydon CR2 8JJ) : Vanguards Rambling Club, 1980. — 47p : ill,maps ; 21cm
£0.90 (pbk) B81-11519

796.5′1′094221 — Surrey. North Downs. Long-distance footpaths: North Downs Way. Recreations: Walking *— Visitors′ guides*

Allen, David J.. Discovering the North Downs Way / David J. Allen and Patrick R. Imrie. — Princes Risborough : Shire, 1980. — 80p : 1ill,maps ; 18cm. — (Discovering series ; no.252)
Includes index
ISBN 0-85263-512-5 (pbk) : £0.95
Primary classification 796.5′1′094223
B81-09220

796.5′1′094221 — Surrey. Recreations: Walking *— Visitors′ guides*

Owen, Susan. Discovering walks in Surrey / Susan Owen and Angela Haine. — Aylesbury : Shire, 1981. — 64p : maps ; 18cm. — (Discovering series ; no.264)
Includes index
ISBN 0-85263-560-5 (pbk) : £1.25 B81-40750

796.5′1′0942219 — Surrey. Waverley *(District)*. **Recreations: Walking** *— Visitors′ guides*

Hyde, George. Ten miles walks in South West Surrey : 12 circular walks / by George Hyde. — Adstock (Adstock Cottage, Adstock, Buckingham MK18 2HZ) : Footpath Publications, c1980. — 31p : 13maps ; 21cm
£0.90 (pbk) B81-11996

796.5′1′094223 — Kent. North Downs. Long-distance footpaths: North Downs Way. Recreations: Walking *— Visitors′ guides*

Allen, David J.. Discovering the North Downs Way / David J. Allen and Patrick R. Imrie. — Princes Risborough : Shire, 1980. — 80p : 1ill,maps ; 18cm. — (Discovering series ; no.252)
Includes index
ISBN 0-85263-512-5 (pbk) : £0.95
Also classified at 796.5′1′094221 B81-09220

796.5′1′094227 — North Hampshire. Recreations: Walking *— Visitors′ guides*

Channer, Nick. North Hampshire walks : ten country rambles near Winchester, Alton, Andover and Basingstoke : with historical notes / Nick Channer. — Newbury : Countryside Books, 1981. — 80p : maps ; 19cm
ISBN 0-905392-09-4 (pbk) : £1.95 B81-40445

796.5′1′0942378 — Cornwall. Falmouth region. Recreations: Walking *— Visitors′ guides*

Six walks around Falmouth. — [Penryn] ([c/o Publicity Officer, 2 Lanaton Rd., Penryn, Cornwall]) : Ramblers′ Association (Cornwall Area)
Cover title
No.1. — 1980. — [16]p : maps ; 22cm
£0.45 (pbk) B81-35535

Six walks around Falmouth. — [Penryn] ([c/o Publicity Officer, 2 Lanaton Rd., Penryn, Cornwall]) : Ramblers′ Association
Cover title
No.2. — 1981. — [12]p : maps ; 22cm
Text and map on inside covers
£0.45 (pbk) B81-35536

796.5′1′0942385 — England. Exmoor. Recreations: Walking *— Visitors′ guides*

Butler, David, *1926-*. Exmoor : walks for motorists / David Butler ; with sketch maps by C.G. Edwards and D.L. Indge. — London : Warne, 1979 (1980 printing). — 107p,[4]p of plates : ill,maps ; 21cm. — (Warne Gerrard guides for walkers. Walks for motorists series ; 26)
ISBN 0-7232-2148-0 (pbk) : £1.50 B81-11204

796.5'1'09424 — England. Severn River region. Recreations: Walking — *Visitors' guides*

Price, Peter A.. Severn Valley : walks for motorists / Peter A. Price ; 30 sketch maps and 10 line drawings by the author ; 6 photographs by the author. — London : Warne, 1981. — 103p,[4]p of plates : ill,maps ; 21cm. — (Warne Gerrard guides for walkers. Walks for motorists series ; 35)
ISBN 0-7232-2168-5 (pbk) : £1.50 B81-16459

796.5'1'0942417 — England. Cotswolds. Recreations: Walking — *Visitors' guides*

Drury, Harry. Walking in the Cotswolds : 41 walks of from 1-1/2 to 15-1/2 miles / by Harry Drury ; illustrations by Alfred Newman. — London : Hale, 1981. — 256p : ill,maps ; 21cm
Includes index
ISBN 0-7091-8587-1 : £6.50
ISBN 0-7091-8595-2 B81-34753

796.5'1'0942511 — England. Peak District. National parks: Peak District National Park. Recreations: Walking — *Visitors' guides*

Parker, William. Short walks in the Peak Park / by William and Vera Parker ; with maps by P.J. Williamson. — Derby : Derbyshire Countryside, c1981. — 64p : 2ill,maps ; 18cm
Ill on inside covers
ISBN 0-85100-074-6 (pbk) : £0.75 B81-28428

796.5'1'0942579 — Oxfordshire. Brightwell-cum-Sotwell. Recreations: Walking — *Visitors' guides*

Leaver, William. Brightwell-cum-Sotwell : perambulations around Sotwell / by Wm. Leaver and Annabel B. Rodda. — [Wallingford] ([Middle Farm, Church La., Brightwell-cum-Sotwell, Wallingford OX10 0SD]) : [K. Owen], c1981. — [14]p : 2maps,facsims ; 15cm
Unpriced (pbk) B81-35506

796.5'1'094264 — Suffolk. Recreations: Walking — *Visitors' guides*

Discovering walks in Suffolk / John Andrews (editor). — Aylesbury : Shire, 1981. — 64p : maps ; 18cm. — (Discovering series ; no.263)
Includes index
ISBN 0-85263-559-1 (pbk) : £1.25 B81-40737

796.5'1'09427 — Northern England. Recreations: Long-distance walking — *Practical information*

Long distance walks. — Lancaster : Dalesman
Vol.1: The North York moors and wolds / by Tony Wimbush. — 1981. — 72p : ill,maps,forms ; 22cm
ISBN 0-85206-626-0 (pbk) : £1.75 B81-17796

796.5'1'094271 — Cheshire. Recreations: Walking — *Visitors' guides*

Edwards, James F.. Further Cheshire : walks for motorists / James F. Edwards ; 31 sketch maps and photographs by the author. — London : Warne, c1981. — 91p,[4]p of plates : ill,maps ; 21cm. — (Warne Gerrard guides for walkers. Walks for motorists series ; 37)
ISBN 0-7232-2166-9 (pbk) : £1.50 B81-16498

796.5'1'094271 — Western Cheshire. Recreations: Walking — *Visitors' guides*

Baker, Jack. Walks in West Cheshire / by Jack Baker. — Adstock (Adstock Cottage, Adstock, Buckingham MK18 2HZ) : Footpath Publications, c1980. — 32p : 14maps ; 21cm
Cover title
£0.90 (pbk) B81-11997

796.5'1'0942783 — Cumbria. Kendal region. Recreations: Walking — *Visitors' guides*

Walks in the Kendal area. — [Kendal] ([6 River Bank Rd., Kendal, Cumbria LA9 5JS]) : Kendal Group of the Ramblers' Association, [1981]. — 44p : ill,maps ; 22cm
Cover title
£0.75 (pbk) B81-26649

796.5'1'094281 — Yorkshire. Long-distance footpaths: Cal-Der-Went Walk. Recreations: Walking - *Visitors' guides*

Carr, Geoffrey. The Cal-Der-Went walk / by Geoffrey Carr. — Clapham, N. Yorkshire : Dalesman, 1979. — 30p : ill,maps ; 19cm. — (A Dalesman mini-book)
ISBN 0-85206-503-5 (pbk) : £0.60 B81-18203

796.5'1'0942819 — West Yorkshire *(Metropolitan County)*. **Bramhope. Recreations: Walking** — *Guidebooks*

Duffield, Joan. Bramhope & North Leeds footpath/bridleway map plus guide to 12 circular walks / Joan Duffield. — Leeds (307 Leeds Rd., Bramhope, Leeds LS16 9JX) : J. & M. Duffield, 1980. — 1folded sheet : 1col.map ; 42x30cm folded to 21x15cm
£0.30c B81-16053

796.5'1'0942846 — North Yorkshire. North York Moors. Recreations: Walking: Bilsdale Circuit — *Visitors' guides*

Teanby, Michael. The Bilsdale Circuit : a 30-mile challenge walk across the North York Moors / by Michael Teanby. — Clapham [N. Yorkshire] : Dalesman, 1981. — 32p : ill,maps ; 19cm
ISBN 0-85206-636-8 (pbk) : £0.60 B81-22925

796.5'1'0942846 — North Yorkshire. North York Moors. Recreations: Walking — *Visitors' guides*

Eskdale and the Cleveland coast / compiled by The Ramblers' Association (North Yorkshire and South Durham Area). — Clapham, N. Yorkshire : Dalesman, 1981. — 48p : maps ; 19cm. — (Walks from your car)
ISBN 0-85206-629-5 (pbk) : £0.85 B81-17834

796.5'1'0942861 — Durham *(County)*. **Teesdale. Recreations: Walking** — *Visitors' guides*

Watson, Keith. Walking in Teesdale / by Keith Watson. — Clapham, N. Yorkshire : Dalesman, 1978. — 64p : ill,maps ; 19cm. — (A Dalesman mini-book)
Bibliography: p62-63
ISBN 0-85206-485-3 (pbk) : £0.75 B81-09165

796.5'1'094288 — Northumberland. Recreations: Walking — *Visitors' guides*

Northumberland : walks for motorists / compiled by members of the Ramblers' Association, Northern Area ; Sketch maps by C.G. Edwards and D.L. Indge ; photographs by I.M.H. Fletcher. — London : Warne, c1981. — 103p,[4]p of plates : ill,maps ; 21cm. — (Warne Gerrard guides for walkers. Walks for motorists series ; 36)
ISBN 0-7232-2167-7 (pbk) : £1.50 B81-16497

796.5'1'094652 — Europe. Pyrenees. Backpacking — *Manuals*

Véron, Georges. Pyrenees high level route : Atlantic to Mediterranean : mountain walking and trekking guide for a complete traverse of the range in 45 day stages with 50 easier or harder alternatives and variations / Georges Véron. — Goring : Gastons-West Col, 1981. — 136p : maps ; 18cm. — (Mountain guides to the Pyrenees)
Translated from the French
£7.50 (pbk) B81-29510

796.5'22 — Cumbria. Lake District. Hill walking — *Visitors' guides*

Bowker, Tom. Exploring the Lakeland fells / by Tom Bowker. — Clapham [N. Yorkshire] : Dalesman, 1981. — 64p : ill,1map ; 19cm
ISBN 0-85206-627-9 (pbk) : £1.10 B81-22920

796.5'22 — Great Britain. Mountainous regions. Hill walking. Navigation — *Manuals*

Cliff, Peter. Mountain navigation / by Peter Cliff ; foreword by F.W.J. Harper. — 2nd ed. — Leicester : Cordee, 1980. — 54p : ill,col.maps ; 21cm
Previous ed.: 1978
ISBN 0-904405-01-x (pbk) : £2.00 B81-04183

796.5'22 — Great Britain. Mountainous regions. Hill walking — *Personal observations*

Brown, Hamish M.. Hamish's Groats End walk : one man and his dog on a hill route through Britain & Ireland / by Hamish M. Brown. — London : Gollancz, 1981. — xiv,301p,[48]p of plates : ill,maps,ports ; 24cm
Bibliography: p289-296. — Includes index
ISBN 0-575-03029-1 : £9.95 B81-38123

796.5'22 — Mountaineering

Cleare, John. Mountaineering / John Cleare. — Poole : Blandford, 1980. — 169p : ill(some col.),ports(some col.) ; 20cm
Bibliography: p162-164. - Includes index
ISBN 0-7137-0946-4 (cased) : £3.95 : CIP rev.
ISBN 0-7137-1082-9 (pbk) : £2.95 B80-18461

Gilbert, Richard, *1937 Nov. 17-*. Mountaineering for all / Richard Gilbert. — London : Batsford, 1981. — 136p : ill ; 26cm
Includes index
ISBN 0-7134-3350-7 : £6.95 B81-15960

796.5'22 — Mountains. Ice pitches & snow pitches. Mountaineering - *Manuals*

Chouinard, Yvon. Climbing ice. — Large print ed. — London : Hodder & Stoughton, Aug.1981. — 1v.
Originally published: 1979
ISBN 0-340-27147-7 (pbk) : £6.95 : CIP entry B81-18112

796.5'22 — Scotland. Highlands. Hill walking — *Manuals*

Gilbert, Richard, *1937 Nov.17-*. Hillwalking in Scotland / by Richard F. Gilbert. — 2nd ed. — Cheltenham : Thornhill, 1979. — 67p : ill,1map ; 19cm. — (A Thornhill guide ; 5)
Previous ed.: 1976
ISBN 0-904110-75-3 (pbk) : £0.95 B81-33109

796.5'22 — Scotland. Tayside. Hill walking — *Visitors' guides*

Tayside : all the life and legend of Scotland. — Dundee (Tayside House, Crichton St., Dundee DD1 3RD) : Tayside Regional Council, Department of Recreation & Tourism
Hill walking : a selection of routes ranging from family walks to longer expeditions / [edited by Ian Brown]. — 1979. — 32p : maps ; 22cm
Cover title. — Bibliography: p32
£0.50 (pbk) B81-32491

796.5'22 — Scotland. Tayside Region. Hill walking — *Visitors' guides*

Tayside : all the life and legend of Scotland : hill walking : a selection of routes ranging from family walks to longer expeditions. — [Dundee] ([Tayside House, Crichton St., Dundee, DD1 3RD]) : [Tayside Regional Council, Department of Recreation & Tourism], [1979]. — 32p : maps ; 21cm
Cover title. — Bibliography: p32
£0.50 (pbk) B81-34442

796.5'22'0922 — Mountaineering, *ca 1860-1970* — *Personal observations — Collections*

Peaks, passes and glaciers : selections from the Alpine journal / compiled and introduced by Walt Unsworth. — London : Allen Lane, 1981. — 284p,[16]p of plates : ill,maps,ports ; 24cm
ISBN 0-7139-1210-3 : £8.95 B81-13916

796.5'22'0924 — Asia. Himalayas. Mountaineering, *1979 — Personal observations*

Hillary, Peter. A sunny day in the Himalayas. — London : Hodder and Stoughton, May 1981. — [166]p
ISBN 0-340-25685-0 : £7.50 : CIP entry B81-04242

796.5'22'0924 — Mountaineering. Buhl, Hermann — *Biographies*

Buhl, Hermann. Nanga Parbat pilgrimage / by Hermann Buhl ; translated by Hugh Merrick. — London : Hodder and Stoughton, 1981. — 360p[16]p of plates : ill,maps,ports ; 22cm
Translation of: Achttausand drüber und drunter. — Originally published: 1956
ISBN 0-340-26498-5 (pbk) : £6.95 : CIP rev. B81-0999

796.5'22'0924 — Mountaineering. Messner, Reinhold — *Biographies*

Faux, Ronald. High ambition. — London : Gollancz, Jan.1982. — [192]p
ISBN 0-575-03069-0 : £9.95 : CIP entry B81-3588

796.5'22'0943642 — Austria. Zillertaler Alps. Mountaineering — *Manuals*

Roberts, Eric, *1945-*. Zillertal Alps : introductory climbing guide / compiled from diaries and notes by Eric Roberts and written by Robin Collomb. — Reading : West Col, 1980. — 94p,[20]p of plates : ill,1map ; 18cm. — (West Col alpine guides)
Includes index
ISBN 0-906227-13-5 (pbk) : £5.95
Also classified at 796.5'22'094538 B81-0232

796.5′22′094538 — Italy. Zillertaler Alps. Mountaineering — *Manuals*

Roberts, Eric, *1945-*. Zillertal Alps : introductory climbing guide / compiled from diaries and notes by Eric Roberts and written by Robin Collomb. — Reading : West Col, 1980. — 94p,[20]p of plates : ill,1map ; 18cm. — (West Col alpine guides)
Includes index
ISBN 0-906227-13-5 (pbk) : £5.95
Primary classification 796.5′22′0943642
B81-02321

796.5′223′0924 — Cumbria. Lake District. Rock climbing — *Personal observations*

Griffin, A. H.. Adventuring in Lakeland : scrambling, ′geriatric′ rock-climbing, gill-climbing, snow-climbing and ski-mountaineering / A.H. Griffin. — London : Hale, 1980. — 189p,[32]p of plates : ill ; 23cm
Includes index
ISBN 0-7091-8586-3 : £7.95 B81-05235

796.5′223′0941 — Great Britain. Rock climbing — *Manuals*

Hard rock : great British rock-climbs / compiled by Ken Wilson with editorial assistance from Mike and Lucy Pearson ; diagrams by Brian Evans. — 2nd ed. — London : Granada, 1981. — xix,236p : ill(some col.) ; 29cm
Previous ed.: London : Hart-Davis MacGibbon, 1974. — Includes index
ISBN 0-246-11192-5 : £17.50 B81-28973

796.5′223′0942461 — Staffordshire. Peak District. Rock climbing — *Manuals*

Staffordshire area / editors of this volume Mike Browell ... [et al.]. — [s.l.] : Peak Committee of the British Mountaineering Council ; Leicester Cordee [distributors], 1981. — 266p,viiip of plates : ill,maps ; 18cm. — (Rock climbs in the Peak. New series ; .6)
Ill on lining papers
ISBN 0-903908-65-4 (pbk) : Unpriced
B81-36196

796.5′223′094251 — Derbyshire. Derwent Valley. Rock climbing — *Manuals*

Derwent Valley / editors Jim Ballard and Ernie Marshall. — [Manchester] : Peak Committee of the British Mountaineering Council, 1981 ; Leicester : Cordee [distributor]. — 240p,[16]p of plates : ill,maps ; 18cm. — (Rock climbs in the Peak ; v.5)
Ill on lining papers
ISBN 0-903908-60-3 (pbk) : £4.50 B81-27497

796.5′223′0942925 — Gwynedd. Llanberis Pass. Rock climbing — *Manuals*

Milburn, Geoff. Llanberis Pass. — 3rd ed., diagrams by Peter Marks, frontispiece by Malc Baxter and map by George Bridge. — [London] : Climbers′ Club with financial assistance from the British Mountaineering Council, 1981. — 180p : ill,2maps ; 17cm. — (Climbers′ Club guides to Wales ; 3)
Previous ed.: 1978. — Maps on lining papers. — Includes index
ISBN 0-901601-16-0 (pbk) : £4.50 B81-37168

796.5′223′094294 — South-east Wales. Rock climbing — *Manuals*

Penning, Tony. New climbs S.E. Wales and the Gower / by Tony Penning. — [S.l.] : T. Penning, [1980] ; [Reading] : [West Col.] [Distributor]. — 44p : ill ; 16cm
Text on inside cover. — Includes index
ISBN 0-906227-16-x (pbk) : £1.50 B81-19285

796.5′223′0942962 — Dyfed. Preseli *(District)* **& South Pembrokeshire** *(District)*. **Rock climbing** — *Manuals*

Littlejohn, Pat. Pembroke / by Pat Littlejohn and Mike Harber ; maps by Don Sargent and Brian Wilkinson ; cover photographs by Chris Griffiths. — [London] ([c/o A.H. Jones, 42 Corring Way, W.5]) : Climbers′ Club with financial assistance from the British Mountaineering Council ; Leicester : Cordee [distributor], 1981. — 268p : ill,maps ; 17cm. — (Climber′s Club guides to Wales)
Maps on lining papers. — Includes index
ISBN 0-901601-15-2 (pbk) : £5.50 B81-22127

796.5′25 — Caves. Exploration — *Amateurs′ manuals*

Judson, David. Caving and potholing / David Judson & Arthur Champion. — London : Granada, 1981. — 192p,[16]p of plates : ill ; 18cm. — (A Mayflower book)
Bibliography: p177-179. - Includes index
ISBN 0-583-13129-8 (pbk) : £1.95 B81-18946

Lovelock, James. A caving manual / Jim Lovelock. — London : Batsford, 1981. — 144p : ill,ports ; 26cm
Bibliography: p142-143. — Includes index
ISBN 0-7134-1904-0 : £7.95 B81-24312

796.54 — Camping — *Manuals*

Williams, P. F.. Adventure camping / Peter F. Williams. — London : Pelham, 1981. — 144p : ill ; 22cm
Includes index
ISBN 0-7207-1333-1 : £6.95 B81-36284

796.54 — Lightweight camping — *Manuals*

Brown, Terry. The Spur book of lightweight camping / by Terry Brown and Rob Hunter. — 2nd ed. — Bourne End : Spurbooks, 1980. — 64p : ill,1map,1plan ; 19cm. — (Spurbook venture guide series)
Previous ed.: published as The Spur book of camping. 1976
ISBN 0-904978-48-6 (pbk) : £0.95 : CIP rev.
B80-04374

796.54′028 — Camping equipment. Construction — *Amateurs′ manuals*

Platten, David. Making camping and outdoor gear : a practical guide to design & construction / David Platten. — Newton Abbot : David & Charles, c1981. — 157p : ill ; 23cm
Includes index
ISBN 0-7153-8023-0 : £4.95 B81-08697

796.6 — CYCLING

796.6 — Cycling — *For children*

Fairclough, Chris. Let′s go cycling / Chris Fairclough ; photography by Chris Fairclough. — London : Watts, c1981. — 32p : col.ill ; 22cm. — (Let′s go series)
ISBN 0-85166-919-0 : £2.99 B81-21749

796.6 — Cycling - *Manuals*

Osman, Tony. The complete cyclist. — London : Collins, May 1981. — [200]p
ISBN 0-00-216880-4 (cased) : £8.50 : CIP entry
ISBN 0-00-216881-2 (pbk) : £4.95 B81-04360

796.6 — Great Britain. Bicycle touring — *Manuals*

Alderson, Frederick. The cyclists′ companion / by Frederick Alderson. — London : Hale, 1981. — 192p,[8]p of plates : ill,1port ; 21cm
Bibliography: p185. - Includes index
ISBN 0-7091-8861-7 : £6.25 B81-18391

796.6 — Sports: Cycling — *For children*

Evans, Ken, *19---*. Cycling / Ken Evans ; colour photographs by All-Sport Limited. — Hove : Wayland, 1980. — 34p : col.ill,col.ports ; 21cm. — (InterSport)
Includes index
ISBN 0-85340-774-6 : £3.75
ISBN 0-85340-772-x B81-06093

796.6 — Western Europe. Bicycle touring

Hughes, Tim. Wheels of choice / Tim Hughes. — Great Missenden (Great Missenden, Bucks. HP16 0HD) : Cyclographic, 1980. — 95p : ill (some col.) ; 22cm
ISBN 0-907191-00-2 (cased) : £5.75
ISBN 0-907191-01-1 (pbk) : Unpriced
B81-08029

796.6060421′4 — North London. Cycling. Clubs: North London Cycling Club, *to 1980*

Smith, A. B.. Along the Great North and other roads. — Gloucester (17a Brunswick Rd, Gloucester GL1 1HG) : Alan Sutton, May 1981. — [192]p
ISBN 0-904387-73-9 : £6.95 : CIP entry
B81-07489

796.6′0941 — Great Britain. Urban regions. Cycling — *Manuals*

Thomas, Nigel, *1950-*. City rider : how to survive with your bike / Nigel Thomas ; cartoons by Maddocks. — London : Elm Tree, 1981. — 128p : ill ; 24cm
Includes index
ISBN 0-241-10574-9 (cased) : £6.95 : CIP rev.
ISBN 0-241-10575-7 (pbk) : £4.50 B81-02366

796.6′09413′4 — Edinburgh. Cycling

Edinburgh for cyclists : a guide to cycling in Edinburgh and Lothian. — Edinburgh : 2 Ainslei Place, Edinburgh EH3 6AR : Spokes, c1980. — 80p : ill,maps,ports ; 21cm
ISBN 0-9507319-0-0 (pbk) : £1.00 B81-15743

796.6′09421 — London. Cycling - *Manuals*

The **Bartholomew/CTC** guide to cycling in and around London. — Edinburgh : Bartholomew, June 1981. — [128]p
ISBN 0-7028-8051-5 (pbk) : £2.50 : CIP entry
B81-13550

796.6′09421 — London. Cycling — *Manuals*

On your bike : the guide to cycling in London. — London (Colombo St. Centre, SE1) : London Cycling Campaign, 1981. — 32p,13p of plates : ill,col.maps ; 21cm
Cover title
ISBN 0-905966-07-4 (pbk) : £0.60 B81-35289

796.6′2′06041 — Great Britain. Bicycles. Racing. Organisations: British Cycling Federation — *Serials*

[Handbook *(British Cycling Federation)***]**. Handbook / British Cycling Federation. — 1981. — London (70 Brompton Rd, SW3 1EN) : The Federation, [1980]. — 256p
£1.25 B81-13105

796.6′2′0924 — England. Bicycles. Racing. Hoban, Barry — *Biographies*

Hoban, Barry. Watching the wheels go round : an autobiography / Barry Hoban with John Wilcockson. — London : Stanley Paul, 1981. — 258p,[8]p of plates : ill,maps,ports ; 23cm
Includes index
ISBN 0-09-145370-4 : £7.95 : CIP rev.
B81-11959

796.7 — MOTORING

796.7 — Motorcycling

Carrick, Peter. The Guinness guide to motorcycling / Peter Carrick ; [editor Anne Marshall]. — London : Guinness Superlatives, c1980. — 223p : ill(some col.),ports(some col.) ; 30cm
Includes index
ISBN 0-85112-210-8 : £10.965 : CIP rev.
B80-12022

796.7 — Motorcycling — *Serials*

[The biker *(Londn)***]**. The biker. — No.1 (June 1980)-. — London (109 Waterloo Road, SE1 8UL) : Business Publications, 1980-. — v. : ill ; 29cm
Monthly. — Description based on: No.3, Aug.1980
ISSN 0260-5147 = Biker (London) : £9.20 per year B81-04043

796.7′075 — Motoring, *to ca 1930*. **Items associated with motoring. Collecting & preservation**, *to ca 1930*

Burgess-Wise, David. Automobile archaeology / David Burgess-Wise ; foreword by Robert A. Lutz. — Cambridge : Stephens, 1981. — 160p : ill,facsims ; 25cm
Includes index
ISBN 0-85059-455-3 : £8.95 B81-18701

796.7′0941 — Great Britain. Motoring — *Serials*

Royal Scottish Automobile Club. The Royal Scottish Automobile Club handbook. — 1975. — Glasgow (11, Blythswood Sq., Glasgow) : [The Club], [1975?]. — 438p
Unpriced B81-06913

Royal Scottish Automobile Club. The Royal Scottish Automobile Club handbook. — 1979. — Glasgow (11, Blythswood Sq., Glasgow G2 4AG) : [The Club], [1979?]. — 456,64p
Unpriced B81-06915

796.7′0941 — Great Britain. Motoring — *Serials continuation*

Royal Scottish Automobile Club. The Royal Scottish Automobile Club handbook. — 1980. — Glasgow (11, Blythswood Sq., G2 4AG) : [The Club], [1980?]. — 415,64p
Unpriced B81-06914

796.72 — MOTOR RACING

796.7′2 — Cars. Rallying. Navigation — *Manuals*

Needham, Les. Navigation for rallies / by Les Needham. — Chislehurst : Lodgemark, [1976]. — 48p : ill ; 19cm
ISBN 0-85077-052-1 (pbk) : Unpriced
B81-01082

796.7′2 — Cars. Rallying — *Serials*

Rothmans world rallying. — 3. — London : Osprey Pub., 1981. — 160p
ISBN 0-85045-391-7 : £7.95
ISSN 0144-6711 B81-29045

796.7′2 — Cars. Rallying, *to 1980*

Robson, Graham. A history of rallying. — London : Osprey, July 1981. — [216]p
ISBN 0-85045-407-7 : £9.95 : CIP entry
B81-14908

796.7′2 — Ferrari racing cars. Racing, *to 1980*

Orsini, Luigi. La Scuderia Ferrari. — London : Osprey, Aug.1981. — [432]p
Translation of: La Scuderia Ferrari
ISBN 0-85045-378-x : £39.95 : CIP entry
B81-18095

796.7′2 — Ford Capri competition cars. Racing, *to 1980*

Walton, Jeremy. Capri / Jeremy Walton. — [Yeovil] : Foulis, 1981. — 285p : ill,ports ; 26cm. — (A Foulis motoring book)
Includes index
ISBN 0-85429-279-9 : Unpriced
Primary classification 629.2′222 B81-31774

796.7′2 — Formula 1 racing cars. Racing. Races: Grand Prix, *1950-*

Lang, Mike. Grand Prix! / by Mike Lang. — [Yeovil] : Foulis. — (A Foulis motoring book)
[Vol.1]: [1950 to 1965]. — 1981. — 288p : ill,ports ; 28cm
ISBN 0-85429-276-4 : £9.95 B81-31118

796.7′2 — Great Britain. Cars. Rallying. Rallies: Lombard-RAC International Rally of Great Britain, *to 1979*

Drackett, Phil. The story of the RAC International Rally / Phil Drackett. — Rev. and enl. ed. — Yeovil : Haynes : Foulis, 1980. — 231p : ill,ports ; 24cm. — (A Foulis motoring book)
Previous ed.: published as Rally of the forests ; London : Pelham, 1970. — Includes index
ISBN 0-85429-270-5 : £7.95 B81-24409

796.7′2 — Racing cars. Racing — *For children*

Gladnik, Roman. Motor racing / [translated from the original German text of Roman Gladnik by Brenda F. Groth]. — St. Albans : Hart-Davis, 1981. — 37p : ill(some col.),col.ports ; 15x16cm. — (Questions answered)
Text on lining paper
ISBN 0-247-13162-8 : £1.50 B81-39466

Lorin, Philippe. All about motor racing / Philippe Lorin, Jean Retailleau ; [translated by Rodney McGough]. — St. Albans : Hart-Davis Educational, 1981. — 53p : col.ill,col.ports ; 27cm
Translation from the French
ISBN 0-247-13084-2 : £3.45 B81-24479

Rickard, Graham. A day with a racing driver / Graham Rickard. — Hove : Wayland, 1980. — 55p : ill,ports ; 24cm. — (A Day in the life)
Bibliography: p55
ISBN 0-85340-792-4 : £3.25 B81-02761

796.7′2 — Racing cars. Racing. Races: Grands Prix, *to 1980*

Hodges, David. Grand prix / David Hodges, Doug Nye, Nigel Roebuck ; [illustrated by Jim Bamber ... et al.]. — London : Joseph, 1981. — 224p : ill(some col.),plans(some col.),ports(some col.) ; 35cm
Includes index
ISBN 0-7181-2024-8 : £19.50 B81-41004

796.7′2 — Stock cars. Racing — *Serials*

Stock car reporter : Britain′s newest stock car racing monthly magazine. — Issue no.1 (June 1980)-. — [Manchester] ([338 Liverpool Rd, Eccles, Manchester M30 0RY]) : [Pan Visuals], 1980-. — v. : ill ; 32cm
Continues: Stock car world
ISSN 0260-4515 = Stock car reporter : £0.40 per issue B81-03298

796.7′2′05 — Racing cars. Racing — *Serials*

L′Année automobile. — 28 (80/81). — Lausanne : Edita SA ; [Cambridge] : [Patrick Stephens] [distributor], c1980. — 253p
ISBN 2-88001-094-2 : Unpriced B81-20075

Annuaire du sport automobile / Fédération internationale de l′automobile. — 1981. — Cambridge : Stephens, c1981. — 864p in various pagings
ISBN 0-85059-497-9 : £11.95
ISSN 0144-4964 B81-14356

796.7′2′09 — Cars. Racing, *to 1980*

Setright, L. J. K.. The Pirelli history of motor sport / L.J.K. Setright. — London : Muller, 1981. — 224p : ill(some col.),ports ; 31cm
Includes index
ISBN 0-584-10385-9 : £15.00 : CIP rev.
B81-07923

796.7′2′0924 — Racing cars. Racing. Ascari, Alberto — *Biographies*

Desmond, Kevin. The man with two shadows : the story of Alberto Ascari / Kevin Desmond. — London : Proteus, 1981. — 178p,[8]p of plates : ill,ports ; 24cm
ISBN 0-906071-09-7 : £6.50 B81-18267

796.7′2′0924 — Racing cars. Racing. Dean, Bruce — *Biographies*

Dean, Bruce. Who dares to dream / Bruce Dean. — Bognor Regis : New Horizon, c1979. — 90p,[20]p of plates : ill,ports ; 21cm
ISBN 0-86116-199-8 : £4.25 B81-21718

796.7′2′0924 — Racing cars. Racing. Jones, Alan, *1946-* — *Biographies*

Jones, Alan, *1946-*. Driving ambition / Alan Jones and Keith Botsford. — London : Stanley Paul, 1981. — 170p,[8]p of plates : ill,ports ; 24cm
ISBN 0-09-146240-1 : £6.95 : CIP rev.
B81-19152

796.7′2′0924 — Racing cars. Racing, *to 1979* — *Personal observations*

Moss, Stirling. Racing and all that / Stirling Moss and Mike Hailwood ; edited by John Thompson. — London : Pelham, 1980. — 155p,[16]p of plates : ill,1facsim,ports ; 23cm
ISBN 0-7207-1276-9 : £6.95 : CIP rev.
Also classified at 796.7′5′0924 B80-23630

796.7′2′0941 — Great Britain. Racing cars. Racing — *Serials*

Royal Automobile ClubMotor sport year book / RAC. — 1978. — London (31 Belgrave Sq., SW1X 8QH) : [RAC], [1977?]. — 64p
£2.00 B81-06701

796.7′2′09415 — Ireland. Racing cars. Racing — *Serials*

Irish motorsport yearbook : cars, rallys, racing, trials & karts. — 197?-. — Dublin (22/23 Moore St., Dublin 1) : Sean Graham, 197-?. — ill,ports ; 30cm
Description based on: 1980 issue
Unpriced B81-09136

796.75 — MOTORCYCLE RACING

796.7′5 — Norton motorcycles. Racing, *to 1979*

Holliday, Bob. Norton story / Bob Holliday. — Rev. 2nd ed. — Cambridge : Stephens, 1981. — 128p : ill,map,ports ; 25cm
Previous ed.: i.e. 2nd ed. 1976. — Includes index
ISBN 0-85059-479-0 : £7.95 B81-24278

796.7′5 — Racing motorcycles. Moto-cross — *Manuals*

Canavesio, Aldo. Motocross / [translated] by Alfred Woolf. — [2nd ed. (rev.)] / Aldo Canavesio with Marvi Cinato, Mario Bignamini and Roberto Genesio. — London : Orbis Publishing, 1981. — 128p : ill(some col.),ports ; 30cm
Translation of: Motocross. — Previous ed.: / by Aldo Canavesio. 1978. — Ill on lining papers
ISBN 0-85613-361-2 : £5.95 B81-14526

796.7′5 — Yamaha motorcycles. Racing, *to 1978*

Macauley, Ted. The Yamaha legend / Ted Macauley. — London : Gentry, 1979. — 247p : ill,ports ; 25cm
ISBN 0-85614-057-0 : £8.95 B81-18894

796.7′5′0321 — Racing motorcycles. Racing, *to 1979* — *Encyclopaedias*

Bishop, George, *1917-*. The encyclopedia of motorcycling / George Bishop. — London : Hamlyn, 1980. — 192p : ill(some col.),ports (some col.) ; 32cm. — (A Bison book)
ISBN 0-600-34941-1 : £5.95
ISBN 0-600-34943-8 B81-10299

796.7′5′0924 — Racing motorcycles. Racing, *to 1979* — *Personal observations*

Moss, Stirling. Racing and all that / Stirling Moss and Mike Hailwood ; edited by John Thompson. — London : Pelham, 1980. — 155p,[16]p of plates : ill,1facsim,ports ; 23cm
ISBN 0-7207-1276-9 : £6.95 : CIP rev.
Primary classification 796.7′2′0924 B80-23630

796.7′5′0941 — Great Britain. Motorcycling, *1930-1939*

Currie, Bob. Motor cycling in the 1930s / Bob Currie. — London : Hamlyn, c1981. — 144p : ill(some col.),facsims,ports ; 27cm
Includes index
ISBN 0-600-34931-4 : £6.00 B81-13961

796.7′5′09422145 — Surrey. Weybridge. Racetracks: Brooklands. Racing motorcycles. Racing, *1920-1929*

Mortimer, Charles. Brooklands : behind the scenes / Charles Mortimer. — Yeovil : Haynes, 1980. — 257p : ill,2facsims,ports ; 24cm. — (A Foulis motorcycling book)
ISBN 0-85429-262-4 : £8.95 B81-05094

796.79 — CARAVANNING

796.7′9 — Motor caravanning — *Manuals*

Bradford, Tony. Caravanning / Tony Bradford. — Oxford : Oxford Illustrated Press, 1979. — v,92p : ill ; 26cm
ISBN 0-902280-63-5 : £4.50 B81-41011

796.8 — COMBAT SPORTS

796.8 — Combat sports — *For children*

Kent, Graeme. Fighting sports / Graeme Kent. — London : Macmillan, 1981. — 96p : ill (some col.),ports(some col.) ; 30cm. — (Macmillan feature books)
Includes index
ISBN 0-333-30866-2 : £4.95 B81-40513

796.8 — Martial arts — *Serials*

[Fighters *(Droitwich)*]. Fighters : the martial arts magazine. — Vol.2, no.1 (Jan. 1979)-. — Droitwich (Peterson House, Northbank, Berryhill Industrial Estate, Droitwich, Worcs. WR9 9BL) : Peterson, 1979-. — v. : ill,ports 30cm
Monthly. — Continues: Fighters′ monthly (1977). — Description based on: Vol.3,no.8 (Aug. 1980)
ISSN 0260-4965 = Fighters (Droitwich) : £8.00 per year B81-0281

796.812 — WRESTLING

796.8'123'0924 — Soviet Union. Free-style wrestling — *Personal observations*

Ivanitskiĭ, A.. Sweet slavery / Alexander Ivanitsky ; [translted from the Russian by Barry Jones]. — Moscow : Progress Publishers ; [London] : Central Books [distributor], 1979. — 180p,[32]p of plates : ill,ports ; 18cm. — (Sport and sportsmen)
Translation of: Sladkaia katorga
£1.95 B81-14011

796.815 — JUJITSUS

796.8'15 — Silat perisai diri — *Manuals*

Chambers, Quintin. Javanese silat : the fighting art of Perisai Diri / Quintin Chambers, Donn F. Draeger. — Tokyo : Kodansha International ; Oxford [distributor], 1978. — 128p : ill
Includes index
ISBN 0-87011-353-4 (pbk) : £4.50 B81-09336

796.83 — BOXING

796.8'3'0924 — Boxing. Muhammad Ali — *Biographies — For children*

Butler, Frank. Muhammad Ali / Frank Butler ; illustrated by Mark Taylor. — London : Hamilton, 1981. — 64p : ill,ports ; 22cm. — (Profiles)
ISBN 0-241-10600-1 : £3.25 : CIP rev.
B81-04215

796.8'3'0924 — Boxing. Refereeing. Gibbs, Harry — *Biographies*

Gibbs, Harry. Box on : the autobiography of Harry Gibbs / as told to John Morris. — London : Pelham, 1981. — 155p,[2]p of plates : ports ; 23cm
ISBN 0-7207-1364-1 : £6.95 : CIP rev.
B81-21512

796.8'3'0924 — Boxing. Watt, Jim — *Biographies*

Watt, Jim. Watt's my name : an autobiography / Jim Watt with Norman Giller. — London : Stanley Paul, 1981. — 172p,[12]p of plates : ill,ports ; 23cm
ISBN 0-09-145380-1 : £6.95 B81-15570

796.8'3'0924 — Heavyweight boxing. Championships: Heavyweight Championship of the World, *1938-1980 — Personal observations*

Wilson, Peter, *1913 Aug.29-*. Boxing's greatest prize : memorable fights for the world heavyweight championship / Peter Wilson. — London : Paul, 1980. — 240p,[16]p of plates : ports ; 23cm
ISBN 0-09-143230-8 : £7.95 B81-28581

796.8'3'0973 — United States. Boxing, *to 1980*

Fleischer, Nat. A pictorial history of boxing / by Nat Fleischer and Sam Andre. — Rev. and enlarged ed / rev. and brought up to date by Sam Andre and Nat Loubet. — London : Hamlyn, 1976, c1975 (1981 [printing]). — 384p : ill,facsims,ports ; 28cm
Originally published: Secaucus, N.J. : Citadel Press, 1975. — Includes index
ISBN 0-600-34665-x (pbk) : £4.95 B81-25542

796.86 — FENCING

796.8'6 — Sports: Foil fencing — *Manuals*

Garret, Maxwell R.. Foil fencing : skills, safety operations, and responsibilities for the 1980s / Maxwell R. Garret and Mary Heinecke Poulson ; with a discussion of legal responibility by Steve Sobel. — University Park, [Pa.] ; London : Pennsylvania State University Press, c1981. — 124p : ill,plans,2forms ; 24cm
Bibliography: p113-117. — Includes index
ISBN 0-271-00273-5 : £4.60
ISBN 0-271-00274-3 (pbk) : Unpriced
B81-34541

796.9 — WINTER SPORTS

796.9 — Snow sports — *For children*

Bloom, Andy. Snow sports / Andy Bloom ; colour photographs by All-Sport Limited. — Hove : Wayland, 1981. — 64p : col.ill,col.ports ; 21cm. — (InterSport)
Includes index
ISBN 0-85340-799-1 : £3.95 B81-07559

796.91 — ICE SKATING

796.91 — Ice skating

Bass, Howard. The love of ice skating and speed skating / Howard Bass ; foreword by Robin Cousins. — [London] : Octopus, [1980]. — 96p : col.ill,col.ports ; 33cm
Includes index
ISBN 0-7064-1203-6 : £3.95 B81-00241

796.91 — Ice skating: Figure skating — *Manuals*

Fassi, Carlo. Figure skating with Carlo Fasi / with Gregory Smith ; editorial consultant, Nina Stark ; illustrated by Walt Spitzmuller. — London : Hale, 1981, c1980. — xi,180p : ill ; 28cm
Originally published: New York : Scribner, 1980
ISBN 0-7091-8825-0 : £9.25 B81-14698

796.91 — Ice skating sports — *For children*

Millard, Clive. Ice sports / Clive Millard and Susan Crimp ; colour photographs by All-Sport Limited. — Hove : Wayland, 1980. — 64p : col.ill,col.ports ; 21cm. — (InterSport)
Includes index
ISBN 0-85340-788-6 : £3.75 B81-01767

796.91'06'041 — Great Britain. Ice skating. Organisations: National Skating Association of Great Britain — *Serials*

National Skating Association of Great Britain. Official handbook / National Skating Association of Great Britain. — 1980-81. — London (117 Charterhouse St., EC1M 6AT) : The Association, [1980]. — 157p
£3.00 (free to Association members)
Also classified at 796.2'1'06041 B81-26383

796.91'092'4 — Ice skating: Figure skating. Cousins, Robin — *Biographies*

Cousins, Robin. Skating for gold / Robin Cousins with Howard Bass. — London : Stanley Paul, 1980. — 158p,[4]p of plates : ill,ports(some col.) ; 25cm
ISBN 0-09-143300-2 : £5.95 : CIP rev.
B80-12475

796.93 — SKIING

796.93 — Skiing — *For children*

Gruneberg, Pierre. Skiing / Pierre Gruneberg ; [translated by Penny Hayman] ; [illustrations Dominique Jouenne and Guy Plomion]. — St Albans : Hart-Davis, 1980. — 61p : ill(some col.),2maps,1facsim,ports(some col.) ; 27cm. — (Signposts series)
Translation of: Le ski. — Includes index
ISBN 0-247-13035-4 : £3.50 B81-04501

796.93 — Skiing - *Manuals*

The **Complete** skiing handbook. — 2nd rev. ed. — London : Martin Dunitz, Aug.1981. — [240]p
Translation of: Das Grosse DSV Skihandbuch
ISBN 0-906348-30-7 : £9.95 : CIP entry
B81-19134

796.93'09426 — Eastern England. Skiing — *Proposals*

Eastern Region Ski Association. Ski-ing in the Eastern region : a plan for development / by the Eastern Region Ski Association. — Bedford (26 Bromham Rd., Bedford MK40 2QP) : Sports Council (Eastern Region), [1981?]. — 24p : 1map ; 30cm
'A memorandum to the Eastern Council for Sport and Recreation'
Unpriced (pbk) B81-29876

796.93'097 — North America. Skiing

Covino, Frank. Skier's digest / by Frank Covino. — 2nd ed. — Northfield : DBI Books ; London : Arms and Armour [distributor], c1976. — 288p : ill,ports ; 28cm
Previous ed.: 1972?
ISBN 0-695-80596-7 (pbk) : £4.00 B81-15700

797.1 — BOATING

797.1 — Boating — *Manuals*

Lane, Carl D.. The boatman's manual : a complete manual of boat handling, operation, maintenance and seamanship / by Carl D. Lane ; drawings by the author. — 4th rev. and enl. ed. — New York ; London : W.W. Norton, c1979. — xii,705p : ill(some col.),1map,1facsim ; 19cm
Previous ed.: i.e. Completely rev. ed., published as The new boatman's manual. London : Coles, 1967. — Text, ill on lining papers. — Includes index
ISBN 0-393-03190-x : £11.50
Also classified at 623.8'208 B81-02451

797.1 — Western Europe. Cruising. Organisations: Cruising Association — *Directories — Serials*

Cruising Association. Cruising Association year book. — 1980. — London (Ivory house, St. Katharine Dock E1 9AT) : The Association, 1980. — 249p
B81-06910

Cruising Association. Cruising Association year book. — 1981. — London (Ivory House, St. Katharine Dock, E1 9AT) : The Association, 1981. — 271p
Free to Association members only B81-23134

797.1'03'21 — Boating — *Encyclopaedias*

Noel, John V.. The boating dictionary : sail and power / John V. Noel, Jr. — New York ; London : Van Nostrand Reinhold, 1981. — viii,295p ; 24cm
ISBN 0-442-26048-2 : £12.70 B81-21172

797.1'0941 — Great Britain. Coastal waters. Boating — *Serials*

Boat world. — 1977. — London : Haymarket Publishing, [1977?]. — 794p in various pagings
£3.00 B81-09086

Boat world. — 1979. — London : Haymarket Publishing, [1979]. — 738p in various pagings
£4.50 B81-09089

Boat world. — 1980. — London : Haymarket Publishing, [1980?]. — 846p in various pagings
£5.00 B81-09088

797.1'0941 — Great Britain. Inland waterways. Boating — *Manuals*

Anderson, Janice. Waterway holidays in Britian / Janice Anderson. — London : Thames/Magnum, 1981. — 203p : ill,maps ; 20cm. — (A 'Wish you were here' guide)
ISBN 0-423-00010-1 (pbk) : £1.75 B81-08743

797.1'0973 — United States. Boating — *Manuals*

Herreshoff, L. Francis. The compleat cruiser : the art, practice and enjoyment of boating / by L. Francis Herreshoff ; illustrated by the author. — Havant : Mason, 1981, c1956. — xii,372p : ill,1plan ; 24cm
Originally published: New York : Sheridan House, 1956. — Includes index
ISBN 0-85937-257-x : 7.95 : CIP rev.
B80-19383

797.1'22 — Canoeing — *Manuals*

Davis, Dennis, *1933-*. Canoeing / Dennis Davis. — [Sevenoaks] : Teach Yourself, 1981. — 129p : ill ; 20cm
Bibliography: p123-125. - Includes index
ISBN 0-340-24883-1 (pbk) : £1.75 B81-16344

Mason, Bill. Path of the paddle / Bill Mason. — Toronto ; London : Van Nostrand Reinhold, c1980. — viii,200p : ill(some col.) ; 23x27cm
Bibliography: p196. — Includes index
ISBN 0-442-29630-4 : £14.95 B81-08714

Richards, Gordon. The complete book of canoeing and kayaking / Gordon Richards with Paul Wade ; edited by Ian Dear. — London : Batsford, 1981. — 142p : ill,2maps,1plan,1form,1port ; 26cm
Includes index
ISBN 0-7134-0761-1 : £7.95 B81-37845

797.1′22′06042619 — Norfolk. Rockland St Mary. Canoeing. Clubs: Rockland St Mary Canoe Club, *to 1979*

Millican, K. D.. A Broadland canoe club / K.D. Millican. — Bognor Regis : New Horizon, c1980. — 145p,[8]p of plates : ill ; 22cm
ISBN 0-86116-181-5 : £4.25 B81-20229

797.1′22′09429 — Wales. Rivers. Canoeing — *Inquiry reports*

Sports Council for Wales. River canoeing in Wales / the Sports Council for Wales, Welsh Water Authority. — [Brecon] ([Cambrian Way, Brecon, Powys LD3 7HP]) : The Authority, [1981]. — 66p : ill,maps,1form ; 30cm
Cover title. — Bibliography: p53
Unpriced (pbk) B81-20816

797.1′22′094295 — England. Wye River. Canoeing — *Practical information*

Shoesmith, R.. The canoeists′ guide to the River Wye. — 4th ed / by R. Shoesmith and R. Devitt ; illustrated by S.M. Thurley. — [Brecon] ([Cambrian Way, Brecon, Powys LD3 7HP]) : Welsh Water Authority, 1980. — 27p : ill,col.maps ; 21cm
Previous ed.: Gloucester : British Publishing Co., 1977
ISBN 0-86097-058-2 (pbk) : Unpriced B81-21997

797.1′24 — Mirror dinghies. Sailing — *Manuals*

Partridge, Roy. Sailing the Mirror / Roy Partridge ; photographs by Tim Hore. — London (13 Fernhurst Rd., S.W.6) : Fernhurst Books, 1980. — 64p : ill ; 25cm
ISBN 0-906754-01-1 (pbk) : £4.50 B81-05202

797.1′24 — Oceans. Yachting — *Manuals*

James, Robert A.. Ocean sailing / Robert A. James. — Lymington : Nautical, 1980. — 224p : ill,plans,ports ; 26cm
Includes index
ISBN 0-245-53582-9 : £10.50 B81-04130

797.1′24 — Sailing

Johnson, Peter. Guinness guide to sailing. — Enfield : Guinness, Nov.1981. — [240]p
ISBN 0-85112-216-7 : £11.95 : CIP entry B81-31199

797.1′24 — Sailing boats. Sailing — *Manuals*

Mudie, Colin. Advanced sailboat cruising / Colin Mudie, Geoff Hales, Michael Handford. — London : Nautical, 1981. — 150p : ill(some col.) ; 21cm
Includes index
ISBN 0-333-31807-2 : £9.95 B81-25986

797.1′24 — Sailing dinghies. Sailing — *Manuals*

Milnes Walker, Nicolette. Introduction to dinghy sailing / Nicolette Milnes Walker. — Newton Abbot : David & Charles, c1981. — xi,104p : ill ; 23cm
Bibliography: p102. — Includes index
ISBN 0-7153-8022-2 : £4.95 B81-08703

797.1′24 — Sailing - *Manuals*

The **Complete** sailing handbook. — 2nd rev. ed. — London : Dunitz, July 1981. — [344]p
Translation of: Das Grosse Handbuch des Segelns. — Previous ed.: 1979
ISBN 0-906348-29-3 : £9.95 : CIP entry B81-14977

797.1′24 — Sailing — *Manuals*

Gliewe, Ramon. Welcome on board : a beginner′s guide to sailing / Ramon Gliewe ; translated and adapted by Barbara Webb. — London : Frederick Muller, 1981. — vii,126p : ill ; 23cm
Translation of: Komm mit an Bord. — Includes index
ISBN 0-584-10384-0 (pbk) : £3.95 : CIP rev. B80-20976

Hedges, Martin. The world of sailing / Martin Hedges. — London : Sidgwick & Jackson, 1981. — 192p : ill(some col.),charts(some col.),maps ; 31cm
Includes index
ISBN 0-283-98725-1 : £6.95 B81-28449

797.1′24 — Sweden. Waste materials. Treatment & disposal

Taylor, Glenn. Tackle windsurfing. — London : Paul, July 1981. — [144]p
ISBN 0-09-145040-3 (cased) : £6.50 : CIP entry
ISBN 0-09-145041-1 (pbk) : £3.95 B81-13718

797.1′24 — Wind surfboards. Racing — *Manuals*

Gutjahr, Rainer. Sailboard racing. — London : Macmillan, Oct.1981. — [120]p
Translation of: Das ist Regatta-Surfen
ISBN 0-333-32213-4 : £7.95 : CIP entry B81-27359

797.1′24 — Wind surfing — *Manuals*

Fuller, Graeme. Let′s go windsurfing / text by Graeme Fuller ; edited by Jim Miles ; illustrations by René Deynis. — London : Octopus, 1981. — 77p : col.ill ; 31cm
Ill on lining papers. — Includes index
ISBN 0-7064-1612-0 : £2.95 B81-20278

Gadd, Mike. The book of windsurfing : a guide to freesailing techniques / Mike Gadd, John Boothroyd, Ann Durrell. — Toronto ; London : Van Nostrand Reinhold, c1980. — 128p : ill (some col.) ; 28cm
Includes index
ISBN 0-442-29729-7 (pbk) : £7.45 B81-01083

Gadd, Mike. The book of windsurfing : a guide to freesailing techniques / Mike Gadd, John Boothroyd, Ann Durrell. — London : Ward Lock, 1981. — 128p : ill(some col.) ; 29cm
Originally published: Toronto : London : Van Nostrand Reinhold, 1980. — Includes index
ISBN 0-7063-6142-3 (pbk) : £2.95 B81-39902

Heath, John, *1944-*. Boardsailing / John Heath ; photographs by Tim Hore. — London : 13 Fernhurst Rd., S.W.6 : Fernhurst, 1981. — 47p : ill ; 25cm
ISBN 0-906754-02-x (pbk) : £2.95 B81-22136

Stickl, Niko. Windsurfing technique. — London : Stanford Maritime, July 1981. — [180]p
Translation of: Windsurfing-Technik
ISBN 0-540-07407-1 : £9.95 : CIP entry B81-14374

797.1′24 — Wind surfing — *Serials*

Board sailing. — No.1 (May 1980)-. — London (34 Buckingham Palace Rd, SW1W 0Re) : Ocean Publications, 1980-. — v. : ill ; 28cm
Monthly. — Description based on: No.9 (May 1981)
ISSN 0261-7447 = Board sailing : £11.00 per year B81-33280

797.1′24 — Yachting

Street, Donald M. (Donald Macqueen), *1930-*. Seawise / Donald M. Street, Jr. — New York ; London : Norton, c1979. — 320p : ill,charts,maps,2plans ; 24cm
Includes index
ISBN 0-393-03232-9 : £9.25 B81-03483

797.1′24 — Yachts. Cruising — *Manuals*

Bond, Bob, *19---*. Cruising / Bob Bond ; illustrations by Dick Everitt. — London : Hodder and Stoughton, 1981. — 182p : ill ; 20cm. — (Teach yourself books)
Bibliography: p177. - Includes index
ISBN 0-340-24791-6 (pbk) : £1.95 B81-21813

797.1′24′0321 — Sailing — *Encyclopaedias*

Shuwall, Melissa. [Running Press glossary of sailing language]. The language of sailing / Melissa Shuwall. — [London] : W.H. Allen, 1981, c1977. — [87]p : ill ; 20cm. — (A Star book)
Originally published: Philadelphia : Running Press, 1977
ISBN 0-352-30944-x (pbk) : £1.50 B81-35606

797.1′24′06041 — Great Britain. Yachting. Clubs — *Directories* — *Serials*

United Kingdom yacht clubs / [Data Research Group]. — [1981]. — Great Missenden : The Group, 1981. — 49leaves
ISBN 0-86099-320-5 : Unpriced B81-29069

797.1′24′060426 — East Anglia. Yachting. Organisations: Royal Norfolk and Suffolk Yacht Club, *to 1979*

Royal Norfolk and Suffolk Yacht Club. 120 years of sailing : the story of the Royal Norfolk and Suffolk Yacht Club / by Charles Goodey. — Lowestoft (Royal Plain, Lowestoft, Suffolk) : The Club, 1980. — 27p,[8]p of plates : ill,1port ; 22cm
Unpriced (pbk) B81-15042

797.1′24′076 — Great Britain. Yachtmasters. Competence. Certification. Examinations set by Royal Yachting Association. Techniques

Fairhall, David. Pass your yachtmaster′s. — London : Macmillan London, Jan.1982. — [104]p
ISBN 0-333-31957-5 : £5.95 : CIP entry B81-34142

797.1′24′0922 — New Zealand. Yachting — *Personal observations* — *Collections*

Before the wind : a New Zealand yachting anthology / compiled by Lorris Chilwell. — Wellington ; London : A.H. & A.W. Reed, 1979. — x,216p,[24]p of plates : ill,1map,ports ; 25cm
Ill on lining papers. — Includes index
ISBN 0-589-01106-5 : £10.75 B81-35363

797.1′24′0924 — Sailing boats. Sailing. Coles, K. Adlard — *Liographies*

Coles, K. Adlard. Sailing years : an autobiography / K. Adlard Coles. — London : Adlard Coles, 1981. — xi,212p : ill,maps,plans,ports ; 26cm
Includes index
ISBN 0-229-11658-2 : £9.95 B81-28943

797.1′25′09422 — England. Thames River. Thames Conservancy reaches. Motorboating — *Regulations* — *Serials*

Thames Water Authority. *Thames Conservancy Division*. Launch digest. — 1981. — Reading (Nugent House, Vastern Rd, Reading RG1 8DB) : Thames Water Authority, 1981. — 49p
Unpriced B81-30841

797.1′4 — England. Solent. Yachts. Racing — *Serials*

Solent year book / Solent Cruising & Racing Association. — 1980/81. — Newport, Isle of Wight (29 High St., Newport, Isle of Wight) : Isle of Wight County Press under the auspices of the Association, c1980. — 318p in various pagings
£1.20 B81-14530

797.1′4 — North Atlantic Ocean. Sailing ships. Racing. Races: Tall Ships Race, *1980* — *Personal observations*

Hollins, Holly. The tall ships are sailing. — Newton Abbot : David & Charles, Jan.1982. — [192]p
ISBN 0-7153-8028-1 : £9.50 : CIP entry B81-3385.

797.1′4 — Yachts. Racing. Races: Nedlloyd Spice Race *(1980)*

Pickthall, Barry. To beat the clipper ships : the story of the Nedlloyd Spice Race / Barry Pickthall. — Glasgow : Brown, Son & Ferguson, 1980. — 127p : ill(some col.),charts,maps,ports ; 31cm
ISBN 0-85174-394-3 : £9.90 B81-2449.

797.1′4 — Yachts. Racing. Rules: International Yacht Racing Union. Yacht racing rules. 1981-1984 — *Texts with commentaries*

Elvström, Paul. Paul Elvström explains — the yacht racing rules : 1981 rules. — Rev. and re-set / edited by Jonathan Bradbeer. — Lymington (7 Station St., Lymington) : Creagh-Osborne, 1981. — 137p : ill(some col.) ; 20cm + 1model(plastic,col ; 12x6cm in pocket 13x7cm)
ISBN 0-229-11660-4 (pbk) : £4.25 B81-2522

Twiname, Eric. The rules book : the 1981-84 International yacht racing rules explained / Eric Twiname. — 2nd ed. / revised by Gerald Sambrooke-Sturgess. — London : Granada, 1981. — 156p : ill ; 19cm
Previous ed.: London : Adlard Coles, 1977
ISBN 0-229-11659-0 (pbk) : £3.95 B81-2522

797.1′4′091631 — North Atlantic Ocean. Yachts. Racing. Races: Observer Singlehanded Transatlantic Race, *to 1980*

Page, Frank, *1930-*. Alone against the Atlantic : the story of The Observer Singlehanded Transatlantic Race 1960-80 / by Frank Page. — London (8 St Andrew's Hill, EC4V 5JA) : The Observer Limited, c1980. — 125p : ill (some col.),col.maps,ports(some col.) ; 28cm
Includes index
ISBN 0-9507034-1-9 : £8.95 B81-24401

797.1′4′0916336 — England. Solent. Yachts. Racing — *Serials*

Solent year book / Solent Cruising & Racing Association. — 1981/82. — Newport (29 High St., Newport, Isle of Wight) : Isle of Wight County Press, c1981. — 322p in various pagings
£1.20 B81-29429

797.1′4′0924 — Great Britain. Coastal waters. Yachts. Racing. Races: Fastnet Yacht Race *(1979) — Personal observations*

Gardner, L. T.. Fastnet '79 : the story of Ailish III / L.T. Gardner. — London : Godwin, 1979. — 102p,[20]p of plates : ill(some col.),1map ; 23cm
ISBN 0-7114-5582-1 : £4.95 : CIP rev. B79-34394

797.1′4′0924 — Great Britain. Coastal waters. Yachts. Racing. Races: Fastnet Yacht Race, *to 1979 — Personal observations*

Dear, Ian. Fastnet : the story of a great ocean race / Ian Dear. — London : Batsford, 1981. — 192p : ill,2maps,plan,ports ; 26cm : pbk
Includes index
ISBN 0-7134-0997-5 : £9.95 B81-33446

797.1′4′0942579 — Oxfordshire. Henley-on-Thames. Thames River. Rowing boats. Racing. Regattas: Henley Royal Regatta, *to 1980*

Dodd, Christopher. Henley Royal Regatta / Christopher Dodd. — London : Stanley Paul, 1981. — 253p,[16]p of plates : ill,2maps,1facsim,ports ; 24cm
Bibliography: p235-237. — Includes index
ISBN 0-09-145160-4 : £9.95 : CIP rev. B81-04259

797.1′72 — Surfing — *Manuals*

McGinness, Laurie. Surfing fundamentals / text by Laurie McGinness ; photographs by Peter Crawford ; additional photographs by Laurie McGinness and Neil Campbell. — Sydney ; London (11 Southampton Row, [WC2]) : A.H. & A.W. Reed, 1978. — 80p : ill(some col.) ; 26cm
ISBN 0-589-50055-4 : £5.35 B81-37366

797.2 — SWIMMING AND DIVING

797.2 — Swimming & diving — *For children*

Duffy, Tony. Swimming and diving / Tony Duffy ; colour photographs by Tony Duffy, All-Sport Limited. — Hove : Wayland, 1981. — 64p : col.ill,col.ports ; 21cm
Includes index
ISBN 0-85340-796-7 : £3.95 B81-07552

797.2′006′041 — Great Britain. Swimming & diving. Organisations: Amateur Swimming Association — *Serials*

Amateur Swimming Association[Handbook *(Amateur Swimming Association)]*. Handbook / Amateur Swimming Association. — 1980. — Loughborough : Amateur Swimming Association, [1980]. — 786p in various pagings
£3.00 B81-09194

797.2′1 — Swimming — *Manuals*

Gorton, Eddie. Swimming. — London : Batsford, Feb.1982. — [64]p. — (Competitive sports series)
ISBN 0-7134-4079-1 : £5.95 : CIP entry B81-37575

797.2′3 — Scuba diving — *Manuals*

Deakin, Joan. Scuba diving / Joan Deakin. — Newton Abbot : David & Charles, c1981. — 160p : ill ; 23cm
Bibliography: p155-156. - Includes index
ISBN 0-7153-7952-6 : £4.95 B81-20807

797.2′3′05 — Recreations: Underwater diving — *Manuals — Serials*

Diving manual / the British Sub-Aqua Club. — 10th ed., 3rd revise (1980). — London (70 Brompton Rd, SW3 1HA) : The Club, 1980. — x,573p
Spine title: BSAC diving manual
ISBN 0-9506786-1-9 : Unpriced B81-27324

797.2′4 — Diving — *Manuals*

Gray, Jennifer, *1950-*. Better diving / by Jennifer Gray ; photographs by Gary Gray. — London : Kaye & Ward, 1981. — 96p : ill ; 23cm
ISBN 0-7182-1473-0 : £3.95 B81-33345

797.2′5 — Water polo — *Manuals*

Barr, David, *1934-*. Water polo / David Barr & Andrew Gordon. — Wakefield : E.P., 1980. — 112p : ill,plan ; 21cm. — (EP sport)
Bibliography: p112
ISBN 0-7158-0684-x : £4.95 B81-33662

797.5 — AIR SPORTS

797.5 — Great Britain. Ballooning. Organisations: British Balloon and Airship Club — *Directories — Serials*

British Balloon and Airship Club. Directory of members / the British Balloon and Airship Club. — 1981. — Leicester (Kimberley House, Vaughan Way, Leicester LE1 4SG) : The Club, [1981]. — 24p
ISSN 0261-8842 : Unpriced B81-35460

797.5 — Light aircraft. Rallying — *Manuals*

Fenton, J. H.. An introduction to air rallying / J.H. Fenton. — Shrewsbury : Airlife, [1981?]. — 62p : ill,charts ; 19cm
ISBN 0-906393-09-4 : Unpriced B81-39166

797.5′2 — Seaplanes. Competitions: Coupe d'aviation maritime Jacques Schneider *(Contest), to 1931*

James, Derek N.. Schneider Trophy aircraft 1913-1931 / Derek N. James. — London : Putnam, 1981. — xiv,304p : ill,ports ; 23cm
Bibliography: p300-301. — Includes index
ISBN 0-370-30328-8 : £12.50 : CIP rev. B81-21626

797.5′4 — Aerobatics — *Manuals*

Williams, Neil, *1934-*. Aerobatics / Neil Williams ; illustrated by L.R. Williams. — Shrewsbury : Airlife, 1975 (1979 [printing]). — 266p : ill ; 22cm
ISBN 0-9504543-0-3 : £7.95 B81-39359

797.5′4′0924 — United States. Light aircraft. Stunt flying — *Personal observations*

Bach, Richard. Nothing by chance : a gypsy pilot's adventures in modern America / Richard Bach ; photographs by Paul E. Hansen. — London : Granada, 1981, c1969. — 220p,[8]p of plates : ill ; 18cm. — (A panther book)
Originally published: New York : Morrow, 1969
ISBN 0-586-05313-1 (pbk) : £1.25 B81-37171

797.5′5 — Recreations: Hang gliding — *Manuals*

Welch, Ann. Soaring hang gliders / Ann Welch and Roy Hill. — London : Murray, 1981. — 160p : ill ; 19cm
Includes index
ISBN 0-7195-3812-2 (pbk) : £5.95 : CIP rev. B81-03832

798 — EQUESTRIAN SPORTS AND ANIMAL RACING

798 — Equestrian sports — *For children*

White-Thomson, Stephen. On horseback / Stephen White-Thomson ; colour photographs by All-Sport Limited. — Hove : Wayland, 1981. — 64p : col.ill,col.ports ; 21cm. — (InterSport)
Includes index
ISBN 0-85340-798-3 : £3.95 B81-07557

798 — Equestrian sports — *Manuals*

Gordon, Sally. The illustrated encyclopaedia of equestrian sports. — London : Pelham, Nov.1981. — [208]p
ISBN 0-7207-1373-0 : £9.95 : CIP entry B81-30393

798′.025′41 — Great Britain. Equestrian sports — *Directories — Serials*

British equestrian directory. — 1981. — Bramham (Wothersome Grange, Bramham, Nr. Wetherby, W. Yorkshire LS23 6LY) : Equestrian Management Consultants, 1981. — 472p
ISBN 0-907029-01-9 : £7.95
ISSN 0144-7203 B81-23492

798′.05 — Equestrian sports — *Serials*

Equestrian year. — 1980-81-. — Richmond, Surrey (1 Church Terrace, Richmond, Surrey TW10 6SE) : Hazleton Pub., 1980-. — v. : ill ; 32cm
Annual
ISSN 0260-8111 = Equestrian year : £11.95 B81-09084

798′092′4 — Great Britain. Equestrian sports. Llewellyn, Harry — *Biographies*

Llewellyn, Harry. Passports to life : journeys into many worlds / Harry Llewellyn ; arranged in conjunction with Pat Lucas. — London : Hutchinson, 1980. — 261p,[6]p of plates : ill,maps,ports ; 25cm
Includes index
ISBN 0-09-143360-6 : £7.95 B81-03426

798.2 — HORSEMANSHIP

798.2 — Horsemanship

Burn, Barbara. [The horseless rider]. A guide to riding, showing and enjoying other people's horses / Barbara Burn ; drawings by Werner Rentsch. — Newton Abbot : David & Charles, c1980. — 221p : ill ; 23cm
Originally published: New York : St. Martin's Press, 1979. — Includes index
ISBN 0-7153-8009-5 : £7.95 : CIP rev. B80-13509

798.2 — Horsemanship — *Amateurs' manuals*

Appleton, John, *1905-*. The horse and pony handbook / John Appleton ; illustrated by Walter Stackpool. — Rev. ed. — London : Angus & Robertson, 1980. — 163p : ill ; 24cm
Previous ed.: 1972. — Ill on lining papers. — Bibliography: p159
ISBN 0-207-14002-2 : £4.95 B81-00242

Gordon, Sally. The rider's handbook / Sally Gordon. — Leicester : Windward, [1980]. — 224p : ill(some col.) ; 28cm. — (A Quarto book)
Includes index
ISBN 0-7112-0031-9 : £7.95 B81-02629

798.2′3 — Horsemanship: Dressage. Manuals — *Critical studies*

Harris, Charles. Riding & dressage : critical reviews with quotes & constructive comments / Charles Harris. — London (9 Skelwith Rd., W6 9EX) : C. Harris, 1981. — xvii,182p : ill ; 19cm
Unpriced (pbk) B81-11551

798.2′3 — Horsemanship: Dressage — *Serials*

Horse & driving : [heavy horses, driving and dressage]. — 3rd year, no.2 (Summer 1979)-. — Bradford : Watmoughs, 1979-. — v. : ill ; 30cm
Quarterly (Summer 1979/Summer 1980), Six issues yearly (Sept./Oct.1980-). — Continues: Heavy horse & driving. — Description based on: 4th year, no.3 (Sept./Oct.1980)
ISSN 0142-7008 = Horse & driving : £13.50 per year
Primary classification 636.1′5 B81-00973

798.2′3 — Livestock: Horses. Riding. Dressage — *Manuals*

Herbermann, Erik F.. The dressage formula / Erik F. Herbermann ; foreword by Egon von Neindorff. — London : J.A. Allen, 1980. — 111p : ill ; 24cm
ISBN 0-85131-348-5 : £5.95 : CIP rev. B80-01711

Marshall, Leonie. Novice to advanced dressage. — London : J.A. Allen, Nov.1981. — [140]p
ISBN 0-85131-373-6 (pbk) : £3.00 : CIP entry B81-34964

798.2´3 — Livestock: Horses. Riding — *For children*

Henrie, Fiona. Let´s go horse riding / Fiona Henrie ; general editor Henry Pluckrose ; photography by Marc Henrie. — London : Watts, c1981. — 32p : col.ill ; 22cm. — (Let´s go series)
ISBN 0-85166-937-9 : £2.99 B81-29194

798.2´3 — Livestock: Horses. Riding — *Manuals*

Hedlund, Gunnar. This is riding : dressage, jumping, eventing in words and pictures / Gunnar Hedlund ; translated by Sigrid Young ; foreword by Elwyn Hartley Edwards. — London : Harrap, 1981. — 143p : ill(some col.) ; 25cm
Translation of: Detta är ridning. — Includes index
ISBN 0-245-53766-x : £6.95 B81-28412

Knox-Thompson, Elaine. Guide to riding and horse care / Elaine Knox-Thompson, Suzanne Dickens. — Rev. and repr. — London : Orbis Publishing, 1980 (1981 [printing]). — 158p : ill ; 27cm
Previous ed.: Auckland : Paul Hamlyn, 1977. — Ill on lining papers. — Includes index
ISBN 0-85613-319-1 : £5.95
Also classified at 636.1´083 B81-23539

798.2´3 — Livestock: Horses. Riding — *Manuals* — *For children*

Drew, Richard. Riding for beginners / Richard and Lavinia Drew ; special photography by Mary Thomas. — Glasgow : Collins, [1980]. — 45p : col.ill ; 29cm
Col. ill on lining papers
ISBN 0-00-138305-1 : £2.95 B81-03620

Owen, Robert, *1918-*. Learning to ride / Robert Owen. — Richmond upon Thames : Country Life Books ; London : Distributed by Hamlyn, 1980. — 111p : ill(some col.) ; 25cm
Includes index
ISBN 0-600-35576-4 : £5.95 B81-15131

Owen, Robert, *1918-*. The young rider / Robert Owen and John Bullock ; illustrated by James Val, Christine Bousfield and Denis Manton. — London : Hamlyn, 1981, c1977. — 143p : ill ; 18cm. — (Beaver books)
Originally published: London : Country Life Books, 1977
ISBN 0-600-20303-4 (pbk) : £0.95 B81-15134

798.2´3 — Livestock: Ponies. Riding — *Manuals* — *For children*

Allen, Jane, *1942-*. Hello to riding / Jane Allen and Mary Danby ; illustrated by Alison Prince. — London : Heinemann, 1980. — 127p : ill ; 21cm
Includes index
ISBN 0-434-92701-5 : £3.95 B81-03540

798.2´3´07 — Livestock: Horses. Riding. Teaching — *Manuals*

Mortimer, Monty. The riding instructor´s handbook / Monty Mortimer. — Newton Abbot : David & Charles, c1981. — 158p : ill,ports ; 23cm
Includes index
ISBN 0-7153-8102-4 : £6.95 B81-33004

798.2´3´071041 — Great Britain. Riding schools. Organisations: Association of British Riding Schools — *Serials*

Association of British Riding Schools. Official handbook / Association of British Riding Schools. — [1981]. — Sawtry (7 Deer Park Rd, Sawtry, Huntingdon, Cambridgeshire PE17 5TT) : The Association, [1981?]. — 92p
ISSN 0260-4469 : £1.50 B81-24152

798.2´3´0924 — Livestock: Horses. Riding — *Personal observations*

McKenna, Christine. Why didn´t they tell the horses? / Christine McKenna ; instruction and commentary by Sue Turner ; illustrated by Mike Peyton ; photographs by Yuon Dorual. — Harmondsworth : Puffin, 1981. — 140p,[8]p of plates : ill,ports ; 18cm
ISBN 0-14-031453-9 (pbk) : £0.95 B81-33610

798.2´4 — Eventing

Baird, Eric. Horse trials / Eric Baird ; illustrated by Heather Sherratt. — London : Teach Yourself, 1980. — 149p,[8]p of plates : ill,ports ; 20cm. — (Teach yourself books)
Includes index
ISBN 0-340-24881-5 (pbk) : £1.50 B81-01643

798.2´4 — Riding competitions: Dressage

Kidd, Jane. A festival of dressage. — London : Stanley Paul, Oct.1981. — 1v.
ISBN 0-09-146190-1 : £7.95 : CIP entry B81-26801

798.2´4´05 — Riding competitions — *Serials*

Pelham horse year. — [No.1]-. — London : Pelham Books in association with Lloyds Bank, 1981-. — v. ; 23cm
Annual
ISSN 0261-300x = Pelham horse year : £6.95 B81-25002

798.2´5 — Show jumping — *Manuals*

Bradley, Caroline. Showjumping with Caroline Bradley / Caroline Bradley and Janet Taylor. — London : Pelham, 1981. — 144p : ill,ports ; 22cm
Includes index
ISBN 0-7207-1247-5 : £6.95 : CIP rev. B81-14902

Draper, Judith. Show jumping / Judith Draper ; illustrated by Vanessa Pancheri. — Sevenoaks : Hodder and Stoughton, 1981. — viii,181p : ill ; 20cm. — (Teach Yourself books)
Bibliography: p175. — Includes index
ISBN 0-340-25108-5 (pbk) : £1.95 : CIP rev. B81-00243

798.2´5´0924 — Show jumping. Broome, David — *Biographies*

Broome, David. Twenty-five years in show jumping / David Broome with Brian Giles ; foreword by Sir Harry Llewellyn. — London : Stanley Paul, 1981. — 124p,[4]p of plates : ill (some col.),ports ; 25cm
Includes index
ISBN 0-09-144410-1 : £6.50 B81-11561

798.2´5´0924 — Show jumping. Gittins, Jack — *Biographies*

Macgregor-Morris, Pamela. Jack Gittins - master horseman / Pamela Macgregor-Morris. — London : Paul, 1980. — 159p,[12]p of plates : ill,ports ; 24cm
Includes index
ISBN 0-09-141640-x : £9.95 : CIP rev. B80-04921

798.2´5´09417 — Ireland *(Republic)*. **Show jumping** — *Serials*

Irish showjumping annual. — 1978-. — Dublin (22, Moore St., Dublin 1) : Ree Enterprises, 1978-. — v. : ill,ports ; 30cm
Description based on: 1980
Unpriced B81-06631

798.4 — HORSE RACING

798.4 — Racehorses. Racing

Horse racing : the complete guide to the world of the turf / [advisory editor Ivor Herbert]. — London : Collins, 1980. — 256p : ill(some col.),maps(some col.),ports(some col.) ; 33cm
Includes index
ISBN 0-00-411649-6 : £15.00 B81-00244

798.4´009 — Racehorses. Racing, *to 1980*

Churchill, Peter, *1933-*. Horse racing / Peter Churchill. — Poole : Blandford, 1981. — 169p : ill(some col.),plans,ports(some col.) ; 20cm
Includes index
ISBN 0-7137-1016-0 (cased) : £4.95
ISBN 0-7137-1115-9 (pbk) : £2.95 B81-15398

798.4´00941 — Great Britain. Racehorses. Racing — *Serials*

Horse racing. — 1981. — London : Queen Anne Press in association with William Hill, c1981. — 222p
ISBN 0-362-02029-9 : £6.95
ISSN 0309-6769 B81-23154

Owners. — Vol.1, no.1 (Oct.1980)-. — Eton (50 High St., Eton, Berkshire) : Whitton Press, 1980-. — v. : ill,ports ; 30cm
Six issues yearly
ISSN 0260-1435 = Owners : £18 per year B81-05533

Ruff's guide to the turf and the Sporting Life annual. — 1981. — London : Mirror Books, [1980?]. — xix,500p
ISBN 0-85939-234-1 : £25.00 B81-12430

798.4´01´0941 — Great Britain. Racehorses. Racing. Betting. Winnings — *Tables*

Raper, Michael. The racing ready reckoner / compiled by Michael Raper and Graham Sharpe. — London : Pan, 1981. — 127p ; 18cm
ISBN 0-330-26421-4 (pbk) : £0.80 B81-20984

798.4´3 — Flat racing. Classic races. Racehorses

Willett, Peter. The Classic racehorse. — London : Stanley Paul, Sept.1981. — 1v.
ISBN 0-09-146110-3 : £9.95 : CIP entry B81-20582

798´.4´30924 — Flat racing. Jockeys: Piggott, Lester - *Biographies*

Lawton, James. Lester Piggott. — Sevenoaks : Hodder & Stoughton, June 1981. — [176]p
Originally published: London : Barker, 1980
ISBN 0-340-26669-4 (pbk) : £1.25 : CIP entry B81-09990

798.4´3´0924 — Great Britain. Flat racing. Jockeys: Baird, George Alexander — *Biographies*

Onslow, Richard. The Squire : a life of George Alexander Baird gentleman rider 1861-1893 / Richard Onslow. — London : Harrap, 1980. — x,178p,[16]p of plates : ill ; 24cm
Ill on lining papers. — Bibliography: p165. — Includes index
ISBN 0-245-53612-4 : £8.95 B81-02403

798.4´3´0941 — Great Britain. Flat racing

Hislop, John. From start to finish : first steps to flat-race riding / John Hislop ; foreword by Sir Gordon Richards ; illustrations by John Skeaping. — 2nd ed. rev. and reset. — London : J.A. Allen, 1980. — 249p : ill,plans,ports ; 22cm
Previous ed.: London : Hutchinson, 1958
ISBN 0-85131-265-9 : £6.95 B81-05245

798.4´3´0941 — Great Britain. Flat racing racehorses — *Performance records* — *Serials*

Racehorses. — 1980. — Halifax : Portway Press, 1981. — 1036p
ISBN 0-900599-31-6 : £30.00 B81-21928

798.4´3´0941 — Great Britain. Flat racing racehorses — *Records of achievement* — *Serials*

100 winners for .... — 1981. — London (55 Curzon St., W1) : The Racehorse, [1981?]. — 48p
£1.25 B81-31897

798.4´3´0941 — Great Britain. Flat racing. Races — *Calendars* — *Serials*

Programmes of flat meetings under the rules of racing. — 1981. — [London] ([42 Portman Sq. W1]) : Jockey Club, c1981. — lxxxi,465p
£14.00 B81-16257

798.4´3´0941 — Great Britain. Flat racing — *Technical data* — *For betting* — *Serials*

Trackwise. — ´81-. — Manchester (Thomson House, Manchester M60 4BJ) : Sporting Chronicle Publications, 1981-. — v. : ill ; 11cm
Annual
ISSN 0261-5223 = Trackwise : £2.00 B81-30826

798.4´3´0941 — Great Britain. Racehorses. Racing

Craig, Dennis. Horse-racing. — 4th ed., rev. — London : J.A. Allen, Dec.1981. — [200]p
Previous ed.: 1963
ISBN 0-85131-357-4 : £9.95 : CIP entry B81-31508

798.4′5 — Great Britain. Point-to-point horses — *Lists — Serials*

Horse and hound hunter chasers and point-to-pointers. — 1981. — London : IPC Magazines, [1981]. — 553p
ISBN 0-85037-507-x : £8.50 B81-10244

798.4′5 — Steeplechasing horses: Monksfield

Powell, Jonathan, *1945-*. Monksfield / Jonathan Powell ; foreword by Brough Scott. — Tadworth : World′s Work, c1980. — 224p : ill,facsims,ports ; 25cm
ISBN 0-437-12800-8 : £6.95 B81-02287

798.4′5′0922 — National Hunt racing. British jockeys

Lee, Alan, *1954-*. Jump jockeys / Alan Lee with Jeff King. — London : Ward Lock, 1980. — 159p : ill,ports ; 23cm
ISBN 0-7063-6064-8 : £5.95 B81-01084

798.4′5′0924 — Great Britain. National Hunt racing. Champion, Bob — *Biographies*

Champion, Bob. Champion′s story : a great human triumph / by Bob Champion and Jonathan Powell. — London : Gollancz, 1981. — 216p,24p of plates : ports ; 23cm
Ill on lining papers. — Includes index
ISBN 0-575-03019-4 : £5.95 B81-40162

798.4′5′0924 — National Hunt racing. Jockeys: Brogan, Barry — *Biographies*

Brogan, Barry. The Barry Brogan story : in his own words. — London : Arthur Barker, c1981. — viii,208p,[8]p of plates : ports ; 23cm
ISBN 0-213-16745-x : £5.95 B81-05104

798.4′5′0941 — Great Britain. National Hunt racehorses — *Records of achievement — Serials*

Chasers & hurdlers. — 1979/80. — Halifax : Portway Press, c1980. — 900p
ISBN 0-900599-30-8 : £26.00 B81-00245

798.4′5′0941 — Great Britain. Racehorses. Racing. National Hunt races. Winners: Racehorses. Dams *— Lists — Serials*

Dams of national hunt winners. — 1975/1977. — London : J.A. Allen, 1979. — [230]p
ISBN 0-85131-342-6 : £7.50 : CIP rev.
B79-30280

Dams of national hunt winners. — 1977/1978. — London : J.A. Allen, 1979. — [176]p
ISBN 0-85131-347-7 : £5.50 : CIP rev.
B79-35462

798.4′5′0941 — Great Britain. Steeplechasing, *1979-1980 — Illustrations*

Byrne, Ed. Ed Byrne′s racing year. — Bridport (Melplash, Bridport, Dorset DT6 3UH) : Trainers Record, c1980. — 192p : chiefly ill (some col.),ports(some col.) ; 22x31cm
ISBN 0-907441-00-9 (cased) : £22.00
ISBN 0-907441-01-7 (Limited ed.) : Unpriced
B81-40165

798.6 — DRIVING AND COACHING

798′.6 — Livestock: Horses. Driving

Hart, Edward. The harness horse / Edward Hart. — Princes Risborough : Shire, 1981. — 32p ; 21cm. — (Shire album ; 53)
ISBN 0-85263-504-4 (pbk) : £0.95 B81-40860

798′.6 — Livestock: Horses. Driving — *Manuals*

Norris, Anne. Driving : how to drive and how not to drive / by Anne Norris and Caroline Douglas ; photographs by Charles Curtis. — London : J.A. Allen, 1981. — 28p : chiefly ill ; 25cm
ISBN 0-85131-368-x (pbk) : £2.50 : CIP rev.
B81-21543

Pape, Max. The art of driving. — London : J.A. Allen, Sept.1981. — [192]p
Translation of: Die Kunst des Fahrens
ISBN 0-85131-339-6 : £15.00 : CIP entry
B81-23787

798′.6′05 — Livestock: Horses. Driving — *Serials*

Horse & driving : [heavy horses, driving and dressage]. — 3rd year, no.2 (Summer 1979)-. — Bradford : Watmoughs, 1979-. — v. : ill ; 30cm
Quarterly (Summer 1979/Summer 1980), Six issues yearly (Sept./Oct.1980-). — Continues: Heavy horse & driving. — Description based on: 4th year, no.3 (Sept./Oct.1980)
ISSN 0142-7008 = Horse & driving : £13.50 per year
Primary classification 636.1′5 B81-00973

798.8 — RACING ANIMALS OTHER THAN HORSES

798′.8 — Racing pigeons. Racing

Aerts, Jan. Pigeon racing : advanced techniques / by Jan Aerts ; translated by Inge Moore. — London : Faber, 1969 (1981 [printing]). — 189p ; 20cm
Translation of: Duivensport op hoger plan
ISBN 0-571-11572-1 (pbk) : £2.50 B81-13041

799 — FIELD SPORTS

799 — Field sports — *Stories, anecdotes*

Cameron, Ewen. Just for fun / Ewen Cameron. — [Blanefield] ([Auchineden, Blanefield, by Glasgow]) : [E. Cameron], c1980. — 81p : ill,ports ; 21cm
Unpriced (pbk) B81-05831

799.1 — RECREATIONS. FISHING

799.1′025′41 — Great Britain. Angling — *Directories*

Where to fish. — 1982-1983. — London : Harmsworth, Sept.1981. — [476]p
ISBN 0-7136-2180-x : £7.95 : CIP entry
B81-22532

799.1′0941 — Great Britain. Angling waters — *Visitors′ guides*

A **Regional** guide to fishing in Britain. — London : Marshall Cavendish, 1979. — 317p : ill(some col.),col.maps ; 23cm
Originally published: in Fisherman′s handbook. — Ill on lining papers. — Includes index
ISBN 0-85685-696-7 : £4.95 B81-18728

799.1′1′0924 — Great Britain. Rivers. Freshwater angling — *Personal observations*

Kenson, Harry. Tales of a dedicated fisherman / by Harry Kenson. — Harrow : Eureditions, 1978. — 119p ; 21cm
ISBN 0-906204-10-0 : Unpriced B81-26666

799.1′1′0941 — Great Britain. Freshwater angling *— Practical information*

Fisherman′s mirror : tackle - tips - tactics : - a great haul of news and views for the start of the season! / [compiled] by Terry Smith. — London : Mirror Books for Mirror Group Newspapers, 1981. — 26p : ill(some col.),1map,ports ; 37cm
"A 'Daily mirror' fishing special". — One sheet (ill) as insert
ISBN 0-85939-255-4 (unbound) : £0.50
B81-31138

799.1′1′094121 — Scotland. Grampian Region. Freshwater angling — *Practical information*

Fishing in Grampian Region. — Aberdeen (Woodhill House, Ashgrove Rd., West, Aberdeen) : Department of Leisure, Recreation & Tourism, Grampian Regional Council, [1981?]. — 18p : 1ill,1map ; 15x22cm
Map on cover. — Includes index
£0.35 (pbk) B81-25505

799.1′1′094132 — Scotland. Lothian Region. Freshwater angling — *Practical information*

Priestley, Graham. Angling in the Lothians : a commentary and detailed guide to the freshwater fishing in the Lothian region of Scotland / by Graham Priestley. — Balerno (22 Cherry Tree Cres., Balerno, Midlothian EH14 5AL) : G. Priestley, c1980. — 48p : ill,maps ; 21cm
ISBN 0-9506926-0-3 (pbk) : £1.00 B81-32489

799.1′1′094295 — England. Wye River. Freshwater angling

Baverstock, Leslie. The Angling times book of the Wye. — Newton Abbot : David & Charles, Nov.1981. — [192]p
ISBN 0-7153-8254-3 : £8.50 : CIP entry
B81-30582

799.1′2 — Angling

The **Fisherman′s** bedside book / edited by David and Gareth Pownall. — [London] : Windward ; London : WHS Distributors, 1980. — 320p : ill ; 24cm
ISBN 0-7112-0065-3 : £7.95 B81-01085

799.1′2 — Angling — *Early works*

Walton, Izaak. The compleat angler. — Oxford : Oxford University Press, Feb.1982. — [384]p. — (The World′s classics)
ISBN 0-19-281511-3 (pbk) : £1.95 : CIP entry
B81-35769

799.1′2 — Angling — *Manuals — For children*

Venables, Bernard. The Piccolo fishing book / written and illustrated by Bernard Venables. — [London] : Piccolo, 1981. — [126]p : ill ; 18cm
ISBN 0-330-26385-4 (pbk) : £0.95 B81-26324

799.1′2 — Coarse fish. Angling — *Manuals*

The **Angler′s** mail guide to basic coarse fishing / consultant editors John Ingham & Roy Westwood ; [contributors John Bailey et al.]. — London : Hamlyn, c1981. — 124p : ill(some col.),col.ports ; 28cm
Includes index
ISBN 0-600-35386-9 : £3.99 B81-22050

799.1′2 — Float fishing

Lane, Billy. The new encyclopaedia of float fishing / Billy Lane & Colin Graham ; line drawings by Jim Randall. — [Rev.ed]. — London : Pelham, 1981. — 144p,[8]p of plates : ill,ports ; 23cm
Previous ed.: published as Billy Lane′s encyclopaedia of float fishing. 1971. — Includes index
ISBN 0-7207-1314-5 : £6.50 B81-15323

799.1′2 — Fly fishing — *Manuals*

The **Complete** book of modern fly-fishing / edited by Larry Solomon. — Northfield : DBI Books ; London : Arms and Armour [distributor], c1979. — 288p : ill ; 28cm
ISBN 0-695-81312-9 (pbk) : £4.00 B81-15698

Harris, Brian, *1937-*. The art of flyfishing / Brian Harris. — London : Ward Lock, 1980. — 184p,[8]p of plates : ill(some col.) ; 26cm
Bibliography: p181-182. — Includes index
ISBN 0-7063-5915-1 : £7.95 : CIP rev.
B80-28644

799.1′2 — Great Britain. Coarse fish. Angling — *Serials*

Coarse fishing monthly. — No.1 (June 1981)-. — Windsor (10 Sheet St., Windsor, Berks. SL4 1BG) : Burlington Pub., 1981-. — v. : ill,maps,ports ; 28cm
ISSN 0261-5312 = Coarse fishing monthly : £9.00 per year B81-33319

799.1′2′05 — Angling — *Serials*

Angler′s mail annual. — 1981. — London : IPC Magazines, [1980?]. — 94p
ISBN 0-85037-514-2 : £2.00 B81-06941

799.1′2′0924 — Angling — *Personal observations*

Lockhart, Logie Bruce. The pleasures of fishing / Logie Bruce Lockhart. — London : Black, 1981. — 104p ; 23cm
ISBN 0-7136-2136-2 : £4.95 : CIP rev.
B81-03831

Taylor, Fred J.. My fishing years. — Newton Abbot : David & Charles, Oct.1981. — [192]p
ISBN 0-7153-8105-9 : £7.50 : CIP entry
B81-30334

799.1′2′0941 — Great Britain. Angling

Angling / [contributors Alan Wrangles ... et al.] ; [introduction by Benny Green]. — London : Hamlyn, 1981. — 96p : ill(some col.),1map,ports ; 25cm. — (Hamlet sports special)
ISBN 0-600-34655-2 (pbk) : £1.99 B81-13918

799.1′2′0941 — Great Britain. Angling — *For children*

The **Beaver** book of fishing / [edited by] Alan Wrangles ; illustrated by John Reynolds. — London : Beaver, 1981. — 143p : ill ; 18cm
ISBN 0-600-20207-0 (pbk) : £0.95 B81-23174

799.1′2′0941 — Great Britain. Angling — *Statistics — Serials*

[National angling survey *(Summary report)*]. National angling survey. — 1970-. — [Marlow] ([Medmenham Laboratory, Henley Rd, P.O. Box 16, Medmenham, Marlow, Bucks., SL7 2HD]) : Water Research Centre, 1970-. — v. : ill ; 30cm
Summarized version of: National angling survey (Main report). — Description based on: 1980 issue
ISSN 0260-0757 = National angling survey (Summary report) : £1.50 B81-04495

799.1′2′0941 — Great Britain. Freshwater angling — *Personal observations*

Sutherland, Douglas. A fisherman's year. — Exeter : Webb & Bower, Feb.1982. — [160]p
ISBN 0-906671-51-5 : £7.95 : CIP entry B81-36057

799.1′2′094137 — Scotland. Borders Region. Angling — *Practical information — Serials*

Angling in the Scottish Borders : (incorporating Visitors guide to Borders angling). — [No.1]-. — Newtown St. Boswells (Regional Headquarters, Newtown St. Boswells, [Roxburghshire]) : Tourism Division, Borders Regional Council, [1980]-. — v. : ill,maps ; 22cm
Annual. — Continues: Visitors guide to Borders angling
ISSN 0262-074x = Angling in the Scottish Borders : £0.30 B81-38196

799.1′2′09417 — Ireland *(Republic)*. **Angling** — *Serials*

Irish rod & gun : Ireland's leading shooting and fishing magazine. — Mar.1978-. — Dublin (21 Main St., Rathfarnham, Dublin 14) : Rod & Gun Magazines Co. Ltd., 1978-. — v. : ill,maps,ports ; 30cm
Monthly. — Description based on: Vol.4, no.2 (Apr.1981)
ISSN 0332-0561 = Irish rod and gun : Unpriced
Also classified at 799.2′13′09417 B81-33051

799.1′2′09423 — South-west England. Angling — *Practical information*

Millman, Mike. Spotlight guide to angling in the South-West / Mike Millman. — London : British Broadcasting Corporation, 1981. — 80p : ill,1map ; 22cm
Map on inside cover. — Includes index
ISBN 0-563-17890-6 (pbk) : £1.95 B81-19588

799.1′4 — Spear fishing — *Manuals*

Way, David. The spearfisherman's handbook / David Way. — London : Hale, 1981. — 160p,[16]p of plates : ill,ports ; 23cm
Bibliography: p151-152. - Includes index
ISBN 0-7091-8588-x : £6.50 B81-17291

799.1′6′028 — Sea angling equipment

Merritt, P. R.. Basic tackle rigs for beach and boat angling / P.R. Merritt. — London : Black, 1980. — 63p : ill ; 21cm
Includes index
ISBN 0-7136-2097-8 : £3.95 B81-01086

799.1′6′0941 — Great Britain. Coastal waters. Sea angling — *Personal observations*

Millman, Mike. Sea angling supreme / Mike Millman. — London : Cassell, 1979. — 157p,[16]p of plates : ill,maps,ports ; 23cm
Includes index
ISBN 0-304-30503-0 : £6.95 B81-01087

799.1′6′0941 — Great Britain. Coastal waters. Sea angling — *Serials*

Sea angling monthly. — No.1 (Dec.1980)-. — Windsor (10 Sheet St., Windsor, Berks. SL4 1BG) : Burlingon, 1980-. — v. : ill ; 28cm
£7.50 per year B81-05684

799.1′6′09422 — Southern England. Coastal waters. Sea angling

Smith, Peter, *1946-*. Sea angling in southern England / Peter Smith. — Newton Abbot : David & Charles, c1981. — 192p : ill,maps,ports ; 23cm
Includes index
ISBN 0-7153-8172-5 : £7.50 : CIP rev. B81-14433

799.1′752 — Great Britain. Carp. Angling — *Manuals*

Hutchinson, Rod. Rod Hutchinson's carp book : tales and tactics from Rod Hutchinson. — [Nottingham] : [88 Goldsmith St., Nottingham] : Hudson-Chadwick, 1981. — 152p : ill,1facsim,ports ; 21cm
£6.50 (pbk) B81-09534

799.1′753 — Pike. Angling

Buller, Fred. Pike and the pike angler. — London : Paul, Nov.1981. — [288]p
ISBN 0-09-146260-6 : £15.95 : CIP entry B81-28148

799.1′755 — Great Britain. Trout. Dry fly fishing — *Manuals*

Wilson, Dermot. Fishing the dry fly / Dermot Wilson. — 2nd ed. — London : Black, 1981. — x,225p : ill ; 23cm
Previous ed.: 1970
ISBN 0-7136-2134-6 : £7.95 : CIP rev. B81-03705

799.1′755 — North America. Trout. Freshwater angling

Trout fishermen's digest / edited by David Richey. — Northfield : DBI Books ; London : Arms and Armour [distributor], c1976. — 288p : ill ; 28cm
ISBN 0-695-80641-6 (pbk) : £4.00 B81-15707

799.1′755 — Salmon & trout. Angling — *Personal observations — Collections*

Trout & salmon fishing / editor : Roy Eaton. — Newton Abbot : David & Charles, 1981. — 212p : ill,ports ; 22cm
ISBN 0-7153-8117-2 : £8.95 B81-15611

799.1′755 — Scotland. Salmon. Freshwater angling

The **Haig** guide to salmon fishing in Scotland / edited by David Barr ; with descriptions of the major salmon rivers and lochs by Bill 'Rogie' Brown. — London : Queen Anne, 1981. — 192p : ill(some col.),maps(some col.),ports(some col.) ; 27cm
Includes index
ISBN 0-362-00554-0 : £11.50 B81-36799

799.1′755 — Still waters. Trout. Fly fishing

Du Broff, Sidney. Fly fishing on still water / Sidney Du Broff. — Bradford-on Avon : Moonraker, 1981. — 119p : ill(some col.) ; 23cm
ISBN 0-239-00199-0 : £6.95 B81-26107

Lapsley, Peter. Trout from stillwaters. — London : A. & C. Black, Oct.1981. — [224]p
ISBN 0-7136-2171-0 : £9.95 : CIP entry B81-24673

799.1′755 — Still waters. Trout. Fly fishing. Flies

Price, Taff. Taff Price's stillwater flies : a modern account of natural history, flydressing and fishing technique. — London : Ernest Benn Bk. 2. — 1981. — p91-185,4p of plates : ill (some col.) ; 25cm
ISBN 0-510-22542-x (pbk) : £5.95
Also classified at 592.092′9 B81-12744

799.1′755 — Trout. Fly fishing — *Manuals*

Sceats, David. Trout fishing. — London : Black, Sept.1981. — [96]p. — (Black's picture sports)
ISBN 0-7136-2111-7 : £2.95 : CIP entry B81-22525

799.2 — RECREATIONS. HUNTING

799.2′13 — Sports: Shooting

Marchington, John. The complete shot. — London : Black, Sept.1981. — [208]p
ISBN 0-7136-2145-1 : £8.95 : CIP entry B81-22527

799.2′13′09417 — Ireland *(Republic)*. **Game animals. Shooting** — *Serials*

Irish rod & gun : Ireland's leading shooting and fishing magazine. — Mar.1978-. — Dublin (21 Main St., Rathfarnham, Dublin 14) : Rod & Gun Magazines Co. Ltd., 1978-. — v. : ill,maps,ports ; 30cm
Monthly. — Description based on: Vol.4, no.2 (Apr.1981)
ISSN 0332-0561 = Irish rod and gun : Unpriced
Primary classification 799.1′2′09417 B81-33051

799.2′13′09426 — East Anglia. Sports: Shooting, *1810-1910*

Johnson, Derek E.. Victorian shooting days. — Woodbridge : Boydell Press, Oct.1981. — [128]p
ISBN 0-85115-156-6 : £8.95 : CIP entry B81-24668

799.2′15′0973 — United States. Game animals. Hunting with bows — *Manuals*

Learn, C. R.. Bowhunter's digest / by C.R. Learn ; edited by Jack Lewis. — Northfield : DBI Books ; London : Arms and Armour [distributor], c1974. — 288p : ill ; 28cm
ISBN 0-695-80451-0 (pbk) : £3.50 B81-15702

799.2′3 — Ferreting — *Manuals*

Wellstead, Graham. The ferret and ferreting guide / Graham Wellstead. — Newton Abbot : David & Charles, 1981. — 157p : ill,1port ; 23cm
Bibliography: p151-152. — Includes index
ISBN 0-7153-8013-3 : £6.50 : CIP rev.
Primary classification 636′.974447 B81-17493

799.2′32 — Falconry — *Manuals — Facsimiles*

Salvin, Francis Henry. Falconry in the British Isles / [by Francis Henry Salvin and William Brodrick]. — Leicester : Windward, 1980. — 147p,xxiv p of plates : col.ill ; 29cm
Facsim of: edition published London : Van Voorst, 1855. — Includes index
ISBN 0-7112-0090-4 : £8.95 B81-01088

799.2′32′0922 — Great Britain. Falconry, *1757-1979 — Biographies*

Upton, Roger. A bird in the hand : celebrated falconers of the park / by Roger Upton ; with a foreword by the Duke of St Albans. — London : Debrett's Peerage, c1980. — 160p : ill(some col.),ports(some col.) ; 28cm
Ill on lining papers. — Bibliography: p158. — Includes index
ISBN 0-905649-34-6 : £12.95 B81-04671

799.2′4 — Game birds. Shooting — *Amateurs' manuals*

Churchill, Robert. [Game shooting]. Churchill's game shooting : the standard text book on the successful use of the shotgun. — 5th rev. ed. / by Macdonald Hastings. — London : Arms and Armour, 1979, c1963. — 252p,24p of plates : ill ; 22cm
Previous ed.: London : Joseph, 1955. — Includes index
ISBN 0-85368-243-7 (pbk) : Unpriced B81-06253

799.2′4′0941 — Great Britain. Game birds. Shooting — *Amateurs' manuals*

Carlisle, G. L.. Shotgun and shooter / by G.L. Carlisle and Percy Stanbury ; photography by G.L. Carlisle. — New rev. ed. — London : Barrie & Jenkins, 1981. — 226,[32]p of plates : ill ; 23cm
Previous ed.: 1970. — Bibliography: p224-226
ISBN 0-09-145050-0 : £6.95 : CIP rev. B81-02552

Kemp, Michael. Shooting games / Michael Kemp. — 2nd ed. — London : Adam & Charles Black, 1980. — 190p : ill ; 22cm
Previous ed.: 1972. — Includes index
ISBN 0-7136-2066-8 : £5.95 B81-19760

799.2′4′0941 — Great Britain. Game birds. Shooting — *Serials*

Shooting & conservation / the British Association for Shooting and Conservation. — Autumn 1981-. — Wrexham (Marford Mill, Rossett, Wrexham, Clwyd LL12 OHL) : The Association, 1981-. — v. : ill ; 28cm
Quarterly. — Continues: WAGBI magazine
ISSN 0262-2378 = Shooting & conservation : Free to Association members only B81-39728

799.2′44′028 — Great Britain. Wildfowl. Shooting. Use of hides, bird calls & decoy wildfowl

Humphreys, John. Hides, calls and decoys / by John Humphreys ; photographs Dave Parfitt. — London (809 High Rd., E.11) : Percival Marshall, c1979. — 94p : ill,ports ; 21cm. — (A Shooting times and country magazine production)
ISBN 0-85242-688-7 (pbk) : £2.95 B81-18984

799.2′4841 — Great Britain. Ducks. Shooting — *Manuals*

Willock, Colin. Duck shooting / Colin Willock. — Rev. ed. — London : Deutsch, 1981. — 127p,[8]p of plates : ill,port ; 21cm
Previous ed.: London : Vista, 1962
ISBN 0-233-97039-8 : £4.95 B81-13595

799.2′597357 — Great Britain. Deer. Stalking — *Manuals*

Luxmoore, Edmund. Deer stalking / Edmund Luxmoore ; drawings by Brian Maxwell ; foreword by Peter Delap. — Newton Abbot : David & Charles, c1980. — 143p : ill ; 25cm
Includes index
ISBN 0-7153-8063-x : £7.50 : CIP rev. B80-18873

799.2′5974442 — Leicestershire. Quorn. Foxes. Hunting. Hunts: Quorn — *Personal observations*

Smith, Ulrica Murray. Magic of the Quorn / Ulrica Murray Smith. — London : J.A. Allen, 1980. — viii,94p,[8]p of plates : ill,ports ; 23cm
ISBN 0-85131-362-0 : £6.95 : CIP rev. B80-22415

799.2′6′097 — North America. Big game. Hunting — *Manuals*

Brakefield, Tom. Big game hunter's digest / by Tom Brakefield. — Northfield : DBI Books ; London : Arms and Armour [distributor], c1977. — 288p : ill ; 28cm
ISBN 0-695-80685-8 (pbk) : £4.00 B81-15701

799.2′92′4 — New Zealand. Hunting, *ca 1945-1980* — *Personal observations*

Holden, Philip. On target. — London : Hodder & Stoughton, July 1981. — [192]p
ISBN 0-340-26506-x : £7.95 : CIP entry B81-20645

799.2942′4′6 — Staffordshire. Hunting — *Personal observations*

Plummer, David Brian. Diary of a hunter. — Woodbridge : Boydell, Sept.1981. — [160]p
ISBN 0-85115-153-1 : £9.95 : CIP entry B81-22588

799.3 — TARGET SHOOTING

799.3′12 — Air gun shooting

Churchill, Bob. Modern airweapon shooting. — Newton Abbot : David & Charles, Sept.1981. — [188]p
ISBN 0-7153-8123-7 : £7.50 : CIP entry B81-22506

799.3′12 — Target pistol shooting — *Amateurs' manuals*

Freeman, P. C.. Target pistol shooting : eliminating the variables / P.C. Freeman. — London : Faber, 1981. — 90p : ill ; 23cm
ISBN 0-571-11662-0 : £4.95 B81-22087

Hinchliffe, K. B.. Target pistol shooting / K.B. Hinchliffe. — Newton Abbot : David & Charles, c1981. — 235p : ill ; 25cm
Includes index
ISBN 0-7153-8160-1 : £10.50 B81-33003

799.32 — ARCHERY

799.3′2 — Sports: Longbow target archery

Foy, Tom. A guide to archery / Tom Foy. — 2nd ed. — London : Pelham, 1980. — 144p : ill,1port ; 22cm
Previous ed.: published as Beginner's guide to archery. 1972. — Includes index
ISBN 0-7207-1245-9 : £6.50 B81-03933

799.3′2′06041 — Archery. Historiology. Organisations: Society of Archer-Antiquaries — *Serials*

Arrow head : the 'new-look' newsletter of the Society of Archer-Antiquaries. — Newsletter no.39 (June 1979)-. — Hertford (c/o Mr A. Webb, 87 Mandeville Rd, Hertford SG13 8JJ) : The Society, 1979-. — v. ; 21cm
Three issues yearly. — Continues: Newsletter (Society of Archer-Antiquaries)
ISSN 0144-7424 = Arrow head : £0.15 per issue (free to Society members) B81-02835

800 — LITERATURE

801 — Literature. Interpretation by readers

Fish, Stanley Eugene. Is there a text in this class? : the authority of interpretive communities / Stanley Fish. — Cambridge, Mass. ; London : Harvard University Press, 1980. — viii,394p ; 24cm
Includes index
ISBN 0-674-46725-6 : £10.50 B81-12629

The **Reader** in the text : essays on audience and interpretation / edited by Susan R. Suleiman and Inge Crosman. — Princeton ; Guildford : Princeton University Press, 1980. — viii,441p : ill ; 23cm
Bibliography: p402-424. - Includes index
ISBN 0-691-06436-9 (cased) : £16.70
ISBN 0-691-10096-9 (pbk) : £5.60 B81-08276

801 — Literature. Interpretation by readers. Semiotic aspects

Eco, Umberto. The role of the reader. — London : Hutchinson Educational, Oct.1981. — [273]p
Originally published: Bloomington ; London : Indiana University Press, 1979
ISBN 0-09-146391-2 (pbk) : £4.95 : CIP entry B81-26800

801 — Literature. Semiotic aspects

Culler, Jonathan. The pursuit of signs : semiotics, literature, deconstruction / Jonathan Culler. — London : Routledge & Kegan Paul, 1981. — xiii, 242p ; 22cm
Includes index
ISBN 0-7100-0757-4 (cased) : £7.95 : CIP rev.
ISBN 0-7100-0758-2 (pbk) : £3.95 B81-16375

Kristeva, Julia. Desire in language : a semiotic approach to literature and art / by Julia Kristeva ; edited by Leon S. Roudiez ; translated by Thomas Gora, Alice Jardine, and Leon S. Roudiez. — Oxford : Blackwell, c1980. — xi,305p : ill ; 24cm
Translation of: Sēmeiōtichē: recherches pour une sémanalyse. — Includes index
ISBN 0-631-12527-2 : £8.95 : CIP rev. B80-24772

801 — Literature. Theories — *Early works*

Aristotle. Poetics / Aristotle ; introduction, commentary and appendixes by D.W. Lucas. — Rep. (with corr.). — Oxford : Clarendon, 1978 (1980 [printing]). — xxviii,313p ; 19cm
English and Greek text. — Originally published: 1968. — Includes index
ISBN 0-19-814024-x (pbk) : £7.50 B81-16496

801 — Literature, *to 1981* — *Philosophical perspectives*

Phillips, D. Z.. Through a darkening glass. — Oxford : Blackwell, Jan.1982. — [224]p
ISBN 0-631-12995-2 : £9.95 : CIP entry B81-34290

801′.3 — Africa. Society. Role of literature. Political aspects

Ngũgĩ wa Thiong'o. Writers in politics : essays / Ngũgĩ wa Thiong'o. — London : Heinemann, 1981. — 142p ; 23cm. — (Studies in African literature)
Includes index
ISBN 0-435-91751-x (cased) : £7.50 : CIP rev.
ISBN 0-435-91752-8 (pbk) : £2.95 B81-06883

801′.3 — Literature - *Sociological perspectives*

Goldmann, Lucien. Essays on method in the sociology of literature. — Oxford : Blackwell, Apr.1981. — [160]p
ISBN 0-631-12769-0 (cased) : £4.95 : CIP entry
ISBN 0-631-12809-3 (pbk) : Unpriced B81-04323

801′.4 — Literature. Linguistic aspects

Literary texts and language study. — London : Edward Arnold, Jan.1982. — [128]p. — (Explorations in language study)
ISBN 0-7131-6263-5 (pbk) : £3.25 : CIP entry B81-33840

801′.4 — Literature. Linguistic aspects — *Phenomenological viewpoints*

Martínez-Bonati, Félix. Fictive discourse and the structures of literature : a phenomenological approach / Félix Martínez-Bonati ; translated by Philip W. Silver with the author's collaboration. — Ithaca ; London : Cornell University Press, 1981. — 176p : ill ; 23cm
Translation from the Spanish. — Includes index
ISBN 0-8014-1308-7 : £9.00 B81-27512

801′.95 — Literature. Criticism

Daiches, David. Critical approaches to literature. — 2nd ed. — Harlow : Longman, Dec.1981. — [416]p
Previous ed.: 1956
ISBN 0-582-49180-0 (pbk) : £5.95 : CIP entry B81-31823

Hartman, Geoffrey H.. Criticism in the wilderness : the study of literature today / Geoffrey H. Hartman. — New Haven ; London : Yale University Press, c1980. — xi,323p : 1ill ; 25cm
Bibliography: p302-314. — Includes index
ISBN 0-300-02085-6 : £11.40 B81-02736

Reader-response criticism : from formalism to post-structuralism / edited by Jane P. Tompkins. — Baltimore ; London : Johns Hopkins University Press, c1980. — xxvi,275p ; 24cm
Bibliography: p233-272
ISBN 0-8018-2400-1 (cased) : £12.00
ISBN 0-8018-2401-x (pbk) : £4.25 B81-21079

801′.95 — Literature. Criticism. Applications of psychoanalysis

Skura, Meredith Anne. The literary use of the psychoanalytic process / Meredith Anne Skura. — New Haven ; London : Yale University Press, c1981. — viii,280p ; 22cm
Includes index
ISBN 0-300-02380-4 : £12.60 B81-21088

801′.95 — Literature. Criticism. Linguistic aspects

Donoghue, Denis. Ferocious alphabets. — London : Faber, Oct.1981. — [211]p
ISBN 0-571-11809-7 : £8.50 : CIP entry B81-27412

801′.95 — Literature. Criticism. Structuralism

Strickland, Geoffrey. Structuralism or criticism? : thoughts on how we read / Geoffrey Stickland. — Cambridge : Cambridge University Press, 1981. — viii,209p ; 23cm
Bibliography: p196-202. - Includes index
ISBN 0-521-23184-1 : £17.50 B81-17026

Untying the text. — London : Routledge & Kegan Paul, July 1981. — [316]p
ISBN 0-7100-0804-x (cased) : £12.50 : CIP entry
ISBN 0-7100-0805-8 (pbk) : £5.95 B81-13725

801′.95 — Literature. Criticism - *Structuralist perspectives*

Todorov, Tzvetan. Introduction to poetics. — Brighton : Harvester Press, Sept.1981. — [128]p
Translation of: Poétique
ISBN 0-7108-0328-1 (cased) : CIP entry
ISBN 0-7108-0333-8 (pbk) B81-20559

801′.95 — Literature. Criticism. Theories

Altieri, Charles. Act & quality : a theory of literary meaning and humanistic understanding / Charles Altieri. — Brighton : Harvester Press, 1981. — vi,343p ; 25cm
Bibliography: p332-340. — Includes index
ISBN 0-7108-0376-1 : £18.95 : CIP rev. B81-18171

801'.95 — Literature. Criticism. Theories *continuation*

Belsey, Catherine. Critical practice / Catherine Belsey. — London : Methuen, 1980. — 168p : 1ill ; 21cm. — (New accents)
Bibliography: p153-165. — Includes index
ISBN 0-416-72940-1 (cased) : £5.95 : CIP rev.
ISBN 0-416-72950-9 (pbk) : £2.75 B80-08906

Sharratt, Bernard. Reading relations : structures of literary production. — Brighton : Harvester Press, Dec.1981. — [352]p
ISBN 0-7108-0059-2 : £25.00 : CIP entry
B81-31641

801'.95 — Literature. Rhetorical criticism

Johnson, Barbara. The critical difference : essays in the contemporary rhetoric of reading / Barbara Johnson. — Baltimore ; London : Johns Hopkins University Press, c1980. — xii,156p : ill ; 24cm
Includes index
ISBN 0-8018-2458-3 : £7.25 B81-34462

801'.95'05 — Literature. Comparative criticism — *Serials*

Comparative criticism. — 3. — Cambridge : Cambridge University Press, Nov.1981. — [352]p
ISBN 0-521-23276-7 : £20.00 : CIP entry
ISSN 0144-7564 B81-31192

801'.95'0903 — Literature. Criticism, ***1750-1950***

Wellek, René. A history of modern criticism 1750-1950. — Cambridge : Cambridge University Press, July 1981
Originally published: London : Cape, 1955
Vol.1: The later eighteenth century. — [358]p
ISBN 0-521-28295-0 (pbk) : £8.95 : CIP entry
B81-20538

Wellek, René. A history of modern criticism 1750-1950. — Cambridge : Cambridge University Press, July 1981
Originally published: London : Cape, 1955
Vol.2: The romantic age. — [459]p
ISBN 0-521-28296-9 (pbk) : £9.95 : CIP entry
B81-20539

801'.95'0924 — Literature. Marxist criticism. Benjamin, Walter — *Critical studies*

Eagleton, Terry. Walter Benjamin, or, Towards a revolutionary criticism / Terry Eagleton. — London : NLB, 1981. — 187p ; 22cm
Includes index
ISBN 0-86091-036-9 (cased) : £8.00 : CIP rev.
ISBN 0-86091-733-9 (pbk) : Unpriced
B81-10495

801'.95'0973 — Literature. American criticism, ***1957-1979 — Critical studies***

Lentricchia, Frank. After the new criticism / Frank Lentricchia. — London : Athlone Press, 1980. — xiv,384p ; 24cm
Originally published: Chicago : University of Chicago Press, 1980. — Includes index
ISBN 0-485-11208-6 : £14.50 : CIP rev.
B80-06055

801'.951'0924 — Poetry. Criticism. Coleridge, Samuel Taylor — *Critical studies*

Marks, Emerson R.. Coleridge on the language of verse / Emerson R. Marks. — Princeton ; Guildford : Princeton University Press, c1981. — xii,117p ; 23cm. — (Princeton essays in literature)
Includes index
ISBN 0-691-06458-x : £5.30 B81-30936

801'.951'0924 — Poetry. Criticism. Johnson, Samuel, ***1709-1784 — Critical studies***

Edinger, William. Samuel Johnson and poetic style / William Edinger. — Chicago ; London : University of Chicago Press, 1977. — xvi,272p ; 23cm
Includes index
ISBN 0-226-18446-3 : £11.90 B81-01089

801'.953 — Fiction in European languages, ***1800-1980.*** **Marxist ciricism. Theories** — *Marxist viewpoints*

Jameson, Fredric. The political unconscious : narrative as a socially symbolic act / Fredric Jameson. — London : Metheun, 1981. — 305p ; 23cm
Includes index
ISBN 0-416-31370-1 : £10.95 B81-20912

802'.8'54 — Literature. Study. Applications of digital computer systems — *Serials*

ALLC journal. — Vol.1, no.1 (Summer 1980)-. — Cambridge (Dr J.L. Dawson, University of Cambridge Literary and Linguistic Computing Centre, Sidgwick Site, Cambridge, CB3 9DA) : Association of Literary and Linguistic Computing, 1980-. — v. : ill ; 30cm
Two issues yearly
Unpriced
Primary classification 410'.28'54 B81-06192

803'.21 — Literature — *Encyclopaedias*

Abrams, M. H.. A glossary of literary terms / M.H. Abrams. — 4th ed. — New York ; London : Holt, Rinehart and Winston, c1981. — vii,220p ; 24cm
Previous ed.: 1971
ISBN 0-03-054166-2 (pbk) : £3.50 B81-22868

805 — Literary magazines in English: New English weekly: Mairet, Philip — *Biographies*

Mairet, Philip. Autobiographical and other papers / by Philip Mairet ; edited by C.H. Sisson. — Manchester : Carcanet, 1981. — xxii,266p ; 22cm
Includes index
ISBN 0-85635-326-4 (pbk) : £7.95 B81-05967

805 — Literature in modern languages — *Serials*

Bradford occasional papers : essays in language, literature and area papers. — Issue no.1 (Autumn 1980)-. — Bradford (Modern Languages Centre, University of Bradford, West Yorks. BD7 1DP) : The Modern Languages Centre, 1980-. — v. ; 20cm
Irregular
ISSN 0261-0353 = Bradford occasional papers : Unpriced B81-13104

808 — English language. Style — *For schools*

Thomson, O. M.. The craft of writing / O.M. Thomson. — Oxford : Oxford University Press, 1981. — 81p ; 22cm
ISBN 0-19-831244-x (pbk) : £1.50 B81-02400

808 — Metaphor

Lakoff, George. Metaphors we live by / George Lakoff and Mark Johnson. — Chicago ; London : University of Chicago Press, 1980. — xiii,242p ; 23cm
Bibliography: p241-242
ISBN 0-226-46800-3 : £7.50 B81-06172

808 — Non-fiction. Writing — *Manuals*

Wells, Gordon. The successful author's handbook / Gordon Wells. — London : Macmillan, 1981. — vi,166p : ill ; 21cm
Includes index
ISBN 0-333-30462-4 (cased) : £3.95 : CIP rev.
ISBN 0-333-30463-2 (pbk) : £3.95 B81-28109

808 — Writers in English: Northern English writers — *Directories*

Directory of northern writers. — 6th ed. / compiled by Elizabeth Jennifer Gordon. — Ashington ([Wansbeck Sq.], Ashington, Northumberland) : Mid Northumberland Arts Group, 1981. — [20]p ; 30cm
Previous ed.: 1979. — Includes index
ISBN 0-904790-15-0 (pbk) : £3.00 (£2.00 to Subscribers) B81-34800

808 — Writers in English. Pseudonyms, ***1900-1980 — Dictionaries***

Atkinson, Frank, *1922-*. Dictionary of literary pseudonyms. — 3rd ed. — London : Bingley, Dec.1981. — [295]p
Previous ed.: 1977
ISBN 0-85157-323-1 : £7.50 : CIP entry
B81-31528

808'.001 — Rhetoric. Philosophical perspectives

Grassi, Ernesto. Rhetoric as philosophy : the humanist tradition / Ernesto Grassi. — University Park ; London : Pennsylvania State University Press, c1980. — 122p ; 24cm
ISBN 0-271-00256-5 : £9.00 B81-01886

808'.001 — Rhetoric — *Philosophical perspectives*

Perelman, Chaïm. The new rhetoric and the humanities : essays on rhetoric and its applications / Ch. Perelman ; with an introduction by Harold Zyskind. — Dordrecht ; London : Reidel, c1979. — xxiii,174p ; 23cm. — (Synthese library, ISSN 0166-6991 ; v.140)
Translated from the French. — Includes index
ISBN 90-277-1018-x (cased) : Unpriced
ISBN 90-277-1019-8 (pbk) : Unpriced
B81-07829

808'.02 — Authorship — *Manuals*

Attwood, Tony. Writing for profit / prepared for R.S. Productions by Tony Attwood. — [Temporary ed., fully updated and revised]. — [Totnes] ([Hamilton House, Nelson Close, Staverton, Totnes, Devon TQ9 6PG]) : [R.S. Productions], [1981]. — [8]leaves ; 30cm
Originally published: as Make money from writing. 19-
ISBN 0-906888-07-7 (unbound) : Unpriced
B81-18214

808'.02 — Authorship — *Manuals — For professional personnel*

Van Til, William. Writing for professional publication / William Van Til. — Boston [Mass] ; London : Allyn and Bacon, c1981. — xv,332p : forms ; 25cm
Includes index
ISBN 0-205-07127-9 : £11.95 B81-05756

808'.02 — New York ***(City).*** **Publishing industries: John Wiley & Sons. House style** — *Manuals*

A **Guide** for Wiley authors / [College Editing Department]. — New York ; Chichester : Wiley, c1980. — 60p : forms ; 28cm
Originally published: 1973. — Text on inside cover. — Includes index
ISBN 0-471-08373-9 (pbk) : Unpriced
B81-24930

808'.02 — Non-book materials. Scripts. Writing — *Manuals*

Swain, Dwight V.. Scripting for video and audiovisual media. — London : Focal Press, Apr.1981. — [190]p
ISBN 0-240-51075-5 : CIP entry B81-02363

808'.02 — Typescripts. Copy-editing — *Manuals*

Butcher, Judith. Copy-editing. — 2nd ed. — Cambridge : Cambridge University Press, Nov.1981. — [352]p
Previous ed.: 1975
ISBN 0-521-23868-4 : £25.00 : CIP entry
B81-31061

808'.02'05 — Authorship — *Serials*

Writers' and artists' yearbook. — 1981. — London : A. & C. Black, c1981. — 497p
ISBN 0-7136-2098-6 : £2.95 : CIP rev.
ISSN 0084-2664 B80-23640

Writers' and artists' yearbook. — 1982. — London : A. & C. Black, Nov.1981. — [500]p
ISBN 0-7136-2178-8 : £3.50 : CIP entry
B81-30362

808'.025 — Serial articles. Writing — *Manuals*

Wilbur, L. Perry. How to write articles that sell / L. Perry Wilbur. — New York ; Chichester : Wiley, c1981. — vi,217p ; 23cm
Bibliography: p210-211. — Includes index
ISBN 0-471-08426-3 (pbk) : £5.00 B81-23716

808'.042 — Creative writing — *Manuals*

Gordon, Helen Heightsman. From copying to creating : controlled compositions and other basic writing exercises / Helen Heightsman Gordon. — New York ; London : Holt, Rinehart and Winston, c1981. — xiv,238p : forms ; 24cm
Text on inside cover. — Includes index
ISBN 0-03-053551-4 (pbk) : £4.95 B81-05879

Leavitt, Hart Day. Stop, look and write! : effective writing through pictures / by Hart Day Leavitt and David A. Sohn. — Rev. ed. — Toronto ; London : Bantam, 1979. — 232p : ill ; 18cm
Previous ed.: 1964
ISBN 0-553-11887-0 (pbk) : £0.95
Also classified at 779 B81-14289

808'.042 — English language. American usage. Composition

Corbett, Edward P. J.. The little English handbook : choices and conventions / Edward P.J. Corbett. — 3rd ed. — New York ; Chichester : Wiley, c1980. — xix,259p : facsims ; 18cm
Text on inside covers. — Previous ed.: 1977. — Includes index
ISBN 0-471-07856-5 (pbk) : £3.75 B81-08065

808'.042 — English language. American usage. Composition — *Manuals*

Weiner, Harvey S.. Creating compositions / Harvey S. Weiner. — 3rd ed. — New York ; London : McGraw-Hill, c1981. — vi,438p : ill,2forms ; 24cm
Previous ed.: c1977
ISBN 0-07-070160-1 (pbk) : £8.75 B81-27523

808'.042 — English language. Composition — *For non-English speaking students — For schools*

Jupp, T. C.. Basic writing skills in English / T.C. Jupp, John Milne, John Davey. — London : Heinemann Educational
Workbook. — 1981. — 43p : ill ; 25cm
ISBN 0-435-28496-7 (corrected : pbk) : £0.60 B81-19376

808'.042 — English language. Composition — *For schools*

Boagey, Eric. Composition choice / Eric Boagey. — Slough : University Tutorial Press, 1981. — x,148p : ill,facsims ; 21cm
ISBN 0-7231-0815-3 (pbk) : £1.65 B81-27069

Use your imagination : an introduction, through mythology, to literature, creative writing and general studies / [compiled by] Hugh McKay, P.R. Smart. — London : Murray, 1980, c1969. — 213p : ill,2geneal.tables ; 22cm
Originally published: Sydney : Reed, 1969 ; London : J. Murray, 1973. — Geneal.tables on inside covers. — Bibliography: p210-211. - Includes index
ISBN 0-7195-2819-4 (pbk) : £2.25 B81-21290

808'.042 — English language. Composition — *For undergraduates*

Marzano, Robert J.. The writing process : prewriting, writing, revising / Robert J. Marzano, Philip DiStefano. — New York ; London : Van Nostrand, c1981. — x,304p ; 23cm
Text on inside covers. — Includes index
ISBN 0-442-26055-5 (pbk) : £9.30 B81-37027

Mattson, Marylu. Help yourself : a guide to writing and rewriting / Marylu Mattson, Sophia Leshing, Elaine Levi. — 2nd ed. — Columbus ; London : Merrill, c1979. — xxviii,313p ; 28cm
Previous ed.: 1972. — Text on inside covers. — Includes index
ISBN 0-675-08295-1 (pbk) : £6.75 B81-02254

808'.042 — English language. Composition — *Manuals*

Butler, Robert A.. Handbook of practical writing / Robert A. Butler. — New York ; London : McGraw-Hill, c1978. — v,234p : ill,facsims ; 23cm
Includes index
ISBN 0-07-009341-5 (pbk) : £3.95 B81-02776

Tedlock, David. Casebook rhetoric : a problem-solving approach to composition / David Tedlock, Paul Jarvie. — New York ; London : Holt, Rinehart and Winston, c1981. — xiv,242p ; 24cm
Includes index
ISBN 0-03-056124-8 (pbk) : £4.95 B81-22997

808'.042 — English language. Writing - *For Non-English speaking students*

Carrier, Mike. Intermediate language skills. — London : Hodder and Stoughton, May 1981. — [96]p
ISBN 0-340-24408-9 (pbk) : £2.75 : CIP entry B81-10437

808'.042 — Verbal communication — *Manuals*

Gubbay, Denise. Speak for yourself : making language work for you / by Denise Gubbay and Sheila Cogill with Nettie Lowenstein and Philip Baker ; edited by Barbara Derkow. — London : British Broadcasting Corporation, 1980. — 96p : ill ; 30cm
ISBN 0-563-16382-8 (pbk) : £2.75 B81-08344

808'.042 — Writing — *For children*

Allington, Richard L.. Beginning to learn about writing. — Oxford : Blackwell, Aug.1981. — [32]p
ISBN 0-86256-043-8 : £2.50 : CIP entry B81-20616

808'.042 — Writing. Techniques — *Manuals*

Dalley, R.. You want to write? : here's how to do it / R. Dalley. — Bognor Regis : New Horizon, c1981. — 44p : ill ; 21cm
ISBN 0-86116-210-2 : £3.25 B81-21815

Hull, Raymond. How to write how-to books and articles. — London (13 Burlington Lodge Studios, Rigault Rd, SW6 4JJ) : Poplar Press, Jan.1982. — [256]p
ISBN 0-907657-01-x : £8.95 : CIP entry B81-33756

Miller, Casey. The handbook of non-sexist writing for writers, editors and speakers. — Rev. ed. — London : Women's Press, Dec.1981. — [144]p
ISBN 0-7043-3878-5 (pbk) : £3.25 : CIP entry B81-31647

Smith, Frank. Writing and the writer. — London : Heinemann Educational, Jan.1982. — [256]p
Originally published: New York : Holt, Rinehart and Winston, 1981
ISBN 0-435-10815-8 (cased) : £8.50 : CIP entry
ISBN 0-435-10816-8 (pbk) : £3.95 B81-35033

808'.042 — Written communication — *Manuals*

Kelsch, Mary Lynn. Writing effectively : a practical guide / Mary Lynn Kelsch, Thomas Kelsch. — Englewood Cliffs ; London : Prentice-Hall, c1981. — xii,163p ; 21cm. — (A Spectrum book)
Bibliography: p157-158. — Includes index
ISBN 0-13-969832-9 (cased) : £7.10
ISBN 0-13-969824-8 (pbk) : £3.50 B81-19652

808'.042'019 — Creative writing. Psychotherapeutic aspects

Brand, Alice Glarden. Therapy in writing : a psycho-educational enterprise / Alice Glarden Brand. — Lexington : Lexington Books, c1980 ; [Farnborough, Hants.] : Gower [distributor], 1981. — xvii,219p : 1 form ; 24cm
Bibliography: p197-213. — Includes index
ISBN 0-669-03232-8 : £14.00 B81-05502

808'.042'07 — Non-English speaking students. Education. Curriculum subjects: English language. Writing skills. Teaching

White, Ronald V.. Teaching written English / Ronald V. White. — London : Allen & Unwin, 1980. — 112p : ill,maps,forms ; 20cm. — (Practical language teaching ; no.3)
Bibliography: p110-112
ISBN 0-04-371068-9 (pbk) : £2.50 : CIP rev. B79-36286

808'.042'071241 — Great Britain. Secondary schools. Curriculum subjects: Writing skills. Teaching

Thornton, Geoffrey. Teaching writing : the development of written language skills / Geoffrey Thornton. — London : Edward Arnold, 1980. — 76p ; 22cm. — (Explorations in language study)
Bibliography: p76
ISBN 0-7131-6282-1 (pbk) : £2.95 : CIP rev. B80-13030

808'.042'076 — English language. Composition — *Questions & answers*

Forbes, Alison, *1950-*. Pen to paper : express yourself in writing / Alison Forbes. — London : Edward Arnold, 1980. — vi,89p : ill,1map,1plan,forms ; 25cm
ISBN 0-7131-0494-5 (pbk) : £2.50 : CIP rev. B80-35392

A writing apprenticeship. — 5th ed / [compiled by] Norman A. Brittin, Ruth L. Brittin. — New York ; London : Holt, Rinehart and Winston, c1981. — xiv,305p ; 24cm
Previous ed.: / compiled by Norman A. Brittin. 1977. — Includes index
ISBN 0-03-055421-7 (corrected : pbk) : £4.95 B81-27096

808'.042'076 — English language. Composition — *Questions & answers — For non-English speaking students*

Johnston, Susan S.. Keys to composition : a guide to writing for students of English as a second language / Susan S. Johnston, Jean Zukowski/Faust. — London : Holt, Rinehart and Winston, c1981. — vii,280p ; 28cm
Includes index
ISBN 0-03-057978-3 (pbk) : £6.95 B81-34532

Land, Geoffrey. Picture stories for composition / Geoffrey Land. — London : Evans, 1981. — 59p : ill ; 28cm
ISBN 0-237-50539-8 (pbk) : Unpriced B81-16132

808'.042'076 — English language. Composition — *Questions & answers — For schools*

Cullup, Michael. Write it in English / Michael Cullup. — Walton-on-Thames : Nelson, 1981. — viii,88p : ill,maps,facsims,forms,1port ; 22cm
Publisher's no.: NCN 010-9207-0
ISBN 0-17-580008-1 (pbk) : £1.65 B81-29499

Finn, F. E. S.. Comprehension and composition / F.E.S. Finn. — London : Murray, c1980. — 88p : ill ; 22cm + Teachers' book(88, T12p : ill ; 22cm)
ISBN 0-7195-3755-x (pbk) : £0.95
ISBN 0-7195-3761-4 (Teachers' book) : : £1.50
Primary classification 428.2 B81-32380

Forsyth, Sandy. Practical composition / Sandy Forsyth & Lesley Hutchinson. — Edinburgh : Oliver & Boyd, 1981. — 104p : ill ; 24cm
ISBN 0-05-003422-7 (corrected : pbk) : £1.50 B81-39144

Mann, F. F.. Englishcraft / F.F. Mann and A.J. Smith. — Slough : University Tutorial Press
3. — 1981. — ix,145p : ill ; 23cm
ISBN 0-7231-0790-4 (pbk) : Unpriced
Primary classification 428.2 B81-19603

808'.042'076 — English language. Composition — *Questions & answers — For West African students*

Tomlinson, Brian. O-level summary and composition / Brian Tomlinson. — Harlow : Longman, 1981. — 108p ; 22cm. — (Study for success)
ISBN 0-582-65502-1 (pbk) : £1.00 B81-38174

808'.042'076 — English language. Writing skills — *Questions & answers — For schools*

Steele, Gary G.. Shortcuts to basic writing skills : an innovative system in composition / Gary G. Steele. — New York ; London : Holt, Rinehart and Winston, c1981. — ix,281p ; 28cm
ISBN 0-03-054036-4 (pbk) : £7.50 B81-22966

808'.042'077 — English language. Writing skills — *Programmed instructions — For non-English speaking students*

Johnson, Keith, *1944-*. Communicate in writing : a functional approach to writing through reading comprehension / Keith Johnson. — Harlow : Longman, 1981. — 125p : ill,map ; 24cm
ISBN 0-582-74811-9 (pbk) : £2.00 B81-22939

808'.0431 — German language. Composition

Hares, R. J.. Der deutsche Aufsatz / R.J. Hares and C.G. Clemmetsen. — London : Hodder and Stoughton, 1981. — 84p ; 22cm
ISBN 0-340-24994-3 (pbk) : £1.95 : CIP rev. B81-02095

808'.0441'076 — French language. Composition — *Questions & answers — For schools*

Bougard, Marie-Thérèse. Photo stop / par Marie-Thérèse Bougard et Sue Cowling ; photos Oliver Stapleton ; illustrations Rowland Howarth ; mise en pages Mike Miller. — London : MGP, c1980. — 43p : ill ; 15x21cm
ISBN 0-86158-625-5 (pbk) : Unpriced B81-23307

Graham, Stuart. Compositions propositions : a guide to composition-writing in French for CSE and GCE Ordinary level / Stuart Graham. — Harlow : Longman, 1981. — 128p : ill ; 24cm
ISBN 0-582-22061-0 (pbk) : £1.50 B81-37410

808'.066 — British government forms. Comprehensibility

Lewis, Alan, *1952-*. The comprehensibility of government forms and pamphlets : means tested benefits and income tax / Alan Lewis. — Bath (Claverton Down, Bath BA2 7AY) : Bath University Centre for Fiscal Studies, c1979. — 13,14p : 1ill ; 30cm. — (Occasional paper / Bath University Centre for Fiscal Studies ; no.9)
Unpriced (pbk) B81-12503

808'.066 — Official documents. Writing. Teaching *— Manuals*

Plain English training kit : a programme of information and exercises to promote the use of plain language and clear design in leaflets, forms, letters and consumer agreements for the public / produced by the Plain English Campaign and the National Consumer Council. — Salford (78 Wiltshire St., Salford M7 0BD) : The Campaign, c1981. — 1portfolio(5,A-M leaves) : facsims,forms ; 30cm
Cover title
£15.00 (unbound) B81-17872

808'.066028 — Oral book reviewing *— Manuals*

Oppenheimer, Evelyn. Oral book reviewing to stimulate reading : a practical guide in technique for lecture and broadcast / by Evelyn Oppenheimer. — Rev. ed. — Metuchen ; London : Scarecrow, 1980. — xi,156p ; 23cm
Previous ed.: published as Book reviewing for an audience. Philadelphia : Chilton, 1962
ISBN 0-8108-1352-1 : £6.30 B81-06565

808'.06607021 — Newspapers with London imprints: Daily mirror. Style *— Manuals*

Waterhouse, Keith. Daily mirror style / Keith Waterhouse. — London : Mirror, 1981. — 111p ; 23cm
ISBN 0-85939-246-5 (pbk) : £3.50 B81-19535

808'.0663 — Social sciences. Essays. Writing — *Manuals*

Rouse, Samuel. Writing essays in social science / by Samuel Rouse. — Cambridge (18 Brooklands Ave., Cambridge CB2 2HN) : National Extension College, 1978. — iii,29p ; 21cm
ISBN 0-86082-122-6 (pbk) : Unpriced B81-05331

808'.066331021 — Great Britain. Personnel. Conditions of service. Company handbooks. Composition *— Manuals — For hotel & catering industries*

A **Guide** to the production and use of staff handbooks. — [Wembley] : HCITB, [1981?]. — 48p ; 15x22cm
Cover title
Unpriced (pbk) B81-33191

808'.06634021 — Legal documents in English. Drafting

Robinson, Stanley. Drafting : its application to conveyancing and commercial documents / Stanley Robinson. — London : Buttterworths, 1980. — xxxiv,428p : forms ; 26cm
Includes index
ISBN 0-406-35890-7 : £30.00 B81-05977

808'.066363021 — United States. Police reports. Writing *— Manuals*

Levie, Robert C.. Criminal justice report writing / Robert C. Levie, Lou E. Ballard. — Boston, Mass. ; London : Allyn and Bacon, c1981. — x,215p : forms ; 24cm. — (Allyn and Bacon criminal Justice series)
Includes index
ISBN 0-205-07224-0 (pbk) : £7.75 B81-11245

808'.066368021 — Scotland. Insurance. Proposal forms. Comprehensibility

Gilmore, Sheila. Forms without fuss : recommendations and criticisms resulting from a survey of insurance proposal forms carried out by the Scottish Consumer Council / report prepared by Sheila Gilmore. — Glasgow (4 Somerset Place, Glasgow, G3 7JT) : Scottish Consumer Council, 1981. — 69p : forms ; 21x27cm
Unpriced (pbk) B81-23302

808'.0665 — Scientific data. Presentation — *Manuals*

Reynolds, Linda. Presentation of data in science : publications, slides, posters, overhead projections, tape-slides, television : principles and practices for authors and teachers / by Linda Reynolds and Doig Simmonds. — The Hague ; London : Hijhoff, 1981. — xxii,209p : ill ; 25cm
Bibliography: p199-202. — Includes index
ISBN 90-247-2398-1 : Unpriced B81-29351

808'.0665021 — Scientific writing *— Manuals*

Turk, Christopher. Effective writing. — London : Spon, Nov.1981. — [200]p
ISBN 0-419-11670-2 (cased) : £8.00 : CIP entry
ISBN 0-419-11680-x (pbk) : £4.00 B81-31165

808'.0666021 — Technical writing *— Manuals*

Hoover, Hardy. [Essentials for the technical writer]. Essentials for the scientific and technical writer / Hardy Hoover. — Rev. and corr. republication. — New York : Dover ; London : Constable, 1980. — viii,216p : ill ; 21cm
Originally published: New York : Chichester : Wiley, 1970. — Includes index
ISBN 0-486-24060-6 (pbk) : £2.60 B81-28882

808'.06661021 — Written communication — *Manuals — For nursing*

Kolin, Philip C.. Professional writing for nurses : in education, practice and research / Philip C. Kolin, Janeen L. Kolin. — St. Louis ; London : Mosby, 1980. — xi,218p : ill,forms ; 24cm
Includes bibliographies and index
ISBN 0-8016-2724-9 (pbk) : £7.75 B81-08538

808'.066651 — Great Britain. Personnel management. Legal aspects. Correspondence - *Forms & precedents*

Janner, Greville. Janner's handbook of draft letters of employment law for employers and personnel managers. — 2nd ed. — London : Business Books, Sept.1981. — [416]p
Previous ed.: published as The Employer's and personnel manager's handbook of draft letters of employment under the name Ewan Mitchell. 1978
ISBN 0-09-145730-0 : £18.50 : CIP entry B81-20561

808'.066651021 — Business correspondence — *Manuals*

Gartside, L.. Model business letters : a classified selection of modern business letters for use in schools and in business / L. Gartside. — 3rd ed. — Plymouth : Macdonald and Evans, 1981. — xiv,530p ; 22cm
Includes index
ISBN 0-7121-1268-5 (pbk) : £4.95 B81-17355

808'.066651021 — Business correspondence - *Manuals - For non-English speaking students*

McKeller, J. S.. Business matters. — Oxford : Pergamon, July 1981. — [128]p. — (Pergamon Institute of English (Oxford) materials for language practice)
ISBN 0-08-025356-3 (pbk) : £2.95 : CIP entry B81-13453

808'.066651021 — Business correspondence. Proofs. Correction *— Manuals*

Camp, Sue C.. Developing proofreading skill / Sue C. Camp. — New York ; London : McGraw-Hill, c1980. — iv,112,4p : forms ; 28cm
Text on inside covers. — Includes index
ISBN 0-07-009635-x (pbk) : £2.10 B81-26654

808'.066651021 — English language. Business English *— For non-English speaking students*

Blundell, J. A.. Career : prospects : English for the business and commercial world / J.A. Blundell, N.M.G. Middlemiss. — Oxford : Oxford University Press, c1981. — 151p : ill ; 25cm
ISBN 0-19-451321-1 (pbk) : £2.95 B81-39262

Blundell, J. A.. Career : prospects : English for the business and commercial world / [Jon Blundell and Nigel Middlemiss]. — Oxford : Oxford University Press
Teacher's book / [Jonathan Higgens]. — 1981. — 186p : ill ; 25cm
ISBN 0-19-451322-x (pbk) : £4.50 B81-39263

808'.066651021 — English language. Business English *— Manuals*

Pryse, B. Elizabeth. Successful communication in business / B. Elizabeth Pryse. — Oxford : Basil Blackwell, 1981. — viii,262p : ill,1form ; 23cm
Includes index
ISBN 0-631-11601-x (pbk) : £3.95 : CIP rev. B80-13895

808'.066651021 — International business correspondence in English *— Manuals*

Sephton, David. English letter-writing guide : a Tick-Tack supplement / [David Sephton]. — Wicklewood : Primrose, c1980. — 62leaves in various pagings ; 30cm
£15.00 (spiral) B81-36424

Sephton, David. Tick-tack : a break-through in any language : tomorrow's instant correspondence kit / David Sephton. — English version, [New 1980 ed.]. — Wicklewood : Primrose Publishing, 1980. — 52leaves in various foliations : 1map ; 30cm + supplement([4]p;21cm)
Previous ed.: 1978
ISBN 0-86235-001-8 (spiral) : £15.00
ISBN 0-86235-031-x (pocket ed.) : £4.00 B81-32456

808'.066651031 — International business correspondence in German *— Manuals — German texts*

Sephton, David. German letter-writing guide : a Tick-Tack supplement / [David Sephton]. — Wicklewood : Primrose, c1980. — 25leaves in various pagings ; 30cm
£10.00 (spiral) B81-36422

Sephton, David. Tick-tack : a break-through in any language : tomorrow's instant correspondence kit / David Sephton. — German version, [New 1980 ed.]. — Wicklewood Publishing, 1980. — 52leaves in varous foliations : 1map ; 30cm + supplement ([4]p;22cm)
German text, English preliminaries. — Previous ed.: 1978
ISBN 0-86235-003-4 (spiral) : £15.00
ISBN 0-86235-033-6 (pocket ed.) : £4.00 B81-32458

808'.0666510397 — International business correspondence in Swedish *— Manuals*

Sephton, David. Tick-Tack : a break-through in any language : tomorrow's instant correspondence kit / David Sephton. — Swedish version, [New 1980 ed. (rev.)]. — Wicklewood : Primrose, c1980. — [50]leaves in various pagings : 1facsim + supplement([4]p; 22cm) ; 30cm
Previous ed. i.e. Rev. ed.: 1978
ISBN 0-86235-006-9 (spiral) : £15.00 B81-36428

808'.066651041 — International business correspondence in French *— Manuals — French texts*

Sephton, David. French letter-writing guide : a Tick-Tack supplement / [David Sephton]. — Wicklewood : Primrose, c1980. — 27leaves in various pagings ; 30cm
£10.00 (spiral) B81-36423

808'.066651041 — International business correspondence in French — *Manuals* — *French texts* *continuation*

Sephton, David. Tick-tack : a break-through in any language : tomorrow's instant correspondence kit / David Sephton. — French version, [New 1980 ed.]. — Wicklewood : Primrose Publishing, 1980. — 52leaves in various foliations : 1map ; 30cm + supplement ([4]p;22cm)
French text, English preliminaries. — Previous ed.: 1978
ISBN 0-86235-002-6 (spiral) : £15.00
ISBN 0-86235-032-8 (Edition de pocke) : £4.00
B81-32457

808'.066651051 — International business correspondence in Italian — *Manuals*

Sephton, David. Tick-Tack : a break-through in any language : tomorrow's instant correspondence kit / David Sephton. — Italian version, [New 1980 ed. (rev.)]. — Wicklewood : Primrose, c1980. — [57]leaves in various pagings : 1map ; 30cm
Previous ed. i.e. Rev. ed.: 1978
ISBN 0-86235-005-0 (spiral) : £15.00
B81-36429

808'.066651061 — International business correspondence in Spanish — *Manuals* — *Spanish texts*

Sephton, David. Tick-tack : a break-through in any language : tomorrow's instant correspondence kit / David Sephton. — Spanish version, [New 1980 ed.]. — Wicklewood : Primrose Publishing, 1980. — 52leaves in various foliations : 1maps ; 30cm + supplement([4]p;21cm)
Spanish text, English preliminaries. — Previous ed.: 1978
ISBN 0-86235-004-2 (spiral) : £15.00
ISBN 0-86235-034-4 (pocket ed.) : £4.00
B81-32459

808'.066651069 — International business correspondence in Portuguese — *Manuals*

Sephton, David. Tick-Tack : a break-through in any language : tomorrow's instant correspondence kit / David Sephton. — Portuguese version, [New 1980 ed. (rev.)]. — Wicklewood : Primrose, c1980. — [50]leaves in various pagings ; 30cm
Previous ed.: 1979
ISBN 0-86235-009-3 (spiral) : £15.00
B81-36427

808'.0666510927 — International business correspondence in Arabic — *Manuals*

Sephton, David. Tick-Tack : a break-through in any language : tomorrow's instant correspondence kit / David Sephton. — Arabic version, New 1980 ed. (rev.). — Wicklewood : Primrose, c1980. — [59]leaves in various pagings ; 30cm
Parallel arabic and romanised script
ISBN 0-86235-010-7 (spiral) : £15.00
ISBN 0-86235-040-9 (arabic pocket ed.)
ISBN 0-86235-011-5 (romanised script)
ISBN 0-86235-041-7 (romanised pocket ed.)
B81-36425

808'.0666510992 — International business correspondence in Malay or Indonesian — *Manuals*

Sephton, David. Tick-Tack : a break-through in any language : tomorrow's instant correspondence kit / David Sephton. — Malay Indonesian version. — Wicklewood : Primrose, c1980. — [29]leaves in various pagings ; 30cm
ISBN 0-86235-012-3 (spiral) : £15.00
B81-36426

808'.066658021 — United States. Business firms. Reports. Writing — *Manuals*

Moyer, Ruth. The research and report handbook : for managers and executives in business, industry, and government / Ruth Moyer, Eleanor Stevens, Ralph Switzer. — New York ; Chichester : Wiley, c1981. — viii,312p : ill,1map,facsims,forms ; 24cm
Bibliography: p304-305. — Includes index
ISBN 0-471-04257-9 (cased) : £9.00
ISBN 0-471-04258-7 (pbk) : £4.40 B81-09783

808'.066791021 — Cinema films. Scripts. Writing

Giustini, Rolando. The filmscript : a writer's guide / Rolando Giustini. — Englewood Cliffs ; London : Prentice-Hall, c1980. — x,243p : ill ; 24cm. — (A Spectrum book)
Includes index
ISBN 0-13-314252-3 (cased) : Unpriced
ISBN 0-13-314245-0 (pbk) : £4.50 B81-12606

808'.066791021 — Scripts. Writing — *Manuals*

Willis, Edgar E.. Writing scripts : for television, radio, and film, / Edgar E. Willis, Camille D'Arienzo. — New York ; London : Holt, Rinehart and Winston, c1981. — xiii,322p : ill ; 24cm
Bibliography: p306-311. — Includes index
ISBN 0-03-052706-6 (pbk) : £7.25 B81-22972

808'.0669021 — Historical events. Serials with American imprints — *Practical information* — *For contributors*

Steiner, Dale R.. Historical journals : a handbook for writers and reviewers / Dale R. Steiner. — Santa Barbara ; Oxford : ABC-Clio, c1981. — x,213p ; 24cm
Includes index
ISBN 0-87436-312-8 : £12.50 B81-28959

808'.06692021 — Curricula vitae. Writing — *Manuals*

Bostwick, Burdette E.. Résumé writing : a comprehensive how-to-do-it guide / Burdette E. Bostwick. — 2nd ed. — New York ; London : Wiley, c1980. — xiii,314p ; 24cm
Previous ed.: 1976. — Includes index
ISBN 0-471-08067-5 : £5.95 B81-11308

808.06'81 — Poetry. Composition by children, to 11 years

Moore, Vardine. The pleasure of poetry with and by children : a handbook / by Vardine Moore. — Metuchen ; London : Scarecrow, 1981. — ix,133p : music ; 23cm
Bibliography: p126-128. — Includes index
ISBN 0-8108-1399-8 : £7.00 B81-25960

808.1 — Great Britain. Schools. Curriculum subjects: Poetry in English. Composition. Teaching

Brownjohn, Sandy. Does it have to rhyme? : teaching children to write poetry / Sandy Brownjohn. — London : Hodder and Stoughton, 1980. — 96p ; 22cm
Bibliography: p94-96
ISBN 0-340-25514-5 (pbk) : £2.75 : CIP rev.
B80-10731

808.1 — Poetry. Aesthetics. Coleridge, Samuel Taylor. Biographia literaria — *Critical studies*

Wheeler, Kathleen M.. Sources, processes and methods in Coleridge's Biographia literaria / Kathleen M. Wheeler. — Cambridge : Cambridge University Press, 1980. — xiii,229p ; 24cm
Bibliography: p212-221. — Includes index
ISBN 0-521-22690-2 : £17.50 B81-05947

808.1 — Poetry. Composition

Riccio, Ottone M.. The intimate art of writing poetry / Ottone M. Riccio ; foreword by Stephen Minot. — Englewood Cliffs ; London : Prentice-Hall, c1980. — xxi,297p ; 21cm. — (A Spectrum book)
Bibliography: p265-273. - Includes index
ISBN 0-13-476846-9 (cased) : Unpriced
ISBN 0-13-476838-8 (pbk) : £3.85 B81-12605

808.1 — Poetry. Imagination — *Philosophical perspectives*

Cardinal, Roger. Figures of reality : a perspective on the poetic imagination / Roger Cardinal. — London : Croom Helm, 1981. — 245p : ill ; 23cm
Includes index
ISBN 0-85664-085-9 : £13.95 B81-07545

808.1 — Poetry in English. Composition — *Interviews* — *Serials*

The **Riverside** interviews. — 1-. — London ([106 Ladbroke Grove, W11]) : Binnacle Press, 1980-. — v. : ill,ports ; 29cm
Irregular
ISSN 0261-3042 = Riverside interviews : Unpriced B81-25003

808.1 — Poetry. Theories

Schiller, Friedrich. On the naive and sentimental in literature / Schiller ; translated with an introduction by Helen Watanabe-O'Kelly. — Manchester : Carcanet, 1981. — 107p ; 20cm
Translation of: Ueber naive und sentimentalische Dichtung
ISBN 0-85635-331-0 (pbk) : £3.95 : CIP rev.
B81-27425

808.1 — Poetry. Theories. Wordsworth, William, *1770-1850.* **Essays upon epitaphs** — *Critical studies*

Devlin, D. D.. Wordsworth and the poetry of epitaphs / D.D. Devlin. — London : Macmillan, 1980. — ix,143p ; 23cm
Bibliography: pix. — Includes index
ISBN 0-333-21783-7 : £12.00 : CIP rev.
B80-18470

808.2'01 — Drama. Semiotic aspects

Elam, Keir. The semiotics of theatre and drama / Keir Elam. — London : Methuen, 1980. — xii,248p : ill ; 21cm. — (New accents)
Bibliography: p221-239. - Includes index
ISBN 0-416-72050-1 : £7.50 : CIP rev.
ISBN 0-416-72060-9 (pbk) : £3.95 B80-08908

808.2'2 — Television drama in English. Scripts. Writing — *Manuals*

Paice, Eric. The way to write for television / Eric Paice. — London : Elm Tree, 1981. — 83p ; 22cm
ISBN 0-241-10650-8 (cased) : £6.50 : CIP rev.
ISBN 0-241-10647-8 (pbk) : £4.25 B81-20519

808.2'2 — Television programmes. Drama. Scripts. Writing — *Manuals*

Bronfeld, Stewart. Writing for film and television / Stewart Bronfeld. — Englewood Cliffs ; London : Prentice-Hall, c1981. — xiv,144p : ill ; 21cm. — (A Spectrum book)
Includes index
ISBN 0-13-970608-9 (cased) : Unpriced
ISBN 0-13-970590-2 (pbk) : £3.20
Also classified at 808.2'3 B81-22755

808.2'3 — Cinema films: Feature films. Scripts. Writing — *Manuals*

Bronfeld, Stewart. Writing for film and television / Stewart Bronfeld. — Englewood Cliffs ; London : Prentice-Hall, c1981. — xiv,144p : ill ; 21cm. — (A Spectrum book)
Includes index
ISBN 0-13-970608-9 (cased) : Unpriced
ISBN 0-13-970590-2 (pbk) : £3.20
Primary classification 808.2'2 B81-22755

808.2'3 — Cinema films. Plots. Construction — *Early works*

Hill, Wycliffe A.. Ten million photography plots / Wycliffe A. Hill. — New York ; London : Garland, 1978, c1919. — 100p : 1form,1port ; 26cm. — (The Garland classics of film literature)
Originally published: Los Angeles : Feature Photodrama Co., 1919
ISBN 0-8240-2879-1 : £16.50 B81-26610

808.3 — Fiction. Bestsellers. Composition — *Manuals*

Koontz, Dean R.. How to write best-selling fiction. — London (13 Burlington Lodge Studios, Rigault Rd., S.W.6.) : Poplar Press, Oct.1981. — [304]p
ISBN 0-907657-00-1 : £8.95 : CIP entry
B81-25742

808.3 — Fiction. Forms: Novels

Robert, Marthe. Origins of the novel / Marthe Robert ; [translated by Sacha Rabinovitch]. — Brighton : Harvester, c1980. — 235p ; 23cm
Translation of: Roman des origines et origines du roman
ISBN 0-85527-577-4 : £18.95 : CIP rev.
B80-22421

808.3 — Fiction. Forms: Novels. Theories

McCarthy, Mary, *1912-.* Ideas and the novel / Mary McCarthy. — London : Weidenfeld and Nicolson, 1981, c1980. — 121p ; 21cm
Originally published: New York : Harcourt Brace Jovanovich, 1980
ISBN 0-297-77896-x : £4.95 B81-05598

808.3 — Fiction. Forms: Novels. Writing — *Manuals*

Doubtfire, Dianne. The craft of novel-writing : a practical guide / Dianne Doubtfire. — Rev. ed. — London : Allison & Busby, 1981. — x,86p : 1form ; 20cm
Previous ed.: 1978. — Bibliography: p85-86. — Includes index
ISBN 0-85031-405-4 (pbk) : £2.50 : CIP rev. B81-13720

Kitchen, Paddy. The way to write novels / Paddy Kitchen. — London : Elm Tree, 1981. — 77p ; 22cm
ISBN 0-241-10648-6 (cased) : £6.50: CIP rev.
ISBN 0-241-10649-4 (pbk) : £14.25 B81-14820

808.3'876 — Science fiction. Religious aspects

Gooch, Stan. Science fiction as religion / Stan Gooch & Christopher Evans. — [Frome] ([45 Milk St., Frome, Somerset]) : Bran's Head, c1981. — 15p ; 22cm
£1.00 (pbk) B81-19422

808.4 — Essays in English. Composition — *For Irish students*

Fearnley, William. English essay-writing for leaving certificate / William Fearnley and Dermot Madden. — Dublin : Gill and Macmillan, 1981. — 35p ; 22cm
ISBN 0-7171-1097-4 (pbk) : £0.90 B81-25571

808.5 — Oral communication — *Manuals*

McCabe, Bernard P.. Speaking is a practical matter / Bernard P. McCabe, Jr, Coleman C. Bender. — 4th ed. — Boston, Mass. ; London : Allyn and Bacon, c1981. — xvi,413p : ill ; 24cm + Instructors manual(51p: forms; 22cm)
Previous ed.: Boston, Mass. : Holbrook Press, 1976. — Bibliography: p342-343. - Includes index
ISBN 0-205-07230-5 (pbk) : Unpriced
ISBN 0-205-07231-3 (Instructors manual) : Unpriced B81-11289

808.5'1 — Public speaking

Ilardo, Joseph A.. Speaking persuasively / Joseph A. Ilardo. — New York : Macmillan ; London : Collier Macmillan, c1981. — xiii,279p : ill ; 24cm
Includes bibliographies and index
ISBN 0-02-359620-1 : £10.50 B81-36169

808.5'1 — Public speaking — *Early works*

Menander, *fl.375-400*. [Treatise 1. English and Greek]. Menander rhetor / edited with translation and commentary by D.A. Russell and N.G. Wilson. — Oxford : Clarendon Press, 1981. — xlvi,390p ; 23cm
Parallel Greek text and English translation. — Bibliography: pix-x. - Includes index
ISBN 0-19-814013-4 : £35.00 : CIP rev. B79-27848

808.5'1 — Public speaking — *Manuals*

Barrett, Harold. Practical uses of speech communication / Harold Barrett. — 5th ed. — New York ; London : Holt, Rinehart and Winston, 1981. — viii,312p : ill,facsims ; 23cm
Previous ed.: 1977. — Includes index
ISBN 0-03-049591-1 (pbk) : £6.25 B81-12691

Barrett, Harold. Speaking practically : an introduction to public speaking / Harold Barrett. — New York ; London : Holt, Rinehart and Winston, c1981. — xi,212p : ill ; 24cm
Brief ed. of the author's Practical uses of speech communication. 5th ed. 1981. — Includes index
ISBN 0-03-054091-7 (pbk) : £5.00 B81-12690

Dixon, Diana. Talking about your research. — Leicester : Primary Communications Research Centre, University of Leicester, Sept.1981. — [44]p. — (Aids to scholarly communication, ISSN 0142-7288)
ISBN 0-906083-19-2 (pbk) : £4.50 : CIP entry B81-21541

Hunt, Gary T.. Public speaking / Gary T. Hunt. — Englewood Cliffs ; London : Prentice-Hall, c1981. — xi,308p : ill,ports ; 23cm
Includes bibliographies and index
ISBN 0-13-738807-1 (pbk) : £8.40 B81-19653

Janner, Greville. Janner's complete speechmaker. — London : Business Books, Oct.1981. — [304]p
ISBN 0-09-142980-3 : £15.00 : CIP entry B81-27372

Rodman, George R.. Public speaking : an introduction to message preparation / George Rodman. — 2nd ed. — New York ; London : Holt, Rinehart and Winston, c1981. — viii,310p : ill ; 24cm
Previous ed.: 1978. — Includes index
ISBN 0-03-051056-2 (pbk) : £6.25 B81-22880

Spencer, Ivor. Speeches and toasts / Ivor Spencer. — London : Ward Lock, 1980. — 189p ; 19cm
ISBN 0-7063-5857-0 (pbk) : £2.50 CIP rev. B80-10200

808.5'1 — Public speaking — *Manuals — For businessmen*

Humes, James C.. Talk your way to the top / James C. Humes. — New York ; London : McGraw-Hill, 1980. — xv,170p ; 21cm
Bibliography: p169-170
ISBN 0-07-031160-9 (pbk) : £3.95 B81-01738

808.5'1'024372 — Public speaking — *Manuals — For teaching*

Estill, Louise. Be confident about speaking / [Louise Estill]. — Gerrards Cross (15 Kingsway, Gerrards Cross, Bucks. SL9 8NS) : Louise Estill Teaching Aids, c1981. — [23]p ; 30cm
In plastic pocket
ISBN 0-907732-02-x (unbound) : £6.50 B81-36265

808.5'1'02461 — Public speaking — *For medicine*

Calnan, James. Speaking at medical meetings : a practical guide / James Calnan and Andras Barabas. — 2nd ed. enlarged and rev. — London : Heinemann Medical, 1981. — xii,184p : ill ; 19cm
Previous ed.: 1972. — Bibliography: p167-171. — Includes index
ISBN 0-433-05001-2 (pbk) : £4.50 B81-36447

808.5'1'0924 — United States. Public speaking. Reid, Loren — *Biographies*

Reid, Loren. Finally it's Friday : school and work in mid-America, 1921-1933 / Loren Reid. — Columbia ; London : University of Missouri Press, 1981. — viii,292p : ill,facsims,ports ; 23cm
Includes index
ISBN 0-8262-0330-2 : £9.80 B81-38215

808.5'1'0975 — United States. Southern states. Public speaking, *1865-1905*

Oratory in the New South / edited by Waldo W. Braden. — Baton Rouge ; London : Louisiana State University Press, c1979. — 286p ; 23cm
Bibliography: p277-280. - Includes index
ISBN 0-8071-0472-8 : £10.50 B81-18268

808.5'43 — Story-telling — *Manuals*

Colwell, Eileen. Storytelling / Eileen Colwell. — London : Bodley Head, 1980. — 83p ; 23cm
Bibliography: p77-83
ISBN 0-370-30228-1 : £3.75 : CIP rev. B80-19881

808.56 — Conversation

Conversation and discourse : structure and interpretation / edited by Paul Werth. — London : Croom Helm, c1981. — 181p ; 23cm
Conference papers. — Includes bibliographies and index
ISBN 0-7099-2717-7 : £13.95 : CIP rev. B81-08829

808.6 — Correspondence in English — *Manuals*

Writing formal letters. — London (1 Aislibie Rd., S.E.12) : Lee Centre, Basic Studies Dept., [1981]. — 57p : facsims,1form ; 30cm
Cover title
Unpriced (spiral) B81-17192

808.6 — Correspondence in Spanish — *Manuals*

Jackson, Mary H.. Guide to correspondence in Spanish. — Cheltenham : Stanley Thornes, Aug.1981. — [62]p
ISBN 0-85950-335-6 (pbk) : £1.95 : CIP entry B81-23802

808.6 — Correspondence — *Manuals*

Carroll, Lewis. Eight or nine wise words about letter writing / by Lewis Carroll. — Esher (Full Point, New Rd., Esher, Surrey KT10 9PG) : Penmiel Press, 1981. — 11p : ill ; 23cm + Prospectus(folded sheet : [4]p : ill ; 22cm)
Originally published: with The Wonderland postage-stamp-case. Oxford : Emberlin, 1891. — Limited ed. of 75 copies
£10.00 (pbk) B81-12119

Lesirge, Ruth. Letter writing / Ruth Lesirge and Roz Ivanič. — Basingstoke : Macmillan Education, 1980. — 23p : ill,facsims ; 30cm
ISBN 0-333-28143-8 (pbk) : £0.85 : CIP rev. B80-13514

808.6 — Postcards & greetings cards. Writing — *Manuals — For slow reading adults*

Moore, Alison. Send a friend a card / Alison Moore, Dona Williams. — [Edinburgh] ([5 Leamington Terrace, Edinburgh EH10 4JW]) : Lothian Region Adult Literacy Scheme, [1980]. — 28p : ill ; 29cm
£0.30 (pbk) B81-09581

808.7 — Jokes *expounded by* **mathematical logic**

Paulos, John Allen. Mathematics and humor / John Allen Paulos. — Chicago ; London : University of Chicago Press, 1980. — 116p : ill ; 22cm
Bibliography: p109-112. — Includes index
ISBN 0-226-65024-3 : £7.80 B81-03529

808.8 — LITERATURE. GENERAL ANTHOLOGIES

808.8 — Literature, *to 1978 — Anthologies — English texts*

The **Norton** anthology of world masterpieces / Maynard Mack, general editor, Bernard M.W. Knox ... [et al.]. — 4th ed. — New York ; London : Norton, c1979. — 2v.(xix,1750p;xix,1881p) ; 22cm
Previous ed.: published as World masterpieces. 1973. — Includes index
ISBN 0-393-95036-0 : £16.50 set
ISBN 0-393-95045-x (v.1:pbk) : £6.95
ISBN 0-393-95040-9 (v.2:cased) : £8.25
ISBN 0-393-95050-6 (v.2:pbk) : £6.95 B81-07789

808.8 — Literature, *to 1979 — Anthologies — English texts*

Hall, Donald, *1928-*. To read literature, fiction, poetry, drama / Donald Hall. — New York ; London : Holt, Rinehart and Winston, c1981. — xxii,1508p : ill,ports ; 25cm
Includes index
ISBN 0-03-021006-2 : £9.95 B81-05393

808.8'0024 — Literature, *ca 1500 — Anthologies — Manuscripts — Facsimiles*

The **Winchester** anthology. — Woodbridge : D.S. Brewer, Oct.1981. — [480]p
ISBN 0-85991-083-0 : £80.00 : CIP entry B81-27430

808.8'033256944 — Literature, *to 1980.* **Special subjects: Jerusalem —** *Anthologies*

Jerusalem : the Holy City in literature. — 2nd ed. — London : Kahn & Averill, Oct.1981. — [244]p
Previous ed.: London : Adam Books, 1968
ISBN 0-900707-65-8 (pbk) : £7.50 : CIP entry B81-30270

808.8'0353 — Literature, *to 1980.* **Special subjects: Sex relations —** *Anthologies*

The **Dirty** bits. — London : Deutsch, Oct.1981. — [160]p
ISBN 0-233-97395-8 : £4.95 : CIP entry B81-26739

808.8'0354 — Literature, *to 1981.* **Special subjects: Love —** *Anthologies — English texts*

A **World** of love. — London : Hamish Hamilton, Jan.1982. — [96]p
ISBN 0-241-10714-8 : £4.95 : CIP entry B81-3466

808.8′036 — Literature, *to 1948.* **Special subjects: Hares** — *Anthologies* — *English texts*
Hares / edited by D. Wyn Hughes. — London : W.H. Allen, 1981. — 55p : ill(some col.) ; 18cm
ISBN 0-491-02634-x : £2.50
Also classified at 760′.04432 B81-05705

808.8′036 — Literature, *to 1980.* **Special subjects: Horses** — *Anthologies*
Horses / edited by Elizabeth Rudd. — London : W.H. Allen, 1981. — 53p : ill(some col.) ; 15cm
ISBN 0-491-02655-2 : £2.50
Also classified at 760′.04432 B81-35739

808.8′0375 — Literature. Special themes: Dragons — *Anthologies*
Dragons / edited by Elizabeth Rudd. — London : W.H. Allen, 1980. — 55p : ill(some col.) ; 18cm
ISBN 0-491-02604-8 : £2.50
Also classified at 760′.0447 B81-02747

808.81 — Poetry, *to 1955* — *Anthologies* — *English texts*
The **Oxford** Book of verse in English translation / chosen and edited by Charles Tomlinson. — Oxford : Oxford University Press, 1980. — xlviii, 608p ; 23cm
Includes index
ISBN 0-19-214103-1 : £12.50 : CIP rev.
B80-18465

808.81 — Poetry, *to 1980* — *Anthologies* — *Welsh texts*
O erddi eraill : cerddi o amrywiol ieithoedd i'r Gymraeg / golygydd D. Myrddin Lloyd. — Caerdydd : Gwasg Prifysgol Cymru ar ran yr Academi Gymreig, 1981. — viii,83p ; 21cm. — (Cyfres barddoniaeth Pwyllgor Cyfieithiadau yr Academi Gymreig ; cyf.2)
ISBN 0-7083-0793-0 (pbk) : £2.95 B81-22963

808.81 — Poetry. Women writers, *to 1977* — *Anthologies* — *English texts*
The **Penguin** book of women poets / edited by Carol Cosman, Joan Keefe, Kathleen Weaver ; consulting editors Joanna Bankier, Doris Earnshaw, Deirdre Lashgari. — Harmondsworth : Penguin, 1979, c1978 (1980 [printing]). — 399p ; 20cm. — (The Penguin poets)
Originally published: London : Allen Lane, 1978. — Includes index
ISBN 0-14-042225-0 (pbk) : £2.50 B81-01090

808.81′9′351 — Poetry in European languages, *ca 1560-1980.* **Special subjects: Mary,** *Queen of Scots* — *Anthologies* — *English texts*
Mary Queen of Scots : an anthology of poetry. — London : Eyre Methuen, Sept.1981. — [64]p
ISBN 0-413-48550-1 : £4.50 : CIP entry
B81-23912

808.81′9358 — Poetry. Special subjects: Frelimo, *1960-1978* — *Anthologies*
Sunflower of hope. — London : Allison & Busby, Nov.1981. — [192]p
ISBN 0-85031-419-4 (cased) : £7.95 : CIP entry
ISBN 0-85031-419-4 (pbk) : £3.50 B81-30574

808.81′9382 — Religious poetry, *to 1979* — *Anthologies* — *English texts*
Playing with fire : a natural selection of religious poetry / edited by Susan Dwyer. — Dublin (55 Dame St., Dublin 2) : Villa, 1980. — 198p ; 23cm
Includes index
ISBN 0-906408-12-1 : £5.95 : CIP rev.
B79-36930

808.83′1 — Children's short stories in European languages, *to 1980* — *Anthologies* — *English texts*
My gold storybook / [illustrated by Val Biro ... et al.]. — London : Hamlyn, 1981. — 111p : col.ill ; 26cm
ISBN 0-600-36659-6 (pbk) : £1.99 B81-38956

My silver storybook / [illustrated by Victor Ambrus ... et al.]. — London : Hamlyn, 1981. — 112p : col.ill ; 26cm
ISBN 0-600-36660-x (pbk) : £1.99 B81-38957

808.83′1 — Short stories. Women writers, *to 1980* — *Anthologies* — *English texts*
Rediscovery : 300 years of stories by and about women. — London : Women's Press, Nov.1981. — [240]p
ISBN 0-7043-3879-3 (pbk) : £3.50 : CIP entry
B81-30351

808.83′9′353 — Fiction, *1750-1980.* **Special subjects: Sex relations** — *Critical studies*
Charney, Maurice. Sexual fiction. — London : Methuen, Oct.1981. — [200]p. — (New accents)
ISBN 0-416-31930-0 (cased) : £6.50 : CIP entry
ISBN 0-416-31940-8 (pbk) : £2.95 B81-27347

808.86′9354 — Love letters, *ca 900-1980* — *Anthologies* — *English texts*
Written with love. — London : Hutchinson, Oct.1981. — [112]p
ISBN 0-09-146620-2 : £2.95 : CIP entry
B81-30207

808.88 — Compliments, *to 1979* — *Anthologies* — *English texts*
Compliments : a treasury of tributes to friends and lovers, relatives and rivals / compiled by Gertrude Buckman ; illustrated by Fiona Almeleh. — London : Unwin, 1980. — 93p : col.ill ; 25cm
Includes index
ISBN 0-04-808028-4 (pbk) : £3.95 : CIP rev.
B80-23643

808.88′2 — Last words, *to 1978* — *Anthologies* — *English texts*
Famous last words / compiled by Jonathon Green. — London : Pan, 1980, c1979. — 317p ; 18cm
Originally published: London : Omnibus Press, 1979. — Includes index
ISBN 0-330-26205-x (pbk) : £1.50 B81-00246

808.88′2 — Quotations, *to 1980* — *Anthologies* — *English texts*
More of who said that?. — Newton Abbot : David & Charles, Oct.1981. — [64]p
ISBN 0-7153-8275-6 : £2.95 : CIP entry
Also classified at 920′.02 B81-28073

808.88′2 — Quotations, *to 1981* — *Anthologies* — *English texts*
Quotations for speakers. — Newton Abbot : David & Charles, Sept.1981. — [64]p
ISBN 0-7153-8111-3 : £2.95 : CIP entry
B81-22505

808.88′2 — Quotations, *to ca 1980* — *Anthologies*
The **concise** Oxford dictionary of quotations. — 2nd ed. — Oxford : Oxford University Press, Sept.1981. — [480]p
Previous ed.: 1964
ISBN 0-19-211588-x (cased) : £5.95 : CIP entry
ISBN 0-19-281324-2 (pbk) : £2.95 B81-22478

808.88′7 — Insults, *to 1980* — *Anthologies* — *English texts*
McPhee, Nancy. The second book of insults / by Nancy McPhee. — London : Deutsch, 1981. — 132p : ports ; 24cm. — (A Ganton Gate book)
Includes index
ISBN 0-233-97374-5 : £3.95 B81-39442

808.88′8 — Fables — *Anthologies* — *English texts*
The **Illustrated** book of world fables / collected by Y.Y Cotterell. — London : Book Club Associates, 1979. — 159p : ill(some col.) ; 25cm
Includes index
Unpriced B81-37882

809 — LITERATURE. HISTORY AND CRITICAL STUDIES

809 — European literature — *Serials*
The **Year's** work in modern language studies. — Vol.41 (1979). — London : The Modern Humanities Research Association, 1980. — 1260p
ISBN 0-900547-73-1 : Unpriced
ISSN 0084-4152
Primary classification 405 B81-09113

809 — Literature — *Critical studies*
Blanchot, Maurice. The siren's song. — Brighton : Harvester Press, Feb.1982. — [256]p
Translated from the French
ISBN 0-85527-738-6 : £9.50 : CIP entry
B81-40263

Robert, Marthe. Inside Writing : a reader's notebook / Marthe Robert ; [translated by Sacha Rabinovitch]. — Brighton : Harvester, 1981. — 139p ; 21cm
Translation of: Livre de lectures
ISBN 0-85527-737-8 : £12.95 B81-31478

Trilling, Lionel. The liberal imagination : essays on literature and society / Lionel Trilling. — Uniform ed. — Oxford : Oxford Univesity Pres. — 284p ; 21cm. — (The works of Lionel Trilling)
Originally published: New York : Viking Press, 1950 ; London : Secker and Warburg, 1951
ISBN 0-19-212218-5 : £8.95 B81-23525

Trilling, Lionel. Prefaces to the experience of literature / Lionel Trilling. — Uniform ed. — Oxford : Oxford University Press, 1981, c1979. — 302p ; 21cm. — (The works of Lionel Trilling)
Originally published: New York : Harcourt Brace Jovanovich, 1979
ISBN 0-19-212219-3 : £8.95 : CIP rev.
B81-01849

809 — Literature — *Critical studies* — *Serials*
Glyph. — 8. — Baltimore ; London : Johns Hopkins University Press, c1981. — 242p
ISBN 0-8018-2481-8 : Unpriced B81-29073

809 — Literature, *to 1980* — *Critical studies*
Literary criticism and myth / edited by Joseph P. Strelka. — University Park ; London : Pennsylvania State University Press, c1980. — xiii,285p ; 24cm. — (Yearbook of comparative criticism ; v.9)
Includes index
ISBN 0-271-00225-5 : Unpriced B81-15567

809′.03 — European literatures, *1558-1900* — *Critical studies*
James, Henry, *1843-1916.* Selected literary criticism / Henry James ; edited by Morris Shapira ; prefaced with a note on 'James as critic' by F.R. Leavis. — Cambridge : Cambridge University Press, 1981. — xxiii,349p ; 22cm
Originally published: London : Heinemann, 1963. — Includes index
ISBN 0-521-28365-5 (pbk) : £6.95 B81-21690

809′.03 — Literature, *1837-1968* — *Critical studies*
Trilling, Lionel. Speaking of literature and society. — Oxford : Oxford University Press, Jan.1982. — [445]p. — (The works of Lionel Trilling)
ISBN 0-19-212221-5 : £9.95 : CIP entry
B81-34373

809′.03 — Western European literatures. Influence of Wagner, Richard, *ca 1880-1980*
Furness, Raymond. Wagner and literature. — Manchester : Manchester University Press, Nov.1981. — [220]p
ISBN 0-7190-0844-1 : £17.50 : CIP entry
B81-31242

809′.034 — European literatures, *1842-1924.* **Influence of Hamlet by Shakespeare, William** — *Critical studies*
Scofield, Martin. The ghosts of Hamlet : the play and modern writers / Martin Scofield. — Cambridge : Cambridge University Press, 1980. — 202p ; 24cm
Includes index
ISBN 0-521-22735-6 : £16.50
Primary classification 822.3′3 B81-07893

809′.034 — Literature, *1800-1945.* **Cultural aspects**
Trilling, Lionel. Beyond culture : essays on literature and learning / Lionel Trilling. — Oxford : Oxford University Press, 1980, c1965. — 204p ; 21cm. — (The Works of Lionel Trilling)
Originally published: New York : Viking Press, 1965 ; London : Secker & Warburg, 1966
ISBN 0-19-212215-0 : £6.95 : CIP rev.
B80-04926

809′.04 — European literatures, *1900-1979* — *Encyclopaedias*

Columbia dictionary of modern European literature. — 2nd ed., fully rev. and enl. / Jean-Albert Bédé and William B. Edgerton general editors. — New York : Guildford : Columbia University Press, 1980. — xxi,895p ; 27cm
Previous ed.: / edited by Horatio Smith. 1947
ISBN 0-231-03717-1 : £28.00 B81-09522

Ward, A. C.. Longman companion to twentieth century literature / A.C. Ward. — 3rd ed. / revised by Maurice Hussey. — Harlow : Longman, 1981. — 598p ; 23cm
Previous ed.: 1975
ISBN 0-582-35307-6 : £12.50 B81-18920

809′.04 — European literatures, *ca 1900-ca 1970* — *Critical studies*

Esslin, Martin. Mediations : essays on Brecht, Beckett, and the media / Martin Esslin. — London : Eyre Methuen, 1980. — 248p ; 24cm
Bibliography: p243-244. — Includes index
ISBN 0-413-47040-7 : £8.95 B81-08533

809′.04 — Literature, *1900-1979* — *Critical studies*

Levin, Harry, *1912-*. Memories of the moderns / Harry Levin. — London : Faber, 1981. — 257p ; 24cm
Includes index
ISBN 0-571-11705-8 : £7.95 B81-10599

809′.041 — European literatures. Modernism, *1890-1930* — *Critical studies*

Modernism : 1890-1930 / edited by Malcolm Bradbury and James McFarlane. — Harmondsworth : Penguin, 1976 (1981 printing). — 683p ; 19cm. — (Pelican guides to European literature)
Bibliography: p641-664. — Includes index
ISBN 0-14-021933-1 (pbk) : £2.25 B81-40474

809.1 — Poetry — *Critical studies*

Raine, Kathleen. The inner journey of the poet. — London : Allen & Unwin, Oct.1981. — [208]p
ISBN 0-04-821054-4 : £10.50 : CIP entry B81-25869

809.1 — Poetry in European languages — *Critical studies*

Hamburger, *Michael*. Art as second nature : occasional pieces 1950-74 / by Michael Hamburger. — Manchester : Carcanet, 1975 (1979 [printing]). — 156p ; 22cm
ISBN 0-85635-292-6 (pbk) : £2.95 B81-05767

809.1 — Poetry *related to* music, *to 1980*

Winn, James Anderson. Unsuspected eloquence. — London : Yale University Press, July 1981. — [384]p
ISBN 0-300-02615-3 : £11.95 : CIP entry
Also classified at 780′.08 B81-22673

809.1′031 — Poetry in European languages, *ca 1500-ca 1700* — *Critical studies*

Hutton, James, *1902-*. Essays on Renaissance poetry / James Hutton ; edited by Rita Guerlac ; foreword by D.P. Walker. — Ithaca, N.Y. ; London : Cornell University Press, 1980. — 378p : 2ill ; 24cm
Includes index
ISBN 0-8014-1253-6 : £17.00 B81-27503

809.1′034 — Poetry, *1800-1980* — *Critical studies*

Perloff, Marjorie. The poetics of indeterminacy : Rimbaud to Cage / Marjorie Perloff. — Princeton ; Guildford, Surrey : Princeton University Press, c1981. — xvi,346p,[8]p of plates : ill ; 23cm
Includes index
ISBN 0-691-06244-7 : £11.70 B81-31679

809.1′034 — Poetry in European languages, *1850-1945* — *Critical studies*

Houston, John Porter. French symbolism and the modernist movement : a study of poetic structures / John Porter Houston. — Baton Rouge ; London : Louisiana State University Press, c1980. — xv,298p : ill ; 24cm
Includes appendix in French. — Includes index
ISBN 0-8071-0593-7 : £12.00 B81-07560

809.1′04 — Poetry in European languages, *1900-ca 1980.* Modernism — *Critical studies*

Hermans, Theo. The structure of modernist poetry. — London : Croom Helm, Jan.1982. — [240]p
ISBN 0-7099-0002-3 : £12.50 : CIP entry B81-34303

809.1′3 — Epic poetry in European languages, *to 1700.* Allegory — *Critical studies*

Murrin, Michael. The allegorical epic : essays in its rise and decline / Michael Murrin. — Chicago ; London : University of Chicago Press, 1980. — xii,275p ; 24cm
Includes index
ISBN 0-226-55402-3 : £13.80 B81-01536

809.1′3 — Epic poetry, *to ca 1980* — *Critical studies*

Traditions of heroic and epic poetry. — London : Modern Humanities Research Association. — (Publications of the Modern Humanities Research Association ; v.9)
Vol.1: The traditions / presented by the late Robert Auty ... [et al.] ; under the general editorship of A.T. Hatto. — 1980. — xiii,376p,[2]leaves of plates : ill,1geneal.table ; 26cm
'Founded upon the Transactions of the London Seminar on Epic 1964-1972' - Half t.p.. — Includes bibliographies
ISBN 0-900547-72-3 : Unpriced B81-29705

809.2′005 — Drama — *Critical studies — Serials*

Themes in drama. — 3. — Cambridge : Cambridge University Press, 1981. — 254p
ISBN 0-521-22180-3 : £15.00 : CIP rev. B81-02109

809.2′512 — Drama in Western European languages. Tragedy, *1506-1694* — *Critical studies*

Reiss, Timothy J.. Tragedy and truth : studies in the development of a Renaissance and neoclassical discourse / Timothy J. Reiss. — New Haven ; London : Yale University Press, c1980. — x,334p ; 25cm
Includes index
ISBN 0-300-02461-4 : £15.45 B81-04673

809.2′927 — Drama in European languages, *1884-1961.* Characters *compared with* Jesus Christ

Ditsky, John. The onstage Christ : studies in the persistence of a theme / by John Ditsky. — London : Vision, 1980. — 188p ; 23cm. — (Vision critical studies)
Includes index
ISBN 0-85478-284-2 : £9.95
Also classified at 232 B81-02713

809.3 — Fiction. Forms: Novels, *to 1979* — *Critical studies*

Novels and novelists : a guide to the world of fiction / editor Martin Seymour-Smith. — London : Windward, 1980. — 288p : ill(some col.),facsims(same col.) ports(same col.) ; 29cm
Text on lining papers. — Includes index
ISBN 0-7112-0015-7 : £8.95 B81-24907

809.3 — Fiction in European languages, *1530-1965* — *Critical studies*

Seymour-Smith, Martin. [An introduction to fifty European novels]. A reader's guide to fifty European novels / by Martin Seymour-Smith. — London : Heinemann, 1980. — 528p ; 21cm. — (Reader's guide series)
Originally published: London : Pan, 1980. — Bibliography: p515-516. - Includes index
ISBN 0-435-18812-7 : £9.50 : CIP rev. B80-13948

809.3 — Fiction in European languages, *to 1960.* Forms: Novels — *Critical studies*

Reed, Walter L.. An exemplary history of the novel : the Quixotic versus the picaresque / Walter L. Reed. — Chicago ; London : University of Chicago Press, 1981. — viii,334p ; 24cm
Includes index
ISBN 0-226-70683-4 : £13.50 B81-29780

809.3′034 — Fiction in European languages, *1800-1945* — *Critical studies*

Nabokov, Vladimir. Lectures on literature / Vladimir Nabokov ; edited by Fredson Bowers ; introduction by John Updike. — London : Weidenfeld and Nicolson, 1980. — xxvii,385p : ill,facsims ; 26cm
ISBN 0-297-77852-8 : £12.50 B81-05193

809.3′81 — Historical novels, *to 1937* — *Critical studies*

Lukács, George. The historical novel / Georg Lukács ; translated from the German by Hannah and Stanley Mitchell. — Harmondsworth : Penguin, 1981, c1962. — 435p ; 20cm. — (A Pelican book)
Translation of: Die theorie des Romans ; ein geschichtsphilosophischer Versuch über die Formen der grossen Epik. — Originally published: London : Merlin, 1962. — Includes index
ISBN 0-14-022372-x (pbk) : £3.95 B81-25080

809′.3′872 — Detective fiction in European languages, *to 1980* — *Critical studies*

Porter, Dennis. The pursuit of crime. — London : Yale University Press, Nov.1981. — [304]p
ISBN 0-300-02722-2 : £14.00 : CIP entry B81-35029

809.3′876 — Science fiction, *to 1979.* Special subjects: Equipment — *Illustrations*

DiFate, Vincent. DiFate's catalog of science fiction hardware / by Vincent DiFate and Ian Summers ; illustrated by Vincent DiFate ; written with Beth Meacham ; diagrams by Gregory Elkin and David Harper. — London : Sidgwick & Jackson, c1980. — 135p : col.ill ; 26cm
Originally published: New York : Workman, 1980. — Includes index
ISBN 0-283-98750-2 (cased) : £8.50 B81-10375

809.3′915 — Fiction in European languages, *1764-1977.* Fantasy — *Critical studies*

Jackson, Rosemary. Fantasy : the literature of subversion / Rosemary Jackson. — London : Methuen, 1981. — viii,211p ; 21cm. — (New accents)
Bibliography: p192-205. - Includes index
ISBN 0-416-71170-7 (cased) : £6.50
ISBN 0-416-71180-4 (pbk) : Unpriced B81-20911

809.3′916 — Horror stories, *to 1980* — *Critical studies*

King, Stephen, *1947-*. Stephen King's danse macabre. — London : Macdonald, 1981. — 400p : ill ; 25cm
Originally published: New York : Everest House, 1980. — Bibliography: p389-391. — List of films: p385-388. — Includes index
ISBN 0-354-04646-2 (cased) : £8.95
ISBN 0-354-04647-0 (pbk) : £5.95 B81-23667

809.3′923 — Fiction, *1700-1900.* Forms: Novels. Endings — *Critical studies*

Miller, D. A.. Narrative and its discontents : problems of closure in the traditional novel / by D.A. Miller. — Princeton ; Guildford : Princeton University Press, c1981. — xv,300p ; 23cm
Bibliography: p285-295. — Includes index
ISBN 0-691-06459-8 : £11.70 B81-26319

809.3′923 — Fiction in European languages, *ca 1850-1930.* Forms: Novels. Endings — *Critical studies*

Torgovnick, Marianna. Closure in the novel / Marianna Torgovnick. — Princeton ; Guildford : Princeton University Press, c1981. — 238p ; 23cm
Bibliography: p225-231. — Includes index
ISBN 0-691-06464-4 : £9.60 B81-32473

809.3′9384 — Fiction, *1550-1800.* Special subjects: Self — *Critical studies*

Weinstein, Arnold L.. Fictions of self : 1550-1800 / Arnold Weinstein. — Princeton ; Guildford : Princeton University Press, c1981. — x,302p ; 23cm
Includes index
ISBN 0-691-06448-2 : £11.20
ISBN 0-691-10107-8 (pbk) : £5.55 B81-26185

809'.889'24 — Jewish literature, *1900-1980* **—** *Critical studies*
Yudkin, Leon I.. Jewish literature and identity in the twentieth century. — London : Croom Helm, Jan.1982. — [176]p
ISBN 0-7099-2900-5 : £9.95 : CIP entry
B81-33889

809'.89282 — Children's literature — *Critical studies — Serials*
[Children's literature *(New Haven)***]**. Children's literature : annual of Modern Language Association Division on Children's Literature and the Children's Literature Association. — Vol.9. — New Haven ; London : Yale University Press, 1981. — 241p
ISBN 0-300-02623-4 : £5.65
ISSN 0092-8208 B81-24113

809'.896 — European literatures. African writers, *1945-1980.* **Implications of structuralism**
Anozie, Sunday O.. Structural models and African poetics : towards a pragmatic theory of literature / Sunday O. Anozie. — London : Routledge & Kegan Paul, 1981. — xi,338p : ill ; 23cm
Bibliography: p289-323. - Includes index
ISBN 0-7100-0467-2 : £13.50 B81-06764

809'.89669 — Literatures. Nigerian writers. Political aspects
Booth, James. Writers and politics in Nigeria / James Booth. — London : Hodder and Stoughton, 1981. — 190p ; 23cm
Bibliography: p186-190. — Includes index
ISBN 0-340-24415-1 (cased) : Unpriced : CIP rev.
ISBN 0-340-24416-x (pbk) : Unpriced
B80-18466

809'.91 — Literature. Irony
Muecke, D. C.. The compass of irony / D.C. Muecke. — London : Methuen, 1969 (1980 printing). — ix,276p : 2ill ; 23cm
Bibliography: p260-269. - Includes index
ISBN 0-416-74360-9 : £15.50 : CIP rev.
B80-08911

809'.912 — Literature. Realism
Levy, David J.. Realism : an essay in interpretation and social reality / David J. Levy. — Manchester : Carcanet New Press, 1981. — 138p ; 23cm
Includes index
ISBN 0-85635-300-0 : £7.95 : CIP rev.
B81-14431

809'.912 — Literature. Realism — *Marxist viewpoints*
Lukács, Georg. Essays on realism / Georg Lukács ; edited and introduced by Rodney Livingstone ; translated by David Fernbach. — London : Lawrence and Wishart, 1980. — 250p ; 23cm
Translation of: Essays über Realismus. — Includes index
£9.95 B81-05733

809'.9145 — European literatures, *1797-1836.* **Romanticism —** *Critical studies — Readings from contemporary sources*
. European romanticism : self-definition : an anthology / compiled by Lilian R. Furst. — London : Methuen, 1980. — xv,167p ; 20cm
Includes index
ISBN 0-416-71870-1 (cased) : £5.95 : CIP rev.
ISBN 0-416-71880-9 (pbk) : £2.50 B79-36444

809'.916 — Literature, *to 1979.* **Tragedy —** *Critical studies*
Tragedy : developments in criticism : a casebook / edited by R.P. Draper. — London : Macmillan, 1980. — 232p ; 23cm. — (Casebook series)
Bibliography: p225. — Includes index
ISBN 0-333-25822-3 (cased) : £12.00 : CIP rev.
ISBN 0-333-25823-1 (pbk) : £4.95 B80-09810

809'.923 — Literature. Narrative. Interpretation by readers
Ruthrof, Horst. The reader's construction of narrative / Horst Ruthrof. — London : Routledge & Kegan Paul, 1981. — xiv,231p ; 23cm
Includes index
ISBN 0-7100-0662-4 : £9.75 : CIP rev.
B81-02378

809'.93352 — Fiction in European languages, *1500-1980.* **Characters: Quixotic heroes —** *Critical studies*
Welsh, Alexander. Reflections on the hero as Quixote / Alexander Welsh. — Princeton ; Guildford : Princeton University Press, c1981. — viii,244p ; 23cm
Includes index
ISBN 0-691-06465-2 : £8.80 B81-30663

809'.93352042 — Literatures. African writers. Special subjects: Sociological perspectives of role of women in African urban communities — *Critical studies*
Little, Kenneth. The sociology of urban women's image in African literature / Kenneth Little. — London : Macmillan, 1980. — x,174p ; 23cm
Bibliography: p159-161. — Includes index
ISBN 0-333-28845-9 : £12.00 : CIP rev.
B80-18874

809'.933520431 — Literature, *to 1980.* **Special subjects: Interpersonal relationships between parents & children —** *Anthologies*
Parents & children / compiled by Claire Tomalin. — Oxford : Oxford University Press, 1981. — viii,91p : ill ; 21cm. — (Small Oxford books)
Includes index
ISBN 0-19-214123-6 : £3.95 : CIP rev.
B81-22650

809'.93353 — Literature. Special subjects: Sex relations — *Critical studies*
Atkins, John, *1916-*. Sex in literature. — London : John Calder
Vol.4: High noon. — Jan.1982. — [320]p
ISBN 0-7145-3756-x : £9.95 : CIP entry
B81-33834

809'.93355 — European literatures, *1100-1500.* **Special subjects: Christian pilgrimages —** *Critical studies*
Howard, Donald R.. Writers and pilgrims : medieval pilgrimage narratives and their posterity / Donald R. Howard. — Berkeley ; London : University of California Press, c1980. — x,133p ; 21cm
Includes index
ISBN 0-520-03926-2 : £6.50 B81-07676

809'.93355 — Literature, *to 1980.* **Special subjects: Cycling —** *Anthologies*
Cycling / compiled by Jeanne Mackenzie. — Oxford : Oxford University Press, 1981. — viii,110p : ill ; 21cm. — (Small Oxford books)
Includes index
ISBN 0-19-214117-1 : £3.95 : CIP rev.
B81-25652

809'.93355 — Literature, *to 1980.* **Special subjects: Food habits —** *Anthologies*
The **Pleasures** of the table / compiled by Theodora Fitzgibbon. — Oxford : Oxford University Press, 1981. — vii,92p : ill ; 21cm. — (Small Oxford books)
Includes index
ISBN 0-19-214120-1 : £3.95 : CIP rev.
B81-25650

809'.93355 — Literature, *to 1980.* **Special subjects: Hospitality —** *Anthologies*
Guests & hosts / compiled by Mari Prichard. — Oxford : Oxford University Press, 1981. — vii,92p : ill ; 21cm. — (Small Oxford books)
Includes index
ISBN 0-19-214115-5 : £3.95 : CIP rev.
B81-25651

809'.93358 — Literature in European languages, *1945-1980.* **Special subjects: Jews. Genocide,** *1939-1945 — Critical studies*
Ezrahi, Sidra DeKoven. By words alone : the Holocaust in literature / Sidra DeKoven Ezrahi ; with a foreword by Alfred Kazin. — Chicago ; London : University of Chicago Press, 1980. — xiii,262p ; 24cm
Bibliography: p245-252. — Includes index
ISBN 0-226-23335-9 : £9.00 B81-05071

809'.9337 — European literatures. Grail legends, *to 1500.* **Ritual aspects**
Weston, Jessie L.. From ritual to romance / by Jessie L. Weston. — Bath : Chivers, 1980. — xv,202p ; 23cm. — (A New Portway book)
Originally published: Cambridge : Cambridge University Press, 1920. — Includes index
ISBN 0-86220-505-0 : £4.50 : CIP rev.
B80-19884

809'.93372 — Fantasy literature, *to 1980.* **Special themes: Places —** *Encyclopaedias*
Manguel, Alberto. The dictionary of imaginary places / Alberto Manguel and Gianni Guadalupi ; illustrated by Graham Greenfield ; maps and charts by James Cook. — London : Granada, 1981, c1980. — 438p : ill,maps,plans ; 31cm
Originally published: New York : Macmillan, 1980. — Includes index
ISBN 0-246-11560-2 : £12.50 B81-21700

809'.93382 — European literatures. Arthurian romances. Special themes: Paganism — *Critical studies*
Darrah, John. The real Camelot : paganism and the Arthurian romances / John Darrah. — London : Thames and Hudson, c1981. — 160p : 1ill ; 23cm
Bibliography: p151-154. — Includes index
ISBN 0-500-01250-4 : £4.95 B81-29478

809'.935221 — Bible. O.T.. Poetry. Parallelism — *Critical studies*
Kugel, James L.. The idea of biblical poetry : parallelism and its history / James L. Kugel. — New Haven ; London : Yale University Press, c1981. — xi,339p ; 24cm
Includes index
ISBN 0-300-02474-6 : £19.20 B81-34085

809'.93592 — Autobiographical prose in European languages, *1900-1966 — Critical studies*
Pilling, John, *1946-*. Autobiography and imagination : studies in self-scrutiny / John Pilling. — London : Routledge & Kegan Paul, 1981. — ix,178p ; 23cm
Includes index
ISBN 0-7100-0730-2 : £10.50 : CIP rev.
B81-10418

810 — AMERICAN LITERATURE

810'.3'21 — English literature. American writers, *to 1900 — Encyclopaedias*
American literature to 1900 / introduction by Lewis Leary. — London : Macmillan, 1980. — vii,328p ; 24cm. — (Great writers student library ; 12)
Includes bibliographies
ISBN 0-333-28336-8 : £10.00 B81-05602

810.8 — English literature. American writers, *to 1978 — Anthologies*
The **Norton** anthology of American literature / [edited by] Ronald Gottesman ... [et al.]. — New York ; London : Norton, c1979. — 2v. ; 22cm
Includes bibliographies and index
ISBN 0-393-95026-3 (cased) : £7.25
ISBN 0-393-95033-6 (v.2)
ISBN 0-393-95030-1 (v.1:pbk)
ISBN 0-393-95035-2 (v.2:pbk) B81-07797

810.8'0327671 — English literature. American writers, *1900-1980.* **Special subjects: United States. Ozark region —** *Anthologies*
Ozark, Ozark : a hillside reader / edited by Miller Williams. — Columbia ; London : University of Missouri Press, 1981. — xi,193p ; 23cm
ISBN 0-8262-0331-0 : £10.40 B81-38386

810.8'0355 — English literature. Caribbean writers, *to 1980.* **Special themes: Social life —** *Anthologies — For Caribbean students*
Heritage : a Caribbean anthology / Esmor Jones, [editor]. — London : Cassell, 1981. — 224p : ill ; 22cm
ISBN 0-304-30648-7 (pbk) : £3.50 B81-18993

810.8′09729 — English literature. West Indian writers, *1945- — Anthologies*

Wasted women, friends and lovers. — London (258 Coldharbour Lane, S.W.9) : Black Ink Collective, 1978 (1980 printing). — 88p : ill ; 21cm. — (Black Ink publications ; no.3)
ISBN 0-9506248-2-9 (pbk) : Unpriced
B81-36095

810.9 — AMERICAN LITERATURE. HISTORY AND CRITICAL STUDIES

810′.9 — English literature. American writers, *1800-1900 — Critical studies*

Lease, Benjamin. Anglo-American encounters. — Cambridge : Cambridge University Press, Jan.1982. — [304]p
ISBN 0-521-23666-5 : £22.50 : CIP entry
B81-34417

810.9 — English literature. American writers, *ca 1750-1976 — Critical studies*

Simpson, Lewis P.. The brazen face of history : studies in the literary consciousness in America / Lewis P. Simpson. — Baton Rouge ; London : Louisiana State University Press, c1980. — xvi,276p ; 24cm
ISBN 0-8071-0752-2 : £12.00 B81-11999

810.9 — English literature. American writers. Influence of Ancient Egyptian hieroglyphs, *ca 1820-ca 1900*

Irwin, John T.. American hieroglyphics : the symbol of the Egyptian hieroglyphics in the American renaissance / John T. Irwin. — New Haven ; London : Yale University Press, c1980. — xii,371p ; 24cm
Includes index
ISBN 0-300-02471-1 : £12.30 : CIP rev.
B80-22425

810.9′001 — English literature. American writers, *1607-1830 — Critical studies*

Early American literature : a collection of critical essays / edited by Michael T. Gilmore. — Englewood Cliffs ; London : Prentice-Hall, c1980. — viii,184p ; 21cm. — (Twentieth century views) (A spectrum book)
Bibliography: p182-184
ISBN 0-13-222513-1 (cased) : £7.10
ISBN 0-13-222463-1 (pbk) : £2.55 B81-02444

810.9′004 — English literature. American writers, *1861-1945 — Critical studies*

Berthoff, Warner. The ferment of realism : American literature, 1884-1919 / Warner Berthoff. — Cambridge : Cambridge University Press, 1981, c1965. — xix,330p ; 22cm
Originally published: New York : Free Press ; London : Collier-Macmillan, 1965. — Bibliography: p299-310. — Includes index
ISBN 0-521-24092-1 (cased) : £25.00 : CIP rev.
ISBN 0-521-28435-x (pbk) : £6.95 B81-19106

810.9′0052 — English literature. American writers, *1900-1979 — Encyclopaedias*

20th-century American literature / introduction by Warren French. — London : Macmillan, 1980. — vii,668p ; 25cm. — (Great writers student library ; 13)
Includes bibliographies
ISBN 0-333-28333-3 : £12.95 B81-05111

810.9′321732 — English literature. American writers. Special subjects: Urban regions

Literature and the American urban experience. — Manchester : Manchester University Press, Nov.1981. — [288]p
ISBN 0-7190-0848-4 (pbk) : £6.95 : CIP entry
B81-31275

810.9′3273 — English literature. American writers, *1700-1980.* **Special subjects: United States —** *Critical studies*

The Literary guide to the United States / Stewart Benedict consultant editor. — Poole : Blandford, 1981. — 246p : ill,maps,facsims,ports ; 24cm
Bibliography: p234-239. — Includes index
ISBN 0-7137-1213-9 : £8.95 : CIP rev.
B81-18164

810.9′351 — English literature. American writers, *1800-1980.* **Special subjects: United States. Burr, Aaron —** *Critical studies*

Nolan, Charles J.. Aaron Burr and the American literary imagination / Charles J. Nolan Jr. — Westport, Conn. ; London : Greenwood Press, 1980. — xiv,210p ; 22cm. — (Contributions in American studies ; no.45)
Bibliography: p187-200. - Includes index
ISBN 0-313-21256-2 : Unpriced B81-05742

810.9′896073 — English literature. American negro writers, *1945-1979 — Critical studies*

Bigsby, C. W. E.. The second black renaissance : essays in black literature / C.W.E. Bigsby. — Westport, Conn. ; London : Greenwood Press, 1980. — vi,332p ; 25cm. — (Contributions in Afro-American and African studies ; n.50)
Includes index
ISBN 0-313-21304-6 : Unpriced B81-07293

810.9′896073 — English literature. American negro writers, *to 1979 — Critical studies*

Baker, Houston A.. The journey back : issues in black literature and criticism / Houston A. Baker, Jr. — Chicago ; London : University of Chicago Press, 1980. — xvii,198p : 2ill,3facsims ; 21cm
Includes index
ISBN 0-226-03534-4 : £7.80 B81-02779

810.9′974 — English literature. New England writers, *1600-1850.* **Semantic aspects**

Lowance, Mason I.. The language of Canaan : metaphor and symbol in New England from the Puritans to the transcendentalists / Mason I. Lowance, Jr. — Cambridge, Mass. ; London : Harvard University Press, 1980. — x,335p ; 24cm
Includes index
ISBN 0-674-50949-8 : £10.50 B81-09350

810.9′974 — English literature. New England writers, *1861-1900 — Critical studies*

Westbrook, Perry D.. Acres of flint : Sarah Orne Jewett and her contemporaries / Perry D. Westbrook. — Rev. ed. — Metuchen ; London : Scarecrow, 1981. — xi,184p,[8]p of plates : ill,ports ; 23cm
Previous ed.: Washington : Scarecrow ; London : Bailey & Swinfen, 1951. — Bibliography: p174-180. - Includes index
ISBN 0-8108-1357-2 : £8.75 B81-17096

810.9′975 — English literature. American writers. Southern states writers, *to 1979 — Biographies*

Southern writers : a biographical dictionary / edited by Robert Bain, Joseph M. Flora and Louis D. Rubin, jr. — Baton Rouge ; London : Louisiana State University Press, c1979. — xxvii,515p ; 25cm. — (Southern literary studies)
ISBN 0-8071-0354-3 : £18.00
ISBN 0-8071-0390-x (pbk) : £5.40 B81-06444

811 — AMERICAN POETRY

811 — Poetry in English. Barbadian writers, *1945- — Texts*

Brathwaite, Edward. The arrivants : a new world trilogy / Edward Brathwaite. — Oxford : Oxford University Press, 1981, c1973. — 275p ; 20cm
Contents: Rights of passage. Originally published: 1967 - Masks. Originally published: 1968 - Islands. Originally published: 1969
ISBN 0-19-911103-0 (pbk) : £2.95 B81-15773

811 — Poetry in English. Barbadian writers. Braithwaite, Edward. Masks — *Critical studies*

Fraser, Robert, *1947-*. Masks : a critical view / by Robert Fraser ; edited by Yolande Cantù. — London : Collings in association with the British Council, 1981. — 40p : 2maps,1port ; 21cm. — (Nexus books ; 04)
Bibliography: p38-39. - List of films p40
ISBN 0-86036-137-3 (pbk) : £1.00 B81-18605

811 — Poetry in English. Jamaican writers, *1945- — Texts*

Johnson, Linton Kwesi. Inglan is a bitch / Linton Kwesi Johnson. — [London] (74 Shakespeare Rd., SE24) : Race Today, 1980. — 30p : ill ; 21cm
ISBN 0-9503498-2-8 (pbk) : £1.50 B81-10523

811 — Poetry in English. Trinidadian writers, *1945-. - Texts*

Walcott, Derek. Selected poetry. — London : Heinemann Educational, Apr.1981. — [160]p. — (Caribbean writers series)
ISBN 0-435-98747-x (pbk) : £2.50 : CIP entry
B81-06886

811 — Poetry in English. Trinidadian writers. Walcott, Derek — *Critical studies*

Thomas, Ned. Derek Walcott : poet of the islands / by Ned Thomas. — [Cardiff] ([53 Charles St., Cardiff]) : Welsh Arts Council, c1980. — 38,39p : 2maps,2ports ; 20cm
Bibliography: p36-37. — Includes text in Welsh, printed tête-bêche, under the title Derek Walcott: bardd yr ynysoedd
ISBN 0-905171-64-0 (pbk) : Unpriced
B81-04602

811 — Poetry in English. West Indian writers, *1945- — Anthologies*

Black-eye perceptions / with an introduction by Danx. — London (258 Coldharbour Lane, S.W.9) : Black Ink Collective, c1980. — 63p : ill ; 21cm. — (Black Ink publications ; no.4)
ISBN 0-9506248-3-7 (pbk) : Unpriced
B81-36096

811′.009 — Poetry in English. American writers, *1840-1970 — Critical studies*

Jones, Peter, *1929 Apr. 25-*. [An introduction to fifty American poets]. A reader′s guide to fifty American poets / by Peter Jones. — London : Heinemann, 1980. — 386p ; 21cm. — (Reader′s guide series)
Originally published: London : Pan Books, 1980. — Bibliography: p361-374. - Includes index
ISBN 0-435-18491-1 : £7.50 : CIP rev.
B80-13950

811.1 — AMERICAN POETRY, 1607-1776

811′.1 — Poetry in English. American writers, *1607-1776 — Texts*

Tompson, Benjamin. Benjamin Tompson : colonial bard : a critical edition / [edited by] Peter White. — University Park ; London : Pennsylvania State University Press, c1980. — xi,218p : facsims ; 24cm
Bibliography: p208-214. — Includes index
ISBN 0-271-00250-6 : £10.00 B81-25644

811′.1 — Poetry in English. American writers. Steere, Richard — *Biographies*

Wharton, Donald P.. Richard Steere : colonial merchant poet / by Donald P. Wharton. — University Park ; London : Pennsylvania State University Press, c1979. — 87p ; 23cm. — (The Pennsylvania State University studies ; no.44)
ISBN 0-271-00207-7 (pbk) : Unpriced
B81-12229

811.2 — AMERICAN POETRY, 1776-1830

811′.2 — Poetry in English. American writers, *1776-1830 — Texts*

Moore, Clement C.. The night before Christmas / by Clement C. Moore ; illustrated by Michael Hague. — London : Benn, 1981. — [10]p : col.ill ; 28cm
Text on lining papers. — Pop-up book
ISBN 0-510-00120-3 : £3.95 B81-37277

Moore, Clement C.. [A visit from St. Nicholas]. The night before Christmas / by Clement Moore ; illustrated by Tomie de Paola. — Oxford : Oxford University Press, 1981, c1980. — [32]p : col.ill ; 29cm
Originally published: New York : Holiday House, 1980
ISBN 0-19-279758-1 : £3.95 : CIP rev.
B81-28188

Stevens, Dorothy. Mary and her little lamb / Dorothy Stevens. — Tadworth : World′s Work, c1980. — [32]p : all col.ill ; 24cm
ISBN 0-437-77577-1 : £2.95 B81-07008

811.3 — AMERICAN POETRY, 1830-1861

811′.3 — Poetry in English. American writers. Whitman, Walt. Influence of French literature, *1715-1900*

Erkkila, Betsy. Walt Whitman among the French : poet and myth / Betsy Erkkila. — Princeton ; Guildford : Princeton University Press, 1980. — x,296p ; 23cm
Bibliography: p275-285. — Includes index
ISBN 0-691-06426-1 : £9.10
Also classified at 840′.9′008 B81-08250

811.4 — AMERICAN POETRY, 1861-1900

811′.4 — Poetry in English. American writers. Dickinson, Emily — *Critical studies*

Homans, Margaret. Women writers and poetic identity : Dorothy Wordsworth, Emily Brontë, and Emily Dickinson / Margaret Homans. — Princeton ; Guildford : Princeton University Press, c1980. — 260p ; 23cm
Includes index
ISBN 0-691-06440-7 : £8.30
Primary classification 821′.8′099287 B81-09257

Porter, David, *1928-*. Dickinson, the modern idiom / David Porter. — Cambridge [Mass.] ; London : Harvard University Press, 1981. — ix,316p ; 24cm
Includes index
ISBN 0-674-20444-1 : £14.00 B81-40025

811.52 — AMERICAN POETRY, 1900-1945

811′.52 — Poetry in English. American writers, *1900-1945 — Texts*

Bishop, Morris. The best of Bishop : light verse from The New Yorker and elsewhere / Morris Bishop ; edited and with an introduction by Charlotte Putman Reppert ; foreword by David McCord ; drawings by Alison Mason Kingsbury and Richard Taylor. — Ithaca ; London : Cornell University Press, 1980. — 221p : ill,2ports ; 23cm
ISBN 0-8014-1310-9 : £7.75 B81-10956

Cummings, E. E.. Complete poems : 1910-1962 / E.E. Cummings. — Rev., corr. and expanded ed., edited by George James Firmage. — London : Granada, 1981. — 2v.(xviii,925p) ; 26cm
Previous ed.: London : MacGibbon & Kee, 1968. — In slip case. — Includes index
ISBN 0-246-10974-2 : Unpriced
ISBN 0-246-11008-2 (v.1) : Unpriced
ISBN 0-246-11009-0 (v.2) : Unpriced
B81-39293

Hunter, Rex. The saga of Sinclair / by Rex Hunter. — North Walsham : Warren House Press, 1981. — 33p ; 22cm
Originally published: New York : S.n., 1927. — Limited ed. of 150 numbered copies of which 100 are for sale
£7.50 B81-27198

Mally, E. Louise. Selected poems / E. Louise Mally ; decorations by Charlotte Mensforth. — St. Albans (12 Cannon St, St. Albans, Herts) : Piccolo Press, 1979. — 21p : ill ; 23cm
Limited ed. of 200 copies
Unpriced (pbk) B81-27694

Nash, Ogden. Custard and company : poems / by Ogden Nash ; selected and illustrated by Quentin Blake. — Harmondsworth : Puffin, 1981, c1979. — 125p : ill ; 20cm
Originally published: Harmondsworth : Kestrel, 1979
ISBN 0-14-031186-6 (pbk) : £0.95 B81-35072

O'Neill, Eugene. Poems 1912-1944 / Eugene O'Neill ; edited by Donald Gallup. — London : Cape, 1980, c1979. — vii,119p ; 22cm
Originally published: New Haven, Conn. : Ticknor and Fields, 1980. — Includes index
ISBN 0-224-01870-1 : £4.50 B81-00247

Simpson, Louis. Caviare at the funeral : poems / by Louis Simpson. — Oxford : Oxford University Press, 1981. — 89p ; 23cm
ISBN 0-19-211943-5 (pbk) : £4.50 B81-17402

Warren, Robert Penn. Being here : poetry 1977-1980 / Robert Penn Warren. — London : Secker & Warburg, 1980. — 108p ; 25cm
Originally published: New York : Random House, 1980
ISBN 0-436-36650-9 : £4.95 B81-02137

811′.52 — Poetry in English. American writers. Frost, Robert, *1874-1963 — Correspondence, diaries, etc.*

Frost, Robert, *1874-1963*. Robert Frost and Sidney Cox : forty years of friendship / [edited by] William R. Evans ; foreword by James M. Cox. — Hanover, N.H. ; London : University Press of New England, 1981. — xiv,297p ; 24cm
Includes index
ISBN 0-87451-195-x : £12.25
Also classified at 818′.5209 B81-39782

811′.52 — Poetry in English. American writers. Loy, Mina — *Critical studies*

Kouidis, Virginia M.. Mina Loy : American modernist poet / Virginia M. Kouidis. — xii,148p,[8]p of plates : ill,1facsim,ports ; 23cm
Bibliography: p141-143. - Includes index
ISBN 0-8071-0672-0 : £9.60 B81-07721

811′.52 — Poetry in English. American writers. Pound, Ezra — *Biographies*

Ackroyd, Peter, *1949-*. Ezra Pound and his world / Peter Ackroyd ; with 111 illustrations. — London : Thames & Hudson, c1980. — 127p : ill,facsims,ports ; 24cm
Bibliography: p120-121. - Includes index
ISBN 0-500-13069-8 : £5.95 B81-19962

811′.52 — Poetry in English. American writers. Pound, Ezra. Cantos, *The — Commentaries*

Terrell, Carroll F.. A companion to the Cantos of Ezra Pound / by Caroll F. Terrell. — Berkeley ; London : University of California Press in co-operation with the National Poetry Foundation, University of Maine at Orono, c1980. — xv,362p ; 26cm
"Volume I (Cantos 1-71)" — jacket. — Bibliography: p361-362
ISBN 0-520-03687-5 : £17.00 B81-29023

811′.52 — Poetry in English. American writers. Pound, Ezra. Cantos, *The. Selected Cantos — Critical studies*

Kearns, George. Guide to Ezra Pound's Selected Cantos / George Kearns. — Folkestone : Dawson, 1980. — x,306p ; 21cm
Bibliography: p300-302. — Includes index
ISBN 0-7129-0988-5 : £16.50 B81-03944

811′.52 — Poetry in English. American writers. Pound, Ezra — *Critical studies*

Bell, Ian F. A.. Critic as scientist : the modernist poetics of Ezra Pound / Ian F.A. Bell. — London : Methuen, 1981. — viii, 302p ; 23cm
Includes index
ISBN 0-416-31350-7 : £14.00 : CIP rev.
B81-14376

Durant, Alan. Ezra Pound, indentity in crisis : a fundamental reassessment of the poet and his work / Alan Durant. — Brighton : Harvester, 1981. — 206p ; 23cm
Bibliography: p191-198. — Includes index
ISBN 0-7108-0036-3 : £18.95 : CIP rev.
B81-00248

811′.52 — Poetry in English. American writers. Sandburg, Carl — *Personal observations*

Perry, Lilla S.. My friend Carl Sandburg : the biography of a friendship / Lilla S. Perry ; edited by E. Caswell Perry. — Metuchen ; London : Scarecrow, 1981. — viii,224p : ill,ports ; 23cm
Includes index
ISBN 0-8108-1367-x : £8.40 B81-14325

811′.52 — Poetry in English. American writers. Tolson, M. B. 'Harlem Gallery' — *Critical studies*

Russell, Mariann. Melvin B. Tolson's Harlem gallery : a literary analysis / Mariann Russell. — Columbia ; London : University of Missouri Press, 1980. — 143p ; 24cm
Bibliography: p124-137. — Includes index
ISBN 0-8262-0309-4 : £9.75 B81-29530

811′.52 — Poetry in English. American writers. Winters, Yvor — *Critical studies*

Powell, Grosvenor. Language as being in the poetry of Yvor Winters / Grosvenor Powell. — Baton Rouge ; London : Louisiana State University Press, c1980. — xii,172p ; 23cm
Includes index
ISBN 0-8071-0585-6 : £8.40 B81-01567

811′.52 — Poetry in English. Canadian writers, *1900-1945 — Texts*

Service, Robert, *1874-1958*. More collected verse / by Robert Service. — London : Benn, 1979, c1953. — 976p in various pagings ; 20cm
Originally published: New York : Dodd, Mead ; London : Benn, 1955
ISBN 0-510-32403-7 : £9.95 : CIP rev.
B79-23428

811′.52′09 — Poetry in English. American writers, *1900-1979 — Critical studies*

Wagner, Linda Welshimer. American modern : essays in fiction and poetry / Linda W. Wagner. — Port Washington, N.Y. ; London : National University Publications : Kennikat, 1980. — 263p ; 23cm. — (Literary criticism series)
ISBN 0-8046-9257-2 : £14.00
Also classified at 813′.52′09 B81-05511

811′.52′09 — Poetry in English. American writers, *1900- — Personal observations*

Tomlinson, Charles. Some Americans : a personal record / Charles Tomlinson. — Berkeley ; London : University of California Press, c1981. — 134p ; 21cm. — (Quantum books)
Includes index
ISBN 0-520-04037-6 : £6.50 B81-27573

811.54 — AMERICAN POETRY, 1945-

811′.54 — Poetry in English. American writers, *1945- — Texts*

Aardema, Verna. Bringing the rain to Kapiti plain : a Nandi tale / retold by Verna Aardema ; pictures by Beatriz Vidal. — London : Macmillan, 1981. — [32]p : col.ill ; 22cm
ISBN 0-333-32009-3 : £3.95 B81-37287

Ashbery, John. As we know : poems / by John Ashbery. — Manchester : Carcanet New Press, c1981. — vi,118p ; 17x22cm
ISBN 0-85635-357-4 : £4.95 B81-32586

Ashbery, John. Shadow train. — Manchester : Carcanet Press, Feb.1982. — [64]p
ISBN 0-85635-424-4 (pbk) : £3.25 : CIP entry
B81-38831

Bensko, John. Green soldiers / John Bensko ; foreword by Richard Hugo. — New Haven ; London : Yale University Press, c1981. — xv,63p ; 21cm. — (Yale series of younger poets ; vol.76)
ISBN 0-300-02637-4 (cased) : Unpriced
ISBN 0-300-02644-7 (pbk) : £3.10 B81-21315

Blackburn, Paul. Against the silences / Paul Blackburn ; preface by Robert Creeley. — London (52 Cascade Ave., N.10) : Permanent Press, 1980. — 69p ; 21cm
Limited ed. of 1000 copies
ISBN 0-905258-07-x : £4.95 : CIP rev.
ISBN 0-905258-06-1 (pbk) : Unpriced
B80-06060

Blessing, Richard. A closed book : poems / by Richard Blessing. — Seattle ; London : University of Washington Press, c1981. — 78p ; 24cm
ISBN 0-295-95757-3 : £6.30 B81-38220

Bradbury, Ray. The haunted computer and the android pope / Ray Bradbury. — London : Granada, 1981. — viii,98p ; 22cm
ISBN 0-246-11745-1 : £7.95 B81-39336

Branin, Jeff. Nam / Jeff Branin. — Torpoint (Knill Cross House, Higher Anderton Rd., Millbrook, Torpoint, Cornwall) : Kawabata Press, 1981. — [32]p ; 21cm
ISBN 0-906110-29-7 (pbk) : £1.00 B81-29921

811′.54 — Poetry in English. American writers, *1945-* — *Texts* *continuation*

Brown, Marc. Witches four / Marc Brown. — London : Hamilton, 1981, c1980. — [36]p : chiefly col.ill ; 24cm
Originally published: New York : Parents Magazine Press, 1980
ISBN 0-241-10545-5 : £3.95 B81-09554

Creeley, Robert. Later / Robert Creeley. — London : Boyars, c1980. — 121p ; 22cm
ISBN 0-7145-2714-9 (cased) : £4.95 : CIP rev.
ISBN 0-7145-2707-6 (pbk) : £2.95 B80-04384

Dacey, Philip. The boy under the bed / Philip Dacey. — Baltimore ; London : Johns Hopkins University Press, c1981. — x,100p ; 24cm. — (Johns Hopkins poetry and fiction)
ISBN 0-8018-2601-2 (cased) : £6.50
ISBN 0-8018-2602-0 (pbk) B81-34851

Dana, Robert. In a fugitive season : a sequence of poems / Robert Dana. — Chicago ; London : Swallow Press, 1980, c1979. — 23cm
Originally published: Iowa City : Windhover Press, 1979
ISBN 0-8040-0804-3 (cased) : Unpriced
ISBN 0-8040-0805-1 (pbk) : Unpriced
B81-11648

Disch, Thomas M.. Abcdefg hijklm nopqrst uvwxyz / Thomas M. Disch. — London : Anvil Press Poetry in association with Wildwood House, 1981. — 79p ; 22cm
ISBN 0-85646-073-7 (pbk) : £3.25 B81-15518

Dodd, Wayne. The names you gave it : poems / by Wayne Dodd. — Baton Rouge ; London : Louisiana State University Press, 1980. — 69p ; 24cm
ISBN 0-8071-0665-8 (cased) : £2.95
ISBN 0-8071-0666-6 (pbk) : Unpriced
B81-11155

Hass, Robert. Praise / Robert Hass. — Manchester : Carcanet, 1981, c1979. — 68p ; 22cm
ISBN 0-85635-356-6 (pbk) : £2.95 : CIP rev.
B81-16897

Hearne, Vicki. Nervous horses / by Vicki Hearne. — Austin ; London : Unversity of Texas Press, c1980. — 70p ; 24cm. — (University of Texas Press poetry series ; no.6)
ISBN 0-292-75517-1 (cased) : £6.00
ISBN 0-292-75518-x (pbk) : £3.00 B81-03475

Kooser, Ted. Sure signs : new and selected poems / Ted Kooser. — Pittsburgh : University of Pittsburgh Press ; London : Feffer and Simons, 1980. — 93p ; 21cm. — (Pitt poetry series)
ISBN 0-8229-3410-8 (cased) : Unpriced
ISBN 0-8229-5313-7 (pbk) : Unpriced
B81-12173

Kresh, David. Love poems / David Kresh. — Nottingham (19 Devonshire Promenade, Lenton. Nottingham) : Slow Dancer, [1981?]. — 48p ; 22cm
Limited ed. of 350 copies, 25 numbered and signed
ISBN 0-9507479-0-4 (pbk) : £1.00 B81-24494

Landesman, Fran. Is it overcrowded in heaven?. — London : Jay Landesman, Sept.1981. — [64]p
ISBN 0-905150-38-4 (pbk) : £2.50 : CIP entry
B81-30271

Lea, Sydney. Searching the drowned man : poems / by Sydney Lea. — Urbana ; London : University of Illinois Press, c1980. — 72p ; 21cm
ISBN 0-252-00796-4 : £6.00 B81-00249

Manley, Frank. Resultances : poems / by Frank Manley. — Columbia ; London : University of Missouri Press, 1980. — 59p ; 22cm. — (A Breakthrough book ; no.34)
ISBN 0-8262-0312-4 : £5.20 B81-28645

Marzollo, Jean. Uproar on Hollercat Hill / by Jean Marzollo ; pictures by Steven Kellogg. — London : Hutchinson, 1980. — [32]p : chiefly col.ill ; 28cm
ISBN 0-09-142750-9 : £3.50 : CIP rev.
B80-13952

Nathan, Leonard. Dear blood / Leonard Nathan. — Pittsburgh : University of Pittsburgh Press ; London : Feffer and Simons, 1980. — 80p ; 21cm. — (Pitt poetry series)
ISBN 0-8229-3407-8 (cased) : Unpriced
ISBN 0-8229-5312-9 (pbk) : Unpriced
B81-12172

Nemerov, Howard. Sentences / Howard Nemerov. — Chicago ; London : University of Chicago Press, 1980. — ix,85p ; 21cm
ISBN 0-226-57260-9 : Unpriced B81-11651

Niatum, Duane. Songs for the harvester of dreams : poems / by Duane Niatum. — Seattle ; London : University of Washington Press, c1981. — viii,64p ; 24cm
ISBN 0-295-95758-1 : £5.55 B81-38219

Olds, Sharon. Satan says / Sharon Olds. — Pittsburgh : University of Pittsburgh Press ; London : Feffer and Simons, 1980. — 72p ; 21cm. — (Pitt poetry series)
ISBN 0-8229-3413-2 (cased) : Unpriced
ISBN 0-8229-5314-5 (pbk) : Unpriced
B81-12171

Peacock, Molly. And we live apart : poems / by Molly Peacock. — Columbia ; London : University of Missouri Press, 1980. — 60p ; 23cm. — (A Breakthrough book ; no.31)
ISBN 0-8262-0288-8 : £4.80 B81-02925

Pine, Edward. A burst of ballades / Edward Pine. — Hunton Bridge (17 Lauderdale Rd., Hunton Bridge, King's Langley, Herts.) : Kit-Cat Press, 1981. — [24]p ; 22cm
Limited ed. of 200 numbered copies
ISBN 0-9500087-1-0 (pbk) : £1.00 B81-29839

Plath, Sylvia. Sylvia Plath : collected poems / edited by Ted Hughes. — London : Faber, 1981. — 351p ; 24cm
Includes index
ISBN 0-571-10573-4 (cased) : £10.00 : CIP rev.
ISBN 0-571-11838-0 (pbk) : Unpriced
B81-21490

Plath, Sylvia. Two uncollected poems / Sylvia Plath. — London : Anvil, 1980. — [6]p ; 18cm
Limited ed. of 450 numbered copies
ISBN 0-85646-075-3 (pbk) : Private circulation
B81-11847

Rakosi, Carl. History. — London (12 Stevenage Rd, SW6 6ES) : Oasis Books, July 1981. — [36]p
ISBN 0-903375-53-2 (pbk) : £1.20 : CIP entry
B81-14391

Roberts, Jane, *1929-*. Dialogues of the soul and mortal self in time / by Jane Roberts ; drawings by Robert F. Butts. — Englewood Cliffs ; London : Prentice-Hall, c1975. — xiv,142p : ill ; 23cm. — (A Reward book)
ISBN 0-13-208546-1 (pbk) : £2.55 B81-39933

Sobin, Gustaf. Caesurae : midsummer. — Plymouth : Blue Guitar Books ; London (12 Stevenage Rd., SW6 6ES) : Independent Press Distribution [distributor], Sept.1981. — [20]p
ISBN 0-907562-00-0 (pbk) : £0.80 : CIP entry
B81-20500

Stafford, William. Absolution / William Stafford. — Knotting (Knotting, Beds.) : Martin Booth, 1980. — [4] leaves ; 16cm
Limited ed. of 125 numbered copies, of which the first 50 are signed by the author
Unpriced (pbk) B81-05894

Stewart, Susan. Yellow stars and ice / by Susan Stewart. — Princeton ; Guildford : Princeton University Press, c1981. — 79p ; 23cm. — (Princeton series of contemporary poets)
ISBN 0-691-06468-7 (cased) : £4.65
ISBN 0-691-01379-9 (pbk) : Unpriced
B81-24741

Stone, John, *1936-*. In all this rain : poems / by John Stone. — Baton Rouge ; London : Louisiana State University Press, 1980. — 69p ; 24cm
ISBN 0-8071-0667-4 (cased) : £6.60
ISBN 0-8071-0668-2 (pbk) : £2.95 B81-07987

Wallace, Ronald. Plums, stones, kisses & hooks : poems / by Ronald Wallace. — Columbia ; London : University of Missouri Press, 1981. — 75p ; 23cm. — (A Breakthrough book ; no.35)
ISBN 0-8262-0314-0 : £5.85 B81-28644

Waterman, Cary. The salamander migration : and other poems / Cary Waterman. — Pittsburgh : University of Pittsburgh Press ; London : Feffer and Simons, 1980. — 66p ; 21cm. — (Pitt poetry series)
ISBN 0-8229-3415-9 (cased) : Unpriced
ISBN 0-8229-5315-3 (pbk) : Unpriced
B81-12170

Yolen, Jane. Dragon night : and other lullabies / Jane Yolen ; illustrated by Demi. — New York ; London : Methuen, 1981, c1980. — [32]p : col.ill ; 21cm
ISBN 0-416-21180-1 : £3.50 B81-12486

811′.54 — Poetry in English. American writers. Roethke, Theodore — *Critical studies*

Ross-Bryant, Lynn. Theodore Roethke : poetry of the earth — poet of the spirit — / Lynn Ross-Bryant. — Port Washington ; London : National University Publications : Kennikat, 1981. — ix,211p ; 22cm. — (Literary criticism series)
Bibliography: p201-206. — Includes index
ISBN 0-8046-9270-x : £12.75 B81-36654

811′.54 — Poetry in English. Canadian writers, *1945-* — *Texts*

Cade, Steven. Slade's marauder / Steven Cade. — [London] : Fontana, 1981, c1980. — 256p : 1map ; 18cm
Originally published: London : Souvenir Press, 1980
ISBN 0-00-616056-5 (pbk) : £1.35 B81-15532

Ondaatje, Michael. The collected works of Billy the Kid : left handed poems / by Michael Ondaatje. — London : Boyars, 1981. — 105p : ill ; 23cm
ISBN 0-7145-2708-4 : £5.95 B81-10153

811′.54′08 — Poetry in English. American writers, *1945-* — *Anthologies*

Seymour, Marjorie. Occasional verse (II) / Marjorie & Douglas Seymour. — [S.l.] : [s.n.], 1980 (Birmingham : University of Birmingham Printing Section). — 16p ; 21cm
Unpriced (pbk) B81-32575

812 — AMERICAN DRAMA

812 — Drama in English. Guyanese writers, *1945-* — *Texts*

Abbensetts, Michael. Samba / Michael Abbensetts. — London : Eyre Methuen, 1980. — 40p ; 21cm. — (A Methuen new theatrescript ; no.29)
Three men, 2 women, supers
ISBN 0-413-48140-9 (pbk) : £1.75 B81-01753

812 — Drama in English. Jamaican writers, *1945-* — *Texts*

Rhone, Trevor D.. Old story time and other plays / Trevor D. Rhone. — Harlow : Longman, 1981. — xxii,225p ; 19cm. — (Drumbeat ; 30)
Contents: Old story time — School's out — Smile orange
ISBN 0-582-78532-4 (pbk) : £1.75 B81-32096

812 — Drama in English. Trinidadian writers, *1945- — Texts*

Matura, Mustapha. Nice ; Rum an' coca cola ; Welcome home Jacko : three plays / by Mustapha Matura. — London : Eyre Methuen, 1980. — 55p ; 21cm. — (A Methuen new theatrescript)
ISBN 0-413-47720-7 (pbk) : £1.75 B81-01749

812.52 — AMERICAN DRAMA, 1900-1945

812'.52 — American cinema films. Screenplays. Writing. Johnson, Nunnally — *Biographies*

Stempel, Tom. Screenwriter : the life and times of Nunnally Johnson / Tom Stempel. — San Diego : Barnes ; London : Tantivy Press, c1980. — 269p : ill,ports ; 24cm
Bibliography: p250-259. — List of films: p202-249. — Includes index
ISBN 0-498-02362-1 : £6.95 B81-35429

812'.52 — Drama in English. American writers, *1900-1945 — Texts*

Kaufman, George S.. Three plays / by Kaufman & Hart ; with introductory essays by Moss Hart and George S. Kaufman. — London : Eyre Methuen, 1981, c1980. — xxiv,307p ; 19cm. — (A Methuen modern play)
Originally published: New York : Grove Press, 1980. — Contents: Once in a lifetime - You can't take it with you - The man who came to dinner
ISBN 0-413-48090-9 (pbk) : £2.95 B81-11151

Miller, Arthur. Collected plays of Arthur Miller / with an introduction. — London : Secker & Warburg
Vol. 2. — 1981. — 531p ; 22cm
Vol.2 has title: Arthur Miller's collected plays
ISBN 0-436-28011-6 : £12.00 B81-24580

Miller, Arthur. The crucible : a play in four acts / Arthur Miller. — Harmondsworth : Penguin, 1968, c1953 (1981 [printing]). — 126p ; 18cm. — (Penguin plays)
Originally published: New York : Viking, 1953 ; London : Cresset, 1956
ISBN 0-14-048078-1 (pbk) : £1.35 B81-35479

Miller, Arthur. Death of a salesman : certain private conversations in two acts and a requiem / Arthur Miller. — Harmondsworth : Penguin, 1961, c1949 (1980 [printing]). — 112p ; 19cm. — (Penguin plays)
Originally published: New York : Viking Press ; London : Cresset Press, 1949
ISBN 0-14-048028-5 (pbk) : £0.75 B81-02844

Miller, Arthur. Death of a salesman / Arthur Miller ; with an introduction by E.R. Wood. — London : Heinemann Educational, 1968 (1981 [printing]). — xxv,108p ; 19cm. — (The Hereford plays)
Originally published: New York : Viking ; London : Cresset, 1949
ISBN 0-435-22576-6 (pbk) : Unpriced B81-24808

Miller, Arthur. A view from the bridge ; All my sons / Arthur Miller. — Harmondsworth : Penguin, 1961, c1981 [printing]. — 171p ; 18cm. — (Penguin plays)
A view from the bridge. Originally published: New York : Viking, 1955 ; London : Cressett, 1957. — All my sons. Originally published: New York : Reynal & Hitchcock, 1947 ; London Cressett, 1958
ISBN 0-14-048029-3 (pbk) : £0.95 B81-34811

Odets, Clifford. Golden boy / Clifford Odets ; with an introduction by E.R. Wood. — London : Heinemann Educational, 1981, c1965. — xxvi,86p ; 19cm. — (The Hereford plays)
Seventeen men, 2 women
ISBN 0-435-22685-1 (pbk) : £1.95 B81-10999

812'.52 — Drama in English. American writers. O'Neill, Eugene. Linguistic aspects

Chothia, Jean. Forging a language. — Cambridge : Cambridge University Press, Oct.1981. — [251]p
Originally published: 1979
ISBN 0-521-28523-2 (cased) : £6.50 : CIP entry B81-32523

812'.52 — Drama in English. American writers. O'Neill, Eugene. Mourning becomes Electra — *Study outlines*

Michel, Pierre. Mourning becomes Electra : notes / by Pierre Michel. — Harlow : Longman, 1981. — 63p ; 21cm. — (York notes ; 130)
Bibliography: p63
ISBN 0-582-78175-2 (pbk) : £0.90 B81-34229

812.54 — AMERICAN DRAMA, 1945-

812'.54 — Drama in English. American writers, *1945- — Texts*

Abbot, Rick. Play on! : a comedy / by Rick Abbott. — London : French, c1980. — 99p : 1plan ; 19cm
Three men, 7 women
ISBN 0-573-61361-3 (pbk) : £1.90 B81-09533

Adams, S. K.. Melancholy baby : a comedy / by S.K. Adams. — New York ; London : French, c1981. — 78p : 1plan ; 19cm
Four men, 4 women
ISBN 0-573-61200-5 (pbk) : £1.90 B81-20216

Ceraso, Christopher. Sittin' : a comedy in one act / by Christopher Ceraso. — New York ; London : French, c1980. — 27p ; 19cm
One man, 2 women
ISBN 0-573-62516-6 (pbk) : £1.00 B81-03071

Denker, Henry. Horowitz and Mrs. Washington : a comedy in two acts / by Henry Denker. — New York ; London : French, c1980. — 74p : 1facsim,1plan ; 19cm
Four men, 2 women
ISBN 0-573-61047-9 (pbk) : £1.90 B81-07716

Fox, Terry Curtis. Justice / by Terry Curtis Fox. — New York ; London : French, c1980. — 79p : 2plans ; 19cm
Six men, 2 women
ISBN 0-573-61110-6 (pbk) : £1.90 B81-02142

Gray, Elizabeth, *1952-*. Lunch or something : a drama in one act / by Elizabeth Gray. — New York ; London : French, c1980. — 23p ; 19cm
Two women, supers
ISBN 0-573-63300-2 (pbk) : £0.90 B81-02960

Hamilton, William, *19---*. Save Grand Canyon : a comedy / by William Hamilton. — London : French, c1981. — 78p ; 19cm
Three men, 3 women
ISBN 0-573-61626-4 (pbk) : Unpriced B81-27199

Johnson, Mike. Return of the maniac : a thriller / by Mike Johnson. — New York ; London : French, c1981. — 116p : 1plan ; 19cm
Two men, 4 women
ISBN 0-573-61506-3 (pbk) : £1.90 B81-15778

Kelly, Terence, *1920-*. The Masterminds : a comedy in two acts / by Terence Kelly. — New York ; London : French, c1980. — 91p ; 19cm
Five men, 3 women
ISBN 0-573-61854-2 (pbk) : £1.90 B81-07713

Lapine, James. Table settings : a comedy / by James Lapine. — New York ; London : French, c1980. — 78p : 2plans ; 19cm
Three men, 4 women
ISBN 0-573-61726-0 (pbk) : £1.90 B81-02691

LaRusso, Louis. Marlon Brando sat right here : a drama in two acts : by Louis LaRusso II. — New York ; London : French, c1980. — 72p : 1plan ; 19cm
Eleven men, 2 women
ISBN 0-573-61290-0 (pbk) : £1.90 B81-03070

Lauck, Carol. Cleo's cafe : a play for children / by Carol Lauck. — New York ; London : French, c1981. — 38p : 1plan ; 19cm
Two men, 4 women
ISBN 0-573-65219-8 (pbk) : £1.20 B81-21058

Leonard, Jim. The diviners : a play in two acts & elegies / by Jim Leonard, Jr. — New York ; London : French, c1981. — 97p ; 19cm
Six men, 5 women
ISBN 0-573-60837-7 (pbk) : £2.25 B81-34620

Levin, Ira. Break a leg : a comedy in two acts / by Ira Levin. — New York ; London : French, c1981. — 70p ; 19cm
Six men, 2 women, supers
ISBN 0-573-60656-0 (pbk) : £1.90 B81-15779

MacArthur, Charles. Johnny on a spot : a comedy in three acts / by Charles MacArthur ; based on a script by Parke Levy & Alan Lipscott ; and derived from a story by George A. Hendon, Jr. & David Peltz. — New York ; London : French, c1981. — 108p ; 19cm
Twenty-five men, 3 women
ISBN 0-573-61111-4 (pbk) : Unpriced B81-34919

McIntyre, Dennis. Modigliani : a play in three acts / by Dennis McIntyre. — New York ; London : French, c1980. — 88p : 1plan ; 19cm
Six men, 1 woman
ISBN 0-573-61853-4 (pbk) : £1.90 B81-03324

Marowitz, Charles. Sex wars : free adaptations of Ibsen and Strindberg. — London : Marion Boyars, Feb.1982. — [192]p
ISBN 0-7145-2721-1 (cased) : £6.95 : CIP entry
ISBN 0-7145-2722-x (pbk) : £3.95 B81-39247

Mastrosimone, William. The woolgatherer : a play in two acts / by William Mastrosimone. — London : French, c1981. — 66p ; 19cm
One man, 1 women
ISBN 0-573-61821-6 (pbk) : Unpriced B81-27200

Merriam, Eve. Dialogue for lovers : sonnets of Shakespeare arranged for dramatic presentation / by Eve Merriam. — New York ; London : French, c1981. — 40p ; 19cm
One man, 2 women
ISBN 0-573-60836-9 (pbk) : £2.25 B81-28652

Nassivera, John. The penultimate problem of Sherlock Holmes : a case for the stage in two acts / by John Nassivera. — New York ; London : French, c1980. — 77p : 1plan ; 19cm
Seven men, 4 women
ISBN 0-573-61448-2 (pbk) : £1.90 B81-07714

Noonan, John Ford. A coupla white chicks sitting around talking : a comedy in two acts / by John Ford Noonan. — New York ; London : French, c1981. — 53p : 1plan ; 19cm
Two women
ISBN 0-573-63017-8 (pbk) : £2.25 B81-21054

Norfolk, William. The lights are warm and coloured : a play / William Norfolk. — London : French, c1980. — 58p : 1plan ; 22cm
Six women, 2 men
ISBN 0-573-11230-4 (pbk) : £1.80 B81-01091

O'Toole, Austin. On the tip of my tongue : a mystery fantasy for children in two acts / by Austin O'Toole. — New York ; London : French, c1980. — 48p : 1plan ; 19cm
Four men, 8 women, supers
ISBN 0-573-65086-1 (pbk) : £1.90 B81-07712

Pine, Robert. Landscape with waitress : a play in one act / by Robert Pine. — New York ; London : French, c1981. — 20p : 1plan ; 19cm
One man, 1 woman. — Plan on inside cover
ISBN 0-573-62289-2 (pbk) : £0.90 B81-20219

Pomerance, Bernard. The elephant man : a drama / by Bernard Pomerance. — New York ; London : French, c1979. — 88p ; 19cm
Five men, 2 women, supers. — Text on inside cover
ISBN 0-573-60874-1 (pbk) : Unpriced B81-24776

Ribalow, Meir Z.. Shrunken heads : a comedy in two acts / by Meir Z. Ribalow. — New York ; London : French, c1980. — 60p : 1plan ; 19cm
Three men, 4 women
ISBN 0-573-61622-1 (pbk) : £1.90 B81-02517

812'.54 — Drama in English. American writers, *1945- — Texts* *continuation*

Sharkey, Jack. 'Honestly, now!' : a crime comedy / by Jack Sharkey. — New York ; London : French, c1981. — 119p : 1plan ; 19cm
Five men, 3 women
ISBN 0-573-61050-9 (pbk) : Unpriced B81-35553

Shem, Samuel. Napoleon's dinner ; and Room for one woman / by Samuel Shem. — New York ; London : French, c1981. — 77p : 2plans ; 19cm
Napoleon's dinner: three men ; Room for one woman : three women
£2.25 (pbk) B81-29960

Shepard, Sam. Four two-act plays / by Sam Shepard. — London : Faber, 1981. — 218p ; 22cm
Contents: La Turista — The tooth of crime — Geography of a horse dreamer — Operation sidewinder
ISBN 0-571-11746-5 (pbk) : £5.50 B81-10146

Shepard, Sam. True West. — London : Faber, Sept.1981. — [64]p
ISBN 0-571-11833-x (pbk) : £2.95 : CIP entry B81-21613

Sills, Paul. More from story theatre / by Paul Sills. — New York ; London : French, c1981. — 72p : 1plan ; 19cm
ISBN 0-573-61855-0 (pbk) : £1.90 B81-16165

Stuart, Nuba-Harold. Hunter! : a light, dark comedy / by Nuba-Harold Stuart. — New York ; London : French, c1980. — 54p : plan ; 19cm
Two men, 2 women
ISBN 0-573-61048-7 (pbk) : £1.90 B81-02059

Thomas, Thom. The interview : a play in two acts / by Thom Thomas. — New York : London, c1981. — 65p ; 19cm
Three men
ISBN 0-573-64030-0 (pbk) : £2.25 B81-21056

Topor, Tom. Nuts : a play in three acts / by Tom Topor. — New York ; London : French, 1981. — 92p : 1plan ; 19cm
six men, 3 women
ISBN 0-573-61325-7 (pbk) : £2.25 B81-21057

Weller, Michael. At home (Split, part 1) / by Michael Weller. — New York ; London : French, c1981. — 25p ; 19cm
One man, 1 woman
ISBN 0-573-62027-x (pbk) : £1.25 B81-21055

Weller, Michael. Loose ends : a play / by Michael Weller. — New York ; London : French, c1980. — 114p : 1facsim,plans ; 19cm
Seven men, 4 women
ISBN 0-573-61197-1 (pbk) : £1.90 B81-07715

White, Betzie Parker. The doublers : a comedy / by Betzie Parker White. — New York ; London : French, c1981. — 16p : 1plan ; 19cm
One man, 1 woman
ISBN 0-573-62133-0 (pbk) : £0.90 B81-20217

White, Edgar. Lament for Rastafari ; and, Like them that dream. — London : Marion Boyars, Jan.1982. — [160]p
ISBN 0-7145-2753-x (cased) : £6.95 : CIP entry
ISBN 0-7145-2756-4 (pbk) : £4.50 B81-37534

Zeman, Jack. Past tense : a drama in two acts / by Jack Zeman. — New York ; London : French, c1981. — 65p : 1plan ; 19cm
Three men, 1 woman
ISBN 0-573-61449-0 (pbk) : £1.90 B81-20218

Ziegler, Tom. Weeds : a comedy in three acts / by Tom Ziegler. — New York ; London : French, c1980. — 98p : plan ; 19cm
Eight men, 2 women
ISBN 0-573-61759-7 (pbk) : £1.90 B81-02060

812'.54'08 — Drama in English. American writers, *1945- — Anthologies*

Daniel, Barbara. Batbrains / by Barbara Daniel. Hello, ma! / by Trude Stone. Me too, then! / by Tom Dudzick & Steven Smith. — New York ; London : French, c1981. — 81p : 3plans ; 19cm
Batbrains: two women. Hello, ma!: two women. Me too, then!: two men, 1 woman
ISBN 0-573-60053-8 (pbk) : £2.25 B81-21051

813 — AMERICAN FICTION

813[F] — Fiction in English. Barbadian writers, *1945- — Texts*

Jackson, Carl. East wind in paradise / by Carl Jackson. — London : New Beacon, 1981. — 147p ; 20cm
ISBN 0-901241-40-7 (cased) : £6.50
ISBN 0-901241-41-5 (pbk) : £2.95 B81-15412

Lamming, George. The emigrants / George Lamming. — London : Allison & Busby, 1980, c1954. — 271p ; 23cm
Originally published: London : Joseph, 1954
ISBN 0-85031-371-6 : £6.50 : CIP rev.
ISBN 0-85031-372-4 (pbk) : £2.95 B80-08420

Lamming, George. Of age and innocence / George Lamming. — London : Allison & Busby, 1981, c1958. — 412p ; 23cm
Originally published: London : Joseph, 1958
ISBN 0-85031-385-6 (cased) : £7.95 : CIP rev.
ISBN 0-85031-386-4 (pbk) : Unpriced B81-14944

813[F] — Fiction in English. Dominican writers, *1900-1945 — Texts*

Rhys, Jean. Good morning, midnight / Jean Rhys. — Harmondsworth : Penguin, 1969 (1980 [printing]). — 158p ; 19cm
ISBN 0-14-002961-3 (pbk) : £0.95 B81-06636

Rhys, Jean. [Postures]. Quartet / Jean Rhys. — Harmondsworth : Penguin, 1973, c1928 (1981 [printing]). — 143p ; 18cm
ISBN 0-14-003610-5 (pbk) : £1.25 B81-32836

Rhys, Jean. [Postures]. Quartet / Jean Rhys. — Large print ed. — Bath : Chivers, 1981. — 233p ; 23cm. — (New Portway)
ISBN 0-85119-102-9 : Unpriced B81-12622

Rhys, Jean. Wide Sargasso sea / Jean Rhys ; introduction by Francis Wyndham. — Large print ed. — Bath : Chivers, 1980, c1966. — xv,217p ; 23cm. — (New Portway)
Originally published: London : Deutsch, 1966
ISBN 0-85997-485-5 : £5.50 : CIP rev. B80-22574

813[F] — Fiction in English. Guyanese writers, *1945- — Texts*

Heath, Roy A. K.. Genetha. — London : Allison and Busby, Oct.1981. — [208]p
ISBN 0-85031-410-0 (cased) : £6.95 : CIP entry
ISBN 0-85031-411-9 (pbk) : £2.95 B81-27981

813[F] — Fiction in English. Jamaican writers, *1945- — Texts*

Brodler, Erna. Jane and Louisa will soon come home / by Erna Brodber. — London : New Beacon, 1980. — 147p ; 20cm
ISBN 0-901241-36-9 (cased) : £6.50
ISBN 0-901241-37-7 (pbk) : £2.95 B81-15411

Hearne, John. The sure salvation / John Hearne. — London : Faber, 1981. — 224p ; 21cm
ISBN 0-571-11670-1 : £6.50 : CIP rev. B81-07448

Mais, Roger. The hills were joyful together / Roger Mais ; introduction by Daphne Morris. — London : Heinemann, 1981, c1953. — xxii,288p ; 19cm. — (Caribbean writers series ; 23)
Originally published: London : Cape, 1953. — Bibliography: pxxii
ISBN 0-435-98586-8 (pbk) : £1.95 : CIP rev. B81-06888

Thelwell, Michael. The harder they come : a novel / by Michael Thelwell. — London : Pluto, 1980. — 399p ; 21cm
Originally published: New York : Grove Press, 1980
ISBN 0-86104-311-1 (cased) : £6.95
ISBN 0-86104-310-3 (pbk) : £2.95 B81-00250

813[F] — Fiction in English. St Christopher-Nevis-Anguilla writers, *1945- — Texts*

Gilchrist, Rupert. Guns of Dragonard / Rupert Gilchrist. — London : Souvenir, 1980. — 223p : 1geneal.table ; 21cm
ISBN 0-285-62453-9 : £6.95 B81-01542

Gilchrist, Rupert. Guns of Dragonard / Rupert Gilchrist. — London : Corgi, 1981, c1980. — 196p ; 18cm : 1geneal.table
Originally published: London : Souvenir, 1980
ISBN 0-552-11761-7 (pbk) : £1.25 B81-35496

Gilchrist, Rupert. The siege of Dragonard Hill / Rupert Gilchrist. — London : Corgi, 1980, c1979. — 241p : 2maps ; 18cm
Originally published: London : Souvenir, 1979
ISBN 0-552-11501-0 (pbk) : £1.50 B81-01551

813[F] — Fiction in English. Trinidadian writers, *1945- — Texts*

Anthony, Michael, *1932-*. All that glitters / Michael Anthony. — London : Deutsch, 1981. — 202p ; 21cm
ISBN 0-233-97369-9 : £5.95 B81-28402

De Boissière, Ralph. Crown jewel : a novel / by Ralph de Boissière. — London : Pan, 1981. — 360p ; 20cm. — (Picador)
Originally published: Melbourne : Australasian Book Society, 1952
ISBN 0-330-26350-1 (pbk) : £2.75 B81-20202

De Boissière, Ralph. Crown jewel : a novel / by Ralph de Boissiere. — London : Allison & Busby, 1981. — 360p ; 23cm
Originally published: Melbourne : Australasian Book Society, 1952
ISBN 0-85031-292-2 : £6.95 : CIP rev.
ISBN 0-85031-293-0 (pbk) : Unpriced B80-17963

De Lima, Clara Rosa. Kilometre nineteen / Clara Rosa De Lima. — Ilfracombe : Stockwell, 1980. — 191p ; 22cm
ISBN 0-7223-1384-5 : £6.30 B81-01092

Hodge, Merle. Crick crack monkey / Merle Hodge ; introduction by Roy Narinesingh. — London : Heinemann, 1981, c1970. — 112p ; 19cm. — (Caribbean writers series ; 24)
Originally published: London : Deutsch, 1970
ISBN 0-435-98401-2 (pbk) : £1.45 : CIP rev. B81-06882

Kydd, Lionel. A breakdown in communications / by Lionel Kydd. — Harrow : Euroeditions, 1979. — 66p ; 21cm
ISBN 0-906204-16-x : Unpriced B81-24759

Lovelace, Earl. The dragon can't dance / Earl Lovelace. — Harlow : Longman, 1981, c1979. — 240p ; 18cm. — (Drumbeat ; 26)
Originally published: London : Deutsch, 1979
ISBN 0-582-64231-0 (pbk) : £1.40 B81-10097

Naipaul, V. S.. A bend in the river / V.S. Naipaul. — Harmondsworth : Penguin, 1980, c1979. — 287p ; 18cm
Originally published: London : Deutsch, 1979
ISBN 0-14-005258-5 (pbk) : £1.50 B81-00251

Naipaul, V. S.. A flag on the island / V.S. Naipaul. — Harmondsworth : Penguin, 1969 c1967 (1981 [printing]). — 213p ; 18cm
Originally published: London : Deutsch, 1967
ISBN 0-14-002939-7 (pbk) : £1.50 B81-35587

813'.009 — Fiction in English. American writers, *1776-1900 — Critical studies*

Bell, Michael Davitt. The development of American romance : the sacrifice of relation / Michael Davitt Bell. — Chicago ; London : University of Chicago Press, 1980. — xiv,291p ; 24cm
Bibliography: p277-279. — Includes index
ISBN 0-226-04211-1 : £13.50 B81-21090

813'.009 — Fiction in English. American writers. Influence of foreign literatures

Kirby, David. America's hive of honey, or, foreign influences on American fiction through Henry James : essays & bibliographies / by David Kirby. — Metuchen ; London : Scarecrow, 1980. — xvii,214p ; 23cm
Bibliography: pxvi-xvii. - Includes index
ISBN 0-8108-1349-1 : £8.75 B81-09374

813'.009'12 — Fiction in English. American writers. Naturalism *— Critical studies*

Kaplan, Harold. Power and order : Henry Adams and the naturalist tradition in American fiction / Harold Kaplan. — Chicago ; London : University of Chicago Press, 1981. — xi,146p : ill ; 24cm
Includes index
ISBN 0-226-42424-3 : £10.50 B81-39823

813'.009'382 — Fiction in English. American writers, *1790-1880.* **Special themes: Religion** *— Critical studies*

Reynolds, David S.. Faith in fiction : the emergence of religious literature in America / David S. Reynolds. — Cambridge, Mass. ; London : Harvard University Press, 1981. — 269p : ill ; 24cm
Bibliography: p219-225. — Includes index
ISBN 0-674-29172-7 : £15.75 B81-39780

813'.01'08[FS] — Short stories in English. American writers, *1830-1861 — Anthologies*

The **Edgar** Allan Poe bedside companion : morgue and mystery tales / edited by Peter Haining. — London : Gollancz, 1980. — 188p : 2facsims ; 21cm
ISBN 0-575-02908-0 : £5.95 B81-05578

813'.01'08[FS] — Short stories in English. Canadian writers, *1800-1979 — Anthologies*

The **Penguin** book of Canadian short stories / edited by Wayne Grady. — Harmondsworth : Penguin, 1980. — viii,455p ; 20cm
ISBN 0-14-005673-4 (pbk) : £1.95 B81-08369

813'.01'0816[FS] — Horror short stories in English. American writers, *1900- — Anthologies*

Alfred Hitchcock's tales to scare you stiff. — London : Reinhardt, Aug.1981. — [352]p
Originally published: New York : Davis Publications, 1978
ISBN 0-370-30298-2 : £5.95 : CIP entry B81-18028

Sinister, strange and supernatural : an anthology / [compiled] by Helen Hoke. — London : Dent, 1981. — 160p ; 24cm
ISBN 0-460-06072-4 : £3.95 B81-17443

813'.01'0816[FS] — Horror short stories in English. American writers, *1945- — Anthologies*

Down by the old bloodstream / Alfred Hitchcock, editor. — London : Severn House, 1981, c1971. — xi,195p ; 21cm
Originally published: S.l. : H.S.D. Publications, 1971
ISBN 0-7278-0683-1 : £5.95 : CIP rev. B81-07608

Happiness is a warm corpse / [compiled by] Alfred Hitchcock. — London : Severn House, 1980, c1969. — 205p ; 21cm
ISBN 0-7278-0665-3 : £5.95 : CIP rev. B80-28787

Having a wonderful crime / [edited by] Alfred Hitchcock. — London : Severn House, 1981, c1977. — 224p ; 21cm
ISBN 0-7278-0717-x : £6.95 : CIP rev. B81-17508

813'.01'08352042[FS] — Short stories in English. American negro women writers, *1945-.* **Special subjects: Negro women** *— Anthologies*

[Midnight birds]. Any woman's blues : stories by contemporary black women writers / edited and with an introduction by Mary Helen Washington. — London : Virago, c1980. — xxv,274p ; 20cm
Originally published: Garden City, N.Y. : Anchor, 1980
ISBN 0-86068-204-8 (pbk) : £3.50 : CIP rev. B81-22512

813'.01'089282[J] — Children's short stories in English, *1945-.* **Caribbean writers** *— Anthologies*

Over our way : a collection of Caribbean short stories for youngsters / edited by Jean D'Costa and Velma Pollard. — Trinidad : Longman Caribbean ; London : Longman, 1980. — x,173p : ill ; 19cm. — (Horizons)
ISBN 0-582-76567-6 (pbk) : Unpriced B81-09283

813'.01'089729[FS] — Short stories in English. West Indian writers, *1900- — Anthologies*

West Indian stories / chosen by John Wickham. — London : Ward Lock Educationl, 1981. — 136p ; 21cm. — (WLE short stories ; 19)
ISBN 0-7062-4082-0 (cased) : £2.95
ISBN 0-7062-4081-2 (pbk) : £1.35 B81-14020

813'.0872[FS] — Detective short stories in English. American writers, *1945- — Anthologies*

Ellery Queen's secrets of mystery / edited by Ellery Queen. — [London] : [Hale], 1981, c1979. — 285p ; 21cm
Originally published: New York : Dial, c1979
ISBN 0-7091-9171-5 : £6.75 B81-35230

Ellery Queen's veils of mystery / edited by Ellery Queen. — London : Hale, 1981, c1980. — 285p ; 21cm
Originally published: New York : Dial, c1980
ISBN 0-7091-9172-3 : £6.75 B81-35227

813'.0874'09 — Fiction in English. American writers. Westerns *— Critical studies*

Milton, John R.. The novel of the American West / John R. Milton. — Lincoln [Ne.] ; London : University of Nebraska Press, c1980. — xvi,341p : ill ; 23cm
Bibliography: p325-332. - Includes index
ISBN 0-8032-0980-0 : £10.80 B81-01093

813'.0876'08[FS] — Science fiction in English. American writers, *1945- — Anthologies*

Butler, Octavia E.. Survivor / Octavia E. Butler. Under a calculating star / John Morressy. The anarchistic colossus / A.E. Van Vogt. — London : Sidgwick & Jackson, 1981. — 248p ; 21cm. — (Science fiction special ; 32)
Contents: Survivor originally published: Garden City, N.Y. : Doubleday ; London : Sidgwick and Jackson, 1978
ISBN 0-283-98510-0 : £8.95 B81-12656

Dickson, Gordon R. (Gordon Rupert). The far call / Gordon R. Dickson. In the hall of the Martian kings / John Varley. — London : Sidgwick & Jackson, 1981. — 316p ; 21cm. — (Quantum special ; 2)
Contents: The far call originally published: New York : Dial Press ; London : Sidgwick and Jackson, 1978
ISBN 0-283-98585-2 : £8.95 B81-12657

Lanier, Sterling E.. The peculiar exploits of Brigadier Ffellows / Sterling E. Lanier. Xeno / D.F. Jones. Frostworld and dreamfire / John Morressy. — London : Sidgwick & Jackson, 1981. — 611p in various pagings ; 20cm. — (Science fiction special ; 35)
The peculiar exploits of Brigadier Ffellows originally published: New York : Walker, 1971 ; London : Sidgwick & Jackson, 1979 — Xeno originally published : as 'Earth has been found', New York : Dell, 1979 ; and, 'Xeno', London : Sidgwick & Jackson, 1979 — Frostworld and dreamfire originally published : New York : Doubleday, 1977 ; London : Sidgwick & Jackson, 1979
ISBN 0-283-98806-1 : £8.95 B81-36177

813'.0876'08[FS] — Science fiction short stories in English. American writers, *1900- — Anthologies*

Nebula winners. — London : W.H. Allen, 1981, c1980
14. — xi,259p ; 21cm
Originally published: New York : Harper & Row, 1980
ISBN 0-491-02754-0 : £6.95 B81-11814

813'.0876'08[FS] — Science fiction short stories in English. American writers, *1945- — Anthologies*

After the fall : an anthology / edited by Robert Sheckley. — London : Sphere, 1980. — x,178p ; 18cm. — (Sphere science fiction)
ISBN 0-7221-7762-3 (pbk) : £1.30 B81-11706

The **Great** science fiction series : stories from the best of the series from 1944 to 1980 by twenty all-time favorite writers / edited by Frederik Pohl, Martin Harry Greenberg and Joseph Olander. — New York ; London : Harper & Row, c1980. — x,419p ; 25cm
Includes bibliographies
ISBN 0-06-013382-1 : £6.95 B81-26528

Reamy, Tom. Blind voices / Tom Reamy. The ultimax man / Keith Laurier. — London : Sidgwick & Jackson, 1981. — 254,217p ; 21cm. — (Science fiction special ; 37)
Blind voices originally published: New York : Berkley Pub. Corp, 1978 ; London : Sidgwick & Jackson, 1979 — The ultimax man originally published: New York : St Martins Press, 1978 ; London : Sidgwick & Jackson, 1979
ISBN 0-283-98808-8 : £8.95 B81-35660

Starry messenger : the best of Galileo / edited by Charles C. Ryan. — London : Hale, 1981, c1979. — 198p ; 21cm. — (Hale SF)
Originally published: New York : St. Martin's Press, 1979
ISBN 0-7091-9118-9 : £6.75 B81-17315

813.3 — AMERICAN FICTION, 1830-1861

813'.3 — Fiction in English. American writers. Hawthorne, Nathaniel *— Correspondence, diaries, etc.*

Hawthorne, Nathaniel. Hawthorne's lost notebook 1835-1841 : facsimile from the Pierpont Morgan Library / transcipt and preface by Barbara S. Mouffe ; introduction by Hyatt H. Waggoner ; foreword by Charles Ryskamp. — University Park ; London : Pennsylvania State University Press, c1980. — 30,86(ie.172)p : facsims,1port ; 24cm
Bibliography: p17-18
ISBN 0-271-00549-1 : £6.90 B81-09018

813'.3 — Fiction in English. American writers. Hawthorne, Nathaniel. Scarlet letter *— Study outlines*

Brown, Suzanne. The scarlet letter : notes / by Suzanne Brown. — Harlow : Longman, 1981. — 80p ; 21cm. — (York notes ; 134)
Bibliography: p73-74
ISBN 0-582-78197-3 (pbk) : £0.90 B81-33690

813'.3 — Fiction in English. American writers. Melville, Herman. Moby Dick *— Study outlines*

Engel, Wilson F.. Moby Dick : notes / by Wilson F. Engel. — Harlow : Longman, 1981. — 94p ; 21cm. — (York notes ; 126)
Bibliography: p92-94
ISBN 0-582-78177-9 (pbk) : £0.90 B81-34236

813'.3 — Fiction in English. American writers. Melville, Herman. Typee *— Sociological perspectives*

Herbert, T. Walter (Thomas Walter), *1938-.* Marquesan encounters : Melville and the meaning of civilization / T. Walter Herbert, Jr. — Cambridge, Mass. ; London : Harvard University Press, 1980. — viii,237p : ill,ports ; 24cm
Bibliography: p227-230. - Includes index
ISBN 0-674-55066-8 : £9.00 B81-09352

813'.3[F] — Fiction in English. American writers, *1830-1861 — Texts*

Melville, Herman. Moby-Dick / by Herman Melville ; edited and with an introduction by Charles Child Walcutt. — Toronto ; London : Bantam, 1967 (1981 [printing]). — xii,594p ; 18cm. — (A Bantam classic)
Bibliography: p594
ISBN 0-553-21007-6 (pbk) : £1.00 B81-39110

813′.3[F] — Fiction in English. American writers, *1830-1861 — Texts* *continuation*

Stowe, Harriet Beecher. Uncle Tom′s cabin, or, Life among the lowly / Harriet Beecher Stowe ; edited with an introduction by Ann Douglas. — Harmondsworth : Penguin, 1981. — 629p : 1port ; 18cm
Port on inside cover
ISBN 0-14-039003-0 (pbk) : £1.95 B81-38358

813′.3′09 — Fiction in English. American writers. Hawthorne, Nathaniel; Melville, Herman & Poe, Edgar Allan — *Critical studies*

Levin, Harry, *1912-*. The power of blackness : Hawthorne, Poe, Melville / Harry Levin. — Chicago ; London : Ohio University Press, 1980, c1958. — xii,263,ixp ; 21cm
Originally published: New York : Knopf, 1958. — Bibliography: p249-255. — Includes index
ISBN 0-8214-0581-0 (pbk) : £3.60 B81-22360

813′.3′09321732 — Fiction in English. American writers, *1830-1861.* **Special themes: Cities** — *Critical studies*

Siegel, Adrienne. The image of the American city in popular literature, 1820-1870 / Adrienne Siegel. — Port Washington ; London : National University Publications : Kennikat, 1981. — 211p ; 22cm. — (Interdisciplinary urban series)
Bibliography: p186-205. — Includes index
ISBN 0-8046-9271-8 : £12.75 B81-36655

813.4 — AMERICAN FICTION, 1861-1900

813′.4 — Fiction in English. American writers, *1861-1900 — Texts with commentaries*

Twain, Mark. The adventures of Tom Sawyer ; Tom Sawyer, abroad ; Tom Sawyer, detective / edited by John C. Gerber, Paul Baender and Terry Firkins. — Berkeley ; London : Published for the Iowa Center for Textual Studies by the University of California Press, 1980. — xvii,717p : ill,facsims,port ; 24cm. — (The Works of Mark Twain ; v.4)
ISBN 0-520-03353-1 : £16.50 B81-04129

Twain, Mark. A Connecticut yankee in King Arthur′s court / edited by Bernard L. Stein ; with an indroduction by Henry Nash Smith. — Berkeley ; London : Published for the Iowa Center for Textual Studies by the University of California Press, 1979. — xvii,827p : ill,facsims ; 24cm. — (The Works of Mark Twain ; v.9)
ISBN 0-520-03621-2 : £19.50 B81-04128

Twain, Mark. The prince and the pauper / edited by Victor Fischer and Lin Salamo with the assistance of Mary Jane Jones. — Berkeley ; London : Published for the Iowa Center for Textual Studies by the University of California Press, 1979. — xvi,533p : ill,facsim ; 24cm. — (The Works of Mark Twain ; v.6)
ISBN 0-520-03622-0 : £15.00 B81-04121

813′.4 — Fiction in English. American writers. Chesnutt, Charles W. — *Critical studies*

Andrews, William L.. The literary career of Charles W. Chesnutt / William L. Andrews. — Baton Rouge ; London : Louisiana State University Press, c1980. — xiii,292p : 1port ; 24cm. — (Southern literary studies)
Bibliography: p279-286. - Includes index
ISBN 0-8071-0673-9 : £12.00 B81-07648

813′.4 — Fiction in English. American writers. Crane, Stephen. Impressionism

Nagel, James. Stephen Crane and literary impressionism / James Nagel. — University Park ; London : Pennsylvania State University Press, c1980. — x,190p ; 24cm
Includes index
ISBN 0-271-00267-0 (corrected) : £9.90 B81-29950

813′.4 — Fiction in English. American writers. James, Henry, *1843-1916 — Critical studies*

Kappeler, Susanne. Writing and reading in Henry James / Susanne Kappeler ; foreword by Tony Tanner. — London : Macmillan, 1980. — xiv,242p ; 23cm
Bibliography: p234-240. - Includes index
ISBN 0-333-29104-2 : £15.00 : CIP rev. B80-24780

813′.4 — Fiction in English. American writers. James, Henry, *1843-1916.* **Europeans, The** — *Study outlines*

McEwan, Neil. The Europeans : notes / by Neil McEwan. — Harlow : Longman, 1981, c1980. — 70p ; 21cm. — (York notes ; 120)
Bibliography: p69-70
ISBN 0-582-78251-1 (pbk) : £0.90 B81-34226

813′.4 — Fiction in English. American writers. James, Henry, *1843-1916.* **Portrait of a lady** — *Study outlines*

Walker, Marshall. The portrait of a lady : notes / by Marshall Walker. — Harlow : Longman, 1981. — 80p ; 21cm. — (York notes ; 117)
ISBN 0-582-78256-2 (pbk) : £0.90 B81-33688

813′.4 — Fiction in English. American writers. James, Henry, *1843-1916.* **Special subjects: Civilization** — *Critical studies*

Berland, Alwyn. Culture and conduct in the novels of Henry James / Alwyn Berland. — Cambridge : Cambridge University Press, 1981. — xi,231p ; 23cm
Includes index
ISBN 0-521-23343-7 : £17.50 B81-17023

813′.4 — Fiction in English. American writers. Twain, Mark. Huckleberry Finn — *Study outlines*

Donnelly, Brian. The adventures of Huckleberry Finn : notes / by Brian Donnelly. — London : Longman, 1980. — 79p ; 21cm. — (York notes ; 49)
Bibliography: p75
ISBN 0-582-78222-8 (pbk) : £0.90 B81-07099

813′.4 — Short stories in English. American writers. Twain, Mark — *Critical studies*

Critical approaches to Mark Twain′s short stories / edited by Elizabeth McMahan. — Port Washington ; London : National University Publications : Kennikat, 1981. — 147p ; 23cm. — (Literary criticism series)
Bibliography: p143-145. — Includes index
ISBN 0-8046-9274-2 : £12.75 B81-29474

813′.4[F] — Fiction in English. American writers, *1861-1900 — Texts*

Alger, Horatio. [The new schoolma′am]. A fancy of hers ; The disagreeable woman : two lost novels for adults by the man loved for his rags-to-riches tales for juveniles / Horatio Alger ; with an introduction by Ralph D. Gardner. — New York ; London : Van Nostrand Reinhold, c1981. — 179p,[19]p of plates : ill,1facsim ; 24cm
Includes index
ISBN 0-442-24716-8 : £11.20 B81-17190

Gilman, Charlotte Perkins. The yellow wallpaper / Charlotte Perkins Gilman ; afterword by Elaine R. Hedges. — London : Virago, 1981, c1973. — 63p ; 20cm. — (Virago modern classics)
ISBN 0-86068-201-3 (pbk) : £1.50 : CIP rev. B81-04349

Glasgow, Ellen. The sheltered life / Ellen Glasgow ; with a new introduction by Paul Binding. — London : Virago, 1981, c1964. — xxviii,292p ; 20cm. — (Virago modern classics)
ISBN 0-86068-191-2 (pbk) : £2.95 : CIP rev. B81-22468

Glasgow, Ellen. Virginia / Ellen Glasgow ; with a new introduction by Paul Binding. — London : Virago, 1981, c1966. — xiii,392p ; 22cm. — (Virago modern classics)
ISBN 0-86068-182-3 (pbk) : £2.95 : CIP rev. B81-22499

James, Henry, *1843-1916.* The Europeans ; Daisy Miller ; Washington Square ; The Aspern papers ; The turn of the screw ; The portrait of a lady / Henry James. — London : Heinemann, 1981. — 829p ; 24cm
ISBN 0-905712-55-2 : £6.95 B81-33732

James, Henry, *1843-1916.* The portrait of a lady. — Oxford : Oxford University Press, Nov.1981. — [688]p. — (The World′s classics)
ISBN 0-19-281514-8 (pbk) : £1.95 : CIP entry B81-28856

James, Henry, *1843-1916.* The turn of the screw / Henry James. — Large print ed. — Bath : Chivers, 1981. — 198p ; 23cm. — (A New Portway large print book)
ISBN 0-85119-108-8 : Unpriced B81-12131

Twain, Mark. The adventures of Huckleberry Finn / by Mark Twain ; afterword by Alfred Kazin. — Toronto ; London : Bantam, 1965 (1981 [printing]). — 292p ; 18cm. — (A Bantam classic)
ISBN 0-553-21000-9 (pbk) : £0.85 B81-39113

Twain, Mark. The adventures of Tom Sawyer / by Mark Twain ; afterword by Alfred Kazin. — Toronto ; London : Bantam, 1966 (1981 [printing]). — 233p ; 18cm. — (Bantam classics)
ISBN 0-553-21001-7 (pbk) : £0.85 B81-39795

813′.4[F] — Short stories in English. American writers, *1861-1900 — Texts*

Gilman, Charlotte Perkins. The Charlotte Perkins Gilman reader : the Yellow wallpaper and other fiction / edited and introducted by Ann J. Lane. — London : Woman′s Press, 1981, c1980. — xlii,208p ; 20cm
Originally published: New York : Pantheon, 1980
ISBN 0-7043-3866-1 (pbk) : £2.95 B81-15645

813′.4[J] — Children′s stories in English. American writers, *1861-1900 — Texts*

Alcott, Louisa M.. Good wives. — London : Octopus, 1981. — 215p : ill ; 22cm
ISBN 0-7064-1563-9 : £1.90 B81-17399

Burnett, Frances Hodgson. Little Lord Fauntleroy / Frances Hodgson Burnett ; illustrated by Mentor Huebner. — Harmondsworth : Penguin, 1981. — 190p : ill ; 20cm
ISBN 0-14-005877-x (pbk) : £0.95 B81-06799

Burnett, Frances Hodgson. Little Lord Fauntleroy / Frances Hodgson Burnett ; illustrated by Mentor Huebner. — [Harmondsworth] : Puffin, 1981. — 190p : ill ; 20cm
ISBN 0-14-031411-3 (pbk) : £0.85 B81-06800

Coolidge, Susan. What Katy did / Susan Coolidge. — London : Octopus, 1981. — 152p : ill ; 22cm
ISBN 0-7064-1562-0 : £1.95 B81-17400

Twain, Mark. The adventures of Huckleberry Finn / Mark Twain. — London : Octopus, 1981. — 246p : ill ; 22cm
ISBN 0-7064-1559-0 : £1.95 B81-17397

813.52 — AMERICAN FICTION, 1900-1945

813′.52 — Fiction in English. American writers. Caspary, Vera — *Biographies*

Caspary, Vera. Secrets of grown-ups / Vera Caspary. — South Yarmouth, Mass. : J. Curley ; [Skipton] : distributed by Magna Print, c1979. — 540p ; 23cm
Published in large print
ISBN 0-89340-264-8 : £5.75 B81-28962

813′.52 — Fiction in English. American writers. Chandler, Raymond — *Correspondence, diaries, etc.*

Chandler, Raymond. Selected letters of Raymond Chandler. — London : Cape, Oct.1981. — [496]p
ISBN 0-224-01962-7 : £12.50 : CIP entry B81-27341

813′.52 — Fiction in English. American writers. Chandler, Raymond. Long goodbye — *Critical studies*

Whitley, John S.. Detectives and friends : Dashiell Hammett′s The glass key and Raymond Chandler′s The long goodbye / by John S. Whitley. — Exeter : University of Exeter. American Arts Documentation Centre, c1981. — 38p ; 22cm. — (American arts pamphlet ; no.6)
Bibliography: p35-38
ISBN 0-85989-157-7 (pbk) : £1.00
Also classified at 813′.52 B81-24191

13′.52 — Fiction in English. American writers. Faulkner, William. Absalom, Absalom! — *Study outlines*

Ross, Mary. Absalom, Absalom! : notes / by Mary Ross. — Harlow : Longman, 1981. — 62p ; 21cm. — (York notes ; 124)
Bibliography: p62
ISBN 0-582-78214-7 (pbk) : £0.90 B81-34240

13′.52 — Fiction in English. American writers. Faulkner, William. As I lay dying — *Study outlines*

Ross, Mary. As I lay dying / notes by Mary Ross. — London : Longman, 1980. — 96p ; 21cm. — (York notes ; 44)
Bibliography: p92
ISBN 0-582-78144-2 (pbk) : £0.90 B81-24972

13′.52 — Fiction in English. American writers. Faulkner, William — *Biographies*

Minter, David L.. William Faulkner : his life and work / David Minter. — Baltimore ; London : Johns Hopkins University Press, c1980. — xvi,325p : 1map,3geneal.tables ; 24cm
Bibliography: p261-265. - Includes index
ISBN 0-8018-2347-1 : £9.50 B81-19787

13′.52 — Fiction in English. American writers. Faulkner, William — *Interviews*

Faulkner, William. Lion in the garden : interviews with William Faulkner 1926-1962 / edited by James B. Meriwether and Michael Millgate. — Lincoln [Neb.] ; London : University of Nebraska Press, 1980, c1968. — xvi,298p ; 21cm. — (Bison book)
Originally published: New York : Random House, 1968. — Includes index
ISBN 0-8032-3068-0 (cased) : Unpriced
ISBN 0-8032-8108-0 (pbk) : £3.60 B81-12466

13′.52 — Fiction in English. American writers. Faulkner, William. Special themes: United States. Negroes — *Critical studies*

Jenkins, Lee. Faulkner and Black-White relations : a psychoanalytic approach / Lee Jenkins. — New York ; Guildford : Columbia University Press, 1981. — v,301p ; 21cm
Bibliography: p291-293. - Includes index
ISBN 0-231-04744-4 : £11.55 B81-18927

13′.52 — Fiction in English. American writers. Fitzgerald, F. Scott — *Biographies*

Bruccoli, Matthew J.. Some sort of epic grandeur : the life of F. Scott Fitzgerald. — London : Hodder & Stoughton, Oct.1981. — [640]p
ISBN 0-340-27579-0 : £14.95 : CIP entry B81-26735

13′.52 — Fiction in English. American writers. Glasgow, Ellen — *Critical studies*

Raper, Julius Rowan. From the sunken garden : the fiction of Ellen Glasgow, 1916-1945 / Julius Rowan Raper. — Baton Rouge ; London : Louisiana State University Press, c1980. — xiii,220p ; 23cm. — (Southern literary studies)
Bibliography: p209-213. — Includes index
ISBN 0-8071-0653-4 : £9.00 B81-01943

813′.52 — Fiction in English. American writers. Hammett, Dashiell. Glass key — *Critical studies*

Whitley, John S.. Detectives and friends : Dashiell Hammett's The glass key and Raymond Chandler's The long goodbye / by John S. Whitley. — Exeter : University of Exeter. American Arts Documentation Centre, c1981. — 38p ; 22cm. — (American arts pamphlet ; no.6)
Bibliography: p35-38
ISBN 0-85989-157-7 (pbk) : £1.00
Primary classification 813′.52 B81-24191

813′.52 — Fiction in English. American writers. Hemingway, Ernest — *Correspondence, diaries, etc.*

Hemingway, Ernest. Ernest Hemingway selected letters 1917-1961 / edited by Carlos Baker. — London : Granada, 1981. — xxvii,948p : 1ill,facsims ; 24cm
Facsims on lining papers. — Includes index
ISBN 0-246-11576-9 : £15.00 B81-21681

813′.52 — Fiction in English. American writers. Hemingway, Ernest. For whom the bell tolls — *Study outlines*

Sanderson, Stewart. For whom the bell tolls : notes / by Stewart Sanderson. — London : Longman, 1980. — 72p ; 21cm. — (York notes ; 95)
Bibliography: p69
ISBN 0-582-78236-8 (pbk) : £0.90 B81-20012

813′.52 — Fiction in English. American writers. Hurston, Zora Neale — *Biographies*

Hemenway, Robert E.. Zora Neale Hurston : a literary biography / Robert E. Hemenway ; with a foreword by Alice Walker. — Urbana ; London : University of Illinois Press, c1977 (1980 printing). — xxiii,371p,[10]p of plates : ill,ports ; 24cm
Bibliography: p355-359. - Includes index
ISBN 0-252-00807-3 (pbk) : £5.40 B81-07146

813′.52 — Fiction in English. American writers. O'Hara, John — *Biographies*

MacShane, Frank. The life of John O'Hara / Frank MacShane. — London : Cape, 1980. — xii,274p,[16]p of plates : ill,ports ; 25cm
Includes index
ISBN 0-224-01885-x : £10.00 B81-14587

813′.52 — Fiction in English. American writers. Steinbeck, John, *1902-1968*. Pearl, *The* — *Study outlines*

Yong, Margaret. The pearl : notes / by Margaret Yong. — Harlow : Longman, 1981. — 88p ; 21cm. — (York notes ; 99)
Bibliography: p85-86
ISBN 0-582-78127-2 (pbk) : £0.90 B81-19632

813′.52 — Fiction in English. American writers. Wharton, Edith — *Critical studies*

Wolff, Cynthia Griffin. A feast of words : the triumph of Edith Wharton / Cynthia Griffin Wolf. — Oxford : Oxford University Press, 1978,c1977. — viii,453p : ports ; 21cm
Originally published: New York : Oxford University Press, 1977. — Bibliography: p443-446. — Includes index
ISBN 0-19-502434-6 (pbk) : Unpriced B81-09653

813′.52 — Fiction in English. Canadian writers. MacLennan, Hugh, *1907-* — *Biographies*

Cameron, Elspeth, *1943-*. Hugh MacLennan : a writer's life / Elspeth Cameron. — Toronto ; London : University of Toronto Press, c1981. — xv,421p : ill,ports ; 24cm
Includes index
ISBN 0-8020-5556-7 : £15.00 B81-36565

813′.52[F] — Fiction in English. American writers, *1900-1945* — *Texts*

Bagby, George. Country and fatal / George Bagby. — London : Hale, 1981, c1980. — 181p ; 20cm
Originally published: Garden City, N.Y. : Doubleday, 1980
ISBN 0-7091-8944-3 : £5.75 B81-11784

Bagby, George. Mugger's day / George Bagby. — London : Hale, 1980, c1979. — 184p ; 20cm
Originally published: Garden City, N.Y. : Doubleday, 1979
ISBN 0-7091-8509-x : £5.75 B81-00263

Bagby, George. A question of quarry / George Bagby. — London : Hale, 1981. — 181p ; 20cm
Originally published: New York : Doubleday, 1981
ISBN 0-7091-9208-8 : £6.25 B81-28877

Baker, Dorothy. Cassandra at the wedding. — London : Virago, Jan.1982. — [238]p. — (Virago modern classics)
Originally published: Boston, Mass. : Houghton Mifflin ; London : Gollancz, 1962
ISBN 0-86068-244-7 (pbk) : £2.95 : CIP entry B81-38301

Boyle, Kay. Plagued by the nightingale / Kay Boyle ; with a new preface by the author. — London : Virago, 1981. — 190p : ill ; 20cm. — (Virago modern classics)
ISBN 0-86068-167-x (pbk) : £2.50 B81-11274

Brand, Max. Gunfighter's return / Max Brand. — London : Hale, 1980, c1950. — 200p ; 20cm
ISBN 0-7091-8383-6 : £4.75 B81-00252

Brand, Max. Six-gun country / Max Brand. — London : Hale, 1981, x1953. — 164p ; 20cm
ISBN 0-7091-8854-4 : £4.95 B81-19292

Brand, Max. Six gun country / Max Brand. — London : Prior, 1981, c1953. — 309p ; 25cm
Published in large print
ISBN 0-86043-604-7 : £5.95 B81-32772

Brand, Max. Tiger / by Max Brand. — London : Remploy, 1979. — 288p ; 20cm
ISBN 0-7066-0793-7 : £4.00 B81-18792

Brand, Max. Trouble kid / Max Brand. — South Yarmouth, Mass. : Curley ; [Long Preston] : Distributed by Magna Print, [1981?], c1959. — 361p ; 23cm
Published in large print
ISBN 0-89340-322-9 : Unpriced B81-35734

Brand, Max. Valley vultures / by Max Brand. — London : Remploy, 1979, c1932. — 318p ; 20cm
ISBN 0-7066-0792-9 : £4.20 B81-02527

Buck, Pearl S.. The angry wife / by Pearl S. Buck. — London : Severn House, 1980. — 238p ; 21cm
Originally published: under the name John Sedges. New York : J. Day, 1947. London : Methuen, 1948
ISBN 0-7278-0690-4 : £5.95 : CIP rev. B80-23689

Cain, James M.. Double indemnity and ; The Embezzler / by James M. Cain. — London : Hale, 1981, c1971. — 218p ; 21cm
ISBN 0-7091-9255-x : £5.75 B81-40466

Cain, James M.. Mildred Pierce / James M. Cain. — London : Hale, 1981, c1969. — 286p ; 21cm
Originally published: New York : Knopf, 1941 ; London : Hale, 1943
ISBN 0-7091-9256-8 : £5.75 B81-40533

Cain, James M.. The postman always rings twice / James M. Cain. — London : Pan, 1981, c1934. — 124p ; 18cm
ISBN 0-330-26312-9 (pbk) : £0.95 B81-17986

Cain, James M.. Serenade / James M. Cain. — London : Pan, 1981, c1938. — 173p ; 18cm
ISBN 0-330-26341-2 (pbk) : £1.25 B81-20199

Caldwell, Taylor. Answer as a man / Taylor Caldwell. — London : Collins, 1981, c1980. — 445p ; 25cm
Originally published: New York : Putnam, 1981
ISBN 0-00-222073-3 : £6.95 B81-05711

Cather, Willa. Death comes for the Archbishop / Willa Cather ; new introduction by A.S. Byatt. — London : Virago, 1981. — 299p ; 20cm. — (Virago modern classics)
ISBN 0-86068-183-1 (pbk) : £2.95 : CIP rev. B81-14436

Cather, Willa. The professor's house / Willa Cather ; new introduction by A.S. Byatt. — London : Virago, 1981. — 283p ; 20cm. — (Virago modern classics)
ISBN 0-86068-184-x (pbk) : £2.95 : CIP rev. B81-14437

Cheever, John. The Wapshot chronicle / John Cheever. — London : Abacus, 1981, c1957. — 296p ; 20cm
Originally published: New York : Harper ; London : Gollancz, 1957
ISBN 0-349-10503-0 (pbk) : £1.95 B81-39745

813'.52[F] — Fiction in English. American writers, *1900-1945 — Texts* *continuation*

Cole, Jackson. Mesquite marauders ; and, Outlaw hell / Jackson Cole. — Large print ed. — Leicester : Ulverscroft, 1980. — 402p ; 22cm. — (Ulverscroft large print series)
ISBN 0-7089-0546-3 : £4.25 : CIP rev. B80-28735

Cole, Jackson. Peril rides the Pecos ; and, Lost river loot / Jackson Cole. — Large print ed. — Leicester : Ulverscroft, 1981. — 402p ; 23cm. — (Ulverscroft large print series)
ISBN 0-7089-0602-8 : Unpriced B81-14226

Cole, Jackson. Shootout trail ; The land pirates. — Large print ed. — Anstey : Ulverscroft, Dec.1981. — [400]p. — (Ulverscroft large print series)
ISBN 0-7089-0729-6 : £5.00 : CIP entry B81-32608

Coleman, Emily Holmes. The shutter of snow / Emily Holmes Coleman ; introduction by Carmen Callil and Mary Siepmann. — London : Virago, 1981, c1974. — 219p ; 20cm. — (Virago modern classics)
ISBN 0-86068-173-4 (pbk) : £2.50 B81-09556

Cunningham, E. V.. The case of the one-penny orange. — Large print ed. — Bath : Chivers, Nov.1981. — [232]p. — (A New Portway large print book)
ISBN 0-85119-140-1 : £5.25 : CIP entry B81-30570

De Camp, L. Sprague. [Wall of serpents]. The enchanter completed / L. Sprague de Camp & Fletcher Pratt ; foreword by Catherine Crook de Camp. — London : Sphere, 1980, c1978. — 157p ; 18cm
Originally published: New York : Avalon Books, 1960
ISBN 0-7221-2229-2 (pbk) : £1.00 B81-07665

De Vries, Peter. Consenting adults or the duchess will be furious : a novel / by Peter De Vries. — London : Gollancz, 1981, c1980. — 221p ; 23cm
ISBN 0-575-02934-x : £5.95 B81-03495

Dickson, Carter. The plague court murders / Carter Dickson. — London : Remploy, 1979. — 234p ; 19cm
ISBN 0-7066-0825-9 : £4.00 B81-09402

Dreiser, Theodore. Sister Carrie / by Theodore Dreiser ; historical editors John C. Berkey, Alice Winters ; textual editor James L.W. West ; general editor Neda M. Westlake ; introduction by Alfred Kazin. — Harmondsworth : Penguin, 1981. — xviii,499p : 1port ; 18cm. — (The Penguin American library)
Port on inside cover. — Bibliography: pxvii-xviii
ISBN 0-14-039002-2 (pbk) : £1.75 B81-38355

Eberhart, Mignon G.. Dead men's plans / by M.G. Eberhart. — Hornchurch : Henry, 1980, c1952. — 176p ; 21cm
Originally published: London : Collins, 1953
ISBN 0-86025-176-4 : £4.75 B81-21206

Eberhart, Mignon G.. Family affair. — London : Collins, Nov.1981. — [224]p. — (Crime Club)
ISBN 0-00-231292-1 : £6.50 : CIP entry B81-28773

Farrell, James T.. Studs Lonigan / James T. Farrell. — London : Granada, 1979 (1980 [printing]). — 819p ; 18cm. — (A Panther book)
Contents: Young Lonigan — The young manhood of Studs Lonigan — Judgement day
ISBN 0-586-05021-3 (pbk) : £2.50 B81-06372

Fast, Howard. Agrippa's daughter / Howard Fast. — London : Granada, 1968, c1964 (1981 [printing]). — 318p ; 18cm. — (A Mayflower book)
Originally published: New York : Doubleday, 1964 ; London : Methuen, 1965
ISBN 0-583-11244-7 (pbk) : £1.50 B81-19918

Fast, Howard. Freedom road / Howard Fast ; with a foreword by W.E.B. Dubois. — London : Severn House, 1980, c1972. — viii,246p ; 21cm
ISBN 0-7278-0686-6 : £5.95 : CIP rev. B80-17974

Fast, Howard. The legacy. — London : Hodder & Stoughton, Nov.1981. — [400]p
ISBN 0-340-25750-4 : £6.95 : CIP entry B81-30138

Fast, Howard. Spartacus / Howard Fast. — London : Granada, 1974 (1981 [printing]). — 285p ; 18cm. — (A Mayflower book)
Originally published: London : J. Lane, 1952
ISBN 0-583-12501-8 (pbk) : £1.50 B81-17408

Faulkner, William. Sanctuary : the original text / William Faulkner ; edited, with an afterword and notes, by Noel Polk. — London : Chatto & Windus, 1981. — 311p ; 22cm
Originally published: New York : Random House, 1981. — Bibliography: p311
ISBN 0-7011-3900-5 : £9.95 B81-26477

Field, Peter. Couger Canyon / Peter Field. — Large print ed. — Leicester : Ulverscroft, 1980. — 285p ; 23cm. — (Ulverscroft large print series)
Originally published: New York : Jefferson House, 1962 ; London : Muller, 1964
ISBN 0-7089-0503-x : £4.25 : CIP rev. B80-11610

Floren, Lee. High border riders / Lee Floren. — London : Hale, 1981, c1979. — 175p ; 20cm
Originally published: New York : Manor Books, 1979
ISBN 0-7091-8827-7 : £4.95 B81-19295

Floren, Lee. Powdersmoke lawyer / Lee Floren. — London : Hale, 1981, c1979. — 204p ; 20cm
Originally published: [S.l.] : Manor Books, 1979
ISBN 0-7091-8828-5 : £4.95 B81-35210

Floren, Lee. The rawhide men / Lee Floren. — London : Hale, 1980, c1979. — 192p ; 20cm
Originally published: New York : Manor, 1979
ISBN 0-7091-8677-0 : £4.95 B81-06317

Franken, Rose. Claudia. — Large print ed. — Anstey : Ulverscroft, Jan.1982. — [430]p. — (Ulverscroft large print series : romance)
ISBN 0-7089-0734-2 : £5.00 : CIP entry B81-33964

Gallico, Paul. Beyond the Poseidon adventure. — Large print ed. — Bath : Chivers, Nov.1981. — [344]p. — (A New Portway large print book)
Originally published: London : Heinemann, 1978
ISBN 0-85119-141-x : £5.50 : CIP entry B81-30571

Gallico, Paul. Coronation. — Large print ed. — Bath : Chivers Press, Nov.1981. — [168]p. — (A New Portway large print book)
ISBN 0-85119-142-8 : £5.25 : CIP entry B81-30572

Gallico, Paul. Love of seven dolls ; and The lonely / Paul Gallico. — Large print ed. — Bath : Chivers, 1981. — 316p ; 23cm. — (A New Portway large print book)
Love of seven dolls. Originally published: London : Joseph, 1954. The lonely. Originally published: London : Joseph, 1947
ISBN 0-85119-125-8 : Unpriced : CIP rev. B81-14919

Gallico, Paul. Mrs Harris goes to Moscow. — Large print ed. — Bath : Chivers Press, Dec.1981. — [264]p. — (A New Portway large print book)
Originally published: London : Heinemann, 1974
ISBN 0-85119-145-2 : £5.25 : CIP entry B81-31836

Gallico, Paul. Mrs Harris, M.P.. — Large print ed. — Bath : Chivers, Dec.1981. — [208]p. — (A New Portway large print book)
Originally published: London : Heinemann, 1965
ISBN 0-85119-146-0 : £4.95 : CIP entry B81-3183

Gann, Ernest K.. The aviator / Ernest K. Gann. — London : Hodder, c1981. — 189p ; 22cm
ISBN 0-340-26755-0 : £5.95 : CIP rev. B81-2015

Gann, Ernest K.. Brain 2000 / by Ernest K. Gann. — London : Hodder and Stoughton, 1980. — 372p ; 23cm
ISBN 0-340-25722-9 : £6.95 B81-1013

Gardner, Erle Stanley. The case of the angry mourner / Erle Stanley Gardner. — London : Granada, 1970, c1958 (1981 [printing]). — 158p ; 18cm. — (A Mayflower book)
Originally published: New York : Morrow, 1951 ; London : Heinemann, 1958
ISBN 0-583-11810-0 (pbk) : £0.85 B81-2343

Gardner, Erle Stanley. The case of the fugitive nurse / Erle Stanley Gardner. — London : Granada, 1970, c1954 (1981 [printing]). — 203p ; 18cm. — (A Mayflower book)
Originally published: New York : Morrow, 1954 ; London : Heinemann, 1959
ISBN 0-583-11632-9 (pbk) : £0.95 B81-3742

Gardner, Erle Stanley. The case of the glamorous ghost / Erle Stanley Gardner. — London : Granada, 1969, c1955 (1981 [printing]). — 207p ; 18cm. — (A Mayflower book)
Originally published: New York : Marrow, 1955 ; London : Heinemann, 1960
ISBN 0-583-11615-9 (pbk) : £0.95 B81-1740

Gardner, Erle Stanley. The case of the green-eyed sister / Erle Stanley Gardner. — London : Granada, 1970, c1953 (1981 [printing]). — 190p ; 18cm. — (A Mayflower book)
Originally published: New York : Morrow, 1953 ; London : Heinemann, 1959
ISBN 0-583-11631-0 (pbk) : £0.95 B81-3218

Gardner, Erle Stanley. The case of the ice-cold hands / Erle Stanley Gardner. — London : Prior, 1981, c1962. — 321p ; 25cm
Originally published: New York : W.J. Black, 1962 ; London : Heinemann, 1968. — Published in large print
ISBN 0-86043-594-6 : £5.95 B81-3276

Gardner, Erle Stanley. The case of the mischievous doll / Erle Stanley Gardner. — London : Prior, 1981, c1963. — vii,333p ; 25cm
Originally published: New York : Morrow, 1963 ; London : Heinemann, 1968. — Published in large print
ISBN 0-86043-601-2 : £5.95 B81-32765

Gardner, Erle Stanley. The case of the moth-eaten mink / Erle Stanley Gardner. — London : Granada, 1981, c1952. — 186p ; 18cm. — (A Mayflower book)
Originally published: New York, Morrow, 1952 ; London : Heinemann, 1958
ISBN 0-583-11617-5 (pbk) : £0.95 B81-13297

Gardner, Erle Stanley. The case of the negligent nymph / Erle Stanley Gardner. — London : Granada, 1969 (1981 [printing]). — 173p ; 18cm. — (A Mayflower book)
Originally published: New York : Morrow, 1950 ; London : Heinemann, 1956
£0.95 (pbk) B81-28908

Gardner, Erle Stanley. The case of the restless redhead / Erle Stanley Gardner. — London : Granada, 1969, c1954 (1981 [printing]). — vi,190p ; 18cm. — (A Mayflower book)
Originally published: New York : Morrow, 1954 ; London : Heinemann, 1960
ISBN 0-583-11543-8 (pbk) : £0.95 B81-30778

813'.52[F] — Fiction in English. American writers, *1900-1945 — Texts* *continuation*

Gardner, Erle Stanley. The case of the substitute face / Erle Stanley Gardner. — London : Severn House, 1980, c1938. — 226p ; 21cm
ISBN 0-7278-0613-0 : £5.95 : CIP rev. B80-22516

Gardner, Erle Stanley. The case of the sunbather's diary / Erle Stanley Gardner. — London : Granada, 1970, c1955 (1981 [printing]). — 222p ; 18cm. — (A Mayflower book)
Originally published: New York : Morrow, 1955 ; London : Heinemann, 1961
£0.95 (pbk) B81-26540

Grey, Zane. Fighting caravans. — Large print ed. — Anstey : Ulverscroft, Oct.1981. — [480]p. — (Ulverscroft large print series)
ISBN 0-7089-0701-6 : £5.00 : CIP entry B81-28095

Grey, Zane. King of the range. — Large print ed. — Anstey : Ulverscroft, Jan.1982. — [459] p. — (Ulverscroft large print series : Western)
ISBN 0-7089-0743-1 : £5.00 : CIP entry B81-33952

Grey, Zane. Light of the western stars / Zane Grey. — Hornchurch : Henry, 1981, c1942. — 159p ; 21cm
ISBN 0-86025-184-5 : £4.95 B81-31996

Grey, Zane. Prairie gold / by Zane Grey. — Hornchurch : Henry, 1981, c1940. — 157p ; 21cm
This abridged version of Desert gold originally published: London : World Distributors, 1965
ISBN 0-86025-185-3 : £5.25 B81-31997

Grey, Zane. Riders of vengeance / Zane Grey. — Hornchurch : Henry, 1981, c1939. — 158p ; 21cm
Abridged version of Riders of the purple sage
ISBN 0-86025-190-x : £5.25 B81-26458

Grey, Zane. The trail driver / by Zane Grey. — Hornchurch : Ian Henry, 1981, c1936. — 157p ; 21cm
ISBN 0-86025-186-1 : £4.95 B81-16032

Grey, Zane. The westerner / Zane Grey ; edited by Loren Grey. — London : Prior, c1981, 1977. — 133p ; 25cm
Published in large print
ISBN 0-86043-580-6 : £4.95 B81-24573

Hammett, Dashiell. The thin man / Dashiell Hammett. — Harmondsworth : Penguin, 1935, c1932 (1979 [printing]). — 189p ; 18cm
ISBN 0-14-000014-3 (pbk) : £0.85 B81-03243

Hayes, Joseph. Island on fire : a true saga / Joseph Hayes. — London : Sphere, 1981, c1979. — 374p ; 18cm
Originally published: New York : Grosset & Dunlap, 1978 ; London : Deutsch, 1979
ISBN 0-7221-0479-0 (pbk) : £1.50 B81-11727

H.D.. Hedylus / H. D.. — London : Carcanet New Press, c1980. — 156p : 1port ; 23cm
ISBN 0-85635-358-2 : £4.95 B81-19293

Hellman, Lillian. Maybe : a story / Lillian Hellman. — London : Quartet, 1981, c1980. — 102p ; 20cm
Originally published: London : Macmillan, 1980
ISBN 0-7043-3357-0 (pbk) : £1.95 B81-24370

Hemingway, Ernest. The old man and the sea / Ernest Hemingway. — London : Granada, 1976 (1980 [printing]). — 109p ; 18cm. — (A Triad Panther book)
Originally published: London : Cape, 1952
ISBN 0-586-04468-x (pbk) : £0.95 B81-21289

Kanin, Garson. Smash. — London : Macmillan, 1981, c1980. — 522p ; 23cm
Originally published: New York : Viking, 1980
ISBN 0-333-31867-6 : £6.95 B81-20694

L'Amour, Louis. Bendigo Shafter / Louis L'Amour. — London : Prior, c1981, 1979. — 583p ; 25cm
Originally published: New York : Dutton, 1979. — Published in large print
ISBN 0-86043-586-5 : £7.95 B81-24578

L'Amour, Louis. The burning hills / by Louis L'Amour. — London : Hale, 1981, c1956. — 159p ; 20cm
Originally published.: New York : Jason, 1956 ; London : Hammond, 1965
ISBN 0-7091-4355-9 : £4.95 B81-15379

L'Amour, Louis. The Californios / Louis L'Amour. — London : Corgi, 1974 (1980 [printing]). — 188p ; 18cm
Originally published: New York : Saturday Review Press, 1974
ISBN 0-552-09696-2 (pbk) : £0.95 B81-01094

L'Amour, Louis. Callaghen / Louis L'Amour. — London : Hale, 1980, c1972. — 208p ; 20cm
Originally published: New York : Bantam ; London : Corgi, 1972
ISBN 0-7091-4309-5 : £4.95 B81-03333

L'Amour, Louis. Catlow. — Large print ed. — Anstey : Ulverscroft, Feb.1982. — [272]p. — (Ulverscroft large print series)
Originally published: New York : Bantam ; London : Transworld, 1963
ISBN 0-7089-0757-1 : £5.00 : CIP entry B81-36935

L'Amour, Louis. Comstock lode / Louis L'Amour. — Toronto ; London : Bantam, 1981. — 378p ; 23cm
ISBN 0-553-01307-6 (pbk) : £2.95 B81-32116

L'Amour, Louis. Fair blows the wind / Louis L'Amour. — London : Corgi, 1979, c1978. — 280p ; 18cm
Originally published: New York : Dutton, 1978
ISBN 0-552-11028-0 (pbk) : £0.95 B81-09313

L'Amour, Louis. Galloway; Sackett's land. — Large print ed. — Anstey : Ulverscroft, Nov.1981. — [528]p. — (Ulverscroft large print series)
Contents: Galloway. Originally published: New York : Saturday Review Press, 1974 ; London : Corgi, 1975 — Sackett's land. Originally published: New York : Bantam Books ; London : Corgi, 1970
ISBN 0-7089-0715-6 : £5.00 : CIP entry B81-30508

L'Amour, Louis. Last stand at Papago Wells ; and, The tall stranger / Louis L'Amour. — Large print ed. — Leicester : Ulverscroft, 1981, c1957. — 411p ; 23cm. — (Ulverscroft large print series)
Originally published: New York : Fawcett, 1957
ISBN 0-7089-0630-3 : £5.00 : CIP rev. B81-07442

L'Amour, Louis. The lonely men / Louis L'Amour. — London : Hale, 1981, c1969. — 171p : ill ; 20cm
Originally published: New York : Bantam, 1969 ; London : Corgi, 1971
ISBN 0-7091-4357-5 : £4.95 B81-40539

L'Amour, Louis. Matagorda / Louis L'Amour. — London : Corgi, 1968, c1967 (1980 [printing]). — 140p ; 18cm
Originally published: New York : Bantam, 1967
ISBN 0-552-07815-8 (pbk) : £0.95 B81-02465

L'Amour, Louis. North to the rails / Louis L'Amour. — London : Corgi, 1980, c1971. — 200p ; 18cm
Originally published: New York : Bantam ; London : Corgi, 1971
ISBN 0-552-08673-8 (pbk) : £0.95 B81-00254

L'Amour, Louis. Over on the dry side / Louis L'Amour. — London : Corgi, 1976, c1975 (1980 [printing]). — 184p ; 18cm
Originally published: New York : Saturday Review Press, 1975
ISBN 0-552-10231-8 (pbk) : £0.95 B81-02827

L'Amour, Louis. Radigan / by Louis L'Amour. — London : Hale, 1981, c1958. — 157p ; 20cm
Originally published: New York : Bantam, 1958 ; London : Hammond, 1964
ISBN 0-7091-4356-7 : £4.95 B81-24433

L'Amour, Louis. Ride the dark trail / Louis L'Amour. — London : Hale, 1980. — 190p ; 20cm
Originally published: New York : Bantam, 197-? ; London : Corgi, 1972
ISBN 0-7091-4308-7 : £4.75 B81-00255

L'Amour, Louis. War party / Louis L'Amour. — London : Corgi, 1975 (1980 [printing]). — 152p ; 18cm
Originally published: New York : Bantam, 1975
ISBN 0-552-09787-x (pbk) : £0.95 B81-02828

L'Amour, Louis. The warrior's path / Louis L'Amour. — [London] : Corgi, 1981, c1980. — 226p ; 18cm
Originally published: United States : s.n., 1980?
ISBN 0-552-11618-1 (pbk) : £0.95 B81-10965

L'Amour, Louis. The warrior's path / Louis L'Amour. — London : Prior, 1981, c1980. — 404p ; 25cm
Originally published: London : Corgi, 1980. — Published in large print
ISBN 0-86043-598-9 : £6.95 B81-32771

L'Amour, Louis. Yondering / Louis L'Amour. — [London] : Corgi, 1980. — 177p ; 18cm
ISBN 0-552-11561-4 (pbk) : £0.95 B81-03321

Le Sueur, Meridel. The girl. — London : Women's Press, Jan.1982. — [156]p
Originally published: Cambridge, Mass. : West End Press, 1978
ISBN 0-7043-3880-7 (pbk) : £2.50 : CIP entry B81-37539

Longstreet, Stephen. Storm watch / Stephen Longstreet. — London : W.H. Allen, 1980, c1979 (1981 [printing]). — 300p : ill ; 18cm. — (A Star book)
Originally published: New York : Plenum, 1979
ISBN 0-352-30894-x (pbk) : £1.60 B81-35157

Loring, Emilie. Forever and a day / Emilie Loring. — London : Prior, 1980, c1965. — 403p ; 25cm
Originally published: Boston : Little, Brown, 1965 ; London : Hale, 1968. — Published in large print
ISBN 0-86043-494-x : £5.95 B81-12196

Loring, Emilie. In times like these / Emilie Loring. — London : Prior, 1980, c1968. — 388p ; 24cm
Originally published: Boston, Mass. : Little, Brown, 1968. — Published in large print
ISBN 0-86043-493-1 : £5.95 B81-00256

Loring, Emilie. Spring always comes / Emilie Loring. — London : Prior, 1980, c1966. — 407p ; 25cm
Originally published: Boston, Brown, 1966 ; London : Hale, 1968. — Published in large print
ISBN 0-86043-563-6 : £5.95 B81-12197

McCarthy, Mary, *1912-*. The group / Mary McCarthy. — Harmondsworth : Penguin, 1966 (1981 [printing]). — 348p ; 19cm
Originally published: New York : Harcourt, Brace and World ; London : Weidenfeld & Nicolson, 1963
ISBN 0-14-002184-1 (pbk) : £1.95 B81-34754

McCloy, Helen. Burn this : a novel of suspense / Helen McCloy. — London : Gollancz, 1980. — 182p ; 21cm
ISBN 0-575-02915-3 : £4.95 B81-01652

813'.52[F] — Fiction in English. American writers, *1900-1945* — *Texts* *continuation*

McCullers, Carson. The mortgaged heart / Carson McCullers. — Harmondsworth : Penguin, 1975 (1981 [printing]). — 299p ; 18cm
Originally published: Boston : Houghton Mifflin ; London : Barrie and Jenkins, 1972
ISBN 0-14-003875-2 (pbk) : £1.95 B81-22347

McCullers, Carson. Reflections in a golden eye / Carson McCullers. — Harmondsworth : Penguin, 1967, c1942 (1981 [printing]). — 124p ; 18cm
Originally published: Boston : Houghton, 1941 ; London : Cresset, 1958
ISBN 0-14-002692-4 (pbk) : £1.25 B81-22341

Macdonald, Ross, *1915-*. The instant enemy / Ross Macdonald. — South Yarmouth, Mass. : Curley ; Long Preston : Magna [distributor], [1981?], c1968. — 455p ; 22cm
Originally published: London : Collins, 1968. — Published in large print
ISBN 0-89340-333-4 : Unpriced B81-37092

MacInnes, Helen. Friends and lovers / Helen MacInnes. — [London] : Fontana, 1972 (1981 [printing]). — 336p ; 18cm
Originally published: London : Harrap, 1948
ISBN 0-00-616251-7 (pbk) : £1.50 B81-15529

MacInnes, Helen. The hidden target / Helen MacInnes. — London : Collins, 1980. — 405p ; 22cm
ISBN 0-00-222282-5 : £6.95 B81-00257

MacInnes, Helen. Prelude to terror / Helen MacInnes. — Large print ed. — Leicester : Ulverscroft, 1980, c1978. — 606p ; 23cm. — (Ulverscroft large print series)
Originally published: London : Collins, 1978
ISBN 0-7089-0499-8 : £4.25 : CIP rev. B80-11620

MacInnes, Helen. Rest and Be Thankful / Helen MacInnes. — London : Fontana, 1973 (1981 [printing]). — 317p ; 18cm
Originally published: London : Harrap, 1949
ISBN 0-00-616379-3 (pbk) : £1.50 B81-28217

Mason, F. van Wyck. Armored giants : a novel of the Civil War / F. van Wyck Mason. — London : Hutchinson, 1981, c1980. — 339p ; 24cm
Originally published: Boston, Mass. : Little, Brown, 1980
ISBN 0-09-144170-6 : £6.95 B81-00258

Mulford, Clarence E.. Buck Peters, ranchman / Clarence E. Mulford. — London : Remploy, 1979. — 252p ; 20cm
Facsim. of ed. published London : Hodder & Stoughton, 1921
ISBN 0-7066-0813-5 : £3.90 B81-07656

Mulford, Clarence E.. The orphan / Clarence E. Mulford. — London : Remploy, 1979. — 284p ; 19cm
ISBN 0-7066-0814-3 : Unpriced B81-38051

Nye, Nelson. Breed of the chaparral / Nelson Nye. — Large print ed. — Leicester : Ulverscroft, 1981, c1946. — 261p ; 23cm. — (Ulverscroft large print)
Originally published: New York : McBride, 1946
ISBN 0-7089-0574-9 : £5.00 B81-11615

Owen, Philip. Mystery at a country inn / Philip Owen. — London : Hale, 1981, c1979. — 186p ; 20cm
Originally published: Stockbridge, Mass. : Berkshire Traveller Press, c1979
ISBN 0-7091-8697-5 : £5.75 B81-03020

Paul, Charlotte. The image. — London : Hodder & Stoughton, Nov.1981. — [304]p. — (Coronet books)
ISBN 0-340-27271-6 (pbk) : £1.75 : CIP entry B81-30142

Pentecost, Hugh. Beware young lovers / Hugh Pentecost. — London : Hale, 1981. — 176p ; 20cm
Originally published: New York : Dodd, Mead & Co., 1980
ISBN 0-7091-8842-0 : £5.75 B81-14091

Pentecost, Hugh. Death mask / Hugh Pentecost. — London : Hale, 1981, c1980. — 198p ; 20cm
ISBN 0-7091-9268-1 : £6.25 B81-35194

Pentecost, Hugh. The homicidal horse / Hugh Pentecost. — London : Hale, 1980, c1979. — 192p ; 20cm
Originally published: New York : Dodd, Mead, 1979
ISBN 0-7091-8605-3 : £5.75 B81-01095

Philips, Judson. Death is a dirty trick / Judson Philips. — London : Hale, 1981, c1980. — 187p ; 20cm
ISBN 0-7091-8669-x : £5.75 B81-11105

Philips, Judson. A murder arranged / Judson Philips. — Large print ed. — Leicester : Ulverscroft, 1981, c1978. — 282p ; 23cm. — (Ulverscroft large print)
Originally published: New York : Dodds, Mead, 1978 ; London : Gollancz, 1979
ISBN 0-7089-0591-9 : Unpriced B81-17674

Queen, Ellery. The French powder mystery / Ellery Queen. — London : Hamlyn Paperbacks, 1981, c1930. — 285p ; 18cm. — (A Hamlyn whodunnit)
ISBN 0-600-20073-6 (pbk) : £1.25 B81-28650

Queen, Ellery. The Roman hat mystery : a problem in deduction / Ellery Queen. — Large print ed. — Leicester : Ulverscroft, 1981. — 508p : 1plan ; 23cm. — (Ulverscroft large print series)
ISBN 0-7089-0521-8 : Unpriced B81-14222

Queen, Ellery. The Spanish cape mystery : a problem in deduction / Ellery Queen. — Feltham : Hamlyn, 1981, c1935. — 221p ; 18cm. — (A Hamlyn whodunnit)
ISBN 0-600-20077-9 (pbk) : £1.10 B81-11430

Sandoz, Mari. Slogum House / Mari Sandoz. — London : University of Nebraska Press, 1981. — 336p ; 21cm. — (A Bison book)
ISBN 0-8032-4126-7 (cased) : Unpriced
ISBN 0-8032-9123-x (pbk) : £2.00 B81-23203

Schulberg, Budd. Everything that moves / by Budd Schulberg. — London : Robson, 1981. — 251p ; 23cm
ISBN 0-86051-152-9 : £6.95 : CIP rev. B81-16872

Schulberg, Budd. What makes Sammy run? / Budd Schulberg ; with a new afterword. — Harmondsworth : Penguin, 1978, c1941 (1981 [printing]). — 252p ; 19cm
Originally published: New York : Random House ; London : Jarrolds, 1941
ISBN 0-14-004795-6 (pbk) : £1.50 B81-15366

Seifert, Elizabeth. Army doctor. — London : Severn House, May 1981. — [272]p
ISBN 0-7278-0705-6 : £6.50 : CIP entry B81-07622

Seifert, Elizabeth. A certain Doctor French / by Elizabeth Seifert. — London : Severn House, 1980, c1943. — 302p ; 21cm
ISBN 0-7278-0695-5 : £5.95 : CIP rev. B80-12113

Seifert, Elizabeth. The doctor's affair / Elizabeth Seifert. — South Yarmouth, Mass. : J. Curley ([Skipton] : Distributed by Magna Print), c1975. — 398p ; 23cm
Originally published: New York : Dodd, Mead, 1975 ; London : Collins, 1977. — Published in large print
ISBN 0-89340-295-8 : £5.75 B81-17991

Seifert, Elizabeth. The doctor's promise. — London : Collins, Nov.1981. — [236]p
ISBN 0-00-222135-7 : £6.95 : CIP entry B81-28772

Seifert, Elizabeth. The doctors were brothers / Elizabeth Seifert. — London : Collins, 1980. — 245p ; 22cm
ISBN 0-00-222178-0 : £6.25 B81-00259

Seifert, Elizabeth. Hillbilly doctor / by Elizabeth Seifert. — London : Severn House, 1981, c1940. — 260p ; 21cm
ISBN 0-7278-0697-1 : £5.95 B81-02535

Seifert, Elizabeth. Legacy for a doctor. — London : Severn House, Sept.1981. — [288]p
Originally published: London : Collins, 1964
ISBN 0-7278-0726-9 : £5.95 : CIP entry B81-23816

Seifert, Elizabeth. The problems of Dr. A / Elizabeth Seifert. — South Yarmouth, Mass. : Joun Curley, c1979 ; [Long Preston] : Magna [distributor]. — 384p ; 23cm
Originally published: New York : Dodd, Mead, 1979
ISBN 0-89340-296-6 : £5.75 B81-22119

Seifert, Elizabeth. The problems of Dr. A. / Elizabeth Seifert. — London : Collins, 1981, c1979. — 229p ; 22cm
Originally published: New York : Dodd, Mead, 1979
ISBN 0-00-222352-x (corrected) : £6.95 B81-17623

Seton, Anya. Avalon. — Large print ed. — Anstey : Ulverscroft, Feb.1982. — [592]p. — (Ulverscroft large print series : historical romance)
ISBN 0-7089-0750-4 : £5.00 : CIP entry B81-36941

Shaw, Irwin. Bread upon the waters / Irwin Shaw. — London : Weidenfeld and Nicolson, 1981. — 391p ; 23cm
ISBN 0-297-77945-1 : £6.95 B81-28688

Sinclair, Upton. The jungle / Upton Sinclair. — Harmondsworth : Penguin, 1936 (1979 printing). — 411p ; 18cm. — (Penguin modern classics)
ISBN 0-14-001999-5 (pbk) : £1.50 B81-23419

Smith, E. E. Doc. Lord Tedric / E.E. 'Doc' Smith. — London : W.H. Smith, 1978. — 159p ; 18cm. — (A Star book)
ISBN 0-352-39550-8 (pbk) : £0.75 B81-26451

Smith, E. E. Doc. Planet of treachery / E.E. Doc Smith with Stephen Goldin. — London : Granada, 1981. — 221p ; 18cm. — (The Family d'Alembert series ; v.7) (A Panther book) (Granada science fiction)
ISBN 0-586-04340-3 (pbk) : £1.25 B81-07195

Stegner, Wallace. [The preacher and the slave]. Joe Hill : a biographical novel / Wallace Stegner. — Lincoln [Neb.] ; London : University of Nebraska Press, 1980 , c1950. — 381p ; 21cm
Originally published: Boston, Mass. : Houghton Mifflin, 1950 ; London : Hammond, 1951
ISBN 0-8032-4116-x (cased) : £11.70
ISBN 0-8032-9115-9 (pbk) : £3.60 B81-06425

Stegner, Wallace. The women on the wall / by Wallace Stegner. — Lincoln, Neb. ; London : University of Nebraska Press, 1981. — 277p ; 21cm. — (A Bison book)
Originally published: Boston, Mass. : Houghton Mifflin, 1950
ISBN 0-8032-4111-9 (cased) : Unpriced
ISBN 0-8032-9110-8 (pbk) : £3.30 B81-19979

Stein, Aaron Marc. The cheating butcher / Aaron Marc Stein. — London : Hale, 1981. — 184p ; 20cm
Originally published: New York : Doubleday, 1980
ISBN 0-7091-8731-9 : £5.75 B81-11167

813'.52[F] — Fiction in English. American writers, *1900-1945 — Texts* *continuation*

Stein, Aaron Marc. A nose for it / Aaron Marc Stein. — London : Hale, 1981, c1980. — 180p ; 20cm
Originally published: Garden City, N.Y. : Doubleday, 1980
ISBN 0-7091-9126-x : £5.95 B81-24850

Stein, Aaron Marc. One dip dead / Aaron Marc Stein. — London : Hale, 1980, c1979. — 183p ; 20cm
Originally published: Garden City, N.Y. : Doubleday, 1979
ISBN 0-7091-8510-3 : £5.75 B81-00260

Stout, Rex. A right to die / Rex Stout. — [London] : Fontana, 1965, c1964 (1980 [printing]). — 191p ; 18cm
Originally published: New York : Viking, 1964 ; London : Collins, 1965
ISBN 0-00-616170-7 (pbk) : £1.00 B81-07667

Swarthout, Glendon. The eagle and the iron cross / Glendon Swarthout. — Large print ed. — Leicester : Ulverscroft, 1981, c1966. — 412p ; 23cm. — (Ulverscroft large print)
Originally published: New York : New American Library, 1966 ; London : Heinemann, 1967
ISBN 0-7089-0570-6 : £5.00 B81-11609

Swarthout, Glendon. Skeletons / Glendon Swarthout. — London : Pan in association with Secker and Warburg, 1980, c1979. — 248p ; 18cm
Originally published: London : Secker & Warburg, 1979
ISBN 0-330-26235-1 (pbk) : £1.25 B81-03433

Trilling, Lionel. The middle of the journey / Lionel Trilling ; with an introduction by the author. — Uniform ed.. — Oxford : Oxford University Press, 1981, c1975. — xxv,342p ; 21cm
Originally published: New York : Viking Press, 1947 ; London : Secker and Warburg, 1948
ISBN 0-19-212226-6 : £8.95 B81-20929

Turnbull, Agnes Sligh. The two bishops / Agnes Sligh Turnbull. — London : Collins, 1980. — 279p ; 22cm
ISBN 0-00-221979-4 : £5.95 B81-01096

Turnbull, Agnes Sligh. The two bishops / Agnes Sligh Turnbull. — London : Prior, 1981, c1980. — 524p ; 25cm
Originally published: London : Collins, 1980. — Published in large print
ISBN 0-86043-585-7 : £6.95 B81-24366

White, E. B.. Charlotte's web / E.B. White ; illustrated by Garth Williams. — Basingstoke : Macmillan Education, 1981, c1952. — 174p : ill ; 21cm. — (M books)
Originally published: London : Hamilton, 1952. — For adolescents
ISBN 0-333-29488-2 : £1.50 B81-18693

Whitney, Phyllis A.. Domino / Phyllis A. Whitney. — London : Prior, 1980, c1979. — 522p ; cm
Originally published: Garden City, N.Y. : Doubleday, 1979 ; London : Heinemann, 1980. — Published in large print
ISBN 0-86043-489-3 : £6.95 B81-01097

Whitney, Phyllis A.. Domino. — London : Hodder and Stoughton, Jan.1982. — [320]p. — (Coronet books)
Originally published: Garden City, N.Y. : Doubleday, 1979 ; London : Hutchinson, 1980
ISBN 0-340-27537-5 (pbk) : £1.50 : CIP entry B81-34134

Whitney, Phyllis A.. The glass flame. — London : Hodder and Stoughton, Jan.1982. — [320]p. — (Coronet books)
Originally published: Garden City, N.Y. : Doubleday ; London : Heinemann, 1979
ISBN 0-340-27536-7 (pbk) : £1.50 : CIP entry B81-34130

Whitney, Phyllis A.. Listen for the whisper / Phyllis A. Whitney. — London : Pan in association with Heinemann, 1981, c1972. — 256p ; 18cm
Originally published: Garden City : Doubleday ; London : Heinemann, 1972
ISBN 0-330-26149-5 (pbk) : £1.25 B81-36700

Whitney, Phyllis A.. Poinciana / Phyllis A. Whitney. — London : Heinemann, 1980. — 345p ; 23cm
ISBN 0-434-86502-8 : £6.95 B81-13125

Whitney, Phyllis A.. Poinciana / Phyllis A. Whitney. — London : Prior, 1981, c1980. — 617p ; 25cm
Originally published: London : Heinemann, 1980. — Published in large print
ISBN 0-86043-597-0 : £7.50 B81-32769

Whitney, Phyllis A.. The red carnelian / Phyllis A. Whitney. — Loughton : Piatkus, 1981, c1971. — 254p ; 21cm
ISBN 0-86188-029-3 : £6.50 : CIP rev. B81-04282

Whitney, Phyllis A.. Seven tears for Apollo / Phyllis A. Whitney. — Loughton : Piatkus, 1981, c1963. — 224p ; 21cm
Originally published: New York : Appleton-Century-Crofts, 1963
ISBN 0-86188-033-1 : £6.50 : CIP rev. B81-15851

Whitney, Phyllis A.. Skye Cameron. — Loughton : Piatkus, Feb.1982. — [224]p
Originally published: London : Hurst & Blackett, 1959
ISBN 0-86188-151-6 : £5.95 : CIP entry B81-36019

Whitney, Phyllis A.. The trembling hills / Phyllis A. Whitney. — Loughton ([17 Brook Rd.,] Loughton, Essex) : Piatkus, 1981, c1976. — 312p ; 21cm
Originally published: New York : Appleton Century Crofts, 1956 ; London : Coronet, 1974
ISBN 0-86188-032-3 : £6.50 B81-08624

Williamson, Jack. Brother to demons, brother to gods / Jack Williamson. — London : Sphere, 1981, c1979. — 184p ; 18cm. — (Sphere science fiction)
Originally published: Indianapolis : Bobbs-Merrill, 1979
ISBN 0-7221-9179-0 (pbk) : £1.25 B81-11708

813'.52[F] — Short stories in English. American writers, *1900-1945 — Texts*

Carr, John Dickson. The door to doom : and other detections / John Dickson Carr ; edited & with an introduction by Douglas G. Greene. — London : Hamilton, 1981, c1980. — 352p ; 23cm
Originally published: New York : Harper & Row, 1980. — List of works: p327-352
ISBN 0-241-10535-8 : £8.95 : CIP rev. B81-02092

Eberhart, Mignon G.. Deadly is the diamond / by Mignon G. Eberhart. — Hornchurch : Henry, 1981, c1958. — 134p ; 21cm
Originally published: New York : Random House, 1958
ISBN 0-86025-188-8 : £4.95 B81-17389

Fitzgerald, F. Scott. The price was high / F. Scott Fitzgerald ; edited by Matthew J. Bruccoli. — London : Pan, 1981, c1979. — (Picador) (The Last uncollected stories of F. Scott Fitzgerald)
Originally published: New York : Harcourt Brace Jovanovich, 1979 ; London : Quartet, 1979
Vol.1. — 427p ; 20cm
ISBN 0-330-26286-6 (pbk) : £2.95 B81-20200

London, Jack. The call of the wild ; White fang, : and other stories / Jack London ; edited by Andrew Sinclair ; introduction by James Dickey. — Harmondsworth : Penguin, 1981. — 410p : 1port ; 18cm. — (The Penguin American library)
Port on inside cover. — Bibliography: p409-410
ISBN 0-14-039001-4 (pbk) : £1.25 B81-38354

Queen, Ellery. A fine and private place / Ellery Queen. — Feltham : Hamlyn, 1981, c1971. — 159p ; 18cm. — (A Hamlyn whodunnit)
Originally published: Cleveland : Ward Publishing ; London : Gollancz, 1971
ISBN 0-600-20078-7 (pbk) : £1.00 B81-41000

Trilling, Lionel. Of this time, of that place and other stories / Lionel Trilling ; selected by Diana Trilling. — Uniform ed.. — Oxford : Oxford University Press, 1981, c1979. — 116p ; 21cm
Originally published: New York : Harcourt Brace Jovanovich, 1979
ISBN 0-19-212217-7 : £8.95 : CIP rev. B81-02355

813'.52[J] — Children's short stories in English. American writers, *1900-1945 - Texts*

Brown, Margaret Wise. Once upon a time in a pigpen. — London : Hutchinson Junior, Sept.1981. — [64]p
ISBN 0-09-146150-2 : £4.95 : CIP entry B81-20556

813'.52[J] — Children's short stories in English. American writers, *1900-1945 — Texts*

Dixon, Franklin W.. The Hardy Boys survival handbook / Franklin W. Dixon in collaboration with survival instructor Sheila Link ; illustrated by Leslie Morrill. — London : Collins, 1981, c1980. — 143p : ill ; 21cm
Originally published: New York : Wanderer Books, 1980
ISBN 0-00-160558-5 : Unpriced
ISBN 0-00-691909-x (Armada) B81-28979

813'.52[J] — Children's stories in English. American writers, *1900-1945 — Texts*

Arthur, Robert. Alfred Hitchcock and the three Investigators in The mystery of the Moaning Cave / text by Robert Arthur. — [London] : Armada, 1981, c1969. — 127p ; 18cm
Originally published: New York : Random House, 1967 ; London : Collins, 1969
ISBN 0-00-691920-0 (pbk) : £0.85 B81-36832

Arthur, Robert, *1899-*. Alfred Hitchcock and the Three Investigators in the secret of Skelton Island / text by Robert Arthur. — [London] : Armada, 1970, c1968 (1981 [printing]). — 158p : ill ; 19cm
Originally published: New York : Random House, 1966 ; London : Collins, 1968
ISBN 0-00-691918-9 (pbk) : £0.80 B81-24836

Bright, Robert. Georgie and the buried treasure / by Robert Bright. — Tadworth : World's Work Children's, 1981, c1979. — [36]p : ill ; 21x27cm
Originally published: Garden City, N.Y. : Doubleday, 1979
ISBN 0-437-28815-3 : £3.50 B81-11679

Disney, Walt. The adventures of Mickey Mouse / Walt Disney. — [London] : Piccolo, 1981, c1936. — 95p : col.ill ; 20cm
ISBN 0-330-26386-2 : £1.25 B81-20201

Dixon, Franklin W.. The apeman's secret / Franklin W. Dixon ; illustrated by Leslie Morrill. — London : Angus & Robertson, 1980. — 184p : ill ; 20cm. — (The Hardy boys ; 60)
ISBN 0-207-95958-7 : Unpriced B81-08501

Dixon, Franklin W.. The mystery of the Aztec warrior / Franklin W. Dixon. — [London] : Armada, 1974, c1973 (1979 [printing]). — 159p : ill ; 18cm. — (The Hardy Boys mystery stories ; 1)
Originally published: New York : Grosset and Dunlap, 1964 ; London : Collins, 1971
ISBN 0-00-690812-8 (pbk) : £0.60 B81-29858

Dixon, Franklin W.. The mystery of the Samurai sword / Franklin W. Dixon ; illustrated by Leslie Morrill. — [London] : Armada, 1981, c1979. — 179p : ill ; 18cm. — (The Hardy boys mystery stories ; 58)
Originally published: New York : Wanderer Books, 1979 ; London : Angus & Robertson, 1980
ISBN 0-00-691819-0 (pbk) : £0.85 B81-28760

813'.52[J] — Children's stories in English. American writers, *1900-1945 — Texts*
continuation

Dixon, Franklin W.. Night of the werewolf / Franklin W. Dixon ; illustrated by Leslie Morrill. — [London] : Armada, 1981, c1979. — 181p : ill ; 18cm. — (The Hardy boys mystery stories)
Originally published: New York : Wanderer, 1979 ; London : Angus & Robertson, 1980
ISBN 0-00-691818-2 (pbk) : £0.80 B81-15540

Dixon, Franklin W.. The Pentagon spy / Franklin W. Dixon ; illustrated by Leslie Morrill. — London : Angus & Robertson, 1980. — 182p : ill ; 20cm. — (The Hardy boys ; 59)
ISBN 0-207-95957-9 : Unpriced B81-08500

Dixon, Franklin W.. The Pentagon spy / Franklin W. Dixon ; illustrated by Leslie Morrill. — London : Armada, 1981, c1980. — 182p : ill ; 19cm. — (The Hardy boys mystery stories ; 59)
Originally published: New York : Wanderer Books ; London : Angus and Robertson, 1980
ISBN 0-00-691820-4 (pbk) : £0.85 B81-36779

Dixon, Franklin W.. The secret agent on flight 101 / Franklin W. Dixon. — [London] : Armada, 1981, c1967. — 158p : ill ; 19cm. — (The Hardy boys)
Originally published: New York : Grosset & Dunlap, 1967 ; London : Macdonald, 1969
ISBN 0-00-691867-0 (pbk) : £0.85 B81-32634

Enright, Elizabeth. The four-storey mistake / Elizabeth Enright. — Harmondsworth : Puffin, 1967 (1981 [printing]). — 145p ; 19cm
Originally published: London : Heinemann, 1955
ISBN 0-14-030316-2 (pbk) : £0.90 B81-40503

Enright, Elizabeth. The Saturdays / Elizabeth Enright. — Harmondsworth : Puffin in association with Heinemann, 1964, c1955 (1981 [printing]). — 149p ; 19cm
ISBN 0-14-030213-1 (pbk) : £0.90 B81-40416

Gates, Doris. [A morgan for Melinda]. A horse for Melinda / by Doris Gates. — London : Transworld, [1981, c1980]. — 156p ; 18cm. — (A Carousel book)
Originally published: New York : Viking Press, 1980
ISBN 0-552-52138-8 (pbk) : £0.95 B81-32102

Hemingway, Ernest. The faithful bull / Ernest Hemingway ; pictures by Michael Foreman. — London : Hamilton, 1980, c1979. — [30]p : col.ill ; 29cm
ISBN 0-241-10506-4 : £3.95 B81-05619

Keene, Carolyn. The flying saucer mystery / Carolyn Keene ; illustrated by Ruth Sanderson. — London : Armada, 1981, c1980. — 167p : ill ; 18cm. — (The Nancy Drew mystery stories)
Originally published: New York : Wanderer Books ; London : Angus & Robertson, 1980
ISBN 0-00-691839-5 (pbk) : £0.80 B81-18527

Keene, Carolyn. Mystery of the stone tiger / Carolyn Keene. — [London] : Sparrow, 1981, c1972. — 170p ; 18cm. — (Dana girls mystery ; no.1)
Originally published: New York : Grosset and Dunlap, 1963
ISBN 0-09-926430-7 (pbk) : £0.95 B81-28583

Keene, Carolyn. Mystery of the wax queen / Carolyn Keene. — London : Sparrow, 1981, c1972. — 170p ; 18cm. — (Dana girls mystery ; no.4)
Originally published: New York : Grosset & Dunlap, 1966
ISBN 0-09-926550-8 (pbk) : £0.95 B81-39156

Keene, Carolyn. The riddle of the frozen fountain / Carolyn Keene. — [London] : Sparrow, 1981, c1972. — 168p ; 18cm. — (Dana girls mystery ; no.2)
Originally published: New York : Grosset and Dunlap, 1964
ISBN 0-09-926290-8 (pbk) : £0.95 B81-28584

Keene, Carolyn. The ringmaster's secret / Carolyn Keene. — [London] : Armada, 1981, c1973. — 158p ; 18cm. — (The Nancy Drew mystery stories ; 25)
Originally published: New York : Grosset and Dunlap, 1953 ; London : Low, Marston, 1965
ISBN 0-00-691910-3 (pbk) : £0.85 B81-28759

Keene, Carolyn. The secret in the old attic / Carolyn Keene. — London : Armada, 1980, c1944. — 156p : 2ill ; 18cm. — (The Nancy Drew mystery stories ; no.24)
ISBN 0-00-691747-x (pbk) : £0.75 B81-03188

Keene, Carolyn. The secret of the silver dolphin / Carolyn Keene. — London : Sparrow, 1981, c1972. — 170p ; 18cm. — (Dana girls mystery ; no.3)
Originally published: New York : Grosset & Dunlap, 1965
ISBN 0-09-926560-5 (pbk) : £0.95 B81-39157

Keene, Carolyn. The triple hoax / Carolyn Keene ; illustrated by Ruth Sanderson. — London : Armada, 1981, c1979. — 184p : ill ; 18cm. — (The Nancy Drew mystery stories ; no.51)
Originally published: New York : Wanderer Books, 1979 ; London : Angus & Robertson, 1980
ISBN 0-00-691838-7 (pbk) : £0.80 B81-15595

London, Jack. White Fang / Jack London. — London : Octopus, 1981. — 212p : ill ; 22cm
ISBN 0-7064-1560-4 : £1.95 B81-17401

O'Hara, Mary. The catch colt / Mary O'Hara. — London : Magnet, 1980, c1978. — 125p ; 18cm
Originally published: London : Methuen, 1979
ISBN 0-416-88230-7 (pbk) : £0.85 B81-07256

Price, Willard. Arctic adventure / by Willard Price ; illustrated by Pat Marriott. — London : Cape, 1980. — 222p : ill ; 21cm
ISBN 0-224-01819-1 : £4.95 : CIP rev. B80-13604

Walt Disney Productions' the fox and the hound. — Maidenhead : Purnell, 1981, c1980. — [20]p : col.ill ; 24cm
ISBN 0-361-05066-6 : £1.99 B81-32932

Worth, Valerie. Imp and Biscuit. — London : Chatto & Windus, Oct.1981. — [64]p
ISBN 0-7011-2606-x : £3.95 : CIP entry B81-28062

813'.52[J] — Children's stories in English. Canadian writers, *1900-1945 — Texts*

Montgomery, L. M.. The blue castle / L.M. Montgomery. — London : Angus & Robertson, 1980, c1972. — 321p ; 20cm
ISBN 0-207-14340-4 : £2.95 B81-11897

Montgomery, L. M.. Jane of Lantern Hill / L.M. Montgomery. — London : Angus & Robertson, 1980, c1977. — 268p ; 19cm
ISBN 0-207-14348-x : £2.95 B81-11896

813'.52'09 — Fiction in English. American writers, *1900-1979 — Critical studies*

Wagner, Linda Welshimer. American modern : essays in fiction and poetry / Linda W. Wagner. — Port Washington, N.Y. ; London : National University Publications : Kennikat, 1980. — 263p ; 23cm. — (Literary criticism series)
ISBN 0-8046-9257-2 : £14.00
Primary classification 811'.52'09 B81-05511

813'.52'09 — Fiction in English. American writers, *1900- — Critical studies*

Kazin, Alfred. Bright book of life : American novelists and story tellers from Hemingway to Mailer / by Alfred Kazin. — Notre Dame, Ind. ; London : University of Notre Dame Press, 1980, c1973. — 334p ; 21cm
Originally published: Boston, Mass. : Little, Brown, 1973 ; London : Secker and Warburg, 1974. — Includes index
ISBN 0-268-00664-4 (pbk) : £4.15 B81-25563

813'.52'09355 — Fiction in English. American writers, *1900-1980.* Special subjects: Sports & games *— Critical studies*

Berman, Neil David. Playful fictions and fictional players : game, sport, and survival in contemporary American fiction / Neil David Berman. — Port Washington ; London : National University Publications : Kennikat, 1981. — 112p ; 23cm. — (Literary criticism series)
Bibliography: p108-110. - Includes index
ISBN 0-8046-9265-3 : £11.45 B81-12970

813'.52'099287 — Fiction in English. American negro women writers, *1900-1976 — Critical studies*

Christian, Barbara. Black women novelists : the development of a tradition, 1892-1976 / Barbara Christian. — Westport, Conn. ; London : Greenwood Press, 1980. — xiv,275p ; 25cm. — (Contributions in Afro-American and African studies ; no.52)
Bibliography: p265-268. - Includes index
ISBN 0-313-20750-x : £15.95 B81-23644

813'.52'09975 — Fiction in English. American writers. Southern states writers, *1900-1945 — Critical studies*

Young, Thomas Daniel. The past in the present : a thematic study of modern Southern fiction / Thomas Daniel Young. — Baton Rouge ; London : Louisiana State University Press, 1981. — xvii,189p ; 23cm. — (Southern literary studies)
ISBN 0-8071-0768-9 : £8.95 B81-25560

813.54 — AMERICAN FICTION, 1945-

813'.54 — Fiction in English. American writers. Burroughs, William S.. Naked lunch. Censorship, *to 1966*

Goodman, Michael Barry. Contemporary literary censorship : the case history of Burroughs' Naked lunch / by Michael Barry Goodman. — Metuchen ; London : Scarecrow, 1981. — x,330p ; 23cm
Bibliography: p300-317. — Includes index
ISBN 0-8108-1398-x : £14.00 B81-25964

813'.54 — Fiction in English. American writers. Ellison, Ralph *— Critical studies*

O'Meally, Robert G.. The craft of Ralph Ellison / Robert G. O'Meally. — Cambridge, Mass. ; London : Harvard University Press, 1980. — ix,212p ; 25cm
Bibliography: p185-193. — Includes index
ISBN 0-674-17548-4 : £8.40 B81-16561

813'.54 — Fiction in English. American writers. Lee, Harper. To kill a mockingbird *— Study outlines*

Metcalf, Rosamund. To kill a mocking bird : notes / by Rosamund Metcalf. — Harlow : Longman, 1981. — 80p ; 21cm. — (York notes ; 125)
Bibliography: p76
ISBN 0-582-78201-5 (pbk) : £0.90 B81-33693

813'.54 — Fiction in English. American writers. Lee, Harper. To kill a mockingbird *— Study outlines — For schools*

Craigs, Edward. To kill a mockingbird : [guidelines] / by Edward Craigs. — Teacher's ed. — London : Glasgow Publications, c1980. — 16,[4]p : ill(some col.),1col.map ; 30cm. — (Guidelines)
Cover title
ISBN 0-86158-520-8 (pbk) : Unpriced B81-25068

813'.54 — Fiction in English. American writers. Mailer, Norman *— Critical studies*

Begiebing, Robert J.. Acts of regeneration : allegory and archetype in the works of Norman Mailer / Robert J. Begiebing. — Columbia, Mo. ; London : University of Missouri Press, 1980. — 209p ; 24cm
Bibliography: p204-206. — Includes index
ISBN 0-8262-0310-8 : £13.00 B81-29588

813'.54 — Fiction in English. American writers. Nabokov, Vladimir *— Critical studies*

Pifer, Ellen. Nabokov and the novel / Ellen Pifer. — Cambridge, Mass. ; London : Harvard University Press, 1980. — 197p ; 22cm
Includes index
ISBN 0-674-59840-7 : £7.50 B81-16567

813′.54 — Fiction in English. American writers. Oates, Joyce Carol — *Critical studies*

Waller, G. F.. Dreaming America : obsession and transcendence in the fiction of Joyce Carol Oates / G.F. Waller. — Baton Rouge ; London : Louisiana State University Press, c1979. — xii,224p ; 24cm
Bibliography: p221-224
ISBN 0-8071-0478-7 : £7.80 B81-12115

813′.54 — Fiction in English. American writers. O′Connor, Flannery — *Critical studies*

Shloss, Carol. Flannery O′Connor′s dark comedies : the limits of inference / Carol Shloss. — Baton Rouge ; London : Louisiana State University Press, c1980. — 159p ; 23cm. — (Southern literary studies)
Bibliography: p145-152. - Includes index
ISBN 0-8071-0674-7 : £8.95 B81-07720

813′.54 — Fiction in English. American writers. Vonnegut, Kurt — *Biographies*

Vonnegut, Kurt. Palm Sunday : an autobiographical collage / Kurt Vonnegut. — London : Cape, 1981. — xviii,330p ; 22cm
ISBN 0-224-01957-0 : £6.95 : CIP rev. B81-12388

813′.54[F] — Fiction in English. American writers, *1945-* — *Texts*

Adams, Tracy. The moth and the flame. — London : Hodder & Stoughton, Jan.1982. — [192]p. — (Silhouette romance)
ISBN 0-340-27666-5 (pbk) : £0.75 : CIP entry B81-33929

Alexander, Karl. A private investigation / Karl Alexander. — London : Severn House, 1981, c1980. — 326p ; 21cm
Originally published: New York : Delacorte Press, c1980
ISBN 0-7278-0708-0 : £6.95 : CIP rev. B81-13515

Alibrandi, Tom. Custody / Tom Alibrandi. — London : W.H. Allen, 1980, c1979 (1981 [printing]). — 371p ; 18cm. — (A Star book)
Originally published: Los Angeles : Pinnacle, 1979
ISBN 0-352-30784-6 (pbk) : £1.75 B81-26523

Alimo, Guy. The hunting of Salyut 7 / Guy Alimo. — [London] : Corgi, 1981, c1979. — 460p ; 18cm
ISBN 0-552-11620-3 (pbk) : £1.75 B81-15342

Allen, Charlotte Vale. The marmalade man. — London : Hutchinson, Aug.1981. — [400]p
ISBN 0-09-146140-5 : £6.95 : CIP entry B81-16848

Allen, Clay. Cougar Canyon / by Clay Allen. — London : Hale, 1980. — 160p ; 20cm
ISBN 0-7091-8257-0 : £4.50 B81-07168

Allen, Clay. Oxyoke / by Clay Allen. — London : Hale, 1981. — 159p 20cm
ISBN 0-7091-8821-8 : £4.95 B81-11906

Alther, Lisa. Original sins / Lisa Alther. — London : Women′s Press, 1981. — 592p ; 22cm
ISBN 0-7043-2839-9 : £6.95 : CIP rev. B81-04377

Amiel, Joseph. Hawks / Joseph Amiel. — London : Pan in association with Macmillan, 1980, c1979 (1981 printing). — 383p ; 18cm
Originally published: New York : Putnam, 1979 ; London : Macmillan, 1980
ISBN 0-330-26197-5 (pbk) : £1.50 B81-20211

Anderson, Poul. The avatar / Poul Anderson. — London : Sphere, 1981, c1978. — 404p ; 18cm. — (Sphere science fiction)
Originally published: New York : Berkley, 1978 ; London : Sidgwick and Jackson, 1980
ISBN 0-7221-1131-2 (pbk) : £1.95 B81-24541

Anderson, Poul. The high crusade / Poul Anderson. — London : Corgi, 1981. — 143p ; 18cm
Originally published: Garden City, N.Y. : Doubleday, 1960
ISBN 0-552-11706-4 (pbk) : £0.95 B81-27249

Anderson, Poul. The horn of time / Poul Anderson. — London : Corgi, 1981, c1968. — 172p ; 18cm
Originally published: New York : New American Library, 1968
ISBN 0-552-11771-4 (pbk) : £1.25 B81-35500

Anderson, Poul. The Merman′s children : fantasy / by Poul Anderson. — London : Sidgwick & Jackson, 1981, c1979. — 319p ; 21cm
Originally published: New York : Berkley Publishing, 1979
ISBN 0-283-98747-2 : £7.95 B81-21271

Anderson, Poul. There will be time / Poul Anderson. — London : Hale, 1980, c1973. — 189p ; 21cm. — (Hale SF)
Originally published: Garden City, N.Y. ; Doubleday, 1973 ; London : Sphere, 1979
ISBN 0-7091-7969-3 : £5.75 B81-00261

Andrews, Virginia. If there be thorns / Virginia Andrews. — [London] : Fontana, 1981. — 350p ; 18cm
Originally published: New York : Pocket Books, 1981
ISBN 0-00-616370-x (pbk) : £1.65 B81-24838

Andrews, Virginia. Petals on the wind / Virginia Andrews. — [London] : Fontana, 1980. — 409p ; 18cm
Originally published: New York : Simon and Schuster, 1980
ISBN 0-00-616182-0 (pbk) : £1.50 B81-06967

Andrews, Virginia. Petals on the wind / Virginia Andrews. — Loughton ([17 Brookside Rd, Loughton IG10 1BW]) : Piatkus, 1980. — 409 ; 21cm
ISBN 0-86188-063-3 : £6.50 : CIP rev. B80-22611

Anson, Jay. 666. — London : Granada, Jan.1982. — [288]p
ISBN 0-246-11839-3 : £7.95 : CIP entry B81-38304

Arensberg, Ann. Sister wolf : a novel / Ann Arensberg. — London : Sidgwick & Jackson, 1981, c1980. — 209p ; 22cm
Originally published: New York : Knopf, 1980
ISBN 0-283-98731-6 : £6.95 B81-11009

Argo, Ellen. The Crystal Star / Ellen Argo. — London : Futura, 1980, c1979. — 440p ; 18cm. — (A Troubadour spectacular)
Originally published: New York : Putnam, 1979
ISBN 0-7088-1918-4 (pbk) : £1.60 B81-00262

Arlen, Leslie. Love and honour / Leslie Arlen. — London : Macdonald Futura, 1980. — 374p ; 18cm. — (The Borodins ; bk.1)
Originally published: New York : Jove, 1980
ISBN 0-7088-1935-4 (pbk) : £1.50 B81-01103

Armour, John, *1916-*. The longlance plain / by John Armour. — London : Hale, 1981. — 157p ; 20cm
ISBN 0-7091-8855-2 : £4.95 B81-14085

Arnett, Caroline. Clarissa / Caroline Arnett. — South Yarmouth, Ma. : Curley ; Skipton : Magna [distributor], 1979, c1976. — 408p ; 23cm. — (A Regency romance)
Published in large print
ISBN 0-89340-195-1 : £5.25 B81-38085

Arnold, Margot. [Marie]. Marie, voodoo queen / Margot Arnold. — London : Granada, 1981, c1979. — 461p ; 18cm. — (A Mayflower book)
Originally published: New York : Pocket Books, 1979
ISBN 0-583-13399-1 (pbk) : £1.95 B81-19942

Asch, Frank. The last puppy / Frank Asch. — London : Evans, 1981, c1980. — [30]p : col.ill ; 20cm
Originally published: Englewood Cliffs : Prentice-Hall, 1980
ISBN 0-237-45558-7 : £2.75 B81-02047

Auchincloss, Louis. The cat and the king / Louis Auchincloss. — London : Weidenfeld and Nicolson, 1981. — 183p : geneal.tables ; 23cm
ISBN 0-297-77989-3 : £6.50 B81-34835

Auel, Jean M.. The clan of the cave bear / Jean M. Auel. — London : Hodder and Stoughton, 1980. — 491p : maps ; 23cm. — (Earth′s children)
ISBN 0-340-25967-1 (cased) : £7.95 : CIP rev.
ISBN 0-340-25989-2 (pbk) : £4.95 B80-12529

Avel, Jean M.. The clan of the Cave Bear. — London : Hodder & Stoughton, May 1981. — [592]p
Originally published: 1980
ISBN 0-340-26883-2 (pbk) : £1.75 : CIP entry B81-03821

Babson, Marian. Bejewelled death / Marian Babson. — London : Collins, 1981. — 173p ; 20cm. — (The Crime club)
ISBN 0-00-231028-7 : £6.25 : CIP rev. B81-28838

Babson, Marian. Queue here for murder / Marian Babson. — London : Collins, 1980. — 171p ; 21cm. — (The Crime Club)
ISBN 0-00-231677-3 : £5.25 B81-01104

Babson, Marian. Queue here for murder. — Large print ed. — Bath : Chivers Press, Feb.1982. — [272]p. — (A Lythway book)
Originally published: London : Collins, 1980
ISBN 0-85119-781-7 : £6.90 : CIP entry B81-35865

Backer, Dorothy. The Parma legacy / Dorothy Backer. — London : Magnum Books, 1980, c1978. — 472p ; 18cm
Originally published: New York : Norton 1978
ISBN 0-417-04010-5 (pbk) : £1.75 B81-27695

Baehr, Consuelo. Best friends / Consuelo Baehr. — London : Gollancz, 1981. — 339p ; 23cm
ISBN 0-575-02904-8 : £5.95 B81-07036

Bailey, F. Lee. Secrets / F. Lee Bailey. — London : Hamlyn Paperbacks, 1981, c1978. — 253p ; 18cm
Originally published: New York : Stein & Day, 1978 ; London : Melbourne House, 1979
ISBN 0-600-20187-2 (pbk) : £1.25 B81-10044

Baker, A. A.. A noose for the marshal / A.A. Baker. — London : Hale, 1981, 1977. — 160p ; 20cm
Originally published: United States? : s.n., 1977
ISBN 0-7091-8909-5 : £4.95 B81-30070

Baker, A. A. (Albert Allen). Ride for hell / A.A. Baker. — London : Hale, 1981, c1976. — 160p ; 20cm
Originally published: Canoga Park, Calif. : Major Books, 1976
ISBN 0-7091-8904-4 : £4.95 B81-15292

Baldwin, James, *1924-*. Another country / James Baldwin. — London : Corgi, 1965, c1963 (1980 [printing]). — 338p ; 18cm
Originally published: London : Joseph, 1963
ISBN 0-552-11564-9 (pbk) : £1.95 B81-02056

Baldwin, James, *1924-*. Go tell it on the mountain / James Baldwin. — London : Corgi, 1963, c1954 (1980 [printing]). — 253p ; 18cm
Originally published: New York : Knopf, 1953: London : Joseph, 1954
ISBN 0-552-11565-7 (pbk) : £1.50 B81-05739

Baldwin, James, *1924-*. Just above my head / James Baldwin. — London : Corgi, 1980, c1979. — 557p ; 18cm
Originally published: New York : Dial Press ; London : Joseph, 1979
ISBN 0-552-11552-5 (pbk) : £1.95 B81-02912

813'.54[F] — Fiction in English. American writers, 1945- — Texts *continuation*

Baldwin, James, *1924-*. Tell me how long the train's been gone / James Baldwin. — London : Corgi, 1970, c1968 (1980 [printing]). — 410p ; 18cm
Originally published: London : Joseph, 1968
ISBN 0-552-11566-5 (pbk) : £1.95 B81-07751

Ball, John, *1911-*. The killing in the market / John Ball with Bevan Smith. — London : Hamlyn Paperbacks, 1980, c1978. — 185p ; 18cm
Originally published: Garden City, N.Y. : Doubleday, 1978
ISBN 0-600-20064-7 (pbk) : £1.00 B81-02467

Ball, John, *1911-*. Then came violence / John Ball. — London : Joseph, 1981, c1980. — 203p ; 23cm
Originally published: Garden City, N.Y. : Doubleday, 1980
ISBN 0-7181-1988-6 : £6.50 B81-06319

Ballenger, Dean W.. Gunslinger justice / by Dean W. Ballenger. — London : Hale, 1981, 1976. — 176p ; 20cm
Originally published: Canoga Park, Calif. : Major Books, 1976
ISBN 0-7091-8873-0 : £4.95 B81-15290

Banks, Carolyn. Mr. Right / Carolyn Banks. — [London] : Corgi, 1981, c1979. — 212p ; 18cm
Originally published: New York : Viking, 1979
ISBN 0-552-11701-3 (pbk) : £1.25 B81-27238

Barnwell, William. The blessing papers / William Barnwell. — Gerrards Cross : Smythe, 1981, c1980. — 354p ; 23cm
ISBN 0-901072-94-x : Unpriced : CIP rev. B80-19432

Barth, John. The end of the road / John Barth. — London : Granada, 1981, c1958. — 190p ; 18cm. — (A Panther book)
Originally published: New York : Doubleday, 1958 ; London : Secker & Warburg, 1962
ISBN 0-586-05282-8 (pbk) : £1.50 B81-26408

Barth, John. The floating opera / John Barth. — London : Granada, 1981, c1967. — 254p ; 18cm. — (A Panther book)
Originally published: New York : Appleton-Century-Crofts, 1956 ; London : Secker & Warburg, 1968
ISBN 0-586-05422-7 (pbk) : £1.95 B81-34837

Barth, John. Giles Goat-boy : or, the revised new Syllabus / John Barth. — London : Granada, 1981, c1966. — 812p : music ; 18cm. — (A Panther book)
Originally published: New York : Doubleday, 1966 ; London : Secker & Warburg, 1967
ISBN 0-586-05280-1 (pbk) : £2.95 B81-17413

Bartholomew, Cecilia. Second sight / Cecilia Bartholomew. — London : Hale, 1981, c1980. — 285p ; 23cm
Originally published: New York : Putnam, 1980
ISBN 0-7091-8761-0 : £6.75 B81-21304

Batchelor, Reg. Stolen gold / by Reg Batchelor. — London : Hale, 1981. — 160p ; 20cm
ISBN 0-7091-9084-0 : £4.95 B81-27289

Bayer, William. Punish me with kisses / William Bayer. — London : Corgi, 1981, c1980. — 254p ; 18cm
ISBN 0-552-11760-9 (pbk) : £1.50 B81-35499

Bayer, William. Punish me with kisses : a novel / by William Bayer. — London : Severn House, 1981, c1980. — 282p ; 21cm
ISBN 0-7278-0684-x : £6.95 : CIP rev. B81-07609

Beagle, Peter. The last unicorn. — London : Allen and Unwin, Feb.1982. — [176]p
ISBN 0-04-823206-8 (pbk) : £1.95 : CIP entry B81-38293

Beattie, Ann. Falling in place : a novel / by Ann Beattie. — London : Secker & Warburg, 1981, c1980. — 342p ; 24cm
Originally published: New York : Random House, 1980
ISBN 0-436-03800-5 : £6.95 B81-11634

Beckman, Patti. Angry lover. — London : Hodder & Stoughton, Nov.1981. — [192]p. — (Silhouette romance)
ISBN 0-340-27260-0 (pbk) : £0.65 : CIP entry B81-30139

Beckman, Patti. The beachcomber / Patti Beckman. — London : Silhouette, 1981, c1980. — 190p ; 18cm. — (Silhouette romance ; no.36)
ISBN 0-340-26726-7 (pbk) : £0.65 : CIP rev. B81-04220

Beckman, Patti. Captive heart / Patti Beckman. — London (47 Bedford Sq., WC1B 3DP) : Silhouette, 1980. — 190p ; 18cm. — (Silhouette romance ; no.8)
ISBN 0-340-26005-x (pbk) : £0.65 : CIP rev. B80-12532

Beckman, Patti. Louisiana lady / Patti Beckman. — London : Silhouette, 1981. — 189p ; 18cm. — (Silhouette romance ; 53)
ISBN 0-340-27031-4 (pbk) : £0.65 : CIP rev. B81-18138

Benford, Gregory. Shiva descending / Gregory Benford and William Rotsler. — London : Sphere, 1980, c1979. — 394p ; 18cm. — (Sphere science fiction)
Originally published: New York : Avon, 1979
ISBN 0-7221-1573-3 (corrected : pbk) : £1.95 B81-11675

Benford, Gregory. Timescape / Gregory Benford. — London : Gollancz, 1980. — 412p ; 23cm
Originally published: New York : Simon and Schuster, 1980
ISBN 0-575-02793-2 : £7.95 B81-00264

Bennett, Dorothea. The Maynard Hayes affair / Dorothea Bennett. — London : Macmillan, 1981, c1979. — 224p ; 21cm
Originally published: New York : Coward, McCann and Geoghegan, 1979
ISBN 0-333-30768-2 : £5.50 B81-11677

Benton, Will. The Buckskin Hills / by Will Benton. — London : Hale, 1960 (1981 [printing]). — 160p ; 20cm
ISBN 0-7091-8954-0 : £2.95 B81-08639

Berger, Thomas. Neighbors : a novel / by Thomas Berger. — London : Magnum, 1981, c1980. — 275p ; 18cm
Originally published: New York : Delacorte/Seymour Lawrence, 1980
ISBN 0-417-06310-5 (pbk) : £1.50 B81-08426

Bester, Alfred. Golem [to the power] 100 / Alfred Bester ; illustrated by Jack Gaughan. — London : Pan, 1981, c1980. — 382p : ill ; 18cm. — (Pan science fiction)
Originally published: London : Sidgwick and Jackson, 1980
ISBN 0-330-26258-0 (pbk) : £1.75 B81-09736

Bickerton, Derek. King of the sea / Derek Bickerton. — London : Granada, 1980, c1979. — 221p ; 23cm
Originally published: New York : Random House, 1979
ISBN 0-246-11392-8 : £5.95 B81-00265

Bickham, Jack M.. Dinah, blow your horn / Jack M. Bickham. — London : Hale, 1980, c1979. — 201p ; 21cm
Originally published: Garden City, N.Y. : Doubleday, 1979
ISBN 0-7091-8534-0 : £5.95 B81-00266

Bickham, Jack M.. The Regensburg legacy / Jack M. Bickham. — London : Hale, 1981, c1980. — 287p ; 21cm
Originally published: Garden City, N.Y. : Doubleday, 1980
ISBN 0-7091-9180-4 : £7.50 B81-33534

Birdwell, Cleo. Amazons / Cleo Birdwell. — London : Granada, 1980. — 379p ; 24cm
Originally published: New York : Holt, Rinehart and Winston, 1980
ISBN 0-246-11426-6 : £6.95 B81-00267

Bjorgum, Kenneth. The betrayed / Kenneth Bjorgum. — London : Hale, 1980, c1979. — 188p ; 20cm
Originally published: Garden City, N.Y. : Doubleday, 1979
ISBN 0-7091-8664-9 : £4.95 B81-01105

Black, Campbell. Asterisk destiny / Campbell Black. — London : Sphere, 1981, c1978. — 244p ; 18cm
Originally published: New York : Moscow, 1978 ; London : Joseph, 1979
ISBN 0-7221-0528-2 (pbk) : £1.25 B81-09801

Black, Campbell. Raiders of the lost Ark : novel / by Campbell Black ; adapted from a screenplay by Lawrence Kasdan ; based on a story by George Lucas and Philip Kaufman. — London : Corgi, 1981. — 180p ; 18cm
ISBN 0-552-11750-1 (pbk) : £0.95 B81-27251

Blaisdell, Anne. Consequence of crime / by Anne Blaisdell. — London : Gollancz, 1981, c1980. — 178p ; 21cm
ISBN 0-575-02977-3 : £5.95 B81-14196

Blake, Stephanie. Wicked is my flesh / Stephanie Blake. — Feltham : Hamlyn, 1981, c1980. — 348p ; 18cm
Originally published: United States : PEI Books, 1980
ISBN 0-600-20328-x (pbk) : £1.50 B81-27874

Blankenship, William D.. Yukon gold / William D. Blankenship. — Large print ed. — Leicester : Ulverscroft, 1980, c1977. — 506p ; 23cm. — (Ulverscroft large print series)
Originally published: New York : Dutton, 1977 ; London : Souvenir Press, 1978
ISBN 0-7089-0532-3 : £4.25 : CIP rev. B80-23686

Blish, James. Black Easter, (or, Faust aleph-null) ; including The day after judgement / James Blish. — London : Arrow, 1981. — 208p : ill ; 18cm
Black Easter originally published: New York : Doubleday, 1968 ; London : Faber, 1969
ISBN 0-09-925450-6 (pbk) : £1.50 B81-16010

Blish, James. Cities in flight / James Blish. — London : Arrow, 1981. — 605p ; 18cm
ISBN 0-09-926440-4 (pbk) : £2.50 B81-39154

Blish, James. Mission to the Heart Stars / James Blish. — London : Granada, 1980, c1965. — 127p ; 28cm. — (A Panther book) (Granada science fiction)
Originally published: New York : Putnam, 1965 ; London : Faber, 1965
ISBN 0-586-04574-0 (pbk) : £0.95 B81-00269

Bloch, Robert. Such stuff as screams are made of / by Robert Bloch ; introduction by Gahan Wilson. — London : Hale, 1980, c1979. — ix,181p ; 21cm
ISBN 0-7091-8562-6 : £6.25 B81-05736

Block, Lawrence. After the first death / Lawrence Block. — London : Hale, 1981, c1969. — 183p ; 21cm
Originally published: New York : Macmillan, 1969
ISBN 0-7091-7714-3 : £6.25 B81-35229

Block, Lawrence. Ariel : a novel / by Lawrence Block. — London : Hale, 1981, c1980. — 281p ; 23cm
Originally published: New York : Arbor House, 1980
ISBN 0-7091-8742-4 : £6.75 B81-03500

Block, Lawrence. Deadly honeymoon / by Lawrence Block. — London : Hale, 1981, c1967. — 189p ; 20cm
Originally published: New York : Macmillan, 1967
ISBN 0-7091-7713-5 : £5.95 B81-15380

813'.54[F] — Fiction in English. American writers, *1945- — Texts* *continuation*

Block, Lawrence. The girl with the long green heart / Lawrence Block. — London : Hale, 1980. — 206p ; 20cm
ISBN 0-7091-7712-7 : £5.75 B81-02528

Block, Thomas H.. Mayday / Thomas Block. — London : New English Library, 1980, c1979 (1981 [printing]). — 348p ; 18cm
Originally published: New York : Marek, 1979
ISBN 0-450-04946-9 (pbk) : £1.75 B81-28694

Blodgett, Michael. Captain Blood : a novel of epic revenge / Michael Blodgett. — London : New English Library, 1981, c1979. — 335p ; 18cm
Originally published: New York : Stonehill, 1979
ISBN 0-450-05247-8 (pbk) : £1.75 B81-35624

Blume, Judy. Deenie / Judy Blume. — London : Heinemann, 1980, c1973. — 123p ; 23cm
Originally published: Scarsdale, N.Y. : Bradbury, 1973. — For adolescents
ISBN 0-434-92883-6 : £4.50 B81-02514

Blumenfeld, Yorick. Jenny : diary of a survivor. — Arundel : Centaur Press, Oct.1981. — [96]p
ISBN 0-900001-16-x : £2.95 : CIP entry B81-30639

Blyth, Myrna. For better and for worse / Myrna Blyth. — Loughton : Piatkus, 1981, c1979. — 304p ; 21cm
Originally published: New York : Putnam, 1979
ISBN 0-86188-068-4 : £6.50 : CIP rev. B81-15832

Bonds, Parris Afton. Made for each other. — London : Hodder & Stoughton, Nov.1981. — [192]p. — (Silhouette romance)
ISBN 0-340-27258-9 (pbk) : £0.65 : CIP entry B81-30140

Bonham, Barbara. Dance of desire / Barbara Bonham. — London : Sphere, 1980, c1978. — 313p ; 18cm
Originally published: Chicago : Playboy Press, 1978
ISBN 0-7221-1772-8 (pbk) : £1.60 B81-00270

Bonham, Barbara. The dark side of passion / Barbara Bonham. — London : Sphere, 1981, c1980. — 400p ; 18cm
ISBN 0-7221-1766-3 (pbk) : £1.75 B81-36820

Bontly, Thomas. Celestial chess / Thomas Bontly. — London : Magnum, 1981, c1979. — 279p ; 18cm
Originally published: New York : Harper & Row, 1979
ISBN 0-417-06340-7 (pbk) : £1.50 B81-28657

Booth, Pat. Rags to riches / Pat Booth. — London : Sphere, 1981. — 246p ; 18cm
ISBN 0-7221-1776-0 (pbk) : £1.25 B81-17977

Booton, Kage. Who knows Julie Gordon / Kage Booton. — London : Hale, 1981, c1980. — 180p ; 20cm
Originally published: Garden City, N.Y. : Doubleday for the Crime Club, 1980
ISBN 0-7091-9300-9 : £6.25 B81-33527

Bosworth, Frank. Barling's guns / by Frank Bosworth. — London : Hale, 1980. — 158p ; 20cm
ISBN 0-7091-8231-7 : £4.50 B81-00424

Bosworth, Frank. The bountymen / by Frank Bosworth. — London : Hale, 1981. — 160p ; 20cm
ISBN 0-7091-9304-1 : £4.95 B81-37314

Bosworth, Frank. The long-riders / Frank Bosworth. — London : Hale, 1971 (1981 [printing]). — 157p ; 20cm
ISBN 0-7091-1898-8 : £2.95 B81-19316

Bouma, J. L.. Slaughter at Crucifix Canyon / J.L. Bouma. — London : Hale, 1981, c1975. — 175p ; 20cm
Originally published: Canoga Park : Major Books, 1975
ISBN 0-7091-8906-0 : £4.95 B81-11778

Bova, Ben. As on a darkling plain / Ben Bova. — London : Magnum, 1981, c1972. — 189p ; 18cm
Originally published: New York : Walker, 1972
ISBN 0-417-05870-5 (pbk) : £1.25 B81-08425

Bova, Ben. The starcrossed / Ben Bova. — London : Magnum, 1980, c1975. — 223p ; 18cm
Originally published: Radnor : Chilton, 1975
ISBN 0-417-05860-8 (pbk) : £1.25 B81-02853

Bowdler, Roger. Magnum P.I. : a novel / by Roger Bowdler ; from the Universal Television series Magnum P.I. written by Donald P. Bellisario and Glen A. Larson. — London : Granada, 1981. — 223p ; 18cm. — (A Mayflower book)
ISBN 0-583-13516-1 (pbk) : £1.25 B81-19944

Bowie, Donald. Cable Harbor : a novel / by Donald Bowie. — London : W.H. Allen, 1981. — 327p ; 22cm
ISBN 0-491-02615-3 : £7.95 B81-35154

Bowles, Paul. The sheltering sky / Paul Bowles. — London : Owen, 1981, c1977. — 304p ; 20cm
Originally published: London : Lehman, 1949
ISBN 0-7206-0587-3 : £7.95 B81-32791

Box, Edgar. Death before bedtime / Edgar Box. — London : Heinemann, 1953, c1978 (1979 [printing]). — 161p ; 23cm
ISBN 0-434-08251-1 : £5.50 B81-38667

Box, Edgar. Death in the fifth position / Edgar Box. — London : Heinemann, 1952, c1978 (1979 printing). — 150p ; 23cm
ISBN 0-434-08253-8 : £5.50 B81-38668

Bradbury, Ray. [The silver locusts]. The Martian chronicles / Ray Bradbury. — London : Granada, 1977, c1951 (1981 [printing]). — 221p ; 18cm. — (A Panther book)
Originally published: London : Hart-Davis, 1951
ISBN 0-586-04362-4 (pbk) : £1.25 B81-32186

Bradford, Barbara Taylor. A woman of substance / Barbara Taylor Bradford. — London : Granada, 1981, c1979. — 868p ; 18cm. — (A Mayflower book)
Originally published: New York : Doubleday, 1979 ; London : Granada, 1980
ISBN 0-583-13201-4 (pbk) : £2.50 B81-09744

Bradford, Will. Buffalo gun / Will Bradford. — London : Hale, 1980. — 159p ; 20cm
ISBN 0-7091-8169-8 : £4.50 B81-00271

Bradley, Concho. Return to the South Desert / by Concho Bradley. — London : Hale, 1980. — 160p ; 20cm
ISBN 0-7091-8431-x : £4.95 B81-00272

Bradley, Marion Zimmer. Stormqueen! : a Darkover novel / Marion Zimmer Bradley. — London : Arrow, 1980, c1978. — 364p ; 18cm
Originally published: New York : Dan Books, 1978
ISBN 0-09-922210-8 (pbk) : £1.50 B81-01106

Bradshaw, Gillian. Hawk of May / Gillian Bradshaw. — London : Eyre Methuen, 1981, c1980. — 270p : 1map ; 23cm
Originally published: New York : Simon and Schuster, c1980
ISBN 0-413-47560-3 : £6.50 B81-12485

Bradshaw, Gillian. Kingdom of summer. — London : Eyre Methuen, Oct.1981. — [282]p
ISBN 0-413-47640-5 : £6.95 : CIP entry B81-25283

Brady, Maureen. Give me your good ear. — London : Women's Press, Oct.1981. — [144]p
ISBN 0-7043-3874-2 (pbk) : £2.95 : CIP entry B81-28065

Brady, Michael. The coda alliance / Michael Brady. — London : Joseph, 1981. — 254p ; 23cm
ISBN 0-7181-1774-3 : £6.95 B81-11146

Brady, Michael, *1928-*. American surrender / Michael Brady. — London : Sphere, 1980, c1979. — 287p ; 18cm
Originally published: London : Joseph, 1979
ISBN 0-7221-1844-9 (pbk) : £1.25 B81-02488

Brand, Larry. Birthpyre / Larry Brand. — London : Corgi, 1981, c1980. — 239p ; 18cm
ISBN 0-552-11782-x (pbk) : £1.25 B81-39100

Brander, Gary. Death walkers / Gary Brander. — London : Hamlyn Paperbacks, 1980. — 222p ; 18cm
ISBN 0-600-20276-3 (pbk) : £1.00 B81-02620

Breadstone, Carl. The mummy / Carl Dreadstone ; adapted from the screenplay by John L. Balderston. — London : W.H. Allen, 1978, c1977. — 128p ; 18cm. — (The Classic library of horror) (A Universal book)
Originallly published: in The classic library of horror omnibus. United States : MCA, 1977 ; London : Wingate, 1978
ISBN 0-426-18841-1 (pbk) : £0.70 B81-20940

Brennan, Will. The guns of Nevada / by Will Brennan. — London : Hale, 1981. — 160p ; 20cm
Originally published: London : Gresham, 1966
ISBN 0-7091-8961-3 : £2.95 B81-16001

Brent, Audrey. Snowflakes in the sun / Audrey Brent. — London : Silhouette, 1981. — 188p ; 18cm. — (Silhouette romance ; 63)
ISBN 0-340-27118-3 (pbk) : £0.65 : CIP rev. B81-25098

Brent, Madeleine. The capricorn stone / Madeleine Brent. — London : Fontana, c1981, c1979. — 286p ; 18cm
Originally published: London : Souvenir Press, 1979
ISBN 0-00-616183-9 (pbk) : £1.35 B81-28211

Brent, Madeleine. The Capricorn Stone / Madeleine Brent. — Large print ed. — Leicester : Ulverscroft, 1981, c1979. — 474p ; 23cm. — (Ulverscroft large print series)
Originally published: London : Souvenir, 1979
ISBN 0-7089-0638-9 : Unpriced : CIP rev. B81-14792

Brent, Madeleine. Moonraker's bride / Madeleine Brent. — Large print ed. — Leicester : Ulverscroft, 1981, c1973. — 571p ; 22cm. — (Ulverscroft large print series)
Originally published: Garden City, N.Y. : Doubleday ; London : Souvenir Press, 1973
ISBN 0-7089-0522-6 : £5.00 B81-12183

Breslin, Catherine. Unholy child / Catherine Breslin. — London : Sphere, 1981, c1979 (1981 [printing]). — 562p ; 18cm
Originally published: New York : Dial Press, 1979
ISBN 0-7221-1863-5 (pbk) : £1.75 B81-09800

Briskin, Jacqueline. [California generation]. Decade / Jacqueline Briskin. — Redcar : Granada, 1981. — 630p ; 25cm
Originally published: London : Blond, 1970
ISBN 0-246-11152-6 : £7.95 B81-29900

Briskin, Jacqueline. Rich friends / Jacqueline Briskin. — London : Granada, 1980, c1976 (1981 [printing]). — 493p ; 18cm. — (A Mayflower book)
Originally published: New York : Delacorte, 1976
ISBN 0-583-13320-7 (pbk) : £1.95 B81-19943

813'.54[F] — Fiction in English. American writers, 1945- — Texts *continuation*

Brodeur, Paul. The stunt man / Paul Brodeur. — London : Macdonald Futura, 1981, c1970. — 252p ; 18cm
Originally published: New York : Atheneum ; London : Bodley Head, 1970
ISBN 0-7088-2030-1 (pbk) : £1.25 B81-15740

Bronson, Anita. Lucy Emmett, or A lady of quality / Anita Bronson. — London : Futura, 1980, c1978. — 384p ; 18cm. — (A Troubadour book)
Originally published: New York : Coward, McCann and Geoghegan, 1978 ; London : Macdonald and Jane's, 1979
ISBN 0-7088-1921-4 (pbk) : £1.50 B81-01107

Brooks, Adrian. The glass arcade / Adrian Brooks. — London : Star, 1980. — 266p ; 18cm
Originally published: New York : Simon & Schuster, 1980
ISBN 0-352-30777-3 (pbk) : £1.50 B81-00273

Brown, Dee. Creek Mary's blood : a novel / Dee Brown. — London : Arrow, 1981, c1980. — 461p : 1map,1geneal.table ; 18cm
Originally published: Franklin Center, Pa. : Franklin Library ; London : Hutchinson, 1980
ISBN 0-09-924680-5 (pbk) : £1.75 B81-11039

Brown, Rosellen. The autobiography of my mother / Rosellen Brown. — London : Sphere, 1981, c1976. — 254p ; 18cm
Originally published: New York : Doubleday, 1976
ISBN 0-7221-1912-7 (pbk) : £1.35 B81-11707

Brown, Vinson. Return of the Indian spirit / edited by Phyllis Johnson ; illustrated by W. Cameron Johnson. — London : Grosvenor, 1981. — 61p : ill ; 22cm
Author: Vinson Brown. — Includes: Laws of the lodge — Wisdom of the old ones
ISBN 0-901269-58-1 (cased) : £3.75
ISBN 0-901269-59-x (pbk) : £1.75 B81-38218

Browning, Dixie. Chance tomorrow / Dixie Browning. — London : Silhouette, 1981. — 188p ; 18cm. — (Silhouette romance ; 52)
ISBN 0-340-27030-6 (pbk) : £0.65 : CIP rev. B81-18140

Browning, Dixie. East of today. — London : Hodder and Stoughton, Feb.1982. — [192]p. — (Silhouette romance)
ISBN 0-340-27673-8 (pbk) : £0.75 : CIP entry B81-38314

Browning, Dixie. Journey to quiet waters / Dixie Browning. — London : Silhouette, 1981. — 189p ; 18cm. — (Silhouette romance ; 58)
ISBN 0-340-27113-2 (pbk) : £0.65 : CIP rev. B81-22472

Browning, Dixie. Tumbled wall / Dixie Browning. — London : Silhouette, 1981, c1980. — 188p ; 18cm. — (Silhouette romance ; no.37)
ISBN 0-340-26727-5 (pbk) : £0.65 : CIP rev. B81-04207

Browning, Dixie. Unreasonable summer / Dixie Browning. — [London] : Silhouette, 1981, c1980. — 188p ; 18cm. — (Silhouette romance ; no.12)
ISBN 0-340-26009-2 (pbk) : £0.65 : CIP rev. B80-19917

Browning, Dixie. Wren of paradise. — London : Hodder and Stoughton, Nov.1981. — [192]p. — (Silhouette romance)
ISBN 0-340-27261-9 (pbk) : £0.65 : CIP entry B81-30545

Buckley, William F.. Who's on first / William F. Buckley, Jr. — Harmondsworth : Penguin, 1980 (1981 [printing]). — 275p ; 19cm
Originally published: Garden City, N.Y. : Doubleday ; London : Allen Lane, 1980
ISBN 0-14-005611-4 (pbk) : £1.50 B81-27217

Buechner, Frederick. Godric / Frederick Buechner. — London : Chatto & Windus, 1981, c1980. — 178p ; 21cm
Originally published: New York : Atheneum, 1980
ISBN 0-7011-2564-0 : £6.50 B81-10998

Bukowski, Charles. Factotum / Charles Bukowski. — London : W.H. Allen, 1981, c1975. — 205p ; 23cm
Originally published: Los Angeles : Black Sparrow Press, 1975
ISBN 0-491-02805-9 : £6.95 B81-35151

Bukowski, Charles. Women / Charles Bukowski. — London : W.H. Allen, 1981, c1978. — 290p ; 23cm
Originally published: Santa Barbara, Calif. : Black Sparrow Press, 1978
ISBN 0-491-02854-7 : £6.95 B81-19985

Burchardt, Bill. Medicine man / Bill Burchardt. — London : Hale, 1980. — 213p ; 20cm
Originally published: Garden City, N.Y. : Doubleday, 1980
ISBN 0-7091-8487-5 : £4.95 B81-02210

Burns, Rex. Angle of attack / by Rex Burns. — London : Hale, 1980, c1979. — 250p ; 20cm
Originally published: New York : Harper & Row, 1979
ISBN 0-7091-8628-2 : £5.50 B81-00274

Burroughs, William S.. Cities of the red night / by William S. Burroughs. — London : John Calder, 1981. — xviii,332p : ill ; 24cm
ISBN 0-7145-3784-5 : £9.95 : CIP rev. B80-06576

Busch, Frederick. The mutual friend / Frederick Busch. — Harmondsworth : Penguin, 1980, c1978. — 224p ; 19cm
Originally published: New York : Harper and Row ; Harvester, 1978
ISBN 0-14-005244-5 (pbk) : £1.95 B81-10992

Buten, Howard. From little acorns : a novel / Howard Buten. — Brighton : Harvester, 1981. — 156p ; 21cm
ISBN 0-7108-0390-7 : £6.95 : CIP rev. B81-28199

Butler, Albert. Get Judge Parker! / by Albert Butler. — Harmondsworth : Henry, 1980. — 171p ; 21cm
Originally published: New York : Tower Publications, 1980
ISBN 0-86025-171-3 : £4.75 B81-02714

Butler, Octavia E.. Survivor / Octavia E. Butler. — London : Sphere, 1981, c1978. — 187p ; 18cm. — (Sphere science fiction)
Originally published: Garden City, N.Y. : Doubleday ; London : Sidgwick & Jackson, 1978
ISBN 0-7221-2101-6 (pbk) : £1.25 B81-17971

Byars, Betsy. The cartoonist / Betsy Byars. — Basingstoke : Macmillan Education, 1981, c1978. — 111p ; 21cm. — (M books)
Originally published: New York : Viking ; London : Bodley Head, 1978. — For adolescents
ISBN 0-333-28307-4 : £1.50 B81-18689

Caine, Leslie. Bridge of love / Leslie Caine. — [London] : Silhouette, 1981, c1980. — 188p ; 18cm. — (Silhouette romance ; no.10)
ISBN 0-340-26007-6 (pbk) : £0.65 : CIP rev. B80-19919

Calde, Mark A.. Conquest / Mark A. Calde. — London : New English Library, 1980. — xiii,386p ; 22cm
Originally published: New York : St Martin's Press, 1980
ISBN 0-450-04828-4 : £6.95 B81-01108

Cameron, John, *1927-*. The astrologer / John Cameron. — London : Sphere, 1981, c1972. — 316p ; 18cm
Originally published: New York : Random House, 1972 ; London : Bodley Head, 1973
ISBN 0-7221-2228-4 (pbk) : £1.50 B81-20389

Card, Orson Scott. A planet called Treason / Orson Scott Card. — London : Pan, 1981, c1979. — 299p : 1map ; 18cm. — (Pan science fiction)
Originally published: New York : St. Martin's Press, 1979
ISBN 0-330-26239-4 (pbk) : £1.50 B81-03051

Card, Orson Scott. Songmaster. — London : Macdonald Futura, 1981, c1980. — 338p ; 21cm. — (Macdonald science fiction)
Originally published: New York : Dial Press, 1980
ISBN 0-354-04707-8 : £5.95 B81-17395

Card, Orson Scott. Songmaster / Orson Scott Card. — London : Macdonald Futura, 1981. — 337p ; 18cm. — (An Orbit book)
Originally published: New York : Dial Press, 1980
ISBN 0-7088-8080-0 (pbk) : £1.75 B81-24411

Carr, Jayge. Leviathan's deep / Jayge Carr. — London : Macdonald Futura, 1980, c1979. — 256p ; 18cm. — (An Orbit book)
Originally published: Garden City, N.Y. : Doubleday, 1979 ; London : Sidgwick and Jackson, 1980
ISBN 0-7088-8077-0 (pbk) : £1.50 B81-15639

Carroll, James. Madonna red / James Carroll. — [London]. — Sevenoaks : Coronet, Dec. 1978. — 282p ; 18cm
Originally published: Boston, Mass. : Little, Brown ; London : Hodder and Stoughton, 1977
ISBN 0-340-23183-1 : £0.95 : CIP rev. B78-35584

Carroll, Mary. Divide the wind. — London : Hodder and Stoughton, Nov.1981. — [192]p. — (Silhouette romance)
ISBN 0-340-27263-5 (pbk) : £0.65 : CIP entry B81-30540

Carroll, Mary. Shadow and sun : Mary Carroll. — London (47 Bedford Sq., WC1B 3DP) : Silhouette, 1980. — 188p ; 18cm. — (Silhouette romance ; no.2)
ISBN 0-340-25999-x (pbk) : £0.65 : CIP rev. B80-12541

Carroll, Mary. Too swift the morning / Mary Carroll. — London : Silhouette, 1981, c1980. — 190p ; 18cm. — (Silhouette romance ; no.44)
ISBN 0-340-26734-8 (pbk) : £0.65 : CIP rev. B81-10466

Carter, Ashley. Master of Blackoaks / Ashley Carter. — London : Pan, 1978, c1976 (1981 [printing]). — 382p ; 18cm
Originally published: London : W. H. Allen, 1977
ISBN 0-330-25279-8 (pbk) : £1.75 B81-40085

Carter, Ashley. Scandal of Falconhurst / Ashley Carter. — London : W.H. Allen, 1981, c1980. — 446p : ill ; 21cm
Originally published: USA : Fawcett Gold Medal Books, 1980
ISBN 0-491-02664-1 : £7.95 B81-0867[illegible]

Carter, Ashley. Secret of Blackoaks / Ashley Carter. — London : Pan, 1981, c1978. — 462p ; 18cm
Originally published: London : W.H. Allen, 1978
ISBN 0-330-26309-9 (pbk) : £1.50 B81-1798[illegible]

Carter, Ashley. Taproots of Falconhurst / Ashley Carter. — London : Pan, 1980, c1978. — 314p ; 18cm
Originally published: United States? : s.n., 1978 ; London : W.H. Allen, 1979
ISBN 0-330-26169-x (pbk) : £1.50 B81-0027[illegible]

Carver, Jeffrey A.. Panglor. — London : Arrow, 1981, c1980. — 268p ; 18cm
ISBN 0-09-925610-x (pbk) : £1.60 B81-2028[illegible]

813′.54[F] — Fiction in English. American writers, *1945- — Texts continuation*

Chapple, Steve. Dont′t mind dying : a story of counry lust and urban decay / Steve Chapple. — London : New English Library, 1981. — 248p ; 23cm
Originally published: Garden City, N.Y. : Doubleday, 1980
ISBN 0-450-04844-6 : £5.95 B81-03446

Charnas, Suzy McKee. Motherlines. — London : Hodder & Stoughton, Oct.1981. — [256]p. — (Coronet books)
Originally published: 1980
ISBN 0-340-26789-5 (pbk) : £1.50 : CIP entry B81-26727

Charnas, Suzy McKee. Walk to the end of the world. — London : Hodder & Stoughton, Oct.1981. — [256]p. — (Coronet books)
Originally published: 1979
ISBN 0-340-26788-7 (pbk) : £1.50 : CIP entry B81-26734

Cheever, Susan. A handsome man / Susan Cheever. — London : Weidenfeld and Nicolson, 1981. — 234p ; 23cm
ISBN 0-297-77980-x : £6.95 B81-35146

Cherryh, C. J.. The Well of Shiuan / C.J. Cherryh. — [London] : Magnum, 1981, c1978. — 253p ; 18cm
Originally published: New York : Daw, 1978
ISBN 0-417-05940-x (pbk) : £1.50 B81-12039

Chesbro, George C.. An affair of sorcerers / George C. Chesbro. — London : Severn House, 1980, c1979. — 351p ; 21cm
Originally published: New York : Simon and Schuster, 1979
ISBN 0-7278-0647-5 : £6.95 : CIP rev. B80-18887

Chesbro, George C.. City of whispering stone. — London : Severn House, Sept.1981. — [224]p
ISBN 0-7278-0733-1 : £6.95 : CIP entry B81-21615

Chesbro, George C.. Shadow of a broken man / George C. Chesbro. — London : Severn House, 1981, c1977. — 233p ; 21cm. — ([A Mongo mystery])
Originally published: New York : Simon and Schuster, 1977
ISBN 0-7278-0702-1 : £6.95 : CIP rev. B81-04371

Cheyne, N. Gilbert. Queen Emma : the flower of Normandy / N. Gilbert Cheyne. — Bognor Regis : New Horizon, c1980. — 375p : 2geneal.tables ; 21cm
ISBN 0-86116-185-8 : £5.75 B81-19259

Child, Timothy. Cold turkey / Timothy Childs. — London : Hale, 1981, c1979. — 188p ; 20cm
Originally published: New York : Harper & Row, 1979
ISBN 0-7091-9004-2 : £5.95 B81-24441

Christian, Frederick H.. Sudden Apache fighter / Frederick H. Christian. — [London] : Corgi, 1969 (1981 [printing]). — 157p ; 18cm. — (Sudden Westerns)
ISBN 0-552-11800-1 (pbk) : £0.95 B81-18553

Christian, Frederick H.. Sudden at bay : based upon the character created by Oliver Strange / Frederick H. Christian. — [London] : Corgi, 1968 (1981 [printing]). — 142p ; 18cm. — (Sudden Westerns)
ISBN 0-552-11799-4 (pbk) : £0.95 B81-18554

Churchill, Thomas. Centralia dead march / Thomas Churchill. — Sanday (Over the water, Sanday, Orkney KW17 2BL) : Cienfuegos, 1980. — 213p ; 22cm
£4.00 (pbk) B81-27312

Clancy, Ambrose. Blind pilot / by Ambrose Clancy. — London : Macmillan, 1981, c1980. — 384p : 1map ; 23cm
Originally published: New York : Morrow, 1980
ISBN 0-333-31001-2 : £6.95 B81-18571

Clark, Mary Higgins. The cradle will fall / Mary Higgins Clark. — [London] : Fontana, 1981, c1980. — 254p ; 18cm
Originally published: London : Collins, 1980
ISBN 0-00-616273-8 (pbk) : £1.25 B81-22005

Clark, Mary Higgins. A stranger is watching / Mary Higgins Clark. — [London] : Fontana, 1979, c1978. — 190p ; 18cm
Originally published: New York : Simon and Schuster ; London : Collins, 1978
ISBN 0-00-616377-7 (pbk) : £1.25 B81-32163

Clavell, James. Noble House / James Clavell. — London : Hodder and Stoughton, 1981. — 1116p ; 24cm
ISBN 0-340-25954-x : £8.95 : CIP rev. B81-12862

Clement, Henry. Prisoner cell block H : the Frankie Doyle story / Henry Clement. — London : Star, 1981. — 220p ; 18cm
Originally published: New York : Pinnacle, 1981
ISBN 0-352-30895-8 (pbk) : £1.50 B81-28507

Cline, Terry. Cross current / Terry Cline. — London : New English Library, 1980, c1979. — 285p ; 18cm
Originally published: Garden City, N.Y. : Doubleday, 1979
ISBN 0-450-04672-9 (pbk) : £1.25 B81-01109

Cline, Terry. Death knell / Terry Cline. — Large print ed. — Leicester : Ulverscroft, 1981, c1977. — 479p ; 23cm. — (Ulverscroft large print series)
Originally published: London : Collins, 1978
ISBN 0-7089-0561-7 : £5.00 B81-11389

Coburn, Andrew. The babysitter / Andrew Coburn. — London : Sphere, 1981, c1979. — 215p ; 18cm
Originally published: New York : Norton, 1979 ; London : Secker & Warburg, 1980
ISBN 0-7221-2472-4 (pbk) : £1.25 B81-08631

Coburn, Andrew. Off duty / by Andrew Coburn. — London : Secker & Warburg, 1981, c1980. — 256p ; 23cm
Originally published: London : Norton, 1980
ISBN 0-436-10291-9 : £6.95 B81-10134

Coen, Franklin. The plunderers / Franklin Coen. — London : Severn House, 1981, c1980. — 275p ; 21cm
Originally published: New York : Coward, McCann & Geoghegan, c1980
ISBN 0-7278-0719-6 : £6.95 : CIP rev. B81-14840

Coffey, Brian, *19---*. The voice of the night / Brian Coffey. — London : Hale, 1981. — 277p ; 23cm
Originally published: under the name Dean Koontz. Garden City, N.Y. : Doubleday, 1980
ISBN 0-7091-8991-5 : £6.50 B81-19303

Coffey, Frank. The shaman / Frank Coffey. — London : W.H. Allen, 1980. — 240p ; 22cm
Originally published: New York : St. Martin′s Press, 1980
ISBN 0-491-02961-6 : £5.95 B81-00277

Coffey, Frank. The shaman / Frank Coffey. — London : W.H. Allen, 1980 (1981 [printing]). — 240p ; 18cm. — (A Star book)
Originally published: New York : St. Martin′s Press, 1980
ISBN 0-352-30822-2 (pbk) : £1.50 B81-26524

Coffman, Virginia. The alpine coach. — Large print ed. — Anstey : Ulverscroft, Nov.1981. — [352]p. — (Ulverscroft large print series)
Originally published: New York : Dell, 1976 ; London : Souvenir Press, 1980
ISBN 0-7089-0709-1 : £5.00 : CIP entry B81-30502

Coffman, Virginia. The beach house. — Loughton : Piatkus, Feb.1982. — [208]p
ISBN 0-86188-135-4 : £6.50 : CIP entry B81-36020

Coffman, Virginia. The cliffs of dread / Virginia Coffman. — Loughton : Piatkus, 1981, c1972. — 187p ; 21cm
ISBN 0-86188-089-7 : £6.50 : CIP rev. B81-15845

Coffman, Virginia. The dark palazzo / Virginia Coffman. — Feltham : Hamlyn, 1981, c1973. — 208p ; 18cm. — (A moonshadow romance)
Originally published: New York : Arbor House, 1973 ; Loughton : Piatkus, 1980
ISBN 0-600-20206-2 (pbk) : £1.10 B81-41001

Coffman, Virginia. The evil at Queen′s Priory / Virginia Coffman. — Large print ed. — Bath : Chivers, 1981, c1973. — 242p ; 23cm. — (A Lythway romantic thriller)
Originally published: United States? : S.n., 1973 ; Loughton ; Piatkus, 1980
ISBN 0-85119-716-7 : £6.50 : CIP rev. B81-08887

Coffman, Virginia. Fire dawn / Virginia Coffman. — South Yarmouth, Mass. : Curley ; [Clitheroe] : Magna Print [[distributor]], c1977. — 485p ; 23cm
Originally published: New York : Arbor House, 1977 ; Loughton : Piatkus, 1979. — Published in large print
ISBN 0-89340-273-7 : £5.50 B81-02764

Coffman, Virginia. The Gaynor women : a novel / by Virginia Coffman. — London : Souvenir, 1981, c1978. — 486p ; 23cm
Originally published: New York : Arbor House, c1978
ISBN 0-285-62467-9 : £6.95 B81-02182

Coffman, Virginia. Night at Sea Abbey / by Virginia Coffman. — Loughton (Loughton, Essex) : Piatkus, 1981, c1972. — 184p ; 21cm
ISBN 0-86188-071-4 : £5.95 B81-07171

Cohen, Sharleen Cooper. Regina′s song / Sharleen Cooper Cohen. — London : New English Library, 1981, c1980. — 411p ; 18cm
Originally published: New York : Dell, 1980
ISBN 0-450-05248-6 (pbk) : £1.75 B81-35622

Cohler, David Keith. [The gamemaker]. Bloodsport / David Keith Cohler. — London : W.H. Allen, 1981, c1980. — 279p ; 18cm. — (A Star book)
Originally published: Garden City, N.Y. : Doubleday ; London : W.H. Allen, 1980
ISBN 0-352-30826-5 (pbk) : £1.50 B81-28550

Coleman, Lonnie. The legacy of Beulah land / Lonnie Coleman. — London : Arrow, 1981, c1980. — 430p : 2geneal.tables ; 18cm
Originally published: London : Cassel, 1980
ISBN 0-09-926730-6 (pbk) : £1.75 B81-34592

Colleton, John, *1907-*. Between Cloris and Amy / by John Colleton. — New York : New American Library ; [London] : New English Library [[distributor]], c1976. — 224p ; 18cm. — (A Signet book)
ISBN 0-451-09789-0 (pbk) : £1.25 B81-19974

Colleton, John, *1907-*. Two nymphs named Melissa / by John Colleton. — New York : New American Library ; [London] : New English Library [[distributor]], c1979. — 220p ; 18cm. — (A Signet book)
ISBN 0-451-09788-2 (pbk) : £1.25 B81-19973

Collin, Richard Oliver. Imbroglio / Richard Oliver Collin. — London : Gollancz, 1981, 1980. — 292p ; 23cm
ISBN 0-575-02941-2 : £6.95 B81-12300

813′.54[F] — Fiction in English. American writers, *1945- — Texts* *continuation*

Collins, Michael, *1924-*. The Slasher / by Michael Collins. — London : Hale, 1981, c1980. — 192p ; 20cm
ISBN 0-7091-9331-9 : £6.25 B81-40547

Colwin, Laurie. Happy all the time / Laurie Colwin. — London : Fontana, 1981, c1978. — 188p ; 18cm
Originally published: London : Collins, 1979
ISBN 0-00-615930-3 (pbk) : £1.25 B81-28209

Condon, Richard. Death of a politician / Richard Condon. — London : Arrow, 1980, c1978. — 294p : ill,forms ; 18cm
Originally published: New York : R. Marek Publishers, 1978 ; London : Hutchinson, 1979
ISBN 0-09-922950-1 (pbk) : £1.50 B81-01110

Condon, Richard. The entwining / Richard Condon. — London : Hutchinson, 1981. — 287p ; 23cm
ISBN 0-09-144130-7 : £6.95 B81-14237

Condon, Richard. The Manchurian candidate. — Large print ed. — Leicester : Ulverscroft, Sept.1981. — [416]p. — (Charnwood library series)
Originally published: London : Joseph, 1960
ISBN 0-7089-8011-2 : £5.25 : CIP entry B81-22653

Conroy, *19---*. The lords of discipline / Pat Conroy. — London : Secker & Warburg, 1981. — 499p ; 23cm
ISBN 0-436-10600-0 : £6.95 : CIP rev. B81-13480

Cook, Robin, *1940-*. Brain / Robin Cook. — London : Macmillan, 1981. — 283p ; 23cm
ISBN 0-333-31508-1 : £5.95 B81-20285

Cook, Robin, *1940-*. Sphinx / Robin Cook. — Large print ed. — Leicester : Ulverscroft, 1981, c1979. — 516p ; 23cm. — (Ulverscroft large print series)
Originally published: London : Macmillan, 1979
ISBN 0-7089-0625-7 : £5.00 : CIP rev. B81-07436

Cooper, Parley J.. Restaurant / Parley J. Cooper. — London : Magnum, 1981, c1979. — 299p ; 18cm
Originally published: New York : Macmillan, 1979
ISBN 0-417-06160-9 (pbk) : £1.50 B81-28659

Cooper, Simon. [The dirt sandwich]. Big girls don′t cry / Simon Cooper. — London : Sphere, 1981, c1980. — 382p ; 18cm
Originally published: New York : Dial Press, 1980
ISBN 0-7221-2496-1 (pbk) : £1.75 B81-24707

Copper, Basil. Dark entry / Basil Copper. — London : Hale, 1981. — 158p ; 20cm. — (.38 special ; 33)
ISBN 0-7091-8642-8 : £6.25 B81-37302

Copper, Basil. The empty silence / Basil Copper. — London : Hale, 1981. — 159p ; 20cm. — (.38 special ; 32)
ISBN 0-7091-8529-4 : £5.95 B81-19219

Copper, Basil. Flip-side / Basil Copper. — London : Hale, 1980. — 172p ; 20cm. — (38 special ; 30)
ISBN 0-7091-8455-7 : £5.50 B81-01111

Copper, Basil. The great white space / Basil Copper. — London : Sphere, 1980, c1974. — 188p ; 18cm
Originally published: New York : St Martin′s Press ; London : Hale, 1974
ISBN 0-7221-2503-8 (pbk) : £1.10 B81-00278

Copper, Basil. The long rest / Basil Copper. — London : Hale, 1981. — 160p ; 20cm. — (.38 special ; 31)
ISBN 0-7091-8472-7 : £5.75 B81-08951

Copper, Basil. Necropolis / Basil Copper. — London : Sphere, 1981, c1980. — ix,372p ; 18cm
Originally published: Sauk City, Wis. : Arkham House, 1980
ISBN 0-7221-2488-0 (pbk) : £1.50 B81-09795

Corley, Edwin. The Jesus factor / Edwin Corley. — London : Sphere, 1980, c1970. — 318p ; 18cm
Originally published: New York : Stein and Day, 1970 ; London : Joseph, 1971
ISBN 0-7221-2546-1 (pbk) : £1.50 B81-01112

Corman, Avery. The old neighborhood : a novel / by Avery Corman. — London : Collins, 1980. — 219p ; 23cm
ISBN 0-00-221624-8 : £5.95 B81-00279

Cormier, Robert. After the first death / Robert Cormier. — [London] : Fontana, 1979. — 184p ; 18cm. — (Lions)
Originally published: New York : Pantheon ; London : Gollancz, 1979
ISBN 0-00-671705-5 (pbk) : £1.00 B81-03038

Cormier, Robert. After the first death / Robert Cormier. — London : Gollancz, 1979. — 233p ; 21cm
Originally published: New York : Pantheon, 1979
ISBN 0-575-02665-0 : £3.95 B81-00280

Cormier, Robert. The chocolate war / Robert Cormier. — London : Lions, 1978, c1974 (1980 [printing]). — 189p ; 18cm
Originally published: New York : Pantheon, 1974 ; London : Gollancz, 1975
ISBN 0-00-671765-9 (pbk) : £0.95 B81-02990

Cormier, Robert. I am the cheese / Robert Cormier. — London : Lions, 1979, c1977 (1980 [printing]). — 190p ; 18cm
Originally published: New York : Pantheon ; London : Gollancz, 1975
ISBN 0-00-671766-7 (pbk) : £0.95 B81-02991

Cormier, Robert. I am the cheese / Robert Cormier. — Basingstoke : Macmillan Education, 1981, c1977. — 191p ; 21cm. — (M books)
Originally published: New York : Pantheon ; London : Gollancz, 1977. — For adolescents
ISBN 0-333-29452-1 : £1.50 B81-18568

Cottonwood, Joe. Famous potatoes / Joe Cottonwood. — [London] : Corgi, 1981, c1978. — 264p ; 18cm
Originally published: Portola Valley, Calif. : No Dead Lines, 1978
ISBN 0-552-11607-6 (pbk) : £1.65 B81-08415

Coughlin, William J.. The stalking man / William J. Coughlin. — London : Magnum, 1981, c1979. — 319p ; 18cm
Originally published: New York : Delacorte, 1979
ISBN 0-417-05620-6 (pbk) : £1.50 B81-08420

Coyne, John, *1937-*. The searing / John Coyne. — [London] : Fontana, 1981, c1980. — 223p : ill ; 18cm
Originally published: New York : Putnam, 1980
ISBN 0-00-616461-7 (pbk) : £1.35 B81-36834

Crichton, Michael. Congo / Michael Crichton. — London : Allen Lane, 1981, c1980. — 348p ; 23cm
Originally published: New York : Knopf, 1980. — Bibliography: p345-348
ISBN 0-7139-1416-5 : £6.95 B81-17789

Crosby, John, *1912-*. [Nightfall]. Snake / John Crosby. — [London] : Coronet, 1979, c1976. — 224p ; 18cm
Originally published: as Nightfall, New York : Stein and Day, 1976 ; and as Snake, London : Cape, 1977
ISBN 0-340-23227-7 (pbk) : £0.95 : CIP rev. B79-19537

Cross, Amanda. A death in the faculty / Amanda Cross. — London : Gollancz, 1981. — 156p ; 21cm
ISBN 0-575-02982-x : £5.95 B81-21666

Cunningham, E. V.. The case of the poisoned eclairs. — Large print ed. — Bath : Chivers Press, Dec.1981. — [272]p. — (A New Portway large print book)
Originally published: London : Deutsch, 1980
ISBN 0-85119-144-4 : £5.25 : CIP entry B81-31835

Curtiss, Ursula. The poisoned orchard / Ursula Curtiss. — London : Macmillan, 1980. — 185p ; 21cm
Originally published: New York : Dodd Mead, 1980
ISBN 0-333-29111-5 : £5.50 B81-00281

Cussler, Clive. Iceberg / Clive Cussler. — Large print ed. — Leicester : Ulverscroft, 1981, c1975. — 494p ; 23cm
Originally published: New York : Dodd, Mead, 1975 ; London : Sphere, 1976
ISBN 0-7089-0681-8 : £5.00 : CIP rev. B81-25892

Cussler, Clive. Night probe! / Clive Cussler. — London : Hodder, c1981. — 344p : 1ill,maps ; 24cm
ISBN 0-340-25656-7 : £6.95 : CIP rev. B81-22494

Dailey, Janet. Reilly′s woman. — Large print ed. — Bath : Chivers, Jan.1982. — [232]p. — (A Lythway book)
Originally published: London : Mills & Boon, 1977
ISBN 0-85119-776-0 : £6.25 : CIP entry B81-33797

Dailey, Janet. The rogue / Janet Dailey. — Loughton : Piatkus, 1981, c1980. — 282p ; 21cm
ISBN 0-86188-097-8 (pbk) : £6.50 : CIP rev. B81-15863

Daley, Robert. Year of the dragon. — London : Hodder & Stoughton, Feb.1982. — [416]p
ISBN 0-340-27644-4 : £6.95 : CIP entry B81-36366

Dana, Amber. The jade moon / by Amber Dana. — London : Hale, 1981. — 160p ; 20cm
ISBN 0-7091-9193-6 : £5.75 B81-30071

Daniels, Norman, *1910-*. Wyndward fury / Norman Daniels. — London : Hamlyn Paperbacks, 1981, c1979. — 350p ; 18cm
Originally published: New York : Warner Books, 1979 ; Feltham : Hamlyn, 1980
ISBN 0-600-20095-7 (pbk) : £1.50 B81-31915

Danielson, Peter. Children of the lion / Peter Danielson. — [London] : Corgi
Book 1. — 1981, c1980. — 464p : maps ; 18cm
ISBN 0-552-11740-4 (pbk) : £1.50 B81-14126

Darcy, Clare. Letty / Clare Darcy. — London : Macdonald Futura, 1980. — 254p ; 23cm
Originally published: New York : Walker, 1980
ISBN 0-354-04519-9 : £5.50 B81-00282

Darcy, Clare. Letty / Clare Darcy. — London : Macdonald Futura, 1981, c1980. — 254p ; 18cm. — (A Futura book)
Originally published: New York : Walker ; London : Macdonald, 1980
ISBN 0-7088-2058-1 (pbk) : £1.25 B81-24429

Darcy, Clare. Letty / Clare Darcy. — London : Prior, c1981, 1980. — 395p ; 25cm
Originally published: New York : Walker, 1980. — Published in large print
ISBN 0-86043-581-4 : £6.50 B81-24576

Davenport, Diana, *19---*. The desperate season / Diana Davenport. — London : Granada, 1980, c1978. — 318p ; 18cm. — (A Mayflower book)
Originally published: New York : Morrow, London : Hart-Davis, MacGibbon, 1979
ISBN 0-583-13148-4 (pbk) : £1.50 B81-17585

813'.54[F] — Fiction in English. American writers, *1945- — Texts* *continuation*

Davis, Dorothy Salisbury. Scarlet night / by Dorothy Salisbury Davis. — London : Gollancz, 1981, c1980. — 244p ; 21cm
ISBN 0-575-02940-4 : £5.95 B81-12303

Davis, Gwen. Ladies in waiting / Gwen Davis. — Feltham : Hamlyn, 1980, c1979. — 277p ; 22cm
Originally published: New York : Macmillan, 1979
ISBN 0-600-20059-0 : £5.95 B81-01113

Davis, Gwen. Ladies in waiting / Gwen Davis. — London : Hamlyn Paperbacks, 1981, c1979. — 284p ; 18cm
Originally published: New York : Macmillan, 1979 ; Feltham : Hamlyn, 1980
ISBN 0-600-20200-3 (pbk) : £1.50 B81-31912

Davis, Robert P.. [Cat five]. Hurricane / Robert P. Davis. — London : Hale, 1980. — 320p ; 23cm
Originally published: New York : Morrow, 1977
ISBN 0-7091-8468-9 : £6.50 B81-00283

Davis, Robert P.. Control tower / Robert P. Davis. — London : Corgi, 1981, c1980. — 283p ; 18cm
Originally published: London : Hale, 1980
ISBN 0-552-11661-0 (pbk) : £1.25 B81-18672

Davis, Robert P.. The divorce / Robert P. Davis. — London : Hale, 1981, c1980. — 360p ; 23cm
Originally published: New York : Morrow, 1980
ISBN 0-7091-9245-2 : £6.50 B81-33531

Day, Robert, *1941-*. [The last cattle drive]. Road show / Robert Day. — London : Sphere, 1979 (1981 [printing]). — 219p ; 18cm
Originally published: New York : Putnam ; London : Secker and Warburg, 1977
ISBN 0-7221-2822-3 (pbk) : £1.50 B81-36822

De Christoforo, Ron. A small circle of friends : a novelization / by Rou de Christoforo ; from a screenplay written by Ezra Sacks. — [London] : Magnum, 1980. — 204p ; 18cm
Originally published: New York : Pocket Books, 1980
ISBN 0-417-06120-x (pbk) : £1.25 B81-06374

De Felitta, Frank. Sea trial / by Frank De Felitta. — London : Gollancz, 1980. — 270p ; 23cm
Originally published: New York : Avon Books, 1980
ISBN 0-575-02928-5 : £5.95 B81-00284

De Felitta, Frank. Sea Trial / Frank De Felitta. — London : Arrow, 1981, c1980. — 270p ; 18cm
Originally published: London : Gollancz, 1980
ISBN 0-09-924910-3 (pbk) : £1.60 B81-28585

De Mille, Nelson. Cathedral / Nelson De Mille. — London : Granada, 1981. — 556p : 2plans ; 24cm
ISBN 0-246-11356-1 : £6.95 B81-21207

Deane, Leslie. Hero / Leslie Deane. — London : Arrow, 1981, c1980. — 390p ; 18cm
Originally published: New York : Jove, 1980
ISBN 0-09-924980-4 (pbk) : £1.75 B81-11038

Delattre, Pierre, *1930-*. Walking on air / Pierre Delattre. — London : Gollancz, 1980. — 243p ; 21cm
ISBN 0-575-02907-2 : £6.95 B81-00285

DeLillo, Don. Running dog / Don DeLillo. — London : Sphere, 1981, c1978. — 246p ; 18cm
Originally published: New York : Knopf, 1978
ISBN 0-7221-2933-5 (pbk) : £1.50 B81-24711

Denker, Henry. The actress / Henry Denker. — London : Granada, 1981, c1978. — 366p ; 18cm. — (A Mayflower book)
Originally published: New York : Simon and Schuster, 1978 ; London : W.H. Allen, 1979
ISBN 0-583-13152-2 (pbk) : £1.50 B81-10880

DeWeese, Jean. Hour of the cat / Jean DeWeese. — London : Hale, 1980. — 179p ; 20cm
Originally published: Garden City, N.Y. : Doubleday, 1980
ISBN 0-7091-8654-1 : £5.50 B81-02212

Dial, Joan. Lovers and warriors. — London : Hodder & Stoughton, Dec.1981. — [352]p
Originally published: Greenwich, Conn. : Fawcett Gold Medal Books, 1978
ISBN 0-340-27267-8 (pbk) : £1.75 : CIP entry B81-31466

Diamond, Graham. Lady of the Haven / Graham Diamond. — London : Magnum, 1980, c1978. — 382p ; 18cm
Originally published: New York : Playboy Press, 1978
ISBN 0-417-04990-0 (pbk) : £1.50 B81-02688

Dick, Philip K.. Vulcan's hammer / Philip K. Dick. — London : Arrow, 1976, c1960 (1981 [printing]). — 154p ; 18cm
Originally published: New York : Ace Books, 1960
ISBN 0-09-913300-8 (pbk) : £1.25 B81-32325

Dickson, Gordon R. (Gordon Rupert). The alien way / Gordon R. Dickson. — London : Hale, 1981, c1965. — 191p ; 21cm. — (Hale SF)
Originally published: New York : Bantam, 1965 ; London : Corgi, 1973
ISBN 0-7091-8729-7 : £5.95 B81-02964

Dickson, Gordon R. (Gordon Rupert). Masters of Everton / Gordon R. Dickson. — London : Sphere, 1981, c1979. — 244p ; 18cm. — (Sphere science fiction)
Originally published: New York : Ace, 1980
ISBN 0-7221-2997-1 (pbk) : £1.50 B81-35062

DiMona, Joseph. To the eagle's nest / Joseph DiMona. — London : Joseph, 1980. — 311p ; 23cm
ISBN 0-7181-1921-5 : £6.50 B81-02216

Disch, Thomas M.. Neighbouring lives / Thomas M. Disch & Charles Naylor. — London : Hutchinson, 1981. — 397p ; 23cm
ISBN 0-09-144710-0 : £7.95 : CIP rev. B81-04379

Disch, Thomas M.. On wings of song / Thomas M. Disch. — London : Magnum, 1981, c1979. — 315p ; 18cm
Originally published: London : Gollancz, 1979
ISBN 0-417-05580-3 (pbk) : £1.50 B81-28662

Dixon, Diana, *1940-*. Return engagement / Diana Dixon. — [London] : Silhouette, 1980. — 190p ; 18cm. — (Silhouette romance ; 29)
ISBN 0-340-26579-5 (pbk) : £0.65 : CIP rev. B81-02565

Doctorow, E. L.. Loon Lake / E.L. Doctorow. — London : Macmillan, 1980. — 258p ; 23cm
Originally published: New York : Random House, 1980
ISBN 0-333-30641-4 : £6.95 B81-01689

Donaldson, Stephen. The wounded land / Stephen Donaldson. — [London] : Fontana, 1980. — 508p : 1map ; 18cm. — (The Second chronicles of Thomas Covenant ; v.1)
Originally published: United States : Del Rey, 1980
ISBN 0-00-616140-5 (pbk) : £1.75 B81-01628

Donaldson, Stephen. The wounded land / Stephen R. Donaldson. — London : Sidgwick & Jackson, 1980. — xi,497p : 1map ; 22cm. — (The second chronicles of Thomas Covenant ; bk.1)
Originally published: New York : Ballentine, 1980
ISBN 0-283-98690-5 : £6.95 B81-01114

Doty, Carolyn. A day late / Carolyn Doty. — London : Hutchinson, 1981, c1980. — 232p ; 23cm
Originally published: New York : Viking, 1980
ISBN 0-09-144960-x : £6.50 : CIP rev. B81-04380

Douglas, Kathryn. The Cavendish chronicles / Kathryn Douglas. — London : New English Library/Times Mirror, 1981, c1979. — 696p ; 18cm
Originally published: New York : Ballantine, 1979
ISBN 0-450-05154-4 (pbk) : £1.75 B81-19975

Dreadstone, Carl. The werewolf of London / Carl Dreadstone. — London : W.H.Allen, 1978, c1977. — 156p ; 18cm. — (The Classic library of horror) (A Universal book)
Originally published: S.l. : MCA, 1977
ISBN 0-426-19027-0 (pbk) : £0.60 B81-20952

Duane, Diane. The door into fire / Diane Duane. — [London] : Magnum, 1981, c1979. — 304p : 1map ; 18cm
Originally published: New York : Dell, 1979
ISBN 0-417-05850-0 (pbk) : £1.50 B81-28677

Duncan, Lois. Killing Mr Griffin / Lois Duncan. — London : Scholastic, 1981, c1978. — 211p ; 18cm. — (Hippo books)
Originally published: Boston, Mass. : Little Brown, 1978 ; London : Hamilton, 1980. — For adolescents
ISBN 0-590-70070-7 (pbk) : £0.95 B81-34836

Duncan, Lois. Summer of fear / by Lois Duncan. — London : Hamilton, 1981, c1976. — 217p ; 21cm
Originally published: Boston : Little, Brown, c1976
ISBN 0-241-10544-7 : £4.95 B81-07683

Duncan, Robert L.. Brimstone / by Robert L. Duncan. — London : Joseph, 1980. — 310p ; 23cm
Originally published: New York : Morrow, 1980
ISBN 0-7181-1933-9 : £6.50 B81-00286

Durham, John, *1916-*. The horsebreaker / by John Durham. — London : Hale, 1981. — 158pp ; 20cm
ISBN 0-7091-8856-0 : £4.95 B81-19228

Dwyer-Joyce, Alice. The glitter-dust. — Large print ed. — Anstey : Ulverscroft, Feb.1982. — [368]p. — (Ulverscroft large print series : romance)
ISBN 0-7089-0747-4 : £5.00 : CIP entry B81-36943

Edwards, Paula. Bewitching grace / Paula Edwards. — London (47 Bedford Sq., WC1B 3DP) : Silhouette, 1980. — 189p ; 18cm. — (Silhouette romance ; no.23)
ISBN 0-340-26444-6 (pbk) : £0.65 B81-14150

Egan, Judith. Elena : a story of the Russian Revolution / Judith Egan. — London : Collins, 1981, 1981. — 314p : 1map ; 23cm
ISBN 0-00-221679-5 : £6.95 : CIP rev. B81-00449

Egan, Lesley. A choice of crimes / Lesley Egan. — London : Gollancz, 1981, c1980. — 180p ; 21cm
ISBN 0-575-03031-3 : £5.95 B81-26456

Egan, Lesley. Look back on death. — Large print ed. — Leicester : Ulverscroft, Dec.1981. — 1v.
Originally published: Garden City, N.Y. : Doubleday, 1978 ; London : Gollancz, 1979
ISBN 0-7089-0716-4 : £5.00 : CIP entry B81-30409

Ehrlich, Max. Naked beach / Max Ehrlich. — London : Granada, 1981, c1979. — 256p ; 18cm. — (A Mayflower book)
ISBN 0-583-13306-1 (pbk) : £1.50 B81-32187

813′.54[F] — Fiction in English. American writers, *1945- — Texts continuation*

Elegant, Robert S.. Munchu / Robert Elegant. — London : Allen Lane, 1980. — x,560p ; 24cm
ISBN 0-7139-1388-6 : £6.95 B81-05909

Engel, Peter. High gloss / Peter Engel. — [London] : Fontana, 1980, c1979. — 317p ; 18cm
Originally published: New York : St. Martin′s Press, 1979
ISBN 0-00-615928-1 (pbk) : £1.50 B81-01115

Erdman, Paul. The last days of America / Paul E. Erdman. — London : Secker & Warburg, 1981. — 245p ; 23cm
ISBN 0-436-14831-5 : £6.50 : CIP rev.
B81-06618

Erikson, Paul. The money wolves / Paul Erikson. — London : Hamlyn Paperbacks, 1981, c1978. — 346p ; 18cm
Originally published: New York : Morrow, 1978 ; Feltham : Hamlyn, 1980
ISBN 0-600-36397-x (pbk) : £1.50 B81-24750

Estleman, Loren D.. Dr. Jekyll and Mr. Holmes / by John H. Watson, M.D. ; as edited by Loren D. Estleman. — Harmondsworth : Penguin, 1980, c1979 (1981 [printing]). — 252p ; 19cm
Originally published: Garden City, N.Y. : Doubleday, 1979
ISBN 0-14-005665-3 (pbk) : £1.25 B81-26515

Etchison, Dennis. The fog / Dennis Etchison ; based on the motion picture written by John Carpenter and Debra Hill. — [London] : Corgi, 1980. — 180p ; 18cm
ISBN 0-552-11530-4 (pbk) : £1.50 B81-07078

Eulo, Ken. The brownstone / Ken Eulo. — London : Coronet Books, 1981, c1980. — 332p ; 18cm
Originally published: New York : Pocket Books, 1980
ISBN 0-340-26668-6 (pbk) : £1.50 : CIP rev.
B81-12351

Evans, Tabor. Longarm and the highgraders / Tabor Evans. — [London] : Magnum, 1981, c1979. — 234p ; 18cm
Originally published: New York : Jove, 1979
ISBN 0-417-06640-6 (pbk) : £1.25 B81-18255

Evans, Tabor. Longarm and the Nesters / Tabor Evans. — [London] : Magnum, 1981, c1979. — 244p ; 18cm
Originally published: New York : Jove, 1979
ISBN 0-417-06650-3 (pbk) : £1.25 B81-28681

Farmer, Philip José. The dark design / Philip José Farmer. — London : Granada, 1979, c1977 (1980 [printing]). — 464p ; 18cm. — (The Riverworld series ; 3) (Panther science fiction) (A Panther book)
Originally published: New York : Berkeley, 1977
ISBN 0-586-04835-9 (pbk) : £1.50 B81-11205

Farmer, Philip José. Dark is the sun / Philip José Farmer. — London : Granada, 1981. — 400p ; 23cm
Originally published: New York : Ballantine, 1979
ISBN 0-246-11378-2 : £6.95 B81-00287

Farmer, Philip José. The fabulous riverboat / Philip José Farmer. — London : Granada, 1980, c1971. — 252p ; 18cm. — (The Riverworld series ; v.2) (Panther science fiction)
Originally published: New York : Putnam, 1971 ; London : Rapp and Whiting : Deutsch, 1974
ISBN 0-586-03989-9 (pbk) : £1.25 B81-07055

Farmer, Philip José. The magic labyrinth / Philip José Farmer. — London : Granada, 1981, c1980. — 496p ; 18cm. — (The Riverworld series ; 4) (Panther science fiction) (A Panther book)
Originally published: New York : Berkeley Publishing, 1980
ISBN 0-586-05387-5 (pbk) : £1.50 B81-07570

Farmer, Philip José. To your scattered bodies go / Philip José Farmer. — London : Granada, 1974, c1971 (1980 [printing]). — 207p ; 18cm. — (The Riverworld series ; 1) (Panther science fiction) (A Panther book)
Originally published: New York : Putnam, 1971 ; London : Rapp and Whiting : Deutsch, 1973
ISBN 0-586-03939-2 (pbk) : £1.25 B81-11206

Farris, John. Catacombs. — London : Hodder & Stoughton, Jan.1982. — [448]p
ISBN 0-340-27827-7 : £6.95 : CIP entry
B81-34148

Farris, John. Shatter / John Farris. — London : W.H. Allen, 1980 (1981 [printing]). — 283p ; 18cm. — (A Star book)
ISBN 0-352-30761-7 (pbk) : £1.50 B81-20939

Faust, Ron. [The burning sky]. The killing game / Ron Faust. — London : New English Library / Times Mirror, 1981, c1978. — 192p ; 18cm
Originally published: Chicago : Playboy Press, c1978
ISBN 0-450-05003-3 (pbk) : 1.25 B81-07682

Ferguson, Austin. [Random track to Peking]. Random track / Austin Ferguson. — London : Arrow, 1981, c1979. — 251p ; 18cm
Originally published: New York : Morrow, 1979 ; London : Hutchinson, 1980
ISBN 0-09-925440-9 (pbk) : £1.25 B81-11019

Fielding, Joy. Kiss mummy goodbye. — Loughton : Piatkus, Aug.1981. — [288]p
ISBN 0-86188-112-5 : £6.50 : CIP entry
B81-15864

Fish, Robert L.. A gross carriage of justice / Robert L. Fish. — London : Hale, 1981, c1979. — 177p ; 20cm
Originally published: New York : Doubleday, 1979
ISBN 0-7091-8803-x : £5.75 B81-11168

Fish, Robert L.. Pursuit : a novel / Robert L. Fish. — London : Futura, 1979, c1978 (1980 printing). — 379p ; 18cm
Originally published: Garden City : Doubleday, 1978
ISBN 0-7088-1660-6 (pbk) : £1.25 B81-05900

Fisher, David E.. The man you sleep with / David E. Fisher. — London : Quartet, 1981. — 120p ; 23cm. — (Quartet crime)
ISBN 0-7043-2283-8 : £5.95 B81-20286

Fitzhugh, Louise. Nobody′s family is going to change / Louise Fitzhugh. — Basingstoke : Macmillan Education, 1981, c1974. — 156p ; 21cm. — (M books)
Originally published: New York : Farrar, Straus and Giroux, 1974 ; London : Gollancz, 1976. — For adolescents
ISBN 0-333-29450-5 : £1.50 B81-18694

Flanagan, Thomas, *1923-*. The year of the French / Thomas Flanagan. — London : Arrow, 1980, c1979. — 642p ; 18cm
Originally published: London : Macmillan, 1979
ISBN 0-09-923520-x (pbk) : £1.95 B81-16072

Fleming, Thomas. The officers′ wives / Thomas Fleming. — London : W.H. Allen, 1981. — 645p ; 24cm
ISBN 0-491-02925-x : £7.95 B81-35150

Florey, Kitty Burns. Family matters / Kitty Burns Florey. — London : Joseph, 1981, c1979. — 294p ; 23cm
Originally published: New York : Seaview, 1979
ISBN 0-7181-1979-7 : £6.95 B81-05924

Foley, Rae. Where Helen lies / Rae Foley. — Large print ed. — Leicester : Ulverscroft, 1980, c1976. — 306p ; 23cm
Originally published: New York : Dodd, Mead, c1976 ; London : Hale, 1977
ISBN 0-7089-0506-4 : £4.25 : CIP rev.
B80-17976

Forbes, Stanton. The will and last testament of Constance Cobble / Stanton Forbes. — London : Hale, 1980. — 171p ; 20cm
Originally published: Garden City, N.Y. : Doubleday for the Crime Club, 1980
ISBN 0-7091-8656-8 : £5.75 B81-02213

Forrest, Richard, *1932-*. The death at Yew Corner / Richard Forrest. — London : Hale, 1981. — 172p ; 20cm
ISBN 0-7091-9271-1 : £6.25 B81-40532

Foster, Alan Dean. Clash of the Titans : novelization / by Alan Dean Foster ; screenplay by Beverley Cross. — London : Macdonald, 1981. — 223p ; 21cm
ISBN 0-354-04746-9 : £4.95 B81-34867

Foster, Alan Dean. Clash of the titans / novelization by Alan Dean Foster ; screenplay by Beverley Cross. — London : Macdonald Futura, 1981. — 223p,[8]p of plates : col.ill ; 18cm. — (A Futura book)
ISBN 0-7088-2056-5 (pbk) : £1.25 B81-28345

Foster, Alan Dean. Outland / novelization by Alan Dean Foster ; based on the screenplay by Peter Hyams. — London : Sphere, 1981. — 269p,[8]p of plates : ill ; 18cm
ISBN 0-7221-3637-4 (pbk) : £1.50 B81-34807

Foster, Harry, *1916-*. Canbyville / by Harry Foster. — London : Hale, 1980 — 160p ; 20cm
ISBN 0-7091-8467-0 : £4.95 B81-01424

Foster, Harry, *1916-*. The mud wagon / by Harry Foster. — London : Hale, 1981. — 158p ; 20cm
ISBN 0-7091-9292-4 : £4.95 B81-35205

Fowles, Anthony. Rough trade / Anthony Fowles. — [London] : Magnum, 1981. — 256p ; 18cm
ISBN 0-417-06210-9 (pbk) : £1.35 B81-2867

Fox, Charles, *1942-*. The noble enemy / Charles Fox. — London : Granada, 1981, c1980. — 383p ; 23cm
ISBN 0-246-11452-5 : £6.95 B81-1007

Frankel, Sandor. The Aleph solution : a novel / by Sandor Frankel and Webster Mews. — Leighton Buzzard (Glebe Cottage, Glebe House, Station Rd, Cheddington, Leighton Buzzard, Beds. LU7 0SQ) : Melbourne House, c1978. — 212p ; 23cm
Originally published: New York : Stein and Day, 1979
ISBN 0-86161-011-3 : £5.95 B81-0111

Fraser, David, *19---*. Blitz / David Fraser. — London : Pan in association with Macmillan, 1980, c1979. — 558p ; 18cm
Originally published: London : Macmillan, 1979
ISBN 0-330-26168-1 (pbk) : £1.95 B81-0028

Freed, Donald. The spymaster / Donald Freed. — London : Corgi, 1981, c1980. — 447p ; 18cm
Originally published: New York : Arbor, 1980
ISBN 0-552-11715-3 (pbk) : £1.75 B81-3210

Freeman, Cynthia. Come pour the wine : a novel / by Cynthia Freeman. — Lougthon : Piatkus, 1981, c1980. — 390p ; 21cm
£6.95 B81-1985

Freeman, Cynthia. Come pour the wine. — Loughton (17 Brook Rd, Loughton, Essex) : Piatkus, Apr.1981. — [400]p
ISBN 0-86188-095-1 : £6.95 : CIP entry
B81-0760

Freeman, Cynthia. Portraits : a novel / by Cynthia Freeman. — Loughton (Loughton, Essex) : Piatkus, 1980, c1979. — 677p : 1geneal.table ; 21cm
Originally published: New York : Arbor House, 1979
ISBN 0-86188-055-2 : £7.95 : CIP rev.
B80-2251

813'.54[F] — Fiction in English. American writers, *1945- — Texts* *continuation*

Freeman, Cynthia. Portraits : a novel / by Cynthia Freeman. — London : Corgi, 1981, c1979. — 595p ; 18cm
Originally published: New York : Arbor, c1979
ISBN 0-552-11730-7 (pbk) : £1.95 B81-32324

Freeman, Cynthia. A world full of strangers / by Cynthia Freeman. — London : Corgi, 1981, c1975. — 631p ; 18cm
Originally published: London : Bantam, 1976
ISBN 0-552-11775-7 (pbk) : £1.95 B81-35497

French, Michael. Rhythms / Michael French. — London : Hamlyn Paperbacks, 1981, c1980. — 391p ; 18cm
Originally published: Garden City, N.Y. : Doubleday, 1980
ISBN 0-600-20389-1 (pbk) : £1.50 B81-19894

Friedman, Hal. Tunnel / Hal Friedman. — London : Hamlyn Paperbacks, 1981, c1979. — 272p ; 18cm
Originally published: New York : Morrow, 1979
ISBN 0-600-20273-9 (pbk) : £1.35 B81-12492

Friedman, Philip. Termination order. — London : Hodder & Stoughton, Jan.1982. — [256]p. — (Coronet books)
Originally published: New York : Dial Press, 1979 ; London : Hodder & Stoughton, 1980
ISBN 0-340-27545-6 (pbk) : £1.25 : CIP entry B81-34133

Fugate, Stephen E.. Day of the ambushers / Stephen E. Fugate. — London : Hale, 1981, c1979. — 222p ; 20cm
Originally published: New York : Manor Books, 1979
ISBN 0-7091-9081-6 : £4.95 B81-28872

Futch, Ladell J.. Rustlers' justice / Ladell J. Futch. — London : Hale, 1981, c1978. — 159p ; 20cm
Originally published: Canoga Park, Calif. : Major Books, 1976
ISBN 0-7091-8905-2 : £4.95 B81-15294

Gaines, Gharles. Dangler : a novel / by Charles Gaines. — London : Chatto & Windus, 1981, c1980. — 288p ; 21cm
Originally published: New York : Simon and Schuster, 1980
ISBN 0-7011-2560-8 : £6.95 B81-11647

Galloway, David, *1937-*. Melody Jones / David Galloway. — London : Calder, 1980, c1976. — 120p ; 21cm. — (Riverrun writers ; 2)
Originally published: 1976
ISBN 0-7145-3807-8 (cased) : £5.95 : CIP rev.
ISBN 0-7145-3733-0 (pbk) : £2.95 B80-01356

Gangemi, Kenneth. The interceptor pilot / Kenneth Gangemi. — London : Boyars, 1980. — 127p ; 23cm
ISBN 0-7145-2699-1 : £5.95 B81-01117

Garbo, Norman. The spy / Norman Garbo. — London : Star, 1981, c1980. — 272p ; 18cm
Originally published: New York : Norton ; London : W.H. Allen, 1980
ISBN 0-352-30781-1 (pbk) : £1.50 B81-11685

Gardner, John, *1919-*. Freddy's book. — London : Secker & Warburg, Oct.1981. — [186]p
ISBN 0-436-17250-x : £5.95 : CIP entry B81-27421

Gardner, John, *1933-*. Grendel / illustrated by Emil Antonucci. — Harmondsworth : Penguin, 1980, c1971. — 174p : ill ; 19cm
Originally published: New York : Knopf, 1971 ; London : Deutsch, 1972
ISBN 0-14-005820-6 (pbk) : £1.25 B81-10925

Garfield, Brian. The paladin / Brian Garfield. — London : Pan in association with Macmillan, 1981, c1980. — 358p ; 18cm
Originally published: London : Macmillan, 1980
ISBN 0-330-26455-9 (pbk) : £1.75 B81-36696

Garfield, Brian. The paladin : a novel based on fact / by Brian Garfield in collaboration with "Christopher Creighton". — London : Prior, c1981, 1979. — 639p ; 25cm
Originally published: London : Macmillan, 1980. — Published in large print
ISBN 0-86043-583-0 : £7.95 B81-24574

Garland, Nicholas. Buy back the dawn / Nicholas Garland. — [London] : Fontana/Collins, 1981, c1980. — 256p ; 18cm
Originally published: New York : Marek, 1980
ISBN 0-00-615926-5 (pbk) : £1.35 B81-18470

Gatenby, Rosemary. The third identity / Rosemary Gatenby. — London : Hale, 1980, c1979. — 235p ; 20cm
Originally published: New York : Dodd, Mead, 1979
ISBN 0-7091-8681-9 : £5.75 B81-08985

Gentry, Peter. Matanza / Peter Gentry. — London : Arrow, 1980, c1979. — 381p ; 18cm
ISBN 0-09-923730-x (pbk) : £1.75 B81-39152

George, Jean. Julie of the wolves / Jean George ; illustrated by Julek Heller. — Basingstoke : Macmillan Education, 1981, c1972. — 154p : ill ; 21cm. — (M books)
Originally published: New York : Harper and Row, 1919 ; London : Hamilton, 1973. — For adolescents
ISBN 0-333-28408-9 : £1.50 B81-18573

Gerrold, David. Deathbeast / by David Gerrold. — London : Hale, 1981, c1978. — 255p ; 20cm. — (Hale SF)
Originally published: New York : Fawcett, 1978
ISBN 0-7091-9075-1 : £6.25 B81-30075

Gerson, Noel B.. Warhead / Noel B. Gerson. — Loughton : Piatkus, 1980, c1970. — 336p ; 21cm
Originally published: Garden City, N.Y. : Doubleday, 1970
ISBN 0-86188-053-6 : £5.95 : CIP rev. B80-12067

Gidding, Joshua. The old girl / Joshua Giddings [i.e. Gidding]. — South Yarmouth, Mass. : John Curley ; [Long Preston] : Magna [distributor] : c1980. — 522p ; 23cm
Originally published: New York : Holt, Rinehart and Winston, 1980. — Published in large print
ISBN 0-89340-339-3 : £4.95 B81-39299

Gilchrist, Robert. Dragonard rising / Rupert Gilchrist. — London : Corgi, 1979, c1978 (1980 [pinting]). — 251p : ill,1map ; 18cm
Originally published: London : Souvenir Press, 1978
ISBN 0-552-11036-1 (pbk) : £1.50 B81-09314

Gillespie, Robert B.. The crossword mystery / Robert Gillespie. — London : Magnum, 1981, c1979. — 192p : ill ; 18cm
Originally published: London : Constable, 1979
ISBN 0-417-04180-2 (pbk) : £1.35 B81-08424

Gilmore, Christopher Cook. Atlantic City proof / Christopher Cook Gilmour [i.e. Gilmore]. — Harmondsworth : Penguin, 1981, c1978. — 281p ; 18cm
Originally published: New York : Simon & Schuster, 1978 ; London : Gollancz, 1979
ISBN 0-14-005512-6 (pbk) : £1.50 B81-32835

Gilmore, Christopher Cook. Atlantic City Proof / Christopher Cook Gilmore. — Large print ed. — Leicester : Ulverscroft, 1981, c198. — 401p ; 23cm
Originally published: New York : Simon and Schuster, 16978 ; London : Gollancz, 1979
ISBN 0-7089-0683-4 : £5.00 : CIP rev. B81-25889

Gilmour, H. B.. The electronic horseman / H.B. Gilmour. — London : Severn House, 1980, 1979. — 187p ; 21cm
ISBN 0-7278-0623-8 : £5.95 : CIP rev. B80-18891

Gilmour, H. B.. Windows / H.B. Gilmour. — London : Coronet, 1980. — 189p ; 18cm
Originally published: New York : Pocket Books, 1980
ISBN 0-340-25541-2 (pbk) : £1.10 : CIP rev. B80-03852

Gipe, George. Resurrection : a novel / by George Gipe. — London : Granada, 1981, c1980. — 252p ; 18cm. — (A Mayflower book)
"Based on a screenplay by Lewis John Carlino"
ISBN 0-583-13346-0 (pbk) : £1.25 B81-29497

Glass, Frankcina. Marvin and Tige / Frankcina Glass. — [London] : Coronet, 1980, c1977. — 254p ; 18cm
Originally published: New York : St. Martin's Press, 1977 ; London : Hodder and Stoughton, 1978
ISBN 0-340-25957-4 (pbk) : £1.25 : CIP rev. B80-19930

Glass, Isabel. Bedside manners : a novel / by Isabel Glass. — London : W.H. Allen, 1981. — 380p ; 19cm
Originally published: Greenwich, Conn. : Fawcett, 1979
ISBN 0-491-02944-6 : £4.95 B81-26490

Glenn, James. Oregon guns / by James Glenn. — London : Hale, 1981. — 160p ; 20cm
Originally published: London : Gresham, 1966
ISBN 0-7091-8960-5 : £2.95 B81-16002

Gluyas, Constance. Flame of the South / by Constance Gluyas. — London : Hale, 1981, c1979. — 341p ; 21cm
Originally published: U.S. : [s.n.], 1979 ; London : Sphere, 1981
ISBN 0-7091-9247-9 : £6.95 B81-35235

Gluyas, Constance. Flame of the south / Constance Gluyas. — London : Sphere, 1981, c1979. — 342p ; 18cm
Originally published: United States : s.n., 1979
ISBN 0-7221-3912-8 (pbk) : £1.50 B81-11705

Goforth, Ellen. Path of desire / Ellen Goforth. — London (47 Bedford Sq., WC1B 3DP) : Silhouette, 1980. — 188p ; 18cm. — (Silhouette romance ; no.5)
ISBN 0-340-26002-5 (pbk) : £0.65 : CIP rev. B80-12552

Goldberg, Lucianne. Friends in high places / Lucianne Goldberg and Sondra Till Robinson. — London : Pan, 1981, c1979. — 400p ; 18cm
Originally published: New York : R. Marek, 1979 ; London : Macmillan, 1980
ISBN 0-330-26307-2 (pbk) : £1.50 B81-17987

Goldman, James. Myself as witness / James Goldman. — Harmondsworth : Penguin, 1981, c1979. — 381p ; 19cm
Originally published: New York : Random House, 1979 ; London : Hamilton, 1980
ISBN 0-14-005771-4 (pbk) : £1.75 B81-34810

Goldman, William, *1931-*. Tinsel / William Goldman. — London : Pan in association with Macmillan, 1980, c1979. — 349p ; 18cm
Originally published: New York : Delacorte ; London : Macmillan, 1979
ISBN 0-330-26183-5 (pbk) : £1.50 B81-00290

Goldreich, Gloria. Leah's journey / Gloria Holdreich. — London : New English Library, 1979, c1978 (1980 [printing]). — 427p ; 18cm
Originally published: New York : Harcourt Brace Jovanovich, 1978
ISBN 0-450-04571-4 (pbk) : £1.50 B81-06316

Goodrum, Charles A.. Carnage of the realm / Charles A. Goodrum. — South Yarmouth : Curley ; Clitheroe : Magna Print [distributor], c1979. — 338p ; 23cm
Originally published: New York : Crown, 1979. — Published in large print
ISBN 0-89340-265-6 : £5.50 B81-02716

813'.54[F] — Fiction in English. American writers, *1945- — Texts* *continuation*

Goodrum, Charles A.. [Carnage of the realm]. Dead for a penny / by Charles A. Goodrum. — London : Gollancz, 1980, c1979. — 152p ; 21cm
Originally published: New York : Crown, 1979
ISBN 0-575-02909-9 : £5.50 B81-01118

Gordon, Angela. A fabled autumn / by Angela Gordon. — London : Hale, 1981. — 171p ; 20cm
ISBN 0-7091-9138-3 : £5.60 B81-33518

Gordon, Angela. A gentle spring / by Angela Gordon. — London : Hale, 1980. — 172p ; 20cm
ISBN 0-7091-7978-2 : £4.75 B81-00291

Gordon, Mary, *1949-*. The company of women / Mary Gordon. — London : Cape, 1981, c1980. — 291p ; 25cm
ISBN 0-224-01955-4 : £6.50 B81-26478

Gosling, Paula. Loser's blues / Paula Gosling. — London : Macmillan, 1980. — 256p ; 21cm
ISBN 0-333-29459-9 : £5.95 B81-00457

Gosling, Paula. A running duck / Paula Gosling. — Large print ed. — Leicester : Ulverscroft, 1981, c1978. — 368p ; 23cm. — (Ulverscroft large print series)
Originally published: London : Macmillan, 1978
ISBN 0-7089-0618-4 : £5.00 : CIP rev. B81-07432

Gosling, Paula. The zero trap / Paula Gosling. — London : Pan in association with Macmillan, 1980, c1979. — 249p ; 18cm
Originally published: London : Macmillan, 1979
ISBN 0-330-26174-6 (pbk) : £1.25 B81-00458

Gould, Heywood. Fort Apache, the Bronx / Heywood Gould ; based upon a screenplay by Heywood Gould. — London : Sphere, 1981. — 351p ; 18cm
ISBN 0-7221-3970-5 (pbk) : £1.75 B81-28360

Granger, Bill. The November man / Bill Granger. — London : New English Library/Times Mirror, 1981, c1979. — 303p ; 18cm
Originally published: New York : Fawcett, 1979
ISBN 0-450-04679-6 (pbk) : £1.50 B81-19972

Granger, Bill. Public murders / Bill Granger. — London : New English Library, c1980. — 268p ; 23cm
Originally published: United States : Jove, 1980
ISBN 0-450-04854-3 : £5.95 B81-24809

Gray, Vanessa. The lonely earl / Vanessa Gray. — South Yarmouth, Mass. : Curley ; Long Preston : Magna [distributor], [1981]?, c1978. — 535p ; 22cm
Originally published: New York : New American Library, 1978. — Published in large print
ISBN 0-89340-325-3 : Unpriced B81-37091

Gray, Vanessa. The wicked guardian / Vanessa Gray. — South Yarmouth, Mass. : John Curley ; [Long Preston] : Magna [distributor], c1978. — 536p ; 23cm. — (Regency romances)
Originally published: New York : New American Library, 1978. — Published in large print
ISBN 0-89340-326-1 : £4.95 B81-39298

Green, Edith Piñero. Rotten apples / Edith Piñero Green. — South Yarmouth : Curley ; [Bolton by Bowland] : Distributed by Magna Print, c1977. — 552p ; 23cm
Originally published: New York : Dutton, 1977. — Published in large print
ISBN 0-89340-286-9 : £5.00 B81-08023

Green, Edith Piñero. Sneaks / Edith Piñero Green. — South Yarmouth, Mass. : J. Curley ; [Skipton] : Distributed by Magna Print, c1979. — v,514p ; 23cm
Published in large print
ISBN 0-89340-287-7 : £5.75 B81-18295

Greenfield, Irving A.. Tagget / Irving A. Greenfield. — Feltham : Hamlyn, 1981, c1979. — 235p ; 18cm
Originally published: New York : Arbor House, 1979
ISBN 0-600-20326-3 (pbk) : £1.35 B81-24730

Greenleaf, Stephen. Grave error / by Stephen Greenleaf. — London : New English Library, 1981, c1979. — 264p ; 23cm
Originally published: New York : Dial, c1979
ISBN 0-450-04731-8 : £5.95 B81-15422

Greer, Francesca. First fire / Francesca Greer. — London : Sphere, 1980, c1979. — 533p ; 18cm
Originally published: United States : s.n., 1979
ISBN 0-7221-4077-0 (pbk) : £1.75 B81-11722

Grey, Romer Zane. High Valley River ; and, The long trail to nowhere / by Romer Zane Grey. — Hornchurch : Henry, 1980, c1979. — [160]p ; 21cm
ISBN 0-86025-181-0 : £4.95 B81-09680

Grey, Romer Zane. Last stand at Indigo Flats ; and, Last stage to Ballarat / Romer Zane Grey. — Hornchurch : Ian Henry, 1980, c1970. — [142]p ; 21cm
ISBN 0-86025-183-7 : £4.95 B81-11276

Grey, Romer Zane. The other side of the canyon ; and, Showdown at Lone Tree / by Romer Zane Grey. — Hornchurch : Ian Henry, 1980, c1970. — [142]p ; 21cm
ISBN 0-86025-182-9 : £4.95 B81-11277

Grey, Romer Zane. The rider of distant trails : and, The lure of buried gold / by Romer Zane Grey. — Hornchurch : Henry, 1980, c1969. — [184]p : ill ; 21cm
ISBN 0-86025-180-2 : £4.95 B81-09679

Grey, Romer Zane. Siege at forlorn river ; and Heritage of the legion / Romer Zane Grey. — Hornchurch : Henry, 1981, c1972. — 158p ; 21cm
ISBN 0-86025-191-8 : £4.95 B81-38089

Groom, Winston. Better times than these / Winston Groom. — London : Sphere, 1980, c1978. — 477p : 1map ; 18cm
Originally published: New York : Summit, 1978 ; London : Macdonald & Jane's, 1979
ISBN 0-7221-4100-9 (pbk) : £1.75 B81-01119

Gross, Joel. The books of Rachel / Joel Gross. — London : New English Library, 1980, c1979. — 446p : geneal.tables ; 23cm
Originally published: New York : Seaview Books, 1979
ISBN 0-450-04827-6 : £6.50 B81-01120

Gross, Joel. The books of Rachel / Joel Gross. — London : New English Library, 1980, c1979 (1981 [printing]). — 436p ; 18cm
Originally published: New York : Seaview, 1979
ISBN 0-450-05266-4 (pbk) : £1.75 B81-40490

Grumbach, Doris. Chamber music / Doris Grumbach. — London : Sphere, 1981, c1979. — 183p ; 18cm
Originally published: London : Hamilton, 1979
ISBN 0-7221-4115-7 (pbk) : £1.25 B81-35066

Grumbach, Doris. The missing person / Doris Grumbach. — London : Hamish Hamilton, 1981. — 252p ; 23cm
ISBN 0-241-10660-5 : £7.95 : CIP rev. B81-15812

Guest, Judith. Ordinary people / Judith Guest. — [London] : Fontana, 1978, c1976 (1981 [printing]). — 188p ; 18cm
Originally published: New York : Viking, 1976 ; London : Collins, 1977
ISBN 0-00-616360-2 (pbk) : £1.25 B81-11179

Gunn, James E.. The dreamers / James Gunn. — London : Gollancz, 1981, c1980. — 166p ; 21cm
Originally published: New York : Simon and Schuster, c1980
ISBN 0-575-02644-8 : £6.95 B81-14194

Gutcheon, Beth. Still missing / Beth Gutcheon. — London : Joseph, 1981. — 255p ; 23cm
ISBN 0-7181-2066-3 : £6.95 B81-37903

Haase, John. Big red / by John Haase. — London : Secker and Warburg, 1980. — 411p ; 25cm
Originally published: New York : Harper & Row, 1980
ISBN 0-436-19000-1 : £6.50 B81-00293

Halberstam, Michael. The wanting of Levine / Michael Halberstam. — London : Magnum, 1980, c1978. — 458p ; 18cm
Originally published: Philadelphia : Lippincott, 1978
ISBN 0-417-05220 0 (pbk) : £1.50 B81-32578

Hale, Arlene. In love's own fashion / Arlene Hale. — South Yarmouth, Mass. : Curley, c1975 ; [Long Preston] : Magna [distributor]. — 354p ; 23cm
Originally published: New York : New American Library, 1975. — Published in large print
ISBN 0-89340-293-1 : £5.75 B81-18309

Hale, Arlene. The winds of summer / by Arlene Hale. — London : Prior, c1981, 1976. — 375p ; 25cm
Originally published: Boston, Mass. : Little, Brown, 1976. — Published in large print
ISBN 0-86043-588-1 : £6.95 B81-24575

Hallahan, William H.. Keeper of the children / William H. Hallahan. — London : Sphere, 1980, c1978. — 189p ; 18cm
Originally published: New York : Morrow, 1978 ; London : Gollancz, 1979
ISBN 0-7221-4246-3 (pbk) : £1.00 B81-11724

Hallahan, William H.. The trade / William H. Hallahan. — London : Gollancz, 1981. — 324p ; 23cm
ISBN 0-575-03001-1 : £6.95 B81-26455

Halldorson, Phyllis. Temporary bride / Phyllis Halldorson. — [London] : Silhouette, 1981, c1980. — 190p ; 18cm. — (Silhouette romance ; 30)
ISBN 0-340-26580-9 (pbk) : £0.65 : CIP rev. B81-02566

Halldorson, Phyllis. To start again. — London : Hodder & Stoughton, Dec.1981. — [192]p. — (Silhouette romance)
ISBN 0-340-27659-2 (pbk) : £0.65 : CIP entry B81-31472

Halston, Carole. Love legacy. — London : Hodder & Stoughton, Jan.1982. — [192]p. — (Silhouette romance)
ISBN 0-340-27663-0 (pbk) : £0.75 : CIP entry B81-34481

Halston, Carole. Stand-in bride / Carole Halston. — London : Silhouette, 1981. — 188p ; 18cm. — (Silhouette romance ; 62)
ISBN 0-340-27117-5 (pbk) : £0.65 : CIP rev. B81-23917

Hamilton, Virginia. The gathering / Virginia Hamilton. — London : Macrae, 1981. — 179p ; 22cm
ISBN 0-86203-037-4 : £5.25 : CIP rev. B81-0887

813'.54[F] — Fiction in English. American writers, 1945- — Texts *continuation*

Hampson, Anne. Chateau in the palms. — Large print ed. — Bath : Chivers Press, Jan.1982. — [256]p. — (A Seymour book)
Originally published: London : Mills & Boon, 1979
ISBN 0-85119-449-4 : £4.95 : CIP entry B81-33807

Hampson, Anne. The dawn steals softly / Anne Hampson. — London (47 Bedford Sq., WC1B 3DP) : Silhouette, 1980. — 189p ; 18cm. — (Silhouette romance ; no.1)
ISBN 0-340-26404-7 (pbk) : £0.65 : CIP rev. B80-23715

Hampson, Anne. An eagle swooped / by Anne Hampson. — Bolton-by-Bowland : Magna, 1981, c1978. — 296p ; 23cm
Originally published: London : Mills and Boon, 1970. — Published in large print
ISBN 0-86009-303-4 : £5.75 B81-14198

Hampson, Anne. Man of the outback / Anne Hampson. — London (47 Bedford Sq., WC1B 3DP) : Silhouette, 1981, c1980. — 189p ; 18cm. — (Silhouette romance ; no.27)
ISBN 0-340-26457-8 (pbk) : £0.65 B81-14147

Hampson, Anne. Man without a heart / Anne Hampson. — London : Silhouette, 1981, c1980. — 189p ; 18cm. — (Silhouette romance ; 51)
ISBN 0-340-26741-0 (pbk) : £0.65 : CIP rev. B81-18142

Hampson, Anne. Second tomorrow / Anne Hampson. — London (47 Bedford Sq., WC1B 3DP) : Silhouette, 1981, c1980. — 189p ; 18cm. — (Silhouette romance ; no.16)
ISBN 0-340-26120-x (pbk) : £0.65 : CIP rev. B80-23714

Hampson, Anne. Shadow of Apollo. — London : Hodder & Stoughton, Oct.1981. — [192]p. — (Silhouette romance)
ISBN 0-340-27119-1 (pbk) : £0.65 : CIP entry B81-26706

Hampson, Anne. Song of the waves / by Anne Hampson. — Bolton-by-Bowland : Magna, 1981, c1976. — 310p ; 22cm
Originally published: London : Mills & Boon, 1976. — Published in large print
ISBN 0-86009-293-3 : £5.75 B81-14701

Hampson, Anne. Stars over Sarawak / by Anne Hampson. — Bolton-by-Bowland : Magna, 1981, c1974. — 296p ; 23cm
Originally published: London : Mills and Boon, 1974
ISBN 0-86009-315-8 : Unpriced : CIP rev. B81-08890

Hampson, Anne. Stormy masquerade / Anne Hampson. — London (47 Bedford Sq., WC1B 3DP) : Silhouette, 1980. — 189p ; 18cm. — (Silhouette romance ; no.4)
ISBN 0-340-26001-7 (pbk) : £0.65 : CIP rev. B80-12560

Hampson, Anne. Where eagles nest / Anne Hampson. — London : Silhouette, 1981, c1980. — 189p ; 17cm. — (Silhouette romance ; 39)
ISBN 0-340-26729-1 (pbk) : £0.65 : CIP rev. B81-04211

Hansen, Ron. Desperadoes / Ron Hansen. — Large print ed. — Leicester : Ulverscroft, 1981, c1979. — 469p ; 23cm. — (Ulverscroft large print)
Originally published: New York : Knopf, 1979 ; London : Souvenir Press, 1980
ISBN 0-7089-0644-3 : Unpriced B81-26475

Hardwick, Elizabeth. Sleepless nights / Elizabeth Hardwick. — London : Virago, 1980, 1979. — 151p ; 20cm. — (Virago modern classics)
Originally published: New York : Random House ; London : Weidenfeld and Nicolson, 1979
ISBN 0-86068-189-0 (pbk) : £2.50 : CIP rev. B80-22526

Hardy, Laura. Burning memories. — London : Hodder and Stoughton, Dec.1981. — [192]p. — (Silhouette romance)
ISBN 0-340-27656-8 (pbk) : £0.65 : CIP entry B81-31434

Harkleroad, J. D.. Horse thief trail / J.D. Harkleroad. — Large print ed. — Leicester : Ulverscroft, 1981, c1980. — 329p ; 23cm
ISBN 0-7089-0672-9 : £5.00 : CIP rev. B81-19189

Harlow, Enid. Crashing / Enid Harlow. — London : Sphere, 1981, c1980. — 246p ; 18cm
Originally published: New York : St. Martin's Press, 1980
ISBN 0-7221-4491-1 (pbk) : £1.25 B81-24712

Harner, Michael J.. Cannibal / Michael Harner and Alfred Meyer. — London : Methuen Paperbacks, 1981, c1979. — 312p : 1map ; 18cm. — (Magnum books)
Originally published: New York : Morrow, 1979. — Bibliography: p5-7
ISBN 0-417-05990-6 (pbk) : £1.50 B81-18242

Harrington, Joyce. No one knows my name / Joyce Harrington. — London : Macmillan, 1981, c1980. — 250p ; 21cm
Originally published: New York : St Martin's Press, 1980
ISBN 0-333-31990-7 : £5.95 B81-37188

Harrington, R. E.. Death of a patriot / R.E. Harrington. — London : Corgi, 1981, c1979. — 179p ; 18cm
Originally published: London : Secker & Warburg, 1979
ISBN 0-552-11709-9 (pbk) : £1.25 B81-27121

Harrington, R. E.. The doomsday game / R.E. Harrington. — London : Secker & Warburg, 1981. — 221p ; 23cm
ISBN 0-436-19114-8 : £6.50 B81-10131

Harris, Leonard, *1929-*. Don't be no hero / Leonard Harris. — Feltham : Hamlyn, 1979, c1978 (1981 [printing]). — 281p ; 18cm
Originally published: New York : Crown, 1978
ISBN 0-600-34615-3 (pbk) : £1.25 B81-10046

Harris, Marilyn. The Eden Passion / Marilyn Harris. — London : Macdonald Futura, 1981, c1979. — 630p ; 18cm. — (A Troubadour spectacular) (A Troubadour book)
ISBN 0-7107-3002-0 (pbk) : £1.95 B81-15470

Harris, Marilyn. The portent / Marilyn Harris. — London : Magnum, 1981, c1980. — 424p ; 18cm
Originally published: New York : Putnam, 1980
ISBN 0-417-06900-6 (pbk) : £1.75 B81-28661

Harris, Richard, *1926-*. Enemies / Richard Harris. — London : Arrow, 1981, c1979. — 298p ; 18cm
Originally published: New York : R. Marek ; London : Hutchinson, 1979
ISBN 0-09-924010-6 (pbk) : £1.60 B81-11040

Harris, Ruth. The last romantics / Ruth Harris. — London : Eyre Methuen, 1981, c1980. — 368p : col.ill ; 19cm
Originally published: New York : Simon and Schuster, 1980. — Ill on inside cover
ISBN 0-413-48450-5 (cased) : Unpriced
ISBN 0-417-06300-8 (pbk) : £1.50 B81-28673

Harris, Timothy. Kyd for hire / Timothy Harris. — London : Pan, 1981, c1977. — 188p ; 18cm. — (A Thomas Kyd thriller)
Originally published: London : Gollancz, 1977
ISBN 0-330-26097-9 (pbk) : £1.25 B81-37451

Harris, Timothy, *1946-*. Goodnight and goodbye / Timothy Harris. — London : Pan, 1981, c1979. — 218p ; 18cm. — (A Thomas Kyd thriller)
Originally published: New York : Delacorte Press, 1979
ISBN 0-330-26096-0 (pbk) : £1.25 B81-37450

Harrison, Fred, *1916-*. Horse mesa / by Fred Harrison. — London : Hale, 1980. — 160p ; 20cm
ISBN 0-7091-8546-4 : £4.75 B81-00469

Harrison, Harry. One step from earth / Harry Harrison. — London : Arrow, 1975, c1970 (1981 [printing]). — 210p ; 18cm
Originally published: New York : Macmillan, 1970 ; London : Faber, 1972
ISBN 0-09-910460-1 (pbk) : £1.50 B81-29144

Harrison, Harry. The QE2 is missing / Harry Harrison. — London : Macdonald Futura, 1980. — 316p ; 18cm. — (A Futura book)
ISBN 0-7088-1955-9 (pbk) : £1.35 B81-06373

Harrison, Harry. The QE2 is missing / Harry Harrison. — London : Severn House, 1981, c1980. — 316p ; 21cm
Originally published: London : Macdonald Futura, 1980
ISBN 0-7278-0659-9 : £6.95 B81-16031

Harrison, Harry. Wheelworld / Harry Harrison. — London : Granada, 1981. — 188p ; 18cm. — (To the stars ; v.2) (A Panther book) (Granada science fiction)
ISBN 0-586-04968-1 (pbk) : £1.25 B81-10878

Harrison, Jim. Legends of the fall / Jim Harrison. — [Glasgow] : Fontana, 1981, c1979. — 255p ; 18cm
Originally published: New York : Delacorte, 1979 ; London : Collins, 1980
ISBN 0-00-616294-0 (pbk) : £1.50 B81-11068

Harrison, William, *1933-*. Savannah blue / William Harrison. — Feltham : Hamlyn, 1981. — 282p ; 18cm
ISBN 0-600-20459-6 (pbk) : £1.50 B81-41003

Harrowe, Fiona. Fountains of glory / Fiona Harrowe. — London : Magnum, 1981, c1979. — 640p : 1map ; 18cm
Originally published: New York : Fawcett, 1979
ISBN 0-417-06260-5 (pbk) : £1.95 B81-08427

Haskin, Gretchen. An imperial affair / Gretchen Haskin. — London : Gollancz, 1980. — 312p ; 23cm
Originally published: New York : Dial Press, 1980
ISBN 0-575-02872-6 : £6.95 B81-00294

Hassler, Jon. Simon's night / Jon Hassler. — South Yarmouth, Mass. : J. Curley ; [Skipton] : Distributed by Magna Print, c1979. — 559p ; 23cm
Originally published: New York : Atheneum ; London : Deutsch, 1979. — Published in large print
ISBN 0-89340-306-7 : £5.75 B81-18298

Hastings, Brooke. Desert fire / Brooke Hastings. — London : Silhouette, 1981,c1980. — 189p ; 18cm. — (Silhouette romance ; no.43)
ISBN 0-340-26733-x (pbk) : £0.65 : CIP rev. B81-10474

Hastings, Brooke. Innocent fire / Brooke Hastings. — London (47 Bedford Sq., WC1B 3DP) : Silhouette, 1980. — 190p ; 18cm. — (Silhouette romance ; no.26)
ISBN 0-340-26447-0 (pbk) : £0.65 B81-14148

Hastings, Brooke. Island conquest. — London : Hodder & Stoughton, Oct.1981. — [192]p. — (Silhouette romance)
ISBN 0-340-27122-1 (pbk) : £0.65 : CIP entry B81-26776

Hastings, Brooke. Playing for keeps / Brooke Hastings. — [London] : Silhouette, 1981, c1980. — 189p ; 18cm. — (Silhouette romance ; no.13)
ISBN 0-340-26010-6 (pbk) : £0.65 : CIP rev. B80-19934

813′.54[F] — Fiction in English. American writers, *1945- — Texts continuation*

Hautzig, Deborah. Second star to the right / Deborah Hautzig. — London : Julia MacRae Books, 1981. — 151p ; 23cm
Originally published: New York : Greenwillow Books, 1981
ISBN 0-86203-052-8 : £4.95 : CIP rev. B81-20461

Hayes, Raphael. Adventuring / Raphael Hayes. — London : Hale, 1981. — 192p ; 20cm
Originally published: New York : Jones, 1979
ISBN 0-7091-8762-9 : £4.95 B81-08652

Healy, Letitia. Summer storm / Letitia Healy. — London (47 Bedford Sq., WC1B 3DP) : Silhouette, 1980. — 189p ; 18cm. — (Silhouette romance ; no.24)
ISBN 0-340-26445-4 (pbk) : £0.65 B81-14151

Heinemann, Gisella. Cutting it! / Gisella Heinemann. — London : Star, 1981, c1979. — 230p ; 18cm
Originally published: New York : Dial Press 1979
ISBN 0-352-30772-2 (pbk) : £1.50 B81-11689

Heinlein, Robert A.. Citizen of the Galaxy / Robert A. Heinlein. — Harmondsworth : Penguin, 1981, c1957. — 262p ; 19cm. — (Penguin science fiction)
Originally published: New York : Scribner, 1957 ; London : Gollancz, 1969
ISBN 0-14-005749-8 (pbk) : £1.50 B81-34760

Heinlein, Robert A.. [A Heinlein triad]. The puppet masters ; Waldo & Magic inc. / Robert A. Heinlein. — London : New English Library, 1981. — 429p ; 23cm
Originally published: London : Gollancz, 1966. — The puppet masters originally published: Garden City, N.Y. : Doubleday, 1951
ISBN 0-450-04805-5 : £7.95 B81-24806

Heinlein, Robert A.. The number of the beast / Robert A. Heinlein. — London : New English Library, 1981, c1980. — 555p ; 18cm
ISBN 0-450-05127-7 (pbk) : £2.25 B81-15387

Heinlein, Robert A.. Revolt in 2100 / Robert A. Heinlein. — London : New English Library, 1972 (1981 [printing]). — 207p ; 23cm
Originally published: Chicago : Shasta, 1953 ; London : Gollancz, 1964
ISBN 0-450-04802-0 : £5.95 B81-24807

Henry, Will. The gates of the mountains / by Will Henry. — Toronto ; London : Bantam, 1967, c1963 (1979 printing). — 245p : 1map ; 18cm
Originally published: New York : Random House, 1963
ISBN 0-553-12565-6 (pbk) : £0.95 B81-38665

Herbert, Frank. God emperor of Dune / by Frank Herbert. — London : Gollancz, 1981. — 349p ; 23cm
ISBN 0-575-02976-5 : £6.95 B81-19895

Herman, Maxine. Forced feedings / Maxine Herman. — London : Hamlyn Paperbacks, 1980, c1979. — 300p ; 18cm
Originally published: New York : M. Evans, 1979
ISBN 0-600-20100-7 (pbk) : £1.50 B81-02251

Herzog, Arthur. Aries rising / Arthur Herzog. — London : Heinemann, 1981, c1980. — 314p ; 24cm
Originally published: New York: R. Marek, 1980
ISBN 0-434-32769-7 : £6.95 B81-15768

Higgins, George V.. Kennedy for the defense / George V. Higgins. — London : Secker & Warburg, 1980. — 225p ; 23cm
ISBN 0-436-19587-9 : £5.95 B81-03389

Higgins, George V.. The rat on fire / George V. Higgins. — London : Secker & Warburg, 1981. — 183p ; 22cm
ISBN 0-436-19588-7 : £5.95 B81-23193

Highsmith, Patricia. The black house / Patricia Highsmith. — London : Heinemann, 1981. — 258p ; 23cm
ISBN 0-434-33518-5 : £6.95 B81-39294

Highsmith, Patricia. The boy who followed Ripley / Patricia Highsmith. — Harmondsworth : Penguin, 1981, c1980. — 335p ; 18cm
Originally published: London : Heinemann, 1980
ISBN 0-14-005739-0 (pbk) : £1.75 B81-18516

Highsmith, Patricia. A dog's ransom / Patricia Highsmith. — Harmondsworth : Penguin, 1975, c1972 (1980 [printing]). — 255p ; 18cm. — (Penguin crime fiction)
Originally published: London : Heinemann, 1972
ISBN 0-14-003944-9 (pbk) : £1.25 B81-01121

Highsmith, Patricia. Edith's diary / Patricia Highsmith. — Harmondsworth : Penguin, 1980, c1977. — 317p ; 18cm
Originally published: London : Heinemann, 1977
ISBN 0-14-004802-2 (pbk) : £1.50 B81-01122

Highsmith, Patricia. Strangers on a train / Patricia Highsmith. — Harmondsworth : Penguin, 1974, c1950 (1980 [printing]). — 255p ; 18cm. — (Penguin crime fiction)
Originally published: New York : Harper, 1950 ; London : Cresset, 1951
ISBN 0-14-003796-9 (pbk) : £1.25 B81-01123

Highsmith, Patricia. A suspension of mercy / Patricia Highsmith. — Harmondsworth : Penguin, 1972, c1965 (1980 [printing]). — 204p ; 18cm. — (Penguin crime fiction)
Originally published: London : Heinemann, 1965
ISBN 0-14-003470-6 (pbk) : £1.25 B81-01124

Hill, Fiona. The autumn rose / Fiona Hill. — London : Methuen Paperbacks, 1981, c1978. — 255p ; 18cm. — (Magnum books)
Originally published: New York : Putnam, 1978 ; London : Eyre Methuen, 1980
ISBN 0-417-05030-5 (pbk) : £1.50 B81-18245

Hill, Heather. Green paradise / Heather Hill. — London : Silhouette, 1981. — 188p ; 18cm. — (Silhouette romance ; 60)
ISBN 0-340-27115-9 (pbk) : £0.65 : CIP rev. B81-23935

Hill, Roger, *1916-*. Navajo country / Roger Hill. — London : Hale, 1980. — 155p ; 20cm
ISBN 0-7091-8561-8 : £4.95 B81-01437

Hill, Roger, *1916-*. Round-up / by Roger Hill. — London : Hale, 1981. — 160p ; 20cm
ISBN 0-7091-9290-8 : £4.95 B81-24843

Hill, Ruth Beebe. Hanta Yo / Ruth Beebe Hill. — New York : Doubleday ; London : Distributed by Windward, 1979. — 834p : 2geneal.tables ; 25cm
Geneal.tables on lining paper
ISBN 0-385-13554-8 : Unpriced B81-11688

Hilton, Benjamin. Undercover deputy / Benjamin Hilton. — London : Hale, 1981, c1976. — 160p ; 20cm
Originally published: Canoga Park, Calif. : Major Books, 1976
ISBN 0-7091-8908-7 : £4.95 B81-17551

Hinton, S. E.. Tex / S.E. Hinton. — London : Fontana, 1981, c1979. — 194p ; 18cm
Originally published: New York : Delacorte, 1979 ; London : Gollancz, 1980. — For adolescents
ISBN 0-00-671763-2 (pbk) : £1.00 B81-37438

Hirschfeld, Burt. The Ewings of Dallas : a novel / by Burt Hirschfeld ; based on the series created by David Jacobs and on the teleplays written by Rena Down... [et al.]. — [London] : Corgi, 1980. — 275p ;
ISBN 0-552-11606-8 (pbk) : £1.35 B81-06401

Hirschfeld, Burt. The Ewings of Dallas : a novel / by Burt Hirschfeld ; based on the series created by David Jacobs and on the teleplays written by Rena Down ... [et al.]. — London : Severn House, 1981 c1980. — 275p ; 21cm
ISBN 0-7278-0677-7 : £6.50 B81-09865

Hirschfeld, Burt. The women of Dallas : a novel by Burt Hirschfeld / based on the series created by David Jacobs and the teleplays written by Rena Down ... [et al.]. — London : Corgi, 1981, c1980. — 279p ; 18cm
ISBN 0-552-11621-1 (pbk) : £1.35 B81-10964

Hirschfeld, Burt. The women of Dallas : a novel / by Burt Hirschfeld ; based on the series created by David Jacobs and on the teleplays written by Loraine Despres ... [et al.]. — London : Severn House, 1981. — 279p ; 21cm
ISBN 0-7278-0700-5 : £6.95 : CIP rev. B81-13519

Hoban, Russell. Riddley Walker / Russell Hoban. — London : Cape, 1980. — 220p : 1map ; 23cm
ISBN 0-224-01851-5 : £5.95 : CIP rev. B80-21069

Hoffman, Lee. The land killer / Lee Hoffman. — London : Hale, 1981, c1978. — 186p ; 20cm
Originally published: Garden City, N.Y. : Doubleday, 1978
ISBN 0-7091-7571-x : £4.95 B81-17550

Hoffman, Lee. Nothing but a drifter / Lee Hoffman. — London : Hale, 1980, c1976. — 187p ; 20cm
Originally published: Garden City, N.Y. : Doubleday, 1976
ISBN 0-7091-7538-8 : £4.75 B81-00295

Hoffman, Lee. The Yarborough brand / Lee Hoffman. — London : Hale, 1981, c1968. — 191p ; 20cm
ISBN 0-7091-7782-8 : £4.95 B81-37320

Hogan, Ray. The proving gun / Ray Hogan. — London : Prior, 1981, c1975. — 252p ; 25cm
Originally published: Garden City, N.Y. : Doubleday, 1975. — Pubished in large print
ISBN 0-86043-587-3 : £4.95 B81-24368

Holland, Cecelia. City of God / Cecelia Holland. — London : Magnum, 1981, c1979. — 273p ; 18cm
Originally published: London : Gollancz, 1979
ISBN 0-417-05210-3 (pbk) : £1.50 B81-28654

Holland, Cecilia. Home ground / Cecilia Holland. — London : Gollancz, 1981. — 371p ; 23cm
ISBN 0-575-02990-0 : £7.95 B81-32934

Holland, Isabelle. Counterpoint / Isabelle Holland. — London : Collins, 1981, c1980. — 303p ; 22cm
Originally published: New York : Rawson, 1980
ISBN 0-00-222071-7 : £6.95 B81-12931

Holland, Isabelle. Tower Abbey / Isabelle Holland. — [London] : Fontana, 1980, c1978. — 288p ; 18cm
Originally published: New York : Rawson, 1978 ; London : Collins, 1979
ISBN 0-00-616125-1 (pbk) : £1.35 B81-01125

Holland, Isabelle. Tower Abbey / Isabelle Holland. — Large print ed. — Leicester : Ulverscroft, 1981, c1978. — 481p ; 23cm. — (Ulverscroft large print series)
Originally published: New York : Rawson Associates, 1978 ; London : Collins, 1979
ISBN 0-7089-0610-9 : £5.00 : CIP rev. B81-02115

Holzer, Hans. The Amityville curse / Hans Holzer. — London : Macdonald Futura, 1981. — 208p ; 18cm
ISBN 0-7088-2089-1 (pbk) : £1.25 B81-32778

813'.54[F] — Fiction in English. American writers, *1945- — Texts* *continuation*

Hopkins, Robert Sydney. Riviera : a novel about the Cannes Film Festival / Robert Sydney Hopkins. — London : Arrow, 1981. — 348p ; 18cm
ISBN 0-09-925410-7 (pbk) : £1.60 B81-16012

Horner, Lance. Falconhurst fancy / Lance Horner and Kyle Onstott. — London : Pan, 1969, c1966 (1981 [printing]). — 379p ; 18cm
Originally published: Greenwich, Conn. : Fawcett, 1966 ; London : W.H. Allen, 1967
ISBN 0-330-02269-5 (pbk) : £1.75 B81-40084

Hoskins, Robert. Legacy of the stars / Robert Hoskins. — London : Hale, 1981, c1979. — 169p ; 20cm. — (Hale SF)
ISBN 0-7091-9358-0 : £6.25 B81-37454

Houston, Will. Night of the outlaws / by Will Houston. — London : Hale, 1981. — 159p ; 20cm
Originally published: London : Gresham, 1966
ISBN 0-7091-8962-1 : £2.95 B81-16004

Howard, Clark. The wardens / Clark Howard. — London : New English Library, 1980, c1979 (1981 [printing]). — 416p ; 18cm
Originally published: New York : Marek, 1979
ISBN 0-450-04942-6 (pbk) : £1.75 B81-14308

Howard, Joseph. Damien-omen II / Joseph Howard ; from the screenplay of Stanley Mann and Michael Hodges. — London : Macdonald Futura, 1978 (1979 [printing]). — 192p ; 18cm
ISBN 0-7088-1358-5 (pbk) : £0.75 B81-40951

Hunt, John, *1916-*. Guns of revenge / by John Hunt. — London : Hale, 1981, c1963. — 160p ; 20cm
Originally published: London : Gresham, 1963
ISBN 0-7091-9464-1 : £3.25 B81-37294

Hunt, John, *1916-*. Shepler's Spring / by John Hunt. — London : Hale, 1981. — 159p ; 20cm
ISBN 0-7091-8691-6 : £4.95 B81-08638

Hunter, Elizabeth. Written in the stars. — London : Hodder and Stoughton, Feb.1982. — [192]p. — (Silhouette romance)
ISBN 0-340-27671-1 (pbk) : £0.75 : CIP entry B81-38313

Hunter, Evan. Love, dad : a novel / Evan Hunter. — London : Joseph, 1981. — 407p ; 23cm
ISBN 0-7181-2040-x : £7.50 B81-33564

Hunter, Jack D.. The blood order / Jack D. Hunter. — London : Corgi, 1981, c1979. — 321p ; 18cm
Originally published: New York : Times Books, 1979 ; London : Sidgwick and Jackson, 1980
ISBN 0-552-11662-9 (pbk) : £1.25 B81-18673

Hunter, Jack D.. The Blue Max / Jack D. Hunter. — [London] : Corgi, 1966, c1964 (1981 [printing]). — 280p ; 18cm
Originally published: New York : Dutton, 1964 ; London : Muller, 1965
ISBN 0-552-11672-6 (pbk) : £0.95 B81-18550

Hunter, Jack D.. The terror alliance / Jack D. Hunter. — London : Severn House, 1981, c1980. — 318p ; 21cm
ISBN 0-7278-0704-8 : £6.95 : CIP rev. B81-07598

Hunter, Mary Vann. Sassafras / Mary Vann Hunter. — London : Hamilton, 1981, c1980. — 282p ; 23cm
Originally published: New York : NAL, 1980
ISBN 0-241-10519-6 : £7.95 : CIP rev. B81-10434

Hyams, Joe. The pool / Joe Hyams. — London : Sphere, 1981, c1978. — 286p ; 18cm
Originally published: New York : Seaview Books, 1978
ISBN 0-7221-4855-0 (pbk) : £1.50 B81-20244

Ingalls, Rachel. Mrs Caliban. — London : Faber & Faber, Jan.1982. — [128]p
ISBN 0-571-11826-7 : £6.50 : CIP entry B81-33791

Irving, John. The Hotel New Hampshire. — London : Cape, Oct.1981. — [428]p
ISBN 0-224-01961-9 : £6.95 : CIP entry B81-28104

Isaacs, Susan, *1943-*. Close relations / Susan Isaacs. — London : Macdonald Futura, 1981. — 270p ; 25cm
ISBN 0-354-04609-8 : £6.95 B81-03536

Ives, John. The Marchand woman / John Ives. — London : Pan in association with Macmillan, 1981, c1979. — 270p ; 18cm
Originally published: New York : Macmillan, 1979 ; London : Macmillan, 1980
ISBN 0-330-26252-1 (pbk) : £1.25 B81-09746

Jackson, Jon A.. The blind pig / Jon A. Jackson. — London : Hale, 1980, c1978. — 228p ; 20cm
Originally published: New York : Random House, c1979
ISBN 0-7091-8576-6 : £5.75 B81-01126

Jaffe, Rona. Mazes and monsters. — London : Hodder & Stoughton, Feb.1982. — [336]p
ISBN 0-340-27820-x : £6.95 : CIP entry B81-35685

Jahn, Michael. Shearwater / Michael Jahn. — Feltham : Hamlyn, 1980. — 153p ; 18cm
ISBN 0-600-20184-8 (pbk) : £1.00 B81-02752

James, Stephanie. A passionate business. — London : Hodder and Stoughton, Feb.1982. — [192]p. — (Silhouette romance)
ISBN 0-340-27669-x (pbk) : £0.75 : CIP entry B81-38311

James, William M.. Fool's gold / William M. James. — London : New English Library, 1981, c1978. — 155p ; 18cm. — (Apache ; no.12)
Originally published: New York : Pinnacle Books, 1978
ISBN 0-450-05071-8 (pbk) : £1.00 B81-09565

Jennings, Gary. Aztec / Gary Jennings. — London : Macdonald, 1981, c1980. — 754p : maps,1plan ; 24cm
Originally published: New York : Atheneum, 1980. — Maps on lining papers
ISBN 0-354-04635-7 : £7.95 B81-28371

Jessup, Richard. Threat / by Richard Jessup. — London : Gollancz, 1981. — 256p ; 21cm
ISBN 0-575-03034-8 : £6.95 B81-32936

John, Nancy. Outback summer. — London : Hodder & Stoughton, Jan.1982. — [192]p. — (Silhouette romance)
ISBN 0-340-27665-7 (pbk) : £0.75 : CIP entry B81-34484

Johnson, Barbara Ferry. Homeward winds the river / Barbara Ferry Johnson. — London : Sphere, 1980, c1979. — 471p ; 18cm
Originally published: United States : s.n., 1979
ISBN 0-7221-5070-9 (pbk) : £1.60 B81-11721

Johnson, Diane. The shadow knows / Diane Johnson. — [St Albans] : Triad Paperbacks, 1980, c1974. — 277p ; 18cm
Originally published: New York : Knopf, 1974 ; London : Bodley Head, 1975
ISBN 0-586-05179-1 (pbk) : £1.50 B81-07084

Johnson, William Oscar. The zero factor / William Oscar Johnson. — London : Severn House, 1980. — 330p ; 21cm
ISBN 0-7278-0622-x : £6.95 : CIP rev. B80-18894

Johnston, Velda. The hour before midnight : a novel of suspense / Velda Johnston. — London : W.H. Allen, 1981, c1978. — 209p ; 21cm
Originally published: New York : Dodd, Mead, 1978
ISBN 0-491-02943-8 : £5.95 B81-03491

Johnston, Velda. The people from the sea / Velda Johnston. — Oxford : Prior, 1981, c1979. — 374p ; 25cm
Originally published: New York : Dodd, Mead, 1979. — Published in large print
ISBN 0-86043-602-0 : £5.95 B81-34863

Johnston, Velda. The Silver Dolphin / Velda Johnston. — London : Prior, 1981, c1979. — 400p ; 25cm
Originally published: New York : Dodd, Mead, 1979. — Published in large print
ISBN 0-86043-603-9 : £6.50 B81-32764

Jones, Douglas C.. [Winding Stair]. The Winding Stair massacre / Douglas C. Jones. — London : Allen & Unwin, 1980, c1979. — 277p : ill,1map ; 23cm
Originally published: New York : Holt, Rinehart and Winston, 1979. — Maps on lining papers
ISBN 0-04-823180-0 : £5.95 : CIP rev. B80-10806

Jones, James, *1921-*. From here to eternity / James Jones. — Bath : Chivers, 1980. — 766p ; 23cm. — (A New Portway book)
Originally published: London : Collins, 1952
ISBN 0-86220-504-2 : £6.95 : CIP rev. B80-19938

Jong, Erica. Fanny : being the true history of the adventures of Fanny Hackabout-Jones : a novel / by Erica Jong. — London : Granada, [1980]. — 496p ; 24cm
ISBN 0-246-11427-4 : £6.95 B81-02998

Joseph, Ronald S.. The power / Ronald S. Joseph. — London : Magnum, 1981, c1978. — 462p ; 18cm
Originally published: New York : Warner Books, 1979
ISBN 0-417-05320-7 (pbk) : £1.95 B81-08429

Kahn, Steve. NY 10022 / Steve Kahn. — London : Coronet, 1980, c1979. — 311p ; 18cm
Originally published: New York : Pocket Books, 1979
ISBN 0-340-25539-0 (pbk) : £1.50 : CIP rev. B80-10285

Kallen, Lucille. C.B. Greenfield : the Tanglewood murder / Lucille Kallen. — London : Collins, 1980. — 195p ; 21cm. — (The Crime Club)
ISBN 0-00-231843-1 : £5.25 B81-01127

Kamarck, Lawrence. Informed sources / Lawrence Kamarck. — [London] : Fontana, 1981, c1979. — 175p ; 18cm
Originally published: New York : Dial, 1979
ISBN 0-00-615973-7 (pbk) : £1.25 B81-15530

Kaminsky, Stuart M.. Bullet for a star / by Stuart M. Kaminsky. — London : Severn House, 1981, c1977. — 188p ; 21cm. — ([A Toby Peters mystery])
Originally published: New York : St. Martin's Press, 1977
ISBN 0-7278-0701-3 : £6.95 : CIP rev. B81-07597

Kaminsky, Stuart M.. The Howard Hughes affair / by Stuart M. Kaminsky. — London : Severn House, 1980, c1979. — 207p ; 21cm
Originally published: New York : St Martin's Press, 1979
ISBN 0-7278-0604-1 : £5.50 : CIP rev. B80-18895

Kaplan, Andrew. Hour of the assassins / Andrew Kaplan. — Rev. ed. — London : Fontana, 1981. — 287p ; 18cm
Previous ed.: New York : Dell, 1980
ISBN 0-00-616100-6 (pbk) : £1.50 B81-36836

813'.54[F] — Fiction in English. American writers, *1945- — Texts continuation*

Kastle, Herbert. Dirty movies / Herbert Kastle. — London : Granada, 1980, c1979. — 459p ; 18cm. — (A Mayflower book)
Originally published: London : W.H. Allen, 1979
ISBN 0-583-13155-7 (pbk) : £1.50 B81-00296

Kastle, Herbert. Sunset people / Herbert Kastle. — London : W.H. Allen, 1980. — 368p ; 22cm
ISBN 0-491-02802-4 : £7.95 B81-01128

Katz, William. Ghostflight / William Katz. — London : Severn House, 1981, c1980. — 362p ; 21cm
ISBN 0-7278-0546-0 : £6.95 : CIP rev. B81-04368

Katz, William. Visions of terror / William Katz. — London : Arrow, 1981. — 223p ; 18cm
ISBN 0-09-924730-5 (pbk) : £1.25 B81-03373

Kaye, Marvin. The incredible umbrella / Marvin Kaye. — London : Hale, 1980, c1979. — 217p ; 21cm
Originally published: Garden City, N.Y. : Doubleday, 1979
ISBN 0-7091-8439-5 : £5.50 B81-08358

Kemelman, Harry. Monday the rabbi took off / Harry Kemelman. — Harmondsworth : Penguin, 1974, c 1972 (1981 [printing]). — 283p ; 19cm
Originally published: Greenwich, Conn. : Fawcett, 1973
ISBN 0-14-003734-9 (pbk) : £1.25 B81-27204

Kemelman, Harry. Tuesday the rabbi saw red / Harry Kemelman. — Harmondsworth : Penguin, 1977, c1973 (1981 [printing]). — 266p ; 19cm
Originally published: New York : A. Fields; London : Hutchinson, 1974
ISBN 0-14-004249-0 (pbk) : £1.25 B81-30948

Kemelman, Harry. Wednesday the Rabbi got wet / Harry Kemelman. — Harmondsworth : Penguin, 1981, c1976. — 265p ; 19cm. — (Penguin crime fiction)
Originally published: New York : Morrow ; London : Hutchinson, 1976
ISBN 0-14-004706-9 (pbk) : £1.75 B81-26503

Kendall, Carol. The Firelings / Carol Kendall. — London : Bodley Head, 1981. — 255p : ill,1map ; 20cm
ISBN 0-370-30401-2 (pbk) : £3.95 : CIP rev. B81-05171

Kendall, Paul Murray. My brother Chilperic : a chronicle of the Long-Haired Kings / Paul Murray Kendall. — London : Allen & Unwin, 1979. — xii,234p : 1map,geneal.tables ; 23cm
Geneal.tables on lining papers
ISBN 0-04-823161-4 : £5.95 : CIP rev. B79-15630

Kennedy, Raymond. Columbine / Raymond Kennedy. — London : Collins, 1981. — 377p ; 22cm
ISBN 0-00-222142-x : £7.95 B81-23201

Kerouac, Jack. The Dharma bums / Jack Kerouac. — London : Granada, 1972, c1958 (1980 [printing]). — 175p ; 18cm. — (A Panther book)
Originally published: New York : Viking Press, 1958 ; London : Deutsch, 1959
ISBN 0-586-03771-3 (pbk) : £1.25 B81-01129

Kerouac, Jack. On the road / Jack Kerouac. — Harmondsworth : Penguin, 1972, c1957 (1980 [printing]). — 290p ; 19cm
Originally published: New York : Viking, 1957 ; London : Deutsch, 1958
ISBN 0-14-003192-8 (pbk) : £1.25 B81-02830

Ketchum, Jack. Open range / by Jack Ketchum. — London : Hale, 1981. — 159p ; 20cm
ISBN 0-7091-9338-6 : £4.95 B81-37315

Keyes, Daniel. The fifth Sally / Daniel Keyes. — London : Hale, 1981, c1980. — 278p ; 24cm
Originally published: Boston, Mass. : Houghton Mifflin, 1980
ISBN 0-7091-8992-3 : £6.75 B81-27302

Kidwell, Catherine. The woman I am / Catherine Kidwell. — London : Sphere, 1981,c1979. — 218p ; 18cm
ISBN 0-7221-5216-7 (pbk) : £1.25 B81-19692

Kienzle, William. Death wears a red hat. — Sevenoaks : Hodder & Stoughton, June 1981. — [288]p
ISBN 0-340-26742-9 (pbk) : £1.50 : CIP entry B81-12347

Kienzle, William X.. Death wears a red hat / William X. Kienzle. — Large print ed. — Leicester : Ulverscroft, 1981, c1980. — 552p ; 23cm. — (Ulverscroft large print)
Originally published: London : Hodder & Stoughton, 1980
ISBN 0-7089-0647-8 : £5.00 B81-28577

Kienzle, William X.. Mind over murder / William X. Kienzle. — London : Hodder, c1981. — v,296p ; 24cm
ISBN 0-340-26406-3 : £6.95 : CIP rev. B81-13493

Kilgore, John. Topar Rim. — Large print ed. — Bath : Chivers Press, Feb.1982. — [248]p. — (A Lythway book)
Originally published: London : Hale, 1979
ISBN 0-85119-785-x : £6.90 : CIP entry B81-35861

King, Frank. Night vision / Frank King. — London : Sphere, 1980, c1979. — 244p ; 18cm
Originally published: New York : Marek, 1979
ISBN 0-7221-5258-2 (pbk) : £1.25 B81-11729

King, Stephen, *1947-*. Firestarter / Stephen King. — London : Macdonald Futura, 1980. — 428p ; 24cm
ISBN 0-354-04525-3 : £6.50 B81-00297

King, Stephen, *1947-*. Firestarter / Stephen King. — London : Macdonald Futura, 1980 (1981 [printing]). — 510p ; 18cm. — (A Futura book)
ISBN 0-7088-2101-4 (pbk) : £1.95 B81-40955

King, Tabitha. Small world. — London : New English Library, Feb.1982. — [240]p
Originally published: New York : Macmillan, 1981
ISBN 0-450-05368-7 (pbk) : £1.75 : CIP entry B81-36201

Kirsch, Robert. Casino / Robert Kirsch. — London : W.H. Allen, 1981, c1979. — 303p ; 18cm. — (A Star book)
Originally published: Secaucus, N.J. : L. Stuart, 1979 ; London : W.H. Allen, 1980
ISBN 0-352-30841-9 (pbk) : £1.60 B81-28553

Klein, Edward. The parachutists / Edward Klein. — London : Gollancz, 1981. — 392p ; 23cm
ISBN 0-575-02991-9 : £6.95 B81-36829

Klein, Elinov. Dazzle / Elinor Klein and Dora Landey. — London : Macdonald Futura, 1980 (1981 [printing]). — 412p ; 18cm. — (A Futura book)
Originally published: New York : Putnam ; London : Bodley Head, 1980
ISBN 0-7088-1880-3 (pbk) : £1.75 B81-24426

Klein, Norma. Love is one of the choices / Norma Klein. — London : Macdonald Futura, 1981, c1978. — 251p ; 18cm. — (A Futura Book)
Originally published: New York : Dial Press, 1978
ISBN 0-7088-1984-2 (pbk) : £1.25 B81-15643

Knight, Spencer. Revenge of the gambler / Spencer Knight. — London : Hale, 1980, c1979. — 190p ; 20cm
Originally published: New York : Manor Books, 1979
ISBN 0-7091-8547-2 : £4.75 B81-00298

Kohan, Rhea. Hand-me-downs / Rhea Kohan. — London : Secker & Warburg, 1980. — 373p ; 22cm
Originally published: New York : Random House, 1980
ISBN 0-436-23580-3 : £6.95 B81-02458

Konrad, Evelyn. Indiscretions / Evelyn Konrad. — London : Collins, 1979. — 255p ; 22cm
ISBN 0-00-222291-4 : £5.25 B81-12195

Konrad, Evelyn. Indiscretions / Evelyn Konrad. — London : Collins : Fontana, 1981, c1979. — 318p ; 18cm
Originally published: New York : Dial Press ; London : Collins, 1979
ISBN 0-00-616262-2 (pbk) : £1.35 B81-10212

Koontz, Dean R.. A darkness in my soul / Dean R. Koontz. — London : Dobson, 1979, c1972. — 124p ; 21cm
ISBN 0-234-72108-1 : £4.25 B81-02604

Koontz, Dean R.. Whispers / by Dean R. Koontz. — London : W.H. Allen, 1981. — 444p ; 24cm
Originally published: New York : Putnam, 1980
ISBN 0-491-02904-7 : £7.95 B81-26486

Kotzwinkle, William. Fata morgana / William Kotzwinkle. — London : Corgi, 1979, c1977. — 173p : ill ; 18cm
Originally published: London : Hutchinson, 1977
ISBN 0-552-10897-9 (pbk) : £0.85 B81-09306

Krantz, Judith. Princess Daisy / Judith Krantz. — [London] : Corgi, 1981, c1980. — 494p ; 18cm
Originally published: New York : Crown ; London : Sidgwick and Jackson, 1980
ISBN 0-552-11660-2 (pbk) : £1.75 B81-16060

Kronsberg, Jeremy Joe. Every which way but loose / Jeremy Joe Kronsberg. — London : Star, 1980. — 191p ; 18cm
Originally published: London : Hale, 1980
ISBN 0-352-30795-1 (pbk) : £1.25 B81-03052

Kurland, Michael. The infernal device / Michael Kurland. — London : New English Library, 1979, c1978 (1981 [printing]). — 251p ; 18cm
Originally published: New York : New American Library, 1978
ISBN 0-450-04560-9 (pbk) : £1.50 B81-35623

Kurtz, Irma. The grand dragon / Irma Kurtz. — London : Arrow, 1981, c1979. — 218p ; 18cm
Originally published: New York : Dutton ; London : Hutchinson, 1979
ISBN 0-09-922780-0 (pbk) : £1.35 B81-07353

Kyle, David, *1919-*. The dragon Lensman : based on the characters created by E.E. 'Doc' Smith / by David A. Kyle. — [London] : Corgi, 1981, c1980. — xiv,176p ; 18cm. — (E.E. 'Doc' Smith's classic Lensman series)
ISBN 0-552-11669-6 (pbk) : £1.25 B81-22371

La Fountaine, George. The Scott-Dunlap ring / George La Fountaine. — London : Severn House, 1980, c1979. — 285p ; 21cm
Originally published: London : Mayflower, 1979
ISBN 0-7278-0618-1 : £5.95 : CIP rev. B80-22540

Ladame, Cathryn. Winter's heart / ; Cathryn Ladame. — London : Silhouette, 1981. — 188p ; 18cm. — (Silhouette romance ; 54)
ISBN 0-340-27032-2 (pbk) : £0.65 : CIP rev. B81-18137

813'.54[F] — Fiction in English. American writers, *1945- — Texts* *continuation*

Lafferty, R. A.. Not to mention camels : a science fiction fantasy / R.A. Lafferty. — London : Dobson, 1980, c1976. — 215p ; 23cm. — (Originally published: Indianapolis : Bobbs-Merrill, 1976)
ISBN 0-234-72207-x : £5.25 B81-01130

L'Amour, Louis. Galloway / Louis L'Amour. — London : Hale, 1979, c1970. — 157p ; 20cm
Originally published: New York : Bantam ; London : Corgi, 1970
ISBN 0-7091-4305-2 : £3.95 B81-19819

L'Amour, Louis. Lonely on the mountain / Louis L'Amour. — London : Corgi, 1981, c1980. — 194p ; 18cm
Originally published: New York : Bantam Books, 1980
ISBN 0-552-11668-8 (pbk) : £0.95 B81-18670

Land, Jane. Irena / Jane Land. — London : Hale, 1980, c1979. — 182p ; 21cm
Originally published: Garden City, N.Y. : Doubleday, 1979
ISBN 0-7091-8625-8 : £6.25 B81-01131

Landers, Gunnard. [The hunting shack]. The hunting party / Gunnard Landers. — London : Arrow, 1981, c1979. — 218p ; 18cm
Originally published: New York : Arbor House, 1979
ISBN 0-09-923030-5 (pbk) : £1.25 B81-20287

Landorf, Joyce. I came to love you late / Joyce Landorf. — London : Pickering & Inglis, 1981. — 221p ; 18cm
ISBN 0-7208-0496-5 (pbk) : £1.75 B81-27197

Lanier, Sterling E.. Hiero's journey ; The war for The Lot / Sterling E. Lanier. — London : Sidgwick & Jackson, 1981. — 348,[200]p ; 20cm. — (Science fiction special ; 34)
Hiero's journey originally published: Radnor : Chilton, 1973 ; London : Sidgwick & Jackson, 1975 — The War for the Lot originally published : Chicago : Follet, 1969 ; London : Sidgwick & Jackson, 1977
ISBN 0-283-98805-3 : £8.95 B81-36178

Lansing, Alfred. Endurance : Shackleton's incredible voyage / Alfred Lansing. — London : Granada, 1980, c1959. — 302p,[8]p of plates : ill,1map,ports ; 18cm. — (A Panther book)
Originally published: London : Hodder and Stoughton, 1959
ISBN 0-586-05120-1 (pbk) : £1.95 B81-09884

Larkin, Rochelle. Mistress of desire / Rochelle Larkin. — London : Sphere, 1979, c1978 (1981 [printing]). — 311p ; 18cm
Originally published: New York : New American Library, 1978
ISBN 0-7221-5441-0 (pbk) : £1.25 B81-40990

Lathen, Emma. Going for gold / by Emma Lathen. — London : Gollancz, 1981. — 251p ; 21cm
Originally published: New York : Simon and Schuster, 1981
ISBN 0-575-02902-1 : £5.95 B81-16062

Lauben, Philip. A nice sound alibi / by Philip Lauben. — London : Hale, 1981. — 192p ; 20cm
ISBN 0-7091-9007-7 : £5.95 B81-15307

Lavender, William. Children of the river / William Lavender. — London : Sphere, 1981, c1980. — 445p ; 18cm. — (The Hargrave journal ; v.1)
Originally published: United States : s.n., 1980
ISBN 0-7221-5462-3 (pbk) : £1.75 B81-17975

Lavender, William. Journey to quiet waters / William Lavender. — London : Sphere, 1981, c1980. — 486p ; 18cm. — (The Hargrave journal ; v.2)
ISBN 0-7221-5465-8 (pbk) : £1.75 B81-28750

Law, Janice. The shadows of the palms / Janice Law. — London : Hale, 1981, c1979. — 216p ; 20cm
ISBN 0-7091-9011-5 : £5.95 B81-17327

Lay, Bierne. Twelve o'clock high! / Bierne Lay, Jr. and Sy Bartlett. — South Yarmouth, Mass. : Curley ; Long Preston : Magna [distributor], [1981]? c1975. — 504p ; 22cm
Originally published: New York : Harper, 1948. — Published in large print
ISBN 0-89340-332-6 : Unpriced B81-37093

Lazlo, Kate. Forever after : a novel / by Kate Lazlo. — London : Bodley Head, 1981. — 278p ; 22cm
ISBN 0-370-30904-9 (corrected : pbk) : £6.50 B81-27095

Le Guin, Ursula K.. The left hand of darkness / Ursula LeGuin. — London : Macdonald Futura, 1981, c1969. — 256p ; 18cm. — (An orbit book)
Originally published: New York : Walker ; London : Macdonald, 1969
ISBN 0-7088-8081-9 (pbk) : £1.60 B81-28347

Le Guin, Ursula K.. Malafrena / Ursula K. Le Guin. — London : Granada, 1981, c1979. — 380p ; 18cm. — (A Panther book)
Originally published: New York : Berkley, 1979 ; London : Gollancz, 1980
ISBN 0-586-05159-7 (pbk) : £1.50 B81-17405

Lee, Patrick. Six-gun samurai / Patrick Lee. — London : Star, 1981. — 161p ; 18cm
Originally published: Los Angeles : Pinnacle Books, 1980
ISBN 0-352-30823-0 (pbk) : £1.25 B81-11666

Lee, Patrick. Six-gun samurai, bushido vengeance / Patrick Lee. — London : Star, 1981. — 182p ; 18cm. — (The six-gun samurai series ; no.2)
ISBN 0-352-30858-3 (pbk) : £1.25 B81-15783

Leffland, Ella. Rumours of peace / Ella Leffland. — London : Granada, 1981, c1979. — 428p ; 18cm. — (A Panther book)
Originally published: New York : Harper and Row, 1979 ; London : Hamilton, 1979
ISBN 0-586-05180-5 (pbk) : £1.95 B81-26409

Leiber, Fritz. A spectre is haunting Texas / Fritz Leiber. — London : Granada, 1971, c1968 (1981 [printing]). — 221p ; 18cm. — (Granada science fantasy)
Originally published: New York : Walker ; London : Gollancz, 1969
ISBN 0-583-11934-4 (pbk) : £1.25 B81-21288

Leigh, Susannah. Glynda / Susannah Leigh. — Sevenoaks : Coronet Books, 1981, c1979. — 636p ; 18cm
Originally published: New York : New American Library, 1979
ISBN 0-340-24872-6 (pbk) : £1.95 : CIP rev. B80-11181

Leonard, Elmore. City primeval / by Elmore Leonard. — London : W.H. Allen, 1981. — xii,275p ; 23cm
Originally published: New York : Arbor House, 1980
ISBN 0-491-02625-0 : £6.95 B81-26488

Leonard, Elmore. The hunted / Elmore Leonard. — London : Hamlyn, 1978, c1977 (1980 [printing]). — 251p ; 18cm
Originally published: London : Secker & Warburg, 1978
ISBN 0-600-20065-5 (pbk) : £1.25 B81-12255

Leonard, George H.. Alien quest / George H. Leonard. — London : Sphere, 1981, c1977. — 251p ; 18cm
ISBN 0-7221-5488-7 (pbk) : £1.50 B81-20248

Lerner, Richard. Epidemic / Richard Lerner and Max Gunther. — [London] : Corgi, 1981, c1980. — 317p ; 18cm
Originally published: New York : Morrow, 1980
ISBN 0-552-11611-4 (pbk) : £1.35 B81-10961

Leven, Jeremy. Creator / Jeremy Leven. — Harmondsworth : Penguin, 1981, c1980. — 607p ; 18cm
Originally published: London : Hutchinson, 1980
ISBN 0-14-005620-3 (pbk) : £1.95 B81-35487

Levin, Ira. A kiss before dying / Ira Levin. — London : Pan, 1970, c1954 (1981 [printing]). — 238p ; 18cm
Originally published: London : Joseph, 1954
ISBN 0-330-02429-9 (pbk) : £1.50 B81-29143

Levin, Ira. Nightmares : three great suspense novels / by Ira Levin. — London : Michael Joseph, 1981. — 459p ; 22cm
Contents: Rosemary's baby. Originally published : New York : Simon & Schuster, 1953 ; London : Michael Joseph, 1954. — Stepford wives. Originally published : New York : Random House ; London : Michael Joseph, 1972. — A kiss before dying. Originally published : London : Michael Joseph, 1967
ISBN 0-7181-2034-5 : £7.95 B81-37184

Lewerth, Margaret. Hester / Margaret Lewerth. — [London] : Fontana, 1981, c1979. — 319p ; 18cm. — (The Roundtree women ; bk.3)
Originally published: New York : Dell, 1979
ISBN 0-00-616062-x (pbk) : £1.35 B81-12701

Liddy, G. Gordon. Out of control / G. Gordon Liddy. — London : Severn House, 1980, c1979. — 305p ; 25cm
Originally published: New York : St. Martin's Press, 1979
ISBN 0-7278-0671-8 : £6.95 : CIP entry B80-18896

Liddy, George Gordon. Out of control / G. Gordon Liddy. — [London] : Corgi, 1981, c1979. — 345p ; 18cm
Originally published: New York : St. Martins Press, 1979
ISBN 0-552-11594-0 (pbk) : £1.50 B81-08408

Lindquist, Donald. The red gods / Donald Lindquist. — Feltham : Hamlyn, 1981. — 326p ; 18cm
ISBN 0-600-20528-2 (pbk) : £1.50 B81-40994

Lindquist, Donald. The Street / Donald Lindquist. — [London] : Magnum, 1981, c1979. — 405p ; 18cm
Originally published: New York : Dutton, 1979
ISBN 0-417-05920-5 (pbk) : £1.75 B81-18254

Lippincott, David. Black prism / David Lippincott. — London : W.H. Allen, 1980. — 252p ; 23cm
ISBN 0-491-02631-5 : £5.95 B81-01696

Littell, Robert, *1935-*. The amateur : a novel / by Robert Littell. — London : Cape, 1981. — 252p ; 23cm
ISBN 0-224-01937-6 : £6.50 : CIP rev. B81-07425

Littell, Robert, *1935-*. The October Circle / Robert Littell. — [London] : Coronet, 1978, c1975. — 221p ; 18cm
Originally published: Boston, Mass. : Houghton Mifflin ; London : Hodder and Stoughton, 1976
ISBN 0-340-23184-x (pbk) : £0.95 : CIP rev. B78-35621

Littlejohn, David, *1937-*. Going to California / David Littlejohn. — London : Secker & Warburg, 1981. — 336p ; 24cm
ISBN 0-436-24750-x : £6.95 B81-18407

Livingstone, M. Jay. The prodigy / M. Jay Livingstone. — London : Sphere, 1981, c1978. — 241p ; 18cm
Originally published: New York : Coward, McCann & Geoghegan, c1978
ISBN 0-7221-5560-3 : £1.25 B81-24540

813′.54[F] — Fiction in English. American writers, 1945- — Texts *continuation*

Lobel, Brana. The revenant / Brana Lobel. — London : Eyre Methuen, 1981, c1979. — 239p ; 19cm
Originally published: Garden City, N.Y. : Doubleday, 1979
ISBN 0-413-48440-8 (cased) : Unpriced
ISBN 0-417-05430-0 (pbk) : £1.35 B81-12042

Lord, Vivian. The voyagers / Vivian Lord. — London : Sphere, 1981, c1980. — 447p ; 18cm
ISBN 0-7221-5618-9 (pbk) : £1.75 B81-35063

Lortz, Richard. Lovers living, lovers dead / Richard Lortz. — London : Corgi, 1980, c1977. — 187p ; 18cm
Originally published: New York : Putnam, 1977
ISBN 0-552-11555-x (pbk) : £1.00 B81-06763

Lottman, Eileen. All night long : a novel / by Eileen Lottman ; based on a screenplay by W.D. Richter. — London : Granada, 1981. — 188p ; 18cm. — (A Mayflower book)
ISBN 0-583-13527-7 (pbk) : £1.25 B81-28910

Love, Edmund G.. Set a trap / by Edmund G. Love. — London : Hale, 1981, c1980. — 278p ; 20cm
ISBN 0-7091-9335-1 : £6.25 B81-37316

Lovin, Roger. Apostle / by Roger Lovin ; edited and illustrated by Polly and Kelly Freas. — London : Hale, 1980, c1978. — 167p : ill ; 21cm
Originally published: Norfolk, Va : Donning, 1978
ISBN 0-7091-8518-9 : £5.75 B81-00299

Lowry, Lois. Find a stranger, say goodbye / Lois Lowry. — London : Granada, 1981, c1978. — 158p ; 18cm. — (A Dragon book)
Originally published: Boston : Houghton Miffin, 1978 ; Harmondsworth : Kestrel, 1980
ISBN 0-583-30403-6 (pbk) : £0.95 B81-17584

Ludlum, Robert. The Bourne identity / Robert Ludlum. — London : Granada, 1980 (1981 [printing]). — 514p ; 18cm. — (A Panther book)
ISBN 0-586-04934-7 (pbk) : £1.95 B81-26410

Ludlum, Robert. The Scarlatti inheritance. — Large print ed. — Leicester : Ulverscroft, Sept.1981. — [728]p. — (Charnwood library series)
Originally published: London : Hart-Davis, 1971
ISBN 0-7089-8009-0 : £6.50 : CIP entry B81-22668

Luke, Thomas. The Hell candidate / Thomas Luke. — [London] : Corgi, 1981, c1980. — 384p ; 18cm
ISBN 0-552-11663-7 (pbk) : £1.50 B81-22372

Lutz, Giles A.. The echo / Giles A. Lutz. — London : Hale, 1981, c1979. — xi,177p ; 20cm
Originally published: Garden City, N.Y. : Doubleday, 1979
ISBN 0-7091-8903-6 : £4.95 B81-14138

Lutz, Giles A.. Lure of the outlaw trail / Giles A. Lutz. — London : Hale, 1980, c1979. — 185p ; 20cm
Originally published: Garden City, N.Y. : Doubleday, 1979
ISBN 0-7091-8531-6 : £4.95 B81-01132

Lynn, Elizabeth A.. Watchtower / Elizabeth A. Lynn. — London : Hamlyn Paperbacks, 1981, c1979. — 208p : 1map,1plan ; 18cm. — (Hamlyn science fantasy)
Originally published: New York : Berkley, 1979
ISBN 0-600-20222-4 (pbk) : £1.25 B81-20698

Lyon, Buck. Bear valley / Buck Lyon. — London : Hale, 1980. — 160p ; 20cm
ISBN 0-7091-8550-2 : £4.95 B81-16003

Lyon, Buck. Carver valley / by Buck Lyon. — London : Hale, 1981. — 156p ; 20cm
ISBN 0-7091-8815-3 : £4.95 B81-14086

Maas, Peter. Made in America / Peter Maas. — [London] : Corgi, 1981, c1979. — 346p ; 18cm
Originally published: New York : Viking Press, 1979 ; London : H. Hamilton, 1980
ISBN 0-552-11625-4 (pbk) : £1.50 B81-15340

McAleer, John. Unit pride / John McAleer and Billy Dickson. — [London] : Blond & Briggs, 1981. — 515p ; 23cm
ISBN 0-85634-117-7 : £7.95 : CIP rev. B81-15828

McBain, Ed. Bread : an 87th Precinct mystery / Ed McBain. — London : Pan, 1976, c1974 (1980 printing). — 190p ; 18cm
Originally published: New York : Random House ; London : Hamilton, 1974
ISBN 0-330-24850-2 (pbk) : £1.25 B81-11207

McBain, Ed. Calypso : an 87th Precinct mystery / Ed McBain. — London : Pan, 1980, c1979. — 191p ; 18cm
Originally published: New York : Viking ; London : Hamilton, 1979
ISBN 0-330-26200-9 (pbk) : £1.25 B81-01133

McBain, Ed. The empty hours : 87th precinct mysteries / Ed McBain. — London : Pan, 1981, c1962. — 190p ; 18cm
ISBN 0-330-26279-3 (pbk) : £1.25 B81-12077

McBain, Ed. The empty hours : an 87th precinct mystery / Ed McBain. — London : Severn House, 1981, c1962. — 165p ; 21cm
Originally published: New York : Simon and Schuster, 1962 ; London : Boardman, 1963
ISBN 0-7278-0687-4 : £5.95 B81-09868

McBain, Ed. Ghosts : an 87th Precinct novel / Ed McBain. — London : Hamilton, 1980. — 212p ; 21cm
Originally published: New York : Viking, 1980
ISBN 0-241-10307-x : £5.95 : CIP rev. B80-09436

McBain, Ed. Heat. — London : H. Hamilton, Dec.1981. — [224]p
ISBN 0-241-10693-1 : £6.95 : CIP entry B81-31460

McBain, Ed. Let′s hear it for the deaf man : an 87th Precinct mystery / Ed McBain. — London : Pan, 1976, c1973 (1980 printing). — 189p : ill,1plan ; 18cm
Originally published: London : Hamilton, 1973
ISBN 0-330-24307-1 (pbk) : £0.90 B81-04179

McBain, Ed. [Murder in the navy]. Death of a nurse / Ed McBain. — Harmondsworth : Penguin, 1980, c1955. — 187p ; 18cm. — (Penguin crime fiction)
Originally published: under the pseudonym Richard Marsten. New York : Fawcett, 1955 ; London : Muller, 1956
ISBN 0-14-005152-x (pbk) : £0.90 B81-07670

McBain, Ed. Rumpelstiltskin / Ed McBain. — London : Hamilton, 1981. — 241p ; 21cm
ISBN 0-241-10522-6 : £6.95 : CIP rev. B81-15810

McBain, Ed. [Tomorrow′s world]. Tomorrow and tomorrow / Ed McBain. — London : Severn House, 1980, c1956. — 193p ; 21cm
Originally published: under the pseudonym Hunt Collins. New York : Avalon Books, 1956
ISBN 0-7278-0681-5 : £5.50 B81-01135

McBain, Laurie. Chance the winds of fortune / Laurie McBain. — London : Macodnald Futura, 1981, c1980. — 505p ; 18cm. — (A Troubadour book)
ISBN 0-7107-3003-9 (pbk) : £1.75 B81-28346

McCaffrey, Anne. The mark of Merlin / Anne McCaffrey. — London : Macdonald Futura, 1980, c1971. — 180p ; 18cm. — (A Troubadour book)
Originally published: London : Millington, 1977
ISBN 0-7088-1924-9 (pbk) : £0.95 B81-06262

McCaffrey, Anne. Restoree / Anne McCaffrey. — London : Corgi, 1970, c1967 (1980 [printing]). — 223p ; 18cm
Originally published: London : Rapp and Whiting, 1967
ISBN 0-552-10161-3 (pbk) : £1.25 B81-01136

McCaffrey, Anne. Ring of fear / Anne McCaffrey. — London : Macdonald Futura, 1980, c1971. — 252p ; 18cm. — (A Troubadour book)
Originally published: London : Millington, 1979
ISBN 0-7107-3000-4 (pbk) : £1.25 B81-02215

McCammon, Robert R.. Bethany′s Sin / Robert R. McCammon. — London : Sphere, 1980. — 342p ; 18cm
ISBN 0-7221-5869-6 (pbk) : £1.40 B81-00300

McCammon, Robert R.. The night boat / Robert R. McCammon. — London : Sphere, 1981, c1980. — 284p ; 18cm
ISBN 0-7221-5871-8 (pbk) : £1.25 B81-20251

McCarthy, Gary. Mustang fever / Gary McCarthy. — London : Hale, 1981, c1980. — 182p ; 20cm
ISBN 0-7091-8949-4 : £4.95 B81-17334

Mcdonald, Gregory. Fletch and the widow Bradley / by Gregory Mcdonald. — London : Gollancz, 1981. — 158p ; 21cm
ISBN 0-575-03033-x : £5.95 B81-39428

Macdonald, Gregory. Fletch′s fortune / Gregory Macdonald. — Feltham : Hamlyn Paperbacks, 1981, c1978. — 253p ; 18cm
Originally published: New York : Avon, 1978 ; London : Gollancz, 1979
ISBN 0-600-33729-4 (pbk) : £1.25 B81-12082

McDonald, Gregory. [Who took Toby Rinaldi?]. Snatched / by Gregory McDonald. — London : Gollancz, 1980. — 264p ; 21cm
Originally published: New York : Putnam, 1980
ISBN 0-575-02873-4 : £5.50 B81-03211

MacDonald, Patricia. The unforgiven / Patricia MacDonald. — [London] : Fontana, 1981. — 253p ; 18cm
ISBN 0-00-616365-3 (pbk) : £1.50 B81-33485

McDowell, Michael. Cold moon over Babylon / Michael McDowell. — Rev. ed. — [London] : Fontana, 1980. — 253p ; 18cm
Previous ed.: New York : Avon, 1980
ISBN 0-00-616099-9 (pbk) : £1.25 B81-01137

McDowell, Michael. Gilded needles / Michael McDowell. — [London] : Fontana, 1981, c1980. — 315p ; 18cm
Originally published: New York? : Avon Books, 1980
ISBN 0-00-616270-3 (pbk) : £1.50 B81-28687

McGill, Gordon. The final conflict, Omen II / Gordon McGill ; from the screenplay by Andrew Birkin and based on characters created by David Seltzer. — London : Macdonald Futura, 1980. — 190p ; 18cm. — (A Futura book)
ISBN 0-7088-1958-3 (pbk) : £1.10 B81-15640

McGill, Gordon. See no evil / Gordon McGill. — London : Sphere, 1981. — 183p ; 18cm
ISBN 0-7221-5872-6 (pbk) : £1.25 B81-24714

McGivern, William. Soldiers of ′44 / William McGivern. — [London] : Fontana, 1980, c1979. — 318p ; 1map ; 18cm
Originally published: New York : Arbor House ; London : Collins, 1979
ISBN 0-00-616322-x (pbk) : £1.50 B81-01138

813′.54[F] — Fiction in English. American writers, *1945- — Texts continuation*

McInerny, Ralph. Second Vespers : a Father Dowling mystery / by Ralph McInerny. — London : Hale, 1981, c1980. — 224p ; 21cm. — (Father Dowling mysteries)
ISBN 0-7091-8832-3 : £5.75 B81-15771

MacInnes, Helen. The hidden target. — Large print ed. — Anstey : Ulverscroft, Jan.1982. — [558]p. — (Charnwood library series)
ISBN 0-7089-8022-8 : £6.50 : CIP entry B81-33990

MacInnes, Helen. The unconquerable / Helen MacInnes. — [London] : Fontana, 1970 (1979 printing). — 511p ; 18cm
ISBN 0-00-615563-4 (pbk) : £1.25 B81-19810

Mack, Carol K.. The chameleon variant / Carol K. Mack and David Ehrenfeld. — London : Sphere, 1981, c1980. — 256p ; 18cm
Originally published: New York : Dial, 1980
ISBN 0-7221-5689-8 (pbk) : £1.50 B81-36824

McKay, Rena. Bridal trap / Rena McKay. — London : Silhouette, 1981, c1980. — 189p ; 18cm. — (Silhouette romance ; no.35)
ISBN 0-340-26725-9 (pbk) : £0.65 : CIP rev. B81-04219

McKay, Rena. Desert devil. — London : Hodder and Stoughton, Feb.1982. — [192]p. — (Silhouette romance)
ISBN 0-340-27672-x (pbk) : £0.75 : CIP entry B81-38319

Mackenzie-Lamb, Eric. Labyrinth / Eric Mackenzie-Lamb. — Feltham : Hamlyn Paperbacks, 1980, c1979. — 239p ; 18cm
Originally published: New York : Morrow, 1979
ISBN 0-600-20058-2 (pbk) : £1.25 B81-06264

Mackey, Mary. McCarthy′s list / Mary Mackey. — London : Picador, 1981, c1979. — 294p ; 20cm
Originally published: Garden City, NY : Doubleday, 1979 ; London : Eyre Methuen, 1980
ISBN 0-330-26377-3 (pbk) : £1.95 B81-24418

McKillip, Patricia A.. The chronicles of Morgon, Prince of Hed / Patricia A. McKillip. — London : Sidgwick & Jackson, 1981. — 256p : 1map ; 21cm
Contents: The riddle-master of Hed. Originally published: New York : Atheneum, 1976 ; London : Sidgwick and Jackson, 1979 — Heir of sea and fire. Originally published: New York : Atheneum, 1977 ; London : Sidgwick and Jackson, 1979 — Harpist in the wind. Originally published: New York : Atheneum, ; London : Sidgwick and Jackson, 1979
ISBN 0-283-98742-1 : £9.50 B81-12655

McKnight, Carolyn. The house in the shadows / by Carolyn McKnight. — London : Hale, 1980, c1979. — 197p ; 21cm
Originally published: New York : St Martin′s Press, 1979
ISBN 0-7091-8627-4 : £6.25 B81-01139

McLaglen, John J.. Geronimo! / John J. McLaglen. — London : Corgi, 1981. — 125p ; 18cm. — (Herne the hunter ; 16)
ISBN 0-552-11689-0 (pbk) : £0.95 B81-27250

McLaglen, John J.. The hanging / John J. McLaglen. — London : Corgi, 1981. — 127p ; 18cm. — (Herne the hunter ; 17)
ISBN 0-552-11788-9 (pbk) : £0.95 B81-39097

McLaglen, John J.. Till death / John J. McLaglen. — [London] : Corgi, 1981, c1980. — 123p ; 18cm. — (Herne the hunter ; 15)
ISBN 0-552-11585-1 (pbk) : £0.85 B81-08416

Macleod, Charlotte. The family vault / Charlotte Macleod. — South Yarmouth, Mass. : Curley, c1979 ; [Long Preston] : Magna [distributor]. — vii,498p ; 23cm
Originally published: Garden City, N.Y. : Doubleday, 1979 ; London : Collins for the Crime Club, 1980. — Published in large print
ISBN 0-89340-299-0 : £5.75 B81-18311

MacLeod, Charlotte. The luck runs out / Charlotte MacLeod. — London : Collins, 1981, c1979. — 214p ; 21cm. — (The Crime Club)
Originally published: Garden City, N.Y. : Doubleday, 1979
ISBN 0-00-231678-1 : £5.95 B81-02838

MacLeod, Charlotte. The withdrawing room : a Sarah Kelling novel / Charlotte MacLeod. — London : Collins, 1981, c1980. — 210p ; 21cm. — (The Crime club)
Originally published: Garden City, N.Y. : Doubleday, 1980
ISBN 0-00-231919-5 : £6.25 : CIP rev. B81-28837

Macleod, Robert, *1906-*. The running gun / Robert Macleod. — Large print ed. — Leicester : Ulverscroft, 1981, c1969. — 339p ; 23cm
Originally published: New York : Fawcett, 1969 ; London : Coronet, 1970
ISBN 0-7089-0686-9 : £5.00 B81-39851

MacMullen, Mary. But Nellie was so nice / Mary McMullen. — London : Collins, 1981, c1979. — 198p ; 21cm. — (The Crime Club)
Originally published: Garden City, N.Y. : Doubleday, 1979
ISBN 0-00-231042-2 : £5.75 B81-01140

McMullen, Mary. My cousin death / Mary McMullen. — London : Collins, 1981, c1980. — 208p ; 21cm. — (The Crime Club)
Originally published: Garden City, N.Y. : Doubleday, 1980
ISBN 0-00-231662-5 : £6.25 B81-28698

Mcmullen, Mary. Something of the night. — London : Collins, Jan.1982. — [224]p. — (The Crime Club)
ISBN 0-00-231719-2 : £6.95 : CIP entry B81-33927

McMullen, Mary. Welcome to the grave. — Large print ed. — Bath : Chivers, Oct.1981. — [304]p. — (A Lythway book)
Originally published: Garden City : Doubleday, 1979 ; London : Collins, 1980
ISBN 0-85119-754-x : £6.90 : CIP entry B81-25813

McNally, Clare. Ghost house / Clare McNally. — [London] : Corgi, 1980, c1979. — 214p ; 18cm
Originally published: Toronto : London : Bantam, 1979
ISBN 0-552-11652-1 (pbk) : £1.25 B81-03322

McNally, Clare. Ghost house revenge / Clare McNally. — London : Corgi, c1981. — 232p ; 18cm
ISBN 0-552-11825-7 (pbk) : £1.25 B81-35597

McNamara, Michael M.. The sovereign solution / Michael McNamara. — London : Star, 1980, c1979. — 212p ; 18cm
Originally published: New York : Crown ; London : W.H. Allen, 1980
ISBN 0-352-30705-6 (pbk) : £1.50 B81-02135

McNaughton, Brian. Satan′s love child / Brian McNaughton. — London : W.H. Allen, 1981, c1977. — 256p ; 18cm. — (A Star book)
Originally published: New York? : Carlyle Communications, 1977?
ISBN 0-352-30952-0 (pbk) : £1.35 B81-39334

McNaughton, Brian. Satan′s seductress / Brian McNaughton. — London : W.H. Allen, 1981, c1980. — 254p ; 18cm. — (Star)
Originally published: United States : Carlyle Books, 1980
ISBN 0-352-30878-8 (pbk) : £1.25 B81-18889

McNeill, George. The Hellions / George McNeill. — [London] : Corgi, 1981, c1979. — vi,374p ; 18cm
ISBN 0-552-11699-8 (pbk) : £1.50 B81-27240

McNeill, George. The plantation / George McNeill. — [London] : Corgi, 1976, c1975 (1981 [printing]). — 393p ; 18cm
Originally published: New York : Bantam, 1975
ISBN 0-552-11729-3 (pbk) : £1.50 B81-27239

McQuay, Mike. Escape from New York : a novel / by Mike McQuay ; based upon a screenplay by John Carpenter & Nick Castle. — London : Corgi, 1981. — 181p ; 18cm
ISBN 0-552-11826-5 (pbk) : £1.25 B81-39791

Magnuson, Teodore. A small gust of wind / Teodore Magnuson. — London : W.H. Allen, 1981, c1980. — viii,403p ; 21cm
Originally published: Indianapolis : Bobbs-Merrill, 1980
ISBN 0-491-02914-4 : £7.95 B81-28623

Mahan, Colleen. The lodge / Colleen Mahan. — London : New English Library, 1981, c1980. — 280p ; 23cm
Originally published: Garden City, N.Y. : Doubleday, 1980
ISBN 0-450-04847-0 : £6.50 B81-03063

Mailer, Norman. The executioner′s song / Norman Mailer. — London : Arrow, 1980, c1979. — 1056p ; 18cm
Originally published: Boston, Mass. : Little, Brown ; London : Hutchinson, 1979
ISBN 0-09-923060-7 (pbk) : £1.95 B81-01141

Major, Ann. Wild lady. — London : Hodder and Stoughton, Feb.1982. — [192]p. — (Silhouette romance)
For adolescents
ISBN 0-340-27670-3 (pbk) : £0.75 : CIP entry B81-38318

Malamud, Bernard. The assistant / Bernard Malamud. — Harmondsworth : Penguin in association with Eyre & Spottiswoode, 1967, c1957 (1981 [printing]). — 216p ; 18cm
Originally published: New York : Farrar, Straus, 1957 ; London : Eyre & Spottiswoode, 1959
ISBN 0-14-002621-5 (pbk) : £1.35 B81-35471

Malamud, Bernard. Dubin′s lives / Bernard Malamud. — Harmondsworth : Penguin, 1979. — 399p ; 18cm
Originally published: New York : Farrar Straus Giroux ; London : Chatto and Windus, 1979
ISBN 0-14-005242-9 (pbk) : £1.75 B81-02489

Malamud, Bernard. The fixer / Bernard Malamud. — Harmondsworth : Penguin in association with Chatto & Windus, 1968, c1966 (1981 [printing]). — 299p ; 18cm
Originally published: New York : Farrar, Strauss & Giroux, 1966 ; London : Eyre & Spottiswoode, 1967
ISBN 0-14-002714-9 (pbk) : £1.75 B81-22257

Malamud, Bernard. The fixer / Bernard Malamud. — London : Chatto & Windus, 1981, c1966. — 335p ; 21cm. — (The collected works of Bernard Malamud)
Originally published: London : Eyre & Spottiswoode, 1967
ISBN 0-7011-2453-9 : £6.95 B81-11005

Malamud, Bernard. The natural / Bernard Malamud. — Harmondsworth : Penguin in association with Eyre & Spottiswoode, 1967, c1952 (1981 [printing]). — 222p ; 18cm
Originally published: New York : Harcourt, Brace, 1952 ; London : Eyre & Spottiswoode, 1963
ISBN 0-14-002783-1 (pbk) : £1.50 B81-40430

Malamud, Bernard. The tenants. — London : Chatto & Windus, Oct.1981. — [240]p
ISBN 0-7011-2451-2 : £7.50 : CIP entry B81-27999

813'.54[F] — Fiction in English. American writers, *1945-* — Texts *continuation*

Maling, Arthur. The Koberg link / Arthur Maling. — Large print ed. — Leicester : Ulverscroft, 1981, c1979. — 405p ; 23cm. — (Ulvescroft large print)
Originally published: New York : Harper and Row, 1979 ; London : Gollancz, 1980
ISBN 0-7089-0674-5 : £5.00 : CIP rev. B81-25891

Malone, Michael. Dingley Falls / Michael Malone. — Feltham : Hamlyn Paperbacks, 1981, c1980. — xii,496p : 1map ; 18cm
Originally published: New York : Harcourt Brace Jovanovich, 1980
ISBN 0-600-20307-7 (pbk) : £1.95 B81-24729

Marasco, Robert. Parlour games. — London : Hodder & Stoughton, Oct.1981. — [304]p. — (Coronet books)
Originally published: 1979
ISBN 0-340-27264-3 (pbk) : £1.50 : CIP entry B81-25754

Marchant, William. Firebird / William Marchant. — London : W.H. Allen, 1981, c1980. — 274p ; 18cm. — (A Star book)
Originally published: New York : Crown, 1980
ISBN 0-352-30954-7 (pbk) : £1.50 B81-39332

Marchant, William. Firebird : a novel / by William Marchant. — London : W.H. Allen, 1981, c1980. — 273p ; 23cm
Originally published: New York : Crown, 1980
ISBN 0-491-02933-0 : £6.95 B81-03490

Marlowe, Ann. The winnowing winds / Ann Marlowe. — Large print ed. — Leicester : Ulverscroft, 1981, c1977. — 408p ; 22cm. — (Ulverscroft large print series)
Originally published: New York : Dodd, Mead, 1977 ; London : New English Library, 1978
ISBN 0-7089-0580-3 : £5.00 B81-12181

Marsland, Amy. Cache-Cache / Amy Marsland. — London : Hale, 1981, c1980. — 185p ; 20cm
Originally published: Garden City, N.Y. : Published for the Crime Club by Doubleday, 1980
ISBN 0-7091-9127-8 : £5.95 B81-27301

Martin, George R. R.. Windhaven. — London : New English Library, Feb.1982. — [320]p
Originally published: New York : Timescape Books, 1981
ISBN 0-450-04666-4 (pbk) : £1.50 : CIP entry B81-36207

Marton, George. The Janus pope / George Marton. — London : W.H. Allen, 1980,, 1979 (1981 [printing]). — 319p ; 18cm
ISBN 0-352-30759-5 (pbk) : £1.75 B81-35158

Marvin, James W.. Body guard / James W. Marvin. — [London] : Corgi, 1981. — 126p ; 18cm. — (Crow ; 5)
ISBN 0-552-11634-3 (pbk) : £0.85 B81-21201

Maryk, Michael. Deathbite / Michael Maryk, Brent Monahan. — London : Granada, 1981, c1979. — 251p ; 18cm. — (A Mayflower book)
Originally published: Kansas City : Andrews and McMeel, 1979
ISBN 0-583-13382-7 (pbk) : £1.25 B81-17411

Mason, K. N.. Boot Hill cowpoke / K.N. Mason. — London : Hale, 1981, c1978. — 176p ; 20cm
Originally published: Canoga Park, Calif. : Major Books, 1978
ISBN 0-7091-8914-1 : £4.95 B81-15293

Masterson, J. B.. Rudge / J.B. Masterson. — London : Hale, 1980, c1979. — 188p ; 20cm
Originally published: Garden City, N.Y. : Doubleday, 1979
ISBN 0-7091-8549-9 : £4.95 B81-02071

Masterton, Graham. Famine / Graham Masterton. — London : Sphere, 1981. — 376p ; 18cm
ISBN 0-7221-6003-8 (pbk) : £1.75 B81-24713

Masterton, Graham. Famine. — London : Severn House, Aug.1981. — [384]p
ISBN 0-7278-0729-3 : £6.95 : CIP entry B81-18101

Masterton, Graham. Fireflash 5 / Graham Masterton. — London : W.H. Allen, 1977, c1976. — 222p ; 18cm. — (A Star book)
Cover title: A mile before morning
ISBN 0-352-39691-1 (pbk) : £0.75 B81-28582

Masterton, Graham. Railroad / Graham Masterton. — London : Hamilton, 1981. — 569p ; 23cm
ISBN 0-241-10562-5 : £7.95 : CIP rev. B81-13429

Masterton, Graham. Rich / Graham Masterton. — London : Sphere, 1979 (1980 [printing]). — 760p ; 18cm
Originally published: London : H. Hamilton, 1979
ISBN 0-7221-5988-9 (pbk) : £1.95 B81-03502

Masterton, Graham. The Sweetman curve / by Graham Masterton. — London : Sphere, 1980, c1979. — 349p ; 18cm
ISBN 0-7221-5989-7 (pbk) : £1.50 B81-00302

Masterton, Graham. The wells of Hell / Graham Masterton. — London : Sphere, 1981, c1979. — 219p ; 18cm ; pbk
Originally published: United States : s.n., 1979
ISBN 0-7221-5991-9 : £1.10 B81-11712

Masur, Harold Q.. The broker / Harold Q. Masur. — London : Souvenir Press, 1981. — 288p : ill ; 20cm
ISBN 0-285-62489-x : £6.95 B81-36106

Matheson, Richard. What dreams may come / Richard Matheson. — London : Sphere, 1981, c1978. — 264p ; 18cm
Originally published: New York: Putnam, c1978 ; London : Joseph, 1979. — Includes bibliography
ISBN 0-7221-5882-3 (pbk) : £1.50 B81-20247

Matthews, Patricia. Love's raging tide / Patricia Matthews. — [London] : Corgi, 1980. — 410p ; 18cm
ISBN 0-552-11553-3 (pbk) : £1.75 B81-03319

Matthews, Patricia. Love's sweet agony / Patricia Matthews. — [London] : Corgi, 1981, c1980. — 368p ; 18cm
ISBN 0-552-11698-x (pbk) : £1.75 B81-21282

Matthews, *1927-* Patricia. Tides of love / by Patricia Matthews. — Toronto ; London : Bantam, 1981. — 326p ; 21cm
ISBN 0-553-01328-9 (pbk) : £3.95 B81-39103

Matthiessen, Peter. At play in the fields of the Lord / Peter Matthiessen. — London : Granada, 1968, c1965 (1980 [printing]). — 320p ; 18cm. — (A Panther book)
Originally published: New York : Random House, 1965 ; London : Heinemann, 1966
ISBN 0-586-02464-6 (pbk) : £1.50 B81-17412

Maupin, Armistead. Tales of the city / Armistead Maupin. — [London] : Corgi, 1980, c1978. — 313p ; 18cm
Originally published: New York : Harper & Row, 1978
ISBN 0-552-11554-1 (pbk) : £1.50 B81-08018

Mayer, Robert, *1939-*. Superfolks / Robert Mayer. — London : Magnum, 1980, c1977. — 230p ; 18cm
Originally published: New York : Dial Press, 1977 ; London : Angus and Robertson, 1978
ISBN 0-417-05460-2 (pbk) : £1.30 B81-02852

Mayerson, Charlotte. An easy life / Charlotte Mayerson. — London : Arlington, 1981. — 208p ; 21cm
ISBN 0-85140-554-1 : £6.50 B81-19362

Maynard, Joyce, *1953-*. Baby love / Joyce Maynard. — London : Deutsch, 1981. — 243p ; 23cm
ISBN 0-233-97386-9 : £6.50 B81-39792

Meggs, Brown. The war train. — London : H. Hamilton, Sept.1981. — [320]p
ISBN 0-241-10393-2 : £6.50 : CIP entry B81-20176

Meschery, Joanne. In a high place. — London : Bodley Head, Feb.1982. — [368]p
ISBN 0-370-30444-6 : £6.50 : CIP entry B81-36370

Meyer, Nicholas. Confessions of a homing pigeon. — London : Hodder and Stoughton, Feb.1982. — [384]p
ISBN 0-340-27829-3 : £6.95 : CIP entry B81-36368

Michaels, Barbara. The crying child / Barbara Michaels. — Large print ed. — Leicester : Ulverscroft, 1981, c1971. — 349p ; 22cm. — (Ulverscroft large print series)
Originally published: New York : Dodd, Mead, 1971 ; London : Souvenir Press, 1972
ISBN 0-7089-0568-4 : £5.00 B81-12178

Michaels, Barbara. House of many shadows : Barbara Michaels. — Large print ed. — Leicester : Ulverscroft, 1981, c1974. — 404p ; 23cm. — (Ulverscroft large print series)
Originally published: New York : Dodd, Mead, 1974 ; London : Souvenir Press, 1976
ISBN 0-7089-0666-4 : £5.00 : CIP rev. B81-20629

Michaels, Barbara. Patriot's dream / Barbara Michaels. — London : Sphere, 1979, c1976. — 317p ; 18cm : 1geneal.table
Originally published: New York : Dodd, Mead, 1976 ; London : Souvenir, 1978
ISBN 0-7221-6062-3 (pbk) : £1.60 B81-24705

Michaels, Barbara. Wait for what will come. — Large print ed. — Anstey : Ulverscroft, Oct.1981. — [400]p. — (Ulverscroft large print series)
Originally published: New York : Dodd, Mead and Co., 1978
ISBN 0-7089-0695-8 : £5.00 : CIP entry B81-28091

Michaels, Barbara. Wait for what will come / Barbara Michaels. — London : Sphere, 1981, c1978. — 256p ; 18cm
Originally published: New York : Dodd, Mead, 1978 ; London : Souvenir, 1980
ISBN 0-7221-6054-2 (pbk) : £1.50 B81-24542

Michaels, Barbara. The walker in shadows / Barbara Michaels. — London : Souvenir, 1981, c1979. — 242p ; 23cm
Originally published: New York : Dodd, Mead, 1979
ISBN 0-285-62460-1 : £6.95 B81-02181

Michaels, Barbara. Wings of the Falcon / Barbara Michaels. — London : Sphere, c1977. — 286p ; 18cm
Originally published: New York : Dodd, Mead, 1977 ; London : Souvenir, 1979
ISBN 0-7221-6068-2 (pbk) : £1.50 B81-01143

Michaels, Fern. Beyond tomorrow. — London : Hodder & Stoughton, Jan.1982. — [192]p. — (Silhouette romance)
ISBN 0-340-27667-3 (pbk) : £0.75 : CIP entry B81-34482

Michaels, Fern. The delta ladies. — London : Hodder & Stoughton, Oct.1981. — [336]p. — (Coronet books)
Originally published: 1980
ISBN 0-340-27106-x (pbk) : £1.75 : CIP entry B81-26730

Michaels, Fern. Golden lasso / Fern Michaels. — [London] : Silhouette, 1981, c1980. — 190p ; 18cm. — (Silhouette romance ; 31)
ISBN 0-340-26581-7 (pbk) : £0.65 : CIP rev. B81-02096

813'.54[F] — Fiction in English. American writers, *1945-* — *Texts* *continuation*

Michaels, Fern. Sea gypsy / Fern Michaels. — [London] : Silhouette, 1981, c1980. — 189p ; 18cm. — (Silhouette romance ; no.15)
ISBN 0-340-26012-2 (pbk) : £0.65 : CIP rev. B80-19953

Michaels, Fern. Whisper my name / Fern Michaels. — London : Silhouette, 1981. — 190p ; 18cm. — (Silhouette romance ; 61)
ISBN 0-340-27116-7 (pbk) : £0.65 : CIP rev. B81-23936

Michaels, Leonard. The men's club / Leonard Michaels. — London : Cape, 1981. — 181p ; 21cm
ISBN 0-224-02925-8 : £5.95 : CIP rev. B81-20606

Miller, Judi. Save the last dance for me / Judi Miller. — London : W.H. Allen, 1981. — 373p : ill ; 18cm. — (A Star book)
Originally published: New York : Pocket Books, 1981
ISBN 0-352-30890-7 (pbk) : £1.75 B81-35156

Miner, Valerie. Blood sisters : an examination of conscience / Valerie Miner. — London : Women's Press, 1981. — xi,206p ; 20cm
ISBN 0-7043-3872-6 (pbk) : £3.50 : CIP rev. B81-14375

Monaco, Richard. The Grail war / Richard Monaco. — London : Sphere, 1981, c1979. — xi,369p ; 18cm
Originally published: New York : Pocket Books, 1979
ISBN 0-7221-6165-4 (pbk) : £1.75 B81-08633

Monteleone, Thomas F.. The secret sea / by Thomas F. Monteleone. — London : Hale, 1981, c1979. — 222p ; 20cm. — (Hale SF)
ISBN 0-7091-9299-1 : £6.25 B81-35201

Moore, Robin. [The big paddle]. Fast shuffle / Robin Moore with Sid Levine. — London : Arrow, 1981, c1978. — 281p ; 18cm
Originally published: New York : Arbor House, 1978 ; London : Melbourne House, 1979
ISBN 0-09-926310-6 (pbk) : £1.60 B81-39155

Moore, Robin. The Black Sea connection. — London : Severn House, Sept.1981. — [256]p
ISBN 0-7278-0713-7 : £6.95 : CIP entry B81-23814

Moore, Robin. The Italian connection : pulsar no.2 / Robin Moore and Al Dempsey. — London : Severn House, 1981, c1975. — 180p ; 21cm
Originally published: New York : Pinnacle Books, 1975
ISBN 0-7278-0652-1 : £5.95 B81-12130

Moore, Robin. The London connection : Pulsar No.1 / Robin Moore and Al Dempsey. — London : Severn House, 1980, c1974. — 209p ; 21cm
ISBN 0-7278-0627-0 : £5.95 : CIP rev. B80-22552

Moore, Robin. Our missile's missing / Robin Moore with Stan Gebler Davies. — London : Magnum, 1980, c1977. — 290p ; 18cm
Originally published: Loughton : Piatkus, 1980
ISBN 0-417-03810-0 (pbk) : £1.50 B81-08422

Moore, Robin. Our missile's missing / Robin Moore and Stan Gebler Davies. — Loughton : Piatkus, 1980, c1977. — 290p ; 21cm
ISBN 0-86188-054-4 : £5.95 : CIP rev. B80-18000

Morgan, Frank, *1916-*. Tomahawk Range / by Frank Morgan. — London : Hale, 1981. — 159p ; 20cm
ISBN 0-7091-8818-8 : £4.95 B81-19227

Morgan, John, *1916-*. Harper's trail / by John Morgan. — London : Hale, 1981. — 158p ; 20cm
ISBN 0-7091-9179-0 : £4.95 B81-24844

Morgan, Speer. Belle Starr : a novel / by Speer Morgan. — London : Secker & Warburg, 1981, c1979. — 310p ; 23cm
Originally published: Boston, Mass. : Little, Brown, 1979
ISBN 0-436-28803-6 : £6.95 B81-02858

Morgan, Valerie. The lovers / by Valerie Morgan. — London : Hale, 1981. — 157p ; 20cm
ISBN 0-7091-9209-6 : £5.75 B81-35239

Morrell, David. The totem / David Morrell. — London : Pan, 1981, c1979. — 235p ; 18cm
Originally published: New York : M. Evans, 1979
ISBN 0-330-26308-0 (pbk) : £1.25 B81-12078

Morris, Janet E.. Dream dancer / Janet E. Morris. — [London] : Fontana, 1980. — 350p ; 18cm. — (The Kerrion Consortium)
ISBN 0-00-616123-5 (pbk) : £1.50 B81-07357

Morrison, Toni. The bluest eye / Toni Morrison. — [St. Albans] : Triad, 1981, c1970. — 190p : 1port ; 18cm
Originally published: New York : Holt, Rinehart and Winston, 1970 ; London : Chatto and Windus, 1979. — Port on inside cover
ISBN 0-586-04982-7 (pbk) : £1.25 B81-36767

Morrison, Toni. Sula / Toni Morrison. — London : Chatto & Windus, 1980, c1973. — 174p ; 21cm
Originally published: New York : Knopf, 1974
ISBN 0-7011-2423-7 : £6.50 : CIP rev. B80-24860

Morrison, Toni. Tar baby. — London : Chatto & Windus, June 1981. — [320]p
ISBN 0-7011-2596-9 : £6.95 : CIP entry B81-16857

Muir, James A.. Bounty hunter / James A. Muir. — London : Sphere, 1980. — 154p ; 18cm. — (Breed ; no.13) (A Sphere adult western)
ISBN 0-7221-6283-9 (pbk) : £0.85 B81-11725

Muir, James A.. Slaughter time / James A. Muir. — London : Sphere, 1981. — 119p ; 18cm. — (Breed ; no.15)
ISBN 0-7221-8998-2 (pbk) : £1.00 B81-35165

Muir, James A.. Spanish gold / James A. Muir. — London : Sphere, 1981. — 150p ; 18cm. — (Breed ; no.14)
ISBN 0-7221-8996-6 : £1.00 B81-17978

Muller, Charles G.. Bloody sundown / Charles G. Muller. — London : Hale, 1981, c1976. — 159p ; 20cm
Originally published: Canoga Park, Calif. : Major Books, 1976
ISBN 0-7091-8911-7 : £4.95 B81-15297

Murphy, Warren. Atlantic City / Warren B. Murphy and Frank Stevens. — London : Sphere, 1980, c1979. — 495p ; 18cm
Originally published: Los Angeles : Pinnacle Books, 1979
ISBN 0-7221-6277-4 (pbk) : £1.95 B81-00303

Murray, Ed. Muscle Beach / Ed Murray ; illustrated by D.A. Redmond. — London : Arrow, 1980. — 146p : ill ; 20cm
ISBN 0-09-922560-3 (pbk) : £1.50 B81-07661

Mykel, A. W.. The Windchime legacy / by A.W. Mykel. — London : Severn House, 1981, c1980. — 423p ; 24cm
Originally published: New York : St. Martin's Press, 1980
ISBN 0-7278-0689-0 : £6.95 : CIP rev. B81-04278

Nabokov, Vladimir. Bend sinister / Vladimir Nabokov. — Harmondsworth : Penguin, 1974, c1974 (1981 [printing]). — 201p ; 20cm
Originally published: New York : Holt, 1947
ISBN 0-14-003682-2 (pbk) : £1.95 B81-14352

Nabokov, Vladimir. Pale fire / Vladimir Nabokov. — Harmondsworth : Penguin, 1973, c1962 (1981 [printing]). — 248p ; 20cm
Originally published: New York : Putnam ; London : Weidenfeld and Nicolson, 1962. — Includes index
ISBN 0-14-003692-x (pbk) : £2.25 B81-26506

Nabokov, Vladimir. Transparent things / Vladimir Nabokov. — Harmondsworth : Penguin, 1975, c1972, (1981 [printing]). — 106p ; 20cm
Originally published: New York : McGraw Hill, 1972 ; London : Weidenfeld & Nicolson, 1973
ISBN 0-14-003968-6 (pbk) : £1.25 B81-35073

Nabokov, Vladimir. Tyrants destroyed and other stories / Vladimir Nabokov. — Harmondsworth : Penguin, 1981, c1975. — 218p ; 20cm
Translations from the Russian. — Originally published: New York : McGraw-Hill, 1974 ; London : Weidenfeld and Nicolson, 1975
ISBN 0-14-004734-4 (pbk) : £2.50 B81-15392

Nahum, Lucien. Shadow 81 / Lucien Nahum. — Large print ed. — Leicester : Ulverscroft, 1981, c1975. — 445p ; 23cm. — (Ulverscroft large print)
Originally published: Garden City, N.Y. : Doubleday, 1975 ; London : New English Library, 1976
ISBN 0-7089-0556-0 : £5.00 : CIP rev. B80-35453

Nash, N. Richard. Aphrodite's cave : a novel / by N. Richard Nash. — London : W.H. Allen, 1981, c1980. — xi,465p ; 22cm
Originally published: Garden City, N.Y. : Doubleday, 1980
ISBN 0-491-02764-8 : £7.95 B81-15405

Nash, N. Richard. Cry macho / N. Richard Nash. — London : W.H. Allen, 1978, c1975. — 302p ; 18cm. — (A Star book)
Originally published: New York : Delacorte, 1975 ; London : W.H. Allen, 1976
ISBN 0-352-39506-0 (pbk) : £0.95 B81-28547

Naylor, Phyllis Reynolds. Revelations / Phyllis Naylor. — London : Sphere, 1981, c1979. — 393p ; 18cm
Originally published: New York : St. Martin's, 1979
ISBN 0-7221-6323-1 (pbk) : £1.50 B81-29901

Nemec, David. Bright lights, dark rooms / David Nemec. — London : Severn House, 1981, c1980. — 322p ; 21cm
Originally published: Garden City, N.Y. : Doubleday, 1980
ISBN 0-7278-0703-x : £6.50 : CIP rev. B81-13538

Nicholson, C. R.. The Friday spy / C.R. Nicholson. — [London] : Corgi, 1981, c1980. — 410p ; 18cm
ISBN 0-552-11612-2 (pbk) : £1.65 B81-10963

Niven, Larry. A hole in space / Larry Niven. — London : Futura, 1975, c1974 (1980 [printing]). — 196p : ill ; 18cm. — (An Orbit book)
Originally published: New York : Ballantine Books, 1974
ISBN 0-86007-853-1 (pbk) : £1.25 B81-00304

Nolan, Frederick. White nights, red dawn / Frederick Nolan. — London : Hutchinson, 1981, c1980. — 471p : 1geneal.table ; 23cm
Originally published: New York : Macmillan, 1980
ISBN 0-09-144840-9 : £7.50 : CIP rev. B81-04383

813'.54[F] — Fiction in English. American writers, *1945- — Texts* *continuation*

Nolan, William F.. Logan's search / William F. Nolan. — [London] : Corgi, 1981, c1980. — 145p ; 18cm
Originally published: New York : Bantam, 1980
ISBN 0-552-11562-2 (pbk) : £1.00 B81-08412

Norman, John, *19---*. Fighting slave of Gor / John Norman. — London : W.H. Allen, 1981, c1980. — 384p ; 18cm. — (Chronicles of Counter Earth ; v.14) (A Star book)
Originally published: New York : Daw Books, 1980
ISBN 0-352-30838-9 (pbk) : £1.95 B81-26449

Norman, John, *19---*. Time slave / John Norman. — London : W.H. Allen, 1981, c1975. — 380p ; 18cm. — (A Star book)
Originally published: New York : Daw Books, 1975
ISBN 0-352-30825-7 (pbk) : £1.95 B81-26450

Norville, Warren. Death tide / Warren Norville. — London : New English Library, 1981, c1979. — 268p : ill ; 18cm
Originally published: New York : Jove, 1979
ISBN 0-450-05025-4 (pbk) : £1.50 B81-09392

Nova, Craig. Incandescence / Craig Nova. — Henley-on-Thames : Ellis, 1980, c1979. — 312p ; 23cm
Originally published: New York : Harper & Row, 1979
ISBN 0-85628-071-2 : £6.50 : CIP rev.
B80-00911

Oates, Joyce Carol. Angel of light. — London : Cape, Nov.1981. — [448]p
ISBN 0-224-02927-4 : £7.50 : CIP entry
B81-30965

Oates, Joyce Carol. Bellefleur / Joyce Carol Oates. — London : Cape, 1981, c1980. — 558p : 1geneal.table ; 25cm
Originally published: New York : Dutton, 1980
ISBN 0-224-01920-1 : £7.50 B81-10983

O'Connor, Flannery. The violent bear it away / Flannery O'Connor ; with an introduction by Paul Bailey. — London : Faber, 1980. — x,243p ; 19cm
Originally published: New York : Farrar, Strauss ; London : Longman, 1960
ISBN 0-571-11613-2 (pbk) : £2.95 : CIP rev.
B80-18901

O'Connor, Flannery. Wise blood / Flannery O'Connor ; with an introduction by V.S. Pritchett. — London : Faber, 1980. — xi,226p ; 19cm
Originally published: New York : Harcourt Brace, 1952 ; London : Faber, 1968
ISBN 0-571-11612-4 (pbk) : £2.95 : CIP rev.
B80-18902

O'Donnell, Lillian. Falling star / Lillian O'Donnell. — London : Hale, 1981, c1979. — 252p ; 20cm
Originally published: New York : Putnam, 1979
ISBN 0-7091-8932-x : £5.75 B81-11779

Olden, Marc. The book of shadows / Marc Olden. — London : Hamlyn Paperbacks, 1981, c1980. — 275p ; 18cm
ISBN 0-600-38409-8 (pbk) : £1.25 B81-35577

Oliver, Frances, *1933-*. Xargos / Frances Oliver. — London : Secker & Warburg, 1981. — 168p ; 23cm
ISBN 0-436-33998-6 : £6.50 : CIP rev.
B81-16413

Oliver, Tess. Double or nothing. — London : Hodder & Stoughton, Dec.1981. — [192]p. — (Silhouette romance)
ISBN 0-340-27658-4 (pbk) : £0.65 : CIP entry
B81-31447

Oliver, Tess. Red, red rose / Tess Oliver. — [London] : Silhouette, 1981, c1980. — 168p ; 18cm. — (Silhouette romance ; no.14)
ISBN 0-340-26011-4 (pbk) : £0.65 : CIP rev.
B80-19958

Olsen, T. V.. Bonner's stallion. — London : Hodder & Stoughton, Dec.1981. — [256]p
Originally published: Greenwich, Conn. : Fawcett Gold Medal Books, 1977
ISBN 0-340-27557-x (pbk) : £1.25 : CIP entry
B81-31464

Orde, Lewis. The night they stole Manhattan / by Lewis Orde and Bill Michaels. — London : Dent, 1980. — 334p : maps ; 23cm
ISBN 0-460-04522-9 : £6.50 B81-05257

Osborn, David. The French decision / David Osborn. — London : Granada, 1980. — 250p ; 23cm
ISBN 0-246-11372-3 : £6.95 B81-00305

Osborn, David. The French decision / David Osborn. — London : Granada, 1980 (1981 [printing]). — 250p ; 18cm. — (A Panther book)
Originally published: Garden City, N.Y. : Doubleday, 1980
ISBN 0-586-05175-9 (pbk) : £1.50 B81-36768

Owen, Ann, *1926-*. The sands of time / Ann Owen. — London : Silhouette, 1981, c1980. — 188p ; 18cm. — (Silhouette romance ; no.40)
ISBN 0-340-26730-5 (pbk) : £0.65 : CIP rev.
B81-09988

Paine, Lauran. The hammerhead / by Lauran Paine. — London : Hale, 1981. — 160p ; 20cm
ISBN 0-7091-8933-8 : £4.95 B81-24845

Paine, Lauran. Punchbowl range / by Lauran Paine. — London : Hale, 1981. — 160p ; 20cm
ISBN 0-7091-8817-x : £4.95 B81-08645

Panati, Charles. Links / Charles Panati. — London : Magnum, 1981. — 223p ; 18cm
Originally published: Boston, Mass. : Houghton Mifflin, 1978 ; London : Eyre Methuen, 1979
ISBN 0-417-04100-4 (pbk) : £1.50 B81-28647

Pape, Gordon. Chain reaction / Gordon Pape and Tony Aspler. — London : Magnum Books, 1980, c1978. — 246p ; 18cm
Originally published: New York : Viking Press, 1978 ; London : Barrie and Jenkins, 1979
ISBN 0-417-04910-2 (pbk) : £1.25 B81-30703

Pape, Gordon. The scorpion sanction / Gordon Pape and Tony Aspler. — London : Eyre Methuen, 1981, c1980. — 358p ; 19cm
Originally published: New York : Viking, 1980
ISBN 0-413-48460-2 (cased) : Unpriced
ISBN 0-417-06000-9 (pbk) : £1.50 B81-28658

Paterson, Katherine. Jacob have I loved / Katherine Paterson. — London : Gollancz, 1981, c1980. — 216p ; 21cm
Originally published: New York : Crowell, 1980
ISBN 0-575-02961-7 (pbk) : £4.95 B81-16056

Patten, Lewis B.. The law in Cottonwood / Lewis B. Patten. — London : Hale, 1981. — 183p ; 20cm
Originally published: Garden City, N.Y. : Doubleday, 1978
ISBN 0-7091-7811-5 : £4.95 B81-08650

Patten, Lewis B.. The trail of the Apache Kid / Lewis B. Patten. — London : Hale, 1981, c1979. — 154p ; 20cm
Originally published: Garden City, N.Y. : Doubleday, 1979
ISBN 0-7091-8486-7 : £4.95 B81-33541

Patten, Lewis B.. The trial at Apache Junction / Lewis B. Patten. — South Yarmouth : Curley ; [Skipton] : Magna Print [distributor], 1981, c1977. — 254p ; 23cm
Originally published: New York : New American Library, 1977. — Published in large print
ISBN 0-89340-309-1 : £5.75 B81-28684

Patten, Lewis B.. Villa's rifles / Lewis B. Patten. — London : Hale, 1980, c1977. — 183p ; 20cm
Originally published: Garden City, N.Y. : Doubleday, 1977
ISBN 0-7091-7518-3 : £4.95 B81-00306

Paul, Barbara. First gravedigger. — London : Collins, Feb.1982. — [248]p. — (The Crime Club)
ISBN 0-00-231299-9 : £6.50 : CIP entry
B81-35936

Paul, Barbara, *1925-*. An exercise for madmen / by Barbara Paul. — London : Hale, 1981, c1978. — 160p ; 20cm. — (Hale SF)
Originally published: Glenview : Medallion, 1978
ISBN 0-7091-8353-4 : £6.75 B81-15383

Payne, Charlotte. The glitterati / Charlotte Payne. — London : Sphere, 1981, c1980. — 344p ; 18cm
Originally published: New York : Morrow, 1980
ISBN 0-7221-6736-9 (pbk) : £1.50 B81-28637

Peck, Richard, *1934-*. Amanda/Miranda / Richard Peck. — [London] : Corgi, 1981, c1980. — 510p ; 18cm
Originally published: London : Gollancz, 1980
ISBN 0-552-11738-2 (pbk) : £1.60 B81-21204

Peck, Richard, *1934-*. New York time / Richard Peck. — London : Gollancz, 1981. — 212p ; 23cm
ISBN 0-575-03011-9 : £6.95 B81-31695

Pendleton, Don. Executioner 37 : Friday's feast / Don Pendleton. — London : Corgi, 1981, c1979. — 181p ; 18cm
ISBN 0-552-11666-1 (pbk) : £0.95 B81-18671

Pendleton, Don. The Executioner 38 : Satan's Sabbath / by Don Pendleton. — London : Corgi, 1981, c1980. — 175p ; 18cm
ISBN 0-552-11722-6 (pbk) : £0.95 B81-32105

Pendleton, Don. Thermal Thursday / Don Pendleton. — London : Corgi, 1980, c1979. — 176p ; 18cm. — (Executioner ; 36)
ISBN 0-552-11458-8 (pbk) : £0.95 B81-09418

Percy, Walker. The second coming / Walker Percy. — London : Secker & Warburg, 1981, c1980. — 359p ; 22cm
Originally published: Philadelphia : Franklin Library for the First Edition Society, 1980
ISBN 0-436-36664-9 : £6.95 B81-02413

Peters, Elizabeth. Devil-may-care. — London : Coronet, Apr.1981. — [240]p
Originally published: London : Cassell, 1978
ISBN 0-340-25081-x (pbk) : £1.25 : CIP entry
B81-01144

Peters, Elizabeth. [Legend in green velvet]. Ghost in green velvet / Elizabeth Peters. — Large print ed. — Leicester : Ulverscroft, 1980, c1976. — 363p ; 23cm. — (Ulverscroft large print series)
Originally published: New York : Dodd, Mead, 1976 ; London : Cassell and Collier Macmillan, 1977
ISBN 0-7089-0548-x : £4.25 : CIP rev.
B80-35454

Peters, Elizabeth. The love talker / Elizabeth Peters. — London : Souvenir, 1981, c1980. — 266p ; 23cm
Originally published: New York : Dodd, Mead, 1980
ISBN 0-285-62442-3 : £6.95 B81-15741

813'.54[F] — Fiction in English. American writers, *1945- — Texts* *continuation*

Peters, Elizabeth. The love talker. — Large print ed. — Anstey : Ulverscroft, Feb.1982. — [416] p. — (Ulverscroft large print series : romantic suspense)
ISBN 0-7089-0751-2 : £5.00 : CIP entry
B81-36940

Peters, Elizabeth. Summer of the dragon / Elizabeth Peters. — Large print ed. — Leicester : Ulverscroft, 1981, c1979. — 388p ; 23cm. — (Ulverscroft large print series)
Originally published: New York : Dodd, Mead, 1979 ; London : Souvenir Press, 1980
ISBN 0-7089-0624-9 : £5.00 : CIP rev.
B81-07906

Petrakis, Harry Mark. Nick the Greek / Harry Mark Petrakis. — London : New English Library, 1980, c1979. — 302p ; 23cm
Originally published: Garden City, N.Y. : Doubleday, 1979
ISBN 0-450-04821-7 : £5.95 B81-01822

Peyton, Audrey. Ashes / by Audrey Peyton. — London : Hale, 1981. — 191p ; 20cm. — (Hale SF)
ISBN 0-7091-8884-6 : £5.95 B81-14135

Phillips, Steven. Resisting arrest / Steven Phillips. — London : Macmillan, 1980. — 352p ; 21cm
Originally published: Garden City, N.Y. : Doubleday, 1980
ISBN 0-333-29107-7 : £6.50 B81-00308

Picano, Felice. The lure / Felice Picano. — London : New English Library, 1981, c1979. — 415p ; 23cm
Originally published: New York : Delacorte, 1979
ISBN 0-450-04750-4 : £6.95 B81-03392

Pilcer, Sonia. Teen angel / Sonia Pilcer. — London : W.H. Allen, 1981, c1978. — 224p ; 18cm. — (Star)
Originally published: London : Weidenfeld and Nicholson, 1978
ISBN 0-352-30836-2 (pbk) : £1.50 B81-18888

Pintoro, John. The summoning / John Pintoro. — Feltham : Hamlyn, 1980, c1979. — 220p ; 18cm
ISBN 0-600-20272-0 (pbk) : £0.95 B81-00309

Plain. Random winds / Belva Plain. — [London] : Fontana, 1981, c1980. — 512p ; 18cm
Originally published: New York : Delacorte Press ; London : Collins, 1980
ISBN 0-00-616265-7 (pbk) : £1.95 B81-32170

Plain, Belva. Random winds / Belva Plain. — London : Collins, 1980. — 475p ; 22cm
ISBN 0-00-221617-5 : £6.95 B81-01145

Plain, Belva. Random winds / Belva Plain. — London : Prior, 1981, c1980. — 806p ; 25cm
Originally published: New York : Delacorte ; London : Collins, 1980. — Published in large print
ISBN 0-86043-593-8 : £9.50 B81-32763

Plante, David. The country : a novel / by David Plante. — London : Gollancz, 1981. — 159p ; 21cm
ISBN 0-575-02938-2 : £6.95 B81-10692

Pohl, Frederik. The cool war / Frederik Pohl. — London : Gollancz, 1981. — 282p ; 21cm
ISBN 0-575-02942-0 : £5.95 B81-18538

Pollock, Ted. The rainbow man / Ted Pollock. — London : Sphere, 1981, c1979. — 314p ; 18cm
Originally published: New York : McGraw-Hall, 1979
ISBN 0-7221-6929-9 (pbk) : £1.50 B81-20385

Portis, Charles. True grit : a novel / by Charles Portis. — Large print ed. — Bath : Chivers, 1981. — 262p ; 23cm. — (A New Portway large print book)
Originally published: New York : Simon and Schuster, 1968 ; London : Cape, 1969
ISBN 0-85119-131-2 : Unpriced : CIP rev.
B81-20533

Potok, Chaim. The promise / Chaim Potok. — Harmondsworth : Penguin, 1971, c1969 (1980 [printing]). — 348p ; 19cm
Originally published: New York : Knopf, 1969, London : Heinemann, 1970
ISBN 0-14-003330-0 (pbk) : £1.50 B81-10988

Powell, James. A man made for trouble / James Powell. — London : Hale, 1981, c1976. — 175p ; 20cm
Originally published: Canoga Park : Major Books, 1976
ISBN 0-7091-8910-9 : £4.95 B81-27290

Powell, James. Vendetta / James Powell. — London : Hale, 1981, c1980. — 211p ; 20cm
Originally published: New York : Ace, 1980
ISBN 0-7091-8726-2 : £4.95 B81-08966

Powers, Anne, *19---*. Eleanor, the passionate queen / by Anne Powers. — London : Hale, 1981. — 206p ; 21cm
ISBN 0-7091-8882-x : £6.50 B81-21883

Powers, Nora. Affairs of the heart / Nora Powers. — London (47 Bedford Sq., WC1B 3DP) : Silhouette, 1980. — 188p ; 18cm. — (Silhouette romance ; no.3)
ISBN 0-340-26000-9 (pbk) : £0.65 : CIP rev.
B80-13076

Powers, Nora. Design for love / Nora Powers. — London : Silhouette, 1981, c1980. — 190p ; 18cm. — (Silhouette romance ; no.41)
ISBN 0-340-26731-3 (pbk) : £0.65 : CIP rev.
B81-10481

Powers, Ron. Face value / Ron Powers. — London : Arrow, 1981, c1979. — 406p ; 18cm
Originally published: New York : Delacorte Press, 1979
ISBN 0-09-924860-3 (pbk) : £1.75 B81-20283

Poyer, Joe. The Balkan assignment / Joe Poyer. — London : Sphere, 1973, c1971 (1981 [printing]). — 22p ; 18cm
Originally published: Garden City, NY : Doubleday, 1971 ; London : Gollancz, 1972
ISBN 0-7221-6965-5 (pbk) : £1.25 B81-21669

Poyer, Joe. The Chinese agenda / Joe Poyer. — London : Sphere, 1974, c1972 (1981 [printing]). — 253p ; 18cm
Originally published: Garden City, NY : Doubleday, 1972 ; London : Gollancz, 1973
ISBN 0-7221-6958-2 (pbk) : £1.25 B81-21668

Poyer, Joe. The contract / Joe Poyer. — London : Sphere, 1978, (1981 [printing]). — 271p ; 18cm
Originally published: New York : Atheneum, 1979
ISBN 0-7221-6959-0 (pbk) : £1.25 B81-21671

Poyer, Joe. The day of reckoning / Joe Poyer. — London : Sphere, 1977, c1976 (1981 [printing]). — 271p ; 18cm
Originally published: Garden City, NY : Doubleday ; London : Weidenfeld and Nicolson, 1976
ISBN 0-7221-6960-4 (pbk) : £1.25 B81-21674

Poyer, Joe. North Cape / Joe Poyer. — London : Sphere, 1971, c1969 (1981 [printing]). — 231p ; 18cm
Originally published: Garden City, NY : Doubleday, 1969; London : Gollancz, 1970
ISBN 0-7221-6966-3 (pbk) : £1.25 B81-21675

Poyer, Joe. Operation Malacca / Joe Poyer. — London : Sphere, 1976, c1968 (1981 [printing]). — 160p ; 18cm
Originally published: Garden City, NY : Doubleday, 1968
ISBN 0-7221-6961-2 (pbk) : £1.25 B81-21673

Poyer, Joe. [The shooting of the green]. Hell shot / Joe Poyer. — London : Sphere, 1978, c1973 (1981 [printing]). — 222p ; 18cm
Originally published: Garden City, NY : Doubleday, 1973 ; London : Barker, 1974
ISBN 0-7221-7000-9 (pbk) : £1.25 B81-21670

Poyer, Joe. Tunnel war / Joe Poyer. — London : Sphere, 1980, c1979 (1981 [printing]). — xii,368p : ill ; 18cm
Originally published: New York : Atheneum, 1979
ISBN 0-7221-7027-0 (pbk) : £1.50 B81-21672

Poyer, Joe. Vengeance 10 / Joe Poyer. — London : Joseph, 1981, c1980. — 348p : 1map ; 23cm
Originally published: New York : Atheneum, 1980
ISBN 0-7181-2005-1 : £6.95 B81-09886

Preiss, Byron. Dragonworld / Byron Preiss and J. Michael Reaves ; illustrated by Joseph Zucker. — Toronto ; London : Bantam, 1979. — 545p : ill ; 23cm
ISBN 0-553-01077-8 (pbk) : £3.95 B81-03493

Pronzini, Bill. Hoodwink / by Bill Pronzini. — London : Hale, 1981. — 216p ; 22cm
ISBN 0-7091-9342-4 : £6.50 B81-35291

Purdy, James. In a shallow grave / James Purdy. — London : Star, 1981, c1975. — 140p ; 18cm
Originally published: New York : Arbor House, 1975 ; London : W.H. Allen, 1978
ISBN 0-352-30889-3 (pbk) : £1.25 B81-28506

Purdy, James. Malcolm / by James Purdy ; foreword by Edward Albee. — Harmondsworth : Penguin, 1980, c1959. — lx,190p ; 20cm
Originally published: New York : Farrar, Straus & Cudahy, 1959 ; London : Secker & Warburg, 1960
ISBN 0-14-005595-9 (pbk) : £1.95 B81-10924

Racina, Thom. Nine to five / Thom Racina. — London : Pan, 1980. — 139p ; 18cm
ISBN 0-330-26428-1 (pbk) : £0.95 B81-02738

Radcliffe, Janette. White jasmine / Janette Radcliffe. — London : W.H. Allen, 1981, c1976. — 175p ; 18cm. — (A star book)
Originally published: New York : Dell, 1976
ISBN 0-352-30574-6 (pbk) : £1.25 B81-20949

Rae, Patricia. Charge nurse / Patricia Rae. — London : W.H. Allen, 1981, c1980. — 365p ; 18cm. — (Star)
Originally published: New York : Zebra Books, 1980
ISBN 0-352-30860-5 (pbk) : £1.60 B81-18887

Raintree, Lee. Dallas / Lee Raintree. — London : Granada, 1980, c1978. — 351p ; 23cm
Originally published: New York : Dell, 1978
ISBN 0-246-11516-5 : £5.95 B81-02733

Raucher, Herman. Maynard's house / by Herman Raucher. — London : Joseph, 1981, c1980. — 240p ; 23cm
Originally published: New York : Putnam, 1980
ISBN 0-7181-2021-3 : £6.95 B81-16059

Reese, John. Legacy of a land hog / John Reese. — London : Hale, 1980, c1979. — 184p ; 20cm
Originally published: Garden City, N.Y. : Doubleday, 1979
ISBN 0-7091-8483-2 : £4.95 B81-03075

Reese, John. A pair of deuces / John Reese. — London : Hale, 1981, c1978. — 182p ; 20cm
Originally published: Garden City, N.Y. : Doubleday, 1978
ISBN 0-7091-8485-9 : £4.95 B81-11781

Reese, John. Two thieves and a puma / John Reese. — London : Hale, 1981, c1980. — 183p ; 20cm
ISBN 0-7091-8741-6 : £4.95 B81-28870

813'.54[F] — Fiction in English. American writers, *1945-* — *Texts* *continuation*

Reno, Marie R.. When the music changed / Marie R. Reno. — London : Eyre Methuen, 1981, c1980. — x,530p ; 23cm
Originally published: New York : New American Library, c1980
ISBN 0-413-48250-2 : £6.95 B81-12487

Rhodes, Richard, *1937-*. The last safari / Richard Rhodes. — London : Deutsch, 1980. — 349p ; 23cm
ISBN 0-233-97216-1 : £6.95 : CIP rev. B80-18495

Rhodes, Richard, *1937-*. Sons of earth : a novel / Richard Rhodes. — London : Deutsch, 1981. — 238p ; 24cm
ISBN 0-233-97413-x : £6.95 B81-35139

Richards, Leigh. Spring fires / Leigh Richards. — London (47 Bedford Sq., WC1B 3DP) : Silhouette, 1981, c1980. — 190p ; 18cm. — (Silhouette romance ; no.21)
ISBN 0-340-26125-0 (pbk) : £0.65 : CIP rev. B80-23738

Richmond, Roe. War in the Panhandle / Roe Richmond. — London : Hale, 1980, c1979. — 192p ; 20cm
Originally published: New York : Manor Books, 1979
ISBN 0-7091-8548-0 : £4.95 B81-00310

Rifkin, Shepard. McQuaid in August / Shepard Rifkin. — London : Hale, 1980, c1979. — 181p ; 20cm
Originally published: Garden City, N.Y. : Doubleday, 1979
ISBN 0-7091-8393-3 : £5.50 B81-00311

Ripy, Margaret. A second chance on love. — London : Hodder and Stoughton, Nov.1981. — [192]p. — (Silhouette romance)
ISBN 0-340-27259-7 (pbk) : £0.65 : CIP entry B81-30546

Ritter, Margaret. The burning woman / Margaret Ritter. — [London] : Fontana, 1981, c1979. — 281p ; 19cm
Originally published: New York : Putnam, 1979
ISBN 0-00-615844-7 (pbk) : £1.35 B81-22006

Ritter, Margaret. The burning woman / by Margaret Ritter. — London : Hale, 1981, c1979. — 315p ; 21cm
Originally published: New York : Putnam, 1979
ISBN 0-7091-8763-7 : £7.25 B81-08735

Robb, Sandra. Surrender in paradise / Sandra Robb. — London : Silhouette, 1981, c1980. — 189p ; 18cm. — (Silhouette romance ; no.42)
ISBN 0-340-26732-1 (pbk) : £0.65 : CIP rev. B81-10480

Robbins, Harold. 79 Park Avenue. — Large print ed. — Anstey : Ulverscroft, Sept.1981. — [448] p. — (Charnwood library series)
ISBN 0-7089-8010-4 : £5.25 : CIP entry B81-21474

Robbins, Harold. Goodbye, Janette / Harold Robbins. — London : New English Library, 1981. — 384p ; 23cm
ISBN 0-450-04858-6 : £6.95 B81-24810

Robbins, Harold. Never leave me. — Large print ed. — Anstey : Ulverscroft, Jan.1982. — [237] p. — (Charnwood library series)
ISBN 0-7089-8023-6 : £4.50 : CIP entry B81-33989

Robbins, Tom. Another roadside attraction / Tom Robbins. — Harmondsworth : Penguin, 1975 (1981 [printing]). — 346p ; 20cm
Originally published : New York : Ballantine, 1972 ; London : W.H. Allen, 1973
ISBN 0-14-004004-8 (pbk) : £1.95 B81-37428

Robbins, Tom. Still life with woodpecker / Tom Robbins. — London : Sidgwick & Jackson, 1980. — x,277p ; 21cm
Originally published: New York : Bantam, 1980
ISBN 0-283-98713-8 (cased) : £6.95
ISBN 0-283-98714-6 (pbk) : £3.50 B81-02902

Roberts, Nora. Irish thoroughbred. — London : Hodder and Stoughton, Dec.1981. — [192]p. — (Silhouette romance)
ISBN 0-340-27661-4 (pbk) : £0.65 : CIP entry B81-31435

Robinson, Marilynne. Housekeeping / Marilynne Robinson. — London : Faber, 1981. — 219p ; 22cm
Originally published: New York : Farrar, Strauss & Giroux, 1980
ISBN 0-571-11713-9 : £5.25 : CIP rev. B81-01146

Roddick, Ellen. Together / Ellen Roddick. — London : Sphere, 1981, c1979. — 183p ; 18cm
Originally published: New York : St. Martin's Press, c1979
ISBN 0-7221-7431-4 (pbk) : £1.25 B81-20246

Roderick, Robert. The Greek position : a novel / by Robert Roderick. — London : Sidgwick & Jackson, 1981. — 553p ; 25cm
ISBN 0-283-98800-2 : £7.95 B81-37889

Roderus, Frank. Hell creek cabin / Frank Roderus. — London : Hale, 1981, c1979. — 183p ; 20cm
ISBN 0-7091-8716-5 : £4.95 B81-24356

Roderus, Frank. Jason Evers : his own story / Frank Roderus. — London : Hale, 1981, c1980. — 178p ; 20cm
Originally published: Garden City : Doubleday, 1980
ISBN 0-7091-8950-8 : £4.95 B81-40540

Roderus, Frank. Sheepherding man / Frank Roderus. — London : Hale, 1980. — 182p ; 20cm
ISBN 0-7091-8678-9 : £4.95 B81-03405

Rogan, Barbara. Changing states : a novel / by Barbara Rogan. — London : Weidenfeld and Nicolson, c1981. — 186p ; 23cm
ISBN 0-297-77869-2 : £5.95 B81-17342

Rogers, Rosemary. Dark fires / Rosemary Rogers. — London : Futura, 1977, c1975 ([printing]). — 604p ; 18cm. — (A Troubadour book)
Originally published: New York : Avon, 1975
ISBN 0-86007-459-5 (pbk) : £1.95 B81-07654

Rogers, Rosemary. Lost love, last love / Rosemary Rogers. — London : Macdonald Futura, 1981, c1980. — 378p ; 18cm. — (A Troubadour spectacular)
ISBN 0-7107-3010-1 (pbk) : £1.50 B81-15451

Rogers, Rosemary. Sweet savage love / Rosemary Rogers. — London : Macdonald Futura, 1977, c1974 (1980 printing). — 636p ; 18cm. — (A Troubadour book)
Originally published: United States : s.n., 1974?
ISBN 0-86007-466-8 (pbk) : £1.95 B81-07652

Rogers, Rosemary. Wicked loving lies / Rosemary Rogers. — London : Futura, 1977, c1976 (1980 [printing]). — 667p ; 18cm. — (A Troubadour book)
Originally published: United States : s.n., 1976?
ISBN 0-86007-570-2 (pbk) : £1.95 B81-07653

Rogers, Rosemary. The wildest heart / Rosemary Rogers. — London : Futura, 1978, c1974 (1980 [printing]). — 608p ; 18cm. — (A Troubadour spectacular)
Originally published: United States : s.n., 1974?
ISBN 0-86007-504-4 (pbk) : £1.95 B81-07658

Roosevelt, James. A family matter. — London : Severn House, Aug.1981. — [320]p
ISBN 0-7278-0725-0 : £6.95 : CIP entry B81-18102

Rosenberger, Joseph. Chinese conspiracy / Joseph Rosenberger. — London : Corgi, 1981, c1973. — 189p ; 18cm. — (Death merchant ; 4)
ISBN 0-552-11723-4 (pbk) : £1.00 B81-39098

Rosenberger, Joseph. The death merchant / Joseph Rosenberger. — [London] : Corgi, 1981, c1973. — 188p ; 18cm. — (Death merchant ; 1)
Originally published: Los Angeles : Pinnacle, 1973
ISBN 0-552-11599-1 (pbk) : £0.95 B81-08411

Rosenberger, Joseph. Operation overkill / Joseph Rosenberger. — [London] : Corgi, 1981, c1972. — 187p ; 18cm. — (Death merchant ; 2)
Originally published: New York : Pinnacle Books, 1972
ISBN 0-552-11632-7 (pbk) : £0.95 B81-15344

Rosenberger, Joseph. The psychotron plot / Joseph Rosenberger. — [London] : Corgi, 1981, c1972. — 156p ; 18cm. — (Death merchant ; 3)
Originally published: Los Angeles : Pinnacle, 1972
ISBN 0-552-11688-2 (pbk) : £0.95 B81-21281

Rosenblum, Robert, *1938-*. Cover story / Robert Rosenblum. — London : Granada, 1980 (1981 [printing]). — 316p ; 18cm. — (A Panther book)
ISBN 0-586-05424-3 (pbk) : £1.50 B81-36769

Roshwald, Mordecai. Level 7 / by Mordecai Roshwald. — London : Allison & Busby, 1981, c1959. — 136p ; 23cm
Originally published: London : Heinemann, 1959
ISBN 0-85031-286-8 (cased) : £6.50 : CIP rev.
ISBN 0-85031-287-6 (pbk) : Unpriced B80-10323

Rossner, Judith. Emmeline / Judith Rossner. — London : Cape, 1980. — 331p ; 23cm
ISBN 0-224-01884-1 : £5.95 B81-02402

Rossner, Judith. Emmeline. — London : Coronet, July 1981. — [352]p
Originally published: London : Cape, 1980
ISBN 0-340-26785-2 (pbk) : £1.95 : CIP entry B81-13890

Rostand, Robert. The D'Artagnan signature / Robert Rostand. — London : Arrow, 1977, c1975 (1981 [printing]). — 245p ; 18cm
Originally published: New York : Putnam, 1975 ; London : Hutchinson, 1976
ISBN 0-09-914870-6 (pbk) : £1.50 B81-32329

Rostand, Robert. A killing in Rome / Robert Rostand. — London : Arrow, 1978, c1977 (1981 [printing]). — 241p ; 18cm
Originally published: London : Hutchinson, 1977
ISBN 0-09-917490-1 (pbk) : £1.50 B81-32328

Rostov, Mara. Night hunt / by Mara Rostov. — London : Hale, 1980, c1979. — 273p ; 23cm
Originally published: New York : Putnam, c1979
ISBN 0-7091-8552-9 : £7.25 B81-02920

Roth, Philip. The ghost writer / Philip Roth. — Harmondsworth : Penguin, 1980, c1979 (1981 [printing]). — 155p ; 18cm
Originally published: London : Cape, 1979
ISBN 0-14-005517-7 (pbk) : £1.25 B81-18323

Roth, Philip. The great American novel / Philip Roth. — Harmondsworth : Penguin, 1981, c1973. — 398p ; 18cm
Originally published: New York : Holt, Rinehart and Winston ; London : Cape, 1973
ISBN 0-14-005519-3 (pbk) : £1.95 B81-40426

Roth, Philip. A Philip Roth reader. — London : Cape, 1981, c1980. — xxiii,483p ; 22cm
Originally published: New York : Farrar, Straus and Giroux, 1980
ISBN 0-224-01922-8 : £8.95 : CIP rev. B81-00328

813′.54[F] — Fiction in English. American writers, *1945- — Texts* *continuation*

Roth, Philip. Portnoy′s complaint / Philip Roth. — [London] : Corgi, 1971, c1969 (1981 [printing]). — 309p ; 18cm
Originally published: New York : Random House ; London : Cape, 1969
ISBN 0-552-11614-9 (pbk) : £1.50 B81-10962

Roth, Philip. Zuckerman unbound / Philip Roth. — London : Cape, c1981. — 225p ; 21cm
ISBN 0-224-01974-0 : £5.95 : CIP rev.
B81-27337

Rotsstein, Aaron Nathan. Judgment in St Peter′s / Aaron Nathan Rotsstein. — London : Pan Books, 1981, c1980. — 250p ; 18cm
Originally published: New York : Putnam, 1980
ISBN 0-330-26371-4 (pbk) : £1.50 B81-24413

Rowe, Jack. Inyo-Sierra passage / Jack Rowe. — London : Hale, 1981, c1980. — 282p ; 21cm
Originally published: New York : McGraw-Hill, 1980
ISBN 0-7091-8987-7 : £6.75 B81-14205

Ruark, Robert. Something of value / Robert Ruark. — London : Corgi, 1970, c1955 (1980 [printing]). — 557p ; 18cm
Originally published: London : Hamilton, 1955
ISBN 0-552-11491-x (pbk) : £1.75 B81-01147

Russell, Ray. The devil′s mirror / Ray Russell. — London : Sphere, 1980. — 189p ; 18cm
ISBN 0-7221-7556-6 (pbk) : £1.10 B81-06426

Ryerson, Martin. Gunfire : at Purgatory Gate / Martin Ryerson. — London : Hale, 1981, c1976. — 175p ; 20cm
Originally published: Canoga Park : Major Books, 1976
ISBN 0-7091-8871-4 : £4.95 B81-34866

Ryerson, Martin. Sheriff without a gun / Martin Ryerson. — London : Hale, 1981, c1976. — 159p ; 20cm
Originally published: Canoga Park, Calif. : Major Books, 1978
ISBN 0-7091-8907-9 : £4.95 B81-15291

Sakol, Jeannie. New Year′s Eve / Jeannie Sakol. — Feltham : Hamlyn, 1980, c1974. — 384p ; 18cm
Originally published: Philadelphia : Lippincott, 1974
ISBN 0-600-36599-9 (pbk) : £1.50 B81-02470

Salem, Richard. New blood / Richard Salem. — London : Macdonald Futura, 1981. — 221p ; 18cm. — (A Futura book)
ISBN 0-7088-2048-4 (pbk) : £1.25 B81-24412

Salvato, Sharon. Bitter Eden / Sharon Salvato. — London : Macdonald Futura, 1980, c1979. — 672p ; 18cm. — (A Troubadour spectacular)
ISBN 0-7088-1917-6 (pbk) : £1.95 B81-06320

Sandberg, Peter Lars. Stubb′s run / Peter Lars Sandberg. — London : Hale, 1980, c1979. — 179p ; 23cm
Originally published: Boston, Mass. : Houghton Mifflin, 1979
ISBN 0-7091-8936-2 : £6.50 B81-11156

Sanders, Lawrence. The first deadly sin / Lawrence Sanders. — London : Star, 1974, c1973 (1981 [printing]). — 566p ; 18cm
Originally published: New York : Putnam, 1973 ; London : W.H. Allen, 1974
£1.95 (pbk) B81-19315

Sanders, Lawrence. The sixth commandment / Lawrence Sanders. — London : Granada, 1980, c1979. — 348p ; 18cm. — (Panther)
Originally published: New York : Putman ; London : Hart-Davis, 1979
ISBN 0-586-05027-2 (pbk) : £1.25 B81-02196

Sanders, Lawrence. The tenth commandment / Lawrence Sanders. — London : Granada, 1981, c1980. — 385p ; 23cm
Originally published: New York : Putnam, 1980
ISBN 0-246-11154-2 : £6.50 B81-03474

Sanders, Lawrence. The third deadly sin / Lawrence Sanders. — London : Granada, 1981. — 457p ; 23cm
ISBN 0-246-11155-0 : £6.95 B81-38055

Sapir, Richard. Chained reaction / Richard Sapir and Warren Murphy. — [London] : Corgi, 1980, c1978. — 178p ; 18cm. — (The Destroyer ; 34)
Originally published: New York : Pinnacle, 1978
ISBN 0-552-11427-8 (pbk) : £0.95 B81-07290

Sapir, Richard. The destroyer 35 : last call / Richard Sapir and Warren Murphy. — [London] : Corgi, 1981, c1978. — 182p ; 18cm
Originally published: United States : s.n., 1978?
ISBN 0-552-11507-x (pbk) : £0.95 B81-10968

Sapir, Richard. Destroyer 37 : bottom line / Richard Sapir and Warren Murphy. — London : Corgi, 1981, c1979. — 178p ; 18cm
ISBN 0-552-11766-8 (pbk) : £1.00 B81-35501

Sapir, Richard. Power play / Richard Sapir and Warren Murphy. — [London] : Corgi, 1981, c1979. — 180p ; 18cm. — (Destroyer ; 36)
ISBN 0-552-11704-8 (pbk) : £0.95 B81-27242

Sargent, Pamela. Cloned lives / Pamela Sargent. — [London] : Fontana Paperbacks, 1981, c1976 (1981 [printing]). — 319p ; 18cm
Originally published: New York : Fawcett, 1976
ISBN 0-00-615553-7 (pbk) : £1.50 B81-15528

Saul, John. Comes the blind fury / John Saul. — Sevenoaks : Coronet, 1981, c1980. — 218p ; 18cm
Originally published: New York : Dell, 1980
ISBN 0-340-26680-5 (pbk) : £1.50 : CIP rev.
B81-18134

Scarborough, Chuck. The Myrmidon project. — Loughton : Piatkus, Nov.1981. — [320]p
ISBN 0-86188-131-1 : £6.95 : CIP entry
B81-30382

Schiff, Barry. The Vatican target / Barry Schiff and Hal Fishman. — London : Arrow, 1981, c1978. — 273p ; 18cm
Originally published: New York : St. Martin′s Press, 1979
ISBN 0-09-922590-5 (pbk) : £1.50 B81-16014

Schwartz, Lynne Sharon. Rough strife / Lynne Sharon Schwartz. — London : Gollancz, 1981, c1980. — 200p ; 22cm
Originally published: New York : Harper & Row, 1980
ISBN 0-575-02996-x : £6.95 B81-28626

Scott, Joanna. Dusky Rose / Joanna Scott. — London : Silhouette, 1981, c1980. — 189p ; 18cm. — (Silhouette romance ; 49)
ISBN 0-340-26739-9 (pbk) : £0.65 : CIP rev.
B81-13776

Scott, Joanna. The marriage bargain. — London : Hodder & Stoughton, Oct.1981. — [192]p. — (Silhouette romance)
ISBN 0-340-27123-x (pbk) : £0.65 : CIP entry
B81-26775

Segal, Brenda Lesley. Aliya : a love story / Brenda Lesley Segal in association with Marianne Kanter ; edited by Lesley Saxby. — London : Futura, 1980, c1978. — 244p ; 18cm. — (A Troubador spectacular)
Originally published: New York : St Martin′s Press ; London : Macdonald & Jane′s, 1978
ISBN 0-7088-1833-1 (pbk) : £1.00 B81-01148

Segal, Erich. Man, woman and child / Erich Segal. — London : Granada, 1980 (1981 [printing]). — 221p ; 18cm. — (A Panther book)
ISBN 0-586-05173-2 (pbk) : £1.25 B81-19914

Sellers, Con. Sweet Caroline / Con Sellers. — London : Sphere, 1980, c1979. — 521p ; 18cm
Originally published: New York : Pocket Books, 1979
ISBN 0-7221-7706-2 (pbk) : £1.95 B81-00312

Seltzer, David. The omen / David Seltzer. — London : Futura, 1976 (1981 [printing]). — 192p ; 18cm
ISBN 0-86007-371-8 (pbk) : £1.25 B81-40950

Setlowe, Richard. The experiment / Richard Setlowe. — London : Hutchinson, 1980. — 299p ; 23cm
Originally published: New York : Holt, Rinehart and Winston, 1980
ISBN 0-09-143310-x : £6.95 : CIP rev.
B80-12593

Seymour, Janette. Emmie′s love / Janette Seymour. — [Sevenoaks] : Coronet, 1981. — 391p ; 18cm
Originally published: New York : Pocket Books, 1981
ISBN 0-340-26661-9 (pbk) : £1.60 : CIP rev.
B81-03818

Shagan, Steve. The formula : a novel / Steve Shagan. — [London] : Corgi, 1980, c1979. — 335p ; 18cm
Originally published: New York : Morrow, 1979 ; London : Joseph, 1980
ISBN 0-552-11549-5 (pbk) : £1.50 B81-06371

Shannon, Dell. Felony at random / Dell Shannon. — Large print ed. — Leicester : Ulverscroft, 1981, c1979. — 354p ; 23cm. — (Ulverscroft large print)
Originally published: New York : Morrow ; London : Gollancz, 1979
ISBN 0-7089-0660-5 : £5.00 : CIP rev.
B81-20628

Shannon, Dell. Murder most strange / Dell Shannon. — London : Gollancz, 1981. — 228p ; 21cm
ISBN 0-575-03012-7 : £5.95 B81-28625

Shea, Robert. Shiké. — Loughton : Piatkus, Nov.1981. — [352]p
ISBN 0-86188-130-3 : £6.95 : CIP entry
B81-30378

Sheldon, Sidney. Rage of angels. — Large print ed. — Leicester : Ulverscroft, Sept.1981. — [597]p. — (Charnwood library series)
Originally published: New York : W. Morrow, 1980 ; London : Collins, 1980
ISBN 0-7089-8003-1 : £6.50 : CIP entry
B81-22659

Sheppard, Eugenia. Skyrocket / Eugenia Sheppard and Earl Blackwell. — London : W.H. Allen, 1981, c1980. — 352p ; 18cm. — (A Star book)
Originally published: Garden City, N.Y. : Doubleday, 1980
ISBN 0-352-30893-1 (pbk) : £1.75 B81-35161

Sheppard, Eugenia. Skyrocket : a novel about glamour and power / Eugenia Sheppard and Earl Blackwell. — London : W.H. Allen, 1981, c1980. — 352p ; 22cm
Originally published: Garden City, N.Y. : Doubleday, 1980
ISBN 0-491-02693-5 : £7.50 B81-02911

Sheppard, Stephen. The four hundred / Stephen Sheppard. — Large print ed. — Leicester : Ulverscroft, 1980, c1979. — 587p ; 23cm. — (Ulverscroft large print series)
Originally published: New York : Summit ; London : Secker and Warburg, 1979
ISBN 0-7089-0585-4 : £4.25 : CIP rev.
B80-23742

813'.54[F] — Fiction in English. American writers, *1945- — Texts* *continuation*

Sherlock, John. The dream makers / John Sherlock. — Feltham : Hamlyn, 1980, c1979. — 377p ; 18cm
ISBN 0-600-20163-5 (pbk) : £1.50 B81-01149

Sherlock, John. J.B.'s daughter / John Sherlock. — London : W.H. Allen, 1981. — 350p ; 22cm
ISBN 0-491-02654-4 : £7.50 B81-11776

Sherman, Jory. Buzzard bait / by Jory Sherman. — London : Hale, 1981, c1978. — 156p ; 20cm
Originally published: Canoga Park, Calif. : Major Books, 1978
ISBN 0-7091-8913-3 : £4.95 B81-15295

Sherman, William. Times Square / William Sherman. — Toronto ; London : Bantam, 1980. — 359p ; 18cm
ISBN 0-553-13116-8 (pbk) : £1.50 B81-00313

Shobin, David. The unborn / David Shobin. — London : Heinemann, 1981, c1980. — 311p ; 23cm
Originally published: New York : Linden Press, 1980
ISBN 0-434-67863-5 : £6.95 B81-15477

Shyer, Marlene Fanta. Never trust a handsome man / Marlene Fanta Shyer. — London : Hamlyn Paperbacks, 1981, c1979. — 191p ; 18cm
Originally published: New York : Coward, McCann & Geoghegan, 1979
ISBN 0-600-20259-3 (pbk) : £1.25 B81-19915

Shyer, Marlene Fanta. Welcome home, jellybean / Marlene Fanta Shyer. — Redcar : Granada, 1981, c1978. — 128p ; 23cm
Originally published: New York : Scribner, 1978. — For adolescents
ISBN 0-246-11558-0 : £4.50 B81-29899

Siddons, Anne Rivers. Fox's earth / Anne Rivers Siddons. — London : Collins, 1981. — 477p ; 23cm
Originally published: New York : Simon and Schuster, 1981
ISBN 0-00-222601-4 : £7.50 B81-31924

Silverberg, Robert. The second trip / Robert Silverberg. — London : Pan, 1980, c1972. — 188p ; 18cm. — (Pan science fiction)
Originally published: Garden City, N.Y. : Doubleday, 1972 ; London : Gollancz, 1979
ISBN 0-330-26227-0 (pbk) : £1.50 B81-03311

Silverberg, Robert. Shadrach in the furnace / Robert Silverberg. — [London] : Coronet, 1979, c1976. — 245p ; 18cm
Orrginally published: New York : Bobbs-Merrill, 1976 ; London : Gollancz, 1977
ISBN 0-340-23235-8 (pbk) : £0.85 B81-05735

Simak, Clifford D.. Cemetery world / Clifford D. Simak. — London : Magnum Books, 1977, c1973 (1980 printing). — 191p ; 18cm
Originally published: New York : Putnam, 1973 ; London : Sidgwick and Jackson, 1975
ISBN 0-417-02040-6 (pbk) : £1.25 B81-07001

Simak, Clifford D.. Project Pope : science fiction / by Clifford D. Simak. — London : Sidgwick & Jackson, 1981. — 313p ; 21cm
Originally published: New York : Ballantine Books, 1981
ISBN 0-283-98803-7 : £7.95 B81-37057

Simak, Clifford D.. The visitors : science fiction / by Clifford D. Simak. — London : Sidgwick & Jackson, 1981, c1980. — 282p ; 21cm
Originally published: New York : Ballantine, 1980
ISBN 0-283-98718-9 : £7.95 B81-03381

Simpson, George E.. Fair warning / George E. Simpson and Neal R. Burger. — London : New English Library, 1981, c1980. — 443p ; 18cm
Originally published: New York : Delacorte ; London : New English Library, 1980
ISBN 0-450-05138-2 (pbk) : £1.75 B81-24747

Sinclair, Murray. Prisoner : cell block H / Murray Sinclair. — London : W.H. Allen, 1981, c1980. — 212p ; 18cm. — (A Star book)
Originally published: Los Angeles : Pinnacle, 1980
ISBN 0-352-30832-x (pbk) : £1.50 B81-35159

Sinclair, Tracy. Paradise Island / Tracy Sinclair. — London : Silhouette, 1981, c1980. — 188p ; 17cm. — (Silhouette romance ; 38)
ISBN 0-340-26728-3 (pbk) : £0.65 : CIP rev. B81-04208

Singer, Brett. The petting zoo / Brett Singer. — London : Macdonald Futura, 1980, c1979. — 254p ; 18cm
Originally published: New York : Simon and Schuster, 1979 ; London : Raven Books, 1980
ISBN 0-7088-1806-4 (pbk) : £1.25 B81-15458

Skinner, Ainslie. Mind's eye / Ainslie Skinner. — London : Pan in association with Secker & Warburg, 1981, c1980. — 276p ; 18cm
Originally published: London : Secker & Warburg, 1980
ISBN 0-330-26253-x (pbk) : £1.25 B81-09749

Sky, Kathleen. Death's Angel : a Star Trek novel / Kathleen Sky. — Toronto ; London : Bantam, 1981. — 213p ; 18cm
ISBN 0-553-14703-x (pbk) : £1.25 B81-32114

Slade, E. R.. Country full of guns / E.R. Slade. — London : Hale, 1981, c1979. — 186p ; 20cm
Originally published: in the United States : s.n., 1979?
ISBN 0-7091-8830-7 (corrected) : £4.95 B81-33523

Slade, E. R.. Gunman's gold / E.R. Slade. — London : Hale, 1981, c1979. — 203p ; 20cm
Originally published: New York : Manor Books, 1979
ISBN 0-7091-8829-3 : £4.95 B81-11782

Sladek, John. Roderick, or, The education of a young machine / John Sladek. — London : Granada, 1980. — 348p ; 23cm
ISBN 0-246-11437-1 : £6.95 B81-05903

Slepian, Jan. The Alfred summer / Jan Slepian. — Harmondsworth : Kestrel, 1981, c1980. — 119p ; 23cm
Originally published: New York : Macmillan, 1980
ISBN 0-7226-5767-6 : £4.75 B81-40683

Smith, J. C. S.. Jacoby's first case / J.C.S. Smith. — London : Hale, c1980. — 188p ; 20cm
Originally published: New York : Atheneum, 1980
ISBN 0-7091-9005-0 : £5.95 B81-24867

Smith, Joan, *1938-*. Dame Durden's daughter / Joan Smith. — South Yarmouth : Curley ; Clitheroe : Magna Print [distributor], c1978. — 349p ; 23cm
Originally published: New York : Walker, 1978. — Published in large print
ISBN 0-89340-267-2 : £5.50 B81-02717

Smith, Kay Nolte. The watcher / Kay Nolte Smith. — London : Gollancz, 1981, c1980. — 327p ; 21cm
Originally published: New York : Coward, McCann and Geoghegan, 1980
ISBN 0-575-02962-5 : £6.95 B81-12064

Smith, Martin Cruz. Gorky Park / Martin Cruz Smith. — London : Collins, 1981. — 365p : 1map ; 24cm
ISBN 0-00-222278-7 : £6.95 B81-18616

Smith, Steven Phillip. The long riders / Steven Phillip Smith ; based upon a screenplay by Bill Bryden ... [et al.]. — London : Severn House, 1981, c1980. — 191p ; 231cm
Originally published: London : Futura, 1980
ISBN 0-7278-0663-7 : £5.95 B81-08628

Smoodin, Roberta. Ursus major / by Roberta Smoodin. — London : Routledge and Kegan Paul, 1980. — 211p ; 23cm
ISBN 0-7100-0717-5 : £5.95 : CIP rev. B80-20989

Snow, Kathleen. Night walking / Kathleen Snow. — London : Arrow, 1980, c1978. — 314p ; 18cm
Originally published: New York : Simon and Schuster, 1978
ISBN 0-09-922320-1 (pbk) : £1.50 B81-02176

Snyder, Zilpha Keatley. Heirs of darkness / Zilpha Keatley Snyder. — London : Magnum, 1980, c1978. — 248p ; 18cm
Originally published: New York : Atheneum, 1978
ISBN 0-417-04880-7 (pbk) : £1.30 B81-01150

Solmssen, Arthur. A princess in Berlin / Arthur Solmssen. — London : Hutchinson, 1981, c1980. — 374p : ill ; 24cm
Originally published: Boston, Mass. : Little, Brown, 1980
ISBN 0-09-144140-4 : £6.95 B81-10159

Sorrentino, Gilbert. Aberration of starlight / Gilbert Sorrentino. — London : Boyars, 1981. — 211p ; 23cm
Originally published: New York : Random House, 1980
ISBN 0-7145-2731-9 : £6.95 : CIP rev. B81-12803

Spencer, Scott. Endless love / Scott Spencer. — Harmondsworth : Penguin, 1981, c1979. — 377p ; 18cm
Originally published: New York : Knopf, 1979 ; London : Cape, 1980
ISBN 0-14-005603-3 (pbk) : £1.75 B81-18330

Spinrad, Norman. Agent of chaos / Norman Spinrad. — London : Corgi, 1981, c1967. — 186p ; 18cm
ISBN 0-552-11727-7 (pbk) : £1.25 B81-32106

Spinrad, Norman. Songs from the stars : science fiction / by Norman Spinrad. — London : Sidgwick & Jackson, 1981, c1980. — 286p ; 21cm
Originally published: New York : Simon and Schuster, 1980
ISBN 0-283-98733-2 : £6.95 B81-11632

St. George, Edith. West of the moon. — London : Hodder & Stoughton, Oct.1981. — [192]p. — (Silhouette romance)
ISBN 0-340-27124-8 (pbk) : £0.65 : CIP entry B81-26774

Stanford, Sandra. And then came dawn. — London : Hodder and Stoughton, Feb.1982. — [192]p. — (Silhouette romance)
ISBN 0-340-27668-1 (pbk) : £0.75 : CIP entry B81-38312

Stanford, Sondra. Golden tide / Sondra Stanford. — London (47 Bedford Sq., WC1B 3DP) : Silhouette, 1980. — 191p ; 18cm. — (Silhouette romance ; no.6)
ISBN 0-340-26003-3 (pbk) : £0.65 : CIP rev. B80-12594

Stanford, Sondra. Long winter's night / Sondra Stanford. — London : Silhouette, 1981. — 189p ; 18cm. — (Silhouette romance ; 57)
ISBN 0-340-27035-7 (pbk) : £0.65 : CIP rev. B81-18141

Stanford, Sondra. No trespassing / Sondra Stanford. — London : Silhouette, 1981, c1980. — 188p ; 18cm. — (Silhouette romance ; no.45)
ISBN 0-340-26735-6 (pbk) : £0.65 : CIP rev. B81-09991

Stanford, Sondra. Shadow of love / Sondra Stanford. — London (47 Bedford Sq., WC1B 3DP) : Silhouette, 1980. — 188p ; 18cm. — (Silhouette romance ; no.25)
ISBN 0-340-26446-2 (pbk) : £0.65 B81-14149

813'.54[F] — Fiction in English. American writers, *1945- — Texts* *continuation*

Stanford, Sondra. Storm's end / Sondra Stanford. — London : Silhouette, 1981, c1980. — 189p ; 18cm. — (Silhouette romance ; no.24)
ISBN 0-340-26724-0 (pbk) : £0.65 : CIP rev. B81-04221

Steel, Danielle. Golden moments. — Loughton : Piatkus, Dec.1981. — [388]p
ISBN 0-86188-085-4 : £6.95 : CIP entry B81-31636

Steel, Danielle. Loving / Danielle Steel. — London : Sphere, 1981, c1980. — 307p ; 18cm
ISBN 0-7221-8167-1 (pbk) : £1.50 B81-28361

Steel, Danielle. Loving / Danielle Steel. — Loughton : Piatkus, 1981, c1980. — 382p ; 21cm
ISBN 0-86188-106-0 (corrected) : £6.95 : CIP rev. B81-15855

Steel, Danielle. The ring / Danielle Steel. — London : Hodder and Stoughton, 1981, c1980. — 338p ; 23cm
Originally published: New York : Delacorte Press, 1980
ISBN 0-340-26488-8 : £5.95 B81-18683

Steel, Danielle. Summer's end / Danielle Steel. — Large print ed. — Leicester : Ulverscroft, 1981, c1979. — 493p ; 23cm. — (Ulverscroft large print series)
Originally published: London : Sphere, 1979
ISBN 0-7089-0607-9 : £5.00 : CIP rev. B81-02580

Steel, Danielle. Summer's end / Danielle Steel. — Loughton ([17 Brook Rd.,] Loughton, Essex) : Piatkus, 1981, c1979. — 318p ; 21cm
Originally published: London : Sphere, 1979?
ISBN 0-86188-066-8 : £5.95 B81-08629

Steel, Danielle. To love again / Danielle Steel. — London : Sphere, 1980 (1981 [printing]). — 278p ; 18cm
ISBN 0-7221-8107-8 (pbk) : £1.25 B81-11486

Steel, Danielle. To love again / Danielle Steel. — Loughton : Piatkus, 1981, c1980. — 278p ; 21cm
Originally published: London : Sphere, 1980
ISBN 0-86188-077-3 : £6.50 B81-12948

Stein, Benjamin, *1944-*. The Croesus conspiracy / Ben Stein. — Feltham : Hamlyn Paperbacks, 1979, c1978 (1981 [printing]). — 320p ; 18cm
Originally published: New York : Simon and Schuster, 1978
ISBN 0-600-32139-8 (pbk) : £1.25 B81-19913

Stein, Sol. The resort / Sol Stein. — [London] : Fontana, 1981, c1980. — 253p ; 18cm
Originally published: New York : Morrow, 1980
ISBN 0-00-616249-5 (pbk) : £1.35 B81-28435

Steiner, George, *1929-*. The portage to San Cristobal of A.H.. — London : Faber, 1981. — 126p ; 20cm
Author: George Steiner
ISBN 0-571-11741-4 (pbk) : £2.95 : CIP rev. B81-07592

Stephan, Leslie. Murder or not / by Leslie Stephan. — London : Hale, 1981. — 192p ; 20cm
ISBN 0-7091-9015-8 : £5.95 B81-26181

Stephens, Jeanne. Mexican nights / Jeanne Stephens. — London (47 Bedford Sq., WC1B 3DP) : Silhouette, 1980. — 189p ; 18cm. — (Silhouette romance ; no.22)
ISBN 0-340-26443-8 (pbk) : £0.65 B81-14152

Stephens, Jeanne. Wonder and desire. — London : Hodder and Stoughton, Dec.1981. — [192]p. — (Silhouette romance)
ISBN 0-340-27660-6 (pbk) : £0.65 : CIP entry B81-31439

Stern, Richard, *1928-*. [In any case]. The Chaleur Network : a novel / by Richard G. Stern. — Sagaponack : Second Chance ; London : Sidgwick & Jackson, 1981. — 241p ; 23cm
Originally published: New York : McGraw-Hill, 1962
ISBN 0-283-98730-8 : £6.95 B81-24369

Stern, Richard Martin. Flood / Richard Martin Stern. — London : Granada, 1980, c1979. — 314p ; 18cm. — (A Panther book)
Originally published: Garden City, N.Y. : Doubleday ; London : Secker & Warburg, 1979
ISBN 0-586-05108-2 (pbk) : £1.50 B81-00314

Stewart, Fred Mustard. Century : a novel / by Fred Mustard Stewart. — London : Hamilton, 1981. — 576p ; 23cm
ISBN 0-241-10680-x : £7.95 : CIP rev. B81-26777

Stewart, Fred Mustard. Star child / Fred Mustard Stewart. — London : Corgi, 1976, c1974 (1980 [printing]). — 238p ; 18cm
Originally published: New York : Arbor House, 1974 ; London : W.H. Allen, 1975
ISBN 0-552-11654-8 (pbk) : £1.25 B81-07351

Stine, Hank. The prisoner : a day in the life / Hank Stine. — London : New English Library, 1981, c1970. — 155p ; 18cm
Originally published: New York : Ace Books, 1970 ; London : Dobson, 1979
ISBN 0-450-05106-4 (pbk) : £1.25 B81-15410

Stolpacker, Pete. Brand of Yuma / Pete Stolpacker. — London : Hale, 1981, c1979. — 215p ; 20cm
Originally published: New York : Manor Books, 1979
ISBN 0-7091-9082-4 : £4.95 B81-24874

Stone, Robert. A flag for sunrise. — London : Secker & Warburg, Oct.1981. — [448]p
ISBN 0-436-49681-x : £6.95 : CIP entry B81-28003

Stowe, James L.. Winter stalk / James L. Stowe. — London : Hamlyn Paperbacks, 1980, c1979. — 284p ; 18cm
Originally published: New York : Simon and Schuster, 1979 ; London : Hamlyn, 1980
ISBN 0-600-20098-1 (pbk) : £1.25 B81-03453

Strang, William, *1935-*. The Texas inheritance : a novel / William Strang. — London : Macmillan, 1980. — 283p ; 23cm
ISBN 0-333-26773-7 : £6.95 B81-03000

Strang, William, *1935-*. The Texas inheritance / William Strang. — London : Pan in association with Macmillan, 1981, c1980. — 283p ; 18cm
Originally published: London : Macmillan, 1980
ISBN 0-330-26405-2 (pbk) : £1.50 B81-37353

Straub, Peter. Shadow land / Peter Straub. — London : Collins, 1981, c1980. — 417p ; 24cm
Originally published: New York : Coward, McCann & Geoghegan, 1980
ISBN 0-00-222343-0 : £6.95 B81-02493

Strieber, Whitley. The hunger / Whitley Strieber. — London : Bodley Head, 1981, c1980. — 248p ; 23cm
ISBN 0-370-30398-9 : £6.50 : CIP rev. B81-01151

Strobos, Robert. Treading water / Robert Strobos. — Baton Rouge ; London : Louisiana State University Press, 1980. — 150p ; 23cm
ISBN 0-8071-0682-8 : £6.00 B81-01152

Styron, William. The confessions of Nat Turner / William Styron. — [London] : Corgi, 1980, c1967. — 413p ; 18cm
Originally published: New York : Random House, 1967 ; London : Cape, 1968
ISBN 0-552-11527-4 (pbk) : £1.95 B81-06369

Styron, William. Lie down in darkness / William Styron. — London : Corgi, 1951 (1980 [printing]). — 443p ; 18cm
Originally published: Indianapolis: Bobbs-Merrill, 1951 ; London : Hamilton, 1952
ISBN 0-552-11423-5 (pbk) : £1.75 B81-00315

Styron, William. Set this house on fire / William Styron. — London : Corgi, 1963, c1960 (1980 [printing]). — 477p : ; 18cm
Originally published: New York : Random House, 1960 ; London : Hamilton, 1961
ISBN 0-552-11528-2 (pbk) : £1.95 B81-07359

Styron, William. Sophie's choice / William Styron. — [London] : Corgi, 1980 c1979 (1981 [printing]). — 683p ; 18cm
Originally published: New York : Random House ; London : Cape, 1979
ISBN 0-552-11610-6 (pbk) : £1.95 B81-10966

Sullivan, Tim. Glitter street / Tim Sullivan. — London : Hale, 1981, c1979. — 277p ; 22cm
Originally published: New York : Rawson, Wade, 1979
ISBN 0-7091-9254-1 : £6.95 B81-24357

Susann, Jacqueline. Yargo / Jacqueline Susann. — London : Corgi, 1979. — 347p ; 18cm
ISBN 0-552-11019-1 (pbk) : £1.25 B81-09309

Sutton, Jefferson. Cassady / Jefferson Sutton. — London : Hale, 1981, c1979. — 205p ; 20cm
Originally published: New York : St. Martin's Press, 1979
ISBN 0-7091-8928-1 : £5.75 B81-11777

Sutton, Stack. The marshal's gun / Stack Sutton. — London : Hale, 1980, c1978. — 160p ; 20cm
Originally published: New York : Major Books, 1978
ISBN 0-7091-8675-4 : £4.95 B81-03404

Talmy, Shel. Hunter killer / Shel Talmy. — London : Pan, 1981. — 316p ; 18cm. — (Pan original)
ISBN 0-330-26311-0 (pbk) : £1.50 B81-18299

Tanous, Peter. The wheat killing / by Peter Tanous and Paul Rubinstein. — London : Deutsch, 1980, c1979. — 273p ; 23cm
Originally published: Garden City, N.Y. : Doubleday, 1979
ISBN 0-233-97280-3 : £6.50 B81-02895

Tanous, Peter. The wheat killing / by Peter Tanous and Paul Rubinstein. — London : Arrow, 1981, c1979. — 273p ; 18cm
Originally published: Garden City, N.Y. : Doubleday, 1979 ; London : Deutsch, 1980
ISBN 0-09-926060-3 (pbk) : £1.60 B81-24842

Taylor, Charles D.. Show of force / Charles D. Taylor. — London : Macdonald Futura, 1981, c1980. — 281p ; 21cm
ISBN 0-354-04619-5 : £4.95 B81-10163

Teed, Jack Hamilton. Gunships : the killing zone / Jack Hamilton Teed. — London : Star, 1981. — 191p ; 18cm
ISBN 0-352-30708-0 (pbk) : £1.25 B81-11682

Templeton, Charles. Act of God / Charles Templeton. — Large print ed. — Leicester : Ulverscroft, 1980, c1978. — 593p ; 23cm. — (Ulverscroft large print series)
Originally published: Boston : Little, Brown, 1978
ISBN 0-7089-0513-7 : £4.25 : CIP rev. B80-18018

Terman, Douglas. First strike / Douglas Terman. — London : Futura, 1980, c1979. — 368p ; 18cm
Originally published: London : Joseph, 1980
ISBN 0-7088-1809-9 (pbk) : £1.75 B81-28342

813'.54[F] — Fiction in English. American writers, 1945- — Texts *continuation*

Terman, Douglas. Free flight / Douglas Terman. — London : Macdonald, 1981, c1980. — 349p ; 23cm
Originally published: New York : Scribner, c1980
ISBN 0-354-04637-3 : £6.95 B81-14078

Tessier, Thomas. The nightwalker / Thomas Tessier. — London : Pan, 1980, c1979. — 158p ; 18cm
Originally published: London : Macmillan, 1979
ISBN 0-330-26225-4 (pbk) : £0.95 B81-03382

Thayer, Nancy. Stepping / Nancy Thayer. — Loughton ([17 Brook Rd., Loughton, Essex IG10 1BW]) : Piatkus, 1980. — 346p ; 21cm
Originally published: Garden City, N.Y. : Doubleday, 1980
ISBN 0-86188-058-7 : £6.50 : CIP rev. B80-22587

Theroux, Paul. The Mosquito Coast / Paul Theroux. — London : Hamilton, 1981. — 392p ; 23cm
ISBN 0-241-10688-5 : £7.95 : CIP rev. B81-25702

Thomas, Michael M.. Green Monday / Michael M. Thomas. — London : Arrow, 1981, c1980. — 526p ; 18cm
Originally published: New York : Wyndham Books ; London : Hutchinson, 1980
ISBN 0-09-925280-5 (pbk) : £1.75 B81-11036

Thomas, Ross. The eighth dwarf / Ross Thomas. — London : Pan, 1981, c1979. — 255p ; 18cm
Originally published: London : Hamilton, 1979
ISBN 0-330-26234-3 (pbk) : £1.25 B81-03050

Thomas, Ross. The fools in town are on our side / Ross Thomas. — London : Magnum, 1981, c1970. — 338p ; 18cm
Originally published: London : Hodder & Stoughton, 1970
ISBN 0-417-05250-2 (pbk) : £1.50 B81-28660

Thomas, Ross. The mordida man / Ross Thomas. — London : Hamilton, 1981. — 284p ; 23cm
ISBN 0-241-10576-5 : £7.95 : CIP rev. B81-04212

Thompson, Buck. Bull Mountain range / by Buck Thompson. — London : Hale, 1981. — 159p ; 20cm
ISBN 0-7091-9028-x : £4.95 B81-19291

Thompson, Earl. A garden of sand / Earl Thompson. — London : Pan, 1981, c1970. — 55p ; 18cm
Originally published: New York : Putnam, 1970 ; London : W.H. Allen, 1971
ISBN 0-330-26453-2 (pbk) : £1.95 B81-20221

Thompson, Gene. Murder mystery / Gene Thompson. — London : Gollancz, 1981, c1980. — 275p ; 21cm
Originally published: New York : Random House, 1980
ISBN 0-575-03002-x : £5.95 B81-24754

Thompson, Joyce. Willie and Phil / Joyce Thompson. — [London] : Coronet, 1980. — 158p ; 18cm
ISBN 0-340-25857-8 (pbk) : £0.95 : CIP rev. B80-12600

Thompson, Steven L.. Recovery / Steven L. Thompson. — London : New English Library, 1981, c1980. — 222p ; 18cm
Originally published: New York : Warner, 1980
ISBN 0-450-04989-2 (pbk) : £1.25 B81-07083

Thornton, Carolyn. The heart never forgets / Carolyn Thornton. — London (47 Bedford Sq., WC1B 3DP) : Silhouette, 1981, c1980. — 189p ; 18cm. — (Silhouette romance ; no.19)
ISBN 0-340-26123-4 (pbk) : £0.65 : CIP rev. B80-21111

Thorp, Roderick. Nothing lasts forever / Roderick Thorp. — [London] : Corgi, 1981, c1979. — 187p ; 18cm
Originally published: New York : Norton, 1979
ISBN 0-552-11579-7 (pbk) : £1.00 B81-08410

Tokson, Elliot. Appointment in Calcutta / Elliot Tokson. — [London] : Magnum, 1981, c1979. — 256p ; 18cm
Originally published: Greenwich, Conn. : Fawcett, 1979
ISBN 0-417-04850-5 (pbk) : £1.50 B81-28679

Tokson, Elliot. Cavender's Balkan quest / Elliot Tokson. — [London] : Magnum, 1981, c1977. — 287p ; 18cm
Originally published: Greenwich, Conn. : Fawcett, 1977
ISBN 0-417-04860-2 (pbk) : £1.50 B81-28678

Tonner, Leslie. Fortunoff's child / Leslie Tonner. — London : Allen Lane, 1980. — 375p ; 23cm
Originally published: New York : Dial Press, 1980
ISBN 0-7139-1365-7 : £6.50 B81-00316

Toole, John Kennedy. A confederacy of dunces / John Kennedy Toole ; foreword by Walker Percy. — Harmondsworth : Penguin, 1981, c1980. — vii,338p ; 20cm
Originally published: Baton Rouge ; London : Louisiana State University Press, 1980
ISBN 0-14-005889-3 (pbk) : £2.50 B81-20955

Toole, John Kennedy. A confederacy of dunces / John Kennedy Toole ; foreword by Walker Percy. — London : Allen Lane, 1981, c1980. — 338p ; 21cm
Originally published: Baton Rouge ; London : Louisiana State University Press, 1980
ISBN 0-7139-1422-x : £7.95 B81-20954

Tralins, Robert. Chains / Robert Tralins. — London : New English Library, 1981. — 174p ; 18cm
ISBN 0-450-04990-6 (pbk) : £1.00 B81-07081

Trent, Brenda. Rising star / Brenda Trent. — London : Silhouette, 1981. — 189p ; 18cm. — (Silhouette romance ; 55)
ISBN 0-340-27033-0 (pbk) : £0.65 : CIP rev. B81-18139

Trent, Brent. Winter dreams. — London : Hodder & Stoughton, Nov.1981. — [192]p. — (Silhouette romance)
ISBN 0-340-27262-7 (pbk) : £0.65 : CIP entry B81-30141

Trevanian. Shibumi. — Large print ed. — Leicester : Ulverscroft, Sept.1981. — [619]p. — (Charnwood library series)
Originally published: New York : Harcourt Brace Jovanovich, 1976 ; London : Hart-Davis MacGibbon, 1977
ISBN 0-7089-8004-x : £6.50 : CIP entry B81-22656

Trott, Susan. When your lover leaves / Susan Trott. — London : Gollancz, 1981, c1980. — 215pp ; 22cm
Originally published: New York : St. Martin's Press, 1980
ISBN 0-575-02905-6 : £7.95 B81-12067

Truman, Margaret. Murder in the White House : a novel / by Margaret Truman. — London : Severn House, 1981, c1980. — 235p ; 21cm
Originally published: Boston, Mass. : G.K. Hall, 1980
ISBN 0-7278-0718-8 : £6.95 : CIP rev. B81-14929

Tunberg, Karl. The quest of Ben Hur / Karl Tunberg and Owen Walford. — Harmondsworth : Penguin, 1981. — 430p ; 18cm
ISBN 0-14-005373-5 (pbk) : £1.75 B81-18341

Tyler, Anne. Celestial navigation / Anne Tyler. — South Yarmouth, Mass. : John Curley ; [Long Preston] : Magna [distributor], c1974. — 530p ; 23cm
Originally published: New York : Knopf, 1974 ; London : Chatto and Windus, 1975. — Published in large print
ISBN 0-89340-320-2 : £4.95 B81-39301

Tyler, Anne. If morning ever comes / Anne Tyler. — South Yarmouth, Mass. : Curley ; [Long Preston] : Distributed by Magna Print, [1981?], c1964. — 428p ; 23cm
Originally published: New York : Knopf, 1964 ; London : Chatto & Windus, 1965. — Published in large print
ISBN 0-89340-319-9 (corrected) : Unpriced B81-38627

Tyler, Anne. Morgan's passing / Anne Tyler. — London : Chatto & Windus, 1980. — 311p ; 21cm
Originally published: New York : Knopf, 1980
ISBN 0-7011-2532-2 : £6.50 B81-01153

Tyler, Anne. Morgan's passing / Anne Tyler. — Feltham : Hamlyn, 1981, c1980. — 282p ; 18cm
Originally published: New York : Knopf ; London : Chatto and Windus, 1980
ISBN 0-600-20409-x (pbk) : £1.50 B81-40998

Tyler, W. T.. The man who lost the war / W.T. Tyler. — London : Collins, 1980. — 369p ; 22cm
ISBN 0-00-222388-0 : £6.95 B81-01154

Updike, John. Bech : a book / John Updike. — Harmondsworth : Penguin, 1972, c1970 (1980 [printing]). — 154p ; 20cm
Originally published: New York : Knopf ; London : Deutsch, 1970
ISBN 0-14-003331-9 (pbk) : £1.95 B81-01978

Updike, John. Couples / John Updike. — Harmondsworth : Penguin, 1970, c1968 (1981 [printing]). — 506p ; 20cm
ISBN 0-14-002944-3 (pbk) : £2.95 B81-22338

Updike, John. A month of Sundays / John Updike. — Harmondsworth : Penguin, 1976 (1981 [printing]). — 189p ; 20cm
Originally published: New York : Knopf ; London : Deutsch, 1975
ISBN 0-14-004150-8 (pbk) : £1.95 B81-13982

Updike, John. Of the farm / John Updike. — Harmondsworth : Penguin, 1968, c1965 (1980 [printing]). — 154p ; 20cm
Originally published: New York : Knopf, 1965 ; London : Deutsch, 1966
ISBN 0-14-002844-7 (pbk) : £1.50 B81-01155

Updike, John. The poorhouse fair / John Updike. — Harmondsworth : Penguin, 1980, c1958. — 158p ; 20cm
Originally published: New York : Knopf ; London : Gollancz, 1959
ISBN 0-14-002843-9 (pbk) : £1.75 B81-00317

Valin, Jonathan. Final notice. — London : Collins, Oct.1981. — [248]p
ISBN 0-00-231293-x : £6.50 : CIP entry B81-25139

Valin, Jonathan. The lime pit / Jonathan Valin. — London : Collins, 1981, c1980. — 224p ; 21cm. — (The Crime Club)
Originally published: New York : Dodd, Mead, 1980
ISBN 0-00-231483-5 (corrected) : £5.95 B81-13588

Van Hazinga, Cynthia. The Georgians / Cynthia Van Hazinga. — London : Sphere, 1981, c1978. — 476p ; 18cm
ISBN 0-7221-4487-3 (pbk) : £1.75 B81-36825

Van-Loon, Antonia. Katherine / by Antonia Van-Loon. — London : W.H. Allen, 1981, c1979. — 304p ; 22cm
Originally published: New York : St. Martin's Press, c1979
ISBN 0-491-02714-1 : £6.95 B81-08667

813'.54[F] — Fiction in English. American writers, *1945- — Texts* *continuation*

Van Lustbader, Eric. Dai-San / Eric van Lustbader. — London : Star, 1981, c1978. — 246p ; 20cm. — (The Sunset warrior sequence ; v.3)
Originally published: Garden City, N.Y. : Doubleday, 1978 ; London : W.H. Allen, 1980
ISBN 0-352-30677-7 (pbk) : £1.75 B81-11665

Van Lustbader, Eric. The ninja / Eric van Lustbader. — London : Granada, 1980 (1981 [printing]). — 526p ; 18cm. — (A Panther book)
Originally published: New York : Evans ; London : Granada, 1980
ISBN 0-586-05153-8 (pbk) : £1.95 B81-28905

Van Lustbader, Eric. Shallows of night / Eric van Lustbader. — London : Star, 1981, c1978. — 216p ; 20cm. — (The Sunset warrior sequence ; v.2)
Originally published: Garden City, N.Y. : Doubleday, 1978 ; London : W.H. Allen, 1980
ISBN 0-352-30676-9 (pbk) : £1.75 B81-11664

Van Lustbader, Eric. Sirens / Eric van Lustbader. — London : Granada, 1981. — 479p ; 24cm
ISBN 0-246-11646-3 : £6.95 B81-21210

Van Lustbader, Eric. The sunset warrior / Eric van Lustbader. — London : Star, 1981, c1977. — 182p ; 20cm. — (The Sunset warrior sequence ; v.1)
Originally published: Garden City, N.Y. : Doubleday, 1977 ; London : W.H. Allen, 1980
ISBN 0-352-30675-0 (pbk) : £1.75 B81-11663

Van Slyke, Helen. A necessary woman / Helen van Slyke. — London : Corgi, 1980, c1979. — 429p ; 18cm
Originally published: Garden City, N.Y. : Doubleday ; London : Heinemann, 1979
ISBN 0-552-11575-4 (pbk) : £1.50 B81-07350

Van Slyke, Helen. No love lost / Helen van Slyke. — London : Corgi, 1981, c1980. — 474p ; 18cm
Originally published: London : Heinemann, 1980
ISBN 0-552-11779-x (pbk) : £1.75 B81-39099

Vance, Jack. The dying earth / Jack Vance. — London : Granada, 1981, c1950. — 159p ; 18cm. — (A Mayflower book)
Originally published: New York : Hillman Periodicals, 1950
ISBN 0-583-12091-1 (pbk) : £1.25 B81-13014

Vance, William E.. Death stalks the Cheyenne Trail / William E. Vance. — London : Hale, 1981, c1980. — 181p ; 20cm
Originally published: Garden City, N.Y. : Doubleday, 1980
ISBN 0-7091-9027-1 : £4.95 B81-19222

Vance, William E.. Drifter's gold / William E. Vance. — London : Hale, 1980, c1979. — 184p ; 20cm
Originally published: Garden City, N.Y. : Doubleday, 1979
ISBN 0-7091-8488-3 : £4.95 B81-02069

Vandergriff, Aola. Daughters of the far islands / Aola Vandergriff. — London : W.H. Allen, 1980, c1979. — 520p ; 18cm. — (Star)
Originally published: New York : Warner Books, 1979
ISBN 0-352-30850-8 (pbk) : £1.50 B81-18886

Vandergriff, Aola. Daughters of the southwind / Aola Vandergriff. — London : Star, 1980, c1977. — 526p ; 18cm
Originally published: New York : Warner, 1977
ISBN 0-352-30848-6 (pbk) : £1.50 B81-11881

Vandergriff, Aola. Daughters of the wild country / by Aola Vandergriff. — London : W.H. Allen, 1980, c1978. — 496p ; 18cm. — (A Star book)
Originally published: New York : Warner, 1978
ISBN 0-352-30851-6 (pbk) : £1.50 B81-15590

Varley, John, *1947-*. Wizard / John Varley. — London : Macdonald Futura, 1981, c1980. — 354p ; 18cm. — (An Orbit book)
Originally published: New York : Berkley, 1980
ISBN 0-7088-8076-2 (pbk) : £1.75 B81-15641

Veley, Charles. Children of the dark / Charles Veley. — London : Granada, 1980, c1979. — 301p ; 18cm. — (A Mayflower book)
Originally published: Garden City, N.Y. : Doubleday, 1979
ISBN 0-583-13202-2 (pbk) : £1.25 B81-01156

Venter, Al J.. Soldier of fortune / Al J. Venter. — London : W.H. Allen, 1980 (1981 [printing]). — 268p ; 18cm. — (A Star book)
ISBN 0-352-30656-4 (pbk) : £1.50 B81-26525

Vinge, Joan D.. Fireship ; and, Mother and child : science fiction / by Joan D. Vinge. — London : Sidgwick and Jackson, 1981, c1978. — 191p ; 21cm
Originally published: New York : Dell, 1978
ISBN 0-283-98721-9 : £6.95 B81-11635

Vinge, Joan D.. Fireship ; and, Mother and child / Joan D. Vinge. — London : Methuen Paperbacks, 1981. — 191p ; 18cm. — (Magnum books)
Originally published: New York : Dell, 1978 ; London : Sidgwick and Jackson, 1981
ISBN 0-417-06320-2 (pbk) : £1.10 B81-18246

Vinge, Joan D.. The outcasts of Heaven Belt / Joan Vinge. — London : Macdonald Futura, 1980, c1978. — 198p : ill ; 18cm. — (An Orbit book)
ISBN 0-7088-8073-8 (pbk) : £1.25 B81-40952

Vinge, Joan D.. The outcasts of Heaven Belt : science fiction / by Joan D. Vinge. — London : Sidgwick & Jackson, 1981, c1978. — 198p : 1ill,1chart ; 21cm
Originally published: New York : New American Library, 1978
ISBN 0-283-98729-4 : £6.95 B81-05438

Vinge, Joan D.. The snow queen / Joan D. Vinge. — London : Macdonald Futura, 1981, c1980. — 536p : 1col.ill ; 18cm. — (An Orbit book)
Originally published: London : Sidgwick & Jackson, 1980. — Ill on inside cover
ISBN 0-7088-8075-4 (pbk) : £1.95 B81-40953

Vitek, Donna. A different dream / Donna Vitek. — [London] : Silhouette, 1981, c1980. — 188p ; 18cm. — (Silhouette romance ; 32)
ISBN 0-340-26582-5 (pbk) : £0.65 : CIP rev. B81-02567

Vitek, Donna. Promises from the past. — London : Hodder & Stoughton, Oct.1981. — [192]p. — (Silhouette romance)
ISBN 0-340-27121-3 (pbk) : £0.65 : CIP entry B81-27355

Vitek, Donna. Showers of sunlight / Donna Vitek. — London : Silhouette, 1981, c1980. — 190p ; 18cm. — (Silhouette romance ; 46)
ISBN 0-340-26736-4 (pbk) : £0.65 : CIP rev. B81-13895

Vitek, Donna. Veil of gold. — London : Hodder & Stoughton, Jan.1982. — [192]p. — (Silhouette romance)
ISBN 0-340-27664-9 (pbk) : £0.75 : CIP entry B81-34483

Vonnegut, Kurt. Cat's cradle / Kurt Vonnegut, jr. — Harmondsworth : Penguin, 1965, c1963 (1979 [printing]). — 178p ; 18cm. — (Penguin science fiction)
Originally published: New York : Holt, Rinehart & Winston ; London : Gollancz, 1963
ISBN 0-14-002308-9 (pbk) : £1.10 B81-01157

Vonnegut, Kurt. Jailbird / Kurt Vonnegut. — London : Granada, 1981, c1979. — 239p ; 18cm. — (A Panther book)
Originally published: Franklin Center, Pa. : Franklin Library ; London : Cape, 1979. — Includes index
ISBN 0-586-05195-3 (pbk) : £1.50 B81-28907

Wage, Walter. Blue moon / Walter Wager. — London : Macdonald Futura, 1981, c1980. — 289p ; 18cm
Originally published: New York : Arbor House, c1980
ISBN 0-7088-2015-8 (pbk) : £1.50 B81-15454

Wagner, Karl Edward. Dark crusade. — London : Coronet, July 1981. — [224]p
Originally published: New York : Warner Books, 1976
ISBN 0-340-25077-1 (pbk) : £1.40 : CIP entry B81-13897

Wallace, Irving. The second lady / Irving Wallace. — London : Arrow, 1981, c1980. — 383p ; 18cm
Originally published: London : Hutchinson, 1980
ISBN 0-09-925270-8 (pbk) : £1.75 B81-39153

Waller, Leslie. The brave and the free / Leslie Waller. — London : Granada, 1980, c1979 (1981 [printing]). — 624p ; 18cm. — (A Mayflower book)
Originally published: New York : Delacorte Press, 1979
ISBN 0-583-13398-3 (pbk) : £1.95 B81-28909

Walsh, Sheila. Lord Gilmore's bride / Sheila Walsh. — South Yarmouth : Curley ; Bolton-by-Bowland : Magna Print [distributor], 1981, c1978. — 360p ; 23cm
Published in large print
ISBN 0-89340-311-3 : £5.75 B81-28683

Walsh, Sheila. The rose domino. — London : Hutchinson, Jan.1982. — 1v.
ISBN 0-09-146730-6 : £6.50 : CIP entry B81-33988

Walsh, Sheila. The sergeant major's daughter / Sheila Walsh. — South Yarmouth, Mass. : John Curley, c1977 ; [London Preston] : Magna [distributor]. — 350p ; 23cm
Originally published: London : Hurst and Blackett, 1977
ISBN 0-89340-310-5 : £5.75 B81-22118

Wambaugh, Joseph. The glitter dome / by Joseph Wambaugh. — London : Weidenfeld and Nicolson, 1981. — 299p ; 25cm
ISBN 0-297-77998-2 : £6.95 B81-33737

Wangerin, Walter. The book of the dun cow / by Walter Wangerin, Jr. — Harmondsworth : Penguin, 1979, c1978 (1981 [printing]). — ix,241p ; 18cm
Originally published: New York : Harper and Row, 1978 ; London : Allen Lane, 1980
ISBN 0-14-005458-8 (pbk) : £1.25 B81-15367

Waugh, Hillary. The Doria Rafe case. — London : Gollancz, Feb.1982. — [192]p
ISBN 0-575-03047-x : £5.95 : CIP entry B81-37572

Waugh, Hillary. The Glenna Powers case / by Hillary Waugh. — London : Gollancz, 1981 c1980. — 190p ; 21cm
ISBN 0-575-02999-4 : £5.95 B81-31691

Waugh, Hillary. Rivergate House / by Hillary Waugh. — London : Gollancz, 1981, c1980. — 281p ; 21cm
Originally published: / under the name Elissa Grandower. Garden City, N.Y. : Doubleday, 1980
ISBN 0-575-02932-3 : £5.95 B81-02913

Waugh, Hillary. The shadow guest / Hillary Waugh. — London : Gollancz, 1971 (1980 [printing]). — 254p ; 21cm
ISBN 0-575-00647-1 : £5.50 B81-03602

Waugh, Hillary. The young prey / Hillary Waugh. — London : Gollancz, 1970, c1969 (1980 [printing]). — 206p ; 21cm
Originally published: Garden City, N.Y. : Doubleday, 1969
ISBN 0-575-00458-4 : £5.50 B81-04181

813'.54[F] — Fiction in English. American writers, *1945- — Texts* *continuation*

Weaver, Gordon. Circling Byzantium / Gordon Weaver. — Baton Rouge ; London : Louisiana University Press, 1980. — 296p ; 24cm
ISBN 0-8071-0694-1 : £8.95 B81-11208

Webb, Charles, *1939*. The graduate / Charles Webb. — Harmondsworth : Penguin, 1968, c1963 (1981 [printing]). — 191p ; 18cm
Originally published: New York : New American Library, 1963 ; London : Constable 1964
ISBN 0-14-002693-2 (pbk) : £1.25 B81-18340

Webb, Charles H.. The wilderness effect. — London : Chatto & Windus, Sept.1981. — [256]p
ISBN 0-7011-2595-0 : £6.50 : CIP entry B81-23811

Webb, James. Fields of fire : a novel / by James Webb. — London : Granada, 1980, c1978. — 443p : 1map ; 18cm. — (A Mayflower book)
Originally published: Englewood Cliffs, N.J. : Prentice-Hall, 1978-
ISBN 0-583-13331-2 (pbk) : £1.50 B81-07349

Weidman, Jerome. Counselors-at-law / Jerome Weidman. — London : Bodley Head, 1981, c1980. — 401p ; 23cm
Originally published: New York : Doubleday, 1980
ISBN 0-370-30378-4 : £6.50 B81-11153

Weidman, Jerome. A family fortune / Jerome Weidman. — Harmondsworth : Penguin, 1981, c1978. — 440p ; 18cm
Originally published: New York : Simon and Schuster ; London : Bodley Head, 1978
ISBN 0-14-005537-1 (pbk) : £1.95 B81-27216

Weill, Gus. The Führer seed / Gus Weill. — London : New English Library, 1981, c1979. — 288p ; 19cm
Originally published: New York : Morrow, 1979
ISBN 0-450-05018-1 (pbk) : £1.50 B81-35625

Wells, William K.. Effigies / William K. Wells. — London : Granada, 1981, c1980. — 398p ; 18cm. — (A Mayflower book)
ISBN 0-583-13423-8 (pbk) : £1.50 B81-10881

West, Owen. The funhouse : a novel / by Owen West ; based on a screenplay by Larry Block. — London : Sphere, 1981, c1980. — 275p ; 18cm
Originally published: S.l. : MCA Publishing, 1980
ISBN 0-7221-9001-8 (pbk) : £1.25 B81-28747

West, Paul. The very rich hours of Count von Stauffenberg / Paul West. — New York ; London : Harper & Row, c1980. — xii,365p : 3maps ; 24cm
ISBN 0-06-014593-5 : £6.95 B81-32577

Westheimer, David. Rider on the wind / David Westheimer. — London : Sphere, 1980, c1979. — 284p ; 18cm
Originally published: London : Joseph, 1979
ISBN 0-7221-9012-3 (pbk) : £1.25 B81-11709

Westlake, Donald E.. Castle in the air / Donald E. Westlake. — London : Hodder and Stoughton, 1980. — 189p ; 23cm
ISBN 0-340-26238-9 : £6.25 B81-02134

Westlake, Donald E.. [Dancing Aztecs]. A New York dance / Donald E. Westlake. — Large print ed. — Leicester : Ulverscroft, 1981, c1976. — 523p ; 23cm. — (Ulverscroft large print series)
Originally published: as Dancing Aztecs. New York : M. Evans, 1976 ; as A New York dance. London : Hodder and Stoughton, 1979?
ISBN 0-7089-0605-2 : £5.00 : CIP rev. B81-02578

Westlake, Donald E.. Nobody's perfect. — London : Coronet, July 1981. — [288]p
Originally published: New York : M. Evans, 1977 ; London : Hodder & Stoughton, 1978
ISBN 0-340-26677-5 (pbk) : £1.50 : CIP entry B81-13779

Wharton, William. Dad : a novel / by William Wharton. — London : Cape, 1981. — 449p ; 22cm
ISBN 0-224-02926-6 : £6.95 : CIP rev. B81-22451

Wheeler, Richard S.. Beneath the blue mountain / Richard S. Wheeler. — London : Hale, 1980, c1979. — 185p ; 20cm
Originally published: Garden City, N.Y. : Doubleday, 1979
ISBN 0-7091-8458-1 : £4.95 B81-00319

Wheeler, Richard S.. Bushwack / Richard S. Wheeler. — London : Hale, 1981. — 185p ; 20cm
Originally published: Garden City, N.Y. : Doubleday, 1978
ISBN 0-7091-8459-x : £4.95 B81-08651

Whiteson, Leon. David Cronenberg's Scanners : a novel / by Leon Whiteson ; based on the original screenplay by David Cronenberg. — London : Granada, 1981. — 158p ; 18cm. — (A Mayflower book)
ISBN 0-583-13522-6 (pbk) : £1.25 B81-17410

Whitney, Phyllis A.. The quicksilver pool. — Large print ed. — Anstey : Ulverscroft, Dec.1981. — [512]p. — (Ulverscroft large print series)
Originally published: New York : Appleton Century Crofts, 1955 ; London : Coronet, 1973
ISBN 0-7089-0723-7 : £5.00 : CIP entry B81-32032

Wiesel, Elie. The testament : a novel / by Elie Wiesel ; translated from the French by Marion Wiesel. — London : Allen Lane, 1981. — 346p ; 23cm
Translation of: Le testament d'un poète juif assassiné
ISBN 0-7139-1429-7 : £5.95 B81-34617

Wilder, Robert. Wind from the Carolinas / Robert Wilder. — Toronto ; London : Bantam, 1965, c1964 (1978 printing). — 566p ; 18cm
Originally published: New York : Putnam, 1964
ISBN 0-553-12750-0 (pbk) : £1.25 B81-09312

Wilhelm, Kate. Juniper time / Kate Wilhelm. — London : Arrow, 1981, c1980. — 280p ; 18cm
Originally published: New York : Harper and Row, 1979 ; London : Hutchinson, 1980
ISBN 0-09-925550-2 (pbk) : £1.60 B81-32068

Wilhelm, Kate. Where late the sweet birds sang / Kate Wilhelm. — London : Arrow, 1977, c1974 (1981 [printing]). — 250p ; 18cm
Originally published: New York : Harper & Row, 1976
ISBN 0-09-914800-5 (pbk) : £1.50 B81-29157

Wilson, F. Paul. The Keep. — London : New English Library, Feb.1982. — [384]p
ISBN 0-450-04889-6 : £6.95 : CIP entry B81-37583

Wilson, Fran. Where mountains wait / Fran Wilson. — London (47 Bedford Sq., WC1B 3DP) : Silhouette, 1980. — 187p ; 18cm. — (Silhouette romance ; no.9)
ISBN 0-340-26006-8 (pbk) : £0.65 : CIP rev. B80-12608

Wilson, Robert Anton. Masks of the Illuminati / Robert Anton Wilson. — London : Sphere, 1981. — 294p : ill ; 18cm
ISBN 0-7221-9229-0 (pbk) : £1.75 B81-36819

Wilson, Robert Anton. Schrödinger's cat : the universe next door / Robert Anton Wilson. — London : Sphere, 1980, c1979. — 256p ; 18cm
ISBN 0-7221-9226-6 (pbk) : £1.75 B81-24708

Wilson, Robert C. (Robert Charles), *1951-*. Crooked tree / Robert C.Wilson. — London : Arrow, 1981, c1980. — 368p ; 18cm
Originally published: New York : Putnam, 1980
ISBN 0-09-924880-8 (pbk) : £1.50 B81-11888

Winston, Daoma. The devil's princess / Daoma Winston. — Large print ed. — Bath : Chivers, 1981, c1980. — 269p ; 23cm. — (A Lythway romantic thriller)
Originally published: London : Piatkus, 1980
ISBN 0-85119-723-x : Unpriced : CIP rev. B81-13785

Winston, Daoma. House of mirror images. — Loughton : Piatkus, Aug.1981. — [192]p
ISBN 0-86188-088-9 : £5.95 : CIP entry B81-15850

Winston, Daoma. Kingdom's Castle / Daoma Winston. — Loughton : Piatkus, 1981, c1972. — 191p ; 21cm
ISBN 0-86188-039-0 : £52.95 B81-08954

Winston, Daoma. The lotteries / Daoma Winston. — London : Macdonald Futura, 1981, c1980. — 263p ; 18cm. — (A Futura book)
Originally published: London : Macdonald, 1980
ISBN 0-7088-1814-5 (pbk) : £1.35 B81-28341

Winston, Daoma. Shadow of an unknown woman / Daoma Winston. — London : Hamlyn Paperbacks, 1981, c1967. — 188p ; 18cm
Originally published: United States : s.n., 1967? ; Loughton : Piatkus, 1979
ISBN 0-600-20152-x (pbk) : £1.00 B81-10049

Winston, Daoma. Skeleton key / Daoma Winston. — London : Hamlyn Paperbacks, 1981, c1972. — 173p ; 18cm. — (A Moonshadow romance)
Originally published: United States : 1972? ; Loughton : Judy Piatkus (Publishers), 1980
ISBN 0-600-20204-6 (pbk) : £0.95 B81-33494

Wisdom, Linda. Dancer in the shadows / Linda Wisdom. — London : Silhouette, 1981, c1980. — 189p ; 18cm. — (Silhouette romance ; 48)
ISBN 0-340-26738-0 (pbk) : £0.65 : CIP rev. B81-13775

Wise, David. Spectrum / David Wise. — London : Allen Lane, 1981. — 370p ; 25cm
ISBN 0-7139-1397-5 : £6.50 B81-14190

Wissmann, Ruth. Celebration for murder / Ruth Wissmann. — London : Hale, 1980, c1979. — 180p ; 20cm
Originally published: Garden City, N.Y. : Doubleday, 1979
ISBN 0-7091-8441-7 : £5.50 B81-00320

Wissmann, Ruth. Whispers in the wind / Ruth Wissmann. — London : Hale, 1981, c1980. — 182p ; 21cm
Originally published: Garden City, N.Y. : Doubleday, 1980
ISBN 0-7091-8995-8 : £6.50 B81-15766

Wohl, James P.. The blind trust kills : a novel of suspense / James P. Wohl. — London : Hale, 1980, c1978. — 202p ; 20cm
Originally published: Indianapolis : Bobbs-Merrill, 1978
ISBN 0-7091-8557-x : £5.75 B81-0215?

Wold, Allen L.. Star god / Allen L. Wold. — London : Hale, 1981, c1980. — xiv,191p ; 22cm
Originally published: New York : St. Martin's Press, 1980
ISBN 0-7091-9296-7 : £6.50 B81-3352?

Wolf, Chris L.. Fire in the sky / by Chris L. Wolf & Michael F. Maikowski. — London : Hale, 1981, c1978. — 205p 21cm. — (Hale SF
ISBN 0-7091-8802-1 : £5.95 B81-1107

813'.54[F] — Fiction in English. American writers, *1945- — Texts* *continuation*

Wolfe, Gene. The claw of the conciliator : science fiction / by Gene Wolfe. — London : Sidgwick & Jackson, 1981. — 303p ; 21cm. — (The Book of the new sun ; v.2)
Originally published: New York : Simon & Schuster, 1981
ISBN 0-283-98802-9 : £7.95 B81-37056

Wolfe, Gene. The shadow of the torturer / Gene Wolfe. — London : Arrow, 1981, c1980. — 303p ; 18cm. — (The Book of the new sun ; v.1)
Originally published: New York : Simon and Schuster, 1980 ; London : Sidgwick and Jackson, 1981
ISBN 0-09-926320-3 (pbk) : £1.60 B81-39159

Wolfe, Gene. The shadow of the torturer : science fiction / by Gene Wolfe. — London : Sidgwick & Jackson, 1981. — 303p ; 21cm. — (The book of the new sun ; v.1)
Originally published: New York : Simon and Schuster, 1980
ISBN 0-283-98738-3 : £7.95 B81-12299

Wolfe, Linda. Private practices / Linda Wolfe. — London : Star, 1981, c1979. — 316p ; 18cm
Originally published: New York : Simon and Schuster, 1979 ; W.H. Allen, 1980
ISBN 0-352-30793-5 (pbk) : £1.50 B81-16065

Wolfe, Winifred. Josie's way. — Loughton : Piatkus, Nov.1981. — [320]p
ISBN 0-86188-092-7 : £6.95 : CIP entry B81-30402

Wood, Barbara, *1947-*. Night trains / Barbara Wood & Gareth Wootton. — London : Magnum, 1980, c1979. — 320p ; 18cm
Originally published: London : Eyre Methuen, 1979
ISBN 0-417-04780-0 (pbk) : £1.40 B81-01159

Wood, Barbara, *1947-*. The watch gods / Barbara Wood. — London : New English Library, 1981. — 347p ; 23cm
ISBN 0-450-04853-5 : £6.50 B81-24805

Wood, Bari. The tribe / Bari Wood. — London : New English Library, 1981. — 339p ; 23cm
Originally published: New York, : New American Library, 1981
ISBN 0-450-04869-1 : £6.95 B81-24812

Woodiwiss, Kathleen E.. Ashes in the wing / Kathleen Woodiwiss. — London : Macdonald Futura, 1980 (1981 [printing]). — 664p ; 18cm. — (A Troubadour spectacular)
ISBN 0-7088-1792-0 (pbk) : £2.25 B81-40959

Woodiwiss, Kathleen E.. The flame and the flower / Kathleen E. Woodiwiss. — London : Macdonald Futura, 1980. — 430p ; 21cm
Originally published: New York : Avon Books, 1972 ; London : Futura, 1975
ISBN 0-354-04579-2 : £6.50 B81-00321

Woodiwiss, Kathleen E.. The wolf and the dove / Kathleen E. Woodiwiss. — London : Macdonald Futura, 1976, c1974 (1981 [printing]). — 508p ; 18cm. — (A Troubadour book)
Originally published: New York : Avon, 1974
ISBN 0-86007-325-4 (pbk) : £1.95 B81-40958

Woodley, Richard. The jazz singer / Richard Woodley ; based on the screenplay by Herbert Baker ; adaptation by Stephen H. Foreman ; based on the play by Samson Raphaelson. — [London] : Corgi, 1981, c1980. — 184p ; 18cm
Originally published: New York : Bantam, 1980
ISBN 0-552-11741-2 (pbk) : £1.00 B81-08407

Wouk, Herman. War and remembrance / Herman Wouk. — [London] : Fontana, 1980, c1978. — 1170p ; 18cm
Originally published: London : Collins, 1978
ISBN 0-00-616007-7 (pbk) : £2.50 B81-00322

Wouk, Herman. The winds of war / Herman Wouk. — Glasgow : Fontana, 1974, c1971 (1980 [printing]). — 960p : 1map ; 18cm
Originally published: Boston, Mass. : Little Brown ; London : Collins, 1971
ISBN 0-00-616126-x (pbk) : £2.50 B81-02726

Wynne, John. Crime wave. — London : John Calder, Feb.1982. — [256]p
ISBN 0-7145-3870-1 : £6.95 : CIP entry B81-35827

Yablonsky, Yabo. Escape to victory / Yabo Yablonsky ; based on a screenplay by Evan Jones and Yabo Yablonsky ; from a story by Yabo Yablonsky and Djordje Milicevic & Jeff Maguire. — London : Corgi, 1981. — 164p ; 18cm
ISBN 0-552-11655-6 (pbk) : £0.95 B81-35494

Yablonsky, Yabo. Jaguar lives! / Yabo Yablonsky. — London : Futura, 1979. — 159p ; 18cm
ISBN 0-7088-1684-3 (pbk) : £0.85 B81-01160

Yarbro, Chelsea Quinn. Hôtel Transylvania / Chelsea Quinn Yarbro. — London : New English Library, 1981, c1978. — 279p ; 18cm
Originally published: New York : St. Martin's Press, 1978
ISBN 0-450-05202-8 (pbk) : £1.25 B81-24748

Yarbro, Chelsea Quinn. The palace / Chelsea Quinn Yarbro. — London : New English Library, 1981, c1978. — 408p ; 18cm
Originally published: New York : St. Martin's, 1978
ISBN 0-450-05312-1 (pbk) : £1.50 B81-35628

Yerby, Frank. A darkness at Ingraham's Crest : a tale of the slaveholding South / Frank Yerby. — London : Granada, 1981, c1979. — 581p ; 23cm
ISBN 0-246-11586-6 : £8.95 B81-38054

Yerby, Frank. The vixens / Frank Yerby. — Large print ed. — Leicester : Ulverscroft, 1981. — 534p ; 23cm. — (Ulverscroft large print series)
Originally published: London : Heinemann, 1948
ISBN 0-7089-0628-1 : £5.00 : CIP rev. B81-07433

Yglesias, Helen. Sweet sir / Helen Yglesias. — London : Hodder and Stoughton, 1981. — 332p ; 23cm
ISBN 0-340-27042-x : £6.95 : CIP rev. B81-13491

Zaroulis, Nancy. The Poe papers : a tale of passion / Nancy Zaroulis. — London : Hamlyn, 1980, c1977. — 180p ; 18cm
Originally published: New York : Putnam, 1977 ; London : W.H. Allen, 1978
ISBN 0-600-20101-5 (pbk) : £1.25 B81-07631

Zeidner, Lisa. Customs. — London : Cape, Oct.1981. — [264]p
ISBN 0-224-02923-1 : £5.95 : CIP entry B81-28194

Zelazny, Roger. My name is legion / Roger Zelazny. — London : Sphere, 1980, c1979. — 205p ; 18cm. — (Sphere science fiction)
Originally published: New York : Ballantine Books, 1976 ; London : Faber, 1979
ISBN 0-7221-9421-8 (pbk) : £1.50 B81-03562

Zelazny, Roger. Roadmarks / Roger Zelazny. — London : Macdonald Futura, 1981, c1979. — 189p ; 21cm. — (Macdonald science fiction)
Originally published: New York : Ballantine Books, 1979
ISBN 0-354-04664-0 : £4.95 B81-17388

Zelazny, Roger. Roadmarks / Roger Zelazny. — London : Macdonald Futura, 1981, c1979. — 189p ; 18cm. — (A Orbit book)
Originally published: New York : Ballantine Books, 1979
ISBN 0-7088-8079-7 (pbk) : £1.50 B81-32784

Ziffren, Mickey. A political affair / Mickey Ziffren. — London : Methuen, 1981, c1979. — 448p ; 19cm
Originally published: New York : Delacorte Press, 1979
ISBN 0-413-48400-9 (cased) : £4.95
ISBN 0-417-06030-0 (pbk) : Unpriced B81-12483

Ziffren, Mickey. A political affair / Mickey Ziffren. — London : Magnum, 1981, c1979. — 448p ; 18cm
Originally published: New York : Delacorte, 1979
ISBN 0-417-06030-0 (pbk) : £1.50 B81-08421

Zindel, Bonnie. A star for the latecomer / Bonnie Zindel and Paul Zindel. — London : Fontana, 1981, c1980. — 184p ; 18cm. — (Fontana lions)
Originally published: New York : Harper and Row ; London : Bodley Head, 1980. — For adolescents
ISBN 0-00-671787-x (pbk) : £1.00 B81-32173

Zindel, Paul. Confessions of a teenage baboon / Paul Zindel. — London : Fontana, 1979, c1977 (1981 [printing]). — 128p ; 18cm. — (Fontana lions)
Originally published: New York : Harper and Row, 1977 ; London : Bodley Head, 1978. — For adolescents
ISBN 0-00-671951-1 (pbk) : £0.95 B81-32172

Zindel, Paul. The girl who wanted a boy / Paul Zindel. — London : Bodley Head, 1981. — 147p ; 23cm. — (A Book for new adults)
Originally published: New York : Harper and Row, 1981
ISBN 0-370-30905-7 : £3.95 B81-35051

Zindel, Paul. I never loved your mind / Paul Zindel. — [London] : Fontana, 1977, c1970 (1981 [printing]). — 128p ; 18cm. — (Lions)
Originally published: New York : Harper & Row, 1970 ; London : Bodley Head, 1971
ISBN 0-00-671769-1 (pbk) : £0.95 B81-15537

Zindel, Paul. My darling, my hamburger / Paul Zindel. — London : Fontana, 1978, c1969 (1980 [printing]). — 125p : ill ; 18cm. — (Lions)
Originally published: New York : Harper & Row, 1969 ; London : Bodley Head, 1970. — For adolescents
ISBN 0-00-671800-0 (pbk) : £0.90 B81-01161

Zindel, Paul. Pardon me, your'e stepping on my eyeball! / Paul Zindel. — [London] : Fontana, 1978, c1981 (1981 [printing]). — 191p ; 18cm. — (Lions)
Originally published: New York : Harper & Row ; London : Bodley Head, 1976
ISBN 0-00-671904-x (pbk) : £1.00 B81-15538

Zindel, Paul. Pardon me, you're stepping on my eyeball! / Paul Zindel. — Basingstoke : Macmillan Education, 1981, c1976. — 191p ; 21cm. — (M books)
Originally published: New York : Harper and Row ; London : Bodley Head, 1976. — For adolescents
ISBN 0-333-29451-3 : £1.50 B81-18688

Zindel, Paul. The Pigman / Paul Zindel. — [London] : Fontana, 1976, c1968 (1980 [printing]). — 124p : ill ; 18cm. — (Lions)
Originally published: New York : Harper & Row, 1968 ; London : Bodley Head, 1969. — For adolescents
ISBN 0-00-671768-3 (pbk) : £0.90 B81-01162

Zindel, Paul. The Pigman's legacy / Paul Zindel. — London : Bodley Head, 1980. — viii,183p ; 21cm. — (A Book for new adults)
Originally published: New York : Harper & Row, 1980. — For adolescents
ISBN 0-370-30370-9 : £3.95 : CIP rev. B80-18906

Zindel, Paul. The undertaker's gone bananas / Paul Zindel. — [London] : Fontana, 1980, c1978. — 159p ; 18cm
Originally published: New York : Harper & Row, 1978. — For adolescents
ISBN 0-00-671698-9 (pbk) : £0.95 B81-07201

813'.54[F] — Fiction in English. American writers, *1945- — Texts* *continuation*

Zukerman, Eugenia. Deceptive cadence : a novel / by Eugenia Zukerman. — London : Weidenfeld and Nicolson, 1981, c1980. — 262p ; 23cm
ISBN 0-297-77887-0 : £6.50 B81-10133

813'.54[F] — Fiction in English. Canadian writers, *1945- — Texts*

Allen, Charlotte Vale. Love life / Charlotte Vale Allen. — London : New English Library, 1981, c1976. — 367p ; 18cm
Originally published: New York : Delacorte, 1976
ISBN 0-450-05174-9 (pbk) : £1.50 B81-24745

Allen, Charlotte Vale. Promises / Charlotte Vale Allen. — London : Hutchinson, 1980. — 343p ; 25cm
ISBN 0-09-142810-6 : £6.50 : CIP rev.
B80-11155

Anderson, Doris. Two women / Doris Anderson. — London : Magnum, 1980, c1978. — 243p ; 18cm
Originally published: Toronto : Macmillan, 1978
ISBN 0-417-05410-6 (pbk) : £1.40 B81-02189

Atwood, Margaret. Life before man. — London : Virago, Jan.1982. — [320]p
Originally published: Toronto : McClelland and Stewart, 1979
ISBN 0-86068-192-0 (pbk) : £2.95 : CIP entry
B81-33762

Betcherman, Barbara. Suspicions / by Barbara Betcherman. — London : Macdonald Futura, 1980. — 410p ; 23cm
ISBN 0-354-04551-2 : £6.95 B81-02187

Corfield, William E.. Dead spy dead secret / William E. Corfield. — London : Hale, 1981. — 208p ; 20cm
ISBN 0-7091-9159-6 : £6.25 B81-28873

Deverell, William. Needles / William Deverell. — [London] : Corgi, 1981, c1979. — 297p ; 18cm
Originally published: Toronto : McClelland & Stewart-Bantam ; Boston, Mass. : Little, Brown, 1979
ISBN 0-552-11613-0 (pbk) : £1.35 B81-10967

Dunmore, Spencer. Ace / Spencer Dunmore. — London : Heinemann, 1981. — 261p ; 23cm
ISBN 0-434-21668-2 : £6.95 B81-32439

Egan, Lesley. Motive in shadow / Lesley Egan. — London : Gollancz, 1980. — 181p ; 21cm
ISBN 0-575-02870-x : £5.50 B81-01163

Erdman, Paul E.. The crash of '79. — Large print ed. — Leicester : Ulverscroft, Sept.1981. — [576]p. — (Charnwood library series)
Originally published: New York : Simon and Schuster, 1976 ; London : Secker and Warburg, 1977
ISBN 0-7089-8017-1 : £6.50 : CIP entry
B81-22651

Fielding, Joy. Kiss Mummy goodbye / Joy Fielding. — [London] : Fontana, 1981. — 285p ; 18cm
Originally published: Garden City, N.Y. : Doubleday, 1981
ISBN 0-00-616319-x (pbk) : £1.50 B81-17436

Fitzgerald, Valerie. Zemindar / Valerie Fitzgerald. — London : Bodley Head, 1981. — 798p : 3maps ; 23cm
ISBN 0-370-30429-2 : £6.95 : CIP rev.
B81-25661

Fulford, Paula. Island destiny / Paula Fulford. — London (47 Bedford Sq., WC1B 3DP) : Silhouette, 1981, c1980. — 188p ; 18cm. — (Silhouette romance ; no.20)
ISBN 0-340-26124-2 (pbk) : £0.65 : CIP rev.
B80-21063

Gedge, Pauline. The eagle and the raven / Pauline Gedge. — Harmondsworth : Penguin, 1981. — 828p : 1map ; 20cm
Originally published: New York : Dial, 1978 ; London ; Allen Lane, 1979
ISBN 0-14-005374-3 (pbk) : £2.50 B81-27222

Gottlieb, Paul. Agency / Paul Gottlieb. — London : Sphere, 1980, c1974. — 204p ; 18cm
Originally published: Don Mills : Musson, 1974 ; London : Hale, 1975
ISBN 0-7221-3972-1 (pbk) : £1.25 B81-00292

Hill, Douglas. Galactic warlord / Douglas Hill. — London : Piccolo in association with Gollancz, 1980, c1979. — 126p ; 18cm
Originally published: London : Gollancz, 1979
ISBN 0-330-26186-x (pbk) : £0.80 B81-02238

Kilian, Crawford. Icequake / Crawford Kilian. — London : Futura, 1979. — 272p ; 18cm
ISBN 0-7088-1538-3 (pbk) : £0.95 B81-17454

MacKenzie, Donald, *1908-*. The last of the boatriders / Donald MacKenzie. — London : Macmillan, 1981. — 190p ; 21cm
ISBN 0-333-31813-7 : £5.50 B81-37183

MacKenzie, Donald, *1908-*. Raven and the paperhangers / Donald MacKenzie. — London : Macmillan, 1980. — 191p ; 21cm
ISBN 0-333-29214-6 : £5.50 B81-00301

Moore, Brian, *1921-*. The temptation of Eileen Hughes / Brian Moore. — London : Cape, 1981. — 211p ; 22cm
ISBN 0-224-01936-8 : £6.50 : CIP rev.
B81-15830

Onley, David C.. Shuttle / David C. Onley. — London : Macdonald, 1981. — 303p : 1ill ; 21cm
ISBN 0-354-04636-5 : £5.25 B81-37904

Onley, David C.. Shuttle / David C. Onley. — London : Macdonald Futura, 1981. — 303p : 1ill ; 18cm
ISBN 0-7088-2087-5 (pbk) : £1.50 B81-24425

Palmer, C. Everard. Houdini, come home / C. Everard Palmer ; illustrated by Gavin Rowe. — London : Deutsch, 1981. — 96p : ill ; 21cm
ISBN 0-233-97359-1 : £4.95 : CIP rev.
B81-16883

Richler, Mordecai. The apprenticeship of Duddy Kravitz / Mordecai Richler. — Harmondsworth : Penguin, 1964, c1959 (1980 [printing]). — 315p ; 18cm
Originally published: London : Deutsch, 1959
ISBN 0-14-002179-5 (pbk) : £1.50 B81-14013

Richler, Mordecai. Joshua then and now : a novel / by Mordecai Richler. — London : Macmillan, 1980. — 435p ; 22cm
ISBN 0-333-30025-4 : £6.95 B81-01164

Smith, Frank A.. Dragon's breath / Frank Smith. — London : Hale, 1981, c1980. — 334p ; 23cm
ISBN 0-7091-8917-6 : £6.50 B81-05737

Smucker, Barbara Claassen. Days of terror / Barbara Claassen Smucker. — [Harmondsworth] : Puffin, [1981]. — 156p ; 18cm
Originally published: Toronto : Clark, Irwin & Company, c1979. — Bibliography: p155-156
ISBN 0-14-031306-0 (pbk) : £0.95 B81-32831

Stevenson, William, *1924-*. The ghosts of Africa : a novel / by William Stevenson. — London : W.H. Allen, 1981, c1980. — 400p : 1map ; 24cm
Originally published: New York : Harcourt Brace Jovanovich, 1980
ISBN 0-491-02844-x : £7.95 B81-11811

Suthren, Victor. A king's ransom / Victor Suthren. — London : Heinemann, 1980. — 217p : ill,2maps ; 23cm
ISBN 0-434-75253-3 : £6.95 B81-02855

Wildman, Faye. A race for love / Faye Wildman. — London : Silhouette, 1981, c1980. — 189p ; 18cm. — (Silhouette romance ; 47)
ISBN 0-340-26737-2 (pbk) : £0.65 : CIP rev.
B81-13900

Wyllie, John. A tiger in red weather / John Wyllie. — London : Hale, 1981, c1980. — 182p ; 20cm
Originally published: Garden City, N.Y. : Published for the Crime Club by Doubleday, 1980
ISBN 0-7091-9057-3 : £5.95 B81-24982

Wynne-Jones, Tim. Odd's End / Tim Wynne-Jones. — London : Deutsch, c1980. — 228p : 1plan ; 22cm
ISBN 0-233-97323-0 : £5.95 B81-08600

Zola, Meguido. Only the best. — London : Julia MacRae Books, Oct.1981. — [32]p
ISBN 0-86203-047-1 : £4.95 : CIP entry
B81-28058

813'.54[F] — Short stories in English. American writers, *1945- — Texts*

Anderson, Poul. The earth book of Stormgate / Poul Anderson. — London : New English Library
Originally published: in 1v. New York : Berkeley, c1978
3. — 1981, c1978. — 175p ; 18cm
ISBN 0-450-04926-4 (pbk) : £1.25 B81-09567

Banks, Russell. The New World : tales / by Russell Banks. — Urbana ; London : University of Illinois Press, c1978. — 136p ; 21cm. — (Illinois short fiction)
ISBN 0-252-00721-2 (cased) : £6.00
ISBN 0-252-00722-0 (pbk) : £2.40 B81-01685

Blish, James. Galactic cluster / James Blish. — London : Granada, 1980, c1960. — 255p ; 28cm. — (Granada science fiction) (A Panther book)
Originally published: London : Faber, 1960
ISBN 0-586-04573-2 (pbk) : £1.25 B81-00268

Bovey, John. Desirable aliens : stories / by John Bovey. — Urbana ; London : University of Illinois Press, c1980. — 173p ; 21cm. — (Illinois short fiction)
ISBN 0-252-00837-5 (cased) : £6.00
ISBN 0-252-00838-3 (pbk) : Unpriced
B81-15489

Bradbury, Ray. The stories of Ray Bradbury / with an introduction by the author. — London : Granada, c1980. — xx,884p : ill ; 25cm
ISBN 0-246-11540-8 : £12.50 B81-10078

Bradbury, Ray. To sing strange songs / Ray Bradbury ; selected and introduced by the author ; frontispiece by Norma Burgin. — Exeter : Wheaton, 1979. — ix,102p : 1ill ; 21cm. — (Literature for life series)
ISBN 0-08-022910-7 (pbk) : £1.45 B81-09651

Clausen, Jan. Mother, sister, daughter, lover : stories / by Jan Clausen. — London : The Women's Press, 1981, c1980. — 136p ; 20cm
Originally published: Trumansburg : Crossing Press, 1980
ISBN 0-7043-3868-8 (pbk) : £2.50 : CIP rev.
B81-12843

Colwin, Laurie. The lone pilgrim : and other stories / Laurie Colwin. — London : Collins, 1981. — 211p ; 22cm
ISBN 0-00-221437-7 : £6.95 B81-2481

Copper, Basil. Here be daemons : tales of horror and the uneasy / Basil Copper. — London : Sphere, 1981, c1978. — 213p ; 18cm
Originally published: London: Hale, 1978
ISBN 0-7221-2499-6 (pbk) : £1.25 B81-2025.

813'.54[F] — Short stories in English. American writers, *1945- — Texts* *continuation*

Corrington, John William. The actes and monuments : stories / by John William Corrington. — Urbana ; London : University of Illinois Press, c1978. — 145p ; 21cm. — (Urbana short fiction)
ISBN 0-252-00716-6 (cased) : £6.00
ISBN 0-252-00715-8 (pbk) : Unpriced
B81-10315

Dennis, Ralph. MacTaggart's war. — London : Hodder & Stoughton, Sept.1981. — [384]p. — (Coronet books)
Originally published: New York : Fawcett, 1980
ISBN 0-340-26670-8 (pbk) : £1.75 : CIP entry
B81-22544

Dick, Philip K.. The golden man / Philip K. Dick. — London : Eyre Methuen, 1981, c1980. — xxviii,336p ; 19cm
ISBN 0-413-48480-7 (cased) : Unpriced
ISBN 0-417-06200-4 (pbk) : £1.50 B81-28682

Disch, Thomas M.. Fundamental Disch / Thomas M. Disch. — London : Gollancz, 1981, c1980. — 373p ; 21cm
ISBN 0-575-02986-2 : £7.95 B81-14197

Dixon, Stephen. 14 stories / Stephen Dixon. — Baltimore ; London : John Hopkins University Press, c1980. — 145p ; 24cm
ISBN 0-8018-2445-1 : £5.00 B81-10323

Farmer, Philip José. Riverworld and other stories / Philip José Farmer. — London : Granada, 1981, c1979. — 303p ; 18cm. — (A Panther book)
ISBN 0-586-05379-4 (pbk) : £1.50 B81-09741

Francis, H. E. (Herbert Edward). Naming things : stories / by H.E. Francis. — Urbana ; London : University of Illinois Press, c1980. — 149p ; 21cm. — (Illinois short fiction)
ISBN 0-252-00830-8 (cased) : £6.00
ISBN 0-252-00831-6 (pbk) : Unpriced
B81-15488

Garber, Eugene K.. Metaphysical tales / stories by Eugene K. Garber. — Columbia ; London : University of Missouri Press, 1981. — ix,191p ; 23cm
ISBN 0-8262-0325-6 : £9.10 B81-37005

Glavin, Anthony. One for sorrow : and other stories / Anthony Glavin. — [Swords] ([Knocksedan House, Swords, Co. Dublin]) : Poolbeg, [1980]. — 155p ; 18cm
ISBN 0-905169-33-6 (pbk) : £2.00 B81-00289

Hartshorne. Whisper of treason / by Hartshorne. — London : Hale, 1981. — 303p 21cm
ISBN 0-7091-8641-x : £7.50 B81-11899

Helprin, Mark. Ellis Island : & other stories / Mark Helprin. — London : Hamilton, 1981. — 196p ; 22cm
ISBN 0-241-10530-7 : £6.50 B81-15500

Henson, Robert. Transports and disgraces : stories / by Robert Henson. — Urbana ; London : University of Illinois Press, c1980. — 126p ; 21cm. — (Illinois short fiction)
ISBN 0-252-00840-5 (cased) : £6.00
ISBN 0-252-00841-3 (pbk) : Unpriced
B81-15487

Highsmith, Patricia. Little tales of misogyny / Patricia Highsmith. — Harmondsworth : Penguin, 1980. — 110p ; 18cm. — (Penguin crime fiction)
Originally published: London : Heinemann, 1977
£0.90 (pbk) B81-07632

Hoffman, William. Virginia reels : stories / by William Hoffman. — Urbana ; London : University of Illinois Press, c1978. — 144p ; 21cm
ISBN 0-252-00702-6 (cased) : Unpriced
B81-07842

Hughes, Mary Gray. The calling : stories / by Mary Gray Hughes. — Urbana ; London : University of Illinois Press, c1980. — 141p ; 21cm. — (Illinois short fiction)
ISBN 0-252-00842-1 (cased) : £6.00
ISBN 0-252-00843-x (pbk) : Unpriced
B81-15490

Kaminsky, Stuart M.. Murder on the Yellow Brick Road. — London : Severn House, Sept.1981. — [208]p
ISBN 0-7278-0732-3 : £6.95 : CIP entry
B81-23819

Kerr, Baine. Jumping-off place : stories / by Baine Kerr. — Columbia ; London : University of Missouri Press, 1981. — 64p ; 23cm. — (A Breakthrough book ; no.33)
ISBN 0-8262-0311-6 : £7.15 B81-28640

King, Harold, *1945 Feb.27-*. Closing ceremonies / Harold King. — London : Magnum Books, 1980, c1979. — 370p ; 18cm
Originally published: New York : Coward, McCann & Geoghegan, 1979 ; Loughton : Piatkus, 1980
ISBN 0-417-05530-7 (pbk) : £1.40 B81-07404

MacLean, Jane. Deadfall : a novel / by Jane MacLean. — London : Hale, 1981, c1979. — 243p 21cm
Originally published: New York : Dutton, 1979
ISBN 0-7091-8667-3 : £6.95 B81-11902

Malamud, Bernard. The magic barrel / Bernard Malamud. — Harmondsworth : Penguin in association with Chatto & Windus, 1968, c1958 (1980 [printing]). — 188p ; 19cm
Originally published: New York : Farrar, Straus & Cudahy, 1958 ; London : Eyre & Spottiswode, 1960
ISBN 0-14-002558-8 (pbk) : £1.25 B81-01169

Malamud, Bernard. Rembrandt's hat / Bernard Malamud. — Harmondsworth : Penguin, 1976, c1973 (1980 [printing]). — 155p ; 19cm
Originally published: New York : Farrar-Straus-Giroux ; London : Eyre Methuen, 1973
ISBN 0-14-004069-2 (pbk) : £1.00 B81-01166

Oates, Joyce Carol. A sentimental education : stories / Joyce Carol Oates. — London : Cape, 1981, c1980. — 196p ; 21cm
Originally published: New York : Dutton, 1980
ISBN 0-224-01953-8 : £6.50 B81-10982

O'Connor, Flannery. Everything that rises musts converge / Flannery O'Connor ; with an introduction by Hermione Lee. — London : Faber, 1980. — xv,269p ; 19cm
Originally published: New York : Farrar, Strauss, 1965 ; London : Faber, 1966
ISBN 0-571-11614-0 (pbk) : £2.95 : CIP rev.
B80-18907

Paterson, Katherine. [Angels & other strangers]. Star of night : stories for Christmas / Katherine Paterson. — London : Gollancz, 1980, c1979. — 118p ; 21cm
Originally published: New York : Crowell, 1979
ISBN 0-575-02886-6 : £4.95 B81-01167

Peabody, Rick. Monaural / Rick Peabody. — Torpoint (Knill Cross House, Hr Anderton Rd., Millbrook, Torpoint, Cornwall) : Kawabata, 1980. — [19]p ; 21cm
ISBN 0-906110-23-8 (pbk) : £0.20 B81-29918

Phillips, Jayne Anne. Black tickets / Jayne Anne Phillips. — London : Allen Lane, 1980, c1979. — 194p ; 23cm
Originally published: New York : Delacorte Press, 1979
ISBN 0-7139-1354-1 : £5.95 B81-00307

Phillips, Jayne Anne. Black tickets / Jayne Anne Phillips. — Harmondsworth : Penguin, 1981, c1979. — 265p ; 20cm. — (King Penguin)
Originally published: New York : Delacorte Press, 1979 ; London : Allen Lane, 1980
ISBN 0-14-005583-5 (pbk) : £2.25 B81-35483

Pournelle, Jerry. High justice / Jerry Pournelle. — London : Futura, 1980, c1977. — 222p ; 18cm. — (An Orbit book)
ISBN 0-7088-8067-3 (pbk) : £1.25 B81-07657

Russell, Ray. Unholy trinity / Ray Russell. — London : Sphere, 1971, c1967 (1980 [printing]). — 140p ; 18cm
Originally published: New York : Bantam Books, 1967 ; London : Sphere, 1971
ISBN 0-7221-7553-1 (corrected: pbk) : £1.10
B81-05250

Schott, Max. Up where I used to live : stories / by Max Schott. — Urbana ; London : University of Illinois Press, 1979, c1978. — 159p ; 21cm. — (Illinois short fiction)
ISBN 0-252-00719-0 (cased) : £6.00
ISBN 0-252-00720-4 (pbk) : Unpriced
B81-10320

Silverberg, Robert. The songs of summer : and other stories / Robert Silverberg. — London : Pan, 1981, c1979. — 172p ; 18cm. — (Pan science fiction)
Originally published: London : Gollancz, 1979
ISBN 0-330-26315-3 (pbk) : £1.25 B81-18297

Skiles, Don. Miss America and other stories. — London : Marion Boyars, Feb.1982. — [128]p
ISBN 0-7145-2755-6 : £6.95 : CIP entry
B81-35828

Stern, Richard, *1928-*. Packages : stories / by Richard Stern. — London : Sidgwick & Jackson, 1980. — 151p ; 23cm
Originally published: New York : Coward, McCann & Geoghegan, 1980
ISBN 0-283-98689-1 : £5.95 B81-01168

Theroux, Paul. World's end and other stories / Paul Theroux. — London : Hamilton, 1980. — 211p ; 21cm
ISBN 0-241-10447-5 : £6.50 : CIP rev.
B80-23771

Tracy, Lorna. Amateur passions : love stories? / Lorna Tracy. — London : Virago, 1981. — 202p ; 21cm
ISBN 0-86068-197-1 (cased) : £7.95 : CIP rev.
ISBN 0-86068-198-x (pbk) : £3.50 B81-01170

Updike, John. The same door / John Updike. — Harmondsworth : Penguin, 1968 (1981 [printing]). — 185p ; 20cm
Originally published: New York : Knopf, 1959 ; London : Deutsch, 1962
ISBN 0-14-002161-2 (pbk) : £1.95 B81-10931

Updike, John. Your lover just called : stories of Joan and Richard Maple / John Updike. — Harmondsworth : Penguin, 1980. — 140p ; 20cm
Originally published: New York : Fawcett Crest Books, 1979
ISBN 0-14-005655-6 (pbk) B81-06399

Van Vogt, A. E.. Lost : Fifty Suns / A.E. van Vogt. — London : New English Library, 1980, 1972. — 189p ; 18cm
Originally published: New York : Daw, 1972
ISBN 0-450-04949-3 (pbk) : £1.25 B81-07662

Vinge, Joan D.. Eyes of amber : and other stories / Joan D. Vinge ; with an introduction by Ben Bova. — London : Macdonald Futura, 1981, c1979. — 288p ; 21cm
ISBN 0-354-04747-7 (cased) : £5.95
ISBN 0-7088-8082-7 (pbk) : £1.75 B81-28441

Weaver, Gordon. Getting serious : stories / by Gordon Weaver. — Baton Rouge ; London : Louisiana State University Press, 1980. — 118p ; 23cm
ISBN 0-8071-0777-8 (cased) : Unpriced
ISBN 0-8071-0778-6 (pbk) : unpriced
B81-11157

Young, Al. Ask me now / Al Young. — London : Sidgwick & Jackson, 1980. — 294p ; 22cm
Originally published: New York : McGraw-Hill, 1980
ISBN 0-283-98674-3 : £5.95 B81-00323

813'.54[F] — Short stories in English. Canadian writers, *1945-* — *Texts*

Virago, Seán. White lies : and other fictions / Seán Virago. — London : Hamilton, 1981, c1980. — 150p ; 23cm
ISBN 0-241-10546-3 : £6.95 B81-15397

813'.54[J] — Children's short stories in English. American writers, *1945-* — *Texts*

Babbitt, Natalie. The Devil's storybook / stories and pictures by Natalie Babbitt. — [London] : Carousel, 1981, c1974. — 101p : ill ; 20cm
Originally published: New York : Farrar, Straus and Giroux, 1974 ; London : Chatto and Windus, 1976
ISBN 0-552-52128-0 (pbk) : £0.80 B81-14311

Disney, Walt. Walt Disney's stories for all seasons. — Maidenhead : Purnell, 1981, c1978. — 128p : col.ill ; 27cm
ISBN 0-361-05085-2 : £4.50 B81-27179

Holder, Heidi. Aesop's fables. — London : Macmillan Children's, Sept.1981. — [32]p
ISBN 0-333-32202-9 : £4.95 : CIP entry B81-23948

Van Leeuwen, Jean. More tales of Oliver Pig. — London : Bodley Head, Oct.1981. — [64]p. — (Bodley beginners)
ISBN 0-370-30908-1 : £3.25 : CIP entry B81-27955

813'.54[J] — Children's stories in English. American writers, *1945-* — *Texts*

Adler, C. S.. Footsteps on the stairs. — London : Hamilton, Feb.1982. — [128]p
ISBN 0-241-10725-3 : £4.95 : CIP entry B81-36384

Adler, C. S.. The silver coach / by C.S. Adler. — London : Hamilton, 1981, c1979. — 123p ; 23cm
Originally published: New York : Coward, McCann & Geoghegan, c1979
ISBN 0-241-10551-x : £4.95 B81-07247

Adler, David A.. Cam Jansen and the mystery of the stolen diamonds : David A. Adler / illustrated by Susanna Natti. — London : Scholastic, 1981, c1980. — 64p : ill ; 18cm. — (A Hippo book)
Originally published: New York : Viking Press, 1980
ISBN 0-590-70030-8 (pbk) : £0.75 B81-11686

Allard, Harry. I will not go to market today / by Harry Allard ; pictures by James Marshall. — London : Dent, 1981, c1979. — [36]p : col.ill ; 20cm
Originally published: New York : Dial Press, 1979
ISBN 0-460-06075-9 : £2.50 B81-40790

Allen, Laura Jean. Ottie and the star / by Laura Jean Allen. — Tadworth : Worlds Work Childrens Book, 1981, c1979. — 32p : col.ill ; 23cm. — (An Early I can read book ; no.19)
Originally published: New York : Harper and Row, 1979
ISBN 0-437-90519-5 : £3.20 B81-16179

Arden, William. Alfred Hitchcock and the three investigations in the mystery of the shrinking house / text by William Arden ; based on characters created by Robert Arthur. — London : Armada, 1976, c1973 (1981 [printing]). — 157p ; 18cm
Originally published: New York : Random House, 1972 ; London : Collins, 1973
ISBN 0-00-691870-0 (pbk) : £0.80 B81-18524

Arden, William. Alfred Hitchcock and the Three Investigators in the secret of Phantom Lake / text by William Arden ; based on characters created by Robert Arthur. — [London] : Armada, 1980, c1974. — 158p ; 18cm
Originally published: New York : Random House, 1973 ; London : Collins, 1974
ISBN 0-00-691805-0 (pbk) : £0.75 B81-08238

Asch, Frank. MacGooses' grocery / by Frank Asch ; pictures by James Marshall. — London : Scholastic Publications, 1981, c1978. — [32]p : col.ill ; 16x21cm. — (A Hippo book)
Originally published: New York : Dial, 1978 ; Harmondsworth : Kestrel, 1979
ISBN 0-590-72077-5 (pbk) : £0.75 B81-14145

Asch, Frank. Sand cake : a Frank Asch bear story. — London : Carousel, 1980, c 1979. — [32]p : col.ill ; 20cm
Originally published: New York : Parents' Magazine Press, 1979
ISBN 0-552-52123-x (pbk) : £0.75 B81-02466

Baum, Willi. Angelito. — London : Dent, Sept.1981. — [40]p
ISBN 0-460-06083-x : £3.95 : CIP entry B81-22606

Blume, Judy. Are you there, God? It's me, Margaret / Judy Blume. — London : Piccolo, 1980, c1970. — 122p ; 18cm
Originally published: Englewood Cliffs, N.J. : Bradbury Press, 1970 ; London : Gollancz, 1978
ISBN 0-330-26244-0 (pbk) : £0.85 B81-01098

Blume, Judy. Blubber / Judy Blume. — [London] : Piccolo in association with Heinemann, 1981, c1974. — 125p ; 18cm
Originally published: Scarsdale, N.Y. : Bradbury Press, 1974 ; London : Heinemann, 1980
ISBN 0-330-26329-3 (pbk) : £0.95 B81-37358

Blume, Judy. Iggie's house / Judy Blume. — London : Heinemann, 1981, c1970. — 110p ; 23cm
Originally published: Englewood Cliffs : Bradbury Press, 1970
ISBN 0-434-92884-4 : £4.95 B81-36128

Blume, Judy. Superfudge / Judy Blume. — London : Bodley Head, 1980. — 141p ; 23cm
Originally published: New York : Dutton, 1980
ISBN 0-370-30358-x : £3.75 : CIP rev. B80-18507

Blume, Judy. Tales of a fourth grade nothing / Judy Blume. — [London] : Piccolo, 1981, c1972. — 123p ; 18cm
Originally published: New York : Dutton, 1972 ; London : Bodley Head, 1979
ISBN 0-330-26211-4 (pbk) : £0.95 B81-17990

Brown, Marc. Arthur's eyes / by Marc Brown. — [Leeds] : Pepper, 1981, c1979. — [32]p : col.ill ; 27cm
Originally published: Boston, Mass. : Little, Brown, c1979
ISBN 0-560-74517-6 : £3.50 B81-39365

Bunting, Eve. The big cheese / Eve Bunting ; illustrated by Sal Murdocca. — London : Macmillan Children's Books, 1980. — 44p : ill ; 23cm
Originally published: New York : Macmillan, 1977
ISBN 0-333-30071-8 : £3.50 : CIP rev. B80-18508

Bunting, Eve. Mr Pride's umbrella / by Eve Bunting ; illustrated by Maggie Ling. — London : Warne, 1980. — 62p : ill ; 21cm
ISBN 0-7232-2703-9 : £3.95 B81-00324

Byars, Betsy. The cartoonist / Betsy Byars. — [Harmondsworth] : Penguin, 1981, c1978. — 111p ; 18cm
Originally published: New York : Viking: London : Bodley Head, 1978
ISBN 0-14-031182-3 (pbk) : £0.90 B81-35576

Byars, Betsy. The Cybil war / Betsy Byars. — London : Bodley Head, 1981. — 103p ; 23cm
ISBN 0-370-30426-8 : £3.50 : CIP rev. B81-04294

Byars, Betsy. The TV Kid / Betsy Byars. — London : Puffin Books, 1979, c1976 (1980 [printing]). — 108p ; 19cm
Originally published: New York : Viking Press ; London : Bodley Head, 1976
ISBN 0-14-031065-7 (pbk) : £0.75 B81-24878

Calhoun. Snow-cat / Mary Calhoun ; illustrated by Erick Ingraham. — London : Gollancz, 1980, c1979. — [40]p : col.ill ; 26cm
Originally published: New York : Morrow, 1979
ISBN 0-575-02843-2 : £3.50 B81-00325

Camp, Joe. Oh heavenly dog / by Joe Camp ; based upon the screenplay by Rod Browning & Joe Camp. — London : Scholastic, c1980. — 139p,[8]p of plates : col.ill ; 18cm. — (A Hippo book)
ISBN 0-590-72083-x (pbk) : £0.70 B81-18434

Carey, M. V.. Alfred Hitchcock and the Three Investigators in the mystery of the magic circle / text by M.V. Carey ; based on characters created by Robert Arthur. — [London] : Armada, 1981, c1979. — 159p ; 18cm
Spine title: The mystery of the magic circle. — Originally published: New York : Random House, 1978 ; London : Collins, 1979
ISBN 0-00-691911-1 (pbk) : £0.85 B81-28756

Carle, Eric. The honeybee and the robber : a moving picture book / by Eric Carle. — London : Julia MacRae, 1981. — 12p : col.ill ; 30cm
ISBN 0-86203-013-7 : £4.50 B81-11628

Cauley, Lorinda Bryan. Goldilocks and the three bears. — London : Ward Lock, Sept.1981. — [32]p
ISBN 0-7063-6154-7 : £3.50 : CIP entry B81-23809

Cauley, Lorinda Bryan. The ugly duckling : a tale from Hans Christian Andersen / retold and illustrated by Lorinda Bryan Cauley. — New York ; London : Harcourt Brace Jovanovich, c1979. — [46]p : col.ill ; 27cm
ISBN 0-15-292435-3 : £4.50
ISBN 0-15-692528-1 (pbk) : Unpriced B81-15357

Claro, Joe. Herbie goes bananas : a novel / by Joe Claro ; from the Walt Disney Productions film written by Don Tait ; based on characters created by Gordon Buford. — London : Scholastic, 1981, c1980. — 122p : ill,ports ; 18cm. — (A Hippo book)
ISBN 0-590-72217-4 (corrected : pbk) : £0.80 B81-21108

Claro, Joe. My bodyguard / Joe Claro. — London : Scholastic, 1981, c1980. — 86p ; 18cm. — (A Hippo book)
ISBN 0-590-72130-5 (pbk) : £0.70 B81-11684

Cleary, Beverly. Beezus and Ramona / Beverly Cleary ; illustrated by Thelma Lambert. — Harmondsworth : Puffin, 1981, c1955. — 160p : ill ; 19cm
Originally published: New York : Morrow, 1955 ; London : Hamilton, 1978
ISBN 0-14-031249-8 (pbk) : £0.85 B81-15368

Cleary, Beverly. Henry and the clubhouse / Beverly Cleary ; illustrated by Thelma Lambert. — London : Hamilton, 1981, c1962. — 192p : ill ; 21cm
ISBN 0-241-10618-4 : £4.95 : CIP rev. B81-01099

Cleary, Beverly. Ramona Quimby, age 8 / Beverly Cleary ; illustrated by Alan Tiegreen. — London : Hamilton, 1981. — 190p : ill ; 21cm
ISBN 0-241-10665-6 : £4.95 : CIP rev. B81-2386[illegible]

Cleary, Beverly. Runaway Ralph / Beverly Cleary ; illustrated by Louis Darling. — Harmondsworth : Puffin, 1978, c1970 (1981 [printing]). — 140p ; 19cm
Originally published: New York : Morrow, 1970
ISBN 0-14-031020-7 (pbk) : £0.90 B81-2234[illegible]

813'.54[J] — Children's stories in English. American writers, *1945- — Texts*
continuation

Coombs, Patricia. Dorrie and the Screebit ghost / by Patricia Coombs. — Tadworth : World's Work Children's, 1981, c1979. — [48]p : ill (some col.) ; 26cm
Originally published: New York : Lothrop, Lee and Shepard, 1979
ISBN 0-437-32804-x : £3.95 B81-11681

Craft, Ruth. Carrie Hepple's garden / Ruth Craft ; illustrated by Irene Haas. — London : Fontana, 1981, c1979. — 32p : col.ill ; 21cm. — (Picture lions)
Originally published: New York : Atheneum, 1979
ISBN 0-00-661927-4 (pbk) : £0.90 B81-20683

Craft, Ruth. The winter bear / Ruth Craft ; illustrated by Erik Blegvad. — London : Collins, 1974 (1981 [printing]). — [24]p : col.ill ; 22cm
Ill on lining papers
ISBN 0-00-195869-0 : £3.50 B81-38364

De Paola, Tomie. The comic adventures of old Mother Hubbard and her dog / illustrated by Tomie de Paola. — London : Methuen Children's, 1981. — [32]p : chiefly col.ill ; 29cm
ISBN 0-416-21350-2 : £3.95 B81-28618

De Paola, Tomie. Fin M'Coul : the giant of Knockmany Hill / retold and illustrated by Tomie de Paola. — London : Anderson, 1981. — [32]p : col.ill ; 29cm
ISBN 0-86264-000-8 : Unpriced B81-18577

De Paola, Tomie. The hunter and the animals. — London : Andersen Press, Feb.1982. — [32]p
ISBN 0-86264-014-8 : £3.95 : CIP entry B81-36963

De Paola, Tomie. Oliver Button is a sissy / story and pictures by Tomie de Paola. — London : Methuen Children's Books, 1981, c1979. — [48]p : col.ill ; 20cm
ISBN 0-416-89650-2 : £2.50 B81-18249

Disney, Walt. Walt Disney presents Peter and the wolf. — Maidenhead : Purnell, c1973 (1981 [printing]). — 19p : col.ill ; 20cm. — (Walt Disney square story books)
Unpriced (pbk) B81-11115

Disney, Walt. Walt Disney presents Peter Pan. — Maidenhead : Purnell, c1974 (1981 [printing]). — 19p : col.ill ; 20cm. — (Walt Disney square story books)
Unpriced (pbk) B81-11114

Disney, Walt. Walt Disney presents Winnie-the-Pooh. — Maidenhead : Purnell, c1974 (1981 [printing]). — 19p : col.ill ; 20cm. — (Walt Disney square story books)
£0.35 (pbk) B81-11116

Disney, Walt. Walt Disney's story of Mickey and the beanstalk. — Maidenhead : Purnell, c1973 (1981 [printing]). — 19p : col.ill ; 20cm. — (Walt Disney square story books)
Unpriced (pbk) B81-11117

Dubelman, Richard. [The adventures of Holly Hobby]. Holly Hobbie / Richard Dubelman. — London : Granada, 1980, c1979. — 222p : ill,2maps ; 24cm
Originally published: New York : Delacorte / Friede, 1980. — Spine title: The adventures of Holly Hobbie
ISBN 0-246-11439-8 : £4.95 B81-00326

Duncan, Lois. I know what you did last summer. — London : Hamilton, Feb.1982. — [208]p
ISBN 0-241-10723-7 : £4.95 : CIP entry B81-36222

Erickson, Russell E.. Warton and the traders / by Russell E. Erickson ; pictures by Lawrence di Fiori. — London : Hodder and Stoughton, 1981, c1979. — 95p : ill ; 22cm
Originally published: New York : Lothrop, Lee and Shepard, 1979
ISBN 0-340-25615-x : £3.95 : CIP rev. B81-14386

Farrar, Susan Clement. Samantha on stage. — London : Hodder and Stoughton, Dec.1981. — [128]p. — (Knight books)
ISBN 0-340-26542-6 (pbk) : £0.85 : CIP entry B81-31446

Fleischman, Sid. Humbug mountain / by Sid Fleischman ; illustrated by Margaret Chamberlain. — London : Gollancz, 1980, c1978. — 147p : ill ; 21cm
Originally published: Boston, Mass. : Little, Brown, c1978
ISBN 0-575-02893-9 : £4.50 B81-05436

Fleischman, Sid. McBroom and the great race / Sid Fleischman ; illustrated by Quentin Blake. — London : Chatto & Windus, 1981. — 46p : ill ; 24cm
Originally published: Boston, Mass. : Little, Brown, 1980
ISBN 0-7011-2580-2 : £4.50 : CIP rev. B81-09457

Fleischman, Sid. [Me and the man on the moon-eyed horse]. The man on the moon-eyed horse / Sid Fleischman ; illustrated by Margaret Chamberlain. — [London] : Fontana, 1981, c1977. — 63p : ill ; 20cm. — (Lions)
Originally published: as Me and the man on the moon-eyed horse / illustrated by Eric von Schmidt. Boston, Mass. : Little, Brown, 1977 ; and as The man on the moon-eyed horse / illustrated by Margaret Chamberlain. London : Gollancz, 1980
ISBN 0-00-671811-6 (pbk) : £0.85 B81-32164

Fox, Paula. A place apart / Paula Fox. — London : Dent, 1981. — 183p ; 21cm
ISBN 0-460-06082-1 : £4.50 B81-19434

Fujikawa, Gyo. The flyaway kite. — London : Hodder & Stoughton Children's Books, Aug.1981. — [32]p
ISBN 0-340-27080-2 : £1.75 : CIP entry B81-18029

Fujikawa, Gyo. Shag has a dream. — London : Hodder & Stoughton Children's Books, Aug.1981. — [32]p
ISBN 0-340-27079-9 : £1.75 : CIP entry B81-18030

Gackenbach, Dick. Hattie, Tom, and the chicken witch : a play and a story / by Dick Gackenbach. — Tadworth : World's Work, 1981. — 63p : ill ; 22cm. — (An I can read book ; no.132)
ISBN 0-437-90132-7 : £3.95 B81-27588

Ginsburg, Mirra. Where does the sun go at night : adapted from an Armenian song / by Mirra Ginsburg ; pictures by Jose Aruego and Ariane Dewey. — London (8 Cork St., W1X 2HA) : MacRae, 1981. — [32]p : col.ill ; 26cm
Originally published: New York : Greenwillow, 1981
ISBN 0-86203-058-7 : £4.25 B81-09671

Goffstein, M. B.. Goldie the dollmaker / M.B. Goffstein. — Edinburgh : Canongate, 1980, c1969. — 55p : ill ; 16x18cm
Originally published: New York : Farrar, Straus, 1969
ISBN 0-86241-000-2 : £2.50 B81-12239

Harris, Christie. Mouse Woman and the muddleheads / by Christie Harris ; drawings by Douglas Tait. — London : Macmillan, 1980, c1979. — 131p : ill ; 21cm
Originally published: New York : Atheneum, 1979. — Bibliography: p131
ISBN 0-333-30484-5 : £4.95 : CIP rev. B80-18520

Hautzig, Esther. A gift for mama / Esther Hautzig ; illustrated by Donna Diamond. — London : Hamilton, 1981. — 56p : ill ; 22cm
ISBN 0-241-10624-9 : £4.25 B81-32073

Hermes, Patricia. What if they knew? / by Patricia Hermes. — New York ; London : Harcourt Brace Jovanovich, c1980. — 121p ; 21cm
ISBN 0-15-295317-5 : £3.95 B81-15440

Hoban, Lillian. Mr. Pig and family / by Lillian Hoban. — Tadworth : World's Work, 1981, c1980. — 64p : col.ill ; 22cm. — (An I can read book ; no.135) (A World's Work children's book)
ISBN 0-437-90135-1 : £3.95 B81-37898

Hoban, Russell. Ace Dragon Ltd / Russell Hoban ; pictures by Quentin Blake. — London : Cape, 1980. — [40]p : col.ill ; 21cm
Ill on lining papers
ISBN 0-224-01706-3 : £3.25 : CIP rev. B80-21131

Hoban, Russell. The great fruit gum robbery. — London : Methuen, Sept.1981. — [32]p
ISBN 0-416-05790-x : £2.95 : CIP entry B81-23743

Hoban, Russell. They came from aargh!. — London : Methuen, Sept.1981. — [32]p
ISBN 0-416-05840-x : £2.95 : CIP entry B81-23744

Hogan, Paula. Mum will dad ever come home?. — Oxford : Blackwell Raintree, Sept.1981. — [32]p
ISBN 0-86256-002-0 : £2.50 : CIP entry B81-20172

Hoover, H. M.. The lost star / H.M. Hoover. — London : Methuen, 1980, c1979. — 157p ; 21cm
Originally published: New York : Viking, 1979
ISBN 0-416-88610-8 : £4.95 : CIP rev. B80-10803

Hoover, H. M.. Return to earth / H.M. Hoover. — London : Methuen, 1981, c1980. — 159p ; 21cm
Originally published: New York : Viking, 1980
ISBN 0-416-20810-x : £4.95 B81-18250

Hope, Laura Lee. The blue poodle mystery / Laura Lee Hope ; illustrated by Gloria Singer. — London : Transworld, 1981, c1980. — 126p : ill ; 18cm. — (The Bobbsey twins ; 1) (A Carousel book)
Originally published: New York : Wanderer, 1980
ISBN 0-552-52133-7 (pbk) : £0.85 B81-27243

Hope, Laura Lee. The dune buggy mystery / Laura Lee Hope ; illustrated by Ruth Sanderson. — London : Transworld, 1981. — 91p : ill ; 18cm. — (The Bobbsey twins ; 3) (A Carousel book)
ISBN 0-552-52158-2 (pbk) : £0.85 B81-35248

Hope, Laura Lee. The missing pony / Laura Lee Hope ; illustrated by Ruth Sanderson. — London : Transworld, 1981. — 93p : ill ; 18cm. — (The Bobbsey twins ; 4) (A Carousel book)
ISBN 0-552-52151-5 (pbk) : £0.85 B81-32113

Hope, Laura Lee. Secret in the pirates' cave / Laura Lee Hope ; illustrated by Ruth Sanderson. — London : Transworld, 1981. — 126p : ill ; 18cm. — (The Bobbsey twins ; 2) (A Carousel book)
ISBN 0-552-52134-5 (pbk) : £0.85 B81-27244

Isadora, Rachel. Ben's Trumpet / by Rachel Isadora. — London : Angus & Robertson, 1980, c1979. — [32]p : ill ; 21x25cm
Originally published: New York : Greenwillow Books, 1979
ISBN 0-207-95944-7 : £3.95 B81-01100

813'.54[J] — Children's stories in English. American writers, *1945-* — *Texts*
continuation

Isadora, Rachel. Max / story & pictures by Rachel Isadora. — London : Angus & Robertson, 1981, c1976. — [32]p : chiefly ill ; 19x23cm
Originally published: New York : Macmillan ; London : Cassell & Collier Macmillan, 1976
ISBN 0-207-14158-4 : £2.95 B81-15501

Kay, Mara. Restless shadows / Mara Kay. — London : Macmillan Children's Books, 1980. — 157p ; 23cm
ISBN 0-333-28519-0 : £4.95 : CIP rev.
B80-08472

Keats, Ezra Jack. Louie's search / Ezra Jack Keats. — London : 8 Cork St., W1X 2HA : Julia MacRae Books, 1980. — [32]p : chiefly col.ill ; 22x24cm
Originally published: New York : Four Winds Press, 1980
ISBN 0-86203-077-3 : £4.50 : CIP rev.
B80-12134

Kenny, Kevin. Sometimes my mum drinks too much. — Oxford : Blackwell Raintree, Sept.1981. — [32]p
ISBN 0-86256-004-7 : £2.50 : CIP entry
B81-20167

Kerr, M. E.. Dinky Hocker shoots smack! / M.E. Kerr. — London : Heinemann Educational, 1980, c1972. — 160p ; 20cm. — (The New windmill series ; 244)
Originally published: New York : Harper and Row, 1972 ; London : Gollancz, 1973
ISBN 0-435-12244-4 : £1.35 : CIP rev.
B80-10863

Kjelgaard, Jim. Stormy / by Jim Kjelgaard. — [London] : Carousel, 1981, c1959. — 150p ; 20cm
Originally published: New York : Holiday House, 1959
ISBN 0-552-52127-2 (pbk) : £0.80 B81-08597

Krasilovsky, Phyllis. The cow who fell in the canal / by Phyllis Krasilovsky ; illustrated by Peter Spier. — Harmondsworth : Puffin, 1970, c1957 (1980 [printing]). — 36p : chiefly ill (some col.) ; 19x23cm. — (Picture puffins)
Originally published: Kingswood : World's Work, 1958
ISBN 0-14-050034-0 (pbk) : £0.80 B81-06024

Lasker, David. The boy who loved music / David Lasker ; illustrated by Joe Lasker. — London : Hamilton, 1980. — [48]p : col.ill ; 26cm
Originally published: New York : Viking Press, 1979
ISBN 0-241-10407-6 : £3.95 : CIP rev.
B80-18522

Le Guin, Ursula K.. [The beginning place]. Threshold / Ursula K. Le Guin. — London : Gollancz, 1980. — 183p ; 23cm
Originally published: New York : Harper and Row, 1980
ISBN 0-575-02881-5 : £5.50 B81-01101

Le Guin, Ursula K.. Leese Webster / Ursula K. Le Guin ; illustrated by James Brunsman. — London : Gollancz, 1981, c1979. — [29]p : chiefly col.ill ; 27cm
Originally published: New York : Atheneum, 1979
ISBN 0-575-02958-7 : £4.50 B81-34869

L'Engle, Madeline. A swiftly tilting planet / Madeleine L'Engle. — London : Souvenir, 1980, c1978. — 278p ; 23cm
Originally published: New York : Farrar, Straus & Giroux, 1978
ISBN 0-285-62459-8 : £5.95 B81-00327

LeSieg, Theo.. Maybe you should fly a jet! maybe you should be a vet! / by Theo. LeSieg ; illustrated by Michael J. Smollin. — [London] : Collins, 1981, c1980. — [40]p : chiefly col.ill ; 24cm. — (I can read it all by myself. Beginner books)
Originally published: New York : Random House, 1980
ISBN 0-00-171173-3 (cased) : £1.95
ISBN 0-00-171336-1 (pbk) : Unpriced
B81-17669

Leverich, Kathleen. The hungry fox and the foxy duck / Kathleen Leverich ; Paul Galdone drew the pictures. — Tadworth : World's Work, 1981, c1978. — [40]p : col.ill ; 24cm
Originally published: New York : Parents' Magazine Press, 1978
ISBN 0-437-54540-7 : £3.50 B81-13110

Little, Mary E.. Old cat and the kitten / Mary E. Little. — London : Chatto & Windus, 1981, c1979. — 119p : ill ; 21cm
Originally published: New York : Atheneum, 1979
ISBN 0-7011-2576-4 : £4.95 : CIP rev.
B81-07595

Littledale, Freya. Snow White and the Seven Dwarfs / retold by Freya Littledale ; illustrated by Susan Jeffers. — Commonwealth ed. — New York ; London : Scholastic, c1980. — col.ill ; 26cm
ISBN 0-590-72089-9 (pbk) : £0.70 B81-18411

Lobel, Arnold. Days with Frog and Toad / by Arnold Lobel. — Tadworth : World's Work, 1980, c1979. — 64p : col.ill ; 22cm. — (An I can read book ; no.131)
Originally published: New York : Harper & Row, 1979
ISBN 0-437-90131-9 : £3.50 B81-02138

Lorenz, Lee. Scornful Simkin : adapted from Chaucer's The Reeve's tale / retold and illustrated by Lee Lorenz. — London : Dent, 1980. — [32]p : (chiefly col.ill) ; 29cm
Originally published: Englewood Cliffs : Prentice-Hall, 1980
ISBN 0-460-06071-6 : £3.50 B81-02140

Madler, Trudy. Why did grandma die?. — Oxford : Blackwell Raintree, Sept.1981. — [32]p
ISBN 0-86256-001-2 : £2.50 : CIP entry
B81-20170

Marshall, James, *1942-*. George and Martha one fine day / James Marshall. — [Harmondsworth] : Kestrel, 1981, c1978. — 46p : col.ill ; 21cm
Originally published: Boston, Mass. : Houghton Mifflin, 1978
ISBN 0-7226-5733-1 : £3.95 B81-20384

Marshall, James, *1942-*. Portly McSwine / James Marshall. — London : Dent, 1981, c1979. — [40]p : col.ill ; 20cm
Originally published: Boston : Houghton Mifflin, 1979
ISBN 0-460-06074-0 : £2.50 B81-40791

Marzollo, Jean. Amy goes fishing. — London : Bodley Head, Oct.1981. — [64]p. — (Bodley beginners)
ISBN 0-370-30902-2 : £3.25 : CIP entry
B81-27458

Mayer, Mercer. Ah-choo / by Mercer Mayer. — London : Transworld, 1980. — [32]p : chiefly ill ; 13x15cm. — (Storychair books)
Originally published: New York : Dial Press, 1976 ; London : Benn, 1980
ISBN 0-552-50071-2 (pbk) : £0.50 B81-10984

Mayer, Mercer. Hiccup. — London : Transworld, 1980, c1976. — [32]p : chiefly ill ; 13x15cm. — (Storychair books)
Originally published: New York : Dial Press, 1976 ; London : Benn, 1980
ISBN 0-552-50070-4 (pbk) : £0.50 B81-10985

Mayer, Mercer. Oops / by Mercer Mayer. — London : Transworld, 1980, c1977. — [32]p : chiefly ill ; 13x15cm. — (Storychair books)
Originally published: New York : Dial Press, 1977 ; London : Benn, 1980
ISBN 0-552-50069-0 (pbk) : £0.50 B81-13140

Murdocca, Sal. The hero of Hamblett / story and pictures by Sal Murdocca. — London : Macmillan Children's, 1981, c1980. — [46]p : col.ill ; 28cm
Originally published: New York : Delacorte, 1980
ISBN 0-333-32114-6 (cased) : Unpriced : CIP rev.
ISBN 0-333-31997-4 (pbk) : £1.95 B81-07453

Myller, Rolf. [How big is a foot?]. How big is big? / Rolf Myller. — [Exeter] : Wheaton, 1979. — [32]p : ill(some col.) ; 23cm
Originally published: New York : Atheneum, 1962
ISBN 0-08-022886-0 : £1.50 B81-10158

Newman, Robert. The case of the vanishing corpse. — London : Hutchinson, Sept.1981. — [176]p
ISBN 0-09-145750-5 : £4.95 : CIP entry
B81-20183

Newman, Robert, *1909-*. [The case of The Baker Street irregular]. A puzzle for Sherlock Holmes / Robert Newman. — London : Transworld, 1981, c1978. — 168p : 1map ; 18cm. — (A Carousel book)
Originally published: New York : Atheneum, 1978 ; London : Hutchinson, 1979
ISBN 0-552-52139-6 (pbk) : £0.85 B81-35596

Noble, Trinka Hakes. The day Jimmy's boa ate the washing / by Trinka Hakes Noble ; pictures by Steven Kellogg. — London : Hutchinson, 1980, c1979. — [32]p : col.ill ; 28cm
Originally published: New York : Dial, c1980
ISBN 0-09-144180-3 : £3.50 B81-15430

Packard, Edward. The third planet from Altair / Edward Packard ; illustrated by Barbara Carter. — London : Evans Bros, 1980, c1979. — 96p : ill ; 19cm
Originally published: Philadelphia : Lippincott, 1979
ISBN 0-237-45512-9 : £3.25 : CIP rev.
B80-05663

Parish, Peggy. Amelia Bedelia helps out / Peggy Parish ; pictures by Lynn Sweat. — Tadworth : World's Work, 1981, c1979. — 63p : col.ill ; 22cm
Originally published: New York : Greenwillow Books, c1979
ISBN 0-437-66108-3 : £3.95 B81-13368

Paterson, Katherine. The great Gilly Hopkins / Katherine Paterson. — Harmondsworth : Puffin, 1981, c1978. — 139p ; 19cm
Originally published: New York : Crowell, 1978 ; London : Gollancz, 1979
ISBN 0-14-031302-8 (pbk) : £0.95 B81-35486

Philips, Barbara. Don't call me fatty. — Oxford : Blackwell Raintree, Sept.1981. — [32]p
ISBN 0-86256-003-9 : £2.50 : CIP entry
B81-20169

Pinkwater, Daniel Manus. The big orange splot / by Daniel Manus. — New York ; London : Scholastic, c1977. — 30p : col.ill ; 19x23cm
ISBN 0-590-03156-2 (pbk) : £0.50 B81-02143

Quigley, Stacy. Do I have to?. — Oxford : Blackwell Raintree, Sept.1981. — [32]p
ISBN 0-86256-000-4 : £2.50 : CIP entry
B81-20168

Relf, Pat. Muppet manners, (or, The night Gonzo gave a party) : starring Jim Henson's Muppets / by Pat Relf ; illustrated by Tom Leigh. — [London?] : Muppet Press, 1981. — [32]p : col.ill ; 21cm
Originally published: New York : Random House : Muppet Press, 1981
ISBN 0-7221-7269-9 (pbk) : £0.95 B81-28630

813'.54[J] — Children's stories in English. American writers, *1945-* **—** *Texts*

continuation

Rice, Eve. Goodnight, goodnight / Eve Rice. — London : Bodley Head, 1981. — [32]p : col.ill ; 26cm
Originally published: New York : Greenwillow Books, 1980
ISBN 0-370-30402-0 : £2.95 B81-13371

Saunders, Susan, *1945-*. Wales' tale / by Susan Saunders ; illustrated by Marilyn Hirsh. — London : Macmillan Children's, 1981, c1980. — 32p : col.ill ; 24cm
Originally published: New York : Viking, 1980
ISBN 0-333-31573-1 : £3.50 B81-18569

Scarry, Richard. Goldilocks and the three bears / [Richard Scarry]. — Glasgow : Collins, 1981. — [20]p : col.ill ; 22cm. — (Richard Scarry's easy to read books)
Originally published: in Richard Scarry's animal nursery tales. 1975
ISBN 0-00-120482-3 : £1.50 B81-11890

Scarry, Richard. Little Red Riding Hood / [Richard Scarry]. — Glasgow : Collins, 1981. — [20]p : col.ill ; 22cm. — (Richard Scarry's easy to read books)
Originally published: in Richard Scarry's animal nursery tales. 1975
ISBN 0-00-120481-5 : £1.50 B81-11891

Scarry, Richard. Richard Scarry's Peasant Pig and the terrible dragon : with Lowly Worm the jolly jester. — London : Collins, 1981. — [44]p : col.ill ; 28cm
Text and ill on lining papers
ISBN 0-00-138283-7 : £2.95 B81-37276

Scarry, Richard. The three little pigs / [Richard Scarry]. — Glasgow : Collins, 1981. — [20]p : col.ill ; 22cm. — (Richard Scarry's easy to read books)
Originally published: in Richard Scarry's animal nursery tales. 1975
ISBN 0-00-120480-7 : £1.50 B81-11892

Scarry, Richard. The wolf and the seven kids / [Richard Scarry]. — Glasgow : Collins, 1981. — [20]p : col.ill ; 22cm. — (Richard Scarry's easy to read books)
Originally published: in Richard Scarry's animal nursery tales. 1975
ISBN 0-00-120483-1 : £1.50 B81-11889

Schick, Alice. Bram Stoker's Dracula / adapted and illustrated by Alice & Joel Schick. — London : Heinemann, 1981, c1980. — [44]p : col.ill ; 29cm
Originally published: New York : Delacorte, Press, 1980
ISBN 0-434-96241-4 : £3.95 B81-13118

Schick, Alice. Mary Shelley's Frankenstein / adapted and illustrated by Alice & Joel Schick. — London : Heinemann, 1981, c1980. — [44]p : col.ill ; 29cm
Originally published: New York : Delacorte Press, 1980
ISBN 0-434-96240-6 : £3.95 B81-13117

Seidler, Tor. The dulcimer boy / Tor Seidler ; drawings by David Hockney. — London : Cape, 1981, c1979. — 83p : ill ; 25cm
Originally published: New York : Viking Press, 1979
ISBN 0-224-01933-3 : £4.95 : CIP rev. B81-01102

Selig, Sylvie. Kangaroo / Sylvie Selig. — London : Cape, 1980. — [44]p : all col.ill ; 18x27cm
ISBN 0-224-01746-2 : £2.95 : CIP rev. B80-06696

Sendak, Maurice. Outside over there / Maurice Sendak. — London : Bodley Head, c1981. — [40]p : col.ill ; 24x26cm
ISBN 0-370-30403-9 : £5.95 B81-21268

Sharmat, Mitchell. Gregory, the terrible eater / by Mitchell Sharmat ; illustrated by Jose Aruego and Ariane Dewey. — Commonwealth ed. — London : Scholastic, 1980. — [32]p : col.ill ; 20x23cm. — (A Hippo book)
ISBN 0-590-72086-4 (pbk) : £0.70 B81-18412

Spier, Peter. Nothing like a fresh coat of paint / Peter Spier. — Tadworth : World's Work, 1980, c1978. — [49]p : col.ill ; 21x27cm
Previous ed.: S.l. : s.n., 1978. — Ill on lining papers
ISBN 0-437-76515-6 : £3.95 B81-09869

Spillane, Mickey. The day the sea rolled back / Mickey Spillane ; illustrated by Maroto. — London : Methuen Children's, 1980, c1979. — 142p : ill ; 20cm. — (A Pied piper book)
Originally published: New York : Windmill Books, 1979
ISBN 0-416-89620-0 : £3.50 : CIP rev. B80-10871

Spillane, Mickey. The day the sea rolled back / Mickey Spillane ; illustrated by Maroto. — London : Methuen Children's Books, 1981, c1979. — 142p : ill ; 18cm. — (A Magnet Book)
Originally published: New York : Windmill, 1979 ; London : Methuen Children's Books, 1980
ISBN 0-416-21220-4 (pbk) : £0.95 B81-29917

St Tamara. Chickaree : a red squirrel / written and illustrated by St. Tamara. — New York ; London : Harcourt Brace Jovanovich, c1980. — [48]p : col.ill ; 22cm
ISBN 0-15-216612-2 : £3.95 B81-15356

Stevenson, James. Howard / James Stevenson. — London : Gollancz, 1981, c1980. — [32]p : col.ill ; 26cm
Originally published: New York : Greenwillow Books, c1980
ISBN 0-575-02836-x : £3.95 B81-10318

Stevenson, James. Monty / James Stevenson. — London : Scholastic Publications, 1981, c1979. — [32]p : col.ill ; 23cm. — (Hippo books)
Originally published: New York : Greenwillow Books ; London : Gollancz, 1979
ISBN 0-590-72078-3 (pbk) : £0.80 B81-34860

Stevenson, Jocelyn. The great Muppet caper : the story based on the movie starring Jim Henson's Muppets / [storybook adaptation by Jocelyn Stevenson]. — London : Muppet/Joseph, 1981. — 57p : col.ill ; 29cm
ISBN 0-7181-2044-2 : £3.95 B81-33497

Theroux, Paul. London snow : a Christmas story / Paul Theroux ; with wood engravings by John Lawrence. — London : Hamilton, 1980, c1979. — 50p : ill ; 23cm
Originally published: Salisbury : Michael Russell, 1979
ISBN 0-241-10450-5 : £4.95 : CIP rev. B80-18905

Van Allsburg, Chris. The garden of Abdul Gasazi / written and illustrated by Chris Van Allsburg. — London : Hamilton, 1981, c1979. — [31]p : ill ; 25x31cm
Originally published: Boston, Mass. : Houghton Mifflin, 1979
ISBN 0-241-10453-x : £4.50 : CIP rev. B81-13828

Viorst, Judith. The tenth good thing about Barney / Judith Viorst ; illustrated by Erik Blegvad. — London : Collins, 1974, c1971. — 24p : ill ; 19cm
Originally published: New York : Atheneum, 1971 ; London : Collins, 1972
ISBN 0-00-195821-6 : £2.95 B81-28400

Watson, Clyde. How Brown Mouse kept Christmas / Clyde Watson ; pictures by Wendy Watson. — London : Hamilton, 1981, c1980. — [30]p : col.ill ; 17cm
Originally published: New York : Farrar, Straus, Giroux, 1980
ISBN 0-241-10505-6 : £3.95 : CIP rev. B80-23800

Watson, Pauline. The walking coat / story by Pauline Watson ; pictures by Tomie de Paola. — Harmondsworth : Kestrel Books, 1981, c1980. — [32]p : col.ill ; 15x20cm
Originally published: New York : Walker, 1980
ISBN 0-7226-5723-4 : £3.25 B81-14191

Weiss, Joan Talmage. Home for a stranger / Joan Talmage Weiss. — New York ; London : Harcourt Brace Jovanovich, c1980. — 109p ; 21cm
ISBN 0-15-235224-4 : £4.95 B81-15358

Wells, Rosemary, *19---*. Morris's disappearing bag : a Christmas story / by Rosemary Wells. — Harmondsworth : Puffin, 1980, c1975. — [40]p : chiefly col. ; 20cm. — (Picture puffins)
Originally published: New York : Dial, 1975 ; Harmondsworth : Kestrel, 1977
ISBN 0-14-050319-6 (pbk) : £0.80 B81-02446

Wells, Rosemary, *19---*. Stanley & Rhoda : by Rosemary Wells. — [London] : Fontana Picture Lions, 1981, c1978. — 40p : col.ill ; 22cm
Originally published: New York : Dial, 1978 ; London : Kestrel, 1980
ISBN 0-00-661807-3 (pbk) : £0.90 B81-36784

Wells, Rosemary, *19---*. Timothy goes to school / story and pictures by Rosemary Wells. — London : Kestrel, 1981. — [32]p : chiefly col.ill ; 16x20cm
Originally published: New York : Dial Press, 1981
ISBN 0-7226-5740-4 : £3.95 B81-37055

Westcott, Nadine Bernard. The giant vegetable garden. — London : Hutchinson Junior, Oct.1981. — [32]p
ISBN 0-09-146630-x : £3.95 : CIP entry B81-30267

Wiseman, Bernard. Morris tells Boris : Mother Moose stories and rhymes / written and illustrated by Bernard Wiseman. — New York ; London : Scholastic, c1979. — [48]p : col.ill ; 21cm
ISBN 0-590-30999-4 (pbk) : £0.50 B81-18416

Wittman, Sally. [A special trade]. A special swap / by Sally Wittman ; pictures by Karen Gundersheimer. — London : Harper & Row, 1980, c1978. — [32]p : col.ill ; 19cm
Originally published: New York : Harper & Row, 1978
ISBN 0-06-337013-1 : £2.95 : CIP rev. B80-08486

Zion, Gene. Harry by the sea / by Gene Zion ; pictures by Margaret Bloy Graham. — Harmondsworth : Puffin in association with Bodley, 1970, c1965 (1981 [printing]). — 32p : col.ill ; 23cm. — (Picture puffins)
Originally published: New York : Harper and Row, 1965 ; London : Bodley Head, 1966
£0.90 (pbk) B81-15369

Zion, Gene. Harry the dirty dog / by Gene Zion ; pictures by Margaret Bloy Graham. — Harmondsworth : Puffin in association with The Bodley Head, 1968, c1956 (1981 [printing]). — 32p : col.ill ; 23cm. — (Picture puffins)
Originally published: New York : Harper, 1956 ; London : Bodley Head, 1960
ISBN 0-14-050003-0 (pbk) : £0.90 B81-27193

813'.54[J] — Children's stories in English. Canadian writers, *1945-* **—** *Texts*

Hill, Douglas. Day of the starwind / Douglas Hill. — London : Gollancz, 1980. — 123p ; 21cm
ISBN 0-575-02917-x : £4.50 B81-02519

Hill, Douglas. Planet of the Warlord / Douglas Hill. — London : Gollancz, 1981. — 128p ; 21cm
ISBN 0-575-03009-7 : £4.50 B81-35274

813′.54[J] — Children's stories in English. Canadian writers, *1945- — Texts*
continuation

Kellogg, Steven. Pinkerton, behave! / story and pictures by Steven Kellogg. — London : Warne, 1981, c1979. — [32]p : col.ill ; 27cm
Originally published: New York : Dial Press, 1979
ISBN 0-7232-2714-4 : £3.95 B81-32631

Kushner, Donn. The violin-maker's gift / Donn Kushner ; illustrated by Doug Panton. — London : Evans, 1980. — 74p : ill ; 23cm
ISBN 0-237-45521-8 : £4.25 B81-08481

Renard, Gail. Echoes of Louisa / Gail Renard. — [London] : Beaver Books, 1981. — 126p ; 18cm
ISBN 0-600-20433-2 (pbk) : £0.85 B81-19912

Smith, Joan, *1938-*. Babe / Joan Smith. — London : Prior, 1981,, c1980. — 403p ; 25cm
Originally published: New York : Fawcett, 1980?. — Published in large print
ISBN 0-86043-584-9 : £6.95 B81-24365

813′.54′09 — Fiction in English. American writers, *1945- — Critical studies*

Smith, Stan, *1943-*. A sadly contracted hero : the comic self in post-war American fiction / Stan Smith. — Elvet Riverside ([c/o University of Durham, Elvet Riverside, Durham, DH1 3JT]) : British Association for American Studies, 1981. — 39p ; 22cm. — (BAAS pamphlets in American studies ; 5)
Bibliography: p35-37
ISBN 0-9504601-5-x : Unpriced B81-25249

814.4 — AMERICAN ESSAYS, 1861-1900

814′.4 — Essays in English. American writers, *1861-1900 — Texts*

Twain, Mark. Early tales & sketches. — Berkeley ; London : Published for the Iowa Center for Textual Studies by the University of California Press. — (The Works of Mark Twain ; v.15)
Vol.1 : 1851-1864 / edited by Edgar Marquess Branch and Robert H. Hirst with the assistance of Harriet Elinor Smith. — 1979. — xxii,789p : ill,facsims,port ; 24cm
Includes index
ISBN 0-520-03186-5 : £22.50 B81-03492

814.52 — AMERICAN ESSAYS, 1900-1945

814′.52 — Essays in English. American writers, *1900-1945 — Texts*

Miller, Henry, *1891-*. Sextet : six essays / Henry Miller. — London : Calder, 1980. — 188p : ill,facsims ; 23cm
Originally published: Santa Barbara : Capra, 1977. — Contents: On turning eighty — Reflections on the death of Mishima — First impressions of Greece — The waters reglitterized — Reflections on the Maurizius case — Mother, child and the world beyond
ISBN 0-7145-3828-0 (cased) : £7.95 : CIP rev.
ISBN 0-7145-3844-2 (pbk) : £49.5 B80-12485

Nin, Anaïs. In favour of the sensitive man : and other essays / Anaïs Nin. — [London] : W.H. Allen, 1981, c1976. — 169p ; 18. — (A Star book)
Originally published: New York : Harcourt Brace Jovanovich, 1976 ; London : W.H. Allen, 1978
ISBN 0-352-30892-3 (pbk) : £1.35 B81-35611

Trilling, Lionel. The last decade. — Oxford : Oxford University Press, Jan.1982. — [250]p. — (The works of Lionel Trilling)
ISBN 0-19-212220-7 : £8.95 : CIP entry
B81-34372

817 — AMERICAN SATIRE AND HUMOUR

817′.009 — Humour in English. American writers, *to 1977 — Critical studies*

Blair, Walter. America's humor : from Poor Richard to Doonesbury / Walter Blair, Hamlin Hill. — Oxford : Oxford University Press, 1978 (1980 printing). — xvi,559p : ill,facsims ; 21cm
Bibliography: p531-546 — Includes index
ISBN 0-19-502756-6 (pbk) : £4.95 B81-01927

817.54 — AMERICAN SATIRE AND HUMOUR, 1945-

817′.54′08 — Humorous prose in English. American writers, *1945- — Anthologies*

Faber, Harold. The book of laws / Harold Faber. — London : Sphere, 1980, c1979. — xi,113p ; 18cm
Originally published: New York : Times Books, 1979
ISBN 0-7221-3421-5 (pbk) : £1.00 B81-03561

817′.54′0809282 — Children's humour in English. American writers, *1945- — Anthologies*

Fozzie's big book of sidesplitting jokes : (please laugh) : starring Jim Henson's Muppets / illustrated by Tim Kirk. — [London?] : Muppet Press, 1981. — [32]p : col.ill ; 21cm
Originally published: New York : Random House : Muppet Press, 1981
ISBN 0-7221-3606-4 (pbk) : £0.95 B81-28631

818 — AMERICAN MISCELLANY

818′.08 — Prose in English. American writers, *1607-1861.* **Forms: Jeremiads**

Bercovitch, Sacvan. The American jeremiad / Sacvan Bercovitch. — Madison ; London : University of Wisconsin Press, 1978 (1980 [printing]). — xvi,239p ; 21cm
Includes index
ISBN 0-299-07350-5 (pbk) : £3.55 B81-10294

818.1 — AMERICAN MISCELLANY, 1607-1776

818′.102′08 — Anecdotes in English. American writers, *1607-1776 — Anthologies*

Ben Franklin laughing : anecdotes from original sources by and about Benjamin Franklin / edited with an introduction by P.M. Zall. — Berkeley ; London : University of California Press, c1980. — 204p : 1port ; 24cm
Includes index
ISBN 0-520-04026-0 : £7.75
Also classified at 973.2′092′4 B81-27618

818.3 — AMERICAN MISCELLANY, 1830-1861

818′.308 — Prose in English. American writers, *1830-1861 — Texts*

Thoreau, Henry David. Walden / Thoreau ; introduced by Colin Ward ; wood-engravings by Michael Renton. — London : Folio Society, 1980. — 298p : ill ; 23cm
In slip case
£7.50 B81-07228

818′.309 — English literature. American writers, *1830-1861 — Texts*

Poe, Edgar Allan. Tales, poems, essays / Edgar Allan Poe ; with an introduction by Laurence Meynell. — London : Collins, 1981. — 576p : 1port ; 19cm
Bibliography: p573-576
ISBN 0-00-424592-x : £4.95 B81-34879

818′.309 — English literature. American writers. Emerson, Ralph Waldo. Sexuality

Cheyfitz, Eric. The trans-parent : sexual politics in the language of Emerson / Eric Cheyfitz. — Baltimore ; London : Johns Hopkins University Press, c1980. — xv,188p ; 24cm
Includes index
ISBN 0-8018-2450-8 : £8.00 B81-34463

818′.309 — English literature. American writers. Poe, Edgar Allan *— Critical studies*

Hammond, J. R.. An Edgar Allan Poe companion : a guide to the short stories, romances and essays / J.R. Hammond. — London : Macmillan, 1981. — xii,205p,[9]p of plates : ill,map,facsims,port ; 23cm
List of films: p189-192. — Bibliograhpy: p196-201. — Includes index
ISBN 0-333-27571-3 : £15.00 B81-38720

Symons, Julian. The tell-tale heart : the life and works of Edgar Allan Poe / Julian Symons. — Harmondsworth : Penguin, 1981, c1978. — x,259p ; 20cm
Originally published: London : Faber, 1978. — Bibliography: p242-245. — Includes index
ISBN 0-14-005371-9 (pbk) : £1.95 B81-25205

818.4 — AMERICAN MISCELLANY, 1861-1900

818′.403 — Diaries in English. American writers. James, Alice *— Biographies*

Strouse, Jean. Alice James : a biography / Jean Strouse. — London : Cape, 1981, c1980. — xv,367p,[16]p of plates : ill,facsims,ports ; 24cm
Originally published: Boston, Mass. : Houghton Mifflin, 1980. — Facsims on lining papers. — Includes index
ISBN 0-224-01436-6 (pbk) : £9.95 : CIP rev.
B81-01171

818′.403 — Diaries in English. American writers. James, Alice *— Correspondence, diaries, etc.*

James, Alice. The death and letters of Alice James : selected correspondence / edited, with a biographical essay, by Ruth Bernard Yeazell. — Berkeley ; London : University of California Press, c1981. — viii,214p,[16]p of plates : 1facsim,ports,1geneal.table ; 23cm
Includes index
ISBN 0-520-03745-6 : £6.95 B81-15972

818.52 — AMERICAN MISCELLANY, 1900-1945

818′.5209 — English literature. American writers, *1900-1945 — Texts*

Barnes, Djuna. Selected works of Djuna Barnes. — London : Faber, 1980, c1962. — 366p ; 22cm
Originally published: New York : Farrar, Straus and Giroux, 1962. — Contents: Spillway - The Antiphon - Nightwood
ISBN 0-571-11579-9 : £5.50 : CIP rev.
B80-08383

Stein, Gertrude. The Yale Gertrude Stein / selections, with an introduction by Richard Kostelanetz. — New Haven ; London : Yale University Press, c1980. — xxxi,464p ; 24cm
ISBN 0-300-02574-2 (cased) : £18.90
ISBN 0-300-02609-9 (pbk) : £4.40 B81-09388

818′.5209 — English literature. American writers. Cox, Sidney *— Correspondence, diaries, etc*

Frost, Robert, *1874-1963*. Robert Frost and Sidney Cox : forty years of friendship / [edited by] William R. Evans ; foreword by James M. Cox. — Hanover, N.H. ; London : University Press of New England, 1981. — xiv,297p ; 24cm
Includes index
ISBN 0-87451-195-x : £12.25
Primary classification 811′.52 B81-39782

818′.5209 — English literature. American writers. Mac Lane, Mary *— Biographies*

Mac Lane, Mary. The story of Mary Mac Lane / by herself ; with an introduction by Michael Yocum. — London : Cape, 1981. — xi,322p : 1port ; 20cm
Originally published: Chicago : Stone, 1902
ISBN 0-224-01923-6 : £6.50 B81-20769

818′.5209 — English literature. American writers. Wilson, Edmund, *1930-1939 — Correspondence, diaries, etc.*

Wilson, Edmund. The Thirties : from notebooks and diaries of the period / Edmund Wilson ; edited with an introduction by Leon Edel. — London : Macmillan, 1980. — xxxii,753p,[11]p of plates : ill,2facsims,ports ; 19cm
Includes index
ISBN 0-333-21211-8 : £12.50 B81-03952

818′.5209 — Humour in English. American writers. Thurber, James *— Correspondence, diaries, etc*

Thurber, James. The collected letters of James Thurber. — London : Hamish Hamilton, Jan.1982. — [256]p
ISBN 0-241-10706-7 : £8.95 : CIP entry
B81-34317

818.54 — AMERICAN MISCELLANY, 1945-

818′.5407 — Humorous prose in English. American writers, *1945- — Texts*

Allen, Woody. Getting even / Woody Allen. — London : W.H. Allen, [1973, c1971] (1981 printing). — 151p : ill 21cm
Originally published: Random House : New York, 1971
ISBN 0-491-02905-5 : £5.95 B81-36162

818′.5407 — Humorous prose in English. American writers, *1945- — Texts continuation*

Allen, Woody. Side effects / Woody Allen. — London : New English Library, 1981, c1980. — 156p ; 23cm
Originally published: New York ; Toronto : Random House, 1980
ISBN 0-450-04864-0 : £5.50 B81-17708

Beard, Henry. Miss Piggy′s guide to life / by Miss Piggy ; as told to Henry Beard. — London : Muppet Press [i.e. Joseph], 1981. — xii,113p : ill(some col.) ; 27cm
ISBN 0-7181-2062-0 : £5.95 B81-35733

Bombeck, Erma. Aunt Erma′s cope book : how to get from Monday to Friday - in 12 days / Erma Bombeck. — [London] : Magnum, 1980, c1979. — 157p ; 18cm
Originally published: New York : McGraw-Hill, 1979
ISBN 0-417-06130-7 (pbk) : £1.10 B81-13063

Bombeck, Erma. Aunt Erma′s cope book : how to get from Monday to Friday - in 12 days / Erma Bombeck. — London : Eyre Methuen, 1981, c1979. — 157p ; 19cm
Originally published: New York : McGraw-Hill, 1979
ISBN 0-413-48430-0 (cased) : £3.95
ISBN 0-417-01630-7 (pbk) : Unpriced
B81-12037

Donleavy, J. P.. The unexpurgated code : a complete manual of survival and manners / J.P. Donleavy ; with drawings by the author. — Harmondsworth : Penguin, 1976 (1981 [printing]). — 321p : ill ; 19cm
Originally published: New York : Delacorte ; London : Wildwood, 1975
ISBN 0-14-004282-2 (pbk) : £1.95 B81-18518

Fechtner, Leopold. 5000 one and two liners for any and every occasion / by Leopold Fechtner. — Wellingborough : Thomas, 1979, c1973 (1980 [printing]). — vi,15-264p ; 22cm
Originally published: New York : Parker Publishing Company, 1973. — Includes index
ISBN 0-85454-064-4 (pbk) : Unpriced
B81-01172

Murphy′s law book two : more reasons why things go wrong! / [compiled by] Arthur Bloch ; illustrated by Ed Powers. — [London] : Magnum, 1981, c1980. — 96p : ill ; 18cm
Originally published: Los Angeles : Price, Stern, Sloan, 1980
ISBN 0-417-06450-0 (pbk) : £1.10 B81-14209

Parriott, Sara. Sex doesn′t count when— / Sara Parriott. — London : Sphere, 1981, c1979. — [84]p : chiefly.ill ; 20cm
ISBN 0-7221-6715-6 (pbk) : £1.00 B81-30670

818′.5407′08 — Humorous prose in English. American writers, *1945- — Anthologies*

The **Official** rules / [compiled by] Paul Dickson. — [New ed.]. — London : Arrow, 1981. — 220p ; 18cm
Previous ed.: 1980. — Includes index
ISBN 0-09-926490-0 (pbk) : £1.35 B81-18781

818′.5408 — Prose in English. American writers, *1945- — Texts*

Capote, Truman. Music for chameleons : new writing / by Truman Capote. — London : Hamilton, 1981, c1980. — xix,262p ; 23cm
Originally published: New York : Random House, 1980
ISBN 0-241-10541-2 : £7.95 B81-02897

818′.5409 — Humour in English. American writers, *1945- — Texts*

Boulding, Kenneth E.. Beasts, ballads, and Bouldingisms : a collection of writings / by Kenneth E. Boulding ; edited by Richard P. Beilock. — New Brunswick ; London : Transaction, c1980. — 199p : ill,music ; 24cm
Bibliography: p183-196. — Includes index
ISBN 0-87855-339-8 : £7.75 B81-12653

Erskine, Jim. Hug a teddy : and 172 other ways to stay safe and secure / by Jim Erskine and George Moran. — London : Muller, 1981, c1980. — [104]p : chiefly ill ; 18cm
ISBN 0-584-10765-x (pbk) : £1.95 B81-34946

820 — ENGLISH LITERATURE

820′.3′21 — English literature. Writers, *to 1980 — Encyclopaedias*

Eagle, Dorothy. The Oxford illustrated literary guide to Great Britain and Ireland / compiled and edited by Dorothy Eagle and Hilary Carnell. — [New ed.] / revised by Dorothy Eagle. — Oxford : Oxford University Press, 1981. — vi,312p,[47]p of plates : ill(some col.),maps(some col.),ports ; 29cm
Previous ed.: published as The Oxford literary guide to the British Isles. Oxford : Clarendon Press, 1977. — Includes index
ISBN 0-19-869125-4 : £12.50 : CIP rev.
Primary classification 941′.003′21 B81-02647

820′.5 — English literature *— Serials*

[**Writer** *(St Ives)*]. Writer. — Sept./Oct.1980-. — St Ives, Cornwall : United Writers Publications, 1980-. — v. : ill ; 25cm
Six issues yearly. — Continues: Writers′ review (St Ives)
ISSN 0260-2776 = Writer (St. Ives) : £4.60 per year B81-03273

820′.5 — Literary periodicals: Periodicals on English literature: 'Scrutiny' *— Critical studies*

Mulhern, Francis. The moment of Scrutiny. — London : New Left Books, Sept.1981. — [354]p
Originally published: 1979
ISBN 0-86091-745-2 (pbk) : £4.50 : CIP entry
B81-30150

820′.7′1242 — England. Middle schools. Curriculum subjects: English literature. Teaching

Haigh, Gerald. English 8 to 13 / Gerald Haigh. — London : Temple Smith, 1980. — 175p ; 23cm. — (Teaching in practice)
Includes index
ISBN 0-85117-195-8 (cased) : £9.95
ISBN 0-85117-206-7 (pbk) : £3.95
Primary classification 420′.7′1242 B81-00845

820′.7′1242 — England. Secondary schools. Curriculum subjects: English literature. Continuous assessment

Scott, Patrick, *1949-*. Coursework in English : principles and assessment / [written by Patrick Scott on behalf of the NATE working party]. — [Huddersfield] ([10B Thornhill Rd., Edgerton, Huddersfield HD3 3AU]) : National Association for the Teaching of English, 1980. — 25p ; 21cm. — (NATE examinations booklet ; no.3)
£0.60 (pbk)
Primary classification 420′.7′1242 B81-19575

820′.7′1242 — England. Secondary schools. Curriculum subjects: English literature. C.S.E. examinations & G.C.E. (O level) examinations

Barnes, Douglas. Seals of approval : an analysis of English examinations at sixteen plus / Douglas Barnes and John Seed. — [Leeds] : University of Leeds School of Education, c1981. — 36p ; 30cm
Cover title
Unpriced (spiral)
Primary classification 420′.7′1242 B81-14176

820′.76 — English literature: Unseens *— Questions & answers — For West African students*

Moody, H. L. B.. Unseen prose and poetry : a certificate guide / H.L.B. Moody. — London : Longman, 1980. — v,121p : ill ; 22cm
ISBN 0-582-60166-5 (pbk) : £1.15 B81-21683

820.8 — English literature, *1800- — Anthologies — For schools*

New **directions** in English : a first-year English course / [compiled by] Patrick Murray. — Dublin : Educational, 1979. — 136p : ill,facsims,1port ; 21cm
Unpriced (pbk) B81-16628

820.8 — English literature *— Anthologies*

Christmas crackers, 1970-1979 : being ten commonplace selections / by John Julius Norwich. — London : Allen Lane, 1980. — 285p : ill ; 23cm
Includes index
ISBN 0-7139-1383-5 : £8.95 B81-01173

820.8 — English literature *— Anthologies — For schools*

Outlook. — London : Murray, Dec.1981. — [112]p
ISBN 0-7195-3876-9 (pbk) : £1.60 : CIP entry
B81-31533

820.8 — English literature, *to 1978 — Anthologies*

The **Norton** anthology of English literature / M.H. Abrams, general editor, E. Talbot Donaldson ... [et al.]. — 4th ed. — New York ; London : Norton, c1979. — 2v.(xl,2574p;xlii,2582p) : ill,maps ; 22cm
Previous ed.: 1974. — Maps on lining papers. — Includes bibliographies and index
ISBN 0-393-95039-5 : £17.90 set
ISBN 0-393-95048-4 (v.1:pbk) : £6.95
ISBN 0-393-95043-3 (v.2:cased) : £8.95
ISBN 0-393-95051-4 (v.2:pbk) : £6.95
B81-07788

820.8′008 — English literature, *1837-1900 — Anthologies*

The **Brontës** : an illustrated selection of prose and poetry. — Clapham, N. Yorkshire : Dalesman, 1980. — 96p : ill,ports ; 21cm
ISBN 0-85206-611-2 (pbk) : £2.50 B81-05752

820.8′00912 — English literature, *1900- — Anthologies — Serials*

New **writing** and writers. — 18. — London : J. Calder, 1980. — ix,122p
ISBN 0-7145-3773-x : £5.95 : CIP rev.
B80-22446

New **writing** and writers. — 19. — London : J. Calder, Jan.1982. — [248]p
ISBN 0-7145-3815-9 (cased) : £5.95 : CIP entry
ISBN 0-7145-3811-6 (pbk) : £3.50 B81-34644

820′.8′00914 — English literature, *1945- — Anthologies*

Hot air : an anthology of prose, poems and pictures / by members and associates of the Hot Air Society ; edited by Richard Hill ; illustrated by Jean Hill. — [Liverpool] ([23 St Anne′s Rd, Liverpool C17 6BN]) : [The Society], c1980. — 48p : ill ; 21cm
£0.60 (pbk) B81-00329

820.8′00914 — English literature, *1945- — Anthologies*

In a few words : writers workshop Second Chance to Learn, Liverpool 1977-79. — Liverpool (Harrison Jones School, West Derby St., Liverpool 7) : Second Chance, [1980?]. — 37p : ill ; 21cm
Cover title
£0.30 (pbk) B81-28348

Start writing, we did! : a collection of student′s writings from Stone Hall Adult Reading Tuition. — Birmingham (1083 Warwick Rd., Birmingham B27 6QT) : S.T.A.R.T. Adult Literacy Unit, c1980. — 40p : ill ; 21cm
Title taken from cover and title page
£0.30 (pbk) B81-17200

Volunteers / [compiled by] G. Shales Hind. — [St. Andrews] ([21 Kilrymont Rd., St. Andrews, Fife]) : [G. Shales Hind], c1980. — xiii,125p ; 22cm
Includes items in Cornish, Gaelic, Irish, Polish and Welsh with English translations
£1.00 (pbk) B81-28633

820′.8′00914 — English literature, *1945- — Anthologies — For schools*

Elephants are dainty birds : a language and literature experience / [compiled by] Sadler / Hayllar / Powell. — Cheltenham : Thornes, 1980, c1978. — ix,234p : ill,facsims,forms ; 24cm
Originally published: Milton, Qld. : Jacaranda Wiley, 1978
ISBN 0-85950-454-9 (pbk) : £2.95 : CIP rev.
B80-10736

820.8′00914 — English literature, *1945- — Anthologies — Serials*

Aireings. — Leeds (32 Alexandra Grove, Leeds LS6 1QX) : Aireings, [1981]-. — v. ; 22cm
Two issues yearly
ISSN 0261-0124 = Aireings : £0.50 per issue
B81-33278

820.8′00914 — English literature, *1945-* **—** *Anthologies — Serials* *continuation*

[Insight *(Chelmsford)***]**. Insight. — [No.1]-. — Chelmsford (c/o 27 Donald Way, Chelmsford, Essex CM2 9JD) : J. Huscroft, 1980-. — v. ; 30cm
ISSN 0260-5767 = Insight (Chelmsford) : £0.25 per issue B81-08222

Lot 49. — No.1-. — Edinburgh (14a Albany St., Edinburgh) : Exiles Press, 1981-. — v. : ill ; 24cm
Three issues yearly
ISSN 0261-2046 = Lot 49 : £1.20 per year B81-20312

Rock drill. — Issue no.1-. — Norwich (c/o R.G. Sheppard, School of English & American Studies, University of East Anglia, Norwich, Norfolk NR4 7JT) : Supranormal Cassettes, c1980-. — v. ; 30cm
Irregular. — Continues: 1983
ISSN 0144-7262 = Rock drill : £0.95 for 3 issues B81-01774

[Telegram *(London)***]**. Telegram : poetry, fiction, reviews, comment. — 1-. — London (c/o 12 Stevenage Rd., SW6 6ES) : Oasis Books and Oxus Press, 1980-. — v. : ill ; 21cm
Three issues yearly
ISSN 0261-1260 = Telegram (London) : £2.00 per year B81-31048

820.8′00914 — English literature: Compositions by contributors to 'Northern Drift' radio programme, *1945-* **—** *Anthologies*

The **Northern** drift : an anthology of poems, prose and songs from the award-winning BBC series / compiled by Alfred Bradley ; line drawings by Jim Andrew. — Glasgow : Blackie 1980. — 92p : ill,music ; 22cm
Includes index
ISBN 0-216-90917-1 (pbk) : £2.25 B81-07245

820.8′00914 — English literature. Tower Hamlets Worker Writers Group writers, *1945-* **—** *Anthologies*

No dawn in Poplar / The Tower Hamlets Worker Writers Group. — London (178 Whitechapel Rd., E1) : THAP, c1980. — 45p : ill ; 21cm
ISBN 0-906698-01-4 (pbk) : £0.70 B81-09264

820.8′015 — Fantasy literature in English, *1945-.* **Irish writers —** *Anthologies — Serials*

Airgedlámh : an Irish fantasy magazine. — Autumn 1980. — London (c/o 33, Wren House, Tachbrook Estate, SW1V 3QD) : S. Jones : D.A. Sutton, 1980-. — v. : ill ; 30cm
ISSN 0261-0396 = Airgedlámh : £1.50 B81-13089

820.8′015 — Fantasy literature in English — *Serials*

Fantasy macabre. — No.1-. — Chigwell Row (c/o D. Reeder, 32a Lambourne Rd, Chigwell Row, Essex) : Fantasy Macabre, 1980-. — v. : ill ; 22cm
ISSN 0260-8251 = Fantasy macabre : £0.60 per issue B81-09155

820.8′032415 — English literature, *to 1980.* **Special subjects: Western Ireland —** *Anthologies*

The **Bedside** book of West of Ireland / [compiled by] Padraic O'Farrell. — Dublin : Mercier Press, c1981. — 104p : ill ; 18cm
ISBN 0-85342-644-9 (pbk) : £2.00 B81-31755

820.8′0324165 — English literature, *ca 1740-1978.* **Special subjects: Down** *(County)* **—** *Anthologies*

The **Winding** roads : poems and postcards of County Down / compiled by Jack McCoy. — Belfast : Blackstaff, c1980. — 88p : ill,1map,music ; 20cm
ISBN 0-85640-243-5 (pbk) : £4.95 B81-12223

820.8′03242186 — English literature. Special subjects: London. Harrow *(London Borough)* **—** *Anthologies*

As I trace again thy winding hill : Harrow on the Hill : a tapestry of prose and verse / [calligraphy and illustrations by] Dorothy Boux ; [passages chosen and edited by] Eliane Wilson. — London : Shepheard-Walwyn, 1981. — xvii,142p : ill,music,facsims ; 25cm
Includes index
ISBN 0-85683-053-4 : £8.95 B81-33379

820.8′032423 — English literature, *to 1980.* **Special subjects: South-west England —** *Anthologies*

The **West** Country book / foreword by H.R.H. The Prince of Wales, Duke of Cornwall ; edited with an introduction by J.C. Trewin. — Exeter : Webb & Bower, 1981. — 222p : col.ill ; 25cm
Ill on lining papers
ISBN 0-906671-23-x : £7.95 B81-19024

820.8′033 — English literature, *1800-1900.* **Special subjects: Seasons —** *Anthologies*

Lawrence, Louis. The seasons / [compiled and illustrated by] Louis Lawrence ; foreword by Roy Strong. — Exeter : Webb & Bower, c1981. — [123]p : ill(some col.),all facsims ; 25cm
Reproduction of a manuscript compiled between 1887 and 1890
ISBN 0-906671-22-1 : £6.95 : CIP rev.
Primary classification 741.942 B81-00198

820.8′0353 — Children's literature in English, *1837-1900.* **Special themes: Moral development —** *Anthologies*

What I cannot tell my mother is not fit for me to know. — Oxford : Oxford University Press, Oct.1981. — [224]p
ISBN 0-19-212223-1 : £7.95 : CIP entry B81-25854

820.8′0354 — English literature, *1861-1977.* **Special subjects: Parenthood —** *Anthologies — For schools*

The **Experience** of parenthood : an anthology of prose, drama, verse, and pictures / edited by Chris Buckton. — London : Longman, 1980. — vii,152p : ill ; 18cm. — (Longman imprint books)
Bibliography: p145-147
ISBN 0-582-23353-4 (pbk) : £1.30 B81-01175

820.8′0354 — English literature, *1900-1975.* **Special subjects: Love —** *Anthologies — For schools*

The **Experience** of love : a collection of stories portraying early love, with a sequence of poems, photographs and drawings / compiled by Michael Marland and edited by Sarah Ray. — Harlow : Longman, 1980. — iii,153p : ill ; 19cm. — (Longman imprint books)
Bibliography: p151
ISBN 0-582-23338-0 (pbk) : £1.15 B81-05568

820.8′0354 — English literature. Irish writers. Special subjects: Love — *Anthologies*

Some Irish loving : a selection / compiled by Edna O'Brien. — Harmondsworth : Penguin, 1981, c1979. — 251p ; 19cm
Originally published: London : Weidenfeld and Nicolson, 1979. — Includes index
ISBN 0-14-004982-7 (pbk) : £1.50 B81-24511

820.8′0354 — English literature, *to 1979.* **Special subjects: Love —** *Anthologies*

The **British** in love / [compiled by] Jilly Cooper. — Harmondsworth : Penguin, 1981, c1980. — 172p ; 18cm
Originally published: London : Arlington, 1980. — Includes index
ISBN 0-14-005650-5 (pbk) : £1.25 B81-12110

820′.8′0355 — English literature. Special subjects: Society — *Critical studies*

Lerner, Laurence. The literary imagination. — Brighton : Harvester Press, Sept.1981. — [224]p
ISBN 0-7108-0097-5 : £18.95 : CIP entry B81-21497

820.8′0356 — English literature, *to 1974.* **Special subjects: Churches. Bells —** *Anthologies*

A Multiplicity of bells : an anthology / compiled by Margaret Pink. — [Sussex] ([17 Millfield Rise, Bexhill-on-Sea, Sussex TN40 1QY]) : [M. Pink], 1978. — 85p ; 21cm
Unpriced (pbk) B81-10087

820.8′0358 — English literature. Special subjects: World War 1 — *Anthologies*

Voices from the Great War. — London : Cape, Nov.1981. — [336]p
ISBN 0-224-01915-5 : £6.95 : CIP entry B81-30300

820.8′036 — Children's literature in English, *1800-.* **Special subjects: Animals —** *Anthologies*

Johnny Morris's animal story book / illustrated by Tony Morris. — London : Beaver, 1980. — 158p ; 18cm
ISBN 0-600-20235-6 (pbk) : £0.90 B81-04018

820.8′036 — English literature, *to 1979.* **Special subjects: Bees —** *Anthologies*

A Murmur of bees / compiled by Amoret Scott ; with illustrations by Dodie Masterman. — Oxford : Oxford Illustrated, 1980. — 95p : ill ; 20cm
Includes index
ISBN 0-902280-79-1 : £3.95 : CIP rev. B80-19395

820′.8′036 — English literature, *to 1979.* **Special subjects: Monkeys —** *Anthologies*

Monkeys / edited by Lynn Hughes. — London : W.H. Allen, 1980. — 53p : col.ill ; 15cm
ISBN 0-491-02692-7 : £2.50
Also classified at 760′.04432 B81-01549

820.8′036 — English literature, *to 1980.* **Special subjects: Cats —** *Anthologies*

CATegories : cats according to their characters from Sphinx, Gib-Hunter, Grimalkin, Tabby to Puss / chosen and introduced by Rosalie Mander ; foreword by A.L. Rowse ; illustrations by Richard Kennedy. — London : Weidenfeld & Nicolson, c1981. — ix,99p : ill ; 23cm
Includes index
ISBN 0-297-77946-x : £5.95 B81-35404

820.8′036 — English literature, *to 1980.* **Special subjects: Falconiformes —** *Anthologies*

Hawks / edited by Lynn Hughes. — London : W.H. Allen, 1981. — 53p : ill(some col.) ; 15cm
ISBN 0-491-02722-2 (corrected) : £2.50
Also classified at 760′.04432 B81-29965

820.8′036 — English literature, *to 1980.* **Special subjects: Gardens. Flowering plants —** *Anthologies*

Angel, Marie. Cottage flowers / Marie Angel. — London : Pelham, 1980. — 46p : col.ill ; 28cm
ISBN 0-7207-1259-9 : £4.95
Also classified at 635.9′022′2 B81-03115

820.8′036 — English literature, *to 1980.* **Special subjects: Songbirds —** *Anthologies*

Songbirds / edited by Lynn Hughes. — London : W.H. Allen, c1981. — 53p : col.ill ; 15cm
ISBN 0-491-02791-5 : £2.50
Also classified at 760′.04432 B81-15693

820.8′09282 — Children's literature in English, *1300-1979* **—** *Anthologies*

Marshall, Sybil. So big, so small. — Cambridge : Cambridge University Press, Apr.1981. — [48] p. — (Lanterns)
ISBN 0-521-28157-1 (sd) : £1.50 : CIP entry B81-02573

820.8′09282 — Children's literature in English, *1837-1945* **—** *Anthologies*

The **Old-fashioned** children's story-book. — London : Watts, c1979. — 64p : col.ill ; 23cm
Edited by Zena Flax
ISBN 0-85166-697-3 : £3.99 B81-05526

820.8′09282 — Children's literature in English, *1945-* **—** *Anthologies*

The **Edge** of wonder / [compiled by Christopher Herbert]. — [London] : CIO, 1981. — 59p : ill ; 21cm
ISBN 0-7151-4750-1 (pbk) : £1.95 B81-20382

The **Red** book of bedtime stories. — Loughborough : Ladybird, c1981. — 51p : col.ill ; 18cm. — (Nursery rhymes & stories)
ISBN 0-7214-0607-6 : £0.50 B81-19457

820.8′09282 — English literature. Compositions by children, *1945-* **—** *Anthologies — Serials*

Children as writers. — 22nd year. — London : Heinemann Educational, 1981. — iv,140p
ISBN 0-435-13411-6 : £2.50 B81-25036

820.8'09282 — English literature. Northern English child writers, *1945- — Anthologies*
Don't tell my friends / editors: Dave Alton, Gordon Phillips. — Gateshead (15 Woodside Gardens, Dunston, Gateshead, Tyne and Wear NE11 9RB) : Pivot Press, 1981. — 52p : ill ; 21cm
'... a second anthology ...' — cover
ISBN 0-906939-01-1 (pbk) : £0.55 B81-13914

820.8'09282 — English literature. South-east England writers. School student writers, *1945- — Anthologies*
Identity parade : an anthology of poetry and prose from young people in the South East / edited by Hubert Moore and Brian Moses. — Tunbridge Wells (9 Crescent Rd., Tunbridge Wells, Kent) : South East Arts, c1980. — 50p : ill ; 21cm
ISBN 0-905593-04-9 (pbk) : £1.00 B81-08068

820.8'09287 — English literature. Avon women writers: Bristol women writers, *1945- — Anthologies*
Shush, mum's writing again. — [Bristol] (110 Cheltenham Rd., Bristol BS6 5RW) : Bristol Broadsides, c1981. — 36p ; 21cm
ISBN 0-906944-09-0 (pbk) : £0.65 B81-27481

820.8'09287 — English literature. Socialist feminist writers, *1945- — Anthologies*
Smile, smile, smile, smile / Alison Fell ... [et al.]. — London : 488 Kingsland Rd., E.8 : Sheba, 1980. — 128p : ill ; 22cm
ISBN 0-907179-03-7 (pbk) : £1.75 B81-06130

820.8'09411 — English literature. Scottish writers, *to 1975 — Anthologies*
This is my country : a personal blend of the purest Scotch / [compiled by] W. Gordon Smith ; illustrations by Barbara Brown. — Abridged ed. — London : Granada, 1981, c1976. — 297p : ill ; 18cm
Previous ed.: London : Souvenir Press, 1976. — Bibliography: p290-291. — Includes index
ISBN 0-586-05378-6 (pbk) : £1.95 B81-37165

820.8'09411 — English literature. Western Scottish writers, *1945- — Anthologies*
Thomson, Geddes. Identities : an anthology of West of Scotland poetry, prose and drama / edited by Geddes Thomson ; introduction by Edwin Magan. — London : Heinemann Educational, 1981. — xiii,225p : ill ; 22cm
Bibliography: p214-215
ISBN 0-435-14901-6 (pbk) : £3.50 : CIP rev. B80-12487

820.8'0941312 — English literature. Stirling University Literary Society writers, *1945- — Anthologies — Serials*
Hairst. — [No.1 (198?-)]-. — [Dunblane] ([c/o Michael Benenson, 19 The Square, Ashfield, Dunblane, Perthshire FK15 0JN]) : Stirling University Literary Society, [198-?]-. — v. ; 21cm
Description based on: No.3 (Autumn 1980)
ISSN 0260-826x = Hairst : Unpriced B81-09156

820.8'09415 — English literature. Irish writers, *1900-1954 - Anthologies*
Yeats, W. B.. The Celtic twilight. — Gerrards Cross : Smythe, June 1981. — [160]p
ISBN 0-86140-069-0 (cased) : £8.50 : CIP entry
ISBN 0-86140-070-4 (pbk) : £2.75 B81-15825

820.8'09415 — English literature. Irish writers, *to 1979 — Anthologies*
The **Irish** bedside book / edited by John M. Feehan. — Dublin : Mercier, c1980. — 128p ; 18cm
ISBN 0-85342-630-9 (pbk) : £2.30 B81-16089

820.8'0942195 — English literature. Richmond upon Thames College writers, *1945- — Anthologies — Serials*
Richmond collage. — No.1 (Summer 1978)-. — [Twickenham] ([c/o College Librarian, Egerton Rd, Twickenham, Middx TW2 7SJ]) : Richmond upon Thames College, 1978-. — v. ; 30cm
Annual. — Description based on: No.3 (Summer 1980)
ISSN 0261-6505 = Richmond collage : Unpriced B81-32899

820.8'09422315 — English literature. Kent writers: Gravesham writers, *1945- — Anthologies*
Rivers of life : a Gravesham anthology / edited by Richard Burns. — Gravesend (Victoria Centre for Adult Education, Darnley Rd, Gravesend, Kent DA11 0RX) : Victoria Press, 1980. — viii,141p : ill ; 21cm
ISBN 0-907165-00-1 (pbk) : £1.50 B81-32161

820.8'094253 — English literature. Lincolnshire writers, *1945- — Anthologies*
Proof : anthology 2 : new writing from Lincolnshire and Humberside collected in 1980 / edited by Patrick O'Shaughnessy. — [Lincoln] : Lincolnshire and Humberside Arts, 1980. — 24p ; 28cm
ISBN 0-906465-20-6 (pbk) : Unpriced
Also classified at 820.8'094283 B81-14566

820.8'094283 — English literature. Humberside writers, *1945- — Anthologies*
Proof : anthology 2 : new writing from Lincolnshire and Humberside collected in 1980 / edited by Patrick O'Shaughnessy. — [Lincoln] : Lincolnshire and Humberside Arts, 1980. — 24p ; 28cm
ISBN 0-906465-20-6 (pbk) : Unpriced
Primary classification 820.8'094253 B81-14566

820.8'15 — English science fiction literature, *1945- — Anthologies — Serials*
Enterprise— personal log : a Star Trek fanzine. — 1-. — Strathmartine (6 Craigmill Cottages, Strathmartine, by Dundee) : ScoTpress, 1981-. — v. ; 30cm
Irregular
ISSN 0261-8621 = Enterprise personal log : £1.15 per issue B81-34039

Stag con. — [No.1]-. — Strathmartine (c/o Ms S. Clark, 6 Craigmill Cottages, Strathmartine, by Dundee [DD3 0PH]) : Star Trek Action Group, [198-]-. — v. : ill ; 30cm
Description based on: '81
ISSN 0261-5835 = Stag con : £1.15 B81-34038

820.9 — ENGLISH LITERATURE. HISTORY AND CRITICAL STUDIES

820.9 — English literature, *1558-1980 — Critical studies*
Hewett, Peter. English language & literature O Level : a course leading to the special NEC O Level examinations set by the Associated Examining Board in English Language O Level and English literature O Level / Peter Hewett and Jack Roberts. — Cambridge : National Extension College, c1979. — 3v. : ill ; 30cm. — (National Extension College correspondence texts ; course no. E18)
ISBN 0-86082-141-2 (pbk) : Unpriced
Primary classification 420 B81-13942

Knights, L. C.. Selected essays in criticism / L.C. Knights. — Cambridge : Cambridge University Press, 1981. — viii,232p ; 23cm
ISBN 0-521-23628-2 (cased) : £19.50
ISBN 0-521-28083-4 (pbk) : £6.30 B81-25924

820.9 — English literature, *1625-1837.* **Implication** *— Critical studies*
Ehrenpreis, Irvin. Acts of implication : suggestion and covert meaning in the works of Dryden, Swift, Pope and Austen / Irvin Ehrenpreis. — Berkeley ; London : University of California Press, c1980. — x,158p ; 23cm. — (The Beckman lectures ; 1978)
Includes index
ISBN 0-520-04047-3 : £9.00 B81-27568

820'.9 — English literature, *1642 - Critical studies - Conference proceedings*
1642 : literature and power in the seventeenth century. — Colchester (Department of Literature, University of Essex, Colchester) : Essex Sociology of Literature Conference Committee, May 1981. — [340]p
Conference papers
ISBN 0-901726-18-4 (pbk) : £4.85 : CIP entry B81-14965

820.9 — English literature, *1764—1930.* **Influence of Italy**
Churchill, Kenneth. Italy and English literature 1764-1930 / Kenneth Churchill. — London : Macmillan, 1980. — viii,230p ; 23cm
Bibliography: p212-227. - Includes index
ISBN 0-333-26444-4 : £20.00 : CIP rev. B80-09813

820.9 — English literature, *1775-1965 — Critical studies*
Hough, Graham. Selected essays / Graham Hough. — Cambridge : Cambridge University Press, 1980, c1978. — 247p ; 22cm
ISBN 0-521-29918-7 (pbk) : £4.50 B81-11190

820.9 — English literature, *1800-1945 — Critical studies*
Trilling, Lionel. The opposing self : nine essays in criticism / Lionel Trilling. — Oxford : Oxford University Press, 1980, c1978. — 204p ; 21cm. — (The Works of Lionel Trilling)
Originally published: New York : Viking Press ; London : Secker & Warburg, 1955
ISBN 0-19-212216-9 : £6.95 : CIP rev. B80-04934

820.9 — English literature, *ca 1390-1930 — Critical studies*
English A Level : a course leading to the English literature GCE A Level exam. of the Associated Examining Board. — Cambridge : National Extension College, 1979-1980. — 5v. : ill,maps,ports ; 30cm. — (National Extension College correspondence texts ; course no. 21)
Includes index
ISBN 0-86082-159-5 (pbk) : Unpriced B81-13943

820.9 — English literature *— Critical studies — Serials*
Essays and studies : being ... of the new series of essays and studies collected for the English Association. — Vol.34 (1981). — London : J. Murray, c1981. — 147p
ISBN 0-7195-3828-9 : Unpriced : CIP rev. B81-06607

The **Yearbook** of English studies. — Vol.11 (1981). — London : Modern Humanities Research Association, c1981. — x,366p
ISBN 0-900547-74-x : Unpriced
ISSN 0306-2473 B81-20310

The **year's** work in English studies. — Vol.59 (1978). — London : Published for the English Association by John Murray, [1981]. — xvi,556p
ISBN 0-7195-3821-1 : Unpriced : CIP rev.
ISSN 0084-4144 B81-06606

820.9 — English literature. Criticism. Eliot, T. S. *— Critical studies*
Lobb, Edward. T.S. Eliot and the Romantic critical tradition / Edward Lobb. — London : Routledge & Kegan Paul, 1981. — xiii,194p ; 22cm
Includes index
ISBN 0-7100-0636-5 : £10.50 B81-19959

820.9 — English literature. Influence of emblem books, *1500-1700*
Daly, Peter M.. Literature in the light of the emblem : structural parallels between the emblem and literature in the sixteenth and seventeenth centuries / Peter M. Daly. — Toronto ; London : University of Toronto Press, c1979. — xiv,245p : ill,facsims ; 24cm
Bibliography: p224-233. — Includes index
ISBN 0-8020-5390-4 : £11.35
Also classified at 830.9 B81-05825

820.9 — English literature. Social aspects — *History*
English literature in history. — London : Hutchinson, 1981
1350-1400, medieval readers and writers / Janet Coleman. — 337p ; 23cm
Includes index
ISBN 0-09-144100-5 (cased) : £12.00 : CIP rev.
ISBN 0-09-144101-3 (pbk) : £5.95 B81-06058

820.9 — English literature, *to 1975* **—** *Critical studies*

Evans, Ifor. A short history of English literature / Ifor Evans. — 4th rev. and enl. ed. / with additional material by Bernard Bergonzi. — Harmondsworth : Penguin, 1976 (1981 [printing]). — 400p ; 18cm. — (Pelican books)
Previous ed.: 1970. — Includes index
ISBN 0-14-020072-x (pbk) : £1.95 B81-40097

820′.9 — English literature, *to 1980.* **Linguistic aspects**

Blake, N. F.. Language variety in English literature. — London : Deutsch, Nov.1981. — [224]p. — (Language library)
ISBN 0-233-97311-7 (cased) : £8.95 : CIP entry
ISBN 0-233-97422-9 (pbk) : £5.50 B81-28800

820′.9 — Great Britain. Society *expounded by* **English literature,** *1066-*

The **context** of English literature. — London : Methuen, Nov.1981
The later Middle Ages. — [288]p
ISBN 0-416-85990-9 (cased) : £10.50 : CIP entry
ISBN 0-416-86000-1 (pbk) : £5.50 B81-32535

820.9′001 — English literature, *to 1558* **—** *Encyclopaedias*

The **beginnings** to 1558 / [editor James Vinson] ; introduction by Allan H. MacLaine. — London : Macmillan, 1980. — vii,86p ; 24cm. — (Great writers student library ; 1)
Bibliography: p24-28
ISBN 0-333-28344-9 : £6.95 B81-12089

820.9′003 — English literature, *1558-1625* **—** *Critical studies*

Greenblatt, Stephen J.. Renaissance self-fashioning : from More to Shakespeare / Stephen Greenblatt. — Chicago ; London : University of Chicago Press, 1980. — 321p ; 24cm
Includes index
ISBN 0-226-30653-4 : £12.00 B81-12682

820.9′003 — English literature, *1558-1702* **—** *Critical studies*

The **Age** of Milton : backgrounds to seventeenth-century literature / C.A. Patrides, Raymond B. Waddington, editors. — Manchester : Manchester University Press, 1980. — x,438p,[8]p of plates : ill,music,ports ; 24cm
Bibliography: p393-427. — Includes index
ISBN 0-7190-0770-4 : £22.50 : CIP rev.
Also classified at 942.06 B80-06532

Slights, Camille Wells. The casuistical tradition : in Shakespeare, Donne, Herbert and Milton / Camille Wells Slights. — Princeton ; Guildford : Princeton University Press, c1981. — xix,307p ; 25cm
Includes index
ISBN 0-691-06463-6 : £12.20 B81-28432

820.9′004 — English literature. Influence of Bible, *1625-1702*

Knott, John R. (John Ray). The sword of the spirit : Puritan responses to the Bible / John R. Knott. — Chicago ; London : University of Chicago Press, 1980. — ix,194p : 2ill,1facsim ; 24cm
Includes index
ISBN 0-226-44848-7 : £10.80 B81-04802

820.9′005 — English literature, *1702-1800* **—** *Critical studies*

Landa, Louis A.. Essays in eighteenth-century English literature / Louis A. Landa. — Princeton ; Guildford : Princeton University Press, c1980. — viii,241p ; 25cm. — (Princeton series of collected essays)
Includes index
ISBN 0-691-06449-0 (cased) : £11.20
ISBN 0-691-01375-6 (pbk) : £4.95 B81-03402

820.9′006 — English literature, *1745-1837* **—** *Critical studies*

Aers, David. Romanticism and ideology : studies in English writing 1765-1830 / David Aers, Jonathan Cook, David Punter. — London : Routledge & Kegan Paul, 1981. — v,194p ; 24cm
Text on inside covers. — Includes index
ISBN 0-7100-0781-7 (pbk) : £6.95 : CIP rev. B81-25732

820.9′007 — English literature, *1800-1837* **—** *Critical studies* **—** *Festschriften*

High romantic argument : essays for M.H. Abrams / essays by Geoffrey Hartman ... [et al.] ; with a reply by M.H. Abrams ; a preface by Stephen M. Parrish ; and a bibliography by Stuart A. Ende ; edited by Lawrence Lipking. — Ithaca ; London : Cornell University Press, 1981. — 182p : 1port ; 23cm
Conference papers. — List of works of M.H. Abrams: p177-182
ISBN 0-8014-1307-9 : £9.00 B81-36448

820.9′007 — English literature, *1800-1837* **—** *Encyclopaedias*

The **Romantic** period : excluding the novel / introduction by Kenneth Muir. — London : Macmillan, 1980. — vii,131p ; 24cm. — (Great writers student library ; 6)
Includes bibliographies
ISBN 0-333-28338-4 : £7.95 B81-05108

820.9′008 — English literature, *1837-1900* **—** *Critical studies*

Buckler, William E.. The Victorian imagination : essays in aesthetic exploration / William E. Buckler. — Brighton : Harvester, 1980. — 382p ; 24cm
Includes index
ISBN 0-7108-0006-1 : £22.00 B81-02628

Buckley, Jerome Hamilton. The Victorian temper : a study in literary culture / Jerome Hamilton Buckley. — Cambridge : Cambridge University Press, 1981, c1951. — x,282p,[8]p of plates : ill,ports ; 22cm
Originally published: Cambridge, Mass. : Harvard University Press, 1951 ; London : Allen & Unwin, 1952. — Includes index
ISBN 0-521-28448-1 (pbk) : £7.95 : CIP rev. B81-30445

820.9′008 — English literature, *1837-1945.* **Imagination. Theological aspects**

Coulson, John. Religion and imagination : 'in aid of a grammar of assent' / by John Coulson. — Oxford : Clarendon, 1981. — x,193p ; 23cm
Bibliography: p170-176. — Includes index
ISBN 0-19-826656-1 : £12.50 : CIP rev. B81-02090

820.9′008 — English literature, *1837-1980* **—** *Structuralist perspectives*

Lodge, David. Working with structuralism : essays and reviews on nineteenth- and twentieth-century literature / David Lodge. — Boston : Routledge & Kegan Paul, 1981. — xii,207p ; 23cm
Includes index
ISBN 0-7100-0658-6 : £10.95 B81-25349

820.9′00912 — English literature, *1900-1945* **—** *Critical studies* **—** *Serials*

VII : an Anglo-American literary review. — Vol.1-. — [Wheaton], Ill. : Wheaton College ; Cambridge : Distributed by Heffers Printers, 1980-. — v. ; 24cm
Annual
ISSN 0271-3012 = VII (Wheaton) : £5.00 per year B81-05537

820.9′00912 — English literature, *1900-* **—** *Critical studies*

Trilling, Lionel. A gathering of fugitives / Lionel Trilling. — Oxford : Oxford University Press, 1980, c1956. — 179p ; 21cm. — (The Works of Lionel Trilling)
Originally published: Boston, Mass. : Beacon Press, 1956 ; London : Secker & Warburg, 1957
ISBN 0-19-212214-2 : £6.95 : CIP rev. B80-05570

820.9′00912 — English literature. Aldington, Richard & Durrell, Lawrence — *Correspondence, diaries, etc*

Aldington, Richard. Literary lifelines : the Richard Aldington-Lawrence Durrell correspondence / edited by Ian S. MacNiven and Harry T. Moore. — London : Faber, 1981. — xvii,236p ; 24cm
Includes index
ISBN 0-571-11501-2 : £8.95 : CIP rev.
Also classified at 828′.91209 B81-13570

820.9′00912 — English literature. Influence of Dadaism & surrealism in European arts, *to 1980*

Young, Alan, *19---.* Dada and after : extremist modernism and English literature / Alan Young. — Manchester : Manchester University Press, c1981. — 247p ; 24cm
Bibliography: p223-236. — Includes index
ISBN 0-7190-0822-0 : £17.50 B81-39878

820.9′00912 — English literature. Oxfordshire writers: Oxford writers. Inklings — *Critical studies*

Carpenter, Humphrey. The Inklings : C.S. Lewis, J.R.R. Tolkein, Charles Williams and their friends / Humphrey Carpenter. — London : Unwin Paperbacks, 1981. — xii,287p,[8]p of plates : ill,facsim,ports ; 20cm
Originally published: London : Allen and Unwin, 1978. — Bibliography: p260-265. - Includes index
ISBN 0-04-809013-1 (pbk) : £2.95 B81-10626

820.908′0355 — English literature. Special subjects: Cricket — *Anthologies*

Summer days. — London : Eyre Methuen, Sept.1981. — [224]p
ISBN 0-413-49060-2 : £6.95 : CIP entry B81-23913

820.9′1 — English literature, *1800-1837.* **Romantic irony —** *Critical studies*

Mellor, Anne Kostelanetz. English romantic irony / Anne K. Mellor. — Cambridge, Mass. ; London : Harvard University Press, 1980. — ix,219p ; 25cm
Includes index
ISBN 0-674-25690-5 : £9.00 B81-04562

820.9′1 — English literature, *1900-1980.* **Irony —** *Critical studies*

Wilde, Alan. Horizons of assent : modernism, postmodernism, and the ironic imagination / Alan Wilde. — Baltimore ; London : Johns Hopkins University Press, c1981. — xii,209p ; 24cm
Includes index
ISBN 0-8018-2449-4 : £9.00 B81-36569

820.9′145 — English literature, *1745-1837.* **Romanticism —** *Critical studies*

Butler, Marilyn. Romantics, rebels and reactionaries : English literature and its background 1976-1830 / Marilyn Butler. — Oxford : Oxford University Press, 1981. — 213p ; 20cm. — (OPUS)
Bibliography: p198-204. — Includes index
ISBN 0-19-219144-6 (cased) : £7.95 : CIP rev.
ISBN 0-19-289132-4 (pbk) : Unpriced B81-13483

820.9′16 — English literature, *1762-1980.* **Special themes: Horror —** *Critical studies*

Horror literature : a core collection and reference guide / edited by Marshall B. Tymn. — New York ; London : Bowker, 1981. — xviii,559p ; 24cm
Includes bibliographies and index
ISBN 0-8352-1341-2 (cased) : Unpriced
ISBN 0-8352-1405-2 (pbk) : Unpriced B81-39041

820.9′3 — English literature, *1558-1625.* **Special themes: Grotesque —** *Critical studies*

Rhodes, Neil. Elizabethan grotesque / Neil Rhodes. — London : Routledge & Kegan Paul, 1980. — xiv,207p ; 23cm
Bibliography: p189-202. - Includes index
ISBN 0-7100-0599-7 : £12.50 : CIP rev. B80-20995

820.9′32 — English literature, *1780-1970.* **Special subjects: Human geographical features —** *Critical studies*

Humanistic geography and literature : essays on the experience of place / edited by Douglas C.D. Pocock. — London : Croom Helm, 1981. — 224p : ill,3maps ; 23cm. — (Croom Helm series in geography and environment)
Includes index
ISBN 0-7099-0193-3 : £14.95 : CIP rev. B80-35399

820.9′352042 — English literature, *1625-1702*. Special themes: Society. Role of women — *Critical studies*
Malekin, Peter. Liberty and love : English literature and society 1640-88 / Peter Malekin. — London : Hutchinson, 1981. — x,219p ; 23cm
Bibliography: p209-210. — Includes index
ISBN 0-09-143040-2 (cased) : £10.00 : CIP rev.
ISBN 0-09-143041-0 (pbk) : 1981
Primary classification 820.9′355 B80-20996

820.9′353 — English literature, *1066-1400*. Special themes: Interpersonal relationships between mothers & daughters — *Critical studies*
Stiller, Nikki. Eve′s orphans : mothers and daughters in medieval English literature / Nikki Stiller. — Westport, Conn. ; London : Greenwood Press, 1980. — xiii,152p ; 22cm. — (Contributions in women′s studies, ISSN 0147-104x ; no.16)
Bibliography: p145-148. — Includes index
ISBN 0-313-22067-0 : £12.95 B81-23475

820.9′355 — English literature, *1500-1980*. Special themes: Capitalism — *Critical studies*
McVeagh, John. Tradeful merchants : the portrayal of the capitalist in literature / John McVeagh. — London : Routledge & Kegan Paul, 1981. — xvi,221p ; 23cm
Bibliography: p213-214. — Includes index
ISBN 0-7100-0729-9 : £11.95 : CIP rev. B81-14926

820.9′355 — English literature, *1625-1702*. Special themes: Great Britain. Constitution — *Critical studies*
Malekin, Peter. Liberty and love : English literature and society 1640-88 / Peter Malekin. — London : Hutchinson, 1981. — x,219p ; 23cm
Bibliography: p209-210. — Includes index
ISBN 0-09-143040-2 (cased) : £10.00 : CIP rev.
ISBN 0-09-143041-0 (pbk) : 1981
Also classified at 820.9′352042 B80-20996

820.9′355 — English literature, *to 1900*. Special themes: Tales. Special subjects: Families. Interpersonal relationships — *Critical studies*
Brewer, Derek. Symbolic stories : traditional narratives of the family drama in English literature / Derek Brewer. — Woodbridge : Brewer, c1980. — ix,190p ; 21cm
ISBN 0-85991-063-6 : £15.00 : CIP rev. B80-17921

820.9′358 — English literature, *1900-1945*. Special subjects: World War 1 — *Critical studies*
Bergonzi, Bernard. Heroes′ twilight : a study of the literature of the Great War / Bernard Bergonzi. — 2nd ed. — London : Macmillan, 1980. — 241p ; 23cm
Previous ed.: London : Constable, 1965. — Bibliography: p229-232. - Includes index
ISBN 0-333-28126-8 : £15.00 : CIP rev.
ISBN 0-333-28157-8 (pbk) : £5.95 B80-13959

820.9′9171241 — English literature. Commonwealth writers, *1900-* — *Critical studies*
King, Bruce, *1933-*. The new English literatures : cultural nationalism in a changing world / Bruce King. — London : Macmillan, 1980. — xi,248p ; 20cm. — (Macmillan new literature handbooks)
Includes index
ISBN 0-333-24070-7 (cased) : £12.00 : CIP rev.
ISBN 0-333-24071-5 (pbk) : £4.50 B80-06533

820.9′9171241′0321 — English literature. Commonwealth writers, *ca 1830-1978* — *Encyclopaedias*
Commonwealth literature / introduction by William Walsh. — London : Macmillan, 1980. — vii,281p ; 25cm. — (Great writers student library ; 14)
Includes bibliographies
ISBN 0-333-28356-2 : £8.95 B81-06642

820.9′9287 — English literature. Women writers, *1775-1886* — *Critical studies*
Gilbert, Sandra M.. The madwoman in the attic : the woman writer and the nineteenth-century literary imagination / Sandra M. Gilbert and Susan Gubar. — New Haven ; London : Yale University Press, 1980, c1979. — xiv,719p : ill,ports ; 24cm
Includes index
ISBN 0-300-02539-4 (cased) : £15.75
ISBN 0-300-02286-7 B81-10290

820.9′9287 — English literature. Women writers. Creative writing. Problems
Olsen, Tillie. Silences / Tillie Olsen. — London : Virago, 1980, c1978. — xviii,298p ; 21cm
Originally published: New York : Delacorte Press/S. Lawrence, 1978. — Includes index
ISBN 0-86068-157-2 (cased) (pbk) : £3.50 B81-08370

820′.9′941 — English literature. Irish writers, *1900-* - *Critical studies*
. Literature and the changing Ireland. — Gerrards Cross : Smythe, June 1981. — [200]p. — (Irish literary studies, ISSN 0140-895x ; 9)
ISBN 0-86140-043-7 : £9.00 : CIP entry B81-09478

820.9′9415 — English literature. Irish writers, *1837-1900* — *Critical studies*
Hall, Wayne E.. Shadowy heroes. — Brighton : Harvester Press, Apr.1981. — lv.p
ISBN 0-7108-0053-3 : Unpriced : CIP entry B81-01855

820.9′9415 — English literature. Irish writers, *to 1978* — *Festschriften*
. Image & illusion : Anglo-Irish literature and its contexts : a festschrift for Roger McHugh / edited by Maurice Harmon. — Portsmouth (98 Ardilaun, Portmarnock, Co, Dublin) : Wolfhound, c1979. — 174p : 1port ; 25cm
Bibliography: p163-166. — Includes index
ISBN 0-905473-42-6 : £10.00 B81-01577

820.9′9422′025 — English literature. South-east England writers — *Directories*
. Directory of writers in the South East of England. — Tunbridge Wells (9-10 Cresecent Rd., Tunbridge Wells, Kent TN1 2LU) : South East Arts, 1979. — 12p ; 30cm
Cover title. — Text on inside cover
Unpriced (pbk) B81-09573

820.9′9429 — English literature. Welsh writers, *1837-1980* — *Biographies*
Jones, Glyn, *1905-*. Profiles : a visitors′ guide to writing in twentieth century Wales / Glyn Jones and John Rowlands. — Llandysul : Gomer, 1980. — xxxi,382p : maps,ports ; 22cm
Maps on lining papers. — Bibliography: p380-382
ISBN 0-85088-713-5 : £9.95
Primary classification 891.6′6′09002 B81-40041

820.9′96 — English literature. African writers, *1945-* — *Critical studies*
Irele, Abiola. The African experience in literature and ideology / Abiola Irele. — London : Heinemann, 1981. — 216p ; 22cm. — (Studies in African literature)
Includes index
ISBN 0-435-91630-0 (cased) : Unpriced
ISBN 0-435-91631-9 (pbk) : £5.95
Also classified at 840.9′96 B81-31963

Irele, Abiola. The African experience in literature and ideology. — London : Heinemann Educational, Sept.1981. — [224]p. — (Studies in African literature)
ISBN 0-435-91631-9 (pbk) : £5.95 : CIP entry
Also classified at 840.9′96 B81-22601

Moore, Gerald, *1924-*. Twelve African writers / Gerald Moore. — London : Hutchinson University Library for Africa, 1980. — 327p ; 23cm
Bibliography: p301-317. - Includes index
ISBN 0-09-141850-x (cased) : £12.00 : CIP rev.
ISBN 0-09-141851-8 (pbk) : £4.95
Also classified at 840.9′96 B80-09364

820.9′96 — English literature. African writers, *1945-* — *Critical studies — Serials*
African literature today. — 11. — London : Heinemann, 1980
No.11: Myth and history. — Sept. 1980. — 231p
ISBN 0-435-91651-3 : Unpriced : CIP rev.
ISBN 0-435-91652-1 (pbk) : £4.50
Also classified at 840.9′96 B80-12488

African literature today. — London : Heinemann Educational
No.12: New writing, new approaches. — Oct.1981. — [224]p
ISBN 0-435-91648-3 (cased) : £9.95 : CIP entry
ISBN 0-435-91649-1 (pbk) : £4.95
Also classified at 840.9′96 B81-28035

821 — ENGLISH POETRY

821 — Poetry in English. Australian writers, *1945-* — *Texts*
Gilbert, Kevin. People are legends : Aboriginal poems / by Kevin Gilbert. — St. Lucia : University of Queensland Press ; Hemel Hempstead : Distributed by International Book Distributors, 1978. — 70p ; 23cm
ISBN 0-7022-1238-5 (cased) : £4.25
ISBN 0-7022-1239-3 (pbk) B81-21190

James, Clive. Charles Charming′s challenges on the pathway to the throne : a royal poem in rhyming couplets / Clive James ; with illustrations by Marc. — London : Cape, 1981. — 103p : ill ; 25cm
ISBN 0-224-01954-6 : £4.95 : CIP rev. B81-08853

Malouf, David. First things last / by David Malouf. — London : Chatto & Windus, 1981, c1980. — 58p ; 22cm
ISBN 0-7011-2562-4 (pbk) : £4.75 B81-11393

821 — Poetry in English. Australian writers. Hope, A. D. (Alec Derwent) — *Critical studies*
Kramer, Leonie. A.D. Hope / by Leonie Kramer. — Melbourne ; Oxford : Oxford University Press, c1979. — 48p ; 22cm. — (Australian writers and their work)
Bibliography: p46-48
ISBN 0-19-550511-5 (pbk) : £1.95 B81-39490

821 — Poetry in English. Gambian writers, *1960-* — *Texts*
Peters, Lenrie. Selected poetry / Lenrie Peters. — London : Heinemann, 1981. — 143p ; 19cm. — (African writers series ; 238)
ISBN 0-435-90238-5 (pbk) : £2.75 B81-11322

821 — Poetry in English. Indian writers, *1858-1947* — *Texts*
Krishnamurti, J.. Poems and parables / J. Krishnamurti. — London : Gollancz, 1981. — xii,164p : 1port ; 24cm
Originally published: in the United States, 1980
ISBN 0-575-02978-1 : £5.95 B81-16055

821 — Poetry in English. Malawian writers, *1960-* — *Texts*
Mapanje, Jack. Of chameleons and gods / Jack Mapanje. — London : Heinemann, 1981. — 80p ; 19cm. — (African writers series ; 236)
ISBN 0-435-90236-9 (pbk) : £1.95 B81-13616

821 — Poetry in English. New Zealand writers, *1907-* — *Texts*
Baxter, James K.. Collected poems / James K. Baxter ; edited by J.E. Weir. — Wellington, [N.Z.] ; Oxford : Oxford University Press, c1979. — xxvii,656p ; 25cm
Includes index
ISBN 0-19-558037-0 : £17.00 B81-24786

821 — Poetry in English. Nigerian writers, *1960-* — *Texts*
Clark, John Pepper. A decade of tongues : selected poems 1958-1968 / J.P. Clark. — London : Longman, 1981. — vii,101p ; 18cm. — (Drumbeat)
ISBN 0-582-64288-4 (pbk) : £1.75 B81-19951

Ofeimun, Odia. The poet lied : and other poems / Odia Ofeimun. — London : Longman, 1980. — 57p : ill ; 18cm. — (Drumbeat)
ISBN 0-582-64000-8 (pbk) : £1.15 B81-11498

821 — Poetry in English. Nigerian writers. Clark, John Pepper — *Critical studies*
Petersen, Kirsten Holst. Selected poems : a critical view / by Kirsten Holst Petersen ; edited by Yolande Cantù. — London : Collings in association with the British Council, 1981. — 32p : ill,1port ; 21cm. — (Nexus books ; 03)
Bibliography: p30-31. - List of films: p32
ISBN 0-86036-136-5 (pbk) : £1.00 B81-18604

821 — Poetry in English. Sierra Leonean writers, *1960- — Texts*

Taylor, Wilfred H.. Black rhapsody / by Wilfred H. Taylor. — Walton-on-Thames : Outposts, c1980. — 36p ; 21cm
£1.20 (pbk) B81-02342

821 — Poetry in English. South African writers, *1961- — Anthologies*

Poets to the people : South African freedom poems / edited by Barry Feinberg. — Enl. ed. — London : Heinemann, 1980. — xiii,194p ; 19cm. — (African writers series)
Previous ed.: London : Allen & Unwin, 1974
ISBN 0-435-90230-x (pbk) : £1.70 B81-07147

821 — Poetry in English. South African writers, *1961- — Texts*

Aylen, Leo. Red alert : this is a God warning : a poem / Leo Aylen. — London : Sidgwick & Jackson, 1981. — iv,43p : music ; 22cm
ISBN 0-283-98818-5 (pbk) : £3.50 B81-36180

821 — Poetry in English. West Indian writers in Great Britain, *1945- — Anthologies*

Bluefoot traveller : poetry by Westindians in Britain / edited by James Berry. — [Rev. ed.]. — London : Harrap, 1981. — 64p ; 22cm
Previous ed.: London : Limestone Publications, 1976
ISBN 0-245-53639-6 (pbk) : £1.50 B81-20383

821 — Poetry in English. Zambian writers, *1945- — Texts*

Durant, Ian. A river in our depths / Ian Durant. — London : Quarto, [1980]. — xviip ; 21cm
£0.95 (pbk) B81-10848

821'.008 — Poetry in English, *1066-1979 — Anthologies*

The **New** golden treasury of English verse / chosen by Edward Lesson. — London : Macmillan, 1980. — xxi,506p ; 23cm
Includes index
ISBN 0-333-30660-0 : £7.95 B81-03733

821'.008 — Poetry in English, *1550-1830 - Anthologies - For non-English speaking students*

Introducing English verse. — London : Longman, May 1981. — [672]p
ISBN 0-582-49014-6 (pbk) : £7.95 : CIP entry B81-07909

821'.008 — Poetry in English *— Anthologies*

An **Anthology** of mine. — London : H. Hamilton, Sept.1981. — [64]p
ISBN 0-241-10667-2 : £3.95 : CIP entry B81-22676

821'.008 — Poetry in English *— Anthologies — Serials*

The **Fireside** book / chosen by David Hope. — 1981. — London : D.C. Thomson, c1980. — [98]p
ISBN 0-85116-195-2 : £1.05 B81-02536

821'.008 — Poetry in English, *to 1945 — Anthologies*

Everyman's book of evergreen verse. — London : Dent, Oct.1981. — [432]p. — (Everyman's library)
ISBN 0-460-00246-5 (cased) : £6.95 : CIP entry
ISBN 0-460-01246-0 (pbk) : £3.95 B81-25820

821'.008 — Poetry in English, *to 1977 — Anthologies*

Everyman's book of English verse / edited by John Wain. — London : Dent, 1981. — 672p ; 24cm
Includes index
ISBN 0-460-04369-2 : £8.95 B81-17866

821'.008 — Poetry in English, *to 1980 — Anthologies*

The **Faber** book of useful verse / edited with an introduction Simon Brett. — London : Faber, 1981. — 254p ; 21cm
ISBN 0-571-11781-3 (cased) : £6.95 : CIP rev.
ISBN 0-571-11782-1 (pbk) : Unpriced B81-25328

Have you heard the sun singing. — London : Evans Bros, Apr.1981. — [288]p
ISBN 0-237-45552-8 (pbk) : £6.95 : CIP entry B81-00330

821'.008 — Poetry in English, *to ca 1970 — Anthologies*

A **book** of faith. — London : Hodder & Stoughton, Jan.1982. — [352]p
ISBN 0-340-27470-0 (pbk) : £2.50 : CIP entry B81-34139

821'.008'015 — Children poetry in English, *1558-.* **Special themes: Fantasy** *— Anthologies*

The **Magic** tree : poems of fantasy and mystery / chosen by David Woolger. — Oxford : Oxford University Press, 1981. — 160p : ill ; 24cm
Includes index
ISBN 0-19-276046-7 (pbk) : £4.95 : CIP rev. B81-22497

821'.008'03241 — Poetry in English, *1557-1979.* **Special subjects: Great Britain. Countryside** *— Anthologies*

A **Country** calendar of rural rhymers / poems chosen by Robin Holmes ; wood engravings by Reynolds Stone. — London : Eyre Methuen, 1980. — 64p : ill(some col.) ; 21cm
ISBN 0-413-47540-9 : £3.50 : CIP rev. B80-18467

821'.008'03241 — Poetry in English, *to 1980.* **Special subjects: Great Britain** *— Anthologies*

The **Faber** book of poems and places / edited with an introduction by Geoffrey Grigson. — London : Faber, 1980. — 387p ; 23cm
Includes index
ISBN 0-571-11647-7 : £6.95 : CIP rev. B80-12490

821'.008'03242 — Poetry in English, *to 1975.* **Special subjects: England** *— Anthologies*

Poet's England. — London : Brentham Press
Includes index
4: Avon and Somerset / compiled by Guy Stapleton ; illustrated by Gillian Durrant. — c1981. — vi,66p : ill,1map ; 23cm
ISBN 0-905772-05-9 (pbk) : £2.00 B81-33480

821'.008'0324248 — Poetry in English, *ca 1590-1974.* **Special subjects: Warwickshire** *— Anthologies*

Poems of Warwickshire : an anthology / edited by Roger Pringle. — Kineton : Roundwood, 1980. — xii,149p ; 23cm
Bibliography: p139-141. — Includes index
ISBN 0-906418-05-4 : £6.95 B81-08385

821'.008'03538 — Orally transmitted bawdy poetry in English, *to 1980 — Anthologies*

The **Gentlefolks** book of naughty verse / [compiled] by Denzil Thomas. — London : John Clare, [1981]. — [94]p : ill ; 23cm
ISBN 0-906549-19-1 (cased) : £4.95
ISBN 0-906549-20-5 (pbk) : Unpriced B81-38388

821'.008'0354 — Poetry in English, *1564-1965.* **Special subjects: Childhood** *— Anthologies*

The **Poetry** of childhood / edited by Samuel Carr. — London : Batsford, 1981. — 92p : ill (some col.) ; 23cm
ISBN 0-7134-3445-7 : £5.95 B81-29472

821'.008'0355 — Poetry in English. Special themes: Exile *— Anthologies*

How strong the roots : poems of exile / collected by Howard Sergeant ; illustrated by Christopher Corr. — London : Evans, 1981. — 96p : ill ; 23cm
Includes index
ISBN 0-237-45559-5 : £3.95 : CIP rev. B81-00331

821'.008'0355 — Poetry in English, *to 1980.* **Special subjects: Schools** *— Anthologies — For children*

The **Beaver** book of school verse / chosen by Jennifer Curry ; illustrated by Graham Thompson. — Harmondsworth : Beaver, 1981. — 151p : ill ; 18cm
Includes index
ISBN 0-600-20321-2 (pbk) : £0.95 B81-38390

821'.008'036 — Poetry in English. Special subjects: Farmyards *- Anthologies*

A **Farmyard** companion. — London : Jill Norman, Sept.1981. — [160]p
ISBN 0-906908-51-5 : £7.95 : CIP entry B81-20525

821'.008'036 — Poetry in English, *to 1979.* **Special subjects: Flowering plants** *— Anthologies*

The **Fairest** flowers : a selection of verses / illustrated by Barbara Sampson. — Kingswood, Surrey : World's Work, c1980. — 48p : col.ill ; 24cm
Includes index
ISBN 0-437-73000-x : £3.95 B81-03743

821'.008'036 — Poetry in English, *to 1979.* **Special subjects: Gardens** *— Anthologies*

Sanders, Rosanne. Portrait of a country garden / Rosanne Sanders. — London : Aurum, c1980. — [93]p : col.ill ; 31cm
ISBN 0-906053-16-1 : £7.95
Also classified at 635.9'0942 B81-03134

821'.008'036 — Poetry in English, *to ca 1950.* **Special subjects: Great Britain. Birds** *— Anthologies*

The **Penguin** book of bird poetry / edited with an introduction by Peggy Munsterberg. — London : Allen Lane, 1980. — 361p : ill ; 21cm
Bibliography: p339-341. — Includes index
ISBN 0-7139-1334-7 : £8.95 B81-01176

821'.008'0375 — Children's poetry in English, *ca 1605-1976.* **Special themes: Witches** *— Anthologies*

Witch poems / edited by Daisy Wallace ; illustrated by Trina Schart Hyman. — Leeds : Pepper, 1980, c1976. — 30p : ill ; 24cm
Originally published: New York : Holiday House, 1976
ISBN 0-560-74506-0 : £3.50 B81-04852

821'.008'0375 — Children's poetry in English, *ca 1700-1979.* **Special themes: Giants** *— Anthologies*

Giant poems / edited by Daisy Wallace ; illustrated by Margot Tomes. — Leeds : Pepper, 1980, c1978. — 32p : ill ; 24cm
Originally published: New York : Holiday House, 1978
ISBN 0-560-74507-9 : £3.50 B81-04851

821'.008'0382 — Christian poetry in English, *ca 650-1979 — Anthologies*

The **New** Oxford book of Christian verse / chosen and edited by Donald Davie. — Oxford : Oxford University Press, 1981. — xxix,319p ; 23cm
Includes index
ISBN 0-19-213426-4 : £7.95 : CIP rev. B81-02356

821'.008'0382 — Religious poetry in English, *to 1980 — Anthologies*

The **Batsford** book of religious verse / edited by Elizabeth Jennings. — London : Batsford, 1981. — 92p : ill(some col.) ; 23cm
Ill on lining papers
ISBN 0-7134-3889-4 : £5.95 B81-24565

821'.008'09282 — Children's poetry in English, *to 1968 — Anthologies*

The **Swinging** rainbow : poems for the young / selected by Howard Sergeant ; illustrations by Brian Denyer. — London : Evans, 1969 (1979 [printing]). — 128p : ill ; 19cm
Includes index
ISBN 0-237-44961-7 : £2.50
ISBN 0-237-44962-5 (pbk) : Unpriced B81-15583

821'.008'09282 — Children's poetry in English, *to 1979 — Anthologies*

A **Child's** treasury of verse / compiled by Eleanor Doan ; illustrated by Nancy Munger. — London : Hodder and Stoughton, 1980, c1977. — 188p : ill ; 26cm
Originally published: Grand Rapids : Zondervan, 1977. — Includes index
ISBN 0-340-24952-8 : £5.95 : CIP rev. B80-13036

821'.008'09282 — Poetry in English, *1500-1979 — Anthologies — For schools*

Gallery : poets past and present / selected by John Blackburn. — Edinburgh : Oliver & Boyd, c1980. — vi,266p ; 20cm
ISBN 0-05-003323-9 (pbk) : Unpriced
B81-08367

821'.008'09282 — Poetry in English, *1558-1945 — Anthologies — For schools*

. Work with verse : a working anthology of older poetry / [compiled by] Sydney Hill. — London : Edward Arnold, 1980. — [80]p ; 22cm
ISBN 0-7131-0495-3 (pbk) : £1.50 : CIP rev.
B80-34049

821'.008'09282 — Poetry in English, *1800-1980 — Anthologies — For African students*

A **Poetry** anthology for junior secondary schools / Rosina Umelo. — London : Macmillan, 1978 (1980 [printing]). — x,118p ; 22cm
Includes index
ISBN 0-333-22693-3 (pbk) : £0.88 B81-05512

821'.008'09282 — Poetry in English, *ca 1500-1918 — Anthologies — For schools*

Echoes / edited by Eric Williams. — London : Edward Arnold, 1980. — 88p : ill ; 18x24cm
Includes index
ISBN 0-7131-0497-x (pbk) : £2.60 : CIP rev.
B80-27473

821'.008'09282 — Poetry in English. Irish writers, *to 1974 — Anthologies — For children*

The **Wolfhound** book of Irish poems for young people / selected by Bridie Quinn & Seamus Cashman ; drawings by Terence O'Connell ; photographs by Dermot Larkin and Michael Cashman. — Dublin : Wolfhound, 1977, c1975. — 192p : ill ; 22cm
Includes index
ISBN 0-9503454-3-1 : £2.50 B81-10671

821'.008'09282 — Poetry in English, *to 1980 — Anthologies — For schools*

Benton, Michael. Watchwords / Michael & Peter Benton. — London : Hodder and Stoughton 2. — c1981. — 96p : ill ; 18x25cm
ISBN 0-340-21230-6 (pbk) : £1.85 : CIP rev.
B81-08919

821'.008'0941486 — Poetry in English. Scottish writers: Dumfries and Galloway Region writers: Nithsdale *(District) writers, 1577-1920 — Catalogues*

A **Very** parochial anthology / [compiled by] T.A. Johnston. — [Sanquhar] ([Sanquhar, Dumfriesshire]) : Museum of Royal Burgh of Sanquhar, [1980]. — 187p : ill,ports ; 22cm
Unpriced B81-15416

821'.008'09415 — Poetry in English. Irish writers, *to 1980 — Anthologies*

The **Penguin** book of Irish verse / introduced and edited by Brendan Kennelly. — 2nd ed. — Harmondsworth : Penguin, 1981. — 470p ; 19cm. — (Penguin poets)
Previous ed.: 1970. — Includes index
ISBN 0-14-042121-1 (pbk) : £2.50 B81-28398

821'.009 — Poetry in English, *1300-1900 — Critical studies*

Schmidt, Michael. [An introduction to fifty British poets, 1300-1900]. A reader's guide to fifty British poets 1300-1900 / by Michael Schmidt. — London : Heinemann, 1980. — 430p ; 21cm. — (Reader's guide series)
Originally published: London : Pan, 1979. — Bibliography: p.405-421. — Includes index
ISBN 0-435-18811-9 : £7.50 : CIP rev.
B80-13960

821'.009 — Poetry in English, *1558-1980.* **Sociological perspectives**

Ward, J. P.. Poetry and the sociological idea / J.P. Ward. — Brighton : Harvester, 1981. — 242p ; 23cm. — (Harvester studies in contemporary literature and culture ; 6)
Includes index
ISBN 0-85527-363-1 : £20.00
ISBN 0-391-02321-7 (U.S.) B81-30665

821'.009 — Poetry in English, *1600-1979 — Study outlines — For Irish students*

Ducke, Joseph. Poetry 3 : shorter poems of the Leaving Certificate / Joseph Ducke. — Dublin : Educational Company, 1981. — 51p ; 21cm. — (Inscapes ; 18)
Unpriced (pbk) B81-37399

821'.009 — Poetry in English, *1660-1780 — Critical studies*

Rothstein, Eric. Restoration and eighteenth century poetry 1660-1780 / Eric Rothstein. — Boston ; London : Routledge & Kegan Paul, 1981. — xiv,242p ; 24cm. — (The Routledge history of English poetry ; v.3)
Bibliography: p166-232. — Includes index
ISBN 0-7100-0660-8 : £13.95 B81-32517

821'.009 — Poetry in English, *1800-1977 — Critical studies*

Heaney, Seamus. Preoccupations : selected prose 1968-1978 / Seamus Heaney. — London : Faber, 1980. — 224p ; 23cm
ISBN 0-571-11638-8 : £7.95 : CIP rev.
B80-18072

821'.009 — Poetry in English, *ca 1600-ca 1980 — Critical studies*

Gunn, Thom. The occasions of poetry. — London : Faber, Feb.1982. — [188]p
ISBN 0-571-11733-3 : £6.95 : CIP entry
Also classified at 821'.914 B81-38308

821'.009 — Poetry in English. Criticism. Blackmur, R. P. *— Critical studies*

Boyers, Robert. R.P. Blackmur : poet-critic : toward a view of poetic objects / Robert Boyers. — Columbia [Mo.] ; London : University of Missouri Press, 1980. — 87p ; 21cm. — (A Literary frontiers edition)
Bibliography: 1p
ISBN 0-8262-0315-9 (pbk) : £4.20 B81-17895

821'.009 — Poetry in English. Criticism *— History*

Needham, John. The completest mode : I.A. Richards and the continuity of English literary criticism. — Edinburgh : Edinburgh University Press, Jan.1982. — [208]p
ISBN 0-85224-387-1 : £12.00 : CIP entry
B81-37528

821'.009 — Poetry in English. Metre

Attridge, Derek. The rhythms of English poetry. — London : Longman, Feb.1982. — [approx.352]p. — (English language series ; 14)
ISBN 0-582-55106-4 (cased) : £13.00 : CIP entry
ISBN 0-582-55105-6 (pbk) : £6.50 B81-38336

821'.009 — Poetry in English. Poets laureate, *1631-1981 — Biographies*

Poets by appointment : Britain's Laureates / [edited by] Nick Russel. — Poole : Blandford, 1981. — vi,201p ; 23cm
Includes index
ISBN 0-7137-1161-2 : £5.95 B81-40659

821'.009 — Poetry in English. Practical criticism *— Manuals*

Bloom, Harold. A map of misreading / Harold Bloom. — Oxford : Oxford University Press, 1975 (1980 [printing]). — 206p ; 21cm
ISBN 0-19-502809-0 (pbk) : £2.50 B81-02278

821'.009 — Poetry in English. Versification — *Critical studies*

Hollander, John. Rhyme's reason : a guide to English verse. — London : Yale University Press, Nov.1981. — [64]p
ISBN 0-300-02735-4 (cased) : £9.00 : CIP entry
ISBN 0-300-02740-0 (pbk) : £2.75 B81-34717

821'.009'358 — Poetry in English. Special themes: Historical events *— Critical studies*

Toliver, Harold E.. The past that poets make / Harold Toliver. — Cambridge, Mass. ; London : Harvard University Press, 1981. — 256p : ill ; 24cm
Includes index
ISBN 0-674-65676-8 : £16.80 B81-39830

821'.03'08 — Narrative poetry in English, *to ca 1970 — Anthologies — For schools*

Narrative poems / edited by Michael Harrison, Christopher Stuart-Clark. — Oxford : Oxford University Press, 1981. — 188p : ill,music ; 20cm
ISBN 0-19-831245-8 (pbk) : £2.25 B81-26143

821'.04 — Folk poetry in English *— Critical studies*

Renwick, Roger deV.. English folk poetry : structure and meaning / Roger deV. Renwick. — London : Batsford Academic and Educational, 1980. — xii,276p ; 24cm
Bibliography: p259-268. - Includes index
ISBN 0-7134-3681-6 : £12.50 : CIP rev.
B80-13961

821'.07 — Humorous poetry in English. Monologues, *1898-1981 — Anthologies*

The **Book** of monologues. — London : H. Hamilton, Nov.1981. — [192]p
ISBN 0-241-10670-2 : £5.95 : CIP entry
B81-28796

821'.07'08 — Humorous poetry in English, *to 1980 — Anthologies*

Comic Irish recitations / [compiled by] James N. Healy. — Dublin : Mercier Press, c1981. — 110p ; 18cm
ISBN 0-85342-645-7 (pbk) : £2.30 B81-31752

The **Penguin** book of light verse / edited with an introduction by Gavin Ewart. — Harmondsworth : Penguin, 1980. — 639p ; 18pcm. — (Penguin poets)
Also published: London : Allen Lane, 1980. — Includes index
ISBN 0-14-042270-6 (pbk) : £2.95 B81-29754

[Unrespectable verse]. The Penguin book of unrespectable verse / edited by Geoffrey Grigson. — Harmondsworth : Penguin, 1980, c1971. — xxiv,334p ; 18cm. — (The Penguin poets)
Originally published: as Unrespectable verse. London : Allen Lane, 1971
ISBN 0-14-042142-4 (pbk) : £1.75 B81-01177

821'.07'08 — Satirical poetry in English, *1660-1980 — Anthologies*

I have no gun but I can spit : an anthology of satirical and abusive verse / selected by Kenneth Baker. — London : Eyre Methuen, 1980. — 204p ; 23cm
Includes index
ISBN 0-413-47500-x : £5.95 B81-00332

821'.07'08 — Satirical poetry in English, *1900- — Anthologies*

A **Vein** of mockery : twentieth-century verse satire / chosen and introduced by James Reeves. — London : Heinemann, 1973 (1979 printing). — vii,120p ; 22cm
Includes index
ISBN 0-435-14773-0 (pbk) : £2.50 B81-23613

821'.07'08 — Satirical poetry in English, *1945- — Anthologies — Serials*

Ving. — No.1-. — Maidstone (73 Ware St., Bearsted, Maidstone, Kent ME14 4PG) : Outcrowd, 1980-. — v. : ill ; 21cm
Irregular
ISSN 0260-0390 = Ving : Unpriced
B81-06790

821'.07'08 — Satirical poetry in English, *ca 1480-1979 — Anthologies*

The **Oxford** book of satirical verse / chosen by Geoffrey Grigson. — Oxford : Oxford University Press, 1980. — xvii,454p ; 23cm
Includes index
ISBN 0-19-214110-4 : £8.50 : CIP rev.
B80-18468

821'.07'089282 — Children's humorous poetry in English, *to 1978 — Anthologies*

The **Children's** book of funny verse / compiled by Julia Watson. — London : Book Club Associates, 1981, c1979. — 127p : ill ; 24cm
Originally published: London : Faber, 1979
Unpriced B81-37888

821'.07'089282 — Children's humorous poetry in English, *to 1978 — Anthologies*
continuation

The **Children's** book of funny verse / compiled by Julia Watson. — Harmondsworth : Puffin in association with Faber, 1981, c1979. — 127p : ill ; 20cm
Originally published: London : Faber, 1979
ISBN 0-14-031333-8 (pbk) : £0.85 B81-40686

821'.07'089282 — Humorous poetry in English, *1837-1945 — Anthologies — For children*

The **Children's** book of comic verse / chosen by Christopher Logue ; illustrated by Bill Tidy. — London : Piccolo, 1980, c1979. — 174p : ill ; 18cm. — (Piccolo)
Originally published: London : Batsford, 1979. — Includes index
ISBN 0-330-26273-4 (pbk) : £0.95 B81-02411

821'.07'0899411 — Humorous poetry in English. Scottish writers, *ca 1425-1980 — Anthologies*

Scottish comic verse : an anthology / compiled by Maurice Lindsay. — London : Hale, 1981. — 254p ; 23cm
Includes index
ISBN 0-7091-8593-6 : £8.50 B81-18508

821.1 — ENGLISH POETRY, 1066-1400

821'.1 — Poetry in English, *1066-1400 — English texts*

[Bodleian Library. Manuscript. Laud Misc. 108]. Havelok the Dane : a tale of the 13th century / put in modern English by R.N. Benton. — [Louth] ([42a Westgate, Louth, Lincs. LN11 9YD]) : [R.N. Benton], c1981. — 11p : 1map ; 37cm
Unpriced (unbound) B81-11994

Langland, William. The vision of Piers Plowman / by William Langland ; a translation into modern English verse with introduction and notes by Terence Tiller. — London : British Broadcasting Corporation, 1981. — 287p ; 23cm
ISBN 0-563-17892-2 (cased) : £9.50 B81-24543

821'.1 — Poetry in English, *1066-1400 — Texts*

Langland, William. Piers Plowman / by William Langland ; an edition of the C-text by Derek Pearsall. — London : Edward Arnold, 1978 (1981 [printing]). — 416p ; 23cm. — (York medieval texts. Second series)
Middle English text, English introduction and notes. — Bibliography: p5-7
ISBN 0-7131-6341-0 (pbk) : £5.95 B81-10518

821'.1 — Poetry in English. Chaucer, Geoffrey. Canterbury tales. Knight's tale *— Study outlines*

Alexander, Michael, *1941-*. The knight's tale / by Michael Alexander. — Harlow : Longman, 1981. — 104p ; 21cm. — (York notes ; 97)
Bibliography: p96
ISBN 0-582-78238-4 (pbk) : £0.90 B81-19663

821'.1 — Poetry in English. Chaucer, Geoffrey. Canterbury tales. Pardoner's tale *— Study outlines*

Windeatt, B. A.. The pardoner's tale : notes / by B.A. Windeatt. — London : Longman, 1980. — 72p ; 21cm. — (York notes ; 50)
Bibliography: p67-68
ISBN 0-582-78140-x (pbk) : £0.90 B81-07098

821'.1 — Poetry in English. Chaucer, Geoffrey. Canterbury tales. Prologue *— Questions & answers — For schools*

Gibbons, F. L.. Chaucer's General prologue / by F.L. Gibbons and D.C. Perkins. — Walton-on-Thames : Celtic Revision Aids, 1981. — iv,124p ; 19cm. — (Literature revision notes and examples)
ISBN 0-17-751301-2 (pbk) : £1.25 B81-15505

821'.1 — Poetry in English. Chaucer, Geoffrey. Canterbury tales. Wife of Bath's prologue and tale *— Study outlines*

East, W. G.. The Wife of Bath's prologue and tale : notes / by W.G. East. — Harlow : Longman, 1981. — 80p ; 21cm. — (York notes ; 109)
Bibliography: p79-80
ISBN 0-582-78210-4 (pbk) : £0.90 B81-34237

821'.1 — Poetry in English. Chaucer, Geoffrey *— Critical studies*

Hussey, S. S.. Chaucer. — 2nd ed. — London : Methuen, Sept.1981. — [246]p
Previous ed.: 1971
ISBN 0-416-72130-3 (cased) : £10.00 : CIP entry
ISBN 0-416-72140-0 (pbk) : £4.95 B81-25668

Roscow, Gregory. Style and syntax in Chaucer's poetry. — Woodbridge : D.S. Brewer, Nov.1981. — [192]p. — (Chaucer studies ; 6)
ISBN 0-85991-080-6 : £15.00 : CIP entry
B81-32022

821'.1 — Poetry in English. Chaucer, Geoffrey. Menippean satire *— Critical studies*

Payne, F. Anne. Chaucer and Menippean satire / F. Anne Payne. — Madison ; London : University of Wisconsin Press, 1981. — xii,290p ; 22cm
Includes index
ISBN 0-299-08170-2 : £15.70 B81-38209

821'.1 — Poetry in English. Chaucer, Geoffrey. Troilus and Criseyde *— Critical studies*

Bishop, Ian. Chaucer's Troilus and Criseyde : a critical study / Ian Bishop. — [Bristol] ([Information Office, 9 Woodland Rd., Bristol BS8 1TB]) : University of Bristol, c1981. — 116p ; 22cm
Bibliography: p115-116
ISBN 0-906515-84-x (pbk) : £4.95 B81-23105

Chaucer's Troilus : essays in criticism / edited by Stephen A. Barney. — London : Scolar Press, 1980. — x,323p ; 24cm
Originally published: Hamden, Conn. : Archon Books, 1980. — Includes index
ISBN 0-85967-607-2 : £12.50 : CIP rev.
B80-12028

821'.1 — Poetry in English. Langland, William. Piers Plowman *— Critical studies*

Goldsmith, Margaret E.. The figure of Piers Plowman. — Woodbridge : Brewer, Oct.1981. — [128]p. — (Piers Plowman studies ; 2)
ISBN 0-85991-077-6 : £15.00 : CIP entry
B81-30448

821'.1 — Poetry in English. Langland, William. Piers Plowman. Special themes: Politics *— Critical studies*

Baldwin, Anna P.. The theme of government in Piers Plowman / Anna P. Baldwin. — Cambridge : Brewer, 1981. — vi,107p ; 24cm. — (Piers Plowman studies ; 1)
Bibliography: p83-91. — Includes index
ISBN 0-85991-073-3 : £15.00 B81-27148

821'.1 — Poetry in English. Morte Arthure *— Critical studies*

The **Alliterative** Morte Arthure : a reassessment of the poem / edited by Karl Heinz Goller. — Cambridge : Brewer, c1981. — 186p ; 24cm. — (Arthurian studies ; 2)
Includes index
ISBN 0-85991-075-x : £17.50 : CIP rev.
B81-01299

821'.1'08 — Poetry in English, *1066-1400 — Anthologies*

[British Library. Manuscript. Cotton Nero AX]. The poems of the Pearl manuscript : Pearl, Cleanness, Patience, Sir Gawain and the Green Knight / edited by Malcolm Andrew and Ronald Waldron. — London : Edward Arnold, 1978 (1981 [printing]). — 376p ; 23cm. — (York medieval texts. Second series)
Middle English text, English introduction and notes, Latin appendix. — Bibliography: p5-13
ISBN 0-7131-6343-7 (pbk) : £5.95 B81-13084

821.2 — ENGLISH POETRY, 1400-1558

821'.2 — Poetry in English, *1400-1558 — Texts*

Henryson, Robert. Selected poems / Robert Henryson ; edited with an introduction by W.R.J. Barron. — Manchester : Carcanet, 1981. — 125p ; 18cm. — (Fyfield books)
ISBN 0-85635-301-9 (pbk) : £1.95 B81-12733

Hoccleve, Thomas. Selections from Hoccleve / edited by M.C. Seymour. — Oxford : Clarendon Press, 1981. — xxxvi,151p ; 22cm
ISBN 0-19-871083-6 (cased) : £10.00 : CIP rev.
ISBN 0-19-871084-4 (pbk) : £4.95 B81-15814

Occleve, Thomas. Selected poems. — Manchester : Carcanet, Oct.1981. — [128]p. — (Fyfield books)
ISBN 0-85635-321-3 (pbk) : £2.50 : CIP entry
B81-27397

Skelton, John, *1460?-1529*. Selected poems / John Skelton ; edited with an introduction by Gerald Hammond. — Manchester : Carcanet, 1980. — 142p ; 18cm. — (Fyfield books)
ISBN 0-85635-308-6 (pbk) : £1.95 B81-00333

Wyatt, *Sir* **Thomas.** The complete poems / Sir Thomas Wyatt ; edited by R.A. Rebholz. — New Haven ; London : Yale University Press, 1981, c1978. — 558p ; 21cm. — (The English poets)
Originally published: Harmondsworth : Penguin, 1978. — Bibliography: p59-67. — Includes index
ISBN 0-300-02681-1 (cased) : £12.50
ISBN 0-300-02688-9 (pbk) : Unpriced
B81-32557

821'.2 — Poetry in English. Skelton, John, *1460?-1529 — Critical studies*

Skelton : the critical heritage / edited by Anthony S.G. Edwards. — London : Routledge & Kegan Paul, 1981. — ix,224p ; 23cm. — (The Critical heritage series)
Bibliography: p217. - Includes index
ISBN 0-7100-0724-8 : £10.50 : CIP rev.
B81-06581

821'.2'0809411 — Poetry in English. Scottish writers, *1400-1625 — Anthologies — Manuscripts — Facsimiles*

[The Bannatyne manuscript]. The Bannatyne manuscript : National Library of Scotland Advocates' M.S.1.1.6 / with an introduction by Denton Fox and William A. Ringler. — London : Scolar Press in association with the National Library of Scotland, 1980. — xlv,60p,375 leaves ; 35cm
Facsimile. — Leaves printed on both sides
ISBN 0-85967-540-8 : Unpriced : CIP rev.
B80-12491

821.3 — ENGLISH POETRY, 1558-1625

821'.3 — Poetry in English, *1558-1625 — Texts*

Greville, Fulke, *Baron Brooke*. Fulke Greville : poems / selected by Anthony Astbury ; [drawing by David Stoker]. — Warwick : Greville, c1980. — 24p : 1port ; 23cm
Unpriced B81-21284

Jonson, Ben. The complete poems / Ben Jonson ; edited by George Parfitt. — Harmondsworth : Penguin, 1975 (1980 [printing]). — 634p ; 20cm. — (Penguin English poets)
Bibliography: p27-29. — Includes index
ISBN 0-14-042277-3 (pbk) : £4.95 B81-22190

Shakespeare, William. The rape of Lucrece / William Shakespeare ; edited by J.W. Lever. — Harmondsworth : Penguin, 1971 (1981 (printing)). — 150p ; 19cm. — (New Penguin Shakespeare)
Bibliography: p29-31
ISBN 0-14-070723-9 (pbk) : £1.25 B81-30950

Spenser, Edmund. The faerie queene / Edmund Spenser ; edited by Thomas P. Roche, Jr. with the assistance of C. Patrick O'Donnell, Jr. — New Haven ; London : Yale University Press, 1981. — 246p ; 21cm. — (The English poets)
Originally published: Harmondsworth : Penguin, 1978. — Bibliography: p11-13
ISBN 0-300-02705-2 (cased) : £20.00
ISBN 0-300-02706-0 (pbk) : Unpriced
B81-33498

821'.3 — Poetry in English. Donne, John *— Critical studies*

Carey, John. John Donne : life, mind and art / John Carey. — London : Faber, 1981. — 303p ; 22cm
Includes index
ISBN 0-571-11636-1 : £9.50 B81-20800

Novarr, David. The disinterred muse : Donne's texts and contexts / David Novarr. — Ithaca ; London : Cornell University Press, 1980. — 218p ; 23cm
Includes index
ISBN 0-8014-1309-5 : £11.75 B81-10958

821'.3 — Poetry in English. Donne, John — *Critical studies* *continuation*

Winny, James. A preface to Donne. — Revised ed. — London : Longman, Sept.1981. — [192] p. — (Preface books)
Previous ed.: 1970
ISBN 0-582-35246-0 : £3.25 : CIP entry B81-28060

821'.3 — Poetry in English. Herbert, George, *b.1593.* **Temple, The** — *Christian viewpoints*

Nuttall, A. D.. Overheard by God : fiction and prayer in Herbert Milton Dante and St John / A.D. Nuttall. — London : Methuen, 1980. — x,147p ; 22cm
Includes index
ISBN 0-416-73980-6 : £8.95 : CIP rev.
Also classified at 821'.4 B80-07483

821'.3 — Poetry in English. Jonson, Ben — *Critical studies*

Peterson, Richard S.. Imitation and praise in the poems of Ben Jonson / Richard S. Peterson. — New Haven ; London : Yale University Press, c1981. — xxi,247p : ill,2facsims,1port ; 22cm
Includes index
ISBN 0-300-02586-6 : £12.95 : CIP rev. B81-22685

821'.3 — Poetry in English. Shakespeare, William. Sonnets. 7-126 — *Critical studies*

Hammond, Gerald, *1945-*. The reader and Shakespeare's young man sonnets / Gerald Hammond. — London : Macmillan, 1981. — viii,247p ; 23cm
Includes index
ISBN 0-333-28851-3 : £12.00 : CIP rev. B80-22451

821'.3 — Poetry in English. Shakespeare, William. Sonnets — *Critical studies*

Middlebrook, Douglas. Sweet my love : a study of Shakespeare's sonnets / Douglas Middlebrook. — Adelaide : New World ; London (93 Talfourd Rd., S.E. 15), c1980. — 159p ; 22cm
Previous ed.: 1978. — Includes index
ISBN 0-908268-02-5 (pbk) : £2.50 B81-17641

Padel, John. New poems by Shakespeare : order and meaning restored to the Sonnets / John Padel. — London (65 Belsize La., NW3 5AU) : Herbert Press, 1981. — 286p ; 23cm
Bibliography: p133-134. — Includes index
ISBN 0-906969-10-7 : £9.95 B81-33233

821'.3 — Poetry in English. Spenser, Edmund — *Critical studies — Serials*

Spenser studies : a Renaissance poetry annual. — 1-. — Pittsburgh : University of Pittsburgh Press ; London : Feffer and Simons [[distributor]], 1980-. — v. : ill ; 24cm
Unpriced B81-27911

821'.3 — Poetry in English. Spenser, Edmund. Faerie queene. Special themes: Praise

Cain, Thomas H.. Praise in The faerie queene / Thomas H. Cain. — Lincoln, Neb. ; London : University of Nebraska Press, c1978. — 229p : ill ; 23cm
Includes index
ISBN 0-8032-1405-7 : £8.40 B81-08073

821'.3 — Poetry in English. Spenser, Edmund. Faerie Queene — *Study outlines*

Barnish, Valerie L.Notes on Spenser's The faerie gueene / compiled by Valerie L. Barnish. — London : Methuen, 1980. — 107p : 1ill ; 20cm. — (Methuen notes)
ISBN 0-417-20340-3 (pbk) : £0.95 B81-07856

821'.3'08 — Poetry in English, *1600-1660 — Anthologies*

Jacobean and Caroline poetry. — London : Methuen, Sept.1981. — [352]p
ISBN 0-416-31060-5 (cased) : £9.50 : CIP entry
ISBN 0-416-31070-2 (pbk) : £4.95 B81-21571

821'.3'09 — Metaphysical poetry in English, *1558-1702 — Study outlines*

Handley, Graham. Brodie's notes on the metaphysical poets / Graham Handley. — London : Pan, 1981. — 123p ; 20cm. — (Pan study aids) (Brodie's notes)
Based on the Penguin edition of The Metaphysical poets
ISBN 0-330-50179-8 (pbk) : £0.80 B81-20397

821.4 — ENGLISH POETRY, 1625-1702

821'.4 — Poetry in English, *1625-1702 — Texts*

Milton, John, *1608-1674.* On the morning of Christ's Nativity : Milton's hymn / with illustrations by William Blake ; and a note on the illustrations by Martin Butlin. — Andoversford : Whittington Press & Angscot Productions, c1981. — xii,24p : col.ill ; 33cm
In slip case. — Limited ed. of 350 numbered copies
ISBN 0-904845-34-6 (cased) : £130.00
ISBN 0-904845-35-4 (leather) : Unpriced B81-28285

Oldham, John, *1653-1683.* Selected poems / John Oldham ; edited with an introduction by Ken Robinson. — Newcastle upon Tyne (1 North Jesmond Ave., Jesmond, Newcastle upon Tyne NE2 3JX) : Bloodaxe, 1980. — 87p ; 22cm. — (Bloodaxe English poets)
Bibliography: p25
ISBN 0-906427-12-6 (pbk) : £2.50 B81-00334

Shipton, William. Dia, a poem (1659) / by William Shipton ; selected and edited by Frederic Clitheroe. — London : Lymes Press, 1981. — 32p ; 20cm
Facsim. of: 1st ed., London : s.n., 1659. — Bibliography: p4
£1.00 (pbk) B81-28282

Vaughan, Henry. The complete poems / Henry Vaughan ; edited by Alan Rudrum. — New Haven ; London : Yale University Press, 1981, c1976. — 718p ; 21cm. — (The English poets)
Originally published: Harmondsworth : Penguin, 1976. — Bibliography: p23-26. — Includes index
ISBN 0-300-02680-3 (cased) : £15.00 : CIP rev.
ISBN 0-300-02687-0 (pbk) : Unpriced B81-22674

821'.4 — Poetry in English. Milton, John, *1608-1674.* **Paradise lost** — *Critical studies*

Fiore, Peter Amadeus. Milton and Augustine : patterns of Augustinian thought in Paradise lost / Peter A. Fiore. — University Park ; London : Pennsylvania State University Press, c1981. — 118p ; 22cm
Bibliography: p107-114. — Includes index
ISBN 0-271-00269-7 : £9.40 B81-34454

821'.4 — Poetry in English. Milton, John, *1608-1674.* **Puns** — *Dictionaries*

Le Comte, Edward. A dictionary of puns in Milton's English poetry / Edward Le Comte. — London : Macmillan, 1981. — xx,238p ; 23cm
Bibliography: p211-219. — Includes index
ISBN 0-333-30085-8 : £15.00 B81-22378

821'.4 — Poetry in English. Milton, John, *1608-1674 — Sociological perspectives*

Milner, Andrew. John Milton and the English revolution : a study in the sociology of literature / Andrew Milner. — London : Macmillan, 1981. — vii,248p ; 23cm
Bibliography: p235-242. — Includes index
ISBN 0-333-27134-3 : £15.00 : CIP rev. B80-20998

821'.4 — Poetry in English. Milton, John. Paradise lost. Books 1 & 2 — *Study outlines*

Beck, Richard James. Paradise lost, books I & II : notes / by Richard James Beck. — London : Longman, 1980. — 72p ; 21cm. — (York notes ; 94)
Bibliography: p67-68
ISBN 0-582-78218-x (pbk) : £0.90 B81-14576

821'.4 — Poetry in English. Milton, John. Paradise lost. Books 4 & 9 — *Study outlines*

Beck, Richard James. Paradise lost, books IV & IX : notes / by Richard James Beck. — London : Longman, 1980. — 80p ; 21cm. — (York notes ; 87)
Bibliography: p75
ISBN 0-582-78219-8 (pbk) : £0.90 B81-14577

821'.4 — Poetry in English. Milton, John. Paradise lost — *Christian viewpoints*

Nuttall, A. D.. Overheard by God : fiction and prayer in Herbert Milton Dante and St John / A.D. Nuttall. — London : Methuen, 1980. — x,147p ; 22cm
Includes index
ISBN 0-416-73980-6 : £8.95 : CIP rev.
Primary classification 821'.3 B80-07483

821'.4 — Poetry in English. Milton, John. Paradise lost — *Critical studies*

Empson, William. Milton's god / William Empson. — Rev. ed., with additional material. — Cambridge : Cambridge University Press, 1981. — 343p ; 22cm
Previous ed.: London : Chatto & Windus, 1965. — Includes index
ISBN 0-521-29910-1 (pbk) : £6.95 B81-18228

821'.4 — Poetry in English. Milton, John. Paradise lost — *Special themes: War — Critical studies*

Freeman, James A.. Milton and the martial muse : Paradise lost and European traditions of war / James A. Freeman. — Princeton ; Guildford : Princeton University Press, c1980. — xiii,253p,[16]p of plates : ill,1facsim,ports ; 23cm
Bibliography: p227-250. — Includes index
ISBN 0-691-06435-0 : £9.80 B81-08368

821'.4 — Poetry in English. Milton, John — *Philosophical perspectives — Critical studies*

Dawes, Winifred H.. Milton : eagle-sighted prophet / by Winifred H. Dawes. — Bristol (8 Merchant Venturers' House, King St., Bristol BS1 4EO) : [W.H. Dawes], [1981]. — 21p ; 22cm
Unpriced (pbk) B81-21902

821'.4 — Poetry in English. Rochester, John Wilmot, *Earl of — Correspondence, diaries, etc.*

Rochester, John Wilmot, *Earl of.* The letters of John Wilmot, Earl of Rochester / edited and annotated with an introduction by Jeremy Treglown. — Oxford : Blackwell, 1980. — xii,275p,8p of plates : ill,facsims,ports ; 24cm
Facsims on lining papers. — Includes index
ISBN 0-631-12831-x : £21.00 : CIP rev. B80-10207

821'.4 — Poetry in English. Rochester, John Wilmot, *Earl of — Critical studies*

Spirit of wit. — Oxford : Basil Blackwell, Nov.1981. — [256]p
ISBN 0-631-12897-2 : £12.00 : CIP entry B81-30169

821'.4 — Poetry in English. Vaughan, Henry — *Critical studies*

Rudrum, Alan. Henry Vaughan. — Cardiff : University of Wales Press, Apr.1981. — [132]p. — (Writers of Wales, ISSN 0141-5050)
ISBN 0-7083-0787-6 (pbk) : £2.50 : CIP entry B81-02375

821'.4 — Sonnets in English. Milton, John — *Critical studies*

Nardo, Anna K.. Milton's sonnets & the ideal community / Anna K. Nardo. — Lincoln [Neb.] ; London : University of Nebraska Press, c1979. — xii,213p ; 23cm
Includes index
ISBN 0-8032-3302-7 : £9.60 B81-01711

821'.4'08 — Poetry in English, *1625-1702 — Anthologies*

Henry King & Richard Crashaw : selected poems / edited by R.L. Cook ; frontispiece illustration by George Bowie. — Kinnesswood (4 Whitecraigs, Kinnesswood, Kinross) : Lomond Press, 1981. — 32p : 1 ill ; 21cm. — (A Turnstone booklet)
Limited ed. of 300 copies
ISBN 0-9506424-3-6 (pbk) : £1.50 B81-21109

821.5 — ENGLISH POETRY, 1702-1745

821'.5 — Poetry in English, *1702-1745 — Texts*

Ramsay, Allan. Allan Ramsay : poems, fables, dramatic sketches and songs : book of the Carlops festival. — Penicuik (Jess Cottage, Carlops, Penicuik, Midlothian, EH26 9NF) : Scots Secretariat, [1980]. — 46p : 2ill ; 21cm. — (Scots Secretariat publications, ISSN 0141-4216)
Bibliography: p8
£0.40 (unbound) B81-32148

Thomson, James, *1700-1748*. The seasons / James Thomson ; edited with an introduction and commentary by James Sambrook. — Oxford : Clarendon Press, 1981. — xcv,405p,[6]p of plates : ill,facsims ; 23cm
Bibliography: pxiii-xv. — Includes index
ISBN 0-19-812713-8 : £45.00 : CIP rev. B80-19398

821'.5 — Poetry in English. Pope, Alexander. Special themes: London *(City)*. Grub Street — *Critical studies*

Rogers, Pat. Hacks and dunces : Pope, Swift and Grub Street / Pat Rogers. — London : Methuen, 1980. — xvi,239p : 2maps ; 22cm
Abridgement of: Grub Street. 1972. — Bibliography: pxi-xiv. - Includes index
ISBN 0-416-74240-8 (pbk) : £4.50 : CIP rev.
Also classified at 828'.509 B80-13038

821'.5 — Poetry in English. Swift, Jonathan — *Critical studies*

Schakel, Peter J.. The poetry of Jonathan Swift : allusion and the development of a poetic style / Peter J. Schakel. — Madison ; London : University of Wisconsin Press, 1978. — x,218p ; 22cm
Includes index
ISBN 0-299-07650-4 : £16.25 B81-32478

821'.5'08 — Poetry in English, *1702-1745 — Anthologies*

Joseph Addison, William Broome, Richard Savage : selected poems / edited by M.L. McCarthy ; frontispiece illustration by Barbara Reid. — Kinnesswood (4 Whitecraigs, Kinnesswood, Kinross) : Lomond Press, 1981. — 28p : 1ill ; 21cm. — (A Turnstone booklet)
Limited ed. of 300 copies
ISBN 0-9506424-4-4 (pbk) : £1.30 B81-20788

821'.5'0809415 — Poetry in English. Irish writers, *1702-1745 — Anthologies*

Swift, Jonathan. The place of the damn'd / by Jonathan Swift. The Devil's reply. — Dublin (Trinity College Library, College St., Dublin 2) : Trinity Closet Press, 1980. — [4]p ; 26cm
Limited ed. of 15O copies
£1.50 (unbound) B81-10936

821.6 — ENGLISH POETRY, 1745-1800

821'.6 — Poetry in English, *1745-1800 — Texts*

Bowles, William Lisle. Fourteen sonnets ; Sonnets written on picturesque spots ; Verses to John Howard ; The grave of Howard ; Verses on the Philanthropic Society ; Elegy written at the Hot Wells ; Monody written at Matlock ; A poetical address to Edmund Burke ; Elegaic stanzas ; Coombe Ellen / William Lisle Bowles ; with an introduction for the Garland edition by Donald H. Reiman. — New York ; London : Garland, 1978. — 191p in various pagings ; 24cm. — (Romantic context)
Facsim. of: eds. published 1789-1798
ISBN 0-8240-2118-5 : Unpriced B81-23198

Gray, Thomas. Selected poems / Thomas Gray ; edited by John Heath-Stubbs. — Manchester : Carcanet, 1981. — 86p ; 18cm. — (Fyfield books)
ISBN 0-85635-317-5 (pbk) : £2.50 : CIP rev. B81-13712

821'.6 — Poetry in English, *1745-1800 — Texts — Facsimiles*

Hayley, William. An essay on sculpture / William Hayley ; with an introduction for the Garland edition by Donald H. Reiman. — New York ; London : Garland, 1978. — xvi,358p : 1ill ; 23cm. — (Romantic context)
Facsim. of edition published London : T. Cadell and W. Davies, 1800
ISBN 0-8240-2160-6 : Unpriced B81-25530

Hayley, William. The eulogies of Howard ; Ballads founded on anecdotes relating to animals ; Poems on serious and sacred subjects / William Hayley ; with an introduction for the Garland edition by Donald H. Reiman. — New York ; London : Garland, 1978. — xvi,86,212,97p : ill ; 21cm. — (Romantic context)
Facsim. of: edition published: London, 1791
ISBN 0-8240-2159-2 : £43.00 B81-14705

821'.6 — Poetry in English. Burns, Robert, *1759-1796 — Critical studies*

Angus-Butterworth, L. M.. The immortal memory of Robert Burns / proposed by L.M. Angus-Butterworth at a Burns Supper held in Manchester. — [Buxton] ([Old Hall Hotel, Buxton, Derbyshire SK17 6BD]) : L.M. Angus-Butterworth, 1981. — 8p : ports ; 21cm
£1.00 (pbk) B81-39051

821'.6 — Poetry in English. Cowper, William — *Correspondence, diaries, etc.*

Cowper, William. The letters and prose writings of William Cowper. — Oxford : Clarendon Press
Vol.2: Letters 1782-1786 / edited by James King and Charles Ryskamp. — 1981. — xxviii,652p,[4]leaves of plates : 1facsim,3ports ; 23cm
Includes index
ISBN 0-19-812607-7 : £35.00 : CIP rev.
Primary classification 828'.608 B80-20999

821'.6'09 — Poetry in English, *1745-1837 — Critical studies*

Harvey, A. D.. English poetry in a changing society 1780-1825 / A.D. Harvey. — London : Allison & Busby, 1980. — 195p ; 23cm
Includes index
ISBN 0-85031-365-1 : £12.00 : CIP rev. B80-12029

821.7 — ENGLISH POETRY, 1800-1837

821'.7 — European countries. Intellectual life. Influence of Byron, George Gordon Byron, *Baron — Conference proceedings*

Byron's political and cultural influence and nineteenth-century Europe : a symposium / edited by Paul Graham Trueblood. — London : Macmillan, 1981. — xix,210p : 1port ; 23cm
Includes index
ISBN 0-333-29389-4 : £15.00 : CIP rev. B80-36297

821'.7 — Poetry in English, *1800-1837 — Texts*

Betham, Matilda. Poems ; and, Elegies / Matilda Betham ; with an introduction for the Garland edition by Donald H. Reiman. — New York ; London : Garland, 1978. — x,116,xii,128p ; 19cm. — (Romantic context)
Facsim. of: Poems, published: London : Hatchard, 1808
ISBN 0-8240-2111-8 : Unpriced B81-26496

Byron, George Gordon Byron, *Baron*. The complete poetical works / Lord Byron ; edited by Jerome J. McGann. — Oxford : Clarendon
Vol.1. — 1980. — xlvii,464p,[3]leaves of plates : ill,1facsim ; 22cm
Includes index
ISBN 0-19-812763-4 (pbk) : £20.00 B81-18500

Byron, George Gordon Byron, *Baron*. The complete poetical works / Lord Byron ; edited by Jerome J. McGann. — Oxford : Clarendon
Vol.2: Childe Harold's pilgrimage. — 1980. — 341p,[3]leaves of plates : ill,facsims ; 23cm
ISBN 0-19-812754-5 : £35:00 : CIP rev.
ISBN 0-19-812764-2 (pbk) : £20.00 B79-26587

Clare, John, *1793-1864*. The shepherd's calendar / John Clare ; edited by Eric Robinson and Geoffrey Summerfield ; with wood engravings by David Gentleman. — Oxford : Oxford University Press, 1964, c1973 (1980 [printing]). — xiv,139p : ill ; 21cm
ISBN 0-19-211249-x (cased) : £5.95
ISBN 0-19-281142-8 (pbk) : Unpriced B81-21133

Claris, John Chalk. Poems (1816) (Juvenile pieces) ; Poems (1818) ; Durovernum / John Chalk Claris ; with an introduction for the Garland edition by Donald H. Reiman. — New York ; London : Garland, 1978. — 393p in various pagings ; 21cm. — (Romantic context)
Facsim. of: Poems (1816), published under the name Arthur Brooke: Canterbury : Rouse, Kirkby and Lawrence, 1816
ISBN 0-8240-2130-4 : Unpriced B81-26495

Reynolds, John Hamilton. The Eden of imagination ; Safie ; The Naiad / John Hamilton Reynolds ; with an introduction for the Garland edition by Donald H. Reiman. — New York ; London : Garland, 1978. — 214p in various pagings ; 24cm. — (Romantic context)
The Eden of imagination facsim. of: ed. published London : James Cawthorn ; John Martin, 1814
ISBN 0-8240-2198-3 : Unpriced B81-23197

Thurlow, Edward Hovell-Thurlow, *Baron*. Poems on several occasions ; An appendix to Poems on several occasions / Edward Thurlow, second Baron Thurlow ; with an introduction for the Garland edition by Donald H. Reiman. — New York ; London : Garland, 1978. — xi,240,109p ; 21cm
Facsim of: ed. published London : For White, Cochrane, and Co., 1813
ISBN 0-8240-2211-4 : Unpriced B81-24826

Wordsworth, William, *1770-1850*. Benjamin the Waggoner / by William Wordsworth ; edited by Paul F. Betz. — Ithaca, N.Y. : Cornell University ; Brighton : Harvester, 1981. — xii,356p : facsims ; 25cm. — (The Cornell Wordsworth)
ISBN 0-85527-513-8 : £40.00 : CIP rev. B80-19399

Wordsworth, William, *1770-1850*. The prelude, 1799, 1805, 1850 : authoritative texts, context and reception, recent crtitucal essays / William Wordsworth ; [edited by] Jonathan Wordsworth, M.H. Abrams, Stephen Gill. — New York ; London : Norton, c1979. — xix,684p ; 22cm. — (A Norton critical edition)
Bibliography: p679-684
ISBN 0-393-09071-x (pbk) : £3.50 B81-07747

Wordsworth, William, *1770-1850*. The Wordsworth poetical guide to the Lakes : an illustrated anthology / compiled and introduced by Richard J. Hutchings. — Brightstone (Corner Cottage, Hunnyhill, Brightstone, Isle of Wight) : Hunnyhill Publications, [1981, c1977]. — iv,33p,[5]p of plates : ill,1port ; 21cm
Cover title. — Bibliography: pi
ISBN 0-9504736-1-8 (pbk) : £0.75 B81-26483

821'.7 — Poetry in English. Blake, William — *Correspondence, diaries, etc.*

Blake, William, *1757-1827*. The letters of William Blake : with related documents / edited by Geoffrey Keynes, Kt. — 3rd ed., rev. and amplified. — Oxford : Clarendon, 1980. — xxviii,235p,[25]p of plates : ill,facsims,ports ; 24cm
Previous ed.: London : Hart-Davis, 1968. — Includes index
ISBN 0-19-812654-9 : £18.50 : CIP rev. B80-18469

821'.7 — Poetry in English. Blake, William — *Critical studies*

Damrosch, Leopold. Symbol and truth in Blake's myth / Leopold Damrosch, Jr. — Princeton ; Guildford : Princeton University Press, c1980. — xiv,395p : ill ; 25cm
Includes index
ISBN 0-691-06433-4 (cased) : £14.00
ISBN 0-691-10095-0 (pbk) : £5.20 B81-12572

821'.7 — Poetry in English. Blake, William. Psychological aspects *compared with* psychoanalytical theories of Freud, Sigmund

George, Diana Hume. Blake and Freud / Diana Hume George. — Ithaca ; London : Cornell University Press, 1980. — 253p : ill ; 23cm
Includes index
ISBN 0-8014-1286-2 : £9.00
Also classified at 150.19'52 B81-06791

821'.7 — Poetry in English. Blake, William. Songs of innocence and experience — *Critical studies*

Leader, Zachary. Reading Blake's Songs / Zachary Leader. — Boston, Mass. ; London : Routledge & Kegan Paul, 1981. — xxiii,259p,[16]p of plates : ill,facsims ; 22cm
Bibliography: p204-206. - Includes index
ISBN 0-7100-0635-7 : £13.50 B81-18481

821'.7 — Poetry in English. Byron, George Gordon Byron, *Baron* — *Correspondence, diaries, etc.*

Byron, George Gordon Byron, *Baron*. Byron's letters and journals : the complete and unexpurgated text of all the letters available in manuscript and the full printed version of all others / edited by Leslie A. Marchand. — London : Murray
Vol.11. 1823-1824: For freedom's battle. — 1981. — 243p,[1]leaf of plates : 1facsim ; 23cm
Bibliography: p199-212. - Includes index
ISBN 0-7195-3792-4 : £11.50 B81-18853

821'.7 — Poetry in English. Coleridge, Samuel Taylor — *Critical studies*

Wheeler, Kathleen M.. The creative mind in Coleridge's poetry / by K.M. Wheeler. — London : Heinemann, 1981. — 189p ; 24cm
Bibliography: p186-189
ISBN 0-435-18925-5 : £10.50 B81-36790

821'.7 — Poetry in English. Hogg, James, *1770-1835* — *Biographies*

Parr, Norah. James Hogg at home : being the domestic life and letters of the Ettrick Shepherd / Norah Parr. — Dollar (31 Craiginnan Gardens, Dollar, Clackmannanshire FK14 7JA) : D.S. Mack, 1980. — 142p : 2maps,1plan,2geneal.tables ; 21cm
Includes index
ISBN 0-9505416-2-1 (pbk) : £6.90 B81-05978

821'.7 — Poetry in English. Keats, John, *1795-1821* — *Biographies*

Richardson, Joanna. The life and letters of John Keats / by Joanna Richardson. — London : Folio Society, 1981. — 170p,[7]leaves of plates : ill,ports ; 23cm
Includes index
£7.85 B81-27163

821'.7 — Poetry in English. Keats, John, *1795-1821* — *Critical studies*

Jones, John, *1924 May 6-*. John Keats's dream of truth / John Jones. — London : Chatto & Windus, 1969 (1980 [printing]). — 302p ; 22cm
Includes index
ISBN 0-7011-2538-1 (pbk) : £3.95 B81-01178

Walsh, William, *1916-*. Introduction to Keats / William Walsh. — London : Methuen, 1981. — 141p ; 22cm
Bibliography: p134-136. — Includes index
ISBN 0-416-30490-7 (cased) : Unpriced : CIP rev.
ISBN 0-416-30500-8 (pbk) : £3.25 B81-13786

821'.7 — Poetry in English. Keats, John, *1795-1821.* **Special themes: Metamorphoses**

Gradman, Barry. Metamorphosis in Keats / Barry Gradman. — Brighton : Harvester, c1980. — xx,140p ; 24cm
Originally published: New York : New York University Press, c1980. — Bibliography: p137. - Includes index
ISBN 0-7108-0052-5 : £15.95 : CIP rev.
B80-19888

21'.7 — Poetry in English. Shelley, Percy Bysshe — *Critical studies*

Cronin, Richard. Shelley's poetic thoughts / Richard Cronin. — London : Macmillan, 1981. — xii,263p ; 23cm
Includes index
ISBN 0-333-30009-2 : £15.00 : CIP rev.
B80-24791

Essays on Shelley. — Liverpool : Liverpool University Press, Nov.1981. — [294]p. — (Liverpool English texts and studies ; 19)
ISBN 0-85323-294-6 : £12.50 : CIP entry
B81-30420

Hall, Jean, *1941-*. The transforming image : a study of Shelley's major poetry / Jean Hall. — Urbana ; London : University of Illinois Press, c1980. — 176p ; 21cm
Includes index
ISBN 0-252-00766-2 : £7.80 B81-05738

821'.7 — Poetry in English. Shelley, Percy Bysshe. Special subjects: Politics — *Critical studies*

Foot, Paul. Red Shelley / Paul Foot. — London : Sidgwick & Jackson in association with Michael Dempsey, 1980. — 293p ; 24cm ; cased
Bibliography: p274-275. - Includes index
ISBN 0-283-98679-4 : £12.95
ISBN 0-283-98691-3 (pbk) : £5.95 B81-21076

821'.7 — Poetry in English. Southey, Robert. Local associations: Avon

Cottle, Basil. Robert Southey and Bristol / by Basil Cottle. — Bristol : Bristol Branch of the Historical Association, 1980. — 20p,4p of plates : 3ill,1port ; 22cm. — (Local history pamphlets / Bristol Branch of the Historical Association ; 47)
Cover title
£0.60 (pbk) B81-05732

821'.7 — Poetry in English. Wordsworth, Dorothy — *Critical studies*

Homans, Margaret. Women writers and poetic identity : Dorothy Wordsworth, Emily Brontë, and Emily Dickinson / Margaret Homans. — Princeton ; Guildford : Princeton University Press, c1980. — 260p ; 23cm
Includes index
ISBN 0-691-06440-7 : £8.30
Primary classification 821'.8'099287 B81-09257

821'.7 — Poetry in English. Wordsworth, William, *1770-1850* — *Critical studies*

Adams, Anthony. Wordsworth / Anthony Adams. — Glasgow : Blackie, 1981. — 166p : ill,1map,ports ; 22cm. — (Authors in their age)
Bibliography: p159-162. - Includes index
ISBN 0-216-90747-0 (pbk) : £3.95 B81-19589

Hodgson, John A.. Wordsworth's philosophical poetry, 1797-1814 / John A. Hodgson. — Lincoln [Neb.] ; London : University of Nebraska Press, c1980. — xxi,216p ; 23cm
Includes index
ISBN 0-8032-2310-2 : £9.90 B81-06662

Rehder, Robert M.. Wordsworth and the beginnings of modern poetry / Robert Rehder. — London : Croom Helm, 1981. — 245p ; 23cm
Includes index
ISBN 0-85664-368-8 : £12.95 B81-18833

821'.7 — Poetry in English. Wordsworth, William, *1770-1850.* **Persons associated with Wordsworth, William,** *1770-1850*

Woof, Robert. The Wordsworth circle : studies of twelve members of Wordsworth's circle of friends : twelve portraits from the National Portrait Gallery / Robert Woof. — Ambleside : Trustees of Dove Cottage, c1979. — 56p : ports ; 21cm
Unpriced (pbk) B81-35534

821'.7 — Poetry in English. Wordsworth, William. Interpersonal relationships with Wordsworth, Mary — *Correspondence, diaries, etc.*

Wordsworth, William, *1770-1850*. The love letters of William and Mary Wordsworth. — London : Chatto & Windus, Oct.1981. — [256]p
ISBN 0-7011-2570-5 : £10.95 : CIP entry
B81-27960

821'.7'08 — Poetry in English, *1800-1837* — *Anthologies*

West Country poems of Wordsworth & Coleridge / illustrated and selected by Richard J. Hutchings. — Brightstone (Corner Cottage, Hunnyhill, Brightstone, Isle of Wight) : Hunnyhill Publications, 1979 (c1979). — 36p,[4]p of plates : ill ; 21cm
ISBN 0-9504736-4-2 (pbk) : £0.75 B81-26482

821'.7'09 — Poetry in English, *1800-1837.* **Romanticism** — *Critical studies*

The **Romantics**. — London : Methuen, Oct.1981. — [288]p. — (The context of English literature)
ISBN 0-416-72010-2 (cased) : £10.50 : CIP entry
ISBN 0-416-72020-x (pbk) : £4.95 B81-25295

821'.7'09145 — Poetry in English, *1800-1837.* **Romanticism** — *Critical studies*

Rajan, Tilottama. Dark interpreter : the discourse of romanticism / by Tilottama Rajan. — Ithaca ; London : Cornell University Press, 1980. — 281p ; 23cm
Bibliography: p273-276. — Includes index
ISBN 0-8014-1292-7 : £9.00 B81-07107

821'.7'09145 — Poetry in English. Coleridge, Samuel Taylor & Wordsworth, William, *1770-1850.* **Romanticism** — *Critical studies*

McFarland, Thomas. Romanticism and the forms of ruin : Wordsworth, Coleridge, and modalities of fragmentation / Thomas McFarland. — Princeton ; Guildford : Princeton University Press, c1981. — xxxiv,423p ; 25cm
Bibliography: pxv-xxxiv. — Includes index
ISBN 0-691-06437-7 (cased) : £16.40
ISBN 0-691-01373-x (pbk) : £5.30 B81-22194

821.8 — ENGLISH POETRY, 1837-1900

821'.8 — Poetry in English, *1837-1900* — *Texts*

Barlas, John. Six sonnets / by John Barlas ; edited with an introductory note by Ian Fletcher. — London : 74 Fortune Green Rd., N.W.6 : Eric & Joan Stevens, 1981. — [10]p ; 23cm
Limited ed. of 95 numbered copies
£3.00 (pbk) B81-05887

Barnes, William, *1801-1886*. Poems from William Barnes / selected and edited by Walter Partridge ; with a preface by Mark Franklin. — Sutton Mandeville (Church Farm, Sutton Mandeville, Salisbury, Wilts.) : Perdix Press, c1981. — 34p : ill ; 27cm
Limited ed. of 100 copies signed by the printer and engraver, of which 5 copies are printed on handmade paper, bound in quarter calf at £27.00; 15 on Japanese vellum, quarter buckram at £21.00 ; 30 on antique wove, quarter buckram at £18.00 and 50 with limp covers at £9.00
ISBN 0-907596-01-0 (pbk) : £9.00 B81-27201

Barnes, William, *1801-1886*. Poems in the Dorset dialect / William Barnes. — Oxford (29 Home Close, Wolvercote, Oxford OX2 8PS) : Atlantis Press, 1980. — 11p : ill ; 25cm
Limited ed. of 96 copies
ISBN 0-907425-00-3 (pbk) : Unpriced
B81-02172

Brown, Oliver Madox. Sonnet written at the age of thirteen for a picture by Mrs Stillman, and other poems / Oliver Madox Brown. — [London] ([74 Fortune Green Rd, NW6 1DS]) : Eric Joan Stevens, 1981. — [6]p ; 26cm
Cover title: Some verses
£3.00 (pbk) B81-28562

Browning, Robert. The ring and the book / Robert Browning ; edited by Richard D. Altick. — New Haven ; London : Yale University Press, 1981. — 707p ; 21cm. — (The English poets)
Originally published: Harmondsworth : Penguin, 1971. — Bibliography: p17-20
ISBN 0-300-02677-3 (cased) : £15.00
ISBN 0-300-02685-4 (pbk) : Unpriced
B81-33499

Browning, Robert, *1812-1889*. The poems / Robert Browning ; edited by John Pettigrew, supplemented and completed by Thomas J. Collins. — Harmondsworth : Penguin, 1981. — 2v. ; 20cm. — (Penguin English poets)
Includes bibliographies and index
ISBN 0-14-042259-5 (pbk) : Unpriced
ISBN 0-14-042260-9 (v.2) : £10.00 B81-38350

821′.8 — Poetry in English, *1837-1900 — Texts continuation*

Browning, Robert, *1812-1889*. The ring and the book / Robert Browning ; edited by Richard D. Altick. — Harmondsworth : Penguin, 1971 (1981 printing). — 707p ; 20cm. — (Penguin English poets)
Bibliography: p17-20
ISBN 0-14-042294-3 (pbk) : £10.00 B81-38351

Chaplin, M. A.. Poems : of Mrs. M.A. Chaplin / selected from Stray chards, Sunlit spray, Chimes for the times. — Ossett (44 Queen's Drive, Ossett, W. Yorks. WF5 0ND) : Zoar, 1975. — 44p ; 19cm
Text on inside cover
Unpriced (pbk) B81-31697

Dolben, Digby Mackworth. The poems and letters of Digby Mackworth Dolben 1848-1867. — Amersham : Avebury, Dec.1981. — [176]p
ISBN 0-86127-219-6 : £10.00 : CIP entry B81-31811

Falkner, John Meade. A Roman villa, Chedworth / John Meade Falkner. — Oxford (29 Home Close, Wolvercote, Oxford OX2 8PS) : Atlantis Press, 1981. — 7p ; 25cm
Limited ed. of 100 copies
ISBN 0-907425-01-1 (pbk) : £1.50 B81-32630

Flint, Violet. A golfing idyll, or, The skipper's round with the Deil on the Links of St Andrews / [Violet Flint]. — [Cutnall Green] ([Cutnall Green, Droitwich, Worchestershire WR9 0PQ]) : [Grant Books], [1978]. — 35p,[7] leaves of plates : ill ; 25cm
Facsim of: 3rd ed. St. Andrews : Henderson, 1897. — Limited ed. of 250 numbered copies
Unpriced B81-26459

Hardy, Thomas, *1840-1928*. [Poems. Selections]. Selected poems of Thomas Hardy / edited with an introduction and notes by James Reeves and Robert Gittings. — London : Heinemann, 1981. — xxvi,113p ; 20cm. — (The Poetry bookshelf)
ISBN 0-435-15076-6 : £4.95 : CIP rev. B80-13518

Langbridge, Frederick. Wagtail : the story of a naughty lamb, and other rhymes for little folks / by Frederick Langbridge ; illustrated by Helena Maguire, etc. — London : Macmillan Children's, 1981. — [8]p : ill(some col.) ; 11x12cm
Facsim. of: 1st ed., London : Raphael Tuck
ISBN 0-333-30915-4 (pbk) : Unpriced B81-38944

Lear, Edward. The pelican chorus; and, The Quangle Wangle's hat. — London : Ash & Grant, Sept.1981. — [32]p
ISBN 0-904069-40-0 : £3.50 : CIP entry B81-25871

Lear, Edward. The Quangle Wangle's hat / by Edward Lear ; pictures by Helen Oxenbury. — Harmondsworth : Puffin, 1973, c1969 (1980 [printing]). — 32p : col.ill ; 23cm. — (Picture puffins)
Originally published: London : Heinemann, 1969
ISBN 0-14-050062-6 (pbk) : £0.80 B81-05220

McGonagall, William. Last poetic gems / William McGonagall. — London : Duckworth, 1980. — 80p ; 19cm
ISBN 0-7156-0613-1 (pbk) : £1.00 B81-01179

McGonagall, William. McGonagall : a library omnibus / William McGonagall. — London : Duckworth, 1980. — 555p in various pagings : 1port ; 20cm
£9.80 B81-11212

McGonagall, William. More poetic gems / William McGonagall. — London : Duckworth, 1980. — 79p ; 19cm
ISBN 0-7156-0220-9 (pbk) : £1.00 B81-01180

McGonagall, William. Poetic gems / William McGonagall. — London : Duckworth, 1980. — 79p ; 19cm
ISBN 0-7156-0265-9 (pbk) : £1.00 B81-04184

McGonagall, William. Still more poetic gems / William McGonagall. — London : Duckworth, 1980. — 80p ; 19cm
ISBN 0-7156-1513-0 (pbk) : £1.00 B81-01182

McGonagall, William. Yet further poetic gems / William McGonagall. — London : Duckworth, 1980. — 78p ; 19cm
ISBN 0-7156-1512-2 (pbk) : £1.00 B81-01183

McGonagall, William. Yet more poetic gems / William McGonagall. — London : Duckworth, 1980. — 79p ; 19cm
ISBN 0-7156-1511-4 (pbk) : £1.00 B81-01184

Morris, William, *1834-1896*. A book of verse. — London : Scolar Press, Apr.1981. — [80]p
ISBN 0-85967-605-6 : £6.95 : CIP entry B81-04284

. Mrs. Duck and family. — London : Macmillan Children's, 1981. — [8]p : ill(some col.) ; 9x14cm
Facsim. of: 1st ed., London : Ernest Nister
ISBN 0-333-30911-1 (pbk) : Unpriced B81-38942

Newbolt, Henry. Selected poems of Henry Newbolt / edited and with an introduction by Patric Dickinson. — London : Hodder & Stoughton, c1981. — 157p : 1port ; 23cm
ISBN 0-340-26388-1 : £6.95 : CIP rev. B81-10467

Nister, Ernest. [In wonderland]. Magic windows : an antique revolving picture book / by Ernest Nister. — [London] : Collins, 1981, c1980. — [10]p : ill(some col.) ; 24cm
Cover title. — Originally published: London : E. Nister, 1895. — Text, ill on lining papers
ISBN 0-00-195654-x : £3.50 B81-26576

Oh, for the wings of a dove. — London : Macmillan Children's, 1981. — [8]p : ill(some col.) ; 7x15cm
Facsim. of : 1st ed., London : Ernest Nister
ISBN 0-333-30914-6 (pbk) : Unpriced B81-38940

Old friends in new dresses / illustrated by W.J. Wiegand. — London : Macmillan Children's, 1981. — [8]p : ill(some col.) ; 11cm
Facsim. of: 1st ed., London : Raphael Tuck
ISBN 0-333-30916-2 (pbk) : Unpriced B81-38945

Pinkie, Winkie and Wee. — London : Macmillan Children's, 1981. — [8]p : col.ill ; 8x11cm
Cover title. — Facsim. of: 1st ed., London : Ernest Nister
ISBN 0-333-30913-8 (pbk) : Unpriced B81-38941

[Puppy dogs]. — London : Macmillan Children's, 1981. — [8]p : col.ill ; 9x11cm
Title provided by publisher. — Facsim. of: 1st ed., London : Castell
ISBN 0-333-30910-3 (pbk) : Unpriced B81-38943

Stevenson, Robert Louis. A child's garden of verses / by Robert Louis Stevenson ; with wood engravings by Joan Hassall. — London : Blackie, 1958 (1975 [printing]). — 84p : ill ; 23cm
Pbk: £0.95
£2.50 (cased) B81-03606

Swinburne, Algernon Charles. Selected poems. — Manchester : Carcanet, Oct.1981. — [144]p. — (Fyfield books)
ISBN 0-85635-137-7 (pbk) : £3.95 : CIP entry B81-27946

Tennyson, Alfred. Tennyson's In memoriam. — Oxford : Clarendon, Feb.1982. — [432]p
ISBN 0-19-812747-2 : £25.00 : CIP entry B81-35803

Wilde, Oscar. The sphinx. — London : Century, Sept.1981. — 2v.
Facsim. of: 1st ed. London : Elkin Mathews & John Lane, 1894
ISBN 0-907492-00-2 : £250.00 : CIP entry B81-20501

Wordsworth. — Brighton : Harvester Press, Oct.1981. — [224]p. — (Cornell Wordsworth)
ISBN 0-7108-0315-x : £30.00 : CIP entry B81-30329

821′.8 — Poetry in English. Arnold, Matthew — *Biographies*

Honan, Park. Matthew Arnold : a life / Park Honan. — London : Weidenfeld and Nicolson, 1981. — xii,496p,[16]p of plates : ill,1facsim,ports ; 24cm
Includes index
ISBN 0-297-77824-2 : £9.95 B81-36268

Trilling, Lionel. Matthew Arnold. — Oxford : Oxford University Press, Jan.1982. — [504]p. — (The works of Lionel Trilling)
Originally published: London : Allen & Unwin, 1975
ISBN 0-19-212222-3 : £9.95 : CIP entry B81-34374

821′.8 — Poetry in English. Bridges, Robert — *Critical studies*

Stanford, Donald E.. In the classic mode : the achievement of Robert Bridges / Donald E. Stanford. — Newark : University of Delaware Press ; London : Associated University Presses, c1978. — 343p : ill,ports ; 24cm
Bibliography: p327-333. - Includes index
ISBN 0-87413-118-9 : £14.50 B81-06751

821′.8 — Poetry in English. Brontë, Emily — *Critical studies*

Homans, Margaret. Women writers and poetic identity : Dorothy Wordsworth, Emily Brontë, and Emily Dickinson / Margaret Homans. — Princeton ; Guildford : Princeton University Press, c1980. — 260p ; 23cm
Includes index
ISBN 0-691-06440-7 : £8.30
Primary classification 821′.8′099287 B81-09257

821′.8 — Poetry in English. Hardy, Thomas, *1840-1928 — Critical studies*

The **Poetry** of Thomas Hardy / edited by Patricia Clements and Juliet Grindle. — London : Vision, c19802. — ix,194p ; 23cm. — (Vision critical studies)
Includes index
ISBN 0-85478-334-2 : £10.95 B81-01715

Taylor, Dennis. Hardy's poetry, 1860-1928 / Dennis Taylor. — London : Macmillan, 1981. — xx,204p,[17]p of plates : ports,1geneal.table ; 23cm
Bibliography: p189-192. — Includes index
ISBN 0-333-27632-9 : £15.00 B81-21858

821′.8 — Poetry in English. Hopkins, Gerard Manley — *Critical studies*

MacKenzie, Norman H.. A reader's guide to Gerard Manley Hopkins / Norman H. MacKenzie. — London : Thames and Hudson, 1981. — 256p ; 21cm
Bibliography: p241-244. - Includes index
ISBN 0-500-14024-3 : £6.95 B81-19750

Sprinker, Michael. A counterpoint of dissonance : the aesthetics and poetry of Gerard Manley Hopkins / Michael Sprinker. — Baltimore ; London : Johns Hopkins University Press, c1980. — 149p ; 24cm
Includes index
ISBN 0-8018-2402-8 : £6.50 B81-19824

Storey, Graham. A preface to Hopkins / Graham Storey. — London : Longman, 1981. — ix,150p : ill,3facsims,port,1geneal.table ; 22cm. — (Preface books)
Bibliography: p146-147. — Includes index
ISBN 0-582-35251-7 (cased) : Unpriced
ISBN 0-582-35252-5 (pbk) : £3.25 B81-29393

821'.8 — Poetry in English. Meynell, Alice — *Biographies*
Badeni, June. The slender tree : a life of Alice Meynell / June Badeni. — Padstow (11 Church St., Padstow, Cornwall) : Tabb House, 1981. — xiii,269p,[11]p of plates : 1ill,1facsim,ports ; 24cm
Bibliography: p253. - Includes index
ISBN 0-907018-01-7 : £10.95

821'.8 — Poetry in English. Morris, *Sir* Lewis — *Biographies*
Phillips, Douglas, *1929-*. Sir Lewis Morris / Douglas Phillips. — [Cardiff] : University of Wales Press on behalf of the Welsh Arts Council, 1981. — 117p,[1]leaf of plates : 1port ; 25cm. — (Writers of Wales, ISSN 0141-5050)
Limited ed. of 1000 copies
ISBN 0-7083-0788-4 (pbk) : Unpriced
B81-19383

821'.8 — Poetry in English. Rossetti, Christina — *Biographies*
Battiscombe, Georgina. Christina Rossetti : a divided life / Georgina Battiscombe. — London : Constable, 1981. — 223p : ill,2facsims,ports ; 24cm
Bibliography: p220-221. - Includes index
ISBN 0-09-461950-6 : £9.50 : CIP rev.
B80-13963

821'.8 — Poetry in English. Rossetti, Dante Gabriel — *Critical studies*
Rees, Joan, *1923-*. The poetry of Dante Gabriel Rossetti : modes of self-expression / Joan Rees. — Cambridge : Cambridge University Press, 1981. — vii,204p ; 23cm
Includes index
ISBN 0-521-23537-5 : £16.50 B81-14501

821'.8 — Poetry in English. Tennyson, Alfred, *Baron Tennyson — Correspondence*
Tennyson, Alfred Tennyson, *Baron*. The letters of Alfred Lord Tennyson. — Oxford : Clarendon Press, Apr.1981
Vol.1 : 1821-1850. — [520]p
ISBN 0-19-812569-0 : £25.00 : CIP entry
B81-02089

821'.8 — Poetry in English. Tennyson, Alfred Tennyson, *Baron — Biographies*
Wheatcroft, Andrew. The Tennyson album : a biography in original photographs / by Andrew Wheatcroft ; introduction by Sir John Betjeman. — London : Routledge & Kegan Paul, 1980. — 160p : ill,facsims,ports ; 28cm
Ill on lining papers
ISBN 0-7100-0494-x : £10.50 : CIP rev.
B80-06538

821'.8 — Poetry in English. Tennyson, Alfred Tennyson, *Baron — Critical studies*
Tennyson : a collection of critical essays / edited by Elizabeth A. Francis. — Enlgewood Cliffs ; London : Prentice-Hall, c1980. — iv,220p ; 21cm. — (Twentieth century views) (A Spectrum book)
Bibliography: p217-218
ISBN 0-13-902353-4 (cased) : £7.10
ISBN 0-13-902346-1 (pbk) : £2.55 B81-09333

821'.8 — Poetry in English. Tennyson, Alfred Tennyson, *Baron.* **Special themes: Family life —** *Critical studies*
Hair, Donald S.. Domestic and heroic in Tennyson's poetry / Donald S. Hair. — Toronto ; London : University of Toronto Press, c1981. — vi,251p : 2ill ; 24cm
Bibliography: p239-245. — Includes index
ISBN 0-8020-5530-3 : £15.00 B81-36566

821'.8 — Poetry in English. Tennyson, Alfred Tennyson, *Baron.* **Special themes: Historical events —** *Critical studies*
Kozicki, Henry. Tennyson and Clio : history in the major poems / Henry Kozicki. — Baltimore ; London : Johns Hopkins University Press, c1979. — xvii,185p : port ; 24cm
Bibliography: p171-178. - Includes index
ISBN 0-8018-2197-5 : £7.50 B81-01185

821'.8 — Poetry in English. Tennyson, Alfred Tennyson, *Baron.* **Style —** *Critical studies*
Trickett, Rachel. Tennyson's craft / Rachel Trickett. — Lincoln : Tennyson Society, 1981. — 16p ; 22cm. — (Tennyson Society occasional paper ; no.4)
Unpriced (pbk) B81-33583

821'.8 — Poetry in English. Yeats, W. B.. Autobiographies — *Critical studies*
O'Hara, Daniel T.. Tragic knowledge : Yeats's Autobiography and hermeneutics / Daniel T. O'Hara. — New York ; Guildford : Columbia University Press, 1981. — x,192p ; 24cm
Includes index
ISBN 0-231-05204-9 : £13.95 B81-25623

821'.8 — Poetry in English. Yeats, W. B. — *Critical studies*
Watkins, Vernon. Yeats & Owen : two essays / Vernon Watkins. — Frome (45 Milk St., Frome, Somerset) : The Hunting Raven, c1981. — 30p ; 22cm
ISBN 0-905220-11-0 (pbk) : £1.75 B81-19419

Yeats, Sligo and Ireland : essays to mark the 21st Yeats International Summer School / edited by A. Norman Jeffares. — Gerrard Cross : Smythe, 1980. — x,267p ; 23cm. — (Irish literary studies, ISSN 0140-895x ; 6)
Includes index
ISBN 0-86140-041-0 : £8.95 : CIP rev.
B80-12030

821'.8 — Poetry in English. Yeats, W. B.. Influence of Irish folklore
Thuente, Mary Helen. W.B. Yeats and Irish folklore / Mary Helen Thuente. — Dublin : Gill and Macmillan, 1980. — x,286p ; 23cm
Bibliography: p274-284. - Includes index
ISBN 0-7171-1020-6 : £13.00 B81-03649

821'.8 — Poetry in English. Yeats, W. B.. Interpersonal relationships with Horton W. T.
Harper, George Mills. W.B. Yeats and W.T. Horton : the record of an occult friendship / George Mills Harper. — [London] : [Macmillan], [1980]. — x,160p : ill ; 23cm
Includes index
ISBN 0-333-27165-3 : £12.00 : CIP rev.
Also classified at 759.2'915 B79-25899

821'.8 — Poetry in English. Yeats, W. B.. Introductions — *Critical studies*
Yeats, W. B.. Yeats on Yeats : the last introductions and the 'Dublin' edition / [edited with a commentary by] Edward Callan. — Mountrath : Dolmen in association with Humanities Press, 1981. — 112p : facsims ; 25cm. — (New Yeats papers ; 20)
Bibliography: p111-112
ISBN 0-85105-370-x (pbk) : Unpriced : CIP rev. B80-13040

821'.8 — Poetry in English. Yeats, W. B.. Special themes: Politics — *Critical studies*
Cullingford, Elizabeth. Yeats, Ireland and fascism / Elizabeth Cullingford. — London : Macmillan, 1981. — viii,251p ; 23cm
Bibliography: p239-244. — Includes index
ISBN 0-333-26199-2 : £15.00 : CIP rev.
B80-21003

821'.8'08 — Poetry in English, *1837-1945 — Anthologies*
Poetry 1870 to 1914 / [edited by] Bernard Bergonzi. — London : Longman, 1980. — xvii,190p ; 20cm. — (Longman English series)
Bibliography: p187-189
ISBN 0-582-35147-2 (pbk) : £2.75 B81-06095

821'.8'0809282 — Children's poetry in English, *1837-1945 — Anthologies*
Favorite poems for children : coloring book / selected & illustrated by Susan Gaber. — New York : Dover ; London : Constable, 1980. — 40p : ill(some col.) ; 28cm. — (Dover coloring book) (Dover pictorial archive series)
Ill on inside covers
ISBN 0-486-23923-3 (pbk) : £1.30 B81-05916

821'.8'09145 — Poetry in English. Swinburne, Algernon Charles & Tennyson, Alfred Tennyson, *Baron.* **Romanticism —** *Critical studies*
McSweeney, Kerry. Tennyson and Swinburne as romantic naturalists / Kerry McSweeney. — Toronto ; London : University of Toronto Press, c1981. — xvii,222p ; 24cm
Includes index
ISBN 0-8020-2381-9 : £15.00 B81-36564

821'.8'09382 — Christian poetry in English, *1837-1900 — Critical studies*
Tennyson, G. B.. Victorian devotional poetry : the Tractarian mode / G.B. Tennyson. — Cambridge, Mass. ; London : Harvard University Press, 1981. — xiv,268p : ill,facsims ; 24cm
Includes index
ISBN 0-674-93586-1 : £10.50 B81-21059

821'.8'099287 — Poetry in English. Women writers, *1800-1900 — Critical studies*
Homans, Margaret. Women writers and poetic identity : Dorothy Wordsworth, Emily Brontë, and Emily Dickinson / Margaret Homans. — Princeton ; Guildford : Princeton University Press, c1980. — 260p ; 23cm
Includes index
ISBN 0-691-06440-7 : £8.30
Also classified at 821'.7 ; 821'.8 ; 811'.4
B81-09257

821.912 — ENGLISH POETRY, 1900-1945

821'.912 — Poetry in English, *1900-1945 — Texts*
Allen, Jonathan, *1957-*. A bad case of animal nonsense / by Jonathan Allen. — London : Dent, 1981. — [58]p : chiefly ill ; 25cm
ISBN 0-460-06077-5 : £2.95 : CIP rev.
B81-18089

Auden, W. H.. Norse poems. — London : Athlone Press, Sept.1981. — [272]p
ISBN 0-485-11226-4 : £7.95 : CIP entry
B81-22649

Baker, Barbara. This singing world : poems / by Barbara Baker. — London (14 Barlly Rd. W10 6AR) : Autolycus, c1978. — 16p ; 21cm
Unpriced (pbk) B81-33509

Barker, Cicely Mary. Flower fairies : poems and pictures / by Cicely Mary Barker. — Miniature library ed. — London : Blackie, c1981. — 4v. : col.ill ; 11cm
In slipcase. — Contents: Berry flower fairies — Blossom flower fairies — Spring flower fairies — Summer flower fairies
ISBN 0-216-91110-9 : Unpriced B81-28482

Betjeman, John. Church poems / John Betjeman ; illustrated by John Piper. — London : Murray, 1981. — 65p : ill ; 22cm
ISBN 0-7195-3784-3 : £5.95
ISBN 0-7195-3797-5 (limited ed.) : Unpriced
B81-16208

Bowes Lyon, Lilian. Uncollected poems / by Lilian Bowes Lyon. — Edinburgh (137 Warrneder Park Rd., Edinburgh EH9 1DS) : Tragara, 1981. — [15]p ; 21cm
Limited ed. of 95 copies
ISBN 0-902616-67-6 (pbk) : £7.50 B81-24987

Bye, Jon. Lore of looking : poems / Jon Bye. — Gravesend (Victoria Centre for Adult Education, Darnley Rd., Gravesend, Kent) : Victoria Press, 1981. — 26p ; 21cm. — (Writers of South East England series ; no.2)
ISBN 0-907165-02-8 (pbk) : £0.75 B81-34855

Cocker, W. D.. New poems / by W.D. Cocker. — Glasgow : Brown, Son & Ferguson, 1949 (1981 [printing]). — 98p ; 19cm
Includes index
ISBN 0-85174-404-4 : £6.00 B81-21142

Collins, Cecil. In the solitude of this land : poems 1940-81 / Cecil Collins. — Ipswich (3 Cambridge Drive, Ipswich IP2 9EP) : Golgonooza Press, c1981. — xixp ; 24cm
Limited ed. of 100 numbered copies, each containing a signed autolithograph by the author
Unpriced (pbk) B81-35410

Colum, Padraic. The poet's circuits. — Centenary ed. — Portlaoise : Dolmen Press, Nov.1981. — [168]p
ISBN 0-85105-390-4 : £6.00 : CIP entry
ISBN 0-85105-391-2 (limited ed.) : £40.00
B81-33650

821′.912 — Poetry in English, ***1900-1945 — Texts continuation***

Crisford, John. A poet′s gift : readable poems that rhyme and scan with a metrigraph for each / John Crisford. — Winsford (Winsford, Minehead, Somerset) : Nether Halse Books, 1981. — 39p : ill ; 21cm
ISBN 0-9507469-0-8 (pbk) : Unpriced : CIP rev. B81-16347

Durrell, Lawrence. Collected poems 1931-1974 / Lawrence Durrell. — Completely rev. ed., edited by James A. Brigham. — London : Faber, 1980. — 350p ; 23cm
Previous ed.: 1968. — Includes index
ISBN 0-571-18009-4 : £9.00 : CIP rev. B79-31344

Edgar, Marriott. Albert comes back / Marriott Edgar ; pictures by Caroline Holden. — London : Methuen, 1980. — [32]p : col.ill ; 28cm
ISBN 0-416-89290-6 : £4.25 B81-01186

Farjeon, Eleanor. Invitation to a mouse and other poems / Eleanor Farjeon ; chosen by Annabel Farjeon ; illustrated by Antony Maitland. — London : Pelham, 1981. — 96p : ill ; 23cm
Includes index
ISBN 0-7207-1322-6 : £4.95 B81-22317

Flecker, James Elroy. Poems : a new selection / James Elroy Flecker ; edited and introduced by Stephen Parry. — London (14 Barlly Rd. W10 6AR) : Autolycus, c1980. — 63p ; 21cm
ISBN 0-903413-36-1 (pbk) : £3.50 B81-33505

Fraser, G. S.. Poems of G.S. Fraser / edited by Ian Fletcher and John Lucas. — Leicester : Leicester University Press, 1981. — 208p ; 24cm
ISBN 0-7185-1214-6 (pbk) : £7.50 : CIP rev. B81-07919

Fuller, Roy. More about Tompkins : and other light verse / by Roy Fuller. — Edinburgh (137 Warrender Park Rd., Edinburgh EH9 1DS) : Tragara, 1981. — [19]p ; 24cm
Limited ed. of 135 copies of which 25 are signed by the author
ISBN 0-902616-69-2 (pbk) : £6.50 B81-24985

Hamburger, Michael. Variations / Michael Hamburger. — Manchester : Carcanet, 1981. — 110p ; 20cm
ISBN 0-85635-354-x (pbk) : £2.95 : CIP rev. B81-16896

Heath, Isobel. Reflexions / by Isobel Heath. — [St. Ives] ([Bosunsnest, Orange La., St. Ives, Cornwall]) : [I. Heath], [1981]. — 10p : 1ill ; 20cm
Cover title
Unpriced (pbk) B81-18380

Hewitt, John. The selected John Hewitt. — Belfast : Blackstaff Press, July 1981. — [120]p
ISBN 0-85640-244-3 (pbk) : £3.50 : CIP entry B81-24646

Hopkins, Kenneth. Collected poems 1935-1965 / Kenneth Hopkins. — North Walsham : Warren House, 1981, c1964. — xvi,232p ; 25cm
Originally published: Carbondale : Southern Illinois University Press, 1964. — Limited ed. of 200 numbered copies . — In slip case. — Includes index
£10.50 B81-37377

Jones, David, *1895-1974*. The narrows / David Jones ; with an introduction by Roland Mathias. — Devon : Interim Press, 1981. — [23]p ; 22cm
Includes: ′Narrows′ and the Western Empire / by Eric Ratcliffe
ISBN 0-904675-18-1 : Unpriced B81-38052

Joyce, James, *1882-1941*. Chamber music / James Joyce. — London : Cape, 1980. — 44p ; 22cm. — (Cape poetry paperbacks)
ISBN 0-224-01860-4 (pbk) : £1.95 : CIP rev. B80-18877

Lawrence, D. H.. [Poems]. The complete poems of D.H. Lawrence / collected and edited with an introduction and notes by Vivian de Sola Pinto and Warren Roberts. — Harmondsworth : Penguin, 1977, c1971 (1980 [printing]). — 1079p ; 20cm
Originally published: in 2v. London : Heinemann, 1964. — Includes index
ISBN 0-14-042220-x (pbk) : £5.00 B81-10995

Lewis, Alun. Selected poems of Alun Lewis / selected by Jeremy Hooker and Gweno Lewis ; foreword by Robert Graves ; afterword by Jeremy Hooker. — London : Unwin Paperbacks, 1981. — 112p ; 20cm
ISBN 0-04-821048-x (pbk) : £2.50 B81-26454

Lindsay, Maurice. Collected poems / by Maurice Lindsay. — Edinburgh : Harris, 1979. — 128p ; 23cm
ISBN 0-904505-71-5 : £6.00 B81-35138

MacDiarmid, Hugh, *1892-1978*. Complete poems 1920-1976 : Hugh MacDiarmid / edited by Michael Grieve and W.R. Aitken. — London : Martin Brian & O′Keeffe, 1978. — 2 (xxii,1485p) ; 23cm
Includes index
ISBN 0-85616-440-2 : £15.00 B81-10591

Manning, Elfrida. Growing tall / by Elfrida Manning ; illustrations by Eileen Bradpiece. — [Farnham] ([18 Upper South View, Farnham, Surrey]) : [W. O. Manning], [1980?]. — [26] leaves : ill ; 21cm
Unpriced (pbk) B81-01995

Milne, Ewart. Spring offering / by Ewart Milne. — Isle of Skye : Aquila, c1981. — [18]p ; 21cm. — (Aquila pamphlet poetry. Second series)
Limited ed. of 250 copies of which 50 are signed, cased and numbered
ISBN 0-7275-0208-5 (cased) : £10.00 B81-37008

Nicholson, Hubert. Selected poems 1930-80 / Hubert Nicholson. — London (14 Barlly Rd. W10 6AR) : Autolycus, c1981. — 52p ; 21cm
ISBN 0-903413-45-0 (pbk) : £2.50 B81-33513

Nicholson, Hubert. Ventriloquists and dolls : fifty poems / by Hubert Nicholson. — London (14 Barlby Rd, W10 6AR) : Autolycus, [c1978]. — 44p ; 21cm
ISBN 0-903413-24-8 (pbk) : £1.75 B81-33514

Nicholson, Norman. Sea to the west / Norman Nicholson. — London : Faber, 1981. — 64p ; 21cm
ISBN 0-571-11745-7 (cased) : £5.95 B81-20930

Nott, Kathleen. Elegies : and other poems / by Kathleen Nott. — [Richmond] : Keepsake, 1981. — 28p ; 21cm
Limited ed. of 275 copies, 50 signed and numbered
ISBN 0-901924-54-7 (pbk) : £0.95 B81-29902

Noyes, Alfred. The highwayman / Alfred Noyes ; illustrated by Charles Keeping. — Oxford : Oxford University Press, 1981. — [32p]p : ill ; 29cm
Ill on lining papers
ISBN 0-19-279748-4 : £4.50 B81-24785

Raine, Kathleen. Collected poems 1935-1980 / Kathleen Raine. — London : Allen & Unwin, 1981. — 312p ; 23cm
ISBN 0-04-821050-1 : Unpriced : CIP rev. B81-01196

Rowse, A. L.. A life : collected poems / A.L. Rowse. — Edinburgh : Blackwood, 1981. — xvi,413p ; 23cm
ISBN 0-85158-141-2 : £9.95 B81-21318

Sitwell, Sacheverell. Catalysts in collusion : a book of catalysts / Sacheverell Sitwell. — [Badby] ([Pennywick, Badby, Daventry, Northants.]) : [M. Battison], [1980]. — [19]p ; 22cm
Unpriced (pbk) B81-01187

Spencer, Bernard. Collected poems / Bernard Spencer ; edited and with an introduction by Roger Bowen. — Oxford : Oxford University Press, 1981. — xxxiii,149p ; 23cm
Includes index
ISBN 0-19-211930-3 : £8.50 : CIP rev. B81-12336

Tessimond, A. S. J.. Morning meeting : poems / by A.S.J. Tessimond ; introduced by Hubert Nicholson. — London (14 Barlly Rd. W10 6AR) : Autolycus, c1980. — 64p : ill,2ports ; 21cm
ISBN 0-903413-41-8 (pbk) : £3.00 B81-33507

Tessimond, A. S. J.. Not love perhaps — : poems / by A.S.J. Tessimond ; selected and introduced by Hubert Nicholson. — London (14 Barlly Rd. W10 6AR) : Autolycus, c1978. — 52p ; 21cm
ISBN 0-903413-18-3 (pbk) : £3.00 B81-33508

Thomas, Evan J.. The solitary place / by Evan J. Thomas. — Triangle (The Old Co-op Shop, Mill Bank, Triangle, W. Yorkshire HX6 3DX) : Sparrow Press, 1981. — 32p : ill ; 21cm
Limited ed. of 500 numbered copies
ISBN 0-9507642-0-5 (pbk) : £1.50 B81-36806

Woolsey, Gamel. The weight of human hours / by Gamel Woolsey. — North Walsham (12 New Rd., North Walsham, Norfolk NR28 9DF) : Warren House Press, 1980. — 45p ; 22cm
Limited edition of 150 numbered copies
£6.00 B81-03598

821′.912 — Poetry in English. Auden, W. H. — ***Biographies***

Carpenter, Humphrey. W.H. Auden : a biography / Humphrey Carpenter. — London : Allen & Unwin, 1981. — xvi,495p,[12]p of plates : ill,1facsim,ports ; 24cm
Bibliography: p459-462. — Includes index
ISBN 0-04-928044-9 : Unpriced : CIP rev. B81-04195

821′.912 — Poetry in English. Auden, W. H. — ***Critical studies***

Mendelson, Edward. Early Auden / Edward Mendelson. — London : Faber, 1981. — xxiii,407p ; 24cm
Includes index
ISBN 0-571-11193-9 : £10.00 : CIP rev. B81-28026

821′.912 — Poetry in English. Auden, W. H. — ***Study outlines***

Ashworth, Clive V.. Notes on the poetry of W.H. Auden / compiled by Clive V. Ashworth. — London : Methuen Paperbacks, 1979. — 71p ; 20cm. — (Methuen notes)
Bibliography: p70. — Includes index
ISBN 0-417-21660-2 (pbk) : £0.75 B81-11595

821′.912 — Poetry in English. Brooke, Rupert — ***Biographies***

Lehmann, John. Rupert Brooke : his life and his legend / John Lehmann. — London : Quartet, 1981, c1980. — xi,178p : 2ill,ports ; 20cm
Originally published: London : Weidenfeld and Nicolson, 1980. — Bibliography: p170-171. — Includes index
ISBN 0-7043-3362-7 (pbk) : £2.95 B81-29533

821′.912 — Poetry in English. Cruikshank, Helen B. — ***Biographies***

Cruickshank, Helen B.. Octobiography / Helen B. Cruickshank. — Montrose : Standard Press, 1976. — 181p : ill,facsims,ports ; 26cm
Includes index
ISBN 0-900871-37-7 (pbk) : £2.95 B81-20767

821′.912 — Poetry in English. Davies, W. H. (William Henry), ***1871-1940 — Biographies***

Hollingdrake, Sybil. The super-tramp : a biography of W.H. Davies / by Sybil Hollingdrake. — 2nd ed. (with appendices). — [Newport, Gwent] ([c/o S. Hollingdrake, 51 Stockton Rd., Newport, Gwent]) : [Hollydragon Books], [1980]. — 42p ; 21cm
Previous ed.: 1971
£1.00 (pbk) B81-15196

821′.912 — Poetry in English. Davies, W.H. (William Henry), *ca 1918-1920 — Biographies*
Davies, W. H. (William Henry). Young Emma / W.H. Davies ; with a foreword by C.V. Wedgwood. — London : Cape, 1980. — 158p ; 23cm
ISBN 0-224-01853-1 : £5.95 : CIP rev.
B80-24795

821′.912 — Poetry in English. Eliot, T. S., *1909-1922 — Critical studies*
Gray, Piers. T.S. Eliot′s intellectual and poetic development, 1909-1922. — Brighton : Harvester Press, Dec.1981. — [416]p
ISBN 0-7108-0046-0 : £22.00 : CIP entry
B81-34018

821′.912 — Poetry in English. Eliot, T. S. — *Critical studies*
Moody, A. D.. Thomas Stearns Eliot : poet / A. D. Moody. — Cambridge : Cambridge University Press, 1979 (1980 [printing]). — xv,381p ; 23cm
Includes index
ISBN 0-521-29968-3 (pbk) : £6.95 B81-02616

821′.912 — Poetry in English. Eliot, T. S.. Selected poems — *Commentaries*
Southam, B. C.. A student′s guide to the Selected poems of T.S. Eliot / B.C. Southam. — 4th ed. — London : Faber, 1981. — 158p ; 19cm
Previous ed.: 1977
ISBN 0-571-18030-2 (pbk) : £1.95 B81-13044

821′.912 — Poetry in English. Eliot, T. S.. Special subjects: Time — *Critical studies*
Gish, Nancy K.. Time in the poetry of T.S. Eliot : a study in structure and theme / Nancy K. Gish. — London : Macmillan, 1981. — viii,150p ; 23cm
Bibliography: p140-147. — Includes index
ISBN 0-333-28994-3 : £15.00 : CIP rev.
B80-36300

821′.912 — Poetry in English. Eliot, T. S.. Waste land — *Study outlines*
Macrae, Alasdair D. F.. The waste land : notes / Alasdair D.F. Macrae. — London : Longman, 1980. — 69p ; 21cm. — (York notes ; 45)
Bibliography: p68-69
ISBN 0-582-78212-0 (pbk) : £0.90 B81-06258

821′.912 — Poetry in English. Fuller, Roy — *Biographies*
Fuller, Roy. Souvenirs / Roy Fuller. — London : London Magazine Editions, 1980. — 191p ; 20cm
ISBN 0-904388-30-1 : £4.95 B81-03662

821′.912 — Poetry in English. Gascoyne, David, *1916-, 1936-1937 — Correspondence, diaries, etc.*
Gascoyne, David, *1916-*. Journal 1936-37 ; Death of an explorer ; Léon Chestov / David Gascoyne. — London : Enitharmon, 1980. — 144p ; 23cm
Also available in a limited ed. of 95 signed copies
ISBN 0-905289-66-8 : £6.75 B81-03803

821′.912 — Poetry in English. Gibbon, Monk — *Biographies*
Gibbon, Monk. The pupil. — Dublin : Wolfhound Press, Sept.1981. — [128]p
ISBN 0-905473-68-x : £5.40 : CIP entry
B81-24652

821′.912 — Poetry in English. Gogarty, Oliver St. John — *Biographies*
O′Connor, Ulick. Oliver St John Gogarty : a poet and his times / Ulick O′Connor. — London : Granada, 1981, c1963. — 348p,[8]p of plates : ports ; 18cm. — (A Panther book)
Originally published: London : Cape, 1964. — Bibliography: p331-337. - Includes index
ISBN 0-586-05119-8 (pbk) : £2.25 B81-22297

821′.912 — Poetry in English. Graves, Robert — *Biographies*
Graves, Robert. Goodbye to all that / Robert Graves ; introduced by Raleigh Trevelyan. — Rev. ed. — London : Folio Society, 1981, c1957. — 295p : ill,1map,facsims,ports ; 23cm
Previous ed.: London : Cape, 1929. — In slip case. — Map on lining papers
£8.50 B81-17696

821′.912 — Poetry in English. Housman, A. E. — *Biographies*
Graves, Richard Perceval. A.E. Housman : the scholar-poet / Richard Perceval Graves. — Oxford : Oxford University Press, 1981. — xv,304p,[16]p of plates : ill,ports ; 20cm
Bibliography: p291-292. — Includes index
ISBN 0-19-281309-9 (pbk) : £3.95 B81-15670

821′.912 — Poetry in English. Jones, David, *1895-1974 — Personal observations*
Blissett, William. The long conversation : a memoir of David Jones / by William Blissett. — Oxford : Oxford University Press, 1981. — 159p,[8]p of plates : ill,1facsim,ports ; 23cm
Includes index
ISBN 0-19-211778-5 : £9.75 : CIP rev.
B81-27361

821′.912 — Poetry in English. Lawrence, D. H. — *Study outlines*
Ashworth, Clive V.. Notes on D.H. Lawrence′s peoms and stories / compiled by Clive V. Ashworth. — London : Methuen Paperbacks, 1981, c1980. — 90p ; 20cm. — (Methuen notes)
Bibliography: p90
ISBN 0-417-21750-1 (pbk) : £0.95
Also classified at 823′.912 B81-19613

821′.912 — Poetry in English. MacDiarmid, Hugh, *1892-1978 — Critical studies*
Boutelle, Ann Edwards. Thistle and rose : a study of Hugh MacDiarmid′s poetry / Ann Edwards Boutelle. — Loanhead : Macdonald, c1980. — 258p ; 22cm
Bibliography: p246-252. — Includes index
ISBN 0-904265-25-0 : £12.50 B81-25588

821′.912 — Poetry in English. MacDiarmid, Hugh, *1892-1978.* **Special subjects: Fishing —** *Critical studies*
McQuillan, Ruth. In line with the Ramna Stacks : a study of the fishing poems of Hugh McDiarmid / by Ruth McQuillan & Agnes Shearer. — Edinburgh (17 St Clair Terrace, Edinburgh EH10 5NW) : Challister, c1980. — 11p ; 21cm
£0.35 (pbk) B81-01989

821′.912 — Poetry in English. Muir, Edwin — *Critical studies*
Knight, Roger. Edwin Muir : an introduction to his work / Roger Knight. — London : Longman, 1980. — 210p ; 23cm
Bibliography: p204-206. - Includes index
ISBN 0-582-48901-6 (cased) : £8.50 : CIP rev.
ISBN 0-582-48906-7 (pbk) : £4.95 B80-10746

821′.912 — Poetry in English. Sitwell, Edith — *Biographies*
Glendinning, Victoria. Edith Sitwell : a unicorn among lions / Victoria Glendinning. — London : Weidenfeld and Nicolson, 1981. — 393p,[20]p of plates : ill(some col.),ports(some col.) ; 24cm
Includes index
ISBN 0-297-77801-3 : £9.95 B81-29677

821′.912 — Poetry in English. Strong, Patience — *Biographies*
Strong, Patience. With a poem in my pocket : the autobiography of Patience Strong. — London : Muller, 1981. — 258p,[16]p of plates : ill,ports ; 23cm
Includes index
ISBN 0-584-10613-0 : £5.95 : CIP rev.
B81-21492

821′.912 — Poetry in English. Thomas, Edward, *1878-1917 — Critical studies*
Motion, Andrew. The poetry of Edward Thomas / Andrew Motion. — London : Routledge & Kegan Paul, 1980. — x,193p ; 23cm
Bibliography: p183-188. — Includes index
ISBN 0-7100-0471-0 : £8.95 : CIP rev.
B80-35403

821′.912 — Poetry in English. Thomas, Edward — *Correspondence, diaries, etc.*
Thomas, Edward, *1878-1917*. A selection of letters to Edward Garnett / Edward Thomas. — Edinburgh : Tragara, 1981. — 34p ; 26cm
Limited ed. of 175 numbered copies
ISBN 0-902616-66-8 (pbk) : Unpriced
B81-11833

821′.912′08 — Poetry in English, *1900-1945 — Anthologies*
Georgian poetry / selected and introduced by James Reeves. — Harmondsworth : Penguin, 1962 (1981 [printing]). — 172p ; 20cm
ISBN 0-14-042059-2 (pbk) : £1.50 B81-37255

821′.912′08 — Poetry in English, *1900-1945.* **Imagism —** *Anthologies*
Imagist poetry / introduced and edited by Peter Jones. — Harmondsworth : Penguin, 1972 (1981 [printing]). — 187p ; 20cm
Includes index
ISBN 0-14-042147-5 (pbk) : £2.50 B81-25445

821′.912′08 — Poetry in English, *1900- — Anthologies*
The **Music** of what happens : poems from The Listener 1965-1980 / edited by Derwent May. — London : British Broadcasting Corporation, 1981. — 151p ; 22cm
ISBN 0-563-17864-7 : £5.50 B81-19388

The **Music** of what happens : poems from the Listener 1965-1980 / edited by Derwent May. — London : British Broadcasting Corporation, 1981. — 151p ; 21cm
ISBN 0-563-17869-8 (pbk) : £3.95 B81-10354

821′.912′08 — Poetry in English, *1900- — Anthologies — Festschriften*
A **garland** for Jack Lindsay / Doris Lessing ... [et al.] ; decorations by Charlotte Mensforth. — [St. Albans] (12 Cannon St., St. Albans, Herts.) : Piccolo Press, 1980. — 14p : ill ; 21cm
Limited ed. of 150 copies
ISBN 0-906667-02-x (pbk) : Unpriced
B81-07854

821′.912′08 — Poetry in English, *1900- — Anthologies — For schools*
Topics in modern poetry. — London : Murray, Feb.1982. — [144]p
ISBN 0-7195-3932-3 (pbk) : £1.95 : CIP entry
B81-35850

821′.912′080358 — Poetry in English, *1900-1945.* **Special subjects: World War 1 —** *Anthologies*
The **Penguin** book of First World War poetry / edited and with an introduction by Jon Silkin. — 2nd ed. — Harmondsworth : Penguin, 1981. — 282p ; 18cm. — (The Penguin poets)
Previous ed.: 1979. — Bibliography: p265-269. — Includes index
ISBN 0-14-042255-2 (pbk) : £1.75 B81-40016

821′.912′080358 — Poetry in English, *1900-1945.* **Special subjects: World War 2 —** *Anthologies*
Hands to action stations! : naval poetry and verse from World War Two / chosen by John Winton ; illustrated by Jack Broome. — Denbigh (Bryn Clwyd, Llandyrnog, Denbigh, Clwyd LL16 4HP) : Bluejacket, c1980. — 143p : ill ; 21cm
Bibliography: p143
ISBN 0-907001-00-9 (pbk) : £2.95 B81-00351

821′.912′080358 — Poetry in English. Women writers, *1900-1945.* **Special themes: World War 1 —** *Anthologies*
Scars upon my heart. — London : Virago, Nov.1981. — [208]p
ISBN 0-86068-226-9 (pbk) : £3.75 : CIP entry
B81-30398

821′.912′0809415 — Poetry in English. Irish writers, *1900- — Anthologies*
Contemporary Irish poetry : an anthology / edited with introduction and notes, by Anthony Bradley. — Berkeley ; London : University of California Press, c1980. — xvii,430p : ports ; 24cm
Includes index
ISBN 0-520-03389-2 : £8.95 B81-00352

Irish poetry after Yeats : seven poets : Austin Clarke, Richard Murphy, Patrick Kavanagh, Thomas Kinsella, Denis Devlin, John Montague, Seamus Heaney / edited by Maurice Harmon. — Portmarnock (98 Ardilaum, Portmarnock, Co. Dublin) : Wolfhound, 1979. — 231p : ports ; 22cm
Bibliography: p227-231
ISBN 0-905473-23-x : £6.05 B81-00353

821'.912'080942574 — Poetry in English.
Oxfordshire writers: Oxford writers, *1900-1945 — Anthologies*
Ten Oxford poets : an anthology. — Oxford (4 The Green, Horspath, Oxford OX9 1RP) : Charles Brand, 1978. — vii,54p ; 22cm
ISBN 0-9506176-0-1 (pbk) : £1.35 B81-38576

821'.912'089282 — Children's poetry in English, *1900-1980 — Anthologies*
When a goose meets a moose. — London : Evans Bross, Apr.1981. — [160]p
Originally published: Sydney : Methuen, 1980
ISBN 0-237-45561-7 : £5.95 : CIP entry
B81-02091

821'.912'09 — Free verse in English, *1900-1980 — Critical studies*
Hartman, Charles O.. Free verse : an essay on prosody / Charles O. Hartman. — Princeton ; Guildford : Princeton University Press, c1980. — x,199p ; 23cm
Bibliography: p187-193. - Includes index
ISBN 0-691-06438-5 : £7.70 B81-09941

821'.912'09 — Poetry in English, *1900-1950 — Critical studies*
Sisson, C. H.. English poetry 1900-1950. — London : Methuen, Nov.1981. — [268]p
ISBN 0-416-32100-3 (pbk) : £3.50 : CIP entry
B81-30518

Sisson, C. H.. English poetry, 1900-1950. — 2nd ed. — Manchester : Carcanet, Nov.1981. — [276]p
Previous ed.: 1971
ISBN 0-85635-393-0 : £9.95 : CIP entry
B81-31202

821'.912'09 — Poetry in English, *1900-1977.*
Political aspects
Craig, Cairns. Yeats, Eliot, Pound and the politics of poetry. — London : Croom Helm, Aug.1981. — [302]p
ISBN 0-85664-997-x : £12.95 : CIP entry
B81-15905

821'.912'09 — Poetry in English, *1900- — Critical studies*
Jarrell, Randall. Kipling, Auden & co. : essays and reviews 1935-1964 / Randall Jarrell. — Manchester : Carconet, 1981, c1980. — xii,381p ; 23cm
Includes index
ISBN 0-85635-346-9 : £9.95 B81-05805

821'.912'09358 — Poetry in English, *1900-1945.*
Special subjects: World War 1 *— Critical studies*
Lehmann, John. The English poets of the First World War / John Lehmann. — [London] : Thames and Hudson, c1981. — 144p,[32]p of plates : ill,facsims,ports ; 25cm
Bibliography: p139-140. — Includes index
ISBN 0-500-01256-3 : £6.95 B81-36508

Poetry of the First World War : a casebook / edited by Dominic Hibberd. — London : Macmillan, 1981. — 247p ; 23cm. — (Casebook series)
Bibliography: p241. - Includes index
ISBN 0-333-26120-8 (cased) : £12.00 : CIP rev.
ISBN 0-333-26121-6 (pbk) : Unpriced
B80-21005

821'.912'09358 — Poetry in English, *1900-1945.*
Special subjects: World War 1 *— Study outlines*
Schlesinger, G.. Notes on the war poets / compiled by G. Schlesinger. — London : Methuen Paperbacks, 1979. — 87p ; 20cm. — (Methuen notes)
Bibliography: p87
ISBN 0-417-21650-5 (pbk) : £0.75 B81-17596

821.914 — ENGLISH POETRY, 1945-

821'.914 — Poetry in English, *1945- — English-French parallel texts*
White, Kenneth, *1936-*. Earth dance / Kenneth White ; with a screenprint by John Christie. — Guildford ([22 Sydney Rd., Guildford, Surrey GU1 3LL]) : Circle Press, 1978. — [4]leaves : col.ill ; 31 cm
Parallel English text and French translation. — Limited ed. of 140 copies of which 125 are signed and 15 are marked Artists Proof
Unpriced (pbk)
Also classified at 769.92'4 B81-09384

821'.914 — Poetry in English, *1945- — English-Spanish parallel texts*
Paz, Octavio. Airborn = Hijos del aire / Octavio Paz & Charles Tomlinson. — London : Anvil Press Poetry, 1981. — 29p ; 22cm
Parallel Spanish text and English translation
ISBN 0-85646-072-9 (pbk) : £1.95
Primary classification 861 B81-15516

821'.914 — Poetry in English, *1945- — Texts*
Abrahams, John. A crown of sonnets : poems / by John Abrahams. — Clacton-on-Sea (91 Thoroughgood Rd., Clacton-on-Sea, Essex CO15 6DP) : Magna, c1980. — [8]p ; 11x15cm
£0.30 (pbk) B81-10300

Abse, Dannie. Way out in the centre / Dannie Abse. — London : Hutchinson, 1981. — 56p ; 23cm
ISBN 0-09-144850-6 (cased) : £5.95 : CIP rev.
ISBN 0-09-144851-4 (pbk) : £2.95 B81-04338

Adam, James S.. Biblical ballads and verses / by James S. Adam. — Edinburgh (10/24 Burlington St., Edinburgh EH6 5JH) : Claymore, c1981. — 46p ; 21cm
ISBN 0-9507492-0-6 (pbk) : £1.75 B81-20938

Adler, Jeremy. Even in April, Ferrara, and liberty / by Jeremy Adler. — Cambridge (280 Cherry Hinton Rd, Cambridge CB1 4AU) : Lobby Press, c1978. — 48p : ill ; 21cm
ISBN 0-906547-14-8 (pbk) : Unpriced
B81-19851

Ahlberg, Allan. The history of a pair of sinners : forgetting not their Ma who was one also / Allan Ahlberg & John Lawrence. — London : Granada, 1980. — 41p : ill(some col.) ; 22cm
ISBN 0-246-11325-1 : £2.95 B81-02682

Allan, Mabel Esther. The haunted valley : and other poems / by Mabel Esther Allan. — [Heswall] ([Glengarth, 11 Oldfield Way, Heswall, Wirral, Merseyside, L60 6RQ]) : M.E. Allan, c1981. — 44p ; 21cm
Unpriced (pbk) B81-24497

Amis, Kingsley. Collected poems 1944-1979 / Kingsley Amis. — Harmondsworth : Penguin, 1980, c1979. — 153p ; 19cm. — (The Penguin poets)
Originally published: London : Hutchinson, 1979
ISBN 0-14-042285-4 (pbk) : £1.50 B81-00335

Anderson, Martin. The kneeling room. — Plymouth : Blue Guitar Books ; London (12 Stevenage Rd., SW6 6ES) : Independent Press Distribution [distributor], Sept.1981. — [20]p
ISBN 0-907562-03-5 (pbk) : £0.80 : CIP entry
B81-20497

Anderson, William, *1935-*. Haddow sonata / William Anderson ; drawings by Kaffe Fassett. — Chipping Norton (35, West St., Chipping Norton, Oxon) : Anthony Kedros, 1981. — 14p : ill ; 22cm
ISBN 0-907454-00-3 (pbk) : £1.50 B81-34624

Angus, William Stephenson. Christmas cards and other verses. — Aberdeen : Aberdeen University Press, Nov.1981. — [74]p
ISBN 0-08-028462-0 (pbk) : £1.15 : CIP entry
B81-34715

Archer, Francis. Baker's dozen : poems / by Francis Archer. — London (14 Barlly Rd. W10 6AR) : Autolycus, [1978?]. — 16p ; 21cm
Unpriced (pbk) B81-33510

Archer, Nuala. Whale on the line / Nuala Archer. — Dublin : Gallery Books, 1981. — 41p ; 22cm
ISBN 0-904011-21-6 (cased) : £4.95
ISBN 0-904011-22-4 (pbk) : £1.98 B81-32938

Armstrong, James. Shadows and silence / by James Armstrong. — Walton-on-Thames : Outposts, 1981. — 11p ; 21cm
£0.60 (pbk) B81-27857

Armstrong, Paul, *1913-*. Word-webs and echoes : a book of poems / by Paul Armstrong. — Walton-on-Thames (70 Holly Ave., Walton-on-Thames, Surrey KT12 3AU) : Paul Newlin, c1981. — 2v. : ill ; 21cm
Vol.1=£1.20, Vol.2=£1.20
Unpriced (pbk) B81-24783

Arrowsmith, Pat. On the brink — : poems / by Pat Arrowsmith. — London (11, Goodwin St., N4 3HQ) : Campaign for Nuclear Disarmament, 1981. — 23p : ill ; 16x21cm
Text on inside covers
ISBN 0-907321-00-3 (pbk) : £0.60 B81-26652

Ash, John. The bed. — London : Oasis, Aug.1981. — [56]p
ISBN 0-903375-58-3 (pbk) : £1.50 : CIP entry
B81-22603

Ayres, Pam. The ballad of Bill Spinks' bedstead. — London : Severn House, Oct.1981. — [64]p
ISBN 0-7278-2018-4 (pbk) : £1.75 : CIP entry
B81-31096

Baines, Peter G.. Concrete : poems / by Peter G. Baines. — London (71 St. Augustines Rd., NW1 9RR) : Street Talk Press, c1979. — 51p ; 21cm
Limited ed. of 100 numbered copies signed by the author
£3.00 (pbk) B81-03607

Baldwin, Marjorie. English summer / by Marjorie Baldwin. — Walton-on-Thames : Outposts, 1981. — 36p ; 21cm
Unpriced (pbk) B81-27856

Baldwin, Michael. Snook / by Michael Baldwin. — London : Phoenix-Springwood, 1980. — 47p ; 25cm
ISBN 0-905947-87-8 (pbk) : £3.00 B81-08033

Banks, William. Sing me a song / William Banks. — Ilfracombe : Stockwell, 1981. — 30p ; 19cm
ISBN 0-7223-1444-2 : £2.40 B81-16772

Barker, M. M. W.. Golden haze / by M.M.W. Barker. — [London] : Regency, c1981. — 25p ; 19cm
Unpriced (pbk) B81-05883

Barker, Sebastian. Epistles, or, Final pagan poems / Sebastian Barker. — London : Martin Brian & O'Keeffe, 1980. — 57p ; 23cm
ISBN 0-85616-181-0 : £3.00 B81-02076

Barkochba, Adam. A brief account of life in a foreign kingdom / Adam Barkochba. — Coatbridge (3 Rannoch Ave., Coatbridge, Lanarkshire ML5 2JF) : A. Barkochba, c1981. — 15leaves ; 30cm
ISBN 0-9507545-0-1 (pbk) : Unpriced
B81-28281

Barnes, Keith. Devolution, evolution and revolution / Keith Barnes. — Bognor Regis : New Horizon, c1981. — 62p ; 21cm
Originally published: Ilfracombe : Stockwell, 1976
ISBN 0-86116-231-5 : £3.95 B81-19553

Barnett, Anthony. A white mess / Anthony Barnett. — London (25 Woodhall Drive, SE21 7HJ) : The Literary Supplement, 1981. — 19p : ill ; 15cm + 1 leaflet(3p ; 15cm)
Limited ed. of 120 copies
ISBN 0-901494-18-6 (pbk) : £2.10 B81-16493

Baxter, S. G.. Modern times / S.G. Baxter. — Bognor Regis : New Horizon, c1980. — 59p ; 21cm
ISBN 0-86116-310-9 : £2.95 B81-19065

Baybars, Taner. Pregnant shadows : poems / Taner Baybars. — London : Sidgwick & Jackson, 1981. — 44p ; 22cm
ISBN 0-283-98757-x (pbk) : £3.50 B81-36179

821'.914 — Poetry in English, *1945-* — Texts *continuation*

Beard, I.. Poetic images / I. Beard. — Ilfracombe : Stockwell, 1981. — 20p ; 15cm
ISBN 0-7223-1523-6 (pbk) : £0.55 B81-39395

Beckinsale, Richard. With love / Richard Beckinsale ; foreword by Judy Beckinsale. — London : Muller, 1980. — 80p : ill,ports ; 23cm
Includes index
ISBN 0-584-10387-5 : £3.50 : CIP rev.
B80-22642

Bendon, Chris. In praise of low music / Chris Bendon. — Lampeter : Outcrop, c1981. — 56p ; 21cm
Cover title. — Text on inside covers
Unpriced (pbk) B81-38682

Bennett, Roy, *1925-*. Images of summer / Roy Bennett. — Sutton (26 Cedar Rd., Sutton, Surrey) : Hippopotamus Press, 1981. — 87p ; 22cm
ISBN 0-904179-25-7 (pbk) : £4.50 : CIP rev.
ISBN 0-904179-26-5 (signed ed) : Unpriced
B80-35405

Beresford, Anne. Songs a Thracian taught me / Anne Beresford. — London : Boyars, 1980. — 63p : 22 ; 22cm
ISBN 0-7145-2724-6 (cased) : £4.95 : CIP rev.
ISBN 0-7145-2725-4 (pbk) : £2.95 B80-17926

Berry, Pual, *1953-*. Legacies / Paul Berry. — King's Lynn ([7 Walsingham Close, Priory Park, South Wootton, King's Lynn PE30 3TF]) : Scree, [1981]. — 47p ; 21cm
ISBN 0-907421-00-8 (pbk) : £1.50 B81-15420

Bevis, John. Four seasons & two minutes at the Swan / John Bevis. — London (49 Danbury St., N1) : Suet Pudding, 1980. — [10]leaves ; 13cm
Limited ed. of 100 copies
Unpriced (pbk) B81-36417

Bielski, Alison. Night sequence / Alison Bielski. — Tenby (3 Harbour Court, Bridge St., Tenby, Dyfed) : A. Bielski, c1981. — 12p ; 22cm
Cover title
ISBN 0-9502562-5-0 (pbk) : £0.65 B81-21192

Bielski, Alsion. Seth : a poem sequence / by Alsion Bielski. — [Bakewell] ([Youlgrave, Bakewell, Derbyshire DE4 1WL]) : Hub Publications, c1980. — 28p ; 21cm
ISBN 0-905049-66-7 (pbk) : £0.80 B81-07239

Bingham, Grace. The undefeated / by Grace Bingham. — Walton-on-Thames : Outposts, 1981. — 12p ; 21cm
£0.60 (pbk) B81-39335

Binny, Bert. What's it all about? / Bert Binny. — Ilfracombe : Stockwell, 1980. — 84p ; 15cm
ISBN 0-7223-1406-x : £2.75 B81-03023

Birch, Clarice A.. 'Lampo' and other poems / Clarice A. Birch. — Ilfracombe : Stockwell, 1981. — 32p ; 15cm
ISBN 0-7223-1511-2 : £2.40 B81-39390

Bissell, Winifred. Sequel : a collection of poems / by Winifred Bissell. — [Wallasey] ([2 College Close, Wallasey, Merseyside]) : [S.J. Hughes], [1981?]. — 32p ; 21cm
Cover title
Unpriced (pbk) B81-39429

Blair-Giles, Brian. Open air poems / by Brian Blair-Giles. — 2nd ed. — 16p ; 15cm
Previous ed.: 1968
£0.30 (pbk) B81-17009

Blake, Quentin. Mister Magnolia / Quentin Blake. — [London] : Fontana Picture Lions, 1981, c1980. — [32]p : col.ill ; 22cm
Originally published: London : Cape, 1980
ISBN 0-00-661879-0 (pbk) : £0.90 B81-36776

Bland, Peter. Stone tents / Peter Bland. — London : London Magazine Editions, 1981. — vi,60p ; 22cm
ISBN 0-904388-40-9 (pbk) : £3.50 B81-02540

Boadella, David. Baptism of fire / by David Boadella. — Weymouth (Abbotsbury, Weymouth, Dorset) : Abbotsbury Publications, 1981. — 40p ; 21cm
Unpriced (pbk) B81-17665

Bocks, Sheila M. L.. A journey through the year : and other poems for young people / Sheila M.L. Bocks. — Ilfracombe : Stockwell, 1981. — 30p ; 15cm
ISBN 0-7223-1499-x : £2.40 B81-39396

Booth, Martin, *1944-*. Devil's wine / poems by Martin Booth. — Gerrards Cross : Smythe, 1980. — 112p ; 22cm
Also available in a limited signed ed
ISBN 0-86140-039-9 (cased) : £6.25 : CIP rev.
ISBN 0-86140-044-5 (pbk) : £3.25
ISBN 0-86140-066-6 (signed ed.) : £12.50
B80-08371

Bowes, T. A.. A collection of poems and lyrics / by T.A. Bowes. — [Guisborough] ([19, Woodhouse Rd, Guisborough, Cleveland TS14 6 LH]) : T.A. Bowes, 1981. — 12p ; 21cm
Unpriced (pbk) B81-21984

Brackenbury, Alison. Dreams of power : and other poems / Alison Brackenbury. — Manchester : Coronet New Press, 1981. — 103p ; 20cm
ISBN 0-85635-352-3 (pbk) : £2.95 B81-12167

Bray, David A.. The poetry of steam / by David A. Bray. — [Nazeing] ([16 Long Green, Nazeing, Nr Waltham Abbey, Essex EN9 2LS]) : D.A. Bray, 1980. — [16]p : ill ; 21cm
Cover title. — Text on inside cover
£1.50 (pbk) B81-06478

Brooking, Doris. Random Rhymes / Doris Brooking. — Ilfracombe : Stockwell, 1981. — 32p ; 15cm
ISBN 0-7223-1502-3 (pbk) : £0.97 B81-35042

Brown, George, *1944-*. Sam Martin and the pigeon club / George Brown ; illustrated by Julie Ann Noad. — Yoxford ([Yoxford Bookshop, High St.,] Yoxford, nor Saxmundham, Suffolk) : Yoxford Publications, 1981. — 35p : 1ill ; 21cm
ISBN 0-907265-02-2 (pbk) : £1.00 B81-29836

Browne, Margaret. Rook country / by Margaret Browne. — Gravesend (Victoria Centre for Adult Education, Darnley Rd., Gravesend, Kent) : Victoria Press, 1981. — 19p ; 21cm. — (Writers of South East England ; no.1)
ISBN 0-907165-01-x (pbk) : £0.75 B81-34854

Browning, Stella. Adventures of Hoodie the crow / by Stella Browning. — New Romney (2 Highfield, Sussex Rd., New Romney, Kent) : Stella Browning Productions, 1972 (1977 [Printing]). — [77]p : ill,1port ; 21cm
Unpriced (pbk) B81-24762

Browning, Stella. Butter in the buttercups : pt.3 winter sequence ; Notail at Wesley : tail of a blackbird : Summer 1976 / Stella Browning. — [Elstree] (55 Barham Ave., Elstree, Herts.) : [Stella Browning Productions], [1977]. — 94p : ill,ports ; 21cm
Unpriced (pbk) B81-24761

Browning, Stella. Butter in the buttercups : pts 1, 2 and 3 / Stella Browning. — 3rd ed. — Elstree (55 Barham Ave., Elstree, Herts.) : Stella Browning Productions, [1978]. — [69]p : ill,ports ; 21cm
Previous ed.: 1977
Unpriced (pbk) B81-24760

Brownjohn, Alan. A night in the gazebo / Alan Brownjohn. — London : Secker & Warburg, 1980. — 64p ; 23cm
ISBN 0-436-07114-2 : £3.00 B81-02136

Bruley, Elaine. Sea, with ships / by Elaine Bruley. — Walton-on-Thames : Outposts, 1981. — 16p ; 21cm
£0.70 (pbk) B81-20900

Bryant, Victor, *1943-*. Traveller's tales / Victor Bryant. — Bognor Regis : New Horizon, c1981. — 95p ; 21cm
ISBN 0-86116-394-x : £2.95 B81-26493

Buchanan, Derek. Looking forward / by Derek Buchanan. — Walton-on-Thames : Outposts, 1980. — 24p ; 21cm
£1.00 (pbk) B81-03257

Bura, Paul. The space between the syllables / Paul Bura. — Edinburgh : Evergreen Books, c1979. — 64p ; 21cm
ISBN 0-284-98631-3 : £2.10 B81-30699

Burchell, Betty. The poems of a country lady : — about village people, nature, birds and animals / compiled by Betty Burchell of the village of Great Tew, Oxfordshire. — 2nd ed. — Oxford : Hannon, 1980. — [20]p : ill ; 21cm
Cover title. — Previous ed.: 1979. — Text on inside cover
Unpriced (pbk) B81-33546

Burchett, Philip J.. Farewell to travellers : verses including two librettos / Philip J. Burchett. — London : Howard Baker, 1980. — 135p ; 23cm
ISBN 0-7030-0193-0 : £1.95 B81-32094

Burnett, David, *1937-*. Jackdaw / David Burnett ; with engravings by Kirill Sokolov. — Durham ([33 Hastings Ave., Durham]) : Black Cygnet Press, 1980. — 64p : ill ; 15x21cm
Unpriced (pbk) B81-08052

Burnett, David, *1937-*. Jackdaw / David Burnett ; with engravings by Kirill Sokolov. — Edinburgh ([137 Warrender Park Rd., Edinburgh EH9 1DS]) : Tragara, 1980, c1979. — 67p : ill ; 20cm
Limited ed. of 150 copies
ISBN 0-902616-57-9 (pbk) : £3.00 B81-00336

Burnett, David, *1937-*. Thais / David Burnett. — London : Black Cygnet, 1981. — 54p ; 15cm
Limited ed. of 150 copies
ISBN 0-9504352-3-6 (pbk) : Unpriced
B81-33733

Caddick, Arthur. Chance medley / Arthur Caddick ; with drawings by Rigby Graham. — [Leicester] ([78 Cambridge St., Leicester LE3 2JP]) : Toni Savage at New Broom, c1981. — [18]p : ill ; 21cm
Limited ed. of 100 numbered copies
ISBN 0-901870-52-8 (pbk) : £6.00 B81-19432

Caddick, Arthur. The jester / Arthur Caddick ; drawings by Pantopuck. — [Leicester] (c/o Toni Savage, 78 Cambridge St., Leicester [LE3 0JP]) : New Broom Private Press, 1981. — [7]p : 2ill ; 21cm
Limited ed. of 100 numbered copies
ISBN 0-901870-50-1 (unbound) : £2.00
B81-10530

Caddick, Arthur. The singing heart / Arthur Caddick ; drawings by Rigby Graham. — Leicester (78 Cambridge St., Leicester) : Toni Savage, 1981. — [10]p : ill ; 21cm
Limited ed. of 90 numbered copies signed by the publisher
ISBN 0-901870-55-2 (pbk) : £2.00 B81-24584

Caddick, Arthur. Windswept / poems by Arthur Caddick ; drawings by Kathie Layfield. — Leicester (78 Cambridge St., Leicester) : New Broom Private Press, 1981. — [14]p : ill ; 21cm
Limited ed. of 90 numbered copies
ISBN 0-901870-56-0 (pbk) : £3.00 B81-35585

Caddy, Eileen. The dawn of change : selections from daily guidance on human problems / Eileen Caddy ; edited by Roy McVicar. — Forres : Findhorn Publications, 1979. — xvi,172p ; 21cm
ISBN 0-905249-39-9 (pbk) : £2.40 B81-36405

821′.914 — Poetry in English, *1945-* — *Texts continuation*

Cairncross, *Sir* Alec. Snatches / Alec Cairncross. — Gerrards Cross : Smythe, 1980. — 43p ; 22cm
ISBN 0-86140-051-8 (pbk) : Unpriced : CIP rev. B80-05582

Cameron, Bella. Sardonic taskmaster / by Bella Cameron. — St Annes-on-Sea (Flat 2, 22 York Rd., St Annes-on-Sea FY8 1HP, Lancashire) : B. Cameron, c1981. — 15p ; 21cm
Cover title
£0.50 (pbk) B81-15956

Carlson, Michael. Winter lovers / Michael Carlson. — Frome (45 Milk St., Frome, Somerset) : Bran′s Head, 1981. — 23p ; 15cm. — (Hunting Raven chapbooks ; 4)
Limited ed. of 325 copies of which the first 20 are signed by the author
£0.90 (pbk) B81-32101

Carr, David, *1943-*. Fruit & veg : poems / by David Carr ; with drawings by Tony Burrell. — Clacton-on-Sea (91 Thoroughgood Rd., Clacton-on-Sea, Essex) : Magma, c1980. — [13]p : ill ; 15cm
£0.30 (pbk) B81-07117

Carradice, Phil. Night walking / Phil Carradice. — [Shoeburyness] ([71, Cunningham Close, Shoeburyness, Essex]) : Sol Publications, [c1981]. — 10p ; 21cm
Cover title
ISBN 0-907376-10-x (pbk) : £0.40 B81-34192

Caws, Ian. Boy with a kite : poems / Ian Caws. — London : Sidgwick & Jackson, 1981. — 59p ; 22cm
ISBN 0-283-98707-3 (pbk) : £3.95 B81-09363

Challis, Chris. William of Cloudeslee / Chris Challis. — Leicester (67 Prospect-Hill, Leicester LE5 3RT) : Daft Lad Press, 1980. — [8]p : ill ; 21cm
ISBN 0-86155-900-2 (pbk) : Unpriced B81-07857

Chapman, Ethel. The gift & other poems / Ethel Chapman. — Bognor Regis : New Horizon, c1979. — 38p : facsims ; 21cm
ISBN 0-86116-195-5 : £1.95 B81-19066

Charles, Emma. Darkness-Light / Emma Charles. — Ilfracombe : Stockwell, 1981. — 14p ; 15cm
ISBN 0-7223-1471-x (pbk) : £0.50 B81-22334

Cherjo. Swan song / Cherjo. — Edwardstown : Cherjo ; Ilfracombe : Stockwell [[distributor]], 1981. — 12p ; 15cm
ISBN 0-7223-1460-4 (pbk) : Unpriced B81-35034

Childish, Billy. 2 minits walk from 10 am / Billy Childish. — Chatham (181 Walderslade Rd, Chatham, Kent) : Phyroid Press, c1981. — 13p ; 21cm
Unpriced (unbound) B81-40674

Childish, Billy. Back on red lite rd. / Billy Childish. — Chatham (181 Walderslade Rd, Chatham, Kent) : Phyroid Press, c1981. — 18p : 1port ; 22cm
Unpriced (unbound) B81-40675

Childish, Billy. The dog jaw woman / Billy Childish. — Chatham (181 Walderslade Rd., Chatham, Kent) : Phyroid, 1980. — 22p : ill,1port ; 21cm
Cover title. — Port on cover
Unpriced (pbk) B81-09954

Childish, Billy. The man with weels / [Billy Childish] ; [photographs by o′Neal]. — [Chatham] ([181 Walderslade Rd, Chatham, Kent]) : Phyroid Press, 1980 (1981 [printing]). — [8]p : ill ; 22cm
Cover title. — Text and ill on inside covers
Unpriced (pbk) B81-40676

Claessen, George. Poems about nothing / George Claessen. — Ilfracombe : Stockwell, 1981. — 40p ; 15cm
ISBN 0-7223-1466-3 (pbk) : £2.50 B81-22333

Clennell, Claire. Enjoy every day / Claire Clennell. — Douglas (1 Hope St., Douglas, Isle of Man) : C. Clennell, 1980. — 32p ; 21cm
Unpriced (pbk) B81-28636

Clifton, Harry. Office of the salt merchant / Harry Clifton. — Dublin : Gallery Books, c1979. — 49p ; 22cm
Also available in pbk : £1.98
£3.96 B81-15409

Clitheroe, Frederic. Forsbrook / by Frederic Clitheroe. — Walton-on-Thames : Outposts, 1980. — 25p ; 21cm
£0.90 (pbk) B81-07230

Coady, Michael. Two for a woman, three for a man / Michael Coady. — Dublin (19 Oakdown Rd., Dublin 14) : Gallery Books, 1980. — 34p ; 23cm
ISBN 0-902996-98-3 (cased) : £3.60(Irish) B81-14277

Cocker, W. D.. Poems : Scots and English / by W.D. Cocker. — Glasgow : Brown, Son & Ferguson, 1979. — 220p ; 19cm
Originally published: 1932. — Includes index
ISBN 0-85174-301-3 : £5.50 B81-20690

Colman, Dan. I never saw my father nude / by Dan Colman. — London : A.Baker, c1981. — [72]p : ill ; 21cm
ISBN 0-213-16791-3 : £3.50 B81-16058

Compton Miller, John. The Chinese saucer / John Compton Miller. — [London] (Sylvias, 25 Beauchamp Place, S.W.1) : [J. Compton Miller], 1980. — 27p ; 21cm
Limited ed. of 100 numbered copies signed by the author
£1.95 (pbk) B81-32377

Constantine, David J.. A brightness to cast shadows / David Constantine. — Newcastle upon Tyne (1 North Jesmond Avenue, Jesmond, Newcastle upon Tyne NE2 3JX) : Bloodaxe, 1980. — 55p ; 22cm
Also available in limited edition of 25 numbered and signed copies
ISBN 0-906427-14-2 (pbk) : £2.50 (signed ed.) : £2.50 B81-09546

Conway, Hilda M.. Songs in the evening / by Hilda Conway. — [s.l.] : [H. Conway], c1980. — 32p ; 19cm
Unpriced (pbk) B81-05886

Conway, Karen. Thoughts of a dreamer / Karen Conway. — Bognor Regis : New Horizon, c1979. — 56p ; 21cm
ISBN 0-86116-375-3 : £2.50 B81-18873

Corbett, William. Schedule rhapsody / William Corbett. — Durham (7 Cross View Terrace, Neville′s Cross, Durham DH1 4JY) : Pig, 1980. — 23p ; 22cm
ISBN 0-903997-48-7 (pbk) : £1.90
ISBN 0-903997-55-x (signed) : £6.00 B81-09873

Cotton, John, *1925-*. Day book / John Cotton. — Berkhamstead (37 Lombardy Drive, Berkhamstead, Herts.) : J. Cotton, c1981. — [12]leaves ; 23cm. — (Priapus poets)
Cover title
Unpriced (pbk) B81-09682

Cotton, John, *1925-*. Day book / John Cotton. — [Berkhamsted] : Priapus Poets, c1981. — 12 leaves ; 26cm
Cover title. — Limited ed. of 80 copies
Unpriced (pbk) B81-13680

Cotton, John, *1925-*. The Totleigh riddles / John Cotton. — Berkhamsted (Berkhamsted, Herts.) : Priapus Poets, c1981. — [13]p ; 16cm
Limited ed. of 200 copies, of which 40 are numbered and signed by the author
£0.50 (pbk) B81-32580

Cox, C. B.. Every common sight / C.B. Cox. — [London] : London Magazine Editions, 1981. — vii,43p ; 23cm
ISBN 0-904388-37-9 (cased) : Unpriced
ISBN 0-904388-38-7 (pbk) : £3.00 B81-02884

Cox, Lilian. Christmas candles : an anthology of verse / by Lilian Cox. — Redhill : National Christian Education Council, 1981. — 24p ; 19cm
ISBN 0-7197-0291-7 (pbk) : £0.60 B81-28396

Crampton, Sean. Humans, beasts, birds / sculptures, Sean Crampton ; photographs, Clive Hicks ; poems, William Anderson. — Chipping Norton (35 West St., Chipping Norton,) : Kedros, 1981. — v,26p : ill ; 21cm
ISBN 0-907454-01-1 (pbk) : £3.60
Also classified at 730′.92′4 B81-35016

Crick, Philip. Episodes. — Plymouth : Blue Guitar Books ; London (12 Stevenage Rd., SW6 6ES) : Independent Press Distribution [distributor], Sept.1981. — [16]p
ISBN 0-907562-02-7 (pbk) : £0.80 : CIP entry B81-20498

Crowhurst, Gordon G.. Mixed spice / Gordon G. Crowhurst. — Ilfracombe : Stockwell, 1981. — 79p ; 15cm
ISBN 0-7223-1459-0 (pbk) : £2.86 B81-22332

Cullingford, Ada. Collection of poems / Ada Cullingford. — Ilfracombe : Stockwell, 1981
Vol.VII. — 1981. — 72p : 1port ; 15cm
ISBN 0-7223-1462-0 (pbk) : £2.86 B81-22331

Curwen, Ursula J.. Stranger at home / Ursula J. Curwen. — Pilling (Bambino, Smallwood Hey, Pilling, Preston, Lancs. PR3 6HJ) : Seek You Enterprises, 1981. — [66]p : ill(some col.) ; 22cm
Limited ed. of 160 numbered copies
ISBN 0-9507644-0-x (spiral) : Unpriced B81-34068

Dale, Douglas. The collected works of Douglas Dale. — London : Regency, c1980. — 32p ; 19cm
Unpriced (pbk) B81-05830

Davie, Donald. Three for water-music ; and, The shires / Donald Davie. — Manchester : Carcanet, 1981. — 69p ; 20cm
ISBN 0-85635-363-9 (pbk) : £2.95 : CIP rev. B81-14454

Davies, H. B.. Light and liberty / H.B. Davies. — Ilfracombe : Stockwell, 1981. — 32p : ill ; 15cm
ISBN 0-7223-1454-x (pbk) : £0.97 B81-18415

Davies, John, *1944 Mar.28-*. At the edge of town / John Davies. — Llandysul : Gomer, 1981. — 75p : ill ; 22cm
ISBN 0-85088-923-5 : £3.50 B81-16472

Davies, Rosaleen. A titter of wit / Rosaleen Davies. — Belfast : Blackstaff, c1980. — 66p : ill ; 22cm
ISBN 0-85640-236-2 (pbk) : £2.50 B81-01189

Davis, Betty. What d′you think′s wrong with our Betty? : down to earth poems for down to earth women / by Betty Davis ; with illustrations by Vivian Adcock. — Solihull (90, Mill La., Bentley Heath, Solihull) : Real Life, c1980. — 40p : ill ; 22cm
Unpriced (pbk) B81-03258

821'.914 — Poetry in English, *1945-* — *Texts continuation*

Dawson, Patricia. La lanterne des morts : lines written in Ludlow after visiting Blaenau Ffestiniog / by Patricia Dawson. — London (142, Elgin Ave, Maida Vale, W9 2NS) : Ram Press, 1980. — [22]p : ill ; 21cm
Limited ed. of 200 signed and numbered copies
ISBN 0-9507117-0-5 (pbk) : Unpriced B81-35661

De Alteriis, Peter. Reflections / Peter de Alteriis. — [London] ([33 Colin Cres., NW9 6EU]) : Midsummer Press, c1981. — [20]p ; 24cm
Unpriced (pbk) B81-34622

Deane, John F.. High sacrifice. — Portlaoise : Dolmen Press, June 1981. — [56]p
ISBN 0-85105-383-1 (cased) : £10.00 : CIP entry
ISBN 0-85105-382-3 (pbk) : £3.00 B81-18071

Deeks, Elizabeth. Crossroads : Christian verse / by Elizabeth Deeks. — Ilkeston : Moorley, [1980]. — 31p ; 21cm
ISBN 0-86071-098-x (pbk) : £0.50 B81-02165

Denning, T. H.. Too deep for tears / T.H. Denning. — Bognor Regis : New Horizon, c1979. — 72p,[12]leaves of plates : ill ; 21cm
ISBN 0-86116-100-9 : £2.95 B81-19244

Denson, Alan. Personal inflexions / by Alan Denson. — [Aberdeen] : [A. Denson] ; [Aberdeen] ([Basement Right, 4 Spital, Aberdeen]) : Distributed by Oliver Alden, 1981. — 24p ; 15cm
Limited ed. of 150 numbered copies
£3.00 (pbk) B81-24817

Denson, Alan. Sardonic fancies / by Alan Denson. — [Aberdeen] : [A. Denson] ; [Aberdeen] ([Basement Right, 4 Spital, Aberdeen]) : Distributed by Oliver Alden, 1981. — xi,14p ; 15cm
Limited ed. of 150 numbered copies
£3.00 (pbk) B81-24818

Dent, Peter. Distant lamps / Peter Dent. — Sutton (26 Cedar Rd., Sutton, Surrey) : Hippopotamus, 1980. — 68p ; 22cm
Limited ed. of 625 copies. — Also available in a limited ed. of 25 numbered copies signed by the author
ISBN 0-904179-23-0 (pbk) : £2.70 : CIP rev.
ISBN 0-904179-24-9 (signed ed.) : unpriced B80-00873

Dewar, Hugo. Arsy-versy world : poems / by Hugo Dewar ; with an introduction by Paul Foot and drawings by Phil Evans. — London (265 Seven Sisters Rd., N4 2DE) : Bookmarks, 1981. — 43p : ill ; 21cm
ISBN 0-906224-05-5 (pbk) : £1.00 B81-28489

Digance, Richard. Animal alphabet / Richard Digance ; with illustrations by Diana Gold. — London : Joseph, 1980. — 75p : ill ; 21cm
ISBN 0-7181-1960-6 : £4.50 B81-00337

Dodsworth, Nellie. Selected poems / Nellie Dodsworth. — [York?] : Barbara Whitehead, 1979. — 37p : ill ; 23cm
Includes index
£1.00 (pbk) B81-39388

Dollar, Ivor. Refractions : random poems before and in Battle 1938-75 / by Ivor Dollar. — Battle (House-Carl House, 2 Lower Lake, Battle, East Sussex) : I.W.M. Dollar, 1975. — 12p ; 21cm
Cover title
£0.25 (pbk) B81-38662

Dollar, Ivor. Refractions II : random poems before and in Battle 1938-77 / by Ivor Dollar. — Battle (House-Carl House, 2 Lower Lake, Battle, East Sussex) : I.W.M. Dollar, 1977. — 12p ; 21cm
Cover title
Unpriced (pbk) B81-38661

Dollar, Ivor. Thinks : Sri Lanka, Malta, Battle 1978 / by Ivor Dollar. — Battle (House-Carl House, 2 Lower Lake, Battle, East Sussex) : I.W.M. Dollar, 1978. — 19p ; 21cm
Cover title. — Ill on inside cover
Unpriced (pbk) B81-38663

Downie, Freda. Plainsong. — London : Secker & Warburg, June 1981. — [64]p
ISBN 0-436-13251-6 : £4.50 : CIP entry B81-09467

Drobniewska, Maria. Rain will fall : poems / by Maria Drobniewska. — West Hanney (The White Cottage, Main St., West Hanney, Oxon) : Whycot Press, 1980. — [24]p ; 21cm
ISBN 0-9506764-1-1 (pbk) : Unpriced B81-06671

Dunn, Douglas. St. Kilda's parliament / Douglas Dunn. — London : Faber, 1981. — 87p ; 20cm. — (Faber paperbacks)
ISBN 0-571-11770-8 (pbk) : £3.00 : CIP rev. B81-28025

East, D. G.. Life in the valley / D.G. East ; illustrated by Cora E.M. Paterson. — Ilfracombe : Stockwell, 1981. — 41p : ill ; 15cm
ISBN 0-7223-1481-7 (pbk) : Unpriced B81-35044

Edgell, David. A book of melancholy : verse and illustration / by David Edgell. — London (14 Barlby Rd, W10 6AR) : Autolycus, [1981?]. — 48p : ill ; 21cm
Unpriced (pbk) B81-33512

Edwards, Frederick, *1909-*. Rambling and rhyming / Frederick Edwards ; [illustrations by Hilary Jackson-Edwards]. — Bognor Regis : New Horizon, c1979. — 43p : ill ; 21cm
ISBN 0-86116-341-9 : £2.50 B81-18877

Elertowicz, Lisa Jozefa. Between the juggler and the fool : poems / by Lisa Jozefa Elertowicz ; with illustrations by Barbara Robertson. — S.l. : S.n., 1979 (Edinburgh : R&R Clark). — 37p : ill ; 22cm
£3.25 B81-12482

Elsberg, John. Walking, as a controlled fall / by John Elsberg. — Torpoint (Knill Cross House, Higher Anderton Rd., Millbrook, Torpoint, Cornwall) : Kawabata, 1980. — [18]p ; 21cm
ISBN 0-906110-24-6 (pbk) : £0.20 B81-11283

Emmott, Stewart Earl. Fading innocence / Stewart Earl Emmott. — Dorking (9 Lakeview Cottage, Westcott, Dorking, Surrey) : S.E. Emmott, 1980. — 48p : 1port ; 18cm
ISBN 0-7223-1416-7 (pbk) : Unpriced B81-07983

Ennis, John. A drink of spring / John Ennis. — Dublin (19 Oakdown Rd., Dublin 14) : Gallery Books, c1979. — 49p ; 23cm
Also available in paperback at £1.80(Irish)
£3.60(Irish) (cased) B81-14275

Enright, D. J.. Collected poems / D.J. Enright. — Oxford : Oxford University Press, 1981. — x,262p ; 23cm
ISBN 0-19-211941-9 : £10.00 : CIP rev. B81-23741

Enters, Ian. Calendar of the Greeks / by Ian Enters. — Walton-on-Thames : Outposts, 1981. — 37p ; 21cm
£1.20 (pbk) B81-09367

Entwistle, Stella. The latent power / by Stella Entwistle. — Walton-on-Thames : Outposts, 1980. — 12p ; 21cm
£0.50 (pbk) B81-00338

Evans, Douglas, *1945-*. Part of my ray / by Douglas Evans. — Reading (19 Downshire Sq., Reading, Berks.) : Self Press, c1981. — [28] leaves ; 30cm
ISBN 0-9507674-0-9 (unbound) : £0.50 B81-35134

Fainlight, Ruth. Two wind poems / Ruth Fainlight. — Knotting (Knotting, Beds.) : Martin Booth, [1980]. — [7]p ; 17cm
Limited ed. of 125 numbered copies, of which the first 50 are signed by the author
£3.50 (£10.50 signed) (pbk) B81-06639

Fearn, Susan. Sixteen poems / Susan Fearn. — Wolverhampton : Handaxe Press, c1981. — [24]p ; 21cm
ISBN 0-9507572-0-9 (pbk) : £0.50 B81-28293

Fenton, James. A German requiem : a poem / by James Fenton. — Edinburgh (73 Morningside Park, Edinburgh, EH10 5EZ) : Salamander Press, 1981, c1980. — 9p ; 28cm
Unpriced (pbk) B81-10397

Fenton, Peter. The leaf burners / Peter Fenton. — Beverley (28 Railway St., Beverley [North Humberside HU17 0DX]) : Paston Press, 1980. — 36p ; 21cm
ISBN 0-907217-00-1 (pbk) : £1.10 : CIP rev. B80-11151

Fetherston, Patrick. Tremens / by Patrick Fetherston. — London (14 Frognal, London N.W.3) : Tetralith, c1978. — [16]p : ill ; 26cm
ISBN 0-9501160-8-4 (spiral) : Unpriced B81-01190

Ffinch, Michael. Simon's garden / Michael Ffinch. — Kendal (28 Highgate, Kendal) : Titus Wilson, 1981. — [34p] : ill ; 30cm
ISBN 0-900811-14-5 (pbk) : £3.00 B81-15799

Ffinch, Michael. Westmorland poems / by Michael Ffinch ; with drawings by Caroline A. Metcalfe-Gibson. — Kendal (28 Highgate, Kendal [Cumbria]) : Titus Wilson, 1980. — 40p : ill ; 25cm
ISBN 0-900811-11-0 (pbk) : £3.50 B81-02484

Finlay, Ian Hamilton. Romances, emblems, enigmas / Ian Hamilton Finlay. — [Carnwarth] : Wild Hawthorn Press, [1981]. — [14]leaves ; 15cm
Unpriced (pbk) B81-10714

Fish, Pete. Swallowtale : and other birdverse / by Pete Fish ; illustrated by Patrick Franks. — Padstow ([11 Church St., Padstow, Cornwall PL28 8BG]) : Tabb House, 1981. — 47p : ill ; 21cm
ISBN 0-907018-08-4 (pbk) : £1.30 B81-34873

Fisher, Roy. Poems 1955-1980 / Roy Fisher. — Oxford : Oxford University Press, 1980. — 193p ; 23cm
ISBN 0-19-211935-4 : £7.95 : CIP rev. B80-21009

Fisher, Stanley. Scenes from a love life — the greatest : and other poems / Stanley Fisher. — Grantham (Irnham, Grantham, Lincs. [NG33 4JG]) : S. Fisher, c1981. — 54leaves ; 21cm
ISBN 0-905143-04-3 (pbk) : £1.25 B81-37375

Flynn, Tony, *1951-*. A strange routine / Tony Flynn. — Newcastle upon Tyne (1 North Jesmond Avenue, Jesmond, Newcastle upon Tyne NE2 3JX) : Bloodaxe, 1980. — 55p ; 22cm
Also available in limited edition of 25 numbered and signed copies
ISBN 0-906427-20-7 (pbk) : £2.50
ISBN 0-906427-21-5 (signed ed.) : £2.50 B81-09547

Foord, Kathleen Hilton. Poems / by Kathleen Hilton Foord. — Ramsgate : Island Print, 1981. — 20p ; 21cm
Unpriced (pbk) B81-28294

Forrester, Alan. Pocketbook poetry / by Alan Forrester. — [Stirling] ([Unit of Aquatic Pathobiology, University of Stirling, Stirling, Scotland]) : [A. Forrester], c1979. — 19p ; 15cm
ISBN 0-9506857-0-4 (pbk) : Unpriced B81-08493

821′.914 — Poetry in English, *1945-* — *Texts continuation*

Fowler, Alastair. From the Domain of Arnheim. — London : Secker and Warburg, Feb.1982. — [64]p
ISBN 0-436-16180-x : £4.50 : CIP entry
B81-35726

Fraser, Olive. The pure accounts. — Aberdeen : Aberdeen University Press, July 1981. — [56]p
ISBN 0-08-025755-0 (pbk) : £3.50 : CIP entry
B81-14912

Fraser, W. R. (William Rae). Some poems 1960-1980 / W.R. Fraser. — Stroud (Newhurst, Walkley Hill, Stroud [Glos. GL5 3TX]) : W.R. Fraser, c1981. — 48p ; 21cm
£2.00 (pbk) B81-37007

Fridge, Jessie Bremner. First book of poems / by Jessie Bremner Fridge. — S.l. : s.n., [1980?]. — [36]p ; 22cm
Cover title
£0.60 (pbk) B81-11858

Fuller, John, *1937-*. The illusionists : a tale / John Fuller. — London : Secker & Warburg, 1980. — 138p ; 22cm
ISBN 0-436-16810-3 (pbk) : £3.95 B81-01191

Fuller, John, *1937-*. The January divan : poems / John Fuller ; illustrations George Szirtes. — Hitchin (2 Taylor′s Hill, Hitchin, Herts SG4 9AD) : Mandeville, c1980. — [11]p : ill ; 23cm
Limited ed. of 300 copies, of which 35 have been signed by the author and the artist
ISBN 0-904533-51-4 (pbk) : £1.00 B81-02170

Fuller, Roy. The reign of sparrows / Roy Fuller. — London : London Magazine Editions, 1980. — 69p ; 23cm
ISBN 0-904388-29-8 : £3.95 B81-01784

Fulton, Gwen. Did you ever? / Gwen Fulton. — London : Cape, 1981. — [22]p : chiefly col.ill ; 25cm
ISBN 0-224-01740-3 : £3.50 : CIP rev.
B80-13343

Gibson, Margaret Munro. The spinning disc : a small selection of the hundreds of poems / by Margaret Munro Gibson. — Bolton (21 Ruins La., Harwood, Bolton BL2 3JQ) : Tell Tale, c1981. — 36p ; 22cm
ISBN 0-906347-01-7 (pbk) : Unpriced
B81-24550

Giles, Eric. Letters / by Eric Giles. — Walton-on-Thames : Outposts, 1980. — 44p ; 21cm
£1.30 (pbk) B81-06640

Gillies, Margaret. Hares on the horizon / by Margaret Gillies. — Walton-on-Thames : Outposts, 1981, c1980. — 32p ; 21cm
£1.00 (pbk) B81-05729

Gogarty, Paul. The accident adventure : 1975-77 / Paul Gogarty. — London (62 North View Rd., N.8) : X Press, c1979. — [43]p : ill ; 30cm
Unpriced (pbk) B81-35666

Goulding, Fil. Where dogs are concerned / Fil Goulding. — Tisbury (2 Cuffs La., Tisbury, Wilts.) : Guthlaxton Wordsmith, 1981. — [24]p : ill ; 21cm
Limited ed. of 250 copies
ISBN 0-907470-02-5 (pbk) : Unpriced
B81-32636

Gowar, Mick. Swings and roundabouts : poems / by Mick Gowar ; illustrated by Alan Curless. — London : Collins, 1981. — 80p : ill ; 22cm
ISBN 0-00-184527-6 : £4.50 B81-19986

Gransden, K. W.. The last picnic / K.W. Gransden. — Hitchin (2 Taylor′s Hill, Hitchin, Herts) : Mandeville, 1981. — [19]p ; 23cm
Limited ed. of 250 copies, of which 35 are signed by the author
ISBN 0-904533-53-0 (pbk) : £0.50 B81-28393

Griffin, Jonathan. Outsing the howling : an interlude / Jonathan Griffin. — London (52 Cascade Ave., N.10) : Permanent Press, 1979. — 29p ; 21cm
Limited ed. of 400 copies, of which 50 are signed and numbered by the author
ISBN 0-905258-05-3 (pbk) : £1.25 B81-28344

Griffiths, Steve. Anglesey material : poems 1975-78 / Steve Griffiths. — London : Collings, 1980. — 48p ; 20cm
ISBN 0-86036-139-x (pbk) : £4.50 B81-00339

Grigson, Geoffrey. Twists of the way / Geoffrey Grigson. — Hitchin (2 Taylor′s Hill, Hitchin, Herts SG4 9AD) : Mandeville, 1980. — [14]p ; 23cm
Limited ed. of 250 copies, of which 30 are signed by the author
ISBN 0-904533-50-6 (pbk) : £0.50 B81-02169

Grounsell, D. J.. Expensive bi focals / [Dougie Grounsell]. — Guernsey (Casa-Mia, Les Sauvagées, St. Sampsons, Guernsey, Channel Islands) : Castel, c1981. — 32p ; 21cm
ISBN 0-9506866-1-1 (pbk) : Unpriced
B81-32584

Grubb, David H. W.. Stone moon poems : a sequence for radio : letters from Cornwall to American friends / David H.W. Grubb. — Torpoint (Knill Gross House, Higher Anderton Road, Millbrook, Torpoint, Cornwall) : Kawabata Press, c1981. — [13]p ; 21cm
ISBN 0-906110-26-2 (pbk) : £0.50 B81-29838

Guest, Harry. Elegies / Harry Guest. — Durham (7 Cross View Terrace, Neville′s Cross, Durham DH1 4JY) : Pig, 1980. — [21]p ; 21cm
ISBN 0-903997-57-6 : £0.80 B81-09872

Hagan-Smith, Pamela. Tales from Desmond dormouse / by Pamela Hagan-Smith. — [Falmouth] ([5 Park Cres., Falmouth, Cornwall TR11 2DL]) : P. Hagan-Smith, c1981. — [17]p : ill ; 22cm. — (A Larnaca publication)
Cover title
£0.75 (pbk) B81-37290

Halsey, Alan. Perspectives on the reach / Alan Halsey. — Newcastle-upon-Tyne (45 Salisbury Gardens, Newcastle upon Tyne, NE2 1HP) : Galloping Dog, 1981. — 56p ; 28cm
Limited ed. of 250 copies, 10 numbered and signed
ISBN 0-904837-41-6 (pbk) : Unpriced
ISBN 0-904837-42-4 (signed ed) B81-33562

Hamilton, Iain. The Kerry Kyle / Iain Hamilton ; and [illustrated by] Ann Thomas. — [London] ([125 Middlesex St., Bishopsgate, E1 7JF]) : Campbell & Hamilton, [1980]. — 55p : ill ; 21cm
ISBN 0-907185-00-2 (pbk) : Unpriced
B81-33487

Hampson, Ida. My bunch of keys : Christian verse / by Ida Hampson. — Ilkeston : Moorley′s, [1981?]. — 36p ; 21cm
ISBN 0-86071-099-8 (pbk) : £0.50 B81-15798

Hanks, Peter. Adrift in an open mind : a collection of poems : 1977-1980 / Peter Hanks. — [Walton Stone] ([149 Manor Rise, Walton Stone, Staffs ST1S 0HY]) : [P. Hanks], c1980. — [20]p : ill ; 21cm
Unpriced (pbk) B81-24571

Harrison, Jay. Anxieties of life / Jay Harrison. — Bognor Regis : New Horizon, c1980. — 89p : ill ; 21cm
ISBN 0-86116-281-1 : £2.95 B81-19068

Harrison, Roy. Babel : a symphonic poem / Roy Harrison. — London (19 South Hill Park, NW3 2ST) : Red Candle Press, 1981. — 19p ; 21cm. — (A Red Candle Press pamphlet)
£1.20 (pbk) B81-35651

Harvey, Andrew. A full circle : poems / by Andrew Harvey. — London : Deutsch, 1981. — 56p ; 23cm
ISBN 0-233-97289-7 (corrected) : £3.95
B81-23128

Harvey, Sally F.. The collected poetry of Sally F. Harvey. — [s.l.] : [S.F. Harvey], c1980. — 32p ; 19cm
Unpriced (pbk) B81-05881

Hassan, David. On a serious note, book / David Hassan. — Bognor Regis : New Horizon, c1981. — 31p ; 21cm
ISBN 0-86116-584-5 : Unpriced B81-39432

Hawkins, Ralph. The word from the one / Ralph Hawkins. — Newcastle upon Tyne (3 Otterburn Terrace, Newcastle upon Tyne NE2 3AP) : Galloping Dog, c1980. — 29 leaves ; 28cm
Limited ed. of 200 copies of which 10 are signed
ISBN 0-904837-33-5 (pbk) : Unpriced
ISBN 0-904837-34-3 (signed) : Unpriced
B81-09683

Hazelton, Alexander. Hazelton′s alternative history of Scotland. — Edinburgh (6 St. Colne St., Edinburgh) : Published under the auspices of the Armstrong Trust Limited, [1981?]. — 56p ; 21cm
Author is: Alexander Hazelton
Unpriced (pbk) B81-33545

Heaney, Seamus. Selected poems 1965-1975 / Seamus Heaney. — London : Faber, 1980. — 136p ; 21cm
ISBN 0-571-11644-2 (pbk) : £3.95 : CIP rev.
ISBN 0-571-11617-5 (pbk) : £1.95 B80-17928

Heaton, John W.. The minstrel book 2 / John W. Heaton. — Bognor Regis : New Horizon, c1980. — 46p ; 21cm
ISBN 0-86116-425-3 : £3.25 B81-19067

Hemmings, Louis. In exile : poems of an emigrant / Louis Hemmings ; drawings by D.W.. — [Dalkey] ([Wolverton, Barnhill Rd., Dalkey Co. Dublin]) : L. Hemmings, 1979. — 30p : ill ; 21cm
Limited ed. of 1,000 signed copies
£0.65 (pbk) B81-06446

Hennessy, Colm. Palpitations : poems / by Colm Hennessy. — [London] ([33 Colin Cres., NW9 6EU]) : Midsummer Press, c1981. — [18]p ; 24cm
Unpriced (pbk) B81-34623

Hewitt, John. Mosaic. — Belfast : Blackstaff Press, Nov.1981. — [56]p
ISBN 0-85640-253-2 (pbk) : £2.95 : CIP entry
B81-30490

Higgins, Ann S.. Private thoughts made public / Ann S. Higgins. — Edinburgh ([137 Warrender Park Rd., Edinburgh EH9 1DS]) : Tragara, 1980. — [79]p ; 25cm
Limited ed. of 200 copies
ISBN 0-902616-64-1 : Unpriced B81-11113

Hill, Eileen J.. Poetry of life / Eileen J. Hill. — Ilfracombe : Stockwell, 1981. — 80p ; 15cm
ISBN 0-7223-1508-2 : £2.85 B81-39389

Hilton-Foord, Kathleen. Grannie′s girl : born 1903 / Kathleen Hilton-Foord. — Thanet : Graphic Art & Print, [1981]. — [40]p : ill ; 21cm
Cover title. — Ill on inside cover
Unpriced (pbk) B81-39553

Hirst, Malcolm. Letters to Dixie, requiems and other poems / by Malcolm Hirst. — Sidcup (95 Walton Rd., Sidcup, Kent DA14 4LL) : Erwood, 1981. — 34p ; 21cm
ISBN 0-907322-05-0 (pbk) : £1.00 B81-16042

821'.914 — Poetry in English, *1945-* **—** *Texts continuation*

Hoadley, J. M.. Something unspoken / by J.M. Hoadley. — London ([32 Portland Rd., W.11]) : [J.M. Hoadley], 1980. — [27]p ; 21cm
Limited ed. of 200 numbered copies
Unpriced (pbk) B81-00340

Holbrook, David. Selected poems : 1961-1978 / David Holbrook. — London : Anvil Press in association with Wildwood House, 1980. — 143p ; 23cm
ISBN 0-85646-066-4 : £5.95 B81-12112

Horovitz, Frances. Water over stone / Frances Horovitz. — London : Enitharmon, 1980. — 48p ; 23cm
ISBN 0-905289-51-x (cased) : £3.75
ISBN 0-905289-46-3 (pbk) : £2.25 B81-00341

Houston, Libby. At the mercy : poems / by Libby Houston. — London : Allison & Busby, 1981. — 46p ; 23cm
ISBN 0-85031-347-3 : £4.95 : CIP rev. B80-09373

Howe, Peter, *1943-*. Origins / by Peter Howe. — London : Chatto and Windus, 1981. — 48p ; 22cm. — (The Phoenix living poets)
ISBN 0-7011-2573-x (pbk) : £3.50 : CIP rev. B81-14388

Howell, Jim. Five poems for Christmas / Jim Howell. — Hitchin (2 Taylor's Hill, Hitchin, Herts. SG4 9AD) : Mandeville, 1980. — [8]p ; 23cm
Limited ed. of 300 copies, of which 30 have been signed by the author
£0.50 (pbk) B81-02328

Howells, Joshua. Of life and love / by Joshua Howells. — [Harpenden] ([4 Connaught Rd, Harpenden, Herts.]) : [J. Howells], [c1979]. — [82p] : 1ill ; 18cm
Unpriced (pbk) B81-02832

Hudson, M. I.. I gather rainbows / M.I. Hudson. — Ilfracombe : Stockwell, 1980. — 32p ; 15cm
ISBN 0-7223-1372-1 : £2.20 B81-03022

Hughes, Ted. Under the North Star / Ted Hughes ; drawings by Leonard Baskin. — London : Faber, 1981. — 44p : col.ill ; 29cm
ISBN 0-571-11721-x : £5.95 : CIP rev. B81-07590

Hulse, Michael. Knowing and forgetting. — London : Secker & Warburg, June 1981. — [64]p
ISBN 0-436-20965-9 : £4.50 : CIP entry B81-09454

Hunt, Irvine. Tyson / Irvine Hunt. — Ashington (Wansbeck Sq., Ashington, Northd.) : Mid NAG, 1978. — 23p ; 22cm. — (North now ; no.6)
ISBN 0-904790-06-1 (pbk) : £1.00 B81-01725

Hunter, Louise. A few of my favourite poems / Louise Hunter. — Ilfracombe : Stockwell, 1981. — 16p ; 15cm
ISBN 0-7223-1427-2 (pbk) : £0.50 B81-03025

Hurley, Jon. The wicked wind / by Jon Hurley. — Hoarwithy (Upper Orchard, Hoarwithy, Hereford) : Vine Leaf, 1980. — 55p ; 22cm
ISBN 0-9507362-0-1 (pbk) : Unpriced B81-02936

Huscroft, John. Hugo's room / by John Huscroft. — Chelmsford ([27 Donald Way] Chelmsford, Essex CM2 9JD) : J. Huscroft, 1981. — 10p ; 16cm
Limited ed. of 200 copies
£0.50 (pbk) B81-33478

Huscroft, John. We travelled back aways, awhile / by John Huscroft. — Chelmsford (27 Donald Way, Chelmsford, Essex CM2 9JD) : J. Huscroft, 1981. — 26p ; 16cm
Published in a limited ed. of 338 copies
£0.60 (pbk) B81-16043

Iqbal, Maryam K.. Reflections : from darkness to light / [Maryam K. Iqbal]. — [Huddersfield] ([252 Almondbury Bank, Huddersfield, HD5 8EL]) : Dar-Ul-Ehsan, [1980]. — 20p ; 20cm
ISBN 0-905773-12-8 (pbk) : Unpriced B81-09271

Iremonger, Edmund. With rhyme and reason / Edmund Iremonger. — Sidlesham (Durley, Sidlesham, Sussex) : Durley Press, 1980. — 93p ; 22cm
ISBN 0-9507143-0-5 (pbk) : £2.10 B81-06654

Irving, Grace. Whispers in the wind : poems / by Grace Irving. — [Annan] ([13 Three Trees Rd, Newbie, Annan, Dumfriesshire]) : George S. Irving, [1980]. — 44p,[1]leaf of plates : 1port ; 19cm
Unpriced (pbk) B81-09863

Ivimy, May. Late swings / Mary Ivimy. — Hitchin (2 Taylor's Hill, Hitchin, Herts SG4 9AD) : Mandeville, 1980. — [8]p ; 23cm
ISBN 0-904533-49-2 (pbk) : £0.50 B81-02168

Jackson, Norman. Waking in the dark / Norman Jackson. — Beverley (28 Railway St., Beverley, [Humberside]) : Paston, 1980. — 34p ; 21cm
ISBN 0-907217-01-x (pbk) : £1.10 : CIP rev. B80-12505

Jackson, T. N.. Show business rhymes / by T.N. Jackson. — Bolton (38 Chorley New Rd., Bolton, Lancs.) : T.N. Jackson, 1980. — 63p ; 21cm
Unpriced (pbk) B81-07836

Jacobs, David, *1949-*. Believing in the silence : poems / by David Jacobs. — [Shoeburyness] ([71, Cunningham Close, Shoeburyness, Essex]) : SOL Publications, [c1980]. — 19p ; 21cm
Cover title
£0.60 (pbk) B81-11002

Jacobs, David, *1949-*. Marlowe Court / David Jacobs. — Hunton Bridge (17 Lauderdale Rd., Hunton Bridge, King's Langley-Herts. [WD4 8QA]) : Kit-Cat Press, 1981. — [20]p ; 21cm
Limited ed. of 200 copies
ISBN 0-9500087-2-9 (pbk) : £1.25 B81-29837

Jemmett, Joan. The angel and Ich dien / Joan Jemmett. — Bognor Regis : New Horizon, c1980. — 33p ; 21cm
ISBN 0-86116-398-2 : £3.25 B81-21825

Jenkins, Gwyn, *1938-*. Border song / Gwyn Jenkins. — Birmingham ([c/o G.B. Jenkins, 7 Morlings Drive, Chase Terrace, Burntwood, Staffs]) : [G. Jenkins], 1981. — [6]p ; 11x13cm
Limited ed. of 50 copies
Private circulation (pbk) B81-17668

Jennings, Elizabeth. A dream of spring : poems / by Elizabeth Jennings ; with illustrations by Anthony Rossiter. — Stratford-upon-Avon (51 Banbury Road, Stratford-upon-Avon, [Warwickshire CV37 7HW]) : Celandine, c1980. — [20]p,[5] leaves of plates : ill ; 26cm
Limited ed. of 150 signed and numbered copies
£14.00 B81-03266

Jenson, John. The collected poetry of John Jenson. — [s.l.] : [J. Jenson], c1980. — 32p ; 19cm
Unpriced (pbk) B81-05885

Jesson, Keith. Monday terrace / Keith Jesson. — [Leicester] ([78 Cambridge St., Leicester, LE3 OJP]) : New Broom, c1981. — [10]p : ill ; 21cm
Published in a limited ed. of 90 numbered and signed copies
ISBN 0-901870-53-6 (pbk) : £2.00 B81-20901

Jimi. The works of Jimi. — Leith (20 Fort Place, Leith, Edinburgh) : T.C. Leopard Productions, c1981. — [28]p : ill ; 22cm
Unpriced (unbound) B81-34069

John, Roland. The child bride's diary. — London (12 Stevenage Rd, SW6 6ES) : Oasis Books, July 1981. — [24]p. — (O Books series ; no.2)
ISBN 0-903375-55-9 (pbk) : £0.50 : CIP entry B81-14392

Johnson, Garry. Boys of the empire : modern rock lyrics / by Garry Johnson. — [S.l.] : [S.n.], [1981?] (printing by Babylon Books). — [16]p ; 21cm
Unpriced (pbk) B81-22018

Johnston, Charles, *1912-*. Talk about the last poet : a novella in verse and other poems including Potted memoirs / Charles Johnston. With new verse translations of The bronze horseman / by Alexander Pushkin. & The novice / by Michael Lermontov ; and an introduction by Kyril Fitzlyon. — London : Bodley Head for C. Johnston, c1981. — 78p ; 19cm
Talk about the last poet adapted from Eucharisticus / Paulinus. - The bronze horseman and The novice translated from the Russian
ISBN 0-370-30434-9 : £4.50
Also classified at 891.71'3'08 B81-24447

Jope, Norman. Primal solutions / [by Norman Jope]. — Lampeter (New Rymers Club, S.D.U.C. Lampeter, Dyfed) : Outcrop Publications, c1981. — 50p ; 21cm
£0.30 (pbk) B81-31788

Kelly, Hannah. The game of cards : and other poems / by Hannah Kelly. — London (14 Barlly Rd. W10 6AR) : Autolycus, c1981. — 36p ; 21cm
ISBN 0-903413-47-7 (pbk) : £2.25 B81-33511

Kennedy, Geraldeen. Moving rainbows / Geraldeen Kennedy. — King's Lynn (Centre Press, Fermoy Centre, King St., King's Lynn, Norfolk) : Centre Poets, 1981. — [16]p : 1port ; 22cm
£0.50 (pbk) B81-35653

Kennelly, Brendan. The boats are home / Brendan Kennelly. — Dublin (19 Oakdown Rd., Dublin 14) : Gallery Books, 1980. — 54p ; 23cm
ISBN 0-904011-08-9 (cased) : £4.50(Irish) B81-14274

Kenward, Jean. Theme and variations : fifty poems / by Jean Kenward. — London (14 Barlly Rd. W10 6AR) : Autolycus, c1981. — 44p ; 21cm
ISBN 0-903413-42-6 (pbk) : £2.50 B81-33506

Kenworthy, Nina. Impressions / by Nina Kenworthy. — Walton-on-Thames : Outposts, 1981. — 12p ; 21cm
£0.50 (pbk) B81-16015

King, Jenny. Letting the dark through / Jenny King ; illustration Mary Norman. — Hitchin (2 Taylor's Hill, Hitchin, Herts.) : Mandeville, 1981. — [18]p : ill ; 23cm
Limited ed. of 200 copies of which 30 are signed by the author and the artist
ISBN 0-904533-52-2 (pbk) : £0.50 B81-28394

Kinsella, Thomas. Poems 1956-1976 / Thomas Kinsella. — Portlaoise : Dolmen, 1980. — 192p ; 23cm
ISBN 0-85105-365-3 (cased) : £7.50 : CIP rev.
ISBN 0-85105-366-1 (pbk) : £4.50 B80-03799

Kramer, Lotte. Family arrivals : a collection of seventeen poems and a dedication / by Lotte Kramer. — Hatch End : Poet & Printer, 1981. — 25p ; 21cm
ISBN 0-900597-29-1 (pbk) : £0.90 B81-24819

Kudian, Mischya. Candy floss : witricks / by Mischa Kudian. — London : Mashtots, 1980. — 48p ; 23cm
ISBN 0-903039-08-7 : £3.60 B81-02167

Lampèrt, Jacqueline. The magic adventures of Harriet Hogmog / Jacqueline Lampèrt. — Bognor Regis : New Horizon, c1979. — 41p,[12]p of plates : ill ; 21cm
ISBN 0-86116-139-4 : £3.50 B81-19264

821'.914 — Poetry in English, *1945-* — *Texts continuation*

Landor, Alfred. Muheza Station / by Alfred Landor. — Walton-on-Thames : Outposts, 1981. — 12p : ill ; 21cm
£0.60 (pbk) B81-17447

Laver, Pete. Water, glass, the toad of guilt / Pete Laver. — Durham (7 Cross View Terr., Neville's Cross, Durham DH1 4JY) : Pig, 1981. — [8]p,[6]leaves : ill ; 30cm
ISBN 0-903997-60-6 (pbk) : £0.80 B81-11287

Lester, Paul. Changing channels : poetical gems / Paul Lester ; cartoons by Les Roadhouse. — Edgbaston (Flat 4, 34 Summerfield Cres., Edgbaston, Birmingham B16) : Protean, c1980. — 15p : ill ; 21cm
Cover title
£0.30 (pbk) B81-02826

Lester, Paul. Mirror on megalopolis / poetry by Paul Lester ; drawings by Les Roadhouse. — Birmingham (Flat 4, 34 Summerfield Cres., Edgbaston, Birmingham) : Protean, c1981. — 23p : ill ; 15x22cm
£0.30 (unbound) B81-17752

Liddane, Norah. The collected works of Norah Liddane. — London : Regency, c1980. — 32p ; 16cm
Unpriced (pbk) B81-05889

Liggins, L. P.. Looking forward gazing back / Len Liggins. — Hornchurch (92 Sutton Ave., Hornchurch, Essex RM12 4NF) : [L. Liggins], c1981. — 20p : 2ill,1port ; 21cm
ISBN 0-9507478-0-7 (pbk) : £0.75 B81-24763

Linden, Heather. Love and battle / by Heather Linden. — [London] : [H. Linden], c1978. — 340p ; 21cm
Private circulation (pbk) B81-21453

Linden, Peter. Slimmer than most : a selection of 25 poems / by Peter Linden. — London (2A Hampstead Hill Gardens, NW3 2PL) : Creative Enterprises, [c1981]. — 89p ; 20cm
ISBN 0-907449-00-x (pbk) : £1.80 B81-15765

Lindin, Eddie. City of razors : and other poems / Eddie Linden. — London : Landesman, 1980. — 63p ; 22cm
ISBN 0-905150-22-8 (pbk) : £2.50 B81-07173

Little, Edith. Pink rock and postcards : more poems / by Edith Little. — Milngavie : Heatherbank, 1981. — 43p : ill ; 22cm
ISBN 0-905192-28-1 (pbk) : £1.50 B81-08492

Littler, K. R.. The shattering of the glass / K.R. Littler. — Ilfracombe : Stockwell, 1981. — 48p ; 15cm
ISBN 0-7223-1451-5 (pbk) : £2.47 B81-22335

Livingstone, Dinah. Ultrasound / by Dinah Livingstone. — London : Katabasis, 1974 (1979 [printing]). — 63p ; 22cm
ISBN 0-904872-06-8 (pbk) : Unpriced B81-38541

Lochhead, Liz. The Grimm sisters / Liz Lochhead. — London (21 Colville Terrace, W.11) : Next Editions in association with Faber, 1981. — 53p ; 23cm
ISBN 0-907147-04-6 (spiral) : £2.50 B81-11650

Lock, Margaret. Fading dreams and other poems / Margaret Lock. — Bognor Regis : New Horizon, c1980. — 100p ; 21cm
ISBN 0-86116-132-7 : Unpriced B81-19265

Logue, Christopher. Ode to the dodo : poems from 1953 to 1978 / Christopher Logue. — London : Cape, 1981. — 176p ; 23cm
ISBN 0-224-01892-2 (cased) : £6.95
ISBN 0-224-01893-0 (pbk) : £4.50 B81-18410

Logue, Christopher. War music : an account of books 16 to 19 of Homer's Iliad / Christopher Logue. — London : Cape, 1981. — 83p ; 23cm
ISBN 0-224-01534-6 : £4.50 : CIP rev. B80-21164

Lomas, Herbert. Public footpath / Herbert Lomas. — London : Anvil Press Poetry in association with Wildwood House, 1981. — 79p ; 22cm
ISBN 0-85646-062-1 (pbk) : £3.25 B81-15519

Long, Richard, *1945-*. Five, six, pick up sticks, seven, eight, lay them straight / Richard Long. — [London] ([c/o 9 North St., Plaistow, E13 9HJ]) : [A. d'Offay], 1980. — 1folded sheet([6] p) ; 30cm
Published to accompany an exhibition
Unpriced B81-19994

Long, Richard, *1945-*. Twelve works 1979-1981 / Richard Long. — London (233, Camberwell New Rd., London SE5) : Coracle Press for Anthony d'Offay, 1981. — [13]leaves ; 14x19cm
Unpriced (pbk) B81-40784

Lovejoy, George. The art of printing / George Lovejoy. — Abingdon (Steventon Vicarage, Abingdon, Oxfordshire [OX13 6SL]) : Rocket Press, 1981. — [6]leaves : 1port ; 15cm
Limited ed. of 150 numbered copies
Unpriced (pbk) B81-35654

Loveridge, John. God save the Queen : sonnets of Elizabeth 1. — London (34 Middleton Rd, E8 4BS) : Clement Publishers, Oct.1981. — [80]p
ISBN 0-907027-03-2 : £6.50 : CIP entry B81-31101

Lowenstein, Tom. La Tempesta's X-ray / Tom Lowenstein. — London (15 Norcott Rd., N.16) : Many, 1980. — 19p ; 29cm
Unpriced (pbk) B81-05779

Lucas, Tony. A private land / Tony Lucas. — [Belper] (c/o D. Greenwood, Chapel House, Belper Lane End, Belper, Derbyshire DE5 2DL) : Nottingham Poetry Society, 1980. — 15p ; 21cm. — (Poetry Nottingham publications, ISSN 0143-3202 ; no.3)
ISBN 0-906842-04-2 (pbk) : £0.65 B81-05748

Lucy, Seán. Unfinished sequence and other poems / Seán Lucy. — Portmarnock (98 Ardilaun, Portmarnock, Co. Dublin) : Wolfhound, c1979. — 63p ; 22cm
ISBN 0-905473-37-x (cased) : £4.25
ISBN 0-905473-38-8 (pbk) : £2.00 B81-00342

MacBeth, George. Typing a novel about the War / George MacBeth. — Knotting (Knotting, Beds.) : Martin Booth, 1980. — [6]p ; 17cm
Limited ed. of 125 numbered copies, of which the first 50 are signed by the author
£3.50 (£11.50 signed) (pbk) B81-06637

McCarthy, Michael H. P.. Stanzas / by Michael H.P. McCarthy. — West Wickham ([105a Station Rd., West Wickham, Kent]) : Belvedere Printing, 1976. — [38]p ; 21cm
£1.25 (pbk) B81-05899

McCrory, Donald. Wind on the skin / by Donald McCrory. — Walton-on-Thames : Outposts, 1981. — 56p ; 21cm
£2.50 (pbk) B81-08572

McDermott, Mustafa Yusuf. Muslim nursery rhymes / Mustafa Yusuf McDermott ; [illustration Mary Clements]. — Leicester (223 London Rd., Leicester) : Islamic Foundation, c1981. — 40p : col.ill ; 21cm. — (Muslim children's library)
ISBN 0-86037-075-5 (pbk) : Unpriced B81-14732

Mace, Patrick. Selected poems / by Patrick Mace. — Walton-on-Thames : Outposts, 1981. — 40p ; 21cm
£1.50 (pbk) B81-16041

McGough, Roger. Unlucky for some / by Roger McGough. — London (43 Floral St., Covent Garden, WC2E 9DW) : Bernard Stone, 1980. — [16]leaves ; 19cm
Limited ed. of 1000 copies of which the first 100 are specially bound, numbered and signed by the author
£1.50 (pbk) B81-13167

McGrath, Leslie. Season to season / Leslie McGrath. — Ilfracombe : Stockwell, 1980. — 32p ; 18cm
ISBN 0-7223-1362-4 (pbk) : £2.20 B81-16769

McGuckian, Medbh. Single ladies : sixteen poems / Medbh McGuckian. — Budleigh Salterton (3 Thornton Close, Budleigh Salterton, Devon EX9 6PJ) : Interim, c1980. — 23p ; 22cm
ISBN 0-904675-17-3 (pbk) : Unpriced B81-16044

Mackay, Alan. The floating world of science : poems / by Alan Mackay. — London (22 Lanchester Rd., N6 4TA) : RAM Press, 1980. — 76p : ill ; 21cm
Unpriced (pbk) B81-18685

MacKay, Lucinda. Poems / Lucinda MacKay. — London (13 Bute St., S.W.7) : Tuba, 1980. — 31p : ill ; 20cm
ISBN 0-907155-00-6 (cased) : £4.50
ISBN 0-907155-01-4 (pbk) : £1.50 B81-02271

McNaughton, Colin. If dinosaurs were cats and dogs / Colin McNaughton. — London : Ernest Benn, 1981. — [32]p : chiefly col.ill ; 28cm
ISBN 0-510-00116-5 : £4.75 B81-35275

Madams, H. H.. Dark encounter : a narrative concerning Arthur and the witch of Kernick / H.H. Madams ; illustrations by Rob Johnson. — Bodmin : Fairhaven, c1980. — 120p : ill ; 21cm
ISBN 0-9507173-0-4 : £3.35 B81-05921

Maddern, Ralph. Off mainstream / Ralph Maddern. — Windsor (9 Priors Rd, Windsor, Berks. SL4 4PD) : Focus, 1978. — 72p : ill ; 21cm
ISBN 0-9505053-1-5 (pbk) : £1.00 B81-01192

Magee, Wes. A dark age. — Belfast : Blackstaff Press, Dec.1981. — [56]p
ISBN 0-85640-256-7 (pbk) : £2.95 : CIP entry B81-34966

Magee, Wes. The space beasts : a set of poems for young children / by Wes Magee. — [Maidstone] ([Springfield, Maidstone, Kent ME14 2LH]) : Kent County Library, [1980]. — [4]p : ill ; 30cm
ISBN 0-905155-31-9 (unbound) : £0.15 B81-10325

Mahon, Derek. Courtyards in Delft / Derek Mahon. — Dublin (19 Oakdown Rd., Dublin 14) : Gallery Books, 1981. — 29p ; 23cm
Limited ed. of 1000 copies, 325 of which are bound in cloth
ISBN 0-904011-19-4 (cased) : £4.50(Irish) B81-14278

Makepeace, Eleanor. Images / by Eleanor Makepeace. — [Gateshead] ([86 Salcombe Gardens, Low Fell, Gateshead NE9 6XZ]) : Shadowcat, c1980. — [4]leaves : col.ill ; 24cm. — (Shadowcat editions ; 3)
Cover title. — Text on inside cover
Unpriced (pbk) B81-17446

Makepeace, Eleanor. Uprooting / by Eleanor Makepeace. — Ashton under Lyne (23 Gambrel Bank Rd., Ashton under Lyne, OL6 8TW) : New Hope International, 1981. — 12p ; 21cm
ISBN 0-903610-02-7 (pbk) : £0.40 B81-20388

Marshall, Frances. Not the only pebble / by Frances Marshall. — Walton-on-Thames : Outposts, 1981. — 20p ; 21cm
£0.70 (pbk) B81-16016

821'.914 — Poetry in English, *1945-* — *Texts continuation*

Matteson, Barbara Haggard. Ringing the changes / Barbara Haggard Matteson. — [Middleton-on-Sea] ([172 Elmer Rd, Middleton-on-Sea, Sussex]) : [B.H. Matteson], [1981]. — [32]p ; 23cm
ISBN 0-9507341-0-1 (pbk) : Unpriced
B81-37090

Matthews, John, *19---*. Merlin in Calydon / John Matthews. — Frome (45 Milk St., Frome, Somerset) : Bran's Head, 1981. — [18]p : ill ; 15cm. — (Hunting Raven chapbooks ; 3)
Limited ed. of 325 copies, of which the first 20 are signed by the author
£0.90 (pbk) B81-32099

Meakin, Viola. Jam for sticky fingers : and other verses for children / by Viola Meakin. — Ipswich : East Anglia Magazine, c1981. — 39p : ill ; 21cm
ISBN 0-900227-56-7 (pbk) : £1.95 B81-40993

Meakin, Viola. Poems of wind and wave / by Viola Meakin. — Ipswich : East Anglian Magazine Ltd, c1980. — 32p ; 21cm
ISBN 0-900227-49-4 (pbk) : £1.95 B81-01193

Mee, Walter. Contributions to the Clerihew dictionary of national biography : with index of names and dates / by Walter Mee ; illustrated by Ann Spano. — [London] (26 Sydney Rd, Richmond, Surrey) : Keepsake, c1980. — 22p : ill ; 16cm. — (Mee's Clerihews)
Unpriced (corrected : pbk) B81-12459

Melling, Frances E.. To hold the pen / by Frances E. Melling. — Sherborne, Glos. : Coombe Springs, 1978. — 38p ; 21cm
ISBN 0-900306-60-2 (pbk) : Unpriced
B81-10324

Mercier, Leigh. The tears of Eve, and other poems / by Leigh Mercier ; illustrations by Eve Watson (with the exception of Sea Witch by John Leigh). — Cardigan (Canllefaes Ganol, Penparc, Cardigan, Dyfed) : L. Mercier, [1981]. — 25p : ill ; 20cm
ISBN 0-9507490-0-1 (pbk) : £1.25 B81-27248

Middleton, Christina Forbes. The dance in the village and other poems. — Aberdeen : Aberdeen University Press, Sept.1981. — [88]p
ISBN 0-08-028438-8 (pbk) : £4.50 : CIP entry
B81-21640

Milligan, Spike. Chill air / Spike Milligan ; drawings by Rigby Graham. — [Leicester] ([78 Cambridge St., Leicester LE3 0JP]) : New Broom, c1981. — [4]p ; 21cm
Cover title. — Limited edition of 150 copies
ISBN 0-901870-49-8 (pbk) : £2.00 B81-13231

Milligan, Spike. Unspun socks from a chicken's laundry / written and illustrated by Spike Milligan and, occasionally, Jane and Laura. — Walton-on-Thames : Hobbs in association with Joseph, 1981. — 72p : ill ; 22cm
ISBN 0-7181-1999-1 : £4.50 B81-19897

Milne, J. Crawford. Breaks there star-fire / by J. Crawford Milne ; cover design and illustrations by Colin Gibson. — Arbroath : Herald, 1981. — 20p : ill ; 22cm
Unpriced (pbk) B81-12043

Milne, Les. I've been singing : poems for everyone / by Les Milne. — Birmingham (11, Gosta Green, Birmingham B4 7ER) : Arts Lab, 1977 (1978 [printing]). — 48p ; 23cm
Text on inside cover
£0.50 (pbk) B81-38540

Ming, Sexton. Lady Ottolin Morrel vs Virgina Woolf / by Sexton Ming. — Gravesend (33 Lower Range Rd., Gravesend, Kent) : Phyroid Press, [1981?]. — [12]p : ill ; 26cm
Unpriced (unbound) B81-26476

Mitter, E.. Because the mind is a flower and speech a fancy bird / E. Mitter. — Bognor Regis : New Horizon, c1981. — 218p ; 21cm
ISBN 0-86116-401-6 : £2.95 B81-32572

Moat, John. Fiesta / by John Moat. — London : Enitharmon, 1980. — 34p ; 23cm
ISBN 0-905289-16-1 (cased) : £3.30
ISBN 0-905289-11-0 (pbk) : £1.95 B81-02171

Mole, John. Feeding the lake / John Mole. — London : Secker & Warburg, 1981. — 58p ; 23cm
ISBN 0-436-28040-x : £4.50 : CIP rev.
B81-21642

Moody, J.. Poems / J. Moody. — Ilfracombe : Stockwell, 1981. — 42p ; 15cm
ISBN 0-7223-1472-8 (pbk) : £0.58 B81-35043

Moorhill, Mollie. Chaffinch Brook and other poems / by Mollie Moorhill. — Kinnesswood (4, Whitecraigs, Kinnesswood, Kinross) : Lomond Press, 1981. — 16p ; 21cm
Limited ed. of 350 copies
ISBN 0-9506424-9-5 (pbk) : £0.75 B81-34621

Morgan, Edwin. Collected poems. — Manchester : Carcanet Press, Nov.1981. — [392]p
ISBN 0-85635-365-5 : £7.95 : CIP entry
B81-30435

Morrice, Kenneth. For all I know. — Aberdeen : Aberdeen University Press, July 1981. — [72]p
ISBN 0-08-025756-9 (pbk) : £3.50 : CIP entry
B81-13822

Morris, Brian, *1930-*. Stones in the brook : poems / by Brian Morris. — Llandysul : Gomer Press, 1978. — 53p ; 22cm
ISBN 0-85088-790-9 : £2.00 B81-01194

Mottram, Eric. Elegies / Eric Mottram. — Newcastle-upon-Tyne (45 Salisbury Gardens, Newcastle upon Tyne, NE2 1HP) : Galloping Dog, 1981. — 100p ; 28cm
Limited edition of 426 copies, 26 lettered and signed
ISBN 0-904837-39-4 (pbk) : Unpriced
ISBN 0-904837-40-8 (signed ed) B81-33563

Moules, Sue. Echoes. — Lampeter ([Timberdine, Station Terrace], Lampeter SA48 7HH) : Outcrop, c1981. — 25p ; 21cm
Cover title
£0.40 (pbk) B81-32070

Moyes, Winifred. Meditations in verse / by Winifred Moyes. — London (3 Lansdowne Rd., W.11) : Greater World Association, [1981?]. — [16]p ; 15cm
£0.50 (pbk) B81-32637

Murch, Edward. Space and line / Edward Murch ; drawing by Rigby Graham. — [Leicester] ([78 Cambridge St., Leicester LE3 0JP]) : New Broom, 1981. — [4]p : ill ; 21cm
Cover title. — Published in a limited ed. of 80 copies
ISBN 0-901870-51-x (pbk) : £2.00 B81-16794

Murray, Charles G.. A long night's journey into day. — [Arduaine] ([Craigfeam, Arduaine, by Oban, Argyll PA34 4XQ]) : [C.G. Murray]
Author: Charles G. Murray
2: Nachtschicht. — [1978]. — [32]p ; 22cm
Cover title. — Part 1 published: as Warm-up for A long night's journey into day
Unpriced (pbk) B81-20937

Murray, Charles G.. Warm-up for A long night's journey into day. — [Arduaine] ([Craigfeam, Arduaine, by Oban, Argyll PA34 4XQ]) : [C. G. Murray], [1978]. — [16]p ; 22cm
Cover title. — Author: Charles G. Murray
Unpriced (pbk) B81-20936

Neish, John. A poet confined / by John Neish. — Walton-on-Thames : Outposts, 1981. — 16p ; 21cm
£0.70 (pbk) B81-27853

Nelson, Geoffrey K.. Butterflys eye / Geoffrey K. Nelson. — Birmingham (32 Clun Rd, Northfield, Birmingham B31 1NU) : Butterfly Books, c1980. — 16p ; 21cm
Cover title
ISBN 0-907312-01-2 (pbk) : Unpriced
B81-02769

Ní Chuilleanáin, Eiléan. The rose-geranium / Eiléan Ní Chuilleanáin. — Dublin : Gallery Books, 1981. — 44p ; 22cm
ISBN 0-904011-23-2 (cased) : £4.95
ISBN 0-904011-24-0 (pbk) : £2.47 B81-32937

Nicholls, Joan. Memory's / Joan Nicholls. — Ilfracombe : Stockwell, 1981. — 16p ; 15cm
ISBN 0-7223-1458-2 (pbk) : £0.50 B81-22337

Nichols, John, *1912-*. In retrospect : a collection of poems / by John Nichols. — [Worthing] ([316 Findon Rd, Worthing, W. Sussex BN14 0HB]) : [J. Nichols], 1980. — 24p ; 21cm
ISBN 0-9507320-0-1 (pbk) : £0.50 B81-01195

Nicholson, E. Sheila. Some thoughts of heaven and other verse / E. Sheila Nicholson. — Bognor Regis : New Horizon, c1981. — 39p ; 21cm
ISBN 0-86116-666-3 : £3.95 B81-39605

Nicola, Andreas. Thoughts from images : poems / by Andreas Nicola ; preface and cover design by Criton Tomazos. — London (12A Ennis Rd., N.E) : Environmental Forum, 1981. — 24p ; 21cm
£0.50 (pbk) B81-27247

The Night before Christmas. — London : Dean, c1980. — [12]p : col.ill ; 21cm. — (A Dean board book)
Cover title
ISBN 0-603-00233-1 : £0.55 B81-10834

Nixon, Colin. With all angles equal : poems / by Colin Nixon ; with drawings by Tony Burrell. — Clacton-on-Sea (91 Thoroughgood Rd., Clacton-on-Sea, Essex) : Magma, c1980. — [20]p : ill ; 11x15cm
£0.40 (pbk) B81-05727

Nottage, Sheila. No longer oneself / Sheila Nottage ; edited by Margaret George. — Kingston Upon Thames ([1 Rayleigh Court, Kingston-upon-Thames KT1 3NF]) : Court Poetry Press, [1981]. — 28p ; 21cm
ISBN 0-906010-26-8 (pbk) : £0.60 B81-16034

O'Brien, Gerry. Moon over the the Mersey / Gerry O'Brien. — Ilfracombe : Stockwell, 1980. — 28p ; 19cm
ISBN 0-7223-1354-3 : £0.55 B81-03021

O'Connor, Philip. Arias of water : poems 1978-1980 / Philip O'Connor. — London : Sidgwick & Jackson, 1981. — ix,66p ; 22cm
ISBN 0-283-98710-3 (pbk) : £4.50 B81-09400

O'Flynn, Criostoir. Banana / Criostoir O'Flynn. — Baile Átha Cliath (29 Sráid Uí Chonaill Íochtair, Baile Átha Cliath, 1) : Foilseacháin Náisiúnta Teoranta, 1979. — 76p ; 22cm
£2.00 B81-21733

O'Grady, Desmond, *1935-*. His skaldcrane's nest / Desmond O'Grady. — Dublin (19 Oakdown Rd., Dublin 14) : Gallery Books, c1979. — 51p ; 23cm
Also available in paperback at £1.80(Irish)
£3.60(Irish) (cased) B81-14276

Orchard, William. Evocative tapestry / William Orchard. — Ilfracombe : Stockwell, 1981. — 192p : ill ; 22cm
ISBN 0-7223-1453-1 : £4.50 B81-35049

Ország-Land, Thomas. The seasons / by Thomas Ország-Land ; with woodcuts by Nicholas Parry. — Market Drayton : Tern, 1980. — [32]p : ill ; 21cm
Limited ed. of 500 copies
ISBN 0-906057-12-4 (pbk) : £3.90 B81-07031

821'.914 — Poetry in English, *1945-* — *Texts continuation*

Owen, Rosemary. Universal nursery rhymes / Rosemary Owen ; illustrated by Eric Rees. — Ilfracombe : Stockwell
Vol.4. — 1981. — 31p : ill,1map ; 18cm
ISBN 0-7223-1492-2 (pbk) : Unpriced
B81-35045

Owens, Philip, *1947-*. Look, Christ / Philip Owens. — Llandysul : Gomer, 1979. — 47p ; 19cm
ISBN 0-85088-601-5 (pbk) : £1.00 B81-39363

Palmer, Graham. Moon shots : a selection of poems / by Graham Palmer. — London ([11 Golden Manor, Hanwell, W7 3EE]) : G. Palmer, 1981. — [28]p ; 21cm
Limited ed. of 200 numbered copies
Unpriced (pbk) B81-34096

Park, Michael. Arabian snapshots / Michael Park. — Scarborough (51 Stepney Ave., Scarborough, N. Yorkshire YO12 5BW) : Rannoch Gillamoor Poets, 1981. — 31p,[2]of plates : ill,2maps ; 21cm
ISBN 0-9507488-0-3 (pbk) : £0.50 B81-19611

Partridge, Kathleen. Wishing you well : a pictorial selection, with verse / by Kathleen Partridge. — Norwich : Jarrold & Sons, [1981?]. — [62]p : ill(some col.) ; 19cm
Ill on inside covers
ISBN 0-85306-450-4 (pbk) : Unpriced
B81-30777

Parvin, Betty. The book of Daniel : poems / Betty Parvin. — Nottingham (9 College St., Nottingham) : Em-Press, 1980. — [20]leaves : 2ill ; 15x21cm
Cover title
ISBN 0-9506621-1-9 (pbk) : Unpriced
B81-10292

Paterson, Alasdair. Alps. — London (12 Stevenage Rd, SW6 6ES) : Oasis Books, July 1981. — [16]p. — (O Books series ; no.1)
ISBN 0-903375-54-0 (pbk) : £0.50 : CIP entry
B81-14393

Patler, Louis. Eloísa / Louis Patler. — Bishop's Stortford (25 Portland Rd., Bishop's Stortford, Herts.) : Great Works Editions, 1979. — [21] leaves ; 30cm
Limited ed. of 300 copies
ISBN 0-905383-10-9 (pbk) : £0.60 B81-00343

Patten, Brian. The irrelevant song / Brian Patten. — 2nd ed. — London : Unwin Paperbacks, 1975, 1980 [printing]. — 63p ; 20cm
Previous ed.: London : Allen & Unwin, 1971
ISBN 0-04-821046-3 (pbk) : £1.75 : CIP rev.
B80-18472

Patten, Brian. Love poems. — London : Allen & Unwin, Sept.1981. — [96]p
ISBN 0-04-821052-8 : £6.95 : CIP entry
B81-22556

Patten, Brian. Notes to the hurrying man / Brian Patten. — London : Unwin Paperbacks, 1980. — 66p ; 20cm
Originally published: London : Allen & Unwin, 1969
ISBN 0-04-821047-1 (pbk) : £1.75 : CIP rev.
B80-23669

Pearce, Brian Louis. The vision of Piers Librarian / Brian Louis Pearce. — Twickenham (72 Heathfield South, Twickenham, Middx) : Woodruff, 1981. — [32]p ; 20cm
Limited ed. of 150 numbered copies
ISBN 0-9501639-7-x (pbk) : £1.20 B81-34067

Pearson, Kenn. Other tides / Kenn Pearson. — Ilfracombe : Stockwell, 1981. — 32p ; 15cm
ISBN 0-7223-1480-9 (pbk) : £0.58 B81-35041

Peden, David C. D.. Clouds before the sun / David C.D. Peden. — Bognor Regis : New Horizon, c1980. — 145p ; 21cm
ISBN 0-86116-282-x : £2.95 B81-19027

Perkins, Harold W.. Touch of magic : poems / by Harold W. Perkins. — Harwood (21 Ruins La., Harwood, Bolton BL2 3JQ) : Harwood Publishing Co., c1981. — 24p ; 21cm
ISBN 0-906692-12-1 (pbk) : £0.65 B81-10833

Phillips, Herbert. Jokuba : being the adventures of Joe Cooper, sea-captain / by Herbert Phillips ; illustrations by the author. — Walton-on-Thames : Outposts, 1981. — 59p : ill ; 21cm
£2.00 (pbk) B81-18545

Phillips, Peter, *19---*. Signs of the times / [by Peter Phillips]. — Plymouth (3 Blenheim Rd, Plymouth PL4 8LJ) : P. Phillips, c1981. — 37p : ill ; 20cm
ISBN 0-9507456-0-x (pbk) : Unpriced
B81-28628

Pickard, Tom. O.K. tree! / Tom Pickard. — Durham (7 Cross View Terrace, Neville's Cross, Durham DH1 4JY) : Pig Press, c1980. — [25]p ; 21cm
Also available in a limited ed. of 26 lettered copies signed by the poet
ISBN 0-903997-56-8 (pbk) : £0.80 B81-06132

Porter, Peter. English subtitles / Peter Porter. — Oxford : Oxford University Press, 1981. — 56p ; 22cm
ISBN 0-19-211942-7 (pbk) : £3.50 B81-17066

Pratt, Thomas Alan. A variety of verse / Thomas Alan Pratt. — Bognor Regis : New Horizon, c1980. — 76p ; 21cm
ISBN 0-86116-066-5 : £2.50 B81-19086

Prendergast, Steve. Riviera Blues / Steve Prendergast. — Southampton (Bassett, Southampton, Hants) : S. Prendergast, 1981. — 15p ; 15cm
ISBN 0-7223-1475-2 (pbk) : Unpriced
B81-35035

Preston, Barbara, *1937-*. Gleanings of truth : a collection of inspired poems / Barbara Preston. — London (29 Furzedown Drive, Tooting, S.W.17) : B.Preston, [1981?]. — [17]p ; 21cm
Unpriced (pbk) B81-31909

Price, Isabel. Testimony to my town : poems / Isabel Price. — [Shildon?] : [I. Price], c1980. — 36p ; 21cm
Cover title
£1.00 (pbk) B81-05896

Pryor, William. Unearth / William Pryor. — Newcastle-upon-Tyne (3 Otterburn Terrace, Newcastle-upon-Tyne NE2 3AP) : Galloping Dog, 1980. — [16] leaves ; 26cm
Limited ed. of 200 copies, 10 of which are signed by the author
ISBN 0-904837-31-9 (pbk) : £0.75
ISBN 0-904837-32-7 (signed ed.) : £2.00
B81-00345

Purser, John. A share of the wind / by John Purser. — Isle of Skye : Aquila, c1980. — [19]p ; 21cm. — (Aquila pamphlet poetry. Second series)
Limited ed. of 250 copies of which 50 are signed, cased and numbered
ISBN 0-7275-0204-2 (cased) : £10.00
ISBN 0-7275-0203-4 (pbk£1.50) B81-37009

Pybus, Rodney. At the stone junction / Rodney Pybus. — Newcastle-upon-Tyne : Northern House, 1978. — [16]p ; 21cm. — (Northern House poets ; 26)
Also available in limited ed. of 25 numbered copies signed by the author
ISBN 0-900570-23-7 (pbk) : £0.60
ISBN 0-900570-24-5 (Signed ed.) : Unpriced
B81-06275

Pybus, Rodney. The loveless letters / by Rodney Pybus. — London : Chatto & Windus, 1981. — 48p ; 22cm
ISBN 0-7011-2563-2 (pbk) : £3.95 B81-11392

Pyper, Betty. Reflections : Christian verse / by Betty Pyper. — Ilkeston : Moorley's Bible & Bookshop, [1980]. — 35p
ISBN 0-86071-092-0 (22cmpbk) : £0.50
B81-06139

Radavich, David. Slain species : a selection of poems / by David Radavich. — Kingston upon Thames ([1 Rayleigh Court, Kingston upon Thames KT1 3NF]) : Court Poetry Press, [c1980]. — 30p ; 21cm
ISBN 0-906010-25-x (pbk) : £0.60 B81-07409

Raine, Craig. A free translation / Craig Raine. — Edinburgh : Salamander, 1981. — 29p ; 22cm
ISBN 0-907540-01-5 (cased) : £4.50
ISBN 0-907540-02-3 (pbk) : Unpriced
B81-28704

Reading, Peter. Tom O'Bedlam's beauties. — London : Secker & Warburg, Nov.1981. — [64]p
ISBN 0-436-40850-3 : £4.50 : CIP entry
B81-30305

Reale-Mad. Fleaman! / by Reale-Mad & Loudgas. — Hanworth (183 Fernside Ave., Hanworth, Middx., TW13 7BQ) : Sweaty Publications, c1980. — [6]p : ill ; 27cm
Cover title
£0.50 (pbk) B81-23189

Reinhardt, Rosamond. The listening silence / by Rosamond Reinhardt. — Walton-on-Thames : Outposts, 1980. — 20p ; 21cm
£0.70 (pbk) B81-05730

Reynolds, Rosetta. In all these things / Rosetta Reynolds. — Bognor Regis : New Horizon, c1979. — 88p ; 21cm
ISBN 0-86116-076-2 : £2.95 B81-19076

Rigg, Pete. Long time ago / Pete & Sheila Rigg ; cats [drawn by] Kathie Layfield. — Leicester (78, Cambridge St., Leicester, LE3 0JP) : New Broom, 1981. — [4]p : ill ; 21cm
Cover title. — Published in a limited ed. of 90 numbered copies. — "Phoenix broadsheet 201" (1 sheet) as insert
ISBN 0-901870-54-4 (pbk) : £2.00 B81-20902

Rigley, David A.. Derbyshire born / by David A. Rigley. — Ely (29 Longfields, Ely, Cambs. CB6 3DN) : Poetry into Print, 1981. — 24p ; 22cm
Unpriced (pbk) B81-32640

Rigley, David A.. Reach into the silence / by David A. Rigley. — Ely (29 Longfields, Ely, Cambridge CB6 3DN) : Poetry into Print, 1981. — 24p ; 22cm
Unpriced (pbk) B81-32638

Rigley, David A.. You follow balloons / by David A. Rigley. — Ely (29 Longfields, Ely, Cambridge CB6 3DN) : Poetry into Print, 1981. — 24p ; 22cm
Unpriced (pbk) B81-32639

Riley, Peter, *1940-*. Lines on the Liver / Peter Riley. — London : Ferry Press, 1981. — [71]p ; 23cm
£3.00 (pbk) B81-34875

Rippier, Jo. Seasons and remembrance. — Gerrards Cross : Colin Smythe, Nov.1981. — [24]p
Limited ed. of 50 copies
ISBN 0-86140-113-1 (pbk) : £9.00 : CIP entry
B81-34959

Roberts, Graham. Sorry it's only me : selected poems / Graham Roberts. — Whitehaven (c/o Graham Roberts Studio, 30 Roper St., Whitehaven, Cumbria CA28 7BS) : Melville Promotions, c1981. — [28]p ; 21cm
Cover title
Unpriced (pbk) B81-37376

21'.914 — Poetry in English, *1945- — Texts continuation*

Robins, Alan. From ballad to verse / by Alan Robins. — Ipswich : East Anglian Magazine Ltd., c1980. — 40p ; 21cm
ISBN 0-900227-50-8 (pbk) : £1.95 B81-00346

Robins, Ivor. Above the stars / Ivor Robins. — Bognor Regis : New Horizon, c1981. — 26p : ill ; 21cm
ISBN 0-86116-172-6 : £2.95 B81-26494

Robinson, Alan, *1929-*. The following spring / by Alan Robinson. — Walton-on-Thames : Outposts, 1980. — 40p ; 21cm
£1.20 (pbk) B81-05888

Robinson, Helen, *1960-*. Hellenic verses / by Helen Robinson. — Sutton Coldfield (Coles La., Sutton Coldfield, W. Midlands) : M.E.P.S., c1980. — 8p : 1port ; 22cm
Unpriced (pbk) B81-00347

Rolls, John Ashby. More poems for lovers / by John Ashby Rolls. — [Epsom] ([18 Treemount Court, Grove Ave., Epsom, Surrey KT17 4DU]) : [Ashby Press], [1980]. — 48p ; 21cm
ISBN 0-9507323-1-1 (pbk) : Unpriced B81-03468

Rose, Margaret E.. The glass ships and other poems / by Margaret E. Rose. — Walton-on-Thames : Outposts, 1981. — 32p ; 21cm
£1.25 (pbk) B81-20903

Rosen, Michael. You can't catch me! / poems by Michael Rosen ; pictures by Quentin Blake. — London : Deutsch, 1981. — [32]p : col.ill ; 27cm
ISBN 0-233-97345-1 : £4.95 : CIP rev. B81-28836

Rozlyn. Rozlyn's book of verse / with a foreword by John J. Keyes. — Ilfracombe : Stockwell, 1981. — 61p ; 15cm
ISBN 0-7223-1500-7 : £2.84 B81-39397

Ryan-Miller, Kathleen. Eden re-visited : collected illustrated poems / by Kathleen Ryan-Miller and Keith Cresswell ; with illustrations by Keith Cresswell. — Worcester (8 Rainbow Hill Terrace, Worcester) : K. Ryan-Miller, 1980. — 64p : ill ; 28cm
Limited ed. of 1000 copies
£4.95 (pbk) B81-19429

Sagar, Keith. The reef : and other poems / by Keith Sagar ; with an introduction by Ted Hughes. — Ilkley (Festival Office, Ilkley, W. Yorks. LS29 8HF) : Proem Pamphlets, 1980. — [20]p ; 22cm
ISBN 0-905125-05-3 (pbk) : £0.50 B81-02541

Sail, Lawrence. The Kingdom of Atlas / Lawrence Sail. — London : Secker & Warburg, 1980. — 64p ; 23cm
ISBN 0-436-44080-6 : £3.95 B81-00348

Saunders, D. J. M.. Bad friends / D.J.M. Saunders. — Cardiff (55 Melrose Ave., Penylan, Cardiff) : Long Spider, c1981. — 24p : ill ; 21cm
ISBN 0-9507529-0-8 (pbk) : £0.95 B81-24548

Schiller, Daphne. In my element / by Daphne Schiller. — Walton-on-Thames : Outposts, 1981. — 20p ; 21cm
(pbk) B81-27854

Seal, Graham. Flowers for the living / by Graham Seal. — Walton-on-Thames : Outposts, 1981. — 28p ; 21cm
£0.90 (pbk) B81-05585

Searle, Chris. Red earth : poems / by Chris Searle. — London : Journeyman, 1980. — 72p ; 21cm
ISBN 0-904526-48-8 (pbk) : £1.95 B81-00349

Sedgwick, Fred. From another part of the island / Fred Sedgwick. — Berkhamsted (Berkhamsted, Herts.) : Priapus, 1981. — [8]p : 1ill ; 22cm. — (Priapus poets)
Limited ed. of 120 copies, 30 of which are signed and numbered by the author
£0.40 (pbk) B81-20943

Sergeant, Howard. Selected poems / Howard Sergeant ; with illustrations by Cherrill Sergeant. — London : Fuller D'Arch Smith, 1980. — 63p : ill ; 22cm
£2.80 B81-35137

Serraillier, Ian. The challenge of the Green Knight : with seven ballads from Robin in the Greenwood / Ian Serraillier ; illustrated by Victor G. Ambrus. — London : Heinemann Educational, 1981. — 85p : ill ; 20cm. — (The New windmill series ; 215)
The Challenge of the Green Knight originally published: London : Oxford University Press, 1966
ISBN 0-435-12215-0 : £1.50 : CIP rev. B80-26235

Shah, Munaver Whusain. Atomic woman : poems / by Munaver Whusain Shah. — Birmingham (516 Coventry Rd, Small Heath, Birmingham 10) : Trininty Arts Association, [1981]. — 20p ; 21cm
£0.60 (pbk) B81-37442

Sharpe, Olive G.. Our friend : recitations on a theme / Olive G. Sharpe. — Ilkeston : Moorley's Bible & Bookshop, [1981?]. — 11p ; 21cm. — (Recitations on a theme)
ISBN 0-86071-108-0 (pbk) : £0.25 B81-26896

Sharpe, Olive G.. Reaching out : children's recitation / Olive G. Sharpe. — Ilkeston : Moorley's Bible & Bookshop, [1981?]. — 35p ; 21cm
ISBN 0-86071-111-0 (pbk) : £0.45 B81-32635

Sharpe, Olive G.. To be a pilgrim / Olive G. Sharpe. — Ilkeston : Moorley's Bible & Bookshop Ltd, [1981?]. — 11p ; 21cm. — (Recitations on a theme)
ISBN 0-86071-109-9 (pbk) : £0.25 B81-26897

Shaw, Robert, *1933-*. The Wrath Valley anthology : epigrams & poems / by Robert Shaw ; with an appendix on the literary geography of the area and map by Wilson Goarfoot. — Hatch End ([30 Grinsdyke Rd., Hatch End, Middlesex HA5 4PW]) : Poet & Printer, 1981. — 40p : 1map ; 23cm
Limited ed. of approx. 500 copies
ISBN 0-900597-28-3 (pbk) : £0.90 B81-16157

Sheppard, Robert G.. The frightened summer / Robert G. Sheppard. — Durham (7 Cross View Terr., Neville's Cross, Durhalm DH1 4JY) : Pig, 1981. — [30]p ; 29cm
ISBN 0-903997-58-4 (pbk) : £0.80 B81-11286

Shuttle, Penelope. The orchard upstairs / Penelope Shuttle. — Oxford : Oxford University Press, 1980. — 52p ; 22cm
ISBN 0-19-211938-9 (pbk) : £3.95 : CIP rev. B80-21019

Silkin, Jon. Selected poems / Jon Silkin. — London : Routledge & Kegan Paul, 1980. — xii,204p ; 22cm
Includes index
ISBN 0-7100-0614-4 (pbk) : £4.95 : CIP rev. B80-17931

Sillitoe, Alan. More Lucifer / Alan Sillitoe. — Knotting : Booth, [1980]. — [7]p ; 17cm
Limited ed. of 125 numbered copies, of which the first 50 are signed by the author
Unpriced (pbk) B81-03251

Simms, Colin. Movement / Colin Simms. — Durham (7 Cross View Terrace, Neville's Cross, Durham) : Pig, 1980. — [6] leaves ; 20x29cm
Limited ed. of 200 copies of which 10 are numbered and signed by the author
£0.60 (pbk) B81-05486

Simpson, Joan Murray. Landscape and inscape : poems / by Joan Murray Simpson ; introduced by Phoebe Hesketh. — London (14 Barlly Rd. W10 6AR) : Autolycus, c1980. — 40p ; 21cm
ISBN 0-903413-46-9 (pbk) : £2.00 B81-33503

Sisson, C. H.. Selected poems. — Manchester : Carcanet Press, Nov.1981. — [144]p
ISBN 0-85635-381-7 (pbk) : £3.95 : CIP entry B81-30436

Smith, Ann, *1947-*. Measure of darkness / Ann Smith. — Ilfracombe : Stockwell, 1980. — 24p ; 15cm
ISBN 0-7223-1417-5 (pbk) : £0.58 B81-03024

Smith, Elsabe Campbell. Collected poems : poems of the Passion and Eastertide and other poems / by Elsabe Campbell Smith. — Ilfracombe : Stockwell, 1980. — 44p ; 15cm
ISBN 0-7223-1432-9 (pbk) : £0.80 B81-03027

Smith, Gavin D.. Without your presence / by Gavin D. Smith. — Stanhope in Weardale : [G.D. Smith], 1979. — [27]p : ill ; 22cm
Unpriced (unbound) B81-38542

Smith, Grahame C.. Poems / Grahame C. Smith. — London (13 Bute St., S.W.7) : Tuba Press, 1981. — 77p ; 20cm
ISBN 0-907155-02-2 (cased) : £4.50 : CIP rev.
ISBN 0-907155-03-0 (pbk) : £1.95 B81-13466

Smith, Ken, *1938-*. Fox running / Ken Smith. — Newcastle upon Tyne : Bloodaxe, 1981. — 22p ; 19x25cm
Originally published: London : Rolling Moss, 1980
ISBN 0-906427-25-8 (pbk) : £1.50 B81-32869

Smith, Ken, *1938-*. What I'm doing now : (and for the Rose Lady) (30/4/80) : eighteen poems / by Ken Smith. — London : Oasis Books, 1980. — 33p ; 21cm
ISBN 0-903375-50-8 (pbk) : Unpriced : CIP rev. B80-12514

Smith, Margery. In transit / by Margery Smith. — Walton-on-Thames : Outposts, 1981. — 36p ; 21cm
£1.35 (pbk) B81-27858

Smith, Tom, *1924-*. Rural rhymes / Tom Smith. — [Minster Lovell] (['Mineath', Brize Norton Rd., Minster Lovell, Oxon OX8 5SG]) : [T. Smith], [1981]. — 32p : ill ; 21cm
Cover title
Unpriced (pbk) B81-15780

Snow, Myke. Requiem for a proud people / [poems by Myke Snow] ; [illustrations by Kate Hopley]. — [Great Britain] : Guthlaxton Wordsmith, 1981. — [23]p : ill ; 21cm
Limited ed. of 250 copies
ISBN 0-907470-00-9 (pbk) : Unpriced B81-15782

Squire, Bob. A breath of fresh air / poems by Bob Squire. — Bolton ([21 Ruins Lane, Harwood, Bolton BL2 3JQ]) : Farnworth Writers, c1981. — 44p ; 21cm
ISBN 0-906347-03-3 (pbk) : Unpriced B81-33477

St. Aubin de Téran, Lisa. The streak / Lisa St. Aubin de Téran. — Knotting (Knotting, Beds.) : Martin Booth, [1980]. — [6]p ; 17cm
Limited ed. of 125 numbered copies, of which the first 50 are signed by the author
£4.35 (£12.50 signed) (pbk) B81-06638

Stafford, William. Absolution / William Stafford. — Bedford : Martin Booth, [1980]. — [4]leaves ; 17cm
Limited ed.: of 125 numbered copies the first 50 of which are signed by the author
Unpriced (pbk) B81-13973

Stanford, Gladys M.. Small fry and other verses / Gladys M. Stanford. — Bognor Regis : New Horizon, c1980. — 89p ; 21cm
ISBN 0-86116-519-5 : £2.95 B81-21842

821'.914 — Poetry in English, *1945-* **—** *Texts continuation*

Stanton, Marion. Life's tapestry : poems / by Marion Stanton. — Shipston-on-Stour : Published for the author by Mr. P. Drinkwater, c1980. — [24]p ; 24cm
Unpriced (pbk) B81-12169

Stevens, Jean Marian. Led by kingfishers / by Jean Marian Stevens. — Walton-on-Thames : Outposts, 1980. — 20p ; 21cm
£0.70 (pbk) B81-01197

Stimson, Nick. In magnet air : poems / by Nick Stimson. — London : Phoenix Springwood, 1980. — 30p ; 22cm
ISBN 0-905947-92-4 (pbk) : £2.50 B81-08032

Stir-about : rhymes to read from then and now / chosen by Nancy Chambers ; illustrated by Carolyn Bull. — London : MacRae, 1981. — 46p : ill ; 21cm. — (Blackbird books)
ISBN 0-86203-041-2 : £2.75 : CIP rev.
B81-20158

Stokes, Adrian. With all the views : the collected poems of Adrian Stokes / edited with an introduction by Peter Robinson. — Manchester : Carcanet, 1981. — 183p ; 23cm
ISBN 0-85635-334-5 : £8.95 : CIP rev.
B81-16895

Suff, David. Knot fire : some notes for painting / David Suff. — [London] ([86 Wickham La., SE2 0XN]) : [D. Suff], c1981. — [55]p : ill (some col.) ; 21cm
Limited ed. of 250 copies
£2.95 (pbk) B81-21208

Suleiman, Ed. Separations. — [London] ([26, Lynmouth Rd, N.2]) : E. Suleiman, [1981?]. — [38]leaves : ill ; 26cm
Author: Ed Suleiman
Unpriced (unbound) B81-39847

Swan, Guida. Angels to zero / Guida Swan ; with four line drawings by Charlie Sidgwick. — Ashburton : Cock Robin Press, c1980. — [28]leaves : ill ; 22cm
Limited ed. of 50 copies
Unpriced (pbk) B81-10051

Sweetman, David. Looking into the deep end / David Sweetman. — London : Faber, 1981. — 47p ; 20cm
ISBN 0-571-11730-9 (pbk) : £3.00 : CIP rev.
B81-01198

Swift, Theophilus. The judgement of Hercules / Theophilus Swift. — Frome (45 Milk St., Frome, Somerset) : Bran's Head, 1981. — 22p : ill ; 15cm : pbk. — (Hunting Raven chapbooks ; 2)
Limited ed. of 325 copies, of which the first 20 are signed by the author
£0.90 (pbk) B81-32100

Szirtes, George. Homage to Cheval : poems & a drawing / by George Szirtes. — Berkhamsted (Berkhamsted, Herts.) : Priapus Poets, c1980. — [9]p : 1ill ; 22cm
Limited ed. of 150 copies of which 30 are numbered and signed by the author
£0.45 (pbk) B81-06635

Szirtes, George. November and May. — London : Secker and Warburg, Nov.1981. — [64]p
ISBN 0-436-50998-9 : £4.50 : CIP entry
B81-30308

Tarn, Nathaniel. The land songs. — Plymouth : Blue Guitar Books ; London (12 Stevenage Rd., SW6 6ES) : Independent Press Distribution [distributor], Sept.1981. — [16]p
ISBN 0-907562-01-9 (pbk) : £0.80 : CIP entry
B81-20499

Taylor, Roma. The Spanish hacienda & other poems / Roma Taylor. — Bognor Regis : New Horizon, c1978. — 42p ; 21cm
ISBN 0-86116-037-1 : £2.50 B81-18881

Thell, William. Varied poetic thoughts / by William Thell. — London : Regency Press, c1980. — 92p ; 23cm
ISBN 0-7212-0588-7 : £3.00 B81-03501

Thomas, D. M.. Dreaming in bronze / D.M. Thomas. — London : Secker & Warburg, 1981. — 71p ; 23cm
ISBN 0-436-51891-0 : £4.50 : CIP rev.
B81-21644

Thomas, H. J. (Howard James). Everyday thoughts / H.J. Thomas. — Bognor Regis : New Horizon, c1979. — 54p ; 21cm
ISBN 0-86116-077-0 : £2.50 B81-19075

Thompson, Keith, *1942-*. An ancient melody / Keith Thompson. — Ruthin (3 Upper Clwyd St., Ruthin, Clwyd) : Spread Eagle, c1979. — 32p ; 21cm
£0.75 (pbk) B81-19431

Thomson, Elizabeth M.. Complete poems / by Elizabeth M. Thomson. — Paisley : J. Thomson, 1979. — 64p ; 21cm
ISBN 0-86122-019-6 (pbk) : £0.50 B81-40972

Thomson, Geddes. A spurious grace / by Geddes Thomson. — Walton-on-Thames : Outposts, 1980. — 28p ; 21cm
£0.90 (pbk) B81-02825

Thwaite, Anthony. Victorian voices / Anthony Thwaite. — Oxford : Oxford University Press, 1980. — 42p ; 22cm
ISBN 0-19-211937-0 (pbk) : £3.95 : CIP rev.
B80-13046

Tomlinson, Charles. The flood / Charles Tomlinson. — Oxford : Oxford University Press, 1981. — 55p ; 22cm
ISBN 0-19-211944-3 (pbk) : £3.95 : CIP rev.
B81-12860

Topley, Peter. Wings of darkness, wings of joy : poems / by Peter Topley ; illustrated with 'tobies', a design by Pat McGrory. — West Wickham ([36, The Grove,] West Wickham, Kent [BR4 9JS]) : Topley Books, c1981. — 24p : ill ; 22cm
Limited ed. of 50 copies
£0.75 (pbk) B81-38087

Touquet, Rowena. So to speak : selected poems / by Rowena Touquet. — Ipswich : East Anglian Magazine, c1981. — 18p ; 22cm
ISBN 0-900227-55-9 (pbk) : £1.95 B81-37279

Tse, C.. Shadows / C. Tse. — Ilfracombe : Stockwell, 1981. — 16p ; 15cm
ISBN 0-7223-1482-5 (pbk) : £0.50 B81-22336

Tunley, Tim. Against the grain : a collection of poems / by Tim Tunley. — London (28 Earlham Grove, Forest Gate, E7 9AW) : Sea Dream Music, 1981. — 18p ; 21cm
£0.10 (pbk) B81-20950

Turton, Godfrey. Shorter poems / Godfrey Turton. — Oxford (10 Benson Place, Oxford) : [G. Turton], 1981. — 35p ; 19cm
£1.50 (pbk) B81-32717

Vanson, Frederic. More miniatures / by Frederic Vanson. — Shoeburyness (71, Cunningham Close, Shoeburyness, Essex) : Sol Publications, c1981. — 8p ; 15cm
ISBN 0-907376-09-6 (pbk) : £0.35 B81-36143

Vaughan, Dorothy. Nantwich : simple tales - simply told / by Dorothy Vaughan. — [Bolton] : Farnworth Writers, c1981. — 32p : ill ; 20cm
ISBN 0-906347-02-5 (pbk) : Unpriced
B81-38088

Veness, Eliza. Poems / Eliza Veness. — Ilfracombe : Stockwell, 1981. — 48p ; 15cm
ISBN 0-7223-1455-8 : £2.47 B81-18306

Veronique. Into the twilight / Veronique. — Auckland : Veronique ; Ilfracombe : Stockwell, 1981. — 14p ; 19cm
ISBN 0-7223-1509-0 (pbk) : Unpriced
B81-39394

Veronique. Two worlds / Veronique. — Auckland : Veronique ; Ilfracombe : Stockwell, 1981. — 22p ; 19cm
ISBN 0-7223-1529-5 (pbk) : Unpriced
B81-39393

Wain, John. Aquarius / John Wain. — London (77 Burghley Rd., N.W.5) : Pisces Press, 1980. — [4]p : 1ill ; 20cm. — (Poems for the zodiac)
Limited ed. of 100 numbered and signed copies
Unpriced (unbound) B81-19929

Wain, John. Aries / John Wain. — London (77 Burghley Rd., N.W.5) : Pisces Press, 1980. — [4]p : 1ill ; 20cm. — (Poems for the zodiac)
Limited ed. of 100 numbered and signed copies
Unpriced (unbound) B81-19928

Wain, John. Cancer / John Wain. — London (77 Burghley Rd., N.W.5) : Pisces Press, 1980. — [4]p : 1ill ; 20cm. — (Poems for the zodiac)
Limited ed. of 100 numbered and signed copies
Unpriced (unbound) B81-19931

Wain, John. Capricorn / John Wain. — London (77 Burghley Rd., N.W.5) : Pisces Press, 1980. — [4]p : 1ill ; 20cm. — (Poems for the zodiac)
Limited ed. of 100 numbered and signed copies
Unpriced (unbound) B81-19927

Wain, John. Gemini / John Wain. — London (77 Burghley Rd., N.W.5) : Pisces Press, 1980. — [4]p : 1ill ; 20cm. — (Poems for the zodiac)
Limited ed. of 100 numbered and signed copies
Unpriced (unbound) B81-19922

Wain, John. Leo / John Wain. — London (77 Burghley Rd., N.W.5) : Pisces Press, 1980. — [4]p : 1ill ; 20cm. — (Poems for the zodiac)
Limited ed. of 100 numbered and signed copies
Unpriced (unbound) B81-19930

Wain, John. Libra / John Wain. — London (77 Burghley Rd., N.W.5) : Pisces Press, 1980. — [4]p : 1ill ; 20cm. — (Poems for the zodiac)
Limited ed. of 100 numbered and signed copies
Unpriced (unbound) B81-19925

Wain, John. Pisces / John Wain. — London (77 Burghley Rd., N.W.5) : Pisces Press, 1980. — [4]p : 1ill ; 20cm. — (Poems for the zodiac)
Limited ed. of 100 numbered and signed copies
Unpriced (unbound) B81-19926

Wain, John. Poems 1949-1979 / John Wain. — London : Macmillan, 1980. — 182p ; 23cm
Includes index
ISBN 0-333-28789-4 (cased) : £9.95
ISBN 0-333-31356-9 (pbk) : Unpriced
B81-26571

Wain, John. Sagittarius / John Wain. — London (77 Burghley Rd., N.W.5) : Pisces Press, 1980. — [4]p : 1ill ; 20cm. — (Poems for the zodiac)
Limited ed. of 100 numbered and signed copies
Unpriced (unbound) B81-19933

Wain, John. Scorpio / John Wain. — London (77 Burghley Rd., N.W.5) : Pisces Press, 1980. — [4]p : 1ill ; 20cm. — (Poems for the zodiac)
Limited ed. of 100 numbered and signed copies
Unpriced (unbound) B81-19923

Wain, John. Taurus / John Wain. — London (77 Burghley Rd., N.W.5) : Pisces Press, 1980. — [4]p : 1ill ; 20cm. — (Poems for the zodiac)
Limited ed. of 100 numbered and signed copies
Unpriced (unbound) B81-19924

Wain, John. Virgo / John Wain. — London (77 Burghley Rd., N.W.5) : Pisces Press, 1980. — [4]p : 1ill ; 20cm. — (Poems for the zodiac)
Limited ed. of 100 numbered and signed copies
Unpriced (unbound) B81-19932

821'.914 — Poetry in English, ***1945-*** **— *Texts continuation***

Waite, Margaret M.. Showers upon the grass : devotional poetry / Margaret M. Waite ; illustrations by Steven Law. — Ilkeston : Moorley's, [1980]. — 35p : ill ; 21cm
ISBN 0-86071-081-5 (pbk) : £0.50 B81-02539

Walker, Hugh Graham. O, valiant heart : a poetical impression / by Hugh Graham Walker. — [Farnsfield] ([Beauna Vista, Chapel La., Farnsfield, Newark on Trent, Notts.) : [H.G. Walker], [1980]. — [21]p ; 20cm
Cover title
£2.50 (pbk) B81-17387

Walker, Hugh Graham. "O valiant heart" : a poetical impression / by Hugh Graham Walker. — [Newark on Trent] ([Beauna Vista, Chapel La., Farnsfield, Newark on Trent, Notts. NG22 8JW]) : [H. Walker], [1981]. — [21]p ; 20cm
Cover title. — Text on inside cover
Unpriced (pbk) B81-19852

Walpole, Jenny. Raven Stone Cross and other poems / Jenny Walpole. — Bognor Regis : New Horizon, c1981. — 44p ; 21cm
ISBN 0-86116-690-6 : £2.95 B81-28951

Walrond, Glyne. The children's voice / Glyne Walrond ; illustrations by Omowale Stewart. — Ilfracombe : Stockwell, 1981. — 48p : ill ; 23cm
ISBN 0-7223-1400-0 : £3.00 B81-03080

Walton, Patricia. A trust of belief / Patricia Walton. — Bognor Regis : New Horizon, c1981. — 115p ; 21cm
ISBN 0-86116-525-x : £3.95 B81-27590

Walton, Robert. Workings / Robert Walton. — Llandysul : Gomer Press, 1979. — 61p ; 22cm
ISBN 0-85088-940-5 : £2.50 B81-07843

Ward, Donald. Border country / Donald Ward. — London : Anvil Press Poetry, 1981. — 70p ; 22cm
ISBN 0-85646-074-5 (pbk) : £3.25 B81-15520

Ward, Philip. Lost songs : political and other poems / Philip Ward. — Cambridge : Oleander, 1981. — 48p ; 21cm. — (Oleander modern poets ; 11)
ISBN 0-902675-51-6 (pbk) : £1.95 B81-16288

Warner, Joseph. A rendezvous of questions & question marks / Joseph Warner. — London (5 Parsifal Rd., N.W.6) : Cacophony Press, 1981. — [20]p : ill ; 26cm
Limited ed. of 100 signed and numbered copies
Unpriced (pbk) B81-15788

Warner, Silvie. Sonnets / Silvie Warner. — London : S. Warner, c1981 (Ilfracombe : Stockwell, 1981). — 47p ; 19cm
Includes index
ISBN 0-7223-1424-8 : Private circulation B81-16773

Warriner, Gary. Confessions of an anarchist disguised as a poet : (poems 1979-80) / Gary Warriner. — Cirencester (Chester St., Cirencester, Glos) : Warriner, 1981. — 22p ; 15cm
ISBN 0-7223-1476-0 (pbk) : Unpriced B81-35036

Waterman, Andrew. Out for the elements / Andrew Waterman. — Manchester : Carcanet, 1981. — 151p ; 22cm
ISBN 0-85635-377-9 (pbk) : £3.95 : CIP rev. B81-22456

Wayles, Florence. Hills and hollows / Florence Wayles. — Ilfracombe : Stockwell, 1980. — 24p ; 15cm
ISBN 0-7223-1431-0 (pbk) : £0.58 B81-03026

Weir, Anthony. Cinema of the blind / Anthony Weir. — [Belfast] : Blackstaff, c1981. — 42p ; 21cm
ISBN 0-85640-235-4 (pbk) : £2.95 B81-27245

Welch, John, *1942-*. Grieving signal / John Welch. — London (15 Norcott Rd., N16 7BJ) : The Many Press, 1980. — 19p ; 21cm
Limited ed. of 200 copies
ISBN 0-907326-00-5 (pbk) : £0.75 B81-02723

Wells, Nigel. The winter festivals / Nigel Wells. — Newcastle upon Tyne (1 North Jesmond Avenue, Jesmond, Newcastle upon Tyne NE2 3JX) : Bloodaxe, 1980. — 80p ; 22cm
Also available in limited edition of 25 numbered and signed copies
ISBN 0-906427-18-5 (pbk) : £3.00
ISBN 0-903427-19-3 (signed ed) : £3.00 B81-09545

Wells, Peter, *1919-*. Poems / by Peter Wells. — Halesworth (Model Farm, Linstead Magna, Halesworth, Suffolk IP19 0DT) : Badelesmere, 1981. — [18]p : ill ; 27cm
Unpriced B81-19430

Whateley, Nell. Poetic reveries / by Nell Whateley. — [s.l.] : [N. Whateley], c1980. — 32p ; 19cm
Unpriced (pbk) B81-05884

Wheeler, V. F.. The collected works of V.F. Wheeler. — London : Regency, c1980. — 32p ; 19cm
Unpriced (pbk) B81-05882

White, B. C.. Poems from the West country / B.C. White. — New ed. — Frome : B.C. White, 1981. — 160p : 1port ; 15cm
Previous ed.: 1976. — Includes index
ISBN 0-7223-1457-4 B81-39387

Whitney, E.. A pocket book of verse / by E. Whitney. — London : Regency, c1980. — 32p ; 19cm
Unpriced (pbk) B81-05890

Whitney, Leonard. Cumbrian poems / by Leonard Whitney. — Clapham, N. Yorkshire : Dalesman, 1980. — 62p : ill ; 22cm
ISBN 0-85206-621-x (pbk) : £1.50 B81-13681

Wild, Mark. The trembling of harebells / by Mark Wild. — Walton-on-Thames : Outposts, 1981. — 52p ; 21cm
£1.80 (pbk) B81-27855

Wilkinson, Gladys Doreena. Poems of the North Country / by Gladys Doreena Wilkinson. — Clapham, N. Yorkshire : Dalesman, 1980. — 64p : ill ; 22cm
ISBN 0-85206-616-3 (pbk) : £1.50 B81-15612

Williams, Patrick, *19---*. Trails / by Patrick Williams. — London : Sidgwick & Jackson, 1981. — 44p ; 22cm
ISBN 0-283-98724-3 (pbk) : £3.50 B81-36181

Wood, Marguerite. A line drawn in water / by Marguerite Wood. — Walton-on-Thames : Outposts, 1980. — 24p ; 21cm
£0.80 (pbk) B81-00350

Woolley, D. F.. A little bit of heaven : and other poems / by D.F. Woolley. — Bognor Regis : New Horizon, c1979. — 77p ; 21cm
ISBN 0-86116-097-5 : £2.50 B81-19229

Wright, Kit. Hot dog : and other poems / Kit Wright ; illustrated by Posy Simmonds. — [Harmondsworth] : Kestrel, 1981. — 72p : ill ; 21cm
ISBN 0-7226-5722-6 : £3.75 B81-24827

Wun-Lug (One Ear). A few rhymes — mainly about man / Wun-Lug (One Ear). — Bognor Regis : New Horizon, c1980. — 62p ; 21cm
ISBN 0-86116-298-6 : £2.95 B81-21716

821'.914 — Poetry in English. Gunn, Thom — ***Biographies***

Gunn, Thom. The occasions of poetry. — London : Faber, Feb.1982. — [188]p
ISBN 0-571-11733-3 : £6.95 : CIP entry
Primary classification 821'.009 B81-38308

821'.914 — Poetry in English. Henn, T. R. — ***Biographies***

Henn, T. R.. Five arches : a sketch for an autobiography ; and, Philoctetes and other poems / T.R. Henn ; with illustrations by Alan Freer. — Gerrard Cross : Smythe, 1980. — 326p : ill,1geneal.table ; 23cm
Includes index
ISBN 0-901072-92-3 : £9.50 : CIP rev. B80-00878

821'.914 — Poetry in English. Hughes, Ted — ***Critical studies***

Gifford, Terry. Ted Hughes : a critical study / Terry Gifford and Neil Roberts. — London : Faber, 1981. — 288p ; 23cm
Bibliography: p264-280. - Includes index
ISBN 0-571-11701-5 : £9.50 : CIP rev. B81-01199

821'.914'08 — Poetry in English, ***1945-*** **—** ***Anthologies***

Codex Bandito 3 : sex & death. — Maidstone (3 Pleasant Villias, 189 Kent St., Mereworth, Maidstone, Kent ME18 5QN) : Outcrowd, 1981. — 2sheets : ill ; 21x30cm folded to 11x15cm
Unpriced (unbound) B81-21283

Contemporary British and North American verse : an introductory anthology / edited by Martin Booth. — Oxford : Oxford University Press, 1981. — 192p ; 22cm
Bibliography: p185-187. - Includes index
ISBN 0-19-831243-1 (pbk) : £2.50 B81-15651

Continuities : new poems / by Byron Press Poets. — [Nottingham] ([c/o Allan Rodway, Dept. of English Studies, University of Nottingham, University Park, Nottingham NG7 2RD]) : [The Poets], [1981?]. — 51p ; 19cm
£2.95 (pbk) B81-32147

Full Z-Zip : side & bottom. — Minoty (The Cottage, Lower Moor Farm, Minoty, nr Malmesbury, Wilts.) : Zip Dinnor, 1981. — [21]p : ill ; 30cm
Limited ed. of 100 copies
ISBN 0-907663-00-1 (pbk) : Unpriced B81-28484

Harwood, Lee. Wish you were here / Lee Harwood & Anthony Lopez. — Deal : Transgravity, 1979. — 24p ; 21cm
ISBN 0-85682-103-9 (pbk) : £0.90 B81-16447

Jarvis, Paul. Triptych : poems / by Paul Jarvis, Alasdair Enticknap, Val Humphreys. — [Harrogate] ([41a Grove Rd., Harrogate HG1 5EP, N. Yorkshire]) : Albatross Emprints, [1980]. — [50]p ; 21cm
ISBN 0-9507116-0-8 (pbk) : £0.60 B81-07858

Lindop, Jim. A blue journey : poems / by Jim Lindop and Rodney Wood. — Brentwood (9 Wingrave Cres., Brentwood, Essex) : Mistral, c1981. — 32p : ill ; 21cm
£0.80 (pbk) B81-37191

Magee, Wes. Poems for a course / Wes Magee & John Cotton. — Berkhamsted (Berkamsted, Herts.) : Priapus, 1980. — [10]p : 1 ill ; 22cm. — (Priapus poets)
£0.25 B81-20942

Mandeville dragoncards eleven / Jonathan Bye ... [et al.]. — [Hitchin] ([2 Taylor's Hill, Hitchin, Herts.]) : [Mandeville], [c1981]. — 1v.(12cards in envelope) ; 11x16cm
£0.50 B81-28395

Modern poets five / edited by Jim Hunter. — London : Faber, 1981. — 149p ; 19cm
ISBN 0-571-11567-5 (pbk) : Unpriced B81-08593

Outcrop / [Norman Jope editor]. — [Lampeter] (Timberdene, Station Terrace, Lampeter, Dyfed SA48 7HH) : N. Jope, 1980. — 64p ; 30cm
Cover title
£0.30 (pbk) B81-17682

821'.914'08 — Poetry in English, *1945-* — *Anthologies* *continuation*

A **Pocket** book of poems : a selection of poems from the Richmond Poetry Group, 1981 / edited by Ron Aberdeen ; illustrated by Graham Rose. — Sunbury-on-Thames (57 Kenyngton Drive, Sunbury-on-Thames, Middx) : The Group, c1981. — 55p : ill ; 21cm
£1.20 (pbk) B81-19989

Poetry introductions. — London : Faber
5. — Jan.1982. — [121]p
ISBN 0-571-11914-x (pbk) : £2.95 : CIP entry B81-34667

Voices of today : an anthology of recent verse / selected by F.E.S. Finn. — London : Murray, c1980. — ix,118p ; 22cm
Includes index
ISBN 0-7195-3757-6 (pbk) : £1.75 B81-01200

821'.914'08 — Poetry in English, *1945-* — *Anthologies — Serials*

Gangsters, ghosts and dragonflies. — London : Allen & Unwin, Oct.1981. — [160]p
ISBN 0-04-821053-6 : £5.95 : CIP entry B81-25107

The **Gregory** awards : poems. — 1980-. — London : Secker & Warburg, 1981-. — v. ; 23cm
Annual
ISSN 0261-5576 = Gregory awards : £4.50 B81-31047

The **Gregory** Awards 1980. — London : Secker & Warburg, June 1981. — [64]p
ISBN 0-436-37812-4 : £4.50 : CIP entry B81-10427

Molly Bloom. — [No.1]-. — Goole (Back 34 Pasture Rd, Goole, North Humberside) : Molly Bloom, c1980-. — v. ; 22cm
Irregular
ISSN 0260-8413 = Molly Bloom : £1.00 per issue B81-21344

New hope international. — 1980/81-. — Ashton-under-Lyne (23 Gambrel Bank Rd, Ashton-under-Lyne OL6 8TW) : New Hope International, 1980-. — v. ; 21cm
Two issues yearly
ISSN 0260-7948 = New hope international : £2.00 for four issues B81-09214

New poetry. — 7. — London : Hutchinson, Oct.1981. — [144]p
ISBN 0-09-146450-1 : £6.50 : CIP entry B81-26794

Other poetry. — [1?]-. — Hay-on-Wye (c/o The Poetry Bookshop, 22 Broad St., Hay-on-Wye, Powys HR3 5DG) : [s.n.], 1979-. — v. ; 21cm
Three issues yearly. — Description based on: 4
ISSN 0144-5847 = Other poetry : £2.40 per year B81-00354

Outcrop. — Vol.2 (1981). — [Lampeter] (New Rhymers Club, St. David's University College, Lampeter, Dyfed) : Outcrop Publications, c1981. — 57p
ISBN 0-907600-00-x : £0.60 (£1.00 to libraries)
ISSN 0260-9657 B81-29645

Poetry into print. — Mar.1981-. — Ely (c/o D.A. Rigley, 29 Longfields, Ely, Cambridge CB6 3DN) : [S.n.], 1981-. — v. ; 22cm
Quarterly
ISSN 0261-0795 = Poetry into print : £2.00 per year B81-29993

Poetry London/apple magazine. — Vol.1, no.1 (Autumn 1979). — London : Mather in association with Editions Poetry London, 1979. — 1v. : ill,ports ; 25cm
Continues: Poetry London-New York. — Only one issue published
£2.50 per issue B81-16231

821'.914'0803242343 — Poetry in English, *1945-*. Special subjects: Alderney — *Anthologies*

Alderney : a book of poems / edited by Felicity Crump and Nina Steane ; with an introduction by Kevin Crossley-Holland ; illustrations by Nina Carroll, Jacqueline Langridge and Barbara Whitelaw, cover design by Barbara Whitelaw. — Alderney (Blanchard, Alderney, Channel Islands) : Blanchard Books, [1981]. — 51p : ill ; 19cm
ISBN 0-9507458-0-4 (pbk) : Unpriced B81-29290

821'.914'08036 — Poetry in English, *1945-*. Special themes: Walls — *Anthologies*

Wall : an exploration through poems and images / Rodney Pybus ... [et al.] in collaboration with Simon McRoyall ... [et al.]. — Brampton (Banks, Brampton, Cumbria) : L.Y.C. Press, 1981. — 51p : ill ; 19x23cm
Published to accompany an exhibition by the artists held at the L.Y.C. Gallery, May 1981
ISBN 0-9504571-1-6 (pbk) : £2.00 B81-23490

821'.914'0809282 — Children's poetry in English, *1945-* — *Anthologies*

Bennett, Jill. Days are where we live. — London : Bodley Head, Oct.1981. — [48]p
ISBN 0-370-30432-2 : £3.50 : CIP entry B81-27395

McGough, Roger. You tell me : poems / by Roger McGough and Michael Rosen ; illustrated by Sara Midda. — Harmondsworth : Puffin, 1981, c1979. — 72p : ill ; 20cm
Originally published: London : Kestrel, 1979
ISBN 0-14-031286-2 (pbk) : £0.75 B81-10688

Over the bridge / edited by John Loveday ; illustrated by Michael Foreman. — Harmondsworth : Puffin, 1981. — 110p : ill ; 20cm
Includes index
ISBN 0-14-031402-4 (pbk) : £0.95 B81-16144

Over the bridge / edited by John Loveday ; illustrated by Michael Foreman. — Harmondsworth : Kestrel, 1981. — 110p : ill ; 21cm
Includes index
ISBN 0-7226-5742-0 : £4.25 B81-16143

821'.914'0809282 — Poetry in English, *1945-* — *Anthologies — For children*

Strictly private : an anthology of poetry / chosen by Roger McGough ; illustrated by Graham Dean. — [Harmondworth] : Kestrel, 1981. — 185p : ill ; 21cm
Includes index
ISBN 0-7226-5694-7 : £4.95 B81-10524

821'.914'0809282 — Poetry in English. Child writers, *1945-* — *Anthologies*

Poets in school / edited by Alasdair Aston ; preface by Stephen Spender. — London : Book Club Associates, 1977. — xv,87p : ill ; 21cm
Unpriced B81-39124

821'.914'0809282 — Poetry in English. Child writers: Berkshire writers: Bracknell writers, *1945-* — *Anthologies*

Poems by the children and people of Bracknell. — Bracknell (Bracknell, Berks.) : South Hill Park Arts Centre, 1980. — 92p ; 21cm
ISBN 0-9507205-0-x (pbk) : £1.50 B81-21121

821'.914'0809287 — Poetry in English. Scottish feminist writers, *1945-* — *Anthologies*

Hens in the hay / poems by Chris Cherry ... [et al.] ; drawings Dianne Barry, Suzie Innes. — Edinburgh (43 Candlemaker Row, Edinburgh EH1 2QB) : Stramullion, 1980. — 79p : ill,ports ; 21cm
ISBN 0-907343-00-7 (pbk) : £1.60 B81-04748

821'.914'0809415 — Poetry in English. Irish writers, *1945-* — *Anthologies*

A **Dream** recurring : and other stories and poems : Maxwell House winners 2. — Dublin (2 Strand Rd., Baldoyle, Dublin 13) : Arlen House, [1980?]. — 112p ; 18cm
ISBN 0-905223-23-3 (pbk) : £1.95
Primary classification 823'.01'089287[FS] B81-09538

821'.914'0809416 — Poetry in English. Northern Irish writers, *1945-* — *Anthologies*

Trio poetry. — Belfast : Blackstaff
2 / Damian Gorman, Medbh McGuckian, Douglas Marshall. — c1981. — 65p ; 21cm
ISBN 0-85640-216-8 (pbk) : £2.95 B81-19688

821'.914'080942142 — Poetry in English. London writers: Highgate writers, *1945-* — *Anthologies*

Kites four : the Highgate poets / editor Fleur Bowers ; with an introduction by Leonard Clark. — London (10a South Grove, N.6) : Highgate Society, 1980. — iv,44p ; 21cm
£0.95 (pbk) B81-08772

821'.914'080942176 — Poetry in English. London writers: Newham *(London Borough)* writers: Stratford writers, *1945-* — *Anthologies*

The **Stratford** poets. — [London] ([c/o Olive Newton, 52b Eastwood Rd., Ilford, Essex IG3 8XA]) : Stratford Poets
Bk 2. — c1980. — 48p ; 21cm
Cover title
ISBN 0-9506495-1-1 (pbk) : £0.80 B81-28492

821'.914'080942319 — Poetry in English. Wiltshire writers: Salisbury writers, *1945-* — *Anthologies — Serials*

Salisbury circle poets. — 1980. — Salisbury (c/o Miss P. Ameg, 5 Belle Vue Rd., Salisbury, Wiltshire) : Salisbury Circle Poets, 1980. — 23p
ISBN 0-9507308-0-7 : Unpriced B81-18798

821'.914'080942496 — Poetry in English. West Midlands *(Metropolitan County)* writers: Birmingham writers: Small Heath writers, *1945-* — *Anthologies*

Khan, Pervaiz. Behind brown eyes / poems by Pervaiz Khan & Munaver Whusain Shah ; drawings by John O'Dowd. — Birmingham (516 Coventry Rd., Small Heath, Birmingham 10) : Trinity Arts, c1981. — 29p : ill ; 22cm. — (Small Heath writers)
£0.60 (pbk) B81-34630

821'.914'08094256 — Poetry in English. Bedfordshire writers, *1945-* — *Anthologies*

Progress in Bunyan's town and other poems / collected by Bill Turner. — [Bedford] ([Central Library, Bedford]) : North Bedfordshire District Libraries, Bedfordshire Country Library, [1980]. — [24]p ; 21cm
Cover title
ISBN 0-901051-90-x (pbk) : £0.50 B81-12017

821'.914'08094258 — Poetry in English. Hertfordshire writers, *1945-* — *Anthologies — Serials*

Hartforde Poets journal. — No.5 (June 1979)-. — Hertford (1c Broad Green Wood, Bayford, Hertford SG13 8PS) : Hartforde Poets Publications, 1979-. — v. ; 21cm
Six issues yearly. — Continues: Hartforde Poets newsletter. — Description based on: No.122 (Aug.1980)
ISSN 0260-3640 = Hartforde Poets journal : £0.25 per issue B81-09028

821'.914'080942735 — Poetry in English. Greater Manchester *(Metropolitan County)* writers: Ashton-under-Lyne region writers, *1945-* — *Anthologies — Serials*

Zip : poetry magazine : supported by N.W. Arts. — [No.1]-. — Mossley ([c/o the Editor,] 17 Anthony St., Mossley, Lancs.) : [s.n.], [1980?]-. — v. : ill ; 21cm
ISSN 0260-7654 = Zip : £0.20 per issue B81-34041

821'.914'08094276 — Poetry in English: Poetry in Lancashire dialects, *1945-* — *Anthologies*

The **Bolton** festival book of dialect and local poetry / selected by Tom Dunne and Pat Entwisle ; edited by Tom Dunne. — [Bolton] ([Le Mans Cres., Bolton BL1 1SA]) : Published for the Bolton Festival 1981, by the Arts Department of Bolton Metropolitan Borough, 1981. — 47p ; 23cm
ISBN 0-906585-03-1 (pbk) : Unpriced B81-37825

821′.914′08094278 — Poetry in English. Cumbrian writers, *1945-* **—** *Anthologies*
Adam′s dream : poems from Cumbria and Lakeland / edited by William Scammell and Rodney Pybus. — Ambleside (Charlotte Mason College, Ambleside, Cumbria) : Cumbria Literature, 1981. — 64p ; 21cm
ISBN 0-9507509-0-5 (pbk) : £1.50 B81-30819

821′.914′0809428 — Poetry in English. North-east English writers, *1945-* **—** *Anthologies*
Ten north-east poets : an anthology / edited by Neil Astley. — Newcastle upon Tyne (1 North Jesmond Avenue, Jesmond, Newcastle upon Tyne NE2 3JX) : Bloodaxe, 1980. — 102p ; 22cm
ISBN 0-906427-13-4 (pbk) : £3.00 B81-09543

821′.914′0809428 — Poetry in English. Pennine writers, *1945-* **—** *Anthologies*
Pennine anthology 1980. — Huddersfield (94 Woodhead Rd., Huddersfield, Yorks.) : Woodhead, [1981]. — 35p : ill ; 22cm
Cover title
£2.00 (pbk) B81-09639

821′.914′080942821 — Poetry in English. South Yorkshire *(Metropolitan County)* **writers: Sheffield writers,** *1945-* **—** *Anthologies*
Scarp 1 / Sheffield Poetry Workshop. — Sheffield (53 Chase Rd., Loxley, Sheffield S6 6RA) : Sheffield Poetry Workshop, 1981. — 38p : ill ; 26cm
Cover title
ISBN 0-9505641-2-5 (pbk) : £0.40 B81-34771

821′.914′080942847 — Poetry in English. North Yorkshire writers. Scarborough writers, *1945-* **—** *Anthologies — Serials*
Spindrift : poems by Scarborough Poetry Workshop. — [1] (1977)-. — Pickering (c/o Ms D. Whalley, 14 Littledale, Pickering, North Yorkshire) : The Workshop, 1977-. — v. ; 21cm
Irregular. — Description based on: 2 (1980)
ISSN 0260-4531 = Spindrift : £0.50
B81-06289

821′.914′09 — Poetry in English, *1945-1980* **—** *Critical studies — Interviews*
Viewpoints : poets in conversation with John Haffenden. — London : Faber and Faber, 1981. — 189p ; 23cm
Bibliography: p186-189
ISBN 0-571-11689-2 : £7.50 B81-24906

821′.914′09 — Poetry in English, *1945-* **—** *Critical studies*
Brown, Merle E.. Double lyric : divisiveness and communal creativity in recent English poetry / Merle E. Brown. — London : Routledge & Kegan Paul, 1980. — xv,236p ; 24cm
Originally published : New York : Columbia University Press, 1980. — Includes index
ISBN 0-7100-0449-4 : £11.50 B81-01201

822 — ENGLISH DRAMA

822 — Drama in English. Ghanaian writers. Aidoo, Ama Ata. Dilemma of a Ghost — *Study outlines*
Grant, Jane W.. Ama Ata Aidoo : the dilemma of a ghost / Jane W. Grant. — Harlow : Longman, 1980. — ix,49p ; 20cm. — (Longman guides to literature)
ISBN 0-582-65075-5 (pbk) : Unpriced
B81-08499

822 — Drama in English. Iranian writers, *1947-* **—** *Texts*
Ataie, Iraj Jannatie. Our wounds / by Iraj Jannatie Ataie. — London (67, Larch Road, Cricklewood Broadway, NW2) : Inter-CUT, c1981. — 30p ; 22cm
Unpriced (pbk) B81-39204

822 — Drama in English. New Zealand writers, *1907-* **—** *Texts*
Hall, Roger, *1939-*. Middle-age spread : a play / Roger Hall. — London : French, c1980. — 51p : plans ; 21cm
Three men, 3 women
ISBN 0-573-11273-8 (pbk) : £2.20 B81-07763

822 — Drama in English. New Zealand writers. Thompson, Mervyn — *Biographies*
Thompson, Mervyn. All my lives / Mervyn Thompson. — Christchurch [N.Z.] ; London : Whitcoulls, 1980. — 185p,[12]p of plates : ill,ports ; 25cm
ISBN 0-7233-0643-5 : Unpriced B81-05062

822 — Drama in English. Nigerian writers. Soyinka, Wole. Lion and the jewel — *Critical studies*
Banham, Martin. The lion and the jewel : a critical view / by Martin Banham ; edited by Yolande Cantù. — London : Collings in association with the British Council, 1981. — 36p : ill,1port ; 21cm
Bibliography: p34-35. - List of films: p36
ISBN 0-86036-135-7 (pbk) : £1.00 B81-18601

822 — Drama in English. Nigerian writers. Soyinka, Wole. Road, The — *Study outlines*
Probyn, Clive T.. The road : notes / by Clive T. Probyn. — Harlow : Longman, 1981. — 63p ; 21cm. — (York notes ; 133)
Bibliography: p62-63
ISBN 0-582-78258-9 (pbk) : £0.90 B81-34231

822 — Drama in English. Nigerian writers, *to 1960* **—** *Texts*
Soyinka, Wole. Opera Wonyosi / Wole Soyinka. — London : Collings, 1981. — 86p ; 21cm
Seventeen men, 6 women, supers
ISBN 0-86036-133-0 (pbk) : £2.25 B81-15997

822 — Drama in English. South African writers, *1909-1961* **—** *Texts*
Fugard, Athol. A lesson from aloes. — Oxford : Oxford University Press, Sept.1981. — [96]p. — (Oxford paperbacks)
ISBN 0-19-281307-2 (pbk) : £1.50 : CIP entry
B81-22475

822 — Drama in English. South African writers, *1961-* **—** *Anthologies*
South African people′s plays : ons phola hi / selected with introductory material by Robert Mshengu Kavanagh. — London : Heinemann, 1981. — xxxi,176p : ill ; 19cm. — (African writers series)
Contents: Unosilimela / by Credo V. Mutwa — Shanti / by Mthuli Shezi — Too late / by Gibson Kente — Survival / by Workshop ′71 Theatre Company
ISBN 0-435-90224-5 (pbk) : £2.95 : CIP rev.
B81-11955

822 — Drama in English. South African writers, *1961-* **—** *Texts*
Aron, Geraldine. Bar and Ger : a drama in one act / by Geraldine Aron. — New York ; London : French, c1980. — 18p ; 19cm
One man, 1 women
ISBN 0-573-62065-2 (pbk) : £1.10 B81-07717

822′.003′21 — Drama in English, *1625-1800* **—** *Encylopaedias*
Restoration and 18th-century drama / introduction by Arthur H. Scouten. — London : Macmillan, 1980. — vii,151p ; 25cm. — (Great writers student library ; 5) (Great writers of the English language)
Includes bibliographies
ISBN 0-333-28340-6 : £8.95 B81-05110

822′.008 — Drama in English, *1606-1777* **—** *Anthologies*
Morrell, J. M.. Four English comedies : of the 17th and 18th centuries / edited by J.M. Morrell. — Harmondsworth : Penguin, 1950, 1980 [printing]. — 414p ; 19cm. — (Penguin English library)
Contents: Volpone / by Ben Jonson — The way of the world / by William Congreve — She stoops to conquer / by Oliver Goldsmith — The school for scandal / by R.B. Sheridan
ISBN 0-14-043158-6 (pbk) : £1.75 B81-27644

822′.009 — Drama in English, *1660-1900* **—** *Critical studies*
Thompson, John Cargill. [An introduction to fifty British plays, 1660-1900]. A reader′s guide to fifty British plays 1660-1900 / by John Cargill Thompson. — London : Heinemann, 1980. — 448p ; 21cm. — (Reader′s guide series)
Originally published: London : Pan, 1980. — Bibliography: p433-439. - Includes index
ISBN 0-435-18881-x : £7.50 : CIP rev.
B80-13968

822′.009 — Drama in English. Criticism. Scott, Clement. Local associations: North Norfolk *(District)*
Stibbons, P. J. R.. Poppyland : strands of Norfolk history / Peter Stibbons and David Cleveland. — Norfolk : Poppyland Publishing, 1981. — 24p : ill,ports ; 21cm
Cover title. — Text on inside covers
ISBN 0-9504300-6-4 (pbk) : £0.90 B81-41030

822′.009 — Drama in English, *to 1979* **—** *Critical studies*
Salgādo, Gāmini. English drama : a critical introduction / Gāmini Salgādo. — London : Edward Arnold, 1980. — vi,234p ; 23cm
Bibliography: p221-226. — Includes index
ISBN 0-7131-6272-4 (pbk) : £4.95 : CIP rev.
B80-18880

822′.009 — Drama in English, *to ca 1975* **—** *Critical studies*
The **Revels** history of drama in English. — London : Methuen
Vol.4: 1613-1660. — Nov.1981. — [300]p
ISBN 0-416-13050-x : £25.00 : CIP entry
Also classified at 792′.0942 B81-30321

822′.02′08 — Radio plays in English, *1945-* **—** *Anthologies*
Soundscene : ten fifteen-minute plays for radio / selected and edited by Alfred Bradley. — Glasgow : Blackie, 1981. — 117p ; 22cm
ISBN 0-216-91073-0 (pbk) : £2.95 B81-36639

822′.02′08 — Radio plays in English, *1945-* **—** *Anthologies — For schools*
Cook, Marianne. Winning through. — London : Edward Arnold, Dec.1981. — [64]p
ISBN 0-7131-0527-5 (pbk) : £1.50 : CIP entry
B81-31548

822′.02′08 — Radio plays in English, *1945-* **—** *Anthologies — Serials*
Best radio plays of .... — 1980. — London : Eyre Methuen, 1981. — 112p
ISBN 0-413-48600-1 : £6.95 B81-31570

822′.02′08 — Television plays in English, *1945-* **—** *Anthologies — For schools*
Power. — London : Hutchinson Educational, Nov.1981. — [160]p. — (Studio scripts)
ISBN 0-09-146771-3 (pbk) : £1.75(non-net) : CIP entry B81-31234

822′.02′089282 — Radio & television plays in English, *1945-* **—** *Anthologies — For schools*
Love and marriage / edited by David Self. — London : Hutchinson, 1981. — 168p : ports ; 19cm. — (Studio scripts)
ISBN 0-09-144521-3 (pbk) : Unpriced : CIP rev. B81-22553

822′.02′089282 — Television plays in English, *1945-* **—** *Anthologies — For schools*
Communities / edited by David Self. — London : Hutchinson, 1980. — 139p : ill ; 19cm. — (Studio scripts)
ISBN 0-09-142511-5 (pbk) : £1.50 : CIP rev.
B81-05583

822′.02′09 — Radio plays in English, *1945-* **—** *Critical studies*
British radio drama / edited by John Drakakis. — Cambridge : Cambridge University Press, 1981. — vii,288p ; 23cm
Bibliography: p278-280. - Includes index
ISBN 0-521-22183-8 (cased) : £19.50
ISBN 0-521-29383-9 (pbk) : £6.95 B81-17932

Radio drama / edited by Peter Lewis. — London : Longman, 1981. — 278p ; 22cm
Bibliography: p260-263. — Includes index
ISBN 0-582-49052-9 (cased) : Unpriced
ISBN 0-582-49053-7 (pbk) : £5.75 B81-29375

822′.02′09 — Television plays in English, *1945-* **—** *Critical studies*
British television drama / edited by George W. Brandt. — Cambridge : Cambridge University Press, 1981. — x,275p : ill,ports ; 23cm
Bibliography: p260-271. - Includes index
ISBN 0-521-22186-2 (cased) : £19.50 : CIP rev.
(pbk) : £6.95 B81-07946

822′.041′08 — Drama in English, *1945-.* **One-act plays** — *Anthologies — For schools*

Plays of humour and suspense / edited by Sadler, Hayllar, Powell ; illustrated by Bruce Baldwin. — South Melbourne [Vic.] ; London : Macmillan, 1980. — 211p : ill ; 22cm
ISBN 0-333-29944-2 (pbk) : £2.75 B81-21874

822′.041′08 — One-act plays in English, *1945-* — *Anthologies*

Play nine : nine short plays / by John Bowen ... [et al.] ; edited by Robin Rook. — London : Edward Arnold, 1981. — 104p ; 22cm
ISBN 0-7131-0561-5 (pbk) : £1.95 : CIP rev. B81-22489

Reakes, Paul. Night intruder / by Paul Reakes. Twenty candles / by Ed Gilmorgan. Dead secret / by Jack Whitfield. — Macclesfield : New Playwrights′ Network, [1980]. — 31,16,16p : 3plans ; 19cm. — (Triad ; 34)
Night intruder: 6 men, 2 women
£1.75 (pbk) B81-05931

Triad 35. — Macclesfield : New Playwrights′ Network, [1981]. — 61p in various pagings : 1plan ; 18cm
Contents: But with a whimper / by Pat Trevor - Cruise for two / by Terry Ellis - Bringing home the ashes / by Dorothy Pollard
£1.75 (pbk) B81-20920

822′.0512′09 — Drama in English. Tragedies, *1558-1625* — *Critical studies*

Bradbrook, M. C.. Themes and conventions of Elizabethan tragedy / M.C. Bradbrook. — 2nd ed. — London : Cambridge University Press, 1980. — vii,270p ; 23cm
Previous ed.: 1935. — Bibliography: p261-266. - Includes index
ISBN 0-521-22770-4 (cased) : £17.50 (pbk) : £5.50 B81-00355

822′.0512′0927 — Drama in English. Chapman, George, *1559-1634* **& Shakespeare, William. Tragedies. Characters: Heroes** — *Critical studies*

Ide, Richard S.. Possessed with greatness : the heroic tragedies of Chapman and Shakespeare / Richard S. Ide. — London : Scolar, 1980. — xvi,253p ; 24cm
Originally published: Chapel Hill : University of North Carolina Press, 1980. — Bibliography: p231-243. - Includes index
ISBN 0-85967-619-6 : £12.50 : CIP rev. B80-08925

822′.0512′09353 — Drama in English. Tragedies, *1558-1625.* **Special themes: Revenge** — *Critical studies*

Hallett, Charles A.. The revenger′s madness : a study of revenge tragedy motifs / Charles A. Hallett and Elaine S. Hallett. — Lincoln, [Neb.] ; London : University of Nebraska Press, c1980. — xi,349p ; 23cm
Bibliography: p323-341. — Includes index
ISBN 0-8032-2309-9 : Unpriced B81-22361

822′.0512′09358 — Drama in English. Tragedies, *1558-1625.* **Special themes: Absolutism** — *Critical studies*

Lever, J. W.. The tragedy of state : a study in Jacobean drama / J.W. Lever. — London : Methuen, 1980, c1971. — ix,100p ; 23cm
Includes index
ISBN 0-416-30550-4 : £12.50 : CIP rev. B80-27490

822′.0516 — Miracle plays in English, *1400-1588* — *Anthologies — For schools*

Medieval mystery plays / edited by Robert Leach & Martyn Briggs. — London : Harrap, 1981. — 31p : music ; 25cm. — (Harrap′s theatre workshop)
Contents: The deluge - The shepherds pageant - The crucifixion
ISBN 0-245-53500-4 (pbk) : £1.25 B81-14622

822′.0516′08 — Religious drama in English, *1945-* — *Anthologies*

Two street plays from Canterbury. — London (St. Paul′s Church, Covent Garden, Bedford St, WC2E 9ED) : Radius, 1980. — 20p ; 21cm. — (Plays for the eighties ; no.2)
Cover title. — Contents: The fruit of the tree / Peter English — Leap of faith / Sheila Fairbairn
ISBN 0-907174-02-7 (pbk) : Unpriced B81-33024

822′.0516′09 — Religious drama in English, *1928-1978* — *Critical studies*

Browne, E. Martin. Fifty years of religious drama : a lecture given at Vaughan College, Leicester on 10th November, 1978 / by E. Martin Browne ; edited with an introduction by Richard Foulkes. — [Leicester] : Department of Adult Education, University of Leicester in association with RADIUS, 1979. — [15]p ; 21cm. — (Vaughan paper, ISSN 0308-9258 ; no.23)
ISBN 0-901507-14-8 (pbk) : Unpriced B81-13228

822′.0523′09 — Drama in English. Comedies, *1558-1702* — *Critical studies*

Farley-Hills, David. The comic in Renaissance comedy / David Farley-Hills. — London : Macmillan, 1981. — x,189p ; 23cm
Includes index
ISBN 0-333-27514-4 : £15.00 B81-31845

822′.0523′09 — Drama in English. Comedies, *1702-1800* — *Critical studies*

Bevis, Richard. The laughing tradition : stage comedy in Garrick′s day / Richard Bevis. — London : Prior, 1981, c1980. — 282p ; 24cm
Originally published: Athens, Ga. : University of Georgia Press, 1979. — Includes index
ISBN 0-86043-503-2 : £12.50 B81-07519

822′.0523′09 — Drama in English. Jonson, Ben & Shakespeare, William. Comedies — *Critical studies*

Grene, Nicholas. Shakespeare, Jonson, Molière : the comic contract / Nicholas Grene. — London : Macmillan, 1980. — xvii,246p ; 23cm
Bibliography: p235-242. — Includes index
ISBN 0-333-23308-5 : £15.00 : CIP rev.
Also classified at 842′.4 B80-02541

822.2 — ENGLISH DRAMA, 1400-1558

822′.2′08 — Drama in English, *1400-1558* — *Anthologies*

Three late medieval moralities. — London : Benn, Nov.1981. — [208]p. — (The New mermaids)
ISBN 0-510-33505-5 (pbk) : £2.95 : CIP entry B81-30525

822′.′2′08 — Drama in English, *1400-1558* — *Anthologies*

Two Tudor interludes ; The interlude of youth ; Hick Scorner / edited by Ian Lancashire. — Manchester : Manchester University Press, 1980. — xix,283p : 1map,facsim ; 21cm. — (The revels plays)
Bibliography: pxiv-xix. - Includes index
ISBN 0-7190-1523-5 : £12.95 : CIP rev. B79-32754

822.3 — ENGLISH DRAMA, 1558-1625

822′.3 — Drama in English, *1558-1625 — Texts*

Chapman, George, *1559?-1634.* Bussy d′Ambois. — London : Benn, Nov.1981. — [160]p
Originally published: 1965
ISBN 0-510-33306-0 : £2.50 : CIP entry B81-30557

Jonson, Ben. [Selections]. The complete plays of Ben Jonson / edited by G.A. Wilkes ; based on the edition edited by C.H. Herford and Percy and Evelyn Simpson. — Oxford : Clarendon
Vol.1. — 1981. — xv,411p ; 23cm
ISBN 0-19-812599-2 : £35.00 : CIP rev. B79-24646

Jonson, Ben. [Selections]. The complete plays of Ben Jonson / edited by G.A. Wilkes ; based on the edition edited by C.H. Herford and Percy and Evelyn Simpson. — Oxford : Clarendon
Vol.2. — 1981. — 431p ; 23cm
ISBN 0-19-812601-8 : £40.00 : CIP rev. B79-24647

Jonson, Ben. Volpone. — London : Ernest Benn, May 1981. — [208]p. — (The new mermaids)
ISBN 0-510-34157-8 (pbk) : £2.50 : CIP entry B81-05173

Marlowe, Christopher, *1564-1593.* The complete works of Christopher Marlowe / edited by Fredson Bowers. — 2nd ed. — Cambridge : Cambridge University Press, 1981
Previous ed.: 1973
Vol.1. — v,543p ; 23cm
ISBN 0-521-22757-7 : £32.50
ISBN 0-521-22759-3 (Set of 2 vols) : £55.00 B81-15337

Marlowe, Christopher, *1564-1593.* The complete works of Christopher Marlowe / edited by Fredson Bowers. — 2nd ed. — Cambridge : Cambridge University Press, 1981
Previous ed.: 1973
Vol.2. — xi,418p : facsims ; 23cm
ISBN 0-521-22758-5 : £30.00
ISBN 0-521-22759-3 (Set of 2 vols) : £55.00 B81-15338

Marlowe, Christopher, *1564-1593.* Tamburlaine the Great / Christopher Marlowe ; edited by J.S. Cunningham. — Manchester : Manchester University Press, c1981. — xiv,338p ; 21cm. — (The Revels plays)
Includes index
ISBN 0-7190-1528-6 : £21.50 : CIP rev. B81-08804

Massinger, Philip. A new way to pay old debts. — London : Benn, Sept.1981. — [128]p. — (The new mermaids)
ISBN 0-510-34021-0 (pbk) : £2.50 : CIP entry B81-20127

Peele, George. The old wives / George Peele ; edited by Patricia Binnie. — Manchester : Manchester University Press, 1980. — xi,95p : 1ill ; 21cm. — (The Revels plays)
Bibliography: px-xi. — Includes index
ISBN 0-7190-1525-1 : £11.50 : CIP rev. B79-37455

Shakespeare, William. Troilus and Cressida. — London : Heinemann Educational, Sept.1981. — [256]p. — (The Player′s Shakespeare)
ISBN 0-435-19015-6 : £2.50 : CIP entry B81-22600

Tourneur, Cyril. The revenger′s tragedy. — London : Benn, May 1981. — [144]p. — (The new mermaids)
ISBN 0-510-34206-x (pbk) : £2.25 : CIP entry B81-05160

822′.3 — Drama in English. Dekker, Thomas — *Commentaries*

Hoy, Cyrus. Introductions, notes, and commentaries to texts in ′The dramatic works of Thomas Dekker′ edited by Fredson Bowers / Cyrus Hoy. — Cambridge : Cambridge University Press, 1980
Vol.III. — xx,313p ; 23cm
ISBN 0-521-22336-9 : Unpriced
ISBN 0-521-23648-7 (set) : £40.00 B81-37140

Hoy, Cyrus. Introductions, notes, and commentaries to texts in ′The dramatic works of Thomas Dekker′ edited by Fredson Bowers / Cyrus Hoy. — Cambridge : Cambridge University Press, c1980
Vol.IV. — xx,205p ; 23cm
Includes index
ISBN 0-521-22506-x : Unpriced
ISBN 0-521-23648-7 (set) : £40.00 B81-37141

822′.3 — Drama in English. Jonson, Ben. Alchemist, *The* — *Study outlines*

Gurr, Andrew. The alchemist : notes / by Andrew Gurr. — Harlow : Longman, 1981. — 72p ; 21cm. — (York notes ; 102)
Bibliography: p64-65
ISBN 0-582-78136-1 (pbk) : £0.90 B81-19637

822'.3 — Drama in English. Jonson, Ben — *Critical studies*

Leggatt, Alexander. Ben Jonson : his vision and his art / Alexander Leggatt. — London : Methuen, 1981. — xvi,300p ; 23cm
Includes index
ISBN 0-416-74660-8 : Unpriced B81-11509

822'.3 — Drama in English. Jonson, Ben. Role of music

Chan, Mary. Music in the theatre of Ben Jonson / by Mary Chan. — Oxford : Clarendon Press, 1980. — xii,397p,[7]p of plates : ill,facsims,music ; 24cm
Bibliography: p366-391. — Includes index
ISBN 0-19-812632-8 : £25.00 : CIP rev. B80-18473

822'.3 — Drama in English. Marlowe, Christopher, *1564-1593.* **Doctor Faustus** — *Study outlines*

Murray, Christopher. Doctor Faustus : notes / by Christopher Murray. — Harlow : Longman, 1981. — 82p ; 21cm. — (York notes ; 127)
Bibliography: p81-82
ISBN 0-582-78250-3 (pbk) : £0.90 B81-34239

822'.3 — Drama in English. Webster, John, *1580?-1625? - Critical studies*

Bradbrook, M. C.. John Webster : citizen and dramatist / M.C. Bradbrook. — London : Weidenfeld and Nicolson, c1980. — xiii,218p : 1geneal.table,1map ; 23cm
Bibliography: p199-203. - Includes index
ISBN 0-297-77813-7 : £10.00 B81-04010

822'.3 — Drama in English. Webster, John, *1580?-1625?.* **Duchess of Malfi & White devil** — *Study outlines*

Moffett, Valerie A.. Notes on Webster's The white devil and The Duchess of Malfi / compiled by Valerie A. Moffett. — London : Methuen Paperbacks, 1979. — 88p ; 20cm. — (Methuen notes)
Bibliography: p88
ISBN 0-417-21670-x (pbk) : £0.75 B81-11596

822'.3 — Drama in English. Webster, John, *b. ca 1580 — Critical studies*

Pearson, Jacqueline. Tragedy and tragicomedy in the plays of John Webster / Jacqueline Pearson. — Manchester : Manchester University Press, 1980. — 151p ; 23cm
Bibliography: p145-147. — Includes index
ISBN 0-7190-0786-0 : £12.50 : CIP rev. B80-06549

822'.3'0321 — Drama in English, *1558-1625 — Encyclopaedias*

Renaissance drama / introduction by Derek Traversi. — London : Macmillan, 1980. — vi,122p ; 24cm. — (Great writers student library ; 3)
Includes bibliographies
ISBN 0-333-28351-1 : £7.95 B81-05109

822'.3'08 — Revels in English, *1558-1625 — Anthologies*

Three revels from the Inns of Court. — Amersham : Avebury, Nov.1981. — [128]p
ISBN 0-86127-402-4 : £9.00 : CIP entry B81-30429

822'.3'080351 — Masques in English, *1558-1625.* **Special subjects: England. Elizabeth I,** *Queen of England — Anthologies*

Wilson, Jean, *1945-*. Entertainments for Elizabeth I / Jean Wilson. — Woodbridge : Brewer, 1980. — 179p : 1ill ; 23cm. — (Studies in Elizabethan and Renaissance culture ; 2)
Bibliography: p171-173. - Includes index. — Includes the text of The four foster children of desire (1581), and those at Cowdray (1591), Elvetham (1591), and Ditchley (1592)
ISBN 0-85991-048-2 : £12.00 : CIP rev.
Also classified at 394'.5'0942 B80-06550

822'.3'09 — Drama in English, *1558-1625 — Critical studies*

Bradbrook, M. C.. A history of Elizabethan drama / M.C. Bradbrook. — Cambridge : Cambridge University Press, [1981]. — 6v. : ill,facsims ; 23cm
In slipcase. — Contents: v.1. Themes and conventions of Elizabethan tragedy. 2nd ed., 1980. Previous ed.: 1935 — v.2. The growth and structure of Elizabethan comedy. New ed., 1979. Previous ed.: London : Chatto & Windus, 1955 — v.3. The rise of the common player. 1979. Originally published: London : Chatto & Windus, 1962 — v.4. Shakespeare and Elizabethan poetry. 1979. Originally published: London : Chatto & Windus, 1951 — v.5. Shakespeare the craftsman. 1979. Originally published: London : Chatto & Windus, 1969 — v.6. The living monument. 1979. Originally published: 1976
ISBN 0-521-29531-9 (pbk) : £23.50
ISBN 0-521-29695-1 (v.1)
ISBN 0-521-29526-2 (v.2)
ISBN 0-521-29527-0 (v.3)
ISBN 0-521-29528-9 (v.4)
ISBN 0-521-29529-7 (v.5)
ISBN 0-521-29530-0 (v.6) B81-25927

Putt, S. Gorley. The golden age of English drama. — Cambridge : Brewer, Sept.1981. — [240]p
ISBN 0-85991-076-8 : £15.00 : CIP entry B81-22540

822'.3'09356 — Drama in English, *1558-1625.* **Special themes: Alchemy** — *Critical studies*

Nicholl, Charles. The chemical theatre / Charles Nicholl. — London : Routledge & Kegan Paul, 1980. — ix,292p : ill,facsims,2ports ; 24cm
Bibliography: p278-284. — Includes index
ISBN 0-7100-0515-6 : £13.50 : CIP rev. B80-21026

822.3'3 — Drama in English. Shakespeare, William. All's well that ends well & Measure for measure — *Critical studies*

Wheeler, Richard P.. Shakespeare's development and the problem comedies : turn and counter-turn / Richard P. Wheeler. — Berkeley ; London : University of California Press, c1981. — xiv,229p ; 25cm
Includes index
ISBN 0-520-03902-5 : £12.00 B81-34334

822.3'3 — Drama in English. Shakespeare, William. Antony and Cleopatra — *Study outlines*

Gotch, Paul. Antony and Cleopatra : notes / by Paul Gotch. — London : Longman, 1980. — 80p : 2 ill ; 21cm. — (York notes ; 82)
Bibliography: p78
ISBN 0-582-78116-7 (pbk) : £0.90 B81-14584

822.3'3 — Drama in English. Shakespeare, William. As you like it — *Study outlines*

Barber, Charles. As you like it : notes / by Charles Barber. — Harlow : Longman, 1981. — 88p ; 21cm. — (York notes ; 108)
Bibliography: p84-86
ISBN 0-582-78142-6 (pbk) : £0.90 B81-19636

822.3'3 — Drama in English. Shakespeare, William — *Biographies*

Schoenbaum, S.. William Shakespeare : records and images / S. Schoenbaum. — London : Scolar Press, 1981. — xviii,276p(2fold.) : ill,facsims,ports ; 36cm
Ill on lining papers. — Bibliography: p247-262. — Includes index
ISBN 0-85967-625-0 : £70.00 B81-17703

822.3'3 — Drama in English. Shakespeare, William. Characters: Men — *Psychoanalytical perspectives*

Kahn, Coppélia. Man's estate : masculine identity in Shakespeare / Coppélia Kahn. — Berkeley ; London : University of California Press, c1981. — xiii,238p ; 23cm
Includes index
ISBN 0-520-03899-1 : £10.50 B81-27566

822.3'3 — Drama in English. Shakespeare, William. Characters: Women

Cook, Judith. Women in Shakespeare / Judith Cook. — London : Harrap, 1980. — xii,156p,[16]p of plates : ill ; 23cm
Bibliography: p147-148. — Includes index
ISBN 0-245-53607-8 (cased) : £8.50
ISBN 0-245-53631-0 (pbk) : £4.50 B81-01202

Pitt, Angela. Shakespeare's women / Angela Pitt. — Newton Abbot : David & Charles, c1981. — 224p : ill,ports ; 24cm
Bibliography: p219-220. — Includes index
ISBN 0-7153-7848-1 : £9.95 B81-08700

822.3'3 — Drama in English. Shakespeare, William. Comedies — *Critical studies*

Riemer, A. P.. Antic fables : patterns of evasion in Shakespeare's comedies / A.P. Riemer. — Manchester : Manchester University Press, 1980. — ix,229p ; 23cm
Originally published: Sydney : Sydney University Press, 1980. — Includes index
ISBN 0-7190-0812-3 : £12.50 B81-01706

822.3'3 — Drama in English. Shakespeare, William. Comedies. Structure

Hart, John A.. Dramatic structure in Shakespeare's romantic comedies / John A. Hart. — Pittsburgh ; London : Carnegie-Mellon University Press, c1980. — iv,126p ; 22cm. — (Carnegie series in English. New series ; no.2)
ISBN 0-915604-23-x (pbk) : Unpriced B81-08060

822.3'3 — Drama in English. Shakespeare, William — *Critical studies*

Allman, Eileen Jorge. Player-king and adversary : two faces of play in Shakespeare / Eileen Jorge Allman. — Baton Rouge ; London : Louisiana State University Press, c1980. — 347p ; 24cm
Bibliography: p335-341. — Includes index
ISBN 0-8071-0592-9 : £15.00 B81-18659

Aspects of Shakespeare's 'problem plays'. — Cambridge : Cambridge University Press, Jan.1982. — [148]p
ISBN 0-521-23959-1 (cased) : £17.50 : CIP entry
ISBN 0-521-28371-x (pbk) : £5.50 B81-37536

Berry, Ralph. Shakespearean structures / Ralph Berry. — London : Macmillan, 1981. — x,151p ; 23cm
Includes index
ISBN 0-333-30774-7 : £15.00 B81-31850

Chaudhuri, Sukanta. Infirm glory : Shakespeare and the Renaissance image of man / Sukanta Chaudhuri. — Oxford : Clarendon Press, 1981. — xiv,231p ; 22cm
Includes index
ISBN 0-19-812801-0 : £12.50 B81-19782

Clemen, Wolfgang. Shakespeare's dramatic art : collected essays / Wolfgang Clemen. — London : Methuen, 1972 (1980 [printing]). — 236p : ill ; 23cm
Includes index. — Includes 4 essays translated from the German
ISBN 0-416-30580-6 : £15.00 : CIP rev. B80-36331

Edwards, Philip. Shakespeare and the confines of art. — London : Methuen, Oct.1981. — [178]p. — (Methuen library reprints)
Originally published: 1968
ISBN 0-416-32200-x : £10.50 : CIP entry B81-24644

Frye, Roland Mushat. Shakespeare. — London : Allen & Unwin, Oct.1981. — [288]p
ISBN 0-04-822043-4 (cased) : £6.95 : CIP entry
ISBN 0-04-822044-2 (pbk) : £2.95 B81-27344

Hirsh, James E.. The structure of Shakespearean scenes. — London : Yale University Press, Oct.1981. — [224]p
ISBN 0-300-02650-1 : £12.60 : CIP entry B81-31943

Manlove, Colin N.. The gap in Shakespeare : the motif of division from Richard II to The tempest / by Colin N. Manlove. — London : Vision, 1981. — 200p ; 23cm. — (Critical studies series)
Includes index
ISBN 0-85478-444-6 : £10.95 B81-36507

822.3'3 — Drama in English. Shakespeare, William — *Critical studies* *continuation*

Rabkin, Norman. Shakespeare and the problem of meaning / Norman Rabkin. — Chicago ; London : University of Chicago, c1981. — x,165p ; 21cm
Includes index
ISBN 0-226-70177-8 : £9.60 B81-28260

Rowse, A. L.. Shakespeare's globe : his intellectual and moral outlook / A.L. Rowse. — London : Weidenfeld and Nicolson, c1981. — ix,210p ; 23cm
Includes index
ISBN 0-297-77897-8 : £8.95 B81-20241

Williams, Gwyn. Person and persona : studies in Shakespeare / by Gwyn Williams. — Cardiff : University of Wales Press, c1981. — 141p : ill ; 21cm
ISBN 0-7083-0784-1 (pbk) : Unpriced : CIP rev. B81-04264

822.3'3 — Drama in English. Shakespeare, William — *Critical studies — Early works*

Shakespeare : the critical heritage / edited by Brian Vickers. — London : Routledge & Kegan Paul. — (The critical heritage series)
Vol.6: 1774-1801. — 1981. — xiv,650p ; 23cm
Bibliography: p637-638. — Includes index
ISBN 0-7100-0629-2 : £22.50 B81-32479

822.3'3 — Drama in English. Shakespeare, William — *Critical studies — For schools*

Leach, Robert, *1942-*. Shakespeare's theatre / Robert Leach. — London : Harrap, 1981. — 48p : ill,1plan,ports ; 25cm. — (Harrap's theatre workshop)
Bibliography: p48
ISBN 0-245-53622-1 (pbk) : £1.25 B81-18982

822.3'3 — Drama in English. Shakespeare, William — *Critical studies — Serials*

Shakespeare survey. — 33. — Cambridge : Cambridge University Press, 1980. — 217p
ISBN 0-521-23249-x : £17.50 B81-11229

Shakespeare survey. — 34. — Cambridge : Cambridge University Press, Dec.1981. — [214]p
ISBN 0-521-23240-6 : £18.50 : CIP entry B81-34015

822.3'3 — Drama in English. Shakespeare, William. Criticism, *to 1979*

Powell, Raymond. Shakespeare and the critics' debate : a guide for students / Raymond Powell. — London : Macmillan, 1980. — vii,167p ; 23cm
Includes index
ISBN 0-333-27666-3 (cased) : £9.00 : CIP rev. B80-03806

822.3'3 — Drama in English. Shakespeare, William. Cymbeline — *Study outlines*

Draper, R. P.. Cymbeline : notes / by R.P. Draper. — London : Longman, 1980. — 104p : 2ill ; 21cm. — (York notes ; 93)
Bibliography: p101-102
ISBN 0-582-78151-5 (pbk) : £0.90 B81-14581

822.3'3 — Drama in English. Shakespeare, William - *Encyclopaedias*

Wells, Stanley, *1930-*. Shakespeare. — Oxford : Oxford University Press, Apr.1981. — [224]p
ISBN 0-19-871074-7 (pbk) : £4.50 : CIP entry B81-18178

822.3'3 — Drama in English. Shakespeare, William. Endings. Influence of European romances, *to 1500 — Critical studies*

White, R. S.. Shakespeare and the romance ending / by R.S. White. — Newcastle upon Tyne (School of English, The University, Newcastle upon Tyne) : R.S. White, c1981. — 139p ; 21cm
Includes index
ISBN 0-9507521-0-x (pbk) : Unpriced B81-24174

822.3'3 — Drama in English. Shakespeare, William. Hamlet — *Critical studies*

Scofield, Martin. The ghosts of Hamlet : the play and modern writers / Martin Scofield. — Cambridge : Cambridge University Press, 1980. — 202p ; 24cm
Includes index
ISBN 0-521-22735-6 : £16.50
Also classified at 809'.034 B81-07893

822.3'3 — Drama in English. Shakespeare, William. Hamlet — *Critical studies — German texts*

Reutter, Hermann. Zur Dramaturgie meines Hamlet / Hermann Reutter. — Mainz ; London : Schott, c1980. — 10p ; 20cm
ISBN 3-7957-2627-1 (pbk) : £0.60 B81-15209

822.3'3 — Drama in English. Shakespeare, William. Hamlet — *Study outlines*

Todd, Loreto. Hamlet : notes / by Loreto Todd. — London : Longman, 1980. — 128p : 1ill ; 21cm. — (York notes ; 84)
Bibliography: p123
ISBN 0-582-78227-9 (pbk) : £0.90 B81-14583

822.3'3 — Drama in English. Shakespeare, William. Henry IV. Part 1 — *Study outlines*

Mares, F. H.. Henry IV, part 1 : notes / by F.H. Mares. — London : Longman, 1980. — 104p : 2ill ; 21cm. — (York notes ; 83)
Bibliography: p98-99
ISBN 0-582-78237-6 (pbk) : £0.90 B81-14582

Toner, Alan. Henry IV Part 1 / Alan Toner. — Dublin : Gill and Macmillan, 1981. — 20p : 1ill ; 22cm. — (Study-guide notes)
Bibliography: p20
ISBN 0-7171-1127-x (pbk) : £0.90 B81-25556

822.3'3 — Drama in English. Shakespeare, William. Imagery — *Critical studies*

Armstrong, Edward A.. Shakespeare's imagination : a study of the psychology of association and inspiration / by Edward A. Armstrong. — [Rev. ed.]. — Lincoln [Neb.] ; London : University of Nebraska Press, 1979, c1963. — 230p ; 23cm
Previous ed.: London : L. Drummond, 1946. — Includes index
ISBN 0-8032-1005-1 : £8.70 B81-17896

822.3'3 — Drama in English. Shakespeare, William. Influence of English royal court, *1603-1612*

Schmidgall, Gary. Shakespeare and the courtly aesthetic / Gary Schmidgall. — Berkeley ; London : University of California Press, c1981. — xxiv,299p : ill ; 23cm : ports
Bibliography: p273-289. — Includes index
ISBN 0-520-04130-5 (pbk) : £17.00 B81-36412

822.3'3 — Drama in English. Shakespeare, William. Julius Caesar — *Questions & answers — For schools*

Perkins, D. C.. Julius Caesar / D.C. Perkins. — Walton-on-Thames : Celtic Revision Aids, 1981. — iv,118p : ill,2plans ; 19cm. — (Literature revision notes and examples)
ISBN 0-17-751303-9 (pbk) : £1.25 B81-15503

822.3'3 — Drama in English. Shakespeare, William. Julius Caesar — *Study outlines — For schools*

Griffin, John, *1935-*. Julius Caesar : an interpretation for the student at O-Level / by John Griffin ; edited by Philippa Bush. — Huntingdon : Cambridge Learning Enterprises, c1979. — 98p ; 21cm
ISBN 0-905946-06-5 (pbk) : Unpriced B81-39374

822.3'3 — Drama in English. Shakespeare, William. King Lear — *Textual criticisms*

Stone, P. W. K.. The textual history of King Lear / P.W.K. Stone. — London : Scolar Press, c1980. — viii,280p ; 25cm
Bibliography: pvi
ISBN 0-85967-536-x : £27.50 : CIP rev. B80-03305

Urkowitz, Steven. Shakespeare's revision of King Lear / Steven Urkowitz. — Princeton, N.J. ; Guildford : Princeton University Press, c1980. — 170p ; 23cm. — (Princeton essays in literature)
Bibliography: p151-152. — Includes index
ISBN 0-691-06432-6 : £7.50 B81-02626

822.3'3 — Drama in English. Shakespeare, William. Macbeth — *Questions & answers — For schools*

Self, David. Macbeth / by David Self. — Teacher's ed. — London : Glasgow Publications, c1980. — 15,[4]p : ill(some col.) ; 30cm. — (Guidelines)
ISBN 0-86158-513-5 (unbound) : Unpriced B81-33170

Self, David. Macbeth / by David Self. — London : Glasgow, c1980. — 15p : ill(some col.) ; 30cm. — (Guidelines)
ISBN 0-86158-513-5 (unbound) : Unpriced B81-21966

822.3'3 — Drama in English. Shakespeare, William. Merchant of Venice — *Questions & answers — For schools*

Perkins, D. C.. The merchant of Venice / D.C. Perkins. — Walton-on-Thames : Celtic Revision Aids, 1981. — iv,124p : ill,2plans ; 19cm. — (Literature revision notes and examples)
ISBN 0-17-751302-0 (pbk) : £1.25 B81-15502

822.3'3 — Drama in English. Shakespeare, William. Merchant of Venice — *Study outlines*

Kiberd, Declan. The merchant of Venice : notes / by Declan Kiberd. — Harlow : Longman, 1981. — 80p ; 21cm. — (York notes ; 107)
Bibliography: p76
ISBN 0-582-78092-6 (pbk) : £0.90 B81-23612

822.3'3 — Drama in English. Shakespeare, William. Midsummer night's dream — *Questions & answers — For schools*

Perkins, D. C.. A midsummer night's dream / by D.C. Perkins and I. Huke. — Walton-on-Thames : Celtic Revision Aids, 1981. — iv,119p : ill,2plans ; 19cm. — (Literature revision notes and examples)
ISBN 0-17-751305-5 (pbk) : £1.25 B81-15506

822.3'3 — Drama in English. Shakespeare, William. Much ado about nothing — *Study outlines*

Drakakis, John. Much ado about nothing : notes / by John Drakakis. — London : Longman, 1980. — 116p : 1ill,1plan ; 21cm. — (York notes ; 73)
Bibliography: p116
ISBN 0-582-78180-9 (pbk) : £0.90 B81-06435

822.3'3 — Drama in English. Shakespeare, William. Othello — *Critical studies*

Adamson, Jane. Othello as tragedy : some problems of judgment and feeling / Jane Adamson. — Cambridge : Cambridge University Press, 1980. — ix,300p ; 23cm
ISBN 0-521-22368-7 (cased) : £15.00 : CIP rev.
ISBN 0-521-29760-5 (pbk) : £4.95 B80-26100

822.3'3 — Drama in English. Shakespeare, William — *Psychoanalytical perspectives*

Representing Shakespeare : new psychoanalytic essays / edited by Murray M. Schwartz and Coppélia Kahn. — Baltimore ; London : Johns Hopkins University Press, c1980. — xxi,296p ; 24cm
Bibliography: p265-286. — Includes index
ISBN 0-8018-2302-1 : £11.50 B81-01611

822.3'3 — Drama in English. Shakespeare, William. Richard II — *Questions & answers — For schools*

Perkins, D. C.. Richard II / D.C. Perkins and I. Huke. — Walton-on-Thames : Celtic Revision Aids, 1981. — iv,123p ; 19cm. — (Literature revision notes and examples)
ISBN 0-17-751304-7 (pbk) : £1.25 B81-15504

822.3'3 — Drama in English. Shakespeare, William. Richard II — *Study outlines*

Keeble, N. H.. Richard II : notes / by by N.H. Keeble. — London : Longman, 1980. — 118p : 2ill ; 21cm. — (York notes ; 41)
Bibliography: p117
ISBN 0-582-78188-4 (pbk) : £0.90 B81-07095

822.3'3 — Drama in English. Shakespeare, William Richard III — *Critical studies*

Gunby, D. C.. Shakespeare: Richard III / by D.C. Gunby. — London : Edward Arnold, 1980. — 62p ; 19cm. — (Studies in English literature ; no.71)
Bibliography: p59. - Includes index
ISBN 0-7131-6284-8 (pbk) : £1.65 : CIP rev. B80-13048

822.3'3 — Drama in English. Shakespeare, William. Richard III — *Study outlines*
Barber, Charles. Richard III : notes / by Charles Barber. — Harlow : Longman, 1981. — 88p : ill,1geneal.table ; 21cm. — (York notes ; 119)
Bibliography: p83-84
ISBN 0-582-78192-2 (pbk) : Unpriced
B81-33685

822.3'3 — Drama in English. Shakespeare, William. Romeo and Juliet — *Study outlines*
Corr, Patricia. Romeo and Juliet / Patricia Corr. — Dublin : Gill and Macmillan, 1981. — 34p : 2ill ; 22cm. — (Study-guide notes)
Bibliography: p34
ISBN 0-7171-1001-x (pbk) : £0.90 B81-25555

822.3'3 — Drama in English. Shakespeare, William. Special subjects: Dancing — *Critical studies*
Brissenden, Alan. Shakespeare and the dance / Alan Brissenden. — London : Macmillan, 1981. — xii,145p,8p of plates : ill ; 23cm
Bibliography: p128-135. — Includes index
ISBN 0-333-28523-9 : £12.00 : CIP rev.
B80-03808

822.3'3 — Drama in English. Shakespeare, William. Special themes: Coming of age — *Critical studies*
Garber, Marjorie B.. Coming of age in Shakespeare. — London : Methuen, July 1981. — [320]p
ISBN 0-416-30350-1 : £12.50 : CIP entry
B81-14858

822.3'3 — Drama in English. Shakespeare, William. Special themes: Flowering plants
De Bray, Lys. Fantastic garlands. — Poole : Blandford Press, Oct.1981. — [143]p
ISBN 0-7137-1066-7 : £9.95 : CIP entry
B81-30326

822.3'3 — Drama in English. Shakespeare, William. Special themes: Pregnancy
Sacks, Elizabeth. Shakespeare's images of pregnancy / Elizabeth Sacks. — London : Macmillan, 1980. — x,148p ; 23cm
Bibliography: p124-142. - Includes index
ISBN 0-333-30004-1 : £12.00 : CIP rev.
B80-36334

822.3'3 — Drama in English. Shakespeare, William. Special themes: Solitariness — *Critical studies*
Dillon, Janette. Shakespeare and the solitary man / Janette Dillon. — London : Macmillan, 1981. — xiv,183p ; 23cm
Includes index
ISBN 0-333-27468-7 : £15.00 : CIP rev.
B80-22468

822.3'3 — Drama in English. Shakespeare, William. Swear-words — *Critical studies*
Shirley, Frances A.. Swearing and perjury in Shakespears's plays / Frances A. Shirley. — London : Allen & Unwin, 1979. — xiv,174p ; 23cm
Bibliography: p163-170. - Includes index
ISBN 0-04-822040-x : 10.00 : CIP rev.
B78-39843

822.3'3 — Drama in English. Shakespeare, William. Taming of the shrew — *Study outlines*
Ridden, Geoffrey M.. The taming of the shrew : notes / by G.M. Ridden. — Harlow : Longman, 1981. — 71p : 2ill ; 21cm. — (York notes ; 118)
Bibliography: p69-71
ISBN 0-582-78198-1 (pbk) : £0.90 B81-34232

822.3'3 — Drama in English. Shakespeare, William. Tempest, *The* — *Study outlines*
Fanagan, John. The tempest / John Fanagan. — Tallaght : Folens, c1979. — 28p ; 22cm. — (Folens' student aids leaving certificate)
Bibliography: p28
ISBN 0-86121-086-7 (pbk) : Unpriced
B81-21920

822.3'3 — Drama in English. Shakespeare, William — *Texts*
Shakespeare, William. All's well that ends well / William Shakespeare ; edited by Barbara Everett. — Harmondsworth : Penguin, 1970 (1981 [printing]). — 228p ; 19cm. — (New Penguin Shakespeare)
Bibliography: p43-46
ISBN 0-14-070720-4 (pbk) : £1.10 B81-35484

Shakespeare, William. All's well that ends well / [William Shakespeare]. — London : British Broadcasting Corporation, 1981. — 128p,[4]p of plates : ports(some col.) ; 21cm
'The text ... used on this volume is the Alexander text, edited by the late Professor Alexander' - title page verso
ISBN 0-563-17874-4 (pbk) : £2.00 B81-18535

Shakespeare, William. Anthony and Cleopatra / William Shakespeare ; edited by Emrys Jones. — Harmondsworth : Penguin, 1977 (1980 [printing]). — 298p ; 19cm. — (The new Penguin Shakespeare)
Bibliography: p49-53
ISBN 0-14-070731-x (pbk) : £0.85 B81-06395

Shakespeare, William. As you like it / William Shakespeare ; edited by H.J. Oliver. — Harmondsworth : Penguin, 1968 (1980 [printing]). — 201p : music ; 19cm. — (The new Penguin Shakespeare)
Bibliography: p43-45
ISBN 0-14-070714-x (pbk) : £0.75 B81-06413

Shakespeare, William. The comedy of errors / William Shakespeare ; edited by Stanley Wells. — Harmondsworth : Penguin, 1972 (1980 [printing]). — 189p ; 19cm. — (The new Penguin Shakespeare)
Bibliography: p39-41
ISBN 0-14-070725-5 (pbk) : £1.25 B81-06393

Shakespeare, William. Coriolanus / William Shakespeare ; edited by G.R. Hibbard. — Harmondsworth : Penguin, 1967 (1980 [printing]). — 263p ; 19cm. — (The new Penguin Shakespeare)
Bibliography: p49-52
ISBN 0-14-070703-4 (pbk) : £1.25 B81-06416

Shakespeare, William. Hamlet / William Shakespeare ; edited by T.J.B. Spencer ; with an introduction by Anne Barton. — Harmondsworth : Penguin, 1980. — 383p ; 19cm. — (The new Penguin Shakespeare)
Bibliography: p55-57
ISBN 0-14-070734-4 (pbk) : £0.95 B81-06419

Shakespeare, William. Hamlet. — London : Methuen, Feb.1982. — [500]p. — (The Arden Shakespeare)
ISBN 0-416-17910-x (cased) : £12.00 : CIP entry
ISBN 0-416-17920-7 (pbk) : £2.95 B81-36391

Shakespeare, William. Henry V / William Shakespeare ; edited by A.R. Humphreys. — Harmondsworth : Penguin, 1968 (1979 [printing]). — 234p : geneal.tables ; 19cm. — (The new Penguin Shakespeare)
Bibliography: p50-54
ISBN 0-14-070708-5 (pbk) : £0.95 B81-06417

Shakespeare, William. [King Henry IV]. The first part of King Henry the Fourth / William Shakespeare ; edited by P.H. Davison. — Harmondsworth : Pengiun, 1968 (1980 [printing]). — 254p : 1geneal.table ; 19cm. — (The new Penguin Shakespeare)
Bibliography: p39-42
ISBN 0-14-070718-2 (pbk) : £0.80 B81-06406

Shakespeare, William. [King Henry IV]. The second part of King Henry the Fourth / William Shakespeare ; edited by P.H. Davison. — Harmondsworth : Penguin, 1977 (1980 [printing]). — 310p : music ; 19cm. — (The new Penguin Shakespeare)
Bibliography: p41-45
ISBN 0-14-070728-x (pbk) : £0.95 B81-06394

Shakespeare, William. [King Henry IV. part 2]. King Henry IV, part 2 / [William Shakespeare] ; edited by Tony Parr. — Basingstoke : Macmillan Education, 1981. — 281p ; 18cm. — (The Macmillan Shakespeare)
ISBN 0-333-17656-1 (pbk) : £0.95 : CIP rev.
B81-13522

Shakespeare, William. [King Henry VI. Part 1]. The first part of King Henry the Sixth / William Shakespeare ; edited by Norman Sanders. — Harmondsworth : Penguin, 1981. — 249p : geneal.tables ; 19cm. — (New Penguin Shakespeare)
ISBN 0-14-070735-2 (pbk) : £1.95 B81-18329

Shakespeare, William. [King Henry VI. Part 2]. The second part of King Henry the Sixth / William Shakespeare ; edited by Norman Sanders. — Harmondsworth : Penguin, 1981. — 301p : 2geneal.tables ; 19cm. — (New Penguin Shakespeare)
ISBN 0-14-070736-0 (pbk) : £2.25 B81-18519

Shakespeare, William. [King Henry VI. Part 3]. Third part of King Henry the Sixth / William Shakespeare ; edited by Norman Sanders. — Harmondsworth : Penguin, 1981. — 297p : ill,2geneal.tables ; 19cm. — (New Penguin Shakespeare)
ISBN 0-14-070737-9 (pbk) : £2.25 B81-18515

Shakespeare, William. [King Henry VIII]. King Henry the Eighth / William Shakespeare ; edited by A.R. Humphreys. — Harmondsworth : Penguin, 1971 (1981 [printing]). — 271p ; 19cm. — (New Penguin Shakespeare)
£1.50 (pbk) B81-22276

Shakespeare, William. King John / William Shakespeare ; edited by R.L. Smallwood. — Harmondsworth : Penguin, 1974 (1981 [printing]). — 373p : geneal.table ; 19cm
ISBN 0-14-070727-1 (pbk) : £1.50 B81-30779

Shakespeare, William. King Lear / William Shakespeare ; edited by G.K. Hunter. — Harmondsworth : Penguin, 1972 (1980 [printing]). — 343p : music ; 19cm. — (The new Penguin Shakespeare)
Bibliography: p53-55
ISBN 0-14-070724-7 (pbk) : £0.85 B81-06392

Shakespeare, William. King Richard III / William Shakespeare ; edited by E.A.J. Honigmann. — Harmondsworth : Penguin, 1968 (1980 [printing]). — 253p : geneal.tables ; 19cm. — (The new Penguin Shakespeare)
Bibliography: p47-50
ISBN 0-14-070712-3 (pbk) : £0.95 B81-06409

Shakespeare, William. King Richard III. — London : Methuen, Nov.1981. — [300]p. — (The Arden Shakespeare)
ISBN 0-416-17970-3 (cased) : £10.50 : CIP entry
ISBN 0-416-17980-0 (pbk) : £2.50 B81-30157

Shakespeare, William. King Richard the Second / William Shakespeare ; edited by Stanley Wells. — Harmondsworth : Penguin, 1969 (1981 [printing]). — 282p ; 18cm : 1geneal.table. — (New Penguin Shakespeare)
ISBN 0-14-070719-0 (pbk) : £1.00 B81-35468

Shakespeare, William. Macbeth / William Shakespeare ; edited by G.K. Hunter. — Harmondsworth : Penguin, 1967 (1980 [printing]). — 199p ; 19cm. — (The new Penguin Shakespeare)
Bibliography: p46-48
ISBN 0-14-070705-0 (pbk) : £0.75 B81-06408

Shakespeare, William. Measure for measure / William Shakespeare ; edited by J.M. Nosworthy. — Harmondsworth : Penguin, 1968 (1980 [printing]). — 189p ; 19cm. — (The new Penguin Shakespeare)
Bibliography: p47-50
ISBN 0-14-070715-8 (pbk) : £0.85 B81-06412

Shakespeare, William. The merchant of Venice / William Shakespeare ; edited by W. Moelwyn Merchant. — Harmondsworth : Penguin, 1967 (1980 [printing]). — 213p ; 19cm. — (The new Penguin Shakespeare)
ISBN 0-14-070706-9 (pbk) : £0.75 B81-06414

822.3'3 — Drama in English. Shakespeare, William — *Texts* *continuation*

Shakespeare, William. The merry wives of Windsor / William Shakespeare ; edited by G.R. Hibbard. — Harmondsworth : Penguin, 1973 (1981 [printing]). — 223p ; 19cm. — (New Penguin Shakespeare)
£1.25 (pbk) B81-22275

Shakespeare, William. A midsummer night's dream / William Shakespeare ; edited by Stanley Wells. — Harmondsworth : Penguin, 1967 (1980 [printing]). — 170p ; 19cm. — (The new Penguin Shakespeare)
Bibliography: p39-40
ISBN 0-14-070702-6 (pbk) : £0.75 B81-06418

Shakespeare, William. A midsummer night's dream. — London : Ash & Grant, Oct.1981. — [96]p
ISBN 0-904069-41-9 : £6.95 : CIP entry B81-27401

Shakespeare, William. Much ado about nothing / William Shakespeare ; edited by R.A. Foakes. — Harmondsworth : Penguin, 1968 (1980 [printing]). — 173p ; 19cm. — (The new Penguin Shakespeare)
Bibliography: p28-32
ISBN 0-14-070709-3 (pbk) : £0.75 B81-06415

Shakespeare, William. Much ado about nothing. — London : Methuen, Nov.1981. — [275]p. — (The Arden Shakespeare)
ISBN 0-416-17990-8 (cased) : £9.00 : CIP entry
ISBN 0-416-19430-3 (pbk) : £2.50 B81-30463

Shakespeare, William. Much ado about nothing. — London : Macmillan Education, Feb.1982. — [232]p. — (The Macmillan Shakespeare)
ISBN 0-333-28628-6 : £0.75 : CIP entry B81-35787

Shakespeare, William. Othello / William Shakespeare ; edited by Kenneth Muir. — Harmondsworth : Penguin, 1968 (1980 [printing]). — 238p : music ; 19cm. — (The new Penguin Shakespeare)
Bibliography: p45-46
ISBN 0-14-070707-7 (pbk) : £0.75 B81-06411

Shakespeare, William. Pericles, Prince of Tyre / William Shakespeare ; edited by Philip Edwards. — Harmondsworth : Penguin, 1976 (1981 [printing]). — 207p : 1map ; 19cm. — (New Penguin Shakespeare)
Bibliography: p43-44
ISBN 0-14-070729-8 (pbk) : £1.25 B81-35485

Shakespeare, William. [Plays. Selections]. Shakespeare playtexts / edited by Robert Leach. — London : Harrap, 1981. — iii,35p : ill,music ; 25cm. — (Harrap's theatre workshop)
Contents: What you will (from Twelfth night) — Confusion's masterpiece (from Macbeth) — The pedlar at the door (from the Winter's tale)
ISBN 0-245-53621-3 (pbk) : £1.95 B81-18987

Shakespeare, William. [Plays. Selections]. Complete Pelican Shakespeare / general editor Alfred Harbage. — Rev. ed. — Harmondsworth : Penguin, 1969 (1981 [printing])
Originally published in one vol.
The Comedies and the Romances. — 529p ; 25cm
ISBN 0-14-071439-1 (pbk) : £3.95 B81-35491

Shakespeare, William. [Plays. Selections]. Complete Pelican Shakespeare / general editor Alfred Harbage. — Rev. ed. — Harmondsworth : Penguin, 1969 (1981 [printing])
Originally published in one vol.
The Tragedies. — 442p ; 25cm
ISBN 0-14-071441-3 (pbk) : £3.95 B81-35492

Shakespeare, William. Romeo and Juliet / William Shakespeare ; edited by T.J.B. Spencer. — Harmondsworth : Penguin, 1967 (1980 [printing]). — 294p ; 19cm. — (New Penguin Shakespeare)
Bibliography: p45-47
ISBN 0-14-070701-8 (pbk) : £0.85 B81-01634

Shakespeare, William. [Selections]. Complete Pelican Shakespeare / general editor Alfred Harbage. — Rev. ed. — Harmondsworth : Penguin, 1969 (1981 [printing])
Originally published in one vol.
The Histories and the non-dramatic poetry. — 477p ; 25cm
ISBN 0-14-071440-5 (pbk) : £3.95 B81-35493

Shakespeare, William. The taming of the shrew / William Shakespeare ; edited by G.R. Hibbard. — Harmondsworth : Penguin, 1968 (1980 [printing]). — 254p ; 19cm. — (The new Penguin Shakespeare)
ISBN 0-14-070710-7 (pbk) : £0.90 B81-06407

Shakespeare, William. The taming of the shrew. — London : Methuen, Dec.1981. — [300]p. — (The Arden Shakespeare)
ISBN 0-416-47580-9 (cased) : £11.50 : CIP entry
ISBN 0-416-17800-6 (pbk) : £2.40 B81-31714

Shakespeare, William. The tempest / William Shakespeare ; edited by Anne Righter (Anne Barton). — Harmondsworth : Penguin, 1968 (1979 [printing]). — 186p : music ; 19cm. — (The new Penguin Shakespeare)
Bibliography
ISBN 0-14-070713-1 (pbk) : £0.80 B81-06420

Shakespeare, William. [Timon of Athens]. The life of Timon of Athens / William Shakespeare ; edited by G.R. Hibbard. — Harmondsworth : Penguin, 1970 (19811981 [printing]). — 271p ; 19cm. — (New Penguin Shakespeare)
£1.50 (pbk) B81-22274

Shakespeare, William. Twelfth night / William Shakespeare ; edited by M.M. Mahood. — Harmondsworth : Penguin, 1968 (1980 [printing]). — 204p : music ; 19cm. — (The new Penguin Shakespeare)
Bibliography: p40-42
ISBN 0-14-070711-5 (pbk) : £0.80 B81-06410

Shakespeare, William. The two gentlemen of Verona / William Shakespeare ; edited by Norman Sanders. — Harmondsworth : Penguin, 1968 (1981 [printing]). — 212p ; 19cm. — (New Penguin Shakespeare)
ISBN 0-14-070717-4 (pbk) : £1.10 B81-26514

Shakespeare, William. The two noble kinsmen / William Shakespeare and John Fletcher ; edited by N.W. Bawcutt. — Harmondsworth : Penguin, 1977 (1981 [printing]). — 248p ; 18cm. — (New Penguin Shakespeare)
ISBN 0-14-070730-1 (pbk) : £1.50 B81-38359

Shakespeare, William. The winter's tale / William Shapespeare ; edited by Ernest Schanzer. — Harmondsworth : Penguin, 1969 (1981 [printing]). — 541p ; 19cm. — (New Penguin Shakespeare)
ISBN 0-14-070716-6 (pbk) : £0.95 B81-30780

Shakespeare, William. The winter's tale. — London : Macmillan Education, Feb.1982. — [280]p. — (The Macmillan Shakespeare)
ISBN 0-333-28627-8 : £0.75 : CIP entry B81-35788

822.3'3 — Drama in English. Shakespeare, William. Tragedies — *Critical studies*

Bayley, John. Shakespeare and tragedy / John Bayley. — London : Routledge & Kegan Paul, 1981. — 228p ; 23cm
Bibliography: p221-228
ISBN 0-7100-0632-2 (cased) : £9.75 : CIP rev.
ISBN 0-7100-0607-1 (pbk) : £4.95 B81-08814

Ribner, Irving. Patterns in Shakespearian tragedy / Irving Ribner. — London : Methuen, 1960 (1979 [printing]). — xii,205p ; 23cm. — (Methuen library reprints)
Includes index
ISBN 0-416-72520-1 : £11.50 : CIP rev. B79-20327

822.3'3 — Drama in English. Shakespeare, William. Troilus and Cressida — *Study outlines*

Massa, Daniel. Troilus and Cressida : notes / by Daniel Massa. — London : Longman, 1980. — 86p : ill ; 21cm. — (York notes ; 47)
Bibliography: p81-82
ISBN 0-582-78225-2 (pbk) : £0.90 B81-07103

822.3'3 — Drama in English. Shakespeare, William. Twelfth night — *Critical studies*

Gregson, J. M.. Shakespeare: Twelfth night / by J.M. Gregson. — London : Edward Arnold, 1980. — 62p ; 19cm. — (Studies in English literature ; no.72)
Bibliography: p59. — Includes index
ISBN 0-7131-6286-4 (pbk) : £1.65 B80-13969

822.3'3 — Drama in English. Shakespeare, William. Twelfth night — *Study outlines*

Todd, Loreto. Twelfth night : notes / by Loreto Todd. — London : Longman, 1980. — 79p : 2ill ; 21cm. — (York notes ; 42)
Bibliography: p75
ISBN 0-582-78108-6 (pbk) : £0.90 B81-07092

822.3'3 — Drama in English. Shakespeare, William. Versification — *Critical studies*

Baxter, John, *1945-*. Shakespeare's poetic styles : verse into drama / John Baxter. — London : Routledge & Kegan Paul, 1980. — 255p ; 22cm
Includes index
ISBN 0-7100-0581-4 : £12.50 : CIP rev. B80-21027

822.3'3 — Drama in English. Shakespeare, William. Winter's tale — *Critical studies*

Frey, Charles. Shakespeare's vast romance : a study of The winter's tale / Charles Frey. — Columbia ; London : University of Missouri Press, c1980. — 174p ; 23cm
Includes index
ISBN 0-8262-0286-1 : £11.40 B81-04011

822.3'3 — Drama in English. Shakespeare, William. Words. Pronunciation

Cercignani, Fausto. Shakespeare's works and Elizabethan pronunciation / Fausto Cercignani — Oxford : Clarendon, 1981. — xxii,432p ; 22cm
Bibliography: p397-375. — Includes index
ISBN 0-19-811937-2 : £37.50 : CIP rev. B79-26603

822.4 — ENGLISH DRAMA, 1625-1702

822'.4 — Drama in English, *1625-1702* — *Texts*

Congreve, William, *1670-1729*. The double dealer — London : Benn, Nov.1981. — [160]p. — (The New mermaids)
ISBN 0-510-33504-7 (pbk) : £2.95 : CIP entry B81-3052

Dryden, John, *1631-1700*. Marriage a la mode. — London : E. Arnold, Sept.1981. — [144]p. — (Regents restoration drama series)
ISBN 0-7131-6356-9 (pbk) : £3.95 : CIP entry B81-2378

Vanbrugh, *Sir* **John**. The provoked wife. — Manchester : Manchester University Press, Feb.1982. — [224]p. — (The Revels Plays)
ISBN 0-7190-1526-x : £17.50 : CIP entry B81-3572

Wycherley, William. The plays of William Wycherley / edited by Peter Holland. — Cambridge : Cambridge University Press, 1981 — xvi,492p : facsims ; 22cm. — (Plays by Renaissance and Restoration dramatists)
Bibliography: pxiii-xvi. — Contents: Love in a wood — The gentleman dancing-master — Th country wife — The plain-dealer
ISBN 0-521-23250-3 (cased) : £22.50 : CIP rev
ISBN 0-521-29880-6 (pbk) : £6.95 B81-1379

822'.4 — Drama in English. Congreve, William, *1670-1729.* **Special themes: Christian doctrine**

Williams, Aubrey L.. An approach to Congreve / Aubrey L. Williams. — New Haven ; London Yale University Press, 1979. — xiii,234p ; 22cm
Includes index
ISBN 0-300-02304-9 : £11.05 B81-1200

822'.4 — Drama in English. Congreve, William, *1670-1729.* **Way of the world** — *Study outlines*
Kelsall, Malcolm. Congreve, The way of the world / by Malcolm Kelsall. — London : Edward Arnold, 1981. — 64p ; 19cm. — (Studies in English literature ; 73)
Bibliography: p62. — Includes index
ISBN 0-7131-6342-9 (pbk) : £1.65 B81-18854

822'.4 — Drama in English. Dryden, John, *1631-1700.* **Heroic plays** — *Critical studies*
Hughes, Derek. Dryden's heroic plays / Derek Hughes. — London : Macmillan, 1981. — xi,195p ; 23cm
Includes index
ISBN 0-333-28584-0 : £15.00 : CIP rev. B80-24802

822'.4'0809287 — Drama in English. Women writers, *1625-1745* — *Anthologies*
The **Female** wits : women playwrights on the London stage 1660-1720 / [selected by] Fidelis Morgan. — London : Virago, 1981. — xi,468p ; 22cm
Bibliography: p467-468. — Contents: The lucky chance, or An alderman's bargain / by Aphra Behn - The fatal friendship / by Catherine Trotter - The royal mischief / by Mary Delarivier Manley - The innocent mistress / by Mary Pix - The wonder! a woman keeps a secret / by Susannah Centlivre - The female wits / Anonymous
ISBN 0-86068-231-5 (pbk) : £8.50 : CIP rev. B81-04310

822'.4'09 — Drama in English, *1625-1745* — *Critical studies*
Brown, Laura. English dramatic form, 1660-1760 : an essay in generic history / Laura Brown. — New Haven ; London : Yale University Press, c1981. — xvi,240p ; 25cm
Includes index
ISBN 0-300-02585-8 : £12.30 B81-24534

822.6 — ENGLISH DRAMA, 1745-1800

822'.6 — Drama in English. Sheridan, Richard Brinsley. Rivals, *The* — *Study outlines*
Jeffares, A. N.. The rivals : notes / by A.N. Jeffares. — Harlow : Longman, 1981. — 72p ; 21cm. — (York notes ; 104)
ISBN 0-582-78272-4 (pbk) : £0.90 B81-19658

822'.6 — Drama in English. Sheridan, Richard Brinsley. School for scandal — *Study outlines*
Jeffares, Bo. The school for scandal : notes / by Bo Jeffares. — London : Longman, 1980. — 72p ; 21cm. — (York notes ; 55)
Bibliography: p68
ISBN 0-582-78106-x (pbk) : £0.90 B81-07091

822.7 — ENGLISH DRAMA, 1800-1837

822'.7 — Drama in English, *1800-1837* — *Texts*
Austen, Jane. Jane Austen's 'Sir Charles Grandison' / transcribed and edited by Brian Southam ; foreword by Lord David Cecil. — Oxford : Clarendon, c1981. — 150p : ill ; 20cm
ISBN 0-19-812637-9 : £7.95 B81-15233

Austen, Jane. Sir Charles Grandison, or, The happy man : a comedy in five acts / by Jane Austen ; [with] a foreword ... by David Cecil. — Burford (18 High St., Burford, Oxfordshire) : David Astor at Jubilee Books, c1981. — 3v. ; 22cm
Seven men, 5 women. — Boxed set. — Limited ed. of 250 copies
£150.00 B81-20017

822'.7'09 — Drama in English, *1800-1900* — *Critical studies*
Booth, Michael R.. Prefaces to English nineteenth-century theatre / Michael Booth. — Manchester : Manchester University Press, [1980]. — xii,231p : 2ill,ports ; 23cm
Originally published in: English plays of the nineteenth century, edited by Michael Booth. In 5 vols. Oxford : Oxford University Press, 1969-1976. — Bibliography: p213-219. - Includes index
ISBN 0-7190-0813-1 (cased) : £15.00 : CIP rev.
ISBN 0-7190-0823-9 (pbk) : £5.50 B80-12517

822.8 — ENGLISH DRAMA, 1837-1900

822'.8 — Drama in English, *1837-1900* — *Texts*
Robertson, T. W.. Six plays / T.W. Robertson ; with an introduction by Michael R. Booth. — Ashover : Amber Lane Press, 1980. — xxiii,324p : 1port ; 23cm
Bibliography: pxxii. — Contents: Society — Ours — Caste — Progress — School — Birth
ISBN 0-906399-16-5 (cased) : £7.95
ISBN 0-906399-17-3 (pbk) : Unpriced B81-28490

Taylor, Tom, *1817-1880.* The ticket-of-leave man / Tom Taylor ; introduction by John Russell Brown. — London : Heinemann, 1981. — x,80p ; 19cm
ISBN 0-435-23830-2 (pbk) : £1.75 B81-16486

Wilde, Oscar. The importance of being Earnest : a trivial comedy for serious people : the original four-act version / Oscar Wilde. — New York ; London : French, [1980], c1956. — 117p : 2plans ; 19cm
Eight men, 4 women
ISBN 0-573-11198-7 (pbk) : £2.00 B81-07674

Wilde, Oscar. Lady Windermere's fan : a play about a good woman / Oscar Wilde ; edited by Ian Small. — London : Ernest Benn, 1980. — xxxiii,102p ; 20cm. — (The New mermaids) (A Benn study. Drama)
Bibliography: pxxxiii
ISBN 0-510-34153-5 (pbk) : £2.95 : CIP rev. B80-17932

822'.8 — Drama in English. Albery, James — *Biographies*
Trewin, Wendy. All on stage : Charles Wyndham and the Alberys / Wendy Trewin. — London : Harrap, 1980. — x,244,[16]p of plates : ill,facsims,ports,geneal.tables ; 24cm
Bibliography: p225-230. - Includes index. — Geneal.tables on lining papers
ISBN 0-245-53444-x : £9.95
Primary classification 792'.028'0922 B81-04135

822'.8 — Drama in English. Wilde, Oscar. Importance of being earnest — *Questions & answers* — *For schools*
Self, David. The importance of being earnest / by David Self. — London : Glasgow, c1980. — 15p : ill(some col.) ; 30cm. — (Guidelines)
ISBN 0-86158-515-1 (unbound) : Unpriced B81-21965

Self, David. The importance of being earnest : [guidelines] / by David Self. — Teacher's ed. — London : Glasgow Publications, c1980. — 16,[4]p : ill(some col.),1port ; 30cm. — (Guidelines)
Cover title
ISBN 0-86158-516-x (pbk) : Unpriced B81-33168

822.912 — ENGLISH DRAMA, 1900-1945

822'.912 — Drama in English, *1900-1945* — *Polish texts*
Thomas, Dylan. [Under Milk Wood. Polish]. Pod Mleczn a Drog a : sztuka na głosy / Dylan Thomas ; adaptacja Tymona Terleckiego. — Londyn (146 Bridge Arch, Sutton Walk, SE1 8XU) : Oficyna Poetów i Malarzy, 1981. — 49p : 1port ; 22cm
Translation of: Under Milk Wood
Unpriced (pbk) B81-17664

822'.912 — Drama in English, *1900-1945* — *Texts*
Beckett, Samuel. Three occasional pieces. — London : Faber, Feb.1982. — [32]p
ISBN 0-571-11800-3 (pbk) : £1.95 : CIP entry B81-36214

Dunbar, Dorothy, *1915-*. Cutty Sark / by Dorothy Dunbar. — Glasgow : Brown, Son & Ferguson, 1981. — 30p ; 18cm. — (Scottish plays ; no.132)
Three men, 4 women
ISBN 0-85174-410-9 (pbk) : £0.70 B81-20692

Dunbar, Dorothy, *1915-*. The Warlock and the gipsy / by Dorothy Dunbar. — Glasgow : Brown, Son & Ferguson, 1981. — 25p ; 18cm. — (Scottish plays ; no.125)
Four men, 3 women
ISBN 0-85174-413-3 (pbk) : £0.70 B81-20693

Greene, Graham. The great Jowett. — London : Bodley Head, Oct.1981. — [32]p
ISBN 0-370-30439-x : CIP entry B81-27433

Groves, Paul. The glittering seeds : a serial play to read or record and develop / Paul Groves, Nigel Grimshaw. — London : Arnold, 1981. — 80p ; 22cm
ISBN 0-7131-0582-8 (pbk) : £1.50 : CIP rev. B81-22514

Lawrence, D. H.. Three plays / by D.H. Lawrence ; with an introduction by Raymond Williams. — Harmondsworth : Penguin, 1969 (1981 [printing]). — 199p ; 18cm
Contents: A collier's Friday night — The daughter-in-law — The widowing of Mrs Holroyd
ISBN 0-14-048086-2 (pbk) : £1.75 B81-26498

McLellan, Robert. Collected plays / Robert McLellan. — London : Calder
Vol.1. — 1981. — ix,278p ; 21cm. — (The Scottish library)
Text on inside covers. — Contents : Torwatletie — Jamie the Saxt — The flouers o Edinburgh — The carlin moth — The changeling
ISBN 0-7145-3818-3 (pbk) : £3.95 : CIP rev. B81-08857

O'Casey, Sean. Three plays / Sean O'Casey. — London : Pan in association with Macmillan, 1980. — 218p ; 18cm. — (Pan classics)
Originally published: London : Macmillan, 1957. — Contents: Juno and the paycock. - The shadow of a gunman. - The plough and the stars
ISBN 0-330-26271-8 (pbk) : £1.50 B81-03434

Priestley, J. B.. Time and the Conways, and other plays / J.B. Priestley. — Harmondsworth : Penguin, 1969 (1981 [printing]). — 302p ; 18cm. — (Penguin plays)
Contents: Time and the Conways — I have been here before — The linden tree — An inspector calls
ISBN 0-14-048094-3 (pbk) : £1.95 B81-35482

Shaw, Bernard. Plays pleasant : Arms and the man, Candida, The man of destiny, You never can tell : definitive text / Bernard Shaw. — Harmondsworth : Penguin, 1946 (1981 [printing]). — 315p ; 19cm. — (Penguin plays)
Originally published: London : Grant Richards, 1898
ISBN 0-14-048004-8 (pbk) : £1.35 B81-32833

Shaw, Bernard. Pygmalion : a romance in five acts / Bernard Shaw ; with over a hundred drawings by Feliks Topolski. — Harmondsworth : Penguin, 1941 (1981 [printing]). — 155p : ill ; 19cm. — (Penguin plays)
'Definitive text'. — Originally published: London : Constable, 1918
ISBN 0-14-048003-x (pbk) : £0.95 B81-35481

Shaw, Bernard. Saint Joan : a chronicle play in six scenes and an epilogue / by Bernard Shaw. — Harmondsworth : Penguin, 1946, (1981 [printing]). — 158p ; 18cm. — (Penguin plays)
ISBN 0-14-048005-6 (pbk) : £1.00 B81-34812

Shaw, Bernard. Three plays for puritans / by Bernard Shaw. — Harmondsworth : Penguin, 1946 (1981 [printing]). — 346p ; 19cm. — (Penguin plays)
Originally published: London : Grant Richards, 1901. — Contents: The devil's disciple — Caesar and Cleopatra — Captain Brassbound's conversion
ISBN 0-14-048002-1 (pbk) : £1.75 B81-27223

Stokes, Arthhur M.. Checkmate! : a Sherlock Holmes burlesque / by Arthur M. Stokes ; with ten illustrations by Ian Gray Schoenherr. — Windsor (29 Temple Rd., Windsor, [Berks.]) : Gaby Goldscheider, 1980. — [22]p : ill,1port ; 22x32cm
Limited ed. of 750 numbered copies. — Text, ill, port on covers
ISBN 0-9505725-4-3 (pbk) : £5.00 B81-12190

822′.912 — Drama in English, *1900-1945* — *Texts continuation*

Synge, J. M.. The playboy of the Western world ; and, Riders to the sea / J.M. Synge. — London : Unwin, 1979. — 93p ; 18cm
Originally published: London : Allen & Unwin, 1962. - The playboy of the Western world originally published: Dublin : Maunsel, 1907
ISBN 0-04-822041-8 (pbk) : £0.85 : CIP rev. B79-17819

822′.912 — Drama in English. Beckett, Samuel. Waiting for Godot — *Study outlines*

Pountney, Rosemary. Waiting for Godot : notes / by Rosemary Pountney and Nicholas Zurbrugg. — Harlow : Longman, 1981. — 71p ; 21cm. — (York notes ; 115)
Bibliography: p70-71
ISBN 0-582-78211-2 (pbk) : £0.90 B81-34233

822′.912 — Drama in English. Bridie, James — *Critical studies*

Low, John Thomas. Doctors, devils, saints and sinners : a critical study of the major plays of James Bridie / John Thomas Low. — Edinburgh (36 North Castle St., Edinburgh EH2 3BN) : Ramsay Head Press, 1980. — 156p ; 20cm
Bibliography: p154-156
ISBN 0-902859-59-5 : £3.95 B81-14306

822′.912 — Drama in English. Johnston, Denis — *Critical studies*

Denis **Johnston** : a retrospective / edited by Joseph Ronsley. — Garrards Cross : Smythe, 1981. — xii,276p,[8]p of plate : ill,ports ; 23cm. — (Irish literary studies, ISSN 0140-895x ; 8)
Bibliography: p245-262. — Incudes index
ISBN 0-86140-078-x : £11.95 B81-29751

822′.912 — Drama in English. O′Casey, Sean. Autobiographies — *Critical studies*

Essays on Sean O′Casey′s autobiographies / edited by Robert G. Lowery. — London : Macmillan, 1981. — xviii,249p ; 23cm
Includes index
ISBN 0-333-26841-5 : £15.00 B81-23078

822′.912 — Drama in English. O′Casey, Sean — *Biographies*

O′Casey, Sean. Autobiographies / Sean O′Casey. — London : Macmillan, 1963 (1981 [printing]). — 2v. ; 25cm
Includes index. — Contents: v.1 : I knock at the door - Pictures in the hallway - Drums under the windows. V.2: Inishfallen, fare thee well - Rose and crown - Sunset and evening star
ISBN 0-333-28451-8 : Unpriced
ISBN 0-333-28542-5 (v.2) : £15.00 B81-21831

822′.912 — Drama in English. O′Casey, Sean — *Critical studies*

Sean **O′Casey** centenary essays / edited by David Krause and Robert G. Lowery. — Gerrards Cross : Smythe, 1980. — 257p ; 23cm. — (Irish literary studies, ISSN 0140-895x ; 7)
Includes index
ISBN 0-86140-008-9 : £9.50 : CIP rev. B80-17933

822′.912 — Drama in English. Shaw, Bernard. Androcles and the lion — *Study outlines*

Maxwell, D. E. S.. Androcles and the lion : notes / by D.E.S. Maxwell. — London : Longman, 1980. — 59p ; 21cm. — (York notes ; 56)
Bibliography: p55
ISBN 0-582-78119-1 (pbk) : £0.90 B81-07093

822′.912 — Drama in English. Shaw, Bernard — *Critical studies*

The **Genius** of Shaw : a symposium / edited by Michael Holroyd. — London : Hodder and Stoughton, c1979. — 238p,[16]p of plates : ill (some col.),music,facsims,ports(some col.) ; 26cm
Includes index
ISBN 0-340-24146-2 : £9.95 : CIP rev. B79-22739

Wilson, Colin. Bernard Shaw : a reassessment / Colin Wilson. — London : Macmillan, 1981, c1969. — xiv,314p ; 23cm
Originally published: London : Hutchinson, 1969. — Includes index
ISBN 0-333-31016-0 : £11.00 B81-24091

822′.912 — Drama in English. Shaw, Bernard — *Critical studies — Serials*

Shaw : the annual of Bernard Shaw studies. — Vol.1-. — University Park [Pa.] ; London : Pennsylvania State University Press, 1981-. — v. ; 24cm
Continues: The Shaw review
£11.20 B81-39510

822′.912 — Drama in English. Synge, J. M.. Playboy of the western world — *Study outlines*

Mortimer, Mark. The playboy of the Western world : notes / by Mark Mortimer. — Harlow : Longman, 1981. — 48p ; 21cm. — (York notes ; 111)
Bibliography: p47-48
ISBN 0-582-78278-3 (pbk) : £0.90 B81-34227

822.914 — ENGLISH DRAMA, 1945-

822′.914 — Drama in English, *1945-* — *Texts*

Adam, Agnes. The wedding presents : a one-act play for seven women / by Agnes Adam. — Glasgow : Brown, Son & Ferguson. — 27p ; 19cm. — (Scottish plays ; no.196)
£0.30 (pbk) B81-17448

Albery, Peter. Brother Francis : the legend of Assisi / by Peter Albery and William Fry. — London (St. Paul′s Church, Covent Garden, Bedford St, WC2E 9ED) : Radius, 1981. — 89p : music ; 21cm. — (Plays for the eighties ; no.3)
ISBN 0-907174-03-5 (spiral) B81-33022

Aron, Geraldine. Joggers : a play / Geraldine Aron. — London : French, c1981. — 19p ; 19cm
Two men, 2 women
ISBN 0-573-12124-9 (pbk) : £0.60 B81-19847

Austin, Brian. The beecher file : a play in one act / by Brian Austin. — Macclesfield : New Playwrights′ Network, [1981?]. — 20p ; 18cm
Three men, 2 women
£0.55 (pbk) B81-32065

Ayckbourn, Alan. Sisterly feelings : a related comedy / Alan Ayckbourn. — London : French, c1981. — 123p ; 22cm
Eight men, 4 women
ISBN 0-573-11420-x (pbk) : £2.20 B81-17343

Ayckbourn, Alan. Sisterly feelings ; and, Taking steps / Alan Ayckbourn. — London : Chatto & Windus, 1981. — 239p ; 21cm
ISBN 0-7011-2561-6 : £6.95 B81-11646

Ayckbourn, Alan. Taking steps : a farce / Alan Ayckbourn. — London : French, c1981. — 78p : 1plan ; 22cm
Four men, 2 women
ISBN 0-573-11425-0 (pbk) : £2.20 B81-15763

Banyard, Edmund. The flame / by Edmund Banyard. — London (St. Paul′s Church, Covent Garden, Bedford St, WC2E 9ED) : Radius, 1980. — 20p : music ; 22cm. — (Plays for the eighties ; no.1)
Text and music on inside covers
ISBN 0-907174-01-9 (pbk) : Unpriced B81-33025

Barker, Howard. The love of a good man ; All bleeding / Howard Barker. — London : John Calder, 1980. — 106p ; 21cm. — (Playscript ; 93)
ISBN 0-7145-3802-7 (cased) : Unpriced : CIP rev.
ISBN 0-7145-3767-5 (pbk) : £4.95 B80-01785

Barker, Howard. No end of blame : scenes of overcoming / Howard Barker. — London : Calder, 1981. — vi,55p ; 21cm. — (Playscript ; 99)
Text on inside covers
ISBN 0-7145-3912-0 (pbk) : £3.95 : CIP rev. B81-21485

Barker, Howard. That good between us ; Credentials of a sympathizer / Howard Barker. — London : John Calder, 1980. — 98p ; 21cm. — (Playscript ; 92)
ISBN 0-7145-3799-3 (cased) : Unpriced : CIP rev.
ISBN 0-7145-3765-9 (pbk) : £4.95 B80-00882

Barker, Lawrence. The birds stopped singing : a play / Lawrence Barker. — London : French, c1981. — 26p : ill,1plan ; 19cm
Three men, 3 women
ISBN 0-573-12028-5 (pbk) : £0.60 B81-15764

Barnes, Peter, *1931-*. Collected plays : with Barnes people : seven monologues, and an introduction / Peter Barnes. — London : Heinemann, c1981. — ix,468p ; 22cm
ISBN 0-435-18281-1 (pbk) : £8.50 : CIP rev. B81-13823

Barnes, Peter, *1931-*. The ruling class / Peter Barnes ; with an introduction by Harold Hobson. — London : Heinemann, 1969 (1980 [printing]). — xi,114p ; 19cm. — (Heinemann plays)
Seventeen men, 5 women
ISBN 0-435-20965-5 (pbk) : £1.75 B81-01203

Barron, Charles. As the bat at noon / by Charles Barron. — Glasgow : Brown, Son & Ferguson, 1981. — 19p ; 18cm. — (Scottish plays ; no.123)
Two men
ISBN 0-85174-412-5 (pbk) : £0.70 B81-20691

Barton, John, *1928-*. The Greeks : ten Greek plays given as a trilogy / adapted by John Barton and Kenneth Cavander ; the adaptation is based on original translations by Kenneth Cavander. — London : Heinemann, 1981. — xx,294p : ill ; 22cm
ISBN 0-435-23068-9 (pbk) : £7.50 : CIP rev. B81-22634

Bell, A. Craig. Charades : a play in three acts / by A. Craig Bell. — Macclesfield : New Playwrights′ Network, [1981]. — 60p : 2plans ; 18cm
Six men, 4 women, supers
£1.75 (pbk) B81-20899

Benfield, Derek. In for the kill : a thriller / Derek Benfield. — London : French, c1981. — 82p : 1plan ; 22cm
Three men, 2 women
ISBN 0-573-11180-4 (pbk) : £2.00 B81-24779

Bennett, Alan, *1934-*. Enjoy / Alan Bennett. — London : Faber, 1980. — 77p ; 20cm
Nine men, 4 women
ISBN 0-571-11734-1 (pbk) : £2.95 : CIP rev. B80-23680

Bennett, Alan, *1934-*. Office suite : two one-act plays / by Alan Bennett. — London : Faber, 1981. — 57p ; 20cm
Contents: Green forms - A visit from Miss Prothero
ISBN 0-571-11744-9 (pbk) : £2.95 : CIP rev. B81-07593

Benton, R. N.. Louth Church long ago. — [Louth] ([42 Alveatgate, Louth, Lincs. LN11 9YD]) : [R.N. Benton], c1981. — 24p : ill,maps ; 33cm
Author: R.N. Benton
Unpriced (unbound) B81-3278

Berkoff, Steven. The trial, and, Metamorphosis : two theatre adaptations from Franz Kafka / Steven Berkoff. — Ambergate : Amber Lane Press, 1981. — 143p : 2ill ; 19cm
ISBN 0-906399-15-7 (pbk) : £2.75 B81-2848

Bleasdale, Alan. No more sitting on the old school bench / Alan Bleasdale. — Todmorden : Woodhouse, c1979. — 77p ; 21cm
Six men, 3 women, supers
ISBN 0-906657-05-9 (pbk) : £1.50 B81-0776

822'.914 — Drama in English, *1945-* **—** *Texts continuation*

Bolt, Robert. A man for all seasons / Robert Bolt. — London : Heinemann, 1960 (1980 [printing]). — xxv,118p ; 19cm. — (Heinemann plays)
Eleven men, 3 women
ISBN 0-435-20961-2 (pbk) : £1.75 B81-01818

Bond, Edward. A-A-America! ; &, Stone / Edward Bond. — Re-set and rev. ed. — London : Eyre Methuen, 1981. — 115p : ill ; 19cm. — (Methuen modern plays)
Previous ed.: 1976
ISBN 0-413-48320-7 (pbk) : £2.75 B81-17995

Boyd, John. Collected plays. — Belfast : Blackstaff Press
Vol.1: The Flats; The Farm; Guests. — Oct.1981. — [240]p
The Flats originally published: 1973
ISBN 0-85640-250-8 (pbk) : £5.50 : CIP entry B81-30981

Breeze, Tony. 5T rules - O.K.! : a play / by Tony Breeze. — Macclesfield : New Playwrights' Network, [1980]. — 48p : 1plan ; 18cm
Ten men, 3 women
£0.75 (pbk) B81-03254

Brenton, Howard. Plays for the poor theatre / Howard Brenton. — London : Eyre Methuen, 1980. — 104p ; 19cm. — (A Methuen modern play)
Contents: The saliva milkshake — Christie in love — Gum and Goo — Heads — the education of Skinny Spew
ISBN 0-413-47080-6 (pbk) : £2.25 B81-03387

Brenton, Howard. The Romans in Britain / Howard Brenton. — London : Eyre Methuen, 1980. — 105p ; 19cm. — (A Methuen modern play)
Twenty-six men, 5 women, supers
ISBN 0-413-46590-x (pbk) : £2.50 B81-01748

Brown, Alan, *1951-*. The babes in the wood : a Victorian pantomime / Alan Brown. — London : French, c1981. — 45p ; 22cm
Nineteen men, 6 women, supers
ISBN 0-573-16432-0 (pbk) : £2.00 B81-24778

Burbridge, Paul. Lightning sketches / Paul Burbridge and Murray Watts. — London : Hodder and Stoughton, 1981. — 192p : music ; 18cm. — (Hodder Christian paperbacks)
ISBN 0-340-26710-0 (pbk) : £1.75 : CIP rev. B81-17531

Burrell, Michael, *1937-*. Hess / Michael Burrell. — Ashover : Amber Lane, 1980, c1978. — 45p ; 19cm
Bibliography: p13
ISBN 0-906399-18-1 (pbk) : £1.50 B81-28699

Burton, Brian J.. Being of sound mind : a play / Brian J. Burton. — London : French, c1981. — 56p : 1plan ; 22cm
Two men, 3 women
ISBN 0-573-11022-0 (pbk) : £2.25 B81-32069

Burton, Brian J.. Murder play : a play / Brian J. Burton. — London : French, c1981. — 24p : 1plan ; 19cm
Two men, 2 women
ISBN 0-573-12171-0 (pbk) : £0.60 B81-11487

Caddy, Leonard H.. Jekyll and Hyde : a play / Leonard H. Caddy. — London : French, c1981. — 61p : 1plan ; 22cm
Four men, 4 women, super
ISBN 0-573-11186-3 (pbk) : £2.00 B81-11378

Campbell, Donald, *1940-*. The widows of Clyth : a play / by Donald Campbell. — Edinburgh : Paul Harris, 1979. — 76p ; 23cm
ISBN 0-904505-79-0 (cased) : £3.50
ISBN 0-904505-80-4 (pbk) : £1.95 B81-35142

Campton, David. Attitudes / by David Campton. — [Leicester] ([35 Liberty Rd., Glenfield, Leicester LE3 8JF]) : [D. Campton], c1980. — 24p ; 21cm
Ten characters
ISBN 0-901615-39-0 (pbk) : £0.45 B81-01670

Campton, David. Dark wings / by David Campton. — Leicester (35 Liberty Rd, Glendfield, Leicester LE3 8JF) : D. Campton, c1981. — 97p : 1plan ; 21cm
Three men, 4 women
ISBN 0-901615-41-2 (pbk) : £1.50 B81-11636

Campton, David. Freedom log / by David Campton. — Leicester (35 Liberty Rd, Glenfield, Leicester LE3 8JF) : D. Campton, c1980. — 21p ; 21cm
Five men, 3 women, supers
ISBN 0-901615-40-4 (pbk) : £0.45 B81-01671

Campton, David. Look - sea ; and Great whales / by David Campton. — Leicester (35 Liberty Rd., Glenfield, Leicester LE3 8JF) : Campton, c1981. — 47p ; 22cm
ISBN 0-901615-42-0 (pbk) : £0.60 B81-16957

Campton, David. An outline of history / by David Campton. — Leicester (35 Liberty Rd., Glenfield, Leicester LE3 8JF) : D.Compton, c1981. — 35p ; 22cm
Eight men, 1 woman, supers. — Originally published: 1974
ISBN 0-901615-28-5 (pbk) : £0.60 B81-16954

Campton, David. Who's a hero, then? / by David Campton. — Leicester (35 Liberty Rd., Glenfield, Leicester LE3 8JF) : D. Campton, c1981. — 22p ; 22cm
Four men, 2 women, supers
ISBN 0-901615-43-9 (pbk) : £0.50 B81-23192

Carpenter, Frank. Plays for tomorrow : Leonardo ; The fire of heaven ; The traveller's tale / by Frank Carpenter. — Brentwood (39 Crescent Rd., Brentwood, Essex) : F. Carpenter, c1981. — 163leaves ; 30cm
Unpriced (pbk) B81-23190

Clark, Gwyn. Anyone for tennis? : a farce / Gwyn Clark. — London : French, c1981. — 28p : 1plan ; 19cm
Two men, 2 women
ISBN 0-573-12008-0 (pbk) : £0.60 B81-11488

Conn, Stewart. Thistlewood / Stewart Conn. — Todmorden : Woodhouse, c1979. — 58p ; 21cm
Seven men, 3 women
ISBN 0-906657-00-8 (pbk) : £1.50 B81-07771

Cox, Constance. What brutes men are : a comedy / Constance Cox. — London : French, c1980. — 21p : plan ; 19cm
Four women
ISBN 0-573-13337-9 (pbk) : £0.60 B81-01204

Dale, Adrian. A slight misunderstanding : a light comedy / Adrian Dale. — London : French, c1980. — 18p ; 19cm
Six women
ISBN 0-573-13308-5 (pbk) : £0.60 B81-01205

Davis, Wyn. Mademoiselle Rousset / by Wyn Davis. — Macclesfield : New Playwrights' Network, [1981?]. — 29p ; 18cm
Five men, 5 women
£0.55 (pbk) B81-15180

Dempster, John. Goodnewsgirls : youth play script / by John Dempster. — Ilkeston : Moorley's Bible and Bookshop, [1981?]. — 42-62p ; 21cm. — (The Sunshine gang)
Six women. — Originally published: 1979
ISBN 0-86071-044-0 (pbk) : £0.28 B81-28751

Dunn, Sheila. The gypsies' Christmas : a play / by Sheila Dunn. — Ilkeston : Moorley's, [1980]. — 27p ; 21cm
Eighteen characters
ISBN 0-86071-097-1 (pbk) : £0.30 B81-00358

Ellis, Terry, *1947-*. Cruise for two / by Terry Ellis. — Macclesfield : New Playwrights' Network, [1981]. — 16p : 1plan ; 18cm
Three men, 2 women
£0.55 (pbk) B81-20906

English, Peter. The colour of the wind / by Peter English. — Macclesfield : New Playwrights' Network, [1981?]. — 24p : 2plans ; 18cm
Eleven men, 5 women
£0.55 (pbk) B81-32064

Flannery, Peter. Heartbreak Hotel / Peter Flannery. — Todmorden : Woodhouse, c1979. — 55p ; 21cm
Two men, 2 women
ISBN 0-906657-01-6 (pbk) : £1.50 B81-07769

Francis, Paul. Power plays : five plays to read and perform / Paul Francis. — London : Edward Arnold, 1981. — 98p ; 21cm
ISBN 0-7131-0514-3 (pbk) : £1.95 : CIP rev. B81-00359

Franks, Richard, *1947-*. Tick, tock, tick : a one-act play / by Richard Franks. — Macclesfield : New Playwrights' Network, [1980]. — 29p : 1plan ; 18cm
Two men, 4 women
£0.55 (pbk) B81-03250

Frayn, Michael. Make and break / Michael Frayn. — London : Eyre Methuen, 1980. — 104p ; 19cm
ISBN 0-413-47790-8 (pbk) : £2.75 B81-01206

Friel, Brian. Aristocrats : a play in three acts / Brian Friel. — Dublin (19 Oakdown Rd., Dublin 14) : Gallery Books, 1980. — 85p ; 23cm
ISBN 0-904011-10-0 (cased) : £4.50(Irish) B81-14270

Friel, Brian. The enemy within / Brian Friel ; with introductory notes by the author and Thomas Kilroy. — Dublin (19 Oakdown Rd., Dublin 14) : Gallery Books, c1979. — 72p ; 23cm
Also available in paperback at £2.25(Irish)
£4.50(Irish) (cased) B81-14269

Friel, Brian. Translations / Brian Friel. — London : Faber, 1981. — 70p ; 20cm
ISBN 0-571-11742-2 (pbk) : £2.50 : CIP rev. B81-04239

Gilmorgan, Ed. Twenty candles : a dramatic play / by Ed Gilmorgan. — Macclesfield : New Playwrights' Network, [1980]. — 16p : 1plan ; 18cm
Three men, 5 women
£0.55 (pbk) B81-05891

Gray, Simon. Close of play ; & Pig in a poke / Simon Gray. — London : Eyre Methuen, 1980. — 92p ; 19cm. — (A Methuen modern play)
ISBN 0-413-46960-3 (pbk) : £2.50 B81-21140

Gray, Simon. Quartermaine's terms / Simon Gray. — London : Eyre Methuen, 1981. — 79p ; 19cm. — (A Methuen modern play)
ISBN 0-413-49140-4 (pbk) : £2.50 B81-29840

Green, Michael, *1927-*. The coarse acting show 2 : (further plays for coarse actors) / Michael Green. — London : French, c1980. — viii,74p ; 22cm
ISBN 0-573-10005-5 (pbk) : £1.80 B81-01830

Griffiths, Trevor. Occupations / Trevor Griffiths. — Rev. ed. — London : Faber, 1980. — 74p ; 20cm
Seven men, 2 women. — Previous ed.: London : Calder and Boyars, 1972
ISBN 0-571-11667-1 (pbk) : £2.95 : CIP rev. B80-23681

Groves, Paul. All action : seven plays to read or record / Paul Groves, Nigel Grimshaw. — London : Edward Arnold, 1981. — 64p ; 22cm
ISBN 0-7131-0585-2 (pbk) : £1.20 : CIP rev. B81-22515

822'.914 — Drama in English, *1945- — Texts continuation*

Groves, Paul. The Tufton Hill lot : plays to read or record / by Paul Groves and Nigel Grimshaw. — London : Murray, c1981. — viii,64p ; 22cm
Bibliography: p64
ISBN 0-7195-3801-7 (pbk) : £1.20 B81-10147

Guinness, Owen. The Mayor of Casterbridge. — London : Macmillan Education, Feb.1982. — [64]p. — (Dramascripts)
ISBN 0-333-30833-6 (pbk) : £0.85 : CIP entry B81-35801

Hampton, Christopher. Total eclipse. — 2nd ed. — London : Faber, May 1981. — [96]p
Previous ed.: 1969
ISBN 0-571-18048-5 (pbk) : £2.95 : CIP entry B81-12917

Harrison, Vivienne. By sun and candlelight / by Vivienne Harrison. — Macclesfield : New Playwrights' Network, [1980]. — 24p : 1plan ; 18cm
Four men, 4 women
£0.55 (pbk) B81-03252

Harrison, Vivienne. Heaven and all this too : a comedy / by Vivienne Harrison. — Macclesfield : New Playwrights' Network, [1980]. — 16p : 1plan ; 18cm
Four men, 3 women, super
£0.55 (pbk) B81-03253

Harvey, Jonathan, *1939-*. Passion and resurrection : a liturgical drama : text / Jonathan Harvey. — London : Faber Music, 1981. — 21p ; 20cm
Unpriced (pbk) B81-17915

Harwood, Ronald. The dresser / Ronald Harwood. — Ambergate : Amber Lane Press, 1980. — 95p ; 19cm
ISBN 0-906399-21-1 (pbk) : £2.25 B81-28488

Hastings, Michael, *1938-*. Carnival war ; Midnite at the Starlite / Michael Hastings. — Harmondsworth : Penguin, 1981. — 145p ; 20cm
Carnival war: six men, 3 women — Midnite at the Starlite: three men, 3 women
ISBN 0-14-048164-8 (pbk) : £1.95 B81-35488

Haworth, Elizabeth. John Mark : a play for Easter / by Betty Haworth. — Redhill : National Christian Education Council, c1980. — 31p ; 21cm
Four men, 3 women
ISBN 0-7197-0266-6 (pbk) : £0.75 : CIP rev. B80-18881

Henderson, W. J.. Esther : a Bible play / by W.J. Henderson. — Ilkeston : Moorley's, [1981?]. — 24p ; 21cm
Ten men, 3 women, supers
ISBN 0-86071-113-7 (pbk) : £0.30 B81-15792

Henderson, W. J.. The scarlet cord : a Bible play / W.J. Hendersen. — Ilkeston : Moorley's, [1981?]. — 23p ; 21cm
Nine men, 5 women, supers
ISBN 0-86071-112-9 (pbk) : £0.30 B81-15797

Hill, Ken, *1937-*. The Mummy's tomb : a play / Ken Hill ; songs by Alan Klein and Ken Hill. — London : French, 1981. — 92p : 1plan ; 22cm
Seven men, 2 women
ISBN 0-573-11288-6 (pbk) : £2.25 B81-35272

Hillman, Barry L.. A few minor dischords : a play for seven females / by Barry L. Hillman & Robert G. Newton. — [Northampton] ([48 Louise Rd., Northampton]) : B.L. Hillman, R.G. Newton, 1978. — 24p ; 22cm
£0.35 (pbk) B81-05898

Hillman, Barry L.. The guests : a vignette on truth / by Barry L. Hillman. — [Northampton] ([48 Louise Rd., Northampton]) : B.L. Hillman, c1980. — 25p ; 21cm
Two men, 1 woman
Unpriced (pbk) B81-05673

Home, William Douglas. The kingfisher : a comedy in two acts / by William Douglas Home. — New York ; London : French, c1981. — 62p : 1facsim ; 19cm
Two men, 1 woman
ISBN 0-573-61130-0 (pbk) : £1.90 B81-15995

Horsler, Peter. Christmas Incorporated : a satirical comedy / Peter Horsler. — London : French, c1981. — 22p : 1plan ; 19cm
Six men, 3 women
ISBN 0-573-12034-x (pbk) : £0.70 B81-35552

Howard, Roger. A break in Berlin / Roger Howard ; introduction by Maro Germanou. — Colchester (c/o Department of Literature, University of Essex, Wivenhoe Park, Colchester) : Theatre Action Press, [1981]. — 32p : 1plan ; 30cm. — (Essex University new plays)
£1.00 (pbk) B81-22327

Howard, Roger. The violent irruption and terrible convulsions of the siege during the late lamentable Civil War at Colchester in the year 1648 / Roger Howard. — Colchester (c/o Theatre Underground, Department of Literature, University of Essex, Colchester CO4 3SQ) : Theatre Action Press, 1981. — 28p ; 22cm
ISBN 0-900575-10-7 (pbk) : £1.25 B81-22325

Jackson, Douglas. Episode : a moment in the lives of the Brontes' / by Douglas Jackson. — Macclesfield : New Playwrights' Network, [1980]. — 16p : 1plan ; 18cm
One man, 4 women
£0.50 (pbk) B81-03249

Johnson, Peter, *1933-*. Cause and effect / by Peter Johnson. — Macclesfield : New Playwrights' Network, [1980]. — 93p : ill,1plan ; 19cm
Five men, 4 women
£1.75 (pbk) B81-07672

Johnson, Peter, *1933-*. One of the family / by Peter Johnson. — Macclesfield : New Playwrights' Network, [1980]. — 24p : 1plan ; 18cm
Three men, 2 women
£0.50 (pbk) B81-03245

Johnson, Peter, *1933-*. Travellers rest : a play in two scenes / by Peter Johnson. — Macclesfield : New Playwrights' Network, [1980]. — 26p : 1plan ; 18cm
One man, 2 women
£0.50 (pbk) B81-03263

Johnston, Christine. The Easter tree : a play / by Christine Johnston. — Ilkeston : Moorley's, [1981?]. — 15p ; 21cm
Twelve men, 6 women
ISBN 0-86071-106-4 (pbk) : £0.25 B81-10150

Johnston, Jennifer. The nightingale and not the lark : a play / Jennifer Johnston. — London : French, c1980. — 17p : 1plan ; 18cm
Two men, 2 women
ISBN 0-573-12178-8 (pbk) : £0.60 B81-32585

Jones, Graham, *1930-*. Escargots / by Graham Jones. — Macclesfield : New Playwrights' Network, [1980]. — 17p : 1plan ; 18cm
Three men, 1 woman
£0.50 (pbk) B81-03247

Josipovici, Gabriel. Vergil dying / by Gabriel Josipovici. — Windsor (40 Grove Rd., Windsor, Berks. SL4 1JQ) : SPAN, 1981. — 43p ; 21cm
One man
ISBN 0-907479-00-6 (pbk) : £1.50 B81-08494

Joynson-Wreford, P.. A house divided : a three-act play / by P. Joynson-Wreford. — Glasgow : Brown, Son & Ferguson, 1981. — 80p : 1ill,1plan ; 18cm
Three men, 5 women
£2.00 (pbk) B81-27196

Kannan, Allan. When the scales fell / by Allan Kannan. — 2nd (rev.) ed. — [Edinburgh] ([2 Quality Street La., Edinburgh EH4 5BU]) : A. Kannan, 1981, c1980. — 90p ; 20cm
Twenty men, 6 women. — Previous ed.: 1980
£1.50 (pbk) B81-33479

Keane, John B.. The chastitute : a play in two acts / John B. Keane. — Dublin : Mercier, c1981. — 71p ; 18cm
ISBN 0-85342-643-0 (pbk) : £1.50 B81-17666

Kempinski, Tom. Duet for one : a play / Tom Kempinski. — London : French, c1981. — 39p : 1plan ; 22cm
One man, 1 woman
ISBN 0-573-11091-3 (pbk) : £2.20 B81-16445

Kilroy, Thomas. Talbot's box : a play in two acts / Thomas Kilroy. — Dublin (19 Oakdown Rd., Dublin 14), Gallery Books, c1979. — 63p ; 23cm
Also available in paperback at £2.25(Irish)
£4.50(Irish) (cased) B81-14273

Knight, Alanna. Girl on an empty swing : a 30-minute one act stage play for 3 women / by Alanna Knight. — Macclesfield : New Playwright's Network, [1980]. — 18p ; 18cm
£0.35 (pbk) B81-07000

Lawrence, Colin. Disturbance : a play in one act / by Colin Lawrence. — Macclesfield : New Playwrights' Network, [1981?]. — 29p : 1plan ; 19cm
Three men, 1 women
Unpriced (pbk) B81-15794

Lawrence, Colin. Harry Simpson, where are you? : a play in one act / by Colin Lawrence. — Macclesfield : New Playwrights' Network, [1981?]. — 22p : 1plan ; 19cm
Three women
£0.55 (pbk) B81-15795

Leonard, Hugh. Da ; A life ; and Time was / Hugh Leonard. — Harmondsworth : Penguin, 1981. — 250p ; 20cm. — (Penguin plays)
Da. Rev. ed. Originally published: London : French, 1978 — A Life. Originally published: London : French, 1980
ISBN 0-14-048161-3 (pbk) : £2.50 B81-22186

Leonard, Hugh. A life : a play / Hugh Leonard. — London : French, c1980. — 64p : 1plan ; 21cm
Four men, 4 women
ISBN 0-573-11244-4 (pbk) : £2.00 B81-07773

Lovering, Taylor. Single fare only : a one-act comedy play, 2F 3M / by Taylor Lovering. — Macclesfield : New Playwrights' Network, [1980]. — 26p : 1plan ; 19cm
Three men, 2 women
£0.50 (pbk) B81-03248

Lowe, Stephen, *1947-*. Touched / Stephen Lowe. — Todmorden : Woodhouse, c1977. — 60p ; 21cm
Three men, 7 women
ISBN 0-906657-03-2 (pbk) : £1.50 B81-07766

Lowe, Stephen, *1947-*. Touched / Stephen Lowe. — Rev. ed. — London : Eyre Methuen in association with the Royal Court Theatre, 1981. — 40p ; 21cm. — (The Royal Court writers series)
Seven women, 3 men. — Previous ed.: Todmorden : Woodhouse Books, 1979
ISBN 0-413-48510-2 (pbk) : £1.75 B81-10974

McCabe, Eugene. Pull down a horseman ; Gale day / Eugene McCabe. — Dublin (19 Oakdown Rd., Dublin 14) : Gallery Books, 1979. — 70p ; 23cm
Also available in paperback at £2.25(Irish)
£4.50(Irish) (cased) B81-14272

822'.914 — Drama in English, *1945-* — *Texts continuation*

McEwan, Ian. The imitation game : three plays for television / Ian McEwan. — London : Cape, 1981. — 175p ; 21cm
ISBN 0-224-01889-2 : £5.95 B81-09589

McMillan, Michael. The school leaver / by Michael McMillan. — London (1 Gresham Rd., S.W.9) : Black Ink Collective, 1978 (1979 [printing]). — 60p : ill ; 22cm
ISBN 0-9506248-1-0 (pbk) : Unpriced B81-36099

McMillan, Roddy. All in good faith / by Roddy McMillan. — Glasgow (34 Sauchiehall St., Glasgow) : Scottish Society of Playwrights, 1979. — 99p,[8]p of plates : facsims ; 22cm
Limited ed. of 500 numbered copies
ISBN 0-906799-01-5 : Unpriced B81-02935

Mander, Charles. Monmouth : a comedy / Charles Mander. — London : French, c1980. — 22p : 1plan ; 19cm
Three men, 2 women
ISBN 0-573-12166-4 (pbk) : £0.60 B81-02057

Mander, Charles. Sparrows : a comedy / Charles Mander. — London : French, c1980. — 22p : 1plan ; 19cm
Two men, 2 women
ISBN 0-573-12258-x (pbk) : £0.60 B81-02058

Manktelow, Bettine. Couples : a play / Bettine Manktelow. — London : French, c1981. — 57p : plans ; 22cm
Five men, 6 women
ISBN 0-573-11541-9 (pbk) : £2.25 B81-37278

Mercer, David, *1928-1980*. Collected T.V. plays / David Mercer. — London : Calder, 1981
Vol.1. — 282p ; 21cm
Originally published: 1964. — Contents: Where the difference begins — A climate of fear — The birth of a private man
ISBN 0-7145-3722-5 (cased) : £6.95
ISBN 0-7145-3723-3 (pbk) : £3.95 B81-10799

Mercer, David, *1928-1980*. Collected T.V. plays / David Mercer. — London : Calder, 1981
Vol.2. — 290p ; 21cm
Contents: A suitable case for treatment — For tea on Sunday — And did those feet — Let's murder Vivaldi — In two minds — The parachute
ISBN 0-7145-3814-0 (cased) : £6.95
ISBN 0-7145-3817-5 (pbk) : £3.95 B81-10798

Miles, Keith. The Coventry mystery plays / adapted by Keith Miles. — London : Heinemann, 1981. — 86p ; 19cm
ISBN 0-435-23600-8 (pbk) : £2.50 B81-35136

Nichols, Peter, *1927-*. Passion play / Peter Nichols. — London : Eyre Methuen, 1981. — 106p ; 20cm. — (A Methuen modern play)
Two men, 4 women
ISBN 0-413-47910-2 (cased) : £2.50
ISBN 0-413-47800-9 (pbk) : £2.50 B81-11150

O'Brien, Edna. Virginia : a play / by Edna O'Brien. — London : Hogarth, 1981. — 63p ; 22cm
One man, 2 women
ISBN 0-7012-0539-3 (pbk) : £2.95 B81-08482

Palin, Michael. More ripping yarns / Michael Palin and Terry Jones ; art direction & design Kate Helpburn ; photographs Bertrand Polo & AMO. — London : Eyre Methuen, 1980. — 95p : ill,1port ; 26cm
Ill on lining papers
ISBN 0-413-47520-4 : £3.95 B81-01207

Parker, Stewart. Catchpenny twist / Stewart Parker. — Dublin (19 Oakdown Rd., Dublin 14) : Gallery Books, 1980. — 72p ; 23cm
ISBN 0-904011-12-7 (cased) : £4.50(Irish) B81-14271

Partos, Glyn. September storm : a play in one act for IOW / by Glyn Partos. — Macclesfield : New Playwrights' Network, [1981?]. — 18p ; 19cm
Ten women
Unpriced (pbk) B81-15793

Pickering, Kenneth. Ulysses / by Ken Pickering and Keith R. Cole. — [London] : Evans, [c1981]. — 42p : ill ; 21cm
Ill on inside covers
ISBN 0-237-75063-5 (pbk) : Unpriced B81-36418

Pinter, Harold. Family voices : a play for radio / Harold Pinter ; with 7 paintings by Guy Vaesen. — London (21 Colville Terrace, W.11) : Next Editions in association with Faber, 1981. — 26p,[7]p of plates : col.ill ; 23cm
ISBN 0-907147-03-8 (spiral) : £2.95 B81-11649

Pinter, Harold. The screenplay of The French lieutenant's woman. — London : Cape, Sept.1981. — [110]p
ISBN 0-224-01983-x : £5.50 : CIP entry B81-22450

Pollard, Dorothy. Bringing home the ashes : a one act play / by Dorothy Pollard. — Macclesfield : New Playwrights' Network ([1981]). — 15p ; 18cm
Five men, 2 women
£0.55 (pbk) B81-20907

Price, Stanley, *1931-*. Moving : a comedy / Stanley Price. — London : French, c1981. — 75p : 1plan ; 22cm
Six men, 5 women
ISBN 0-573-11286-x (pbk) : £2.25 B81-39331

Reakes, Paul. Bang, your dead! : a comedy thriller / Paul Reakes. — London : French, c1981. — 27p : 1plan ; 19cm
2 Women, 3 men
ISBN 0-573-12023-4 (pbk) : £0.65 B81-32792

Reakes, Paul. Night intruder : a one act thriller / by Paul Reakes. — Macclesfield : New Playwrights' Network, [1980]. — 31p : 1plan ; 18cm
Six men, 2 women
£0.65 (pbk) B81-05892

Robbins, Norman. The grand old Duke of York : a pantomime / Norman Robbins. — London : French, c1981. — 71p ; 22cm
Ten men, 3 women, supers
ISBN 0-573-16423-1 (pbk) : £2.00 B81-16446

Rudkin, David. Hippolytus / Euripides ; a version by David Rudkin. — London : Heinemann, 1980. — vi,97p ; 19cm
ISBN 0-435-23780-2 (pbk) : £3.50 : CIP rev. B80-13523

Russell, Willy. Educating Rita : a comedy / Willy Russell. — London : French, c1981. — 58p : 1plan ; 22cm
One man, 1 woman
ISBN 0-573-11115-4 (pbk) : £2.20 B81-11379

Scotland, James. Hogmanay : a ne'erday Saturnalia / by James Scotland. — Glasgow : Brown, Son & Ferguson, 1981. — 30p ; 19cm. — (Scottish plays ; no.119)
Four men, 5 women
ISBN 0-85174-358-7 (pbk) : £0.75 B81-28397

Scott, Noel. Came a dealer in dreams : a play / Noel Scott. — London : French, c1980. — 9p ; 19cm
Eight men, 1 women, supers
ISBN 0-573-15211-x (pbk) : £0.50 B81-07711

Shaffer, Peter. Amadeus : a play / by Peter Shaffer. — Rev. ed. — Harmondsworth : Penguin, 1981. — 109p : music ; 20cm. — (Penguin plays)
Previous ed.: London : Deutsch, 1980
ISBN 0-14-048160-5 (pbk) : £1.95 B81-35076

Shaffer, Peter. Four plays / Peter Shaffer. — Harmondsworth : Penguin, 1981. — 206p ; 20cm
Contents: The private ear - The public eye - White liars - Black comedy
ISBN 0-14-048159-1 (pbk) : £2.25 B81-10693

Shaffer, Peter. The royal hunt of the sun : a play concerning the conquest of Peru / Peter Shaffer. — Harmondsworth : Penguin, 1981, c1964. — 96p : ill,music ; 20cm. — (Penguin plays)
Originally published: London : Hamilton, 1964
ISBN 0-14-048163-x (pbk) : £1.35 B81-10699

Shaffer, Peter. Three plays / Peter Shaffer. — Harmondsworth : Penguin, 1976 (1981 [printing]). — 300p ; 20cm. — (Penguin plays)
Contents: Five finger exercise. Originally published: London : Hamilton, 1958 — Shrivings. Originally Published: London : Deutsch, 1974 — Equus. Originally published: London : Deutsch, 1973
ISBN 0-14-048128-1 (pbk) : £1.95 B81-35075

Sharp, Ian. Genesis. — London : Edward Arnold, Dec.1981. — [48]p
ISBN 0-7131-0615-8 (pbk) : £0.90 : CIP entry B81-31553

Sharpe, Ted. Too many pebbles : a one-act play / by Ted Sharpe. — Macclesfield : New Playwrights' Network, [1981?]. — 21p ; 18cm
Six men, 3 women, supers
£0.55 (pbk) B81-15796

Sharpe, Ted. When we practise to deceive : a one-act play / by Ted Sharpe. — Macclesfield : New Playwrights' Network, [1981]. — 24p : 1plan ; 18cm
Three men, 2 women
£0.55 (pbk) B81-32066

Shirley, Rae. Bus stop : a comedy / Rae Shirley. — London : Evans, [1981]. — 20p : 1plan ; 21cm. — (Evans one act plays)
ISBN 0-237-75062-7 (pbk) : Unpriced B81-12194

Shirley, Rae. Sherry in the trifle : a comedy / Rae Shirley. — London : Evans plays, c1980. — 21p : 1plan ; 21cm. — (Evans one act plays)
ISBN 0-237-75061-9 (pbk) : Unpriced B81-12201

Simpson, John G.. The Milman strain : a play in three acts / by John G. Simpson. — [Ilkeston] ([366 Nottingham Rd., Ilkeston, Derbyshire DE7 5BN]) : [J.G. Simpson], [1981]. — 69p ; 20cm
£1.25 (spiral) B81-35652

Simpson, John G.. Refuge for a square peg : a play in three acts / by John G. Simpson. — [Ilkeston] ([366 Nottingham Rd, Ilkeston, Derbyshire DE7 5BN]) : [J.G. Simpson], [1981]. — 61p : ill ; 21cm
Four men, 2 women
£1.20 (spiral) B81-10659

Smith, Mavis. Nightmare : a play in one act / by Mavis Smith. — Macclesfield : New Playwrights' Network, [1980]p. — 26p : 1plan ; 18cm
One man, 2 women
£0.50 (pbk) B81-03246

Snelgrove, Michael. Hidden meanings : a comedy / Michael Snelgrove. — London : French, c1980. — 29p : 1plan ; 19cm
Four men, 5 women
ISBN 0-573-12098-6 (pbk) : £0.60 B81-07770

Southworth, John. David Copperfield : a play / by John Southworth ; based on the novel by Charles Dickens. — London : Heinemann Educational, 1981. — xi,116p : music ; 19cm
Twentyone men, 10 women, supers
ISBN 0-435-23806-x (pbk) : £1.50 B81-09528

822′.914 — Drama in English, *1945- — Texts continuation*

Spurling, John. The British Empire, part one. — London : Marion Boyars, Sept.1981. — [160]p
ISBN 0-7145-2743-2 (cased) : £5.95 : CIP entry
ISBN 0-7145-2732-7 (pbk) B81-25135

St. George, A. M.. The wheels of darkness : a radio play / by A.M. St. George. — London (38 Woodfield Ave., W5 1PA) : Spook Enterprises, c1981. — 18p ; 26cm
Eleven men, nine women
£0.40 (pbk) B81-23199

Stoppard, Tom. Night and day : a play / Tom Stoppard. — London : French, c1979. — 60p : 1plan ; 22cm
Seven men, 1 woman
ISBN 0-573-11308-4 (pbk) : £2.00 B81-11377

Stoppard, Tom. Night and day : a comedy / by Tom Stoppard. — Rev. & rewritten. — New York ; London : French, c1980. — 94p ; 18cm
Seven men, 1 woman, 1 boy. — Previous ed.: London : Faber, 1978
ISBN 0-573-61324-9 (pbk) : £1.90 B81-09676

Stoppard, Tom. On the razzle / by Tom Stoppard ; adapted from Einen Jux will er sich machen by Johann Nestroy. — London : Faber, 1981. — 79p ; 20cm. — (Faber paperbacks)
ISBN 0-571-11835-6 (pbk) : £2.50 : CIP rev. B81-23777

Storey, David. Early days ; Sisters ; and Life class / David Storey. — Harmondsworth : Penguin, 1980. — 236p ; 20cm. — (Penguin plays)
ISBN 0-14-048165-6 (pbk) : £2.50 B81-06646

Stott, Mike. Lenz : a play based (loosely) on the story by Georg Büchner / Mike Stott. — Todmorden : Woodhouse, c1979. — 65p ; 21cm
Four men, 6 women
ISBN 0-906657-02-4 (pbk) : £1.50 B81-07768

Sumner, Jill. Murder at the mill : a Victorian melo-drama in four scenes / by Jill Sumner. — Macclesfield : New Playwrights' Network, [1981?]. — 17p : plans ; 18cm
Six men, 6 women
£0.50 (pbk) B81-10847

Sustins, Nigel. Holiday in Jerusalem : an Easter play / by Nigel Sustins. — Ilkeston : Moorley's, [1981?]. — 14p ; 21cm
Seven men, 6 women
ISBN 0-86071-107-2 (pbk) : £0.25 B81-10149

Sustins, Nigel. Star search : a play for Christmas / by Nigel Sustins. — Ilkeston : Moorley's Bible & Bookshop, [1980]. — 16p ; 22cm
Seven men, 2 women, supers
ISBN 0-86071-100-5 (pbk) : £0.20 B81-00360

Symonds, John. The bicycle play / John Symonds ; introduced by the author's Reflections on an alternative theatre. — London (35 Palace Court, W2 4LS) : Pindar Press, 1981. — 186p ; 22cm. — (Plays ; v.1)
Series also titled: The collected dramatic works of John Symonds
ISBN 0-907132-01-4 : £10.00 B81-17068

Tally, Ted. Terra Nova : a play / Ted Tally. — Acting ed. — London : French, c1981. — 64p ; 22cm
Six men, 1 woman
ISBN 0-573-11448-x (pbk) : £2.20 B81-19855

Taylor, Don, *19---*. The exorcism : a play / Don Taylor. — London : French, c1981. — 60p : 1plan ; 22cm
Two men, 2 women
ISBN 0-573-11120-0 (pbk) : £2.20 B81-11380

Terson, Peter. The 1861 Whitby lifeboat disaster / Peter Terson. — Todmorden : Woodhouse, c1979. — 64p ; 21cm
Sixteen men, 8 women
ISBN 0-906657-04-0 (pbk) : £1.50 B81-07772

Trevor, Pat. But with a whimper : a one act play / by Pat Trevor. — Macclesfield : New Playwrights' Network, [1981]. — 30p ; 18cm
One man, 1 woman, 1 boy, 1 girl
£0.70 (pbk) B81-20905

Two Gay Sweatshop plays. — London (27 Priory Ave., N8 7RN) : Gay Men's Press, 1981. — 142p ; 20cm
Contents: As time goes by / by Noel Greig & Drew Griffiths - The dear love of comrades / by Noel Greig
ISBN 0-907040-06-3 (pbk) : £2.50 B81-18374

Vickery, Frank. Breaking of the string / by Frank Vickery. — Macclesfield : New Playwrights' Network, [1981?]. — 72p ; 18cm
Two men, 2 women
£1.95 (pbk) B81-32063

Walker, David, *1947-*. Kith and kin / David Walker. — London : Edward Arnold, 1981. — 79p ; 22cm
ISBN 0-7131-0562-3 (pbk) : £1.35 : CIP rev. B81-07492

Waterhouse, Steve. Shades of reckoning : a play / by Steve Waterhouse. — Macclesfield : New Playwrights' Network, [1981]. — 69p : 1plan ; 19cm
Six men, 2 women
£1.90 (pbk) B81-20904

Way, Brian. The Christmas carol / by Charles Dickens ; adapted by Brian Way. — Boston, Mass. : Baker's Plays ; London : French [distributor], c1977. — 73p ; 28cm
Play in 2 acts. — 7 men, 1 woman, supers
£2.35 (pbk) B81-01208

Weldon, Fay. Action replay : a play / Fay Weldon. — London : French, 1980. — 39p ; 22cm
Three men, 3 women
ISBN 0-573-11001-8 (pbk) : £1.80 B81-01209

Wells, John, *1936-*. 'Anyone for Denis'. — London : Faber, Jan.1982. — [72]p
ISBN 0-571-11920-4 : £2.95 : CIP entry B81-34654

Wesker, Arnold. Caritas. — London : Cape, Oct.1981. — [64]p
ISBN 0-224-02020-x (pbk) : £2.50 : CIP entry B81-30963

Wesker, Arnold. The Wesker trilogy / Arnold Wesker. — Harmondsworth : Penguin, 1964 (1981 [printing]). — 217p : music ; 20cm. — (Arnold Wesker ; vol.1)
Originally published: London : Cape, 1960. — Contents: Chicken soup with barley. Originally published: Harmondsworth : Penguin, 1959 — Roots. Originally published: Harmondsworth : Penguin, 1959 — I'm talking about Jerusalem. Originally published: Harmondsworth, Penguin, 1960
ISBN 0-14-048048-x (pbk) : £1.75 B81-40500

Whitfield, Jack. Dead secret : a play in one act / by Jack Whitfield. — Macclesfield : New Playwrights' Network, [1980]. — 16p : 1plan ; 18cm
Five women
£0.55 (pbk) B81-05893

Williams, Guy. Romeo and Juliet. — London : Macmillan Education, Feb.1982. — [64]p. — (Dramascript classics)
ISBN 0-333-32503-6 (pbk) : £0.85 : CIP entry B81-35802

Williams, Hugh Steadman. Everywoman : a verse drama / Hugh Steadman Williams. — London : French, c1981. — 21p ; 19cm
Nine men, 5 women
ISBN 0-573-06253-6 (pbk) : £0.70 B81-35554

Williams, Nigel. Line 'em / Nigel Williams. — London : Eyre Methuen, 1980. — 62p ; 19cm. — (A Methuen modern play)
Thirteen men, 1 woman
ISBN 0-413-47890-4 (pbk) : £2.25 B81-01210

Witt, Mary. Path to liberty : a play / Mary Witt. — London : French, c1981. — 22p : 1plan ; 19cm
Six women
ISBN 0-573-13294-1 (pbk) : £0.60 B81-21193

Wroe, Malcolm. The student and the cockatoo : a comedy / Malcolm Wroe. — London : French, c1981. — 22p : 1plan ; 19cm
Two men, 1 women
ISBN 0-573-12256-3 (pbk) : £0.60 B81-17437

822′.914 — Drama in English. Ayckbourn, Alan — *Interviews*

Watson, Ian. Conversations with Ayckbourn / Ian Watson. — London : Macdonald, 1981. — 189p : ill,ports ; 26cm
ISBN 0-354-04649-7 : £8.95 B81-26983

822′.914 — Drama in English. Barnes, Peter, *1931- — Critical studies*

Dukore, Bernard F.. The theatre of Peter Barnes / by Bernard F. Dukore. — London : Heinemann, 1981. — ix,158p ; 22cm
Bibliography: p156-158
ISBN 0-435-18280-3 (pbk) : £5.50 : CIP rev. B81-11971

822′.914 — Drama in English. Bolt, Robert. Man for all seasons — *Study outlines*

Bareham, Tony. A man for all seasons : notes / by Tony Bareham. — London : Longman, 1980. — 69p ; 21cm. — (York notes ; 51)
Bibliography: p64-65
ISBN 0-582-78181-7 (pbk) : £0.90 B81-07094

822′.914 — Drama in English. Bond, Edward — *Critical studies*

Hay, Malcolm. Bond : a study of his plays / by Malcolm Hay and Philip Roberts. — London : Eyre Methuen, 1980. — 319p,[16]p of plates : ill,ports ; 20cm. — ([Modern theatre profiles])
Bibliography: p301-315. — Includes index
ISBN 0-413-38290-7 (cased) : £8.50
ISBN 0-413-47060-1 (pbk) : £3.95 B81-00361

822′.914 — Drama in English. Leonard, Hugh, *to ca 1945 — Biographies*

Leonard, Hugh. Home before night / Hugh Leonard. — Harmondsworth : Penguin, 1981, c1979. — 170p ; 18cm
Originally published: London : Deutsch, 1979
ISBN 0-14-005540-1 (pbk) : £1.25 B81-25078

822′.914 — Drama in English. Osborne, John, *1929-*. **Look back in anger —** *Study outlines*

Griffiths, Gareth. Look back in anger : notes / by Gareth Giffiths. — Harlow : Longman, 1981. — 71p ; 21cm. — (York notes ; 128)
ISBN 0-582-78239-2 (pbk) : £0.90 B81-33691

822′.914 — Drama in English. Osborne, John — *Biographies*

Osborne, John. A better class of person. — London : Faber, Oct.1981. — [288]p
ISBN 0-571-11785-6 : £7.95 : CIP entry B81-28159

822′.914 — Drama in English. Pinter, Harold. Caretaker, *The — Study outlines*

Stephen, Martin. The caretaker : notes / by G.M. Stephen. — Harlow : Longman, 1981. — 79p ; 21cm. — (York notes ; 106)
Bibliography: p76-77
ISBN 0-582-78155-8 (pbk) : £0.90 B81-19630

822′.914 — Drama in English. Pinter, Harold — *Critical studies*

Hayman, Ronald. Harold Pinter / by Ronald Hayman. — 4th ed. — London : Heinemann, 1980. — xvi,127p,[4]p of plates : ill ; 19cm. — (Contemporary playwrights)
Previous ed.: 1975. — Bibliography: px-xii
ISBN 0-435-18438-5 (pbk) : £2.50 B81-01754

822′.914 — Drama in English. Stoppard, Tom — *Critical studies*

Dean, Joan Fitzpatrick. Tom Stoppard : comedy as a moral matrix / Joan Fitzpatrick Dean. — Columbia ; London : University of Missouri Press, 1981. — 109p ; 21cm. — (A Literary frontiers edition)
ISBN 0-8262-0332-9 (pbk) : £5.60 B81-38217

822′.914 — Drama in English. Warner, Francis - *Critical studies*

Pursglove, Glyn. Francis Warner and tradition. — Gerrards Cross : Smythe, Sept.1980. — [250]p
ISBN 0-86140-083-6 : £9.50 : CIP entry
B81-20159

822′.914 — Drama in English. Warner, Francis. Requiem and its maquettes — *Critical studies*

Jeffrey, Rosalind. Chess in the mirror : a study of theatrical cubism in Francis Warner′s Requiem and its Maquettes / by Roselind Jeffrey. — Oxford : Thornton, 1980. — 145p,[3]leaves of plates : ill(some col.) ; 23cm
Includes index
ISBN 0-85455-020-8 : Unpriced : CIP rev.
B80-12036

822′.914 — Great Britain. Television drama in English. Scripts. Writing. Stewart, A. J. — *Biographies*

Stewart, A. J.. King′s memory : the autobiography of A.J. Stewart. — 2nd ed. — Glasgow : Maclellan, 1981. — 311p ; 22cm. — (An Embryo book)
Previous ed.: published as Died 1813 - born 1929. London : Macmillan, 1978. — Bibliography: p6
ISBN 0-85335-245-3 : £6.95 B81-40983

822′.914 — Scripts. Writing. Shaughnessy, Alfred — *Biographies*

Shaughnessy, Alfred. Both ends of the candle / Alfred Shaughnessy. — Milton Keynes : Robin Clark, 1979, c1978. — 167p,[4]p of plates : ill,ports ; 18cm
Originally published: London : Owen, 1978. — List of works: p159-160. — Includes index
ISBN 0-86072-018-7 (pbk) : £1.25 B81-39720

822′.914′080353 — Drama in English, *1945-*. Special subjects: Sex relations — *Anthologies*

Strike while the iron is hot : three plays on sexual politics / edited and introduced by Michelene Wandor. — London : Journeyman, 1980. — 141p ; 22cm
Contents: Strike while the iron is hot - Care and control - My mother says I never should
ISBN 0-904526-47-x (pbk) : £2.95 B81-03665

822′.914′08037 — Drama in English. West Country writers, *1945-*. Special subjects: Supernatural — *Anthologies*

West country tales. — Exeter : Webb & Bower, Nov.1981. — [128]p
ISBN 0-906671-65-5 : £4.95 : CIP entry
B81-34208

822′.914′09 — Drama in English, *1945-* — *Critical studies*

Contemporary English drama / associate editor C.W.E. Bigsby. — London : Edward Arnold, 1981. — 192p ; 22cm. — (Stratford-upon-Avon studies ; 19)
Includes index
ISBN 0-7131-6335-6 (cased) : Unpriced
ISBN 0-7131-6336-4 (pbk) : £4.95 B81-28316

822′.914′0926 — Drama in English, *1945-*. Dialogue — *Sociolinguistic perspectives*

Burton, Deirdre. Dialoque and discourse : a sociolinguistic approach to modern drama dialogue and naturally occurring conversation / Deirdre Burton. — London : Routledge & Kegan Paul, 1980. — xi,210p : ill ; 23cm
Bibliography: p190-202. - Includes index
ISBN 0-7100-0560-1 : £12.50 : CIP rev.
Also classified at 401′.9 B80-17940

822′.914′09358 — Drama in English, *1945-*. Special subjects: Politics — *Critical studies*

Itzin, Catherine. Stages in the revolution : political theatre in Britain since 1968 / Catherine Itzin. — London : Eyre Methuen, 1980. — xv,399p ; 21cm
Bibliography: p390-392. - Includes index
ISBN 0-413-39180-9 (cased) : £9.95
ISBN 0-413-46150-5 (pbk) : £4.50
Primary classification 792′.0941 B81-03786

823 — ENGLISH FICTION

823 — Fiction in English. African writers, *1945-* — *Critical studies*

Ngara, Emmanuel. Stylistic criticism and the African novel. — London : Heinemann Educational, Jan.1982. — [192]p. — (Studies in African literature)
ISBN 0-435-91720-x (pbk) : £3.95 : CIP entry
B81-34504

823 — Fiction in English. Australian writers. Cambridge, Ada; Praed, Rosa & Tasma — *Critical studies*

Beilby, Raymond. Ada Cambridge, Tasma and Rosa Praed / by Raymond Beilby and Cecil Hadgraft. — Melbourne ; Oxford : Oxford University Press, 1979. — 48p ; 22cm. — (Australian writers and their work)
Bibliography: p45-48
ISBN 0-19-550509-3 (pbk) : £1.75 B81-39492

823 — Fiction in English. Australian writers. Furphy, Joseph — *Critical studies*

Barnes, John, *1931-*. Joseph Furphy / by John Barnes. — Melbourne ; Oxford : Oxford University Press, 1979. — 46p ; 22cm. — (Australian writers and their work)
Bibliography: p45-46
ISBN 0-19-550533-6 (pbk) : £1.75 B81-39493

823 — Fiction in English. Australian writers. White, Patrick — *Biographies*

White, Patrick. Flaws in the glass : a self-portrait / Patrick White. — London : Cape, 1981. — 260p,[12]p of plates : ill,ports ; 23cm
ISBN 0-224-02924-x : £7.95 : CIP rev.
B81-28076

823 — Fiction in English. Australian writers. White, Patrick — *Critical studies*

Kiernan, Brian. Patrick White / Brian Kiernan. — London : Macmillan, 1980. — 147p ; 20cm. — (Macmillan commonwealth writers series)
Bibliography: p143-144. — Includes index
ISBN 0-333-26549-1 (cased) : £7.95 : CIP rev.
ISBN 0-333-06550-5 (pbk) : £3.50 B80-06092

823 — Fiction in English. Kenyan writers. Ngugi wa Thiong′o — *Critical studies*

Killam, G. D.. An introduction to the writings of Ngugi / G.D. Killam. — London : Heinemann, 1980. — vi,122p ; 22cm
Bibliography: p119-120. — Includes index
ISBN 0-435-91669-6 (pbk) : £2.95 : CIP rev.
B80-32363

Robson, Clifford B.. Ngugi wa Thiog′o / Clifford B. Robson. — London : Macmillan, 1979. — vi,164p ; 20cm. — (Macmillan Commonwealth writers series)
Bibliography: p158-162. — Includes index
ISBN 0-333-25470-8 (cased) : £6.95 : CIP rev.
ISBN 0-333-25471-6 (pbk) : £2.50 B79-06774

823 — Fiction in English. New Zealand writers. Ashton-Warner, Sylvia — *Biographies*

Ashton-Warner, Sylvia. I passed this way / Syliva Ashton-Warner. — London : Virago, 1980, c1979. — ix,499p : ill,maps,ports ; 25cm
Originally published: New York : Knopf, 1979. — Maps on lining papers
ISBN 0-86068-160-2 : £12.00 B81-03758

823 — Fiction in English. New Zealand writers. Mansfield, Katherine — *Critical studies*

Hanson, Clare. Katherine Mansfield / Clare Hanson and Andrew Gurr. — London : Macmillan, 1981. — 146p ; 20cm
Bibliography: p140-143. — Includes index
ISBN 0-333-27056-8 (cased) : £10.00
B81-23015

823 — Fiction in English. Nigerian writers. Achebe, Chinua. Arrow of God — *Study outlines*

Carroll, David, *1932-*. Arrow of God : notes / by David Carroll. — Harlow : Longman, 1980. — 80p ; 21cm. — (York notes ; 92)
Bibliography: p74
ISBN 0-582-78145-0 (pbk) : £0.90 B81-19634

823 — Fiction in English. Nigerian writers. Achebe, Chinua. Man of the people — *Study outlines*

Probyn, Clive T.. A man of the people : notes / by Clive T. Probyn. — Harlow : Longman, 1981. — 64p ; 21cm. — (York notes ; 116)
ISBN 0-582-78179-5 (pbk) : £0.90 B81-33692

823 — Fiction in English. Nigerian writers. Achebe, Chinua. Things fall apart — *Study outlines*

Dunn, T. A.. Things fall apart : notes / by T.A. Dunn. — Harlow : Longman, 1981. — 64p ; 21cm. — (York notes ; 96)
ISBN 0-582-78204-x (pbk) : £0.90 B81-19662

823 — Fiction in English. Nigerian writers. Amadi, Elechi. Concubine — *Critical studies*

Niven, Alastair. The concubine : a critical view / by Alastair Niven ; edited by Yolande Cantù. — London : Collings in association with the British Council, 1981. — 32p : ill,1port ; 21cm. — (Nexus books ; 01)
Bibliography: p30-31. - List of films: p32
ISBN 0-86036-134-9 (pbk) : £1.00 B81-18603

823 — Fiction in English. South African writers. Abrahams, Peter, *1919-*. Biographies: Tell freedom — *Study outlines*

Daniels, Russell. Tell freedom / Russell Daniels. — Harlow : Longman, 1981. — vii,86p ; 20cm. — (Longman guides to literature)
ISBN 0-582-65534-x (pbk) : £0.88 B81-13975

823[F] — Fiction in English. Australian writers, *1890-1945* — *Texts*

Franklin, Miles. My career goes bung : purporting to be the autobiography of Sybilla Penelope Melvyn Miles Franklin / with a foreword by Verna Coleman. — London : Virago, 1981. — 234p ; 20cm. — (Virago modern classics)
Originally published: Melbourne : Georgian House, 1946
ISBN 0-86068-220-x (pbk) : £2.95 : CIP rev.
B81-04346

Mitchell, Elyne. The colt from Snowy River / Elyne Mitchell ; illustrated by Victor Ambrus. — London : Granada, 1981, c1980. — 157p : ill ; 18cm. — (A Dragon book)
Originally published: London : Hutchinson, 1980
ISBN 0-583-30475-3 (pbk) : £0.85 B81-26405

Richardson, Henry Handel. The getting of wisdom / Henry Handel Richardson ; with a new introduction by Germaine Greer. — London : Virago, 1981, c1946. — 233p ; 20cm. — (Virago modern classics)
ISBN 0-86068-179-3 (pbk) : £2.95 : CIP rev.
B81-01212

Richardson, Henry Handel. Maurice Guest / Henry Handel Richardson ; with a new introduction by Karen Macleod. — London : Virago, 1981, c1940. — 562p ; 20cm. — (Virago modern classics)
ISBN 0-86068-196-3 (pbk) : £3.50 : CIP rev.
B81-02592

Stead, Christina. A Christina Stead reader / selected by Jean B. Read. — London : Virago, 1981. — viii,369p ; 19cm
ISBN 0-86068-224-2 (pbk) : £3.95 B81-35144

Stead, Christina. A little tea, a little chat / Christina Stead ; with a new introduction by Hilary Bailey. — London : Virago, 1981, c1948. — 394p ; 20cm. — (Virago modern classics)
Originally published: New York : Harcourt Brace, 1948
ISBN 0-86068-176-9 (pbk) : £3.50 : CIP rev.
B81-16912

Stead, Christina. The people with the dogs / Christina Stead ; with a new introduction by Judith Kegan Gardiner. — London : Virago, 1981, c1952. — 345p ; 19cm. — (Virago modern classics)
Originally published: Boston, Mass. : Little, Brown, 1952
ISBN 0-86068-177-7 (pbk) : £3.50 : CIP rev.
B81-16913

White, Patrick. Voss / Patrick White. — Harmondsworth : Penguin, 1960 (1981 [printing]). — 447p ; 20cm. — (King penguin)
Originally published: London : Eyre & Spottiswoode, 1957
ISBN 0-14-006008-1 (pbk) : £2.95 B81-34755

823[F] — Fiction in English. Australian writers, *1945-* — *Texts*

Bail, Murray. Homesickness / Murray Bail. — South Melbourne ; London : Macmillan, 1980. — 317p ; 21cm
ISBN 0-333-29896-9 : £6.95 B81-00362

Braddon, Russell. The naked island. — Large print ed. — Anstey : Ulverscroft, Feb.1982. — [456]p. — (Charnwood library series)
ISBN 0-7089-8024-4 : £5.25 : CIP entry B81-36956

Braddon, Russell. The predator / Russell Braddon. — London : Joseph, 1980. — 191p ; 23cm
ISBN 0-7181-1958-4 : £5.95 B81-00363

Carey, Peter. Bliss. — London : Faber, Sept.1981. — [304]p
ISBN 0-571-11769-4 : £6.50 : CIP entry B81-24591

Carey, Peter. The fat man in history / Peter Carey. — London : Faber, 1980, c1979. — 186p ; 23cm
ISBN 0-571-11619-1 : £4.95 : CIP rev. B80-18034

Cato, Nancy. Brown sugar. — London : New English Library, Feb.1982. — [256]p
Originally published: London : Heinemann, 1974
ISBN 0-450-05362-8 (pbk) : £1.50 : CIP entry B81-36204

Cato, Nancy. North-West by south / Nancy Cato. — London : New English Library, 1980, c1965. — 313p ; 18cm
Originally published: London : Heinemann, 1965
ISBN 0-450-04932-9 (pbk) : £1.75 B81-02192

Cleary, Jon. The faraway drums / Jon Cleary. — London : Collins, 1981. — 288p ; 22cm
ISBN 0-00-222283-3 : £6.95 : CIP rev. B81-28771

Cleary, Jon. The golden sabre / Jon Cleary. — London : Collins, 1981. — 300p ; 22cm
ISBN 0-00-222269-8 : £6.50 B81-01213

Cleary, Jon. The high commissioner / by Jon Cleary. — Bolton-by-Bowland : Magna, 1979, c1966. — 479p ; 23cm
Originally published: London : Collins, 1966. — Published in large print
ISBN 0-86009-208-9 : £5.25 : CIP rev. B79-30329

Cleary, Jon. A very private war / Jon Cleary. — [London] : Fontana, 1981, c1980. — 287p ; 18cm
Originally published: London : Collins, 1980
ISBN 0-00-616244-4 (pbk) : £1.50 B81-11878

Denton, Kit. The breaker / by Kit Denton. — Long Preston : Magna Print, 1981, c1973. — 547p ; 22cm
Originally published: Sydney : Angus and Robertson, 1973 ; London : Angus and Robertson, 1979. — Published in large print
ISBN 0-86009-329-8 : Unpriced : CIP rev. B81-14447

Foreman, Russell. Long pig / Russell Foreman. — London : Granada, 1981, c1958. — 248p ; 18cm. — (A Mayflower book)
Originally published: London : Heinemann, 1959
ISBN 0-583-13305-3 (pbk) : £1.50 B81-32579

Gibson, Tom. The last crusader / Tom Gibson. — London : Hale, 1981. — 253p ; 21cm
ISBN 0-7091-8876-5 : £6.25 B81-14203

Grant, Maxwell. Inherit the sun. — London : Hodder and Stoughton, Feb.1982. — [448]p. — (Coronet books)
Originally published: 1981
ISBN 0-340-27539-1 (pbk) : £1.95 : CIP entry B81-36362

Grant, Maxwell, *1937-*. Inherit the sun / Marshall Grant. — London : Hodder and Stoughton, 1981. — 414p ; 22cm
ISBN 0-340-25968-x : £6.95 B81-11271

Ireland, David. A woman of the future / David Ireland. — Ringwood, Vic. ; Harmondsworth : Penguin, 1980, c1979 (1981 [printing]). — 351p ; 19cm
Originally published: Melbourne : Allen Lane, 1979
ISBN 0-14-005657-2 (pbk) : £1.95 B81-40417

Kata, Elizabeth. Child of the holocaust / Elizabeth Kata. — Sydney ; London : Collins, 1979. — 189p ; 22cm
ISBN 0-00-221599-3 : £5.25 B81-02725

Kelly, Gwen. Always afternoon / Gwen Kelly. — Sydney ; London : Collins, 1981. — 263p ; 22cm
ISBN 0-00-222217-5 : £6.95 B81-23200

Kenrick, Tony. The 81st site / Tony Kenrick. — London : Granada, 1980. — 288p ; 23cm
ISBN 0-246-11230-1 : £5.95 B81-00364

Kenrick, Tony. The 81st Site / Tony Kenrick. — London, 1980 (1981 [printing]). — 288p ; 18cm. — (A Panther book)
ISBN 0-586-05066-3 (pbk) : £1.50 B81-21983

Kenrick, Tony. Two lucky people / Tony Kenrick. — London : Star, 1980, c1978. — 191p ; 18cm
Originally published: London : Joseph, 1978
ISBN 0-352-30546-0 (pbk) : £1.25 B81-02186

Leonard, Alison. An inch of candle / Alison Leonard. — London : Angus & Robertson, 1980. — 174p ; 23cm
For adolescents
ISBN 0-207-95936-6 : £4.95 B81-00365

Marshall, William, *1944-*. Perfect end / William Marshall. — London : Hamilton, 1981. — 198p ; 21cm. — (A Yellowthread Street mystery)
ISBN 0-241-10638-9 : £7.50 : CIP rev. B81-25782

Marshall, William, *1944-*. Sci Fi : a Yellowthread Street mystery / William Marshall. — London : Hamilton, 1981. — 202p ; 21cm
ISBN 0-241-10536-6 : £6.50 : CIP rev. B81-02556

Marshall, William, *1944-*. Shanghai / William Marshall. — London : Pan, 1980, c1979. — 234p ; 18cm
Originally published: London : Hamilton, 1979
ISBN 0-330-26251-3 (pbk) : £1.25 B81-09742

Marshall, William, *1944-*. Skulduggery : a Yellowthread Street mystery / William Marshall. — London : Pan, 1981, c1979. — 174p ; 18cm
Originally published: London : Hamilton, 1979
ISBN 0-330-26342-0 (pbk) : £1.00 B81-20209

Moorhouse, Frank. The everlasting secret family and other secrets / Frank Moorhouse. — London : Angus & Robertson, 1980. — 213p ; 19cm
ISBN 0-207-14275-0 : £4.95 B81-00366

Peters, Lance. The dirty half mile / Lance Peters. — London : Granada, 1981, c1979. — 347p ; 18cm. — (A Mayflower book)
ISBN 0-583-13232-4 (pbk) : £1.50 B81-06370

Stow, Randolph. Visitants / Randolph Stow. — London : Picador in association with Secker & Warburg, 1981,c1979. — 182p ; 20cm
Originally published: London : Secker & Warburg, 1979
ISBN 0-330-26378-1 (pbk) : £1.95 B81-24417

Walker, Lucy. The distant hills / Lucy Walker. — [Glasgow] : Fontana, 1981, c1962. — 187p ; 18cm
Originally published: London : Collins, 1962
ISBN 0-00-616162-6 (pbk) : £0.90 B81-11063

Walker, Lucy. Joyday for Jodi / Lucy Walker. — Large print ed. — Leicester : Ulverscroft, 1980, c1972. — 344p ; 23cm. — (Ulverscroft large print series)
Originally published: London : Collins, 1971
ISBN 0-7089-0508-0 : £4.25 : CIP rev. B80-18023

Walker, Lucy. The loving heart / Lucy Walker. — [London] : Fontana, 1962, c1960 (1981 [printing]). — 223p ; 19cm
Originally published: London : Collins, 1960
ISBN 0-00-616261-4 (pbk) : £0.95 B81-22014

Walker, Lucy. Reaching for the stars / Lucy Walker. — Large print ed. — Leicester : Ulverscroft, 1981, c1964. — 374p ; 23cm. — (Ulverscroft large print series)
Originally published: London : Collins, 1966
ISBN 0-7089-0636-2 : Unpriced : CIP rev. B81-13512

Walker, Lucy. Ribbons in her hair / Lucy Walker. — Large print ed. — Leicester : Ulverscroft, 1981, c1972. — 467p : 1geneal.table ; 23cm. — (Ulverscroft large print series)
Originally published: under the name Dorothy Lucie Sanders. London : Hodder and Stoughton, 1957 ; and under the name Lucy Walker. London : Collins, 1972
ISBN 0-7089-0594-3 : Unpriced B81-14221

Walker, Lucy. Six for heaven / Lucy Walker. — Glasgow : Collins ; [London] : Fontana, 1970, c1969 (1979 printing). — 189p ; 18cm
Originally published: under the name Dorothy Lucie Sanders. London : Hodder and Stoughton, 1952
ISBN 0-00-615834-x (pbk) : £0.80 B81-19815

Walker, Lucy. Six for heaven / Lucy Walker. — Large print ed. — Leicester : Ulverscroft, 1981, c1969. — 377p ; 23cm. — (Ulverscroft large print series)
Originally published: London : Hodder & Stoughton, 1953
ISBN 0-7089-0650-8 : £5.00 B81-28575

West, Morris. The clowns of God / Morris West. — London : Hodder and Stoughton, 1981. — 400p ; 23cm
ISBN 0-340-26512-4 : £6.95 : CIP rev. B81-01853

West, Morris. The clowns of God. — London : Hodder & Stoughton, Feb.1982. — [432]p. — (Coronet Books)
ISBN 0-340-27638-x (pbk) : £1.95 : CIP entry B81-36365

West, Morris. The clowns of God. — Large print ed. — Anstey : Ulverscroft, Feb.1982. — [566] p. — (Charnwood library series)
ISBN 0-7089-8029-5 : £6.50 : CIP entry B81-36961

West, Morris. Kundu / Morris West. — Large print ed. — Leicester : Ulverscroft, 1980. — 305p ; 23cm. — (Ulverscroft large print series)
Originally published: London : Angus & Robertson, 1957
ISBN 0-7089-0530-7 : £4.25 : CIP rev. B80-23754

West, Morris. Proteus / Morris West. — Large print ed. — Leicester : Ulverscroft, 1981, c1979. — 509p ; 23cm. — (Ulverscroft large print series)
Originally published: London : Collins, 1979
ISBN 0-7089-0642-7 : Unpriced : CIP rev. B81-13514

West, Morris. Summer of the red wolf / Morris West. — Glasgow : Fontana/Collins, 1981, c1971. — 220p ; 18cm
Originally published: London : Heinemann, 1971
ISBN 0-00-615839-0 (pbk) : £1.35 B81-18474

823[F] — Fiction in English. Australian writers, *1945- — Texts* *continuation*

West, Morris. The tower of Babel / Morris West. — [London] : Fontana, 1981, c1971. — 288p ; 18cm
Originally published: New York : Morrow ; London : Heinemann, 1968
ISBN 0-00-615840-4 (pbk) : £1.50 B81-39340

823[F] — Fiction in English. Cameroon writers, *1960- — Texts*

Jumbam, Kenjo. The white man of God / Kenjo Jumbam. — London : Heinemann, 1980. — 151p ; 19cm. — (African writers series ; no.231)
ISBN 0-435-90231-8 (pbk) : £1.40 : CIP rev. B80-12562

823[F] — Fiction in English. Chinese writers, *1945- — Texts*

Chen, Yuan-tsung. The dragon's village : an autobiographical novel of Revolutionary China / Yuan-tseng Chen. — London : Women's Press, 1981, c1980. — 285p ; 20cm
Originally published: New York : Pantheon, c1980
ISBN 0-7043-3865-3 (pbk) : £3.50 B81-26852

823[F] — Fiction in English. Dutch writers, *1945-*

Van de Wetering, Janwillem. The Maine massacre / Janwillem van de Wetering. — London : Corgi, 1981, c1974. — 236p ; 18cm
Originally published: London : Heinemann, 1979
ISBN 0-552-11767-6 (pbk) : £1.25 B81-37654

Van de Wetering, Janwillem. The mind-murders / Janwillem van de Wetering. — London : Heinemann, 1981. — 186p ; 21cm
ISBN 0-434-85927-3 : £6.95 B81-37655

823[F] — Fiction in English. Greek writers, *1945- — Texts*

Wilden, Theodore. The exchange / Theodore Wilden. — London : Collins, 1981. — 272p ; 22cm
ISBN 0-00-222229-9 : £6.95 B81-31925

823[F] — Fiction in English. Indian writers, *1858-1947 — Texts*

Narayan, R. K.. The guide / R.K. Narayan. — London : Heinemann, 1980, c1958. — 246p ; 21cm
Originally published: London : Methuen, 1958
ISBN 0-434-49611-1 : £6.95 B81-03741

Narayan, R. K.. The man-eater of Malgudi / R.K. Narayan. — London : Heinemann, 1961 (1980 [printing]). — 182p ; 21
ISBN 0-434-49601-4 : £6.95 B81-03313

Narayan, R. K.. The vendor of sweets / R.K. Narayan. — London : Heinemann, 1980, c1967. — 191p ; 21cm
Originally published: London : Bodley Head, 1967
ISBN 0-434-49610-3 : £6.95 B81-03740

823[F] — Fiction in English. Indian writers, *1947- — Texts*

Desai, Anita. Fire on the mountain / Anita Desai. — Harmondsworth : Penguin, 1981, c1977. — 145p ; 20cm. — (A King Penguin)
Originally published: London : Heinemann, 1977
ISBN 0-14-005347-6 (pbk) : £1.95 B81-40496

Lidchi, Maggi. The first wife : a novel / by Maggi Lidchi. — London : Gollancz, 1981. — 207p ; 23cm
ISBN 0-575-02786-x : £6.95 B81-14192

Rushdie, Salman. Midnight's children / Salman Rushdie. — London : Cape, 1981. — 446p ; 25cm
ISBN 0-224-01823-x : £6.95 : CIP rev. B80-21104

823[F] — Fiction in English. Israeli writers, *1947- — Texts*

Bar-Zohar, Michael. The phantom conspiracy / by Michael Bar-Zohar. — London : Weidenfeld and Nicolson, 1981, c1980. — 336p ; 23cm
Originally published: New York : Morrow, 1980
ISBN 0-297-77892-7 : £6.50 B81-30702

Elon, Amos. Timetable : the story of Joel Brand / Amos Elon. — London : Hutchinson, 1981, c1980. — 349p ; 23cm
Originally published: Garden City, N.Y.: Doubleday, 1980
ISBN 0-09-144230-3 : £6.95 B81-15659

Louvish, Simon. A moment of silence : journeys through a counterfeit mezuza / Simon Louvish. — London : Martin Brian & O'Keeffe, 1979. — 264p ; 21cm
ISBN 0-85616-131-4 : £4.95 B81-00369

Portugali, Menachem. Khamsin / M. Portugali. — London : Macdonald Futura, 1981. — 272p ; 18cm. — (A Futura book)
ISBN 0-7088-1972-9 (pbk) : £1.25 B81-15642

823[F] — Fiction in English. Kenyan writers, *1960- — Texts*

Akare, Thomas. The slums / Thomas Akare. — London : Heinemann, 1981. — 182p ; 19cm. — (African writers series ; 241)
ISBN 0-435-90241-5 (pbk) : £1.95 B81-28754

823[F] — Fiction in English. New Zealand writers, *1907- — Texts*

Ashton-Warner, Sylvia. Spinster : a novel / Sylvia Ashton-Warner ; introduction by Fleur Adcock. — London : Virago, 1980. — xiii,269p ; 21cm
Originally published: London : Secker and Warburg, 1958
ISBN 0-86068-161-0 : £2.95 B81-00370

Batistich, Amelia. Another mountain, another song. — London : Hodder and Stoughton, Oct.1981. — [244]p
ISBN 0-340-26496-9 : £6.95 : CIP entry B81-30493

Calder, Jason. Target Margaret Thatcher / by Jason Calder. — Palmerston North, N.Z. : Dunmore ; London : Hale, 1981. — 175p : ill ; 21cm
ISBN 0-7091-9272-x : £6.25
ISBN 0-908564-71-6 (N.Z.) B81-40528

Cook, Hugh, *1956-*. Plague summer : a novel / by Hugh Cook. — London : Hale, 1980. — 224p ; 22cm
ISBN 0-7091-8707-6 : £5.50 B81-05435

Eden, Dorothy. The American heiress / Dorothy Eden. — London : Hodder and Stoughton, 1980. — 218p ; 23cm
ISBN 0-340-25896-9 : £5.95 : CIP rev. B80-13992

Eden, Dorothy. The American heiress. — London : Coronet, May 1981. — [256]p
Originally published: 1980
ISBN 0-340-26743-7 (pbk) : £1.25 : CIP entry B81-04209

Eden, Dorothy. The American heiress. — Large print ed. — Anstey : Ulverscroft, Jan.1982. — [445]p. — (Ulverscroft large print series : romance)
ISBN 0-7089-0733-4 : £5.00 : CIP entry B81-33965

Eden, Dorothy. Melbury Square / Dorothy Eden. — Large print ed. — Leicester : Ulverscroft, 1981, c1970. — 551p ; 23cm
Originally published: London : Hodder & Stoughton, 1970
ISBN 0-7089-0663-x : £5.00 : CIP rev. B81-20634

Eden, Dorothy. Never call it loving. — Large print ed. — Anstey : Ulverscroft, Nov.1981. — [560]p. — (Ulverscroft large print series)
Originally published: London : Hodder and Stoughton, 1966
ISBN 0-7089-0708-3 : £5.00 : CIP entry B81-30504

Eden, Dorothy. Sleep in the woods / Dorothy Eden. — Large print ed. — Leicester : Ulverscroft, 1980, c1960. — 521p ; 23cm. — (Ulverscroft large print series)
Originally published: London : Hodder & Stoughton, 1960
ISBN 0-7089-0509-9 : £4.25 : CIP rev. B80-17971

Eden, Dorothy. The Storrington papers / Dorothy Eden. — Large print ed. — Leicester : Ulverscroft, 1980, c1979. — 379p ; 23cm. — (Ulverscroft large print series)
Originally published: London : Hodder and Stoughton, 1979
ISBN 0-7089-0540-4 : £4.25 : CIP rev. B80-24827

Eden, Dorothy. The vines of Yarabee / Dorothy Eden. — Large print ed. — Leicester : Ulverscroft, 1980, c1969. — 516p ; 23cm. — (Ulverscroft large print series)
Originally published: New York : McCann ; London : Hodder and Stoughton, 1969
ISBN 0-7089-0550-1 : £4.25 : CIP rev. B80-35442

Frame, Janet. Faces in the water / Janet Frame. — London : Women's Press, 1980, c1961. — 254p ; 20cm
Originally published: Christchurch, N.Z. : Pegasus Press, 1961 ; London : W.H. Allen, 1962
ISBN 0-7043-3861-0 (pbk) : £2.75 B81-00371

Frame, Janet. Living in the Maniototo / Janet Frame. — London : Women's Press in association with Hutchinson Group (NZ) Ltd, 1981, c1979. — 240p ; 20cm
Originally published: New York : Braziller, 1979
ISBN 0-7043-3867-x (pbk) : £3.25 B81-21980

Gee, Maurice. Meg. — London : Faber, Oct.1981. — [256]p
ISBN 0-571-11783-x : £5.95 : CIP entry B81-25302

Harrison, Craig. The quiet earth. — London : Hodder & Stoughton, Nov.1981. — [242]p
ISBN 0-340-26507-8 : £6.95 : CIP entry B81-30132

Jeffery, Margaret. The black shore / Margaret Jeffery. — London : Heinemann, 1980. — 217p ; 23cm
ISBN 0-434-37250-1 : £6.50 B81-00372

Kalman, Yvonne. Greenstone land / Yvonne Kalman. — London : Macdonald, 1981. — 475p ; 23cm
ISBN 0-354-04672-1 : £7.95 B81-37906

Kidman, Fiona. A breed of women / Fiona Kidman. — London : Macmillan, 1980, c1979. — 345p ; 22cm
Originally published: Sydney : Harper & Row, 1979
ISBN 0-333-31177-9 : £5.95 B81-19949

Mantell, Laurie. Murder and chips / by Laurie Mantell. — London : Gollancz, 1980. — 157p ; 23cm
ISBN 0-575-02882-3 : £6.95 B81-10691

Marsh, Ngaio. Black as he's painted / Ngaio Marsh. — [London] : Fontana, 1975, c1974 (1980 [printing]). — 221p : 1map ; 18cm
Originally published: London : Collins, 1974
ISBN 0-00-616163-4 (pbk) : £1.00 B81-01214

Marsh, Ngaio. Colour scheme / Ngaio Marsh. — [London] : Fontana, 1960, c1943 (1981 [printing]). — 256p ; 19cm
ISBN 0-00-616376-9 (pbk) : £1.25 B81-39342

823[F] — Fiction in English. New Zealand writers, *1907- — Texts* *continuation*

Marsh, Ngaio. Died in the wool / Ngaio Marsh. — London : Fontana, 1963 (1981 [printing]). — 256p ; 18cm
Originally published: London : Collins, 1945
ISBN 0-00-616151-0 (pbk) : £1.35 B81-28213

Marsh, Ngaio. Died in the wool / by Ngaio Marsh. — Long Preston : Magna Print, 1981, c1945. — 488p ; 23cm
Originally published: London : Collins, 1945. — Published in large print
ISBN 0-86009-326-3 : £5.75 : CIP rev. B81-14379

Marsh, Ngaio. Final curtain / Ngaio Marsh. — [London] : Fontana, 1956 (1980 [printing]). — 250p ; 18cm
Originally published: London : Collins, 1947
ISBN 0-00-615957-5 (pbk) : £1.25 B81-01805

Marsh, Ngaio. The nursing home murder / Ngaio Marsh and Henry Jellett. — [London] : Fontana, 1961, c1935 (1981 [printing]). — 190p ; 18cm
ISBN 0-00-616164-2 (pbk) : £1.25 B81-15534

Marsh, Ngaio. Scales of justice / Ngaio Marsh. — [London] : Fontana, 1958 (1979 printing). — 255p ; 18cm
Originally published: London : Collins, 1955
ISBN 0-00-615777-7 (pbk) : £0.85 B81-19813

Marsh, Ngaio. Swing, brother, swing / Ngaio Marsh. — [London] : Fontana, 1956 (1981 [printing]). — 255p ; 18cm
Originally published: London : Collins, 1949
ISBN 0-00-616441-2 (pbk) : £1.25 B81-39343

Marsh, Ngaio. Vintage murder / Ngaio Marsh. — [London] : Fontana, 1961, c1937 (1980 [printing]). — 223p : 1plan ; 18cm
ISBN 0-00-616152-9 (pbk) : £1.00 B81-00373

Sandys, Elspeth. The broken tree / Elspeth Sandys. — London : Hutchinson, 1981. — 386p ; 23cm
ISBN 0-09-143790-3 : £6.95 B81-11272

Saunders, G. K.. The stranger / G.K. Saunders. — Sydney ; London : Whitcombe & Tombs, 1978. — 217p ; 21cm
ISBN 0-7233-5304-2 : £3.25 B81-21188

Shadbolt, Maurice. The Lovelock version / Maurice Shadbolt. — London : Hodder and Stoughton, 1980. — 568p ; 25cm
ISBN 0-340-25718-0 : £9.95 : CIP rev. B80-14027

Simons, Wendy. Odd woman out / Wendy Simons. — London : Angus & Robertson, c1980. — 196p ; 20cm
Originally published: Sydney : Angus & Robertson, 1980
ISBN 0-207-14037-5 : £5.5 B81-08502

Stevens, David, *1933-*. White for danger / David Stevens. — [London] : Fontana, 1980, c1979. — 221p : 1map ; 18cm
Originally published: London : Collins, 1979
ISBN 0-00-616155-3 (pbk) : £1.00 B81-06266

Summers, Essie. Autumn in April / by Essie Summers. — London : Mills & Boon, 1981. — 187p ; 19cm
ISBN 0-263-09837-0 : £4.55 B81-10891

Summers, Essie. Daughter of the misty gorges / by Essie Summers. — London : Mills & Boon, 1981. — 190p ; 20cm
ISBN 0-263-09920-2 : £4.55 B81-34097

Summers, Essie. Heir to Windrush Hill. — Large print ed. — Anstey : Ulverscroft, Nov.1981. — [400]p. — (Ulverscroft large print series)
Originally published: London : Mills and Boon, 1966
ISBN 0-7089-0707-5 : £5.00 : CIP entry B81-30503

Summers, Essie. The house of the shining tide. — Large print ed. — Anstey : Ulverscroft, Oct.1981. — [368]p. — (Ulverscroft large print series)
Originally published: London : Mills & Boon, 1962
ISBN 0-7089-0692-3 : £5.00 : CIP entry B81-28103

Wilder, Cherry. The luck of Brin's five / Cherry Wilder. — Londn : Angus & Robertson, 1979. — vii,230p ; 23cm
Originally published: New York : Atheneum, 1977
ISBN 0-207-13823-0 (cased) : £4.95
ISBN 0-207-14368-4 (Australia) B81-17444

823[F] — Fiction in English. Nigerian writers, *1960- — Texts*

Aluko, T. M.. Wrong ones in the dock. — London : Heinemann Educational, Feb.1982. — [192]p. — (African writers series ; 242)
ISBN 0-435-90242-3 (pbk) : £1.95 : CIP entry B81-36226

Ekwuru, Andrew. Going to storm / Andrew Ekwuru. — Walton-on-Thames : Nelson, 1980. — 148p ; 19cm. — (Panafrica library)
ISBN 0-17-511619-9 (pbk) : £1.25 : CIP rev. B80-18484

Emecheta, Buchi. The moonlight bride / Buchi Emecheta. — Oxford : Oxford University Press in association with University Press Limited, 1980. — 77p ; 20cm. — (Masquerade books)
ISBN 0-19-271435-x (pbk) : £1.50 : CIP rev. B80-18913

Emecheta, Buchi. The wrestling match / Buchi Emecheta. — Oxford : Oxford University Press in association with University Press Limited, c1980. — 74p ; 20cm. — (Masquerade Books)
ISBN 0-19-271436-8 (pbk) : £1.50 : CIP rev. B80-18514

Emecheta, Buchni. Destination Biafra. — London : Allison & Busby, Oct.1981. — [224]p
ISBN 0-85031-409-7 : £6.95 : CIP entry B81-28087

Garba, Mohmed Tukur. The black temple / Mohmed Tukur Garba. — London : Macmillan, 1981. — 100p ; 18cm. — (Pacesetters)
ISBN 0-333-31147-7 (pbk) : £0.80 B81-38785

Ighavini, Dickson. Bloodbath at Lobster Close / Dickson Ighavini. — London : Macmillan, 1980. — 152p ; 18cm. — (Pacesetters)
ISBN 0-333-28498-4 (pbk) : Unpriced B81-01215

Ike, Vincent Chukwuemeka. Expo '77 / Chukwuemeka Ike. — [London] : Fontana, 1980. — 190p ; 18cm
ISBN 0-00-616063-8 (pbk) : £1.25 B81-10213

Onyeama, Dillibe. Revenge of the medicine man / Dillibe Onyeama. — London : Sphere, 1980. — 184p ; 18cm
ISBN 0-7221-6545-5 (pbk) : £1.00 B81-11730

Soyinka, Wole. Aké : the years of childhood / Wole Soyinka. — London : Collings, c1981. — 230p,[1]leaf of plates : ports ; 24cm
ISBN 0-86036-155-1 : £7.50 B81-26457

Soyinka, Wole. The forest of a thousand daemons. — Walton-on-Thames : Nelson, Jan.1982. — [144]p. — (Panafrica library)
Originally published: 1968
ISBN 0-17-511288-6 (pbk) : £1.25 : CIP entry B81-34390

Tutuola, Amos. The witch-herbalist of the remote town. — London : Faber, Oct.1981. — [208]p
ISBN 0-571-11703-1 (cased) : £6.50 : CIP entry
ISBN 0-571-11704-x (pbk) : £2.50 B81-25304

823[F] — Fiction in English. Nigerian writers, *to 1960 — Texts*

Soyinka, Wole. Season of anomy / Wole Soyinka. — Walton-on-Thames : Nelson, 1980. — 313p ; 19cm. — (Panafrica library)
Originally published: London : Collings, 1973
ISBN 0-17-511618-0 (pbk) : £1.95 : CIP rev. B80-18498

823[F] — Fiction in English. Norwegian writers, *1945- — Texts*

Sharman, Nick, *1952-*. Childmare / Nick Sharman. — London : Hamlyn Paperbacks, 1980. — 205p ; 18cm
ISBN 0-600-20182-1 (pbk) : £1.00 B81-05492

823[F] — Fiction in English. Somali writers, *1960- — Texts*

Farah, Nuruddin. Sweet and sour milk / Nuruddin Farah. — London : Heinemann, 1980, c1979. — 237p ; 19cm. — (African writers series ; 226)
Originally published: London : Allison and Busby, 1979
ISBN 0-435-90226-1 (pbk) : £1.60 : CIP rev. B80-06113

823[F] — Fiction in English. Somalian writers, *1960- — Texts*

Farah, Nuruddin. Sardines. — London : Allison & Busby, Oct.1981. — [286]p
ISBN 0-85031-408-9 : £6.95 : CIP entry B81-27940

823[F] — Fiction in English. South African writers, *1909-1961 — Texts*

Gordimer, Nadine. Burger's daughter / Nadine Gordimer. — Harmondsworth : Penguin, 1980, c1979. — 361p ; 20cm
Originally published: London : Cape, 1979
ISBN 0-14-005593-2 (pbk) : £1.95 B81-10991

Gordimer, Nadine. July's people / Nadine Gordimer. — London : Cape, 1981. — 160p ; 23cm
ISBN 0-224-01932-5 : £5.95 B81-36161

Gordimer, Nadine. A world of strangers / Nadine Gordimer. — Harmondsworth : Penguin, 1962, c1958 (1981 [printing]). — 265p ; 20cm
Originally published: London : Gollancz, 1958
ISBN 0-14-001704-6 (pbk) : £1.75 B81-10990

Jenkins, Geoffrey. A bridge of magpies / Geoffrey Jenkins. — [London] : Fontana, 1977, c1974 (1981 [printing]). — 222p : 1map ; 18cm
Originally published: London : Collins, 1974
ISBN 0-00-616197-9 (pbk) : £1.25 B81-15524

Jenkins, Geoffrey. A ravel of waters / Geoffrey Jenkins. — London : Collins, 1981. — 252p ; 22cm
ISBN 0-00-221618-3 : £6.95 : CIP rev. B81-12908

Jenkins, Geoffrey. The river of diamonds / Geoffrey Jenkins. — [London] : Fontana, 1966, c1964 (1980 [printing]). — 221p ; 18cm
Originally published: London : Collins, 1964
ISBN 0-00-616144-8 (pbk) : £1.15 B81-06268

Jenkins, Geoffrey. Southtrap / Geoffrey Jenkins. — Large print ed. — Leicester : Ulverscroft, c1979. — 481p ; 23cm. — (Ulverscroft large print series)
Originally published: London : Collins, 1979
ISBN 0-7089-0611-7 : £5.00 : CIP rev. B81-02582

Jenkins, Geoffrey. A twist of sand / Geoffrey Jenkins. — [London] : Fontana, 1961, c1959 (1981 [printing]). — 252p : 1map ; 18cm
Originally published: London : Collins, 1959
ISBN 0-00-616198-7 (pbk) : £1.25 B81-15526

Mphahlele, Es'kia. Chirundu / Es'kia Mphahlele. — Walton-on-Thames : Nelson, 1980. — 220p ; 19cm. — (Panafrica library)
Originally published: Johannesburg : Ravan, 1979
ISBN 0-17-511621-0 (pbk) : £1.50 : CIP rev. B80-18492

823[F] — Fiction in English. South African writers, *1909-1961* **— Texts** *continuation*

Packer, Joy. The dark curtain / by Joy Packer. — Long Preston : Magna, 1981, c1977. — 357p ; 23cm. — (Large type series)
Originally published: London : Eyre Methuen, 1977
ISBN 0-86009-316-6 : Unpriced : CIP rev. B81-08891

Packer, Joy. Veronica / by Joy Packer. — Bolton-by-Bowland : Magna, 1981, c1970. — 303p ; 22cm
Originally published: London : Eyre and Spottiswoode, 1970. — Published in large print
ISBN 0-86009-294-1 : £5.75 B81-08684

823[F] — Fiction in English. South African writers, *1961-* **— Texts**

Abrahams, Peter. Wild conquest. — Walton-on-Thames : Nelson, Feb.1982. — [384]p. — (Panafrica library)
Originally published: London : Faber, 1951
ISBN 0-17-511623-7 (pbk) : £2.50 : CIP entry B81-35794

Axe, Eric. South enchanted Africa and a stare from a mountain / Eric Axe. — Bognor Regis : New Horizon, c1980. — 129p ; 21cm
ISBN 0-86116-447-4 : £4.50 B81-19060

Brink, André. A dry white season / André Brink. — London : Star, 1980, c1979. — 316p ; 20cm
Originally published: London : W.H. Allen, 1979
ISBN 0-352-30703-x (pbk) : £1.95 B81-00367

Burmeister, Jon. The glory hunters / Jon Burmeister. — Large print ed. — Leicester : Ulverscroft, 1981, c1979. — 355p ; 23cm. — (Ulverscroft large print series)
Originally published: London : Joseph, 1979
ISBN 0-7089-0569-2 : £5.00 B81-21335

Cockburn, Terry. The Altoran creed / by Terry Cockburn. — London : Dobson, 1980. — 233p ; 21cm
ISBN 0-234-72208-8 : £5.25 B81-01216

Coetzee, J. M.. Waiting for the barbarians / J.M. Coetzee. — London : Secker & Warburg, 1980. — 156p ; 23cm
ISBN 0-436-10295-1 : £5.95 B81-01217

Divigny, Dion. Adrift : a novel / Dion Divigny. — London : Collins, 1981. — 139p ; 21cm
ISBN 0-00-261004-3 : £4.95 B81-12072

Ebersohn, Wessel. Divide the night : a Yudel Gordon story / by Wessel Ebersohn. — London : Gollancz, 1981. — 224p ; 21cm
ISBN 0-575-02937-4 : £6.95 B81-12301

Ebersohn, Wessel. A lonely place to die / Wessel Ebersohn. — Feltham : Hamlyn, 1981, c1979. — 205p ; 18cm. — (A Hamlyn whodunnit)
Originally published: London : Gollancz, 1979
ISBN 0-600-20264-x (pbk) : £1.10 B81-11428

Gray, Stephen, *1941-*. Caltrop's desire / Stephen Gray. — London : Collings in association with Philip, 1980. — 135p ; 23cm
ISBN 0-86036-108-x : £5.50 B81-00368

Hope, Christopher. A separate development / Christopher Hope. — London : Routledge & Kegan Paul, 1981. — 199p ; 22cm
ISBN 0-7100-0954-2 : £6.95 : CIP rev. B81-28009

Jute, André. Sinkhole. — London : Secker & Warburg, Feb.1982. — [160]p
ISBN 0-436-22982-x : £6.95 : CIP entry B81-39245

Laffeaty, Christina. Count Antonov's heir / Christina Laffeaty. — Large print ed. — Bath : Chivers, 1981 c1980. — 255p ; 23cm. — (A Seymour book)
Originally published: London : Mills & Boon, 1980
ISBN 0-85119-421-4 : Unpriced : CIP rev. B81-13586

Laffeaty, Christina. For love or Lorenzo / Christina Laffeaty. — London : Hale, 1981. — 175p ; 20cm
ISBN 0-7091-9177-4 : £5.60 B81-27297

Laffeaty, Christina. Zulu sunset / Christina Laffeaty. — London : Mills & Boon, 1980. — 188p ; 20cm. — (Masquerade)
ISBN 0-263-09799-4 : £3.85 B81-01218

McClure, James. The blood of an Englishman. — Large print ed. — Anstey : Ulverscroft, Feb.1982. — [512]p. — (Ulverscroft large print series : mystery)
ISBN 0-7089-0744-x : £5.00 : CIP entry B81-36945

McClure, James. Snake / James McClure. — Harmondsworth : Penguin, 1977, c1975. — 191p ; 18cm
Originally published: London : Gollancz, 1975
ISBN 0-14-004472-8 (pbk) : £1.75 B81-35566

McClure, James. The Sunday hangman / James McClure. — Harmondsworth : Penguin, 1981, c1977. — 254p ; 18cm
Originally published: London : Macmillan, 1977
ISBN 0-14-004768-9 (pbk) : £1.50 B81-35567

Ngcobo, Lauretta G.. Cross of gold : a novel / by Lauretta G. Ngcobo. — London : Longman, 1981. — 289p ; 19cm. — (Drumbeat ; 25)
ISBN 0-582-78519-7 (pbk) : £1.75 B81-22324

Paton, Alan. Ah, but your land is beautiful. — London : Cape, Oct.1981. — [272]p
ISBN 0-224-01981-3 : £6.95 : CIP entry B81-27410

Rive, Richard. Emergency. — Walton-on-Thames : Nelson, Feb.1982. — [256]p. — (Panafrica library)
Originally published: London : Faber, 1964
ISBN 0-17-511625-3 (pbk) : £2.00 : CIP entry B81-35795

Scholefield, Alan. The stone flower. — London : Hamilton, Feb.1982. — [384]p
ISBN 0-241-10739-3 : £7.95 : CIP entry B81-37588

Sepamla, Sipho. The root is one. — Walton-on-Thames : Nelson, Jan.1982. — [144] p. — (Panafrica library)
Originally published: London : Collings, 1979
ISBN 0-17-511624-5 (pbk) : £1.25 : CIP entry B81-34392

Smith, Wilbur. The sound of thunder. — Large print ed. — Long Preston : Magna Print Books, Jan.1982. — [525]p
Originally published: London : Heinemann, 1966
ISBN 0-86009-367-0 : £4.50 : CIP entry B81-33995

Trew, Antony. The Moonraker mutiny / by Antony Trew. — Bolton-by-Bowland : Magna, 1981, c1972. — 492p : ill ; 23cm
Originally published: London : Collins, 1972. — Published in large print
ISBN 0-86009-313-1 : £5.75 : CIP rev. B81-03714

Wingate, William. Hardacre's way / William Wingate. — London : Macmillan, 1980. — 250p ; 23cm
Originally published: New York : St Martin's Press, 1980
ISBN 0-333-29086-0 : £5.50 B81-01211

823[F] — Fiction in English. Spanish writers, *1945-* **— Texts**

Pombal. Wena wekaneni, or, O you of the right / Pombal. — Bognor Regis : New Horizon, c1980. — 96p ; 21cm
ISBN 0-86116-387-7 (corrected) : £3.50 B81-19260

823[F] — Fiction in English. Western Samoan writers, *1945-* **— Texts**

Wendt, Albert. Leaves of the banyan tree / Albert Wendt. — Harmondsworth : Penguin, 1981, c1979. — 416p ; 20cm
Originally published: New Zealand : Longman Paul, 1979 ; London : Allen Lane, 1980
ISBN 0-14-005473-1 (pbk) : £2.95 B81-27578

823[F] — Fiction in English. Zimbabwean writers, *1960-* **— Texts**

Davis, John Gordon. Leviathan / John Gordon Davis. — London : Pan, 1977, c1976 (1978 printing). — 347p ; 18cm
Originally published: New York : Dutton, 1976 ; London : Joseph, 1977
ISBN 0-330-25278-x (pbk) : £1.50 B81-37351

Marechera, Dambudzo. Black sunlight / Dambudzo Marechera. — London : Heinemann, 1980. — 117p ; 19cm. — (African writers series ; 237)
ISBN 0-435-90237-7 (pbk) : £2.60 : CIP rev. B80-26170

Nieseswand, Peter. The word of a gentleman : a novel / by Peter Niesewand. — London : Secker & Warburg, 1981. — 314p ; 23cm
ISBN 0-436-31021-x : £6.95 B81-12237

Niesewand, Peter. A member of the club / Peter Niesewand. — London : Pan in association with Secker and Warburg, 1981, c1979. — 185p ; 18cm
Originally published: London : Secker and Warburg, 1979
ISBN 0-330-26340-4 (pbk) : £1.25 B81-20212

823[F] — Fiction in English. Zimbabwean writers, *1961-* **— Texts**

Nyamfukudza, S.. The non-believer's journey / S. Nyamfukudza. — London : Heinemann, 1980. — 113p ; 19cm. — (African writers series ; no.233)
ISBN 0-435-90233-4 (pbk) : £1.95 : CIP rev. B80-14021

823[F] — Short stories in English. Indian writers, *1947-* **— Texts**

Dhondy, Farrukh. Poona company / by Farrukh Dhondy. — London : Gollancz, 1980. — 149p ; 21cm
ISBN 0-575-02901-3 : £4.95 B81-00374

823[F] — Short stories in English. New Zealand writers, *1907-* **— Texts**

Davin, Dan. Selected stories / Dan Davin. — Wellington : Victoria University Press with Price Milburn ; London : Hale, 1981. — 319p ; 23cm
ISBN 0-7091-9094-8 : £6.95 B81-21305

Mansfield, Katherine. Selected stories / Katherine Mansfield ; edited with an introduction by D.M. Davin. — Oxford : Oxford University Press, 1953 (1981 [printing]). — xxiv,362p ; 19cm. — (The World's classics)
Bibliography: pxviii-xix
ISBN 0-19-281561-x (pbk) : £1.75 : CIP rev. B81-12865

823[J] — Children's short stories in English. New Zealand writers, *1945-.* **— Texts**

Mahy, Margaret. The chewing-gum rescue and other stories. — London : Dent, Jan.1982. — [128]p
ISBN 0-460-06084-8 : £4.95 : CIP entry B81-38337

823[J] — Children's stories in English. Australian writers, *1890-1945* **— Texts**

Mitchell, Elyne. Snowy River brumby / Elyne Mitchell ; illustrated by Victor Ambrus. — London : Hutchinson, c1981. — 122p : ill ; 23cm
ISBN 0-09-143940-x : £4.95 B81-08015

823[J] — Children's stories in English. Australian writers, *1945-* **— Texts**

Baker, Ivy. The dingo summer / Ivy Baker. — London : Angus & Robertson, 1980. — 108p ; 23cm
ISBN 0-207-14210-6 : £3.95 B81-01219

823[J] — Children's stories in English. Australian writers, *1945-* **—** *Texts* *continuation*

Bidwell, Dafne. The tiger gang and the car thieves / Dafne Bidwell ; illustrated by Graham Bryce. — London : Methuen, 1980, c1977. — 184p : ill ; 18cm. — (A Magnet book)
Originally Published: Sydney : Methuen of Australia, 1977
ISBN 0-416-89550-6 (pbk) : £0.85 B81-29755

Dalgleish, Joan. The latchkey dog / Joan Dalgleish ; illustrated by Stephen Axelsen. — Sydney ; London : Hodder and Stoughton, 1980. — 172p : ill ; 22cm
ISBN 0-340-26129-3 : £4.50 B81-10045

Edwards, Hazel. The pancake olympics / Hazel Edwards ; [illustrations by Tony Oliver]. — London : Arnold, 1981. — 67p : ill ; 20cm. — (Young magpie library)
ISBN 0-7131-0600-x (pbk) : £1.25 B81-39423

Edwards, Hazel. There's a hippopotamus on our roof eating cake / by Hazel Edwards ; illustrated by Deborah Niland. — Sydney ; London : Hodder and Stoughton, c1980. — [32]p : col.ill ; 27cm
Originally published: Lane Cove : Hodder and Stoughton (Australia), 1980
ISBN 0-340-25780-6 : £3.95 B81-10335

Edwards, Hugh, *1933-*. Sim the sea lion / Hugh Edwards ; [illustrations by Stephen Hederics]. — London : Arnold, 1981. — 59p : ill ; 20cm. — (Young magpie library)
ISBN 0-7131-0595-x (pbk) : £1.25 B81-39419

Fatchen, Max. Closer to the stars / Max Fatchen. — London : Methuen, 1981. — 119p ; 21cm
ISBN 0-416-20630-1 : £4.50 B81-17993

Fatchen, Max. Conquest of the river / Max Fatchen ; illustrated by Clyde Pearson. — [London] : Magnet, 1981, c1970. — 158p : ill ; 18cm
Originally published: London : Methuen, 1970
ISBN 0-416-87620-x (pbk) : £0.95 B81-12491

Graham, Bob. Pete and Roland / Bob Graham. — Sydney ; London : Collins, 1981. — 38p : ill (some col.) ; 22cm
ISBN 0-00-184344-3 : £3.50 B81-37901

Mattingley, Christobel. Black dog / Christobel Mattingley ; illustrations by Craig Smith. — London : Bodley Head, 1980, c1979. — [32]p : ill ; 22cm
Originally published: Sydney : Collins, 1979
ISBN 0-370-30349-0 : £3.25 : CIP rev. B80-18524

Park, Ruth. Playing Beatie Bow / Ruth Park. — Harmondsworth : Kestrel, 1981, c1980. — 196p ; 23cm
Originally published: West Melbourne : Nelson, 1980
ISBN 0-7226-5771-4 : £5.50 B81-40684

Pausacker, Jenny. Fat & Skinny / Jenny Pausacker ; [illustrations by Tony Oliver]. — London : Arnold, 1981. — 60p : ill ; 20cm. — (Young magpie library)
ISBN 0-7131-0599-2 (pbk) : £1.25 B81-39420

Pavey, Peter. One dragon's dream / Peter Pavey. — Ringwood, Vic ; Harmondsworth : Puffin, 1981, c1978. — [32]p : chiefly col.ill ; 21x28cm. — (Picture puffins)
Originally published: West Melbourne, Vic. : Nelson, 1978 ; London : Hamish Hamilton, 1979
ISBN 0-14-050359-5 (pbk) : £1.00 B81-27195

Phipson, Joan. [Keep calm]. When the city stopped / Joan Phipson. — [London] : Piccolo, 1980, c1978 (1981 printing). — 155p ; 18cm
Originally published: London : Macmillan, 1978
ISBN 0-330-26032-4 (pbk) : £0.90 B81-17981

Rose, Madeline. Witch over the water / Madeline Rose ; with illustrations by Trevor Weekes. — London : Angus & Robertson, 1980. — 106p : ill ; 23cm
ISBN 0-207-14251-3 : £3.95 B81-08595

Roy, Thomas Albert. The vengeance of the dolphin / Thomas Albert Roy ; illustrated by Rex Backhaus-Smith. — London : Bodley Head, 1980. — 183p : ill,maps ; 23cm
ISBN 0-370-30215-x : £4.50 : CIP rev. B79-37055

Sammon, Stella. Nifty : the sugar glider / Stella Sammon ; [illustrations by Stephen Hederics]. — London : Arnold, 1981. — 66p : ill ; 20cm. — (Young magpie library)
ISBN 0-7131-0597-6 (pbk) : £1.25 B81-39421

Smith, Peter, *1943 Dec.20-*. Jenny's baby brother / Peter Smith ; illustrations by Bob Graham. — Sydney ; London : Collins, 1981. — 28p : col.ill ; 22cm
ISBN 0-00-184345-1 : £3.50 B81-37900

Spence, Eleanor. The seventh pebble / Eleanor Spence ; illustrated by Sisca Verwoert. — Melbourne ; Oxford : Oxford University Press, 1980. — 172p : ill ; 23cm
ISBN 0-19-554262-2 : £3.95 B81-01220

Stevens, Kathleen. The beast in the bathtub / story by Kathleen Stevens ; illustrated by Ray Bowler. — Leeds : Pepper, 1981, c1980. — [31]p : col.ill ; 22x27cm
Originally published: Victoria, Australia : Childerset Pty., 1980
ISBN 0-560-74515-x : £3.25 B81-15994

Thiele, Colin. The fire in the stone / Colin Thiele. — Harmondsworth : Puffin, 1981, c1973. — 227p ; 18cm
Originally published: Adelaide : Rigby, 1973
ISBN 0-14-031360-5 (pbk) : £0.95 B81-34809

Thiele, Colin. Magpie Island / Colin Thiele ; illustrated by Roger Haldane. — Harmondsworth : Puffin, 1981, c1974. — 47p : ill ; 18cm
Originally published: London : Collins, 1974
ISBN 0-14-031399-0 (pbk) : £0.60 B81-35593

Treloar, Bruce. Bumble's dream / Bruce Treloar. — London : Bodley Head, 1981. — [29]p : col.ill ; 27cm
ISBN 0-370-30424-1 : £4.50 : CIP rev. B81-27934

Weldrick, Valerie. The Blakeley ghost / Valerie Weldrick ; illustrated by Sylvia Isaac. — Richmond [Australia] ; London : Hutchinson, 1980. — 112p : ill ; 23cm
ISBN 0-09-137260-7 : £4.50 B81-01221

Worthy, Judith. Garden in the sky / Judith Worthy ; illustrated by Murray Frederick. — London : Angus & Robertson, 1980. — 84p : ill ; 19cm
ISBN 0-207-14092-8 : £3.95 B81-11895

Worthy, Judith. The incredible runaway pumpkin / Judith Worthy ; [illustrations by Geoff Hocking]. — London : Arnold, 1981. — 67p : ill ; 20cm. — (Young magpie library)
ISBN 0-7131-0596-8 (pbk) : £1.25 B81-39424

Wrightson, Patricia. Behind the wind / Patricia Wrightson. — London : Hutchinson, 1981. — 156p ; 23cm
Maps on lining papers
ISBN 0-09-144620-1 : £4.95 : CIP rev. B81-04384

823[J] — Children's stories in English. Guyanese writers, *1945-* **—** *Texts*

Agard, John. Dig away two-hole Tim / John Agard ; illustrated by Jennifer Northway. — London : Bodley Head, 1981. — [25]p : col.ill ; 21x24cm
ISBN 0-370-30421-7 : £3.95 : CIP rev. B81-25841

823[J] — Children's stories in English. Indian writers, *1947-* **—** *Texts*

Mitchell, Elyne. Brumby racer. — London : Hutchinson Junior Books, Jan.1982. — [120]p
ISBN 0-09-137560-6 : £4.95 : CIP entry B81-39213

823[J] — Children's stories in English. New Zealand writers, *1907-* **—** *Texts*

Corney, Estelle. Pa's top hat / Estelle Corney ; pictures by Hilary Abrahams. — London : Deutsch, 1980. — [32]p : col.ill ; 26cm
ISBN 0-233-97255-2 : £4.95 B81-01222

Cowley, Joy. The silent one / Joy Cowley ; illustrated by Sherryl Jordan. — Christchurch, N.Z. ; London : Whitcoulls, 1981. — 96p : ill ; 24cm
ISBN 0-7233-0630-3 : Unpriced B81-40987

Holden, Philip. Stag / Philip Holden ; illustrated by Tony Oliver. — Sydney ; London : Hodder and Stoughton, 1980. — 154p : ill ; 22cm
ISBN 0-340-24651-0 : £4.50 B81-00375

Mitcalfe, Barry. The Square Gang / Barry Mitcalfe. — London : Faber, 1981. — 158p ; 21cm
ISBN 0-571-11681-7 : £4.95 : CIP rev. B81-06884

Sutton, Eve. My cat likes to hide in boxes / by Eve Sutton ; illustrated by Lynley Dodd. — Harmondsworth : Puffin, 1978 (1981 [printing]). — [30]p : chiefly col.ill ; 23cm. — (Picture puffins)
Originally published: London : Hamilton Childrens, 1973
ISBN 0-14-050242-4 (pbk) : £0.95 B81-40672

823[J] — Children's stories in English. Nigerian writers, *1960-* **—** *Texts*

Afolalu, Idowu. The runaway drummer / Idowu Afolalu. — [London] : Collins, 1981. — 64p : ill ; 21cm
£1.05 (pbk) B81-32935

Fulani, Dan. Sauna and the bank robbers. — Sevenoaks : Hodder & Stoughton, May 1981. — [128]p
ISBN 0-340-20853-8 (pbk) : £1.50 : CIP entry B81-08920

823[J] — Children's stories in English. South African writers, *1909-1961* **—** *Texts*

Seed, Jenny. The year one / by Jenny Seed ; illustrated by Susan Sansome. — London : Hamilton, 1980. — 92p : ill ; 19cm. — (Antelope books)
ISBN 0-241-10550-1 : £2.25 B81-06312

823[J] — Children's stories in English. Swiss writers, *1945-* **—** *Texts*

Brandenberg, Franz. Nice new neighbours / Franz Brandenberg ; illustrated by Aliki. — London : Scholastic, 1981, c1977. — 62p : col.ill ; 21cm. — (A Hippo book)
Originally published: New York : Greenwillow, 1977 ; London : Deutsch, 1979
ISBN 0-590-72060-0 (pbk) : £0.75 B81-19536

823'.003 — Fiction in English, *to 1900* **—** *Encyclopaedias*

The **Novel** to 1900 / introduction by A.O.J. Cockshut. — London : Macmillan, 1980. — vi,313p ; 25cm. — (Great writers student library ; 8)
Includes bibliographies
ISBN 0-333-28331-7 : £8.95 B81-05601

823'.009 — Fiction in English, *1700-1980.* **Forms: Novels** *compared with* **German novels,** *1700-1980*

Klieneberger, H. R.. The novel in England and Germany. — London : Wolff, Aug.1981. — [254]p
ISBN 0-85496-079-1 (pbk) : £8.00 : CIP entry
Also classified at 833'.009 B81-18114

823'.009 — Fiction in English, *1745-1915* — *Critical studies*
McMaster, Juliet. The novel from Sterne to James : essays on the relation of literature to life / by Juliet and Rowland McMaster. — London : Macmillan, 1981. — x,218p : ill ; 22cm
Includes index
ISBN 0-333-27658-2 : £15.00 B81-38727

823'.009 — Fiction in English, *1800-1945* — *Critical studies*
Levine, George. The realistic imagination : English fiction from Frankenstein to Lady Chatterley / George Levine. — Chicago ; London : University of Chicago Press, 1981. — x,357p ; 24cm
Includes index
ISBN 0-226-47550-6 : £15.00 B81-29778

823'.009 — Fiction in English, *1800-1967* — *Critical studies*
Fleishman, Avrom. Fiction and the ways of knowing : essays on British novels / by Avrom Fleishman. — Austin ; London : University of Texas Press, c1978. — x,224p ; 24cm
ISBN 0-292-72422-5 : £9.00 B81-09291

823'.009 — Fiction in English. Women writers, *1625-1980 — Critical studies*
Pratt, Annis. Archetypal patterns in women's fiction. — Brighton : Harvester Press, Jan.1982. — [280]p
ISBN 0-7108-0381-8 : £18.95 : CIP entry B81-33851

823'.009'27 — Children's stories in English. Characters — *Encyclopaedias*
Mortimore, Arthur D.. Children's literary characters index 1981 : the first supplement to Index to characters in children's literature / by Arthur D. Mortimore. — Bristol (72 Friary Grange Park, Winterbourne, Bristol BS17 1NB) : D. Mortimore, c1981. — 78p ; 22cm
ISBN 0-9505665-1-9 : £4.95 B81-15063

823'.009'353 — Fiction in English, *to 1965*. Special themes: Confession — *Critical studies*
Doody, Terrence. Confession and community in the novel / Terrence Doody. — Baton Rouge ; London : Louisiana State University Press, c1980. — 200p ; 24cm
Includes index
ISBN 0-8071-0662-3 : £8.95 B81-08288

823'.009'896 — Fiction in English. Negro writers, *to 1979 — Critical studies*
Barthold, Ronnie J.. Black time : fiction of Africa, the Caribbean and the United States / Ronnie J. Barthold. — New Haven ; London : Yale University Press, c1981. — x,209p : ill ; 22cm
Bibliography: p199-202. — Includes index
ISBN 0-300-02573-4 : £11.00 B81-18213

823'.009'9282 — Children's stories in English: Stories for children, 9-13 years — *Critical studies*
Inglis, Fred. The promise of happiness : value and meaning in children's fiction / Fred Inglis. — Cambridge : Cambridge University Press, 1981. — xiv,333p ; 23cm
Bibliography: p312-324. — Includes index
ISBN 0-521-23142-6 : £17.50 B81-16418

823'.01'08[FS] — Short stories in English, *1800-1900 — Anthologies*
Keating, P. J.. Nineteenth century short stories / edited with an introduction by Peter Keating. — Harlow : Longman, 1981. — v,232p ; 20cm. — (Longman English series)
Bibliography: p218
ISBN 0-582-35233-9 (pbk) : £2.10 B81-38385

823'.01'08[FS] — Short stories in English, *1800-1980 - Anthologies*
The **Oxford** book of short stories. — Oxford : Oxford University Press, June 1981. — [720]p
ISBN 0-19-214116-3 : £12.50 : CIP entry B81-14414

823'.01'08[FS] — Short stories in English, *1900- — Anthologies*
In short : an anthology of short stories / chosen by F.E.S. Finn. — London : Murray, c1981. — viii,152p ; 20cm
ISBN 0-7195-3756-8 (pbk) : £1.25 : CIP rev. B81-06055

Twisters : stories of the sinister and the macabre / edited by Steve Bowles. — London : Fontana, 1981. — 121p ; 18cm
ISBN 0-00-671798-5 (pbk) : £0.90 B81-10337

The **Way** things happen : eighteen short stories / selected by Arnold Thompson and Vanda Thompson ; illustrations by Gerry Manson. — London : Edward Arnold, 1981. — 94p : ill ; 22cm
ISBN 0-7131-0557-7 (pbk) : £1.60 : CIP rev. B81-18157

823'.01'08[FS] — Short stories in English, *1900- - Anthologies - Serials*
Punch short stories. — 3. — London : Robson, July 1981. — [192]p
ISBN 0-86051-136-7 : £5.95 : CIP entry B81-14453

823'.01'08[FS] — Short stories in English, *1945- — Anthologies*
Cracks in the image : stories by gay men / [Simon Burt ... et al.]. — London (27 Priory Ave., N8 7RN) : Gay Men's Press, 1981. — 134p ; 20cm
ISBN 0-907040-08-x (pbk) : £2.50 : CIP rev. B81-04317

Introduction. — 7. — London : Faber, 1981. — 255p
ISBN 0-571-11680-9 : £4.95 : CIP rev. B81-03696

New stories 6 / edited by Beryl Bainbridge. — London : Hutchinson in association with the Arts Council of Great Britain and PEN, 1981. — 208p ; 23cm
ISBN 0-09-145230-9 : £6.95 : CIP rev. B81-03677

Winter's tales. — 26. — London : Macmillan, 1980. — 223p
ISBN 0-333-26836-9 : £5.95 B81-10581

You can't keep out the darkness : an anthology of short stories / edited by Peggy Woodford. — London : Bodley Head, 1980. — 173p ; 23cm
ISBN 0-370-30293-1 : £4.50 : CIP rev. B80-19987

823'.01'08[FS] — Short stories in English, *1945- — Anthologies — For Caribbean students*
Sunshine and shadow : an anthology of short stories / edited by Roy Narinesingh and Clifford Narinesingh. — London : Cassell, 1980 (1981 [printing]). — v,120p : ill ; 21cm
ISBN 0-304-30713-0 (pbk) : Unpriced B81-26302

823'.01'08036[FS] — Animal short stories in English, *1837-1980 — Anthologies*
Richard Adams's favourite animal stories / [illustrated by Beverley Butcher]. — London : Octopus, 1981. — 254p : ill ; 22cm
ISBN 0-7064-1276-1 : £1.99 B81-19423

823'.01'0809415[FS] — Short stories in English. Irish writers, *1900- — Anthologies*
The **Bodley** Head book of Irish short stories / selected and introduced by David Marcus. — London : Bodley Head, 1980. — 378p ; 20cm
ISBN 0-370-30225-7 : £8.50 : CIP rev. B80-08456

Modern Irish short stories / edited by Ben Forkner ; preface by Anthony Burgess. — London : Joseph, 1981, c1980. — 557p ; 21cm
ISBN 0-7181-1983-5 : £7.95 B81-12273

Short stories from Ireland / selected and introduced by Kenyon Calthrop ; frontispiece by Norma Burgin. — Exeter : Wheaton, 1979. — viii,103p : 1ill ; 21cm. — (Literature for life series)
ISBN 0-08-022876-3 (pbk) : £1.70 B81-09650

823'.01'0809415[FS] — Short stories in English. Irish writers, *to 1980 — Anthologies*
The **Penguin** book of Irish short stories / edited by Benedict Kiely. — Harmondsworth : Penguin, 1981. — 544p ; 19cm
ISBN 0-14-005340-9 (pbk) : £1.95 B81-25345

823'.01'0815[FS] — Fantasy short stories in English. Irish writers, *1800-1900 — Anthologies*
Irish masters of fantasy : an anthology with introduction and biographical essays / edited by Peter Tremayne ; illustrations by Jeanette Dunne. — Portmarnock (98 Ardilaun, Portmarnock, Co. Dublin) : Wolfhound, c1979. — 220p : ill,ports ; 22cm
ISBN 0-905473-13-2 : £6.05 B81-01223

823'.01'0816[FS] — Horror short stories in English, *1900- — Anthologies*
Alfred Hitchcock's monster museum. — [London] : Fontana, 1973, c1965 (1981 [printing]). — 190p ; 18cm. — (Lions)
Originally published: New York : Random House, 1965 ; London : Reinhardt, 1971
ISBN 0-00-671873-6 (pbk) : £0.95 B81-11175

Alfred Hitchcock's spellbinders in suspense. — London : Fontana, 1974, c1967 (1981 [printing]). — 221p ; 18cm. — (Lions)
Originally published: New York : Random House, 1967 ; London : Reinhardt, 1972
ISBN 0-00-671874-4 (pbk) : £0.95 B81-11882

The **Fourteenth** Fontana book of great horror stories / edited by Mary Danby. — London : Fontana, c1981. — 189p ; 18cm
ISBN 0-00-616196-0 (pbk) : £1.00 B81-28212

Stories of fear / edited by Denys Val Baker. — London : Kimber, 1980. — 237p ; 23cm
ISBN 0-7183-0337-7 : £5.75 B81-01225

823'.01'0816[FS] — Horror short stories in English, *1945- — Anthologies*
The **21st** Pan book of horror stories / edited by Herbert van Thal. — London : Pan, 1980. — 174p ; 18cm
ISBN 0-330-26192-4 (pbk) : £0.90 B81-01224

Alfred Hitchcock presents the master's choice. — London : Hodder & Stoughton. — (Coronet books)
Book 2. — Dec.1981. — [336]p
ISBN 0-340-26771-2 (pbk) : £1.25 : CIP entry B81-31471

Alfred Hitchcock's alive and screaming. — London : Severn House, Dec.1981. — [240]p
ISBN 0-7278-0745-5 : £6.95 : CIP entry B81-31625

Alfred Hitchcock presents the master's choice. — London : Coronet, July 1981
Originally published: London : Reinhardt, 1979
Book 1. — [192]p
ISBN 0-340-26678-3 (pbk) : £1.23 : CIP entry B81-13778

New tales of terror / edited by Hugh Lamb. — London : Magnum : 1980. — 192p ; 18cm
ISBN 0-417-05690-7 (pbk) : £1.10 B81-03057

New tales of terror / edited by Hugh Lamb. — London : Severn House, 1981, c1980. — 192p ; 20cm
Originally published: London : Magnum, 1980
ISBN 0-7278-0716-1 : £5.95 : CIP rev. B81-17507

823'.01'0816[J] — Children's horror short stories in English, *1900- — Anthologies*
The **Beaver** book of horror stories / [edited by] Mark Ronson. — London : Beaver, 1981. — 157p ; 18cm
ISBN 0-600-20383-2 (pbk) : £0.95 B81-40991

Skylark ghost and monster stories / collected by Jill Bennett ; illustrated by Julek and Adam Heller. — London : Book Club Associates, 1980. — 191p : ill(some col.) ; 24cm
Unpriced B81-37885

Twisters : stories of the sinister and macabre / edited by Steve Bowles. — London : Collins, 1981. — 121p ; 22cm
ISBN 0-00-195843-7 : £4.50 B81-04746

823'.01'0832[FS] — Short stories in English, *1900-.* **Special subjects: Cities. Social life —** *Anthologies — For schools*
City stories / chosen by David Self. — London : Ward Lock Educational, 1980. — 109p ; 21cm. — (WLE short stories ; 10)
ISBN 0-7062-3775-7 (cased) : £2.95
ISBN 0-7062-3774-9 (pbk) : £1.35 B81-06649

823'.01'0832162[FS] — Short stories in English, *1719-1977.* **Special subjects: Oceans —** *Anthologies*
Sea stories / edited by Patricia J. Robertson ; illustrated by Reginald Gray. — London : Octopus, 1981. — 299p : ill ; 22cm
ISBN 0-7064-1572-8 : £1.99 B81-34735

823'.01'0833[J] — Children's short stories in English, *1945-.* **Special subjects: Christmas —** *Anthologies*
New stories for Christmas : short stories reflecting various aspects of Christmas for today's children / compiled by Hazel Snashall. — Redhill : National Education Council, 1980. — 112p ; 20cm
ISBN 0-7197-0262-3 (pbk) : £2.00 : CIP rev. B81-99999

Powers, Mala. Follow the star / Mala Powers ; illustrations by Suzy-Jane Tanner. — London : Hodder and Stoughton, 1981, c1980. — [112]p : col.ill ; 26cm
Originally published: Millbrae : Dawne-Leigh, 1980
ISBN 0-340-26696-1 : £4.95 : CIP rev. B81-26707

823'.01'083527913[FS] — Short stories in English, *1886-1979.* **Special subjects: Persons: Freaks —** *Anthologies*
The **Elephant** Man and other freaks / edited by Sean Richards. — London : Macdonald Futura, 1980. — 192p,[24]p of plates : ill,facsims,ports ; 18cm
ISBN 0-7088-1927-3 (pbk) : £1.25 B81-05567

823'.01'08353[FS] — Short stories in English, *1900-.* **Special themes: Heroism —** *Anthologies*
Jewels of wonder : an anthology of heroic fantasies / edited by Mike Ashley. — London : Kimber, 1981. — 203p ; 23cm
ISBN 0-7183-0457-8 : £5.75 B81-28693

Stories of courage / chosen by Mike Samuda. — London : Ward Lock Educational, 1981. — 123p ; 21cm. — (WLE short stories ; 17)
ISBN 0-7062-4077-4 (cased) : £2.95
ISBN 0-7062-4074-x (pbk) : £1.35 B81-14019

823'.01'0836[J] — Children short stories in English, *1700-1981.* **Special subjects: Livestock: Horses —** *Anthologies*
More horse and pony stories / edited by Janet Sachs ; illustrated by Reginald Gray. — London : Octopus, 1981. — 296p : ill ; 22cm
ISBN 0-7064-1549-3 : £1.99 B81-28324

823'.01'0837[FS] — Short stories in English, *1837-1980.* **Special subjects: Supernatural —** *Anthologies*
Mystery stories / edited by Patricia J. Robertson ; illustrated by Sam Thompson. — London : Octopus, 1981. — 299p : ill ; 22cm
ISBN 0-7064-1571-x : £1.99 B81-35015

823'.01'08375[FS] — Ghost short stories in English, *1900- — Anthologies*
Cornish ghost stories : and other tales of the macabre / edited by Denys Val Baker. — London : Kimber, 1981. — 196p ; 23cm
ISBN 0-7183-0208-7 : £5.75 B81-28643

823'.01'08375[FS] — Ghost short stories in English. Irish writers, *1837- — Anthologies*
The **Bedside** book of Irish ghost stories / collected and edited by Patrick F. Byrne. — Dublin : Mercier, c1980. — 112p ; 18cm
ISBN 0-85342-623-6 (pbk) : £2.30 B81-22308

823'.01'08375[J] — Children's animal ghost short stories in English, *1945- — Anthologies*
Animal ghosts / edited by Carolyn Lloyd ; illustrated by Martin White. — Rev. ed. — London : Armada, 1980. — 128p : ill ; 18cm
Previous ed.: London : Fontana, 1971
ISBN 0-00-691814-x (pbk) : £0.75 B81-01226

Animal ghosts : a new collection / edited and compiled by Richard Davis. — London : Hutchinson, 1980. — 143p ; 23cm
ISBN 0-09-142700-2 : £4.95 : CIP rev. B80-19478

823'.01'08375[J] — Children's ghost short stories in English, *1900- — Anthologies*
Spooky stories / edited by Barbara Ireson. — London : Carousel, 1979 (1980 [printing]) No.2 / illustrated by Les Matthews. — 127p : ill ; 20cm
ISBN 0-552-52104-3 (pbk) : £0.65 B81-39384

823'.01'08375[J] — Children's ghost short stories in English, *1945- — Anthologies*
Spooky stories 3 / edited by Barbara Ireson ; illustrated by Carolyn Bull. — London : Transworld, 1981. — 149p : ill ; 17cm. — (A Carousel book)
ISBN 0-552-52140-x (pbk) : £0.85 B81-37204

823'.01'08375[J] — Children's humorous ghost short stories in English, *1945- — Anthologies*
Ghostly laughter / edited by Barbara Ireson. — [London] : Beaver, 1981. — 159p ; 18cm
ISBN 0-600-20322-0 (pbk) : £0.95 B81-12489

823'.01'08375[J] — Children's short stories in English, *1900-.* **Special subjects: Witches —** *Anthologies*
[Witches brew]. Alfred Hitchcock's witch's brew. — Harmondsworth : Puffin, 1980, c1977. — 157p : 1port ; 19cm
This collection originally published: as Witches brew, New York : Random House, 1977 ; and as Alfred Hitchcock's witch's brew, London : Reinhardt, 1978. — Port on inside cover
ISBN 0-14-031209-9 (pbk) : £0.80 B81-02843

823'.01'0891821[FS] — Short stories in English. Caribbean writers, *1945- — Anthologies*
Fraser, Robert, *1947-.* This island place / Robert Fraser. — London : Harrap, 1981. — ix,115p : 1map ; 19cm
ISBN 0-245-53569-1 (pbk) : £1.95 B81-09759

823'.01'089282[J] — Children's short stories in English, *1702-1945 — Anthologies*
Hamlyn all-colour story bok. — London : Hamlyn, c1979. — 224p : col.ill ; 27cm
ISBN 0-600-38300-8 : £3.75 B81-02695

823'.01'089282[J] — Children's short stories in English, *1837- — Anthologies*
Stories for nine-year-olds : and other young readers / edited by Sara and Stephen Corrin ; illustrated by Shirley Hughes. — Harmondsworth : Puffin in association with Faber, 1981, c1979. — 217p : ill ; 20cm
Originally published: London : Faber, 1979
ISBN 0-14-031342-7 (pbk) : £1.25 B81-15388

823'.01'089282[J] — Children's short stories in English, *1900-1945 — Anthologies*
Marshall, Sybil. Wings. — Cambridge : Cambridge University Press, Apr.1981. — [48] p. — (Lanterns)
ISBN 0-521-28155-5 (pbk) : £1.50 : CIP entry B81-01227

Mysterious, menacing and macabre. — London : Dent, Oct.1981. — [160]p
ISBN 0-460-06086-4 : £4.50 : CIP entry B81-25818

823'.01'089282[J] — Children's short stories in English, *1900- — Anthologies*
The **Faber** book of modern fairy tales. — London : Faber, Sept.1981. — [311]p
ISBN 0-571-11768-6 : £5.95 : CIP entry B81-21531

823'.01'089282[J] — Children's short stories in English, *1945- — Anthologies*
100 magical stories / [stories by Margaret Conroy ... et al.] ; [illustrations by Shirley Bellwood ... et al.]. — London : Hamlyn, 1981. — 157p : col.ill ; 22cm
ISBN 0-600-36494-1 : £2.95 B81-33561

American. — London : J. Murray, Nov.1981. — [128]p. — (The Short story series)
ISBN 0-7195-3870-x (pbk) : £1.10 : CIP entry B81-30958

The **best** of shadows / illustrated by Les Matthews. — [London] : Carousel, 1979 (1980 [printing]). — 174p : ill ; 20cm
ISBN 0-552-52096-9 (pbk) : £0.65 B81-07080

Country. — London : J. Murray, Nov.1981. — [128]p. — (The Short story series)
ISBN 0-7195-3873-4 (pbk) : £1.10 : CIP entry B81-30961

Crime. — London : J. Murray, Nov.1981. — [128]p. — (The Short story series)
ISBN 0-7195-3869-6 (pbk) : £1.10 : CIP entry B81-30959

Fantasy. — London : J. Murray, Nov.1981. — [128]p. — (The Short story series)
ISBN 0-7195-3874-2 (pbk) : £1.10 : CIP entry B81-30583

The **Magnet** book of strange tales / edited by Jean Russell ; illustrated by Tony Ross. — London : Methuen Children's, 1980 (1981 [printing]). — 144p : ill ; 20cm. — (A Magnet book)
ISBN 0-416-21190-9 (pbk) : £1.00 B81-34907

My bedtime library. — [London] : Hamlyn, [1981]. — 7v. : col.ill ; 23cm
ISBN 0-600-36634-0 : £9.95 B81-28580

Rainbow storybook. — London : Thames, 1981. — 125p : col.ill ; 25cm
ISBN 0-423-00030-6 : £3.95 B81-28634

Skylark short stories / collected by Jill Bennett ; illustrated by Julek Heller. — London : Book Club Associates, 1979. — 190p : ill ; 24cm
Unpriced B81-39771

Suspense. — London : J. Murray, Nov.1981. — [128]p. — (The Short story series)
ISBN 0-7195-3872-6 (pbk) : £1.10 : CIP entry B81-30962

A **Treasury** of bedtime stories. — London (Elsley Court, 20 Great Titchfield St., W1P 7AD) : Kingfisher, Sept.1981. — [160]p
ISBN 0-86272-001-x : £3.95 : CIP entry B81-20171

War. — London : J. Murray, Nov.1981. — [128] p. — (The Short story series)
ISBN 0-7195-3871-8 (pbk) : £1.10 : CIP entry B81-30957

A **Wonderful** dream : and other stories / written by pupils of all ages at inner London schools ; edited by Alasdair Aston ; preface by Peter Newsam. — [London] : [ILEA], 1981. — 128p ; 19cm
Includes index
£2.00 (pbk) B81-23680

823'.01'089287[FS] — Short stories in English. Irish women writers, *1945- — Anthologies*
Barr, Fiona. Sisters / Fiona Barr, Barbara Haycock Walsh, Stella Mahon. — Belfast : Blackstaff, c1980. — 103p ; 23cm. — (Blackstaff short stories)
ISBN 0-85640-165-x : £5.95 : CIP rev. B80-18501

A **Dream** recurring : and other stories and poems : Maxwell House winners 2. — Dublin (2 Strand Rd., Baldoyle, Dublin 13) : Arlen House, [1980?]. — 112p ; 18cm
ISBN 0-905223-23-3 (pbk) : £1.95
Also classified at 821'.914'0809415 B81-09538

823'.01'089411[FS] — Short stories in English. Scottish writers, *1800-1900 — Anthologies*
Scottish short stories 1800-1900 / edited by Douglas Gifford. — London : Calder, 1981. — 350p ; 21cm. — (The Scottish library)
Originally published: London : Calder and Boyars, 1971
ISBN 0-7145-0657-5 (pbk) : £5.75 B81-13289

823'.01'089411[FS] — Short stories in English. Scottish writers, *1945-* **—** *Anthologies*

Scottish short stories. — London : Collins 1981 / preface by Willis Pickard. — 1981. — 196p ; 22cm
ISBN 0-00-222400-3 : £6.25 : CIP rev. B81-15893

823'.01'08968[FS] — Short stories in English. South African writers, *1961-* **—** *Anthologies*

Africa South contemporary writings / edited by Mothobi Mutloatse. — London : Heinemann, 1981, c1980. — 208p ; 19cm. — (African writers series ; 243)
ISBN 0-435-90243-1 (pbk) : £1.95 : CIP rev. B81-12916

823'.01'099282 — Children's short stories in English. Anthologies. 'So big, so small' — *For teaching*

Marshall, Sybil. 'So big, so small' teaching notes. — Cambridge : Cambridge University Press, Apr.1981. — [29]p. — (Lanterns)
ISBN 0-521-28341-8 (pbk) : £1.20 : CIP entry B81-12857

823'.081'09 — Historical fiction in English, *1800-1900* **—** *Critical studies*

Lascelles, Mary. The story-teller retrieves the past : historical fiction and fictitious history in the art of Scott, Stevenson, Kipling, and some others / Mary Lascelles. — Oxford : Clarendon, 1980. — xii,167p ; 23cm
Includes index
ISBN 0-19-812802-9 : £9.75 B81-04803

823'.085'08[FS] — Romantic short stories in English, *1945-* **—** *Anthologies*

Loving couples : stories of love and marriage / edited by Alfred Bradley and Kay Jamieson. — London : Joseph, 1981. — 201p ; 23cm
ISBN 0-7181-2037-x : £6.95 B81-37905

823'.085'08[FS] — Romantic short stories in English, *1945-* **—** *Anthologies* **—** *Serials*

The **People's** friend annual. — 1981. — Dundee : D.C. Thomson, c1981. — 186p
ISBN 0-85116-194-4 : £1.05 B81-02635

823'.087'08[J] — Children's adventure short stories in English, *1848-1981* **—** *Anthologies*

More adventure stories / edited by Hayden McAllister ; illustrated by Sam Thompson. — London : Octopus, 1981. — 297p : ill ; 22cm
ISBN 0-7064-1550-7 : £1.99 B81-28336

823'.087'0892827[J] — Girls' adventure stories in English, *1945-* **—** *Anthologies*

Girls' adventure stories. — Maidenhead : Purnell, 1981. — 223p : ill ; 21cm
ISBN 0-361-05058-5 : £2.25 B81-22185

823'.0872 — Crime fiction in English, *1773-ca 1970* **—** *Critical studies*

Knight, Stephen, *1940-*. Form and ideology in crime fiction / Stephen Knight. — London : Macmillan, 1980. — viii,202p ; 23cm
Includes bibliographies and index
ISBN 0-333-28876-9 : £15.00 : CIP rev. B80-24807

823'.0872 — Detective fiction in English, *1840-1979* **—** *Critical studies*

Detective fiction : a collection of critical essays / edited by Robin W. Winks. — Englewood Cliffs ; London : Prentice-Hall, c1980. — vi,246p ; 21cm. — (Twentieth century views) (A Spectrum book)
Bibliography: p234-246
ISBN 0-13-202689-9 (cased) : Unpriced
ISBN 0-13-202671-6 (pbk) : £3.20 B81-04725

823'.0872 — Detective fiction in English, *1861-1979.* **Characters: Women detectives —** *Critical studies*

Craig, Patricia. The lady investigates : women detectives and spies in fiction / by Patricia Craig and Mary Cadogan. — London : Gollancz, 1981. — 252p : ill ; 23cm
Bibliography: p247. - Includes index
ISBN 0-575-02885-8 : £9.95 B81-15236

823'.0872 — Detective fiction in English. Women writers, *1900-1945* **—** *Critical studies*

Mann, Jessica. Deadlier than the male : an investigation into feminine crime writing / Jessica Mann. — Newton Abbot : David & Charles, c1981. — 256p ; 23cm
Bibliography: p245-252. - Includes index
ISBN 0-7153-7877-5 : £9.50 B81-20806

823'.0872 — Gothic fiction in English, *1765-1930* **—** *Critical studies*

Wilt, Judith. Ghosts of the Gothic : Austen, Eliot & Lawrence / Judith Wilt. — Princeton ; Guildford : Princeton University Press, c1980. — xii,307p,[4]p of plates : ill ; 23cm
Includes index
ISBN 0-691-06439-3 : £10.30 B81-03750

823'.0872 — Gothic fiction in English, *1765-1978* **—** *Critical studies*

Punter, David. The literature of terror : a history of Gothic fictions from 1765 to the present day / David Punter. — London : Longman, 1980. — 449p ; 23cm
Bibliography: p428-443. — Includes index
ISBN 0-582-48920-2 (cased) : £12.00 : CIP rev.
ISBN 0-582-48921-0 (pbk) : £5.95 B79-34426

823'.0872[FS] — Crime short stories in English, *1945-* **—** *Anthologies* **—** *Serials*

Winter's crimes. — 12. — London : Macmillan, 1980. — 224p
ISBN 0-333-28987-0 : £5.50 B81-09237

823'.0872[FS] — Detective short stories in English, *1837-1980* **—** *Anthologies*

The **Fifth** bedside book of great detective stories / edited by Herbert van Thal. — London : Barker, c1981. — 189p ; 23cm
ISBN 0-213-16788-3 : £6.50 B81-09537

823'.0872[FS] — Detective short stories in English, *1900-* **—** *Anthologies*

Ellery Queen's : scenes of the crime / edited by Ellery Queen. — London : Hale, 1981, c1979. — 286p ; 21cm
ISBN 0-7091-9170-7 : £6.75 B81-33537

The **Fourth** bedside book of great detective stories / edited by Herbert van Thal. — London : Barker, c1979. — 221p ; 22cm
ISBN 0-213-16704-2 : £5.50 B81-10050

John Creasey's crime collection 1981 : an anthology by members of the Crime Writers' Association / edited by Herbert Harris. — London : Gollancz, 1981. — 189p ; 21cm
ISBN 0-575-03022-4 : £6.95 B81-35128

Verdict of thirteen : a Detection Club anthology / introduction by Julian Symons. — South Yarmouth, Mass. : John Curley, c1978 ; [London Preston] : Magna [distributors]. — xv,491p ; 23cm
Originally published: London : Faber, 1979
ISBN 0-89340-300-8 : £5.75 B81-22117

Verdict of thirteen : a Detection Club anthology. — Harmondsworth : Penguin, 1981. — 234p ; 19cm
Originally published: London : Faber, 1979
ISBN 0-14-005159-7 (pbk) : £1.50 B81-22033

823'.0872[FS] — Detective short stories in English, *1945-* **—** *Anthologies*

Crime wave. — London : Collins, Dec.1981. — [298]p. — (The Crime Club)
ISBN 0-00-231030-9 : £6.95 : CIP entry B81-31524

823'.0872[FS] — Spy short stories in English, *1837-1980* **—** *Anthologies*

Favourite spy stories / [illustrated by Mark Thomas]. — London : Octopus, 1981. — 249p : ill ; 22cm
ISBN 0-7064-1277-x : £1.99 B81-19418

823'.0874'08 — Short stories in English, *1945-*: **Westerns —** *Anthologies* **—** *Serials*

[Western magazine *(London)*]. Western magazine. — No.1 (Oct.1980)-. — London : IPC Magazines, 1980-. — v. : ill,ports ; 29cm
Monthly
ISSN 0144-848x = Western magazine (London) : £0.70 per issue
Also classified at 978'.02'05 B81-04761

823'.0876'05 — Science fiction in English — *Serials*

Extro. — Vol.1, no.4-. — Manchester (127a Oxford Rd, All Saints, Manchester) : Constellation Publications, 1979-. — v. : ill,ports ; 31cm
Continues: Popular music and science fiction journal
ISSN 0260-5414 = Extro : £4.50 for 8 issues B81-02022

823'.0876'08[FS] — Science fiction short stories in English, *1900-* **—** *Anthologies*

Alien worlds : stories of adventure on other planets / edited by Douglas Hill. — London : Heinemann, 1981. — 121p ; 23cm
ISBN 0-434-94285-5 : £4.50 B81-02856

Mysterious visions : great science fiction by masters of the mystery / edited by Charles G. Waugh, Martin Harry Greenberg and Joseph Olander. — London : Hale, 1980. — xxvi,516p ; 23cm. — (Hale SF)
ISBN 0-7091-8640-1 : £6.95 B81-01661

823'.0876'08[FS] — Science fiction short stories in English, *1945-* **—** *Anthologies*

The **Golden** age of science fiction. — London : Hutchinson, Sept.1981. — [288]p
ISBN 0-09-145770-x : £6.95 : CIP entry B81-20182

Isaac Asimov's marvels of science fiction : [stories] / [by Isaac Asimov ... et al.] ; edited by George Scithers. — London : Hale, 1981, c1979. — 287p : ill ; 21cm
ISBN 0-7091-9169-3 : £6.95 B81-35186

Space : a collection of science fiction stories. — London : Hutchinson
7 / chosen by Richard Davis. — 1981. — 159p ; 23cm
ISBN 0-09-144350-4 : £5.50 : CIP rev. B81-01228

823'.0876'089282[J] — Children's science fiction short stories in English, *1900-* **—** *Anthologies*

Fantasy tales / edited by Barbara Ireson. — [London] : Beaver, 1981, c1977. — 190p ; 18cm
Originally published: London : Faber, 1977
ISBN 0-600-20056-6 (pbk) : £1.10 B81-36752

823'.0876'089282[J] — Children's science fiction short stories in English, *1945-* **—** *Anthologies*

Skylark science fiction stories / collected by Jill Bennett ; illustrated by Peter Gregory + Arthur Ransom. — London : Book Club Associates, 1980. — 191p : ill ; 24cm
Unpriced B81-37886

823'.0876'09 — Science fiction in English — *Reviews* **—** *Anthologies* **—** *Serials*

SF horizons. — No.1 (Sept.1979)-. — Lancaster (2 Daisy Bank, Quernmore Rd, Lancaster LA1 3JW) : Keith A. Walker, 1979-. — v. : ill ; 30cm
First issue includes a supplement entitled: SFanzine review
ISSN 0144-641x = SF horizons : Unpriced B81-06781

823'.0876'09 — Science fiction in English, *to 1979* **—** *Critical studies*

Griffiths, John, *1934-*. Three tomorrows : American, British and Soviet science fiction / John Griffiths. — London : Macmillan, 1980. — 217p ; 23cm
Includes index
ISBN 0-333-26910-1 (cased) : £10.00 : CIP rev.
ISBN 0-333-26912-8 (pbk) : £3.95
Also classified at 891.73'0876'09 B80-18883

823'.0876'09 — Science fiction in English, *to 1979* — *Critical studies* : *continuation*

Parrinder, Patrick. Science fiction : its criticism and teaching / Patrick Parrinder. — London : Methuen, 1980. — xix,166p ; 21cm. — (New accents)
Bibliography: p154-161. — Includes index
ISBN 0-416-71390-4 (cased) : £5.95 : CIP rev.
ISBN 0-416-71400-5 (pbk) : £2.75 B80-13974

823'.0876'0927 — Science fiction in English, *1900-*. **Characters**

Wingrove, David. The immortals of science fiction / David Wingrove. — London (60 Greek St., W.1) : Pierrot, 1980. — 113 : col.ill ; 29cm
ISBN 0-905310-37-3 (pbk) : £5.95 B81-05383

823.2 — ENGLISH FICTION, 1400-1558

823'.2 — Fiction in English. Malory, ***Sir*** **Thomas** — *Critical studies*

Aspects of Malory / edited by Toshiyuki Takamiya and Derek Brewer. — Cambridge : Brewer, c1981. — x,232p : ill,facsims ; 23cm. — (Arthurian studies ; 1)
Bibliography: p179-186. — Includes index
ISBN 0-85991-068-7 : £17.50 : CIP rev.
B81-03836

823'.2[F] — Fiction in English, *1400-1558* — *Texts*

Malory, ***Sir*** **Thomas**. [Le Morte d'Arthur]. Sir Thomas Malory's tales of King Arthur / edited and abridged with an introduction by Michael Senior. — London : Book Club Associates, 1980. — 351p : ill(some col.),facsims(some col.) ; 25cm
Ill on lining papers. — Includes index
Unpriced B81-37881

823.3 — ENGLISH FICTION, 1558-1625

823'.3 — Fiction in English. Sidney, ***Sir Philip.*** *Special themes: Rebellion*

McCoy, Richard C.. Sir Philip Sidney : rebellion in Arcadia / Richard C. McCoy. — [Brighton] : Harvester Press, 1979. — xiii,230p ; 24cm
Originally published: New Brunswick, N.J. : Rutgers University Press, 1979. — Bibliography: p218-223. — Includes index
ISBN 0-85527-855-2 : £18.50 B81-01573

823'.3 — Short stories in English, *1558-1625* — *Texts with commentaries*

Greene, Robert. [Planetomachia]. Robert Greene's Planetomachia and the text of the third tragedy : a bibliographical explanation and a new edition of the text / edited with an introduction and notes by D.F. Bratchell. — Amersham : Avebury, 1979. — ix,82p ; 23cm
ISBN 0-86127-201-3 : £8.00 : CIP rev.
B79-21925

823.4 — ENGLISH FICTION, 1625-1702

823'.4 — Fiction in English, *1625-1702* — *Texts with commentaries*

Bunyan, John. The Holy War : made by Shaddai upon Diabolus. For the regaining of the metropolis of the world. Or, the losing and taking again of the town of Mansoul / John Bunyan ; edited by Roger Sharrock and James F. Forrest. — Oxford : Clarendon, 1980. — xlviii,288p,[1] leaf of plates : 1facsim ; 23cm
Includes index
ISBN 0-19-811887-2 : £25.00 : CIP rev.
B80-01789

Bunyan, John. A treatise of the fear of God ; The greatness of the soul ; A holy life / John Bunyan ; edited by Richard L. Greaves. — Oxford : Clarendon Press, 1981. — xlv,365p,[1] leaf of plates : 1facsim ; 23cm. — (The Miscellaneous works of John Bunyan ; v.9)
A treatise of the fear of God originally published: London : N.Ponder, 1679. — Bibliography: pxiii
ISBN 0-19-812737-5 : £35.00 B81-30650

823'.4 — Fiction in English. Bunyan, John — *Critical studies* — *Quotations*

What they said about John Bunyan / [compiled] by H.G. Tibbutt. — [Bedford] ([County Hall, Bedford MK42 9AP]) : Arts and Recreation Department, Bedfordshire County Council, 1981. — 19p,[8]p of plates : ill,facsims ; 21cm
Unpriced (pbk) B81-40289

823'.4 — Fiction in English. Bunyan, John. Pilgrim's progress — *Critical studies*

The **Pilgrim's** progress : critical and historical views / edited by Vincent Newey. — Liverpool : Liverpool University Press, 1980. — xiii,302p ; 23cm. — (Liverpool English texts and studies)
Includes index
ISBN 0-85323-194-x : £12.00 : CIP rev.
B80-07953

823.5 — ENGLISH FICTION, 1702-1745

823'.5 — Fiction in English. Defoe, Daniel — *Biographies*

Bastian, F.. Defoe's early life / F. Bastian. — London : Macmillan, 1981. — xii,377p,8p of plates : ill,1map,1facsim,ports ; 22cm
Includes index
ISBN 0-333-27432-6 : £15.00 B81-38725

823'.5 — Fiction in English. Fielding, Henry. Joseph Andrews — *Study outlines*

King, Bruce, *1933-*. Joseph Andrews : notes / by Bruce King. — Harlow : Longman, 1981. — 72p ; 21cm. — (York notes ; 105)
Bibliography: p68-69
ISBN 0-582-78174-4 (pbk) : £0.90 B81-19660

823'.5 — Fiction in English. Fielding, Henry. Tom Jones — *Study outlines*

Butler, Lance St John. Tom Jones : notes / by Lance St John Butler. — Harlow : Longman, 1981. — 120p ; 21cm. — (York notes ; 113)
Bibliography: p114-115
ISBN 0-582-78205-8 (pbk) : £0.90 B81-33689

823'.5 — Fiction in English. Swift, Jonathan. Gulliver's travels & Tale of a tub — *Critical studies*

Louis, Frances Deutsch. Swift's anatomy of misunderstanding : a study of Swift's epistemological imagination in A tale of a tub and Gulliver's travels / Frances Deutsch Louis. — London : Prior, 1981. — xxvi,193p ; 23cm
Bibliography: p188-193
ISBN 0-86043-521-0 : £9.50 B81-27756

823'.5[F] — Fiction in English, *1702-1745* — *Texts*

Defoe, Daniel. The fortunes and misfortunes of the famous Moll Flanders, etc... — Oxford : Oxford University Press, Nov.1981. — [408]p. — (The World's classics)
ISBN 0-19-281570-9 (pbk) : £1.95 : CIP entry
B81-28857

Defoe, Daniel. The life and strange surprizing adventures of Robinson Crusoe, of York, mariner ... / Daniel Defoe ; edited with an introduction by J. Donald Crowley. — Oxford : Oxford University Press, 1972 (1981 [printing]). — xxx,316p : 2maps ; 19cm. — (The World's classics)
Bibliography: pxxvii-xxviii
ISBN 0-19-281555-5 (pbk) : £0.95 : CIP rev.
B81-25666

Defoe, Daniel. Roxana : the fortunate mistress, or, a History of the life and vast variety of fortunes of Mademoiselle de Beleau afterwards called the Countess de Wintselsheim in Germany being the person known by the name of the Lady Roxana in the time of Charles II / Daniel Defoe ; edited with an introduction and notes by Jane Jack. — Oxford : Oxford University Press, 1981, c1964. — xviii,333p ; 19cm. — (The World's classics)
ISBN 0-19-281563-6 (pbk) : £1.50 : CIP rev.
B81-12859

Goldsmith, Oliver. The vicar of Wakefield. — Oxford : Oxford University Press, Nov.1981. — [232]p. — (The World's classics)
ISBN 0-19-281560-1 (pbk) : £1.50 : CIP entry
B81-28855

823.6 — ENGLISH FICTION, 1745-1800

823'.6 — Fiction in English, *1745-1800* — *Texts with commentaries*

Sterne, Laurence. Tristram Shandy : an authoritative text, the author on the novel, criticism / Laurence Sterne ; edited by Howard Anderson. — New York ; London : Norton, c1980. — xv,650p ; 22cm. — (A Norton critical edition)
Bibliography: p649-650
ISBN 0-393-95034-4 (pbk) : £3.25 B81-08359

823'.6 — Fiction in English. Goldsmith, Oliver. Vicar of Wakefield — *Study outlines*

Donnelly, Brian. Oliver Goldsmith The vicar of Wakefield : notes / by Brian Donnelly. — London : Longman, 1980. — 72p : ill ; 21cm. — (York notes ; 79)
Bibliography: p72
ISBN 0-582-78114-0 (pbk) : £0.90 B81-07679

823'.6[F] — Fiction in English, *1745-1800* — *Texts*

Cleland, John. [Genuine memoirs of the celebrated Miss Maria Brown]. Memoirs of Maria Brown / John Cleland ; edited and with an introduction by Maurice Renfrew. — London : Hamlyn Paperbacks, c1981. — 158p ; 18cm
ISBN 0-600-20393-x (pbk) : £1.25 B81-31916

Radcliffe, Ann. The Italian, or, The confessional of the black penitents. — Oxford : Oxford University Press, Nov.1981. — [420]p. — (The World's classics)
ISBN 0-19-281572-5 (pbk) : £1.95 : CIP entry
B81-28858

Richardson, Samuel. Pamela, or Virtue rewarded / Samuel Richardson ; edited by Peter Sabor ; with an introduction by Margaret A. Doody. — Harmondsworth : Penguin, 1980. — 537p : 1facsim ; 18cm. — (Penguin English library)
Bibliography: p23-24
ISBN 0-14-043140-3 (pbk) : £1.95 B81-01633

Smollett, Tobias. The adventures of Roderick Random / Tobias Smollett ; edited with an introduction and notes by Paul-Gabriel Boucé. — Oxford : Oxford University Press, 1979 (1981 [printing]). — xxxviii,481p ; 19cm. — (The World's classics)
Bibliography: pxxvii-xxix
ISBN 0-19-281261-0 (pbk) : £2.50 : CIP rev.
B81-04299

823.7 — ENGLISH FICTION, 1800-1837

823'.7 — Fiction in English, *1800-1837* — *Texts with commentaries*

Edgeworth, Maria. Castle Rackrent / Maria Edgeworth ; edited with an introduction by George Watson. — Oxford : Oxford University Press, 1964 (1980 [printing]). — xxxv,127p ; 19cm. — (The World's classics)
Bibliography: pxxix-xxx
ISBN 0-19-281539-3 (pbk) : £1.50 : CIP rev.
B80-13528

Scott, ***Sir*** **Walter**. Waverley, or, 'Tis sixty years since / Sir Walter Scott ; edited by Claire Lamont. — Oxford : Clarendon Press, 1981. — xlii,470p ; 23cm
ISBN 0-19-812643-3 : £20.00 : CIP rev.
B80-10757

823'.7 — Fiction in English, *1800-1837* — *Texts with commentaries* — *For schools*

Austen, Jane. Pride and prejudice. — London : Macmillan Education, Jan.1982. — [336]p. — (Macmillan students' novels)
ISBN 0-333-32132-4 (pbk) : £0.95 : CIP entry
B81-34145

823'.7 — Fiction in English. Austen, Jane — *Biographies*

Cecil, David. A portrait of Jane Austen / David Cecil. — Harmondsworth : Penguin, 1980, c1978. — 208p : ill(some col.),maps,facsims,ports(some col.) ; 24cm
Originally published: London : Constable, 1978. — Includes index
ISBN 0-14-005411-1 (pbk) : £3.95 B81-06487

823'.7 — Fiction in English. Austen, Jane — *Critical studies*

Jane Austen in a social context / edited by David Monaghan. — London : Macmillan, 1981. — x,199p ; 23cm
Includes index
ISBN 0-333-27189-0 : £12.00 : CIP rev. B80-09826

Odmark, John. An understanding of Jane Austen's novels : character, value and ironic perspective / John Odmark. — Oxford : Blackwell, 1981. — xvi,224p : ill ; 23cm
Ill on lining papers. — Bibliography: p207-215. — Includes index
ISBN 0-631-12494-2 : £9.95 B81-31852

823'.7 — Fiction in English. Austen, Jane. Pride and prejudice — *Study outlines — For schools*

Neill, Heather. Pride and prejudice : [guidelines] / by Heather Neill. — Teacher's ed. — London : Glasgow Publications, c1980. — 16,[4]p : ill(some col.),1map,1port ; 30cm. — (Guidelines)
Cover title
ISBN 0-86158-518-6 (pbk) : Unpriced B81-25069

823'.7 — Fiction in English. Austen, Jane. Sense and sensibility — *Study outlines*

Gooneratne, Yasmine. Sense and sensibility : notes / by Yasmine Gooneratne. — London : Longman, 1980. — 88p ; 21cm. — (York notes ; 91)
Bibliography: p84
ISBN 0-582-78107-8 (pbk) : £0.90 B81-14578

823'.7 — Fiction in English. Edgeworth, Maria. Castle Rackrent — *Study outlines*

O'Flaherty, G.. Castle Rackrent / G. O'Flaherty. — Dublin : Folens, c1979. — 32p ; 22cm. — (Folens' student aids leaving certificate)
Bibliography: p32
ISBN 0-86121-071-9 (pbk) : Unpriced B81-23974

823'.7 — Fiction in English. Scott, *Sir* Walter — *Critical studies*

Anderson, James, *1918-*. Sir Walter Scott and history : with other papers / by James Anderson. — Edinburgh (1 Albyn Place, Edinburgh EH2 4NG) : Edina, 1981. — viii,199p ; 23cm
Includes index
ISBN 0-905695-12-7 : £6.75 B81-29136

823'.7 — Fiction in English. Scott, *Sir* Walter. *Ivanhoe — Study outlines*

Low, Donald A.. Sir Walter Scott Ivanhoe : notes / by Donald A. Low. — London : Longman, 1980. — 69p ; 21cm. — (York notes ; 58)
Bibliography: p69
ISBN 0-582-78095-0 (pbk) : £0.90 B81-06440

823'.7 — Fiction in English. Scott, *Sir* Walter. *Quentin Durward — Study outlines*

Engel, Wilson F.. Quentin Durward : notes / by Wilson F. Engel. — London : Longman, 1980. — 79p ; 21cm. — (York notes ; 54)
Bibliography: p74-75
ISBN 0-582-78120-5 (pbk) : £0.90 B81-07102

823'.7 — Fiction in English. Scott, *Sir* Walter. Waverley — *Study outlines*

Lamont, Claire. Waverley : notes / by Claire Lamont. — Harlow : Longman, 1981. — 78p ; 21cm. — (York notes ; 122)
Bibliography: p77-78
ISBN 0-582-78263-5 (pbk) : £0.90 B81-34238

823'.7 — Fiction in English. Trollope, Frances — *Biographies*

Johnston, Johanna. The life, manners and travels of Fanny Trollope : a biography / Johanna Johnston. — London : Quartet, 1980, c1978. — 271p ; 20cm
Originally published: New York : Hawthorn Books, 1978 ; London : Constable, 1979. — Bibliography: p259-262. — Includes index
ISBN 0-7043-3325-2 (pbk) : £2.95 B81-29240

823'.7[F] — Fiction in English, *1800-1837 — Texts*

Austen, Jane. Mansfield Park / Jane Austen ; with an introduction by Monica Dickens and notes by W.A. Craik. — London : Pan, 1972 (1980 printing). — xiii,384p ; 18cm. — (A Pan classic)
£0.95 (pbk) B81-03612

Austen, Jane. Northanger Abbey ; Lady Susan ; The Watsons ; and Sanditon / Jane Austen ; edited by John Davie. — Oxford : Oxford University Press, 1980. — xxxii,388p ; 20cm. — (Oxford classics)
ISBN 0-19-251023-1 (cased) : £4.99 : CIP rev.
ISBN 0-19-281525-3 (pbk) : Unpriced B80-13526

Austen, Jane. Persuasion / Jane Austen ; edited by John Davie. — Oxford : Oxford University Press, c1971 (1980 [printing]). — xx,255p ; 20cm. — (Oxford classics)
Bibliography: pxv-xvii
ISBN 0-19-251022-3 (cased) : £4.00 : CIP rev. B80-13527

Austen, Jane. Pride and prejudice / Jane Austen ; illustrated by Lynette Hemmant. — Kingswood : World's Work, 1980. — 303p : ill (some col.) ; 25cm
ISBN 0-437-24575-6 : £5.95 B81-00377

Austen, Jane. Pride and prejudice / by Jane Austen. — Toronto ; London : Bantam, 1981. — 292p ; 18cm. — (A Bantam classic)
ISBN 0-553-21018-1 (pbk) : £0.85 B81-39104

Austen, Jane. Sense and sensibility / Jane Austen ; introduction and notes by W.A. Craik. — London : Pan, 1972 (1980 printing). — 315p ; 18cm. — (A Pan classic)
Bibliography: p315
ISBN 0-330-02949-5 (pbk) : £0.95 B81-01230

Austen, Jane. Sense and sensibility / Jane Austen. — Harmondsworth : Penguin, 1981. — 333p ; 18cm
ISBN 0-14-005791-9 (pbk) : £0.85 B81-07403

Austen, Jane. Sense and sensibility / Jane Austen. — [Sevenoaks] : Coronet, 1981. — 320p ; 18cm
ISBN 0-340-26394-6 (pbk) : £1.40 B81-07087

Banim, John. Tales by the O'Hara Family : Crohoore of the bill-hook, The fetches, John Doe / John Banim, Michael Banim. — New York ; London : Garland, 1978. — (Ireland)
Facsim of: ed. published: London : For W. Simpkin and R. Marshall, 1825
ISBN 0-8240-3465-1 : Unpriced B81-24831

Carleton, William. The black prophet / William Carleton. — New York ; London : Garland, 1979. — 320p ; 19cm. — (Ireland)
Facsim of: edition published Belfast : Simms and M'Intyre, 1847
ISBN 0-8240-3490-2 : £50.60 B81-24720

Edgeworth, Maria. Ennui / Maria Edgeworth ; with an introduction by Robert Lee Wolff. — New York ; London : Garland, 1978. — xxvii,vii,400p ; 19cm. — (Ireland)
Facsim of: edition published as Vol.1 of Tales of fashionable life. London : Printed for J. Johnson, 1809
ISBN 0-8240-3452-x : Unpriced B81-26484

Hogg, James, *1770-1835*. The private memoirs and confessions of a justified sinner / James Hogg ; edited with an introduction by John Carey. — Oxford : Oxford University Press, 1981, c1969. — xxxiii,262p ; 19cm. — (The World's classics)
ISBN 0-19-281556-3 (pbk) : £1.95 : CIP rev. B81-12864

Scott, *Sir* Walter. Waverley / Sir Walter Scott ; edited with an introduction by Andrew Hook. — Harmondsworth : Penguin, 1972 (1980 printing). — 608p : 1port ; 18cm. — (Penguin English library)
Port on inside cover
ISBN 0-14-043071-7 (pbk) : £1.95 B81-03238

823'.7'09 — Fiction in English, *1800-1900.* **Obscurity** — *Critical studies*

White, Allon. The uses of obscurity : the fiction of early modernism / Allon White. — London : Routledge & Kegan Paul, 1981. — vii,190p : ill ; 23cm
Bibliography: p181-186. — Includes index
ISBN 0-7100-0751-5 : £12.00 : CIP rev. B81-14925

823'.7'09355 — Fiction in English, *1800-1900.* **Special themes: Great Britain. Industrialisation** — *Critical studies*

Fryckstedt, Monica Correa. The early industrial novel : Mary Barton and its predecessors / by Monica Correa Fryckstedt. — Manchester : John Rylands University Library of Manchester, 1980. — p11-30 ; 25cm
£1.25 (pbk) B81-35540

823.8 — ENGLISH FICTION, 1837-1900

823'.8 — Children's stories in English, *1837-1900 — Gaelic texts*

Wilde, Oscar. [The selfish giant. Gaelic]. Am famhaire mosach / eadar-theangaichte le Ruairidh MacLeoid ; rinn Tormod MacLeoid na dealbhannan nuair a bha e ann an Ard Sgol Phort-righ. — [Lochmaddy] ([Lochmaddy, North Uist, PA82 5BD]) : [Crùisgean], 1980. — 27p : ill ; 21cm
£1.90 (pbk) B81-09632

823'.8 — Children's stories in English. Bannerman, Helen — *Biographies*

Hay, Elizabeth. Sambo Sahib : the story of Little Black Sambo and Helen Bannerman / Elizabeth Hay. — Edinburgh : Harris, 1981. — x,194p : ill,facsims,ports ; 23cm
Bibliography: p176. - Includes index
ISBN 0-904505-91-x : £7.50 B81-23364

823'.8 — Children's stories in English. Liddell, Alice — *Biographies*

Clark, Anne, *1933-*. The real Alice / Lewis Carroll's dream child ; Anne Clark. — London : Joseph, 1981. — 271p : ill,music,facsims,ports,geneal.tables ; 24cm
Geneal. tables on lining papers. — Bibliography: p264-265. — Includes index
ISBN 0-7181-2064-7 : £12.50 B81-39117

823'.8 — Fiction in English, *1837-1900 — Texts — Facsimiles*

Linskill, Mary. Cleveden / by Mary Linskill. — Whitby : Caedmon, 1980. — viii,341p : ill ; 20cm
Facsim. of: 1st ed., S.l. : s.n., 1875. — Ill on lining papers
ISBN 0-905355-14-8 : £7.50 B81-28477

823'.8 — Fiction in English, *1837-1900 — Texts with commentaries*

Dickens, Charles, *1812-1870*. David Copperfield / Charles Dickens ; edited by Nina Burgis. — Oxford : Clarendon, 1981. — lxv,781p,[33] leaves of plates : ill,facsims ; 22cm. — (The Clarendon Dickens)
ISBN 0-19-812492-9 : £40.00 : CIP rev. B79-16145

Hardy, Thomas, *1840-1928*. Tess of the D'Urbervilles : an authoritative text : Hardy and the novel : criticism / Thomas Hardy ; edited by Scott Elledge. — 2nd ed. — New York ; London : W.W. Norton, c1979. — 467p ; 21cm
Previous ed.: 1965. — Bibliography: p465-467
ISBN 0-393-09044-2 (pbk) : £3.50 B81-04736

Hardy, Thomas, *1840-1928*. The woodlanders / Thomas Hardy ; edited by Dale Kramer. — Oxford : Clarendon Press, 1981. — ix,430p ; 23cm
Bibliography: pix
ISBN 0-19-812504-6 : £25.00 B81-17587

823'.8 — Fiction in English, *1837-1900 — Texts with commentaries — For schools*

Brontë, Charlotte. Jane Eyre. — London : Macmillan Education, Jan.1982. — [480]p. — (Macmillan students' novels)
ISBN 0-333-32131-6 (pbk) : £0.95 : CIP entry B81-33979

823'.8 — Fiction in English, *1837-1900 — Texts with commentaries — For schools*
continuation

Brontë, Emily. Wuthering heights. — London : Macmillan Education, Jan.1982. — [336]p. — (Macmillan students' novels)
ISBN 0-333-32128-6 (pbk) : £0.95 : CIP entry
B81-33980

Dickens, Charles, *1912-1870.* Great expectations. — London : Macmillan Education, Jan.1982. — [480]p. — (Macmillan students' novels)
ISBN 0-333-32127-8 (pbk) : £0.95 : CIP entry
B81-34143

823'.8 — Fiction in English. Blackmore, R. D.. Lorna Doone. Local associations: England. Exmoor

Elliott-Cannon, Arthur. In quest of the Doones / by A. Elliott-Cannon. — Dulverton : Breakaway, 1981. — 48p : ill,2maps ; 20cm
ISBN 0-907506-01-1 (pbk) : £0.75 B81-24080

823'.8 — Fiction in English. Brontë, Charlotte. Jane Eyre. Local associations: Derbyshire. Hathersage

Hulbert, Martin F. H.. Jane Eyre and Hathersage / by Martin F.H. Hulbert. — [Hathersage] ([The Vicarage, Hathersage, Sheffield S30 1AB]) : [Hathersage Parochial Church Council], [1980]. — [8]p : ill,1port ; 22cm
£0.15 (unbound) B81-18657

823'.8 — Fiction in English. Brontë, Charlotte. Special themes: Death — *Critical studies*

Keefe, Robert. Charlotte Brontë's world of death / Robert Keefe. — Austin ; London : University of Texas Press, c1979. — xxi,224p ; 23cm
Bibliography: p213-216. — Includes index
ISBN 0-292-75043-9 : £7.20 B81-19667

823'.8 — Fiction in English. Brontë, Emily. Wuthering Heights — *Study outlines*

Smith, Angela. Wuthering Heights : notes / by Angela Smith. — London : Longman, 1980. — 70p : 1geneal.table ; 21cm. — (York notes ; 43)
Bibliography: p66
ISBN 0-582-78091-8 (pbk) : £0.90 B81-07101

823'.8 — Fiction in English. Dickens, Charles, *1812-1870 — Critical studies*

Lambert, Mark, *1942-*. Dickens and the suspended quotation / Mark Lambert. — New Haven ; London : Yale University Press, 1981. — xii,186p : ill ; 22cm
Bibliography: pxi-xiii. - Includes index
ISBN 0-300-02555-6 : £10.40 B81-17293

Newman, S. J.. Dickens at play / S.J. Newman. — London : Macmillan, 1981. — x,131p ; 23cm
Includes index
ISBN 0-333-26153-4 : £12.00 : CIP rev.
B80-27500

823'.8 — Fiction in English. Dickens, Charles, *1812-1870.* **Great expectations** — *Study outlines — For schools*

Fozzard, Peter. Great expectations : [guidelines] / by Peter Fozzard. — Teacher's ed. — London : Glasgow Publications, c1980. — 16,[4]p : ill(some col.) ; 30cm. — (Guidelines)
Cover title
ISBN 0-86158-522-4 (pbk) : Unpriced
B81-25070

823'.8 — Fiction in English. Dickens, Charles, *1812-1870.* **Oliver Twist** — *Study outlines*

Brown, Suzanne. Oliver Twist : notes / by Suzanne Brown. — Harlow : Longman, 1981. — 88p ; 21cm. — (York notes ; 101)
Bibliography: p76
ISBN 0-582-78254-6 (pbk) : £0.90 B81-33686

823'.8 — Fiction in English. Dickens, Charles, *1812-1870.* **Our mutual friend** — *Critical studies*

David, Deirdre. Fictions of resolution in three Victorian novels : North and South, Our mutual friend, Daniel Deronda / Deirdre David. — London : Macmillan, 1981. — xii,209p ; 23cm
Includes index
ISBN 0-333-28732-0 : £15.00
Primary classification 823'.8'09 B81-19714

823'.8 — Fiction in English. Dickens, Charles, *1812-1870.* **Pickwick papers** — *Study outlines*

Wheeler, Michael, *1947-*. Pickwick papers : notes / by Michael Wheeler. — Harlow : Longman, 1981. — 70p ; 21cm. — (York notes ; 110)
Bibliography: p69-70
ISBN 0-582-78255-4 (pbk) : £0.90 B81-34234

823'.8 — Fiction in English. Dickens, Charles, *1812-1870.* **Special themes: Religion** — *Critical studies*

Walder, Dennis. Dickens and religion. — London : Allen & Unwin, Nov.1981. — [256]p
ISBN 0-04-800006-x : £12.50 : CIP entry
B81-28782

823'.8 — Fiction in English. Dickens, Charles, *1812-1870.* **Style** — *Critical studies*

Horton, Susan R.. The reader in the Dickens world : style and response / Susan R. Horton. — London : Macmillan, 1981. — xiii,136p ; 23cm
Includes index
ISBN 0-333-27692-2 : £15.00 : CIP rev.
B80-11153

823'.8 — Fiction in English. Disraeli, Benjamin — *Critical studies*

Braun, Thom. Disraeli the novelist / Thom Braun. — London : Allen & Unwin, 1981. — vii,149p ; 23cm
Includes index
ISBN 0-04-809017-4 : Unpriced : CIP rev.
B81-15870

823'.8 — Fiction in English. Eliot, George — *Critical studies*

Newton, K. M.. George Eliot : romantic humanist : a study of the philosophical structure of her novels / K.M. Newton. — [London] : Macmillan, 1981. — vii,215p ; 23cm
Includes index
ISBN 0-333-28101-2 : £12.00 : CIP rev.
B80-09380

823'.8 — Fiction in English. Eliot, George. Daniel Deronda — *Critical studies*

David, Deirdre. Fictions of resolution in three Victorian novels : North and South, Our mutual friend, Daniel Deronda / Deirdre David. — London : Macmillan, 1981. — xii,209p ; 23cm
Includes index
ISBN 0-333-28732-0 : £15.00
Primary classification 823'.8'09 B81-19714

823'.8 — Fiction in English. Eliot, George *expounded by* **her attitudes to visual arts**

Witemeyer, Hugh. George Eliot and the visual arts / Hugh Witemeyer. — New Haven ; London : Yale University Press, 1979. — xiii,238p : ill,ports ; 22cm
Bibliography: pxiii. - Includes index
ISBN 0-300-02281-6 : £12.30 B81-11314

823'.8 — Fiction in English. Eliot, George. Organisations: George Eliot Fellowship — *Serials*

[Review, George Eliot Fellowship]. Review / the George Eliot Fellowship. — No.9 (June 1978). — [Coventry] ([71 Stepping Stones Rd., Coventry CV5 8JT]) : The Fellowship, 1978. — 29p
Unpriced B81-13206

[Review, George Eliot Fellowship]. Review / the George Eliot Fellowship. — No.10 (June 1979). — [Coventry] ([71 Stepping Stones Rd, Coventry CV5 8JT]) : The Fellowship, 1979. — 35p
Unpriced B81-13205

[Review *(George Eliot Fellowship)***]**. Review / the George Eliot Fellowship. — No.8 (June 1977). — Coventry (71 Stepping Stones Rd., Coventry CV5 8JT) : The Fellowship, 1977. — 28p
Unpriced B81-13207

[Review *(George Eliot Fellowship)***]**. Review / the George Eliot Fellowship. — No.11 (1980). — [Coventry] ([71 Stepping Stones Rd., Coventry CV5 8JT]) : The Fellowship, 1980. — 59p
Unpriced B81-13208

823'.8 — Fiction in English. Eliot, George. Organisations: George Eliot Fellowship, *to 1980*

Adams, Kathleen. The story of the George Eliot Fellowship / by Kathleen Adams. — [Coventry] ([71 Stepping Stone Rd, Coventry CV5 8JT]) : The Fellowship, 1980. — 30p ; 22cm
£1.00 (unbound) B81-06476

823'.8 — Fiction in English. Eliot, George. Silas Marner — *Study outlines*

Rutherford, Anna. Silas Marner : notes / by Anna Rutherford. — Harlow : Longman, 1981. — 72p ; 21cm. — (York notes ; 98)
Bibliography: p66-67
ISBN 0-582-78118-3 (pbk) : £0.90 B81-19629

823'.8 — Fiction in English. Eliot, George. Silas Marner — *Study outlines — For schools*

Murray, Patrick, *1935*. Silas Marner / Patrick Murray. — Dublin : Educational Company, 1981. — 37p ; 22cm. — (Inscapes ; 19)
Bibliography: p34
Unpriced (pbk) B81-34445

823'.8 — Fiction in English. Gaskell, Elizabeth — *Correspondence, diaries, etc.*

Chapple, J. A. V.. Elizabeth Gaskell : a portrait in letters / J.A.V. Chapple assisted by John Geoffrey Sharps. — Manchester : Manchester University Press, c1980. — xviii,172p,[8]p of plates : ill,facsims,ports ; 24cm
Includes index
ISBN 0-7190-0799-2 : £8.75 : CIP rev.
B80-13536

823'.8 — Fiction in English. Gaskell, Elizabeth — *Critical studies*

Duthie, Enid L.. The themes of Elizabeth Gaskell / Enid L. Duthie. — London : Macmillan, 1980. — xii,217p ; 23cm
Bibliography: p209-211. — Includes index
ISBN 0-333-27851-8 : £12.00 : CIP rev.
B80-03814

823'.8 — Fiction in English. Gaskell, Elizabeth. Mary Barton & North and south — *Study outlines*

Parsons, E. M.. Notes on Elizabeth Gaskell's Mary Barton and North and south / compiled by E.M. Parsons. — London : Methuen Paperbacks, 1981. — 103p ; 20cm. — (Methuen notes)
Bibliography: p103
ISBN 0-417-20900-2 (pbk) : £0.95 B81-19616

823'.8 — Fiction in English. Gaskell, Elizabeth. North and south — *Critical studies*

David, Deirdre. Fictions of resolution in three Victorian novels : North and South, Our mutual friend, Daniel Deronda / Deirdre David. — London : Macmillan, 1981. — xii,209p ; 23cm
Includes index
ISBN 0-333-28732-0 : £15.00
Primary classification 823'.8'09 B81-19714

823'.8 — Fiction in English. Gissing, George — *Biographies*

Halperin, John. Gissing. — Oxford : Oxford University Press, Oct.1981. — [375]p
ISBN 0-19-812677-8 : £17.50 : CIP entry
B81-25844

823'.8 — Fiction in English. Gissing, George — *Critical studies*

George Gissing : critical essays / edited by Jean-Pierre Michaux. — London : Vision, c1981. — 214p ; 23cm. — (Critical studies series)
Includes index
ISBN 0-85478-404-7 : £11.95 B81-15731

823'.8 — Fiction in English. Haggard, H. Rider — *Biographies*

Higgins, D. S.. Rider Haggard : the great storyteller / D. S. Higgins. — London : Cassell, 1981. — 266p,[16]p of plates : ill,2facsims,ports ; 24cm
Bibliography: p250-256. — Includes index
ISBN 0-304-30827-7 : £9.95 B81-34607

823'.8 — Fiction in English. Hardy, Florence Emily — *Biographies*

Gittings, Robert. The second Mrs Hardy / Robert Gittings and Jo Manton. — Rev. ed. — Oxford : Oxford University Press, 1981, c1979. — x,150p : ill,facsims,ports ; 20cm
Previous ed.: London : Heinemann, 1979. — Bibliography: p145. — Includes index
ISBN 0-19-281322-6 (pbk) : £2.50 : CIP rev. B81-06612

823'.8 — Fiction in English. Hardy, Thomas, *1840-1928* — *Biographies*

Hawkins, Desmond. Hardy : novelist and poet / Desmond Hawkins. — London : Macmillan, 1981, c1976. — 247p : ill,ports ; 20cm
Originally published: Newton Abbot : David & Charles, 1976. — Bibliography: p237-240. — Includes index
ISBN 0-333-31644-4 (pbk) : £3.95 B81-31851

823'.8 — Fiction in English. Hardy, Thomas, *1840-1928* — *Critical studies*

Bayley, John. An essay on Hardy / John Bayley. — Cambridge : Cambridge University Press, 1978 (1979 [printing]). — 237p ; 22cm
ISBN 0-521-28462-7 (pbk) : £5.95 B81-38980

Page, Norman. Thomas Hardy / by Norman Page. — London : Routledge & Kegan Paul, 1977 (1981 [printing]). — xiii,195p ; 22cm
Bibliography: p184-186. - Includes index
ISBN 0-7100-8615-6 (pbk) : £3.75 B81-14284

Salter, C. H.. Good little Thomas Hardy. — London : Macmillan, June 1981. — [192]p
ISBN 0-333-29387-8 : CIP entry B81-13788

Sumner, Rosemary. Thomas Hardy : psychological novelist / Rosemary Sumner. — London : Macmillan, 1981. — 216p : 2ill ; 23cm
Bibliography: p212-216. — Includes index
ISBN 0-333-29085-2 : £15.00 B81-23014

A **Thomas** Hardy miscellany / edited by J. Stevens Cox. — St. Peter Port : Toucan, 1981. — [20]p : 1map ; 20cm
Contents: Thomas Hardy's Wessex / anonymous. Originally published : in The Bookman, Vol.1, No.1, Oct.1891 — Letter from Hardy to the editor of The Bookman. Originally published : in The Bookman, Vol.1, No.3, Dec. 1891 — The work of Thomas Hardy / by Professor Minto. Originally published : in The Bookman, Vol.1, No.3, Dec.1891
ISBN 0-85694-247-2 (unbound) : Unpriced
Also classified at 823'.8 B81-37075

Willis, Irene Cooper. An essay on Thomas Hardy / by Irene Cooper Willis ; edited with introduction and notes by F.B. Pinion. — Langport (8 Brooklands Rd., Langport, Somerset, TA10 9SZ) : Thomas Hardy Society, 1981. — 22p : ill ; 22cm. — (Monograph / The Thomas Hardy Society ; no.1)
Cover title
ISBN 0-904398-28-5 (pbk) : £0.50 B81-33082

823'.8 — Fiction in English. Hardy, Thomas, *1840-1928* — *Encyclopaedias*

Hurst, Alan, *19---*. Hardy : an illustrated dictionary / Alan Hurst. — London : Kaye & Ward, 1980. — 215p : ill,map,facsims,ports ; 23cm
Bibliography: p214-215
ISBN 0-7182-1245-2 : £5.95 B81-01561

823'.8 — Fiction in English. Hardy, Thomas, *1840-1928.* **Local associations: Wessex**

A **Thomas** Hardy miscellany / edited by J. Stevens Cox. — St. Peter Port : Toucan, 1981. — [20]p : 1map ; 20cm
Contents: Thomas Hardy's Wessex / anonymous. Originally published : in The Bookman, Vol.1, No.1, Oct.1891 — Letter from Hardy to the editor of The Bookman. Originally published : in The Bookman, Vol.1, No.3, Dec. 1891 — The work of Thomas Hardy / by Professor Minto. Originally published : in The Bookman, Vol.1, No.3, Dec.1891
ISBN 0-85694-247-2 (unbound) : Unpriced
Primary classification 823'.8 B81-37075

823'.8 — Fiction in English. Hardy, Thomas, *1840-1928.* **Special themes: Women** — *Critical studies*

Boumelha, Penny. Thomas Hardy and women. — Brighton : Harvester Press, Dec.1981. — [208]p
ISBN 0-7108-0018-5 : £18.95 : CIP entry B81-31546

823'.8 — Fiction in English. Hardy, Thomas, *1840-1928.* **Tess of the d'Urbervilles** — *Study outlines*

Lindley, David. Tess of the d'Urbervilles : notes / by David Lindley. — London : Longman, 1980. — 88p ; 21cm. — (York notes ; 80)
Bibliography: p83
ISBN 0-582-78094-2 (pbk) : £0.90 B81-14655

823'.8 — Fiction in English. Hardy, Thomas, *1840-1928.* **Under the greenwood tree** — *Study outlines*

Karkalas, Ann. Under the greenwood tree : notes / by Ann Karkalas. — Harlow : Longman, 1981. — 72p : 1ill,1map ; 21cm. — (York notes ; 129)
Bibliography: p71-72
ISBN 0-582-78206-6 (pbk) : £0.90 B81-34235

823'.8 — Fiction in English. Hope, Anthony, *1863-1933.* **Prisoner of Zenda** — *Study outlines*

Munro, John M. (John Murchison). The prisoner of Zenda : notes / by John M. Munro and Leon Raikes. — London : Longman, 1980. — 64p ; 21cm. — (York notes ; 88)
Bibliography: p61
ISBN 0-582-78241-4 (pbk) : £0.90 B81-14585

823'.8 — Fiction in English. Kipling, Rudyard. Kim — *Study outlines*

Gillies, Valerie. Kim : notes / by Valerie Gillies. — Harlow : Longman, 1981. — 72p ; 21cm. — (York notes ; 114)
Bibliography: p67-68
ISBN 0-582-78117-5 (pbk) : £0.90 B81-19631

823'.8 — Fiction in English. Kipling, Rudyard. Puck of Pook's Hill. Special subjects: England, *100-400* — *Critical studies*

Rivet, A. L. F.. Rudyard Kipling's Roman Britain : fact and fiction : an inaugural lecture / by A.L.F. Rivet ; given in the University of Keele on Thursday 6th November 1976. — [Keele] : [University of Keele], [1978]. — 19p : 1ill ; 22cm
Unpriced (pbk) B81-06519

823'.8 — Fiction in English. Meredith, George, *1828-1909* — *Critical studies*

Shaheen, Mohammad. George Meredith : a reappraisal of the novels / Mohammad Shahen. — London : Macmillan, 1981. — ix,150p ; 23cm
Bibliography: p139-147. — Includes index
ISBN 0-333-24007-3 : £15.00 : CIP rev. B80-07492

823'.8 — Fiction in English. Phillpotts, Eden. Dartmoor cycle — *Critical studies*

Day, Kenneth F.. Eden Phillpotts on Dartmoor / Kenneth F. Day. — Newton Abbot : David & Charles, c1981. — 248p : ill,1map,2facsims,2ports ; 23cm
ISBN 0-7153-8118-0 : £6.95 B81-25340

823'.8 — Fiction in English. Steel, Flora Annie — *Biographies*

Powell, Violet. Flora Annie Steel : novelist of India / Violet Powell. — London : Heinemann, 1981. — 173p,[12]p of plates : ill,ports ; 23cm
Includes index
ISBN 0-434-59957-3 : £8.50 B81-15182

823'.8 — Fiction in English. Stevenson, Robert Louis. Dr. Jekyll and Mr. Hyde — *Study outlines*

Campbell, Ian, *1942-*. Dr Jekyll and Mr Hyde : notes / by Ian Campbell. — Harlow : Longman, 1981. — 64p ; 21cm. — (York notes ; 132)
ISBN 0-582-78157-4 (pbk) : £0.90 B81-33687

823'.8 — Fiction in English. Stevenson, Robert Louis. Kidnapped — *Study outlines*

Hannah, Donald. Kidnapped : notes / by Donald Hannah. — London : Longman, 1980. — 63p ; 21cm. — (York notes ; 90)
Bibliography: p63
ISBN 0-582-78121-3 (pbk) : £0.90 B81-14579

823'.8 — Fiction in English. Stevenson, Robert Louis. Treasure island — *Study outlines*

Jeffares, Bo. Robert Louis Stevenson Treasure Island / notes by Bo Jeffares. — London : Longman, 1980. — 85p ; 21cm. — (York notes ; 48)
Bibliography p81
ISBN 0-582-78105-1 (pbk) : £0.90 B81-08294

823'.8 — Fiction in English. Stoker, Bram. Local associations: North Yorkshire. Whitby

Stamp, Cordelia. Dracula discovered / Cordelia Stamp. — Whitby : Caedmon, 1981. — 13p,[6]p of plates : ill,1port ; 21cm. — (A Caedmon cameo)
ISBN 0-905355-21-0 (pbk) : £0.65 B81-24537

823'.8 — Fiction in English. Trollope, Anthony — *Critical studies*

Lansbury, Coral. The reasonable man : Trollope's legal fiction / Coral Lansbury. — Princeton ; Guildford : Princeton University Press, 1981. — xii,227p ; 23cm
Includes index
ISBN 0-691-06457-1 : £9.60 B81-32558

823'.8 — Fiction in English. Trollope, Anthony — *Critical studies, 1883-1978*

The **Trollope** critics / edited by N. John Hall. — London : Macmillan, 1981. — xxxix,248p ; 23cm
Bibliography: p226-242. — Includes index
ISBN 0-333-26298-0 : £15.00 : CIP rev. B80-11154

823'.8[F] — Fiction in English, *1837-1900* — *Texts*

Beerbohm, Max. Zuleika Dobson, or, An Oxford love story / Max Beerbohm. — Harmondsworth : Penguin in association with Heinemann, 1952 (1981 [printing]). — 251p ; 19cm. — (Penguin modern classics)
ISBN 0-14-000895-0 (pbk) : £1.50 B81-27224

Brontë, Anne. The tenant of Wildfell Hall / Anne Brontë ; with an introduction by Phyllis Bentley. — London : Granada, 1969 (1981 [printing]). — 398p ; 18cm. — (A Panther book)
ISBN 0-586-02657-6 (pbk) : £2.25 B81-37426

Brontë, Charlotte. Jane Eyre / by Charlotte Brontë. — 3rd ed. — Toronto ; London : Bantam, 1981. — xi,433p ; 18cm. — (Bantam classics)
ISBN 0-553-21020-3 (pbk) : £1.00 B81-39794

Brontë, Charlotte. Jane Eyre. — Large print ed. — Leicester : Ulverscroft, Sept.1981. — [752]p. — (Charnwood library series)
ISBN 0-7089-8015-5 : £6.50 : CIP entry B81-22664

Brontë, Charlotte. Shirley / Charlotte Brontë ; edited by Herbert Rosengarten and Margaret Smith. — Oxford : Oxford University Press, 1981, c1979. — xxxiv,684p ; 19cm. — (The World's classics)
ISBN 0-19-281562-8 (pbk) : £2.50 : CIP rev. B81-21608

Brontë, Emily. Wuthering Heights / Emily Brontë ; edited with an introduction by Ian Jack. — Oxford : Oxford University Press, 1981. — xxvii,370p : 1facsim,1geneal.table ; 20cm
ISBN 0-19-251026-6 : £4.50 B81-38501

Brontë, Emily. Wuthering Heights / Emily Brontë ; edited with an introduction by Ian Jack. — Oxford : Oxford University Press, 1981. — xxvii,370p : geneal.table ; 19cm. — (The World's classics)
ISBN 0-19-281543-1 (pbk) : £0.95 B81-24775

823'.8[F] — Fiction in English, *1837-1900* — Texts *continuation*

Collins, Wilkie. Basil / Wilkie Collins. — New York : Dover ; London : Constable, 1980. — viii,344p ; 21cm
ISBN 0-486-24015-0 (pbk) : £2.50 B81-05608

Dickens, Charles. Nicholas Nickleby / Charles Dickens ; introduction and notes by Arthur Calder-Marshall. — London : Pan, 1968 (1981 [printing]). — xxx,785p ; 18cm. — (A Pan classic)
ISBN 0-330-26424-9 (pbk) : £1.75 B81-05708

Dickens, Charles, *1812-1870*. A Christmas carol ; The Cricket on the hearth / Charles Dickens. — London : Octopus, 1981. — 199p : ill ; 22cm
ISBN 0-7064-1561-2 : £1.95 B81-17396

Dickens, Charles, *1812-1870*. Dombey and Son. — Oxford : Oxford University Press, Feb.1982. — [784]p. — (The World's classics)
ISBN 0-19-281565-2 (pbk) : £2.25 : CIP entry B81-36955

Dickens, Charles, *1812-1870*. Great expectations / Charles Dickens ; edited by Angus Calder. — Harmondsworth : Penguin, 1965 (1981 [printing]). -- 511p ; 19cm
ISBN 0-14-005934-2 (pbk) : £0.90 B81-40431

Dickens, Charles, *1812-1870*. Hard times / Charles Dickens ; new introduction by Philip Collins. — London : Dent, c1978 (1979 printing). — xxiv,268p ; 19cm. — (Everyman's library ; no.292)
Bibliography: pxviii-xx
ISBN 0-460-10292-3 : £4.50
ISBN 0-460-11292-9 (pbk) : Unpriced B81-10145

Dickens, Charles, *1812-1870*. The mystery of Edwin Drood / by Charles Dickens ; with illustrations. — [Canterbury] ([Canterbury, Kent]) : [Faculty of Humanities, University of Canterbury], [1980]. — 6v. : ill ; 22cm
Facsim. of: ed. issued in six parts: London : Chapman & Hall, Apr.-Sept.1870
£3.60 (pbk) B81-32812

Dickens, Charles, *1812-1870*. The mystery of Edwin Drood / Charles Dickens concluded by Leon Garfield ; illustrated by Antony Maitland ; with an introduction by Edward Blishen. — London : Deutsch, 1980. — xv,327p : ill ; 25cm
ISBN 0-233-97257-9 : £7.95 B81-01231

Dickens, Charles, *1812-1870*. Oliver Twist. — Oxford : Oxford University Press, Feb.1982. — [384]p. — (The World's classics)
ISBN 0-19-281591-1 (pbk) : £1.25 : CIP entry B81-35765

Dickens, Charles, *1812-1870*. Oliver Twist. — Large print ed. — Anstey : Ulverscroft, Jan.1982. — [696]p. — (Charnwood library series)
ISBN 0-7089-8019-8 : £6.50 : CIP entry B81-33992

Dickens, Charles, *1812-1870*. [Pickwick papers]. The posthumous papers of the Pickwick Club / Charles Dickens ; introduction by Christopher Hibbert ; drawings by Charles Keeping. — London : Folio Society, 1981. — xxvi,740p : ill ; 25cm
In a slip case
£15.50 B81-26485

Dickens, Charles, *1812-1870*. A tale of two cities / Charles Dickens ; introduction and notes by Ian Ousby. — London : Pan, 1980. — 383p ; 18cm. — (A Pan classic)
ISBN 0-330-26305-6 (pbk) : £1.25 B81-01232

Dickens, Charles, *1812-1870*. A tale of two cities / by Charles Dickens. — Toronto ; London : Bantam, 1981. — viii,352p ; 18cm. — (A Bantam classic)
ISBN 0-553-21017-3 (pbk) : £1.00 B81-39105

Eliot, George. The mill on the Floss / George Eliot ; edited and introduced by Gordon S. Haight. — Oxford : Oxford University Press, 1981, c1980. — xxii,528p ; 19cm. — (The World's classics)
Bibliography: pxix
ISBN 0-19-281567-9 (pbk) : £1.95 : CIP rev. B81-22555

Eliot, George. Silas Marner / George Eliot ; with an introduction by Michael Harrington ; and notes by James Gordon. — London : Pan, 1972 (1980 printing). — 204p ; 18cm. — (A Pan classic)
ISBN 0-330-23258-4 (pbk) : £0.80 B81-03610

Eliot, George. Silas Marner / George Eliot. — Large print ed. — Bath : Chivers, 1981. — 318p ; 23cm. — (A New Portway large print book)
ISBN 0-85119-114-2 : £5.25 : CIP rev. B81-04236

Gaskell, Elizabeth. North and south. — Oxford : Oxford University Press, Feb.1982. — [472]p. — (The World's classics)
ISBN 0-19-281595-4 (pbk) : £1.50 : CIP entry B81-35764

Gissing, George. Eve's ransom / George Gissing. — New York : Dover ; London : Constable, 1980. — 125p ; 22cm
ISBN 0-486-24016-9 (pbk) : £1.75 B81-16071

Gissing, George. The town traveller. — Brighton : Harvester Press, Sept.1981. — [336]p
ISBN 0-85527-902-8 : £7.50 : CIP entry B81-24622

Gissing, George. Will Warburton. — Brighton : Harvester Press, Nov.1981. — [384]p
ISBN 0-85527-882-x : £9.50 : CIP entry B81-30367

Grossmith, George. The diary of a nobody / George Grossmith and Weedon Grossmith ; with an introduction by Patrick Hanks ; illustrated by Weedon Grossmith. — London : Collins, 1955 (1981 [printing]). — 254p : ill ; 19cm
ISBN 0-00-424543-1 : £3.25 B81-37924

Hardy, Thomas, *1840-1928*. The mayor of Casterbridge / by Thomas Hardy. — Toronto ; London : Bantam, 1981. — 326p ; 18cm. — (A Bantam classic)
ISBN 0-553-21024-6 (pbk) : £1.00 B81-39107

Hardy, Thomas, *1840-1928*. The Mayor of Casterbridge. — Large print ed. — Anstey : Ulverscroft, Jan.1982. — [473]p. — (Charnwood library series)
ISBN 0-7089-8021-x : £5.25 : CIP entry B81-33991

Hardy, Thomas, *1840-1928*. The return of the native / by Thomas Hardy. — Toronto ; London : Bantam, 1981. — 371p ; 18cm. — (A bantam classic)
ISBN 0-553-21025-4 (pbk) : £1.00 B81-39106

Hardy, Thomas, *1840-1928*. The woodlanders / Thomas Hardy ; introduced by Ian Gregor ; and edited by James Gibson. — Harmondsworth : Penguin, 1981. — 463p ; 18cm. — (Penguin English library)
ISBN 0-14-043145-4 (pbk) : £1.25 B81-10994

Jefferies, Richard. After London, or, Wild England : in two parts : I. The relapse into barbarism : II. Wild England / Richard Jeffries ; with an introduction by John Fowles. — Oxford : Oxford University Press, 1980. — xxi,248p ; 19cm. — (The Worlds classics)
ISBN 0-19-281266-1 (pbk) : £1.50 B79-15600

Jefferies, Richard. Bevis the story of a boy / Richard Jefferies ; introduction by Henry Williamson. — London : Dent, 1981. — 430p : 1map ; 19cm. — (Everyman's library ; 850)
Originally published in 3 vols: London : Sampson Low & Co., 1882
ISBN 0-460-01850-7 : Unpriced
ISBN 0-460-01850-7 (pbk) : £2.75 B81-13129

Jefferies, Richard. The dewy morn. — London : Wildwood House, Jan.1982. — [416]p. — (Rediscovery)
Originally published: London : Bentley, 1884
ISBN 0-7045-0461-8 (pbk) : £3.50 : CIP entry B81-37546

Jerome, Jerome K.. Three men on the bummel. — Large print ed. — Bath : Chivers, Oct.1981. — [320]p. — (A New Portway large print book)
ISBN 0-85119-138-x : £5.50 : CIP entry B81-25801

Kipling, Rudyard. Proofs of holy writ / by Rudyard Kipling ; with an introduction by Philip Mason. — Edinburgh : Tragara, 1981. — xi,20p ; 24cm
Limited ed. of 125 numbered copies
ISBN 0-902616-70-6 (pbk) : £9.00 B81-32790

Le Fanu, Sheridan. Uncle Silas / Sheridan Le Fanu ; edited and with an introduction and notes by W.J. McCormack assisted by Andrew Swarbrick. — Oxford : Oxford University Press, 1981. — xxviii,433p ; 19cm
Bibliography: pxxi-xxii
ISBN 0-19-281541-5 (pbk) : £2.95 : CIP rev. B81-21607

Mason, A. E. W.. The dean's elbow / A.E.W. Mason. — London : Remploy, 1979. — 312p ; 19cm
ISBN 0-7066-0818-6 : £4.30 B81-34853

Moore, George, *1852-1933*. A drama in muslin : a realistic novel / by George Moore ; with an introduction by A. Norman Jeffares. — Gerrards Cross : Smythe, 1981. — xv,329p ; 23cm
ISBN 0-86140-055-0 : Unpriced : CIP rev.
ISBN 0-86140-056-9 (pbk) : Unpriced B80-17944

Moore, George, *1852-1933*. The Lake / by George Moore ; with an afterword by Richard Allen Cave. — Gerrards Cross : Smythe, 1980. — xi,274p ; 22cm
ISBN 0-900675-75-6 (cased) : £9.50 : CIP rev.
ISBN 0-901072-82-6 (pbk) : £3.25 B80-12523

Morris, William, *1834-1896*. The wood beyond the world / by William Morris ; introducation by Tom Shippey. — Oxford : Oxford University Press, 1980. — xix,168p : 1ill ; 20cm
ISBN 0-19-281301-3 (pbk) : £1.95 : CIP rev. B80-07038

Scott, *Sir* **Walter**. Kenilworth. — Large print ed. — Anstey : Ulverscroft, Feb.1982. — [746]p. — (Charnwood library series)
ISBN 0-7089-8028-7 : £6.50 : CIP entry B81-36960

Shiel, M. P.. The lord of the sea / M.P. Shiel. — London : Souvenir, 1981. — 320p ; 21cm. — (Nightowl books)
ISBN 0-285-62482-2 : £6.95 B81-07402

Stevenson, Robert Louis. Catriona : a sequel to Kidnapped : being memoirs of the further adventures of David Balfour at home and abroad... / by Robert Louis Stevenson. — Centenary ed. / with an introduction by Jenni Calder. — Edinburgh : W & R Chambers, 1980. — xxv,265p ; 23cm. — (The Works of Robert Louis Stevenson)
ISBN 0-550-20452-0 : £6.95 B81-02421

Stevenson, Robert Louis. Kidnapped : being memoirs of the adventures of David Balfour in the year 1751 ... / by Robert Louis Stevenson. — Chambers centenary ed. / with an introduction by Jenni Calder. — Ediburgh : Chambers, 1980. — xxiv,211p : 1map ; 23cm. — (The Works of Robert Louis Stevenson)
ISBN 0-550-20451-2 : £6.95 B81-07709

823'.8[F] — Fiction in English, *1837-1900 — Texts continuation*

Surtees, Robert Smith. Mr. Sponge's sporting tour. — Craddock (Craddock Cleve, Craddock, Cullompton, Devon EX15 3LW) : R.S. Surtees Society, Sept.1981. — [432]p
Facsim. of: 1st ed. London : Bradbury and Evans, 1854
ISBN 0-9507697-0-3 : £12.95 : CIP entry
B81-28715

Trollope, Anthony. Doctor Thorne / Anthony Trollope ; with an introduction and notes by David Skilton. — Oxford : Oxford University Press, 1980. — xxii,639p : 1map ; 19cm. — (The world's classics)
ISBN 0-19-281508-3 (pbk) : £2.50 : CIP rev.
B80-13531

Trollope, Anthony. Doctor Thorne / Anthony Trollope ; with an introduction and notes by David Skilton. — Oxford : Oxford University Press, 1981, c1980. — xxii,639p : 1map ; 20cm. — (Oxford classics)
ISBN 0-19-251025-8 : £6.00 B81-38500

Trollope, Anthony. Framley Parsonage / Anthony Trollope ; with an introduction and notes by P.D. Edwards. — Oxford : Oxford University Press, 1926 (1980 [printing]). — xxvii,592p : 1map ; 19cm. — (The World's classics)
ISBN 0-19-281545-8 (pbk) : £2.50 : CIP rev.
B80-18884

Trollope, Anthony. The last chronicle of Barset / Anthony Trollope ; edited by Stephen Gill. — Oxford : Oxford University Press, 1932 (1980 [printing]). — xxiii,900p : 1map ; 19cm. — (The world's classics)
ISBN 0-19-281544-x (pbk) : £2.95 : CIP rev.
B80-13532

Trollope, Anthony. The last chronicle of Barset / Anthony Trollope ; introduction by Kathleen Tillotson. — London : Dent, 1978. — xv,389p ; 19cm. — (Everyman's library ; no.391)
ISBN 0-460-00391-7 : £7.50 B81-11412

Trollope, Anthony. The last chronicle of Barset / Anthony Trollope ; introduction by Julian Symons ; drawings by Peter Reddick. — London : Folio Society, 1980. — 772p : ill,maps ; 23cm
Maps on lining papers. - In a slip cased
£14.92 B81-07951

Trollope, Anthony. The last chronicle of Barset / Anthony Trollope ; edited by Stephen Gill. — Oxford : Oxford University Press, 1981, c1980. — xxiii,900p : 1map ; 20cm
ISBN 0-19-251029-0 : £7.00 B81-38497

Trollope, Anthony. Rachel Ray / by Anthony Trollope. — New York : Dover ; London : Constable, 1980. — vi,391p ; 22cm
ISBN 0-486-23930-6 (pbk) : £3.15 B81-05248

Trollope, Anthony. The Small House at Allington / Anthony Trollope ; edited by James R. Kincaid. — Oxford : Oxford University Press, 1981, c1980. — 674p ; 20cm. — (Oxford classics)
ISBN 0-19-251030-4 : £6.00 B81-38499

Trollope, Anthony. The three clerks / by Anthony Trollope. — New York : Dover ; London : Constable, 1981. — 497p ; 22cm
ISBN 0-486-24099-1 (pbk) : £4.15 B81-37895

Trollope, Anthony. The warden / Anthony Trollope ; with an introduction and notes by David Skilton ; illustrations by Edward Ardizzone. — Oxford : Oxford University Press, 1980 (1981 [printing]). — xxii,274p : ill,1map ; 20cm
ISBN 0-19-251005-3 : £3.50 B81-39850

Trollope, Anthony. The way we live now. — Oxford : Oxford University Press, Feb.1982. — [1000]p. — (The World's classics)
ISBN 0-19-281576-8 (pbk) : £2.95 : CIP entry
B81-35768

Wilde, Oscar. The picture of Dorian Gray / Oscar Wilde ; edited with an introduction by Isobel Murray. — Oxford : Oxford University Press, 1981. — 236p ; 19cm. — (The World's classics)
ISBN 0-19-281553-9 (pbk) : £1.25 : CIP rev.
B81-04300

823'.8[F] — Short stories in English, *1837-1900 — Texts*

Allen, Grant. An African millionaire : episodes in the life of the illustrious Colonel Clay / Grant Allen ; with an introduction by Norman Donaldson. — New York : Dover ; London : Constable, 1980. — xviii,317p : ill ; 22cm
ISBN 0-486-23992-6 (pbk) : £2.50 B81-20044

Gaskell, Elizabeth. Cousin Phillis and other tales / Elizabeth Gaskell ; edited with an introduction and notes by Angus Easson. — Oxford : Oxford University Press, 1981. — xix,364p ; 19cm. — (The World's classics)
Bibliography: pxv-xvi
ISBN 0-19-281554-7 (pbk) : £2.95 : CIP rev.
B81-21623

Graham, R. B. Cunninghame. Tales of horsemen / R.B. Cunninghame Graham ; edited and illustrated by Alexander Maotland. — Edinburgh : Canongate, 1981. — 137p : ill ; 23cm
ISBN 0-903937-92-1 : £5.95 B81-24545

Haggard, H. Rider. The best short stories of Rider Haggard / edited and introduced by Peter Haining ; foreword by Hammond Innes. — London : Joseph, 1981. — 254p ; 23cm
ISBN 0-7181-2010-8 : £7.50 B81-34632

Munro, Neil. Para handy tales / Neil Munro ('Hugh Foulis'). — London : Pan, 1969 (1981 printing). — 380p ; 18cm
Originally published: London : Blackwood, 1955
ISBN 0-330-02277-6 (pbk) : £1.50 B81-34266

Power, Victor O'D.. Some strange experiences of Kitty the Hare : the famous travelling woman of Ireland / Victor O'D. Power. — Dublin : Mercier Press, c1981. — 104p ; 19cm
ISBN 0-85342-661-9 (pbk) : Unpriced
B81-34876

Trollope, Anthony. The two heroines of Plumplington and other stories / Anthony Trollope ; introduction by Julian Symons ; drawings by Peter Reddick. — London : Folio Society, 1981. — 276p : ill ; 23cm
In slip case
Unpriced B81-32075

Yeats, W. B.. The secret rose : stories by W.B. Yeats : a variorum edition / edited by Phillip L. Marcus, Warwick Gould and Michael J. Sidnell. — Ithaca ; London : Cornell University Press, 1981. — xxxiv,271p ; 24cm
Bibliography: p265-271
ISBN 0-8014-1194-7 : £15.00 B81-34850

823'.8[J] — Children's short stories in English, *1837-1900 — Texts*

Grahame, Kenneth. The golden age / Kenneth Grahame ; with illustrations and decorations by Ernest H. Shepard ; and a foreword by Naomi Lewis. — London (27 Goodge St., W1P 1FD) : Robin Clark, 1928 (1980 [printing]). — 143p : ill ; 20cm
ISBN 0-86072-046-2 (pbk) : £1.95 B81-03917

Nesbit, E.. The magic world / by E. Nesbit ; with illustrations by H.R. Millar and Spencer Pryse. — London : Macmillan, 1980. — viii,280p,[23]p of plates ; 20cm
Facsim. of: edition published London : Macmillan, 1912
ISBN 0-333-30783-6 : £3.95 B81-02904

823'.8[J] — Children's stories in English, *1837-1900 — Texts*

Ardizzone's English fairy tales : twelve classic tales / selected and illustrated by Edward Ardizzone ; from the collection of Joseph Jacobs. — London : Deutsch, 1980. — 78p : ill ; 25cm
ISBN 0-233-97306-0 : £3.95 B81-28392

Barrie, J. M.. Peter Pan. — London : Hodder & Stoughton, Sept.1981. — [192]p
ISBN 0-340-26430-6 : £7.95 : CIP entry
B81-23924

Carroll, Lewis. Alice's adventures in Wonderland / by Lewis Carroll ; with forty-two illustrations by John Tenniel. — New children's ed. — London : Macmillan Children's Books, 1980. — xi,179p,[8]leaves of plates : ill(some col.) ; 21cm
Previous ed.: 1927
ISBN 0-333-29038-0 : £4.95 B81-13107

Carroll, Lewis. Through the looking glass : and what Alice found there / Lewis Carroll ; with fifty illustrations by John Tenniel. — London : Octopus, 1981. — 216p : ill ; 22cm
ISBN 0-7064-1558-2 : £1.90 B81-17398

Crane, Walter. Flora's feast : a masque of flowers / penned & pictured by Walter Crane. — [Leicester] : Windward, 1980. — 40p : chiefly col.ill ; 26cm
Facsim of: edition published London : Cassell, 1889
ISBN 0-7112-0102-1 : £3.95 B81-01233

Dickens, Charles, *1812-1870*. Captain Boldheart : (Holiday romance, Part III from the pen of Col. Robert Redforth, aged nine) / by Charles Dickens ; illustrated by Philippe Dumas. — London : Dent, 1980. — 40p : col.ill ; 26cm
ISBN 0-460-06751-6 : £3.95 B81-03543

Grahame, Kenneth. The wind in the willows. — Large print ed. — Leicester : Ulverscroft, Sept.1981. — [260]p. — (Charnwood library series)
ISBN 0-7089-8007-4 : £4.50 : CIP entry
B81-22662

Grahame, Kenneth. [The wind in the willows. Selections]. The river bank : from The wind in the willows / Kenneth Grahame ; illustrated by Adrienne Adams. — London : Magnet, 1981. — [32]p : col.ill ; 19cm
Originally published: London : Methuen, 1978
ISBN 0-416-24270-7 (pbk) : £1.10 B81-12479

Hardy, Thomas, *1840-1928*. Our exploits at West Poley / Thomas Hardy ; illustrated by John Lawrence ; with an introduction by Richard L. Purdy. — Oxford : Oxford University Press, 1952 (1981 [printing]). — x,77p : ill ; 20cm. — (Oxford paperbacks)
ISBN 0-19-281323-4 (pbk) : £1.25 : CIP rev.
B81-02553

Kingsley, Charles. The water babies. — London : Hodder and Stoughton Children's Books, Oct.1981. — [256]p
ISBN 0-340-27458-1 (cased) : £10.95 : CIP entry
ISBN 0-340-27465-4 (limited ed.) : £30.00
B81-30252

Nister, Ernest. Animal tales : a reproduction from an antique book / by Ernest Nister. — London : Ernest Benn, 1981, c1980. — [10]p : ill(some col.) ; 24x30cm
Originally published: New York : Collins, 1980
ISBN 0-510-00121-1 : £3.95 B81-35276

Wilde, Oscar. The happy prince : a fairy tale / by Oscar Wilde ; illustrated by Joanna Isles. — [Slightly abridged ed.]. — London : Evans, 1981. — [28]p : col.ill ; 29cm
Col.ill on lining papers
ISBN 0-237-45528-5 : £3.95 : CIP rev.
B81-20119

Wilde, Oscar. The nightingale and the rose / Oscar Wilde ; illustrated by Freire Wright and Michael Foreman. — London : Kaye & Ward, 1981. — [32]p : col.ill ; 22x27cm
ISBN 0-7182-1259-2 : £3.75 B81-32871

823'.8'09 — Fiction in English, *1837-1900 — Critical studies*

Carlisle, Janice. The sense of an audience. — Brighton : Harvester Press, Oct.1981. — [256]p
ISBN 0-7108-0338-9 : £18.95 : CIP entry
B81-28072

823'.8'09 — Fiction in English, *1837-1900 — Critical studies* *continuation*

David, Deirdre. Fictions of resolution in three Victorian novels : North and South, Our mutual friend, Daniel Deronda / Deirdre David. — London : Macmillan, 1981. — xii,209p ; 23cm
Includes index
ISBN 0-333-28732-0 : £15.00
Also classified at 823'.8 ; 823'.8 ; 823'.8
B81-19714

823'.8'09 — Fiction in English, *1837-1980.* **Socialist writers** *— Critical studies*

The **Socialist** novel in Britain. — Brighton : Harvester, Nov.1981. — [224]p
ISBN 0-7108-0340-0 : £18.95 : CIP entry
B81-30603

823'.8'09 — Fiction in English. Brontë *(Family) — Biographies*

Lane, Margaret, *1907-.* The drug-like Brontë dream / Margaret Lane ; illustrated by Joan Hassall. — London : Murray, 1980. — 100p : ill ; 23cm
Ill on lining papers
ISBN 0-7195-3768-1 : £6.50 B81-03560

823'.8'09 — Fiction in English. Brontë *(Family) — Biographies — Readings from contemporary sources*

The **Brontës** : their lives recorded by their contemporaries / compiled with an introduction by E.M. Delafield. — Stroud (Mount Vernon, Rodborough, Stroud, Gloucester GL5 2LP) : Ian Hodgkins, 1979. — 274p : ports ; 23cm
Originally published: London : Leonard & Virginia Woolf, 1935
ISBN 0-906460-03-4 : £9.75 : CIP rev.
B79-31356

823'.8'09 — Fiction in English. Brontë *(Family).* **Local associations**

Bainbridge, Cyril. The Brontës and their country / by Cyril Bainbridge. — East Bergholt (East Bergholt, Sussex) : Hugh Tempest Radford, 1978. — 46p : ill,2maps,ports,1geneal.table ; 21cm
Bibliography: p45-46
ISBN 0-906290-01-5 (pbk) : Unpriced
B81-09587

823'.8'09145 — Fiction in English, *1837-1900.* **Romanticism** *— Critical studies*

Stone, Donald D.. The romantic impulse in Victorian fiction / Donald D. Stone. — Cambridge, Mass. ; London : Harvard University Press, 1980. — viii,396p ; 25cm
Includes index
ISBN 0-674-77932-0 : £10.50 B81-03553

823'.8'0916 — Sensation fiction in English, *1837-1900 — Critical studies*

Hughes, Winifred. The maniac in the cellar : sensation novels of the 1860s / Winifred Hughes. — Princeton ; Guildford : Princeton University Press, c1980. — x,211p ; 23cm
Includes index
ISBN 0-691-06441-5 : £8.40 B81-11795

823'.8'0917 — Fiction in English. Comedy, *1800-1945 — Critical studies*

Polhemus, Robert M.. Comic faith : the great tradition from Austen to Joyce / Robert M. Polhemus. — Chicago ; London : University of Chicago Press, 1980. — x,398p ; 24cm
Bibliography: p359-391. — Includes index
ISBN 0-226-67320-0 : £15.00 B81-06544

823'.8'093242 — Fiction in English, *1837-1900.* **Special subjects: England. Working classes. Social conditions** *— Critical studies*

Smith, Sheila M.. The other nation : the poor in English novels of the 1840s and 1850s / Sheila M. Smith. — Oxford : Clarendon, 1980. — xvi,282p,[24]p of plates : ill,facsims,ports ; 23cm
Bibliography: p270-273. - Includes index
ISBN 0-19-812642-5 : £12.00 : CIP rev.
B80-07041

823'.8'09352042 — Fiction in English, *1837-1945.* **Special themes: Great Britain. Society. Role of women** *— Critical studies*

Stubbs, Patricia. Women and fiction : feminism and the novel 1880-1920 / Patricia Stubbs. — London : Methuen, 1981, c1979. — xvi,263p ; 22cm
Originally published: Brighton : Harvester, 1979. — Bibliography: p249-257. — Includes index
ISBN 0-416-30640-3 (pbk) : £4.95 B81-21326

823'.8'093520621 — Fiction in English, *1837-1900.* **Special themes: England. Gentlemen. Social values** *— Critical studies*

Gilmour, Robin, *1943-.* The idea of the gentleman in the Victorian novel / Robin Gilmour. — London : Allen & Unwin, 1981. — 190p ; 23cm
Bibliography: p185. — Includes index
ISBN 0-04-800005-1 : Unpriced : CIP rev.
B81-28788

823'.8'09353 — Fiction in English. Women writers, *1837-1977.* **Special themes: Interrelationships of insanity & femininity** *— Critical studies*

Rigney, Barbara Hill. Madness and sexual politics in the feminist novel. Studies in Brontë, Woolf, Lessing and Atwood / Barbara Hill Rigney. — Madison ; London : University of Wisconsin Press, 1978 (1980 printing). — 148p ; 22cm
Bibliography: p137-141. - Includes index
ISBN 0-299-07714-4 (corrected : pbk) : £3.55
B81-11766

823'.8'0936 — Fiction in English, *1837-1945.* **Special subjects: Nature** *— Critical studies*

Ebbatson, Roger. Lawrence and the nature tradition : a theme in English fiction 1859-1914 / Roger Ebbatson. — Brighton : Harvester, 1980. — xiii,271p ; 23cm
Includes index
ISBN 0-85527-343-7 : £20.00 : CIP rev.
B80-07955

823'.8'099282 — Children's stories in English, *1837-1900.* **Social aspects**

Bratton, J. S.. The impact of Victorian children's fiction / J.S. Bratton. — London : Croom Helm, c1981. — 230p ; 23cm
Bibliography: p218-222. — Includes index
ISBN 0-85664-777-2 : £11.95 : CIP rev.
B81-10011

823.91 — ENGLISH FICTION, 1900-

823'.9'1[F] — Fiction in English, 1900- *Texts*

Koestler, Arthur. Bricks to Babel : selected writings with comments by the author / Arthur Koestler. — London : Hutchinson, 1980. — 697p : ill ; 25cm
Bibliography: p687-688. — Includes index
ISBN 0-09-143670-2 : £12.50 : CIP rev.
Primary classification 192 B80-22862

823.912 — ENGLISH FICTION, 1900-1945

823'.912 — Children's stories in English, *1900-1945 — Latin texts*

Milne, A. A.. [The house at Pooh Corner. Latin]. Domus Anguli Puensis / A.A. Milnei ; librum exornavit E.H. Shepard ; liber alter de Urso Puo de anglico sermone in Latinum conversus auctore Briano Staplesio. — Londinii : Sumptibus Methueni, 1980. — 159p : ill ; 20cm
Translation of: The house at Pooh Corner
ISBN 0-416-88550-0 : £3.95 : CIP rev.
B80-09500

823'.912 — Children's stories in English. Potter, Beatrix. Organisations: Beatrix Potter Society *— Serials*

[Newsletter *(Beatrix Potter Society)*]. Newsletter / the Beatrix Potter Society. — No.1 (Nov. 1980)-. — Teddington (c/3 Ms A. Clarke, The Dell's House, 110 Kingston Rd, Teddington, Middx.) : The Society, 1980-. — v. ; 21cm
Quarterly
ISSN 0260-3780 = Newsletter — Beatrix Potter Society : Unpriced B81-07313

823'.912 — Children's stories in English. Potter, Beatrix *— Personal observations*

Parker, Ulla Hyde, *Lady.* Cousin Beatie : a memory of Beatrix Potter / by Ulla Hyde Parker. — London : Warne, 1981. — 40p : ill (some col.),facsims,ports,1geneal.table ; 20cm
Geneal. table on lining papers
ISBN 0-7232-2793-4 : £3.50 B81-32970

823'.912 — Children's stories in English. Potter, Beatrix, *to 1913 — Biographies*

Lane, Margaret, *1907-.* The magic years of Beatrix Potter / by Margaret Lane. — London : Fontana, 1980, c1978. — 216p : ill(some col.),facsims,ports ; 25cm
Originally published: London : Warne, 1978. — Bibliography: p211-212. — Includes index
ISBN 0-00-635990-6 (pbk) : £5.95 B81-01630

823'.912 — Fiction in English, *1900-1945 — Texts — Manuscripts — Facsimiles*

Joyce, James, *1882-1941.* The James Joyce archive / general editor Michael Groden ; associate editors ... [others]. — [New York] ; [London] : Garland
[Ulysses] : [notes & 'Telemachus' - 'Scylla and Charybdis'] : [a facsimile of notes for the book & manuscripts & typescripts for episodes 1-9] / [prefaced & arranged by Michael Groden]. — 1978. — xxx,374p : chiefly facsims(some col.) ; 32cm
Bibliography: pxx-xxiii
ISBN 0-8240-2822-8 : Unpriced B81-27255

823'.912 — Fiction in English, *1900-1945 — Texts with commentaries — For schools*

Conrad, Joseph. Lord Jim. — London : Macmillan Education, Jan.1982. — [336]p. — (Macmillan students' novels)
ISBN 0-333-32129-4 (pbk) : £0.95 : CIP entry
B81-34144

823'.912 — Fiction in English. Bagnold, Enid *— Correspondence, diaries, etc*

Bagnold, Enid. Letters to Frank Harris, & other friends / Enid Bagnold ; edited & with an introduction by R.P. Lister. — Andoversford : Whittington Press & Heinemann, c1980. — xxv,77p : facsim,ports(some col.) ; 26cm
Facsim. on lining papers. — Limited ed. of 440 numbered copies, of which the first 30 are bound in Nigerian goatskin and the remainder in cloth. — In slip case
£35.00 B81-28426

823'.912 — Fiction in English. Bennett, Arnold *— Biographies*

Roberts, Thomas R.. Arnold Bennett's Five Towns origins / by Thomas R. Roberts. — [Stoke-on-Trent] ([Bethesda St., Hanley, Stoke-on-Trent, ST1 4HS]) : Libraries, Museums and Information Committee, City of Stoke-on-Trent Museum and Art Gallery, [1981?]. — 15p ; 22cm
Cover title
£0.20 (pbk) B81-37523

823'.912 — Fiction in English. Bennett, Arnold *— Critical studies*

Arnold Bennett : the critical heritage / edited by James Hepburn. — London : Routledge & Kegan Paul, 1981. — xx,554p ; 23cm. — (The Critical heritage series)
Bibliography: p530-534. — Includes index
ISBN 0-7100-0512-1 : £18.50 B81-07059

823'.912 — Fiction in English. Bowen, Elizabeth *— Critical studies*

Lee, Hermione. Elizabeth Bowen : an estimation / Hermione Lee. — London : Vision, c1981. — 255p ; 23cm. — (Critical studies series)
Bibliography: p245-251. — Includes index
ISBN 0-85478-344-x : £12.95 B81-33381

823'.912 — Fiction in English. Buchan, John, *1875-1940 — Critical studies — Serials*

The **John** Buchan journal. — Vol.1, no.1 (Spring 1980)-. — Edinburgh (c/o R.J. Angus [12 Torphin Rd, Edinburgh EH13 0HW]) : John Buchan Society, 1980-. — v. ; 21cm
Two issues yearly
ISSN 0260-3225 = John Buchan journal : Free to Society members B81-04752

823'.912 — Fiction in English. Buchan, John, *1875-1940.* **Thirty-nine steps** — *Study outlines*

Gray, Martin, *1945-*. The Thirty-nine steps : notes / by Martin Gray. — London : Longman, 1980. — 64p ; 21cm. — (York notes ; 89)
Bibliography: p55-56
ISBN 0-582-78244-9 (pbk) : £0.90 B81-14575

823'.912 — Fiction in English. Cartland, Barbara — *Biographies*

Cloud, Henry. Barbara Cartland : crusader in pink / Henry Cloud. — London : Pan, 1981, c1979. — 175p,[4]p of plates : ports ; 18cm
Originally published: London : Weidenfeld & Nicolson, 1979. — Includes index
ISBN 0-330-26407-9 (pbk) : £1.50 B81-39009

Cloud, Henry. [Barbara Cartland]. Crusader in pink / by Henry Cloud. — Long Preston : Magna, 1981, c1979. — 305p ; 23cm
Originally published: London : Weidenfeld and Nicolson, 1979. — Published in large print
ISBN 0-86009-361-1 : £4.95 : CIP rev.
B81-23738

823'.912 — Fiction in English. Cary, Joyce. Political ideologies: Liberalism

Cook, Cornelia. Joyce Cary : liberal principles / by Cornelia Cook. — London : Vision, 1981. — 242p ; 23cm. — (Critical studies series)
Bibliography: p235-240. — Includes index
ISBN 0-85478-414-4 : £12.95 B81-26048

823'.912 — Fiction in English. Christie, Agatha — *Biographies*

Gregg, Hubert. Agatha Christie and all that mousetrap / Hubert Gregg. — London : Kimber, 1980. — 170p,[16]p of plates : ill,facsims,ports, ; 25cm
Includes index
ISBN 0-7183-0427-6 : £8.50 B81-12632

823'.912 — Fiction in English. Conrad, Joseph, *1909-1924* — *Childhood reminiscences*

Conrad, John. Joseph Conrad : times remembered, 'Ojciec jest tutaj' / John Conrad. — Cambridge : Cambridge University Press, 1981. — xiv,218p : ill,ports ; 24cm
ISBN 0-521-22805-0 : £10.50 : CIP rev.
B81-01234

823'.912 — Fiction in English. Conrad, Joseph — *Critical studies*

Bonney, William W.. Thorns & arabesques : contexts for Conrad's fiction / William W. Bonney. — Baltimore ; London : Johns Hopkins University Press, 1980. — xii,244p ; 24cm
Includes index
ISBN 0-8018-2345-5 : £10.00 B81-00378

Watts, Cedric. A preface to Conrad. — London : Longman, Feb.1982. — [208]p. — (Preface books)
ISBN 0-582-35273-8 (cased) : £5.25 : CIP entry
ISBN 0-582-35274-6 (pbk) : £3.25 B81-36979

823'.912 — Fiction in English. Conrad, Joseph. Heart of darkness, Nostromo & Under western eyes — *Critical studies*

Heart of darkness, Nostromo and Under western eyes : a casebook / edited by C.B. Cox. — London : Macmillan, 1981. — 224p ; 23cm. — (Casebook series)
Bibliography: p218. — Includes index
ISBN 0-333-26823-7 (cased) : £12.00 : CIP rev.
ISBN 0-333-26824-5 (pbk) : Unpriced
B80-21142

823'.912 — Fiction in English. Conrad, Joseph. Youth & Typhoon — *Study outlines*

Spear, Hilda D.. Youth and typhoon : notes / by Hilda D. Spear. — London : Longman, 1980. — 64p ; 21cm. — (York notes ; 100)
ISBN 0-582-78199-x (pbk) : £0.90 B81-19661

823'.912 — Fiction in English. Doyle, *Sir* **Arthur Conan. Characters: Sherlock Holmes. Higher education**

Utechin, Nicholas. Sherlock Holmes at Oxford. — 2nd ed. — Oxford (Corpus Christi College, Oxford OX1 4JF) : Robert Dugdale, July 1981. — [32]p
Previous ed.: 1977
ISBN 0-9503880-8-4 (pbk) : £1.25 : CIP entry
B81-23894

823'.912 — Fiction in English. Doyle, *Sir Arthur Conan. Hound of the Baskervilles — Study outlines*

Brown, Terence. The hound of the Baskervilles : notes / by Terence Brown. — London : Longman, 1980. — 69p ; 21cm. — (York notes ; 53)
Bibliography: p65
ISBN 0-582-78128-0 (pbk) : £0.90 B81-07100

823'.912 — Fiction in English. Doyle, *Sir Arthur Conan. Sherlock Holmes stories — Critical studies*

A **Sherlock** Holmes compendium / edited by Peter Haining. — London : W.H. Allen, 1980. — 216p : ill,facsims,forms,maps,ports ; 24cm
ISBN 0-491-02843-1 : £8.95 B81-02861

823'.912 — Fiction in English. Ford, Ford Madox. Special themes: Politics — *Critical studies*

Green, Robert, *1940-*. Ford Madox Ford : prose and politics / Robert Green. — Cambridge : Cambridge University Press, 1981. — xv,218p ; 23cm
Bibliography: p204-214. — Includes index
ISBN 0-521-23610-x : £16.50 B81-29350

823'.912 — Fiction in English. Forster, E. M. — *Critical studies*

Trilling, Lionel. E.M. Forster. — Oxford : Oxford University Press, Jan.1982. — [162]p. — (The works of Lionel Trilling)
Originally published: London : Hogarth Press, 1967
ISBN 0-19-212227-4 : £7.95 : CIP entry
B81-34375

823'.912 — Fiction in English. Forster, E. M.. Howard's End & Where angels fear to tread — *Study outlines*

Schlesinger, G.. Notes on E.M. Forster's Where angels fear to tread and Howard's End / compiled by G. Schlesinger. — London : Methuen, 1981, c1980. — 72p ; 20cm. — (Methuen notes)
ISBN 0-417-21710-2 (pbk) : £0.95 B81-07855

823'.912 — Fiction in English. Greene, Graham — *Biographies*

Greene, Graham. A sort of life / Graham Greene. — Harmondsworth : Penguin, 1974, c1971 (1981 [printing]). — 156p ; 19cm
Originally published: London : Bodley Head, 1971
ISBN 0-14-003495-1 (pbk) : £1.25 B81-37209

Greene, Graham. A sort of life. — Large print ed. — Bath : Chivers, Nov.1981. — [256]p. — (A New Portway large print book)
Originally published: London : Bodley Head, 1971
ISBN 0-85119-143-6 : £4.95 : CIP entry
B81-31255

Greene, Graham. Ways of escape / Graham Greene. — London : Bodley Head, 1980. — 308p ; 21cm
ISBN 0-370-30356-3 : £6.95 : CIP rev.
B80-20005

823'.912 — Fiction in English. Hall, Radclyffe — *Critical studies*

Franks, Claudia Stillman. Radclyffe Hall : beyond The well of loneliness. — Amersham : Avebury Publishing, Dec.1981. — [160]p
ISBN 0-86127-210-2 (cased) : £10.95 : CIP entry
ISBN 0-86127-221-8 (pbk) : £6.95 B81-32600

823'.912 — Fiction in English. Holtby, Winifred — *Biographies*

Brittain, Vera. Testament of friendship : the story of Winifred Holtby / Vera Brittain ; afterword by Rosalind Delmar. — London : Fontana in association with Virago, 1981, c1940. — 453p ; 18cm
Originally published: London : Macmillan, 1940
ISBN 0-00-636353-9 (pbk) : £2.50 B81-38286

823'.912 — Fiction in English. Joyce, James, *1882-1941* — *Critical studies*

Bolt, Sydney. A preface to James Joyce / Sydney Bolt. — London : Longman, 1981. — xiii,202p : ill,1map,1facsim,ports ; 22cm. — (Preface books)
Bibliography: p195-198. — Includes index
ISBN 0-582-35194-4 (cased) : Unpriced : CIP rev.
ISBN 0-582-35195-2 (pbk) : £3.95 B80-00441

Cope, Jackson I.. Joyce's cities : archaeologies of the soul / Jackson I. Cope. — Baltimore ; London : Johns Hopkins University Press, c1981. — xii,144p ; 24cm
Includes index
ISBN 0-8018-2543-1 : £7.75 B81-37459

A **starchamber** quiry : a James Joyce centennial volume, 1882-1982. — London : Methuen, Feb.1982. — [200]p
ISBN 0-416-31560-7 : £9.00 : CIP entry
B81-35715

823'.912 — Fiction in English. Joyce, James, *1882-1941 — Critical studies — Serials*

James Joyce broadsheet. — No.1 (Jan. 1980)-. — London (University College, Gower St., WC1E 6BT) : James joyce Centre, 1980-. — v. : ill ; 42cm
Three issues yearly
ISSN 0143-6333 = James Joyce broadsheet : £3.00 per year B81-02002

823'.912 — Fiction in English. Joyce, James, *1882-1941.* **Dubliners & Portrait of the artist as a young man** — *Critical studies*

Bidwell, Bruce. The Joycean way. — Dublin : Wolfhound Press, Sept.1981. — [160]p
ISBN 0-905473-39-6 : £8.00 : CIP entry
B81-23795

823'.912 — Fiction in English. Joyce, James, *1882-1941.* **Finnegans wake** — *Commentaries*

McHugh, Roland. Annotations to Finnegans wake / Roland McHugh. — London : Routledge & Kegan Paul, 1980. — xii,628p ; 26cm
ISBN 0-7100-0661-6 (cased) : £17.95 : CIP rev.
ISBN 0-7100-0666-7 (pbk) : £5.95 B80-21143

823'.912 — Fiction in English. Joyce, James, *1882-1941.* **Influence of Dante Alighieri**

Reynolds, Mary T.. Joyce and Dante : the shaping imagination / by Mary T. Reynolds. — Princeton, N.J. ; Guildford : Princeton University Press, c1981. — xix,375p : facsims ; 24cm
Includes index
ISBN 0-691-06446-6 : £13.90 B81-37731

823'.912 — Fiction in English. Joyce, James, *1882-1941.* **Local associations: Dublin**

Delaney, Frank. James Joyce's odyssey. — London : Hodder & Stoughton, Nov.1981. — [256]p
ISBN 0-340-26885-9 : £8.95 : CIP entry
B81-31088

823'.912 — Fiction in English. Joyce, James, *1882-1941 — Personal observations — Collections*

Portraits of the artist in exile : recollections of James Joyce by Europeans / edited by Willard Potts. — Portmarnock (98 Ardilaun, Portmarnock, Co. Dublin) : Wolfhound, 1979. — xvi,304p : ill,ports ; 25cm
Originally published: Seattle : University of Washington Press, 1979. — Includes index
ISBN 0-905473-41-8 : Unpriced B81-01780

823'.912 — Fiction in English. Joyce, James, *1882-1941 — Psychological perspectives*
Brivic, Sheldon. Joyce between Freud and Jung / Sheldon Brivic. — Port Washington, N.Y. ; London : National University Publications : Kennikat, 1980. — 226p ; 22cm. — (Literary criticism series)
Includes index
ISBN 0-8046-9249-1 : £12.75 B81-05724

823'.912 — Fiction in English. Joyce, James, *1882-1941.* **Special themes: Politics** *— Critical studies*
Manganiello, Dominic. Joyce's politics / Dominic Manganiello. — London : Routledge & Kegan Paul, 1980. — xii,260p ; 23cm
Includes index
ISBN 0-7100-0537-7 : £12.50 : CIP rev. B80-21144

823'.912 — Fiction in English. Joyce, James, *1882-1941.* **Ulysses** *— Critical studies*
Brown, Carole. Bloomsday, the eleventh hour : the quest for the vacant place / Carol Brown and Leo Knuth. — Colchester (c/o Department of Literature, University of Essex, Wivenhoe Park, Colchester, Essex CO4 3SQ) : A Wake Newslitter, 1981. — 16p : ill ; 23cm
Unpriced (pbk) B81-30105

823'.912 — Fiction in English. Joyce, James, *1882-1941.* **Ulysses. Syntax**
Gottfried, Roy K.. The art of Joyce's syntax in Ulysses / by Roy K. Gottfried. — London : Macmillan, 1980. — 191p ; 23cm
Bibliography: p181-185. — Includes index
ISBN 0-333-30648-1 : £12.00 : CIP rev. B80-09901

823'.912 — Fiction in English. Lawrence, D. H. — *Biographies*
Carswell, Catherine. The savage pilgrimage. — Cambridge : Cambridge University Press, Oct.1981. — [352]p
Originally published: London : Chatto and Windus, 1932
ISBN 0-521-23975-3 (cased) : £17.50 : CIP entry
ISBN 0-521-28386-8 (pbk) : £5.95 B81-30446

Neville, G. H.. A memoir of D.H. Lawrence. — Cambridge : Cambridge University Press, Jan.1982. — [208]p
ISBN 0-521-24097-2 : £18.00 : CIP entry B81-34664

823'.912 — Fiction in English. Lawrence, D. H. — *Correspondence, diaries, etc.*
Lawrence, D. H.. Letters / D.H. Lawrence ; selected by Richard Aldington ; with an introduction by Aldous Huxley. — Harmondsworth : Penguin, 1950 (1981 [printing]). — 182p ; 18cm
ISBN 0-14-000759-8 (pbk) : £1.75 B81-38421

823'.912 — Fiction in English. Lawrence, D. H. — *Critical studies*
A D.H. Lawrence handbook. — Manchester : Manchester University Press, Nov.1981. — [400]p
ISBN 0-7190-0780-1 : £14.50 : CIP entry B81-31274

Hobsbaum, Philip. A reader's guide to D.H. Lawrence / Philip Hobsbaum. — London : Thames and Hudson, c1981. — 160p ; 21cm
Bibliography: p152-156. — Includes index
ISBN 0-500-14023-5 : £6.95 B81-29276

Leavis, F. R.. D.H. Lawrence : novelist / F.R. Leavis. — Harmondsworth : Penguin, in association with Chatto & Windus 1964, c1955 (1981 [printing]). — 384p ; 18cm. — (Pelican Books)
Originally published: London : Chatto & Windus, 1955. — Includes index
ISBN 0-14-021491-7 (pbk) : £3.25 B81-35509

823'.912 — Fiction in English. Lawrence, D. H.. Special themes: Nature & culture *— Critical studies*
Burns, Aidan. Nature and culture in D.H. Lawrence / by Aidan Burns. — London : Macmillan, 1980. — ix,137p ; 23cm
Bibliography: p131-133. - Includes index
ISBN 0-333-28444-5 : £12.00 : CIP rev. B80-18932

823'.912 — Fiction in English. Lindsay, David — *Critical studies*
Sellin, Bernard. The life and works of David Lindsay / Bernard Sellin ; translated by Kenneth Gunnell. — Cambridge : Cambridge University Press, c1981. — xxiii,257p ; 23cm
Translated from the French. — Bibliography: p249-251. — Includes index
ISBN 0-521-22768-2 : £17.50 : CIP rev. B81-19175

823'.912 — Fiction in English. Lowry, Malcolm — *Critical studies*
Cross, Richard K.. Malcolm Lowry : a preface to his fiction / Richard K. Cross. — London : Athlone Press, 1980. — xiii,146p ; 21cm
Originally published: Chicago ; London : University of Chicago Press, 1980. — Bibliography: p107-111. - Includes index
ISBN 0-485-11202-7 : £7.95 : CIP rev. B80-02228

823'.912 — Fiction in English. O'Flaherty, Liam — *Biographies*
O'Flaherty, Liam. Share the devil. — Dublin : Wolfhound Press, July 1981. — [288]p
Originally published: London : Grayson & Grayson, 1934
ISBN 0-905473-64-7 : £8.00 : CIP entry B81-24651

823'.912 — Fiction in English. Orwell, George, *1933-1937 — Biographies*
Stansky, Peter. Orwell : the transformation / Peter Stansky and William Abrahams. — London : Granada, 1981, c1979. — 253p,[8]p of plates : ill,ports ; 20cm. — (Paladin Book)
Originally published: London : Constable, 1979. — Includes index
ISBN 0-586-08375-8 (pbk) : £2.25 B81-32922

823'.912 — Fiction in English. Orwell, George — *Biographies*
Crick, Bernard. George Orwell : a life / Bernard Crick. — London : Secker & Warburg, 1980. — 473p : ill,ports ; 24cm
Includes index
ISBN 0-436-11450-x : £10.00 B81-03742

Crick, Bernard. George Orwell. — 2nd ed. — London : Secker & Warburg, Sept.1981. — [504]p
ISBN 0-436-11451-8 : £12.50 (£10.00 until 31/12/81) : CIP entry B81-23792

Lewis, Peter, *1928-*. George Orwell : the road to 1984 / Peter Lewis. — London : Heinemann, 1981. — 122p : ill,facsims,ports ; 25cm
Bibliography: p117. — Includes index
ISBN 0-434-98021-8 (cased) : £7.95
ISBN 0-434-98007-2 (pbk) : £4.95 B81-40206

823'.912 — Fiction in English. Orwell, George, *to 1933 — Biographies*
Stansky, Peter. The unknown Orwell / Peter Stansky and William Abrahams. — London : Granada, 1974, c1972 (1981 [printing]). — xviii,287p,[4]p of plates : ill,ports ; 20cm. — (A Paladin Book)
Originally published: London : Constable, 1972. — Includes index
ISBN 0-586-08178-x (pbk) : £2.25 B81-32921

823'.912 — Fiction in English. Priestley, John Boynton *— Critical studies*
Atkins, John, *1916-*. J.B. Priestley : the last of the sages / by John Atkins. — London : Calder, 1981. — ix,309p : ports ; 23cm
Bibliography: p295-300. - Includes index
ISBN 0-7145-3804-3 : £13.95 : CIP rev. B80-01880

823'.912 — Fiction in English. Reid, Forrest — *Critical studies*
Taylor, Brian, *1950-*. The green avenue : the life and writings of Forrest Reid, 1875-1947 / Brian Taylor. — Cambridge : Cambridge University Press, 1980. — xiv,218p,[32]p of plates : ill,facsims,ports ; 23cm
Bibliography: p191-211. — Includes index
ISBN 0-521-22801-8 : £12.50 : CIP rev. B80-26246

823'.912 — Fiction in English. Saki, *1870-1916 — Biographies*
Langguth, A. J.. Saki. — London : Hamish Hamilton, Oct.1981. — [288]p
ISBN 0-241-10678-8 : £9.95 : CIP entry B81-24612

823'.912 — Fiction in English. Sayers, Dorothy L. *— Biographies*
Brabazon, James. Dorothy L Sayers : the life of a courageous woman / by James Brabazon ; with a preface by Anthony Fleming and a foreword by P.D. James. — London : Gollancz, 1981. — xviii,308p,[12]p of plates : ill,1facsim,ports ; 24cm
Bibliography: p297-303. - Includes index
ISBN 0-575-02728-2 : £9.95 B81-18397

823'.912 — Fiction in English. Stephens, James, *1882-1950.* **Charwoman's daughter** *— Study outlines*
Spring, Brian. The charwoman's daughter / Brian Spring. — Dublin : Helicon, 1979. — 28p ; 21cm. — (Helicon notes)
£0.76 (pbk) B81-38689

823'.912 — Fiction in English. Tolkien, J. R. R. — *Correspondence, diaries, etc.*
Tolkien, J. R. R.. Letters of J.R.R. Tolkien : a selection / edited by Humphrey Carpenter with the assistance of Christopher Tolkien. — London : Allen & Unwin, 1981. — 463p,[1]leaf of plates : 1facsim ; 23cm
ISBN 0-04-826005-3 : Unpriced : CIP rev. B81-09495

823'.912 — Fiction in English. Tolkien, J. R. R. — *Critical studies — Serials*
The New Tolkien newsletter : a review of the works of J.R.R. Tolkien. — Vol.1, no.1 (Aug. 1st 1980)-. — [Bath] ([16 Prior Park Buildings, Bath, Avon BA2 4NP]) : [Widcome Press], 1980-. — v. : ill ; 29cm
Three issues yearly
ISSN 0260-3268 = New Tolkien newsletter : £1.15 per issue B81-01235

823'.912 — Fiction in English. Tolkien, J. R. R.. Hobbit, *The — Study outlines*
Ridden, Geoffrey M.. The hobbit : notes / by Geoffrey M. Ridden. — Harlow : Longman, 1981. — 70p ; 21cm. — (York notes ; 121)
Bibliography: p69-70
ISBN 0-582-78230-9 (pbk) : £0.90 B81-34228

823'.912 — Fiction in English. Tolkien, J. R. R.. Lord of the Rings *— Atlases*
Strachey, Barbara. Journeys of Frodo : an atlas of J.R.R. Tolkien's The Lord of the rings / Barbara Strachey. — London : Unwin Paperbacks, 1981. — 50[i.e.109]p : col.maps ; 19x25cm
ISBN 0-04-912011-5 (pbk) : £2.95 B81-25635

823'.912 — Fiction in English. Tolkien, J. R. R. — *Questions & answers*
Robinson, Nigel. The Tolkien quiz book / compiled by Nigel Robinson & Linda Wilson. — London : Star, 1981. — 115p ; 18cm. — (A Star book)
Bibliography: p114
ISBN 0-352-30951-2 (pbk) : £1.25 B81-27559

823'.912 — Fiction in English. Tolkien, J. R. R.. Silmarillion *— Critical studies*
Helms, Randel. Tolkien and the Silmarils / Randel Helms. — [London] : Thames and Hudson, c1981. — xiii,104p ; 22cm
Includes index
ISBN 0-500-01264-4 : £5.50 B81-36808

823'.912 — Fiction in English. Tolkien, J. R. R.. Silmarillion, *The — Critical studies*
Kocher, Paul H.. A reader's guide to The silmarillion / Paul H. Kocher. — London : Thames and Hudson, 1980. — 286p ; 22cm
Bibliography: p273-275. - Includes index
ISBN 0-500-14022-7 : £5.50 B81-07138

823'.912 — Fiction in English. Toynbee, Philip — *Correspondence, diaries, etc.*
Toynbee, Philip. Part of a journey : an autobiographical journal 1977-1979 / Philip Toynbee. — London : Collins, 1981. — 398p ; 23cm
ISBN 0-00-211696-0 : £9.95 B81-12465

823′.912 — Fiction in English. Vaughan, Hilda — *Critical studies*
Newman, Christopher W.. Hilda Vaughan / Christopher W. Newman. — [Cardiff] : University of Wales Press on behalf of the Welsh Arts Council, 1981. — 91p : 1port ; 25cm. — (Writers of Wales, ISSN 0141-5050)
Limited ed. of 1000 copies. — Bibliography: p83-88
ISBN 0-7083-0796-5 (pbk) : £2.50 : CIP rev. B81-14896

823′.912 — Fiction in English. Wells, H. G.. History of Mr Polly — *Study outlines*
Stephen, Martin. The history of Mr Polly : notes / by Martin Stephen. — London : Longman, 1980. — 72p ; 21cm. — (York notes ; 86)
Bibliography: p68-69
ISBN 0-582-78132-9 (pbk) : £0.90 B81-14580

823′.912 — Fiction in English. Wells, H. G.. Invisible man — *Study outlines*
Stephen, Martin. The invisible man : notes / by Martin Stephen. — London : Longman, 1980. — 79p ; 21cm. — (York notes ; 52)
Bibliography: p74-75
ISBN 0-582-78172-8 (pbk) : £0.90 B81-07097

823′.912 — Fiction in English. Wells, H. G. — *Personal observations — Collections*
H.G. Wells : interviews and recollections / edited by J.R. Hammond. — London : Macmillan, 1980. — xii,121p ; 23cm
Includes index
ISBN 0-333-27416-4 : £12.00 B81-09789

823′.912 — Fiction in English. Wells, H. G.. War of the worlds — *Study outlines*
Parrinder, Patrick. The war of the worlds : notes / by Patrick Parrinder. — Harlow : Longman, 1981. — 64p ; 21cm. — (York notes ; 103)
Bibliography: p63
ISBN 0-582-78134-5 (pbk) : £0.90 B81-19633

823′.912 — Fiction in English. Wodehouse, P. G. — *Biographies*
Green, Benny. P.G. Wodehouse : a literary biography / Benny Green. — London : Pavilion, 1981. — 256p,[16]p of plates : ill,facsims,ports ; 24cm
Includes index
ISBN 0-907516-04-1 : £8.95 : CIP rev. B81-25739

Wodehouse, P. G.. Wodehouse on Wodehouse / P.G. Wodehouse. — Harmondsworth : Penguin, 1981. — 655p ; 20cm
Originally published: London : Hutchinson, 1980. — Includes index. — Contents: Bring on the girls. Originally published: London : Jenkins, 1954. — Performing flea. Originally published: London : Jenkins, 1953. — Over seventy. Originally published: London : Jenkins, 1957
ISBN 0-14-005245-3 (pbk) : £2.95 B81-40499

Wodehouse, P. G.Pelham Grenville. Wodehouse on Wodehouse / P.G. Wodehouse. — London : Hutchinson, 1980. — 655p ; 23cm
Bibliography: p2. - Includes index. — Contents: Bring on the girls / by P.G. Wodehouse and Guy Bolton - Performing flea - Over seventy
ISBN 0-09-143210-3 : £9.95 : CIP rev. B80-12623

823′.912 — Fiction in English. Wodehouse, P. G. — *Critical studies*
Morris, J. H. C.. Thank you, Wodehouse / by J.H.C. Morris with contributions by A.D. Macintyre ; introduction by Frances Donaldson. — London : Weidenfeld and Nicolson, c1981. — 152p ; 23cm
Includes index
ISBN 0-297-78001-8 : £6.95 B81-35143

Usborne, Richard. A Wodehouse companion. — London : H. Hamilton, Oct.1981. — [224]p
ISBN 0-241-89955-9 : £9.95 : CIP entry B81-26748

Wind, Herbert Warren. The world of P.G. Wodehouse. — London : Hutchinson, Oct.1981. — 1v.
ISBN 0-09-145670-3 : £5.95 : CIP entry B81-26769

823′.912 — Fiction in English. Woolf, Virginia. Alleged insanity
Poole, Roger. The unknown Virginia Woolf. — Brighton : Harvester Press, July 1981. — [304]p
Originally published: Cambridge : Cambridge University Press, 1978
ISBN 0-7108-0366-4 (pbk) : £5.50 : CIP entry B81-18174

Trombley, Stephen. 'All that summer she was mad' : Virginia Woolf and her doctors. — London : Junction Books, Oct.1981. — [352]p
ISBN 0-86245-039-x : £12.50 : CIP entry B81-30265

823′.912 — Fiction in English. Woolf, Virginia — *Biographies*
Bell, Quentin. Virginia Woolf. — London : Hogarth, Jan.1982. — [560]p
Originally published: 1972
ISBN 0-7012-0461-3 : £12.50 : CIP entry B81-34298

823′.912 — Fiction in English. Woolf, Virginia — *Correspondence, diaries, etc.*
Woolf, Virginia. A change of perspective : the letters of Virginia Woolf / editor Nigel Nicolson, assistant editor Joanne Trautmann. — London : Chatto & Windus, 1981, c1977. — xxii,600p,8p of plates : ports ; 24cm. — (The Letters of Virginia Woolf ; v.3, 1923-1928)
Originally published: London : Hogarth Press, 1977. — Includes index
ISBN 0-7011-2481-4 (pbk) : £4.50 B81-18736

Woolf, Virginia. The diary of Virginia Woolf. — Harmondsworth : Penguin
Vol.2: 1920-24 / edited by Anne Olivier Bell ; assisted by Andrew McNeillie. — 1981, c1978. — xii,371p : 2maps ; 20cm
Originally published: London : Hogarth Press, 1978. — Includes index
ISBN 0-14-005283-6 (pbk) : £2.95 B81-37205

Woolf, Virginia. The diary of Virginia Woolf. — London : Hogarth Press
Vol.4: 1931-1935. — Jan.1982. — [400]p
ISBN 0-7012-0467-2 : £12.50 : CIP entry B81-34299

Woolf, Virginia. The letters of Virginia Woolf. — London : Chatto & Windus. — (A Chatto & Windus paperback ; CWP63)
Vol.4: 1929-1931. A reflection of the other person. — Oct.1981. — [464]p
Originally published: London : Hogart, 1978
ISBN 0-7011-2597-7 (pbk) : £4.50 : CIP entry B81-27928

823′.912 — Fiction in English. Woolf, Virginia. Special subjects: Death & grief — *Critical studies*
Spilka, Mark. Virginia Woolf's quarrel with grieving / Mark Spilka. — Lincoln [Neb.] ; London : University of Nebraska Press, c1980. — xii,142p ; 23cm
Bibliography: p135-137. - Includes index
ISBN 0-8032-4120-8 : £8.00 B81-17301

823′.912 — Fiction in English. Woolf, Virginia. Voyage out — *Critical studies*
DeSalvo, Louise A.. Virginia Woolf's first voyage : a novel in the making / Louise A. DeSalvo. — London : Macmillan, 1980. — xiii,202p ; 22cm
Bibliography: p181-187. — Includes index
ISBN 0-333-29353-3 : £12.00 : CIP rev. B80-08038

823′.912 — Fiction in English. Yates, Dornford — *Biographies*
Smithers, A. J.. Dornford Yates. — London : Hodder & Stoughton, Feb.1982. — [288]p
ISBN 0-340-27547-2 : £9.95 : CIP entry B81-36363

823′.912 — Fiction in European languages. Translations into English language. Lawrence, D. H. — *Critical studies*
Hyde, G. M.. D.H. Lawrence and the art of translation / G.M. Hyde. — London : Macmillan, 1981. — 101p ; 23cm
Bibliography: p96-98. — Includes index
ISBN 0-333-28599-9 : £12.00 B81-38644

823′.912 — Short stories in English. Lavin, Mary — *Critical studies*
Kelly, A. A.. Mary Lavin : quiet rebel : a study of her short stories / A.A. Kelly. — Portmarnock (98 Ardilaun, Portmarnock, Co. Dublin) : Wolfhound, c1980. — 200p : 1port ; 21cm
Bibliography: p187-195. — Includes index
ISBN 0-905473-46-9 : £8.00 B81-01624

823′.912 — Short stories in English. Lawrence, D. H. — *Study outlines*
Ashworth, Clive V.. Notes on D.H. Lawrence's peoms and stories / compiled by Clive V. Ashworth. — London : Methuen Paperbacks, 1981, c1980. — 90p ; 20cm. — (Methuen notes)
Bibliography: p90
ISBN 0-417-21750-1 (pbk) : £0.95
Primary classification 821′.912 B81-19613

823′.912[F] — Fiction in English, *1900-1945 — Texts*
Allingham, Margery. Sweet danger / Margery Allingham. — Large print ed. — Leicester : Ulverscroft, 1981. — 390p : 1plan ; 23cm. — (Ulverscroft large print series)
ISBN 0-7089-0589-7 : Unpriced B81-14229

Ames, Jennifer. The two of us / Jennifer Ames. — Large print ed. — Bath : Chivers, 1981, c1964. — 271p ; 23cm. — (A Lythway book)
Originally published: London : Collins, 1964
ISBN 0-85119-740-x : £6.70 : CIP rev. B81-20106

Audemars, Pierre. Gone to her death / by Pierre Audemars. — London : Hale, 1981. — 206p ; 20cm
ISBN 0-7091-9135-9 : £5.95 B81-27300

Avenell, Donne. Leslie Charteris' Count on the Saint / original outlines by Donne Avenell ; developed by Graham Weaver. — London : Hodder and Stoughton, 1980. — 174p ; 20cm
ISBN 0-340-25384-3 : £5.50 : CIP rev. B80-19920

Ayres, Ruby M.. Missing the tide. — Large print ed. — Bath : Chivers, Feb.1982. — [248]p. — (A Seymour book)
Originally published: London : Hodder & Stoughton, 1948
ISBN 0-85119-452-4 : £4.95 : CIP entry B81-36050

Ayres, Ruby M.. [The story of fish and chips]. The mists of love / Ruby M. Ayres. — Large print ed. — Bath : Chivers, 1980, c1951. — 194p ; 23cm. — (A Seymour book)
Originally published: London : Macdonald, 1951
ISBN 0-86220-020-2 : £4.95 : CIP rev. B80-22486

Ayres, Ruby M.. Wallflower. — London : Severn House, Nov.1981. — [192]p
ISBN 0-7278-0748-x : £5.95 : CIP entry B81-30589

Baker, Denys Val. Rose : a novel of Cornwall / Denys Val Baker. — London : Kimber, 1980. — 172p ; 23cm
ISBN 0-7183-0357-1 : £5.50 B81-01259

Bates, H. E.. The best of H.E. Bates : a selection of novels and short stories. — London : Joseph, 1980. — 634p ; 23cm
ISBN 0-7181-1943-6 : £6.95 B81-07169

Bates, H. E.. A breath of French air / H.E. Bates. — Harmondsworth : Penguin in association with Joseph, 1962, c1959 (1980 [printing]). — 158p ; 19cm
Originally published: London : Joseph, 1959
ISBN 0-14-001685-6 (pbk) : £0.95 B81-00379

Bates, H. E.. The darling buds of May / H.E. Bates. — Harmondsworth : Penguin in association with Joseph, 1961, c1958 (1980 [printing]). — 157p ; 19cm
Originally published: London : Joseph, 1958
ISBN 0-14-001602-3 (pbk) : £0.85 B81-01236

823'.912[F] — Fiction in English, *1900-1945* — *Texts* *continuation*

Bates, H. E.. Fair stood the wind for France / H.E. Bates. — Harmondsworth : Penguin in association with Joseph, 1980, c1944. — 254p ; 18cm
Originally published: London : Joseph, 1944
ISBN 0-14-001279-6 (pbk) : £1.25 B81-00380

Bates, H. E.. A little of what you fancy / H.E. Bates. — Harmondsworth : Penguin, 1973, c1970 (1980 [printing]). — 183p ; 19cm
Originally published: London : Joseph, 1970
ISBN 0-14-003702-0 (pbk) : £0.90 B81-04177

Bates, H. E.. Love for Lydia / H.E. Bates. — Harmondsworth : Penguin in association with Joseph, 1956 (1981 [printing]). — 301p ; 18cm
Originally published: London : Joseph, 1952
£1.75 (pbk) B81-18517

Bates, H. E.. The nature of love / by H.E. Bates. — London : Severn House, 1981, c1953. — 190p ; 21cm
Originally published: London : Joseph, 1953
ISBN 0-7278-0735-8 : £5.95 : CIP rev.
B81-18099

Bates, H. E.. Oh! to be in England / H.E. Bates. — Harmondsworth : Penguin in association with Joseph, 1966, c1963 (1980 printing). — 142p ; 18cm
Originally published: London : Joseph, 1963
ISBN 0-14-002477-8 (pbk) : £0.80 B81-00381

Bates, H. E.. The triple echo / H.E. Bates ; drawings by Ron Clarke. — Harmondsworth : Penguin, 1972, c1970 (1981 [printing]). — 89p : ill ; 18cm
Originally published: London : Joseph, 1970
ISBN 0-14-003563-x (pbk) : £0.95 B81-34815

Bates, H. E.. When the green woods laugh / H.E. Bates. — Harmondsworth : Penguin in association with Joseph, 1963, c1960 (1980 [printing])
Originally published: London : Joseph, 1960
ISBN 0-14-001975-8 (pbk) : £0.85 B81-06396

Baxter, Olive. Invitation to romance / Olive Baxter. — Large print ed. — Bath : Lythway, 1980, c1966. — 209p ; 23cm
Originally published: London : Wright & Brown, 1966
ISBN 0-85046-902-3 : £5.90 : CIP rev.
B80-22488

Beckett, Samuel. Murphy / Samuel Beckett. — London : Pan in association with Calder & Boyars, 1973, c1938 (1980 printing). — 158p : 1port ; 20cm. — (Picador)
Port on inside cover
£1.50 (pbk) B81-05677

Bell, Neil. Pinkney's garden / by Neil Bell. — Hornchurch : Henry, 1980, c1939. — 160p ; 21cm
ISBN 0-86025-179-9 : £4.95 B81-02537

Bennett, Arnold. Helen with the high hand : an idyllic diversion / by Arnold Bennett. — London : Remploy, 1979. — vi,311p ; 19cm
ISBN 0-7066-0820-8 : £4.50 B81-09397

Bishop, L.. News-hawk / L. Bishop. — Bognor Regis : New Horizon, c1980. — 115p,[1]leaf of plates : 1port ; 21cm
ISBN 0-86116-642-6 : £4.25 B81-18955

Black, Hermina. Portrait of Sarah / by Hermina Black. — Bolton-By-Bowland : Magna Print, 1980, c1967. — 339p ; 23cm
Originally published: London : Hodder and Stoughton, 1967. — Published in large print
ISBN 0-86009-274-7 : £5.25 : CIP rev.
B80-22490

Black, Hermina. Spoilt music / Hermina Black. — London : Sphere, 1980, c1968. — 152p ; 18cm
Originally published: London : Hodder & Stoughton, 1968
ISBN 0-7221-1699-3 (pbk) : £1.10 B81-01238

Black, Hermina. Spoilt music / by Hermina Black. — Bolton-by-Bowland : Magna Print, 1981, c1968. — 323p ; 23cm
Originally published: London : Hodder & Stoughton, 1968. — Published in large print
ISBN 0-86009-298-4 : £5.75 B81-12231

Black, Hermina. Stardust for dreams / Hermina Black. — [London] : Coronet, 1962 (1979 [printing]). — 192p ; 18cm
Originally published: London : Hodder & Stoughton, 1957
ISBN 0-340-02478-x (pbk) : £0.60 B81-35373

Black, Hermina. Two ways of loving / Hermina Black. — London : Hodder and Stoughton, 1981. — 192p ; 21cm
ISBN 0-340-25973-6 : £6.50 : CIP rev.
B81-18133

Black, Lionel. The penny murders / Lionel Black. — Large print ed. — Leicester : Ulverscroft, 1980, c1979. — 294p ; 23cm. — (Ulverscroft large print series)
Originally published: London : Collins, 1979
ISBN 0-7089-0534-x : £4.25 : CIP rev.
B80-24815

Black, Lionel. The Rumanian circle / Lionel Black. — London : Collins, 1981. — 182p ; 20cm. — (The Crime club)
ISBN 0-00-231870-9 : £5.75 : CIP rev.
B81-13464

Blackmore, Jane. Flames of love / Jane Blackmore. — Loughton : Piatkus, 1981. — 202p ; 21cm
ISBN 0-86188-084-6 : £6.25 : CIP rev.
B81-04372

Blackmore, Jane. Wildfire love / Jane Blackmore. — Loughton : Piatkus, 1980. — 222p ; 21cm
ISBN 0-86188-045-5 : £5.50 : CIP rev.
B80-17948

Blake, Nicholas. The case of the abominable Snowman / Nicholas Blake. — Feltham : Hamlyn, 1981, c1941. — 190p ; 18cm. — (A Hamlyn whodunnit)
ISBN 0-600-20161-9 (pbk) : £1.10 B81-11431

Blake, Nicholas. The smiler with the knife / Nicholas Blake. — Large print ed. — Leicester : Ulverscroft, 1981, c1939. — 388p ; 23cm. — (Ulverscroft large print series)
ISBN 0-7089-0645-1 : £5.00 B81-28566

Blake, Nicholas. Thou shell of death / Nicholas Blake. — London : Hamlyn Paperbacks, 1981. — 187p ; 18cm. — (A Hamlyn whodunnit)
ISBN 0-600-20162-7 (pbk) : £1.25 B81-28649

Bloom, Ursula. The abiding city / Ursula Bloom. — Large print ed. — Bath : Chivers, 1981, c1958. — 296p ; 23cm. — (A Lythway romance)
Originally published: London : Hutchinson, 1958
ISBN 0-85119-713-2 : £6.60 : CIP rev.
B81-04235

Bloom, Ursula. The dandelion clock. — Large print ed. — Bath : Chivers, Feb.1982. — [312] p. — (A Seymour book)
Originally published: London : Hutchinson, 1966
ISBN 0-85119-453-2 : £4.95 : CIP entry
B81-36049

Bloom, Ursula. The doctor who fell in love. — Large print ed. — Bath : Chivers, Oct.1981. — [208]p. — (A Lythway book)
Originally published: London : Hale, 1974
ISBN 0-85119-749-3 : £6.50 : CIP entry
B81-25807

Bloom, Ursula. Edwardian day-dream / Ursula Bloom. — Large print ed. — Bath : Chivers, 1980, c1972. — 250p ; 23cm. — (A Seymour book)
Originally published: London : Hutchinson, 1972
ISBN 0-86220-021-0 : £4.95 : CIP rev.
B80-22491

Bloom, Ursula. The girl who loved Crippen / Ursula Bloom. — Large print ed. — Bath : Chivers, 1981. — 292p ; 23cm. — (A Lythway book)
Originally published: London : Hutchinson, 1955
ISBN 0-85119-733-7 : Unpriced : CIP rev.
B81-19171

Bloom, Ursula. Marriage in heaven / Ursula Bloom. — Large print ed. — Bath : Lythway, 1980. — 222p ; 23cm
ISBN 0-85046-903-1 : £5.90 : CIP rev.
B80-22492

Bloom, Ursula. The old Adam / Ursula Bloom. — Large print ed. — Bath : Chivers, 1981, c1967. — 286p ; 23cm. — (A Seymour book)
Originally published: London : Hutchinson, 1967
ISBN 0-85119-404-4 : Unpriced B81-08982

Bloom, Ursula. Two pools in a field / Ursula Bloom. — Large print ed. — Bath : Chivers, 1981, c1967. — 291p ; 23cm. — (A Lythway romance)
Originally published: London : Hutchinson, 1967
ISBN 0-85119-729-9 : Unpriced : CIP rev.
B81-13716

Bowen, Elizabeth. The hotel. — London : Cape, Nov.1981. — [270]p
ISBN 0-224-60057-5 : £6.50 : CIP entry
B81-28840

Bowen, Elizabeth. A world of love. — London : Cape, Nov.1981. — [224]p
Originally published: 1955
ISBN 0-224-60051-6 : £6.50 : CIP entry
B81-30323

Brand, Christianna. Heads you lose / by Christianna Brand. — Hornchurch : Ian Henry, 1981. — 190p ; 20cm
ISBN 0-86025-170-5 : £5.25 B81-34880

Brand, Christianna. Tour de force / Christianna Brand. — Feltham : Hamlyn, 1980, c1955. — 190p ; 18cm. — (A Hamlyn whodunnit)
Originally published: London : Michael Joseph, 1955
ISBN 0-600-20196-1 (pbk) : £1.10

Bridge, Ann. Illyrian spring / Ann Bridge. — [St. Albans] : Triad, 1981, c1935. — 353p ; 18cm
ISBN 0-586-05220-8 (pbk) : £2.25 B81-09883

Bridge, Ann. Peking picnic / Ann Bridge. — [St. Albans] : Triad, 1981, c1932. — 328p ; 18cm
ISBN 0-586-05219-4 (pbk) : £1.95 B81-07356

Buchan, John, *1875-1940*. The island of sheep / John Buchan. — Harmondsworth : Penguin, 1956 (1981 [printing]). — 244p : 1map ; 18cm
ISBN 0-14-001131-5 (pbk) : £1.50 B81-14344

Buchan, John, *1875-1940*. Mr Standfast / John Buchan. — Harmondsworth : Penguin, 1956 (1981 [printing]). — 347p ; 19cm
ISBN 0-14-001134-x (pbk) : £1.50 B81-40495

Buchan, John, *1875-1940*. Prester John / John Buchan. — Harmondsworth : Penguin, 1956 (1981 [printing]). — 202p : 1map ; 18cm
ISBN 0-14-001138-2 (pbk) : £1.25 B81-14343

Buchan, John, *1875-1940*. A prince of the captivity / John Buchan. — Feltham : Hamlyn, 1981. — 271p ; 18cm
ISBN 0-600-20564-9 (pbk) : £1.50 B81-40997

823'.912[F] — Fiction in English, *1900-1945* — *Texts* *continuation*

Buchan, John, *1875-1940*. Sick Heart river / by John Buchan ; with an introduction by Trevor Royle. — Loanhead (Edgefield Rd., Loanhead, Midlothian) : Macdonald, 1981. — 228p ; 23cm
ISBN 0-904265-43-9 : £6.95 B81-29834

Buchan, John, *1875-1940*. The three hostages / John Buchan. — Harmondsworth : Penguin, 1953 (1981 [printing]). — 282p ; 18cm
ISBN 0-14-000908-6 (pbk) : £1.50 B81-14345

Burns, Sheila. The dark-eyed sister. — Large print ed. — Bath : Chivers Press, Feb.1982. — [280]p. — (A Lythway book)
Originally published: London : Hale, 1968
ISBN 0-85119-782-5 : £6.90 : CIP entry B81-35864

Burns, Sheila. Surgeon at sea. — Large print ed. — Bath : Chivers, Oct.1981. — [280]p. — (A Lythway book)
Originally published: London : Hale, 1969
ISBN 0-85119-748-5 : £6.90 : CIP entry B81-25806

Burns, Sheila. A surgeon's sweetheart. — Large print ed. — Bath : Chivers Press, Dec.1981. — [288]p. — (A Lythway book)
Originally published: London : Hale, 1966
ISBN 0-85119-765-5 : £6.80 : CIP entry B81-31796

Butler, William Vivian. Gideon's law / J.J. Marric ; as told by William Vivian Butler. — London : Hodder and Stoughton, 1981. — 191p ; 21cm
ISBN 0-340-25304-5 : £5.95 : CIP rev. B81-04340

Caddell, Elizabeth. Return match / Elizabeth Cadell. — Large print ed. — Leicester : Ulverscroft, 1981, c1979. — 355p ; 23cm. — (Ulverscroft large print series)
Originally published: London : Hodder and Stoughton, 1979
ISBN 0-7089-0592-7 : Unpriced B81-14228

Cadell, Elizabeth. Any two can play / Elizabeth Cadell. — London : Hodder and Stoughton, 1981. — 221p ; 21cm
ISBN 0-340-26234-6 : £5.95 B81-10143

Cadell, Elizabeth. Iris in winter / Elizabeth Cadell. — London : Hale, 1951 (1980 [printing]). — 272p ; 21cm
ISBN 0-7091-8624-x : £5.95 B81-01239

Cadell, Elizabeth. My dear Aunt Flora / Elizabeth Cadell. — London : Hale, 1946, c1976 (1982 [printing]). — 252p ; 21cm
ISBN 0-7091-5675-8 : £5.50 B81-40537

Cadell, Elizabeth. Parson's house / Elizabeth Cadell. — [London] : Coronet, 1978, c1977. — 189p ; 18cm
Originally published: London : Hodder and Stoughton, 1977
ISBN 0-340-23097-5 (pbk) : £0.80 : CIP rev. B78-34821

Canning, Victor. The boy on platform one / Victor Canning. — London : Heinemann, 1981. — 177p ; 23cm
ISBN 0-434-10796-4 : £6.95 B81-39296

Canning, Victor. The circle of the gods / Victor Canning. — Large print ed. — Leicester : Ulverscroft, 1981, c1977. — 383p ; 23cm. — (Ulverscroft large print)
Originally published: London : Heinemann, 1977
ISBN 0-7089-0571-4 : £5.00 B81-11617

Canning, Victor. The crimson chalice / Victor Canning. — Large print ed. — Leicester : Ulverscroft, 1980, c1976. — 378p : 1map ; 23cm. — (Ulverscroft large print series)
Originally published: London : Heinemann, 1976
ISBN 0-7089-0543-9 : £4.25 : CIP rev. B80-26124

Canning, Victor. Doubled in diamonds / Victor Canning. — Large print ed. — Bath : Chivers, 1980, c1966. — 314p ; 23cm
Originally published: London : Heinemann, 1966
ISBN 0-85997-471-5 : £5.00 : CIP rev. B80-17956

Canning, Victor. Fall from grace / Victor Canning. — London : Heinemann, 1980. — 214p ; 23cm
ISBN 0-434-10795-6 : £6.95 B81-00382

Canning, Victor. Fall from grace. — Large print ed. — Anstey : Ulverscroft, Feb.1982. — [416] p. — (Ulverscroft large print series : general fiction)
ISBN 0-7089-0754-7 : £5.00 : CIP entry B81-36936

Canning, Victor. The immortal wound / Victor Canning. — Large print ed. — Leicester : Ulverscroft, 1981, c1978. — 372p ; 23cm. — (Ulverscroft large print series)
Originally published: London : Heinemann, 1978
ISBN 0-7089-0600-1 : Unpriced B81-14188

Canning, Victor. The rainbird pattern / by Victor Canning. — Bolton-by-Bowland : Magna, 1979, c1972. — 472p ; 23cm
Originally published: London : Heinemann, 1972. — Published in large print
ISBN 0-86009-202-x : £4.95 : CIP rev. B79-30324

Carr, Philippa. The drop of the dice / Philippa Carr. — London : Collins, 1981. — 360p : geneal.table ; 22cm. — (Daughters of England)
ISBN 0-00-222144-6 : £6.95 B81-14075

Carr, Philippa. The lion triumphant / Philippa Carr. — [London] : Collins : Fontana, 1975, c1974 (1980 [printing]). — 351p ; 18cm. — (Daughters of England)
Originally published: London : Collins, 1974
ISBN 0-00-616246-0 (pbk) : £1.50 B81-14524

Carr, Philippa. The love-child / Philippa Carr. — [London] : Fontana, 1979, c1978 (1981 [printing]). — 314p ; 18cm
Originally published: London : Collins, 1978
ISBN 0-00-616412-9 (pbk) : £1.50 B81-36837

Carr, Philippa. The love-child / Philippa Carr. — Large print ed. — Leicester : Ulverscroft, 1981, c1978. — 465p : 1geneal.table ; 23cm. — (Ulverscroft large print series)
Originally published: London : Collins, 1978. — Geneal.table on lining papers
ISBN 0-7089-0523-4 : Unpriced B81-14227

Carr, Philippa. The miracle at St Bruno's / Philippa Carr. — [London] : Collins : Fontana, 1974, c1972 (1981 [printing]). — 352p ; 18cm. — (Daughters of England)
Originally published: London : Collins, 1972
ISBN 0-00-616245-2 (pbk) : £1.50 B81-11176

Carr, Philippa. Saraband for two sisters / Philippa Carr. — Large print ed. — Leicester : Ulverscroft, 1981, c1976. — 563p : 2 geneal.tables ; 23cm. — (Ulverscroft large print series)
Originally published: London : Collins, 1976. — Geneal.tables on lining papers
ISBN 0-7089-0609-5 : £5.00 : CIP rev. B81-02581

Carr, Philippa. The song of the siren / Philippa Carr. — [London] : Fontana, 1981, c1980. — 315p : geneal.table ; 18cm. — (Daughters of England)
Originally published: London : Collins, 1980
ISBN 0-00-616243-6 (pbk) : £1.50 B81-11174

Carr, Philippa. The song of the siren / Philippa Carr. — Large print ed. — Leicester : Ulverscroft, 1981, c1980. — 478p ; 23cm. — (Ulverscroft large print series)
Originally published: London : Collins, 1980
ISBN 0-7089-0651-6 : £5.00 B81-28572

Cartland, Barbara. Afraid / Barbara Cartland. — London : Arrow, 1981. — 159p ; 18cm
ISBN 0-09-924740-2 (pbk) : £0.80 B81-03427

Cartland, Barbara. Again this rapture / by Barbara Cartland. — Long Preston : Magna, 1981, c1947. — 426p ; 23cm
Originally published: London : Hutchinson, 1947. — Published in large print
ISBN 0-86009-327-1 : £4.95 : CIP rev. B81-16905

Cartland, Barbara. An angel in hell. — London : Severn House, Sept.1981. — [176]p
Originally published: London : Pan, 1976
ISBN 0-7278-0722-6 : £5.95 : CIP entry B81-23815

Cartland, Barbara. Armour against love / by Barbara Cartland. — Bolton-by-Bowland : Magna, 1981, c1945. — 485p ; 23cm. — (Large type series)
Originally published: London : Hutchinson, 1945
ISBN 0-86009-304-2 : Unpriced : CIP rev. B81-08885

Cartland, Barbara. Count the stars / Barbara Cartland. — London : New English Library, 1981. — 158p ; 23cm
ISBN 0-450-04846-2 : £4.95 B81-15426

Cartland, Barbara. Count the stars / Barbara Cartland. — London : New English Library, 1981. — 158p ; 18cm
ISBN 0-450-05233-8 (pbk) : £1.00 B81-40493

Cartland, Barbara. Dollars for the Duke / Barbara Cartland. — London : Corgi, 1981. — 156p : ill ; 18cm
ISBN 0-552-11787-0 (pbk) : £0.95 B81-39096

Cartland, Barbara. The dream within / by Barbara Cartland. — Bolton-by-Bowland : Magna Print, 1981, c1947. — 497p ; 23cm
Originally published: London : Hutchinson 1947. — Published in large print
ISBN 0-86009-318-2 : £5.75 : CIP rev. B81-10447

Cartland, Barbara. Dreams do come true / Barbara Cartland. — London : Pan, 1981. — 138p ; 18cm
ISBN 0-330-26403-6 (pbk) : £0.90 B81-03384

Cartland, Barbara. The frightened bride. — Large print ed. — Long Preston : Magna Print Books, Jan.1982. — [320]p
Originally published: London : Hurst and Blackett, 1979
ISBN 0-86009-368-9 : £5.25 : CIP entry B81-33769

Cartland, Barbara. From hell to heaven / Barbara Cartland. — [London] : Corgi, 1981. — 157p ; 18cm
ISBN 0-552-11600-9 (pbk) : £0.95 B81-10986

Cartland, Barbara. A gamble with hearts. — Large print ed. — Long Preston : Magna Print Books, Dec.1981. — [420]p
Originally published: London : Hurst and Blackett, 1979
ISBN 0-86009-363-8 : £4.95 : CIP entry B81-31818

Cartland, Barbara. Gift of the gods / Barbara Cartland. — London : Pan, 1981. — 140p ; 18cm
ISBN 0-330-26490-7 (pbk) : £0.95 B81-20213

Cartland, Barbara. The heart of the clan / Barbara Cartland. — London : Arrow, 1981. — 166p ; 18cm
ISBN 0-09-925930-3 (pbk) : £0.95 B81-20273

Cartland, Barbara. The horizons of love / Barbara Cartland. — London : Pan, 1980. — 144p ; 18cm
ISBN 0-330-26355-2 (pbk) : 0.90 B81-02184

823'.912[F] — Fiction in English, *1900-1945* — *Texts continuation*

Cartland, Barbara. In the arms of love. — London : Hutchinson, Nov.1981. — [160]p
ISBN 0-09-146410-2 : £5.95 : CIP entry B81-28768

Cartland, Barbara. An innocent in Russia / Barbara Cartland. — London : Pan, 1981. — 141p ; 18cm
ISBN 0-330-26529-6 (pbk) : £0.95 B81-37356

Cartland, Barbara. The judgement of love / by Barbara Cartland. — Bolton-by-Bowland : Magna Print, 1980, c1979. — 278p ; 23cm
Originally published: London : Hutchinson, 1979. — Published in large print
ISBN 0-86009-282-8 : £2.25 : CIP rev. B80-34103

Cartland, Barbara. The kiss of life. — London : Hutchinson, May 1981. — [160]p
ISBN 0-09-143770-9 : £5.50 : CIP entry B81-04233

Cartland, Barbara. The leaping flame / Barbara Cartland. — Rev. ed. — London : Hale, 1973 (1981 [printing]). — 215p ; 21cm
Previous ed.: 1942
ISBN 0-7091-3118-6 : £5.25 B81-32321

Cartland, Barbara. The lioness and the lily / Barbara Cartland. — London : Corgi, 1981. — 155p ; 18cm
ISBN 0-552-11705-6 (pbk) : £0.95 B81-27252

Cartland, Barbara. Look, listen and love / Barbara Cartland. — London : Severn House, 1980. — 155p ; 21cm
Originally published: London : Pan, 1977
ISBN 0-7278-0421-9 : £5.25 : CIP rev. B80-17958

Cartland, Barbara. Love at the helm / Barbara Cartland ; inspired and helped by Earl Mountbatten of Burma. — London : Pan, 1981, c1980. — 136 : ill ; 18cm
Originally published: London : Weidenfeld and Nicolson, 1980
ISBN 0-330-26520-2 (pbk) : £0.95 B81-37355

Cartland, Barbara. Love at the helm / by Barbara Cartland ; inspired and helped by Earl Mountbatten of Burma. — Bolton-by-Bowland : Magna, 1981, c1980. — 272p ; 22cm
Originally published: London : Weidenfeld and Nicolson, 1980. — Published in large print
ISBN 0-86009-290-9 : £5.75 B81-08686

Cartland, Barbara. Love in the dark / Barbara Cartland. — London : Arrow, 1981, c1979. — 159p ; 18cm
Originally published: London : Hutchinson, 1979
ISBN 0-09-926280-0 (pbk) : £0.95 B81-34591

Cartland, Barbara. Love in the moon / Barbara Cartland. — London : New English Library, 1980. — 160p ; 23cm
ISBN 0-450-04745-8 : £4.95 B81-00383

Cartland, Barbara. Love in the moon / Barbara Cartland. — London : New English Library/Times Mirror, 1981, c1980. — 160p ; 18cm
Originally published: 1980
ISBN 0-450-05192-7 (pbk) : £1.00 B81-19978

Cartland, Barbara. Love leaves at midnight / by Barbara Cartland. — Bolton-by-Bowland : Magna, 1980, c1978. — 293p ; 23cm
Originally published: London : Hutchinson, 1978. — Published in large print
ISBN 0-86009-267-4 : £5.25 : CIP rev. B80-19436

Cartland, Barbara. Love wins / Barbara Cartland. — London : Pan, 1981. — 136p ; 18cm. — (Pan original)
ISBN 0-330-26564-4 (pbk) : £0.95 B81-36699

Cartland, Barbara. Lucifer and the angel / Barbara Cartland. — London : Hutchinson, 1980. — 151p ; 21cm
ISBN 0-09-142270-1 : £5.50 : CIP rev. B80-23692

Cartland, Barbara. Money, magic and marriage / Barbara Cartland. — London : Arrow, 1980. — 159p ; 18cm
ISBN 0-09-924150-1 (pbk) : £0.85 B81-07514

Cartland, Barbara. The mysterious maid-servant / by Barbara Cartland. — Bolton-by-Bowland : Magna, 1981, c1977. — 283p ; 23cm
Originally published: London : Hutchinson, 1977. — Published in large print
ISBN 0-86009-291-7 : £5.75 B81-14207

Cartland, Barbara. A night of gaiety / Barbara Cartland. — London : Pan, 1981. — 141p ; 18cm
ISBN 0-330-26419-2 (pbk) : £0.90 B81-05907

Cartland, Barbara. Passions in the sand / Barbara Cartland. — London : Severn House, 1981, c1976. — 157p ; 21cm
Originally published: London : Pan, 1976
ISBN 0-7278-0678-5 : £5.95 : CIP rev. B81-07623

Cartland, Barbara. Pride and the poor princess / Barbara Cartland. — [London] : Corgi, 1980. — 160p ; 18cm
ISBN 0-552-11583-5 (pbk) : £0.95 B81-03451

Cartland, Barbara. The river of love. — London : Pan, 1981. — 138p ; 18cm
ISBN 0-330-26489-3 (pbk) : £0.95 B81-20214

Cartland, Barbara. The runaway heart / Barbara Cartland. — London : Sphere, 1967, c1961 (1980 [printing]). — 150p ; 18cm
Originally published: / by Barbara Cartland writing as Barbara McCorquodale. London : Jenkins, 1961
ISBN 0-7221-2272-1 (pbk) : £0.75 B81-01240

Cartland, Barbara. The smuggled heart / by Barbara Carland. — Bolton-by-Bowland : Magna Print, 1979, c1959. — 427p ; 23cm
Originally published: London : Hutchinson, 1959. — Published in large print
ISBN 0-86009-198-8 : £4.95 : CIP rev. B79-30327

Cartland, Barbara. Towards the stars. — Large print ed. — Long Preston : Magna, Oct.1981. — [480]p
ISBN 0-86009-323-9 : £4.95 : CIP entry B81-27387

Cartland, Barbara. The waltz of hearts / Barbara Cartland. — London : Pan, 1980. — 154p ; 18cm
ISBN 0-330-26365-x (pbk) : £1.90 B81-01241

Cartland, Barbara. The wild, unwilling wife / Barbara Cartland. — London : Severn House, 1981, c1977. — 155p ; 21cm
Originally published: London : Pan Books, 1977
ISBN 0-7278-0426-x : £5.25 B81-05740

Cartland, Barbara. The wings of ecstasy / Barbara Cartland. — London : Pan, 1981. — 143p ; 18cm. — (Pan original)
ISBN 0-330-26581-4 (pbk) : £0.95 B81-36698

Castle, Wilfrid T. F.. The imitator / Wilfrid T.F. Castle. — Bognor Regis : New Horizon, c1979. — 178p ; 21cm
ISBN 0-86116-264-1 : £4.75 B81-19085

Charteris, Leslie. Count on the Saint. — London : Hodder & Stoughton, Oct.1981. — [176]p. — (Coronet books)
Originally published: 1980
ISBN 0-340-27105-1 (pbk) : £1.25 : CIP entry B81-26725

Charteris, Leslie. The Saint bids diamonds / Leslie Charteris. — London : Severn House, 1980. — 255p ; 21cm
ISBN 0-7278-0639-4 : £5.50 : CIP rev. B80-30252

Charteris, Leslie. The Saint to the rescue / Leslie Charteris. — [Sevenoaks] : Coronet, 1963, c1959 (1978 [printing]). — 188p ; 18cm
Originally published: London : Hodder & Stoughton, 1961
ISBN 0-340-01729-5 (pbk) : £0.75 : CIP rev. B78-25480

Chase, James Hadley. Believed violent / James Hadley Chase. — London : Corgi, 1980, c1968. — 184p ; 18cm
Originally published: London : Hale, 1968
ISBN 0-552-11506-1 (pbk) : £0.95 B81-00384

Chase, James Hadley. A can of worms / James Hadley Chase. — [London] : Corgi, 1981, c1979. — 190p ; 18cm
Originally published: London : Hale, 1979
ISBN 0-552-11598-3 (pbk) : £0.95 B81-08413

Chase, James Hadley. Consider yourself dead / James Hadley Chase. — London : Corgi, 1979, c1978 (1980 [printing]). — 189p ; 18cm
Originally published: London : Hale, 1978
ISBN 0-552-11042-6 (pbk) : £0.85 B81-13112

Chase, James Hadley. An ear to the ground / James Hadley Chase. — [London] : Corgi, 1981, c1968. — 189p ; 18cm
Originally published: London : Hale, 1968
ISBN 0-552-11631-9 (pbk) : £0.95 B81-15343

Chase, James Hadley. Figure it out for yourself / James Hadley Chase. — London : Hale, 1950 (1979 [printing]). — 256p ; 21cm
ISBN 0-7091-7223-0 : £3.95 B81-02868

Chase, James Hadley. More deadly than the male / James Hadley Chase. — London : Hale, c1981. — 223p ; 23cm
Originally published: under the name Ambrose Grant. London : Eyre and Spottiswoode, 1946
ISBN 0-7091-8649-5 : £6.50 B81-11162

Chase, James Hadley. Try this one for size / James Hadley Chase. — London : Hale, 1980. — 160p ; 23cm
ISBN 0-7091-8553-7 : £5.50 B81-01242

Chase, James Hadley. Try this one for size / James Hadley Chase. — Large print ed. — London : Hale, 1980. — 286p ; 23cm
ISBN 0-7091-8563-4 : £6.50 B81-07090

Chase, James Hadley. Well now, my pretty / James Hadley Chase. — London : Corgi, 1980, c1967. — 187p ; 18cm
Originally published: London : Hale, 1967
ISBN 0-552-11558-4 (pbk) : £0.95 B81-02690

Chase, James Hadley. The whiff of money / James Hadley Chase. — [London] : Corgi, 1981, c1969. — 192p ; 18cm
Originally published: London : Hale, 1969
ISBN 0-552-11703-x (pbk) : £0.95 B81-27241

Chase, James Hadley. You can say that again / James Hadley Chase. — [London] : Corgi, 1981, c1980. — 187p ; 18cm
Originally published: London : Hale, 1980
ISBN 0-552-11687-4 (pbk) : £0.95 B81-21197

Christian, Catherine. The sword and the flame : variations on a theme of Sir Thomas Malory / Catherine Christian. — London : Pan in association with Macmillan, 1979, c1978 (1981 printing). — 505p : 2maps ; 18cm
Originally published: as The sword and the flame, London : Macmillan, 1978 ; and as The Pendragon, London : Pan, 1979
ISBN 0-330-26492-3 (pbk) : £1.95 B81-36773

Christie, Agatha. The ABC murders / Agatha Christie. — Large print ed. — Leicester : Ulverscroft, 1980, c1936. — 344p ; 23cm. — (Ulverscroft large print series)
ISBN 0-7089-0590-0 : £4.25 B81-00385

823′.912[F] — Fiction in English, *1900-1945 — Texts* *continuation*

Christie, Agatha. After the funeral / Agatha Christie. — [London] : Fontana, 1956, c1953 (1981 [printing]). — 192p : 1geneal.table ; 18cm
Originally published: London : Collins, 1953
ISBN 0-00-616275-4 (pbk) : £1.00 B81-15535

Christie, Agatha. At Bertram′s hotel / Agatha Christie ; featuring Miss Marple, the original character as created by Agatha Christie. — [London] : Fontana, 1968, 1965 (1981 [printing]). — 192p ; 18cm
Originally published: London : Collins, 1965
ISBN 0-00-616171-5 (pbk) : £1.00 B81-11181

Christie, Agatha. The best of Poirot / by Agatha Christie. — London : Collins, 1980. — 862p ; 23cm. — (Collins′ collectors′ choice)
Contents: Murder on the Orient Express - Cards on the table - Hercule Poirot′s Christmas - Five little pigs - The labours of Hercules
ISBN 0-00-244685-5 : £5.95 B81-08026

Christie, Agatha. Cards on the table / Agatha Christie. — [London] : Fontana, 1957, c1936 (1981 [printing]). — 192p ; 18cm
Originally published: London : Collins, 1936
ISBN 0-00-616281-9 (pbk) : £1.00 B81-22008

Christie, Agatha. A Caribbean mystery / Agatha Christie. — [London] : Fontana, 1981, c1964 (1981 [printing]). — 158p ; 18cm
Originally published: London : Collins, 1964
ISBN 0-00-616435-8 (pbk) : £1.00 B81-39748

Christie, Agatha. Cat among the pigeons / Agatha Christie. — [London] : Fontana, 1962, c1959 (1981 [printing]). — 187p ; 18cm
Originally published: London : Collins, 1959
ISBN 0-00-616174-x (pbk) : £1.00 B81-10214

Christie, Agatha. The clocks / Agatha Christie. — [London] : Fontana, 1966, c1963 (1981 [printing]). — 221p ; 18cm
Originally published: London : Collins, 1963
ISBN 0-00-616173-1 (pbk) : £1.00 B81-10217

Christie, Agatha. Death comes as the end / Agatha Christie. — [London] : Fontana, 1960, c1945 (1981 [printing]). — 191p ; 18cm
Originally published: London : Collins, 1945
ISBN 0-00-616373-4 (pbk) : £1.00 B81-36830

Christie, Agatha. Elephants can remember / Agatha Christie. — [London] : Fontana, 1975, c1972 (1981 [printing]). — 160p ; 18cm
Originally published: London : Collins, 1972
ISBN 0-00-616264-9 (pbk) : £1.00 B81-10215

Christie, Agatha. Five little pigs / Agatha Christie. — [London] : Fontana, 1959, c1942 (1981 printing). — 188p ; 19cm
ISBN 0-00-616372-6 (pbk) : £1.00 B81-28691

Christie, Agatha. Hercule Poirot′s Christmas / Agatha Christie. — London : Pan in association with Collins, 1967, c1939 (1980 [printing]). — 203p ; 18cm
ISBN 0-330-10721-6 (pbk) : £0.95 B81-07040

Christie, Agatha. The mirror crack′d from side to side / Agatha Christie. — [London] : Fontana, 1965, c1962 (1981 [printing]). — 191p ; 18cm
Originally published: London : Collins, 1962
ISBN 0-00-616135-9 (pbk) : £1.25 B81-11182

Christie, Agatha. Mrs. McGinty′s dead / Agatha Christie. — [Glasgow] : Fontana, 1955, c1952 (1981 [printing]). — 188p ; 18cm
Originally published: London : Collins, 1952
ISBN 0-00-616371-8 (pbk) : £1.00 B81-18475

Christie, Agatha. The murder at the vicarage / Agatha Christie. — [London] : Fontana, 1961, c1930 (1981 [printing]). — 189p ; 18cm
ISBN 0-00-616130-8 (pbk) : £1.00 B81-32166

Christie, Agatha. Murder in Mesopotamia / by Agatha Christie. — London : Collins, 1936 (1978 [printing]). — 284p ; 19cm. — (The Crime Club)
ISBN 0-00-244506-9 : £3.20 B81-01243

Christie, Agatha. Murder in Mesopotamia / Agatha Christie. — London : Pan in association with Collins, 1952 (1981 [printing]). — 190p ; 18cm
ISBN 0-330-26322-6 (pbk) : £0.95 B81-18293

Christie, Agatha. N or M? / Agatha Christie. — London : Fontana, 1962, c1941 (1981 [printing]). — 189p ; 18cm
ISBN 0-00-616301-7 (pbk) : £1.00 B81-28215

Christie, Agatha. Ordeal by innocence / Agatha Christie. — [London] : Fontana, 1981, c1958, (1981 [printing]). — 192p ; 18cm
Originally published: London : Collins, 1958
ISBN 0-00-616424-2 (pbk) : £1.00 B81-39747

Christie, Agatha. The Sittaford mystery / by Agatha Christie. — London : Crime Club, 1978. — 191p ; 20cm
ISBN 0-00-244753-3 : £3.00 B81-08107

Christie, Agatha. Sparkling cyanide / Agatha Christie. — [London] : Fontana, 1960, c1945 (1981 [printing]). — 189p ; 18cm
Originally published: London : Collins, 1945
ISBN 0-00-616263-0 (pbk) : £1.00 B81-10216

Clinton-Baddeley, V. C.. To study a long silence / V.C. Clinton-Baddeley. — Large print ed. — Bath : Chivers, 1981, c1972. — 257p ; 23cm. — (A New Portway large print book)
Originally published: London : Gollancz, 1972
ISBN 0-85119-112-6 : £4.95 : CIP rev.
B81-03181

Collins, Norman. Little Nelson. — London : Collins, Nov.1981. — [154]p
ISBN 0-00-222610-3 : £5.95 : CIP entry
B81-30297

Compton-Burnett, I.. A heritage and its history / by I. Compton-Burnett. — London : Gollancz, 1959 (1979 [printing]). — 190p ; 21cm
ISBN 0-575-02723-1 : £4.95 B81-38548

Connolly, Cyril. The rock pool / Cyril Connolly ; with an introduction by Peter Quennell. — Oxford : Oxford University Press, 1981. — xxi,138p ; 20cm. — (Oxford paperbacks)
ISBN 0-19-281327-7 (pbk) : £2.50 : CIP rev.
B81-25794

Conrad, Joseph. Lord Jim / by Joseph Conrad. — Toronto ; London : Bantam, 1957 (1981 [printing]). — ix,271p ; 18cm. — (A Bantam classic)
ISBN 0-553-21027-0 (pbk) : £0.85 B81-39114

Conrad, Joseph. Lord Jim. — Large print ed. — Leicester : Ulverscroft, Sept.1981. — [512]p. — (Charnwood library series)
ISBN 0-7089-8014-7 : £5.25 : CIP entry
B81-22665

Conway, Laura. Dearest Mamma / Laura Conway. — Large print ed. — Bath : Chivers, 1981, c1969. — 288p ; 23cm. — (A Lythway general novel)
Originally published: London : Collins, 1969
ISBN 0-85119-730-2 : Unpriced : CIP rev.
B81-13715

Cowen, Frances. The elusive lover / by Frances Cowen. — London : Hale, 1981. — 191p ; 20cm
ISBN 0-7091-9354-8 : £5.75 B81-37319

Cowen, Frances. House of Larne / by Frances Cowen. — London : Hale, 1980. — 174p ; 20cm
ISBN 0-7091-8429-8 : £5.25 B81-02475

Creasey, John, *1908-1973*. Affair for the Baron / John Creasey as Anthony Morton. — Large print ed. — Bath : Lythway, 1980, c1976. — 257p ; 23cm
Originally published: London : Hodder and Stoughton, 1967
ISBN 0-85046-894-9 : £6.25 : CIP rev.
B80-10820

Creasey, John, *1908-1973*. Bad for the Baron / John Creasey as Anthony Morton. — Large print ed. — Bath : Lythway, 1980, c1962. — 274p ; 23cm
Originally published: London : Hodder and Stoughton, 1962
ISBN 0-85046-904-x : £6.25 : CIP rev.
B80-22555

Creasey, John, *1908-1973*. The Baron and the Chinese puzzle. — Large print ed. — Bath : Chivers, Oct.1981. — [320]p. — (A Lythway book)
Originally published: London : Hodder and Stoughton, 1965
ISBN 0-85119-750-7 : £6.90 : CIP entry
B81-25808

Creasey, John, *1908-1973*. The Baron and the missing old masters / John Creasey as Anthony Morton. — Large print ed. — Bath : Lythway, 1980, c1968. — 228p ; 23cm
Originally published: London : Hodder and Stoughton, 1968
ISBN 0-85046-895-7 : £5.95 : CIP rev.
B80-10821

Creasey, John, *1908-1973*. Burgle the Baron / John Creasey as Anthony Morton. — Large print ed. — Bath : Lythway, 1980, c1973. — v,266p ; 23cm
Originally published: London : Hodder and Stoughton, 1973
ISBN 0-85046-888-4 : £5.80 : CIP rev.
B80-08431

Creasey, John, *1908-1973*. A kind of prisoner : a Department Z adventure / by John Creasey. — Hornchurch : Henry, 1981, c1954. — 191p ; 21cm
Originally published: London : Hodder & Stoughton, 1954
ISBN 0-86025-187-x : £4.95 B81-17394

Creasey, John, *1908-1973*. The prophet of fire / John Creasey. — Hornchurch : Henry, 1980, c1951. — 192p ; 21cm
Originally published: London : Evans, 1951
ISBN 0-86025-177-2 : £4.95 B81-07176

Creasey, John, *1908-1973*. A sharp rise in crime / John Creasey. — Large print ed. — Leicester : Ulverscroft, 1981, c1978. — 253p ; 23cm. — (Ulverscroft large print series)
Originally published: London : Collins, 1978
ISBN 0-7089-0562-5 : £5.00 B81-11388

Creasey, John, *1908-1973*. Sport for the Baron / John Creasey as Anthony Morton. — Large print ed. — Bath : Chivers, 1980, c1966. — 217p ; 23cm
Originally published: London : Hodder & Stoughton, 1966
ISBN 0-85046-905-8 : £5.90 : CIP rev.
B80-22556

Creasey, John, *1908-1973*. The Toff and the Golden Boy / by John Creasey. — Bolton-by-Bowland : Magna, 1980, c1969. — 263p ; 23cm
Originally published: London : Hodder & Stoughton, 1969. — Published in large print
ISBN 0-86009-222-4 : £5.25 : CIP rev.
B79-37470

Crisp, Quentin. Chog : a Gothic fantasy / Quentin Crisp ; illustrations Jo Lynch. — London : Magnum, 1981, c1979. — 164p : ill ; 20cm
Originally published: London : Eyre Methuen, 1979
ISBN 0-417-03520-9 (pbk) : £2.50 B81-08419

823'.912[F] — Fiction in English, *1900-1945 — Texts* *continuation*

Crispin, Edmund. Love lies bleeding / Edmund Crispin. — Large print ed. — Bath : Chivers, 1980, c1948. — 354p ; 23cm
Originally published: London : Gollancz, 1948
ISBN 0-85997-479-0 : Unpriced : CIP rev.
B80-22505

Crispin, Edmund. The moving toyshop / Edmund Crispin. — Large print ed. — Bath : Chivers, 1981, c1946. — 317p ; 1map ; 23cm. — (New Portway)
Originally published: London : Gollancz, 1946
ISBN 0-85119-100-2 : Unpriced B81-08510

Crispin, Edward. The glimpses of the moon / Edward Crispin. — Harmondsworth : Penguin, 1981, c1977. — 301p ; 18cm
Originally published: London : Gollancz, 1977
ISBN 0-14-005047-7 (pbk) : £1.50 B81-35568

Cronin, A. J.. The citadel. — Large print ed. — Leicester : Ulverscroft, Sept.1981. — [592]p. — (Charnwood library series)
ISBN 0-7089-8005-8 : £6.50 : CIP entry
B81-22660

Cronin, A. J.. The Judas tree. — Large print ed. — Anstey : Ulverscroft, Feb.1982. — [420]p. — (Charnwood library series)
ISBN 0-7089-8025-2 : £5.25 : CIP entry
B81-36957

De Polnay, Peter. A minor giant. — Loughton : Piatkus, Aug.1981. — [224]p
ISBN 0-86188-075-7 : £6.50 : CIP entry
B81-15865

De Polnay, Peter. A stone throw / Peter de Polnay. — Loughton : Piatkus, 1981. — 228p ; 21cm
ISBN 0-86188-070-6 : £5.95 B81-16033

De Polnay, Peter. The talking horse / Peter de Polnay. — London : W.H. Allen, 1980. — 191p ; 21cm
ISBN 0-491-02753-2 : £5.95 B81-00386

De Selincourt, Hugh. The cricket match / Hugh de Selincourt ; with an introduction by Benny Green. — Oxford : Oxford University Press, 1979, c1924 (1980 printing). — xiii,193p ; 21cm
ISBN 0-19-281299-8 : £1.95 : CIP rev.
B80-07065

Deane, Sonia. Red roses from the doctor / Sonia Deane. — Large print ed. — Bath : Chivers, 1980, c1979. — 204p ; 23cm. — (A Seymour book)
Originally published: London : Hurst & Blackett, 1979
ISBN 0-86220-016-4 : £4.50 : CIP rev.
B80-17964

Delderfield, R. F.. Give us this day. — London : Hodder and Stoughton, Dec.1981. — [768]p
Originally published: 1973
ISBN 0-340-25354-1 (pbk) : £1.75 : CIP entry
B81-31444

Dell, Ethel M.. The obstacle race / Ethel M. Dell ; condensed by Barbara Cartland. — New York ; London : Bantam, 1980. — 152p ; 18cm. — (Barbara Cartland's library of love)
ISBN 0-553-13912-6 (pbk) : £0.95 B81-06458

Dell, Ethel M.. Tetherstones / by Ethel M. Dell ; condensed by Barbara Cartland. — London : Duckworth, 1981, c1978. — 200p ; 23cm. — (Barbara Cartland's library of love ; 21)
ISBN 0-7156-1532-7 : £6.95 B81-13124

Doyle, *Sir* Arthur Conan. The complete Sherlock Holmes / Arthur Conan Dolyle ; with a preface by Christopher Morley. — Harmondsworth : Penguin, 1981, c1930. — 1122p : ill,maps ; 21cm
ISBN 0-14-005694-7 (pbk) : £2.95 B81-30068

Doyle, *Sir* Arthur Conan. The complete Sherlock Holmes / by Sir Arthur Conan Doyle ; with a preface by Julian Symons. — London : Secker & Warburg, 1981. — viii,1122p : ill ; 25cm
ISBN 0-436-13300-8 : £9.95 B81-11630

Doyle, *Sir* Arthur Conan. The hound of the Baskervilles / Arthur Conan Doyle. — Harmondsworth : Penguin, 1981. — 174p ; 19cm
ISBN 0-14-000111-5 (pbk) : £0.95 B81-26500

Doyle, *Sir* Arthur Conan. The lost world : being an account of the recent amazing adventures of Professor E. Challenger ... / Sir Arthur Conan Doyle ; illustrated by Ian Newsham. — Harmondsworth : Puffin, 1981. — 263p : ill,maps ; 18cm
ISBN 0-14-031385-0 (pbk) : £0.95 B81-29490

Doyle, *Sir* Arthur Conan. The valley of fear / Sir Arthur Conan Doyle. — Harmondsworth : Penguin, 1981. — 179p : ill ; 19cm
ISBN 0-14-005710-2 (pbk) : £1.25 B81-34759

Du Maurier, Daphne. [The breaking point]. The blue lenses and other stories / Daphne du Maurier. — Harmondsworth : Penguin, 1970, c1959 (1980 printing). — 287p ; 18cm
Originally published: London : Gollancz, 1959
ISBN 0-14-003085-9 (pbk) : £1.25 B81-01244

Du Maurier, Daphne. The flight of the falcon / Daphne du Maurier. — Harmondsworth : Penguin, 1969, c1965 (1980 [printing]). — 282p ; 18cm
Originally published: London : Gollancz, 1965
ISBN 0-14-002946-x (pbk) : £1.25 B81-00387

Du Maurier, Daphne. The glass-blowers / by Daphne du Maurier. — London : Gollancz, 1963 (1981 [printing]). — 320p ; 23cm
ISBN 0-575-02922-6 : £6.95 B81-08670

Du Maurier, Daphne. Hungry Hill / Daphne du Maurier. — Harmondsworth : Penguin, 1965, c1943 (1979 [printing]). — 414p ; 19cm
ISBN 0-14-002344-5 (pbk) : £1.50 B81-01245

Du Maurier, Daphne. The King's General. — Large print ed. — Anstey : Ulverscroft, Jan.1982. — [504]p. — (Charnwood library series)
Originally published: London : Gollancz, 1946
ISBN 0-7089-8020-1 : £5.25 : CIP entry
B81-33994

Du Maurier, Daphne. Rebecca. — Large print ed. — Leicester : Ulverscroft, Sept.1981. — [599]p. — (Charnwood library series)
ISBN 0-7089-8006-6 : £6.50 : CIP entry
B81-22661

Du Maurier, Daphne. The scapegoat / by Daphne du Maurier. — London : Gollancz, 1957 (1981 [printing]). — 368p ; 25cm
ISBN 0-575-02921-8 : £6.95 B81-03452

Dunsany, Edward Plunkett, *Baron*. The king of Elfland's daughter. — London : Allen & Unwin, Feb.1982. — [192]p
ISBN 0-04-823207-6 (pbk) : £2.50 : CIP entry
B81-35917

Durbridge, Francis. Bat out of hell / Francis Durbridge. — Hornchurch : Henry, 1981, c1972. — 189p ; 21cm
Originally published: London : Hodder and Stoughton, 1972
ISBN 0-86025-189-6 : £5.25 B81-26461

Durbridge, Francis. Breakaway / Francis Durbridge. — London : Hodder and Stoughton, 1981. — 191p ; 21cm
ISBN 0-340-27023-3 : £5.95 : CIP rev.
B81-14842

Durbridge, Francis. The passenger / Francis Durbridge. — Sevenoaks : Coronet Books, 1978, c1977. — 160p ; 18cm
ISBN 0-340-22704-4 (pbk) : £0.75 : CIP rev.
B78-34842

Durrell, Lawrence. Livia, or, Buried alive : a novel / by Lawrence Durrell. — London : Faber, 1978 (1981 [printing]). — 265p ; 20cm. — (Faber paperbacks)
ISBN 0-571-11780-5 (pbk) : £2.50 : CIP rev.
B81-21611

Edgar, Josephine. The Lady of Wildersley. — Large print ed. — Bath : Chivers, Nov.1981. — [208]p. — (A Lythway book)
Originally published: London : Macdonald and Jane's, 1975
ISBN 0-85119-757-4 : £6.20 : CIP entry
B81-31249

Edgar, Josephine. My sister Sophie. — Large print ed. — Bath : Chivers, Oct.1981. — [296]p. — (A Lythway book)
Originally published: London : William Collins, 1964
ISBN 0-85119-751-5 : £6.90 : CIP entry
B81-25809

Elsna, Hebe. Cast a long shadow / Hebe Elsna. — Large print ed. — Bath : Lythway, c1976. — 248p ; 23cm
Originally published: London : Collins, 1976
ISBN 0-85046-913-9 : £6.30 : CIP rev.
B80-34110

Elsna, Hebe. The elusive crown / by Hebe Elsna. — Long Preston : Magna Print, 1981, c1973. — 321p ; 22cm
Originally published: London : Collins, 1973. — Published in large print
ISBN 0-86009-330-1 : Unpriced : CIP rev.
B81-14448

Elsna, Hebe. Gallant lady / by Hebe Elsna. — Bolton-by-Bowland : Magna Print, 1979, c1968. — 340p ; 23cm
Originally published: London : Collins, 1968. — Published in large print
ISBN 0-86009-194-5 : £4.95 : CIP rev.
B79-30338

Elsna, Hebe. The long years of loving / Hebe Elsna. — London : Hale, 1981. — 224p ; 21cm
Revised version of: Clemency Page. London : Collins, 1947
ISBN 0-7091-8826-9 : £6.50 B81-11740

Elsna, Hebe. Red-headed bastard / Hebe Elsna. — London : Hale, 1981. — 208p ; 21cm
ISBN 0-7091-9253-3 : £6.75 B81-40536

Essex, Mary. A doctor's love. — Large print ed. — Bath : Chivers Press, Jan.1982. — [248]p. — (A Lythway book)
Originally published: London : Hale, 1974
ISBN 0-85119-774-4 : £6.70 : CIP entry
B81-33809

Farnol, Jeffery. The amateur gentleman / by Jeffrey [i.e. Jeffery] Farnol ; condensed by Barbara Cartland. — London : Duckworth, 1981, c1978. — 247p ; 23cm. — (Barbara Cartland's library of love ; 22)
ISBN 0-7156-1536-x : £6.95 : CIP rev.
B81-06057

Farnol, Jeffery. The broad highway / by Jeffrey [i.e. Jeffery] Farnol ; condensed by Barbara Cartland. — London : Duckworth, 1980, c1978. — 213p ; 23cm. — (Barbara Cartland's library of love ; 16)
ISBN 0-7156-1476-2 : £6.95 : CIP rev.
B80-0750

Ferrars, Elizabeth. The cup and the lip / Elizabeth Ferrars. — Large print ed. — Bath : Lythway, 1980, c1975. — 253p ; 23cm
Originally published: London : Collins for the Crime Club, 1975
ISBN 0-85046-914-7 : £6.30 : CIP rev.
B80-3240

Ferrars, Elizabeth. Experiment with death / Elizabeth Ferrars. — London : Collins, 1981. — 182p ; 21cm. — (The crime club)
ISBN 0-00-231288-3 : £5.75 : CIP rev.
B81-1285

823'.912[F] — Fiction in English, ***1900-1945*** **—**
Texts *continuation*

Ferrars, Elizabeth. Frog in the throat / Elizabeth Ferrars. — London : Collins, 1980. — 176p ; 21cm. — (The Crime Club)
ISBN 0-00-231281-6 : £5.25 B81-01246

Ferrars, Elizabeth. Last will and testament / Elizabeth Ferrars. — Large print ed. — Leicester : Ulverscroft, 1980, c1978. — 283p ; 23cm. — (Ulverscroft large print series)
Originally published: London : Collins, 1978
ISBN 0-7089-0505-6 : £4.25 : CIP rev.
B80-17975

Ferrars, Elizabeth. Thinner than water. — London : Collins, Dec.1981. — [208]p. — (Crime Club)
ISBN 0-00-231895-4 : £6.25 : CIP entry
B81-31526

Ferrars, Elizabeth. Witness before the fact. — Large print ed. — Anstey : Ulverscroft, Oct.1981. — [304]p. — (Ulverscroft large print series)
Originally published: London : Collins, 1979
ISBN 0-7089-0688-5 : £5.00 : CIP entry
B81-28093

Forester, C. S.. The Commodore / C.S. Forester. — Harmondsworth : Penguin in association with Joseph, 1956, c1945 (1980 [printing]). — 271p ; 19cm
Originally published: London : Joseph, 1945
ISBN 0-14-001116-1 (pbk) : £1.25 B81-06402

Forester, C. S.. Hornblower in the West Indies / C.S. Forester. — London : Sphere, 1980, c1958. — 254p ; 18cm
Originally published: London : Joseph, 1958
ISBN 0-7221-0508-8 (pbk) : £1.25 B81-01247

Forester, C. S.. The peacemaker / C.S. Forester. — Large print ed. — Bath : Chivers, 1981, c1934. — 303p ; 23cm. — (A New Portway large print book)
ISBN 0-85119-115-0 : £5.25 : CIP rev.
B81-03834

Forester, C. S.. Plain murder / C.S. Forester. — Large print ed. — Bath : Chivers, 1981. — 298p ; 23cm. — (A New Portway large print book)
ISBN 0-85119-128-2 : Unpriced : CIP rev.
B81-06036

Forester, C. S.. The ship / C.S. Forester. — Harmondsworth : Penguin in association with Joseph, 1949, c1943 (1980 [printing]). — 187p ; 19cm
Originally published: London : Joseph, 1943
ISBN 0-14-000698-2 (pbk) : £0.95 B81-06403

Forster, E. M.. Passage to India. — Large print ed. — Leicester : Ulverscroft, Sept.1981. — [436]p. — (Charnwood library series)
ISBN 0-7089-8000-7 : £5.25 : CIP entry
B81-22657

Freeman, R. Austin. The red thumb mark / by R. Austin Freeman. — London : Remploy, 1979. — 248p ; 19cm
ISBN 0-7066-0816-x : £4.10 B81-38047

Gerhardie, William. Futility : a novel on Russian themes / William Gerhardie ; preface by Michael Holroyd. — Revised definitive collected ed. — Harmondsworth : Penguin, 1974, c1971 (1981 [printing]). — 183p ; 18cm. — (Penguin modern classics)
Originally published: London : Macdonald, 1971
ISBN 0-14-000391-6 (pbk) : £1.75 B81-14014

Gilbert, Anthony. Death takes a wife / Anthony Gilbert. — Large print ed. — Bath : Chivers, 1981, c1959. — 337p ; 23cm. — (New Portway)
Originally published: London : Collins, 1959
ISBN 0-85119-101-0 : Unpriced B81-08509

Gilbert, Anthony. The mouse who wouldn't play ball / Anthony Gilbert. — Large print ed. — Bath : Chivers, 1980. — 250p ; 23cm
ISBN 0-85997-482-0 : £5.50 : CIP rev.
B80-22517

Glyn, Elinor. The price of things / by Elinor Glyn ; condensed by Barbara Cartland. — London : Duckworth, 1980, c1978. — 182p ; 23cm. — (Barbara Cartland's library of love ; 20)
ISBN 0-7156-1480-0 : £6.95 B81-07291

Godden, Rumer. The battle of the Villa Fiorita / Rumer Godden. — London : Macdonald Futura, 1981, c1963. — 237p ; 18cm
Originally published: London : Macmillan, 1963
ISBN 0-7088-2018-2 (pbk) : £1.35 B81-15742

Godden, Rumer. A candle for St Jude / Rumer Godden. — London : Futura, 1980, c1973. — 186p ; 18cm. — (A Troubadour book)
Originally published: London : Joseph, 1948
ISBN 0-7088-1913-3 (pbk) : £1.10 B81-00388

Godden, Rumer. Five for sorrow, ten for joy / Rumer Godden. — London : Futura, 1980, c1979. — 237p ; 18cm. — (Troubadour)
Originally published: London : Macmillan, 1979
ISBN 0-7088-1842-0 (pbk) : £1.25 B81-00389

Godden, Rumer. In this house of Brede / Rumer Godden. — London : Futura, 1980, c1969. — 424p ; 18cm. — (A Troubadour book)
Originally published: London : Macmillan, 1969
ISBN 0-7088-1909-5 (pbk) : £1.75 B81-00390

Godden, Rumer. The peacock spring / Rumer Godden. — Large print ed. — Leicester : Ulverscroft, 1980, c1975. — 451p ; 23cm. — (Ulverscroft large print)
Originally published: London : Macmillan, 1975
ISBN 0-7089-0512-9 : £4.25 : CIP rev.
B80-17979

Goolden, Barbara. Before the flame is lit / Barbara Goolden. — Large print ed. — Bath : Chivers, 1981, c1971. — 208p ; 23cm. — (A Lythway book)
Originally published: London : Heinemann, 1971
ISBN 0-85119-736-1 : Unpriced : CIP rev.
B81-16112

Goolden, Barbara. The crystal and the dew. — Large print ed. — Bath : Chivers, Oct.1981. — [256]p. — (A Lythway book)
Originally published: London : William Heinemann, 1975
ISBN 0-85119-752-3 : £6.70 : CIP entry
B81-25810

Goolden, Barbara. A law for lovers / Barbara Goolden. — Large print ed. — Bath : Chivers, 1981, c1973. — 259p ; 23cm. — (A Lythway book)
Originally published: London : Heinemann, 1973
ISBN 0-85119-744-2 : £6.70 : CIP rev.
B81-20102

Goolden, Barbara. Sanctuary / Barbara Goolden. — London : Heinemann, 1980. — 175p ; 21cm
ISBN 0-434-30213-9 : £5.50 B81-01248

Goolden, Barbara. Sanctuary / Barbara Goolden. — Large print ed. — Bath : Chivers, 1981, c1980. — 238p ; 23cm. — (A Lythway general novel)
Originally published: London : Heinemann, 1980
ISBN 0-85119-724-8 : Unpriced : CIP rev.
B81-14923

Graeme, Bruce. Mather investigates / by Bruce Graeme. — London : Hale, 1980. — 175p ; 20cm
ISBN 0-7091-8606-1 : £5.95 B81-00391

Graeme, Bruce. The snatch. — Large print ed. — Bath : Chivers, Oct.1981. — [280]p. — (A Lythway book)
Originally published: London : Hutchinson, 1976
ISBN 0-85119-753-1 : £6.90 : CIP entry
B81-25811

Graeme, Bruce. Two-faced / Bruce Graeme. — Large print ed. — Bath : Chivers, 1981, c1977. — 280p ; 23cm. — (A Lythway thriller)
Originally published: London : Hutchinson, 1977
ISBN 0-85119-708-6 : Unpriced B81-10874

Graham, Winston. The stranger from the sea : a novel of Cornwall 1810-1811. — London : Collins, Oct.1981. — [424]p. — (Poldark ; 8)
ISBN 0-00-222616-2 : £7.95 : CIP entry
B81-25137

Greene, Graham. Brighton rock / Graham Greene. — Harmondsworth : Penguin in association with Heinemann, 1975 (1980 printing). — 246p ; 19cm
ISBN 0-14-000442-4 (pbk) : £1.10 B81-02229

Greene, Graham. A burnt-out case / Graham Greene. — Harmondsworth : Penguin in association with Heinemann, 1975 (1981 [printing]). — 198p ; 18cm
Originally published: London : Heinemann, 1961
ISBN 0-14-001894-8 (pbk) : £1.25 B81-22342

Greene, Graham. The comedians / Graham Greene. — Harmondsworth : Penguin, 1967, c1966 (1980 [printing]). — 286p ; 18cm
Originally published: London : Bodley Head, 1966
ISBN 0-14-002766-1 (pbk) : £1.25 B81-03377

Greene, Graham. The confidential agent : an entertainment / Graham Greene. — Harmondsworth : Penguin in association with Heinemann, 1963, c1971 (1980 [printing]). — 205p ; 18cm
ISBN 0-14-001895-6 (pbk) : £1.25 B81-03376

Greene, Graham. Doctor Fischer of Geneva, or, The bomb party / Graham Greene. — Harmondsworth : Penguin, 1981, c1980 (1981 [printing]). — 142p ; 18cm
Originally published: London : Bodley Head, 1980
ISBN 0-14-005588-6 (pbk) : £1.25 B81-35574

Greene, Graham. The end of the affair / Graham Greene. — Harmondsworth : Penguin in association with Heinemann, 1962, c1951 (1980 [printing]). — 191p ; 18cm
Originally published: London : Heinemann, 1951
ISBN 0-14-001785-2 (pbk) : £1.25 B81-03374

Greene, Graham. England made me / Graham Greene. — Harmondsworth : Penguin, 1943, c1962 (1981 [printing]). — 206p ; 19cm
ISBN 0-14-003146-4 (pbk) : £1.25 B81-10993

Greene, Graham. A gun for sale : an entertainment / Graham Greene. — Harmondsworth : Penguin in association with Heinemann, 1963 (1981 [printing]). — 186p ; 19cm
ISBN 0-14-001896-4 (pbk) : £1.25 B81-26510

Greene, Graham. The heart of the matter / Graham Greene. — Harmondsworth : Penguin in association with Heinemann, 1962, c1971 (1980 [printing]). — 271p ; 19cm
Originally published: London : Heinemann, 1948
ISBN 0-14-001789-5 (pbk) : £1.25 B81-01974

Greene, Graham. The honorary consul / Graham Greene. — Harmondsworth : Penguin, 1974, c1973 (1980 [printing]). — 267p ; 18cm
Originally published: London : Bodley Head, 1973
ISBN 0-14-003911-2 (pbk) : £1.25 B81-00392

823'.912[F] — Fiction in English, *1900-1945* —
Texts *continuation*

Greene, Graham. The honorary consul / Graham Greene. — London : Heinemann, 1980, c1973. — 334p ; 20cm. — (The collected edition / Graham Greene ; 21)
Originally published: London : Bodley Head, 1973
ISBN 0-434-30571-5 (corrected) : £6.95
ISBN 0-370-30347-4 (Bodley Head) B81-11764

Greene, Graham. It's a battlefield / Graham Greene. — Harmondsworth : Penguin, 1940, c1962 (1980 [printing]). — 201p ; 19cm
ISBN 0-14-000257-x (pbk) : £1.25 B81-02831

Greene, Graham. It's a battlefield / Graham Greene. — Large print ed. — Bath : Chivers, 1980. — 295p ; 23cm. — (New Portway)
ISBN 0-85997-473-1 : £5.50 : CIP rev. B80-18487

Greene, Graham. Loser takes all / Graham Greene. — Harmondsworth : Penguin, 1971, c1955 (1980 [printing]). — 123p ; 19cm
Originally published: London : Heinemann, 1955
ISBN 0-14-003277-0 (pbk) : £0.95 B81-08087

Greene, Graham. Our man in Havana : an entertainment / Graham Greene. — Harmondsworth : Penguin in association with Heinemann, 1962, c1958 (1981 [printing]). — 21.p ; 18cm
Originally published: London : Heinemann, 1958
ISBN 0-14-001790-9 (pbk) : £1.25 B81-06429

Greene, Graham. Our man in Havana. — Large print ed. — Bath : Chivers, Jan.1982. — [336] p. — (A New Portway large print book)
Originally published: London : Heinemann, 1958
ISBN 0-85119-151-7 : £5.35 : CIP entry B81-33811

Greene, Graham. The power and the glory / Graham Greene. — Harmondsworth : Penguin in association with Heinemann, 1962, c1971 (1980 [printing]). — 221p ; 18cm
ISBN 0-14-001791-7 (pbk) : £1.25 B81-03375

Greene, Graham. The quiet American / Graham Greene. — Harmondsworth : Penguin in association with Heinemann, 1962, c1973 (1980 [printing]). — 188p ; 18cm
Originally published: London : Heinemann, 1955
ISBN 0-14-001792-5 (pbk) : £1.25 B81-07200

Greene, Graham. A sense of reality / Graham Greene. — Harmondsworth : Penguin in association with the Bodley Head, 1968, c1963 (1981 [printing]). — 111p ; 18cm
Originally published: London : Bodley Head, 1963
ISBN 0-14-002821-8 (pbk) : £1.25 B81-40418

Greene, Graham. Stamboul train : an entertainment / Graham Greene. — Harmondsworth : Penguin in association with Heinemann, 1963, c1932 (1980 [printing]). — 215p ; 19cm
ISBN 0-14-001898-0 (pbk) : £1.25 B81-02677

Greene, Graham. The third man and The fallen idol / Graham Greene. — Harmondsworth : Penguin in association with Heinemann, 1971, c1977 (1981 [printing]). — 156p ; 18cm
Originally published: London : Heinemann, 1950
ISBN 0-14-003278-9 (pbk) : £0.95 B81-07369

Greene, Graham. Travels with my aunt / Graham Greene. — Harmondsworth : Penguin in association with the Bodley Head, 1971, c1969 (1980 [printing]). — 264p ; 18cm
Originally published: London : Bodley Head, 1969
£1.25 (pbk) B81-07512

Greig, Maysie. The golden garden / Maysie Greig. — Rev. ed. — Large print ed. — Bath : Chivers, 1981 c1968. — 271p ; 23cm. — (A Seymour book)
ISBN 0-85119-420-6 : Unpriced B81-24816

Hartley, L. P.. The go-between. — Large print ed. — Leicester : Ulverscroft, Sept.1981. — [401]p. — (Charnwood library series)
Originally published: London : H. Hamilton, 1953
ISBN 0-7089-8001-5 : £5.25 : CIP entry B81-22658

Harvey, Rachel. Dearest doctor. — Large print ed. — Bath : Chivers, Dec.1981. — [272]p. — (A Lythway book)
Originally published: London : Hurst & Blackett, 1968
ISBN 0-85119-764-7 : £6.80 : CIP entry B81-31795

Haycox, Ernest. The border trumpet / Ernest Haycox. — Large print ed. — Leicester : Ulverscroft, 1980, c1966. — 441p ; 22cm. — (Ulverscroft large print series)
ISBN 0-7089-0560-9 : £4.25 : CIP rev B80-35447

Haycox, Ernest. Chaffee of Roaring Horse / Ernest Haycox. — Large print ed. — Leicester : Ulverscroft, 1981, c1957. — 403p ; 23cm. — (Ulverscroft large print series)
ISBN 0-7089-0658-3 : £5.00 B81-28570

Heppenstall, Rayner. The blaze of noon / Rayner Heppenstall. — London : Allison & Busby, 1980. — 166p ; 23cm
ISBN 0-85031-288-4 (cased) : £6.50 : CIP rev.
ISBN 0-85031-298-2 (pbk) : £2.50 B80-02558

Heyer, Georgette. Bath tangle / Georgette Heyer. — Large print ed. — Leicester : Ulverscroft, 1980. — 562p ; 23cm. — (Ulverscroft large print series)
Originally published: London : Heinemann, 1955
ISBN 0-7089-0496-3 : £4.25 : CIP rev. B80-11612

Heyer, Georgette. Beauvallet / Georgette Heyer. — London : Pan in association with Heinemann, 1963 (1981 [printing]). — 219p ; 18cm
ISBN 0-330-10254-0 (pbk) : £1.50 B81-24733

Heyer, Georgette. The black moth. — London : Pan in association with Heinemann, 1965 (1981 [printing]). — 284p ; 18cm
ISBN 0-330-20092-5 (pbk) : £1.50 B81-17980

Heyer, Georgette. The conqueror / Georgette Heyer. — London : Pan in association with Heinemann, 1962 (1981 printing). — 348p ; 18cm
ISBN 0-330-20063-1 (pbk) : £1.50 B81-09735

Heyer, Georgette. Devil's cub / Georgette Heyer. — London : Pan in association with Heinemann, 1969 (1980 printing). — 285p ; 18cm
ISBN 0-330-02361-6 (pbk) : £1.50 B81-02133

Heyer, Georgette. The foundling / Georgette Heyer. — London : Pan in association with Heinemann, 1963 (1981 printing). — 350p ; 18cm
Originally published: London : Heinemann, 1948
ISBN 0-330-20031-3 (pbk) : £1.50 B81-18292

Heyer, Georgette. Frederica / Georgette Heyer. — London : Pan, 1968, c1965 (1981 [printing]). — 329p ; 18cm
Originally published: London : Bodley Head, 1965
ISBN 0-330-20272-3 (pbk) : £1.50 B81-24739

Heyer, Georgette. An infamous army / Georgette Heyer. — London : Pan in association with Heinemann, 1961 (1981 printing). — 411p ; 18cm
Bibliography: p410-412
ISBN 0-330-20062-3 (pbk) : £1.50 B81-09734

Heyer, Georgette. Regency buck. — Large print ed. — Anstey : Ulverscroft, Oct.1981. — [512] p. — (Ulverscroft large print series)
ISBN 0-7089-0694-x : £5.00 : CIP entry B81-28096

Hilton, James. Lost horizon / James Hilton. — London : Pan in association with Macmillan, 1947 (1980 [printing]). — 185p ; 18cm
ISBN 0-330-10558-2 (pbk) : £0.95 B81-06397

Hodgson, William Hope. The ghost pirates / William Hope Hodgson. — London : Sphere, 1981. — 139p ; 18cm
ISBN 0-7221-4679-5 : £1.10 B81-17979

Holt, Victoria. The devil on horseback / Victoria Holt. — London : Fontana, 1979, c1977 (1981 [printing]). — 315p ; 18cm
Originally published: London : Collins, 1977
ISBN 0-00-616278-9 (pbk) : £1.50 B81-28216

Holt, Victoria. The Judas kiss / Victoria Holt. — London : Collins, 1981. — 378p ; 22cm
ISBN 0-00-222295-7 : £7.50 : CIP rev. B81-25138

Holt, Victoria. The mask of the enchantress / Victoria Holt. — Large print ed. — Leicester : Ulverscroft, 1981, c1980. — 489p ; 23cm. — (Ulverscroft large print series)
Originally published: London : Collins, 1980
ISBN 0-7089-0652-4 : £5.00 B81-28568

Holt, Victoria. My enemy the Queen / Victoria Holt. — [London] : Fontana, 1980, c1978. — 351p ; 18cm
Originally published: London : Collins, 1978. — Bibliography: p350-351
ISBN 0-00-616450-1 (pbk) : £1.65 B81-32167

Holt, Victoria. The spring of the tiger / Victoria Holt. — [Glasgow] : Collins : Fontana, 1981, c1979. — 373p ; 18cm
Originally published: London : Collins, 1979
ISBN 0-00-616408-0 (pbk) : £1.50 B81-18478

Holt, Victoria. The spring of the tiger / Victoria Holt. — Large print ed. — Leicester : Ulverscroft, 1981, c1979. — 512p ; 23cm. — (Ulverscroft large print)
Originally published: London : Collins, 1979
ISBN 0-7089-0572-2 : £5.00 B81-11613

Holtby, Winifred. Anderby Wold. — London : Virago, Nov.1981. — [320]p. — (Virago modern classics)
ISBN 0-86068-207-2 (pbk) : £2.95 : CIP entry B81-30400

Holtby, Winifred. The crowded street. — London : Virago, Nov.1981. — [288]p. — (Virago modern classics)
ISBN 0-86068-208-0 (pbk) : £2.95 : CIP entry B81-30399

Holtby, Winifred. South Riding : an English landscape / Winifred Holtby. — [London] : Fontana, 1954, 1981 [printing]. — 510p ; 19cm
ISBN 0-00-616451-x (pbk) : £1.95 B81-3678

Holtby, Winifred. South Riding : an English landscape / Winifred Holtby ; with a new introduction by Kenneth Young. — New ed. — London : Collins, 1966 (1979 printing). — xvi,448p ; 22cm
ISBN 0-00-221761-9 : £5.50 B81-3866

Household, Geoffrey. The last two weeks of Georges Rivac / Geoffrey Household. — London : Sphere, 1980, c1978. — 187p ; 18cm
Originally published: London : Joseph, 1978
ISBN 0-7221-4672-8 (pbk) : £1.10 B81-0124

Household, Geoffrey. Summon the bright water / Geoffrey Household. — London : Joseph, 1981 — 190p ; 1map ; 23cm
ISBN 0-7181-2052-3 : £6.95 B81-3513

823'.912[F] — Fiction in English, *1900-1945* —
Texts *continuation*

Howard, Mary, *1907-*. Mr. Rodriguez / Mary Howard. — Large print ed. — Leicester : Ulverscroft, 1980, c1979. — 497p ; 23cm. — (Ulverscroft large print series)
Originally published: London : Collins, 1979
ISBN 0-7089-0551-x : £4.25 : CIP rev.
B80-35449

Howard, Mary, *1907-*. The Spanish summer / Mary Howard. — Large print ed. — Leicester : Ulverscroft, 1980, c1977. — 431p ; 23cm. — (Ulverscoft large print series)
Originally published: London : Collins, 1977
ISBN 0-7089-0524-2 : £4.25 : CIP rev.
B80-23720

Hull, E. M.. The lion tamer. — London : Duckworth, Sept.1981. — [188]p. — (Barbara Cartland's library of love ; no.24)
ISBN 0-7156-1539-4 : £4.95 : CIP entry
B81-22455

Hutchinson, R. C.. [Journey with strangers]. Recollection of a journey / R.C. Hutchinson. — London : Joseph, 1981, c1952. — 399p ; 21cm
Originally published: New York : Rinehart ; London : Cassell, 1952
ISBN 0-7181-1995-9 : £6.95 B81-08484

Huxley, Aldous. Island / Aldous Huxley ; with an introduction and notes by M.J. Russell. — Harlow : Longman, 1980. — xi,291p ; 19cm. — (The Heritage of literature series)
Bibliography: p291
ISBN 0-582-35154-5 (pbk) : £1.75 B81-07207

Huxley, Elspeth. The mottled lizard / Elspeth Huxley. — Harmondsworth : Penguin, 1981, c1962. — 334p ; 18cm
Originally published: London : Chatto & Windus, 1962
ISBN 0-14-005958-x (pbk) : £1.50 B81-35569

Innes, Hammond. Dead and alive / Hammond Innes. — [London] : Fontana, 1958 (1981 [printing]). — 158p ; 18cm
Originally published: London : Collins, 1946
ISBN 0-00-616247-9 (pbk) : £1.00 B81-17439

Innes, Hammond. Levkas Man / Hammond Innes. — [London] : Fontana, 1973, c1971 (1981 [printing]). — 285p : 3maps ; 18cm
Originally published: London : Collins, 1971
ISBN 0-00-616347-5 (pbk) : £1.50 B81-17440

Innes, Hammond. The lonely skier / Hammond Innes. — [London] : Fontana, 1957 (1981 [printing]). — 192p ; 19cm
Originally published: London : Collins, 1947
ISBN 0-00-615966-4 (pbk) : £1.25 B81-32168

Innes, Hammond. [The Mary Deare]. The wreck of the Mary Deare / Hammond Innes. — [London] : Fontana, 1959, c1956 (1981 [printing]). — 254p : 2maps ; 18cm
Originally published: London : Collins, 1956
ISBN 0-00-616248-7 (pbk) : £1.50 B81-36780

Innes, Hammond. North Star / Hammond Innes. — [London] : Fontana, 1977, c1974 (1981 [printing]). — 256p : maps ; 18cm
Originally published: London : Collins, 1974
ISBN 0-00-615953-2 (pbk) : £1.35 B81-32169

Innes, Hammond. Solomons seal / Hammond Innes. — Large print ed. — Leicester : Ulverscroft, 1981, c1980. — 555p : maps ; 23cm. — (Ulverscroft large print series)
Originally published: London : Collins, 1980. — Maps on lining papers
ISBN 0-7089-0654-0 : £5.00 B81-28569

Innes, Hammond. The strange land / Hammond Innes. — London : Collins, 1954 (1979 [printing]). — 286p ; 21cm
ISBN 0-00-221768-6 : £4.95 B81-38543

Innes, Michael. The Ampersand papers / Michael Innes. — Harmondsworth : Penguin, 1980, c1978. — 192p ; 18cm. — (Penguin crime fiction)
Originally published: London : Gollancz, 1978
ISBN 0-14-005163-5 (pbk) : £0.95 B81-10927

Innes, Michael. Appleby at Allington / Michael Innes. — Large print ed. — Bath : Chivers, 1981, c1968. — 264p ; 23cm. — (A New Portway large print book)
Originally published: London : Gollancz, 1968
ISBN 0-85119-122-3 : Unpriced : CIP rev.
B81-13584

Innes, Michael. Appleby's answer / Michael Innes. — Large print ed. — Bath : Chivers, 1981, c1963. — 274p ; 23cm. — (A New Portway large print book)
Originally published: London : Gollancz, 1973
ISBN 0-85119-127-4 : Unpriced : CIP rev.
B81-13711

Innes, Michael. Appleby's End / Michael Innes. — Harmondsworth : Penguin, 1969, 1945 (1980 [printing]). — 188p ; 18cm
Originally published: London : Gollancz, 1945
ISBN 0-14-003002-6 (pbk) : £0.95 B81-07511

Innes, Michael. Appleby's other story. — Large print ed. — Bath : Chivers, Oct.1981. — [296] p. — (A New Portway large print book)
Originally published: London : Gollancz, 1974
ISBN 0-85119-137-1 : £5.40 : CIP entry
B81-25800

Innes, Michael. Lord Mullion's secret / by Michael Innes. — London : Gollancz, 1981. — 192p ; 21cm
ISBN 0-575-02903-x : £5.95 B81-21667

Innes, Michael. Silence observed / Michael Innes. — Feltham : Hamlyn, 1981, c1961. — 154p ; 18cm
Originally published: London : Gollancz, 1961
ISBN 0-600-20147-3 (pbk) : £1.00 B81-40999

Innes, Michael. The weight of the evidence : a detective story / by Michael Innes. — Feltham : Hamlyn, 1980, c1944. — 254p : 2plans ; 18cm. — (A Hamlyn whodunnit)
ISBN 0-600-20149-x (pbk) : £1.10 B81-00393

Irvine, Alexander. My lady of the chimney corner / Alexander Irvine. — Long Preston : Magna Print, 1981. — 226p ; 23cm
Published in large print
ISBN 0-86009-333-6 : Unpriced : CIP rev.
B81-14452

Isherwood, Christopher. Mr Norris changes trains / Christopher Isherwood ; with an introduction and notes by Geoffrey Halson. — Harlow : Longman, 1980, c1935. — xxviii,212p ; 19cm. — (The Heritage of literature series)
ISBN 0-582-33053-x (pbk) : £1.30 B81-03496

Jeffries, Roderic. Murder begets murder / Roderic Jeffries. — Large print ed. — Bath : Chivers, 1981, c1979. — 268p ; 23cm. — (A Lythway book)
Originally published: London : Colins for the Crime Club, 1979
ISBN 0-85119-745-0 : £6.70 : CIP rev.
B81-20101

Jesse, F. Tennyson. Moonraker / by F. Tennyson Jesse ; with a new introduction by Bob Leeson. — London : Virago, 1981, c1927. — 162p : ill ; 20cm. — (Virago modern classics)
ISBN 0-86068-186-6 (pbk) : £2.50 : CIP rev.
B81-03716

Johnson, Pamela Hansford. A bonfire / Pamela Hansford Johnson. — London : Macmillan, 1981. — 190p ; 23cm
ISBN 0-333-31138-8 : £5.95 B81-18570

Jones, Jack, *1884-*. Bidden to the feast / by Jack Jones. — London : Remploy, 1979. — 446p ; 22cm
ISBN 0-7066-0827-5 : £5.00 B81-38046

Keane, Molly. Good behaviour / Molly Keane. — London : Deutsch, 1981. — 245p ; 22cm
ISBN 0-233-97332-x : £6.50 B81-35376

Kennedy, Margaret, *1896-1967*. The ladies of Lyndon / Margaret Kennedy ; with a new introduction by Nicola Beauman. — London : Virago, 1981, c1967. — xix,320p ; 20cm. — (Virago modern classics)
ISBN 0-86068-215-3 (pbk) : £2.95 : CIP rev.
B81-27470

Kennedy, Margaret, *1896-1967*. Together and apart / Margaret Kennedy ; with a new introduction by Julia Birley. — London : Virago, 1981, c1967. — x,342p ; 20cm. — (Virago modern classics)
ISBN 0-86068-216-1 (pbk) : £2.95 : CIP rev.
B81-27469

Kyle, Elisabeth. All the nice girls / Elisabeth Kyle. — Bolton-by-Bowland : Magna Print, 1981, c1976. — 320p ; 23cm
Originally published: London : P. Davies, 1976. — Published in large print
ISBN 0-86009-300-x : £5.75 B81-12233

Kyle, Elisabeth. The burning hill. — Large print ed. — Long Preston : Magna, Sept.1981. — [356]p
ISBN 0-86009-343-3 : £4.95 : CIP entry
B81-22460

Kyle, Elisabeth. The deed box / Elisabeth Kyle. — London : Hale, 1981. — 159p ; 21cm
ISBN 0-7091-9250-9 : £6.50 B81-40543

Kyle, Elisabeth. Down the water / by Elisabeth Kyle. — Bolton-by-Bowland : Magna, 1980, c1975. — 327p ; 23cm
Originally published: London : P. Davies, 1975. — Published in large print
ISBN 0-86009-272-0 : £5.25 : CIP rev.
B80-22539

Lawrence, D. H.. Aaron's rod / D.H. Lawrence. — Harmondsworth : Penguin in association with Heinemann, 1950 (1981 [printing]). — 346p ; 19cm
ISBN 0-14-000755-5 (pbk) : £1.95 B81-27228

Lawrence, D. H.. The boy in the bush / D.H. Lawrence and M.L. Skinner. — Harmondsworth : Penguin, 1963, c1924 (1981 [printing]). — 391p ; 18cm
ISBN 0-14-001935-9 (pbk) : £1.95 B81-18335

Lawrence, D. H.. The first Lady Chatterley : the first version of Lady Chatterley's lover / D.H. Lawrence ; with a foreword by Frieda Lawrence. — Harmondsworth : Penguin, 1973 (1981 [printing]). — 253p ; 18cm
ISBN 0-14-003731-4 (pbk) : £1.50 B81-07370

Lawrence, D. H.. Kangaroo / D.H. Lawrence. — Harmondsworth : Penguin in association with Heinemann, 1950, c1951 (1981 [printing]). — 394p ; 19cm
ISBN 0-14-000751-2 (pbk) : £1.50 B81-22039

Lawrence, D. H.. Lady Chatterley's lover / D.H. Lawrence ; with an introduction by Richard Hoggart. — Harmondsworth : Penguin in association with Heinemann, 1961 (1980 [printing]). — xiv,316p ; 19cm
ISBN 0-14-001484-5 (pbk) : £1.00 B81-01868

Lawrence, D. H.. [Lady Chatterley's lover]. John Thomas and Lady Jane : the second version of Lady Chatterley's lover / D.H. Lawrence. — Harmondsworth : Penguin, 1973, c1972 (1981 [printing]). — 376p ; 18cm
Originally published: London : Heinemann, 1972
ISBN 0-14-003732-2 (pbk) : £1.95 B81-26552

Lawrence, D. H.. The lost girl / D.H. Lawrence. — Harmondsworth : Penguin in association with Heinemann, 1950, c1920 (1980 [printing]). — 400p ; 19cm
ISBN 0-14-000752-0 (pbk) : £1.25 B81-01250

823'.912[F] — Fiction in English, *1900-1945* **—**
Texts *continuation*

Lawrence, D. H.. The lost girl. — Cambridge ed. — Cambridge : Cambridge University Press, Sept.1981. — 1v.
ISBN 0-521-22263-x : CIP entry
ISBN 0-521-29423-1 (pbk) : Unpriced
B81-23765

Lawrence, D. H.. The plumed serpent / D.H. Lawrence. — Harmondsworth : Penguin in association with Heinemann, 1950, c1926 (1981 [printing]). — 462p ; 18cm
ISBN 0-14-000754-7 (pbk) : £1.25 B81-14347

Lawrence, D. H.. The Prussian officer / D.H. Lawrence. — Harmondsworth : Penguin in association with Heinemann, 1945 (1981 [printing]). — 224p ; 18cm
ISBN 0-14-000513-7 (pbk) : £1.00 B81-14348

Lawrence, D. H.. The rainbow / D.H. Lawrence ; introduction by Richard Hoggart ; illustrations by Charles Raymond. — London : Folio Society, 1981. — 430p,[19]leaves of plates : ill ; 26cm
In slip case
Unpriced B81-32071

Lawrence, D. H.. Sons and lovers / D.H. Lawrence. — Harmondsworth : Penguin, 1948, c1913 (1981 [printing]). — 511p ; 18cm
ISBN 0-14-000668-0 (pbk) : £1.25 B81-11028

Lawrence, D. H.. Sons and lovers. — Large print ed. — Leicester : Ulverscroft, Sept.1981. — [681]p. — (Charnwood library series)
ISBN 0-7089-8008-2 : £6.50 : CIP entry
B81-22663

Lawrence, D. H.. St Mawr ; and, The virgin and the gipsy / D.H. Lawrence. — Harmondsworth : Penguin, 1950 (1981 [printing]). — 251p ; 18cm
ISBN 0-14-000757-1 (pbk) : £0.95 B81-11034

Lawrence, D. H.. Three novellas / D.H. Lawrence. — Harmondsworth : Penguin in association with Heinemann, 1960 (1981 [printing]). — 250p ; 18cm
Contents: The ladybird - The fox - The captains doll
ISBN 0-14-001483-7 (pbk) : £1.00 B81-14346

Lawrence, D. H.. The trespasser / D.H. Lawrence. — Harmondsworth : Penguin in association with Heinemann, 1960 (1981 [printing]). — 216p ; 19cm
ISBN 0-14-001480-2 (pbk) : £1.25 B81-22038

Lawrence, D. H.. The white peacock / D.H. Lawrence ; with an introduction by Richard Aldington. — Harmondsworth : Penguin, 1950 (1981 [printing]). — 368p ; 18cm
ISBN 0-14-000760-1 (pbk) : £1.25 B81-11035

Lawrence, D. H.. Women in love / D.H. Lawrence. — Harmondsworth : Penguin in association with Heinemann, 1960, c1921 (1980 [printing]). — 540p ; 18cm
ISBN 0-14-001485-3 (pbk) : £1.00 B81-01251

Lawrence, D. H. David Herbert. The rainbow / D.H. Lawrence ; edited with an introduction and notes by John Worthen. — Harmondsworth : Penguin, 1981. — 574p ; 18cm
Bibliography: p574
ISBN 0-14-043155-1 (pbk) : £1.50 B81-38352

Lawrence, D. H. David Herbert. Sons and lovers / D.H. Lawrence ; edited with an introduction and notes by Keith Sagar. — Harmondsworth : Penguin, 1981. — 506p ; 18cm. — (The Penguin English library)
Bibliography: p505-506
ISBN 0-14-043154-3 (pbk) : £1.50 B81-38353

Lehmann, Rosamond. Dusty answer / Rosamond Lehmann. — Harmondsworth : Penguin, 1936 (1981 [printing]). — 303p ; 20cm. — (Penguin modern classics)
ISBN 0-14-000053-4 (pbk) : £2.95 B81-35074

Lehmann, Rosamond. The echoing grove / Rosamond Lehmann. — Harmondsworth : Penguin, 1958 (1981 [printing]). — 300p ; 20cm. — (Penguin modern classics)
Originally published: London : Collins, 1953
ISBN 0-14-001262-1 (pbk) : £2.95 B81-34761

Lehmann, Rosamund. Invitation to the waltz / by Rosamund Lehmann ; with a new introduction by Janet Watts. — London : Virago, 1981, c1932. — 302p ; 20cm. — (Virago modern classics)
ISBN 0-86068-202-1 (pbk) : £2.95 : CIP rev.
B81-09459

Lehmann, Rosamund. The weather in the streets / Rosamund Lehmann ; with a new introduction by Janet Watts. — London : Virago, 1981, c1936. — 383p ; 20cm. — (Virago modern classics)
ISBN 0-86068-203-x (pbk) : £2.95 B81-09458

Lewis, C. S.. Out of the silent planet / C.S. Lewis. — Large print ed. — Bath : Chivers, 1981. — 275p ; 23cm. — (A New Portway large print book)
ISBN 0-85119-132-0 : £5.25 : CIP rev.
B81-20114

Lewis, Wyndham, *1882-1957*. Mrs. Dukes' million / Wyndham Lewis. — London : Prior, 1980, c1977. — 365p ; 22cm
Originally published: Toronto : Coach House, 1977
ISBN 0-86043-505-9 : £7.95 B81-05440

Lindsay, David. A voyage to Arcturus / David Lindsay. — London : Sphere, 1980, c1920. — 287p ; 18cm
ISBN 0-7221-5541-7 (pbk) : £1.50 B81-11704

Linklater, Eric. Laxdale Hall / by Eric Linklater. — Loanhead (Edgefield Rd., Loanhead, Midlothian) : Macdonald, c1981. — 301p ; 23cm
ISBN 0-904265-44-7 : £6.95 B81-29835

Linklater, Eric. Position at noon / by Eric Linklater ; with decorations by Hans Tisdall. — Loanhead (Edgefield Rd, Loanhead, Midlothian) : Macdonald Publishers, c1980. — 252p : ill,1geneal.table ; 23cm
Originally published: London : Cape, 1958
ISBN 0-904265-38-2 (cased) : £5.95
ISBN 0-904265-42-0 (pbk) B81-00394

Llewellyn, Richard. A night of bright stars / Richard Llewellyn. — London : New English Library, 1980, c1979. — 203p ; 18cm
Originally published: London : Joseph, 1979
ISBN 0-450-04947-7 (pbk) : £1.50 B81-01252

Llewellyn, Richard. Up, into the singing mountain / Richard Llewellyn. — London : New English Library, 1976, c1960 (1978 [printing]). — 287p ; 18cm
Originally published: Garden City, N.Y. : Doubleday, 1960 ; London : Joseph, 1963
ISBN 0-450-03849-1 (pbk) : £0.90 B81-01253

Lofts, Norah. A calf for Venus. — London : Hodder & Stoughton, Feb.1982. — [240]p
ISBN 0-340-25468-8 : £6.95 : CIP entry
B81-35686

Lofts, Norah. The claw / Norah Lofts. — London : Hodder and Stoughton, 1981. — 220p ; 23cm
ISBN 0-340-26409-8 : £6.95 : CIP rev.
B81-13891

Lofts, Norah. Day of the butterfly / Norah Lofts. — Large print ed. — Leicester : Ulverscroft, 1981, c1979. — 502p ; 23cm. — (Ulverscroft large print series)
Originally published: London : Bodley Head, 1979
ISBN 0-7089-0623-0 : £5.00 : CIP rev.
B81-07428

Lofts, Norah. Requiem for idols / Norah Lofts. — [London] : Corgi, 1972 (1980 [printing]). — 141p ; 18cm
ISBN 0-552-11488-x (pbk) : £0.95 B81-03450

Lofts, Norah. Silver nutmeg / Norah Lofts. — [London] : Corgi, 1968 (1980 [printing]). — 447p ; 18cm
Originally published: London : Joseph, 1947
ISBN 0-552-11490-1 (pbk) : £1.75 B81-05910

Lofts, Norah. To see a fine lady / Norah Lofts. — London : Corgi, 1968 (1980 [printing]). — 223p ; 18cm
Originally published: London : Joseph, 1946
ISBN 0-552-11397-2 (pbk) : £1.25 B81-03010

Lofts, Norah. White hell of pity / Norah Lofts. — London : Corgi, 1970 (1980 [printing]). — 187p ; 18cm
ISBN 0-552-11489-8 (pbk) : £1.00 B81-02863

Lofts, Norah, *1904-*. The old priory / Norah Lofts. — London : Bodley Head, 1981. — 213p ; 21cm
ISBN 0-370-30391-1 : £5.95 : CIP rev.
B81-00395

Lymington, John. The power ball / by John Lymington. — London : Hale, 1981. — 192p ; 20cm
ISBN 0-7091-9155-3 : £6.25 B81-27315

Macaulay, Rose. They were defeated. — Oxford : Oxford University Press, Oct.1981. — [448]p. — (Oxford paperbacks)
ISBN 0-19-281316-1 (pbk) : £2.50 : CIP entry
B81-25793

Macdonald, William Colt. [The devil's drum]. Hellgate / William Colt MacDonald. — Hornchurch : Henry, 1980, c1956. — 157p ; 21cm
Originally published: Philadelphia : Lippincott, 1956
ISBN 0-86025-178-0 : £4.95 B81-09681

MacDonald, William Colt. Peaceful Jenkins / William Colt MacDonald. — London : Remploy, 1979. — 192p ; 19cm
ISBN 0-7066-0805-4 : £3.70 B81-17336

MacDonald, William Colt. Sombrero / William Colt MacDonald. — Large print ed. — Leicester : Ulverscroft, 1980. — 372p ; 23cm. — (Ulverscroft large print series)
ISBN 0-7089-0517-x : £4.25 : CIP rev.
B80-17993

MacDonald, William Colt. The three mesquiteers / William Colt MacDonald. — London : Remploy, 1979. — 253p ; 19cm
Originally published: London : Hodder & Stoughton, 1947
ISBN 0-7066-0808-9 : £3.90 B81-17337

McLaverty, Michael. In this thy day / Michael McLaverty. — Swords (Knocksedan House, Swords, Co. Dublin) : Poolbeg, 1981. — 200p ; 18cm
Originally published: London : Cape, 1945
ISBN 0-905169-45-x (pbk) : £2.75 B81-20386

Macpherson, Ian, *1905-1944*. Wild harbour / by Ian Macpherson ; introduction by Donald Campbell. — Edinburgh : Harris, 1981. — xi,251p ; 23cm. — (The Scottish fiction reprint library)
ISBN 0-86228-022-2 : £6.95 B81-28359

Manning, Marsha. The heart alone / by Marsha Manning. — London : Hale, 1981. — 158p ; 20cm
ISBN 0-7091-8805-6 : £5.50 B81-14092

Marric, J. J.. Gideon's badge / J.J. Marric. — Large print ed. — Leicester : Ulverscroft, 1980. — 353p ; 23cm. — (Ulverscroft large print series)
Originally published: London : Hodder and Stoughton, 1966
ISBN 0-7089-0535-8 : £4.25 : CIP rev.
B80-24855

823'.912[F] — Fiction in English, *1900-1945* — *Texts* *continuation*

Marric, J. J.. Gideon's vote. — Large print ed. — Anstey : Ulverscroft, Feb.1982. — [368]p. — (Ulverscroft large print series : mystery)
ISBN 0-7089-0745-8 : £5.00 : CIP entry B81-36942

Marsh, Jean, *1897*. Unbidden dream / by Jean Marsh. — London : Hale, 1981. — 192p ; 20cm
ISBN 0-7091-9176-6 : £5.60 B81-24443

Marsh, Jean, *1897-*. Mistress of Tanglewood / by Jean Marsh. — London : Hale, 1981. — 191p ; 20cm
ISBN 0-7091-8632-0 : £5.50 B81-03016

Meynell, Laurence. Hooky goes to blazes : a Hooky Hefferman story / Laurence Meynell. — London : Macmillan, 1981. — 188p ; 21cm
ISBN 0-333-30040-8 : £5.50 B81-11680

Meynell, Lawrence. Hooky gets the wooden spoon. — Large print ed. — Bath : Chivers, Jan.1982. — [272]p. — (A Lythway book)
Originally published: London : Macmillan, 1977
ISBN 0-85119-778-7 : £6.90 : CIP entry B81-33795

Mitchell, Gladys. The death-cap dancers / Gladys Mitchell. — London : Joseph, 1981. — 192p ; 21cm
ISBN 0-7181-1984-3 : £6.50 B81-09888

Mitchell, Gladys. The death cap dancers. — Large print ed. — Long Preston : Magna Print Books, Feb.1982. — [420]p
Originally published: London: Michael Joseph, 1981
ISBN 0-86009-379-4 : £5.25 : CIP entry B81-36026

Mitchell, Gladys. Lovers, make moan / Gladys Mitchell. — London : Joseph, 1981. — 192p ; 21cm
ISBN 0-7181-2031-0 : £6.95 B81-33474

Mitchell, Gladys. Mingled with venom. — Large print ed. — Long Preston : Magna, Sept.1981. — [412]p
ISBN 0-86009-339-5 : £4.95 : CIP entry B81-22465

Mitchell, Gladys. My father sleeps. — London : Severn House, Aug.1981. — [208]p
ISBN 0-7278-0724-2 : £5.95 : CIP entry B81-18103

Mitchell, Gladys. Nest of vipers / by Gladys Mitchell. — Long Preston : Magna, 1981, c1979. — 379p ; 23cm
Originally published: London : Joseph, 1979. — Published in large print
ISBN 0-86009-306-9 : £5.75 : CIP rev. B81-03710

Mitchell, Gladys. The worsted viper / Gladys Mitchell. — London : Severn House, 1980, c1943. — 191p ; 21cm
ISBN 0-7278-0603-3 : £5.25 : CIP rev. B80-18898

Mitchell, Gladys. Wraiths and changelings / by Gladys Mitchell. — Bolton-by-Bowland : Magna, 1980. — 367p ; 23cm
Originally published: London : Joseph, 1978. — Published in large print
ISBN 0-86009-276-3 : £5.25 : CIP rev. B80-22551

Mitchell, J. Leslie. The thirteenth disciple / J. Leslie Mitchell ; introduction by Douglas F. Young. — Edinburgh : Harris, c1981. — 286p ; 23cm. — (The Scottish fiction reprint library)
ISBN 0-86228-008-7 : £6.95 B81-28358

Mitford, Nancy. The blessing / Nancy Mitford. — Harmondsworth : Penguin in association with Hamish Hamilton, 1957, c1951 (1981 [printing]). — 221p ; 18cm
Originally published: London : Hamish Hamilton, 1951
ISBN 0-14-001211-7 (pbk) : £1.25 B81-14015

Mitford, Nancy. The pursuit of love ; and, Love in a cold climate / Nancy Mitford. — Harmondsworth : Penguin in association with Hamilton, 1980. — 456p ; 19cm
The pursuit of love originally published: London : Hamilton, 1945
ISBN 0-14-005696-3 (pbk) : £1.50 B81-01254

Monsarrat, Nicholas. The Kappillan of Malta / Nicholas Monsarrat. — London : Pan, 1975, c1973 (1980 printing). — xxxi,524p : 2maps ; 18cm
Originally published: London : Cassell, 1973
ISBN 0-330-24266-0 (pbk) : £2.25 B81-03617

Monsarrat, Nicholas. Three corvettes / Nicholas Monsarrat. — Large print ed. — Bath : Chivers, 1980, c1945. — 392p ; 23cm. — (New Portway)
Originally published: London : Cassell, 1945
ISBN 0-85997-484-7 : £5.50 : CIP rev. B80-22605

Monsarrat, Nicholas. The white rajah / Nicholas Monsarrat. — London : Pan, 1964, c1961 (1980 printing). — 365p : 1map ; 18cm
Originally published: London : Cassell, 1961
ISBN 0-330-20046-1 (pbk) : £1.75 B81-00517

Morton, Anthony. The Baron on board / John Creasey as Anthony Morton. — Large print ed. — Bath : Chivers, 1981, c1964. — 266p ; 23cm. — (A Lythway book)
Originally published: London : Hodder & Stoughton, 1964
ISBN 0-85119-734-5 : Unpriced : CIP rev. B81-18146

Morton, Anthony. A sword for the Baron / John Creasey as Anthony Morton. — Large print ed. — Bath : Chivers, 1981, c1963. — 274p ; 23cm. — (A Lythway book)
Originally published: London : Hodder and Stoughton, 1963
ISBN 0-85119-743-4 : £6.70 : CIP rev. B81-20103

Muskett, Netta. After rain. — Large print ed. — Anstey : Ulverscroft, Jan.1982. — [480]p. — (Ulverscroft large print series : romance)
ISBN 0-7089-0735-0 : £5.00 : CIP entry B81-33963

Muskett, Netta. Blue haze. — Loughton : Piatkus, Jan.1982. — [256]p
ISBN 0-86188-158-3 : £5.95 : CIP entry B81-34641

Muskett, Netta. Cloudbreak / Netta Muskett. — London : Remploy, 1979. — 207p ; 19cm
Originally published: London : Hutchinson, 1964
ISBN 0-7066-0833-x : £3.80 B81-38048

Muskett, Netta. The high fence / Netta Muskett. — Loughton : Piatkus, 1980. — 253p ; 21cm
Originally published: London : Hutchinson, 1959
ISBN 0-86188-047-1 : £4.95 : CIP rev. B80-18003

Muskett, Netta. Love and Deborah / Netta Muskett. — Loughton : Piatkus, 1981. — 254p ; 21cm
Originally published: London : Hutchinson, 1963
ISBN 0-86188-101-x : £5.95 : CIP rev. B81-04370

Muskett, Netta. Love in amber / by Netta Muskett. — Long Preston : Magna Print, 1981, c1942. — 419p ; 22cm
Published in large print
ISBN 0-86009-328-x : Unpriced : CIP rev. B81-14446

Muskett, Netta. Scarlet heels. — Large print ed. — Long Preston : Magna Print Books, Dec.1981. — [420]p
ISBN 0-86009-364-6 : £4.95 : CIP entry B81-31819

Muskett, Netta. Tamarisk. — Loughton : Piatkus, Sept.1981. — [216]p
ISBN 0-86188-113-3 : £5.95 : CIP entry B81-24596

Muskett, Netta. Through many waters / by Netta Muskett. — Bolton-by-Bowland : Magna Print, 1981, c1961. — 410p ; 23cm
Originally published: London : Hutchinson, 1961. — Published in large print
ISBN 0-86009-301-8 : £5.75 B81-12232

Muskett, Netta. Today is ours / Netta Muskett. — Loughton : Piatkus, 1981. — 255p ; 21cm
ISBN 0-86188-051-x : £5.50 B81-02483

Muskett, Netta. Wide and dark / Netta Muskett. — Large print ed. — Leicester : Ulverscroft, 1981, c1954. — 479p ; 23cm
ISBN 0-7089-0664-8 : £5.00 : CIP rev. B81-20630

O'Brian, Patrick. The Ionian mission / Patrick O'Brian. — London : Collins, 1981. — 346p ; 22cm
ISBN 0-00-222365-1 : £6.95 : CIP rev. B81-15914

O'Brien, Kate. The ante-room / Kate O'Brien. — Dublin (P.O. Box 1113, Baldoyle, Dublin 13) : Arlen, c1980. — xi,306p ; 18cm
ISBN 0-905223-22-5 (pbk) : £2.60 B81-09678

O'Flaherty, Liam. The black soul. — Dublin : Wolfhound Press, July 1981. — [200]p
ISBN 0-905473-63-9 : £6.00 : CIP entry B81-24641

O'Flaherty, Liam. Famine / Liam O'Flaherty. — Portmarnock (98 Ardilaun, Portmarnock, Co. Dublin) : Wolfhound, 1979, c1937. — 448p ; 22cm
Originally published: London : Gollancz, 1937
ISBN 0-905473-25-6 : £6.30 B81-00397

O'Flaherty, Liam. The wilderness / Liam O'Flaherty ; illustrations by Jeanette Dunne ; edited for publication by A.A. Kelly. — Dublin : Wolfhound, 1978. — 212p : ill ; 22cm
ISBN 0-905473-19-1 : £4.50 B81-01255

Oliver, Edith. The love child / Edith Oliver ; with a new introduction by Hermione Lee. — London : Virago, 1981, c1948. — 208p ; 20cm. — (Virago modern classics)
ISBN 0-86068-168-8 (pbk) : £2.50 B81-11273

Orwell, George. Nineteen eighty-four. — Large print ed. — Anstey : Ulverscroft, Feb.1982. — [428]p. — (Charnwood library series)
ISBN 0-7089-8027-9 : £5.25 : CIP entry B81-36959

Pargeter, Edith. This rough magic : a novel / by Edith Pargeter. — London : Remploy, 1979, c1953. — 329c : ill ; 19cm
Originally published: London : Heinemann, 1953
ISBN 0-7066-0802-x : £4.30 B81-34852

Parkinson, C. Northcote. So near so far / C. Northcote Parkinson. — London : John Murray, 1981. — 227p : i maps ; 22cm
ISBN 0-7195-3813-0 : £6.95 B81-03174

Peake, Mervyn. Mr Pye / Mervyn Peake ; with drawings by the author. — Harmondsworth : Penguin, 1972, c1969 (1981 [printing]). — 254p : ill ; 18cm
Originally published: London : Heinemann, 1953
ISBN 0-14-003372-6 (pbk) : £1.50 B81-32838

823'.912[F] — Fiction in English, *1900-1945 — Texts* *continuation*

Peake, Mervyn. Titus alone / Mervyn Peake. — Rev. ed. — Harmondsworth : Penguin in association with Eyre & Spottiswoode, 1970 (1981 [printing]). — 262p : ill ; 20cm
Previous ed.: London : Eyre & Spottiswoode, 1959
ISBN 0-14-006051-0 (pbk) : £1.95 B81-35589

Peters, Ellis. The knocker on death's door / Ellis Peters. — Large print ed. — Leicester : Ulverscroft, 1981, c1970. — 330p ; 23cm. — (Ulverscroft large print series)
Originally published: London : Macmillan, 1970
ISBN 0-7089-0633-8 : Unpriced : CIP rev. B81-13511

Peters, Ellis. The leper of Saint Giles : the fifth chronicle of Brother Cadfael / Ellis Peters. — London : Macmillan, 1981. — 223p : 1map ; 21cm
ISBN 0-333-31985-0 : £5.50 B81-39440

Peters, Ellis. Monk's-hood : the third chronicle of Brother Cadfael / Ellis Peters. — London : Macmillan, 1980. — 223p : 1plan ; 21cm
ISBN 0-333-29410-6 : £5.95 B81-01640

Peters, Ellis. A morbid taste for bones : a mediaeval whodunnit / Ellis Peters. — Large print ed. — Leicester : Ulverscroft, 1981, c1977. — 343p ; 23cm. — (Ulverscroft large print series)
Originally published: London : Macmillan, 1977
ISBN 0-7089-0659-1 : £5.00 : CIP rev. B81-20632

Peters, Ellis. Mourning raga / Ellis Peters. — Large print ed. — Leicester : Ulverscroft, 1981, c1969. — 319p ; 23cm. — (Ulverscroft large print series)
Originally published: London : Macmillan, 1969
ISBN 0-7089-0576-5 : £5.00 B81-11391

Peters, Ellis. Saint Peter's Fair / Ellis Peters. — London : Macmillan, 1981. — 220p : 1plan ; 21cm. — (The fourth chronicle of Brother Cadfael)
ISBN 0-333-31050-0 : £5.50 B81-21139

Plaidy, Jean. The Queen and Lord M / Jean Plaidy. — London : Pan, 1981. — 269p ; 18cm
Originally published: London : Robert Hale, 1973
ISBN 0-330-26016-2 (pbk) : £1.50 B81-12079

Plaidy, Jean. The star of Lancaster / Jean Plaidy. — London : Hale, 1981. — 320p : ill,geneal.tables ; 23cm. — (Plantagenet saga ; [v.11])
ISBN 0-7091-7996-0 : £6.95 B81-28874

Plaidy, Jean. The vow on the heron / Jean Plaidy. — London : Hale, 1980. — 350p : geneal.table ; 23cm. — (Plantagenet saga ; 9)
Bibliography: p8
ISBN 0-7091-7092-0 : £6.25 B81-01256

Porter, Gene Stratton. Freckles : by Gene Stratton Porter / condensed by Barbara Cartland. — Toronto ; London : Bantam, 1978. — 210p ; 18cm. — (Barbara Cartland's library of love ; 26)
Full ed. published: New York : London : Doubleday, Page, 1904
ISBN 0-553-12392-0 (pbk) : £0.70 B81-07562

Priestley, J. B.. Bright day / J.B Priestley. — London : Granada, 1980. — 303p ; 18cm. — (A panther book)
Originally published: London : William Heinemann, 1946
ISBN 0-586-05204-6 (pbk) : £2.25 B81-01257

Priestley, J. B.. The good companions / J.B. Priestley. — London : Granada, 1981. — 618p ; 18cm. — (A Panther book)
ISBN 0-586-05196-1 (pbk) : £2.50 B81-10877

Priestley, J. B.. It's an old country / J.B. Priestley. — London : Granada, 1981, c1967. — 254p ; 18cm. — (A Panther book)
Originally published: London : Heinemann, 1967
ISBN 0-586-05203-8 (pbk) : £1.95 B81-29489

Priestley, J. B.. Lost empires : being Richard Herncastle's account of his life on the variety stage from November 1913 to August 1914 together with a prologue and epilogue / J.B. Priestley. — London : Granada, 1980, c1965. — 346p ; 18cm. — (A Panther book)
Originally published: London : Heinemann, 1965
ISBN 0-586-05199-6 (pbk) : £1.95 B81-01702

Priestley, J. B.. The shapes of sleep : a topical tale / J.B. Priestley. — London : Granada, 1981, c1962. — 190p : ill ; 18cm. — (A Panther book)
Originally published: London : Heinemann, 1962
ISBN 0-586-05201-1 (pbk) : £1.75 B81-09889

Prole, Lozania. Judas Iscariot - traitor? / Ursula Bloom as Lozania Prole. — Large print ed. — Bath : Chivers, 1981, c1971. — 302p ; 23cm. — (A Lythway book)
Originally published: London : Hale, 1971
ISBN 0-85119-741-8 : £6.70 : CIP rev. B81-20105

Raymond, Ernest. We, the accused / Ernest Raymond. — [London] : Corgi, 1973, c1935 (1980 [printing]). — 509p ; 18cm
ISBN 0-552-11479-0 (pbk) : £1.75 B81-08024

Redwood, Alec. Wine with Veronica / Alec Redwood. — Bognor Regis : New Horizon, c1979. — 141p ; 21cm
ISBN 0-86116-058-4 : £3.50 B81-18867

Renault, Mary. Funeral games. — London : J. Murray, Oct.1981. — [272]p
ISBN 0-7195-3883-1 : £7.50 : CIP entry B81-27409

Richmond, Grace. Air ambulance nurse / by Grace Richmond. — London : Hale, 1981. — 160p ; 21cm
ISBN 0-7091-8813-7 : £5.50 B81-11658

Richmond, Grace. Haunted love / by Grace Richmond. — London : Hale, 1980. — 159p ; 20cm
ISBN 0-7091-8395-x : £5.25 B81-00398

Richmond, Grace. Nurse Hanson's strange case / by Grace Richmond. — London : Hale, 1981. — 160p ; 20cm
ISBN 0-7091-9035-2 : £5.75 B81-30072

Robins, Denise. Climb to the stars. — Large print ed. — Long Preston : Magna, Nov.1981. — [456]p
ISBN 0-86009-351-4 : £4.95 : CIP entry B81-30434

Robins, Denise. It wasn't love / by Denise Robins. — Bolton-by-Bowland : Magna Print, 1980, c1930. — 265p ; 22cm
Published in large print
ISBN 0-86009-331-x : Unpriced : CIP rev. B81-14450

Robins, Denise. Jezebel / Denise Robins. — Rev. ed.. — [London] : Coronet, 1979, c1977. — 256p ; 18cm
Previous ed.: published as She-devil under the name of Francesca Wright. London : Corgi, 1970
ISBN 0-340-23320-6 (pbk) : £0.85 B81-07355

Robins, Denise. Let me love. — London : Hodder & Stoughton, Oct.1981. — [224]p. — (Coronet books)
Originally published: 1979
ISBN 0-340-27108-6 (pbk) : £1.25 : CIP entry B81-26729

Robins, Denise. Light the candles / Denise Robins. — London : Severn House, 1981, c1959. — 188p ; 21cm
Originally published: London : Hurst & Blackett, 1959
ISBN 0-7278-0731-5 : £5.95 : CIP rev. B81-14930

Robins, Denise. Lightning strikes twice / by Denise Robins. — Bolton-by-Bowland : Magna, 1981, c1966. — 379p : ill ; 22cm
Originally published: London : Hodder and Stoughton, 1966. — Published in large print
ISBN 0-86009-295-x : £5.75 B81-08681

Robins, Denise. Loving and giving / by Denise Robins. — Bolton-by-Bowland : Magna, 1981, c1965. — 411p ; 23cm
Originally published: London : Hodder and Stoughton, 1966. — Published in large print
ISBN 0-86009-310-7 : £5.75 : CIP rev. B81-03711

Robins, Denise. Nightingale's song. — Large print ed. — Long Preston : Magna, Sept.1981. — [380]p
ISBN 0-86009-340-9 : £4.95 : CIP entry B81-22464

Robins, Denise. Second best / by Denise Robins. — Bolton-by-Bowland : Magna Print, 1981, c1931. — 400p ; 23cm
Published in large print
ISBN 0-86009-321-2 : £5.75 : CIP rev. B81-10450

Robins, Denise. Slave women. — Large print ed. — Long Preston : Magna Print Books, Feb.1982. — [440]p
Originally published: London : Hodder and Stoughton, 1961
ISBN 0-86009-374-3 : £5.25 : CIP entry B81-35702

Robins, Denise. Strange rapture / by Denise Robins. — Bolton-by-Bowland : Magna Print, 1980, c1933. — 306p ; 23cm
Published in large print
ISBN 0-86009-220-8 : £5.25 : CIP rev. B79-37497

Robins, Denise. Sweet Cassandra / by Denise Robins. — Bolton-by-Bowland : Magna Print, 1979, c1970. — 383p ; 23cm
Originally published: London : Hodder and Stoughton, 1970. — Published in large print
ISBN 0-86009-185-6 : £4.95 : CIP rev. B79-30365

Ruck, Berta. His official fiancée / by Berta Ruck ; condensed by Barbara Cartland. — London : Duckworth, 1981, c1978. — 246p ; 23cm. — (Barbara Cartland's library of love ; 23)
ISBN 0-7156-1538-6 : £6.95 : CIP rev. B81-14432

Rush, Philip. Pierce Allard / Philip Rush. — London : Hale, 1981. — 207p ; 21cm
ISBN 0-7091-8771-8 : £6.25 B81-11739

Sadleir, Michael. Fanny by gaslight / Michael Sadleir. — Harmondsworth : Penguin, 1981, c1940. — 382p ; 18cm
Originally published: New York : Appleton-Century ; London : Constable, 1940
ISBN 0-14-006005-7 (pbk) : £1.50 B81-35474

Sava, George. A change of heart / by George Sava. — London : Hale, 1981. — 222p ; 21cm
ISBN 0-7091-9133-2 : £6.50 B81-35237

Shann, Renée. Everyone needs a rainbow / Renée Shann. — Large print ed. — Bath : Chivers, 1981, c1976. — 242p ; 23cm. — (A Seymour book)
Originally published: Collins, 1976
ISBN 0-85119-413-3 : £4.95 : CIP rev. B81-04231

823'.912[F] — Fiction in English, ***1900-1945*** **—**
Texts *continuation*

Shann, Renée. Light of heart / Renée Shann. — Large print ed. — Bath : Chivers, 1981, c1976. — 244p ; 23cm. — (A Seymour book)
Originally published: London : Collins, 1976
ISBN 0-85119-417-6 : £4.95 : CIP rev. B81-08894

Shann, Renée. Not wisely but too well / Renée Shann. — Large print ed. — Bath : Chivers, 1981, c1970. — 264p ; 23cm. — (A Seymour book)
Originally published: London : Collins, 1970
ISBN 0-85119-407-9 : Unpriced B81-08981

Shann, Renée. Pound foolish / Renée Shann. — Rev.ed., large print ed. — Bath : Lythway, 1980, c1973. — 309p ; 23cm
Originally published: London : Collins, 1973
ISBN 0-85046-900-7 : £6.25 : CIP rev. B80-10838

Shann, Renée. Time to go / Renée Shann. — Large print ed. — Leicester : Ulverscroft, 1981, c1938. — 413p ; 23cm. — (Ulverscroft large print series)
ISBN 0-7089-0677-x : £5.00 : CIP rev. B81-25672

Short, Christopher. The Saint and the Hapsburg necklace / written by Christopher Short. — Bolton-by-Bowland : Magna Print, 1980, c1975. — 347p ; 23cm
At head of title: Leslie Charteris. — Originally published: Garden City, N.Y. : Doubleday ; London : Hodder and Stoughton, 1976. — Published in large print
ISBN 0-86009-223-2 : £5.25 : CIP rev. B79-37499

Sinclair, May. The three sisters. — London : Virago, Feb.1982. — [400]p. — (Virago modern classics)
ISBN 0-86068-243-9 (pbk) : £3.50 : CIP entry B81-36022

Stacpoole, H. de Vere. The blue lagoon / H. de Vere Stacpoole. — London : Macdonald Futura, 1980, c1908. — 252p ; 18cm. — (A Futura book)
ISBN 0-7088-1985-0 (pbk) : £1.25 B81-15637

Stacpoole, H. de Vere. The blue lagoon / H. de Vere Stacpoole. — London : Macdonald Futura, 1981. — 252p ; 21cm
ISBN 0-354-04659-4 : £4.95 B81-10164

Standish, Robert. Honourable ancestor : a novel / by Robert Standish. — London : Remploy, 1979, c1956. — 315p ; 19cm
Originally published: London : Davies, 1956
ISBN 0-7066-0806-2 : £4.30 B81-05437

Stapledon, Olaf. Sirius : a fantasy of love and discord / Olaf Stapledon. — Harmondsworth : Penguin, 1964, c1944 (1979 printing). — 188p ; 18cm
ISBN 0-14-001999-5 (pbk) : £0.85 B81-23417

Stevenson, D. E.. Green money / D.E. Stevenson. — Large print ed. — Leicester : Ulverscroft, 1981, c1939. — 481p : 1map ; 23cm. — (Ulverscroft large print series)
ISBN 0-7089-0649-4 : £5.00 B81-28571

Stevenson, D. E.. The house of the deer / D.E. Stevenson. — London : Collins, 1978, c1970. — 221p ; 21cm
ISBN 0-00-243325-7 : £3.50 B81-07179

Stevenson, D. E.. Mrs. Tim flies home / D.E. Stevenson. — London : Prior, 1980, c1952. — xiv,474p ; 24cm
Originally published: London : Collins, 1952. — Published in large print
ISBN 0-86043-427-3 : £6.95 B81-01258

Stewart, J. I. M.. Andrew and Tobias / J.I.M. Stewart. — London : Gollancz, 1980. — 221p ; 22cm
ISBN 0-575-02878-5 : £5.50 B81-02518

Strange, Oliver. The Marshal of Lawless : an adventure of Sudden, the outlaw / Oliver Strange. — [London] : Corgi, 1961 (1981 [printing]). — 157p ; 18cm. — (Sudden Westerns)
ISBN 0-552-11795-1 (pbk) : £0.95 B81-18546

Strange, Oliver. Sudden / Oliver Strange. — [London] : Corgi, 1961 (1981 [printing]). — 222p ; 18cm. — (Sudden Westerns)
ISBN 0-552-11797-8 (pbk) : £0.95 B81-18548

Strange, Oliver. Sudden outlawed / Oliver Strange. — Abridged ed. — [London] : Corgi, 1960 (1981 [printing]). — 157p ; 18cm. — (Sudden Westerns)
ISBN 0-552-11796-x (pbk) : £0.95 B81-18547

Strange, Oliver. Sudden plays a hand / Oliver Strange. — [London] : Corgi, 1961 (1981 [printing]). — 157p ; 18cm. — (Sudden Westerns)
Originally published: London : Newnes, 1950
ISBN 0-552-11798-6 (pbk) : £0.95 B81-18549

Symons, Julian. The Blackheath poisonings : a Victorian murder mystery / by Julian Symons. — Harmondsworth : Penguin, 1980, c1978. — 302p ; 18cm. — (Penguin crime fiction)
Originally published: New York : Harper & Row ; London : Collins, 1978
ISBN 0-14-005171-6 (pbk) : £1.25 B81-07035

Thompson, Flora, *1877-1947.* Still glides the stream / Flora Thompson ; drawings by Lynton Lamb. — Oxford : Oxford University Press, 1948 (1981 [printing]). — 233p : ill ; 21cm
ISBN 0-19-217414-2 : £4.95 B81-22184

Tolkien, J. R. R.. The Lord of the Rings. — London : Unwin Paperbacks, Apr.1981
Originally published: 1954
Part 1: The Fellowship of the Ring. — [536]p
ISBN 0-04-823185-1 (pbk) : £1.50 : CIP entry B81-00399

Tolkien, J. R. R.. The Lord of the Rings. — London : Unwin Paperbacks, Apr.1981
Originally published: 1954
Part 2: The two towers. — [446]p
ISBN 0-04-823186-x (pbk) : £1.50 : CIP entry B81-00400

Tolkien, J. R. R.. The Lord of the Rings. — London : Unwin Paperbacks, Apr.1981
Originally published: 1954
Part 3: The return of the king. — [560]p
ISBN 0-04-823187-8 (pbk) : £1.50 : CIP entry B81-00401

Tranter, Nigel. Balefire / Nigel Tranter. — London : Remploy, 1979, c1958. — 223p,[1] folded leaf : 1map ; 22cm
Originally published: London : Hodder & Stoughton, 1958
ISBN 0-7066-0799-6 : £4.20 B81-03557

Tranter, Nigel. The enduring flame / by Nigel Tranter. — London : Remploy, 1979. — 255p ; 20cm
Originally published: London : Hodder & Stoughton, 1957
ISBN 0-7066-0800-3 : £4.20 B81-07659

Tranter, Nigel. Macbeth the king. — London : Coronet, Apr.1981. — [400]p
Originally published: 1978
ISBN 0-340-26544-2 (pbk) : £1.75 : CIP entry B81-01838

Tranter, Nigel. Margaret the queen. — London : Hodder and Stoughton, Apr.1981. — [432]p
Originally published: London : Hodder and Stoughton, 1979
ISBN 0-340-26545-0 (pbk) : £1.75 : CIP entry B81-01842

Tranter, Nigel. True Thomas / Nigel Tranter. — London : Hodder and Stoughton, 1981. — 432p ; 23cm
ISBN 0-340-25619-2 : £6.95 B81-10144

Turk, Frances. A flush of scarlet / Frances Turk. — Large print ed. — Bath : Chivers, 1981, c1963. — 270p ; 23cm. — (A Lythway romance)
Originally published: London : Wright & Brown, 1963
ISBN 0-85119-731-0 : Unpriced : CIP rev. B81-13714

Turk, Frances. The Lesley affair / Frances Turk. — Large print ed. — Bath : Lythway, 1980, c1968. — 287p ; 23cm
Originally published: London : Wright & Brown, 1968
ISBN 0-85046-917-1 : Unpriced : CIP rev. B80-34138

Turk, Frances. Salutation. — Large print ed. — Anstey : Ulverscroft, Oct.1981. — [480]p. — (Ulverscroft large print series)
Originally published: London : Wright and Brown, 1949
ISBN 0-7089-0693-1 : £5.00 : CIP entry B81-28102

Turnbull, Patrick. Some scared slope / Patrick Turnbull. — London : Hale, 1981. — 206p 21cm
ISBN 0-7091-8732-7 : £6.25 B81-11900

Upfield, Arthur W.. The widows of Broome / Arthur W. Upfield. — Large print ed. — Leicester : Ulverscroft, 1980. — 353p ; 23cm. — (Ulverscroft large print series)
Originally published: London : Heinemann, 1951
ISBN 0-7089-0490-4 : £4.25 : CIP rev. B80-11631

Walsh, Maurice. And no quarter / Maurice Walsh. — Edinburgh : W. & R. Chambers, 1980. — 317p ; 19cm
ISBN 0-550-20418-0 : £3.95 B81-00402

Walsh, Maurice. The road to nowhere / Maurice Walsh. — [Edinburgh] : W & R Chambers, c1980. — 285p ; 20cm
ISBN 0-550-20417-2 : £3.95 B81-02420

Walsh, Maurice. The Spanish lady / Maurice Walsh. — [Edinburgh] : W & R Chambers, c1980. — 367p : 1 map ; 20cm
ISBN 0-550-20419-9 : £3.95 B81-02464

Waugh, Evelyn. Black mischief / Evelyn Waugh ; illustrations by Quentin Blake ; introduction by William Deedes. — London : Folio Society, 1980. — 206p : ill,maps ; 23cm
Maps on lining papers. — In slip case
Unpriced B81-09394

Waugh, Evelyn. Brideshead revisited : the sacred and profane memories of Captain Charles Ryder / Evelyn Waugh. — Harmondsworth : Penguin, 1951, c1945 (1981 [printing]). — 394p ; 20cm
Originally published: London : Chapman & Hall, 1945
ISBN 0-14-005915-6 (pbk) : £2.50 B81-40428

Waugh, Evelyn. Men at arms / Evelyn Waugh. — Harmondsworth : Penguin, 1964, c1952 (1981 [printing]). — 245p ; 18cm
Originally published: London : Chapman & Hall, 1952
ISBN 0-14-002123-x (pbk) : £1.50 B81-22189

Waugh, Evelyn. Officers and gentlemen / Evelyn Waugh. — Harmondsworth : Penguin, 1964, c1955 (1981 [printing]). — 248p ; 18cm
Originally published: London : Chapman & Hall, 1955
ISBN 0-14-002121-3 (pbk) : £1.50 B81-22042

Waugh, Evelyn. Unconditional surrender : the conclusion of Men at arms and Officers and gentlemen / Evelyn Waugh. — [Harmondsworth] : Penguin, 1964, c1961 (1980 [printing]). — 239p ; 18cm
Originally published: London : Chapman & Hall, 1961
ISBN 0-14-002122-1 (pbk) : £1.50 B81-22041

823'.912[F] — Fiction in English, ***1900-1945*** **—** *Texts* *continuation*

Webb, Mary. Precious bane / Mary Webb. — Harmondsworth : Penguin, 1981. — 270p ; 18cm
ISBN 0-14-005299-2 (pbk) : £1.50 B81-34814

Webb, Mary, *1881-1927*. The house in Dormer Forest / Mary Webb ; with a new introduction by Michèle Barale. — London : Virago, 1981. — 292p ; 20cm. — (Virago modern classics)
ISBN 0-86068-180-7 (pbk) : £2.50 : CIP rev. B81-04347

Wells, H. G.. The invisible man / H.G. Wells. — [London] : Fontana, 1959, c1897 (1981 [printing]). — 223p ; 18cm
Bibliography: p219-223
ISBN 0-00-616419-6 (pbk) : £1.50 B81-36833

Wentworth, Patricia. The clock strikes twelve / Patricia Wentworth. — Leicester : Ulverscroft, 1981, c1945. — 423p ; 23cm. — (Ulverscroft large print series)
Originally published: London : Hodder & Stoughton, 1945
ISBN 0-7089-0604-4 : £5.00 : CIP rev. B81-02577

Wentworth, Patricia. The listening eye / Patricia Wentworth. — Large print ed. — Leicester : Ulverscroft, 1981. — 404p ; 23cm. — (Ulverscroft large print)
Originally published: London : Hodder & Stoughton, 1957
ISBN 0-7089-0661-3 : £5.00 : CIP rev. B81-20627

Wheatley, Dennis. Herewith the clues. — Exeter : Webb & Bower, Feb.1982. — [152]p
ISBN 0-906671-49-3 (unbound) : £9.95 : CIP entry B81-36038

Wheatley, Dennis. Murder off Miami. — Exeter : Webb & Bower, July 1981. — [328]p
ISBN 0-906671-63-9 (pbk) : £9.95 : CIP entry B81-20578

Wheatley, Dennis. The satanist / Dennis Wheatley. — London : Arrow (1962, c1960) (1981 [printing]). — 511p ; 18cm
Originally published: London : Hutchinson, 1960
ISBN 0-09-908910-6 (pbk) : £1.50 B81-14035

Williams, Emlyn, *1905-*. Headlong : a novel / Emlyn Williams. — London : Heinemann, 1980. — 287p ; 23cm
ISBN 0-434-86605-9 : £6.95 B81-00403

Williamson, Henry. A test to destruction / by Henry Williamson. — Bath : Chivers, 1980, c1960. — 461p ; 23cm. — (A New Portway book)
Originally published: London : Macdonald, 1960
ISBN 0-86220-503-4 : £4.95 : CIP rev. B80-09878

Willis, Ted. The naked sun / Ted Willis. — London : Macmillan, 1980. — 209p ; 23cm
ISBN 0-333-30437-3 : £5.95 B81-01260

Wodehouse, P. G.. Big money / P.G. Wodehouse. — London : Hutchinson, 1981. — 208p ; 20cm
ISBN 0-257-65656-1 : £6.95 : CIP rev. B81-13904

Wodehouse, P. G.. Eggs, beans and crumpets / P.G. Wodehouse. — Harmondsworth : Penguin, 1971 (1981 [printing]). — 189p ; 18cm
ISBN 0-14-003351-3 (pbk) : £1.25 B81-26501

Wodehouse, P. G.. Ice in the bedroom / P.G. Wodehouse. — London : Hutchinson, 1981, c1961. — 223p ; 20cm
Originally published: London : Jenkins, 1961
ISBN 0-257-65944-7 : £6.95 : CIP rev. B81-13902

Wodehouse, P. G.. Indiscretions of Archie / P.G. Wodehouse. — Harmondsworth : Penguin, 1963, c1921 (1981 [printing]). — 223p ; 18cm
ISBN 0-14-002046-2 (pbk) : £1.25 B81-35592

Wodehouse, P. G.. Meet Mr Mulliner / P.G. Wodehouse. — Harmondsworth : Penguin, 1962, c1927 (1981 [printing]). — 170p ; 19cm
ISBN 0-14-001815-8 (pbk) : £1.25 B81-22344

Wodehouse, P. G.. Much obliged, Jeeves / P.G. Wodehouse. — Harmondsworth : Penguin, 1981, c1971. — 173p ; 18cm
Originally published: London : Barrie and Jenkins, 1971
ISBN 0-14-005102-3 (pbk) : £1.25 B81-18526

Wodehouse, P. G.. The Old Reliable. — London : Hutchinson, July 1981. — [240]p
Originally published: London : Jenkins, 1951
ISBN 0-257-66125-5 : £6.95 : CIP entry B81-13886

Wodehouse, P. G.. Pearls, girls and Monty Bodkin / P.G. Wodehouse. — London : Hutchinson, 1981, c1972. — 191p ; 20cm
Originally published: London : Barrie & Jenkins, 1972
ISBN 0-214-66815-0 : £6.95 B81-10670

Wodehouse, P. G.. Pigs have wings / P.G. Wodehouse. — Harmondsworth : Penguin, 1957, c1952 (1981 [printing]). — 234p ; 18cm
Originally published: London : Jenkins, 1952
ISBN 0-14-001170-6 (pbk) : £1.25 B81-11033

Wodehouse, P. G.. Psmith in the city / P.G. Wodehouse. — Harmondsworth : Penguin, 1970 (1981 [printing]). — 157p ; 18cm
ISBN 0-14-003207-x (pbk) : £0.95 B81-14032

Wodehouse, P. G.. Service with a smile / P.G. Wodehouse. — Harmondsworth : Penguin, 1966, c1961 (1981 [printing]). — 175p ; 19cm
Originally published: New York : Simon and Schuster, 1961 ; London : Jenkins, 1962
ISBN 0-14-002532-4 (pbk) : £1.25 B81-27215

Wodehouse, P. G.. Service with a smile / P.G. Wodehouse. — London : Hutchinson, 1980, c1961. — 192p ; 20cm
Originally published: New York : Simon and Schuster, 1961 ; London : Jenkins, 1962
ISBN 0-09-142890-4 : £6.50 : CIP rev. B80-14042

Wodehouse, P. G.. The small bachelor / P.G. Wodehouse. — London : Hutchinson, 1981. — 204p ; 20cm
ISBN 0-257-65236-1 : £6.95 B81-05221

Wodehouse, P. G.. Spring fever / P.G. Wodehouse. — Harmondsworth : Penguin, 1969, c1948 (1981 [printing]). — 207p ; 18cm
Originally published: London : Jenkins, 1948
ISBN 0-14-003040-9 (pbk) : £1.25 B81-22256

Wodehouse, P. G.. Summer lightning / P.G. Wodehouse. — Harmondsworth : Penguin, 1954,, c1929 (1981 [printing]). — 255p ; 18cm
ISBN 0-14-000995-7 (pbk) : £1.50 B81-22345

Wodehouse, P. G.. Uncle Dynamite / P.G. Wodehouse. — London : Hutchinson, 1981. — 249p ; 20cm
Originally published: London : Jenkins, 1948
ISBN 0-257-66390-8 : £6.95 B81-03430

Wodehouse, P. G.. Young men in spats / P.G. Wodehouse. — Harmondsworth : Penguin, 1971 (1981 [printing]). — 215p ; 18cm
ISBN 0-14-003352-1 (pbk) : £1.25 B81-35591

Wood, Margaret, *1910-*. The sun over the high mountains / Margaret Wood. — Large print ed. — Bath : Chivers, 1980, c1970. — 193p ; 23cm. — (A Seymour book)
Originally published: London : Hale, 1970
ISBN 0-86220-019-9 : £4.50 : CIP rev. B80-18031

Woodward, Lilian. Design for loving / by Lilian Woodward. — London : Hale, 1980. — 157p ; 20cm
ISBN 0-7091-8513-8 : £5.75 B81-02700

Woodward, Lilian. Flight to Sandaha / by Lilian Woodward. — London : Hale, 1981. — 152p ; 20cm
ISBN 0-7091-8852-8 : £5.60 B81-21301

Woodward, Lillian. Love's a magician / by Lil[l]ian Woodward. — London : Hale, 1981. — 175p ; 20cm
ISBN 0-7091-9175-8 : £5.75 B81-40462

Woolf, Leonard. The village in the jungle / Leonard Woolf ; with an introduction by E.F.C. Ludowyk. — Oxford : Oxford University Press, 1981. — xv,179p ; 20cm. — (Oxford paperbacks)
ISBN 0-19-281312-9 (pbk) : £2.50 : CIP rev. B81-25791

Wright, Esther Terry. A vacant chair / Esther Terry ; illustrated by J.P. Sayer. — London : Martin Brian & O'Keeffe, 1979. — 128p : ill ; 21cm
ISBN 0-85616-061-x : £4.00 B81-02930

Wyndham, John, *1903-1969*. The day of the Triffids / John Wyndham. — Harmondsworth : Penguin in association with Joseph, 1954, c1951 (1981 [printing]). — 272p ; 18cm
Originally published: London : Joseph, 1951
ISBN 0-14-000993-0 (pbk) : £1.25 B81-35573

Wynne, Pamela. Ashes of desire / by Pamela Wynne ; condensed by Barbara Cartland. — London : Duckworth, 1980, c1978. — 185p ; 23cm. — (Barbara Cartland's library of love ; 19)
ISBN 0-7156-1479-7 : £6.95 B81-07561

Yates, Dornford. Adèle and Co. / Dornford Yates. — Harmondsworth : Penguin, 1981, c1931. — 254p ; 18cm
ISBN 0-14-005660-2 (pbk) : £1.50 B81-35570

Yates, Dornford. Berry and Co. / Dornford Yates. — Harmondsworth : Penguin, 1981, c1920. — 275p ; 18cm : 1geneal.table
ISBN 0-14-005658-0 (pbk) : £1.50 B81-35572

Yates, Dornford. Jonah and Co. / Dornford Yates. — Harmondsworth : Penguin, 1981, c1922. — 269p ; 18cm
ISBN 0-14-005659-9 (pbk) : £1.50 B81-35571

823'.912[F] — Short stories in English, ***1900-1945*** **—** *Texts*

Acton, *Sir* Harold. The soul's gymnasium and other stories. — London : Hamilton, Feb.1982. — [192]p
ISBN 0-241-10740-7 : £7.50 : CIP entry B81-36386

Allingham, Margery. The Allingham case-book / Margery Allington. — Large print ed. — Bath : Chivers, 1981, c1969. — 345p ; 23cm. — (A New Portway large print book)
Originally published: London : Chatto & Windus, 1969
ISBN 0-85119-104-5 : Unpriced B81-08626

Bates, H. E.. The four beauties / H.E. Bates. — Harmondsworth : Penguin, 1972, c1968 (1981 [printing]). — 152p ; 19cm
Originally published: London : Joseph, 1968
ISBN 0-14-003420-x (pbk) : £1.25 B81-32834

Bates, H. E.. The grapes of paradise : eight novellas / H.E. Bates. — Harmondsworth : Penguin in association with Joseph, 1974 (1981 [printing]). — 315p ; 19cm
ISBN 0-14-003820-5 (pbk) : £1.75 B81-26551

Bates, H. E.. Seven by five : a collection of stories 1926-61 / H.E. Bates ; with a preface by Henry Miller. — Harmondsworth : Penguin, 1972, c1963 (1981 [printing]). — 484p ; 18cm
Originally published: London : Joseph, 1963
ISBN 0-14-003419-6 (pbk) : £1.75 B81-17428

823'.912[F] — Short stories in English, *1900-1945*
— Texts *continuation*

Bates, H. E.. The stories of Flying Officer 'X' / H.E. Bates. — Large print ed. — Bath : Chivers, 1981. — 239p ; 23cm. — (A New Portway large print book)
Originally published: London : Cape, 1952
ISBN 0-85119-120-7 : Unpriced : CIP rev.
B81-13783

Bowen, Elizabeth. The collected stories of Elizabeth Bowen / with an introduction by Angus Wilson. — London : Cape, 1980. — 784p : ill ; 22cm
ISBN 0-224-01838-8 : £8.50 : CIP rev.
B80-06668

Canning, Victor. Delay on Turtle. — Large print ed. — Bath : Chivers, Jan.1982. — [320]p. — (A New Portway large print book)
Originally published: London : NEL, 1962
ISBN 0-85119-149-5 : £5.35 : CIP entry
B81-33813

Chesterton, G. K.. [The Father Brown stories]. The Penguin complete Father Brown / G.K. Chesterton. — Harmondsworth : Penguin, 1981. — 718p ; 21cm
ISBN 0-14-005977-6 (pbk) : £3.95 B81-40685

Christie, Agatha. The Listerdale mystery / Agatha Christie. — [London] : Fontana, 1961, c1934 (1981 [printing]). — 192p ; 18cm
ISBN 0-00-616425-0 (pbk) : £1.00 B81-32165

Christie, Agatha. Miss Marple's final cases / Agatha Christie. — [London] : Fontana, 1980, c1979. — 154p ; 18cm
ISBN 0-00-616207-x (pbk) : £0.95 B81-01629

Christie, Agatha. The thirteen problems / Agatha Christie. — [London] : Fontana, 1965, c1933 (1981 [printing]). — 192p ; 18cm
ISBN 0-00-616274-6 (pbk) : £1.00 B81-15531

Creasey, John, *1908-1973*. Murder in the stars / by John Creasey. — Hornchurch : Henry, 1980, c1953. — 190p ; 21cm
Originally published: under the name Michael Halliday. London : Hodder & Stoughton, 1953
ISBN 0-86025-175-6 : £4.95 B81-06367

Dahl, Roald. [More Roald Dahl tales of the unexpected]. Further tales of the unexpected / Roald Dahl. — Large print ed. — Bath : Chivers, 1981. — 228p ; 23cm. — (A New Portway large print book)
Originally published: London : Joseph, 1980
ISBN 0-85119-116-9 : £4.95 : CIP rev.
B81-08888

Dahl, Roald. More tales of the unexpected / Roald Dahl. — Large print ed. — Bath : Chivers, 1981, c1980. — 205p ; 23cm. — (A New Portway large print book)
Originally published: London : Joseph, 1980
ISBN 0-85119-121-5 : Unpriced : CIP rev.
B81-14381

Dahl, Roald. A Roald Dahl selection : nine short stories / by Roald Dahl ; edited and introduced by Roy Blatchford ; with photographs by Catherine Shakespeare Lane. — Harlow : Longman in association with Joseph, 1980. — vi,160p : ill ; 19cm. — (Longman imprint books)
Bibliography: p159-160
ISBN 0-582-22281-8 (pbk) : £1.15 B81-06670

Dahl, Roald. Tales of the unexpected / Roald Dahl. — Large print ed. — Bath : Chivers, 1981, c1979. — 231p ; 23cm. — (A New Portway large print book)
Originally published: London : Joseph, 1979
ISBN 0-85119-113-4 : £4.55 : CIP rev.
B81-03182

Doyle, ***Sir*** **Arthur Conan**. The adventures of Sherlock Holmes / Arthur Conan Doyle. — Harmondsworth : Penguin, 1981. — 285p ; 18cm
ISBN 0-14-005724-2 (pbk) : £1.25 B81-26517

Doyle, ***Sir*** **Arthur Conan**. The case-book of Sherlock Holmes / Sir Arthur Conan Doyle. — Harmondsworth : Penguin in association with J. Murray and Cape, 1951 (1981 [printing]). — 254p ; 18cm
ISBN 0-14-000805-5 (pbk) : £1.25 B81-26516

Doyle, ***Sir*** **Arthur Conan**. His last bow : some reminiscences of Sherlock Holmes / Sir Arthur Conan Doyle ; with an introduction and notes by Felicia Gordon and Richard Adams. — London : Longman, 1980. — xli,227p ; 19cm. — (The Heritage of literature series)
ISBN 0-582-34914-1 (pbk) : £1.60 B81-07177

Doyle, ***Sir*** **Arthur Conan**. The memoirs of Sherlock Holmes / Sir Arthur Conan Doyle. — Harmondsworth : Penguin in association with John Murray and Cape, 1950 (1981 [printing]). — 255p ; 19cm
ISBN 0-14-000785-7 (pbk) : £1.25 B81-34758

Doyle, ***Sir*** **Arthur Conan**. The Penguin complete Sherlock Holmes / Sir Arthur Conan Doyle ; with a preface by Christopher Morley. — London : Allen Lane, 1981. — 1122p ; 22cm
ISBN 0-7139-1444-0 : £7.95 B81-34615

Doyle, ***Sir*** **Arthur Conan**. The return of Sherlock Holmes / Sir Arthur Conan Doyle ; with an introduction and notes by Richard Adams. — London : Longman, 1980. — xxxix,371p : ill,1map ; 19cm. — (The Heritage of literature series)
ISBN 0-582-34913-3 (pbk) : £1.95 B81-07178

Doyle, ***Sir*** **Arthur Conan**. Sherlock Holmes meets the Sussex vampire : and other cases of the world's most famous detective / Sir Arthur Conan Doyle ; selected and introduced by Peter Haining. — [London] : Armada, 1981. — 159p : ill ; 18cm
ISBN 0-00-691885-9 (pbk) : £0.80 B81-11879

Du Maurier, Daphne. The birds and other stories / Daphne du Maurier ; selected and edited with an introduction by Richard Adams ; and a foreword by Daphne du Maurier ; with photographs by Catherine Shakespeare Lane. — Harlow : Longman, 1980. — ix,138p : ill,1port ; 18cm. — (Longman imprint books)
Bibliography: p135-6
ISBN 0-582-22290-7 (pbk) : £1.15 B81-05553

Du Maurier, Daphne. Don't look now : and other stories / Daphne du Maurier. — Harmondsworth : Penguin, 1981. — 267p ; 18cm
ISBN 0-14-003590-7 (pbk) : £1.50 B81-30942

Du Maurier, Daphne. The rendezvous : and other stories / Daphne du Maurier. — Large print ed. — Bath : Chivers, 1981, c1980. — xi,211p ; 23cm. — (A New Portway large print book)
Originally published: London : Gollancz, 1980
ISBN 0-85119-129-0 : Unpriced : CIP rev.
B81-18075

Du Maurier, Daphne. The rendezvous and other stories / Daphne du Maurier. — London : Gollancz, 1980. — 287p ; 23cm
ISBN 0-575-02845-9 : £5.95 B81-00404

Du Maurier, Daphne. Split second : and other stories / Daphne du Maurier. — Large print ed. — Bath : Chivers, 1981, c1980. — 244p ; 23cm. — (A New Portway large print book)
Originally published: London : Gollancz, 1980
ISBN 0-85119-130-4 : Unpriced : CIP rev.
B81-18076

Ellis, H. F.. [The world of A.J. Wentworth B.A.]. A.J. Wentworth, B.A. / H.F. Ellis. — London : Arrow, 1981, c1980. — 215p ; 18cm
Originally published: Harmondsworth : Penguin, 1964. — Contents: The papers of A.J. Wentworth, B.A. Originally published: London : Evans, 1949 — The papers of A.J. Wentworth, B.A. (Ret'd). Originally published: London : Bles, 1962
ISBN 0-09-925990-7 (pbk) : £1.25 B81-28753

Ferrars, Elizabeth. Designs on life : a collection of short stories / Elizabeth Ferrars. — Large print ed. — Bath : Chivers, 1981, c1980. — 258p ; 23cm. — (A Lythway mystery)
Originally published: London : Collins, 1980
ISBN 0-85119-717-5 : £6.50 : CIP rev.
B81-08889

Forster, E. M.. Arctic summer : and other fiction / E.M. Forster. — London : Edward Arnold, 1980. — xxxv,342p ; 23cm. — (The Abinger edition of E.M. Forster ; v.9)
ISBN 0-7131-6290-2 : £18.50 : CIP rev.
B80-14048

Greene, Graham. Across the bridge : and other stories / Graham Greene. — Large print ed. — Bath : Chivers, 1981. — 220p ; 23cm. — (A New Portway large print book)
Originally published: as part of Twenty one stories. London : Heinemann, 1954
ISBN 0-85119-126-6 : Unpriced : CIP rev.
B81-15899

Greene, Graham. Loser takes all, and other stories / Graham Greene. — Large print ed. — Bath : Chivers, 1981. — 215p ; 23cm. — (A New Portway large print book)
ISBN 0-85119-133-9 : £4.95 : CIP rev.
B81-20113

Greene, Graham. May we borrow your husband? : and other comedies of the sexual life / Graham Greene. — Harmondsworth : Penguin, c1969, c1972 (1980 [printing]). — 141p ; 19cm
Originally published: London : Bodley Head, 1967
£0.95 (pbk) B81-10987

Greene, Graham. Twenty-one stories / Graham Greene. — Harmondsworth : Penguin in association with Heinemann, 1970, c1975 (1980 [printing]). — 199p ; 18cm
Originally published: London : Heinemann, 1954
ISBN 0-14-003093-x (pbk) : £1.25 B81-07509

Household, Geoffrey. Capricorn and Cancer / Geoffrey Household. — London : Joseph, c1981. — 254p ; 21cm
ISBN 0-7181-2003-5 : £6.95 B81-35133

Lawrence, D. H.. D.H. Lawrence : short stories. — London : Dent, June 1981. — [400]p. — (Everyman's library)
ISBN 0-460-01190-1 (pbk) : £2.50 : CIP entry
B81-05165

Lawrence, D. H.. England, my England / D.H. Lawrence. — Harmondsworth : Penguin in association with Heinemann, 1960, c1980 [printing]. — 189p ; 18cm
ISBN 0-14-001482-9 (pbk) : £0.90 B81-01261

Lawrence, D. H.. Love among the haystacks : and other stories / D.H. Lawrence. — Harmondsworth : Penguin, 1960 (1981 [printing]). — 172p ; 18cm
ISBN 0-14-001512-4 (pbk) : £0.90 B81-11027

Lawrence, D. H.. The princess, and other stories / D.H. Lawrence ; edited by Keith Sager. — Harmondsworth : Penguin in association with Heinemann, 1971 (1981 [printing]). — 248p : ill ; 19cm
ISBN 0-14-003263-0 (pbk) : £1.25 B81-18514

Lawrence, D. H.. Short stories / D.H. Lawrence ; selected and introduced by Stephen Gill. — London : Dent, 1981. — xliii,456p ; 18cm. — (Everyman's library)
ISBN 0-460-01229-0 (pbk) : £2.75 B81-35269

Lawrence, D. H.. The woman who rode away : and other stories / D.H. Lawrence. — Harmondsworth : Penguin in association with Heinemann, 1950, c1934 (1981 [printing]). — 256p ; 18cm
ISBN 0-14-000758-x (pbk) : £0.95 B81-11026

Levin, Mary. Selected stories / Mary Lavin. — Harmondsworth : Penguin, 1981. — 272p ; 20cm
ISBN 0-14-005602-5 (pbk) : £2.75 B81-22108

823′.912[F] — Short stories in English, *1900-1945* — *Texts* *continuation*

MacDonald, William Colt. Tombstone for a troubleshooter / by William Colt MacDonald. — Hornchurch : Henry, 1980, c1960. — 157p ; 21cm
Originally published: Philadelphia : Lippincott, 1960 ; London : Hodder & Stoughton, 1961
ISBN 0-86025-173-x : £4.55 B81-21205

Monsarrat, Nicholas. The ship that died of shame : and other stories / Nicholas Monsarrat. — Large print ed. — Bath : Chivers, 1980, c1959. — 357p ; 23cm
Originally published: London : Cassell, 1959
ISBN 0-85997-483-9 : £5.50 : CIP rev. B80-22604

O′Connor, Frank. The cornet-player who betrayed Ireland / Frank O′Connor. — Swords (Knocksedan House, Swords, Co. Dublin) : Poolbeg, 1981. — 238p ; 22cm
ISBN 0-905169-37-9 : Unpriced B81-20381

O′Connor, Frank. The cornet-player who betrayed Ireland / Frank O′Connor. — Swords (Knocksedan House, Swords, Co. Dublin) : Poolbeg Press, 1981. — 238p ; 18cm
ISBN 0-905169-48-4 (pbk) : Unpriced B81-20700

O′Flaherty, Liam. Liam O′Flaherty′s short stories. — London : New English Library/Times Mirror, 1970 (1981 [printing])
Vol.1. — 126p ; 18cm
ISBN 0-450-05089-0 (pbk) : £1.25 B81-19977

O′Flaherty, Liam. Short stories. — Dublin : Wolfhound Press, July 1981. — [224]p
ISBN 0-905473-51-5 (pbk) : £2.50 : CIP entry B81-24643

O′Flaherty, Liam. [The short stories of Liam O′Flaherty]. Liam O′Flaherty′s short stories. — Abridged. — London : New English Library
Vol.2. — 1970 (1981 [printing]). — 128p ; 18cm
ISBN 0-450-05136-6 (pbk) : £1.25 B81-19988

Saki. The complete works of Saki. — London : Bodley Head, 1980. — 944p ; 22cm
ISBN 0-370-30360-1 : £10.00 : CIP rev. B80-19985

Stephens, James, *1882-1950*. Desire : and other stories / James Stephens ; selected and introduced by Augustine Martin. — Swords (Knocksedan House, Swords, Co. Dublin) : Poolbeg Press, 1980. — 223p ; 18cm
ISBN 0-905169-41-7 (pbk) : £2.50 B81-12954

Tolkien, J. R. R.. Unfinished tales of Númenor and Middle-earth / by J.R.R. Tolkien ; edited with introduction, commentary, index and maps by Christopher Tolkien. — London : Allen & Unwin, 1980. — 472p : geneal.table,maps(some col.) ; 23cm
Col. map on folded leaf attached to inside cover. — Includes index
ISBN 0-04-823179-7 : £7.50 : CIP rev. B80-18503

Wallace, Edgar. Two stories ; and, The Seventh man / Edgar Wallace. — Oxford (4 Bradmore Rd., Oxford OX2 6QW) : Penelope Wallace, 1981. — 23p ; 22cm
Fascsim. reprints from Novel magazine. — Bibliography: p23
Unpriced (unbound) B81-24784

Warner, Sylvia Townsend. Scenes of childhood : and other stories / by Sylvia Townsend Warner. — London : Chatto & Windus, 1981. — 177p ; 23cm
ISBN 0-7011-2516-0 : £6.50 : CIP rev. B81-10487

West, Rebecca. The harsh voice. — London : Virago, Feb.1982. — [256]p
ISBN 0-86068-249-8 (pbk) : £2.95 : CIP entry B81-40236

White, Antonia. Strangers / by Antonia White ; new introduction by Hermione Lee. — London : Virago, 1981, c1980. — vii,173p ; 20cm. — (Virago modern classics)
Originally published: London : Harvill Press, 1954
ISBN 0-86068-171-8 (pbk) : £2.50 B81-09555

White, T. H.. The Maharajah and other stories / T.H. White ; collected and with an introduction by Kurth Sprague. — London : Macdonald, 1981. — 192p ; 23cm
ISBN 0-354-04670-5 : £6.95 B81-16066

Wills, Chester. Silver on the sage / Chester Wills. — London : Collins, 1949 (1978 [printing]). — 192p ; 19cm
ISBN 0-00-247810-2 : £2.95 B81-07400

Wodehouse, P. G.. The golf omnibus / P.G. Wodehouse. — London : Hutchinson, 1980, c1973. — 467p ; 23cm
Originally published: London : Barrie and Jenkins, 1973
ISBN 0-09-143960-4 : £7.95 B81-01262

Wodehouse, P. G.. Mulliner nights / P.G. Wodehouse. — Harmondsworth : Penguin, 1971 (1981 [printing]). — 188p ; 19cm
ISBN 0-14-003354-8 (pbk) : £1.25 B81-30772

Wodehouse, P. G.. The world of Jeeves / P.G. Wodehouse. — London : Hutchinson, 1980, c1967. — ix,564p ; 23cm
Originally published: London : Jenkins, 1967
ISBN 0-09-143810-1 : £7.95 B81-02044

Wyndham, John. The seeds of time / John Wyndham. — Harmondsworth : Penguin in association with Michael Joseph, 1959, c1956 (1981 [printing]). — 222p ; 18cm
Originally published: London : Joseph, 1956
£1.25 (pbk) B81-14350

Wyndham, John, *1903-1969*. Consider her ways : and others / John Wyndham. — Harmondsworth : Penguin in association with Joseph, 1965, c1961 (1979 printing). — 189p ; 18cm
Originally published: London : Joseph, 1961
ISBN 0-14-002231-7 (pbk) : £0.95 B81-19818

Wyndham, John, *1903-1969*. Sleepers of Mars / John Wyndham writing as John Beynon Harris ; introduction by Walter Gillings. — London : Severn House, 1980. — 155p ; 21cm
Originally published: London : Coronet, 1973
ISBN 0-7278-0670-x : £5.50 : CIP rev. B80-18038

823′.912[J] — Children′s short stories in English, *1900-1945* — *Texts*

Bisset, Donald. The hedgehog who rolled uphill. — London : Methuen Children′s Books, Feb.1982. — [96]p
ISBN 0-416-24310-x : £3.50 : CIP entry B81-35710

Bisset, Donald. What time is it, when it isn′t? / Donald Bisset ; illustrated by the author. — London : Methuen Children′s Books, 1981, c1980. — 94p : ill ; 20cm. — (A Magnet book)
ISBN 0-416-20830-4 (pbk) : £0.85 B81-18256

Blyton, Enid. The big Noddy book / [Enid Blyton]. — Maidenhead : Purnell Books, 1980. — [44]p : col.ill ; 27cm
Ill on lining papers
ISBN 0-361-04659-6 : £1.95 B81-00405

Blyton, Enid. [Mister Meddle′s mischief]. Mr Meddle′s mischief / Enid Blyton ; illustrated by Rene Cloke. — Rev. ed. — London : Beaver Books, 1981, c1970. — 111p : ill ; 18cm
Originally published: as Mister Meddle′s mischief. London : Dean, 1970
ISBN 0-600-20420-0 (pbk) : £0.70 B81-27877

Blyton, Enid. [Mister Meddle′s muddles]. Mr Meddle′s muddles / Enid Blyton ; illustrated by Rene Cloke. — Rev. ed. — London : Beaver Books, 1981, c1970. — 126p : ill ; 18cm
Originally published: as Mister Meddle′s muddles. London : Dean, 1970
ISBN 0-600-20419-7 (pbk) : £0.70 B81-27878

Brisley, Joyce Lankester. The Joyce Lankester Brisley book : an anthology of her stories / selected and edited by Frank Waters. — London : Harrap, 1981. — 189p : ill,facsims ; 23cm
Facsims. on lining papers
ISBN 0-245-53610-8 : £4.95 B81-40330

Dahl, Roald. George′s marvellous medicine / Roald Dahl ; illustrations by Quentin Blake. — London : Cape, 1981. — 96p : ill ; 24cm
ISBN 0-224-01901-5 : £3.95 B81-19426

Farjeon, Eleanor. The old nurse′s stocking-basket / Eleanor Farjeon ; illustrated by Edward Ardizzone. — Harmondsworth : Puffin in association with Oxford University Press, 1981. — 77p : ill ; 20cm. — (A Young Puffin)
ISBN 0-14-031220-x (pbk) : £0.80 B81-10697

Hunter, Norman. The best of Branestawm / Norman Hunter. — London : Bodley Head, 1980. — 254p : ill ; 22cm
ISBN 0-370-30362-8 : £4.95 : CIP rev. B80-19993

Johns, W. E. (William Earl). Biggles flies north / W.E. Johns. — London : Armada, 1966 (1980 [printing]). — 157p : ill ; 18cm
ISBN 0-00-691752-6 (pbk) : £0.75 B81-02042

Johns, W. E. (William Earl). Biggles in Australia / W.E. Johns. — [London] : Armada, 1970 (1981 [printing]). — 126p 18cm
Originally published: London : Hodder & Stoughton, 1955
ISBN 0-00-691868-9 (pbk) : £0.80 B81-11071

Manning-Sanders, Ruth. A book of cats and creatures / Ruth Manning-Sanders ; illustrated by Robin Jacques. — London : Methuen Children′s, 1981, c1980. — 126p : ill ; 24cm
ISBN 0-416-87970-5 : £4.50 : CIP rev. B80-07565

Manning-Sanders, Ruth. Oh really, rabbit! / Ruth Manning-Sanders ; illustrated by James Hodgson. — London : Methuen Children′s Books, 1981, c1980. — 92p : ill ; 20cm. — (A Magnet book)
ISBN 0-416-24220-0 (pbk) : £0.85 B81-18257

Richard, Frank, *1875-1961*. Bunter the bad lad / by Frank Richards. — London : Howard Baker, c1979. — 224p : ill,1map ; 23cm
ISBN 0-7030-0163-9 : £3.95 B81-15512

Richards, Frank, *1875-961*. Billy Bunter′s convict / by Frank Richards. — London : H. Baker, c1979. — 196p. in various pagings : ill(some col.),facsims,1port ; 28cm. — (Howard Baker Magnet ; v.70)
Facsimile reprints. — Contents: Magnet issues 834, 1035, 1039, 1040, 1041, 1056 and 1057
ISBN 0-7030-0173-6 : £5.95 B81-08062

Richards, Frank, *1875-1961*. The bully of Greyfriars / by Frank Richards. — London : Howard Baker, c1979. — 204p in various pagings : ill(some col.),facsims,3ports ; 28cm. — (The Magnet ; no.69)
Facsimile reprints of Magnet issues 1111-1117
ISBN 0-7030-0162-0 : £5.95 B81-19686

Robinson, Joan G.. Mary-Mary stories / written and illustrated by Joan G. Robinson. — London : Harrap, 1965 (1980 [printing]). — 176p : ill ; 23cm
ISBN 0-245-53626-4 : £4.95 B81-07079

Trease, Geoffrey. A wood by moonlight : and other stories / Geoffrey Trease. — London : Chatto & Windus, 1981. — 126p ; 21cm
ISBN 0-7011-2575-6 : £3.95 : CIP rev. B81-11966

823'.912[J] — Children's short stories in English, *1900-1945 — Texts* *continuation*

Uttley, Alison. Little Grey Rabbit's second storybook / by Alison Uttley ; pictures by Margaret Tempest. — London : Collins, 1981. — 141p : col.ill ; 25cm
Ill on lining papers
ISBN 0-00-194163-1 : £4.95 B81-28494

Vipont, Elfrida. The elephant and the bad baby / story by Elfrida Vipont ; illustrations by Raymond Briggs. — Harmondsworth : Puffin in association with Hamilton, 1971, c1969 (1980 [printing]). — [32]p : ill(some col.) ; 17x23cm. — (Picture puffins)
Originally published: London : Hamilton, 1969
£0.80 (pbk) B81-01265

823'.912[J] — Children's stories in English, *1900-1945 — Texts*

Almedingen, E. M.. The crimson oak / E.M. Almedingen ; illustrated by Kate Mellor. — London : Methuen Children's Books, 1981. — 127p : ill ; 20cm. — (A pied piper book)
ISBN 0-416-20720-0 : £3.50 B81-12250

Ardizzone, Edward. Johnny the clockmaker / by Edward Ardizzone. — Oxford : Oxford University Press, 1960 (1980 [printing]). — [48p] : ill(some col.) ; 26cm
ISBN 0-19-279587-2 (pbk) : Unpriced
ISBN 0-19-272120-8 (pbk) : £1.75 B81-12124

Ardizzone, Edward. Tim to the rescue / by Edward Ardizzone. — Harmondsworth : Puffin, 1981. — [48]p : ill(some col.) ; 24cm. — (Picture Puffins)
Originally published: Oxford : Oxford University Press, 1949
ISBN 0-14-050338-2 (pbk) : £0.95 B81-40504

Baker, Margaret, *1890-*. [The Black cats and the tinker's wife]. Black cats ; and, The silver crown / Margaret Baker ; illustrated by Mary Baker. — Harmondsworth : Kestrel Books, c1981. — 96p : ill ; 21cm
ISBN 0-7226-5709-9 : £3.95 B81-32824

'BB'. Bill Badger's winter cruise / 'BB' ; illustrated by D.J. Watkins-Pitchford. — London : Methuen Children's Books, 1981. — 119p : ill ; 20cm
Originally published: London : Hamilton, 1959
ISBN 0-416-87890-3 : £3.50 B81-11147

'BB'. [Wanderig wind]. Bill Badger and the wandering wind / 'BB' ; illustrated by D.J. Watkins-Pitchford. — London : Methuen Children's, 1981. — 121p : ill ; 20cm
Originally published: London : Hamilton, 1957
ISBN 0-416-87900-4 : £3.50 : CIP rev. B80-19479

Biro, Val. Gumdrop and the secret switches / story and pictures by Val Biro. — London : Hodder and Stoughton, 1981. — 28p : col.ill ; 25cm
Ill on lining papers
ISBN 0-340-26276-1 : £3.50 : CIP rev. B81-13529

Blyton, Enid. The adventures of Mr Pink-Whistle / Enid Blyton ; illustrated by Rene Cloke. — Rev. ed. — London : Beaver, 1981, c1969. — 111p : ill ; 18cm
Originally published: London : Dean, 1969
ISBN 0-600-20418-9 (pbk) : £0.70 B81-19899

Blyton, Enid. Big Noddy book / by Enid Blyton. — London : Sampson Low, Marston, 1977 (1981 [printing]). — [42]p : col.ill ; 27cm
ISBN 0-361-05089-5 : £2.20 B81-35216

Blyton, Enid. Bimbo and Topsy / Enid Blyton. — Rev. ed. — [London] : Beaver, 1981, c1969. — 126p : ill ; 18cm
Originally published: London : Dean, 1969
ISBN 0-600-20423-5 (pbk) : £0.70 B81-19909

Blyton, Enid. The boy who wanted a dog / Enid Blyton ; illustrated by Joyce Smith and David Dowland. — London (3 Fitzroy Sq. W1P 6JD) : Sparrow, 1980, c1963. — 94p : ill ; 18cm
Originally published: Guildford : Lutterworth, 1963
ISBN 0-09-924110-2 (pbk) : £0.65 B81-00406

Blyton, Enid. Brer Rabbit and his friends / retold by Enid Blyton ; illustrated by Graham Percy. — [London] : Windward, [1980]. — 29p : ill (some col.) ; 29cm
Ill on lining papers
ISBN 0-7112-4932-6 : £1.99 B81-12929

Blyton, Enid. The Buttercup Farm family / Enid Blyton ; illustrated by Joyce Smith and David Dowland. — London : Sparrow, 1981. — 95p : ill ; 18cm
Originally published: London : Lutterworth, 1951
ISBN 0-09-926050-6 (pbk) : £0.75 B81-16075

Blyton, Enid. The caravan family / Enid Blyton ; illustrated by Joyce Smith and David Dowland. — London (3 Fitzroy Sq., W1P 6JD) : Sparrow, 1980. — 93p : ill ; 18cm
Originally published: Guildford : Lutterworth, 1953
ISBN 0-09-924530-2 (pbk) : £0.65 B81-00407

Blyton, Enid. The family at Red-Roofs / Enid Blyton. — [London] : Armada, 1967, c1945 (1981 [printing]). — 160p : ill ; 18cm
Originally published: London : Lutterworth, 1945
ISBN 0-00-691871-9 (pbk) : £0.75 B81-11880

Blyton, Enid. Gulliver's adventures in the land of Lilliput / retold by Enid Blyton ; illustrated by Graham Percy. — [London] : Windward, [1980?]. — 29p : ill(some col.) ; 29cm
Ill on lining papers
ISBN 0-7112-4930-x : £1.99 B81-12928

Blyton, Enid. Mr Pink-Whistle interferes / Enid Blyton ; illustrated by Rene Cloke. — Rev. ed. — [London] : Beaver, 1981, c1970. — 127p : ill ; 18cm
Originally published: London : Dean, 1970
ISBN 0-600-20417-0 (pbk) : £0.70 B81-19908

Blyton, Enid. Robin Hood and his merry men / retold by Enid Blyton ; illustrated by Edward Mortelmans. — [London] : Windward, [1980?]. — 29p : ill(some col.) ; 29cm
Originally published: London : Johnston & Bacon, 1955. — Ill on lining papers
ISBN 0-7112-4931-8 : £1.99 B81-12930

Blyton, Enid. Run-about's holiday / Enid Blyton ; illustrated by Joyce Smith and David Dowland. — London : Sparrow, 1981. — 95p : ill ; 18cm
Originally published: London : Lutterworth, 1951
ISBN 0-09-926040-9 (pbk) : £0.75 B81-16076

Blyton, Enid. Those dreadful children / Enid Blyton. — [London] : Armada, 1967 (1980 [printing]). — 158p : ill ; 18cm
Originally published: London : Lutterworth, 1949
ISBN 0-00-691804-2 (pbk) : £0.75 B81-08020

Blyton, Enid. Up the Faraway Tree / Enid Blyton ; illustrated by Dorothy M. Wheeler. — [London] : Beaver, 1981, c1951. — 95p : ill ; 18cm
Originally published: London : Newnes, 1951
ISBN 0-600-20521-5 (pbk) : £0.70 B81-35662

Blyton, Enid. The very big secret / Enid Blyton ; illustrated by Joyce Smith and David Dowland. — London (3 Fitzroy Sq., W1P 6JD) : Sparrow, 1980. — 88p : ill ; 18cm
Originally published: Guildford : Lutterworth, 1952
ISBN 0-09-924540-x (pbk) : £0.65 B81-00408

Bowen, Elizabeth. The good tiger / Elizabeth Bowen ; illustrated by Quentin Blake. — London : Methuen Children's Books, 1981, c1965. — [25]p : col.ill ; 19cm. — (A Magnet book)
Originally published: New York : Knopf, 1965 ; London : Cape, 1970
ISBN 0-416-21230-1 (pbk) : £0.95 B81-29920

Brent-Dyer, Elinor M.. Excitements at the Chalet school / Elinor M. Brent-Dyer. — London : Armada, 1981. — 192p ; 19cm
Originally published: Edinburgh : Chambers, 1957
ISBN 0-00-691915-4 : £0.85 B81-20682

Clifford, Martin, *1875-1961*. Tom Merry's party / by Martin Clifford. — London : Howard Baker, c1979. — 202p in various pagings : ill (some col.),facsims(some col.) ; 28cm. — (Howard Baker Gem ; v.9)
Facsim of: Weekly issues of the Gem 14 August-11 December, 1937
ISBN 0-7030-0174-4 : £5.95 B81-17232

Dahl, Roald. The Twits / Roald Dahl ; illustrations by Quentin Blake. — London : Cape, 1980. — 80p : ill ; 24cm
ISBN 0-224-01855-8 : £3.50 : CIP rev. B80-18513

Derwent, Lavinia. The boy in the Bible / Lavinia Derwent ; illustrated by Gareth Floyd. — [London] : Piccolo, 1981, c1973. — 141p : ill ; 18cm
Originally published: Glasgow : Blackie, 1973
ISBN 0-330-26264-5 (pbk) : £0.95 B81-09743

Emanuel, Walter. A dog day, or, The angel in the house / by Walter Emanuel ; pictured by Cecil Aldin. — London : Transworld, [1981?]. — [64]p : col.ill ; 17cm. — (A Carousel book)
ISBN 0-906008-20-4 (pbk) : £0.90 B81-21276

Fidler, Kathleen. The ghosts of Sandeel Bay / Kathleen Fidler ; illustrated by Annabel Large. — London : Blackie, 1981. — 128p : ill,1map ; 21cm
ISBN 0-216-91060-9 : £4.95 B81-08235

Fuller, Ronald. Pilgrim : the story of The Pilgrim's progress by John Bunyan / written by Ronald Fuller ; pictures by Pat Marriott. — London : Deutsch, 1980. — 47p : col.ill ; 32cm
ISBN 0-233-97252-8 : £4.50 : CIP rev. B80-18518

Gág, Wanda. Millions of cats / by Wanda Gág. — Harmondsworth : Puffin in association with Faber and Faber, 1976 (1981 [printing]). — [32]p : ill ; 19cm. — (Picture puffins)
ISBN 0-14-050168-1 (pbk) : £0.85 B81-33481

Godden, Rumer. Little Plum / Rumer Godden ; with drawings by Jean Primrose. — Harmondsworth : Puffin, 1975, c1963 (1981 [printing]). — 134p : ill ; 20cm. — (A Young Puffin)
Originally published : London : Macmillan, 1963
ISBN 0-14-030737-0 (pbk) : £0.95 B81-22339

Goodall, Nan. Donkey's glory / by Nan Goodall. — 3rd new ed. / with illustrations by Adriana Saviozzi. — London : Mowbray, 1980. — 111p : ill ; 21cm
ISBN 0-264-66752-2 (cased) : £3.22
ISBN 0-264-66712-3 (pbk) : £1.95 B81-02236

Graves, Robert. An ancient castle / Robert Graves ; illustrated by Elizabeth Graves ; with an afterword by William David Thomas. — London : Peter Owen, 1980. — 69p : ill ; 23cm
ISBN 0-7206-0567-9 : £3.95 B81-01263

Hennell, Thomas. Lady Filmy Fern, or, The voyage of the window box / by Thomas Hennell ; illustrated by Edward Bawden. — London : Hamilton, 1980. — [41]p : col.ill ; 22x28cm
ISBN 0-241-10468-8 : £4.95 : CIP rev. B80-12619

823′.912[J] — Children′s stories in English, *1900-1945 — Texts continuation*

Hunter, Norman. Professor Branestawm and the wild letters / Norman Hunter ; illustrated by Gerald Rose. — London : Bodley Head, 1981. — [36]p : ill ; 22cm
ISBN 0-370-30361-x : £3.25 B81-13373

Hunter, Norman. Professor Branestawm′s pocket motor car / Norman Hunter ; illustrated by Gerald Rose. — London : Bodley Head, 1981. — [32]p : ill ; 22cm
ISBN 0-370-30363-6 : £3.25 B81-13372

Johns, W. E. (William Earl). Biggles defies the Swastika / W.E. Johns. — London : Armada, 1965 (1980 [printing]). — 159p ; 18cm
ISBN 0-00-691796-8 (pbk) : £0.75 B81-01786

Johns, W. E. (William Earl). Biggles goes to war / W.E. Johns. — London : Severn House, 1980. — 159p : ill ; 21cm
ISBN 0-7278-0574-6 : £3.95 : CIP rev.
B80-09480

Johns, W. E. (William Earl). Biggles in the jungle / W.E. Johns. — London : Armada, 1981. — 157p : ill ; 18cm
ISBN 0-00-691869-7 (pbk) : £0.80 B81-18525

Johns, W. E. (William Earl). The death rays of Ardilla : an interplanetry adventure / W. E. Johns. — London : Piccolo, 1981, c1959. — 159p ; 18cm
Originally published: London : Hodder and Stoughton, 1959
ISBN 0-330-26289-0 (pbk) : £0.95 B81-12126

Johns, W. E. (William Earl). The edge of beyond : an interplanetary adventure / W.E. Johns. — London : Piccolo, 1981, c1958. — 157p ; 18cm
Originally published: London : Hodder and Stoughton, 1958
ISBN 0-330-26288-2 (pbk) : £0.95 B81-12125

Knight, Eric. Lassie come-home / Eric Knight ; illustrated by Marguerite Kirmse. — Harmondsworth : Puffin Books, 1981, c1942. — 232p : ill ; 18cm
ISBN 0-14-031293-5 (pbk) : £0.95 B81-30697

Lewis, C. S.. The horse and his boy / C.S. Lewis ; illustrated by Pauline Baynes. — [London] : Fontana, 1980, c1954. — 188p : ill,1map ; 18cm. — (The Chronicles of Narnia ; 3) (Lions)
Originally published: London : Bles, 1954
ISBN 0-00-671666-0 (pbk) : £0.85 B81-07567

Lewis, C. S.. The last battle / C.S. Lewis ; illustrated by Pauline Baynes. — London : Lions, 1980, c1956. — 173p : ill ; 18cm. — (The Chronicles of Narnia)
Originally published: London : J. Lane, 1956
ISBN 0-00-671669-5 (pbk) : £2.75 B81-02989

Lewis, C. S.. The lion, the witch and the wardrobe / C.S. Lewis ; illustrated by Pauline Baynes. — [London] : Fontana, 1980, c1950. — 171p : ill ; 18cm. — (The Chronicles of Narnia ; 2) (Lions)
Originally published: London : Bles, 1950
ISBN 0-00-671663-6 (pbk) : £0.85 B81-07565

Lewis, C. S.. The magician′s nephew / C.S. Lewis ; illustrated by Pauline Baynes. — London : Fontana, 1980, c1955. — 171p : ill ; 18cm. — (The Chronicles of Narnia ; 1) (Lions)
Originally published: London : J. Lane, 1955
ISBN 0-00-671667-9 (pbk) : £0.95 B81-02125

Lewis, C. S.. Prince Caspian : the return to Narnia / C.S. Lewis ; illustrated by Pauline Baynes. — [London] : Fontana, 1980, c1951. — 190p : ill,1map ; 18cm. — (The Chronicles of Narnia ; 4) (Lions)
Originally published: London : Bles, 1951
ISBN 0-00-671664-4 (pbk) : £0.85 B81-07563

Lewis, C. S.. The silver chair / C.S. Lewis ; illustrated by Pauline Baynes. — [London] : Fontana, 1980, c1953. — 206p : map ; 18cm. — (Lions)
Originally published: London : Bles, 1953
ISBN 0-00-671668-7 (pbk) : £0.85 B81-07564

Lewis, C. S.. The voyage of the Dawn Treader / C.S. Lewis ; illustrations by Pauline Baynes. — [London] : Fontana, 1980, c1952. — 189p : ill ; 18cm. — (The Chronicles of Narnia ; 5) (Lions)
Originally published: London : Bles, 1952
ISBN 0-00-671665-2 (pbk) : £0.85 B81-07566

Lofting, Hugh. Doctor Dolittle and the secret lake / by Hugh Lofting ; illustrated by the author. — Harmondsworth : Puffin, 1969, c1949 (1981 [printing]). — 328p : ill ; 18cm
Originally published: Philadelphia : Lippincott, 1948 ; London : Cape, 1949
ISBN 0-14-030369-3 (pbk) : £1.50 B81-38361

Lofting, Hugh. Doctor Dolittle′s caravan / written and illustrated by Hugh Lofting. — Harmondsworth : Puffin, 1968, c1927 (1981 [printing]). — 234p : ill ; 18cm
ISBN 0-14-030367-7 (pbk) : £1.10 B81-26499

Lofting, Hugh. Doctor Dolittle′s circus / told and illustrated by Hugh Lofting. — Harmondsworth : Puffin, 1968 (1981 [printing]). — 277p : ill ; 19cm
ISBN 0-14-030366-9 (pbk) : £1.10 B81-27221

Lofting, Hugh. Doctor Dolittle′s garden / told & pictured by Hugh Lofting. — Harmondsworth : Puffin, 1968 (1981 [printing]). — 220p : ill ; 18cm
ISBN 0-14-030368-5 (pbk) : £1.25 B81-18512

Lofting, Hugh. Doctor Dolittle′s Puddleby adventures / written & illustrated by Hugh Lofting. — Harmondsworth : Penguin, 1969, c1953 (1981 [printing]). — 217p : ill ; 18cm
Originally published: Philadelphia : Lippincott, 1952 ; London : Cape, 1953
ISBN 0-14-030409-6 (pbk) : £1.10 B81-38360

Lofting, Hugh. Doctor Dolittle′s zoo / written & illustrated by Hugh Lofting. — Harmondsworth : Penguin, 1967 (1981 [printing]). — 228p : ill ; 18cm
ISBN 0-14-030292-1 (pbk) : £1.25 B81-18511

Robinson, Joan G.. [Meg and Maxie]. The sea witch / Joan G. Robinson. — [London] : Beaver, 1981, c1979. — 125p ; 18cm
Originally published: London : Gollancz, 1979
ISBN 0-600-20232-1 (pbk) : £0.80 B81-11850

Sava, George. The magician of Medeena / George Sava. — Bognor Regis : New Horizon, c1978. — 98p,[7]p of plates : ill,1map
ISBN 0-86116-106-8 : £2.95 B81-18868

Sava, George. Mickey & his friends / George Sava. — Bognor Regis : New Horizon, c1978. — 72p : ill ; 21cm
ISBN 0-86116-105-x : £2.95 B81-19064

Smith, Dodie. The midnight kittens / Dodie Smith. — London (3 Fitzroy Sq., W1P 6JD) : Sparrow, 1980, c1979. — 119p : ill ; 18cm
Originally published: London : W.H. Allen, 1978
ISBN 0-09-924060-2 (pbk) : £0.80 B81-01264

Todd, Barbara Euphan. Worzel Gummidge and the treasure ship / Barbara Euphan Todd. — London : Sparrow, 1980, c1958. — 187p ; 18cm
Originally published: London : Evans, 1958
ISBN 0-09-924070-x (pbk) : £0.85 B81-02499

Tolkien, J. R. R.. The hobbit, or, There and back again. — London : Unwin Paperbacks, Apr.1981. — [288]p
Originally published: 1937
ISBN 0-04-823188-6 (pbk) : £1.25 : CIP entry
B81-00409

Treadgold, Mary. Journey from the Heron / Mary Treadgold. — London : Cape, 1981. — 160p ; 21cm
ISBN 0-224-01970-8 : £4.95 : CIP rev.
B81-20624

Trease, Geoffrey. Mandeville / Geoffrey Trease. — London : Macmillan, 1980. — 190p ; 21cm
ISBN 0-333-30574-4 : £4.95 : CIP rev.
B80-18527

Williams, Ursula Moray. Bogwoppit / Ursula Moray Williams ; illustrated by Shirley Hughes. — [London] : Beaver, 1980, c1979. — 157p : ill ; 18cm
Originally published: London : Hamilton Children′s Books, 1978
ISBN 0-600-20060-4 (pbk) : £0.85 B81-01266

Williams, Ursula Moray. Gobbolino : the witch′s cat / written and illustrated by Ursula Moray Williams ; with a preface by the author to this reissue of the original edition. — London : Harrap, 1981. — 192p : ill ; 21cm
ISBN 0-245-53768-6 : £4.95 B81-28440

Williams, Ursula Moray. Jeffy, the burglar′s cat / Ursula Moray Williams ; illustrated by David McKee. — London : Andersen, 1981. — 141p : ill ; 21cm
ISBN 0-905478-95-9 : £3.95 B81-14245

823′.912′09 — Fiction in English, *1900-1945.* **Forms: Novels** - *Critical studies*

Batchelor, John. The Edwardian novelists. — London : Duckworth, July 1981. — [260]p
ISBN 0-7156-1109-7 : £20.00 : CIP entry
B81-14862

823′.912′09 — Fiction in English. Influence of Wagner, Richard, *1900-1970*

DiGaetani, John Louis. Richard Wagner and the modern British novel / John Louis DiGaetani. — Rutherford : Fairleigh Dickinson University Press ; London : Associated University Presses, c1978. — 179p : music ; 22cm
Bibliography: p164-175. — Includes index
ISBN 0-8386-1955-x : Unpriced B81-35326

823′.912′09 — Fiction in English. Joyce, James, *1882-1941* **; Woolf, Virginia & Lawrence, D. H.** *— Critical studies*

Kiely, Robert. Beyond egotism : the fiction of James Joyce, Virginia Woolf, and D.H. Lawrence / Robert Kiely. — Cambridge, Mass. ; London : Harvard University Press, 1980. — 244p ; 25cm
Includes index
ISBN 0-674-06896-3 : £8.40 B81-04403

823′.912′09 — Fiction in English. Non-British writers. Influence of exile, *1900-1980*

Gurr, Andrew. Writers in exile : the identity of home in modern literature / Andrew Gurr. — Brighton : Harvester Press, 1981. — 160p ; 23cm. — (Harvester studies in contemporary literature and culture ; 4)
Bibliography: p154-160
ISBN 0-85527-836-6 : £15.95 B81-22381

823′.912′09326 — Fiction in English. English & West African writers, *1900-.* **Special subjects: West Africa. European & African stereotypes —** *Critical studies*

Milbury-Steen, Sarah L.. European and African stereotypes in twentieth-century fiction / Sarah L. Milbury-Steen. — London : Macmillan, 1980. — xiii,188p ; 23cm
Bibliography: p178-183. - Includes index
ISBN 0-333-29143-3 : £15.00 : CIP rev.
Also classified at 843′.912′09326 B80-22636

823′.912′099287 — Fiction in English. Women writers, *1900-1980 — Critical studies*

Crosland, Margaret. Beyond the lighthouse : English women novelists in the twentieth century / Margaret Crosland. — London : Constable, 1981. — xi,260p ; 23cm
Bibliography: p231-252. — Includes index
ISBN 0-09-462410-0 : £7.50 B81-38691

823.914 — ENGLISH FICTION, 1945-

823'.914 — Children's stories in English, *1945-* — *Welsh texts*
Cole, Tamasin. [The last trick. Welsh]. Y tric olaf / darlunian gan Tamasin Cole ; stori gan James Cressey ; addasiad Cymraeg gan Ifor Wyn Williams. — Durham (55 Hallgarth St., Durham) : Ivan Corbett, 1980. — [28]p : chiefly col.ill ; 27cm
Translation of: The last trick
ISBN 0-904836-09-6 : £2.50 B81-10208

823'.914 — Children's stories in English. Garner, Alan — *Critical studies*
Philip, Neil. A fine anger : a critical introduction to the work of Alan Garner / Neil Philip. — London : Collins, 1981. — 191p ; 22cm
Bibliography: p167-188. — Includes index
ISBN 0-00-195043-6 : £5.95 B81-15656

823'.914 — Fiction in English. Cookson, Catherine, *to 1968* — *Biographies*
Cookson, Catherine. Our Kate / Catherine Cookson. — [London] : Corgi, 1974, c1969 (1980 [printing]). — 252p,[8]p of plates : ill,ports ; 18cm
Originally published: London : Macdonald, 1969
ISBN 0-552-11676-9 (pbk) : £1.25 B81-22176

823'.914 — Fiction in English. Davis, Margaret Thomson — *Biographies*
Davis, Margaret Thomson. The making of a novelist. — London : Allison & Busby, Oct.1981. — [176]p
ISBN 0-85031-434-8 : £6.50 : CIP entry B81-27964

823'.914 — Fiction in English. Drabble, Margaret — *Critical studies*
Rose, Ellen Cronan. The novels of Margaret Drabble : equivocal figures / Ellen Cronan Rose. — London : Macmillan, 1980. — xi,141p : 1ill ; 23cm
Bibliography: p130-134. — Includes index
ISBN 0-333-28568-9 : £12.00 : CIP rev. B80-13609

823'.914 — Fiction in English. Farrell, J. G.. Siege of Krishnapur — *Study outlines*
Farrar, David. Brodie's notes on J.G. Farrell's The siege of Krishnapur / David Farrar. — London : Pan, 1981. — 76p ; 20cm. — (Pan study aids) (Brodie's notes)
ISBN 0-330-50178-x (pbk) : £0.80 B81-07539

823'.914 — Fiction in English. Golding, William. Lord of the Flies — *Study outlines — For schools*
Self, David. Lord of the flies : [guidelines] : by David Self. — Teacher's ed. — London : Glasgow Publications, c1980. — 16,[4]p : ill (some col.),1port ; 30cm. — (Guidelines)
Cover title
ISBN 0-86158-524-0 (pbk) : Unpriced B81-25071

823'.914 — Fiction in English. Golding, William. Spire, *The* — *Study outlines*
Bunnell, W. S.. Notes on William Golding's The spire / compiled by W.S. Bunnell. — London : Methuen Paperbacks, 1981, c1980. — 60p : 1ill ; 20cm. — (Methuen notes)
ISBN 0-417-21760-9 (pbk) : £0.95 B81-19612

823'.914 — Fiction in English. Gunn, Neil M. — *Biographies*
Hart, Francis Russell. Neil M. Gunn. — London : J. Murray, Oct.1981. — [320]p
ISBN 0-7195-3856-4 : £15.00 : CIP entry B81-27382

823'.914 — Fiction in English. Murdoch, Iris — *Critical studies*
Dipple, Elizabeth. Iris Murdoch : work for the spirit. — London : Methuen, Jan.1982. — [384]p
ISBN 0-416-31290-x : £12.50 : CIP entry B81-34401

823'.914 — Fiction in English. Scott, Paul — *Critical studies*
Swinden, Patrick. Paul Scott : images of India / Patrick Swinden. — London : Macmillan, 1980. — xii,123p ; 23cm
Includes index
ISBN 0-333-27740-6 : £8.95 : CIP rev. B80-08039

823'.914[F] — Fiction in English, *1945-* — *Texts*
Ableman, Paul. Shoestring's finest hour : an original novel / by Paul Ableman ; based on the BBC-TV series created by Robert Banks Stewart and Richard Harris. — London : British Broadcasting Corporation, 1980. — 204p ; 23cm
ISBN 0-563-17866-3 : £5.95 B81-07041

Ableman, Paul. Shoestring's finest hour : an original novel / by Paul Ableman ; based on the BBC-TV series created by Robert Banks Stewart and Richard Harris. — London : British Broadcasting Corporation, 1980. — 204p ; 18cm
ISBN 0-563-17867-1 (pbk) : £1.00 B81-03494

Ackroyd, Peter, *1949-*. The great fire of London. — London : Hamish Hamilton, Jan.1982. — [192]p
ISBN 0-241-10704-0 : £7.50 : CIP entry B81-34318

Adams, Douglas. The restaurant at the end of the universe / Douglas Adams. — London : Arthur Barker, c1980. — 185p ; 23cm
Originally published: London : Pan, 1980
ISBN 0-213-16792-1 : £5.50 B81-11007

Adams, Richard, *1920-*. The girl in a swing / Richard Adams. — London : Allen Lane, 1980. — 396p ; 23cm
ISBN 0-7139-1407-6 : £5.95 B81-00416

Adams, Richard, *1920-*. The girl in a swing / Richard Adams. — Harmondsworth : Penguin, 1980 (1981 [printing]). — 396p ; 18cm
Originally published: London : Allen Lane, 1980
ISBN 0-14-005533-9 (pbk) : £1.50 B81-28700

Agry, Ed. Assault force : O'Reilly / by Ed Agry. — London : Hale, 1981. — 188p ; 21cm
ISBN 0-7091-8833-1 : £6.25 B81-08986

Ahmed, Abul. Remember 'Rietta for ever / Abul Ahmed. — Bognor Regis : New Horizon, c1981. — 248p ; 21cm
ISBN 0-86116-729-5 : £5.75 B81-18740

Aikiku. Kaguya Hime / by Aikiku ; illustrations by Mizu. — London (28, Russell Rd., W.14) : Rafael Barrett, 1980. — 55p : ill ; 26cm
£1.75 (pbk) B81-18368

Aikiku. Momotaro : (peachuboyo) / by Aikiku ; collage of scenes from Japanese adult comics approved by the official censor and additional illustrations by Mizu. — London (28, Russell Rd., W.14) : Rafael Barrett, 1980. — 61p : ill ; 26cm
£1.85 (pbk) B81-18367

Aird, Catherine. The religious body / Catherine Aird. — Hornchurch : Henry, 1980, c1966. — 173p ; 21cm
Originally published: London : Macdonald, 1966
ISBN 0-86025-167-5 : £4.55 B81-05925

Aird, Catherine. Some die eloquent / Catherine Aird. — London : Hamlyn Paperbacks, 1981. — 190p ; 18cm. — (A Hamlyn whodunnit)
Originally published: London : Collins, 1979
ISBN 0-600-20379-4 (pbk) : £1.25 B81-28648

Aird, Catherine. Some die eloquent / Catherine Aird. — Large print ed. — Leicester : Ulverscroft, 1981, c1979. — 327p ; 23cm. — (Ulverscroft large print series)
Originally published: London : Collins, 1979
ISBN 0-7089-0631-1 : Unpriced : CIP rev. B81-14791

Airth, Rennie. Once a spy / Rennie Airth. — London : Cape, 1981. — 245p ; 21cm
ISBN 0-224-01902-3 : £6.50 : CIP rev. B81-01267

Alding, Peter. A man condemned / by Peter Alding. — London : Hale, 1981. — 176p ; 20cm
ISBN 0-7091-8889-7 : £5.75 B81-15382

Aldiss, Brian W.. Enemies of the system : a tale of homo uniformis / Brian Aldiss. — [St Albans] : Triad, 1980, c1978 (1981 [printing]). — 124p ; 18cm. — (Panther science fiction)
Originally published: London : Cape, 1978
ISBN 0-586-04996-7 (pbk) : £1.25 B81-32326

Aldiss, Brian W.. Galaxies like grains of sand / Brian Aldiss ; with an introduction by Norman Spinard. — London : Granada, 1979, c1960. — 188p ; 18cm. — (Panther)
£1.25 (pbk) B81-34740

Aldiss, Brian W.. Helliconia spring. — London : Cape, Oct.1981. — [320]p
ISBN 0-224-01843-4 : £6.95 : CIP entry B81-27364

Alexander, Faith. Storm in my heart / by Faith Alexander. — London : Hale, 1981. — 160p ; 20cm
ISBN 0-7091-8646-0 : £5.50 B81-02870

Alexander, Kate. Fields of battle / Kate Alexander. — London : Macdonald, 1981. — 442p ; 22cm
ISBN 0-354-04640-3 : £7.95 B81-35375

Alexander, Robert. The soul eater / Robert Alexander. — [London] : Corgi, 1980, c1979. — 189p ; 18cm
Originally published: London : Souvenir, 1979
ISBN 0-552-11576-2 (pbk) : £1.00 B81-07082

Alexander, Susan, *19---*. Wedding in the family / by Susan Alexander. — London : Mills & Boon, 1981. — 188p ; 20cm
ISBN 0-263-09908-3 : £4.55 B81-35645

Alexander-Cox, Barbara. The face of all people / Barbara Alexander-Cox. — Bognor Regis : New Horizon, c1978. — 116p ; 21cm
ISBN 0-86116-025-8 : £2.95 B81-19039

Alington, Gabriel. The stars are upside down / Gabriel Alington. — London : Heinemann, 1980. — 170p ; 23cm
For adolescents
ISBN 0-434-92672-8 : £4.95 B81-07253

Allan, Margaret, *1922-*. For love of Colin / by Margaret Allan. — London : Hale, 1980. — 173p ; 20cm
ISBN 0-7091-8520-0 : £5.25 B81-01268

Allan, Margaret, *1922-*. The valley of rainbows / by Margaret Allan. — London : Hale, 1981. — 176p ; 20cm
ISBN 0-7091-9068-9 (corrected) : £5.60 B81-29944

Allan, Stella. A dead giveaway / Stella Allan. — London : Collins, 1980. — 221p ; 20cm. — (The Crime Club)
ISBN 0-00-231280-8 : £5.25 B81-01269

Allbeury, Ted. Consequences of fear / Ted Allbeury. — London : Granada, 1979 (1981 [printing]). — 190p ; 18cm. — (A Mayflower book)
ISBN 0-583-12937-4 (pbk) : £1.25 B81-19920

Allbeury, Ted. The other side of silence / Ted Allbeury. — London : Granada, 1981. — 320p ; 23cm
ISBN 0-246-11449-5 : £5.95 B81-10077

Allbeury, Ted. The secret whispers / Ted Allbeury. — London : Granada, 1981. — 221p ; 23cm
ISBN 0-246-11108-9 : £6.95 B81-38057

Allbeury, Ted. Shadow of shadows. — London : Granada, Feb.1982. — [240]p
ISBN 0-246-11601-3 : £6.95 : CIP entry B81-36227

823'.914[F] — Fiction in English, ***1945- — Texts continuation***

Allbeury, Ted. The twentieth day of January / Ted Allbeury. — London : Granada, 1980 (1981 [printing]). — 221p ; 18cm. — (A Mayflower book)
ISBN 0-583-12935-8 (pbk) : £1.25 B81-34838

Allen, Maggie. The walls of Jericho : a novel based on the life of Sophia Jex-Blake / by Maggie Allen and Michael Elder ; derived from the BBC-TV serial. — London : British Broadcasting Corporation, 1981. — 255p ; 18cm
ISBN 0-563-17917-1 (cased) : £6.75
ISBN 0-563-17929-5 (pbk) : £1.95 B81-11008

Allen, Michael. Spence in Petal Park / Michael Allen. — Large print ed. — Leicester : Ulverscroft, 1980, c1977. — 344p ; 23cm. — (Ulverscroft large print series)
Originally published: London : Constable, 1977
ISBN 0-7089-0533-1 : £4.25 : CIP rev. B80-24810

Alleston, Margaret. Three for luck? / by Margaret Alleston. — London : Hale, 1981. — 187p ; 20cm
ISBN 0-7091-8807-2 : £5.50 B81-11660

Allfrey, P. Shand. The orchid house. — London : Virago, Feb.1982. — [256]p. — (Virago modern classics)
Originally published: London : Constable, 1953
ISBN 0-86068-242-0 (pbk) : £2.95 : CIP entry B81-36023

Allison-Williams, Jean. Cry 'God for Richard' / by Jean Allison-Williams. — London : Hale, 1981. — 191p ; 20cm
ISBN 0-7091-9111-1 : £6.50 B81-24870

Allon, Frank X.. Super-fox / Frank X. Allon. — Bognor Regis : New Horizon, c1981. — 174p ; 21cm
ISBN 0-86116-686-8 : £5.25 B81-18741

Allyne, Kerry. Across the great divide / Kerry Allyne. — Large print ed. — Bath : Chivers, 1981, c1979. — 207p ; 23cm. — (A Seymour book)
Originally published: London : Mills and Boon, 1979
ISBN 0-85119-432-x : £4.95 : CIP rev. B81-20110

Allyne, Kerry. Coral cay / by Kerry Allyne. — London : Mills and Boon, 1981. — 187p ; 19cm
ISBN 0-263-09943-1 : £4.55 B81-40868

Allyne, Kerry. Mixed feelings / by Kerry Allyne. — London : Mills & Boon, 1981. — 188p ; 19cm
ISBN 0-263-09867-2 : £4.55 B81-18343

Allyne, Kerry. Reunion at Pitereeka / by Kerry Allyne. — London : Mills & Boon, 1980. — 188p ; 19cm
ISBN 0-263-09754-4 : £3.85 B81-00417

Alverson, Charles. The time bandits. — London : Severn House, Oct.1981. — [128]p
ISBN 0-7278-0737-4 : £5.95 : CIP entry B81-30177

Amis, Kingsley. Russian hide and seek : a melodrama / Kingsley Amis. — Harmondsworth : Penguin, 1981, c1980. — 250p ; 19cm
Originally published: London : Hutchinson, 1980
ISBN 0-14-005738-2 (pbk) : £1.50 B81-32837

Amis, Martin. Other people : mystery story / Martin Amis. — London : Cape, 1981. — 223p ; 21cm
ISBN 0-224-01766-7 : £5.95 : CIP rev. B81-01270

Andersen, Ian. The big night / Ian Andersen. — London : Hale, 1981, c1979. — 205p ; 20cm
Originally published: New York : Simon and Schuster, 1979
ISBN 0-7091-9090-5 : £5.95 B81-21295

Anderson, J. R. L.. Death in a greenhouse. — Large print ed. — Anstey : Ulverscroft, Jan.1982. — [408]p. — (Ulverscroft large print series : mystery)
ISBN 0-7089-0730-x : £5.00 : CIP entry B81-33953

Anderson, J. R. L.. Death in a high latitude / by J.R.L. Anderson. — London : Gollancz, 1981. — 221p ; 21cm
ISBN 0-575-02995-1 : £5.95 B81-24753

Anderson, J. R. L.. Death in the desert / J.R.L. Anderson. — Large print ed. — Leicester : Ulverscroft, 1980, c1976. — 337p ; 23cm. — (Ulverscroft large print series)
Originally published: London : Gollancz, 1976
ISBN 0-7089-0504-8 : £4.50 : CIP rev. B80-17945

Anderson, J. R. L.. The nine-spoked wheel / J.R.L. Anderson. — Large print ed. — Leicester : Ulverscroft, 1981, c1975. — 325p ; 23cm. — (Ulverscroft large print series)
Originally published: London : Gollancz, 1975
ISBN 0-7089-0617-6 : £5.00 : CIP rev. B81-07438

Andrews, Jane. Takeover at St Peter's / by Jane Andrews. — London : Hale, 1981. — 175p ; 20cm
ISBN 0-7091-8026-8 (corrected) : £5.50 B81-06427

Andrews, Jane. The tender tyrant / by Jane Andrews. — London : Hale, 1981. — 160p ; 20cm
ISBN 0-7091-8241-4 : £5.60 B81-19220

Andrews, Jane. To Jonathan a father / by Jane Andrews. — London : Hale, 1980. — 156p ; 20cm
ISBN 0-7091-7951-0 : £4.95 B81-00418

Andrews, Lucilla. Edinburgh excursion / Lucilla Andrews. — [London] : Corgi, 1971, c1970 (1980 [printing]). — 189p ; 18cm
Originally published: London : Harrap, 1970
ISBN 0-552-11546-0 (pbk) : £0.95 B81-08019

Andrews, Lucilla. One night in London / Lucilla Andrews. — [London] : Corgi, 1980, c1979. — 175p ; 18cm
Originally published: London : Heinemann, 1979
ISBN 0-552-11538-x (pbk) : £0.95 B81-03317

Andrews, Lucilla. Silent song / Lucilla Andrews. — [London] : Corgi, 1975, c1973 (1981 [printing]). — 207p ; 18cm
Originally published: London : Harrap, 1973
ISBN 0-552-11547-9 (pbk) : £0.95 B81-14125

Andrews, Lucilla. A weekend in the garden / Lucilla Andrews. — London : Heinemann, 1981. — 170p ; 23cm
ISBN 0-434-02127-x : £6.50 B81-11633

Andrews, Lucilla. A weekend in the garden. — Large print ed. — Bath : Chivers, Jan.1982. — [312]p. — (A Lythway book)
Originally published: London : Heinemann, 1981
ISBN 0-85119-772-8 : £6.60 : CIP entry B81-37535

Andrews, Virginia. If there be thorns. — Loughton (17 Brook Rd, Loughton, Essex) : Piatkus, Apr.1981. — [288]p
ISBN 0-86188-099-4 : £6.95 : CIP entry B81-04283

Anthony, Evelyn. The assassin / by Evelyn Anthony. — Long Preston : Magna, 1981, c1970. — 476p ; 23cm
Originally published: London : Hutchinson, 1970. — Published in large print
ISBN 0-86009-337-9 : £4.95 : CIP rev. B81-16909

Anthony, Evelyn. The avenue of the dead. — London : Hutchinson, Oct.1981. — [224]p
ISBN 0-09-145830-7 : £6.95 : CIP entry B81-24613

Anthony, Evelyn. The defector / Evelyn Anthony. — London : Hutchinson, 1980. — 367p ; 23cm
ISBN 0-09-142950-1 : £5.95 : CIP rev. B80-12526

Anthony, Evelyn. The defector. — Large print ed. — Anstey : Ulverscroft, Jan.1982. — [524] p. — (Ulverscroft large print series : adventure, suspense)
ISBN 0-7089-0738-5 : £5.00 : CIP entry B81-33959

Anthony, Evelyn. The grave of truth / Evelyn Anthony. — London : Arrow, 1980, c1979. — 242p ; 18cm
Originally published: London : Hutchinson, 1979
ISBN 0-09-924180-3 (pbk) : £1.25 B81-01271

Anthony, Evelyn. The grave of truth / Evelyn Anthony. — Leicester : Ulverscroft, 1981, c1979. — 426p ; 23cm
Originally published: London : Hutchinson, 1979
ISBN 0-7089-0667-2 : £5.00 : CIP rev. B81-18116

Anthony, Evelyn. The legend / by Evelyn Anthony. — Long Preston : Magna Print, 1981, c1968. — 485p ; 23cm
Originally published: London : Hutchinson, 1969. — Published in large print
ISBN 0-86009-325-5 : £5.75 : CIP rev. B81-14827

Arbor, Jane. Invisible wife / by Jane Arbor. — London : Mills & Boon, 1981. — 188p ; 19cm
ISBN 0-263-09877-x : £4.55 B81-26420

Arbor, Jane. One brief sweet hour / by Jane Arbor. — London : Mills & Boon, 1980. — 188p ; 19cm
ISBN 0-263-09771-4 : £3.85 B81-07196

Arbor, Jane. Two pins in a fountain. — Large print ed. — Bath : Chivers, Oct.1981. — [240] p. — (A Seymour book)
Originally published: London : Mills & Boon, 1977
ISBN 0-85119-436-2 : £4.95 : CIP entry B81-25802

Arbor, Jane. Where the wolf leads / Jane Arbor. — Large print ed. — Bath : Chivers, 1981, c1980. — 224p ; 23cm. — (A Seymour book)
Originally published: London : Mills & Boon, 1980
ISBN 0-85119-428-1 : Unpriced : CIP rev. B81-19173

Archer, Jeffrey. Not a penny more, not a penny less / Jeffrey Archer. — London : Hodder and Stoughton, 1981, c1976. — 255p ; 23cm
Originally published: London : Cape, 1976
ISBN 0-340-26245-1 : £6.95 : CIP rev. B81-16882

Archer, Jeffrey. A quiver full of arrows / Jeffrey Archer. — London : Hodder and Stoughton, c1980. — 190p ; 23cm
ISBN 0-340-25752-0 : £4.95 : CIP rev. B80-2488

Arden, Judith. Golden promises / Judith Arden. — London : Macdonald Futura, 1981. — 254p ; 21cm
ISBN 0-354-04758-2 : £4.95 B81-3486

823'.914[F] — Fiction in English, *1945-* — *Texts continuation*

Arden, Judith. Golden promises / Judith Arden. — London : Macdonald Futura, 1981. — 254p ; 18cm. — (A Minstrel book ; 14)
ISBN 0-7088-2065-4 (pbk) : £0.95 B81-32782

Armitage, Aileen. Hawksmoor / Aileen Armitage. — London : Hamlyn Paperbacks, 1981. — 448p ; 18cm
ISBN 0-600-20116-3 (pbk) : £1.75 B81-19904

Armitage, Aileen. Jacob's Well / Aileen Armitage. — London : Hamlyn Paperbacks, 1981. — 185p ; 18cm. — (A Moonshadow romance)
ISBN 0-600-20373-5 (pbk) : £1.10 B81-33495

Armstrong, Lindsay. My dear innocent / by Lindsay Armstrong. — London : Mills & Boon, 1981. — 186p ; 20cm
ISBN 0-263-09933-4 : £4.55 B81-35635

Armstrong, Lindsay. Spitfire / by Lindsay Armstrong. — London : Mills & Boon, 1981. — 188p ; 20cm
ISBN 0-263-09860-5 : £4.55 B81-18349

Armstrong, Robert, *1940-*. The Alfriston Gang / by Robert Armstrong. — [Eastbourne] ([20 Pevensey Rd, Eastbourne, E. Sussex]) : [Sound Forum], c1980. — [46]p ; 21cm
Text on inside cover
£0.65 (unbound) B81-02829

Armstrong, Tilly. Lightly like a flower / Tilly Armstrong. — Large print ed. — Bath : Chivers, 1981, c1978. — 271p ; 23cm. — (A Lythway romance)
Originally published: London : Collins, 1978
ISBN 0-85119-728-0 : Unpriced : CIP rev. B81-13713

Arnold, Bruce. The muted swan. — London : H. Hamilton, Oct.1981. — [224]p
ISBN 0-241-10687-7 : £7.95 : CIP entry B81-26785

Arnold, Bruce. The song of the nightingale / Bruce Arnold. — London : Hamilton, 1980. — 272p ; 21cm
ISBN 0-241-10497-1 : £6.95 : CIP rev. B80-18478

Arnold, Margot. The officers' woman. — Large print ed. — Anstey : Ulverscroft, Jan.1982. — [447]p. — (Charnwood library series)
Originally published: London : Wingate, 1972
ISBN 0-7089-8018-x : £5.25 : CIP entry B81-33993

Ashby, Carter. Pine Ridge / by Carter Ashby. — London : Hale, 1980. — 160p ; 20cm
ISBN 0-7091-8319-4 : £4.50 B81-00419

Ashford, Jeffrey. Hostage to death. — Large print ed. — Long Preston : Magna Print Books, Feb.1982. — [320]p
Originally published: London : Long, 1977
ISBN 0-86009-377-8 : £5.25 : CIP entry B81-35701

Ashford, Jeffrey. The loss of the Culion / Jeffrey Ashford. — London : Collins, 1981. — 160p ; 21cm. — (The Crime Club)
ISBN 0-00-231482-7 : £5.75 B81-14080

Ashford, Jeffrey. A recipe for murder. — Large print ed. — Long Preston : Magna Print Books, Jan.1982. — [320]p
Originally published: London : Long, 1980
ISBN 0-86009-372-7 : £5.25 : CIP entry B81-33766

Ashton, Elizabeth. Egyptian honeymoon / by Elizabeth Ashton. — London : Mills & Boon, 1981. — 189p ; 19cm
ISBN 0-263-09874-5 : £4.55 B81-26419

Ashton, Elizabeth. Rebel against love / by Elizabeth Ashton. — London : Mills & Boon, 1981. — 190p ; 20cm
ISBN 0-263-09827-3 : £4.55 B81-09412

Ashton, Elizabeth. Silver arrow / by Elizabeth Ashton. — London : Mills & Boon, 1980. — 189 ; 20cm
ISBN 0-263-09772-2 (corrected) : £3.85 B81-06315

Ashton, Mark. A gilded frame / by Mark Ashton. — London : Hale, 1981. — 188p ; 20cm
ISBN 0-7091-9274-6 : £6.25 B81-35192

Ashton, Mark. That infernal triangle / by Mark Ashton. — London : Hale, 1981. — 190p ; 20cm
ISBN 0-7091-8931-1 : £5.75 B81-15381

Ashton, Stephen. The pitiless sky / Stephen Ashton. — London : New English Library, 1981, c1979. — 150p ; 18cm
Originally published: London : Muller, 1979
ISBN 0-450-04575-7 (pbk) : £1.25 B81-02909

Aspinall, Ruth. Lambs in the wind / [Ruth Aspinall]. — [London] (38 Abingdon Rd., W8 6AS) : Twangings Press, 1980. — 466p ; 22cm
ISBN 0-904915-11-5 : £3.00 B81-02721

Aspinall, Ruth. The sand clock / by Ruth Aspinall. — [London] ([38 Abingdon Rd, W8 6AS]) : [Twangings Press], [1980]. — 357p ; 22cm
ISBN 0-904915-08-5 : £2.00 B81-02767

Atkins, Meg Elizabeth. Palimpsest. — London : Quartet, Oct.1981. — [224]p. — (Quartet crime)
ISBN 0-7043-2310-9 : £6.50 : CIP entry B81-25710

Attenborough, John. One man's inheritance / John Attenborough. — London : Pan, 1981, c1979. — 239p ; 18cm
Originally published: London : Hodder and Stoughton, 1979
ISBN 0-330-26281-5 (pbk) : £1.25 B81-12075

Attenborough, John. One man's inheritance / John Attenborough. — Large print ed. — Leicester : Ulverscroft, 1981, c1979. — 448p : 1map ; 23cm. — (Ulverscroft large print)
Originally published: London : Hodder & Stoughton, 1979
ISBN 0-7089-0599-4 : Unpriced B81-14189

Austin, Geoffrey. The fireships of Ushant / Geoffrey Austin. — London : Hale, 1981. — 173p ; 21cm
ISBN 0-7091-9059-x : £6.25 B81-24431

Ayling, Rose. Love on the agenda / by Rose Ayling. — London : Hale, 1981. — 207p ; 20cm
ISBN 0-7091-8714-9 : £5.50 B81-11837

Ayling, Rose. Trials of love / by Rose Ayling. — London : Hale, 1981. — 208p ; 20cm
ISBN 0-7091-9237-1 : £5.75 B81-28868

Baber, Jocelyn. Crescendo / J. Baber. — Bognor Regis : New Horizon, c1980. — 271p ; 22cm
ISBN 0-86116-215-3 : £4.25 B81-19249

Back, R. P.. The runes are cast / R.P. Back. — Ilfracombe : Stockwell, 1980. — 43p ; 18cm
ISBN 0-7223-1368-3 (pbk) : £1.75 B81-07982

Bacon, Lyn. A turbulent courtship / by Lyn Bacon. — London : Hale, 1981. — 192p ; 20cm
ISBN 0-7091-8996-6 : £6.50 B81-21878

Bacon, Margaret. The kingdom of the rose. — Loughton : Piatkus, Jan.1982. — [544]p
ISBN 0-86188-117-6 : £7.50 : CIP entry B81-33760

Baddeley, Pam. Weaver of dreams / by Pam Baddeley ; illustrated by Martin Delaney. — Strathmartine (c/o Sheila Clark, 6 Craigmill Cottages, Strathmartine, by Dundee DD3 0PH) : ScoTpress, 1981. — 46p : ill ; 30cm. — (A Star Trek fanzine)
£1.15 (pbk) B81-35650

Bagley, Desmond. Bahama crisis / Desmond Bagley. — London : Collins, 1980. — 250p : 1map ; 22cm
ISBN 0-00-222358-9 : £6.50 B81-01272

Bagley, Desmond. Bahama crisis. — Large print ed. — Anstey : Ulverscroft, Feb.1982. — [432] p. — (Ulverscroft large print series : adventure, suspense)
ISBN 0-7089-0752-0 : £5.00 : CIP entry B81-36939

Bagley, Desmond. The snow tiger / Desmond Bagley. — [London] : Fontana, 1976, c1975 (1979 [printing]). — 253p ; 18cm
Originally published: London : Collins, 1975
ISBN 0-00-615684-3 (pbk) : £0.95 B81-02988

Bailey, Stephen. The teddy bear / Stephen Bailey. — Bognor Regis : New Horizon, c1981. — 214p ; 22cm
ISBN 0-86116-630-2 : £5.75 B81-20701

Bainbridge, Beryl. Another part of the wood / Beryl Bainbridge. — Rev. ed. — London : Fontana, 1980, c1979. — 159p ; 19cm
Previous ed.: London : Hutchinson, 1968
ISBN 0-00-616061-1 (pbk) : £1.15 B81-01273

Bainbridge, Beryl. Harriet said - / Beryl Bainbridge. — [London] : Fontana, 1977, c1972 (1980 [printing]). — 158p ; 18cm
Originally published: London : Duckworth, 1972
ISBN 0-00-616154-5 (pbk) : £1.00 B81-01274

Bainbridge, Beryl. A weekend with Claude. — London : Duckworth, Aug.1981. — [160]p
Originally published: London : Hutchinson, 1967
ISBN 0-7156-1596-3 : £6.95 : CIP entry B81-16389

Bainbridge, Beryl. Winter garden / Beryl Bainbridge. — London : Duckworth, 1980. — 157p ; 21cm
ISBN 0-7156-1495-9 : £5.95 B81-00420

Baines, Ruth. Sing love's secret / by Ruth Baines. — London : Hale, 1981. — 159p ; 21cm
ISBN 0-7091-8814-5 : £5.50 B81-11653

Baker, Christine. Dark giant / by Christine Baker. — London : Hale, 1981. — 160p ; 20cm
ISBN 0-7091-9283-5 : £5.75 B81-30077

Baker, Christine. Love's dream / by Christine Baker. — London : Hale, 1981. — 170p ; 20cm
ISBN 0-7091-8897-8 : £5.60 B81-17328

Ballard, J. G.. Hello America / J.G. Ballard. — London : Cape, 1981. — 224p ; 21cm
ISBN 0-224-01914-7 : £6.50 : CIP rev. B81-04296

Balmain, Lydia. Caribbean nurse / by Lydia Balmain. — London : Mills and Boon, 1981. — 190p ; 19cm
ISBN 0-263-09955-5 : £4.55 B81-40873

Banks, Lynne Reid. Children at the gate / Lynne Reid Banks. — Harmondsworth : Penguin in association with Chatto & Windus, 1971, c1968 (1979 printing). — 279p ; 18cm
Originally published: London : Chatto and Windus, 1968
ISBN 0-14-003236-3 (pbk) : £1.25 B81-23418

823'.914[F] — Fiction in English, *1945-* — *Texts continuation*

Banks, Lynne Reid. Defy the wilderness / Lynne Reid Banks. — London : Chatto & Windus, 1981. — 277p ; 21cm
ISBN 0-7011-2593-4 : £6.95 : CIP rev. B81-23810

Banks, Lynne Reid. Path to the silent country : Charlotte Brontë's years of fame / Lynne Reid Banks. — London : Corgi, 1979, c1977. — 236p ; 18cm
Originally published: London : Weidenfeld and Nicolson, 1977
ISBN 0-552-11038-8 (pbk) : £0.85 B81-03069

Banks, Lynne Reid. Sarah and after / Lynne Reid Banks. — Tring : Lion, 1981, c1975. — 169p ; 18cm
Originally published: London : Bodley Head, 1975
ISBN 0-85648-357-5 (pbk) : £1.50 B81-24983

Banks, Lynne Reid. Two is lonely / Lynne Reid Banks. — Harmondsworth : Penguin, 1976, c1974 (1981 [printing]). — 249p ; 18cm
Originally published: London : Chatto & Windus, 1974
ISBN 0-14-004109-5 (pbk) : £1.50 B81-22255

Banks, Lynne Reid. The writing on the wall / Lynne Reid Banks. — London : Chatto & Windus, 1981. — 192p ; 21cm
For adolescents
ISBN 0-7011-2568-3 : £5.50 : CIP rev. B81-01847

Bannatyne, Jack. Strike force squadron / Jack Bannatyne. — London : Hale, 1981. — 190p ; 21cm
ISBN 0-7091-8880-3 : £6.25 B81-16006

Bannister, Don. Long day at Shiloh / Don Bannister. — London : Routledge & Kegan Paul, 1981. — 277p ; 22cm
ISBN 0-7100-0727-2 : £6.95 : CIP rev. B81-07596

Bannister, Jo. The matrix / Jo Bannister. — London : Hale, 1981. — 191p 21cm. — (Hale SF)
ISBN 0-7091-8801-3 : £5.95 B81-11905

Banville, John. Kepler : a novel / by John Banville. — London : Secker & Warburg, 1981. — 192p ; 23cm
ISBN 0-436-03264-3 : £5.95 B81-10141

Barber, Dulan. Beasts / Dulan Barber. — London : Macmillan, 1980. — 106p ; 21cm. — (Topliner tridents)
For adolescents
ISBN 0-333-28990-0 : £3.95 : CIP rev. B80-11160

Barber, Frank Douglas. The last white man / Frank Douglas Barber. — London : W.H. Allen, 1981. — 222p ; 21cm
ISBN 0-491-02824-5 : £6.95 B81-19981

Barber, Noel. Tanamera. — London : Hodder & Stoughton, Oct.1981. — [800]p
ISBN 0-340-26516-7 : £7.95 : CIP entry B81-30145

Barclay, Tessa. The stony places / Tessa Barclay. — London : W.H. Allen, 1981. — 383p ; 21cm
ISBN 0-491-02724-9 : £6.95 B81-11813

Bargate, Verity. Tit for tat / Verity Bargate. — London : Cape, 1981. — 167p ; 21cm
ISBN 0-224-01908-2 : £5.95 : CIP rev. B81-04331

Barker, D. A.. A question of reality / D.A. Barker. — London : Hale, 1981. — 205p ; 20cm. — (Hale S.F.)
ISBN 0-7091-9199-5 : £6.25 B81-35238

Barlay, Stephen. Crash course. — London : Hodder and Stoughton, July 1981. — [320]p
Originally published: London : Hamilton, 1979
ISBN 0-340-25075-5 (pbk) : £1.25 : CIP entry B81-13889

Barlay, Stephen. Cuban confetti / by Stephen Barlay. — London : Hamilton, 1981. — 320p ; 23cm
ISBN 0-241-10233-2 : £7.50 : CIP rev. B81-01275

Barlay, Stephen. The ruling passion. — London : H. Hamilton, Jan.1982. — [256]p
ISBN 0-241-10695-8 : £7.95 : CIP entry B81-34151

Barling, Tom. Bikini red north / Tom Barling. — London : Eyre Methuen, 1981. — 286p ; 23cm
ISBN 0-413-48160-3 : £6.95 : CIP rev. B81-05163

Barling, Tom. Goodbye Piccadilly / Tom Barling. — [London] : Magnum, 1981, c1980. — 343p : 2maps ; 18cm
Originally published: London : Eyre Methuen, 1980
ISBN 0-417-05680-x (pbk) : £1.50 B81-12041

Barnard, Robert. Mother's boys / Robert Barnard. — London : Collins, 1981. — 188p ; 21cm. — (The Crime Club)
ISBN 0-00-231589-0 : £5.75 B81-02174

Barnard, Robert. Sheer torture / Robert Barnard. — London : Collins, 1981. — 186p ; 21cm. — (The Crime Club)
ISBN 0-00-231871-7 : £6.25 : CIP rev. B81-13768

Barnes, Julian, *1946-*. Metroland / Julian Barnes. — London : Robin Clark, 1981, c1980. — 176p ; 20cm
Originally published: London : Cape, 1980
ISBN 0-86072-048-9 (pbk) : £2.95 B81-28646

Barnes, Keith. Sunrise and sunset / Keith Barnes. — Bognor Regis : New Horizon, c1980. — 160p ; 21cm
ISBN 0-86116-182-3 : £4.75 B81-19072

Barnett, Rebecca. Mellie / Rebecca Barnett. — Bognor Regis : New Horizon, c1978. — 198p ; 22cm
ISBN 0-86116-023-1 : £3.95 B81-11010

Barnett, Tony, *1921-*. The Head of Ocrin / Tony Barnett. — London : Hale, 1981. — 224p ; 21cm
ISBN 0-7091-8743-2 : £7.25 B81-08738

Baron, Stephanie. Animals under the stone / Stephanie Baron. — London : Arlington, 1981. — 160p ; 21cm
ISBN 0-85140-524-x : £5.50 B81-18432

Barr, Elizabeth. Lord of Tresarnack / by Elizabeth Barr. — London : Hale, 1981. — 191p ; 20cm
ISBN 0-7091-9183-9 : £6.75 B81-33519

Barrett, Max. Dark in the morning / by Max Barrett. — London : Hale, 1981. — 187p ; 20cm
ISBN 0-7091-8799-8 : £6.25 B81-11107

Barrett, Max. Roxie Blane / by Max Barrett. — London : Hale, 1981. — 191p ; 20cm
ISBN 0-7091-9122-7 : £6.50 B81-33533

Barrett, Susan. The beacon / by Susan Barrett. — London : Hamilton, 1981. — 217p ; 23cm
ISBN 0-241-10528-5 : £7.50 B81-11626

Barry, Eileen. The wayward heart / by Eileen Barry. — London : Hale, 1980. — 157p ; 20cm
ISBN 0-7091-8447-6 : £5.25 B81-01276

Barstow, Stan. A brother's tale / Stan Barstow. — [London] : Corgi, 1981, c1980. — 250p ; 18cm
Originally published: London : Joseph, 1980
ISBN 0-552-11682-3 (pbk) : £1.50 B81-21196

Barwick, James. The hangman's crusade / James Barwick. — London : Macmillan, 1980. — 318p ; 23cm
ISBN 0-333-27838-0 : £6.95 B81-01809

Baumann, Margaret. Bridal flowers / by Margaret Baumann. — London : Mills & Boon, 1980. — 190p ; 20cm
ISBN 0-263-09738-2 : £3.85 B81-00421

Baumann, Margaret. Rendezvous with a dream / by Margaret Baumann. — London : Mills & Boon, 1981. — 190p ; 20cm
ISBN 0-263-09894-x : £4.55 B81-28513

Bawden, Nina. Walking naked / Nina Bawden. — London : Macmillan, 1981. — 221p ; 23cm
ISBN 0-333-31304-6 : £5.95 B81-18572

Baxter, Alida. Amazing grace / Alida Baxter. — London : Arrow, 1980, c1979. — 204p ; 18cm
Originally published: London : Arlington, 1979
ISBN 0-09-924170-6 (pbk) : £1.00 B81-02994

Baxter, David, *1916-*. Winds of change / David Baxter. — Bognor Regis : New Horizon, c1981. — 240p ; 22cm
ISBN 0-86116-733-3 : £6.25 B81-27530

Beastall, Ann. The camping cantata / by Ann Beastall. — Bognor Regis : New Horizon, c1979. — 186p ; 21cm
ISBN 0-86116-068-1 : £3.50 B81-19029

Beaton, Janet. Flower o' the broom / Janet Beaton. — London : Hale, 1981. — 160p ; 20cm
ISBN 0-7091-9178-2 : £5.60 B81-24439

Beaton, Janet. Gift of Aphrodite / by Janet Beaton. — London : Hale, 1981. — 155p ; 20cm
ISBN 0-7091-8690-8 : £5.50 B81-03019

Beattie, Tasman. Judas flight. — Large print ed. — Long Preston : Magna, Nov.1981. — [480]p
ISBN 0-86009-354-9 : £4.95 : CIP entry B81-30428

Beattie, Tasman. The Tillinger codicil / Tasman Beattie. — London : Magnum, 1980 (1981 [printing]). — 366p ; 18cm
ISBN 0-417-05900-0 (pbk) : £1.50 B81-28656

Bebb, Prudence. The eleventh emerald / by Prudence Bebb. — London : Hale, 1981. — 240p ; 20cm
ISBN 0-7091-8941-9 : £6.25 B81-15946

Beckford, Grania. Catch the fire / Grania Beckford. — London : Granada, 1981. — 367p ; 18cm. — (A Mayflower book)
ISBN 0-583-13476-9 (pbk) : £1.95 B81-34906

Beckwith, Robert. The faithful years / Robert Beckwith ; illustrations by George Hooker. — Bognor Regis : New Horizon, c1980. — 167p : ill ; 21cm
ISBN 0-86116-293-5 : £5.75 B81-19041

Bedford, Kenneth. The Mexican treasure / by Kenneth Bedford. — London : Hale, 1981. — 159p ; 20cm
ISBN 0-7091-8816-1 : £4.95 B81-11838

Beeching, Jack. Death of a terrorist : a novel / Jack Beeching. — London : Constable, 1981. — 236p ; 23cm
ISBN 0-09-464220-6 : £6.95 B81-20702

823'.914[F] — Fiction in English, *1945-* — Texts *continuation*

Beevor, Antony. For reasons of state / Antony Beevor. — London : Cape, 1980. — 231p ; 21cm
ISBN 0-224-01930-9 : £6.50 : CIP rev.
B81-14843

Behan, Brian. Time to go / Brian Behan. — London : Martin Brian & O'Keefe, 1979. — 158p ; 21cm
ISBN 0-85616-121-7 : £4.95 B81-09677

Belic, Ziva. The endless search / by Ziva Belic. — Harrow : Euroeditions, 1979. — 62p ; 21cm
ISBN 0-906204-31-3 : Unpriced B81-24756

Bell, Anne. Wake the brave / Anne Bell. — London : Hale, 1980. — 176p ; 20cm
ISBN 0-7091-8684-3 : £5.95 B81-03018

Bell, Ken, *19---*. Black pudden republic / by Ken Bell. — Newcastle upon Tyne : Graham, 1981. — 358p ; 23cm
ISBN 0-85983-175-2 : £7.50 B81-32865

Bell, Mary Hayley. Him, her & me : the autobiography of Mr Chips, a Yorkshire terrier / Mary Hayley Bell ; with drawings by Molly Blake. — London : Weidenfeld and Nicolson, 1981. — 114p : ill ; 23cm
Ill. on lining papers
ISBN 0-297-77956-7 : £5.50 B81-35149

Bellingham, Leo. Oxford : the novel / Leo Bellingham. — London (111 High Holborn, WC1V 6JS) : Nold Jonson, 1981. — 236p ; 23cm
ISBN 0-907538-01-0 : £6.00 B81-17390

Benator, Stephen. The man on the bridge / Stephen Benator. — Brighton : Harvester, 1981. — 218p ; 21cm
ISBN 0-7108-0025-8 : £7.50 : CIP rev.
B80-12533

Benedictus, David. Lloyd George / David Benedictus. — London : Weidenfeld and Nicolson, c1981. — 222p ; 23cm
Based on a BBC TV series written by Elaine Morgan
ISBN 0-297-77766-1 : £5.95 B81-02847

Benedictus, David. Lloyd George / David Benedictus. — London : Sphere, 1981. — 222p ; 18cm
Originally published: London : Weidenfeld and Nicolson, c1981
ISBN 0-7221-1590-3 (pbk) : £1.25 B81-14593

Bennett, Barbara. A rough music. — Large print ed. — Anstey : Ulverscroft, Dec.1981. — [432] p. — (Ulverscroft large print series)
Originally published: London : Heinemann, 1980
ISBN 0-7089-0719-9 : £5.00 : CIP entry
B81-32031

Bennett, Barbara. There is a season. — Large print ed. — Bath : Chivers Press, Jan.1982. — [312]p. — (A Lythway book)
Originally published: London : Heinemann, 1976
ISBN 0-85119-773-6 : £6.90 : CIP entry
B81-33810

Bennett, R. A.. A short walk to death / by R.A. Bennett. — London : Hale, 1981. — 176p ; 20cm
ISBN 0-7091-9032-8 : £5.95 B81-21879

Bennetts, Pamela. Beau Barron's lady / Pamela Bennetts. — London : Hale, 1981. — 175p ; 23cm
ISBN 0-7091-8567-7 : £5.95 B81-08994

Bennetts, Pamela. Lucy's cottage / Pamela Bennetts. — London : Hale, 1981. — 160p ; 21cm
ISBN 0-7091-9051-4 : £6.25 B81-21300

Bennetts, Pamela. The quick and the dead / Pamela Bennetts. — Large print ed. — London : Hale, 1980, c1979. — 256p ; 23cm
ISBN 0-7091-8613-4 : £5.00 B81-01277

Benson, Nella. Compact of fire / by Nella Benson. — London : Hale, 1981. — 191p ; 20cm
ISBN 0-7091-8634-7 : £5.50 B81-15948

Benson, Nella. A time and place / by Nella Benson. — London : Hale, 1981. — 190p ; 20cm
ISBN 0-7091-8658-4 : £5.60 B81-24877

Benson, Valerie. Outback Cinderella / by Valerie Benson. — London : Hale, 1981. — 190p ; 20cm
ISBN 0-7091-8790-4 : £5.50 B81-17329

Benson, Valerie. Today is not forever / by Valerie Benson. — London : Hale, 1981. — 187p ; 20cm
ISBN 0-7091-9211-8 : £5.75 B81-30078

Bentine, Michael. Smith & Son removers / Michael Bentine. — London : Robson, 1981. — 167p ; 23cm
ISBN 0-86051-153-7 : £6.75 : CIP rev.
B81-27456

Bentley, Elizabeth, *1947-*. The York quest / Elizabeth Bentley. — London : Hale, 1980. — 192p ; 21cm
ISBN 0-7091-8391-7 : £6.25 B81-00422

Bentley, Joyce. The ring of fate / Joyce Bentley. — Large print ed. — Leicester : Ulverscroft, 1980, c1979. — 369p ; 23cm. — (Ulverscroft large print series. historical romance) (Ulverscroft large print series)
Originally published: London : Macdonald and Jane's, 1979
ISBN 0-7089-0553-6 : £4.25 : CIP rev.
B80-35436

Beresford, Elisabeth. The silver chain / by Elisabeth Beresford. — London : Hale, 1980. — 158p ; 20cm
ISBN 0-7091-8621-5 : £5.25 B81-02425

Beresford, Leigh. Fantocine / Leigh Beresford. — London : Hale, 1981. — 191p ; 21cm. — (Hale SF)
ISBN 0-7091-8719-x : £5.95 B81-08984

Berg, Rilla. Decision for Nurse Lewis / Rilla Berg. — Large print ed. — Bath : Chivers, 1981, c1978. — 289p ; 23cm. — (A Seymoour book)
Originally published: London : Hale, 1978
ISBN 0-85119-424-9 : Unpriced : CIP rev.
B81-13707

Berg, Rilla. A doctor's marriage / by Rilla Berg. — London : Hale, 1980. — 158p ; 20cm
ISBN 0-7091-8418-2 : £5.25 B81-02206

Berger, John. The foot of Clive / John Berger. — [London] : Writers and Readers, [1979, c1962]. — 156p : 1port ; 20cm
Originally published: London : Methuen, 1962
ISBN 0-904613-88-7 (pbk) : £1.95 B81-24821

Bergonzi, Bernard. The Roman persuasion : a novel / Bernard Bergonzi. — London : Weidenfeld and Nicolson, 1981. — 192p ; 23cm
ISBN 0-297-77927-3 : £6.95 B81-11111

Bermant, Chaim. Now Newman was old : a novel / by Chaim Bermant. — London : Allen & Unwin, 1978. — 197p ; 23cm
ISBN 0-04-823145-2 : £4.95 : CIP rev.
B78-31651

Bermant, Chaim. The patriarch / Chaim Bermant. — London : Weidenfeld and Nicolson, c1981. — 424p ; 23cm
ISBN 0-297-77990-7 : £6.95 B81-31998

Betteridge, Anne. A place for everyone / Anne Betteridge. — Large print ed. — Bath : Lythway [1980, c1977]. — 228p ; 23cm
Originally published: London : Hurst & Blackett, 1977
ISBN 0-85046-910-4 : Unpriced : CIP rev.
B80-34144

Bevan, Gloria. Emerald cave / by Gloria Bevan. — London : Mills & Boon, 1981. — 189p ; 20cm
ISBN 0-263-09895-8 : £4.55 B81-28514

Bianchin, Helen. Devil in command / by Helen Bianchin. — London : Mills & Boon, 1980. — 186p ; 19cm
ISBN 0-263-09761-7 : £3.85 B81-01637

Bianchin, Helen. The savage touch / by Helen Bianchin. — London : Mills & Boon, 1981. — 188p ; 19cm
ISBN 0-263-09866-4 : £4.55 B81-18345

Bickers, Richard Townshend. Battle climb / by Richard Townshend Bickers. — London : Hale, 1981. — 192p ; 20cm
ISBN 0-7091-8449-2 : £6.50 B81-24434

Bickers, Richard Townshend. Operation Thunderflash / Richard Townshend Bickers. — London : Hale, 1981. — 189p 21cm
ISBN 0-7091-8379-8 : £6.25 B81-11898

Bickers, Richard Townshend. Sea strike / Richard Townshend Bickers. — London : Hale, 1980. — 188p ; 21cm
ISBN 0-7091-8410-7 : £5.95 B81-00423

Biggar, Joan. The maiden voyage / Joan Biggar. — Glasgow : Molendinar, 1977. — 155p ; 23cm
ISBN 0-904002-21-7 : £3.50 B81-38666

Billington, Rachel. A woman's age / Rachel Billington. — Harmondsworth : Penguin, 1981, c1979. — 588p ; 18cm
Originally published: London : H. Hamilton, 1979
ISBN 0-14-005605-x (pbk) : £1.95 B81-22027

Bingham, John. Brook : a novel / by John Bingham. — London : Gollancz, 1981. — 187p ; 21cm
ISBN 0-575-02981-1 : £5.95 B81-18544

Bingham, John. Deadly picnic / John Bingham. — Large print ed. — Bath : Chivers, 1981, c1980. — 209p ; 23cm. — (A Lythway thriller)
Originally published: London : Macmillan, 1980
ISBN 0-85119-712-4 : £5.90 : CIP rev.
B81-04229

Bishop, Martin. Evergreen / by Martin Bishop. — London : Hale, 1980. — 159p ; 20cm
ISBN 0-7091-8532-4 : £4.95 B81-02156

Bishop, Sheila. Long summer shadows / Sheila Bishop. — Large print ed. — Bath : Lythway, 1980, c1978. — 254p ; 23cm
Originally published: London : Hurst & Blackett, 1978
ISBN 0-85046-911-2 : £6.30 : CIP rev.
B80-34098

Black, Campbell. Raiders of the lost ark. — London : Severn House, Aug.1981. — [176]p
ISBN 0-7278-0736-6 : £5.95 : CIP entry
B81-18098

Black, Jett. Thunder range / by Jett Black. — London : Hale, 1980. — 160p ; 20cm
ISBN 0-7091-8448-4 : £4.95 B81-02152

Black, Laura. Strathgallant. — London : H. Hamilton, July 1981. — [320]p
ISBN 0-241-10442-4 : £7.50 : CIP entry
B81-14854

823'.914[F] — Fiction in English, *1945-* **—** *Texts continuation*

Blackburn, Elsie. Lonely cottage / Elsie Blackburn. — Bognor Regis : New Horizon, c1980. — 64p ; 21cm
ISBN 0-86116-437-7 : £3.75 B81-19082

Blackstock, Charity. Dream towers / Charity Blackstock. — London : Hodder and Stoughton, c1981. — 224p ; 21cm
ISBN 0-340-25903-5 : £6.95 B81-02185

Blackstock, Charity. The encounter / Charity Blackstock. — Loughton : Piatkus, 1981, c1971. — 222p ; 21cm
Originally published: New York : Coward-McCann, 1970
ISBN 0-86188-078-1 : £6.50 : CIP rev. B81-07624

Blackwood, Caroline. The fate of Mary Rose / Caroline Blackwood. — London : Cape, 1981. — 208p ; 21cm
ISBN 0-224-01791-8 : £5.95 B81-11000

Blair, Janey. The menace of Forwood / by Janey Blair. — London : Hale, 1981. — 191p ; 20cm
ISBN 0-7091-9088-3 : £6.50 B81-24355

Blair, Janey. The wisdom of love / by Janey Blair. — London : Hale, 1981. — 188p ; 20cm
ISBN 0-7091-9303-3 : £5.75 B81-40465

Blake, Jennifer. Tender betrayal / Jennifer Blake. — London : Sphere, 1981, c1979. — 416p ; 18cm
ISBN 0-7221-1743-4 (pbk) : £1.50 B81-09802

Blake, Ken. Cry wolf / Ken Blake ; based on the original screenplays by Ronald Graham and Paul Wheeler. — London : Sphere, 1981. — 155p ; 18cm. — (The Professionals ; 10)
ISBN 0-7221-1659-4 (pbk) : £1.00 B81-39750

Blake, Ken. No stone / Ken Blake ; based on the original sceenplays by Tony Barwick and Roger Marshall. — London : Sphere, 1981. — 121p ; 18cm. — (The Professionals ; 9)
ISBN 0-7221-1658-6 (pbk) : £1.00 B81-39751

Blake, M. Glaiser. The Peterloo inheritance / M. Glaiser Blake. — London : Hale, 1981. — 92p ; 20cm
ISBN 0-7091-9000-x : £6.50 B81-17316

Blake, Sally. The devil's kiss / Sally Blake. — London : Macdonald Futura, 1981. — 255p ; 18cm. — (A Minstrel book ; 17)
ISBN 0-7088-2098-0 (pbk) : £0.95 B81-40946

Blanshard, Audrey. Countess incognito / Audrey Blanshard. — London : Hale, 1981. — 189p ; 20cm
ISBN 0-7091-8986-9 : £6.50 B81-24869

Blomfield, Richard. Looking for love / Richard Blomfield. — Bognor Regis : New Horizon, c1981. — 161p ; 21cm
ISBN 0-86116-302-8 : £4.75 B81-18743

Bogarde, Dirk. A gentle occupation / Dirk Bogarde. — [London] : Triad, 1981, c1980. — 447p : 4maps ; 18cm
Originally published: London : Chatto & Windus, 1980
ISBN 0-586-05360-3 (pbk) : £1.95 B81-37285

Bogarde, Dirk. Voices in the garden / Dirk Bogarde. — London : Chatto & Windus, 1981. — 337p ; 21cm
ISBN 0-7011-2572-1 : £6.95 : CIP rev. B81-23742

Boland, John. The Midas touch. — Large print ed. — Bath : Chivers Press, Dec.1981. — [280] p. — (A Lythway book)
Originally published: London : Boardman, 1960
ISBN 0-85119-766-3 : £6.80 : CIP entry B81-31797

Boland, John. Mysterious way. — Large print ed. — Bath : Chivers, Nov.1981. — [280]p. — (A Lythway book)
Originally published: London : Boardman, 1959
ISBN 0-85119-756-6 : £6.70 : CIP entry B81-31250

Bolt, David. Samson. — Loughton : Piatkus, Jan.1982. — [336]p
ISBN 0-86188-129-x : £6.95 : CIP entry B81-34640

Bonnett, Stanley. Jump, boy, jump / Stanley Bonnett. — London : New English Library, 1981, c1979. — 176p ; 18cm
Originally published: London : Joseph, 1979
ISBN 0-450-05021-1 (pbk) : £1.25 B81-11161

Bowden, Jean. Wendy Craig's Nanny : a novel / by Jean Bowden. — London : Granada, 1981. — 239p ; 18cm. — (A Mayflower book)
ISBN 0-583-13479-3 (pbk) : £1.25 B81-07879

Bowden, Jim. Gunfight at Elm Creek / by Jim Bowden. — London : Hale, 1980. — 158p ; 20cm
ISBN 0-7091-8577-4 : £4.95 B81-06318

Bowers, Raymond. The spark. — London : Hutchinson, Feb.1982. — [432]p
ISBN 0-09-145820-x : £7.95 : CIP entry B81-35932

Bowes, Florence. The MacOrvan curse / Florence Bowes. — London : Hale, 1981. — 178p ; 20cm
ISBN 0-7091-9264-9 : £6.75 B81-35214

Boyce, K. A.. Revenge / K.A. Boyce. — Bognor Regis : New Horizon, c1979. — 102p ; 21cm
ISBN 0-86116-067-3 : £2.95 B81-18874

Boyd, Derek. The man who was blind / Derek Boyd. — Bognor Regis : New Horizon, c1980. — 236p : 1map ; 21cm
ISBN 0-86116-467-9 : £4.75 B81-19257

Boyd, William, *1952-*. A good man in Africa / by William Boyd. — London : Hamilton, 1981. — 251p ; 23cm
ISBN 0-241-10516-1 : £6.95 B81-02507

Boyd, William, *1952-*. On the Yankee station : and other stories / by William Boyd. — London : Hamilton, 1981. — 184p ; 21cm
ISBN 0-241-10426-2 : £7.95 : CIP rev. B81-13813

Bradford, Michael. Counter-coup / Michael Bradford. — London : Frederick Muller, 1980. — 337p ; 23cm
ISBN 0-584-31052-8 : £7.50 : CIP rev. B80-09385

Bradford, Roy. The last ditch. — Belfast : Blackstaff Press, Nov.1981. — [224]p
ISBN 0-85640-258-3 (cased) : £6.95 : CIP entry
ISBN 0-85640-259-1 (pbk) : £2.95 B81-31229

Brady, William S.. Comanche! / William S. Brady. — [London] : Fontana/Collins, 1981. — 124p ; 18cm. — (Peacemaker ; 1)
ISBN 0-00-615938-9 (pbk) : £0.95 B81-15523

Brady, William S.. Dead man's hand / William S. Brady. — [London] : Fontana, 1981. — 126p ; 18cm. — (Hawk ; 10)
ISBN 0-00-616204-5 (pbk) : £0.95 B81-39341

Brady, William S.. Desperadoes / William S. Brady. — [London] : Fontana, 1981. — 124p ; 18cm. — (Hawk ; no.8)
ISBN 0-00-616075-1 (pbk) : Unpriced B81-12700

Brady, William S.. The gates of death / William S. Brady. — [London] : Fontana, 1980. — 124p ; 19cm. — (Hawk ; 7)
ISBN 0-00-616074-3 (pbk) : £0.85 B81-05356

Brady, William S.. Killing time / William S. Brady. — [London] : Fontana, 1980. — 124p ; 18cm. — (Hawk ; 4)
ISBN 0-00-615618-5 (pbk) : £0.75 B81-03371

Brady, William S.. Outlaws / William S. Brady. — [London] : Fontana, 1981. — 126p ; 18cm. — (Peacemaker ; 2)
ISBN 0-00-615939-7 (pbk) : £0.852 B81-22315

Brady, William S.. Whiplash / William S. Brady. — [London] : Fontana, 1981. — 127p ; 19cm. — (Peacemaker ; 3)
ISBN 0-00-615940-0 (pbk) : £0.95 B81-36778

Brady, William S.. The widowmaker / William S. Brady. — Glasgow : Fontana, 1981. — 124p ; 18cm. — (Hawk ; 9)
ISBN 0-00-616203-7 (pbk) : £0.95 B81-18793

Braine, John. One and last love / John Braine. — London : Eyre Methuen, c1981. — 175p : ill ; 23cm
ISBN 0-413-47990-0 : £6.50 B81-29916

Braine, John. The queen of a distant country / John Braine. — [London] : Magnum, 1981, c1972. — 224p ; 18cm
Originally published: London : Eyre Methuen, 1972
ISBN 0-417-06020-3 (pbk) : £1.50 B81-28680

Braine, John. Room at the top / John Braine. — Harmondsworth : Penguin, 1959, c1957 (1981 [printing]). — 234p ; 18cm
Originally published: London : Eyre & Spottiswoode, 1957
ISBN 0-14-001361-x (pbk) : £1.50 B81-26504

Breed, Bryan. Match / by Bryan Breed & Mary St. George. — London : Clare, c1980. — 208p ; 23cm
ISBN 0-906549-00-0 : £4.95 B81-10319

Breeze, Paul. While my guitar gently weeps / Paul Breeze. — London : Macdonald Futura, 1980, c1979. — 222p ; 18cm
Originally published: London : Joseph, 1979
ISBN 0-7088-1840-4 (pbk) : £1.25 B81-01279

Breton-Smith, Clare. The ten-year gap / Clare Breton Smith. — Large print ed. — Bath : Chivers, 1981, c1969. — 259p ; 23cm. — (A Seymour book)
Originally published: London : Hurst & Blackett, 1969
ISBN 0-85119-414-1 : £4.95 : CIP rev. B81-00555

Brett, Rosalind. The girl at White Drift / Rosalind Brett. — Large print ed. — Leicester : Ulverscroft, 1981, c1962. — 329p ; 22cm. — (Ulverscroft large print series)
Originally published: London : Mills and Boon, 1962
ISBN 0-7089-0564-1 : £5.00 B81-12176

Brett, Simon, *1945-*. Situation tragedy : a crime novel / by Simon Brett. — London : Gollancz, 1981. — 170p ; 21cm
ISBN 0-575-02973-0 : £5.95 B81-16063

Briar, Bridget. Shannondene / by Bridget Briar. — London : Regency, c1980. — 73p ; 23cm
ISBN 0-7212-0591-7 : £3.50 B81-03407

Bridge, S. R.. The golden locust / by S.R. Bridge. — London : Hale, 1981. — 191p ; 20cm
ISBN 0-7091-8985-0 : £6.50 B81-17332

Bridgman, Jane. Arbella / Jane Bridgman. — Bognor Regis : New Horizon, c1981. — 213p ; 21cm
ISBN 0-86116-276-5 : £5.75 B81-19256

Brierley, David. Big bear, little bear / David Brierley. — London : Faber, 1981. — 223p ; 21cm
ISBN 0-571-11598-5 : £6.25 : CIP rev. B81-06874

823'.914[F] — Fiction in English, *1945-* — *Texts continuation*

Briggs, Raymond. Jim and the beanstalk / Raymond Briggs. — Harmondsworth : Penguin in association with Hamilton, 1980, c1970. — 40p : ill(some col.) ; 23cm. — (Picture puffins)
Originally published: London : H.Hamilton, 1970
ISBN 0-14-050077-4 (pbk) : £0.80 B81-02816

Britt, Katrina. Another time, another place / by Katrina Britt. — London : Mills & Boon, 1981. — 189p ; 20cm
ISBN 0-263-09863-x : £4.55 B81-18352

Britt, Katrina. A girl called Tegi / by Katrina Britt. — London : Mills & Boon, 1980. — 190p ; 19cm
ISBN 0-263-09797-8 : £3.85 B81-07199

Britt, Katrina. The wrong man / by Katrina Britt. — London : Mills & Boon, 1980. — 190p ; 20cm
ISBN 0-263-09731-5 : £3.85 B81-01278

Britten Austin, Paul. The organ maker's wife : being the literary remains of John Palmer ... / by Paul Britten Austin. — London : Duckworth, 1981. — 387p ; 20cm
ISBN 0-7156-1599-8 : £8.95 : CIP rev.
B81-25130

Broderick, John. London Irish / John Broderick. — London : Pan, 1981, c1979. — 220p ; 18cm
Originally published: Barrie and Jenkins, 1979
ISBN 0-330-26282-3 (pbk) : £1.25 B81-12071

Broderick, John. The trial of Father Dillingham. — London : Marion Boyars, Sept.1981. — [192]p
ISBN 0-7145-2747-5 : £6.95 : CIP entry
B81-21614

Bromige, Iris. Alex and the Raynhams / Iris Bromige. — Large print ed. — Leicester : Ulverscroft, 1981, c1961. — 335p ; 22cm. — (Ulverscroft large print series)
Originally published: London : Hodder and Stoughton, 1961
ISBN 0-7089-0578-1 : £5.00 B81-12179

Bromige, Iris. A distant song / Iris Bromige. — Large print ed. — Leicester : Ulverscroft, 1980, c1977. — 282p ; 23cm. — (Ulverscroft large print series)
Originally published: London : Hodder and Stoughton, 1977
ISBN 0-7089-0536-6 : £4.25 : CIP rev.
B80-24816

Bromige, Iris. A house without love / Iris Bromige. — London : Severn House, 1980, c1964. — 189p ; 21cm
Originally published: London : Hodder & Stoughton, 1964
ISBN 0-7278-0614-9 : £4.95 : CIP rev.
B80-22495

Bromige, Iris. A house without love. — Large print ed. — Anstey : Ulverscroft, Nov.1981. — [384]p. — (Ulverscroft large print series)
Originally published: London : Hodder & Stoughton, 1964
ISBN 0-7089-0705-9 : £5.00 : CIP entry
B81-30499

Bromige, Iris. The paths of summer. — London : Coronet, Apr.1981. — [208]p
Originally published: 1979
ISBN 0-340-26098-x (pbk) : £1.10 : CIP entry
B81-01280

Bromige, Iris. A sheltering tree : a Rainwood family novel / Iris Bromige. — Large print ed. — Leicester : Ulverscroft, 1980, c1970. — 317p : 2geneal.tables ; 23cm. — (Ulverscroft large print series)
Originally published: London : Hodder & Stoughton, 1970. — Geneal. tables on lining papers
ISBN 0-7089-0507-2 : £4.25 : CIP rev.
B80-17953

Bromige, Iris. Stay but till tomorrow / Iris Bromige. — Large print ed. — Leicester : Ulverscroft, 1981, c1946. — 344p ; 23cm
Originally published: London : Longman, 1946
ISBN 0-7089-0662-1 : £5.00 : CIP rev.
B81-19183

Bromige, Iris. The tangled wood / Iris Bromige. — Large print ed. — Leicester : Ulverscroft, 1981, c1969. — 328p : 1geneal.table ; 23cm. — (Ulverscroft large print series)
Originally published: London : Hodder and Stoughton, 1969
ISBN 0-7089-0620-6 : £5.00 : CIP rev.
B81-07437

Brook, Esther. Ashcombe Park / by Esther Brook. — London : Hale, 1980. — 191p ; 21cm
ISBN 0-7091-8451-4 : £6.25 B81-01281

Brooke, Jocelyn. The orchid trilogy / Jocelyn Brooke ; introduction by Anthony Powell. — London : Secker and Warburg, 1981. — 437p ; 23cm
Contents: The military orchid. Originally published: London : Bodley Head, 1948 - A mine of serpents. Originally published : London : Bodley Head, 1949 - The goose cathedral. Originally published : London : Bodley Head, 1950
ISBN 0-436-06950-4 : £9.95 B81-19704

Brookner, Anita. A start in life / Anita Brookner. — London : Cape, 1981. — 176p ; 21cm
ISBN 0-224-01899-x : £5.95 B81-19428

Broome, Susannah. The amulet of fortune / Susannah Broome. — Large print ed. — Leicester : Ulverscroft, 1981, c1978. — 544p ; 23cm
Originally published: London : Heinemann, 1978
ISBN 0-7089-0665-6 : £5.00 : CIP rev.
B81-19199

Brown, Alan, *1951-*. A wind up the willow / Alan Brown. — London : Calder, 1980, c1978. — 95p ; 21cm. — (Riverrun writers ; 3)
Originally published: 1978
ISBN 0-7145-3808-6 (cased) : £5.95 : CIP rev.
ISBN 0-7145-3734-9 (pbk) : £2.95 B80-01348

Brown, Olivia. The lily and the bull / Olivia Brown. — Rev. ed. — [London] : Corgi, 1980. — 160p ; 18cm
Previous ed.: London : Collins, 1979
ISBN 0-552-11556-8 (pbk) : £1.00 B81-02959

Brown, Robin, *1937-*. Megalodon / Robin Brown. — London : Joseph, 1981. — 223p ; 23cm
ISBN 0-7181-2042-6 : £6.95 B81-35132

Browne, Christabel. The story of Harriet Bland. — London : Hutchinson, Feb.1982. — [320]p
ISBN 0-09-146740-3 : £6.50 : CIP entry
B81-38335

Browne, Peter Francis. Land's end / Peter Francis Browne. — London : Secker & Warburg, 1981. — 247p ; 23cm
ISBN 0-436-07098-7 : £6.50 B81-10140

Brunner, John. Times without number / John Brunner. — Completely rev. and considerably expanded. — Feltham : Hamlyn Paperbacks, 1974 (1981 [printing]). — 233p ; 18cm. — (Hamlyn science fiction)
Previous ed.: New York : Ace Books, 1962
ISBN 0-600-20086-8 (pbk) : £1.10 B81-20680

Buchan, Kate. Black Fox / Kate Buchan. — London : Mills & Boon, 1980, c1979. — 188p ; 20cm. — (Masquerade)
ISBN 0-263-09677-7 : £3.85 B81-01282

Buchan, Kate. The flame stone / Kate Buchan. — London : Mills & Boon, 1981. — 188p ; 20cm. — (Masquerade)
ISBN 0-263-09782-x : £4.55 B81-14244

Buckingham, Nancy. The house called Edenhythe / Nancy Buckingham. — Bolton-by-Bowland : Magna Print Books, 1980, c1970. — 295p ; 23cm
Originally published: London : Hale, 1970. — Published in large print
ISBN 0-86009-275-5 : £5.25 : CIP rev.
B80-22497

Buckingham, Nancy. The jade dragon / by Nancy Buckingham. — Large print ed. — Long Preston : Magna, 1981, c1976. — 385p ; 23cm
Originally published: London : Hale, 1976. — Published in large print
ISBN 0-86009-335-2 : £4.95 : CIP rev.
B81-16907

Buckingham, Nancy. Marianna / Nancy Buckingham. — London : Eyre Methuen, 1981. — 283p ; 23cm
ISBN 0-413-47440-2 : £6.25 : CIP rev.
B80-18480

Buckingham, Nancy. The other Cathy. — Large print ed. — Long Preston : Magna, Oct.1981. — [448]p
ISBN 0-86009-345-x : £4.95 : CIP entry
B81-27386

Buckingham, Nancy. Quest for Alexis / by Nancy Buckingham. — Long Preston : Magna, 1981, c1973. — 351p ; 23cm. — (Large type series)
Originally published: New York : Hawthorn Books, 1973 ; London : Hale, 1974
ISBN 0-86009-317-4 : Unpriced : CIP rev.
B81-08886

Buckingham, Nancy. Valley of the ravens / by Nancy Buckingham. — Bolton-by-Bowland : Magna Print, 1981, c1973. — 339p ; 23cm
Originally published: New York : Hawthorn Books, 1973 ; London : Hale, 1975. — Published in large print
ISBN 0-86009-297-6 : £5.75 B81-12236

Buckingham, Nancy. Vienna summer. — Large print ed. — Long Preston : Magna Print Books, Jan.1982. — [480]p
Originally published: London : Eyre Methuen, 1979
ISBN 0-86009-371-9 : £5.25 : CIP entry
B81-33767

Buffery, Judith. Gringol weed / Judith L. Buffery. — London : Dobson, 1980. — 240p ; 21cm. — (Star Lords saga)
ISBN 0-234-72209-6 : £5.25 B81-01283

Bulmer, Kenneth. Blind run / Kenneth Bulmer ; based on the original screenplays by Ranald Graham ... [et al.]. — London : Severn House, 1980, c1979. — 159p ; 21cm. — (The Professionals ; [no.5])
Originally published: London : Sphere, 1979
ISBN 0-7278-0602-5 : £4.95 : CIP rev.
B80-18886

Bulmer, Kenneth. Fall girl / Kenneth Bulmer ; based on the original screenplays by Ronald Graham, Edmund Ward and Don Houghton. — London : Severn House, 1981, c1979. — 156p ; 21cm. — (The Professionals ; [6])
ISBN 0-7278-0730-7 : £5.50 : CIP rev.
B81-14838

Bulmer, Kenneth1921-. Shark Africa / Kenneth Bulmer. — London : Severn House, 1981. — 156p ; 21cm. — (Sea wolf)
Originally published / by Bruno Krauss. London : Sphere, 1980?
ISBN 0-7278-0632-7 : £5.25 B81-32573

Burchell, Mary. Nightingales / Mary Burchell. — Large print ed. — Bath : Chivers, 1981, c1980. — 247p ; 23cm. — (A Seymour book)
Originally published: London : Mills and Boon, 1980
ISBN 0-85119-433-8 : £4.95 : CIP rev.
B81-20108

823'.914[F] — Fiction in English, *1945-* — *Texts continuation*

Burgess, Anthony. Earthly powers / Anthony Burgess. — London : Hutchinson, 1980. — 678p ; 24cm
ISBN 0-09-143910-8 : £6.95 : CIP rev. B80-26122

Burgess, Anthony. The eve of Saint Venus / Anthony Burgess ; illustrated by Edward Pagram ; with a special new preface. — London : Hamlyn Paperbacks, 1981, c1964. — 125p : ill ; 18cm
Originally published: London : Sidgwick & Jackson, 1964
ISBN 0-600-20525-8 (pbk) : £1.10 B81-34871

Burgess, Anthony. Man of Nazareth / Anthony Burgess. — London : Magnum, 1980, c1979. — 357p ; 18cm
Originally published: New York : McGraw-Hill, 1979
ISBN 0-417-05810-1 (pbk) : £1.50 B81-05877

Burghley, Rose. The garden of Don José. — Large print ed. — Bath : Chivers, Jan.1982. — [216]p. — (A Lythway book)
Originally published: London : Mills & Boon, 1964
ISBN 0-85119-775-2 : £6.25 : CIP entry B81-33804

Burke, John, *1922-*. The devil's footsteps / John Burke. — [Sevenoaks] : Coronet, 1978, c1976. — 173p ; 18cm
Originally published: London : Weidenfeld and Nicolson, 1976
ISBN 0-340-22947-0 (pbk) : £0.85 : CIP rev. B78-25472

Burke, Owen. The figurehead / Owen Burke. — [London] : Fontana, 1981, c1979. — 333p ; 18cm
Originally published: London : Collins, 1979
ISBN 0-00-616176-6 (pbk) : £1.65 B81-32174

Burley, W. J.. The house of Care : a novel / by W.J. Burley. — London : Gollancz, 1981. — 182p ; 21cm
ISBN 0-575-02965-x : £5.95 B81-12069

Burlinson, Richard. Concerto / Richard Burlinson. — Bognor Regis : New Horizon, c1981. — 209p 21cm
ISBN 0-86116-555-1 : £5.75 B81-32127

Burnett, David, *1946-*. The Cranborne chase : a novel / David Burnett. — London : Hamilton, 1981. — 339p ; 23cm
ISBN 0-241-10418-1 : £7.50 B81-02896

Burns, Patricia. Moonshadow / Patricia Burns. — London : Corgi, 1981. — 269p ; 18cm
ISBN 0-552-11786-2 (pbk) : £1.25 B81-39101

Burton, Ian J.. The runner / Ian J. Burton. — London : Weidenfeld and Nicolson, c1981. — 145p ; 23cm
ISBN 0-297-77986-9 : £6.50 B81-33736

Bushby, John. The Spanish general / John Bushby. — London : Hale, 1981. — 223p ; 21cm
ISBN 0-7091-9252-5 : £7.50 B81-35232

Butler, David, *1927-*. Lusitania / David Butler. — London : Macdonald, 1981. — 734p ; 24cm
ISBN 0-354-04183-5 : £7.95 B81-34870

Butler, Gwendoline. The red staircase / Gwendoline Butler. — London : Collins, 1980. — 422p ; 22cm
ISBN 0-00-221621-3 : £6.50 B81-01284

Butler, Gwendoline. The red staircase / Gwendoline Butler. — [London] : Fontana, 1981, c1979. — 378p ; 18cm
Originally published: London : Collins, 1980
ISBN 0-00-616382-3 (pbk) : £1.50 B81-39746

Butler, Richard, *1925-*. A blood-red sun at noon / Richard Butler. — London : Hale, 1981, c1980. — 263p : 1map ; 22cm
Originally published: Sydney : Collins, 1980. — Map on lining papers
ISBN 0-7091-8806-4 : Unpriced B81-14137

Byatt, A. S.. The virgin in the garden / A.S. Byatt. — Harmondsworth : Penguin, 1981, c1978. — 428p ; 20cm. — (A King penguin)
Originally published: London : Chatto and Windus, 1978
ISBN 0-14-005494-4 (pbk) : £2.95 B81-22188

Calhoun, Rory. The man from Padera / Rory Calhoun. — London : Hale, 1980, c1978. — 172p ; 20cm
ISBN 0-7091-8674-6 : £4.95 B81-02257

Callan, Leo. Black rebel / Leo Callan. — London : New English Library, 1981. — 158p ; 18cm
ISBN 0-450-05267-2 (pbk) : £1.00 B81-40494

Callan, Michael Feeney. The falcon ring / by Michael Feeney Callan. — London : Hale, 1981. — 207p ; 20cm
ISBN 0-7091-9003-4 : £5.75 B81-17324

Callan, Michael Feeney. Lovers and dancers / Michael Fenney Callan. — Feltham : Hamlyn, 1981. — 399p ; 18cm
ISBN 0-600-38405-5 (pbk) : £1.50 B81-11433

Callison, Brian. The Auriga madness / Brian Callison. — London : Collins, 1980. — 223p ; 22cm
ISBN 0-00-222069-5 : £5.95 B81-00435

Callison, Brian. The Auriga madness / Brian Callison. — [London] : Fontana, 1981, c1980. — 223p ; 18cm
Originally published: London : Collins, 1980
ISBN 0-00-616386-6 (pbk) : £1.25 B81-28690

Callison, Brian. The dawn attack / by Brian Callison. — Bolton-by-Bowland : Magna, 1981, c1972. — 504p ; 22cm
Originally published: London : Collins, 1972. — Published in large print
ISBN 0-86009-292-5 : £5.75 B81-08685

Callison, Brian. A flock of ships / by Brian Callison. — Bolton-by-Bowland : Magna, 1980, c1970. — 409p ; 23cm
Originally published: London : Collins, 1970. — Published in large print
ISBN 0-86009-216-x : £5.25 : CIP rev. B79-34447

Callison, Brian. The Judas ship. — Large print ed. — Long Preston : Magna, Dec.1981. — [480]p
ISBN 0-86009-358-1 : £4.95 : CIP entry B81-31817

Callison, Brian. The sextant / Brian Callison. — London : Collins, 1981. — 252p ; 22cm
ISBN 0-00-222296-5 : £7.25 : CIP rev. B81-20621

Callison, Brian. A ship is dying. — Large print ed. — Long Preston : Magna, Sept.1981. — [480]p
ISBN 0-86009-344-1 : £4.95 : CIP entry B81-22461

Callison, Brian. Trapp's peace. — Large print ed. — Long Preston : Magna Print Books, Jan.1982. — [380]p
Originally published: London : Collins, 1979
ISBN 0-86009-385-9 : £5.25 : CIP entry B81-38855

Callison, Brian. A web of salvage / by Brian Callison. — Long Preston : Magna Print, 1981, c1973. — 344p ; 23cm
Originally published: London : Collins, 1973. — Published in large print
ISBN 0-86009-324-7 : £5.75 : CIP rev. B81-14831

Cameron, D. Y.. A touch of spring / by D.Y. Cameron. — London : Hale, 1981. — 160p ; 20cm
ISBN 0-7091-9092-1 : £5.60 B81-24873

Cameron, Lorna. Summer in France / by Lorna Cameron. — London : Mills & Boon, 1981. — 189p ; 20cm
ISBN 0-263-09917-2 : £4.55 B81-35643

Campbell, K. M.. Honours of war / by K.M. Campbell. — London : Allen & Unwin, 1981. — 205p ; 23cm
ISBN 0-04-823176-2 : Unpriced : CIP rev. B80-18481

Campbell, Laura. Heart in danger / by Laura Campbell. — London : Hale, 1981. — 207p ; 20cm
ISBN 0-7091-8894-3 : £5.60 B81-19223

Campbell, Ramsey. The doll who ate his mother : a novel of modern terror / by Ramsey Campbell. — London : W.H. Allen, 1978, c1976 (1980 [printing]). — 209p ; 19cm. — (A Star book)
Originally published: Indianapolis : Bobbs-Merrill, 1976 ; London : Millington, 1977
ISBN 0-352-30498-7 (pbk) : £0.95 B81-15593

Campbell, Ramsey. The nameless / Ramsey Campbell. — [London] : Fontana, 1981. — 253p ; 18cm
ISBN 0-00-616179-0 (pbk) : £1.25 B81-39749

Campbell, Ramsey. Through the walls / Ramsey Campbell. — Rochdale (79 Rochdale Rd., Milnrow, Rochdale, Lancs. OL16 4DT) : British Fantasy Society, 1981. — [16]p : ill ; 21cm. — (B.F.S. booklet ; no.5)
Limited ed. of 500 copies
£0.50 (pbk) B81-35665

Campbell, Ramsey. To wake the dead / Ramsey Campbell. — [London] : Fontana, 1980, c1979. — 316p ; 18cm
Originally published: London : Millington, 1980
ISBN 0-00-615734-3 (pbk) : £1.35 B81-01285

Canaway, W. H.. The solid gold Buddha / W.H. Canaway. — Large print ed. — Leicester : Ulverscroft, 1981, c1979. — 315p ; 23cm. — (Ulverscroft large print)
Originally published: London : Hutchinson, 1979
ISBN 0-7089-0597-8 : Unpriced B81-14193

Cannon, Elliott. A foe to sleep / by Elliott Cannon. — London : Hale, 1980. — 176p ; 20cm
ISBN 0-7091-7829-8 : £5.50 B81-00275

Cannon, Elliott. The life-adjuster / Elliott Cannon. — London : Hale, 1981. — 190p ; 20cm
ISBN 0-7091-8512-x : £5.75 B81-08644

Cannon, Elliott. A question of survival / by Elliott Cannon. — London : Hale, 1981. — 191p ; 20cm
ISBN 0-7091-8733-5 : £5.95 B81-24348

Cannon, John, *1929-*. Stranger to Sereno / John Cannon. — London : Bodley Head, 1981. — 157p ; 21cm
ISBN 0-370-30431-4 : £6.50 : CIP rev. B81-21620

Capsey, Anne. Strawberry / Anne Capsey. — Bognor Regis : New Horizon, c1980. — 106p ; 21cm
ISBN 0-86116-167-x : £3.50 B81-19239

Carder, Peter. The well-wisher / Peter Carder. — Bognor Regis : New Horizon, c1981. — 191p ; 21cm
ISBN 0-86116-621-3 : £5.75 B81-26492

823'.914[F] — Fiction in English, *1945-* **—** *Texts continuation*

Carlisle, D. M.. The secret of the chateau / by D.M. Carlisle. — London : Hale, 1981. — 158p ; 20cm
ISBN 0-7091-8728-9 : £5.95 B81-08961

Carnac, Nicholas. Indigo. — London : H. Hamilton, Jan.1982. — [352]p
ISBN 0-241-10146-8 : £7.95 : CIP entry B81-34150

Carpenter, Richard. Smuggler / Richard Carpenter ; illustrated by Graham Humphries. — London : Fontana, 1981. — 155p : ill ; 19cm. — (An Armada original)
ISBN 0-00-691949-9 (pbk) : £0.85 B81-18790

Carr, Glyn. Lewker in Tirol / Glyn Carr. — Large print ed. — Bath : Chivers, 1980, c1967. — 308p : 1 map ; 23cm. — (New Portway)
Originally published: London : Bles, 1967
ISBN 0-85997-472-3 : £5.50 : CIP rev. B80-17957

Carr, Margaret. Daggers drawn / by Margaret Carr. — London : Hale, 1980. — 171p ; 20cm
ISBN 0-7091-8544-8 : £5.75 B81-02157

Carter, Angela. Heroes and villains / Angela Carter. — Harmondsworth : Penguin, 1981, c1969. — 150p ; 20cm. — (A King Penguin)
Originally published: London : Heinemann, 1969
ISBN 0-14-005652-1 (pbk) : £1.95 B81-27202

Carter, Angela. The magic toyshop / Angela Carter. — London : Virago, 1981, c1967. — 199p ; 20cm. — (Virago modern classics)
Originally published: London : Heinemann, 1967
ISBN 0-86068-190-4 (pbk) : £2.50 B81-24833

Carter, Brian. A black fox running / Brian Carter ; illustrated by the author. — London : Dent, c1981. — iv,264p : ill,2maps ; 23cm
ISBN 0-460-04523-7 : £6.95 : CIP rev. B81-12784

Carter, D. Mark. The sky is burning / D. Mark Carter. — London : Hale, 1981. — 189p ; 20cm
ISBN 0-7091-9097-2 (corrected) : £6.50 B81-27296

Carter, Peter, *1929-*. The sentinels / Peter Carter. — Oxford : Oxford University Press, 1980. — 247p : 1map ; 23cm
ISBN 0-19-271438-4 : £4.75 : CIP rev. B80-23691

Carter, R. M. H.. The dream killers / by R.M.H. Carter. — London : Hale, 1981. — 192p ; 20cm
ISBN 0-7091-9002-6 : £6.25 B81-19302

Carter, Rosemary. Another life / by Rosemary Carter. — London : Mills & Boon, 1981. — 187p ; 20cm
ISBN 0-263-09910-5 : £4.55 B81-34101

Carter, Rosemary. Face in the portrait / by Rosemary Carter. — London : Mills & Boon, 1980. — 186p ; 19cm
ISBN 0-263-09757-9 : £3.85 B81-01286

Carter, Rosemary. Kelly's man. — Large print ed. — Bath : Chivers Press, Jan.1982. — [256] p. — (A Seymour book)
Originally published: London : Mills & Boon, 1980
ISBN 0-85119-448-6 : £4.95 : CIP entry B81-33808

Carter, Rosemary. Safari encounter / by Rosemary Carter. — Lonson : Mills & Boon, 1981. — 186p ; 20cm
ISBN 0-263-09849-4 : £4.55 B81-17429

Carteret, Cindy. Prison of love / by Cindy Carteret. — London : Hale, 1981. — 192p ; 20cm
ISBN 0-7091-9093-x : £5.60 B81-21292

Case, Tom. Cook / Tom Case. — Reading : T. Case, 1981. — 190p ; 18cm
ISBN 0-907431-00-3 (pbk) : £1.00 B81-37899

Cass, Zoë. The silver leopard / Zoë Cass. — Large print ed. — Leicester : Ulverscroft, 1980, c1976. — 378p ; 23cm. — (Ulverscroft large print series)
Originally published: New York : Random House, 1976 ; London : Elek, 1978
ISBN 0-7089-0554-4 : £4.25 : CIP rev. B80-35438

Castle, Brenda. The pines of Monterey / by Brenda Castle. — London : Hale, 1981. — 156p ; 20cm
ISBN 0-7091-9024-7 : £5.60 B81-15298

Castle, Ronald. Back to Bandola / Ronald Castle. — Bognor Regis : New Horizon, c1981. — 178p ; 21cm
ISBN 0-86116-695-7 : £5.75 B81-18870

Caudwell, Sarah. Thus was Adonis murdered / Sarah Caudwell. — London : Collins, 1981. — 246p : ill ; 21cm. — (The Crime Club)
ISBN 0-00-231854-7 : £5.95 B81-08669

Cave, Emma. Cousin Henrietta / Emma Cave. — London : Collins, 1981. — 251p ; 22cm
ISBN 0-00-221971-9 : £7.95 B81-33566

Cave, Peter. Fireflood / Peter Cave. — London : Macdonald Futura, 1980. — 252p ; 18cm
ISBN 0-7088-1750-5 (pbk) : £1.25 B81-05717

Cave, Peter. Fireflood / Peter Cave. — London : Severn House, 1981, c1980. — 252p ; 21cm
Originally published: London : MacDonald Futura, 1980
ISBN 0-7278-0734-x : £6.95 : CIP rev. B81-18100

Cave, Peter. Siege / Peter Cave. — London : Severn House, 1980. — 274p ; 21cm
Originally published: Feltham : Hamlyn, 1980
ISBN 0-7278-0628-9 : £5.95 : CIP rev. B80-22500

Cave, Peter. Slow burn / Peter Cave. — Feltham : Hamlyn, 1981. — 287p ; 18cm
ISBN 0-600-36376-7 (pbk) : £1.50 B81-27879

Cavendish, Clare. Doctor's family / by Clare Cavendish. — London : Hale, 1980. — 191p ; 20cm
ISBN 0-7091-8559-6 : £4.95 B81-01659

Cavendish, Clare. Nurse in the Highlands / by Clare Cavendish. — London : Hale, 1981. — 169p ; 20cm
ISBN 0-7091-8930-3 : £5.60 B81-27309

Chalmers, Garet. Homo-hetero / Garet Chalmers. — London : Hale, 1980. — 189p ; 21cm. — (Hale SF)
ISBN 0-7091-8343-7 : £5.50 B81-00427

Chambers, Peter, *1924-*. The deep blue cradle / by Peter Chambers. — London : Hale, 1980. — 176p ; 20cm
ISBN 0-7091-7971-5 : £5.75 B81-01287

Chambers, Peter, *1924-*. The lady who never was / by Peter Chambers. — London : Hale, 1981. — 191p ; 20cm
ISBN 0-7091-9190-1 : £6.25 B81-35195

Chambers, Peter, *1924-*. A long time dead / by Peter Chambers. — London : Hale, 1981. — 191p ; 20cm
ISBN 0-7091-8688-6 : £5.75 B81-14088

Chance, John Newton. The black widow / by John Newton Chance. — London : Hale, 1981. — 175p ; 20cm
ISBN 0-7091-7412-8 : £5.75 B81-08953

Chance, John Newton. The death importer / by John Newton Chance. — London : Hale, 1981. — 202p ; 20cm
ISBN 0-7091-7719-4 : £5.95 B81-24440

Chance, John Newton. The mayhem madchen / by John Newton Chance. — London : Hale, 1980. — 172p ; 20cm
ISBN 0-7091-7376-8 : £5.50 B81-02203

Chand, Meira. Last quadrant / Meira Chand. — London : John Murray, 1981. — 194p ; 23cm
ISBN 0-7195-3826-2 : £6.95 : CIP rev. B81-14378

Chandler, A. Bertram. Bring back yesterday. — London : Allison and Busby, Nov.1981. — [128]p
ISBN 0-85031-406-2 : £5.95 : CIP entry B81-30575

Chandler, A. Bertram. [Rendezvous on a lost world]. When the dream dies / A. Bertram Chandler. — London : Sphere, 1981. — 123p ; 18cm. — (The Rim world series ; v.2)
Originally published: New York : Ace, 1961 ; London : Allison & Busby, 1981
ISBN 0-7221-2252-7 (pbk) : £1.25 B81-36821

Chandler, A. Bertram. [Rendezvous on a lost world]. When the dream dies / A. Bertram Chandler. — London : Allison & Busby, 1981. — 128p ; 23cm. — (The Rim world series ; v.2)
Originally published: New York : Ace Books, 1961
ISBN 0-85031-361-9 : £5.95 : CIP rev. B80-23693

Chandler, A. Bertram. The Rim of space / A. Bertram Chandler. — London : Sphere, 1981, c1961. — 127p ; 18cm. — (The Rim world series) (Sphere science fiction)
ISBN 0-7221-2247-0 (pbk) : £1.25 B81-20243

Chandler, A. Bertram. The rim of space / A. Bertram Chandler. — London : Allison & Busby, 1981. — 127p ; 23cm. — (The Rim world series ; v.1)
Originally published: New York : Bouregy, 1961
ISBN 0-85031-360-0 : £5.95 : CIP rev. B80-10241

Chandler, Glenn. The sanctuary / Glenn Chandler. — London : Hamlyn Paperbacks, 1981. — 171p ; 18cm
ISBN 0-600-20069-8 (pbk) : £1.00 B81-12490

Chandler, Glenn. The tribe / Glenn Chandler. — Feltham : Hamlyn, 1981. — 187p ; 18cm
ISBN 0-600-20343-3 (pbk) : £1.10 B81-27876

Chapman, Jean, *1929-*. The unreasoning earth / Jean Chapman. — London : Hutchinson, 1981. — 192p ; 23cm
ISBN 0-09-143480-7 (pbk) : £5.95 B81-12949

Chapman, Margaret, *1923-*. Orchid isle / by Margaret Chapman. — London : Hale, 1981. — 158p ; 20cm
ISBN 0-7091-9105-7 : £5.60 B81-24862

Chapman, Margaret, *1923-*. Symphony for a surgeon / by Margaret Chapman. — London : Hale, 1981. — 158p ; 20cm
ISBN 0-7091-8638-x : £5.50 B81-03017

Chappell, Mollie. Dearest neighbour / by Mollie Chappell. — London : Hale, 1981. — 192p ; 20cm
ISBN 0-7091-9184-7 : £6.75 B81-33544

Chard, Judy. The darkening skies / by Judy Chard. — London : Hale, 1981. — 172p 20cm
ISBN 0-7091-8558-8 : £5.50 B81-14139

823'.914[F] — Fiction in English, *1945-* — *Texts continuation*

Chard, Judy. Seven lonely years / Judy Chard. — London : Hale, 1980. — 175p ; 20cm
ISBN 0-7091-8290-2 : £4.95 B81-00428

Charles, Robert, *1923-*. Flowers of evil / Robert Charles. — London : Macdonald Futura, 1981. — 254p : ill ; 18cm
ISBN 0-7088-2004-2 (pbk) : £1.25 B81-15459

Charles, Theresa. With somebody else / by Theresa Charles. — London : Hale, 1981. — 157p ; 20cm
ISBN 0-7091-8810-2 : £5.50 B81-14133

Chatham, Larry. Smith's canyon / by Larry Chatham. — London : Hale, 1981. — 160p ; 20cm
ISBN 0-7091-8900-1 : £4.95 B81-15296

Chatwin, Bruce. The Viceroy of Ouidah / Bruce Chatwin. — London : Cape, 1980. — 155p : ill,1map ; 22cm
Map on lining papers
ISBN 0-224-01820-5 : £5.95 : CIP rev. B80-21050

Cheatham, Lillian. The Saxon inheritance / Lillian Cheatham. — London : Hale, 1981, c1980. — 222p ; 20cm
ISBN 0-7091-9260-6 : £6.75 B81-35207

Cheatham, Lillian. Shadowed reunion / by Lillian Cheatham. — London : Mills & Boon, 1981. — 188p ; 20cm
ISBN 0-263-09913-x : £4.55 B81-34104

Chesham, Henry. The angry atoll / by Henry Chesham. — London : Hale, 1981. — 189p ; 20cm
ISBN 0-7091-9085-9 : £6.50 B81-35656

Chesney, Marion. Annabelle / Marion Chesney. — London : Macdonald Futura, 1981. — 158p ; 21cm. — (Macdonald regency)
ISBN 0-354-04662-4 : £4.25 B81-17393

Chesney, Marion. Annabelle / Marion Chesney. — London : Macdonald Futura, c1981. — 158p ; 18cm. — (A Regency romance)
ISBN 0-7088-2035-2 (pbk) : £1.10 B81-28340

Chesney, Marion. The constant companion / Marion Chesney. — London : Macdonald Futura, 1981, c1980. — 160p ; 21cm
ISBN 0-354-04735-3 : £4.50 B81-28372

Chesney, Marion. The constant companion / Marion Chesney. — London : Macdonald Futura, 1981, c1980. — 160p ; 18cm. — (A Futura book)
Originally published: S.l. : S.n., 1980
ISBN 0-7088-2043-3 (pbk) : £1.10 B81-24428

Chesney, Marion. Daisy / Marion Chesney. — London : Macdonald Futura, 1981, c1980. — 256p ; 21cm
ISBN 0-354-04660-8 : £4.95 B81-10165

Chesney, Marion. Henrietta / Marion Chesney. — London : Macdonald Futura, 1980, c1979. — 222p ; 21cm
ISBN 0-354-04803-1 : £4.95 B81-28442

Chesney, Marion. Kitty / Marion Chesney. — London : Futura, 1980, c1979. — 256p ; 18cm. — (A Troubadour book)
ISBN 0-7088-1923-0 (pbk) : £1.10 B81-06265

Chesney, Marion. My dear Duchess / Marion Chesney. — London : Macdonald Futura, 1980, c1979. — 192p ; 21cm
Originally published: S.l. : s.n., 1979
ISBN 0-354-04756-6 : £4.50 B81-34865

Chester, Deborah. A love so wild / Deborah Chester. — London : Sphere, 1981, c1980. — 312p ; 18cm
Originally published: London : Joseph, 1980
ISBN 0-7221-2281-0 (pbk) : £1.50 B81-20245

Chester, Roy. The Damocles factor / Roy Chester. — Large print ed. — Bath : Chivers, 1981, c1977. — 242p ; 23cm. — (A Lythway book)
Originally published: London : Long : 1977
ISBN 0-85119-742-6 : £6.70 : CIP rev. B81-20104

Chester, Roy. The winds of Pentecost / by Roy Chester. — London : Hale, 1981. — 175p ; 20cm
ISBN 0-7091-9270-3 : £6.25 B81-37310

Chetwynd-Hayes, R.. The monster club / R. Chetwynd-Hayes. — London : New English Library, 1976, c1975 (1981 [printing]). — 192p ; 18cm
ISBN 0-450-05109-9 (pbk) : £1.25 B81-11160

Chevalier, Paul. The grudge / Paul Chevalier. — London : Hodder and Stoughton, 1980. — 345p ; 23cm
ISBN 0-340-25754-7 : £7.50 : CIP rev. B80-13985

Cheyne, N. Gilbert. The story of Anne Ange / N. Gilbert Cheyne. — Bognor Regis : New Horizon, c1981. — 239p ; 22cm
ISBN 0-86116-572-1 : £6.25 B81-18684

Chisholm, Matt. The Cheyenne trap / Matt Chisholm. — London : Hamlyn Paperbacks, 1980. — 144p ; 18cm. — (Blade westerns ; 10)
ISBN 0-600-20139-2 (pbk) : £0.95 B81-10047

Chisholm, Matt. The Indian incident / Matt Chisholm. — London : Hale, 1981, c1978. — 169p ; 20cm
Originally published: Feltham : Hamlyn, 1978
ISBN 0-7091-8705-x : £4.95 B81-08955

Chisholm, Matt. The last act / Matt Chisholm. — London : Hamlyn Paperbacks, 1981. — 140p ; 18cm. — (Blade westerns ; 12)
ISBN 0-600-20355-7 (pbk) : £0.95 B81-24751

Chisholm, Matt. The Navaho Trail / Matt Chisholm. — London : Hamlyn Paperbacks, 1981. — 144p ; 18cm. — (Blade westerns ; 11)
ISBN 0-600-20354-9 (pbk) : £0.95 B81-19947

Chisholm, Matt. The Tucson conspiracy / Matt Chisholm. — London : Hale, 1981, c1978. — 172p ; 20cm
Originally published: Feltham : Hamlyn, 1978
ISBN 0-7091-8702-5 : £4.95 B81-21302

Christie, Anne. My secret gorilla / Anne Christie. — Loughton : Piatkus, c1981. — 201p ; 21cm
ISBN 0-86188-069-2 : £6.50 : CIP rev. B81-09477

Christopher, Cathy. Blue winter smoke / by Cathy Christopher. — London : Hale, 1981. — 158p ; 20cm
ISBN 0-7091-8406-9 : £5.60 B81-21309

Christopher, Cathy. Warnings of thunder / by Cathy Christopher. — London : Hale, 1980. — 157p ; 20cm
ISBN 0-7091-8400-x : £5.50 B81-08991

Christopher, John, *1922-*. Fireball / by John Christopher. — London : Gollancz, 1981. — 148p ; 21cm
ISBN 0-575-02974-9 : £4.95 B81-24755

Christopher, John, *1922-*. The prince in waiting / John Christopher. — Harmondsworth : Puffin in association with Hamilton, 1973, c1970 (1981 [printing]). — 155p ; 18cm
Originally published: London : Hamilton, 1970
ISBN 0-14-030617-x (pbk) : £0.85 B81-35594

Christopher, John 1922-. The sword of the spirits / John Christopher. — [Harmondsworth] : Penguin in association with Hamilton, 1973, c1972 (1981 [printing]). — 153p ; 18cm
Originally published: London : Hamilton, 1972
ISBN 0-14-030630-7 (pbk) : £0.85 B81-35575

Cimino, Moyra. A letter to Cecilia / Moyra Cimino. — Bognor Regis : New Horizon, c1980. — 104p,[5]p of plates : ill,1facsim,ports ; 22cm
ISBN 0-86116-463-6 : £3.50 B81-19250

Clair, Daphne. Dark remembrance / by Daphne Clair. — London : Mills & Boon, 1981. — 188p ; 19cm
ISBN 0-263-09872-9 : £4.55 B81-26574

Clair, Daphne. The loving trap / by Daphne Clair. — London : Mills & Boon, 1980. — 188p ; 19cm
ISBN 0-263-09759-5 : £3.85 B81-01288

Clair, Daphne. Never count tomorrow / by Daphne Clair. — London : Mills & Boon, 1980. — 189p ; 19cm
ISBN 0-263-09796-x : £3.85 B81-05904

Clancy, Leo. Fix / Leo Clancy. — London : Sphere, 1980, c1979. — 218p ; 18cm
Originally published: London : Secker & Warburg, 1979
ISBN 0-7221-2384-1 (pbk) : £1.10 B81-11728

Clare, Elizabeth. By the golden waters / by Elizabeth Clare. — London : Hale, 1981. — 160p ; 20cm
ISBN 0-7091-9284-3 : £5.75 B81-37309

Clark, Douglas, *1919-*. Roast eggs / by Douglas Clark. — London : Gollancz, 1981. — 175p ; 21cm
ISBN 0-575-02963-3 : £5.95 B81-10696

Clark, Douglas, *1919-*. Table d'hote / Douglas Clark. — Large print ed. — Leicester : Ulverscroft, 1981, c1977. — 315p ; 23cm. — (Ulverscroft large print series)
Originally published: London : Gollancz, 1977
ISBN 0-7089-0603-6 : £5.00 : CIP rev. B81-02576

Clark, Eric, *1937-*. Black gambit / Eric Clark. — [London] : Coronet, 1979, c1978. — 229p ; 18cm
Originally published: New York : Morrow ; London : Hodder and Stoughton, 1978
ISBN 0-340-24271-x (pbk) : £0.95 : CIP rev. B79-21247

Clark, Eric, *1937-*. Send in the lions / Eric Clark. — London : Hodder and Stoughton, c1981. — 208p ; 23cm
ISBN 0-340-25966-3 : £6.95 B81-02740

Clarke, Arthur C.. Islands in the sky / Arthur C. Clarke. — Harmondsworth : Penguin, 1981, c1954. — 208p ; 18cm
Originally published: London : Sidgwick & Jackson, 1952
ISBN 0-14-005766-8 (pbk) : £1.25 B81-27192

Clarke, Brenda. The lofty banners / Brenda Clarke. — Feltham : Hamlyn, 1980. — 416p ; 22cm
ISBN 0-600-20214-3 : £5.95 B81-01289

Clarke, Brenda. The lofty banners / Brenda Clarke. — London : Hamlyn Paperbacks, 1981, c1980. — 416p ; 18cm
Originally published: Feltham : Hamlyn, 1980
ISBN 0-600-31564-9 (pbk) : £1.75 B81-31913

Claughton, Russell. The long Good Friday / Russell Claughton ; based on the original story and screenplay by Barrie Keeffe. — [London] : Magnum, 1981. — 176p ; 18cm
ISBN 0-417-05960-4 (pbk) : £1.25 B81-18252

Clavell, James. Noble house. — London : Coronet, June 1981. — [1632]p
ISBN 0-340-26877-8 (pbk) : £2.95 : CIP entry B81-12350

823'.914[F] — Fiction in English, ***1945-*** **—** ***Texts continuation***

Cleary, Denis. [The Capricorn run]. The hook / Denis Cleary and Frank Maher. — London : Severn House, 1980, c1979. — 155p ; 21cm
Originally published: London : New English Library, 1978
ISBN 0-7278-0634-3 : £4.95 : CIP rev. B80-28734

Cleary, Denis. Sahara strike / Denis Cleary and Frank Maher. — London : Severn House, 1981, c1980. — 159p ; 21cm
ISBN 0-7278-0654-8 : £5.25 B81-16068

Cleary, Denis. Wipe-out / Denis Cleary and Frank Maher. — London : Severn House, 1981, c1980. — 188p ; 21cm
Originally published: London : New English Library, 1980
ISBN 0-7278-0715-3 : £5.95 : CIP rev. B81-14839

Clews, Roy. Young Jethro. — Large print ed. — Anstey : Ulverscroft, Jan.1982. — [493]p. — (Ulverscroft large print series : general fiction)
Originally published: London : Heinemann, 1975
ISBN 0-7089-0740-7 : £5.00 : CIP entry B81-33957

Clifford, Francis. The naked runner / by Francis Clifford. — Bolton-by-Bowland : Magna Print, 1979, c1966. — 403p ; 23cm
Originally published: London : Hodder and Stoughton, 1966. — Published in large print
ISBN 0-86009-207-0 : £4.95 : CIP rev. B79-30330

Clifford, Kay. Love at second sight / by Kay Clifford. — London : Mills & Boon, 1981. — 191p ; 20cm
ISBN 0-263-09911-3 : £4.55 B81-34100

Clifford, Kay. The tycoon's lady / by Kay Clifford. — London : Mills & Boon, 1980. — 190p ; 20cm
ISBN 0-263-09730-7 : £3.85 B81-00429

Cockburn, Claud. Ballantyne's folly / Claud Cockburn. — London : Quartet, 1981, c1970. — 208p ; 20cm
Originally published: London : Weidenfeld and Nicolson, 1970
ISBN 0-7043-3384-8 (pbk) : £2.95 : CIP rev. B81-16877

Cockburn, Claud. The peace-seeker's tale / Claud Cockburn ; illustrations by Rebecca Fraser. — London (21 Colville Terrace, W.11) : Next Editions in association with Faber, 1981. — 27p : ill ; 23cm
ISBN 0-907147-05-4 (spiral) : £2.50 B81-34862

Cody, Liza. Dupe / Liza Cody. — London : Collins, 1980. — 238p ; 21cm. — (The Crime Club)
ISBN 0-00-231272-7 : £5.50 B81-01801

Coffman, Virginia. Marsanne / Virginia Coffman. — Large print ed. — Leicester : Ulverscroft, 1980, c1976. — 308p : ill ; 23cm. — (Ulverscroft large print series)
Originally published: New York : Abor House, 1976
ISBN 0-7089-0539-0 : £4.25 : CIP rev. B80-24824

Cohen, Sandee. All we know of heaven / Sandee Cohen. — London : Collins, 1980. — 251p ; 22cm
ISBN 0-00-222055-5 : £5.95 B81-00430

Cohen, Sandee. All we know of heaven / Sandee Cohen. — [London] : Fontana, 1981, c1980. — 251p ; 18cm
Originally published: London : Collins, 1980
ISBN 0-00-616384-x (pbk) : £1.35 B81-32175

Cole, Adrian. The LUCIFER experiment / by Adrian Cole. — London : Hale, 1981. — 208p ; 20cm. — (Hale SF)
ISBN 0-7091-9198-7 : £6.25 B81-35189

Cole, Adrian. Wargods of Ludorbis / by Adrian Cole. — London : Hale, 1981. — 206p ; 20cm. — (Hale SF)
ISBN 0-7091-8886-2 : £6.75 B81-17325

Coleman, Terry. Thanksgiving. — London : Hutchinson, Oct.1981. — [353]p
ISBN 0-09-146530-3 : £7.95 : CIP entry B81-28168

Coles, Janis. Counterfeit countess / Janis Coles. — London : Hale, 1980. — 173p ; 20cm
ISBN 0-7091-8471-9 : £5.95 B81-01290

Coles, Janis. The Craigdarroch girl / by Janis Coles. — London : Hale, 1981. — 192p ; 20cm
ISBN 0-7091-9314-9 : £6.75 B81-40464

Colin, Ann. A different class of doctor / Ann Colin. — London : Corgi, 1980. — 147p ; 18cm
ISBN 0-552-11460-x (pbk) : £0.85 B81-01291

Colin, Ann. Doctor Jamie / Ann Colin. — London : Corgi, 1980. — 159p ; 18cm
ISBN 0-552-11509-6 (pbk) : £0.85 B81-01651

Colley, Barbara, ***1918-***. Unintentional / Barbara Colley. — Bognor Regis : New Horizon, c1978. — 136p ; 21cm
ISBN 0-86116-046-0 : £3.95 B81-19038

Collier, Margaret. The scars remained / by Margaret Collier. — London : Hale, 1981. — 204p ; 20cm
ISBN 0-7091-8835-8 : £5.95 B81-14202

Collins, Carol. Almost a stranger / Carol Collins. — London : Hale, 1981. — 191p ; 20cm
ISBN 0-7091-9021-2 : £5.60 B81-27294

Collins, Jackie. Chances / Jackie Collins. — London : Pan, 1981. — 599p ; 23cm
ISBN 0-00-222127-6 : £7.50 : CIP rev. B81-22648

Collins, Jackie. The world is full of divorced women / Jackie Collins. — London : W.H. Allen, 1981, c1980. — 267p ; 21cm
Originally published: 1975
ISBN 0-491-02884-9 : £6.95 B81-19984

Collins, Jackie. The world is full of married men / Jackie Collins. — London : W.H. Allen, 1968 (1981 [printing]). — 157p ; 18cm. — (A Star book)
ISBN 0-352-39875-2 (pbk) : £1.50 B81-35160

Collins, Jackie. The world is full of married men / Jackie Collins. — London : W.H. Allen, 1981, c1968. — 157p ; 21cm
Originally published: Cleveland : World Publishing, 1968
ISBN 0-491-02894-6 : £5.95 B81-19983

Collins, Lynne. The sister and the surgeon / by Lynne Collins. — London : Mills & Boon, 1981. — 188p ; 20cm
ISBN 0-263-09907-5 : £4.55 B81-34105

Collins, Patricia. Mary. — Loughton : Piatkus, Aug.1981. — [208]p
ISBN 0-86188-115-x : £6.50 : CIP entry B81-15852

Collins, Rae. Bouquet of wild robins / by Rae Collins. — London : Hale, 1980. — 191p ; 20cm
ISBN 0-7091-8479-4 : £5.25 B81-01292

Collins, Rae. Distant thunder / by Rae Collins. — London : Hale, 1981. — 160p ; 20cm
ISBN 0-7091-8689-4 : £5.50 B81-11662

Collins, Rae. North of springtime / by Rae Collins. — London : Hale, 1981. — 205p ; 20cm
ISBN 0-7091-9108-1 : £5.75 B81-30079

Colman, David, ***1931-***. The savage pair / David Colman. — Bognor Regis : New Horizon, c1979. — 94p ; 21cm
ISBN 0-86116-039-8 : £3.95 B81-19078

Colquhoun, Keith. Goebbels and Gladys / Keith Colquhoun. — London : Murray, 1981. — 188p ; 23cm
ISBN 0-7195-3787-8 : £6.95 B81-16210

Compton, D. G.. [The continuous Katherine Mortenhoe]. Death watch / D.G. Compton. — London : Magnum, 1981, c1974. — 255p ; 18cm
Originally published: London : Gollancz, 1974
ISBN 0-417-06580-9 (pbk) : £1.50 B81-28609

Conlon, Kathleen. Consequences / Kathleen Conlon. — London : Macdonald Futura, 1981. — 191p ; 23cm
ISBN 0-354-04713-2 : £6.95 B81-31920

Conlon, Kathleen. A forgotten season / Kathleen Conlon. — London : Hamlyn Paperbacks, 1981. — 176p ; 18cm
Originally published: London : Collins, 1980
ISBN 0-600-20226-7 (pbk) : £1.10 B81-33496

Connolly, Ray. A Sunday kind of woman / Ray Connolly. — Glasgow : Fontana/Collins, 1981, c1980. — 189p ; 18cm
Originally published: London : Collins, 1980
ISBN 0-00-616277-0 (pbk) : £1.25 B81-18471

Conway, Laura. Heiress apparent / by Laura Conway. — Bolton-by-Bowland : Magna, 1980, c1966. — 347p ; 23cm
Originally published: London : Collins, 1966. — Published in large print
ISBN 0-86009-215-1 : £5.25 : CIP rev. B79-34453

Conway, Laura. The night of the party / by Laura Conway. — Bolton-by-Bowland : Magna, 1979, c1969. — 355p ; 23cm
Originally published: London : Collins, 1969. — Published in large print
ISBN 0-86009-206-2 : £4.95 : CIP rev. B79-30331

Conway, Peter, ***1929-***. Needle track / by Peter Conway. — London : Hale, 1981. — 175p ; 21cm
ISBN 0-7091-9233-9 : £6.25 B81-29866

Conway, Peter, ***1929-***. Nut case / by Peter Conway. — London : Hale, 1980. — 159p ; 20cm
ISBN 0-7091-8639-8 : £5.75 B81-01293

Cooke, Emma. A single sensation / Emma Cooke. — Dublin : Poolbeg, 1981. — 157p ; 18cm
ISBN 0-905169-44-1 (pbk) : £2.50 B81-39367

Cookson, Catherine. The blind miller. — Large print ed. — Anstey : Ulverscroft, Jan.1982. — [558]p. — (Ulverscroft large print series : general fiction)
ISBN 0-7089-0741-5 : £5.00 : CIP entry B81-33956

Cookson, Catherine. Fenwick Houses / Catherine Cookson. — London : Corgi, 1970, c1960 (1980 [printing]). — 251p ; 18cm
Originally published: London : Macdonald, 1960
ISBN 0-552-11336-0 (pbk) : £1.00 B81-03009

Cookson, Catherine. Fenwick houses. — Large print ed. — Anstey : Ulverscroft, Dec.1981. — [480]p. — (Ulverscroft large print series)
Originally published: London : Macdonald, 1960
ISBN 0-7089-0726-1 : £5.00 : CIP entry B81-32607

Cookson, Catherine. The invitation / Catherine Cookson. — London : Corgi, 1972, c1970 (1979 printing). — 251p ; 18cm
Originally published: London : MacDonald, 1970
ISBN 0-552-11260-7 (pbk) : £0.95 B81-19814

823'.914[F] — Fiction in English, *1945- — Texts continuation*

Cookson, Catherine. Lanky Jones / Catherine Cookson. — London : Macdonald Futura, 1980. — 151p ; 21cm
ISBN 0-354-08116-0 : £3.95 B81-02906

Cookson, Catherine. Lanky Jones / Catherine Cookson. — London : Transworld, 1981, c1980. — 138p ; 18cm. — (A Carousel book)
Originally published: London : Macdonald Futura, 1980
ISBN 0-552-52141-8 (pbk) : £0.85 B81-39095

Cookson, Catherine. The Mallen girl / Catherine Cookson. — Large print ed. — Leicester : Ulverscroft, 1981, c1973. — 457p ; 23cm. — (Ulverscroft large print series)
Originally published: London : Heinemann, 1974
ISBN 0-7089-0641-9 : Unpriced : CIP rev. B81-14794

Cookson, Catherine. The Mallen litter / Catherine Cookson. — Large print ed. — Leicester : Ulverscroft, 1981, c1974. — 528p ; 23cm
Originally published: London : Heinemann, 1974
ISBN 0-7089-0669-9 : £5.00 : CIP rev. B81-19184

Cookson, Catherine. The Mallen streak / Catherine Cookson. — Large print ed. — Leicester : Ulverscroft, 1981, c1973. — 468p ; 23cm. — (Ulverscroft large print series)
Originally published: London : Heinemann, 1973
ISBN 0-7089-0613-3 : £5.00 : CIP rev. B81-02116

Cookson, Catherine. The man who cried / Catherine Cookson. — Large print ed. — Leicester : Ulverscroft, 1980, c1979. — 512p ; 22cm. — (Ulverscroft large print series)
Originally published: London : Heinemann, 1979
ISBN 0-7089-0527-7 : £4.25 : CIP rev. B80-27514

Cookson, Catherine. The Mary Ann omnibus / Catherine Cookson. — London : Macdonald, 1981. — 756p ; 24cm
ISBN 0-354-04604-7 : £6.95 B81-28375

Cookson, Catherine. Pure as the lily / Catherine Cookson. — London : Macdonald Futura, 1972 (1980 [printing]). — 315p ; 21cm
ISBN 0-356-03986-2 : £5.95 B81-01294

Cookson, Catherine. Tilly Trotter / Catherine Cookson. — [London] : Corgi, 1981, c1980. — 398p ; 18cm
Originally published: London : Heinemann, 1980
ISBN 0-552-11737-4 (pbk) : £1.50 B81-24828

Cookson, Catherine. Tilly Trotter. — Large print ed. — Anstey : Ulverscroft, Oct.1981. — [576] p. — (Ulverscroft large print series)
Originally published: London : Heinemann, 1980
ISBN 0-7089-0698-2 : £5.00 : CIP entry B81-28098

Cooper, Ann. Maclean's woman / by Ann Cooper. — London : Mills & Boon, 1981. — 189p ; 20cm
ISBN 0-263-09823-0 : £4.55 B81-09403

Cooper, Edmund, *1926-*. A world of difference / by Edmund Cooper. — London : Hale, 1980. — 192p ; 21cm
ISBN 0-7091-8686-x : £5.75 B81-01295

Cooper, Louise. Crown of Horn / Louise Cooper. — London : Hamlyn Paperbacks, 1981. — 256p ; 18cm
ISBN 0-600-20238-0 (pbk) : £1.25 B81-19902

Cooper, Margaret Chilvers. It's about time : a witches' brew of comedy, tragedy and ghosts / Margaret Chilvers Cooper. — London : Kimber, 1980. — 192p ; 23cm
ISBN 0-7183-0347-4 : £5.50 B81-01296

Cooper, Richard. Codename Icarus. — London : Hodder & Stoughton, Dec.1981. — [160]p. — (Knight books)
ISBN 0-340-27535-9 (pbk) : £0.95 : CIP entry
ISBN 0-563-20040-5 (BBC) B81-31438

Cordell, Alexander. Rogue's march / Alexander Cordell. — London : Hodder and Stoughton, c1981. — 511p ; 23cm
ISBN 0-340-25351-7 : £7.50 B81-11270

Cordell, Alexander. To slay the dreamer. — London : Hodder & Stoughton, Aug.1981. — [320]p. — (Coronet books)
Originally published: London : Hodder & Stoughton, 1980
ISBN 0-340-26675-9 (pbk) : £1.75 : CIP entry B81-18131

Cork, Dorothy. First passion / by Dorothy Cork. — London : Mills & Boon, 1980. — 191p ; 20cm
ISBN 0-263-09768-4 : £3.85 B81-01297

Cork, Dorothy. Secret marriage. — London : Hodder & Stoughton, Dec.1981. — [192]p. — (Silhouette romance)
ISBN 0-340-27657-6 (pbk) : £0.65 : CIP entry B81-31433

Corley, James. Sundrinker / by James Corley. — London : Hale, 1980. — 192p ; 21cm. — (Hale SF)
ISBN 0-7091-8335-6 : £5.25 B81-00431

Cornwell, Bernard. Sharpe's Eagle : Richard Sharpe and the Talavera Campaign July 1809 / Bernard Cornwell. — London : Collins, 1981. — 266p ; 22cm
ISBN 0-00-221997-2 : £6.50 B81-01298

Cornwell, Bernard. Sharpe's eagle : Richard Sharpe and the Talavera Campaign July 1809 / Bernard Cornwell. — [London] : Fontana, 1981. — 255p ; 18cm
ISBN 0-00-616455-2 (pbk) : £1.35 B81-37897

Cornwell, Bernard. Sharpe's gold : Richard Sharpe and the destruction of Almeida, August 1810 / Bernard Cornwell. — London : Collins, 1981. — 250p ; 22cm
ISBN 0-00-222129-2 : £6.95 B81-37444

Corrie, Jane. Bride for sale / by Jane Corrie. — London : Mills & Boon, 1981. — 189p ; 19cm
ISBN 0-263-09834-6 : £4.55 B81-10882

Corrie, Jane. Pirates' lair / by Jane Corrie. — London : Mills & Boon, 1980. — 190p ; 20cm
ISBN 0-263-09766-8 : £3.85 B81-01299

Corrie, Jane. The station boss. — Bath : Chivers Press, Dec.1981. — [232]p. — (A Seymour book)
Originally published: London : Mills & Boon, 1980
ISBN 0-85119-444-3 : £4.95 : CIP entry B81-31839

Couper, Elspeth. Bride for a Viking / by Elspeth Couper. — London : Hale, 1981. — 207p ; 20cm
ISBN 0-7091-8971-0 : £6.75 B81-40469

Couper, Elspeth. The gold and the rainbow / by Elspeth Couper. — London : Hale, 1981. — 158p ; 20cm
ISBN 0-7091-8851-x : £5.75 B81-35242

Couper, Elspeth. The lonely sky / by Elspeth Couper. — London : Hale, 1981. — 172p ; 20cm
ISBN 0-7091-8793-9 : £5.50 B81-14073

Courtney, Caroline. Dangerous engagement / Caroline Courtney. — London : Corgi, 1981, c1979. — 221p ; 18cm
Originally published: London : Arlington, 1979
ISBN 0-552-11724-2 (pbk) : £0.95 B81-32108

Courtney, Caroline. Dangerous engagement / Caroline Courtney. — London : Prior, c1981, 1979. — 355p ; 25cm
Originally published: London : Arlington, 1980. — Published in large print
ISBN 0-86043-582-2 : £6.50 B81-24577

Courtney, Caroline. Duchess in disguise / Caroline Courtney. — [London] : Corgi, 1981, c1979. — 172p ; 18cm
Originally published: London : Arlington, 1979
ISBN 0-552-11514-2 (pbk) : £0.95 B81-08414

Courtney, Caroline. The fortunes of love / Caroline Courtney. — London : Arlington, 1980. — 229p ; 21cm
ISBN 0-85140-497-9 : £5.95 B81-02218

Courtney, Caroline. The fortunes of love / Caroline Courtney. — London : Prior, 1981, c1980. — 379p ; 25cm
Originally published: London : Arlington, 1980. — Published in large print
ISBN 0-86043-592-x : £6.50 B81-32768

Courtney, Caroline. Guardian of the heart / Caroline Courtney. — London : Prior, 1980, c1979. — 336p ; 25cm
Originally published: London : Arlington, 1980. — Published in large print
ISBN 0-86043-575-x : £5.95 B81-21970

Courtney, Caroline. Guardian of the heart / Caroline Courtney. — London : Corgi, 1981, c1979. — 220p ; 18cm
Originally published: London : Arlington, 1979
ISBN 0-552-11605-x (pbk) : £0.95 B81-18773

Courtney, Caroline. Heart of honour. — London : Arlington Books, Feb.1982. — [224]p
ISBN 0-85140-569-x : £6.50 : CIP entry B81-39223

Courtney, Caroline. Love triumphant. — London : Arlington Books, June 1981. — [224]p
ISBN 0-85140-534-7 : £5.95 : CIP entry B81-12793

Courtney, Caroline. Love unmasked / Caroline Courtney. — [London] : Corgi, 1981, c1979. — 239p ; 18cm
Originally published: London : Arlington Books, 1979
ISBN 0-552-11604-1 (pbk) : £0.95 B81-18555

Courtney, Caroline. Love unmasked / Caroline Courtney. — London : Prior, 1981, c1979. — 321p ; 25cm
Originally published: London : Arlington, 1979. — Published in large print
ISBN 0-86043-579-2 : £5.95 B81-28320

Courtney, Caroline. Love's masquerade. — London : Arlington Books, Sept.1981. — [224]p
ISBN 0-85140-547-9 : £5.95 : CIP entry B81-20185

Courtney, Caroline. The romantic rivals / Caroline Courtney. — London (3 Clifford St., Mayfair, W.1) : Columbine House, 1981. — 256p ; 21cm
ISBN 0-85140-523-1 : £5.95 B81-11499

Courtney, Caroline. A wager for love / Caroline Courtney. — [London] : Corgi, 1981, c1979. — 208p ; 18cm
Originally published: London : Arlington, 1979
ISBN 0-552-11515-0 (pbk) : £0.95 B81-08417

Cowley, Stewart. Starliners : commercial spacetravel in 2200 AD / Stewart Cowley. — London : Hamlyn, 1980. — 90p : ill,col.charts,plans ; 31cm
Ill, plans on lining papers
ISBN 0-600-35357-5 : £3.95 B81-01300

823'.914[F] — Fiction in English, ***1945- — Texts continuation***

Cowper, Richard. Clone / Richard Cowper. — London : Pan Books, 1981, c1972. — 167p ; 18cm. — (Pan science fiction)
Originally published: London : Gollancz, 1972
ISBN 0-330-26179-7 (pbk) : £1.25 B81-24415

Cowper, Richard. A dream of kinship / by Richard Cowper. — London : Gollancz, 1981. — 239p ; 21cm
ISBN 0-575-02969-2 : £6.95 B81-12062

Cowper, Richard. Profundis / Richard Cowper. — London : Pan, 1980, c1979. — 158p ; 18cm. — (Pan science fiction)
Originally published: London : Gollancz, 1979
ISBN 0-330-26178-9 (pbk) : £1.25 B81-00432

Cox, Richard, *1931-*. The KGB directive / Richard Cox. — London : Hutchinson, 1981. — 335p ; 23cm
ISBN 0-09-145270-8 : £6.95 : CIP rev. B81-12317

Coyle, J. B.. The man from the S.A.S. / J.B. Coyle. — Bognor Regis : New Horizon, c1979. — iii,167p ; 22cm
ISBN 0-86116-040-1 : £3.95 B81-36111

Craddock, Rosemary. The Abbey governess / by Rosemary Craddock. — London : Hale, 1980. — 176p ; 20cm
ISBN 0-7091-8571-5 : £5.95 B81-02160

Cradock, Fanny. Thunder over Castle Rising / Fanny Cradock. — London : W.H. Allen, 1980. — vii,227p : 1 geneal.table ; 22cm
ISBN 0-491-02763-x : £5.95 B81-02193

Craig, Mark. The secret of Blackrock Falls / Mark Craig. — Bognor Regis : New Horizon, 1979. — 176p : ill ; 21cm
ISBN 0-86116-173-4 : £4.25 B81-18864

Craven, Sara. Moon of Aphrodite / by Sara Craven. — London : Mills & Boon, 1980. — 187p ; 19cm
ISBN 0-263-09762-5 : £3.85 B81-01301

Craven, Sara. Summer of the raven / by Sara Craven. — London : Mills & Boon, 1981. — 190p ; 19cm
ISBN 0-263-09842-7 : £4.55 B81-10975

Craven, Sara. Witching hour / by Sara Craven. — London : Mills & Boon, 1981. — 187p ; 20cm
ISBN 0-263-09897-4 : £4.55 B81-28522

Crawford, Anna. Every other Tuesday / Anna Crawford. — Bognor Regis : New Horizon, c1981. — 214p 22cm
ISBN 0-86116-667-1 : £5.25 B81-32123

Crawley, Aidan. Dial 200-200 / Aidan Crawley. — Large print ed. — Bath : Chivers, 1981, c1980. — 334p ; 23cm. — (A New Portway large print book)
Originally published: London : Weidenfeld & Nicolson, 1980
ISBN 0-85119-105-3 : Unpriced B81-08627

Crawley, Aileen. The bride of Suleiman / Aileen Crawley. — London : Hutchinson, 1981. — 272p ; 23cm. — ([A Window on time] ; [pt.1])
Bibliography: p271-272
ISBN 0-09-143780-6 : £6.95 B81-11413

Creed, David. Death watch / David Creed. — London : Methuen Paperbacks, 1981, c1979. — 207p ; 18cm. — (Magnum books)
Originally published: London : Secker and Warburg, 1979
ISBN 0-417-05540-4 (pbk) : £1.35 B81-18241

Creed, David. The scarab / David Creed. — London : Secker & Warburg, 1980. — 215p ; 23cm
ISBN 0-436-11412-7 : £5.95 B81-00433

Cresswell, Jasmine. The Danewood legacy / by Jasmine Cresswell. — London : Hale, 1981. — 208p ; 20cm
ISBN 0-7091-8999-0 : £6.50 B81-17311

Cresswell, Jasmine. The reluctant viscountess / Jasmine Cresswell. — London : Hale, 1981. — 192p ; 20cm
ISBN 0-7091-9203-7 : £6.75 B81-37303

Cresswell, Jesmine. Caroline / by Jasmine Cresswell. — London : Hale, 1980. — 224p ; 20cm
ISBN 0-7091-8657-6 : £6.95 B81-02214

Crisp, N. J.. Buccaneer / N.J. Crisp and Eric Paice. — London : Severn House, 1980. — 206p ; 21cm
ISBN 0-7278-0643-2 : £5.95 : CIP rev. B80-22563

Critchlow, Dorothy. The house in the holly / by Dorothy Critchlow. — London : Hale, 1980. — 158p ; 20cm
ISBN 0-7091-8609-6 : £5.25 B81-02530

Croft, Eve. Brainchild / by Eve Croft. — London (38 Mount Pleasant, WC1X 0AP) : Onlywomen, [1981]. — 287p ; 20cm
ISBN 0-906500-06-0 (corrected : pbk) : £2.95 B81-20908

Cronin, Michael, *1907-*. Epitaph for a lady / Michael Cronin. — London : Hale, 1980. — 192p ; 21cm
ISBN 0-7091-8464-6 : £6.25 B81-00436

Cronin, Michael, *1907-*. The killing in Quemada / by Michael Cronin. — London : Hale, 1981. — 191p ; 20cm
ISBN 0-7091-9124-3 : £5.95 B81-24871

Crook, William. Four days. — London : Magnum, 1981, c1979. — 171p ; 18cm
Originally published: London : Eyre Methuen, 1979
ISBN 0-417-03680-9 (pbk) : £1.25 B81-08423

Crowther, Bruce. Black Wednesday / by Bruce Crowther. — London : Hale, 1981. — 207p ; 20cm
ISBN 0-7091-9276-2 : £6.25 B81-35211

Crowther, Bruce. Unholy alliance / by Bruce Crowther. — London : Hale, 1981. — 188p ; 20cm
ISBN 0-7091-8783-1 : £5.75 B81-03334

Cummins, Frederick. Shulima and Jesus / Frederick Cummins. — Bognor Regis : New Horizon, c1980. — 169p ; 21cm
ISBN 0-86116-459-8 : £4.75 B81-19033

Cummins, Mary. Forgotten bride / by Mary Cummins. — London : Hale, 1981. — 192p ; 20cm
ISBN 0-7091-9202-9 : £6.75 B81-33516

Cummins, Mary. Glenallyn's bride / by Mary Cummins. — London : Hale, 1981. — 191p ; 20cm
ISBN 0-7091-8745-9 : £6.25 B81-11165

Cummins, Mary. Towers in the mist / Mary Cummins. — London : Hale, 1980. — 190p ; 21cm
ISBN 0-7091-8469-7 : £6.25 B81-00437

Curtin, Michael. The replay / Michael Curtin. — London : Deutsch, 1981. — 271p ; 23cm
ISBN 0-233-97327-3 : £6.95 : CIP rev. B81-21624

Curtis, Jean. The Harwood inheritance / by Jean Curtis. — London : Hale, 1981. — 157p ; 20cm
ISBN 0-7091-9347-5 : £5.75 B81-40463

Curtis, Jean. The house on Craig's Corner / by Jean Curtis. — London : Hale, 1980. — 160p ; 20cm
ISBN 0-7091-8457-3 : £5.25 B81-02209

Curtis, Marjorie. Fortunes of love / by Marjorie Curtis. — London : Hale, 1981. — 160p ; 20cm
ISBN 0-7091-8795-5 : £5.50 B81-14373

Curtis, Marjorie. New man at St. Giles / by Marjorie Curtis. — London : Hale, 1981. — 158p ; 20cm
ISBN 0-7091-9289-4 : £5.75 B81-35247

Curtis, Marjorie. Staff nurse in Fiji / Marjorie Curtis. — London : Hale, 1980. — 159p ; 20cm
ISBN 0-7091-8315-1 : £4.95 B81-00434

Curzon, Clare. Special occasion / Clare Curzon. — London : Collins, 1981. — 206p ; 21cm. — (The Crime Club)
ISBN 0-00-231661-7 : £5.95 B81-10162

Curzon, Linda. Nurse in the house / Linda Curzon. — Large print ed. — Bath : Lythway, 1980. — 251p ; 23cm
Originally published: London : Hale, 1968
ISBN 0-85046-906-6 : £5.90 : CIP rev. B80-22506

D'Agneau, Marcel. The curse of the Nibelung : being the last case of Lord Holmes of Baker Street and Sir John Watson / re-constructed by Marcel d'Agneau. — London : Arlington, 1981. — 304p ; 23cm
ISBN 0-85140-561-4 : £6.95 : CIP rev. B81-20186

D'Agneau, Marcel. Eeny meeny miny mole / Marcel D'Agneau. — London : Arlington, 1980. — 298p ; 23cm
ISBN 0-85140-521-5 : £6.50 : CIP rev. B80-22507

D'Agneau, Marcel. Eeny meeny miny mole / Marcel d'Agneau. — London : Arrow, 1981, c1980. — 298p ; 18cm
Originally published: London : Arlington, 1980
ISBN 0-09-926300-9 (pbk) : £1.50 B81-34589

Dailey, Janet. Dakota dreamin' / by Janet Dailey. — London : Mills & Boon, 1981. — 187p ; 19cm
ISBN 0-263-09835-4 : £4.55 B81-10886

Dailey, Janet. Difficult decision / by Janet Dailey. — London : Mills & Boon, 1980. — 186p ; 20cm
ISBN 0-263-09734-x : £3.85 B81-01302

Dailey, Janet. The hostage bride. — London : Hodder & Stoughton, Jan.1982. — [192]p. — (Silhouette romance)
ISBN 0-340-27662-2 (pbk) : £0.75 : CIP entry B81-34480

Dailey, Janet. A land called Deseret / Janet Dailey. — Large print ed. — Bath : Chivers, 1981, c1979. — 228p ; 23cm. — (A Seymour book)
Originally published: London : Mills and Boon, 1979
ISBN 0-85119-434-6 : £4.95 : CIP rev. B81-20109

Dailey, Janet. One of the boys / Janet Dailey. — London : Mills & Boon, 1981. — 186p ; 19cm
ISBN 0-263-09865-6 : £4.55 B81-18344

Dailey, Janet. Ride the thunder / Janet Dailey. — [London] : Fontana, 1981, c1980. — 320p ; 18cm
Originally published: New York : Pocket Books, 1980
ISBN 0-00-616336-x (pbk) : £1.50 B81-20687

Dailey, Janet. Ride the thunder. — Loughton : Piatkus, Dec.1981. — [320]p
ISBN 0-86188-132-x : £6.95 : CIP entry B81-31638

823'.914[F] — Fiction in English, *1945- — Texts continuation*

Dailey, Janet. Southern nights / by Janet Dailey. — London : Mills & Boon, 1980. — 188p ; 20cm
ISBN 0-263-09746-3 : £3.85 B81-00438

Dailey, Janet. The thawing of Mara / Janet Dailey. — Large print ed. — Bath : Chivers, 1981, c1980. — 220p ; 23cm. — (A Seymour book)
Originally published: London : Mills & Boon, 1980
ISBN 0-85119-429-x : Unpriced : CIP rev. B81-20503

Dailey, Janet. Touch the wind / Janet Dailey. — London : Fontana, 1980, c1979. — 320p ; 18cm
Originally published: New York : Pocket Books, 1979
ISBN 0-00-616443-9 (pbk) : £1.50 B81-28758

Dailey, Janet. Touch the wind / Janet Dailey. — Loughton : Piatkus, 1981, c1979. — 320p ; 21cm
Originally published: New York : Pocket Books, 1979 ; London : Fontana, 1980
ISBN 0-86188-076-5 : £6.50 B81-12951

Dailey, Janet. The travelling kind / by Janet Dailey. — London : Mills & Boon, 1981. — 187p ; 20cm
ISBN 0-263-09826-5 : £4.55 B81-09411

Dailey, Janet. Wild and wonderful / by Janet Dailey. — London : Mills & Boon, 1980. — 186p ; 19cm
ISBN 0-263-09758-7 : £3.85 B81-01636

Daniel, Elaine. Dangerous to know / by Elaine Daniel. — London : Hale, 1981. — 176p ; 20cm
ISBN 0-7091-9115-4 : £5.60 B81-33521

Daniels, Philip. Alibi of guilt / Philip Daniels. — London : Hale, 1980. — 176p ; 20cm
ISBN 0-7091-8527-8 : £5.75 B81-01303

Daniels, Philip. Foolproof / by Philip Daniels. — London : Hale, 1981. — 175p ; 20cm
ISBN 0-7091-9062-x : £5.95 B81-27305

Dann, Colin. The animals of Farthing Wood / by Colin Dann. — Long Preston : Magna, 1981, c1979. — 495p ; 23cm
Originally published: London : Heinemann, 1979. — Published in large print
ISBN 0-86009-338-7 : £4.95 : CIP rev. B81-16910

Darby, Catherine. Falcon's claw / by Catherine Darby. — London : Hale, 1981. — 222p ; 21cm
ISBN 0-7091-6863-2 : £6.75 B81-33543

Darby, Catherine. Moon in Pisces / Catherine Darby. — London : Hale, 1980. — 192p ; 21cm
ISBN 0-7091-6465-3 : £6.25 B81-01304

Darby, Catherine. Seed of the falcon / Catherine Darby. — London : Hale, 1981. — 238p ; 21cm
ISBN 0-7091-6738-5 : £6.50 B81-11737

Darke, Marjorie. Comeback / Marjorie Darke. — Harmondsworth : Kestrel Books, 1981. — 184p ; 23cm
For adolescents
ISBN 0-7226-5743-9 : £5.50 B81-32825

Darke, Susan. Love is a circle / by Susan Darke. — London : Hale, 1981. — 158p ; 20cm
ISBN 0-7091-9362-9 : £5.75 B81-40549

Darke, Susan. Then come kiss me / by Susan Darke. — London : Hale, 1981. — 160p ; 20cm
ISBN 0-7091-9043-3 : £5.60 B81-24352

Darrell, Elizabeth. The gathering wolves / Elizabeth Darrell. — London : Hodder and Stoughton, 1981. — 342p ; 23cm
ISBN 0-340-26332-6 : £6.95 B81-15784

Daveson, Mons. Land of tomorrow / by Mons Daveson. — London : Mills & Boon, 1980. — 189p ; 20cm
ISBN 0-263-09767-6 : £3.85 B81-01413

Davis, Howard Charles. Poodle's grave / Howard Charles Davis. — London : Hale, 1981. — 175p ; 20cm
ISBN 0-7091-9173-1 : £5.95 B81-33522

Davis, Howard Charles. The Selsey gold / by Howard Charles Davis. — London : Hale, 1980. — 192p ; 20cm
ISBN 0-7091-8508-1 : £5.50 B81-00439

Davis, Joseph A.. Samaki : the story of an otter in Africa : a true-to-life novel / written and illustrated by J.A. Davis. — London : Sphere, 1981, c1979. — 213p : ill ; 20cm
Originally published: London : Joseph, 1979
ISBN 0-7221-2849-5 (pbk) : £1.95 B81-35070

Davis, Margaret Thomson. A baby might be crying / by Margaret Thomson Davis. — London : Allison & Busby, 1973 (1980 [printing]). — 219p ; 23cm
ISBN 0-85031-094-6 : £5.95 B81-04172

Davis, Margaret Thomson. The breadmakers / Margaret Thomson Davis. — London : Allison & Busby, c1972 (1980 [printing]). — 222p ; 23cm
ISBN 0-85031-081-4 : £5.95 B81-04171

Davis, Margaret Thomson. The dark side of pleasure : a novel / by Margaret Thomson Davis. — London : Allison & Busby, 1981. — 234p ; 23cm
ISBN 0-85031-387-2 : £6.50 : CIP rev. B80-18888

Davis, Margaret Thomson. A sort of peace / by Margaret Thomson Davis. — London : Allison & Busby, 1973 (1980 [printing]). — 217p ; 23cm
ISBN 0-85031-105-5 : £5.95 B81-04159

Davis, Michael, *1956-*. Young Kim / Michael Davis. — Bognor Regis : New Horizon, c1980. — 153p ; 22cm
ISBN 0-86116-388-5 : £4.25 B81-19269

De Breffny, Brian. My first naked lady / Brian de Breffny. — London : Hamilton, 1981. — 208p ; 20cm
ISBN 0-241-10614-1 : £7.95 : CIP rev. B81-13814

De Larrabeiti, Michael. The bunce / Michael de Larrabeiti. — London : Sphere, 1981, c1980. — 180p ; 18cm
Originally published: London : Joseph, 1980
ISBN 0-7221-5351-1 : £1.25 B81-24539

De Montfort, Guiy. All the Queen's men / Guiy de Monfort. — London : Hamlyn Paperbacks, 1980. — 288p ; 18cm
ISBN 0-600-20338-7 (pbk) : £1.25 B81-02468

De Montfort, Guiy. All the Queen's men. — London : Severn House, Sept.1981. — [288]p
Originally published: London : Hamlyn, 1980
ISBN 0-7278-0727-7 : £6.95 : CIP entry B81-23817

De Quincy, Alix. The indifferent heart / by Alix de Quincy. — London : Hale, 1981. — 191p ; 20cm
ISBN 0-7091-8895-1 : £5.60 B81-21881

Dean, Dinah. The eagle's fate / Dinah Dean. — London : Mills & Boon, 1981. — 190p ; 19cm. — (Masquerade)
ISBN 0-263-09869-9 : £4.55 B81-26414

Deighton, Len. XPD / Len Deighton. — London : Hutchinson, 1981. — 396p ; 23cm
ISBN 0-09-144570-1 : £6.95 B81-08014

Delancey, Diney. The slopes of love / Diney Delancey. — London : Hale, 1981. — 192p ; 20cm
ISBN 0-7091-9020-4 : £5.60 B81-21294

Delroy, Margaret. Love never fails / by Margaret Delroy. — London : Hale, 1981. — 159p ; 20cm
ISBN 0-7091-8896-x : £5.60 B81-17331

Denham, A. V.. The bandit / by A.V. Denham. — London : Hale, 1980. — 191p ; 20cm
ISBN 0-7091-8419-0 : £5.25 B81-00440

Denis, John. Air Force One is down / written by John Denis ; [story outline by] Alistair MacLean. — [London] : Fontana, 1981. — 224p ; 18cm
ISBN 0-00-616335-1 (pbk) : £1.25 B81-33486

Denison, Mary. At Madam Muriel's / Mary Denison. — London : Dobson, 1979. — 185p ; 21cm
ISBN 0-234-72099-9 : £3.25 B81-01417

Dennison, Diana. Tory Frampton / Diana Dennison. — London : Hale, 1981. — 175p ; 20cm
ISBN 0-7091-9025-5 : £5.60 B81-24864

Dennison, Diana. The Tregonnyth inheritance / by Diana Dennison. — London : Hale, 1980. — 187p ; 21cm
ISBN 0-7091-8412-3 : £6.25 B81-00441

Denny, Lesley. Snap judgement / by Lesley Denny. — London : Hale, 1981. — 191p ; 20cm
ISBN 0-7091-9009-3 : £5.95 B81-27317

Derwent, Lavinia. Macpherson's caravan. — London : Hodder and Stoughton, May 1981. — [128]p
Originally published: London : Burke Publishing, 1968
ISBN 0-340-26527-2 (pbk) : £0.85 : CIP entry B81-04243

Dessau, Joanna. Amazing Grace / Joanna Dessau. — London. — 159p ; 21cm
ISBN 0-7091-8626-6 : £5.95 B81-09719

Devine, D. M.. This is your death / Dominic Devine. — London : Collins, 1981. — 221p ; 21cm. — (The Crime Club)
ISBN 0-00-231866-0 : £6.50 : CIP rev. B81-15892

Devon, Sarah. Bridehaven. — Large print ed. — Bath : Chivers, Jan.1982. — [256]p. — (A Lythway book)
Originally published: London : Hale, 1970
ISBN 0-85119-777-9 : £6.70 : CIP entry B81-33796

Dewa, Roberta J.. Lackland's lady / Roberta J. Dewa. — London : Hale, 1980. — 224p ; 21cm
ISBN 0-7091-8652-5 : £6.95 B81-03499

Dewhurst, Eileen. Trio in three flats / Eileen Dewhurst. — London : Collins, 1981. — 245p ; 21cm. — (The Crime Club)
ISBN 0-00-231864-4 : £5.95 B81-02494

Dewhurst, Eileen. Whoever I am. — London : Collins, Feb.1982. — [224]p. — (The Crime Club)
ISBN 0-00-231920-9 : £6.50 : CIP entry B81-35939

Dewhurst, Keith. Captain of the sands. — London : Cape, Nov.1981. — [400]p
ISBN 0-224-01619-9 : £6.95 : CIP entry B81-28831

823'.914[F] — Fiction in English, *1945-* — Texts *continuation*

Dexter, Colin. The dead of Jericho / Colin Dexter. — London : Macmillan, 1981. — 224p ; 21cm
ISBN 0-333-31728-9 : £5.95 B81-22323

Dexter, Ted. Deadly putter / by Ted Dexter and Clifford Makins. — London : Allen & Unwin, 1979. — 151p ; 23cm
ISBN 0-04-823167-3 : £4.95 : CIP rev. B79-30336

Dickinson, Margaret. Adelina / Margaret Dickinson. — London : Hale, 1981. — 190p ; 21cm. — (The Abbeyford trilogy)
ISBN 0-7091-8939-7 : £6.50 B81-29862

Dickinson, Margaret. Sarah / by Margaret Dickinson. — London : Hale, 1981. — 174p ; 21cm
ISBN 0-7091-8836-6 : £5.95 B81-14072

Dickinson, Peter, *1927-*. The seventh raven / Peter Dickinson. — London : Gollancz, 1981. — 192p : ill,1plan ; 21cm
ISBN 0-575-02960-9 : £4.95 B81-18539

Dickinson, Peter, *1927-*. [Skin deep]. The glass-sided ants' nest / by Peter Dickinson. — Harmondsworth : Penguin, 1981, c1968. — 157p ; 18cm
Originally published: London : Hodder & Stoughton, 1968
ISBN 0-14-005864-8 (pbk) : £0.95 B81-34813

Dickinson, Peter, *1927-*. A summer in the Twenties. — London : Hodder and Stoughton, Apr.1981. — [256]p
ISBN 0-340-26407-1 : £6.95 : CIP entry B81-02368

Diffey, Myrna. Search for happiness / by Myrna Diffey. — London : Hale, 1981. — 192p ; 20cm
ISBN 0-7091-8659-2 : £5.50 B81-02871

Diffey, Myrna. Uncertain love / by Myrna Diffey. — London : Hale, 1981. — 158p ; 20cm
ISBN 0-7091-9337-8 : £5.75 B81-40538

Dillin, William. Strike / by William Dillin. — London : Hale, 1981. — 192p ; 20cm
ISBN 0-7091-9109-x : £6.50 B81-24847

Dillon, Catherine. Beloved prisoner / Catherine Dillon. — Large print ed. — Leicester : Ulverscroft, 1980, c1979. — 429p ; 23cm. — (Ulverscroft large print series)
Originally published: London : Hodder and Stoughton, 1979
ISBN 0-7089-0557-9 : £4.25 : CIP rev. B80-35441

Dillon, Eilís. The bitter glass / Eilis Dillon. — Dublin (Knocksedan House, Swords, Co. Dublin) : Ward River, 1981. — 220p ; 18cm
Originally published: London : Faber, 1958
ISBN 0-907085-07-5 (pbk) : £2.50 B81-17445

Dillon, Eilís. Wild geese / Eilís Dillon. — London : Hodder and Stoughton, 1981, c1980. — 352p ; 25cm
ISBN 0-340-24983-8 : £6.95 B81-15785

Dingwell, Joyce. The all-the-way man / by Joyce Dingwell. — London : Mills and Boon, 1980. — 188p ; 20cm
ISBN 0-263-09773-0 : £3.85 B81-06423

Dingwell, Joyce. A man like Brady / by Joyce Dingwell. — London : Mills & Boon, 1981. — 189p ; 19cm
ISBN 0-263-09831-1 : £4.55 B81-10884

Dingwell, Joyce. Second chance. — Large print ed. — Anstey : Ulverscroft, Dec.1981. — [352] p. — (Ulverscroft large print series)
Originally published: London : Mills and Boon, 1956
ISBN 0-7089-0720-2 : £5.00 : CIP entry B81-32035

Dixon, Frederick. Nothing, dreary nothing / Frederick Dixon. — Bognor Regis : New Horizon, c1979. — 156p ; 21cm
ISBN 0-86116-317-6 : £4.25 B81-19074

Domatilla, John. The last crime / John Domatilla. — London : Heinemann, 1980. — 155p ; 23cm
ISBN 0-434-20090-5 : £5.95 B81-01814

Donald, Robyn. Iceberg / by Robyn Donald. — London : Mills and Boon, 1980. — 189p ; 20cm
ISBN 0-263-09769-2 : £3.85 B81-06422

Donald, Robyn. The interloper / by Robyn Donald. — London : Mills & Boon, 1981. — 188p ; 19cm
ISBN 0-263-09839-7 : £4.55 B81-10978

Donald, Robyn. Summer at Awakopu / by Robyn Donald. — London : Mills & Boon, 1979, c1978. — 186p ; 17cm
ISBN 0-263-72861-7 (pbk) : £0.55 B81-06404

Donaldson, Margaret. The moon's on fire / Margaret Donaldson ; illustrated by Joanna Stubbs. — London : Deutsch, 1980. — 138p : ill ; 22cm
ISBN 0-233-97249-8 : £4.50 : CIP rev. B80-19990

Donleavy, J. P.. The beastly beatitudes of Balthazar B / J.P. Donleavy. — Harmondsworth : Penguin in association with Eyre & Spottiswoode, 1969, c1968 (1980 [printing]). — 399p ; 18cm
Originally published: New York : Delacorte Press, 1968 ; London : Eyre & Spottiswoode, 1969
ISBN 0-14-003056-5 (pbk) : £1.95 B81-01418

Donleavy, J. P.. The ginger man / J.P. Donleavy. — Harmondsworth : Penguin, 1968 (1979 [printing]). — 346p ; 18cm
Originally published: Paris : Olympia Press, 1955 ; London : Transworld, 1963
ISBN 0-14-002705-x (pbk) : £1.50 B81-01419

Donleavy, J. P.. Schultz / J.P. Donleavy. — Harmondsworth : Penguin, 1981, c1980. — 375p ; 18cm
Originally published: London : Allen Lane, 1980
ISBN 0-14-005008-6 (pbk) : £1.50 B81-11031

Donnelly, Jane. Flash point / by Jane Donnelly. — London : Mills & Boon, 1981. — 187p ; 20cm
ISBN 0-263-09901-6 : £4.55 B81-34103

Donnelly, Jane. So long a winter / by Jane Donnelly. — London : Mills & Boon, 1981. — 188p ; 20cm
ISBN 0-263-09821-4 : £4.55 B81-09393

Doré, Henry Michael. The racialists / Henry Michael Doré. — Bognor Regis : New Horizon, c1979. — 220p ; 21cm
ISBN 0-86116-188-2 : £4.25 B81-18875

Doubtfire, Dianne. Sky lovers / Dianne Doubtfire. — London : Macmillan, 1981. — 85p ; 21cm. — (Topliner tridents)
For adolescents
ISBN 0-333-28055-5 : £3.95 : CIP rev. B81-04230

Douglas, Colin, *1945-*. The houseman's tale / Colin Douglas. — [London] : Fontana, 1977, c1975 (1980 [printing]). — 222p ; 18cm
Originally published: Edinburgh : Canongate, 1975
ISBN 0-00-616240-1 : £1.00 B81-00442

Douglas, Colin, *1945-*. Wellies from the Queen / Colin Douglas. — London : Hutchinson, 1981. — 251p ; 23cm
ISBN 0-09-143760-1 : £6.95 B81-11275

Douglas, Iain. The hearth of Ruvaig / by Ia[i]n Douglas. — London : Hale, 1981. — 192p ; 20cm. — (Hale SF)
ISBN 0-7091-9066-2 : £6.25 B81-24435

Douglas, Iain. Saturn's missing rings / by Iain Douglas. — London : Hale, 1980. — 173p ; 21cm. — (Hale SF)
ISBN 0-7091-8415-8 : £5.50 B81-00443

Douglas, Iain. The world of the sower / Iain Douglas. — London : Hale, 1981. — 160p ; 21cm. — (Hale SF)
ISBN 0-7091-8774-2 : £5.95 B81-05959

Douglas, Peter, *1932-*. About this village / Peter Douglas. — Woodbridge : Boydell Press, 1980. — 175p : ill ; 21cm
ISBN 0-85115-133-7 : £4.95 B81-07038

Douglas, Peter, *1932-*. Village life. — Woodbridge : Boydell, Oct.1981. — [128]p
ISBN 0-85115-155-8 : £5.50 : CIP entry B81-30483

Douglas, Sheila. Surgery by the sea / by Sheila Douglas. — London : Mills & Boon, 1979, c1978. — 187p ; 17cm
ISBN 0-263-72864-1 (pbk) : £0.55 B81-06398

Doyle, Amanda. The year at Yattabilla / Amanda Doyle. — Large print ed. — Leicester : Ulverscroft, 1980, c1970. — 305p ; 23cm. — (Ulverscroft large print series)
Originally published: London : Mills and Boon, 1970
ISBN 0-7089-0537-4 : £4.25 : CIP rev. B80-24825

Drabble, Margaret. The waterfall / Margaret Drabble. — Harmondsworth : Penguin, 1971, c1969 (1980 [printing]). — 239p ; 18cm
Originally published: London : Weidenfeld & Nicolson, 1969
ISBN 0-14-003317-3 (pbk) : £1.25 B81-01420

Dransfield, Evelyn. The mark of Cain / Evelyn Dransfield. — Bognor Regis : New Horizon, c1978. — 108p ; 21cm
ISBN 0-86116-045-2 : £3.50 B81-18861

Draper, Alfred. Grey Seal / Alfred Draper. — London : Macdonald, 1981. — 255p ; 23cm
ISBN 0-354-04641-1 : £6.95 B81-26575

Driscoll, Peter. In connection with Kilshaw / Peter Driscoll. — London : Granada, 1981, c1974. — 256p ; 18cm. — (A Panther book)
Originally published: London : Macdonald, 1974
ISBN 0-586-05208-9 (pbk) : £1.50 B81-28953

Driscoll, Peter. The white lie assignment / Peter Driscoll. — London : Granada, 1981, c1971. — 221p ; 18cm. — (A Panther book)
Originally published: London : Macdonald, 1971
ISBN 0-586-05209-7 (pbk) : £1.25 B81-17409

Drummond, June. Slowly the poison / June Drummond. — Large print ed. — Bath : Lythway, 1980, c1975. — 313p ; 23cm
Originally published: London : Gollancz, 1975
ISBN 0-85046-912-0 : CIP rev. B80-34108

Drummond, June. Such a nice family / June Drummond. — Large print ed. — Bath : Chivers, 1981, c1980. — 251p ; 23cm. — (A Lythway mystery)
Originally published: London : Gollancz, 1980
ISBN 0-85119-720-5 : Unpriced : CIP rev. B81-13784

Duffy, Maureen. Gor saga. — London : Eyre Methuen, Oct.1981. — [224]p
ISBN 0-413-49190-0 : £6.95 : CIP entry B81-25309

823'.914[F] — Fiction in English, *1945-* — *Texts continuation*

Duker, Peter. Given half a chance / Peter Duker. — Bognor Regis : New Horizon, 1981. — 231p ; 21cm
ISBN 0-86116-508-x : £6.25 B81-26491

Dunbar, Catherine. The nuthatch tree / Catherine Dunbar. — London : Hodder and Stoughton, 1981. — 312p ; 23cm
ISBN 0-340-26246-x : £7.50 : CIP rev. B81-19142

Duncan, Alex. God and the doctor / Alex Duncan. — London : W.H. Allen, 1981. — 208p ; 21cm
ISBN 0-491-02784-2 : £5.95 B81-15406

Duncan, George, *1927-*. The bloody legionnaires / George Duncan. — [London] : Magnum, 1981. — 279p ; 18cm
ISBN 0-417-05950-7 (pbk) : £1.50 B81-12040

Duncan, Rafe. Ebony Island / Rafe Duncan. — London : Arrow, 1981. — 303p ; 18cm
ISBN 0-09-923070-4 (pbk) : £1.60 B81-28590

Dunn, Christopher. Deadlines / Christopher Dunn. — London : Heinemann, 1981. — 213p ; 23cm
ISBN 0-434-21670-4 : £6.50 B81-18406

Dunne, Colin. The landsbird / Colin Dunne. — [Glasgow] : Fontana, 1981, c1979. — 252p ; 18cm
Originally published: London : Collins, 1979
ISBN 0-00-616256-8 (pbk) : £1.50 B81-11066

Durman, Hilda. Artist in love / Hilda Durman. — London : Hale, 1980. — 157p ; 20cm
ISBN 0-7091-8228-7 : £4.95 B81-00444

Durman, Hilda. A heart of stone / by Hilda Durman. — London : Hale, 1981. — 160p ; 20cm
ISBN 0-7091-8514-6 : £5.50 B81-14084

Durman, Hilda. His favourite girl / by Hilda Durman. — London : Hale, 1981. — 160p ; 20cm
ISBN 0-7091-8521-9 : £5.60 B81-21296

Durman, Hilda. Kit's benefactor / by Hilda Durman. — London : Hale, 1981. — 158p ; 20cm
ISBN 0-7091-9036-0 : £5.75 B81-37298

Durrell, Gerald. The mockery bird. — London : Collins, Nov.1981. — [210]p
ISBN 0-00-222603-0 : £6.95 : CIP entry B81-28780

Dwyer, Winifred. The falling star / Winifred Dwyer. — Bognor Regis : New Horizon, c1978. — 123p ; 22cm
ISBN 0-86116-014-2 : £2.95 B81-19266

Dwyer-Joyce, Alice. Danny boy / Alice Dwyer-Joyce. — Large print ed. — Leicester : Ulverscroft, 1981, c1979. — 345p : 1geneal.table ; 22cm. — (Ulverscroft large print series)
Originally published: London : Hale, 1979. — Geneal.table on lining papers
ISBN 0-7089-0579-x : £5.00 B81-12177

Dwyer-Joyce, Alice. Lachlan's woman / Alice Dwyer-Joyce. — Large print ed. — London : Hale, 1980, c1979. — 285p ; 23cm
Originally published: New York : St. Martin's Press ; London : Hale, 1979
ISBN 0-7091-8616-9 : £5.40 B81-02921

Dwyer-Joyce, Alice. The penny box / Alice Dwyer-Joyce. — New York : St Martin's ; London : Hale, 1980. — 188p ; 21cm
ISBN 0-7091-8535-9 : £6.25 B81-02919

Dyer, Alfred. The Gabriel inheritance / by Alfred Dyer. — London : Hale, 1981. — 176p ; 20cm. — (Hale SF)
ISBN 0-7091-8773-4 : £5.95 B81-21298

Dyer, Alfred. The symbiotic mind / Alfred Dyer. — London : Hale, 1980. — 223p ; 21cm. — (Hale SF)
ISBN 0-7091-8275-9 : £5.25 B81-00445

Dyke, Carol Hamilton. The clouded summer / by Carol Hamilton Dyke. — London : Hale, 1981. — 159p ; 20cm
ISBN 0-7091-8738-6 : £5.50 B81-08643

Dyke, Carol Hamilton. A girl like Lucy / by Carol Hamilton Dyke. — London : Hale, 1981. — 157p ; 20cm
ISBN 0-7091-9037-9 : £5.60 B81-27306

Dyke, Carol Hamilton. The last days of loving / Carol Hamilton Dyke. — London : Hale, 1980. — 159p ; 20cm
ISBN 0-7091-8075-6 : £4.95 B81-00446

Dymoke, Juliet. A kind of warfare / by Juliet Dymoke. — London : Dobson, 1981. — 176p : 1geneal.table ; 23cm
ISBN 0-234-72271-1 : £5.95
ISBN 0-234-72284-3 (Stonor ed.) B81-18543

Dymoke, Juliet. The lion of Mortimer / Juliet Dymoke. — London : Dobson, 1979. — 190p ; 23cm. — (The Plantagenets)
ISBN 0-234-72094-8 : £3.95 B81-02234

Early, Richard E.. Master weaver / Richard E. Early. — London : Routledge and Kegan Paul, 1980. — 214p ; 23cm
ISBN 0-7100-0641-1 : £7.50 : CIP rev. B80-17969

Earth, Thomas E.. The Shalashi project / Thomas E. Earth. — Bognor Regis : New Horizon, c1978. — 170p ; 21cm
ISBN 0-86116-017-7 : £3.95 B81-19079

Eastvale, Margaret. Change of heart / Margaret Eastvale. — London : Mills & Boon, 1981. — 189p ; 20cm
ISBN 0-263-09778-1 : £4.55 B81-09308

Ebel, Suzanne. Julia's sister. — London : Severn House, Apr.1981. — [160]p
ISBN 0-7278-0693-9 : £5.95 : CIP entry B81-07610

Ebel, Suzanne. Music in winter / Suzanne Ebel. — Large print ed. — Leicester : Ulverscroft, 1981, c1975. — 298p ; 23cm. — (Ulverscroft large print series)
Originally published: London : Collins, 1975
ISBN 0-7089-0634-6 : Unpriced : CIP rev. B81-14837

Ebel, Suzanne. A rose in the heather / Suzanne Ebel. — Large print ed. — Leicester : Ulverscroft, 1980, c1978. — 307p ; 23cm. — (Ulverscroft large print series)
Originally published: London : Collins, 1977
ISBN 0-7089-0510-2 : £4.25 : CIP rev. B80-17970

Eckersley, Jill. A little loving / Jill Eckersley. — Feltham : Hamlyn Paperbacks, 1981. — 172p ; 18cm. — (A Sapphire romance)
ISBN 0-600-20154-6 (pbk) : £0.75 B81-12084

Eckhardt, Kurt. Achtung: Normandy! / Kurt Eckhardt. — London (Old Mission Hall, Dewar St., S.E.15) : Magread, 1980. — 238p ; 18cm. — (A Moat Hall book)
ISBN 0-427-00463-2 (pbk) : £1.25 B81-03003

Edgeworth, Ann. Runaway maid / Ann Edgeworth. — London : Mills and Boon, 1980, c1979. — 188p ; 20cm. — (Masquerade)
ISBN 0-263-09679-3 : £3.85 B81-06421

Edson, J. T.. Back to the bloody border / by J.T Edson. — London : Hale, 1980, c1970. — 158p ; 20cm
Originally published: London : Corgi, 1970
ISBN 0-7091-8183-3 : £4.95 B81-0044

Edson, J. T.. Beguinage is dead! / by J.T. Edson — London : Severn House, 1980, c1978. — 187p ; 21cm
Originally published: London : Corgi, 1978
ISBN 0-7278-0540-1 : £4.95 : CIP rev. B80-1888

Edson, J. T.. Calamity, Mark and Belle / J.T. Edson. — [London] : Corgi, 1980. — 207p ; 18cm. — (Calamity Jane series)
ISBN 0-552-11542-8 (pbk) : £0.95 B81-0719

Edson, J. T.. Chuchilo / by J.T. Edson. — London : Hale, 1981, c1969. — 158p ; 20cm
ISBN 0-7091-8190-6 : £4.95 B81-2129

Edson, J. T.. Cold deck, hot lead / by J.T. Edson. — London : Hale, 1981, c1969. — 141p ; 20cm
Originally published: London : Corgi, 1969
ISBN 0-7091-8192-2 : £4.95 B81-3353

Edson, J. T.. Cuchilo. — London : Corgi, 1969 (1981 [printing]). — 158p ; 18cm
£0.95 (pbk) B81-2228

Edson, J. T.. The fortune hunters / J.T. Edson. — [London] : Corgi, 1969 (1981 [printing]). — 157p ; 18cm
Originally published: London : Brown Watson, 1965
ISBN 0-552-08241-4 (pbk) : £0.95 B81-2543

Edson, J. T.. From hide and horn / by J.T. Edson. — London : Hale, 1980, c1969. — 158p ; 20cm
Originally published: London : Corgi, 1969
ISBN 0-7091-8184-1 : £4.95 B81-0775

Edson, J. T.. Go back to hell / by J.T. Edson. — London : Hale, 1980, c1972. — 159p ; 20cm
Originally published: London : Corgi, 1972
ISBN 0-7091-5320-1 : £4.50 B81-0142

Edson, J. T.. Gun wizard / J.T. Edson. — [London] : Corgi, 1969 (1981 [printing]). — 158p ; 18cm
Originally published: London : Brown Watson, 1963
ISBN 0-552-08065-9 (pbk) : £0.95 B81-2543

Edson, J. T.. The hard riders / J.T. Edson. — [London] : Corgi, 1968 (1981 [printing]). — 157p ; 18cm. — (A Corgi western)
Originally published: London : Watson, 1962
ISBN 0-552-07890-5 (pbk) : £0.95 B81-2120

Edson, J. T.. Hell in the Palo Duro / J.T. Edson — London : Hale, 1981, c1971. — 175p ; 20cm
Originally published: London : Corgi, 1971
ISBN 0-7091-8186-8 : £4.95 B81-0291

Edson, J. T.. The hooded riders / by J.T. Edson. — London : Hale, 1981, c1968. — 158p ; 20cm
Originally published: London : Corgi, 1968
ISBN 0-7091-8188-4 : £4.95 B81-1178

Edson, J. T.. Kill Dusty Fog! / by J.T. Edson. — London : Hale, 1981, c1970. — 157p ; 20cm
Originally published: London : Corgi, 1970
ISBN 0-7091-8187-6 : £4.95 B81-1183

Edson, J. T.. Master of triggernometry / J.T. Edson. — [London] : Corgi, 1981, c1980. — 202p ; 18cm
ISBN 0-552-11638-6 (pbk) : £0.95 B81-1534

Edson, J. T.. McGraw's inheritance / J.T. Edson. — London : Corgi, 1968 (1981 [printing]). — 140p : ill ; 18cm. — (A Corgi western)
ISBN 0-552-07900-6 (pbk) : £0.95 B81-18772

823'.914[F] — Fiction in English, *1945-* **— Texts** *continuation*

Edson, J. T.. Old moccasins on the trail / J.T. Edson. — London : Corgi, 1981. — 191p ; 18cm
ISBN 0-552-11770-6 (pbk) : £1.00 B81-35598

Edson, J. T.. Ole Devil and the caplocks / J.T. Edson. — London : Severn House, 1981, c1976. — 203p ; 21cm
Originally published: London : Corgi, 1976
ISBN 0-7278-0721-8 : £5.95 : CIP rev. B81-14800

Edson, J. T.. Ole devil and the mule train / by J.T. Edson. — London : Hale, 1981. — 158p ; 20cm
Originally published: London : Corgi, 1976
ISBN 0-7091-8245-7 : £4.95 B81-40535

Edson, J. T.. The quest for Bowie's blade / J.T. Edson. — [London] : Corgi, 1974 (1981 [printing]). — 206p ; 18cm
ISBN 0-552-09607-5 (pbk) : £0.95 B81-25434

Edson, J. T.. Rangeland Hercules / J.T. Edson. — London : Corgi, 1968 (1981 [printing]). — 141p ; 18cm
ISBN 0-552-07963-4 (pbk) : £0.95 B81-18778

Edson, J. T.. The Rio Hondo kid / by J.T. Edson. — London : Hale, 1980, c1963. — 159p ; 20cm
Originally published: London : Wright & Brown, 1966
ISBN 0-7091-5321-x : £4.50 B81-07515

Edson, J. T.. Sagebrush sleuth / J.T. Edson. — London : Corgi, 1968 (1981 [printing]). — 142p ; 18cm
ISBN 0-552-08012-8 (pbk) : £0.95 B81-18774

Edson, J. T.. Set a-foot / by J.T. Edson. — London : Hale, 1981, c1977. — 205p ; 20cm
Originally published: London : Corgi, 1978
ISBN 0-7091-8244-9 : £4.95 B81-35191

Edson, J. T.. The small Texan / J.T. Edson. — London : Corgi, 1969 (1981 [printing]). — 157p ; 18cm
£0.95 (pbk) B81-22278

Edson, J. T.. The small Texan / by J.T. Edson. — London : Hale, 1981, c1969. — 157p ; 20cm
Originally published: London : Corgi, 1969
ISBN 0-7091-8191-4 : £4.95 B81-27299

Edson, J. T.. Terror valley / J.T. Edson. — London : Corgi, 1968 (1981 [printing]). — 157p ; 18cm
ISBN 0-552-08018-7 (pbk) : £0.95 B81-18775

Edson, J. T.. The Texan / J.T. Edson. — Large print ed. — Leicester : Ulverscroft, 1981, c1968. — 304p ; 23cm. — (Ulverscroft large print series)
Originally published: London : Wright & Brown, 1964
ISBN 0-7089-0616-8 : £5.00 : CIP rev. B81-02117

Edson, J. T.. The town tamers / by J.T. Edson. — London : Hale, 1980, c1969. — 142p ; 20cm
Originally published: London : Corgi, 1969
ISBN 0-7091-8182-5 : £4.75 B81-02204

Edson, J. T.. Waco rides in / by J.T. Edson. — London : Hale, 1981, c1969. — 158p ; 20cm
Originally published: London : Wright & Brown, 1967
ISBN 0-7091-8189-2 : £4.95 B81-15999

Edson, J. T.. Waco's debt / by J.T. Edson. — London : Hale, 1980, c1968. — 160p ; 20cm
Originally published: London : Wright & Brown, 1964
ISBN 0-7091-4446-6 : £4.50 B81-01422

Edson, J. T.. Young ole devil / J.T. Edson. — [London] : Corgi, 1975 (1981 [printing]). — 170p ; 18cm
ISBN 0-552-09650-4 (pbk) : £0.95 B81-25435

Edson, J. T.. Young ole Devil / J.T. Edson. — London : Severn House, 1981, c1975. — 170p ; 21cm
Originally published: London : Corgi, 1975
ISBN 0-7278-0676-9 : £5.95 B81-16069

Edson, J. T.. You're in command now, Mr. Fog / by J.T. Edson. — London : Hale, 1980, c1973. — 189p ; 20cm
Originally published: London : Corgi, 1973
ISBN 0-7091-8185-x : £4.95 B81-03073

Edson, J. T.. [The Ysabel Kid]. Sidewinder / J.T. Edson. — [London] : Corgi, 1969 (1981 [printing]). — 156p ; 18cm
Originally published: London : Wright & Brown, 1967
ISBN 0-552-08279-1 (pbk) : £0.95 B81-25439

Edwardes, Michael, *1923-*. The man from the other shore / Michael Edwardes. — London : Hamilton, 1981. — 186p ; 23cm
Based on the life of Basil Zacharias Zaharoff
ISBN 0-241-10615-x : £6.95 B81-13116

Edwards, G. B.. The book of Ebenezer Le Page / by G.B. Edwards ; introduction by John Fowles. — London : Hamilton, 1981. — 400p : 1map ; 24cm
ISBN 0-241-10477-7 : £7.50 B81-15733

Edwards, Rachelle. Fortune's child / by Rachelle Edwards. — London : Hale, 1981. — 176p ; 20cm
ISBN 0-7091-8711-4 : £6.25 B81-08642

Edwards, Rachelle. The marriage bargain / by Rachelle Edwards. — London : Hale, 1981. — 159p ; 20cm
ISBN 0-7091-9100-6 : £6.25 B81-27320

Edwards, Rachelle. The Smithfield bargain / by Rachelle Edwards. — London : Hale, 1980. — 157p ; 20cm
ISBN 0-7091-8460-3 : £5.95 B81-00448

Edwards, Ruth Dudley. Corridors of death. — London : Quartet Books, Oct.1981. — 1v.
ISBN 0-7043-2311-7 : £5.95 : CIP entry B81-28118

Egleton, Clive. Seven days to a killing / Clive Egleton. — Large print ed. — Leicester : Ulverscroft, 1980, c1973. — 342p ; 23cm. — (Ulverscroft large print series)
Originally published: London : Hodder and Stoughton, 1973
ISBN 0-7089-0528-5 : £4.25 : CIP rev. B80-23703

Egleton, Clive. The winter touch / Clive Egleton. — London : Hodder, c1981. — 238p ; 23cm
ISBN 0-340-26250-8 : £6.95 : CIP rev. B81-17533

Elder, A. J.. The Rubicon file : a successor to Honeywood / A.J. Elder ; illustrations by Ionicus. — London : Architectural, 1980. — xvi,239p : ill ; 23cm
ISBN 0-85139-168-0 (cased) : £10.95
ISBN 0-85139-132-x
ISBN 0-85139-107-9 (pbk) : £5.95 B81-04013

Elgin, Elizabeth. Mistress of Luke's Folly / Elizabeth Elgin. — London : Hale, 1981. — 192p ; 21cm
ISBN 0-7091-8770-x : £6.25 B81-11659

Ellerbeck, Rosemary. Rose, Rose, where are you? / Rosemary Ellerbeck. — Large print ed. — Leicester : Ulverscroft, 1981, c1978. — 359p ; 23cm. — (Ulverscroft large print series)
Originally published: London : Hale, 1978
ISBN 0-7089-0596-x : Unpriced B81-14225

Elliot, Elisabeth. No graven image. — London : Hodder & Stoughton, Oct.1981. — [256]p
Originally published: 1966
ISBN 0-340-26355-5 (pbk) : £1.95 : CIP entry B81-25750

Elliott, Janice. Secret places / Janice Elliott. — London : Hodder and Stoughton, 1981. — 192p ; 23cm
ISBN 0-340-26247-8 : £6.50 B81-10139

Elsna, Hebe. The mask of comedy. — Large print ed. — Long Preston : Magna, Dec.1981. — [448]p
ISBN 0-86009-355-7 : £4.95 : CIP entry B81-31815

Emerson, Sally. Second sight / Sally Emerson. — London : Robin Clark, 1981, c1980. — 239p ; 20cm
Originally published: London : Joseph, 1980
ISBN 0-86072-052-7 (pbk) : £2.95 B81-28578

Emery, Denise. Sunrise in Hong Kong / Denise Emery. — London : Severn House, 1981, c1980. — 120p ; 21cm
ISBN 0-7278-0691-2 : £4.95 : CIP rev. B80-12064

Emery, Denise. The sweet bells of Utrecht / Denise Emery. — London : Hamlyn Paperbacks, 1981, c1979. — 137p ; 18cm. — (A Sapphire romance)
Originally published: London : Severn House, 1980
ISBN 0-600-20092-2 (pbk) : £0.75 B81-31917

England, Edward. Chateau Rocca / Edward England. — Bognor Regis : New Horizon, c1979. — 85p ; 21cm
ISBN 0-86116-041-x : £3.95 B81-19267

English, Jean. Rosie of the Lane : a Regency romance / by Jean English. — London : Hale, 1981. — 208p ; 20cm
ISBN 0-7091-9278-9 : £6.75 B81-35240

Eskapa, Shirley. Blood fugue / Shirley Eskapa. — London : Quartet, 1981. — 135p ; 23cm. — (Quartet crime)
ISBN 0-7043-2284-6 : £5.95 B81-20284

Essex, Francis. Shillingbury tales / Francis Essex. — London : New English Library, 1981. — 229p ; 18cm
ISBN 0-450-05164-1 (pbk) : £1.25 B81-19987

Evans, Alan, *1930-*. Dauntless / Alan Evans. — London : Hodder and Stoughton, 1980. — 252p : 1map ; 23cm
ISBN 0-340-25305-3 : £6.50 : CIP rev. B80-13062

Evans, Alan, *1930-*. Ship of force / Alan Evans. — Large print ed. — Leicester : Ulverscroft, 1980, c1979. — 452p ; 23cm. — (Ulverscroft large print series)
Originally published: London : Hodder and Stoughton, 1979
ISBN 0-7089-0555-2 : £4.25 : CIP rev. B80-35444

Evans, Alan, *1930-*. Thunder at dawn / Alan Evans. — Large print ed. — Leicester : Ulverscroft, 1980, c1978. — 399p ; 22cm. — (Ulverscroft large print)
Originally published: London : Hodder and Stoughton, 1978
ISBN 0-7089-0541-2 : £4.25 : CIP rev. B80-24828

Evans, Christopher. The insider. — London : Faber, Nov.1981. — [192]p
ISBN 0-571-11774-0 : £6.95 : CIP entry B81-31090

Evans, Jean. Hospital in the mountains / by Jean Evans. — London : Mills & Boon, 1981. — 188p ; 20cm
ISBN 0-263-09928-8 : £4.55 B81-35634

823'.914[F] — Fiction in English, *1945- — Texts continuation*

Evans, Jean. Maria d'Este : the second duchess / Jean Evans. — Large print ed. — Bath : Chivers, 1981, c1978. — 224p ; 23cm. — (A Lythway book)
Originally published: London : Hale, 1978
ISBN 0-85119-735-3 : Unpriced : CIP rev. B81-18147

Evans, Jonathan. The midas men / Jonathan Evans. — London : Joseph, 1981. — 314p ; 23cm
ISBN 0-7181-2043-4 : £7.50 B81-33565

Evans, Russell. Survival / Russell Evans. — Harmondsworth : Puffin, 1981, c1979. — 150p ; 19cm. — (Puffin plus)
Originally published: London : Dobson, 1979. — For adolescents
ISBN 0-14-031284-6 (pbk) : £1.10 B81-26505

Everett, Nick. Shock wave / Nick Everett. — London : New English Library, 1981. — 143p ; 18cm
ISBN 0-450-05096-3 (pbk) : £1.10 B81-14312

Faid, Mary. The summer of the wedding / by Mary Faid. — London : Hale, 1980. — 191p ; 20cm
ISBN 0-7091-8456-5 : £5.25 B81-02208

Fairfax, Kate. Wild honey / Kate Fairfax. — London : Macdonald Futura, 1981. — 254p ; 21cm
ISBN 0-354-04655-1 (corrected) : £4.95 B81-29945

Fairless, Stephanie. That incredible summer / by Stephanie Fairless. — London : Hale, 1981. — 157p ; 20cm
ISBN 0-7091-8633-9 : £5.50 B81-02531

Falconer, Noel. Spitfire sharpshooter / Noel Falconer. — London : Hale, 1980. — 207p ; 21cm
ISBN 0-7091-8526-x : £6.25 B81-02070

Fantoni, Barry. Mike Dime. — Large print ed. — Anstey : Ulverscroft, Jan.1982. — [270]p. — (Ulverscroft large print series : mystery)
ISBN 0-7089-0731-8 : £5.00 : CIP entry B81-33962

Farelane, Alexan. The quest of Aah. — Thornton Heath (908 London Rd., Thornton Heath, Surrey CR4 7PE) : Lashbrook & Knight, Nov.1981. — [615]p
ISBN 0-9507559-0-7 : £7.95 : CIP entry B81-31201

Farely, Alison. Archduchess arrogance / by Alison Farely. — London : Hale, 1980. — 187p ; 20cm
ISBN 0-7091-8599-5 : £6.25 B81-11106

Farrell, J. G.. A girl in the head / J.G. Farrell. — [London] : Fontana, 1981, c1967. — 221p ; 18cm
Originally published: London : Cape, 1967
ISBN 0-00-616194-4 (pbk) : £1.50 B81-11180

Farrell, J. G.. The hill station : an unfinished novel ; and An Indian diary / J.G. Farrell ; edited by John Spurling. — London : Weidenfeld and Nicolson, 1981. — x,228p ; 23cm
ISBN 0-297-77922-2 : £6.50
Also classified at 828'.91409 B81-19321

Farrell, J. G.. Troubles / J.G. Farrell. — Harmondsworth : Penguin, 1975, c1970 (1981 [printing]). — 410p ; 18cm
ISBN 0-14-003973-2 (pbk) : £1.75 B81-07367

Farren, Mick. The song of Phaid the gambler / Mick Farren. — London : New English Library, 1981. — 537p ; 19cm
ISBN 0-450-05343-1 (pbk) : £1.75 B81-40487

Farron, Daniel. Transplant / Daniel Farron. — London : Hamlyn Paperbacks, 1981. — 190p ; 18cm
ISBN 0-600-20233-x (pbk) : £1.00 B81-19903

Feely, Terence. Rich little poor girl / Terence Feely. — [London] : Hamlyn Paperbacks, 1981. — 352p ; 18cm
ISBN 0-600-20201-1 (pbk) : £1.50 B81-19907

Feild, Reshad. The invisible way : a time to love - a time to die / Reshad Feild. — Salisbury : Element, 1979. — 187p ; 22cm
ISBN 0-906540-04-6 (pbk) : £4.50 B81-40973

Ferrand, Georgina. The beckoning dawn / by Georgina Ferrand. — London : Hale, 1981. — 159p ; 20cm
ISBN 0-7091-9279-7 : £5.75 B81-30073

Ferrand, Georgina. Reluctant lover. — London : Hale, 1980. — 155p ; 20cm
ISBN 0-7091-8277-5 : £5.25 B81-02473

Field, Sandra. The storms of spring / by Sandra Field. — London : Mills & Boon, 1981. — 187p ; 20cm
ISBN 0-263-09916-4 : £4.55 B81-34106

Figes, Eva. Waking / Eva Figes. — London : Hamilton, 1981. — 88p ; 21cm
ISBN 0-241-10520-x : £3.95 B81-08239

Finch, John. Cuddon return / John Finch. — Large print ed. — Leicester : Ulverscroft, 1981, c1979. — 538p ; 23cm. — (Ulverscroft large print)
Originally published: London : Souvenir, 1979
ISBN 0-7089-0586-2 : £5.00 B81-11616

Finch, John. Flesh and blood / John Finch. — Loughton ([17 Brook Rd.,] Loughton, Essex [IG10 IBW]) : Piatkus, 1980. — 222p ; 21cm
ISBN 0-86188-048-x : £5.25 : CIP rev. B80-10261

Finch, Simon. Voyager in bondage / by Simon Finch. — London : Souvenir, 1981. — 207p : 1map ; 21cm
ISBN 0-285-62463-6 : £6.95 B81-21189

Findlow, Evo. Gypsy fire / by Evo Findlow. — London : Hale, 1981. — 192p ; 20cm
ISBN 0-7091-8893-5 : £5.60 B81-17326

Firth, Susanna. Master of shadows / by Susanna Firth. — London : Mills & Boon, 1981. — 187p ; 20cm
ISBN 0-263-09824-9 : £4.55 B81-09409

Fish, Olive. Web of treason / by Olive Fish. — London : Hale, 1981. — 192p ; 20cm
ISBN 0-7091-9387-4 : £6.75 B81-40530

Fisher, Alan E.. The midnight men / by Alan E. Fisher. — London : Hale, 1980. — 190p ; 20cm
ISBN 0-7091-8648-7 : £5.75 B81-02073

Fisher, Hazel. Major Mike / by Hazel Fisher. — London : Mills & Boon, 1981. — 187p ; 20cm
ISBN 0-263-09896-6 : £4.55 B81-28515

Fiske, Sharon. Summer cypress / by Sharon Fiske. — London : Hale, 1981. — 160p ; 21cm
ISBN 0-7091-8881-1 : £5.95 B81-17320

Fitzgerald, George. The Devil & Co Ltd / George Fitzgerald. — Bognor Regis : New Horizon, c1979. — 108p ; 21cm
ISBN 0-86116-062-2 : £3.50 B81-18862

Fitzgerald, Julia. Fallen woman / Julia Fitzgerald. — London : Macdonald Futura, 1981. — 254p ; 18cm. — (A Minstrel book ; 3)
ISBN 0-7088-2006-9 (pbk) : £0.95 B81-15463

Fitzgerald, Julia. Salamander / Julia Fitzerald. — London : Macdonald Futura, 1981. — 416p ; 18cm. — (A Troubadour spectacular)
ISBN 0-7107-3007-1 (pbk) : £1.75 B81-15453

Fitzgerald, Penelope. Human voices / Penelope Fitzgerald. — London : Collins, 1980. — 176p ; 22cm
ISBN 0-00-222280-9 : £5.25 B81-00450

Fitzgerald, Penelope. Offshore / Penelope Fitzgerald. — London : Magnum Books, 1980, c1979. — 141p ; 18cm
Originally published: London : Collins, 1979
ISBN 0-417-06010-6 (pbk) : £1.10 B81-30701

Fitzgerald, Penelope. Offshore. — Large print ed. — Bath : Chivers Press, Feb.1982. — [232]p. — (A Lythway book)
Originally published: London : Collins, 1979
ISBN 0-85119-783-3 : £6.90 : CIP entry B81-35863

Fitzroy, Rosamond. The manor of Braye / Rosamond Fitzroy. — Large print ed. — Leicester : Ulverscroft, 1980. — 387p ; 23cm. — (Ulverscroft large print series)
Originally published: London : Arlington, 1979
ISBN 0-7089-0544-7 : £4.25 : CIP rev. B80-26139

Fitzroy, Rosamond. The widow's might. — Large print ed. — Anstey : Ulverscroft, Feb.1982. — [416]p. — (Ulverscroft large print series : general fiction)
ISBN 0-7089-0755-5 : £5.00 : CIP entry B81-36937

Fitzsimons, Christopher. Reflex action / Christopher Fitzsimons. — London : Hodder and Stoughton, 1980. — 271p ; 23cm
ISBN 0-340-25276-6 : £6.50 : CIP rev. B80-12551

Fleetwood, Hugh. A young fair god. — London : Hamilton, Feb.1982. — [192]p
ISBN 0-241-10715-6 : £7.95 : CIP entry B81-36387

Fleming, Ian, *1908-1964*. Dr. No. — Large print ed. — Bath : Chivers, Jan.1982. — [304]p. — (A New Portway large print book)
Originally published: London : Cape, 1958
ISBN 0-85119-150-9 : £5.35 : CIP entry B81-33812

Foley, Lorette. Murder in Burgos / by Lorette Foley. — London : Hale, 1981. — 173p ; 20cm
ISBN 0-7091-9041-7 : £5.95 B81-24349

Follett, James. Churchill's gold. — Sevenoaks : Hodder & Stoughton, June 1981. — [224]p
ISBN 0-340-26674-0 (pbk) : £1.50 : CIP entry B81-12352

Follett, James. Earth search / James Follett. — London : British Broadcasting Corporation, 1981. — 208p ; 22cm
ISBN 0-563-20005-7 : £7.50 B81-35582

Follett, James. Earthsearch / James Follett. — London : British Broadcasting Corporation, 1981. — 208p ; 18cm
ISBN 0-563-17943-0 (pbk) : £1.65 B81-34878

Follett, Ken. The key to Rebecca / Ken Follett. — London : Hamilton, 1980. — 311p ; 23cm
ISBN 0-241-10492-0 : £5.95 B81-06966

Follett, Ken. Triple / Ken Follett. — London : Macdonald Futura, 1980, c1979. — 377p ; 18cm
Originally published: London : Macdonald, 1979
ISBN 0-7088-1804-8 (pbk) : £1.50 B81-01658

Follett, Ken. Triple. — Large print ed. — Anstey : Ulverscroft, Sept.1981. — [544]p. — (Charnwood library series)
ISBN 0-7089-8013-9 : £6.50 : CIP entry B81-21473

823'.914[F] — Fiction in English, *1945-* — Texts *continuation*

Forbes, Colin. The Stockholm syndicate. — London : Collins, Nov.1981. — [378]p
ISBN 0-00-222299-x : £7.95 : CIP entry B81-28769

Forde, Nicholas. Urgent conference / by Nicholas Forde. — London : Hale, 1981. — 158p ; 20cm
ISBN 0-7091-8777-7 : £5.75 B81-14132

Forster, Margaret. The bride of Lowther Fell : a romance / Margaret Forster. — London : Secker & Warburg, 1980. — 310p ; 23cm
ISBN 0-436-16111-7 : £6.95 B81-00451

Forster, Margaret. Marital rites / Margaret Forster. — London : Secker & Warburg, 1981. — 182p ; 23cm
ISBN 0-436-16112-5 : £6.95 : CIP rev. B81-13479

Forster, Margaret. Mother can you hear me? / Margaret Forster. — Harmondsworth : Penguin, 1981, c1979. — 268p ; 18cm
Originally published: London : Secker & Warburg, 1979
ISBN 0-14-005599-1 (pbk) : £1.75 B81-35586

Forsyth, Frederick. The Devil's alternative / Frederick Forsyth. — Large print ed. — Leicester : Ulverscroft, 1980, c1979. — 660p ; 23cm. — (Ulverscroft large print series)
Originally published: London : Hutchinson, 1979
ISBN 0-7089-0529-3 : £4.25 : CIP rev. B80-23706

Forsyth, Frederick. The four novels of Frederick Forsyth. — London : Hutchinson, Sept.1981. — [1120]p
ISBN 0-09-145720-3 : £8.95 : CIP entry B81-20180

Forsyth, Frederick. The Odessa file. — Large print ed. — Anstey : Ulverscroft, Nov.1981. — [560]p. — (Ulverscroft large print series)
Originally published: London : Hutchinson, 1972
ISBN 0-7089-0710-5 : £5.00 : CIP entry B81-30506

Foster, Delia. Treasure of love / by Delia Foster. — London : Hale, 1980. — 159p ; 20cm
ISBN 0-7091-8364-x : £5.25 B81-00452

Fox, Caroline, *1935-*. Scorpio / Caroline Fox. — London : Deutsch, 1981. — 238p ; 23cm
ISBN 0-233-97371-0 : £6.50 : CIP rev. B81-13432

Fox, Peter, *1946-*. Satan's messenger / Peter Fox. — London : Macmillan, 1981. — 221p ; 23cm
ISBN 0-333-30598-1 : £5.50 B81-20271

Foxall, P. A.. The silent informer / P.A. Foxall. — London : Hale, 1981. — 170p ; 20cm
ISBN 0-7091-8850-1 : £5.75 B81-15998

Foxall, P. A.. Testament of violence / by P.A. Foxall. — London : Hale, 1980. — 174p ; 20cm
ISBN 0-7091-8555-3 : £5.75 B81-01425

Foxall, P. A.. The wild card / by P.A. Foxall. — London : Hale, 1981. — 176p ; 20cm
ISBN 0-7091-9207-x : £6.25 B81-35209

Foxall, Raymond. The last Jacobite / Raymond Foxall. — London : Hale, 1980. — 224p ; 21cm
ISBN 0-7091-8636-3 : £7.25 B81-08987

Francis, Dick. Reflex / Dick Francis. — Large print ed. — Leicester : Ulverscroft, 1981, c1980. — 463p ; 23cm. — (Ulverscroft large print series)
Originally published: London : Joseph, 1980
ISBN 0-7089-0653-2 : £5.00 B81-28574

Francis, Dick. Twice shy / Dick Francis. — London : Joseph, 1981. — 248p ; 23cm
ISBN 0-7181-2056-6 : £6.95 B81-39426

Francis, Dick. Whip hand / Dick Francis. — Large print ed. — Leicester : Ulverscroft, 1980, c1979. — 458p ; 22cm. — (Ulverscroft large print series)
Originally published: London : Joseph, 1979
ISBN 0-7089-0542-0 : £4.25 : CIP rev. B80-24830

Francis, Dick. Whip hand / Dick Francis. — London : Pan, 1981, c1979. — 255p ; 18cm
Originally published: London : Joseph, 1979
ISBN 0-330-26306-4 (pbk) : £1.50 B81-17984

Francis, Richard H.. Blackpool vanishes / Richard Francis. — London : Granada, 1980, c1979. — 191p ; 18cm. — (A Panther book)
Originally published: London : Faber, 1979
ISBN 0-586-04579-1 (pbk) : £1.25 B81-03011

Francis, Richard H.. Daggerman / Richard H. Francis. — London : Granada, 1981, c1980. — 223p ; 18cm. — (A Panther book)
Originally published: London : Faber, 1980
ISBN 0-586-05405-7 (pbk) : £1.25 B81-32180

Frank, Alan. Galactic aliens / by Alan Frank. — London : Angus & Robertson in conjunction with the International Agency for Scientific Intelligence, 1979. — [98]p : col.ill ; 31cm
ISBN 0-207-95890-4 : £4.95 B81-40939

Fraser, Antonia. A splash of red / Antonia Fraser. — London : Weidenfeld and Nicolson, 1981. — 229p ; 23cm
ISBN 0-297-77937-0 : £5.95 B81-17385

Fraser, George MacDonald. Mr American / George MacDonald Fraser. — London : Collins, 1980. — 573p ; 23cm
ISBN 0-00-221996-4 : £6.95 B81-05239

Fraser, Guy. Monster / by Guy Fraser. — London : Hale, 1981. — 175p ; 20cm
ISBN 0-7091-9188-x : £6.25 B81-33528

Fraser, Mary. Time of change / Mary Fraser. — London : Sphere, 1980. — 249p ; 18cm. — (The Village)
ISBN 0-7221-3647-1 (pbk) : £1.25 B81-01426

Frayn, Michael. Towards the end of the morning / Michael Frayn. — [Glasgow] : Fontana, 1977, c1967 (1981). — 223p ; 18cm
Originally published: London : Collins, 1967
ISBN 0-00-616159-6 (pbk) : £1.50 B81-18476

Frayn, Michael. A very private life / Michael Frayn. — [Glasgow] : Fontana, 1981, c1968. — 192p ; 18cm
Originally published: London : Collins, 1968
ISBN 0-00-616156-1 (pbk) : £1.35 B81-18477

Free, Colin. Brannan. — London : Eyre Methuen, Oct.1981. — [320]p
ISBN 0-413-47460-7 : £6.95 : CIP entry B81-25289

Freeling, Nicolas. One damn thing after another / Nicolas Freeling. — London : Heinemann, 1981. — 237p ; 23cm
ISBN 0-434-27186-1 : £6.95 B81-12953

Freeman, Gillian. An Easter egg hunt : a novel / by Gillian Freeman. — London : Hamilton, 1981. — 143p ; 20cm
ISBN 0-241-10568-4 : £6.95 : CIP rev. B81-04381

Freemantle, Brian. [Charlie Muffin]. Charlie M / Brian Freemantle. — South Yarmouth, Mass. : Curley, c1977 ; [Long Preston] : Magna [distributor]. — 361p ; 23cm
Originally published: London : Cape, 1977. — Published in large print
ISBN 0-89340-312-1 : £5.75 B81-18308

Freemantle, Brian. Here comes Charlie M. / Brian Freemantle. — South Yarmouth, Mass. : John Curley, 1978 ; [Long Preston] : Magna [distributor]. — 382p ; 23cm
Originally published: as Here comes Charlie M. Garden City, N.Y. : Doubleday, 1978 and as Clap hands, here comes Charlie, London : Cape, 1978
ISBN 0-89340-313-x : £5.75 B81-22116

Freemantle, Brian. The inscrutable Charlie Muffin / Brian Freemantle. — London : Arrow, 1981, c1979. — 192p ; 18cm
Originally published: London : Cape, 1979
ISBN 0-09-925460-3 (pbk) : £1.25 B81-16011

Freemantle, Brian. The inscrutable Charlie Muffin / Brian Freemantle. — South Yarmouth : Curley ; Bolton-by-Bowland : Magna Print [distributor], 1981, c1979. — 344p ; 23cm
Originally published: London : Cape, 1979. — Published in large print
ISBN 0-89340-314-8 : £5.75 B81-28685

Freemantle, Brian. Madrigal for Charlie Muffin. — London : Hutchinson, Oct.1981. — 1v.
ISBN 0-09-145260-0 : £6.95 : CIP entry B81-26795

Freemantle, Brian. The man who wanted tomorrow / Brian Freemantle. — London : Sphere, 1980, c1975. — 256p ; 18cm
Originally published: London : Cape, 1975
ISBN 0-7221-3663-3 (pbk) : £1.25 B81-11710

Fresson, I. M.. Walk alone no more / I.M. Fresson. — London : Hale, 1980. — 191p ; 20cm
ISBN 0-7091-8279-1 : £5.50 B81-05251

Fullbrook, Gladys. The seeing hands / Gladys Fullbrook. — Large print ed. — Bath : Chivers, 1981, c1967. — 226p ; 23cm. — (A Seymour book)
Originally published: London : Mills & Boon, 1967
ISBN 0-85119-430-3 : Unpriced : CIP rev. B81-20505

Fullerton, Alexander. All the drowning seas / Alexander Fullerton. — London : Joseph, 1981. — 262p ; 23cm
Maps on lining papers
ISBN 0-7181-1998-3 : £6.95 B81-17593

Fullerton, Alexander. Storm force to Narvik / Alexander Fullerton. — London : Pan, 1981, c1979. — 269p : 2maps ; 18cm
Originally published: London : Joseph, 1979
ISBN 0-330-26310-2 (pbk) : £1.25 B81-17982

Gair, Malcolm. The Schultz money / Malcolm Gair. — Hornchurch : Ian Henry, 1981, c1960. — 139p ; 21cm
Originally published: London : Collins, 1960
ISBN 0-86025-121-7 : £4.55 B81-21270

Gall, Sandy. Chasing the dragon / Sandy Gall. — London : Collins, 1981. — 285p ; 22cm
ISBN 0-00-222125-x : £6.95 B81-14082

Gandolfi, Simon. France-Security / Simon Gandolfi. — London : Blond & Briggs, 1981. — 185p ; 23cm
ISBN 0-85634-116-9 : £6.95 B81-34194

Gandolfi, Simon. The reluctant stud / Simon Gandolfi. — London : Sphere, 1981, c1980. — 216p ; 18cm
ISBN 0-7221-3803-2 (pbk) : £1.25 B81-28632

Garabet, Marilyn. Dearest of princes / by Marilyn Garabet. — London : Hale, 1981. — 190p ; 21cm
ISBN 0-7091-9371-8 : £6.75 B81-40529

Garden, Graeme. The seventh man. — London : Eyre Methuen, Sept.1981. — [160]p
ISBN 0-413-49080-7 : £6.50 : CIP entry B81-23773

823'.914[F] — Fiction in English, *1945-* — *Texts continuation*

Gardiner, Judy. My love, my land / Judy Gardiner. — Felthan : Hamlyn Paperbacks, 1980, c1970. — 223p ; 18cm
ISBN 0-600-20123-6 (pbk) : £1.25 B81-06321

Gardiner, Judy. My love, my land / Judy Gardiner. — London : Severn House, 1981, c1970. — 223p ; 21cm
Originally published: Feltham : Hamlyn, 1980
ISBN 0-7278-0657-2 : £5.95 B81-07172

Gardiner, Judy. The quick and the dead / Judy Gardiner. — London : Hamlyn Paperbacks, 1981. — 144p ; 18cm
ISBN 0-600-20225-9 (pbk) : £1.00 B81-19901

Gardiner, Judy. The quick and the dead / Judy Gardiner. — London : Severn House, 1981. — 144p ; 21cm
ISBN 0-7278-0710-2 : £5.50 : CIP rev. B81-12910

Gardner, John. Licence renewed. — London : Hodder & Stoughton, Feb.1982. — [272]p
ISBN 0-340-26873-5 (pbk) : £1.75 : CIP entry B81-36351

Gardner, John, *1919-*. The garden of weapons. — London : Hodder & Stoughton, Oct.1981. — [400]p. — (Coronet books)
Originally published: 1980
ISBN 0-340-27107-8 (pbk) : £1.75 : CIP entry B81-26726

Gardner, John, *1926-*. The airline pirates / by John Gardner. — London : Star, 1981, c1970. — 192p ; 18cm
Originally published: London : Hodder and Stoughton, 1970
ISBN 0-352-30804-4 (pbk) : £1.25 B81-11670

Gardner, John, *1926-*. The garden of weapons / John Gardner. — London : Hodder and Stoughton, 1980. — 393p ; 23cm
ISBN 0-340-24820-3 : £6.95 : CIP rev. B80-13064

Gardner, John, *1926-*. A killer for a song : a Boysie Oakes entertainment / John Gardner. — London : W.H. Allen, 1981, c1975. — 191p ; 18cm. — (Star)
Originally published: London : Hodder and Stoughton, 1975
ISBN 0-352-30837-0 (pbk) : £1.25 B81-18885

Gardner, John, *1926-*. Licence renewed / John Gardner. — London : Cape, 1981. — 270p ; 21cm
ISBN 0-224-01941-4 : £6.50 : CIP rev. B81-11961

Garfield, Leon. The house of cards. — London : Bodley Head, Oct.1981. — [256]p
ISBN 0-370-30380-6 : £6.50 : CIP entry B81-25771

Garlick, Nicholas. California dreaming / by Nicholas Garlick. — London : Hale, 1981. — 188p ; 20cm. — (Hale SF)
ISBN 0-7091-9267-3 : £6.25 B81-35202

Garnar, Pauline. Against the stream / by Pauline Garnar. — London : Hale, 1981. — 208p ; 20cm
ISBN 0-7091-9080-8 : £5.60 B81-33538

Garrett, Charles C.. Blood target / Charles C. Garrett. — London : Sphere, 1981. — 152p ; 18cm. — (Gunslinger) (A Sphere adult western)
ISBN 0-7221-5035-0 (pbk) : £1.00 B81-09797

Garrick, Kate. Picture of Julie. — Large print ed. — Bath : Chivers, Oct.1981. — [256]p. — (A Seymour book)
Originally published: London : Mills & Boon, 1979
ISBN 0-85119-437-0 : £4.95 : CIP entry B81-25803

Gash, Jonathan. Gold from Gemini / Jonathan Gash. — Large print ed. — London : Ulverscroft, 1981, c1978. — 339p ; 23cm. — (Ulverscroft large print)
Originally published: London : Collins, 1978
ISBN 0-7089-0575-7 : £5.00 B81-11387

Gash, Jonathan. The grail tree / Jonathan Gash. — Feltham : Hamlyn, 1981, c1979. — 190p ; 18cm. — (A Hamlyn whodunnit)
Originally published: London : Collins, 1979
ISBN 0-600-20241-0 (pbk) : £1.00 B81-40995

Gash, Jonathan. Spend game / Jonathan Gash. — Large print ed. — Leicester : Ulverscroft, 1981, c1980. — 359p ; 23cm. — (Ulverscroft large print series)
Originally published: London : Collins, 1980
ISBN 0-7089-0673-7 : £5.00 : CIP rev. B81-25686

Gash, Jonathan. The Vatican rip : a Lovejoy narrative / Jonathan Gash. — London : Collins, 1981. — 221p ; 21cm. — (The Crime Club)
ISBN 0-00-231868-7 : £6.50 : CIP rev. B81-15891

Gaskin, Catherine. Blake's Reach / Catherine Gaskin. — [London] : Fontana, 1961, c1958 (1981 [printing]). — 318p ; 18cm
Originally published: London : Collins, 1958
ISBN 0-00-616375-0 (pbk) : £1.50 B81-36775

Gaskin, Catherine. Blake's Reach. — Large print ed. — Anstey : Ulverscroft, Feb.1982. — [508] p. — (Charnwood library series)
ISBN 0-7089-8026-0 : £5.25 : CIP entry B81-36958

Gaskin, Catherine. Corporation wife / Catherine Gaskin. — [London] : Fontana, 1963, c1960 (1981 [printing]). — 320p ; 18cm
Originally published: London : Collins, 1960
ISBN 0-00-616280-0 (pbk) : £1.50 B81-22010

Gaskin, Catherine. Daughter of the house / Catherine Gaskin. — [Glasgow] : Fontana, 1971, c1952 (1980 [printing]). — 223p ; 18cm
Originally published: London : Collins, 1952
ISBN 0-00-616134-0 (pbk) : £1.00 B81-02839

Gaskin, Catherine. Edge of glass / Catherine Gaskin. — [London] : Fontana, 1969, c1967 (1981 [printing]). — 252p ; 18cm
Originally published: London : Collins, 1967
ISBN 0-00-616279-7 (pbk) : £1.25 B81-22009

Gaskin, Catherine. A falcon for a queen / Catherine Gaskin. — [London] : Collins : Fontana, 1974, c1972 (1980 [printing]). — 317p ; 18cm
Originally published: London : Collins, 1972
ISBN 0-00-616133-2 (pbk) : £1.25 B81-03372

Gaskin, Catherine. Family affairs / Catherine Gaskin. — London : Collins, 1980. — 475p ; 24cm
ISBN 0-00-222232-9 : £6.95 B81-05241

Gaskin, Catherine. Family affairs / Catherine Gaskin. — [London] : Fontana, 1981, c1980. — 511p ; 18cm
Originally published: Glasgow : Collins, 1980
ISBN 0-00-616462-5 (pbk) : £1.95 B81-36831

Gaskin, Catherine. The file on Devlin / Catherine Gaskin. — [London] : Fontana, 1967, c1965 (1981 [printing]). — 256p ; 18cm
Originally published: London : Collins, 1965
ISBN 0-00-616374-2 (pbk) : £1.35 B81-36777

Gaskin, Catherine. Fiona / Catherine Gaskin. — [London] : Collins, 1972, c1970 (1980 [printing]). — 285p ; 18cm
Originally published: London : Collins, 1970
ISBN 0-00-615305-4 (pbk) : £1.25 B81-03422

Gaskin, Catherine. Fiona / Catherine Gaskin. — Large print ed. — Leicester : Ulverscroft, 1981, c1970. — 467p ; 23cm. — (Ulverscroft large print series)
Originally published: London : Collins, 1970
ISBN 0-7089-0565-x : Unpriced B81-14224

Gaskin, Catherine. I know my love / Catherine Gaskin. — [London] : Fontana, 1964, c1962 (1980 [printing]). — 318p ; 18cm
Originally published: London : Collins, 1962
ISBN 0-00-616242-8 (pbk) : £1.35 B81-07660

Gaskin, Catherine. The Lynmara legacy / Catherine Gaskin. — [London] : Fontana, 1976, c1975 (1981 [printing]). — 348p ; 18cm
Originally published: London : Collins, 1975
ISBN 0-00-616241-x (pbk) : £1.50 B81-06968

Gaskin, Catherine. The property of a gentleman / Catherine Gaskin. — [London] : Collins, 1976, c1974 (1980 [printing]). — 316p ; 18cm
Originally published: London : Collins, 1974
ISBN 0-00-616132-4 (pbk) : £1.25 B81-03423

Gater, Dilys. The dark star / by Dilys Gater. — London : Hale, 1981. — 190p ; 20cm
ISBN 0-7091-9073-5 : £6.50 B81-24350

Gaud, Priscilla. Dreams to sell / by Priscilla Gaud. — London : Hale, 1980. — 190p ; 20cm
ISBN 0-7091-8670-3 : £6.25 B81-01428

Gaunt, Graham. The incomer / Graham Gaunt. — London : Collins, 1981. — 208p ; 21cm. — (The Crime Club)
ISBN 0-00-231357-x : £5.95 : CIP rev. B81-00453

Gavin, Catherine. How sleep the brave. — London : Hodder & Stoughton, Jan.1982. — [304]p. — (Coronet books)
Originally published: London : Hodder & Stoughton, 1980
ISBN 0-340-27077-2 (pbk) : £1.50 : CIP entry B81-34132

Gay, Virginia. The rector / Virginia Gay. — South Yarmouth, Mass. : Curley, c1980 ; [Long Preston] : Magna [distributor]. — 480p ; 23cm
Originally published: Garden City, N.Y. : Doubleday, 1980. — Published in large print
ISBN 0-89340-305-9 : £5.75 B81-18310

Gay, Virginia. The rector / Virginia Gay. — London : Hale, 1981. — 234p ; 21cm
Originally published: Garden City, N.Y. : Doubleday, 1980
ISBN 0-7091-9134-0 : £6.50 B81-29864

Gayle, Emma. Frenchman's harvest / Emma Gayle. — London : Mills & Boon, 1980. — 191p ; 20cm. — (Masquerade)
ISBN 0-263-09680-7 : £3.85 B81-07085

Geare, Michael. Cyril Pure's diary / Michael Geare ; with a foreword by Jilly Cooper. — London : Weidenfeld and Nicolson, 1981. — vii,141p ; 23cm
ISBN 0-297-77939-7 : £6.95 B81-35649

Gee, Maggie. Dying, in other words / Maggie Gee. — Brighton : Harvester, 1981. — 214p ; 23cm
ISBN 0-7108-0030-4 : £7.50 B81-28686

Georgeson, Valerie. Angels on the move / Valerie Georgeson ; based on the BBC series. — London : New English Library, 1981. — 190p ; 18cm
ISBN 0-450-05387-3 (pbk) : £1.25 B81-40489

Germany, Jo. City of golden cages / Jo Germany. — Large print ed. — Bath : Chivers, 1981, c1978. — 250p ; 23cm. — (A Lythway historical romance)
Originally published: London : Hurst & Blackett, 1978
ISBN 0-85119-721-3 : Unpriced B81-24782

823'.914[F] — Fiction in English, *1945- — Texts continuation*

Gibbard, T. S. J.. The Torold core / by T.S.J. Gibbard. — London : Hale, 1980. — 189p ; 21cm. — (Hale SF)
ISBN 0-7091-8601-0 : £5.75 B81-01660

Gibbs, Mary Ann. Dinah / Mary Ann Gibbs. — Loughton : Piatkus, 1981, c1980. — 223p ; 21cm
ISBN 0-86188-104-4 : £6.50 : CIP rev. B81-09472

Gibbs, Mary Ann. The milliner's shop. — Loughton : Piatkus, Nov.1981. — [224]p
ISBN 0-86188-118-4 : £6.50 : CIP entry B81-30376

Gibbs, Mary Ann. The tempestuous petticoat / Mary Ann Gibbs. — [Sevenoaks] : Coronet, 1979, c1977. — 184p ; 18cm
Originally published: London : Hurst and Blackett, 1977
ISBN 0-340-24494-1 (pbk) : £0.85 : CIP rev. B79-26633

Gibbs, Mary Ann. A young lady of fashion / by Mary Ann Gibbs. — Bolton-by-Bowland : Magna, 1980, c1978. — 326p ; 23cm
Originally published: London : Hurst & Blackett, 1978. — Published in large print
ISBN 0-86009-269-0 : £5.25 : CIP rev. B80-19448

Gidley, Charles. The river running by / Charles Gidley. — London : Deutsch, 1981. — 500p ; 24cm
ISBN 0-233-97333-8 : £6.95 B81-28404

Gifford, Thomas, *1937-*. Hollywood gothic / Thomas Gifford. — London : Sphere, 1980, c1979. — 311p ; 18cm
Originally published: London : Hamilton, 1980
ISBN 0-7221-3839-3 (pbk) : £1.50 B81-17983

Gilbert, Anna. The leavetaking. — London : Coronet, Aug.1981. — [192]p
Originally published: London : Hodder & Stoughton, 1980
ISBN 0-340-26683-x : £1.25 : CIP entry B81-18033

Gilbert, Anna. The look of innocence / by Anna Gilbert. — Large print ed. — Bolton-by-Bowland : Magna Print, 1980, c1975. — 427p ; 23cm
Originally published: London : Hodder and Stoughton, 1975. — Published in large print
ISBN 0-86009-203-8 : £4.95 : CIP rev. B79-30341

Gilbert, Harry. Sarah's nest / Harry Gilbert. — London : Faber, 1981. — 138p ; 21cm
For adolescents
ISBN 0-571-11596-9 : £4.50 B81-10148

Gilbert, Jacqueline. Autumn in Bangkok / by Jacqueline Gilbert. — London : Mills & Boon, 1980. — 191p ; 19cm
ISBN 0-263-09755-2 : £3.85 B81-01429

Gilbert, Michael. Blood and judgement / Michael Gilbert. — Feltham : Hamlyn, 1980, c1959. — 189p ; 18cm. — (A Hamlyn whodunnit)
Originally published: London : Hodder & Stoughton, 1959
ISBN 0-600-20129-5 (pbk) : £1.10 B81-00454

Gilbert, Michael. The empty house / Michael Gilbert. — Harmondsworth : Penguin, 1981, c1978. — 220p ; 18cm. — (Penguin crime fiction)
Originally published: Sevenoaks : Hodder & Stoughton, 1978
ISBN 0-14-005142-2 (pbk) : £1.10 B81-15389

Gilbert, Michael. The empty house. — Large print ed. — Anstey : Ulverscroft, Nov.1981. — [400]p. — (Ulverscroft large print series)
Originally published: London : Hodder and Stoughton, 1978
ISBN 0-7089-0702-4 : £5.00 : CIP entry B81-30478

Gill, B. M. (Barbara M.). Victims / B.M. Gill. — London : Hodder and Stoughton, c1981. — 199p ; 23cm
ISBN 0-340-25353-3 : £6.50 B81-22412

Gill, Bartholomew. McGarr at the Dublin Horse Show / Bartholomew Gill. — London : Hale, 1981, c1979. — 192p ; 20cm
Originally published: New York : Scribner, c1979
ISBN 0-7091-9006-9 : £5.95 B81-24981

Gillen, Lucy. The storm eagle / by Lucy Gillen. — London : Mills & Boon, 1980. — 190p ; 20cm
ISBN 0-263-09764-1 : £3.85 B81-01430

Gilligan, Patrick. The Spike / Patrick Gilligan. — Dublin : Published in collaboration with Radio Telefís Éireann by Mercier, 1978. — 128p : ill ; 19cm
ISBN 0-85342-533-7 (pbk) : £1.80 B81-05923

Gillott, Jacky. The head case / Jacky Gillott. — London : Granada, 1980, c1979. — 366p ; 18cm. — (A Panther book)
Originally published: London : Hodder and Stoughton, 1979
ISBN 0-586-05088-4 (pbk) : £1.50 B81-00455

Gillott, Jacky. Salvage / Jacky Gillott. — London : Granada, 1981, c1968. — 270p ; 18cm. — (A Panther book)
Originally published: London : Gollancz, 1968
ISBN 0-586-05289-5 (pbk) : £1.50 B81-34904

Gillott, Jacky. War baby / Jacky Gillott. — London : Granada, 1981, c1971. — 318p ; 18cm. — (A Panther book)
Originally published: London : Gollancz, 1971
ISBN 0-586-05290-9 (pbk) : £1.50 B81-28906

Gilman, George G.. Black as death / George G. Gilman. — London : New English Library, 1981. — 159p ; 18cm. — (The Undertaker ; 1)
ISBN 0-450-05157-9 (pbk) : £1.00 B81-28481

Gilman, George G.. Destined to die / George G. Gilman. — London : New English Library, 1981. — 158p ; 18cm. — (The Undertaker ; 2)
ISBN 0-450-05195-1 (pbk) : £1.00 B81-28483

Gilman, George G.. Edge 40: Montana melodrama. — London : New English Library, Feb.1982. — [160]p
ISBN 0-450-05364-4 (pbk) : £1.25 : CIP entry B81-36202

Gilman, George G.. Funeral by the sea / George G. Gilman. — London : New English Library, 1981. — 160p ; 19cm. — (The Undertaker ; 3)
ISBN 0-450-05269-9 (pbk) : £1.00 B81-40491

Gilman, George G.. Steele's war : the storekeeper / George G. Gilman. — London : New English Library, 1981. — 155p ; 18cm. — (Adam Steele ; no.27)
ISBN 0-450-05095-5 (pbk) : £1.00 B81-14313

Gilman, George G.. Steele's war : the stranger / George G. Gilman. — London : New English Library, 1981. — 157p ; 19cm. — (Adam Steele ; no.28)
ISBN 0-450-05250-8 (pbk) : £1.00 B81-35631

Gilman, George G.. Town on trial / George G. Gilman. — London : New English Library, 1981. — 156p ; 18cm. — (Edge ; 36)
ISBN 0-450-04671-0 (pbk) : £1.00 B81-11159

Gilman, George G.. Vengeance at Ventura / George G. Gilman. — London : New English Library/Times Mirror, 1981. — 144p ; 18cm. — (The Edge series ; no.37)
ISBN 0-450-05093-9 (pbk) : £1.00 B81-19976

Gilman, Hilary. Gamble with hearts / Hilary Gilman. — London : Hale, 1980. — 160p ; 21cm
ISBN 0-7091-8554-5 : £5.95 B81-02158

Glanville, Brian. Never look back / Brian Glanville. — London : Joseph, 1980. — 239p ; 23cm
ISBN 0-7181-1953-3 : £5.95 B81-00456

Gloag, Julian. Sleeping dogs lie / Julian Gloag. — London : Secker & Warburg, 1980. — 314p ; 22cm
Originally published: New York : Dutton, 1980
ISBN 0-436-18203-3 : £6.95 B81-02457

Golding, William. Rites of passage / William Golding. — London : Faber, 1980. — 278p ; 23cm
ISBN 0-571-11639-6 : £5.95 : CIP rev. B80-26143

Goodwin, Suzanne. Emerald / Suzanne Goodwin. — London : Severn House, 1980. — 159p ; 21cm
ISBN 0-7278-0637-8 : £5.50 : CIP rev. B80-28746

Goodwin, Suzanne. The winter spring / Suzanne Goodwin. — London : Magnum, 1980, c1978. — 268p ; 18cm
Originally published: London : Bodley Head, 1978
ISBN 0-417-04650-2 (pbk) : £1.40 B81-01431

Goodwin, Suzanne. The winter spring. — Large print ed. — Anstey : Ulverscroft, Jan.1982. — [547]p. — (Ulverscroft large print series : historical romance)
ISBN 0-7089-0736-9 : £5.00 : CIP entry B81-33961

Gordon, Katharine. Peacock in flight / Katharine Gaskin. — Large print ed. — Leicester : Ulverscroft, 1981, c1979. — 309p ; 22cm. — (Ulverscroft large print series)
Originally published: New York : Morrow ; London : Hodder and Stoughton, 1979
ISBN 0-7089-0567-6 : £5.00 B81-12175

Gordon, Katherine. The peacock ring / Katherine Gordon. — London : Hodder and Stoughton, 1981. — 320p ; 23cm
ISBN 0-340-23007-x : £6.95 B81-11269

Gordon, Richard, *1921-*. Doctors' daughters / Richard Gordon. — London : Heinemann, 1981. — 137p ; 21cm
ISBN 0-434-30258-9 : £5.95 B81-35599

Gordon, Richard, *1921-*. The private life of Dr Crippen : a novel / Richard Gordon. — London : Heinemann, 1981. — 184p ; 23cm
ISBN 0-434-30257-0 : £6.95 B81-32000

Gordon, Victoria. Always the boss / by Victoria Gordon. — London : Mills & Boon, 1981. — 188p ; 19cm
ISBN 0-263-09882-6 : £4.55 B81-26422

Gordon, Victoria. Dream house / by Victoria Gordon. — London : Mills & Boon, 1981. — 188p ; 20cm
ISBN 0-263-09925-3 : £4.55 B81-35640

Gordon, Victoria. The everywhere man / by Victoria Gordon. — London : Mills & Boon, 1981. — 189p ; 20cm
ISBN 0-263-09846-x : £4.55 B81-14182

Gordon, Victoria. The sugar dragon / by Victoria Gordon. — London : Mills & Boon, 1980. — 188p ; 19cm
ISBN 0-263-09794-3 : £3.85 B81-07198

Gordon, Victoria. Wolf at the door / by Victoria Gordon. — London : Mills & Boon, 1981. — 188p ; 20cm
ISBN 0-263-09816-8 : £4.55 B81-09398

Gordon, Yvonne. Love reborn / by Yvonne Gordon. — London : Hale, 1981. — 174p ; 20cm
ISBN 0-7091-8698-3 : £5.60 B81-17312

823′.914[F] — Fiction in English, *1945-* — *Texts continuation*

Gordon, Yvonne. Too many kisses / by Yvonne Gordon. — London : Hale, 1981. — 159p ; 20cm
ISBN 0-7091-9161-8 : £5.75 B81-35295

Gordon, Yvonne. Try to forget him / by Yvonne Gordon. — London : Hale, 1980. — 155p ; 20cm
ISBN 0-7091-8428-x : £5.25 B81-02474

Gosling, Paula. The zero trap. — Large print ed. — Anstey : Ulverscroft, Dec.1981. — [432]p. — (Ulverscroft large print series)
Originally published: London : Macmillan, 1979
ISBN 0-7089-0724-5 : £5.00 : CIP entry B81-32605

Gouriet, John. Checkmate Mr President. — Glasgow : Maclellan, Sept.1981. — [228]p
ISBN 0-85335-250-x : £7.95 : CIP entry B81-25116

Gower, Iris. Beloved captive / Iris Gower. — London : Macdonald Futura, 1981. — 251p ; 21cm
ISBN 0-354-04621-7 : £4.95 B81-12070

Gower, Iris. Beloved captive / Iris Gower. — London : Macdonald Futura, 1981. — 251p ; 18cm. — (A Minstrel book ; 2)
ISBN 0-7088-2010-7 (pbk) : £0.95 B81-15462

Gower, Iris. Beloved traitor / Iris Gower. — London : Macdonald, 1981. — 252p ; 21cm
ISBN 0-354-04667-5 : £4.95 B81-37909

Gower, Iris. Beloved traitor / Iris Gower. — London : Macdonald Futura, 1981. — 252p ; 18cm. — (A Minstrel book ; 15)
ISBN 0-7088-2073-5 (pbk) : £0.95 B81-32780

Graham, David, *1919-*. Down to a sunless sea / David Graham. — London : Pan, 1980, c1979 (1981 printing). — 316p ; 18cm
Originally published: London : Hale, 1979
ISBN 0-330-26184-3 (pbk) : £1.50 B81-06267

Graham, Elizabeth. Devil on horseback. — Large print ed. — Bath : Chivers, Nov.1981. — [264] p. — (A Seymour book)
ISBN 0-85119-440-0 : £5.25 : CIP entry B81-31254

Graham, Elizabeth. King of Copper Canyon / by Elizabeth Graham. — London : Mills & Boon, 1980. — 187p ; 19cm
ISBN 0-263-09743-9 : £3.85 B81-00459

Graham, Elizabeth. Madrona Island / by Elizabeth Graham. — London : Mills & Boon, 1981. — 186p ; 20cm
ISBN 0-263-09848-6 : £4.55 B81-14183

Graham, Helen Scott. Rings and roundelays / Helen Scott Graham. — London : Hale, 1980. — 191p ; 21cm
ISBN 0-7091-8337-2 : £5.95 B81-01432

Graham, Winston. The Japanese girl. — Large print ed. — Bath : Chivers, Dec.1981. — [200] p. — (A New Portway large print book)
Originally published: London : Collins, 1971
ISBN 0-85119-147-9 : £4.95 : CIP entry B81-31838

Granger, Bill. Public murders. — London : New English Library, Feb.1982. — [272]p
Originally published: New York : Jove, 1980 ; London : N.E.L., 1980
ISBN 0-450-05370-9 (pbk) : £1.75 : CIP entry B81-36200

Grant, David, *1942-*. Emerald decision / David Grant. — London : Fontana, c1981, c1980. — 384p ; 18cm
Originally published: London : Joseph, 1980
ISBN 0-00-615988-5 (pbk) : £1.50 B81-28210

Grant, James, *1933-*. Don′t shoot the pianist / by James Grant. — Loughton ([17 Brook Rd.], Loughton, Essex, IG10 1BW) : Piatkus, 1980. — 204p ; 21cm
ISBN 0-86188-040-4 : £5.50 : CIP rev. B80-12071

Grant, James, *1933-*. Victims / James Grant. — Large print ed. — Bath : Chivers, 1981, c1980. — 269p ; 23cm. — (A Lythway thriller)
Originally published: Loughton : Piatkus, 1980
ISBN 0-85119-714-0 : £5.90 : CIP rev. B81-04232

Granville, Lynn. The witch child / Lynn Granville. — London : Hale, 1980. — 174p ; 21cm
ISBN 0-7091-8463-8 : £5.95 B81-00461

Gratus, Jack. The redneck rebel / Jack Gratus. — London : Corgi, 1980. — 284p ; 18cm
ISBN 0-552-11535-5 (pbk) : £1.50 B81-00460

Gray, Alasdair. Lanark : a life in four books / by Alasdair Gray. — Edinburgh : Canongate, 1981. — 560p : ill ; 25cm
ISBN 0-903937-74-3 : £7.95 B81-24547

Gray, Edwyn. Crash dive 500 / Edwyn Gray. — London : Macdonald Futura, 1981. — 220p : 1map ; 18cm. — (A Futura book)
ISBN 0-7088-1943-5 (pbk) : £1.25 B81-15636

Gray, Edwyn. Diving stations / Edwyn Gray. — London : Macdonald Futura, 1980. — 222p ; 18cm
ISBN 0-7088-1947-8 (pbk) : £1.25 B81-00462

Gray, Juliet. Bride for a Benedict / by Juliet Gray. — London : Hale, 1981. — 192p ; 20cm
ISBN 0-7091-8540-5 : £5.50 B81-08726

Gray, Juliet. Enter a lover / by Juliet Gray. — London : Hale, 1980. — 191p ; 20cm
ISBN 0-7091-8180-9 : £5.25 B81-00463

Gray, Juliet. This side of heaven / by Juliet Gray. — London : Hale, 1981. — 160p ; 19cm
ISBN 0-7091-9318-1 : £5.75 B81-40461

Grayson, Laura. A bouquet of irony / by Laura Grayson. — London : Hale, 1981. — 207p ; 20cm
ISBN 0-7091-9113-8 : £6.50 B81-24863

Grayson, Laura. Dimity / by Laura Grayson. — London : Hale, 1980. — 192p ; 20cm
ISBN 0-7091-8536-7 : £6.25 B81-00464

Grayson, Richard. The death of Abbé Didier : a novel / by Richard Grayson. — London : Gollancz, 1981. — 175p ; 21cm
ISBN 0-575-02935-8 : £5.95 B81-02914

Greaves, Jimmy. The ball game. — London : Hodder & Stoughton, Nov.1981. — [160]p. — (Coronet books)
Originally published: London : Barker, 1980
ISBN 0-340-26663-5 (pbk) : £1.25 : CIP entry B81-30547

Greaves, Jimmy. The boss. — London : Arthur Barker, c1981. — 154p ; 23cm
ISBN 0-213-16784-0 : £5.95 B81-11011

Green, Marjorie. Flowers for Kathie / by Marjorie Green. — London : Hale, 1980. — 160p ; 20cm
ISBN 0-7091-8465-4 : £5.25 B81-02153

Greenhough, Terry. The alien contract / Terry Greenhough. — London : Hale, 1980. — 159p ; 21cm. — (Hale SF)
ISBN 0-7091-8517-0 : £5.75 B81-00465

Greenwald, Harry J.. Chinaman′s chance / by Harry J. Greenwald. — London : Hale, 1981. — 192p ; 20cm. — (Hale SF)
ISBN 0-7091-9186-3 : £6.25 B81-27303

Grey, Belinda. Daughter of Isis / Belinda Grey. — London : Mills & Boon, 1981. — 189p ; 19cm. — (Masquerade)
ISBN 0-263-09784-6 : £4.55 B81-18347

Grey, Belinda. Glen of frost / Belinda Grey. — London : Mills & Boon, 1981. — 190p ; 20cm. — (Masquerade)
ISBN 0-263-09781-1 : £4.55 B81-10976

Grey, Belinda. Sweet wind of morning / Belinda Grey. — London : Mills & Boon, 1980, c1979. — 188p ; 20cm. — (Masquerade)
Originally published: Chatswood, N.S.W. : Mills and Boon, 1979
ISBN 0-263-09681-5 : £3.85 B81-08010

Grey, Charlotte. Summer in Hanover Square / by Charlotte Grey. — London : Hale, 1981. — 186p ; 20cm
ISBN 0-7091-8970-2 : £6.50 B81-19296

Grey, Francesca. Fire at the heart / by Francesca Grey. — London : Hale, 1980. — 189p ; 20cm
ISBN 0-7091-8048-9 : £4.75 B81-00466

Gribble, Leonard. Dead end in Mayfair / by Leonard Gribble. — London : Hale, 1981. — 208p ; 20cm
ISBN 0-7091-9230-4 : £6.25 B81-37312

Griffin, John, *1934-*. A flame from Persepolis / by John Griffin. — London : Hale, 1981. — 224p ; 20cm. — (Richard Raven series)
ISBN 0-7091-9012-3 : £5.95 B81-17335

Grove, Peter J.. The Levellers / by Peter J. Grove. — London : Hale, 1981. — 189p ; 20cm. — (Hale SF)
ISBN 0-7091-9156-1 : £6.25 B81-33539

Guest, Lynn. Children of Hachiman / Lynn Guest. — London : Corgi, 1981, c1980. — 309p : 1map ; 18cm
Originally published: London : Bodley Head, 1980
ISBN 0-552-11683-1 (pbk) : £1.50 B81-32110

Gulliver, Nicol. Roses in the night / Nicol Gulliver. — Bognor Regis : New Horizon, c1979. — 101p ; 21cm
ISBN 0-86116-149-1 : £4.25 B81-18872

Gulliver, Nicol. Tomorrow lasts forever / Nicol Gulliver. — Bognor Regis : New Horizon, c1981. — 88p ; 21cm
ISBN 0-86116-465-2 : £3.50 B81-19247

Gunn, Alec. The silver Mercedes / Alec Gunn. — Bognor Regis : New Horizon, 1981. — 225p ; 21cm
ISBN 0-86116-681-7 : £5.75 B81-27587

Guy, Elizabeth. There′s no one here but me / Elizabeth Guy. — Ilfracombe : Stockwell, 1981. — 77p ; 19cm
ISBN 0-7223-1448-5 (pbk) : £2.00 B81-18413

Hagar, Judith. Don′t run from love / by Judith Hagar. — London : Hale, 1981. — 160p ; 20cm
ISBN 0-7091-8645-2 : £5.50 B81-13127

Hagenbach, Keith. The fox potential / Keith Hagenbach. — London : Star, 1981, c1980. — 303p ; 18cm
Originally published: London : W.H. Allen, 1980
ISBN 0-352-30760-9 (pbk) : £1.50 B81-11668

Hagenbach, Keith. The rat quotient / Keith Hagenbach. — London : W.H. Allen, 1981. — 280p ; 23cm
ISBN 0-491-02834-2 : £7.95 B81-19980

Haggard, William. The mischief-makers. — London : Hodder & Stoughton, Feb.1982. — [192]p
ISBN 0-340-27718-1 : £6.50 : CIP entry B81-36367

823'.914[F] — Fiction in English, ***1945-*** **— Texts** *continuation*

Haggard, William. The money men / William Haggard. — London : Hodder and Stoughton, 1981. — 175p ; 23cm
ISBN 0-340-25881-0 : £5.95 B81-03312

Haines, Pamela. The kissing gate / Pamela Haines. — London : Collins, 1981. — 572p ; 24cm
ISBN 0-00-222356-2 : £7.95 B81-12192

Hainsworth, Annette. The jewelled crown / Annette Hainsworth. — London : Hale, 1981. — 191p ; 21cm
ISBN 0-7091-8695-9 : £6.25 B81-08732

Hainsworth, Annette. Tomorrow's child / Annette Hainsworth. — London : Hale, 1981. — 185p : ill ; 21cm
ISBN 0-7091-9121-9 : £6.50 B81-27304

Hall, Adam. The Pekin target. — London : Collins, Oct.1981. — [320]p
ISBN 0-00-222606-5 : £7.50 : CIP entry B81-25867

Hall, Adam. The scorpion signal / Adam Hall. — [Glasgow] : Fontana, 1981, c1979. — 238p ; 18cm
Originally published: London : Collins, 1979
ISBN 0-00-615995-8 (pbk) : £1.25 B81-11062

Hall, Shirley. The comfortable cage / Shirley Hall. — Bognor Regis : New Horizon, c1979. — 137p ; 21cm
ISBN 0-86116-092-4 (corrected) : £3.50 B81-23610

Hall, Unity. Secrets / Unity Hall. — London : Pan, 1981. — 318p ; 18cm
ISBN 0-330-26339-0 (pbk) : £1.50 B81-20204

Hallums, James. Bodysnatch / James Hallums. — London : Macdonald Futura, 1980. — 253p ; 18cm
ISBN 0-7088-1949-4 (pbk) : £1.25 B81-02067

Hallums, James. Coup d'etat / James Hallums. — London : Eyre Methuen, 1981. — 188p ; 19cm
ISBN 0-417-06430-6 (pbk) : £1.50 B81-32177

Hamilton, Alistair. Holding pattern / Alistair Hamilton. — Feltham : Hamlyn Paperbacks, 1981. — 251p ; 18cm
ISBN 0-600-34622-6 (pbk) : £1.35 B81-12083

Hamilton, Claire. All for the love of you / by Claire Hamilton. — London : Hale, 1981. — 160p ; 20cm
ISBN 0-7091-8715-7 : £5.50 B81-11103

Hamilton, Claire. A summer for strangers / by Claire Hamilton. — London : Hale, c1980. — 160p ; 20cm
ISBN 0-7091-8009-8 : £4.95 B81-01433

Hamilton, Jessica. Childgrave / Jessica Hamilton. — London : Sphere, 1981. — vii,278p ; 18cm
ISBN 0-7221-4212-9 (pbk) : £1.50 B81-37283

Hamilton, Tamsin. Paris in the fall / Tamsin Hamilton. — London : Granada, 1981. — 351p ; 23cm
ISBN 0-246-11390-1 : £7.95 B81-15360

Hamley, Dennis. Landings / Dennis Hamley. — London : Granada, 1981, c1979. — 190p ; 18cm. — (A Dragon book)
Originally published: London : Deutsch, 1979
ISBN 0-583-30422-2 (pbk) : £0.75 B81-09737

Hammond, Gerald. The reward game. — Large print ed. — Anstey : Ulverscroft, Dec.1981. — 1v.
Originally published: London : Macmillan, 1980
ISBN 0-7089-0717-2 : £5.00 : CIP entry B81-30408

Hammond, Gerald, *1926-*. Dead game / Gerald Hammond. — Large print ed. — Leicester : Ulverscroft, 1980, c1979. — 388p ; 23cm. — (Ulverscroft large print series)
Originally published: London : Macmillan, 1979
ISBN 0-7089-0547-1 : £4.25 : CIP rev. B80-35446

Hammond, Gerald, *1926-*. The revenge game / Gerald Hammond. — London : Macmillan, 1981. — 191p : 1map ; 21cm
ISBN 0-333-31058-6 : £2.50 B81-18566

Hammond, Marc. Fathom / Marc Hammond. — London : Severn House, 1980, c1978. — 345p ; 21cm
Originally published: London : Futura, 1978
ISBN 0-7278-0675-0 : £6.95 : CIP rev. B80-22525

Hammond, Marc. Killer mountain. — London : Severn House, Aug.1981. — [320]p
Originally published: London : Futura, 1980
ISBN 0-7278-0714-5 : £6.95 : CIP entry B81-17506

Hammond, Marc. The Theseus Code / Marc Hammond. — London : Severn House, 1981, c1979. — 318p ; 21cm
Originally published: London : Futura, 1978
ISBN 0-7278-0682-3 : £6.95 B81-11279

Hampson, Anne. Reap the whirlwind. — Large print ed. — Long Preston : Magna, July 1981. — [320]p
ISBN 0-86009-360-3 : £4.95 : CIP entry B81-14435

Hampton, Mia. Girl without a shadow / by Mia Hampton. — London : Hale, 1981. — 191p ; 20cm
ISBN 0-7091-8892-7 : £5.60 B81-17318

Handley, Alfred. The scorpion trap / by Alfred Handley. — London : Hale, 1980. — 192p ; 20cm
ISBN 0-7091-8607-x : £5.75 B81-02701

Hankin, Elizabeth R.. Farewell to the enemy / by Elizabeth R. Hankin. — London : Hale, 1981. — 192p ; 20cm
ISBN 0-7091-8838-2 : £6.25 B81-11109

Hankin, Elizabeth R.. The phantom hills / by Elizabeth R. Hankin. — London : Hale, 1981. — 192p ; 20cm
ISBN 0-7091-9263-0 : £6.75 B81-35193

Hann, Elizabeth. Love's traders / Elizabeth Hann. — London : Macdonald Futura, 1981. — 256p ; 18cm. — (A Minstrel book ; 8)
ISBN 0-7088-2007-7 (pbk) : £0.95 B81-15468

Hann, Elizabeth. Walburga's eve / Elizabeth Hann. — Feltham : Hamlyn Paperbacks, 1981. — 256p ; 18cm
ISBN 0-600-20067-1 (pbk) : £1.35 B81-12086

Hansel, Josephine. Daughter of Eve / by Josephine Hansel. — London : Hale, 1981. — 160p ; 20cm
ISBN 0-7091-8788-2 : £5.50 B81-15302

Hanson, Vic J.. Amos Crowle, widow-maker / by Vic J. Hanson. — London : Hale, 1981. — 160p ; 20cm
ISBN 0-7091-9195-2 : £4.95 B81-37452

Hanson, Vic J.. The end of the kill / by Vic J. Hanson. — London : Hale, 1980. — 155p ; 20cm
ISBN 0-7091-8545-6 : £5.75 B81-07170

Hanson, Vic J.. Guns of Black Heart / Vic J. Hanson. — London : Hale, 1980. — 157p ; 20cm
ISBN 0-7091-8206-6 : £4.50 B81-00467

Hanson, Vic J.. The hands of Amos Crowle / by Vic J. Hanson. — London : Hale, 1981. — 159p 20cm
ISBN 0-7091-8701-7 : £4.95 B81-11072

Hanson, Vic J.. Men on a dusty street / by Vic J. Hanson. — London : Hale, 1981. — 158p ; 20cm
ISBN 0-7091-8948-6 : £4.95 B81-21307

Harbinson, W. A.. Deadlines / W.A. Harbinson. — London : New English Library, 1981. — 221p ; 18cm
ISBN 0-450-05126-9 (pbk) : £1.25 B81-11163

Harbinson, W. A.. Genesis / W.A. Harbinson. — London : Corgi, 1980. — 612p ; 18cm
Bibliography: p609-612
ISBN 0-552-11533-9 (pbk) : £1.75 B81-02055

Harbinson, W. A.. Genesis / W.A. Harbinson. — Loughton : Piatkus, 1981, c1980. — 611p ; 21cm
Originally published: London : Corgi, 1980
ISBN 0-86188-086-2 : £7.95 B81-12950

Harcourt, Palma. Climate for conspiracy. — Large print ed. — Anstey : Ulverscroft, Nov.1981. — [352]p. — (Ulverscroft large print series)
Originally published: London : Collins, 1974
ISBN 0-7089-0703-2 : £5.00 : CIP entry B81-30479

Harcourt, Palma. A fair exchange / Palma Harcourt. — Large print ed. — Leicester : Ulverscroft, 1980, c1975. — 378p ; 23cm. — (Ulverscroft large print series)
Originally published: London : Collins, 1975
ISBN 0-7089-0492-0 : £4.25 : CIP rev. B80-10794

Harcourt, Palma. Tomorrow's treason / Palma Harcourt. — Large print ed. — Leicester : Ulverscroft, 1981, c1980. — 343p ; 23cm. — (Ulverscroft large print series)
Originally published: London : Collins, 1980
ISBN 0-7089-0619-2 : £5.00 : CIP rev. B81-07435

Harcourt, Palma. A turn of traitors / Palma Harcourt. — London : Collins, 1981. — 204p ; 22cm
ISBN 0-00-222398-8 : £6.50 B81-02440

Harcourt, Palma. The twisted tree / Palma Harcourt. — London : Collins, 1982. — 238p ; 22cm
ISBN 0-00-222139-x : £7.50 : CIP rev. B81-33967

Hardwick, Michael. The Chinese detective : a novel / by Michael Hardwick ; from the TV serial created by Ian Kennedy Martin. — London : British Broadcasting Corporation, 1981. — 189p ; 22cm
ISBN 0-563-17939-2 (cased) : £6.25
ISBN 0-563-17941-4 (pbk) : £1.50 B81-17442

Hardwick, Michael. Endings and beginnings / Michael Hardwick. — London : Prior, 1980, c1965. — 289p ; 25cm. — (Upstairs, downstairs series ; 6)
Originally published: London : Sphere, 1975. — Published in large print
ISBN 0-86043-498-2 : £4.95 B81-12198

Hardwick, Michael. On with the dance / Michael Hardwick. — London : Prior, 1980, c1975. — 281p ; 25cm. — (Upstairs, downstairs series ; 5)
Originally published: London : Sphere, 1975. — Published in large print
ISBN 0-86043-499-0 : £4.95 B81-12199

Hardwick, Michael. Regency rake / Michael Hardwick. — London : Sphere, 1981, c1979. — 249p ; 18cm
Originally published: London : Joseph, 1979
ISBN 0-7221-4228-5 (pbk) : £1.35 B81-28749

823′.914[F] — Fiction in English, *1945- — Texts continuation*

Hardwick, Michael. Regency revenge / Michael Hardwick. — London : Joseph, c1980. — 222p ; 23cm
ISBN 0-7181-1948-7 : £6.50 B81-00468

Hardwick, Mollie. The Atkinson century / Mollie Hardwick. — London : Severn House, 1980. — 313p ; 21cm. — (The Atkinson heritage ; v.3)
ISBN 0-7278-0640-8 : £5.95 : CIP rev. B80-08409

Hardwick, Mollie. The Atkinson heritage / Mollie Hardwick. — Large print ed. — Leicester : Ulverscroft, 1981, c1978. — 454p ; 23cm. — (Ulverscroft large print series)
Originally published: New York : Bantam Books ; London : Troubadour, 1978
ISBN 0-7089-0670-2 : £5.00 : CIP rev. B81-20633

Hardwick, Mollie. Calling Juliet Bravo : new arrivals / by Mollie Hardwick ; from the TV series created by Ian Kennedy Martin. — London : British Broadcasting Corporation, 1981. — 174p ; 23cm
ISBN 0-563-17956-2 : £6.75 B81-39427

Hardwick, Mollie. Juliet Bravo / Mollie Hardwick. — London : Severn House
1. — 1981, c1980. — 143p ; 21cm
Originally published: London : Pan, 1980
ISBN 0-7278-0669-6 : £5.95 B81-11278

Hardwick, Mollie. Juliet Bravo / Mollie Hardwick. — London : Severn House
2. — 1981, c1980. — 126p ; 20cm
Originally published: London : Pan, 1980
ISBN 0-7278-0728-5 : £5.95 : CIP rev. B81-23818

Hardwick, Mollie. Lovers meeting / Mollie Hardwick. — Large print ed. — Leicester : Ulverscroft, 1981, c1979. — 497p ; 22cm. — (Ulverscroft large print series)
Originally published: New York : St. Martin′s Press ; Eyre Methuen, 1979
ISBN 0-7089-0581-1 : £5.00 B81-12174

Hardwick, Mollie. The war to end wars / Mollie Hardwick. — London : Prior, 1980, c1974. — 423p ; 24cm. — (Upstairs downstairs series ; 4)
Originally published: London : Sphere, 1975. — Published in large print
ISBN 0-86043-497-4 (corrected) : £6.95 B81-15142

Hardwick, Mollie. The years of change / Mollie Hardwick. — London : Prior, 1980, c1974. — 491p ; 24cm. — (Upstairs, downstairs series ; 3)
Originally published: London : Sphere, 1974. — Published in large print
ISBN 0-86043-496-6 : £6.95 B81-11982

Hardy, Alex. Patch of hell / by Alex Hardy. — London : Hale, 1981. — 207p ; 20cm
ISBN 0-7091-9262-2 : £6.75 B81-40542

Hardy, Robin. The education of Don Juan / Robin Hardy. — London : W.H. Allen, 1981, c1980. — 482p ; 18cm. — (Star)
Originally published: New York : Wyndham Books, 1979 ; London : Macmillan, 1980
ISBN 0-352-30829-x (corrected : pbk) : £1.95 B81-24963

Hardy, Robin. The Wicker Man / Robin Hardy and Anthony Shaffer. — Feltham : Hamlyn Paperbacks, 1980, c1978. — 213p ; 18cm
Originally published: New York : Crown, 1978 ; Feltham : Hamlyn, 1979
ISBN 0-600-39477-8 (pbk) : £1.25 B81-02145

Hardy, Ronald. Rivers of darkness / Ronald Hardy. — London : Corgi, 1981, c1979. — 509p ; 18cm
Originally published: New York : Putnam ; London : Hamilton, 1979
ISBN 0-552-11609-2 (pbk) : £1.75 B81-15386

Harness, Charles L.. The rose / Charles L. Harness. — London : Granada, 1969, c1968 (1981 [printing]). — 158p ; 18cm. — (A Panther book) (Granada science fiction)
Originally published: London : Sidgwick and Jackson, 1968
ISBN 0-586-02879-x (pbk) : £1.25 B81-13015

Harold, Edmund. Vision tomorrow / Edmund Harold. — [U.K.] : Spiritual Venturers Association ; Ilfracombe : Stockwell [distributor], 1981. — 210p ; 22cm
ISBN 0-7223-1516-3 (pbk) : £2.95 B81-35052

Harpwood, Diane. Tea and tranquillisers. — London : Virago, Oct.1981. — [168]p
ISBN 0-86068-123-8 (cased) : £5.95 : CIP entry
ISBN 0-86068-124-6 (pbk) : £2.95 B81-27471

Harrel, Linda. Arctic enemy / by Linda Harrel. — London : Mills & Boon, 1981. — 189p ; 20cm
ISBN 0-263-09914-8 : £4.55 B81-34107

Harriott, Ted. The last proud rider / Ted Harriott. — London : Secker & Warburg, 1981. — [vi],185p ; 23cm
ISBN 0-436-19111-3 : £6.95 : CIP rev. B81-20465

Harris, Catherine. Monkshill / by Catherine Harris. — London : Hale, 1981. — 190p ; 20cm
ISBN 0-7091-8737-8 : £5.50 B81-08733

Harris, Evelyn. Deadly green / by Evelyn Harris. — London : Hale, 1981. — 187p ; 20cm
ISBN 0-7091-8888-9 : £5.75 B81-14090

Harris, Evelyn. Down among the dead men / Evelyn Harris. — Large print ed. — Leicester : Ulverscroft, 1980, c1979. — 295p ; 23cm. — (Ulverscroft large print series)
Originally published: London : Hale, 1979
ISBN 0-7089-0519-6 : £4.25 : CIP rev. B80-23716

Harris, John, *1916-*. Live free or die!. — London : Hutchinson, Feb.1982. — [288]p
ISBN 0-09-147150-8 : £6.95 : CIP entry B81-38845

Harris, John, *1916-*. North strike : a novel of the Narvik campaign / John Harris. — London : Hutchinson, 1981. — 271p : 1map ; 23cm
Map on lining papers
£6.95 B81-10160

Harris, John, *1916-*. Swordpoint : a novel of Cassino / John Harris. — London : Arrow, 1981, c1980. — 284p : 1map ; 18cm
Originally published: London : Hutchinson, 1980
ISBN 0-09-925950-8 (pbk) : £1.50 B81-28586

Harris, John, *1916-*. Take or destroy! / John Harris. — London : Arrow, 1977, c1976 (1981 [printing]). — 285p ; 18cm
Originally published: London : Hutchinson, 1976
ISBN 0-09-914210-4 (pbk) : £1.50 B81-32323

Harrison, Elizabeth. A doctor called Caroline / Elizabeth Harrison. — Large print ed. — Bath : Chivers, 1981, c1979. — 251p ; 23cm. — (A Lythway romance)
Originally published: London : Hurst and Blackett, 1979
ISBN 0-85119-718-3 : £6.50 : CIP rev. B81-11974

Harrison, Elizabeth. The Ravelston affair. — Large print ed. — Anstey : Ulverscroft, Feb.1982. — [320]p. — (Ulverscroft large print series : romance)
ISBN 0-7089-0749-0 : £5.00 : CIP entry B81-36946

Harrison, Harry. In our hands, the stars / Harry Harrison. — London : Arrow, c1975, c1970 (1981 [printing]). — 217p ; 18cm
Originally published: London : Faber, 1970
ISBN 0-09-910450-4 (pbk) : £1.50 B81-37429

Harrison, M. John. A storm of wings : being the second volume of the Viriconium sequence ... / M. John Harrison. — London : Sphere, 1980. — 185p ; 18cm
ISBN 0-7221-4442-3 (pbk) : £1.35 B81-11723

Harrison, Sarah, *1946-*. Flowers of the field / Sarah Harrison. — London : Macdonald Futura, 1980 (1981 [printing]). — 666p ; 18cm. — (A Futura book)
Originally published: London : Macdonald and Jane′s, 1980
ISBN 0-7088-1812-9 (pbk) : £1.75 B81-15469

Harrod-Eagles, Cynthia. The dark rose / Cynthia Harrod-Eagles. — London : Macdonald, 1981. — 559p : 1geneal.table ; 23cm. — (Dynasty ; 2)
ISBN 0-354-04594-6 : £7.95 B81-03002

Harrod-Eagles, Cynthia. Dynasty II : the dark rose / Cynthia Harrod-Eagles. — London : Macdonald Futura, 1981. — 559p ; 18cm. — (A Troubadour spectacular)
Cover title: The dark rose
ISBN 0-7107-3006-3 (pbk) : £1.75 B81-15460

Harrod-Eagles, Cynthia. The Princeling / Cynthia Harrod-Eagles. — London : Macdonald, 1981. — 410p : 2plans,geneal.table ; 23cm. — (Dynasty ; 3)
Bibliography: p5
ISBN 0-354-04731-0 : £7.95 B81-35374

Hart, Tom. Cradle song. — London : Quartet, Feb.1982. — [128]p
ISBN 0-7043-2322-2 : £5.95 : CIP entry B81-35724

Hart, Tom. Don′t tell your mother / Tom Hart. — London : Quartet, 1979. — 187p ; 21cm
ISBN 0-7043-3372-4 (pbk) : £3.95 B81-24820

Hart-Davis, Duff. Level five. — London : Cape, Jan.1982. — [288]p
ISBN 0-224-01828-0 : £6.50 : CIP entry B81-33976

Harte, Marjorie. Doctors in conflict / Marjorie Harte. — Large print ed. — Bath : Chivers, 1981, c1963. — 275p ; 23cm. — (A Seymour book)
Originally published: London : Hale, 1963
ISBN 0-85119-405-2 : Unpriced B81-08980

Hartley, Travis. Shawnee County / by Travis Hartley. — London : Hale, 1980. — 160p ; 20cm
ISBN 0-7091-8168-x : £4.50 B81-00470

Hartmann, Michael. Leap for the sun / by Michael Hartmann. — Bolton-by-Bowland : Magna Print, 1981, c1976. — 469p ; 23cm
Originally published: London : Heinemann, 1976. — Published in large print
ISBN 0-86009-299-2 : £5.75 B81-12235

Hartmann, Michael. Shadow of the leopard. — Large print ed. — Long Preston : Magna, Nov.1981. — [480]p
ISBN 0-86009-350-6 : £4.95 : CIP entry B81-30431

Hartnup, Paula. Garfield / by Paula Hartnup. — London : Hale, 1980. — 160p ; 20cm
ISBN 0-7091-8476-x : £5.95 B81-00471

Harvey, John, *1938-*. Blind / John Harvey. — London : Eyre Methuen, 1981, c1980. — 176p ; 19cm
ISBN 0-413-48420-3 (cased) : £3.95
ISBN 0-417-05380-0 (pbk) : Unpriced B81-12044

823′.914[F] — Fiction in English, *1945-* — Texts *continuation*

Harvey, John, *1938-*. Blind / John Harvey. — London : Magnum, 1981, c1980. — 176p ; 18cm
ISBN 0-417-05380-0 (pbk) : £1.25
ISBN 0-413-48420-3 (Eyre Methuen) : £3.95
B81-08428

Harvey, John, *1938-*. Blood on the border / John B. Harvey. — London : Pan, 1981. — 127p ; 18cm. — (Hart ; 5)
ISBN 0-330-26313-7 (pbk) : £0.85 B81-18436

Harvey, John, *1938-*. Cherokee outlet / by John B. Harvey. — London : Hale, 1980. — 160p ; 20cm
ISBN 0-7091-8663-0 : £4.95 B81-00472

Harvey, John, *1938-*. Blood trail / by John B. Harvey. — London : Hale, 1981, c1980. — 160p 20cm
Originally published: London : Pan, 1980
ISBN 0-7091-8611-8 : £4.95 B81-11073

Harvey, John, *1938-*. Ride the wide country / John B. Harvey. — London : Pan, 1981. — 127p ; 18cm. — (Hart ; 6)
ISBN 0-330-26314-5 (pbk) : £0.85 B81-18437

Harvey, John, *1938-*. The silver lie / by John B. Harvey. — London : Hale, 1981, c1980. — 176p ; 20cm
Originally published: London : Pan, 1980
ISBN 0-7091-8756-4 : £4.95 B81-37313

Harvey, John, *1938-*. Tago / John B. Harvey. — London : Hale, 1981, c1980. — 160p ; 20cm
Originally published: London : Pan Books, 1980
ISBN 0-7091-8725-4 : £4.95 B81-24872

Harvey, Marianne. The proud hunter / Marianne Harvey. — London : Futura, 1980. — 348p ; 18cm. — (A Troubadour spectacular)
ISBN 0-7088-1936-2 (pbk) : £1.50 B81-07033

Harvey, Samantha. The driftwood beach / by Samantha Harvey. — London : Mills & Boon, 1981. — 190p ; 19cm
ISBN 0-263-09885-0 : £4.55 B81-28561

Hashemi, Louise. Quiet as a nun / Antonia Fraser ; adapted by Louise Hashemi. — Oxford : Oxford University Press, c1980. — 95p ; 18cm. — (Alpha crime)
ISBN 0-19-424227-7 (pbk) : £0.65 B81-02131

Hastings, Macdonald. Cork on the telly / Macdonald Hastings. — London : Remploy, 1979. — 231p ; 19cm
Originally published: London : Joseph, 1966
ISBN 0-7066-0840-2 : £4.10 B81-38045

Hastings, Phyllis. Buttercup Joe / Phyllis Hastings. — London : Hale, 1980. — 172p ; 21cm
ISBN 0-7091-8597-9 : £5.95 B81-08993

Hastings, Phyllis. A delight of angels / by Phyllis Hastings. — London : Hale, 1981. — 240p ; 21cm
ISBN 0-7091-9110-3 : £6.75 B81-35228

Hastings, Phyllis. Field of the forty footsteps / by Phyllis Hastings. — Large print ed. — London : Hale, 1980, c1978. — 320p ; 23cm
Originally published: 1978
ISBN 0-7091-8615-0 : £5.80 B81-00473

Hatfield, Michael. Spy fever. — London : Quartet Books, Oct.1981. — [192]p. — (Quartet qrime)
ISBN 0-7043-2309-5 : £6.50 : CIP entry
B81-31095

Haward, Winifred I.. Banners against the wind / Winifred Haward. — Bognor Regis : New Horizon, c1980. — 232p ; 21cm
ISBN 0-86116-227-7 : £5.25 B81-19031

Hawkesworth, John. In my lady's chamber / John Hawkesworth. — London : Prior, 1980, c1972. — 336p ; 24cm. — (Upstairs, downstairs series ; 2)
Originally published: London : Sphere, 1973. — Published in large print
ISBN 0-86043-495-8 : £5.95 B81-11983

Hawkesworth, John. Upstairs, downstairs / John Hawkesworth. — London : Prior, 1980, c1971. — 425p : ill ; 24cm. — (Upstairs downstairs series ; 1)
Originally published: London : Sphere, 1972. — Published in large print
ISBN 0-86043-491-5 (corrected) : £6.95
B81-15141

Haydn, Richard, *1931-*. The silent valley / Richard Haydn. — London : Hale, 1981. — 173p ; 23m
ISBN 0-7091-8940-0 : £6.25 B81-19299

Haythorne, John. The Strelsau dimension / John Haythorne. — London : Quartet, 1981. — 137p ; 23cm. — (Quartet crime)
ISBN 0-7043-2285-4 : £5.95 B81-20288

Hayward, David. The Strasbourg connection / by David Hayward. — London : Hale, 1981. — 192p ; 20cm
ISBN 0-7091-9205-3 : £6.25 B81-37317

Heald, Tim. Blue blood will out / Tim Heald. — London : Arrow, 1981, c1974. — 205p ; 18cm. — (A Bognor mystery)
Originally published: London : Hutchinson, 1974
ISBN 0-09-913290-7 (pbk) : £1.10 B81-14033

Heald, Tim. Deadline / Tim Heald. — London : Arrow, 1981, c1974. — 183p ; 18cm. — (A Bognor mystery)
Originally published: London : Hutchinson, 1975
ISBN 0-09-924700-3 (pbk) : £1.10 B81-11022

Heald, Tim. Just desserts / Tim Heald. — London : Arrow, 1981, c1974. — 190p ; 18cm. — (A Bognor mystery)
Originally published: London : Hutchinson, 1977
ISBN 0-09-924850-6 (pbk) : £1.10 B81-11024

Heald, Tim. Let sleeping dogs die / Tim Heald. — London : Arrow, 1981, c1976. — 190p ; 18cm. — (A Bognor mystery)
Originally published: London : Hutchinson, 1976
ISBN 0-09-924710-0 (pbk) : £1.10 B81-11020

Heald, Tim. Masterstroke. — London : Hutchinson, Feb.1982. — [176]p
ISBN 0-09-146760-8 : £6.95 : CIP entry
B81-38334

Heald, Tim. Murder at Moose Jaw / Tim Heald. — London : Hutchinson, 1981. — 187p ; 23cm
ISBN 0-09-144610-4 : £6.50 B81-14238

Heald, Tim. Unbecoming habits / Tim Heald. — London : Arrow, 1974, c1973 ([1981 printing]). — 223p ; 18cm. — (A Bognor mystery)
Originally published: London : Hutchinson, 1973
ISBN 0-09-909110-0 (pbk) : £1.10 B81-14034

Healey, Ben. Last ferry from the lido / Ben Healey. — London : Hale, 1981. — 189p ; 20cm
ISBN 0-7091-8781-5 : £5.75 B81-14206

Healey, Ben. The most wicked Bianca : a late Renaissance chronicle based on the life of Bianca Capello of Venice, Grand Duchess of Tuscany 1579 to 1587 / Ben Healey. — Feltham : Hamlyn, 1980. — 252p ; 18cm
ISBN 0-600-31541-x (pbk) : £1.25 B81-00474

Healey, Ben. The week of the scorpion / by Ben Healey. — London : Hale, 1981. — 191p ; 20cm
ISBN 0-7091-9277-0 : £6.25 B81-33517

Hearn, Peter. From the high skies / Peter Hearn. — London : Hale, 1981. — 188p ; 21cm
ISBN 0-7091-9132-4 : £6.75 B81-40548

Heaton, Kathleen. The sorceress / Kathleen Heaton. — London : Hale, 1980. — 191p ; 21cm
ISBN 0-7091-8339-9 : £6.25 B81-00475

Heaven, Constance. Heir to Kuragin / Constance Heaven. — London : Pan in association with Heinemann, 1981, c1978. — 252p ; 18cm
Originally published: London : Heinemann, 1978
ISBN 0-330-26124-x (pbk) : £1.50 B81-20196

Heaven, Constance. The house of Kuragin / Constance Heaven. — London : Pan in association with Heinemann, 1973, c1972 (1981 printing). — 205p ; 18cm
Originally published: London : Heinemann, 1972
£1.25 (pbk)
ISBN 0-330-23724-1 B81-27665

Heaven, Constance. The Wildcliffe bird / Constance Heaven. — London : Heinemann, 1981. — 248p ; 23cm
ISBN 0-434-32617-8 : £6.95 B81-13126

Hebden, Mark. Pel is puzzled / Mark Hebden. — London : Hamilton, 1981. — 232p ; 21cm
ISBN 0-241-10646-x : £7.50 : CIP rev.
B81-13815

Helm, P. J.. The brainpicker / by Peter Helm. — London : Hale, 1981. — 192p ; 20cm
ISBN 0-7091-9128-6 (corrected) : £5.95
B81-33515

Henaghan, Rosalie. Coppers girl / by Rosalie Henaghan. — London : Mills & Boon, 1981. — 189p ; 20cm
ISBN 0-263-09854-0 : £4.55 B81-18348

Hendrick, Vincent J.. Not many millionaires / Vincent J. Hendrick. — Bognor Regis : New Horizon, c1981. — 265p ; 21cm
ISBN 0-86116-318-4 : £5.75 B81-39604

Hendricks, Sonia. Dinsvale / by Sonia Hendricks. — Bognor Regis : New Horizon, c1980. — 64p ; 21cm
ISBN 0-86116-213-7 : £4.50 B81-19026

Hennessy, Max. Blunted lance. — London : H. Hamilton, Sept.1981. — [224]p
ISBN 0-241-10606-0 : £6.95 : CIP entry
B81-25681

Hennessy, Max. The dangerous years / Max Hennessy. — London : Sphere, 1981, c1978. — 312p ; 18cm
Originally published: London : Hamilton, 1978
ISBN 0-7221-0451-0 (pbk) : £1.50 B81-35067

Hennessy, Max. The dangerous years. — Large print ed. — Anstey : Ulverscroft, Jan.1982. — [572]p. — (Ulverscroft large print series : adventure, suspense)
ISBN 0-7089-0739-3 : £5.00 : CIP entry
B81-33958

Hennessy, Max. The lion at sea. — Large print ed. — Anstey : Ulverscroft, Oct.1981. — [480] p. — (Ulverscroft large print series)
Originally published: London : Hamilton 1977
ISBN 0-7089-0696-6 : £5.00 : CIP entry
B81-28094

Hennessy, Max. Soldier of the Queen / Max Hennessy. — London : Hamilton, 1980. — 279p ; 23cm
ISBN 0-241-10241-3 : £6.50 : CIP rev.
B80-18488

Herbert, James. The jonah / James Herbert. — London : New English Library, 1981. — 253p ; 23cm
ISBN 0-450-04855-1 : £6.50 B81-15425

823'.914[F] — Fiction in English, *1945-* — *Texts continuation*

Herbert, Julia. Bond-woman / Julia Herbert. — London : Mills & Boon, 1980, c1979. — 188p ; 20cm. — (Masquerade)
Originally published: Australia : s.n., 1979
ISBN 0-263-09675-0 : £3.85 B81-00476

Herbert, Nan. A buccaneer's nurse / by Nan Herbert. — London : Hale, 1980. — 191p ; 20cm
ISBN 0-7091-8264-3 : £4.95 B81-01434

Herbert, Nan. The Sinclair heir / by Nan Herbert. — London : Hale, 1981. — 192p ; 20cm
ISBN 0-7091-9101-4 : £6.50 B81-27319

Herley, Richard. The Flint Lord / Richard Herley. — London : Heinemann/Peter Davies, 1981. — 219p ; 23cm
ISBN 0-434-32762-x : £6.95 B81-24582

Herley, Richard. The stone arrow / Richard Herley. — London : Granada, 1981, c1978. — 250p ; 18cm. — (A Mayflower book)
Originally published: London : P. Davies, 1978
ISBN 0-583-13239-1 (pbk) : £1.50 B81-32182

Hermon, Celia. Commuter's pastimes / Celia Hermon. — Bognor Regis : New Horizon, c1980. — 101p ; 21cm
ISBN 0-86116-359-1 : £3.50 B81-19254

Herring, Christine. The Castell affair / by Christine Herring. — London : Hale, 1981. — 189p ; 20cm
ISBN 0-7091-8998-2 : £6.50 B81-24851

Herring, Christine. The treasure of La Buse / by Christine Herring. — London : Hale, 1980. — 190p ; 20cm
ISBN 0-7091-8683-5 : £6.25 B81-08965

Hersom, Kathleen. Maybe it's a tiger. — London : Macmillan Children's Books, Aug.1981. — [32]p
ISBN 0-333-32382-3 : £3.95 : CIP entry B81-15815

Higgins, Jack. Passage by night / Jack Higgins. — Large print ed. — Leicester : Ulverscroft, 1980, c1964. — 269p ; 23cm. — (Ulverscroft large print series)
Originally published: under the name of Hugh Marlowe. London : Abelard-Schumann, 1964
ISBN 0-7089-0514-5 : £4.25 : CIP rev. B80-17983

Higgins, *Jack*. Solo / Jack Higgins. — Large print ed. — Leicester : Ulverscroft, 1981, 1980. — 383p : ill ; 26cm. — (Ulverscroft large print series)
Originally published: London : Collins, 1980
ISBN 0-7089-0626-5 : £5.00 : CIP rev. B81-07434

Higgins, Jack. A fine night for dying / Jack Higgins. — London : Arrow, 1977, c1969 (1981 [printing]). — 183p ; 18cm
Originally published: under the name Martin Fallon. London : Long, 1969
ISBN 0-09-915900-7 (pbk) : £1.25 B81-32775

Higgins, Jack. Four great thrillers. — London : Collins, Nov.1981. — [750]p. — (Collins' collectors' club)
Contents: Storm warning — The violent enemy — Day of judgement — Wrath of the lion
ISBN 0-00-243345-1 : £6.95 : CIP entry B81-28770

Higgins, Jack. A Jack Higgins quartet. — London : Collins, 1980. — 781p ; 23cm. — (Collins' collectors' choice)
Contents: The last place God made - The savage day - A prayer for the dying - The eagle has landed
ISBN 0-00-243344-3 : £5.95 B81-08025

Higgins, Jack. Luciano's luck / Jack Higgins. — London : Collins, 1981. — 215p ; 24cm
ISBN 0-00-222335-x : £6.95 : CIP rev. B81-13507

Higgins, Jack. Solo / Jack Higgins. — London : Pan in association with Collins, 1981, c1980. — 255p ; 18cm
Originally published: London : Collins, 1980
ISBN 0-330-26368-4 (pbk) : £1.50 B81-24737

Higgins, Jack. The testament of Caspar Schultz / Jack Higgins. — Large print ed. — Bath : Chivers, 1981, c1962. — 226p ; 23cm. — (A Lythway thriller)
Originally published: New York : Fawcett, 1962
ISBN 0-85119-704-3 : £5.25 B81-08678

High, Monique Raphel. Encore / Monique Raphel High. — London : Granada, 1981. — 665p ; 24cm
ISBN 0-246-11645-5 : £7.95 B81-38058

High, Monique Raphel. The four winds of Heaven / Monique Raphel High. — London : Granada, 1980. — 686p : 1geneal.table ; 24cm
ISBN 0-246-11415-0 : £6.95 B81-01435

High, Monique Raphel. The four winds of heaven / Monique Raphel High. — London : Granada, 1980. — 686p ; 18cm. — (A Mayflower book)
ISBN 0-583-13378-9 (pbk) : £1.95 B81-21987

Hildick, E. W.. The loop. — London : Hodder and Stoughton, May 1981. — [224]p
Originally published: London : Hamilton, 1977
ISBN 0-340-25089-5 (pbk) : £1.25 : CIP entry B81-03816

Hill, Archie. Dark pastures / Archie Hill. — London : Macmillan, 1981. — vii,115p : 1map ; 21cm. — (Topliner tridents)
For adolescents
ISBN 0-333-30692-9 : £3.95 B81-21136

Hill, Archie. Prison bars / Archie Hill. — London : Hutchinson, 1980. — 255p ; 21cm
ISBN 0-09-143070-4 : £6.95 B81-01436

Hill, Graham, *1943-*. Chance encounter / Graham Hill. — London ([89, Notting Hill Gate, W11 3JZ]) : Amulet, 1980. — 191p ; 18cm
ISBN 0-9507160-2-2 (pbk) : £1.50 B81-08635

Hill, Pamela. Homage to a rose / by Pamela Hill. — Large print ed. — London : Hale, 1980, c1979. — 347p ; 23cm
ISBN 0-7091-8614-2 : £6.10 B81-06647

Hill, Pamela. Knock at a star / Pamela Hill. — London : Hale, 1981. — 239p ; 23cm
ISBN 0-7091-8937-0 : £6.50 B81-28876

Hill, Pamela. A place of ravens / Pamela Hill. — London : Hale, 1980. — 223p : ill ; 23cm
ISBN 0-7091-8570-7 : £6.50 B81-11158

Hill, Peter, *1937-*. The savages / Peter Hill. — London : Heinemann, 1980. — 184p ; 23cm
ISBN 0-434-33610-6 : £6.50 B81-02908

Hill, Reginald. A killing kindness / Reginald Hill. — London : Collins, 1980. — 269p ; 21cm. — (The Crime Club)
ISBN 0-00-231406-1 : £5.50 B81-07516

Hill, Susan. In the springtime of the year / Susan Hill. — Harmondsworth : Penguin, 1977, c1974 (1981 [printing]). — 169p ; 18cm
Originally published: London : Hamilton, 1974
ISBN 0-14-004110-9 (pbk) : £1.25 B81-22346

Hilton, Christopher. Moves on an old board / by Christopher Hilton. — London : Hale, 1981. — 188p ; 20cm
ISBN 0-7091-9008-5 : £5.95 B81-24846

Hilton, John Buxton. The anathema store. — Large print ed. — Anstey : Ulverscroft, Oct.1981. — [352]p. — (Ulverscroft large print series)
Originally published: London : Collins, 1980
ISBN 0-7089-0689-3 : £5.00 : CIP entry B81-28097

Hilton, John Buxton. The green frontier. — London : Collins, Jan.1982. — [192]p. — (Crime Club)
ISBN 0-00-231029-5 : £6.50 : CIP entry B81-33973

Hilton, John Buxton. Playground of death / John Buxton Hilton. — London : Collins, 1981. — 160p ; 21cm. — (The Crime Club)
ISBN 0-00-231650-1 : £5.75 B81-02441

Hilton, John Buxton. Surrender value : a Superintendent Kenworthy novel / John Buxton Hilton. — London : Collins, 1981. — 153p ; 21cm
ISBN 0-00-231795-8 : £6.25 B81-18615

Hinde, Thomas. Daymare / Thomas Hinde. — London : Macmillan, 1980. — 243p : 2 maps ; 23cm
Maps on lining papers
ISBN 0-333-30427-6 : £6.95 B81-00477

Hinde, Thomas. Mr Nicholas / Thomas Hinde. — London : Macmillan London, 1980, c1952. — 271p ; 23cm
Originally published: London : MacGibbon & Kee, 1952
ISBN 0-333-29539-0 : £6.95 B81-01438

Hines, Barry. Looks and smiles / Barry Hines. — London : Joseph, 1981. — 219p ; 22cm
ISBN 0-7181-1877-4 : £6.95 B81-35735

Hirst, William. Kid gunslinger / by William Hirst. — London : Hale, 1980. — 159p ; 20cm
ISBN 0-7091-8230-9 : £4.50 B81-01439

Hislop, Richard. A rose in the banyan tree / Richard Hislop. — London : Corgi, 1980, c1979. — 187p ; 18cm
Originally published: London : Heinemann, 1979
ISBN 0-552-11476-6 (pbk) : £1.15 B81-02141

Hitchcock, Lydia. The Ducetti lair / Lydia Hitchcock. — London : Columbine House, 1981. — 206p ; 23cm
ISBN 0-85140-532-0 : £6.50 : CIP rev. B81-12794

Hitchcock, Raymond. Attack the Lusitania! / Raymond Hitchcock. — London : Sphere, 1981, c1979. — 215p ; 18cm
Originally published: London : Joseph, 1979
ISBN 0-7221-4596-9 (pbk) : £1.25 B81-17973

Hobson, Mary. Oh Lily / Mary Hobson. — London : Heinemann, 1981. — 186p ; 23cm
ISBN 0-434-34020-0 : £6.95 B81-11631

Hocking, Mary. March House / Mary Hocking. — London : Chatto & Windus, 1981. — 221p ; 21cm
ISBN 0-7011-2586-1 : £6.95 : CIP rev. B81-16935

Hodge, Jane Aiken. Marry in haste / Jane Aiken Hodge. — London : Hodder and Stoughton, 1969 (1980 printing). — 223p ; 21cm
Originally published: 1969
ISBN 0-340-25942-6 : £5.95 : CIP rev. B80-24839

Hodge, Jane Aiken. Maulever Hall / Jane Aiken Hodge. — Large print ed. — Leicester : Ulverscroft, 1980, c1964. — 486p ; 23cm. — (Ulverscroft large print series)
Originally published: London : Hale, 1964
ISBN 0-7089-0495-5 : £4.25 : CIP rev. B80-11614

823'.914[F] — Fiction in English, *1945- — Texts continuation*

Hodge, Jane Aiken. Red sky at night / Jane Aiken Hodge. — Large print ed. — Leicester : Ulverscroft, 1980, c1978. — 480p ; 23cm. — (Ulverscroft large print series)
Originally published: New York : Coward, McCann & Geoghegan, 1977 ; London : Hodder and Stoughton, 1978
ISBN 0-7089-0595-1 : £4.25 B81-11125

Hodge, Jane Aiken. Savannah Purchase / Jane Aitken Hodge. — London : Hodder and Stoughton, 1980, c1971. — 256p ; 21cm
ISBN 0-340-25941-8 : £5.95 : CIP rev. B80-24840

Hodge, Jane Aiken. Wide is the water / Jane Aiken Hodge. — London : Hodder, c1981. — 240p ; 22cm
ISBN 0-340-26244-3 : £6.95 : CIP rev. B81-10473

Hogan, Desmond. The leaves on grey / Desmond Hogan. — London : Pan, 1981, c1980. — 118p ; 20cm. — (Picador)
Originally published: London : Hamilton, 1980
ISBN 0-330-26287-4 (pbk) : £1.50 B81-18409

Holden, Albert. The death of Hammerstein / Albert Holden. — Bognor Regis : New Horizon, c1979. — 253p ; 21cm
ISBN 0-86116-091-6 : £4.25 B81-18959

Holden, Matthew, *1939-*. Scramble Dieppe / Matthew Holden. — London : Severn House, 1981, c1980. — 157p ; 21cm. — (Squadron ; 3)
Originally published: London : Sphere, 1980
ISBN 0-7278-0720-x : £5.50 : CIP rev. B81-17509

Holden, Matthew, *1939-*. Sons of the morning / Matthew Holden. — London : Severn House, 1980, c1978. — 171p ; 21cm. — (Squadron ; 1)
Originally published: London : Sphere, 1978
ISBN 0-7278-0633-5 : £4.95 : CIP rev. B80-28752

Holden, Matthew, *1939-*. The sun climbs slowly / Matthew Holden. — London : Severn House, 1981, c1978. — 160p ; 21cm. — (Squadron ; 2)
Originally published: London : Sphere, 1978
ISBN 0-7278-0653-x : £5.95 B81-16067

Holden, Matthew, *1939-*. Whirlwind at Arromanches / Matthew Holden. — London : Sphere, 1981. — 156p ; 18cm. — (Squadron ; 5)
ISBN 0-7221-6681-8 (pbk) : £1.00 B81-11713

Holden, Ursula. Sing about it. — London : Eyre Methuen, Feb.1982. — [160]p
ISBN 0-413-47730-4 : £6.50 : CIP entry B81-36380

Holding, James G.. Death hunt / James G. Holding. — London : Hale, 1980. — 187p ; 20cm
ISBN 0-7091-8668-1 : £4.95 B81-02923

Holdstock, Robert. Where time winds blow / Robert Holdstock. — London : Faber, 1981. — 286p ; 21cm
ISBN 0-571-11679-5 : £6.95 : CIP rev. B81-07594

Holland, Lillie. The rightful heir. — Large print ed. — Bath : Chivers Press, Dec.1981. — [264] p. — (A Lythway book)
Originally published: London : Hurst & Blackett, 1975
ISBN 0-85119-768-x : £6.80 : CIP entry B81-31799

Holles, Robert. I'll walk beside you / Robert Holles. — London : Sphere, 1980, c1979. — 124p ; 18cm
Originally published: London : Hamilton, 1979
ISBN 0-7221-4617-5 (pbk) : £0.95 B81-00478

Holme, Timothy. The Neapolitan streak / Timothy Holme. — Large print ed. — Leicester : Ulverscroft, 1981, c1980. — 377p ; 23cm. — (Ulverscroft large print)
Originally published: London : Macmillan, 1980
ISBN 0-7089-0646-x : £5.00 B81-28565

Holmes, B. J.. Gunfall / by B.J. Holmes. — London : Hale, 1980. — 160p ; 20cm
ISBN 0-7091-8384-4 : £4.95 B81-01440

Holmes, B. J.. A noose for Yanqui / by B.J. Holmes. — London : Hale, 1981. — 160p ; 20cm
ISBN 0-7091-9165-0 : £4.95 B81-27298

Holt, Kathleen. Harlequinade / by Kathleen Holt. — London : Hale, 1981. — 208p ; 20cm
ISBN 0-7091-8766-1 : £5.50 B81-11656

Honeycombe, Gordon. The edge of heaven. — London : Hutchinson, May 1981. — [416]p
ISBN 0-09-143030-5 : £6.95 : CIP entry B81-04256

Honeywood, John. The dying breath / by John Honeywood. — London : Hale, 1981. — 192p ; 20cm
ISBN 0-7091-8780-7 : £5.75 B81-08964

Honeywood, John. The terrorist's woman / by John Honeywood. — London : Hale, 1981. — 189p ; 20cm
ISBN 0-7091-9359-9 : £6.25 B81-37297

Hornsby, Ken. The padded sell / Ken Hornsby. — London : Hale, 1980. — 175p ; 23cm
ISBN 0-7091-8433-6 : £6.25 B81-00479

Hornsby, Ken. Wet behind the ears / Ken Hornsby. — London : Dobson, 1980. — 200p ; 21cm
ISBN 0-234-72202-9 : £3.95 B81-02731

Horrex, John. One little ship / John Horrex. — Bognor Regis : New Horizon, c1980. — 235p ; 21cm
ISBN 0-86116-569-1 : £6.25 B81-18863

Horsley, David. Salt Creek killing / by David Horsley. — London : Hale, 1981. — 160p ; 20cm
ISBN 0-7091-8796-3 : £4.95 B81-11840

Horsley, David. Troubleshooter on trial / David Horsley. — London : Hale, 1980. — 158p ; 20cm
ISBN 0-7091-8382-8 : £4.75 B81-02149

Horst, Karl. Arctic mutiny / Karl Horst. — London : Corgi, 1981. — 174p ; 18cm
ISBN 0-552-11721-8 (pbk) : £1.25 B81-32111

Horton, Gordon T.. X-Isle / by Gordon T. Horton. — London : Hale, 1980. — 207p ; 21cm. — (Hale SF)
ISBN 0-7091-8422-0 : £5.50 B81-01441

Horwood, William. Duncton Wood : a novel / by William Horwood. — Richmond upon Thames : Country Life, 1980. — 543p ; 24cm
ISBN 0-600-36794-0 : £7.95 B81-00480

Horwood, William. Duncton Wood : a novel / by William Horwood. — Feltham : Hamlyn, 1981, c1980. — 733p ; 18cm
Originally published: Richmond upon Thames : Country Life, 1980
ISBN 0-600-20434-0 (pbk) : £1.95 B81-33484

Hough, Richard. Buller's guns / Richard Hough. — London : Weidenfeld and Nicolson, c1981. — 297p ; 22cm
ISBN 0-297-77908-7 : £6.50 B81-35147

Howard, Elizabeth Jane. Something in disguise / Elizabeth Jane Howard. — Harmondswoth : Penguin, 1971, c1969 (1980 [printing]). — 282p ; 18cm
Originally published: London : Cape, 1969
ISBN 0-14-003288-6 (pbk) : £1.25 B81-11211

Howard, Hartley. Routine investigation / Hartley Howard. — Large print ed. — Leicester : Ulverscroft, 1980, c1967. — 308p ; 23cm. — (Ulvercroft large print series)
Originally published: London : Collins, 1967
ISBN 0-7089-0491-2 : £4.25 : CIP rev. B80-10804

Howard, Linden. The Devil's lady / Linden Howard. — London : Magnum, 1981, c1980. — 226p ; 18cm
Originally published: London : Millington, 1980
ISBN 0-417-05610-9 (pbk) : £1.50 B81-28610

Howard, Lynde. All I ever wanted / by Lynde Howard. — London : Hale, 1981. — 159p ; 21cm
ISBN 0-7091-8749-1 : £5.50 B81-11654

Hoy, Linda. Your friend, Rebecca / Linda Hoy. — London : Bodley Head, c1981. — 154p ; 20cm. — (A Book for new adults)
For adolescents
ISBN 0-370-30418-7 (pbk) : £3.25 : CIP rev. B81-04382

Hoyland, Michael. A love affair with war / Michael Hoyland. — London : Collins, 1981. — 258p : plans ; 22cm
ISBN 0-00-222351-1 : £6.50 : CIP rev. B81-04228

Hoyle, Fred. Seven steps to the sun / Fred Hoyle and Geoffrey Hoyle ; edited by Barbara Hoyle. — Harmondsworth : Penguin, 1981, c1970. — 188p ; 18cm. — (Penguin science fiction)
Originally published: London : Heinemann, 1970
ISBN 0-14-005132-5 (pbk) : £1.25 B81-22040

Hoyle, Jill. Another moon / by Jill Hoyle. — London : Hale, 1981. — 159p ; 20cm
ISBN 0-7091-8635-5 : £5.50 B81-13115

Hughes, Alison. Escape to happiness / by Alison Hughes. — London : Hale, 1980. — 160p ; 20cm
ISBN 0-7091-8060-8 : £4.75 B81-00481

Hughes, Alison. Meeting with a stranger / by Alison Hughes. — London : Hale, 1981. — 175p ; 20cm
ISBN 0-7091-8929-x : £5.60 B81-21884

Hughes, Edward, *1913-*. Earth's second chance / Edward Hughes. — Bognor Regis : New Horizon, c1980. — 48p ; 21cm
ISBN 0-86116-243-9 : £2.95 B81-19242

Hughes, Elena. Island of whispers / by Elena Hughes. — London : Hale, 1980. — 192p ; 20cm
ISBN 0-7091-8444-1 : £5.25 B81-02151

Hughes, Glyn. Where I used to play on the green. — London : Gollancz, Jan.1982. — [192]p
ISBN 0-575-02997-8 : £7.95 : CIP entry B81-35886

Hughes, Michael, *1940-*. Kommando 55 / Michael Hughes. — London : New English Library, 1980 (1981 [printing]). — 221p ; 18cm
ISBN 0-450-05173-0 (pbk) : £1.25 B81-28697

Hughes, Michael, *1940-*. The sleeper awakes / Michael Hughes. — London : W.H. Allen, 1980. — 202p ; 22cm
ISBN 0-491-02863-6 : £5.95 B81-01442

823'.914[F] — Fiction in English, *1945-* — *Texts continuation*

Hughes, Michael, *1940-*[The Sleeper awakes]. The sleeper / Michael Hughes. — London : W.H. Allen, 1980 (1981 [printing]). — 202p ; 18cm. — (A Star book)
ISBN 0-352-30818-4 (pbk) : £1.50 B81-26526

Hulme, Ann. Summer heiress / Ann Hulme. — London : Mills & Boon, 1981. — 191p ; 20cm. — (Masquerade)
ISBN 0-263-09893-1 : £4.55 B81-28517

Humphreys, Emyr. A toy epic / Emyr Humphreys. — London : Severn House, 1981, c1958. — 160p ; 21cm
Originally published: London : Eyre & Spottiswoode, 1958
ISBN 0-7278-0712-9 : £5.95 : CIP rev. B81-12782

Humphreys, James. 'Through the eyes of a pig' / James Humphreys. — London : Sphere, 1981. — 155p ; 18cm
ISBN 0-7221-4786-4 (pbk) : £1.25 B81-37293

Hunt, Alethia. Girl in the dark / by Alethia Hunt. — London : Hale, 1981. — 192p ; 20cm
ISBN 0-7091-9281-9 : £5.75 B81-35206

Hunt, Alethia. The Hadleigh inheritance / Alethia Hunt. — London : Hale, 1980. — 190p ; 20cm
ISBN 0-7091-8405-0 : £5.25 B81-00482

Hunter, Alan. Gabrielle's way / Alan Hunter. — London : Constable, 1981, c1980. — 145p ; 23cm. — (Constable crime)
ISBN 0-09-463910-8 : £5.95 B81-03041

Hunter, Alan. The Honfleur decision / Alan Hunter. — Large print ed. — Bath : Chivers, 1981, c1980. — 273p ; 23cm. — (A Lythway thriller)
Originally published: London : Constable, 1980
ISBN 0-85119-702-7 : £5.25 B81-08680

Hunter, Claire. Island of stone / Claire Hunter. — Tisbury : Longstone, 1981. — viii,223p : 2maps ; 22cm
Maps on lining papers
ISBN 0-9507526-0-6 : £6.95 B81-40974

Hunter, Elizabeth. A touch of magic. — London : Hodder & Stoughton, Oct.1981. — [192]p. — (Silhouette romance)
ISBN 0-340-27120-5 (pbk) : £0.65 : CIP entry B81-27356

Hunter, Elizabeth, *1934-*. Bride of the sun / Elizabeth Hunter. — London : Silhouette, 1981, c1980. — 188p ; 18cm. — (Silhouette romance ; 50)
ISBN 0-340-26740-2 (pbk) : £0.65 : CIP rev. B81-13777

Hunter, Elizabeth, *1934-*. The lion's shadow / Elizabeth Hunter. — London (47 Bedford Sq., WC1B 3DP) : Silhouette, 1981, c1980. — 188p ; 18cm. — (Silhouette romance ; no.18)
ISBN 0-340-26122-6 (pbk) : £0.65 : CIP rev. B80-21073

Hurren, Louise. The living majority / Louise Hurren. — Bognor Regis : New Horizon, c1980. — 391p : ill ; 22cm
ISBN 0-86116-605-1 : £6.75 B81-18963

Hutson, Shaun. Blood and honour / by Shaun Hutson. — London : Hale, 1981. — 207p ; 20cm
ISBN 0-7091-8994-x : £6.50 B81-17330

Hutt, Decia. A handful of earth / Decia Hutt. — Large print ed. — Bath : Chivers, 1981, c1979. — 266p ; 23cm. — (A Lythway historical romance)
Originally published: London : Hurst and Blackett, 1979
ISBN 0-85119-715-9 : £6.50 : CIP rev. B81-04227

Hutton, Ann. The ivory slave / by Ann Hutton. — London : Hale, 1981. — 174p ; 20cm
ISBN 0-7091-8713-0 : £5.50 B81-08963

Hutton, Malcolm. Address unknown / by Malcolm Hutton. — London : Hale, 1981. — 192p ; 22cm
ISBN 0-7091-9095-6 : £6.50 B81-24848

Huxham, Gerry. Say goodbye to dragons / Gerry Huxham. — London : Macmillan, 1978 (1979 [printing]). — 103p ; 18cm. — (Toplines)
Originally published: 1978. — For adolescents
ISBN 0-333-24663-2 (pbk) : £1.12 : CIP rev. B79-22795

Hyatt, Betty Hale. The jade pagoda / Betty Hale Hyatt. — London : Hale, 1981, c1980. — 182p ; 20cm
Originally published: Garden City, N.Y. : Doubleday, 1980
ISBN 0-7091-9372-6 : £6.75 B81-37296

Hyatt, Betty Hale. Love's untold secret / Betty Hale Hyatt. — London : Hale, 1981, c1978. — 176p ; 20cm
ISBN 0-7091-8734-3 : £5.95 B81-13113

Hyde, Christopher. The wave. — London : Hodder & Stoughton, Dec.1981. — [240]p
Originally published: 1980
ISBN 0-340-27270-8 (pbk) : £1.10 : CIP entry B81-31465

Hyde, Eleanor. Tudor mansion / Eleanor Hyde. — Large print ed. — Bath : Lythway, 1980, c1978. — 182p ; 23cm
Originally published: London : Hale, 1978
ISBN 0-85046-907-4 : £5.50 : CIP rev. B80-22532

Hyde, Jennifer. A handful of shadows / by Jennifer Hyde. — London : Hale, 1980. — 175p ; 20cm
ISBN 0-7091-8074-8 : £5.25 B81-01443

Hylton, Sara. Caprice / Sara Hylton. — London : Arrow, 1981, c1980. — 349p ; 18cm
Originally published: London : Hutchinson, 1980
ISBN 0-09-925980-x (pbk) : £1.60 B81-28592

Hylton, Sara. The Carradice chain. — London : Hutchinson, Oct.1981. — [300]p
ISBN 0-09-145280-5 : £6.95 : CIP entry B81-26764

Inchbald, Peter. Tondo for short / Peter Inchbald. — London : Collins, 1981. — 221p ; 21cm. — (The Crime Club)
ISBN 0-00-231040-6 : £6.50 : CIP rev. B81-13769

Innes, Brian. The Red Baron lives! : a rattling good yarn / Brian Innes. — London : New English Library, 1981. — 282p ; 23cm
Bibliography: p281-282
ISBN 0-450-04870-5 : £6.50 B81-37436

Innes, Hammond. The last voyage : Captain Cook's lost diary / Hammond Innes. — [London] : Fontana, 1981, c1978. — 254p ; 19cm
Originally published: London : Collins, 1978
ISBN 0-00-616195-2 (pbk) : £1.50 B81-20686

Innes, Jean. Silver lady / by Jean Innes. — London : Hale, 1981. — 176p ; 20cm
ISBN 0-7091-8752-1 : £5.50 B81-14089

Innes, Jean. White blooms of Yarrow / Jean Innes. — Large print ed. — Bath : Chivers, 1981, c1976. — 232p ; 23cm. — (A Seymour book)
Originally published: London : Hale, 1976
ISBN 0-85119-406-0 : Unpriced B81-08983

Ireland, Timothy. To be looked for / Timothy Ireland. — London : Bodley Head, 1981. — 188p ; 20cm. — (A Book for new adults)
ISBN 0-370-30440-3 (pbk) : £3.50 : CIP rev. B81-28828

Irving, Clive. Axis / Clive Irving. — London : Corgi, 1981, c1980. — 381p ; 18cm
Originally published: London : Hamilton, 1980
ISBN 0-552-11780-3 (pbk) : £1.75 B81-39102

Jackman, Stuart. A game of soldiers / by Stuart Jackman. — London : Hamish Hamilton, 1981. — 302p : 1plan ; 21cm
ISBN 0-241-10655-9 : £7.95 : CIP rev. B81-13428

Jackson, Robert, *1941-*. Mosquito Sguadron : Yeoman in the battle over Germany / Robert Jackson. — Lodnon : Barker, c1981. — 148p : ill ; 23cm
ISBN 0-213-16771-9 : £5.50 B81-08693

Jackson, Robert, *1941-*. Operation diver : Yeoman on special missions / Robert Jackson. — London : Barker, c1981. — 149p ; 23cm
ISBN 0-213-16793-x : £5.95 B81-22115

Jackson, Robert, *1941-*. Target Tobruk : Yeoman in the Western Desert / Robert Jackson. — [London] : Corgi, 1980, c1979. — 158p : maps ; 18cm
Originally published: London : A. Barker, 1979
ISBN 0-552-11557-6 (pbk) : £1.00 B81-03320

Jackson, Robert, *1941-*. Tempest squadron : Yeoman in the Battle of the Ardennes / Robert Jackson. — London : Barker, c1981. — 137p ; 23cm
ISBN 0-213-16804-9 : £5.50 B81-39398

Jackson, Tony, *1945-*. The café ; les romans chauds / Tony Jackson. — Durham (7 Cross View Terrace, Nevilles Cross, Durham DH1 4JY) : Pig Press, 1980. — 108p ; 18cm
ISBN 0-903997-49-5 (pbk) : £3.90
ISBN 0-903997-54-1 (signed ed.) : £10.00 B81-11893

Jaggard, Robert W.. Minitax motoring / Robert W. Jaggard. — Ilfracombe : Stockwell
Vol.1. — 1981. — 59p ; 18cm
ISBN 0-7223-1461-2 (pbk) : £3.00 B81-35047

Jagger, Brenda. The clouded hills / Brenda Jagger. — London : Macdonald Futura, 1980. — 593p ; 23cm
ISBN 0-354-04522-9 : £6.95 B81-01444

Jagger, Brenda. The clouded hills / Brenda Jagger. — London : Macdonald Futura, 1980 (1981 [printing]). — 590p ; 18cm. — (A Futura book)
ISBN 0-7088-1827-7 (pbk) : £1.95 B81-40954

Jagger, Brenda. Daughter of Aphrodite / Brenda Jagger. — London : Constable, 1981. — 277p ; 23cm
ISBN 0-09-463840-3 : £6.95 B81-10074

Jagger, Brenda. Flint and roses / Brenda Jagger. — London : Macdonald Futura, 1981. — 479p ; 23cm
ISBN 0-354-04738-8 : £7.95 B81-31922

Jallim, Collins. The St Lucian / by Collins Jallim. — [Wembley] : Selectededitions, [1980]. — 45p ; 21cm
ISBN 0-86237-005-1 (pbk) : £0.85 B81-20195

James, Anna. Kissing cousins / Anna James. — London : Hale, 1981. — 191p 21cm
ISBN 0-7091-8764-5 : £6.25 B81-11903

James, Anna. The rebel heart / Anna James. — London : Hamlyn Paperbacks, 1980. — 236p ; 18cm
ISBN 0-600-32076-6 (pbk) : £1.25 B81-02144

James, Margaret, *1922-*. Marionette / Margaret James. — London : Prior, c1981, 1979. — v,330p ; 25cm
Originally published: London : Hale, 1979. — Published in large print
ISBN 0-86043-578-4 : £5.95 B81-24579

823'.914[F] — Fiction in English, *1945-* — *Texts continuation*

James, P. D.. Cover her face / P.D. James. — London : Prior, 1980, c1962. — 426p ; 25cm
Originally published: London : Faber, 1962. — Published in large print
ISBN 0-86043-492-3 : £5.95 B81-01452

James, P. D.. Innocent blood / P.D. James. — London : Prior, 1981, c1980. — 570p ; 25cm
Originally published: London : Faber, 1980. — Published in large print
ISBN 0-86043-599-7 : £7.50 B81-32767

James, P. D.. A mind to murder / P.D. James. — Harmondsworth : Penguin, 1974, c1963 (1980 [printing]). — 220p ; 18cm. — (Penguin crime fiction)
Originally published: London : Faber, 1963
£0.95 (pbk) B81-00483

James, P. D.. A mind to murder / by P.D. James. — London : Prior, 1980, c1963. — 437p ; 25cm
Originally published: London : Faber, 1963. — Published in large print
ISBN 0-86043-500-8 : £5.95 B81-12200

James, P. D.. Unnatural causes / by P.D. James. — London : Prior, 1980, c1967. — 448p ; 25cm
Originally published: London : Faber, 1967. — Published in large print
ISBN 0-86043-501-6 : £5.95 B81-09811

James, P. D.. An unsuitable job for a woman / by P.D. James. — London : Hall, c1981, 1972. — 435p ; 25cm
Originally published: London : Faber, 1972. — Published in large print
ISBN 0-86043-577-6 : £6.95 B81-24572

James, Peter, *19---*. Dead letter drop / Peter James. — London : W.H. Allen, 1981. — 203p ; 21cm
ISBN 0-491-02704-4 : £6.50 B81-19982

James, Saffron. Love is for the brave / by Saffron James. — London : Hale, 1980. — 160p ; 20cm
ISBN 0-7091-8427-1 : £5.25 B81-01445

James, Sally. Fortune at stake / by Sally James. — London : Hale, 1981. — 190p ; 20cm
ISBN 0-7091-8834-x : £6.25 B81-15952

James, Sally. Heir to Rowanlea / by Sally James. — London : Hale, 1980. — 192p ; 20cm
ISBN 0-7091-8568-5 : £6.25 B81-01466

James, Vanessa. Piers Clarendon / Vanessa James. — London : Hale, 1980. — 175p ; 20cm
ISBN 0-7091-8389-5 : £5.25 B81-01447

Jeal, Tim. A marriage of convenience / Tim Jeal. — London : Sphere, 1981, c1979. — 446p ; 18cm
Originally published: London : Hamilton, 1979
ISBN 0-7221-0413-8 (pbk) : £1.75 B81-24709

Jeffrey, Elizabeth. Web of destiny. — Large print ed. — Bath : Chivers Press, Jan.1982. — [256]p. — (A Seymour book)
Originally published: London : Mills & Boon, 1979
ISBN 0-85119-450-8 : £4.95 : CIP entry B81-33806

Jeffries, Roderic. Unseemly end : an Inspector Alvarez novel / Roderic Jeffries. — London : Collins, 1981. — 199p ; 21cm. — (The Crime Club)
ISBN 0-00-231867-9 : £6.25 : CIP rev. B81-25101

Jenkins, Judith. The black lily / by Judith Jenkins. — London : Hale, 1981. — 191p ; 20cm
ISBN 0-7091-8946-x : £5.60 B81-19221

Jenkins, Judith. The temporary bride / Judith Jenkins. — London : Hale, 1980. — 176p ; 20cm
ISBN 0-7091-8575-8 : £5.50 B81-15770

Jerome, Hilary. A woman's world : 138-9 Chri plus / by Hilary Jerome. — Wells (The Old Vicarage, Godney, Wells, Somerset, BA5 1RX) : Thorn, c1980. — 232p ; 22cm
ISBN 0-906374-02-2 : £5.50 : CIP rev. B80-12077

Jhabvala, Ruth Prawer. Get ready for battle / Ruth Prawer Jhabvala. — Harmondsworth : Penguin, 1981, c1962. — 160p ; 20cm
Originally published: London : Murray, 1962
ISBN 0-14-005289-5 (pbk) : £1.75 B81-27698

Jinman, Keith. Joss / Keith Jinman. — Bognor Regis : New Horizon, c1981. — 98p : ill 21cm
ISBN 0-86116-527-6 : £3.75 B81-32126

Jobson, Hamilton. Don't tell the press / by Hamilton Jobson. — London : Hale, 1981. — 206p ; 20cm
ISBN 0-7091-9067-0 : £5.95 B81-24984

Jobson, Hamilton. Exit to violence / Hamilton Jobson. — Large print ed. — Bath : Chivers, 1981, c1979. — 248p ; 23cm. — (A Lythway thriller)
Originally published: London : Collins, 1979
ISBN 0-85119-705-1 : £5.25 B81-08682

Jobson, Hamilton. To die a little / Hamilton Jobson. — Large print ed. — Bath : Chivers, 1981, c1978. — 271p ; 23cm. — (A Lythway thriller)
Originally published: London : Collins for the Crime Club, 1978
ISBN 0-85119-725-6 : Unpriced : CIP rev. B81-14920

John, Nancy. The Spanish house / Nancy John. — [London] : Silhouette, 1981, c1980. — 190p ; 18cm. — (Silhouette romance ; 33)
ISBN 0-340-26583-3 (pbk) : £0.65 : CIP rev. B81-02568

John, Nancy. To trust tomorrow / Nancy John. — London : Silhouette, 1981. — 189p ; 18cm. — (Silhouette romance ; 56)
ISBN 0-340-27034-9 (pbk) : £0.65 : CIP rev. B81-18119

John, Nancy. Tormenting flame / Nancy John. — London (47 Bedford Sq., WC1B 3DP) : Silhouette, 1981, c1980. — 188p ; 18cm. — (Silhouette romance ; no.17)
ISBN 0-340-26121-8 (pbk) : £0.65 : CIP rev. B80-21077

Johns, Larry. Czechmate / by Larry Johns. — London : Hale, 1980. — 156p ; 20cm
ISBN 0-7091-8519-7 : £5.75 B81-05734

Johns, Larry. The Dongola script / by Larry Johns. — London : Hale, 1981. — 191p ; 20cm
ISBN 0-7091-9189-8 : £6.25 B81-39161

Johns, Larry. Thunder island / by Larry Johns. — London : Hale, 1980. — 192p ; 20cm
ISBN 0-7091-8313-5 : £5.25 B81-00484

Johnson, Elisabeth. The fires of love / by Elisabeth Johnson. — London : Hale, 1980. — 176p ; 20cm
ISBN 0-7091-8317-8 : £4.95 B81-00485

Johnson, Elisabeth. Tropical wildcat / by Elisabeth Johnson. — London : Hale, 1981. — 189p ; 20cm
ISBN 0-7091-9137-5 : £5.60 B81-35246

Johnson, Sheila. Suffer little children / Sheila Johnson. — London : Collins, 1981. — 181p ; 20cm
ISBN 0-00-231796-6 : £6.25 : CIP rev. B81-15883

Johnston, Jennifer. The Christmas tree / Jennifer Johnston. — London : Hamilton, 1981. — 167p ; 21cm
ISBN 0-241-10673-7 : £6.95 : CIP rev. B81-23866

Johnston, Jennifer. The old jest / Jennifer Johnston. — [London] : Fontana, 1980, c1979. — 158p ; 18cm
Originally published: London : Hamilton, 1979
ISBN 0-00-615850-1 (pbk) : £1.00 B81-01453

Johnston, Ronald. Sea story / Ronald Johnston. — London : Macdonald Futura, 1980. — 309p ; 23cm
ISBN 0-354-04555-5 : £6.50 B81-00486

Johnston, Ronald. Sea story / Ronald Johnston. — South Yarmouth, Mass. : John Curley ; [Long Preston] : Magna [distributor], c1980. — 624p ; 23cm
Originally published: London : Macdonald Futura, 1980. — Published in large print
ISBN 0-89340-336-9 : £4.95 B81-39300

Jon, Montague. A question of law / Montague Jon. — London : Macmillan, 1981. — 192p ; 21cm
ISBN 0-333-31729-7 : £5.50 B81-37185

Jon, Montague. The Wallington case / Montague Jon. — London : Macmillan, 1981. — 222p ; 21cm
ISBN 0-333-30526-4 : £5.50 B81-18692

Jones, Andromeda. The peach princess / by Andromeda Jones. — London : Hale, 1980. — 188p ; 20cm
ISBN 0-7091-8300-3 : £5.25 B81-00487

Jones, Eva. Taboo / Eva Jones. — London : Cape, 1981. — 199p ; 21cm
ISBN 0-224-01863-9 : £6.50 B81-02894

Jones, Gareth, *1951-*. [Lord of misrule]. The disinherited / by Gareth Jones. — London : Gollancz, 1981, c1980. — 352p ; 23cm
Originally published: New York : Farrar, Straus, Giroux, 1980
ISBN 0-575-02770-3 : £6.95 B81-12304

Jones, Gareth Lovett. Valley with a bright cloud / Gareth Lovett Jones. — London : Methuen, 1980. — 189p ; 21cm
ISBN 0-416-87780-x : £4.95 : CIP rev. B80-11617

Jones, Gwyn, *1952-*. Up will go Parliament / Gwyn Jones. — Bognor Regis : New Horizon, c1981. — 205p ; 21cm
ISBN 0-86116-718-x : £4.75 B81-19258

Jones, Jonah. A tree may fall / Jonah Jones. — London : Bodley Head, 1980. — 213p ; 23cm
ISBN 0-370-30320-2 : £5.95 : CIP rev. B80-18489

Jones, Peggy Loosemore. Moon over Mexico / by Peggy Loosemore Jones. — London : Hale, 1981. — 190p ; 20cm
ISBN 0-7091-8700-9 : £5.50 B81-02533

Jones, Tristan. Dutch treat : a novel of World War II / Tristan Jones. — London : Bodley Head, 1980, c1979. — 270p : 1map,1plan ; 23cm
Originally published: Kansas City : Andrews & McMeel, 1979
ISBN 0-370-30307-5 : £6.50 : CIP rev. B80-14011

Jons, Hal. Assassin trail / by Hal Jons. — London : Hale, 1981. — 160p ; 20cm
ISBN 0-7091-9291-6 : £4.95 B81-33542

Jons, Hal. Gringo gold / by Hal Jons. — London : Hale, 1981. — 160p ; 20cm
ISBN 0-7091-8622-3 : £4.95 B81-11780

823'.914[F] — Fiction in English, ***1945- — Texts continuation***

Jons, Hal. Guns of justice / by Hal Jons. — London : Hale, 1980. — 157p ; 20cm
ISBN 0-7091-8475-1 : £4.95 B81-00488

Jordan, David, *1939-*. Double red / David Jordan. — London : Deutsch, 1981. — 156p ; 23cm
ISBN 0-233-97329-x : £5.95 : CIP rev. B81-08881

Jordan, Lee. Cat's eyes. — London : Hodder & Stoughton, Nov.1981. — [176]p
ISBN 0-340-27244-9 : £5.95 : CIP entry B81-31160

Jordan, Neil. The past / Neil Jordan. — London : Cape, 1980. — 232p ; 21cm
ISBN 0-224-01845-0 : £6.50 : CIP rev. B80-13559

Jordan, Penny. Falcon's prey / by Penny Jordan. — London : Mills & Boon, 1981. — 188p ; 20cm
ISBN 0-263-09906-7 : £4.55 B81-34109

Jordan, Penny. Tiger man / by Penny Jordan. — London : Mills & Boon, 1981. — 186p ; 20cm
ISBN 0-263-09918-0 : £4.55 B81-35642

Joseph, Marie. Emma Sparrow. — London : Hutchinson, Nov.1981. — [300]p
ISBN 0-09-146360-2 : £6.95 : CIP entry B81-28766

Joseph, Marie. A leaf in the wind / Marie Joseph. — London : Hutchinson, 1980. — 302p ; 21cm
ISBN 0-09-142380-5 : £5.95 B81-00489

Joseph, Marie. Maggie Craig / Marie Joseph. — London : Arrow, 1981, c1979. — 268p ; 18cm
Originally published: London : Hutchinson, 1980
ISBN 0-09-925390-9 (pbk) : £1.35 B81-16013

Josipovici, Gabriel. The air we breathe. — Brighton : Harvester Press, Oct.1981. — [128]p
ISBN 0-7108-0056-8 : £7.95 : CIP entry B81-30330

Joyce, Cyril. A calculated risk / by Cyril Joyce. — London : Hale, 1981. — 160p ; 20cm
ISBN 0-7091-9206-1 : £6.25 B81-29859

Joyce, Cyril. Errant witness / by Cyril Joyce. — London : Hale, 1981. — 191p ; 20cm
ISBN 0-7091-8721-1 : £5.75 B81-08962

Judd, Alan. A breed of heroes. — London : Hodder and Stoughton, May 1981. — [288]p
ISBN 0-340-26334-2 : £7.25 : CIP entry B81-04388

Judge, Sara. The gypsy's return / by Sara Judge. — London : Hale, 1981. — 192p ; 20cm
ISBN 0-7091-9228-2 : £6.75 B81-33526

Kamada, Annelise. A love so bold / by Annelise Kamada. — London : Hale, 1981. — 352p ; 21cm
Originally published: United States? : s.n., 1978
ISBN 0-7091-8989-3 : £7.50 B81-19297

Kamada, Annelise. Richer than a crown / by Annelise Kamada. — London : Hale, 1981, c1968. — 238p ; 20cm
ISBN 0-7091-9039-5 : £6.50 B81-37308

Kartun, Derek. I, Norman Harris / Derek Kartun. — London : Bodley Head, 1980. — 223p ; 21cm
ISBN 0-370-30365-2 : £5.50 : CIP rev. B80-19939

Kavanagh, Dan. Fiddle city. — London : Cape, Oct.1981. — [176]p
ISBN 0-224-01977-5 : £5.95 : CIP entry B81-27335

Kay, George, *1915-*. The secret life of Mr. Beauty / George Kay. — Bognor Regis : New Horizon, c1979. — 100p ; 21cm
ISBN 0-86116-189-0 : £2.50 B81-19243

Kaye, M. M.. Shadow of the moon : M.M. Kaye. — Harmondsworth : Penguin, 1979 (1980 [printing]). — 614p : 1geneal.table ; 20cm
Originally published: London : Longmans, 1957
ISBN 0-14-005316-6 (pbk) : £2.50 B81-02130

Kea, Neville. The glass school / Neville Kea. — London : Hale, 1980. — 159p ; 21cm. — (Hale SF)
ISBN 0-7091-8440-9 : £5.95 B81-03074

Kea, Neville. The rats of Megaera / Neville Kea. — London : Hale, 1980. — 192p ; 21cm. — (Hale SF)
ISBN 0-7091-8105-1 : £5.50 B81-01488

Kea, Neville. Scorpion / by Neville Kea. — London : Hale, 1981. — 158p ; 20cm. — (Hale SF)
ISBN 0-7091-9266-5 : £6.25 B81-35198

Keating, H. R. F.. Go West, Inspector Ghote. — London : Collins, 1981. — 213p ; 20cm. — (The Crime Club)
ISBN 0-00-231289-1 : £25.95 : CIP rev. B81-04237

Keating, H. R. F.. Inspector Ghote breaks an egg / H.R.F. Keating. — Large print ed. — Bath : Lythway, 1981, c1970. — 320p ; 23cm. — (A Lythway mystery)
Originally published: London : Collins, 1970
ISBN 0-85119-709-4 : Unpriced B81-10873

Keating, H. R. F.. Inspector Ghote draws a line. — Large print ed. — Bath (Lythway), 1980, c1979. — 300p ; 23cm
Originally published: London : Collins, 1979
ISBN 0-85046-908-2 : £6.25 : CIP rev. B80-22535

Keating, H. R. F.. Inspector Ghote draws a line / H.R.F. Keating. — Feltham : Hamlyn, 1981. — 195p ; 18cm. — (A Hamlyn whodunnit)
Originally published: London : Collins, 1979
ISBN 0-600-20249-6 (pbk) : £1.10 B81-11429

Keating, H. R. F.. Inspector Ghote plays a joker / H.R.F. Keating. — London : Hamlyn Paperbacks, 1981. — 189p ; 18cm. — (A Hamlyn whodunnit)
Originally published: London : Collins, 1969
ISBN 0-600-20310-7 (pbk) : £1.25 B81-28651

Keating, H. R. F.. Inspector Ghote trusts the heart / H.R.F. Keating. — Large print ed. — Bath : Chivers, 1981, c1972. — 303p ; 23cm. — (A Lythway mystery)
Originally published: London : Collins for the Crime Club, 1972
ISBN 0-85119-726-4 : Unpriced : CIP rev. B81-14922

Keating, H. R. F.. The murder of the Maharajah / H.R.F. Keating. — Feltham : Hamlyn, 1981, c1980. — 223p ; 18cm. — (A Hamlyn whodunnit)
Originally published: London : Collins, 1980
ISBN 0-600-20320-4 (pbk) : £1.25 B81-40996

Keating, H. R. F.. The murder of the Maharajah / H.R.F. Keating. — London : Prior, 1981, c1980. — 469p ; 25cm
Originally published: London : Collins [for] the Crime Club, 1980. — Published in large print
ISBN 0-86043-591-1 : £7.50 B81-32770

Keating, H. R. F.. The perfect murder / H.R.F. Keating. — Feltham : Hamlyn, 1980, c1964. — 256p ; 18cm. — (A Hamlyn whodunnit)
Originally published: London : Collins, 1964
ISBN 0-600-20240-2 (pbk) : £1.10 B81-00490

Kebbell, Janet. Shadow of darkness / by Janet Kebbell. — London : Hale, 1980. — 158p ; 20cm
ISBN 0-7091-8061-6 : £4.75 B81-00491

Keene, Tom. Spyship / Tom Keene with Brian Haynes. — London : Allen Lane, 1980. — 315p ; 23cm
ISBN 0-7139-1266-9 : £5.95 B81-00492

Keene, Tom. Spyship / Tom Keene with Brian Haynes. — Harmondsworth : Penguin, 1981, c1980. — 347p ; 18cm
Originally published: New York : R. Marak ; London : Allen Lane, 1980
ISBN 0-14-005216-x (pbk) : £1.50 B81-15372

Kelaart, Piers. Midas / Piers Kelaart. — London : Macdonald Futura, 1981. — 240p ; 18cm
ISBN 0-7088-1988-5 (pbk) : £1.25 B81-15738

Kelly, Patrick, *1917-*. The lonely margins / Patrick Kelly. — London : Granada, 1981. — 267p ; 23cm
ISBN 0-246-11107-0 : £6.95 B81-21212

Kemp, Sarah. Goodbye, pussy. — Large print ed. — Bath : Chivers Press, Dec.1981. — [256]p. — (A Lythway book)
Originally published: London : Collins, 1979
ISBN 0-85119-769-8 : £6.80 : CIP entry B81-31800

Kemp, Shirley E.. A house in the country / by Shirley E. Kemp. — London : Hale, 1980. — 160p ; 20cm
ISBN 0-7091-8474-3 : £5.25 B81-01449

Kennedy, Lena. Autumn Alley / Lena Kennedy. — London : Macdonald Futura, 1981, c1980. — 394p ; 18cm. — (A futura book)
Originally published: London : Macdonald, 1980
ISBN 0-7088-1978-8 (corrected : pbk) : £1.60 B81-30932

Kennedy, Lena. Nelly Kelly / Lena Kennedy. — London : Macdonald, 1981. — 277p ; 23cm
ISBN 0-354-04712-4 : £6.95 B81-28373

Kennemore, Tim. The fortunate few / Tim Kennemore. — London : Faber, 1981. — 107p ; 21cm
ISBN 0-571-11732-5 : £3.95 : CIP rev. B81-23764

Kent, Alexander. Richard Bolitho - midshipman / Alexander Kent. — London : Sparrow Books, 1981, c1975. — 158p ; 18cm
Originally published: London : Hutchinson, 1975
ISBN 0-09-915200-2 (pbk) : £0.80 B81-13304

Kent, Alexander. Stand into danger / Alexander Kent. — London : Arrow, 1981, c1980. — 296p ; 18cm. — (A Richard Bolitho story)
Originally published: London : Hutchinson, 1980
ISBN 0-09-925380-1 (pbk) : £1.50 B81-11025

Kent, Alexander. Stand into danger. — Large print ed. — Anstey : Ulverscroft, Feb.1982. — [496]p. — (Ulverscroft large print series : adventure, suspense)
ISBN 0-7089-0753-9 : £5.00 : CIP entry B81-36938

Kent, Alexander. A tradition of victory / Alexander Kent. — London : Hutchinson, 1981. — 296p : maps ; 23cm
Maps on lining papers
ISBN 0-09-145810-2 : £6.95 : CIP rev. B81-20557

Kent, Pamela. Flight to the stars. — Large print ed. — Bath : Chivers Press, Feb.1982. — [240] p. — (A Lythway book)
Originally published: London : Mills & Boon, 1977
ISBN 0-85119-784-1 : £6.90 : CIP entry B81-35862

Kent, Sarah, *1924-*. The Spanish jewel / by Sarah Kent. — London : Hale, 1981. — 192p ; 20cm
ISBN 0-7091-8693-2 : £6.25 B81-08653

823'.914[F] — Fiction in English, *1945-* — *Texts continuation*

Kent, Stella, *1927-*. All her lovely companions / by Stella Kent. — London : Hale, 1981. — 190p ; 20cm
ISBN 0-7091-9078-6 : £5.60 B81-24351

Kenworthy, Christopher. In the dark of the moon / by Christopher Kenworthy. — London : Hale, 1981. — 237p ; 21cm
ISBN 0-7091-9200-2 : £7.25 B81-35231

Kenyon, Michael. Zigzag / Michael Kenyon. — London : Collins, 1981. — 218p ; 20cm. — (The Crime Club)
ISBN 0-00-231981-0 : £6.50 : CIP rev. B81-25102

Keppel, Charlotte. The ghosts of Fontenoy / Charlotte Keppel. — Loughton : Piatkus, 1981. — 247p ; 21cm
ISBN 0-86188-107-9 : £6.50 : CIP rev. B81-15824

Keppel, Charlotte. The villains : a haunting tale of the marshes / Charlotte Keppel. — Loughton ([17 Brook Rd,] Loughton, Essex [IG10 2BW]) : Piatkus, 1980. — 226p ; 21cm
ISBN 0-86188-049-8 : £5.50 : CIP rev. B80-12079

Kerr, Carole. Stolen heart / by Carole Kerr. — London : Hale, 1981. — 191p ; 20cm
ISBN 0-7091-8853-6 : £5.60 B81-15949

Kersey, Clare. The eagle's bride / by Clare Kersey. — London : Hale, 1981. — 158p ; 20cm
ISBN 0-7091-9344-0 : £6.50 B81-40546

Kershaw, Valerie. The bank manager's wife / Valerie Kershaw. — London : Duckworth, 1981. — 160p ; 23cm
ISBN 0-7156-1600-5 : £7.95 : CIP rev. B81-21582

Kershaw, Valerie. Rosa / Valerie Kershaw. — London : Duckworth, 1980. — 139p ; 23cm
ISBN 0-7156-1506-8 : £6.95 : CIP rev. B80-13067

Kessler, Leo. Cauldron of blood / Leo Kessler. — London : Macdonald Futura, 1981. — 223p ; 21cm
ISBN 0-354-04661-6 : £4.50 B81-12065

Kessler, Leo. Cauldron of blood / Leo Kessler. — London : Macdonald Futura, 1981. — 223p ; 18cm. — (Wotan/Panzer)
ISBN 0-7088-1997-4 (pbk) : £0.95 B81-15452

Kessler, Leo. Ghost division / Leo Kessler. — London : Severn House, 1981, c1978. — 189p ; 21cm
Originally published: London : Futura, c1978
ISBN 0-7278-0679-3 : £5.95 : CIP rev. B81-07613

Kessler, Leo. Otto's phoney war / Leo Kessler. — London : Macdonald Futura, 1981. — 224p ; 21cm. — (Otto Stahl ; 1) (Macdonald war)
ISBN 0-354-04665-9 : £4.50 B81-17392

Kessler, Leo. Panzer hunt / Leo Kessler. — London : Futura, 1979. — 188p ; 18cm. — (Wotan series)
ISBN 0-7088-1520-0 (pbk) : £0.80 B81-17460

Kessler, Leo. Schirmer's headhunters / Leo Kessler. — London : Macdonald Futura, 1981. — 189p ; 21cm
ISBN 0-354-04666-7 : £4.50 B81-21317

Kessler, Leo. Schirmer's headhunters / Leo Kessler. — London : Macdonald Futura, 1981. — 189p : 1map ; 18cm. — (A Futura book) (Wotan ; 16)
ISBN 0-7088-2063-8 (pbk) : £1.10 B81-40949

Kessler, Leo. Sink the Scharnhorst / Leo Kessler. — London : Macdonald Futura, 1981. — 256p ; 18cm. — (The Sea wolves ; 1)
ISBN 0-7088-2060-3 (pbk) : £1.25 B81-28343

Kessler, Leo. Valley of the assassins / Leo Kessler. — London : Futura, 1979. — 206p : 1map,1plan ; 18cm. — (Stormtroop)
ISBN 0-7088-1485-9 (pbk) : £0.85 B81-17459

Kidd, Flora. Bride for a captain / Flora Kidd. — London : Mills and Boon, 1981. — 188p ; 19cm
ISBN 0-263-09935-0 : £4.55 B81-40871

Kidd, Flora. Passionate stranger / by Flora Kidd. — London : Mills & Boon, 1981. — 187p ; 20cm
ISBN 0-263-09899-0 : £4.55 B81-28520

Kidd, Flora. Personal affair / by Flora Kidd. — London : Mills & Boon, 1981. — 188p ; 20cm
ISBN 0-263-09853-2 : £4.55 B81-14247

Kilner, Geoffrey. Kingfisher / Geoffrey Kilner. — London : Dobson, 1980. — 151p ; 21cm
For adolescents
ISBN 0-234-72205-3 : £3.95 B81-00493

Kilworth, Garry. Gemini god / Garry Kilworth. — London : Faber, 1981. — 240p ; 21cm
ISBN 0-571-11661-2 : £6.50 : CIP rev. B81-10468

Kilworth, Garry. Split second / Gary [i.e. Garry] Kilworth. — Harmondsworth : Penguin, 1981, c1979. — 191p ; 19cm. — (Penguin science fiction)
Originally published: London : Faber, 1979
ISBN 0-14-005203-8 (pbk) : £1.50 B81-32832

Kimball, Frank. The Saginaw Hills / by Frank Kimball. — London : Hale, 1981. — 154p ; 20cm
ISBN 0-7091-8915-x : £4.95 B81-24875

Kimball, Ralph. Manning / by Ralph Kimball. — London : Hale, 1981. — 160p ; 20cm
ISBN 0-7091-8692-4 : £4.95 B81-06376

Kincaid, Stephanie. The heart has reasons / Stephanie Kincaid. — London : Hale, 1981. — 186p ; 20cm
ISBN 0-7091-8736-x : £5.50 B81-11169

Kinder, Kathleen, *1932- (Oct.)*. The raven and the dove / Kathleen Kinder. — [London] : Fontana, 1981, c1979. — 188p ; 18cm
Originally published: London : Collins, 1979
ISBN 0-00-616413-7 (pbk) : £1.25 B81-36782

King, Betty. Claybourn / Betty King. — London : Hale, 1980. — 173,[1]p ; 21cm
Bibliography: p[1]
ISBN 0-7091-8220-1 : £5.50 B81-00494

Kingham, Janet M.. The eyes of a child / Janet M. Kingham. — Bognor Regis : New Horizon, c1979. — 45p ; 21cm
ISBN 0-86116-248-x : £2.50 B81-19241

Kinsley, Peter. The VATCHMAN switch / by Peter Kinsley. — London : Hale, 1980. — 255p ; 20cm
ISBN 0-7091-8328-3 : £5.75 B81-01450

Kirsten, Angela. The devil's ring / Angela Kirsten. — London : Hale, 1980. — 191p ; 20cm
ISBN 0-7091-8566-9 : £6.25 B81-00495

Kitchen, Paddy. The Golden Veil : a novel based on the life of Elizabeth Siddall / by Paddy Kitchen. — London : Hamilton, 1981. — 286p ; 23cm
ISBN 0-241-10584-6 : £7.95 : CIP rev. B81-04301

Knight, Alanna. Castle Clodha. — Large print ed. — Long Preston : Magna, Aug.1981. — [412]p
ISBN 0-86009-336-0 : £4.95 : CIP entry B81-16908

Knowles, Anne. The raven tree / Anne Knowles. — London : Erye Methuen, 1981. — 156p ; 23cm
ISBN 0-413-46730-9 : £5.95 : CIP rev. B81-00496

Knox, Bill. A killing in antiques / Bill Knox. — London : Hutchinson, 1981. — 185p ; 21cm
ISBN 0-09-144420-9 : £5.95 B81-10161

Konrad, Klaus. First blood / Klaus Konrad. — London : Macdonald Futura, 1980. — 223p ; 18cm
ISBN 0-7088-1904-4 (pbk) : £1.10 B81-07655

Konrad, Klaus. March on Moscow / Klaus Konrad. — London : Macdonald Futura, 1981. — 222p ; 21cm. — ([Russian series] ; [2])
ISBN 0-354-04745-0 : £4.95 B81-28374

Kostov, K. N.. Baptism of blood / K.N. Kostov. — London : Arrow, 1980. — 221p : 1map ; 18cm
ISBN 0-09-922580-8 (pbk) : £1.10 B81-02498

Kostov, K. N.. Baptism of blood. — London : Severn House, Oct.1981. — [224]p
ISBN 0-7278-0739-0 : £5.95 : CIP entry B81-24637

Kostov, K. N.. Blood on the Baltic / K.N. Kostov. — London : Arrow, 1981. — 217p ; 18cm
ISBN 0-09-925560-x (pbk) : £1.25 B81-16008

Kostov, K. N.. The gulag rats / K.N. Kostov. — London : Arrow, 1981. — 206p ; 18cm
ISBN 0-09-924000-9 (pbk) : £1.10 B81-11042

Krauss, Bruno. Shark hunt / Bruno Krauss. — London : Sphere, 1980. — 160p ; 18cm. — (Sea wolf ; 4)
ISBN 0-7221-5291-4 (pbk) : £0.95 B81-07664

Krisman, Sue. Ducks and drakes / Sue Krisman. — London : Heinemann, 1981. — 185p ; 23cm
ISBN 0-434-39756-3 : £6.95 B81-10076

Kroll, Burt. Flaming range / by Burt Kroll. — London : Hale, 1981. — 160p ; 20cm
ISBN 0-7091-8717-3 : £4.95 B81-07749

Kruse, John. Red Omega. — London : Bodley Head, Oct.1981. — [288]p
ISBN 0-370-30336-9 : £6.95 : CIP entry B81-25768

Kyle, Duncan. Green river high / Duncan Kyle. — [London] : Fontana, 1980, c1979. — 251p ; 18cm
Originally published: London : Collins, 1979
ISBN 0-00-616001-8 (pbk) : £1.25 B81-01451

Kyle, Duncan. Green river high. — Large print ed. — Long Preston : Magna, Oct.1981. — [480]p
ISBN 0-86009-348-4 : £4.95 : CIP entry B81-27383

Kyle, Duncan. Stalking point / Duncan Kyle. — London : Collins, 1981. — 288p ; 22cm
ISBN 0-00-222297-3 : £7.50 : CIP rev. B81-25099

Lacey, Pat. Rosemary Cottage / by Pat Lacey. — London : Hale, 1981. — 176p ; 20cm
ISBN 0-7091-8765-3 : £5.50 B81-14070

Laffeaty, Christina. To reap a bitter harvest / by Christina Laffeaty. — London : Hale, 1980. — 187p ; 20cm
ISBN 0-7091-8574-x : £5.25 B81-01454

823′.914[F] — Fiction in English, *1945-* — *Texts continuation*

Laine, Annabel. The melancholy virgin / Annabel Laine. — London : Macdonald, 1981. — 220p ; 23cm
ISBN 0-354-04616-0 : £6.95 B81-14081

Lajeunesse, C. R.. Dead man running / by C.R. Lajeunesse. — London : Hale, 1981. — 191p ; 20cm
ISBN 0-7091-8839-0 : £5.75 B81-08640

Lake, Nara. Goldrush girl / Nara Lake. — London : Hale, 1981. — 190p ; 21cm
ISBN 0-7091-9182-0 : £6.75 B81-35236

Lake, Patricia. Untamed witch / by Patricia Lake. — London : Mills & Boon, 1981. — 188p ; 20cm
ISBN 0-263-09912-1 : £4.55 B81-34108

Laker, Rosalind. Banners of silk. — London : Eyre Methuen, Sept.1981. — [480]p
ISBN 0-413-48120-4 : £6.95 : CIP entry B81-23910

Laker, Rosalind. The Warwycks of Easthampton / Rosalind Laker. — London : Eyre Methuen, 1980. — 350p ; 23cm
ISBN 0-413-46700-7 : £6.50 B81-01455

Lamb, Charlotte. Abduction / by Charlotte Lamb. — London : Mills & Boon, 1981. — 188p ; 19cm
ISBN 0-263-09814-1 : £4.55 B81-09401

Lamb, Charlotte. Compulsion / by Charlotte Lamb. — London : Mills & Boon, 1980. — 189p ; 20cm
ISBN 0-263-09748-x : £3.85 B81-00497

Lamb, Charlotte. Dangerous / by Charlotte Lamb. — London : Mills & Boon, 1981. — 188p ; 20cm
ISBN 0-263-09900-8 : £4.55 B81-34102

Lamb, Charlotte. Desire / by Charlotte Lamb. — London : Mills and Boon, 1981. — 188p ; 19cm
ISBN 0-263-09934-2 : £4.55 B81-40870

Lamb, Charlotte. Duel of desire / by Charlotte Lamb. — London : Mills & Boon, 1979, c1978. — 190p ; 17cm
ISBN 0-263-72852-8 (pbk) : £0.55 B81-06405

Lamb, Charlotte. Heartbreaker / by Charlotte Lamb. — London : Mills & Boon, 1981. — 188p ; 20cm
ISBN 0-263-09923-7 : £4.55 B81-35639

Lamb, Charlotte. Illusion / by Charlotte Lamb. — London : Mills & Boon, 1981. — 187p ; 20cm
ISBN 0-263-09888-5 : £4.55 B81-28555

Lamb, Charlotte. Seduction : by Charlotte Lamb. — London : Mills & Boon, 1980. — 187p ; 19cm
ISBN 0-263-09792-7 : £3.85 B81-05905

Lamb, Charlotte. Storm centre. — Large print ed. — Bath : Chivers Press, Dec.1981. — [248] p. — (A Seymour book)
ISBN 0-85119-445-1 : £4.95 : CIP entry B81-31727

Lamb, Charlotte. Stranger in the night / by Charlotte Lamb. — London : Mills & Boon, 1980. — 187p ; 20cm
ISBN 0-263-09740-4 : £3.85 B81-00498

Lambert, Derek. I, said the spy / Derek Lambert. — London : Arlington, 1980. — 453p ; 23cm
ISBN 0-85140-490-1 : £6.50 : CIP rev. B80-17987

Lambert, Derek. I, said the spy / Derek Lambert. — London : Sphere, 1981, c1980. — 435p ; 18cm
Originally published: London : Arlington, 1980
ISBN 0-7221-5346-5 (pbk) : £1.75 B81-37284

Lambert, Derek. Trance / Derek Lambert. — London : Arlington, 1981. — 270p ; 23cm
ISBN 0-85140-549-5 : £6.95 : CIP rev. B81-20156

Lamont, Marianne. Horns of the moon / Marianne Lamont. — London : Pan, 1981, c1979. — 268p ; 18cm
Originally published: London : Constable, 1979
ISBN 0-330-26254-8 (pbk) : £1.25 B81-09738

Lancaster, David. Caroline R / David Lancaster. — London : Hutchinson, 1980. — 319p ; 23cm
ISBN 0-09-144360-1 (corrected) : £6.95 B81-02497

Lancaster, Graham. Seward′s folly / Graham Lancaster. — London : Methuen, 1980. — 159p ; 23cm
ISBN 0-413-47360-0 : £5.95 B81-02242

Lancaster, Sheila. Dark sweet wanton / Sheila Lancaster. — Large print ed. — Leicester : Ulverscroft, 1981, c1979. — 494p ; 23cm. — (Ulverscroft large print)
Originally published: London : Hodder & Stoughton, 1979
ISBN 0-7089-0637-0 : Unpriced B81-26474

Landy, Mary. A letter from Lyla / by Mary Landy. — London : Hale, 1981. — 173p ; 20cm
ISBN 0-7091-8660-6 : £5.50 B81-15303

Landy, Mary. Profile of a stranger / by Mary Landy. — London : Hale, 1981. — 176p ; 20cm
ISBN 0-7091-9288-6 : £5.75 B81-35245

Lane, Roumelia. Dream island / by Roumelia Lane. — London : Mills & Boon, 1981. — 186p ; 20cm
ISBN 0-263-09857-5 : £4.55 B81-18353

Lane, Roumelia. Second spring / by Roumelia Lane. — London : Mills & Boon, 1980. — 190p ; 20cm
ISBN 0-263-09726-9 : £3.85 B81-00499

Lang, Frances. The filigree bird / by Frances Lang. — London : Hale, 1981. — 190p ; 20cm
ISBN 0-7091-8847-1 : £5.95 B81-15306

Lang, Frances. Fortune′s favourite / by Frances Lang. — London : Hale, 1981. — 191p ; 20cm
ISBN 0-7091-9060-3 : £6.50 B81-37295

Langley, Bob. Autumn tiger / Bob Langley. — London : Joseph, 1981. — 251p ; 23cm
ISBN 0-7181-2030-2 : £6.95 B81-39295

Langley, Bob. Warlords / Bob Langley. — London : Sphere, 1981, c1979. — 222p ; 18cm
Originally published: London : Joseph, 1979
ISBN 0-7221-5409-7 (pbk) : £1.25 B81-09798

Langley, Tania. Mademoiselle Madeleine / Tania Langley. — London : Corgi, 1981. — 253p ; 18cm
ISBN 0-552-11684-x (corrected : pbk) : £1.25 B81-30709

Lant, Harvey. Gun thunder / Harvey Lant. — London : Hale, 1981. — 160p ; 20cm
ISBN 0-7091-9307-6 : £4.95 B81-37322

Lant, Harvey. Gunsmoke marshal / by Harvey Lant. — London : Hale, 1981. — 159p ; 20cm
ISBN 0-7091-8739-4 : £4.95 B81-08958

Lapington, G. E.. Warm on a cold night / G.E. Lapington. — London : Eyre Methuen, 1980. — 347p ; 22cm
ISBN 0-413-47170-5 : £5.95 : CIP rev. B80-11619

Laqueur, Walter. Farewell to Europe : a novel / by Walter Laqueur. — London : Weidenfeld and Nicolson, 1981. — 310p ; 23cm
ISBN 0-297-77870-6 : £6.50 B81-11110

Lash, Jennifer. From May to October / Jennifer Lash. — London : Hamilton, 1980. — 216p ; 21cm
ISBN 0-241-10470-x : £6.95 B81-00500

Latouche, Harriet. Tarot cards in Thessaly / Harriet Latouche. — Bognor Regis : New Horizon, c1980. — 268p ; 21cm
ISBN 0-86116-546-2 : £6.75 B81-19042

Laurance, Andrew. The hiss / Andrew Laurance. — London : W.H. Allen, 1981. — 191p ; 18cm. — (A star book)
ISBN 0-352-30842-7 (pbk) : £1.25 B81-15591

Lauren, Linda. Honesty / Linda Lauren. — London : New English Library, 1980 (1981 [printing]). — 192p ; 18cm
ISBN 0-450-05111-0 (pbk) : £1.25 B81-14315

Lauren, Linda. Pretties / Linda Lauren. — London : New English Library, 1981. — 212p ; 23cm
ISBN 0-450-04835-7 : £5.95 B81-03393

Laurence, Joseph. For the love of a ladye / Joseph Laurence. — Bognor Regis : New Horizon, c1980. — v,373p ; 22cm
ISBN 0-86116-184-x : £5.75 B81-19248

Lawrence, Arthur. The Duke and the tailor / by Arthur Lawrence. — Wembley : Selecteditions, 1980. — 396p ; 21cm
ISBN 0-86237-010-8 (pbk) : £2.00 B81-20193

Lawson, Joan, *1925-*. Flint Cottage / Joan Lawson. — London : Dobson, 1981. — 192p ; 21cm
ISBN 0-234-72263-0 : £4.25 B81-31923

Layberry, L. G. J.. Gleanings : a farming love story / L.G.J. Layberry. — Tunbridge Wells : Midas, 1981. — 173p ; 23cm
ISBN 0-85936-274-4 : £5.95 B81-32072

Le Carré, John. The honourable schoolboy / John le Carré. — London : Pan, 1978, c1977 (1981 printing). — 542p : 1map ; 18cm
Originally published: London : Hodder and Stoughton, 1977
ISBN 0-330-25356-5 (pbk) : £1.95 B81-24455

Le Carré, John. Smiley′s people / John le Carré. — London : Pan, 1980 (1981 printing). — 334p ; 18cm
Originally published: New York : Knopf, 1979 ; London : Hodder and Stoughton, 1980
ISBN 0-330-26272-6 (pbk) : £1.75 B81-20206

Le Carré, John. Smiley′s people / John Le Carré. — Large print ed. — Leicester : Ulverscroft, 1981, c1979. — 530p ; 23cm. — (Ulverscroft large print series)
Originally published: New York : Knopf, 1979 ; London : Hodder and Stoughton, 1980
ISBN 0-7089-0639-7 : Unpriced : CIP rev. B81-13513

Le Carré, John. Tinker, tailor, soldier, spy / John le Carré. — London : Pan, 1975, c1974 (1981 printing). — 316p ; 18cm
Originally published: London : Hodder and Stoughton, 1974
ISBN 0-330-24407-8 (pbk) : £1.75 B81-24456

Leach, Christopher, *1925-*. Blood games : a novel / Christopher Leach. — London : Dent, 1981. — 227p ; 23cm
ISBN 0-460-04536-9 : £6.95 : CIP rev. B81-14921

823'.914[F] — Fiction in English, *1945-* — *Texts continuation*

Leamer, Laurence. Assignment. — London : Hodder & Stoughton, Aug.1981. — [224]p
ISBN 0-340-27038-1 : £6.95 : CIP entry
B81-21645

Lear, Peter. Goldengirl / Peter Lear. — London : Granada, 1978, c1977 (1979 [printing]). — 377p ; 18cm. — (Mayflower)
Originally published: London : Cassell, 1977
ISBN 0-583-12858-0 (pbk) : £1.50 B81-24454

Leasor, James. The Unknown Warrior / James Leasor. — London : Heinemann, 1980. — 264p ; 23cm
Bibliography: p262-264
ISBN 0-434-41028-4 : £6.95 B81-00501

Leather, Edwin. The Duveen letter / Edwin Leather. — London : Macmillan, 1980. — 191p ; 21cm
ISBN 0-333-28973-0 : £5.50 B81-01456

Leavitt, Marianne Marshall. Ambassador's lady / by Marianne Marshall Leavitt. — London : Hale, 1980. — 206p ; 21cm
ISBN 0-7091-8598-7 : £6.25 B81-01457

Lecomber, Brian. Dead weight / by Brian Lecomber. — Bolton-by-Bowland : Magna, 1981, c1976. — 522pp ; 23cm
Originally published: London : Hodder and Stoughton, 1976. — Published in large print
ISBN 0-86009-311-5 : £5.75 : CIP rev.
B81-03712

Lee, K. R.. Rendezvous with battleship / by K.R. Lee. — London : Hale, 1981. — 204p : 1map ; 21cm
ISBN 0-7091-8846-3 : £6.25 B81-08990

Lee, Tanith. Volkhavaar / Tanith Lee. — London : Hamlyn Paperbacks, 1981, c1977. — 202p ; 18cm. — (Hamlyn science fiction)
ISBN 0-600-39453-0 (pbk) : £1.25 B81-33491

Lees, R. H.. A question of murder / by R.H. Lees. — London : Hale, 1981. — 192p ; 20cm
ISBN 0-7091-9235-5 : £6.25 B81-35200

Leeson, Robert. It's my life / Robert Leeson. — [London] : Fontana, 1981, c1980. — 140p ; 18cm. — (Lions)
Originally published: London : Collins, 1980. — For adolescents
ISBN 0-00-671783-7 (pbk) : £0.95 B81-15522

Legat, Michael. Mario's vineyard / Michael Legat. — London : Souvenir, 1980. — 455p ; 21cm
ISBN 0-285-62452-0 : £6.95 B81-00502

Leigh, James, *1937-*. The ludi victor / James Leigh. — London : Bodley Head, 1981. — 287p ; 23cm
Originally published: New York : Coward, McCann & Geoghegan, 1980
ISBN 0-370-30373-3 : £5.95 B81-11154

Leigh, Petra. Garnet / Petra Leigh. — London : Star, 1978. — 348p ; 18cm
ISBN 0-352-30242-9 (pbk) : £1.25 B81-28508

Leigh, Rhoda. Cry for the moon / by Rhoda Leigh. — London : Hale, 1981. — 160p ; 20cm
ISBN 0-7091-8266-x : £5.50 B81-08952

Leigh, Rhoda. A love worth waiting for / by Rhoda Leigh. — London : Hale, 1981. — 158p ; 20cm
ISBN 0-7091-9163-4 : £5.60 B81-35243

Leigh, Rhoda. The right man / by Rhoda Leigh. — London : Hale, 1980. — 157p ; 20cm
ISBN 0-7091-8265-1 : £4.95 B81-00503

Leigh, Roberta. Confirmed bachelor / by Roberta Leigh. — London : Mills & Boon, 1981. — 190p ; 19cm
ISBN 0-263-09883-4 : £4.55 B81-26412

Leitch, Maurice. Silver's city. — London : Secker & Warburg, Oct.1981. — [192]p
ISBN 0-436-24413-6 : £6.50 : CIP entry
B81-25319

Lemarchand, Elizabeth. Change for the worse / Elizabeth Lemarchand. — Loughton (17 Brook Rd, Loughton, Essex IG10 1BW) : Piatkus, 1980. — 185p : 1map ; 21cm
ISBN 0-86188-041-2 : £5.50 : CIP rev.
B80-10294

Lemarchand, Elizabeth. Change for the worse. — Large print ed. — Anstey : Ulverscroft, Feb.1982. — [336]p. — (Ulverscroft large print series : mystery)
ISBN 0-7089-0773-3 : £5.00 : CIP entry
B81-36934

Lemarchand, Elizabeth. Nothing to do with the case / Elizabeth Lemarchand. — Loughton ([17 Brook Rd.,] Loughton, Essex) : Piatkus, 1981. — 187p : 1map ; 21cm
ISBN 0-86188-067-6 B81-08625

Lemarchand, Elizabeth. Troubled waters. — Loughton : Piatkus, Jan.1982. — [192]p
ISBN 0-86188-133-8 : £6.50 : CIP entry
B81-34639

Lennox, Terry. Cowboys / Terry Lennox ; based on the series by Peter Learmouth. — London : New English Library, 1981. — 158p ; 19cm
ISBN 0-450-05286-9 (pbk) : £1.25 B81-40488

Leonard, Jason. Meet Mrs Piercey / Jason Leonard. — London : Hale, 1981. — 160p 23cm
ISBN 0-7091-8524-3 : £6.25 B81-11901

Leopold, Christopher. The night fishers of Antibes / Christopher Leopold. — London : Hamilton, 1981. — 211p ; 23cm
ISBN 0-241-10413-0 : £6.95 B81-15499

Leslie, Peter. The Andersen assault / Peter Leslie. — London : Hamlyn Paperbacks, 1981. — 239p ; 18cm
ISBN 0-600-20256-9 (pbk) : £1.25 B81-19911

Leslie, Peter. Killers under a cruel sky / Peter Leslie. — Feltham : Hamlyn, 1981. — 220p ; 18cm
ISBN 0-600-20255-0 (pbk) : £1.25 B81-11432

Leslie, Richard. Dusk patrol / Richard Leslie. — London : Hale, 1980. — 192p ; 21cm
ISBN 0-7091-8631-2 : £6.25 B81-02162

Leslie, Richard. Dusk patrol. — Large print ed. — Bath : Chivers Press, Feb.1982. — [288]p. — (A Lythway book)
Originally published: London : Hale, 1980
ISBN 0-85119-786-8 : £6.90 : CIP entry
B81-35860

Leslie, Richard. The sky aflame / by Richard Leslie. — London : Hale, 1981. — 190p ; 20cm
ISBN 0-7091-9120-0 : £6.50 B81-29943

Lessing, Doris. The memoirs of a survivor / Doris Lessing. — [London] : Picador, 1976, c1974 (1981 printing). — 189p ; 20cm
Originally published: London : Octagon, 1974
ISBN 0-330-24623-2 (pbk) : £1.95 B81-40088

Lessing, Doris. Shikasta : re: colonised Planet 5 : personal, psychological, historical documents relating to visit by Johor (George Sherban), emissary (Grade 9), 87th of the period of the last days / Doris Lessing. — London : Granada, 1981, c1979. — 447p ; 18cm. — (Canopus in Argos) (A Panther book)
Originally published: London : Cape, 1979
ISBN 0-586-05310-7 (pbk) : £1.95 B81-19941

Lessing, Doris. The Sirian experiments : the report by Ambien II, of the Five / Doris Lessing. — London : Cape, 1981, c1980. — 288p ; 23cm. — (Canopus in Argos)
Originally published: New York : Knopf, 1980
ISBN 0-224-01891-4 : £6.95 B81-14502

Lester, Jane. Love's golden touch / Jane Lester. — London : Hale, 1981. — 160p ; 20cm
ISBN 0-7091-8787-4 : £5.50 B81-15300

Lewis, J. R. (John Royston). A relative distance / Roy Lewis. — London : Collins, 1981. — 192p ; 20cm
ISBN 0-00-231717-6 : £5.75 B81-12927

Lewis, J. R. (John Royston). Seek for justice / Roy Lewis. — London : Collins, 1981. — 196p ; 20cm. — (The Crime Club)
ISBN 0-00-231872-5 : £6.25 : CIP rev.
B81-25103

Lewis, Maynah. Barren Harvest / by Maynah Lewis. — London : Hale, 1981. — 159p ; 20cm
ISBN 0-7091-9282-7 : £5.75 B81-35244

Lewis, Maynah. Love has two faces / Maynah Lewis. — Feltham : Hamlyn Paperbacks, 1981. — 158p ; 18cm. — (A sapphire romance)
ISBN 0-600-20040-x (pbk) : £0.75 B81-12085

Lewis, Richard, *1945-*. Parasite / Richard Lewis. — Feltham : Hamlyn, 1980. — 187p ; 18cm
ISBN 0-600-20066-3 (pbk) : £0.95 B81-00504

Lewis, Roy Harley. The manuscript murders / by Roy Harley Lewis. — London : Hale, 1981. — 208p ; 20cm
ISBN 0-7091-9136-7 : £5.95 B81-40544

Lewis, Sheila. Silver bird of prey / by Sheila Lewis. — London : Hale, 1981. — 158p ; 20cm
ISBN 0-7091-9063-8 : £5.60 B81-30080

Lewis, Sheila. Stars in her eyes / by Sheila Lewis. — London : Hale, 1980. — 159p ; 20cm
ISBN 0-7091-8446-8 : £5.25 B81-01458

Lewty, Marjorie. Beyond the lagoon / by Marjorie Lewty. — London : Mills & Boon, 1981. — 187p ; 19cm
ISBN 0-263-09841-9 : £4.55 B81-10973

Light, John. The well of time / John Light. — London : Hale, 1981. — 222p ; 21cm. — (Hale SF)
ISBN 0-7091-8776-9 : £5.95 B81-11500

Lillis, Molly. Flame in the wind / by Molly Lillis. — London : Hale, 1981. — 192p ; 20cm
ISBN 0-7091-8891-9 : £5.60 B81-19305

Lillis, Molly. Palace of the winds / by Molly Lillis. — London : Hale, 1981. — 157p ; 20cm
ISBN 0-7091-9191-x : £5.75 B81-37301

Lillis, Molly. South with the swallows / by Molly Lillis. — London : Hale, 1980. — 188p ; 20cm
ISBN 0-7091-8289-9 : £5.25 B81-02529

Linaker, Michael R.. Scorpion : second generation. — London : New English Library, Feb.1982. — [160]p
ISBN 0-450-05363-6 (pbk) : £1.25 : CIP entry
B81-36203

Linaker, Michael R.. The touch of hell / Michael R. Linaker. — London : New English Library, 1981. — 158p ; 18cm
ISBN 0-450-05125-0 (pbk) : £1.10 B81-09557

Linden, Heather. Love in a seminary / by Heather Linden. — [London] : [H. Linden], c1981. — 81leaves ; 21cm
Private circulation (pbk) B81-21455

823'.914[F] — Fiction in English, *1945- — Texts continuation*

Linden, Heather. They come to destroy / by Heather Linden. — [London] : [H. Linden], c1978. — 81p ; 21cm
Private circulation (pbk) B81-21454

Linden, Heather. To save my country England / by Heather Linden. — [London] : [H. Linden], c1981. — 111leaves ; 21cm
Private circulation (pbk) B81-21456

Lindsay, Rachel. Mask of gold. — Large print ed. — Anstey : Ulverscroft, Nov.1981. — [416] p. — (Ulverscroft large print series)
Originally published: London : Hutchinson, 1956
ISBN 0-7089-0706-7 : £5.00 : CIP entry B81-30505

Lindsay, Rachel. Untouched wife / by Rachel Lindsay. — London : Mills & Boon, 1981. — 188p ; 19cm
ISBN 0-263-09890-7 : £4.55 B81-28560

Lindsay, Richard. The moon is the key / by Richard Lindsay. — London : Hale, 1980. — 174p ; 21cm. — (Hale SF)
ISBN 0-7091-8420-4 : £5.50 B81-03014

Lindsey, Johanna. Fires of winter / Johanna Lindsey. — Feltham : Hamlyn Paperbacks, 1981, c1980. — 362p ; 18cm
ISBN 0-600-20397-2 (pbk) : £1.50 B81-20681

Lindsey, Olive. Ring of destiny / by Olive Lindsey. — London : Hale, 1980. — 159p ; 20cm
ISBN 0-7091-8572-3 : £5.25 B81-00505

Lingard, Joan. Across the barricades / Joan Lingard. — [Harmondsworth] : Puffin in association with Hamilton, 1973, c1972 (1981 [printing]). — 173p ; 19cm. — (Puffin plus)
Originally published: London : Hamilton, 1972. — For adolescents
ISBN 0-14-030637-4 (pbk) : £1.00 B81-32830

Lingard, Joan. The clearance / Joan Lingard. — [London] : Beaver, 1981, c1974. — 143p ; 18cm. — (Maggie ; 1)
Originally published: London : Hamilton, 1974. — For adolescents
ISBN 0-600-20299-2 (pbk) : £0.95 B81-13144

Lingard, Joan. Greenyards / Joan Lingard. — London : Hamilton, 1981. — 295p ; 22cm
ISBN 0-241-10523-4 : £7.50 B81-15396

Lingard, Joan. The pilgrimage / Joan Lingard. — [London] : Beaver, 1981, c1976. — 174p ; 18cm. — (Maggie ; 3)
Originally published: London : Hamilton, 1976. — For adolescents
ISBN 0-600-20301-8 (pbk) : £0.95 B81-13146

Lingard, Joan. The resettling / Joan Lingard. — [London] : Beaver, 1981, c1975. — 175p ; 18cm. — (Maggie ; 2)
Originally published: London : Hamilton, 1975. — For adolescents
ISBN 0-600-20300-x (pbk) : £0.95 B81-13145

Lingard, Joan. The reunion / Joan Lingard. — [London] : Beaver, 1981, c1977. — 159p ; 18cm. — (Maggie ; 4)
Originally published: London : Hamilton, 1977. — For adolescents
ISBN 0-600-20302-6 (pbk) : £0.95 B81-13147

Lively, Penelope. Judgement day / Penelope Lively. — London : Heinemann, 1980. — 167p ; 23cm
ISBN 0-434-42738-1 : £6.95 B81-02854

Llewellyn, Sam. Gurney's release. — Large print ed. — Anstey : Ulverscroft, Dec.1981. — [560] p. — (Ulverscroft large print series)
Originally published: London : Arlington Books, 1979
ISBN 0-7089-0727-x : £5.00 : CIP entry B81-32609

Llewellyn, Sam. Gurney's revenge / Sam Llewellyn. — Large print ed. — Leicester : Ulverscroft, 1981, c1977. — 402p ; 23cm. — (Ulverscroft large print)
Originally published: London : Arlington, 1977
ISBN 0-7089-0655-9 : £5.00 B81-28573

Llewellyn, Sam. Gurney's reward. — Large print ed. — Anstey : Ulverscroft, Oct.1981. — [480] p. — (Ulverscroft large print series)
Originally published: London : Arlington Books, 1978
ISBN 0-7089-0699-0 : £5.00 : CIP entry B81-28100

Llewellyn, Sam. Hell Bay / Sam Llewellyn. — London : Arlington, 1980. — 495p : maps ; 22cm
Maps on lining papers
ISBN 0-85140-504-5 : £6.50 : CIP rev. B80-09857

Llewellyn, Sam. The last will and testament of Robert Louis Stevenson. — London : Arlington, Sept.1981. — [288]p
ISBN 0-85140-544-4 : £6.95 : CIP entry B81-20096

Lloyd, Alan. Trade imperial / Alan Lloyd. — Feltham : Hamlyn Paperbacks, 1981, c1979. — 268p ; 18cm
Originally published: London : Cassell, 1979
ISBN 0-600-20237-2 (pbk) : £1.35 B81-24728

Lloyd, Levanah. Cauldron of desire / Levanah Lloyd. — London : Macdonald Futura, 1981. — 255p ; 21cm
ISBN 0-354-04757-4 : £4.95 B81-34872

Lloyd, Levanah. Cauldron of desire / Levanah Lloyd. — London : Macdonald Futura, 1981. — 255p ; 18cm. — (A Minstrel book ; 13)
ISBN 0-7088-2074-3 (pbk) : £0.95 B81-32779

Lloyd, Levanah. A maid called Wanton / Levanah Lloyd. — London : Macdonald Futura, 1981. — 255p ; 21cm
ISBN 0-354-04623-3 : £4.95 B81-12063

Lloyd, Levanah. A maid called Wanton / Levanah Lloyd. — London : Macdonald Futura, 1981. — 255p ; 18cm. — (A Minstrel book ; 4)
ISBN 0-7088-1998-2 (pbk) : £0.95 B81-15464

Lloyd, Levanah. Mail order bride / Levanah Lloyd. — London : Macdonald Futura, 1981. — 252p ; 21cm
ISBN 0-354-04657-8 : £4.95 B81-21316

Lloyd, Ross. The eternal seed / Ross Lloyd. — Bognor Regis : New Horizon, c1979. — 194p ; 21cm
ISBN 0-86116-130-0 : £3.50 B81-18958

Lodge, David. The British Museum is falling down / David Lodge ; with an introduction by the author. — London : Secker & Warburg, 1981. — 176p ; 23cm
Originally published: London : MacGibbon & Kee, 1965
ISBN 0-436-25530-8 : £6.95 : CIP rev. B81-07467

Lodge, David. How far can you go? / David Lodge. — Harmondsworth : Penguin, 1981, c1980. — 243p ; 18cm
Originally published: London : Secker and Warburg, 1980
ISBN 0-14-005746-3 (pbk) : £1.50 B81-40432

Long, Freda M.. Ever-loving Adelaide / Freda M. Long. — London : Hale, 1980. — 192p ; 21cm
ISBN 0-7091-8671-1 : £6.25 B81-02532

Long, Freda M.. Poison in Putney / Freda M. Long. — London : Hale, 1981. — 192p ; 21cm
ISBN 0-7091-9072-7 : £6.50 B81-24493

Long, Jean M.. Cornish rhapsody / by Jean M. Long. — London : Hale, 1981. — 176p ; 20cm
ISBN 0-7091-9018-2 : £5.50 B81-21311

Long, William Stuart. The exiles / by Vivian Stuart writing as William Stuart Long. — London : Macdonald Futura, 1980, c1979. — 683p : maps ; 18cm. — (A Troubadour spectacular)
Originally published: New York : Dell, 1980
ISBN 0-7088-1914-1 (pbk) : £1.95 B81-02202

Lorch, Irene. Devil's field / by Irene Lorch. — Harrow : Eureditions, 1978. — 92p ; 22cm
ISBN 0-906204-25-9 : Unpriced B81-28549

Lord, Graham. The Nostradamus horoscope / Graham Lord. — London : Hutchinson, 1981. — 251p : ill ; 22cm
ISBN 0-09-145840-4 : £6.95 : CIP rev. B81-19135

Lorrimer, Claire. Chantal / Claire Lorrimer. — [London] : Corgi, 1981. — x,429p ; 18cm
Originally published: London : Arlington, 1980
ISBN 0-552-11726-9 (pbk) : £1.50 B81-27237

Lorrimer, Claire. The chatelaine. — London : Arlington Books, May 1981. — [496]p
ISBN 0-85140-531-2 : £6.95 : CIP entry B81-08806

Lovell, Marc. The spy game / Marc Lovell. — London : Hale, 1981, c1980. — 186p ; 20cm
Originally published: Garden City, N.Y. : Doubleday, 1980
ISBN 0-7091-8890-0 : £5.75 B81-11783

Lovesey, Peter. Abracadaver / by Peter Lovesey. — Harmondsworth : Penguin, 1981, c1972. — 220p ; 18cm
Originally published: New York : Dodd, Mead, 1972
ISBN 0-14-005803-6 (pbk) : £1.25 B81-18331

Lovesey, Peter. Invitation to a dynamite party / Peter Lovesey. — Harmondsworth : Penguin, 1976, c1974 (1980 [printing])
Originally published: London : Macmillan, 1974
ISBN 0-14-004029-3 : £0.90 B81-07368

Lovesey, Peter. Mad Hatter's holiday / Peter Lovesey. — Harmondsworth : Penguin, 1981, c1973. — 192p ; 18cm. — (Penguin crime fiction)
Originally published: London : Macmillan, 1973
ISBN 0-14-005804-4 (pbk) : £1.25 B81-18327

Lowden, Desmond. Boudapesti 3 / Desmond Lowden. — London : Pan in association with Macmillan, 1980, c1979. — 190p ; 18cm
Originally published: London : Macmillan, 1979
ISBN 0-330-26042-1 (pbk) : £0.95 B81-02509

Lowden, Desmond. Sunspot / Desmond Lowden. — London : Macmillan, 1981. — 219p ; 21cm
ISBN 0-333-19619-8 : £5.50 B81-28954

Lowe-Watson, Dawn. The good morrow. — Large print ed. — Long Preston : Magna Print Books, Jan.1982. — [512]p
Originally published: London : Heinemann, 1980
ISBN 0-86009-370-0 : £5.25 : CIP entry B81-33768

Lowing, Anne. The branch and the briar. — Large print ed. — Bath : Chivers Press, Feb.1982. — [232]p. — (A Lythway book)
Originally published: London : Hale, 1976
ISBN 0-85119-787-6 : £6.90 : CIP entry B81-35859

Lucas, Jeremy. Whale / Jeremy Lucas. — London : Cape, 1981. — 172p : maps ; 23cm
Maps on lining papers
ISBN 0-224-01921-x : £5.50 : CIP rev. B81-14793

823'.914[F] — Fiction in English, *1945-* — *Texts continuation*

Lustgarten, Edgar. Turn the light out as you go / Edgar Lustgarten. — Large print ed. — Bath : Chivers, 1981, c1978. — 268p ; 23cm. — (A Lythway mystery)
Originally published: London : Elek, 1978
ISBN 0-85119-706-x : £5.25 B81-08683

Lutz, Gunther. Panzer platoon, blood and ice / Gunther Lutz. — London : Severn House, 1981, c1978. — 204p ; 21cm
Originally published: London : Sphere, 1978
ISBN 0-7278-0673-4 : £5.95 B81-12132

Lyall, Gavin. The secret servant / Gavin Lyall. — Large print ed. — Leicester : Ulverscroft, 1981, c1980. — 412p ; 23cm. — (Ulverscroft large print series)
Originally published: New York : Viking ; London : Hodder & Stoughton, 1980
ISBN 0-7089-0682-6 : £5.00 : CIP rev. B81-25890

Lyle, Elizabeth. Cassy / Elizabeth Lyle. — London : Joseph, 1981. — 254p ; 23cm
ISBN 0-7181-2006-x : £6.75 B81-16061

Lyman, Irene Ponting. House of the golden cupid / Irene Ponting Lyman. — Large print ed. — Bath : Chivers, 1980, c1959. — 258p ; 23cm. — (A Seymour book)
Originally published: London : Jenkins, 1959
ISBN 0-86220-022-9 : £4.95 : CIP rev. B80-22545

Lyne, de Castro. Empty scabbard / de Castro Lyne. — London : Hale, 1981. — 222p ; 21cm
ISBN 0-7091-9167-7 : £7.50 B81-35233

Lynne, James Broom. Rogue diamond / James Broom Lynne. — London : Macdonald Futura, 1981, c1980. — 350p ; 18cm. — (A Futura book)
Originally published: London : Joseph, 1980
ISBN 0-7088-2029-8 (pbk) : £1.50 B81-24427

Lyons, Elena. The hunting of Abbotsgarth. — Large print ed. — Bath : Chivers, Nov.1981. — [288]p. — (A Lythway book)
Originally published: Loughton : Piatkus, 1980
ISBN 0-85119-758-2 : £6.70 : CIP entry B81-31248

McArthur, Catherine. The flight of the dove. — Large print ed. — Anstey : Ulverscroft, Feb.1982. — [352]p. — (Ulverscroft large print series : romance)
ISBN 0-7089-0791-1 : £5.00 : CIP entry B81-36933

MacArthur, Wilson. Touch a tender spot / by Wilson MacArthur. — London : Hale, 1981. — 159p ; 20cm
ISBN 0-7091-9287-8 : £5.75 B81-35294

MacBeth, George. A kind of treason. — London : Hodder & Stoughton, Feb.1982. — [224]p
ISBN 0-340-26490-x : £6.95 : CIP entry B81-38329

MacBeth, George. The samurai / George MacBeth. — London : New English Library, 1981, c1975. — 248p ; 18cm. — (Cadbury)
Originally published: New York : Harcourt Brace Jovanovich, 1975 ; London : Quartet, 1976
ISBN 0-450-05100-5 (pbk) : £1.25 B81-14310

MacBeth, George. [The seven witches]. Cadbury and the seven witches / George MacBeth. — London : New English Library, 1981, c1978. — 233p ; 18cm
Originally published: New York : Harcourt, Brace, Jovanovich ; London : W.H. Allen, 1978
ISBN 0-450-05112-9 (pbk) : £1.25 B81-24746

McBrearty, Kathleen. Caribbean pink / by Kathleen McBrearty. — London : Mills & Boon, 1980. — 191p ; 20cm
ISBN 0-263-05044-0 : £3.85 B81-00512

McCarty, Nick. Jacky's battlefield / Nick McCarty. — London : Macmillan, 1981. — 108p ; 21cm. — (Topliner tridents)
For adolescents
ISBN 0-333-26540-8 : £3.95 : CIP rev. B81-04226

McColm, Alec. Something missing / by Alec McColm. — London : Hale, 1981. — 192p ; 20cm
ISBN 0-7091-8935-4 : £5.95 B81-17333

McConnell, James, *1915 Oct.14-*. The Benedictine commando / James McConnell. — London : Hamilton, 1981. — 331p ; 23cm
ISBN 0-241-10613-3 : £7.95 : CIP rev. B81-10464

McConnell, Nellie D.. At the Miranda / Nellie D. McConnell. — Ilfracombe : Stockwell, 1981. — 149p ; 23cm
ISBN 0-7223-1436-1 : £6.75 B81-03410

McCrum, Robert. In the secret state / Robert McCrum. — London : Fontana, 1981, c1980. — 254p ; 18cm
Originally published: London : H. Hamilton, 1980
ISBN 0-00-616108-1 (pbk) : £1.50 B81-12478

McCrum, Robert. A loss of heart. — London : Hamilton, Feb.1982. — [256]p
ISBN 0-241-10705-9 : £7.95 : CIP entry B81-35818

McCulloch, Sarah. A lady for Ludovic / Sarah McCulloch. — London : Corgi, 1981. — 189p ; 18cm. — (A Georgian romance)
ISBN 0-552-11769-2 (pbk) : £0.95 B81-35495

McCulloch, Sarah. A most insistent lady / Sarah McCulloch. — [London] : Corgi, 1981, c1980. — 174p ; 18cm. — (A Georgian romance)
ISBN 0-552-11601-7 (pbk) : £0.95 B81-10979

McCutchan, Philip. Bowering's breakwater / by Philip McCutchan. — Bolton-by-Bowland : Magna Print, 1980, c1964. — 424p ; 23cm
Originally published: London : Harrap, 1964. — Published in large print
ISBN 0-86009-270-4 : £5.25 : CIP rev. B80-22546

McCutchan, Philip. Cameron comes through / Philip McCutchan. — Large print ed. — Bath : Chivers, 1981, c1980. — 246p ; 23cm. — (A Lythway general novel)
Originally published: London : A. Barker, 1980
ISBN 0-85119-727-2 : Unpriced : CIP rev. B81-14850

McCutchan, Philip. Cameron of the Castle Bay / Philip McCutchan. — London : A. Barker, c1981. — 166p ; 23cm
ISBN 0-213-16785-9 : £5.95 B81-16064

McCutchan, Philip. Cameron, Ordinary Seaman / Philip McCutchan. — Bolton-by-Bowland : Magna, 1981, c1980. — 247p ; 23cm. — (A Lythway general novel)
Originally published: London : A. Barker, 1980
ISBN 0-85119-703-5 : £5.25 B81-08687

McCutchan, Philip. Half a bag of stringer / by Philip McCutchan. — Bolton-by-Bowland : Magna Print, 1981, c1970. — 359p ; 23cm
Originally published: London : Harrap, 1970. — Published in large print
ISBN 0-86009-302-6 : £5.75 B81-12234

McCutchan, Philip. Halfhyde on the Yangtze / Philip McCutchan. — London : Weidenfeld and Nicolson, c1981. — 178p ; 23cm
ISBN 0-297-77954-0 : £5.95 B81-28283

McCutchan, Philip. Shard calls the tune : a 'Simon Shard' novel / Philip McCutchan. — London : Hodder and Stoughton, 1981. — 190p ; 23cm
ISBN 0-340-25004-6 : £5.95 B81-10142

McCutchan, Philip. Sunstrike. — Large print ed. — Long Preston : Magna, Oct.1981. — [480]p
ISBN 0-86009-347-6 : £4.95 : CIP entry B81-27384

McCutchan, Philip, *1920-*. Lieutenant Cameron RNVR / Philip McCutchan. — London : Barker, c1981. — 159p ; 23cm
ISBN 0-213-16812-x : £5.95 B81-39391

McDermott, F. C.. The horizon's always twisted somehow / F.C. McDermott. — Bognor Regis : New Horizon, c1979. — 117p ; 21cm
ISBN 0-86116-110-6 : £2.95 B81-19230

MacDonald, Malcolm, *1932-*. Abigail. — London : Coronet, Apr.1981. — [448]p
Originally published: 1979
ISBN 0-340-26216-8 (pbk) : £1.95 : CIP entry B81-01459

Macdonald, Malcolm, *1932-*. Goldeneye / Malcolm Macdonald. — London : Hodder and Stoughton, 1981. — 504p ; 23cm
ISBN 0-340-25457-2 : £7.50 : CIP rev. B81-13888

Macdonald, Peter. One way street / Peter Macdonald. — London : Hale, 1981. — 191p ; 21cm
ISBN 0-7091-8878-1 : £6.50 B81-21877

Macdonald, Peter. Wide horizons / by Peter Macdonald. — London : Hale, 1980. — 206p ; 21cm
ISBN 0-7091-8685-1 : £6.25 B81-02163

McEvoy, Marjorie. Dusky cactus / Marjorie McEvoy. — Large print ed. — Leicester : Ulverscroft, 1980, c1968. — 271p ; 23cm. — (Ulverscroft large print series)
Originally published: London : Jenkins, 1968
ISBN 0-7089-0525-0 : £4.25 : CIP rev. B80-23725

McEvoy, Marjorie. No castle of dreams / Marjorie McEvoy. — Large print ed. — Bath : Lythway, 1980, c1960. — 253p ; 23cm
Originally published: London : Jenkins, 1960
ISBN 0-85046-909-0 : £6.25 : CIP rev. B80-22547

McEvoy, Marjorie. Ravensmount / by Marjorie McEvoy. — Bolton-by-Bowland : Magna, 1981, c1974. — 340p ; 23cm
Originally published: S.l : s.n., 1974. — Published in large print
ISBN 0-86009-305-0 : £5.75 B81-14199

McEwan, Angus J.. The secret ghost town / Angus J. McEwan ; with illustrations by Derek Lucas. — London : Hale, 1981. — 158p ; 21cm
ISBN 0-7091-9152-9 : £4.25 B81-29865

McEwan, Ian. The comfort of strangers / Ian McEwan. — London : Cape, 1981. — 134p ; 21cm
ISBN 0-224-01931-7 : £5.50 : CIP rev. B81-26721

McGahern, John. The pornographer / John McGahern. — London : Quartet, 1980. — 252p ; 20cm
Originally published: London : Faber, 1979
ISBN 0-7043-3329-5 (pbk) : £2.25 B81-05908

McGrath, Pat. Stray cats from a wayward world / Pat McGrath. — London : W.H. Allen, 1981. — 220p ; 23cm
ISBN 0-491-02498-3 : £7.95 B81-35155

McGuire, Sarah. The daughters of the house / Sarah McGuire. — New York : St Martin's ; London : Hale, 1980. — 240p ; 21cm
ISBN 0-7091-8093-4 : £6.50 B81-01468

McGuire, Steve. The operator / Steve McGuire. — Bognor Regis : New Horizon, c1978. — 220p ; 21cm
ISBN 0-86116-123-8 : £3.50 B81-18961

823'.914[F] — Fiction in English, *1945- — Texts continuation*

Mackelworth, R. W.. Shakehole / by R.W. Mackelworth. — London : Hale, 1981. — 208p ; 20cm. — (Hale SF)
ISBN 0-7091-9265-7 : £6.25 B81-40545

McKenzie, Helen B.. The Sassenach / written and illustrated by Helen B. McKenzie. — Edinburgh : Canongate, 1980. — 165p : ill ; 23cm
ISBN 0-903937-72-7 : £4.95 B81-12038

MacKenzie, Lee. False witness / Lee MacKenzie ; based on the successful Yorkshire Television series originated by Kevin Laffan. — [London] : Fontana, 1981. — 190p ; 18cm. — (Emmerdale Farm ; bk.15)
ISBN 0-00-616292-4 (pbk) : 0.95 B81-36783

Mackenzie, Lee. Innocent victim / Lee Mackenzie. — London : Fontana, 1981. — 160p ; 18cm. — (Emmerdale Farm ; book 14)
ISBN 0-00-616291-6 (pbk) : £0.95 B81-18791

Mackie, Charles. Mariota / Charles Mackie. — London : Hale, 1981. — 191p ; 21cm
ISBN 0-7091-8877-3 : £6.50 B81-15772

Mackie, Mary. Counterfeit love / by Mary Mackie. — London : Hale, 1981. — 159p ; 20cm
ISBN 0-7091-8040-3 : £5.50 B81-11661

Mackie, Mary. Dark ruby / by Mary Mackie. — London : Hale, 1980. — 160p ; 20cm
ISBN 0-7091-7977-4 : £5.25 B81-01460

Mackie, Mary. Season of mists / by Mary Mackie. — London : Hale, 1981. — 160p ; 20cm
ISBN 0-7091-8661-4 : £5.75 B81-30069

Mackinlay, Margaret. The pawns of kings / Margaret Mackinlay. — London : Hale, 1981. — 222p ; 21cm
ISBN 0-7091-9201-0 : £7.25 B81-33540

McLaren, Colin Andrew. Mother of the free / Colin Andrew McLaren. — London : Collings, 1980. — 161p ; 23cm
ISBN 0-86036-044-x : £5.00 B81-00513

MacLaverty, Bernard. Lamb / Bernard MacLaverty. — Harmondsworth : Penguin, 1981, c1980. — 152p ; 20cm. — (A King penguin)
Originally published: New York : Braziller ; London : Cape, 1980
ISBN 0-14-005769-2 (pbk) : £1.95 B81-22110

Maclean, Alistair. Athabasca / Alistair Maclean. — [London] : Fontana, 1981, c1980. — 252p : 1map ; 18cm
Originally published: Garden City, N.Y. : Doubleday ; London : Collins, 1980
ISBN 0-00-616266-5 (pbk) : £1.35 B81-39339

Maclean, Alistair. Athabasca / Alistair Maclean. — Large print ed. — Leicester : Ulverscroft, 1981. — 284p : 1map ; 23cm. — (Ulverscroft large print series)
Originally published: London : Collins, 1980. — Map on lining papers
ISBN 0-7089-0668-0 : £5.00 : CIP rev. B81-20631

Maclean, Alistair. Bear Island / Alistair Maclean. — [London] : Fontana, 1973, c1971 (1981 [printing]). — 288p : 1map ; 19cm
Originally published: Garden City, N.Y. ; Doubleday ; London : Collins, 1971
ISBN 0-00-616434-x (pbk) : £1.50 B81-39344

Maclean, Alistair. Five great thrillers / by Alistair Maclean. — London : Collins, 1980. — 1109p ; 23cm. — (Collins' collectors' choice)
Contents: Fear is the key - The dark crusader - The Satan bug - Ice station Zebra - Bear Island
ISBN 0-00-243018-5 : £5.95 B81-08012

Maclean, Alistair. Force 10 from Navarone / Alistair Maclean. — [London] : Fontana, 1970, c1968 (1979 [printing]). — 223p : 1map ; 18cm
Originally published: Garden City, N.Y. : Doubleday ; London : Collins, 1968
ISBN 0-00-616433-1 (pbk) : £1.25 B81-39345

MacLean, Alistair. Four great adventure stories. — London : Collins, Nov.1981. — [750]p. — (Collins' collectors' choice)
Contents: When eight bells toll — The golden gate — Caravanto Vaccarès — Circus
ISBN 0-00-243347-8 : £6.95 : CIP entry B81-28765

MacLean, Alistair. The golden rendezvous / Alistair MacLean. — [London] : Fontana, 1964, c1962 (1981 [printing]). — 222p ; 18cm
Originally published: London : Collins, 1962
ISBN 0-00-616259-2 (pbk) : £1.25 B81-15525

MacLean, Alistair. The guns of Navarone / Alistair MacLean. — [London] : Fontana, 1980. — 254p : 2maps ; 18cm
Previously published: London : Collins, 1957
ISBN 0-00-616160-x (pbk) : £1.25 B81-01461

MacLean, Alistair. Ice Station Zebra / Alistair Maclean. — [London] : Fontana, 1963 (1980 [printing]). — 253p : 1plan ; 18cm
Originally published: London : Collins, 1963
ISBN 0-00-616141-3 (pbk) : £1.25 B81-02040

MacLean, Alistair. The last frontier / Alistair MacLean. — [London] : Fontana, 1963, c1959 (1981 [printing]). — 253p ; 18cm
Originally published: London : Collins, 1959
ISBN 0-00-615749-1 (pbk) : £1.25 B81-15539

Maclean, Alistair. Puppet on a chain / Alistair Maclean. — [London] : Fontana, 1971, c1969 (1981 [printing]). — 222p ; 19cm
Originally published: London : Collins, 1969
ISBN 0-00-615751-3 (pbk) : £1.25 B81-22013

MacLean, Alistair. River of death / Alistair MacLean. — London : Collins, 1981. — 192p ; 22cm
ISBN 0-00-222348-1 : £7.50 : CIP rev. B81-20527

Maclean, Alistair. The satan bug / Alistair Maclean. — [London] : Fontana, 1964, c1962 (1981 [printing]). — 222p ; 19cm
Originally published: under the name Ian Stuart. London : Collins, 1962
ISBN 0-00-615750-5 (pbk) : £1.25 B81-22012

McLeave, Hugh. Second time round / by Hugh McLeave. — London : Hale, 1981. — 239p : ill ; 20cm
ISBN 0-7091-9016-6 : £5.95 B81-15769

MacLeod, Jean S.. Black sand, white sand / by Jean S. MacLeod. — London : Mills & Boon, 1981. — 186p ; 20cm
ISBN 0-263-09745-5 : £4.55 B81-14186

Macleod, Jean S.. Cruel deception / by Jean S. Macleod. — London : Mills & Boon, 1981. — 191p ; 20cm
ISBN 0-263-09922-9 : £4.55 B81-34111

MacLeod, Jean S.. Meeting in Madrid. — Large print ed. — Bath : Chivers, Nov.1981. — [312] p. — (A Lythway book)
Originally published: London : Mills & Boon, 1979
ISBN 0-85119-759-0 : £6.90 : CIP entry B81-31247

MacLeod, Robert, *1928-*. The Californio / Robert MacLeod. — Large print ed. — Leicester : Ulverscroft, 1981, c1966. — 326p ; 23cm. — (Ulverscroft large print)
Originally published: New York : Fawcett, 1966 ; London : Hodder Fawcett, 1968
ISBN 0-7089-0588-9 : £5.00 B81-11610

MacLeod, Robert, *1928-*. A problem in Prague. — London : Hutchinson, Aug.1981. — [184]p
ISBN 0-09-145800-5 : £6.50 : CIP entry B81-19141

McMaster, Alison. The rose hedge / by Alison McMaster. — London : Hale, 1981. — 206p ; 20cm
ISBN 0-7091-8972-9 : £5.50 B81-14136

MacNeil, Duncan. The train at Bundarbar : a 'James Ogilvie' novel / Duncan MacNeil. — London : Hodder and Stoughton, 1981. — 191p ; 20cm
ISBN 0-340-26322-9 : £6.50 : CIP rev. B81-02367

McNeil, John. Spy game / John McNeil. — London : Weidenfeld and Nicolson, 1980. — 300p ; 23cm
ISBN 0-297-77844-7 : £6.50 B81-00514

McQueen, Ronald A.. The man who knew time / Ronald A. McQueen. — London : Hale, 1981. — 186p ; 20cm. — (Hale SF)
ISBN 0-7091-9168-5 : £6.50 B81-33524

McQueen, Ronald A.. The Sorcerer of Marakaan / Ronald A. McQueen. — London : Hale, 1980. — 190p ; 21cm. — (Hale SF)
ISBN 0-7091-8680-0 : £5.75 B81-08992

McVean, James. Seabird Nine / James NcVean. — London : Macdonald, 1981. — 316p ; 23cm
ISBN 0-354-04314-5 : £5.95 B81-22016

Maddocks, Margaret. Dance barefoot / Margaret Maddocks. — Feltham : Hamlyn, 1980, c1966. — 158p ; 18cm
Originally published: London : Hurst & Blackett, 1966
ISBN 0-600-31568-1 (pbk) : £0.95 B81-03401

Maddocks, Margaret. [Fair shines the day]. The open door / Margaret Maddocks. — London : Hamlyn Paperbacks, 1980, c1952. — 222p ; 18cm
Originally published: London : Hurst & Blackett, 1952
ISBN 0-600-33735-9 (pbk) : £1.25 B81-02065

Madison, Hank. Lawless range / by Hank Madison. — London : Hale, 1980. — 158p ; 20cm
ISBN 0-7091-8515-4 : £4.95 B81-02154

Maitland, Sara. Daughter of Jerusalem / Sara Maitland. — London : Sphere, 1981, c1978. — 249p ; 18cm
Originally published: London : Blond and Briggs, 1978
ISBN 0-7221-5777-0 (pbk) : £1.25 B81-17972

Malcolm, Aleen. The taming / Aleen Malcolm. — London : Macdonald Futura, 1981, c1979. — 480p : ill,1map ; 18cm. — (A Troubadour book)
Originally published: S.l. : S.n., 1979
ISBN 0-7107-3017-9 (pbk) : £1.60 B81-24430

Malcolm, Margaret. Eagles fly alone / by Margaret Malcolm. — London : Mills & Boon, 1981. — 189p ; 20cm
ISBN 0-263-09927-x : £4.55 B81-35644

Mallanson, Todd. Ladykiller / Todd Mallanson. — London : W.H. Allen, 1981, c1980. — 203p ; 18cm. — (A Star book)
Originally published: London : Weidenfeld & Nicolson, 1980
ISBN 0-352-30824-9 (pbk) : £1.50 B81-28551

Mallory, Lewis. Gate of fear / Lewis Mallory. — London : Hamlyn Paperbacks, 1981. — 156p ; 18cm
ISBN 0-600-20257-7 (pbk) : £1.00 B81-11848

Mallory, Lewis. The nursery / Lewis Mallory. — London : Hamlyn Paperbacks, 1981. — 157p ; 18cm
ISBN 0-600-20340-9 (pbk) : £1.10 B81-31911

Mallory, Peter. A killing matter / by Peter Mallory. — London : Hale, 1981. — 192p ; 20cm
ISBN 0-7091-9013-1 : £5.95 B81-19298

823'.914[F] — Fiction in English, *1945-* — Texts *continuation*

Malloy, Lester. Jo Jo and the private eye / by Lester Malloy. — London : Hale, 1981. — 159p ; 20cm
ISBN 0-7091-8782-3 : £5.75 B81-11732

Manley-Tucker, Audrie. The piper in the hills. — Large print ed. — Long Preston : Magna, Oct.1981. — [456]p
ISBN 0-86009-346-8 : £4.95 : CIP entry B81-27385

Manley-Tucker, Audrie. Shadow of yesterday. — Large print ed. — Long Preston : Magna Print Books, Feb.1982. — [380]p
Originally published: London : Mills & Boon, 1965
ISBN 0-86009-375-1 : £5.25 : CIP entry B81-35699

Manley-Tucker, Audrie. Tamberlyn / by Audrie Manley-Tucker. — London : Mills & Boon, 1981. — 189p ; 19cm
ISBN 0-263-09833-8 : £4.55 B81-10890

Mann, Ann L.. Glorious in the Wednesday House / Ann L. Mann. — Bognor Regis : New Horizon, c1980. — 74p ; 21cm
ISBN 0-86116-214-5 : £4.75 B81-19231

Mann, James. Endgame / James Mann. — London : New English Library, 1981, c1982. — 255p ; 23cm
ISBN 0-450-04848-9 : £5.95 B81-37437

Manners, Alexandra. The singing swans / Alexandra Manners. — [London] : Coronet, 1979, c1975. — 256p ; 18cm
Originally published: New York : Putnam, 1975 ; London : Millington, 1976
ISBN 0-340-23836-4 (pbk) : £0.95 : CIP rev. B79-13152

Manning, Olivia. The sum of things : a novel / by Olivia Manning. — London : Weidenfeld and Nicolson, 1980. — 203p ; 23cm
ISBN 0-297-77816-1 : £5.95 B81-00506

Manning, Val. Fertility queen / by Val Manning. — London : Hale, 1980. — 191p ; 21cm
Bibliography: p191
ISBN 0-7091-8260-0 : £5.50 B81-00507

Mansfield, Estrith. Gallows close / by Estrith Mansfield. — Ilfracombe : Stockwell, [1981?]. — 236p ; 19cm
ISBN 0-7223-1497-3 : Unpriced B81-39601

Mantle, Winifred. Summer at Temple Quentin / Winifred Mantle. — Large print ed. — Bath : Chivers, 1981, c1967. — 245p ; 23cm. — (A Lythway book)
Originally published: London : Collins, 1967
ISBN 0-85119-746-9 : £6.70 : CIP rev. B81-20100

March, Stella. Because of yesterday / Stella March. — Large print ed. — Bath : Chivers, 1981, c1959. — 276p ; 23cm. — (A Seymour book)
Originally published: London : Wright & Brown, 1959
ISBN 0-85119-425-7 : Unpriced : CIP rev. B81-13710

March, Stella. A carriage for Fiona / by Stella March. — London : Hale, 1981. — 156p ; 20cm
ISBN 0-7091-8883-8 : £6.25 B81-17313

March, Stella. A cloud in the sky / Stella March. — Large print ed. — Bath : Chivers, 1981, c1958. — 264p ; 23cm. — (A Seymour book)
Originally published: London : Wright & Brown, 1958
ISBN 0-85119-412-5 : £4.95 : CIP rev. B81-04224

March, Stella. Dear pretender / by Stella March. — London : Hale, 1981. — 160p ; 20cm
ISBN 0-7091-9087-5 : £6.50 B81-35197

March, Stella. The flickering flame / by Stella March. — London : Remploy, 1979. — 176p ; 19cm
Originally published: London : Wright & Brown, 1968
ISBN 0-7066-0831-3 : Unpriced B81-38049

March, Stella. Sentimental journey / Stella March. — Large print ed. — Bath : Chivers, 1981, c1966. — 238p ; 23cm. — (A Seymour book)
Originally published: London : Wright & Brown, 1966
ISBN 0-85119-400-1 : Unpriced B81-08507

March, Stella. Sing high, sing low / by Stella March. — London : Remploy, 1979. — 175p ; 19cm
Originally published: London: Wright & Brown, 1961
ISBN 0-7066-0830-5 : £3.80 B81-38050

Marchant, Catherine. [Evil at Rogers Cross]. The iron facade / Catherine Marchant. — London : Corgi, 1978, c1976 (1980 [printing]). — 175p ; 18cm
Originally published: United States : s.n., 1965 ; London : Heinemann, 1976
ISBN 0-552-11521-5 (pbk) : £1.00 B81-07668

Marcus, Joanna. Marsh blood / Joanna Marcus. — [London] : Corgi, 1981, c1980. — 190p ; 18cm
On cover: 'Lucilla Andrews writing as Joanna Marcus'. — Originally published: London : Hutchinson, 1980
ISBN 0-552-11633-5 (pbk) : £1.00 B81-15347

Mariner, David. Sinister charade / David Mariner. — Feltham : Hamlyn, 1981, c1979. — 189p ; 18cm
Originally published: London : Hale, 1979
ISBN 0-600-20157-0 (pbk) : £1.00 B81-11426

Markstein, George. Ultimate issue / George Markstein. — London : New English Library, 1981. — 380p ; 23cm
ISBN 0-450-04876-4 : £6.95 B81-33735

Marquis, Max. The traitor machine / Max Marquis. — Feltham : Hamlyn, 1980. — 284p ; 18cm
ISBN 0-600-32989-5 (pbk) : £1.25 B81-07166

Marriott, Emma Jane. Double jeopardy / Emma Jane Marriott. — London : Hale, 1981. — 191p ; 21cm
ISBN 0-7091-9204-5 : £6.75 B81-35187

Marriott, Thomas. The pagan land / Thomas Marriott. — London : Joseph, 1981. — xii,391p ; 23cm
ISBN 0-7181-2000-0 : £7.50 B81-33500

Marsh, Carol. Nurse under suspicion / by Carol Marsh. — London : Hale, 1981. — 192p ; 20cm
ISBN 0-7091-8898-6 : £5.60 B81-19300

Marshall, James Vance. A walk to the hills of dreamtime / James Vance Marshall ; illustrated by Lydia Rosier. — London : Heinemann Educational, 1981, c1970. — 158p : ill ; 20cm. — (The New windmill series ; 255)
Originally published: London : Hodder & Stoughton, 1970
ISBN 0-435-12255-x : £1.50 B81-22109

Martin, Caroline. Man with a falcon / Caroline Martin. — London : Mills & Boon, 1981. — 191p ; 19cm. — (Masquerade)
ISBN 0-263-09786-2 : £4.55 B81-26413

Martin, David, *1937-*. The road to Ballyshannon / David Martin. — London : Secker & Warburg, 1981. — 155p ; 23cm
ISBN 0-436-27333-0 : £6.95 : CIP rev. B81-15921

Martin, Graham Dunstan. Catchfire / by Graham Dunstan Martin. — London : Allen & Unwin, 1981. — 183p : 1map ; 23cm
Map on lining papers
ISBN 0-04-823184-3 : Unpriced B81-15491

Martin, Ian Kennedy. Billions / Ian Kennedy Martin. — London : Pan in association with Heinemann, 1980, c1979. — 182p ; 18cm
Originally published: London : Heinmann, 1979
ISBN 0-330-26201-7 (pbk) : £1.25 B81-00508

Martin, John, *1893-*. Portrait of a King / by John Martin. — Ipswich : East Anglia Magazine Ltd, [1980?]. — 228p ; 22cm
ISBN 0-900227-43-5 : £7.95 B81-01462

Martin, Rhona. Gallows wedding / Rhona Martin. — London : Corgi, 1979, c1978. — 303p ; 18cm
Originally published: London : Bodley Head, 1978
ISBN 0-552-11037-x (pbk) : £0.9k B81-09311

Martin, Vicky. Seeds of the sun / Vicky Martin. — Leicester : Ulverscroft, 1981, c1979. — 478p ; 23cm. — (Ulverscroft large print series)
Originally published: London : Macdonald, 1979
ISBN 0-7089-0635-4 : Unpriced B81-26480

Mason, Anita. Bethany : a novel / by Anita Mason. — London : Hamilton, 1981. — 219p ; 21cm
ISBN 0-241-10513-7 : £7.50 B81-06224

Mason, Chuck. Hell on the range / Chuck Mason. — London : Hale, 1980. — 158p ; 20cm
ISBN 0-7091-8408-5 : £4.95 B81-00509

Mason, Douglas R.. Horizon Alpha / Douglas R. Mason. — London : Hale, 1981, c1971. — 168p 21cm. — (Hale SF)
Originally published: New York : Ballantine, 1971
ISBN 0-7091-8775-0 : £5.95 B81-11904

Mason, Douglas R.. The Typhon intervention / by Douglas R. Mason. — London : Hale, 1981. — 206p ; 20cm. — (Hale SF)
ISBN 0-7091-9030-1 : £6.25 B81-27307

Mason, Hilary. Blood royal / Hilary Mason. — London : Coronet, 1980. — 270p ; 18cm
ISBN 0-340-26095-5 (pbk) : £1.40 : CIP rev. B80-36392

Mason, Hilary. Morisco / Hilary Mason. — London : Pan in association with Collins, 1981, c1979. — 268p ; 18cm
Originally published: London : Collins, 1979
ISBN 0-330-26372-2 (pbk) : £1.50 B81-24738

Massie, Allan. The death of men. — London : Bodley Head, Sept.1981. — [256]p
ISBN 0-370-30339-3 : £6.50 : CIP entry B81-21618

Masters, John. Heart of war : a novel / by John Masters. — London : Joseph, 1980. — 617p : geneal.tables ; 23cm. — (Loss of Eden ; 2)
ISBN 0-7181-1947-9 : £7.95 B81-01463

Masters, John. Heart of war / John Masters. — London : Sphere, 1981, c1980. — 695p : geneal.tables ; 18cm
Originally published: London : Joseph, 1980
ISBN 0-7221-0467-7 (pbk) : £1.95 B81-35069

Masters, John. Now, God be thanked : a novel / by John Masters. — London : Sphere, 1979 (1980 [printing]). — 699p : 4geneal.tables ; 18cm. — (Loss of day ; 1)
Originally published: London : Michael Joseph, 1979
ISBN 0-7221-0553-3 (pbk) : £1.95 B81-07671

823'.914[F] — Fiction in English, *1945-* — *Texts continuation*

Mather, Anne. The autumn of the witch. — Large print ed. — Long Preston : Magna, Sept.1981. — [320]p
ISBN 0-86009-341-7 : £4.95 : CIP entry B81-22463

Mather, Anne. Castles of sand / by Anne Mather. — London : Mills & Boon, 1981. — 189p ; 20cm
ISBN 0-263-09859-1 : £4.55 B81-18357

Mather, Anne. Charlotte's hurricane. — Large print ed. — Long Preston : Magna Print Books, Feb.1982. — [350]p
Originally published: London : Mills and Boon, 1970
ISBN 0-86009-376-x : £5.25 : CIP entry B81-35698

Mather, Anne. Forbidden flame / by Anne Mather. — London : Mills & Boon, 1981. — 190p ; 20cm
ISBN 0-263-09838-9 : £4.55 B81-14184

Mather, Anne. A haunting compulsion / by Anne Mather. — London : Mills & Boon, 1981. — 188p ; 19cm
ISBN 0-263-09830-3 : £4.55 B81-10887

Mather, Anne. Images of love / by Anne Mather. — London : Mills & Boon, 1980. — 187p ; 20cm
ISBN 0-263-09729-3 : £3.85 B81-00510

Mather, Anne. Innocent obsession / by Anne Mather. — London : Mills & Boon, 1981. — 188p ; 20cm
ISBN 0-263-09892-3 : £4.55 B81-28521

Mather, Anne. Lure of eagles. — Large print ed. — Bath : Chivers, Nov.1981. — [312]p. — (A Lythway book)
Originally published: London : Mills & Boon, 1979
ISBN 0-85119-760-4 : £6.90 : CIP entry B81-31273

Mather, Anne. Proud harvest / by Anne Mather. — Bolton-by-Bowland : Magna, 1981, c1978. — 303p ; 23cm
Originally published: London : Mills and Boon, 1978. — Published in large print
ISBN 0-86009-312-3 : £5.75 : CIP rev. B81-03713

Mather, Berkely. The midnight gun / Berkely Mather. — London : Collins, 1981. — 336p : 1map ; 22cm
ISBN 0-00-222334-1 : £6.95 B81-28692

Matthew, Christopher. The Crisp report. — London : Hutchinson, Oct.1981. — 1v.
ISBN 0-09-146350-5 : £5.50 : CIP entry B81-27373

Maugham, Robin. The corridor : a novel / by Robin Maugham. — London : Kimber, 1980. — 174p ; 23cm
ISBN 0-7183-0417-9 : £5.50 B81-01464

Maugham, Robin. The deserters : a novel / Robin Maugham. — London : Kimber, 1981. — 172p : ill ; 23cm
ISBN 0-7183-0198-6 : £5.50 B81-32098

Maxwell, Vicky. The way of the Tamarisk / Vicky Maxwell. — Large print ed. — Leicester : Ulverscroft, 1980, c1974. — 317p ; 23cm. — (Ulverscroft large print)
Originally published: London : Collins, 1974
ISBN 0-7089-0593-5 : £4.25 B81-01465

May, Peter, *1951-*. Hidden faces / Peter May. — Loughton : Piatkus, 1981. — 300p ; 21cm
ISBN 0-86188-061-7 : £6.50 B81-16035

Maybury, Anne. Jessamy Court. — Large print ed. — Anstey : Ulverscroft, Jan.1982. — [580] p. — (Ulverscroft large print series : romantic suspense)
ISBN 0-7089-0737-7 : £5.00 : CIP entry B81-33960

Maybury, Anne. Radiance / Anne Maybury. — [London] : Fontana, 1981, c1979. — 255p ; 19cm
Originally published: London : Collins, 1979
ISBN 0-00-616387-4 (pbk) : £1.35 B81-33488

Maybury, Anne. Radiance / Anne Maybury. — Large print ed. — Leicester : Ulverscroft, 1981, c1979. — 466p ; 23cm. — (Ulverscroft large print series)
Originally published: London : Collins, 1979
ISBN 0-7089-0648-6 : £5.00 B81-28576

Mayhew, Margaret. The flame and the furnace / Margaret Mayhew. — London : Hamilton, 1981. — 176p ; 23cm
ISBN 0-241-10525-0 : £7.50 : CIP rev. B81-02555

Mayhew, Margaret. The railway king / Margaret Mayhew. — Large print ed. — Leicester : Ulverscroft, 1980, c1979. — 422p ; 22cm. — (Ulverscroft large print)
Originally published: London : H. Hamilton, 1979
ISBN 0-7089-0558-7 : £4.25 : CIP rev. B80-35451

Maynard, Nan. The last dawn / Nan Maynard. — London : Hale, 1981. — 224p ; 21cm
ISBN 0-7091-8988-5 : £6.50 B81-21303

Mayne, Cora. The Roylake Ruby / by Cora Mayne. — London : Hale, 1980. — 160p ; 20cm
ISBN 0-7091-8482-4 : £5.25 B81-01466

Mayo, Margaret. Afraid to love. — Large print ed. — Bath : Chivers, Oct.1981. — [256]p. — (A Seymour book)
Originally published: London : Mills & Boon, 1978
ISBN 0-85119-438-9 : £4.95 : CIP entry B81-25804

Mayo, Margaret. Burning desire / Margaret Mayo. — Large print ed. — Bath : Chivers, 1981, c1980. — 226p ; 23cm. — (A Seymour book)
Originally published: London : Mills & Boon, 1980
ISBN 0-85119-431-1 : Unpriced : CIP rev. B81-18077

Mayo, Margaret. Charming enemy / by Margaret Mayo. — London : Mills & Boon, 1981. — 190p ; 20cm
ISBN 0-263-09856-7 : £4.55 B81-18351

Mayo, Margaret. Innocent bride / by Margaret Mayo. — London : Mills & Boon, 1980. — 191p ; 20cm
ISBN 0-263-09728-5 : £3.85 B81-00511

Mayo, Margaret. Mistaken marriage. — Large print ed. — Bath : Chivers, Dec.1981. — [272] p. — (A Seymour book)
Originally published: London : Mills & Boon, 1979
ISBN 0-85119-446-x : £4.95 : CIP entry B81-31728

Mayo, Margaret. Stormy affair. — Large print ed. — Bath : Chivers, Nov.1981. — [264]p. — (A Seymour book)
Originally published: London : Mills & Boon, 1979
ISBN 0-85119-441-9 : £5.25 : CIP entry B81-31253

Mayo, Margaret. Tormented love / by Margaret Mayo. — London : Mills & Boon, 1980. — 189p ; 20cm
ISBN 0-263-09763-3 : £3.85 B81-01467

Meadows, Rose. The prude / by Rose Meadows. — London : Hale, 1981. — 207p ; 20cm
ISBN 0-7091-9258-4 : £6.75 B81-35241

Melville, Anne. The Lorimer legacy / Anne Melville. — [London] : Corgi, 1980, c1979. — 309p : 1geneal.table
Originally published: London : Heinemann, 1979
ISBN 0-552-11478-2 (pbk) : £1.25 B81-01142

Melville, Anne. Lorimers at war / Anne Melville. — London : Heinemann, 1980. — 271p : 1geneal.table ; 23cm
ISBN 0-434-46272-1 : £6.95 B81-03539

Melville, James, *1931-*. A sort of Samurai / James Melville. — London : Secker & Warburg, 1981. — 167p ; 23cm
ISBN 0-436-27692-5 : £6.95 : CIP rev. B81-09456

Melville, James, *1931-*. The wages of Zen / James Melville. — [London] : Magnum, 1981, c1979. — 174p ; 18cm
Originally published: London : Secker & Warburg, 1979
ISBN 0-417-05650-8 (pbk) : £1.25 B81-12035

Melville, Jennie. Murder has a pretty face / Jennie Melville. — London : Macmillan, 1981. — 253p ; 21cm
ISBN 0-333-30060-2 : £5.95 B81-11678

Melville-Ross, Antony. Backlash / Antony Melville-Ross. — [London] : Fontana, 1981, c1979. — 189p ; 18cm
Originally published: London : Collins, 1979
ISBN 0-00-616366-1 (pbk) : £1.25 B81-22316

Melville-Ross, Antony. Tightrope / Antony Melville-Ross. — London : Collins, 1981. — 251p ; 22cm
ISBN 0-00-221968-9 : £6.95 B81-02888

Melville-Ross, Antony. Trigger. — London : Collins, Feb.1982. — [288]p
ISBN 0-00-221969-7 : £6.95 : CIP entry B81-36980

Melvin, Frances. The boughs of innocence / Frances Melvin. — London : Hutchinson, 1981. — 191p ; 23cm
ISBN 0-09-143800-4 : £6.95 B81-20290

Melwood, Mary. The watcher bee. — London : Deutsch, Feb.1982. — [200]p
ISBN 0-233-97432-6 : £4.95 : CIP entry B81-36389

Mercer, June. The clearing mists / by June Mercer. — London : Hale, 1981. — 191p ; 20cm
ISBN 0-7091-8973-7 : £5.50 B81-11170

Merrill, Jean, *19---*. Marah / Jean Merrill. — London : Macdonald, 1981. — 191p ; 23cm
ISBN 0-354-04607-1 : £5.95 B81-10166

Merrill, Jean, *19---*. Seraphina / Jean Merrill. — London : Futura, 1980, c1979. — 246p ; 18cm. — (A Troubadour book)
Originally published: London : Raven Books, 1979
ISBN 0-7088-1911-7 (pbk) : £1.10 B81-00515

Messer, Diana. Labours of love / Diana Messer. — London : New Horizon, c1981. — 211p ; 22cm
ISBN 0-86116-675-2 : £5.75 B81-39438

Messiter, Ian. The judgement / Ian Messiter. — London : Joseph, 1981. — 222p ; 23cm
ISBN 0-7181-2038-8 : £7.95 B81-33473

Mewburn, Robert. The tangled skein / Robert Mewburn. — Bognor Regis : New Horizon, c1981. — 118p ; 21cm
ISBN 0-86116-678-7 : £4.50 B81-18745

823'.914[F] — Fiction in English, *1945-* — Texts *continuation*

Meyler, Désirée. Forget tomorrow / Désirée Meyler. — London : Macdonald Futura, 1981. — 508p ; 18cm. — (A Troubadour book)
ISBN 0-7107-3015-2 (pbk) : £1.60 B81-15456

Meynell, Laurence. Parasol in the park / Laurence Meynell. — London : Hale, 1981. — 221p ; 21cm
ISBN 0-7091-8879-x : £6.50 B81-17314

Meyrick, Polly. The reluctant match / Polly Meyrick. — London : Mills & Boon, 1981. — 189p ; 20cm. — (Masquerade)
ISBN 0-263-09780-3 : £4.55 B81-10972

Michel, Freda. Crucible of knaves / by Freda Michel. — London : Hale, 1980. — 223p ; 20cm
ISBN 0-7091-8453-0 : £6.50 B81-00516

Middlemas, E. M.. Where eagles soar / by E.M. Middlemas. — London : Hale, 1981. — 190p ; 20cm
ISBN 0-7091-8923-0 : £5.60 B81-27292

Middleton, Stanley. The other side / Stanley Middleton. — London : Hutchinson, 1980. — 191p ; 21cm
ISBN 0-09-143750-4 : £5.95 B81-01469

Midgley, John, *1931-*. The Kremlin directive / by John Midgley. — London : Hale, 1981. — 188p ; 20cm
ISBN 0-7091-9089-1 : £5.95 B81-27313

Milburn, Constance. Castles on sand / by Constance Milburn. — London : Hale, 1981. — 173p ; 20cm
ISBN 0-7091-8794-7 : £5.50 B81-15953

Mildiner, Leslie. Getting the eagle / Leslie Mildiner. — London : Macmillan, 1981. — 122p ; 21cm. — (Topliner tridents)
For adolescents
ISBN 0-333-27578-0 : £3.95 : CIP rev. B81-04225

Miles, Keith. Crossroads : a family affair : a novel / by Keith Miles. — London : Arrow, 1981, c1980. — 80p : ill ; 30cm
Originally published: London : Barker, 1980
ISBN 0-85939-146-9 (pbk) : £0.75 B81-34595

Miles, Keith. The spoils of war / Keith Miles ; based on the Granada television series by John Finch. — [London] : Fontana
2: The promised land. — 1981. — 190p ; 18cm
ISBN 0-00-616234-7 (pbk) : £1.25 B81-28437

Miller, Denis, *1935-*. Diplomatic traffic / Denis Miller. — London : New English Library, 1979, c1978. — 208p ; 18cm
ISBN 0-450-03831-9 (pbk) : £1.00 B81-03062

Miller, Peter. The square leopard / Peter Miller. — London : Muller, c1980. — 155p ; 18cm
ISBN 0-584-31080-3 : £0.90 : CIP rev. B79-29002

Mills, Elizabeth McHolm. The lemming / Elizabeth McHolm Mills. — Bognor Regis : New Horizon, c1978. — 148p ; 21cm
ISBN 0-86116-024-x : £3.95 B81-01470

Milne, Roseleen. The major's lady. — London : Coronet, July 1981. — [224]p
Originally published: London : Hodder & Stoughton, 1979
ISBN 0-340-26672-4 (pbk) : £1.40 : CIP entry B81-13818

Mitchell, Ian. Dove of war / by Ian Mitchell. — London : Hale, 1980. — 191p ; 20cm
ISBN 0-7091-8478-6 : £5.50 B81-01471

Mitchell, Pat. Full circle / by Pat Mitchell ; illustrated by Roo. — Strathmartine (6 Craigmill Cottages, Strathmartine, by Dundee) : ScoTpress, c1981. — 73p : ill ; 30cm
Unpriced (pbk) B81-11112

Mitford, William. Lovely she goes! / William Mitford. — London : Sphere, 1981, c1969. — 206p ; 18cm
ISBN 0-7221-6126-3 (pbk) : £1.25 B81-35065

Moffat, Gwen. The buckskin girl. — London : Gollancz, Feb.1982. — [192]p
ISBN 0-575-03049-6 : £6.95 : CIP entry B81-37571

Molyneux-Carter, Patricia. Clovers / Patricia Molyneux-Carter. — Bognor Regis : New Horizon, c1980. — 178p ; 21cm
ISBN 0-86116-272-2 : £5.25 B81-19030

Montague, Jeanne. Flower of my heart / Jeanne Montague. — London : Macdonald Futura, 1981. — 255p ; 18cm. — (A Minstrel book ; 18)
ISBN 0-7088-2102-2 (pbk) : £0.95 B81-40947

Montague, Jeanne. Touch me with fire / Jeanne Montague. — London : Macdonald, 1981. — 253p ; 21cm
ISBN 0-354-04739-6 : £4.95 B81-37908

Montague, Jeanne. Touch me with fire / Jeanne Montague. — London : Macdonald Futura, 1981. — 253p ; 18cm. — (A Minstrel book ; 16)
ISBN 0-7088-2066-2 (pbk) : £0.95 B81-32781

Montague, Lisa. Fortune's folly / Lisa Montague. — London : Mills and Boon, 1981. — 190p ; 19cm. — (Masquerade)
ISBN 0-263-09949-0 : £4.55 B81-40874

Montague, Lisa. Lady of darkness / Lisa Montague. — Large print ed. — Bath : Chivers, 1981, c1978. — 264p ; 23cm. — (A Seymour book)
Originally published: Australia : s.n., 1978 ; London : Mills & Boon, 1980
ISBN 0-85119-426-5 : Unpriced : CIP rev. B81-13709

Montague, Richard. Frank faces of the dead / Richard Montague. — Bognor Regis : New Horizon, c1979. — 191p ; 22cm
ISBN 0-86116-074-6 : £3.50 B81-27064

Moody, Ron. The devil you don't / Ron Moody. — London : Sphere, 1981, c1980. — 187p ; 18cm
Originally published: London : Robson, 1980
ISBN 0-7221-6179-4 (pbk) : £1.25 B81-35064

Moorcock, Michael. Byzantium endures / Michael Moorcock. — London : Secker & Warburg, 1981. — 404p : 1map ; 23cm
ISBN 0-436-28458-8 (corrected) : £6.95 B81-28546

Moorcock, Michael. Byzantium endures. — London : Secker & Warburg, May 1981. — [420]p
ISBN 0-436-28459-6 : £6.95 : CIP entry B81-10507

Moorcock, Michael. The dancers at the end of time / Michael Moorcock. — London : Granada, 1981. — viii,603p ; 23cm
Conents: An alien heat. Originally published: London : MacGibbon and Kee, 1972 - The hollow lands. Originally published: London : Hart-Davis MacGibbon, 1975 - The end of all songs. Originally published: St. Albans : Hart-Davis MacGibbon, 1976
ISBN 0-246-11606-4 : £7.95 B81-21215

Moorcock, Michael. The entropy tango : a comic romance / Michael Moorcock ; pictures by Romain Slocombe ; lyrics by Michael Moorcock. — London : New English Library, 1981. — 153p : ill ; 23cm
ISBN 0-450-04886-1 : £5.95 B81-37441

Moorcock, Michael. The Land Leviathan : a new scientific romance / Michael Moorcock. — London : Granada, 1981, c1974. — 173p ; 18cm. — (A Mayflower book)
Originally published: London : Quartet Books, 1974
ISBN 0-583-13102-6 (pbk) : £1.25 B81-37282

Moorcock, Michael. The oak and the ram / Michael Moorcock. — London : Granada, 1981, c1973. — 157p ; 18cm. — (The Books of Corum ; v.5) (A Mayflower book) (Mayflower science fantasy)
Originally published: London : Allison & Busby, 1973
ISBN 0-583-12985-4 (pbk) : £0.95 B81-19945

Moorcock, Michael. The sailor on the seas of fate / Michael Moorcock. — London : Granada, 1981, c1976. — 190p ; 18cm. — (A Mayflower book)
Originally published: London : Quartet Books, 1976
ISBN 0-583-13099-2 (pbk) : £0.95 B81-21986

Moorcock, Michael. The transformation of Miss Mavis Ming : a romance of the end of time / by Michael Moorcock. — London : Star, 1980, c1977. — 159p ; 18cm
Originally published: London : W.H. Allen, 1977
ISBN 0-352-30649-1 (pbk) : £0.95 B81-00518

Moorcock, Michael. The war lord of the air / Michael Moorcock. — London : Granada, 1981, c1971. — 156p ; 18cm. — (A Mayflower book)
Originally published: London : New English Library, 1971
ISBN 0-583-13434-3 (pbk) : £0.95 B81-26406

Moorcock, Michael. Warrior of Mars / Michael Moorcock. — London : New English Library, 1981. — 384p ; 23cm
Contents: The city of the beast. Originally published as Warriors of Mars. S.l. : Compact Books, 1965 - Lord of the spiders. Originally published as Blades of Mars. S.l. : Compact Books, 1968 - Masters of the pit. Originally published as Barbarians of Mars. S.l. : Compact Books, 1969
ISBN 0-450-04830-6 : £7.95 B81-08101

Moore, Eric L.. The S.H.A.P.E. affair / Eric L. Moore. — Bognor Regis : New Horizon, c1981. — 292p 21cm
ISBN 0-86116-456-3 : £6.75 B81-32125

Moore, Mary, *19---*. Hill of amethyst / by Mary Moore. — London : Mills & Boon, 1981. — 188p ; 20cm
ISBN 0-263-09898-2 : £4.55 B81-28519

Moore, Mary, *19---*. Middle of nowhere / by Mary Moore. — London : Mills & Boon, 1980. — 190p ; 20cm
ISBN 0-263-09788-9 : £3.85 B81-07206

Moray, Helga. Beacon of gold / Helga Moray. — [London] : Corgi, 1981, c1980. — 277p ; 18cm
Originally published: London : Hale, 1980
ISBN 0-552-11580-0 (pbk) : £1.65 B81-08409

Moray, Helga. Sunny days / Helga Moray. — London : Hale, 1981. — 191p ; 20cm
ISBN 0-7091-8798-x : £6.50 B81-24436

Moray, Helga. Sweet and bitter fancy / by Helga Moray. — London : Hale, 1980. — 229p ; 21cm
ISBN 0-7091-8173-6 : £6.25 B81-02698

Morecambe, Eric. Mr Lonely / Eric Morecambe. — London : Eyre Methuen, 1981. — 189p,[4]p of plates : ill,music,ports ; 23cm
ISBN 0-413-48170-0 : £5.95 B81-15139

Morgan, Denise. Kingmaker's knight / Denise Morgan. — London : Hale, 1981. — 208p ; 21cm
ISBN 0-7091-8565-0 : £6.25 B81-11734

823'.914[F] — Fiction in English, *1945- — Texts continuation*

Morgan, Denise. Second son / Denise Morgan. — London : Hale, 1980. — 208p ; 21cm
ISBN 0-7091-8537-5 : £6.25 B81-01472

Morgan, Denise. Sons and roses / Denise Morgan. — London : Hale, 1981. — 222p ; 21cm
ISBN 0-7091-8696-7 : £6.50 B81-29867

Morgan, Glebe. The rail rogues / Glebe Morgan. — London : Hale, 1981, c1980. — 208p ; 20cm
Originally published: New York : Tower Publications, 1980
ISBN 0-7091-9294-0 : £4.95 B81-30074

Morgan, Hal C.. Jinglebob spurs / by Hal C. Morgan. — London : Hale, 1981. — 159p ; 20cm
ISBN 0-7091-9026-3 : £4.95 B81-17321

Morgan, Hal C.. Thunder trail / by Hal C. Morgan. — London : Hale, 1980. — 158p ; 20cm
ISBN 0-7091-8267-8 : £4.50 B81-01473

Morgan, Stanley. Russ Tobin in Hollywood / Stanley Morgan. — London : W.H. Allen, 1978. — 173p ; 19cm. — (A Star book)
ISBN 0-352-30168-6 (pbk) : £0.70 B81-28548

Morgan, Stanley. Russ Tobin up tight / Stanley Morgan. — London : Star, 1978. — 171p ; 19cm
Originally published: London : W.H. Allen, 1977
ISBN 0-352-30118-x (pbk) : £0.70 B81-28510

Morice, Anne. The men in her death / Anne Morice. — London : Macmillan, 1981. — 188p ; 21cm
ISBN 0-333-31286-4 : £5.50 B81-28955

Morrice, Anne. Death in the round. — Large print ed. — Bath : Chivers Press, Dec.1981. — [296]p. — (A Lythway book)
Originally published: London : Macmillan, 1980
ISBN 0-85119-770-1 : £6.80 : CIP entry
B81-31801

Morrison, Emma. Love is the conqueror / Emma Morrison. — Bognor Regis : New Horizon, c1980. — 151p ; 22cm
ISBN 0-86116-397-4 : £4.25 B81-18962

Mortimer, Carole. Brand of possession / by Carole Mortimer. — London : Mills & Boon, 1980. — 187p ; 19cm
ISBN 0-263-09732-3 : £3.85 B81-00519

Mortimer, Carole. Deceit of a pagan. — Large print ed. — Bath : Chivers, Nov.1981. — [256] p. — (A Seymour book)
Originally published: London : Mills & Boon, 1980
ISBN 0-85119-442-7 : £5.25 : CIP entry
B81-31252

Mortimer, Carole. Devil lover / by Carole Mortimer. — London : Mills & Boon, 1981. — 188p ; 20cm
ISBN 0-263-09844-3 : £4.55 B81-14185

Mortimer, Carole. Engaged to Jarrod Stone / Carole Mortimer. — London : Mills & Boon, 1980. — 186p ; 20cm
ISBN 0-263-09749-8 : £3.85 B81-00520

Mortimer, Carole. First love, last love / by Carole Mortimer. — London : Mills & Boon, 1981. — 186p ; 20cm
ISBN 0-263-09924-5 : £4.55 B81-35641

Mortimer, Carole. The flame of desire / by Carole Mortimer. — London : Mills & Boon, 1981. — 188p ; 20cm
ISBN 0-263-09864-8 : £4.55 B81-18355

Mortimer, Carole. Freedom to love / by Carole Mortimer. — London : Mills & Boon, 1981. — 186p ; 20cm
ISBN 0-263-09902-4 : £4.55 B81-34099

Mortimer, Carole. Ice in his veins / by Carole Mortimer. — London : Mills & Boon, 1981. — 187p ; 19cm
ISBN 0-263-09829-x : £4.55 B81-10885

Mortimer, Carole. Living together / by Carole Mortimer. — London : Mills & Boon : 1980. — 190p ; 20cm
ISBN 0-263-09790-0 : £3.85 B81-05906

Mortimer, Carole. Point of no return / by Carole Mortimer. — London : Mills and Boon, 1981. — 186p ; 19cm
ISBN 0-263-09947-4 : £4.55 B81-40869

Mortimer, Carole. Satan's master / by Carole Mortimer. — London : Mills & Boon, 1981. — 187p ; 20cm
ISBN 0-263-09886-9 : £4.55 B81-28559

Mortimer, June. Return a stranger / by June Mortimer. — London : Hale, 1980. — 159p ; 20cm
ISBN 0-7091-8620-7 : £5.50 B81-08957

Mosco, Maisie. Children's children / Maisie Mosco. — London : New English Library, 1981. — 382p : 2geneal.tables ; 22cm
ISBN 0-450-04871-3 : £6.95 B81-34058

Mosley, Nicholas. Serpent. — London : Secker & Warburg, Oct.1981. — [192]p
ISBN 0-436-28847-8 : £6.95 : CIP entry
B81-25320

Moss, Baron. The big wall / Baron Moss ; drawings by Ken Sprague. — London : Methuen Paperbacks, 1980, c1979. — 286p : ill ; 18cm. — (Magnum books)
Originally published: Maidstone : Bachman & Turner, 1979. — Bibliography: p283-286
ISBN 0-417-04800-9 (pbk) : £1.40 B81-18244

Moss, Baron. Chains / Baron Moss. — London : Bachman & Turner, 1978. — 352p ; 22cm
ISBN 0-85974-071-4 : £5.50 B81-11883

Moss, Ernest. Hannibal's last elephant / Ernest Moss. — Harrow : Eureditions, 1979. — 150p : ill,1map ; 20cm
ISBN 0-906204-35-6 : Unpriced B81-26664

Moules, Joan. Passionate enchantment / by Joan Moules. — London : Hale, 1980. — 172p ; 20cm
ISBN 0-7091-8480-8 : £5.52 B81-01474

Moyes, Patricia. Angel death. — Large print ed. — Anstey : Ulverscroft, Jan.1982. — [501]p. — (Ulverscroft large print series : mystery)
ISBN 0-7089-0746-6 : £5.00 : CIP entry
B81-33954

Moyes, Patricia. Black widower / Patricia Moyes. — Large print ed. — Leicester : Ulverscroft, 1981, c1975. — 397p ; 23cm. — (Ulverscroft large print series)
Originally published: London : Collins, 1975
ISBN 0-7089-0675-3 : £5.00 : CIP rev.
B81-25684

Moyes, Patricia. To kill a coconut / Patricia Moyes. — Leicester : Ulverscroft, 1981, c1977. — 335p ; 23cm. — (Ulverscroft large print)
Originally published: London : Collins, 1977
ISBN 0-7089-0632-x : Unpriced B81-26479

Muir, Helen. Many men & talking wives / Helen Muir. — London : Duckworth, 1981. — 156p ; 23cm
ISBN 0-7156-1613-7 : £7.95 : CIP rev.
B81-25129

Mullen, Dore. All we know of heaven / Dore Mullen. — London : Hamlyn, 1981. — 316p ; 18cm
ISBN 0-600-20365-4 (pbk) : £1.25 B81-12256

Mullen, Michael. Kelly. — Dublin : Wolfhound Press, Oct.1981. — [176]p
ISBN 0-905473-69-8 : £6.00 : CIP entry
B81-27478

Muller, Mary. Cloud across the moon / Mary Muller. — Large print ed. — Leicester : Ulverscroft, 1981, c1970. — 387p ; 23cm. — (Ulverscroft large print series)
Originally published: London : Souvenir Press, 1970
ISBN 0-7089-0676-1 : £5.00 : CIP rev.
B81-25683

Muller, Mary. Flagdown / Mary Muller. — Large print ed. — Leicester : Ulverscroft, 1981, c1974. — 400p ; 22cm. — (Ulverscroft large print series)
Originally published: Ontario : Dent ; London : Souvenir Press, 1974
ISBN 0-7089-0566-8 : £5.00 B81-12182

Muller, Mary. Tree in the wind / Mary Muller. — Large print ed. — Leicester : Ulverscroft, 1981, c1969. — 393p ; 23cm. — (Ulverscroft large print series)
Originally published: London : Souvenir, 1969
ISBN 0-7089-0606-0 : £5.00 : CIP rev.
B81-02579

Murdoch, Iris. The sea, the sea / Iris Murdoch. — St Albans : Triad Panther, 1979, c1978. — 501p ; 18cm
Originally published: London : Chatto and Windus, 1978
ISBN 0-586-04976-2 (pbk) : £1.50 B81-00521

Murphy, Christopher. Scream at the sea / Christopher Murphy. — London : Secker & Warburg, 1981. — 206p ; 23cm
ISBN 0-436-29685-3 : £5.95 : CIP rev.
B81-09455

Murray, Frances. Castaway / by Frances Murray. — Bolton-by-Bowland : Magna Print, 1981, c1978. — 388p ; 23cm
Originally published: London : Hodder and Stoughton, 1978. — Published in large print
ISBN 0-86009-322-0 : £5.75 : CIP rev.
B81-14385

Murray, Julia. Town bronze / Julia Murray. — London : Hale, 1980. — 189p ; 20cm
ISBN 0-7091-8682-7 : £5.95 B81-08956

Murray, Julia. Traitor's ransom / by Julia Murray. — London : Hale, 1981. — 190p ; 20cm
ISBN 0-7091-9074-3 : £6.50 B81-35188

Murray, Rachel. Design for enchantment / by Rachel Murray. — London : Hale, 1981. — 189p ; 20cm
ISBN 0-7091-9280-0 : £5.75 B81-37300

Murray, Rachel. Thread of scarlet / by Rachel Murray. — London : Hale, 1980. — 192p ; 20cm
ISBN 0-7091-8318-6 : £5.25 B81-01475

Murrey, Jeneth. The bright side of dark / by Jeneth Murrey. — London : Mills & Boon, 1981. — 189p ; 19cm
ISBN 0-263-09891-5 : £4.55 B81-28558

Murrey, Jeneth. Hell is my heaven / by Jeneth Murrey. — London : Mills & Boon, 1981. — 190p ; 20cm
ISBN 0-263-09926-1 : £4.55 B81-35633

Murrey, Jeneth. More than yesterday / by Jeneth Murrey. — London : Mills & Boon, 1981. — 190p ; 20cm
ISBN 0-263-09862-1 : £4.55 B81-18350

823'.914[F] — Fiction in English, *1945-* — Texts *continuation*

Myall, Doris E.. The queen's lute player / by Doris E. Myall. — London : Hale, 1981. — 176p ; 20cm
ISBN 0-7091-9099-9 : £6.25 B81-24868

Nabb, Magdalen. Death of an Englishman. — London : Collins, Dec.1981. — [240]p. — (The Crime Club)
ISBN 0-00-231298-0 : £6.50 : CIP entry B81-31525

Napier, Mary. Blind chance / Mary Napier. — [London] : Fontana, 1981, c1980. — 190p ; 18cm
Originally published: London : Collins, 1980
ISBN 0-00-616276-2 (pbk) : £1.25 B81-15533

Napier, Mary. Forbidden places / Mary Napier. — London : Collins, 1981. — 222p ; 22cm
ISBN 0-00-222171-3 : £6.50 B81-12274

Nassauer, Rudolf. Reparations / Rudolf Nassauer. — London : Cape, 1981. — 254p ; 21cm
ISBN 0-224-01882-5 : £6.50 B81-09665

Neels, Betty. An apple from Eve / by Betty Neels. — London : Mills & Boon, 1981. — 187p ; 19cm
ISBN 0-263-09875-3 : £4.55 B81-26421

Neels, Betty. Hannah / by Betty Neels. — London : Mills & Boon, 1980. — 187p ; 20cm
ISBN 0-263-09736-6 : £3.85 B81-00522

Neels, Betty. Heaven round the corner / by Betty Neels. — London : Mills and Boon, 1981. — 188p ; 19cm
ISBN 0-263-09944-x : £4.55 B81-40866

Neels, Betty. Not once but twice / by Betty Neels. — London : Mills & Boon, 1981. — 187p ; 20cm
ISBN 0-263-09822-2 : £4.55 B81-09404

Neels, Betty. When May follows / by Betty Neels. — London : Mills & Boon, 1980. — 186p ; 20cm
ISBN 0-263-09789-7 : £3.85 B81-07086

Neilan, Sarah. Paradise / Sarah Neilan. — London : Hodder, c1981. — 350p : 3maps ; 23cm
ISBN 0-340-23389-3 : £6.95 : CIP rev. B81-15820

Neill, Robert. The Devil's door / Robert Neill. — London : Arrow, 1981, c1979. — 182p ; 18cm
Originally published: London : Hutchinson, 1979
ISBN 0-09-925420-4 (pbk) : £1.25 B81-11037

Neill, Robert. The devil's door / Robert Neill. — Large print ed. — Bath : Chivers, 1981, c1979. — 292p ; 23cm. — (A New Portway large print book)
Originally published: London : Hutchinson, 1979
ISBN 0-85119-109-6 : Unpriced B81-12129

Nelson, Gillian. Charity's child / Gillian Nelson. — London : New English Library, 1981, c1980. — 245p ; 19cm
Originally published: London : W.H. Allen, 1980
ISBN 0-450-05026-2 (pbk) : £1.50 B81-35627

Nelson, Gillian. The cypress room / Gillian Nelson. — London : Bodley Head, 1981. — 235p ; 23cm
ISBN 0-370-30420-9 : £6.95 : CIP rev. B81-02569

Neville, Anne. A perfect wife / Anne Neville. — London : Hale, 1981, c1980. — 158p ; 21cm
ISBN 0-7091-8008-x : £5.50 B81-11657

Neville, Anne. The wakening time / by Anne Neville. — London : Hale, 1980. — 157p ; 20cm
ISBN 0-7091-7853-0 : £5.25 B81-01476

Newby, P. H.. Feelings have changed. — London : Faber, Oct.1981. — [266]p
ISBN 0-571-11823-2 : £7.25 : CIP entry B81-25330

Newman, Andrea. Mackenzie. — London : Severn House, 1981, c1980. — 441p ; 21cm
Originally published: Harmondsworth : Penguin, 1980
ISBN 0-7278-0692-0 : £6.95 B81-13229

Newman, Christopher. Convicted for love / Christopher Newman. — Bognor Regis : New Horizon, c1980. — 160p ; 22cm
ISBN 0-86116-268-4 : £4.75 B81-16245

Newman, Edgar. Bullion and old brass : the Cader Idris adventures / by Edgar Newman ; illustrated by Jacqueline Tettmar. — Wendover : Goodchild, 1979. — 192p : ill,1map ; 18cm
ISBN 0-903445-54-9 (pbk) : £0.65 B81-11887

Newman, G. F.. Charlie and Joanna / G.F. Newman. — London : Granada, 1981. — 199p ; 23cm
ISBN 0-246-11385-5 : £6.95 B81-38060

Newman, G. F.. The list / G.F. Newman. — London : Sphere, 1981, c1979. — vii,244p ; 18cm
Originally published: London : Secker and Warburg, 1979
ISBN 0-7221-6365-7 (pbk) : £1.50 B81-28638

Newman, G. F.. The obsession / G.F. Newman. — London : Granada, 1981, c1980. — 247p ; 18cm. — (A Panther book)
ISBN 0-586-04664-x (pbk) : £1.50 B81-09747

Newman, Mona. The Hong Kong triangle / Mona Newman. — London : Hale, 1981. — 191p ; 20cm
ISBN 0-7091-9023-9 : £5.60 B81-21308

Newman, Mona. To Vienna with love / by Mona Newman. — London : Hale, 1980. — 173p ; 20cm
ISBN 0-7091-8291-0 : £4.95 B81-00523

Newson, Geoffrey. The glory hole / Geoffrey Newson. — London : Muller, 1980. — 305p ; 23cm
ISBN 0-584-31074-9 : £7.50 : CIP rev. B80-09439

Newton, William. It never comes easy / by William Newton. — London : Hale, 1981. — 157p ; 20cm
ISBN 0-7091-8778-5 : £6.25 B81-29860

Newton, William. Nothing is for free / by William Newton. — London : Hale, 1980. — 188p ; 20cm
ISBN 0-7091-8392-5 : £5.75 B81-02150

Newton, William. The set-up / by William Newton. — London : Hale, 1981. — 174p ; 20cm
ISBN 0-7091-8556-1 : £5.75 B81-11785

Nicholas, James, *19---*. Blind drop / by James Nicholas. — London : Hale, 1981. — 176p ; 20cm
ISBN 0-7091-8887-0 : £5.75 B81-16007

Nichols, Mary. The end of Queen Street / by Mary Nichols. — London : Hale, 1981. — 157p ; 20cm
ISBN 0-7091-8808-0 : £5.50 B81-15950

Nichols, Mary. When the bough breaks / by Mary Nichols. — London : Hale, 1981. — 160p ; 20cm
ISBN 0-7091-9319-x : £5.75 B81-37321

Nicholson, Michael, *1937-*. Red joker / Michael Nicholson. — London : Granada, 1981, c1980. — 252p ; 18cm. — (A Panther book)
ISBN 0-586-05340-9 (pbk) : £1.25 B81-10879

Nicole, Christopher. The Friday spy. — London : Severn House, Nov.1981. — [416]p
Originally published: London : Corgi, 1981
ISBN 0-7278-0743-9 : £6.95 : CIP entry B81-30588

Nicole, Christopher. Haggard / Christopher Nicole. — London : Corgi, 1981, c1980. — 399p ; 18cm
Originally published: London : Joseph, 1980
ISBN 0-552-11717-x (pbk) : £1.75 B81-32104

Nicole, Christopher. Haggard's inheritance / Christopher Nicole. — London : Joseph, 1981. — 394p : 1geneal.table ; 23cm
Geneal.table on lining papers
ISBN 0-7181-1987-8 : £7.95 B81-16057

Nicole, Christopher. The thunder and the shouting / Christopher Nicole. — London : Corgi, 1980. c1969. — 281p : ; 18cm
Originally published: Garden City, N.Y. : Doubleday ; London : Hutchinson, 1969
ISBN 0-552-11581-9 (pbk) : £1.50 B81-07358

Nield, Howard. Year of four Caesars / Howard Nield. — New York : St Martin's ; London : Hale, 1981. — 287p ; 21cm
ISBN 0-7091-9049-2 : £6.95 B81-21306

Niesewand, Peter. Fallback. — London : Granada Publishing, Feb.1982. — [512]p
ISBN 0-246-11772-9 : £7.95 : CIP entry B81-38323

Nisbet, Hugh A.. Farewell to Krondahl / by Hugh A. Nisbet. — London : Hale, 1980. — 192p ; 21cm. — (Hale SF)
ISBN 0-7091-8516-2 : £5.75 B81-02155

Niven, David. Go slowly, come back quickly / by David Niven. — London : Hamilton, 1981. — 382p ; 22cm
ISBN 0-241-10690-7 : £6.50 : CIP rev. B81-23888

Norman, Barry. Have a nice day. — London : Quartet, Sept.1981. — [192]p
ISBN 0-7043-2292-7 : £6.50 : CIP entry B81-25764

Norman, Barry. A series of defeats / Barry Norman. — London : Arrow, 1979, c1977. — 169p ; 18cm
Originally published: London : Quartet, 1977
ISBN 0-09-919640-9 (pbk) : £0.85 B81-01477

Norman, Diana. King of the last days. — London : Hodder & Stoughton, Nov.1981. — [192]p
ISBN 0-340-27039-x : £6.95 : CIP entry B81-30131

Norman, Frank. The dead butler caper / Frank Norman. — Large print ed. — Bath : Chivers, 1981, c1978. — 284p ; 23cm. — (A Lythway book)
Originally published: London : Macdonald and Jane's, 1978
ISBN 0-85119-747-7 : £6.70 : CIP rev. B81-20099

North, Elizabeth. Dames / Elizabeth North. — London : Cape, 1981. — 273p ; 22cm
ISBN 0-224-01900-7 : £6.95 : CIP rev. B81-07948

North, Michael. Mission to Ulster / Michael North. — London : Dobson, 1981. — 192p ; 21cm
ISBN 0-234-72281-9 : £4.95 B81-31696

North, Sam. Ramapo!. — London : Arlington, Sept.1981. — [300]p
ISBN 0-85140-533-9 : £6.95 : CIP entry B81-20098

823'.914[F] — Fiction in English, *1945- — Texts continuation*

Northan, Irene. Miss Astbury and Milordo / by Irene Northan. — London : Hale, 1981. — 192p ; 20cm
ISBN 0-7091-9040-9 : £6.50 B81-27314

Northmore, Irma. Wanderlust / Irma Northmore. — Bognor Regis : New Horizon, c1980. — 275p ; 21cm
ISBN 0-86116-656-6 : £6.75 B81-19073

Norton, Joan. Brier rose / by Joan Norton. — London : Hale, 1981. — 207p ; 20cm
ISBN 0-7091-9259-2 : £6.75 B81-40460

Nowak-Soliński, Witold. Krysia : a romantic trilogy / Witold Nowak-Soliński. — Glasgow : Maclellan, 1981
Book 1: A girl on the train. — 149p : ill ; 22cm
ISBN 0-85335-242-9 : £5.95 B81-40976

Nye, Robert. Faust : being the historia von D. Johann Fausten ... / by Robert Nye. — London : Hamilton, 1980. — 277p ; 23cm
ISBN 0-241-10202-2 : £5.95 : CIP rev. B80-18900

O'Brian, Patrick. The surgeon's mate / Patrick O'Brian. — [London] : Fontana, 1981, c1980. — 314p ; 18cm
Originally published: London : Collins, 1980
ISBN 0-00-616411-0 (pbk) : £1.50 B81-22007

O'Brien, Edna. The country girls / Edna O'Brien. — London : Weidenfeld and Nicolson, 1981, c1960. — 187p ; 23cm
Originally published: London : Hutchinson, 1960
ISBN 0-297-77983-4 : £6.50 B81-22112

Occram. The ark of the sun / Occram. — Bognor Regis : New Horizon, c1980. — 195p ; 21cm
ISBN 0-86116-582-9 : £5.75 B81-18865

O'Donnell, Peter. The Xanadu Talisman / by Peter O'Donnell. — London : Souvenir Press, 1981. — 288p ; 21cm. — (Modesty Blaise)
ISBN 0-285-62412-1 : £6.95 B81-15737

Ogle, Josephine. Triple circle / Josephine Ogle. — Bognor Regis : New Horizon, c1979. — 145p ; 21cm
ISBN 0-86116-118-1 : £3.95 B81-15789

O'Grady, Leslie. Lady Jade. — Loughton : Piatkus, Feb.1982. — [320]p
ISBN 0-86188-160-5 : £6.95 : CIP entry B81-36047

Oldfield, Pamela. This ravished land / Pamela Oldfield. — London : Macdonald Futura, 1981. — 428p ; 18cm. — (The Heron saga ; 2)
ISBN 0-7088-2082-4 (pbk) : £1.75 B81-32785

Oliver, Marina. Lord Hugo's bride / Marina Oliver. — London : Hale, 1980. — 188p ; 21cm
ISBN 0-7091-8411-5 : £6.25 B81-00524

Oliver, Marina. Lord Hugo's wedding / by Marina Oliver. — London : Hale, 1981. — 173p ; 20cm
ISBN 0-7091-9181-2 : £6.50 B81-35190

Oliver, Marina. Runaway Hill / Marina Oliver. — London : Hale, 1981. — 190p ; 20cm
ISBN 0-7091-8694-0 : £6.25 B81-13114

Oliver, Winifred. Operation Interpuss / Winifred Oliver. — Bognor Regis : New Horizon, c1981. — 106p,[15]leaves of plates 21cm
ISBN 0-86116-510-1 : £3.95 B81-32124

Olivia. Olivia / by Olivia. — London : Hogarth, 1949 (1981 [printing]). — 109p ; 21cm
ISBN 0-7012-0177-0 : £4.50 B81-17620

O'Neill, Olivia. Dragon star / Olivia O'Neill. — London : Macdonald, 1981. — 335p ; 21cm
ISBN 0-354-04715-9 : £6.95 B81-28370

Oosthuizen, Ann. Loneliness and other lovers / Ann Oosthuizen. — London (488 Kingsland Rd., E.8.) : Sheba Feminist Publishers, 1981. — 160p ; 20cm
ISBN 0-907179-08-8 (pbk) : £2.75 B81-35579

Oram, Neil. The warp / Neil Oram. — London : Sphere
2: Lemmings on the edge. — 1981. — 311p ; 18cm
ISBN 0-7221-6553-6 (pbk) : £1.75 B81-28752

Ord, Irene. Island of dreams / by Irene Ord. — London : Hale, 1980. — 158p ; 20cm
ISBN 0-7091-8198-1 : £5.25 B81-02148

Ord, Irene. Man of granite / by Irene Ord. — London : Hale, 1981. — 173p ; 20cm
ISBN 0-7091-8316-x : £5.50 B81-13128

Ord, Irene. Stand-in for love / by Irene Ord. — London : Hale, 1981. — 160p ; 20cm
ISBN 0-7091-8481-6 : £5.60 B81-24496

Orgill, Douglas. [The day of darkness]. Man in the dark / by Douglas Orgill. — Hornchurch : Henry, 1980, c1965. — 128p ; 21cm
Originally published: London : P. Davies, 1965
ISBN 0-86025-172-1 : £4.55 B81-07037

Ormerod, Roger. Double take / by Roger Ormerod. — London : Hale, 1980. — 192p ; 20cm
ISBN 0-7091-8528-6 : £5.75 B81-00525

Ormerod, Roger. One deathless hour : a Mallin & Coe story / by Roger Ormerod. — London : Hale, 1981. — 190p ; 20cm
ISBN 0-7091-8841-2 : £5.75 B81-11164

Ormesher, Elizabeth. The silver web / by Elizabeth Ormesher. — London : Hale, 1981. — 159p ; 20cm
ISBN 0-7091-8968-0 : £6.25 B81-19289

Ormsby, Patricia. The elusive marriage. — Large print ed. — Long Preston : Magna, Dec.1981. — [448]p
ISBN 0-86009-356-5 : £4.95 : CIP entry B81-31814

Ormsby, Patricia. Heir presumptive / by Patricia Ormsby. — Bolton-by-Bowland : Magna, 1981, c1978. — 361p ; 23cm
Originally published: London : P.Davies, 1978. — Published in large print
ISBN 0-86009-307-7 : £5.75 B81-14200

Ormsby, Patricia. Set to partners / Patricia Ormsby. — Bolton-by-Bowland : Magna, 1980, c1978. — 419p ; 23cm
Originally published: London : P. Davies, 1978. — Published in large print
ISBN 0-86009-268-2 : £5.25 : CIP rev. B80-19461

Orwig, Sara. Camilla / Sara Orwig. — London : Mills and Boon, 1981. — 190p ; 19cm
ISBN 0-263-09777-3 : £4.55 B81-40872

Osman, George. Friends and neighbours / George Osman. — Bognor Regis : New Horizon, c1980. — 183p ; 21cm
ISBN 0-86116-258-7 : £4.75 B81-19037

Oxley, Ian. A brief glimpse of tartan / Ian Oxley. — Bognor Regis : New Horizon, c1980. — 72p ; 21cm
ISBN 0-86116-232-3 : £3.50 B81-18871

Page, Emma. Every second Thursday / Emma Page. — London : Collins, 1981. — 186p ; 20cm. — (The Crime Club)
ISBN 0-00-231290-5 : £6.25 : CIP rev. B81-20552

Page, Vicki. Love and nurse Jeni / by Vicki Page. — London : Hale, 1981. — 158p ; 20cm
ISBN 0-7091-8789-0 : £5.60 B81-24495

Page, Vicki. Nurse in deep water / by Vicki Page. — London : Hale, 1981. — 160p ; 20cm
ISBN 0-7091-8292-9 : £5.50 B81-02869

Page, Vicki. Portrait of a woman / by Vicki Page. — London : Hale, 1980. — 159p ; 20cm
ISBN 0-7091-8181-7 : £4.95 B81-00526

Pargeter, Margaret. At first glance / by Margaret Pargeter. — London : Mills and Boon, 1981. — 186p ; 19cm
ISBN 0-263-09946-6 : £4.55 B81-40867

Pargeter, Margaret. Collision / by Margaret Pargeter. — London : Mills & Boon, 1981. — 187p ; 20cm
ISBN 0-263-09870-2 : £4.55 B81-26573

Pargeter, Margaret. Dark surrender / Margaret Pargeter. — London : Mills & Boon, 1980. — 187p ; 20cm
ISBN 0-263-09750-1 : £3.85 B81-01478

Pargeter, Margaret. Deception / by Margaret Pargeter. — London : Mills & Boon, 1980. — 188p ; 20cm
ISBN 0-263-09742-0 : £3.85 B81-00527

Pargeter, Margaret. The loving slave / by Margaret Pargeter. — London : Mills & Boon, 1981. — 188p ; 20cm
ISBN 0-263-09845-1 : £4.55 B81-14178

Pargeter, Margaret. Substitute bride / by Margaret Pargeter. — London : Mills & Boon, 1981. — 187p ; 20cm
ISBN 0-263-09889-3 : £4.55 B81-28557

Parker, F. M.. Skinner / by F.M. Parker. — London : Hale, 1981. — 182p ; 20cm
ISBN 0-7091-9522-2 : £4.95 B81-40531

Parker, Olwen. The truest joy / by Olwen Parker. — London : Hale, 1981. — 160p ; 20cm
ISBN 0-7091-8812-9 : £5.50 B81-14069

Parkes, Patricia. Devil by candlelight / Patricia Parkes. — London : Macdonald Futura, 1981. — 252p ; 21cm
ISBN 0-354-04656-x : £4.95 B81-21313

Parkin, Molly. A bite of the apple : a novel / by Molly Parkin. — London : W.H. Allen, 1981. — 165p ; 22cm
ISBN 0-491-02814-8 : £5.95 B81-15408

Parkin, Molly. Up and coming / by Molly Parkin. — London : Star, 1981, c1980. — 159p ; 18cm
Originally published: London : W.H. Allen, 1980
ISBN 0-352-30758-7 (pbk) : £1.00 B81-11669

Parkinson, Elsie. Coffee coloured / Elsie Parkinson. — Bognor Regis : New Horizon, c1981. — 114p ; 21cm
ISBN 0-86116-517-9 : £3.75 B81-39606

Parrish, Frank. Sting of the honeybee / Frank Parrish. — Large print ed. — Leicester : Ulverscroft, 1980, c1978. — 338p ; 23cm. — (Ulverscroft large print seris)
Originally published: London : Constable, 1978
ISBN 0-7089-0520-x : £4.25 : CIP rev. B80-23735

Parrish, Patt. Feather in the wind / by Patt Parrish. — London : Hale, 1981. — 160p ; 20cm
ISBN 0-7091-9019-0 : £5.60 B81-35212

Parrish, Patt. The sheltered haven / by Patt Parrish. — London : Hale, 1981. — 190p ; 20cm
ISBN 0-7091-9361-0 : £5.75 B81-40468

823'.914[F] — Fiction in English, *1945-* **— *Texts***
continuation

Parsons, Tony. Platinum logic / Tony Parsons. — London : Pan, 1981. — 509p ; 18cm
ISBN 0-330-26457-5 (pbk) : £1.75 B81-36695

Parvin, Brian. Then there was murder / by Brian Parvin. — London : Hale, 1980. — 159p ; 20cm
ISBN 0-7091-8388-7 : £5.75 B81-11171

Parvin, Brian. Wreath for a ragman / by Brian Parvin. — London : Hale, 1981. — 160p ; 20cm
ISBN 0-7091-8511-1 : £5.75 B81-14093

Patterson, Harry. Brought in dead. — Large print ed. — Bath : Chivers, Nov.1981. — [256] p. — (A Lythway book)
Originally published: London : Long, 1967
ISBN 0-85119-761-2 : £6.50 : CIP entry
B81-31272

Patterson, Harry. Sad wind from the sea / Harry Patterson. — London : Arrow, 1981, c1959. — 191p ; 18cm
Originally published: London : Long, 1959
ISBN 0-09-926260-6 (pbk) : £1.25 B81-24841

Patterson, Harry. To catch a king / Harry Patterson. — London : Arrow, 1980, c1979. — 222p ; 18cm
Originally published: London : Hutchinson, 1979
ISBN 0-09-921900-x (pbk) : £1.10 B81-02127

Patterson, Harry. To catch a king / Harry Patterson. — Large print ed. — Leicester : Ulverscroft, 1981, c1979. — 323p ; 23cm. — (Ulverscroft large print series)
Originally published: London : Hutchinson, 1979
ISBN 0-7089-0612-5 : £5.00 : CIP rev.
B81-02583

Pattinson, James. The Antwerp appointment / James Pattinson. — London : Hale, 1981. — 191p ; 21cm
ISBN 0-7091-6791-1 : £6.25 B81-14067

Pattinson, James. Busman's holiday / James Pattinson. — London : Hale, 1980. — 190p ; 20cm
ISBN 0-7091-6589-7 : £6.25 B81-01479

Pattinson, James. Stride / James Pattinson. — London : Hale, 1981. — 220p ; 21cm
ISBN 0-7091-7041-6 : £6.50 B81-37453

Pattison, Ruth. The hanging legend / by Ruth Pattison. — London : Hale, 1981. — 192p ; 20cm
ISBN 0-7091-8947-8 : £6.50 B81-15304

Paxton, Lois. The man who died twice / Lois Paxton. — Large print ed. — Bath : Chivers, 1981, c1968. — 230p ; 23cm. — (A Seymour book)
Originally published: London : Hurst & Blackett, 1968
ISBN 0-85119-408-7 : Unpriced B81-12134

Payton, Coral. Tarrant Hall / by Coral Payton. — London : Hale, 1981. — 192p ; 20cm
ISBN 0-7091-9061-1 : £6.50 B81-21882

Peake, Lilian. A secret affair / by Lilian Peake. — London : Mills & Boon, 1980. — 187p ; 19cm
ISBN 0-263-09733-1 : £3.85 B81-00528

Peake, Lilian. Strangers into lovers / by Lilian Peake. — London : Mills & Boon, 1981. — 188p ; 20cm
ISBN 0-263-09861-3 : £4.55 B81-18354

Pearsall, Ronald. Tides of war. — Large print ed. — Long Preston : Magna Print Books, Jan.1982. — [650]p
Originally published: London : Joseph, 1978
ISBN 0-86009-365-4 : £5.25 : CIP entry
B81-33771

Pearson, John, *1930-*. Biggles : the authorized biography / John Pearson. — Feltham : Hamlyn, 1980, c1978. — 311p ; 18cm
Originally published: London : Sidgwick and Jackson, 1978
ISBN 0-600-20062-0 (pbk) : £1.50 B81-01480

Pearson, Michael, *1924-*. The store / Michael Pearson. — London : Macmillan, 1980. — 432p ; 23cm
ISBN 0-333-25765-0 : £6.95 B81-01481

Pellow, John. Parson's progress / by John Pellow. — London : John Clare Books, c1981. — 146p ; 23cm
ISBN 0-906549-18-3 : £6.95 B81-21314

Pemberton, Margaret. Harlot / Margaret Pemberton. — London : Arrow, 1981. — 392p ; 18cm
ISBN 0-09-926400-5 (pbk) : £1.60 B81-39160

Pemberton, Margaret. Lion of Languedoc / Margaret Pemberton. — London : Mills & Boon, 1981. — 189p ; 19cm. — (Masquerade historical romances)
ISBN 0-263-09779-x : £4.55 B81-09310

Pembroke, Peter. The Cuban connection / by Peter Pembroke. — London : Hale, 1980. — 191p ; 20cm
ISBN 0-7091-8327-5 : £5.50 B81-00529

Penn, Margaret. The foolish virgin / Margaret Penn. — Cambridge : Cambridge University Press, 1981. — 253p ; 22cm
Originally published: London : Cape, 1951
ISBN 0-521-28297-7 (pbk) : £3.75 : CIP rev.
B81-06891

Penn, Margaret. Manchester fourteen miles / Margaret Penn. — Cambridge : Cambridge University Press, 1947 (1981 [printing]). — 340p ; 22cm
ISBN 0-521-28065-6 (pbk) : £3.75 : CIP rev.
B81-06611

Penn, Margaret. Young Mrs. Burton / Margaret Penn. — Cambridge : Cambridge University Press, 1981. — 256p ; 22cm
Originally published: London : Cape, 1954
ISBN 0-521-28298-5 (pbk) : £3.75 : CIP rev.
B81-06890

Perriam, Wendy. Absinthe for elevenses / Wendy Perriam. — London : Macdonald Futura, 1981, c1980. — 320p : ill ; 18cm
Originally published: London : Joseph, 1980
ISBN 0-7088-2011-5 (pbk) : £1.50 B81-15457

Perry, Anne. Callander square. — Large print ed. — Anstey : Ulverscroft, Dec.1981. — [464]p. — (Ulverscroft large print series)
Originally published: London : Hale, 1980
ISBN 0-7089-0718-0 : £5.00 : CIP entry
B81-32033

Perry, Hilda. Between two loves / by Hilda Perry. — London : Hale, 1981. — 173p ; 20cm
ISBN 0-7091-8753-x (corrected) : £5.50
B81-11733

Perry, Hilda. Depth of love / by Hilda Perry. — London : Hale, 1980. — 160p ; 20cm
ISBN 0-7091-8445-x : £5.25 B81-02207

Perry, Hilda. I believe in you / by Hilda Perry. — London : Hale, 1980. — 158p ; 20cm
ISBN 0-7091-8058-6 : £4.75 B81-00530

Perry, Ritchie. Fool's mate / Ritchie Perry. — London : Collins, 1981. — 196p ; 21cm. — (The Crime Club)
ISBN 0-00-231286-7 : £5.75 B81-11006

Perry, Roger, *1928-*. Esper's War / Roger Perry. — London : Hale, 1981. — 188p ; 20cm. — (Hale SF)
ISBN 0-7091-9154-5 : £6.25 B81-28875

Perry, Roger, *1928-*. The making of Jason / Roger Perry. — London : Hale, 1980. — 158p ; 21cm. — (Hale SF)
ISBN 0-7091-8454-9 : £5.25 B81-00531

Perry, Roland. Programme for a puppet / Roland Perry. — Feltham : Hamlyn, 1980, c1979. — 318p ; 18cm
Originally published: London : W.H. Allen, 1979
ISBN 0-600-20333-6 (pbk) : £1.25 B81-01482

Peters, Caroline. The castle of the cormorants / by Caroline Peters. — London : Hale, 1981. — 192p ; 20cm
ISBN 0-7091-8997-4 : £6.50 B81-24353

Peters, Maureen. Beggar maid, queen / Maureen Peters. — London : Hale, 1980. — 190p ; 21cm
ISBN 0-7091-8272-4 : £6.25 B81-00532

Peters, Maureen. Night of the willow / by Maureen Peters. — London : Hale, 1981. — 206p ; 21cm
ISBN 0-7091-8421-2 : £6.25 B81-02699

Peters, Maureen. Ravenscar / Maureen Peters. — London : Hale, 1981. — 172p ; 21cm
ISBN 0-7091-8966-4 : £6.25 B81-21880

Peters, Sue. Dangerous rapture / by Sue Peters. — London : Mills & Boon, 1981. — 189p ; 20cm
ISBN 0-263-09905-9 : £4.55 B81-34110

Petrie, Glen. The Tondeau of Chartres / Glen Petrie. — London : Macmillan, 1981. — 445p ; 23cm
ISBN 0-333-31134-5 : £7.95 B81-18567

Peyton, K. M.. Dear Fred / K.M. Peyton. — London : Bodley Head, 1981. — 232p ; 23cm
ISBN 0-370-30350-4 : £4.95 B81-16981

Peyton, K. M.. Flambards divided / K.M. Peyton. — Oxford : Oxford University Press, 1981. — 263p : 1ill ; 23cm
ISBN 0-19-271452-x : £5.95 B81-18215

Phillips, Dee. The coconut kiss. — London : Hodder & Stoughton, Jan.1982. — [192]p
ISBN 0-340-27468-9 : £6.95 : CIP entry
B81-34138

Phillips, Dee. No, not I / Dee Phillips. — London : Robin Clark, 1981, c1980. — 190p ; 20cm
Originally published: London : Hodder and Stoughton, 1980
ISBN 0-86072-049-7 (pbk) : £2.95 B81-28639

Phillips, Leon. Ritual fire dance / by Leon Phillips. — London : Hale, 1981. — 176p ; 20cm
ISBN 0-7091-8804-8 : £5.75 B81-14134

Phipps, Grace M.. Nurse Penny's patients / by Grace M. Phipps. — London : Hale, 1981. — 176p ; 20cm
ISBN 0-7091-8792-0 : £5.50 B81-15305

Pike, Charles R.. Angel of death / Charles R. Pike. — London : Granada, 1980. — 156p ; 18cm. — (Jubal Cade : 15) (A Mayflower book)
ISBN 0-583-13174-3 (pbk) : £0.85 B81-02195

Pike, Charles R.. Mourning is red / Charles R. Pike. — London : Granada, 1981. — 141p ; 18cm. — (Jubal Cade ; 16) (A Mayflower book)
ISBN 0-583-13175-1 (pbk) : £0.95 B81-08237

Pilcher, Rosamunde. Wild mountain thyme / Rosamunde Pilcher. — London : New English Library, 1980, c1978 (1981 [printing]). — 249p ; 18cm
Originally published: New York : St. Martin's Press, 1978
ISBN 0-450-04770-9 (pbk) : £1.25 B81-02910

823'.914[F] — Fiction in English, *1945- — Texts continuation*

Pilcher, Rosamunde. Wild mountain thyme / Rosamunde Pilcher. — Large print ed. — Leicester : Ulverscroft, 1981, c1978. — 455p ; 23cm. — (Ulverscroft large print series)
Originally published: New York : St Martin's Press, 1978 ; London : New English Library, 1980
ISBN 0-7089-0621-4 : £5.00 : CIP rev. B81-07907

Pincher, Chapman. Dirty tricks / Chapman Pincher. — London : Sidwick & Jackson, 1980 (1981 [printing]). — 207p ; 18cm
ISBN 0-283-98753-7 (pbk) : £1.50 B81-18381

Pirie, David. Mystery story / David Pirie. — London : Frederick Muller, 1980. — 167p ; 23cm
ISBN 0-584-31103-6 : £6.50 : CIP rev. B80-18009

Pitstow, Margaret. Candia / by Margaret Pitstow. — London : Hale, 1981. — 192p ; 20cm
ISBN 0-7091-9326-2 : £5.75 B81-37306

Pitstow, Margaret. Dangerous labyrinth / by Margaret Pitstow. — London : Hale, 1981. — 191p ; 20cm
ISBN 0-7091-8754-8 : £5.50 B81-08728

Pitstow, Margaret. Past love / by Margaret Pitstow. — London : Hale, 1980. — 188p ; 20cm
ISBN 0-7091-8380-1 : £5.25 B81-00533

Plaidy, Jean. Passage to Pontefract / Jean Plaidy. — London : Hale, 1981. — 366p ; 23cm. — (Plantagenet saga ; 10)
ISBN 0-7091-7764-x : £6.50 B81-14066

Plumb, R. T.. A house called Madrid / R.T. Plumb. — London : Duckworth, 1980. — 149p ; 23cm
ISBN 0-7156-1484-3 : £6.95 : CIP rev. B80-13075

Plummer, David Brian. Lepus : the story of a hare / D. Brian Plummer ; illustrated by Martin Knowelden. — Woodbridge : Boydall Press, c1981. — 119p : ill ; 23cm
ISBN 0-85115-142-6 : £5.50 B81-17044

Polland, Madeleine. All their kingdoms / Madeleine A. Polland. — London : Collins, 1981. — 412p ; 24cm
ISBN 0-00-221439-3 : £6.50 : CIP rev. B81-07626

Polland, Madeleine. Sabrina / Madeleine Polland. — Large print ed. — Leicester : Ulverscroft, 1981, c1978. — 505p ; 23cm. — (Ulverscroft large print series)
Originally published: New York : Delacorte Press ; London : Collins, 1979
ISBN 0-7089-0679-6 : £5.00 : CIP rev. B81-25656

Ponsonby, D. A.. Kaye's Walk / D.A. Ponsonby. — Large print ed. — Bath : Chivers, 1981, c1977. — 236p ; 23cm. — (A Seymour book)
Originally published: London : Hurst & Blackett, 1977
ISBN 0-85119-409-5 : Unpriced B81-12133

Poole, Elizabeth Garfield. Destiny : a novel / by Elizabeth Garfield Poole. — Bognor Regis : New Horizon, c1981. — 63p ; 21cm
ISBN 0-86116-461-x : £3.50 B81-18742

Pope, Dudley. Buccaneer : a novel / by Dudley Pope. — London : Secker & Warburg, 1981. — 277p : 1map ; 23cm
ISBN 0-436-37740-3 : £6.95 B81-15767

Pope, Dudley. Ramage and the renegades. — London : Secker & Warburg, Oct.1981. — [300]p. — (An Alison Press book)
ISBN 0-436-37741-1 : £6.95 : CIP entry B81-25321

Pope, Dudley. Ramage's signal : a novel / by Dudley Pope. — London : Secker & Warburg, 1980. — 255p : ill,map ; 23cm
ISBN 0-436-37739-x : £6.50 B81-00534

Pope, Dudley. Ramage's signal / Dudley Pope. — [London] : Fontana, 1981, c1980. — 286p : 2maps ; 18cm
Originally published: London : Secker & Warburg, 1980
ISBN 0-00-616307-6 (pbk) : £1.50 B81-32171

Porter, Alvin. Devil's Breed / by Alvin Porter. — London : Hale, 1980. — 158p ; 20cm
ISBN 0-7091-8221-x : £4.50 B81-00535

Porter, Alvin. Gunsmoke and rawhide / by Alvin Porter. — London : Hale, 1981. — 160p ; 20cm
ISBN 0-7091-9194-4 : £4.95 B81-33530

Porter, Joyce. Dover beats the band / Joyce Porter. — Large print ed. — Bath : Chivers, 1981, c1980. — 240p ; 23cm. — (A Lythway mystery)
Originally published : London : Weidenfeld and Nicolson, 1980
ISBN 0-85119-722-1 : Unpriced B81-24781

Porter, R. W.. Kiss and kill / by R.W. Porter. — London : Hale, 1981. — 206p ; 20cm
ISBN 0-7091-8687-8 : £5.75 B81-03077

Potter, Dennis. Pennies from heaven. — London : Quartet, Nov.1981. — 1v.
ISBN 0-7043-2300-1 : CIP entry B81-30407

Potter, Jay Hill. The bitter trail / by Jay Hill Potter. — London : Hale, 1981. — 159p ; 20cm
ISBN 0-7091-8755-6 : £4.95 B81-08649

Potter, Jay Hill. Jasper and Hack / by Jay Hill Potter. — London : Hale, 1981. — 160p ; 20cm
ISBN 0-7091-9116-2 : £4.95 B81-24432

Powell, Margaret. First love, last love / Margaret Powell. — London : Duckworth, 1980. — 164p ; 23cm
ISBN 0-7156-1505-x : £6.95 B81-01663

Powell, Margaret. Maids and mistresses / Margaret Powell. — London : Joseph, 1981. — 192p ; 23cm
ISBN 0-7181-2023-x : £6.50 B81-22318

Powers, Tim. The drawing of the dark / Tim Powers. — London : Granada, 1981, c1979. — 383p ; 18cm. — (A Mayflower book)
ISBN 0-583-13319-3 (pbk) : £1.95 B81-27696

Pownall, David. Beloved latitudes / by David Pownall. — London : Gollancz, 1981. — 140p ; 23cm
ISBN 0-575-02988-9 : £6.95 B81-19892

Pratchett, Terry. Strata / Terry Pratchett. — Gerrards Cross : Smythe, 1981. — 192p ; 23cm
ISBN 0-901072-91-5 : £5.95 : CIP rev. B80-18010

Preston, Ivy. Summer at Willowbank / by Ivy Preston. — London : Hale, 1980. — 159p ; 20cm
ISBN 0-7091-8417-4 : £5.25 B81-00536

Preston, Ivy. Where ratas twine / Ivy Preston. — Large print ed. — Bath : Chivers, 1981, c1960. — 241p ; 23cm. — (A Seymour book)
Originally published: London : Wright & Brown, 1960
ISBN 0-85119-401-x : Unpriced B81-08506

Price, Anthony. The labyrinth makers. — Large print ed. — Anstey : Ulverscroft, Nov.1981. — [384]p. — (Ulverscroft large print series)
Originally published: London : Gollancz, 1970
ISBN 0-7089-0711-3 : £5.00 : CIP entry B81-30498

Price, Anthony. Soldier no more : a novel / by Anthony Price. — London : Gollancz, c1981. — 277p ; 22cm
ISBN 0-575-03028-3 : £6.95 B81-36827

Price, Les. A crowded silence / Les Price. — Bognor Regis : New Horizon, c1980. — 161p ; 21cm
ISBN 0-86116-287-0 : £5.25 B81-19025

Priest, Christopher. The affirmation / Christopher Priest. — London : Faber, 1981. — 213p ; 21cm
ISBN 0-571-11684-1 : £6.25 B81-19363

Priest, Christopher. The space machine : a scientific romance / Christopher Priest. — London : Pan, 1981, c1976. — 363p ; 18cm
Originally published: London : Faber, 1976
ISBN 0-330-26345-5 (pbk) : £1.50 B81-20208

Prior, Allan. Never been kissed in the same place twice / Allan Prior. — London : Arrow, 1980, c1978. — 477p ; 18cm
Originally published: London : Cassell, 1978
ISBN 0-09-922340-6 (pbk) : £1.75 B81-02177

Prior, Allan. Theatre : a novel / by Allan Prior. — London : Hamilton, 1981. — 303p ; 23cm
ISBN 0-241-10437-8 : £6.95 : CIP rev. B81-20175

Prowse, Catherine. The flight from love / Catherine Prowse. — London : Magnum Books, 1980. — 222p ; 18cm
ISBN 0-417-05150-6 (pbk) : £1.25 B81-02907

Pym, Barbara. Excellent women / Barbara Pym. — Harmondsworth : Penguin, 1980. — 237p ; 18cm
Originally published: London: Cape, 1952
ISBN 0-14-005383-2 (pbk) : £1.25 B81-00538

Pym, Barbara. A glass of blessings / Barbara Pym. — Harmondsworth : Penguin, 1980, c1958. — 251p ; 19cm
Originally published: London : Cape, 1958
ISBN 0-14-005382-4 (pbk) : £1.35 B81-00539

Pym, Barbara. Jane and Prudence / Barbara Pym. — London : Granada, 1981. — 252p ; 18cm. — (A Panther book)
Originally published: London : Cape, 1953
ISBN 0-586-05370-0 (pbk) : £1.50 B81-36771

Pym, Barbara. Less than angels / Barbara Pym. — London : Granada, 1980. — 253p ; 18cm. — (A Panther book)
Originally published: London : Cape, 1955
ISBN 0-586-05368-9 (pbk) : £1.50 B81-02063

Pym, Barbara. No fond return of love / Barbara Pym. — London : Granada, 1981, c1961. — 287p ; 18cm. — (A Panther book)
Originally published: London : Cape, 1961
ISBN 0-586-05371-9 (pbk) : £1.50 B81-32184

Pym, Barbara. Some tame gazelle / Barbara Pym. — London : Granada, 1981. — 253p ; 18cm. — (A Panther book)
Originally published: London : Cape, 1950
ISBN 0-586-05369-7 (pbk) : £1.50 B81-05911

Quinnell, A. J.. Man of fire / A.J. Quinnell. — London : Macmillan, 1981, c1980. — 284p ; 23cm
Originally published: New York : Morrow, 1980
ISBN 0-333-30742-9 : £5.95 B81-19950

Radley, Sheila. The chief inspector's daughter / Sheila Radley. — London : Constable, 1981. — 208p ; 22cm. — (Constable crime)
ISBN 0-09-463320-7 : £5.95 B81-02993

Radley, Sheila. Death in the morning / Sheila Radley. — London : Prior, 1981, c1978. — 426p ; 25cm
Published in large print
ISBN 0-86043-600-4 : £6.95 B81-32773

823'.914[F] — Fiction in English, *1945- — Texts continuation*

Rae, Doris. The spell of solitude / by Doris Rae. — London : Hale, 1981. — 191p ; 20cm
ISBN 0-7091-9077-8 : £5.60 B81-30076

Rae, Hugh C.. The haunting at Waverley Falls / Hugh C. Rae. — London : New English Library, 1981, c1980. — 288p ; 18cm
Originally published: London : Constable, 1980
ISBN 0-450-05156-0 (pbk) : £1.25 B81-28696

Rance, Joseph. Bullet train / Joseph Rance and Arei Kato. — London : Pan, 1981, c1980. — 233p : 1ill,1map ; 18cm
Originally published: London : Souvenir Press, 1980
ISBN 0-330-26277-7 (pbk) : £1.50 B81-37348

Rance, Joseph. Bullet train. — Large print ed. — Anstey : Ulverscroft, Oct.1981. — [416]p. — (Ulverscroft large print series)
Originally published: London : Souvenir Press, 1980
ISBN 0-7089-0697-4 : £5.00 : CIP entry B81-28092

Randall, Hugh. Body & soul : the story of Marcus, slave under Rome / Hugh Randall. — London : Hale, 1980. — 253p ; 23cm
ISBN 0-7091-7773-9 : £6.95 B81-00540

Randall, Rona. The ladies of Hanover Square. — London : H. Hamilton, Sept.1981. — [320]p
ISBN 0-241-10661-3 : £7.95 : CIP entry B81-20514

Randall, Rona. The mating dance / Rona Randall. — London : Macdonald Futura, 1980, c1979. — 503p ; 18cm. — (A Troubadour spectacular)
Originally published: London : Hamilton, 1979
ISBN 0-7088-1776-9 (pbk) : £1.75 B81-01657

Raphael, Jane. Next year in Jerusalem / Jane Raphael. — London : Hale, 1980. — 224p ; 21cm
ISBN 0-7091-8346-1 : £6.50 B81-00541

Rathbone, Julian. Base case / Julian Rathbone. — London : Joseph, 1981. — 186p ; 21cm
ISBN 0-7181-1993-2 : £6.50 B81-14077

Raven, Simon. The roses of Picardie : a romance / Simon Raven. — London : Granada, 1981, c1980. — 443p ; 18cm. — (A Panther book)
Originally published: London : Blond & Briggs, 1980
ISBN 0-586-05126-0 (pbk) : £1.50 B81-02694

Raymond, Diana. Emma Pride. — Loughton : Piatkus, Dec.1981. — [256]p
ISBN 0-86188-128-1 : £6.95 : CIP entry B81-31637

Raymond, Mary. April promise / by Mary Raymond. — London : Hale, 1980. — 156p ; 20cm
ISBN 0-7091-8381-x : £5.25 B81-00542

Raymond, Patrick. The white war / Patrick Raymond. — London : Pan, 1981, c1978. — 205p ; 18cm
Originally published: London : Cassell, 1978
ISBN 0-330-26202-5 (pbk) : £1.25 B81-37349

Rayner, Claire. Bedford Row / Claire Rayner. — [London] : Corgi, 1978, c1977 (1980 [printing]). — 314p : 1geneal.table ; 18cm. — (The Performers saga ; bk.5)
Originally published: London : Cassell, 1977
ISBN 0-552-11504-5 (pbk) : £1.50 B81-00544

Rayner, Claire. The meddlers / by Claire Rayner. — Loughton : Piatkus, 1981, c1970. — 314p ; 21cm
Originally published: London : Cassell, 1970
ISBN 0-86188-103-6 : £5.95 : CIP rev. B81-09473

Rayner, Claire. Reprise / Claire Rayner. — London : Arrow, 1981, c1980. — 270p ; 18cm
Originally published: London : Hutchinson, 1980
ISBN 0-09-924890-5 (pbk) : £1.35 B81-14124

Rayner, Claire. The running years. — London : Hutchinson, Oct.1981. — [656]p
ISBN 0-09-146510-9 : £7.95 : CIP entry B81-24618

Rayner, Claire. Soho Square / Claire Rayner. — London : Corgi, 1977, c1976 (1980 printing). — 347p : 1geneal.table ; 18cm. — (The Performers ; bk.4)
Originally published: London : Cassell, 1976
ISBN 0-552-11503-7 (pbk) : £1.50 B81-00543

Rayner, Claire. A time to heal. — Loughton : Piatkus, Nov.1981. — [268]p
Originally published: 1972
ISBN 0-86188-105-2 : £5.95 : CIP entry B81-30626

Rayner, D. A.. The enemy below / D.A. Rayner. — [London] : Fontana, 1958, (1981 [printing]). — 191p ; 18cm
Originally published: London : Collins, 1956
ISBN 0-00-616380-7 (pbk) : £1.25 B81-36835

Rayner, William, *1929-*. Wheels of fortune / William Rayner. — London : Collins, 1979. — 255p ; 22cm
ISBN 0-00-221975-1 : £5.50 B81-01876

Read, *Miss*. News from Thrush Green / Miss Read. — Harmondsworth : Penguin, 1973, c1970 (1981 [printing]). — 192p ; 18cm
Originally published: London : Joseph, 1970
ISBN 0-14-003659-8 (pbk) : £1.25 B81-35588

Read, *Miss*. No holly for Miss Quinn / 'Miss Read' ; illustrations by J.S. Goodall. — Harmondsworth : Penguin, 1978, c1976 (1980 [printing]). — 124p : ill ; 18cm
Originally published: London : Joseph, 1976
ISBN 0-14-004725-5 (pbk) : £0.95 B81-02324

Read, *Miss*. Return to Thrush Green / Miss Read ; illustrated by J.S. Goodall. — Harmondsworth : Penguin, 1980, c1978. — 208p : ill ; 18cm
Originally published: London : Joseph, 1978
ISBN 0-14-005255-0 (pbk) : £1.25 B81-09261

Read, *Miss*. Thrush Green / by 'Miss Read' ; illustrated by J.S. Goodall. — Harmondsworth : Penguin in association with Joseph, 1962, c1959 (1981 [printing]). — 219p : ill ; 19cm
Originally published: London : Joseph, 1959
ISBN 0-14-001802-6 (pbk) : £1.00 B81-35476

Read, *Miss*. Tyler's Row / 'Miss Read' ; illustrated by J.S. Goodall. — Harmondsworth : Penguin, 1975, c1972 (1980 [printing]). — 185p : ill ; 18cm
Originally published: London : Joseph, 1972
ISBN 0-14-003917-1 (pbk) : £0.95 B81-02325

Read, *Miss*. Village affairs / 'Miss Read' ; illustrations by J.S. Goodall. — Harmondsworth : Penguin, 1979, c1977 (1980 [printing]). — 218p : ill ; 18cm
Originally published: London : Joseph, 1977
ISBN 0-14-004966-5 (pbk) : £0.95 B81-02326

Read, *Miss*. Village affairs / by Miss Read ; illustrations by J.S. Goodall. — Bolton-by-Bowland : Magna Print, 1980, c1977. — 357p : ill ; 23cm
Originally published: London : Joseph, 1977. — Published in large print
ISBN 0-86009-245-3 : £5.25 : CIP rev. B79-37488

Read, *Miss*. Village centenary / by Miss Read ; illustrated by J.S. Goodall. — London : Joseph, c1980. — 236p : ill ; 21cm
Ill on lining papers
ISBN 0-7181-1954-1 : £5.95 B81-00545

Read, *Miss*. Village diary / 'Miss Read'. — Harmondsworth : Penguin, 1970, c1957 (1980 [printing]). — 250p : ill ; 18cm
Originally published: London : Joseph, 1957
ISBN 0-14-003215-0 (pbk) : £0.95 B81-02322

Read, *Miss*. Village school / 'Miss Read' ; with drawings by J.S. Goodall. — Harmondsworth : Penguin in association with Michael Joseph, 1960, c1955 (1980 [printing]). — 238p : ill ; 18cm
Originally published: London : Joseph, 1955
ISBN 0-14-001462-4 (pbk) : £0.95 B81-02323

Read, Piers Paul. A married man / Piers Paul Read. — London : Pan in association with The Alison Press-Secker & Warburg, 1981, c1979. — 285p ; 18cm
Originally published: New York : Lippincott ; London : Secker & Warburg, 1979
ISBN 0-330-26369-2 (pbk) : £1.50 B81-24416

Read, Piers Paul. The Villa Golitsyn : a novel / by Piers Paul Read. — London : Secker & Warburg, 1981. — 192p ; 23cm. — (An Alison Press book)
ISBN 0-436-40968-2 : £6.95 : CIP rev. B81-25322

Redmon, Anne. Emily Stone / Anne Redmon. — London : Methuen Paperbacks, 1981, c1974. — 238p ; 18cm. — (Magnum books)
Originally published: London : Secker and Warburg, 1974
ISBN 0-417-05090-9 (pbk) : £1.50 B81-12493

Redmon, Anne. Music and silence / Anne Redmon. — London : Secker & Warburg, 1979. — 251p ; 23cm
ISBN 0-436-40991-7 : £4.95 B81-07175

Redmon, Anne. Music and silence / Anne Redmon. — London : Magnum, 1980, c1979. — 251p ; 18cm
Originally published: London : Secker & Warburg, 1979
ISBN 0-417-05080-1 (pbk) : £1.40 B81-03487

Reeman, Douglas. A ship must die / Douglas Reeman. — Large print ed. — Leicester : Ulverscroft, 1981, c1979. — 491p ; 23cm. — (Ulverscroft large print)
Originally published: London : Hutchinson, 1979
ISBN 0-7089-0584-6 : £5.00 B81-11612

Reeman, Douglas. Torpedo run / Douglas Reeman. — London : Hutchinson, 1981. — 290p : maps ; 23cm
Maps on lining papers
ISBN 0-09-144700-3 : £6.95 : CIP rev. B81-01483

Rees, A. H.. The latter days / A.H. Rees. — Bognor Regis : New Horizon, c1978
Vol.1. — 145p,[5]leaves of plates : col.maps ; 21cm
ISBN 0-86116-047-9 : £3.95 B81-18957

Rees, David, *1936-*. Miss Duffy is still with us / David Rees. — London : Dobson, 1980. — 153p : geneal.table ; 21cm
For adolescents
ISBN 0-234-72214-2 : £4.25 B81-01484

Rees, Joan, *1927-*. The queen of hearts / Joan Rees. — Large print ed. — Bath : Chivers, 1980, c1974. — 260p ; 23cm. — (A Seymour book)
Originally published: London : Hale, 1974
ISBN 0-86220-023-7 : £4.95 : CIP rev. B80-22572

Rees, Lucy. Take it to the limit. — Hale (7 Carver Rd., Hale, Altrincham, Cheshire) : Draden Books, Oct.1981. — [204]p
ISBN 0-906371-80-5 : £6.00 : CIP entry B81-28173

Reeve, Elaine. Lady in the lion's den / Elaine Reeve. — London : Mills & Boon, 1980. — 188p ; 20cm. — (Masquerade)
ISBN 0-263-09678-5 : £3.85 B81-02734

823'.914[F] — Fiction in English, *1945-* **—** *Texts continuation*

Reeve, Linda-Dawn. Condemned / Linda-Dawn Reeve. — London : Hale, 1981. — 190p ; 20cm
ISBN 0-7091-9370-x : £6.75 B81-37307

Reeve, Linda-Dawn. The early years / Linda-Dawn Reeve. — London : Hale, 1980. — 221p ; 21cm
Bibliography: p221
ISBN 0-7091-8342-9 : £6.50 B81-00547

Reeve, Linda-Dawn. The royal suitor / by Linda-Dawn Reeve. — London : Hale, 1981. — 320p ; 21cm
ISBN 0-7091-8653-3 : £7.50 B81-08729

Reeves, L. P.. If it's blue, it's plague / by L.P. Reeves. — London : Hale, 1981. — 160p ; 20cm. — (Hale SF)
ISBN 0-7091-9056-5 : £6.25 B81-19225

Reid, Henrietta. Lord of the Isles / by Henrietta Reid. — London : Mills & Boon, 1981. — 186p ; 20cm
ISBN 0-263-09847-8 : £4.55 B81-14187

Rena, Sally. A painless death : a novel / by Sally Rena. — London : Weidenfeld and Nicolson, 1981. — 155p ; 22cm
ISBN 0-297-77999-0 : £5.95 B81-39752

Rendell, Ruth. A guilty thing surprised / Ruth Rendell. — London : Arrow, 1980, c1970. — 191p ; 18cm
Originally published: London : Hutchinson, 1970
ISBN 0-09-923500-5 (pbk) : £1.00 B81-00546

Rendell, Ruth. The lake of darkness / Ruth Rendell. — London : Arrow, 1981, c1980. — 200p ; 18cm
Originally published: London : Hutchinson, 1980
ISBN 0-09-925530-8 (pbk) : £1.10 B81-16009

Rendell, Ruth. The lake of darkness / Ruth Rendell. — Large print ed. — Bath : Chivers, 1981, c1980. — 318p ; 23cm. — (A New Portway large print book)
Originally published: London : Hutchinson, 1980
ISBN 0-85119-118-5 : £5.35 : CIP rev.
B81-08899

Rendell, Ruth. Make death love me / Ruth Rendell. — London : Prior, 1980, c1979. — 460p ; 25cm
Originally published: London : Hutchinson, 1979. — Published in large print
ISBN 0-86043-490-7 : £6.95 B81-02538

Rendell, Ruth. Put on by cunning / Ruth Rendell. — London : Hutchinson, 1981. — 207p ; 23cm
ISBN 0-09-144120-x : £5.95 : CIP rev.
B81-04298

Rhea, Nicholas. Constable around the village / Nicholas Rhea. — London : Hale, 1981. — 191p ; 23cm
ISBN 0-7091-9130-8 : £6.95 B81-35290

Rhea, Nicholas. Constable on the prowl / Nicholas Rhea. — London : Hale, 1980. — 192p ; 23cm
ISBN 0-7091-8432-8 : £6.25 B81-01485

Rhodes, Leland. Eagle mountain range / by Leland Rhodes. — London : Hale, 1981. — 160p ; 20cm
ISBN 0-7091-8706-8 : £4.95 B81-06375

Rhodes, Ted. Triangle : a novel / by Ted Rhodes ; from the BBC-TV series created by Ted Rhodes and Bill Sellars based on scripts written by Michael Armstrong ... [et al.]. — London : British Broadcasting Corporation, 1981. — 288p ; 22cm
ISBN 0-563-17925-2 : £6.00 B81-18687

Rhodes, Ted. Triangle : a novel / by Ted Rhodes ; from the BBC-TV series created by Ted Rhodes and Bill Sellars ; based on scripts written by Michael Armstrong ... [et al.]. — London : British Broadcasting Corporation, 1981. — 288p ; 18cm
ISBN 0-563-17926-0 (pbk) : £1.50 B81-15790

Rhys, Jack. The eternity merchants / by Jack Rhys. — London : Hale, 1981. — 175p ; 20cm. — (Hale SF)
ISBN 0-7091-8902-8 : £6.75 B81-15384

Rhys, Jack. The five doors / by Jack Rhys. — London : Hale, 1981. — 175p ; 20cm. — (Hale SF)
ISBN 0-7091-9053-0 : £6.25 B81-35196

Rich, Meredith. Bare essence / Meredith Rich. — London : Sphere, 1980. — 316p ; 18cm
ISBN 0-7221-7333-4 (pbk) : £1.35 B81-11711

Richards, Carol. The serpent's cove / by Carol Richards. — London : Hale, 1981. — 176p ; 20cm
ISBN 0-7091-9261-4 : £6.50 B81-37455

Richards, Guy. Red kill / Guy Richards. — London : Dent in association with Arrow Books, 1980. — 249p ; 23cm
ISBN 0-460-04532-6 : £6.50 B81-01486

Richards, Guy. Red kill / Guy Richards. — London : Arrow, 1981, c1980. — 249p ; 18cm
Originally published: London : Dent, 1980
ISBN 0-09-926270-3 (pbk) : £1.50 B81-34339

Richards, Maura. Two to tango / Maura Richards. — Dublin (Knocksedan House, Swords, Co. Dublin) : Ward River Press, 1981. — 185p ; 18cm
ISBN 0-907085-09-1 (pbk) : £2.20 B81-28495

Riding, Julia. Deep space warriors / Julia Riding. — London : Hale, 1981. — 175p ; 20cm. — (Hale SF)
ISBN 0-7091-8885-4 : £5.95 B81-19224

Ridyard, Richard D.. The final destiny / by Richard D. Ridyard. — London : Hale, 1980. — 160p ; 20cm
ISBN 0-7091-8604-5 : £5.75 B81-00548

Rigby, Ray. Hill of sand / Ray Rigby. — London : W.H. Allen, 1981. — 286p ; 23cm
ISBN 0-491-02974-8 : £7.95 B81-28624

Riley, Joe, *1945-*. The long firm / Joe Riley. — Bognor Regis : New Horizon, c1978. — 164p ; 21cm
ISBN 0-86116-063-0 : £3.50 B81-18866

Robbins, Rae. Michael O'Brien / Rae Robins [i.e. Robbins]. — Bognor Regis : New Horizon, c1979. — 133p ; 21cm
ISBN 0-86116-155-6 : £2.95 B81-19080

Roberts, Geoffrey K. (Geoffrey Keith), *1929-*. A game of Troy / Geoffrey K. Roberts. — London : Collings, 1980. — 191p ; 23cm
ISBN 0-86036-122-5 : £5.25 B81-01487

Roberts, George B. J.. Assignment in Almería / George B.J. Roberts. — Bognor Regis : New Horizon, c1980. — 244p ; 21cm
ISBN 0-86116-500-4 : £5.25 B81-19238

Roberts, Irene. The golden pagoda / Irene Roberts. — Large print ed. — Bath : Chivers, 1981, c1972. — 241p ; 23cm. — (A Seymour book)
Originally published: London : Hale, 1972
ISBN 0-85119-416-8 : £4.95 : CIP rev.
B81-11975

Roberts, Janet Louise. Golden Lotus / Janet Louise Roberts. — London : Sphere, 1981, c1979. — 406p ; 18cm
ISBN 0-7221-7407-1 (pbk) : £1.75 B81-36826

Robinson, Derek, *1932 Apr. 12-*. The Eldorado network / Derek Robinson. — London : Sphere, 1981, c1979. — 443p ; 18cm
Originally published: London : Hamilton, 1979
ISBN 0-7221-7421-7 (pbk) : £1.50 B81-11726

Robinson, Derek, *1932 Apr.12-*. Goshawk Squadron / Derek Robinson. — London : Sphere, 1981, c1971. — 221p ; 18cm
Originally published: London : Heinemann, 1971
ISBN 0-7221-7422-5 (pbk) : £1.25 B81-20250

Robson, James, *1944-*. The last prisoner / James Robson. — Feltham : Hamlyn, 1980. — 386p ; 23cm
ISBN 0-600-20052-3 : £5.95 B81-01488

Robson, James, *1944-*. The last prisoner / James Robson. — London : Hamlyn Paperbacks, 1981, c1980. — 386p ; 18cm
Originally published: Feltham : Hamlyn, 1980
ISBN 0-600-20211-9 (pbk) : £1.50 B81-31918

Roche, Nicola. No armour for a woman / Nicola Roche. — London : Hale, 1981. — 159p ; 21cm
ISBN 0-7091-8993-1 : £6.25 B81-35293

Rome, Margaret. Castle in Spain / by Margaret Rome. — London : Mills & Boon, 1981. — 186p ; 19cm
ISBN 0-263-09879-6 : £4.55 B81-26418

Rome, Margaret. Isle of calypso. — Large print ed. — Bath : Chivers, Dec.1981. — [224]p. — (A Seymour book)
Originally published: London : Mills & Boon, 1979
ISBN 0-85119-447-8 : £4.95 : CIP entry
B81-31794

Rome, Margaret. Miss high and mighty. — Large print ed. — Bath : Chivers, Oct.1981. — [248] p. — (A Seymour book)
Originally published: London : Mills & Boon, 1980
ISBN 0-85119-439-7 : £4.95 : CIP entry
B81-25805

Rome, Margaret. Second-best bride / by Margaret Rome. — London : Mills & Boon, 1981. — 188p ; 20cm
ISBN 0-263-09815-x : £4.55 B81-09399

Rome, Margaret. Son of Adam. — Large print ed. — Bath : Chivers Press, Jan.1982. — [240] p. — (A Seymour book)
Originally published: London : Mills & Boon, 1978
ISBN 0-85119-451-6 : £4.95 : CIP entry
B81-33805

Rome, Margaret. The wild man / by Margaret Rome. — London : Mills & Boon, 1980. — 187p ; 20cm
ISBN 0-263-09735-8 : £3.85 B81-00549

Ronson, Mark. Plague pit / Mark Ronson. — Feltham : Hamlyn, 1981. — 191p ; 18cm
ISBN 0-600-20230-5 (pbk) : £1.00 B81-41002

Roscoe, Charles. Killer trail / by Charles Roscoe. — London : Hale, 1981. — 159p ; 20cm
ISBN 0-7091-9046-8 : £4.95 B81-28615

Rose-Anne, Vee. A day in the life of Maximilian / Vee Rose-Anne. — Bognor Regis : New Horizon, c1979. — 64p : ill ; 21cm
ISBN 0-86116-069-x : £1.95 B81-21969

Ross, Cameron. Case for compensation / Cameron Ross. — London : Hale, 1980. — 176p ; 20cm
ISBN 0-7091-8425-5 : £5.50 B81-06222

Ross, Cameron. Villa plot, counterplot / by Cameron Ross. — London : Hale, 1981. — 174p ; 20cm
ISBN 0-7091-9160-x : £6.25 B81-29863

823'.914[F] — Fiction in English, ***1945- — Texts continuation***

Ross, Caroline. Miss Nobody / Caroline Ross. — [Loughton] : Piatkus, 1981. — 319p ; 21cm
ISBN 0-86188-111-7 (cased) : £6.95
ISBN 0-86188-119-2 (pbk) : £1.50 B81-18472

Ross, John, *1912-*. Public eye Appleyard : a health inspector at large / by John Ross. — London : Hale, 1981. — 174p ; 23cm
ISBN 0-7091-8525-1 : £6.25 B81-16798

Ross, Jonathan. Dark blue and dangerous / Jonathan Ross. — London : Constable, 1981. — 160p ; 23cm. — (Constable crime)
ISBN 0-09-464080-7 : £5.95 B81-19294

Ross, Stella. Cruel heritage / by Stella Ross. — London : Hale, 1981. — 159p ; 21cm
ISBN 0-7091-8809-9 : £5.50 B81-11655

Rossiter, John. Dark flight / John Rossiter. — London : Eyre Methuen, 1981. — 214p ; 22cm
ISBN 0-413-47420-8 : £5.95 B81-28608

Rouch, James. Blindfire / James Rouch. — London : New English Library, 1980. — 157p ; 18cm. — (The Zone ; 2)
ISBN 0-450-04769-5 (corrected : pbk) : £1.00 B81-06223

Rouch, James. Hard target / James Rouch. — London : New English Library, 1980. — 158p ; 18cm. — (The Zone ; 1)
ISBN 0-450-04768-7 (pbk) : £1.00 B81-06221

Rowe, Ron. The vase / Ron Rowe. — Bognor Regis : New Horizon, c1979. — 153p,[2]p of plates : 2ill ; 22cm
ISBN 0-86116-193-9 : £4.75 B81-19255

Rowlands, V. M. D.. The Duke and Rebecca / by V.M.D. Rowlands. — London : Hale, 1981. — 208p ; 20cm
ISBN 0-7091-8800-5 : £6.25 B81-14204

Royce, Kenneth. Ten thousand days. — Sevenoaks : Hodder & Stoughton, June 1981. — [272]p
ISBN 0-340-26249-4 : £6.95 : CIP entry B81-10471

Royce, Kenneth. The third arm. — London : Hodder & Stoughton, Nov.1981. — [208]p
Originally published: 1980
ISBN 0-340-26671-6 (pbk) : £1.50 : CIP entry B81-30542

Royce, Kenneth. The XYY man / Kenneth Royce. — Large print ed. — Leicester : Ulverscroft, 1981, c1970. — 356p ; 23cm. — (Ulverscroft large print)
Originally published: London : Hodder & Stoughton, 1970
ISBN 0-7089-0598-6 : Unpriced B81-14195

Rubens, Bernice. Birds of passage / by Bernice Rubens. — London : Hamish Hamilton, 1981. — 215p ; 22cm
ISBN 0-241-10664-8 : £7.50 : CIP rev. B81-20513

Rubens, Bernice. The elected member / Bernice Rubens. — London : Sphere, 1980, c1969. — 205p ; 18cm
Originally published: Andover : Eyre & Spottiswoode, 1969
ISBN 0-7221-7529-9 (pbk) : £1.00 B81-01489

Rubens, Bernice. A five year sentence / Bernice Rubens. — London : Sphere, 1981, c1978. — 185p ; 18cm
Originally published: London : W.H. Allen, 1978
ISBN 0-7221-7522-1 (pbk) : £1.10 B81-08632

Rubens, Bernice. I sent a letter to my love / Bernice Rubens. — London : Sphere, 1980, c1975. — 197p ; 18cm
Originally published: London : W.H. Allen, 1975
ISBN 0-7221-7521-3 (pbk) : £1.00 B81-01490

Rubens, Bernice. Spring sonata : a fable / Bernice Rubens. — London : Sphere, 1981,c1979. — 215p ; 18cm
Originally published: London : W.H. Allen, 1979
ISBN 0-7221-7530-2 (pbk) : £1.25 B81-35736

Rubens, Robert. The Cosway miniature / by Robert Rubens. — Maidstone : Bachman & Turner, 1980. — 114p ; 22cm
ISBN 0-85974-097-8 : £4.65 B81-01491

Rudorff, Raymond. The house of the Brandersons / Raymond Rudorff. — London : Corgi, 1978, c1973 (1980 [printing]). — 270p ; 18cm
Originally published: New York : Arbor House, 1973 ; London : Barrie & Jenkins, 1976
ISBN 0-552-11653-x (pbk) : £1.25 B81-02516

Rufffell, Ann. Pyramid power / Ann Ruffell. — London : Julia MacRae, 1981. — 159p ; 23cm
ISBN 0-86203-038-2 : £5.25 B81-11627

Rush, Alison. The last of Danu's children. — London : Allen & Unwin, Oct.1981. — [300]p
ISBN 0-04-823201-7 : £5.50 : CIP entry B81-25284

Russell, Evelyn. A mixed marriage / Evelyn Russell. — Bognor Regis : New Horizon, c1980. — 168p ; 22cm
ISBN 0-86116-315-x : £4.75 B81-19083

Russell, Martin. Rainblast. — London : Collins, Feb.1982. — [224]p. — (The Crime Club)
ISBN 0-00-231721-4 : £6.50 : CIP entry B81-35937

Russell, Martin, *1934-*. Backlash / Martin Russell. — London : Collins, 1981. — 167p ; 21cm. — (The Crime Club)
ISBN 0-00-231025-2 : £5.75 B81-12298

Russell, Martin, *1934-*. Catspaw / Martin Russell. — London : Collins, 1980. — 175p ; 21cm. — (The Crime Club)
ISBN 0-00-231862-8 : £5.25 B81-07089

Russell, Martin, *1934-*. Daylight robbery / by Martin Russell. — Large print ed. — Long Preston : Magna, 1981, c1978. — 338p ; 23cm
Originally published: London : Collins, 1978
ISBN 0-86009-319-0 : Unpriced : CIP rev. B81-08892

Russell, Martin, *1934-*. Death fuse. — Large print ed. — Long Preston : Magna Print Books, Jan.1982. — [360]p
Originally published: London : Collins, 1980
ISBN 0-86009-373-5 : £5.25 : CIP entry B81-33765

Russell, Martin, *1934-*. Mr T / Martin Russell. — Large print ed. — Bath : Chivers, 1981, c1977. — 267p ; 23cm. — (A Lythway mystery)
Originally published: London : Collins, 1977
ISBN 0-85119-719-1 : £6.50 : CIP rev. B81-08893

Russell, Martin, *1934-*. Murder by the mile / Martin Russell. — Bolton-by-Bowland : Magna, 1980, c1975. — 298p ; 23cm
Originally published: London : Collins, 1975. — Published in large print
ISBN 0-86009-271-2 : £5.25 : CIP rev. B80-22577

Ryman, Ras. Weavers of death / by Ras Ryman. — London : Hale, 1981. — 192p ; 20cm. — (Hale SF)
ISBN 0-7091-9065-4 : £6.25 B81-24980

Sadler, Jeff. Arizona blood trail / by Jeff Sadler. — London : Hale, 1981. — 160p ; 20cm
ISBN 0-7091-9293-2 : £4.95 B81-37318

Salaman, Nicholas. The frights : a novel / by Nicholas Salaman. — London : Secker & Warburg, 1981. — 169p ; 23cm. — (An Alison Press Book)
ISBN 0-436-44085-7 : £6.95 : CIP rev. B81-21643

Salisbury, Carola. Count Vronsky's daughter / Carola Salisbury. — London : Collins, 1981. — 300p ; 22cm
ISBN 0-00-222298-1 : £6.95 B81-39435

Salisbury, Carola. The shadowed spring / Carola Salisbury. — London : Pan in association with Collins, 1981, c1980. — 303p ; 18cm
Originally published: London : Collins, 1980
ISBN 0-330-26406-0 (pbk) : £1.25 B81-37354

Salisbury, Carola. The shadowed spring / Carola Salisbury. — Large print ed. — Leicester : Ulverscroft, 1981, c1980. — 522p ; 23cm. — (Ulverscroft large print series)
Originally published: New York : Doubleday ; London : Collins, 1980
ISBN 0-7089-0680-x : £5.00 : CIP rev. B81-25682

Salisbury, Carole. The winter bride / Carola Salisbury. — Large print ed. — Leicester : Ulverscroft, 1981, c1977. — 434p ; 22cm. — (Ulverscroft large print series)
Originally published: Garden City, N.Y. : Doubleday ; London : Collins, 1978
ISBN 0-7089-0582-x : £5.00 B81-12180

Sampson, Fay. The chains of sleep / Fay Sampson. — London : Dobson, 1981. — 121p ; 21cm
ISBN 0-234-72250-9 (corrected) : £4.25 B81-17374

Sampson, Fay. The hungry snow / Fay Sampson. — London : Dobson, 1980. — 184p ; 21cm
ISBN 0-234-72262-2 : £4.25 B81-02732

Sanders, James. Frontiers of fear / James Sanders. — London : Hale, 1980. — 206p ; 21cm
ISBN 0-7091-8424-7 : £6.25 B81-00550

Sanderson, Jill. Never forget me / Jill Sanderson. — London : Hamlyn Paperbacks, 1981. — 175p ; 18cm. — (A Sapphire romance)
ISBN 0-600-20181-3 (pbk) : £0.75 B81-34845

Sandon, J. D.. One too many mornings / J.D. Sandon. — London : Granada, 1981. — 159p ; 18cm. — (The Gringos ; no.7) (A Mayflower book)
ISBN 0-583-13245-6 (pbk) : £0.95 B81-09885

Sandwell, Beryl. The price of love / by Beryl Sandwell. — London : Remploy, 1979, c1969. — 188p ; 19cm
Originally published: London : Hale, 1969
ISBN 0-7066-0811-9 : £4.00 B81-09396

Sargent, Marshall. High and lowly / Marshall Sargent. — Bognor Regis : New Horizon, c1980. — 196p ; 21cm
ISBN 0-86116-244-7 : £5.25 B81-19234

Sargent, Ruth. Roses on the water / by Ruth Sargent. — London : Hale, 1981. — 190p ; 20cm
ISBN 0-7091-8791-2 : £5.50 B81-15951

Saunders, Peter, *1930-*. The Serbian triangle / Peter Saunders. — Feltham : Hamlyn, 1981. — 160p : ill ; 18cm
ISBN 0-600-20258-5 (pbk) : £1.10 B81-27875

Saxton, Judith. The pride / Judith Saxton. — Feltham : Hamlyn Paperbacks, 1981. — 352p ; 18cm
ISBN 0-600-20227-5 (pbk) : £1.50 B81-28401

Schlee, Ann. The vandal / Ann Schlee. — London : Macmillan Children's, 1979. — 173p ; 21cm
ISBN 0-333-26068-6 : £4.50 : CIP rev. B79-06831

823'.914[F] — Fiction in English, *1945-* — *Texts continuation*

Scholefield, Alan. Lion in the evening / Alan Scholefield. — Large print ed. — Leicester : Ulverscroft, 1980, c1974. — 307p ; 23cm. — (Ulverscroft large print series)
Originally published: London : Heinemann, 1974
ISBN 0-7089-0515-3 : £4.25 : CIP rev. B80-18014

Scott, A. (Albert). And Judy O'Grady / A. Scott. — Bognor Regis : New Horizon, c1980. — 441p ; 20cm
ISBN 0-86116-140-8 : £5.75 B81-19040

Scott, Douglas, *1926-*. Die for the Queen / Douglas Scott. — London : Secker & Warburg, 1981. — xvii,300p ; 23cm
ISBN 0-436-44426-7 : £6.95 B81-10138

Scott, Douglas, *1926-*. In the face of the enemy. — London : Secker & Warburg, Feb.1982. — [312]p
ISBN 0-436-44427-5 : £6.95 : CIP entry B81-35725

Scott, Isobel. Find me a dream / by Isobel Scott. — London : Hale, 1981. — 160p ; 20cm
ISBN 0-7091-8644-4 : £5.60 B81-24438

Scott, Isobel. Love's remedy / by Isobel Scott. — London : Hale, 1980. — 174p ; 20cm
ISBN 0-7091-8430-1 : £5.25 B81-05247

Scott, Isobel. A wild sweetness / by Isobel Scott. — London : Hale, 1981. — 174p ; 20cm
ISBN 0-7091-8473-5 : £5.50 B81-15954

Scott, Jack. An uprush of mayhem. — London : Collins, Feb.1982. — [204]p. — (The Crime Club)
ISBN 0-00-231894-6 : £6.95 : CIP entry B81-35938

Scott, Jack, *1922-*. A distant view of death / Jack Scott. — London : Collins, 1981. — 199p ; 21cm. — (The Crime Club)
Previous ed.:
ISBN 0-00-231863-6 : £5.95 B81-05714

Scott, Jeremy. [Angels in your beer]. Escape / Jeremy Scott. — London : W.H. Allen, 1981, c1979. — 277p ; 18cm. — (A Star book)
£1.50 (pbk) B81-20956

Scott, Mary, *1888-*. Breakfast at six / Mary Scott. — Large print ed. — Leicester : Ulverscroft, 1981. — 421p ; 23cm. — (Ulverscroft large print series)
Originally published: London : Hurst & Blackett, 1953
ISBN 0-7089-0622-2 : £5.00 : CIP rev. B81-07904

Scott, Norford. Hard range / by Norford Scott. — London : Hale, 1981. — 18p ; 20cm
ISBN 0-7091-9295-9 : £4.95 B81-35204

Scott, Peter Graham. Dragonfire / Peter Graham Scott. — London : Macdonald Futura, 1981. — 239p ; 18cm. — (A Futura book)
ISBN 0-7088-1962-1 (pbk) : £1.25 B81-15638

Scruton, Roger. Fortnight's anger / Roger Scruton. — Manchester : Carcanet, 1981. — 224p ; 23cm
ISBN 0-85635-376-0 : £6.95 : CIP rev. B81-27944

Seaman, Donald. Chase Royal : a novel / Donald Seaman. — London : Hamilton, 1980. — 319p : 1ill ; 23cm
ISBN 0-241-10356-8 : £6.95 : CIP rev. B80-24864

Secombe, Harry. Welsh Fargo / Harry Secombe. — London : Robson, 1981. — 224p ; 23cm
ISBN 0-903895-87-0 : £6.50 : CIP rev. B81-27402

Sefton, Juliet. Heir to Trevayan / Juliet Sefton. — London : Hamlyn Paperbacks, 1981. — 187p ; 18cm
ISBN 0-600-20156-2 (pbk) : £1.25 B81-10043

Sellar, Maurice. The allies / Maurice Sellar. — London : Sphere, 1981, c1979. — 232p ; 18cm
Originally published: London : Cassell, 1979
ISBN 0-7221-7707-0 (pbk) : £1.25 B81-09796

Sellers, Michael. From eternity to here / Michael Sellers. — London : Macmillan, 1981. — 173p ; 21cm
ISBN 0-333-29347-9 : £5.50 B81-10130

Serafín, David. Saturday of glory / David Serafín. — Large print ed. — Leicester : Ulverscroft, 1981, c1979. — 357p ; 23cm. — (Ulverscroft large print)
Originally published: London : Collins, 1979
ISBN 0-7089-0577-3 : £5.00 B81-11386

Sewart, Alan. In that rich earth / by Alan Sewart. — London : Hale, 1981. — 192pp ; 20cm
ISBN 0-7091-8045-4 : £5.75 B81-11166

Sewart, Alan. Loop current / by Alan Sewart. — London : Hale, 1980. — 190p ; 20cm
ISBN 0-7091-7733-x : £5.75 B81-01492

Sewart, Alan. A romp in green heat / Alan Sewart. — London : Hale, 1981. — 188p ; 20cm
ISBN 0-7091-8210-4 : £5.95 B81-24849

Seymour, Gerald. The contract / Gerald Seymour. — London : Collins, 1980. — 347p ; 22cm
ISBN 0-00-221998-0 : £6.50 B81-00551

Seymour, Gerald. Red fox / Gerald Seymour. — [London] : Fontana, 1980, c1979. — 283p ; 18cm
Originally published: London : Collins, 1979
ISBN 0-00-616003-4 (pbk) : £1.25 B81-01880

Seymour, Miranda. Medea / Miranda Seymour. — London : Joseph, 1981. — 247p ; 23cm
ISBN 0-7181-2007-8 : £7.50 B81-22319

Shann, Renée. Only time will tell. — Large print ed. — Bath : Chivers, Feb.1982. — [248]p. — (A Seymour book)
Originally published: London : Collins, 1977
ISBN 0-85119-454-0 : £4.95 : CIP entry B81-36048

Sharpe, Tom. The Wilt alternative / Tom Sharpe. — London : Pan in association with Secker and Warburg, 1981, c1979. — 218p ; 18cm
Originally published: London : Secker and Warburg, 1979
ISBN 0-330-26338-2 (pbk) : £1.25 B81-09740

Shaul, Frank. Sixgun bait / by Frank Shaul. — London : Hale, 1981. — 176p ; 20cm
ISBN 0-7091-9239-8 : £4.95 B81-33532

Shaw, Bob. The Ceres solution / by Bob Shaw. — London : Gollancz, 1981. — 191p ; 21cm
ISBN 0-575-02966-8 : £5.95 B81-28627

Shaw, Bob. Dagger of the mind / Bob Shaw. — London : Pan, 1981, c1979. — 172p ; 18cm
Originally published: London : Gollancz, 1979
ISBN 0-330-26284-x (pbk) : £1.25 B81-12076

Shaw, Catherine. Beloved buccaneer / by Catherine Shaw. — London : Mills & Boon, 1980. — 189p ; 20cm
ISBN 0-263-09739-0 : £3.85 B81-01493

Shaw, Catherine. Chateau of dreams / by Catherine Shaw. — London : Mills & Boon, 1981. — 191p ; 19cm
ISBN 0-263-09871-0 : £4.55 B81-26572

Shaw, Howard. Death of a don. — London : Hodder & Stoughton, Jan.1982. — [160]p
ISBN 0-340-27643-6 : £6.50 : CIP entry B81-34123

Shear's, Sarah. Annie's kingdom / Sarah Shears. — Loughton : Piatkus, c1980. — 150p ; 21cm
ISBN 0-86188-056-0 : £5.50 : CIP rev. B80-22580

Shears, Sarah. The apprentice / Sarah Shears. — Loughton : Piatkus, c1981. — 220p ; 21cm
ISBN 0-86188-083-8 : £6.50 : CIP rev. B81-07629

Shears, Sarah. Deborah Hammond. — Loughton : Piatkus, Sept.1981. — [224]p
ISBN 0-86188-110-9 : £6.50 : CIP entry B81-21617

Shears, Sarah. The landlady / Sarah Shears. — [Littlehampton] ([Arnadale Rd, Lineside Industrial Estate, Littlehampton, W. Sussex BN17 7EN]) : Piatkus, [1980]. — 204p ; 21cm
ISBN 0-86188-044-7 : £5.95 : CIP rev. B80-12114

Shears, Sarah. Tapioca for tea. — Loughton (17 Brook Rd, Loughton, Essex) : Piatkus, June 1981. — [256]p
Originally published: London : Elek, 1971
ISBN 0-86188-100-1 : £6.95 : CIP entry B81-09475

Sheffield, Charles. Sight of Proteus / Charles Sheffield. — London : Arrow, 1981, c1978. — 282p ; 18cm
Originally published: New York : Ace, 1978
ISBN 0-09-925960-5 (pbk) : £1.60 B81-36913

Shelby, Graham. The Cannaway concern / Graham Shelby. — London : Hodder and Stoughton, 1981, c1980. — 297p : 1map ; 23cm
Originally published: New York : Doubleday, 1980
ISBN 0-340-23435-0 : £6.95 B81-10137

Shelyn, Jack. Joker in a stacked deck / by Jack Shelynn. — London : Hale, 1981. — 190p 20cm
ISBN 0-7091-8643-6 : £5.75 B81-11074

Shelynn, Jack. Epilogue for Selena / by Jack Shelynn. — London : Hale, 1980. — 155p ; 20cm
ISBN 0-7091-8225-2 : £5.75 B81-00553

Sheppard, Stephen. The four hundred / Stephen Sheppard. — Harmondsworth : Penguin, 1980, c1979. — 413p ; 19cm
Originally published: London : Secker and Warburg, 1979
ISBN 0-14-005505-3 (pbk) : £1.25 B81-03379

Sherman, D. R.. Old Mali and the boy / D.R. Sherman. — Harmondsworth : Penguin, 1968, c1964 (1981 [printing]). — 107p ; 18cm
Originally published: London : Gollancz, 1964
ISBN 0-14-002813-7 (pbk) : £0.95 B81-22340

Sherry, Sylvia. South of Red River / by Sylvia Sherry. — London : Hamish Hamilton, 1981. — 221p ; 21cm
ISBN 0-241-10579-x : £7.95 : CIP rev. B81-15813

Sherwood, Anne. House of lost secrets / by Anne Sherwood. — London : Hale, 1981. — 176p ; 20cm
ISBN 0-7091-8724-6 : £5.50 B81-11172

Sherwood, Anne. Yesterday's children / by Anne Sherwood. — London : Hale, 1981. — 160p ; 20cm
ISBN 0-7091-9076-x : £5.60 B81-40534

Shoesmith, Kathleen A.. Autumn escapade / by Kathleen A. Shoesmith. — London : Hale, 1981. — 206p ; 20cm
ISBN 0-7091-8875-7 : £5.95 B81-19290

823'.914[F] — Fiction in English, *1945-* — *Texts continuation*

Short, Agnes. Miss Jenny / Anges Short. — London : Constable, 1981. — 210p ; 23cm
ISBN 0-09-464040-8 : £6.95 B81-31995

Sillitoe, Alan. The second chance : and other stories / Alan Sillitoe. — London : Cape, 1981. — 219p ; 21cm
ISBN 0-224-01877-9 : £5.95 B81-02506

Simmons, Jeffrey. Lucky fellow / Jeffrey Simmons. — London : Sphere, 1981, c1979. — 286p ; 18cm
Originally published: London : W.H. Allen, 1979
ISBN 0-7221-7863-8 (pbk) : £1.50 B81-17974

Simonds, Paula. Daughter of violence / Paula Simonds. — London : Hale, 1981. — 224p ; 21cm
ISBN 0-7091-8990-7 : £7.50 B81-21312

Simpson, Dorothy, *1933-*. The night she died / Dorothy Simpson. — London : Joseph, c1981. — 187p ; 23cm
ISBN 0-7181-1978-9 : £6.50 B81-08011

Simpson, John, *1944-*. Moscow requiem / John Simpson. — London : Robson, 1981. — 279p ; 23cm
ISBN 0-86051-135-9 : £6.50 B81-24724

Simpson, Margaret, *1913-*. Love in disguise / by Margaret Simpson. — London : Hale, 1981. — 176p ; 20cm
ISBN 0-7091-8723-8 : £5.50 B81-08736

Sims, George, *1923-*. Who is Cato? / George Sims. — London : Macmillan, 1981. — 169p ; 21cm
ISBN 0-333-30630-9 : £5.50 B81-18691

Sinclair, Andrew. Sea of the dead / Andrew Sinclair. — London : Sphere, 1981, c1978. — 186p ; 18cm
Originally published: London : Joseph, 1978
ISBN 0-7221-0485-5 (pbk) : £1.10 B81-17976

Sinclair, Joanna. Dark buccaneer / by Joanna Sinclair. — London : Hale, 1981. — 160p ; 20cm
ISBN 0-7091-8437-9 : £6.25 B81-11104

Sinclair, Joanna. A man from Byzantium / by Joanna Sinclair. — London : Hale, 1980. — 188p ; 21cm
ISBN 0-7091-8413-1 : £6.25 B81-07750

Sinclair, Olga. Bitter-sweet summer / Olga Sinclair. — Large print ed. — Bath : Chivers, 1981, c1970. — 254p ; 23cm. — (A Seymour book)
Originally published: London : Hale, 1970
ISBN 0-85119-402-8 : Unpriced B81-08511

Skilleter, John. Keep it going, Sir / John Skilleter. — Bognor Regis : New Horizon, c1980. — 228p ; 22cm
ISBN 0-86116-431-8 : £5.25 B81-19070

Slater, Nigel. Falcon / Nigel Slater. — London : Granada, 1980, c1979. — 223p ; 18cm. — (Panther)
Originally published: London : Collins, 1979
ISBN 0-586-04970-3 (pbk) : £1.25 B81-00554

Slaughter, Carolyn. Dreams of the Kalahari / Carolyn Slaughter. — London : Granada, 1981. — 394p ; 23cm
ISBN 0-246-11517-3 : £6.95 B81-18575

Smart, Olga. Woman on a pedestal / Olga Smart. — Bognor Regis : New Horizon, c1980. — 109p ; 21cm
ISBN 0-86116-451-2 : £3.50 B81-19069

Smith, A. C. H.. Extra cover : a novel / by A.C.H. Smith. — London : Weidenfeld and Nicolson, 1981. — 151p ; 23cm
ISBN 0-297-77924-9 : £5.95 B81-12919

Smith, Anne, *1944-*. The magic glass / Anne Smith. — London : Joseph, 1981. — 173p ; 23cm
ISBN 0-7181-1986-x : £6.50 B81-11148

Smith, Doris E.. Back o' the moon / by Doris E. Smith. — London : Mills & Boon, 1981. — 189p ; 19cm
ISBN 0-263-09868-0 : £4.55 B81-18339

Smith, Doris E.. Catch a kingfisher / by Doris E. Smith. — London : Hale, 1981. — 190p ; 20cm
ISBN 0-7091-9114-6 : £5.60 B81-40550

Smith, Frederick E. (Frederick Escreet). 633 Squadron : Operation Cobra. — London : Severn House, Nov.1981. — [240]p
ISBN 0-7278-0744-7 : £6.95 : CIP entry B81-30254

Smith, Frederick E. (Frederick Escreet). The war god / Frederick E. Smith. — London : Corgi, 1981, c1980. — 340p ; 18cm
Originally published: London : Cassell, 1980
ISBN 0-552-11697-1 (pbk) : £1.50 B81-27246

Smith, George Henry. Witch queen of Lochlann / George Henry Smith. — London : Hale, 1981. — 159p ; 20cm
Originally published: United States : s.n., 1969
ISBN 0-7091-8943-5 : £6.25 B81-19301

Smith, Guy N.. Caracal / Guy N. Smith. — London : New English Library, 1980. — 172p ; 18cm
ISBN 0-450-04771-7 (pbk) : £1.10 B81-06428

Smith, Guy N.. Crabs on the rampage / Guy N. Smith. — London : New English Library, 1981. — 157p ; 19cm
ISBN 0-450-05251-6 (pbk) : £1.25 B81-35630

Smith, Guy N.. Doomflight / Guy N. Smith. — London : Hamlyn Paperbacks, 1981. — 221p ; 18cm
ISBN 0-600-20277-1 (pbk) : £1.10 B81-10048

Smith, Guy N.. Manitou doll / Guy N. Smith. — London : Hamlyn Paperbacks, 1981. — 236p ; 18cm
ISBN 0-600-20352-2 (pbk) : £1.10 B81-19910

Smith, Guy N.. Satan's snowdrop / Guy N. Smith. — Feltham : Hamlyn, 1980. — 219p ; 18cm
ISBN 0-600-20171-6 (pbk) : £0.95 B81-01494

Smith, Guy N.. Wolfcurse / Guy N. Smith. — London : New English Library, 1981. — 176p ; 18cm
ISBN 0-450-05158-7 (pbk) : £1.25 B81-24744

Smith, Harriet. All my love / by Harriet Smith. — London : Hale, 1981. — 160p ; 20cm
ISBN 0-7091-9091-3 : £5.60 B81-24879

Smith, Harriet. Australian nurse / by Harriet Smith. — London : Hale, 1980. — 160p ; 20cm
ISBN 0-7091-8619-3 : £5.25 B81-02211

Smith, Jonathan. In flight / Jonathan Smith. — London : Allen Lane, 1980. — 178p ; 23cm
ISBN 0-7139-1347-9 : £5.50 B81-01662

Smith, Mason McCann. When the Emperor dies. — London : Hamish Hamilton, Jan.1982. — [384]p
ISBN 0-241-10697-4 : £7.95 : CIP entry B81-34319

Smith, Pamela. The search / by Pamela Smith. — London : Hale, 1981. — 191p ; 20cm
ISBN 0-7091-8709-2 : £5.95 B81-11108

Smith, Walter J.. Fourth gear / by Walter J. Smith. — London : Hale, 1981. — 174p ; 21cm. — (Hale SF)
ISBN 0-7091-8539-1 : £5.75 B81-08989

Smith, Wilbur. The dark of the sun / by Wilbur Smith. — Long Preston : Magna Print, 1981, c1965. — 510p ; 22cm
Originally published: London : Heinemann, 1965. — Published in large print
ISBN 0-86009-332-8 : Unpriced : CIP rev. B81-14451

Smith, Wilbur. A falcon flies / Wilbur Smith. — London : Pan in association with Heinemann, 1981, c1979. — 543p ; 18cm
Originally published: London : Heinemann, 1980
ISBN 0-330-26412-5 (pbk) : £1.95 B81-37448

Smith, Wilbur. Shout at the devil / by Wilbur Smith. — Bolton-by-Bowland : Magna, 1981, c1968. — 668p ; 22cm
Originally published: London : Heinemann, 1968. — Published in large print
ISBN 0-86009-296-8 : £6.75 B81-08688

Smith, Wilbur. The sound of thunder / Wilbur Smith. — London : Pan in association with Heinemann, 1968, c1966 (1981 printing). — 429p ; 18cm
Originally published: London : Heinemann : 1966
ISBN 0-330-02135-4 (pbk) : £1.50 B81-37446

Smith, Wilbur. A sparrow falls / Wilbur Smith. — London : Pan in association with Heinemann, 1978, c1977 (1980 printing). — 540p ; 18cm
Originally published: London : Heinemann, 1977
ISBN 0-330-25394-8 (pbk) : £1.75 B81-40768

Smith, Wilbur. When the lion feeds / Wilbur Smith. — London : Pan in association with Heinemann, 1966, c1964 (1981 printing). — 420p ; 18cm
Originally published: London : Heinemann, 1964
ISBN 0-330-20139-5 (pbk) : £1.50 B81-37449

Smith, Wilbur. When the lion feeds / by Wilbur Smith. — Bolton-by-Bowland : Magna, 1981, c1974. — 2v. ; 23cm
Originally published: London : Heinemann, 1964. — Published in large print
ISBN 0-86009-308-5
ISBN 0-86009-309-3 (v.2) : £4.50 B81-14201

Somerville-Large, Peter. A living dog / by Peter Somerville-Large. — London : Gollancz, 1981. — 204p ; 21cm
ISBN 0-575-02919-6 : £5.95 B81-03325

Spark, Muriel. Loitering with intent / Muriel Spark. — London : Bodley Head, 1981. — 221p ; 21cm
ISBN 0-370-30900-6 : £6.50 : CIP rev. B81-06627

Spark, Muriel. Not to disturb / Muriel Spark. — London : Granada, 1981. — 95p ; 18cm. — (A Panther book)
Originally published: London : Macmillan, 1971
ISBN 0-586-05234-8 (pbk) : £0.95 B81-10875

Spark, Muriel. Territorial rights / Muriel Spark. — London : Granada, 1980, c1979. — 187p ; 18cm. — (A Panther book)
Originally published: London : Macmillan, 1979
ISBN 0-586-05194-5 (pbk) : £1.25 B81-01701

Sparks, Christine. The elephant man / Christine Sparks. — London : Macdonald Futura, 1980. — 272p,[8]p of plates : ill ; 23cm
ISBN 0-354-04573-3 : £6.95 B81-03436

Sparks, Christine. Open all hours / Christine Sparks ; based on the television series by Roy Clarke. — London : British Broadcasting Corporation, 1981. — 159p ; 22cm
ISBN 0-563-17440-4 : £6.25 B81-12121

823'.914[F] — Fiction in English, *1945-* — *Texts continuation*

Sparks, Christine. Open all hours / Christine Sparks ; based on the television series by Roy Clarke. — London : British Braodcasting Corporation, 1981. — 159p ; 18cm
ISBN 0-563-17924-4 (pbk) : £1.25 B81-11012

Spence, Bill. Bomber's moon / by Bill Spence. — London : Hale, 1981. — 224p ; 20cm
ISBN 0-7091-9257-6 : £6.95 B81-35213

Spence, Peter. To the manor born / Peter Spence. — London : Severn House Bk.2. — 1981, c1980. — 169p ; 21cm
Originally published: London : Arrow Books, 1980
ISBN 0-7278-0711-0 : £5.95 : CIP rev. B81-12783

Spicer, Michael. Final act / Michael Spicer. — London : Severn House, 1981. — 160p ; 25cm
ISBN 0-7278-2012-5 : £6.95 : CIP rev. B81-13702

Spurr, Clinton. Railroad marshal / by Clinton Spurr. — London : Hale, 1980. — 158p ; 20cm
ISBN 0-7091-8398-4 : £4.75 B81-00556

St Clair, Joy. Heart under siege / by Joy St Clair. — London : Mills & Boon, 1981. — 190p ; 19cm
ISBN 0-263-09881-8 : £4.55 B81-26424

St. James, Ian. The Balfour conspiracy / Ian St. James. — London : Heinemann, 1981. — 274p ; 23cm
ISBN 0-434-66621-1 : £5.95 B81-11629

Stableford, Brian. War games / Brian Stableford. — London : Pan, 1981. — 205p ; 18cm
ISBN 0-330-26410-9 (pbk) : £1.50 B81-37350

Stables, Mira. Golden barrier / by Mira Stables. — London : Hale, 1981. — 175p ; 21cm
ISBN 0-7091-8772-6 : £5.95 B81-11735

Stables, Mira. Miss Mouse / Mira Stables. — London : Hale, 1980. — 158p ; 21cm
ISBN 0-7091-8414-x : £5.95 B81-00557

Stables, Mira. No impediment / Mira Stables. — [London] : Corgi, 1980, c1979. — 151p ; 18cm. — (A Georgian romance)
Originally published: London : Hale, 1979
ISBN 0-552-11559-2 (pbk) : £0.95 B81-07088

Stafford, Lee. Louisiana lady / by Lee Stafford. — London : Hale, 1981. — 191p ; 20cm
ISBN 0-7091-8967-2 : £5.95 B81-15955

Stafford, Lee. Passionate torment / Lee Stafford. — London : Hale, 1980. — 176p ; 21cm
ISBN 0-7091-8403-4 : £5.75 B81-02256

Stall, Mike. The Belshazzar affair / by Mike Stall. — London : Hale, 1981. — 174p ; 20cm
ISBN 0-7091-9010-7 : £5.95 B81-17323

Stall, Mike. The deadly charade / by Mike Stall. — London : Hale, 1980. — 188p ; 20cm
ISBN 0-7091-8543-x : £5.75 B81-00558

Stall, Mike. Kill Hitler! / by Mike Stall. — London : Hale, 1981. — 175p ; 20cm
ISBN 0-7091-9034-4 : £6.25 B81-35296

Standish, Caroline. Sweet temptation / Caroline Standish. — London : Macdonald Futura, 1981. — 253p ; 18cm. — (A Minstrel book ; 5)
ISBN 0-7088-2013-1 (pbk) : £0.95 B81-15465

Stanier, Hilda Brookman. Plantagenet Princess / Hilda Brookman Stanier. — London : Hale, 1981. — 188p ; 21cm
ISBN 0-7091-8718-1 : £6.25 B81-08988

Stanton, Anna. Journey's end / Anna Stanton. — Feltham : Hamlyn Paperbacks, 1981. — 154p ; 18cm. — (A Sapphire romance)
ISBN 0-600-20068-x (corrected : pbk) : £0.75 B81-13590

Stanton, Gerald. Beyond the fourth house / Gerald Stanton. — Bognor Regis : New Horizon, c1979. — 198p ; 21cm
ISBN 0-86116-064-9 : £3.95 B81-21802

Statham, Wallace. Running from me / Wallace Statham. — Bognor Regis : New Horizon, c1979. — 128p ; 21cm
ISBN 0-86116-138-6 : £3.25 B81-18876

Stead, Kathleen. Dark love / Kathleen Stead. — Bognor Regis : New Horizon, c1979. — 134p ; 22cm
ISBN 0-86116-085-1 : £3.50 B81-19262

Stearn, Kelly. Compromises / Kelly Stearn. — London : Star, 1981. — 317p ; 18cm
ISBN 0-352-30802-8 (pbk) : £1.50 B81-11687

Steele, Hunter. McCandy : the partial screening of a character in question / Hunter Steele. — London : Murray, 1981. — 235p ; 23cm
ISBN 0-7195-3771-1 : £6.95 B81-12206

Steele, Jessica. Bachelor's wife / by Jessica Steele. — London : Mills & Boon, 1981. — 188p ; 19cm
ISBN 0-263-09878-8 : £4.55 B81-26417

Steele, Jessica. Devil in disguise / by Jessica Steele. — London : Mills & Boon, 1980. — 190p ; 19cm
ISBN 0-263-09795-1 : £3.85 B81-06269

Steele, Jessica. Gallant antagonist / by Jessica Steele. — London : Mills & Boon, 1981. — 190p ; 20cm
ISBN 0-263-09919-9 : £4.55 B81-35636

Steele, Jessica. Innocent abroad / by Jessica Steele. — London : Mills & Boon, 1981. — 189p ; 20cm
ISBN 0-263-09825-7 : £4.55 B81-09405

Steele, Jessica. Price to be met / by Jessica Steele. — London : Mills & Boon, 1980. — 191p ; 20cm
ISBN 0-263-09737-4 : £3.85 B81-00559

Steene, Alton. Maybury / Alton Steene. — London : Severn House, 1981. — 155p ; 21cm
ISBN 0-7278-0723-4 : £5.95 : CIP rev. B81-14841

Stein, Mel. Danger zone / Mel Stein. — [London] : Fontana, 1980. — 318p ; 18cm
ISBN 0-00-615638-x (pbk) : £1.35 B81-00560

Stein, Mel. Rags to riches / Mel Stein. — Loughton : Piatkus, c1981. — 407p ; 21cm
ISBN 0-86188-052-8 : £6.95 : CIP rev. B81-07607

Stephens, Frances. River girl / by Frances Stephens. — London : Hale, 1981. — 192p ; 20cm
ISBN 0-7091-8443-3 : £5.50 B81-08730

Stephens, Frances. Wings of the morning / by Frances Stephens. — London : Hale, 1980. — 189p ; 20cm
ISBN 0-7091-8442-5 : £5.25 B81-01495

Stevens, Lynsey. Terebori's gold / by Lynsey Stevens. — London : Mills & Boon, 1981. — 191p ; 20cm
ISBN 0-263-09818-4 : £4.55 B81-09408

Stevenson, Anne. The French inheritance / Anne Stevenson. — Large print ed. — Leicester : Ulverscroft, 1980, c1974. — 400p ; 23cm. — (Ulverscroft large print series)
Originally published: New York : Putnam ; London : Collins, 1974
ISBN 0-7089-0538-2 : £4.25 : CIP rev. B80-24869

Stevenson, Anne. Mask of treason / by Anne Stevenson. — Loughton : Piatkus, 1981, c1979. — 262p ; 21cm
Originally published: New York : Putnam, 1979
ISBN 0-86188-073-0 : £6.50 B81-12952

Stevenson, Anne. Turkish rondo. — Loughton : Piatkus, Sept.1981. — [256]p
ISBN 0-86188-096-x : £6.50 : CIP entry B81-21616

Stewart, A. C.. Wandering star / by A.C. Stewart. — London : Hale, 1981. — 159p ; 20cm
ISBN 0-7091-9164-2 : £5.60 B81-27293

Stewart, A. J.. Falcon. — Glasgow : MacLellan, Dec.1981. — [248]p
Originally published: London : P. Davies, 1970
ISBN 0-85335-246-1 : £6.95 : CIP entry B81-33881

Stewart, Bruce. A disorderly girl / Bruce Stewart. — London : Arrow, 1980, c1978. — 284p ; 18cm
Originally published: Victoria, Australia : Hutchinson, 1978
ISBN 0-09-922180-2 (pbk) : £1.35 B81-01496

Stewart, Ian, *1928-*. Deadline in Jakarta / Ian Stewart. — Feltham : Hamlyn, 1981. — 222p ; 18cm
ISBN 0-600-33004-4 (pbk) : £1.25 B81-11427

Stewart, Ian, *1928-*. An H-bomb for Alice / Ian Stewart. — Feltham : Hamlyn Paperbacks, 1981. — 329p ; 18cm
ISBN 0-600-20329-8 (pbk) : £1.50 B81-19917

Stewart, Isobel. Give back the years / by Isobel Stewart. — London : Hale, 1981. — 175p ; 20cm
ISBN 0-7091-8843-9 : £5.60 B81-38608

Stewart, Isobel. The glory and the gold / Isobel Stewart. — London : Hale, 1981. — 164p ; 22cm
ISBN 0-7091-8858-7 : £5.95 B81-11736

Stewart, Isobel. The heather on the hills / by Isobel Stewart. — London : Hale, 1980. — 157p ; 20cm
ISBN 0-7091-8401-8 : £5.25 B81-02205

Stewart, Isobel. Stranger in the glen / Isobel Stewart. — London : Mills & Boon, 1981. — 191p ; 19cm. — (Masquerade)
ISBN 0-263-09785-4 : £4.55 B81-18346

Stirling, Jessica. The blue evening gone / Jessica Stirling. — London : Hodder, c1981. — 413p ; 23cm
ISBN 0-340-25990-6 : £7.50 : CIP rev. B81-09461

Stirling, Jessica. The deep well at noon / Jessica Stirling. — London : Pan, 1981, c1979. — 573p ; 18cm
Originally published: London : Hodder and Stoughton, 1979
ISBN 0-330-26233-5 (pbk) : £1.75 B81-03049

Stirling, Jessica. [The Dresden finch]. Beloved sinner / Jessica Stirling. — London : Severn House, 1981, c1976. — 238p ; 21cm
Originally published: New York : Delacorte, 1976
ISBN 0-7278-0658-0 : £5.95 B81-08622

823'.914[F] — Fiction in English, *1945-* **—** *Texts continuation*

Stoker, M. Brooke. Court of deceit / M. Brooke Stoker. — London : Hale, 1981. — 192p ; 20cm
ISBN 0-7091-9112-x : £6.50 B81-24865

Stone, Richard, *1940-*. The devil's engineering / Richard Stone. — Sevenoaks (25 Quakers Hall La., Sevenoaks, Kent TN13 3TU) : Ashgrove, 1980. — 256p ; 21cm
ISBN 0-906798-07-8 : £5.95 B81-01497

Stordy, Ann. My sweet Liverpool / Ann Stordy. — Bognor Regis : New Horizon, c1980. — 232p ; 21cm
ISBN 0-86116-313-3 : £5.25 B81-19084

Storey, B. G.. Cabin six / B.G. Storey. — Bognor Regis : New Horizon, c1980. — 201p ; 21cm
ISBN 0-86116-203-x : £4.75 B81-18879

Stranger, Joyce. Double trouble : vet up the wall / Joyce Stranger. — [London] : Carousel, c1981. — 116p ; 18cm
ISBN 0-552-52132-9 (pbk) : £0.75 B81-21280

Stranger, Joyce. The January Queen / Joyce Stranger. — London : Corgi, 1980, c1979. — 189p ; 18cm
Originally published: London : Joseph, 1979
ISBN 0-552-11536-3 (pbk) : £1.25 B81-02194

Stranger, Joyce. The stallion / Joyce Stranger. — London : Joseph, 1981. — 223p ; 21cm
ISBN 0-7181-2032-9 : £6.95 B81-33501

Strathern, William. Don't look for me — I'm dead / by William Strathern. — London : Hale, 1981. — 192p ; 20cm
ISBN 0-7091-8785-8 : £5.75 B81-08648

Stratton, Alan. The empire builders / Alan Stratton. — London : Macdonald Futura, 1981. — 539p ; 18cm
ISBN 0-7088-1839-0 (pbk) : £1.75 B81-32783

Stratton, Rebecca. The black invader / by Rebecca Stratton. — London : Mills & Boon, 1981. — 189p ; 19cm
ISBN 0-263-09873-7 : £4.55 B81-26416

Stratton, Rebecca. Dark enigma / by Rebecca Stratton. — London : Mills & Boon, 1981. — 187p ; 20cm
ISBN 0-263-09915-6 : £4.55 B81-34098

Stratton, Rebecca. The silken cage / by Rebecca Stratton. — London : Mills & Boon, 1981. — 192p ; 19cm
ISBN 0-263-09832-x : £4.55 B81-10889

Street, Mary. A friendly star / by Mary Street. — London : Hale, 1981. — 189p ; 20cm
ISBN 0-7091-8921-4 : £5.60 B81-17317

Street, Pamela. Light of evening : a novel / by Pamela Street. — London : Hale, 1981. — 191p ; 21cm
ISBN 0-7091-9251-7 : £6.50 B81-35234

Strong, Michael. The wolves came down from the mountain / Michael Strong. — London : Hamlyn Paperbacks, 1980, c1979. — 183p ; 18cm
Originally published: London : Long, 1979
ISBN 0-600-20010-8 (pbk) : £1.00 B81-06263

Strutt, Sheila. The master of Craighill / Sheila Strutt. — Large print ed. — Bath : Chivers, 1981, c1979. — 215p ; 23cm. — (A Seymour book)
Originally published: London : Mills and Boon, 1979
ISBN 0-85119-435-4 : £4.95 : CIP rev. B81-20107

Strutt, Sheila. No yesterdays / by Sheila Strutt. — London : Mills & Boon, 1981. — 189p ; 20cm
ISBN 0-263-09887-7 : £4.55 B81-28556

Strutt, Sheila. On the edge of love / by Sheila Strutt. — London : Mills & Boon, 1981. — 189p ; 20cm
ISBN 0-263-09820-6 : £4.55 B81-09406

Stuart, Anthony. Force play / Anthony Stuart. — Large print ed. — Bath : Chivers, 1981, c1979. — 298p ; 23cm. — (A New Portway large print book)
Originally published: New York : Arbor House, 1979 ; London : Macdonald and Jane's, 1980
ISBN 0-85119-119-3 : £5.35 : CIP rev. B81-12867

Stuart, Ian, *1927-*. End on the rocks / by Ian Stuart. — London : Hale, 1981. — 175p ; 20cm
ISBN 0-7091-9017-4 : £5.95 B81-23611

Stuart, Ian, *1927-*. The Renshaw strike / by Ian Stuart. — London : Hale, 1980. — 189p ; 20cm
ISBN 0-7091-8650-9 : £5.75 B81-01498

Stuart, Robyn. Buccaneer's lady / Robyn Stuart. — London : Mills & Boon, 1981. — 190p ; 20cm. — (Masquerade)
ISBN 0-263-09787-0 : £4.55 B81-28516

Stuart, Vivian. The exiles / Vivian Stuart. — [Henley-on-Thames] : Ellis, 1980. — 548p ; 23cm
Originally published: New York : Dell, 1979
ISBN 0-85628-100-x : £8.50 : CIP rev. B80-19467

Stuart, Vivian. The settlers / by Vivian Stuart writing as William Stuart Long. — London : Macdonald Futura, 1981, c1980. — 541p : 1map ; 18cm. — (The Australians ; bk.2) (A Futura book)
Originally published: New York : Dell, 1980
ISBN 0-7088-2086-7 (pbk) : £1.95 B81-40944

Stuart, Vivian. The settlers / Vivian Stuart. — [Henley-on-Thames] : Ellis, 1981, c1980. — 544p ; 23cm. — (The Australians ; v.2) (The Australians)
ISBN 0-85628-103-4 : £8.50 : CIP rev. B81-19153

Stubbs, Jean. The ironmaster / Jean Stubbs. — London : Macmillan, 1981. — 415p ; 23cm
ISBN 0-333-27311-7 : £6.95 B81-20268

Stubbs, Jean. Kit's Hill / Jean Stubbs. — Large print ed. — Leicester : Ulverscroft, 1981, c1978. — 542p ; 23cm. — (Brief chronicles ; v.1) (Ulverscroft large print series)
Originally published: London : 1978
ISBN 0-7089-0627-3 : £5.00 : CIP rev. B81-07905

Stubbs, Susie. Recipe for love / by Susie Stubbs. — London : Hale, 1981. — 192p ; 20cm
ISBN 0-7091-9106-5 : £5.60 B81-35292

Sturrock, Jeremy. Suicide most foul / Jeremy Sturrock. — London : Hale, 1981. — 204p ; 20cm
ISBN 0-7091-8600-2 : £6.50 B81-17319

Styles, Showell. The Baltic convoy. — Large print ed. — Bath : Chivers, Dec.1981. — [296] p. — (A Lythway book)
Originally published: London : Faber, 1979
ISBN 0-85119-771-x : £6.80 : CIP entry B81-31802

Styles, Showell. A kiss for Captain Hardy / Showell Styles. — Large print ed. — Bath : Chivers, 1981, c1979. — 277p ; 23cm. — (A Lythway historical novel)
Originally published: London : Faber, 1979
ISBN 0-85119-711-6 : Unpriced B81-10872

Styles, Showell. Mr Fitton's commission. — Large print ed. — Bath : Chivers, Oct.1981. — [296]p. — (A Lythway book)
Originally published: London : Faber, 1977
ISBN 0-85119-755-8 : £6.90 : CIP entry B81-25812

Styles, Showell. A sword for Mr. Fitton / Showell Styles. — Large print ed. — Bath : Chivers, 1981, c1975. — 270p : 1map ; 23cm. — (A Lythway book)
Originally published: London : Faber, 1975
ISBN 0-85119-737-x : Unpriced : CIP rev. B81-19110

Suckling, Nigel. The clothmerchant's apprentice : the first volume in the tale of Rufus, the clothmerchant's apprentice, showing his early days and the beginning of his acquaintance with the Golden Wheel / written and illustrated by Nigel Suckling. — London (219 Eversleigh Rd. SW11 5UY) : Big O, 1979. — 143p : ill ; 25cm
ISBN 0-905664-07-8 (cased) : Unpriced B81-02220

Summers, Essie. Spring in September / Essie Summers. — Large print ed. — Leicester : Ulverscroft, 1980, c1978. — 303p ; 23cm. — (Ulverscroft large print series)
Originally published: London : Mills and Boon, 1978
ISBN 0-7089-0552-8 : £4.25 : CIP rev. B80-35458

Summers, Rowena. Blackmaddie / Rowena Summers. — Feltham : Hamlyn, 1980. — 319p ; 18cm
ISBN 0-600-20172-4 (pbk) : £1.35 B81-01499

Summerson, Rachel. Hearts are trumps, or, She would be a lady : a novel / by Rachel Summerson. — London : Sidgwick & Jackson, 1981. — 295p ; 23cm
ISBN 0-283-98749-9 : £6.95 B81-17338

Sunderland, C. J.. Marshal Carney's riddle / by C.J. Sunderland. — London : Hale, 1980. — 160p ; 20cm
ISBN 0-7091-8610-x : £4.95 B81-00561

Suster, Gerald. The Elect / Gerald Suster. — London : Sphere, 1980. — 244p ; 18cm
ISBN 0-7221-8285-6 (pbk) : £1.35 B81-01500

Suster, Gerald. The scar / Gerald Suster. — Feltham : Hamlyn, 1981. — 219p ; 18cm
ISBN 0-600-20357-3 (pbk) : £1.25 B81-27873

Sutcliff, Rosemary. The rider of the white horse / Rosemary Sutcliff. — London : Hodder and Stoughton, 1981, c1959. — 320p : ill ; 23cm
ISBN 0-340-26549-3 : £6.95 : CIP rev. B81-01846

Sutcliff, Rosemary. The sword and the circle : King Arthur and the knights of the Round Table / Rosemary Sutcliff ; decorations by Shirley Felts. — London : Bodley Head, 1981. — 260p : ill ; 23cm
ISBN 0-370-30387-3 : £4.95 B81-13374

Swan, Rose. So near my love / Rose Swan. — London : Hale, 1981. — 156p ; 20cm
ISBN 0-7091-9210-x : £5.75 B81-33535

Swan, Rose. A time to love / by Rose Swan. — London : Hale, 1980. — 155p ; 20cm
ISBN 0-7091-8263-5 : £4.95 B81-00562

Swift, Graham. Shuttlecock / Graham Swift. — London : Allan Lane, 1981. — 219p ; 23cm
ISBN 0-7139-1413-0 : £6.95 B81-35409

Synge, Ursula. Swan's wing / Ursula Synge. — London : Bodley Head, c1981. — 155p ; 23cm
For adolescents
ISBN 0-370-30425-x : £4.95 : CIP rev. B81-03822

823'.914[F] — Fiction in English, *1945-* — *Texts continuation*

Tabor, Percy. Seven little sinner boys / Percy Tabor. — Bognor Regis : New Horizon, c1980. — 237p ; 21cm
ISBN 0-86116-240-4 : £5.25 B81-18878

Tangye, Derek. When the winds blow / Derek Tangye. — Large print ed. — Bath : Chivers, 1981, c1980. — 254p ; 23cm. — (A New Portway large print book)
Originally published: London : Joseph, 1980
ISBN 0-85119-135-5 : £5.25 : CIP rev. B81-20111

Tanner, Janet. The black mountains / Janet Tanner. — London : Macdonald, 1981. — 469p ; 22cm
ISBN 0-354-04606-3 : £7.95 B81-35377

Tattersall, Jill. Damnation Reef / Jill Tatterall. — South Yarmouth, Mass. : Curley ; [Bolton by Bowland] : Magna Print [distributor], c1979. — 557p ; 23cm
Originally published: New York : Morrow, 1979 ; London : Hodder and Stoughton, 1980
ISBN 0-89340-270-2 : £5.50 B81-02219

Tattersall, Jill. Dark at noon / Jill Tattersall. — South Yarmouth, Mass. : Curley ; [Bolton-by-Bowland] : Magna Print [distributor], c1978. — 521p ; 23cm
Originally published: New York : Morrow, 1978 ; London : Hodder and Stoughton, 1979. — Published in large print
ISBN 0-89340-271-0 : £5.50 B81-02880

Taylor, Bernard, *1934-*. The reaping / by Bernard Taylor. — London : Souvenir, 1980. — 237p ; 21cm
ISBN 0-285-62436-9 : £5.95 : CIP rev. B80-12599

Taylor, Margaret Stewart. The forced deception / by Margaret Stewart Taylor. — London : Hale, 1981. — 205p ; 20cm
ISBN 0-7091-9374-2 : £6.75 B81-37304

Taylor, Margaret Stewart. The hidden king / by Margaret Stewart Taylor. — London : Hale, 1980. — 191p ; 21cm
ISBN 0-7091-8538-3 : £6.25 B81-00563

Taylor, Margaret Stewart. The wayward jilt / Margaret Stewart Taylor. — Large print ed. — Bath : Chivers, 1980, c1974. — 258p ; 23cm. — (A Seymour book)
Originally published: London : Hale, 1971
ISBN 0-86220-017-2 : £4.95 : CIP entry B80-18017

Taylor, William Carr. Dr Smith-Simpkin's first job / by William Carr Taylor. — Harrow : Euroeditions, 1979. — 188p ; 21cm
ISBN 0-906204-33-x : Unpriced B81-24758

Tennant, Emma. Alice fell / Emma Tennant. — London : Cape, 1980. — 124p ; 21cm
ISBN 0-224-01872-8 : £5.50 : CIP rev. B80-24871

Tennant, Emma. Wild nights / Emma Tennant. — London : Pan, 1981, c1979. — 127p ; 20cm. — (Picador)
Originally published: London : Cape, 1979
ISBN 0-330-26241-6 (pbk) : £1.95 B81-03479

Thirkell, Alison. Now the king's come / Alison Thirkell. — London : Hale, 1981. — 205p ; 20cm
ISBN 0-7091-9123-5 : £6.50 B81-28871

Thomas, Alexandra. The Takamaka tree / Alexandra Thomas. — London : Hamlyn Paperbacks, 1981. — 156p ; 18cm. — (A Sapphire romance)
ISBN 0-600-20174-0 (pbk) : £0.75 B81-31914

Thomas, Craig. Sea Leopard / Craig Thomas. — London : Joseph, 1981. — 315p ; 23cm
Maps on lining papers
ISBN 0-7181-1957-6 : £6.95 B81-17594

Thomas, Craig. Wolfsbane / Craig Thomas. — London : Sphere, 1979, c1978 (1981 [printing]). — 332p ; 18cm
Originally published: London : Joseph, 1978
ISBN 0-7221-8452-2 (pbk) : £1.50 B81-40989

Thomas, D. M.. The white hotel : a novel / by D.M. Thomas. — London : Gollancz, 1981. — 240p ; 23cm
ISBN 0-575-02889-0 : £6.95 B81-02692

Thomas, Donald. The blindfold game / Donald Thomas. — London : Deutsch, 1981. — 294p ; 24cm
ISBN 0-233-97366-4 : £6.95 B81-35140

Thomas, Leslie, *1931*. Stand up virgin soldiers / Leslie Thomas. — London : Pan, 1976, c1975 (1981 printing). — 250p ; 18cm
Originally published: London : Eyre Methuen, 1975
ISBN 0-330-24776-x (pbk) : £1.50 B81-36701

Thomas, Leslie, *1931-*. Bare Nell / Leslie Thomas. — London : Pan, 1978, c1977 (1981 [printing]). — 333p ; 18cm
Originally published: London : Eyre Methuen, 1977
£1.50 (pbk) B81-22284

Thomas, Leslie, *1931-*. Come to the war / Leslie Thomas. — London : Pan, 1971, c1969 (1981 [printing]). — 219p ; 18cm
Originally published: London : Joseph, 1969
ISBN 0-330-02741-7 (pbk) : £1.50 B81-29128

Thomas, Leslie, *1931-*. His lordship / Leslie Thomas. — London : Pan, 1972, c1970 (1981 printing). — 238p ; 18cm
Originally published: London : Joseph, 1970
ISBN 0-330-02943-6 (pbk) : £1.50 B81-24457

Thomas, Leslie, *1931-*. The magic army. — London : Eyre Methuen, Oct.1981. — [450]p
ISBN 0-413-46560-8 : £7.50 : CIP entry B81-25316

Thomas, Leslie, *1931-*. The man with the power / Leslie Thomas. — London : Pan, 1975, c1973 (1981 printing). — 251p ; 18cm
Originally published: London : Eyre Methuen, 1973
ISBN 0-330-24408-6 (pbk) : £1.60 B81-40712

Thomas, Leslie, *1931-*. Onward virgin soldiers / Leslie Thomas. — London : Pan, 1973, c1971 (1981 printing). — 300p ; 18cm
Originally published: London : Joseph, 1971
ISBN 0-330-23620-2 (pbk) : £1.50 B81-13020

Thomas, Leslie, *1931-*. Ormerod's landing. — Large print ed. — Long Preston : Magna Print Books, Feb.1982. — [480]p
Originally published: London : Eyre Methuen, 1978
ISBN 0-86009-378-6 : £5.25 : CIP entry B81-35700

Thomas, Leslie, *1931-*. The virgin soldiers / Leslie Thomas. — London : Pan, 1967, c1966 (1980 printing). — 204p ; 18cm
Originally published: London : Constable, 1966
ISBN 0-330-20191-3 (pbk) : £1.25 B81-09739

Thompson, Anne Armstrong. The Swiss legacy. — London : Hodder and Stoughton, Aug.1981. — [256]p
Originally published: New York : Simon and Schuster, 1974 ; London : Hodder and Stoughton, 1979
ISBN 0-340-26684-8 (pbk) : £1.50 : CIP entry B81-18135

Thompson, E. V.. Ben Retallick / E.V. Thompson. — London : Macmillan, 1980. — 400p : 1map ; 23cm
ISBN 0-333-30611-2 : £6.95 B81-01501

Thompson, E. V.. The music makers / E.V. Thompson. — London : Pan in association with Macmillan, 1981, c1979. — 445p ; 18cm
Originally published: London : Macmillan, 1979
ISBN 0-330-26276-9 (pbk) : £1.50 B81-12074

Thompson, Kathleen Lumley. While shepherding / by Kathleen Lumley Thompson. — [Wembley] : [Selecteditions], [1980]. — 263p ; 21cm
ISBN 0-86237-007-8 (pbk) : £2.00 B81-23123

Thomson, Daisy. The eve of love / by Daisy Thomson. — London : Hale, 1981. — 191p ; 20cm
ISBN 0-7091-8699-1 : £5.50 B81-03406

Thomson, Daisy. To love and be wise / by Daisy Thomson. — London : Hale, 1980. — 191p ; 20cm
ISBN 0-7091-8002-0 : £4.95 B81-00564

Thomson, June. Deadly relations / June Thomson. — London : Magnum, 1980, c1979. — 232p ; 18cm
Originally published: London : Constable, 1979
ISBN 0-417-04950-1 (pbk) : £1.50 B81-28655

Thorne, Nicola. The daughters of the house / Nicola Thorne. — London : Granada, 1981. — 684p ; 22cm
Bibliography: p682-684
ISBN 0-246-11359-6 : £6.95 B81-10980

Thorne, Nicola. The perfect wife and mother / Nicola Thorne. — London : Heinemann, 1980. — 248p ; 23cm
ISBN 0-434-77902-4 : £6.95 B81-02513

Thornley, Richard. Zig-zag / Richard Thornley. — London : Cape, 1981. — 172p ; 21cm
ISBN 0-224-01909-0 : £6.50 : CIP rev. B81-04297

Thorpe, Kay. Cooper Lake / by Kay Thorpe. — London : Mills & Boon, 1981. — 186p ; 19cm
ISBN 0-263-09876-1 : £4.55 B81-26423

Thorpe, Sylvia. The Avenhurst inheritance / Sylvia Thorpe. — London : Hutchinson, 1981. — 253p ; 23cm
ISBN 0-09-143470-x : £5.95 B81-02496

Thorpe, Sylvia. No more a-roving / Sylvia Thorpe. — [London] : Corgi, 1981, c1970. — 172p ; 18cm
Originally published: London : Hurst & Blackett, 1970
ISBN 0-552-11617-3 (pbk) : £1.00 B81-15346

Thorpe, Sylvia. The sword and the shadow / Sylvia Thorpe. — London : Corgi, 1981. — 287p ; 18cm
Originally published: London : Hutchinson, 1951
ISBN 0-552-11768-4 (pbk) : £1.25 B81-35498

Thynn, Alexander. Pillars of the establishment / Alexander Thynn. — London : Hutchinson, 1980. — 283p : music,1geneal.table ; 23cm
ISBN 0-09-141980-8 : £6.95 B81-01502

Tilbury, Quenna. Sweet conquest / Quenna Tilbury. — London : Hale, 1980. — 175p ; 20cm
ISBN 0-7091-8227-9 : £4.95 B81-00565

Timperley, Rosemary. Homeward bound / by Rosemary Timperley. — London : Hale, 1980. — 190p ; 23cm
ISBN 0-7091-8200-7 : £6.25 B81-01503

Timperley, Rosemary. Miss X / by Rosemary Timperley. — Large print ed. — London : Hale, 1980. — 322p ; 23cm
ISBN 0-7091-8603-7 : £5.80 B81-01504

823'.914[F] — Fiction in English, *1945-* **—** *Texts continuation*

Timperley, Rosemary. The secret dancer / Rosemary Timperly. — London : Hale, 1981. — 190p ; 21cm
ISBN 0-7091-9329-7 : £6.75 B81-40467

Timperley, Rosemary. The spell of the Hanged Man / Rosemary Timperley. — London : Hale, 1981. — 192p ; 21cm
ISBN 0-7091-8964-8 : £6.50 B81-29861

Timperley, Rosemary. That year at the office / Rosemary Timperley. — London : Hale, 1981. — 160p ; 23cm
ISBN 0-7091-8618-5 : £6.25 B81-14065

Tinniswood, Peter. Shemerelda : by the incredibly beautiful H.H. Washbrook / as told to [i.e. by] Peter Tinniswood. — London : Hodder and Stoughton, 1981. — 157p ; 23cm
ISBN 0-340-22718-4 : £5.95 B81-15786

Tinsley, Nina. Quenton's Island / by Nina Tinsley. — London : Hale, 1981. — 176p ; 20cm
ISBN 0-7091-8637-1 : £5.50 B81-02922

Todd, Catherine. Bond of honour / Catherine Todd. — New York : St. Martin's ; London : Hale, 1981. — 223p ; 20cm
ISBN 0-312-08763-2 : £6.95 B81-37311

Toft, John. The dew / John Toft. — London : W.H. Allen, 1981. — 235p ; 23cm
ISBN 0-491-02745-1 : £7.95 B81-28622

Toms, Patricia. Mrs Sherwood's summer / Patricia Toms. — Large print ed. — Bath : Chivers, 1981, c1965. — 288p ; 23cm. — (A Seymour book)
Originally published: London : Collins, 1965
ISBN 0-85119-422-2 : Unpriced B81-24813

Torrance, Lee. Only on Friday / Lee Torrance. — New York : St. Martin's Press ; London : Hale, 1980. — 207p ; 21cm
ISBN 0-7091-8402-6 : £6.25 B81-02755

The **Tourist's** guide to Transylvania. — London : Octopus, c1981. — 78p : col.ill,1col.map ; 33cm
Ill on lining papers
ISBN 0-7064-1602-3 : £3.95 B81-17456

Tree, Norma R.. Tale for a minstrel / by Norma R. Tree. — London : Hale, 1981. — 191p ; 21cm
ISBN 0-7091-8969-9 : £6.25 B81-14071

Tremain, Rose. The cupboard / Rose Tremain. — London : Macdonald, 1981. — 251p ; 23cm
ISBN 0-354-04769-8 : £6.95 B81-37907

Tremain, Rose. Letter to Sister Benedicta / Rose Tremain. — London : Arrow, 1981, c1978. — 175p ; 18cm
Originally published: London : Macdonald and Jane's, 1978
ISBN 0-09-924900-6 (pbk) : £1.25 B81-11886

Tremayne, Peter. Dracula, my love / Peter Tremayne. — [London] : Magnum, 1980. — 154p ; 18cm
Originally published: Folkestone : Bailey & Swinfen, 1980
ISBN 0-417-05040-2 (pbk) : £1.25 B81-06368

Tremayne, Peter. Dracula my love / Peter Tremayne. — Folkestone : Bailey & Swinfen, 1980. — iv,154p ; 23cm
ISBN 0-561-00309-2 : £4.95 B81-00566

Tremayne, Peter. The fires of Lan-Kern / Peter Tremayne. — London : Magnum Books, 1980. — 272p ; 18cm
Originally published: Folkestone : Bailey Bros and Swinfen, 1980
ISBN 0-417-04270-1 (pbk) : £1.40 B81-27697

Tremayne, Peter. Zombie! / Peter Tremayne. — London : Sphere, 1981, c1981. — 183p ; 18cm
ISBN 0-7221-8599-5 (pbk) : £1.25 B81-35068

Trenhaile, John. Kyril. — London : Severn House, Oct.1981. — [240]p
ISBN 0-7278-0741-2 : £6.95 : CIP entry B81-24636

Tresillian, Richard. Fleur / Richard Tresillian. — London : Sphere, 1981, c1979. — 307p ; 18cm
Originally published: London : Arlington, 1979
ISBN 0-7221-8600-2 (pbk) : £1.75 B81-24710

Trevelyan, Robert. Pendragon — seeds of mutiny. — London : Hodder & Stoughton, Oct.1981. — [192]p. — (Coronet books)
Originally published: 1979
ISBN 0-340-26682-1 (pbk) : £1.10 : CIP entry B81-26728

Treves, Kathleen. Nurse Lyle of Wayne's Ward / Kathleen Treves. — Large print ed. — Bath : Chivers, 1980, c1966. — 252p ; 23cm. — (A Seymour book)
Originally published: London : Ward Lock, 1966
ISBN 0-86220-018-0 : £4.95 : CIP entry B80-18020

Treves, Kathleen. Prior's Holt / by Kathleen Treves. — London : Hale, 1981. — 176p ; 20cm
ISBN 0-7091-8844-7 : £5.60 B81-15299

Trevor, Alison. Bride of deception / Alison Trevor. — [London] : Magnum, 1981. — 333p ; 18cm
ISBN 0-417-05780-6 (pbk) : £1.50 B81-28675

Trevor, Elleston. The Damocles sword / Elleston Trevor. — London : Collins, 1981. — 314p ; 22cm
ISBN 0-00-222179-9 : £6.95 B81-03421

Trevor, Elleston. The sibling / Elleston Trevor. — London : New English Library, 1981, c1979. — 286p ; 18cm
Originally published: Chicago Playboy Press, 1979 ; London : New English Library, 1980
ISBN 0-450-04682-6 (pbk) : £1.50 B81-09558

Trevor, Meriol. The civil prisoners / Meriol Trevor. — Large print ed. — Leicester : Ulverscroft, 1980, c1977. — 349p : geneal.tables ; 23cm. — (Ulverscroft large print series)
Originally published: London : Hodder and Stoughton, 1977. — Geneal. tables on lining papers
ISBN 0-7089-0526-9 : £4.25 : CIP rev. B80-23746

Trevor, Meriol. The wanton fires. — Large print ed. — Anstey : Ulverscroft, Dec.1981. — [368] p. — (Ulverscroft large print series)
Originally published: London : Hodder and Stoughton, 1979
ISBN 0-7089-0722-9 : £5.00 : CIP entry B81-32034

Trevor, William. The children of Dynmouth / William Trevor. — London : Heinemann Educational, 1981, c1976. — 221p ; 20cm. — (The New windmill series ; 250)
Originally published: London : Bodley Head, 1976
ISBN 0-435-12250-9 : £1.60 : CIP rev. B80-26241

Trevor, William. Elizabeth alone / William Trevor. — London : Bodley Head, 1973 (1981 [printing]). — 335p ; 21cm
ISBN 0-370-01493-6 : £6.95 B81-16266

Trevor, William. The love department / William Trevor. — Harmondsworth : Penguin, 1970, c1966 (1981 [printing]). — 262p ; 20cm. — (A King Penguin)
Originally published: London : Bodley Head, 1966
ISBN 0-14-006010-3 (pbk) : £2.50 B81-40497

Trew, Antony. The Antonov project / Antony Trew. — [Glasgow] : Fontana, 1981, c1979. — 224p ; 18cm
Originally published: London : Collins, 1979
ISBN 0-00-616136-7 (pbk) : £1.25 B81-11070

Trew, Antony. Kleber's convoy. — Large print ed. — Long Preston : Magna, Nov.1981. — [480]p
ISBN 0-86009-352-2 : £4.95 : CIP entry B81-30433

Tripp, Donald. Secret connections / Donald Tripp. — Bognor Regis : New Horizon, c1980. — 172p ; 22cm
ISBN 0-86116-344-3 : £4.25 B81-18882

Tripp, Miles. Going solo / Miles Tripp. — London : Macmillan, 1981. — 174p ; 21cm
ISBN 0-333-30436-5 : £5.50 B81-11676

Trollope, Joanna. The city of gems. — London : Hutchinson, Sept.1981. — 1v.
ISBN 0-09-145690-8 : £6.95 : CIP entry B81-22598

Trollope, Joanna. Eliza Stanhope. — Large print ed. — Long Preston : Magna, Sept.1981. — [380]p
ISBN 0-86009-342-5 : £4.95 : CIP entry B81-22462

Trollope, Joanna. Parson Harding's daughter / Joanna Trollope. — London : Arrow, 1980, c1979. — 284p ; 18cm
Originally published: London : Hutchinson, 1979
ISBN 0-09-922290-6 (pbk) : £1.25 B81-02128

Troop, Elizabeth. Darling daughters / Elizabeth Troop. — London : Granada, 1981. — 252p ; 23cm
ISBN 0-246-11458-4 : £6.95 B81-21214

Troop, Elizabeth. Woolworth Madonna / Elizabeth Troop. — Harmondsworth : Penguin, 1980, c1976. — 107p ; 20cm
Originally published: London : Duckworth : 1976
ISBN 0-14-004818-9 (pbk) : £1.50 B81-01505

Tubb, E. C.. Prison of night / E.C. Tubb. — London : Arrow, 1980, c1977. — 160p ; 18cm. — (The Dumarest saga ; 17)
Originally published: New York : Daw, 1977
ISBN 0-09-923970-1 (pbk) : £1.10 B81-07663

Tubb, E. C.. The winds of Gath / E.C. Tubb. — London : Arrow, 1973, c1967 (1981 [printing]). — 191p ; 18cm. — (The Dumarest saga ; 1)
Originally published: New York : Ace Books, 1967
ISBN 0-09-907610-1 (pbk) : £1.15 B81-17624

Turnbull, Peter. Deep and crisp and even / Peter Turnbull. — London : Collins, 1981. — 216p ; 21cm. — (The Crime Club)
ISBN 0-00-231287-5 : £5.95 B81-10210

Turner, George. Vaneglory. — London : Faber, Oct.1981. — [320]p
ISBN 0-571-11664-7 : £6.95 : CIP entry B81-28028

Turner, Janet œc 1952-. Shades of love / Janet Turner. — London : Hale, 1981. — 159p ; 20cm
ISBN 0-7091-9022-0 : £5.60 B81-21291

Turner, Judy. A gift for Pamela / Judy Turner. — London : Mills & Boon, 1981. — 188p ; 20cm. — (Masquerade)
ISBN 0-263-09783-8 : £4.55 B81-14246

Turner, Mary. Runaway lady / Mary Turner. — London : Hale, 1980. — 223p ; 20cm
ISBN 0-7091-8438-7 : £6.50 B81-00567

823'.914[F] — Fiction in English, *1945-* **— Texts** *continuation*

Turner, Pearl. Comrades in death / by Pearl Turner. — London : Hale, 1980. — 156p ; 20cm
ISBN 0-7091-8630-4 : £5.75 B81-02161

Tynan, Kathleen. Agatha : the Agatha Christie mystery / Kathleen Tynan. — London : Star, 1978 (1979 [printing]). — 189p ; 18cm
Originally published: New York : Ballantine ; London : Weidenfeld and Nicolson, 1978
ISBN 0-352-30296-8 (pbk) : £0.75 B81-28511

Underwood, Michael. Crime upon crime / Michael Underwood. — London : Macmillan, 1980. — 190p ; 21cm
ISBN 0-333-29552-8 : £5.50 B81-01506

Underwood, Michael. Double jeopardy / Michael Underwood. — London : Macmillan, 1981. — 189p ; 21cm
ISBN 0-333-31097-7 : £5.50 B81-21137

Underwood, Michael. Murder with malice. — Large print ed. — Anstey : Ulverscroft, Nov.1981. — [352]p. — (Ulverscroft large print series)
Originally published: London : Macmillan, 1977
ISBN 0-7089-0704-0 : £5.00 : CIP entry B81-30500

Upton, Peter. The eve of April twenty / Peter Upton. — London : Arrow, 1980, c1978. — 397p ; 18cm
Originally published: London : Arlington Press, 1978
ISBN 0-09-921740-6 (pbk) : £1.50 B81-02126

Ure, Jean. Curtain fall / Jean Ure. — Large print ed. — Leicester : Ulverscroft, 1981, c1978. — 307p ; 23cm. — (Ulverscroft large print series)
Originally published: London : Corgi, 1978
ISBN 0-7089-0608-7 : £5.00 : CIP rev. B81-02114

Ure, Jean. Dress rehearsal / Jean Ure. — London : Severn House, 1981, c1977. — 140p ; 21cm
Originally published: London : Corgi, 1978
ISBN 0-7278-0699-8 : £4.95 B81-08623

Ure, Jean. Masquerade / Jean Ure. — London : Severn House, 1980, c1979. — 153p ; 21cm
Originally published: London : Corgi, 1979
ISBN 0-7278-0696-3 : £4.95 : CIP rev. B80-18022

Ure, Jean. No precious time / Jean Ure. — London : Severn House, 1981, c1976. — 142p ; 21cm
Originally published: London : Corgi, 1976
ISBN 0-7278-0707-2 : £5.50 : CIP rev. B81-13539

Ure, Jean. See you Thursday / Jean Ure. — Harmondsworth : Kestrel, 1981. — 174p ; 23cm
For adolescents
ISBN 0-7226-5724-2 : £4.95 B81-28641

Uren, Rhona. Nurse Foster / by Rhona Uren. — London : Hale, 1980. — 160p ; 20cm
ISBN 0-7091-8560-x : £4.95 B81-01507

Uren, Rhona. The stranger at the castle / by Rhona Uren. — London : Hale, 1981. — 176p ; 20cm
ISBN 0-7091-9139-1 : £5.60 B81-27291

Vacha, Robert. The proton plot / Robert Vacha. — London : Star, 1980. — 204p ; 18cm
ISBN 0-352-30502-9 (pbk) : £0.95 B81-01508

Van Greenaway, Peter. 'Cassandra' Bell : a novel / Peter Van Greenaway. — London : Gollancz, 1981. — 192p ; 21cm
ISBN 0-575-02874-2 : £5.95 B81-03550

Van Greenaway, Peter. Manrissa man. — London : Gollancz, Feb.1982. — [208]p
ISBN 0-575-03100-x : £6.95 : CIP entry B81-40244

Van Hassen, Amy. Menace / Amy van Hassen. — London : New English Library, 1981. — 192p ; 23cm
ISBN 0-450-04836-5 : £5.50 B81-15423

Van Zwanenberg, Micky. The Cambridge four / Micky van Zwanenberg ; with a foreword by Dorian Williams. — Bognor Regis : New Horizon, c1981. — 201p ; 22cm
ISBN 0-86116-559-4 : £5.75 B81-34841

Vance, Jack. The face. — Sevenoaks : Coronet Books, June 1981. — [224]p
ISBN 0-340-26666-x (pbk) : £1.10 : CIP entry B81-12348

Vanner, Lyn. Jessie / Lyn Vanner. — [London] : Corgi, 1980. — 366p ; 18cm
ISBN 0-552-11537-1 (pbk) : £1.75 B81-08022

Vanner, Lyn. Rannoch Chase / Lyn Vanner. — London : Corgi, 1981. — 320p ; 18cm
ISBN 0-552-11664-5 (pbk) : £1.50 B81-32107

Vansittart, Peter. The death of Robin Hood : a novel / Peter Vansittart. — London : Owen, 1981. — 224p ; 23cm
ISBN 0-7206-0576-8 : £7.50 B81-03079

Venables, Hubert. The Frankenstein diaries / translated from the original German and edited [i.e. written] by Hubert Venables. — London : Hutchinson, 1980. — 120p : ill ; 25cm
ISBN 0-09-142670-7 : £4.95 : CIP rev. B80-13547

Venters, Archie. Death below zero / by Archie Venters. — London : Hale, 1981. — 191p ; 20cm
ISBN 0-7091-9158-8 : £5.95 B81-35215

Vern, Sarah. Forbidden desires / by Sarah Vern. — London : Hale, 1981. — 191p ; 20cm
ISBN 0-7091-8945-1 : £5.60 B81-27308

Vern, Sarah. Mutinous heart / by Sarah Vern. — London : Hale, 1980. — 188p ; 20cm
ISBN 0-7091-8010-1 : £4.95 B81-00568

Vern, Sarah. An unconditional love / by Sarah Vern. — London : Hale, 1981. — 175p ; 20cm
ISBN 0-7091-8747-5 : £5.50 B81-14087

Vernon, Claire. Doctor on safari / Claire Vernon. — Large print ed. — Bath : Chivers, 1981, c1964. — 275p ; 23cm. — (A Lythway book)
Originally published: London : Hale, 1964
ISBN 0-85119-738-8 : Unpriced : CIP rev. B81-19111

Vernon, Dorothy. Awaken the heart / Dorothy Vernon. — [London] : Silhouette, 1981, c1980. — 189p ; 18cm. — (Silhouette romance ; no.11)
ISBN 0-340-26008-4 (pbk) : £0.65 : CIP rev. B80-19974

Vernon, Dorothy. Kissed by moonlight / Dorothy Vernon. — London : Silhouette, 1981. — 188p ; 18cm. — (Silhouette romance ; 59)
ISBN 0-340-27114-0 (pbk) : £0.65 : CIP rev. B81-23934

Vernon, Marjorie. But is it love? / by Marjorie Vernon. — London : Hale, 1981. — 208p ; 20cm
ISBN 0-7091-9069-7 : £5.60 B81-27318

Vernon, Marjorie. The desperate search / by Marjorie Vernon. — London : Hale, 1981. — 208p ; 20cm
ISBN 0-7091-8712-2 : £5.50 B81-08734

Veronese, Gina. House of Satan / Gina Veronese. — London : Mills & Boon, 1980. — 188p ; 20cm. — (Masquerade)
ISBN 0-263-09674-2 : £3.85 B81-00569

Veryan, Patricia. [The Lord and the gypsy]. Debt of honour / Patricia Veryan. — [London] : Fontana/Collins, 1981, c1978. — 283p ; 18cm
Originally published: New York : Walker, 1978 ; London : Souvenir, 1980
ISBN 0-00-616250-9 (pbk) : £1.50 B81-15527

Veryan, Patricia. [Love's duet]. A perfect match / Patricia Veryan. — London : Souvenir, 1981, c1979. — 317p ; 21cm
Originally published: New York : Walker, 1979
ISBN 0-285-62472-5 : £7.95 B81-19433

Vivian, Anna. Gypsy Hollow / by Anna Vivian. — London : Hale, 1981. — 190p ; 20cm
ISBN 0-7091-9185-5 : £6.75 B81-33520

Von Waldon, Suzanne. The heart leads the way / Suzanne von Waldon. — Bognor Regis : New Horizon, c1981. — 149p ; 22cm
ISBN 0-86116-702-3 : £5.25 B81-29958

Vyse, Michael. Overworld / Michael Vyse. — London : Faber, 1980. — 154p ; 21cm
ISBN 0-571-11621-3 : £5.95 : CIP rev. B80-26198

Wagner, Geoffrey. The killing time / Geoffrey Wagner. — London : Sphere, 1981. — 316p ; 18cm
ISBN 0-7221-8780-7 (pbk) : £1.75 B81-24706

Wainwright, John. An urge for justice / John Wainwright. — London : Macmillan, 1981. — 192p ; 21cm
ISBN 0-333-32231-2 : £5.50 B81-39441

Wainwright, John, *1921-*. All on a summer's day / John Wainwright. — London : Macmillan, 1981. — 290p ; 21cm
ISBN 0-333-31310-0 : £5.95 B81-22322

Wainwright, John, *1921-*. Duty elsewhere / John Wainwright. — Large print ed. — Leicester : Ulverscroft, 1981, c1979. — 302p ; 23cm. — (Ulverscroft large print series)
Originally published: London : Collins, 1979
ISBN 0-7089-0563-3 : £5.00 B81-11390

Wainwright, John, *1921-*. A kill of small consequence / John Wainwright. — London : Macmillan, 1980. — 222p ; 21cm
ISBN 0-333-30041-6 : £5.50 B81-01509

Wainwright, John, *1921-*. Landscape with violence. — Large print ed. — Anstey : Ulverscroft, Oct.1981. — [496]p. — (Ulverscroft large print series)
Originally published: London : Macmillan, 1975
ISBN 0-7089-0690-7 : £5.00 : CIP entry B81-28101

Wainwright, John, *1921-*. Man of law / John Wainwright. — London : Macmillan, 1980. — 222p ; 21cm
ISBN 0-333-29175-1 : £5.50
ISBN 0-333-29175-1 B81-03481

Wainwright, John, *1921-*. The reluctant sleeper. — Large print ed. — Bath : Chivers, Jan.1982. — [264]p. — (A Lythway book)
Originally published: London : Macmillan, 1979
ISBN 0-85119-779-5 : £6.70 : CIP entry B81-33794

Wainwright, John, *1921-*. The tainted man / John Wainwright. — London : Macmillan, 1980. — 178p ; 21cm
ISBN 0-333-30969-3 : £5.50 B81-14242

823'.914[F] — Fiction in English, *1945- — Texts continuation*

Wainwright, John, *1921-*. Tension / John Wainwright. — London : Magnum, 1981, c1979. — 192p ; 18cm
Originally published: London : Macmillan, 1979
ISBN 0-417-06110-2 (pbk) : £1.50 B81-28611

Wainwright, John, *1921-*. Tension / John Wainwright. — Large print ed.. — Bath : Chivers, 1981, c1979. — 246p ; 23cm. — (A Lythway thriller)
Originally published: Macmillan, 1979
ISBN 0-85119-707-8 : £5.25 B81-08679

Wainwright, John, *1921-*. The Venus Fly-Trap / John Wainwright. — Large print ed. — Bath : Chivers, 1981, c1980. — 286p ; 23cm. — (A Lythway book)
Originally published: London : Macmillan, 1980
ISBN 0-85119-739-6 : Unpriced : CIP rev. B81-19113

Wakeley, Dorothy. Mercy's story / by Dorothy Wakeley. — London : Hale, 1981. — 191p ; 20cm
ISBN 0-7091-8676-2 : £6.25 B81-08960

Walker, Henry. Sunrise, sunset / Henry Walker. — Bognor Regis : New Horizon, c1980. — 353p ; 22cm
ISBN 0-86116-580-2 : £5.75 B81-20953

Walker, Peter N.. Siege for Panda One / by Peter N. Walker. — London : Hale, 1981. — 192p ; 20cm
ISBN 0-7091-8786-6 : £5.75 B81-08647

Wallace, Jane. Fugitive summer / Jane Walace. — London : New English Library, 1981. — 253p ; 23cm
ISBN 0-450-04840-3 : £5.50 B81-15424

Walsh, Bill, *1933-*. Live bait / by Bill Walsh. — London : Hale, 1981. — 187p ; 20cm
ISBN 0-7091-9014-x : £5.95 B81-15385

Warby, Marjorie. The stars are fire / Marjorie Warby. — Large print ed. — Bath : Chivers, 1981, c1973. — 236p ; 23cm. — (A Seymour book)
Originally published: London : Collins, 1973
ISBN 0-85119-410-9 : Unpriced B81-12127

Ward, Edmund. The Baltic emerald / Edmund Ward. — London : Eyre Methuen, 1981. — 217p ; 23cm
ISBN 0-413-47780-0 : £6.50 B81-12252

Ward, Kate. Bid time delay / by Kate Ward. — London : Hale, 1981. — 190p ; 20cm
ISBN 0-7091-9079-4 : £5.60 B81-35208

Ward, Kate. Causeway to happiness / by Kate Ward. — London : Hale, 1981. — 206p ; 20cm
ISBN 0-7091-8722-x : £5.50 B81-11173

Warde, Joan. Casualty doctor / Joan Warde. — London : Hale, 1981. — 160p ; 20cm
ISBN 0-7091-8542-1 : £5.25 B81-08959

Warde, Joan. Flower of love / by Joan Warde. — London : Hale, 1981. — 160p ; 20cm
ISBN 0-7091-9044-1 : £5.60 B81-24437

Warmington, Mary Jane. Bought for gold / Mary Jane Warmington. — London : Macdonald Futura, 1981. — 252p ; 21cm
ISBN 0-354-04628-4 : £4.95 B81-12061

Warmington, Mary Jane. Bought for gold / Mary Jane Warmington. — London : Macdonald Futura, 1981. — 252p : ill ; 18cm. — (A Minstrel book ; 6)
ISBN 0-7088-2016-6 (pbk) : £0.95 B81-15466

Warmington, Mary Jane. Bride in sables / Mary Jane Warmington. — London : Macdonald Futura, 1981. — 252p ; 18cm. — (A Minstrel book ; 20)
ISBN 0-7088-2099-9 (pbk) : £0.95 B81-40948

Warmington, Mary Jane. Velvet rose / Mary Jane Warmington. — London : Macdonald Futura, 1981. — 254p ; 21cm. — (Minstrel romance)
ISBN 0-354-04654-3 : £4.95 B81-24830

Warnock, William. The Samurai kites / Williams Warnock. — London : Sphere, 1981. — 250p ; 18cm
ISBN 0-7221-8903-6 (pbk) : £1.50 B81-28748

Waterhouse, Keith. Maggie Muggins, or, Spring in Earl's Court / Keith Waterhouse. — London : Joseph, c1981. — 220p ; 23cm
ISBN 0-7181-2014-0 : £6.95 B81-20941

Watkins, Ivor. The blood snarl / Ivor Watkins. — London : Macdonald Futura, 1980. — 347p ; 18cm
ISBN 0-7088-1729-7 (pbk) : £1.50 B81-02472

Watkins, Jean. The impatient heart / Jean Watkins. — London : Hale, 1980. — 176p ; 20cm
ISBN 0-7091-8301-1 : £5.25 B81-00571

Watkins, Michael. The gift : an East Anglian fable / by Michael Watkins ; [illustrated by Oona Harte]. — Ipswich : East Anglian Magazine, [1981?]. — 30p : ill ; 18cm
ISBN 0-900227-53-2 (pbk) : £1.50 B81-17403

Watson, Colin, *1920-*. Plaster sinners / Colin Watson. — London : Eyre Methuen, 1980. — 159p ; 23cm
ISBN 0-413-39040-3 : £5.95 : CIP rev. B80-18499

Watson, Ian. Deathhunter / by Ian Watson. — London : Gollancz, 1981. — 173p ; 21cm
ISBN 0-575-03023-2 : £6.95 B81-39425

Watson, Ian. The embedding / Ian Watson. — London : Granada, 1980, c1973. — 185p ; 18cm. — (A Panther book) (Panther science fiction)
Originally published: London : Gollancz, 1973
ISBN 0-586-05190-2 (pbk) : £1.25 B81-19916

Watson, Ian. Under heaven's bridge / by Ian Watson and Michael Bishop. — London : Gollancz, 1980. — 159p ; 21cm
ISBN 0-575-02927-7 : £6.95 B81-12305

Watson, Julia, *1943-*. Love song / Julia Watson. — London : Macdonald Futura, 1981. — 254p ; 21cm
ISBN 0-354-04627-6 : £4.95 B81-12068

Watson, Julia, *1943-*. Love song / Julia Watson. — London : Macdonald Futura, 1981. — 254p : ill ; 18cm. — (A Minstrel book ; 7)
ISBN 0-7088-2023-9 (pbk) : £0.95 B81-15467

Watts, A. F.. Life in the raw is seldom mild / A.F. Watts. — Bognor Regis : New Horizon, c1980. — 385p ; 22cm
ISBN 0-86116-541-1 : £5.75 B81-18883

Way, Margaret. King Country / Margaret Way. — Large print ed. — Leicester : Ulverscroft, 1981, c1970. — 340p ; 23cm
Originally published: London : Mills & Boon, 1970
ISBN 0-7089-0678-8 : £5.00 : CIP rev. B81-25673

Way, Margaret. The McIvor affair / by Margaret Way. — London : Mills & Boon, 1981. — 188p ; 19cm
ISBN 0-263-09828-1 : £4.55 B81-10883

Way, Margaret. A season for change / by Margaret Way. — London : Mills & Boon, 1981. — 189p ; 20cm
ISBN 0-263-09852-4 : £4.55 B81-14241

Way, Margaret. Shadow dance / by Margaret Way. — London : Mills & Boon, 1981. — 187p ; 20cm
ISBN 0-263-09819-2 : £4.55 B81-09410

Way, Margaret. Temple of fire / by Margaret Way. — London : Mills and Boon, 1981, c1980. — 189p ; 19cm
ISBN 0-263-09770-6 (cased) : £3.85
ISBN 0-263-73428-5 (pbk) : unpriced B81-06430

Weale, Anne. Bed of roses / by Anne Weale. — London : Mills & Boon, 1981. — 191p ; 19cm
ISBN 0-263-09840-0 : £4.55 B81-10977

Weale, Anne. Blue days at sea / by Anne Weale. — London : Mills & Boon, 1981. — 189p ; 20cm
ISBN 0-263-09921-0 : £4.55 B81-35646

Weale, Anne. The last night at paradise / by Anne Weale. — London : Mills & Boon, 1980. — 187p ; 20cm
ISBN 0-263-09747-1 : £3.85 B81-00572

Weale, Anne. Rain of diamonds / by Anne Weale. — London : Mills & Boon, 1981. — 188p ; 20cm
ISBN 0-263-09843-5 : £4.55 B81-14180

Weale, Anne. A touch of the devil / Anne Weale. — Large print ed. — Bath : Chivers, 1981, c1980. — 261p ; 23cm. — (A Seymour book)
Originally published: London : Mills & Boon, 1980
ISBN 0-85119-423-0 : Unpriced : CIP rev. B81-13542

Weale, Anne. Until we meet / Anne Weale. — Large print ed. — Leicester : Ulverscroft, 1980, c1961. — 317p ; 23cm. — (Ulverscroft large print series)
Originally published: London : Mills & Boon, 1961
ISBN 0-7089-0511-0 : £4.25 : CIP rev. B80-18024

Webb, Michael, *1954-*. Club — mink lined murder / Michael Webb. — Bognor Regis : New Horizon, c1978. — 132p ; 22cm
ISBN 0-86116-073-8 : £3.50 B81-19246

Webb, Neil. Hardcase law / by Neil Webb. — London : Hale, 1981. — 160p ; 20cm
ISBN 0-7091-8820-x : £4.95 B81-08737

Webster, Ernest. The Friulan plot / by Ernest Webster. — London : Hale, 1980. — 192p ; 20cm
ISBN 0-7091-8530-8 : £5.75 B81-00573

Webster, Ernest. Madonna of the black market / by Ernest Webster. — London : Hale, 1981. — 158p ; 20cm
ISBN 0-7091-9102-2 : £5.95 B81-24442

Webster, Jan. Beggarman's country. — Large print ed. — Anstey : Ulverscroft, Nov.1981. — [528]p. — (Ulverscroft large print series)
Originally published: London : Collins, 1979
ISBN 0-7089-0713-x : £5.00 : CIP entry B81-30366

Webster, Jan. Colliers Row / Jan Webster. — Large print ed. — Leicester : Ulverscroft, 1981, c1977. — 474p ; 23cm. — (Ulverscroft large print series)
Originally published: London : Collins, 1977
ISBN 0-7089-0656-7 : £5.00 B81-28567

Webster, Jan. Due South. — London : Collins, Jan.1982. — [360]p
ISBN 0-00-221435-0 : £7.25 : CIP entry B81-33966

823'.914[F] — Fiction in English, *1945- — Texts continuation*

Webster, Jan. Saturday city / Jan Webster. — Large print ed. — Leicester : Ulverscroft, 1981, c1978. — 479p : 1geneal.table ; 23cm. — (Ulverscroft large print series)
Originally published: New York : St. Martin's Press ; London : Collins, 1978
ISBN 0-7089-0684-2 : £5.00 : CIP rev. B81-25765

Webster, Joanne. Kissing time / Joanne Webster. — London : Hodder and Stoughton, c1981. — 110p ; 23cm
ISBN 0-340-25889-6 : £4.95 B81-33482

Weigh, Iris. A shared legacy / by Iris Weigh. — London : Hale, 1981. — 174p ; 20cm
ISBN 0-7091-8899-4 : £5.60 B81-21293

Weldon, Fay. The fat woman's joke / Fay Weldon. — London : Hodder and Stoughton, 1981, c1967. — 136p ; 23cm
Originally published: London : MacGibbon, 1967
ISBN 0-340-26130-7 : £6.50 B81-18682

Weldon, Fay. Puffball. — London : Hodder and Stoughton, May 1981. — [272]p
Originally published: 1980
ISBN 0-340-26662-7 (pbk) : £1.25 : CIP entry B81-03819

Wellesbourne, Peter. Operation Albatross / Peter Wellesbourne. — London : Hale, 1981. — 222p ; 21cm
ISBN 0-7091-8845-5 : £7.50 B81-14068

Welsh, Ken. Fear for the hero! / Ken Welsh. — London : Eyre Methuen, 1981. — 282p ; 19cm
ISBN 0-413-48390-8 : £3.95 B81-12253

Welsh, Ken. Fear for the hero! / Ken Welsh. — London : Magnum, 1981. — 282p ; 18cm
ISBN 0-417-05570-6 (pbk) : £1.50 B81-08418

Wentworth, Patricia. The silent pool / Patricia Wentworth. — Large print ed. — Leicester : Ulverscroft, 1980, c1956. — 423p ; 23cm. — (Ulverscroft large print series)
Originally published: London : Hodder & Stoughton, 1956
ISBN 0-7089-0549-8 : £4.25 : CIP rev. B80-35461

Wentworth, Sally. The Judas kiss / by Sally Wentworth. — London : Mills & Boon, 1981. — 187p ; 20cm
ISBN 0-263-09932-6 : £4.55 B81-35638

Wentworth, Sally. King of Culla / by Sally Wentworth. — London : Mills & Boon, 1981. — 186p ; 19cm
ISBN 0-263-09880-x : £4.55 B81-26415

Wentworth, Sally. Race against love / by Sally Wentworth. — London : Mills & Boon, 1980. — 186p ; 19cm
ISBN 0-263-09741-2 : £3.85 B81-00574

Wentworth, Sally. Summer fire / by Sally Wentworth. — London : Mills & Boon, 1981. — 187p ; 20cm
ISBN 0-263-09858-3 : £4.55 B81-18356

Wessex, Raymond. It's a dog's life / Raymond Wessex ; illustrated by Jayne Southfield. — Bognor Regis : New Horizon, c1980. — 110p,[10] leaves of plates : ill ; 21cm
ISBN 0-86116-274-9 : £4.50 B81-19028

West, Anna. A ring at the ready / by Anna West. — London : Hale, 1981. — 159p ; 20cm
ISBN 0-7091-8811-0 : £5.50 B81-15947

Westall, Robert. The devil on the road / Robert Westall. — Harmondsworth : Puffin, 1981, c1978. — 247p : 1ill ; 18cm. — (Puffin plus)
Originally published: London : Macmillan, 1978
ISBN 0-14-031358-3 (pbk) : £1.15 B81-35470

Westall, Robert. The scarecrows / Robert Westall. — London : Chatto & Windus, 1981. — 159p ; 21cm
ISBN 0-7011-2556-x : £5.50 B81-11645

Weston, Sophie. Tomorrow starts at midnight / by Sophie Weston. — London : Mills & Boon, 1980. — 189p ; 20cm
ISBN 0-263-09744-7 : £3.85 B81-00575

Westwood, Gwen. Dangerous to love / by Gwen Westwood. — London : Mills and Boon, 1981. — 192p ; 19cm
ISBN 0-263-09945-8 : £4.55 B81-40865

Westwood, Gwen. Keeper of the heart. — Large print ed. — Anstey : Ulverscroft, Dec.1981. — [384]p. — (Ulverscroft large print series)
Originally published: London : Mills and Boon, 1969
ISBN 0-7089-0721-0 : £5.00 : CIP entry B81-32036

Westwood, Gwen. Zulu moon / by Gwen Westwood. — London : Mills & Boon, 1980. — 189p ; 19cm
ISBN 0-263-09760-9 : £3.85 B81-01510

Whalen, Steve. Deep water. — London : Arlington Books, Sept.1981. — [320]p
ISBN 0-85140-546-0 : £6.95 : CIP entry B81-20095

Wheatley, Dennis. The Malinsay masacre : a murder mystery / Dennis Wheatley ; planned by J.G. Links. — Exeter : Webb & Bower, 1981. — 92leaves : ill,maps,facsims,plans,1geneal.table ; 27cm
Facsim of: edition published London : Hutchinson, 1938. — Leaves vary in size ; some printed on both sides
ISBN 0-906671-40-x (pbk) : £9.95 B81-12947

Whitby, Sharon. The houseless one / Sharon Whitby. — London : Hale, 1981. — 220p ; 21cm
ISBN 0-7091-8963-x : £6.25 B81-19226

Whitby, Sharon. No song at Morningside / Sharon Whitby. — London : Hale, 1981. — 205p ; 20cm
ISBN 0-7091-9119-7 : £6.75 B81-37305

Whitby, Sharon. The silky / Sharon Whitby. — London : Hale, 1980. — 191p ; 21cm
ISBN 0-7091-8569-3 : £6.25 B81-02072

White, Alan, *1924-*. Cassidy's Yard. — Large print ed. — Bath : Chivers, Nov.1981. — [304] p. — (A Lythway book)
Originally published: London : Granada, 1980
ISBN 0-85119-763-9 : £6.90 : CIP entry B81-31270

White, Alan, *1924-*. The homeward tide / Alan White. — London : Granada, 1981. — 443p ; 23cm
ISBN 0-246-11393-6 : £6.95 B81-21213

White, Alan, *1924-*. Ravenswyke / Alan White. — London : Granada, 1981, c1980. — 380p ; 18cm. — (A Mayflower book)
Originally published: London : Hutchinson, 1980
ISBN 0-583-13231-6 (pbk) : £1.95 B81-26411

White, James, *1928-*. Ambulance ship / James White. — London : Corgi, 1980. — 224p ; 18cm
ISBN 0-552-11511-8 (pbk) : £1.25 B81-07354

Whitehead, Barbara, *1930-*. The caretaker wife / by Barbara Whitehead. — Bolton-By-Bowland : Magna Print, 1980, c1977. — 345p ; 23cm
Originally published: London : Heinemann, 1977. — Published in large print
ISBN 0-86009-273-9 : £5.25 : CIP rev. B80-22596

Whitehead, Barbara, *1930-*. Quicksilver lady / by Barbara Whitehead. — Bolton-by-Bowland : Magna, 1981, c1979. — 471p ; 23cm
Originally published: London : Heinemann, 1979. — Published in large print
ISBN 0-86009-314-x : £5.75 : CIP rev. B81-03715

Whiting, Dajmar L.. The wings of the sun / Dajmar L. Whiting. — London : Hale, 1980. — 208p ; 21cm
ISBN 0-7091-8470-0 : £6.25 B81-00576

Whittal, Yvonne. East to Barryvale. — Large print ed. — Bath : Chivers Press, Feb.1982. — [240]p. — (A Lythway book)
Originally published: London : Mills & Boon, 1976
ISBN 0-85119-788-4 : £6.90 : CIP entry B81-35858

Whittal, Yvonne. The light within / by Yvonne Whittal. — London : Mills & Boon, 1981. — 189p ; 20cm
ISBN 0-263-09817-6 : £4.55 B81-09407

Whittal, Yvonne. The lion of La Roche / by Yvonne Whittal. — London : Mills & Boon, 1981. — 190p ; 20cm
ISBN 0-263-09884-2 : £4.55 B81-28518

Whittal, Yvonne. Season of shadows / by Yvonne Whittal. — London : Mills & Boon, 1980. — 187p ; 19cm
ISBN 0-263-09752-8 : £3.85 B81-00577

Whittal, Yvonne. The spotted plume / by Yvonne Whittal. — London : Mills & Boon, 1981. — 188p ; 20cm
ISBN 0-263-09931-8 : £4.55 B81-35637

Whittal, Yvonne. Where two ways meet / by Yvonne Whittal. — London : Mills & Boon, 1981. — 187p ; 20cm
ISBN 0-263-09850-8 : £4.55 B81-14179

Whittle, Norah. Above the shadows / Norah Whittle. — Large print ed. — Bath : Chivers, 1981, c1965. — 243p ; 23cm. — (A Seymour book)
Originally published: London : Hurst & Blackett, 1965
ISBN 0-85119-411-7 : Unpriced B81-12128

Whittle, Norah. After the ball / Norah Whittle. — Large print ed. — Bath : Chivers, 1981, c1967. — 250p ; 23cm. — (A Seymour book)
Originally published: London : Hurst & Blackett, 1967
ISBN 0-85119-403-6 : Unpriced B81-08508

Whittle, Norah. Crowsfell / Norah Whittle. — Large print ed. — Bath : Chivers, 1981, c1967. — 280p ; 23cm. — (A Seymour book)
Originally published: London : Hurst & Blackett, 1967
ISBN 0-85119-427-3 : Unpriced : CIP rev. B81-13708

Whittle, Norah. In search of a name. — Large print ed. — Bath : Chivers, Feb.1982. — [224] p. — (A Seymour book)
Originally published: London : Hurst and Blackett, 1972
ISBN 0-85119-455-9 : £4.95 : CIP entry B81-36058

Whittle, Norah. Listener's folly / Norah Whittle. — Large print ed. — Bath : Chivers, 1981, c1968. — 276p ; 23cm. — (A Seymour book)
Originally published: London : Hurst & Blackett, 1968
ISBN 0-85119-418-4 : £4.95 : CIP rev. B81-08895

Whittle, Tyler. The house of Flavell / Tyler Whittle. — Loughton : Piatkus, 1981. — 327p ; 21cm
ISBN 0-86188-102-8 : £6.95 : CIP rev. B81-09474

823'.914[F] — Fiction in English, *1945-* — *Texts continuation*

Wiat, Philippa. The golden chariot / Philippa Wiat. — Large print ed. — London : Hale, 1980, c1979. — 320p ; 23cm
Originally published: 1979
ISBN 0-7091-8612-6 : £5.80 B81-00578

Wiat, Philippa. The king's vengeance / Philippa Wiat. — London : Hale, 1980. — 175p ; 23cm
ISBN 0-7091-8390-9 : £6.25 B81-11738

Wiat, Philippa. Lord of the Wolf / by Philippa Wiat. — London : Hale, 1980. — 270p : 2geneal.tables ; 23cm
ISBN 0-7091-8208-2 : £5.95 B81-00579

Wiat, Philippa. Shadow of Samain / Philippa Wiat. — Large print ed. — London : Hale, 1980. — 272p ; 23cm
ISBN 0-7091-8617-7 : £5.20 B81-02702

Wibberley, Mary. A dangerous man. — Large print ed. — Bath : Chivers, Nov.1981. — [256] p. — (A Seymour book)
Originally published: London : Mills & Boon, 1979
ISBN 0-85119-443-5 : £5.25 : CIP entry B81-31251

Wibberley, Mary. Devil's causeway / by Mary Wibberley. — London : Mills & Boon, 1981. — 187p ; 19cm
ISBN 0-263-09836-2 : £4.55 B81-10888

Wibberley, Mary. A dream of thee / by Mary Wibberley. — London : Mills & Boon, 1980. — 186p ; 20cm
ISBN 0-263-09751-x : £3.85 B81-00580

Wibberley, Mary. Fire and steel / by Mary Wibberley. — London : Mills & Boon, 1980. — 187p ; 19cm
ISBN 0-263-09765-x : £3.85 B81-01511

Wibberley, Mary. Gold to remember / by Mary Wibberley. — London : Mills & Boon, 1981. — 188p ; 20cm
ISBN 0-263-09851-6 : £4.55 B81-14240

Wigan, Christopher. Buckboard Barber / Christopher Wigan. — London : Hale, 1981. — 160p ; 20cm
ISBN 0-7091-9129-4 : £4.95 B81-27295

Wight, E. B.. Tangled web / E.B. Wight. — Ilfracombe : Stockwell, 1980. — 150p ; 19cm
ISBN 0-7223-1421-3 : £6.00 B81-03340

Wilcox, Ronald. The centre of the wheel / by Ronald Wilcox. — London : Hale, 1981. — 224p ; 20cm
ISBN 0-7091-8665-7 : £6.25 B81-15301

Wildman, Faye. Rain lady / Faye Wildman. — [London] : Silhouette, 1981, c1980. — 190p ; 18cm. — (Silhouette romance ; 28)
ISBN 0-340-26578-7 (pbk) : £0.65 : CIP rev. B81-02564

Wiles, Domini. The Betrayer / Domini Wiles. — London : Pan in association with Collins, 1981, c1979. — 158p ; 18cm
Originally published: London : Collins, 1979
ISBN 0-330-26280-7 (pbk) : £1.25 B81-12073

Wilkinson, Margaret. The shadow of Marissa / by Margaret Wilkinson. — London : Hale, 1980. — 160p ; 20cm
ISBN 0-7091-8407-7 : £5.25 B81-00581

Williams, Alan, *1935 Aug.-*. Dead secret / Alan Williams. — London : Granada, 1980 (1981 [printing]). — 281p ; 18cm. — (A Panther book)
ISBN 0-586-04533-3 (pbk) : £1.50 B81-07401

Williams, Alan, *1935 Aug.-*. Holy of holies / Alan Williams. — London : Granada, 1981. — 382p ; 23cm
ISBN 0-246-11307-3 : £6.95 B81-10075

Williams, David, *1926-*. Treasure up in smoke / David Williams. — London : Granada, 1980, c1978. — 192p ; 18cm. — (A Panther book)
Originally published: London : Collins, 1978
ISBN 0-586-05101-5 (pbk) : £0.95 B81-06400

Williams, David, *1931-*. Bluebirds over / David Williams. — London : New English Library, 1981. — 158p ; 18cm. — (Fighter ; 1)
ISBN 0-450-04670-2 (pbk) : £1.00 B81-09566

Williams, David, *1931-*. Bluebirds over. — London : Severn House, Dec.1981. — [160]p. — (Fighter ; 1)
ISBN 0-7278-0753-6 : £5.95 : CIP entry B81-31626

Williams, Eric, *1911 July 13-*. Dragoman Press : an adventure in the Balkans / Eric Williams. — London : Remploy, 1979. — 255p ; 22cm
Originally published : London: Collins, 1959
ISBN 0-7066-0829-1 : £4.20 B81-38044

Williams, Eric C.. Homo telekins / by Eric C. Williams. — London : Hale, 1981. — 208p ; 20cm. — (Hale SF)
ISBN 0-7091-8848-x : £6.75 B81-16005

Williams, Gordon, *1934-*. [The microcolony]. Micronaut world / Gordon Williams. — London : New English Library, 1981, c1979. — 221p ; 18cm
Originally published: New York : Bantam, 1979
ISBN 0-450-05133-1 (pbk) : £1.50 B81-24743

Williams, Gordon, *1934-*. The micronauts / Gordon Williams. — London : New English Library, 1981, c1977. — 218p : 1ill ; 18cm
Originally published: New York : Bantam, 1977
ISBN 0-450-05023-8 (pbk) : £1.50 B81-03064

Williams, Gordon, *1934-*. Revolt of the micronauts / Gordon Williams. — London : New English Library, 1981. — 192p ; 19cm
ISBN 0-450-05239-7 (pbk) : £1.50 B81-35626

Williams, Jennifer. Isabelle / by Jennifer Williams. — London : Hale, 1980. — 207p ; 21cm
ISBN 0-7091-8673-8 : £6.25 B81-03403

Williams, Lawrence, *1915-*. A copper snare / by Lawrence Williams. — London : Hale, 1980. — 190p ; 20cm
ISBN 0-7091-8332-1 : £5.25 B81-01512

Williams, Louie. Doctor's house / by Louie Williams. — London : Hale, 1980. — 157p ; 20cm
ISBN 0-7091-8049-7 : £4.75 B81-00582

Williams, Louie. I'll marry a doctor / by Louie Williams. — London : Hale, 1980. — 175p ; 20cm
ISBN 0-7091-8541-3 : £5.25 B81-00583

Williams, Louie. Nurse's diary / by Louie Williams. — London : Hale, 1981. — 176p ; 20cm
ISBN 0-7091-9391-2 : £5.75 B81-37299

Williams, Malcolm. Poor little rich girl / by Malcolm Williams. — London : Hale, 1981. — 156p ; 20cm
ISBN 0-7091-9045-x : £5.60 B81-24876

Williams, Mary. Return to Carnecrane / Mary Williams. — London : Kimber, 1981. — 238p ; 23cm
ISBN 0-7183-0088-2 : £5.95 B81-21191

Williams, Mary. Trenhawk : a romantic novel of Cornwall / Mary Williams. — London : Kimber, 1980. — 317p ; 23cm
ISBN 0-7183-0437-3 : £6.50 B81-01513

Williams, Mary-Beth. The glorious Grahams / by Mary-Beth Williams. — London : Hale, 1981. — 176p ; 20cm
ISBN 0-7091-8922-2 : £5.60 B81-21299

Williams, Mary-Beth. Mistress of Ravensmere / by Mary-Beth Williams. — London : Hale, 1981. — 176p ; 20cm
ISBN 0-7091-8466-2 : £5.50 B81-03015

Williams, Mary-Beth. Rose Marten — adventuress / by Mary-Beth Williams. — London : Hale, 1980. — 188p ; 20cm
ISBN 0-7091-8229-5 : £4.95 B81-00584

Williams, Veronica. A house in shadow / Veronica Williams. — London : Hale, 1981. — 174p ; 21cm
ISBN 0-7091-8769-6 : £5.95 B81-11731

Williamson, Tony. The connector / Tony Williamson. — [London] : Fontana, 1977, c1976 (1980 [printing]). — 192p ; 18cm
Originally published: London : Collins, 1976
ISBN 0-00-615775-0 (pbk) : £1.00 B81-11884

Williamson, Tony. The Samson strike / Tony Williamson. — [London] : Fontana, 1980, c1979. — 220p ; 18cm
Originally published: London : Collins, 1979
ISBN 0-00-616002-6 (pbk) : £1.25 B81-11885

Williamson, Tony. Technicians of death / by Tony Williamson. — Long Preston : Magna, 1981, c1978. — 527p ; 23cm
Originally published: New York : Atheneum ; London : Collins 1978
ISBN 0-86009-320-4 : Unpriced : CIP rev. B81-11972

Williamson, Tony. Warhead. — London : Collins, Jan.1982. — [222]p
ISBN 0-00-222626-x : CIP entry B81-34584

Wilson, A. N.. Who was Oswald Fish?. — London : Secker & Warburg, Oct.1981. — [320]p
ISBN 0-436-57606-6 : £6.95 : CIP entry B81-25324

Wilson, Anna. Cactus / by Anna Wilson. — London (38 Mount Pleasant, W.C.1) : Onlywomen, c1980. — 155p ; 20cm
ISBN 0-906500-04-4 (pbk) : £2.25 B81-00585

Wilson, David, *19---*. Witches' cauldron / David Wilson. — London : Hale, 1981. — 192p ; 20cm
ISBN 0-7091-8797-1 : £6.25 B81-24866

Wilson, Derek. Bear rampant. — London : H. Hamilton, Sept.1981. — [320]p
ISBN 0-241-10147-6 : £7.50 : CIP entry B81-20580

Wilson, Gina. A friendship of equals / Gina Wilson. — London : Faber, 1981. — 156p ; 21cm
For adolescents
ISBN 0-571-11632-9 : £4.50 : CIP rev. B81-07490

Wilson, Jeanne. Troubled heritage / Jeanne Wilson. — London : Arrow, 1979, c1977. — 271p : 3geneal.tables ; 18cm. — (An island chronicle ; v.2)
Originally published: London : Macmillan, 1977
ISBN 0-09-920150-x (pbk) : £0.95 B81-13133

Wilson, Scott. The copper city / by Scott Wilson. — London : Hale, 1981. — 159p ; 20cm. — (Quantro ; 2)
ISBN 0-7091-8522-7 : £4.95 B81-08641

Wilson, Scott. Desperadoes / by Scott Wilson. — London : Hale, 1981. — 160p ; 20cm
ISBN 0-7091-8819-6 : £4.95 B81-24986

823'.914[F] — Fiction in English, *1945-* — *Texts continuation*

Wilson, Scott. The fight at Hueco Tanks / by Scott Wilson. — London : Hale, 1980. — 158p ; 20cm
Bibliography: p158
ISBN 0-7091-8399-2 : £4.95 B81-01514

Wilson, Steve. Dealer's war / Steve Wilson. — London : Macmillan, 1980. — 255p ; 21cm
ISBN 0-333-27121-1 : £5.95 B81-00586

Wilson Guinne de Martyn (Vaux) et Crevecoeur, Iain. Knight to Queen's castle / Iain Wilson Guinne de Martyn (Vaux) et Crevecoeur. — Bognor Regis : New Horizon, c1979. — 183p ; 21cm
ISBN 0-86116-165-3 : £2.95 B81-19235

Wiltshire, David, *1935-*. [Child of Vodyanoi]. The nightmare man / David Wiltshire. — London : Hamlyn Paperbacks, c1978. — 192p ; 18cm
Originally published: London : Hale, 1978
ISBN 0-600-20447-2 (pbk) : £1.10 B81-19893

Wiltshire, David, *1935-*. Genesis II / by David Wiltshire. — London : Hale, 1981. — 189p ; 20cm. — (Hale SF)
ISBN 0-7091-9157-x : £6.25 B81-35203

Winch, Arden. Blood money / Arden Winch. — London : British Broadcasting Corporation, c1981. — 284p ; 22cm
ISBN 0-563-17879-5 : £8.25 B81-36828

Winch, Arden. Blood money / Arden Winch. — London : B.B.C., 1981. — 284p ; 18cm
ISBN 0-563-17880-9 (pbk) : £1.50 B81-35648

Winchester, Jack. The solitary man / Jack Winchester. — London : Sphere, 1981, c1980. — 184p ; 18cm
Originally published: London : Hamish Hamilton, 1980
ISBN 0-7221-3664-1 (pbk) : £1.25 B81-36823

Winchester, Kay. For love of you / Kay Winchester. — Large print ed. — Bath : Chivers, 1981, c1958. — 271p ; 23cm. — (A Seymour book)
Originally published: London : Ward, Lock, 1958
ISBN 0-85119-419-2 : £4.95 : CIP rev. B81-08896

Winchester, Kay. Return to Rowanstoke / by Kay Winchester. — London : Hale, 1980. — 158p ; 20cm
ISBN 0-7091-8573-1 : £5.25 B81-01515

Wingate, John. Carrier / John Wingate. — London : Weidenfeld and Nicolson, 1981. — 192p : 1map ; 23cm
ISBN 0-297-77861-7 : £5.50 B81-10132

Winslow, Pauline Glen. The Windsor plot / Pauline Glen Winslow. — London : Arlington, 1981. — 365p ; 23cm
ISBN 0-85140-545-2 : £6.95 : CIP rev. B81-18085

Winspear, Violet. Desire has no mercy / Violet Winspear. — Large print ed. — Bath : Chivers, 1981, c1979. — 258p ; 23cm. — (A Seymour book)
Originally published: London : Mills and Boon, 1979
ISBN 0-85119-415-x : £4.95 : CIP rev. B81-00632

Winspear, Violet. A girl possessed / by Violet Winspear. — London : Mills & Boon, 1980. — 188p ; 19cm
ISBN 0-263-09793-5 : £3.85 B81-05926

Winspear, Violet. Love's agony / by Violet Winspear. — London : Mills & Boon, 1981. — 186p ; 20cm
ISBN 0-263-09855-9 : £4.55 B81-14239

Winstanley, Tom. On the mountain / Tom Winstanley. — Harrow : Euroeditions, 1978. — 92p ; 21cm
ISBN 0-906204-13-5 : Unpriced B81-24757

Winter, Patrick. The goad / Patrick Winter. — London : Arrow, 1981. — 286p ; 18cm
ISBN 0-09-924720-8 (pbk) : £1.60 B81-24837

Winter, Sarah. Pamela's passions / Sarah Winter. — London : Macdonald Futura, 1981. — 251p ; 18cm. — (A Minstrel book ; 1)
ISBN 0-7088-2005-0 (pbk) : £0.95 B81-15461

Winward, Walter. The Ball Bearing Run / by Walter Winward. — London : Hamilton, 1981. — 280p ; 23cm
ISBN 0-241-10601-x : £6.95 : CIP rev. B81-04293

Winward, Walter. Seven minutes past midnight / Walter Winward. — [London] : Corgi, 1980, c1979. — 336p : 1map,1plan ; 18cm
Originally published: London : Hamilton, 1979
ISBN 0-552-11551-7 (pbk) : £1.25 B81-03318

Wiseman, Thomas. Savage day / Thomas Wiseman. — London : Cape, 1981. — 438p ; 23cm
ISBN 0-224-01928-7 : £6.95 : CIP rev. B81-27365

Wishart, Nan. Fatal entrance / Nan Wishart. — Bognor Regis : New Horizon, c1979. — 124p ; 21cm
ISBN 0-86116-116-5 : £2.95 B81-19036

Wood, Christopher, *1935-*. Taiwan / Christopher Wood. — London : Michael Joseph, 1981. — 251p ; 23cm
ISBN 0-7181-2051-5 : £6.95 B81-38086

Wood, Kenneth, *1922-*. Shadows / by Kenneth Wood. — London : Dobson, 1979. — 185p ; 21cm
ISBN 0-234-72096-4 : £3.75 B81-02680

Woodford, Peggy. The girl with a voice / Peggy Woodford. — London : Bodley Head, c1981. — 186p ; 20cm. — (A Book for new adults)
For adolescents
ISBN 0-370-30423-3 (pbk) : £3.50 : CIP rev. B81-12346

Woodman, Richard. An eye of the fleet / Richard Woodman. — London : Murray, 1981. — 185p ; 23cm
ISBN 0-7195-3788-6 : £6.95 : CIP rev. B80-18032

Woods, Sara. Cry guilty / Sara Woods. — London : Macmillan, 1981. — 190p ; 21cm
ISBN 0-333-30976-6 : £5.50 B81-20269

Woods, Sara. Dearest enemy / Sara Woods. — London : Macmillan, 1981. — 191p ; 21cm
ISBN 0-333-31847-1 : £5.50 B81-37182

Woods, Sara. Weep for her / Sara Woods. — London : Macmillan, 1980. — 222p ; 21cm
ISBN 0-333-30027-0 : £5.50 B81-01516

Worboys, Anne. The Bhunda jewels / Anne Worboys. — London : Severn House, 1980. — 224p ; 21cm
ISBN 0-7278-0638-6 : £5.95 : CIP rev. B80-28781

Worboys, Anne. The lion of Delos / Anne Worboys. — Large print ed. — Leicester : Ulverscroft, 1980, c1974. — 406p ; 23cm. — (Ulverscroft large print series)
Originally published: London : Hodder & Stoughton, 1975
ISBN 0-7089-0500-5 : £4.25 : CIP rev. B80-11632

Worth, Margaret. I want a hero / Margaret Worth. — London (14 Queens Rd, Southwold, Suffolk IP18 6EQ) : Peacock Press, 1980. — 112p ; 22cm
ISBN 0-9507081-0-0 (pbk) : Unpriced B81-02173

Wright, Glover. The torch / Glover Wright. — London : Hutchinson, 1981, c1980. — 231p ; 23cm
Originally published: New York : Putnam, 1980
ISBN 0-09-143240-5 : £5.95 : CIP rev. B80-23760

Wright, James, *1925-*. The Devil's parole / James Wright. — London : Allen Lane, 1981. — 349p ; 23cm
ISBN 0-7139-1385-1 : £6.95 B81-15735

Wright, Lilian. The Mack family / Lilian Wright. — Bognor Regis : New Horizon, c1978. — 201p ; 22cm
ISBN 0-86116-044-4 : £2.95 B81-18960

Wright, Meg. The tribe of Jen-Wae : Meg Wright / illustrated by Lee Sullivan. — Dundee (c/o Sheila Clark, 6 Craigmill Cottages, Strathmartine by Dundee, Scotland) : Scotpress, 1981. — 92p : ill ; 30cm
Limited ed. of 350 copies
£1.80 (pbk) B81-28284

Wright, Meg. With hoops of steel / by Meg Wright. — Strathmartine (6 Craigmill Cottages, Strathmartine, by Dundee) : Scotpress, c1981. — 61p ; 30cm
Limited ed. of 300 copies
£1.25 (pbk) B81-15791

Wright, Melinda. The Concorde affair / Melinda Wright. — London : Columbine House, 1981. — 224p ; 23cm
ISBN 0-85140-556-8 : £6.50 : CIP rev. B81-18086

Wright, Patricia. Storm harvest / Particia Wright. — [London] : Fontana, 1980, c1979. — 313p ; 18cm
Originally published: London : Collins, 1979
ISBN 0-00-616124-3 (pbk) : £1.35 B81-01518

Wright, Patricia. This, my city / Patricia Wright. — London : Collins, 1981. — 442p ; 22cm
ISBN 0-00-222366-x : £6.95 B81-08636

Wykham, Helen. Ottoline Atlantica / Helen Wykham. — London : Boyars, 1980. — 220p ; 23cm
ISBN 0-7145-2686-x : £6.95 : CIP rev. B80-08454

Wynd, Oswald. The ginger tree / Oswald Wynd. — Large print ed. — Leicester : Ulverscroft, 1981, c1977. — 562p ; 23cm. — (Ulverscroft large print series)
Originally published: London : Collins, 1977
ISBN 0-7089-0614-1 : £5.00 : CIP rev. B81-02584

Wynn, Emily. The passionate prude / by Emily Wynn. — London : Hale, 1981. — 190p ; 20cm
ISBN 0-7091-8744-0 : £5.95 B81-08646

Wynne, Annabel. The Fanshawe Folly / Annabel Wynne. — London : Macdonald Futura, 1981. — 219p ; 18cm. — (A Victorian romance)
ISBN 0-7088-1855-2 (pbk) : £1.10 B81-15739

Wynne, F. C.. Fourpence a day and all found / F.C. Wynne. — Bognor Regis : New Horizon, c1981. — 195p ; 21cm
ISBN 0-86116-458-x : £5.75 B81-18744

Yankali. The day London was invaded by grass / Yankali ; illustrations by Mizu. — [London] ([28, Russell Rd., W14 8HT]) : Barrett, 1979. — 28p : ill ; 26cm
£1.60 (pbk) B81-18370

823'.914[F] — Fiction in English, *1945-* — *Texts continuation*

Yankali. The phallidomite scandal / by Yankali ; pretty pretty pictures by Mizu Jr.. — London (28, Russell Rd., W.14) : Rafael Barrett, 1980. — 51p : ill ; 26cm
£1.75 (pbk) B81-18371

Yankali. The sooo-ftening of Buckingham Palace / by Yankali ; brush visuals by Mizu. — London (28, Russell Rd., W.14) : Rafael Barrett, 1980. — 47p : ill ; 26cm
£1.75 (pbk) B81-18369

York, Alison. The scented sword / Alison York. — London : Star, 1980. — 348p ; 18cm
Originally published: London : W.H. Allen, 1980
ISBN 0-352-30706-4 (pbk) : £1.95 B81-01519

York, Amanda. Somewhere in the whirlwind / Amanda York. — London : Hamlyn Paperbacks, 1981, c1980. — 288p ; 18cm
ISBN 0-600-20179-1 (pbk) : £1.35 B81-35578

Yorke, Margaret. Death on account / Margaret Yorke. — London : Arrow, 1980, c1979. — 159p ; 18cm
Originally published: London : Hutchinson, 1979
ISBN 0-09-924590-6 (pbk) : £1.00 B81-01520

Yorke, Margaret. The hand of death / Margaret Yorke. — London : Hutchinson, 1981. — 217p ; 21cm
ISBN 0-09-145140-x : £6.50 : CIP rev.
B81-12324

Yorke, Margaret. No medals for the Major / Margaret Yorke. — London : Arrow, 1981, c1974. — 174p ; 18cm
Originally published: London : Bles, 1974
ISBN 0-09-925400-x (pbk) : £1.10 B81-11044

Yorke, Margaret. No medals for the Major. — Large print ed. — Long Preston : Magna, Dec.1981. — [412]p
ISBN 0-86009-357-3 : £4.95 : CIP entry
B81-31816

Zec, Donald. The face / Donald Zec. — London : New English Library, 1980. — 317p ; 23cm
ISBN 0-450-04752-0 : £5.95 B81-02139

Zec, Donald. The face / Donald Zec. — London : New English Library, 1980 (1981 [printing]). — 317p ; 18cm
ISBN 0-450-05226-5 (pbk) : £1.60 B81-35629

Zeno. The four sergeants / Zeno. — Large print ed. — Leicester : Ulverscroft, 1981, c1976. — 395p : 2maps ; 23cm. — (Ulverscroft large print)
Originally published: London : Macmillan, 1976. — Maps on lining papers
ISBN 0-7089-0640-0 : Unpriced B81-26481

823'.914[F] — Short stories in English, *1945-* — *Texts*

Aiken, Joan. A touch of chill : stories of horror, suspense & fantasy / Joan Aiken. — London : Fontana, 1981, c1979. — 190p ; 18cm
Originally published: London : Gollancz, 1979
ISBN 0-00-671764-0 (pbk) : £0.95 B81-22321

Amis, Kingsley. Collected short stories / Kingsley Amis. — London : Hutchinson, 1980. — 303p ; 23cm
ISBN 0-09-143430-0 : £6.95 B81-00410

Archer, Jeffrey. A quiver full of arrows. — London : Hodder & Stoughton, Nov.1981. — [192]p. — (Coronet books)
Originally published: 1980
ISBN 0-340-27272-4 (pbk) : £1.25 : CIP entry
B81-30136

Ballard, J. G.. The Venus hunters / J.G. Ballard. — London : Granada, 1980. — 144p ; 18cm. — (A Panther book)
ISBN 0-586-05187-2 (pbk) : £0.95 B81-00415

Barker, A. L. (Audrey Lilian). Life stories / by A.L. Barker. — London : Hogarth, 1981. — 319p ; 21cm
ISBN 0-7012-0538-5 : £6.95 : CIP rev.
B81-23812

Behan, Brendan. After the wake. — Dublin : O'Brien Press, Sept.1981. — 1v. — (Irish classic fiction, ISSN 0332-1347)
ISBN 0-905140-97-4 : £6.00 : CIP entry
B81-20653

Bell, A. Craig. The last man : and other stories / by A. Craig Bell. — [Wembley] : Selecteditions, [1981?]. — 149p ; 18cm
ISBN 0-86237-006-x (pbk) : £1.25 B81-20194

Boyd, Neil. Bless me again, father / Neil Boyd. — London : Joseph, 1981. — 220p ; 23cm
ISBN 0-7181-1985-1 : £6.50 B81-12272

Boyd, Neil. Father under fire / Neil Boyd. — [London] : Corgi, 1981, c1980. — 240p ; 18cm
Originally published: London : Joseph, 1980
ISBN 0-552-11628-9 (pbk) : £1.25 B81-15339

Burke, Helen Lucy. A season for mothers and other stories / Helen Lucy Burke. — Swords (Knocksedan House, Swords, Co. Dublin) : Poolbeg, 1980. — 160p ; 18cm
ISBN 0-905169-32-8 (pbk) : £2.00 B81-00411

Campbell, Ramsey. The height of the scream / Ramsey Campbell. — London : Star, 1981, c1976. — 208p ; 18cm
Originally published: Sauk City : Arkham House, 1976 ; London : Millington, 1978
ISBN 0-352-30803-6 (pbk) : £1.50 B81-11690

Carter, Angela. The bloody chamber and other stories / Angela Carter. — Harmondsworth : Penguin, 1981, c1979. — 125p ; 20cm. — (A King Penguin)
Originally published: London : Gollancz, 1979
ISBN 0-14-005404-9 (pbk) : £1.95 B81-27225

Chetwynd-Hayes, R.. The fantastic world of Kamtellar : a book of vampires and ghouls / R. Chetwynd-Hayes. — London : Kimber, 1980. — 189p ; 23cm
ISBN 0-7183-0367-9 : £5.50 B81-01521

Clarke, Arthur C.. Of time and stars : the worlds of Arthur C. Clarke / with an introduction by J.B. Priestley. — Harmondsworth : Penguin in association with Victor Gollancz, 1981, c1972. — 205p ; 18cm
Originally published: London : Gollancz, 1972
ISBN 0-14-005750-1 (pbk) : £1.25 B81-27191

Cooper, Jilly. Love and other heartaches. — London : Arlington, Oct.1981. — [224]p
ISBN 0-85140-558-4 : £6.50 : CIP entry
B81-27388

Crowe, W. Haughton. The star of the County Down : and other romantic tales from the Ring of Mourne / told or re-told by W. Haughton Crowe. — Dundalk ([Francis St., Dundalk, Co. Louth]) : Dundalgan Press, 1974. — 61p : 1col.ill ; 19cm
ISBN 0-85221-037-x (pbk) : £0.65 B81-18414

Dearle, Marjorie. We remember yesterday / Marjorie Dearle. — [Littlehampton] ([51c Norfold Rd., Littlehampton, West Sussex, BN17 5HE]) : [M. Dearle], 1981. — 84p ; 19cm
£2.00 (pbk) B81-31921

Donleavy, J. P.. Meet my maker the mad molecule / J.P. Donleavy. — Harmondsworth : Penguin, 1967, c1964 (1981 [printing]). — 169p ; 18cm
Originally published: Boston, Mass. : Little, Brown, 1964 ; London : Bodley Head, 1965
ISBN 0-14-002719-x (pbk) : £1.25 B81-18574

Fleming, Ian. For your eyes only : five secret occasions in the life of James Bond / Ian Fleming. — London : Triad : Granada, 1979, c1960 (1981 [printing]). — 190p ; 18cm
Originally published: London : Cape, 1960
ISBN 0-586-04596-1 (pbk) : £1.25 B81-26544

Friel, Brian. Selected stories / Brian Friel ; with an introduction by Seamus Deane. — Dublin : Gallery Books, 1979. — 121p ; 23cm
£3.75 B81-15407

Gardam, Jane. The Sidmouth letters / Jane Gardam. — London : Abacus, 1981, c1980. — 147p ; 20cm
Originally published: London : Hamilton, 1980
ISBN 0-349-11408-0 (pbk) : £1.75 B81-39743

Hall, K. W.. Terror watched : and other stories / K.W. Hall. — London : New Horizon, 1981. — 129p ; 21cm
ISBN 0-86116-522-5 : £4.50 B81-39437

Hardwick, Mollie. Calling Juliet Bravo : new arrivals / by Mollie Hardwick ; from the TV series created by Ian Kennedy Martin. — London : B.B.C., 1981. — 174p ; 18cm
ISBN 0-563-17961-9 (pbk) : £1.25 B81-35647

Hogan, Desmond. Children of Lir : stories from Ireland / by Desmond Hogan. — London : Hamilton, 1981. — 163p ; 21cm
ISBN 0-241-10608-7 : £6.95 : CIP rev.
B81-02093

Hoyle, Fred. The Westminster disaster / Fred Hoyle, Geoffrey Hoyle ; edited by Barbara Hoyle. — Harmondsworth : Penguin, 1980, c1978. — 188p ; 19cm
Originally published: London : Heinemann, 1978
ISBN 0-14-005301-8 (pbk) : £1.25 B81-01522

Hutchinson, David, *1960-*. The paradise equation / David Hutchinson. — London : Abelard, 1981. — 95p ; 23cm
ISBN 0-200-72717-6 : £4.75 : CIP rev.
B80-19483

Ireland, Walter. Rusty & 4 other stories / Walter Ireland. — Bognor Regis : New Horizon, c1978. — 66p : ill ; 22cm
ISBN 0-86116-038-x : £2.95 B81-19081

Jhabvala, Ruth Prawer. [An experience of India]. How I became a holy mother and other stories / Ruth Prawer Jhabvala. — Harmondsworth : Penguin, 1981, c1976. — 267p ; 20cm
Originally published: London : J. Murray, 1971
ISBN 0-14-004829-4 (pbk) : £2.50 B81-22026

Keane, John B.. More Irish short stories / John B. Keane. — Dublin : Mercier Press, c1981. — 120p ; 18cm
ISBN 0-85342-660-0 (pbk) : Unpriced
B81-34877

Kelly, Maeve. A life of her own : and other stories / Maeve Kelly. — [Swords] : Poolbeg Press, [1976] ([1979] printing). — 144p ; 18cm
ISBN 0-905169-04-2 (pbk) : £1.50 B81-19817

Kelly, Owen. Tales out of school / Owen Kelly. — Belfast : Blackstaff, c1980. — 87p ; 23cm
ISBN 0-85640-199-4 : £5.95 : CIP rev.
B80-19473

King, Francis, *1923-*. Indirect method and other stories / Francis King. — London : Hutchinson, 1980. — 185p ; 21cm
ISBN 0-09-143690-7 : £6.50 B81-00412

Linden, Heather. Roses to stay the tears of the dead / by Heather Linden. — [London] : [H. Linden], c1978. — 169p ; 21cm
Private circulation (pbk) B81-21457

Lloyd, L. E.. Twisted echoes / L.E. Lloyd. — Ilfracombe : Stockwell, 1981. — 85p ; 19cm
ISBN 0-7223-1495-7 : £3.90 B81-39392

823'.914[F] — Short stories in English, ***1945- — Texts*** *continuation*

Lohan, Katharine. de Vassart, DA/Q / by Katharine Lohan. — Harrow : Eureditions, 1979. — 77p ; 20cm
ISBN 0-906204-27-5 : Unpriced B81-26665

Lohan, Katharine. Two yo-yos and a furbody / Katharine Lohan. — Bognor Regis : New Horizon, c1980. — 99p ; 21cm
ISBN 0-86116-159-9 : £3.75 B81-19236

McArdle, John. It's handy when people don't die : and other stories / John McArdle. — Swords (Knocksedan House, Swords, Co. Dublin) : Poolbeg, 1981. — 158p ; 18cm
ISBN 0-905169-43-3 (pbk) : Unpriced B81-24581

McAughtry, Sam. Belfast / Sam McAughtry. — Dublin : Ward River Press, 1981. — 157p ; 18cm
ISBN 0-907085-10-5 (pbk) : £2.20 B81-32128

McBratney, Sam. Lagan Valley details : short stories / by Sam McBratney. — Belfast : Blackstaff, c1980. — 23cm
ISBN 0-85640-189-7 : £6.95 B81-01523

Mars-Jones, Adam. Lantern lecture : and other stories / Adam Mars-Jones. — London : Faber, 1981. — 197p ; 23cm
ISBN 0-571-11813-5 : £6.95 : CIP rev. B81-21612

Milo, A.. Reflections from a star spangled sky / A. Milo. — Bognor Regis : New Horizon, c1978. — 82p ; 21cm
ISBN 0-86116-135-1 : £2.95 B81-18869

Moorcock, Michael. Moorcock's book of martyrs / Michael Moorcock. — London : Granada, 1981, c1976. — 175p ; 18cm. — (A Mayflower book)
Originally published: London : Quartet Books, 1976
ISBN 0-583-13107-7 (pbk) : £1.25 B81-28952

Moorcock, Michael. The singing citadel : four tales of heroic fantasy / Michael Moorcock. — London : Granada, 1981, c1970. — 125p ; 18cm. — (Granada science fantasy) (A Mayflower book)
Originally published: St Albans : Mayflower, 1970
ISBN 0-583-11670-1 (pbk) : £0.95 B81-09799

Mortimer, John. Rumpole. — Large print ed. — Bath : Chivers Press, Feb.1982. — [256]p. — (A New Portway large print book)
ISBN 0-85119-153-3 : £5.25 : CIP entry B81-35836

Mortimer, John. Rumpole of the Bailey. — Large print ed. — Bath : Chivers Press, Feb.1982. — [256]p. — (A New Portway large print book)
ISBN 0-85119-154-1 : £5.25 : CIP entry B81-36053

Mortimer, John. Rumpole's return. — Large print ed. — Bath : Chivers Press, Feb.1982. — [296]p. — (A New Portway large print book)
Originally published: Harmondsworth : Penguin, 1980
ISBN 0-85119-156-8 : £5.25 : CIP entry B81-36051

Mortimer, John. The trials of Rumpole. — Large print ed. — Bath : Chivers Press, Feb.1982. — [256]p. — (A New Portway large print book)
ISBN 0-85119-155-x : £5.25 : CIP entry B81-36052

Mulkerns, Val. An idle woman and other stories / Val Mulkerns. — Swords (Knocksedan House, Swords, Co. Dublin) : Poolbeg, 1980. — 144p ; 18cm ; pbk
ISBN 0-905169-34-4 : £2.00 B81-01524

Norris, Leslie. Sliding : fourteen short stories and eight poems / by Leslie Norris ; with photographs by Jessie Ann Matthew ; edited by Geoffrey Halson. — Harlow : Longman, 1981. — x,165p : ill ; 19cm. — (Longman imprint books)
ISBN 0-582-22066-1 (pbk) : £1.30 B81-39600

Owen, William, *1931-*. Strange Scottish stories / retold and illustrated by William Owen. — Norwich : Jarrold Colour Publications, c1981. — 143p : ill ; 21cm
ISBN 0-85306-919-0 (pbk) : Unpriced B81-24546

Piacentini, Valerie. The wheel of fate / by Valerie Piacentini ; with poetry by Sheila Clark. — Strathmartine by Dundee (6 Craigmill Cottages, Strathmartine by Dundee) : ScoTpress, c1980. — 47p ; 30cm. — (A Star trek fanzine)
Limited ed. of 100 copies
£1.15 (pbk) B81-39684

Quinn, Niall. Voyovic : and other stories / by Niall Quinn. — Portmarnock : Wolfhound, 1980. — 163p ; 23cm
ISBN 0-905473-61-2 : £5.95 : CIP rev. B80-28790

Raphael, Frederic. Oxbridge blues : and other stories / Frederic Raphael. — London : Cape, 1980. — 213p ; 21cm
ISBN 0-224-01871-x : £5.95 B81-05242

Rendell, Ruth. Means of evil / Ruth Rendell. — South Yarmouth, Mass. : J. Curley ([Skipton] : Distributed by Magna Print), c1979. — 314p ; 23cm
Originally published: London : Hutchinson, 1979. — Published in large print
ISBN 0-89340-315-6 : £5.75 B81-17992

Rowlands, D. G.. Eye hath not seen — : supernatural anecdotes from the reminiscences of Father D. O'Connor / D.G. Rowlands ; illustrated by David Lloyd. — Runcorn (11B, Cote Lea Sq., Southgate, Runcorn, Cheshire WA7 2SA) : R.A. Pardoe, c1980. — 38p : ill ; 22cm
Text on inside covers
£1.15 (pbk) B81-29031

Scott, J. M.. Red hair and moonwater / by J.M. Scott. — London : Hale, 1980. — 201p ; 21cm
ISBN 0-7091-8409-3 : £6.25 B81-00552

Shah, Amina. The Assemblies of Al-Hariri : fifty encounters with the Shaykh Abu Zayd of Servj / retold by Amina Shah from the Makamat of Al-Hariri of Basra. — London : Octagon, 1980. — xviii,267p ; 22cm
ISBN 0-900860-86-3 : £7.50 B81-11253

Shaw, Bob. A better mantrap. — London : Gollancz, Jan.1982. — [192]p
ISBN 0-575-03083-6 : £6.95 : CIP entry B81-35885

Smith, Iain Crichton. Murdo : and other stories / by Iain Crichton Smith. — London : Gollancz, 1981. — 141p ; 21cm
ISBN 0-575-02983-8 : £4.95 B81-18536

Strong, Eithne. Patterns : and other stories / Eithne Strong. — Swords (Knocksedan House, Swords, Co. Dublin, Ireland) : Poolbeg, 1981. — 144p ; 18cm
ISBN 0-905169-52-2 (pbk) : Unpriced B81-35164

Tindall, Gillian. The China egg : and other stories / Gillian Tindall. — London : Hodder and Stoughton, 1981. — 192p ; 23cm
ISBN 0-340-25970-1 : £6.95 B81-10136

Trevor, William. Beyond the pale and other stories. — London : Bodley Head, Oct.1981. — [256]p
ISBN 0-370-30442-x : £6.95 : CIP entry B81-28829

Van Greenaway, Peter. Edgar Allan who-? / by Peter Van Greenaway. — London : Gollancz, 1981. — 173p ; 21cm
ISBN 0-575-02998-6 : £5.95 B81-31692

Wade, Rosalind. Red letter day : twelve stories of Cornwall / Rosalind Wade. — London : Kimber, 1980. — 253p ; 23cm
ISBN 0-7183-0377-6 : £5.75 B81-00413

Walsh, Luella. Fish out of water and worse / Luella Walsh. — Ilfracombe : Stockwell, 1981. — 64p ; 18cm
ISBN 0-7223-1468-x (pbk) : £1.81 B81-35048

Watson, Ian. The very slow time machine : science fiction stories / Ian Watson. — London : Granada, 1981, c1979. — 222p ; 18cm. — (Panther science fiction)
Originally published: London : Gollancz, 1979
ISBN 0-586-05064-7 (pbk) : £1.25 B81-34909

Weldon, Fay. Watching me, watching you : and other stories / Fay Weldon. — London : Hodder and Stoughton, c1981. — 208p ; 23cm
ISBN 0-340-25600-1 : £6.95 : CIP rev. B81-04295

West, Anthony C.. All the king's horses : and other stories / Anthony C. West. — Swords (Knocksedan House, Swords, Co. Dublin, Ireland) : Poolbeg, 1981. — 144p ; 18cm
ISBN 0-905169-51-4 (pbk) : Unpriced B81-35163

White, Terence de Vere. Birds of prey : stories / by Terence de Vere White. — London : Gollancz, 1980. — 157p ; 22cm
ISBN 0-575-02911-0 : £5.95 B81-00414

Whitelaw, Stella. Cat stories / Stella Whitelaw. — London : Hamlyn Paperbacks, 1981. — 159p : ill ; 18cm
ISBN 0-600-20229-1 (pbk) : £1.10 B81-35580

Williams, Barnaby. The racers / Barnaby Williams. — London : New English Library, 1981. — 188p ; 18cm
ISBN 0-450-05194-3 (pbk) : £1.25 B81-24749

Williams, Mary. Ghostly carnival : Cornish ghost stories / Mary Williams. — London : Kimber, 1980. — 175p ; 23cm
ISBN 0-7183-0407-1 : £5.50 B81-01525

823'.914[J] — Children's short stories in English, ***1945- — Texts***

100 day by day stories. — London : Hamlyn, 1981. — 157p : col.ill ; 22cm
ISBN 0-600-36471-2 : £2.95 B81-19889

100 playtime stories. — London : Hamlyn, 1981. — 156p : col.ill ; 22cm
ISBN 0-600-36470-4 : £2.95 B81-19888

Ainsworth, Ruth. The pirate ship : and other stories / Ruth Ainsworth ; illustrated by Shirley Hughes. — London : Heinemann, c1980. — 158p : ill ; 24cm
ISBN 0-434-92589-6 : £4.95 B81-00587

Aird, Mary. The Browns come to St Mark's / Mary Aird. — London : CIO, 1980. — 49p : ill ; 22cm
ISBN 0-7151-0395-4 (pbk) : £1.50 B81-33502

Allan, Mabel Esther. A strange enchantment / Mabel Esther Allan. — [London] : Abelard, 1981. — 126p ; 22cm
ISBN 0-200-72737-0 : £4.95 B81-05747

Althea. Desmond and the monsters / by Althea ; illustrated by Maureen Galvani. — Over : Dinosaur, c1975. — [32]p : col.ill ; 16x19cm. — (Dinosaur's Althea books)
ISBN 0-85122-286-2 (cased) : £1.85
ISBN 0-85122-285-4 (pbk) : £0.70 B81-17386

823'.914[J] — Children's short stories in English, *1945- — Texts* *continuation*

Ambrus, Victor. Dracula's : bedtime storybook : tales to keep you awake at night / Victor G. Ambrus. — Oxford : Oxford University Press, c1981. — [32]p : col.ill ; 33cm
ISBN 0-19-279762-x : £4.50 B81-39845

Ambrus, Victor. Dracula's bedtime storybook. — Oxford : Oxford University Press, Sept.1981. — [32]p
ISBN 0-19-272122-4 : £4.50 : CIP entry B81-22498

Bannerman, A.. Magical moments : short stories / by A. Bannerman ; illustrated by Julian Moore. — Ilfracombe : Stockwell, 1980. — 27p : ill ; 18cm
ISBN 0-7223-1351-9 (pbk) : £0.66 B81-16770

Barklem, Jill. The big book of Brambly Hedge / Jill Barklem. — London : Collins, 1981. — [24]p : col.ill ; 41cm
ISBN 0-00-195758-9 (pbk) : £3.95 B81-35407

Bird, Maria. Andy Pandy story book. — Sevenoaks : Hodder and Stoughton Children's Books, Aug.1981. — [64]p
ISBN 0-340-26764-x : £2.50 : CIP entry B81-18143

Biro, Val. The magic doctor. — Oxford : Oxford University Press, May 1981. — [32]p
ISBN 0-19-279752-2 : £3.95 : CIP entry B81-06050

Bisset, Donald. Johnny here and there / Donald Bisset ; illustrated by the author. — London : Methuen Children's, 1981. — 111p : ill ; 21cm. — ([A Read aloud book])
ISBN 0-416-20770-7 : £3.50 B81-12484

Bowman, David T.. Ramble Wood tales / David T. Bowman ; illustrated by Cora E.M. Paterson. — Ilfracombe : Stockwell, 1981. — 24p : ill ; 19cm
ISBN 0-7223-1470-1 (pbk) : £0.72 B81-22330

Box, Janette Marie. Five delightful stories / Janette Marie Box. — Bognor Regis : New Horizon, c1979. — 80p,[16]p of plates : ill ; 21cm
ISBN 0-86116-403-2 : £3.50 B81-19268

Brambleby, Ailsa. More tales for Brownies / by Ailsa Brambleby. — Rev. [ed.]. — Glasgow : Brown, Son & Ferguson, 1973 (1978 [printing]). — vii,85p : ill ; 19cm
ISBN 0-85174-333-1 (pbk) : Unpriced B81-18912

Campbell, Rod. Charlie Clown ; Nigel Knight / Rod Campbell. — London : Abelard, [1981]. — [32]p : chiefly col.ill ; 17cm. — (Little people)
Cover title. — Also published separately
ISBN 0-200-72761-3 : £1.95 : CIP rev. B81-14849

Campbell, Rod. Eddie Enginedriver ; Freddie Fireman / Rod Campbell. — London : Abelard, [1981]. — [32]p : chiefly col.ill ; 17cm. — (Little people)
Cover title. — Also published separately
ISBN 0-200-72759-1 : £1.95 : CIP rev. B81-14845

Campbell, Rod. Nancy Nurse ; Gertie Gardener / Rod Campbell. — London : Abelard, [1981]. — [32]p : chiefly col.ill ; 17cm. — (Little people)
Cover title. — Also published separately
ISBN 0-200-72760-5 : £1.95 : CIP rev. B81-14801

Chambers, Robin. The fight of neither century : and other stories / Robin Chambers ; illustrated by Shirley Soar. — London : Granada, 1981, c1980. — 121p : ill ; 18cm. — (A Dragon book)
ISBN 0-583-30338-2 (pbk) : £0.85 B81-19940

Clare, Helen. Bel the giant and other stories / Helen Clare ; illustrated by Peggy Fortnum. — Harmondsworth : Puffin in association with the Bodley Head, 1971, c1956 (1981 [printing]). — 122p : ill ; 20cm. — (A Young Puffin)
Originally published: London : Bodley Head, 1956
ISBN 0-14-030471-1 (pbk) : £0.95 B81-22253

Cookson, Catherine. The nipper / Catherine Cookson. — Harmondsworth : Puffin, 1973, c1970 (1980 [printing]). — 156p ; 19cm
Originally published: London : Macdonald, 1970
ISBN 0-14-030580-7 (pbk) : £0.75 B81-02327

Cooper, Lawrence J.. The schoolboy avengers / Lawrence J. Cooper. — Bognor Regis : New Horizon, c1981. — 145p ; 21cm
ISBN 0-86116-353-2 : £3.50 B81-19237

Coren, Alan. Arthur and the purple panic. — London : Robson, Sept.1981. — [64]p. — (Arthur books)
ISBN 0-86051-141-3 : £1.95 : CIP entry B81-22457

Cresswell, Helen. At the stroke of midnight : traditional fairy tales / retold by Helen Cresswell ; illustrated by Carolyn Dinan. — London : Fonatana, 1981,c1971. — 96p : ill ; 20cm
Originally published: 1973
ISBN 0-00-671902-3 (pbk) : £0.90 B81-22313

Cresswell, Helen. A kingdom of riches : traditional fairy tales retold by Helen Cresswell / illustrated by Carolyn Dinan. — London : Fontana, 1981, c1971. — 96p : ill ; 20cm
Originally published: 1973
ISBN 0-00-671903-1 (pbk) : £0.90 B81-22314

Cubitt, Winnie. More teeny stories / Winnie Cubitt. — Bognor Regis : New Horizon, c1981. — 32p : ill ; 21cm
ISBN 0-86116-679-5 : £3.25 B81-20696

Cubitt, Winnie. The teeny stories / Winnie Cubitt. — Bognor Regis : New Horizon, c1978. — 44p : ill ; 21cm
ISBN 0-86116-032-0 : £2.50 B81-19034

Dickens, Frank. Albert Herbert Hawkins (the naughtiest boy in the world) and the Olympic Games / by Frank Dickens. — [London] : Carousel, 1980. — [32]p : col.ill ; 21x26cm
ISBN 0-552-52116-7 (pbk) : £0.75 B81-02749

Doherty, Berlie. How green you are!. — London : Methuen Children's Books, Jan.1982. — [144] p. — (A Pied piper book)
ISBN 0-416-20940-8 : £3.95 : CIP entry B81-33789

Dunnett, Margaret. No pets allowed : and other animal stories / Margaret Dunnett ; illustrated by Peter Rush. — London : Deutsch, 1981. — 140p : ill ; 21cm
ISBN 0-233-97103-3 : £4.95 : CIP rev. B81-01526

Eyton, Wendy. The ghost of Christmas present : and other stories / by Wendy Eyton ; illustrated by Ken Langstaff. — London : Warne, 1980. — 120p : ill ; 21cm
ISBN 0-7232-2705-5 : £4.95 B81-00588

Freemantle, Karen. Travel in time and other stories / by Karen Freemantle. — Bognor Regis : New Horizon, c1979. — 37p : ill,ports ; 19cm
ISBN 0-86116-196-3 (pbk) : £0.95 B81-19035

Gardam, Jane. The hollow land / Jane Gardam ; illustrated by Janet Rawlins. — London : Julia MacRae, 1981. — 152p : ill ; 23cm
ISBN 0-86203-023-4 : £5.25 : CIP rev. B81-14441

Gregory, Susan, *1945 May 28-*. Magic! / Susan Gregory ; illustrated by Simon Willby. — London : Cassell, 1981. — 126p : ill ; 19cm. — (Cassell compass books)
ISBN 0-304-30791-2 (pbk) : Unpriced : CIP rev. B81-09463

Hardcastle, Michael. Half a team / Michael Hardcastle ; illustrated by Trevor Stubley. — London : Methuen Children's, 1980. — 108p : ill ; 20cm. — (A Pied Piper book)
ISBN 0-416-87740-0 : £3.50 : CIP rev. B80-19482

Hughes, Penny. Kelligant pig : & other stories / written by Penny Hughes ; illustrated by Sarah Kensington. — London : Sackett & Marshall, 1979. — [32]p : col.ill ; 26cm
Cover title
ISBN 0-86109-046-2 : £2.50 B81-07330

Hull, Ernest. Troublesome Sammy / Ernest Hull. — Bognor Regis : New Horizon, c1978. — 44p,[6]leaves of plates : ill ; 21cm
ISBN 0-86116-061-4 : £2.95 B81-19251

Jones, Ray, *19---*. The mouse that roared : and other animal fables / Ray Jones ; illustrated by Shirley Felts. — [London] : Piccolo in association with Heinemann, 1981, c1979. — 110p : ill ; 18cm
Originally published: London : Heinemann, 1979
ISBN 0-330-26383-8 (pbk) : £0.90 B81-24734

Jones, Terry. Fairy tales. — London (8 Cork St., W1X 2HA) : Pavilion Books, Sept.1981. — [128]p
ISBN 0-907516-03-3 : £6.95 : CIP entry B81-20188

Julie-Dawn. Roly-Poly stories / Julie-Dawn. — Bognor Regis : New Horizon, c1981. — 58p : ill ; 21cm
ISBN 0-86116-440-7 : £2.95 B81-28949

Kemp, Gene. The clock tower ghost. — London : Faber, Oct.1981. — [89]p
ISBN 0-571-11767-8 : £3.95 : CIP entry B81-25327

Kemp, Gene. Dog days and cat naps / Gene Kemp ; illustrated by Carolyn Dinan. — London : Faber, 1980. — 110p : ill ; 21cm
ISBN 0-571-11595-0 : £4.50 : CIP rev. B80-18917

Kramin, Anne. On the hot line to Santa / Anne Kramin. — Bognor Regis : New Horizon, c1979. — 50p : ill ; 21cm
ISBN 0-86116-390-7 : £2.50 B81-18956

Layton, George. [The balaclava story]. The fib : and other stories / George Layton. — London : Fontana, 1981, c1978. — 144p ; 18cm. — (Lions)
Originally published: in 2 vols. London : Longman, 1975
ISBN 0-00-671808-6 (pbk) : £0.95 B81-15598

Mark, Jan. Hairs in the palm of the hand / by Jan Mark ; illustrated by Jan Ormerod. — Harmondsworth : Kestrel, 1981. — 96p : ill ; 23cm
ISBN 0-7226-5728-5 : £4.25 B81-28485

Millington, J.. Fantasy tales for children / J. Millington. — Bognor Regis : New Horizon, c1981. — 67p : ill ; 21cm
ISBN 0-86116-427-x : £3.25 B81-26460

Molony, Eileen. Giant, spriggan and buccaboo / Eileen Molony ; illustrated by Gareth Floyd. — London : Kaye & Ward, 1980. — vii,111p : ill,1map ; 23cm
ISBN 0-7182-1238-x : £4.50 B81-00589

Morris, Jean, *1924-*. Twist of eight / Jean Morris ; illustrated by Jolyne Knox. — London : Chatto & Windus, 1981. — 128p : ill ; 21cm
ISBN 0-7011-2557-8 : £4.95 : CIP rev. B81-07611

823'.914[J] — Children's short stories in English, *1945-* — *Texts* *continuation*

My little colour gift book of animal funtime stories. — London : Dean, 1979, c1973. — 117p : col.ill ; 18cm
ISBN 0-603-00165-3 : Unpriced B81-15787

My little animal storybook. — London : Hamlyn, 1981. — 45p : col.ill ; 16cm
ISBN 0-600-36490-9 : £0.99 B81-19953

My little book of magic tales. — London : Hamlyn, 1981. — 44p : col.ill ; 16cm
ISBN 0-600-36485-2 : £0.99 B81-19898

Needle, Jan. A sense of shame : and other stories / Jan Needle. — London : Deutsch, 1980. — 125p ; 21cm
ISBN 0-233-97266-8 : £4.50 B81-02178

Pandya, Michael. Mohit, the bear beater / Michael Pandya. — Cardiff (139 Hill Rise, Llanedeyrn, Cardiff CF2 6UN) : Preeti Publishing, c1981. — 40p : ill ; 21cm
Ill on inside covers
ISBN 0-9507595-0-3 (pbk) : £0.80 B81-32097

Pandya, Michael. Mohit, the bear beater / Michael Pandya. — [2nd ed.]. — Cardiff : Preeti, [1981]. — 48p : ill ; 21cm. — (Children's tales from the East)
Previous ed.: 1981
ISBN 0-9507595-2-x (pbk) : £0.85 B81-39602

Price, Susan. The carpenter : and other stories / retold by Susan Price. — London : Faber, 1981. — 126p ; 21cm
ISBN 0-571-11731-7 : £4.95 : CIP rev. B81-23763

Ryan, John, *1921-*. Captain Pugwash : a pirate story / by John Ryan. — Harmondsworth : Puffin in association with the Bodley Head, 1980, c1957. — 32p : col.ill,1col.map ; 23cm. — (Picture puffins)
Originally published: London : Lane, 1957
£0.80 (pbk) B81-02817

Sheen, Paul. Bitter sweet. — Chester (173 Butterbache Rd, Huntington, Chester CH3 6DE) : Paul Sheen, c1980. — 6 leaves in various pagings ; 30cm
Author: Paul Sheen. — Contents: Once upon a dime - The blue lagoon of Mythveld - Once upon a wasted time
Unpriced (unbound) B81-01527

Siverns, Ruth. Barlow Dale's casebook / Ruth Siverns. — London : Macmillan, 1981. — 141p : ill ; 21cm
ISBN 0-333-31023-3 : £4.95 B81-19954

Smith, Claire. Big book of children's stories / Claire Smith ; illustrated by Helen Haynes. — Ilfracombe : Stockwell, 1981. — 156p : ill ; 19cm
ISBN 0-7223-1463-9 : £3.00 B81-35046

Softly, Barbara. Ponder and William / Barbara Softly ; with drawings by Diana John. — Harmondsworth : Puffin, 1981, c1966. — 125p : ill ; 20cm. — (A Young Puffin original)
Originally published: Harmondsworth : Penguin, 1966
ISBN 0-14-030261-1 (pbk) : £0.85 B81-18520

Summerfield, Geoffrey. The king of the cats : & other short tales / told by Geoffrey Summerfield. — London : Ward Lock Educational, 1980. — 94p : ill(some col.) ; 23cm
ISBN 0-7062-4023-5 : £5.95 B81-02200

Summerfield, Geoffrey. Run for your life : & other short tales / told by Geoffrey Summerfield. — London : Ward Lock Educational, 1980. — 96p : ill(some col.) ; 23cm
ISBN 0-7062-4022-7 : £5.95 B81-07167

Todd, H. E.. The dial-a-story book / H.E. Todd ; pictures by Val Biro. — Harmondsworth : Puffin, 1981. — 63p : ill ; 20cm. — (A Young puffin)
ISBN 0-14-031332-x (pbk) : £0.75 B81-18513

Waterhouse, Keith. Worzel Gummidge's television adventures / Keith Waterhouse and Willis Hall ; based upon the characters created by Barbara Euphan Todd. — Harmondsworth : Kestrel, 1981, c1979. — 298p ; 23cm
Originally published: in 2 bks. as The television adventures of Worzel Gummidge, and More television adventures of Worzel Gummidge. Harmondsworth : Puffin, 1979
ISBN 0-7226-5773-0 : £5.25 B81-40682

Wilson, David Henry. The fastest gun alive : and other night adventures / David Henry Wilson ; illustrated by Anne Mieke. — [London] : Piccolo, 1981, c1978. — 95p : ill ; 18cm
Originally published: London : Chatto & Windus, 1978
ISBN 0-330-26053-7 (pbk) : £0.85 B81-03048

Wingfield, Harry. The fox turned wolf and other stories / retold and illustrated by Harry Wingfield. — Loughborough : Ladybird, c1981. — 51p : col.ill ; 18cm. — (Myths, tables and legends)
Based on stories by Jean de la Fontaine
ISBN 0-7214-0605-x : £0.50 B81-17441

Wood, Anne, *1937-*. A first fairy story book. — London : Hodder and Stoughton Children's Books, July 1981. — [192]p
ISBN 0-340-25297-9 : £3.95 : CIP entry B81-14939

823'.914[J] — Children's stories in English, *1945-* — *Texts*

Adams, Pam. The gingerbread man / illustrated by Pam Adams. — [Swindon] : Child's Play, c1980. — [20]p : chiefly col.ill ; 19cm. — ([Child's Play action book])
Cover title. — Text, ill on inside covers
ISBN 0-85953-107-4 : Unpriced B81-34858

Adams, Pam. If I weren't me — who would I be? / illustrated by Pam Adams. — [Swindon] : Child's Play, c1981. — [20]p : chiefly col.ill ; 19cm. — (Child's Play double mirror action book)
Cover title. — Text, ill on inside cover
ISBN 0-85953-108-2 : Unpriced B81-32137

Adams, Pam. Mrs Honey's hat / written and illustrated by Pam Adams. — [Swindon] : Child's Play, c1980. — [28]p : chiefly col.ill ; 19cm
Ill on inside cover
ISBN 0-85953-099-x : Unpriced B81-32138

Adams, Pam. There were ten in the bed / illustrated by Pam Adams. — [Swindon] : Child's Play, c1979. — [20] : col.ill ; 19cm
Cover title. — Text, ill on inside covers
ISBN 0-85953-095-7 : Unpriced B81-32139

Adams, Richard, *1920-*. Watership Down. — Large print ed. — Leicester : Ulverscroft, Sept.1981. — [704]p. — (Charnwood library series)
Originally published: London : Rex Collings, 1972
ISBN 0-7089-8012-0 : £6.50 : CIP entry B81-22669

Adamson, Jean. Topsy and Tim at the seaside / Jean and Gareth Adamson. — Glasgow : Blackie, c1981. — [24]p : col.ill ; 18cm
ISBN 0-216-91156-7 (cased) : Unpriced : CIP rev.
ISBN 0-216-91157-5 (pbk) : £0.60 B81-18041

Adamson, Jean. Topsy and Tim at the zoo / Jean and Gareth Adamson. — Glasgow : Blackie, c1981. — [24]p : col.ill ; 18cm
ISBN 0-216-91139-7 (cased) : Unpriced : CIP rev.
ISBN 0-216-91138-9 (pbk) : £0.60 B81-18044

Adamson, Jean. Topsy and Tim can cook / Jean and Gareth Adamson. — Glasgow : Blackie, c1981. — [24]p : col.ill ; 25cm. — (Topsy and Tim activity books)
ISBN 0-216-90987-2 (cased) : £2.75
ISBN 0-216-90986-4 (pbk) : £0.95 B81-12080

Adamson, Jean. Topsy and Tim can look after pets / Jean and Gareth Adamson. — Glasgow : Blackie, c1981. — [24]p : col.ill ; 25cm. — (Topsy and Tim activity books)
ISBN 0-216-91122-2 : £2.75 : CIP rev.
ISBN 0-216-91123-0 (pbk) : £0.95 B81-22470

Adamson, Jean. Topsy and Tim can play party games / Jean and Gareth Adamson. — Glasgow : Blackie, c1981. — [24]p : col.ill ; 25cm. — (Topsy and Tim activity books)
ISBN 0-216-91124-9 : £2.75 : CIP rev.
ISBN 0-216-91125-7 (pbk) : £0.95 B81-22471

Adamson, Jean. Topsy and Tim can sing and play / Jean and Gareth Adamson. — Glasgow : Blackie, c1980. — [24]p : col.ill ; 25cm. — (Topsy and Tim activity books)
ISBN 0-216-90989-9 (cased) : £2.75 : CIP rev.
ISBN 0-216-90988-0 (pbk) : £0.95 B80-19476

Adamson, Jean. Topsy and Tim go to hospital. — London : Blackie, Feb.1982. — [24]p. — (Topsy and Tim handy books)
ISBN 0-216-91137-0 (cased) : £1.75 : CIP entry
ISBN 0-216-91136-2 (pbk) : £0.60 B81-36031

Adamson, Jean. Topsy and Tim go to playschool / Jean and Gareth Adamson. — [Glasgow] : Blackie, c1981. — [11]p : col.ill ; 15cm
ISBN 0-216-91090-0 (unbound) : £0.95 B81-26521

Adamson, Jean. Topsy and Tim go to the dentist. — London : Blackie, Feb.1982. — [24]p. — (Topsy and Tim handy books)
ISBN 0-216-91135-4 (cased) : £1.75 : CIP entry
ISBN 0-216-91134-6 (pbk) : £0.60 B81-36030

Adamson, Jean. Topsy and Tim go to the doctor. — London : Blackie, Feb.1982. — [24]p. — (Topsy and Tim handy books)
ISBN 0-216-91133-8 (cased) : £1.75 : CIP entry
ISBN 0-216-91132-x (pbk) : £0.60 B81-36029

Adamson, Jean. Topsy and Tim have their eyes tested. — London : Blackie, Feb.1982. — [24] p. — (Topsy and Tim handy books)
ISBN 0-216-91154-0 (cased) : £1.75 : CIP entry
ISBN 0-216-91155-9 (pbk) : £0.60 B81-36390

Adamson, Jean. Topsy and Tim learn to swim / Jean and Gareth Adamson. — Glasgow : Blackie, c1981. — [24]p : col.ill ; 18cm
ISBN 0-216-91143-5 (cased) : Unpriced : CIP rev.
ISBN 0-216-91140-0 (pbk) : £0.60 B81-18042

Adamson, Jean. Topsy and Tim's birthday / Jean and Gareth Adamson. — [Glasgow] : Blackie, c1981. — [11]p : col.ill ; 15cm
ISBN 0-216-91120-6 (unbound) : £0.95 B81-26519

Adamson, Jean. Topsy and Tim's birthday party / Jean and Gareth Adamson. — Glasgow : Blackie, c1981. — [24]p : col.ill ; 18cm
ISBN 0-216-91141-9 (cased) : Unpriced : CIP rev.
ISBN 0-216-91140-0 (pbk) : £0.60 B81-18043

Adamson, Jean. Topsy and Tim's country day / Jean and Gareth Adamson. — [Glasgow] : Blackie, c1981. — [11]p : col.ill ; 15cm
ISBN 0-216-91119-2 (unbound) : £0.95 B81-26522

Adamson, Jean. Topsy and Tim's new pet / Jean and Gareth Adamson. — [Glasgow] : Blackie, c1981. — [11]p : col.ill ; 15cm
ISBN 0-216-91091-9 (unbound) : £0.95 B81-26520

823'.914[J] — Children's stories in English, *1945- — Texts* *continuation*

Ahlberg, Allan. Fred's dream / [words by] Allan Ahlberg, pictures by Janet Ahlberg. — London : Fontana Picture Lions, 1981, c1976. — [32]p : chiefly col.ill ; 21cm. — (The Brick Street boys)
ISBN 0-00-661930-4 (pbk) : £0.90 B81-28406

Ahlberg, Allan. The great marathon football match / [words by] Allan Ahlberg, pictures by Janet Ahlberg. — London : Fontana Picture Lions, 1981, c1976. — [32]p : chiefly col.ill ; 21cm. — (The Brick Street boys)
ISBN 0-00-661931-2 (pbk) : £0.90 B81-28407

Ahlberg, Janet. Each peach pear plum / Janet and Allan Ahlberg. — London : Fontana, 1980, c1978. — [30]p : col.ill ; 16x22cm. — (Picture lions)
Originally published: Harmondsworth : Kestrel, 1978
ISBN 0-00-661678-x (pbk) : £0.85 B81-01305

Ahlberg, Janet. Funnybones / Janet and Allan Ahlberg. — London : Heinemann, 1980. — [32]p : col.ill ; 26cm
ISBN 0-434-92503-9 : £3.95 B81-02455

Aiken, Joan. Mice and Mendelson / Joan Aiken ; illustrated by Babette Cole ; music by John Sebastian Brown. — Harmondsworth : Puffin, 1981, c1978. — 108p : ill,music ; 20cm
Originally published: London : Cape, 1978
ISBN 0-14-031253-6 (pbk) : £0.85 B81-35071

Aiken, Joan. The stolen lake / Joan Aiken ; illustrated by Pat Marriott. — London : Cape, 1981. — 272p : ill ; 21cm
ISBN 0-224-01924-4 : £5.50 : CIP rev.
B81-00590

Akrill, Caroline. Eventer's dream / Caroline Akrill. — London : Arlington, 1981. — 167p ; 23cm
ISBN 0-85140-535-5 : £4.50 : CIP rev.
B81-10479

Alcock, Vivien. The stonewalkers / Vivien Alcock. — London : Methuen Children's Books, c1981. — 142p ; 21cm
ISBN 0-416-20700-6 : £4.95 : CIP rev.
B81-08945

Alexander, Ewart. The salmon / Ewart Alexander. — Harlow : Longman, 1979 (1981 [printing]). — 79p : ill ; 20cm. — (Knockouts)
ISBN 0-582-39101-6 : £2.95 B81-35130

Alexander, Marygold. The adventures of Maggot and Spong : and other members of the Coven of the Unholy Sisterhood of the Cloven Hoof / by Marygold Alexander ; illustrations by Karen Belsey. — Bognor Regis : New Horizon, c1980. — 426p,[24]leaves of plates : ill,music ; 21cm
ISBN 0-86116-125-4 : £5.75 B81-19233

Allan, Mabel Esther. Goodbye to Pine Street. — London : Abelard-Schuman, Feb.1982. — [128]p
ISBN 0-200-72770-2 (cased) : £3.95 : CIP entry
ISBN 0-200-72771-0 (pbk) : £1.25 B81-36228

Allan, Mabel Esther. The Pine Street problem / Mabel Esther Allan ; illustrated by Patricia Drew. — London : Abelard, 1981. — 115p : ill ; 21cm
ISBN 0-200-72738-9 : £3.95 B81-10128

Allan, Mabel Esther. Strangers in Wood Street / Mabel Esther Allan ; illustrated by Lesley Smith. — London : Methuen Children's, 1981. — 125p : ill ; 20cm. — (A Pied Piper book)
ISBN 0-416-89890-4 : £3.50 B81-08692

Allen, Joy. Cup final for Charlie / Joy Allen ; illustrated by Janet Duchesne. — London : Hamilton, 1981. — 47p : ill ; 19cm. — (Gazelle books)
ISBN 0-241-10691-5 : £1.95 B81-40788

Allen, Joy. Stitches for Charlie / Joy Allen ; [illustrated by Janet Duchesne]. — London : Hamilton, 1980. — 48p : ill ; 19cm. — (Gazelle books)
ISBN 0-241-10511-0 : £1.80 : CIP rev.
B80-23773

Allen, Peter M.. Hasan and the bag of salt. — Sevenoaks : Hodder and Stoughton Children's Books, Apr.1981. — [32]p
ISBN 0-340-25293-6 : £3.50 : CIP entry
B81-01306

Althea. Jeremy Mouse was hungry / by Althea ; illustrated by the author. — Cambridge : Dinosaur, 1981. — [24]p : chiefly col.ill ; 16x19cm. — (Dinosaur's Althea books)
ISBN 0-85122-275-7 (cased) : £1.85 : CIP rev.
ISBN 0-85122-259-5 (pbk) : £0.70 B81-12853

Althea. Listen to your feet / by Althea ; illustrated by Ann Rees. — London : Souvenir, c1981. — [22]p : col.ill ; 19cm. — (Althea's brightstart books)
ISBN 0-285-62491-1 : £1.50 B81-34625

Althea. My sister / by Althea ; illustrated by Susan Morgan. — London : Souvenir, c1981. — [22]p : col.ill ; 19cm. — (Althea's brightstart books)
ISBN 0-285-62490-3 : £1.50 B81-34626

Alverson, Charles. Time bandits / Charles Alverson ; based on a screenplay by Michael Palin and Terry Gilliam. — London : Sparrow, 1981. — 123p,[8]p of plates : ill ; 18cm
ISBN 0-09-926020-4 (pbk) : £0.95 B81-24834

Anderson, Verily. Brownies on wheels. — London : Hodder and Stoughton, Apr.1981. — [128]p
ISBN 0-340-26546-9 (pbk) : £0.85 : CIP entry
B81-01307

Andrews, Allen. The pig Plantagenet / Allen Andrews ; with drawings by Michael Foreman. — London : Hutchinson, 1980. — 199p : ill ; 25cm
Ill on lining papes
ISBN 0-09-142740-1 : £5.95 : CIP rev.
B80-13539

Archer, Jeffrey. By royal appointment / Jeffrey Archer ; illustrated by Peter Longden. — London : Octopus, 1980. — [42]p : col.ill ; 29cm
ISBN 0-7064-1383-0 : £2.50 B81-32147

Archer, Jeffrey. Willy and the killer kipper. — London : Hodder and Stoughton Children's Books, Oct.1981. — [48]p
ISBN 0-340-27057-8 : £3.95 : CIP entry
B81-25695

Archer, Jeffrey. Willy visits the square world / Jeffrey Archer ; illustrated by Derek Matthews. — London : Octopus, 1980. — [42]p : col.ill ; 29cm
ISBN 0-7064-1200-1 : £2.50 B81-00591

Arkle, Phyllis. The adventures of Blunter Button / Phyllis Arkle ; illustrated by Linda Birch. — London : Hodder and Stoughton, 1980. — 47p : ill ; 23cm. — (Hopscotch)
ISBN 0-340-25208-1 : £2.50 : CIP rev.
B80-08461

Arkle, Phyllis. Two village dinosaurs / Phyllis Arkle ; illustrated by Eccles Williams. — Harmondsworth : Penguin, 1981, c1969. — 92p : ill ; 19cm
Originally published: Leicester : Brockhampton Press, 1969
ISBN 0-14-031304-4 (pbk) : £0.75 B81-10698

Armitage, Ronda. [The bossing of Josie]. The birthday spell / Ronda and David Armitage. — London : Scholastic, 1981, c1980. — [32]p : col.ill ; 23cm. — (A Hippo book)
Originally published: London : Deutsch, 1980
ISBN 0-590-70039-1 (pbk) : £0.85 B81-18417

Armitage, Ronda. 'Don't forget, Matilda!' / Ronda and David Armitage. — London : Scholastic, 1980, c1978. — [32]p : col.ill ; 20cm. — (A Hippo book)
Originally published: London : Deutsch, 1979
ISBN 0-590-70038-3 (pbk) : £0.95 B81-00592

Armitage, Ronda. Ice creams for Rosie / Ronda and David Armitage. — London : Deutsch, 1981. — [32]p : col.ill,1col.map ; 26cm
Map on lining papers
ISBN 0-233-97361-3 : £4.50 : CIP rev.
B81-22647

Armitage, Ronda. The lighthouse keeper's lunch / Ronda and David Armitage. — Harmondsworth : Puffin, 1980, c1977. — [32]p : col.ill ; 23cm. — (Picture puffins)
Originally published: London : Deutsch, 1977
ISBN 0-14-050327-7 (corrected : pbk) : £0.80
B81-10303

Arthur, Ruth M.. Requiem for a princess. — London : Hodder & Stoughton, Dec.1981. — [128]p
Originally published: London : Gollancz, 1967
ISBN 0-340-26597-3 (pbk) : £0.85 : CIP entry
B81-31737

Ashley, Bernard. Break in the sun / Bernard Ashley ; illustrated by Charles Keeping. — Harmondsworth : Puffin Books, 1980. — 185p : ill ; 18cm
ISBN 0-14-031341-9 (pbk) : £0.85 B81-30700

Ashley, Bernard. Dinner ladies don't count / Bernard Ashley ; illustrated by Janet Duchesne. — London (8 Cork St., W1X 2HA) : MacRae, 1981. — 44p : ill ; 21cm. — (Blackbird books)
ISBN 0-86203-017-x : £2.75 B81-09672

Ashley, Bernard. Dodgem / Bernard Ashley. — London : MacRae, c1981. — 222p ; 23cm
ISBN 0-86203-048-x : £5.25 : CIP rev.
B81-01308

Ashley, Bernard. I'm trying to tell you / Bernard Ashley ; illustrated by Lyn Jones. — [Harmondsworth] : Kestrel, 1981. — 78p : ill ; 21cm
ISBN 0-7226-5725-0 : £3.75 B81-20215

Ashley, Bernard. A kind of wild justice / Bernard Ashley. — London : Heinemann Educational, 1980, c1978. — 182p ; 20cm. — (The New windmill series ; 249)
Originally published: Oxford : Oxford University Press, 1978
ISBN 0-435-12249-5 : £1.60 : CIP rev.
B80-26212

Augarde, Steve. January Jo and friends. — London : Deutsch, Nov.1981. — [32]p
ISBN 0-233-97364-8 : £4.50 : CIP entry
B81-28839

Augarde, Steve. Mr. Mick / written and illustrated by Steve Augarde. — London : Deutsch, 1980. — [32]p : col.ill ; 26cm
ISBN 0-233-97254-4 : £4.95 : CIP rev.
B80-18506

Avery, Gillian. Mouldy's orphan / Gillian Avery ; illustrated by Faith Jaques. — Harmondsworth : Puffin, 1981, c1978. — 79p : ill ; 20cm
Originally published: London : Collins, 1978
ISBN 0-14-031269-2 (pbk) : £0.75 B81-29495

Baker, Alan, *1951-*. Benjamin's dreadful dream / story and pictures by Alan Baker. — [London] : Fontana, 1981, c1980. — [32]p : chiefly col.ill ; 16x22cm. — (Picture lions)
Originally published: London : Deutsch, 1980
ISBN 0-00-661784-0 (pbk) : £0.85 B81-11281

Baker, Margaret J.. The gift horse. — London : Hodder & Stoughton Children's Books, Feb.1982. — [96]p
ISBN 0-340-26434-9 : £3.50 : CIP entry
B81-36349

823'.914[J] — Children's stories in English, *1945- — Texts continuation*

Banks, Lynne Reid. I, Houdini : the autobiography of a self-educated hamster / Lynne Reid Banks ; illustrated by Terry Riley. — London : Granada, 1981, c1978. — 128p : ill ; 18cm. — (A Dragon book)
Originally published: London : Dent, 1978
ISBN 0-583-30482-6 (pbk) : £0.85 B81-35217

Banks, Lynne Reid. The Indian in the cupboard / Lynne Reid Banks ; illustrated by Robin Jacques. — London : Dent, 1980. — 160p : ill ; 23cm
ISBN 0-460-06992-6 : £4.95 : CIP rev. B80-07557

Banks, Lynne Reid. The Indian in the cupboard / Lynne Reid Banks ; illustrated by Robin Jacques. — London : Granada, 1981. — 160p : ill ; 18cm. — (A Dragon book)
ISBN 0-583-30461-3 (pbk) : £0.85 B81-21985

Barry, Margaret Stuart. Maggie Gumption / Margaret Stuart Barry ; illustrated by Gunvor Edwards. — [London] : Fontana, 1981, c1979. — 74p : ill ; 20cm. — (Lions)
Originally published: London : Hutchinson, 1979
ISBN 0-00-671786-1 (pbk) : £0.85 B81-18479

Barry, Margaret Stuart. Maggie Gumption flies high / Margaret Stuart Barry ; illustrated by Gunvor Edwards. — London : Hutchinson, 1981. — 63p : ill ; 23cm
ISBN 0-09-143450-5 : £3.50 B81-10155

Barry, Margaret Stuart. The witch of Monopoly Manor / Margaret Stuart Barry ; illustrated by Linda Birch. — London : Fontana, c1981, c1980. — 80p : ill ; 20cm. — (Lions)
Originally published: London : Collins, 1980
ISBN 0-00-671788-8 (pbk) : £0.90 B81-28214

Bawden, Nina. William Tell / story told by Nina Bawden ; pictures by Pascale Allamand. — London : Cape, 1981. — [32]p : col.ill ; 28cm
ISBN 0-224-01940-6 : £3.95 : CIP rev. B81-00593

Bayley, Nicola. The patchwork cat / Nicola Bayley & William Mayne. — London : Cape, 1981. — [32]p : ill(some col.) ; 26cm
ISBN 0-224-01925-2 : £3.95 : CIP rev. B81-25687

Beckwith, Lillian. The spuddy / Lillian Beckwith ; decorations by Victor Ambrus. — [London] : Sparrow Books, 1980, c1974. — 95p : ill ; 18cm
Originally published: London : Hutchinson, 1974
ISBN 0-09-913330-x (pbk) : £0.85 B81-13305

Bennett, Thea. A little silver trumpet / Thea Bennett ; illustrated by Priscilla Lamont. — London : BBC, 1980. — 110p : ill ; 21cm
Based on the BBC series of the same name
ISBN 0-563-17884-1 : £5.25 B81-02864

Bennett, Thea. A little silver trumpet. — London : Hodder and Stoughton, Jan.1982. — [112]p. — (Knight Books)
ISBN 0-340-28041-7 (pbk) : £0.95 : CIP entry
ISBN 0-563-17886-8 (BBC) B81-33930

Bentley, Anne. The Groggs' day out / by Anne and Roy Bentley. — London : Deutsch, 1981. — [32]p : chiefly col.ill ; 26cm
ISBN 0-233-97348-6 : £4.50 : CIP rev. B81-04390

Bentley, Theresa M.. Willowy / by Theresa M. Bentley. — Wembley : Selecteditions, c1980. — [19]p : col.ill ; 22cm
ISBN 0-86237-008-6 (pbk) : £0.60 B81-20198

Beresford, Elisabeth. The four of us / Elisabeth Beresford ; illustrated by Trevor Stubley. — London : Hutchinson, 1981. — 110p : ill ; 23cm
ISBN 0-09-144760-7 : £3.95 : CIP rev. B81-04339

Bermant, Chaim. Belshazzar : a cat's story for humans / by Chaim Bermant ; illustrated by Meg Rutherford. — London : Allen & Unwin, 1979. — 67p : ill ; 23cm
ISBN 0-04-823172-x (cased) : £3.50 : CIP rev. B79-32865

Berridge, Celia. Grandmother's tales / story and pictures by Celia Berridge. — London : Deutsch, 1981. — [30]p : col.ill ; 26cm
ISBN 0-233-97357-5 : £4.95 : CIP rev. B81-11938

Berridge, Celia. What did you do in the holiday? / words and pictures by Celia Berridge. — London : Scholastic Publications, 1981, c1979. — [32]p : col.ill ; 16x22cm. — (A Hippo book)
Originally published: London : Deutsch, 1979
ISBN 0-590-70059-6 (pbk) : £0.95 B81-14144

Berridge, Elizabeth. Run for home / Elizabeth Berridge. — London : Pelham, 1981. — 144p ; 21cm
ISBN 0-7207-1294-7 : £4.50 B81-11152

Berrisford, Judith M.. Jackie and the pony rivals / Judith M. Berrisford ; illustrated by Geoffrey Whittam. — London : Hodder and Stoughton, 1981. — 103p : ill ; 19cm
ISBN 0-340-25206-5 : £3.50 B81-33483

Berrisford, Judith M.. Pony-trekkers, go home!. — London : Hodder & Stoughton, July 1981. — [128]p
ISBN 0-340-26599-x (pbk) : £0.85 : CIP entry B81-14915

Bidwell, Dafne. The Tiger Gang and the hijackers / Dafne Bidwell ; illustrated by Graham Bryce. — London : Magnet, 1980, c1976. — 167p : ill ; 18cm
Originally published: Sydney : Methuen of Australia 1976
ISBN 0-416-89560-3 (pbk) : £0.85 B81-06424

Billington, Rachel. Rosanna and the wizard-robot. — London : Methuen Children's Books, Oct.1981. — [192]p
ISBN 0-416-21840-7 : £4.50 : CIP entry B81-25838

Blake, Quentin. Angelo / written and illustrated by Quentin Blake. — Harmondsworth : Penguin, 1972, c1970 (1980 [printing]). — 28p : col.ill ; 23cm. — (Picture puffins)
Originally published: London : Cape, 1970. — Text on inside covers
ISBN 0-14-050059-6 (pbk) : £0.80 B81-06079

Blakeley, Peggy. Oscar on the moon / words by Peggy Blakeley ; paintings by Taxi Kitada. — London : Black, c1980. — [25]p : col.ill ; 25cm. — (Read together books)
ISBN 0-7136-2090-0 : £3.95 B81-02476

Blakeley, Peggy. The smallest Christmas tree / words by Peggy Blakeley ; paintings by Masahiro Kasuya. — London : Black, c1980. — [26]p : col.ill ; 25cm. — (Read together books)
ISBN 0-7136-2091-9 : £3.95 B81-02477

Blanch, Graham. The dragon who couldn't fly / story by Graham Blanch ; pictures by Katy Sleight. — Winchester : Hambleside, c1981. — [24]p : col.ill ; 26cm. — (A Terrapin book)
ISBN 0-86042-035-3 : Unpriced B81-24364

Blyth, Alan. Cinderella : (La cenerentola) the story of Rossini's opera. — London : Julia MacRae, Aug.1981. — [30]p
ISBN 0-86203-073-0 : £4.50 : CIP entry B81-17530

Blyth, Alan. Lohengrin : the story of Wagner's opera. — London : Julia MacRae, Aug.1981. — [30]p
ISBN 0-86203-068-4 : £4.50 : CIP entry B81-17529

Bolt, David. Adam / David Bolt. — Tring : Lion Publishing, 1981, 1960. — 143p ; 18cm
Originally published: London : Dent, 1960
ISBN 0-85648-372-9 (pbk) : £1.50 B81-37058

Bond, Gill. Zooey and Hazel / written by Gill Bond and Chris Austin ; illustrated by Gill Bond. — London : H. Hamilton, 1981. — 42p : col.ill ; 18x21cm
ISBN 0-241-10589-7 : £4.25 B81-14083

Bond, Michael. Here comes Thursday / Michael Bond ; illustrated by Daphne Rowles. — London : Harrap, 1981, c1966. — 126p : ill ; 23cm
ISBN 0-245-58688-1 : £4.75 B81-28438

Bond, Michael. J.D. Polson and the Liberty Head dime / by Michael Bond ; illustrated by Roger Wade Walker ; [hand lettering by Leslie Lee]. — London : Octopus, 1980. — [42]p : chiefly col.ill ; 29cm
ISBN 0-7064-1381-4 : £2.50 B81-00594

Bond, Michael. Paddington at home / Michael Bond. — London : Collins, c1980. — [12]p : col.ill ; 20cm
ISBN 0-00-138264-0 : £0.95 B81-07846

Bond, Michael. Paddington goes out / Michael Bond. — London : Collins, c1980. — [12]p : col.ill ; 20cm
ISBN 0-00-138265-9 : £0.95 B81-07845

Bond, Michael. Paddington takes the test / Michael Bond ; illustrated by Peggy Fortnum. — [London] : Fontana, 1981, c1979. — 125p : ill ; 20cm. — (Lions)
Originally published: London : Collins, 1979
ISBN 0-00-671876-0 (pbk) : £0.90 B81-18473

Bond, Michael. Thursday in Paris / Michael Bond ; illustrated by Leslie Wood. — London : Harrap, 1981, c1971. — 127p : ill,1map ; 23cm
ISBN 0-245-50647-0 : £4.75 B81-32320

Bond, Ruskin. Flames in the forest / Ruskin Bond ; illustrated by Valerie Littlewood. — London (8 Cork St., W1X 2HA) : MacRae, 1981. — 44p : ill ; 21cm. — (Blackbird books)
ISBN 0-86203-027-7 : £2.75 B81-09669

Bonsall, Crosby. The case of the double cross / written and illustrated by Crosby Bonsall. — Tadworth : World's Work, 1981, c1980. — 64p : col.ill ; 22cm. — (An I can read mystery ; no.136) (A World's Work children's book)
ISBN 0-437-90136-x : £3.95 B81-37902

Bonsall, Crosby. Who's afraid of the dark? / by Crosby Bonsall. — Tadworth : World's Work, 1981, c1980. — 32p : col.ill ; 22cm. — (An Early I can read book ; no.20)
ISBN 0-437-90520-9 : £3.20 B81-20935

Boorer, Lesley. The house in the forest / written and illustrated by Lesley Boorer. — London : Hodder and Stoughton, 1981. — 95p : ill ; 20cm. — (Leapfrog)
ISBN 0-340-25616-8 : £3.95 B81-21876

Boyle, Vera. Toby, Peetie, Harry and Fred were here / Vera Boyle ; illustrated by Michael Charlton. — London : Macmillan Children's Books, 1981. — 114p : ill ; 21cm
ISBN 0-333-31529-4 : £4.95 : CIP rev. B81-00425

Brandreth, Gyles. Frankenstein's monster fun book. — London : Hodder & Stoughton, July 1981. — [128]p
ISBN 0-340-26532-9 (pbk) : £0.85 : CIP entry B81-13508

Brewster, Patience. Ellsworth and the cats from Mars / by Patience Brewster. — London : Hutchinson, 1981. — 32p : col.ill ; 27cm
ISBN 0-09-144800-x : £3.95 : CIP rev. B81-03676

823'.914[J] — Children's stories in English, *1945-* — *Texts* *continuation*

Brierley, Louise. King Lion and his cooks. — London : Andersen, Oct.1981. — [32]p
ISBN 0-86264-008-3 : £3.50 : CIP entry B81-27416

Briggs, Raymond. The snowman / Raymond Briggs. — Harmondsworth : Puffin, 1980, c1978. — [32]p : all col.ill ; 30cm. — (Picture puffins)
Originally published: London : H. Hamilton, 1978
ISBN 0-14-050350-1 (pbk) : £1.25 B81-01310

Brock, Carey. The golden chain : a story illustrative of the Lord's prayer / by Carey Brock. — Ossett (44 Queen's Drive, Ossett, W. Yorks. WF5 0ND) : Zoar, [1981?]. — 116p,[6]p of plates : ill(some col.),col.maps ; 19cm
Maps on lining papers
£2.00 B81-31698

Brown, George Mackay. Six lives of Fankle the cat / George Mackay Brown ; illustrated by Ian MacInnes. — London : Chatto & Windus, 1980. — 120p : ill ; 23cm
ISBN 0-7011-2534-9 : £4.95 B81-00595

Brown, Lindsay. The treasure of Dubarry Castle / Lindsay Brown ; illustrated by Val Biro. — London : Piccolo, 1980, c1978. — 144p : ill ; 18cm
Originally published: London : Hale, 1978
ISBN 0-330-26210-6 (pbk) : £0.85 B81-02239

Brown, Roy. Chips and the river rat. — London : Andersen Press, Oct.1981. — [96]p
ISBN 0-86264-007-5 : £3.95 : CIP entry B81-27415

Brown, Roy, *1921-*. Chips and the crossword gang / Roy Brown ; illustrated by Pauline Carr. — London : Granada, 1980, c1979. — 90p : ill ; 18cm. — (A Dragon book)
Originally published: London : Anderson Press, 1979
ISBN 0-583-30356-0 (pbk) : £0.75 B81-00596

Brown, Roy, *1921-*. Cover drive / Roy Brown. — London : Granada, 1981, c1979. — 93p ; 18cm. — (A Dragon book)
Originally published: London : Abelard, 1979
ISBN 0-583-30458-3 (pbk) : £0.85 B81-17586

Brown, Roy, *1921-*. Octopus / Roy Brown. — London : Andersen, 1981. — 190p ; 23cm
ISBN 0-905478-92-4 : £4.95 B81-14243

Brown, Roy, *1921-*. Undercover boy / Roy Brown ; illustrated by Pauline Carr. — London : Granada, 1980, c1978. — 94p : ill ; 18cm. — (A Dragon book)
Originally published: London : Anderson Press, 1978
ISBN 0-583-30355-2 (pbk) : £0.75 B81-01311

Brown, Ruth. A dark, dark tale. — London : Andersen, Sept.1981. — [32]p
ISBN 0-86264-001-6 : £3.95 : CIP entry B81-23899

Browne, Anthony. Hansel and Gretel / The brothers Grimm ; illustrated [and adapted] by Anthony Browne ; ... from the translation by Eleanor Quarrie. — London : MacRae, 1981. — 32p : col.ill ; 26cm
ISBN 0-86203-042-0 : £4.95 : CIP rev. B81-20635

Bull, Angela. The bicycle parcel / Angela Bull ; illustrated by Jane Paton. — London : Hamilton, 1980. — 48p : ill ; 20cm. — (Gazelle books)
ISBN 0-241-10489-0 : £1.80 : CIP rev. B80-11209

Burch, T. R.. Tig's crime / T.R. Burch. — London : Fontana, 1981, c1979. — 149p ; 18cm. — (Lions)
Originally published: London : Heinemann, 1979
ISBN 0-00-671748-9 (pbk) : £0.90 B81-15599

Burkett, Molly. Look for the buzzards / Molly Burkett ; illustrated by Hilary Abrahams. — London : Deutsch, 1981. — 127p : ill ; 22cm
ISBN 0-233-97360-5 : £4.95 : CIP rev. B81-18118

Burnap, Jennifer. The tale of a tail : and other animal fables / Jennifer Burnap ; illustrated by Susan Bridger. — London : Blackie, 1980. — 64p : ill ; 21cm
ISBN 0-216-91039-0 : £3.95 : CIP rev. B80-18909

Burnham, Jeremy. Mystery of the tower / Jeremy Burnham and Trevor Ray ; illustrated by Pauline Carr. — [London] : Carousel, 1981. — 206p : ill ; 18cm
ISBN 0-552-52130-2 (pbk) : £0.85 B81-14309

Burningham, John. Mr Gumpy's motor car / John Burningham. — Harmondsworth : Puffin, 1979, c1973 (1981 [printing]). — [32]p : col.ill ; 23cm. — (Picture puffins)
Originally published: London : Cape, 1973. — Text on inside cover
ISBN 0-14-050300-5 (pbk) : £0.95 B81-35490

Burns, Peggy. Killer Dog / Peggy Burns ; [illustrations by David Astin]. — Tring : Lion, 1981. — 94p : ill ; 18cm
ISBN 0-85648-383-4 (pbk) : £0.95 B81-33489

Burt, Anne. Once upon a star / Anne Burt ; illustrated by Cora E.M. Paterson. — Ilfracombe : Stockwell, 1981. — 16p : ill ; 19cm
ISBN 0-7223-1452-3 (pbk) : £0.55 B81-05922

Burton, Hester. Five August days / Hester Burton ; illustrated by Trevor Ridley. — Oxford : Oxford University Press, 1981. — 176p : ill ; 21cm
ISBN 0-19-271454-6 : £5.95 : CIP rev. B81-04341

Butterworth, Ben. A fly in his eye / written by Ben Butterworth ; illustrated by Martin Salisbury. — Loughborough : Ladybird, c1981. — 25p : col.ill ; 19x20cm. — (Early learning)
ISBN 0-7214-0672-6 : £0.95 B81-20925

Butterworth, Ben. Oliver Octopus / written by Ben Butterworth ; illustrated by Kathie Layfield. — Loughborough : Ladybird, c1981. — 25p : col.ill ; 19x20cm. — (Early learning)
ISBN 0-7214-0670-x : £0.95 B81-20921

Butterworth, Ben. Tommy's tuba / written by Ben Butterworth ; illustrated by Martin Aitchison. — Loughborough : Ladybird, c1981. — 25p : col.ill ; 19x20cm. — (Early learning)
ISBN 0-7214-0674-2 : Unpriced B81-20924

Butterworth, Ben. The weathervane / written by Ben Butterworth ; illustrated by Martin Aitchison. — Loughborough : Ladybird, c1981. — 25p : col.ill ; 19x20cm. — (Early learning)
ISBN 0-7214-0673-4 : £0.95 B81-20926

Buzby goes skateboarding. — London : Severn House Paperbacks, 1979. — [32]p : col.ill ; 13x14cm
ISBN 0-906461-00-6 (pbk) : £0.40 B81-13135

Buzby's challenge. — London : Severn House Paperbacks, 1979. — [32]p : col.ill ; 13x14cm
ISBN 0-906461-03-0 (pbk) : £0.40 B81-13137

Buzby's girlfriend. — London : Severn House Paperbacks, 1979. — [32]p : ill ; 13x14cm
ISBN 0-906461-01-4 (pbk) : £0.40 B81-13134

Buzby's rock group. — London : Severn House Paperbacks, 1979. — [32]p : col.ill ; 13x14cm
ISBN 0-906461-02-2 (pbk) : £0.40 B81-13136

Caldecott, Moyra. The king of shadows / Moyra Caldecott ; illustrated by Oliver Caldecott. — London (19 Turney Road) : M. Caldecott, c1981. — 177p : ill ; 21cm
Unpriced (pbk) B81-35550

Campbell, Rod. Charlie Clown. — London : Abelard-Schuman, July 1981. — [16]p. — (Little people)
ISBN 0-200-72753-2 (pbk) : £0.50 : CIP entry B81-14802

Campbell, Rod. Eddie Engine-driver. — London : Abelard-Schuman, July 1981. — [16]p. — (Little people)
ISBN 0-200-72755-9 (pbk) : £0.50 : CIP entry B81-14846

Campbell, Rod. Freddie Fireman. — London : Abelard-Schuman, July 1981. — [16]p. — (Little people)
ISBN 0-200-72756-7 (pbk) : £0.50 : CIP entry B81-14847

Campbell, Rod. Gertie Gardener. — London : Abelard-Schuman, July 1981. — [16]p. — (Little people)
ISBN 0-200-72758-3 (pbk) : £0.50 : CIP entry B81-14805

Campbell, Rod. Nancy Nurse. — London : Abelard-Schuman, July 1981. — [16]p. — (Little people)
ISBN 0-200-72754-0 (pbk) : £0.50 : CIP entry B81-14804

Campbell, Rod. Nigel Knight. — London : Abelard-Schuman, July 1981. — [16]p. — (Little people)
ISBN 0-200-72757-5 (pbk) : £0.50 : CIP entry B81-14803

Carrick, Malcolm. Mr. Tod's trap / Malcolm Carrick. — Tadworth : World's Work, 1981, c1980. — 64p : col.ill ; 22cm
ISBN 0-437-90134-3 : £3.95 B81-20932

Carter, Peter, *1929-*. Under Goliath / Peter Carter. — Harmondsworth : Puffin in association with Oxford University Press, 1980, c1977. — 169p ; 18cm
Originally published: Oxford : Oxford University Press, 1977
ISBN 0-14-031132-7 (pbk) : £0.90 B81-01312

Cartlidge, Michelle. Teddy Trucks / Michelle Cartlidge. — London : Heinemann, 1981. — [36]p : col.ill ; 27cm
Ill on lining papers
ISBN 0-434-93143-8 : £3.95 B81-39338

Carus, Zena. Smuggler's castle. — Sevenoaks : Hodder & Stoughton, Aug.1981. — [192]p
Originally published: London : Blackie, 1980
ISBN 0-340-26536-1 (pbk) : £0.85 : CIP entry B81-18132

Cash, Dave. Miss Mouse and Cosmic Turtle / by Dave Cash ; and drawn by John Farman. — [Leeds] : Pepper, 1981. — [32]p : col.ill ; 25cm
ISBN 0-560-74514-1 : Unpriced B81-18617

Casley, Nina. The dogs of Dogton Villa / by Nina Casley. — [Torrington] ([11 Yarde, Petersmarland, Torrington N. Devon]) : Henscath, c1981. — 39p : ill ; 21cm
ISBN 0-907646-00-x (pbk) : £0.95 : CIP rev. B81-25119

Cass, Joan. The four surprises / Joan Cass ; pictures by Tony Linsell. — London : Abelard, c1981. — [25]p : col.ill ; 24cm
ISBN 0-200-72681-1 : £4.50 : CIP rev. B81-01313

Cecil, Mirabel. Ruby the donkey : a winter story / written by Mirabel Cecil ; illustrated by Christina Gascoigne. — London : Methuen/Walker Books, 1980. — [26]p : col.ill ; 22cm
Ill on lining papers
ISBN 0-416-89190-x : £1.95 : CIP rev. B80-18910

823'.914[J] — Children's stories in English, *1945-* — *Texts* *continuation*

Cecil, Mirabel. Spiky the hedgehog : an autumn story / written by Mirabel Cecil ; illustrated by Christina Gascoigne. — London : Methuen, 1980. — [28]p : col.ill ; 22cm
ISBN 0-416-89170-5 : £1.95 : CIP rev. B80-18911

Chambers, Nancy. Wildcat Wendy and the Peekaboo Kid / Nancy Chambers ; illustrated by James Hodgson. — London : Fontana, 1981, c1979. — 58p : ill ; 20cm
Originally published: London : Hamilton, 1979
ISBN 0-00-671928-7 (pbk) : £0.85 B81-22320

Chard, Brigid. Voices on the wind / Brigid Chard. — London : Collings, 1980. — 188p ; 23cm
ISBN 0-86036-127-6 : £4.95 B81-00597

Charles, *Prince of Wales*. The old man of Lochnagar / H.R.H. the Prince of Wales ; illustrations by Sir Hugh Casson. — London : Hamilton, 1980. — [46]p : col.ill ; 21x27cm
ISBN 0-241-10527-7 : £3.95 B81-00598

Chauncy, Nan. Tangara : 'Let us set off again' / Nan Chauncy ; illustrated by Brian Wildsmith. — Oxford : Oxford University Press, 1960 (1979 printing). — 180p : ill ; 21cm. — (New Oxford library)
ISBN 0-19-277094-2 : £2.25 : CIP rev. B79-17899

Cheeky Teddy at the circus. — London : Dean, c1980. — [24]p : col.ill ; 13cm. — (Dean's little tots' series)
ISBN 0-603-00191-2 (pbk) : £0.15 B81-06340

Cheeky Teddy at the seaside. — London : Dean, c1980. — [24]p : col.ill ; 13cm. — (Dean's little tots' series)
ISBN 0-603-00189-0 (pbk) : £0.15 B81-06342

Cheeky Teddy at the zoo. — London : Dean, c1980. — [24]p : col.ill ; 13cm. — (Dean's little tots' series)
ISBN 0-603-00192-0 (pbk) : £0.15 B81-06338

Cheeky Teddy on the farm. — London : Dean, c1980. — [24]p : col.ill ; 13cm. — (Dean's little tots' series)
ISBN 0-603-00190-4 (pbk) : £0.15 B81-06339

Childs, Rob. Sandford on the run. — London : Blackie, Oct.1981. — [128]p
ISBN 0-216-91131-1 : £4.75 : CIP entry B81-27354

Christopher, John, *1922-*. Beyond the Burning Lands / John Christopher. — [Harmondsworth] : Puffin in association with Hamilton, 1973, c1971 (1981 [printing]). — 153p ; 19cm
Originally published: London : Hamilton, 1971
ISBN 0-14-030625-0 (pbk) : £0,85 B81-35478

Christopher, John, *1922-*. The city of gold and lead / John Christopher. — London : Beaver, 1977, c1967 (1981 [printing]). — 159p ; 18cm. — (The Tripods trilogy ; 2)
Originally published: London : Hamilton, 1967
ISBN 0-600-31931-8 (pbk) : £0.90 B81-29129

Christopher, John, *1922-*. The pool of fire / John Christopher. — London : Beaver, 1977, c1968 (1981 [printing]). — 156p ; 18cm. — (The Tripods trilogy ; 3)
Originally published: London : Hamilton, 1968
ISBN 0-600-37134-4 (pbk) : £0.90 B81-29142

Christopher, John, *1922-*. The white mountains / John Christopher. — London : Beaver, 1976, c1967 (1981 [printing]). — 153p ; 18cm. — (The Tripods trilogy ; 1)
Originally published: London : Hamilton, 1967
ISBN 0-600-39367-4 (pbk) : £0.90 B81-29141

Cleveland-Peck, Patricia. The birthday cake / Patricia Cleveland-Peck ; illustrated by Maureen Bradley. — London : Hamilton, 1981. — 47p : ill ; 19cm. — (Gazelle books)
ISBN 0-241-10626-5 : £1.80 : CIP rev. B81-02560

Cleveland-Peck, Patricia. The String family / Patricia Cleveland-Peck. — [London] : Piccolo in association with Heinemann, 1981, c1979. — 76p : ill ; 18cm
Originally published: London : Heinemann, 1979
ISBN 0-330-26414-1 (pbk) : £0.90 B81-37357

Cleveland-Peck, Patricia. William the wizard / by Patricia Cleveland-Peck ; illustrated by Sophie Kittredge. — London : Hamilton, 1980. — 94p : ill ; 19cm. — (Antelope books)
ISBN 0-241-10514-5 : £2.25 : CIP rev. B80-23779

Cockett, Mary. The cat and the castle. — Sevenoaks : Hodder and Stoughton Children's Books, Oct.1981. — [32]p
ISBN 0-340-26575-2 : £2.50 : CIP entry B81-26710

Cole, Babette. Nungu and the elephant / written and illustrated by Babette Cole. — London : Macdonald General, 1980. — [28]p : col.ill ; 24cm
ISBN 0-354-08097-0 : £2.95 B81-07034

Cole, Babette. Promise and the monster / by Babette Cole ; bubble calligraphy by Monica Gripaios. — London : Granada, 1981. — [26]p : chiefly col.ill ; 28cm
Ill on lining papers
ISBN 0-246-11610-2 : £3.95 B81-28619

Cole, Tamasin. The last trick / illustrated by Tamasin Cole ; story by James Cressey. — London : Black, 1980. — [28]p : chiefly col.ill ; 27cm
ISBN 0-7136-2040-4 : £3.50 : CIP rev. B80-18912

Coleman, Leslie. Fort Wilberforce / Leslie Coleman ; illustrated by John Laing. — [London] : Beaver, 1980, c1977. — 79p : ill ; 20cm
Originally published: Glasgow : Blackie, 1977
ISBN 0-600-20136-8 (pbk) : £0.75 B81-01314

Collins, Joan, *1917-*. The lost world / by Sir Arthur Conan Doyle ; retold in simple language by Joan Collins ; illustrated by Martin Aitchison. — Loughborough : Ladybird, c1981. — 51p : col.ill ; 18cm. — (Ladybird children's classics)
ISBN 0-7214-0711-0 : £0.50 B81-37879

Collins, Joan, *1917-*. A tale of two cities / by Charles Dickens ; retold in simple language by Joan Collins ; with illustrations by Frank Humphris. — Loughborough : Ladybird, c1981. — 51p : col.ill ; 18cm. — (Ladybird children's classics)
ISBN 0-7214-0710-2 : £0.50 B81-37878

Conway, Anne. A dragon for a friend / Anne Conway. — Winchester : Hambleside, c1980. — 185p : ill ; 23cm. — (A Terrapin book)
ISBN 0-86042-022-1 : Unpriced B81-24359

Cook, Patrick. Elmer the rat / Patrick Cook. — Harmondsworth : Puffin, 1981, c1980. — 54p : ill ; 20cm
Originally published: Ringwood, Vic. : Penguin, 1980
ISBN 0-14-031394-x (pbk) : £0.75 B81-22028

Cookson, Catherine. Joe and The Gladiator / Catherine Cookson ; illustrated by Gillian Shanks. — Harmondsworth : Puffin, 1971, c1968 (1980 [printing]). — 154p : ill ; 18cm
Originally published: London : Macdonald, 1968
ISBN 0-14-030484-3 (pbk) : £0.75 B81-01315

Cooper, Clare. The black horn / Clare Cooper ; illustrated by Trevor Stubley. — London : Hodder and Stoughton, 1981. — 128p : ill ; 23cm
ISBN 0-340-25556-0 : £4.95 B81-26448

Cooper, Jilly. Little Mabel's great escape / Jilly Cooper ; illustrated by Timothy Jaques. — London : Granada, 1981. — [32p] : col.ill ; 26cm
ISBN 0-246-11160-7 : £3.95 B81-21211

Cooper, Susan. Silver on the tree / Susan Cooper. — London : Chatto & Windus, 1977 (1978 [printing]). — 269p ; 23cm
ISBN 0-7011-2230-7 : £4.95 B81-35162

Coren, Alan. Arthur and the Bellybutton Diamond / Alan Coren ; illustrated by John Astrop. — Harmondsworth : Puffin, 1981, c1979. — 60p : ill ; 18cm
Originally published: London : Robson, 1979
ISBN 0-14-031346-x (pbk) : £0.80 B81-15393

Coren, Alan. Arthur and the great detective / Alan Coren ; illustrated by John Astrop. — Harmondsworth : Puffin, 1981, c1979. — 60p : ill ; 18cm
Originally published: London : Robson, 1979
ISBN 0-14-031345-1 (pbk) : £0.80 B81-15394

Coren, Alan. Arthur v the rest. — London : Robson, Sept.1981. — [64]p. — (Alan Coren's Arthur books ; 10th)
ISBN 0-86051-142-1 : £1.95 : CIP entry B81-22467

Corlett, William. Barriers. — London : Hamish Hamilton, Oct.1981. — [160]p
ISBN 0-241-10718-0 : £5.25 : CIP entry B81-30206

Cowley, Stewart. The space warriors / Stewart Cowley. — London : Dean, c1980. — 122p : col.ill ; 28cm
ISBN 0-603-00197-1 : £2.95 B81-32344

Cresswell, Helen. The bongleweed / Helen Cresswell ; illustrated by Ann Strugnell. — [Harmondsworth] : Puffin in association with Faber, 1981, c1973. — 172p : ill ; 18cm
Originally published: London : Faber, 1973
ISBN 0-14-031272-2 (pbk) : £0.95 B81-22036

Cresswell, Helen. My Aunt Polly by the sea / Helen Cresswell ; illustrated by Margaret Gordon. — Exeter : Wheaton, 1980. — [24]p : col.ill ; 21x22cm
ISBN 0-08-025621-x (cased) : £2.75
ISBN 0-08-025622-8 (pbk) : £0.90 B81-00599

Cross, Gillian. Save our school / Gillian Cross ; illustrated by Gareth Floyd. — London : Methuen Children's, 1981. — 111p : ill ; 20cm. — (A Pied Piper book)
ISBN 0-416-89800-9 : £3.50 B81-08691

Cross, Gillian. A whisper of lace / Gillian Cross. — Oxford : Oxford University Press, 1981. — 143p ; 23cm
ISBN 0-19-271447-3 : £4.50 : CIP rev. B81-01316

Crouch, Marcus. Rainbow Warrior's bride. — London : Pelham, Oct.1981. — [24]p
ISBN 0-7207-1296-3 : £3.25 : CIP entry B81-27888

Cunliffe, John. Postman Pat and the mystery thief / story by John Cunliffe ; pictures by Celia Berridge from the original television design by Ivor Wood. — London : Deutsch, 1981. — [36]p : col.ill ; 17x20cm
ISBN 0-233-97418-0 : £1.95 : CIP rev. B81-30281

Cunliffe, John. Postman Pat's treasure hunt / story by John Cunliffe ; pictures by Celia Berridge from the original television designs by Ivor Wood. — London : Deutsch, 1981. — [36]p : col.ill ; 17x20cm
ISBN 0-233-97417-2 : £1.95 : CIP rev. B81-26719

823'.914[J] — Children's stories in English, *1945-* — *Texts* *continuation*

Cunningham, Donald. Bron the Hunter / Donald Cunningham. — Bognor Regis : New Horizon, c1981. — 92p : ill ; 21cm
ISBN 0-86116-217-x : £3.25 B81-28948

Curry, Peter. The glass hat / Peter Curry. — Tadworth : World's Work, c1981. — [32]p : col.ill ; 21cm
ISBN 0-437-32940-2 : £4.50 B81-36142

Curtis, Anthony. Spillington and the whitewash clowns / by Anthony Curtis ; illustrated by Rosemary Bullen. — Leeds : Pepper Press, c1981. — 64p : ill ; 20cm
ISBN 0-560-74513-3 : £3.50 B81-19854

Curtis, Philip. Mr Browser and the comet crisis. — London : Andersen, Aug.1981. — [128]p. — (Andersen young readers' library)
ISBN 0-86264-004-0 : £3.95 : CIP entry B81-23788

Curtis, Philip. Mr Browser meets the Burrowers / Philip Curtis ; illustrated by Tony Ross. — London : Anderson, 1980. — 128p : ill ; 21cm. — (Anderson young readers' library)
ISBN 0-905478-88-6 : £3.95 B81-00600

Da Pavlova, Chrisi É.. A tortoise tale / Chrisi É. da Pavlova. — Bognor Regis : New Horizon, c1980. — 32p : ill ; 21cm
ISBN 0-86116-438-5 : £2.95 B81-19252

Daniels, Meg. Out of doors. — London : Blackie, Feb.1982. — [12]p. — (Blackie concertina books)
ISBN 0-216-91130-3 : £0.95 : CIP entry B81-36028

Dann, Colin. The animals of Farthing Wood / Colin Dann ; illustrated by Jacqueline Tettmar. — London : Piccolo in association with Heinemann, 1980, c1979. — 302p : ill ; 18cm
Originally published: London : Heinemann, 1979
ISBN 0-330-26187-8 (pbk) : £1.50 B81-01317

Dann, Colin. The animals of Farthing Wood / by Colin Dann ; illustrated by Jacqueline Tettmar. — Wendover : Goodchild, 1979
ISBN 0-903445-55-7 (pbk) : Unpriced B81-03230

Dann, Colin. In the grip of winter. — London : Hutchinson, Oct.1981. — [144]p
ISBN 0-09-146340-8 : £5.95 : CIP entry B81-26763

Davies, Andrew. Conrad's war / Andrew Davies. — London : Heinemann Educational, 1981, c1978. — 126p ; 20cm. — (The New Windmill series ; 253)
Originally published: London : Blackie, 1978
ISBN 0-435-12253-3 : £1.35 B81-22111

Davies, Andrew. Marmalade Atkins in space. — London : Abelard-Schuman, Nov.1981. — [96]p
ISBN 0-200-72773-7 : £4.95 : CIP entry B81-30220

Davies, Pauline. The southern hill and the land beyond / Pauline Davies ; illustrations by Rachel Miles. — Tring : Lion, 1973 (1981 [printing]). — 157p : ill ; 18cm
ISBN 0-86760-345-3 (pbk) : £1.25 B81-33490

Davis, Gerry. Doctor Who and the cybermen : based on the BBC television serial Doctor Who and the moon base by Kit Pedler and Gerry Davis by arrangement with the British Broadcasting Corporation / Gerry Davis ; illustrated by Alan Willow. — London : W.H. Allen, 1981, c1974. — 150p : ill ; 21cm
ISBN 0-491-02915-2 : £4.50 B81-28607

De Fossard Esta. When Floyd went down to the farm / story by Esta de Fossard ; photography by Haworth Bartram. — Leeds : E.J. Arnold, 1981. — [32]p : col.ill ; 27cm. — (Scamps)
ISBN 0-560-03630-2 (pbk) : Unpriced B81-10359

De Hamel, Joan. Take the long path / Joan de Hamel ; with illustration and maps by Gareth Floyd. — Harmondsworth : Puffin, 1980, c1978. — 128p : ill,maps ; 19cm
Originally published: Guildford : Lutterworth Press, 1978
ISBN 0-14-031257-9 : £0.85 B81-10690

Deary, Terry. The Lambton worm / Terry Deary ; illustrated by Charlotte Firmin. — London : A&C Black, 1981. — 64p : ill ; 23cm
ISBN 0-7136-2055-2 : £3.50 B81-19896

Degen, Bruce. The little witch and the riddle / by Bruce Degen. — Tadworth : World's Work, 1981, c1980. — 62p : col.ill ; 22cm. — (An I can read book ; no.133)
ISBN 0-437-90133-5 : £3.95 B81-20934

Dennant, Richard. The video affair / by Richard Dennant ; illustrated by Janet Duchesne. — London : Hamilton, 1981. — 90p : ill ; 19cm. — (Antelope books)
ISBN 0-241-10621-4 : £2.25 B81-15775

Denton, Michael. The eggbox brontosaurus / Michael Denton ; illustrated by Hilda Offen. — London : Granada, 1980. — 94p,[1]leaf of plates : ill(some col.) ; 23cm
ISBN 0-246-11493-2 : £3.95 B81-12926

Derwent, Lavinia. Macpherson's mystery adventure. — London : Blackie, Feb.1982. — [128]p
ISBN 0-216-91148-6 : £4.95 : CIP entry B81-36034

Dick, Paul. Henry Beaver / by Paul Dick ; illustrated by Doreen Edmonds [i.e. Edmond]. — Winchester : Hambleside, c1980. — [24]p : ill(some col.) ; 18x22cm. — (A Terrapin book)
ISBN 0-86042-027-2 (pbk) : £0.75 B81-24363

Dick Turpin. — Maidenhead : Purnell, 1980. — 61p : col.ill ; 27cm
Ill on lining papers
ISBN 0-361-04613-8 : £3.50 B81-18247

Dickinson, Mary. Alex and Roy / story by Mary Dickinson ; pictures by Charlotte Firmin. — London : Deutsch, 1981. — [32]p : col.ill ; 18x22cm
ISBN 0-233-97347-8 : £3.95 B81-39793

Dickinson, Mike. My Dad doesn't even notice. — London : Deutsch, Feb.1982. — [32]p
ISBN 0-233-97385-0 : £4.50 : CIP entry B81-37579

Dickinson, Peter, *1927-*. Tulku / Peter Dickinson. — Harmondsworth : Puffin, 1981, c1979. — 286p ; 18cm
Originally published: London : Gollancz, 1979
ISBN 0-14-031357-5 (pbk) : £1.50 B81-34808

Dicks, Terrance. The case of the blackmail boys : the Baker Street irregulars / Terrance Dicks. — [London] : Piccolo, 1981, c1979. — 108p ; 18cm
Originally published: London : Blackie, 1979
ISBN 0-330-26265-3 (pbk) : £0.80 B81-09745

Dicks, Terrance. The case of the cop catchers / Terrance Dicks. — London : Blackie, 1981. — 127p ; 21cm. — (The Baker Street irregulars)
ISBN 0-216-91062-5 (corrected) : £4.50 B81-13589

Dicks, Terrance. Cry vampire!. — London : Blackie, Oct.1981. — [128]p
ISBN 0-216-91126-5 : £5.25 : CIP entry B81-26760

Dicks, Terrance. Doctor Who and the day of the Daleks : based on the BBC television serial by Louis Marks by arrangement with the British Broadcasting Corporation / Terrance Dicks. — London : W.H. Allen, 1981. — 126p ; 21cm
ISBN 0-491-02975-6 : £4.50 B81-35153

Dicks, Terrance. Doctor Who and the monster of Peladon : based on the BBC television serial by Brian Hayles by arrangement with the British Broadcasting Corporation / Terrance Dicks. — London : Target, 1980. — 124p ; 18cm
ISBN 0-426-20132-9 (pbk) : £0.85 B81-10209

Dicks, Terrance. Star quest, terrorsaur! / Terrance Dicks. — London : W.H. Allen, 1981. — 125p ; 21cm
ISBN 0-491-02701-x : £4.50 B81-35152

Digby, Anne, *1935-*. Boy trouble at Trebizon / Anne Digby. — London : Granada, 1980. — 125p : ill ; 21cm
ISBN 0-246-11421-5 : £3.95 B81-00601

Digby, Anne, *1935-*. Boy trouble at Trebizon / Anne Digby ; illustrated by Gavin Rowe. — London : Granada, 1981, c1980. — 125p : ill ; 18cm. — (A Dragon book)
ISBN 0-583-30430-3 (pbk) : £0.85 B81-19948

Digby, Anne, *1935-*. More trouble at Trebizon / Anne Digby ; illustrated by Gavin Rowe. — London : Granada, 1981. — 159p : ill ; 21cm
ISBN 0-246-11425-8 : £3.95 B81-12932

Digby, Anne, *1935-*. Quicksilver horse / Anne Digby. — London : Granada, 1979 (1981 printing). — 94p ; 18cm. — (A Dragon book)
£0.75 (pbk) B81-33391

Dobson, Julia. The ivory poachers : a Crisp twins adventure / Julia Dobson ; illustrated by Gary Rees. — London : Methuen Children's Books Ltd. — 123p : ill ; 19cm. — (A Magnet Book)
ISBN 0-416-24340-1 (cased) : £3.50 : CIP rev.
ISBN 0-416-24200-6 (pbk) : Unpriced B81-10457

Dobson, Julia. The tomb robbers : a Crisp twins adventure / Julia Dobson ; illustrated by Gary Rees. — London : Methuen Children's Books, 1981. — 125p : ill ; 19cm. — (A Magnet book)
ISBN 0-416-24350-9 (cased) : £3.50 : CIP rev.
ISBN 0-416-24210-3 (pbk) : Unpriced B81-10456

Docherty, Hugh. The day Ollie broke down. — Glasgow : MacLellan, Jan.1982. — [20]p. — (Embryo)
ISBN 0-85335-253-4 : £2.50 : CIP entry B81-38830

Dowling, Patrick. Birthday party / Patrick Dowling ; illustrated by Richard Draper ; based on the characters created by David Sproxton and Peter Lord. — London : Heinemann/Quixote, 1980. — [24]p : col.ill ; 20cm. — (The Amazing adventures of Morph)
ISBN 0-434-98003-x : £2.95 B81-08360

Dowling, Patrick. Birthday party / Patrick Dowling ; illustrated by Richard Draper ; based on the characters created by David Sproxton and Peter Lord. — London : Piccolo in association with Heinemann/Quixote, 1981, c1980. — [24]p : col.ill ; 19cm. — (The Amazing adventures of Morph) (Piccolo picture books)
Originally published: London : Heinemann/Quixote, 1980
ISBN 0-330-26482-6 (pbk) : £0.90 B81-18373

Dowling, Patrick. Swimming pool / Patrick Dowling ; illustrated by Richard Draper ; based on the characters created by David Sproxton and Peter Lord. — London : Heinemann/Quixote, 1980. — [24]p : col.ill ; 20cm. — (The Amazing adventures of Morph)
ISBN 0-434-98002-1 : £2.95 B81-07699

823'.914[J] — Children's stories in English, *1945-* — *Texts continuation*

Dowling, Patrick. Swimming pool / Patrick Dowling ; illustrated by Richard Draper ; based on the characters created by David Sproxton and Peter Lord. — London : Piccolo in association with Heinemann/Quixote, 1981, c1980. — [24]p : col.ill ; 19cm. — (The Amazing adventures of Morph) (Piccolo picture books)
Originally published: London : Heinemann/Quixote, 1980
ISBN 0-330-26483-4 (pbk) : £0.90 B81-18372

Drake, Tony. Playing it right / Tony Drake. — Harmondsworth : Puffin, 1981, c1979. — 123p ; 18cm
Originally published: London : Collins, 1979
ISBN 0-14-031298-6 (pbk) : £0.80 B81-26502

Drazin, Judith. The midsummer picnic. — London : H. Hamilton, Jan.1982. — [96]p. — (Antelope books)
ISBN 0-241-10716-4 : £2.50 : CIP entry
B81-34322

Drew, Janie. Sandra at Pebbleridge / Janie Drew. — Bognor Regis : New Horizon, c1980. — 43p : ill ; 21cm
ISBN 0-86116-356-7 : £3.50 B81-19263

Dunbar, Joyce. Jugg / Joyce and James Dunbar. — London : Scolar Press, 1980. — 111p : ill ; 25cm
ISBN 0-85967-596-3 : £4.95 : CIP rev.
B80-18042

Dyke, Jennifer. Lost in the supermarket / written by Jennifer Dyke ; illustrated by Sally Long. — Loughborough : Ladybird, c1981. — 25p : col.ill ; 19x20cm. — (Early learning)
ISBN 0-7214-0671-8 : £0.95 B81-20922

Dyke, John. Pigwig / John Dyke. — London : Magnet, 1978 (1981 [printing]). — [32]p : col.ill ; 19cm
ISBN 0-416-20980-7 (pbk) : £0.95 B81-28613

Dyke, John. Pigwig and the crusty diamonds. — London : Methuen Children's Books, Feb.1982. — [32]p
ISBN 0-416-21380-4 : £3.50 : CIP entry
B81-35713

Eadington, Joan. Jonny Briggs and the giant cave. — London : Hodder & Stoughton, Feb.1982. — [96]p. — (Knight books)
ISBN 0-340-28042-5 (pbk) : £0.95 : CIP entry
B81-37573

Edmond, Doreen. Frog's wooing / by Doreen Edmund. — Winchester : Hambleside, c1981. — [24]p : col.ill ; 26cm. — (A Terrapin book)
ISBN 0-86042-034-5 : Unpriced B81-24499

Edmond, Doreen. Ronald Rabbit's white coat / Doreen Edmond. — Winchester : Hambleside, c1980. — [24]p : ill(some col.) ; 18x22cm. — (A Terrapin book)
ISBN 0-86042-031-0 (pbk) : £0.75 B81-24361

Edwards, Dorothy. Here's Sam / Dorothy Edwards ; illustrated by David Higham. — [London] : Magnet, 1981, c1979. — 93p : ill ; 20cm
Originally published: London : Methuen, 1979
ISBN 0-416-89520-4 (pbk) : £0.80 B81-08599

Edwards, Dorothy. The magician who kept a pub : and other stories / Dorothy Edwards ; illustrated by Jill Bennett. — [London] : Fontana, 1981, c1975. — 159p : ill ; 20cm. — (Lions)
Originally published: Harmondsworth : Kestrel, 1975
ISBN 0-00-671785-3 (pbk) : £0.90 B81-11064

Edwards, Dorothy. My naughty litte sister goes fishing / Dorothy Edwards & Shirley Hughes. — London : Methuen's Children's Books, 1976 (1980 [printing]). — [24]p : col.ill ; 19cm. — (A Magnet book)
Originally published: in My naughty little sister. London : Methuen, 1952
ISBN 0-416-89910-2 (pbk) : £0.90 B81-32581

Edwards, Dorothy. The witches and the grinnygog / Dorothy Edwards. — London : Faber, 1981. — 176p ; 21cm
ISBN 0-571-11720-1 : £4.95 : CIP rev.
B81-24592

Egan, Frank. The fairy Isle of Coosanure. — Dublin : Wolfhound Press, Oct.1981. — [96]p
ISBN 0-905473-70-1 : £3.75 : CIP entry
B81-27479

Elliot, Margaret. To trick a witch / Margaret Elliot ; illustrated by Colin Dunbar. — London : Abelard, 1981. — 89p : ill ; 21cm
ISBN 0-200-72749-4 (pbk) : £3.50
ISBN 0-200-72748-6 (pbk) : Unpriced
B81-18433

Elvey, Amy. The day the animals talk. — Telford (156 Woodrows, Woodside, Telford, Shropshire) : Woody Books, Dec.1981. — [20]p
ISBN 0-907751-01-6 (pbk) : £1.50 : CIP entry
B81-32052

Erickson, Russell E.. Warton and Morton. — London : Hodder and Stoughton, Aug.1981. — [64]p
Originally published: New York : Lothrop, Lee and Shepard, 1976 ; London : Hodder and Stoughton, 1979
ISBN 0-340-26535-3 (pbk) : £0.85 : CIP entry
B81-18136

Escott, John. Alarm bells / by John Escott ; illustrated by Maureen Bradley. — London : Hamilton, 1981. — 96p : ill ; 19cm. — (Antelope books)
ISBN 0-241-10700-8 : £2.50 : CIP rev.
B81-26733

Escott, John. A walk down the pier / John Escott ; illustated by Frances Phillips. — Harmondsworth : Puffin, 1981, c1977. — 77p : ill ; 20cm. — (A young puffin)
Originally published: London : Hamish Hamilton, 1977
ISBN 0-14-031325-7 (pbk) : £0.80 B81-35475

Fanning, Peter. Nobody's hero / Peter Fanning. — London : Dobson, 1981. — 128p ; 21cm
ISBN 0-234-72247-9 : £4.25 B81-18537

Faunce-Brown, Daphne. Snuffles' house / by Daphne Faunce-Brown ; illustrated by Frances Thatcher. — Winchester : Hambleside, c1980. — [32]p : col.ill ; 24x26cm. — (A Terrapin book)
ISBN 0-86042-023-x : Unpriced B81-24500

Fell, Alison. The grey dancer / Alison Fell. — London : Collins, 1981. — 89p ; 22cm
ISBN 0-00-184267-6 : £4.50 B81-13108

Fennell, Ian. Robottom the robot / Ian Fennell and David Higham. — London : Methuen Children's, 1980. — [28]p : chiefly col.ill ; 22cm. — (A Methuen picture-story book)
ISBN 0-416-89660-x : £2.95 : CIP rev.
B80-18515

Fisher, David. Doctor Who and the creature from the pit / David Fisher. — London : W.H. Allen, 1981. — 121p ; 18cm. — (A Target book)
ISBN 0-426-20123-x (pbk) : £0.90 B81-11502

Fisher, David, *1929 Apr. 13-*. Doctor Who and the creature from the pit : based on the BBC television serial by David Fisher by arrangement with the British Broadcasting Corporation / David Fisher. — London : W.H. Allen, 1981. — 121p ; 21cm
ISBN 0-491-02991-8 : £4.25 B81-03394

Fisk, Nicholas. Calfang. — London : Hodder & Stoughton, July 1981. — [112]p
ISBN 0-340-26529-9 (pbk) : £0.85 : CIP entry
B81-13820

Fisk, Nicholas. [Escape from Splatterbang]. Flamers / Nicholas Fisk. — [Sevenoaks] : Knight, 1979, c1978. — 95p ; 18cm
Originally published: London : Pelham, 1978
ISBN 0-340-24028-8 (pbk) : £0.60 : CIP rev.
B79-20453

Fisk, Nicholas. Robot revolt / Nicholas Fisk. — London : Pelham, 1981. — 128p ; 21cm
ISBN 0-7207-1332-3 : £4.50 : CIP rev.
B81-10484

Flack, Marjorie. Angus and the ducks / told and pictured by Marjorie Flack. — Harmondsworth : Puffin in association with Bodley Head, 1971 (1981 [printing]). — 32p : ill(some col.) ; 16x23cm. — (Picture puffins)
Originally published: Garden City, N.Y. : Doubleday Doran, 1930 ; London : John Lane, 1933
ISBN 0-14-050036-7 (pbk) : £0.90 B81-18384

Flack, Marjorie. Angus and Wag-Tail-Bess / told and pictured by Marjorie Flack. — Harmondsworth : Puffin in association with Bodley Head, 1973 (1981 [printing]). — 32p : ill(some col.) ; 16x23cm. — (Picture puffins)
£0.90 (pbk) B81-22272

Flint, F. Barrie. The adventures of Mr. Pip / F. Barrie Flint ; illustrated by Karen Belsey. — Bognor Regis : New Horizon, c1979. — 85p : ill ; 21cm
ISBN 0-86116-081-9 : £2.50 B81-19240

Flint, F. Barrie. A garden of tits / F. Barrie Flint ; illustrated by Karen Belsey. — Bognor Regis : New Horizon, 1979. — 66p : ill ; 21cm
ISBN 0-86116-049-5 : £2.50 B81-18884

Foreman, Michael, *1938-*. Dinosaurs : and all that rubbish / Michael Foreman. — Harmondsworth : Puffin Books in association with Hamilton, 1974, c1972 (1981 printing). — [32]p : col.ill ; 23cm. — (Picture puffins)
Originally published: London : Hamilton, 1972
ISBN 0-14-050098-7 (pbk) : £0.90 B81-30941

Foreman, Michael, *1938-*. Moose / Michael Foreman. — Harmondsworth : Puffin, 1973, c1971 (1981 [printing]). — [32]p : col.ill ; 23cm. — (Picture puffins)
Originally published: London : Hamilton, 1971
ISBN 0-14-050073-1 (pbk) : £0.90 B81-26538

Foreman, Michael, *1938-*. Panda and the odd lion / Michael Foreman. — London : Hamilton, 1981. — [32]p : chiefly col.ill ; 29cm
ISBN 0-241-10081-x : £3.95 : CIP rev.
B80-03947

Foreman, Michael, *1938-*. Trick a tracker / Michael Foreman. — London : Gollancz, 1981. — [30]p : chiefly col.ill ; 29cm
ISBN 0-575-02975-7 : £3.95 B81-21209

Forsyth, Anne. Baxter the travelling cat / Anne Forsyth ; illustrated by Sally Holmes. — London : Hodder and Stoughton, 1981. — 47p : ill ; 23cm. — (Hopscotch)
ISBN 0-340-26273-7 : £2.50 : CIP rev.
B81-13527

Forsyth, Anne. Sam's wonderful shell. — London : H. Hamilton, Jan.1982. — [48]p. — (Gazelle books)
ISBN 0-241-10708-3 : £1.95 : CIP entry
B81-34321

Freeman, Barbara C.. Clemency in the moonlight / Barbara C. Freeman ; with decorations by the author. — London : Macmillan Children's Books, 1981. — 156p : ill ; 21cm
ISBN 0-333-31176-0 : £4.95 : CIP rev.
B81-01427

823'.914[J] — Children's stories in English, *1945-* *— Texts continuation*

French, Fiona. The princess and the musician : a Persian tale / story and pictures by Fiona French. — London : Evans, 1981. — [24]p : col.ill ; 35cm
ISBN 0-237-45522-6 : £4.75 B81-20928

Freud, Clement. Clicking Vicky / Clement Freud ; illustrated by Glenys Ambrus. — London : Pelham, 1980. — [32]p : ill(some col.) ; 26cm
ISBN 0-7207-1176-2 : £3.25 B81-00603

Frewer, Glyn. Bryn of Brockle Hanger : the saga of a badger / Glyn Frewer. — London : Dent, 1980. — 128p ; 23cm
ISBN 0-460-06050-3 : £4.95 : CIP rev. B80-18045

Furminger, Jo. Blackbirds at the gallop / Jo Furminger ; illustrations by Susan Hunter. — London : Hodder and Stoughton, 1981. — 120p : ill ; 23cm
ISBN 0-340-26223-0 : £4.95 : CIP rev. B81-25660

Furminger, Jo. Blackbirds' pony trek. — London : Hodder and Stoughton, July 1981. — [120]p
Originally published: 1977
ISBN 0-340-26528-0 (pbk) : £0.85 : CIP entry B81-13866

Furminger, Jo. Mrs Boffy's birthday / by Jo Furminger ; illustrated by Sally Holmes. — London : Hodder and Stoughton, 1980. — 88p : ill ; 20cm
ISBN 0-340-24586-7 : £3.95 : CIP rev. B80-14054

Furminger, Jo. Saddle up, Blackbirds! / Jo Furminger ; illustrations by Susan Hunter. — London : Hodder and Stoughton, c1980. — 126p : ill ; 23cm
ISBN 0-340-24275-2 : £3.95 : CIP rev. B80-18519

Furminger, Justine. Bobbie takes the reins / Justine Furminger ; illustrations by Douglas Phillips. — London : Hodder and Stoughton, 1981. — 138p : ill ; 23cm
ISBN 0-340-26436-5 : £4.95 : CIP rev. B81-25659

Gardam, Jane. Bridget and William / Jane Gardam ; illustrated by Janet Rawlins. — London (8 Cork St., W1X 2HA) : MacRae, 1981. — 46p : ill ; 21cm. — (Blackbird books)
ISBN 0-86203-012-9 : £2.75 B81-09673

Gardam, Jane. Horse. — London : MacRae, Feb.1982. — [48]p. — (Blackbird books)
ISBN 0-86203-066-8 : £2.75 : CIP entry B81-36044

Garfield, Leon. Fair's fair / Leon Garfield ; pictures by Margaret Chamberlain. — London : Macdonald Futura, 1981. — [28]p : col.ill ; 29cm
ISBN 0-354-08126-8 : £3.25 B81-40793

Garner, Alan. The Moon of Gomrath / Alan Garner. — [London] : Fontana, 1972, c1963 (1981 [printing]). — 156p ; 18cm. — (Lions)
Originally published: London : Collins, 1963
ISBN 0-00-671673-3 (pbk) : £0.95 B81-15536

Garner, Alan. The owl service / Alan Carner. — [London] : Fontana, 1981, c1967. — 156p ; 19cm. — (Lions)
Originally published: London : Collins, 1967
ISBN 0-00-671675-x (pbk) : £0.90 B81-11067

Garner, Alan. The weirdstone of Brisingamen : a tale of Alderley / Alan Garner. — [London] : Fontana, 1971, c1960 (1981 [printing]). — 224p : 2maps ; 18cm. — (Lions)
Originally published: London : Collins, 1960
ISBN 0-00-671672-5 (pbk) : £1.00 B81-15521

Garnett, William. Farmer Gribbins and Farmer Green / by William Garnett ; illustrated by Susan Cutting. — Padstow (11 Church St., Padstow, Cornwall) : Tabb House, 1981. — 65p : ill ; 21cm
ISBN 0-907018-05-x (pbk) : £1.95 B81-18529

Gascoigne, Bamber. Why the rope went tight. — London : Methuen/Walker, June 1981. — [32]p
ISBN 0-416-05700-4 : £3.95 : CIP entry B81-14387

Gathorne-Hardy, Jonathan. Cyril Bonhamy v Madam Big / Jonathan Gathorne-Hardy ; illustrations by Quentin Blake. — London : Cape, 1981. — 80p : ill ; 24cm
ISBN 0-224-01991-0 : £4.50 : CIP rev. B81-27342

Geras, Adèle. The rug that grew / Adèle Geras ; illustrated by Priscilla Lamont. — London : Hamilton, 1981. — 47p : ill ; 20cm. — (Gazelle books)
ISBN 0-241-10533-1 : £1.80 B81-08009

Gerrard, Jean. Matilda Jane / story by Jean Gerrard ; pictures by Roy Gerrard. — London : Gollancz, 1981. — [32]p : col.ill ; 29cm
ISBN 0-575-02897-1 : £4.95 B81-19891

Gettings, Fred. The salamander tales. — Edinburgh : Floris, Sept.1981. — [96]p
ISBN 0-903540-48-7 : £3.95 : CIP entry B81-25124

Gifford, Griselda. Because of Blunder / Griselda Gifford ; illustrated by Mary Rayner. — Harmondsworth : Puffin in association with Gollancz, 1979, c1977. — 109p : ill ; 18cm
Originally published: London : Gollancz, 1977
ISBN 0-14-031105-x (pbk) : £0.60 B81-08630

Gifford, Griselda. Earwig and Beetle / Griselda Gifford ; illustrated by Jill Bennett. — London : Gollancz, 1981. — 96p : ill ; 21cm
ISBN 0-575-03007-0 : £4.50 B81-31693

Gili, Phillida. Demon Daisy's dreadful week / Phillida Gili. — London (8 Cork St., W1X 2HA) : Julia McRae, c1980. — [30]p : col.ill ; 21cm
ISBN 0-86203-025-0 : £3.75 : CIP rev. B80-12132

Gili, Phillida. The lost ears / Phillida Gili. — London : Julia MacRae, c1981. — [24]p : col.ill ; 19cm
ISBN 0-86203-033-1 : £3.95 : CIP rev. B81-14390

Gillham, Bill. My brother Barry. — London : Deutsch, Sept.1981. — [96]p
ISBN 0-233-97358-3 : £4.50 : CIP entry B81-22666

Gillham, Bill. Septimus Fry F.R.S., or, How Mrs. Fry had the cleverest baby in the world / Bill Gillham ; illustrations by Steve Augarde. — London : Deutsch, 1980. — [32]p : col.ill ; 26cm
ISBN 0-233-97253-6 : £4.95 B81-00604

Gilmore, Maeve. Captain Eustace and the magic room. — London : Methuen Children's Books, Oct.1981. — [32]p. — (A Methuen picture-story book)
ISBN 0-416-89020-2 : £3.25 : CIP entry B81-25282

Godden, Rumer. The dragon of Og. — London : Macmillan, Sept.1981. — [64]p
ISBN 0-333-31731-9 : £3.95 : CIP entry B81-23946

Godfrey, Elsa. Susan Sunshine and the hedgehog tree / pictures by Elsa Godfrey ; words by Gerard Macdonald. — London : Souvenir, 1981. — [32]p : col.ill ; 27cm
ISBN 0-285-62466-0 : Unpriced B81-15429

Goffe, Toni. Toby's animal rescue service. — London : H. Hamilton, Apr.1981. — [48]p
ISBN 0-241-10580-3 : £3.25 : CIP entry B81-02557

Goldsmith, John, *1947-*. Mrs Babcary's diving-machine / John Goldsmith ; illustrated by Eleanor Newton. — London : Pelham, 1981. — [24]p : col.ill ; 17cm
ISBN 0-7207-1357-9 : £2.50 B81-39399

Goldsmith, John, *1947-*. Mrs Babcary's steam-cart / John Goldsmith ; illustrated by Eleanor Newton. — London : Pelham, 1981. — [24]p : col.ill ; 17cm
ISBN 0-7207-1356-0 : £2.50 B81-39401

Goldsmith, John, *1947-*. Mrs Babcary's treat / John Goldsmith ; illustrated by Eleanor Newton. — London : Pelham, 1981. — [26]p : col.ill ; 17cm
ISBN 0-7207-1355-2 : £2.50 B81-39400

Goodall, John S.. The adventures of Paddy Pork / John S. Goodall. — 2nd ed. — London : Macmillan Children's, 1980. — [60]p : all ill ; 14x18cm
Previous ed.: 1968
ISBN 0-333-01115-5 : £1.95 B81-01318

Goodall, John S.. The ballooning adventures of Paddy Port / John S. Goodall. — 2nd ed. — London : Macmillan Children's, 1980. — [60]p : col.ill ; 14x18cm
Previous ed.: 1969
£1.95 B81-04180

Goodall, John S.. Paddy's new hat / John S. Goodall. — London : Macmillan Children's, c1980. — [60]p : col.ill ; 14x18cm
ISBN 0-333-27977-8 : £2.50 B81-01320

Grant, Gwen. Knock and wait / Gwen Grant ; illustrated by Gareth Floyd. — London : Fontana, 1981. — 142p : ill ; 18cm. — (Lions)
ISBN 0-00-671762-4 (pbk) : £0.95 B81-28436

Grant, John. Littlenose's birthday. — London : Hodder & Stoughton, Nov.1981. — [96]p
Originally published: London : British Broadcasting Corporation, 1979
ISBN 0-340-27531-6 (pbk) : £0.85 : CIP entry B81-30125

Gray, John. There are dragons. — Belfast : Appletree Press, Oct.1981. — [24]p
ISBN 0-904651-85-1 (pbk) : £0.95 : CIP entry B81-30997

Greaves, Margaret. Charlie, Emma and the dragon family. — London : Methuen Children's Books, Feb.1982. — [96]p. — (Read aloud books)
ISBN 0-416-21580-7 : £3.50 : CIP entry B81-35712

Greenway, Shirley. The Emperor's nightingale / Hans Andersen ; retold by Shirley Greenway ; pictures by Sandy Nightingale. — [London] : Piccolo, 1981. — [24]p : col.ill ; 22cm. — (Piccolo picture classics)
ISBN 0-330-26354-4 (pbk) : £0.80 B81-20197

Grender, Iris. Did I ever tell you about my Irish great grandmother?. — London : Hutchinson, Oct.1981. — [64]p
ISBN 0-09-146570-2 : £3.95 : CIP entry B81-28170

Gretz, Susanna. The bears who went to the seaside / Susanna Gretz. — Harmondsworth : Puffin, 1975, c1972 (1981 [printing]). — [31]p : col.ill ; 20x23cm. — (Picture puffins)
Originally published: London : Benn, 1972
£0.90 (pbk) B81-22273

Gretz, Susanna. Teddybears moving day / Susanna Gretz. — London : Benn, 1981. — [32]p : col.ill ; 23cm
Ill on lining papers
ISBN 0-510-12402-x : £3.95 B81-23191

823'.914[J] — Children's stories in English, *1945-* **— Texts** *continuation*

Griffiths, Helen. Dancing horses. — London : Hutchinson, Sept.1981. — [160]p
ISBN 0-09-146160-x : £5.50 : CIP entry
B81-20184

Haigh, Sheila. Watch for the champion / Sheila Haigh ; illustrated by Barry Wilkinson. — London : Methuen Children's, 1980. — 140p : ill ; 20cm. — (A Pied Piper book)
ISBN 0-416-87390-1 : £3.50 : CIP rev.
B79-37518

Halam, Ann. Ally, Ally, Aster / by Ann Halam. — London : Allen & Unwin, 1981. — 118p ; 23cm
ISBN 0-04-823192-4 : Unpriced : CIP rev.
B81-13450

Hall, Amanda. The gossipy wife / Amanda Hall, adapted from a Russian folk tale. — Glasgow : Blackie, 1981. — [25]p : col.ill ; 30cm
ISBN 0-216-91092-7 : £4.95 : CIP rev.
B81-23871

Hallihan, Barbara. Pitfall / by Barbara Hallihan. — Ossett (44 Queen's Drive, Ossett, W. Yorks. WF5 0ND) : Zoar, 1974, c1972. — 35p,[8] leaves of plates : ill ; 19cm
Originally published: s.l. : s.n., 1972
ISBN 0-904435-05-9 : £1.50 B81-31699

Hallihan, Barbara. Rich toward God / by Barbara Hallihan ; (based on Driven into exile by A.L.O.E.) ; illustrated by Timothy Abbot. — [Ossett] ([44 Queen's Drive, Ossett, W. Yorks. WF5 0ND]) : [Zoar], [1981?]. — 110p : ill ; 19cm
£2.00 B81-31700

Hallworth, Grace. The carnival kite / Grace Hallworth ; illustrated by Patrice Aitken. — London : Methuen Children's, 1980. — [28]p : col.ill ; 22cm
Text, col.ill on inside covers
ISBN 0-416-87880-6 : £2.95 B81-01321

Hanbury Tenison, Marika. The princess and the unicorn / by Marika Hanbury Tenison ; illustrated by Ann Evans. — London : Granada, 1981. — 64p : ill ; 22cm
ISBN 0-246-11529-7 (cased) : £4.95
ISBN 0-583-30474-5 (pbk) : Unpriced
B81-38059

Hardcastle, Michael. Behind the goal / Michael Hardcastle. — London : Pelham, c1980. — 120p ; 21cm
ISBN 0-7207-1252-1 : £3.95 : CIP rev.
B80-18048

Hardcastle, Michael. Breakaway : a Mark Fox story / Michael Hardcastle. — [London] : Armada, c1976 (1980 [printing]). — 125p ; 18cm. — (A Mark Fox book ; 2)
ISBN 0-00-691795-x (pbk) : £0.75 B81-03088

Hardcastle, Michael. Breakaway / Michael Hardcastle. — London : Severn House, 1980, c1976. — 125p ; 21cm. — (A Mark Fox story)
Originally published: London : Armada, 1976
ISBN 0-7278-0607-6 : £3.95 : CIP rev.
B80-18915

Hardcastle, Michael. On the ball : a Mark Fox story / Michael Hardcastle. — London : Severn House, 1981, c1977. — 125p ; 21cm. — ([Mark Fox] ; [v.3])
Originally published: London : Armada, 1977
ISBN 0-7278-0612-2 : £3.95 B81-09866

Hardcastle, Michael. Roar to victory. — London : Methuen Children's Books, Jan.1982. — [128] p. — (A Pied Piper book)
ISBN 0-416-20960-2 : £3.95 : CIP entry
B81-34398

Hargreaves, Roger. An apple for Oink / by Roger Hargreaves. — London : Hamlyn, 1981. — [12]p : chiefly col.ill ; 21cm. — (Timbuctoo)
ISBN 0-600-38819-0 (unbound) : £0.75
B81-19991

Hargreaves, Roger. Hiss and the storm / by Roger Hargreaves. — London : Hamlyn, 1981. — [12]p : chiefly col.ill ; 21cm. — (Timbuctoo)
ISBN 0-600-38816-6 (unbound) : £0.75
B81-19993

Hargreaves, Roger. Little Miss Bossy / by Roger Hargreaves. — London : Thurman, c1981. — [32]p : col.ill ; 13x14cm
ISBN 0-85985-182-6 (pbk) : £0.50 B81-18281

Hargreaves, Roger. Little Miss Helpful / by Roger Hargreaves. — London : Thurman, c1981. — [32]p : col.ill ; 13x14cm
ISBN 0-85985-185-0 (pbk) : £0.50 B81-18290

Hargreaves, Roger. Little Miss Late / by Roger Hargreaves. — London : Thurman, c1981. — [32]p : col.ill ; 13x14cm
ISBN 0-85985-184-2 (pbk) : £0.50 B81-18291

Hargreaves, Roger. Little Miss Naughty / by Roger Hargreaves. — London : Thurman, c1981. — [32]p : col.ill ; 13x14cm
ISBN 0-85985-179-6 (pbk) : £0.50 B81-18289

Hargreaves, Roger. Little Miss Neat / by Roger Hargreaves. — London : Thurman, c1981. — [32]p : col.ill ; 13x14cm
ISBN 0-85985-181-8 (pbk) : £0.50 B81-18282

Hargreaves, Roger. Little Miss Plump / by Roger Hargreaves. — London : Thurman, c1981. — [32]p : col.ill ; 13x14cm
ISBN 0-85985-188-5 (pbk) : £0.50 B81-18280

Hargreaves, Roger. Little Miss Scatterbrain / by Roger Hargreaves. — London : Thurman, c1981. — [32]p : col.ill ; 13x14cm
ISBN 0-85985-187-7 (pbk) : £0.50 B81-18288

Hargreaves, Roger. Little Miss Shy / by Roger Hargreaves. — London : Thurman, c1981. — [32]p : col.ill ; 13x14cm
ISBN 0-85985-189-3 (pbk) : £0.50 B81-18283

Hargreaves, Roger. Little Miss Splendid / by Roger Hargreaves. — London : Thurman, c1981. — [32]p : col.ill ; 13x14cm
ISBN 0-85985-180-x (pbk) : £0.50 B81-18287

Hargreaves, Roger. Little Miss Sunshine / by Roger Hargreaves. — London : Thurman, c1981. — [32]p : col.ill ; 13x14cm
ISBN 0-85985-183-4 (pbk) : £0.50 B81-18286

Hargreaves, Roger. Little Miss Tiny / by Roger Hargreaves. — London : Thurman, c1981. — [32]p : col.ill ; 13x14cm
ISBN 0-85985-186-9 (pbk) : £0.50 B81-18285

Hargreaves, Roger. Little Miss Trouble / by Roger Hargreaves. — London : Thurman, c1981. — [32]p : col.ill ; 13x14cm
ISBN 0-85985-178-8 (pbk) : £0.50 B81-18284

Hargreaves, Roger. Moo's fancy hats / by Roger Hargreaves. — London : Hamlyn, 1981. — [12]p : chiefly col.ill ; 21cm. — (Timbuctoo)
ISBN 0-600-38818-2 (unbound) : £0.75
B81-19990

Hargreaves, Roger. Roar's day of mistakes / by Roger Hargreaves. — London : Hamlyn, 1981. — [12]p : chiefly col.ill ; 21cm. — (Timbuctoo)
ISBN 0-600-38817-4 (unbound) : £0.75
B81-19992

Hargreaves, Roger. Things. — London : Hodder & Stoughton Children's Books, Sept.1981. — [32]p
ISBN 0-340-27445-x : £2.50 : CIP entry
B81-20581

Harnett, Cynthia. Stars of fortune / written and illustrated by Cynthia Harnett. — [London] : Methuen Children's Books, 1981, c1956. — 223p : ill,coats of arms,geneal.table ; 18cm. — (A Magnet book)
Originally published: London : Methuen, 1956
ISBN 0-416-89880-7 (pbk) : £0.95 B81-18253

Harris, Rosemary, *1923-*. The enchanted horse / Rosemary Harris ; illustrated by Pauline Baynes. — Harmondsworth : Kestrel, 1981. — [32]p : col.ill ; 28cm
ISBN 0-7226-5630-0 : £5.95 B81-28491

Harris, Rosemary, *1923-*. Tower of the stars / Rosemary Harris. — London : Faber, 1980. — 272p ; 21cm
ISBN 0-571-11607-8 : £5.95 : CIP rev.
B80-26224

Harrison, Sarah, *1946-*. In Granny's garden / Sarah Harrison & Mike Wilks. — London : Cape, 1980. — [32]p : col.ill ; 29cm
ISBN 0-224-01867-1 : £3.50 B81-01322

Hart, Tom. Fairies and friends / Tom Hart ; illustrated by Michelle Pearson Cooper. — London : Quartet, 1981. — 57p : col.ill ; 24cm
ISBN 0-7043-2280-3 : £4.95 B81-24371

Harvey, Anne. A present for Nellie. — London : MacRae, Feb.1982. — [48]p. — (Blackbird books)
ISBN 0-86203-067-6 : £2.75 : CIP entry
B81-36043

Hastings, Selina. Sir Gawain and the Green Knight. — London : Methuen/Walker, Aug.1981. — [32]p
ISBN 0-416-05860-4 : £3.95 : CIP entry
B81-20642

Hayden, Eric W. (Eric William). The adventures of Bobby Wildgoose / E.W. Hayden. — Bognor Regis : New Horizon, c1980. — 25p,[7]p of plates : ill,1map,1port ; 21cm
ISBN 0-86116-448-2 : £3.50 B81-19063

Hayes, Richard. The Xenon File / Richard Hayes. — London : Macmillan, 1980. — 190p ; 21cm
ISBN 0-333-26899-7 : £4.95 : CIP rev.
B80-11218

Haywood, Marion. Spud and the jokers / Marion Haywood. — London : Dobson, 1980. — 137p ; 21cm
ISBN 0-234-72206-1 : £3.50 B81-00605

Hewett, Anita. Mrs Mopple's washing line / written by Anita Hewett ; drawn by Robert Broomfield. — Harmondsworth : Puffin in association with Bodley Head, 1970, c1966 (1981 [printing]). — 29p : col.ill ; 17x23cm. — (Picture puffins)
Originally published: London : Bodley Head, 1966
ISBN 0-14-050028-6 (pbk) : £0.90 B81-22271

Hickson, Joan. The seven sparrows and the motor car picnic. — London : Deutsch, Oct.1981. — [32]p
ISBN 0-233-97363-x : £4.25 : CIP entry
B81-26716

Higham, David, *1949-*. G was a giant who knocked down a house. — London : Methuen Children's Books, Oct.1981. — [32]p. — (A Methuen picture-story book)
ISBN 0-416-21790-7 : £3.25 : CIP entry
B81-25728

Hildick, E. W.. The case of the invisble dog : a McGurk mystery / E.W. Hildick ; illustrated by Val Biro. — London : Granada, 1980, c1977. — 93p : ill ; 18cm. — (A McGurk mystery) (A Dragon book)
Originally published: London : Hodder and Stoughton, 1977
ISBN 0-583-30360-9 (pbk) : £0.75 B81-06457

Hildick, E. W.. The case of the secret scribbles : a McGurk mystery / E.W. Hildick ; illustrated by Val Biro. — London : Granada, 1980, c1978. — 96p : ill ; 18cm. — (A Dragon book)
Originally published: New York : Macmillan ; London : Hodder and Stoughton, 1978
ISBN 0-583-30361-7 (pbk) : £0.75 B81-06314

823'.914[J] — Children's stories in English, *1945-* — *Texts* *continuation*

Hill, Denise. The wrong side of the bed / Denise Hill ; illustrated by Doreen Caldwell. — London : Hamilton, 1981. — 47p : ill ; 19cm. — (Gazelle books)
ISBN 0-241-10622-2 : £1.80 : CIP rev.
B81-02558

Hill, Eric. Where's Spot? / Eric Hill. — London : Heinemann, 1980. — [20]p : col.ill ; 22x23cm
Cover title. — Ill on lining papers
ISBN 0-434-94288-x : £2.95 B81-00606

Hinton, Nigel. The witch's revenge. — London : Abelard-Schuman, Oct.1981. — [112]p
ISBN 0-200-72765-6 : £4.95 : CIP entry
B81-26758

Hoban, Tana. One little kitten / photographs by Tana Hoban ; text by Mary Rowe. — London : Angus & Robertson, 1981. — [24]p : chiefly ill ; 24cm
Originally published: without text : New York : Greenwillow, 1979. — Ill on lining papers
ISBN 0-207-95943-9 : £2.95 B81-23058

Holiday, Jane. Chun's Chinese dragon / by Jane Holiday ; illustrated by Elaine McGregor Turney. — London : Hamilton, 1981. — 86p ; 19cm. — (Antelope books)
ISBN 0-241-10627-3 : £2.25 : CIP rev.
B81-02561

Holiday, Jane. Merman in Maids Moreton / Jane Holiday ; illustrated by Maureen Bradley. — London : Hodder and Stoughton, 1980. — 47p : ill ; 23cm. — (Hopscotch)
ISBN 0-340-25677-x : £2.50 B81-01323

Horowitz, Anthony. Misha, the magician and the mysterious amulet / Anthony Horowitz ; with illustrations by John Woodgate. — London : Arlington, 1981. — 204p : ill ; 24cm
ISBN 0-85140-507-x : £4.50 : CIP rev.
B80-09889

Hough, Richard. Razor eyes / Richard Hough. — London : Dent, 1981. — v,113p : ill ; 23cm
ISBN 0-460-06053-8 : £4.95 : CIP rev.
B81-22599

Hourihane, Ursula. Stumpy and Scatty make peppermint creams / written by Ursula Hourihane ; illustrated by Sara Silcock. — London : Transworld, 1971 (1979 [printing]). — [22]p : ill(some col.) ; 13x20cm. — (A Storychair book)
ISBN 0-552-50066-6 (pbk) : £0.50 B81-38546

Hourihane, Ursula. Stumpy finds a home / Ursula Hourihane ; illustrated by Sara Silcock. — London : Transworld, 1971 (1979 [printing]). — [22]p : ill(some col.) ; 13x20cm. — (A storychair book)
ISBN 0-552-50065-8 (pbk) : £0.50 B81-38545

Huddy, Delia. The tale of the Crooked Crab / Delia Huddy ; illustrated by Linda Birch. — London (8 Cork St., W1X 2HA) : MacRae, 1981. — 45p : ill ; 21cm. — (Blackbird books)
ISBN 0-86203-022-6 : £2.75 B81-09670

Hudson, May Isabel. The tale of Micky and Sandy / May Isabel Hudson. — London : New Horizon, c1981. — 32p : col.ill ; 21cm
ISBN 0-86116-183-1 : £2.95 B81-39436

Hughes, Monica. Crisis on Conshelf Ten / Monica Hughes. — [London] : Magnet, 1981, c1975. — 143p ; 18cm
Originally published: London : Hamilton, 1975
ISBN 0-416-89990-0 (pbk) : £0.90 B81-08594

Hughes, Monica. Earthdark / Monica Hughes. — [London] : Magnet, 1981, c1977. — 122p : 1map ; 18cm
Originally published: London : Hamilton, 1977
ISBN 0-416-21070-8 (pbk) : £0.95 B81-12036

Hughes, Monica. The guardian of Isis / Monica Hughes. — London : Hamilton, 1981. — 140p ; 23cm
ISBN 0-241-10597-8 : £5.25 : CIP rev.
B81-03684

Hughes, Monica. The keeper of the Isis Light / Monica Hughes. — [London] : Magnet, 1981, c1980. — 136p ; 18cm
Originally published: London : Hamilton Children's, 1980
ISBN 0-416-21030-9 (pbk) : £0.95 B81-18405

Hughes, Shirley. Alfie gets in first / Shirley Hughes. — London : Bodley Head, 1981. — [36]p : col.ill ; 21cm
ISBN 0-370-30417-9 : £3.50 : CIP rev.
B81-25772

Hughes, Shirley. Here comes Charlie Moon / written and illustrated by Shirley Hughes. — London : Bodley Head, 1980. — 142p : ill ; 23cm
ISBN 0-370-30335-0 : £3.75 : CIP rev.
B80-19992

Hughes, Shirley. Lucy & Tom at the seaside / [Shirley Hughes]. — [London] : [Carousel], [1981?, c1976]. — [32]p : chiefly ill(some col.) ; 26x19cm
Originally published: London : Gollancz, 1976
ISBN 0-552-52144-2 (pbk) : £0.95 B81-21277

Hughes, Shirley. Lucy & Tom go to school / written and drawn by Shirley Hughes. — London : Transworld, 1981, c1973. — [32]p : chiefly ill(some col.) ; 26x19cm. — (A Carousel book)
Originally published: London : Gollancz, 1973
ISBN 0-552-52145-0 (pbk) : £0.95 B81-21278

Hughes, Shirley. Moving Molly / Shirley Hughes. — [London] : Fontana, 1981, c1978. — [32]p : col.ill ; 16x22cm. — (Picture lions)
Originally published: London : Bodley Head, 1978
ISBN 0-00-661782-4 (pbk) : £0.85 B81-11282

Hulke, Malcolm. Doctor Who and the Green death : based on the BBC television serial by Robert Sloman by arrangement with the British Broadcasting Corporation / Malcolm Hulke ; illustrated by Alan Willow. — London : W.H. Allen, 1981. — 142p : ill ; 21cm
ISBN 0-491-02874-1 : £4.25 B81-11812

Hulke, Malcolm. Doctor Who and the sea-devils : based on the BBC television serial by Malcolm Hulke by arrangement with the British Broadcasting Corporation / Malcolm Hulke ; illustrated by Alan Willow. — London : W.H. Allen, 1981, c1974. — 139p : ill ; 21cm
ISBN 0-491-02954-3 : £4.25 B81-28606

Hunter, Mollie. You never knew her as I did / Mollie Hunter. — London : Hamilton, 1981. — 214p : geneal.tables ; 23cm
ISBN 0-241-10643-5 : £5.25 : CIP rev.
B81-10440

Hurford, John. The dormouse. — Barnstaple : Spindlewood, Nov.1981. — [25]p
Originally published: London: Cape, 1974
ISBN 0-907349-20-x (cased) : £3.95 : CIP entry
ISBN 0-907349-25-0 (pbk) : £1.35 B81-35891

Hutchins, Pat. Don't forget the bacon! / Pat Hutchins. — Harmondsworth : Puffin, 1978, c1976 (1980 [printing]). — [32]p : chiefly col.ill ; 19x23cm. — (Picture Puffin)
Originally published: London : Bodley Head, 1976
£0.80 (pbk) B81-03593

Hutchins, Pat. Good-night, Owl! / Pat Hutchins. — Harmondsworth : Puffin in association with Bodley Head, 1975, c1972 (1980 [printing]). — [31p] : chiefly col.ill ; 23cm. — (Picture puffins)
Originally published: New York : Macmillan, 1972 ; London : Bodley Head, 1973
£0.80 (pbk) B81-06082

Hutchins, Pat. Happy birthday, Sam / by Pat Hutchins. — Harmondsworth : Puffin, 1981, c1978. — [32]p : col.ill ; 23cm. — (Picture puffins)
Originally published: New York : Greenwillow, London : Bodley Head, 1978
ISBN 0-14-050339-0 (pbk) : £0.90 B81-27220

Hutchins, Pat. The Mona Lisa mystery / Pat Hutchins ; illustrated by Laurence Hutchins. — London : Bodley Head, c1981. — 191p : ill ; 22cm
ISBN 0-370-30310-5 : £4.50 : CIP rev.
B81-04292

Hutchins, Pat. Rosie's walk / [by Pat Hutchins]. — Harmondsworth : Puffin, 1970, c1968 (1980 [printing]). — [32]p : chiefly col.ill ; 18x23cm. — (Picture puffins)
Originally published: New York : Macmillan ; London : Bodley Head, 1968
ISBN 0-14-050032-4 (pbk) : £0.80 B81-13296

Hutchins, Pat. The surprise party / Pat Hutchins. — Harmondsworth : Puffin Books in association with the Bodley Head, 1972 (1981 [printing]). — [28]p : chiefly col.ill ; 19cm. — (Picture puffins)
Originally published: London : Bodley Head, 1970
ISBN 0-14-050055-3 (pbk) : £0.95 B81-40673

Hutchins, Pat. Tom and Sam / by Pat Hutchins. — Harmondsworth : Puffin in association with Bodley Head, 1972, c1968 (1981 [printing]). — 32p : col.ill ; 18x23cm. — (Picture puffins)
Originally published: New York : Macmillan, 1968 ; London : Bodley Head, 1969
ISBN 0-14-050042-1 (pbk) : £0.90 B81-13290

Hutchins, Pat. The wind blew / Pat Hutchins. — Harmondsworth : Puffin, 1978, c1974 (1980 [printing]). — [32]p : chiefly col.ill ; 18x23cm. — (Picture puffins)
Originally published: London : Bodley Head, 1974
£0.80 (pbk) B81-03594

Hynard, Stephen. Snowy the rabbit / by Stephen Hynard ; illustrated by Frances Thatcher. — Winchester : Hambleside, c1980. — [32]p : col.ill ; 23x26cm. — (A Terrapin book)
ISBN 0-86042-033-7 : Unpriced B81-24501

Ireland, Kenneth. The cove / by Kenneth Ireland. — London : Dobson, 1979. — 157p ; 21cm
ISBN 0-234-72135-9 : £3.75 B81-01684

Ireland, Kenneth. The pigeon hole / by Kenneth Ireland. — London : Dobson, 1980. — 192p : 1ill ; 21cm
ISBN 0-234-72215-0 : £3.95 B81-01324

Jeffries, Roderic. Voyage into danger / Roderic Jeffries. — London : Hodder and Stoughton, 1981. — 119p ; 23cm
ISBN 0-340-26427-6 : £3.95 : CIP rev.
B81-18160

Jezard, Alison. Albert on the farm / Alison Jezard ; illustrated by Margaret Gordon. — Harmondsworth : Puffin, 1981, c1979. — 78p : ill ; 20cm. — (A young puffin)
Originally published: London : Gollancz, 1979
ISBN 0-14-031281-1 (pbk) : £0.85 B81-34757

Johnson, Jane, *1951-*. Bertie on the beach / Jane Johnson. — London : Ernest Benn, 1981. — [32]p : chiefly col.ill ; 26cm
ISBN 0-510-00112-2 : £3.95 B81-35277

Jones, Diana Wynne. The four grannies / Diana Wynne Jones ; illustrated by Thelma Lambert. — London : Beaver, 1981, c1980. — 79p : ill ; 18cm
Originally published: London : Hamilton, 1980
ISBN 0-600-20406-5 (pbk) : £0.75 B81-40992

Jones, Diana Wynne. The homeward bounders / Diana Wynne Jones. — London : Macmillan, 1981. — 224p ; 21cm
ISBN 0-333-30979-0 : £4.95 B81-19955

823'.914[J] — Children's stories in English, *1945-* — *Texts* *continuation*

Jones, Diana Wynne. The time of the ghost. — London : Macmillan Children's Books, Oct.1981. — [192]p
ISBN 0-333-32012-3 : £4.95 : CIP entry
B81-26759

Jones, Gwyneth A.. Dear Hill / Gwyneth A. Jones. — London : Macmillan Children's, 1980. — 187p ; 21cm
ISBN 0-333-30106-4 : £4.95 : CIP rev.
B80-22623

Jones, Harold. Tales from Aesop / written and illustrated by Harold Jones. — London : MacRae, 1981. — 40p : col.ill ; 26cm
ISBN 0-86203-018-8 : £5.95 : CIP rev.
B81-20467

Kavanagh, P. J.. Scarf Jack / P.J. Kavanagh. — Harmondsworth : Puffin, 1980, c1978. — 190p ; 18cm
Originally published: London : Bodley Head, 1978
ISBN 0-14-031208-0 (pbk) : £0.95 B81-18510

Kay, Mara. Lolo. — London : Macmillan Children's Books, Sept.1981. — [160]p
ISBN 0-333-31732-7 : £4.95 : CIP entry
B81-23947

Kaye, Geraldine. The day after yesterday / Geraldine Kaye ; illustrated by Glenys Ambrus. — London : Deutsch, 1981. — 93p : ill ; 21cm
ISBN 0-233-97344-3 : £4.25 : CIP rev.
B81-04389

Kaye, Geraldine. The plum tree party. — London : Hodder and Stoughton Children's Books, Oct.1981. — [48]p
ISBN 0-340-26574-4 : £2.50 : CIP entry
B81-26711

Kaye, M. M.. The ordinary princess / M.M. Kaye ; text illustrations by Faith Jaques. — Harmondsworth : Puffin, 1981, c1980. — 122p : ill ; 18cm
Originally published: London : Kestrel, 1980
ISBN 0-14-031384-2 (pbk) : £0.85 B81-40433

Keef, Chloë. Melanie Mall and the circus animals / written and illustrated by Chloë Keef. — London : Warne, 1979. — [26]p : col.ill ; 26cm
ISBN 0-7232-2179-0 : £3.25 B81-15781

Kelleher, Victor. The hunting of Shadroth / Victor Kelleher. — [Harmondsworth] : Kestrel, 1981. — 192p ; 23cm
ISBN 0-7226-5688-2 : £4.95 B81-10316

Kemp, Gene. Gowie Corby plays chicken / Gene Kemp. — [Harmondsworth] : Puffin in association with Faber, 1981, c1979. — 136p ; 19cm
Originally published: London : Faber, 1979
ISBN 0-14-031322-2 (pbk) : £0.90 B81-35480

Kennemore, Tim. The middle of the sandwich / Tim Kennemore. — London : Faber, 1981. — 112p ; 21cm
ISBN 0-571-11678-7 : £4.25 : CIP rev.
B81-06873

Kenward, Jean. Ragdolly Anna stories / by Jean Kenward ; illustrated by Zoë Hall. — London : Warne, 1979. — 95p : ill ; 21cm
ISBN 0-7232-2278-9 : £2.95 B81-03458

Kerven, Rosalind. Mysteries of the seals / Rosalind Kerven. — London : Abelard-Schuman, c1981. — 123p ; 21cm
ISBN 0-200-72736-2 : £4.95 B81-15596

Kesteven, G. R.. The awakening water / G.R. Kesteven. — Sevenoaks : Knight Books, 1979, c1977. — 160p ; 18cm
Originally published: London : Chatto and Windus, 1977
ISBN 0-340-24033-4 (pbk) : £0.75 : CIP rev.
B79-25426

Kev. The rescue mission : adventures from Hurlindaine / conceived, written, and illustrated by Kev. — [Llanelli] ([Merrivale, Penygaer Rd., Llanelli, Dyfed SA14 8RU]) : [K. Morris], c1981. — [40]p : chiefly ill,1map ; 30cm
£1.00 (pbk) B81-37876

Kimura, Yasuko. Cuthbert and the good ship Thingamabob / pictures by Yasuko Kimura ; story by Kim Chesher. — London : Evans, 1981. — [33]p : col.ill ; 20x21cm
Originally published: Japan : Shika-sha Co., 1980
ISBN 0-237-45564-1 : £3.95 : CIP rev.
B81-00652

King, Clive. Stig of the dump / by Clive King ; illustrated by Edward Ardizzone. — Harmondsworth : Puffin, 1963 (1981 [printing]). — 156p : ill ; 18cm
ISBN 0-14-030196-8 (pbk) : £0.90 B81-38362

King, Deborah. Sirius and Saba. — London : Hamilton, Apr.1981. — [32]p
ISBN 0-241-10599-4 : £4.50 : CIP entry
B81-01325

King, Eve. Farmyard troubles / Eve King ; illustrated by Cora E.M. Paterson. — Ilfracombe : Stockwell, 1981. — 32p : ill ; 18cm
ISBN 0-7223-1464-7 (pbk) : £0.70 B81-35050

King-Smith, Dick. The mouse butcher / Dick King-Smith ; illustrated by Wendy Smith. — London : Gollancz, 1981. — 126p : ill ; 21cm
ISBN 0-575-02899-8 : £4.95 B81-12066

Knights, Roger. The lettermen go to a party / by Roger Knights. — [London] ([5 Elvaston Mews SW7 5HY]) : Hathercliff, [1981?]. — [32]p : chiefly col.ill ; 14cm
ISBN 0-907048-05-6 (pbk) : £0.45 B81-19906

Knights, Roger. The lettermen go to the fair / by Roger Knights. — [London] ([5 Elvaston Mews SW7 5HY]) : Hathercliff, [1981?]. — [32]p : chiefly.col.ill ; 15x14cm
ISBN 0-907048-04-8 (pbk) : £0.45 B81-19905

Koelling, Caryl. Whose house is this? / written by Caryl Koelling ; designed and illustrated by Carol Wynne. — [Swindon] : Child's Play, 1978. — [20]p : chiefly col.ill ; 19cm. — (Child's Play action books)
Text, ill on inside cover
ISBN 0-85953-090-6 : Unpriced B81-32134

Koralek, Jenny. John Logan's rooster / by Jenny Koralek ; illustrated by Sally Holmes. — London : Hamilton, 1981. — 45p : ill ; 20cm
ISBN 0-241-10617-6 : £1.80 B81-15776

Krailing, Tessa. A dinosaur called Minerva / Tessa Krailing ; illustrated by Maggie Ling. — London : Scholastic, 1980. — 128p : ill ; 18cm. — (Hippo books)
ISBN 0-590-70031-6 (pbk) : £0.70 B81-11683

Lane, Margaret, *1907-*. Operation hedgehog. — London : Methuen/Walker, Oct.1981. — [32]p
ISBN 0-416-05920-1 : £4.50 : CIP entry
B81-28119

Lang, Andrew. The chronicles of Pantouflia. — London : Methuen Children's Books, Jan.1982. — [196]p
ISBN 0-416-21940-3 : £4.95 : CIP entry
B81-34397

Langholm, A. D.. The Clover Club and the house of mystery / A.D. Langholm ; illustrated by Reginald Gray. — London : Methuen Children's Books, 1980, c1978. — 141p : ill ; 21cm
Originally published: London : W.H. Allen, 1978
ISBN 0-416-89860-2 : £3.95 : CIP rev.
B80-18919

Langholm, A. D.. Queen rider / A.D. Langholm. — London : Methuen Children's Books, 1980, c1979. — 120p ; 21cm
Originally published: London : W.H. Allen, 1979
ISBN 0-416-89820-3 : £3.50 : CIP rev.
B80-10865

Langholm, A. D.. Queen rider / A.D. Langholm. — London : Methuen, 1980, c1979. — 120p ; 18cm. — (A Magnet book)
Originally published: London : W.H. Allen, 1979
ISBN 0-416-89830-0 (pbk) : £0.85 B81-29492

Lavelle, Sheila. Ursula bear / Sheila Lavelle ; illustrated by Thelma Lambert. — London : Beaver Books, 1981, c1977. — 78p : ill ; 18cm
Originally published: London : Hamish Hamilton's Children's Books, 1977. — Contents: Ursula Bear - Ursula dancing
ISBN 0-600-20072-8 (pbk) : £0.75 B81-12254

Lavelle, Sheila. Ursula exploring / Sheila Lavelle ; illustrated by Thelma Lambert. — London : Hamilton, 1980. — 45p : ill ; 20cm. — (Gazelle books)
ISBN 0-241-10490-4 : £1.80 : CIP rev.
B80-11219

Lavelle, Sheila. Ursula flying. — London : H. Hamilton, July 1981. — [48]p. — (Gazelle series)
ISBN 0-241-10651-6 : £1.80 : CIP entry
B81-14956

Lawrence, Ann. The hawk of May / Ann Lawrence ; illustrated by Shirley Felts. — London : Macmillan Children's, 1980. — 192p : ill ; 21cm
ISBN 0-333-28396-1 : £4.95 : CIP rev.
B80-13599

Lawrence, Ann. Oggy and the holiday / Ann Lawrence ; illustrated by Hans Helweg. — [London] : Piccolo, 1981, c1979. — 95p : ill ; 18cm
Originally published: London : Gollancz, 1979
ISBN 0-330-26353-6 (pbk) : £0.90 B81-20220

Leavy, Una. Shoes for Tom. — London : Abelard-Schuman, Sept.1981. — [24]p
ISBN 0-200-72767-2 : £3.50 : CIP entry
B81-23870

Leavy, Una. Tom's garden. — London : Abelard-Schuman, Sept.1981. — [24]p
ISBN 0-200-72766-4 : £3.50 : CIP entry
B81-23869

Lee, Robert, *1950-*. Fishy business / Robert Lee ; illustrated by Caroline Holden. — London : Methuen Children's Books, 1981. — 141p : ill ; 20cm. — (A Pied Piper book)
ISBN 0-416-20660-3 : £3.50 B81-10970

Lee, Simon, *1943-*. The giant's paw / Simon Lee. — Bognor Regis : New Horizon, c1979. — 147p[10]p of plates : ill ; 22cm
ISBN 0-86116-216-1 : £3.50 B81-19061

Leeson, Robert. Grange Hill for sale / Robert Leeson ; based on the BBC television series Grange Hill by Phil Redmond. — London : Fontana, 1981. — 128p ; 18cm. — (Fontana Lions)
ISBN 0-00-671813-2 (pbk) : £0.85 B81-37896

Leeson, Robert. Grange Hill goes wild / Robert Leeson ; based on the BBC television series Grange Hill by Phil Redmond. — London : Fontana, 1980. — 141p ; 18cm. — (Lions)
ISBN 0-00-671812-4 (pbk) : £0.80 B81-02442

Leeson, Robert. Grange Hill goes wild / Robert Leeson ; based on the BBC television series Grange Hill by Phil Redmond. — London : British Broadcasting Corporation, 1980. — 141p ; 22cm
ISBN 0-563-17865-5 : £4.50 B81-07748

823'.914[J] — Children's stories in English, ***1945-*** ***— Texts*** *continuation*

Leeson, Robert. Harold and Bella, Jammy and me. — London : Hamilton, Feb.1982. — [128]p
Originally published: London : Fontana, 1980
ISBN 0-241-10722-9 : £4.95 : CIP entry
B81-36383

Leeson, Robert. The third class genie / Robert Leeson. — London : Hamilton Children's Books, 1981, c1975. — 128p : 1map ; 21cm
Originally published: London : Collins, 1975
ISBN 0-241-10623-0 : £4.95 : CIP rev.
B81-01326

Leitch, Patricia. [Jacky jumps to the top]. Jump to the top / Patricia Leitch. — London : Armada, 1981, c1972. — 127p ; 18cm. — (An Armada pony book)
Originally published: London : Collins, 1973
ISBN 0-00-691886-7 (pbk) : £0.80 B81-15588

Leitch, Patricia. The summer riders / Patricia Leitch. — London : Severn House, 1980, c1977. — 128p : ill ; 21cm
Originally published: London : Armada, 1977
ISBN 0-7278-0568-1 : £3.95 : CIP rev.
B80-18052

Lewis, Naomi. Anna and the rainbow. — London : Cape, Oct.1981. — [32]p
ISBN 0-224-01842-6 : £4.50 : CIP entry
B81-27339

Lewis, Naomi. Come with us. — London : Andersen Press, Feb.1982. — [32]p
ISBN 0-86264-011-3 : £3.95 : CIP entry
B81-36962

Lewis, Naomi. Hare and badger go to town / by Naomi Lewis & Tony Ross. — London : Andersen, 1981. — [28]p : col.ill ; 20cm
ISBN 0-905478-94-0 : £2.95 B81-24823

Lewis, Naomi. The snow queen / a new adapted version by Naomi Lewis ; illustrated by Errol Le Cain. — Harmondsworth : Puffin, 1981, c1979. — [32]p : col.ill ; 24cm. — (Picture Puffins)
Originally published: London : Constable, 1968
ISBN 0-14-050294-7 (pbk) : £0.95 B81-40505

Lindsay, Elizabeth. Heggerty Haggerty and the dreadful drought / Elizabeth Lindsay ; illustrated by Pam Jarvis. — London : Hamilton, 1980. — 47p : ill ; 19cm. — (Gazelle books)
ISBN 0-241-10515-3 : £1.80 : CIP rev.
B80-23794

Ling, Sheilah Ward. Final set / Sheilah Ward Ling. — London : Dobson, 1981. — 191p ; 21cm
ISBN 0-234-72245-2 : £4.50 B81-18540

Lingard, Joan. Hostages to fortune / Joan Lingard. — [Harmondsworth] : Puffin, 1981, c1976. — 174p ; 19cm. — (A Kevin and Sadie story) (Puffin plus)
Originally published: London : Hamilton, 1976. — For adolescents
ISBN 0-14-031350-8 (pbk) : £0.95 B81-22035

Lingard, Joan. Into exile / Joan Lingard. — Harmondsworth : Puffin in association with Hamish Hamilton, 1974, c1973 (1981 [printing]). — 172p ; 19cm
Originally published: London : Hamilton, 1973
ISBN 0-14-030702-8 (pbk) : £0.95 B81-26550

Lingard, Joan. A proper place / Joan Lingard. — [Harmondsworth] : Puffin, 1979, c1975 (1981 [printing]). — 174p ; 19cm. — (A Kevin and Sadie story) (Puffin plus)
Originally published: London : Hamilton, 1975. — For adolescents
ISBN 0-14-031036-3 (pbk) : £0.95 B81-26553

Lingard, Joan. Strangers in the house. — London : H. Hamilton, Oct.1981. — [144]p
ISBN 0-241-10671-0 : £4.95 : CIP entry
B81-25701

Little, Patrick. A court for owls. — London : Macmillan Children's Books, Oct.1981. — [160]p
ISBN 0-333-31076-4 : £4.95 : CIP entry
B81-25780

Lively, Penelope. The stained glass window / Penelope Lively ; illustrated by Michael Pollard. — London : Abelard in association with Richard Sadler, 1976 (1980 [printing]). — 58p : ill ; 21cm. — (A Grasshopper book)
ISBN 0-200-72264-6 (cased) : £2.95: CIP rev.
ISBN 0-200-72263-8 (pbk) : £0.75 B81-01327

Lloyd, Errol. Nini on time / Errol Lloyd. — London : Bodley Head, 1981. — [26]p : col.ill ; 21x26cm
ISBN 0-370-30301-6 : £3.95 B81-13370

Lloyd, Jeremy. Captain Beaky / by Jeremy Lloyd ; illustrated by Keith Michell. — London : Chappell Music
Vol.2. — 1981. — 64p : col.ill,2ports ; 30cm
ISBN 0-903443-51-1 (pbk) : £2.95 B81-24880

Lockwood, Jennifer. Friday every day. — London : H. Hamilton, July 1981. — [48]p. — (Gazelle series)
ISBN 0-241-10652-4 : £1.80 : CIP entry
B81-17523

Longden, Peter. The bottleneck ; and the mole hole. — Loughborough : Ladybird, c1981. — 51p : col.ill ; 18cm. — (The fun guys)
Cover title. — Written and illustrated by Peter Longden
ISBN 0-7214-0689-0 : £0.50 B81-29904

Longden, Peter. The hen coat ; The ship shape. — Loughborough : Ladybird, 1981. — 51p : col.ill ; 18cm. — (The fun guys)
Cover title. — Written and illustrated by Peter Longden
ISBN 0-7214-0677-7 : £0.50 B81-13122

Longden, Peter. The mouse trap ; and the cricket team. — Loughborough : Ladybird, c1981. — 51p : col.ill ; 18cm. — (The fun guys)
Cover title. — Written and illustrated by Peter Longden
ISBN 0-7214-0691-2 : £0.50 B81-29905

Longden, Peter. The mush rooms ; and the fox glove. — Loughborough : Ladybird, c1981. — 51p : col.ill ; 18cm. — (The fun guys)
Cover title. — Written and illustrated by Peter Longden
ISBN 0-7214-0690-4 : £0.50 B81-29903

Longden, Peter. The rat race ; The sky lark. — Loughborough : Ladybird, 1981. — 51p : col.ill ; 18cm. — (The fun guys)
Cover title. — Written and illustrated by Peter Longden
ISBN 0-7214-0678-5 : £0.50 B81-13121

Longden, Peter. The spring time ; The moth ball. — Loughborough : Ladybird, 1981. — 51p : col.ill ; 18cm. — (The fun guys)
Cover title. — Written and illustrated by Peter Longden
ISBN 0-7214-0676-9 : £0.50 B81-13123

Longhurst, Joy. The butter mountain / by Joy Longhurst ; illustrations, Diane Rosher. — [Canterbury] ([22 Best La., Canterbury, Kent]) : [Joy Longhurst], [1981?]. — 44p : ill(some col.) ; 16cm
Unpriced B81-17391

Lorenz, Lee. The feathered ogre. — London : Dent, Feb.1982. — [32]p
ISBN 0-460-06098-8 : £3.95 : CIP entry
B81-38309

Lurie, Morris. The Twenty-seventh Annual African Hippopotamus Race / Morris Lurie ; illustrated by Elizabeth Honey. — Harmondsworth : Puffin, 1977 (1981 [printing]). — 100p : ill ; 20cm. — (A young puffin)
Originally published: London : Collins, 1969
ISBN 0-14-030991-8 (pbk) : £0.85 B81-34756

Macaulay, David. Unbuilding / David Macaulay. — London : Hamilton, 1981, c1980. — 78p : ill ; 32cm
Originally published: Boston : Houghton Mifflin, 1980
ISBN 0-241-10609-5 : £4.95 : CIP rev.
B81-04216

McCaffrey, Mary. Smoke-drift to heaven. — London : Abelard-Schuman, Sept.1981. — [128]p
ISBN 0-200-72763-x : £4.50 : CIP entry
B81-23867

McCann, Sean. Hot shot!. — London : Hodder & Stoughton, Sept.1981. — [96]p
Originally published: 1979
ISBN 0-340-26539-6 (pbk) : £0.85 : CIP entry
B81-23926

McCann, Sean. Shoot on sight / Sean McCann ; illustrated by Barry Raynor. — London : Hodder and Stoughton, 1981. — 72p : ill ; 21cm
ISBN 0-340-26428-4 : £4.25 : CIP rev.
B81-18151

McDonald, Jill. The Happyhelper Engine / Jill McDonald. — London : Methuen Children's Books, 1980. — [28]p : chiefly col.ill ; 23cm. — (A Methuen picture-story book)
ISBN 0-416-89240-x : £2.95 : CIP rev.
B80-18523

McIntosh, Mabel Wilson. Journey to the moon / by Mabel Wilson McIntosh ; illustrated by Graham Morris. — Winchester : Hambleside, c1980. — [24]p : ill(some col.) ; 18x22cm. — (A Terrapin book)
ISBN 0-86042-032-9 (pbk) : £0.75 B81-24362

McKee, David. King Rollo and King Frank. — London : Andersen, Oct.1981. — [32]p
ISBN 0-905478-96-7 : £0.95 : CIP entry
B81-27465

McKee, David. King Rollo and the bath. — London : Andersen, Oct.1981. — [32]p
ISBN 0-905478-97-5 : £0.95 : CIP entry
B81-27464

McKee, David. King Rollo and the search. — London : Andersen, Oct.1981. — [32]p
ISBN 0-905478-98-3 : £0.95 : CIP entry
B81-27420

McKee, David. The magician and double trouble / story and pictures by David Hope. — London : Arnold, 1981. — [25]p : col.ill ; 28cm
ISBN 0-200-72747-8 : £4.95 : CIP rev.
B81-25685

McKee, David. Not now, Bernard / David McKee. — London : Arrow, 1980. — [26]p : chiefly col.ill ; 23cm. — (A Sparrow book)
ISBN 0-09-924050-5 (pbk) : £1.25 B81-13109

McNaughton, Colin. Football crazy / Colin McNaughton. — London : Heinemann, 1980. — [32]p : col.ill ; 29cm
ISBN 0-434-94991-4 : £4.95 B81-03059

McNaughton, Colin. King Nonn the Wiser / Colin McNaughton. — London : Heinemann, 1981, c1980. — [32]p : col.ill ; 25cm
ISBN 0-434-94990-6 : £4.50 B81-18408

McNaughton, Colin. The rat race : the amazing adventures of Anton B. Stanton / by Colin McNaughton. — Harmondsworth : Puffin, 1980, c1978. — [32]p : col.ill ; 19x23cm. — (Picture puffins)
Originally published: London : Benn, 1978
ISBN 0-14-050311-0 (pbk) : £0.80 B81-00616

McPhail, David. Where can an elephant hide? / by David McPhail. — London : Deutsch, 1981, c1979. — [32]p : col.ill ; 20x24cm
Originally published: Garden City, N.Y. : Doubleday, 1979
ISBN 0-233-97349-4 : £3.50 B81-20951

823'.914[J] — Children's stories in English, *1945-* — *Texts* *continuation*

Magorian, Michelle. Goodnight Mister Tom / Michelle Magorian. — Harmondsworth : Kestrel, 1981. — 304p ; 23cm
ISBN 0-7226-5701-3 : £5.50 B81-15390

Mahy, Margaret. The great piratical rumbustification ; & The librarian and the robbers / Margaret Mahy ; with pictures by Quentin Blake. — Harmondsworth : Puffin, 1981, c1978. — 71p : ill ; 20cm. — (A young Puffin)
Originally published: London : Dent, 1978
ISBN 0-14-031261-7 (pbk) : £0.80 B81-40502

Mahy, Margaret. Raging robots & unruly uncles / Margaret Mahy ; illustrated by Peter Stevenson. — London : Dent, 1981. — 93p : ill ; 24cm
ISBN 0-460-06073-2 : £3.95 B81-32823

Mair, Craig. The lighthouse boy / Craig Mair ; illustrated by Ray Evans. — London : John Murray, 1981. — 113p : ill,1map ; 23cm
ISBN 0-7195-3824-6 : £4.95 B81-20931

Manning, Rosemary. Dragon on the harbour / Rosemary Manning ; illustrated by Peter Rush. — [Harmondsworth] : Kestrel, 1980. — 184p : ill,music ; 21cm
ISBN 0-7226-5690-4 : £3.95 B81-01328

Mark, Jan. The Ennead / Jan Mark. — Harmondsworth : Puffin, 1981, c1978. — 252p ; 19cm. — (Puffin plus)
Originally published: Harmondsworth : Kestrel, 1978
ISBN 0-14-031354-0 (pbk) : £1.35 B81-26511

Mark, Jan. The short voyage of the Albert Ross / Jan Mark ; illustrated by Gavin Rowe. — London : Granada, 1981, c1980. — 77p : ill ; 18cm. — (A Dragon book)
Originally published: 1980
ISBN 0-583-30373-0 (pbk) : £0.85 B81-17406

Mark, Jan. Under the autumn garden / Jan Mark. — Harmondsworth : Puffin, 1980, c1977. — 154p ; 18cm
Originally published: London : Kestrel, 1977
ISBN 0-14-031248-x (pbk) : £0.90 B81-01329

Marshall, Frances. Princess Kalina and the hedgehog. — London : Faber, Sept.1981. — [18]p
ISBN 0-571-11844-5 : £3.95 : CIP entry B81-23756

Marshall, Yvonne. The bird. — London : Evans Bros, Apr.1981. — [24]p. — (Hide-and-seek series)
ISBN 0-237-45535-8 : £1.95 : CIP entry B81-00611

Marshall, Yvonne. The bumble-bee. — London : Evans Bros, Apr.1981. — [24]p. — (Hide-and-seek series)
ISBN 0-237-45537-4 : £1.95 : CIP entry B81-00612

Marshall, Yvonne. The cat. — London : Evans Bros, Apr.1981. — [24]p. — (Hide-and-seek series)
ISBN 0-237-45536-6 : £1.95 : CIP entry B81-00613

Marshall, Yvonne. Nasim. — London : Evans Bros, Apr.1981. — [24]p. — (Hide-and-seek series)
ISBN 0-237-45534-x : £1.95 : CIP entry B81-00614

Marter, Ian. Doctor Who and the enemy of the world / Ian Marter. — London : Target, 1981. — 127p ; 18cm
ISBN 0-426-20126-4 (pbk) : £0.95 B81-11667

Martin, David, *1935-*. K9 and the beasts of Vega / David Martin. — London : Sparrow, [1980]. — [32]p : col.ill ; 19cm. — (The Adventures of K9 ; no.2)
ISBN 0-09-924470-5 (pbk) : £3.65 B81-00617

Martin, David, *1935-*. K9 and the missing planet / David Martin. — London : Sparrow, [1980]. — [32]p : col.ill ; 19cm. — (The Adventures of K9 ; no.4)
ISBN 0-09-924490-x (pbk) : £0.65 B81-11061

Martin, David, *1935-*. K9 and the Zeta rescue / David Martin. — London : Arrow, [1980?]. — [32]p : col.ill ; 19cm. — (The Adventures of K9 ; no.3) (Sparrow books)
ISBN 0-09-924460-8 (corrected : pbk) : £0.65 B81-11674

Mattingley, Christopher. The jetty. — Sevenoaks : Hodder & Stoughton, June 1981. — [128]p
ISBN 0-340-26530-2 (pbk) : £0.85 : CIP entry B81-09989

Mayle, Peter. The amazing adventures of Chilly Billy / by Peter Mayle & Arthur Robins. — Leeds : Pepper Press, c1980. — 64p : col.ill ; 20cm
ISBN 0-560-74503-6 : £3.95 B81-19853

Mayne, William. It / William Mayne. — Harmondsworth : Puffin, 1980, c1977. — 191p ; 19cm
Originally published: London : Hamilton, 1977
ISBN 0-14-031174-2 (pbk) : £1.25 B81-10689

Mayne, William. The mouse and the egg / William Mayne ; with pictures by Krystyna Turska. — London (8 Cork St., W1X 2HA) : MacRae, c1980. — [32]p : col.ill ; 26cm
ISBN 0-86203-035-8 : £3.95 : CIP rev. B80-22628

Meredith, Lucy. The paper aeroplane. — London : Faber, Sept.1981. — [26]p
ISBN 0-571-11845-3 : £3.95 : CIP entry B81-20555

Michael, Enid. The runaway National / Enid Michael. — [London] : Corgi, 1981. — 155p ; 18cm
ISBN 0-552-11629-7 (pbk) : £0.95 B81-15341

Milburn, Constance. Sasha : -looking after your first puppy- / written by Constance Milburn ; illustrated by Frank Rodgers. — [London] : Blackie, 1981. — [46]p : col.ill ; 25cm
ISBN 0-216-90861-2 (cased) : £3.95
ISBN 0-216-90966-x (pbk) : £1.50 B81-12081

Miles, Judith. Beauty & the beast / [text Judith Miles] ; [illustrations Martina Selway]. — Harlow : Longman by arrangement with the British Broadcasting Corporation, 1981. — 14p : col.ill ; 14x16cm. — (You and me storybooks)
ISBN 0-582-39137-7 (pbk) : £0.40 B81-28364

Miles, Judith. The birthday party / ; [text Judith Miles] ; [illustrations Sara Cole]. — Harlow : Longman by arrangement with the British Broadcasting Corporation, 1981. — 14p : col.ill ; 14x16cm. — (You and me storybooks)
ISBN 0-582-39138-5 (pbk) : £0.40 B81-28365

Miles, Judith. Needles, nuts & nails / [text Judith Miles] ; [illustrations Martina Selway]. — Harlow : Longman by arrangement with the British Broadcasting Corporation, 1981. — 14p : col.ill ; 14x16cm. — (You and me storybooks)
ISBN 0-582-39133-4 (pbk) : £0.40 B81-28362

Miles, Ken. Lawrence the lifeboat / by Ken Miles ; illustrated by Pam Wilson, Jim Morrison. — [Dover] ([96 Templeside, Temple Ewell, Dover, Kent CT16 3BD]) : White Cliffs, c1980. — [12]p : ill(chiefly col.) ; 15x21cm
Cover title
ISBN 0-907327-00-1 (pbk) : £0.75 B81-00618

Miles, Patricia. Louther Hall / Patricia Miles. — London : Hamilton, 1981. — 144p ; 23cm
ISBN 0-241-10595-1 : £4.95 : CIP rev. B81-04214

Miller, Margaret J.. The mad muddle. — London : Hodder and Stoughton Children's Books, Feb.1982. — [96]p
ISBN 0-340-27253-8 : £3.50 : CIP entry B81-36358

Miller, Moira. Oh Abigail! / Moira Miller ; illustrated by Doreen Caldwell. — London : Methuen Children's, 1981. — 96p : ill ; 21cm. — ([A Read aloud book])
ISBN 0-416-20640-9 : £3.50 : CIP rev. B81-10459

Miller, Mona. Julie : a bedtime story for young children in eight instalments / by Mona Miller ; illustrations by Ann Holehouse. — London (14 Barlly Rd. W10 6AR) : Autolycus, c1978. — 27p : ill ; 21cm
ISBN 0-903413-19-1 (pbk) : Unpriced B81-33504

Moon, Heather. Winklepicker. — Sevenoaks : Hodder & Stoughton, July, 1981. — [160]p
ISBN 0-340-26534-5 (pbk) : £0.85 : CIP entry B81-13816

Mooney, Bel. Liza's yellow boat / by Bel Mooney. — London : Quartet, 1980. — [55]p : col.ill ; 31cm
ISBN 0-7043-2268-4 : £4.95 B81-02754

Moore, John. Granny Stickleback. — London : Hamish Hamilton, Oct.1981. — [32]p
ISBN 0-241-10635-4 : £4.25 : CIP entry B81-26781

Moore, Katherine. The little stolen sweep. — London : Allison & Busby, Sept.1981. — [128]p
ISBN 0-85031-414-3 : £4.95 : CIP entry B81-20130

Moore, Patrick. The secret of the black hole : a Scott Saunders space adventure / Patrick Moore. — London : Armada, 1980. — 125p ; 18cm. — (Scott Saunders space adventure series ; 6)
ISBN 0-00-691736-4 (pbk) : £0.75 B81-02992

Morgan, Alison. Paul's kite / Alison Morgan. — London : Chatto & Windus, 1981. — 112p ; 21cm
ISBN 0-7011-2594-2 : £4.95 : CIP rev. B81-27926

Morgan, Helen, *1921-*. The sketchbook crime / Helen Morgan ; illustrated by Jim Russell. — Exeter : Wheaton, 1980. — 64p : ill ; 22cm
ISBN 0-08-025608-2 : £2.50 B81-01330

Morris, Neil. Find the canary. — London : Hodder and Stoughton Children's Books, Feb.1982. — [24]p. — (Mystery pictures)
ISBN 0-340-27463-8 : £1.75 : CIP entry B81-36360

Morris, Neil. Hide and seek. — London : Hodder and Stoughton Children's Books, Feb.1982. — [24]p. — (Mystery pictures)
ISBN 0-340-27464-6 : £1.75 : CIP entry B81-36361

Morris, Neil. Search for Sam. — London : Hodder and Stoughton Children's Books, Feb.1982. — [24]p. — (Mystery pictures)
ISBN 0-340-27461-1 : £1.75 : CIP entry B81-36357

Morris, Neil. Where's my hat?. — London : Hodder and Stoughton Children's Books, Feb.1982. — [24]p. — (Mystery pictures)
ISBN 0-340-27462-x : £1.75 : CIP entry B81-36359

Moss, Ernest. Hannibal's last elephant / Ernest Moss. — 2nd ed. — Wembley : Selecteditions, 1980. — 150p : ill,1map ; 19cm
Previous ed.: 1979
ISBN 0-86237-001-9 (pbk) : £1.75 B81-23124

823'.914[J] — Children's stories in English, *1945- — Texts* *continuation*

Muir, Frank. Super What-a-mess / Frank Muir ; illustrated by Joseph Wright. — London : Ernest Benn, 1980. — [32]p : col.ill ; 28cm
ISBN 0-510-00097-5 : £3.50 B81-00619

Muir, Frank. What-a-mess and the cat-next-door / Frank Muir ; illustrated by Joseph Wright. — London : Ernest Benn, 1981. — [32]p : chiefly col.ill ; 28cm
ISBN 0-510-00107-6 : £3.95 B81-39433

Muir, Frank. What-a-mess the good / Frank Muir ; illustrated by Joseph Wright. — [London] : Carousel, 1980, c1978. — [32]p : col.ill ; 28cm
Originally published: London : Benn, 1978
ISBN 0-552-52111-6 (pbk) : £0.85 B81-00620

Munro, Alan. Moby's magic mirror / Alan Munro. — Glasgow : Blackie, 1981. — 93p ; 21cm
ISBN 0-216-91087-0 : £4.75 : CIP rev. B81-04391

Munthe, Adam John. Anna and the echo-catcher / Adam John Munthe, Elizabeth Falconer. — London : Chatto & Windus, 1981. — [28]p : chiefly ill(some col.) ; 29cm
Ill on end papers
ISBN 0-7011-2498-9 : £4.50 B81-10997

Murphy, Jill. Peace at last / Jill Murphy. — London : Macmillan, 1980. — [25]p : chiefly ill (some col.) ; 26cm
ISBN 0-333-30642-2 : £2.95 B81-00621

Murphy, Jill. The worst witch / written and illustrated by Jill Murphy. — Harmondsworth : Puffin, 1978, c1974 (1981 [printing]). — 106p : ill ; 20cm. — (A Young puffin)
Originally published: London : Allison and Busby, 1974
ISBN 0-14-031108-4 (pbk) : £0.80 B81-26554

Murphy, Jill. The worst witch strikes again / written and illustrated by Jill Murphy. — Harmondsworth : Puffin, 1981, c1980. — 91p : ill ; 20cm. — (A Young puffin)
Originally published: London : Allison and Busby, 1980
ISBN 0-14-031348-6 (pbk) : £0.85 B81-22030

Napier, Lena. Nat : the school cat / story by Lena Napier ; photography by Haworth Bartram. — Leeds : E.J. Arnold, 1981. — [32]p : col.ill ; 27cm. — (Scamps)
ISBN 0-560-03629-9 (pbk) : Unpriced B81-10358

Needle, Jan. Albeson and the Germans / by Jan Needle. — London : Fontana Lions, 1981, c1977. — 127p ; 18cm
Originally published: London : Deutsch, 1977
ISBN 0-00-671900-7 (pbk) : £0.95 B81-37443

Needle, Jan. Another fine mess. — London : Deutsch, Nov.1981. — [160]p
ISBN 0-233-97370-2 : £3.95 : CIP entry B81-28827

Needle, Jan. Losers weepers. — London : Methuen Children's Books, Nov.1981. — [128] p. — (A Pied Piper book)
ISBN 0-416-21510-6 : £3.50 : CIP entry B81-30158

Needle, Jan. Wild wood. — London : Deutsch, May 1981. — [192]p
ISBN 0-233-97346-x : £4.95 : CIP entry B81-04385

Newman, Nanette. That dog! / Nanette Newman ; illustrated by Penny Simon. — London : Heinemann, 1980. — [49]p : ill ; 19cm
ISBN 0-434-98001-3 : £3.95 B81-02456

Nichols, Grace. Trust you, Wriggly!. — Sevenoaks : Hodder and Stoughton, Apr.1981. — [128]p
ISBN 0-340-25555-2 : £3.25 : CIP entry B81-01331

Nicoll, Helen. Mog's mumps / by Helen Nicoll and Jan Pieńkowski. — Harmondsworth : Puffin, 1981, c1976. — [32]p : chiefly col.ill ; 21cm
Originally published: London : Heinemann, 1976
ISBN 0-14-050357-9 (pbk) : £0.90 B81-08106

Nye, Robert. The bird of the golden land / by Robert Nye ; illustrated by Krystyna Turska. — London : Hamilton, 1980. — 96p : ill ; 24cm
ISBN 0-241-10315-0 : £4.95 : CIP rev. B80-18921

Nye, Robert. Harry Pay the pirate / Robert Nye. — London : Hamilton, 1981. — 154p ; 23cm
ISBN 0-241-10672-9 : £4.95 : CIP rev. B81-20460

Ó Corrbuí, Máirtín. The adventures of Danny Joe / Mairtin O Corrbui ; illustrated by Karen Belsey. — Bognor Regis : New Horizon, c1980. — 154p,[9]leaves of plates : ill ; 21cm
ISBN 0-86116-176-9 : £3.50 B81-19232

Ó Corrbuí, Máirtín. A dog's life / Mairtin O Corrbui. — Bognor Regis : New Horizon, c1981. — 68p ; 21cm
ISBN 0-86116-460-1 : £3.25 B81-28950

Oakden, David. Buttercup Willie / David Oakden ; illustrated by Maggie Ling. — Exeter : Wheaton, 1980. — 63p : ill ; 22cm
ISBN 0-08-025005-x : £2.50 B81-00622

Oakley, Graham. The church mice at Christmas / Graham Oakley. — London : Macmillan Children's, 1980. — [36]p : col.ill ; 21x26cm
ISBN 0-333-30549-3 : £3.95 B81-01821

Oakley, Graham. Hetty and Harriet. — London : Macmillan Children's Books, Oct.1981. — [32]p
ISBN 0-333-32373-4 : £3.95 : CIP entry B81-27357

O'Brien, Edna. The dazzle / Edna O'Brien ; illustrated by Peter Stevenson. — London : Hodder and Stoughton, 1981. — 44p : col.ill ; 26cm
ISBN 0-340-26491-8 : £3.95 : CIP rev. B81-23925

Offen, Hilda. Rita the Rescuer / words and pictures by Hilda Offen. — London : Methuen Children's Books, 1981. — [28]p : col.ill ; 22cm. — (A Methuen picture-story book)
ISBN 0-416-21150-x : £3.25 : CIP rev. B81-01854

Oldfield, Pamela. Cloppity / by Pamela Oldfield ; illustrated by Linda Birch. — London : Hamilton, 1981. — 74p : ill ; 20cm. — (Gazelle books)
ISBN 0-241-10616-8 : £1.80 B81-15774

Oldfield, Pamela. The Gumby Gang strikes again / Pamela Oldfield ; illustrated by Lesley Smith. — Glasgow : Blackie, c1980. — 90p : ill ; 21cm
ISBN 0-216-91038-2 : £3.95 : CIP rev. B80-13105

Oldfield, Pamela. More about the Gumby Gang. — London : Hodder and Stoughton, Jan.1982. — [96]p. — (Knight books)
Originally published: London : Blackie, 1979
ISBN 0-340-27530-8 (pbk) : £0.85 : CIP entry B81-34136

Oldfield, Pamela. The Willerbys and the burglar / Pamela Oldfield ; illustrated by Shirley Bellwood. — London : Blackie, 1981. — 89p : ill ; 21cm
ISBN 0-216-91061-7 : £4.25 B81-12248

Oldfield, Pamela. The Willerbys and the haunted mill / Pamela Oldfield ; illustrated by Shirley Bellwood. — London : Blackie, 1981. — 61p : ill ; 21cm
ISBN 0-216-91114-1 : £4.25 : CIP rev. B81-17526

Osborne, Maureen. The Kettlewitch / Maureen Osborne ; illustrated by Eileen Browne. — London : Heinemann, 1981. — 126p : ill ; 23cm
ISBN 0-434-95584-1 : £4.95 B81-36131

Paddington and the snowbear. — London : Collins, 1981. — [10]p : col.ill ; 16cm. — (A mini pop-up book)
Text and ill on lining papers
ISBN 0-00-144202-3 : £0.95 B81-21131

Paddington at the launderette. — London : Collins, 1981. — [10]p : col.ill ; 16cm. — (A mini pop-up book)
Text and ill on lining papers
ISBN 0-00-144203-1 : £0.95 B81-21132

Paddington's birthday treat. — London : Collins, 1981. — [10]p : col.ill ; 16cm. — (A mini pop-up book)
Text and ill on lining papers
ISBN 0-00-144204-x : £0.95 B81-21130

Paddington's shopping adventure. — London : Collins, 1981. — [10]p : col.ill ; 16cm. — (A mini pop-up book)
Text and ill on lining papers
ISBN 0-00-144205-8 : £0.95 B81-21129

Parker, Barbara. Ossie the ostrich / [text Barbara Parker] ; [illustrations Sara Cole]. — Harlow : Longman by arrangement with the British Broadcasting Corporation, 1981. — 14p : col.ill ; 14x16cm. — (You and me storybooks)
ISBN 0-582-39136-9 (pbk) : £0.40 B81-28366

Parker, Barbara. Town mouse, country mouse / [text Barbara Parker] ; [illustrations Ruth Brown]. — Harlow : Longman by arrangement with the British Broadcasting Corporation, 1981. — 14p : col.ill ; 14x16cm. — (You and me storybooks)
ISBN 0-582-39134-2 (pbk) : £0.40 B81-28367

Partridge, Jenny. Colonel Grunt / Jenny Patridge. — Tadworth : World's Work Children's, c1980. — [24]p : col.ill ; 17cm
ISBN 0-437-66171-7 : £1.50 B81-03442

Partridge, Jenny. Hopfellow / Jenny Patridge. — Tadworth : World's Work Children's, c1980. — [26]p : col.ill ; 17cm
ISBN 0-437-66172-5 : £1.50 B81-03443

Partridge, Jenny. Mr Squint / Jenny Patridge. — Tadworth : World's Work Children's, c1980. — [24]p : col.ill ; 17cm
ISBN 0-437-66170-9 : £1.50 B81-03441

Partridge, Jenny. Peterkin Pollensnuff / Jenny Partridge. — Tadworth : World's Work Children's, c1980. — [26]p : col.ill ; 17cm
ISBN 0-437-66173-3 : £1.50 B81-03444

Peet, Bill. Cowardly Clyde / Bill Peet. — London : Deutsch, 1980, c1979. — 38p : col.ill ; 25cm
Originally published: Boston, Mass. : Houghton, Mifflin, 1979
ISBN 0-233-97251-x : £4.50 : CIP rev. B80-24903

Peppé, Rodney. The mice who lived in a shoe / Rodney Peppé. — Harmondsworth : Kestrel, 1981. — [32]p : chiefly col.ill ; 28cm
ISBN 0-7226-5737-4 : £4.25 B81-37374

Perry, Ritchie. George H. Ghastly / Ritchie Perry ; illustrated by Priscilla Lamont. — London : Hutchinson, 1981. — 76p : ill ; 21cm
ISBN 0-09-143590-0 : £3.95 B81-10156

Phillips, Ann. The multiplying glass / Ann Phillips ; illustrated by Liz Moyes. — Oxford : Oxford University Press, 1981. — 157p : ill ; 21cm
ISBN 0-19-271455-4 : £5.95 : CIP rev. B81-05170

823'.914[J] — Children's stories in English, *1945-* **—** *Texts* *continuation*

Pieck, Anton. A day to remember / words by Bernard Stone ; illustrations by Anton Pieck ; music composed by Wallace Southam. — London : Ernest Benn, 1981. — [32]p : chiefly col.ill,music ; 22cm
ISBN 0-510-00113-0 : £3.95 B81-39434

Piers, Helen. Frog and Water Shrew / Helen Piers ; pictures by Pauline Baynes. — Harmondsworth : Kestrel, 1981. — [42]p : col.ill ; 22cm
Ill on lining papers
ISBN 0-7226-5731-5 : £4.25 B81-37281

Piers, Helen. How foal forgot to be frightened / Helen Piers. — London : Methuen's Children's Books, 1980. — [24]p : col.ill ; 19cm. — (A Magnet book)
ISBN 0-416-89380-5 (pbk) : £0.75 B81-32583

Piers, Helen. Mouse looks for a house / Helen Piers. — [London] : Magnet, 1979. — [16]p : chiefly col.ill ; 19cm
Originally published: London : Methuen, 1966
ISBN 0-416-57880-2 (pbk) : £0.55 B81-09675

Piers, Helen. The naughty little goat / Helen Piers. — London : Methuen's Children's Books, 1980. — [24]p : col.ill ; 19cm. — (A Magnet book)
ISBN 0-416-89370-8 (pbk) : £0.75 B81-32582

Piers, Helen. Two hungry mice / Helen Piers. — [London] : Magnet, 1979. — [16]p : chiefly col.ill ; 19cm
Originally published: London : Methuen, 1966
ISBN 0-416-57940-x (pbk) : £0.35 B81-09674

Pinocchio : an exciting new version of a popular fairy tale / designed by Jonathan and Lynn Shook ; illustrated by Linda Griffith ; paper engineering by Tor Lokvig. — Maidenhead : Purnell Books, 1981. — [10]p : col.ill ; 28cm. — (A Purnell pop-up book)
Text, ill on lining papers
ISBN 0-361-05145-x : £2.50 B81-18541

Pinocchio / [illustrated by Jane Yamata]. — London : Chatto & Windus, c1981. — [12]p : col.ill ; 18cm. — (A Peepshow book)
ISBN 0-7011-2567-5 : £2.25 B81-35061

Poole, Josephine. Kings, ghosts and highwaymen / Josephine Poole ; illustrated by Barbara Swiderska. — London : Carousel, 1981, c1978. — 149p : ill ; 18cm
Originally published: London : Ernest Benn, 1978
ISBN 0-552-52137-x (pbk) : £0.95 B81-32112

Powling, Chris. The mustang machine. — London : Abelard-Schuman, Sept.1981. — [128]p
ISBN 0-200-72764-8 : £4.50 : CIP entry B81-23868

Price, Susan. Christopher Uptake / Susan Price. — London : Faber, 1981. — 189 ; 21cm
For adolescents
ISBN 0-571-11660-4 : £4.75 : CIP rev. B81-00537

Prince, Alison. The sinister airfield. — London : Methuen Children's Books, Feb.1982. — [128] p. — (A Pied Piper book)
ISBN 0-416-21440-1 : £3.95 : CIP entry B81-35711

Prince, Maggie. Dragon in the drainpipe / by Maggie Prince ; illustrated by Val Biro. — London : Hodder and Stoughton, 1981. — 92p : ill ; 20cm. — (Leapfrog)
ISBN 0-340-25914-0 : £3.95 : CIP rev. B81-13526

Provensen, Alice. An owl and three pussycats / Alice and Martin Provensen. — London : Cape, 1981. — [32]p : col.ill ; 33cm
ISBN 0-224-01821-3 : £4.25 : CIP rev. B81-01332

Pullein-Thompson, Christine. Phantom horse goes to Scotland / Christine Pullein-Thompson. — London : Armada, 1981. — 127p ; 18cm. — (An Armada original)
ISBN 0-00-691778-x (pbk) : £0.80 B81-15592

Pullein-Thompson, Christine. Pony patrol and the mystery horse / Christine Pullein-Thompson. — London : Severn House, 1981, c1980. — 157p ; 21cm
ISBN 0-7278-0706-4 : £4.95 : CIP rev. B81-04369

Pullein-Thompson, Diana. Black Beauty's family / Diana and Christine Pullein-Thompson ; illustrated by Elisabeth Grant. — [London] : Beaver. — 1981, c1978
Originally published in 1 vol.: London : Hodder & Stoughton, 1978
1. — 175p : ill,1geneal.table ; 18cm
ISBN 0-600-20451-0 (pbk) : £0.95 B81-31910

Pullein-Thompson, Diana. Cassidy in danger / Diana Pullein-Thompson. — London : Armada, 1981, c1979. — 126p ; 18cm. — (An Armada pony book)
Originally published: London : Dent 1979
ISBN 0-00-691777-1 (pbk) : £0.80 B81-15601

Pullein-Thompson, Diana. Ponies in the valley / Diana Pullein-Thompson. — [London] : Armada, 1976 (1980 [printing]). — 128p ; 19cm. — (An Armada pony book)
ISBN 0-00-691806-9 (pbk) : £0.75 B81-08021

Pullein-Thompson, Diana. The pony seekers / Diana Pullein-Thompson. — London : Severn House, 1981. — 117p ; 21cm
ISBN 0-7278-0694-7 : £4.95 : CIP rev. B81-07599

Pullein-Thompson, Josephine. Ghost horse on the moor / Josephine Pullein-Thompson ; illustrated by Eric Rowe. — London : Hodder and Stoughton, 1980. — 116p : ill ; 23cm
ISBN 0-340-25430-0 : £3.95 : CIP rev. B80-24907

Pullein-Thompson, Josephine. The no-good pony / Josephine Pullein-Thompson. — [London] : Sparrow, 1981. — 127p ; 18cm
ISBN 0-09-926080-8 (pbk) : £0.90 B81-20272

Pullein-Thompson, Josephine. The no-good pony. — London : Severn House, Nov.1981. — [128]p
ISBN 0-7278-0751-x : £4.25 : CIP entry B81-30253

Pullein-Thompson, Josephine. Show jumping secret / Josephine Pullein-Thompson. — London : Armada, 1969, c1955 (1981 [printing]). — 126p : ill ; 18cm. — (An Armada pony book)
Originally published: London : Collins, 1955
ISBN 0-00-691887-5 (pbk) : £0.80 B81-15594

Pullein-Thompson, Josephine. Treasure on the moor. — London : Hodder & Stoughton Children's Books, Feb.1982. — [128]p
ISBN 0-340-26889-1 : £3.95 : CIP entry B81-36352

Rayner, Mary. Mrs Pig's bulk buy / written and illustrated by Mary Rayner. — London : Macmillan Children's, 1981. — [32]p : col.ill ; 28cm
ISBN 0-333-30978-2 : £3.95 : CIP rev. B81-06037

Reed, Giles. Meet the Munch Bunch / illustrations by Angela Mitson ; written by Giles Reed. — Ipswich : Studio, 1979. — [32]p : col.ill ; 21cm
ISBN 0-904584-54-2 (cased) : £1.50
ISBN 0-904584-76-3 (pbk) : Unpriced B81-40678

Reed, Giles. The Munch Bunch at the seaside / illustrations by Angela Mitson ; written by Giles Reed. — Ipswich : Studio, 1979. — [32]p : col.ill ; 21cm
ISBN 0-904584-56-9 (cased) : £1.50
ISBN 0-904584-78-x (pbk) : Unpriced B81-40679

Rees, David, *1936-*. A beacon for the Romans / David Rees ; illustrated by Peter Kesteven. — Exeter : Wheaton, 1981. — 77p : ill ; 22cm
ISBN 0-08-025651-1 : £3.25 B81-22017

Rees, David, *1936-*. Holly, Mud and Whisky / David Rees ; illustrated by David Grosvenor. — London : Dobson, 1981. — 112p : ill ; 21cm
ISBN 0-234-72229-0 : £4.95 B81-31694

Rees, David, *1936-*. The night before Christmas Eve / David Rees ; illustrated by Peter Kesteven. — Exeter : Wheaton, 1980. — 59p : ill ; 22cm
ISBN 0-08-025006-8 : £2.50 B81-01333

Riley, Terry, *1941-*. The witch and the owl / illustrated by Terry Riley ; story by Rosemary Day. — London : Dent, 1981. — [26]p : col.ill ; 27cm
ISBN 0-460-06886-5 : £4.50 : CIP rev. B79-26039

Robertson, J. Macleod. Sammy's super T-shirt / H. Macleod Robertson ; illustrated by Paul Wright. — London : Methuen Children's Books, 1981. — 127p : ill ; 20cm. — (A Pied Piper book)
ISBN 0-416-88070-3 : £3.50 B81-10971

Rock, Nora. Rope around the wind / Nora Rock ; illustrated by Victor Ambrus. — London : Anderson, 1980. — 114p : ill,1map ; 21cm. — (Anderson young readers' library)
ISBN 0-905478-89-4 : £3.95 B81-00623

Rock, Nora. The silver dolphin / Nora Rock ; illustrated by Penny Simon. — London : Hamilton, 1981. — 80p : ill ; 19cm. — (Antelope books)
ISBN 0-241-10653-2 : £2.25 : CIP rev. B81-13819

Roennfeldt, Robert. Tiddalick : the frog who caused a flood : an adaptation of an Aboriginal dreamtime legend / by Robert Roennfeldt. — Harmondsworth : Puffin, 1980. — [32]p : col.ill ; 20cm. — (Picture puffins)
ISBN 0-14-050349-8 (pbk) : £0.80 B81-27218

Rogers, Margaret, *1941-*. The doomsday experiment : Margaret Rogers. — London : Andersen, 1981. — 143p ; 21cm
ISBN 0-905478-93-2 : £3.95 B81-21053

Rogers, Marilyn Erica. Willem's golden bone / Marilyn Erica Rogers ; illustrated by Jonathan Allen. — London : Macmillan, 1980. — 139p : ill ; 21cm
ISBN 0-333-26161-5 : £4.95 : CIP rev. B80-08477

Roose-Evans, James. The adventures of Odd & Elsewhere / by James Roose-Evans ; with pictures by Brian Robb. — London : Magnet, 1981, c1972. — 94p : ill ; 20cm
Originally published: London: Deutsch, 1971
ISBN 0-416-24290-1 (pbk) : £0.85 B81-28614

Roose-Evans, James. The secret of the seven bright shiners : an Odd & Elsewhere story / James Roose-Evans ; pictures by Brian Robb. — [London] : Magnet, 1981, c1972. — 94p : ill ; 20cm
Originally published: London : Deutsch, 1972
ISBN 0-416-24300-2 (pbk) : £0.85 B81-28674

Ropnor, Pamela. Helping Mr Paterson. — London : Chatto & Windus, Jan.1982. — [144]p
ISBN 0-7011-2605-1 : £4.95 : CIP entry B81-34297

823'.914[J] — Children's stories in English, *1945-* — *Texts* *continuation*

Rose, Gerald, *1935-*. How George lost his voice / Gerald Rose. — London : Bodley Head, 1981. — [30]p : col.ill ; 26cm
ISBN 0-370-30435-7 : £3.95 : CIP rev.
B81-27434

Rose, Gerald, *1935-*. The tiger-skin rug / Gerald Rose. — Harmondsworth : Puffin, 1981, c1979. — [32]p : col.ill ; 23cm. — (Picture puffins)
Originally published: London : Faber, 1979
ISBN 0-14-050323-4 (pbk) : £0.90 B81-27219

Ross, Tony. The enchanted pig. — London : Andersen, Nov.1981. — [32]p
ISBN 0-86264-002-4 : £3.95 : CIP entry
B81-30616

Ross, Tony. Hugo and the Ministry of Holidays / Tony Ross. — London : Andersen, 1980. — [26]p : col.ill ; 24cm
ISBN 0-905478-86-x : £2.95 B81-06496

Ross, Tony. Little red riding hood / retold by Tony Ross. — Harmondsworth : Puffin, 1981, c1978. — [32]p : col.ill ; 23cm. — (Picture puffins)
Originally published: London : Andersen Press, 1978
ISBN 0-14-050314-5 (pbk) : £0.95 B81-33475

Ross, Tony. Puss in boots : the story of a sneaky cat / by Tony Ross. — London : Andersen, 1981. — [28]p : chiefly.col.ill ; 26cm
ISBN 0-905478-91-6 : £3.95 B81-14249

Rowlands, Avril. God's wonderful railway : fire on the line / Avril Rowlands. — London : British Broadcasting Corporation, 1981. — 112p : ill,1map ; 21cm
ISBN 0-563-17893-0 (cased) : £4.95
ISBN 0-563-17895-7 (pbk) : Unpriced
B81-35551

Ruffell, Ann. Dragon air / Ann Ruffell ; illustrated by Nicole Goodwin. — London : Hamilton, 1981. — 47p : ill ; 19cm. — (Gazelle books)
ISBN 0-241-10692-3 : £1.95 B81-40789

Ruffell, Ann. The horse tree / by Ann Ruffell ; illustrated by Sally Holmes. — London : Hamilton, 1980. — 94p : ill ; 19cm. — (Antelope books)
ISBN 0-241-10526-9 : £2.25 : CIP rev.
B80-23798

Ryan, John, *1921-*. Crockle adrift / written and illustrated by John Ryan. — London : Hamlyn, 1981. — [32]p : col.ill ; 21cm. — (Beaver books)
ISBN 0-600-20461-8 (pbk) : £0.90 B81-24367

Ryan, John, *1921-*. Crockle and the kite / written and illustrated by John Ryan. — London : Hamlyn, 1981. — [32]p : col.ill ; 21cm. — (Beaver books)
ISBN 0-600-20348-4 (pbk) : £0.90 B81-12480

Ryan, John, *1921-*. Crockle takes a swim / written and illustrated by John Ryan. — London : Hamlyn, 1980. — [32]p : col.ill ; 21cm. — (Beaver books)
ISBN 0-600-20243-7 (pbk) : £0.70 B81-01334

Ryan, John, *1921-*. The floating jungle / written and illustrated by John Ryan. — London : Hamlyn, 1981. — [32]p : col.ill ; 21cm. — (Beaver books)
ISBN 0-600-20462-6 (pbk) : £0.90 B81-24372

Ryan, John, *1921-*. The haunted Ark / written and illustrated by John Ryan. — London : Hamlyn, 1980. — [32]p : col.ill ; 21cm. — (Beaver books)
ISBN 0-600-20244-5 (pbk) : £0.70 B81-01335

Ryan, John, *1921-*. Mr Noah's birthday / written and illustrated by John Ryan. — London : Hamlyn, 1981. — [32]p : col.ill ; 21cm. — (Beaver books)
Text on inside front cover
ISBN 0-600-20347-6 (pbk) : £0.90 B81-12481

Ryan, John, *1921-*. Pugwash and the buried treasure : a pirate story / by John Ryan. — London : Bodley Head, 1980. — [32]p : col.ill ; 26cm
ISBN 0-370-30338-5 : £3.95 : CIP rev.
B80-20001

Ryan, John, *1921-*. Pugwash in the Pacific : a pirate story / by John Ryan. — Harmondsworth : Puffin in association with Bodley Head, 1975, c1973 (1981 [printing]). — [32]p : col.ill ; 23cm
Originally published: London : Bodley Head, 1973
£0.90 (pbk) B81-22258

Saddler, Allen. The clockwork monster. — Sevenoaks : Hodder and Stoughton Children's Books, Apr.1981
ISBN 0-340-25593-5 : £3.50 : CIP entry
B81-01336

Sampson, Derek, *1932-*. Grump and that mammoth again! / Derek Sampson ; illustrated by Simon Stern. — London : Methuen Children's Books, 1981. — 91p : ill ; 21cm
ISBN 0-416-20710-3 : £3.50 B81-12249

Santa Claus is coming to town / [illustrated by Anne Grahame Johnstone]. — London : Dean, c1980. — [12]p : col.ill ; 21cm. — (A Dean board book)
Cover title. — Originally published: 1979
ISBN 0-603-00232-3 : £0.55 B81-07707

Santa's toy shop / [illustrated by Anne Grahame Johnstone]. — London : Dean, c1980. — [12]p : col.ill ; 21cm. — (A Dean board book)
Cover title. — Originally published: 1979
ISBN 0-603-00234-x : £0.55 B81-07706

Saunders, Jean, *1932-*. Anchor man / Jean Saunders. — London : Heinemann, 1980. — 91p ; 21cm
ISBN 0-434-95837-9 : £3.20 B81-02515

Scott, Peter Graham. Into the labyrinth / Peter Graham Scott. — London : Muller, 1981. — 192p ; 23cm
ISBN 0-584-31086-2 : £5.95 B81-20685

Scott, Sally. The Elf King's bride, or, How prince Armandel prevailed against the Twilight Realms / Sally Scott. — London : MacRae, c1981. — 87p : ill ; 24cm
ISBN 0-86203-028-5 : £4.95 : CIP rev.
B81-11970

Secombe, Harry. Katy and the Nurgla / Harry Secombe ; illustrated by Priscilla Lamant. — Harmondsworth : Puffin, 1980, c1978. — 61p : ill ; 20cm. — (A young puffin)
Originally published: London : Robson, 1980
ISBN 0-14-031189-0 (pbk) : £0.65 B81-01337

Sefton, Catherine. Emer's ghost / Catherine Sefton. — London : Hamilton, 1981. — 137p ; 21cm
ISBN 0-241-10619-2 : £4.95 : CIP rev.
B81-10496

Sefton, Catherine. The Finn gang / by Catherine Sefton ; illustrated by Sally Holmes. — London : Hamilton, 1981. — 95p : ill ; 19cm. — (Antelope books)
ISBN 0-241-10694-x : £2.50 : CIP rev.
B81-26732

Sefton, Catherine. A puff of smoke. — London : H. Hamilton, Jan.1982. — [48]p. — (Gazelle books)
ISBN 0-241-10707-5 : £1.95 : CIP entry
B81-34320

Shannon, George. Lizard's song. — London : Macrae, Jan.1982. — [32]p
ISBN 0-86203-057-9 : £4.95 : CIP entry
B81-34663

Shannon, George. The Piney Woods peddler. — London : MacRae, Feb.1982. — [32]p
ISBN 0-86203-061-7 : £4.95 : CIP entry
B81-37584

Shapiro, Arnold. All kinds of cats / written by Arnold Shapiro ; illustrated by Larry Moore ; designed by John Strejin ; paper engineering by Tor Lokvig. — Maidenhead : Purnell Books, 1981. — [10]p : col.ill ; 28cm. — (A Purnell pop-up book)
Text, ill on lining papers
ISBN 0-361-05146-8 : £2.50 B81-18542

Shapiro, Arnold. Hide and seek / written by Arnold Shapiro ; designed and illustrated by Karen Acosta. — [Swindon] : Child's Play, 1978. — [20]p : chiefly col.ill ; 19cm. — (A lift-up surprise book) (Child's Play action books)
Ill on inside cover
ISBN 0-85953-086-8 : Unpriced B81-32135

Shapiro, Arnold. Mr Cuckoo's clock shop / written by Arnold Shapiro ; designed and illustrated by Linda Griffith. — [Swindon] : Child's Play, 1978. — [20]p : col.ill ; 19cm. — (Child's Play action books)
Ill on inside cover
ISBN 0-85953-089-2 : Unpriced B81-32327

Shennan, Victoria. Ben / by Victoria Shennan ; illustrations by Michael Charlton. — London : Bodley Head, 1980. — [28]p : chiefly col.ill ; 16x17cm
ISBN 0-370-30300-8 : £3.25 : CIP rev.
B80-20002

Sibley, Jacqueline. Jonathan Mark and the puppies / Jacqueline Sibley ; illustrated by Walter Rieck. — London : Scripture Union, 1979. — [32]p : ill(some col.) ; 25cm
ISBN 0-85421-779-7 (pbk) : Unpriced
B81-17341

Sibley, Jacqueline. Jonathan Mark at aunties / Jacqueline Sibley ; illustrated by Walter Rieck. — London : Scripture Union, 1979. — [32]p : ill(some col.) ; 25cm
ISBN 0-85421-778-9 (pbk) : Unpriced
B81-17340

Sibley, Jacqueline. Jonathan Mark at the zoo / Jacqueline Sibley ; illustrated by Walter Rieck. — London : Scripture Union, 1979. — [32]p : ill(some col.) ; 25cm
ISBN 0-85421-777-0 (pbk) : Unpriced
B81-17339

Silcock, Ruth. Albert John in disgrace / by Ruth Silcock ; illustrated by Barry Wilkinson. — Harmondsworth : Kestrel, 1981. — [32]p : col.ill ; 20x25cm
ISBN 0-7226-5643-2 : £4.50 B81-28493

Sinclair, Olga. Gypsy girl / Olga Sinclair ; illustrated by Jane Bottomley. — London : Collins, 1981. — 128p : ill ; 21cm
ISBN 0-00-184271-4 : £4.50 B81-07708

Sivers, Brenda. Count Dobermann of Pinscher / Brenda Sivers ; illustrations by Frank Rodgers. — London : Abelard, 1981. — 95p : ill ; 21cm. — (The Adventures of Sherlock Hound)
ISBN 0-200-72741-9 : £4.25 B81-12034

Sivers, Brenda. Hound and the Perilous Pekes / Brenda Sivers ; illustrations by Frank Rodgers. — London : Abelard-Schuman, 1981. — 94p ; 21cm. — (The adventures of Sherlock Hound)
ISBN 0-200-72721-4 : £4.25 : CIP rev.
B81-17525

Slater, Jim. The boy who saved earth. — London : Hodder and Stoughton, Jan.1982. — [96]p. — (Knight books)
Originally published: 1979
ISBN 0-340-26541-8 (pbk) : £0.85 : CIP entry
B81-33924

823'.914[J] — Children's stories in English, *1945-* — *Texts* *continuation*

Slater, Jim. Goldenrod / Jim Slater ; illustrated by Christopher Chamberlain. — London : Heinemann Educational, 1981, c1978. — 118p : ill ; 20cm. — (The New windmill series)
Originally published: London : Cape, 1978
ISBN 0-435-12254-1 : £1.35 B81-22113

Slater, Jim. Grasshopper and the pickle factory / Jim Slater ; illustrated by Babette Cole. — London : Granada, 1980. — 94p : ill ; 23cm. — (A Dragon book)
ISBN 0-246-11226-3 : £3.50 B81-00624

Slater, Jim. Grasshopper and the unwise owl / Jim Slater ; illustrated by Babette Cole. — London : Granada, 1979 (1981 printing). — 94p : ill ; 18cm. — (A Dragon book)
ISBN 0-583-30368-4 (pbk) : £0.75 B81-29491

Sleigh, Barbara. Broomsticks and beasticles. — London : Hodder & Stoughton, Oct.1981. — [160]p
ISBN 0-340-25948-5 : £4.50 : CIP entry B81-28055

Sloan, Carolyn. Further inventions of Mr Cogg / Carolyn Sloan. — London : Macmillan Children's, 1981. — 184p : ill ; 21cm
ISBN 0-333-31125-6 : £4.95 : CIP rev. B81-00625

Sloan, Carolyn. Mr Cogg and his computer / Carolyn Sloan ; illustrated by Glenys Ambrus. — London : Piccolo in association with Macmillan, 1981, c1979. — 187p : ill ; 18cm
Originally published: London : Macmillan, 1979
ISBN 0-330-26493-1 (pbk) : £1.25 B81-36766

Smith, *Mr.*. Jacko's play / by Ray Smith. — London : Macmillan Children's Books, 1980. — [24]p : chiefly col.ill ; 25x27cm
ISBN 0-333-30609-0 : £3.95 B81-02739

Smith, Alan, *1933-*. Snowy / Alan Smith ; illustrations by David Barnett. — Richmond upon Thames : Country Life Books, 1980. — 128p ; 23cm
ISBN 0-600-38430-6 : £4.95 B81-12238

Smith, Alexander McCall. The perfect hamburger. — London : H. Hamilton, Jan.1982. — [96]p. — (Antelope books)
ISBN 0-241-10717-2 : £2.50 : CIP entry B81-34406

Smith, Bryan, *1938-*. Blizzard! / Bryan Smith. — Glasgow : Blackie, 1981. — 96p : 1map ; 20cm
ISBN 0-216-91055-2 : £4.75 B81-05902

Smith, Graham St. John. The thieving magpie / Graham St. John Smith. — Winchester : Hambleside, c1980. — 150p : ill ; 23cm. — (A Terrapin book)
ISBN 0-86042-025-6 : Unpriced B81-28617

Smith, Jim. The Frog Band and the owlnapper / Jim Smith. — Tadworth : World's Work, c1980. — [32]p : col.ill ; 30cm
ISBN 0-437-75914-8 : £3.95 B81-00626

Smith, Moira. The fastest snail on earth / written by Moira Smith ; illustrated by Keith Logan. — Loughborough : Ladybird, c1981. — 25p col.ill ; 19x20cm
ISBN 0-7214-0669-6 : £0.95 B81-20923

Smyth, Gwenda. A pet for Mrs Arbuckle / text by Gwenda Smyth ; pictures by Ann James. — London : Hamilton, 1981. — [32]p : col.ill ; 29cm
ISBN 0-241-10543-9 : £4.25 B81-37054

Snapes, Joan. Buffy / by Joan Snapes. — London : Pelham, 1981. — [24]p : col.ill ; 24x25cm
ISBN 0-7207-1297-1 : £3.50 : CIP rev. B81-03833

Solomon, Helen. Stranded at Staffna / Helen Solomon ; illustrated by Gareth Floyd. — London : Good Reading, 1979. — 112p,[4]p of plates : ill ; 23cm
ISBN 0-904223-36-1 : £3.45 B81-08598

Solomon, Joan, *19---*. Gifts and almonds / Joan Solomon ; photographs by Joan Solomon & Ryan Solomon. — London : Hamilton, 1980. — [32]p : col.ill ; 21cm
ISBN 0-241-10422-x : £3.50 : CIP rev. B80-18923

Solomon, Joan, *19---*. A present for mum / Joan Solomon ; photographs by Joan Solomon & Ryan Solomon. — London : Hamish Hamilton, 1981. — [32]p : col.ill ; 22cm
ISBN 0-241-10553-6 : £3.50 : CIP rev. B81-01338

Solomon, Joan, *19---*. Shabnam's day out / Joan Solomon ; photographs by Joan Solomon & Ryan Solomon. — London : Hamilton, c1980. — [32]p : col.ill ; 21cm
ISBN 0-241-10420-3 : £3.50 : CIP rev. B80-18924

Solomon, Joan, *19---*. Wedding day / Joan Solomon ; photographs by Joan Solomon. — London : Hamish Hamilton : 1981. — [32]p : col.ill ; 22cm
ISBN 0-241-10552-8 : £3.50 : CIP rev. B81-01339

Southall, Ivan. The fox hole / Ivan Southall ; illustrated by Ian Ribbons. — London : Magnet, 1980, c1967. — 117p : ill ; 18cm
Originally published: London : Methuen, 1967
ISBN 0-416-89440-2 (pbk) : £0.85 B81-01340

Southall, Ivan. King of the sticks / Ivan Southall. — [Harmondsworth] : Puffin, 1981, c1979. — 139p ; 19cm
Originally published: London : Methuen, 1979
ISBN 0-14-031395-8 (pbk) : £0.95 B81-32829

Southall, Ivan. Over the top / Ivan Southall ; illustrated by Ian Ribbons. — [London] : Magnet, 1980, c1972. — 94p ; 18cm
Originally published: London : Methuen Children's, 1972
ISBN 0-416-89430-5 (pbk) : £0.85 B81-03056

Spalding, Tony. The summer house / written and illustrated by Tony Spalding. — London : Galliard, 1981. — 255p : ill ; 23cm
ISBN 0-85249-467-x : £4.95 B81-09008

Spencer-Smith, Sheila. The Wheal Teague mystery / Sheila Spencer-Smith. — Padstow ([11 Church St., Padstow, Cornwall PL28 8BG]) : Tabb House, 1981. — 80p : ill ; 21cm
ISBN 0-907018-06-8 (pbk) : £1.95 B81-18686

Spicer, Venetia. The adventures of Chatrat / written and illustrated by Venetia Spicer. — London : Quartet, 1980. — 48p : col.ill ; 24x27cm
ISBN 0-7043-2264-1 : £4.95 B81-02866

Spooner, Alan. Rainbow cake / Alan Spooner ; illustrated by David Parkins. — [Harmondsworth] : Kestrel, 1981. — 183p : ill ; 23cm
ISBN 0-7226-5675-0 : £4.95 B81-10317

Stemp, Robin. Guy and the flowering plum tree / Robin Stemp ; illustrated by Carolyn Dinan. — London : Faber, 1980. — [32]p : col.ill ; 26cm
ISBN 0-571-11576-4 : £3.75 : CIP rev. B80-18926

Stevenson, Peter, *1953-*. Braithwaite's original brass band / Peter Stevenson. — London : Dent, 1981. — [32]p : col.ill ; 27cm
ISBN 0-460-06956-x : £3.95 B81-08119

Stevenson, Robert, *1920-*. Vet in Tibet / by Robert Stevenson. — Melksham : Venton, c1980. — 182p : 1map ; 20cm
Map on lining paper
ISBN 0-85993-002-5 : £6.25 B81-23187

Stewart, Mary, *1916-*. A walk in Wolf Wood. — London : Hodder & Stoughton, Oct.1981. — [128]p
ISBN 0-340-26537-x (pbk) : £0.85 : CIP entry B81-25751

Stinton, Judith. Boo to a goose / Judith Stinton ; illustrated by Janet Duchesne. — London : MacRae, 1981. — 46p : ill ; 21cm. — (Blackbird books)
ISBN 0-86203-056-0 : £2.75 : CIP rev. B81-30318

Stobbs, William. This little piggy. — London : Bodley Head, Oct.1981. — [32]p
ISBN 0-370-30428-4 : £3.50 : CIP entry B81-27396

Stone, Bernard. The tale of Admiral Mouse. — London : Andersen, Oct.1981. — [32]p
ISBN 0-86264-009-1 : £3.50 : CIP entry B81-27463

Stone, Bernard, *1920-*. Emergency mouse : a story / by Bernard Stone ; illustrated by Ralph Steadman. — London : Arrow, 1981, c1978. — [28]p : col.ill ; 23cm. — (A Sparrow book)
Originally published: London : Andersen, 1978
ISBN 0-09-926630-x (pbk) : £1.35 B81-39430

Storr, Catherine. The bugbear / by Catherine Storr ; illustrated by Elaine McGregor Turney. — London : Hamilton, 1981. — 91p : ill ; 19cm. — (Antelope books)
ISBN 0-241-10549-8 : £2.25 B81-07684

Storr, Catherine. February yowler. — London : Faber, Feb.1982. — [76]p
ISBN 0-571-11854-2 : £3.50 : CIP entry B81-36223

Storr, Catherine. Marianne dreams / Catherine Storr ; illustrated by Marjorie-Ann Watts. — Rev. ed. — Harmondsworth : Puffin, 1964 (1981 [printing]). — 203p : ill ; 19cm
ISBN 0-14-030209-3 (pbk) : £1.10 B81-40420

Storr, Catherine. Vicky. — London : Faber, Oct.1981. — [160]p
ISBN 0-571-11762-7 : £4.95 : CIP entry B81-24640

Strachan, Ian, *1938-*. Moses Beech / Ian Strachan. — Oxford : Oxford University Press, 1981. — 155p ; 23cm
ISBN 0-19-271451-1 : £5.25 B81-19427

Stranger, Joyce. Jason, nobody's dog / Joyce Stranger ; illustrated by Douglas Phillips. — London : Carousel, 1980, c1970. — 92p : ill,1map ; 18cm
Originally published: London : Dent, 1970
ISBN 0-552-52113-2 (pbk) : £0.60 B81-01341

Stranger, Joyce. Vet on call. — London : Severn House, Oct.1981. — [128]p
Originally published: London : Carousel, 1981
ISBN 0-7278-0738-2 : £4.25 : CIP entry B81-24635

Strong, Jeremy. Lightning Lucy. — London : A. & C. Black, Feb.1982. — [80]p
ISBN 0-7136-2164-8 : £3.50 : CIP entry B81-35832

Styles, Showell. Centurion comes home / Showell Styles. — London : Faber, 1980. — 192p ; 19cm
ISBN 0-571-11610-8 : £5.95 : CIP rev. B80-18904

Sussex, Rayner. The magic apple / by Rayner Sussex ; illustrated by David Higham. — London : Magnet, 1979 (1981 [printing]). — [32]p : col.ill ; 19cm
ISBN 0-416-21040-6 (pbk) : £0.95 B81-28612

Sutcliff, Rosemary. Eagle's egg / by Rosemary Sutcliff ; illustrated by Victor Ambrus. — London : Hamilton, 1981. — 94p : ill ; 19cm. — (Antelope books)
ISBN 0-241-10620-6 : £2.25 B81-15777

823'.914[J] — Children's stories in English, *1945- — Texts* *continuation*

Sutcliff, Rosemary. Frontier wolf / Rosemary Sutcliff ; cover illustration by Ivan Lapper ; map by Leslie Marshall. — Oxford : Oxford University Press, 1980. — ix,196p : 1map ; 23cm
ISBN 0-19-271448-1 : £4.75 : CIP rev. B80-18928

Sutcliff, Rosemary. The lantern bearers / Rosemary Sutcliff. — Harmondsworth : Puffin in association with Oxford University Press, 1981, c1959. — 272p : 1map ; 19cm
Originally published: Oxford : Oxford University Press, 1959
ISBN 0-14-031222-6 (pbk) : £1.50 B81-15371

Sutcliff, Rosemary. The road to Camlann / Rosemary Sutcliff ; decorations by Shirley Felts. — London : Bodley Head, 1981. — 142p : ill ; 23cm
ISBN 0-370-30384-9 : £4.50 : CIP rev. B81-21619

Sutcliff, Rosemary. Sun horse, moon horse / Rosemary Sutcliff ; decorations by Shirley Felts. — Basingstoke : Macmillan Education, 1981, c1977. — 111p : ill ; 21cm. — (M books)
Originally published: London: Bodley Head, 1977
ISBN 0-333-28310-4 : £1.30 B81-18690

Sutcliff, Rosemary. Three legions / Rosemary Sutcliff. — Oxford : Oxford University Press, 1980. — 216,179,225p : maps ; 22cm
Map on lining papers. — Contents: The eagle of the ninth. Originally published : 1954 - The silver branch. Originally published: 1957 - The lantern bearers. Originally published: 1959
ISBN 0-19-271450-3 : £7.95 : CIP rev. B80-14059

Svendsen, Elisabeth D.. Eeyore helps a badger / Elisabeth D. Svendson ; pictures by Eve Bygrave. — London : Piccolo, 1981. — [24]p : ill(some col.) ; 21cm. — (Piccolo original)
ISBN 0-330-26327-7 (pbk) : £0.80 B81-12123

Svendsen, Elisabeth D. The great escape / Elisabeth D. Stevenson ; pictures by Eve Bygrave. — London : Piccolo, 1981. — [24]p : ill(some col.) ; 21cm. — (Piccolo original)
ISBN 0-330-26326-9 (pbk) : £0.80 B81-12122

Swindells, Robert. Ghost ship to Ganymede / Robert Swindells ; illustrated by Jeff Burns. — Exeter : Wheaton, 1980. — 76p : ill ; 22cm
ISBN 0-08-025007-6 : £2.95 B81-01342

Swindells, Robert. World-eater. — Sevenoaks : Hodder and Stoughton, Oct.1981. — [96]p
ISBN 0-340-26576-0 : £4.25 : CIP entry B81-26709

Szudek, Agnes. Specs forever / by Agnes Szudek ; illustrated by Susan Sansome. — London : Hamilton, 1981. — 90p : ill ; 19cm. — (Antelope books)
ISBN 0-241-10625-7 : £2.25 : CIP rev. B81-02559

Tate, Joan. Turn again, Whittington / Joan Tate. — London : Pelham, 1980. — 109p ; 21cm
ISBN 0-7207-1285-8 : £3.95 B81-00627

The **Telebugs** at the tennis match. — London (41 Buckingham Palace Rd., SW1W 0PP) : Video Sonic Productions, c1981. — 32p : col.ill ; 21cm
Text on inside cover
Unpriced (pbk) B81-35664

Tennant, Emma. The search for Treasure Island / Emma Tennant ; illustrated by Andrew Skilleter. — [Harmondsworth] : Puffin, 1981. — 102p : ill ; 19cm. — (A Puffin original)
ISBN 0-14-031400-8 (pbk) : £0.85 B81-35477

Thomas, Leslie, *1931-*. Midnight clear / Leslie Thomas ; illustrated by Shirley Felts. — London : Arlington Books, 1978 (1979 printing). — 27p : ill ; 22cm
ISBN 0-85140-331-x (pbk) : £0.95 : CIP rev. B79-26700

Thomson, Ruth. Detective Peabody up in the air / story by Ruth Thomson ; illustrations by Ken Kirkwood. — London : Dent, 1980. — [29]p : col.ill ; 25cm. — (A Detective Peabody casebook)
ISBN 0-460-06875-x : £2.95 B81-05715

Thorne, Jenny. The voyage of Prince Fuji / Jenny Thorne. — London : Macmillan Children's, 1980. — [33]p : col.ill ; 31cm
ISBN 0-333-29003-8 : £3.95 B81-01817

Thornton, David, *1935-*. Alfie and the magic puddle / by David Thornton. — Leeds : D & J Thornton, [1981]. — [23]p : col.ill ; 11x15cm. — (The Adventures of Alfie Apple)
ISBN 0-907339-09-3 (pbk) : £0.50 B81-36108

Thornton, David, *1935-*. Alfie and the ruined mill / by David Thornton. — Leeds : D & J Thornton, [1981]. — [23]p : col.ill ; 11x15cm. — (The Adventures of Alfie Apple)
ISBN 0-907339-11-5 (pbk) : £0.50 B81-36107

Thornton, David, *1935-*. Alfie and the wishing well / by David Thornton. — Leeds : D & J Thornton, [1981]. — [23]p : col.ill ; 11x15cm. — (The Adventures of Alfie Apple)
ISBN 0-907339-10-7 : £0.50 B81-36109

Timothy, M. L.. The Obadiah stories : as daddy told them to Briony / M.L. Timothy ; illustrated by Pauline Sollis. — Ilfracombe : Stockwell, 1981. — 150p : ill ; 19cm
ISBN 0-7223-1426-4 : £3.65 B81-05901

Todd, H. E.. The big sneeze / story by H.E. Todd ; pictures by Val Biro. — London : Hodder and Stoughton, 1980. — [26]p : col.ill ; 25cm
ISBN 0-340-25207-3 : £3.95 : CIP rev. B80-14061

Todd, H. E.. The crawly crawly caterpillar / H.E. Todd ; illustrated by Val Biro. — London : Carousel, 1981. — [32]p : col.ill ; 19cm
ISBN 0-552-52129-9 (pbk) : £0.95 B81-18776

Todd, H. E.. Jungle silver / story by H.E. Todd ; pictures by Val Biro. — London : Hodder and Stoughton, 1981. — [28]p : col.ill ; 25cm
ISBN 0-340-26399-7 : £3.50 : CIP rev. B81-18158

Todd, H. E.. The sick cow / story by H.E. Tood ; pictures by Val Biro. — Harmondsworth : Puffin, 1979, c1979 (1980 [printing]). — [31]p : col.ill ; 23cm. — (Picture puffins)
Originally published: London : Brockhampton, 1974
ISBN 0-14-050269-6 (pbk) : £0.80 B81-01343

Tomlinson, Jill. The otter who wanted to know / Jill Tomlinson ; illustrated by Joanna Cole. — [London] : Magnet, 1981. — 79p : ill ; 20cm
Originally published: London : Methuen, 1979
ISBN 0-416-89460-7 (pbk) : £0.85 B81-08601

Townsend, John Rowe. Good-bye to Gumble's Yard / John Rowe Townsend. — Harmondsworth : Puffin, 1981. — 158p : 1map ; 18cm
Previous ed.: published as Widdershins Crescent. London : Hutchinson, 1965
ISBN 0-14-031403-2 (pbk) : £0.95 B81-18325

Townsend, John Rowe. The intruder / John Rowe Townsend ; illustrated by Graham Humphreys. — London : Heinemann Educational, 1980, c1969. — 176p : ill,1map ; 20cm. — (The New windmill series ; 248)
Originally published: London : Oxford University Press, 1969
ISBN 0-435-12248-7 : £1.60 : CIP rev. B80-26240

Townsend, John Rowe. The islanders / John Rowe Townsend. — Oxford : Oxford University Press, 1981. — 192p ; 23cm
ISBN 0-19-271449-x : £5.25 B81-18789

Townson, Hazel. The great ice-cream crime / Hazel Townson ; illustrated by Philippe Dupasquier. — London : Andersen, 1981. — 72p : ill ; 21cm. — (Andersen young readers' library)
ISBN 0-86264-005-9 : £2.95 : CIP rev. B81-23898

Tozer, Mary. Queen Yesno / Mary Tozer. — Tadworth : World's Work, c1981. — [32]p : col.ill ; 26cm
ISBN 0-437-79422-9 : £3.95 B81-32777

Treece, Henry. The dream time. — London : Hodder and Stoughton, Nov.1981. — [96]p
Originally published: Leicester : Brockhampton Press, 1967
ISBN 0-340-17464-1 (pbk) : £0.95 : CIP entry B81-30249

Trevor, Elleston. Sweethallow Valley / Elleston Trevor ; with drawings by Leslie Atkinson. — Nashville ; London : Charter House, c1978. — 222p : ill ; 21cm. — (The Woodlander series)
Originally published: London : Falcon Press, 1950
ISBN 0-905947-16-9 : £3.25 B81-06645

Trimby, Elisa. Mr Plum's oasis / Elisa Trimby. — London : Faber, 1981. — [32]p : chiefly col.ill,col.maps ; 26cm
ISBN 0-571-11481-4 : £3.95 B81-15602

Tulip, Joan. Ruth's swing / by Joan Tulip ; illustrated by Sue McMaster. — Cambridge : Dinosaur, c1981. — [24]p : chiefly col.ill ; 16x19cm. — (Dinosaur's Althea books)
ISBN 0-85122-276-5 (corrected : cased) : £1.85 : CIP rev.
ISBN 0-85122-260-9 (pbk) : £0.70 B81-12854

Tully, Tom. Ed at large / Tom Tully ; illustrated by Lesley Smith. — London : Beaver Books, 1981, c1980. — 110p : ill ; 18cm
Originally published: London : Warne, 1980
ISBN 0-600-20473-1 (pbk) : £0.85 B81-28405

Tully, Tom. Little Ed / by Tom Tully ; illustrated by Lesley S.J. Smith. — London : Warne, 1979. — 118p : ill ; 21cm
ISBN 0-7232-2188-x : £2.95 B81-08634

Tully, Tom. Look out - it's little Ed! / by Tom Tully ; illustrated by Lesley S.J. Smith. — London : Warne, 1981. — 121p : ill ; 21cm
ISBN 0-7232-2767-5 : £3.95 B81-37927

Tully, Tom. The space-waifs / Tom Tully ; illustrated by Penny Ives. — Exeter : Wheaton, 1980. — 58p : ill ; 22cm
ISBN 0-08-025612-0 : £2.50 B81-00629

Turska, Krystyna. The prince and the firebird. — London : Hodder and Stoughton Children's Books, Oct.1981. — [32]p
ISBN 0-340-25557-9 : £3.95 : CIP entry B81-25779

Van der Meer, Ron. I'm fed up! / Ron and Atie van der Meer. — London : Hamilton, 1981. — [30]p : chiefly col.ill ; 26cm
ISBN 0-241-10483-1 : £3.95 : CIP rev. B81-04213

Van der Meer, Ron. Joey / Ron and Atie Van der Meer ; afterword by Esther Rantzen. — London : Heinemann in association with the National Foster Care Association, 1980. — [32]p : chiefly ill ; 26cm
ISBN 0-434-97102-2 : £3.95 B81-03388

Van der Meer, Ron. Monster Island / [Ron van der Meer] ; assistant illustrator Atie van der Meer ; paper engineers Tor Lokvig, John Strejan. — London : Hamilton, 1981. — [10]p : all col.ill ; 28cm
Pop-up book. — Text, ill. on lining papers
ISBN 0-241-10582-x : £4.95 B81-36112

823'.914[J] — Children's stories in English, *1945-* *— Texts* *continuation*

Vendrell, Carme Solé. The boy with the umbrella / Carme Solé Vendrell. — London : Blackie, 1981. — [28]p : chiefly col.ill ; 19cm
ISBN 0-216-91086-2 : £3.00 B81-15597

Venture, Peter. Sidney's friend / Peter Venture. — London : Granada, 1981, c1980. — 37p : col.ill ; 28cm
ISBN 0-246-11590-4 : £3.95 B81-38053

Venture, Peter. Sidney's house / Peter Venture. — London : Granada, 1981, c1980. — 37p : col.ill ; 28cm
ISBN 0-246-11589-0 : £3.95 B81-28621

Vesey, A.. Cousin Blodwyn's visit / words and pictures by A. Vesey. — London : Methuen Childrens, 1980. — [28]p : ill(some col.) ; 23cm. — (A Methuen picture-story book)
ISBN 0-416-89580-8 : £2.95 : CIP rev. B80-08996

Vicary, Tim. Alfred's oak / by Tim Vicary. — Winchester : Hambleside, c1979. — 104p ; 23cm
ISBN 0-86042-021-3 : £2.95 B81-24358

Waddell, Martin. The great green mouse disaster. — London : Andersen, Oct.1981. — [24]p
ISBN 0-86264-006-7 : £3.95 : CIP entry B81-27414

Waddell, Martin. Napper goes for goal / Martin Waddell ; illustrated by Barrie Mitchell. — Harmondsworth : Puffin, 1981. — 103p : ill ; 18cm
ISBN 0-14-031318-4 (pbk) : £0.80 B81-10695

Waddington-Feather, John. Quill's adventures in the great beyond / by John Waddington-Feather. — Winchester : Hambleside, c1980. — 94p : ill ; 23cm. — (A Terrapin book)
ISBN 0-86042-024-8 : Unpriced B81-24498

Wain, John. Lizzie's floating shop. — London : Bodley Head, Oct.1981. — [224]p
ISBN 0-370-30906-5 (pbk) : £3.50 : CIP entry B81-27956

Waller, Jane. Below the green pond. — London : Abelard-Schuman, Feb.1982. — [128]p
ISBN 0-200-72762-1 : £5.95 : CIP entry B81-36246

Walsh, Jill Paton. Babylon. — London : Deutsch, Oct.1981. — [32]p
ISBN 0-233-97362-1 : £4.25 : CIP entry B81-26714

Walsh, Jill Paton. The green book. — London : Macmillan Children's Books, Oct.1981. — [128]p
ISBN 0-333-31910-9 : £4.95 : CIP entry B81-27358

Walt Disney's Bambi and his friends and Little Hiawatha. — Maidenhead : Purnell, 1981. — 1folded sheet([18]p) : col.ill ; 80x90mm
Cover title
ISBN 0-361-04916-1 : Unpriced B81-12581

Walt Disney's Donald on safari and On the farm. — Maidenhead : Purnell, 1981. — 1folded sheet([18]p) : col.ill ; 80x90mm
Cover title
ISBN 0-361-04915-3 : Unpriced B81-12579

Walt Disney's Mickey's train ride and The picnic. — Maidenhead : Purnell, 1981. — 1folded sheet([18]p) : col.ill ; 80x90mm
Cover title
ISBN 0-361-04917-x : Unpriced B81-12580

Walt Disney's Pluto at the zoo and The Circus. — Maidenhead : Purnell, 1981. — 1folded sheet([18]p) : col.ill ; 80x90mm
Cover title
ISBN 0-361-04918-8 : Unpriced B81-12582

Walters, Hugh. The dark triangle / Hugh Walters. — London : Faber, 1981. — 125p ; 21cm
ISBN 0-571-11584-5 : £4.95 B81-08512

Walters, Hugh. School on the moon / Hugh Walters ; illustrated by Trevor Ridley. — London : Abelard, 1981. — 74p : ill ; 21cm. — (A Grasshopper book)
ISBN 0-200-72744-3 (cased) : £3.50
ISBN 0-200-72743-5 (pbk) : unpriced B81-10129

Warner, Marina. The impossible day. — London : Methuen, Oct.1981. — [24]p
ISBN 0-416-05770-5 : £3.50 : CIP entry B81-28081

Warner, Marina. The impossible night. — London : Methuen, Oct.1981. — [24]p
ISBN 0-416-05850-7 : £3.50 : CIP entry B81-27931

Warner Hooke, Nina. A donkey called Paloma / Nina Warner Hooke ; illustrated by Laszlo Acs. — London : Methuen Children's Books, 1981. — 141p : ill ; 20cm. — (A Pied Piper book)
ISBN 0-416-89980-3 : £3.50 : CIP rev. B81-01344

Warner Hooke, Nina. The moon on the water. — London : Methuen Children's Books, Jan.1982. — [144]p. — (A Pied Piper book)
Originally published: London : British Broadcasting Corporation, 1975
ISBN 0-416-88060-6 : £3.50 : CIP entry B81-34396

Waterhouse, Keith. Worzel Gummidge at the fair / Keith Waterhouse and Willis Hall ; based on the characters created by Barbara Todd ; illustrated by Gerry Downes. — Harmondsworth : Puffin, 1980. — 95p : ill ; 20cm. — (A young puffin original)
ISBN 0-14-031381-8 (pbk) : £0.65 B81-01345

Waterhouse, Keith. Worzel Gummidge goes to the seaside / Keith Waterhouse and Willis Hall ; based on characters created by Barbara Euphan Todd ; photographs by Barry Rickman and Tony Nutley. — Harmondsworth : Puffin, 1980. — [32]p : col.ill ; 23cm. — (Picture puffins)
ISBN 0-14-050364-1 (pbk) : £0.90 B81-07039

Waterman, Jill. Harry's stripes / Jill Waterman. — London : Burke, 1981. — [32]p : chiefly col.ill ; 28cm
ISBN 0-222-00760-5 : £3.95 : CIP rev. B80-11227

Watson, Jean, *1936-*. The pilgrim's progress / retold in modern English by Jean Watson ; from the original story by John Bunyan ; illustrated by Peter Wane. — London : Ark, 1980, c1978. — 141p : ill ; 23cm
Originally published: London : Scripture Union, 1978
ISBN 0-86201-071-3 (pbk) : £1.95 B81-03512

Watts, Marjorie-Ann. Zebra goes to school / Marjorie-Ann Watts. — London : Deutsch, 1981. — 32p : col.ill ; 26cm
ISBN 0-233-97241-2 : £4.50 B81-20927

Webster, Joanne. Horse on a hilltop / Joanne Webster ; illustrated by Trevor Parkin. — London : Beaver, 1981, c1976. — 95p : ill ; 18cm
Originally published: London : Hodder and Stoughton, 1976
ISBN 0-600-20401-4 (pbk) : £0.85 B81-20699

Webster, Joanne. Horses is like people / Joanne Webster ; illustrated by Trevor Parkin. — London : Beaver, 1981, c1979. — 48p : ill ; 18cm. — (Beaver books)
Originally published: London : Hodder and Stoughton, 1979
ISBN 0-600-20400-6 (pbk) : £0.85 B81-20697

Webster, Joanne. The love genie / Joanne Webster. — London : Scholastic, 1981, c1978. — 128p ; 18cm. — (A Hippo book)
Originally published: London : Hodder and Stoughton, 1978
ISBN 0-590-70073-1 (pbk) : £0.80 B81-18435

Weir, Rosemary. Pyewacket and son / Rosemary Weir ; illustrated by Charles Pickard. — London : Abelard, 1980. — 105p : ill ; 21cm. — (A Grasshopper book)
ISBN 0-200-72708-7 (cased) : £3.50 : CIP rev.
ISBN 0-200-72707-9 (pbk) : £0.95 B80-18931

Welfare, Mary. Witchdust / Mary Welfare ; illustrated by Shirley Hughes. — London : John Murray, 1980. — 78p : ill ; 23cm
ISBN 0-7195-3789-4 : £4.95 B81-00630

Welfare, Mary. Witchdust / Mary Welfare ; illustrated by Shirley Hughes. — London : Methuen Children's, 1981, c1980. — 78p : ill ; 19cm. — (A Magnet book)
Originally published: London : Murray, 1980
ISBN 0-416-21390-1 (pbk) : £0.85 B81-34902

Weller, June. The jester : a story for children / June Weller ; illustrated by Elaine Jones. — Cheshire : J. Weller, c1980. — 29p : ill,1map,plans ; 23cm. — (The Gawsworth series)
ISBN 0-9506947-0-3 (unbound) : Unpriced B81-39753

Weller, June. The wizard : the legend of Alderley Edge retold for children / June Weller ; illustrated by Elaine Jones. — Stone : Panda Press, 1979, c1978. — 27p : ill,1map ; 22cm. — (The Gawsworth series)
Text on lining papers
ISBN 0-906689-01-5 (corrected pbk) : £0.95 B81-40166

Westall, Robert. The Watch House / Robert Westall. — Harmondsworth : Puffin, 1980, c1977. — 203p ; 18cm
Originally published: London : Macmillan, 1977
ISBN 0-14-031285-4 (pbk) : £0.95 B81-02230

Whitaker, David. [Doctor who in an exciting adventure with the Daleks]. Doctor Who and the Daleks : based on the BBC television serial by Terry Nation by arrangement with the BBC / David Whitaker ; illustrated by Arnold Schwartzman. — London : W.H. Allen, 1973, c1964 (1980 [printing]). — 157p : ill ; 18cm. — (A Target book)
Originally published: London : Muller, 1964
ISBN 0-426-10110-3 (pbk) : £0.85 B81-15589

White, Mary. Mindwave / Mary White. — London : Methuen, 1980. — 145p ; 21cm
ISBN 0-416-20680-8 : £4.50 B81-08668

White, Mary. Three cheers for nineteen! / Mary White ; [illustrations by Rosemary Wilson]. — London : Arnold, 1981. — 59p : ill ; 20cm. — (Young magpie library)
ISBN 0-7131-0598-4 (pbk) : £1.25 B81-39422

Whizz & Co. / illustrated by Christopher Masters. — Exeter : Wheaton, c1981. — 32p : col.ill ; 22cm
ISBN 0-08-024963-9 (cased) : £2.95
ISBN 0-08-024962-0 (pbk) : £0.90 B81-22022

Whizz & Co. and the ghost / illustrated by Christopher Masters. — Exeter : Wheaton, c1981. — 32p : col.ill ; 22cm
ISBN 0-08-024969-8 (cased) : £2.95
ISBN 0-08-024968-x (pbk) : £0.90 B81-22019

Whizz & Co. at the fair / illustrated by Christopher Masters. — Exeter : Wheaton, c1981. — 32p : col.ill ; 22cm
ISBN 0-08-024967-1 (cased) : £2.95
ISBN 0-08-024966-3 (pbk) : £0.90 B81-22021

Whizz and Co. and Nutley's horse / illustrated by Christopher Masters. — Exeter : Wheaton, c1981. — 32p : col.ill ; 22cm
ISBN 0-08-024973-6 (cased) : £2.95
ISBN 0-08-024972-8 (pbk) : £0.90 B81-22023

823'.914[J] — Children's stories in English, *1945-* — *Texts* *continuation*

Whizz and the old clock / illustrated by Christopher Masters. — Exeter : Wheaton, c1981. — 32p : col.ill ; 22cm
ISBN 0-08-024965-5 (cased) : £2.95
ISBN 0-08-024964-7 (pbk) : £0.90 B81-22020

Wild, Robin. Spot's dogs and the kidnappers / Robin and Jocelyn Wild. — London : Heinemann, 1981. — [32]p : col.ill ; 25cm
ISBN 0-434-97264-9 : £3.95 B81-13119

Wildsmith, Brian. Bear's adventure / Brian Wildsmith. — Oxford : Oxford University Press, c1981. — [30]p : col.ill ; 32cm
ISBN 0-19-279757-3 : £4.50 : CIP rev.
B81-25747

Wildsmith, Brian. Professor Noah's spaceship / Brian Wildsmith. — Oxford : Oxford University Press, 1980. — [32]p : col.ill ; 31cm
ISBN 0-19-279741-7 : £3.50 : CIP rev.
B80-18528

Wilkinson, Nora. The snow house / Nora Wilkinson ; illustrated by Martin J. Cottam. — Harmondsworth : Kestrel, 1980. — 187p ; 23cm
ISBN 0-7226-5687-4 : £4.75 B81-00631

Wilkinson, Nora. The snow house / Nora Wilkinson ; illustrated by Martin J. Cottam. — Harmondsworth : Puffin, 1981, c1980. — 187p : ill ; 19cm
Originally published: London : Kestrel, 1980
ISBN 0-14-031289-7 (pbk) : £1.25 B81-10694

Willard, Barbara. The keys of Mantlemass / Barbara Willard. — [Harmondsworth] : Kestrel, 1981. — 175p ; 23cm. — (The Mantlemass novels)
ISBN 0-7226-5699-8 : £5.50 B81-20387

Willard, Barbara. The pocket mouse / Barbara Willard ; illustrated by M. Harford-Cross. — London : MacRae, 1981, c1969. — 44p : ill ; 21cm. — (Blackbird books)
Originally published: London : Hamilton, 1969
ISBN 0-86203-039-0 : £2.75 : CIP rev.
B81-20636

Willard, Barbara. Spell me a witch. — London : Hodder and Stoughton, Sept.1981. — [144]p
Originally published: 1979
ISBN 0-340-26540-x (pbk) : £0.95 : CIP entry
B81-23927

Willard, Barbara. Summer season / Barbara Willard. — London : Julia MacRae, c1981. — 160p : ill ; 23cm
For adolescents
ISBN 0-86203-053-6 : £5.25 : CIP rev.
B81-04222

Willis, Jeanne. The tale of Georgie Grub. — London : Andersen, Nov.1981. — [32]p
ISBN 0-86264-003-2 : £3.95 : CIP entry
B81-30617

Wills, Jean. May day hullabaloo / Jean Wills ; illustrated by Priscilla Lamont. — London : Hamilton, 1981. — 95p : ill ; 19cm. — (Antelope books)
ISBN 0-241-10654-0 : £2.25 : CIP rev.
B81-13908

Wilson, Bob. Stanley Bagshaw. — London : H. Hamilton, Oct.1981. — [32]p
ISBN 0-241-10634-6 : £4.50 : CIP entry
B81-26778

Wilson, F. G.. Greenland Products / F.G. Wilson. — Bognor Regis : New Horizon, c1979. — 52p : ill ; 21cm
ISBN 0-86116-235-8 : £2.95 B81-19062

Wilson, Forrest, *1934-*. Super Gran rules O.K.! / Forrest Wilson ; illustrated by David McKee. — Harmondsworth : Puffin, 1981. — 142p : ill ; 18cm
ISBN 0-14-031427-x (pbk) : £0.85 B81-40423

Wood, Audrey. Magic shoelaces / [text and illustrations] Audrey Wood. — [Swindon] : Child's Play, c1980. — [28]p : chiefly col.ill ; 19cm
Cover title. — Text, ill on inside covers
ISBN 0-85953-109-0 : Unpriced B81-32142

Wood, Audrey. Orlando's little-while friends : a scrapbook story / by Audrey Wood. — [Swindon] : Child's Play, c1980. — [32]p : col.ill ; 30cm
Cover title
ISBN 0-85953-111-2 (cased) : Unpriced
ISBN 0-85953-106-6 (pbk) : Unpriced
B81-32143

Wood, Audrey. Scaredy cats / [text and illustrations] Audrey Wood. — [Swindon] : Child's Play, c1980. — [28]p : chiefly col.ill ; 19cm
Cover title. — Text, ill on inside covers
ISBN 0-85953-110-4 : Unpriced B81-32140

Wood, Audrey. Twenty-four robbers / written and illustrated by Audrey Wood. — [Swindon] : Child's Play, c1980. — [28]p : chiefly col.ill ; 19cm
Cover title. — Text, ill on inside covers
ISBN 0-85953-100-7 : Unpriced B81-32141

Wood, Kenneth. Shining armour. — London : Julia MacRae Books, Jan.1982. — [192]p
ISBN 0-86203-059-5 : £4.95 : CIP entry
B81-33758

Wood, Leslie. Six silly cyclists / Leslie Wood. — [Exeter] : Wheaton, 1979. — [24]p : col.ill ; 21x20cm
ISBN 0-08-024162-x (cased) : £1.95
ISBN 0-08-024161-1 (pbk) : Unpriced
B81-18618

Worthington, Phoebe. Teddy Bear postman / by Phoebe and Selby Worthington. — London : Warne, 1981. — [16]p : col.ill ; 19x24cm
ISBN 0-7232-2768-3 : Unpriced B81-37925

Youldon, Gillian. Homes / [designed by Gillian Youldon and illustrated by James Hodgson]. — [London] : Watts, [1981]. — [14]p : chiefly col.ill ; 21cm. — (All a-board story books)
Cover title. — Ill and text on lining papers
ISBN 0-85166-894-1 : £1.99 B81-10151

Young, Mike, *1945-*. Superted and the helicopter pirates / Mike Young ; illustrations by Philip Watkins. — London : Muller, 1980. — [23]p : col.ill ; 14x16cm
ISBN 0-584-64122-2 (pbk) : £0.50 B81-01346

Young, Mike, *1945-*. Superted and the lost ponies / Mike Young ; illustrations by Philip Watkins. — London : Muller, 1980. — [23]p : col.ill ; 14x16cm
ISBN 0-584-64123-0 (pbk) : £0.50 B81-01347

Young, Mike, *1945-*. Superted in Creepy Castle / Mike Young ; illustrations by Philip Watkins. — London : Muller, 1980. — [24]p : col.ill ; 14x16cm
ISBN 0-584-64121-4 (pbk) : £0.50 B81-01348

Young, Mike, *1945-*. Superted in space / Mike Young ; illustrations by Philip Watkins. — London : Muller, 1980. — [24]p : col.ill ; 14x16cm
ISBN 0-584-64120-6 (pbk) : £0.50 B81-01349

Zabel, Jennifer. Miss Priscilla scares 'em stiff / story by Jennifer Zabel ; pictures by Christopher Masters. — London : Warne, 1981. — [23]p : col.ill ; 26cm
ISBN 0-7232-2780-2 : £3.95 B81-37926

Zabel, Jennifer. Pickle's revenge / Jennifer Zabel ; illustrated by Lyn Mitchell. — Exeter : Wheaton, 1981. — 62p : ill ; 22cm
ISBN 0-08-025620-1 : £3.25 B81-32866

Zeissl, Francesca. King Gargantua / [text Fancesca Zeissl] ; [illustrations Ruth Brown]. — Harlow : Longman by arrangement with the British Broadcasting Corporation, 1981. — 14p : col.ill ; 14x16cm. — (You and me storybooks)
ISBN 0-582-39135-0 (pbk) : £0.40 B81-28363

823'.914'09 — Fiction in English, *1945-*. **Style**

Phelan, James, *1951-*. Worlds from words : a theory of language in fiction / James Phelan. — Chicago ; London : University of Chicago Press, c1981. — xi,259p ; 22cm
Bibliography: p245-251. — Includes index
ISBN 0-226-66690-5 (pbk) : £14.00 B81-39644

823'.914'09 — Fiction in English. Bestsellers, *1945-* — *Critical studies*

Sutherland, J. A. (John Andrew). Bestsellers : popular fiction of the 1970's / John Sutherland. — London : Routledge & Kegan Paul, 1981. — xii,268p : ill ; 23cm
Bibliography: p249-259. — Includes index
ISBN 0-7100-0750-7 : £8.95 B81-16797

823'.914'0924 — Fiction in English, *1945-*: **Books with British imprints** — *Plot outlines* — *For acquisition of cinema film rights* — *Serials*

Film rights. — [Issue 127(1)?]-. — London : Jaguar, c1978-. — v. ; 21x33cm
Monthly. — Continues: Synopses (London). — With: Filmlog. — Description based on: Issue 120(5)
ISSN 0142-6087 = Film rights : Joint subscription with Filmlog, £12.00 per year
B81-06778

823'.914'093 — Fiction in English. Irish writers, *1945-1973*. **Special subjects: Religion & sex** *compared with* **religion & sex as special subjects in fiction in French,** *1945-1973*

O'Rourke, Brian. The conscience of the race : sex and religion in Irish and French novels 1941-1973 / Brian O'Rourke. — Dublin (3 Serpentine Ave., Dublin 4) : Four Courts Press, c1980. — 70p ; 22cm
Bibliography: p68-70. — Includes index
ISBN 0-906127-22-x : £5.00
Also classified at 843'.914'093 B81-06543

823'.914'09355 — Girls' serials in English: Serials with British imprints: 'Schoolgirl' & 'Schoolgirls own'. Stories. Special subjects: Morcove School — *Critical studies*

Cadogan, Mary. The Morcove companion / by Mary Cadogan and Tommy Keen. — Maidstone (30 Tonbridge Rd., Maidstone, Kent) : Museum Press, [1981]. — 29p,[25]p of plates : ill,music,facsims ; 22cm
Ill. on inside covers
Unpriced (pbk) B81-27692

824 — ENGLISH ESSAYS

824 — Essays in English. South African writers, *1837-1900* — *Texts*

Schreiner, Olive. Dreams. — London : Wildwood House, Jan.1982. — [184]p. — (Rediscovery)
Originally published: 1891
ISBN 0-7045-0454-5 (pbk) : £2.95 : CIP entry
B81-37531

824'.008 — Essays in English, *1558-1945* — *Anthologies*

A Book of English essays / selected by W.E. Williams. — New and enl. ed. — Harmondsworth : Penguin, 1951 (1980 [printing]). — 378p ; 18cm. — (Penguin English library)
Previous ed.: 1942
ISBN 0-14-043153-5 (pbk) : £1.25 B81-04099

824.7 — ENGLISH ESSAYS, 1800-1837

824'.7 — Essays in English. Smith, Sydney, *1771-1845* — *Biographies*

Bell, Alan, *1942-*. Sydney Smith / Alan Bell. — Oxford : Clarendon Press, 1980. — x,250p,[4]p of plates : ill ; ports ; 23cm
Includes index
ISBN 0-19-812050-8 : £9.95 : CIP rev.
B80-22637

824.8 — ENGLISH ESSAYS, 1837-1900

824'.8 — Essays in English, *1837-1900 — Texts*
Wilde, Oscar. Essays and lectures / Oscar Wilde. — New York ; London : Garland, 1978. — xii,244p ; 19cm. — (The Aesthetic movement & the arts and crafts movement)
Facsim. of: edition published London : Methuen, 1908
ISBN 0-8240-2455-9 : Unpriced B81-25531

824'.8 — Essays in English. Rolfe, Frederick William. Artist's models of modern Babylon & New local industry — *Critical studies*
Weeks, Donald. Frederick William Rolfe and artists' models / by Donald Weeks. — Edinburgh ([137 Warrender Park Rd., Edinburgh EH9 1DS]) : Tragara, 1981. — 22p ; 24cm
Limited ed. of 115 numbered copies. — Includes the text of one article by Rolfe, and one attributed to him
ISBN 0-902616-71-4 (pbk) : £7.50 B81-37642

824.912 — ENGLISH ESSAYS, 1900-1945

824'.912 — Essays in English, *1900-1945 — Texts*
Greene, Graham. Collected essays / Graham Greene. — Harmondsworth : Penguin in association with Bodley Head, 1970, c1969 (1981 [printing]). — 344p ; 20cm
Originally published: London : Bodley Head, 1969
ISBN 0-14-003159-6 (pbk) : £2.50 B81-14351

Lawrence, D. H.. Selected essays / D.H. Lawrence. — Harmondsworth : Penguin in association with Heinemann, 1950 (1981 [printing]). — 351p ; 20cm
ISBN 0-14-000753-9 (pbk) : £3.95 B81-14528

Orwell, George. Down and out in Paris and London ; The road to Wigan Pier ; Homage to Catalonia ; Essays and journalism : 1931-1940 ; Essays and journalism : 1940-1943 ; Essays and journalism : 1944-1945 ; Essays and journalism : 1945-1949 / George Orwell. — London : Secker & Warburg, 1980. — 840p ; 24cm
ISBN 0-905712-45-5 : £5.95 B81-03517

Thomas, Edward, *1878-1917*. The chessplayer : & other essays / Edward Thomas ; with an introduction by R. George Thomas ; and with two wood-engravings by Hellmuth Weissenborn. — Andoversford : Whittington Press, c1981. — viii,28p : ill ; 26cm
Limited ed. of 375 numbered copies
ISBN 0-904845-36-2 : £14.50 B81-28479

Webb, Mary, *1881-1927*. The spring of joy. — London : Wildwood House, Jan.1982. — [152] p. — (Rediscovery)
Originally published: London : Dent, 1917
ISBN 0-7045-0455-3 (pbk) : £2.95 : CIP entry B81-37545

824.914 — ENGLISH ESSAYS, 1945-

824'.914 — Essays in English, *1945- — Texts*
McInnes, Colin. Out of the way : later essays / Colin MacInnes ; with a foreword by Ray Gosling. — London : Martin Brian & O'Keeffe, 1979. — 344p : 1ill ; 22cm
ISBN 0-85616-091-1 : £9.50 B81-01350

825.914 — ENGLISH SPEECHES, 1945-

825'.914 — Speeches in English, *1945- — Texts*
Muggeridge, Malcolm. Muggeridge : ancient & modern / Malcolm Muggeridge ; with drawings by Trog. — [Expanded ed.] / edited by Christopher Ralling and Jane Bywaters. — London : British Broadcasting Corporation, 1981. — 256p,[12]p of plates : ill,ports ; 22cm
Previous ed.: published as Muggeridge through the microphone. 1967
ISBN 0-563-17905-8 : £8.95 B81-19592

826 — ENGLISH LETTERS

826'.008 — Abusive letters in English, *to 1978 — Anthologies*
Dear sir, drop dead! / edited by Donald Carroll. — London : Eyre Methuen, 1979. — 152p ; 21cm
Originally published: New York : Collier, 1979
ISBN 0-413-39560-x : £4.50 : CIP rev. B79-25437

826.912 — ENGLISH LETTERS, 1900-1945

826'.912 — Letters in English, *1900-1945 — Texts*
Stark, Freya. Letters / Freya Stark ; edited by Lucy Moorehead. — Salisbury : Michael Russell
Vol.6: The Broken road 1947-52. — 1981. — 288p ; 24cm
Includes index
ISBN 0-85955-081-8 : £9.50 B81-11702

826'.912'08 — Letters in English, *1900- — Anthologies*
The **First** cuckoo. — 2nd ed. — Hemel Hempstead : Allen & Unwin, Oct.1981. — [320]p
Previous ed.: 1978
ISBN 0-04-808031-4 : £7.95 : CIP entry B81-28180

826.914 — ENGLISH LETTERS, 1945-

826'.914 — Humorous letters in English, *1945- — Texts*
Root, Henry. The Henry Root letters / Henry Root. — London : Macdonald Futura, 1981, c1980. — 252p,[14]p of plates : facsims ; 18cm
Originally published: London : Weidenfeld and Nicolson, 1980
ISBN 0-7088-1888-9 (pbk) : £1.25 B81-17430

826'.914'08 — Letters in English, *1945- — Anthologies*
Lyttelton, George. The Lyttelton Hart-Davis letters : correspondence of George Lyttelton and Rupert Hart-Davis / edited and introduced by Rupert Hart-Davis. — London : Murray
Vol.3: 1958. — 1981. — v,185p ; 23cm
Includes index
ISBN 0-7195-3770-3 : £12.50 B81-16209

826'.914'080351 — Letters in English. Compositions by children, *1945-*. **Special subjects: Santa Claus** *— Anthologies*
Dear Santa : a collection of children's letters to Santa Claus / compiled by Stan Jones. — London : Muller, 1981. — [44]p : ill(some col.),facsims ; 21cm
Text on lining papers
ISBN 0-584-10432-4 : Unpriced B81-36091

827 — ENGLISH SATIRE AND HUMOUR

827 — Humour in English. New Zealand writers, *1907-*. **Special subjects: New Zealand. Politics** — *Anthologies*
Up the poll : the perplexed person's guide to elections / Bruce Ansley ... [et al.] ; illustrated by Simon Darby. — Christchurch, N.Z. ; London : Whitcoulls, 1981. — 63p : ill,facsims,ports ; 24cm
ISBN 0-7233-0667-2 (pbk) : Unpriced B81-40979

827'.008 — Humour in English, *1641-1979 — Anthologies*
Everyman's book of nonsense / edited by John Davies ; foreword by Spike Milligan. — London : Dent, 1981. — 252p : ill ; 24cm
Includes index
ISBN 0-460-04479-6 : £8.95 B81-13591

827'.008 — Humour in English — *Anthologies — For children*
The **Illustrated** treasury of humour for children. — London : Hodder and Stoughton Children's Books, Oct.1981. — [256]p
ISBN 0-340-27456-5 : £4.95 : CIP entry B81-27362

827'.008 — Humour in English, *to 1976 — Anthologies*
The **Book** of nonsense : an anthology / edited by Paul Jennings. — London : Futura, 1979, c1977. — 543p ; 18cm
Originally published: London : Raven Books, 1977
ISBN 0-7088-1417-4 (pbk) : £1.95 B81-17452

827'.008'09282 — Children's humour in English — *Anthologies*
The **Ladybird** book of jokes riddles and rhymes / compiled by Joyce and Peter Young ; with illustrations by Martin Aitchison ... [et al.]. — Loughborough : Ladybird, c1981. — 57p : col.ill ; 31cm
Ill on lining papers
ISBN 0-7214-7516-7 : £1.95 B81-28744

More crazy jokes / compiled by Janet Rogers ; illustrated by Robert Nixon. — [London] : Beaver, 1980. — 122p : ill ; 18cm
ISBN 0-600-20285-2 (pbk) : £0.75 B81-07281

827'.008'09282 — Humour in English — *Anthologies — For children*
Brandreth, Gyles. How to be funny : an A to Z of amazing and astonishing ways to make people laugh / Gyles Brandreth ; illustrated by Colin Hawkins. — London : Hippo, [1981?]. — 112p : ill ; 18cm
ISBN 0-590-70022-7 (pbk) : £0.70 B81-37095

827.912 — ENGLISH SATIRE AND HUMOUR, 1900-1945

827'.912'080355 — Humour in English, *1900-1980*. **Special subjects: Cinema films** - *Anthologies*
Powell, Dilys. Punch at the cinema. — London : Robson, July 1981. — [192]p
ISBN 0-86051-145-6 : £6.95 : CIP entry B81-14434

827.914 — ENGLISH SATIRE AND HUMOUR, 1945-

827'.914 — Humour in English, *1945- — Texts*
I'm sorry I haven't a clue / Tim Brooke-Taylor ... [et al.]. — London : Robson, 1980. — 122p : ill,1 map,music,ports ; 24cm
ISBN 0-86051-108-1 : £3.95 B81-01351

827'.914'08 — Humour in English, *1945- — Anthologies*
1,001 logical laws / compiled by John Peers ; illustrated by George Booth ; edited by Gordon Bennett. — London : Hamlyn Paperbacks, 1981, c1979. — 160p : ill ; 18cm
Originally published: Garden City, N.Y. : Doubleday, 1979
ISBN 0-600-20281-x (pbk) : £0.95 B81-28992

The **best** of Shrdlu / [compiled by] Denys Parsons. — London : Pan, 1981. — 174p : ill ; 18cm
ISBN 0-330-26375-7 (pbk) : £0.95 B81-26330

Cuttings 2 : the pick of country life from Punch / compiled by Carole Mansur ; cartoons by Geoffrey Dickinson. — London : Elm Tree Books, 1981. — 60p : ill ; 20cm
ISBN 0-241-10656-7 (pbk) : £1.25 : CIP rev. B81-15811

Cyril Fletcher's oddities from That's life! / foreword by Esther Rantzen. — London : British Broadcasting Corporation, 1981. — 64p : ill,facsims ; 20cm
ISBN 0-563-17940-6 (pbk) : £1.25 B81-25256

Logue, Christopher. Christopher Logue's bumper book of true stories / drawings by Bert Kitchen. — London (34 Greek St., W.1) : Private Eye, 1980. — 192p : ill ; 19cm
ISBN 0-233-97305-2 (pbk) : £2.25 B81-12599

Not 1982 : Not the Nine O'Clock News rip-off annual / [written by Douglas Adams et al.]. — London : Faber, 1981. — [732]p : ill,ports ; 15x18cm
ISBN 0-571-11853-4 (unbound) : £2.95 B81-36642

Take no notice : a riotous collection of signs, notices and graffiti / [compiled by] Gordon Irving ; [illustrated by Ian Heath]. — London : Star, 1980. — 109p : ill ; 18cm
ISBN 0-352-30689-0 (pbk) : £1.00 B81-03895

827'.914'08 — Humour in English, *1945- — Anthologies — For conjurors*
Merry, Richard. Merry bits & patter quips / by Richard Merry ; with guest Val Andrews and others. — Bideford (64 High St., Bideford, Devon) : Supreme Magic, c1981. — 68p : ports ; 25cm
Includes a series of three articles on the task of the compere by Clifford Davis
Unpriced (pbk) B81-40596

827'.914'08 — Humour in English, *1945- — Anthologies — For entertainers*
Laughs!. — Bideford (64 High St., Bideford, Devon) : Supreme Magic, c1976. — 32p ; 20cm
Unpriced (pbk) B81-40638

827'.914'08 — Humour in English, *1945- — Anthologies — Serials*
Grown-up's Christmas annual. — 1980-. — London : Pan Books, 1980-. — v. : ill ; 30cm
ISSN 0261-0418 = Grown up's Christmas annual : £2.95 B81-15078

827'.91408 — Humour in English, *1945- — Anthologies — Serials*
Pick of Punch. — London : Hutchinson, Sept.1981. — [192]p
ISBN 0-09-146580-x : £7.50 : CIP entry B81-25131

827'.914'08 — Puns in English, *1945- — Anthologies*
Pun fun / compiled by Paul Jennings. — Feltham : Hamlyn, 1980. — 127p ; 18cm
ISBN 0-600-20001-9 (pbk) : £0.95 B81-03641

827'.914'080355 — Humour in English, *1945-*. **Special subjects: Offices** — *Anthologies*
Office graffiti / [compiled by] Nicholas Locke. — London : Proteus
2. — 1981. — [176]p : ill ; 25cm
ISBN 0-906071-87-9 (pbk) : £2.95 B81-37641

827'.914'0809282 — Humour in English, *1945- — Anthologies — For children*
Cole, William, *1919-*. New knock knocks / William Cole ; illustrated by Mike Thaler. — London : Granada, 1981. — [76]p : ill ; 20cm. — (A Dragon book)
ISBN 0-583-30491-5 (pbk) : £0.80 B81-38228

828 — ENGLISH MISCELLANY

828 — English literature. Nigerian writers. Soyinka, Wole — *Critical studies*
Critical perspectives on Wole Soyinka / edited by James Gibbs. — London : Heinemann, 1981, c1980. — 274p ; 22cm. — (Critical perspectives)
Originally published: Washington, D.C. : Three Continents Press, 1980. — Bibliography: p253-272
ISBN 0-435-91613-0 (pbk) : £3.95 : CIP rev. B81-11956

828 — Humour in English. New Zealand writers, *1907- — Texts*
Scott, Tom, *19---*. Shakes and leaders / Tom Scott. — Christchurch, N.Z. ; London : Whitcoulls, 1981. — 72p : ill ; 30cm
ISBN 0-7233-0663-x (pbk) : Unpriced B81-40978

828'.02 — Graffiti in English — *Anthologies*
Rees, Nigel. The graffiti file. — London : Allen & Unwin, Oct.1981. — [352]p
ISBN 0-04-827049-0 (pbk) : £5.95 : CIP entry B81-25870

828'.08 — Prose in English — *Critical studies*
Gardner, Helen. In defence of the imagination. — Oxford : Clarendon Press, Oct.1981. — [208]p
ISBN 0-19-812639-5 : £6.00 : CIP entry B81-25855

828'.08 — Prose in English, *to 1980.* **Special subjects: Scotland** — *Anthologies — For schools*
The Scottish experience : a prose anthology / [selection and editorial matter Strathclyde Regional Council]. — Edinburgh : Oliver and Boyd, c1981. — 181p ; 21cm
Includes bibliographies
ISBN 0-05-003454-5 (pbk) : Unpriced B81-11481

828.2 — ENGLISH MISCELLANY, 1400-1558

828'.2 — Graffiti in English - *Anthologies*
Barker, Mark. The writing on the wall. — Sevenoaks : Hodder & Stoughton, June 1981. — [144]p
ISBN 0-340-26981-2 (pbk) : £0.95 : CIP entry B81-09992

828.3 — ENGLISH MISCELLANY, 1558-1625

828'.308'09 — Prose in English, *1558-1702 — Critical studies*
Poetry and drama 1570-1700. — London : Methuen, Nov.1981. — [256]p
ISBN 0-416-74470-2 : £13.50 : CIP entry B81-30627

828.4 — ENGLISH MISCELLANY, 1625-1702

828'.408 — Prose in English, *1625-1702 — Texts*
Milton, John. [Prose works]. Complete prose works of John Milton. — New Haven ; London : Yale University Press
Vol.7. 1659-1660 / [editor Robert W. Ayers] ; [author of historical introduction Austin Woolrych]. — Rev. ed. — c1980. — xiii,547p : 1facsim ; 24cm
Previous ed.: 1974. — Includes index
ISBN 0-300-02015-5 : £23.35 B81-11700

828.5 — ENGLISH MISCELLANY, 1702-1745

828'.509 — English literature. Swift, Jonathan — *Critical studies*
Reilly, Patrick. Jonathan Swift. — Manchester : Manchester University Press, Sept.1981. — [280]p
ISBN 0-7190-0850-6 : £12.50 : CIP entry B81-23825

828'.509 — English literature. Swift, Jonathan. Special themes: London *(City).* **Grub Street** — *Critical studies*
Rogers, Pat. Hacks and dunces : Pope, Swift and Grub Street / Pat Rogers. — London : Methuen, 1980. — xvi,239p : 2maps ; 22cm
Abridgement of: Grub Street. 1972. — Bibliography: pxi-xiv. - Includes index
ISBN 0-416-74240-8 (pbk) : £4.50 : CIP rev.
Primary classification 821'.5 B80-13038

828.6 — ENGLISH MISCELLANY, 1745-1800

828'.608 — Prose in English, *1745-1800 — Texts*
Cobbett, William. Advice to young men : and (incidentally) to young woman : in the middle and higher ranks of life in a series of letters addressed to a youth, a bachelor, a lover, a husband, a father, and a citizen or a subject / by William Cobbett ; with a preface by George Spater. — Oxford : Oxford University Press, 1980. — xvi,335p ; 21cm
ISBN 0-19-212212-6 (cased) : £5.50 : CIP rev.
ISBN 0-19-281297-1 (pbk) : £2.50 B80-13109

Cowper, William. The letters and prose writings of William Cowper. — Oxford : Clarendon Press
Vol.2: Letters 1782-1786 / edited by James King and Charles Ryskamp. — 1981. — xxviii,652p,[4]leaves of plates : 1facsim,3ports ; 23cm
Includes index
ISBN 0-19-812607-7 : £35.00 : CIP rev.
Also classified at 821'.6 B80-20999

828'.6'08 — Prose in English. Cobbett, William — *Biographies*
Spater, George. William Cobbett. — Cambridge : Cambridge University Press
Vol.1. — Jan.1982. — [310]p
ISBN 0-521-22216-8 : £15.00 : CIP entry B81-37552

828'.609 — English literature, *1745-1800 — Texts*
Landor, Walter Savage. Walter Savage Landor : selected poetry and prose / edited by Keith Hanley. — Manchester : Carcanet, 1981. — xlii,275p : ill,1port ; 23cm
Bibliography: p262-264. — Includes index
ISBN 0-85635-272-1 : £8.95 B81-33560

828'.609 — English literature. Godwin, William - *Critical studies*
Tysdahl, B. J.. William Godwin as novelist. — London : Athlone Press, Sept.1981. — [224]p
ISBN 0-485-11223-x : £15.00 : CIP entry B81-20459

828'.609 — English literature. Johnson, Samuel, *1709-1784.* **Biographies: Boswell, James,** *1740-1795.* **Life of Samuel Johnson** — *Critical studies*
Dowling, William C.. Language and logos in Boswell's Life of Johnson / William C. Dowling. — Princeton ; Guildford : Princeton University Press, 1981. — xix,185p ; 23cm
Includes index
ISBN 0-691-06455-5 : £9.30 B81-29197

828.7 — ENGLISH MISCELLANY, 1800-1837

828'.708'080358 — Prose in English, *1800-1837.* **Special subjects: Napoleonic Wars** — *Anthologies*
English literature and the Great War with France : an anthology and commentary / [compiled by] A.D. Harvey. — London (111 High Holborn, WC1V 6JS) : Nold Jonson, 1981. — 162p ; 23cm
ISBN 0-907538-02-9 : £9.00 B81-19725

828'.709 — English literature, *1800-1837 — Texts*
Shelley, Percy Bysshe. Shelley on love : an anthology / edited by Richard Holmes. — London : Anvil Press in association with Wildwood House, 1980. — 247p : ill,ports ; 23cm
Bibliography: p239-243
ISBN 0-85646-063-x : £9.95 B81-12111

828'.709 — English literature. Landor, Walter Savage. Local associations: Gwent. Llanthony
Hopkins, Gordon. Llanthony Abbey and Walter Savage Landor / by Gordon Hopkins. — [s.l.] : C.H.G. Hopkins ; Cowbridge ([Prebends Gate Cottage, Quarry Heads La., Durham DH1 3DZ]) : D. Brown [distributor], 1979. — 48p : 1ill,1map ; 21cm
ISBN 0-905928-04-0 (pbk) : £0.90
Primary classification 942.9'98 B81-09536

828'.709 — English literature. Scott, *Sir* **Walter** — *Correspondence, diaries, etc.*
Scott, *Sir* **Walter.** Scott on himself : a selection of the autobiographical writings of Sir Walter Scott / edited by David Hewitt. — Edinburgh : Scottish Academic Press, 1981. — xxx,297p : 1geneal.table ; 23cm. — (The Association for Scottish Literary Studies ; no.10)
ISBN 0-7073-0283-8 : £6.75 B81-29460

828'.709 — English literature. Scott, *Sir* **Walter** — *Critical studies*
McMaster, Graham. Scott and society. — Cambridge : Cambridge University Press, Dec.1981. — [264]p
ISBN 0-521-23769-6 : £19.50 : CIP entry B81-32532

828'.709 — English literature. Scott, *Sir* **Walter. Influence of Scotland**
Scott, Paul Henderson. Walter Scott and Scotland / Paul Henderson Scott. — Edinburgh : W. Blackwood, 1981. — xi,99p : 1port ; 23cm
Bibliography: p98-99
ISBN 0-85158-143-9 : £5.95 B81-39066

828'.709 — English literature. Scott, *Sir Walter. Language*
Tulloch, Graham. The language of Walter Scott : a study of his Scottish and period language / Graham Tulloch. — London : Deutsch, 1980. — 350p ; 23cm. — (The language library)
Bibliography: p337-342. - Includes index
ISBN 0-233-97223-4 : £12.95 : CIP rev. B80-10884

828'.709 — English literature. Scott, *Sir Walter. Special themes: Landscape — Critical studies*
Reed, James. Sir Walter Scott : landscape and locality / James Reed. — London : Athlone, 1980. — 188p,[6]p of plates : ill,1map,1port ; 25cm
Bibliography: p178-181. — Includes index
ISBN 0-485-11197-7 : £15.50 : CIP rev. B80-21148

828′.709 — English literature. Wordsworth, Dorothy — *Biographies*

Gunn, Elizabeth. A passion for the particular : Dorothy Wordsworth : a portrait / by Elizabeth Gunn. — London : Gollancz, 1981. — 246p,[8]p of plates : ill,1facsim,ports ; 24cm
Bibliography: p236-238. — Includes index
ISBN 0-575-02700-2 : £12.50 B81-07106

828′.709 — English literature. Wordsworth, Dorothy - *Correspondence, diaries, etc*

Wordsworth, Dorothy. Letters of Dorothy Wordsworth. — Oxford : Oxford University Press, July 1981. — [240]p. — (Oxford paperbacks)
ISBN 0-19-281318-8 (pbk) : £2.50 : CIP entry B81-14867

828.8 — ENGLISH MISCELLANY, 1837-1900

828′.808 — Autobiographical prose in English. Pate, Walter — *Critical studies*

Monsman, Gerald. Walter Pater's art of autobiography / Gerald Monsman. — New Haven ; London : Yale University Press, c1980. — ix,174p ; 22cm
Includes index
ISBN 0-300-02533-5 : Unpriced B81-06168

828′.808 — Prose in English. Carlyle, Thomas — *Critical studies*

Daiches, David. Carlyle : the paradox reconsidered : lecture delivered to the Carlyle Society, session 1980-1981 as part of the Carlyle Centenary Conference, February 1981 / by David Daiches. — [Edinburgh] ([38 Grange Rd., Edinburgh 9]) : [Carlyle Society], [1981?]. — 15p ; 22cm. — (The Thomas Green lecture ; no.6)
Unpriced (pbk) B81-36904

828′.808 — Prose in English. De Quincey, Thomas — *Biographies*

Lindop, Grevel. The opium-eater : a life of Thomas De Quincey / Grevel Lindop. — London : Dent, 1981. — xiv,433p,[12]p of plates : ill,1facsim,ports ; 24cm
Bibliography: p409-415. — Includes index
ISBN 0-460-04358-7 : £12.00 B81-28923

828′.808 — Prose in English. Pater, Walter — *Critical studies*

Walter Pater : an imaginative sense of fact / edited by Philip Dodd. — London : Cass, 1981. — 95p ; 23cm
ISBN 0-7146-3183-3 : £9.95 : CIP rev. B81-14807

828′.808 — Scotland. National libraries: National Library of Scotland. Exhibits: Items associated with Carlyle, Thomas — *Catalogues*

Bell, A. S.. Thomas Carlyle, 1795-1881 / [A.S. Bell]. — Edinburgh : National Library of Scotland, 1981. — 37p : ill,facsims,ports ; 25cm. — (Exhibition catalogue ; no.18)
Catalogue of an exhibition to mark the centenary of the death of Thomas Carlyle
ISBN 0-902220-43-8 (pbk) : Unpriced B81-38461

828′.808′08 — Prose in English, *1837-1900* — *Anthologies*

The **Portable** Victorian reader / edited with an introduction by Gordon S. Haight. — Harmondsworth : Penguin, 1976 (1981 [printing]). — xlvi,658p : ill ; 19cm
Originally published: New York : Viking Press, 1972. — Bibliography: p xlvi
ISBN 0-14-015069-2 (pbk) : £2.95 B81-30943

828′.808′09 — Prose in English. Reynolds *(Family)***,** *1808-1815 - Correspondence, diaries, etc.*

Reynolds *(Family)*. Letters from Lambeth. — Woodbridge : Boydell Press, Aug.1981. — [224]p
ISBN 0-85115-150-7 : £12.00 : CIP entry B81-18091

828′.809 — English literature. Benson, Arthur Christopher — *Correspondence, diaries, etc.*

Benson, Arthur Christopher. Edwardian excursions : from the diaries of A.C. Benson 1898-1904 / selected, edited and introduced by David Newsome. — London : Murray, 1981. — ix,190p,[8]p of plates : ill,1port ; 23cm
Includes index
ISBN 0-7195-3769-x : £12.50 B81-21422

828′.809 — English literature. Linskill, Mary — *Biographies*

Stamp, Cordelia. Mary Linskill / Cordelia Stamp. — Whitby : Caedmon, c1980. — 118p,[7] leaves of plates : ill,ports ; 23cm
Ill on lining papers
ISBN 0-905355-15-6 : £6.50 B81-07733

828′.809 — English literature. Macaulay, Thomas Babington Macaulay, *Baron* — *Correspondence, diaries, etc.*

Macaulay, Thomas Babington Macaulay, *Baron*. The letters of Thomas Babington Macaulay / edited by Thomas Pinney. — Cambridge : Cambridge University Press
Vol.5: January 1849-December 1855. — 1981. — xiv,484p,[1]leaf of plates : 1port ; 24cm
ISBN 0-521-22749-6 : £40.00 B81-37613

Macaulay, Thomas Babington Macaulay, *Baron*. The letters of Thomas Babington Macaulay / edited by Thomas Pinney. — Cambridge : Cambridge University Press
Vol.6: January 1856-December 1859. — 1981. — xii,484p,[1]leaf of plates : 2ports ; 24cm
Bibliography: p289-302. — Includes index
ISBN 0-521-22750-x : £40.00 B81-37614

828′.809 — English literature. Ruskin, John — *Biographies*

Hunt, John Dixon. The wider sea. — London : Dent, , Sept.1981. — [320]p
ISBN 0-460-12009-3 : £8.25 : CIP entry B81-25859

828′.809 — English literature. Ruskin, John — *Critical studies*

The **Ruskin** polygon. — Manchester : Manchester University Press, Aug.1981. — [224]p
ISBN 0-7190-0834-4 : £25.00 : CIP entry B81-19160

828′.809 — English literature. Ruskin, John. Local associations: South Yorkshire *(Metropolitan County)***. Sheffield**

Hewison, Robert. Art and Society : Ruskin in Sheffield 1876 / Robert Hewison. — London (137 Fowler's Walk, W5 1BQ) : Published for the Guild of St George by Brentham, 1981. — 23p ; 22cm. — (Guild of St George Ruskin lecture ; 1979)
ISBN 0-905772-06-7 (pbk) : Unpriced B81-31686

828′.809 — English literature. Stevenson, Robert Louis — *Critical studies*

Robert Louis Stevenson : the critical heritage / edited by Paul Maixner. — London : Routledge & Kegan Paul, 1981. — xxiii,532p ; 23cm. — (The Critical heritage series)
Bibliography: p519. - Includes index
ISBN 0-7100-0505-9 : £17.50 : CIP rev. B81-14928

828′.809 — English literature. Stevenson, Robert Louis — *Critical studies* — *Conference proceedings*

Stevenson and Victorian Scotland / edited by Jenni Calder. — Edinburgh : Edinburgh University Press, c1981. — 141p ; 20cm
Conference papers. — Includes bibliographies
ISBN 0-85224-399-5 : £5.00 B81-39175

828′.809 — English literature. Wilde, Oscar. Local associations: France. Berneval — *Correspondence, diaries, etc*

Wilde, Oscar. Berneval : an unpublished letter / by Oscar Wilde ; with notes and introduction by Jeremy Mason. — Edinburgh ([24 Putney Bridge Rd., London S.W.18]) : [J.Mason], 1981. — [23]p : ill,1map ; 28cm
Limited ed. of 70 numbered copies
Unpriced (pbk) B81-30664

828.91 — ENGLISH MISCELLANY, 1900-

828′.91 — English literature. Williams, Raymond — *Critical studies*

Ward, J. P.. Raymond Williams. — Cardiff : University of Wales Press, Nov.1981. — [96]p. — (Writers of Wales, ISSN 0141-5050)
ISBN 0-7083-0807-4 (pbk) : £2.50 : CIP entry B81-32020

828.912 — ENGLISH MISCELLANY, 1900-1945

828′.91207 — Humorous prose in English, *1900-1945* — *Texts*

Morley, Robert. Morley marvels / Robert Morley. — [Sevenoaks] : Coronet, 1978, c1976 (1980 [printing]). — 220p ; 18cm
Originally published: London: Robson Books, 1976
ISBN 0-340-22331-6 (pbk) : £1.10 : CIP rev. B78-25640

Parkinson, C. Northcote. The law : or still in pursuit / C. Northcote Parkinson ; illustrated by Osbert Lancaster. — Harmondsworth : Penguin, 1981, c1979. — 220p : ill ; 18cm
Originally published: London : Murray, 1979
ISBN 0-14-005714-5 (pbk) : £1.75 B81-33603

828′.91207 — Humorous prose in English. Potter, Stephen, *1900-1969* — *Biographies*

Jenkins, Alan, *1914-*. Stephen Potter : inventor of gamesmanship / Alan Jenkins. — London : Weidenfeld and Nicolson, 1980. — 263p,[8]p of plates : ill,2facsims,ports ; 24cm
Bibliography: p250. — Includes index
ISBN 0-297-77817-x : £8.50 B81-02607

828′.91207′0803241 — Humorous prose in English, *1900-***. Special subjects: Great Britain. Social life,** *1930-1979* — *Anthologies*

Laughing matter / [compiled by] Janet Dunbar & Clifford Webb ; foreword by Richard Baker ; illustrated by John Minnion. — London : Joseph, 1980. — 143p : ill ; 21cm
ISBN 0-7181-1951-7 : £4.50 B81-02631

828′.91208 — Prose in English, *1900-1945* — *Texts*

Morley, Robert. Morley matters / Robert Morley ; with a preface by Peter Bull. — London : Robson, 1980. — 174p ; 24cm
ISBN 0-86051-115-4 : £5.95 B81-00633

Morley, Robert. Morley matters. — London : Hodder & Stoughton, Nov.1981. — [176]p. — (Coronet books)
Originally published: London : Robson, 1980
ISBN 0-340-26774-7 (pbk) : £1.50 : CIP entry B81-30541

Thomas, Edward, *1879-1917*. A language not to be betrayed : selected prose of Edward Thomas / selected and with introduction by Edna Longley. — Manchester : Carcanet in association with Mid-Northumberland Arts Group, 1981. — xxii,290p ; 23cm
Bibliography: p282-285. — Includes index
ISBN 0-85635-336-1 : £9.95 B81-25909

828′.91208 — Prose in English. Nicolson, Harold — *Biographies*

Lees-Milne, James. Harold Nicolson. — London : Chatto & Windus
Vol.2: 1930-1968. — Oct.1981. — [448]p
ISBN 0-7011-2602-7 : £15.00 : CIP entry B81-27927

Lees-Milne, James. Harold Nicolson : a biography / by James Lees-Milne. — London : Chatto & Windus
1886-1926. — 1980. — xii,429p,[15]p of plates : ill,ports ; 23cm
Includes index
ISBN 0-7011-2520-9 : £15.00 : CIP rev. B80-07576

828′.91208 — Prose in English. Williamson, Henry. Organisations: Henry Williamson Society — *Serials*

Henry Williamson Society journal. — No.1 (July 1980)-. — Freshwater (c/o J. Homan, Ryburn House, Camp Rd, Freshwater, Isle of Wight PO40 9HJ) : The Society, 1980-. — v. ; 21cm
Two issues yearly
ISSN 0144-9338 = Henry Williamson Society journal : £0.50 per issue (free to Society members) B81-26756

828'.91209 — Biographical prose in English. Pope-Hennessy, James — *Correspondence, diaries, etc.*

Pope-Hennessy, James. A lonely business : a self-portrait of James Pope-Hennessy / edited by Peter Quennell. — London : Weidenfeld and Nicolson, 1981. — 278p ; 24cm
Includes index
ISBN 0-297-77918-4 : £12.50 B81-18400

828'.91209 — English literature, *1900-1945 — Texts*

Du Maurier, Daphne. The Rebecca notebook and other memories / Daphne Du Maurier. — London : Gollancz, 1981. — 173p : 1facsim ; 23cm
ISBN 0-575-02994-3 : £6.95 B81-35273

Lawrence, D. H.. A D.H. Lawrence selection / selected and edited by Geoffrey Halson. — London : Longman, 1981. — 149p : ill,ports ; 19cm. — (Longman imprint books)
ISBN 0-582-22279-6 (pbk) : £1.20 B81-12577

Mew, Charlotte. Collected poems and prose / Charlotte Mew ; edited and with an introduction by Val Warner. — Manchester : Carcanet in association with Virago, 1981. — xxiv,445p ; 23cm
ISBN 0-85635-260-8 : £9.95 : CIP rev.
B81-22481

Mew, Charlotte. Collected poems and prose. — London : Virago, Feb.1982. — [480]p
ISBN 0-86068-223-4 (pbk) : £4.95 : CIP entry
B81-36024

Smith, Stevie. Me again : uncollected writings of Stevie Smith / illustrated by herself ; edited by Jack Barbera & William McBrien ; with a preface by James MacGibbon. — London : Virago, 1981. — xvi,360p : ill,facsims,ports ; 23cm
Facsims on lining papers. — Includes index
ISBN 0-86068-217-x : £9.95 : CIP rev.
B81-27438

Thomas, Edward, *1878-1917*. Selected poems and prose / Edward Thomas ; edited with an introduction by David Wright. — Harmondsworth : Penguin, 1981. — 295p ; 18cm. — (The Penguin English library)
ISBN 0-14-043144-6 (pbk) : £1.25 B81-38357

828'.91209 — English literature. Beckett, Samuel — *Biographies*

Bair, Deirdre. Samuel Beckett : a biography / Deirdre Bair. — London : Picador, 1980, c1978. — 624p,[16]p of plates : ill,ports ; 20cm
Originally published: London : Cape, 1978. — Includes index
ISBN 0-330-26163-0 (pbk) : £3.95
Also classified at 848'.91409 B81-06995

828'.91209 — English literature. Brittain, Vera, *1913-1917 — Correspondence, diaries, etc.*

Brittain, Vera. Chronicle of youth : war diary 1913-1917 / Vera Brittain ; edited by Alan Bishop with Terry Smart. — London : Gollancz, 1981. — 382p,[8]p of plates : ill,1map,1facsim,ports ; 24cm
Includes index
ISBN 0-575-02888-2 : £8.50 B81-38122

828'.91209 — English literature. Brooke, Jocelyn — *Biographies*

Brooke, Jocelyn. The orchid trilogy / Jocelyn Brooke ; introduction by Anthony Powell. — Harmondsworth : Penguin, 1981. — 437p ; 20cm. — (A King Penguin)
Contents: The military orchid. Originally published: London : Bodley Head, 1948 — A mine of serpents. Originally published: London : Bodley Head, 1949 — The goose cathedral. Originally published: London : Bodley Head, 1950
ISBN 0-14-005545-2 (pbk) : £2.95 B81-25075

828'.91209 — English literature. Durrell, Lawrence — *Correspondence*

Aldington, Richard. Literary lifelines : the Richard Aldington-Lawrence Durrell correspondence / edited by Ian S. MacNiven and Harry T. Moore. — London : Faber, 1981. — xvii,236p ; 24cm
Includes index
ISBN 0-571-11501-2 : £8.95 : CIP rev.
Primary classification 820.9'00912 B81-13570

828'.91209 — English literature. Ross, Adelaide — *Biographies*

Ross, Adelaide. Reverie : an autobiography / by Adelaide Ross. — London : Hale, 1981. — 250p,[8]p of plates : ill,ports ; 23cm
Includes index
ISBN 0-7091-8822-6 : £8.50 B81-24555

828'.91209 — Humour in English, *1900-1945 — Texts*

Bentley, E. Clerihew. The complete clerihews of E. Clerihew Bentley. — Oxford : Oxford University Press, Oct.1981. — [160]p
ISBN 0-19-212978-3 : £3.95 : CIP entry
B81-25795

Miller, Max, *1895-1963*. The Max Miller blue book / compiled by Barry Took ; illustrations by Trog. — London : Robson, 1975 (1981 [printing]). — [96p] : ill,music,1facsim,ports ; 21cm
ISBN 0-903895-53-6 (pbk) : £2.50 B81-40785

Robinson, W. Heath. How to build a new world / by W. Heath Robinson and Cecil Hunt. — London : Duckworth, 1981. — viii,136p : ill ; 23cm
Originally published: London : Hutchinson, 1941. — Ill on lining papers. — Includes index
ISBN 0-7156-1534-3 : £5.95 : CIP rev.
B81-04314

Robinson, W. Heath. How to make the best of things / W. Heath Robinson and Cecil Hunt. — London : Duckworth, 1980. — viii,120p : ill ; 23cm
Ill on lining papers
ISBN 0-7156-1533-5 : £5.95 : CIP rev.
B81-07618

828.914 — ENGLISH MISCELLANY, 1945-

828'.91402 — Anecdotes in English, *1945- — Texts*

Wyatt, Woodrow. To the point / Woodrow Wyatt. — London : Weidenfeld and Nicolson, c1981. — ix,155p ; 23cm
ISBN 0-297-77938-9 : £6.95 B81-18402

828'.91402 — Aphorisms in English, *1945- — Texts*

Oxley, William. The synopthegms of a prophet / William Oxley. — Brixham (6 The Mount, Furzeham, Brixham, Devon) : Ember, c1981. — [12]p ; 21cm
£0.30 (pbk) B81-40301

828'.914'02 — Aphorisms in English, *1945- — Texts*

Ussher, Arland. The juggler. — Portlaoise : Dolmen Press, July 1981. — [128]p
ISBN 0-85105-374-2 : £9.00 : CIP entry
B81-20579

828'.91407 — Experimental writing in English, *1945- — Texts*

Phillips, Tom. A humument : a treated Victorian novel / Tom Phillips. — London : Thames and Hudson, 1980. — 367p : all col.ill ; 19cm
ISBN 0-500-09146-3 : £12.00 B81-05949

828'.91407 — Humorous prose in English, *1945- — Texts*

Boothroyd, Basil. In my state of health / Basil Boothroyd. — London : Robson, 1981. — 150p ; 23cm
ISBN 0-86051-148-0 : £6.50 : CIP rev.
B81-22458

Briers, Richard. Natter natter / Richard Briers ; cartoons by Larry. — London : Dent, 1981. — 160p : ill ; 24cm
ISBN 0-460-04508-3 : £4.95 : CIP rev.
B81-13761

Buckman, Rob. Jogging from memory, or, Letters to Sigmund Freud Vol.II / Rob Buckman ; illustrations by Martin Honeysett. — London : Heinemann/Quixote, 1980. — 137p : ill ; 23cm
ISBN 0-434-98000-5 : £5.95 B81-02689

Cooper, Jilly. Jolly super / Jilly Cooper. — London : Corgi, 1981, c1971. — 147p ; 18cm
Originally published: London : Methuen, 1971
ISBN 0-552-11751-x (pbk) : £1.25 B81-32923

Cooper, Jilly. Jolly super too / Jilly Cooper. — London : Corgi, 1981, c1973. — 166p ; 18cm
Originally published: London : Methuen, 1973
ISBN 0-552-11752-8 (pbk) : £1.25 B81-32924

Cooper, Jilly. Jolly superlative / Jilly Cooper. — London : Corgi, 1981, c1975. — 157p ; 18cm
Originally published: London : Eyre Methuen, 1979
ISBN 0-552-11801-x (pbk) : £1.25 B81-39660

Cooper, Jilly. Supercooper / Jilly Cooper. — London : Eyre Methuen, 1980. — 159p ; 23cm
ISBN 0-413-47860-2 : £5.50 : CIP rev.
B80-22640

Cooper, Jilly. Supercooper. — Large print ed. — Bath : Chivers, Dec.1981. — [296]p. — (A Lythway book)
Originally published: London : Eyre Methuen, 1980
ISBN 0-85119-767-1 : £6.80 : CIP entry
B81-31798

Cooper, Jilly. Superjilly / Jilly Cooper. — London : Corgi, 1981, c1977. — 175p ; 18cm
Originally published: London : Eyre Methuen, 1977
ISBN 0-552-11802-8 (pbk) : £1.25 B81-39659

Coren, Alan. The best of Alan Coren. — London : Robson, 1980. — 416p ; 23cm
ISBN 0-86051-121-9 : £7.50 : CIP rev.
B80-18068

Davies, Hunter. Father's day : scenes from domestic life / Hunter Davies ; illustrated by Geoffrey Dickinson. — London : Weidenfeld & Nicolson, c1981. — viii,151p : ill ; 24cm
ISBN 0-297-77936-2 : £5.50 B81-21269

Foley, Donal. Man bites dog / Donal Foley. — Dublin (11 D'Oliver St., Dublin 2) : Irish Times
ISBN 0-907011-02-0 (pbk) : £2.00 B81-08067

Ingrams, Richard. Dear Bill : the collected letters of Denis Thatcher / written by Richard Ingrams & John Wells ; illustrated by George Adamson. — London : Private Eye : Deutsch, c1980. — 80p ; 22cm
ISBN 0-233-97303-6 (pbk) : £1.95 B81-02179

Ingrams, Richard. The other half : further letters of Denis Thatcher / written by Richard Ingrams & John Wells ; illustrated by George Adamson. — London (34 Greek St., W.1.) : Private Eye, c1981. — 80p : ill ; 22cm
ISBN 0-233-97420-2 (pbk) : £1.95 B81-35584

Krin, Sylvie. Born to be Queen / Sylvie Krin ; illustrated by Barry Glynn. — Harmondsworth : Penguin in association with Private eye, 1981. — 48p : ill ; 21cm
'First published in Private Eye 1980-81' - title page verso
ISBN 0-14-006057-x (pbk) : £0.95 B81-28689

McCall, Andrew. The ghastly guest book / Andrew McCall ; illustrations by Joanna Carrington. — London : Hamilton, 1981. — 121p : ill ; 23cm
ISBN 0-241-10325-8 : £5.95 : CIP rev.
B81-25704

McSherry, Charles. Sex instruction for Irish farmers / Charles McSherry. — Dublin : Mercier, c1980. — 92p ; 18cm
£2.00 (pbk) B81-29963

828'.91407 — Humorous prose in English, *1945-* — *Texts* *continuation*

Marshall, Arthur, *1910-*. I'll let you know : musings from Myrtlebank / Arthur Marshall ; illustrated by Tim Jaques. — London : Hamilton, 1981. — 181p : ill ; 23cm
ISBN 0-241-10644-3 : £5.95 : CIP rev. B81-23863

Muir, Frank. The fourth Frank Muir goes into- / Frank Muir and Simon Brett. — London : Robson, 1981. — 144p : ill,facsims ; 24cm
ISBN 0-86051-147-2 : £4.50 : CIP rev. B81-22466

Muir, Frank. Take my word for it : still more stories from "My word!" ... / Frank Muir & Denis Norden. — London : Methuen Paperbacks, 1981, c1978. — 108p : ill ; 18cm. — (Magnum books)
Originally published: London : Eyre Methuen, 1978
ISBN 0-417-06230-3 (pbk) : £1.10 B81-18243

Muir, Frank. The third Frank Muir goes into - / Frank Muir and Simon Brett. — London : Robson, 1980. — 144p : ill,ports ; 24cm
ISBN 0-86051-112-x : £3.95 : CIP rev. B80-18070

Robert Morley's second book of bricks / cartoons by John Minnion. — London : Weidenfeld & Nicolson, 1981. — 144p : ill ; 24cm
£4.95 B81-37934

Simple, PeterThe **Stretchford** chronicles : 25 years of Peter Simple : extracts from the Way of the World column of the Daily telegraph / selected by Michael Wharton ; illustrated by Ffolkes. — London : Daily Telegraph, c1980. — 288p : ill ; 23cm
ISBN 0-901684-59-7 : £6.75 B81-02718

Springer-Mlajsi, Janez. Jokes for bright people / by Janez Springer-Mlajsi. — London : Regency, c1980. — 32p : ill ; 16cm
Unpriced (pbk) B81-05895

Tovey, Doreen. Cats in the belfry / Doreen Tovey ; illustrated by Maurice Wilson ; introduction by Michael Joseph. — Large print ed. — Bath : Chivers, 1981, c1957. — 198p : ill ; 23cm. — (A New Portway large print book)
Originally published: London : Elek, 1957
ISBN 0-85119-106-1 : Unpriced B81-09007

Ward, Christopher. Our cheque is in the post / Christopher Ward ; illustrated by Frank Dickens. — London : Secker & Warburg, 1980. — vi,87p : ill ; 21cm
ISBN 0-436-56164-6 : £3.95 : CIP rev. B80-32534

Williams, Kenneth. Kenneth Williams' acid drops. — London : Hodder & Stoughton, Oct.1981. — [208]p
Originally published: London : Dent, 1980
ISBN 0-340-26782-8 (pbk) : £1.25 : CIP entry B81-26708

828'.91407 — Prose in English, *1945-*. Special subjects: Pets: Cats — *Texts*

Tovey, Doreen. A comfort of cats / Doreen Tovey. — Large print ed. — Bath : Chivers, 1980, c1979. — 227p ; 23cm. — (New Portway)
Originally published: London : Joseph, 1979
ISBN 0-85997-486-3 : £5.50 : CIP rev. B80-22641

828'.91407 — Prose in English, *1945-*. Special subjects: Siamese cats — *Texts*

Tovey, Doreen. Cats in May / Doreen Tovey. — Large print ed. — Bath : Chivers, 1981, c1959. — 168p ; 23cm. — (A New Portway large print book)
Originally published: London : Elek, 1959
ISBN 0-85119-111-8 : Unpriced B81-15222

828'.91407'08 — Experimental writing in English, *1945-* — *Anthologies* — *Serials*

[Caprice *(Watford Heath)*]. Caprice. — No.1 (Apr.1980)-. — Watford Heath (2 Bucks Ave., Watford Heath, Herts. WD1 4AS) : K. Seddon, c1980-. — v. : ill ; 30cm
Irregular
£2.40 for 4 issues B81-07007

828'.91407'08 — Humorous prose in English, *1945-* — *Anthologies*

Barker, Mark. The rag mag collection / by Mark Barker and Larry. — London : Clare, [1981?]. — [96]p : ill ; 23cm
ISBN 0-906549-22-1 (cased) : £4.95
ISBN 0-906549-24-8 (pbk) : Unpriced B81-40900

Gorrah, Seamus B.. Ireland strikes back! / Seamus B. Gorrah. — London : Hamlyn Paperbacks, 1981. — 78p ; 18cm
ISBN 0-600-20412-x (pbk) : £0.85 B81-19900

High life, low life / Taki, Jeffrey Bernard ; introduction by Richard West ; edited by Cosmo Landesman. — London : Jay Landseman, 1981. — 207p ; 23cm
ISBN 0-905150-27-9 : £6.95 : CIP rev. B81-18052

White tie tales : a collection of after-dinner stories / [compiled by] John H. Morecroft. — Folkestone : Bailey & Swinfen, 1974 (1981 [printing]). — 101p ; 19cm
ISBN 0-561-00314-9 (pbk) : £1.35 B81-40551

Yarwood, Mike. Family joke book / Mike Yarwood. — London : Hamlyn Paperbacks, 1980. — 125p ; 18cm
ISBN 0-600-20104-x (pbk) : £0.85 B81-03213

828'.91407'08 — Humorous prose in English, *1945-*. Special subjects: English literature — *Anthologies* — *Serials*

Transactions of the Literary Drivel Society. — Vol.1, no.1-. — [London] ([c/o John Firth, 276 Maida Ave., W2]) : [The Society], 1981-. — v. ; 21cm
Quarterly
ISSN 0261-1066 = Transactions of the Literary Drivel Society : Unpriced B81-27910

828'.91407'080352039162 — Humorous prose in English, *1945-*. Special subjects: Irishmen — *Anthologies*

The **Last** complete Irish gag book / compiled by Garry Chambers ; illustrated by Bill Tidy. — [London] : Star, 1981. — 125p : ill ; 18cm
ISBN 0-352-30679-3 (pbk) : £1.25 B81-22286

828'.91407'080356 — Humorous prose in English. Compositions by secondary school students, *1945-*. Special subjects: Chemistry — *Anthologies*

H2O and all that / [compiled by] Martyn Berry. — London : Heinemann Educational, c1980. — 82p : ill ; 22cm
ISBN 0-435-64100-x (pbk) : £1.95 : CIP rev. B80-32535

828'.91408 — Prose in English, *1945-* — *Texts*

Willock, Colin. Town gun. — London : Deutsch, Nov.1981
2. — [272]p
ISBN 0-233-97399-0 : £7.95 : CIP entry B81-30217

828'.91408'08 — Prose in English, *1945-* — *Anthologies*

Not poetry : contemporary prose writing. — Issue 1 (Spring 1980)-. — Newcastle upon Tyne (3 Otterburn Terrace, Newcastle upon Tyne) : Galloping Dog Press, 1980-. — v ; 30cm
Quarterly
£3.00 per year B81-07157

828'.91408'080354 — Prose in English. London writers: Hackney *(London Borough)* writers, *1945-*. Special subjects: Childbirth — *Anthologies*

Every birth it comes different : writings from Hackney Reading Centre. — London (136 Kingsland High St., E8) : Centerprise, c1980. — 72p : ill ; 21cm
ISBN 0-903738-47-3 (pbk) : £1.20 B81-07650

828'.91408'0809287 — Prose in English. London writers: Southwark *(London Borough)* writers: Peckham women writers, *1945-* — *Anthologies*

I want to write it down / writing by women in Peckham. — London (The Bookplace, 13 Peckham High St., S.E.15) : Peckham Publishing Project, c1980. — 68p : ill,ports ; 21cm
ISBN 0-906464-70-6 (pbk) : £1.00 B81-05643

828'.91409 — English literature, *1945-* — *Texts*

Allnutt, Gillian. Spitting the pips out / Gillian Allnutt. — London (488 Kingshead Rd., E8) : Sheba Feminist Publishers, 1981. — 140p ; 20cm
ISBN 0-907179-06-1 (pbk) : £2.25 B81-29611

Bush, Noel Hazel. Just another day! : — a day in the life of a teaching nun, with some of her stories and verses / by Noel Hazel Bush (Sister Anthony). — Market Harborough (5 St. Mary's Rd., Market Harborough, Leics. LE16 7DS) : Green and Co., c1981. — 45p,[2]leaves of plates : 2ill,1port ; 21cm
Unpriced (pbk) B81-28635

Freeman, John, *1946-*. A vase of honesty / John Freeman. — Bishop's Stortford (25 Portland Rd., Bishop's Stortford, Herts.) : Great Works Editions, 1979. — [46]leaves ; 30cm
Limited ed. of 200 copies
ISBN 0-905383-11-7 (pbk) : £0.75 B81-00634

Goodwin, David. The other side / David Goodwin. — Bognor Regis : New Horizon, c1981. — 97p : ill ; 21cm
ISBN 0-86116-685-x : £3.75 B81-34842

Nolan, Christopher, *1965-*. Dam-burst of dreams : the writings of Christopher Nolan / introduction by Marjorie Wallace. — London : Weidenfeld and Nicolson, 1981. — xv,128p ; 23cm
ISBN 0-297-77978-8 : £3.95 B81-25270

Pinter, Harold. Poems and prose 1949-1977 / by Harold Pinter. — London : Eyre Methuen, 1978 (1980 [printing]). — viii,101p ; 24cm
ISBN 0-413-47190-x (pbk) : £2.95 B81-01352

Toczek, Nick. Rock'n'roll terrorism / Nick Toczek. — Isle of Skye : Aquila, c1981. — [20]p ; 21cm
ISBN 0-7275-0205-0 (pbk) : £0.75
ISBN 0-7275-0206-9 (Limited signed ed.) : £1.50 B81-38387

Troostwyk, David. National Day / David Troostwyk. — London (10 Martello St., London Fields, E.8) : Matt's Gallery, c1981. — 61p ; 21cm
To accompany an exhibition at Matt's Gallery. — Limited ed. of 300 copies
ISBN 0-907623-00-x (pbk) : Unpriced B81-33734

828'.91409 — English literature. Blishen, Edward, *to 1939* — *Biographies*

Blishen, Edward. Shaky relations / Edward Blishen. — London : Hamish Hamilton, 1981. — 202p ; 23cm
ISBN 0-241-10348-7 : £8.95 : CIP rev. B81-13530

828'.91409 — English literature. Farrell, J. G. — *Correspondence, diaries, etc.*

Farrell, J. G.. The hill station : an unfinished novel ; and An Indian diary / J.G. Farrell ; edited by John Spurling. — London : Weidenfeld and Nicolson, 1981. — x,228p ; 23cm
ISBN 0-297-77922-2 : £6.50
Primary classification 823'.914[F] B81-19321

828'.91409 — Humour in English, *1945-* — *Texts*

Big Daddy. Big Daddy's joke book / with cartoons by Graham Round. — London : Armada, 1981. — 125p : ill ; 18cm. — (An Armada original)
ISBN 0-00-691908-1 (pbk) : £0.85 B81-22011

828′.91409 — Humour in English, *1945- — Texts continuation*

Brandreth, Gyles. The crazy encyclopaedia / Gyles Brandreth ; illustrated by Bobbie Craig. — [London] : Carousel, 1981. — 126p : ill ; 20cm
ISBN 0-552-54174-5 (pbk) : £0.75 B81-08473

Brandreth, Gyles. Total nonsense Z to A / by Gyles Brandreth ; with drawings by Lucy Robinson. — New York ; Sterling ; London : Oak Tree, 1981. — 96p : ill ; 21cm
Includes index
Unpriced B81-39901

Cowley, Stewart. Do it yourself brain surgery & other home skills / Stewart Cowley. — London : Muller, 1981. — 127p : ill ; 29cm
Includes index
ISBN 0-584-97073-0 (cased) : Unpriced
ISBN 0-584-97104-4 (pbk) : £3.95 B81-39185

Creme, Lol. The fun starts here : out-takes from a rock memoir / Lol Creme and Kevin Godley. — London : Arrow, 1981. — [76]p : ill ; 24x30cm
Ill on inside covers
ISBN 0-09-926070-0 (pbk) : £4.95 B81-40557

Hardie, Sean. Not the royal wedding / [written and edited by Sean Hardie and John Lloyd, with Laurie Rowley ... et al.]. — London : Pavilion, 1981. — 48p : ill,1map,plans,ports (some col.),geneal.table ; 27cm
Ports on lining papers
ISBN 0-907516-07-6 (cased) : £4.95
ISBN 0-7221-6468-8 (Sphere) : Unpriced B81-34163

Harding, Mike. The armchair anarchist′s almanac. — London : Robson, Oct.1981. — [144]p
ISBN 0-86051-124-3 : £5.95 : CIP entry B81-27451

James, Paul. The laugh-a-minute joke book / Paul James. — [London] : Sparrow, 1981. — 170p ; 18cm
ISBN 0-09-926030-1 (pbk) : £0.90 B81-27118

Just joking / compiled by Mike Yarwood with the help of a few friends ; drawings by David Myers. — London : Dent, 1981. — 146p : ill ; 23cm
ISBN 0-460-04524-5 : £4.95 : CIP rev. B81-27982

Lennon, John. John Lennon in his own write ; and a Spaniard in the works / by John Lennon. — London : Cape, 1981. — 154p : ill (some col.) ; 21cm
Originally published: 1964
ISBN 0-224-02921-5 : £5.50 B81-11001

Lindley, Geoff. [A funny thing happened to me on the way to the settee]. A funny thing happened on the way to the settee / Geoff Lindley. — Bognor Regis : New Horizon, c1980. — 252p ; 22cm
Originally published: Grimsby : G. Lindley, 1977
ISBN 0-86116-124-6 : £3.50 B81-19077

Maggot Incorporated publications. — Hanworth (183 Fernside Ave., Hanworth, Middx., TW13 7BQ) : Sweaty Publications, c1980. — [24]p : ill(some col.) ; 28cm
Cover title
£1.00 (pbk) B81-23188

Marshall, Andrew. Bestseller ! : the life and death of Eric Pode of Croydon. — London : Allen & Unwin, Sept.1981. — [128]p
ISBN 0-04-827036-9 : £4.95 : CIP entry B81-20480

Nationalists of Nazareth : what really happened in the Bible : pigs spiral downward. — Carlops by Penicuik (Jess Cottage, Carlops by Penicuik, Midlothian, EH 26 9NF) : Scots Secretariat, [198-?]. — 13p : ill ; 22cm
£0.20 (unbound) B81-29893

The **Naughty** diary of an Edwardian lady : a facsimile reproduction of a naturist′s diary for the year 1906 ... / [Ethel Hordle]. — London : Macdonald, 1981. — [78]p : col.ill ; 24cm
ISBN 0-354-04690-x : £4.95 B81-38367

Rowley, Laurie. The news Huddlines : Roy Hudd laughs at the news with Janet Brown and Chris Emmett / written by Laurie Rowley, Andy Hamilton, Terry Ravenscroft ; lyrics by Jeremy Browne, Richard Quick and Andy Wilson ... ; line drawings created and drawn by Safu-Maria Gilbert. — London : New English Library, c1980. — [144]p : ill ; 18cm
ISBN 0-450-05051-3 (corrected : pbk) : £1.25 B81-07030

Sharma, S. K. (Surendra Kumar). Laughter : is good for health / by S.K. Sharma. — Firswood (19 Warwick Court, Firswood, Manchester M16 3JG) : S.K. Sharma, [1981]. — [44]p : 1ill ; 21cm
Cover title
£1.25 (pbk) B81-21657

Stilgoe, Richard. The Richard Stilgoe letters : a jumble of anagrams / with cartoons by Richard Willson. — London : Allen & Unwin, 1981. — vii,201[i.e. 120]p : ill ; 23cm
ISBN 0-04-827035-0 : Unpriced : CIP rev. B81-20481

Weller, Don. Promiscuous purchaser / Don Weller ; illustrated by Joan McFadyen. — Stone : Panda Press, c1979. — 175p : ill ; 21cm
ISBN 0-906689-00-7 (pbk) : Unpriced B81-39873

Wogan, Terry. The day job / Terry Wogan ; illustrations by Hector Breeze. — London : Queen Anne, 1981. — 88p : col.ill ; 26cm
ISBN 0-362-00558-3 : £5.25 B81-37815

829 — OLD ENGLISH LITERATURE

829′.1 — Orally transmitted poetry in Old English *— Critical studies*

Opland, Jeff. Anglo-Saxon oral poetry : a study of the traditions / Jeff Opland. — New Haven ; London : Yale University Press, 1980. — xi,289p ; 24cm
Bibliography: p267-282. - Includes index
ISBN 0-300-02426-6 : £12.60 B81-04908

829′.1 — Poetry in Old English. Battle of Maldon *— Critical studies*

The **Battle** of Maldon. — Manchester : Manchester University Press, Oct.1981. — [117]p. — (Old and Middle English texts)
ISBN 0-7190-0838-7 (pbk) : £3.50 : CIP entry B81-25830

829′.1 — Poetry in Old English. Exedous — *Critical studies*

Tolkien, J. R. R.. The Old English Exodus. — Oxford : Clarendon Press, Nov.1981. — [128]p
ISBN 0-19-811177-0 : £8.00 : CIP entry B81-28850

829′.8 — Prose in Old English *— Critical studies*

Bately, Janet M.. The literary prose of King Alfred′s reign : translation or transformation? : an inaugural lecture in the Chair of English Language and Medieval Literature delivered at University of London King′s College on 4th March 1980 / by Janet M. Bately. — [London] ([Strand, WC2R 2LS]) : [Kings College, University of London], [1980]. — 26p ; 21cm
Cover title
Unpriced (pbk) B81-19858

830 — GERMANIC LITERATURES

830′.09 — Germanic literatures. Characters: Brynhilde *— Critical studies*

Andersson, Theodore M.. The legend of Brynhild / Theodore M. Andersson. — Ithaca ; London : Cornell University Press, 1980. — 268p ; 23cm. — (Islandica ; 43)
Bibliography: p250-257. — Includes index
ISBN 0-8014-1302-8 : £13.50 B81-11818

830′.8 — German literature, *1770-1980 - Anthologies - For schools*

Gefunden. — London : Heinemann Educational, July 1981. — [192]p
ISBN 0-435-38860-6 (pbk) : £3.95 : CIP entry B81-13475

830.8′09436 — German literature. Austrian writers, *1945- — Anthologies — English texts*

Anthology of modern Austrian literature. — London : Oswald Wolff, Oct.1981. — [200]p
ISBN 0-85496-077-5 : £8.00 : CIP entry B81-27462

830.9 — GERMAN LITERATURE. HISTORY AND CRITICAL STUDIES

830.9 — German literature, *1750-1980 — Critical studies*

Parry, Idris. Hand to mouth and other essays / Idris Parry. — Manchester : Carcanet, 1981. — 173p ; 23cm
ISBN 0-85635-375-2 : £6.95 : CIP rev. B81-28189

830.9 — German literature. Influence of emblem books, *1500-1700*

Daly, Peter M.. Literature in the light of the emblem : structural parallels between the emblem and literature in the sixteenth and seventeenth centuries / Peter M. Daly. — Toronto ; London : University of Toronto Press, c1979. — xiv,245p : ill,facsims ; 24cm
Bibliography: p224-233. — Includes index
ISBN 0-8020-5390-4 : £11.35
Primary classification 820.9 B81-05825

830.9′007 — German literature, *1830-1900 — Critical studies*

Stern, J. P.. Re-interpretations : seven studies in nineteenth-century German literature / J.P. Stern. — Cambridge : Cambridge University Press, 1981, c1964. — 370p ; 23cm
Originally published: London : Thames & Hudson, 1964. — Includes index
ISBN 0-521-23983-4 (cased) : £25.00 : CIP rev.
ISBN 0-521-28366-3 (pbk) : £7.95 B81-19120

830.9′00912 — German literature. Influence of social conditions, *1900-1945*

Taylor, Ronald, *1924-*. Literature and society in Germany 1918-1945 / Ronald Taylor. — Brighton : Harvester, 1980. — xiii,363p ; 25cm. — (Harvester studies in contemporary literature and culture ; 3)
Bibliography: p346-353. — Includes index
ISBN 0-85527-898-6 : £22.00 : CIP rev. B80-08041

830.9′145 — German literature, *1750-1830.* **Romanticism** *— Critical studies*

Menhennet, Alan. The Romantic movement / Alan Menhennet. — London : Croom Helm, 1981. — 276p ; 23cm. — ([Literary history of Germany] ; 6)
Bibliography: p262-269. — Includes index
ISBN 0-7099-0381-2 : £15.95 : CIP rev. B80-35394

830.9′9436 — German literature. Austrian writers, *1900-1975 — Conference proceedings*

Studies in modern Austrian literature : eight papers / edited by B.O. Murdoch and M.G. Ward. — Glasgow (8 Crawford Cres., Uddingston, Glasgow G71 7DP) : Scottish Papers in Germanic Studies, 1981. — vi,122p ; 21cm. — (Scottish papers in Germanic studies ; v.1)
Conference papers. — Includes 3 papers in German
ISBN 0-907409-00-8 (pbk) : £3.50 B81-15754

831 — GERMAN POETRY

831′.03′09 — Narrative poetry in German, *to 1517.* **Literary sources** *— Critical studies*

Lofmark, Carl. The authority of the source in Middle High German narrative poetry / Carl Lofmark. — London : Institute of Germanic Studies, University of London, 1981. — x,161p ; 22cm. — (Bithell series of dissertations ; v.5)
Bibliography: p149-153. — Includes index
ISBN 0-85457-098-5 (pbk) : Unpriced B81-12498

831'.04'09 — Lyric poetry in German, *1150-1300 — Critical studies*

Sayce, Olive. The medieval German lyric, 1150-1300. — Oxford : Clarendon Press, July 1981. — [400]p
ISBN 0-19-815772-x : £25.00 : CIP entry
B81-16887

831.2 — GERMAN POETRY, 1150-1300

831'.2 — Poetry in German. Albrecht, *von Scharfenberg.* **Jüngerer Titurel. Narrative —** *Critical studies*

Parshall, Linda B.. The art of narration in Wolfram's Parzifal and Albrecht's Jüngerer Titurel / Linda B. Parshall. — Cambridge : Cambridge University Press, 1981. — vi,289p ; 23cm. — (Anglica Germanica. Series 2)
Bibliography: p275-285. — Includes index
ISBN 0-521-22237-0 : £25.00
Primary classification 831'.2 B81-38285

831'.2 — Poetry in German. Wolfram, *von Eschenbach.* **Parzival. Narrative —** *Critical studies*

Parshall, Linda B.. The art of narration in Wolfram's Parzifal and Albrecht's Jüngerer Titurel / Linda B. Parshall. — Cambridge : Cambridge University Press, 1981. — vi,289p ; 23cm. — (Anglica Germanica. Series 2)
Bibliography: p275-285. — Includes index
ISBN 0-521-22237-0 : £25.00
Also classified at 831'.2 B81-38285

831.5 — GERMAN POETRY, 1625-1750

831'.5'09 — Poetry in German, *1625-1750 — Critical studies*

Browning, Robert M. (Robert Marcellus). German poetry in the Age of Enlightenment : from Brockes to Klopstock / Robert M. Browning. — University Park ; London : Pennsylvania State University Press, c1978. — xi,336p ; 23cm. — (The Penn State series in German literature)
Bibliography: p319-328. — Includes index
ISBN 0-271-00541-6 : £9.60 B81-04735

831.6 — GERMAN POETRY, 1750-1830

831'.6 — Poetry in German. Goethe, Johann Wolfgang von — *Critical studies*

Papers read before the Society : 1979-80 / edited by Frank M. Fowler, Brian A. Rowley and Ann C. Weaver. — [London] ([c/o German Department, University College, Gower St., WC1E 6BT]) : [English Goethe Society], 1980. — 165p ; 22cm. — (Publications of the English Goethe Society. New series ; vol.L)
Unpriced (pbk) B81-32496

831'.6 — Poetry in German. Goethe, Johann Wolfgang von. Influence of Greek civilization

Trevelyan, Humphry. Goethe and the Greeks. — Cambridge : Cambridge University Press, Oct.1981. — [368]p
Originally published: 1941
ISBN 0-521-24137-5 (cased) : £25.00 : CIP entry
ISBN 0-521-28471-6 (pbk) : £8.95 B81-31285

831'.6 — Poetry in German. Müller, Wilhelm — *Biographies*

Baumann, Cecilia C.. Wilhelm Müller : the poet of the Schubert song cycles : his life and work / Cecilia C. Baumann. — University Park ; London : Pennsylvania State University Press, c1981. — xv,191p : ill,1port ; 24cm. — (The Penn State series in German literature)
Bibliography: p171-184. — Includes index
ISBN 0-271-00266-2 : £4.85 B81-36197

831.8 — GERMAN POETRY, 1856-1900

831'.8 — Poetry in German, *1856-1900 — English texts*

Meggendorfer, Lothar. [Nur für brave Kinder. English]. Trick or treat : a reproduction of an antique moving picture book full of surprises / by Lothar Meggendorfer. — London : Benn, 1981. — [8]p : col.ill ; 22x25cm
Translation of: Nur für brave Kinder. — Cover title. — Text, ill. on inside covers
ISBN 0-510-00110-6 : £3.50 B81-20789

831.912 — GERMAN POETRY, 1900-1945

831'.912 — Poetry in German, *1900-1945 — English texts*

Brecht, Bertolt. Bertolt Brecht poems / edited by John Willett and Ralph Manheim with the co-operation of Erich Fried. — 2nd corr. ed. — London : Eyre Methuen, 1979 (1981 [printing]). — xxvii,627p ; 22cm. — (Bertolt Brecht plays, poetry and prose)
Cover title: Poems 1913-1956. — Previous ed.: published in 3 vols. 1976. — Includes index
ISBN 0-413-48790-3 (pbk) : £4.95 B81-30822

831'.912 — Poetry in German, *1900-1945 — German-English parallel texts*

Kaschnitz, Marie Luise. Selected later poems of Marie Luise Kaschnitz / translated by Lisel Mueller. — Princeton ; Guildford : Princeton University Press, c1980. — xii,111p ; 23cm. — (The Lockert library of poetry in translation)
Parallel German text and English translation
ISBN 0-691-06442-3 (cased) : £5.55
ISBN 0-691-01374-8 (pbk) : £2.75 B81-07761

Rilke, Rainer Maria. Selected poems of Rainer Maria Rilke / a translation from the German and commentary by Robert Bly. — New York ; London : Harper & Row, c1981. — xi,224p ; 24cm
Includes index
ISBN 0-06-010432-5 (cased) : Unpriced
ISBN 0-06-090727-4 (pbk) : £3.95 B81-26527

831'.912 — Poetry in German. Austrian writers. Trakl, Georg — *Critical studies*

Sharp, Francis Michael. The poet's madness : a reading of George Trakl / Francis Michael Sharp. — Ithaca ; London : Cornell University Press, 1981. — 252p ; 23cm
Includes poems in German with parallel English translations. — Bibliography: p239-247. — Includes index
ISBN 0-8014-1297-8 : £10.50 B81-27262

831'.912 — Poetry in German. French writers, *1900-1945 — English texts*

Kandinsky, Wassily. Sounds / Wassily Kandinsky ; translated and with an introduction by Elizabeth R. Napier. — New Haven ; London : Yale University Press, c1981. — vii,136p : ill ; 22cm
Translation of: Klänge. — English and German text
ISBN 0-300-02510-6 (cased) : £21.00 : CIP rev.
ISBN 0-300-02664-1 (pbk) : £8.35
Also classified at 769.92'4 B81-17534

831'.912 — Poetry in German. Hofmannsthal, Hugo von — *Correspondence, diaries, etc.*

Strauss, Richard. The correspondence between Richard Strauss and Hugo von Hofmannsthal / translated by Hanns Hammelmann and Ewald Osers ; introduction by Edward Sackville-West. — Cambridge : Cambridge University Press, 1980, c1961. — xx,558p : 2facsims,3ports ; 24cm
Translation of: Richard Strauss und Hugo von Hofmannsthal: Briefwechsel. — Originally published: London : Collins, 1961. — Includes index
ISBN 0-521-23476-x (cased) : £29.50 : CIP rev.
ISBN 0-521-29911-x (pbk) : £7.95
Primary classification 780'.92'4 B80-28594

831'.912 — Poetry in German. Rilke, Rainer Maria. Special themes: Landscape

Sandford, John. Landscape and landscape imagery in R.M. Rilke / John Sandford. — London : Institute of Germanic Studies, University of London, 1980. — x,159p ; 22cm. — (Bithell series of dissertations ; v.4)
Bibliography: p154-159
ISBN 0-85457-096-9 (pbk) : £8.00 B81-04126

831.914 — GERMAN POETRY, 1945-

831'.914 — Poetry in German, *1945- — English texts*

Enzensberger, Hans Magnus. The sinking of the Titanic : a poem / Hans Magnus Enzensberger ; translated by the author. — Manchester : Carcanet, 1981. — 98p ; 23cm
Translation of: Der Untergang der Titanic. — Originally published: Boston, Mass. : Houghton Mifflin, 1980
ISBN 0-85635-372-8 : £3.95 B81-14002

Gernhardt, Almut. What a day! / pictures by Almut Gernhardt ; with verses by Robert Gernhardt ; translated from the German by Kathrine Talbot. — London : Cape, 1980. — [32]p : col.ill ; 25cm
Translation of: Was für ein Tag
ISBN 0-224-01844-2 : £3.50 : CIP rev.
B80-13612

Klinge, Günther. Drifting with the moon / Günther Klinge ; selected and adapted into English by Ann Atwood. — Rutland, Vt. : Tuttle ; London : Prentice-Hall [distributor], 1978. — 120p : col.ill ; 20cm
Translated from the German. — In slip case
ISBN 0-8048-1296-9 : Unpriced B81-24453

831'.914 — Poetry in German, *1945- — Texts*

Richthofen, Patrick von. Drei Frauen / von Patrick von Richthofen. — [Durham] (University of Durham, [Old Shire Hall, Durham DH1 3HP]) : North Gate Press, [1981?]. — [4]p ; 21cm
Text in English and German. — Limited ed. of 102 numbered copies
Unpriced (pbk) B81-32629

832.6 — GERMAN DRAMA, 1750-1830

832'.6 — Drama in German, *1750-1830 — English texts*

Goethe, Johann Wolfgang von. Goethe's plays / Johann Wolfgang von Goethe ; translated with introductions by Charles E. Passage. — London : Benn, 1980. — x,626p : ill ; 22cm
Translation from the German
ISBN 0-510-00087-8 : £12.95 : CIP rev.
B80-04566

Tieck, Ludwig. The land of upside down / Ludwig Tieck ; translated by Oscar Mandel in collaboration with Maria Kelsen Feder. — Rutherford : Fairleigh Dickinson University ; London : Associated University Presses, c1978. — 123p ; 22cm
Translation of the 3rd version of Die verkehrte Welt, from v.5 of the author's Schriften, published 1828-1846. — Bibliography: p27-28
ISBN 0-8386-2061-2 : £7.25 B81-08431

832'.6 — Drama in German, *1750-1830 — Texts*

Grillparzer, Franz. Des Meeres und der Liebe Wellen / Franz Grillparzer ; edited by Martin Ward. — Driffield : Hutton Press, 1981. — xxix,151p ; 21cm
German text, English introduction and notes. — Bibliography: p149
ISBN 0-907033-04-0 (pbk) : Unpriced
B81-27589

832'.6 — Drama in German. Goethe, Johann Wolfgang von. Faust — *Critical studies*

Gearey, John. Goethe's Faust : the making of Part 1 / John Gearey. — New Haven ; London : Yale University Press, c1981. — xi,228p ; 22cm
Bibliography: p217-222. — Includes index
ISBN 0-300-02571-8 : £11.95 : CIP rev.
B81-09983

832'.6 — Drama in German. Goethe, Johann Wolfgang von. Influence of European visual arts, *to 1788*

Robson-Scott, W. D.. The younger Goethe and the visual arts / W.D. Robson-Scott. — Cambridge : Cambridge University Press, 1981. — xii,175p,[7]p of plates : ill ; 23cm. — (Anglica Germanica series ; 2)
Bibliography: p162-168. — Includes index
ISBN 0-521-23321-6 : Unpriced : CIP rev.
B81-07575

832'.6 — Drama in German. Lessing, Gotthold Ephraim, *1729-1781 — Critical studies*

Lamport, F. J.. Lessing and the drama / F.J. Lamport. — Oxford : Clarendon, 1981. — 247p ; 23cm
Bibliography: p236-241. — Includes index
ISBN 0-19-815767-3 : £15.00 : CIP rev.
B81-13830

832.8 — GERMAN DRAMA, 1856-1900

832'.8 — Drama in German, ***1856-1900 — English texts***

Hauptmann, Gerhart. The weavers / Gerhart Hauptmann ; translated and introduced by Frank Marcus. — London : Eyre Methuen, 1980. — xii,88p ; 19cm. — (Methuen's theatre classics)
Translation of: Die Waber
ISBN 0-413-47630-8 (pbk) : £2.75 B81-35400

Schnitzler, Arthur. The round dance. — Manchester : Carcanet Press, Jan.1982. — [232]p
Translation of the German
ISBN 0-85635-398-1 : £6.95 : CIP entry
B81-38832

Wedekind, Frank. The Lulu plays & other sex tragedies / Frank Wedekind translated from the German by Stephen Spender. — London : Calder, 1977, c1952 (1981 [printing]). — 281p ; 21cm. — (German expressionism)
Originally published: London : Vision, 1952. — Contents: Earth spirit - Pandora's box - Death and devil - Castle Wetterstein
ISBN 0-7145-0868-3 (pbk) : £4.50 B81-12772

Wedekind, Frank. Spring awakening / Frank Wedekind ; translated by Edward Bond ; with introductions by Edward Bond and Elisabeth Bond. — London : Eyre Methuen, 1980. — xxxv,59p ; 19cm. — (Methuen's theatre classics)
Thirty men, 7 women. — Translation of: Frühlings Erwachen. — Bibliography: pxxiii-xxiv
ISBN 0-413-47620-0 (pbk) : £2.25 B81-07718

832.912 — GERMAN DRAMA, 1900-1945

832'.912 — Drama in German, ***1900-1945 - English texts***

Kaiser, Georg. Kaiser plays. — London : John Calder, Aug.1981. — (German expressionism ; 2)
Vol.2. — [224]p
ISBN 0-7145-3763-2 (cased) : £6.95 : CIP entry
ISBN 0-7145-3899-x (pbk) B81-18104

832'.912 — Drama in German, ***1900-1945 — Texts***

Brecht, Bertolt. Leben des Galilei / Bertolt Brecht ; edited by H.F. Brookes and C.E. Fraenkel. — 2nd ed. — London : Heinemann Educational, 1981. — xxxi,204p : ill ; 19cm. — (Heinemann German texts)
German text, English introduction, appendices and notes. — Previous ed.: 1958. — Text on inside covers. — Bibliography: p180-182. — Includes index
ISBN 0-435-38123-7 (pbk) : £2.50 B81-30057

832'.912 — Drama in German, ***1900-1945 - Texts with commentaries***

Brecht, Bertolt. Der aufhaltsame Aufsteig des Arturo Ui. — London : Methuen, June 1981. — [220]p. — (Methuen's twentieth century texts)
ISBN 0-423-90180-x (pbk) : £2.50 : CIP entry
B81-12868

832'.912 — Drama in German. Brecht, Bertolt, ***1941-1947 — Biographies***

Lyon, James K.. Bertolt Brecht in America / James K. Lyon. — Princeton ; Guildford : Princeton University Press, c1980. — xiv,408p,[16]p of plates : ill,ports ; 24cm
Bibliography: p383-396. — Includes index
ISBN 0-691-06443-1 : £11.00 B81-05396

832'.912 — Drama in German. Brecht, Bertolt — ***Conference proceedings***

Bertolt Brecht : political theory and literary practice / edited by Betty Nance Weber and Hubert Heinen. — Manchester : Manchester University Press, c1980. — 209p ; 24cm
Conference papers. — Originally published: Athens, Georgia : University of Georgia Press, 1980. — Includes index
ISBN 0-7190-0806-9 : £15.00 : CIP rev.
B80-18074

832'.912 — Drama in German. Brecht, Bertolt — ***Critical studies***

Esslin, Martin. Brecht : a choice of evils : a critical study of the man, his work and his opinions / Martin Esslin. — 3rd, rev. ed.. — London : Eyre Methuen, 1980. — xvi,315p ; 20cm. — ([Mordern theatre profiles])
Previous ed.: London : Heinemann Educational, 1965. — Bibliography: p290-301. - Includes index
ISBN 0-413-47050-4 (cased) : £7.50
ISBN 0-413-46650-7 (pbk) : £3.95 B81-02241

Needle, Jan. Brecht. — Oxford : Blackwell, 1981. — xvi,235p : ill,ports ; 24cm
Bibliography: p226-228. - Includes index
ISBN 0-631-19610-2 : £9.00 : CIP rev.
B80-12628

832'.912 — Drama in German. Swiss writers, ***1900-1945 — Texts***

Frisch, Max. Triptych : three scenic panels / Max Frisch ; translated by Geoffrey Skelton. — London : Eyre Methuen, 1981. — 73p ; 19cm. — (A Methuen modern play)
Translation of: Triptychon
ISBN 0-413-47850-5 (pbk) : £2.50 B81-19723

832'.912'08 — Drama in German, ***1900-1945 — Anthologies — English texts***

Seven expressionist plays : Kokoschka to Barlach / translated from the German by J.M. Ritchie and H.F. Garten. — London : John Calder, 1980. — 201p ; 22cm. — (German expressionism)
Translations from the German. — Originally published: London : Calder & Boyars, 1968
ISBN 0-7145-0520-x (cased) : £6.95 : CIP rev.
ISBN 0-7145-0521-8 (pbk) : £3.50 B79-32125

832.914 — GERMAN DRAMA, 1945-

832'.914 — Drama in German, ***1945- — English texts***

König, Karl. Plays for Christmas / Karl König. — Botton Village (Botton Village, Danby, Whitby, N. Yorks Y021 2NJ) : Camphill, c1980. — 59p ; 19cm
Translations from the German
ISBN 0-904145-20-4 (pbk) : Unpriced
B81-32574

833 — GERMAN FICTION

833[F] — Fiction in German. Japanese writers, ***1945- — English texts***

Matsubara, Hisako. Samurai / Hisako Matsubara ; translated from the German by Ruth Hein. — London : Bodley Head, 1980. — 217p ; 23cm
Translation of: Brokatrausch
ISBN 0-370-30348-2 : £5.95 : CIP rev.
B80-20012

833'.009 — Fiction in German, ***1700-1980.*** **Forms: Novels** ***compared with*** **English novels,** ***1700-1980***

Klieneberger, H. R.. The novel in England and Germany. — London : Wolff, Aug.1981. — [254]p
ISBN 0-85496-079-1 (pbk) : £8.00 : CIP entry
Primary classification 823'.009 B81-18114

833'.01'076 — Short stories in German, ***to 1980 — Questions & answers — For schools***

Cahillane, Monica. Das wrack and other stories / Monica Cahillane. — Tallaght : Folens, c1979. — 54p ; 22cm. — (Folens' student aids leaving certificate)
ISBN 0-86121-063-8 (pbk) : £0.72 B81-18622

833.6 — GERMAN FICTION, 1750-1830

833'.6[F] — Fiction in German, ***1750-1830 — English texts***

Goethe, Johann Wolfgang von. Wilhelm Meister : the years of travel. — London : John Calder
Translation of: Wilhelm Meisters Wanderjahre
Book 2. — Nov.1981. — [224]p
ISBN 0-7145-3838-8 : £6.95 : CIP entry
B81-30597

833.8 — GERMAN FICTION, 1856-1900

833'.8 — Fiction in German. Fontane, Theodor — ***Critical studies***

Garland, Henry. The Berlin novels of Theodor Fontane / Henry Garland. — Oxford : Clarendon Press, 1980. — viii,296p ; 23cm
Bibliography: p284-288. — Includes index
ISBN 0-19-815765-7 : £14.00 : CIP rev.
B80-09000

833.912 — GERMAN FICTION, 1900-1945

833'.912 — Fiction in German. Austrian writers. Musil, Robert — ***Critical studies***

Luft, David S.. Robert Musil and the crisis of European culture 1880-1942 / David S. Luft. — Berkeley ; London : University of California Press, c1980. — xii,323p : 1ports ; 24cm
Bibliography: p299-312. - Includes index
ISBN 0-520-03852-5 : £11.45 B81-12162

833'.912 — Fiction in German. Czechoslovak writers. Kafka, Franz — ***Critical studies***

The World of Franz Kafka / edited by J.P. Stern. — London : Weidenfeld and Nicolson, c1980. — vii,263p,[24]p of plates : ill,1facsim,ports ; 25cm
Includes index
ISBN 0-297-77845-5 : £9.95 B81-08383

833'.912 — Fiction in German. Hesse, Hermann. Steppenwolf — ***Study outlines***

Jillings, Lewis. Steppenwolf : notes / by Lewis Jillings and Margaret Jillings. — Harlow : Longman, 1981. — 73p ; 21cm. — (York notes ; 135)
Bibliography: p72-73
ISBN 0-582-78274-0 (pbk) : £0.90 B81-34230

833'.912 — Fiction in German. Mann, Thomas — ***Critical studies***

Heller, Erich. Thomas Mann : the ironic German / by Erich Heller. — Rev. ed. — Cambridge : Cambridge University Press, 1981. — 314p ; 23cm
Originally published: South Bent : Regnery/Gateway, 1979. — Bibliography: p299-301
ISBN 0-521-23546-4 (cased) : £17.50
ISBN 0-521-28022-2 (pbk) : £4.95 B81-15334

833'.912[F] — Fiction in German, ***1900-1945 — English texts***

Brecht, Bertolt. Threepenny novel / Bertolt Brecht ; translated by Desmond I. Vesey, verses translated by Christopher Isherwood ; introduction by John Willett. — London : Granada, 1981. — xii,369p ; 23cm
Translation of: Dreigroschenroman
ISBN 0-246-11605-6 : £9.95 B81-38056

Heym, Stefan. Collin / Stefan Heym. — London : Hodder and Stoughton, c1980. — 315p ; 22cm
Translation of: Collin. — Originally published: in German. West Germany : s.n., 1979
ISBN 0-340-25721-0 : £7.95 : CIP rev.
B80-10886

Remarque, Erich Maria. Spark of life / Erich Maria Remarque ; translated from the German by James Stern. — London : Granada, 1981, c1952. — 383p ; 18cm. — (A Mayflower book)
Translation of: Der Funke Leben. — Originally published: New York : Appleton ; London : Hutchinson, 1952
ISBN 0-583-13246-4 (pbk) : £1.95 B81-32183

Remarque, Erich Maria. A time to love and a time to die / Erich Maria Remarque ; translated from the German by Denver Lindley. — London : Granada, 1981, c1954. — 366p ; 18cm. — (A Mayflower book)
Translation of: Zeit zu leben und Zeit zu sterben. — This translation originally published: New York : Harcourt, Brace ; London : Hutchinson, 1954
ISBN 0-583-13247-2 (pbk) : £1.95 B81-28911

833'.912[F] — Fiction in German. Swiss writers, ***1900-1945 — English texts***

Frisch, Max. Man in the Holocene : a story / Max Frisch ; translated from the German by Geoffrey Skelton. — London : Eyre Methuen, 1980. — 113p ; 21cm
Translation of: Der Mensch erscheint im Holozän
ISBN 0-413-46820-8 : £5.50 B81-04880

833'.912[F] — Short stories in German, *1900-1945 — English texts*
Marut, Ret. To the honourable Miss S and other stories from the Brickburner. — Sanday (Over the Water, Sanday, Orkney) : Cienfuegos Press, Oct.1981. — [184]p
Translated from the German
ISBN 0-904564-45-2 : £5.95 : CIP entry
B81-27423

833'.912[J] — Children's stories in German, *1900-1945 — English texts*
Seidmann-Freud, Tom. The magic boat / by Tom Seidmann-Freud. — London : Benn, 1981. — [10]p : col.ill ; 22cm
A book to turn and move. — Translation from the German. — Cover title. — Text on inside front cover. — Picture frame card in pocket
ISBN 0-510-00104-1 : £2.95 B81-20796

833.912[J] — Short stories in German, *1900-1945 — English texts*
Zweig, Stefan. The royal game and other stories. — London : Cape, Nov.1981. — [300]p
ISBN 0-224-01984-8 : £6.95 : CIP entry
B81-30964

833'.912'09 — Fiction in German. Mann, Heinrich & Mann, Thomas — *Biographies*
Hamilton, Nigel, *1944-*. The brothers Mann : the lives of Heinrich and Thomas Mann, 1871-1950 and 1875-1955 / Nigel Hamilton. — New Haven ; London : Yale University Press, 1979, c1978. — 422p ; 24cm
Originally published: London : Secker & Warburg, 1978. — Bibliography: p340-398. - Includes index
ISBN 0-8000-2348-x (cased) : Unpriced
ISBN 0-300-02668-4 (pbk) : £6.25 B81-20967

833.914 — GERMAN FICTION, 1945-

833'.914 — Fiction in German, *1945- — Texts*
Böll, Heinrich. Die verlorene Ehre der Katharina Blum / Heinrich Böll ; edited with introduction and notes by Ulrike Hanna Meinhof and Ruth Rach. — London : Harrap, 1980. — xlii,134p : 2ports ; 19cm. — (Modern world literature series)
ISBN 0-245-53547-0 (pbk) : £2.40 B81-07047

833'.914 — Short stories in German, *1945- — Texts with commentaries*
Schnurre, Wolfdietrich. Mann sollte dagegen sein. — London : Heinemann Educational, Feb.1982. — [176]p
ISBN 0-435-38750-2 (pbk) : £2.95 : CIP entry
B81-38846

833'.914[F] — Fiction in German, *1945- — English texts*
Berthold, Will. Eagles of the Reich / Will Berthold ; translated by Fred Taylor. — London : Sphere, 1980. — 281p ; 18cm
Translation of: Von Himmel zur Hölle
ISBN 0-7221-1624-1 (pbk) : £1.50 B81-01709

Braunburg, Rudolf. Betrayed skies : a novel / by Rudolf Braunburg ; translated from the German by J. Maxwell Brownjohn. — London : Severn House, 1981, c1980. — xviii,366p ; 21cm
Translation of: Der verratene Himmel. — Originally published: Garden City, N.Y. : Doubleday, 1980
ISBN 0-7278-0709-9 : £6.95 : CIP rev.
B81-12802

Dörfla, Eugen. [Die zenzorierte Mistel. English]. Censored mistletoe / by Eugen Dörfla and Friedrich Seifert ; translated from the German by Freddie Sail. — Feltham (11 Richmond Ave., Feltham Middlesex TW14 9SG) : S.Editions, c1980. — 21p ; 20cm
Translation of: Die zenzorierte Mistel
ISBN 0-907037-00-3 (pbk) : Unpriced
B81-05716

Grass, Günter. Dog years / Günter Grass ; translated by Ralph Manheim. — Harmondsworth : Penguin in association with Secker & Warburg, 1969, c1965 (1981 [printing]). — 616p ; 18cm
Translation of: Hundejahre. — Originally published: New York : Harcourt, Brace & World ; London : Secker & Warburg, 1965
ISBN 0-14-002838-2 (pbk) : £2.95 B81-40425

Grass, Günter. The meeting at Telgte / Günter Grass ; translated by Ralph Manheim ; afterword by Leonard Forster. — London : Secker & Warburg, 1981. — 147p ; 21cm
Translation of: Das Treffen in Telgte
ISBN 0-436-18778-7 : £5.95 B81-28552

Handke, Peter. The goalie's anxiety at the penalty kick / Peter Handke ; translated by Michael Roloff. — London : Quartet, 1978, c1972. — 91p ; 18cm
Translation of: Die Angst des Tormanns beim Elfmeter. — Originally published: New York : Farrar, Straus and Giroux, 1972 ; London : Eyre Methuen, 1977
ISBN 0-86072-050-0 (pbk) : £1.50 B81-33493

Handke, Peter. Short letter, long farewell / Peter Handke ; translated by Ralph Manheim. — London : Quartet, 1978, c1974. — 167p : 1map ; 18cm
Translation of: Der kurze Brief zum langen Abschied. — Originally published: New York : Farrar, Straus and Giroux, 1974 ; London : Eyre Methuen, 1977
ISBN 0-86072-051-9 (pbk) : £1.50 B81-33492

Hochhuth, Rolf. A German love story / Rolf Hochhuth ; translated by John Brownjohn. — London : Abacus, 1981, c1980. — 269p ; 20cm
Translation of: Eine leibe in Deutschland. — Originally published: London : Weidenfeld and Nicolson, 1980
ISBN 0-349-11698-9 (pbk) : £1.95 B81-39744

Kirst, Hans Hellmut. Gunner Asch goes to war / Hans Hellmut Kirst ; translated from the German by Robert Kee. — [London] : Fontana, 1965 (1981 [printing]). — 287p ; 18cm
This translation originally published: London : Weidenfeld & Nicolson, 1956
ISBN 0-00-616258-4 (pbk) : £1.25 B81-10336

Kirst, Hans Hellmut. Heroes for sale. — London : Collins, Feb.1982. — [288]p
Translation of: Ausverkauf der Helden
ISBN 0-00-222396-1 : £7.50 : CIP entry
B81-35930

Kirst, Hans Hellmut. The night of the generals. — Large print ed. — Anstey : Ulverscroft, Nov.1981. — [480]p. — (Ulverscroft large print series)
Translation of: Die Nacht der Generale. — Originally published: London : Collins, 1965
ISBN 0-7089-0712-1 : £5.00 : CIP entry
B81-30507

Kirst, Hans Hellmut. The Revolt of Gunner Asch / Hans Hellmut Kirst ; translated from the German by Robert Kee. — [Glasgow] : Fontana, 1981. — 253p ; 18cm
Translation of: Null Acht Funfzehn. — Originally published: as Zero eight fifteen. London : Weidenfeld & Nicolson, 1955
ISBN 0-00-616257-6 (pbk) : £1.25 B81-11065

Konsalik, Heinz G.. Certified insane / Heinz Konsalik ; translated by Anthea Bell. — Henley-on-Thames : Aidan Ellis, 1980. — 213p ; 23cm
Translation of: Entmüendigt
ISBN 0-85628-092-5 : £7.50 : CIP rev.
B80-08493

Konsalik, Heinz G.. The desert doctor / Heinz Konsalik ; translated by Anthea Bell. — London : Pan, 1981, c1979. — 218p ; 18cm
Translation of: Der Wuestendoktor. — Originally published: Henley-on-Thames : A. Ellis, 1979
ISBN 0-330-26431-1 (pbk) : £0.95 B81-17988

Konsalik, Heinz G.. Diagnosis. — Henley-on-Thames : A. Ellis, Apr.1981. — [224]p
Translation of: Diagnose
ISBN 0-85628-102-6 : £7.50 : CIP entry
B81-04234

Konsalik, Heinz G.. Doctor Erica Werner / Heinz Konsalik ; translated by Anthea Bell. — London : Pan, 1981, c1979. — 201p ; 18cm
Translation of: Doktor Med E. Werner. — Originally published: Henley-on-Thames : A. Ellis, 1979
ISBN 0-330-26430-3 (pbk) : £0.95 B81-17989

Konsalik, Heinz G.. The heart of the 6th Army / Heinz G. Konsalik ; tranlated from the German by Oliver Coburn. — London : Macdonald Futura, 1981, c1977. — 298p ; 18cm. — (A Futura book)
Translation of: Herz der 6. Armee. — Originally published: Walton-on-Thames : A. Ellis, 1977
ISBN 0-7088-1961-3 (pbk) : £1.25 B81-15635

Konsalik, Heinz G.. Highway to hell / Heinz G. Konsalik ; translated by Robert Vacha. — London : Macdonald Futura, 1981. — 235p ; 18cm. — (A Futura book)
Translation of: Die Rollbahn. — Originally published: Henley-on-Thames, A. Ellis, 1976
ISBN 0-7088-1965-6 (pbk) : £1.25 B81-15634

Konsalik, Heinz G.. The last Carpathian wolf / Heinz G. Konsalik ; translated from the German by Oliver Coburn. — London : Macdonald Futura, 1981, c1978. — 177p ; 18cm. — (A Futura book)
Translation of: Der letzte Karpaten Wolf. — Originally published: Henley on Thames : A. Ellis, 1978
ISBN 0-7088-2050-6 (pbk) : £1.10 B81-24410

Konsalik, Heinz G.. The last Carpathian wolf / Heinz G. Konsalik ; translated from the German by Oliver Coburn. — Large print ed. — Leicester : Ulverscroft, 1981, c1978. — 313p ; 23cm. — (Ulverscroft large print)
Translation of: Der letzte Karpaten Wolf. — Originally published: Henley-on-Thames : A. Ellis, 1978
ISBN 0-7089-0583-8 : £5.00 B81-11611

Konsalik, Heinz G.. The ravishing doctor / Heinz Konsalik ; translated by Anthea Bell. — London : Pan, 1981, c1979. — 217p ; 18cm
Translation of: Die schoene Aertzin. — Originally published: Henley-on-Thames : Ellis, 1980
ISBN 0-330-26433-8 (pbk) : £0.95 B81-24736

Konsalik, Heinz G.. The ravishing doctor. — Large print ed. — Anstey : Ulverscroft, Oct.1981. — [384]p. — (Ulverscroft large print series)
Translation of: Die schöne Ärztin. — Originally published: Henley-on-Thames: A. Ellis, 1980
ISBN 0-7089-0691-5 : £5.00 : CIP entry
B81-28099

Konsalik, Heinz G.. Strike force 10 / Heinz Konsalik ; translated from the German by Anthea Bell. — London : Macmillan, 1981. — 316p ; 23cm
Translation of: Sie waren Zehn
ISBN 0-333-30600-7 : £6.95 B81-21138

Konsalik, Heinz G.. Summer with Danica / Heinz Konsalik ; translated by Anthea Bell. — London : Pan, 1981, c1979. — 201p ; 18cm
Translation of: Ein Sommer mit Danica. — Originally published: Henley-on-Thames : A. Ellis, 1979
ISBN 0-330-26432-x (pbk) : £0.95 B81-24414

Palmer, Lilli. The red raven / Lilli Palmer. — Feltham : Hamlyn, 1981, c1978. — 265p ; 18cm
Translation of: Der rote Rabe. — Originally published: New York : Macmillan, 1978 ; London : W.H. Allen, 1979
ISBN 0-600-20133-3 (pbk) : £1.25 B81-11434

Palmer, Lilli. A time to embrace / Lilli Palmer ; translated by Carey Harrison. — London : Weidenfeld and Nicolson, 1980. — 342p ; 25cm
Translation of: Umarmen hat seine Zeit. — Originally published: New York : Macmillan, 1980
ISBN 0-297-77837-4 : £6.50 B81-00635

833'.914[F] — Fiction in German, *1945- — English texts* *continuation*

Palmer, Lilli. A time to embrace / Lilli Palmer ; translated by Carey Harrison. — London : Macdonald Futura, 1981. — 400p ; 18cm. — (A Futura book)
Translation of: Umarmen hat seine Zeit. — Originally published: New York : Macmillan, 1980 ; London : Weidenfeld and Nicolson, 1980
ISBN 0-7088-1982-6 (pbk) : £1.95 B81-40956

Paretti, Sandra. The magic ship / Sandra Paretti ; translated from the German by Ruth Hein. — London : New English Library, 1980, c1979 (1981 [printing]). — 350p ; 18cm
Translation of: Das Zauberschiff. — Originally published: New York : St. Martin's Press, 1979
ISBN 0-450-05188-9 (pbk) : £1.75 B81-28695

Paretti, Sandra. Maria Canossa. — London : Hodder & Stoughton, Feb.1982. — [308]p
ISBN 0-340-27449-2 : £6.95 : CIP entry B81-35684

Pešek, Luděk. Trap for Perseus / Ludek Pesek ; translated from the German by Anthea Bell. — Harmondsworth : Kestrel, 1981, c1980. — 168p ; 23cm
Translation of: Falle für Perseus. — Originally published: Scarsdale, N.Y. : Bradbury, 1980
ISBN 0-7226-5748-x : £4.95 B81-35145

Schneider, Rolf. November : a novel / by Rolf Schneider ; translated from the German by Michael Bullock. — London : Hamilton, 1981. — 235p ; 23cm
Translation of: November
ISBN 0-241-10347-9 : £7.95 : CIP rev. B80-07578

Wolf, Christa. A model childhood. — London : Virago, Feb.1982. — [408]p
Translation of: Kindheitsmuster
ISBN 0-86068-253-6 : £8.95 : CIP entry B81-36021

Wolf, Christa. The quest for Christa T.. — London : Virago, Feb.1982. — [192]p. — (Virago modern classics)
Translation of: Nachdenken über Christa T.
ISBN 0-86068-221-8 (pbk) : £2.95 : CIP entry B81-36025

Wölfel, Ursula. Shooting Star / Ursula Wölfel ; illustrated by Heiner Rothfuchs ; translated by Anthea Bell. — London : Andersen, 1979. — 93p : ill ; 21cm. — (Andersen young readers' library)
Translation of: Fliegender Stern
ISBN 0-905478-52-5 : £2.95 B81-09395

833'.914[F] — Fiction in German. Czechoslovak writers, *1945- — English texts*

Demetz, Hana. The house on Prague Street / Hana Demetz ; translated from the German by the author. — London : W.H. Allen, 1981, c1980. — 186p ; 18cm. — (A Star book)
Translation of: Ein Haus in Böhmen. — Originally published: 1980
ISBN 0-352-30780-3 (pbk) : £1.25 B81-28554

833'.914[J] — Children's short stories in German, *1945- — English texts*

Ecke, Wolfgang. [The case of the invisible witness]. The Magnet detective book 3 / Wolfgang Ecke ; illustrated by Rolf Rettich ; translated from the German by Stella and Vernon Humphries. — London : Magnet, 1980 (1981 [printing]). — 125p : ill ; 18cm
ISBN 0-416-21370-7 (pbk) : £0.90 B81-30101

833'.914[J] — Children's stories in German, *1945- — English texts*

Bolliger, Max. The king and the flute player / story by Max Bolliger ; illustrations by Jindra Capek. — London : Gollancz, 1981. — [25]p : col.ill ; 30cm
Translation from the German
ISBN 0-575-02950-1 : £3.95 B81-02521

Bolliger, Max. The shepherd's tune / written by Max Bolliger ; illustrated by Štěpán Zavřel. — London : Macdonald Futura, 1981. — [26]p : col.ill ; 30cm
Translation of: Das Hirtenlied
ISBN 0-354-08134-9 : £4.25 B81-29857

Bolliger, Max. A winter story / Max Bolliger ; illustrated by Beatrix Schären ; translated from the German by Anthea Bell. — Harmondsworth : Kestrel, 1976 (1980 printing). — [24]p : ill(some col.) ; 29cm
Translation of: Eine Wintergeschichte
ISBN 0-7226-5295-x : £4.50 B81-01353

Bröger, Achim. The happy dragon / Achim Bröger and Gisela Kalow ; English version by Olive Jones. — London : Methuen Children's Books, 1980. — [28]p : col.ill,2ports ; 24cm
Translation of: Ich War Einmal
ISBN 0-416-21050-3 : £3.50 B81-11149

Fuchshuber, Annegert. The joker and the lion / Annegert Fuchshuber ; translated by Gwen Marsh. — London : Dent, 1981. — [28]p : col.ill ; 24cm
Translation of: Fidibus
ISBN 0-460-06076-7 : £3.95 B81-11810

Gantschev, Ivan. The volcano / story and pictures by Ivan Gantschev. — London : Neugebauer, c1981. — [30]p : col.ill ; 29cm
Translation of: Ivan, der Vulkan
ISBN 0-907234-03-8 : £3.95 B81-12574

Gernhardt, Robert. A pig that is kind won't be left behind. — London : Cape, Oct.1981. — [32]p
ISBN 0-224-01973-2 : £4.50 : CIP entry B81-27394

Hann, Penelope. Edward the elephant / story by Penelope Hann ; illustrated by Dominique Leclaire. — London : Neugebauer, c1981. — [26]p : col.ill ; 22x29cm
Translation of: Eduard, der Elefant
ISBN 0-907234-04-6 : £3.95 B81-12575

Hauptmann, Tatjana. Adelina Schlime : a snail tale / Tatjana Hauptmann. — London : Ernest Benn, 1981. — 27p : chiefly col.ill ; 28cm
Translation of: Adelheid Schleim
ISBN 0-510-00105-x : £3.95 B81-11003

Heine, Helme. Mr Miller the dog / written and illustrated by Helme Heine. — London : Dent, 1980. — [56]p : col.ill ; 21cm
Translation of: Der Hund Herr Müller
ISBN 0-460-06057-0 : £3.50 B81-08013

Hellberg, Hans-Eric. Ben's lucky hat / Hans-Eric Hellberg ; illustrated by David Parkins ; translated by Patricia Crampton. — London : Methuen Children's Books, 1980. — 143p : ill ; 20cm. — (A Pied Piper book)
Translation of: Björn med Trollhatten
ISBN 0-416-87770-2 : £3.75 : CIP rev. B80-11656

Janosch. A letter for tiger / Janosch. — London : Anderson, 1981. — [47]p : col.ill ; 25cm
Translation of: Post für den Tiger
ISBN 0-905478-99-1 : £3.95 B81-18576

Kočí, Marta. Blackard / Marta Kočí. — London : Neugebauer, c1981. — [28]p : col.ill ; 29cm
Translation of: Schwarzack
ISBN 0-907234-02-x : £3.95 B81-12576

Lobe, Mira. The snowman who went for a walk : a story / by Mira Lobe ; illustrated by Winfried Opgenoorth ; and translated by Peter Carter. — Oxford : Oxford University Press, c1981. — [22]p : col.ill ; 29cm
Translation from the German
ISBN 0-19-279759-x : £3.95 : CIP rev. B81-22496

Manches, Marie-Hélène. The lonely rhinoceros / illustrated by Marie-Hélène Manches ; story by Patrick Barthélémi. — Oxford : Oxford University Press, c1980. — [24]p : col.ill ; 24x27cm
Translation of: Das kunterbunte Rhinozeros
ISBN 0-19-279754-9 : £3.95 B81-24822

Olden, Ingrid. The frog with pink glasses / Ingrid Olden. — London : Macdonald, 1981. — [26]p : chiefly col.ill ; 21x29cm
Translation of: Der Frosch mit der rosaroten Brille
ISBN 0-354-08133-0 : Unpriced B81-35380

Rettich, Margret. The voyage of the jolly boat / Margret Rettich ; English version by Olive Jones. — London : Methuen, 1981. — [32]p : col.ill ; 27cm
Translation of: Die Reise mit der Jolle
ISBN 0-416-30791-4 : Unpriced : CIP rev. B81-01354

Schaffer, Ulrich. Zilya's secret plan / Ulrich Schaffer ; illustrated by Takashi Shoji. — Tring : Lion, 1978 (1980 [printing]). — [31]p : col.ill ; 24cm
Translated from the German
ISBN 0-85648-086-x (cased) : Unpriced
ISBN 0-85648-338-9 (pbk) : £0.95 B81-13031

Scheffler, Ursel. The man with the tomato nose / story by Ursel Scheffler ; illustrated by Friedrich Kohlsaat ; [English version by Barbara Parray]. — Oxford : Oxford University Press, c1981. — [26]p : col.ill ; 29cm
Translated from the German
ISBN 0-19-279756-5 : £3.95 B81-17453

Uebe, Ingrid. Hurrah for Dizzy Lizzy! / Ingrid Uebe ; translated from the German by Stella and Vernon Humphries ; illustrated by Joan Beales. — London : Methuen Children's, 1980. — 143p : ill ; 21cm
Translation of: Lillekille
ISBN 0-416-88380-x : £4.50 : CIP rev. B80-13613

Ungerer, Tomi. Moon man / Tomi Ungerer. — London : Methuen Children's, 1980. — 39p : col.ill ; 32cm
Translation of: Der Mondmann. — Originally published: London : Whiting & Wheaton, 1966
ISBN 0-416-20670-0 : £4.50 B81-03055

Who are you afraid of-? / pictures by Hanne Türk ; translated by Oliver E. Gadsby after an idea by Christa Tauss. — London : Neugebauer, c1981. — [24]p : col.ill ; 22x29cm
Translation of: Wer fürchtet sich vor-?
ISBN 0-907234-01-1 : £3.95 B81-12573

833'.914[J] — Children's stories in German. Austrian writers, *1945- — English texts*

Nostlinger, Christine. Lollipop. — London : Andersen Press, Feb.1982. — [128]p. — (Andersen young readers' library)
Translation of: Lollipop
ISBN 0-86264-015-6 : £3.95 : CIP entry B81-36964

833'.914[J] — Children's stories in German. Swiss writers, *1945- — English texts*

Baumann, Kurt. Piro and the fire brigade. — London : Faber, Sept.1981. — [30]p
Translation of: Piro und die Feuerwehr
ISBN 0-571-11843-7 : £3.95 : CIP entry B81-22623

Nikly, Michelle. The princess on the nut. — London : Faber, Sept.1981. — [26]p
Translation of: Die Prinzessin auf der Nuss
ISBN 0-571-11846-1 : £3.95 : CIP entry B81-22624

837.8 — GERMAN SATIRE AND HUMOUR, 1856-1900

837'.8 — Satire in German. Tucholsky, Kurt - *Critical studies*

Grenville, Bryan P.. Kurt Tucholsky. — London : Oswald Wolff, 4une 1981. — [112]p. — (German literature and society ; v.1)
ISBN 0-85496-074-0 (pbk) : £4.00 : CIP entry
B81-10018

838.6 — GERMAN MISCELLANY, 1750-1830

838'.609 — German literature. Kleist, Heinrich von, *1803-1804 — Biographies*

Brown, H. M.. Kleist's 'lost' year and the quest for 'Robert Guiskard'. — Leamington Spa (2a Upper Grove St., Leamington Spa, Warwickshire, CV32 5AN) : James Hall, Oct.1981. — [128]p
ISBN 0-907471-02-1 (pbk) : £5.95 : CIP entry
B81-31238

838.912 — GERMAN MISCELLANY, 1900-1945

838'.91208 — Prose in German, *1900-1945 — English texts*

Walser, Robert. Selected shorter prose. — Manchester : Carcanet Press, Oct.1981. — [224]p
ISBN 0-85635-370-1 : £6.95 : CIP entry
B81-28848

838.914 — GERMAN MISCELLANY, 1945-

838'.91409 — German literature, *1945- — English texts*

Janosch. The big Janosch book of fun and verse / Janosch ; translated by Anthea Bell. — London : Andersen, 1980. — 125p : col.ill ; 28cm
Translation of: Die Maus hat rote Strümpfe an
ISBN 0-905478-87-8 : £6.50 B81-04478

839.09 — YIDDISH LITERATURE

839'.0913'08 — Poetry in Yiddish, *1860- — Anthologies — Polish texts*

Antologia poezji żydowskiej (1868-1968) / wybór, przekład i opracowanie Ewa Szepsa. — Londyn : Oficyna Poetów i Malarzy, 1980. — 368p ; 22cm
Unpriced (pbk) B81-31397

839'.0933[F] — Fiction in Yiddish, *1860- — English texts*

Singer, Isaac Bashevis. Gimpel the Fool and other tales / Isaac Bashevis Singer. — Harmondsworth : Penguin, 1981, c1957. — 174p ; 18cm
Translated from the Yiddish. — Originally published: New York : Noonday, 1957 ; London : Owen, 1958
ISBN 0-14-005176-7 (pbk) : £1.50 B81-35590

Singer, Isaac Bashevis. Satan in Goray / Isaac Bashevis Singer ; translated from the Yiddish by Jacob Sloan. — Harmondsworth : Penguin Books, 1981, c1958. — 158p ; 18cm
Translation of: ha-Satan be Gore. — Originally published: New York : Noonday Press, 1955 ; London : P. Owen, 1958
ISBN 0-14-005389-1 (pbk) B81-30698

Singer, Isaac Bashevis. Shosha / Isaac Bashevis Singer. — Harmondsworth : Penguin, 1979, c1978 (1980 [printing]). — 250p ; 19cm
Translated from the Yiddish MS. — Originally published: New York : Farrar, Strous and Giroux, 1978 ; London : Cape, 1979
ISBN 0-14-005390-5 (pbk) : £1.50 B81-03626

839'.0933[F] — Short stories in Yiddish, *1860- — English texts*

Singer, Isaac Bashevis. Old love / Isaac Bashevis Singer. — South Yarmouth, Ma. : Curley ; [Bolton-by-Bowland] : Magna Print [distributor], c1979. — viii,519p ; 23cm
Translation from the Yiddish. — Originally published: New York : Farrar, Straus & Giroux, 1979 ; London : Cape, 1980. — Published in large print
ISBN 0-89340-266-4 : £5.50 B81-03945

Singer, Isaac Bashevis. The Spinoza of Market Street / Isaac Bashevis Singer. — Harmondsworth : Penguin, 1981, c1961. — 190p ; 19cm
Originally published: New York : Farrar, Straus & Cudahy, 1961 : London : Secker & Warburg, 1962
ISBN 0-14-005175-9 (pbk) : £1.75 B81-27686

839.31 — DUTCH LITERATURE

839.3'1164 — Poetry in Dutch, *1945- — English texts*

Polet, Sybren. Xman / Sybren Polet ; translated by Peter Nijmeijer. — Deal, Kent : Transgravity, 1979. — [10]p ; 21cm
Translation of: Adam X
ISBN 0-85682-109-8 (pbk) : Unpriced
B81-16670

839.3'1364 — Fiction in Dutch, *1945- — Welsh texts*

Gijsen, Marnix. Galarnad Annes / Marnix Gijsen ; cyfieithiad o Klaaglied om Agnes gan Elin Garlick. — Abertawe : C. Davies, 1979. — 103p ; 19cm
ISBN 0-7154-0499-7 : £3.95 B81-17573

839.3'1364[F] — Fiction in Dutch, *1945- — English texts*

Mulisch, Harry. Two women / Harry Mulisch ; translated from the Dutch by Els Early. — London : John Calder, 1980. — 125p ; 23cm
Translation of: Twee vrouwen
ISBN 0-7145-3810-8 : £6.95 : CIP rev.
ISBN 0-7145-3839-6 (pbk) : £2.95 B80-06711

839.3'1364[J] — Children's short stories in Dutch, *1945- — English texts*

Kuijer, Guus. Daisy's new head / Guus Kuijer ; illustrated by Mance Post ; translated by Patricia Crampton. — Harmondsworth : Kestrel, 1980. — 105p : ill ; 21cm
Translation of: Met de Poppen Gooien
ISBN 0-7226-5571-1 : £3.95 B81-04674

839.3'1364[J] — Children's stories in Dutch, *1945- — English texts*

Biegel, Paul. The curse of the werewolf / Paul Biegel ; illustrated by Frank Rogers. — London : Blackie, 1981. — 143p : ill ; 23cm
Translation of: De vloek van woestewolf
ISBN 0-216-90992-9 : £5.25 : CIP rev.
B80-18535

Biegel, Paul. The tin can beast and other stories / Paul Biegel ; translated by Patricia Crampton ; illustration by Babs van Wely. — London (Kings Place, 329 Chiswick High Road, London W4) : Glover & Blair, 1980. — 165p : ill ; 21cm
Translated from the Dutch
ISBN 0-906681-05-7 : £4.95 B81-11004

Biegel, Paul. Virgil Nosegay and the cake hunt / Paul Biegel ; translated by Patricia Crampton ; illustrated by Babs van Wely. — London : Blackie, 1981. — 125p : ill ; 24cm
Translation of: Virgilius van Tuil op zoek naar een taart
ISBN 0-216-91088-9 : £4.95 : CIP rev.
B81-16890

Fossey, Koen. The mysterious railway / Koen Fossey. — London : Macdonald, 1981. — [24]p : chiefly col.ill ; 29cm
Translation of: Het spoortje in het bos
ISBN 0-354-08138-1 : £3.95 B81-35379

Schubert, Ingrid. The magic bubble trip / Ingrid and Dieter Schubert. — London : Hutchinson, 1981. — [27]p : col.ill ; 27cm
Translation of: Helemaal verkikkerd
ISBN 0-09-137780-3 : £3.95 B81-35278

839.3'18109 — Dutch literature, *to 1450 — English texts*

Hadewijch. Hadewijch : the complete works / translation and introduction by Mother Columba Hart ; preface by Paul Mommaers. — London : SPCK, 1981, c1980. — xxiv,412p ; 23cm. — (The Classics of Western spirituality)
Originally published: New York : Paulist Press, 1980. — Bibliography: p389-391. - Includes index
ISBN 0-281-03793-0 (pbk) : £8.50 B81-20783

839.36 — AFRIKAANS LITERATURE

839.3'6'09352 — Afrikaans literature. Special subjects: South Africa. Coloured persons — *Critical studies*

February, Venie A.. Mind your colour : the 'coloured' stereotype in South African literature / V.A. February. — London : Kegan Paul International, 1981. — viii,248p ; 23cm. — (Monographs from the African Studies Centre, Leyden)
Bibliography: p222-235. — Includes index
ISBN 0-7103-0002-6 : £10.50 B81-17259

839.3'635[F] — Fiction in Afrikaans, *1961- — English texts*

Joubert, Elsa. Poppie / Elsa Joubert. — London : Hodder and Stoughton, 1980. — 359p : 1map,1geneal.table ; 22cm
Translation of: Die Swerfjare van Poppie Nongena
ISBN 0-340-25047-x : £6.50 : CIP rev.
B80-08494

Joubert, Elsa. Poppie. — London : Hodder & Stoughton, Dec.1981. — [368]p
Translation of: Die swerfjare van Poppie Nongena. — Originally published: 1980
ISBN 0-340-27269-4 (pbk) : £1.25 : CIP entry
B81-31365

839.5 — SCANDINAVIAN LITERATURES

839'.6'08 — Old Norse literature — *Anthologies*

Gordon, E. V.. An introduction to Old Norse / by E.V. Gordon. — 2nd ed. / rev. by A.R. Taylor. — Oxford : Clarendon Press, 1981. — lxxxii,412p : ill,1map,1facsim ; 19cm
Old Norse text, English introduction and notes. — Previous ed.: 1927. — Includes index
ISBN 0-19-811184-3 (pbk) : £7.50 : CIP rev.
B81-06574

839'.68 — Prose in Old Norse — *English texts*

Orkneyinga saga : the history of the Earls of Orkney / translated with an introduction by Hermann Pàlsson and Paul Edwards. — Harmondsworth : Penguin, 1981, c1978. — 251p : 3maps,1geneal.table ; 18cm. — (Penguin classics)
Translated from the Icelandic. — Includes index
ISBN 0-14-044383-5 (pbk) : £1.95 B81-21014

839'.6991'008 — Poetry in Faeroese — *Anthologies — English texts*

Rocky shores : an anthology of Faroese poetry / compiled and translated from the Faroese and the Danish (William Heinesen), and with an introduction and notes on the poems by George Johnston. — Paisley (12 Townhead Terrace, Paisley, Renfrewshire PA1 2AX, Scotland) : Wilfion, 1981. — vi,124p ; 21cm. — (UNESCO collection of representative works. European series) (A Ronkon paperback)
Bibliography: p115-124
ISBN 0-905075-10-2 (pbk) : £4.00 B81-18507

839.7 — SWEDISH LITERATURE

839.7'172 — Poetry in Swedish, *1900-1945 — English texts*

Lundkvist, Artur. Agadir / by Artur Lundkvist ; translated and with a preface by William Jay Smith and Leif Sjöberg. — Chicago ; London : Ohio University Press, 1980, c1979. — xiii,55p : ill ; 24cm. — (International poetry series ; v.2)
Translation of: Agadir. — Originally published: Pittsburgh : International Poetry Forum, 1979
ISBN 0-8214-0444-x (cased) : £6.60
ISBN 0-8214-0561-6 (pbk) : £3.60 B81-14688

839.7'172'08 — Poetry in Swedish, *1900-1979 — Anthologies*

An **Anthology** of Swedish poetry from 1880 to the present day / edited by Irene Scobbie & Philip Holmes. — Hull : Department of Scandinavian Studies, University of Hull, 1980. — v,169p ; 30cm
Swedish text, English introduction. — Includes index
ISBN 0-85958-526-3 (spiral) : £1.00
B81-15644

839.7'1'74 — Poetry in Swedish, *1945- - English texts*

Aspenström, Werner. The blue whale & other pieces. — London (12 Stevenage Rd, SW6 6ES) : Oasis Books, July 1981. — [96]p
ISBN 0-903375-48-6 (pbk) : £1.80 : CIP entry B81-14401

839.7'174 — Poetry in Swedish, *1945- — English texts*

Edfelt, Johannes. Family tree and other prose poems. — London : Oasis, Sept.1981. — [20]p. — (O books series ; 4)
Translated from the Swedish
ISBN 0-903375-56-7 (pbk) : £0.60 : CIP entry B81-22604

Tranströmer, Tomas. Baltics / Tomas Tranströmer ; translated from the Swedish by Robin Fultan. — London : Oasis Books, 1980. — 17p : 1map ; 21cm
Translations of: Östersjöar
ISBN 0-903375-51-6 (pbk) : Unpriced : CIP rev. B80-14063

839.7'26 — Drama in Swedish, *1800-1900 — English texts*

Strindberg, August. Apologia and two folk plays / by August Strindberg ; translations and introductions by Walter Johnson. — Seattle ; London : University of Washington Press, c1981. — 225p,[4]p of plates : ill,music,1port ; 23cm. — (The Washington Strindberg)
Contents: The great highway. Translation of: Stora landsvägen — The crownbride. Translation of: Kronbruden — Swanwhite. Translation of: Svanevit
ISBN 0-295-95760-3 : £13.60 B81-38615

839.7'274 — Drama in Swedish, *1945- — English texts*

Adams-Ray, Bride. Noah's ark : and other sound and movement plays for the under-sevens / Bride Adams-Ray. — Pinner (125 Waxwell La., Pinner, Middx HA5 3ER) : Grail, 1981. — 71p ; 25cm
ISBN 0-901829-60-9 (pbk) : £2.00 B81-26445

Blunder, Bluebell, Baby and Birdie : a play for the ages of ten through fourteen / with music by Gunnar Edander ; translated by Catherine Enge and Peter Böök. — New York ; London : French, c1981. — 52p : 1plan ; 19cm
Two men, 2 women. — Translation of: Bellman, Blomman, Baby och Bruden
ISBN 0-573-65001-2 (pbk) : £2.25 B81-21052

839.7'36 — Fiction in Swedish. Söderberg, Hjalmar. Doktor Glas *— Critical studies*

Geddes, Tom. Hj. Söderberg, Doktor Glas / by Tom Geddes. — 2nd (rev.) ed. — Hull : Department of Scandinavian Studies, University of Hull, 1980, c1975. — 60p : 2maps ; 21cm. — (Studies in Swedish literature ; no.3)
Previous ed.: 1975. — Bibliography: p56-60
ISBN 0-85958-516-6 (pbk) : Unpriced B81-11697

839.7'374 — Children's stories in Swedish, *1945- — Welsh texts*

Bergström, Gunilla. Ifan Bifan a'i ffrind dirgel / Gunilla Bergström ; addasiad Cymraeg gan Juli Phillips ; ymgynghorwr iaith Elen Ogwen. — Caerdydd : Gwasg y Dref Wen, c1980. — [25]p : col.ill ; 24cm
Translation of: Alfons och hemlige Mallgan
£1.95 B81-04186

Bergström, Gunilla. Ifan Bifan a'r anghenfil / Gunilla Bergström ; addasiad Cymraeg gan Juli Phillips ; ymgynghorwr iaith Elen Ogwen. — Caerdydd : Gwasg y Dref Wen, c1980. — [28]p : col.ill ; 24cm
Translation of: Alfons och odjuret
£1.95 B81-04188

Bergström, Gunilla. Pwy all achub Ifan Bifan? / Gunilla Bergström ; addasiad Cymraeg gan Juli Phillips ; ymgynghorwr iaith Elen Ogwen. — Caerdydd : Gwasg y Dref Wen, c1980. — [25]p : col.ill ; 24cm
Translation of: Vem räddar Alfons Aberg?
£1.95 B81-04189

Bergström, Gunilla. Un cyfrwys wyt ti, Ifan Bifan! / Gunilla Bergström ; addasiad Cymraeg Juli Phillips ; ymgynghorwr iaith Elen Ogwen. — Caerdydd : Gwasg y Dref Wen, c1980. — [25]p : col.ill ; 24cm
Translation of: Listigt, Alfons Aberg!
£1.95 B81-04187

839.7'374 — Children's stories in Swedish. Jansson, Tove. Pappan och havet *— Critical studies*

Jones, W. Glyn. Tove Jansson : Pappan och havet / by Glyn Jones. — Hull (c/o Department of Scandinavian Studies, University of Hull) : Gavin Orton, c1979. — 38p ; 21cm. — (Studies in Swedish literature ; no.11)
Bibliography: p38
ISBN 0-85958-526-3 (pbk) : £0.30 B81-03657

839.7'374[J] — Children's stories in Swedish, *1945- — English texts*

Hägerström, Solveig. The journey to Fleecy Mountain / Solveig Hägerström ; translated from the Swedish by Particia Crampton ; illustrated by Joanna Carey. — London : Methuen Children's, 1980. — 174p : ill,1map ; 21cm
Translation of: Resan till Ulliga Bergen
ISBN 0-416-88270-6 : £4.50 : CIP rev. B80-19497

Lamerand, J.-P.. The queen of the whales / J.-P. Lamerand. — London : Kaye & Ward, 1981. — [32]p : col.ill ; 27cm
Translation from the Swedish?
ISBN 0-7182-3720-x : £3.50 B81-28579

Lindgren, Astrid. I want to go to school too / Astrid Lindgren ; illustrated by Ilon Wikland. — London : Methuen Children's Books, 1980. — [30]p : col.ill ; 27cm
Translation of: Jag vill också gå I skolan
ISBN 0-416-88990-5 : £3.75 : CIP rev. B80-10889

Lindgren, Astrid. Mardie to the rescue / Astrid Lindgren ; illustrated by Ilon Wikland ; translated by Patricia Crampton. — London : Methuen Children's, 1981. — 184p : ill ; 21cm
Translation of: Madicken och Junibackens Pims
ISBN 0-416-20650-6 : £4.95 B81-34908

Lindgren, Astrid. The six Bullerby children / Astrid Lindgren ; translated from the Swedish by Evelyn Ramsden ; illustrated by Ilon Wikland. — [London] : Magnet, 1980, c1963. — 91p : ill ; 20cm
Translation of: Alla vi barn i Bullerbyn. — Originally published: London : Methuen, 1963
ISBN 0-416-89500-x (pbk) : £0.85 B81-01355

Lindgren, Astrid. Springtime in Bullerby / Astrid Lindgren ; illustrated by Ilon Wikland ; translated by Patricia Crampton. — London : Methuen Children's Books, 1980. — [32]p : col.ill ; 22x29cm
Translation of: Vår i Bullerbyn
ISBN 0-416-88710-4 : £3.50 : CIP rev. B80-01883

Lindgren, Barbro. The wild baby / Barbro Lindgren, Eva Eriksson ; English text by Alison Winn. — London : Hodder and Stoughton, 1981. — [27]p : col.ill ; 27cm
Translation of: Mamman och den vilda Bebin
ISBN 0-340-26573-6 : £3.50 : CIP rev. B81-18179

Löfgren, Ulf. Hans Andersen's The Emperor's new clothes / Ulf Löfgren ; English version by Linda M. Jennings. — London : Hodder and Stoughton, 1980. — [26]p : col.ill ; 25x27cm
Translation from the Swedish. — Spine title: The Emperor's new clothes
ISBN 0-340-25676-1 : £3.50 : CIP rev. B80-24919

Löfgren, Ulf. Hans Andersen's The tinder box / Ulf Löfgren ; English version by Linda M. Jennings. — London : Hodder and Stoughton, 1980. — [26]p : col.ill ; 25x27cm
Translation from the Swedish. — Spine title: The tinder box
ISBN 0-340-25604-4 : £3.50 : CIP rev. B80-24920

Mählqvist, Stefan. Come into my night, come into my dream, / text, Stefan Mählqvist ; illustrations, Tord Nygren ; English translation and adaptation, Anthea Bell. — Leeds : Pepper, 1981. — 26p : chiefly col.ill ; 27cm
Translation from the Swedish
ISBN 0-560-74510-9 : £3.75 B81-28703

Pettersson, Allan Rune. Frankenstein's aunt / Allan Rune Pettersson ; translated by Joan Tate. — London : Hodder & Stoughton, 1980. — 125p ; 23cm
Translation of: Frankensteins faster
ISBN 0-340-24933-1 : £3.95 : CIP rev. B80-24904

Rydberg, Viktor. The Christmas tomten. — London : Hodder & Stoughton Children's Books, Aug.1981. — [32]p
ISBN 0-340-27065-9 : £3.50 : CIP entry B81-18031

839.81 — DANISH LITERATURE

839.8'136 — Children's stories in Danish, *1800-1900 — Welsh texts*

Andersen, H. C.. Y blwch tân / Hans Christian Andersen ; lluniau gan Ulf Löfgren. — Caerdydd : Gwasg y Dref Wen, c1980. — [28]p : col.ill ; 25x27cm
Translation of: Fyrtiet
£2.50 B81-04175

Andersen, H. C.. Dillad newydd yr Ymerawdwr / Hans Christian Andersen ; lluniau gan Ulf Löfgren. — Caerdydd : Gwasg y Dref Wen, c1980. — [28]p : col.ill ; 25x27cm
Translation of: Kejserens nye klaeder
£2.50 B81-04174

839.8'136[J] — Children's short stories in Danish, *1800-1900 — English texts*

Andersen, H. C.. Fairy tales of Hans Christian Andersen. — London : Hodder & Stoughton, Oct.1981. — [160]p
Translated from the Danish
ISBN 0-340-27025-x : £6.95 : CIP entry B81-28164

Andersen, H. C.. Hans Andersen's fairy tales : a new translation with introduction and notes / by Naomi Lewis ; illustrated by Philip Gough. — Harmondsworth : Puffin, 1981. — 174p : ill ; 18cm
Translations from the Danish
ISBN 0-14-030333-2 (pbk) : £0.95 B81-21332

839.8'136[J] — Children's stories in Danish, *1800-1900 — English texts*

Andersen, H. C.. The little mermaid. — London : Faber, Sept.1981. — [48]p
Translation of: Die kleine Seejungfrau
ISBN 0-571-11847-x : £4.95 : CIP entry B81-21496

Galdone, Paul. The steadfast tin soldier / [illustrated by] Paul Galdone ; story by Hans Christian Andersen. — Tadworth : World's Work Children's, 1981, c1979. — [32]p : col.ill ; 26cm
Originally published: Boston, Mass. : Houghton Mifflin, 1979
ISBN 0-437-23061-9 : £3.95 B81-14052

839.8'1372 — Fiction in Danish. Dinesen, Isak *— Correspondence, diaries, etc.*

Dinesen, Isak. Letters from Africa 1914-1931 / Isak Dinesen ; edited for the Rungstedlund Foundation by Frans Lasson ; translated by Anne Born. — London : Weidenfeld and Nicolson, c1981. — xli,474p,[56]p of plates : ill,ports ; 24cm
Translation of: Breve fra Afrika. — Includes index
ISBN 0-297-78000-x : £12.95 B81-36664

839.8'1374[F] — Fiction in Danish, *1945- — English texts*

Hassel, Sven. Blitzfreeze / Sven Hassel ; [translated from the Danish by Tim Bowie]. — London : Severn House, 1981, c1975. — 357p ; 21cm
Translation of: Jeg sa dem do. — Originally published: London : Corgi, 1975
ISBN 0-7278-0674-2 : £6.95 B81-09867

839.8′1374[F] — Fiction in Danish, *1945- — English texts* *continuation*

Hassel, Sven. Liquidate Paris / Sven Hassel ; translated from the French by Jean Ure. — London : Severn House, 1980, c1971. — 285p ; 21cm
Translation of: Liquidez Paris!
ISBN 0-7278-0667-x : £5.95 : CIP rev.
B80-18934

839.8′1374[J] — Children′s stories in Danish, *1945- — English texts*

Hansen, Hans. Jenny moves house / Hans Hansen ; illustrated by Svend Otto S ; English version by Joan Tate. — London : Pelham, 1981. — [26]p : col.ill ; 26cm
Translation of: Vi er flyett
ISBN 0-7207-1306-4 : £3.50 : CIP rev.
B81-03176

Holm, Anne. The hostage / Anne Holm ; translated from the Danish by Patricia Crampton. — London : Methuen, 1980. — 172p ; 21cm
Translation from the Danish MS
ISBN 0-416-88540-3 : £4.50 : CIP rev.
B80-19498

Mogensen, Jan. Just before dawn. — London : Hamilton, Feb.1982. — [32]p
Translated from the Danish
ISBN 0-241-10719-9 : £3.95 : CIP entry
B81-35819

Stage, Mads. The greedy blackbird / Mads Stage. — London : Burke, 1981. — [26]p : chiefly col.ill ; 27cm
ISBN 0-222-00808-3 : £3.95 B81-37439

Svend, Otto S.. Jon′s big day / Svend Otto S. ; translated by Joan Tate. — London : Pelham, 1980. — [26]p : col.ill ; 26cm
Translation of: Helgis store dag
ISBN 0-7207-1304-8 : £3.25 B81-08016

839.82 — NORWEGIAN LITERATURE

839.8′226 — Drama in Norwegian, *1800-1900 — English texts*

Ibsen, Henrik. Four major plays / Henrik Ibsen ; translated by James McFarlane and Jens Arup ; with an introduction by James McFarlane. — Oxford : Oxford University Press, 1981. — xviii ; 19cm. — (The World′s classics)
Bibliography: pxv-xvi. — Contents: A doll′s house / translated by James McFarlane. This translation originally published: 1961. Translation of: Et dukkehjem — Ghosts / translated by James McFarlane. This translation originally published: 1961. Translation of: Gengangere — Hedda Gabler / translated by Jens Arup. This translation originally published: 1966. Translation of: Hedda Gabler — The master builder / translated by James McFarlane. This translation originally published: 1966. Translation of: Bygmester Solness
ISBN 0-19-281568-7 (pbk) : £1.95 : CIP rev.
B81-31258

Ibsen, Henrik. The wild duck / by Henrik Ibsen ; a new version by Christopher Hampton. — New York ; London : French, c1980. — 131p ; 19cm
Translation of: Vildanden
ISBN 0-573-61820-8 (pbk) : £2.25 B81-37280

839.8′226 — Drama in Norwegian. Ibsen, Henrik *— Critical studies*

Ibsen and the theatre : essays in celebration of the 150th anniversary of Henrik Ibsen′s birth / edited by Errol Durbach. — London : Macmillan, 1980. — viii,144p : 1ill ; 23cm
Includes index
ISBN 0-333-28425-9 : £15.00 : CIP rev.
B80-03978

839.8′226 — Drama in Norwegian. Ibsen, Henrik. Dukkehjem, *Et — Study outlines*

King, Bruce, *1933-*. A doll′s house : notes / by Bruce King. — London : Longman, 1980. — 64p ; 21cm. — (York notes ; 85)
Bibliography: p56-57
ISBN 0-582-78156-6 (pbk) : £0.90 B81-17673

839.8′226 — Drama in Norwegian. Ibsen, Henrik. Gengangere *— Study outlines*

King, Adele. Ghosts : notes / by Adele King. — Harlow : Longman, 1981. — 64p ; 21cm. — (York notes ; 131)
Bibliography: p58
ISBN 0-582-78229-5 (pbk) : £0.90 B81-33694

839.8′2372[F] — Fiction in Norwegian, *1900-1945 — English texts*

Vesaas, Tarjei. The bleaching yard / Tarjei Vesaas ; translated from the Norwegian by Elizabeth Rokkan. — London : Peter Owen, 1981. — 156p ; 20cm. — (Unesco collection of representative works. Norwegian series)
Translation of: Bleikeplassen
ISBN 0-7206-0560-1 : £7.95 B81-38738

839.8′2374[F] — Fiction in Norwegian, *1945- — English texts*

Masterson, Louis. Harder than steel / Louis Masterson. — London : Corgi, 1979. — 141p ; 18cm
Translated from the Norwegian
ISBN 0-552-11046-9 (pbk) : £0.65 B81-09307

839.8′2374[J] — Children′s stories in Norwegian, *1945- — English texts*

Prøysen, Alf. Mrs Pepperpot′s busy day / story by Alf Prøysen ; illustrated by Björn Berg ; translated by Marianne Helweg. — Harmondsworth : Puffin, 1975, c1968 (1980 [printing]). — 32p : col.ill ; 18x23cm. — (Picture puffins)
Translation from the Norwegian
ISBN 0-14-050112-6 (pbk) : £0.80 B81-01356

839.83 — NEW NORSE LITERATURE

839.8′3172 — Poetry in New Norse: Poetry in Telemark dialects, *1900-1945 — English texts*

Vesaas, Tarjei. Evening. — London : Oasis, Sept.1981. — [16]p. — (O books series ; 3)
Translation of selections from Dikt i samling
ISBN 0-903375-57-5 : £0.60 : CIP entry
B81-23904

840 — ROMANCE LITERATURES

840.8′0354 — French literature. Women writers, *1100-1975.* **Special themes: Love** *— Anthologies — English texts*

Sullerot, Evelyne. Women on love : eight centuries of feminine writing / Evelyne Sullerot ; translated by Helen R. Lane. — London (90 Great Russell St., WC1B 3PY) : Norman, 1980. — xi,334p : ill ; 24cm
Translation of: Histoire et mythologie de l′amour. — Originally published: Garden City, N.Y. : Doubleday, 1979. — Includes index
ISBN 0-906908-13-2 (cased) : £8.50 : CIP rev.
ISBN 0-906908-24-8 (pbk) : Unpriced
B80-08499

840.9 — FRENCH LITERATURE. HISTORY AND CRITICAL STUDIES

840.9 — French literature, *1800-1970 — Critical studies — Festschriften*

Literature and society : studies in nineteenth and twentieth century French literature : presented to R.J. North / edited by C.A. Burns. — Birmingham (Cardigan St, Birmingham) : Published for the University of Birmingham by John Goodman & Sons (Printers) Limited, 1980. — vii,247p : 1port ; 22cm
ISBN 0-7044-0413-3 : Unpriced B81-38473

840′.9 — French literature - *Critical studies*

Barthes, Roland. A Barthes reader. — London : Cape, June 1981. — [450]p
ISBN 0-224-01944-9 : £12.50 : CIP entry
B81-11939

840.9 — French literature. Criticism. Baudelaire, Charles *— Critical studies*

Lloyd, Rosemary. Baudelaire′s literary criticism. — Cambridge : Cambridge University Press, Dec.1981. — [350]p
ISBN 0-521-23552-9 : £29.50 : CIP entry
B81-31830

840.9′007 — French literature, *1815-1900 — Critical studies*

Fairlie, Alison. Imagination and language : collected essays on Constant, Baudelaire, Nerval and Flaubert / Alison Fairlie ; edited by Malcolm Bowie. — Cambridge : Cambridge University Press, 1981. — xi,47p : ill,facsims,ports ; 23cm
Bibliography: p461-470. — Includes index
ISBN 0-521-23291-0 : £30.00 B81-35600

840′.9′008 — French literature, *1848-1971.* **Influence of Whitman, Walt**

Erkkila, Betsy. Walt Whitman among the French : poet and myth / Betsy Erkkila. — Princeton ; Guildford : Princeton University Press, 1980. — x,296p ; 23cm
Bibliography: p275-285. — Includes index
ISBN 0-691-06426-1 : £9.10
Primary classification 811′.3 B81-08250

840.9′00912 — French literature, *1900- — Critical studies*

Robinson, Christopher. French literature : in the twentieth century / Christopher Robinson. — Newton Abbot : David & Charles, c1980. — 288p ; 23cm. — (Comparative literature)
Bibliography: p284-285. - Includes index
ISBN 0-7153-8076-1 : £10.50 : CIP rev.
B80-21156

840.9′142 — French literature. Classicism *— Critical studies — French texts*

Mourgues, Odette de. Quelques paradoxes sur le classicisme / by Odette de Mourgues. — Oxford : Clarendon Press, 1981. — 15p ; 22cm. — (The Zaharoff lecture ; 1980-1)
ISBN 0-19-951531-x (pbk) : £1.95 : CIP rev.
B81-25115

840.9′96 — French literature. African writers, *1945- — Critical studies*

Irele, Abiola. The African experience in literature and ideology / Abiola Irele. — London : Heinemann, 1981. — 216p ; 22cm. — (Studies in African literature)
Includes index
ISBN 0-435-91630-0 (cased) : Unpriced
ISBN 0-435-91631-9 (pbk) : £5.95
Primary classification 820.9′96 B81-31963

Irele, Abiola. The African experience in literature and ideology. — London : Heinemann Educational, Sept.1981. — [224]p. — (Studies in African literature)
ISBN 0-435-91631-9 (pbk) : £5.95 : CIP entry
Primary classification 820.9′96 B81-22601

Moore, Gerald, *1924-*. Twelve African writers / Gerald Moore. — London : Hutchinson University Library for Africa, 1980. — 327p ; 23cm
Bibliography: p301-317. - Includes index
ISBN 0-09-141850-x (cased) : £12.00 : CIP rev.
ISBN 0-09-141851-8 (pbk) : £4.95
Primary classification 820.9′96 B80-09364

840.9′96 — French literature. African writers, *1945- — Critical studies — Serials*

African literature today. — 11. — London : Heinemann, 1980
No.11: Myth and history. — Sept. 1980. — 231p
ISBN 0-435-91651-3 : Unpriced : CIP rev.
ISBN 0-435-91652-1 (pbk) : £4.50
Primary classification 820.9′96 B80-12488

African literature today. — London : Heinemann Educational
No.12: New writing, new approaches. — Oct.1981. — [224]p
ISBN 0-435-91648-3 (cased) : £9.95 : CIP entry
ISBN 0-435-91649-1 (pbk) : £4.95
Primary classification 820.9′96 B81-28035

840.9′9714 — French literature. Quebec *(Province)* **writers,** *to 1980 — Critical studies*

May, Cedric. Breaking the silence : the literature of Québec / by Cedric May. — [Birmingham] : University of Birmingham, Regional Canadian Studies Centre, 1981. — 186p ; 30cm
Includes 10 poems and extracts from Refus global in French. — Includes bibliographies and index
ISBN 0-7044-0515-6 (spiral) : Unpriced
B81-28878

841.1 — FRENCH POETRY, TO 1400

841′.1 — Poetry in Franco-Italian — *Texts*

The **Franco-Italian** Roland (V4) / edited by Geoffrey Robertson-Mellor. — Salford (Salford M5 4WT) : University of Salford, Department of Modern Languages, 1980. — xxxii,296p ; 30cm
Franco-Italian text and English introduction and notes
Unpriced (spiral) B81-26244

841′.1 — Poetry in Old French. Chrétien, *de Troyes* — *Critical studies*

Topsfield, L. T.. Chrétien de Troyes : a study of the Arthurian romances / L.T. Topsfield. — Cambridge : Cambridge University Press, 1981. — 367p ; 23cm
Bibliography: p341-351. — Includes index
ISBN 0-521-23361-5 : £27.50 : CIP rev.
B81-06039

841′.1 — Poetry in Old French — *Old French-English parallel texts*

Fantosme, Jordan. Jordan Fantosme's Chronicle / edited with an introduction, translation and notes [by] R.C. Johnston. — Oxford : Clarendon, 1981. — liv,214p,[1]leaf of plates : 1facsim, ; 23cm
Parallel Anglo-Norman text and English translation. — Bibliography: pliii-liv
ISBN 0-19-815758-4 : £20.00 : CIP rev.
B80-02236

841.3 — FRENCH POETRY, 1500-1600

841′.3 — Poetry in French, *1500-1600* — *Texts*

Matthieu, Pierre. Tablettes de la vie et de la mort / Pierre Matthieu ; edition critique par C.N. Smith. — [Exeter] : University of Exeter, 1981. — xxii,60p : ill ; 21cm. — (Textes littéraires, ISSN 0309-6998 ; 40)
Bibliography: pxxi-xxii
ISBN 0-85989-196-8 (pbk) : Unpriced
B81-19440

841′.3 — Poetry in French. Ronsard, Pierre de — *Critical studies*

Quainton, Malcolm. Ronsard's ordered chaos : visions of flux and stability in the poetry of Pierre de Ronsard / Malcolm Quainton. — Manchester : Manchester Univeristy Press, c1980. — 252p ; 24cm
Bibliography: p227-235. - Includes index
ISBN 0-7190-0760-7 : £17.50 : CIP rev.
B79-32127

841.8 — FRENCH POETRY, 1848-1900

841′.8 — Poetry in French, *1848-1900* — *French-English parallel texts*

Rimbaud, Arthur. Une saison en Enfer = A season in Hell ; Les illuminations = The illuminations / Arthur Rimbaud ; a new translation by Enid Rhodes Peschel. — New York ; London : Oxford University Press, 1974, c1973 (1979 [printing]). — vii,181p : ill,1facsim,ports ; 21cm
Parallel French text and English translation. — Originally published: New York ; London : Oxford University Press, 1973. — Includes index
ISBN 0-19-501760-9 (pbk) : £1.75 B81-40782

841′.8 — Poetry in French. Baudelaire, Charles — *Biographies*

Hyslop, Lois Boe. Baudelaire : man of his time / Lois Boe Hyslop. — New Haven ; London : Yale University Press, c1980. — xviii,207p ; 22cm
Includes index
ISBN 0-300-02513-0 : £10.40 : CIP rev.
B80-22647

841′.8 — Poetry in French. Mallarmé, Stéphane — *Critical studies*

Bersani, Leo. The death of Stéphane Mallarmé. — Cambridge : Cambridge University Press, Feb.1982. — [112]p. — (Cambridge studies in French)
ISBN 0-521-23863-3 : £9.95 : CIP entry
B81-36240

841′.8 — Poetry in French. Rimbaud, Arthur — *Critical studies*

Hackett, C. A.. Rimbaud : a critical introduction / C.A. Hackett. — Cambridge : Cambridge University Press, 1981. — x,167p ; 23cm. — (Major European authors)
Bibliography: p162-163. — Includes index
ISBN 0-521-22976-6 (cased) : £17.50
ISBN 0-521-29756-7 (pbk) : £5.95 B81-25926

841′.8′08 — Poetry in French, *1848-1900* — *Anthologies* — *Welsh texts*

Beirdd simbolaidd Ffrainc / [cyfieithwyd gan] Euros Bowen. — Caerdydd : Gwasg Prifysgol Cymru ar ran yr Academi Gymreig, 1980. — vii,81p ; 21cm. — (Cyfres barddoniaeth Pwyllgor Cyfieithiadau yr Academi Gymreig ; cyf.1)
ISBN 0-7083-0731-0 (pbk) : £2.95 : CIP rev.
B80-05118

841.912 — FRENCH POETRY, 1900-1945

841′.912 — Poetry in French, *1900-1945* — *French-English parallel texts*

Apollinaire, Guillaume. Caligrammes : poems of peace and war (1913-1916) / Guillaume Apollinaire ; translated by Anne Hyde Greet with an introduction by S.I. Lockerbie and commentary by Anne Hyde Greet and S.I. Lockerbie. — Berkeley ; London : University of California Press, c1980. — xii,513p ; 25cm
Parallel French text and English translation, English introduction and notes. — Bibliography: p509-513
ISBN 0-520-01968-7 : £12.00 B81-12692

Eluard, Paul. Last love poems of Paul Eluard / translated with an introduction, by Marilyn Kallet. — Bilingual ed. — Baton Rouge ; London : Louisiana State University Press, c1980. — xxiii,91p ; 24cm
Parallel French text and English translation
ISBN 0-8071-0681-x : £7.20 B81-01770

841′.912 — Poetry in French. Apollinaire, Guillaume. Interpersonal relationships with Playden, Annie

Adlard, John. One evening of light mist in London : the story of Annie Playden and Guillaume Apollinaire / by John Adlard. — Edinburgh : Tragara, 1980. — 33p,[2]leaves of plates : ill,ports ; 23cm
Limited ed.: of 145 numbered copies
Unpriced (pbk)
Also classified at 942.083′092′4 B81-14745

841.914 — FRENCH POETRY, 1945-

841′.914 — Poetry in French, *1945-* — *Texts*

Michael-Titus, C.. Moires de ciel / C. Michael Titus ; illustrés par Ionas. — London : Panopticum, 1981. — 45p : ill ; 20cm
ISBN 0-9504138-8-7 (pbk) : Unpriced
B81-20695

842 — FRENCH DRAMA

842′.0512′09 — Drama in French, *1600-1715.* **Tragedies** — *Critical studies*

Gossip, C. J.. An introduction to French classical tragedy / C.J. Gossip. — London : Macmillan, 1981. — 193p ; 22cm
Includes index
ISBN 0-333-26168-2 : £15.00 B81-38723

842.3 — FRENCH DRAMA, 1500-1600

842′.3 — Drama in French, *1500-1600* — *Texts*

[Biblioteca Capitular Colombina. Manuscript. 15-2-1]. Le Mystère de Sainte Venice / texte établi et présenté par Graham A. Runnalls. — [Exeter] : University of Exeter, 1980. — xxii,38p ; 21cm. — (Textes littéraires, ISSN 0309-6998 ; 38)
Bibliography: pxxi-xxii
ISBN 0-85989-186-0 (pbk) : Unpriced
B81-13340

842.4 — FRENCH DRAMA, 1600-1715

842′.4 — Drama in French, *1600-1715* — *Texts*

Crébillon, Prosper Jolyot de. Electre / Prosper Jolyot de Crébillon ; edition critique par John Dunkley. — [Exeter] : University of Exeter, 1980. — lxii,66p : ill,2facsims ; 21cm. — (Textes littéraires, ISSN 0309-6998 ; 39)
Bibliography: p64-66
ISBN 0-85989-191-7 (pbk) : £2.00 B81-21257

Dancourt, Florent Carton. Le chevalier à la mode / Florent Carton Dancourt ; edition critique par Robert H. Crawshaw. — [Exeter] ([Northcote House, The Queen's Drive, Exeter, EX4 4QJ]) : University of Exeter, 1980. — xxxii,98p : ill,music,1port ; 21cm. — (Textes littéraires, ISSN 0309-6998 ; 37)
Bibliography: pxxx-xxxii
ISBN 0-85989-101-1 (pbk) : £2.00 B81-11327

842′.4 — Drama in French. Corneille, Pierre. Horace — *Critical studies*

Knight, R. C.. Corneille, Horace / R.C. Knight. — London : Grant & Cutler, 1981. — 80p ; 20cm. — (Critical guides to French texts ; 4)
Bibliography: p76-80
ISBN 0-7293-0094-3 (pbk) : Unpriced
B81-31756

842′.4 — Drama in French. Molière — *Critical studies*

Grene, Nicholas. Shakespeare, Jonson, Molière : the comic contract / Nicholas Grene. — London : Macmillan, 1980. — xvii,246p ; 23cm
Bibliography: p235-242. — Includes index
ISBN 0-333-23308-5 : £15.00 : CIP rev.
Primary classification 822′.0523′09 B80-02541

842′.4 — Drama in French. Racine, Jean. Mithridate — *Critical studies*

O'Regan, M. J.. The mannerist aesthetic : a study of Racine's Mithridate / Michael O'Regan. — [Bristol] : University of Bristol, c1980. — 95p : ill,1port ; 22cm
Bilbiography: p93-95
ISBN 0-906515-76-9 (pbk) : £3.75 B81-10410

842′.4 — Drama in French. Racine, Jean. Tragedies. Style — *Critical studies*

Flowers, Mary Lynne. Sentence structure and characterization in the tragedies of Jean Racine : a computer-assisted study / Mary Lynne Flowers. — Rutherford : Fairleigh Dickinson University Press ; London : Associated University Presses, c1979. — 223p ; 23cm
Bibliography: p216-220. — Includes index
ISBN 0-8386-2056-6 : Unpriced B81-35327

842.5 — FRENCH DRAMA, 1715-1789

842′.5 — Drama in French, *1715-1789* — *Texts*

Voltaire. Thérèse : a fragment / Voltaire ; edited with an introduction by Desmond Flower. — Cambridge : [D. Flower], 1981. — 20p,[8]p of plates : facsims ; 29cm
French text, English introduction
Private circulation B81-36190

842.8 — FRENCH DRAMA, 1848-1900

842′.8 — Drama in French, *1848-1900* — *English texts*

Rostand, Edmond. Cyrano de Bergerac : an heroic comedy in five acts / by Edmond Rostand ; translated into English verse by Brian Hooker ; prepared for Walter Hampden. — Toronto ; London : Bantam, 1950, c1951 (1981 [printing]). — 195p ; 18cm. — (A Bantam classic)
ISBN 0-553-21030-0 (pbk) : £0.85 B81-39109

842.912 — FRENCH DRAMA, 1900-1945

842′.912 — Drama in French, *1900-1945 — English texts*

Sartre, Jean-Paul. Altona ; Men without shadows ; The flies / Jean-Paul Sartre. — Harmondsworth : Penguin in association with Hamilton, 1962 (1981 [printing]). — 316p ; 20cm
Altona / translated by Sylvia and George Leeson. This translation originally published: London : Hamilton, 1960. Translation of: Les séquestres d′Altona — Men without shadows / translated by Kitty Black. This translation originally published: London : Hamilton, 1949. Translation of: Morts sans sépulture — The flies / translated by Stuart Gilbert. This translation originally published: London : Hamilton, 1946. Translation of: Les mouches
ISBN 0-14-048014-5 (pbk) : £2.95 B81-37250

842′.912 — Drama in French, *1900-1945 — Texts*

Pagnol, Marcel. Topaze : pièce en quatre actes / Marcel Pagnol ; edited with an introduction and notes by David Coward. — London : Harrap, 1981, c1930. — xlvii,155p : 1port ; 20cm. — (Modern world literature series)
Ten men, 7 women, supers. — French text, English introduction and notes
ISBN 0-245-53370-2 (pbk) : £2.95 B81-32062

842′.912 — Drama in French. Anouilh, Jean — *Critical studies*

McIntyre, H. G.. The theatre of Jean Anouilh / H.G. McIntyre. — London : Harrap, 1981. — 165p : 1port ; 23cm
Bibliography: p157-162. — Includes index
ISBN 0-245-53221-8 : £5.50 B81-25922

842.914 — FRENCH DRAMA, 1945-

842′.914 — Drama in French, *1945- — English texts*

Obaldia, René de. Obaldia plays. — London : John Calder
Translated from the French
Vol.3. — Jan.1982. — [256]p
ISBN 0-7145-3559-1 (pbk) : £4.95 : CIP entry B81-33835

Sarraute, Nathalie. Collected plays / Nathalie Sarraute ; translated from the French by Maria Jolas and Barbara Wright. — London : Calder, 1980. — 107p ; 21cm
Translation of: Théâtre. — Contents: It is there — its beautiful — Izzum — The lie — Silence
ISBN 0-7145-3713-6 (pbk) : £4.95 B80-00927

842′.914 — Drama in French. Planchon, Roger — *Critical studies*

Daoust, Yvette. Roger Planchon : director and playwright / Yvette Daoust. — Cambridge : Cambridge University Press, 1981. — xi,252p : ill,1port ; 24cm
Bibliography: p240-243
ISBN 0-521-23414-x : £18.50
Primary classification 792′.0233′0924
B81-24764

843 — FRENCH FICTION

843 — Fiction in French. Cameroon writers. Oyono, Ferdinand. Vieux nègre et la médaille — *Study outlines*

Oyono, Ferdinand. The old man and the medal / Ferdinand Oyono. — Harlow : Longman, 1981. — vii,40p ; 20cm. — (Longman guides to literature)
ISBN 0-582-65074-7 (pbk) : £0.70 B81-32979

843 — Fiction in French. Guinean writers. Laye, Camara — *Critical studies*

King, Adele. The writings of Camara Laye / Adele King. — London : Heinemann, [1980]. — 132p ; 23cm. — (Studies in African literature)
Bibliography: p126-128. — Includes index
ISBN 0-435-91680-7 (cased) : £7.50
ISBN 0-435-91681-5 (pbk) : £3.90 B81-30783

843 — Fiction in French. Guinean writers. Laye, Camara. Enfant noir — *Study outlines*

Dibba, Ebou. Camara Laye The African child / Ebou Dibba. — Harlow : Longman, 1980. — ix,49p ; 20cm. — (Longman guides to literature)
ISBN 0-582-65076-3 (pbk) : £0.70 B81-06008

843[F] — Fiction in French. Algerian writers, *1960- — English texts*

Kourouma, Ahmadou. The suns of independence / Ahmadou Kourouma ; translated from the French by Adrian Adams. — London : Heinemann, 1981. — vii,136p ; 19cm. — (African writers series ; 239)
Translation of: Les soleils des indépendances
ISBN 0-435-90239-3 (pbk) : £2.50 : CIP rev. B80-32556

843[F] — Fiction in French. Guadelopean writers — *English texts*

Schwarz-Bart, Simone. The bridge of beyond. — London : Heinemann Educational Books, Nov.1981. — [192]p. — (Caribbean writers series ; 27)
Translation of: Pluie et vent sur Télumée miracle
ISBN 0-435-98770-4 (pbk) : £1.95 : CIP entry B81-31163

843[F] — Fiction in French. Guinean writers, *1960- — English texts*

Fantouré, Alioum. Tropical circle / Alioum Fantouré ; adapted into English by Dorothy S. Blair. — Harlow : Longman, 1981. — 259p ; 19cm. — (Longman drumbeat ; 28)
Translation of: Le cercle des tropiques
ISBN 0-582-64282-5 (pbk) : £1.60 B81-39337

843[F] — Fiction in French. Guinean writers, *to 1960 — English texts*

Laye, Camara. The guardian of the word : Kouma Lafôlô Kouma / Camara Laye ; translated from the French by James Kirkup. — London : Fontana, 1980. — 223p ; 18cm
Translation of: Le maître de la parole
ISBN 0-00-615946-x (pbk) : £1.35 B81-10218

843[F] — Fiction in French. Martinique writers, *1945- — English texts*

Zobel, Joseph. Black shack alley / Joseph Zobel ; translated and introduced by Keith Q. Warner. — London : Heinemann, 1980. — 182p ; 19cm. — (Caribbean writers series ; 21)
Translation of: La rue cases-nègres
ISBN 0-435-98800-x (pbk) : £1.90 : CIP rev. B80-13114

843[F] — Fiction in French. Senegalese writers, *1960- — English texts*

Fall, Aminata Sow. The beggar′s strike, or, The dregs of society / Aminata Sow Fall ; translated by Dorothy S. Blair. — Harlow : Longman, 1981. — 99p ; 18cm. — (Drumbeat ; 31)
Translation of: La Grève des bàttu
ISBN 0-582-78530-8 (pbk) : £1.25 B81-32095

843′.009 — Fiction in French, *1700-1800 — Critical studies*

Mylne, Vivienne. The eighteenth-century French novel. — 2nd ed. — Cambridge : Cambridge University Press, Nov.1981. — [292]p
Previous ed.: Manchester : Manchester University Press, 1965
ISBN 0-521-23864-1 (cased) : £19.50 : CIP entry
ISBN 0-521-28266-7 (pbk) : £6.95 B81-31261

843′.01′0896[FS] — Short stories in French. African writers, *1945- — Anthologies — English texts*

Jazz and palm wine : and other stories / edited with an introduction by Willfried F. Feuser. — Harlow : Longman, 1981. — 214p ; 18cm. — (Drumbeat ; 33)
ISBN 0-582-64248-5 (pbk) : £1.60 B81-39833

843.4 — FRENCH FICTION, 1600-1715

843′.4[F] — Fiction in French, *1600-1715 — English texts*

La Fayette, *Madame de.* The Princesse de Clèves / Madame de Lafayette ; translated by Nancy Mitford. — Rev. ed., repr. with further revisions / by Leonard Tancock. — Harmondsworth : Penguin, 1978, c1962 (1980 [printing]). — 204p ; 19cm. — (Penguin classics)
Translation of: La Princesse de Clèves. — Previous ed.: London : Euphorion Books, 1950. — Bibliography: p203-204
ISBN 0-14-044337-1 (pbk) : £1.50 B81-10989

843′.4[J] — Children′s stories in French, *1600-1715 — English texts*

Perrault, Charles. Cinderella, or, The little glass slipper / Charles Perrault ; illustrated by Errol Le Cain. — Harmondsworth : Puffin, 1978, c1972 (1981 [printing]). — [32]p : ill(some col.) ; 18x23cm. — (Picture puffins)
Originally published: London : Faber, 1972
£0.90 (pbk) B81-15365

843.5 — FRENCH FICTION, 1715-1789

843′.5 — Fiction in French, *1715-1789 — Texts*

Hilliard d′Auberteuil, M.. Miss Mac Rea / Hilliard d′Auberteuil. — New York ; London : Garland, 1978. — 243p in various pagings ; 19cm. — (The Garland library of narratives of North American Indian captivities ; v.16)
Facsimile reprints. - Contents: Miss Mac Rea / Hilliard d′Auberteuil, Originally published: Philadelphia : s.n., 1784 - Narrative of Mrs. Scott and Capt. Stewart′s captivity 1786. Originally published: S.l. : s.n., 1786 - A Remarkable narrative of the captivity and escape of Mrs. Frances Scott 1799. Originally published: S.n. : s.n., 1799 - A Remarkable narrative of the captivity and escape of Mrs. Frances Scott 1800. Originally published: S.l. : Whitcome, 1800 - A premarkable narrative of the captivity and escape of Mrs. Frances Scott. Originally published: Leominster : s.n, 1811
ISBN 0-8240-1640-8 : £40.00 B81-15270

843′.5[F] — Fiction in French, *1715-1789 — English texts*

Voltaire. Candide / by Voltaire ; translated by Lowell Bair ; with an appreciation by André Maurois ; illustrations by Sheilah Beckett. — Toronto ; London : Bantam, 1959 (1981 [printing]). — 122p : ill ; 18cm. — (A Bantam classic)
ISBN 0-553-21028-9 (pbk) : £0.85 B81-39108

843.7 — FRENCH FICTION, 1815-1848

843′.7 — Fiction in French. Balzac, Honoré de. Cousine Bette — *Critical studies*

Bellos, David. Honoré de Balzac, la cousine Bette / David Bellos. — London : Grant & Cutler, 1980. — 94p ; 20cm. — (Critical guides to French texts ; 1)
Bibliography: p93-94
ISBN 0-7293-0092-7 (pbk) : £1.80 B81-17021

843′.7 — Fiction in French. Sand, George. Interpersonal relationships with Turgenev, I. S., *1845-1870*

Waddington, Patrick. Turgenev and George Sand : an improbable entente / Patrick Waddington. — London : Macmillan, 1981. — 176p,[8]p of plates : ill,ports ; 23cm
Bibliography: p133-139. — Includes index
ISBN 0-333-29147-6 : £12.00
Primary classification 891.73′3 B81-15673

843′.7 — Short stories in French, *1815-1848 — Texts*

Mérimée, Prosper. Carmen et autres nouvelles choisies : Mateo Falcone, Tamango, La Vénus d′Ille / Prosper Mérimée ; edited by M.J. Tilby. — London : Harrap, 1981. — 176p : 1port ; 22cm
French text, English introduction and notes. — Bibliography: p45-46
ISBN 0-245-53546-2 (pbk) : £2.95 B81-29284

843′.7[F] — Fiction in French, *1815-1848 — English texts*

Gautier, Théophile. Mademoiselle de Maupin / Théophile Gautier ; translated with an introduction by Joanna Richardson. — Harmondsworth : Penguin, 1981. — 347p ; 18cm. — (Penguin classics)
Translation of: Mademoiselle de Maupin
ISBN 0-14-044398-3 (pbk) : £2.25 B81-11029

843.8 — FRENCH FICTION, 1848-1900

843′.8 — Fiction in French, *1848-1900 — English texts — Texts with commentaries*

Flaubert, Gustave. [La tentation de Saint Antoine. English]. The temptation of Saint Antony / Gustave Flaubert ; translated with an introduction and notes by Kitty Mrosovsky. — London : Secker & Warburg, 1980. — 293p,[8]p of plates : ill ; 23cm
Translation of: La tentation de Saint Antione
ISBN 0-436-15998-8 : £10.00 B81-05575

843'.8 — Fiction in French. Flaubert, Gustave, *1830-1857 — Correspondence, diaries, etc.*

Flaubert, Gustave. The letters of Gustave Flaubert 1830-1857. — London : Faber, Sept.1981. — [270]p
ISBN 0-571-11814-3 : £3.50 : CIP entry
B81-21463

843'.8 — Fiction in French. Flaubert, Gustave — *Critical studies — French texts*

Flaubert. — Manchester : Manchester University Press, Jan.1982. — [280]p
ISBN 0-7190-0842-5 (pbk) : £7.50 : CIP entry
B81-34553

843'.8 — Short stories in French, *1848-1900 — Texts*

Flaubert, Gustave. Trois contes de jeunesse / Gustave Flaubert ; edition critique par T.A. Unwin. — [Exeter] : University of Exeter, 1981. — xxi,76p : 1facsim,1port ; 21cm. — (Textes littéraires, ISSN 0309-6998 ; 41)
Bibliography: pxxi
ISBN 0-85989-102-x (pbk) : Unpriced
B81-29230

843'.8[F] — Fiction in French, *1848-1900 — English texts*

Flaubert, Gustave. Madame Bovary / by Gustave Flaubert ; translated by Lowell Blair ; edited and with an introduction by Leo Bersani. — Toronto ; London : Bantam, 1959, c1972 (1981 [printing]). — 424p : ill ; 18cm. — (A Bantam classic)
Bibliography: p421-424
ISBN 0-553-21033-5 (pbk) : £1.00 B81-39112

Flaubert, Gustave. Madame Bovary. — Oxford : Oxford University Press, Nov.1981. — [384]p. — (The World's classics)
ISBN 0-19-281564-4 (pbk) : £1.95 : CIP entry
B81-30514

Maupassant, Guy de. Une vie / Guy de Maupassant ; translated by Katharine Vivian ; introduction by Mervyn Horder ; lithographs by Laszlo Acs. — London : Folio Society, 1981. — 238p,[9]leaves of plates : ill(some col.) ; 23cm
Translation of: Une vie. — In slip case
£7.75 B81-17699

Maupassant, Guy de. Une vie / Guy de Maupassant ; translated by Katharine Vivian ; introduction by Mervyn Horder ; lithographs by Laszlo Acs. — London : Folio Society, 1981. — 238p,[8]leaves of plates : col.ill ; 23cm
In slip case
Unpriced B81-32074

Verne, Jules. Carpathian Castle / Jules Verne ; edited by I.O. Evans. — London : Granada, 1979, c1963. — 189p ; 21cm
Translation of: Le Château des Carpathes. — Originally published: London : Arco, 1963
ISBN 0-246-11139-9 : £4.95 B81-15736

Verne, Jules. The clipper of the clouds / Jules Verne edited by I.O. Evans. — London : Granada, 1979, c1962. — 191p ; 21cm
Translation of: Robur-le-Conquérant. — Originally published: London : Arco, 1962
ISBN 0-246-11138-0 : £4.95 B81-15734

Verne, Jules. From the earth to the moon / Jules Verne. — London : Granada, 1979, c1959. — 157p ; 21cm
Translation of: De la terre à la lune. — Originally published: London : Hanison, 1959
ISBN 0-246-11137-2 : £4.95 B81-39297

843'.8'09 — Fiction in French, *1848-1900 — Biographies*

Williams, Roger L.. The horror of life / Roger L. Williams. — London : Weidenfeld and Nicolson, c1980. — xiii,381p : 6ports ; 24cm
Originally published: Chicago : University of Chicago Press, 1980. — Bibliography: p357-374. - Includes index
ISBN 0-297-77883-8 : £15.00 B81-05854

843'.8'09358 — Fiction in French. Loti, Pierre & Mille, Pierre — *Special themes: Colonialism — Critical studies*

Hargreaves, Alec G.. The colonial experience in French fiction : a study of Pierre Loti, Ernest Psichari and Pierre Mille / Alec G. Hargreaves. — London : Macmillan, 1981. — ix,193p ; 23cm
Bibliography: p181-191. — Includes index
ISBN 0-333-28854-8 : £20.00 : CIP rev.
Also classified at 843'.912 B80-36472

843.912 — FRENCH FICTION, 1900-1945

843'.912 — Fiction in French, *1900-1945 — Texts*

Beauvoir, Simone de. Les belles images / Simone de Beauvoir ; edited with an introduction and notes by Blandine Stefanson. — London : Heinemann Educational, 1980. — 290p : 1map ; 19cm
French text, English introduction and notes. — Les belles images originally published: Paris : Gallimard, 1966. — Bibliography: p269-271
ISBN 0-435-37070-7 (pbk) : £3.50 : CIP rev.
B80-02962

Colette. Le blé en herbe / Colette ; edited with an introduction by Brian Stimpson. — London : Hodder and Stoughton, 1980. — 160p : 1map ; 20cm. — (Textes francais classiques et modernes)
French text, English introduction and notes. — Bibliography: p61-62
ISBN 0-340-23302-8 (pbk) : £2.95 : CIP rev.
B80-19499

Troyat, Henri. Grandeur nature / Henri Troyat ; edited by Nicholas Hewitt. — London : Methuen Educational, 1980. — xli,203p ; 20cm. — (Methuen's twentieth century texts)
French text, English introduction and notes. — Bibliography: pxxxix-xli
ISBN 0-423-90110-9 (pbk) : £2.75 : CIP rev.
B80-07584

843'.912 — Fiction in French, *1900-1945 — Texts with commentaries*

Sartre, Jean-Paul. Les mots. — London : Methuen Educational, Sept.1981. — [200]p. — (Methuen's twentieth century texts)
ISBN 0-423-50560-2 (pbk) : £2.50 : CIP entry
B81-22642

843'.912 — Fiction in French. Beauvoir, Simone de. Political commitment

Whitmarsh, Anne. Simone de Beauvoir and the limits of commitment / Anne Whitmarsh. — Cambridge : Cambridge University Press, 1981. — xii,212p ; 23cm
Bibliography: p199-207. — Includes index
ISBN 0-521-23669-x : £14.50 : CIP rev.
B81-19190

843'.912 — Fiction in French. Bernanos, Georges. Religious beliefs

Cooke, John E.. Georges Bernanos : a study of Christian commitment / John E. Cooke. — [Amersham] : Avebury, 1981. — 197p ; 23cm
Bibliography: p155-197
ISBN 0-86127-202-1 : £10.00 B81-37133

843'.912 — Fiction in French. Camus, Albert — *Biographies*

Lottman, Herbert R.. Albert Camus : a biography / Herbert R. Lottman. — London : Pan, 1981, c1979. — xii,753p,[8]p of plates : 1ill,ports ; 20cm. — (Picador)
Originally published: London : Weidenfeld and Nicolson, 1979. — Includes index
ISBN 0-330-26262-9 (pbk) : £3.95 B81-09953

McCarthy, Patrick. Camus. — London : Hamilton, Feb.1982. — [288]p
ISBN 0-241-10603-6 : £9.95 : CIP entry
B81-35820

843'.912 — Fiction in French. Camus, Albert. Chute, *La* **& Etranger,** *L'* — *Critical studies*

Jones, Rosemarie. Camus, L'étranger and La chute / Rosemarie Jones. — London : Grant & Cutler, 1980. — 94p ; 20cm. — (Critical guides to French texts ; 2)
Bibliography: p93-94
ISBN 0-7293-0093-5 (pbk) : £1.80 B81-17019

843'.912 — Fiction in French. Camus, Albert. Etranger, *L'* — *Study outlines*

King, Adele. L'étranger = The Stranger, or, The outsider : notes / by Adele King. — London : Longman, 1980. — 61p ; 21cm. — (York notes ; 46)
Bibliography: p56-57
ISBN 0-582-78159-0 (pbk) : £0.90 B81-07096

843'.912 — Fiction in French. Colette — *Biographies*

Sarde, Michèle. Colette : free and fettered / by Michèle Sarde ; translated from the French by Richard Miller. — London : Joseph, [1981]. — 479p,[32]p of plates : ports ; 24cm
Translation of: Colette, libre et entravée. — Originally published: New York : Morrow, 1980. — Bibliography: p467-471. — Includes index
ISBN 0-7181-2058-2 : £12.95 B81-37683

843'.912 — Fiction in French. Mauriac, François. Political beliefs

Scott, Malcolm. Mauriac : the politics of a novelist / Malcolm Scott. — Edinburgh : Scottish Academic Press, 1980. — xi,158p ; 23cm
Bibliography: p141-143
ISBN 0-7073-0262-5 : £7.50 B81-04009

843'.912 — Fiction in French. Proust, Marcel. A la recherche du temps perdu — *Psychoanalytical perspectives*

Splitter, Randolph. Proust's Recherche : a psychoanalytic interpretation / Randolph Splitter. — Boston ; London : Routledge & Kegan Paul, 1981. — ix,148p ; 22cm
Includes index
ISBN 0-7100-0664-0 : £10.50 B81-08127

843'.912 — Fiction in French. Proust, Marcel. A la recherche du temps perdu. Special themes: Man. Sexuality

Rivers, J. E.. Proust & the art of love : the aesthetics of sexuality in the life, times, & art of Marcel Proust / J.E. Rivers. — New York ; Guildford : Columbia University Press, 1980. — xii,327p ; 24cm
Bibliography: p297-309. - Includes index
ISBN 0-231-05036-4 : £12.45 B81-09517

843'.912 — Fiction in French. Psichari, Ernest — *Special themes: Colonialism — Critical studies*

Hargreaves, Alec G.. The colonial experience in French fiction : a study of Pierre Loti, Ernest Psichari and Pierre Mille / Alec G. Hargreaves. — London : Macmillan, 1981. — ix,193p ; 23cm
Bibliography: p181-191. — Includes index
ISBN 0-333-28854-8 : £20.00 : CIP rev.
Primary classification 843'.8'09358 B80-36472

843'.912 — Fiction in French. Queneau, Raymond. Zazie dans le métro — *Critical studies*

Redfern, W. D.. Queneau, Zazie dans le métro / W.D. Redfern. — London : Grant & Cutler, 1980. — 70p ; 20cm. — (Critical guides to French texts ; 3)
Bibliography: p68-70
ISBN 0-7293-0086-2 (pbk) : £1.50 B81-17020

843'.912 — Fiction in French. Sarraute, Nathalie — *Critical studies*

Minogue, Valerie. Nathalie Sarraute and the war of the words : a study of five novels / Valerie Minogue. — Edinburgh : Edinburgh University Press, 1981. — v,230p ; 22cm
Bibliography: p219-225. - Includes index
ISBN 0-85224-405-3 : £10.00 B81-10085

843'.912[F] — Fiction in French, *1900-1945 — English texts*

Camus, Albert. The outsider. — London : Hamish Hamilton, Jan.1982. — [128]p
Translation of : L'étranger
ISBN 0-241-10778-4 : £5.95 : CIP entry
B81-34567

843′.912[F] — Fiction in French, *1900-1945 — English texts* *continuation*

Proust, Marcel. Remembrance of things past / [Marcel Proust] ; [translated by C.K. Scott Moncrieff, Terence Kilmartin and Andreas Mayor]. — [London] : [Chatto & Windus], [1981]. — 3v. ; 21cm
Translation of: A la recherche du temps perdu. — Contents: Swann′s way - Within a budding grove - The Guermantes way - Cities of the plain - The Captive - The fugitive - Time regained
ISBN 0-7011-2477-6 : £55.00 : set
ISBN 0-7011-2478-4 (v.2) : £19.00
ISBN 0-7011-2479-2 (v.3) : £18.50 B81-10338

Queneau, Raymond. We always treat women too well : a novel / by Raymond Queneau ; translated from the French by Barbara Wright. — London : John Calder, 1981. — 174p : ill,1map ; 21cm
Translation of: On est toujours trop bon avec les femmes / published under the name Sally Mara
ISBN 0-7145-3687-3 : £8.95 : CIP rev. B80-23813

Renard, Maurice. The hands of Orlac / Maurice Renard ; translated from the French by Iain White. — London : Souvenir, 1980. — 301p ; 21cm. — (Nightowl books)
Translation of: Les mains d′Orlac
ISBN 0-285-62461-x : £6.95 B81-09882

Roché, Henri-Pierre. Jules and Jim / Henri-Pierre Roché ; translated by Patrick Evans. — London : Boyars, 1981. — 239p ; 22cm
Translation of: Jules et Jim. — Originally published: London : Calder & Boyars, 1963
ISBN 0-7145-2749-1 : £6.95 : CIP rev. B81-18105

Simenon, Georges. Maigret & the flea. — Large print ed. — Long Preston : Magna, Nov.1981. — [320]p
Translation of: Maigret et l′indicateur
ISBN 0-86009-353-0 : £4.95 : CIP entry B81-30432

Simenon, Georges. Maigret and the Concarneau murders / Georges Simenon. — London : Severn, 1980, c1939. — 140p ; 21cm
Translation of: Le chien jaune
ISBN 0-7278-0666-1 : £4.95 : CIP rev. B80-12148

Simenon, Georges. Maigret and the dosser / by Georges Simenon ; translated from the French by Jean Stewart. — Bolton-by-Bowland : Magna, 1980, c1963. — 231p ; 23cm
Translation of: Maigret et le clochard. — This translation originally published: London : Hamilton, 1973. — Published in large print
ISBN 0-86009-278-x : £5.25 : CIP rev. B80-22648

843′.912′09326 — Fiction in French. French & African writers, *1900-*. **Special subjects: Africa. European & African stereotypes** — *Critical studies*

Milbury-Steen, Sarah L.. European and African stereotypes in twentieth-century fiction / Sarah L. Milbury-Steen. — London : Macmillan, 1980. — xiii,188p ; 23cm
Bibliography: p178-183. - Includes index
ISBN 0-333-29143-3 : £15.00 : CIP rev.
Primary classification 823′.912′09326 B80-22636

843.914 — FRENCH FICTION, 1945-

843′.914 — Children′s short stories in French, *1945- — Irish texts*

Laramée, Ghislaine. Trí fhabhalsceál / Ghislaine Laramée a d′aithris ; Romain Simon a mhaisigh ; Siobhán Denman a d′aistrigh. — Baile Atha Cliath : Oifig an tSoláthair, c1980. — 11p : col.ill
Contents: An madra rua agus an chorr bhán - An préachán agus an madra rua - An leon agus an francach
£1.20 (30cm) B81-15189

843′.914 — Childrens′ stories in French, *1945- — Irish texts*

Ó Colla, Eoghan. Breagain Dhaidi na Nollag / teacs Evelyne Passegand ; learaidi Marie-Josee [i.e. Marie-José] Sacre ; curtha in oiriuint do phaisti 7-9 bliana ag Eoghan O Colla. — Baile Atha Cliath : Oifig an tSoláthair, 1980. — [26]p : col.ill ; 27cm
Unpriced B81-15190

843′.914 — Fiction in French, *1945- — Texts with commentaries*

Lainé, Pascal. La dentellière. — London : Methuen, Nov.1981. — [250]p. — (Methuen′s twentieth century French texts)
ISBN 0-423-50820-2 (pbk) : £2.50 : CIP entry B81-30156

843′.914[F] — Fiction in French, *1945- — English texts*

Arsan, Emmanuelle. Vanna / Emmanuelle Arsan ; translated from the French by Celeste Piano. — London : Granada, 1981. — 249p ; 18cm. — (A Mayflower book)
Translation of: Vanna
ISBN 0-583-13294-4 (pbk) : £1.50 B81-32576

Beer, Olivier. Pas de deux / Olivier Beer. — Large print ed. — Bath : Chivers, 1981, c1980. — 170p ; 23cm. — (A Lythway book)
Translation of: Le chant des enfants morts. — Originally published: London : Gollancz, 1980
ISBN 0-85119-732-9 : Unpriced : CIP rev. B81-19172

Bensen, Bernard. The peace book. — London : Cape, Oct.1981. — [192]p
Translation of: Le livre de la paix
ISBN 0-224-01989-9 (cased) : £6.95 : CIP entry
ISBN 0-224-02928-2 (pbk) : Unpriced B81-27363

Curval, Philippe. Brave old world. — London : Allison & Busby, Aug.1981. — [288]p
Translation of: Cette chère humanité
ISBN 0-85031-407-0 : £6.95 : CIP entry B81-18097

Danton, Pierre. No river so wide / Pierre Danton ; translated by Jean Raggan. — London : W.H. Allen, 1981, c1978. — 379p ; 18cm. — (A Star book)
Translation of: Antilope n′Tcheri. — Originally published: New York? : Dell?, 1978?
ISBN 0-352-30979-2 (pbk) : £1.75 B81-39333

Hemingway, Joan. Rosebud. — Large print ed. — Anstey : Ulverscroft, Dec.1981. — [448]p. — (Ulverscroft large print series)
Translation of: Rosebud. — Originally published: Henley-on-Thames: Aidan Ellis, 1974
ISBN 0-7089-0725-3 : £5.00 : CIP entry B81-32604

Jacquemard, Yves. The body vanishes. — Large print ed. — Bath : Chivers, Nov.1981. — [232] p. — (A Lythway book)
Translation of: La crime de la maison Grün. — This translation originally published: London : Collins, 1980
ISBN 0-85119-762-0 : £6.50 : CIP entry B81-31271

Remy, Pierre-Jean. Orient express : a novel of love and adventure / Pierre-Jean Remy ; translated by St John Field. — London : Collins, 1981, c1980. — 335p ; 22cm
Translation of: Orient express. — Originally published: New York : Morrow, 1980
ISBN 0-00-221976-x : £7.50 B81-10211

Robbe-Grillet, Alain. In the labyrinth : a novel / by Alain Robbe-Grillet ; translated by Christine Brooke-Rose. — London : Calder, 1967, c1980 (1980 [printing]). — 188p ; 21cm
Translation of: Dans le labyrinthe
ISBN 0-7145-0297-9 (cased) : £5.95 : CIP rev.
ISBN 0-7145-0298-7 (pbk) : £3.95 B80-00928

Robbe-Grillet, Alain. The voyeur / Alain Robbe-Grillet ; translated by Richard Howard. — London : Calder, 1959, c1958 (1980 [printing]). — 219p ; 20cm
Translation of: Le voyeur. — Originally published: New York : Grove Press, 1958
ISBN 0-7145-0601-x (pbk) : £3.95 B81-10321

Tournier, Michael. Gemini / Michael Tournier ; translated by Anne Carter. — London : Collins, 1981. — 452p ; 22cm
Translation of: Les météores
ISBN 0-00-221448-2 : £8.95 B81-35408

Volkoff, Vladimir. The turn-around / Vladimir Volkoff ; translated from the French by Alan Sheridan. — London : Bodley Head, 1981. — 410p ; 23cm
Translation of: Le retournement
ISBN 0-370-30323-7 : £6.95 : CIP rev. B81-01357

843′.914[F] — Short stories in French, *1945- — English texts*

Ward Jouve, Nicole. Shades of grey / Nicole Ward Jouve ; translated by the author. — London : Virago, 1981. — 176p ; 21cm
Translation of: Le spectre du gris
ISBN 0-86068-228-5 (cased) : £7.95 : CIP rev.
ISBN 0-86068-229-3 (pbk) : £2.95 B81-09479

Yourcenar, Marguerite. Fires. — Henley on Thames : Aidan Ellis, Dec.1981. — [160]p
Translation of: Feux
ISBN 0-85628-109-3 : £6.95 : CIP entry B81-31650

843′.914[J] — Children′s stories in French, *1945- — English texts*

Brunhoff, Laurent de. Babar and the ghost. — London : Methuen, May 1981. — [32]p. — (Babar books)
ISBN 0-416-21480-0 : £3.95 : CIP entry B81-04249

Chessex, Jacques. Mary & the wild cat / story by Jacques Chessex ; illustrations by Danièle Bour. — London : Gollancz, 1980. — [24]p : col.ill ; 23cm
Translation of: Marie et le chat sauvage
ISBN 0-575-02800-9 : £3.25 B81-11085

Dumas, Philippe. Laura : Alice′s new puppy / Philippe Dumas. — [London] : Fontana, 1981, c1976. — 59p : ill ; 20cm. — (Lions)
Translation of: Laura. — Originally published: London : Gollancz, 1979
ISBN 0-00-671770-5 (pbk) : £0.80 B81-11069

Dumas, Philippe. Laura loses her head / Philippe Dumas. — London : Gollancz, 1981. — [56]p : col.ill ; 22cm
Translation of: Laura perd la tête
ISBN 0-575-03016-x : £3.50 B81-32933

Goscinny. Curing the Daltons. — London : Hodder & Stoughton Children′s Books, Jan.1982. — [48]p
Translation of: La guérison des Dalton
ISBN 0-340-27473-5 : £1.50 : CIP entry B81-34125

Goscinny. The dashing white cowboy. — London : Hodder & Stoughton Children′s Books, Jan.1982. — [48]p
Translation of: Le cavalier blanc
ISBN 0-340-27474-3 : £1.50 : CIP entry B81-34124

Lamorisse, Albert. The red balloon / illustrated with photographs from the film The red balloon ; written, directed and produced by Albert Lamorisse ; translated by Malcolm Barnes. — London : Unwin, 1980. — [63]p : ill (some col.) ; 19cm
Translation of: La ballon rouge. — Originally published: London : Allen & Unwin, 1957
ISBN 0-04-823178-9 (pbk) : £1.50 : CIP rev. B80-18536

Sacré, Marie-José. The rowdies / Marie-José Sacré. — London : Macdonald, 1981. — [25]p : chiefly col.ill ; 26x27cm
Translation of: Le tribu du malotrus
ISBN 0-354-08120-9 : £3.75 B81-30696

843'.914[J] — Children's stories in French, *1945-* — *English texts* *continuation*

Timmermans, Gommaar. The rabbit who tried. — London : Methuen, Sept.1981. — [32]p. — (Methuen picture story books)
Translation of: Albin le lapin
ISBN 0-416-21750-8 : £3.25 : CIP entry
B81-23774

Voilier, Claude. The Famous Five and the missing cheetah. — London : Hodder and Stoughton, Nov.1981. — [128]p
Translation of: Les cinq au Cap des Tempêtes
ISBN 0-340-27248-1 (pbk) : £0.75 : CIP entry
B81-30250

Voilier, Claude. The famous five and the mystery of the emeralds. — London : Hodder and Stoughton, Apr.1981. — 1v.
Translation of: Les cinq sont les plus forts
ISBN 0-340-26524-8 : £0.75p : CIP entry
B81-00637

Voilier, Claude. The Famous Five and the stately homes gang. — London : Hodder and Stoughton, Apr.1981. — [128]p
Translation of: Le marquis appelle les cinq
ISBN 0-340-26525-6 (pbk) : £0.85 : CIP entry
B81-02562

Voilier, Claude. The Famous Five go on television. — London : Hodder and Stoughton, Nov.1981. — [128]p
Translation of: Les cinq à la télévision
ISBN 0-340-27247-3 (pbk) : £0.75 : CIP entry
B81-30251

843'.914'09 — Fiction in French. Butor, Michel; Robbe-Grillet, Alain & Sarraute, Nathalie — *Critical studies*

Jefferson, Ann. The nouveau roman and the poetics of fiction / Ann Jefferson. — Cambridge : Cambridge University Press, 1980. — lx,218p ; 23cm
Bibliography: p210-216. — Includes index
ISBN 0-521-22239-7 : £12.50 : CIP rev.
B80-28649

843'.914'093 — Fiction in French, *1945-1973.* **Special subjects: Religion & sex** *compared with* **religion & sex as special subjects of Irish fiction in English,** *1945-1973*

O'Rourke, Brian. The conscience of the race : sex and religion in Irish and French novels 1941-1973 / Brian O'Rourke. — Dublin (3 Serpentine Ave., Dublin 4) : Four Courts Press, c1980. — 70p ; 22cm
Bibliography: p68-70. — Includes index
ISBN 0-906127-22-x : £5.00
Primary classification 823'.914'093 B81-06543

844.3 — FRENCH ESSAYS, 1500-1600

844'.3 — Essays in French. Montaigne, Michel de — *Critical studies*

Burke, Peter. Montaigne / Peter Burke. — Oxford : Oxford University Press, 1981. — 81p : ill ; 19cm. — (Past masters)
Bibliography: p75-78. — Includes index
ISBN 0-19-287523-x (cased) : Unpriced : CIP rev.
ISBN 0-19-287522-1 (pbk) : £1.25 B81-25746

Montaigne and his age / edited by Keith Cameron. — [Exeter] : University of Exeter, c1981. — ix,202p : ill,maps,1port ; 21cm
Includes index
ISBN 0-85989-167-4 (pbk) : £3.50 B81-34270

848.4 — FRENCH MISCELLANY, 1600-1715

848'.402 — Aphorisms in French, *1600-1715* — *English texts*

La Rochefoucauld, François, *duc de.* Maxims / La Rochefoucauld ; translated with an introduction by Leonard Tancock. — Harmondsworth : Penguin, 1959 (1981 [printing]). — 126p ; 19cm. — (The Penquin classics)
ISBN 0-14-044095-x (pbk) : £1.50 B81-27641

848.5 — FRENCH MISCELLANY, 1715-1789

848'.507 — Prose in French. Voltaire. Dictionnaire philosophique — *Critical studies*

Todd, Christopher. Voltaire, Dictionnaire philosophique / Christopher Todd. — London : Grant & Cutler, 1980. — 72p ; 20cm. — (Critical guides to French texts ; 5)
ISBN 0-7293-0101-x (pbk) : Unpriced
B81-31754

848'.509 — French literature. Voltaire — *Biographies*

Mason, Haydn. Voltaire : a biography / Haydn Mason. — London : Elek : Granada, 1981. — xiii,194p,[8]p of plates : ill,ports ; 24cm
Bibliography: p186-187. — Includes index
ISBN 0-236-40184-x : £9.95 B81-32720

848.8 — FRENCH MISCELLANY, 1848-1900

848'.808 — Prose in French, *1848-1900* — *English texts*

Satie, Erik. Memoirs of an amnesiac : to be read far from the herd and the mummified dead, those great scourges of humanity / Eric Satie ; [new translation by Max Paddison]. — [London] ([18 Carlisle St., W1]) : [M. Paddison], c1981. — 32p : 1port ; 22cm
Translated from the French. — Limited ed. of 500 numbered copies. — Includes Observations of an idiot (myself) / Eric Satie
Unpriced (pbk) B81-37634

848'.809 — French literature, *1848-1900* — *English texts*

Jarry, Alfred. Selected works of Alfred Jarry / edited by Roger Shattuck and Simon Watson Taylor. — London : Eyre Methuen, 1965 (1980 [printing]). — 281p,[26]p of plates : ill,music,facsims,ports ; 21cm
Includes five poems in French. — Bibliography: p281
ISBN 0-413-47400-3 (pbk) : £3.95 B81-04797

848'.809 — French literature. Villiers de l'Isle-Adam, Auguste — *Biographies*

Raitt, A. W.. The life of Villiers de l'Isle-Adam / A.W. Raitt. — Oxford : Clarendon Press, 1981. — xviii,452p of plates : ill,ports ; 22cm
Bibliography: p425-437. — Includes index
ISBN 0-19-815771-1 : £25.00 B81-38503

848.912 — FRENCH MISCELLANY, 1900-1945

848'.91207 — Experimental writing in French. Romanian writers, *1900-1945* — *English texts*

Tzara, Tristan. Seven Dada manifestos and lampisteries / Tristan Tzara ; translated by Barbara Wright ; illustrations by Francis Picabia. — London : Calder, 1977 (1981 [printing]). — 118p : ill,1port ; 20cm
Translation of: Lampisteries, précédées des Sept manifestes Dada. — Bibliography: p115-118
ISBN 0-7145-3762-4 (pbk) : £3.50 B81-32391

848'.91209 — French literature. Artaud, Antonin — *Biographies*

Knapp, Bettina L.. Antonin Artaud : man of vision / by Bettina L. Knapp ; with a preface by Anaïs Nin. — Chicago ; London : Swallow Press, 1980. — xiv,233p : 1port ; 22cm
Originally published: New York : D. Lewis, 1969. — Bibliography: p225-228. — Includes index
ISBN 0-8040-0809-4 (pbk) : £3.60 B81-25643

848.914 — FRENCH MISCELLANY, 1945-

848'.91407 — Experimental writing in French, *1945-* — *English texts*

Queneau, Raymond. Exercises in style / Raymond Queneau ; translated by Barbara Wright. — London : Calder, 1981. — 197p ; 21cm
Translation of: Exercises de style. — Originally published: London : Gaberbocchus, 1958
ISBN 0-7145-3793-4 (pbk) : £3.50 B81-38807

848'.91407 — Humorous prose in Franglais, *1945-* — *Texts*

Kington, Miles. Let's parler Franglais! / Miles Kington ; illustrations by Merrily Harpur. — Harmondsworth : Penguin, 1981, c1979. — 96p : ill ; 20cm
Originally published: London : Robson, 1979
ISBN 0-14-005625-4 (pbk) : £0.95 B81-27647

Kington, Miles. Parlez vous Franglais? / Miles Kington ; illustrations by Merrily Harpur. — London : Robson, 1981. — 95p : ill ; 23cm. — (Let's parlez Franglais ; 3)
ISBN 0-86051-150-2 : £3.50 : CIP rev.
B81-22459

848'.91409 — French literature. Beckett, Samuel — *Biographies*

Bair, Deirdre. Samuel Beckett : a biography / Deirdre Bair. — London : Picador, 1980, c1978. — 624p,[16]p of plates : ill,ports ; 20cm
Originally published: London : Cape, 1978. — Includes index
ISBN 0-330-26163-0 (pbk) : £3.95
Primary classification 828'.91209 B81-06995

850.9 — ITALIAN LITERATURE. HISTORY AND CRITICAL STUDIES

850.9 — Italian literature, *to 1979* — *Critical studies*

Whitfield, J. H.. A short history of Italian literature / by J.H. Whitfield. — with a new chapter from 1922 to the present by J.R. Woodhouse. — Manchester : Manchester University Press, 1980. — 335p ; 22cm
Previous ed.: Harmondsworth : Penguin , 1960. — Bibliography: p322-325. - Includes index
ISBN 0-7190-0782-8 (pbk) : £4.75 : CIP rev.
B80-13617

850.9'001 — Italian literature, *to 1375* — *Critical studies* — *Early works*

Dante Alighieri. [De vulgari eloquentia. English]. Literature in the vernacular / Dante ; translated with an introduction by Sally Purcell. — Manchester : Carcanet, 1981. — 84p ; 20cm
Translation of De vulgari eloquentia
ISBN 0-85635-274-8 (pbk) : £2.95
Also classified at 851'.1'08 B81-25221

851.1 — ITALIAN POETRY, TO 1375

851'.1 — Poetry in Italian. Dante Alighieri — *Critical studies*

Anderson, William, *1935-*. Dante the maker / William Anderson. — London : Routledge & Kegan Paul, 1980. — xii,497p : ill,2maps ; 24cm
Bibliography: p460-471. — Includes index
ISBN 0-7100-0322-6 : £18.00 : CIP rev.
B80-01886

Boyde, Patrick. Dante, philomythes and philosopher. — Cambridge : Cambridge University Press, June 1981. — [404]p
ISBN 0-521-23598-7 : £30.00 : CIP entry
B81-13795

Dante : soundings : eight literary and historical essays / edited by David Nolan. — Dublin : Published for the Foundation for Italian Studies, University College, Dublin [by] Irish Academic Press, c1981. — 192p ; 22cm. — (Publications of the Foundation for Italian Studies University College Dublin ; 1)
Includes index
ISBN 0-7165-0058-2 : £12.00 B81-40904

851'.1 — Poetry in Italian. Dante Alighieri. Divina commedia. Inferno — *Critical studies*

Fowlie, Wallace. A reading of Dante's Inferno / Wallace Fowlie. — Chicago ; London : University of Chicago Press, 1981. — vii,237p : ill ; 24cm
Bibliography: p231-232. — Includes index
ISBN 0-226-25887-4 (cased) : £10.80
ISBN 0-226-25888-2 (pbk) : Unpriced
B81-28353

851'.1 — Poetry in Italian, *to 1375* — *English texts*

Boccaccio, Giovanni. Chaucer's Boccaccio : sources of Troilus and the Knight's and Franklin's tales / edited and translated by N.R. Havely. — Woodbridge : Brewer, 1980. — 225p ; 25cm. — (Chaucer studies ; 3)
Bibliography: p215-220. — Includes index
ISBN 0-85991-036-9 : £15.00 : CIP rev.
B80-10394

Dante Alighieri. [Divina commedia. English]. The Divine comedy / Dante Alighieri ; the John Ciardi translation. — New York ; London : Norton, c1970. — xvii,602p : ill ; 22cm
ISBN 0-393-04472-6 : £8.50 B81-09720

851′.1 — Poetry in Italian, *to 1375 — English texts continuation*

Dante Alighieri. [La divina commedia. English]. The divine comedy / Dante ; a new verse translation by C.H. Sisson ; introduction, commentary, notes and bibliography by David H. Higgins. — London : Pan, 1981. — 688p : map,2geneal.tables ; 20cm. — (Pan classics)
Bibliography: p686-688
ISBN 0-330-26261-0 (pbk) : £3.50 B81-12495

Petrarca, Francesco. Song and sonnets from Laura′s lifetime / Francis Petrarch ; translated by Nicholas Kilmer. — London : Anvil Press Poetry, 1980. — 78p ; 22cm. — (Poetica ; 8)
Bibliography: p77-78
ISBN 0-85646-060-5 (pbk) : £3.50 B81-13360

851′.1 — Poetry in Italian, *to 1375 — Italian-English parallel texts*

Dante Alighieri. The divine comedy of Dante Alighieri : a verse translation / with introductions & commentary by Allen Mandelbaum ; drawings by Barry Moser. — Berkeley ; London : University of California Press, c1980. — xxiv,307p : ill ; 29cm
Parallel Italian text and English translation and introduction. — Spine title: Inferno
ISBN 0-520-02712-4 : £12.00 B81-29001

851′.1′08 — Poetry in Italian, *to 1375 — Anthologies — English texts*

Dante Alighieri. [De vulgari eloquentia. English]. Literature in the vernacular / Dante ; translated with an introduction by Sally Purcell. — Manchester : Carcanet, 1981. — 84p ; 20cm
Translation of De vulgari eloquentia
ISBN 0-85635-274-8 (pbk) : £2.95
Primary classification 850.9′001 B81-25221

851.4 — ITALIAN POETRY, 1542-1585

851′.4 — Poetry in Italian, *1542-1585 — English texts*

Tasso, Torquato. Godfrey of Bulloigne : a critical edition of Edward Fairfax′s translation of Tasso′s Gerusalemme liberata, together with Fairfax′s original poems / edited by Kathleen M. Lea and T.M. Gang. — Oxford : Clarendon Press, 1981. — 23cm
ISBN 0-19-812480-5 : £55.00 : CIP rev. B80-13618

851.6 — ITALIAN POETRY, 1748-1814

851′.6 — Poetry in Italian. Foscolo, Ugo — *Critical studies*

Cambon, Glauco. Ugo Foscolo : poet of exile / Glauco Cambon. — Princeton ; Guildford : Princeton University Press, c1980. — x,356p : 2facsims ; 23cm
Bibliography: p345-349. - Includes index
ISBN 0-691-06424-5 : £11.80 B81-04003

851.912 — ITALIAN POETRY, 1900-1945

851′.912 — Poetry in Italian, *1900-1945 — Italian-English parallel texts*

Gozzano, Guido. The man I pretend to be : The colloquies ; and selected poems of Guido Gozzano / translated and edited by Michael Palma ; with an introductory essay by Eugenio Montale. — Princeton ; Guildford : Princeton University Press, c1981. — xxv,254p ; 23cm. — (The Lockert library of poetry in translation)
Parallel Italian text and English translation. — Translation of: I colloqui ; and other selected poems. — Bibliography: p251-253
ISBN 0-691-06467-9 (cased) : £9.30
ISBN 0-691-01378-0 (pbk) : Unpriced B81-34364

851′.912′08 — Poetry in Italian, *1900-1945 — Anthologies — English texts*

The **Blue** moustache : some futurist poets / [selection and] translation by Felix Stefanile. — Manchester : Carcanet New Pres, 1981. — 58p ; 22cm
Translation from the Italian
ISBN 0-85635-355-8 (pbk) : £2.95 : CIP rev. B81-06593

851.914 — ITALIAN POETRY, 1945-

851′.914 — Poetry in Italian, *1945- — Italian-English parallel texts*

Scotellaro, Rocco. The dawn is always new : selected poetry of Rocco Scotellaro / translated by Ruth Feldman and Brian Swann. — Princeton, N.J. ; Guildford : Princeton University Press, c1980. — xiii,202p ; 23cm. — (The Lockert library of poetry in translation)
ISBN 0-691-06423-7 : £8.00
ISBN 0-691-01370-5 (pbk) : Unpriced B81-03216

851′.914′08 — Poetry in Italian, *1945- — Anthologies — Italian-English parallel texts*

The **New** Italian poetry : 1945 to the present : a bilingual anthology / edited and translated by Lawrence R. Smith. — Berkeley ; London : University of California Press, c1981. — xvii,483p ; 24cm
ISBN 0-520-03859-2 : £17.00 B81-27483

852.4 — ITALIAN DRAMA, 1542-1585

852′.4 — Drama in Italian, *1542-1585 — Italian-English parallel texts*

Porta, Giambattista Della. Gli duoi fratelli rivali = The two rival brothers / Giambattista Della Porta ; edited and translated by Louise George Clubb. — Berkeley ; London : University of California Press, c1980. — 329p ; 21cm. — (Biblioteca Italiana)
Parallel Italian text and English translation. — Bibliography: p327-329
ISBN 0-520-03786-3 : £13.50 B81-15971

852.912 — ITALIAN DRAMA, 1900-1945

852′.912 — Drama in Italian. Pirandello, Luigi — *Critical studies*

Ragusa, Olga. Luigi Pirandello : an approach to his theatre / Olga Ragusa. — Edinburgh : Edinburgh University Press, c1980. — x,198p : 1ill ; 22cm. — (Writers of Italy series ; 8)
Bibliography: p184-191. - Includes index
ISBN 0-85224-373-1 : £7.00 B81-09640

852′.9′12 — Drama in Italian. Pirandello, Luigi - *Critical studies - Serials*

The **Yearbook** of the British Pirandello Society. — No.1 (1981)-. — Bristol (c/o Dept. of Italian, University of Bristol, 95 Woodland Rd, Bristol BS8 1US) : British Pirandello Society, Apr.1981. — [110]p
ISBN 0-907564-00-3 (pbk) : £2.95 : CIP entry
ISSN 0260-9215 B81-10503

853.1 — ITALIAN FICTION, TO 1375

853′.1[F] — Short stories in Italian, *to 1375 — English texts*

Boccaccio, Giovanni. The decameron / Giovanni Boccaccio ; translated by J.M. Rigg ; introduction by Edward Hutton. — London : Dent, 1978. — xxi,350p : 1ill ; 19cm. — (Everyman′s library ; no.845)
Translation of: Il decamerone
ISBN 0-460-00845-5 (cased) : £5.95
ISBN 0-460-01845-0 (pbk) : Unpriced B81-19489

Boccaccio, Giovanni. [Decamerone. English. Selections]. Stories from the Decameron of Boccaccio : stories told during ten days by ten young people who left Florence to save themselves from the great plague which struck their city in 1348 / edited by Colin Bennett ; illustrations by Andrew Skilleter. — [London] : Peter Lowe, c1980. — 160p : ill(some col.) ; 28cm
£6.95 (corrected) B81-12457

853.8 — ITALIAN FICTION, 1859-1900

853′.8[F] — Fiction in Italian, *1859-1900 — English texts*

Verga, Giovanni. Mastro-don Gesualdo : a novel / Giovanni Verga ; translated, with an introduction, by Giovanni Cecchetti. — Berkeley ; London : University of California Press, c1979. — xix,329p ; 24cm
Translation of: Mastro-don Gesualdo
ISBN 0-520-03598-4 : £8.75 B81-11079

853.912 — ITALIAN FICTION, 1900-1945

853′.912[F] — Fiction in Italian, *1900-1945 — English texts*

Tomasi di Lampedusa, Giuseppe. The leopard / Giuseppe di Lampedusa ; translated by Archibald Colquhoun. — [London] : Fontana, 1963, c1961 (1981 [printing]). — 223p ; 19cm
Translation of: Il Gattopardo. — Originally published: London : Collins, 1960
ISBN 0-00-616437-4 (pbk) : £1.50 B81-36785

853′.912[F] — Short stories in Italian, *1900-1945 — English texts*

Moravia, Alberto. The voice of the sea : and other stories / Alberto Moravia ; translated from the Italian by Angus Davidson. — London : Granada, 1981, c1978. — 223p ; 18cm. — (A Panther book)
Translation of: Boh. — Originally published: London : Secker and Warburg, 1978
ISBN 0-586-04792-1 (pbk) : £1.95 B81-22842

853.914 — ITALIAN FICTION, 1945-

853′.914[F] — Fiction in Italian, *1945- — English texts*

Calvino, Italo. If on a winter′s night a traveller / Italo Calvino ; translated from the Italian by William Weaver. — London : Secker & Warburg, 1981. — 260p ; 22cm
Translation of: Se una motte d′inverno un viaggiatore
ISBN 0-436-08271-3 : £6.95 B81-31999

Fallaci, Oriana. A man / Oriana Fallaci ; translated from the Italian by William Weaver. — London : Bodley Head, 1981, c1980. — 463p ; 25cm
Translation of: Un uomo. — Originally published: New York : Simon and Schuster, c1980
ISBN 0-370-30385-7 : £6.50 B81-13376

Sciascia, Leonardo. Candido. — Manchester : Carcanet Press, Feb.1982. — [144]p
Translation of: Candido. — Originally published: New York : Harcourt Press, 1979
ISBN 0-85635-404-x : £5.95 : CIP entry B81-40262

853′.914[F] — Short stories in Italian, *1945- — English texts*

Guareschi, Giovanni. Tales from the little world of Don Camillo / Giovanni Guareschi. — Harmondsworth : Penguin, 1980. — 221p ; 19cm
Translations from the Italian
ISBN 0-14-005770-6 (pbk) : £1.25 B81-10932

Guareschi, Giovanni. The world of Don Camillo / Giovanni Guareschi. — London : Gollancz, 1980. — 559p ; 24cm
Translated from the Italian. — Contents: The little world of Don Camillo — Don Camillo and the prodigal son — Don Camillo′s dilemma — Don Camillo and the Devil — Comrade Don Camillo
ISBN 0-575-02933-1 : £5.95 B81-02520

860.9 — SPANISH LITERATURE. HISTORY AND CRITICAL STUDIES

860.9′003 — Spanish literature, *1516-1700 — Critical studies*

Wilson, Edward M.. Spanish and English literature of the 16th and 17th centuries : studies in discretion, illusion and mutability / Edward M. Wilson. — Cambridge : Cambridge University Press, 1980. — xix,281p ; 24cm
Bibliography: pxiii-xix. — Includes index
ISBN 0-521-22844-1 : £15.50 : CIP rev. B80-26262

860′.9′0062 — Spanish literature, *1900-1945.* **Influence of cinema films,** *1920-1936*

Morris, C. B.. This loving darkness : the cinema and Spanish writers, 1920-1936 / C.B. Morris. — Oxford : Published for the University of Hull by the Oxford University Press, 1980. — 196p ; 23cm. — (University of Hull publications)
Bibliography: p184-186. - Includes index
ISBN 0-19-713440-8 : £12.95 : CIP rev. B80-23817

860.9′0064 — Spanish literature, *1945-*. Influence of alienation

Ilie, Paul. Literature and inner exile : authoritarian Spain, 1939-1975 / Paul Ilie. — Baltimore ; London : Johns Hopkins University Press, c1980. — ix,197p ; 24cm
Bibliography: p177-187. — Includes index
ISBN 0-8018-2424-9 : £8.95 B81-34331

861 — SPANISH POETRY

861 — Poetry in Spanish. Argentinian writers. Lugones, Leopoldo. Influence of Laforgue, Jules — *Spanish texts*

Ferguson, Raquel Halty. Laforgue y Lugones : dos poetas de la luna / Raquel Halty Ferguson. — London : Tamesis, c1981. — 128p ; 25cm
Bibliography: p121-125
ISBN 0-7293-0097-8 : Unpriced B81-32482

861 — Poetry in Spanish. Mexican writers, *1910-1945 — Spanish-English parallel texts*

Paz, Octavio. Airborn = Hijos del aire / Octavio Paz & Charles Tomlinson. — London : Anvil Press Poetry, 1981. — 29p ; 22cm
Parallel Spanish text and English translation
ISBN 0-85646-072-9 (pbk) : £1.95
Also classified at 821′.914 B81-15516

861 — Poetry in Spanish. Nicaraguan writers, *1945- — Texts*

Cardenal, Ernesto. Psalms / Ernesto Cardenal ; translated by Thomas Blackburn ... [et al.]. — London : Sheed and Ward, 1981. — 80p ; 22cm
Translation of Salmos
ISBN 0-7220-7016-0 (pbk) : £3.00 B81-27810

861.3 — SPANISH POETRY, 1516-1700

861′.3 — Poetry in Spanish, *1516-1700 — Texts*

Cueva, Juan de la. [Los Inventores de las cosas]. Juan de la Cueva′s Los inventores de las cosas : a critical edition and study / [edited by] Beno Weiss and Louis C. Pérez. — University Park ; London : Pennsylvania State University Press, c1980. — 197p : 1port ; 24cm
Spanish text, English introduction and notes. — Bibliography: p149-151. — Includes index
ISBN 0-271-00279-4 : £10.50 B81-25646

Estrada, Diego, *Duque de.* Octavas rimas a la insigne victoria conseguida por el Marqués de Santa Cruz / Diego Duque de Estrada ; edición y estudio de Henry M. Ettinghausen. — [Exeter] : University of Exeter, 1980. — xxxii,75p : 1map,1facsim ; 21cm. — (Exeter Hispanic texts, ISSN 0305-8700 ; 26)
Bibliography: p73. - Includes index
ISBN 0-85989-131-3 (pbk) : Unpriced B81-11543

861′.3 — Poetry in Spanish. Garcilaso de la Vega, *1503-1536 — Critical studies*

Rivers, Elias L.. Garcilaso de la Vega, Poems : a critrical guide / Elias L. Rivers. — London : Grant & Cutler in association with Tamesis, 1980. — 100p ; 20cm. — (Critical guides to Spanish texts ; 27)
Bibliography: p95-100
ISBN 0-7293-0087-0 (pbk) : Unpriced B81-31973

861′.3 — Poetry in Spanish. Herrera, Fernando de. Versification — *Critical studies — Spanish texts*

Ferguson, William, *1943-*. La versificación en Fernando de Herrera / William Ferguson. — London : Tamesis, c1981. — 136p ; 25cm
Bibliography: p127-131
ISBN 0-7293-0098-6 : Unpriced B81-32481

861.5 — SPANISH POETRY, 1800-1900

861′.5 — Poetry in Spanish, *1800-1900 — Texts*

Espronceda, José de. El estudiante de Salamanca and other poems / Jose de Espronceda ; edited and selected, with an introduction and notes by Richard A. Cardwell. — London : Tamesis Texts, c1980. — 187p ; 21cm
Spanish text, introduction and notes in English. — Bibliography: p71-72. — Includes index
ISBN 0-7293-0096-x (pbk) : Unpriced B81-31758

Zayas, Antonio de. Antología poética / Antonio de Zayas ; selección e introducción de J.M. Aguirre. — [Exeter] : University of Exeter, 1980. — xxvi,73p : 1port ; 21cm. — (Exeter Hispanic texts, ISSN 0305-8700 ; 27)
Includes index
ISBN 0-85989-136-4 (pbk) : Unpriced B81-11544

861.62 — SPANISH POETRY, 1900-1945

861′.62 — Poetry in Spanish. Jiménez, Juan Ramón. Influence of Blake, William; Shelley, Percy Bysshe & Yeats, W. B.

Young, Howard T.. The line in the margin : Juan Ramón Jiménez and his readings in Blake, Shelley and Yeats / Howard T. Young. — Madison ; London : University of Wisconsin Press, 1980. — xxiii,295p : ill,facsims,2ports ; 24cm
Bibliography: p257-258. — Includes index
ISBN 0-299-07950-3 : £6.00 B81-02848

861′.62′08 — Poetry in Spanish, *1900- — Anthologies — Spanish-English parallel texts — Serials*

Ecuatorial : poetry : poecia. — No.1 (Spring 1978)-. — London (Dr William Rowe, Dept. of Spanish, King′s College, Strand, WC2R 2LS) : [s.n.], 1978-. — v. ; 30cm
Irregular. — Parallel text in English and Spanish or Portuguses. — Subtitle varies
Unpriced B81-05836

861′.62′09 — Poetry in Spanish, *1900-1945 — Critical studies*

Morris, C. B.. A generation of Spanish poets 1920-1936 / C.B. Morris. — Cambridge : Cambridge University Press, 1969 (1978 [printing]). — xi,301p,vileaves of plates : ports ; 21cm
Bibliography: p273-288. — Includes index
ISBN 0-521-29481-9 (pbk) : £4.50 B81-38486

861.64 — SPANISH POETRY, 1945-

861′.64 — Poetry in Spanish, *1945- — Texts*

Quinta, Carla. Número májico / Carla Quinta. — Bognor Regis : New Horizon, c1980. — 72p ; 21cm
ISBN 0-86116-643-4 : £3925 B81-19071

Quintanilla, Manuel. Enigma fenix / M.F. Quintanilla. — London (c/o 27 Powis Sq., W11) : M. Quintanilla, 1981. — 100p : ill ; 22cm
ISBN 0-9507504-0-9 (pbk) : Unpriced B81-25636

862.3 — SPANISH DRAMA, 1516-1700

862′.3 — Drama in Spanish, *1516-1700 — Texts*

Vega, hope de. El perro del hortelano / hope de Vega ; a critical edition, with introduction and notes by Victor Dixon. — London : Tamesis Texts, c1981. — 216p ; 21cm
Spanish text, introduction and notes in English. — Bibliography: p68-74
ISBN 0-7293-0095-1 (pbk) : Unpriced B81-31757

862′.3′09 — England. Pepys, Samuel. Private collections: Drama in Spanish, *1516-1700.* **Texts** — *Critical studies*

Wilson, Edward M.. Samuel Pepys′s Spanish plays / Edward M. Wilson & Don W. Cruickshank. — London : Bibliographical Society, 1980. — 196p : ill ; 25cm. — (Bibliographical Society Publications for the years 1977 and 1978)
Includes index
ISBN 0-19-721793-1 : £20.00 : CIP rev. B80-30413

862.62 — SPANISH DRAMA, 1900-1945

862′.62 — Drama in Spanish. García Lorca, Federico. Bodas de sangre — *Critical studies*

Morris, C. B.. Garcia Lorca, Bodas de sangre / C.B. Morris. — London : Grant & Cutler in association with Tamesis Books, 1980. — 93p ; 20cm. — (Critical guides to Spanish texts ; 26)
Bibliography: p91-93
ISBN 0-7293-0083-8 (pbk) : £1.80 B81-17022

862′.62 — Drama in Spanish. García Lorca, Federico — *Critical studies*

Edwards, Gwynne. Lorca : the theatre beneath the sand / Gwynne Edwards. — London : Boyars, 1980. — 310p ; 22cm. — ([Critical appraisals])
Bibliography: p297-301. — Includes index
ISBN 0-7145-2698-3 : £12.00 : CIP rev. B80-06215

863 — SPANISH FICTION

863 — Fiction in Spanish. Argentian writers, *1945- — Texts*

Farrando, Julio. El negro marques / Julio Farrando. — [Fareham] ([10 Talland Rd., Titchfield, Fareham, Hants. PO14 4NJ]) : [J. Farrando], [1918]. — 53p ; 18cm
Cover title
£3.80 (pbk) B81-30938

863 — Fiction in Spanish. Argentinian writers. Cortázar, Julio - *Critical studies*

Boldy, Steven. The novels of Julio Cortázar / Steven Boldy. — Cambridge : Cambridge University Press, 1980. — ix,220p ; 24cm. — (Cambridge Iberian and Latin American studies)
Bibliography: p210-213. - Includes index
ISBN 0-521-23097-7 : £12.95 B81-04773

863 — Fiction in Spanish. Colombian writers, *1945- — Texts*

García Márquez, Gabriel. El coronel no tiene quien le escriba / Gabriel Garcia Marquez ; edited with introduction, notes and vocabulary by Giovanni Pontiero. — Manchester : Manchester University Press, 1981, c1958. — xlvii,90p ; 20cm. — (Spanish texts)
El coronel no tiene quien le escriba. Originally published: Medellín : Aguirre, 1961
ISBN 0-7190-0836-0 (pbk) : £3.95 : CIP rev. B81-08871

863 — Fiction in Spanish. Colombian writers. García Márquez, Gabriel — *Critical studies*

Janes, Regina. Gabriel García Márquez : revolutions in wonderland / Regina Janes. — Columbia, [Mo.] ; London : University of Missouri Press, 1981. — 115p ; 21cm
ISBN 0-8262-0337-x (pbk) : £5.60 B81-38242

863 — Fiction in Spanish. Cuban writers. Carpentier, Alejo — *Critical studies*

Janney, Frank. Alejo Carpenter and his early works / Frank Janney. — London : Tamesis, c1981. — 141p ; 25cm
Bibliography: p133-141
ISBN 0-7293-0062-5 : Unpriced B81-31759

863 — Fiction in Spanish. Latin American writers, *1910-1975 — Critical studies*

Brotherston, Gordon. The emergence of the Latin American novel / Gordon Brotherston. — Cambridge : Cambridge University Press, 1977 (1979 [printing]). — viii,164p ; 22cm
Bibliography: p150-160. - Includes index
ISBN 0-521-29565-3 (pbk) : £3.95 B81-04023

863 — Fiction in Spanish. Latin American writers, *1945- — Critical studies*

Schwartz, Ronald. Nomads, exiles, & émigrés : the rebirth of the Latin American narrative, 1960-80 / Ronald Schwartz. — Metuchen ; London : Scarecrow, 1980. — xiii,153p ; 23cm
Bibliography: p131-141. - Includes index
ISBN 0-8108-1359-9 : £6.65 B81-06278

863[F] — Fiction in Spanish, *1945-.* **Mexican writers** — *English texts*

Fuentes, Carlos. The death of Artemio Cruz / Carlos Fuentes ; translated by Sam Hileman. — Harmondsworth : Penguin, 1978, c1964. — 264p ; 18cm
Translation of: La muerte de Artemio Cruz. — Originally published: London : Collins, 1964
ISBN 0-14-004921-5 (pbk) : £0.95 B81-04776

863[F] — **Short stories in Spanish. Argentinian writers,** *1910-1945 — English texts*

Borges, Jorge Luis. Labyrinths : selected stories and other writings / Jorge Luis Borges ; edited by Donald A. Yates and James E. Irby ; preface by André Maurois. — Harmondsworth : Penguin, 1980, c1964 (1981 [printing]). — 287p ; 20cm. — (A King penguin)
Translated from the Spanish. — Originally published: New York : New Directions, 1964
ISBN 0-14-002981-8 (pbk) : £2.50 B81-29741

Borges, Jorge Luis. Six problems for Don Isidro Parodi / Jorge Luis Borges, Adolfo Bioy-Casares ; translated by Norman Thomas di Giovanni. — London : Allen Lane, 1981. — 160p ; 24cm
Translation of: Seis problemas para don Isidro Parodi / H. Bustos Domecq
ISBN 0-7139-1421-1 : £5.95 B81-23989

Borges, Jorge Luis. A universal history of infamy / Jorge Luis Borges ; translated by Norman Thomas di Giovanni. — Harmondsworth : Penguin, 1975, c1972 (1981 [printing]). — 137p ; 20cm
Translation of: Historia universal de la infamia. — Originally published: New York : Dutton, 1972 ; London : Allen Lane, 1973. — Bibliography: p133-137
ISBN 0-14-003959-7 (pbk) : £1.95 B81-25446

863[F] — **Short stories in Spanish. Mexican writers,** *1945- — English texts*

Fuentes, Carlos. Burnt water : stories / by Carlos Fuentes ; translated from the Spanish by Margaret Sayers Peden. — London : Secker & Warburg, 1981, c1980. — 231p ; 21cm
Originally published: New York : Farrar, Straus, and Giroux, 1980
ISBN 0-436-16763-8 : £6.50 B81-03932

863'.01'08 — **Short stories in Spanish,** *1369-1516 — Anthologies*

Dos **Opúsculos** Isabelinos / edición y estudio de Keith Whinnom. — [Exeter] : University of Exeter, 1979. — liv,112p : 1geneal.table ; 21cm. — (Exeter Hispanic texts, ISSN 0305-8700, ISSN 22)
Bibliography: p106-112. — Includes index. — Contents: La Coronación de la Señora Gracisla. — Cárcel de amor Nicolás Núñez
ISBN 0-85989-069-4 (pbk) : Unpriced B81-23973

863.1 — SPANISH FICTION, TO 1369

863'.1 — **Fiction in Spanish,** *to 1369 — Texts*

Juan Manuel, *Infante of Castile.* Juan Manuel, a selection / edited, with introduction and notes by Ian Macpherson. — London : Tamesis Texts, 1980. — xliii,167p : 3geneal.tables ; 21cm
Spanish text, English introduction and notes. — Includes bibliographies
ISBN 0-7293-0084-6 (pbk) : £5.40 B81-17651

863.5 — SPANISH FICTION, 1800-1900

863'.5 — **Fiction in Spanish. Alas, Leopoldo. Regenta,** *La* **& Su único hijo** *— Critical studies*

Valis, Noël Maureen. The decadent vision in Leopoldo Alas : a study of La Regenta and Su único hijo / Noël Maureen Valis. — Baton Rouge ; London : Louisiana State University Press, c1981. — 215p ; 23cm
Bibliography: p195-209. — Includes index
ISBN 0-8071-0769-7 : £11.35 B81-29526

863'.5 — **Fiction in Spanish. Pérez Galdós, Benito** *— Critical studies*

Urey, Diane F.. Galdós and the irony of language. — Cambridge : Cambridge University Press, Feb.1982. — [138]p. — (Cambridge Iberian and Latin American studies)
ISBN 0-521-23756-4 : £17.50 : CIP entry B81-39209

863.64 — SPANISH FICTION, 1945-

863'.64[F] — **Fiction in Spanish,** *1945- — English texts*

García Márquez, Gabriel. Innocent Eréndira : and other stories / Gabriel García Márquez ; translated from the Spanish by Gregory Rabassa. — [London] : Picador, 1981, c1978. — 125p ; 20cm
Translations from the Spanish. — Originally published: New York : Harper & Row, 1978 ; London : Cape, 1979
£1.75 (pbk) B81-37352

868.62 — SPANISH MISCELLANY, 1900-1945

868'.6208 — **Prose in Spanish,** *1900-1945 — English texts*

García Lorca, Federico. Deep song : and other prose / Federico García Lorca ; edited and translated by Christopher Maurer. — London : Boyars, 1980. — xiii,143p ; 21cm
ISBN 0-7145-2723-8 : £6.95 : CIP rev. B80-14065

868'.6209 — **Spanish literature,** *1900-1945 Texts*

García Lorca, Federico. Autógrafos / Federico García Lorca. — Oxford : Dolphin Book Co. [111]: Así que pasen cinco aõs / transcripción, notas y estudio por Rafael Martinez Nadal. — 1979. — 253p ; 28cm
Contents: Facsimile and transcription of Así que pasen cinco años
ISBN 0-85215-065-2 (pbk) : £28.00 B81-24255

869.1 — PORTUGUESE POETRY

869.1 — **Poetry in Portuguese. Brazilian writers,** *1921- — English texts*

Andrade, Carlos Drummond de. The minus sign : a selection from the Poetic anthology / Carlos Drummond de Andrade ; translated from the Portuguese by Virginia de Araujo. — Manchester : Carcanet, 1981. — 168p ; 22cm
Translation of: selections from Antologia poética. — Bibliography: p165. - Includes index
ISBN 0-85635-296-9 (pbk) : £3.95 B81-28956

869.1'2 — **Poetry in Portuguese,** *1500-1800 — Texts*

Camões, Luiz de. Os Lusiadas / Luís de Camões ; edited with an introduction and notes by Frank Pierce. — Oxford : Clarendon, 1973 (1981 [printing]). — xiv,271p ; 22cm
Portuguese text, English introduction and notes. — Includes index
ISBN 0-19-815782-7 (pbk) : £3.50 B81-40511

869.1'2 — **Poetry in Portuguese. Miranda, Francisco de Sá de** *— Critical studies*

Earle, T. F.. Theme and image in the poetry of Sá de Miranda / T.F. Earle. — Oxford : Oxford University Press, 1980. — 153p ; 23cm. — (Oxford modern languages and literature monographs)
Bibliography: p143-150. — Includes index
ISBN 0-19-815754-1 : £9.00 : CIP rev. B80-07155

869.3 — PORTUGUESE FICTION

869.3[F] — **Fiction in Portuguese. Brazilian writers,** *1921- — English texts*

Amado, Jorge. Tieta : the goat girl, or the return of the prodigal daughter : a melodramatic serial novel in five sensational episodes, with a touching epilogue : thrills and suspense! / by Jorge Amado ; translated from the Portuguese by Barbara Shelby Merollo. — London : Souvenir, 1981. — xi,671p ; 22cm
Translation of: Tieta do Agreste. — Originally published: New York : Knopf, 1979
ISBN 0-285-62507-1 : £7.95 B81-34616

Dourado, Autran. The voices of the dead : a novel / Autran Dourado ; translated from the Portuguese by John M. Parker. — London : Peter Owen, 1980. — 248p ; 20cm. — (UNESCO collection of representative works. Brazilian series)
Translation of: Ópera dos mortos
ISBN 0-7206-0558-x : £6.95 B81-04885

Olinto, Antonio. The water house. — Walton-on-Thames : Nelson, Jan.1982. — [416] p. — (Panafrica library)
Translation of: A casa da agua. — Originally published: London : Rex Collings, 1970
ISBN 0-17-511622-9 (pbk) : £2.75 : CIP entry B81-34391

870 — ITALIC LITERATURES

870'.7'1042 — **England. Educational institutions. Curriculum subjects: Latin literature**

Goodyear, F. R. D.. The future of Latin studies in English education : an inaugural lecture / by F.R. D. Goodyear. — London ([Regent's Park, NW1 4NS]) : Bedford College, University of London, [1981?]. — 14p ; 26cm
Delivered Nov.21, 1967
Unpriced (pbk)
Primary classification 470'.7'1042 B81-35416

870.9 — LATIN LITERATURE. HISTORY AND CRITICAL STUDIES

870.9 — **Latin literature,** *to ca 1400 — Critical studies — Conference proceedings — Serials*

Papers of the Liverpool Latin Seminar. — 1976-. — Liverpool (School of Classics, Abercromby Sq., University of Liverpool, P.O. Box 147, Liverpool L69 3BX) : F. Cairns, 1977-. — v. ; 21cm. — (Arca)
Issued every two years
ISSN 0261-0698 = Papers of the Liverpool Latin Seminar : £10.00
Also classified at 880.9'001 B81-17477

Papers of the Liverpool Latin Seminar. — 1979. — Liverpool (School of Classics, Abercromby Sq., University of Liverpool, P.O. Box 147, Liverpool L69 3BX) : F. Cairns, c1979. — 360p. — (Arca, ISSN 0309-5541 (corrected) ; 3)
ISBN 0-905205-03-0 : £12.50
ISSN 0261-0698
Also classified at 880.9'001 B81-17478

870.9'9429 — **Latin literature. Welsh writers,** *1350- — Critical studies*

Davies, Ceri. Latin writers of the Renaissance / Ceri Davies. — [Cardiff] : University of Wales Press on behalf of the Welsh Arts Council, 1981. — 67p : 1facsim ; 25cm. — (Writers of Wales, ISSN 0141-5050)
Limited ed. of 1000 copies. — Bibliography: p55-63
ISBN 0-7083-0792-2 (pbk) : £2.50 : CIP rev. B81-04275

871 — LATIN POETRY

871'.008 — **Poetry in Latin,** *200-1300 — Anthologies*

The **Oxford** book of medieval Latin verse / newly selected and edited by F.J.E. Raby. — Repr. from corr. sheets of 1st ed. — Oxford : Clarendon Press, 1981, c1959. — xix,511p ; 17cm
Medieval Latin text, English introduction and notes. — Includes index
ISBN 0-19-812119-9 : £9.50 B81-28963

871'.009 — **Poetry in Latin. Scansion**

Ritchie, Frank. First steps in Latin scansion / by Frank Ritchie. — St Peter Port : Toucan, 1981. — [12]p ; 19cm. — (Blanchelande College classics series ; no.1)
Cover title. — Originally published: in Easy Ovid
ISBN 0-85694-241-3 (pbk) : Unpriced B81-39973

871'.01 — **Poetry in Latin. Juvenal** *— Commentaries*

Courtney, E.. A commentary on the Satires of Juvenal / by E. Courtney. — London : Athlone, 1980. — x,650p : maps ; 23cm
Bibliography: p61-71. — Includes index
ISBN 0-485-11190-x : £35.00 : CIP rev. B80-04577

871′.01 — Poetry in Latin, *to ca 500 — Latin-English parallel texts*

Persius Flaccus, Aulus. [Satires. English & Latin]. The satires / Persius ; text with translation and notes by J.R. Jenkinson. — Warminster : Aris & Phillips, c1980. — vii,131p ; 22cm. — (Classical texts)
Bibliography: p126-131
ISBN 0-85668-159-8 (cased) : £10.00 : CIP rev.
ISBN 0-85668-173-3 (pbk) : £5.00 B80-07585

Virgil. [Eclogues. English]. Virgil's Eclogues : the Latin text with a verse translation and brief notes / by Guy Lee. — Liverpool (School of Classics, Abercromby Sq., University of Liverpool, P.O. Box 147) : F.Cairns, 1980. — vii,88p ; 21cm. — (Liverpool Latin texts, ISSN 0144-9451 ; 1)
Parallel Latin text and English translation
ISBN 0-905205-04-9 (pbk) : £4.00 B81-20002

Virgil. The georgics / Virgil ; with John Dryden's translation ; notes and introduction by Alistair Elliot. — Ashington (Wansbeck Sq., Ashington, Northumberland) : Mid Northumberland Arts Group, 1981. — 198p ; 22cm
Includes parallel Latin text and English translation. — Bibliography: p195
ISBN 0-904790-13-4 (pbk) : £3.95 B81-15119

871′.01 — Poetry in Latin, *to ca 500 — Texts with commentaries*

Horace. The Odes / Horace ; edited with introduction, revised text and commentary by Kenneth Quinn. — Basingstoke : Macmillan, 1980. — xviii,333p ; 22cm. — (Classical series)
Latin text, English introduction and notes. — Bibliography: pxvii-xviii. — Includes index
ISBN 0-333-11876-6 (pbk) : £8.95 : CIP rev.
B80-02595

872 — LATIN DRAMATIC POETRY AND DRAMA

872′.01 — Drama in Latin, *to ca 500 — English texts*

Plautus, Titus Maccius. Rudens ; Curculio ; Casina. — Cambridge : Cambridge University Press, Nov.1981. — [157]p. — (Translations from Greek and Roman authors)
ISBN 0-521-28046-x (pbk) : £2.50 : CIP entry
B81-38813

Plautus, Titus Maccius. A villa at Cyrene : the Rudens of Plautus in translation (with some omissions) / R.N. Benton. — [Louth] ([42a Westgate, Louth, Lincs., LN11 9YD]) : R.N. Benton, 1981. — 24p : ill,1chart,1map ; 30cm
Translated from the Latin translation of the original Greek
£2.50 (unbound) B81-23617

872′.01 — Drama in Latin, *to ca 500 — Texts*

Terence. Phormio / Terence ; edited by R.H. Martin. — Letchworth : Bradda, 1981, c1959. — vii,208p ; 20cm
Latin text, English introduction and commentary. — Originally published: London : Methuen, 1959. — Bibliography: p79-80
£2.95 (pbk) B81-35418

872′.01′08 — Drama in Latin, *to ca 500 — Anthologies — English texts*

The **Tenth** muse : classical drama in translation / edited with an introduction by Charles Doria. — Chicago ; London : Ohio University Press, c1980. — 587p ; 23cm
Translations from the Greek and Latin
ISBN 0-8040-0781-0 : Unpriced
ISBN 0-8040-0813-2 (pbk) : Unpriced
Primary classification 882′.01′08 B81-12141

873 — LATIN EPIC POETRY AND FICTION

873′.01 — Epic poetry in Latin. Virgil. Aeneid — *Critical studies*

Quinn, Kenneth. 'But the queen - ' : conceptual fields in Virgil's Aeneid / by Kenneth Quinn. — Exeter : University of Exeter, 1981. — 20p ; 22cm. — (Jackson Knight memorial lecture ; 13)
Unpriced (pbk) B81-33328

874 — LATIN LYRIC POETRY

874′.008 — Lyric poetry in Latin, *B.C.70-A.D.1674 — Anthologies — Latin-English parallel texts*

More Latin lyrics : from Virgil to Milton / translated by Helen Waddell ; edited & with and introduction by Dame Felicitas Corrigan. — London : Gollancz, 1976 (1980). — 392p,[4]p of plates : facsims,ports ; 22cm
Parallel Latin text and English translation. — Includes index
ISBN 0-575-02177-2 : £8.95 B81-03604

876 — LATIN LETTERS

876′.01 — Letters in Latin, *to ca 500 — Texts*

Cicero, Marcus Tullius. Epistulae ad Quintum fratrem et M. Brutum / Cicero ; edited by D.R. Shackleton Bailey. — Cambridge : Cambridge University Press, 1980. — xi,274p ; 23cm. — (Cambridge classical texts and commentaries ; 22)
Latin text, English introduction and commentary. — Bibliography: pix-xi. — Includes index
ISBN 0-521-23053-5 : £25.00 B81-14648

878 — LATIN MISCELLANY

878′.0102 — Epigrams in Latin. Martial. Epigrams. Bk 1 — *Commentaries*

Howell, Peter. A commentary on Book One of the Epigrams of Martial / Peter Howell. — London : Athlone, 1980. — vi,369p : ill,3maps,1plan ; 23cm
Bibliography: p20-24. — Includes index
ISBN 0-485-11191-8 : £28.00 : CIP rev.
B80-08508

878′.0108 — Prose in Latin, *to ca 500 — English texts*

Cicero, Marcus Tullius. On the good life / Cicero ; translated with an introduction by Michael Grant. — Harmondsworth : Penguin, 1971 (1979 [printing]). — 381p : maps,2geneal.tables ; 18cm. — (Penguin classic)
Translation from the Latin. — Bibliography: p359. — Includes index
ISBN 0-14-044244-8 (pbk) : £1.75 B81-39938

878′.0109 — Latin literature. Rhetoric. Criticism. Seneca, Lucius Annaeus, *ca.55 B.C.-ca.39 — Critical studies*

Fairweather, Janet. Seneca the Elder / Janet Fairweather. — Cambridge : Cambridge University Press, 1981. — xii,418p ; 23cm. — (Cambridge classical studies)
Bibliography: p377-383. — Includes index
ISBN 0-521-23101-9 : £20.00 : CIP rev.
B81-00639

880 — CLASSICAL AND MODERN GREEK LITERATURES

880′.07 — Education. Curriculum subjects: Classics

Dietrich, B. C. A sense of guilt : an inaugural lecture delivered at the University College of Wales, Aberystwyth on 24 October 1979 / by B.C. Dietrich. — Cardiff : University of Wales Press, 1980. — 24p ; 21cm
ISBN 0-7083-0781-7 (pbk) : £0.90 : CIP rev.
B80-18935

880.09 — Classical literatures — *Critical studies*

Pegasus : classical essays from the University of Exeter / edited and with an introduction by H.W. Stubbs. — [Exeter] : University of Exeter, 1981. — x,133p,[12]p of plates : ill,1port ; 21cm
Includes index
ISBN 0-85989-117-8 (pbk) : £4.50 B81-20847

880.09 — Classical literatures — *Critical studies — Serials*

Yale classical studies / edited for the Department of Classics. — Vol.26. — Cambridge : Cambridge University Press, 1980. — 237p
ISBN 0-521-23120-5 : £15.00 B81-35962

880.9 — CLASSICAL GREEK LITERATURE. HISTORY AND CRITICAL STUDIES

880.9′001 — Greek literature, *to ca 500 — Critical studies — Conference proceedings — Serials*

Papers of the Liverpool Latin Seminar. — 1976-. — Liverpool (School of Classics, Abercromby Sq., University of Liverpool, P.O. Box 147, Liverpool L69 3BX) : F. Cairns, 1977-. — v. ; 21cm. — (Arca)
Issued every two years
ISSN 0261-0698 = Papers of the Liverpool Latin Seminar : £10.00
Primary classification 870.9 B81-17477

Papers of the Liverpool Latin Seminar. — 1979. — Liverpool (School of Classics, Abercromby Sq., University of Liverpool, P.O. Box 147, Liverpool L69 3BX) : F. Cairns, c1979. — 360p. — (Arca, ISSN 0309-5541 (corrected) ; 3)
ISBN 0-905205-03-0 : £12.50
ISSN 0261-0698
Primary classification 870.9 B81-17478

881 — CLASSICAL GREEK POETRY

881′.009 — Poetry in Greek, *to 1600 — Critical studies*

Trypanis, Constantine Athanasius. Greek poetry. — London : Fraser, May 1981. — [896]p
ISBN 0-571-08346-3 : £25.00 : CIP entry
Also classified at 889′.1′009 B81-12821

881′.01′08 — Epigrammatic poetry in Greek, *to ca 500 — Anthologies*

Further Greek epigrams. — Cambridge : Cambridge University Press, Feb.1982. — [598]p
ISBN 0-521-22903-0 : £82.50 : CIP entry
B81-40269

881′.01′08 — Poetry in Greek, *to ca 500 — Anthologies — English texts*

The **Greek** anthology : and other ancient epigrams : a selection in modern verse translations / edited with an introduction by Peter Jay. — Rev. ed. — Harmondsworth : Penguin, 1981. — 442p : maps ; 18cm. — (Penguin classics)
Previous ed.: London : Allen Lane, 1973. — Bibliography: p423-424. — Includes index
ISBN 0-14-044285-5 (pbk) : £2.50 B81-40010

882 — CLASSICAL GREEK DRAMATIC POETRY AND DRAMA

882′.01 — Drama in Greek. Euripides — *Critical studies*

Collard, C.. Euripides / by C. Collard. — Oxford : Clarendon for the Classical Association, 1981. — 39p ; 24cm. — (New surveys in the classics ; no.14)
Bibliography: p37-39
ISBN 0-903035-11-1 (pbk) : £2.50 B81-22369

882′.01 — Drama in Greek. Euripides — *Textual criticisms*

Diggle, James. Studies on the text of Euripides : Supplices, Electra, Heracles, Troades, Iphigenia in Tauris, Ion / James Diggle. — Oxford : Clarendon, 1981. — x,127p ; 22cm
Bibliography: pxi-xv. - Includes index
ISBN 0-19-814019-3 : £12.50 : CIP rev.
B80-06216

882′.01 — Drama in Greek. Menander — *Critical studies*

Goldberg, Sander M.. The making of Menander's comedy / Sander M. Goldberg. — London : Athlone, 1980. — vi,148p ; 23cm
Bibliography: p122-124. - Includes index
ISBN 0-485-11189-6 : £12.50 : CIP rev.
B80-04578

882′.01 — Drama in Greek. Menander. Misoumenos — *Textual criticisms*

Turner, E. G.. The lost beginning of Meander Misoumenos / by E.G. Turner. — London : British Academy, c1978. — P.315-331 ; 25cm
Includes Greek text and English translation
ISBN 0-85672-162-x (pbk) : £1.00 B81-09263

882′.01 — Drama in Greek. Sophocles. Tragedies — *Critical studies*

Segal, Charles. Tragedy and civilization : an interpretation of Sophocles / Charles Segal. — Cambridge, Mass. ; London : Published for Oberlin College by Harvard University Press, 1981. — xii,506p ; 24cm. — (Martin classical lectures ; v.26)
Bibliography: p489-497. — Includes index
ISBN 0-674-90206-8 : £21.00 B81-39778

882′.01 — Drama in Greek, *to ca 500* — *English texts*

Euripides. Helen, The Trojan women, The Bacchae. — Cambridge : Cambridge University Press, Sept.1981. — [176]p. — (Translations from Greek and Roman authors)
ISBN 0-521-28047-8 (pbk) : £2.50 : CIP entry B81-30312

882′.01 — Drama in Greek, *to ca 500* — *Greek-English parallel texts*

Aristophanes. [Acharnians. Greek and English]. Acharnians / edited with translation and notes by Alan H. Sommerstein. — Warminster : Aris & Phillips, c1980. — viii,215p ; 21cm. — (The Comedies of Aristophanes ; v.1)
Parallel Greek text and English translation, English introduction and notes. — Bibliography: pvii-viii
ISBN 0-85668-167-9 (cased) : £10.00 : CIP rev.
ISBN 0-85668-172-5 (pbk) : £5.00 B80-10895

Aristophanes. Knights. — Warminster : Aris & Phillips, Nov.1981. — [232]p. — (The Comedies of Aristophanes ; v.2)
ISBN 0-85668-177-6 (cased) : £10.00 : CIP entry
ISBN 0-85668-178-4 (pbk) : £5.00 B81-30405

882′.01 — Drama in Greek. Tragedies, *to ca 500* — *Critical studies*

Bain, David. Masters, servants and orders in Greek tragedy. — Manchester : Manchester University Press, Nov.1981. — [96]p. — (Publications of the Faculty of Arts of the University of Manchester ; no.26)
ISBN 0-7190-1296-1 : £10.00 : CIP entry B81-31244

882′.01′01 — Drama in Greek, *to ca 500.* **Theories. Nietzsche, Friedrich. Geburt der Tragödie aus dem Geiste der Musik** — *Critical studies*

Silk, M. S.. Nietzsche on tragedy / M.S. Silk and J.P.Stern. — Cambridge : Cambridge University Press, 1981. — 441p ; 24cm
Bibliography: p430-431. — Includes index
ISBN 0-521-23262-7 : £27.50 B81-14660

882′.01′08 — Drama in Greek, *to ca 500* — *Anthologies — English texts*

The **Tenth** muse : classical drama in translation / edited with an introduction by Charles Doria. — Chicago ; London : Ohio University Press, c1980. — 587p ; 23cm
Translations from the Greek and Latin
ISBN 0-8040-0781-0 : Unpriced
ISBN 0-8040-0813-2 (pbk) : Unpriced
Also classified at 872′.01′08 B81-12141

882′.01′09 — Drama in Greek. Tragedies, *to ca 500 expounded by* **Aristotle′s theories of dramatic tragedy**

Jones, John, *1924 May 6-*. On Aristotle and Greek tragedy / John Jones. — London : Chatto & Windus, 1962 (1980 [printing]). — 284p ; 22cm
Includes index
ISBN 0-7011-1379-0 (pbk) : £3.95 B81-07225

882′.01′09 — Drama in Greek. Tragedies, *to ca 500.* **Social aspects**

Vernant, Jean-Pierre. Tragedy and myth in ancient Greece / Jean-Pierre Vernant and Pierre Vidal-Naquet ; translated from the French by Janet Lloyd. — Brighton : Harvester, 1981. — xi,199p,[4]p of plates : ill ; 23cm. — (European philosophy and the human sciences ; 7)
Translation of: Myth et tragedie en Grèce Ancienne
ISBN 0-85527-916-8 : £28.00 B81-16175

883 — CLASSICAL GREEK EPIC POETRY AND FICTION

883′.01 — Epic poetry in Greek. Homer. Iliad & Odyssey — *Critical studies*

Griffin, Jasper. Homer / Jasper Griffin. — Oxford : Oxford University Press, 1980. — 82p ; 18cm. — (Past masters)
Bibliography: p80. - Includes index
ISBN 0-19-287533-7 (cased) : £4.50 : CIP rev.
ISBN 0-19-287532-9 (pbk) : £0.95 B80-13619

883′.01 — Epic poetry in Greek, *to ca 500* — *English texts*

Homer. [Odyssey. English]. The illustrated Odyssey / translated from Homer by E.V. Rieu ; introduction by Jacquetta Hawkes ; original photographs by Tim Mercer. — London : Sidgwick & Jackson, 1980. — 255p : ill(some col.),1map ; 26cm
Originally published: Harmondsworth : Penguin, 1945
ISBN 0-283-98588-7 : £8.95 B81-20398

883′.01 — Epic poetry in Greek, *to ca 500* — *Texts*

Homer. [Iliad. Book 11]. The Iliad of Homer, book XI / edited by E.S. Forster. — Letchworth : Bradda, 1981. — ix,99p : ill,maps ; 20cm
Text in English and Greek. — Originally published : Methuen, 1939
£1.95 (pbk) B81-16958

884 — CLASSICAL GREEK LYRIC POETRY

884′.01′08 — Lyric poetry in Greek, *to ca 500* — *Anthologies — English texts*

Archilochos, Sappho, Alkman : three lyric poets of the Late Greek Bronze Age / translated, with an introduction, by Guy Davenport. — Berkeley ; London : University of California Press, c1980. — 176p ; 24cm
ISBN 0-520-03823-1 : £8.75 B81-05760

Campbell, D. A.. The golden lyre. — London : Duckworth, Sept.1981. — [300]p
ISBN 0-7156-1563-7 : £24.00 : CIP entry B81-22576

888 — CLASSICAL GREEK MISCELLANY

888′.0108 — Prose in Greek, *to ca 500* — *English texts*

Aesop. The fables of Aesop / illustrated by Edward J. Detmold. — Sevenoaks : Hodder & Stoughton, 1981. — xvi,152p,[23]p of plates : ill (some col.) ; 26cm
Facsim. of: 1909
ISBN 0-340-26766-6 : £10.95
ISBN 0-340-26769-0 (leather) : Unpriced B81-27778

888′.01′08 — Prose in Greek, *to ca 500* — *English texts*

Arrian. Life of Alexander the Great. — Cambridge : Cambridge University Press, Nov.1981. — [112]p. — (Translations from Greek and Roman authors)
ISBN 0-521-28195-4 (pbk) : £2.20 : CIP entry B81-30524

889 — MODERN GREEK LITERATURE

889′.1′009 — Poetry in Modern Greek, *to 1980* — *Critical studies*

Trypanis, Constantine Athanasius. Greek poetry. — London : Fraser, May 1981. — [896]p
ISBN 0-571-08346-3 : £25.00 : CIP entry
Primary classification 881′.009 B81-12821

889′.132 — Poetry in Modern Greek, *1900-1945* — *English texts*

Ritsos, Yannis. Subterranean horses / by Yannis Ritsos ; illustrations by the author ; translated by Minas Savvas ; introduction by Vassilis Vassilikos. — Chicago ; London : Ohio University Press, c1980. — xii,63p : ill ; 24cm. — ([International poetry series ; v.3])
Translated from the Greek
ISBN 0-8214-0579-9 (cased) : Unpriced
ISBN 0-8214-0580-2 (pbk) : Unpriced B81-19971

889′.134 — Poetry in Modern Greek, *1945-* — *English texts*

Sinopoulos, Takis. Stones / Takis Sinopoulos ; translated from the Greek by John Stathatos. — London : Oasis Books, 1980. — 26p ; 20cm
Translation of: Petres. Athens : Kedres, 1972
ISBN 0-903375-46-x (pbk) : Unpriced : CIP rev. B79-37067

889′.32[F] — Fiction in Modern Greek, *1821-1900* — *English texts*

Rohoïdēs, Emmanouēl. Pope Joan / Lawrence Durrell ; translated and adapted from the Greek of Emmanuel Royidis. — London : Owen, 1981, c1960. — 164p ; 20cm
Translation of: Papissa Iōanna. — Previous ed.: London : D. Verschoyle, 1954. —
Bibliography: p164
ISBN 0-7206-0585-7 : £6.95 B81-17371

891.2/4 — INDIC LITERATURES

891′.22′008 — Drama in Sanskrit — *Anthologies — English texts*

VíśākhadattaThree Sanskrit plays / translated with an introduction by Michael Coulson. — Harmondsworth : Penguin, 1981. — 429p ; 20cm. — (Penguin classics)
Contents: Śakuntalā / by Kālidāsa. Translation of Şakuntala — Rāshasa′s ring / by Viśākhadatta. Translation of Mudrārākshasa — Mālatī and Mādhava / by Bhavabhūti Translation of Mālatī-mādhava
ISBN 0-14-044374-6 (pbk) : £4.95 B81-40012

891′.3 — Nīti literature in Pali — *Anthologies*

Pāli nīti texts of Burma : Dhammanīti, Lokanīti, Mahārahanīti, Rājanīti : critical edition and study / by Heinz Bechert and Heinz Braun. — London : Pali Text Society, 1981. — lxxxv,230p ; 23cm. — (Text series ; no.171)
Bibliography: pxi-xix. — Includes index
ISBN 0-7100-0918-6 : £22.50 B81-26353

891′.3 — Poetry in Pali — *Texts*

Buddharakkhita. Jinâlaṅkâra, or, Embellishments of Buddha / by Buddharakkhita ; edited, with introduction, notes, and translation by James Gray. — London : Pali Text Society ; London : Distributed by Routledge & Kegan Paul, 1981. — 112p ; 23cm. — (Sacred books of the Buddhists ; v.36)
Pali text, English introduction, notes and translation. — Originally published: London : Luzac, 1894
ISBN 0-7100-0609-8 : Unpriced B81-32378

891′.3 — Short stories in Pali — *Anthologies*

Paññ a sa-J a taka, or, Zimme Pa n n a sa (in the Burmese recension) / edited by Padmanabh S. Jaini. — London : Pali Text Society ; London : Distributed by Routledge & Kegan Paul. — (Text series / Pali Text Society ; no.172)
ISBN 0-7100-0919-4 : £22.50 B81-27020

891′.4 — Indian literatures, *1940-1977* — *Critical studies*

Contemporary Indian literature and society / editor Motilal Jotwani. — New Delhi : Heritage ; London [distributor], c1979. — xi,251p ; 23cm
£9.00 B81-09300

891.5 — IRANIAN LITERATURES

891′.5511 — Poetry in Persian, *1000-1389* — *English texts*

Imar Khayyám. [Rubaiyat. English]. The Ruba′iyat of Omar Khayyam / translated by Peter Avery and John Heath-Stubbs. — London : Allen Lane, 1979. — 128p : col.ill,maps ; 24cm
Maps on lining papers. — Bibliography: p128
ISBN 0-7139-1134-4 : £6.95 B81-40013

Omar Khayyám. [Rubaiyat. English]. Omar Khayyam / [translated by] Edward Fitzgerald ; illustrated by Karen Belsey. — Bognor Regis : New Horizon, c1978. — 90p : ill ; 22cm
Translation of: Rubaiyat
ISBN 0-86116-056-8 : £3.50 B81-40941

891'.5511 — Poetry in Persian, *1000-1389 — English texts* *continuation*

Omar Khayyám. [Rubaiyat. English]. The Ruba'iyat of Omar Khayyam / translated by Peter Avery and John Heath-Stubbs. — Harmondsworth : Penguin, 1981, c1979. — 116p : 1map ; 18cm. — (Penguin classics)
Translated from the Persian. — This translation orignally published: London : Allen Lane, 1979. — Bibliography: p115-116
ISBN 0-14-044384-3 (pbk) : £1.25 B81-40011

891'.5511 — Poetry in Persian, *1000-1389 — Esperanto-English parallel texts*

Omar Khayyám. [Rubaiyat. English & Esperanto]. La Robajoj de Omar Kajam = The Rubáiyát of Omar Khayyám / elangligita de William Auld ; [translated by] Edward Fitzgerald ; kovrildesegno kaj ilustraĵoj de Jean Bomford. — Glasgow ([16 Woodlands Drive, Coatbridge ML5 1LE]) : Eldonejo Kardo, 1980. — 49p,[6]leaves of plates : ill ; 21cm
Translation of: Rubaiyat. — Text in Esperanto and English
ISBN 0-905149-14-9 (pbk) : £2.80 B81-40942

891'.5511 — Poetry in Persian. Jalāl al-Dīn, Rūmī *— Critical studies*

Schimmel, Annemarie. The triumphal sun : a study of the works of Jalāloddin Rumi / Annemarie Schimmel. — Rev. ed. — London : East-West, c1980. — xviii,513p : ill,facsims ; 24cm. — (Persian studies series)
Previous ed.: London : Fine Books, 1978. — Bibliography: p481-492. — Includes index
ISBN 0-85692-006-1 : £12.50 B81-26824

891'.5512 — Poetry in Persian, *1389-1900 — English texts*

Jāmī. Yusuf and Zulaikha : an allegorical romance / by Hakim Nuruddin Abdurrahman (Jami) ; edited, abridged and translated by David Pendlebury. — London : Octagon Press, 1980. — ix,185p ; 21cm
Translation from the Persian
ISBN 0-900860-77-4 : £8.00 B81-40302

891'.5513 — Poetry in Persian, *1900- — Persian-English parallel texts*

Nurbakhsh, Javad. Divani Nurbakhsh : Sufi poetry / Javad Nurbakhsh. — London (41 Chepstow Place, W.2) : Khaniqahi-Nimatullahi, c1980. — 265p ; 24cm
Parallel English and Persian text
Unpriced B81-11652

891'.5513 — Poetry in Persian, *1900- — Polyglot texts*

Khalili, Khalilullah. Quatrains of Khalilullah Khalili. — London : Octagon Press, 1981. — 82p ; 21cm
Parallel Persian, Arabic and English text
ISBN 0-900860-84-7 : Unpriced B81-26832

891.62 — IRISH LITERATURE

891.6'2'09 — Irish literature, *to 1800 — Critical studies*

Hyde, Douglas, *1860-1949.* A literary history of Ireland : from earliest times to the present day / by Douglas Hyde. — New ed. / with introduction by Brian Ó Cuív. — London : Benn, 1967 (1980 [printing]). — xlii,654p ; 23cm
Bibliography: pxxvii-xxxii. - Includes index
ISBN 0-510-31701-4 : £12.95 : CIP rev. B79-36084

891.6'2'0936 — Irish literature, *to 1980.* **Special themes: Nature** *— Critical studies — Irish texts*

Léachtaí cholm cille XI : an dúlra sa litríocht / in eagar ag Pádraig Ó Fiannachta. — Má Nuad : An Sagart, 1980. — 178p ; 22cm
Includes bibliographies
Unpriced (pbk) B81-13285

891.6'21'008 — Poetry in Irish, *1600-1900 — Anthologies — Irish-English parallel texts*

An **Duanaire,** 1600-1900 : poems of the dispossessed / curtha i láthair ag Seán ó Tuama ; with translations into English verse by Thomas Kinsella. — Portlaoise : Dolmen, 1981. — xxxix,382p : ill,2maps,1port ; 23cm
Parallel Irish text and English translation
ISBN 0-85105-363-7 (cased) : £12.00 : CIP rev.
ISBN 0-85105-364-5 (pbk) : £4.50 B80-03407

891.6'211'08 — Poetry in Old Irish *— Anthologies — English texts*

Voices from ancient Ireland : a book of early Irish poetry / photographs and English translation by Bob Willoughby ; Irish advisor: John Cabell. — London : Pan, 1981. — [64]p : ill(some col.) ; 25cm. — (Pan original)
ISBN 0-330-26274-2 (pbk) : £2.95 B81-13917

891.6'212 — Poetry in Irish, *1171-1700 — English texts*

Dán na mBráthar Mionúr / Cuthbert Mhág Craith a chuir in eagar. — Baile Átha Cliath : Institiúid Ard-Léinn Bhaile Átha Cliath. — 1980
Cuid 2: Aistriúcháin, nótaí etc.. — viii,440p ; 23cm. — (Scríbhinní Gaeilge na mBráthar Mionúr ; 8)
English text, Irish notes. — Includes index
Unpriced B81-23390

891.6'214 — Poetry in Irish, *1850- — Texts*

Ellis, Conleth. Aimsir fháistineach / Conleth Ellis ; maisith ag Pádraig Ó Cuimín. — Baile Átha Cliath (6 Sráid Fhearchair, Baile Átha Cliath 2) : Clódhanna, 1981. — 40p ; 22cm
£1.50 (pbk) B81-26557

Mac an tSaoi, Máire. An galar dubhach / Máire mac an tSaoi. — Baile Átha Cliath ([26 Céide Fearann Dara, Br. Na hArdphairce Ath Cliath 6]) : Sáirséal agus Dill, 1980. — 29p ; 17cm
Includes index
ISBN 0-902563-71-8 : £2.00 B81-20267

Mac Síomóin, Tomás, Codarsnai / Tomás Mac Síomóin. — Baile Átha Cliath (6 Sráid Fhearchair, Baile Átha Cliath 2) : Clódhanna, 1981. — 47p ; 22cm
Unpriced (pbk) B81-26558

Ó Ríordáin, Seán. Scáthán véarsaí : rogha dánta / le Seán Ó Ríordáin. — Baile Átha Cliath : Sáirséal agus Dill, 1980. — 123p : 1port ; 18cm
Includes index
ISBN 0-902563-72-6 : £6.00 B81-15191

Tóibín, Tomás. Fuinneoga / Tomás Tóibín. — Baile Átha Cliath, [i.e. Dublin] (29 Sr. Uí Chonaill Íoch, Baile Átha Cliath 1) : Foilseacháin Náisiúnta Teoranta, c1980. — viii,80p : ill ; 19cm
£2.00 B81-18880

891.6'224 — Drama in Irish, *1850- — Texts*

Ó Tuairisc, Eoghan. Fornocht do chonac / Eoghan Ó Tuairisc. — Baíle Átha Cliath [ie. Dublin] : Oifig an tSoláthair, c1981. — 95p : ill ; 19cm
£1.50 B81-37795

891.6'234 — Children's stories in Irish, *1850- — Texts*

Mac Cárthaigh, Tadhg. An solas draíochta / léaráidí le Mary Lowther. — Baile Átha Cliath : Oifig an tSoláthair, 1980. — 81p : col.ill ; 17x19cm
Unpriced (pbk) B81-15192

891.6'234[F] — Short stories in Irish, *1850- — English texts*

Ó Cadhain, Máirtín. The road to Brightcity : and other stories / Máirtín Ó Cadhain ; translated from the Irish by Eoghan O Tuairisc. — Swords (Knocksedan House, Swords, Co. Dublin) : Poolbeg Press, 1981. — 111p ; 18cm
ISBN 0-905169-47-6 (pbk) : £1.93 B81-32129

891.6'28208 — Prose in Irish, *1171-1700 — Irish-English parallel texts*

Pairlement Chloinne Tomáis / edited by N.J.A. Williams. — Dublin ([10 Burlington Rd., Dublin 4]) : Dublin Institute for Advanced Studies, 1981. — lxvi,196p ; 20cm
Irish text with English translation, introduction and notes. — Bibliography: pix. - Includes index
Unpriced B81-23168

891.63 — GAELIC LITERATURE

891.6'313 — Scotland. National libraries: National Library of Scotland. Exhibits: Items associated with MacLean, Sorley *— Catalogues*

Matheson, Ann. Somhairle Macgill-eain = Sorley MacLean / [Ann Matheson]. — Edinburgh : National Library of Scotland, 1981. — 40p : ill,facsims,ports ; 25cm. — (Exhibition catalogue ; no.19)
Catalogue of an exhibition to mark the 70th birthday of Sorley MacLean
ISBN 0-902220-45-4 (pbk) : Unpriced B81-38460

891.6'333 — Children's stories in Gaelic, *1830- — Texts*

Fearghusdan, Iain. Turus a' chriosdaidh / Iain Fearghusdan. — [Lochmaddy] ([Lochmaddy, North Uist, PA82 5BD]) : Crùisgean, 1979. — 29p : ill ; 21cm
Adaptation of: Pilgrim's progress / by John Bunyan
£1.20 (pbk) B81-09633

891.66 — WELSH LITERATURE

891.6'6'08002 — Welsh literature awarded prizes at Eisteddfodau Teulu Pantyfedwen, Pontrhydfendigaid *— Anthologies*

O fedel Pantyfedwen : cyfansoddiadau llenyddol buddugol / Eisteddfodau Teulu Pantyfedwen, Pontrhydfendigaid. — Pantyfedwen : Eisteddfodau Teulu Pantyfedwen, Pontrhydfendigaid, Pwyllgor Llen ; Llandysul : Gwasg Gomer [distributor], 1981. — 26p ; 22cm
Cover title
£0.50 (pbk) B81-36337

891.6'6'08002 — Welsh literature awarded prizes at Urdd Gobaith Cymru. *Eisteddfod Genedlaethol — Anthologies*

Cyfansoddiadau llenyddol buddugol / Eisteddfod Genedlaethol Urdd Gobaith Cymru, Dyffryn Teifi a'r Cylch 1981. — Aberystwyth : Urdd Gobaith Cymru, [1981]. — 133p ; 21cm
£1.10 (pbk) B81-27259

891.6'6'08092289 — Welsh literature. Puritan writers, *1600- — Anthologies*

Thomas, Oliver. Gweithiau Oliver Thomas ac Evan Roberts : dau Biwritan cynnar / golygwyd gyda rhagymadrodd gan Merfyn Morgan. — Caerdydd : Cyhoeddwyd ar ran Bwrrd Gwybodau Celtaidd Prifysgol Cymru [gan] Wasg Prifysgol Cymru, 1981. — lxxxix,318p ; 23cm
ISBN 0-7083-0729-9 : Unpriced B81-26839

891.6'6'09 — Welsh literature *— Critical studies*

Jones, Gwyn, *1907-.* Babel and the dragon's tongue : the eighth Gwilym James Memorial Lecture of the University of Southampton : delivered at the University on Thursday, 19th February, 1981 / by Gwyn Jones. — [Southampton] : University of Southampton, 1981. — 21p ; 21cm. — (The Eighth Gwilym James memorial lecture)
ISBN 0-85432-217-5 (pbk) : Unpriced B81-30692

891.6'6'09 — Welsh literature *— Critical studies — Serials*

Welsh books & writers = Llên a llyfrau Cymru = Bücher und Schriftsteller von Wales. — Autumn 1979-. — Aberystwyth (Queen's Sq., Aberystwyth, Dyfed) : Cyngor Llfrau Cymraeg, 1979-. — v. : ill,ports ; 30cm
Annual. — Description based on: Autumn 1980 issue
ISSN 0261-5711 = Welsh books & writers : Unpriced B81-31053

891.6'6'09 — Welsh literature, *to 1978 — Critical studies — Welsh texts*

Lewis, Saunders. Meistri a'u crefft : ysgrifau llenyddol / gan Saunders Lewis ; golygwyd gan Gwynn ap Gwilym. — Caerdydd : Gwasg Prifysgol Cymru ar ran yr Academi Gymreig, 1981. — ix,292p ; 23cm. — (Clasuron yr Academi ; 2)
ISBN 0-7083-0791-4 : Unpriced B81-29507

891.6′6′09002 — Welsh literature, *1600- — Biographies*

Jones, Glyn, *1905-*. Profiles : a visitors′ guide to writing in twentieth century Wales / Glyn Jones and John Rowlands. — Llandysul : Gomer, 1980. — xxxi,382p : maps,ports ; 22cm
Maps on lining papers. — Bibliography: p380-382
ISBN 0-85088-713-5 : £9.95
Also classified at 820.9′9429 B81-40041

891.6′609′002 — Welsh literature. Gwent writers, *1800-1900 - Critical studies*

Thomas, Mair Elvet. Agweddau ar weithgarwch llenyddol Gwent yn y ganrif ddiwethaf. — Cardiff : University of Wales Press, May 1981. — 1v.. — (Darlith goffa Islwyn)
ISBN 0-7083-0800-7 (pbk) : £0.90 : CIP entry B81-07416

891.6′61′009 — Poetry in Welsh, *to ca 1980 - Critical studies - Festschriften - Welsh texts*

Bardos. — Cardiff : University of Wales Press, June 1981. — [256]p
ISBN 0-7083-0799-x : £15.00 : CIP entry B81-12833

891.6′611 — Poetry in Welsh, *to 1600 — Texts*

Siôn Tudur. Gwaith Siôn Tudur / wedi ei olygu gan Enid Roberts. — Caerdydd : Gwasg Prifysgol Cymru, 1980. — 2v. : facsims,geneal.tables ; 27cm
Includes bibliographies and index
ISBN 0-7083-0740-x : Unpriced
ISBN 0-7083-0752-3 (v.1) : Unpriced
ISBN 0-7083-0753-1 (v.2) : Unpriced B81-19056

891.6′611′08 — Poetry in Welsh, *to 1600 — Anthologies*

Cywyddau serch y tri bedo. — Cardiff : University of Wales Press, Sept.1981. — [85]p. — (Clasuron yr academi ; 3)
ISBN 0-7083-0795-7 : £4.95 : CIP entry B81-21495

891.6′61109 — Poetry in Welsh, *to 1600 — Critical studies*

Jarman, A. O. H.. The Cynfeirdd : early Welsh poets and poetry. — Cardiff : University of Wales Press, Dec.1981. — [144]p. — (Writers of Wales)
ISBN 0-7083-0813-9 (pbk) : £2.50 : CIP entry B81-35890

891.6′612 — Poetry in Welsh, *1600- — English texts*

Hooson, I. D.. Poems / by I.D. Hooson ; translated from the Welsh by Blodwen Edwards. — [Wales?] : [s.n.], 1980 (Denbigh : Gee). — 61p,[1] leaf of plates : 1port ; 19cm
£2.27 B81-01980

Hooson, I. D.. The wine and other poems / by I.D. Hooson ; translated from the Welsh by Blodwen Edwards. — [Wales?] : [s.n.], 1980 (Denbigh : Gee). — 39p,[1] leaf of plates : 1port ; 19cm
£1.84 B81-01979

891.6′612 — Poetry in Welsh, *1600- — Texts*

Bowen, Euros. Amrywion / Euros Bowen. — Llandysul : Gwasg Gomer, 1980. — 116p ; 22cm
ISBN 0-85088-932-4 : £3.50 B81-01358

Dofwy. Dofwy : Richard Jones (1863-1956). — Abertawe : C. Davies, c1979. — 60p ; 18cm. — (Cyfres beirrd bro ; 14)
ISBN 0-7154-0516-0 (pbk) : £1.25 B81-13967

Evans, Donald, *1940-*. Eden / Donald Evans. — Llandysul : Gwasg Gomer, 1981. — 69p ; 22cm
ISBN 0-85088-575-2 (pbk) : £1.75 B81-38345

Evans, Donald, *1940-*. Grawn / Donald Evans. — Llandysul : Gwasg Gomer, 1979. — 73p ; 22cm
ISBN 0-85088-821-2 (pbk) : £1.50 B81-38347

George, W. R. P.. Tân / W.R.P. George. — Llandysul : Gwasg Gomer, 1979. — 72p ; 19cm
ISBN 0-85088-711-9 : £1.75 B81-38341

Iolo Morganwg. Cerddi rhydd Iolo Morganwg / golygwyd gan P.J. Donovan. — Caerdydd : Gwasg Prifysgol Cymru cyhoeddwyd ar ran Bwrdd Gwybodau Celtaidd Prifysgol Cymru, 1980. — xii,175p ; 23cm
Includes index
ISBN 0-7083-0782-5 : Unpriced : CIP rev B80-18936

Isfoel. Cyfoeth awen Isfoel / golygydd T. Llew Jones. — Llandysul : Gwasg Gomer, 1981. — 124p,[1]leaf of plates : 2ports ; 19cm
ISBN 0-85088-505-1 (pbk) : £1.75 B81-38430

Parry, R. Williams. Cerddi Robert Williams Parry : detholiad / gyda rhaygmadrodd gan Thomas Parry. — Y Drefnewydd [Newtown] ([Newtown, Powys SY16 3PW]) : Gwasg Gregynog, 1980. — xiv,112p : ill ; 30cm
Limited ed. of 230 copies of which 215 are for sale. 15 copies are specially bound and numbered I to XV; the remainder are numbered 1-200
Unpriced B81-07832

Perlau′r beirdd / [golygwyd gan] Morgan D. Jones. — Llandysul : Gwasg Gomer, 1981. — 169p ; 18cm
Bibliography: p161. — Includes index
ISBN 0-85088-545-0 (pbk) : £1.95 B81-38343

891.6′612 — Poetry in Welsh. Eifion Wyn — *Biographies — Welsh texts*

Williams, Peredur Wyn. Eifion Wyn / Peredur Wyn Williams. — Llandysul : Gwasg Gomer, 1980. — 263p,[12]p of plates : ill,1facsim,ports ; 22cm
ISBN 0-85088-942-1 : £5.00 B81-01615

891.6′612 — Poetry in Welsh. Parry-Williams, T. H. — *Biographies — Welsh texts*

Syr Thomas Parry-Williams 1887-1975 / golygydd Ifor Rees. — [Cardiff] : Cyngor Celfyddydau Cymru, 1981. — 88p : ill,1map,facsims,forms,ports ; 19x24cm. — (Bro a bywyd ; 1)
ISBN 0-905171-67-5 (pbk) : Unpriced B81-26812

891.6′612′08 — Poetry in Welsh, *1600- — Anthologies*

Cerddi ′79 / golygydd T. Llew Jones. — Llandysul : Gwasg Gomer, 1979. — 122p ; 22cm
ISBN 0-85088-841-7 (pbk) : £1.75 B81-40023

891.6′622 — Drama in Welsh, *1600- — Texts*

Davies, James Kitchener. Gwaith James Kitchener Davies / golygydd gan Mair I. Davies. — Llandysul : Gwasg Gomer, 1980. — 258p,[7]p of plates : 1ill,facsims,ports ; 22cm
Facsims on lining papers
ISBN 0-85088-922-7 : £5.25

Jones, Catherine Pierce. Syrffed : drama fer ar gyfer cwmni o ferched / gan Catherine Pierce Jones. — [Ruthin] ([Station Rd, Ruthin, Clwyd]) : Cyngor Gwasanaethau Gwirfoddol Clwyd, [1980]. — 11p ; 30cm
Unpriced (pbk) B81-01359

Jones, Edgar, *1932-*. Yr alwad : drama fer ar gyfer cwmni o ferched / gan Edgar Jones. — [Ruthin] ([Station Rd., Ruthin, Clwyd]) : Cyngor Gwasanaethau Gwirfoddol Clwyd, c1979. — 19p ; 30cm
Cover title
Unpriced (pbk) B81-10280

Myrddin ap Dafydd. Gormod o stiw : drama un act / gan Myrddin ap Dafydd. — [Ruthin] ([Station Rd, Ruthin, Clwyd]) : Cyngor Gwasanaethau Gwirfoddol Clwyd, c1980. — 23p ; 20cm
Unpriced (pbk) B81-01360

Owen, William, *1935-*. Cynt y cyferfydd : drama / gan William Owen. — [Ruthin] ([Station Rd., Ruthin, Clwyd LL15 1BS]) : Cyngor Gwasanaethau Gwirfoddol Clwyd, [1981]. — 24p ; 30cm
Cover title
Unpriced (pbk) B81-19995

Parry, Gwenlyn. Y tŵr / gan Gwenlyn Parry. — Llandysul : Gwasg Gomer, 1979. — 109p,[9]p of plates : ill ; 22cm
ISBN 0-85088-771-2 : £2.50 B81-39364

891.6′6301′08 — Short stories in Welsh, *1600- — Anthologies*

Storïau awr hamdden. — Abertawe : C.Davies
Cyfrol 5 / casglwyd gan Urien Wiliam. — c1979. — 136p ; 22cm
ISBN 0-7154-0522-5 (pbk) : £2.00 B81-13974

891.6′631 — Fiction in Welsh, *to 1600 — Texts*

Kedymdeithas Amlyn ac Amic. — Caerdydd : Gwasg Prifysgol Cymru, Nov.1981. — [120]p
ISBN 0-7083-0751-5 : £12.50 : CIP entry B81-30374

891.6′632 — Children′s short stories in Welsh, *1600- — Texts*

Exell, Olwen. Y bwgan brain a storïau eraill / Olwen Exell ; addaswyd i′r Gymraeg gan Eifion Williams ; arluniwyd y gyfrol gan Ann Eleri Jones. — Abertawe : C. Davies, 1979. — 56p : ill(some col.) ; 25cm
ISBN 0-7154-0534-9 (pbk) : £0.90 B81-12451

Exell, Olwen. Storïau mundud neu ddwy / Olwen Exell ; cyfieithwyd i′r Gymraeg gan Eifion W. Williams ; arluniwyd y gyfrol gan Ann Eleri Jones. — Abertawe : C. Davies, 1979. — 58p : ill(some col.) ; 25cm
ISBN 0-7154-0527-6 (pbk) : £0.90 B81-12452

Williams, Ifor Wyn. Y dychryn / Ifor Wyn Williams. — [Aberystwyth] : Cwnmi Urdd Gobaith Cymru, c1981. — 47p ; 21cm
Unpriced (pbk) B81-27489

Williams, Megan. Nawr am stori / gan Megan Williams ; arluniwyd gan Sylvia Williams. — 2 argraffiad. — Llandysul : Gwasg Gomer, 1980. — 71p : col.ill ; 25cm
Previous ed.: 1979
ISBN 0-85088-990-1 (pbk) : Unpriced B81-07844

891.6′632 — Children′s stories in Welsh, *1600- — Texts*

Huws, Emily. Caer Criw Crawiau / Emily Huws. — Llandysul : Gwasg Gomer, 1981. — 58p : ill ; 21cm
ISBN 0-85088-764-x (pbk) : £1.00 B81-38426

Huws, Emily. Ceffyl Criw Crawiau / Emily Huws. — Llandysul : Gwasg Gomer, 1981. — 55p : ill ; 21cm
ISBN 0-85088-754-2 (pbk) : £1.00 B81-38427

Huws, Emily. Criw Crawiau a′r cwch / Emily Huws. — Llandysul : Gwasg Gomer, 1981. — 62p : ill ; 21cm
ISBN 0-85088-774-7 (pbk) : £1.00 B81-38428

Ifans, Alun. Barti Ddu / Alun Ifans ; arlunydd Lin Jenkins. — Llandysul : Gwasg Gomer, 1981. — 24p : col.ill ; 20cm. — (Cyfres y môr-ladron ; 1)
ISBN 0-85088-884-0 (pbk) : £0.95 B81-39404

Ifans, Alun. Harri Morgan / Alun Ifans ; arlunydd Lin Jenkins. — Llandysul : Gwasg Gomer, 1981. — 31p : col.ill ; 20cm. — (Cyfres y môr-ladron ; 2)
ISBN 0-85088-894-8 (pbk) : £0.95 B81-39402

Ifans, Alun. Twm Prys / Alun Ifans ; arlunydd Lin Jenkins. — Llandysul : Gwasg Gomer, 1981. — 28p : col.ill ; 20cm. — (Cyfres y môr-ladron ; 3)
ISBN 0-85088-904-9 (pbk) : £0.95 B81-39403

Jones, Dylan N.. Achub y dref / Dylan N. Jones ; dyluniwyd y gyfrol gan Glyn Rees. — Llandysul : Gwasg Gomer, 1981. — 28p : ill (some col.) ; 30cm
ISBN 0-85088-704-6 (pbk) : £0.90 B81-39405

891.6′6′632 — Children's stories in Welsh, *1600- — Texts*

Jones, Dylan N.. Harri'r bws coch / Dylan N. Jones ; arluniwyd y gyfrol gan Diana Sayers. — [Denbigh] : Gwasg Gee, 1980. — 26p : col.ill ; 18x20cm
£1.10 (pbk) B81-00641

891.6′632 — Children's stories in Welsh, *1600- — Texts*

Wynne, Doreen. Sali'r wenynen fach / Doreen Wynne ; darluniwyd y gyfrol gan Enfys Beynon Thomas. — Llandysul : Gwasg Gomer, 1981. — 66p : col.ill ; 23cm
ISBN 0-85088-844-1 (pbk) : £1.60 B81-38340

891.6′632 — Fiction in Welsh, *1600- — Texts*

Hughes, Mair Wynn. Hirddydd haf / Mair Wynn Hughes. — Llandysul : Gwasg Gomer, 1981. — 135p ; 19cm
ISBN 0-85088-535-3 (pbk) : £2.50 B81-38342

Jones, Alun, *1946-*. Pan ddaw'r machlud : nofel / gan Alun Jones. — Llandysul : Gwasg Gomer, 1981. — 280p ; 22cm
ISBN 0-85088-515-9 (pbk) : £4.95 B81-38346

Jones, R. Maldwyn. Dechrau dysgu : stori ar gyfer dysgwyr - i'w helpu i groesi'r bont / R. Maldwyn Jones. — Llandysul : Gwasg Gomer, 1980. — 77p ; 19cm
ISBN 0-85088-533-7 (pbk) : £1.75 B81-00640

Lewis, Robyn. Esgid yn gwasgu / Robyn Lewis. — Llandysul : Cyhoeddwyd ac argraffwyd dros Lys yr Eisteddfod genedlaethol gan Wasg Gomer, 1980. — 84p ; 19cm
Cyfrol y Fedal Ryddiaith Eisteddfod Genedlaethol Frenhinol Cymru
ISBN 0-85088-603-1 (pbk) : £1.50 B81-07337

Lilly, Gweneth. Gaeaf y cerrig / Gweneth Lilly. — Llandysul : Gwasg Gomer, 1981. — 242p ; 19cm
ISBN 0-85088-605-8 (pbk) : £2.75 B81-38429

Lloyd, J. Selwyn. Llygad y daran / J. Selwyn Lloyd. — Llandysul : Gwasg Gomer, 1980. — 140p ; 19cm
ISBN 0-85088-573-6 (pbk) : Unpriced B81-02164

Pritchard, Elfyn. Maes y Carneddau / Elfyn Pritchard. — Llandysul : Gwasg Gomer, 1981. — 175p ; 18cm
ISBN 0-85088-625-2 (pbk) : £2.50 B81-38431

Pritchard, Marged. Enfys y bore / gan Marged Pritchard. — Llandysul : Gwasg Gomer, 1980. — 70p ; 19cm
ISBN 0-85088-623-6 (pbk) : £1.50 B81-00642

Pyrs, Enid. Er mwyn Sara / Enid Pyrs. — Abertawe : Penry, 1980. — 163p ; 18cm. — (Cyfres y fodrwy)
ISBN 0-903701-30-8 (pbk) : £0.50 B81-19849

Roberts, Eigra Lewis. Mis o Fehefin / gan Eigra Lewis Roberts. — Llandysul : Gwasg Gomer, 1980. — 256p ; 22cm
ISBN 0-85088-513-2 (pbk) : £2.75 B81-00643

Roberts, Eigra Lewis. Plentyn yr haul : Katherine Mansfield (1888-1923) / Eigra Lewis Roberts. — Llandysul : Gwasg Gomer, 1981. — 122p ; 19cm
Based on the life of Katherine Mansfield
ISBN 0-85088-954-5 (pbk) : £1.75 B81-40163

Tomos, Angharad. 'Rwy'n gweld yr haul / Angharad Tomos. — [Aberystwyth] : [Cwmni Urdd Gobaith Cymru], 1981. — 27p : 1port ; 22cm
Cover title
Unpriced (pbk) B81-26487

Wyn, Mared. Cwlwm y coed / Mared Wyn. — [Caernarfon] : Gwasg Pantycelyn, 1980. — 140p ; 18cm. — (Cyfres y fodrwy)
£0.50 (pbk) B81-19848

Wynne, Doreen. Plentyn amser / Doreen Wynne. — Llandysul : Gwasg Gomer, 1980. — 163p ; 19cm
ISBN 0-85088-543-4 (pbk) : £1.75 B81-05236

891.6′632 — Fiction in Welsh. Roberts, Kate — *Biographies — Welsh texts*

Kate Roberts / golygydd Derec Llwyd Morgan. — [Cardiff] : Cyngor Celfyddydau Cymru. — 63p : ill,facsims,forms,ports ; 19x24cm. — (Bro a bywyd ; 2)
ISBN 0-905171-68-3 (pbk) : Unpriced B81-26834

891.6′632 — Short stories in Welsh, *1600- — Texts*

Evans, Ennis. Pruddiaith : storïau byrion / gan Ennis Evans. — Llandysul : Gwasg Gomer, 1981. — 82p ; 19cm
ISBN 0-85088-635-x (pbk) : £1.50 B81-38344

891.6′632[F] — Fiction in Welsh, *1600- — English texts*

Roberts, Kate. [Y byw sy'n cysgu. English]. The living sleep / Kate Roberts ; translated from the original Welsh by Wyn Griffith. — [London] : Corgi, 1981, c1976. — 203p ; 18cm
Translation of: Y byw sy'n cysgu. — Originally published: Cardiff : John Jones Cardiff, 1976
ISBN 0-552-11685-8 (pbk) : £1.35 B81-21202

Roberts, Kate. Feet in chains / Kate Roberts ; translated from the original Welsh by John Idris Jones. — London : Corqi, 1980, c1977. — 159p ; 18cm
Translation of: Traed mewn cyffion. — Originally published: Cardiff : Jones Cardiff, 1977
ISBN 0-552-11596-7 (pbk) : £0.95 B81-06313

891.6′632[F] — Short stories in Welsh, *1600- — Texts*

Chilton, Irma. Y syrcas a storïau eraill / Irma Chilton. — Llandysul : Gwasg Gomer, 1980. — 144p ; 19cm
ISBN 0-85088-633-3 (pbk) : £1.85 B81-01569

891.6′642 — Essays in Welsh, *1600- — Texts*

Clwyd, Hafina. Defaid yn chwerthin / Hafina Clwyd. — Llandysul : Gwasg Gomer, 1980. — 96p ; 19cm
ISBN 0-85088-962-6 (pbk) : £1.75 B81-01361

Jones, John Gruffydd. Cysgodion ar y pared : cyfrol o wyth ysgrif / John Gruffydd Jones. — Llandysul : Cyhoeddwyd dros Lys yr Eisteddfod Genedlaethol gan Wasg Gomer, 1981. — 32p ; 19cm. — (Y Fedal ryddiaith / Eisteddfod Genedlaethol Frenhinol Cymru ; 1981)
ISBN 0-85088-585-x (pbk) : £0.50 B81-38425

891.6′68209 — Welsh literature, *1600- — Texts*

Ap Hywel, Elin. Cyfaddawdu / Elin ap Hywel. — [Aberystwyth] : Gwasg yr Urdd, [1980]. — 32p : 1port
Cyfrol arobryn cystadleuaeth y Fedal Lenyddiaeth yn Eisteddfod Genedlaethol Urdd Gobaith Cymru, Bro Colwyn. — Originally published:
Unpriced (pbk) B81-07314

891.7 — RUSSIAN LITERATURE

891.708 — Russian literature, *to ca 1980 — Anthologies — For criticism*

The literary appreciation of Russian writers. — Cambridge : Cambridge University Press, Feb.1982. — [240]p
ISBN 0-521-23498-0 (cased) : £14.50 : CIP entry
ISBN 0-521-28003-6 (pbk) : £5.95 B81-36948

891.708′0044 — Russian literature, *1945-*. **Influence of political events,** *1952-1958 — Study examples: Novyĭ mir*

Frankel, Edith Rogovin. Novy mir. — Cambridge : Cambridge University Press Dec.1981. — [224]p. — (Cambridge studies in Russian literature)
ISBN 0-521-23438-7 : £19.50 : CIP entry B81-34728

891.709 — Russian literature, *to 1979 — Critical studies*

Woodward, James. Russian literature and the Russian language : inaugural lecture delivered at the college on 9 December 1980 / by James Woodward. — Swansea : University College of Swansea, 1981. — 29p ; 22cm
ISBN 0-86076-022-7 (pbk) : Unpriced B81-26314

891.709′003 — Russian literature, *1800- — Critical studies — Russian texts*

Filippov, Boris. Literary essays = Stat'i o literature / Boris Filipoff. — London (40 Elsham Rd, W14 8HB) : Overseas Publications Interchange, 1981. — 236p ; 22cm
Russian text. — Russian title transliterated
ISBN 0-903868-28-8 (pbk) : £6.00 B81-19355

891.7′09′0042 — Russian literature, *1917-1978 — Sociological perspectives*

Hingley, Ronald. Russian writers and Soviet society 1917-1978. — London : Methuen, July 1981. — [320]p
Originally published: London : Weidenfeld and Nicolson, 1979
ISBN 0-416-31390-6 (pbk) : £5.50 : CIP entry B81-13869

891.709′0042 — Russian literature. Formalist movement, *1917-1930 — Critical studies*

Erlich, Victor. Russian formalism : history - doctrine / Victor Erlich. — 3rd ed. — New Haven ; London : Yale University Press, c1981. — 311p ; 24cm
Previous ed.: The Hague : Mouton, 1965. — Bibliography: p287-302. — Includes index
ISBN 0-300-02635-8 (pbk) : £5.65 B81-27033

891.71′3 — Poetry in Russian, *1800-1917 — English texts*

Blok, Aleksandr. Selected poems / Alexander Blok ; [translated from the Russian by Alex Miller]. — Moscow : Progress ; [London] : Distributed by Central Books, c1981. — 326p : ports ; 23cm
Translation of: Aleksandr Blok Izbrannoe
ISBN 0-7147-1652-9 : £4.50 B81-28509

Mandel'shtam, Osip. Osip Mandelstam : poems / chosen and translated by James Greene ; with forewords by Nadezhda Mandelstam and Donald Davie. — New rev. and enl. ed. — London : Elek : Granada, 1980. — 96p ; 23cm
Previous ed.: 1977
ISBN 0-246-11459-2 : £5.95 B81-00645

891.71′3 — Poetry in Russian, *1800-1917 — Polish texts*

Pushkin, A. S.. Eugeniusz Oniegin / Aleksander Puszkin ; przełożył Tadeusz Bobiński. — Londyn (146 Bridge Arch, Sutton Walk, SE1 8XU) : Oficyna Poetów i Malarzy, 1981. — 202p ; 22cm
Translation of: Evgeniĭ Onegin
Unpriced (pbk) B81-18225

891.71′3 — Poetry in Russian, *1800-1917 — Russian-English parallel texts*

Mandel'shtam, Osip. Osip Mandelstam's Stone / translated and introduced by Robert Tracy. — Princeton ; Guildford : Princeton University Press, c1981. — xiii,253p ; 23cm. — (The Lockert library of poetry in translation)
Parallel Russian text and English translation
ISBN 0-691-06444-x (cased) : £9.80
ISBN 0-699-01376-4 (pbk) : £4.25 B81-16184

891.71′3 — Poetry in Russian, *1800-1917 — Texts*

Lermontov, M. ÎU.. Mtsyri / Lermontov = Mtsyri / M. Yu. Lermontov. — Letchworth : Prideaux, 1980. — 27p ; 21cm. — (Russian titles for the specialist, ISSN 0305-3741 ; no.220)
Russian text. — Russian title transliterated
£0.60 (pbk) B81-02019

T͡svetaeva, Marina. Remeslo : kniga stikhov / Marina Tsvetaeva. — Reprint of the 1923 Helikon ed. / with an introduction and notes by Efim Etkind. — Oxford : Meeuws, 1981. — xl,165p : 1port ; 18cm
Russian text. — Includes index
ISBN 0-902672-46-0 (pbk) : Unpriced B81-17045

891.71'3 — Poetry in Russian. Blok, Aleksandr — *Biographies*

Orlov, Vladimir. Hamayun : the life of Alexander Blok / Vladimir Orlov ; [translated from the Russian by Olga Shartse]. — Abridged ed. — Moscow : Progress ; [London] : Central Books [distributor], c1980. — 477p ; 21cm
Translation of: Gamaĭūn
ISBN 0-7147-1651-0 : £4.50 B81-29306

891.71'3 — Poetry in Russian. Blok, Aleksandr — *Critical studies — Festschriften — Russian texts*

In memory of Aleksandr Blok : 1880-1980 = Pamyati Aleksandra Bloka : 1880-1980 / Anna Akhmatova ... [et al.]. — London (40 Elsham Rd., W14 8HB) : Overseas Publications Interchange, 1980. — 157p : 1port ; 22cm
Russian text. — Russian title transliterated
ISBN 0-903868-29-6 (pbk) : £6.00 B81-19354

891.71'3 — Poetry in Russian. Brīūsov, Valeriĭ — *Correspondence, diaries, etc.*

Brīūsov, Valeriĭ. The diary of Valery Bryusov (1893-1905) / with reminiscences by V.F. Khodasevich and Marina Tsvetaeva ; edited, translated, and with an introductory essay by Joan Delaney Grossman. — Berkeley ; London : University of California Press, c1980. — 234p,[8]p of plates : ill,ports ; 22cm. — (Documentary studies in modern Russian poetry ; 1)
Translated from the Russian. — Bibliography: p223-228. — Includes index
ISBN 0-520-03858-4 : £9.50 B81-11827

891.71'3 — Poetry in Russian. Gippius, Z. N. — *Biographies*

Zlobin, Vladimir. A difficult soul : Zinaida Gippius / Vladimir Zlobin ; edited, annotated and with an introductory essay by Simon Karlinsky. — Berkeley ; London : University of California Press, c1980. — 197p,[4]p of plates : ports ; 22cm. — (Documentary studies in modern Russian poetry ; 3)
Translation of: Tīazhelaīa dusha. — Includes index
ISBN 0-520-03867-3 : £8.75 B81-14208

891.71'3'08 — Poetry in Russian, *1800-1917 — Anthologies — English texts*

Johnston, Charles, *1912-*. Talk about the last poet : a novella in verse and other poems including Potted memoirs / Charles Johnston. With new verse translations of The bronze horseman / by Alexander Pushkin. & The novice / by Michael Lermontov ; and an introduction by Kyril Fitzlyon. — London : Bodley Head for C. Johnston, c1981. — 78p ; 19cm
Talk about the last poet adapted from Eucharisticus / Paulinus. - The bronze horseman and The novice translated from the Russian
ISBN 0-370-30434-9 : £4.50
Primary classification 821'.914 B81-24447

891.71'42 — Poetry in Russian, *1917-1945 - English texts*

Tsvetayeva, Marina Ivanovna. Selected poems of Marina Tsvetayeva. — Rev. and enl. ed. — Oxford : Oxford University Press, June 1981. — [160]p
Previous ed.: 1971
ISBN 0-19-211894-3 (pbk) : £4.95 : CIP entry B81-14413

891.7'1'42 — Poetry in Russian. Pasternak, Boris *— Critical studies*

Gifford, Henry. Pasternak : a critical study. — Cambridge : Cambridge University Press, Oct.1981. — [280]p. — (Major European authors)
Originally published: 1977
ISBN 0-521-28677-8 (pbk) : £7.95 : CIP entry B81-28174

891.71'42'09 — Poetry in Russian, *1917-1945 — Critical studies — Russian texts*

Four poets : Blok, Sologub, Gumilev, Mandelshtam : selected essays = O chetyrekh poetakh : sbornik statei / [compiled by] Gleb Struve. — London (40 Elsham Rd., W14 8HB) : Overseas Publications Interchange, 1981. — 185p ; 22cm
Russian text. — Russian title transliterated
ISBN 0-903868-30-x (pbk) : £6.00 B81-19357

891.71'44 — Poetry in Russian, *1945- — English texts*

Evtushenko, Evgeniĭ. Invisible threads. — London : Secker and Warburg, Nov.1981. — [192]p
Translated from the Russian
ISBN 0-436-59220-7 : £10.00 : CIP entry B81-30354

891.71'44 — Poetry in Russian, *1945- — Russian-English parallel texts*

Ziedonis, Imants. Thoughtfully I read the smoke : selected poems / Imants Ziedonis ; [translated by Dorian Rottenberg] ; [designed and illustrated by Yrigori Dauman]. — Moscow : Progress Publishers ; [London] : Central Books [distributor], c1980. — 278pp : ill ; 18cm
Parallel Russian text and English translation. — Includes index
£1.95 B81-14006

891.7'1'4408 — Poetry in Russian, *1945- . - Anthologies - Russian-English parallel texts*

The new Russian poets 1953-1968. — London : Marian Boyars, Apr.1981. — [320]p
Parallel Russian text and English translation
ISBN 0-7145-2715-7 (pbk) : £3.50 : CIP entry B81-07929

891.72'3 — Drama in Russian, *1800-1917 — English texts*

Chekhov, A. P.. [The three sisters]. Anton Chekhov's Three sisters : a translation / Brian Friel. — Dublin : Gallery Books, 1981. — 114p ; 22cm
Translation from the Russian
ISBN 0-904011-25-9 (cased) : £6.21
ISBN 0-904011-26-7 (pbk) : £3.45 B81-39846

Turgenev, I. S.. A month in the country / Ivan Turgenev ; adapted into English by Emlyn Williams ; with an introduction by Michael Redgrave. — London : Heinemann, c1943 (1981 [printing]). — xv,93p ; 19cm. — (Heinemann plays)
Translation of: Mesīats v derevne
ISBN 0-435-20966-3 (pbk) : £1.75 B81-13675

Turgenev, Ivan Sergeevich. A month in the country. — London : Hogarth, Oct.1981. — [128]p
Translation from the Russian
ISBN 0-7012-0540-7 : £4.95 : CIP entry B81-25836

891.72'3 — Drama in Russian. Chekhov, A. P. — *Critical studies*

Chekhov : the critical heritage / edited by Victor Emeljanow. — London : Routledge & Kegan Paul, 1981. — xxii,471p ; 23cm. — (The Critical heritage series)
Bibliography: p457. — Includes index
ISBN 0-7100-0374-9 : £17.50 B81-06969

891.72'3 — Drama in Russian. Griboedov, A. S.. Murder

Harden, Evelyn J.. The murder of Griboedov : new materials / Evelyn J. Harden. — Birmingham : Department of Russian Language & Literature, University of Birmingham, c1979. — viii,96p ; 21cm. — (Birmingham Slavonic monographs, ISSN 0141-3805 ; no.6)
Bibliography: p93-96
ISBN 0-7044-0313-7 (pbk) : £1.60 B81-10090

891.72'42 — Drama in Russian. Shvarts, E. — *Critical studies*

Metcalf, Amanda J.. Evgenii Shvarts and his fairy-tales for adults / Amanda J. Metcalf. — Birmingham : Department of Russian Language & Literature, University of Birmingham, c1979. — v,101p ; 21cm. — (Birmingham Slavonic monographs, ISSN 0141-3805 ; no.8)
Bibliography: p95-101
ISBN 0-7044-0350-1 (pbk) : £2.00 B81-11361

891.73'0876'08[FS] — Science fiction stories in Russian, *1945- — Anthologies — English texts*

New Soviet science fiction / introduction by Theodore Sturgeon ; translated from the Russian by Helen Saltz Jacobson. — New York : Macmillan ; London : Collier Macmillan, 1979. — xi,297p ; 22cm. — (Macmillan's best of Soviet science fiction)
ISBN 0-02-578220-7 : £6.25 B81-20986

891.73'0876'09 — Science fiction in Russian, *to 1979 — Critical studies*

Griffiths, John, *1934-*. Three tomorrows : American, British and Soviet science fiction / John Griffiths. — London : Macmillan, 1980. — 217p ; 23cm
Includes index
ISBN 0-333-26910-1 (cased) : £10.00 : CIP rev.
ISBN 0-333-26912-8 (pbk) : £3.95
Primary classification 823'.0876'09 B80-18883

891.73'2 — Fiction in Russian, *1700-1800 — Texts*

Karamzin, N. M.. Bednaīa Liza = Poor Liza / N.M. Karamzin ; with introduction, notes and vocabulary by W. Harrison. — Letchworth : Prideaux, 1980, c1963. — 75p ; 20cm. — (Russian texts for students ; 9)
Originally published: Letchworth : Bradda Books, 1963
£0.90 (pbk) B81-14004

891.73'3 — Fiction in Russian. Dostoevskiĭ, F. M.. Brothers Karamazov — *Critical studies*

Terras, Victor. A Karamazov companion : commentary on the genesis, language, and style of Dostoevsky's novel / Victor Terras. — Madison ; London : University of Wisconsin Press, 1981. — xiv,482p ; 22cm
Bibliography: p447-456. — Includes index
ISBN 0-299-08310-1 (cased) : £19.50
ISBN 0-299-08314-4 (pbk) : £6.45 B81-29379

891.73'3 — Fiction in Russian. Dostoevskiĭ, F. M.. Influence of Dickens, Charles, *1812-1870*

MacPike, Loralee. Dostoevsky's Dickens : a study of literary influence / Loralee MacPike. — London : Prior, 1981. — viii,223p ; 23cm
Bibliography: p215-223
ISBN 0-86043-449-4 : £9.50 : CIP rev. B80-22659

891.73'3 — Fiction in Russian. Dostoevskiĭ, F. M.. Special themes: Racial discrimination against Jews — *Critical studies*

Goldstein, David I.. Dostoyevsky and the Jews / David I. Goldstein ; foreword by Joseph Frank. — Austin ; London : University of Texas Press, c1981. — xxix,230p ; 24cm. — (University of Texas Press slavic series ; no.3)
Translation of: Dostoïevski et les Juifs. — Includes index
ISBN 0-292-71528-5 : £12.20 B81-40171

891.73'3 — Fiction in Russian. Tolstaīa, S. A. — *Biographies*

Edwards, Anne, *1927-*. Sonya : the life of Countess Tolstoy / Anne Edwards. — London : Hodder and Stoughton, 1981. — 512p,[16]p of plates : ill,ports ; 25cm
Bibliography: p494-497. — Includes index
ISBN 0-340-25002-x : £8.50 : CIP rev. B81-05124

891.73'3 — Fiction in Russian. Tolstoĭ, L. N. — *Critical studies*

Greenwood, E. B.. Tolstoy : the comprehensive vision / E.B. Greenwood. — London : Methuen, 1980, c1975. — v,184p ; 22cm
Originally published: London : Dent, 1975. — Bibliography: p172-176. - Includes index
ISBN 0-416-74130-4 (pbk) : £2.95 : CIP rev. B80-13129

891.73'3 — Fiction in Russian. Turgenev, I. S. — *Critical studies*

Ripp, Victor. Turgenev's Russia : from Notes of a hunter to Fathers and sons / by Victor Ripp. — Ithaca ; London : Cornell University Press, 1980. — 218p ; 23cm
Includes index
ISBN 0-8014-1294-3 : £8.75 B81-18730

891.73'3 — Fiction in Russian. Turgenev, I. S.. Interpersonal relationships, *1845-1870.* **Sand, George**

Waddington, Patrick. Turgenev and George Sand : an improbable entente / Patrick Waddington. — London : Macmillan, 1981. — 176p,[8]p of plates : ill,ports ; 23cm
Bibliography: p133-139. — Includes index
ISBN 0-333-29147-6 : £12.00
Also classified at 843'.7 B81-15673

891.73'3 — Short stories in Russian, ***1800-1917 — Texts***

Odoevskiĭ, V. F.Romanticheskiye povesti / V.F. Odoyevsky ; introduction and selected bibliography by Neil Cornwell. — Oxford : Meeuws, 1975. — xiv,397p : 1ill,music,1port ; 21cm. — (Mouette reprint series. Russian section ; v.4)
Russian text, English introduction. — Added t.p. in Russian. — Facsim. of: edition published Leningrad : Priboĭ Leningrad, 1929. — Bibliography: pxii-xiv
ISBN 0-902672-16-9 : £8.00 B81-10288

891.73'3[F] — Fiction in Russian, ***1800-1917 — English texts***

Dostoevskiĭ, F. M.. Crime and punishment / by Fyodor Dostoevsky ; translated from the Russian by Constance Garnett. — Toronto ; London : Bantam, 1958 (1981 [printing]). — 472p ; 18cm. — (A Bantam classic)
Translation of: Prestuplenie i nakazanie
ISBN 0-553-21038-6 (pbk) : £1.00 B81-39111

LermontovMichael I͡Ur'evich, M. I͡U.. A hero of our time / Mikhail Lermontov ; translated by Reginald Merton ; introduction by Peter Forster ; lithographs by Dodie Masterman. — London : Folio Society, 1980. — 175p : col.ill ; 23cm
Translation of: Geroĭ nashego vremeni. — In slip case
£4.95 B81-07227

891.73'3[F] — Short stories in Russian, ***1800-1917 — English texts***

Tolstoĭ, L. N.. The Raid and other stories. — Oxford : Oxford University Press, Feb.1982. — [416]p. — (The World's classics)
Translated from the Russian
ISBN 0-19-281584-9 (pbk) : £1.95 : CIP entry B81-35766

Turgenev, I. S.. A hunter's sketches / Ivan Turganev ; [edited by Raissa Bobrova] ; [commentary compiled by Nikolai Chernov]. — Moscow : Progress ; London : Distributed by Central Books, 1979. — 372p,[80]p of plates : ill(some col.),facsims(some col.),ports ; 21cm. — (Progress Russian classics series)
Translation of: Zapiski okhotnika. — Originally published: s.l.: s.n., 1955
£3.95 B81-06630

891.73'42 — Fiction in Russian, ***1917-1945 — Texts***

Zami͡atin, Evgeniĭ. Navodnenie / Evg. Zami͡atin = The flood / Zamyatin. — Letchworth : Prideaux, 1978. — 67p : ill ; 21cm. — (Russian titles for the specialist, ISSN 0305-3741)
Russian text. — Added t.p in Russian. — Russian title transliterated. — Originally published: Leningrad : Izdatel'stvo Pisateleĭ, 1930
Unpriced (pbk) B81-11513

891.73'42 — Fiction in Russian. Platonov, Andreĭ Platonovich. Influence of Fedorov, N. F.

Teskey, Ayleen. Platonov and Fyodorov. — Amersham : Avebury, Dec.1981. — [182]p
ISBN 0-86127-214-5 : £12.00 : CIP entry B81-31812

891.73'42[F] — Fiction in Russian, ***1917-1945 — English texts***

Beli͡aev, Aleksandr. Professor Dowell's head / by Alexander Beliaev ; introduction by Theodore Sturgeon ; translated by Antonina W. Bouis. — New York : Collier ; London : Collier Macmillan, 1981, c1980. — viii,157p ; 21cm. — (Macmillan's best of Soviet science fiction series)
Translation of: Golova professora Douėli͡a
ISBN 0-02-016580-3 (pbk) : £1.95 B81-37186

Kollontaĭ, A. M.. A great love / Alexandra Kollontai ; translated and introduced by Cathy Porter. — London : Virago, 1981. — 1563 ; 20cm
Translated from the Russian
ISBN 0-86068-188-2 (pbk) : £2.50 B81-12946

Nabokov, Vladimir. The gift / Vladimir Nabokov ; translated from the Russian by Michael Scammell with the collaboration of the author. — Harmondsworth : Penguin, 1980, c1963. — 332p ; 20cm
Translation of: Dar. — Originally published: New York : Putnam ; London : Weidenfeld & Nicolson, 1963
ISBN 0-14-005475-8 (pbk) : £2.95 B81-10996

Shefner, Vadim. The unman / Vadim Shefner ; translated from the Russian by Alice Stone Nakhimovsky and Alexander Nakhimovsky ; Kovrigin's chronicles / [Vadim Shefner] ; translated from the Russian by Antonina W. Bouis ; introduction by Theodore Sturgeon. — New York : Collier ; London : Collier Macmillan, 1981, c1980. — vi,233p ; 21cm. — (Macmillan's best of Soviet science fiction series)
Translations of: Chelovek s pi͡at'i͡u "ne" ; and of: Devushka u obryva
ISBN 0-02-025230-7 (pbk) : £2.25 B81-37187

891.73'44 — Fiction in Russian, ***1945- — Texts***

Roziner, Feliks. Nekto Finkel'maier : roman / Feliks Roziner = A certain Finkelmaier / Felix Roziner. — London (40 Elsham Rd., W14 8HB) : Overseas Publications Interchange, 1981. — 596p ; 19cm
ISBN 0-903868-31-8 (cased) : £6.00
ISBN 0-903868-32-6 (pbk) : £6.00 B81-26404

891.73'44 — Fiction in Russian. Solzhenit͡syn, Aleksandr ***— Biographies***

Solzhenit͡syn, Aleksandr. The oak and the calf : sketches of literary life in the Soviet Union / Alexander Solzhenitsyn ; translated from the Russian by Harry Willetts. — London : Collins/Fontana, c1980. — vii,568p ; 20cm
Translation of: Bodalsi͡a telenok s dubom. — Originally published: New York : Harper & Row ; London : Collins, 1980. — Includes index
ISBN 0-00-634283-3 (pbk) : £3.95 B81-38282

891.73'44 — Fiction in Russian. Solzhenit͡syn, Aleksandr ***— Critical studies — Russian texts***

Flegon, A.. Bokrug solzhenit͡syna / A. Flegon. — London (30 Baker St. W.1) : Flegon Press, 1981. — 2v.((1008p)) : ill(some col.),music,facsims,ports ; 18cm
Unpriced (pbk) B81-29553

891.73'44 — Fiction in Russian. Solzhenit͡syn, Aleksandr. Special themes: Love ***— Critical studies***

Edna Monica, ***Sister.*** The mystery of love in Solzhenitsyn : a conference given to the novitiate on the vow of chastity / Sister Edna Monica. — Fairacres (Convent of the Incarnation, Fairacres, Oxford OX4 1TB) : SLG Press, c1980. — 12p ; 21cm. — (Fairacres publication, ISSN 0307-1405 ; 73)
Originally published: in the Fairacres Chronicle, vol.12, no.1, Spring 1979
ISBN 0-7283-0084-2 (pbk) : £0.20 B81-18717

891.73'44[F] — Fiction in Russian, ***1945- — English texts***

Efremov, Ivan. Andromeda : a space-age tale / Ivan Yefremov. — Moscow : Progress ; [London] : Distributed by Central Books, 1959 (1981 printing). — 397p : ill ; 21cm. — (Progress Soviet authors library)
Translation of: Tumannost' Andromedy
ISBN 0-7147-1624-3 : £3.95 B81-28512

Gonchar, Oles'. The shore of love / Oles Honchar ; [translated from the Russian by Liv Tudge]. — Moscow : Progress ; [London] : Distributed by Central Books, c1980. — 259p : ill ; 21cm
Translation of: Bereg li͡ubvi
ISBN 0-7147-1630-8 : £2.95 B81-32633

Kasymbekov, Tolegen. The broken sword / Tolegen Kassymbekov ; [translated from the Russian by David Foreman and Sergei Sosinsky]. — Moscow : Progress ; London : distributed by Central Books, c1980. — 517p : ill ; 21cm
Translation of: Slomannyĭ mech
ISBN 0-7147-1611-1 : £4.50 B81-27194

Kolesnikov, Mikhail. School for ministers : a trilogy / Mikhail Kolesnikov ; [translated from the Russian by Liv Tudge]. — Moscow : Progress ; [London] : Distributed by Central Books, c1980. — 501p ; 21cm
Translation of: Shkola ministrov
ISBN 0-7147-1628-6 : £4.25 B81-32632

Rasputin, Valentin. Money for Maria and, Borrowed time : two village tales / Valentin Rasputin ; translated by Kevin Windle and Margaret Wettlin. — St Lucia, Qld. : University of Queensland Press ; Hemel Hempstead : Distributed by Prentice-Hall, c1981. — xxx,374p ; 23cm
Translations of Den'gi dli͡a Mariĭ and Posledniĭ srok
ISBN 0-7043-2274-9 : £6.95 B81-40940

Rybakov, Anatoliĭ. Heavy sand / Anatoli Rybakov ; translated from the Russian by Harold Shukman. — London : Allen Lane, 1981. — 380p ; 24cm
Translation of: Ti͡azhelyĭ pesok
ISBN 0-7139-1343-6 : £7.95 B81-23202

Sharipov, A.. General Chernyakhovsky / A. Sharipov ; [translated from the Russian by Yuri Shirokov]. — Moscow : Progress ; [London] : Distributed by Central Books, c1980. — 507p : ill,ports ; 21cm
Translation of: General Cherni͡akhovskiĭ
ISBN 0-7147-1612-x : £4.50 B81-27680

Strugatskiĭ, Arkadiĭ. Beetle in the anthill / Arkady Strugatsky and Boris Strugatsky ; translated from the Russian by Antonina W. Bouis ; introduction by Theodore Sturgeon. — New York : Macmillan ; London : Collier Macmillan, c1980. — ix,217p ; 22cm. — (Macmillan's best of Soviet science fiction)
Translation of: Zhuk v muraveĭnike
ISBN 0-02-615120-0 : £5.95 B81-18296

Struga͡tskiĭ, Boris. The snail on the slope / Boris and Arkady Strugatsky. — London : Gollancz, 1980. — 243p ; 21cm
Translation of : Ulitka na sklone
ISBN 0-575-02795-9 : £6.50 B81-08230

Vladimov, Georgi. Faithful Ruslan : the story of a guard dog / Georgi Vladimov ; translated from the Russian by Michael Glenny. — Harmondsworth : Penguin, 1979. — 184p ; 18cm
Translation of: Vernyĭ Ruslan. — Originally published: London : Cape, 1979
ISBN 0-14-005252-6 (pbk) : £0.95 B81-11030

Voĭnovich, Vladimir. The Ivankiad, or, The tale of the writer Voinovich's installation in his new apartment / Vladimir Voinovich ; translated by David Lapeza. — Harmondsworth : Penguin, 1979, c1977. — 123p ; 18cm
Translation of: Ivan'kiada, ili raskaz o vselenii pisateli͡a Voĭnovicha v novui͡u kvartiru. — Originally published: New York : Farrar, Straus and Giroux, 1977 ; London : Cape, 1978
ISBN 0-14-004943-6 (pbk) : £0.95 B81-11078

Voĭnovich, Vladimir. The life and extraordinary adventures of private Ivan Chonkin / Vladimir Voinovich ; translated by Richard Lourie. — Harmondsworth : Penguin, 1978, c1977 (1981 [printing]). — 269p ; 20cm. — (A King Penguin)
Translation of: Zhizn' i neobychaĭnye prikli͡uchenii͡a soldata Ivana Chonkina. — Originally published: New York : Farrar, Straus and Giroux ; London : Cape, 1977
ISBN 0-14-006115-0 (pbk) : £2.50 B81-39158

Voĭnovich, Vladimir. Pretender to the throne : the further adventures of Private Ivan Chonkin / Vladimir Voinovich ; translated by Richard Lourie. — London : Cape, 1981. — 357p ; 21cm
Translation of: Pretendent na prestol
ISBN 0-224-01966-x : £7.95 : CIP rev. B81-22452

891.73'44[F] — Fiction in Russian, *1945-* — *English texts* *continuation*

Zinov'ev, Aleksandr. The Yawning heights / Alexander Zinoviev. — Harmondsworth : Penguin, 1981, c1979
Translation of: Ziiaiushchie vysoty. — Originally published: London : Bodley Head, 1979
ISBN 0-14-005415-4 : £4.95 B81-22187

891.73'44[F] — Short stories in Russian, *1945-* — *English texts*

Kolupaev, Viktor. Hermit's swing / Victor Kolupaev ; translated from the Russian by Helen Saltz Jacobson ; introduction by Theodore Sturgeon. — New York : Macmillan ; London : Collier Macmillan, c1980. — xi,199p ; 22cm. — (Macmillan's best of Soviet science fiction)
Translation of: Kacheli Otschel'nika
ISBN 0-02-566350-x : £5.95 B81-20985

891.73'44[J] — Children's short stories in Russian, *1945-* — *English texts*

Pogodin, Radi. Of jolly people and fine weather / Radi Pogodin ; [translated from the Russian by Raissa Bobrova]. — Moscow : Progress ; London : Central Books [[distributor]], c1980. — 131p : col.ill ; 23cm
Translation of: Rasskazy o veselykh lîudîakh i khoroshcheĭ pogode
ISBN 0-7147-1574-3 : £2.25 B81-14010

891.73'44[J] — Children's stories in Russian, *1945-* — *English texts*

Beĭshenaliev, Shukurbek. The horned lamb / Sh. Beyshenaliev ; [translated from the Russian by Gladys Evans]. — Moscow : Progress ; London : Central Books [[distributor]], 1979. — [22]p : col.ill ; 28cm
Translation of: Rogatyĭ îagnënok. — Cover title. — Originally published: 1969. — Ill on inside covers
£0.45 (pbk) B81-14009

Kirshina, K.. The yard of tame birds / K. Kirshina ; translated from the Russian by Jan Butler ; illustrated by G. Nikolsky. — Moscow : Progress ; London : Central Books [[distributor]], 1979. — 19p : col.ill ; 22cm
Translation of: Dvor nepug annykh ptits. — Ill on inside covers
£0.45 (pbk) B81-14008

891.77'44'080355 — Humour in Russian, *1945-*. **Special subjects: Olympic Games** — *Anthologies* — *English texts*

Olympic smiles / [translated from the Russian by David Foreman] ; [designed by Boris Markevich] ; [compiled by N.L. Yelin]. — Moscow : Progress Publishers ; [London] : Central Books [distributor], c1980. — 143p : ill ; 20cm
Translation of: Olimpiada ulybaetsîa
ISBN 0-7147-1631-6 (pbk) : £0.95 B81-32947

891.78'308 — Prose in Russian. Belyĭ, Andreĭ — *Critical studies*

Peterson, Ronald E.. Andrei Bely's short prose / Ronald E. Peterson. — Birmingham : Department of Russian Language & Literature, University of Birmingham, c1980. — ix,93p ; 21cm. — (Birmingham Slavonic monographs, ISSN 0141-3805 ; no.11)
Bibliography: p85-93
ISBN 0-7044-0409-5 (pbk) : £3.00 B81-10092

891.78'308 — Prose in Russian. Leont'ev, Konstantin. Correspondence with Rozanov, V. V.

Leont'ev, Konstantin. Pis'ma k Vasilîîu Rozanovu. — London (28 Lanacre Avenue, NW9 5FN) : Nina Karsov, Aug.1981. — [144]p
ISBN 0-9502324-9-1 (cased) : £7.50 : CIP entry
ISBN 0-907652-00-x (pbk) : £5.40 B81-20479

891.78'308 — Prose in Russian. Mandel'shtam, Osip. Egyptian stamp — *Critical studies*

West, Daphne M.. Mandelstam : the Egyptian stamp / Daphne M. West. — Birmingham : Department of Russian Language & Literature, University of Birmingham, c1980. — v,152p ; 21cm. — (Birmingham Slavonic monographs, ISSN 0141-3805 ; no.10)
Bibliography: p147-152
ISBN 0-7044-0376-5 (pbk) : £3.60 B81-11344

891.78'4209 — Russian literature. Bulgakov, Mikhail — *Critical studies*

Wright, A. Colin. Mikhail Bulgakov : life and interpretations / A. Colin Wright. — Toronto ; London : University of Toronto Press, c1978. — viii,324p,[2]p of plates : 1port ; 24cm
Bibliography: p281-310. — Includes index
ISBN 0-8020-5402-1 : £17.50 B81-25474

891.79 — UKRAINIAN LITERATURE

891.7'912 — Poetry in Ukrainian. Shevchenko, T. H. — *Critical studies*

Shevchenko and the critics 1861-1980 / edited by George S.N. Luckyj ; translations by Dolly Ferguson and Sophia Yurkevich ; introduction by Bohdan Rubchak. — Toronto ; London : Published in association with the Canadian Institute of Ukrainian Studies by University of Toronto Press, c1980. — xi,522p : 1port ; 23cm
Translation from the Ukrainian. — Includes index
ISBN 0-8020-2346-0 (cased) : £18.00
ISBN 0-8020-6377-2 (pbk) : Unpriced B81-34181

891.7'913 — Poetry in Ukrainian, *1917-* — *Texts*

Shalapaÿ, Tonîa. Pelîustky : vybrani poezii / Tonîa Shalapaÿ. — Rochdale ([3 Osborne St Deeplish, Rochadale OL15 1QU]) : T. Shalapaÿ, 1981. — 56p ; 19cm
Title page transliterated. — Includes index
Unpriced (pbk) B81-28369

891.82 — SERBO-CROATIAN LITERATURE

891.8'21'03 — Orally transmitted epic poetry in Serbo-Croatian, *ca 1500-ca 1850* — *Critical studies*

Koljević, Svetozar. The epic in the making / Svetozar Koljević. — Oxford : Clarendon, 1980. — xii,376p,6p of plates : ill,maps,ports ; 23cm
Bibliography: p351-363. — Includes index
ISBN 0-19-815759-2 : £25.00 : CIP rev. B80-02967

891.8'215 — Poetry in Serbo-Croatian, *1900-* — *English texts*

Demirović, Hamdija. Twenty-five poems / by Hamdija Demirović ; English versions and introduction by Charles Causley ; frontispiece and cover graphics by Petar Waldegg. — Richmond (26 Sydney Rd., Richmond, Surrey) : Keepsake Press, 1980. — 44p : 1ill ; 22cm
Translations from the Serbo-Croatian. — Limited ed. of 425 copies, of which 30 are signed by author and translator
£2.25 (corrected : pbk) B81-32726

891.8'235[F] — Fiction in Serbo-Croatian, *1900-* — *English texts*

Ćosić, Dobrica. Reach to eternity / Dobrica Cosić ; translated by Muriel Heppell. — New York ; London : Harcourt Brace Jovanovich, c1980. — 410p ; 25cm
Translation of: Vreme smrti. III
ISBN 0-15-175961-8 : £8.95 B81-19743

891.85 — POLISH LITERATURE

891.8'5'09007 — Polish literature, *1919-* — *Critical studies* — *Polish texts*

Tarnawski, Wit. Od Gombrowicza do Mackiewicza : szkice i portrety literackie / Wit Tarnawski. — Londyn : Oficyna poetów i malarzy, 1980. — 179p ; 22cm
Unpriced (pbk) B81-18266

891.8'5'09007 — Polish literature. Emigré writers, *1919-* — *Critical studies* — *Polish texts*

Laks, Szymon. Szargam świ etości / Szymon Laks. — Londyn : OPiM, 1980. — 111p ; 22cm
Includes index
Unpriced (pbk) B81-22211

891.8'517 — Poetry in Polish, *1919-* — *Polish-English parallel texts*

Pasierb, Janusz St.. Things ultimate and other poems = Rzeczy ostatnie i inne wiersze / Janusz St. Pasierb ; translated by Charles Lambert. — London : Poets and Painters Press, 1980. — 100p ; 22cm
Parallel Polish text and English translation
Unpriced (pbk) B81-20046

Szymborska, Wisława. Sounds, feelings, thoughts : seventy poems / by Wisława Szymborska ; translated and introduced by Magnus J. Krynski and Robert A. Maguire. — Princeton ; Guildford : Princeton University Press, c1981. — 215p ; 23cm
Parallel Polish text and English translation. — Bibliography: p213-214
ISBN 0-691-06469-5 (cased) : £4.90
ISBN 0-691-01380-2 : Unpriced B81-35732

891.8'517 — Poetry in Polish, *1919-* — *Texts*

Bednarczyk, Czesław. Odrastaj aca pami eć / Czesław Bednarczyk. — London : Oficyna Poetów i Malarzy, 1981. — 55p ; 22cm
Limited ed. of 130 copies of which the first 20 are signed and numbered by the author. — Includes index
Unpriced (pbk) B81-15201

Bielobradek, Joanna. Bracia żydzi / Joanna Bielobradek. — Londyn : Oficyna Poetów i Malarzy, 1981. — 54p ; 21cm
Unpriced (pbk) B81-28757

Braun, Jerzy. Prometej Adam / Jerzy Braun. — Londyn [i.e. London] : Odnowa, 1980. — 69p ; 22cm
ISBN 0-903705-27-3 (pbk) : Unpriced B81-17461

Drobnik, Jerzy. Wiersze / Jerzy Drobnik. — London : Veritas, 1980. — 142p : facsims,3ports ; 22cm
Unpriced (pbk) B81-00646

Grynberg, Henryk. Wiersze z Ameryki / Henryk Grynberg. — Londyn : Oficyna poetów i malarzy, 1980. — 62p ; 22cm
Unpriced (pbk) B81-00647

Leszcza, Jan. Trzy ściany / Jan Leszcza. — Londyn : Oficyna poetów i malarzy, 1980. — 61p ; 22cm
£3.00 (pbk) B81-00648

Obertyńska, Beata. Perły-wierzz / Beata Obertyńska. — Brighton (5 Hanover Terrace, Brighton) : Collegium Marianum, 1980. — 32p ; 21cm
Unpriced (pbk) B81-29493

Solski, Wacław. Dym : wiersze osobiste / Wacław Solski. — London : Polska fundacja kulturalna, [1980]. — 74p : 1port ; 22cm
Unpriced (pbk) B81-00649

Suberlak, Jan. Smutek wyśpiewać : wiersze / Jan Suberlak. — London : Veritas, 1980. — 77p ; 22cm
Unpriced (pbk) B81-01362

891.8'5'17 — Poetry in Polish. Milosz, Czeslaw - *Biographies*

Milosz, Czeslaw. Native realm. — Manchester : Carcanet Press, May 1981. — [300]p
Translation of the Polish
ISBN 0-85635-378-7 : £6.95 : CIP entry B81-07918

891.8'517 — Poetry in Polish. Miłosz, Czesław — *Critical studies* — *Polish texts*

Łapinski, Zdzisław. Między polityką a metafizyką : o poezji Ezesława Miłosza Zdzisław Łapiński. — Londyn : Odnowa, 1981. — 45p ; 22cm
ISBN 0-903705-40-0 (pbk) : Unpriced B81-40389

891.8'527 — Drama in Polish, *1919-* — *Texts*

Karren, Tamara. "Kim był ten człowiek?" : rzecz o Januszu Korczaku / Tamara Karren. — Londyn : Oficyna Poetów i Malarzy, 1981. — 47p,[3]leaves of plates : ill ; 22cm
Unpriced (pbk) B81-24752

Pankowski, Marian. Nasz Julo Czerwony i siedem innych sztuk / Marian Pankowski. — Londyn : Oficyna Poetów i Malarzy, 1981. — 301p ; 22cm
Unpriced (pbk) B81-32103

891.8′537 — Fiction in Polish, 1919- — *Texts*
Gonczyński, Franciszek. Vayn nad parsą / Franciszek Gonczyński. — Londyn [London] : Oficyna Poetów i Malarzy, 1980. — 125p ; 22cm
Unpriced (pbk) B81-14722

Janin, Józef. Bywajcie, wiara! : [powieść] / Józef Janin. — Londyn : Oficyna Poetów i Malarzy [1981]. — 116p ; 22cm
Unpriced (pbk) B81-15486

Janin, Józef. Bywajcie, wiara! : (powieść) / Józef Janin. — Londyn [London] (146 Bridge Arch, Sutton Walk, S.E.1) : Oficyna Poetów I Malarzy, 1981. — 116p ; 22cm
Unpriced (pbk) B81-13166

Liebert, Wacław. Ewidencja W.16 : powieść / Wacław Liebert. — Londyn : Polska Fundacja Kulturalna, 1980. — 248p ; 19cm
Unpriced (pbk) B81-10550

Mackiewicz, Józef. Droga donik ad / Józef Mackiewicz. — Londyn [i.e. London] : Kontra, 1981. — 384p ; 18cm
Originally published: London: Orbis, 1955
ISBN 0-9502324-8-3 (pbk) : £7.95 B81-17372

891.8′537 — Fiction in Polish, *1919-* — *Texts*
Mackiewicz, Józef. Lewa wolna. — London (28 Lanacre Ave., NW9 5FN) : Kontra, Sept.1981. — [460]p
Originally published: London, Polska Fundacja Kulturalna, 1965
ISBN 0-907652-02-6 (pbk) : £7.95 : CIP entry B81-28296

Mniszek, Helena. Ordynat michorowski : powieść / Helena Mniszek. — Londyn : Orbis Books, 1977. — 146p ; 22cm
Originally published: Toronto : Polish Alliance Press, 1969
ISBN 0-901149-11-x (pbk) : Unpriced B81-21218

Mniszek, Helena. Trędowata : powieść / Helena Mniszek. — Londyn : Orbis Books, 1977. — 404p ; 22cm
Originally published: Toronto : Polish Alliance Press, 1969
ISBN 0-901149-10-1 (pbk) : Unpriced B81-21217

891.8′537 — Fiction in Polish, 1919- — *Texts*
Moszkowicz, Michał. Punkt zero / Michał Moszkowicz. — Stockholm ; London : Poets′ and Painters′ Press, 1980. — 94p ; 22cm
Unpriced (pbk) B81-01363

Pawełczak, Jadwiga. Burza : powieść / Jadwiga Pawełczak. — Londyn : Polska fundacja kulturalna, 1980. — 107p ; 22cm
Unpriced (pbk) B81-00650

Pawełczak, Jadwiga. Cień / Jadwiga Pawełczak. — Londyn : Polska fundacja kulturalna, 1980. — 64p ; 22cm
Unpriced (pbk) B81-00651

Romanowski, Władysław. Zły znak / Władysław Romanowski. — Londyn : Nakładem Polskiej Fundacji Kulturalnej, 1980. — 168p ; 19cm
Unpriced (pbk) B81-10551

Skorusa, Jan. Bywaj dziewcz e zdrowe / Jan Skorusa. — London : Veritas, 1980. — 251p ; 19cm
£2.70 (pbk) B81-01364

891.8′537 — Fiction in Polish, *1919-* — *Texts*
Toporska, Barbara. Spójrz wstecz, ajonie : powieść / Barbara Toporska. — Londyn : Polska Fundacja Kulturalna, 1981. — 295p ; 22cm
Unpriced (pbk) B81-31966

891.8′537 — Short stories in Polish, *1919-* — *Texts*
Iwańska, Alicja. Karnawały ... / Alicja Iwańska. — Londyn : Oficyna Poetów i Malarzy, 1980. — 112p ; 22cm
Unpriced (pbk) B81-29494

Świdzińska, Halina. Drogi i bezdroża : wspomnienia i opowieści o ludziach i zdarzeniach / Halina Świdzińska. — Londyn : OPiM, 1981. — 238p,[3]leaves of plates : 3ports ; 22cm
£4.00 (pbk)
Primary classification 970.053′6′0924
B81-18265

891.8′537[F] — Fiction in Polish, *1919-* — *English texts*
Andrzejewski, Jerzy. Ashes and diamonds / by Jerzy Andrzejewski ; translated from the Polish by D.J. Welsh ; introduction by Heinrich Böll. — Harmondsworth : Penguin, 1965, c1962 (1980 [printing]). — xiii,238p ; 20cm. — (Writers from the other Europe)
Translation of: Popiót i Diament. — Originally published: London : Weidenfeld & Nicolson, 1962
ISBN 0-14-005277-1 (pbk) : £2.50 B81-02893

Lem, Stanislaw. Return from the stars / Stanislaw Lem ; translated from the Polish by Barbara Marszal and Frank Simpson. — London : Secker & Warburg, 1980. — 247p ; 23cm
Translation of: Powrót z gwiazd
ISBN 0-436-24415-2 : £6.95 B81-06547

Lem, Stanislaw. Solaris ; The chain of chance ; A perfect vacuum / Stanislaw Lem. — Harmondsworth : Penguin, 1981. — 543p ; 20cm. — (A King penguin)
Solaris originally published: New York : Walker, 1970 ; London : Faber & Faber, 1971. — Translation of: Solaris — The chain of chance originally published: London : Secker & Warburg, 1978. — Translation of: Katar — A perfect vacuum originally published: New York : Harcourt Brace Jovanovich ; London : Secker & Warburg, 1979. — Translation of: Doskonała próznia
ISBN 0-14-005539-8 (pbk) : £3.50 B81-34763

Łysek, Paweł. The hard life of Jura Odcesty / Paweł Łysek ; edited by Ludwik Krzyżanowski and Thomas E. Bird ; translated by Ludwik Kryżanowski ; with an introduction by Thomas E. Bird. — London : Poets′ and Painters′ Press, 1980. — 179p,[5]leaves of plates : ill,1col.port ; 22cm
Translation of: Twarde żywobycie Jury Odcesty
Unpriced (pbk) B81-14248

Miłosz, Czesław. The Issa Valley / Czesław Miłosz ; translated from the Polish by Louis Iribarne. — London : Sidgwick & Jackson, 1981. — 288p ; 23cm
Translation of: Dolina Issy
ISBN 0-283-98762-6 : £6.95 : CIP rev.
B81-07619

891.8′537[F] — Short stories in Polish, *1919-* — *Texts*
Reszczyńska-Stypińska, Marta. Nadzieja - matka cierpliwych / Marta Reszczyńska-Stypińska. — Londyn : Polska fundacja kulturalna, 1980. — 76p ; 22cm
Unpriced (pbk) B81-02330

891.8′58702 — Aphorisms in Polish, *1919-* — *Texts*
Litwin, Aleksander. I bogowie błądzili — / Aleksander Litwin. — Londyn : Oficyna Poetów i Malarzy, 1980. — 84p ; 22cm
Unpriced (pbk) B81-29496

891.8′58709 — Polish literature. Miłosz, Czesław — *Biographies*
Miłosz, Czesław. Native realm : a search for self-definition / Czesław Miłosz ; translated from the Polish by Catherine S. Leach. — London : Sidgwick & Jackson, 1981, c1968. — 300p ; 23cm
Originally published: New York : Doubleday, 1968. — Translation of: Rodzinna Europa
ISBN 0-283-98782-0 : £8.95 B81-29181

891.86 — CZECH LITERATURE

891.8′635[F] — Fiction in Czech, *1900-* - *English texts*
Kohout, Pavel. The hangwoman. — London : Hutchinson, July 1981. — [272]p
Translation of : Die Henkerin
ISBN 0-09-139370-1 : £7.50 : CIP entry
B81-13423

891.8′635[F] — Short stories in Czech, *1900-* — *English texts*
Kundera, Milan. Laughable loves / Milan Kundera ; tranlated from the Czech by Suzanne Rappaport ; introduction by Philip Roth. — Harmondsworth : Penguin, 1975, c1974 (1980 [printing]). — xviii,242p ; 20cm. — (Writers from the other Europe)
Translation of: Smesné lásky. — Originally published: New York : Knopf, 1974 ; London : J. Murray, 1978
ISBN 0-14-004044-7 : £2.50 B81-10928

891.8′635[J] — Children′s short stories in Czech, *1900-* — *English texts*
Macourek, Milŏs. Curious tales / Milŏs Macourek ; translated from the Czech by Marie Burg ; illustrated by Adolf Born. — Oxford : Oxford University Press, 1980. — 88p : ill(some col.) ; 25cm
ISBN 0-19-271427-9 : £3.95 : CIP rev.
B79-22040

891.8′635[J] — Children′s stories in Czech, *1900-* — *English texts*
Procházka, Jan. Lenka / Jan Procházka ; translated by Anthea Bell. — London : Abelard, 1981. — 112p ; 21cm
Translation of: Lenka
ISBN 0-200-72710-9 : £4.75 B81-12251

892.4 — HEBREW LITERATURE

892.4′1′008 — Poetry in Hebrew, *to 1980* — *Anthologies — Hebrew-English parallel texts*
The **Penguin** book of Hebrew verse / edited by T. Carmi. — Harmondsworth : Penguin, 1981. — 608p ; 20cm. — (The Penguin poets)
English introduction and notes, parallel Hebrew text and English translation. — Also printed: London : Allen Lane, 1981. — Bibliography: p581-585. — Includes index
ISBN 0-14-042197-1 (pbk) : £6.95 B81-40014

892.4′3509 — Fiction in Hebrew, *1885-1947*. Special subjects: Arabs — *Critical studies*
Domb, Risa. The Arab in Hebrew prose 1911-1948. — London : Vallentine, Mitchell, Oct.1981. — [192]p
ISBN 0-85303-203-3 : £12.50 : CIP entry
B81-27404

892.4′36[F] — Fiction in Hebrew, *1947-* — *English texts*
Appelfeld, Aron. Badenheim 1939 / Aharon Appelfeld ; translated by Dalya Bilu. — London : Dent, 1981, c1980. — 148p : ill ; 20cm
Translation of: Badenheim, ir nofesh. — Originally published: Boston : Godine, 1980
ISBN 0-460-04548-2 : £4.95 : CIP rev
B81-23878

Oz, Amos. The hill of evil counsel : three stories / Amos Oz ; translated from the Hebrew by Nicholas de Lange in collaboration with the author. — [London] : Fontana, 1980, c1978. — 210p ; 18cm
Translation of: Har ha-′etsah ha-ra′ah. — Originally published: London : Chatto and Windus, 1978
ISBN 0-00-615798-x (pbk) : £1.65 B81-11178

892.4′36[F] — Short stories in Hebrew, *1947-* — *English texts*
Oz, Amos. Where the jackals howl : and other stories / Amos Oz ; translated from the Hebrew by Nicholas de Lange & Philip Simpson. — London : Chatto & Windus, c1981. — 217p ; 21cm
ISBN 0-7011-2571-3 : £6.95 : CIP rev.
B81-06052

892.4′36[J] — Children′s stories in Hebrew, *1947-* — *English texts*
Ofek, Uriel. Smoke over Golan / Uriel Ofek ; translated from the Hebrew by Israel I. Tasfitt ; illustrated by Gary Rees. — London : Methuen Children′s, 1980, c1979. — 138p : ill ; 20cm. — (A Pjed Piper book)
Translation of: Ashan kissa et ha-Golan. — Originally published: New York : Harper & Row, c1979
ISBN 0-416-20970-x : £3.50 B81-12488

892.7 — ARABIC LITERATURE

892′.7′09 — Arabic literature, *ca 500-1500 — Critical studies*

Grunebaum, Gustave E. von. Themes in medieval Arabic literature / Gustave E. von Grunebaum ; edited with a foreword by Dunning S. Wilson ; preface by Speros Vryonis Jr. — London : Variorum Reprints, 1981. — 360p in various pagings : 1port ; 24cm. — (Collected studies series ; 133)
Includes index
ISBN 0-86078-079-1 : £22.00 B81-15565

892′.716 — Poetry in Arabic, *1945- — English texts*

Darwish, Mahmoud. The music of human flesh / Mahmoud Darwish ; selected and translated by Denys Johnson-Davies. — London : Heinemann, 1980. — xix,71p : 1facsim. — (Arab authors ; 7)
Includes 1 poem in Arabic
ISBN 0-435-99407-7 (pbk) : £2.80 : CIP rev. B80-36482

892′.7301′08[FS] — Short stories in Arabic, *1945- — Anthologies — English texts*

Modern Arab stories / [translated by Denys Johnson-Davies et al.]. — London (177 Tottenham Court Rd, W1[P 9LF]) : Ur, 1980. — 132p ; 20cm
Translation from the Arabic
ISBN 0-905206-50-9 (pbk) : £1.25 B81-36571

892′.736[F] — Fiction in Arabic. Egyptian writers, *1945- — English texts*

Mahfūz, Najīb. Children of Gebelawi / Naguib Mahfouz ; translated by Philip Stewart. — London : Heinemann, 1981. — ix,355p ; 19cm. — (African writers series ; 225)
Translated from the Arabic
ISBN 0-435-90225-3 (pbk) : £2.95 B81-13618

Mahfūz Najib. Children of Gebelawi / Neguib Mahfouz ; translated by Philip Stewart. — London : Heinemann, 1981. — ix,355p ; 19cm. — (Arab authors ; 15)
Translated from the Arabic
ISBN 0-435-99415-8 (pbk) : £3.75 B81-16282

893 — HAMITIC AND CHAD LITERATURES

893′.5[F] — Fiction in Somali *- English texts*

Cawl, Faarax. Ignorance is the enemy of love. — London : Zed, Sept.1981. — [144]p
Translation of: Aqoondarro waa u nacab jacayr
ISBN 0-905762-86-x : £4.50 : CIP entry B81-20523

894 — URAL-ALTAIC, PALAEOSIBERIAN, DRAVIDIAN LITERATURES

894′.3533[F] — Fiction in Turkish, *1850- — English texts*

Yasar Kemal. The saga of a seagull / Yashar Kemal ; translated from the Turkish by Thilda Kemal. — London : Collins, 1981. — 250p ; 22cm
Translation of: Al Gözüm seyreyle Salih
ISBN 0-00-261748-x : £6.95 B81-25347

894′.51113 — Poetry in Hungarian, *1900- — Texts*

András, Sándor. Mondolatok / András Sándor. — London ([7 St James Mansions, West End Lane, N.W.6]) : Szespsi Csombor Kör, 1981. — 55p ; 21cm
ISBN 0-903565-07-2 (pbk) : £2.50 B81-39385

894′.51133 — Fiction in Hungarian, *1900- — Texts*

Endre, Karátson. Színhelyek / Karátson Endre. — London ([7 St. James Mansions, West End La., N.W.6]) : Szepsi Csombor Kör, 1980. — 104p ; 21cm. — (A Szepsi Csombor Kör kiadvanyai ; 12)
ISBN 0-903565-06-4 (pbk) : Unpriced B81-19890

894′.541301′089282 — Children′s short stories in Finnish, *1900 — Anthologies — Welsh texts*

Storïau o′r Ffinneg / golygydd a chyfieithydd Niclas L. Walker. — Llandysul : Gwasg Gomer, 1979. — 161p ; 22cm. — (Storïau tramor ; 7)
ISBN 0-85088-641-4 : £2.95 B81-39368

895.1 — CHINESE LITERATURE

895.1′08′005 — Chinese literature, *1912- — Anthologies — English texts*

Literature of the Hundred Flowers / edited by Hualing Nieh. — New York ; Guildford : Columbia University Press, 1981. — 2v. ; 24cm. — (Modern Asian literature series)
Translations from the Chinese. — Includes bibliographies
ISBN 0-231-05264-2 : Unpriced
ISBN 0-231-05074-7 (v.1) : £15.45
ISBN 0-231-05276-3 (v.2) : £24.55 B81-18933

895.1′1′0080358 — Poetry in Chinese. Special subjects: China. Politics, *1976-1979 — English texts — Anthologies*

Goodman, David S. G.. Beijing Street voices : the poetry and politics of China′s democracy movement / David S.G. Goodman. — London : Boyars, c1981. — xv,202p : ill ; 23cm. — ([Open Forum])
Poems translated from the Chinese, English introductions and notes. — Bibliography: p185-192. — Includes index
ISBN 0-7145-2703-3 : £9.95 B81-28460

895.1′1′0080382 — Zen Buddhist poetry in Chinese, *ca 1000-1912 — Anthologies — English texts*

The **Penguin** book of Zen poetry / edited and translated by Lucien Stryk and Takashi Ikemoto ; with an introduction by Lucien Stryk. — Harmondsworth : Penguin, 1981, c1977. — 160p : ill ; 20cm. — (Penguin poets)
Translations from the Japanese and Chinese. — Originally published: London : Allen Lane, 1977
ISBN 0-14-042247-1 (pbk) : £1.95
Primary classification 895.6′1′0080382 B81-40019

895.1′104 — Tz′u poetry in Chinese, *700-1000 — Critical studies*

Chang, Kang-i Sun. The evolution of Chinese tz′u poetry : from late T′ang to Northern Sung / Kang-i Sun Chang. — Princeton ; Guildford : Princeton University Press, c1980. — xvi,251p : ill,1facsim,1port ; 23cm
Bibliography: p216-229. — Includes index
ISBN 0-691-06425-3 : £9.70 B81-05529

895.1′12 — Poetry in Chinese, *B.C.200-A.D.545 — Anthologies — English texts*

New songs from a jade terrace. — London : Allen & Unwin, Jan.1982. — [264]p
Translated from the Chinese
ISBN 0-04-895026-2 : £10.00 : CIP entry B81-33898

895.1′13′09 — Poetry in Chinese, *ca 700-ca 1000 — Critical studies*

Owen, Stephen. The great age of Chinese poetry : the High T′ang / Stephen Owen. — New Haven ; London : Yale University Press, c1981. — xv,440p ; 26cm
Bibliography: p427-434. - Includes index
ISBN 0-300-02367-7 : £18.90 B81-09391

895.1′14 — Poetry in Chinese, *ca 1000-1912 — English texts*

Ryōkan. The Zen poems of Ryōkan / selected and translated with an introduction, biographical sketch, and notes by Nobuyuki Yuasa. — Princeton ; Guildford : Princeton University Press, c1981. — 218p : ill,facsims,maps ; 24cm. — (Princeton library of Asian translations)
Translations from the Chinese and Japanese. — Bibliography: p217-218
ISBN 0-691-06466-0 : £11.60
Also classified at 895.6′13 B81-39670

895.1′301′08[FS] — Short stories in Chinese, *1912- — Anthologies — English texts*

Modern Chinese stories and novellas 1919-1949 / edited by Joseph S.M. Lau, C.T. Hsia, and Leo Ou-fan Lee. — New York ; Guildford : Columbia University Press, 1981. — xxvii,578p,[6]p of plates : ports ; 26cm. — (Modern Asian literature series)
Translations from the Chinese. — Bibliography: p561-568
ISBN 0-231-04202-7 (cased) : £25.30
ISBN 0-231-04203-5 (pbk) : £10.85 B81-39724

895.1′34[F] — Fiction in Chinese, *ca 1000-1912 — English texts*

Wu, Cheng′en. Monkey / Wu Ch′êng-ên ; translated by Arthur Waley. — London : Unwin Paperbacks, 1979. — 336p ; 18cm
Translation of: Xi you ji. — Originally published: London : Allen and Unwin, 1942
ISBN 0-04-823173-8 (pbk) : £1.95 : CIP rev. B81-05584

895.1′34′09 — Fiction in Chinese, *ca 1000-1912 — Critical studies*

Hegel, Robert E.. The novel in seventeenth-century China / Robert E. Hegel. — New York ; Guildford : Columbia University Press, 1981. — xx,336p : ill,1map,1facsim ; 24cm
Bibliography: p309-329. — Includes index
ISBN 0-231-04928-5 : £12.40 B81-24016

895.1′35[F] — Fiction in Chinese, *1912- — English texts*

Bajin. Cold nights : a novel / by Pa Chin ; translated by Nathan K. Mao & Liu Ts′un-yan. — Hong Kong : Chinese University Press ; Seattle ; London : University of Washington Press [distributor], 1978. — xxxiv,181p : ill,1map,ports ; 24cm
Translation of: Han ye. — Bibliography: p177-181
ISBN 0-295-95639-9 : £5.95 B81-02606

895.6 — JAPANESE LITERATURE

895.6′1′0080382 — Zen Buddhist poetry in Japanese, *ca 1200-1976 — Anthologies — English texts*

The **Penguin** book of Zen poetry / edited and translated by Lucien Stryk and Takashi Ikemoto ; with an introduction by Lucien Stryk. — Harmondsworth : Penguin, 1981, c1977. — 160p : ill ; 20cm. — (Penguin poets)
Translations from the Japanese and Chinese. — Originally published: London : Allen Lane, 1977
ISBN 0-14-042247-1 (pbk) : £1.95
Also classified at 895.1′1′0080382 B81-40019

895.6′104 — Haiku in Japanese, *1603-1868 — Anthologies — English texts*

Homage to the Haiku masters / [compiled and translated by] S.D.P. Clough. — [Malvern] ([14 St Ann′s Rd., Malvern, Worcs.]) : [S.D.P. Clough], [c1981]. — 114p : 3ill ; 21cm
Cover title. — Originally published: in 4 pamphlets entitled Tanka, haiku, sijo. 1973 ; Homage to the Haiku masters. 1975 ; Further homage to the Haiku masters. 1976 ; Further homage to the Haiku masters. Supplement. 1977. — Includes index
Unpriced (pbk) B81-20665

895.6′11′08 — Poetry in Japanese, *to 1185 — Anthologies — English texts*

[Man′yōshū. *English*]. The ten thousand leaves : a translation of the Man′yōshū, Japan′s premier anthology of classical poetry / Ian Hideo Levy. — Princeton ; Guildford : Princeton University Press. — (Princeton library of Asian translations)
Includes index
Vol.1. — 1981. — 409p : ill ; 23cm
ISBN 0-691-06452-0 : £15.20 B81-40512

895.6′13 — Poetry in Japanese, *1603-1868 — English texts*

Ryōkan. The Zen poems of Ryōkan / selected and translated with an introduction, biographical sketch, and notes by Nobuyuki Yuasa. — Princeton ; Guildford : Princeton University Press, c1981. — 218p : ill,facsims,maps ; 24cm. — (Princeton library of Asian translations)
Translations from the Chinese and Japanese. — Bibliography: p217-218
ISBN 0-691-06466-0 : £11.60
Primary classification 895.1′14 B81-39670

895.6′34 — Fiction in Japanese. Higuchi, Ichiyō — *Biographies*

Danly, Robert Lyons. In the shade of Spring leaves. — London : Yale University Press, Sept.1981. — [352]p
ISBN 0-300-02614-5 : £13.95 : CIP entry B81-30245

895.6′35[F] — Fiction in Japanese, *1945-* — *English texts*
Endō, Shusakū. Volcano / Shusaku Endo ; translated from the Japanese and with an introduction by Richard A. Schuchert. — London : Quartet, 1980, c1978. — 175p ; 20cm
Translation of: Kazan. — Originally published: London : Owen, 1978
ISBN 0-7043-3356-2 (pbk) : £2.50 B81-21279

Endō, Shūsaku. When I whistle / Shusaku Endo ; translated from the Japanese by Van C. Gessel. — London : Quartet, 1980, c1979. — 277p ; 20cm. — (UNESCO collection of representative works. Japanese series)
Translation of: Kuchibue wo fuku toki. — Originally published: London : Owen, 1979
ISBN 0-7043-3340-6 (pbk) : £2.95 B81-03554

Ishiguro, Kazuo. A pale view of hills. — London : Faber, Feb.1982. — [183]p
Translation from Japanese
ISBN 0-571-11866-6 : CIP entry B81-38321

895.6′35[J] — Children′s stories in Japanese, *1945-* — *English texts*
Iguchi, Bunshu. An elephant′s tale. — London : Dent, Oct.1981. — [32]p
ISBN 0-460-06090-2 : £3.95 : CIP entry B81-25819

Kuratomi, Chizuko. Mr Bear, baker / written by Chizuko Kuratomi ; illustrated by Kozo Kakimoto. — London : Macdonald, 1981. — [26]p : col.ill ; 26cm
Translation from the Japanese
ISBN 0-354-08135-7 : £3.95 B81-32931

Kuratomi, Chizuko. Mr Bear′s shadow / written by Chizuko Kuratomi ; illustrated by Kozo Kakimoto. — London ; Macdonald, c1980. — [26]p : col.ill ; 25cm
Translation of: Chiisakunatta Donkumasan
ISBN 0-354-08113-6 : £3.50 B81-03053

Sugita, Yutaka. The treasure box / pictures by Yutaka Sugita ; story by Robin and Inge Hyman. — London : Evans, 1980. — [25]p : chiefly col.ill ; 26cm
These illustrations originally published: with Japanese text. Tokyo : Shiko-sha, 1979
ISBN 0-237-45520-x : £3.95 : CIP rev. B80-03964

Sugita, Yutaka. Whoops, hoops! / Yutaka Sugita. — London : Dent, 1980. — [27]p : col.ill ; 25cm
ISBN 0-460-06052-x : £3.50 B81-03976

Watanabe, Shigeo. How do I put it on? / Shigeo Watanabe ; illustrated by Yasuo Ohtomo. — Harmondsworth : Puffin, 1981, c1979. — [24]p : col.ill ; 23cm
Translation from the Japanese. — Originally published: London : Bodley Head, 1979
ISBN 0-14-050360-9 (pbk) : £0.90 B81-18534

Watanabe, Shigeo. Ready, steady, go! / Shigeo Watanabe ; illustrated by Yasuo Ohtomo. — London : Bodley Head, 1981. — 28p : chiefly ill ; 22cm
Translated from the Japanese
ISBN 0-370-30406-3 : £2.95 B81-15996

896 — AFRICAN LITERATURES

896′.33 — Ballads in Asante-Twi — *Anthologies — Esperanto-English parallel texts*
Nimo, Ko. Ashanti ballads = Baladoj el Asante / [original Asante-Twi by Ko Nimo] ; English by Joe Latham ; Esperanto de Albert Goodheir. — Coatbridge (16 Woodlands Drive, Coatbridge ML5 1LE, Scotland) : KARDO, 1981. — 42p ; 21cm
Parallel Esperanto and English translations and some ballads in Asante-Twi
ISBN 0-905149-17-3 (pbk) : £1.00 B81-21119

896′.39 — Poetry in Zulu — *English texts*
Kunene, Mazisi. Anthem of the decades : a Zulu epic / Mazisi Kunene ; translated from Zulu by the author. — London : Heinemann, 1981. — xl,312p ; 19cm. — (African writers series ; 234)
ISBN 0-435-90234-2 (pbk) : £3.50 B81-23588

896′.39[F] — Fiction in Sotho — *English texts*
Mofolo, Thomas. Chaka / Thomas Mofolo ; new English translation by Daniel P. Kunene. — London : Heinemann, 1981. — xxiii,168p ; 19cm. — (African writers series ; 229)
Translation of: Chaka
ISBN 0-435-90229-6 (pbk) : £1.95 : CIP rev. B80-26274

897 — NORTH AMERICAN INDIAN LITERATURES

897 — North American Indian literatures — *Anthologies — English texts*
Traditional literatures of the American Indian : texts and interpretations / compiled and edited by Karl Kroeber. — Lincoln, [Neb.] ; London : University of Nebraska Press, 1981. — 162p ; 21cm. — (A Bison book)
Includes index
ISBN 0-8032-2704-3 (cased) : Unpriced
ISBN 0-8032-7753-9 (pbk) : £3.60 B81-24015

897 — North American Indian literatures — *Critical studies*
Literature of the American Indians : views and interpretations : a gathering of Indian memories, symbolic contents and literary criticism / edited with an introduction and notes by Abraham Chapman. — New York : New American Library ; London : New English Library, 1975. — x,357p : ill ; 21cm. — (A Meridian book)
ISBN 0-452-00435-7 (pbk) : £2.75 B81-21955

899 — AUSTRONESIAN AND OTHER LITERATURES

899′.22 — Indonesian literatures — *Critical studies — Conference proceedings*
Papers on Indonesian languages and literatures / edited by Nigel Phillips and Khaidir Anwar. — London (School of Oriental and African Studies, Malet St. WC1E 7HP) : Indonesian Etymological Project, 1981. — x,155p : ill,2facsims,maps ; 25cm
Conference papers. — Includes a chapter in French. — Includes bibliographies and index
ISBN 0-9507474-0-8 (pbk) : Unpriced : CIP rev.
Primary classification 499′.22 B81-08855

899′.22 — Orally transmitted narrative poetry in Minangkabau — *Critical studies*
Phillips, Nigel. Sijobang. — Cambridge : Cambridge University Press, Sept.1981. — [261]p. — (Cambridge studies in oral and literate culture)
ISBN 0-521-23737-8 : £22.50 : CIP entry B81-21566

900 — GEOGRAPHY, HISTORY, AND THEIR AUXILIARIES

900 — Historical events. Anniversaries — *For children*
Brandreth, Gyles. Crazy days / Gyles Brandreth ; illustrated by Peter Stevenson. — London : Carousel, 1981. — [144p] : ill ; 20cm
ISBN 0-552-54191-5 (pbk) : £0.85 B81-37345

900 — History — *Festschriften*
History and imagination. — London : Duckworth, Sept.1981. — [394]p
ISBN 0-7156-1570-x : £18.00 : CIP entry B81-22675

900 — History — *For schools*
Lines, C. J.. Exploring the past / authors Clifford Lines, Laurie Bolwell. — London : Macdonald Educational, c1981. — 48p : ill (some col.),maps(some col.),1facsim,1plan ; 22cm. — (Town and around)
Text on inside covers
ISBN 0-356-07190-1 (pbk) : Unpriced B81-26252

901 — HISTORY. PHILOSOPHY AND THEORY

901 — Civilization — *Philosophical perspectives*
Skolimowski, Henryk. Eco-philosophy : designing new tactics for living / Henryk Skolimowski. — Boston, [Mass.] ; London : Boyars, 1981. — viii,117p : ill ; 21cm. — (Ideas in progress)
ISBN 0-7145-2677-0 (cased) : £6.95
ISBN 0-7145-2676-2 (pbk) : £2.95 B81-27168

901 — Historical events — *Philosophical perspectives*
Hegel, Georg Wilhelm Friedrich. Lectures on the philosophy of world history : introduction : reason in history / translated from the German edition of Johannes Hoffmeister by H.B. Nisbet ; with an introduction by Duncan Forbes. — Cambridge : Cambridge University Press, 1975 (1980 [printing]). — xxxviii,252p ; 22cm. — (Cambridge studies in the history and theory of politics)
Translation of: Vorlesungen über die Philosophie der Geschichte. — Bibliography: p234-242. — Includes index
ISBN 0-521-28145-8 (pbk) : £5.50 B81-03398

901 — Historical events. Philosophical perspectives. Theories of Voegelin, Eric
Webb, Eugene, *1938-*. Eric Voegelin : philosopher of history / by Eugene Webb. — Seattle ; London : University of Washington Press, c1981. — xi,320p ; 24cm
Bibliography: p290-310. — Includes index
ISBN 0-295-95759-x : £13.00 B81-29783

901 — History — *Marxist viewpoints*
McLennan, Gregor. Marxism and the methodologies of history. — London : New Left Books, Nov.1981. — [308]p
ISBN 0-86091-045-8 (cased) : £13.50 : CIP entry
ISBN 0-86091-743-6 (pbk) : £4.95 B81-34211

901 — History. Theories of Dilthey, Wilhelm
Bulhof, Ilse N.. Wilhelm Dilthey : a hermeneutic approach to the study of history and culture / by Ilse N. Bulhof. — The Hague ; London : Nijhoff, 1980. — 233p ; 25cm. — (Martinus Nijhoff philosophy library ; v.2)
Bibliography: p218-225. - Includes index
ISBN 90-247-2360-4 : Unpriced B81-05013

901′.9 — Psychohistory — *Festschriften*
New directions in psychohistory : the Adelphi papers in honor of Erik H. Erikson / edited by Mel Albin with the assistance of Robert J. Devlin, Gerald Heeger. — Lexington : Lexington Books ; [Farnborough, Hants.] : Gower [distributor], 1980. — xx,217p : 1ill ; 24cm
Includes index
ISBN 0-669-02350-7 : £15.00 B81-04082

902 — HISTORY. MISCELLANY

902′.02 — World events, *to 1980* — *Chronologies*
365 days to remember. — Maidenhead : Purnell, 1981. — 224p : ill(some col.),col.maps,ports (some col.) ; 27cm
Includes index
ISBN 0-361-04538-7 : £6.99 B81-17739

902′.02 — World, *to 1980* — *Chronologies — For children*
Cooke, Jean. [World of history]. History fact-finder / [authors, Jean Cooke, Ann Kramer, Theodore Rowland-Entwhistle] ; [illustrators, Brian and Constance Dear]. — London : Ward Lock, c1981. — 240p : ill(some col.),maps,ports ; 20cm
Originally published: London : Hamlyn, 1977. — Includes index
ISBN 0-7063-6097-4 : Unpriced : CIP rev. B81-02374

903 — HISTORY. DICTIONARIES, ENCYCLOPAEDIAS, CONCORDANCES

903′.21 — World — *Encyclopaedias — For children*
Tyrrell, Janet. Our world : a first picture encyclopedia / Janet Tyrrell ; illustrated by Chris Shields. — Maidenhead : Purnell, 1980. — 61p : ill ; 33cm
Includes index
ISBN 0-361-04359-7 : £3.99 B81-15203

904 — HISTORY. COLLECTED ACCOUNTS OF SPECIAL KINDS OF EVENTS

904 — Disasters
Whittow, John. Disasters : the anatomy of environmental hazards / John Whittow. — London : Allen Lane, 1980. — 411p : ill,maps ; 22cm
Bibliogrpahy: p403-405. - Includes index
ISBN 0-7139-1253-7 : £8.95 B81-03752

904 — Disasters — *Forecasts*
Tilms, Richard A.. Judgement of Jupiter / by Richard A. Tilms. — London : New English Library, 1980. — 136p : ill ; 23cm
ISBN 0-450-04749-0 : £5.95 B81-01365

904'.5 — Natural disasters. Causes
Whittow, John. Disasters : the anatomy of environmental hazards / John Whittow. — Harmondsworth : Pelican, 1980. — 411p : ill,maps ; 21cm. — (Pelican geography and environmental studies)
Originally published: London : Allen Lane, 1980. — Bibliography: p403-405. — Includes index
ISBN 0-14-022114-x (pbk) : £4.50 B81-01734

904'.5 — Natural disasters — *For children*
Zoeller, Juscha. Natural forces / [translated from the original German text of Juscha Zoeller by Brenda F. Groth]. — St. Albans : Hart-Davis, 1981. — 36p : col.ill ; 15x16cm. — (Questions answered)
ISBN 0-247-13093-1 : £1.50 B81-39461

904'.7 — Battles, *to 1945* — *For children*
Williams, Brian, *1943-*. The wonder book of battles / [Brian Williams]. — London : Ward Lock, 1981. — 37p : ill(some col.),ports(some col.) ; 27cm
Includes index
ISBN 0-7063-6133-4 : £2.50 B81-39964

905 — HISTORY. SERIALS

905 — Historical events — *Serials*
History journal / Middlesex Polytechnic. — June 1980-. — Barnet (S.G. Doree, Middlesex Polytechnic, Trent Park, Cockfosters Rd, Barnet, Herts. EN4 0PT) : Humanities Resource Centre of the Middlesex Polytechnic, 1980-. — v. ; 30cm
Annual
ISSN 0144-2791 = History journal : Unpriced B81-02025

907 — HISTORY. STUDY AND TEACHING

907 — Area studies — *Serials*
Journal of area studies. — No.1 (Spring 1980)-. — Portsmouth (Hampshire Terrace, Portsmouth, Hants. PO1 2EG) : Portsmouth Polytechnic School of Languages and Area Studies, 1980-. — ill,maps ; 30cm
Two issues yearly
£1.75per year B81-24701

907 — Historical sources: Audiovisual media — *Serials*
Historical journal of film, radio and television. — Vol.1, no.1 (Mar.1981)-. — Dorchester-on-Thames (Haddon House, Dorchester-on-Thames, Oxford OX9 8JZ) : Carfax Publishing in association with the International Association for Audio-Visual Media in Historical Research and Education, 1981-. — v. ; 26cm
Two issues yearly
ISSN 0143-9685 = Historical journal of film, radio and television : Unpriced B81-33707

907 — Historical sources: Cinema films
Feature films as history / edited by K.R.M. Short. — London : Croom Helm, c1981. — 192p ; 23cm
Includes index
ISBN 0-7099-0459-2 : £9.95 : CIP rev. B81-01851

907'.1 — Schools. Curriculum subjects: History. Teaching
Reeves, Marjorie. Why history? / Marjorie Reeves. — London : Longman, 1980. — vii,151p ; 22cm
Includes bibliographies and index
ISBN 0-582-36119-2 (cased) : £6.50 : CIP rev.
ISBN 0-582-36120-6 (pbk) : £2.95 B80-12641

907'.1041 — Great Britain. Schools. Curriculum subjects: History. Teaching
Henderson, James L.. The teaching of world history / by James L. Henderson. — London : Historical Association, c1979. — 31p ; 21cm. — (Teaching of history series ; no.42)
Bibliography: p29-31
ISBN 0-85278-204-7 (pbk) : £1.40 B81-23003

Rogers, P. J.. The new history : theory into practice / by P.J. Rogers. — London : Historical Association, c1980. — 63p ; 21cm. — (Teaching of history series ; no.44)
Bibliography: p62-63
ISBN 0-85278-208-x : £1.40 B81-23002

907'.1041 — Great Britain. Schools. Curriculum subjects: History. Teaching. Use of historical sources
Palmer, M.. The source method in history teaching / by M. Palmer, G.R. Batho. — London : Historical Association, c1981. — 32p : 1ill,1map,facsims ; 21cm. — (Teaching of history series ; no.48)
Bibliography: p30-32
ISBN 0-85278-237-3 (pbk) : Unpriced B81-27581

907'.1041 — Great Britain. Schools. Curriculum subjects: History. Teaching. Use of visits to houses of historical importance
Neal, Philip. Heritage education / Philip Neal. — [Birmingham] ([102 Edmunds St., Birmingham B3 3DS]) : National Association for Environmental Education, [c1979]. — 27p : ill ; 30cm. — (Practical guide ; 7)
Cover title
Unpriced (pbk) B81-08269

907'.2 — Historiography
Butterfield, *Sir* **Herbert**. The origins of history / Herbert Butterfield ; edited with an introduction by Adam Watson. — London : Eyre Methuen, 1981. — 252p ; 25cm
Bibliography: p231-244. — Includes index
ISBN 0-413-48370-3 : £12.50 B81-28966

Howard, Michael, *1922-*. The lessons of history : an inaugural lecture delivered before the vice-chancellor and Fellows of the University of Oxford on Friday 6 March 1981 / by Michael Howard. — Oxford : Clarendon, 1981. — 21p ; 22cm
ISBN 0-19-951532-8 (pbk) : £1.95 : CIP rev. B81-12895

907'.2 — Historiography, *700-1500*
The **Writing** of history in the Middle Ages : essays presented to Richard William Southern / edited by R.H.C. Davis & J.M. Wallace-Hadrill with the assistance of R.J.A.I. Catto & M.H. Keen. — Oxford : Clarendon Press, 1981. — xiii,517p,[2]leaves of plates : 1facsim,1port ; 23cm
Bibliography: p495-502. — Includes index
ISBN 0-19-822556-3 : £22.50 B81-35521

907'.2 — Historiography. Implications of political beliefs of historiographers — *Socialist viewpoints*
Sutton, David C.. Point of view in the writing of history / by David C. Sutton. — Coventry (P.O. Box 104, Coventry CV5 8NE) : Chapelfields Press, 1981. — 8p ; 30cm
ISBN 0-86279-009-3 (pbk) : £0.45 B81-25073

907'.2 — Historiology
Braudel, Fernand. On history / Fernand Braudel ; translated by Sarah Matthews. — London : Weidenfeld and Nicolson, c1980. — ix,226p ; 24cm
Translation of: Ecrits sur l'histoire. — Originally published: Chicago : Chicago University Press, 1980. — Includes index
ISBN 0-297-77880-3 : £10.95 B81-02782

Haddock, B. A. (Bruce Anthony). An introduction to historical thought / B.A. Haddock. — London : Edward Arnold, 1980. — 184p ; 22cm
Bibliography: p175-181. - Includes index
ISBN 0-7131-6323-2 (cased) : £9.50 : CIP rev.
ISBN 0-7131-6324-0 (pbk) : £4.75 B80-23838

907'.2 — Historiology. Study techniques
Daniels, Robert V.. Studying history : how and why / Robert V. Daniels. — 3rd ed. — Englewood Cliffs ; London : Prentice-Hall, c1981. — xii,125p : ill ; 21cm
Previous ed.: 1972. — Bibliography: p119-125
ISBN 0-13-858738-8 (pbk) : £4.50 B81-16675

907'.2024 — American historiography. Josephson, Matthew — *Biographies*
Shi, David E.. Matthew Josephson, bourgeois bohemian / David E. Shi. — New Haven ; London : Yale University Press, c1981. — xiii,314p,[14]p of plates : ill,1facsim,ports ; 24cm
Includes index
ISBN 0-300-02563-7 : £12.60 B81-22423

907'.2024 — Historiography. Ibn Khaldūn, 'Abd ar-Raḥmān ibn Muḥammad. Western criticism, *to 1977*
Al-Azmeh, Aziz. Ibn Khaldūn in modern scholarship : a study in orientalism / Aziz Al-Azmeh. — London (117 Piccadilly, W.1) : Third World Centre for Research and Publishing, 1981. — xxi,333p : 1col.ill ; 23cm
Bibliography: p231-318. — Includes index
ISBN 0-86199-003-x : £10.00 B81-36712

907'.2024 — Historiography. Khaldūn, Ibn - *Critical studies*
Azmeh, Aziz. Ibn Khaldūn. — London : Cass, May 1981. — [192]p
ISBN 0-7146-3130-2 : £14.00 : CIP entry B81-08861

907'.2024 — Historiography. Ranke, Leopold von
Dickens, A. G.. Ranke as reformation historian / by A.G. Dickens. — [Reading] : University of Reading, 1980. — 20p ; 24cm. — (The Stenton lectures, ISSN [0309-0469] ; 13, 1979)
Bibliography: p19-20
ISBN 0-7049-0210-9 (pbk) : £1.50 B81-24035

907'.2041 — British historiography. Political aspects
Parker, Christopher. History as present politics / Christopher Parker. — Winchester (Winchester SO22 4NR) : King Alfred's College, 1980. — 38p ; 21cm. — (Contexts and connections ; 6)
Unpriced (pbk) B81-08047

907'.2041 — British Marxist historiology
People's history and socialist theory / edited by Raphael Samuel. — London : Routledge & Kegan Paul, 1981. — lvi,417p : ill ; 23cm. — (History Workshop series)
Includes bibliographies
ISBN 0-7100-0765-5 : £10.95 : CIP rev.
ISBN 0-7100-0652-7 (pbk) : £6.95 B80-35511

907'.2042 — Engligh historiography, *1900-1970*
Tawney, R. H.. The attack. — Nottingham : Spokesman, May 1981. — [200]p
Originally published: London : Allen & Unwin, 1953
ISBN 0-85124-311-8 (cased) : £8.00 : CIP entry
ISBN 0-85124-312-6 (pbk) : £3.00 B81-08838

907'.2'042 — English historiography, *ca 1066-ca 1485*
Galbraith, V. H.. Kings and chroniclers. — London (35 Gloucester Ave., NW1 7AX) : Hambledon Press, Nov.1981. — [320]p. — (History series ; 4)
ISBN 0-9506882-4-x : £20.00 : CIP entry B81-30622

907'.2044 — French historiography, *1929-1979* — *Philosophical perspectives*
Ricœur, Paul. The contribution of French historiography to the theory of history / Paul Ricœur. — Oxford : Clarendon, 1980. — 65p ; 22cm. — (The Zaharoff lecture for ... ; 1978-9)
ISBN 0-19-952249-9 (pbk) : £2.75 : CIP rev. B80-13131

907'.2045 — Italian historiography, *1400-1620*
Cochrane, Eric. Historians and historiography : in the Italian Renaissance / Eric Cochrane. — Chicago ; London : University of Chicago Press, 1981. — xx,649p ; 25cm
Includes index
ISBN 0-226-11152-0 : £26.25 B81-38899

907′.2047 — Soviet historiography, *1928-1932*

Barber, John, *1944-*. Soviet historians in crisis, 1928-1932 / John Barber. — London : Macmillan in association with Centre for Russian and East European Studies, University of Birmingham, 1981. — xiii,194p ; 23cm. — (Studies in Soviet history and society)
Bibliography: p179-185. - Includes index
ISBN 0-333-28196-9 : £15.00 : CIP rev.
B80-22666

907′.206 — African historiography

Temu, Arnold. African historiography. — London : Zed Press, Nov.1981. — [208]p
ISBN 0-905762-78-9 : £12.95 : CIP entry
B81-33627

907′.8 — Great Britain. Secondary schools. Curriculum subjects: History. Teaching. Applications of digital computer systems

Computers in secondary school history teaching / contributions from Ian Killbery, Beverley Labbett, Keith Randell ; edited by Joseph Hunt ; commissioned by the National Development Programme in Computer Assisted Learning. — London : Historical Association, c1980. — 48p : 1map ; 21cm. — (Teaching of history series ; no.40)
ISBN 0-85278-198-9 (pbk) : £1.40 B81-23004

909 — WORLD HISTORY, CIVILIZATION

909 — Civilization

Rüstow, Alexander. Freedom and domination : a historical critique of civilization / Alexander Rüstow ; abbreviated translation from the German by Salvator Attanasio ; edited, and with an introduction, by Dankwart A. Rustow. — Princeton ; Guildford : Princeton University Press, c1980. — xxix,716p ; 25cm
Condensed translation of Ortsbestimmung der Gegenwart, 3 Vols. — Includes index
ISBN 0-681-05604-5 : £19.20 B81-09608

909 — Civilization, *to 1979*

Cooke, Jean. Man-made wonders of the world / Jean Cooke. — London : Octopus, 1980. — 96p : col.ill ; 33cm
Includes index
ISBN 0-7064-1224-9 : £3.95 B81-03332

909 — Human geography — *Encyclopaedias*

The **Dictionary** of human geography. — Oxford : Blackwell, Sept.1981. — [320]p
ISBN 0-631-10721-5 : £15.00 : CIP entry
B81-21493

909 — Peoples — *For children*

People / illustrated by Anna Dzierzek. — London : Hamlyn, 1981. — [42]p : col.ill,col.maps ; 26cm. — (I can learn)
Maps on lining papers
ISBN 0-600-36482-8 : £1.99 B81-24059

Spier, Peter. People / written and illustrated by Peter Spier. — Tadworth : World's Work, 1981, c1980. — [42]p : col.ill ; 24cm
Originally published: Garden City, N.Y. : Doubleday, 1979. — Ill on lining papers
ISBN 0-437-76516-4 : £4.95 B81-15136

909 — World. Effects of sun

Goodavage, Joseph F.. Storm on the sun / Joseph F. Goodavage. — London : Sphere, 1980, c1979. — 192p ; 18cm
Originally published: New York : Simon and Schuster, 1977
ISBN 0-7221-3963-2 (pbk) : £1.35 B81-08335

909 — World events, *1980- expounded by* **Biblical prophecies**

Walvoord, John F.. Armageddon : oil and the Middle East crisis / John F. Walvoord and John E. Walvoord. — London (1 Creed La., EC4V 5BR) : Lamp Press, 1980, c1976. — 207p : ill,maps,2ports ; 18cm
Originally published: Grand Rapids : Zondervan, 1974
ISBN 0-7208-0352-7 (pbk) : £1.75
ISBN 0-7208-0352-7 B81-14552

909 — World, *to 1980*

Roberts, J. M.. The pelican history of the world / J.M. Roberts. — Rev. ed. — Harmondsworth : Penguin, 1980. — 1052p : maps ; 20cm. — (Pelican books)
Previous ed. published as: The Hutchinson history of the world. London : Hutchinson, 1976. — Includes index
ISBN 0-14-022101-8 (pbk) : £3.95 B81-02946

Thomas, Hugh. An unfinished history of the world. — Rev. ed. — London : Hamish Hamilton, Jan.1982. — [816]p
Previous ed.: 1979
ISBN 0-241-10696-6 : £17.50 : CIP entry
B81-34405

Thomas, Hugh, *1931-*. An unfinished history of the world / Hugh Thomas. — Rev. ed. — London : Pan, 1981. — xvii,792p : maps ; 20cm
Previous ed.: London : Hamilton, 1979. — Includes index
ISBN 0-330-26458-3 (pbk) : £3.95 B81-38102

909′.0491497 — Gypsies — *For children*

Acton, Thomas. Gypsies / Thomas Acton. — London : Macdonald Educational, 1981. — 48p : ill(some col.),col.maps,music,1col.port ; 29cm. — (Surviving peoples)
Bibliography: p47. — Includes index
ISBN 0-356-05956-1 : £3.50 B81-29910

909′.049193 — Latvian exiles, *1940-1980*

Grunts, Marita V.. Latvians in exile in the free world, 1940-1980 / Marita V. Grunts. — [London] ([75 Braxted Park, SW16 3AU]) : [M.V. Grunts], [1980]. — 22,[42]leaves : facsims ; 30cm
Bibliography: 2p
Unpriced (spiral) B81-12262

909′.0491992 — Armenians, *to 1980*

Lang, David Marshall. The Armenians : a people in exile / David Marshall Lang. — London : Allen & Unwin, 1981. — xi,203p,[16]p of plates : ill,maps,1facsim,ports ; 24cm
Bibliography: p191-196. — Includes index
ISBN 0-04-956010-7 : Unpriced : CIP rev.
B81-13438

909′.04924 — Diaspora

Comay, Joan. The Diaspora story : the epic of the Jewish people among the nations / Joan Comay in association with Beth Hatefutsoth — the Nahum Goldmann Museum of the Jewish Diaspora, Tel Aviv. — London : Weidenfeld and Nicolson, c1981. — 288p : ill(some col.),maps,facsims,ports(some col.),1geneal.table ; 24cm
Includes index
ISBN 0-297-77854-4 : £15.00 B81-29882

909′.04924082 — Jewish communities. Social life, *1900-1950*

Patai, Raphael. The vanished worlds of Jewry / Raphael Patai ; picture research by Eugene Rosow with Vivien Kleiman. — London : Weidenfeld and Nicolson, 1981. — 192p : ill,ports ; 29cm
Includes index
ISBN 0-297-77856-0 : £12.50 B81-05625

909′.049240828 — Jews — *Serials*

The **Jewish** travel guide. — 1979. — London : Jewish Chronicle Publications, c1979. — 296p in various pagings
ISBN 0-900498-73-0 : £2.00 B81-24148

The **Jewish** travel guide. — 1980. — London : Jewish Chronicle Publications, c1980. — 295p
ISBN 0-900498-76-5 : £2.35 B81-24147

The **Jewish** travel guide. — 1981. — London : Jewish Chronicle Publications, c1981. — 292p
ISBN 0-900498-80-3 : £2.75 B81-24146

The **Jewish** year book. — 1980 = 5740-5741. — London : Jewish Chronicle Publications, 1980. — 305p in various pagings
ISBN 0-900498-77-3 : Unpriced B81-24144

The **Jewish** year book. — 1981 = 5741-5742. — London : Jewish Chronicle Publications, c1981. — 302p in various pagings
ISBN 0-900498-79-x : Unpriced B81-24145

909′.049240828′05 — Jews — *Serials*

The **Jewish** year book. — 1979 = 5739-5740. — London : Jewish Chronicle Publications, c1979. — 296p in various pagings
ISBN 0-900498-69-2 : Unpriced B81-28706

909′.04927 — Arabs, *to 1979*

Rodinson, Maxime. The Arabs / Maxime Rodinson ; translated by Arthur Goldhammer. — London : Croom Helm, 1981. — xvi,187p ; 21cm
Translation of: Les Arabes. — Includes index
ISBN 0-7099-0376-6 (cased) : £8.50
ISBN 0-7099-0377-4 (pbk) : Unpriced
B81-37635

909′.04927′0024737 — Arab civilization, *to 1979 — For numismatics*

Plant, Richard J.. Arabic coins and how to read them / by Richard J. Plant. — 2nd ed.(rev.). — London : Seaby, 1980. — 150p : ill,geneal.tables ; 22cm
English and Arabic text. — Previous ed.: 1973. — Includes index
ISBN 0-900652-52-7 (pbk) : £4.50 : CIP rev.
Primary classification 737.4′0917′4927
B80-04890

909′.04960828′05 — Negro culture — *Serials*

Black seeds : [black world monthly]. — Vol.1, no.1 (Sept.1980)-. — London (Karnak House, 300 Westbourne Park Rd, W11 1EH) : Afla Ink Publishers, 1980-. — v. : ill,ports ; 30cm
ISSN 0144-4530 = Black seeds : £10.00 per year B81-06789

909.07 — Crusades, *1095-1274*

Riley-Smith, Louise. The crusades : idea and reality, 1095-1274 / Louise and Jonathan Riley-Smith. — London : Edward Arnold, 1981. — xiii,191p : 1map ; 24cm. — (Documents of medieval history ; 4)
Bibliography: p178-181. — Includes index
ISBN 0-7131-6348-8 (pbk) : £6.50 : CIP rev.
B81-22521

909.07 — Crusades — *For wargaming*

Heath, Ian. A wargamers' guide to the Crusades / Ian Heath. — Cambridge : Stephens, 1980. — 160p : ill,maps ; 25cm
Bibliography: p159-160
ISBN 0-85059-430-8 : £7.50 : CIP rev.
B80-09926

909.07 — World, *ca 300-1450 — For Irish students*

Gallagher, Peter. Medieval times / Peter Gallagher. — Dublin : Educational Company, 1981. — 251p : ill,maps,facsims,ports ; 21cm
Includes index
Unpriced (pbk) B81-38780

909.07′03′21 — Civilization, *395-1429 — Encyclopaedias*

Grabois, Aryeh. The illustrated encyclopedia of medieval civilization / Aryeh Grabois. — London : Octopus, 1980. — 751p : ill(some col.),maps,facsims,ports ; 25cm
Bibliography: p9-10. — Includes index
ISBN 0-7064-0856-x : £15.00 B81-05058

909.08 — Escapes, *1568-1944*

Lewis, Brenda Ralph. Great escapes! / re-told by Brenda Ralph Lewis. — London : Hamlyn, 1981. — 110p : ill(some col.),col.maps,1facsim,1plan,ports(some col.),1geneal.table ; 28cm
Originally published: in the Hamlyn book of great escapes
ISBN 0-600-36662-6 (pbk) : £1.99 B81-38590

909.08 — Land wars, *1618-1878*

Chandler, David, *1934-*. Atlas of military strategy 1618-1878 / David G. Chandler ; cartography by Hazel R. Watson and Richard A. Watson. — London : Arms & Armour, 1980. — 208p : ill,col.maps,col.plans,ports ; 29cm
Ill on lining papers. — Bibliography: p202-203. — Includes index
ISBN 0-85368-134-1 : £16.50 B81-04970

909.08 — Social conditions, *1400-1800*
Braudel, Fernand. The structures of everyday life : the limits of the possible / Fernand Braudel ; translation from the French [by Miriam Kochan]. — [New ed.] / revised by Siân Reynolds. — London : Collins, 1981. — 623p : ill,port,facsims,ports ; 23cm. — (Civilisation and capitalism ; v.1)
Translation of: Les structures du quotidien. — Previous ed.: published as Capitalism and material life, 1400-1800. London : Weidenfeld and Nicolson, 1973. — Includes index
ISBN 0-00-216303-9 : £15.00 : CIP rev. B81-26756

909.08 — World, *1450-1763 — For children*
Townson, W. D.. Atlas of the world in the Age of Discovery 1453-1763 / [author W.D. Townson] ; [editor Frances M. Clapham] ; [assistant editor Fay Franklin]. — Harlow : Longman, 1981. — 61p : ill(some col.),col.maps,ports(some col.) ; 33cm
Map on lining papers. — Includes index
ISBN 0-582-39117-2 : £4.95 B81-25614

909.08 — World, *1494-1801 — For schools*
Roberts, J. M.. Making one world / J.M. Roberts. — [Harmondsworth] : Penguin, [1981]. — 128p : ill(some col.),maps(some col.),facsims(some col.),ports(some col.) ; 23cm. — (An Illustrated world history ; 5)
Includes index
ISBN 0-14-064005-3 : £3.95 B81-21147

909.08 — World, *1500-1980*
Larousse encyclopedia of modern history : from 1500 to the present day / general editor Marcel Dunan ; English advisory editors John Roberts, Bernard Wasserstein ; [translated by Delano Ames] ; foreword by Hugh Trevor-Roper. — New rev. ed. — London : Hamlyn, 1981. — 437p,[28]p of plates : ill(some col.),maps,ports (some col.) ; 29cm
Translation of: Histoire universelle Larousse. — Previous ed.: 1972. — Includes index
ISBN 0-600-02376-1 (pbk) : £6.95 B81-38557

909′.091670828 — Antarctic Ocean *— For children*
The **Antarctic** / edited by Pat Hargreaves. — Hove : Wayland, 1980. — 69p : ill(some col.),col.maps ; 25cm. — (Seas and oceans)
Bibliography: p68. — Includes index
ISBN 0-85340-747-9 : £3.95 B81-01955

909′.091821 — Caribbean countries, *1450-1960 — For Caribbean students — For schools*
Hall, D.. The Caribbean experience. — London : Heinemann Educational, Nov.1981. — [144]p. — (Heinemann CXC history ; 2)
ISBN 0-435-98300-8 (pbk) : £2.75 : CIP entry B81-30259

909′.091823 — Pacific region. Stone antiquities. Archaeological investigation *— Conference proceedings*
Archaeological studies of Pacific stone resources / edited by Foss Leach and Janet Davidson. — Oxford : B.A.R., 1981. — 237p : ill,maps ; 30cm. — (BAR. International series ; 104)
Conference papers. — Includes 2 papers in Russian. — Includes bibliographies
ISBN 0-86054-122-3 (pbk) : £9.50 B81-36628

909′.0943 — Mountainous regions *— For schools*
Learn about the mountain environment / edited by Duncan Prowse ; contributors and consultants Andrew Goudie ... [et al.] ; research by Ruth Thomson ... [et al.] ; designed by Valerie Sargent ; project development manager for Schools Abroad Barbara Hopper. — Haywards Heath (Grosvenor Hall, Bolnore Rd., Haywards Heath, W. Sussex RH16 4BX) : Schools Abroad, c1980. — 96p : ill(some col.),maps (some col.),1plan,ports ; 27cm
ISBN 0-905703-59-6 (pbk) : Unpriced B81-21155

909′.09630828 — Atlantic Ocean *— For children*
The **Atlantic** / edited by Pat Hargreaves. — Hove : Wayland, 1980. — 68,[4]p : ill(some col.),6maps(some col.),2plans ; 25cm. — (Seas and oceans)
Bibliography: p[4]. — Includes index
ISBN 0-85340-767-3 : £3.95 B81-01956

909′.096320828 — Arctic Ocean *— For children*
The **Arctic** / edited by Pat Hargreaves. — Hove : Wayland, 1981. — 66p : ill(some col.),col.maps ; 25cm. — (Seas and oceans)
Bibliography: p66. — Includes index
ISBN 0-85340-769-x : £4.50 B81-17058

909′.0963640828 — Gulf of Mexico *— For children*
The **Caribbean** and Gulf of Mexico / edited by Pat Hargreaves. — Hove : Wayland, 1980. — 69,[31]p : ill(some col.),4col.maps ; 25cm. — (Seas and oceans)
Bibliography: p[3]. — Includes index
ISBN 0-85340-746-0 : £3.95
Also classified at 909′.0963650828 B81-01954

909′.0963650828 — Caribbean Sea *— For children*
The **Caribbean** and Gulf of Mexico / edited by Pat Hargreaves. — Hove : Wayland, 1980. — 69,[31]p : ill(some col.),4col.maps ; 25cm. — (Seas and oceans)
Bibliography: p[3]. — Includes index
ISBN 0-85340-746-0 : £3.95
Primary classification 909′.0963640828 B81-01954

909′.096380828 — Mediterranean Sea *— For children*
The **Mediterranean** / edited by Pat Hargreaves. — Hove : Wayland, 1980. — 69,[3]p : ill(some col.),4maps(some col.),1col.plan ; 25cm. — (Seas and oceans)
Bibliography: p[3]. — Includes index
ISBN 0-85340-748-7 : £3.95 B81-01957

909′.09640828 — Pacific Ocean *— For children*
The **Pacific** / edited by Pat Hargreaves. — Hove : Wayland, 1981. — 69p : ill(some col.),col.maps ; 25cm. — (Seas and oceans)
Bibliography: p69. — Includes index
ISBN 0-85340-745-2 : £4.50 B81-17059

909′.09650828 — Indian Ocean *— For children*
The **Indian** Ocean / edited by Pat Hargreaves. — Hove : Wayland, 1981. — 67p : col.ill,col.maps,1port ; 25cm. — (Seas and oceans)
Bibliography: p67. — Includes index
ISBN 0-85340-768-1 : £4.50 B81-17057

909′.0965330828 — Red Sea *— For children*
The **Red** Sea and Persian Gulf / edited by Pat Hargreaves. — Hove : Wayland, 1981. — 67p : ill(some col.),col.maps ; 25cm. — (Seas and oceans)
Bibliography: p67. — Includes index
ISBN 0-85340-770-3 : £4.50
Also classified at 909′.0965350828 B81-17056

909′.0965350828 — Persian Gulf *— For children*
The **Red** Sea and Persian Gulf / edited by Pat Hargreaves. — Hove : Wayland, 1981. — 67p : ill(some col.),col.maps ; 25cm. — (Seas and oceans)
Bibliography: p67. — Includes index
ISBN 0-85340-770-3 : £4.50
Primary classification 909′.0965330828 B81-17056

909′.0971241082 — Commonwealth, *1900-1947 — Festschriften*
The **First** British Commonwealth : essays in honour of Nicholas Mansergh / edited by Norman Hillmer and Philip Wigley. — London : Cass, 1980. — 192p,[1] leaf of plates : 1port ; 23cm
Bibliography: p187-190
ISBN 0-7146-3153-1 : £12.50 : CIP rev. B79-30411

909′.0971241082 — Commonwealth countries. Army operations by Great Britain. *Army, 1900-1980*
Lunt, James. Imperial sunset : frontier soldiering in the 20th century / James Lunt. — London : Macdonald Futura, 1981. — 422p,[24]p of plates : ill,maps,ports ; 24cm
Bibliography: p397-402. - Includes index
ISBN 0-354-04528-8 : £15.95 B81-15195

909′.09712410822 — Commonwealth, *1918-1939*
Holland, R. F.. Britain and the Commonwealth Alliance 1918-1939 / R.F. Holland. — London : Macmillan, 1981. — viii,248p : ill ; 23cm. — (Cambridge Commonwealth series)
Bibliography: p237-242. — Includes index
ISBN 0-333-27295-1 : £20.00 : CIP rev. B80-09914

909′.09712410828 — Commonwealth
The **Commonwealth** today / Commonwealth Secretariat. — [New ed.]. — London : The Secretariat, 1981. — 32p : ill,1map,ports ; 15x20cm
Previous ed.: i.e. rev. ed. 1979. — Text on inside covers. — Bibliography: p30-31
Unpriced (pbk) B81-40649

909′.09712410828 — Commonwealth countries *— Serials*
A **Year** book of the Commonwealth / Foreign and Commonwealth Office. — 1980. — London : H.M.S.O., 1980. — vii,526p
ISBN 0-11-580221-5 : £20.00 B81-02602

909′.0972′4 — Developing countries *— Encyclopaedias*
Kurian, George Thomas. Encyclopedia of the Third World. — Rev. ed. — London : Mansell, Jan.1982. — 3v.([1800]p)
Previous ed.: 1978
ISBN 0-7201-1628-7 : £60.00 : CIP entry
ISBN 0-7201-1619-8 (v.1)
ISBN 0-7201-1629-5 (v.2)
ISBN 0-7201-1630-9 (v.3) B81-33844

909′.097240828 — Developing countries
Only one world : the Sheffield declaration / UTU. — Sheffield (210 Abbeyfield Rd., Sheffield S4 7AZ) : Urban Theology Unit, [1974?]. — [4]p : ill ; 31cm
£0.05 (unbound) B81-18004

909′.097240828 — Developing countries. Information sources *— Lists*
Who to ask about the developing countries / edited by David Spark and Adam Harvey. — 2nd ed. — London : 128 Buckingham Palace Rd., SW1W 9SH : Centre for World Development Education (in association with the Development Journalists′ Group), 1980. — iv,64p ; 15x21cm
Previous ed.: 1976
Unpriced (pbk) B81-01863

909′.097240828 — Developing countries *— Practical information — For expatriate British personnel*
Brown, Harry, *19---*. Brits abroad : a guide to working and living in the developing countries / Harry Brown and Rosemary Thomas. — London : Express Books, c1981. — 250p : ill ; 22cm
ISBN 0-85079-108-1 (pbk) : £3.95 B81-32990

909′.097240828 — Developing countries. Social conditions
May, Brian, *1914-*. The third world calamity / Brian May. — London : Routledge & Kegan Paul, 1981. — xii,274p,[16]p of plates : ill,ports ; 23cm
Includes index
ISBN 0-7100-0764-7 : £8.95 B81-09586

909′.097240828 — Developing countries. Social conditions *— Serials*
[Links *(Oxford)***]**. Links : action against poverty and underdevelopment. — No.1-. — Oxford (232 Cowley Rd, Oxford OX4 1UH) : Third World First, [1976]-. — v. : ill ; 30cm
Three issues yearly (Oct.1976-Dec.1980), two issues yearly (Mar.1981-). — Description based on: No.10
ISSN 0261-4014 = Links (Oxford) : Free to Third World First members B81-29092

909′.097240828′05 — Developing countries *— Serials*
[South *(London)***]**. South : the Third World Magazine. — No.1 (Oct.1980)-. — London (13th floor, New Zealand House, 80 Haymarket, SW1Y 4TS) : South Publications, 1980-. — v. : ill,ports ; 28cm
Monthly. — Pilot issue published July 1980
ISSN 0260-6976 = South (London) : £8.00 per year B81-20407

909′.09732 — Lost cities *— For children*
Fagg. Lost cities / by Christopher Fagg ; illustrated by Roger Payne ... [et al.] ; edited by Suzanne le Maitre. — London : Kingfisher, 1980. — 24p : col.ill ; 23cm. — (Kingfisher explorer books. mysteries)
Bibliography: p24. - Includes index
ISBN 0-7063-6067-2 : £1.95 B81-03455

909′.0973′2 — Urban regions *History - Serials*
Urban history yearbook. — 1981. — Leicester : Leicester University Press, July 1981. — [248]p
ISBN 0-7185-6081-7 (pbk) : £14.00 : CIP entry
ISSN 0306-0845 B81-16388

909′.0974927 — Arab countries, *to 1979*
Polk, William R.. The Arab world / William R. Polk. — 4th ed.. — Cambridge, Mass. ; London : Harvard University Press, 1980. — xxix,456p : maps,1facsim ; 25cm. — (The American foreign policy library)
Previous ed.: published as The United States and the Arab world. 1975. — Bibliography: p419-439. — Includes index
ISBN 0-674-04316-2 (cased) : £3.50
ISBN 0-674-04317-0 (pbk) : £5.40 B81-05961

909′.0974927 — Arab countries, *to 1980*
Mansfield, Peter. The Arabs / Peter Mansfield. — Rev. ed. reprinted with postscripts. — Harmondsworth : Penguin, 1980 (1981 [printing]). — 576p : 1map ; 20cm. — (Penguin books)
Previous ed.: London : Allen Lane, 1976. — Includes index
ISBN 0-14-022067-4 (pbk) : £2.95 B81-25444

909′.097521 — English speaking countries. Political events, *1530-1785*
Calder, Angus. Revolutionary empire : the rise of the English-speaking empires from the 15th century to the 1780s / Angus Calder. — London : Cape, 1981. — xxiii,916p,[32]p of plates : ill,maps,ports ; 24cm
Bibliography: p847-885. — Includes index
ISBN 0-224-01452-8 : £16.50 : CIP rev. B80-00465

909′.097671 — Books on Islamic civilization — *Reviews — Anthologies — Serials*
The **Muslim** world book review. — Vol.1, no.1 (Autumn 1980)-. — Leicester (223 London Rd, Leicester) : The Islamic Foundation, 1980-. — v. ; 30cm
Quarterly
ISSN 0260-3063 = Muslim world book review : Unpriced B81-13688

909′.097671 — Islamic civilization, *to 1980*
Nasr, Seyyed Hossein. Islamic life and thought / by Seyyed Hossein Nasr. — London : Allen and Unwin, 1981. — 232p ; 23cm
Includes index
ISBN 0-04-297041-5 : Unpriced : CIP rev. B81-13767

909′.097671 — Islamic countries. Public opinion in Western world
Said, Edward W.. Covering Islam : how the media and the experts determine how we see the rest of the world / Edward W. Said. — London : Rougledge & Kegan Paul, 1981. — xxxi,186p ; 21cm
Includes index
ISBN 0-7100-0840-6 : £8.95 : CIP rev. B81-05138

909′.097671 — Islamic countries. Social conditions, *to 1980*
Gellner, Ernest. Muslim society / Ernest Gellner. — Cambridge : Cambridge University Press, 1981. — ix,264p ; 24cm. — (Cambridge studies in social anthropology ; 32)
Bibliography: p247-251. — Includes index
ISBN 0-521-22160-9 : £18.50 B81-26230

909′.097671 — Islamic studies
Studies on Islam / translated and edited by Merlin L. Swartz. — New York ; Oxford : Oxford University Press, 1981. — xi,284p ; 24cm
Includes index
ISBN 0-19-502716-7 (cased) : £12.00
ISBN 0-19-502717-5 (pbk) : Unpriced B81-32568

909′.0976710827 — Islamic countries. Revolutions, *1976-1980*
Siddiqui, Kalim. 'Al-Harakah Al-Islamiyah : Qadāya wa Ahdāf'. — London (6 Endsleigh St., WC1H 0DS) : Open Press, Sept.1981. — [96]p
ISBN 0-905081-09-9 (pbk) : £2.50 : CIP entry B81-20470

909′.0976710827′0924 — Islamic countries. Social life, *1979-1980 — Personal observations*
Naipaul, V. S.. Among the believers : an Islamic journey / V.S. Naipaul. — London : Deutsch, 1981. — 399p ; 24cm
ISBN 0-233-97416-4 : £7.95 B81-38256

909′.097′6710828 — Islamic countries. Political events, *1980-1981*
Issues in the Islamic movement 1980-1981. — London : Open Press, Dec.1981. — [200]p
ISBN 0-905081-10-2 (cased) : £10.00 : CIP entry
ISBN 0-905081-11-0 (pbk) B81-31544

909′.0976710828 — Islamic countries. Society. Theories of Marxists
Turner, Bryan S.. Marx and the end of orientalism / Bryan S. Turner. — London : Allen & Unwin, 1978. — 98p ; 23cm. — (Controversies in sociology ; 7)
Bibliography: p86-95. — Includes index
ISBN 0-04-321020-1 (cased) : £7.50 : CIP rev. B78-35875

909′.0976710828 — Islamic culture. Applications of systems theory
Siddiqui, Kalim. The Islamic movement : a systems approach / Kalim Siddiqui. — London : Open Press in association with the Muslim Institute, 1980. — 24p ; 22cm
ISBN 0-905081-06-4 (pbk) : £1.00 B81-09004

909′.0977 — ACP countries. Social conditions — *Serials*
Annuaire des Etats ACP : Afrique, Caraïbes, Pacifique = ACP States yearbook : Africa, Caribbean, Pacific. — 80/81-. — Bruxelles : Editions Delta ; Epping : Bowker [distributor], 1980-. — v. ; 29cm
Parallel texts in French and English
Unpriced B81-04496

909′.09812 — Western civilization, *to 1980*
Brinton, Crane. Civilization in the West / Crane Brinton, John B. Christopher, Robert Lee Wolff. — 4th ed. — Englewood Cliffs ; London : Prentice-Hall, c1981
Previous ed.: 1973
Part 1: Prehistory to 1715. — xvi,319,xvii-xxxip,[16]p of plates : ill(some col.),facsims,1geneal.table,maps,ports(some col.) ; 28cm
Includes index
ISBN 0-13-134924-4 (pbk) : £9.75 B81-33144

Brinton, Crane. Civilization in the West / Crane Brinton, John B. Christopher, Robert Lee Wolff. — 4th ed. — Englewood Cliffs ; London : Prentice-Hall, c1981
Previous ed.: 1973
Part 2: 1600 to the present. — xiv,265-614,xv-xxxivp,[16]p of plates : ill(some col.),facsims,maps,ports(some col.) ; 28cm
Includes index
ISBN 0-13-134932-5 (pbk) : £9.75 B81-33145

909′.0981201 — Western culture, *400-1200 — French texts*
Riché, Pierre. Instruction et vie religieuse dans le Haut Moyen Age / Pierre Riché. — London : Variorum Reprints, 1981. — 360p in various pagings : maps,facsims,1port ; 24cm. — (Collected studies series ; CS139)
Includes two papers in English. — Includes index
ISBN 0-86078-086-4 : £24.00 : CIP rev. B81-21632

909′.09812081 — Western world. Women. Social life, *1837-1901 — Readings from contemporary sources*
Victorian woman : a documentary account of women's lives in nineteenth-century England, France, and the United States / edited by Erna Olafson Hellerstein, Leslie Parker Hume, and Karen M. Offen ; associate editors Estelle B. Freedman, Barbara Charlesworth Gelpi and Marilyn Yalom ; prepared under the auspices of the Center for Research on Women at Stanford University. — Brighton : Harvester, 1981. — xvi,534p : ill,2facsims ; 24cm
Bibliography: p511-522. - Includes index
ISBN 0-7108-0084-3 : £25.00 B81-11992

909′.098120828 — Western civilization. Role
Barraclough, Geoffrey. Worlds apart : untimely thoughts on development and development strategies / by Geoffrey Barraclough. — Brighton : Institute of Development Studies, 1980. — 14p ; 21cm. — (Discussion paper / IDS, ISSN 0308-5864 ; DP152)
Unpriced (pbk) B81-06209

909′.098120828 — Western world. Society
Changing images of man. — Oxford : Pergamon, Apr.1981. — [200]p. — (Systems science and world order library) (Pergamon international library)
ISBN 0-08-024314-2 : £19.00 : CIP entry B81-00653

909′.098120828 — Western world. Society. Theories
Sparrow, John. Too much of a good thing / John Sparrow. — Chicago ; London : University of Chicago Press, 1977. — ix,92p ; 21cm. — (A Phoenix book)
ISBN 0-226-76848-1 (cased) : Unpriced
ISBN 0-226-76850-3 (pbk) : £2.10 B81-38142

909′.09821 — Caribbean countries, *1783-1979 — For Caribbean students — For schools*
Greenwood, R. (Robert), *1939-*. Development and decolonisation / R. Greenwood and S. Hamber. — London : Macmillan Caribbean, 1981, c1980. — viii,182p : ill,maps,ports ; 25cm. — (Caribbean certificate history ; Bk.3)
Bibliography: p175-176. — Includes index
ISBN 0-333-30570-1 (pbk) : £2.75 B81-21791

909′.09821 — Caribbean region, *1530-1630*
Andrews, Kenneth R.. The Spanish Caribbean : trade and plunder 1530-1630 / Kenneth R. Andrews. — New Haven ; London : Yale University Press, c1978. — xi,267p,[1]folded leaf of plates : map ; 23cm
Maps on lining papers. — Includes index
ISBN 0-300-02197-6 : £16.00 B81-04796

909′.09821 — Caribbean region, *to 1980 — For Caribbean students*
Claypole, William. Caribbean story / William Claypole, John Robottom. — Trinidad ; Longman Caribbean ; London : Longman
Bk.2: The inheritors. — 1981. — 220p : ill,maps,facsims,ports ; 25cm
Bibliography: p216. — Includes index
ISBN 0-582-76533-1 (pbk) : £2.50 : CIP rev. B81-19166

909′.1 — World, *800-1100 — For children*
Norman, Kathleen. The rise of Christian Europe : A.D.800-A.D. 1100 / Kathleen Norman. — London : Macmillan Children's Books, 1980. — 46p : chiefly ill(some col.),maps,1plan,ports (some col.),1geneal.table ; 32cm. — (History in pictures ; bk.7)
Includes index
ISBN 0-333-25544-5 : £3.95 B81-11625

909′.5 — World events, *1524 expounded by* **Biblical prophecies**
Pastoris, Heinrich. Practica Teütsch = Casting a German horoscope / Heinrich Pastoris ; translated with an introduction and notes by Helga Robinson-Hammerstein. — Dublin ([College St., Dublin 2]) : The Friends of the Library, Trinity College, 1980. — [9]p ; 21cm
German text, English translation. — Facsim of: ed.: published Augsburg : Johann Schonesperger, 1523. — English translation (17p) in pocket
ISBN 0-904720-05-5 (pbk) : Unpriced B81-30099

909.7 — Colonisation by European countries, *1700-1900*
Cairns, Trevor. Europe round the world. — Cambridge : Cambridge University Press, Apr.1981. — 1v. — (Cambridge introduction to the history of mankind ; 9)
ISBN 0-521-22710-0 (pbk) : CIP entry B81-03150

909.7 — Sea battles, *1794-1805 - Readings from contemporary sources*
Jackson, T. Sturges. Logs of the great sea fights 1794-1805. — Havant : K. Mason, Aug.1981
Vol.1. — [346]p
Originally published: London : Navy Records Society, 1899
ISBN 0-85937-266-9 : £15.00 : CIP entry B81-18054

909.7 — Sea battles, *1794-1805 - Readings from contemporary sources* *continuation*

Jackson, T. Sturges. Logs of the great sea fights 1794-1805. — Havant : K. Mason, Aug.1981
Vol.2. — [348]p
Originally published: London : Navy Records Society, 1900
ISBN 0-85937-267-7 : £15.00 : CIP entry B81-18055

909.8 — Intellectual life. Influence of theories of evolution of Darwin, Charles, *1860-1979*

Oldroyd, D. R.. Darwinian impacts : an introduction to the Darwinian revolution / D.R. Oldroyd. — Milton Keynes : Open University Press, 1980. — xiv,399p : ill ; 22cm
Bibliography: p369-379. — Includes indexes
ISBN 0-335-09001-x (pbk) : £7.95 : CIP rev. B80-07590

909.8 — Land battles, *1805-1950*

The **Victors** / edited by Peter Young. — London : Hamlyn, 1981. — 256p : ill(some col.),col.maps,ports(some col.) ; 31cm
Includes index
ISBN 0-600-34166-6 : £9.95 B81-32355

909.8'092'2 — World events, *1860-1980 — Biographies*

Palmer, Alan. Who's who in modern history 1860-1980 / Alan Palmer. — London : Weidenfeld and Nicolson, c1980. — 332p ; 25cm
ISBN 0-297-77642-8 : £8.50 B81-03199

909.81 — Wars. Perception by man, *1861-1945*

Terraine, John. The smoke and the fire : myths and anti-myths of war 1861-1945 / John Terraine. — London : Sidgwick & Jackson, 1980. — 240p,[16]p of plates : ill,1facsim,ports ; 24cm
Bibliography: p228-232. — Includes index
ISBN 0-283-98701-4 : £8.95 B81-02735

909.81 — World, *1801-1918 — For schools*

Roberts, J. M.. One world : Europe the maker / J.M. Roberts. — [Harmondsworth] : Penguin, [1981]. — 128p : ill(some col.),maps(some col.),facsims(some col.),ports(some col.) ; 23cm. — (An Illustrated world history ; 6)
Includes index
ISBN 0-14-064006-1 : £3.95 B81-21146

909.81 — World, *1804-1914 — For schools*

Roberts, J. M.. One world : disappearing barriers / J.M. Roberts. — [Harmondsworth] : Penguin, [1981]. — 128p : ill(some col.),maps (some col.),facsims(some col.),ports(some col.) ; 23cm. — (An Illustrated world history ; 7)
Includes index
ISBN 0-14-064007-x : £3.95 B81-21145

909.81'022'2 — Social life, *1865-1921 — Illustrations*

The **World** as it was : 1865-1921 : a photographic portrait from the Keystone-Mast Collection / edited and with text by Margarett Loke ; foreword by Paul Theroux. — London : Hutchinson, 1980. — 217p : chiefly ill,ports ; 32cm
Originally published: New York : Summit, 1980
ISBN 0-09-143530-7 : £12.95 B81-05442

909.82 — Adventures, *1860-ca 1970*

Brett, Bernard. Daring adventures! / re-told by Bernard Brett. — London : Hamlyn, 1981. — 110p : ill(some col.),col.maps,1plan,ports(some col.) ; 28cm
Originally published: in The Hamlyn book of true adventures
ISBN 0-600-36661-8 (pbk) : £1.99 B81-38594

909.82 — Adventures, *1953-1980*

Bonington, Chris. The quest for adventure. — London : Hodder & Stoughton, Oct.1981. — [448]p
ISBN 0-340-25599-4 : £13.95 : CIP entry B81-26753

909.82 — Political events, *1919-1980*

Watson, Jack B.. Success in twentieth century world affairs since 1919 / Jack B. Watson. — 2nd ed. — London : Murray, 1981. — xii,418p : ill,maps,ports ; 22cm. — (Success studybooker)
Previous ed.: 1974. — Includes bibliographies and index
ISBN 0-7195-2920-4 (cased) : Unpriced
ISBN 0-7195-3841-6 () : £3.50 B81-17449

909.82 — Revolutions. Role of regular military forces, *1900-1970 — Conference proceedings*

Regular armies and insurgency / edited by Ronald Haycock. — London : Croom Helm, c1979. — 101p ; 23cm
Conference papers. — Includes index
ISBN 0-85664-787-x : £7.95 : CIP rev. B79-18787

909.82 — Wars, *1945-1975*

Carver, Michael. War since 1945 / Michael Carver. — London : Weidenfeld and Nicolson, c1980. — x,322p,[16]p of plates : ill,maps ; 24cm
Bibliography: p305-306. - Includes index
ISBN 0-297-77846-3 : £10.50 B81-08312

909.82 — World, *1870-1975 — For schools*

Snellgrove, L. E.. The modern world since 1870 / L.E. Snellgrove. — London : Longman, 1968 (1979 [printing]). — 327p : ill,maps,facsims,ports ; 25cm. — (Longman secondary histories ; 5)
Includes bibliographies and index
ISBN 0-582-20502-6 (pbk) : £3.25 B81-40303

909.82 — World, *1890-1940*

Gerhardie, William. God's fifth column : a biography of the age 1890-1940 / William Gerhardie ; edited and with an introduction by Michael Holroyd & Robert Skidelsky. — London : Hodder and Stoughton, 1981. — 360p ; 25cm
Includes index
ISBN 0-340-26340-7 : £11.95 B81-14553

909.82 — World, *1900-1945*

Leeds, Christopher A.. Twentieth-century history 1900-45 / C.A. Leeds. — Plymouth : Macdonald and Evans, 1979. — ix,207p ; 18cm. — (The M & E handbook series)
Bibliography: p187. — Includes index
ISBN 0-7121-2025-4 (pbk) : £2.75 B81-12294

909.82 — World, *1900-1979*

Cornwell, R. D.. World history in the twentieth century / R.D. Cornwell. — New ed. — Harlow : Longman, 1980. — x,566p : ill,maps,ports ; 22cm
Previous ed.: 1969. — Bibliography: p552-556. — Includes index
ISBN 0-582-33074-2 (cased) : Unpriced
ISBN 0-582-33075-0 (pbk) : unpriced B81-08457

909.82 — World, *1900-1979 — For schools*

O'Callaghan, Bryn. In your century / Bryn O'Callaghan. — London : Longman, 1981. — 128p : ill(some col.),col.maps,facsims(some col.),ports(some col.) ; 24cm. — (The Developing world. History ; no.5)
Bibliography: p126-127. - Includes index
ISBN 0-582-20495-x (pbk) : Unpriced B81-05741

909.82 — World, *1914-1969 — For schools*

Roberts, J. M.. The age of upheaval : the world since 1914 / J.M. Roberts. — Harmondsworth : Penguin, 1981. — 144p : ill(some col.),maps (some col.),facsims(some col.),ports(some col.) ; 23cm. — (An Illustrated world history ; 8)
Includes index
ISBN 0-14-064008-8 : £3.95 B81-21144

909.82 — World, *1939-1979*

Rundle, R. N.. International affairs 1939-1979 / R.N. Rundle. — London : Hodder and Stoughton, 1981. — 208p : ill,maps,ports ; 25cm
Includes index
ISBN 0-340-23709-0 (pbk) : £3.95 : CIP rev. B81-15937

909.82 — World, *1955-1980*

From our own correspondent / edited by Roger Lazer. — London : British Broadcasting Corporation, 1980. — 208p ; 23cm
ISBN 0-563-17858-2 : £6.50 B81-05088

909.82 — World, *ca 1900-1979 — For schools*

Martell, John. The twentieth-century world / by John Martell. — 3rd ed. — London : Harrap, 1980. — 359p : ill,maps,ports ; 25cm
Previous ed.: 1973. — Includes index
ISBN 0-245-53578-0 (pbk) : Unpriced B81-09250

909.82'092'2 — Politicians, *1900-1980 — Personal observations*

Berlin, Isaiah. Personal impressions / Isaiah Berlin ; edited by Henry Hardy ; with an introduction by Noel Annan. — London : Hogarth, 1980. — xxx,219p,[8]p of plates : ports ; 23cm. — (Selected writings / Isaiah Berlin ; 4)
Includes index
ISBN 0-7012-0510-5 : £9.50
Primary classification 305.5'5 B81-10334

909.82'092'4 — Political events, *ca 1945-1980 — Personal observations*

Kissinger, Henry A.. For the record : selected statements 1977-1980 / Henry Kissinger. — London : Weidenfeld and Nicolson and Joseph, 1981. — xiii,332p ; 24cm
Includes index
ISBN 0-7181-2025-6 : £9.95 B81-14683

909.82'1 — Political events, *1917 — Readings from contemporary sources — Facsimiles*

United States. *War Department. General Staff.* Weekly summaries : June 2-October 13, 1917 / introduction by Richard D. Chichester. — New York ; London : Garland, 1978. — xvi,[600]p : 1map ; 24cm. — (United States military intelligence ; v.1)
Facsims. of documents issued by the Military Intellingence Branch of the United States Army, which had the title Weekly intelligence summary
ISBN 0-8240-3000-1 : Unpriced B81-34370

909.82'1 — Political events, *1919 — Readings from contemporary sources*

Daily summaries : January 11-April 30, 1919 / introduction by Richard D. Challener. — New York ; London : Garland, 1978. — vii,ca.530p ; 24cm. — (United States military intelligence ; v.30)
Facsim. of: Weekly intelligence summaries. United States War Dept. General Staff, 1917-1927
ISBN 0-8240-3029-x : Unpriced B81-41012

909.82'1 — World events, *1890-1914*

Tuchman, Barbara W.. The proud tower : a portrait of the world before the war 1890-1914 / Barbara W. Tuchman. — London : Macmillan, 1980, c1966. — xv,528p,[32]p of plates : ill,ports ; 23cm
Originally published: New York : Macmillan ; London : Hamilton, 1966. — Bibliography : p465-510. — Includes index
ISBN 0-333-30645-7 (cased) : £12.50
ISBN 0-333-30646-5 (pbk) : £4.95 B81-01690

909.82'2 — Political events, *1927 — Readings from contemporary sources — Facsimiles*

United States. *War Department. General Staff.* Weekly summaries : 1927 / introduction by Richard D. Challener. — New York ; London : Garland, 1979. — viii,p11435-11916 : maps ; 24cm
Facsims. of documents issued by the Military Intelligence Branch of the United States Army, which had the title Weekly intelligence summary
ISBN 0-8240-3025-7 : Unpriced B81-34371

909.82'3'0202 — World events, *1931-1945 — Chronologies*

Goralski, Robert. World War II almanac, 1931-1945 : a political and military record / Robert Goralsky. — London : Hamilton, 1981. — 486p : ill(some col.),col.maps,1facsim,ports ; 25cm
Bibliography: p456-466. — Includes index
ISBN 0-241-10573-0 : £9.95 B81-24274

909.82'4 — World events, *1941-1962*
Balfour, Michael, *1908-*. The adversaries : America, Russia and the open world 1941-62 / Michael Balfour. — London : Routledge & Kegan Paul, 1981. — xv,259p ; 23cm
Bibliography: p245-252. - Includes index
ISBN 0-7100-0687-x : £10.50 : CIP rev. B81-02379

909.82'5'0924 — World events, *1956 — Personal observations*
Edgar, Donald. Express '56 : a year in the life of a Beaverbrook journalist / by Donald Edgar. — London : Clare, c1981. — 179p ; 23cm
ISBN 0-906549-17-5 : £6.95 B81-22960

909.82'6 — Social conditions, *1968*
Firsoff, George. 1968 : spring of youth / by George Firsoff. — Bath (Bath Community Printshop, 2 Longacre, London Rd., Bath) : G. Firsoff, 1980. — 204p : ill,maps ; 21cm
ISBN 0-9507174-0-1 (pbk) : Unpriced B81-06814

909.82'6'0922 — Women prime ministers, *1960-1980 — Biographies — For children*
Gibbs, Richard. Women prime ministers / Richard Gibbs. — Hove : Wayland, 1981. — 64p : ill(some col.),col.maps,ports(some col.) ; 23cm. — (In profile)
Bibliography: p62. — Includes index
ISBN 0-85340-883-1 : £3.95 B81-40615

909.82'7 — Political events, *1979-1980 — Correspondence, diaries, etc. — Polish texts*
Laks, Szymon. Dziennik pisany w biały dzień / Szymon Laks. — Londyn (i.e. London) : Oficyna Poetów i Malarzy, 1981. — 130p ; 22cm
Includes index
Unpriced (pbk) B81-17078

909.82'7'0207 — Political events, *1970-1979 — Cartoons*
The **1970s** : best political cartoons of the decade / edited by Jerry Robinson. — New York ; London : McGraw-Hill, 1981. — 192p : chiefly ill ; 28cm
Includes index
ISBN 0-07-053281-8 (pbk) : £6.50 B81-22429

909.82'7'05 — Political events *— Communist viewpoints — Serials*
Documents in communist affairs. — 1977. — London : Butterworths, Jan.1982. — [364]p
Originally published: Cardiff : University College Cardiff Press, 1978
ISBN 0-408-10818-5 : £15.00 : CIP entry B81-37542

Documents in communist affairs. — 1979. — London : Butterworths, Jan.1982. — [572]p
Originally published: Cardiff : University College Cardiff Press, 1979
ISBN 0-408-10819-3 : £20.00 : CIP entry B81-37543

909.82'8 — Social conditions. Effects of economic uncertainty *— Conference proceedings*
International Conference on Social Welfare *(20th : 1980 : Hong Kong)*. Social development in times of economic uncertainty : proceedings of the XXth International Conference on Social Welfare, Hong Kong, July 18-22, 1980. — New York ; Guildford : Published for the International Council on Social Welfare by Columbia University Press, 1981. — xix,202p ; 24cm
ISBN 0-231-05326-6 : £17.50 B81-36341

909.82'8 — World events *— Questions & answers*
Greenstone, Danny. The news quiz. — London : Robson, Oct.1981. — [160]p
ISBN 0-86051-155-3 : £4.50 : CIP entry B81-27454

909.82'8'0202 — World events, *1980 — Chronologies*
Waugh, Auberon. Auberon Waugh's yearbook : a news summary and press digest of 1980 / Auberon Waugh. — London : Pan, 1981. — [234]p ; 20cm. — (Pan original)
Includes index
ISBN 0-330-26491-5 (pbk) : £1.95 B81-39608

909.82'8'05 — Political events *— Labour party (Great Britain) Young Socialists viewpoints — Serials*
[Socialist youth *(London)***]**. Socialist youth : paper of the Labour Party Young Socialists. — Feb.1980-. — London (144 Walworth Rd, SE17) : Labour Party Young Socialists National Committee, 1980-. — v. : ill ; 42cm
Monthly. — Continues: Left (London). — Description ased on: Sept.1980
ISSN 0260-7336 = Socialist youth (London) : £0.15 per issue B81-05407

909.82'8'05 — Political events *— Marxist viewpoints — Serials*
[News & letters *(British edition)***]**. News & letters. — British ed. — Summer 1980. — London (Box NL, Rising Free, 182 Upper St., N1) : [News and Letters Publications], 1980. — 1v. : ill ; 37cm
Continued by: Marxist humanism. — One issue only published under this title
Unpriced B81-07798

909.82'8'05 — Political events *— Right-wing political viewpoints — Serials*
[The Phoenix *(Shotton)***]**. The Phoenix. — No.1 (May 1980)-. — Shotton (95a Chester Rd East, Shotton, Deeside, Clwyd, N. Wales) : B.P. Publications, 1980-. — v. : ill ; 45cm
Monthly
ISSN 0261-2852 = Phoenix (Shotton) : £3.00 per year B81-20455

909.82'8'05 — Social conditions *— Serials*
The **International** year book and statesmen's who's who. — 1981. — East Grinstead : Kelly's Directories, 1981. — cviii,752p
ISBN 0-610-00542-1 : Unpriced B81-28707

909.82'8'05 — World events *— Serials*
The **Annual** register. — 1979. — London : Longman, 1980. — xvi,568p
ISBN 0-582-50294-2 : £24.00 : CIP rev. B80-10396

The **Annual** register. — 1980. — Harlow : Longman, 1981. — xvi,556p
ISBN 0-582-50297-7 : £25.00 : CIP rev. B81-14947

Britannica book of the year. — 1977. — Chicago ; London : Encyclopaedia Britannica, c1977. — 768p
ISBN 0-85229-325-9 : Unpriced
ISSN 0068-1156 B81-14538

Britannica book of the year. — 1978. — Chicago ; London : Encyclopaedia Britannica, c1978. — 768p
ISBN 0-85229-342-9 : Unpriced
ISSN 0068-1156 B81-14539

Britannica book of the year. — 1979. — Chicago ; London : Encyclopaedia Britannica, c1979. — 768p
ISBN 0-85229-362-3 : Unpriced
ISSN 0068-1156 B81-18805

Britannica book of the year. — 1980. — Chicago ; London : Encyclopaedia Britannica, c1980. — 766p
ISBN 0-85229-372-0 : Unpriced
ISSN 0068-1156 B81-14541

New dictionary. — New York : Facts on File ; Oxford : Clio Press [distributor], c1980. — vi,390p
ISBN 0-87196-109-1 : Unpriced B81-08289

909.82'8'05 — World *— Serials*
The **Europa** year book. — 1980 (Vol.2, Cameroon-Zimbabwe). — London : Europa, c1980. — xv,1838p
ISBN 0-905118-47-2 : Unpriced : CIP rev.
ISSN 0071-2302 B80-06218

The **Europa** year book. — 1981 (Vol.1, pt.1, International organizations, pt.2, Europe, pt.3, Afghanistan-Burundi). — London : Europa, c1981. — xxii,1789p
ISBN 0-905118-59-6 : £72.00 the set
ISSN 0071-2302 B81-23491

The **Europa** year book. — 1982 (Vol.1, pt.1, International organizations, pt.2, Europe, pt.3, Afghanistan-Burundi). — London : Europa, Feb.1982. — [1800]p
ISBN 0-905118-71-5 : CIP entry
ISSN 0071-2302 B81-38838

909.82'8'0924 — World events, *ca 1980 — Personal observations*
Craven, John, *1940-*. John Craven's newsworld. — Wakefield : EP Publishing, 1980. — 96p : ill(some col.),ports(some col.) ; 30cm
£3.95 (corrected pbk) B81-35658

909.83 — Civilization, *2081 — Forecasts*
O'Neill, Gerard K.. 2081. — London : Cape, Oct.1981. — [288]p
ISBN 0-224-01677-6 : £6.95 : CIP entry B81-27445

909.83 — Civilization *— Forecasts*
Higgins, Ronald. The seventh enemy. — London : Hodder & Stoughton, Sept.1981. — [304]p
Originally published: 1978
ISBN 0-340-27575-8 (pbk) : £3.95 : CIP entry B81-22582

910 — GEOGRAPHY, TRAVEL

910 — Geographical features *— For children*
Bowler, L.. Exploring geography / L. Bowler and B. Waites ; illustrated by Barry Davies. — Huddersfield : Schofield & Sims. — 88p : col.ill,col.maps ; 26cm
ISBN 0-7217-1046-8 (pbk) : Unpriced B81-17567

910 — Geographical features *— For schools*
Bunnett, R. B.. General geography / R.B. Bunnett, A.J. Eaton. — London : Longman, 1970 (1976 printing). — iv,152p : ill,maps ; 20cm. — (Longman certificate notes)
ISBN 0-582-69584-8 (pbk) : £0.95 B81-12686

Jones, David P.. Geography in a changing world / David P. Jones. — London : Hodder and Stoughton, [1981]
Bk.1: Understanding places. — 128p : ill(some col.),col.maps ; 25cm
Includes index
ISBN 0-340-23444-x (pbk) : £2.55 : CIP rev. B80-09508

Speak, P.. Sketch-map geographies / P. Speak, A.H.C. Carter. — London : Longman. — v,90p : ill(some col.),maps(some col.) ; 25cm
Previous ed.: 1966
ISBN 0-582-33078-5 (pbk) : Unpriced B81-17549

910 — Geography
Balchin, W. G. V.. Concern for geography : a selection of the work of W.G.V. Balchin. — Swansea (Swansea, W. Glamorgan, SA2 8PP) : Department of Geography, University College of Swansea, 1981. — vi, 268p : ill,maps,1port ; 25cm
Limited ed. of 500 numbered copies. — Includes bibliographies
ISBN 0-9507384-0-9 : £13.00 B81-21107

Sant, Morgan. Applied geography. — London : Longman, Sept.1981. — [256]p
ISBN 0-582-30040-1 (cased) : £12.95 : CIP entry
ISBN 0-582-30041-x (pbk) : £6.95 B81-25878

910 — Geography. Applications of systems theory
Wilson, A. G.. Geography and the environment. — Chichester : Wiley, Oct.1981. — [304]p
ISBN 0-471-27956-0 (cased) : £13.35 : CIP entry
ISBN 0-471-27957-9 (pbk) : £6.65 B81-30482

910 — Geography *— For schools*
Bateman, R.. Steps in geography / R. Bateman and F. Martin. — London : Hutchinson
Bk.2. — 1981. — 96p : ill,maps,1facsim,plans ; 30cm
Ill and text on inside covers
ISBN 0-09-144471-3 (pbk) : Unpriced : CIP rev. B81-03674

910 — Geography — *For schools*
continuation

Catling, Simon. Outset geography / Simon Catling, Tim Firth, David Rowbotham. — Edinburgh : Oliver & Boyd
1 / mapping consultant Jane Thake ; illustrated by Jon Davis and Tim Smith. — 1981. — 56p : col.ill,col.maps,col.plans ; 27cm
Text and ill on inside covers
ISBN 0-05-003294-1 (pbk) : Unpriced
B81-18921

Dobson, F. R.. Canada and the United States / F.R. Dobson, H.E. Virgo. — London : Hodder and Stoughton, 1980. — 124p : ill(some col.),maps(some col.) ; 18cm. — (A New school geography ; v.5) (New school series)
Previous ed.: London. — Includes index
ISBN 0-340-25772-5 (pbk) : £2.95 : CIP rev.
B80-18089

Lines, C. J.. Exploring the land / authors Clifford Lines, Laurie Bolwell. — London : Macdonald Educational, c1981. — 48p : ill (some col.),maps(some col.) ; 22cm. — (Town and around)
Ill, text on inside covers
ISBN 0-356-07187-1 (pbk) : Unpriced
B81-26254

Martin, F.. Leisure. — London : Hutchinson Education, Nov.1981. — [128]p. — (Core geography ; 1)
ISBN 0-09-144451-9 (pbk) : £2.95 : CIP entry
B81-28830

Slater, Frances. Skills in geography. — London : Cassell
Level 1. — Jan.1982. — [64]p
ISBN 0-304-30377-1 (pbk) : £2.25 : CIP entry
B81-34140

Slater, Frances. Skills in geography. — London : Cassell
Level 2. — Feb.1982. — [64]p
ISBN 0-304-30378-x (pbk) : £2.25 : CIP entry
B81-35786

910 — Geography — *Marxist viewpoints*

Quaini, Massimo. Geography and Marxism. — Oxford : Blackwell, Jan.1982. — [192]p
Translation of 2nd ed. of : Marxismo e geografia
ISBN 0-631-12565-5 (cased) : £11.00 : CIP entry
ISBN 0-631-12816-6 (pbk) : £4.50 B81-34289

910 — Geography. Spatial analysis

Coffey, William J.. Geography : towards a general spatial systems approach. — London : Methuen, Nov.1981
ISBN 0-416-30970-4 : £11.00 : CIP entry
ISBN 0-416-30980-1 (pbk) : £5.50 B81-30552

910 — World. Geographical features

The **Orbis** pocket encyclopedia of the world. — London : Orbis, 1981. — 233p : col.ill,charts,col.maps ; 17cm
Includes index
ISBN 0-85613-339-6 (pbk) : £2.95 B81-39899

910 — World. Geographical features — *For children*

Matthews, Patrick. Round the world with Teddy Edward / by Patrick Matthews and Su Swallow. — Harlow : Longman, 1981. — 41p : ill(some col.),col.maps ; 28cm
Includes index
ISBN 0-582-39054-0 : £3.95 B81-37011

Williamson, Lyn. First picture atlas / author Lyn Williamson ; illustrators Roy Coombs ... [et al.] ; maps drawn by Product (Graphics) Support Limited. — London : Kingfisher, 1980. — 61p : col.ill,col.maps ; 31cm. — (A Kingfisher book)
Maps on lining papers. — Includes index
ISBN 0-7063-6001-x : £2.95 B81-05913

910 — World. Geographical features — *For slow learning students — For schools*

Jenkins, A. J.. Earth our planet / A.J. Jenkins. — London : Edward Arnold, 1980. — 64p : ill,maps ; 30cm
ISBN 0-7131-0217-9 (pbk) : £2.50 : CIP rev.
B79-15118

910'.01 — Geography. Applications of information theory

Thomas, R. W. (Richard Wyn). Information statistics in geography / by R.W. Thomas. — Norwich : Geo Abstracts, c1981. — 42p : ill ; 21cm. — (Concepts and techniques in modern geography, ISSN 0306-6142 ; no.31)
Bibliography: p38-42
ISBN 0-86094-090-x (pbk) : Unpriced
B81-40798

910'.01 — Geography. Concepts, *to 1980*

Holt-Jensen, Arild. Geography : its history and concepts : a student's guide / Arild Holt-Jensen ; English adaptation and translation by Brian Fullerton. — London : Harper & Row, 1981, c1980. — xi,171p : ill ; 22cm
Translation of: Geografiens innhold og metoder. — Bibliography: p149-159. — Includes index
ISBN 0-06-318186-x (cased) : £7.95 : CIP rev.
ISBN 0-06-318187-8 (pbk) : £4.95 B81-13574

910'.01 — Geography — *Philosophical perspectives*

Themes in geographic thought / edited by Milton E. Harvey and Brian P. Holly. — London : Croom Helm, c1981. — 224p : ill ; 23cm. — (Croom Helm series in geography and environment)
Bibliography: p209-221. — Includes index
ISBN 0-7099-0188-7 : £12.95 : CIP rev.
B81-02376

910'.01 — Geography. Spatial analysis

Unwin, D. J.. Introductory spatial analysis. — London : Methuen, Dec.1981. — [250]p
ISBN 0-416-72190-7 (cased) : £10.00 : CIP entry
ISBN 0-416-72200-8 (pbk) : £5.00 B81-31715

910'.01 — Geography. Theories, *1600-1860*

Bowen, Margarita. Empiricism and geographical thought. — Cambridge : Cambridge University Press, Dec.1981. — [350]p. — (Cambridge geographical studies ; 15)
ISBN 0-521-23653-3 : £25.00 : CIP entry
B81-32596

910'.01 — Geography. Theories, *to 1980*

James, Preston E.. All possible worlds : a history of geographical ideas. — 2nd ed. / Preston E. James and Geoffrey J. Martin, maps and illustrations by Eileen W. James. — New York ; Chichester : Wiley, c1981. — xvii,508p : ill,maps,ports ; 24cm
Previous ed.: Indianapolis : Odyssey Press, 1972. — Bibliography: p427-471. — Includes index
ISBN 0-471-06121-2 : £12.60 B81-23719

910'.014 — Eponymous place names — *Lists*

Forrest, A. J.. A dictionary of eponymous places / A.J. Forrest. — Brandon (38 Bury Rd., Brandon, Suffolk IP27 0BT) : A.J. Forrest, c1981. — [18]p ; 16cm
Unpriced (pbk) B81-33243

910'.014 — Place names. Changes, *1900-1979 — Lists*

Room, Adrian. Place-name changes since 1900 : a world gazetteer / compiled by Adrian Room. — London : Routledge & Kegan Paul, 1980. — xxii,202p ; 23cm
Bibliography: p199-202
ISBN 0-7100-0702-7 : £8.95 : CIP rev.
B80-21174

910'.01'8 — Geography. Quantitative methods

Quantitative geography in Britain. — London : Routledge & Kegan Paul, Oct.1981. — [400]p
ISBN 0-7100-0731-0 : £35.00 : CIP entry
B81-25731

910'.02 — Physical geographical features — *For children*

Lambert, David, *1932-*. The active earth. — London : Methuen/Walker, Aug.1981. — [48] p. — (All about earth)
ISBN 0-416-05650-4 : £3.95 : CIP entry
B81-20640

910'.02 — Physical geography

Dury, G. H.. An introduction to environmental systems / George Dury. — London : Heinemann, 1981. — 366p : ill(some col.),col.charts,col.maps ; 29cm
Includes index
ISBN 0-435-35176-1 : £8.75 : CIP rev.
ISBN 0-435-08001-6 (U.S.)
ISBN 0-435-08002-4 (Instruments manual) : £3.50 B81-12343

Knapp, Brian. Earth and man. — London : Allen and Unwin, Feb.1982. — [288]p
ISBN 0-04-551055-5 (pbk) : £4.95 : CIP entry
B81-35918

Navarra, John Gabriel. Contemporary physical geography / John Gabriel Navarra. — Philadelphia ; London : Saunders College, c1981. — vii,523,A66,xvp : ill(some col.),maps (some col.) ; 27cm
Maps on lining papers. — Bibliography: pA57-A66. — Includes index
ISBN 0-03-057859-0 : £13.25 B81-25275

910'.02 — Physical geography — *For schools*

Jackson, Nora. A groundwork of physical geography / Nora Jackson, Philip Penn. — Metric ed. — London : George Philip, 1980. — ix,230p : ill,charts,maps ; 22cm
Previous ed.: i.e. 3rd ed., 1978. — Col. map on folded leaf attached to inside cover
ISBN 0-540-01049-9 (pbk) : £2.95 : CIP rev.
B80-18090

Practical foundations of physical geography / edited by Brian Knapp. — London : Allen & Unwin, 1981. — 138p : ill,charts,maps ; 22x28cm
ISBN 0-04-551035-0 (pbk) : Unpriced : CIP rev. B80-23842

910'.02 — Physical geography — *For West African students*

Bryant, R. V.. Elements of physical geography : for the school certificate / R.V. Bryant, Adekanmi Onibokun. — London : Collins, 1981. — 96p : ill,maps ; 26cm
Includes index
ISBN 0-00-326510-2 (pbk) : £1.50 B81-34247

910'.02'0321 — Physical geography — *Encyclopaedias*

Moore, W. G.. The Penguin dictionary of geography : definitions and explanations of terms used in physical geography / W.G. Moore. — 6th ed. — Harmondsworth : Penguin, 1981. — 256p,[24]p of plates : ill,maps ; 20cm. — (Penguin reference books)
Previous ed.: published as A dictionary of geography. 1974
ISBN 0-14-051002-8 (pbk) : £1.95 B81-40441

910'.02'076 — Physical geography — *Questions & answers — For schools*

Bennetts, J.. Physical geography / by J. Bennetts. — Sunbury on Thames : Celtic Revision Aids, 1980. — 110p : ill,maps ; 19cm. — (Worked examples. A level)
ISBN 0-17-751162-1 (pbk) : £1.40 B81-26133

910'.02'1693 — Rivers & streams. Geographical aspects — *For schools*

Eden, Michael. Rivers. — London : Bodley Head, Oct.1981. — [24]p. — (The Younger geographers)
ISBN 0-370-30388-1 : £2.75 : CIP entry
B81-30489

910'.091 — Regional geography

DeBlij, Harm J.. Geography : regions and concepts / Harm J. deBlij with a chapter by Stephen S. Birdsall. — 3rd ed. — New York ; Chichester : Wiley, c1981. — xii,583p : ill (some col.),col.maps ; 29cm
Previous ed.: 1978. — Includes index
ISBN 0-471-08015-2 : £11.90 B81-10544

Kromm, David E.. World regional geography / David E. Kromm. — Philadelphia ; London : Saunders, c1981. — xvii,510p,[31]p of plates : ill(some col.),col.maps,1port ; 26cm
Includes bibliographies and index
ISBN 0-03-057781-0 : £14.95 B81-22862

910'.0912 — Temperate regions. Geographical features — *For West African student*
Turner, H. P.. The cooler lands / [H.P. Turner]. — [New ed.]. — London : Longman, 1980. — 108p : ill,maps ; 25cm. — (Junior secondary geographies for West Africa ; bk.3)
Previous ed.: 1972
ISBN 0-582-60377-3 (pbk) : £1.75 B81-29684

910'.0913 — Tropical regions. Geographical features — *For West African students*
Turner, H. P.. The warmer lands / [H.P. Turner]. — New ed. — London : Longman, 1981. — 104p : ill,maps ; 25cm. — (Junior secondary geographies for West Africa ; bk.2)
Previous ed.: 1972
ISBN 0-582-60376-5 (pbk) : £1.75 B81-29685

910'.09163 — Atlantic Ocean. Voyages by catamarans, *1971-1973:* **Anneliese** *(Boat) — Personal observations*
Swale, Rosie. Children of Cape Horn / Rosie Swale. — London : Granada, 1981. — 266p,[16]p of plates : ill,1map,ports ; 18cm. — (A Mayflower book)
Originally published: London : Elek, 1974
ISBN 0-583-13343-6 (pbk) : £1.50 B81-38164

910'.091631 — England. Emigration to Quebec *(Province).* **Voyages by steamships,** *1848-1855 — Personal observations — Collections*
Towards Quebec : two mid-19th century emigrants' journals / with introduction and commentary by Anne Giffard. — London : H.M.S.O., 1981. — 70p,[16]p of plates : ill,2maps,1facsim ; 23cm
At head of title: National Maritime Museum
ISBN 0-11-290335-5 : £3.95 B81-29674

910'.091631 — North Atlantic Ocean. Exploration, *ca 700-ca 1600*
Marcus, G. J. (Geoffrey Jules). The conquest of the North Atlantic / G.J. Marcus. — Woodbridge : Boydell, c1980. — xiv,224p : ill,maps ; 25cm
Bibliography: p213-220. — Includes index
ISBN 0-85115-130-2 : £11.95 : CIP rev. B80-22670

910'.091631 — North Atlantic Ocean. Sailing ships: Mary Celeste *(Ship).* **Crew. Disappearance**
Maxwell, John, *1936-*. The Mary Celeste / John Maxwell. — Feltham : Hamlyn, 1980, c1979. — 208p ; 18cm
Originally published: London : Cape, 1979
ISBN 0-600-20050-7 (pbk) : £1.00 B81-07273

910'.091631 — North Atlantic Ocean. Sailing ships: Mary Celeste *(Ship).* **Crew. Disappearance** — *For schools*
The **Mysterious** case of the Mary Celeste / [devised by John Simkin] ; [illustrated by David Simkin] ; [tested and revised by Stephen Ball ... et al.]. — Brighton (139 Carden Ave., Brighton, Sussex) : Tressell Publications, 1981. — 18p : ill,1chart,1plan,ports ; 30cm. — (Active learning in the humanities)
Cover title. — Bibliography: p1
ISBN 0-907586-00-7 (pbk) : Unpriced B81-26146

910'.09163'1 — North Atlantic Ocean. Steam liners: Titanic *(Ship).* **Sinking,** *1912*
Wade, Wyn Craig. The Titanic : end of a dream / Wyn Craig Wade. — London : Futura, 1980, c1979. — 189p,[6]p of plates : ill,plans,ports ; 18cm
Originally published: New York : Rawson, Wade, 1979 ; London : Weidenfeld & Nicolson, 1980. — Bibliography: p456-474. — Includes index
ISBN 0-7088-1864-1 (pbk) : £1.60 B81-02066

910'.091631 — North Atlantic Ocean. Voyages by trimarans, *1979:* **RTL-Timex** *(Ship) — Personal observations*
Angel, Nicolas. Capsize in a trimaran : a story of survival in the North Atlantic / by Nicolas Angel ; with a preface by Alain Bombard ; translated from the original French by Alan Wakeman. — London : Stanford Maritime, 1980. — 178p,viiip of plates : ill,1map,ports ; 22cm
Translation of: Chavirage en trimaran
ISBN 0-540-07401-2 : £6.95 : CIP rev. B80-22671

910'.091632 — Arctic Ocean. Voyages by ketches, *1959-1961:* **Cresswell** *(Boat) — Personal observations*
Jones, Tristan. Ice! / Tristan Jones. — London : Macdonald Futura, 1981, c1978. — 281p : 1map ; 18cm
Originally published: Kansas City : Sheed Andrews and McMeel, 1978 ; London : Bodley Head, 1979
ISBN 0-7088-1968-0 (pbk) : £1.50 B81-17720

910'.0916327 — Northwest Passage. Voyages by ketches, *1977:* **Williwaw** *(Boat) — Personal observations*
Roos, Willy de. North-West passage / Willy de Roos ; translated from the French by Bruce Penman ; foreword by G.S. Ritchie. — London : Hollis & Carter, 1980. — 208p,[8]p of plates : maps,facsims ; 23cm
Translation of: Le passage du nord-ouest
ISBN 0-370-30263-x : £6.50 : CIP rev. B80-20027

910'.09164 — Pacific Ocean. Exploration by ships, *1769-1770:* **St Jean-Baptiste** *(Ship) — Correspondence, diaries, etc*
The **expedition** of the St Jean-Baptiste to the Pacific, 1769-1770. — London (c/o Map Library, British Library, Great Russell St., WC1B 3DG) : Hakluyt Society, Sept.1981. — [301]p. — (Hakluyt Society second series ; 158)
ISBN 0-904180-11-5 : £12.00 : CIP entry B81-28037

910'.09164 — Pacific Ocean. Exploration. Voyages by Cook, James, *1728-1779, 1768-1779*
Cook's voyages and peoples of the Pacific / edited by Hugh Cobbe. — London : Published for the Trustees of the British Museum and the British Library Board by British Museum Publications, c1979. — 143p,[8]p of plates : ill (some col.),charts,maps,facsims,ports ; 26cm
Published to accompany an exhibition. — Bibliography: p143
ISBN 0-7141-1550-9 (cased) : £8.95 : CIP rev.
ISBN 0-7141-1551-7 (pbk) : £3.95
Also classified at 990 B78-40594

910'.09164 — Pacific Ocean. Exploration. Voyages by sailing ships: Roebuck *(Ship), 1699-1701 — Personal observations*
Dampier, William. A voyage to New Holland. — Gloucester : Alan Sutton, Oct.1981. — [232]p
Originally published: London : John Knapton, [1703?]
ISBN 0-904387-75-5 : £9.95 : CIP entry B81-31099

910'.09164 — Pacific Ocean. Exploration. Voyages by Torres, Luis Baéz de, *1606*
Hilder, Brett. The voyage of Torres : the discovery of the Southern coastline of New Guinea and Torres Strait by Captain Luis Baez de Torres in 1606 / Brett Hilder. — St. Lucia : University of Queensland Press ; Hemel Hemptead : Prentice-Hall [distributor], c1980. — xxxii,194p,[8]p of plates : ill,charts,maps (some col.),1port ; 25cm
Maps on lining papers. — Bibliography: p181-188. - Includes index
ISBN 0-7022-1275-x : £12.95 B81-18905

910'.09164 — Pacific Ocean. Seafaring. Sailing, *to 1966*
Morton, Harry. The wind commands : sailors and sailing ships in the Pacific / Harry Morton ; drawings by Don Hermansen and Paul Dwillies from original drawings and research by Peggy Morton. — Greenwich : Conway Maritime, [1980]. — xxvii,498p,[52]p of plates : ill,facsims,2maps,ports ; 27cm
Originally published: Vancouver : University of British Columbia Press, 1975. — Bibliography: p459-479. - Includes index
ISBN 0-85177-214-5 : £9.50 B81-04459

910'.09164 — Pacific Ocean. Voyages by ketches, *1973-1979:* **Sea Foam** *(Boat) — Personal observations*
Payson, Herb. Blown away / Herb Payson. — London : Stanford, 1980. — x,251p : maps ; 24cm
Originally published: Boston, Mass. : Sail Books, 1980. — Maps on lining papers
ISBN 0-540-07403-9 : £6.95 B81-08307

910'.091647 — South-west Pacific Ocean. Voyages by Vietnamese refugees
Townsend, Peter, *1914-*. The girl in the white ship. — London : Collins, Nov.1981. — [176]p
ISBN 0-00-216726-3 : £7.95 : CIP entry B81-28163

910'.091724 — Developing countries. Geographical features — *For schools*
Jones, D. J.Geography in a changing world. — London : Hodder and Stoughton
Bk.2: Understanding developing places / Laurence Kimpton. — c1981. — 128p : ill (some col.),maps(some col.) ; 25cm
ISBN 0-340-23445-8 (pbk) : £2.85 : CIP rev. B80-13133

910'.091732 — Cities. Geographical features — *For schools*
Conolly, Geoff. Cities / Geoff Conolly. — London : Philip, c1980. — 64p : ill(some col.),maps(some col.) ; 27cm. — (World studies)
Ill on lining papers
ISBN 0-540-01054-5 (pbk) : £4.00 B81-26156

910'.091732 — Urban regions. Geographical aspects
Geography and the urban environment. — Chichester : Wiley
Vol.4. — Dec.1981. — [336]p
ISBN 0-471-28051-8 : £19.30 : CIP entry B81-34225

910'.091732 — Urban regions. Geographical features — *For schools*
Gordon, George, *1939-*. Urban geography : models and concepts / George Gordon, William J. Dick ; designed and illustrated by Lewis Eadie. — Edinburgh : Holmes McDougall, 1980. — 128p : ill,maps(some col.) ; 21x26cm
Bibliography: p124. - Includes index
ISBN 0-7157-1964-5 (pbk) : £2.95 B81-18379

910'.091814 — Southern hemisphere. Geographical features — *For schools*
Jackson, Nora. The Southern continents / Nora Jackson, Philip Penn. — 8th, metric ed. — London : Philip, c1981. — ix,270p : ill,maps ; 22cm. — (Groundwork geographies)
Previous ed.: 1978
ISBN 0-540-01060-x (pbk) : £2.60 B81-26155

910'.091821 — Caribbean region — *Practical information — For British businessmen*
Central and South America and the Caribbean / editor Jane Walker ; associate editor Mark Ambrose. — London : Joseph, c1981. — 447p : maps ; 23cm. — (The Business traveller's handbook ; v.2)
Includes index
ISBN 0-7181-1976-2 : £14.95
Primary classification 918'.0438 B81-25633

910'.091822 — Mediterranean region. Description & travel
Beny, Rolfe. Odyssey : mirror of the Mediterranean / photographed and designed by Roloff Beny ; text and anthology by Anthony Thwaite. — London : Thames & Hudson, c1981. — 371p : ill(some col.),maps ; 32cm
Includes index
ISBN 0-500-24111-2 : £30.00 B81-39287

910'.2'02 — International travel — *Practical information — For businessmen*
The **International** guide to business travel / edited by Gene Santoro. — [Leicester] : Windward, c1981. — 135p : ill,maps ; 23cm
ISBN 0-7112-0057-2 (pbk) : £2.50 B81-23063

910'.2'02 — Overland travel — *Practical information — For motorcycling*
Pratt, Paul R.. World understanding on two wheels : an introduction to overland travel / by Paul R. Pratt. — [Cobham] ([80 Tilt Rd., Cobham, Surrey]) : P.R. Pratt, c1980. — 81,[8]p of plates : ill,1col.maps,ports ; 21cm
Ill on inside covers
ISBN 0-9507353-0-2 (pbk) : £2.40 B81-09366

910'.2'02 — Travel. Planning — *For British businessmen — Practical information*
Business travel planner / chief editor and principal author Tony Bush. — London : Oyez, c1981. — 1v. (loose-leaf) ; 26cm
ISBN 0-85120-490-2 : £21.95 B81-17054

910'.22'2 — Geographical features. Illustrations — *Questions & answers — For schools*
Lockey, B.. The interpretation of Ordnance Survey maps and geographical pictures / B. Lockey. — Metric ed. — London : George Philip, c1980. — 36p : ill,col.maps ; 24cm
Previous ed.:1975
ISBN 0-540-01046-4 (pbk) : £1.35 : CIP rev.
Primary classification 912'.01'4 B79-35094

910'.22'2 — World — *Aerial photographs*
Sheffield, Charles. Earth watch : a survey of the world from space / Charles Sheffield. — London : Sidgwick & Jackson, 1981. — 160p : col.ill,maps ; 32cm
Includes index
ISBN 0-283-98737-5 : £10.00 B81-30025

910'.3'21 — Geography — *Encyclopaedias*
Walker, Ann. A basic dictionary of geography. — London : Bell and Hyman, June 1981. — [48]p
ISBN 0-7135-1245-8 (pbk) : £1.60 : CIP entry B81-11919

910'.3'21 — World — *Gazetteers*
Wilcocks, Julie. Countries and islands of the world : a guide to nomenclature / Julie Wilcocks. — London : Bingley, 1981. — 133p ; 23cm
ISBN 0-85157-338-x : Unpriced : CIP rev. B81-12795

910'.3'9162 — Geography — *Irish & English dictionaries*
Foclóir tireolaíochta agus pleanala mar aon le téarmaí seandálaiochta = Dictionary of geography and planning incorporating archeological terms / An Roinn Oideachais. — Cagran nua seo. — Baile Atha Cliath [i.e. Dublin] : Oifig an tSolathair, 1981. — vii,261p ; 24cm
Previous ed.: 1972
Unpriced (pbk) B81-38013

910.4 — Expeditions: Operation Drake *(1978-1980)*
Blashford-Snell, John. In the wake of Drake / John Blashford-Snell and Michael Cable. — London : W.H. Allen, 1980. — 135p,[8]p of plates : ill,ports ; 18cm. — (A Star book)
ISBN 0-352-30750-1 (pbk) : £1.25 B81-21852

910.4 — International travel, *1891-1913 — Personal observations — Correspondence, diaries, etc*
Fountaine, Margaret. Love among the butterflies : the travels and adventures of a Victorian lady / Margaret Fountaine ; edited by W.F. Cater. — London : Collins, 1980. — 223p,[32]p of plates : ill(some col.),facsims(some col.),ports (some col.) ; 26cm
ISBN 0-00-216514-7 : £8.50 B81-01797

910.4 — Journeys on horseback, *to 1979*
Lawrence, Margot. Flyers and stayers : the book of the world's greatest rides / Margot Lawrence. — London : Harrap, 1980. — 256p : ill,ports ; 25cm
Bibliography: p248-249. - Includes index
ISBN 0-245-53549-7 : £9.95 B81-03779

910.4 — Travel, *ca 1920-1980 — Personal observations — Collections*
Travel in Vogue. — London : Macdonald Futura, 1981. — 255p,[16]p of plates : ill(some col.),ports ; 29cm
ISBN 0-354-04600-4 : £10.95 B81-10794

910.4 — Travel, *ca 1959-1979 — Personal observations*
Jones, Bob. Travelling / by Bob Jones. — Christchurch [N.Z.] ; London : Whitcoulls, 1980. — 256p ; 22cm
ISBN 0-7233-0645-1 : £9.95 B81-01916

910.4 — Travel. Fictitious accounts, *1600-1800*
Adams, Percy G.. Travelers and travel liars 1660-1800 / by Percy G. Adams. — New York : Dover ; London : Constable, c1980. — x,292p,[8]p of plates : ill,maps,1 port ; 22cm
Originally published: Berkeley : University of California Press ; London : Cambridge University Press, 1962. — Includes index
ISBN 0-486-23942-x (pbk) : £2.50 B81-03922

910.4 — Travel — *Personal observations*
Hodgkinson, E.. Which way to Shangri-la? / by E. Hodgkinson. — Harrow : Eureditions, 1978. — 247p ; 22cm
ISBN 0-906204-24-0 : Unpriced B81-29465

910.4 — World. Description & travel, *1920-1980 — Personal observations*
Mitchison, Naomi. Mucking around : five continents over fifty years / Naomi Mitchison. — London : Gollancz, 1981. — 147p,[8]p of plates : ill,ports ; 23cm
ISBN 0-575-02945-5 : £7.50 B81-22268

910.4 — World. Description & travel — *Personal observations*
Hammond Innes, Dorothy. What lands are these? / Dorothy Hammond Innes ; drawings by Cavendish Morton. — London : Collins and Harvill Press, c1981. — 202p : ill ; 23cm
Ill on lining papers
ISBN 0-00-262970-4 : £7.95 B81-28718

910.4'092'4 — Travel. Murphy, Dervla — *Biographies*
Murphy, Dervla. Wheels within wheels / Dervla Murphy. — Harmondsworth : Penguin, 1981, c1979. — 236p ; 19cm
Originally published: London : J. Murray, 1979
ISBN 0-14-005448-0 (pbk) : £1.50 B81-25083

910.4'1 — Expeditions: Operation Drake *(Expedition)*
Mitchell, Andrew W.. Operation Drake. — London : Severn House, Oct.1981. — [224]p
ISBN 0-7278-2007-9 : £12.95 : CIP entry B81-24665

910.4'1 — World. Circumnavigation by warships, *1772-1775:* **Resolution** *(Ship) - Personal observations*
Forster, Johann Reinhold. The Resolution Journal of Johann Reinhold Forster, 1772-1775. — London (c/o Map Library, British Library, Great Russell St., WC1B 3DG) : Hakluyt Society, July 1981. — 4v.[(786)]p. — (Hakluyt Society second series ; 152-5)
ISBN 0-904180-10-7 : CIP entry B81-13721

910.4'1 — World. Circumnavigation by yachts, *1972-1980:* **Super Shrimp** *(Yacht) — Personal observations*
Acton, Shane. Shrimpy : a record round-the-world voyage in an 18 foot yacht / Shane Acton. — Cambridge : Stephens, 1981. — 184p : ill,maps,plans,ports ; 24cm
ISBN 0-85059-524-x : £4.95 B81-29273

910.4'1 — World. Circumnavigation by yachts, *1975-1977:* **Ilimo** *(Yacht) — Personal observations*
Gash, Ann. A star to steer her by / Ann Gash. — London : Angus & Robertson, 1980. — 240p,[8]p of plates : ill,maps,2facsims,ports ; 23cm
Map on lining papers
ISBN 0-207-14123-1 : £5.95 B81-08378

910.4'1'0924 — World. Single-handed circumnavigation. James, Naomi, *1978-1980 — Biographies*
James, Naomi. At sea on land / Naomi James. — London : Hutchinson, 1981. — 176p,[12]p of plates : ill,ports ; 23cm
ISBN 0-09-144630-9 : £6.95 : CIP rev. B81-02645

910.4'5 — Sailing, *1520-1914*
The **Adventure** of sail 1520-1914- / by David Macintyre ... [et al.] ; with an introduction by Uffa Fox. — London (Brent House, 24 Friern Park, N.12) : Ferndale, 1979, c1970. — 256p : ill(some col.),maps,ports ; 26x32cm
Originally published: London : Elek, 1970. — Ill on lining papers
ISBN 0-905746-01-5 : £25.00 B81-11236

910.4'5 — Seafaring, *to 1980*
Francis, Clare. The commanding sea / by Clare Francis and Warren Tute. — London : BBC and Pelham, 1981. — 280p : ill(some col.),maps(some col.), facsims(some col.),ports (some col.) ; 30cm
Includes index
ISBN 0-7207-1307-2 : £12.50 B81-16479

910.4'5 — Voyages by ketches, *1962-1968:* **Cresswell** *(Boat) — Personal observations*
Jones, Tristan. Saga of a wayward sailor / Tristan Jones. — London : Sphere, 1981, c1979. — 275p ; 18cm
Originally published: London : Bodley Head, 1980
ISBN 0-7221-5105-5 (pbk) : £1.50 B81-38568

910.4'5 — Voyages by sailing boats, *1959-1966:* **Mary Deare** *(Yacht) — Personal observations*
Innes, Hammond. Sea and island / Hammond Innes. — [London] : Fontana, 1970, c1967 (1981 [printing]). — 285p,[16]p of plates : ill,1map,ports ; 18cm
Originally published: Glasgow : Collins, 1967
ISBN 0-00-636345-8 (pbk) : £1.75 B81-12010

910.4'5 — Voyages by sailing boats, *1974-1980:* **Sea Dart** *(Ship) — Personal observations*
Jones, Tristan. Adrift. — London : Bodley Head, May 1981. — [284]p
ISBN 0-370-30422-5 : £6.95 : CIP entry B81-06587

910.4'5 — Voyages by sailing boats: Barbara *(Ship)* **& Sea Dart** *(Ship), 1969-1974 — Personal observations*
Jones, Tristan. The incredible voyage. — Large print ed. — Leicester : Ulverscroft, Sept.1981. — [558]p. — (Charnwood library series)
Originally published: Mission, Kan. : Sheed, Andrews and McMeel ; London : Bodley Head, 1978
ISBN 0-7089-8002-3 : £6.50 : CIP entry B81-25665

910.4'5 — Voyages by sailing ships: Ladye Doris *(Ship), ca 1908-1914 — Personal observations*
Hay, May. I saw a ship a' sailing / Mary Hay. — London : H.M.S.O., 1981. — x,102p,[16]p of plates : ill ; 23cm
At head of title: National Maritime Museum
ISBN 0-11-290340-1 : £3.95 B81-28993

910.4'5 — Voyages by yachts — *Serials*
Roving commissions / by members of the Royal Cruising Club. — 20 (1979). — London : Angus & Robertson, 1980. — ix,149p
ISBN 0-207-95941-2 : £6.95
ISSN 0485-5175 B81-02233

910.4'5 — Voyages from Australia to Great Britain by liners, *1964:* **Orchardes** *(Ship) — Personal observations*
Potter, R. A.. My trip to England / R.A. Potter. — Ilfracombe : Stockwell, 1981. — 39p ; 19cm
ISBN 0-7223-1449-3 (pbk) : £1.95 B81-26236

910.4'5 — Voyages from Greece to China by boats, *1979-1980 - Personal observations*
Young, Gavin. Slow boats to China. — London : Hutchinson, Sept.1981. — 1v.
ISBN 0-09-146050-6 : £8.95 : CIP entry B81-20583

910.4'5 — Voyages from Ireland to Australia by barques, *1938-1939:* **Moshulu** *(Ship) — Personal observations*
Newby, Eric. The last grain race / Eric Newby. — London : Granada, 1981. — 251,[16]p of plates : ill,1map,ports ; 18cm. — (A Panther book)
Originally published: London : Secker & Warburg, 1956
ISBN 0-586-05117-1 (pbk) : £1.95 B81-25918

910.4'5 — Voyages, *to 1980*
A **Book** of sea journeys. — London : Collins, Oct.1981. — [300]p
ISBN 0-00-216310-1 : £7.95 : CIP entry B81-24587

910.4'5'0922 — Privateering, *ca 1655-1728 — Biographies — For children*
Pascall, Jeremy. Pirates and privateers / Jeremy Pascall. — Hove : Wayland, 1981. — 64p : ill (some col.),maps(some col.),1facsim,ports(some col.) ; 23cm. — (In profile)
Bibliography: p62. — Includes index
ISBN 0-85340-880-7 : £3.95
Also classified at 364.1'64 B81-40616

910.4'5'0924 — Voyages. Slocum, Joshua — *Biographies*

Slocum, Victor. Capt. Joshua Slocum : the life and voyages of America's best known sailor / by Victor Slocum. — Havant : Mason, 1981, c1977. — 384p,[16]p of plates : ill,maps,ports ; 24cm
Originally published: New York : Sheridan House, 1950 ; and as The life and voyages of Captain Joshua Slocum. London. — Includes index
ISBN 0-85937-251-0 : £8.95 : CIP rev. B81-12826

910.4'5'0924 — Voyages. Swale, Rosie — *Biographies*

Swale, Rosie. Libras don't say no / Rosie Swale. — London : Granada, 1981, c1980. — 208p,[8]p of plates : ill,ports ; 18cm. — (A Mayflower book)
Originally published: London : Elek, 1980
ISBN 0-583-13465-3 (pbk) B81-38165

Swale, Rosie. Rosie darling / Rosie Swale. — London : Granada, 1981, c1973. — 237p,[4]p of plates : ill,ports ; 18cm. — (A Mayflower book)
Originally published: London : Pelham, 1973. — Includes index
ISBN 0-583-13348-7 (pbk) : £1.50 B81-38163

910.4'53 — Hidden treasure

Wilson, Derek. The world atlas of treasure / Derek Wilson. — London : Collins, 1981. — 256p : ill,col.maps,facsims,ports ; 30cm
Bibliography: p250-251. - Includes index
ISBN 0-00-216877-4 : £9.95 B81-10721

910.4'53 — Hidden treasure — *For children*

Williams, Adam. Missing treasure / by Adam Williams ; illustrated by Harry Bishop ; edited by Jill Coleman. — London : Kingfisher, 1980. — 23p : col.ill,1col.map ; 23cm. — (Kingfisher explorer books. Mysteries)
Includes index
ISBN 0-7063-6066-4 : £1.95 B81-02201

910.4'53 — Shipwrecks. Excavation of remains — *Personal observations*

Wignall, Sydney. In search of Spanish treasure. — Newton Abbot : David & Charles, Jan.1982. — [256]p
ISBN 0-7153-8244-6 : £9.50 : CIP entry B81-33816

910'.5 — Applied geography — *Serials*

[Applied geography *(Sevenoaks)*]. Applied geography : an international journal. — Vol.1, no.1 (Jan.1981-). — Sevenoaks : Butterworths, 1981-. — v. : ill ; 25cm
Quarterly
ISSN 0143-6228 = Applied geography (Sevenoaks) : £30.00 per year B81-14368

910'.6'042659 — Cambridgeshire. Cambridge. Universities. Exploration clubs: Cambridge University Explorers' and Travellers' Club — *Serials*

Cambridge University Explorers' and Travellers' Club. Cambridge expeditions journal : the journal of the Cambridge University Explorers' and Travellers' Club. — 1980. — [Cambridge] ([c/o I. Mackley, Queen's College, Cambridge]) : The Club, [1980?]. — 64p
ISSN 0575-6790 : Unpriced B81-21945

910'.68 — Travel by British businessmen. Management. Organisations: Institute of Travel Managers — *Serials*

ITM yearbook : the official guide of the Institute of Travel Managers. — 1980-81. — Eastbourne (P.O. Box 64, Eastbourne, East Sussex) : John Offord, c1980. — 224p
ISBN 0-903931-29-x : Unpriced B81-10560

910'.7'1041 — Great Britain. Schools. Curriculum subjects: Geography. Teaching

Jay, L. J.. Geography teaching with a little latitude / L.J. Jay. — London : Allen & Unwin, 1981. — xii,137p : ill,maps ; 23cm. — (Classroom close-ups ; 7)
Bibliography: p132-133. - Includes index
ISBN 0-04-371077-8 (cased) : Unpriced B81-08575

910'.7'1141 — Great Britain. Universities & polytechnics. Curriculum subjects: Geography. Degree courses — *Directories* — *Serials*

A Matter of degree. — 1981/1982. — Norwich (Regency House, Duke St., Norwich NR3 3AP) : Geo Abstracts in association with the Geographical Association, the Institute of British Geographers, the Geographical magazine, c1981. — 40p
ISSN 0140-7961 : £1.50 B81-35958

910'.7'1142142 — London. Camden *(London Borough)*. Universities. Colleges: University College, London. *Department of Geography*. Curriculum. Reform

Wood, Peter A.. The undergraduate teaching review, 1978-80 / Peter A. Wood. — London (26 Bedford Way, WC1H 0AP) : Department of Geography, University College London, 1981. — 28,[17]p : ill ; 30cm. — (Occasional papers / University College, London. Department of Geography ; no.37)
Unpriced (pbk) B81-39037

910'.7'12 — Secondary schools. Curriculum subjects: Geography. Academic achievement of students. Assessment — *For teaching*

Black, H. D.. Diagnostic assessment in geography : a teacher's handbook / by H.D. Black and W.B. Dockrell. — [Edinburgh] ([16 Moray Place, Edinburgh EH3 6DR]) : Scottish Council for Research in Education, c1980. — x,80p : ill,forms ; 22cm
ISBN 0-901116-24-6 (pbk) : £2.20 B81-32301

910'.7'1241 — Great Britain. Middle schools. Curriculum subjects: Geography. Teaching

Geographical work in primary and middle schools / edited by David Mills. — Sheffield : Geographical Association, c1981. — viii,200p : ill,maps ; 25cm
Includes bibliographies and index
ISBN 0-900395-66-4 (pbk) : Unpriced
Primary classification 372.8'91044'0941 B81-25092

910'.7'1241 — Great Britain. Secondary schools. Curriculum subjects: Geography — *Conference proceedings*

Recent university work in geography and its relation to schools : a collection of papers including workshop sessions presented at a conference for sixth form teachers held at the University of London Institute of Education between July 14 and July 18, 1980 / edited by Ashley Kent. — London : Department of Geography, University of London Institute of Education, 1981. — vii,340p : ill,maps,facsims ; 30cm
Includes bibliographies
ISBN 0-85473-103-2 (pbk) : Unpriced B81-23026

910'.7'1241 — Great Britain. Secondary schools. Curriculum subjects: Geography. Teaching — *Conference proceedings*

Geography into the 1980s : the proceedings of a conference 'From 14-19 : the contribution of three Schools Council projects to geography in secondary education' held in Oxford on 19th March 1980 and organized by the Geographical Association Working Group on New Techniques and Methods in the Teaching of Geography / edited by Eleanor Rawling. — Sheffield : Geographical Association, c1980. — 68p : ill ; 30cm
ISBN 0-900395-65-6 (pbk) : Unpriced B81-37269

910'.7'1242 — England. Secondary schools. Students, 16-19 years. Curriculum subjects: Geography. Teaching. Projects: Schools Council Curriculum Development Project, Geography 16-19

Corney, Graham. Teacher education and geography 16-19 / by Graham Corney. — London (20 Bedford Way WC1H 0AL) : Schools Council Curriculum Development Project, Geography 16-19, University of London Institute of Education, 1981. — 32p : ill,maps ; 21cm. — (Schools Council Curriculum Development Project, Geography 16-19 occasional paper ; no.1)
ISBN 0-85473-108-3 (pbk) : Unpriced B81-22414

910'.72 — Geography. Research. Applications of systems theory

Morgan, R. K.. The application of the systems approach in geographical research : a discussion of certain problems / R.K. Morgan. — [Birmingham] : [Department of Geography, University of Birmingham], 1980. — 38p ; 30cm. — (Occasional publication / Department of Geography, University of Birmingham ; no.10)
Bibliography: p36-38
ISBN 0-7044-0398-6 (pbk) : £1.00 B81-39712

910'.72 — Geography. Research. Political aspects — *Conference proceedings*

Geography, ideology and social concern / edited by D.R. Stoddart. — Oxford : Blackwell, 1981. — vi,250p : ill ; 24cm
Includes bibliographies and index
ISBN 0-631-19480-0 (cased) : £12.00 : CIP rev.
ISBN 0-631-12717-8 (pbk) : £5.50 B80-12647

910'.72 — Geography. Research. Statistical inference

Summerfield, M. A.. Approaches to statistical inference in geography : comments on some fundamental problems / M.A. Summerfield. — Oxford (Mansfield Rd., Oxford OX1 3TB) : School of Geography, University of Oxford, 1981. — 19p ; 30cm. — (Working papers / School of Geography, University of Oxford, ISSN 0260-5953 ; no.3)
Bibliography: p19
Unpriced (pbk) B81-22903

910'.724 — Geography. Causal models

Pringle, D. G.. Causal modelling : the Simon-Blalock approach / by D.G. Pringle. — Rev. version. — Norwich : Geo Abstracts, 1980. — 36p : ill ; 22cm. — (Concepts and techniques in modern geography, ISSN 0306-6142 ; no.27)
Bibliography: p35-36
ISBN 0-86094-045-4 (pbk) : £1.00 B81-11338

910'.724 — Geography. Field studies. Methodology

Lounsbury, John F.. Introduction to geographic field methods and techniques / John F. Lounsbury and Frank T. Aldrich. — Columbus ; London : Merrill, c1979. — x,181p : ill,maps ; 25cm
Includes bibliographies and index
ISBN 0-675-08304-4 (pbk) : £7.50 B81-08330

910'.76 — Geography - *Questions & answers - For African students - For schools*

Pritchard, J. M.. Africa. — London : Edward Arnold, July 1981. — [80]p
ISBN 0-7131-8071-4 (pbk) : £1.75 : CIP entry B81-14396

910'.76 — Geography — *Questions & answers* — *For Caribbean students*

Rahil, Vohn A. M.. Multiple choice questions in Caribbean geography / Vohn A.M. Rahil. — London : Macmillan Caribbean, 1981. — 138p : ill,charts,maps(some col.) ; 25cm
ISBN 0-333-30818-2 (pbk) : £1.75 B81-13404

910'.7'8 — Great Britain. Secondary schools. Curriculum subjects: Geography. Teaching aids: Mental maps

Stoltman, Joseph P.. Mental maps : resources for teaching and learning / Joseph P. Stoltman. — Sheffield : Geographical Association, 1980. — 39p : ill,maps,1plan ; 27cm. — (Occasional paper / Geographical Association, ISSN 0305-9464)
Cover title
ISBN 0-900395-64-8 (pbk) : Unpriced B81-38929

910'.8921'0222 — Travel by Britons, *1837-1901* — *Illustrations*

Goodall, John S.. Victorians abroad / by John S. Goodall. — London : Macmillan, 1980. — [64]p : all col.ill ; 14x19cm
ISBN 0-333-28453-4 : £2.95 B81-07900

910'.9 — Exploration, *to 1800* — *For children*

Grant, Neil, *1938-*. The discoverers / [author Neil Grant]. — London : Marshall Cavendish Children's Books, 1979. — 61p : ill(some col.),maps(some col.),ports(some col.) ; 29cm. — (The Living past)
Includes index
ISBN 0-85685-678-9 : Unpriced B81-21745

910′.9 — Exploration, *to 1980 — For children*
Lye, Keith. Explorers / Keith Lye. — London : Macmillan Children′s, c1981. — 49p : col.ill,col.maps,col.facsims,ports(some col.) ; 36cm. — (The Macmillan colour library)
Includes index
ISBN 0-333-30790-9 : £3.95 B81-21785

910′.92′2 — Exploration. Schlagintweit, Adolph von; Schlagintweit-Sakünlünski, Hermann von & Schlagintweit, Robert von — *Biographies*
Alcock, Helga. The Schlagintweit brothers : achievements in high Asia / by Helga Alcock. — [Totnes] ([Wyse House, Haberton, Totnes, Devon]) : [H. Alcock], 1981. — [20]p,folded leaf : ill,maps(some col.) ; 24cm
Limited ed. of 50 copies
Unpriced (pbk) B81-22775

910′.92′2 — Geographers — *Biographies — Serials*
Geographers : biobibliographical studies. — Vol.5. — London : Mansell, Nov.1981. — [150]p
ISBN 0-7201-1635-x : £17.00 : CIP entry B81-30633

910′.92′4 — Exploration. Cook, James, *1728-1779.* **Ships**
Stamp, Tom. Captain Cook and his ships / Tom & Cordelia Stamp. — Whitby : Caedmon, c1981. — 14p : ill,ports ; 21cm. — (A Caedmon cameo)
ISBN 0-905355-17-2 (pbk) : £0.65 B81-24535

910′.92′4 — Travel. Newby, Eric — *Biographies*
Newby, Eric. A traveller′s life. — London : Collins, Oct.1981. — [256]p
ISBN 0-00-211874-2 : £7.95 : CIP entry B81-24606

910′.94 — European maritime exploration, *1200-1500*
Chaunu, Pierre. European expansion in the later Middle Ages / by Pierre Chaunu ; translated by Katharine Bertram. — Amsterdam ; Oxford : North-Holland, 1979. — xiv,326p : ill,maps ; 23cm. — (Europe in the Middle Ages ; v.10)
Translation of: L′expansion européenne du XIIIe au XVe siècle. — Bibliography: p3-48. — Includes index
ISBN 0-444-85132-1 : Unpriced B81-39350

910′.941 — British seafaring, *to 1979 — Readings from contemporary sources*
The **British** seafarer / [compiled by] Michael Mason, Basil Greenhill, Robin Craig. — London : Hutchinson : BBC in association with the National Maritime Museum, 1980. — [160]p : ill(some col.),maps,music,facsims,ports ; 27cm
ISBN 0-09-141950-6 (cased) : £9.95 : CIP rev.
ISBN 0-563-17852-3 (BBC)
ISBN 0-09-141951-4 (pbk) : £5.95 B80-07157

910′.941 — Great Britain. Geography, *ca 1880-1979*
Freeman, T. W.. A history of modern British geography / T.W. Freeman. — London : Longman, 1980. — ix,258p : ill,map ; 23cm
Bibliography: p240-250. - Includes index
ISBN 0-582-30030-4 : £13.50 : CIP rev. B80-09512

910′.942 — Exploration. Voyages by Englishmen, *1556-1591 — Personal observations — Collections*
Hakluyt, Richard. [The principall navigations, voiages and discoveries of the English nation, made by sea or over land. Selections]. Hakluyt′s voyages : a selection / [edited] by Richard David. — London : Chatto & Windus, 1981. — 640p : ill,maps,ports ; 23cm
Maps on lining papers. — Includes index
ISBN 0-7011-2533-0 : £12.50 B81-37922

911 — HISTORICAL GEOGRAPHY

911 — Great Britain. Public boundaries. Mapping by Ordance Survey, *1840-1980*
Booth, J. R. S.. Public boundaries and Ordnance Survey 1840-1980 / by J.R.S. Booth ; edited by R.A.G. Powell. — [Southampton] ([Romsey Rd., Maybush, Southampton SO9 4DH]) : Ordnance Survey, c1980. — 451p : ill,2facsim,maps,forms ; 30cm
Bibliography : p435-438. — Includes index
£17.00 (pbk) B81-37517

911 — World, *to 1980 — Atlases*
The **Hamlyn** historical atlas / general editor R.I. Moore. — London : Hamlyn, 1981. — 176p : col.maps ; 31cm
ISBN 0-600-30361-6 : £12.95
ISBN 0-600-34172-0 (pbk) : Unpriced B81-14264

911′.072 — Historical geography. Research projects — *Directories — Serials*
Register of research in historical geography 1980 / edited by M. Trevor Wild. — Norwich : Geo Abstracts, c1980. — ii,36p ; 22cm. — (Historical geography research series, ISSN 0143-633x ; no.4)
Previous ed.: / edited by Harold Fox. 1976. — Includes index
ISBN 0-86094-054-3 (pbk) : £1.00 B81-08299

911′.1821 — Caribbean region, *to 1978 — Atlases*
Ashdown, Peter. Caribbean history in maps / Peter Ashdown. — Trinidad : Longman Caribbean ; London : Longman, 1979. — iv,84p : maps ; 22x28cm
Includes index
ISBN 0-582-76541-2 (pbk) : £1.80 : CIP rev. B79-23538

911′.411 — Scotland. Geographical features. Historical sources
Whyte, I. D.. Sources for Scottish historical geography : an introductory guide / by I.D. Whyte and K.A. Whyte. — Norwich : Geo Abstracts, 1981. — ii,46p ; 21cm. — (Historical geography research series, ISSN 0143-683x ; no.6)
Text on inside covers
ISBN 0-86094-066-7 (pbk) : Unpriced B81-27284

911′.415 — Ireland, *to 1980 — Atlases*
Edwards, Ruth Dudley. An atlas of Irish history. — 2nd ed. — London : Methuen, July 1981. — [280]p
Previous ed.: 1973
ISBN 0-416-74820-1 (cased) : £11.00 : CIP entry
ISBN 0-416-74050-2 (pbk) : £5.50 B81-13498

911′.415 — Irish civilization, *to 1980.* **Geographical factors**
Evans, E. Estyn. The personality of Ireland : habitat, heritage and history / E. Estyn Evans. — New enl. rev. ed. — Belfast : Blackstaff Press, 1981. — 130p,[16]p of plates : ill,maps ; 22cm
Previous ed.: London : Cambridge University Press, 1973. — Bibliography: p120-124. — Includes index
ISBN 0-85640-238-9 (pbk) : £3.95 B81-27030

911′.42 — England, *700-1066 — Atlases*
Hill, David, *1937 July 15-*. An atlas of Anglo-Saxon England / David Hill. — Oxford : Blackwell, 1981. — xii,180p : ill,maps,facsims ; 29cm
Bibliography: p167. — Includes index
ISBN 0-631-11181-6 : £16.00 B81-40054

911′.423′8 — Somerset. Geographical features, *to 1980*
Havinden, Michael. The Somerset landscape. — London : Hodder & Stoughton, Feb.1982. — [272]p. — (The Making of the English landscape)
ISBN 0-340-20116-9 : £7.95 : CIP entry B81-35689

911′.4257 — Oxfordshire. Geographical features, *to 1974*
Rhodes, John, *1944-*. Oxfordshire : a county and its people / text and design by John G. Rhodes. — Woodstock : Oxfordshire County Museum, c1980. — 37p : ill,maps,facsims,plans,1port ; 20x21cm. — (Oxfordshire Museums Service publication ; no.12)
Bibliography: p37
ISBN 0-901036-05-6 (pbk) : Unpriced B81-05861

911′.428 — England. Central Pennines. Geographical features, *to 1979*
Porter, John, *1946-*. The making of the central Pennines / John Porter. — Ashbourne : Moorland, c1980. — 155p : ill,maps,1facsim,plans ; 22cm
Includes bibliographies and index
ISBN 0-903485-80-x : £6.95 : CIP rev. B80-25001

911′.48 — Scandinavia. Geographical features, *ca 1250-1980*
Mead, W. R.. An historical geography of Scandinavia / W.R. Mead. — London : Academic Press, 1981. — xviii,313p : ill,maps ; 24cm
Includes bibliographies and index
ISBN 0-12-487420-7 : £15.00 : CIP rev. B81-12335

912 — ATLASES AND MAPS

912 — Maps — *Collectors′ guides*
Lister, Raymond. Old maps and globes : with a list of cartographers, engravers, publishers and printers concerned with printed maps and globes from c.1500 to c.1850 / Raymond Lister. — Rev. ed. — London : Bell & Hyman, 1979. — 356p,[48]p of plates : ill,maps ; 26cm
Previous ed.: published as How to identify old maps and globes. London : Bell, 1965. — Bibliography: p109-115. - Includes index
ISBN 0-7135-1146-x : £9.95 B81-18375

912 — Maps — *For schools*
Robertson, Ann. Maps and mapping / Ann Robertson. — London : Hutchinson, 1980. — 32p : ill,maps ; 21x30cm. — (Down to earth)
ISBN 0-09-139811-8 (unbound) : Unpriced : CIP rev. B79-22950

912 — World — *Atlases*
The **library** atlas. — 15th ed. / [Harold Fullard, H.C. Darby, B.M. Willett editors]. — London : Philip, 1981. — xxiii,176,xxxii,140p : col.ill,chiefly col.maps ; 32cm
Previous ed.: 1980. — Includes index
ISBN 0-540-05387-2 : £12.50 B81-26154

Modern home atlas. — 5th ed. — London : G. Philip, May 1981. — [56]p
ISBN 0-540-05390-2 : £1.95 : CIP entry B81-06875

Philips′ concise atlas of the world. — 2nd ed. — London : George Philip & Son, Oct.1981. — [232]p
Previous ed.: 1980
ISBN 0-540-05407-0 : £5.95 : CIP entry B81-28811

Philips′ illustrated atlas of the world / editor Bernard Stonehouse ; consultant editors T.W. Freeman ... [et al.]. — London : George Philip, 1980. — 208p : col.ill,col.maps ; 38cm
Includes indexes
ISBN 0-540-05371-6 : £14.95 : CIP rev. B80-18092

912 — World - *Atlases*
Philip′s new practical atlas. — 9th ed. — London : G. Philip, Aug.1981. — [152]p
Previous ed.: 1980
ISBN 0-540-05394-5 : £4.95 : CIP entry B81-16366

912 — World — *Atlases*
Philips′ new reference atlas. — 2nd ed. — London : Philip, Apr.1981. — [264]p
Previous ed.: 1980
ISBN 0-540-05386-4 : £7.95 : CIP entry B81-02112

Philips′ new world atlas. — 4th ed. — London : George Philip, Oct.1981. — [280]p
Previous ed.: 1980
ISBN 0-540-05406-2 : £7.95 : CIP entry B81-25734

Philips′ universal atlas / edited by Harold Fullard. — London : Philip, c1981. — 176,140p : col.ill,chiefly col.maps ; 32cm
Previous ed.: 1978. — Includes index
ISBN 0-540-05388-0 : £14.95 B81-26152

912 — World — *Atlases* *continuation*

Philips' world atlas. — 2nd ed. — London : Philip, Apr.1981. — [152]p
Previous ed.: 1979
ISBN 0-540-05385-6 : £4.95 : CIP entry
B81-02111

Pocket atlas of the world. — New ed. — London : G. Philip, Jan.1982. — [124]p
Previous ed.: Published as Philips' pocket atlas of the world, 1971
ISBN 0-540-05410-0 (pbk) : £1.50 : CIP entry
B81-34278

Price, Brian P.. The Hamlyn world atlas / Brian P. Price. — London : Hamlyn, c1980. — 196p : col.ill,col.maps ; 37cm
Col. ill on lining papers. — Includes index
ISBN 0-600-30490-6 : £12.95 B81-00654

Purnell's family atlas / authenticator Keith Lye ; editor Wendy Hobson. — Maidenhead : Purnell, 1981. — 128p : col.ill,col.maps,col.ports ; 33cm
Includes index
ISBN 0-361-05156-5 : £4.99 B81-37810

The **Reader's** digest great world atlas. — 3rd ed. — London : Reader's Digest, c1977 (1980 [printing]). — 182p : ill(some col.),1col.chart,col.maps ; 40cm
Previous ed.: i.e. 2nd ed., 6th revise, 1975. — Includes index
£12.95 B81-09842

The **university** atlas. — 21st ed. / [Harold Fullard, H.C. Darby, B.M. Willett editors]. — London : Philip, c1981. — xxiii,176,140p : col.ill,chiefly col.maps ; 32cm
Previous ed.: 1980. — Includes index
ISBN 0-540-05378-3 : £9.95 B81-26153

The **Whole** world / compiled by Charles Thornford. — Huddersfield : Schofield & Sims, 1981. — 48p : col.ill,col.maps ; 32cm
ISBN 0-7217-1050-6 (pbk) : Unpriced
B81-11718

912 — World — *Atlases* — *For children*

Tivers, Jacqueline. [The Bartholomew children's world atlas]. A first Puffin children's world atlas : a book of maps for young children / Jacqueline Tivers and Michael Day. — Harmondsworth : Penguin, 1981, c1980. — 47p : chiefly col.ill,col.maps ; 30cm
Originally published: Edinburgh : Bartholomew, 1980
ISBN 0-14-031344-3 (pbk) : £1.75 B81-16980

Townson, W. D.. Illustrated atlas of the modern world. — London : Longman, Sept.1981. — [64]p
ISBN 0-582-39128-8 : £4.95 : CIP entry
B81-25876

912 — World — *Atlases* — *For schools*

Barker, Ronald S.. Your atlas / Ronald S. Barker ; edited by Harold Fullard, B.M. Willett & Helen McCourt ; with acknowledgements to L. Francis & B. Stringer. — Leeds : Arnold, c1981. — 49p : col.ill,col.maps ; 28cm
Maps on inside cover. — Includes index
ISBN 0-560-00224-6 (pbk) : Unpriced
ISBN 0-540-05381-3 (Philip) : Unpriced
B81-21739

912 — World. Social conditions — *Atlases*

Kidron, Michael. The state of the world atlas / Michael Kidron & Ronald Segal. — London : Pan, 1981. — [173]p : col.ill,maps(some col.) ; 26cm. — (Pan reference)
Includes index
ISBN 0-330-26334-x (pbk) : £5.95 B81-06260

Kidron, Michael. The state of the world atlas / Michael Kidron & Ronald Segal. — London : Heinemann, 1981. — [173]p : col.ill,maps(some col.) ; 26cm
Includes index
ISBN 0-435-35495-7 : £9.50 B81-06259

912'.01'4 — Great Britain. Ordnance Survey maps. Map reading — *For schools*

Lockey, B.. The interpretation of Ordnance Survey maps and geographical pictures / B. Lockey. — Metric ed. — London : George Philip, c1980. — 36p : ill,col.maps ; 24cm
Previous ed.:1975
ISBN 0-540-01046-4 (pbk) : £1.35 : CIP rev.
Also classified at 910'.22'2 B79-35094

Turk, Brian. Map practice / Brian Turk. — Slough : University Tutorial, 1981, c1980. — 32p : ill(some col.),col.maps ; 30cm
ISBN 0-7231-0818-8 (pbk) : £2.60 B81-23089

912'.01'4 — Map reading

Keates, J. S.. Understanding maps. — London : Longman, Feb.1982. — [192]p
ISBN 0-582-30039-8 (pbk) : £8.95 : CIP entry
B81-37602

912'.01'4 — Map reading — *For schools*

Catling, Simon. Your map book / Simon Catling ; with acknowledgements to L. Francis and W. Stringer. — Leeds : Arnold, 1981. — 41p : col.ill,col.maps ; 29cm
Adaptation of Let's make a map / by L. Francis and W. Stringer. Norwood, S.A.: Rigby, 1979. — Text on inside cover
ISBN 0-560-00225-4 (pbk) : Unpriced
ISBN 0-540-05379-1 (Philip) : Unpriced
B81-21738

Kemp, Richard. Mapwork one / Richard Kemp. — London : Edward Arnold, 1981. — 48p : ill (some col.),maps(some col.) ; 25cm
ISBN 0-7131-0350-7 (pbk) : £1.95 : CIP rev.
B79-21455

Speak, P.. Map reading and interpretation / P. Speak, A.H.C. Carter. — New ed., metric. — Harlow : Longman, 1981. — 80p : ill,maps (some col.) ; 28cm
Previous ed.: i.e. 2nd ed. 1970
ISBN 0-582-33076-9 (pbk) : £3.50 B81-37411

912'.028 — Maps. Pattern analysis

Cliff, A. D.. Spatial processes : models & applications / A.D. Cliff & J.K. Ord. — London : Pion, c1981. — 266p : ill,maps ; 24cm
Bibliography: p251-261. — Includes index
ISBN 0-85086-081-4 : £12.50 B81-05951

912'.09 — Maps, *to 1979*

Hodgkiss, Alan G.. Understanding maps : a systematic history of their use and development / A.G. Hodgkiss. — Folkestone : Dawson, 1981. — 209p : ill,maps ; 28cm
Bibliography: p199-203. — Includes index
ISBN 0-7129-0940-0 : £15.00 : CIP rev.
B80-04176

912'.1324941082 — Great Britain. *Parliament. House of Commons.* **Members. Elections,** *1885-1979* — *Atlases*

Kinnear, Michael. The British voter : an atlas and survey since 1885 / Michael Kinnear ; cartography by the author. — 2nd ed. — London : Batsford, 1981. — 172p : maps ; 31cm
Previous ed.: 1968. — Bibliography: p157-159. — Includes index
ISBN 0-7134-3482-1 : £20.00 B81-33366

912'.1385'0941 — Great Britain. Railways — *Atlases*

Baker, S. K.. Rail atlas of Britain / compiled by S.K. Baker. — 3rd ed. — Oxford : Oxford Publishing, 1980. — iii,115p : chiefly col.maps ; 25cm
Previous ed.: 1978. — Includes index
ISBN 0-86093-106-4 : £4.95 B81-06798

912'.1551136 — Continental drift — *Atlases*

Smith, A. G. (Alan Gilbert). Phanerozoic paleocontinental world maps. — Rev. and enl. version / A.G. Smith, A.M. Hurley, J.C. Briden. — Cambridge : Cambridge University Press, 1980. — 98p : chiefly maps ; 27cm. — (Cambridge earth science series)
Previous ed.: published as Mesozoic and cenozoic paleocontinental maps / by A.G. Smith and J.C. Briden. 1977. — Bibliography: p98
ISBN 0-521-23257-0 (cased) : £12.50 : CIP rev.
ISBN 0-521-23258-9 (pbk) : £6.25 B80-26279

912'.15515773 — Great Britain. Drought, *1975-1976* — *Atlases*

Atlas of drought in Britain 1975-76 / edited by J.C. Doornkamp and K.J. Gregory ; cartographic advisor A.S. Burn ; foreword by Denis Howell. — London : 1 Kensington Gore, SW7 2AR : Institute of British Geographers, 1980. — 87p : ill(some col.),maps(some col.) ; 43cm
Includes bibliographies and index
ISBN 0-901989-31-2 : Unpriced B81-08205

912'.15515781241 — Great Britain. Mean monthly rainfall, *1941-1970* — *Atlases*

Woodley, K. E.. Maps of average monthly rainfall over the British Isles for 1941-70 / by K.E. Woodley. — Bracknell (London Rd., Bracknell, Berks RG12 2SZ) : Meteorological Office, 1980. — 25p : all charts ; 30cm. — (Hydrological memorandum ; no.44)
ISBN 0-86180-043-5 (pbk) : Unpriced
B81-13158

912'.1594094228 — Isle of Wight. Freshwater molluscs & land molluscs. Distribution — *Atlases*

Preece, R. C.. An atlas of the non-marine Mollusca of the Isle of Wight / by R.C. Preece. — [Newport] ([County Library, Upper St. James's St., Newport, Isle of Wight PO30 1LL]) : Isle of Wight Council, 1980. — 41p : ill,maps ; 25cm. — (Isle of Wight County Museum Service natural history series ; no.1)
Bibliography: p40. — Includes index
ISBN 0-906328-09-8 (pbk) : Unpriced
B81-23001

912'.1595781'094246 — Staffordshire. Moths. Distribution — *Atlases*

Warren, R. G.. Moths : Noctuidae (Acronictinae-Hyperinae), Hepialidae ; Cossidae, Zygaenidae, Sesiidae / author R.G. Warren ; editor G. Halfpenny. — Stoke-on-Trent : The City Museum & Art Gallery, [1981]. — 55p : maps ; 22cm. — (Atlas of the lepidoptera of Staffordshire ; pt.6) (Publication / Staffordshire Biological Recording Scheme, ISSN 0309-2100 ; no.8)
Includes index
ISBN 0-905080-10-6 (pbk) : Unpriced
B81-31313

912'.1647954235 — Devon. Public houses — *Maps*

Better pubs map of Devon. — Crediton (Red Cross House, Crediton, Devon) : Better Pubs Ltd., [1980?]. — 1folded sheet ; 63x50cm folded to 19x13cm : col.ill,1map
£0.60 B81-17955

912'.41 — Great Britain — *Atlases* — *For motoring*

The **Complete** atlas of Britain. — 3rd ed. — Basingstoke : Automobile Association, 1981. — xiv,256p : ill(some col.),col.maps,plans ; 29cm
Previous ed.: 1980. — Includes index
ISBN 0-86145-062-0 : Unpriced B81-10946

Practical road atlas, Great Britain. — London : Hamlyn, 1981. — 153p : ill,chiefly maps ; 30cm
Includes index
ISBN 0-600-34978-0 (pbk) : £3.50 B81-24058

912'.41 — Great Britain. Towns — *Atlases*

AA town plans / edited Barry Francis. — Updated 2nd ed. — [Basingstoke] : Automobile Association ; London : Hutchinson [distributor], c1979. — 224p : ill,col.maps,col.plans ; 20x21cm
Previous ed.: 1977
ISBN 0-86145-003-5 (pbk) : £2.95 B81-10947

912'.41'05 — Great Britain — *Atlases* — *For motoring* — *Serials*

Collins road atlas. Britain & Ireland. — Rev. ed 1981/1982. — Glasgow : Collins, c1981. — 97p
ISBN 0-00-447410-4 : £2.95 B81-29421

912'.41464 — Scotland. Strathclyde Region. Ayr — *Maps*

Ayr : official street plan. — 3rd ed. — London : Burrow, [1980?]. — 12p : 1map ; 25cm
Previous ed.: 197-?. — Map (folded sheet) attached to inside back cover. — Includes index
£0.75 (pbk) B81-23629

912'.42 — England — *Atlases* — *For motoring*
Navigator / RAC. — [London] : Map Productions
3: East & West Midlands, Birmingham, Nottingham, Hanley, Stoke / [editors Roger Edwards, Pat Sorton] ; [cartography Map Productions Limited]. — [1981?]. — 104p : ill,col.maps ; 32cm
Maps on lining papers. — Includes index
ISBN 0-540-03170-4 (pbk) : £4.95 B81-12477

912'.421 — London — *Atlases*
Kelly's London street atlas. — East Grinstead : Kelly's Directories, c1981. — 305p : ill,col.maps ; 29cm
Includes index
ISBN 0-610-00541-3 : £7.95 B81-17193

912'.42261 — West Sussex. Crawley *(District)* — *Maps*
Borough of Crawley : official street plan. — Wallington : Forward Publicity, [1981]. — 16p,(folded sheets) : ill,1map ; 21cm
Cover title
Unpriced (pbk) B81-36404

912'.423 — South-west England — *Atlases*
West Country : Hamlyn leisure atlas / [compiled and edited by Colin Wilson]. — London : Hamlyn, 1981. — 128p : ill(some col.),col.maps ; 31cm
Maps on lining papers. — Includes index
ISBN 0-600-34957-8 : £5.95 B81-24064

912'.42315 — Wiltshire. Trowbridge — *Maps*
Official street plan, Trowbridge. — Wallington : Forward Publicity, [1981]. — 8p,[2]p of plates (folded sheet) : ill,1map ; 21cm
Cover title. — Includes index
Unpriced (pbk) B81-10705

912'.42512 — Derbyshire. Chesterfield *(District)* — *Atlases*
Borough of Chesterfield : official street & area map. — 3rd ed. — Wallington : Forward Publicity, [1981]. — 56p : ill,maps ; 21cm
Previous ed.:
Unpriced (pbk) B81-39013

912'.42515 — Derbyshire. Bolsover *(District)* — *Atlases*
Bolsover District Council official map : containing town centre maps of Bolsover, Clowne, Creswell, Shirebrook, South Normanton. — Wallington : Forward Publicity, [1981]. — 16p,[2]p of plates(fold sheet) : maps ; 21cm
Cover title. — Includes index
Unpriced (pbk) B81-10712

912'.42517 — Derbyshire. Derby — *Atlases*
City of Derby : official street plan. — Gloucester : Published by British Publishing in conjunction with the Estates Department of Derby City Council, [1981]. — 72p : ill,maps,1plan ; 21cm
Includes index
ISBN 0-7140-1964-x (pbk) : Unpriced B81-28736

912'.42542 — Leicestershire. Leicester — *Atlases*
AZ street atlas of Leicester and district. — Sevenoaks : Geographers' A-Z Map Co., [1981?]. — 40p : all maps ; 21cm
Includes index
ISBN 0-85039-181-4 (pbk) : £1.00 B81-29612

912'.42579 — Oxfordshire. South Oxfordshire *(District)* — *Atlases*
South Oxfordshire. *District Council.* South Oxfordshire : official map book / issued by authority of the South Oxfordshire District Council. — Wallington : Forward Publicity, 1981. — 84p : ill,chiefly maps ; 24cm
Unpriced (pbk) B81-39014

912'.42715 — Cheshire. Vale Royal *(District)* — *Atlases*
Vale Royal : official map. — Wallington : Forward, [1981]. — 16,[2]p of plates : chiefly maps ; 21cm
Includes index
Unpriced (pbk) B81-21104

912'.42731 — Greater Manchester *(Metropolitan County)*. **Trafford** *(District)* — *Atlases*
Metropolitan Borough of Trafford : street atlas and index. — Wallington : Forward, [1981]. — 88p : chiefly maps ; 24cm
Cover title. — Includes index
Unpriced (pbk) B81-21097

912'.42737 — Greater Manchester *(Metropolitan County)*. **Bolton** *(District)* — *Atlases*
Bolton street atlas : including Bolton, Blackrod, Farnworth, Horwich, Kearsley, Little Lever, South Turton and Westhoughton / Bolton Metropolitan Borough. — 3rd ed. — [Bolton] ([c/o Public Relations and Information Officer, Town Hall, Bolton, BL1 1RU]) : Bolton Council, 1980. — 96p : chiefly maps ; 21cm
Includes index
Unpriced (pbk) B81-14550

912'.427625 — Lancashire. Hyndburn *(District)* — *Atlases*
Shurmer, Adrian. Shurmer's street guide (with maps) of Hyndburn / researched and compiled by Adrian Shurmer. — 2nd ed. / maps drawn by James S. Cunningham. — Accrington ([34 Bank St., Accrington]) : Dalton & Co., c1981. — 128p : ill,maps ; 15cm
Unpriced (pbk) B81-32992

912'.42784 — Cumbria. Copeland *(District)* — *Atlases*
Official map : featuring street plans of Whitehaven Cleator Moor, Egremont & Millom : borough of Copeland. — Wallington : Forward Publicity, [1981]. — 16p,[2]p of plates (folded sheet) : ill,maps ; 21cm
Cover title. — Includes index
Unpriced (pbk) B81-10706

912'.42843 — North Yorkshire. York — *Maps*
The **City** of York : official street plan. — Wallington : Forward Publicity, [1981]. — 16p (folded sheet) : 1map ; 21cm
Cover title
Unpriced (pbk) B81-36398

912'.429 — Wales — *Atlases*
Atlas cenedlaethol Cymru / golygydd H. Carter ; is-olygydd H.M. Griffiths ; tynnwyd y mapiau gan David L. Fryer a'r Cwmni a'r Adran Ddaearyddiaeth, Coleg Prifysgol Cymru Aberystwyth. — [Caerdydd] : Cyhoeddwyd gan Wasg Prifysgol Cymru ar ran Pwyllgor Gwyddorau Cymdeithasol. Bwrdd Gwybodau Celtaidd Prifysgol Cymru, [1980-1981], c1980. — 1v : col.ill,chiefly col.maps ; 55x42cm
Parallel Welsh and English text. — Added t.p. in English with the title National atlas of Wales. — Five parts of 42 in a box on publication
ISBN 0-7083-0775-2 : Unpriced : CIP rev. B80-18094

Wales : Hamlyn leisure atlas / [compiled and edited by Colin Wilson]. — London : Hamlyn, 1981. — 128p : ill(some col.),col.maps,1port ; 31cm
Maps on lining papers. — Includes index
ISBN 0-600-34956-x : £5.95 B81-24063

912'.71 — Canada. Official maps
Nicholson, N. L.. The maps of Canada : a guide to official Canadian maps, charts, atlases and gazetteers / N.L. Nicholson, L.M. Sebert. — Folkestone : Dawson, 1981. — x,251p,[1]leaf of plates : ill,maps,ports ; 26cm
Includes index
ISBN 0-7129-0911-7 : £20.00 : CIP rev. B79-32138

912'.9441 — New South Wales. Sydney. Social conditions — *Atlases*
Poulsen, Michael. Sydney : a social and political atlas / Michael Poulsen and Peter Spearritt. — Sydney ; London : Allen & Unwin, 1981. — 163p : maps ; 31x43cm
Two maps (2 transparent sheets) as insert. — Bibliography: p161-163
ISBN 0-86861-202-2 (cased) : £27.50
ISBN 0-86861-210-3 (pbk) : Unpriced B81-26680

914 — EUROPE

914 — European Community countries. Geographical features — *For schools*
Clare, Roger. Europe and the Common Market / Roger Clare. — London : Edward Arnold, 1981. — 32p : ill,maps ; 30cm. — (Meet the world!)
ISBN 0-7131-0487-2 (pbk) : £1.75 B81-15607

914 — North-western Europe. Tourist industries. Personnel: Guides. Training
Cross, Donald A. E.. Some educational aspects of tourist guide training in the British Isles and parts of Europe / Donald A.E. Cross. — London (64 St. James St. SW1A 1NF) : British Travel Educational Trust, [1980], c1979. — ii,375p : ill,maps,facsims,1plan,forms ; 30cm
£2.50 (pbk) B81-40656

914 — Southern Europe. Description & travel, *1971-1977 — Personal observations — Correspondence, diaries, etc.*
Dibble, L. Grace. Return tickets to Southern Europe / L. Grace Dibble. — Ilfracombe : Stockwell, 1980. — 400p,[8]p of plates : ill,1port ; 22cm
ISBN 0-7223-1423-x : £5.75 B81-16784

914 — Southern Europe. Geographical features
Beckinsale, Monica. Southern Europe : the Mediterranean and Alpine lands / Monica and Robert Beckinsale. — London : Hodder and Stoughton, 1975 (1979 [printing]). — 334p : ill,maps ; 29cm
Bibliography: p311-321. - Includes index
ISBN 0-340-24436-4 (pbk) : £5.95 B81-18377

914 — Western Europe. Geographical features
Brunt, Barry. Britain and Western Europe : a regional geography / Barry Brunt ; edited by Desmond Gillmor. — Dublin : Gill and Macmillan, 1980. — 281p : ill,maps ; 27cm
ISBN 0-7171-0874-0 (pbk) : £4.50 B81-02534

914 — Western Europe. Geographical features — *For schools*
Perry, Allen H.. Studying Western Europe : the companion volume to Geography of Western Europe / Allen H. Perry and Vivian C. Perry ; diagrams and maps by G. Lewis. — Dublin : Educational Company of Ireland, 1979. — 91p : ill,maps ; 21cm
Unpriced (pbk) B81-22776

914'.0076 — Western Europe. Geographical features — *Questions & answers — For schools*
Tolley, H.. Data response exercises on North America and Western Europe / H. Tolley, K. Briggs, D. Riley. — Oxford : Oxford University Press, 1981. — 80p : ill,maps ; 30cm
ISBN 0-19-913266-6 (pbk) : £2.50
Also classified at 917'.0076 B81-25951

914'.0452 — Europe. Description & travel, *1924-1939 — Personal observations — Polish texts*
Zaniewicki, Zbigniew. Od Amazonki do Wisły : 1924-1939 / Zbigniew Zaniewicki. — Londyn : Nakładem Polskiej Fundacji Kulturalnej, 1980. — 299p,[8]p of plates : ill,ports ; 19cm
Unpriced (pbk) B81-14723

914'.0455 — Europe. Description & travel — *Personal observations*
Hone, Joseph. Gone tomorrow. — London : Secker & Warburg, Oct.1981. — [156]p
ISBN 0-436-20084-8 : £6.50 : CIP entry B81-27375

914'.04557'0222 — Europe. Description & travel, *1970-1979 — Illustrations*
Evans, Ray, *1920-*. Travelling with a sketchbook / Ray Evans. — London : Murray, 1980. — 110p : chiefly ill ; 26cm
Text, ill on lining papers
ISBN 0-7195-3790-8 : £7.50 : CIP rev. B80-18940

914'.04558 — Europe — *Practical information — For British businessmen*
Europe / editor Jane Walker ; associate editor Mark Ambrose. — London : Joseph, c1981. — 462p : maps ; 23cm. — (The Business traveller's handbook ; v.3)
Includes index
ISBN 0-7181-1982-7 : £12.50 B81-25639

914'.04558 — Europe — *Visitors' guides — For hitch-hiking*

Welsh, Ken. Hitch-hiker's guide to Europe : how to see Europe by the skin of your teeth / Ken Welsh. — 8th ed. — London : Pan, 1981. — 304p : ill,maps ; 20cm
Previous ed.: 1979
ISBN 0-330-26275-0 (pbk) : £1.95 B81-20756

914.1 — GREAT BRITAIN

914.1 — Great Britain. Facilities for school parties — *Directories — Serials*

Schools and colleges welcome. — 1981. — Kingston-upon-Thames (31, Castle Street, Kingston upon Thames, Surrey KT1 1ST) : Lewis Publications, c1980. — 99p
ISSN 0260-7581 : Unpriced B81-10266

914.1 — Great Britain. Geographical features — *For schools*

Clare, Roger. Great Britain / Roger Clare. — London : Edward Arnold, 1981. — 32p : ill,maps ; 30cm. — (Meet the world!)
ISBN 0-7131-0486-4 (pbk) : £1.75 B81-15606

Dobinson, Humphrey M.. Around the U.K. / Humphrey M. Dobinson. — Sunbury-on-Thames : Nelson, 1979. — 48p : ill,maps ; 22cm
Cover title
ISBN 0-17-432147-3 (pbk) : £0.70 B81-22168

Gadsby, Jean. Looking at Britain / Jean and David Gadsby. — 4th ed. — London : A and C Black, 1980. — 96p : ill(some col.),1col.chart,maps(some col.),2col.plans ; 26cm. — (Looking at geography ; 3)
Previous ed.: 1970. — Includes index
ISBN 0-7136-1954-6 (cased) : £2.95 : CIP rev.
ISBN 0-7136-1852-3 (pbk) : £1.45(non-net)
B79-25460

Jackson, Nora. The British Isles. — 8th ed. — Littlehampton : Philip, June 1981. — [304]p. — (Groundwork geographies)
Previous ed.: 1978
ISBN 0-540-01065-0 (pbk) : £2.95 : CIP entry
B81-12309

Kirby, D.A.. Geography of Britain : perspectives and problems / D.A. Kirby & H. Robinson. — Slough : University Tutorial, 1981. — ix,320p : ill,maps,1facsim ; 25cm
Includes index
ISBN 0-7231-0810-2 (pbk) : Unpriced
B81-14636

Lines, C. J.. Land and work / authors Clifford Lines, Laurie Bolwell. — London : Macdonald Educational, 1981. — 48p : ill(some col.),col.maps ; 21cm. — (Town and around. Geography)
Cover title. — Text, ill on covers
ISBN 0-356-07188-x (pbk) : Unpriced
B81-29914

Moore, W. G.. Fundamental geography of the British Isles / W.G. Moore. — Amersham : Hulton Educational, 1981. — 208p : ill,charts,maps ; 25cm
Includes index
ISBN 0-7175-0884-6 (pbk) : £2.95 B81-33599

Sauvain, Philip. First elements of geography : the British Isles / Philip A. Sauvain. — Amersham : Hulton Educational, 1980. — 128p : ill(some col.),maps(some col.) ; 25cm
ISBN 0-7175-0858-7 (pbk) : £2.75 B81-13009

Simmons, W. M.. The British Isles : excluding the Republic of Ireland / W.M. Simmons ; assisted by R.T. Way. — 4th ed. — Plymouth : Macdonald and Evans, 1981. — viii,312p : ill,maps ; 22cm. — (The New Certificate geography series)
Previous ed.: 1976. — Includes index
ISBN 0-7121-0285-x (pbk) : £4.95 B81-09593

914.1 — Great Britain. National Trust properties — *Directories*

The **National** Trust atlas. — London : George Philip, Oct.1981. — [224]p
ISBN 0-540-05398-8 : £9.95 : CIP entry
B81-25837

914.1'00142 — Great Britain. Place names. Etymology — *Dictionaries*

Field, John, *1921-*. Place-names of Great Britain and Ireland / John Field. — Newton Abbot : David & Charles, c1980. — 208p : maps ; 22cm
Bibliography: p207-208
ISBN 0-7153-7439-7 : £8.50 : CIP rev.
B79-20498

914.1'003'21 — Great Britain. Castles — *Gazetteers*

Fry, Plantagenet Somerset. The David & Charles book of castles / Plantagenet Somerset Fry ; drawings and plans by Richard Maguire. — Newton Abbot : David & Charles, c1980. — 512p : ill,maps,plans ; 23cm
Bibliography: p493-502. - Includes index
ISBN 0-7153-7976-3 : £10.95 : CIP rev.
B80-18863

914.1'003'21 — Great Britain. Country houses — *Gazetteers*

Burke's and Savills guide to country houses. — London : Burke's Peerage
Vol.2: Herefordshire, Shropshire, Warwickshire, Worcestershire / Peter Reid. — 1980. — x,245p : ill,maps ; 31cm
Maps on lining papers. — Includes index
ISBN 0-85011-031-9 : £19.50
ISBN 0-85011-032-7 (Collectors ed.) : Unpriced
B81-26105

914.1'003'21 — Great Britain. Places associated with Arthur, *King — Gazetteers*

Ashe, Geoffrey. A guidebook to Arthurian Britain / Geoffrey Ashe ; line drawings by Ian Newsham. — London : Longman, 1980. — xix,234p : ill,maps ; 22cm. — (Longman travellers series)
Bibliography: p227-228. - Includes index
ISBN 0-582-50282-9 : £6.95 : CIP rev.
B80-13625

914.1'003'21 — Great Britain. Towns of historical importance — *Gazetteers*

Braithwaite, Lewis. The historic towns of Britain / Lewis Braithwaite. — London : Black, 1981. — 218p : maps ; 21cm
Includes index
ISBN 0-7136-2118-4 : £6.95 B81-16219

914.1'003'21 — Great Britain. Villages — *Gazetteers*

AA book of British villages : a guide to 700 of the most interesting and attractive villages in Britain / [edited and designed by the Reader's Digest Association]. — London : Drive Publications for the Automobile Association, c1980 (1981 [printing]). — 447p : ill(some col.),maps(some col.),col.facsims ; 29cm
£11.95 B81-30017

914.1'04858 — Great Britain. Castles — *Visitors' guides*

Warner, Philip. A guide to castles in Britain : where to find them and what to look for / Philip Warner. — Rev. and enl. — London : New English Library, 1981. — 192p : ill,maps,plans ; 26cm
Previous ed.: 1976. — Ill on lining papers. — Includes index
ISBN 0-450-04833-0 : Unpriced B81-17426

914.1'04858 — Great Britain. Christian holy places. Description & travel

Pepin, David. Discovering shrines and holy places / David Pepin. — Princes Risborough : Shire, 1980. — 80p : ill,maps ; 18cm. — (Discovering series ; no.254)
Includes index
ISBN 0-85263-514-1 (pbk) : £0.95 B81-05819

914.1'04858 — Great Britain. Coastal regions. Walking journeys, *1978 — Personal observations*

Merrill, John N.. Turn right at Land's End / John Merrill. — Harmondsworth : Penguin, 1981, c1979. — 309p : maps ; 18cm
Originally published: Oxford : Oxford Illustrated Press, 1979
ISBN 0-14-005490-1 (pbk) : £1.95 B81-27648

914.1'04858 — Great Britain. Country parks — *Visitors' guides*

Waugh, Mary. The Shell book of country parks / Mary Waugh. — Newton Abbot : David & Charles, c1981. — 224p : ill,maps ; 24cm
Bibliography: p218-219. — Includes index
ISBN 0-7153-7963-1 : £6.95 B81-23442

914.1'04858 — Great Britain. Description & travel

The **British** Isles : a symphony in colour. — New Malden ([80 Coombe Rd.], New Malden, Surrey) : Colour Library International, 1980. — 383p : col.ill,col.maps,col.ports ; 30cm
Ill on lining papers
ISBN 0-906558-50-6 : £15.00 B81-19374

Burton, Anthony. The David & Charles book of curious Britain. — Newton Abbot : David & Charles, Oct.1981. — [304]p
ISBN 0-7153-8083-4 : £6.50 : CIP entry
B81-27972

914.1'04858 — Great Britain. Description & travel — *For non-English speaking students*

Tite, Peter. Going places / Peter Tite. — London : Mary Glasgow, 1979. — 32p : ill,maps,1facsim,ports + teacher's guide(23p; 21cm). — (Project GB ; 9)
ISBN 0-905999-74-6 (pbk) : Unpriced
B81-37628

914.1'04858 — Great Britain. Description & travel - *Personal observations*

Thomas, Leslie, *1931-*. The hidden places of Britain. — London : Arlington, Sept.1981. — [264]p
ISBN 0-85140-542-8 : £9.95 : CIP entry
B81-20097

914.1'04858 — Great Britain. Gardens — *Visitors' guides*

Sanecki, Kay N.. Discovering gardens in Britain / Kay N. Sanecki. — Princes Risborough : Shire, 1979. — 80p : ill ; 18cm. — (Discovering series ; no.56)
Includes index
ISBN 0-85263-456-0 (pbk) : £0.85 B81-29393

914.1'04858 — Great Britain. Islands. Description & travel

Shea, Michael. The Country life book of Britain's offshore islands / Michael Shea. — Richmond upon Thames : Country Life, 1981. — 272p : ill(some col.),maps ; 25cm
Includes index
ISBN 0-600-36766-5 : £10.00 B81-25545

914.1'04858 — Great Britain. Islands — *Visitors' guides*

Booth, David, *1941-*. The Shell book of the islands of Britain / David Booth and David Perrott. — London : Guideway/Windward, 1981. — 192p : ill,col.maps ; 25cm
Includes index
ISBN 0-7112-0087-4 : £7.95 B81-17786

914.1'04858 — Great Britain. Places associated with graphic artists — *Visitors' guides*

Jacobs, Michael, *1952-*. The Phaidon companion to art and artists in the British Isles / Michael Jacobs and Malcolm Warner. — Oxford : Phaidon, 1980. — 320p : ill(some col.),maps,ports(some col.) ; 26cm
Includes index
ISBN 0-7148-1932-8 : £12.95 B81-02427

914.1'04858 — Great Britain. Places associated with writers of English literature. Description & travel

Peel, J. H. B.. People and places / by J.H.B. Peel ; illustrated by Valerie Croker. — London : Hale, 1980. — 188p : ill ; 23cm
ISBN 0-7091-8583-9 : £7.25 B81-03076

914.1'04858 — Great Britain — *Visitors' guides*

1000 days out in Great Britain and Ireland. — London : Macdonald, 1981. — 300,23p of plates : maps(some col.) ; 22cm
'Revised and expanded from material first published in Great Britain in 1980 in The Sunday times book of the countryside'. — Includes index
ISBN 0-354-04679-9 (cased) : Unpriced
ISBN 0-7088-2026-3 (pbk) : £3.95 B81-26243

914.1′04858 — Great Britain — *Visitors′ guides continuation*

The **Best** of Britain and Ireland. — 2nd ed., rev. and updated. — London : Pitman, 1981. — 447p : ill,maps ; 20cm. — (Pitman touring guides)
Previous ed.: published as : Verstappen′s the best of Britain and Ireland, 1979. — Includes index
ISBN 0-273-01608-3 (pbk) : Unpriced B81-11232

Holiday mirror / in association with English Tourist Board ... [et al.] ; [edited by Paul Hughes]. — [London] : [Mirror Books], [1981]. — 28p : ill(some col.) ; 36cm. — (A Daily mirror holiday special)
£0.50 (unbound) B81-35184

Seeing Britain on a budget. — London : Kogan Page, 1981, c1980. — 264p : ill,maps ; 20cm
Includes index
ISBN 0-85038-423-0 (cased) : £5.95
ISBN 0-85038-412-5 (pbk) : £2.95 B81-08173

Village England / edited by Peter Crookston. — London : Hutchinson, 1980. — 256p : col.ill,col.maps ; 27cm
Includes index
ISBN 0-09-142320-1 : £9.95 : CIP rev. B80-13628

Yeadon, David. Hidden corners of Britain / written and illustrated by David Yeadon. — London : Allen and Unwin, 1981. — 300p : ill,maps ; 23cm
Includes index
ISBN 0-04-914059-0 : £9.95 B81-20854

914.1′04858 — Great Britain — *Visitors′ guides — For organised parties*

Coaches and parties welcome. — 1981. — Kingston-upon-Thames (31, Castle St., Kingston-upon-Thames, Surrey KT2 1ST) : Lewis Publications, c1980. — 195p
Unpriced B81-09093

914.1′04858 — Great Britain — *Walkers′ guides*

Marriott, Michael. The footpaths of Britain : a guide to walking in England, Scotland and Wales / Michael Marriott ; foreword by John Hillaby. — London : Queen Anne Press, 1981. — 176p : ill(some col.),maps(some col.) ; 27cm
Bibliography: p174. — Includes index
ISBN 0-362-00544-3 : £8.95 B81-28503

914.1′04858′0247966 — Great Britain — *Visitors′ guides — For cycling*

Gausden, Christa. The CTC route guide to cycling in Britain and Ireland / Christa Gausden and Nicholas Crane. — Harmondsworth : Penguin in association with Oxford Illustrated Press, 1981, c1980. — 431p : ill,maps ; 20cm. — (Penguin handbooks)
Originally published: Oxford : Oxford Illustrated Press, 1980. — Bibliography: p430-431
ISBN 0-14-046421-2 (pbk) : £2.50 B81-27643

914.1′04858′0321 — Great Britain. Description & travel — *Encyclopaedias*

Treasures of Britain and treasures of Ireland / [edited by Drive Publications Limited for the Automobile Association]. — 4th ed. — London : Drive Publications for the Automobile Association, c1980. — 680p : col.ill,col.maps,col.facsims,col.ports ; 29cm
Previous ed.: 1976. — Col.ill on lining papers
£8.95
Also classified at 709′.41 B81-09879

914.1′04858′05 — Great Britain — *Practical information — For foreign students — Serials*

How to live in Britain. — 1981. — London : Evans Brothers in association with the British Council, 1981. — 55p
ISBN 0-237-45581-1 : £0.95 B81-27125

914.1′04858′05 — Great Britain — *Visitors′ guides — For motoring — Serials*

[Guide and handbook *(Royal Automobile Club)*]. Guide and handbook / the Royal Automobile Club. — 1981. — London (83 Pall Mall [SW1Y 5HS]) : R.A.C., c1981. — 624p
ISBN 0-86211-021-1 : £4.25 B81-27917

914.1′04858′05 — Great Britain — *Visitors′ guides — Serials*

Great value Britain. — 1980-. — London : British Tourist Authority ; [Bainbridge Island, Wash] : Heron House [distributor], 1980-. — v. ; 18cm
Annual. — Description based on: 1981
Unpriced B81-20074

914.11 — SCOTLAND

914.11 — Scotland. Dovecots — *Visitors′ guides*

Peterkin, G. A. G.. Scottish dovecotes / G.A.G. Peterkin ; drawings by W.R.A. Logie. — Coupar Angus : Culross, 1980. — vi,65p,[6]p of plates : ill ; 21cm
Bibliography: p25
ISBN 0-900323-42-6 (pbk) : Unpriced B81-05329

914.11 — Scotland. Gardens open to the public — *Directories — Serials*

Scotland′s gardens / [Scotland′s Gardens Scheme]. — 1981. — Edinburgh (26 Castle Terrace, Edinburgh EH1 2EL) : The Scheme, 1981. — 106p
£0.60 B81-24118

914.11 — Scotland. Geographical features — *For schools*

Macgregor, Alan. Looking at Scotland. — London : A. & C. Black, Oct.1981. — [64]p. — (Looking at geography ; 5)
ISBN 0-7136-2143-5 (cased) : £2.95 : CIP entry
ISBN 0-7136-2142-7 (pbk) : £1.95 B81-30465

914.11 — Western Scotland — *Visitors′ guides — Serials*

The **West** of Scotland visitor : a complete tourist guide to the West of Scotland. — No.1 (Summer 1979)-. — [Edinburgh] ([20 North Bridge, Edinburgh EH1 1YT]) : [Scotsman Publications], 1979-. — v. : ill ; 43cm
Annual. — Description based on: No.2 (Summer 1980)
ISSN 0260-4426 = West of Scotland visitor : £0.20 B81-03581

914.11′0473 — Scotland. Description & travel, *1769 — Early works — Facsimiles*

Pennant, Thomas. A tour in Scotland, MDCCLXIX / [Thomas Pennant]. — Perth (176 High St., Perth, Scotland) : Melven Press, 1979. — xiii,388p,[28]leaves of plates : ill,1map,2ports ; 22cm
Facsim. of 3rd ed. Warrington : W. Eyres, 1774. — Bibliography: pix. — Includes index
ISBN 0-9505884-9-0 : £8.95 B81-11234

914.11′0483 — Scotland. Description & travel, *ca 1935 — Personal observations*

Muir, Edwin. Scottish journey / Edwin Muir ; introduction by T.C. Smout. — Edinburgh : Mainstream, 1979. — xx,250p ; 23cm
Originally published: London : Heinemann, 1935
ISBN 0-906391-04-0 : £4.95 B81-09253

914.11′0485 — Scotland. Description & travel, *1950-1980 — Personal observations*

Weir, Tom. Tom Weir′s Scotland. — Edinburgh : Gordon Wright, c1980. — 208p,[32]p of plates
ISBN 0-903065-31-2 : 7.50 B81-02315

914.11′04857 — Scotland, *1970-1979 — Visitors′ guides — For motoring*

Scotland : the Lowlands and Highlands. — Newly rev. ed. / completely revised by Harry Loftus. — London : Letts, [1980]. — 64p : ill,maps ; 22cm. — (Letts tour)
Previous ed.: published as Touring Scotland, the Lowlands and Highlands. 1979. — Includes index
ISBN 0-85097-311-2 (pbk) : £0.75 B81-09268

914.11′04858 — Scotland. Description & travel — *Personal observations*

Anderson, Moira. Moira Anderson′s Scotland / Moira Anderson with Netta Martin. — Guildford : Lutterworth, 1981. — 160p : col.ill,col.ports ; 27cm
Includes index
ISBN 0-7188-2518-7 : £8.95 B81-31119

914.11′04858 — Scotland. Islands — *Visitors′ guides*

Tindall, Jemima. Scottish island hopping : a handbook for the independent traveller / Jemima Tindall. — London : Macdonald, 1981. — 272p : ill,maps ; 24cm. — (Island hopping series)
Includes index
ISBN 0-354-04700-0 : £7.95 B81-18695

914.11′04858 — Scotland. National Trust properties — *Visitors′ guides*

National Trust for Scotland. The National Trust for Scotland guide / compiled and edited by Robin Prentice. — London : Cape, 1981. — 332p : ill(some col.),maps ; 25cm
Previous ed.: i.e. 2nd ed. 1978. — Includes index
ISBN 0-224-01903-1 : £8.50 B81-18990

914.11′04858 — Scotland — *Visitors′ guides*

Scott, Malcolm A.. Where to go, what to do in Scotland / by Malcolm A. Scott ; illustrations by Robert Frost. — 3rd ed. — Tavistock (Merchants House, Barley Market St., Tavistock, Devon) : Heritage in association with New English Library, 1981. — 144p : ill ; 18cm
Previous ed.: 1980. — Includes index
ISBN 0-903975-13-0 (pbk) : £0.90 B81-17830

914.11′04858 — Scotland — *Visitors′ guides — For motoring*

Mead, Robin. Scotland / Robin Mead ; [illustrations by Ed Perera]. — London (83 Pall Mall) : Travellers Realm, 1981. — 128p : ill,maps ; 19cm. — (RAC going places)
Includes index
ISBN 0-86211-003-3 (pbk) : £2.95 B81-22139

914.11′04858 — Scotland — *Walkers′ guides*

Macinnes, David. Walking through Scotland / David & Kathleen Macinnes. — Newton Abbot : David & Charles published in collaboration with The Ramblers′ Association, c1981. — 192p : ill,maps ; 23cm
Bibliography: p186. — Includes index
ISBN 0-7153-8090-7 : £6.50 : CIP rev. B81-00655

914.11′04858′0222 — Scotland. Description & travel — *Illustrations*

Poucher, W. A.. Scotland / W.A. Poucher. — London : Constable, 1980. — 200p : chiefly col.ill ; 27cm
ISBN 0-09-463860-8 : £9.95 B81-01581

This is Scotland / designed and edited by Jenny Carter. — London : Fontana, 1981. — 92p : chiefly col.ill,1col.map ; 31cm
ISBN 0-00-435670-5 (cased) : £4.95
ISBN 0-00-636423-3 (pbk) : Unpriced B81-26674

914.11′04858′0247971 — Scotland. Rivers — *Practical information — For canoeing*

A **Guide** to Scottish rivers / by Scottish Canoe Association. — [Edinburgh] ([18 Ainslie Place, Edinburgh]) : Scottish Canoe Association, 1981. — 25p in various pagings ; 30cm
Unpriced (unbound) B81-26624

914.11′1 — Scotland. Highlands & Western Isles. Description & travel, *1802-1804 — Correspondence, diaries, etc.*

Hogg, James, *1770-1835*. Highland tours : the Ettrick shepherd′s travels in the Scottish Highlands and Western Isles in 1802, 1803 and 1804 / James Hogg ; with an introduction by Sir Walter Scott ; edited by William F. Laughlan. — Hawick (9 Maxton Court, Hawick, Roxburghshire TD9 7QN) : Byways, 1981. — 160p : ill,maps ; 19cm
Includes index
ISBN 0-907448-00-3 (pbk) : £1.95 B81-34700

914.11′104858′05 — Northern Scotland — *Visitors′ guides — Serials*

The **North** of Scotland visitor : a complete tourist guide to the North of Scotland. — No.1 (Summer 1980)-. — Edinburgh (20 North Bridge, Edinburgh EH1 1YT) : Scotland Publications, 1980-. — v. : ill ; 43cm
Annual
ISSN 0260-2415 = North of Scotland visitor : £0.20 B81-07375

914.11'32 — Scotland. Orkney. Scapa Flow. Germany. *Kriegsmarine.* Warships. Underwater salvage

George, S. C.. Jutland to junkyard : the raising of the scuttled German High Seas Fleet from Scapa Flow — the greatest salvage operation of all time / by S. C. George. — Edinburgh : Harris, 1981. — 176p : ill,map,plans,ports ; 23cm
Originally published: Cambridge : Stephens, 1973. — Ill on lining papers. — Bibliography: p173. — Includes index
ISBN 0-86228-029-x : £7.95 B81-34369

914.11'3204858 — Scotland. Orkney. Antiquities — *Visitors' guides*

Points, G. A.. A concise guide to historic Orkney / by G.A. Points. — Byfleet (Flat 4, The Beeches, High Rd., Byfleet, Surrey) : GAP Publications, 1981. — 16p : ill,maps ; 21cm
Unpriced (pbk) B81-28900

914.11'3204858 — Scotland. Orkney — *Visitors' guides*

Thomson, Gordon. The other Orkney book : a complete pocket guide to the Orkney Islands : with remarks on their physical peculiarities, history, productions, commerce & customs : and gazetteers describing principal archaeological sites, historic monuments, towns, islands, amenities &c., &c., : also a glossary of place-names with their meanings / by Gordon Thomson ; illustrated by Ethel Walker. — Edinburgh : Northabout, 1980. — 110p : ill,maps,1facsim ; 21cm
Bibliography: p89
ISBN 0-907200-00-1 (pbk) : £1.60 B81-34344

914.11'4 — Scotland. Western Isles. Barra & Vatersay — *Visitors' guides*

Charnley, Robert. Barra and Vatersay : a traveller's guide / by Robert Charnley. — [Castlebay] ([Castlebay, Isle of Barra]) : Hebridean Enterprises, c1981. — 40p,[4]p of plates : ill(some col.),maps ; 21cm
Bibliography: p35
ISBN 0-907440-00-2 (pbk) : £0.90 B81-11399

914.11'504858 — Scotland. Highlands. Description & travel

The **Heart** of the Highlands. — Norwich : Jarrold Colour, c1981. — 16p : col.ill,2maps ; 25cm
Cover title. — Maps on inside covers
ISBN 0-85306-959-x (pbk) : Unpriced B81-21895

914.11'65 — Scotland. Highland Region. Golspie. Country houses: Dunrobin Castle — *Visitors' guides*

Dunrobin castle : seat of the Countess of Sutherland / foreword by the Countess of Sutherland. — [Derby] : Pilgrim, c1981. — 16p : ill(some col.),coat of arms,ports,1geneal.table ; 24cm
Ill on inside covers
ISBN 0-900594-61-6 (pbk) : £0.60 B81-32742

914.11'75 — Scotland. Highland Region. Inverness — *Visitors' guides*

Inverness : the Highland capital. — [Inverness] ([23 Church St., Inverness]) : [Published for Inverness District Council by Inverness, Loch Ness and Nairn Tourist Organisation], [1980?]. — 63p : ill(some col.),1col.map,1col.coat of arms,1col.facsim ; 21cm
Cover title. — Map on inside cover
Unpriced (pbk) B81-11753

914.11'75 — Scotland. Highland Region. Strathdearn, *to 1945*

Grant, I. F.. Along a highland road / I.F. Grant. — London : Shepheard-Walwyn, 1980. — 198p : ill,maps,ports ; 25cm
Includes index
ISBN 0-85683-048-8 : £6.95 B81-02975

914.11'82 — Scotland. Highland Region. Skye — *Walkers' guides*

Poucher, W. A.. The magic of Skye / W.A. Poucher ; with 152 photographs by the author. — New ed. — London : Constable, 1980. — 291p : ill,maps ; 18cm
Previous ed.: London : Chapman and Hall, 1949. — Maps on lining papers. — Includes index
ISBN 0-09-463770-9 : £5.95 B81-01732

914.12 — North-eastern Scotland. Description & travel

Peck, Edward H.. North-east Scotland. — Edinburgh : Bartholomew, May 1981. — [200]p
ISBN 0-7028-8021-3 : £8.95 : CIP entry B81-04251

914.12'104858 — Scotland. Grampian Region. Description & travel

Graham, Cuthbert. Portrait of Aberdeen and Deeside : with Aberdeenshire, Banff and Kincardine / Cuthbert Graham. — 2nd ed. — London : Hale, 1980. — 240p,[24]p of plates : ill,3maps ; 23cm
Previous ed.: 1972. — Bibliography: p231-234. — Includes index
ISBN 0-7091-8578-2 : £6.95 B81-01907

914.12'104858'05 — Scotland. Grampian Region — *Visitors' guides — Serials*

[Grampian Region *(Tourist guide)*]. Grampian Region. — 1976-. — Aberdeen (Woodhill House, Ashgrove Rd West, Aberdeen AB9 2LU) : Department of Leisure, Recreation and Tourism, Grampian Regional Council, 1976-. — v. : ill,maps ; 30cm
Annual. — Description based on: 1980 issue
ISSN 0144-6797 = Grampian Region : Unpriced B81-09094

[Grampian Region *(Tourist guide)*]. Grampian Region : Scotland's North East. — 1981. — Aberdeen (Woodhill House, Ashgrove Rd., West, Aberdeen AB9 2LU) : Department of Leisure, Recreation and Tourism, Grampian Regional Council, 1981. — 20p
ISSN 0144-6797 : Unpriced B81-09095

914.12'23 — Scotland. Grampian Region. Elgin. Abbeys: Pluscarden Abbey — *Visitors' guides*

Skinner, Basil C.. Pluscarden Abbey, near Elgin, Moray, Scotland : the story of a XIIIth century monastery — and of how Benedictines of the XXth century returned to restore it / [text by Basil C. Skinner]. — Derby : Pilgrim, c1981. — [24]p : ill(some col.),2maps,1coat of arms,1col.plan
Ill on inside covers
ISBN 0-900594-54-3 : £0.40 B81-16439

914.12'2504858 — Scotland. Grampian Region. Banff and Buchan *(District)* — *Visitors' guides*

Banff and Buchan : official guide. — Gloucester : British Publishing, [1981?]. — 100p : ill(some col.),2maps(1col.) ; 21cm
ISBN 0-7140-1886-4 (pbk) : Unpriced B81-28737

914.12'32 — Scotland. Grampian Region. Ellon. Country houses: Haddo House — *Visitors' guides*

Gordon, Archie, *Marquess of Aberdeen and Temair.* A guide to Haddo House / by Archie Gordon, 5th Marquess of Aberdeen. — [Edinburgh] ([5 Charlotte Sq., Edinburgh EH2 4DU]) : National Trust for Scotland, c1981. — 31p : col.ill,1map,col.ports,1geneal.table ; 21cm
Ill on inside covers
Unpriced (pbk) B81-33682

Haddo House and Country Park, Ellon. — Aberdeen ([Woodhill House, Ashgrove Rd. West, Aberdeen]) : Grampian Regional Council, Department of Leisure, Recreation and Tourism in conjunction with the National Trust for Scotland (North East), [1981]. — 1folded sheet : ill ; 21x39cm folded to 21x10cm
Unpriced B81-31666

National Trust for Scotland. A souvenir of Haddo House. — New enl. ed. / original written by Cosmo Gordon of Ellon and brought up to date by David, 4th Marquess of Aberdeen with an appreciation of the 4th Marquess by Robin Barbour. — Edinburgh : National Trust for Scotland, 1979. — 25p : ill,1port ; 21cm
Previous ed.: 1958. — "A tour of the house" (folder : 6p) as insert
Unpriced (pbk) B81-22166

914.12'32 — Scotland. Grampian Region. Pitmedden. Gardens: Great Garden of Pitmedden — *Visitors' guides*

The **Great** garden of Pitmedden : and its environs. — [Edinburgh] (5 Charlotte Square, Edinburgh EH2 4DU) : National Trust for Scotland, c1981. — [24]p : ill,col.plans ; 22x15cm
Unpriced (pbk) B81-24164

914.12'35 — Scotland. Grampian Region. Peterculter. Castles: Drum Castle — *Visitors' guides*

National Trust for Scotland. Drum Castle : Aberdeenshire / historical text written by Cuthbert Graham ; tour text by David Learmont ; colour photography by Martin Johnston. — [Edinburgh] (Charlotte Square, Edinburgh EH2 4DU) : National Trust for Scotland, c1977 (1981 [printing]). — [28]p : ill (some col.),1coat of arms ; 21cm. — (Guidebook / National Trust for Scotland)
Ill on inside covers
Unpriced (pbk) B81-24167

914.12'3504858 — Scotland. Grampian Region. Aberdeen — *Visitors' guides*

Aberdeen : city for lovers. — [Aberdeen] ([St. Nicholas House, Aberdeen, AB9 1DE]) : [City of Aberdeen, Department of Development & Tourism], [1981]. — 32p : col.ill,col.maps,1port ; 30cm. — (City of Aberdeen tourist guide ; v.8, 1981)
£0.25 (pbk) B81-16998

914.12'4 — Scotland. Grampian Region. Kincardine and Deeside *(District).* Castles: Balmoral Castle — *Visitors' guides*

Balmoral Castle. — Derby : Pilgrim, c1981. — 24p : ill(some col.),1col.map,ports(some col.) ; 24cm
Ill on inside covers
ISBN 0-900594-56-x (pbk) : £0.60 B81-32746

914.12'404858 — Scotland. Grampian Region. Kincardine and Deeside *(District)* — *Visitors' guides*

Kincardine and Deeside District official guide. — Gloucester : British Publishing, 1980. — 64p : ill,1 map ; 21cm
Unpriced (pbk) B81-07954

914.12'504858 — Scotland. Tayside Region — *Visitors' guides*

Tayside : all the life and legend of Scotland : a comprehensive guide to Angus, Dundee, Perth and Kinross districts. How to get there, what to see, where to stay and what to do. — [Dundee] : [Department of Recreation and Tourism, Tayside Regional Council], [1980?]. — 23,xxvii p : ill(some col.),2col.maps ; 30cm
Unpriced (pbk) B81-32365

914.12'8 — Scotland. Tayside Region. Glen Lyon. Description & travel

Wheater, Hilary. Aberfeldy to Glenlyon / by Hilary Wheater ; illustrations by Ferelith Malteno ; cartography by Richard Wheater. — Aberfeldy ([Donafuil Farm] Aberfeldy PH15 2LE) : Appin, c1981. — 45p : ill,1map,1facsim ; 22cm. — (A Guide in hand)
Map on inside cover
ISBN 0-907452-01-9 (pbk) : Unpriced B81-25413

914.12'8 — Scotland. Tayside Region. Kindrogan Hill. History trails — *Walkers' guides*

Kindrogan in Victorian times : an instructive and invigorating walk in picturesque surroundings. — Blairgowrie (Kindrogan Field Centre, Enochdu, Blairgowrie, Perthshire [PH10 7PG]) : Scottish Field Studies Association, [1978]. — [16]p : ill,2maps ; 15x22cm
Cover title. — Text, ill on insided cover
Unpriced (pbk) B81-09578

914.12'8 — Scotland. Tayside Region. Kinross region — *Visitors' guides*

A **Historical** guide to the county of Kinross : tours around some places of historical interest in the shire / edited by Nancy H. Walker ; illustrated by Andrew Thorburn. — Kincross (3 Springfield Rd., Kincross KY13 7BA) : Kincross-shire Antiquarian Society, 1980. — 42p : ill,maps ; 21cm
Bibliography: p42
£1.00 (pbk) B81-09368

914.12′8 — Scotland. Tayside Region. Perth. Street names

What's in a name : a survey of Perth street names / compiled by pupils of Primary VII of Caledonian Road School. — Perth : Perth Civic Trust, [1979]. — 32p : ill ; 22cm
Unpriced (pbk) B81-09342

914.12′90946 — Scotland. Fife Region. Beaches. Geographical aspects

Ritchie, W. The beaches of Fife / commissioned by the Countryside Commission for Scotland, 1978 ; W. Ritchie. — Aberdeen : Department of Geography, University of Aberdeen, 1979. — 92p,[48]p of plates : ill,maps(some col.) ; 30cm
Bibliography: p91-92
Unpriced (pbk) B81-10677

914.12′95 — Scotland. Fife Region. Tarvit Hill — *Visitors' guides*

Hill of Tarvit : visitor trail / the National Trust for Scotland. — [Edinburgh] ([5 Charlotte Square, Edinburgh EH2 4DU]) : The Trust, [1981]. — 1folded sheet(6p) : ill ; 22cm
Unpriced B81-24165

914.12′98 — Scotland. Fife Region. Culross — *Visitors' guides*

National Trust for Scotland. Culross : a short guide to the Royal Burgh / Phil Sked. — Edinburgh : National Trust for Scotland, [1981?]. — 19p : ill(some col.),1col.map ; 21cm
Ill on covers
Unpriced (pbk) B81-36741

914.13′04858 — South-east Scotland — *Walkers' guides*

Smith, Sydney, *1907-*. East of Scotland rambles / Sydney Smith. — Glasgow : Molendinar, 1979. — 128p : maps ; 16cm
Includes index
ISBN 0-904002-29-2 (pbk) : £1.50 B81-08530

914.13′12 — Scotland. Central Region. Trossachs — *Visitors' guides*

Guide to Callander, Trossachs and the Rob Roy Country. — [3rd ed.]. — Callander ([Cross St. Printing Works, Callander, Perthshire, FK17 8EA]) : Fleming, [1981?]. — 68p : ill(some col.),2maps ; 20cm
Previous ed.: 1976
£0.40 (pbk) B81-33259

914.13′204858 — Scotland. Lothian Region — *Visitors' guide*

A guide to Lothian region. — Glouester : British Publishing Co. for Lothian Regional Council, [1981?]. — 116p : ill(some col.),maps(some col.),1port ; 30cm
ISBN 0-7140-1934-8 (pbk) : Unpriced B81-28730

914.13′3 — Scotland. Lothian Region. Livingston — *Visitors' guides*

Livingstone town guide. — London : Burrow, [1980?]. — 72p : ill(some col.),1col.map ; 21cm
£0.75 (pbk) B81-23625

914.13′4 — Edinburgh. Castles: Edinburgh Castle — *Visitors' guides*

Edinburgh Castle. — Carrbridge : Landmark Press, [1980?]. — 31p : ill(some col.),col.coats of arms,facsims,ports(some col.) ; 22cm. — (A Landmark guide)
Cover title. — Text, ill on inside covers
£0.85 (pbk) B81-32337

914.13′40485 — Edinburgh. Description & travel, *1950-1980 — Personal observations*

Jones, Ken, *1927-*. With gold and honey blest : Edinburgh in autumn / Ken Jones ; illustrated by William Inglis. — Peterhead (Peterhead, Scotland) : Volturna, c1979. — xiii,214p,[27]p of plates : ill,2maps,ports ; 27cm
Maps on lining papers
ISBN 0-85606-090-9 : £12.50 B81-03126

914.13′404858′0222 — Edinburgh. Description & travel — *Illustrations*

Goodchild, Doris Ann. Edinburgh portraits / [drawn & scribed by Doris Ann Goodchild]. — [Haddington] ([Low Letham, Haddington, E. Lothian]) : [D.A. Goodchild], c1981. — 68p : ill ; 23x19cm
Includes index
ISBN 0-9506561-4-3 (cased) : Unpriced
ISBN 0-9506561-5-1 (pbk) : Unpriced B81-19424

914.13′404858′05 — Edinburgh — *Visitors' guides — For shoppers — Serials*

Shopping in Edinburgh. — 1981-. — Edinburgh (7 Royal Terrace, Edinburgh EH7 5AB) : Pastime Publications in association with the Edinburgh Chamber of Commerce, 1981-. — v. : ill,maps ; 22cm
Annual. — Continues: Shopping guide (Edinburgh Chamber of Commerce & Manufactures)
ISSN 0261-5517 = Shopping in Edinburgh : £0.70 B81-30870

914.13′404858′05 — Edinburgh — *Visitors' guides — Serials*

Edinburgh civic handbook / prepared by the Department of Public Relations and Tourism. — 1980/81. — [Edinburgh?] : Burrow (Scotland), [1980?]. — 128p B81-06484

914.13′6 — Scotland. Lothian Region. Haddington. Country houses: Lennoxlove — *Visitors' guides*

Lennoxlove : home of the Duke of Hamilton and Brandon. — Derby : Pilgrim Press, c1981. — 16p : ill(some col.),1map,ports,2geneal.tables ; 24cm
Cover title. — Port, geneal. table on inside cover
ISBN 0-900594-55-1 (pbk) : £0.50 B81-25899

914.13′7 — Great Britain. Solway Firth region — *Visitors' guides*

Wood, M. A.. Exploring the Solway / by M.A. Wood. — Clapham [N. Yorkshire] : Dalesman, 1981. — 64p : ill,maps ; 19cm. — (A Dalesman mini-book)
ISBN 0-85206-631-7 (pbk) : £1.10 B81-22924

914.13′704858′05 — Scotland. Borders Region — *Visitors' guides — Serials*

The **Borders** visitor : a complete tourist guide to the Borders. — No.1 (Summer 1980)-. — Edinburgh (20 North Bridge, Edinburgh EH1 1YT) : Scotsman Publications, 1980-. — v. : ill,maps ; 43cm
Annual
ISSN 0260-4442 = Borders visitor : £0.20 per issue B81-07374

The **Scottish** Borders. — 1980-. — [Newtown St. Boswells] ([Newtown St. Boswells, Roxburghshire]) : [Borders Regional Council, Tourism Division], 1980-. — v. : ill ; 21cm
Annual. — Continues: Where to stay in the Scottish Borders. — Description based on: 1981 issue
ISSN 0262-0707 = Scottish Borders : Unpriced B81-38195

914.13′8204858 — Scotland. Borders Region. Tweeddale *(District) — Visitors' guides*

Official guide / Tweeddale District Council. — [Peebles] ([District Offices, Rosetta Rd., Peebles EH45 8HG]) : [The Council], [1981]. — 80p : ill,2maps ; 19cm
Unpriced (pbk) B81-34899

914.13′85 — Scotland. Borders Region. Selkirk. Country houses: Bowhill — *Visitors' guides*

Bowhill, Selkirk, Scotland : border home of the Duke of Buccleuch and Queensberry, K.T.. — Derby : Pilgrim Press, c1981. — 24p : ill(some col.),1map,ports,1geneal.table ; 24cm
Ill, geneal.table on inside cover
ISBN 0-900594-58-6 (pbk) : £0.50 B81-25575

914.13′9204858 — Scotland. Borders Region. Roxburgh *(District) — Visitors' guides*

Roxburgh official guide. — Gloucester : British Publishing, c1980. — 76p : ill(some col.),1col.map,1port ; 21cm
Unpriced (pbk) B81-07967

914.14′2504858 — Scotland. Strathclyde Region. Dumbarton *(District) — Visitors' guides*

Osborne, Brian D.. Discovering Dumbarton district : places of interest to see and visit / Brian D. Osborne & Michael C. Taylor. — Dumbarton (Levenford House, Helenslee Rd., Dumbarton G82 2AH) : Dumbarton District Libraries, 1981. — 32p : ill ; 21cm
ISBN 0-906927-06-4 (pbk) : £1.00 B81-30687

914.14′3604858 — Scotland. Strathclyde Region. Strathkelvin *(District) — Visitors' guides*

Strathkelvin official guide. — [London] : [Burrow], [1980]. — 96p : ill,1map,1coat of arms,ports ; 19cm
Unpriced (pbk) B81-09907

914.14′3804858 — Scotland. Strathclyde Region. Cumbernauld and Kileyth *(District) — Visitors' guides*

Cumberland and Kilsyth official guide. — London : Burrow, [1979]. — 56p : ill(some col.),1coat of arms,1port ; 25cm
Unpriced (pbk) B81-09908

914.14′4104858 — Scotland. Strathclyde Region. Renfrew *(District) — Visitors' guides*

Renfrew District Council : an official guide. — Gloucester : British Publishing, [1981?]. — 136p : ill(some col.),maps,1col.coat of arms,1port ; 25cm
ISBN 0-7140-1874-0 (pbk) : Unpriced B81-11773

914.14′4904858 — Scotland. Strathclyde Region. Motherwell *(District) — Visitors' guides*

Motherwell District official guide : published with the co-operation of Motherwell District Council. — London : Burrow, [1981?]. — 84p : ill,2maps,1coat of arms,1port ; 21cm
Unpriced (pbk) B81-35013

914.14′5404858 — Scotland. Strathclyde Region. East Kilbride *(District) — Visitors' guides — Serials*

The **Official** guide to East Kilbride. — 6th ed.. — London : Burrow, [1979]. — 100p
Unpriced B81-10258

914.14′6104858 — Scotland. Strathclyde Region. Cuninghame *(District).* **Buildings of historical importance —** *Visitors' guides*

The **Cunninghame** heritage. — London : Burrow, [1980?]. — 56p : ill ; 19cm
£0.75 (pbk) B81-23633

914.14′83 — Scotland. Dumfries and Galloway Region. Ecclefechan. Houses: Arched House — *Visitors' guides*

National Trust for Scotland. Thomas Carlyle's 1795-1881 birthplace Ecclefechan : a guide to the Arched House / the National Trust for Scotland. — [Edinburgh] (5 Charlotte Square, Edinburgh EH2 4DU) : The Trust, [1981]. — 1folded sheet(6p) : ill ; 22cm
Unpriced B81-24166

914.15 — IRELAND

914.15′0481 — Ireland. Description & travel, *1804 — Personal observations*

[Journal of a tour in Ireland ... in August 1804]. Ireland in 1804 / [edited] with an introducation by Seamus Grimes. — Dublin (3 Serpentine Ave., Dublin 4) : Four Courts Press, 1980. — 68p : ill,2maps ; 22cm
Originally published: London : R. Phillips, 1806. — Map (folded sheet) attached to back cover
£5.00 B81-04173

914.15′04822 — Ireland. Description & travel, *ca 1935 — Personal observations*

Praeger, Robert Lloyd. The way that I went : an Irishman in Ireland / Robert Lloyd Praeger. — 3rd ed. — Dublin : Figgins, 1947 (1980 [printing]). — xiii,394p,[1],xxxviii leaves of plates : ill,maps,plans,1port ; 21cm
One map as insert. — Includes index
ISBN 0-900372-93-1 (pbk) : Unpriced B81-05289

914.15′04824 — Ireland. Antiquities, *to ca 1200 — Visitors′ guides*
Weir, Anthony. Early Ireland : a field guide / Anthony Weir. — Belfast : Blackstaff, c1980. — 245p : ill,maps ; 21cm
Includes index
ISBN 0-85640-212-5 (pbk) : £7.95 : CIP rev. B80-23854

914.15′04824 — Ireland. Description & travel
Gardiner, Leslie. The love of Ireland / by Leslie Gardiner. — London : Octopus, 1981. — 76p : col.ill,maps,ports ; 33cm
Ill on lining papers. — Includes index
ISBN 0-7064-1505-1 : £3.95 B81-34736

Sheehy, Terence J.. Ireland / by Terence J. Sheehy ; foreword by William MacQuitty. — [New Malden] : Colour Library International, 1979. — 192p : col.ill ; 31cm
ISBN 0-904681-90-4 : £5.95 B81-14333

Veber, May. Ireland observed / May Veber ; translated from the French by Jean Joss. — London : Kaye & Ward, 1980. — 131p : ill (some col.),1map,ports ; 27cm
Translation of: Voir l′Irlande. — Includes index
ISBN 0-7182-1006-9 : £9.50 B81-01823

914.16′0025 — Northern Ireland — *Directories — Serials*
Belfast and Northern Ireland directory / compiled ... by Century Services Limited. — 99th ed. (1980). — Belfast (51 Donegall St., Belfast BT1 2GB) : Century Services Ltd, 1980. — 848p
£25.00 B81-29106

914.16′04824′0222 — Northern Ireland. Description & travel — *Illustrations*
McNally, Kenneth. Ulster rich & rare / text and photographs by Kenneth McNally. — Belfast : Ulster Television, c1980. — 96p : chiefly ill (some col.) ; 20cm
ISBN 0-903152-13-4 (pbk) : Unpriced B81-20964

914.16′1304824 — Ballymena *(District) — Visitors′ guides*
Ballymena official guide. — Wallington : Home Publishing, [1981]. — 55p : ill(some col.),1map ; 21cm
Unpriced (pbk) B81-26642

914.16′1704824 — Carrickfergus *(District) — Visitors′ guides*
Carrickfergus. *Borough Council*. Borough of Carrickfergus : official guide / issued by authority of the Carrickfergus Borough Council. — Wallington : Home Publishing, [1981]. — 64p : ill(some col.),2maps,1coat of arms ; 21cm
Unpriced (pbk) B81-39011

914.16′1904824 — Lisburn *(District) — Visitors′ guides*
The **Borough** of Lisburn official guide. — Wallington : Home Publishing, [1980]. — 88p : ill(some col.),1map,coat of arms ; 21cm
Unpriced (pbk) B81-07968

914.16′5304824 — North Down *(District) — Visitors′ guides*
Borough of North Down : official guide. — Wallington (Falcon House, 20-22 Belmont Rd., Wallington, Surrey, SM6 8TA) : Home, [1981]. — 72p : ill(some col.),1coat of arms, 1map ; 21cm
Unpriced (pbk) B81-21106

914.16′5704824 — Banbridge *(District) — Visitors′ guides*
Banbridge District : official guide. — Wallington : Home Publishing, [1980]. — 68p : ill(some col.),2maps ; 21cm
Unpriced (pbk) B81-07969

914.16′6404824 — Craigavon *(District) — Visitors′ guides*
Craigavon Borough : official guide. — Wallington : Home Publishing, [1981?]. — 76p : ill(some col.),1col.coat of arms,map ; 21cm
Unpriced (pbk) B81-28864

914.17 — Ireland *(Republic)*. **Midland region. Description & travel**
The **Midlands** : Longford, Cavan, Laois, Westmeath, Roscommon, Monaghan, Offaly / [edited by Leo Daly, assisted by Tom Kennedy and Gearoid O′Brien]. — Dublin (5 Henrietta St., Dublin) : Alberrie Kennedy, 1979. — 71p : ill,1map,ports ; 30cm
Cover title
Unpriced (pbk) B81-30648

914.17′04824 — Ireland *(Republic)*. **Literary associations** — *Visitors′ guides*
Cahill, Susan. A literary guide to Ireland / Susan and Thomas Cahill. — Portmarnock (98 Ardilaun, Portmarnock, County Dublin) : Wolfhound, 1979, c1973. — xv,333p : ill,1map ; 21cm
Originally published: New York : Scribner, 1973. — Bibliography: p319-324. - Includes index
ISBN 0-905473-35-3 (cased) : £8.50
ISBN 0-905473-36-1 (pbk) : Unpriced B81-07412

914.17′04824 — Ireland *(Republic) — Practical information*
Facts about Ireland. — Dublin ([80 St Stephen′s Green, Dublin 2]) : Department of Foreign Affairs, 1978. — 258p : ill,col.maps,1col.coat of arms, music,facsims(some col.),ports(some col.) ; 20cm
Bibliography: p245-255
ISBN 0-906404-00-2 (pbk) : Unpriced B81-03805

914.18′22 — Meath *(County)*. **Brugh na Boinne. Neolithic passage graves: Newgrange** — *Visitors′ guides*
O′Kelly, Claire. Illustrated guide to Newgrange and other Boyne monuments / Claire O′Kelly. — 3rd ed. revised, further enlarged and reset. — Blackrock (Ardnalee, Blackrock, Cork) : C. O′Kelly, 1978. — 139p,32p of plates : ill,1map,plans ; 22cm
Previous ed.: 1971. — Bibliography: p133-135 — Includes index
ISBN 0-9506267-0-8 (pbk) : £3.10 B81-25544

914.18′25 — Louth *(County)*. **Newtown Monasterboice. Monasteries: Monasterboice** *(Monastery) — Visitors′ guides*
Roe, Helen M.. Monasterboice and its monuments / Helen M. Roe. — Dundalk (5, Oliver Plunkett Park, Dundalk) : County Louth Archaeological and Historical Society, 1981. — 78p : ill,plans ; 21cm
£1.65 (pbk) B81-35516

914.18′350481 — Dublin, *1825 — Visitors′ guides — Facsimiles*
Wright, G. N.. An historical guide to the City of Dublin / G.N. Wright. — Dublin (3 Serpentine Ave., Dublin 4) : Four Courts Press ; Kill-o′-the-Grange : Irish Academic Press, 1980. — xxxv,260p,[14] leaves of plates : ill ; 21cm
Facsim of: 2nd edition published London : Baldwin, Cradock and Joy, 1825. — Includes index B81-04162

914.19′4 — Limerick *(County)*. **Lough Gur region. Antiquities** — *Visitors′ guides*
O′Kelly, M. J.. Illustrated guide to Lough Gur Co. Limerick / M.J. & C. O′Kelly. — Blackrock (Ardnalee, Blackrock, Cork) : Claire O′Kelly, 1978. — 44p,[4]p of plates : ill,1map ; 21cm
Bibliography: p43-44
Unpriced (pbk) B81-24922

914.19′604824 — Kerry *(County)*. **Coastal regions. Description & travel** — *Personal observations*
Feehan, John M.. The magic of the Kerry Coast / John M. Feehan. — Cork : Mercier, c1979. — 122p ; 18cm
ISBN 0-85342-584-1 (pbk) : £1.80 B81-05697

914.2 — ENGLAND

914.2 — England. Gardens open to the public — *Directories*
Gardens to visit / the Gardeners′ Sunday Organisation. — 1980. — [Dorking] ([Gardeners′ Sunday, White Witches, Claygate Rd, Dorking, Surrey]) : The Organisation, [1980]. — 72p
£0.30 B81-00656

914.2 — England. Gardens open to the public — *Directories — Serials*
Gardens open to the public in England and Wales . — 1981. — London : National Gardens Scheme, 1981. — xvi,160p
ISBN 0-900558-13-x : £0.70
ISSN 0141-2361 B81-20080

Gardens to visit / [the Gardeners′ Sunday Organisation]. — 1981. — [Dorking] : The Organisation, [1981]. — 80p
£0.35 B81-20434

914.2′0014 — England. Place names. Pronunciation, *1875-1980 — Dictionaries*
Forster, Klaus. A pronouncing dictionary of English place-names : including standard local and archaic variants / Klaus Forster. — London : Routledge & Kegan Paul, 1981. — xxxvi,268p ; 22cm
Bibliography: pxiii-xxxvi
ISBN 0-7100-0756-6 : £9.50 B81-16448

914.2′003′21 — England. Prehistoric antiquities — *Gazetteers*
Dyer, James. The Penguin guide to prehistoric England and Wales / James Dyer. — London : Allen Lane, 1981. — 384p,[16]p of plates : ill,maps,plans ; 23cm
Bibliography: p363-366. — Includes index
ISBN 0-7139-1164-6 (corrected) : £9.50 B81-29019

914.2′0472 — England. Description & travel, *1738-1791 — Correspondence, diaries, etc*
Wesley, John. John Wesley′s England : a 19th-century pictorial history based on an 18th-century journal / compiled by Richard Bewes. — London : Hodder and Stoughton, 1981. — [124]p : ill,1map,coat of arms,ports ; 21x28cm
ISBN 0-340-25843-8 (cased) : £8.95 : CIP rev.
ISBN 0-340-25747-4 (pbk) : £5.95
Also classified at 287′.092′4 B80-20031

914.2′0481 — England. Description & travel, *1872-1901 — Personal observations*
Jones, Henry, *1843-1916*. English hours / Henry James ; with an introduction by Leon Edel. — Oxford : Oxford University Press, 1981. — xvi,192p ; 20cm
Originally published: Boston, Mass. : Houghton Mifflin ; London : Heinemann, 1905. — Includes index
ISBN 0-19-281321-8 (pbk) : £1.95 B81-35328

914.2′0481′0924 — England. Visits by Turgenev, I. S.
Waddington, Patrick. Turgenev and England / Patrick Waddington. — London : Macmillan, 1980. — x,382p,16p of plates : ill,facsims,ports ; 23cm
Bibliography: p308-346. - Includes index
ISBN 0-333-22072-2 : £20.00 : CIP rev. B80-14074

914.2′04857 — England. Description & travel — *Personal observations*
West, Richard. An English journey. — London : Chatto & Windus, Sept.1981. — [224]p
ISBN 0-7011-2584-5 : £7.95 : CIP entry B81-23844

914.2′04858 — England. Abbeys & cathedrals — *Visitors′ guides*
Thurlow, Gilbert. Cathedrals and abbeys of England / [written by Gilbert Thurlow]. — Norwich : Jarrold & Sons, c1981. — [32]p : ill (some col.),1plan,1col.port ; 25cm. — (Jarrold Cotman house series)
Text, ill on inside covers
ISBN 0-85306-934-4 (pbk) : Unpriced B81-13366

914.2′04858 — England. Country houses — *Visitors′ guides*
Burton, Neil. The historic houses handbook / Neil Burton. — London : Macmillan, 1981. — xxix,639p : ill,maps,plans ; 21cm
Includes index
ISBN 0-333-27254-4 (cased) : £12.00 B81-23016

914.2'04858 — England. Shrines. Description & travel

Purcell, William. Pilgrim's England : a personal journey / William Purcell ; line drawings by Trevor Stubley. — London : Longman, 1981. — xvi,190p : ill,1map,facsims ; 22cm. — (Longman travellers series)
Bibliography: p185-186. — Includes index
ISBN 0-582-50290-x : £8.50 B81-38266

914.2'04858 — England — *Visitors' guides*

Tingey, Frederick. [Letts go to England & Wales]. England & Wales / main text by Frederick Tingey ; some points worth considering by Harold Dennis-Jones. — London : Letts, 1979 (1981 [printing]). — 96p : ill,maps ; 19cm. — (Letts guide)
ISBN 0-85097-340-6 (pbk) : £1.25 B81-08548

914.2'04858 — England — *Visitors' guides — For bus travel*

Gundrey, Elizabeth. England by bus / Elizabeth Gundrey. — Feltham : Hamlyn Paperbacks, 1981. — 221p : ill,maps ; 20cm
ISBN 0 600 20253 4 (pbk) : £1.25 B81-22710

914.21 — London. Canals — *Visitors' guides*

Pratt, Derek. Discovering London's canals / Derek Pratt. — 2nd ed. — Aylesbury : Shire, 1981. — 56p : ill,maps ; 18cm. — (Discovering series ; no.232)
Previous ed.: 1977. — Bibliography: p54-55. - Includes index
ISBN 0-85263-552-4 (pbk) : £0.95 B81-17424

914.21 — London. Celebrities. Houses — *Visitors' guides*

Carter, Kathy. London and the famous : an historical guide to fifty famous people and their London homes. — London : Frederick Muller, Jan.1982. — [160]p
ISBN 0-584-95005-5 (cased) : £5.95 : CIP entry
ISBN 0-584-95006-3 (pbk) : £3.95 B81-34288

914.21 — London. Cemeteries — *Visitors' guides*

Meller, Hugh. London cemeteries. — Amersham : Avebury Publishing, Dec.1981. — [250]p
ISBN 0-86127-003-7 (cased) : £14.95 : CIP entry
ISBN 0-86127-004-5 (pbk) : £7.95 B81-31644

914.21'0025 — London — *Directories — Serials*

Kelly's Post Office London directory. — 182nd ed. (1981). — East Grinstead : Kelly's Directories, 1981. — 2360p
ISBN 0-610-00538-3 : Unpriced B81-16751

914.21'04858 — Central London. Churchyards — *Visitors' guides*

Hackman, Harvey. Wates's book of London churchyards : a guide to the old churchyards and burial-grounds of the City and Central London / Harvey Hackman. — London : Collins, 1981. — 144p,[24]p of plates : ill ; 23cm
ISBN 0-00-216313-6 (pbk) : £5.00 B81-06755

914.21'04858 — Central London — *Walkers' guides*

Milton, Marc. Frank Cook's strolling through London / [written by Marc Milton]. — [Chislehurst] ([8 Wykeham Court, Old Perry St., Chislehurst, Kent BR7 6PN]) : [Frank Cook Travel Guides], [c1981]. — 96p : ill,col.maps ; 18cm
Includes index
ISBN 0-9506503-1-5 (pbk) : £1.75 B81-34799

914.21'04858 — London. Description & travel

Clayton, Robert. Portrait of London / Robert Clayton. — London : Hale, 1980. — 288p,[32]p of plates : ill,maps ; 23cm
Includes index
ISBN 0-7091-8360-7 : £7.95 B81-01939

Shute, Nerina. More London villages / Nerina Shute. — London : Hale, 1981. — 192p,[16]p of plates : ill,maps,ports ; 23cm
Includes bibliographies and index
ISBN 0-7091-8355-0 : £6.50 B81-07719

914.21'04858 — London. Night life — *Visitors' guides*

Levey, Paula. Dancing in London / Paula Levey. — London : New English Library, 1981. — xii,161p ; 18cm
ISBN 0-450-05213-3 (pbk) : £1.50 B81-26147

914.21'04858 — London. Parks — *Walkers' guides*

Wittich, John. Discovering London's parks and squares / John Wittich. — Aylesbury : Shire, 1981. — 64p : maps ; 18cm. — (Discovering series ; no.259)
Includes index
ISBN 0-85263-550-8 (pbk) : £1.25 B81-40745

914.21'04858 — London — *Practical information*

Rothmans concise guide to London / [editor George Hammond]. — Aylesbury (PO Box 100, Oxford Rd., Aylesbury, Bucks.) : Rothmans Publications, 1981. — 304p : ill (some col.),col. maps ; 22cm
ISBN 0-907574-00-9 (pbk) : £4.50 B81-26883

914.21'04858 — London — *Visitors' guides*

Alternative London 6. — London : Wildwood House, Aug.1981. — [256]p
ISBN 0-7045-0427-8 (pbk) : £2.95 : CIP entry B81-20574

Britain, quick guide to London. — [1981]. — London : British Tourist Authority, c1981. — 48p
ISBN 0-7095-0602-3 : Unpriced B81-09696

Colourful London. — Norwich : Jarrold, c1981. — [64]p : col.ill,1map,col.ports ; 29cm
Map, text on inside covers. — Includes index
ISBN 0-85306-979-4 (pbk) : Unpriced B81-37866

London : a pictorial guide. — Huntingdon : Photo Precision, [1981]. — 64p : chiefly col.ill,col.maps,2col.ports ; 24cm. — (Colourmaster international)
Text on inside cover
ISBN 0-85933-202-0 (pbk) : Unpriced B81-29305

Piper, David. London : an illustrated companion guide / David Piper. — London : Collins, 1980. — 286p : ill(some col),maps,ports(some col.) ; 26cm
Abridged from Companion guide to London. 6th ed., 1977. — Bibliography: p271-272. — Includes index
ISBN 0-00-216287-3 : £9.95 B81-01367

Powell, Anton. Discovering London. — London : Ward Lock, Apr.1981. — [96]p
ISBN 0-7063-6099-0 : £2.95 : CIP entry B81-00657

Twort, David. London / [revised by David Twort and Gabrielle Varro]. — London : Octopus, 1980. — 176p : maps ; 10x21cm. — (Guide in jeans)
Translation of: Guide de Londres en jeans
ISBN 0-7064-1464-0 (pbk) : Unpriced B81-16174

914.21'04858 — London — *Visitors' guides — For industrial development*

London's new deal. — London : Greater London Council, [1981?]. — [20]p : col.ill,2col.maps ; 30cm
Cover title. — Ill on inside covers
ISBN 0-7168-1164-2 (pbk) : Unpriced B81-34881

914.21'04858 — London — *Visitors' guides — For motoring*

RAC motorists' London : and 60 miles around. — Croydon (Box 92, RAC House, Lansdowne Rd., Croydon, CR9 6HN) : Travellers Realm, 1981. — 216p : ill,maps(some col.) ; 18cm
Includes index
ISBN 0-86211-017-3 (pbk) : £2.95 B81-34920

914.21'04858 — London — *Walkers' guides*

Borer, Mary Cathcart. London walks and legends / Mary Cathcart Borer. — London : Granada, 1981. — 224p : ill,maps ; 18cm. — (A Mayflower book)
ISBN 0-583-13308-8 (pbk) : £1.25 B81-22280

Fletcher, Geoffrey. London at my feet / Geoffrey Fletcher. — [London] : The Daily Telegraph, 1980. — 76p : ill ; 20cm
ISBN 0-901684-57-0 (pbk) : £1.85 B81-08262

Pilton, Barry. Miles of London / Barry Pilton ; researched by Sybil Harper ; foreword by Bernard Miles ; illustrations by Sue Scullard ; decorative maps by Sarah Dunkin. — London : Macdonald Futura, 1981. — 91p : ill,maps ; 22cm
ISBN 0-354-04652-7 : £4.95 B81-29673

Williams, Guy R.. London walks / Guy Williams. — London : Constable, 1981. — 283p : ill,maps ; 18cm
Includes index
ISBN 0-09-462740-1 : £5.50 B81-23069

914.21'04858'024388 — London — *Practical information — Serials — For taxi driving*

Taxi drivers compendia. — 1980. — London (184 Gloucester Place, NW1) : Britannic Publicity & Publications, [1980?]. — 160p
Unpriced B81-20079

914.21'04858'05 — London — *Visitors' guides — German texts — Serials*

London rund um die Uhr. — [1981-1982]-. — London (36 Walpole St., SW3 4QS) : Canal Publications, 1981-. — v. : ill(some col.),maps,plans,ports ; 22cm
Annual. — Also published in English and Spanish editions
ISSN 0262-0359 = London rund um die Uhr : £3.50 B81-36548

914.21'04858'05 — London — *Visitors' guides — Serials*

London round the clock. — 1981-1982-. — London (36 Walpole St., SW3 4QS) : Canal Publications, 1981-. — v. : ill(some col.),maps,plans,ports ; 22cm
Annual. — Also published in German and Spanish editions
ISSN 0262-0472 = London round the clock : £3.50 B81-36546

914.21'04858'05 — London — *Visitors' guides — Spanish texts — Serials*

Londres dia y noche. — 1981-1982-. — London ([36 Walpole St., SW3 4QS]) : Canal Publications, 1981-. — v. : ill(some col.),maps,plans,ports ; 22cm
Annual. — Also published in English and German editions
ISSN 0262-0480 = Londres dia y noche : £3.50 B81-36547

914.21'2 — London *(City)*. **Cathedrals: St. Paul's Cathedral** *(London) — Visitors' guides*

St. Paul's Cathedral : a guide / prepared by the Cathedral. — [Norwich] : [Jarrold Colour], c1980. — [28]p : col.ill,1col.plan,col.ports ; 25cm
Also published : in Italian and Spanish
ISBN 0-85306-889-5 (unbound) : Unpriced B81-17416

914.21'2 — London *(City)*. **Cathedrals: St. Paul's Cathedral** *(London) — Visitors' guides — Italian texts*

La Cattedrale di San Paolo : una guida / presenta dalla Cattedrale. — [Norwich] : [Jarrold Colour], c1981. — [28]p : col.ill,1col.plan,col.ports ; 25cm
Also published : in English and Spanish
ISBN 0-85306-932-8 (unbound) : Unpriced B81-17417

914.21'2 — London *(City)*. **Cathedrals: St. Paul's Cathedral** *(London) — Visitors' guides — Spanish texts*

La Catedral de San Pablo : una guia / preparada por la Catedral. — [Norwich] : [Jarrold Colour], c1981. — [28]p : col.ill,1col.plan,col.ports ; 25cm
Also published: in English and Italian
ISBN 0-85306-930-1 (unbound) : Unpriced B81-17418

914.21′2′0025 — London *(City) — Directories — Serials*
City of London directory & livery companies guide. — 1981. — Colchester : City of London Weekly, [1981?]. — 372p
ISBN 0-901129-19-4 : Unpriced
ISSN 0142-5072 B81-09127

914.21′204858 — London *(City) — Visitors′ guides*
Visitors′ guide to the City of London. — [London] : [Burrow], [1981]. — 104p,[2]p of plates : ill,col.maps,1coat of arms ; 19cm
Cover title
£0.50 (pbk) B81-23622

914.21′32 — London. Westminster *(London Borough).* **Parish churches: St John′s Church,** *Hyde Park Crescent, London — Visitor′s guides*
Wittich, John. St John′s Church, Hyde Park Crescent, London W.2 : a guide to the church and the parish / by John Wittich. — Watford : Woodmansterne, 1980. — 16p : ill,1map,1plan ; 21cm
Map, plan on inside covers
ISBN 0-906472-14-8 (pbk) : £0.50 B81-06230

914.21′34 — London. Kensington and Chelsea *(London Borough).* **Palaces: Kensington Palace. State apartments** *— Visitors′ guides*
Hedley, Olwen. Kensington Palace : the State Apartments / [Olwen Hedley]. — London : Pitkin Pictorials, c1976. — 24p : col.ill,1plan,col.ports ; 23cm
Plan on inside cover
ISBN 0-85372-205-6 (pbk) : Unpriced B81-37142

914.21′42 — London. Camden *(London Borough).* **Houses: Fenton House** *— Visitors′ guides*
National Trust. Fenton House, Hampstead. — Rev. — [London] : National Trust, 1981. — 29p,8p of plates : ill,plans ; 22cm
Previous ed.: 1978
Unpriced (pbk) B81-22306

914.21′43 — London. Islington *(London Borough).* **Clerkenwell** *— Walkers′ guides*
Cosh, Mary. An historical walk through Clerkenwell / by Mary Cosh. — London (Central Library, 2 Fieldway Cres., N5 1PF) : Islington Libraries, c1980. — 34p,[1]folded leaf of plates : ill,maps,1plan ; 22cm
Bibliography: p34
ISBN 0-902260-07-3 (pbk) : £0.85 B81-17644

914.21′4304858′05 — London. Islington *(London Borough) — Practical information — For businessmen — Serials*
Business partner. — Jan.1981-. — [London] (Borough Employment Office, Islington, 227 Essex Rd, N1 3PW]) : Hackney & Islington Councils, 1981-. — v. : ill,ports ; 30cm
Five issues yearly
ISSN 0261-3328 = Business partner (corrected) : Unpriced
Also classified at 914.21′4404858′05
B81-32240

914.21′4404858′05 — London. Hackney *(London Borough) — Practical information — For businessmen — Serials*
Business partner. — Jan.1981-. — [London] (Borough Employment Office, Islington, 227 Essex Rd, N1 3PW]) : Hackney & Islington Councils, 1981-. — v. : ill,ports ; 30cm
Five issues yearly
ISSN 0261-3328 = Business partner (corrected) : Unpriced
Primary classification 914.21′4304858′05
B81-32240

914.21′62 — London. Greenwich *(London Borough).* **Eltham. Description & travel**
Looking into Eltham. — London (c/o 22 Larchwood Rd., S.E.9) : Eltham Society, c1980. — 64p : ill,1map,1plan,ports ; 21cm
Includes index
Unpriced (pbk) B81-05302

914.21′6204858 — London. Greenwich *(London Borough) — Visitors′ guides*
London Borough of Greenwich : official guide. — London : Burrow, [1981?]. — 56p : ill(some col.),1col.coat of arms,ports ; 25cm
Unpriced (pbk) B81-35003

London Borough of Greenwich : official guide. — London : Pubished by authority of the London Borough of Greenwich [by] Burrow, [1981]. — 56p : ill(some col.),1coat of arms ; 25cm
£1.25 (pbk) B81-39142

914.21′6304858′05 — London. Lewisham *(London Borough) — Visitors′ guides — Serials*
Lewisham official guide / produced by the Public Relations Division. — 1980/81. — London : Burrow, [1981?]. — 56p
Unpriced B81-09157

914.21′65 — London. Lambeth *(London Borough).* **Parish churches: Church of St. Mary-at-Lambeth** *— Visitors′ guides*
A **Guide** to the history, architecture and current proposals for the Church of St Mary-at-Lambeth, London / edited by Francis Terry for the Vauxhall Society in association with the Tradescant Trust. — London (20 Albert) : Published by the Vauxhall Society in association with the Tradescant Trust, 1980. — 20p : ill,1plan,ports ; 21cm
Bibliography: p15
Unpriced (pbk) B81-24921

914.21′704858 — London. Outer London *— Visitors′ guides*
Jenkins, Simon, *1943-.* The companion guide to outer London / Simon Jenkins. — London : Collins, 1981. — 237p,[24]p of plates : ill,maps,ports ; 22cm. — (The Companion guides)
Maps on lining papers. — Includes index
ISBN 0-00-216186-9 : £8.50 : CIP rev.
B81-05150

914.21′7804858 — London. Bromley *(London Borough) — Visitors′ guides*
The **London** Borough of Bromley : offical guide. — Gloucester : British Publishing Co., [1980]. — 112p : ill(some col.),maps,2coats of arms ; 21cm
Maps (folded sheet) attached to inside back cover
ISBN 0-7140-1869-4 (pbk) : £0.60 B81-26297

914.21′7804858 — London. Bromley *(London Borough) — Walkers′ guides*
Daniell, Philip A.. An afternoon out : in and around Bromley / by Philip Daniell. — London (300 Baring Rd., SE12) : Environment Bromley, [1981]. — [16]p : ill,maps ; 21cm
Cover title
£0.30 (pbk) B81-18669

914.21′82 — London. Hounslow *(London Borough).* **Hanworth. Parish churches: St. George′s Church** *(Hanworth) — Visitors′ guides*
Cameron, Andrea, *1939-.* St George′s Church, Hanworth : a history and guide / by Andrea Cameron. — Heston (16 Orchard Ave., Heston, Middx) : Hounslow and District History Society, 1981. — 29p : ill,1map ; 21cm
£0.60 (pbk) B81-36078

914.21′8504858 — London. Brent *(London Borough) — Visitors′ guides*
Official guide to Brent Borough : its industry and commerce. — London : Published with the co-operation of Brent London Borough Council [by] Burrow, c1981. — 84p : ill(some col.),1coat of arms ; 22cm
£2.00 (pbk) B81-39143

914.21′8804858 — London. Haringey *(London Borough) — Visitors′ guides*
Haringey : official guide. — London : Burrow, [1980]. — 44p : ill,1col.map ; 25cm
Unpriced (pbk) B81-09901

914.21′9104858′05 — London. Croydon *(London Borough) — Visitors′ guides — Serials*
Croydon official guide. — 1981-2. — Gloucester : British Publishing Company, [1981]. — 96p
ISBN 0-7140-1922-4 : Unpriced B81-30740

914.21′9204858 — London. Sutton *(London Borough) — Visitors′ guides*
The **London** Borough of Sutton : official guide. — Wallington : Home Publishing, [1981?]. — 100p : ill(some col.) ; 24cm
Includes index
Unpriced (pbk) B81-23628

914.21′9504858′05 — London. Richmond upon Thames *(London Borough) — Visitors′ guides — Serials*
Richmond guide : Chamber of Commerce yearbook. — [No.1]-. — [Richmond, Surrey] (c/o Geoffrey Mowbray Ltd, 21 Brighton Rd, South Croydon, Surrey CR2 6UL) : Richmond Chamber of Commerce, [1977]-. — v. : ill,coats of arms,maps,ports ; 22cm
Annual. — Continues: Richmond (Surrey) Chamber of Commerce yearbook. — No issue published for 1978. — Description based on: 1981 issue
ISSN 0261-3778 = Richmond guide : £0.30
B81-27919

914.22 — Central Southern England *— Visitors′ guides — For motoring*
Mason, John, *1914-.* Southern England : Hampshire, Isle of Wight, Surrey / John Mason. — [London] ([83 Pall Mall, SW1Y 5HW]) : Travellers Realm, 1981. — 128p : ill,maps ; 19cm. — (RAC going places ; 6)
Includes index
ISBN 0-86211-007-6 (pbk) : £2.95 B81-21184

914.22 — Central Southern England *— Visitors′ guides — Serials*
Where to go, what to do in the South. — 1981 ed. — Tavistock (Merchants House, Barley Market St., Tavistock, Devon) : Heritage Publications in association with New English Library-Times Mirror, c1981. — 127p
ISBN 0-903975-03-3 : £0.90 B81-21949

914.22 — South-east England. Trackways: Pilgrim′s Way *— Walkers′ guides — Early works*
Cartwright, Julia. The Pilgrim′s Way from Winchester to Canterbury. — London : Wildwood House, Feb.1982. — [168]p. — (Rediscovery)
Originally published: London : Virtue, 1893
ISBN 0-7045-0453-7 (pbk) : £3.50 : CIP entry
B81-36973

914.22 — Southern England. Long-distance footpaths: Ridgeway *— Walkers′ guides*
Burden, Vera. Discovering the Ridgeway / Vera Burden with contributions by James Dyer, A.C. Fraser and Stuart Harrison. — [New] ed. — Aylesbury : Shire, 1981. — 48p : ill,maps ; 18cm. — (Discovering series ; no.211)
Previous ed.: 1978. — Includes index
ISBN 0-85263-558-3 (pbk) : £0.95 B81-40749

914.22′04858 — England. Home Counties. Long-distance footpaths: London Countryway *— Walkers′ guides*
Chesterton, Keith. A guide to the London countryway / Keith Chesterton. — 2nd ed. — London : Constable, 1981, c1978. — 280p : ill,maps ; 18cm
Previous ed.: 1978. — Includes index
ISBN 0-09-461740-6 : £5.50 B81-22254

914.22′04858 — England. Thames River region. Description & travel *— Visitors′ guides — For motoring*
Metcalfe, Leon. Discovering the Thames : a motorist′s guide to the best view points and the most interesting features / Leon Metcalfe. — 2nd ed. — Aylesbury : Shire, 1981. — 53p : ill,maps ; 18cm. — (Discovering series ; no.47)
Previous ed.: 1969. — Includes index
ISBN 0-85263-566-4 (pbk) : £1.25 B81-40746

914.22′04858 — England. Thames River *— Visitors′ guides*
Prichard, Mari. A Thames companion / Mari Prichard & Humphrey Carpenter. — 2nd ed. — Oxford : Oxford University Press, 1981. — xxiv,182p : ill,3maps,ports ; 20cm
Previous ed.: Oxford : Oxford Illustrated Press, 1975. — Includes index
ISBN 0-19-285099-7 : £3.95 : CIP rev.
B81-01368

914.22′04858 — South-east England *— Visitors′ guides — For motoring*
Straker, J. F.. Southeast England : Kent, Sussex / J.F. Straker. — [London] ([83 Pall Mall, SW1Y 4HW]) : Travellers Realm, 1981. — 128p : ill,maps ; 19cm. — (RAC going places ; 1)
Includes index
ISBN 0-86211-002-5 (pbk) : £2.95 B81-21185

914.22′04858 — South-east England — *Walkers′ guides*

Gerard-Pearse, Peter. The drinkers′ guide to walking : London and the South East / [researched, walked, photographed, compiled and written by Peter Gerard-Pearse and Nigel Matheson]. — New York ; London : Proteus, 1981. — 158p : ill,maps ; 23cm
ISBN 0-906071-74-7 (cased) : £5.50
ISBN 0-906071-73-9 (pbk) : £3.50
Primary classification 647′.95422 B81-34927

914.22′04858′05 — South-east England — *Visitors′ guides — Serials*

Where to go, what to do in the South-East. — 1981 ed. — Tavistock (Merchants House, Barley Market St., Tavistock, Devon) : Heritage Publications in association with New English Library-Times Mirror, c1981. — 144p
ISBN 0-903975-08-4 : £0.90 B81-21948

914.22′104858 — Surrey — *Visitors′ guides*

Surrey county guide. — Gloucester : British Publishing Co., [1980]. — 104p : ill(some col.),maps(some col.) ; 24cm
Map (folded sheet) attached to lining paper
ISBN 0-7140-1890-2 (pbk) : £0.75 B81-26289

914.22′14204858 — Surrey. Woking — *Visitors′ guides — Serials*

[Official guide ... *(Borough of Woking)*]. Official guide ... / Borough of Woking. — 1980/81-. — Gloucester : British Pub. Company, 1980-. — v. : ill,maps ; 25cm
Every two years. — Continues: Woking
ISSN 0260-4574 = Official guide — Borough of Woking : Unpriced B81-02815

914.22′165 — Surrey. Great Bookham. Country houses: Polesden Lacey — *Visitors′ guides*

National Trust. Polesden Lacey : Surrey / [The National Trust]. — London : The Trust, c1979 ([1981 printing]). — 34p,[8]p of plates : ill,1col.map,1col.plan,1port ; 25cm
Ill on inside cover. — Bibliography: p34
Unpriced (pbk) B81-34546

914.22′1704858 — Surrey. Reigate and Banstead *(District)* — *Visitors guides*

Borough of Reigate and Banstead : official guide / issued by authority of the Reigate and Banstead Borough Council. — Wallington : Home Publishing, [1981]. — 92p : ill(some col.),coat of arms ; 21cm
Unpriced (pbk) B81-39002

914.22′19 — Surrey. Godalming — *Visitors′ guides*

Godalming : official guide. — Wallington : Forward Publicity, [1981]. — 26p,[2]p of plates (folded sheet) : ill,1map ; 21cm
Unpriced (pbk) B81-10704

914.22′304858 — Kent. Description & travel

Church, Richard. Kent. — London : Hale, 1948 (1981 [printing]). — viii,289p,[49]p of plates : ill,1map ; 23cm
Includes index
ISBN 0-7091-2550-x : £7.50 B81-18388

914.22′36 — Kent. Westerham. Houses: Quebec House — *Visitors′ guides*

National Trust. Quebec House : Kent. — [London] : National Trust, 1979, c1978. — 14p,[4]p of plates : ill,2ports ; 22cm
£0.40 (pbk) B81-19804

National Trust. Quebec House : Kent. — [London] : The Trust, 1981, c1978. — 14p,[4]p of plates : 2ill,2ports ; 22cm
Unpriced (pbk) B81-18750

914.22′3604858 — Kent. Sevenoaks *(District)* — *Visitors′ guides*

Sevenoaks district council official guide. — Gloucester : British Publishing Co. for the Sevenoaks District Council, [1981]. — 56p : ill (some col.),1 col.map ; 21cm
ISBN 0-7140-1946-1 (pbk) : £0.60 B81-26288

914.22′37504858 — Kent. Maidstone *(District)* — *Visitors′ guides*

Maidstone official guide. — Gloucester : Published for the Borough Council by British Publishing, 1980. — 132p : ill(some col.),maps (some col.), 1col.coat of arms,1col.plan ; 21cm
English text, French and German sections
ISBN 0-7140-1923-2 (pbk) : Unpriced B81-13188

914.22′38 — Kent. Lamberhurst. Castles: Scotney Castle — *Visitors′ guides*

National Trust. Scotney Castle, Kent. — [London] : National Trust, 1979 (1981 [printing]). — 27p : ill ; 22cm
Unpriced (pbk) B81-22953

914.22′392 — Kent. Small Hythe. Houses: Smallhythe Place — *Visitors′ guides*

National Trust. Ellen Terry′s house : Smallhythe Tenterden, Kent / [The National Trust]. — Rev. — [London] : The Trust, 1981, c1979. — 12p,[4]p of plates : 2ill,1ports,1geneal.table ; 21cm
Unpriced (pbk) B81-34548

914.22′39204858 — Kent. Ashford *(District)* — *Visitors′ guides*

Ashford Borough official guide. — Wallington : Home Publishing, [1980]. — 104p : ill(some col.),2maps,coat of arms ; 21cm
Unpriced (pbk) B81-07957

914.22′395 — Kent. Romney Marsh — *Visitors′ guides*

Godwin, Fay. Romney Marsh / photographs by Fay Godwin ; written by Richard Ingrams. — London : Wildwood House, 1980. — 192p : ill,maps,ports ; 21cm
Bibliography: p189. - Includes index
ISBN 0-7045-3039-2 : £6.95 B81-04520

914.22′504858 — East & West Sussex. Description & travel

Woodford, Cecile. Portait of Sussex / Cecile Woodford ; photographs by Patricia and Lawrence Stevens. — 2nd ed. — London : Hale, 1981. — 224p,[24]p of plates : ill,1map ; 23cm
Previous ed.: 1972. — Includes index
ISBN 0-7091-8979-6 : £6.95 B81-10852

914.22′504858 — East & West Sussex — *Visitors′ guides*

Lowther, Kenneth E.. Sussex : the resorts and villages of East and West Sussex / Kenneth Lowther and Reginald Hammond. — London : Ward Lock, 1981. — 192p : ill,maps ; 18cm. — (Ward Lock′s red guides)
Includes index
ISBN 0-7063-5901-1 (cased) : Unpriced
ISBN 0-7063-5902-x (pbk) : £2.95 B81-27120

914.22′51 — East Sussex. Forest Row — *Visitors′ guides*

Forest Row : official guide. — Wallington : Forward Publicity, [1981]. — 24p,leaf of plates (folded sheet) : ill,1col.map ; 19cm
Unpriced (pbk) B81-13287

914.22′51 — East Sussex. Hailsham — *Visitors′ guides*

Hailsham, Sussex : official guide. — Wallington : Forward Publicity, [1981]. — 36p,[2]p of plates (folded sheet) : ill,1map,2ports ; 19cm
Unpriced (pbk) B81-10703

914.22′57 — East Sussex. Peacehaven — *Visitors′ guides*

Peacehaven : official town guide. — Wallington : Forward Publicity, [1981]. — 28p : ill,plan ; 21cm
Unpriced (pbk) B81-15572

914.22′57 — East Sussex. Seaford — *Visitors′ guides*

Seaford : official guide. — Gloucester : British Publishing, [1981?]. — 72p,[2]p of fold.plates : ill,2maps ; 12x19cm
Cover title
ISBN 0-7140-1978-x (pbk) : £0.20 B81-27731

914.22′6′00723 — East & West Sussex. South Downs. Geography. Field studies. Sites — *For teaching*

Allen, C.M.J.. Brighton and the Downs : (the area of sheet 198 of the O.S. 1:50 000 map series) / by C.M.J. Allen. — Sheffield : Geographical Association, c1981. — 35p ; 21cm. — (Fieldwork location guides ; no.1)
Text on inside covers. — Bibliography: p33-35
ISBN 0-900395-67-2 (pbk) : Unpriced B81-27584

914.22′60481 — East & West Sussex. South Downs. Description & travel, *1899-1900 — Personal observations*

Hudson, W. H.. Nature in downland / W.H. Hudson. — London : Macdonald Futura, 1981. — x,243p ; 18cm. — (Heritage)
Originally published: London : Dent, 1923. — Includes index
ISBN 0-7088-2071-9 (pbk) : £1.60 B81-33206

914.22′62 — West Sussex. Petworth. Country houses: Petworth House — *Visitors′ guides*

National Trust. Petworth House : West Sussex. — Rev. — [London] : National Trust, 1981, c1978. — 47p,[12]p of plates : ill,1plan,1port,1geneal.table ; 25cm
Bibliography: p47
Unpriced (pbk) B81-18425

914.22′62 — West Sussex. South Harting. Country houses: Uppark — *Visitors′ guides*

National Trust. Uppark, Sussex. — Rev. — [London] : National Trust, 1981. — 45p,[4]p of plates : ill,plans,1port ; 22cm
Previous ed.: i.e. New ed. 1976. — Plans on inside covers
Unpriced (pbk) B81-22305

914.22′64 — West Sussex. Pulborough. Country houses: Parham Park — *Visitors′ guides*

Tritton, P. A.. Parham : Pulborough, West Sussex / [text by P.A. Tritton] ; [photography by D.W. Gardiner]. — Derby : English Life Publications, c1981. — 28p : ill(some col.),ports(some col.),geneal.table ; 20cm
Cover title. — Port, genealogical tables on inside cover
ISBN 0-85101-178-0 (pbk) : £0.75 B81-24468

914.22′65 — West Sussex. Burgess Hill — *Visitors′ guides*

Burgess Hill : official guide. — Wallington : Forward Publicity, [1981?]. — 35p : ill,2maps,1col.coat of arms ; 21cm
Map (folded sheet) attached to inside back cover. — Includes index
Unpriced (pbk) B81-23624

914.22′65 — West Sussex. East Grinstead. Buildings of historical importance — *Walkers′ guides*

East Grinstead town trail. — East Grinstead (c/o Barclays Bank, East Grinstead, [West Sussex RH19 3AH]) : East Grinstead Society, c1978 (1980 printing). — 1sheet ; 43x30cm folded to 22x15cm : ill,1map
£0.20 B81-33567

914.22′65 — West Sussex. East Grinstead — *Visitors′ guides*

Leppard, M. J.. East Grinstead official guide. — 3rd ed. / text by M.J. Leppard, N.H. Collins. — London : Burrow, 1981. — 36p : ill,1map,1coat of arms ; 19cm
Previous ed.: 1976
£0.75 (pbk) B81-23632

914.22′65 — West Sussex. Hassocks — *Visitors′ guides*

Hassocks, West Sussex : official guide. — Wallington : Forward Publicity, [1981]. — 24p : ill,1map ; 19cm
Unpriced (pbk) B81-23621

914.22′67 — West Sussex. Bognor Regis — *Visitors′ guides*

Bognor Regis : a brief guide to places of interest. — Bognor Regis (c/o Hon. Sec., 4 Gainsborough Rd., Bognor Regis, PO21 2HT) : Bognor Regis Local History Society, 1981. — 14p : ill,1map ; 21cm
ISBN 0-9507455-0-2 (unbound) : Unpriced B81-22982

914.22'71 — Hampshire. Whitchurch, *ca 1900 — Walkers' guides*

Hawkes, Bea. A walk round old Whitchurch / Bea Hawkes. — Andover (Apollo House, Station Approach, Andover, Hants.) : Figuredene in association with Sunrise Wessex Co., c1981. — 20p,[8]p of plates : ill,1port ; 21cm
ISBN 0-906147-10-7 (pbk) : £0.80 B81-28719

914.22'723 — Hampshire. Hawley — *Visitors' guides*

Hawley parish guide & information handbook. — London : Burrow, [1981]. — 24p : ill,1map ; 19cm
Unpriced (pbk) B81-23623

914.22'732 — Hampshire. Romsey. Country houses: Mottisfont Abbey — *Visitors' guides*

Mottisfont Abbey : Hampshire. — [London] : National Trust, c1978 (1981 [printing]). — 22p[8]p of plates : ill,1facsim,1plan ; 22cm
Bibliography: p22
Unpriced (pbk) B81-26871

914.22'735 — Hampshire. Winchester — *Visitors' guides*

Turner, Barbara Carpenter. City of Winchester : the ancient capital of England / [Barbara Carpenter Turner]. — London : Pitkin Pictorials, c1974. — 24p : ill(some col.),map ; 23cm. — (Pitkin 'Pride of Britain' books)
Map and text on inside covers
ISBN 0-85372-050-9 (pbk) : Unpriced
B81-40767

914.22'7504858 — Hampshire. New Forest — *Walkers' guides*

Edwards, Anne-Marie. The unknown forest : a walker's guide to the New Forest / Anne-Marie Edwards. — Newbury (3 Catherine Rd, Newbury, Berks.) : Countryside Books, 1981. — 95p : maps ; 21cm
Bibliography: p95
ISBN 0-905392-08-6 (pbk) : £2.50 B81-23970

914.22'772 — Hampshire. Hedge End — *Visitors' guides*

Hedge End official guide. — Wallington : Forward Publicity, [1981]. — 20p : ill,1map ; 19cm
Unpriced (pbk) B81-26638

914.22'9304858 — Berkshire. Reading — *Visitors' guides*

Cliffe, David. The stranger in Reading : an unofficial guide / compiled by David Cliffe. — New ed. [expanded and updated]. — [Reading] ([Central Library, Blagrave St., Reading RG1 1QL]) : Reading Libraries, 1980. — 40p : maps ; 21cm
Previous ed.: 1978. — Text on inside cover
ISBN 0-9506044-2-9 (pbk) : £0.90 B81-30686

914.22'94 — Berkshire. Sonning. Description & travel

Conniford, Mike. To Sonning : a book of pen and ink drawings / by Mike Conniford ; with accompanying narrative by Sybil Conniford. — [Caversham] ([12 Westdene Cres., Caversham, Reading RG4 7HD]) : Inkpen Art Productions, c1981. — 12p : ill,1map ; 15x22cm
Cover title. — Text, map on inside covers
ISBN 0-907403-07-7 (pbk) : £1.50 B81-28502

914.22'96 — Berkshire. Windsor. Castles: Windsor Castle — *Visitors' guides*

Innes-Smith, Robert. Windsor Castle / by Robert Innes-Smith ; foreword by Sacheverell Sitwell. — Derby : English Life, c1981. — 24p : ill (some col.),ports ; 28cm
Text, ill on inside cover
ISBN 0-85101-182-9 (pbk) : £0.70 B81-36877

914.22'96 — Berkshire. Windsor — *Visitors' guides*

Royal Windsor. — St. Ives, Cambs. : Photo Precision, [1981]. — 32p : col.ill ; 24cm. — (Colourmaster international)
Text on inside cover
ISBN 0-85933-165-2 (pbk) : Unpriced
B81-40287

914.23 — South-west England. Coastal regions. Seafaring, *1558-1979*

Parker, Derek. The West Country and the sea / Derek Parker ; line drawings by Peter Green. — London : Longman, 1980. — x,246p : ill,maps,facsims,ports ; 22cm
ISBN 0-582-41181-5 : £7.50 : CIP rev.
Primary classification 914.23'04858 B80-21188

914.23'04858 — South-west England. Coastal regions — *Visitors' guides*

Parker, Derek. The West Country and the sea / Derek Parker ; line drawings by Peter Green. — London : Longman, 1980. — x,246p : ill,maps,facsims,ports ; 22cm
ISBN 0-582-41181-5 : £7.50 : CIP rev.
Also classified at 914.23 B80-21188

914.23'04858 — South-west England. Long-distance footpaths — *Walkers' guides*

Proctor, Alan. A Severn to Solent walk / Alan Proctor ; drawings by Dennis Brierley. — Cheltenham : Thornhill, c1981. — xxi,41p : ill,maps ; 19cm
ISBN 0-904110-91-5 (pbk) : £0.95 B81-38080

914.23'04858 — South-west England — *Visitors' guides — For motoring*

Le Messurier, Brian. The West Country. — London : Ward Lock, Dec.1981. — [192]p. — (Regional guides to Britain)
ISBN 0-7063-5893-7 (cased) : £4.95 : CIP entry
ISBN 0-7063-5892-9 (pbk) : £2.50 B81-31648

914.23'04858 — South-west England — *Visitors' guides — For picnicking*

Forde, Nicholas. The West Country picnic book / by Nicholas Forde. — Dulverton : Breakaway, 1981. — 47p : ill ; 20cm
ISBN 0-907506-00-3 (pbk) : £0.75 B81-24082

914.23'04858 — South-west England — *Walkers' guides*

Matheson, Nigel. The drinker's guide to walking : the South West / [researched, walked, photographed, compiled and written by Nigel Matheson and Peter Gerard-Pearse]. — New York ; London : Proteus, 1981. — 159p : ill,maps ; 23cm
ISBN 0-906071-76-3 (cased) : £6.50
ISBN 0-906071-75-5 (pbk) : £3.50
Primary classification 647'.95423 B81-34932

914.23'04858'05 — South-west England — *Visitors' guides — Serials*

On holiday in the west country. — 1981. — London : IPC Magazines, c1981. — 64p
£0.80 B81-34035

West Country holidays. — 1981. — Gloucester : British Pub. Co., [1981?]. — 144p
ISBN 0-7140-1955-0 : £0.40 B81-13701

Where to go, what to do in the South West. — 1981 ed. — Tavistock (Merchants House, Barley Market St., Tavistock, Devon) : Heritage Publications in association with New English Library-Times Mirror, c1981. — 160p
ISBN 0-903975-97-1 : £0.90 B81-21943

914.23'12 — Wiltshire. Calne — *Visitors' guides*

Calne, Wiltshire : official guide. — Gloucester : British Publishing Co., [1981]. — 56p : ill,maps,1coat of arms ; 19cm
Map (folded sheet) attached to back cover
ISBN 0-7140-1965-8 (pbk) : £0.40 B81-26291

914.23'12 — Wiltshire. Corsham — *Visitors' guides*

Corsham, Wiltshire : the official guide. — Gloucester : British Publishing, [1981?]. — 20p : ill,ill,maps ; 19cm
Maps on folded sheet attached to inside cover
ISBN 0-7140-1967-4 (pbk) : Unpriced
B81-28740

914.23'1304858 — Wiltshire. Thamesdown *(District) — Visitors' guides*

Borough of Thamesdown : official guide. — London : Burrow, [1981?]. — 112p : ill(some col.),maps,1col.coat of arms ; 21cm
Unpriced (pbk) B81-35001

914.23'15 — Wiltshire. Bradford-on-Avon. Country houses: Great Chalfield Manor — *Visitors' guides*

National Trust. Great Chalfield Manor : Wiltshire. — [London] : The Trust, 1980. — 18p,[4]p of plates : ill,1plan ; 22cm
Author: Robert Floyd. — Bibliography: p17
Unpriced (pbk) B81-18753

914.23'19 — Wiltshire. Amesbury. Megalithic henge monuments: Stonehenge — *Visitors' guides*

Newall, R. S.. Stonehenge : Wiltshire / by the late R.S. Newall. — 3rd ed. — London : H.M.S.O., 1959 (1981 [printing]). — 34p : ill,plans ; 22cm. — (Ancient monuments and historic buildings) (Official handbook / Department of the Environment)
Plan on folded leaf attached to inside cover
ISBN 0-11-670068-8 (pbk) : £1.00 B81-21247

914.23'19 — Wiltshire. Stourton. Country houses: Stourhead House — *Visitors' guides*

National Trust. Stourhead : Wiltshire : an illustrated souvenir / [The National Trust]. — London : The Trust, c1979 ([1981 printing]). — [24]p : ill(some col.),col.ports ; 23cm
Text: Dudley Dodd
Unpriced (pbk) B81-34543

914.23'3904858 — Dorset. Christchurch *(District) — Visitors' guides*

Christchurch : ' - where time is pleasant' : official borough guide / [compiled and edited by Roger Morris and Wendy Summerhayes]. — Wallington : Home Publishing, [1981]. — 64p : ill,maps,1coat of arms ; 21cm
Unpriced (pbk) B81-21253

914.23'404858 — Channel Islands — *Visitors' guides*

Eadie, Peter McGregor. The Channel Islands / Peter McGregor Eadie ; atlas and maps and plans by John Flower. — London : Benn, 1981. — 154p : ill,maps(some col.) ; 20cm. — (Blue guide)
Includes index
ISBN 0-510-01640-5 (cased) : £8.95
ISBN 0-510-01641-3 (pbk) : £4.95 B81-03990

914.23'41'0025 — Jersey — *Directories — Serials*

Jersey evening post almanac & trade directory. — 1981/82. — St Saviour (Jersey Evening Post, Five Oaks, St Saviour, Jersey, C.I.) : W.E. Guiton, [1981]. — 272,80p
£2.00 B81-30760

914.23'420473 — Guernsey, *ca 1820 — Visitors' guides*

Pictures from early Guernsey books / edited by J. Stevens Cox. — St. Peter Port (Mount Durand, St. Peter Port, Guernsey) : Toucan Press, 1981. — 16p : ill ; 15cm
ISBN 0-85694-249-9 (unbound) : Unpriced
B81-36885

914.23'4204858 — Guernsey — *Visitors' guides*

Guernsey. — [Norwich] : [Jarrold], c1981. — [32]p : col.ill,1map ; 19cm
English text, captions in English and French. — Cover title. — Text and map on inside covers
ISBN 0-85306-962-x (pbk) : Unpriced
B81-19358

914.23'5 — South Devon — *Visitors' guides*

Lowther, Kenneth E.. South Devon : Sidmouth, Exmouth, Dawlish, Teignmouth, Torbay, Dartmouth, Salcombe / Kenneth Lowther and Reginald Hammond. — London : Ward Lock, 1981. — 159p : ill,maps ; 18cm. — (Ward Lock's red guides)
Includes index
ISBN 0-7063-6095-8 (pbk) : £2.95 : CIP rev.
B81-03702

914.23'504857 — Devon, *1970-1979 — Visitors' guides — For motoring*

Devon and Cornwall. — Newly rev. ed. / completely revised by Harry Loftus. — London : Loftus, [1980]. — 64p : ill,maps ; 22cm. — (Letts tour)
Previous ed.: published as Touring Devon and Cornwall. 1980
ISBN 0-85097-310-4 (pbk) : £0.75
Also classified at 914.23'704857 B81-09267

914.23'5'04857 — Devon — *Visitors' guides*
Jellicoe, Ann. Devon : a Shell guide. — London : Faber, Sept.1981. — [180]p
Originally published: 1975
ISBN 0-571-11818-6 : £2.95 : CIP entry
B81-22619

914.23'504858 — Devon — *Visitors' guides*
Devon. — [Exeter] : Devon Tourism Officer, [1981?]. — [20]p : chiefly ill(some col.),2maps (some col.) ; 21cm
Cover title
ISBN 0-86114-292-6 (pbk) : Unpriced
B81-29384

Devon's places of interest. — Exeter ([c/o Local Government Library, Room G53], County Hall, Exeter [EX2 4QB]) : Devon Tourism Office, [1981?]. — 64p : ill,1map ; 21cm
Cover title. — Text on inside covers
ISBN 0-86114-291-8 (pbk) : £0.40 B81-11772

914.23'504858 — Devon — *Visitors' guides* — *Dutch texts*
Devon : voor een geweldige Britse vacantie!. — [Exeter] ([County Hall, Exeter]) : [Devon Tourism Office], [1981?]. — [24]p : ill (some col.),maps (some col.) ; 21cm
Also available in French and German versions
ISBN 0-86114-295-0 (unbound) : Unpriced
B81-31413

914.23'504858 — Devon — *Visitors' guides* — *French texts*
Devon : lieu idéal pour vacances idéales!. — [Exeter] ([County Hall, Exeter]) : [Devon Tourism Office], [1981?]. — [24]p : ill (some col.),maps (some col.) ; 21cm
Also available in German and Dutch versions
ISBN 0-86114-293-4 (unbound) : Unpriced
B81-31411

914.23'504858 — Devon — *Visitors' guides* — *German texts*
Devon : für einmalige Ferien in England!. — [Exeter] ([County Hall, Exeter]) : Devon Tourism Office, [1981?]. — [24]p : ill (some col.),maps (some col.) ; 21cm
Also available in French and Dutch versions
ISBN 0-86114-294-2 (unbound) : Unpriced
B81-31412

914.23'52 — Devon. Braunton — *Visitors' guides*
Ellacott, S. E.. Here is Braunton / by S.E. Ellacott. — South Molton (The Industrial Estate, Cooks Cross, South Molton, N. Devon) : Quest (Western) Publications, [1981?]. — 102p : ill,1map,ports ; 21cm
Map (46x62cm folded to 17x11cm) attached to inside cover
ISBN 0-905297-13-x (pbk) : Unpriced
B81-36419

914.23'530481 — Devon. Dartmoor. Description & travel, *ca 1900* — *Personal observations*
Baring-Gould, S.. A book of Dartmoor. — London : Wildwood House, Feb.1982. — [304] p. — (Rediscovery)
Originally published: London : Methuen, 1900
ISBN 0-7045-0465-0 (pbk) : £3.95 : CIP entry
B81-36972

914.23'53'0483 — Devon. Dartmoor - *Visitors' guides - Early works - Facsimiles*
Crossing, William. Crossing's guide to Dartmoor. — Newton Abbott : David & Charles, Apr.1981. — [530]p
Originally published: 1965. - Facsim. of: 2nd ed. of Guide to Dartmoor. Plymouth : Western Morning News, 1912
ISBN 0-7153-4034-4 : £4.95 : CIP entry
B81-08926

914.23'55 — Devon. Newton Abbot — *Visitors' guides*
Official guide to Newton Abbot : the ideal centre. — Gloucester : British Publishing for Newton Abbot Town Council, [1981]. — 220p + 1folded sheet : ill(some col.),coats of arms,1facsim ; 17cm
Street map and index to street plan of Newton Abbot (1folded sheet) as insert
ISBN 0-7140-1963-1 (pbk) : Unpriced
B81-24965

914.23'5504858 — Devon. Teign River region. Description & travel — *Personal observations*
Chard, Judy. Along the Teign / Judy Chard. — Bodmin : Bossiney, 1981. — 104p : ill,maps,ports ; 21cm
Text on inside cover
ISBN 0-906456-55-x (pbk) : £1.75 B81-36839

914.23'56 — Devon. Exeter. Cathedrals: Exeter Cathedral — *Visitors' guides*
Exeter Cathedral. — London : Pitkin Pictorials, c1981. — 24p : ill(some col.),1plan ; 23cm. — (Pitkin 'Pride of Britain' books)
Plan and text on inside covers
ISBN 0-85372-087-8 (pbk) : Unpriced
B81-37335

914.23'56'0025 — Devon. Exeter — *Directories* — *Serials*
Bray's Exeter street directory. — 1981-82 ed.-. — [Exmouth] ([209 Exeter Rd, Exmouth EX8 3DZ]) : Exe Publishing Company, c1980-. — v. : maps ; 24cm
ISSN 0262-0111 = Bray's Exeter street directory : £3.50 B81-38519

914.23'5604858 — Devon. Exeter — *Visitors' guides* — *For industrial development*
Development opportunities in Exeter. — London (Publicity House, Streatham Hill, SW2 4TR) : Pyramid, 1980. — 56p : ill,1map ; 21cm
Unpriced (pbk) B81-09911

914.23'57 — Devon. Otter Valley — *Walkers' guides*
Twelve walks in the Otter Valley : around Budleigh Salterton, East Budleigh, Otterton, Colaton Raleigh & Newton Poppleford. — [Budleigh Salterton] ([12 Marine Parade, Budleigh Salterton, Devon]) : Otter Valley Association, 1981. — 36p : ill,maps ; 21cm
Cover title. — Bibliography: p36
ISBN 0-9507534-0-8 (pbk) : £0.60 B81-24304

914.23'59204858 — Devon. South Hams *(District)*. Description & travel
Chard, Judy. The South Hams / Judy Chard. — Bodmin : Bossiney, 1980. — 104p : ill,1map,ports ; 21cm
ISBN 0-906456-41-x (pbk) : £1.50 B81-08775

914.23'595 — Devon. Brixham. Place names. Etymology
Saxton, William A.. Brixham before the Conquest, or, The story told by place names / given on 7th October 1980 by William A. Saxton. — [Brixham] ([Higher St., Brixham, Devon]) : [Brixham Museum & History Society], [1980]. — 16p : 1map ; 21cm. — (Occasional lecture papers / Brixham Museum & History Society ; no.1)
Cover title. — Map on back cover
Unpriced (pbk) B81-10106

914.23'7 — Cornwall. Atlantic coastal regions. Description & travel
Tangye, Nigel. The living breath of Cornwall / Nigel Tangye. — London : Kimber, 1980. — 178p ; 23cm
Bibliography: p170-172. — Includes index
ISBN 0-7183-0008-4 : £5.50 B81-03114

914.23'704857 — Cornwall, *1970-1979* — *Visitors' guides* — *For motoring*
Devon and Cornwall. — Newly rev. ed. / completely revised by Harry Loftus. — London : Loftus, [1980]. — 64p : ill,maps ; 22cm. — (Letts tour)
Previous ed.: published as Touring Devon and Cornwall. 1980
ISBN 0-85097-310-4 (pbk) : £0.75
Primary classification 914.23'504857
B81-09267

914.23'704858 — Cornwall. Rural regions. Social life — *Personal observations*
Baker, Denys Val. Upstream at the mill / Denys Val Baker. — London : Kimber, 1981. — 192p : ill ; 23cm
ISBN 0-7183-0098-x : £5.50 B81-26142

914.23'71 — Cornwall. Padstow region — *Walkers' guides*
Palmer, Alfred J.. Walks around Padstow / Alfred J. Palmer. — [Bodmin] ([1 Whitley Barn, Tresarrett, Bodmin, Cornwall PL0 4QH]) : [A.J. Palmer], [1980]. — [8]p : maps ; 22cm
Cover title
£0.30 (pbk) B81-01998

914.23'72 — Cornwall. Lostwithiel. Castles: Restormel Castle — *Visitors' guides*
Great Britain. *Department of the Environment.* Restormel Castle / Department of the Environment ; [written by C.A. Ralegh Radford]. — 2nd ed. — [London] : H.M.S.O., 1980. — 7p : 1plan ; 21cm
Previous ed.: 1947
ISBN 0-11-671067-5 (unbound) : £0.20
B81-07324

914.23'7404858 — Cornwall. Caradon *(District)*. Coastal regions — *Walkers' guides*
Harris, W. Best. From Cremyll to Crafthole / W. Best Harris. — [Plymouth] ([10 Queens Rd., Lipson, Plymouth, Devon]) : W.B. Harris, 1981. — 51p : ill,1map ; 21cm
Unpriced (pbk) B81-36863

914.23'7504858 — Cornwall. Penwith *(District)*. Antiquities. Sites — *Visitors' guides*
Weatherhill, Craig. Belerion : ancient sites of Land's End / Craig Weatherhill. — Penzance (5 Chapel St., Penzance, Cornwall) : Alison Hodge, 1981. — 87p : ill,maps ; 19x21cm
Bibliography: p86. — Includes index
ISBN 0-906720-01-x (pbk) : £3.25 B81-16654

914.23'7604858 — Cornwall. Kerrier *(District)* — *Visitors' guides*
Official guide / Kerrier District Council. — Gloucester : British Publishing, [1981?]. — 160p : ill(some col.),maps(some col.) ; 22cm
Includes index
ISBN 0-7140-1937-2 (pbk) : Unpriced
B81-15517

914.23'78 — Cornwall. Falmouth. Waterfronts — *Visitors' guides*
Lochrie, Peter. Look at the Falmouth waterfront / with Peter Lochrie and Derek Toyne ; designed and illustrated at Falmouth School of Art by Derek Toyne ... [et al.]. — Falmouth (24 Penmere Cres., Falmouth, Cornwall) : Marina Press Society, c1981. — [24]p : ill,1map ; 21cm
Unpriced (corrected pbk) B81-35528

914.23'7904858'05 — Isles of Scilly — *Visitors' guides* — *Serials*
The **Isles** of Scilly standard guidebook. — 39th ed. (1979/1980). — St. Mary's : Bowley Publications, [1980?]. — 71p
ISBN 0-900184-16-7 : £0.60 B81-09714

914.23'85 — Somerset. Dunster. Country houses: Dunster Castle — *Visitors' guides*
Dunster Castle : Somerset. — Rev.. — [London] : National Trust, 1981, c1979. — 61p : ill,2plans,ports,1geneal.table ; 25cm
Bibliography: p61
Unpriced (pbk) B81-26874

914.23'89 — Somerset. Wincanton — *Visitors' guides*
Wincanton, queen of the vale : a guide to the district. — Wallington : Forward, [1981]. — 44p : ill,maps ; 15x21cm
Includes introductions in French and German. — Includes index
Unpriced (pbk) B81-21100

914.23'89 — Somerset. Yeovil. Country houses: Montacute House — *Visitors' guides*
National Trust. Montacute House : Somerset. — [London] : National Trust, 1981, c1979. — 48p : ill,plans,ports,1geneal.table ; 25cm
Bibliography: p46
Unpriced (pbk) B81-18426

914.23'89 — Somerset. Yeovil *(District)*. Country houses: Lytes Cary — *Visitors' guides*
National Trust. Lytes Cary : Somerset. — [London] : The Trust, 1981, c1977. — 30p : ill,1plan ; 22cm
Author: Dudley Dodd. — Bibliography: p30
Unpriced (pbk) B81-18751

914.23'904858 — Avon. Description & travel
Haddon, John, *1919-*. Portrait of Avon / John Haddon. — London : Hale, 1981. — 221p,[24]p of plates : ill,maps ; 23cm
Includes index
ISBN 0-7091-8361-5 : £6.95 B81-14700

914.23'9104858 — Avon. Northavon *(District) — Description & travel*
Wilshire, Lewis. Berkeley Vale and Severn Shore / Lewis Wilshire. — New ed. — London : Hale, 1980. — xx,236p,[24]p of plates : ill,1map,2ports ; 23cm
Previous ed.: published as The Vale of Berkeley. 1954. — Includes index
ISBN 0-7091-8533-2 : £6.95
Primary classification 914.24'1904858 B81-04398

914.23'93 — Avon. Bristol region. Activities for children
Children's Bristol : where to go and what to do in and around Bristol / compiled and written by Merilyn Chambers ... [et al.] ; illustrated by Alan Hurst. — Rev. and enl. ed. — Bristol (14 Dowry Sq., Bristol 8) : Redcliffe Press, 1979. — 152p : ill ; 20cm
Previous ed.: 1976. — Includes index
ISBN 0-905459-14-8 (pbk) : £1.50 B81-08393

914.23'93 — Avon. Henbury. Estates: Blaise Castle Estate. Buildings of historical importance — *Visitors' guides*
Temple, Nigel. The Garden History Society, Bristol Meeting, 6 June 1981 : a brief guide to supplement the programme & introduction / [prepared by] Nigel Temple. — [London] ([24 Woodlands North Side, SW4 0RJ]) : Garden History Society, 1981. — [3]leaves : ill,maps ; 21cm
Unpriced (unbound) B81-33576

914.24 — England. North Midlands — *Visitors' guides — For motoring*
The **Peak** District, the Dales and the North Midlands. — Newly rev. ed. / completely revised by Harry Loftus. — London : Letts, [1980]. — 64p : ill,maps ; 22cm. — (Letts tour)
Previous ed.: 1979. — Includes index
ISBN 0-85097-314-7 (pbk) : £0.75 B81-09265

914.24'04858 — England. Midlands. Description & travel
Reese, Anna. Cricket tours, the Midlands and East Anglia / by Anna Reese. — [Upper Heyford] ([c/o RAF Upper Heyford, Upper Heyford Oxon. OX5 3LW]) : [A. Reese], [1981?]. — 48p : ill ; 22cm
Bibliography: p46. — Includes index
Unpriced (pbk)
Also classified at 914.26'04858 B81-32738

914.24'04858 — England. West Midlands. Canals: Birmingham Canal Navigations — *Visitors' guides*
Beavon, J. R. G.. Along the Birmingham canals : a boating and walking guide / by J.R.G. Beavon ; canal sketches by Zette Braithwaite. — Warley : Tetradon, 1981. — 94p : ill,maps,music ; 21cm. — (Tetradon outdoor guides)
Bibliography: p94. — List of sound recording : p94
ISBN 0-906070-06-6 (pbk) : £3.50 B81-39813

914.24'04858 — England. West Midlands. Canals. Description & travel
Elwin, Geoff. The Stratford upon Avon and Warwick canals : the canals from Birmingham centre to Stratford-upon-Avon, Warwick, Leamington Spa and Braunston : a detailed illustrated survey / Geoff Elwin & Cathleen King. — Northolt (44 Moat Farm Rd., Northolt, Middx UB5 5DR) : Blackthorn, c1981. — 44p : ill,maps ; 30cm
Cover title. — Text on inside covers. — Includes index
ISBN 0-9507303-1-9 (pbk) : £3.50 B81-35307

914.24'04858 — London. Places associated with poets — *Visitors' guides*
Kitchen, Paddy. Poets' London / Paddy Kitchen ; line drawings by Wendy Dowson. — London : Longman, 1980. — 213p : ill,1facsim,ports ; 22cm. — (Longman travellers series)
Includes index
ISBN 0-582-50283-7 : £6.95 : CIP rev. B80-13630

914.24'04858'0247966 — England. West Midlands *— Practical information — For cycle touring*
Shaw, Matthew. Byway cycling : in the West Midlands / by Matthew Shaw. — Shrewsbury (40 London Rd., Shrewsbury, Shropshire SY2 6NX) : M. Shaw, [1981?]. — 48p : ill,maps (some col.) ; 22cm
Cover title. — Bibliography: p48
£1.50 (pbk) B81-30015

914.24'04858'05 — England. Midlands — *Visitors' guides — Serials*
Places to visit from Leicester. — 1981. — Leicester (12 Bishop St., Leicester LE1 6AA) : Information and Publicity Section, Recreation and Arts Department, Leicester City Council, 1981. — 88p
ISBN 0-901675-35-0 : £0.50 B81-28709

914.24'10482'0922 — Gloucestershire. Visits by British royal families, *1922-1980 — Illustrations*
The **Royal** Family in Glo'shire / [editor Derek Archer]. — Dursley (Reliance Works, Dursley, Glos.) : F. Bailey & Son, [1981?]. — 50p : chiefly ill,ports ; 21cm. — (Pages from the past)
£1.00 (pbk) B81-27480

914.24'104858 — Gloucestershire — *Visitors' guides*
Gloucestershire County guide. — Gloucester : British Publishing, [1981]. — 144p,[2]folded p of plates : ill(some col.),maps(some col.),plan,ports(some col.) ; 21cm
ISBN 0-7140-1916-x (pbk) : Unpriced B81-27622

914.24'12 — Gloucestershire. Tewkesbury — *Visitors' guides*
Tewkesbury : official guide. — Rev. — Gloucester : British Publishing, 1981. — 96p : ill(some col.),maps ; 22cm
Previous ed.: 1979
£0.25 (pbk) B81-28739

914.24'14 — Gloucestershire. Gloucester. Cathedrals: Gloucester Cathedral — *Visitors' guides — French texts*
Evans, Seiriol. La cathedrale de Gloucester / [Seiriol Evans] ; [adapté pour traduction par Gilbert Thurlow]. — London : Pitkin Pictorials, c1981. — 24p : ill(some col.),1plan ; 23cm. — (Pitkin 'Pride of Britain' books)
Plan and text on inside covers
ISBN 0-85372-308-7 (pbk) : Unpriced B81-37829

914.24'16'0481 — Gloucestershire. Cheltenham — *Visitors' guides — Early works*
Rowe, George. George Rowe's illustrated Cheltenham guide. — Gloucester : Alan Sutton, Dec.1981. — [176]p
Facsim. of: 1845 ed. Cheltenham : s.n.
ISBN 0-904387-95-x (pbk) : £3.95 : CIP entry B81-33879

914.24'17 — England. Cotswold Edge — *Visitors' guides*
Barraclough, Marian. Exploring the Cotswold edge / Marian Barraclough ; illustrations by Mona Hubbard. — Cheltenham : Thornhill, c1979. — 52p : ill,maps ; 19cm
ISBN 0-904110-77-x (pbk) : £0.85 B81-19863

914.24'17 — Gloucestershire. Cirencester — *Visitors' guides*
Cirencester : the Roman Corinium : the official guide / with contributions on The history of the Roman town by J.S. Wacher [and] The Corinium Museum by D.J. Viner. — Gloucester : British Publishing Co., [1980]. — 88p : ill(some col.),maps ; 22cm
Bibliography: p75
ISBN 0-7140-1902-x (pbk) : £0.60 B81-26292

914.24'1704858 — England. Cotswolds. Long-distance footpaths: Cotswold Way — *Walkers' guides*
Sale, Richard, *1946-*. A guide to the Cotswold Way / Richard Sale. — London : Constable, 1980. — 246p : ill,maps ; 18cm
Map on lining papers. — Includes index
ISBN 0-09-463210-3 : £5.95 : CIP rev. B80-14075

914.24'19 — Gloucestershire. Nailsworth — *Visitors' guides*
Nailsworth, Gloucestershire : the official guide / revised by M.E.H. Mills. — Gloucester : British Publishing Co., 1980. — 44p : ill,maps ; 19cm
Originally published: 1978
ISBN 0-7140-1954-2 (pbk) : £0.25 B81-26293

914.24'19 — Gloucestershire. Stroud *(District)*. **Castles: Berkeley Castle —** *Visitors' guides*
Sackville-West, V.. Berkeley Castle : the historic Gloucestershire seat of the Berkeley family since the eleventh century : the home of Mr. and Mrs. R.J.G. Berkeley : an illustrated survey / history and description of contents by V. Sackville West. — Derby : English Life, c1981. — 32p : chiefly ill(some col.),1col.coat of arms 1geneal.table 1 col.map,ports(some col.) ; 24cm
Cover title. — Text, ill on covers
ISBN 0-85101-176-4 (pbk) : Unpriced B81-31142

914.24'1904858 — Gloucestershire. Stroud *(District) — Description & travel*
Wilshire, Lewis. Berkeley Vale and Severn Shore / Lewis Wilshire. — New ed. — London : Hale, 1980. — xx,236p,[24]p of plates : ill,1map,2ports ; 23cm
Previous ed.: published as The Vale of Berkeley. 1954. — Includes index
ISBN 0-7091-8533-2 : £6.95
Also classified at 914.23'9104858 B81-04398

914.24'4304858 — Hereford and Worcester. Redditch *(District) — Visitors' guides*
Redditch Borough Council official guide. — Gloucester : British Publishing, [1981?]. — 64p : ill(some col.),2maps ; 22cm
Map on folded sheet attached to inside cover
ISBN 0-7140-1898-8 (pbk) : Unpriced B81-11771

914.24'44 — Hereford and Worcester. Leominster *— Visitors' guides*
The **Official** guide to Leominster / photographs by Crosby Photography. — 3rd ed. — Gloucester : British Publishing Co., [1981]. — 44p : ill,maps ; 19cm
Previous ed.: 1978
ISBN 0-7140-1962-3 (pbk) : £0.30 B81-26296

914.24'47 — Hereford and Worcester. Ledbury — *Directories — Serials*
Tilley's Ledbury almanack. — 1981. — Ledbury (16, High Street, Ledbury, Herefordshire) : Tilley & Son, [1980?]. — 194p
£0.75 B81-10577

914.24'49 — Hereford and Worcester. Evesham. Abbeys: Evesham Abbey — *Visitors' guides*
Cox, D. C.. Evesham Abbey and the parish churches : a guide / by D.C. Cox. — Evesham : Vale of Evesham Historical Society, c1980. — 25p : ill,plans ; 25cm
ISBN 0-907353-01-0 (pbk) : Unpriced
Also classified at 914.24'49 B81-10808

914.24'49 — Hereford and Worcester. Evesham. Parish churches: All Saints *(Church : Evesham)* **& St. Lawrence's** *(Church : Evesham) — Visitors' guides*
Cox, D. C.. Evesham Abbey and the parish churches : a guide / by D.C. Cox. — Evesham : Vale of Evesham Historical Society, c1980. — 25p : ill,plans ; 25cm
ISBN 0-907353-01-0 (pbk) : Unpriced
Primary classification 914.24'49 B81-10808

914.24'5'0014 — Shropshire. Fields. Names
Foxall, H. D. G.. Shropshire field-names / by H.D.G. Foxall. — Shrewsbury (23 Oak St., Shrewsbury SY3 7RQ) : Shropshire Archaeological Society, 1980. — xi,98p : ill,maps ; 22cm
Includes index
ISBN 0-9501227-3-4 (pbk) : £2.45 B81-07988

914.24'504858 — Shropshire. Hilly regions. Description & travel
Waite, Vincent. Shropshire hill country / by Vincent Waite. — London : Phillimore, c1981. — xxi,162p,[16]p of plates : ill,1map,ports ; 22cm
Originally published: London : Dent, 1970. — Includes index
ISBN 0-85033-365-2 (pbk) : £3.95 B81-19307

914.24'51 — Shropshire. Weston Rhyn. Country houses: Tyn-y-Rhos Hall — *Visitors' guides*

Tyn-y-Rhos Hall. — Oswestry (Tyn-y-Rhos Hall, Weston Rhyn, Oswestry, Salop) : [M. Thompson-Butler-Lloyd], [1981?]. — [4]p : 1port ; 21cm
Unpriced (unbound) B81-33553

914.24'54 — Shropshire. Pontesbury — *Visitors' guides*

Pontesbury Shropshire official guide. — Wallington : Forward Publicity, [1981]. — 20p : ill,1map ; 19cm
Unpriced (pbk) B81-26641

914.24'59 — Shropshire. Bridgnorth — *Visitors' guides*

Bridgnorth. *Town Council*. Bridgnorth : official guide / issued by the authority of the Bridgnorth Town Council. — Wallington : Forward Publicity, [1981]. — 32p,[1]leaf of plates : ill,1map,1coat of arms ; 21cm
Unpriced (pbk) B81-39015

914.24'59 — Shropshire. Shifnal — *Visitors' guides*

Shifnal official guide. — [Gloucester] : [British Publishing], [1981?]. — 43p : ill,1map ; 19cm
ISBN 0-7140-1948-8 (pbk) : Unpriced B81-27732

914.24'6304858 — Staffordshire. Stoke-on-Trent — *Visitors' guides*

The **City** of Stoke-on-Trent official handbook. — [London] : [Burrow], [1980]. — 180p : ill(some col.),coats of arms,port ; 25cm
Unpriced (pbk) B81-09905

914.24'64 — Staffordshire. Stone — *Visitors' guides*

Stone : official guide. — Wallington : Forward, [1981]. — 44p : ill,1map ; 21cm
Includes index
Unpriced (pbk) B81-21102

914.24'6504858 — Staffordshire. East Staffordshire *(District)* — *Visitors' guides*

East Staffordshire : official map — : containing street maps of Burton upon Trent, Uttoxeter, Rolleston, Tutbury, Barton under Needwood. — Wallington : Forward Publicity, [1981]. — 28p : maps ; 21cm
Cover title. — Includes index
£0.35 (pbk) B81-26643

914.24'8304858 — Warwickshire. Nuneaton and Bedworth *(District)* — *Visitors' guides*

Nuneaton & Bedworth, Warwickshire : official guide. — Wallington : Home Publicity, [1981]. — 86p,[2]p of plates(folded sheet) : ill(some col.),3maps,1port ; 21cm
Unpriced (pbk) B81-10710

914.24'89 — Warwickshire. Charlecote. Country houses: Charlecote Park — *Visitors' guides*

National Trust. Charlecote Park : Warwickshire / [The National Trust]. — Rev. — [London] : The Trust, 1981, c1979. — 38p,[8]p of plates : ill,1map,1geneal.table ; 22cm
Unpriced (pbk) B81-34549

914.24'904858 — West Midlands *(Metropolitan County)*. **Black Country. Parish churches** — *Lists*

Billington, Eric R.. Parish registers and churches of the West Midlands and Black Country : including district locations of churches, commencement date of registers and guide to their whereabouts / compiled by Eric R. Billington. — Birmingham (69 Hollydale Rd., Erdington, Birmingham B24 9LS) : Birmindex, 1980. — 17p ; 30cm
Bibliography: p9
Unpriced (pbk)
Primary classification 016.929'34249
B81-28881

914.24'904858 — West Midlands *(Metropolitan County)* — *Visitors' guides*

The **County** of West Midlands. — [Birmingham] ([County Hall, 1 Lancaster Circus, Queensway, Birmingham B4 7DJ]) : [West Midlands County Council], 1980. — 140p : ill(some col.),col.maps,2col.coats of arms ; 30cm
Unpriced (pbk) B81-11836

914.24'91 — West Midlands *(Metropolitan County)*. **Wolverhampton. Country houses: Wightwick Manor** — *Visitors' guides*

National Trust. Wightwick Manor : West Midlands / [photographs: A.F. Kersting, Jonathan Gibson and Alex Starkey]. — Rev. — [London] : The Trust, 1981. — 22p,[4]p of plates : ill,1facsim ; 22cm
Previous ed.: 1978. — Bibliography: p22
Unpriced (pbk) B81-18754

914.24'9804858 — West Midlands *(Metropolitan County)*. **Coventry. Description & travel**

Coventry : city and cathedral. — Norwich : Jarrold, c1981. — [16]p : ill(some col.),1map ; 20cm. — (Jarrold Cotman-color-series)
Map on inside cover
ISBN 0-85306-940-9 (pbk) : Unpriced
B81-19415

914.25 — England. Northern East Midlands — *Visitors' guides — Serials*

Out and about : 300 ideas for outings within 40 miles of Derby. — 7th ed.. — Derby (c/o Mrs J. Steer, 478 Duffield Rd, Allestree, Derby) : Derby and District Consumer Group, c1981. — 32p
£0.45 B81-31892

914.25 — England. Southern East Midlands — *Visitors' guides — For motoring*

Tingey, Frederick. Home Counties : Bedfordshire, Berkshire, Buckinghamshire, Hertfordshire, Oxfordshire / Frederick Tingey. — London (83 Pall Mall [S.W.1]) : Travellers Realm, 1981. — 128p : ill,maps ; 20cm. — (RAC going places ; 7)
Includes index
ISBN 0-86211-008-4 (pbk) : £2.95 B81-37369

914.2504858 — England. Chilterns — *Visitors' guides*

Lands, Neil. Visitor's guide to the Chilterns. — Ashbourne : Moorland Publishing, Jan.1982. — [128]p
ISBN 0-86190-029-4 (cased) : £5.95 : CIP entry
ISBN 0-86190-028-6 (pbk) : £3.95 B81-38834

914.25'04858 — England. East Midlands — *Visitors' guides*

East Midland counties : Derby, Nottingham, Leicester and Lincoln .... — London : Geographia, 1981. — 128p,[8]p of plates : ill,maps(some col.) ; 19cm. — (A Geographia guide)
Map (folded sheet) attached to inside cover. — Includes index
£1.50 (pbk)
ISBN 0-09-205540-0 B81-34265

914.25'1 — Derbyshire. Trackways — *Walkers' guides*

Toulson, Shirley. Derbyshire : exploring the ancient tracks and mysteries of Mercia / Shirley Toulson ; illustrated by Oliver Caldecott ; maps drawn by Sue Lawes. — London : Wildwood, 1980. — 173p : ill,maps ; 21cm
Bibliography: p.172-173. — Includes index
ISBN 0-7045-3048-1 : Unpriced B81-36525

914.25'1104858 — England. Peak District — *Visitors' guides*

Porter, C. L. M.. Visitor's guide to the Peak District. — Ashbourne : Moorland Publishing, Feb.1982. — [144]p
ISBN 0-86190-038-3 (cased) : £5.95 : CIP entry
ISBN 0-86190-037-5 (pbk) : £3.95 B81-39242

914.25'1104858 — England. Peak District — *Walkers' guides*

Bellamy, Rex. The Peak District companion : a walker's guide to its fells, dales and history / Rex Bellamy ; photographs by Don Bellamy. — Newton Abbot : David & Charles, c1981. — 239p,[16]p of plates : ill,maps ; 23cm
Bibliography: p227. — Includes index
ISBN 0-7153-8140-7 : £7.95 B81-23082

914.25'1104858 — England. South Pennines. Description & travel

Parry, Keith. Trans-Pennine heritage : hills, people and transport / Keith Parry. — Newton Abbot : David & Charles, c1981. — 199p : ill,maps ; 23cm
Bibliography: p192-193. - Includes index
ISBN 0-7153-8019-2 : £7.95 B81-19711

914.25'13 — Derbyshire. Ashbourne — *Visitors' guides*

Merrill, John N.. Ashbourne : a practical guide for visitors / compiled by John N. Merrill ; illustrated by J.J. Thomlinson. — Clapham, N. Yorkshire : Dalesman, 1979. — 32p : ill,2maps ; 19cm
Maps on inside covers
ISBN 0-85206-509-4 (pbk) : £0.60 B81-39589

914.25'13 — Derbyshire. Over Haddon. Country houses: Haddon Hall — *Visitors' guides*

Mantell, Keith H.. Haddon Hall / [text by Keith H. Mantell] ; [photographs by Sydney W. Newbery et al.]. — Derby : English Life Publications, c1980. — 32p : ill(some col.) ; 24cm
Cover title. — Originally published: 1974. — Ill on lining papers
ISBN 0-85101-159-4 (pbk) : £0.50 B81-11525

914.25'13 — Derbyshire. Sudbury. Country houses: Sudbury Hall — *Visitors' guides*

National Trust. Sudbury Hall : Derbyshire. — [London] : National Trust, 1981, c1978. — 23p[8]p of plates : ill,1plan ; 25cm
Bibliography: p23
Unpriced (pbk) B81-18422

914.25'13 — England. Peak District. Dovedale — *Visitors' guides*

Mantell, Keith H.. Dovedale guide / [text written by Keith Mantell] ; [photography by Andy Williams assisted by Susan Beaton Bramwell] ; [map drawn by D.G. Mackay]. — Derby : Derbyshire Countryside, c1981. — 24p : col.ill,1col.map ; 20cm
Ill on inside covers
ISBN 0-85100-075-4 (pbk) : £0.50 B81-38766

914.25'14 — Derbyshire. North East Derbyshire *(District)*. **Country houses: Hardwick Hall** — *Visitors' guides*

National Trust. Hardwick Hall, Derbyshire. — [London] : National Trust, c1979 (1981 [printing]). — 62p : ill,plans,1port,1geneal.table ; 22cm
Bibliography: p50
Unpriced (pbk) B81-22302

914.25'1404858 — Derbyshire. North East Derbyshire *(District)* — *Visitors' guides*

North East Derbyshire District Council official guide. — Gloucester : British Publishing, [1981]. — 76p : ill(some col.),maps(some col.),coat of arms ; 25cm
Unpriced (pbk) B81-27620

914.25'19 — Derbyshire. Melbourne — *Visitors' guides*

Blunt, John. Melbourne / [written by John Blunt, Robert Innes-Smith and Eric Sample]. — Derby : Derbyshire Countryside, c1980. — 16p : ill,1map ; 24cm
ISBN 0-85100-068-1 (pbk) : £0.40 B81-02436

914.25'204858 — Nottinghamshire — *Visitors' guides*

Walker, Christine. Hello Nottingham / Christine Walker & John Lake. — Nottingham (18a Cavendish Cres. North, Nottingham NG7 1BA) : Peebles, 1981. — 28p : ill,1map,ports ; 31x22cm
Cover title. — Text on inside cover
ISBN 0-9507632-0-9 (pbk) : £0.60 B81-34976

914.25'27 — Nottingham. Sneinton — *Walkers' guides*

Ablitt, Dave. A guide to old Sneinton / by Dave Ablitt ; drawings by Jim Wright ; photography and cover design by Bill Vincent. — Nottingham (101 Skipton Circus, Sneinton Dale, [Nottingham NG3 7DT]) : Sneinton Environmental Society, 1980. — [28]p : ill,1map ; 21cm
£0.50 (pbk) B81-05355

914.25′2904858 — Nottinghamshire. Rushcliffe *(District) — Visitors′ guides*
Rushcliffe offical guide. — Gloucester : British Publishing, [1981?]. — 84p : ill(some col.),maps (some col.),1col.coat of arms ; 21cm
Map on folded sheet attached to inside cover
ISBN 0-7140-1928-3 (pbk) : Unpriced B81-11774

Rushcliffe official guide. — Gloucester : British Publishing, [1980]. — 84p,[2]p of plates(folded sheet) : ill(some col.),maps(some col.),col.coat of arms ; 21cm
Unpriced (pbk) B81-07966

914.25′32 — Lincolnshire. Tattershall. Castles: Tattershall Castle *— Visitors′ guides*
Tattershall Castle : Lincolnshire. — [London] : National Trust, 1981. — 20p,[4]p of plates : ill (some col.),plans ; 25cm
Bibliography: p20
Unpriced (pbk) B81-26873

914.25′3404858 — Lincolnshire. Lincoln — *Visitors′ guides*
Lincoln. — St. Ives, Huntingdon : Photo Precision, [1980]. — 32p : ill(some col.),1map,1plan ; 24cm. — (Colourmaster publication)
ISBN 0-85933-187-3 (pbk) : Unpriced B81-10393

914.25′3704858 — Lincolnshire. Boston *(District) — Visitors′ guides*
Boston : official guide. — London : Burrow, [1981?]. — 36p : ill ; 21cm
Unpriced (pbk) B81-35000

Boston official guide / issued by authority of the Council of the Borough of Boston. — London : Burrow, [1981]. — 36p : ill ; 21cm
£1.00 (pbk) B81-39140

914.25′38 — Lincolnshire. Woolsthorpe. Country houses: Woolsthorpe Manor *— Visitors′ guides*
National Trust. Woolsthorpe Manor : Lincolnshire / [The National Trust]. — [London] : The Trust, c1979. — 13p,[4]p of plates : ill,2ports ; 22cm
Bibliography: p13
Unpriced (pbk) B81-34545

914.25′4′00321 — Leicestershire. Place names — *Encyclopaedias*
Bourne, Jill. Place-names of Leicestershire & Rutland / Jill Bourne. — 2nd ed. — [Leicester] ([1st Floor, Thames Tower, Navigation St., Leicester LE1 3TZ]) : Leicestershire Libraries and Information Service, 1981. — 80p : ill,maps ; 21cm
Prevous ed.: 1977. — Bibliography: p73-74
ISBN 0-85022-085-8 (pbk) : £1.50 B81-25576

914.25′404858′05 — Leicestershire *— Visitors′ guides — Serials*
Leicestershire : the county handbook. — 1980-82. — London : Burrow, [1980?]. — 76p
ISBN 0-85022-065-3 : Unpriced B81-09179

914.25′4104858 — Leicestershire. Blaby *(District) — Visitors′ guides*
Blaby Leicestershire : official guide. — Wallington : Home Publishing, [1981]. — 52p : ill,coat of arms,maps ; 21cm
Unpriced (pbk) B81-36401

914.25′42 — Leicestershire. Leicester. Guildhalls: Guildhall, *Leicester - Visitors′ guides*
Pegden, N. A.. Leicester Guildhall : a short history and guide / N.A. Pegden ; with contributions by Robin Emmerson and Patrick J. Boylan. — Leicester (96 New Walk, Leicester LE1 6TD) : Leicestershire Museums, Art Galleries and Records Service, c1981. — 23p : ill,plans ; 15x21cm. — (Leicestershire Museums publication ; no.17)
ISBN 0-85022-066-1 (pbk) : Unpriced B81-18932

914.25′4204858 — Leicestershire. Leicester — *Visitors′ guides*
City of Leicester. — Gloucester : British Publishing, [1981]. — 100p : ill(some col.),2maps(some col.),col.coat of arms ; 25cm
ISBN 0-7140-1938-0 (pbk) : Unpriced B81-27623

914.25′46 — Leicestershire. Belvoir. Castles: Belvoir Castle *— Visitors′ guides*
Belvoir Castle : The Leicester home of the Dukes of Rutland. — Derby : English Life, c1981. — 28p : ill(some col.),ports(some col.),1geneal.table ; 24cm
Ill on inside covers
ISBN 0-85101-181-0 (pbk) : £0.50 B81-39050

914.25′48 — Leicestershire. North West Leicestershire *(District).* **Country houses. Private chapels: Staunton Harold Church** *— Visitors′ guides*
National Trust. Staunton Harold Church : Leicestershire. — [London] : The Trust, 1981, c1975. — 15p,[4]p of plates : ill ; 22cm
Bibliography: p15
Unpriced (pbk) B81-21320

914.25′5204858 — Northamptonshire. Kettering *(District) — Visitors′ guides*
Borough of Kettering official guide. — London : Burrow, [1980]. — 40p : ill,2col.maps,1coat of arms ; 15x21cm
Unpriced (pbk) B81-09906

914.25′54 — Northamptonshire. Oundle. Country houses: Lyveden New Bield *— Visitors′ guides*
National Trust. Lyveden New Bield : Northamptonshire. — [London] : The Trust, 1981, c1973. — 14p,[4]p of plates : 1ill,2plans,1port ; 22cm
Author: Gyles Isham
Unpriced (pbk) B81-18752

914.25′54 — Northamptonshire. Raunds & Stanwick *— Visitors′ guides*
Raunds and Stanwick : official guide. — Wallington : Forward Publicity, [1981]. — 36p : ill,1map ; 19cm
Unpriced (pbk) B81-36402

914.25′5404858 — Northamptonshire. East Northamptonshire *(District) — Visitors′ guides*
East Northamptonshire : official guide / photographs by Stanley Cutmore. — Wallington : Home Publicity, [1981]. — 64p,[2]p of plates(folded sheet) : ill,maps ; 21cm
Unpriced (pbk) B81-10709

914.25′6104858 — Bedfordshire. North Bedfordshire *(District) — Visitors′ guides*
Borough of North Bedfordshire : official guide. — Wallington : Home Publishing, [1981]. — 116p : ill(some col.) ; 21cm
Unpriced (pbk) B81-15571

914.25′6304858 — Bedfordshire. Mid Bedfordshire *(District) — Visitors′ guides*
Mid Bedfordshire District : official guide & street plans. — Wallington : Home Publishing, [1981?]. — 71p : ill,maps ; 21cm
Includes index
Unpriced (pbk) B81-23630

914.25′6504858 — Bedfordshire. South Bedfordshire *(District) — Visitors′ guides*
South Bedfordshire : official guide. — Wallington : Home Publishing, 1981. — 84p : ill(some col.),1map ; 21cm
Unpriced (pbk) B81-36399

914.25′704858 — Oxfordshire *— Visitors′ guides*
Oxfordshire County handbook. — London : Burrow, [1981]. — 52p : ill(some col.),1map,1coat of arms ; 26cm
£3.25 (pbk) B81-39138

914.25′71 — Oxfordshire. Carterton & Black Bourton *— Visitors′ guides*
Carterton and Black Bourton : official guide. — Wallington : Forward, [1981]. — 40p : ill,1map ; 19cm
Includes index
Unpriced (pbk) B81-21103

914.25′73 — Oxfordshire. Bicester *— Visitors′ guides*
Bicester. *Town Council*. Bicester, Oxford : official town guide / issued by authority of the Bicester Town Council. — Wallington : Forward Publicity, 1981. — 48p,[1]leaf of plates : ill,1map,2coats of arms,1port ; 21cm
Unpriced (pbk) B81-39012

914.25′7404858 — Oxfordshire. Oxford *— Visitors′ guides*
Hall, Michael, *1957-*. Oxford / text by Michael Hall ; with photographs by Ernest Frankl. — Cambridge (6 De Freville Ave., Cambridge CB4 1HR) : Pevensey, 1981. — 99p : col.ill,maps(some col.) ; 25cm
ISBN 0-907115-03-9 (cased) : Unpriced B81-24423

Heyworth, Peter, *1931-*. The Oxford guide to Oxford / Peter Heyworth ; with photographs by Hunter Cordaiy. — Oxford : Oxford University Press, 1981. — 156p : ill,2maps ; 21cm
Bibliography: p14-15. — Includes index
ISBN 0-19-211581-2 (cased) : £6.95
ISBN 0-19-285095-4 (pbk) : £3.50 B81-22140

Ingpen, Elizabeth. Oxford in colour / by Elizabeth Ingpen and A.N. Court. — Norwich : Jarrold, c1981. — [32]p : col.ill,1map ; 19cm. — (Jarrold Cotman-color series)
Map, text on inside covers
ISBN 0-85306-956-5 (pbk) : Unpriced B81-24317

914.25′76 — Oxfordshire. Abingdon *— Directories — Serials*
Abingdon who′s who and directory. — 1981-82. — [Abingdon] ([Stratton Lodge, Bath St., Abingdon, Oxon]) : Abingdon Town Council, [1981?]. — 240p
ISBN 0-900012-44-7 : £1.50 B81-29043

914.25′79 — Oxfordshire. Stonor. Country houses: Stonor House *— Visitors′ guides*
Stonor. — Stonor Park (Stonor Park, Henley-on-Thames, Oxon.) : Stonor Enterprises, [1981?]. — 24p : ill(some col.),ports,geneal.tables ; 21cm + Hand list of contents(14p : ill,map,coat of arms ; 21cm)
Cover title. — Bibliography: p24
Unpriced (pbk) B81-30016

914.25′79 — Oxfordshire. Watlington *— Visitors′ guides*
Watlington Oxfordshire : official guide. — Wallington : Forward Publicity, [1981]. — 28p : ill,maps ; 19cm
Unpriced (pbk) B81-36400

914.25′804858 — Hertfordshire *— Visitors′ guides*
Hertfordshire county handbook. — Wallington : Home Publishing, [1981]. — 129p : ill(some col.),coat of arms,ports ; 24cm
Unpriced (pbk) B81-15573

914.25′82 — Hertfordshire. Stevenage. Country houses: Knebworth House *— Visitors′ guides*
Flower, Sibylla Jane. Knebworth House : home of the Lytton family since 1492. — [Derby] : [English Life Publications], c[1981]. — 24p : ill (some col.),ports,1geneal.table ; 24cm
Text by Sibylla Jane Flower. — Ill on inside covers
ISBN 0-85101-175-6 (pbk) : £0.50 B81-25574

914.25′8304858 — Hertfordshire. East Hertfordshire *(District) — Visitors′ guides*
East Hertfordshire industrial and general information handbook. — London : Burrow, [1979]. — 80p : ill,1port ; 22cm
Unpriced (pbk) B81-09909

914.25′895 — Hertfordshire. Bushey. Parish churches: St. James the Apostle *(Church : Bushey) — Visitors′ guides*
St James : the Apostle. — [Watford] ([Parish Office, High St., Bushey, Watford]) : Bushey Parish Church, [1981]. — 22p : ill(some col.),1plan ; 21cm
Ill on inside covers
£0.50 (pbk) B81-21426

914.25′89504858 — Hertfordshire. Hertsmere *(District) — Visitors′ guides*
Borough of Hertsmere official guide. — Gloucester : British Publishing, [1981?]. — 104p : ill,1col.map,1col.coat of arms,1facsim ; 21cm
English text, English, French and German introductions and photographic captions
ISBN 0-7140-1912-7 (pbk) : Unpriced B81-11770

914.25′904857 — Buckinghamshire — *Visitors′ guides*

Watkin, Bruce. Buckinghamshire : a Shell guide. — London : Faber, Sept.1981. — [192]p
ISBN 0-571-11784-8 : £5.95 : CIP entry
B81-21532

914.25′91 — Buckinghamshire. Olney — *Visitors′ guides*

Styles, Jim. Let′s talk about Olney : a conversational guide / by Jim Styles ; with illustrations by Reg Perkins. — Bradwell (Bradwell, Milton Keynes, MK13 9AP) : Bradwell Abbey Field Centre, 1981. — 27p,21p of plates : ill ; 21cm. — (Occasional paper / Bradwell Abbey Field Centre, ISSN 0306-8838 ; no.6)
Cover title
Unpriced (pbk) B81-37944

914.25′9304858 — Buckinghamshire. Aylesbury Vale *(District)* — *Visitors′ guides*

Aylesbury Vale : official guide. — Wallington : Home Publishing, [1981?]. — 63p : ill(some col.),1map,1coat of arms ; 21cm
Includes index
Unpriced (pbk) B81-23631

914.25′95 — Buckinghamshire. Princes Risborough — *Visitors′ guides*

Princes Risborough : official guide / photographs by A. Rigby. — Wallington : Home Publishing, [1980]. — 36p,[2]folded p of plates : ill,1map ; 21cm
Unpriced (pbk) B81-28862

914.25′95 — Buckinghamshire. West Wycombe. Country houses: West Wycombe Park — *Visitors′ guides*

National Trust. West Wycombe Park : Buckinghamshire / [The National Trust]. — Rev. — [London] : The Trust, 1981, c1978. — 30p,[8]p of plates : ill(some col.),1map,1plan ; 25cm
Bibliography: p30
Unpriced (pbk) B81-34547

914.25′9704858 — Buckinghamshire. Chiltern *(District)* — *Visitors′ guides*

Chiltern District Council official guide. — Gloucester : British Publishing, [1980]. — 88p : ill,maps ; 21cm
Unpriced (pbk) B81-07965

914.25′98 — Buckinghamshire. Taplow. Country houses: Cliveden — *Visitors′ guides*

National Trust. Cliveden : Buckinghamshire. — [London] : National Trust, 1978 (1980 [printing]). — 38p : ill,maps,ports ; 25cm
Bibliography: p38
Unpriced (pbk) B81-18427

914.26′04858 — East Anglia. Description & travel

Reese, Anna. Cricket tours, the Midlands and East Anglia / by Anna Reese. — [Upper Heyford] ([c/o RAF Upper Heyford, Upper Heyford Oxon. OX5 3LW]) : [A. Reese], [1981?]. — 48p : ill ; 22cm
Bibliography: p46. — Includes index
Unpriced (pbk)
Primary classification 914.24′04858 B81-32738

914.26′04858 — East Anglia — *Visitors′ guides — For motoring*

Clark, K. D.. East Anglia & Essex : Cambridge, Essex, Norfolk, Suffolk / K.D. Clark. — [London] ([83 Pall Mall, SW1Y 5HW]) : Travellers Realm, 1981. — 128p : ill,maps ; 19cm. — (RAC going places ; 8)
Includes index
ISBN 0-86211-009-2 (pbk) : £2.95 B81-21183

914.26′04858 — East Anglia — *Walkers′ guides*

Galloway, Bruce. Walks in East Anglia / Bruce Galloway. — Woodbridge : Boydell
1: Norfolk and Suffolk. — c1981. — 182p : maps ; 25cm
Bibliography: p182
ISBN 0-85115-131-0 (cased) : £9.95 : CIP rev.
ISBN 0-85115-135-3 (pbk) : Unpriced
B81-16875

914.26′04858′0222 — East Anglia. Description & travel — *Illustrations*

Bloemendal, F. A. H.. England in cameracolour, East Anglia / photographs by F.A.H. Bloemendal ; text by Francesca Barran. — London : Ian Allan, 1981. — 110p : chiefly col.ill,maps ; 30cm
Maps on lining papers
ISBN 0-7110-1101-x : £7.95 B81-32806

914.26′04858′05 — East Anglia — *Visitors′ guides — Serials*

East Anglia guide / East Anglia Tourist Board. — 1981. — Ipswich (14 Museum St., Ipswich, Suffolk) : The Board, c1981. — 59p
£1.00 B81-20072

914.26′12 — Norfolk. Mundesley — *Walkers′ guides*

Mundesley. — Norwich (County Planning Dept., County Hall, Martineau La., Norwich) : Norfolk County Council, c1980. — 1folded sheet : 1ill,1map ; 22cm. — (Norfolk parish walks)
Unpriced B81-37763

914.26′12 — Norfolk. Walsingham. Shrines: Shrine of Our Lady of Walsingham *(Catholic)* — *Visitors′ guides*

Pyle-Bridges, Dominic. Guide to the sanctuary of Our Lady of Walsingham : England′s Nazareth / Dominic Pyle-Bridges ; foreword by Alan Carefull. — 4th ed., rev. — Maidstone (1 Hastings Rd., Maidstone, Kent) : L.A.L., 1981. — 20p : 1plan ; 22cm
Previous ed.: 1979. — Plan on inside cover
£0.30 (pbk) B81-18272

914.26′12 — Norfolk. Wells-next-the-Sea — *Walkers′ guides*

Banham, Eleanor. Wells town trail / [text by Eleanor Banham]. — Norwich (County Hall, Martineau La., Norwich NR1 2DH) : Norfolk County Planning Department, c1980. — [15]p : ill,1map ; 21cm
Cover title
Unpriced (pbk) B81-19558

914.26′13 — Norfolk. Sandringham. Parish churches: St Mary Magdalene *(Church: Sandringham)* — *Visitors′ guides*

Ashton, Patrick. Sandringham Church : St Mary Magdalene / [by Patrick Ashton]. — [New ed.]. — London : Pitkin Pictorials, c1981. — 24p : ill(some col.) ; 23cm. — (Pitkin ′Pride of Britain′ books)
Previous ed. published: as ′A brief history of Sandringham Church′. 1958. — Text and ill on inside covers
ISBN 0-85372-065-7 (pbk) : Unpriced
B81-37828

914.26′14 — Norfolk. East Dereham — *Walkers′ guides*

East Dereham. — Norwich (County Planning Dept., County Hall, Martineau La., Norwich) : Norfolk County Council, c1981. — 1folded sheet : 1ill,1map 22cm. — (Norfolk parish walks)
Unpriced B81-37764

914.26′14 — Norfolk. Oxborough. Country houses: Oxburgh Hall — *Visitors′ guides*

Oxburgh Hall : Norfolk. — Rev.. — [London] : National Trust, 1980, c1978 (1981 [printing]). — 31p : ill,1plan,1geneal.table ; 22cm
Unpriced (pbk) B81-26872

914.26′1404858 — East Anglia. Breckland region. Description & travel

Cook, Olive. Breckland / Olive Cook. — 2nd ed. — London : Hale, 1980. — xvi,176p,[16]p of plates : ill,1map ; 23cm
Previous ed.: 1956. — Bibliography: p174. — Includes index
ISBN 0-7091-8365-8 : £6.95 B81-05728

914.26′1504858 — Norfolk. Norwich — *Visitors′ guides*

Ingpen, Elizabeth. Colourful Norwich / [text by Elizabeth Ingpen]. — Norwich : Jarrold, c1981. — [16]p : col.ill,1map,ports ; 25cm
Cover title. — Ill on inside covers
ISBN 0-85306-954-9 (pbk) : £0.80 B81-21333

914.26′1704858′05 — Norfolk Broads — *Visitors′ guides — For boating — Serials*

What to do on the Norfolk Broads. — 1981. — Norwich : Jarrold Colour Publications, c1981. — 96p
ISBN 0-85306-922-0 : £1.50 B81-10270

914.26′18 — Norfolk. Bradwell — *Walkers′ guides*

Bradwell. — Norwich (County Planning Dept., County Hall, Martineau La., Norwich) : Norfolk County Council, c1981. — 1folded sheet : 1ill,1map ; 22cm. — (Norfolk parish walks)
Unpriced B81-37765

914.26′1804858′05 — Norfolk. Great Yarmouth *(District)* — *Visitors′ guides — Serials*

Great Yarmouth official holiday guide. — 1981. — Great Yarmouth (14 Regent St., Great Yarmouth, NR30 1RW) : [Great Yarmouth District Council] Department of Publicity, 1981. — 240p
Unpriced B81-13094

914.26′19 — Norfolk. South Norfolk *(District)*. Billingford. Windmills: Billingford Mill — *Visitors′ guides*

Billingford Windmill. — Norwich (c/o The Technical Adviser, County Planning Department, County Hall, Martineau La., Norwich NR1 2DH) : Norfolk Windmills Trust, 1980. — 26p : ill ; 22cm
£0.50 (pbk) B81-19557

914.26′19 — Norfolk. Wicklewood. Windmills: Wicklewood Windmill — *Visitors′ guides*

Wicklewood Windmill / written for the Norfolk Windmills Trust by the Norfolk County Council Planning Department. — Norwich (c/o County Planning Department, County Hall, Martineau La., Norwich NR1 2DH) : Norfolk Windmills Trust, 1981. — 12p ; 21cm
£0.15 (pbk) B81-33549

914.26′404857 — Suffolk — *Visitors′ guides*

Scarfe, Norman. Suffolk : a Shell guide. — 3rd ed. — London : Faber, Sept.1981. — [192]p
Previous ed.: 1966
ISBN 0-571-11821-6 (pbk) : £2.95 : CIP entry
B81-22622

914.26′4504858 — Suffolk. Mid Suffolk *(District)* — *Visitors′ guides*

Mid Suffolk district : official guide. — Wallington : Home Publishing, [1981]. — 64p : ill(some col.),maps ; 21cm
Unpriced (pbk) B81-23618

914.26′48 — Suffolk. East Bergholt. Buildings of historical importance — *Visitors′ guides*

Elam, Jack. Looking at East Bergholt, Suffolk / [text, Jack Elam] ; [general editor, Kevin Armstrong] ; [illustrations, A.Q. Haythornthwaite] ; [introduction, Celia Jennings]. — [East Bergholt] ([c/o Mrs Gillian Walker, Little Cowt, East Bergholt, Suffolk]) : East Bergholt Society, c1981. — [16]p : ill,1map ; 21x9cm
Cover title. — Map on inside cover
£0.65 (pbk) B81-34343

914.26′48 — Suffolk. Sudbury — *Visitors′ guides*

Sudbury and district, Suffolk : the official guide. — London : Burrow, [1981]. — 32p,[1]folded leaf of plates : ill,1map ; 19cm
Unpriced (pbk) B81-35002

914.26′5 — Cambridgeshire. Places associated with ′The Old Vicarage, Grantchester′ by Brooke, Rupert. Description & travel

Cheason, Danis. The Cambridgeshire of Rupert Brooke : an illustrated guide / written and illustrated by Denis Cheason. — [Waterbeach] (4 Primrose La., Waterbeach, Cambs. CB5 9JZ) : D. Cheason, c1980. — [44]p : ill,1map ; 18x24cm
Map on cover
ISBN 0-9506614-1-4 (pbk) : Unpriced
B81-05979

914.26'56 — Cambridgeshire. Ely. Cathedrals: Ely Cathedral. Steeple Gate — *Visitors' guides*
Holmes, Reg. Steeple Gate Ely / by Reg Holmes. — [Ely] (Resource and Technology Centre, Back Hill, Ely, CB7 4DA) : EARO, c1980. — [8]p : ill,1map ; 21cm
Cover title
ISBN 0-904463-74-5 (pbk) : £0.25 B81-06213

914.26'56 — Cambridgeshire. Ely. Cathedrals: Ely Cathedral — *Visitors' guides*
Franklin, Alan V.. May I show you round? : Ely Cathedral : under the guidance of Alan Franklin / foreword by the Dean (H.S. Carey). — Derby ([Lodge La., Derby DE1 3HE]) : English Life Publications, c1981. — 20p : col.ill,1plan ; 20cm
Previous ed.: St Ives, Cambs. : Photo Precision, 1973. — Ill, plan on inside covers
ISBN 0-85101-179-9 (pbk) : £0.40 B81-23158

914.26'56 — Cambridgeshire. Stretham region. Description & travel
Cheason, Denis. Cambridge to Ely : a guide to the region between two fine cities / written and illustrated by Denis Cheason. — [Waterbeach] (Primrose La., Waterbeach, Cambs. CB5 9JZ) : D. Cheason, [1979]. — ill,1map ; 16x21cm
Map on cover
ISBN 0-9506614-0-6 : Unpriced
Also classified at 914.26'57 B81-06663

914.26'57 — Cambridgeshire. Waterbeach region. Description & travel
Cheason, Denis. Cambridge to Ely : a guide to the region between two fine cities / written and illustrated by Denis Cheason. — [Waterbeach] (Primrose La., Waterbeach, Cambs. CB5 9JZ) : D. Cheason, [1979]. — ill,1map ; 16x21cm
Map on cover
ISBN 0-9506614-0-6 : Unpriced
Primary classification 914.26'56 B81-06663

914.26'5904 — Cambridgeshire. Cambridge. Visits by royal families, *1564-1955*
Colthorpe, Marion. Royal Cambridge : royal visitors to Cambridge, Queen Elizabeth I-Queen Elizabeth II / Marion Colthorpe. — [Cambridge] ([Tourist Information Centre, Wheeler St., Cambridge CB2 3QD]) : Cambridge City Council, c1977. — 120p : ill,1map,facsims,1plan,ports ; 21cm
Text on inside cover. — Bibliography: p116. — Includes index
ISBN 0-906086-00-0 : £1.95 B81-17600

914.26'5904858 — Cambridgeshire. Cambridge — *Visitors' guides — French texts*
Cambridge : un guide illustré des séries Colourmaster. — St. Ives, Huntingdon : Photo Precision, [1980]. — 32p : ill(some col.),1map ; 24cm. — (Colourmaster publication)
Includes index
ISBN 0-85933-198-9 (pbk) : Unpriced B81-10395

914.26'5904858 — Cambridgeshire. Cambridge — *Visitors' guides — German texts*
Cambridge : ein illustrierter Führer aus der Colourmaster Reihe. — St. Ives, Huntingdon : Photo Precision, [1980]. — 32p : ill(some col.),1map ; 24cm. — (Colourmaster publication)
Includes index
ISBN 0-85933-197-0 (pbk) : Unpriced B81-10394

914.26'7 — South Essex. Rivers — *Visitors' guides*
Clarke, Vernon. Rivers of South Essex / Vernon Clarke. — Colchester (The Lodge, Mill La., Colne Engaine, Colchester CO6 2HX) : V. Clarke, c1981. — 20p : ill,2maps ; 22cm
Cover title. — Includes index
£0.55 (pbk) B81-10404

914.26'7 — West Essex. Rivers — *Visitors' guides*
Clarke, Vernon. Rivers of West Essex / Vernon Clarke. — Colchester (The Lodge, Mill La., Colne Engaine, Colchester CO6 2HX) : V. Clarke, c1981. — 20p : ill,2maps ; 22cm
Cover title. — Includes index
£0.55 (pbk) B81-10405

914.26'704857 — Essex — *Visitors' guides*
Scarfe, Norman. Essex : a Shell guide. — London : Faber, Sept.1981. — [211]p
Originally published: 1968
ISBN 0-571-11819-4 (pbk) : £2.95 : CIP entry B81-22620

914.26'712 — Essex. Saffron Walden — *Visitors' guides*
Saffron Walden : official guide. — Wallington : Forward Publicity, [1981]. — 32p,[2]p of plates : ill,1map ; 21cm
Unpriced (pbk) B81-23619

914.26'76 — Essex. Bentley Common. Parish churches: St Paul's Church *(Bentley Common)* — *Visitors' guides*
Lewis, Lesley. Saint Paul's Church : Bentley Common near Brentwood, Essex / by Lesley Lewis. — [London] ([38 Whitelands House, Cheltenham Terrace, SW3 4QY]) : [E.R. Lewis], [1981]. — 15p : ill,1map,1plan ; 22cm
Ill on covers
Unpriced (pbk) B81-34257

914.26'76 — Essex. Brentwood *(District)*. **Country parks: Thorndon Country Park** — *Visitors' guides*
Duchars, A.. Thorndon Country Park / [A. Duchars]. — [Chelmsford] ([County Hall, Chelmsford CM1 1LX]) : [Essex County Council], 1976 (1979 [printing]). — 22p : ill,maps ; 22cm
Cover title. — Map on inside cover. — Bibliography: p22
Unpriced (pbk) B81-24766

914.26'76 — Essex. Brentwood *(District)*. **Country parks: Weald Country Park** — *Visitors' guides*
Duchars, A.. Weald Country Park / A. Duchars. — [Chelmsford] ([Estates & Valuation Department, Clarendon House, Parkway, Chelmsford CM2 0NT]) : [Essex County Council], 1977 (1979 [printing]). — 36p,1leaf of plates : ill,maps,plans ; 21cm
Cover title. — Map on inside cover. — Bibliography: p35
Unpriced (pbk) B81-24767

914.26'7604858 — Essex. Brentwood *(District)* — *Visitors' guides*
Brentwood : official guide. — Gloucester : British Publishing Co., [1980]. — 104p : ill,maps(some col.) ; 22cm
Maps (folded sheet) attached to back cover
ISBN 0-7140-1920-8 (pbk) : £0.50 B81-26294

914.26'77204858 — Essex. Basildon *(District)* — *Visitors' guides*
Basildon District guide. — Wallington : Forward Publicity, [1981]. — 72p : ill(some col.),3maps ; 22cm
Unpriced (pbk) B81-10707

914.27'005 — North-west England. Geographical features — *Serials*
The **Manchester** geographer : journal of the Manchester Geographical Society. — Vol.1, no.1 (Autumn 1980)-. — Manchester (274 The Corn Exchange Building, Manchester) : The Society, 1980-. — v. : ill ; 21cm
Two issues yearly
ISSN 0260-5503 = Manchester geographer : £3.50 per year B81-06825

914.27'04857 — Northern England, *1970-1979* — *Visitors' guides — For motoring*
The **Lake** District, the Pennines and Yorkshire Dales / completely revised by Harry Loftus. — London : Letts, [1980]. — 64p : ill,maps ; 22cm
Previous ed.: published as Letts tour the Lake District, the Pennines and Yorkshire Dales. 1974. — Includes index
ISBN 0-85097-141-1 (pbk) : £0.45 B81-13016

914.27'04858'05 — Northern England — *Visitors' guides — Serials*
England's northcountry / English Tourist Board. — 1980-. — London (4 Grosvenor Gardens, SW1W 0DU) : The Board, 1979-. — v. : ill,maps,ports ; 30cm
Annual. — Description based on: 1981 issue
ISSN 0261-0566 = England's northcountry : Unpriced B81-14547

914.27'14 — Cheshire. Chester. Description & travel
Bethell, David. Portrait of Chester / by David Bethell. — London : Hale, 1980. — 192p, [24]p of plates : 1map ; 23cm
Includes index
ISBN 0-7091-8359-3 : £6.95 B81-00658

914.27'15 — Cheshire. Northwich — *Visitors' guides*
Northwich official guide. — Gloucester : British Publishing, [1981?]. — 40p : ill,maps ; 18cm
Map on folded sheet attached to inside cover
ISBN 0-7140-1925-9 (pbk) : Unpriced B81-11769

914.27'16 — Cheshire. Alderley Edge — *Visitors' guides*
Alderley Edge : official guide. — Wallington : Forward Publicity, [1981]. — 27p : ill,map,coat of arms ; 19cm
Unpriced (pbk) B81-23620

914.27'16 — Cheshire. Knutsford — *Visitors' guides*
Knutsford, Cheshire : the official guide. — 19th ed. — Gloucester : British Publishing, 1980. — 72p,leaf of plates (folded sheet) : ill,1map,coat of arms,1facsim ; 19cm
Previous ed.: 1978
Unpriced (pbk) B81-07956

914.27'1604858 — Cheshire. Macclesfield *(District)* — *Visitors' guides*
Macclesfield : Borough Council official guide, including the Wilmslow and Knutsford areas / issued by authority of the Macclesfield Borough Council. — Wallington : Home Publishing, [1980?]. — 84p : ill(some col.),coat of arms ; 24cm
Unpriced (pbk) B81-20223

914.27'35 — Greater Manchester *(Metropolitan County)*. **Ashton-under-Lyne. Parish churches: Ashton Parish Church** — *Visitors' guides*
Radcliffe, Albert E.. A history and guide of Ashton Parish Church : to celebrate the 700th anniversary of our parish 1281-1981 / [Albert E. Radcliffe]. — [Ashton-under-Lyne] ([The Rectory, Caroline St., Ashton-under-Lyne, Lancs. OL6 6NS]) : [The Church], [1980]. — 36p : ill,1port ; 21cm
Cover title
£0.60 (pbk) B81-04643

914.27'3804858 — Greater Manchester *(Metropolitan County)*. **Bury** *(District)* — *Visitors' guides*
Bury : Metropolitan Borough official guide. — Wallington : Home Publishing, [1980?]. — 84p : ill,maps,coats of arms(some col.) ; 24cm
Cover title
Unpriced (pbk) B81-20222

914.27'392 — Greater Manchester *(Metropolitan County)*. **Rochdale** — *Walkers' guides*
Trails around Rochdale 1980. — [Rochdale] ([10, Ashley Close, Rochdale, OL11 3EP]) : Rochdale Civic Society, [1980]. — 1portfolio (5items) : ill,maps ; 30cm
Contents: Introduction and history — Town centre trail — Churches — Waterways — Housing trail
£2.25 B81-37333

914.27'392 — Greater Manchester *(Metropolitan County)*. **Smithy Bridge** — *Walkers' guides*
Smithy Bridge / Littleborough Local Historical and Archaeological Society. — [Rochdale] ([Denehurst, Edenfield Rd., Rochdale]) : Rochdale Recreation and Amenities Department, 1980. — 15p,[2]p of plates : 2maps ; 21cm. — (History trail ; no.6)
Cover title
£0.20 (pbk) B81-33092

914.27'504858 — Merseyside *(Metropolitan County)* — *Visitors' guides — For industrial development*
Merseyside : a guide to industrial and distribution services / MERCEDO Merseyside County Economic Development Office. — [London] : Burrow, [1981]. — 156p : ill(some col.),col.maps ; 30cm
Spine title: Merseyside industrial guide
Unpriced (pbk) B81-23999

914.27'5404858 — Merseyside *(Metropolitan County).* **Knowsley** *(District) — Practical information — For businessmen*

Knowsley : industrial and commercial guide. — London : Burrow, [1981]. — 44p : ill,1coat of arms ; 25cm
£1.25 (pbk) B81-39139

914.27'62304858 — Lancashire. Blackburn *(District) — Visitors' guides*

The **Borough** of Blackburn : official handbook. — Gloucester : British Publishing Co., [1981?]. — 204p : ill(some col.),maps,ports ; 25cm
Includes index
ISBN 0-7140-1845-7 (pbk) : £1.20 B81-26298

914.27'68504858'0222 — Lancashire. Forest of Bowland. Description & travel — *Illustrations*

Wainwright, A.. A Bowland sketchbook / A. Wainwright. — Kendal : Westmorland Gazette, 1981. — [180]p : ill ; 18x24cm
£3.30 B81-39183

914.27'804857 — Cumbria. Lake District. Description & travel, *1970-1979 — Personal observations*

Davies, Hunter. A walk around the Lakes : observations relative chiefly to the picturesque beauty ... / by Hunter Davies. — Feltham : Hamlyn Paperbacks, 1980, c1979. — xi,339p,[8]p of plates : ill,maps,ports ; 20cm
Originally published: London : Weidenfeld and Nicolson, 1979. — Bibliography: p329-330. — Includes index
ISBN 0-600-20012-4 (pbk) : £1.50 B81-04738

914.27'804858 — Cumbria. Description & travel

Marshall, J. D.. Portrait of Cumbria / by J.D. Marshall. — London : Hale, 1981. — 224p,[24]p of plates : ill ; 23cm
Bibliography: p215-218. — Includes index
ISBN 0-7091-9142-1 : £7.95 B81-26944

914.27'804858 — Cumbria. Lake District. Description & travel

Goddard, Frank. Foothills of the fells / Frank Goddard ; photographs by Geoffrey Berry. — London : Hale, 1981. — 208p,[24]p of plates : ill,1map ; 23cm
Includes index
ISBN 0-7091-9341-6 : £8.25 B81-38916

914.27'804858 — Cumbria. Lake District. National Trust properties — *Visitors' guides*

The **National** Trust in the Lake District : a colour guide to National Trust properties in the Lake District and Cumbria. — 2nd ed. — Clapham, N. Yorkshire : Dalesman, 1980. — 40p : ill(some col.),1col.map ; 21cm
Previous ed.: 1975
ISBN 0-85206-579-5 (pbk) : £0.75 B81-04521

914.27'804858 — Cumbria. Lake District. Places associated with Lake District legends — *Walkers' guides*

Bailey, Brian J.. Lakeland walks and legends / Brian J. Bailey. — London : Granada, 1981. — 172p : ill,1map ; 18cm. — (A Mayfower book)
ISBN 0-583-13249-9 (pbk) : £1.50 B81-19091

914.27'804858 — Cumbria. Lake District — *Visitors' guides*

The **English** Lakes. — Huntingdon : Photo Precision, [1981?]. — 32p : col.ill,1col.map ; 24cm. — (Colourmaster international)
ISBN 0-85933-175-x (pbk) : Unpriced B81-21273

The **Lakes** : a pictorial guide. — Huntingdon : Photo Precision, 1981. — 64p : col.ill,1col.map ; 24cm. — (Colourmaster international)
Text on inside front cover
ISBN 0-85933-203-9 (pbk) : Unpriced B81-18907

On holiday in the Lake District. — Clapham [N. Yorkshire] : Dalesman, 1981. — 96p : ill,maps ; 21cm
ISBN 0-85206-640-6 (pbk) : £1.00 B81-37160

914.27'804858 — Cumbria. Lake District — *Walkers' guides*
Hart, Tony. The freedom of the fells : an introduction to fell-walking in the English Lake District / written and illustrated by Tony Hart. — Wembley : Selecteditions, 1980. — 193p,[37] leaves of plates : ill,maps ; 21cm
Bibliography: p167-173
ISBN 0-86237-002-7 (pbk) : £2.00 B81-23118

Spencer, Brian, *19---*. A visitor's guide to the Lake District / Brian Spencer. — Ashbourne : Moorland, c1981. — 144p : ill,maps ; 22cm
Includes index
ISBN 0-86190-013-8 (cased) : Unpriced : CIP rev.
ISBN 0-86190-010-3 (pbk) : £3.95 B81-08862

914.27'83 — Cumbria. Bowness & Windermere — *Visitors' guides*
Mitchell, W. R. (William Reginald). Bowness and Windermere : a guide for visitors and residents / by W.R. Mitchell ; illustrated by Tom Sykes. — Clapham, N. Yorkshire : Dalesman, 1980. — 32p : ill,2plans ; 19cm. — (A Dalesman mini-book)
Plans on inside covers
ISBN 0-85206-580-9 (pbk) : £0.60 B81-01571

914.27'83 — Cumbria. Kendal. Country houses: Sizergh Castle — *Visitors' guides*
National Trust. Sizergh Castle, Cumbria. — [Rev. ed.]. — [London] : National Trust, 1979 (1981 [printing]). — 26p,[8]p of plates : ill,plans,ports ; 22cm
Unpriced (pbk) B81-22952

914.27'83 — Cumbria. Ulverston — *Visitors' guides*
Ulverston official guide 1981-1982. — Wallington : Forward Publicity, [1981?]. — 52p : ill,2maps,1coat of arms ; 22cm
Two maps (folded sheet) attached to inside back cover. — Includes index
Unpriced (pbk) B81-23626

914.28'1'0014 — Yorkshire. Place names
Morris, R. W.. Yorkshire through place names. — Newton Abbot : David & Charles, Feb.1982. — [192]p
ISBN 0-7153-8230-6 : £9.50 : CIP entry B81-35824

914.28'104858 — West Yorkshire *(Metropolitan County) — Practical information — For businessmen*
Services for industry and commerce in West Yorkshire / West Yorkshire Metropolitan County Council. — Gloucester : British Publishing, [1981]. — 176p : ill(some col.),maps(some col.),2plans,ports ; 30cm
ISBN 0-7140-1980-1 (pbk) : Unpriced B81-27621

914.28'104858 — Yorkshire — *Visitors' guides*
On holiday in Yorkshire / compiled by The Dalesman. — Clapham [N. Yorkshire] : Dalesman, 1981. — 94p : ill,maps ; 21cm
ISBN 0-85206-638-4 (pbk) : £1.00 B81-37159

914.28'104858'0222 — Yorkshire. Description & travel — *Illustrations*
Bloemendal, F. A. H.. Yorkshire : England in cameracolour / photographs by F.A.H. Bloemendal ; text by Alan Hollingsworth. — London : Ian Allan, 1980. — 110p : chiefly col.ill,maps ; 30cm
Maps on lining papers
ISBN 0-7110-1031-5 : £7.95 B81-01370

914.28'12 — West Yorkshire *(Metropolitan County).* **Hebden Bridge** — *Visitors' guides*
Official guide to Hebden Bridge : 'the Pennine Centre', West Yorkshire. — Gloucester : British Publishing, [1980]. — 68p,[2]p of plates (folded sheet) : ill,maps ; 21cm
Unpriced (pbk) B81-07958

914.28'1304858 — West Yorkshire *(Metropolitan County).* **Kirklees** *(District) — Visitors' guides*
Kirklees civic guide / compiled and designed by Kirklees Metropolitan Council. — 2nd ed. / editors M.J. Fay and Patricia Bagley. — Wallington : Home Publishing, 1981. — 132p : ill(some col.),maps,1col.coat of arms,ports ; 24cm
Previous ed.: 1978
Unpriced (pbk) B81-26644

914.28'15 — West Yorkshire *(Metropolitan County).* **Wakefield. Country houses: Nostell Priory** — *Visitors' guides*
National Trust. Nostell Priory, Yorkshire. — [New ed.]. — [London] : National Trust, 1978 (1981 [printing]). — 34p,12p of plates : ill (some col.),1plan,ports,1geneal.table ; 25cm
Bibliography: p34
Unpriced (pbk) B81-22955

914.28'17 — West Yorkshire *(Metropolitan County).* **Keighley. Houses: East Riddlesden Hall** — *Visitors' guides*
National Trust. East Riddlesden Hall : Keighley, Yorkshire. — [London] : The Trust, 1981, c1979. — 17p,[4]p of plates : ill ; 22cm
Bibliography: p17
Unpriced (pbk) B81-18749

914.28'19 — West Yorkshire *(Metropolitan County).* **Leeds** — *Walkers' guides*
Broadhead, Ivan E.. Exploring Leeds : a guided tour / by Ivan E. Broadhead. — Warley : Tetradon, 1981. — 52p : ill,maps ; 21cm. — (Tetradon outdoor guides)
ISBN 0-906070-05-8 (pbk) : £1.30 : CIP rev. B81-21589

914.28'19 — West Yorkshire *(Metropolitan County).* **Little Woodhouse. Houses: Claremont** — *Visitors' guides*
Yorkshire Archaeological Society. Claremont Leeds / Brian and Dorothy Payne ; foreword by Maurice Beresford ; postscript by Herman Ramm. — Leeds (23 Clarendon Rd., Leeds LS2 9NZ) : Yorkshire Archaeological Society, 1980. — ix,44p : ill,maps,plans ; 15x21cm
Map on inside back cover
ISBN 0-902122-31-2 (pbk) : Unpriced B81-05571

914.28'19 — West Yorkshire *(Metropolitan County).* **Otley** — *Visitors' guides*
Otley : official guide. — Wallington : Forward, [1981]. — 40p,[1]folded leaf of plates : ill,1coat of arms,1map ; 21cm
Includes index
Unpriced (pbk) B81-21098

914.28'304858 — Humberside — *Visitors' guides*
Humberside county handbook : the offical guide to the county. — Gloucester : British Publishing, [1981?]. — 224p : ill(some col.),maps(some col.),1col.coat of arms, ports ; 24cm
Map on folded sheet attached to inside cover
ISBN 0-7140-1871-6 (pbk) : Unpriced B81-11775

914.28'3304858 — Humberside. Cleethorpes *(District) — Visitors' guides*
Cleethorpes Borough Council official area guide the history, information, local services, commerce and industry in the towns and villages of the borough. — Gloucester : British Publishing Co., [1981]. — 80p : ill(some col.),col.maps ; 21cm
ISBN 0-7140-1811-2 (pbk) : £0.40 B81-26295

914.28'3404858 — Humberside. Great Grimsby *(District) — Visitors' guides*
Great Grimsby : official guide. — Wallington : Home Publishing, [1981]. — 120p : ill(some col.),1map,coat of arms,1port ; 21cm
Unpriced (pbk) B81-36403

914.28'3704858 — Humberside. Hull — *Visitors' guides*
Where in Hull are we? : a guide / produced by the Hull Junior Chamber of Commerce & Shipping. — [Hull] (Samman House, Bowlalley La., Hull) : Hull Junior Chamber of Commerce & Shipping, [1980]. — 40p : ill,1col.map,1port ; 21cm
Cover title
Unpriced (pbk) B81-32466

914.28'3704858 — Humberside. Hull — *Walkers' guides*
. A walk round the old town of Hull / City Information Service. — 2nd ed. — Hull (Central Library, Albion St,. Hull, HU1 3TF) : Kingston upon Hull City Information Service, 1981. — 6p : ill,1map ; 30cm
Previous ed.: 1976?
Free (unbound) B81-27614

914.28'38 — Humberside. Welwick. Parish churches: Parish Church of St. Mary, Welwick — *Visitors' guides*

Wardle, Chris. The parish church of St. Mary, Welwick : the history and local legend concerning the church / compiled by Chris Wardle. — [Withernsea] ([The Vicarage, Main St., Hollym, Withernsea, N. Humberside HU19 2RS]) : C. Wardle, 1978. — 5 leaves : ill ; 26cm
Cover title
£0.15 (pbk) B81-17360

Wardle, Chris. The parish church of St. Mary, Welwick : the history and local legend concerning the church. — New illustrated ed. / compiled by Chris Wardle and I.R. Dowse. — [Withernsea] ([The Vicarage, Main St., Hollym, Withernsea, N. Humberside, HU19 2RS]) : [I.R. Dowse], 1981. — 8p : ill,1geneal.table ; 22cm
Cover title. — Previous ed.: / by Chris Wardle. 1978
£0.35 (pbk) B81-17359

914.28'404858 — North Yorkshire. Dales — *Visitors' guides*

Gower, Edward. Exploring the Yorkshire Dales / by Edward Gower. — 4th ed. — Clapham, N. Yorkshire : Dalesman, 1980. — 72p : maps ; 19cm. — (A Dalesman mini-book)
Previous ed.: 1978. — Maps on inside covers. — Includes bibliographies
ISBN 0-85206-603-1 (pbk) : £1.00 B81-08776

914.28'41 — North Yorkshire. Upper Wharfedale. Description & travel

Houghton, F. W.. Upper Wharfedale : from Bolton Bridge to the head-waters / by F.W. Houghton. — Clapham, N.Yorkshire : Dalesman, 1980. — 168p : ill,1map ; 22cm
Bibliography: p163. — Includes index
ISBN 0-85206-600-7 (pbk) : £3.95 B81-06975

914.28'43 — North Yorkshire. York. Town houses: Treasurer's House — *Visitors' guides*

National Trust. Treasurer's House : York / [photographs by W. Farnsworth]. — [London] : The Trust, 1981, c1978. — 23p,[4]p of plates : ill,1plan ; 22cm
Unpriced (pbk) B81-18748

914.28'4304858 — North Yorkshire. York — *Visitors' guides — French texts*

Rotheray, Brian. La ville de York / de Brian Rotheray. — St. Ives, Huntingdon : Photo Precision, [1980]. — 32p : col.ill,1col.map ; 24cm. — (Colourmaster publication)
ISBN 0-85933-199-7 (pbk) : Unpriced B81-10392

914.28'4304858 — North Yorkshire. York — *Visitors' guides — German texts*

Rotheray, Brian. Die Stadt York / von Brian Rotheray. — St. Ives, Huntingdon : Photo Precision, [1980]. — 32p : col.ill,1col.map ; 24cm. — (Colourmaster publication)
ISBN 0-85933-200-4 (pbk) : Unpriced B81-10391

914.28'4304858 — North Yorkshire. York — *Walkers' guides*

Broadhead, Ivan E.. Walkabout York : a guided tour through a historic city / by Ivan E. Broadhead. — Warley (40 Hazdor Rd., Oldbury, Warley, W. Midlands B68 9LA) : Tetradon, 1980. — 47p : ill,maps ; 21cm
ISBN 0-906070-03-1 (pbk) : £1.50 B81-04971

914.28'45 — North Yorkshire. Selby — *Visitors' guides*

Selby : official guide. — Wallington : Forward Publicity, [1981?]. — 56p,[2]folded p of plates : ill(some col.),maps ; 21cm
Unpriced (pbk) B81-28861

914.28'46 — North Yorkshire. Kirkham. Priories: Kirkham Priory — *Visitors' guides*

Great Britain. *Department of the Environment*. Kirkham Priory / Department of the Environment. — 2nd ed. — [London] : H.M.S.O., 1980. — 7p : 1plan ; 21cm
Previous ed.: 1960
ISBN 0-11-671061-6 (unbound) : £0.20 B81-07325

914.28'46 — North Yorkshire. Malton & Norton — *Visitors' guides*

Malton and Norton-on-Derwent : official guide. — Wallington : Forward Publicity, [1981]. — 56p : ill,maps ; 21cm
£0.10 (pbk) B81-36397

914.28'49 — North Yorkshire. Northallerton region — *Visitors' guides*

Northallerton & district : Chamber of Trade and Commerce handbook. — Wallington : Forward Publicity, [1981]. — 35p,[2]p of plates(folded sheet) : ill,1map ; 21cm
Unpriced (pbk) B81-10711

914.28'54 — Cleveland. Guisborough — *Visitors' guides*

Guisborough official guide. — Wallington : Forward, [1981]. — 44p : ill,2maps ; 21cm
Includes index
Unpriced (pbk) B81-21101

914.28'604858 — Durham *(County)* — *Visitors' guides*

Thorold, Henry. County Durham / by Henry Thorold. — London : Faber, 1980. — 192p,[2]p of plates : ill,1col.map ; 24cm. — (A Shell guide)
Ill on lining papers. — Includes index
ISBN 0-571-11640-x : £4.95 : CIP rev. B80-26292

914.28'6304858 — Durham *(County)*. **Darlington** *(District)* — *Visitors' guides*

The **Borough** of Darlington : official guide. — Wallington : Forward, [1981]. — 80p : ill(some col.),coats of arms,maps ; 24cm
Bibliography: p67
Unpriced (pbk) B81-21099

914.28'6404858 — Durham *(County)*. **Wear Valley** *(District)* — *Visitors' guides*

Discover the Wear Valley. — London : Burrow, [1981]. — 32p : ill,maps ; 22cm
Unpriced (pbk) B81-24081

914.28'6504858 — Durham *(County)*. **Durham** — *Walkers' guides*

Walk. — Durham (Hon. Secretary, c/o Department of Geography, The University, Durham) : City of Durham Trust
2: The river banks. — Rev. ed. — 1981. — 1sheet : ill,1maps ; 21x38cm folded to 10x21cm
Previous ed.: S.l. : s.n., 197-
Unpriced B81-32484

914.28'6904858 — Durham *(County)*. **Chester-le-Street** *(District)* — *Visitors' guides*

Chester-le-Street District official guide. — Wallington : Home Publishing, [1980]. — 30p,[2]p of plates(folded sheet) : ill,maps ; 22cm
Unpriced (pbk) B81-07955

914.28'804858 — Northumberland — *Visitors' guides*

Northumberland : County handbook : issued by authority of Northumberland County Council. — London : Burrow, [1981]. — 108p : ill,maps ; 25cm
Unpriced (pbk) B81-35012

Northumberland County handbook / issued by authority of Northumberland County Council. — London : Burrow, [1981]. — 108p : ill,1map,1coat of arms,1port ; 25cm
£2.00 (pbk) B81-39136

914.28'83 — Northumberland. Cambo. Country houses: Wallington Hall — *Visitors' guides*

National Trust. Wallington : Northumberland. — Rev. — [London] : National Trust, 1981, c1979. — 27p,[1] leaf of plates : ill(some col.),1plan ; 25cm
Unpriced (pbk) B81-18423

914.28'87 — Northumberland. Alnwick. Castles: Alnwick Castle — *Visitors' guides*

Alnwick Castle : home of the Duke of Northumberland. — Derby : English Life, 1980. — 32p : ill(some col.),plan,ports(some col.) ; 24cm
Text, ill on inside covers
ISBN 0-85101-157-8 (pbk) : £0.60 B81-16221

914.28'8704858 — Northumberland. Alnwick *(District)* — *Visitors' guides*

District of Alnwick : offical guide. — Wallington (Falcon House, 20-22 Belmont Rd., Wallington, Surrey, SM6 8TA) : Home, [1981]. — 64p : ill,1coat of arms,1map ; 21cm
Unpriced (pbk) B81-21105

914.28'89 — Northumberland. Holy Island. Castles: Lindisfarne Castle — *Visitors' guides*

National Trust. Lindisfarne Castle / by Peter Orde. — Rev. — [London] : National Trust, 1981. — 15p,[8]p of plates : ill,plans,2ports ; 25cm
Previous ed.: 1978. — Bibliography: p15
Unpriced (pbk) B81-22304

914.29 — WALES

914.29'04857 — Wales, *1970-1979* — *Visitors' guides — For motoring*

Wales. — Newly rev. ed. / completely revised by Harry Loftus. — London : Letts, [1980]. — 64p : ill,maps ; 22cm. — (Letts tour)
Previous ed.: published as Touring Wales. 1980. — Includes index
ISBN 0-85097-315-5 (pbk) : £0.75 B81-09266

914.29'04858 — Wales. Description & travel — *Personal observations*

Vaughan-Thomas, Wynford. Wynford Vaughan-Thomas's Wales / with photographs by Derry Brabbs. — London : Joseph, 1981. — 223p : col.ill,maps,ports(some col.) ; 25cm
Ill on lining papers. — Includes index
ISBN 0-7181-2055-8 : £9.95 B81-39855

914.29'04858'0222 — Wales. Description & travel — *Illustrations*

Thomas, Roger, *1947-*. The Country life picture book of Wales / Roger Thomas. — Richmond upon Thames : Country Life Books, 1981. — 128p : col.ill ; 31cm
ISBN 0-600-36807-6 : £7.95 B81-22839

914.29'04858'0222 — Wales. Mountains. Description & travel — *Illustrations*

Poucher, W. A.. Wales / W.A. Poucher. — London : Constable, 1981. — 203p : chiefly col.ill ; 27cm
ISBN 0-09-464310-5 : £9.95 B81-37724

Wainwright, A.. Welsh mountain drawings / A. Wainwright. — Kendall ([22 Stricklandgate, Kendal, Westmorland LA9 4NE]) : Westmorland Gazette, 1981. — [210]p : all ill ; 23x28cm
£6.00 B81-18459

914.29'104858 — North Wales. Caves — *Visitors' guides — For exploration*

Oldham, Tony. The caves of North Wales. — Crymych (Rhychydŵr, Crymych, Dyfed SA41 3RB) : Anne Oldham, 1980, c1981. — xii,69p : ill,maps ; 26cm
Previous ed.: 1977. — Includes bibliographies and index
£3.00 (pbk) B81-21922

914.29'204858 — Gwynedd — *Visitors' guides*

Gwynedd. — Gloucester : British Publishing, [1981?]. — 128p : ill,maps(some col.),coat of arms ; 21cm
Includes some articles in Welsh and some in English, forewords in Welsh and English, prefaces in French, Dutch, German, Welsh and English
ISBN 0-7140-1969-0 (pbk) : Unpriced B81-27624

914.29'25 — Gwynedd. Bangor. Country houses: Penrhyn Castle — *Visitors' guides*

National Trust. Penrhyn Castle : Gwynedd. — [London] : National Trust, 1979 (1980 [printing]). — 16p : ill,1plan ; 25cm
Unpriced (pbk) B81-18424

914.29'2504858 — Gwynedd. Snowdonia — *Walkers' guides*

Maddern, Ralph. Walk in magnificent Snowdonia / Ralph Maddern. — Windsor (9 Priors Rd, Windsor, Berks. SL4 4PD) : Focus, 1979. — 102p : ill,maps ; 20cm
Bibliography: p102
ISBN 0-9505053-2-3 (pbk) : £1.50 B81-06837

914.29′27 — Gwynedd. Conwy Valley — *Walkers′ guides*

Maddern, Ralph. Walk in the beautiful Conway Valley / Ralph Maddern. — 3rd ed. — Windsor (9 Priors Rd, Windsor, Berks. SL4 4PD) : Focus, 1979. — 82p : ill,maps ; 20cm
Previous ed.: 1978. — Bibliography: p82
ISBN 0-9505053-0-7 (pbk) : £1.20 B81-10674

914.29′27 — Gwynedd. Gwybrnant Valley. Farmhouses: Tŷ Mawr — *Visitors′ guides*

National Trust. Tŷ Maur : Gwynedd. — [London] : The Trust, 1979. — 20p : 1ill,facsims,1port ; 22cm
Text in English and Welsh
Unpriced (pbk) B81-18746

914.29′37 — Clwyd. Carrog — *Walkers′ guides*

Carrog, near Corwen, Clwyd, village trail. — [Mold] ([Shire Hall, Mold, CH7 6NG]) : Clwyd County Planning and Estates Department in association with the Carrog Womens Institute, 1981. — 20p : ill,maps ; 21cm
Cover title
ISBN 0-904444-45-7 (pbk) : Unpriced B81-36135

914.29′37 — Clwyd. Country parks: Moel Famau Country Park — *Walkers′ guides*

Thompson, Keith, *1942-*. Walks in the Moel Famau Country Park / Keith Thompson. — [Ruthlin?] (Ruthlin, Clwyd) : Spread Eagle, c1980. — [24]p : ill,1map ; 21cm
Bibliography: p[23]
ISBN 0-907207-03-0 (pbk) : Unpriced B81-21846

914.29′37 — Clwyd. Llangollen — *Visitors′ guides*

Llangollen official guide. — Gloucester : British Publishing, [1981]. — 44p : ill(some col.),1map ; 19cm
ISBN 0-7140-1993-3 (pbk) : Unpriced B81-27619

914.29′4′04857 — South-west Wales — *Visitors′ guides*

Rees, Vyvyan. South-west Wales : a Shell guide. — 2nd ed. — London : Faber, Sept.1981. — [190]p
Previous ed.: 1963
ISBN 0-571-11820-8 (pbk) : £2.95 : CIP entry B81-22621

914.29′404858 — South Wales — *Visitors′ guides*

Hammond, Reginald J. W.. South Wales : Wye Valley, Newport, Cardiff, Porthcawl, Swansea and Gower, Tenby, St David′s / Reginald Hammond ; edited and revised by Kenneth Lowther. — London : Ward Lock, 1981. — 160p : ill,maps ; 18cm. — (Ward Lock′s red guides)
Includes index
ISBN 0-7063-6078-8 (pbk) : £2.95 B81-27121

914.29′51 — Powys. Welshpool. Castles: Powis Castle. Gardens — *Visitors′ guides*

National Trust. Powis Castle gardens : Powys. — [London] : The Trust, 1980, c1972. — 24p : 1plan ; 22cm
Unpriced (pbk) B81-18747

914.29′5604858 — South Wales. National parks: Brecon Beacons National Park — *Walkers′ guides*

Barber, Chris, *1941-*. Exploring the Brecon Beacons National Park : a walker′s guide to the Brecon Beacons, waterfall country and Black Mountains / Chris Barber. — Bristol (2nd Floor, Clifton Heights, Bristol BS8 1EW) : Regional Publications, 1980. — 96p : ill,maps ; 21cm
ISBN 0-906570-05-0 (pbk) : £3.80 B81-04519

914.29′604858 — Dyfed. Railway services. Disused routes. Description & travel — *Personal observations — Welsh texts*

Thomas, Dewi W.. Wrth ymdaith / Dewi W. Thomas. — Llandysul : Gwasg Gomer, 1980. — 185p : ill,maps,1facsim,ports ; 19cm
ISBN 0-85088-523-x (pbk) : £2.25 B81-04718

914.29′82 — West Glamorgan. Gower — *Visitors′ guides*

A **Pocket** guide to Gower / [West Glamorgan County Council]. — [Swansea] : [The Council], [1980]. — [24]p : ill,2maps ; 22cm. — (West Glamorgan county series ; no.1)
£0.20 (unbound) B81-07840

914.29′82 — West Glamorgan. Mumbles — *Visitors′ guides*

A **Pocket** guide to Mumbles / [West Glamorgan County Council]. — [Swansea] : [The Council], [1980]. — [28]p : ill,2maps ; 21cm. — (West Glamorgan county series ; no.2)
£0.25 (unbound) B81-07839

914.29′8304858 — West Glamorgan. Lliw Valley *(District)* — *Visitors′ guides*

A **Pocket** guide to Lower Lliw Valley / [West Glamorgan County Council]. — [Swansea] : [The Council], [1980]. — [20]p : ill,3maps ; 21cm. — (West Glamorgan county series ; no.3)
£0.25 (unbound) B81-07841

914.29′904858 — Gwent. Churches — *Visitors′ guides*

Guy, John R.. Ancient Gwent churches / John R. Guy and Ewart B. Smith. — 2nd ed. — Risca : Starling Press, 1980. — 72p,[40]p of plates : ill,1map ; 21cm
Previous ed.: 1979. — Bibliography: p72
ISBN 0-903434-42-3 (pbk) : Unpriced B81-11844

914.29′91 — Gwent. Newport *(District)*. **Country houses: Tredegar House** — *Visitors′ guides*

Tredegar House. — [Newport, Gwent] ([John Frost Sq., Newport, Gwent NPT 1PA]) : Newport Museum and Art Gallery, [1981?]. — 1sheet ; 30x63cm folded to 30x21cm : ill,1plan
Unpriced B81-36068

914.29′98 — Gwent. Grosmont. Castles: Grosmont Castle — *Visitors′ guides*

Great Britain. *Welsh Office*. Grosmont Castle, Gwent / prepared by the Welsh Office ; [by] J.K. Knight = Castell y Grysmwnt / paratowyd gan y Swyddfa Gymreig. — Cardiff : H.M.S.O., 1980. — 35p : ill,1plan ; 21cm
Parallel English and Welsh text. — Plan (1 folded sheet) attached to back cover
ISBN 0-11-790128-8 (pbk) : £0.85 B81-07549

914.3 — CENTRAL EUROPE, GERMANY

914.3′04878 — Germany — *Visitors′ guides*

Kane, Robert S.. Germany : A to Z guide / by Robert S. Kane. — Chicago : McNally ; London : Distributed by Pitman, c1980. — vii,344p,[16]p of plates : col.ill,col.maps ; 21cm
Includes index
ISBN 0-273-01677-6 (pbk) : £2.95 B81-11235

914.3′04878 — West Germany. Description & travel — *For children*

Fairclough, Chris. Let′s go to West Germany / text and photographs by Chris Fairclough. — London : Watts, c1981. — 32p : col.ill,col.maps ; 22cm
Includes index
ISBN 0-85166-927-1 : £2.99 B81-32452

914.3′04878 — West Germany — *Visitors′ guides*

Tingey, Nancy. Germany / main text by Nancy Tingey ; facts at your fingertips by Harold Dennis-Jones. — London : Letts, 1979 (1981 [printing]). — 96p : ill ; 19cm. — (Letts guide)
ISBN 0-85097-345-7 (pbk) : £1.25 B81-08550

914.3′4046 — West Germany. Rhine River region. Description & travel, *ca 1790 — Polyglot texts — Early works — Facsimiles*

Janscha, L.. Collection de cinquante vues du Rhin les plus intéressantes et les plus pittoresques, depuis Spire jusqu′à Düsseldorf : dessinées sur les lieux d′après nature = Fünfzig malerische nach der Natur gezeichnet / von L. Janscha und von Ziegler gestochen. — Edinburgh : Harris, 1980. — [53]leaves[50] leaves of plates : col.ill ; 59cm + Booklet([8]p : ill(some col.) ; 25cm)
Text in French and German. — Facsim reprint. Originally published: Vienna : Artaria, 1978. — Limited ed. of 775 numbered copies. - Half bound in goatskin blocked in gold. - In box
ISBN 0-86228-000-1 : £950.00 : CIP rev.
Primary classification 769.92′4 B80-12004

914.36 — AUSTRIA

914.36′0453 — Austria — *Visitors′ guides*

Austria. — Rev. [ed.]. — London : Letts, 1979 (1981 [printing]). — 96p : ill ; 19cm. — (Letts guide)
Previous ed.: i.e. Completely rev. ed. published as: Letts go to Austria. 1977
ISBN 0-85097-396-1 (pbk) : £1.25 B81-11842

914.37 — CZECHOSLOVAKIA

914.37′0443 — Czechoslovakia — *Practical information — For British businessmen*

Czechoslovakia. — London (50 Ludgate Hill, EC4M 7HU) : British Overseas Trade Board, 1981. — 52p : ill,2maps ; 21cm. — (Hints to exporters)
Bibliography: p41-43
Unpriced (pbk) B81-17690

914.39 — HUNGARY

914.39′0453 — Hungary, *1981 — Personal observations*

Porter, Monica. The paper bridge. — London : Quartet, Oct.1981. — [272]p
ISBN 0-7043-2296-x : £9.95 : CIP entry B81-25708

914.4 — FRANCE

914.4′0434 — France. Description & travel, *1763-1765 — Correspondence, diaries, etc.*

Smollett, Tobias. Travels through France and Italy / Tobias Smollett ; edited by Frank Felsenstein. — London : Oxford University Press, 1979. — lxv,523p : 1facsim ; 23cm
Bibliography: p502-504. — Includes index
ISBN 0-19-812611-5 : £17.50 : CIP rev.
Also classified at 914.5′047 B79-11326

Smollett, Tobias. Travels through France and Italy. — Oxford : Oxford University Press, Nov.1981. — [512]p. — (The World′s classics)
Originally published: London : s.n., 1766
ISBN 0-19-281569-5 (pbk) : £2.50 : CIP entry
Also classified at 914.5′047 B81-30566

914.4′04838 — France. Description & travel

The **Book** of France / consultant editor John Ardagh. — Leicester : Windward, 1980. — 256p : ill(some col.),maps ; 31cm
Includes index
ISBN 0-7112-0059-9 : £9.95 B81-11643

914.4′04838 — France — *Visitors′ guides*

The **Best** of France. — 2nd ed., rev. and updated. — London : Pitman, 1981. — 294p : ill,maps ; 20cm. — (Pitman touring guides)
Previous ed.: published as: Verstappen′s the best of France, 1979. — Includes index
ISBN 0-273-01609-1 (pbk) : Unpriced B81-19463

914.4′04838 — France — *Visitors′ guides — For motoring*

Eperon, Arthur. Travellers′ France : a guide to six major routes through France / Arthur Eperon ; introduction by John Carter ; maps and drawings by Ken Smith. — 6th printing (rev.). — London : Pan, 1980. — 160p : ill,col.maps ; 20cm
Previous ed.: 1979. — Includes index
ISBN 0-330-25982-2 (pbk) : £2.50 B81-10293

914.4'04838 — France — *Visitors' guides — For motoring* *continuation*

Eperon, Arthur. Travellers' France : a guide to six major routes through France / Arthur Eperon ; introduction by John Carter ; maps and drawings by Ken Smith. — Rev. ed. — London : BBC, 1980. — 160p : ill,col.maps ; 21cm
Previous ed.: London : Pan, 1979. — Includes index
ISBN 0-563-17915-5 : £5.50 B81-05286

914.4'04838 — France — *Visitors' guides — For schools*

McLagan, Pat. In France / written and edited by Pat McLagan, contributions from Spencer Thomas ... [et al.] ; designed by Valerie Sargent ; cartoons by David Lock ; illustrations by David Palmer, John Harries. — Walton on Thames : Nelson, 1981. — 96p : ill(some col.),maps(some col.),ports,forms ; 25cm
ISBN 0-17-439081-5 (pbk) : £1.95 B81-16438

McLagan, Pat. In France / written and edited by Pat McLagan ; contributions from Spencer Thomas ... [et al.] ; designed by Valerie Sargent ; cartoons by David Lock ; illustrations by David Palmer, John Harries. — Haywards Heath (Grosvenor Hall, Bolnore Rd., Haywards Heath, West Sussex RH16 4BX), Schools Abroad, c1981. — 96p : ill(some col.),maps(some col.),facsims,ports ; 25cm
Also published: London : Nelson, 1981
ISBN 0-905703-55-3 (pbk) : Unpriced B81-26066

914.4'204838'05 — France. Normandy — *Visitors' guides — Serials*

Tourist guide. Normandy / Michelin. — 5th ed. — London : Michelin Tyre Co., c1980. — 170p
ISBN 2-06-013480-3 : Unpriced B81-29094

914.4'25 — France. Dieppe — *Visitors' guides — For children*

Bienvenue à Dieppe / [compiled by Alma Gray] ; [edited by Joan Henry]. — London (Publishing Centre, Highbury Station Rd, Islington, N1 1SB) : Learning Materials Service in association with Mary Glasgow, c1979. — 20p : ill ; 15x21cm
ISBN 0-86158-504-6 (unbound) : Unpriced B81-29153

914.4'3404838 — France. Seine River region. Description & travel — *For children*

Hills, C. A. R.. The Seine / C.A.R. Hills. — Hove : Wayland, 1981. — 67p : ill(some col.),col.maps ; 21x22cm. — (Rivers of the world)
Map on lining papers. — Bibliography: p66. - Includes index
ISBN 0-85340-807-6 : £4.25 B81-12977

914.4'3604838 — France. Paris — *Practical information — For visual artists*

Paris art guide / editor Fiona Dunlop. — London (89 Notting Hill Gate, W11 3JZ) : Art Guide, c1981. — 72p : ill,maps ; 21cm
Maps on inside covers
ISBN 0-9507160-1-4 (pbk) : £1.95 B81-23993

914.4'3604838 — France. Paris — *Visitors' guides*

Le More, Henri. Paris / [compiled by Henri Le More]. — London : Octopus, 1980. — 187p : maps ; 10x21cm. — (Guide in jeans)
Translation of: Guide de Paris en jeans
ISBN 0-7064-1466-7 (pbk) : Unpriced B81-14057

914.4'3604838'05 — France. Paris — *Visitors' guides — Serials*

Tourist guide. Paris / Michelin. — 3rd ed.. — London : Michelin Tyre Co., c1979. — 178p
ISBN 2-06-013540-0 : Unpriced B81-09230

914.5 — ITALY

914.5'047 — Italy. Description & travel, *1763-1765 — Correspondence, diaries, etc.*

Smollett, Tobias. Travels through France and Italy / Tobias Smollett ; edited by Frank Felsenstein. — London : Oxford University Press, 1979. — lxv,523p : 1facsim ; 23cm
Bibliography: p502-504. — Includes index
ISBN 0-19-812611-5 : £17.50 : CIP rev.
Primary classification 914.4'0434 B79-11326

Smollett, Tobias. Travels through France and Italy. — Oxford : Oxford University Press, Nov.1981. — [512]p. — (The World's classics)
Originally published: London : s.n., 1766
ISBN 0-19-281569-5 (pbk) : £2.50 : CIP entry
Primary classification 914.4'0434 B81-30566

914.5'049 — Italy. Description & travel, *ca 1915 — Personal observations*

Lawrence, D. H.. Twilight in Italy / D.H. Lawrence. — Harmondsworth : Penguin in association with Heinemann, 1960 (1981 [printing]). — 174p ; 19cm
Originally published: London : Duckworth, 1916
ISBN 0-14-001481-0 (pbk) : £1.25 B81-27664

914.5'04928 — Italy. Description & travel

Keates, Jonathan. The love of Italy / Jonathan Keates. — [London] : Octopus, [1980]. — 93p : col.ill,col.map ; 33cm
Col. ill on lining papers. — Includes index
ISBN 0-7064-1237-0 : £3.95 B81-01371

914.5'04928 — Italy. Description & travel — *For children*

Fairclough, Chris. Let's go to Italy / text and photographs by Chris Fairclough. — London : Watts, c1981. — 32p : col.ill,col.maps ; 22cm
Includes index
ISBN 0-85166-920-4 : £2.99 B81-32451

914.5'04928 — Italy. Islands — *Visitors' guides*

Facaros, Dana. Mediterranean island hopping : the Italian islands, Corsica/Malta : a handbook for the independent traveller / Dana Facaros and Michael Pauls. — London : Macdonald, 1981. — 491p : maps ; 24cm. — (Island hopping series)
Bibliography: p488-490. - Includes index
ISBN 0-354-04701-9 : £7.95 B81-18698

914.5'04928 — Italy — *Practical information — For British businessmen*

Italy. — [London] : British Overseas Trade Board, 1980. — 60p ; 21cm. — (Hints to exporters)
Bibliography: p48-50
Unpriced (pbk) B81-38618

914.5'04928 — Italy — *Visitors' guides*

. Italy. — Rev. [ed.]. — London : Letts, 1979 (1981 [printing]). — 96p : ill,1 map ; 19cm. — (Letts guide)
Previous ed.: i.e. Completely rev. ed. published as: Letts go to Italy
ISBN 0-85097-346-5 (pbk) : £1.25 B81-08546

914.5'04928 — Italy — *Visitors' guides — For motoring*

Eperon, Arthur. Travellers' Italy : a guide to eight major routes throughout Italy / Arthur Eperon ; introduction by Frank Bough ; maps and drawings by Ken Smith. — London : Pan, 1980. — 169p : ill,col.maps ; 20cm
Includes index
ISBN 0-330-26302-1 (pbk) : £2.50 B81-04105

Eperon, Arthur. Travellers' Italy : a guide to eight major routes throughout Italy / Arthur Eperon ; introduction by Frank Bough ; maps and drawings by Ken Smith. — London : British Broadcasting Corporation, 1980. — 169p : ill(some col.),maps(some col.) ; 21cm
Includes index
ISBN 0-563-17914-7 : £5.50 B81-11485

914.5'63204928 — Italy. Rome — *Visitors' guides*

Willey, David. Rome : welcome to Rome / David and Marie-Claire Willey. — Glasgow : Collins, 1981. — 127p : ill(some col.),maps,plans ; 18cm. — (A Collins travel guide)
Includes index
ISBN 0-00-447314-0 (pbk) : £1.95 B81-10653

914.5'804928 — Italy. Sicily — *Visitors' guides*

Kininmonth, Christopher. Sicily / by Christopher Kininmonth. — 3rd ed. — London : Cape, 1981. — 312p : maps,1plan ; 18cm. — (Travellers' guide)
Previous ed.: 1972. — Col. maps on inside covers. — Bibliography: p301-304. — Includes index
ISBN 0-224-01854-x (pbk) : £5.95 B81-18447

Macadam, Alta. Sicily. — 2nd ed. / Alta Macadam ; 32 maps and plans by John Flower. — London : Ernest Benn, 1981. — 191p,[15]p of plates : ill,maps(some col.),plans ; 21cm. — (Blue guide)
Previous ed.: / edited by Alta Macadam. 1975. — Bibliography: p21-22. — Includes index
ISBN 0-510-01638-3 (cased) : £10.95
ISBN 0-510-01639-1 (pbk) : £5.95 B81-01597

914.585 — MALTA

914.5'8504 — Malta — *Visitors' guides*

Balls, Bryan. Travellers' guide to Malta : a concise guide to the Mediterranean islands of Malta, Gozo and Comino. — 4th ed. / text by Brian [i.e. Bryan] Balls and Richard Cox. — St Albans : Geographia, 1981. — 118p : ill(some col.),maps ; 22cm. — (Thornton Cox travellers guides)
Previous ed.: London : Thornton Cox, 1978. — Includes index
ISBN 0-09-208210-6 (pbk) : £3.50 B81-32322

Severin, Inge. See Malta & Gozo : a complete guide with maps and gazetteer / Inge Severin. — Rev. ed. — London : Format, 1979. — 144p : ill,maps,plans ; 20cm
Previous ed.: 1978. — Ill on lining papers. — Bibliography: p144
ISBN 0-903372-04-5 : £3.50 B81-39617

914.59 — SARDINIA

914.5'90491 — Italy. Sardinia. Description & travel, *ca 1920 — Personal observations*

Lawrence, D. H.. Sea and Sardinia / D.H. Lawrence. — Harmondsworth : Penguin in association with Heinemann, 1944 (1981 [printing]). — 212p ; 19cm
Originally published: London : Heinemann, 1923-
ISBN 0-14-000465-3 (pbk) : £1.50 B81-27659

914.6 — IBERIAN PENINSULA, SPAIN

914.6 — Southern Spain. Description & travel

De Stroumillo, Elisabeth. The tastes of travel : Southern Spain / Elisabeth de Stroumillo. — London : Collins, 1981. — 268p : maps ; 21cm
Bibliography: p259. — Includes index
ISBN 0-00-262829-5 : £6.50 B81-19512

914.6'0483 — Spain — *Practical information — For British businessmen*

Spain : (including the Canary Islands). — London (50 Ludgate Hill, EC4M 7HU) : British Overseas Trade Board, 1981. — 56p : ill ; 21cm. — (Hints to exporters)
Bibliography: p47-49
Unpriced (pbk) B81-17686

914.6'0483 — Spain — *Visitors' guides*

Kane, Robert S.. Spain : A to Z guide / by Robert S. Kane. — Chicago : Rand McNally ; London : Distributed by Pitman, c1980. — vii,294p,[16]p of plates : col.maps ; 21cm
Includes index
ISBN 0-273-01679-2 (pbk) : £2.95 B81-11233

914.6'0483'05 — Spain — *Visitors' guides — Serials*

Tourist guide. Spain / Michelin. — 2nd ed. — London : Michelin Tyre Co., c1980. — 289p
ISBN 2-06-015210-0 : Unpriced B81-29095

914.6'750483 — Spain. Balearic Islands — *Visitors' guides*

Facaros, Dana. Mediterranean island hopping : the Spanish islands : a handbook for the independent traveller / Dana Facaros and Michael Pauls. — London : Macdonald, 1981. — 264p : maps ; 24cm. — (Island hopping series)
Bibliography: p263-264
ISBN 0-354-04702-7 : £7.95 B81-18696

914.69 — PORTUGAL

914.69'0444'05 — Portugal — *Visitors' guides — Serials*

Tourist guide. Portugal, Madeira / Michelin. — 2nd ed. — London : Michelin Tyre Co., c1980. — 146p
ISBN 2-06-015570-3 : Unpriced B81-08747

914.7 — EASTERN EUROPE, SOVIET UNION

914.7′0482 — Russia *(RSFSR)*. Description & travel, *1890 — Personal observations — Facsimiles*

Stevens, T.. [Through Russia on a mustang]. Travelling through Russia in 1890 / by T. Stevens. — Letchworth (P.O. Box 1, Letchworth, Herts.) : Short-Run Reprints, 1981. — ix,334p,[16]leaves of plates : ill,1port ; 20cm. — (Reprints for researchers ; no.3)
Facsim of: edition published London : Cassell, 1891
£4.50 (pbk) B81-22260

914.7′31204853 — Russia *(RSFSR)*. Moscow. Description & travel

Levin, Deana. Moscow / written by Deana Levin ; picture researcher Kathy Brandt ; commissioned photography by Deana Levin. — London : Marshall Cavendish, 1978. — 99p : ill(some col.),1map,ports ; 28cm. — (The World′s cities)
Ill on lining papers
ISBN 0-85685-502-2 : £3.95 B81-01717

914.81 — NORWAY

914.81′0448 — Norway — *Practical information — For British businessmen*

Norway. — London (50 Ludgate Hill, EC4M 7HU) : British Overseas Trade Board, 1981. — 47p : ill ; 21cm. — (Hints to exporters)
Bibliography: p37-40
Unpriced (pbk) B81-17684

914.81′0448 — Norway — *Visitors′ guides*

Nicole, Gladys. Norway & Sweden / main text by Gladys Nicol ; facts at your fingertips by Harold Dennis-Jones. — London : Letts, 1979 (1981 [printing]). — 96p : ill ; 19cm. — (Letts guides)
ISBN 0-85097-335-x (pbk) : £1.25
Also classified at 914.85′0458 B81-08547

914.85 — SWEDEN

914.85′0458 — Sweden — *Visitors′ guides*

Nicole, Gladys. Norway & Sweden / main text by Gladys Nicol ; facts at your fingertips by Harold Dennis-Jones. — London : Letts, 1979 (1981 [printing]). — 96p : ill ; 19cm. — (Letts guides)
ISBN 0-85097-335-x (pbk) : £1.25
Primary classification 914.81′0448 B81-08547

914.91 — ICELAND AND FAEROE ISLANDS

914.91′2045 — Iceland — *Practical information — For British businessmen*

Iceland / British Overseas Trade Board. — [London] : [The Board], 1981. — 39p : ill,1map ; 21cm. — (Hints to exporters)
Text on inside covers. — Bibliography: p32-34
Unpriced (pbk) B81-13280

914.95 — GREECE

914.95′045 — Greece. Travel by Western Europeans, *1798-1840*

Tsigakou, Fani-Maria. The rediscovery of Greece : travellers and painters of the romantic era / Fani-Maria Tsigakou ; introduction by Sir Steven Runciman. — London : Thames and Hudson, c1981. — 208p : ill(some col.) ; 28cm
Includes index
ISBN 0-500-23336-5 : £16.00 B81-37650

914.95′047 — Greece. Description & travel, *1931-1973 — Personal observations*

Moore, Jack, *1905-*. Taming ancient rivers of Greece / by Jack Moore. — London : Faraway, 1981. — 344p,[8]p of plates : ill(some col.),maps,ports(some col.) ; 23cm
Includes index
ISBN 0-9507476-0-2 : £12.00 B81-40981

914.95′0476 — Greece. Description & travel — *For schools*

Selwyn, Antony. Classical and modern Greece / Antony Selwyn ; illustrations by Richard Reid ; map by David Palmer ; edited by Picot Cassidy ; designed by John Leath ; Schools Abroad project development manager Barbara Hopper. — London (40 Tavistock St., WC2E 7PB) : Chancerel, c1980. — 126p : ill,1map,1plan ; 20cm
ISBN 0-905703-51-0 : Unpriced B81-21157

914.95′0476 — Greece. Islands — *Visitors′ guides*

Facaros, Dana. Greek island hopping : a handbook for the independent traveller / Dana Facaros. — Repr., rev. and updated. — London : Macdonald, 1980, c1979 (1981 [printing]). — 352p : maps ; 24cm. — (Island hopping series)
Originally published: London : Wilton House Gentry, 1979. — Includes index
ISBN 0-354-04703-5 : £7.95 B81-18697

Mead, Robin. The Greek Islands / main text by Robin Mead. — Completely rev. ed / facts at your fingertips by Harold Dennis-Jones. — London : Letts, 1979 (1981 [printing]). — 96p : ill,col.maps ; 19cm. — (Letts guide)
Previous ed.: i.e. Completely rev. ed. published as: Letts go to the Greek islands. 1977
ISBN 0-85097-366-x (pbk) : £1.25 B81-08551

914.95′0476 — Greece. Mainland — *Visitors′ guides*

Sidgwick, Christopher. Greece / main text by Christopher Sidgwick. — Further rev. ed. / facts at your fingertips by Harold Dennis-Jones. — London : Letts, 1979 (1981 [printing]). — 96p : ill ; 19cm. — (Letts guide)
Previous ed.: i.e. Completely rev. ed. published as: Letts go to Greece. 1977
ISBN 0-85097-356-2 (pbk) : £1.25 B81-08543

914.95′0476 — Greece — *Practical information — For British businessmen*

Greece. — [London] : British Overseas Trade Board, 1981. — 51p ; 21cm. — (Hints to exporters)
Bibliography: p40-42
Unpriced (pbk) B81-38619

914.95′0476 — Greece — *Visitors′ guides*

De Stroumillo, Elisabeth. Greece : a concise guide to Greece and the Greek islands / Elisabeth de Stroumillo. — 2nd rev. ed. — St. Albans : Geographia, 1980. — 127p,[8]p of plates : ill(some col.),maps ; 22cm. — (Thornton Cox travellers guides)
Previous ed.: London : Thornton Cox, 1974. — Includes index
ISBN 0-09-208300-5 (pbk) : £2.95 B81-12637

Harrison, John, *1928-*. Greece : welcome to Greece / John and Shirley Harrison. — Glasgow : Collins, 1981. — 128p : col.ill,col.maps,plans ; 18cm. — (A Collins travel guide)
Includes index
ISBN 0-00-447310-8 (pbk) : £1.95 B81-07213

Rossiter, Stuart. Greece. — 4th ed. / Stuart Rossiter, atlas of Greece, street atlas of Athens, and 91 maps and plans by John Fowler. — London : Benn, 1981. — 768p : ill,maps(some col.),plans ; 21cm. — (Blue guide)
Previous ed.: 1977. — Includes index
ISBN 0-510-01642-1 : £14.95
ISBN 0-510-01643-x (pbk) : £7.95 B81-16758

Stylianoudi, L.. Greece / [compiled by L. Stylianoudi and Yiorgos Stamelos]. — London : Octopus, 1980. — 186p : 1map ; 10x21cm. — (Guide in jeans)
Translation of: Guide de la Grèce en jeans
ISBN 0-7064-1467-5 (pbk) : Unpriced B81-14056

914.95′0476′05 — Greece — *Visitors′ guides — Serials*

Fodor′s Greece. — 1981. — London : Hodder and Stoughton, c1981. — 378p
ISBN 0-340-26050-5 : £5.50 B81-16739

914.95′120476 — Greece. Athens — *Visitors′ guides*

Rossiter, Stuart. Athens and environs / Stuart Rossiter ; street atlas of Athens, and 14 maps and plans by John Flower. — 2nd ed. — London : Ernest Benn, 1981. — 189p,24p of plates : ill,col.maps,plans ; 20cm. — (Blue guide)
Previous ed.: 1962. — Includes index
ISBN 0-510-01636-7 (cased) : £10.95
ISBN 0-510-01637-5 (pbk) : £5.95 B81-05231

914.95′5′0476 — Greece. Ionian Islands — *Visitors′ guides*

Young, Martin. Corfu and the other Ionian islands. — 3rd ed. — London : Cape, July 1981. — [324]p. — (Travellers′ guide)
Previous ed.: 1976
ISBN 0-224-01952-x (pbk) : £5.95 : CIP entry B81-15908

914.97 — YUGOSLAVIA

914.97′0423 — Yugoslavia. Description & travel

Yugoslavia : republics and provinces / [authors Veljko Kojovic et al.]. — London : Muller, 1980, c1979. — 256p : ill(some col.) ; 31cm
Translation of: Jugoslavija. — Ill on lining papers
ISBN 0-584-97105-2 : Unpriced B81-11802

914.97′0423 — Yugoslavia — *Visitors′ guides*

Mason, John, *1914-*. Yugoslavia / main text by John and Anne Mason. — Rev. [ed.] / facts at your fingertips by Harold Dennis-Jones. — London : Letts, 1979 (1981 [printing]). — 96p : ill ; 19cm. — (Letts guide)
Previous ed.: i.e. Completely rev. ed. published as: Letts go to Yugoslavia. 1979
ISBN 0-85097-376-7 (pbk) : £1.25 B81-08545

914.99 — AEGEAN ISLANDS

914.99′0476 — Greece. Aegean Islands. Description & travel, *1975-1978 — Personal observations*

Ebdon, John. Ebdon′s odyssey / John Ebdon ; illustrations by Michael Ffolkes. — London : Peter Davies, 1979. — 177p : ill ; 23cm
ISBN 0-432-04020-x : £5.95 B81-10742

914.99′6 — Greece. Rhodes — *Visitors′ guides*

Currie, Jean. Rhodes and the Dodecanese / by Jean Currie. — 3rd ed. — London : Cape, 1981. — 272p : maps,plans ; 18cm. — (Travellers′ guide)
Previous ed.: 1975. — Col. maps on inside covers. — Bibliography: p263-264 . — Includes index
ISBN 0-224-01927-9 (pbk) : £5.95 B81-18445

914.998 — CRETE

914.99′80446 — Greece. Crete — *Visitors′ guides*

Bowman, John, *1931-*. Crete / by John Bowman. — 5th ed. — London : Cape, 1981. — 323p : maps(some col.),plans ; 17cm. — (Travellers′ guide)
Previous ed.: 1978. — Map on inside covers. — Bibliography: p308-311. — Includes index
ISBN 0-224-01951-1 (pbk) : £5.95 : CIP rev. B81-11960

915 — EURASIA, ASIA

915′.04427 — Asia. Description & travel, *1970-1979 — Personal observations*

Dickson, Mora. Assignment in Asia / by Mora Dickson. — London : Dobson, 1979. — 185p : ill,maps,ports ; 23cm
Maps on lining papers
ISBN 0-234-72039-5 : £6.95 B81-04720

915′.04427 — Asia. Description & travel, *1976 — Personal observations*

Stansfield, Derek. Journey of a lifetime / Derek Stansfield. — Bognor Regis : New Horizon, c1979. — 117,[27]p[7]p of plates : ill,1map ; 21cm
ISBN 0-86116-114-9 : £3.50 B81-21777

915′.04427 — Asia. Journeys by railways, *1970-1979 — Personal observations*

Lamplugh, Barbara. Trans-Siberia by rail and a month in Japan / by Barbara Lamplugh. — London (16 Holland Park Gardens, W14 8DY) : Lascelles, 1979 (1980 [printing]). — 155p : ill,maps,2facsims,plans,1port ; 19cm
Unpriced (pbk)
Also classified at 915.2′0447 B81-05938

Theroux, Paul. The great railway bazaar : by train through Asia / Paul Theroux. — Harmondsworth : Penguin, 1977, c1975 (1981 [printing]). — 379p : 1map ; 18cm
Originally published: London : Hamilton, 1975
ISBN 0-14-004235-0 (pbk) : £1.50 B81-13060

915'.04428'05 — Asia — *Visitors' guides — Serials*

The **On-your-own** guide to Asia. — Revised 5th ed. — Rutland, Vt. : Tuttle ; London : Prentice-Hall [distributor], 1981. — 383p
ISBN 0-8048-1353-1 : £2.95
ISSN 0162-5950 B81-31008

915.1 — CHINA AND ADJACENT AREAS

915.1'0425 — China. Description & travel, *1245-ca 1350 — Personal observations — Collections*

[The Mongol mission]. The Mission to Asia : narratives and letters of the Franciscan missionaries in Mongolia and China in the thirteenth and fourteenth centuries / edited by Christopher Dawson ; translated by a Nun of Stanbrook Abbey. — London : Sheed and Ward, 1955 (1980 printing). — xxxix,246p : geneal.tables ; 22cm. — (Spiritual masters)
Bibliography: pxxxvii-xxxviii. — Includes index
ISBN 0-7220-5512-9 (pbk) : £8.00
Also classified at 915.1'70425 B81-05498

915.1'0425'0924 — China. Description & travel, *ca 1270-1295.* **Polo, Marco** — *Biographies — For children*

Thisse, Simone Abraham. Marco Polo / Simone Abraham Thisse ; illustrated by Alain d'Orange ; [translated by Merle Philo]. — St. Albans : Hart-Davis, 1981. — 30p : col.ill,1col.map ; 25cm. — (Junior histories)
Translation of the French. — Text on lining paper
ISBN 0-247-13214-4 : £2.95 B81-39464

915.1'0457 — China. Description & travel, *1978 — Personal observations*

Morath, Inge. Chinese encounters / Inge Morath, Arthur Miller. — London : Secker & Warburg, 1979. — 252p : ill(some col.),ports ; 25cm
Originally published: New York : Farrar, Straus, Giroux, 1979
ISBN 0-436-28007-8 : £12.50 B81-10772

915.1'0458 — China — *Practical information — For British businessmen*

The **People's** Republic of China / British Overseas Trade Board. — [London] : [The Board], 1980. — 54p : ill,maps ; 21cm. — (Hints to exporters)
Text on inside covers. — Bibliography: p47-49
Unpriced (pbk) B81-13282

People's Republic of China : the businessman's guide. — London : Standard Chartered Bank Limited, c1981. — 72p : col.ill,1col.map ; 25cm
Unpriced (pbk) B81-25357

915.1'0458 — China — *Visitors' guides*

Garside, Evelyne. China companion : a guide to 100 cities, resorts and places of interest in the People's Republic of China / Evelyne Garside. — London : Deutsch, 1981. — ix,271p : maps,plans ; 22cm
Bibliography: p270. — Includes index
ISBN 0-233-97270-6 (pbk) : £4.95 B81-24279

Meyer, Charles. China observed / Charles Meyer ; translated from the French by Jean Joss. — London : Kaye & Ward, 1981. — 182p : col.ill,col.maps,ports ; 27cm
Includes index
ISBN 0-7182-1007-7 : £12.95 B81-29334

915.1'15 — China. Peking region. Royal tombs: Shih-san-ling

Paludan, Ann. The imperial Ming tombs. — London : Yale University Press, Nov.1981. — [272]p
ISBN 0-300-02511-4 : £24.50 : CIP entry B81-35024

915.1'504 — Tibet. Description & travel

Allen, Charles. Always a little further. — London : André Deutsch, Sept.1981. — [240]p
ISBN 0-233-97281-1 : £9.95 : CIP entry B81-21627

915.1'60442 — China. Sinkiang-Uighur Autonomous Region. Description & travel, *1935 — Personal observations*

Fleming, Peter. News from Tartary : a journey from Peking to Kashmir / Peter Fleming. — London : Macdonald Futura, 1980. — 394p ; 18cm
Includes index
ISBN 0-7088-1919-2 (corrected : pbk) : £1.75 B81-07022

915.1'70425 — Mongolia. Description & travel, *1245-ca 1350 — Personal observations — Collections*

[The Mongol mission]. The Mission to Asia : narratives and letters of the Franciscan missionaries in Mongolia and China in the thirteenth and fourteenth centuries / edited by Christopher Dawson ; translated by a Nun of Stanbrook Abbey. — London : Sheed and Ward, 1955 (1980 printing). — xxxix,246p : geneal.tables ; 22cm. — (Spiritual masters)
Bibliography: pxxxvii-xxxviii. — Includes index
ISBN 0-7220-5512-9 (pbk) : £8.00
Primary classification 915.1'0425 B81-05498

915.19'50443'05 — South Korea — *Visitors' guides — Serials*

Fodor's Japan and Korea. — 1981. — London : Hodder and Stoughton, c1981. — 468p
ISBN 0-340-26043-2 : £6.95
ISSN 0098-1613
Primary classification 915.2'0448'05 B81-16740

915.2 — JAPAN

915.2 — Japan. Geographical features

Pezeu-Massabuau, Jacques. The Japanese islands : a physical and social geography / Jacques Pezeu-Massabuau ; translated and adapted from the French by Paul C. Blum. — Rutland [Vt.] : Tuttle ; London : Prentice-Hall [distributor], 1978. — 283p,1folded leaf of plates : ill,maps(some col.) ; 20cm
Bibliography: p267-269. — Includes index
ISBN 0-8048-1184-9 : £7.55 B81-24242

915.2'0447 — Japan. Description & travel, *1970-1979 — Personal observations*

Lamplugh, Barbara. Trans-Siberia by rail and a month in Japan / by Barbara Lamplugh. — London (16 Holland Park Gardens, W14 8DY) : Lascelles, 1979 (1980 [printing]). — 155p : ill,maps,2facsims,plans,1port ; 19cm
Unpriced (pbk)
Primary classification 915'.04427 B81-05938

915.2'0448'05 — Japan — *Visitors' guides — Serials*

Fodor's Japan and Korea. — 1981. — London : Hodder and Stoughton, c1981. — 468p
ISBN 0-340-26043-2 : £6.95
ISSN 0098-1613
Also classified at 915.19'50443'05 B81-16740

915.3 — ARABIAN PENINSULA AND ADJACENT AREAS

915.3'0452'0924 — Arabia. Exploration. Philby, H. St. J. B. — *Biographies*

Monroe, Elizabeth. Philby of Arabia / Elizabeth Monroe. — London : Quartet, 1980. — 332p,[8]p of plates : ill,maps,ports ; 22cm
Bibliography: p307-316. — Includes index
ISBN 0-7043-3346-5 (pbk) : £3.95 B81-26463

915.3'5 — Oman. Description & travel

Oman. — London (21 John St., WC1N 2BP) : Middle East Economic Digest, Oct.1981. — [240]p
ISBN 0-7103-0013-1 (pbk) : £12.50 : CIP entry B81-30882

915.3'5 — United Arab Emirates. Description & travel

UAE. — London (21 John St., WC1N 2BP) : Middle East Economic Digest, Nov.1981. — [240]p
ISBN 0-7103-0014-x (pbk) : £12.50 : CIP entry B81-30881

915.3'50453 — Oman & United Arab Emirates — *Practical information — For British businessmen*

United Arab Emirates and the Sultanate of Oman . — London (50 Ludgate Hill, EC4M 7HU) : British Overseas Trade Board, 1981. — 104p : ill,maps ; 21cm. — (Hints to exporters)
Bibliography: p92-97
Unpriced (pbk) B81-17225

915.3'80453 — Saudi Arabia — *Practical information — For British businessmen*

Saudi Arabia / compiled and edited by Trevor Mostyn. — London : Middle East Economic Digest ; Henley-on-Thames : Distributed by Kegan Paul International, c1981. — viii,280p,[8]p of plates : ill(some col.),maps,ports ; 21cm. — (A MEED practical guide)
Ill on inside cover. — Bibliography: p272-276. — Includes index
ISBN 0-7103-0011-5 : £12.50
ISBN 0-9505211-3-2 (Middle East Economic Digest) B81-22094

915.3'80453 — Saudi Arabia — *Practical information — For businessmen*

Mostyn, Trevor. Saudi Arabia / compiled and edited by Trevor Mostyn. — London (21 John St., WC1N 2BP) : Middle East Economic Digest, c1981. — viii,280p,[8]p of plates : ill (some col.),maps,ports ; 21cm. — (A MEED practical guide)
Bibliography: p272-276. — Includes index
ISBN 0-9505211-3-2 (pbk) : Unpriced B81-18313

915.4 — SOUTH ASIA, INDIA

915.4 — Asia. Himalayas. Geographical features

The **Himalaya** : aspects of change / editor J.S. Lall in association with A.D. Moddie. — Delhi ; Oxford : Oxford University Press, 1981. — xix,481p,[12]p of plates : ill(some col.),maps ; 24cm
Includes bibliographies and index
ISBN 0-19-561254-x : £17.50 B81-38504

915.4 — South Asia. Geographical features

Johnson, B. L. C.. South Asia : selective studies of the essential geography of India, Pakistan, Bangladesh, Sri Lanka and Nepal / B.L.C. Johnson. — 2nd ed. — London : Heinemann Educational, 1981. — xi,240p : ill,maps ; 26cm
Previous ed.: 1969. — Includes index
ISBN 0-435-35488-4 : £10.50 B81-32117

915.4'04311'0222 — India. Description & travel, *1786-1794 — Illustrations*

Archer, Mildred. Early views of India : the picturesque journeys of Thomas and William Daniell 1786-1794 : the complete aquatints / Mildred Archer. — London : Thames and Hudson, c1980. — 240p : ill(some col.),maps,1facsim,plan,ports ; 28cm
Bibliography: p238. — Includes index
ISBN 0-500-01238-5 : £16.00 B81-05800

915.4'04359 — India. Description & travel, *1940-1954 — Personal observations*

Swayne-Thomas, April. Indian summer : a Mem-sahib in India and Sind / April Swayne-Thomas ; with illustrations from the author's drawings ; and a foreword by Sir Sidney Ridley. — London : New English Library, 1981. — 175p : ill(some col.) ; 28cm
ISBN 0-450-04850-0 : £8.50 B81-17420

915.4'0451 — Asia. Himalayas. Description & travel, *1973 — Personal observations*

Matthiessen, Peter. The snow leopard / Peter Matthiessen. — London : Pan, 1980, c1978. — 312p : 2maps ; 20cm. — (Picador)
Originally published: New York : Viking Press, 1978 ; London : Chatto and Windus, 1979. — Includes index
ISBN 0-330-26161-4 (pbk) : £1.95 B81-00659

915.4'0452 — Asia. Himalayas. Mountaineering expeditions, *1977 — Personal observations*

Rowell, Galen. Many people come, looking , looking / Galen Rowell. — London : Allen & Unwin, 1980. — ix,164p : col.ill,maps,col.ports ; 31cm
Includes index
ISBN 0-04-910071-8 : £15.00 : CIP rev. B81-02548

915.4′0452′05 — India (Republic) — *Visitors′ guides — Serials*

Fodor′s India and Nepal. — 1979-. — London : Hodder and Stoughton, 1979-. — v. : ill ; 21cm
Annual. — Continues: Fodor′s India. — Description based on: 1981
£7.95
Also classified at 915.49′604′05 B81-16745

915.4′10452 — India *(Republic)*. Ganges River region. Expeditions: Indo-New Zealand Ganga Expedition — *Personal observations*

Hillary, Edmund. From the ocean to the sky / Edmund Hillary. — Large print ed. — Leicester : Ulverscroft, 1980, c1979. — 451p : maps ; 23cm. — (Ulverscroft large print)
Originally published: London : Hodder and Stoughton, 1979
ISBN 0-7089-0587-0 : £4.25 B81-12613

915.491 — PAKISTAN

915.49′13 — Kashmir. Zaskar. Description & travel

Peissel, Michel. Zanskar. — Large print ed. — Anstey : Ulverscroft, Nov.1981. — [416]p. — (Ulverscroft large print series)
Originally published: London : Collins ; Harvill Press, 1979
ISBN 0-7089-0714-8 : £5.00 : CIP entry
B81-30501

915.49′13 — Pakistan. Nanga Parbat. Mountaineering expeditions, *1978 — Personal observations*

Messner, Reinhold. Solo Nanga Parbat / Reinhold Messner ; translated by Audrey Salkeld. — London : Kaye & Ward, 1980. — 276p : ill(some col.),maps(some col.),ports ; 24cm
Translation from the German. — Ill on lining papers
ISBN 0-7182-1250-9 : £7.95 B81-35306

915.493 — SRI LANKA

915.49′3043 — Sri Lanka — *Practical information — For British businessmen*

Sri Lanka. — London (50 Ludgate Hill, EC4M 7HU) : British Overseas Trade Board, 1981. — 46p : ill,1map ; 21cm. — (Hints to exporters)
Bibliography: p39-41
Unpriced (pbk) B81-17688

915.49′3043 — Sri Lanka — *Visitors′ guides*

Wheeler, Tony. Sri Lanka : a travel survival kit / [Tony Wheeler] ; [illustrations by Peter Campbell]. — South Yarra : Lonely Planet ; [London] : [Lascelles] [distributor], 1980 (1981 [printing]). — 176p,[4]p of plates : ill(some col.),maps ; 19cm
ISBN 0-908086-14-8 (pbk) : Unpriced
ISBN 0-908086-12-1 (pbk) : £2.50 B81-37978

915.496 — NEPAL

915.49′6 — Asia. Everest. Expeditions, *1980 — Personal observations*

Tasker, Joe. Everest the cruel way. — London : Eyre Methuen, Oct.1981. — [176]p
ISBN 0-413-48750-4 : £7.50 : CIP entry
B81-25312

915.49′6 — Asia. Everest. Mountaineering expeditions, *to 1979*

Unsworth, Walt. Everest / Walt Unsworth. — London : Allen Lane, 1981. — xiv,578p,[64]p of plates : ill(some col.),maps,ports ; 24cm
Bibliography: p511-527. — Includes index
ISBN 0-7139-1108-5 : £14.95 B81-07065

915.49′6 — Nepal. Annapurna. Mountaineering expeditions by women, *1978*

Blum, Arlene. Annapurna : a woman′s place / Arlene Blum ; foreword by Maurice Herzog. — London : Granada, 1980. — xii,256p,[8]p of plates : ill(some col.),2maps,ports(some col.) ; 26cm
Bibliography: p246-253. - Includes index
ISBN 0-246-11530-0 : £8.95 B81-05478

915.49′6 — Nepal. Kali Gandaki River. Expeditions: Joint Services River Rover Expedition *(1978-1979 : Nepal)*

Cole, Michael, *1935-*. Journey to the fourth world / by Michael Cole. — Tring : Lion, 1981. — 224p : ill,maps,ports ; 19cm
Bibliography: p224
ISBN 0-85648-410-5 (cased) : Unpriced
ISBN 0-85648-361-3 (pbk) : £1.50 B81-27486

915.49′6 — Nepal. Katmandu region. Description & travel — *Personal observations*

Millward, Jack. Himalayan trek / by Jack Millward. — Harrow : Eureditions, 1979. — 124p,[4]p of plates : col.ill ; 21cm
ISBN 0-906204-26-7 : Unpriced B81-26667

915.49′6 — Nepal — *Visitors′ guides*

Raj, Prakash A.. Kathmandu & the Kingdom of Nepal / [Prakash A. Raj]. — Victoria, Australia : Lonely Planet ; London : Lascelles [distributor], 1980. — 159p,[4]p of plates : ill (some col.),maps,1port ; 19cm. — (Lonely Planet guides)
Previous ed.: 197-. — Includes index
ISBN 0-908086-24-5 (pbk) : £2.50 B81-11719

915.49′604 — Nepal. Description & travel — *Personal observations*

Grant, William M. B.. In the search of a snowman : a Himalayan reconnaissance / by William B. Grant. — [Findhorn] ([69 Findhorn Bay Caravan Park, Findhorn, Morayshire]) : [W.M.B. Grant], [1981]. — 20p : ill,1map,ports ; 23cm
Cover title
For private distribution (pbk) B81-27834

Lomax, Judy. Walking in the clouds : impressions of Nepal / Judy Lomax. — London : Hale, c1981. — 189p,[24]p of plates : ill,maps,ports ; 23cm
ISBN 0-7091-8831-5 : £8.95 B81-16443

915.49′604 — Nepal. Plants. Collecting. Expeditions — *Personal observations*

Lancaster, Roy. Plant hunting in Nepal / Roy Lancaster. — London : Croom Helm, c1981. — 194p,[8]p of plates : ill(some col).,maps ; 24cm
Bibliography: p181-182. — Includes index
ISBN 0-7099-1606-x : £8.95 : CIP rev.
B81-14892

915.49′604′05 — Nepal — *Visitors′ guides — Serials*

Fodor′s India and Nepal. — 1979-. — London : Hodder and Stoughton, 1979-. — v. : ill ; 21cm
Annual. — Continues: Fodor′s India. — Description based on: 1981
£7.95
Primary classification 915.4′0452′05 B81-16745

915.6 — MIDDLE EAST

915.6′041′0924 — Middle East. Exploration. Burckhardt, John Lewis — *Biographies*

Sim, Katharine. [Desert traveller]. Jean Louis Burckhardt : a biography / Katharine Sim. — London : Quartet, 1981, c1969. — 447,[8]p of plates : ill,ports ; 22cm
Originally published: London : Gollancz, 1969. — Bibliography: p419-423. — Includes index
ISBN 0-7043-3355-4 (pbk) : £4.95 B81-26995

915.6′044 — Middle East — *Practical information — For British businessmen*

The **Middle** East / editor Jane Walker ; associate editor Mark Ambrose. — London : Joseph, c1981. — 285p : maps ; 23cm. — (The Business traveller′s handbook ; v.4)
Includes index
ISBN 0-7181-1977-0 : £12.50 B81-25637

915.61′0438 — Turkey — *Practical information — For British businessmen*

Turkey. — London (50 Ludgate Hill, EC4M 7HU) : British Overseas Trade Board, 1981. — 56p : ill,1map ; 21cm. — (Hints to exporters)
Bibliography: p47-49
Unpriced (pbk) B81-17685

915.62 — South-west Turkey. Carian antiquities. Sites — *Visitors′ guides*

Bean, George E.. Turkey beyond the Maeander / George E. Bean. — 2nd ed. — London : Benn, 1980. — xx,236p,[48]p of plates : ill,maps,plans ; 23cm. — (A Benn study. Archaeology)
Previous ed.: 1971. — Map on lining paper. — Bibliography: p225-228. - Includes index
ISBN 0-510-03206-0 : £9.95 : CIP rev.
B79-35104

915.645′044 — Cyprus — *Visitors′ guides*

Cyprus / [edited by] Ian Robertson. — London : Ernest Benn, 1981. — 196p,16p of plates : maps(some col.) ; 21cm. — (Blue guide)
Includes index
ISBN 0-510-01634-0 (cased) : £10.95
ISBN 0-510-01633-2 (pbk) : £6.95 B81-03789

915.67′0443 — Iraq — *Practical information — For British businessmen*

Iraq : an introduction to doing business in Iraq. — London (1, Victoria St, SW1 0ET) : Commercial Relations & Exports 5, Department of Trade, [1979?]. — 14p ; 30cm
Unpriced (unbound) B81-38495

915.67′4 — Asia. Euphrates River region. Description & travel — *For children*

Batchelor, John, *1947-*. The Euphrates / John and Julie Batchelor. — Hove : Wayland, 1981. — 67p : ill(some col.),col.maps ; 21x22cm. — (Rivers of the world)
Map on lining papers. — Bibliography: p66. - Includes index
ISBN 0-85340-806-8 : £4.25 B81-12978

915.694′0454 — Israel. Description & travel — *Personal observations*

Pedlow, J. C.. Windows on the Holy Land / J.C. Pedlow. — Cambridge : James Clarke, 1980. — 149p : ill,maps ; 19cm
ISBN 0-227-67839-7 (pbk) : £3.35 : CIP rev.
B80-10902

915.694′0454 — Israel — *Visitors′ guides*

Pitch, Anthony S.. Bazak guide to Israel / produced by Avraham Levi. — [Jerusalem] : [Bazak Israel Guidebook] ; [Network] ; [London] : Distributed by Harper & Row, [c1981]. — 527p : maps(some col.) ; 23cm
Authors: Anthony S. Pitch and Alec Israel. — Includes index
ISBN 0-06-090847-5 (pbk) : Unpriced
B81-22144

Rosenbaum, Maurice. Israel : a concise guide to Israel / Maurice Rosenbaum. — London : Geographia, 1981. — 132p : ill(some col.),maps ; 22cm. — (Thornton Cox travellers guides)
Includes index
ISBN 0-09-207930-x (pbk) : £3.50 B81-39189

915.694′0454 — Palestine. Antiquities. Sites — *Visitors′ guides*

Murphy-O′Connor, Jerome. The Holy Land : an archaeological guide from earliest times to 1700 / Jerome Murphy-O′Connor ; drawings by Alice Sancey. — Oxford : Oxford University Press, 1980. — xvi,320p : ill,maps,plans ; 21cm
ISBN 0-19-217689-7 (cased) : £8.50 : CIP rev.
ISBN 0-19-285088-1 (pbk) : £3.95 B80-13632

915.695′0444 — Jordan. Description & travel

Osborne, Christine, *1940-*. An insight and guide to Jordan / Christine Osborne ; photographs by the author. — Harlow : Longman, 1981. — xiii,218p,[16]p of plates : ill(some col.),maps ; 22cm
Bibliography: p210-211. — Includes index
ISBN 0-582-78307-0 : £7.95 : CIP rev.
B81-09501

915.695′0444 — Jordan — *Practical information — For British businessmen*

Jordan. — London (50 Ludgate Hill, EC4M 7HU) : British Overseas Trade Board, 1981. — 52p : ill,2maps ; 21cm. — (Hints to exporters)
Bibliography: p41-43
Unpriced (pbk) B81-17689

915.7 — ASIATIC SOVIET UNION, SIBERIA

915.7′04853 — Soviet Union. Railway services: Transsibibirskaîâ magistral′. Journeys, *1980* — *Personal observations*

Pond, Elizabeth. Russia perceived : a Trans-Siberian journey / by Elizabeth Pond. — London : Gollancz, 1981. — 296p : maps ; 24cm
Maps on lining papers. — Bibliography: p278-286. — Includes index
ISBN 0-575-02936-6 : £9.95 B81-25254

915.7′04853 — Soviet Union. Railway services: Transsibirskaîâ magistral′. Journeys, *1977* — *Personal observations*

Newby, Eric. The big red train ride / Eric Newby. — Harmondsworth : Penguin, 1980, c1978. — 267p,[16]p of plates : ill,1map,ports ; 20cm
Originally published: London : Weidenfeld & Nicolson, 1978. — Bibliography: p255-258. - Includes index
ISBN 0-14-005243-7 (pbk) : £1.75 B81-06461

915.8 — CENTRAL ASIA

915.8′04 — Central Asia. Description & travel, ***ca 1200-1900* — *Personal observations — Collections***

The **Road** to Kabul : an anthology / edited by Gerald de Gaury and H.V.F. Winstone. — London : Quartet, 1981. — 233p : ill,maps,ports ; 24cm
ISBN 0-7043-2238-2 : £9.95 B81-12220

915.8′604853 — Tadzhikistan. Pamir. Mountaineering expeditions, *1974* — *Personal observations*

Craig, Robert W.. Storm and snow in the high Pamirs / Robert W. Craig. — Rev. ed. — London : Gollancz, 1981, c1980. — 223p,[8]p of plates : ill(some col.),maps,col.ports ; 24cm
Previous ed: New York : The Mountaineers ; Leicester : Cardee, 1977
ISBN 0-575-02773-8 : £6.95 B81-01372

915.9 — SOUTH-EAST ASIA

915.9 — South-east Asia. Geographical features — *For schools*

Jones, Sheila, *1929-*. Contrasts in South East Asia / [Sheila Jones, Pat Cleverley]. — London : Longman, 1981. — 49p : ill(some col.),maps (some col.) ; 23cm. — (Longman revised colour geographies)
Bibliography: p49
ISBN 0-582-22078-5 (pbk) : £1.25 B81-10231

915.9′0453 — South-east Asia. Description & travel — *Personal observations*

Rusher, Leslie. Bamboo notebook / by Leslie Rusher ; drawings by Jim Moss. — London : Salvationist, 1981. — 108p : ill,1port ; 22cm
ISBN 0-85412-363-6 (pbk) : Unpriced
B81-24379

915.9′0453′05 — South-east Asia — *Visitors′ guides — Serials*

Fodor′s Southeast Asia. — 1981. — London : Hodder and Stoughton, c1980. — 517p
Cover title: Fodor′s ... guide to South-East Asia
ISBN 0-340-26038-6 : £6.95
ISSN 0160-8991 B81-20323

915.97 — VIETNAM

915.97′0444 — Asia. Mekong River region. Description & travel — *For children*

Lightfoot, Paul. The Mekong / Paul Lightfoot. — Hove : Wayland, 1981. — 65p : ill(some col.),col.maps ; 21x22cm. — (Rivers of the world)
Map on lining papers. — Bibliography: p64. - Includes index
ISBN 0-85340-808-4 : £4.25 B81-12975

915.98 — INDONESIA

915.98 — Indonesia. Krakatau. Plants. Collecting. Expeditions: Krakatoa Centenary Expedition *(1979)*

The **Krakatoa** centenary expedition : an interim report / edited by J.R. Flenley. — [Hull] : Department of Geography, University of Hull, 1980. — 27p : 1map ; 30cm. — (Miscellaneous series / University of Hull Department of Geography ; no.24)
Bibliography: p24
ISBN 0-85958-110-1 (sprial) : Unpriced
B81-07647

915.98′0438 — Indonesia — *Practical information — For British businessmen*

Indonesia / British Overseas Trade Board. — [London] : [The Board], 1980. — 43p : ill,1map ; 21cm. — (Hints to exporters)
Text on inside covers. — Bibliography: p36-38
Unpriced (pbk) B81-13283

916 — AFRICA

916 — Africa. Geographical features — *For schools*

Steel, Robert W.. Africa / Robert W. Steel, Eileen M. Steel. — 2nd ed. — London : Longman, 1981. — 328p : ill,maps ; 21cm. — (Geographies)
Previous ed: 1974. — Includes index
ISBN 0-582-33079-3 (pbk) : £2.35 B81-07045

916′.0423′0922 — Africa. Exploration by Baker, *Sir* Samuel White & Baker, Florence, *Lady*

Hall, Richard, *1925-*. Lovers on the Nile / Richard Hall ; research associate James A. Casada. — London : Quartet, 1981, c1980. — 254p,[8]p : ill,1map,ports ; 20cm
Originally published: London : Collins, 1980. — Bibliography: p233-237. — Includes index
ISBN 0-7043-3365-1 (pbk) : £3.95 B81-26994

Hall, Richard, *1925-*. Lovers on the Nile / Richard Hall ; research associate James A. Casada. — Large print ed. — Leicester : Ulverscroft, 1981. — 473p : 1map ; 23cm
Originally published: London : Collins, 1980. — Map on lining papers
ISBN 0-7089-0643-5 : Unpriced B81-27184

916′.0423′0924 — Africa. Exploration. Grogan, Ewart Scott — *Biographies*

Farrant, Leda. The legendary Grogan : the only man to trek from Cape to Cairo, Kenya′s controversial pioneer / by Leda Farrant. — London : Hamilton, 1981. — xii,260p,[8]p of plates : ill,2facsims,ports ; 23cm
Bibliography: p250-252. — Includes index
ISBN 0-241-10592-7 : £12.50 : CIP rev.
B81-08906

916′.0431 — Africa. Journeys by cars, *1933* — *Personal observations*

Gilg, A. Cameron. Turn left - the Riffs have risen : from England to Cape Town in a baby car / A. Cameron Gilg ; with some anecdotes contributed by Walter Kay ; edited by Barry Cockcroft ; editorial note by Colin McElduff. — London : Royal Automobile Club, 1981. — 191p : ill,1map,ports ; 23cm
Ill on lining papers. — Includes index
ISBN 0-86211-016-5 : £4.50 B81-09358

916′.04328 — Africa. Description & travel

Gordon, René. Africa : a continent revealed / René Gordon. — Richmond upon Thames : Country Life, 1980. — 280p : col.ill,maps ; 33cm
Bibliography: p280
ISBN 0-600-36782-7 : £17.50 B81-10298

916′.04328 — Africa — *Practical information — For British businessmen*

Africa / regional editor Toby Milner. — London : Joseph, c1981. — 511p : maps ; 23cm. — (The Business traveller′s handbook ; v.1)
Includes index
ISBN 0-7181-1981-9 : £14.95 B81-25638

916′.04328 — Africa — *Visitors′ guides*

Crowther, Geoff. Africa on the cheap / [Geoff Crowther]. — South Yarra : Lonely Planet ; London : Lascelles [distributor], 1980. — 362p : ill,maps,1port ; 19cm
ISBN 0-908086-19-9 (pbk) : £3.95 B81-26683

916.1 — NORTH AFRICA

916.1′0448′05 — North Africa — *Visitors′ guides — Serials*

Traveller′s guide to North Africa. — [No.1]-. — London (P.O. Box 261, 63 Long Acre, WC2 9LR) : IC Magazines, 1981-. — v. : ill,maps ; 19cm
Annual. — Continues in part: Traveller′s guide to Africa
ISSN 0144-7637 = Traveller′s guide to North Africa : £4.95 B81-29435

916.2 — EGYPT

916.2′043′0922 — Nile River region. Exploration. English explorers, *1862-1904* — *Biographies — For children*

Langley, Andrew. Explorers on the Nile / Andrew Langley. — Hove : Wayland, 1981. — 64p : ill(some col.),maps(some col.),ports(some col.) ; 23cm. — (In profile)
Bibliography: p62. — Includes index
ISBN 0-85340-882-3 : £3.95 B81-40618

916.24 — SUDAN

916.24′044 — Sudan — *Practical information — For British businessmen*

Sudan. — London (50 Ludgate Hill, EC4M 7HU) : British Overseas Trade Board, 1980. — 64p : ill,1 map ; 21cm. — (Hints to exporters)
Bibliography: p54-56
Unpriced (pbk) B81-02823

916.4 — MOROCCO

916.4′045 — Morocco — *Visitors′ guides*

Kininmonth, Christopher. Morocco / by Christopher Kininmonth. — 2nd ed. — London : Cape, 1981. — 368p : maps ; 18cm. — (Travellers′ guide)
Previous ed.: 1972. — Col. maps on inside covers. — Bibliography: p359-360. — Includes index
ISBN 0-224-01897-3 (pbk) : £6.50 B81-18446

916.6 — WEST AFRICA

916.6 — West Africa. Geographical features

Church, R. J. Harrison. West Africa : a study of the environment and of man′s use of it / R.J. Harrison Church ; with a chapter on soils and soil management [by] R.P. Moss. — 8th ed. — London : Longman, 1980. — xxxi,526p : ill,maps ; 24cm. — (Geographies for advanced study)
Previous ed.: 1974. — Bibliography: p485-516. — Includes index
ISBN 0-582-30020-7 (pbk) : £9.50 : CIP rev.
B80-04592

916.6 — West Africa. Geographical features — *For schools*

Iloeje, N. P.. A new geography of West Africa / N.P. Iloeje. — New rev. ed. — London : Longman, 1980. — 201p,[8]p of plates : ill (some col.),maps ; 25cm
Previous ed.: i.e. Metricated ed.: 1977. — Includes index
ISBN 0-582-60379-x (pbk) : £3.00 B81-21435

916.6′04 — West Africa. Description & travel, ***1941* — *Personal observations — Correspondence, diaries, etc.***

Greene, Graham. In search of a character : two African journals / Graham Greene. — Harmondsworth : Penguin in association with Bodley Head, 1968, c1961 (1980 [printing]). — 105p ; 18cm
Originally published: London : Bodley Head, 1961
ISBN 0-14-002822-6 (pbk) : £1.25
Also classified at 916.75′1042 B81-06996

916.6′04′05 — West Africa — *Visitors′ guides — Serials*

Traveller′s guide to West Africa. — [No.1]-. — London (P.O. Box 261, 63 Long Ace, WC2 9LR) : IC Magazines, 1981-. — v. : ill,maps ; 19cm
Annual. — Continues in part: Traveller′s guide to Africa
ISSN 0144-7645 = Traveller′s guide to West Africa : £4.95 B81-29434

916.62 — MALI, UPPER VOLTA, NIGER

916.6′2043 — Niger & Upper Volta — *Practical information — For British businessmen*
Ivory Coast, Niger and Upper Volta. — London (50 Ludgate Hill, EC4M 7HU) : British Overseas Trade Board, 1981. — 63p : ill,2maps ; 21cm. — (Hints to exporters)
Bibliography: p54-58
Unpriced (pbk)
Also classified at 916.66′8045 B81-17691

916.6′2043 — West Africa. Niger River region. Exploration, *1976 — Personal observations*
Odili, Herbert A.. My endurance - my conquest : the revealing and incredible story of how one man became the first in exploration history to defeat the River Niger / Herbert A. Odili ; compiled by Charles Thornton. — Bognor Regis : New Horizon, c1979. — vi,148p,[16]p of plates : ill ; 21cm
ISBN 0-86116-392-3 : £4.75 B81-21826

916.651 — GAMBIA

916.6′51043 — Gambia — *Practical information — For British businessmen*
The **Gambia**. — London (50 Ludgate Hill, EC4M 7HU) : British Overseas Trade Board, 1980. — 39p : ill,maps ; 21cm. — (Hints to exporters)
Bibliography: p33-34
Unpriced (pbk) B81-02818

916.662 — LIBERIA

916.66′2042 — Liberia. Description & travel, *1935 — Personal observations*
Greene, Barbara. [Land benighted]. Too late to turn back : Barbara and Graham Greene in Liberia / Barbara Greene ; with an introduction by Paul Theroux. — London (13 Golden Square W1R 3AG) : Settle Bendall, 1981. — xvii,204p : ill,1map,ports ; 22cm
Originally published: London, Geoffrey Bles, 1938
ISBN 0-907070-06-x : £7.95 B81-38975

916.668 — IVORY COAST

916.66′8045 — Ivory Coast — *Practical information — For British businessmen*
Ivory Coast, Niger and Upper Volta. — London (50 Ludgate Hill, EC4M 7HU) : British Overseas Trade Board, 1981. — 63p : ill,2maps ; 21cm. — (Hints to exporters)
Bibliography: p54-58
Unpriced (pbk)
Primary classification 916.6′2043 B81-17691

916.7 — CENTRAL AFRICA

916.7 — Central Africa. Geographical features — *For schools*
Michie, W. D.. The lands and peoples of Central Africa / W.D. Michie, E.D. Kadzombe, M.R. Naidoo. — New ed. — London : Longman, 1981. — iv,202p : ill,maps ; 25cm
Previous ed.: 1973. — Includes index
ISBN 0-582-60380-3 (pbk) : £2.60 B81-15241

916.7′04 — Africa south of the Sahara. Description & travel, *1975-1978 — Personal observations*
Dodwell, Christina. Travels with fortune / Christina Dodwell. — London : Arrow, 1981, c1979. — 315p : maps ; 18
Originally published: London : W.H. Allen, 1979
ISBN 0-09-924640-6 (pbk) : £1.50 B81-11439

916.7′04′0222 — Africa. Central Africa. Description & travel — *Illustrations*
Sleen, Marc. Safari / Marc Sleen. — [London] : New English Library, 1980. — 224p : chiefly ill(some col.),1col.map,col.ports ; 31cm
Ill, col.map on lining papers
ISBN 0-450-04445-9 : £8.95 B81-02289

916.7′04′05 — Central & Southern Africa — *Visitors′ guides — Serials*
Traveller′s guide to Central and Southern Africa. — [No.1]-. — London (P.O. Box 261, 63 Long Acre, WC2 9LR) : IC Magazines, 1981-. — v. : ill,maps ; 19cm
Annual. — Continues in part: Traveller′s guide to Africa
ISSN 0144-7661 = Traveller′s guide to Central and Southern Africa : £4.95 B81-29436

916.751 — ZAIRE

916.75′1042 — Zaire. Description & travel, *1959 — Personal observations — Correspondence, diaries, etc.*
Greene, Graham. In search of a character : two African journals / Graham Greene. — Harmondsworth : Penguin in association with Bodley Head, 1968, c1961 (1980 [printing]). — 105p ; 18cm
Originally published: London : Bodley Head, 1961
ISBN 0-14-002822-6 (pbk) : £1.25
Primary classification 916.6′04 B81-06996

916.76 — EAST AFRICA

916.76′044 — East Africa. Description & travel, *1972 — Personal observations*
Whittingham, John. Shoe-string safari : travels, adventures and experiences in Africa / by John Whittingham. — Oxford : Hannon, [c1978]. — vii,191p : ill,1map,1facsim,ports ; 21cm
ISBN 0-904233-23-5 (cased) : £4.95
ISBN 0-904233-24-3 (pbk) : £2.95
Also classified at 916.8′0462 B81-05723

916.76′044′05 — East Africa — *Visitors′ guides — Serials*
Traveller′s guide to East Africa and the Indian Ocean. — [No.1]-. — London (P.O. Box 261, 63 Long Acre, WC2 9LR) : IC Magazines, 1981-. — v. : ill,maps ; 19cm
Annual. — Continues in part: Traveller′s guide to Africa
ISSN 0144-7653 = Traveller′s guide to East Africa and the Indian Ocean : £4.95
Also classified at 916.9′04′05 B81-29433

916.762 — KENYA

916.76′2044 — Kenya. Description & travel — *Personal observations*
Cubitt, Gerald. The book of Kenya / Gerald Cubitt photographs ; Eric Robins text. — London : Collins and Harvill, 1980. — 208p : ill(some col.),maps,ports ; 32cm
Ill on lining papes. — Bibliography: p208
ISBN 0-00-216044-7 : £15.00 B81-05956

Naipaul, Shiva. North of south : an African journey / Shiva Naipaul. — Harmondsworth : Penguin, 1980, c1979. — 349p : 1map ; 20cm
Originally published: London : Deutsch, 1978
ISBN 0-14-004894-4 (pbk) : £1.95
Also classified at 916.78′044 B81-01373

916.78 — TANZANIA

916.78′044 — Tanzania. Description & travel — *Personal observations*
Naipaul, Shiva. North of south : an African journey / Shiva Naipaul. — Harmondsworth : Penguin, 1980, c1979. — 349p : 1map ; 20cm
Originally published: London : Deutsch, 1978
ISBN 0-14-004894-4 (pbk) : £1.95
Primary classification 916.76′2044 B81-01373

916.79 — MOZAMBIQUE

916.7′9045 — Mozambique. Wildlife reserves: National parks. Description & travel — *Personal observations*
Tinley, Lynne. Drawn from the plains : life in the wilds of Southern Africa / Lynne Tinley. — London : Collins, 1979. — 191p,[4]p of plates : ill(some col.),2maps ; 25cm
ISBN 0-00-211667-7 : £6.95
Also classified at 916.88′043 B81-03621

916.8 — SOUTHERN AFRICA

916.8′0456 — Southern Africa. Description & travel, *1951 — Correspondence, diaries, etc.*
Lister, Douglas S.. Africa calls / Douglas S. Lister. — Bognor Regis : New Horizon, c1980. — 317p,[39]p of plates : ill,1plan,port ; 22cm
ISBN 0-86116-042-8 : £5.75 B81-21807

916.8′0462 — South Africa. Description & travel, *1973 — Personal observations*
Breytenbach, Breyten. A season in paradise / Breyten Breytenbach ; translated from the Afrikaans by Rike Vaughan. — London : Cape, 1980. — 291p : 1 map ; 23cm
Translation of: 'n Seisoen in die paradys
ISBN 0-224-01876-0 : £8.50 : CIP rev
B81-19198

916.8′0462 — Southern Africa. Description & travel, *1972 — Personal observations*
Whittingham, John. Shoe-string safari : travels, adventures and experiences in Africa / by John Whittingham. — Oxford : Hannon, [c1978]. — vii,191p : ill,1map,1facsim,ports ; 21cm
ISBN 0-904233-23-5 (cased) : £4.95
ISBN 0-904233-24-3 (pbk) : £2.95
Primary classification 916.76′044 B81-05723

916.81′1042 — Botswana. Kalahari Desert. Description & travel, *1952.* **Van der Post, Laurens. Lost world of the Kalahari** — *Study outlines*
Kemp, C.. Notes on Van der Post′s Venture to the interior and The lost world of the Kalahari / compiled by C. Kemp. — London : Methuen, 1981, c1980. — 57p ; 20cm. — (Methuen notes)
ISBN 0-417-21680-7 (pbk) : £0.95
Primary classification 916.897′042 B81-08611

916.81′1043 — Southern Africa. Kalahari Desert. Description & travel — *Personal observations*
Luard, Nicholas. The last wilderness : a journey across the great Kalahari Desert / Nicholas Luard. — London : Elm Tree, 1981. — 222p,[32]p of plates : col.ill,1map ; 24cm
ISBN 0-241-10299-5 : £8.95 : CIP rev.
B81-07588

916.88′043 — Namibia. Wildlife reserves: National parks. Description and travel — *Personal observations*
Tinley, Lynne. Drawn from the plains : life in the wilds of Southern Africa / Lynne Tinley. — London : Collins, 1979. — 191p,[4]p of plates : ill(some col.),2maps ; 25cm
ISBN 0-00-211667-7 : £6.95
Primary classification 916.7′9045 B81-03621

916.897 — MALAWI

916.897′042 — Malawi. Description & travel, *ca 1950.* **Van der Post, Laurens. Venture to the interior** — *Study outlines*
Kemp, C.. Notes on Van der Post′s Venture to the interior and The lost world of the Kalahari / compiled by C. Kemp. — London : Methuen, 1981, c1980. — 57p ; 20cm. — (Methuen notes)
ISBN 0-417-21680-7 (pbk) : £0.95
Also classified at 916.81′1042 B81-08611

916.9 — INDIAN OCEAN ISLANDS

916.9′04′05 — South-western Indian Ocean. Islands — *Visitors′ guides — Serials*
Traveller′s guide to East Africa and the Indian Ocean. — [No.1]-. — London (P.O. Box 261, 63 Long Acre, WC2 9LR) : IC Magazines, 1981-. — v. : ill,maps ; 19cm
Annual. — Continues in part: Traveller′s guide to Africa
ISSN 0144-7653 = Traveller′s guide to East Africa and the Indian Ocean : £4.95
Primary classification 916.76′044′05 B81-29433

916.9′804 — Mauritius & Réunion *(Island) — Practical information — For British businessmen*
Mauritius and Réunion. — London (50 Ludgate Hill, EC4M 7HU) : British Overseas Trade Board, 1980. — 60p : ill,2maps ; 21cm. — (Hints to exporters)
Bibliography: p49-51
Unpriced (pbk) B81-02824

917 — NORTH AMERICA

917 — North America. Geographical features — *For schools*
Dunlop, Stewart. North America : a new geography / Stewart Dunlop, Donald MacDonald. — London : Heinemann Educational, 1981. — 186p : ill(some col.),maps(some col.) ; 25cm
Includes index
ISBN 0-435-34250-9 (pbk) : £3.80 : CIP rev.
B81-02103

917'.0076 — North America. Geographical features — *Questions & answers — For schools*

Tolley, H.. Data response exercises on North America and Western Europe / H. Tolley, K. Briggs, D. Riley. — Oxford : Oxford University Press, 1981. — 80p : ill,maps ; 30cm
ISBN 0-19-913266-6 (pbk) : £2.50
Primary classification 914'.0076 B81-25951

917'.04538 — North America — *Practical information — For businessmen*

Executive North America. — London : Pitman, 1981. — 846p : ill,maps ; 21cm. — (A Pitman guide)
Originally published: United States : Heron House, 1981. — Includes index
ISBN 0-273-01293-2 : £7.95 B81-14743

917'.09732 — North America. Cities. Geographical features — *For schools*

Hellyer, Michael J.. North American cities / [Michael J. Hellyer]. — London : Longman, 1981. — 49p : ill(some col.),col.maps ; 23cm. — (Longman revised colour geographies)
Bibliography: p49
ISBN 0-582-22039-4 (pbk) : £1.25 B81-24481

917.1 — CANADA

917.1'04646'05 — Canada — *Visitors' guides — Serials*

Fodor's Canada. — 1978-. — London : Hodder and Stoughton, 1978-. — v. : ill ; 21cm
Annual. — Cover title: Fodor's ... guide to Canada. — Description based on: 1981 issue
ISSN 0160-3906 = Fodor's Canada : £6.95
B81-20322

917.18'044 — Newfoundland. Coastal waters. Voyages by schooners, *1960-1968*: Happy Adventure *(Boat)* — *Personal observations*

Mowat, Farley. The boat who wouldn't float / Farley Mowat. — Large print ed. — Leicester : Ulverscroft, 1981, c1969. — 384p ; 23cm. — (Ulverscroft large print)
Originally published: Toronto : McClelland & Stewart, 1969 ; London : Heinemann, 1970
ISBN 0-7089-0601-x : Unpriced B81-20775

917.2 — MIDDLE AMERICA, MEXICO

917.2'04822'0924 — Mexico. Description & travel, *ca 1924 — Personal observations*

Lawrence, D. H.. Mornings in Mexico ; and Etruscan places / D.H. Lawrence. — Harmondsworth : Penguin in assocation with William Heinemann, 1960 (1981 [printing]). — 214p,[16]p of plates : ill ; 18cm
Mornings in Mexico originally published: London : Martin Secker, 1927
ISBN 0-14-001513-2 (pbk) : £1.75
Also classified at 937'.5 B81-27652

917.2'04825 — Mexico. Description & travel, *1938 — Personal observations*

Greene, Graham. The lawless roads / Graham Greene. — Harmondsworth : Penguin in association with Heinemann, 1947, c1939 (1981 [printing]). — 224p : 1map ; 18cm
Originally published: London : Longman, 1939
ISBN 0-14-000559-5 (pbk) : £1.75 B81-40711

917.2'04833 — Mexico — *Visitors' guides*

Wilhelm, John. The Wilhelms' guide to all Mexico. — 5th ed., rev. and enl. / by John, Lawrence, and Charles Wilhelm. — New York ; London : McGraw-Hill, c1978. — xi,485p : ill,maps ; 22cm
Previous ed.: published as Guide to Mexico / by John Wilhelm. 1973. — Includes index
ISBN 0-07-070289-6 : £9.35 B81-03989

917.2'04833'05 — Mexico — *Visitors' guides — Serials*

Fodor's Mexico. — 1981. — London : Hodder and Stoughton, c1981. — xi,603p
ISBN 0-340-26035-1 : £6.95
ISBN 0-679-00708-3 (David McKay pbk)
B81-09071

917.286 — COSTA RICA

917.286'0452 — Costa Rica — *Practical information — For British businessmen*

Costa Rica. — London (50 Ludgate Hill, EC4M 7HU) : British Overseas Trade Board, 1981. — 39p : ill,1map ; 21cm. — (Hints to exporters)
Bibliography: p32-34
Unpriced (pbk) B81-17687

917.287 — PANAMA

917.287'0452 — Panama — *Practical information — For British businessmen*

Panama. — [London] : British Overseas Trade Board, 1981. — 50p : 1map ; 21cm. — (Hints to exporters)
Bibliography: p43-45
Unpriced (pbk) B81-38616

917.29 — WEST INDIES

917.293'0454 — Dominican Republic — *Practical information — For British businessmen*

The **Dominican** Republic. — London (50 Ludgate Hill, EC4M 7HU) : British Overseas Trade Board, 1981. — 47p : ill,2maps ; 21cm. — (Hints to exporters)
Bibliography: p40-42
Unpriced (pbk) B81-17227

917.299'04'05 — Bermuda — *Visitors' guides — Serials*

Fodor's Bermuda. — 1981. — London : Hodder and Stoughton, c1981. — vi,180p
ISBN 0-340-26048-3 : £5.50
ISSN 0192-3765 B81-20321

917.3 — UNITED STATES

917.3 — United States. Geographical features

Watson, J. Wreford. The United States. — London : Longman, Feb.1982. — [304]p. — (Geographies for advanced study)
ISBN 0-582-30004-5 (cased) : £18.00 : CIP entry
ISBN 0-582-30005-3 (pbk) : £9.95 B81-35920

917.3'04926 — United States, *1977-1981 — Visitors' guides*

Girard, Christian. USA / [compiled by Christian Girard]. — London : Octopus, 1980. — 223p : maps ; 10x21cm. — (Guide in jeans)
Translation of: Guide des U.S.A. en jeans
ISBN 0-7064-1465-9 (pbk) : Unpriced
B81-20016

917.3'04926 — United States. Journeys by bicycles, *1978 — Personal observations*

Miller, Christian. Daisy, Daisy : a journey across America on a bicycle / Christian Miller. — London : Routledge & Kegan Paul, 1980. — viii,180p : maps ; 23cm
ISBN 0-7100-0709-4 : £5.95 : CIP rev.
B80-21204

917.3'04927 — United States. Description and travel - *Personal observations*

Williams, Hugo. No particular place to go. — London : Cape, July 1981. — 1v.
ISBN 0-224-01810-8 : CIP entry B81-13858

917.3'04927 — United States — *Practical information*

Clarke, Nigel J.. Travel U.S.A. / by Nigel J. Clarke. — Charmouth (The Holt, The Street, Charmouth, Dorset) : N.J. Clarke, [1981]. — 232p ; 19cm
Cover title
Unpriced (pbk) B81-24946

917.3'04927'05 — United States, *1981- — Visitors' guides — Serials*

Let's go. The budget guide to the USA / written by Harvard Student Agencies. — 1981-. — Leicester : WHS Distributors, [1981?]-. — v. : ill,maps ; 21cm
ISSN 0260-8650 = Let's go. The budget guide to the USA : £2.95 B81-10279

917.3'04927'05 — United States — *Visitors' guides — Serials*

Fodor's budget travel in America. — 1979-. — London : Hodder and Stoughton, 1979-. — v. : ill ; 21cm
Annual. — Description based on: 1981 issue
ISSN 0192-8287 = Fodor's budget travel in America : £4.95 B81-20330

Fodor's USA. — 1981. — London : Hodder and Stoughton, c1981. — xv,974p
Cover title: Fodor's ... guide to the USA
ISBN 0-340-26036-x : £6.95
ISSN 0147-8745 B81-20329

917.3'09732 — United States. Urban regions. Geographical features

Hartshorn, Truman Asa. Interpreting the city : an urban geography / Truman Asa Hartshorn ; Borden Devon Dent cartographer. — New York ; Chichester : Wiley, c1980. — x,498p : ill,maps ; 29cm
Maps in lining papers. — Includes bibliographies and index
ISBN 0-471-05637-5 : Unpriced B81-08513

917.4 — UNITED STATES. NORTH-EASTERN STATES

917.43'10441 — Vermont. Lake Champlain. Description & travel, *1870 — Personal observations*

James, Henry, *1843-1916*. Lake George to Burlington : two American travel sketches / by Henry James. — Edinburgh (137 Warrender Park Rd., Edinburgh EH9 1DS) : Tragara Press, 1981. — 21p ; 20cm
Limited ed. of 120 numbered copies
ISBN 0-902616-68-4 : £10.50
Primary classification 917.47'51 B81-22432

917.47'10443 — New York *(City)*. Description & travel

Maynard, Chris. New York / written by Chris Maynard and Gail Rebuck ; picture researcher Kathy Brandt ; commissioned photography by Peter Semler. — London : Marshall Cavendish, 1978. — 98p : ill(some col.),1map,col.ports ; 28cm. — (The World's cities)
Ill on lining papers
ISBN 0-85685-500-6 : £3.95 B81-01668

917.47'10443 — New York *(City)* — *Visitors' guides*

Appleberg, Marilyn J.. The I love New York guide / compiled by Marilyn Appleberg ; illustrated by Albert Pfeiffer. — New York : Collier ; London : Collier Macmillan, 1979. — 188p : ill,col.maps ; 18cm
Includes index
ISBN 0-02-097210-5 (pbk) : £1.95 B81-02043

Appleberg, Marilyn J.. I love New York guide / [compiled by] Marilyn J. Appleberg ; illustrated by Albert Pfeiffer. — Rev. ed. — New York : Collier ; London : Collier Macmillan, 1981. — 219p,[16]p : ill,col.maps ; 18cm
Previous ed.: 1979. — Includes index
ISBN 0-02-097220-2 (pbk) : £1.95 B81-33375

Van Peebles, Meggan. New York / [compiled by Meggan Van Peebles and Frank Dexter Brown]. — London : Octopus, 1981. — 192p : maps ; 21x10cm. — (Guide in jeans)
Translation of: Guide de New York en jeans
ISBN 0-7064-1581-7 (pbk) : £1.50 B81-18188

917.47'10443'05 — New York *(City)* — *Visitors' guides — For businessmen — Serials*

The **Business** traveler's survival guide. New York. — 1981 ed.-. — New York : Business Travelers, Inc. ; [London] : [Collins] [[distributor]], 1981-. — v. ; 21cm
Annual
£5.50 B81-30858

917.47'10443'05 — New York *(City)* — *Visitors' guides — Serials*

Tourist guide. New York / Michelin. — 5th ed. — London : Michelin Tyre Co., c1978. — 148p
ISBN 2-06-015510-x : Unpriced B81-29096

917.47'51 — New York *(State)*. Lake George. Description & travel, *1870 — Personal observations*

James, Henry, *1843-1916*. Lake George to Burlington : two American travel sketches / by Henry James. — Edinburgh (137 Warrender Park Rd., Edinburgh EH9 1DS) : Tragara Press, 1981. — 21p ; 20cm
Limited ed. of 120 numbered copies
ISBN 0-902616-68-4 : £10.50
Also classified at 917.43'10441 B81-22432

917.5 — UNITED STATES. SOUTH-EASTERN STATES

917.58′2310443′05 — Georgia ***(State)*****. Atlanta —** *Visitors′ guides — For businessmen — Serials*
The **Business** traveler′s survival guide. Atlanta. — 1981 ed.-. — New York : Business Travelers, Inc. ; [London] : [Collins] [[distributor]], 1981-. — v. ; 21cm
Annual
£4.95 B81-30859

917.6 — UNITED STATES. SOUTH CENTRAL STATES

917.64′40463 — North America. Rio Grande region. Description & travel — *For children*
Johnson, Raymond. The Rio Grande / Raymond Johnson. — Hove : Wayland, 1981. — 69p : ill (some col.),col.maps,ports ; 21x22cm. — (Rivers of the world)
Map on lining papers. — Bibliography: p68. - Includes index
ISBN 0-85340-809-2 : £4.25 B81-12976

917.7 — UNITED STATES. NORTH CENTRAL STATES

917.7′0433 — United States. Mississippi River region. Description & travel, ***1980*** — *Personal observations*
Raban, Jonathan. Old glory : an American voyage / Jonathan Raban. — London : Collins, 1981. — 527p : col.maps ; 23cm
Maps on lining papers
ISBN 0-00-216521-x : £9.95 : CIP rev. B81-25133

917.8 — UNITED STATES. WESTERN STATES

917.8′042′0924 — United States. Western states. Exploration. Role of Jefferson, Thomas
Jackson, Donald. Thomas Jefferson & the Stony Mountains : exploring the West from Monticello / Donald Jackson. — Urbana ; London : University of Illinois Press, c1981. — xii,339p : maps ; 24cm
Bibliography: p311-324. — Includes index
ISBN 0-252-00823-5 : £11.95 B81-22353

917.8′0433 — United States. Western states. Overland travel to California — *Personal observations*
Moffat, Gwen. Hard road West : alone on the California trail / by Gwen Moffat. — London : Gollancz : 1981. — viii,198p,[16]p of plates : ill,maps,1port ; 24cm
Map on lining papers. — Includes index
ISBN 0-575-02943-9 : £9.95 B81-15273

917.9 — UNITED STATES. PACIFIC COAST STATES

917.9′0433 — United States. Pacific coast states — *Visitors′ guides*
Van Dam, Ine. West Coast USA : a guide to California, Oregon & Washington / Ine van Dam. — London : J. Murray, 1981. — 229p : ill,maps ; 22cm
Includes index
ISBN 0-7195-3758-4 (pbk) : £5.95 : CIP rev. B81-13400

917.91′3′045 — United States. Western states. Colorado River region. Description & travel — *For children*
Winks, Robin W.. The Colorado / Robin W. Winks and Honor Leigh Winks. — Hove : Wayland, 1980. — 60,[5]p : ill(some col.),col.maps,ports ; 21x23cm. — (Rivers of the world)
Col.maps on lining papers. — Bibliography: p[4]. — Includes index
ISBN 0-85340-751-7 : £3.95 B81-08390

917.94′0453 — California — *Visitors′ guides*
Robertson, Fyfe. Visit California with Fyfe Robertson : including San Francisco, Los Angeles, San Diego, Hollywood, Disneyland and Yosemite, plus trips to Las Vegas and the Grand Canyon. — [Kingston upon Thame] ([31, Castle St., Kingston-upon-Thames, KI1 1ST]) : [Lewis Publications], [1981]. — 144p : ill,maps,1form,ports ; 21cm. — (Lewis world travel)
Cover title. — Includes index
ISBN 0-901449-10-5 (pbk) : £1.95 B81-16967

917.96′82 — Idaho. Salmon River Mountains. Aeroplanes. Accidents, ***1979*****. Survivors experiences**
Gzowski, Peter. The Sacrament / Peter Gzowski. — London : Hale, 1981, c1980. — 203p : ill,1map,2ports ; 24cm
Originally published: Toronto : McClelland and Stewart, 1980
ISBN 0-7091-8916-8 : £6.95 B81-12185

917.97′940443 — Washington ***(State)*****. Olympic Peninsula** — *Visitors′ guides*
Kirk, Ruth. Exploring the Olympic Peninsula / by Ruth Kirk ; photographs by Ruth and Louis Kirk. — 3rd rev. ed. — Seattle ; London : University of Washington Press ... in cooperation with the Pacific Northwest National Parks Association, c1980. — 118p : ill,maps ; 23cm
Previous ed.: 1976. — Bibliography: p113. — Includes index
ISBN 0-295-95750-6 (pbk) : £4.75 B81-32149

918 — SOUTH AMERICA

918 — South America. Geographical features
Morris, Arthur. South America. — 2nd ed. — London : Hodder & Stoughton, Sept.1981. — [288]p
ISBN 0-340-27205-8 (pbk) : £7.95 : CIP entry B81-22493

918′.0437 — Spanish America. Description & travel, ***1970-1979*** — *Personal observations*
Theroux, Paul. The Old Patagonian Express : by train through the Americas / Paul Theroux. — Harmandsworth : Penguin, 1980, c1979 (1981 [printing]). — 429p ; 18cm
Originally published: London : Hamilton, 1979
ISBN 0-14-005493-6 (pbk) : £1.50 B81-05517

918′.0438 — Latin America — *Practical information — For British businessmen*
Central and South America and the Caribbean / editor Jane Walker ; associate editor Mark Ambrose. — London : Joseph, c1981. — 447p : maps ; 23cm. — (The Business traveller′s handbook ; v.2)
Includes index
ISBN 0-7181-1976-2 : £14.95
Also classified at 910′.091821 B81-25633

918′.0438′05 — South America — *Visitors′ guides — Serials*
The ... South American handbook. — 57th ed. (1981). — Bath (Mendip Press, Parsonage Lane, Bath BA1 1EN) : Trade & Travel Publications, c1981. — 1304p
ISBN 0-900751-17-7 : Unpriced
ISSN 0309-4529 B81-03928

918.1 — BRAZIL

918.1 — Brazil. Geographical features — *For schools*
Vaughan-Williams, Phillip. Brasil : a concise thematic geography / Phillip Vaughan-Williams. — Slough : University Tutorial Press, 1981. — x,166p : ill,maps ; 26cm
Bibliography: p160-161. — Includes index
ISBN 0-7231-0813-7 (pbk) : £3.50 B81-27071

918.2 — ARGENTINA

918.2′70463 — Argentina. Patagonia. Description & travel, ***1963 & 1979*** — *Personal observations*
Earle, John, *1929-*. The springs of enchantment : climbing and exploration in Patagonia / John Earle. — London : Hodder and Stoughton, 1981. — 191p,[16]p of plates : ill,maps,ports ; 23cm
Includes index
ISBN 0-340-24304-x : £7.95 B81-04569

918.4 — BOLIVIA

918.4′0452 — Bolivia. Expeditions to discover El Dorado — *Personal observations*
Salmon, Ross. My quest for El Dorado / Ross Salmon. — Large print ed. — Leicester : Ulverscroft, 1981, c1979. — 468p ; 22cm. — (Ulverscroft large print)
Originally published: London : Hodder & Stoughton, 1979
ISBN 0-7089-0657-5 : £5.00 : CIP rev. B81-16888

918.61 — COLOMBIA

918.61′04632 — Colombia — *Practical information — For British businessmen*
Colombia. — [London] : British Overseas Trade Board, 1981. — 51p : 1map ; 21cm. — (Hints to exporters)
Bibliography: p42-44
Unpriced (pbk) B81-38617

918.66 — ECUADOR

918.66′0474 — Ecuador — *Practical information — For British businessmen*
Ecuador / British Overseas Trade Board. — [London] : [The Board], 1981. — 49p,[1] folded leaf of plates : ill,2maps ; 21cm. — (Hints to exporters)
Text on inside covers. — Bibliography: p42-44
Unpriced (pbk) B81-13281

918.95 — URUGUAY

918.95′0465 — Uruguay — *Practical information — For British businessmen*
Uruguay. — London (50 Ludgate Hill, EC4M 7HU) : British Overseas Trade Board, 1981. — 47p : ill,1map ; 21cm. — (Hints to exporters)
Bibliography: p40-42
Unpriced (pbk) B81-17228

919 — OCEANIA, ATLANTIC OCEAN ISLANDS, POLAR REGIONS, ETC

919′.04 — Pacific islands — *Practical information — For British businessmen*
Fiji, French Polynesia, Kiribati, New Caledonia, Solomon Islands, Tonga, Tuvalu, and Western Samoa. — London (50 Ludgate Hill, EC4M 7HU) : British Overseas Trade Board, 1981. — 143p : ill,1map ; 21cm. — (Hints to exporters)
Bibliography: p136-139
Unpriced (pbk) B81-17226

919.3 — MELANESIA, NEW ZEALAND

919.31 — New Zealand. Geographical features — *For schools*
Knight, Colin L.. New Zealand geography : a systems approach / Colin L. Knight, John F. Buckland, Frank McPherson. — Rev. ed. — Christchurch, N.Z. ; London : Whitcoulls, 1978 (1980 [printing]). — 200p : ill(some col.),maps(some col.),facsims ; 25cm
Previous ed.: 1973. — Maps on lining papers. — Bibliography: p196-198. — Includes index
ISBN 0-7233-0545-5 : Unpriced B81-17898

919.312′2 — New Zealand. National parks: Urewera National Park. Long-distance footpaths: Waikaremoana Track — *Walkers′ guides*
Temple, Philip. The Shell guide to the Waikaremoana Track / by Philip Temple. — Rev. ed. — Christchurch, N.Z. ; London : Whitcoulls, 1980. — 37p : ill,1col.map,1port ; 18cm
Previous ed.: 1977
ISBN 0-7233-0652-4 (pbk) : Unpriced B81-17968

919.315′3 — New Zealand. Heaphy River region. Long-distance footpaths: Heaphy Track — *Walkers′ guides*
Temple, Philip. The Shell guide to the Heaphy track / by Philip Temple. — 2nd ed. — Christchurch, N.Z. ; London : Whitcoulls, 1978. — 37p : ill,1col.map ; 18cm
Previous ed.: 1976
ISBN 0-7233-0587-0 (pbk) : Unpriced B81-17967

919.315′4 — New Zealand. National parks: Mount Cook National Park & Westland National Park. Long-distance footpaths: Copland Track — *Walkers′ guides*
Temple, Philip. The Shell guide to the Copland track / by Philip Temple. — Rev. ed. — Christchurch, N.Z. ; London : Whitcoulls, 1980. — 37p : ill,1col.map,ports ; 18cm
Previous ed.: 1977
ISBN 0-7233-0651-6 (pbk) : Unpriced B81-17965

919.315'7 — New Zealand. National parks: Fiordland National Park. Long-distance footpaths: Hollyford Track — *Walkers' guides*

Temple, Philip. The Shell guide to Hollyford track / by Philip Temple. — Rev. ed. — Christchurch, N.Z. ; London : Whitcoulls, 1980. — 37p : ill,1col.map ; 18cm
Previous ed.: 1977
ISBN 0-7233-0653-2 (pbk) : Unpriced
B81-17966

919.315'7 — New Zealand. National parks: Fiordland National Park. Long-distance footpaths: Milford Track — *Walkers' guides*

Temple, Philip. The Shell guide to the Milford track / by Philip Temple. — 2nd ed. — Christchurch, N.Z. ; London : Whitcoulls, 1978. — 37p : ill,1col.map ; 18cm
Previous ed.: 1976
ISBN 0-7233-0588-9 (pbk) : Unpriced
B81-17964

919.4 — AUSTRALIA

919.4'042'0924 — Australia. Exploration. Buckley, William — *Biographies*

Morgan, John, *fl.1852*. The life and adventures of William Buckley : thirty-two years a wanderer amongst the aborigines of the unexplored country round Port Phillip / John Morgan. — Firle : Caliban, 1979. — 238p : ill,ports ; 19cm
Originally published: Hobart : Macdougall, 1852
ISBN 0-904573-12-5 : £7.50
Also classified at 994'.0049915'0924
B81-32621

919.4'046 — Australia. Deserts. Description & travel — *Personal observations*

Davidson, Robyn. Tracks. — Large print ed. — Anstey : Ulverscroft, Feb.1982. — [416]p. — (Ulverscroft large print series : non-fiction)
ISBN 0-7089-0756-3 : £5.00 : CIP entry
B81-36944

919.4'0463 — Australia. Deserts. Description & travel — *Personal observations*

Davidson, Robyn. Tracks / Robyn Davidson. — London : Cape, 1980. — 256p,[16]p of plates : ill,map,ports ; 23cm
Map on lining papers. — Bibliograhy: p255-256
ISBN 0-224-01861-2 : £5.95 : CIP rev.
B80-21205

919.4'0463 — Australia. National parks — *Visitors' guides*

Fairley, Alan. The Observer's book of national parks of Australia / Alan Fairley. — Sydney : Methuen Australia ; London : Warne, 1981. — xii,168p,[16]p of plates : col.ill,maps ; 15cm. — (A7)
Includes index
ISBN 0-454-00199-1 : £2.50 B81-32973

919.4'0463 — Australia — *Visitors' guides*

Stone, Frank. Australian tour suggestions / Frank Stone. — Ilfracombe : Stockwell, 1981. — 60p : 2maps ; 18cm
ISBN 0-7223-1434-5 (pbk) : £12.10 B81-16767

919.6 — POLYNESIA

919.6'12 — Tonga. Tongatapu — *Visitors' guides*

Packett, C. Neville. Travel and holiday guide to Tongatapu Island / C. Neville Packett. — [Bradford] ([Lloyds Bank Chambers, Hustlergate, Bradford, W.Yorkshire BD1 1PA]) : [C.N. Packett], [1981]. — [28]p : ill,maps,1coat of arms ; 21cm
Unpriced (unbound) B81-23540

919.8 — POLAR REGIONS

919.8'04 — Arctic. Expeditions, *1827* — *Early works*

Scoresby, William, *1789-1857*. The Polar ice ; The North Pole / William Scoresby. — Whitby : Caedmon, 1980. — 102p in various pagings,folded leaf : 1map ; 21cm
Facsims of: 2 articles originally published 1815 and 1825
ISBN 0-905355-09-1 : £7.95
Also classified at 919.8'2 B81-22164

919.8'2 — Greenland. Geographical features — *Early works*

Scoresby, William, *1789-1857*. The Polar ice ; The North Pole / William Scoresby. — Whitby : Caedmon, 1980. — 102p in various pagings,folded leaf : 1map ; 21cm
Facsims of: 2 articles originally published 1815 and 1825
ISBN 0-905355-09-1 : £7.95
Primary classification 919.8'04 B81-22164

919.8'9 — British Antarctic Territory. Elephant Island group. Expeditions, *1976-1977* — *Personal observations*

Furse, Chris. Elephant Island : an Antarctic expedition / Chris Furse. — Shrewsbury (7 St. John's Hill, Shrewsbury SY1 1JE) : Anthony Nelson, 1979. — 256p,[8]p of plates : ill(some col.),maps,ports ; 24cm
Ports. on lining papers. — Bibliography: p252. - Includes index
ISBN 0-904614-02-6 : £9.95 B81-16149

919.8'904 — Antarctic. Coastal regions. Exploration. Voyages by Belgian Antarctic Expedition *(1898-1899)* — *Personal observations*

Cook, Frederick A.. Through the first Antarctic night 1898-1899 : a narrative of the voyage of the Belgica among newly discovered lands and over an unknown sea about the South Pole / by Frederick A. Cook ; with an appendix containing a summary of the scientific results ; with a new introduction by Baron Gaston de Gerlache. — London : C. Hurst, c1980. — xxiv,xv,478p,[74]p of plates : ill,charts,maps,facsims,ports ; 23cm
Facsim of: edition published London : Heinemann, 1900. — Includes index
ISBN 0-905838-40-8 : £17.50 B81-07723

919.8'904 — Antarctic. Description & travel — *Personal observations*

Bailey, Jean. Antarctica : a traveller's tale / Jean Bailey ; with charcoal drawings by Lorraine Hannay. — London : Angus & Robertson, c1980. — 182p,[16]p of plates : ill(some col.),1map ; 25cm
Map on lining papers
ISBN 0-207-13821-4 : £7.95 B81-31655

919.8'904 — Antarctic. Expeditions: British Antarctic Expedition *(1898-1900)* — *Personal observations* — *Facsimiles*

Borchgrevink, C. E.. First on the Antarctic continent : being an account of the British Antarctic expedition 1898-1900 / by C.E. Borchgrevink ; with a new introduction by Tore Gjelsvik. — London : C. Hurst, c1980. — xv,vii,333p,[1] leaf of plates : ill,maps,ports ; 23cm
Facsim of: edition published London : Newnes, 1901. — Three fold. leaves of maps attached to inside cover. — Bibliography: pvii. - Includes index
ISBN 0-905838-41-6 : £17.50 B81-07724

919.8'904 — Antarctic. Exploration by Amundsen, Roald, *1911-1912* — *For children*

Miller, Margaret J.. Roald Amundsen : first to the South Pole / by Margaret J. Miller. — London : Hodder and Stoughton, 1981. — 127p : ill,maps,ports ; 24cm. — (Twentieth century people)
Includes index
ISBN 0-340-25950-7 : £5.50 : CIP rev.
B81-27986

919.9 — EXTRATERRESTRIAL WORLDS

919.9'04 — Outer space. Exploration & research

Adelman, Saul J.. Bound for the stars / Saul J. Adelman, Benjamin Adelman. — Englewood Cliffs ; London : Prentice-Hall, c1981. — xiv,335p : ill,charts ; 24cm. — (A Spectrum book)
Includes index
ISBN 0-13-080390-1 (cased) : Unpriced
ISBN 0-13-080382-0 (pbk) : £5.80 B81-16595

919.9'04 — Outer space. Exploration — *Forecasts* — *For children*

Ardley, Neil. Out into space / Neil Ardley. — London : Watts, [1981]. — 36p : col.ill ; 30cm. — (World of tomorrow)
Includes index
ISBN 0-85166-906-9 : £3.99
Also classified at 609'.99 B81-26677

919.9'04 — Outer space. Exploration, *to 1979*

Ridpath, Ian. Hamlyn encyclopedia of space / Ian Ridpath. — London : Hamlyn, c1981. — 160p : ill,col.charts,1col.map,ports(some col.) ; 29cm
Col. ill on lining papers. — Includes index
ISBN 0-600-38289-3 : £4.95 B81-22049

919.9'04 — Outer space. Exploration, *to 1980*

Gatland, Kenneth. The illustrated encyclopedia of space technology : a comprehensive history of space exploration / Kenneth Garland, consultant and principal author. — London : Salamander, c1981. — 289p : ill(some col.),col.maps,ports(some col.) ; 31cm
Text on lining papers. — Includes index
ISBN 0-86101-075-2 : £11.95 B81-26676

919.9'04 — Solar system. Exploration & research

Sagan, Carl. The cosmic connection : an extraterrestrial perspective / by Carl Sagan ; produced by Jerome Agel. — London : Papermac, 1981, c1973. — xiii,274p : ill ; 20cm
Originally published: Garden City, N.Y. : Doubleday ; London : Hodder and Stoughton, 1973. — Includes index
ISBN 0-333-32474-9 (pbk) : £2.95 B81-31906

920 — BIOGRAPHY

920'.0022'2 — Celebrities — *Illustrations*

Angeli, Daniel. Private pictures / introduced by Anthony Burgess ; photographs by Daniel Angeli and Jean-Paul Dousset. — London : Cape, 1980. — [96]p : chiefly ports ; 31cm
ISBN 0-224-01846-9 (cased) : £8.50
ISBN 0-224-01883-3 (pbk) : £4.95 B81-01374

920'.009'04 — Heroes & heroines, *ca 1900-1977*

Kenyon, James, *1910-*. Heroes and heroines / James and R.J. Kenyon and I.P. Jones ; illustrated by Hilda Offen. — London : Granada, 1981. — 155p : ill ; 18cm. — (A Dragon book)
ISBN 0-583-30309-9 (pbk) : £0.95 B81-11462

920'.009'04 — Western culture. Persons, *1900-1980*

Makers of modern culture / edited by Justin Wintle. — London : Routledge & Kegan Paul, 1981. — xviii,605p ; 24cm
Includes index
ISBN 0-7100-0732-9 : £12.50 : CIP rev.
B81-03362

920'.009'047 — Celebrities — *Biographies*

Stevens, Andy. World of stars : your 200 favourite personalities / Andy Stevens. — London : Armada, 1980. — 128p : ill,ports ; 20cm
ISBN 0-00-691797-6 (pbk) : £0.95 B81-01528

920'.02 — Conquerors — *Biographies*

Grant, Neil, *1938-*. Conquerors / Neil Grant. — London : Macdonald Educational, 1981. — 46p : ill,maps ; 25cm. — (Macdonald new reference library ; 29)
Text on lining papers. — Bibliography: p46. — Includes index
ISBN 0-356-05828-x : £2.75 B81-39118

920'.02 — Persons, *1660-1978*

Foot, Michael. Debts of honour / Michael Foot. — London : Poynter, 1980. — x,240p ; 24cm
Includes index
ISBN 0-7067-0243-3 : £9.50 B81-03072

920'.02 — Persons — *Biographies* — *For children*

Hellicar, Eileen. But who on earth was? / Eileen Hellicar. — Newton Abbot : David & Charles, c1981. — 160p : ports ; 23cm
Includes index
ISBN 0-7153-7962-3 : £4.95 : CIP rev.
B81-11926

920'.02 — Persons, *to 1979* — *Biographies*

Purnell's encyclopedia of famous people / [editor Rosalind Williams] ; [contributors Penny Boumelha et al.] ; [picture research Valerie Walker] ; [compiled by Laurence Urdang Associates]. — Maidenhead : Purnell, 1980. — 156p : ill,facsims,ports ; 30cm
Ports on lining papers
ISBN 0-361-04646-4 : £4.95 B81-01375

920′.02 — Persons, *to 1979* — *Biographies* *continuation*
Who did what : the Mitchell Beazley illustrated biographical dictionary : the lives and achievements of the 5000 men and women - leaders of nations, saints and sinners, artists and scientists - who shaped our world / [general editor Gerald Howat]. — Rev. ed. — [London] : [Mitchell Beazley], 1979. — 387p : ill(some col.),maps(some col.),facsims,ports (some col.) ; 27cm
Previous ed.: 1975. — Facsims on lining papers
ISBN 0-85533-166-6 (cased) : £9.95
ISBN 0-85533-165-8 (pbk) : £5.95 B81-07238

920′.02 — Persons, *to 1980* — *Biographies*
More of who said that?. — Newton Abbot : David & Charles, Oct.1981. — [64]p
ISBN 0-7153-8275-6 : £2.95 : CIP entry
Primary classification 808.88′2 B81-28073

920′.02′05 — Persons — *Biographies* — *Serials*
The **International** who's who. — 44th ed. (1980-81). — London : Europa, 1980. — xix,140p
ISBN 0-905118-48-0 : £30.00 : CIP rev.
ISSN 0074-9613 B80-09016

The **International** who's who. — 45th ed. (1981-82). — London : Europa, June 1981. — [1400]p
ISBN 0-905118-63-4 : £35.00 : CIP entry
ISSN 0074-9613 B81-13807

Who's who. — 1980. — London : A. & C. Black, c1980. — 2915p in various pagings
ISBN 0-7136-2030-7 : £30.00 B81-34042

Who's who. — 1981. — London : A. & C. Black, c1981. — 2958p in various pagings
ISBN 0-7136-2104-4 : £35.00 B81-34043

920′.037 — Ancient Romans — *Biographies*
Who was who in the Roman world 753 BC-AD476 / edited by Diana Bowder. — Oxford : Phaidon, 1980. — 256p : ill,maps,ports,geneal.tables ; 25cm
Bibliography: p243-245
ISBN 0-7148-2049-0 : £8.95 : CIP rev. B80-23870

920′.04 — Europeans, *ca 1920-1975* — *Personal observations*
Rowse, A. L.. Memories of men and women / A.L. Rowse. — London : Eyre Mathuen, 1980. — 258p ; 23cm
ISBN 0-413-47700-2 : £8.50 B81-00660

920′.041 — British eccentrics, *to 1981* — *Biographies*
Caufield, Catherine. The Emperor of the United States of America & other magnificent British eccentrics / by Catherine Caufield ; drawings by Peter Till. — London : Routledge & Kegan Paul, 1981. — viii,223p : ill,1map,port ; 21cm
Bibliography: p218-220
ISBN 0-7100-0957-7 : £6.95 : CIP rev. B81-28008

920′.041 — Britons, *1848-1941* — *Biographies*
Brendon, Piers. Eminent Edwardians / Piers Brendon. — Harmondsworth : Penguin, 1981, c1979. — xvi,255p ; 20cm
Originally published: London : Secker & Warburg, 1979. — Includes bibliographies
ISBN 0-14-005573-8 (pbk) : £2.50 B81-37257

920′.041 — Britons — *Biographies*
The **Concise** dictionary of national biography. — Oxford : Oxford University Press
Part 2: 1901-1970. — Feb.1982. — [704]p
ISBN 0-19-865303-4 : £15.00 : CIP entry B81-36247

920′.041 — Britons, *to 1978* — *Quotations*
The **Penguin** concise dictionary of biographical quotations / edited by Justin Wintle and Richard Kenin. — Abridged ed. — Harmondsworth : Penguin, 1981. — 715p ; 20cm
Previous ed.: published as Dictionary of biographical quotations of British and American subjects. London : Routledge & Kegan Paul, 1978. — Includes index
ISBN 0-14-051099-0 (pbk) : £3.95
Also classified at 920′.073 B81-40824

920′.041′05 — Britons — *Biographies* — *Serials*
The **Dictionary** of national biography. — 1961-1970. — Oxford : Oxford University Press, Oct.1981. — [1100]p
ISBN 0-19-865207-0 : £20.00 : CIP entry B81-30180

920′.042 — English persons, *1588-1623* — *Biographies*
Palmer, Alan. Who's who in Shapespeare's England / Alan & Veronica Palmer. — Brighton : Harvester, 1981. — 280p : maps,ports ; 25cm
ISBN 0-85527-718-1 : £30.00 B81-26175

920′.0421 — Londoners — *Interviews*
Bourne, Richard. Londoners / Richard Bourne ; photographs by John Minihan. — London : Dent, 1981. — 226p : ill,ports ; 26cm
ISBN 0-460-04489-3 : £9.95 : CIP rev. B81-22633

920′.0429 — Welsh persons, *1756-1980* — *Biographies* — *Welsh texts*
Jones, Gwilym R.. Dynion dawnus / gan Gwilym R. Jones. — Y Bala ([County Press Buildings, Baba, Gwynedd LL23 7PG]) : Llyfrau'r Faner, 1980. — 83p : ports ; 19cm
£1.50 (pbk) B81-10283

920′.073 — Americans, *to 1978* — *Quotations*
The **Penguin** concise dictionary of biographical quotations / edited by Justin Wintle and Richard Kenin. — Abridged ed. — Harmondsworth : Penguin, 1981. — 715p ; 20cm
Previous ed.: published as Dictionary of biographical quotations of British and American subjects. London : Routledge & Kegan Paul, 1978. — Includes index
ISBN 0-14-051099-0 (pbk) : £3.95
Primary classification 920′.041 B81-40824

920.71′09′04 — Men, *1900-1975* — *Personal observations*
Cooke, Alistair. Six men / Alistair Cooke. — Harmondsworth : Penguin, 1978, c1977 (1980 [printing]). — 206p ; 19cm
Originally published: London : Bodley Head, 1977
ISBN 0-14-004834-0 (pbk) : £1.25 B81-01376

920.72 — Women, *to 1980* — *Biographies*
Raven, Susan. Women in history : thirty-five centuries of feminine achievement / Susan Raven and Alison Weir ; foreword by Elizabeth Longford. — London : Weidenfeld and Nicolson, c1981. — 288p : ill,facsims,ports ; 24cm
Includes index
ISBN 0-297-77930-3 : £8.95 B81-28988

920.72′05 — Women — *Biographies* — *Serials*
The **World** who's who of women. — 5th ed. (1980). — Cambridge (Cambridge CB2 3QP) : International Biographical Centre, 1980. — 1167p
ISBN 0-900332-54-9 : Unpriced B81-25023

920.72′0941 — British women — *Biographies*
Berkery, Rita. Behind the scenes / Rita Berkery. — Bognor Regis : New Horizon, c1980. — 45p ; 21cm
ISBN 0-86116-245-5 : £4.25 B81-21723

920.72′0942 — England. Women, *1816-1933* — *Biographies*
Longford, Elizabeth. Eminent Victorian women / Elizabeth Longford. — London : Weidenfeld & Nicolson, c1981. — 256p : ill(some col.),facsims,ports ; 25cm
Ill on lining papers. — Bibliography: p249-250. — Includes index
ISBN 0-297-77985-0 : £9.95 B81-39951

929.1 — GENEALOGY

929′.1 — Genealogy — *Amateurs' manuals*
Colwell, Stella. The family history book : a guide to tracing your ancestors / Stella Colwell. — Oxford : Phaidon, 1980. — 176p : ill,map,coat of arms,facsims,forms,ports,geneal.tables ; 29cm
Bibliography: p168-173. — Includes index
ISBN 0-7148-2074-1 : £9.95 B81-00661

929′.1′02541 — Great Britain. Genealogy — *Directories* — *Serials*
National genealogical directory. — 1980. — Brighton (4, Sussex Sq., Brighton, Sussex) : M.J. Burchall and J. Warren, c1980. — ii,224p
ISBN 0-907084-04-4 : £2.50 B81-04722

929′.1′025421 — London. Genealogical societies — *Directories* — *Serials*
The **London** and Middlesex genealogical directory . — 1980-. — Ilford (15 Cavendish Gardens, Ilford, Essex IG1 3EA) : Association of London and Middlesex Family History Societies, 1980-. — v. ; 21cm
ISSN 0160-4914 = London and Middlesex genealogical directory : Unpriced B81-05535

929′.1′0604128 — Scotland. Tay Valley. Genealogy. Organisations: Tay Valley Family History Society — *Serials*
[Newsletter *(Tay Valley Family History Society)*]. Newsletter / Tay Valley Family History Society. — Vol.1, no.1 (Apr.1981)-. — St. Andrews (R.F. Adams, 14 Lucklaw Rd, Balmullo, St. Andrews, Fife KY16 OAY) : The Society, 1981-. — v. ; 30cm
ISSN 0260-7662 = Newletter - Tay Valley Family History Society : Unpriced B81-32904

929′.1′072041 — Great Britain. Genealogy. Research — *Amateurs' manuals*
Chadwick, David Kniveton. Looking for your family history : a brief guide for the absolute beginner / by David Kniveton Chadwick. — [Nottingham] ([43 Sandy La., Bramcote Hill, Nottingham]) : [D.K. Chadwick], [1981]. — [11]p ; 21cm
Cover title
Unpriced (pbk) B81-23028

929′.1′0720411 — Scotland. Genealogy. Research
James, Alwyn. Scottish roots : a step-by-step guide for ancestor hunters in Scotland and overseas / Alwyn James. — Loanhead : Macdonald Publishers, c1981. — 181p : ill,facsims,ports,geneal.table ; 22cm
ISBN 0-904265-45-5 (cased) : £6.95
ISBN 0-904265-46-3 (pbk) : £3.95 B81-35288

929′.1′0922 — Great Britain. Genealogy. Research projects. Coordinators — *Directories*
Directory of family history project co-ordinators / compiled by Pauline A. Saul. — 3rd ed. — [Tollerton] ([Peapkin's End, 2 Stella Grove, Tollerton, NG12 4EY]) : Federation of Family History Societies, 1981. — 27p ; 21cm
Cover title. — Previous ed.: 1980
ISBN 0-907099-08-4 (pbk) : Unpriced B81-34848

929′.1′0941 — Great Britain. Genealogy — *Amateurs' manuals*
Currer-Briggs, Noel. Debrett's family historian. — Exeter : Webb & Bower, Oct.1981. — [208]p
ISBN 0-906671-43-4 : £9.95 : CIP entry B81-30476

929′.1′09415 — Ireland. Genealogy — *Serials*
Family links : past and present : magazine of the Irish Genealogical Association. — Vol.1, no.1 (Jan.1981)-. — Belfast (162a Kingsway, Dunmurry, Belfast BT17 9AD) : The Association, 1981-. — v. : ill,ports ; 30cm
Three issues yearly
ISSN 0260-7816 = Family links : Free to Association members B81-33943

929.2 — FAMILY HISTORIES

929′.2′06042763 — Lancashire. Rossendale *(District)*. **Families. Genealogical aspects. Organisations: Rossendale Society for Genealogy and Heraldry, Lancashire. Members. Interests** — *Lists* — *Serials*
[The Inquisition *(Rossendale Society for Genealogy and Heraldry, Lancashire)*]. The Inquisition ; the official expiscator of the R.S.G.H. ; Lancashire. — [No.1]-. — [Rochdale] ([c/o Mrs J. Pickup, 15 Falcon Close, Norden, Rochdale OL12 7RY]) : [Rossendale Society for Genealogy and Heraldry, Lancashire], [1977]-. — v. ; 30cm
Irregular. — Description based on: [No.2?]
ISSN 0144-7211 = Inquisition (Rossendale Society for Genealogy and History, Lancashire) : £0.60 per issue (free to Society members) B81-06387

929´.2´0604278 — Cumbria. Families. Genealogical aspects. Organisations: Cumbria Family History Society — *Directories* — *Serials*

Cumbria Family History Society. Directory of members interests / Cumbria Family History Society. — 1981. — [Maulds Meaburn] ([Holesfoot, Maulds Meaburn, Near Penrith, Cumbria CA10 3HX]) : The Society, 1981. — [53]p
Unpriced B81-32214

929´.2´06042827 — South Yorkshire *(Metropolitan County).* **Doncaster** *(District).* **Families. Organisations: Doncaster Society for Family History** — *Directories*

Doncaster Society for Family History. Directory of members interests / Doncaster Society for Family History. — Doncaster (210 Bawtry Rd., Doncaster, S. Yorkshire DN4 7BZ) : The Society, 1981. — 20p ; 21cm
Cover title
ISBN 0-9506934-0-5 (pbk) : Unpriced
B81-23157

929´.2´0720427 — North-west England. Families. Genealogical aspects. Research projects — *Lists*

Combined register of members´ interests 1981 : Family History Society of Cheshire, North Cheshire Family History Society, Liverpool Family History Society, Rossendale Society for Genealogy and Heraldry, Lancashire. — [Willaston] ([c/o P. Raven, 35 Field Hay La., Willaston, Wirral, L64 1TQ]) : Family History Society of Cheshire, [1981?]. — v,x,116p ; 30cm
Cover title
£1.25 (pbk) B81-34672

929´.2´094 — Europe. Rothschild *(Family), to 1973* — *Biographies*

Cowles, Virginia. The Rothschilds : a family of fortune / Virginia Cowles. — Rev. ed. — London : Weidenfeld and Nicolson, 1979. — 304p : ill(some col.),coat of arms,ports(some col.),geneal.table ; 26cm
Previous ed.: New York : Knopf ; London : Weidenfeld and Nicolson, 1973. — Ill on lining papers. — Includes index
ISBN 0-297-76538-8 : £10.00 B81-11210

929´.2´0941 — Great Britain. Ballyn *(Family), to 1915*

Roberts, Elizabeth Grace. Mr. Ballyn and the Bunns of St. Albans / Elizabeth Grace Roberts. — Stourbridge (7 Harrow Close, Hagley, Stourbridge, West Midlands, DY9 0PP) : Paulin, c1980. — 192p : ill,ports,geneal.tables ; 22cm
Ill on inside covers
£6.95 (pbk)
Also classified at 929´.2´0942 B81-19757

929´.2´0941 — Great Britain. Caraher *(Family).* **Organisations: Caraher Family History Society** — *Serials*

Journal of the Caraher Family History Society. — Issue 1 (Nov.1980)-. — Muthill (Gowanlea, Willoughby St., Muthill, Perthshire, Scotland PH5 2AB) : The Society, 1980-. — v. ; 22cm
Annual
ISSN 0260-8391 = Journal of the Caraher Family History Society : £2.50 per issue
B81-09043

929´.2´0941 — Great Britain. Families, *to 1980.* **Genealogical aspects**

Personally speaking again : (about this ancestry business) / Birmingham and Midland Society for Genealogy and Heraldry. — [Sedgley] ([21 Larkswood Drive, Sedgley, W. Midlands DY3 3UQ]) : [The Society], [1981]. — 56 [i.e. 112],5p : geneal.tables ; 30cm
Cover title. — Includes index
ISBN 0-905105-46-x (pbk) : £2.50 B81-18656

929´.2´09411 — Donnaichaidh *(Clan)* — *Serials*

Clan Donnachaidh Society. Clan Donnachaidh annual. — 1979-1980. — Edinburgh ([Rose Street Lane South, Edinburgh EH2 4BB]) : The Society, [1980?]. — 48p
Unpriced B81-06240

929´.2´09411 — McVannel *(Clan), to 1980*

Crawford, Kenneth. The history of the McVannel Clan / Kenneth and Jean Crawford. — 2nd ed. — Leek (5 Dainty St., Leek, Staffs. ST13 5PG) : K. and J. Crawford, 1981. — 55p,[20]leaves of plates(some folded) : ill,maps,ports,geneal.tables ; 31cm
Previous ed.: S.l. : Ontario Clan Gathering, 1935. — Bibliography: p19
ISBN 0-9507566-0-1 (pbk) : £10.00 B81-34456

929´.2´09411 — Scotland. Borders Region. Turnbull *(Family), to 1800*

Scott, R. E.. I saved the King : the story of the Turnbulls / by R.E. Scott. — 2nd ed. — Hawick (24 High St., Hawick, Roxburghshire) : Hawick News, 1979. — 17p : ill,1coat of arms ; 22cm
Previous ed.: S.l. : s.n., 1977. — Bibliography: p17
£0.55 (pbk) B81-13046

929´.2´09411 — Scotland. Clans

Moncreiffe, *Sir* **Iain,** *bart.* The Highland clans. — New rev. ed. — London : Barrie and Jenkins, June 1981. — [240]p
Previous ed.: London : Barrie and Rockliff, 1967
ISBN 0-09-144740-2 : £12.50 : CIP entry
B81-12384

929´.2´09411 — Scotland. Clans. Tartans

Bain, Robert. The clans and tartans of Scotland / Robert Bain. — 5th ed. / enlarged and re-edited by Margaret O. MacDougall ; heraldic adviser P.E. Stewart-Blacker ; with a foreword by the Countess of Erroll. — Glasgow : Fontana, 1976 (1981 [printing]). — 320p : col.ill,col.maps,coats of arms ; 18cm
Previous ed.: 1959. — Bibliography: p318-319
ISBN 0-00-636416-0 (pbk) : £2.95 B81-25618

929´.2´09411 — Scotland. Highland Region. Sutherland *(District).* **Sutherland** *(Clan)* — *Serials*

Newsletter of the Clan Sutherland Society in Scotland. — Vol.1, no.1 (Mar.1978)-. — Golspie (Dunrobin Castle, Golspie, Sutherland) : The Society, 1978-. — v. ; 30cm
Three issues yearly. — Description based on: Vol.4, no.1 (Feb.1981)
ISSN 0261-3662 = Newsletter of the Clan Sutherland Society in Scotland : Free to Society members only B81-26584

929´.2´094111 — Scotland. Clans

Grimble, Ian. Clans and chiefs / Ian Grimble. — London : Blond & Briggs, 1980. — 267p,[16]p of plates : ill,1map,ports ; 25cm
Includes index
ISBN 0-85634-111-8 : £10.95 : CIP rev.
B80-22708

929´.2´09415 — Ireland. O Mahony *(Clan).* **Gatherings,** *1981*

The **clan** gathering, 1981 / The O Mahony Records Society. — [Co. Wicklow] (Ardnalee, Putland Rd, Bray, Co. Wicklow) : [Peter Tynan O Mahony], [1981?]. — [4]leaves : 1map ; 30cm
Unpriced (unbound) B81-34686

929´.2´09417 — Ireland *(Republic).* **Goodbody** *(Family), to 1979.* **Genealogical aspects**

Goodbody, Michael I. A.. The Goodbody family of Ireland / by Michael I.A. Goodbody. — [Halstead] ([Barton House, Halstead, Essex, CO9 2AU]) : [M.I.A. Goodbody], [1980]. — 95p ; 25cm
Includes index
Unpriced B81-07115

929´.2´0942 — Avon. Bristol. Browne *(Family), to 1978*

Marshall, Charles W.. The Browne family of Bristol, London, etc. from the mid seventeenth century / compiled by Charles W. Marshall. — [Exeter] ([18a, Church Hill, Pinhoe, Exeter, Devon EX4 9JQ]) : C.W. Marshall, 1979. — 54p[4]p of plates : ill,1coat of arms,ports,geneal.tables ; 21cm
Limited edition of 100 copies
Unpriced (pbk) B81-07262

929´.2´0942 — Brooksby *(Family).* **Genealogical aspects** — *Serials*

Brooksby news / the Brooksby Family Association. — Vol.1, no.1 (Spring 1980-). — Silsoe (21 Elm Drive, Silsoe, Bedford MK45 4EG) : R.A.F. City for the Association, 1980-. — v. ; 30cm
Description based on: Vol.1 no.2 (Summer 1980)
ISSN 0260-7360 = Brooksby news : Free to Association members only B81-07312

929´.2´0942 — Cornwall. Vivian *(Family), ca 1850*

Hughes, M. V.. Vivians / M.V. Hughes. — Oxford : Oxford University Press, 1935 (1980 printing). — 239p ; 20cm
ISBN 0-19-281303-x (pbk) : £1.75 : CIP rev.
B80-12655

929´.2´0942 — Derbyshire. Rivett *(Family), 1538-1909*

Rivett-Carnac, Douglas. The Rivett family of Repton and Derby (1538-1909) / Douglas Rivett-Carnac. — [Halesworth] ([Mill House, Ubbeston Green, Halesworth, Suffolk]) : [D. Rivett-Carnac], 1980. — xii,159p,[4]folded leaves of plates : 2maps,coats of arms,facsims,geneal.tables,ports ; 22cm
Published in a limited ed. of 100 copies. — Maps on lining papers
Unpriced B81-24889

929´.2´0942 — England. Brittain *(Family), to 1974*

Harvie, Alida. Those glittering years / by Alida Harvie. — London : Regency Press, c1980. — 232p,[16]p of plates : ill,ports,1geneal.table ; 23cm
Geneal. table on lining papers
ISBN 0-7212-0597-6 : £4.00 B81-05083

929´.2´0942 — England. Broom *(Family)* — *Serials*

Broom tree. — No.1-. — Elm (c/o Mr W.E.P. Broome, 25 Abington Grove, Elm, Cambridgeshire[Broom Family Group]), 1980-. — v. ; 26cm
Quarterly. — Description based on: No.3
ISSN 0260-7182 = Broom tree : Free to Group members B81-15155

929´.2´0942 — England. Comber *(Family).* **Genealogical aspects**

Barrow, Geoffrey B.. The Comber family : with notes on the various families of the surname Rivers / by Geoffrey B. Barrow. — London : Research Publishing, c1980. — 35p : 1ill,coats of arms,geneal.tables ; 26cm
Coats of arms, geneal.tables on 2 folded leaves attached to inside cover
ISBN 0-7050-0085-0 : £9.00 B81-09318

929´.2´0942 — England. Denning *(Family)*

Denning, Alfred Denning, *Baron.* The family story / by Lord Denning. — Lodon : Butterworths, 1981. — xi,270p,[16]p of plates : ill,ports,1geneal.table ; 24cm
Includes index
ISBN 0-406-17609-4 : £8.50 B81-23095

929´.2´0942 — England. Kemsley *(Family), to 1977*

Thornton-Kemsley, Colin. Kentish Kemsleys and their descendants / by Colin Thornton-Kemsley. — [England?] : S.n., c1980 (Rochester : Staples Printers Rochester Limited). — x,70p : geneal.tables ; 24cm
Includes index
Unpriced B81-17451

929´.2´0942 — England. Paston *(Family)* — *Correspondence, diaries, etc.*

The **Paston** letters. — Rev. ed. / edited with an introduction by John Warrington. — London : Dent, 1956 (1978 [printing]). — xxiii,283p : 1map,geneal.table ; 19cm. — (Everyman´s library ; no.752)
Previous ed.: published in 2 vols. 1924. — Bibliography: pxii. — Includes index
ISBN 0-460-00752-1 : £5.95 B81-13998

The **Pastons** : a family in the Wars of the Roses / edited by Richard Barber. — London : Folio Society, 1981. — 208p,[10]leaves of plates : col.ill,1map,1geneal.table
Map on lining papers. — In a slip case
£10.00 B81-37629

929'.2'0942 — England. Percy *(Family)* — *Genealogies*

Percy, Keith. Percy family tree. — Sutton (6 Devonshire Road, Sutton, Surrey SM2 5HQ) : K. Percy, [1980?]. — 73p : geneal.tables ; 30cm
Cover title. — By Keith Percy. — Limited ed. of 400 copies
£2.50 (pbk) B81-10199

929'.2'0942 — England. Stoddard *(Family)* — *History — Serials*

[Stoddard tribeloid *(UK edition)***]**. Stoddard tribeloid. — UK ed.. — Vol.1, no.1 (June 1980)-. — London (40 Margravine Rd, W6 8HH) : J. Stoddard, 1980-. — v. ; 30cm
Quarterly. — UK edition of: Stoddard tribeloid (US edition). — Pilot issue published: Apr.1980
ISSN 0144-4174 = Stoddard tribeloid. UK edition : £1.00 per year B81-06775

929'.2'0942 — England. Traherne *(Family), 1550-1850*

Purslow, Vera E.. Centuries of Traherne families / Vera E. Purslow. — Claverdon (19 St. Michael's Rd., Claverdon, Warwickshire, CV35 8NT) : V.E. Purslow
Bk.4: The city of Hereford. — c1981. — 30p,[1]folded leaf of plates : 1geneal.table ; 19cm
£2.55 (pbk) B81-21395

929'.2'0942 — Great Britain. Gurney *(Family), 1548-1827*

Anderson, Verily. Friends and relations : three centuries of Quaker families / Verily Anderson. — London : Hodder and Stoughton, 1980. — 320p,[8]p of plates : ill,maps,1facsim,ports,geneal.table ; 23cm
Includes index
ISBN 0-340-22214-x : £9.95 : CIP rev. B80-24959

929'.2'0942 — Hereford and Worcester. Heins *(Family), 1800-1980*

Heins, Nigel. Light at eventide : a history of the Heins family / Nigel Heins. — [Ross-on-Wye] ([11 Kyrle St., Ross-on-Wye, Herefordshire HR9 7DB]) : [N. Heins], 1980. — [52]p : 1facsim,ports ; 30cm
Unpriced (pbk) B81-32741

929'.2'0942 — Hereford and Worcester. Tardebigge. Windsor *(Family), to 1943*

Mabey, Margaret. The Windsors of Hewell / by Margaret Mabey. — Birmingham (7 Reservoir Rd., Cofton Hackett, Birmingham B45 8PJ) : Lickey Hill Local History Society, 1981. — 17p,[2]leaves of plates : 1map,1geneal.table ; 30cm
Bibliography: p17
£0.60 (pbk) B81-31689

929'.2'0942 — Hertfordshire. St Albans. Bunn *(Family), to 1915*

Roberts, Elizabeth Grace. Mr. Ballyn and the Bunns of St. Albans / Elizabeth Grace Roberts. — Stourbridge (7 Harrow Close, Hagley, Stourbridge, West Midlands, DY9 0PP) : Paulin, c1980. — 192p : ill,ports,geneal.tables ; 22cm
Ill on inside covers
£6.95 (pbk)
Primary classification 929'.2'0941 B81-19757

929'.2'0942 — Lancashire. Nelson & Paythorne. Marsden *(Family), to 1981*

Marsden, Peter. The Marsden family of Paythorne and Nelson 1666-1981 / by Peter R.V. Marsden. — [Lindfield] ([21, Meadow La., Lindfield, Sussex RH16 2RJ]) : [P.R.V. Marsden], 1981. — 287 leaves,[4]folded leaves of plate : ill,maps(some col.)facsims,plans(some col.),ports,geneal.tables ; 30cm
Unpriced (spiral) B81-22787

929'.2'0942 — Leicestershire. Wymondham. Berkeley *(Family), to ca 1630*

Taylor, Ralph Penniston. The Berkeleys of Wymondham / Ralph Penniston Taylor. — Melton Mowbray (Wymondham, Melton Mowbray, Leics.) : Brewhouse Private Press, 1980. — 58,[2]p,[1]folded leaf of plates : ill,1map,coats of arms,1geneal.table ; 27cm
Limited ed. of 110 numbered copies. — Bibliography: p[1]
£15.00 B81-04822

929'.2'0942 — Lincolnshire. Holywell. Reynardson *(Family), to ca 1920*

Phillipson, Mildred. Holywell and the Birch Reynardsons / Mildred Phillipson. — [Sleaford] : Society for Lincolnshire History and Archaeology, 1981. — 19p ; 30cm
Cover title
ISBN 0-904680-14-2 (pbk) : Unpriced B81-40693

929'.2'0942 — London. Farjeon *(Family), ca 1850-1900*

Farjeon, Eleanor. A nursery in the nineties / Eleanor Farjeon. — Oxford : Oxford University Press, 1980, c1935. — 534p,[8]p of plates : music,ports ; 20cm
Facsim. of: edition published London : Gollancz, 1935
ISBN 0-19-281308-0 (pbk) : £3.95 : CIP rev.
Primary classification 942.1'081'0924 B80-12667

929'.2'0942 — Newth *(Family)* **& Nuth** *(Family)*. **Genealogical aspects** — *Serials*

Newsletter of the Newth/Nuth Family History Society. — No.2 (Spring 1980)-. — Taunton (c/o Mrs C. Davies, Euston Lodge, Middleway, Taunton, Somerset) : The Society, 1980-. — v. ; 30cm
Two issues yearly. — Continues: Newth Nuth news
Free to Society members B81-06189

Newth Nuth news / Newth Nuth Family History Society. — No.1 (Dec.1979)-. — Taunton (c/o Mrs C. Davies, Euston Lodge, Middleway, Taunton, Somerset) : The Society, 1979-. — 1v. ; 30cm
Continued by: Newsletter of the Newth/Nuth Family History Society. — Only one issue published
Free to Society members B81-06190

929'.2'0942 — Norfolk. King's Lynn. Aickman *(Family), 1827-1896*

Aickman, Dorothy Jean. John Aickman's Foundery MDCCC XXVII, King's Lynn : a fragment of Lynn history / by Dorothy Jean Aickman. — [Cambridge] ([Flat 22, Sherlock Close, Cambridge, CB3 0HW]) : [D.J. Aickman], 1980. — ix,52p,[9]p of plates : ill,maps ; 23cm
Limited ed. of 500 copies. — Includes index
ISBN 0-9507068-0-9 : Unpriced B81-17203

929'.2'0942 — Prendergast *(Family)*. **Genealogical aspects** — *Serials*

The **Prendergast** chronicles. — Mar.1981-. — Taunton (12 Clifford Cres., Taunton, Somerset TA2 6DW) : The Prendergast Association, 1981-. — v. : geneal.tables ; 30cm
Quarterly
ISSN 0260-4183 = Prendergast chronicles : Unpriced B81-29062

929'.2'0942 — Shropshire. Shrewsbury. Darwin *(Family)*

Lerwill, C. J.. The Darwins of Shrewsbury : a brief guide for visitors to Shrewsbury / by Chris Lerwill ; illustrated by Laura Lerwill. — [Colchester] ([26 Chaplin Rd., East Bergholt, Colchester, Essex CO7 6SR]) : C.J. Lerwill, , c1981. — ii,18p : ill,1map,1port ; 21cm
Bibliography: p18
ISBN 0-9507590-0-7 (pbk) : Unpriced B81-33748

929'.2'0942 — Staffordshire. Drayton Bassett. Bassett *(Family), 895-1632*

Smith, Christine, *1941-*. The Drayton dynasty : a history of the Bassetts / by Christine Smith. — Tamworth (10 Drayton La. Drayton Bassett, Tamworth, Staffs.) : C. Smith, [1980]. — 52p : ill,1coat of arms,geneal.tables,maps ; 22cm
Cover title
£1.00 (pbk) B81-06949

929'.2'0942 — Wiltshire. Bratton. Reeves *(Family), ca 1774-1914* **& Whitaker** *(Family), ca 1446-1914*

Reeves, Marjorie. Sheep bell and ploughshare : the story of two village families / Marjorie Reeves. — London : Granada, 1980, c1978. — 256p,[16]p of plates : ill,facsims,ports,geneal.tables ; 20cm. — (A Paladin book)
Originally published: Bradford-on-Avon : Moonraker, 1978. — Includes index
ISBN 0-586-08349-9 (pbk) : £1.95 B81-04890

929'.2'094218 — London. Middlesex. Families. Genealogical aspects — *Serials*

Greentrees : the journal of the Central Middlesex Family History Society. — Vol.1, no.1 (Autumn 1978)-. — [Kenton] ([c/o Mr T. Francis, 4 Addiscombe Close, Kenton, Middx HA3 8JS]) : The Society, 1978-. — v. ; 21cm
Description based on: Vol.2, no.2 (Spring 1981)
ISSN 0261-1139 = Greentrees : Free to Society members B81-36551

929'.2'094231 — Wiltshire. Families. Genealogical aspects — *Serials*

Wiltshire Family History Society. — No.1 (Spring 1981)-. — Swindon (c/o Mrs M. Moore, 17 Blakeney Ave., Nythe, Swindon, Wilts.) : The Society, 1981-. — v. : ill ; 21cm
Quarterly
ISSN 0260-7174 = Wiltshire Family History Society : £4.00 per year B81-31052

929'.2'094244 — Hereford and Worcester. Herefordshire. Families. Genealogical aspects — *Serials*

The **journal** of the Herefordshire Family History Society. — Vol.1, no.1 (Spring 1980)-. — Fownhope (1 Scotch Firs, Fownhope, Herefordshire) : The Society, 1980-. — v. ; 21cm
Quarterly
ISSN 0260-1044 = Journal of the Herefordshire Family History Society : £4.00 per year (free to members) B81-03616

929'.2'094245 — Shropshire. Families. Genealogical aspects — *Serials*

Shropshire family history journal. — Vol.1, pt.1 (Jan.1980)-. — Shrewsbury (c/o S.C. Clifford, Portway, Windsor La., Bomere Heath, Shrewsbury, SY4 3LR) : Shropshire Family History Society, 1980-. — v. ; 30cm
Quarterly
ISSN 0261-135x = Shropshire family history journal : Unpriced B81-31051

929'.2'094275 — Merseyside *(Metropolitan County)*. **Families. Genealogical aspects** — *Serials*

Liverpool Family History Society. — Vol.1, no.1 (Winter 1976)-. — [Liverpool] ([c/o H. Culling, 11 Lisburn La., Liverpool L13 9AE]) : [The Society], [1976]-. — v. ; 30cm
Description based on: Vol.2, no.7
ISSN 0260-7557 = Liverpool Family History Society : £1.50 per year B81-15151

929'.2'0942827 — South Yorkshire *(Metropolitan County)*. **Doncaster** *(District)*. **Families. Genealogical aspects** — *Serials*

The **Doncaster** ancestor : the journal of the Doncaster Society for Family History. — Vol.1, no.1 (Summer 1980)-. — Doncaster (c/o R.A. Bonser, 105 Princess St., Woodlands, Doncaster) : The Society, 1980-. — v. : ill ; 22cm
Two issues yearly
ISSN 0144-459x = Doncaster ancestor : Free to Society members B81-04446

929'.2'094285 — Cleveland. Families. Genealogical aspects — *Serials*

The **Journal** of Cleveland Family History Society. — Vol.1, no.1 (June 1980)-. — Billingham (c/o Mr J.R. Chapman, 16 Belmont Ave., Billingham, Cleveland TS22 5HF) : The Society, 1980-. — v. ; 30cm
Quarterly
ISSN 0260-2679 = Journal of Cleveland Family History Society : Free to Society members only B81-09129

929'.2'09429 — Gwent. Tredegar. Morgan *(Family), to 1962*

James, Leslie, *1944-*. The Morgans of Tredegar / [Leslie W. James]. — [Newport, Gwent] ([John Frost Sq., Newport, Gwent NPT 1PA]) : Newport Museum and Art Gallery, c1977. — [4]p : ports ; 30cm
Unpriced (unbound) B81-36069

929′.2′094293 — Clwyd. Families. Genealogical aspects — *Serials*

Hel achau : cylchgrawn Cymdeithas Hanes Teuluoedd Clwyd : journal of the Clwyd Family History Society. — Rhif 1 (Haf 1980)-. — [Ruthin] ([c/o Mr L.A. Sharrock, 17 Parc-y-llan, Llanfair D.C., Ruthin, Clwyd]) : The Society, 1980-. — v. ; 30cm
Two issues yearly. — Text in English. — With: Rhestr aelodau a diddordebau′r aelodau (Clwyd Family History Society)
ISSN 0260-1753 = Hel achau : Free to Society members B81-07693

929′.2′0944 — France. La Rochelle. Depont *(Family), 1661-1795* — *Biographies*

Forster, Robert. Merchants, landlords, magistrates : the Depont family in eighteenth-century France / Robert Forster. — Baltimore ; London : Johns Hopkins University Press, c1980. — xii,275p : ill,maps,geneal.table ; 24cm
Includes index
ISBN 0-8018-2406-0 : £12.00 B81-13587

929′.2′0954 — India. Graham *(Family)* — *Correspondence, diaries, etc.*

The **Graham** Indian Mutiny papers / edited and introduced by A.T. Harrison ; with an historiographical essay by T.G. Fraser. — Belfast ([66 Balmoral Ave., Belfast 9]) : Public Record Office of Northern Ireland, 1980. — lix,167p : ill,maps,facsims,ports ; 31cm
Includes index
ISBN 0-905691-04-0 : £7.50 B81-10744

929.3 — GENEALOGICAL SOURCES

929′.3′09 — Wills, *to 1976* — *Humour*

Warner, Gerald. Being of sound mind : a book of eccentric wills / Gerald Warner ; illustrations by Albert Rusling. — London : Elm Tree, 1980. — 112p : ill ; 23cm
Bibliography: p112
ISBN 0-241-10471-8 : £4.95 : CIP rev. B80-14081

929′.342 — Parishes included in Boyd′s marriage index — *Lists*

A **List** of parishes in Boyd′s marriage index / the Society of Genealogists. — 4th ed. — London (37 Harrington Gardens, SW7 4JX) : The Society of Genealogists, 1980. — xii,53p ; 21cm
Previous ed.: 1974
ISBN 0-901878-46-4 (pbk) : £1.20 B81-18762

929′.342462 — Staffordshire. Audley. Parish registers, *1538-1712* — *Texts*

Registers of the parish church of St. James the Great, Audley, North Staffs : baptisms, marriages, burials 1538-1712. — [Sedgley] ([21 Larkswood Drive, Sedgley, W. Midlands DY3 3UQ]) : Birmingham and Midland Society for Genealogy and Heraldry, [1980]. — 210,16p ; 30cm
Cover title. — Includes index
ISBN 0-905105-50-8 (pbk) : £3.50 B81-18652

929′.342464 — Staffordshire. Church Eaton. Parish registers, *1538-1812* — *Texts*

Registers of the Church of St. Editha, Church Eaton Staffordshire : baptisms, marriages, burials 1538-1812. — [Sedgley] ([21 Larkswood Drive, Sedgley, W. Midlands, DY3 3UQ]) : [Birmingham & Midland Society for Genealogy & Heraldry], [1980]. — 184,15p ; 30cm
Cover title. — Includes index
ISBN 0-905105-47-8 (pbk) : £3.50 B81-38778

929′.34249 — England. West Midlands. Genealogical sources

Markwell, F. C.. Tracing your ancestors in Warwickshire / F.C. Markwell. — [Sedgley] ([21 Larkswood Drive, Sedgley, W. Midlands DY2 2UQ]) : Birmingham and Midland Society for Genealogy and Heraldry, 1981. — 215p : maps ; 30cm
ISBN 0-905105-45-1 (pbk) : £4.00 B81-18653

929′.342493 — West Midlands *(Metropolitan County).* **Cradley. Presbyterian churches. Park Lane Presbyterian Church** *(Cradley).* **Baptisms,** *1736-1837* — *Lists*

Park Lane Presbyterian Church *(Cradley).* Registers of Park Lane Presbyterian Church, Cradley, Worcs. : baptisms 1736-1837 (includes a few burials). — [Cradley] : [The Church], [1981]. — 64p,4p ; 30cm
Cover title
ISBN 0-905105-40-0 (pbk) : Unpriced B81-08463

929′.342496 — West Midlands *(Metropolitan County).* **King′s Norton. Parish registers,** *1754-1844* — *Texts*

Registers of the Church of St. Nicolas, King′s Norton, Worcs. : baptisms & burials 1792-1844, marriages 1754-1837 (includes banns 1754-1771). — [Birmingham] : [Birmingham and Midland Society for Genealogy and Heraldry], [1981]. — 197p,17p ; 30cm
Cover title. — Includes index
ISBN 0-905105-52-4 (pbk) : £4.00 B81-31657

929′.342497 — West Midlands *(Metropolitan County).* **Elmdon. Parish registers,** *1742-1846* — *Texts*

The **Bishop′s** Transcripts of the registers of the Parish of Elmdon, Warwickshire, 1742-1846. — [Sedgley] ([21 Larkswood Drive, Sedgley, W. Midlands OY3 3UQ]) : [Birmingham and Midlands Society for Genealogy and Heraldry], [1981]. — 30,3p ; 30cm
Cover title. — Includes index
ISBN 0-905105-37-0 (pbk) : £1.30 B81-35262

929′.342521 — Nottinghamshire persons: Clayworth persons. Wills, *1670-1710* — *Collections*

Village life from wills & inventories : Clayworth parish 1670-1710 / edited by Elizabeth R. Perkins. — Nottingham (Publications Unit, Department of Adult Education, 14 Shakespeare St., Nottingham NG1 4FJ) : Centre for Local History, University of Nottingham, c1979. — 25,xxxix p : ill ; 30cm. — (Record series / Centre for Local History, University of Nottingham ; 1)
Unpriced (pbk)
Also classified at 942.5′21 B81-09831

929′.34256 — Bedfordshire persons. Wills, *1383-1548* — *Texts*

Bedfordshire wills proved in the Prerogative Court of Canterbury 1383-1548 / edited by Margaret McGregor. — Bedford (County Record Office, County Hall, Bedford) : Bedfordshire Historical Record Society, 1979. — xxv,237p ; 21cm. — (The Publications of the Bedfordshire Historical Record Society ; v.58)
Includes index
ISBN 0-85155-040-1 (pbk) : £5.00 B81-14504

929′.342574 — Oxfordshire. Oxford. Universities. Colleges: Merton College. Private chapels: St. John the Baptist′s Church *(Oxford).* **Baptisms & marriages. Parish registers** — *Texts*

Baptisms and marriages at Merton College / transcribed from the registers of St. John the Baptist′s Church, Oxford, the College Chapel by Alan Bott. — Oxford ([Oxford OX1 4JD]) : Merton College, 1981. — 165p,[9]leaves of plates : ill,facsims,1plan ; 23cm
Includes index
Unpriced B81-15730

929′.342614 — Norfolk. Attleborough. Parish registers, *1552-1840* — *Texts*

Attleborough parish registers 1552-1840 / translated by E.W. Sanderson ; edited and indexed by Patrick Palgrave-Moore. — Norwich (c/o Palgrave-Moore, 13 West Parade, Norwich NR2 3DN) : Norfolk & Norwich Genealogical Society, [1980?]. — xi,296p ; 25cm. — (Norfolk genealogy ; v.12)
Includes index
£6.00 (£5.00 to members of the Society) B81-14503

929′.3426496 — West Midlands *(Metropolitan County).* **Sutton Coldfield. Householders,** *1663-1674* — *Lists*

The **Quarters** of Sutton : being lists of the households of Sutton Coldfield in the late seventeenth century made by the collectors of the hearth tax / transcribed by the Sutton Coldfield History Research Group ; edited with an introduction by R.M. Lea. — Birmingham (c/o R.M. Lea, 210 Dower Rd., Sutton Coldfield, West Midlands B75 6SZ) : University of Birmingham Department of Extra Mural Studies, 1981. — vi,25p : 1map,facsims ; 30cm
ISBN 0-7044-0432-x (spiral) : £1.00 B81-23438

929′.342719 — Cheshire. Warrington. Unitarian churches. Unitarian Chapel *(Warrington).* **Baptisms,** *1724-1853* — *Lists*

The **Unitarian** Chapel : Cairo Street, Warrington : births & baptisms 1724-1853, deaths & burials 1788-1960, monumental inscriptions 1749-1969 / transcribed, edited and indexed by J.R. Bulmer. — [Warrington] ([c/o Unitarian Chapel, Cairo St., Warrington, Lancs.]) : [J.R. Bulmer], 1980. — v,56p ; 26cm
Includes index
Unpriced (pbk)
Also classified at 929′.342719 ; 929.5′09427′19 B81-29152

929′.342719 — Cheshire. Warrington. Unitarian churches. Unitarian Chapel *(Warrington).* **Burials,** *1788-1960* — *Lists*

The **Unitarian** Chapel : Cairo Street, Warrington : births & baptisms 1724-1853, deaths & burials 1788-1960, monumental inscriptions 1749-1969 / transcribed, edited and indexed by J.R. Bulmer. — [Warrington] ([c/o Unitarian Chapel, Cairo St., Warrington, Lancs.]) : [J.R. Bulmer], 1980. — v,56p ; 26cm
Includes index
Unpriced (pbk)
Primary classification 929′.342719 B81-29152

929′.34281 — Church of England. *Diocese of York.* **Historiology. Organisations: Borthwick Institute of Historical Research. Stock: Genealogical sources for Yorkshire**

Webb, C. C.. A guide to genealogical sources in the Borthwick Institute of Historical Research / C.C. Webb. — [York] : [The Institute], 1981. — ii,73p : 1map ; 21cm
Cover title. — At head of title: University of York, Borthwick Institute of Historical Research. — Bibliography: p65-70
Unpriced (pbk) B81-34910

929′.342839 — Humberside. Skipsea. Marriages. Parish registers, *1750-1837* — *Texts*

Skipsea marriages 1750-1837 / transcribed by P.M. Pattinson. — Cottingham (1 Creyke Close, Cottingham, N. Humberside HU16 4DH) : East Yorkshire Family History Society, [1980?]. — 18p ; 30cm. — (East Riding transcripts ; no.3)
Cover title
Unpriced (pbk) B81-15206

929.4 — PERSONAL NAMES

929.4′2′06 — Persons with same surnames. Genealogical aspects. Organisations. Formation — *Manuals*

Palgrave, Derek A.. Forming a one name group / Derek A. Palgrave. — 2nd ed. — Doncaster (210 Bawtry Rd., Doncaster, S. Yorks. DN4 7BZ) : Federation of Family History Societies, 1981. — 17p ; 21cm
Cover title. — Previous ed.: 1977. — Bibliography: p17
ISBN 0-907099-04-1 (pbk) : Unpriced B81-12986

929.4′2′0941 — British surnames

Verstappen, Peter. The book of surnames : origins and oddities of popular names / compiled by Peter Verstappen. — London : Pelham, 1980. — 256p ; 23cm
Includes index
ISBN 0-7207-1275-0 : £6.95 : CIP rev. B80-23874

929.4′2′0941 — British surnames — *Dictionaries*
Cottle, Basil. The Penguin dictionary of surnames / Basil Cottle. — 2nd ed. — Harmondsworth : Penguin, 1978 (1981 [printing]). — 444p ; 18cm. — (Penguin reference books)
Bibliography: p443-444
ISBN 0-14-051032-x (pbk) : £2.50 B81-40440

929.4′2′094237 — Cornish surnames. Etymology
White, G. Pawley. A handbook of Cornish surnames / compiled by G. Pawley White (Gunwyn) ; foreword by A.L. Rowse. — 2nd ed. — Redruth (Trewolsta, Trewirgie, Redruth, [Cornwall]) : Dyllansow Truran-Cornish Publications, 1981. — 73p ; 22cm
Previous ed.: Camborne : G.P. White, 1972. — Bibliography: p73
ISBN 0-9506431-9-x (pbk) : Unpriced B81-21899

929.4′4 — Forenames. Interpretation
Dunkling, Leslie. Our secret names / Leslie Alan Dunkling. — London : Sidgwick & Jackson, 1981. — 163p ; 18cm
Bibliography: p146-151. — Includes index
ISBN 0-283-98734-0 (cased) : £6.95
ISBN 0-283-98755-3 (pbk) : £1.25 B81-17601

929.4′4′0942 — English forenames — *Dictionaries*
Jones, Merle. The Daily express guide to names / Merle Jones. — [London] : Star, c1981. — 175p ; 18cm
ISBN 0-352-30813-3 (pbk) : £1.25 B81-15067

Wyatt, Katharine. Children's names and horoscopes / Katharine Wyatt and Lesley Burrow ; with horoscopes by Roger Elliot. — London : Ebury, 1980. — 151p : ill(some col.),forms ; 22cm
ISBN 0-85223-181-4 : £4.95 B81-00662

929.5 — EPITAPHS

929.5′0941 — Great Britain. Graveyards. Monumental inscriptions. Recording — *Manuals*
Rayment, J. L.. Notes on the recording of monumental inscriptions / by J.L. Rayment. — 3rd ed. — Plymouth (96 Beaumont St., Milehouse, Plymouth, Devon PL2 3AQ) : Federation of Family History Societies, 1981. — 29p : ill,1plan,1form ; 22cm
Cover title. — Previous ed.: 1978
ISBN 0-907099-03-3 (pbk) : Unpriced B81-09862

929.5′09426′14 — Norfolk. Gressenhall. Parish churches: St. Mary *(Church: Gressenhall).* **Monumental inscriptions** — *Texts*
Carrington, A. C.. A record of the monumental inscriptions in the church and churchyard of St. Mary, Gressenhall, Norfolk / this survey was undertaken by Gressenhall & District Women's Institute for the Norfolk Federation of Women's Institutes Churchyard Project, 1980-1981 ; recording team A.C. Carrington, B.I. Carrington, J.M. Carrington ; churchyard plan A.C. Carrington. — [Gressenhall] ([10 Halls Drive, Gressenhall, East Dereham, Norfolk NR20 4EJ]) : [Gressenhall News & Views], 1981. — iii,61p ; 31cm + 1plan; 42x60cm
ISBN 0-9507631-0-1 (pbk) : Unpriced B81-31994

929.5′09427′19 — Cheshire. Warrington. Unitarian churches. Unitarian Chapel *(Warrington).* **Churchyards. Monumental inscriptions,** *1749-1969*
The **Unitarian** Chapel : Cairo Street, Warrington : births & baptisms 1724-1853, deaths & burials 1788-1960, monumental inscriptions 1749-1969 / transcribed, edited and indexed by J.R. Bulmer. — [Warrington] ([c/o Unitarian Chapel, Cairo St., Warrington, Lancs.]) : [J.R. Bulmer], 1980. — v,56p ; 26cm
Includes index
Unpriced (pbk)
Primary classification 929′.342719 B81-29152

929.5′09428′39 — Humberside. North Frodingham. Parish churches: St. Elgin's Church *(North Frodingham).* **Churchyards. Monumental inscriptions** — *Texts*
North Frodingham monumental inscriptions. — [Beverley] ([23 The Woodlands, Beverley, N. Humberside HU1 8BT]) : East Yorkshire Family History Society, [1981?]. — [17]p ; 30cm
Unpriced (unbound) B81-11517

North Frodingham monumental inscriptions. — [Cottingham] ([1 Creyke Close, Cottingham, North Humberside, HU16 4DH]) : East Yorkshire Family History Society, [1981]. — [17]p : 1ill ; 30cm
Includes index
Unpriced (unbound) B81-19336

929.5′09428′39 — Humberside. Skerne. Parish churches: Skerne Church. Churchyards. Monumental inscriptions — *Texts*
Skerne : monumental inscriptions. — [Beverley] ([23 The Woodlands, Beverley, N. Humberside HU1 8BI]) : East Yorkshire Family History Society, 1981. — 13p ; 22cm
Cover title. — Includes index
Unpriced (pbk) B81-19555

929.5′09429′25 — Gwynedd. Ogwen valley. Cemeteries. Gravestones. Inscriptions: Poetry in Welsh. Englynion, *ca 1800-ca 1955* — *Collections*
Englynion beddau Dyffryn Ogwen / [golygwyd gan] J. Elwyn Hughes. — Llandysul : Gwasg Gomer, 1979. — 139p ; 19cm
Includes index
ISBN 0-85088-861-1 (pbk) : £1.50 B81-40040

929.6 — HERALDRY

929.6 — Heraldry
Dennys, Rodney. Heraldry and the heralds. — London : Cape, Oct.1981. — [288]p
ISBN 0-224-01643-1 : £10.50 : CIP entry B81-26720

Von Volborth, Carl-Alexander. Heraldry : customs, rules and styles / written and illustrated by Carl-Alexander von Volborth. — Poole : Blandford Press, 1981. — 229p : chiefly ill(some col.),coats of arms(some col.) ; 29cm
Bibliography: p219-221. — Includes index
ISBN 0-7137-0940-5 : £19.95 : CIP rev. B81-23835

929.7 — ROYAL HOUSES, PEERAGE, LANDED GENTRY

929.7′094 — Coburg *(House of), to 1980*
Ashdown, Dulcie M.. Victoria and the Coburgs / Dulcie M. Ashdown. — London : Hale, 1981. — 208p,[16]p of plates : ill,ports,4geneal.tables ; 23cm
Includes index
ISBN 0-7091-8582-0 : £8.25 B81-12241

929.7′2 — England. Precedence
Squibb, G. D.. Precedence in England and Wales. — Oxford : Clarendon Press, Nov.1981. — [162]p
ISBN 0-19-825389-3 : £12.50 : CIP entry B81-33643

929.7′2 — England. Royal families. Marriages, *1299-1307.* **Political aspects**
English royal marriages : the French marriages of Edward I and Edward II : 1299-1307 : facsimiles / with introduction by Elizabeth M. Hallam. — London : H.M.S.O., 1981. — 4p,[7]p of plates : all facsims ; 22x30cm. — (Public Records Office Museum pamphlets ; no.11)
ISBN 0-11-440104-7 (pbk) : £1.50 B81-24787

929.7′2 — Great Britain. Bowes-Lyon *(Family), 1767-1980*
Day, James Wentworth. The Queen Mother's family story. — Large print ed., 2nd ed. — Bath : Chivers Press, Oct.1981. — [408]p. — (A New Portway large print book)
Previous ed.: London : Hale, 1967
ISBN 0-85119-165-7 : £5.95 : CIP entry B81-28019

929.7′2 — Great Britain. Queensberry *(Marquesses of), 1818-1945*
Roberts, Brian, *1930-.* The mad bad line : the family of Lord Alfred Douglas / by Brian Roberts. — London : Hamilton, 1981. — x,319p,8p of plates : ill,ports,1geneal.table ; 24cm
Bibliography: p297-299. — Incudes index
ISBN 0-241-10637-0 : £15.00 : CIP rev. B81-13831

929.7′2 — Great Britain. Royal families, *1930-1981* — *Quotations*
Royal quotes / selected and compiled by Noel St George. — Newton Abbot : David & Charles, c1981. — 64p ; 22cm
Bibliography: p64
ISBN 0-7153-8257-8 : £2.95 : CIP rev. B81-13568

929.7′2 — Great Britain. Royal families. Children, *1840-1980* — *Biographies*
Clear, Celia. Royal children : from 1940 to 1980 / Celia Clear. — London : Barker, c1981. — 143p : ill,ports 1geneal.table ; 25cm
Bibliography: p139-142. — Includes index
ISBN 0-213-16786-7 : £6.95 B81-24276

929.7′2 — Scotland. Stuart *(House of)* — *Biographies*
Ridler, Alan. Will ye no come back again / Alan Ridler. — Bognor Regis : New Horizon, c1981. — 84p ; 21cm
Bibliography: p81-84
ISBN 0-86116-712-0 : £4.25 B81-22100

929.7′2′025 — Great Britain. Nobility — *Directories*
G.E.C.. The complete peerage of England, Scotland, Ireland, Great Britain and the United Kingdom, extant, extinct or dormant. — New ed., rev. and much enl. — Gloucester : Alan Sutton, Dec.1981. — 6v.
Facsim. of: New ed., rev. and much enl. London : St Catherine's Press, 1910-1959. — Previous ed.: London : G. Bell & Sons, 1887-1898
ISBN 0-904387-82-8 : £300.00 : CIP entry B81-31543

929.7′5 — Italy. Borgia *(Family)*
Edgington, Harry. The Borgias / Harry Edginton. — Feltham : Hamlyn Paperbacks, c1981. — 203p,[4]p of plates : ill,ports ; 18cm
ISBN 0-600-20318-2 (pbk) : £1.50 B81-26077

Mallett, Michael. The Borgias : the rise and fall of a Renaissance dynasty / Michael Mallett. — London : Granada, 1981, c1969. — 368p : ill,geneal.tables ; 18cm. — (A Panther book)
Originally published: London : Bodley Head, 1969. — Bibliography: p339-354. — Includes index
ISBN 0-586-05428-6 (pbk) : £1.95 B81-14305

929.8 — ORDERS AND DECORATIONS, ARMORIAL BEARINGS, AUTOGRAPHS

929.8′1′05 — Honours: Decorations & orders — *Serials*
The **Miscellany** of honours / the Orders and Medals Research Society. — No.2 (1980). — London (E Block, Duke of York's H.Q., King's Rd, Chelsea, S.W.3) : The Society, 1980. — 106p
Unpriced B81-10571

929.8′2′0942251 — East Sussex. Wadhurst. Parish churches: Wadhurst Church. Coats of arms
Harper, R. W. E.. Heraldry in Wadhurst Church / by R.W.E. Harper. — Pulham Saint Mary ([Crossingford Lodge], Pulham Saint Mary, [Diss, Norfolk] IP21 4RJ) : Noel Nicholls, c1980. — 30p : coats of arms ; 22cm
Unpriced (pbk) B81-18493

929.8′2′0945634 — Vatican. Visitors. Coats of arms — *Lists*
Heim, Bruno Bernard. Armorial / Bruno B. Heim ; edited and introduced by Peter Bander van Duren ; preface by the Duke of Norfolk. — Gerrards Cross ([P.O. Box 6] Gerrards Cross, Bucks. [SL9 7AE]) : Van Duren, 1981. — 223p,[6]p of plates : ill,coats of arms(some col.),facsims,ports(some col.) ; 23cm
"Blazons for the Liber amicorum et illustrorum hospitum by Garioch Pursuivant" i.e. John C.G. George. — Includes index
ISBN 0-905715-16-0 (cased) : £22.00 : CIP rev.
ISBN 0-905715-18-7 (Limited signed ed.) : Unpriced B81-07473

929.9 — FLAGS AND OTHER FORMS OF INSIGNIA AND IDENTIFICATION

929.9′2 — Flags

Flags of the world / edited by E.M.C. Barraclough and W.G. Crampton. — 2nd ed., with revisions and suppl. — London : Warne, 1981. — 262p : ill(some col.),coats of arms (some col.) ; 24cm
Previous ed.: 1978. — Bibliography: p253-254. — Includes index
ISBN 0-7232-2797-7 : £12.50 B81-39291

929.9′2 — Flags — *For children*

Ross, David, *1945-*. Flags / by David Ross ; illustrated by Mike Saunders. — London : Granada, 1981. — 61p : col.ill ; 19cm. — (Granada guides)
Includes index
ISBN 0-246-11563-7 : £1.95 B81-39306

930 — ANCIENT HISTORY, TO CA 500 A. D.

930 — Ancient civilizations

Service, Alastair. Lost worlds. — London : Collins, Oct.1981. — [208]p
ISBN 0-00-216461-2 : £9.95 : CIP entry B81-24621

930 — Ancient civilizations — *For schools*

Garden, Glen. Life B.C. / Glen Garden. — Richmond, Victoria ; London : Heinemann Educational, 1980. — 148p : ill(some col.),col.maps,ports ; 21x28cm
Includes index
ISBN 0-435-31200-6 (pbk) : £1.50 : CIP rev. B80-21208

930 — Ancient world

The **Cambridge** ancient history. — Cambridge : Cambridge University Press
Vol.1 / edited by I.E.S. Edwards, the late C.J. Gadd, N.G.L. Hammond. — 3rd ed
Previous ed.: individual chapters published as fascicles. 1961-1968
Pt.1: Prolegomena and prehistory. — 1970 (1980 [printing]). — xxii,803p : ill,maps(some col.),plans ; 23cm
Bibliography: p619-672. — Includes index
ISBN 0-521-29821-0 (pbk) : £12.50 B81-24487

The **Cambridge** ancient history. — Cambridge : Cambridge University Press
Vol.1 / edited by I.E.S. Edwards, the late C.J. Gadd, N.G.L. Hammond. — 3rd ed
Previous ed.: individual chapters published as fascicles. 1961-1968
Part 2: Early history of the Middle East. — 1971 (1980 [printing]). — xxiii,1058p : ill,maps,plans ; 23cm
Includes index
ISBN 0-521-29822-9 (pbk) : £15.00 B81-11199

The **Cambridge** ancient history. — Cambridge : Cambridge University Press
Vol.2 / edited by I.E.S. Edwards ... [et al.]. — 3rd ed
Previous ed.: individual chapters published as fascicles. 1961-1968
Pt.1: History of the Middle East and the Aegean region c.1800-1380 B.C.. — 1973 (1980 [printing]). — xxi,868p,[1]folded leaf of plates : ill,maps,plans,1geneal.table ; 23cm
Bibliography: p716-817. — Includes index
ISBN 0-521-29823-7 (pbk) : £12.50 B81-24486

The **Cambridge** ancient history. — Cambridge : Cambridge University Press
Vol.2 / edited by I.E.S. Edwards ... [et al.]. — 3rd ed
Previous ed.: individual chapters published as fascicles. 1961-1968
Part 2: History of the Middle East and the Aegean region c.1380-1000 B.C.. — 1975 (1980 [printing]). — xxiii,1128p : ill,maps ; 23cm
Includes index
ISBN 0-521-29824-5 (pbk) : £15.00 B81-11198

930 — Civilization, *to 565*

Robinson, Charles Alexander. Ancient history : from prehistoric times to the death of Justinian. — 3rd ed. / William G. Sinnigen, Charles Alexander Robinson, Jr. — New York : Macmillan ; London : Collier Macmillan, c1981. — xix,563p : ill,maps,plans,ports,2geneal.tables ; 24cm
Previous ed.: 1967. — Maps on lining papers. — Bibliography: p530-544. — Includes index
ISBN 0-02-410810-3 : £12.50 B81-36123

930 — Civilization, *to ca 1400*

Larousse encyclopedia of ancient and medieval history / general editor Marcel Dunan ; English advisory editor John Bowle ; [translated by Delano Ames and Geoffrey Sainsbury]. — London : Hamlyn, 1963, c1964 (1981 [printing]). — 413p,[32]p of plates : ill(some col.),maps,ports ; 29cm
Translation of the French from: Histoire Universelle Larousse. — Includes index
ISBN 0-600-02371-0 (pbk) : £6.95 B81-32360

930 — Prehistory. Theories of Childe, V. Gordon

McNairn, Barbara. The method and theory of V. Gordon Childe : economic, social an cultural interpretations of prehistory / Barbara McNairn. — Edinburgh : Edinburgh University Press, c1980. — vii,184p ; 18cm
Bibliography: p168-181. Includes index
ISBN 0-85224-389-8 (pbk) : £3.75 B81-14694

930′.03′21 — Ancient civilizations — *Encyclopaedias*

The **Encyclopedia** of ancient civilizations / edited by Arthur Cotterell. — [Leicester] : Windward, 1980. — 367p : ill(some col.),maps,plans,ports,2geneal.tables ; 26cm
Bibliography: p356-361. - Includes index
ISBN 0-7112-0036-x : £12.95 B81-01377

930′.07′202 — Ancient world. Historiography. Hieronymus, *of Cardia* — *Critical studies*

Hornblower, Jane. Hieronymus of Cardia. — Oxford : Oxford University Press, Oct.1981. — [288]p. — (Oxford classical and philosophical monographs)
ISBN 0-19-814717-1 : £15.00 : CIP entry B81-25843

930′.09′822 — Mediterranean region. Antiquities, *to B.C.200*

Trump, D. H.. The prehistory of the Mediterranean / D.H. Trump. — Harmondsworth : Penguin, 1981, c1980. — x,310p,[16]p of plates : ill,1map,1plan ; 20cm. — (Pelican books)
Originally published: London : Allen Lane, 1980. — Bibliography: p302. — Includes index
ISBN 0-14-022080-1 (pbk) : £3.95 B81-21111

930.1 — ARCHAEOLOGY

930.1 — Ancient world. Antiquities. Sites

Walker, Charles. Wonders of the ancient world / Charles Walker. — London : Orbis, 1980. — 176p : ill(some col.),plans ; 30cm
Bibliography p172.— Includes index
ISBN 0-85613-265-9 : £7.50 B81-09793

930.1 — Archaeology

Barry, Iris, *1950-*. Discovering archaeology / by Iris Barry. — Harlow : Longman, 1980. — 96p : ill(some col.),col.maps,plans ; 27cm
Includes index
ISBN 0-582-39091-5 : £5.95 : CIP rev. B80-10406

930.1 — Archaeology — *Festschriften*

Antiquity and man : essays in honour of Glyn Daniel / edited by John D. Evans, Barry Cunliffe and Colin Renfrew. — London : Thames and Hudson, c1981. — 256p : ill,maps,plans,ports ; 28cm
Includes bibliographies and index
ISBN 0-500-05040-6 : £25.50 B81-27506

930.1 — Environmental archaeology

Shackley, Myra. Environmental archaeology. — London : Allen & Unwin, Oct.1981. — [256]p
ISBN 0-04-913020-x (cased) : £18.00 : CIP entry (pbk) : £9.95 B81-24604

930.1 — Prehistoric civilization

Charroux, Robert. One hundred thousand years of man′s unknown history / Robert Charroux ; translated from the French by Lowell Bair. — London : Sphere, 1981, c1970. — 191p ; 18cm
Translation of: Histoire inconnue des hommes depuis cent mille ans. — Originally published: New York : Berkley Publishing, 1970
ISBN 0-7221-2266-7 (pbk) : £1.50 B81-35525

930.1 — Prehistoric man

Mazák, Vratislav. Prehistoric man / by Vratislav Mazák ; illustrated by Zdeněk Burian ; [translated by Margot Schierlová ; [line drawings by Vratislav Mazák and Zdeněk Burian]. — London : Hamlyn, c1980. — 191p : ill(some col.) ; 20cm
Translation from the Czech. — Bibliography: p188-189 — Includes Index
ISBN 0-600-37151-4 : £2.95 B81-02199

930.1 — Prehistoric man — *For children*

Millard, Anne. Early man / by Anne Millard. — London : Pan, 1981. — 91p : ill(some col.),maps(some col.),1col.port ; 18cm. — (A Piccolo factbook)
Text on inside cover. — Includes index
ISBN 0-330-26418-4 (pbk) : £1.25 B81-38774

Millard, Anne. Early man / by Anne Millard ; editor Jacqui Bailey. — London : Kingfisher, 1981. — 91p : ill(some col.),col.maps ; 19cm. — (A Kingfisher factbook)
Includes index
ISBN 0-86272-016-8 : £2.50 : CIP rev. B81-14411

930.1′01 — Archaeology. Theories — *Conference proceedings*

Economic archaeology : towards an integration of ecological and social approaches / edited by Alison Sheridan and Geoff Bailey. — Oxford : B.A.R., 1981. — 303p : ill,maps ; 30cm. — (BAR. International series ; 96)
Includes bibliographies
ISBN 0-86054-113-4 (pbk) : £11.00 B81-36623

930.1′01′8 — Archaeology. Methodology — *Festschriften*

Pattern of the past : studies in honour of David Clarke / edited by Ian Hodder, Glynn Isaac, Norman Hammond. — Cambridge : Cambridge Univeristy Press, 1981. — ix,443p : ill,maps ; 26cm
Includes bibliographies and index
ISBN 0-521-22763-1 : £27.50 B81-08120

930.1′028 — Antiquities. Sites. Research. Applications of aerial photography — *Serials*

[Orbit *(London)*]. Orbit. — Vol.1, 1980-. — London (2A,27 Bryanston Sq., W1) : Aerial Archaeology Foundation, 1980-. — v. : ill ; 21cm
Irregular
Unpriced B81-08764

930.1′028 — Archaeological investigation. Applications of soil science — *Conference proceedings*

Soils and archaeology / edited by David A. Jenkins. — Swansea : W.S.D.G., 1978. — 161p : ill,maps ; 21cm. — (Report / Welsh Soils Discussion Group ; no.19)
Conference papers. — Includes bibliographies
Unpriced (pbk) B81-28289

930.1′028 — Archaeology. Applications of aerial photography — *Serials*

Aerial archaeology. — Vol.4 (1979). — London (2A, 27 Bryanston Sq., W1) : Aerial Archaeology Foundation, c1980. — viii,118p
ISSN 0140-9220 : £9.00 B81-15280

930.1′028 — Society. Role of material objects. Archaeological investigation

Modern material culture : the archaeology of us / edited by Richard A. Gould, Michael B. Schiffer. — New York ; London : Academic Press, c1981. — xvii,347p : ill,maps,plans,ports ; 24cm. — (Studies in archaeology)
Bibliography: p323-342. — Includes index
ISBN 0-12-293580-2 : £22.80 B81-38701

930.1′028′04 — Shipwrecks. Archaeological investigation — *Manuals*

Muckelroy, Keith. Discovering a historic wreck : a handbook offering some advice on what to do when you find an archaeological site under water / by Keith Muckelroy. — [London] ([Greenwich, SE10 9NF]) : Trustees of the National Maritime Museum, 1981?. — vii,47p : ill ; 21cm. — (Handbooks in maritime archaeology, ISSN 0260-5570 ; no.1)
Includes bibliographies
ISBN 0-905555-51-1 (pbk) : Unpriced B81-31499

930.1′028′04 — Underwater antiquities. Preservation — *Manuals*

Robinson, Wendy S.. First aid for marine finds / by Wendy S. Robinson. — [London] ([Greenwich, SE10 9NF]) : Trustees of the National Maritime Museum, 1981?. — ix,40p : ill,1form ; 21cm. — (Handbooks in maritime archaeology, ISSN 0260-5570 ; no.2)
ISBN 0-905555-52-x (pbk) : Unpriced
B81-31498

930.1′028′3 — Antiquities. Excavation of remains by personnel of University of Durham & University of Newcastle upon Tyne — *Serials*

Archaeological reports for ... / University of Durham ; University of Newcastle upon Tyne. — 1980. — Durham : the University, 1981. — 60p
ISSN 0141-8971 : £0.50 B81-24135

930.1′028′5 — Antiquities. Dating. Scientific techniques

Progress in scientific dating methods / edited by Richard Burleigh. — London : British Museum, 1980. — 90p : ill ; 30cm. — (Occasional paper / British Museum, ISSN 0142-4815 ; no.21)
Conference papers
ISBN 0-86159-020-1 (pbk) : Unpriced
B81-11328

930.1′028′5 — Archaeological investigation. Sources of evidence: Livestock. Diseases. Sources of evidence: Bones

Baker, J. R.. Animal diseases in archaeology / J. Baker, D. Brothwell. — London : Academic Press, 1980. — ix,235p : ill,1map ; 24cm. — (Studies in archaeological science)
Bibliography: p208-221. — Includes index
ISBN 0-12-074150-4 : £12.80 : CIP rev.
B80-01263

930.1′028′5 — Archaeology. Applications of digital computer systems — *Conference proceedings*

Computer applications in archaeology 1980. — [Birmingham] : [Computer Centre, University of Birmingham], [c1980]. — 48p : ill ; 21cm
Conference papers. — Cover title. — Includes bibliographies
ISBN 0-7044-0412-5 (pbk) : Unpriced
B81-17897

930.1′028′5 — Dendrochronology - *For archaeology*

Baillie, M. G. L.. Tree-ring dating and archaeology. — London : Croom Helm, Aug.1981. — [304]p. — (Croom Helm studies in archaeology)
ISBN 0-7099-0613-7 : £15.95 : CIP entry
B81-16873

930.1′028′5 — Man. Bones — *For archaeology*

Brothwell, D. R.. Digging up bones. — 3rd ed. — London : British Museum (Natural History), Sept.1981. — [208]p
Previous ed.: 1972
ISBN 0-19-858504-7 (cased) : £6.00 : CIP entry
ISBN 0-19-858510-1 (pbk) : Unpriced
B81-30457

930.1′028′5404 — Archaeology. Applications of microcomputer systems — *Conference proceedings*

Microcomputers in archaeology : proceedings of a seminar held in the Institute of Archaeology 18 June 1980 : with related articles / edited by Jennifer D. Stewart. — Duxford (Imperial War Museum, Duxford Airfield, Duxford, Cambs. CB2 4QR) : Museum Documentation Association, 1980. — vii,136p : ill,forms ; 30cm. — (MDA occasional paper, ISSN 0140-7198 ; 4)
Includes 1 chapter in French. — Bibliography: p131-136
ISBN 0-905963-34-2 (spiral) : £5.00 (£3.50 to members of the Museum Documentation Association) B81-25549

930.1′05 — Archaeology — *Serials*

Advances in archaeological method and theory. — Vol.4. — New York ; London : Academic Press, 1981. — xii,443p
ISBN 0-12-003104-3 : £21.40
ISSN 0162-8003 B81-34021

930.1′09 — Archaeology, *to 1980*

Daniel, Glyn. A short history of archaeology / Glyn Daniel. — London : Thames and Hudson, c1981. — 232p : ill(some col.),facsims,ports ; 25cm
Bibliography: p217-219. — Includes index
ISBN 0-500-02101-5 : £9.50 B81-27016

930.1′09 — Archaeology, *to 1980 — Conference proceedings*

Conference on the History of Archaeology *(1st : 1978 : Aarhus)*. Towards a history of archaeology : being the papers read at the first conference on the History of Archaeology in Aarhus, 29 August-2 September 1978 / edited by Glyn Daniel. — London : Thames and Hudson, c1981. — 192p : ill ; 25cm
Includes bibliographies and index
ISBN 0-500-05039-2 : £12.00 B81-23515

930.1′092′2 — Scotland. Antiquaries, *1640-1830*

Brown, Iain Gordon. The hobby-horsical antiquary : a Scottish character 1640-1830 : an essay / by Iain Gordon Brown. — Edinburgh : National Library of Scotland, 1980. — 48p : ill,ports ; 25cm
Bibliography: p47
ISBN 0-902220-38-1 (pbk) : Unpriced
B81-32341

930.1′092′4 — Archaeology. Childe, V. Gordon — *Biographies*

Green, Sally. Prehistorian : a biography of V. Gordon Childe / Sally Green ; with a foreword by Jack Lindsay. — Bradford-on-Avon : Moonraker, 1981. — xxii,200p : 1geneal.table ; 22cm
Bibliography: p176-190. — Includes index
ISBN 0-239-00206-7 : £8.95 B81-24551

930.1′092′4 — Archaeology. Evans, *Sir* **Arthur** — *Biographies*

Horwitz, Sylvia L.. The find of a lifetime : Sir Arthur Evans and the discovery of Knossos / Sylvia L. Horwitz. — London : Weidenfeld and Nicolson, 1981. — ix,278p[8]p of plates : ill,facsims,ports ; 24cm
Bibliography: p267-270. — Includes index
ISBN 0-297-78008-5 : £9.95 B81-40202

930.1′2 — Palaeolithic man. Archaeological investigation. Sources of evidence: Fossil animals. Bones

Binford, Lewis R.. Bones : ancient men and modern myths / Lewis R. Binford ; with a foreword by F. Clark Howell. — New York ; London : Academic Press, c1981. — xxv,320p : ill ; 25cm. — (Studies in archeology)
Bibliography: p299-312. — Includes index
ISBN 0-12-100035-4 : £24.40 B81-37711

930.1′2 — Stone Age civilisation

Wymer, J. J.. The palaeolithic age. — London : Croom Helm, Apr.1981. — [272]p
ISBN 0-7099-2710-x : £10.95 : CIP entry
ISBN 0-7099-2718-5 (pbk) : £5.95 B81-08830

930.2/5 — ANCIENT HISTORY. SPECIAL PERIODS

930′.4 — Ancient civilizations, *B.C.200-A.D.300 — For children*

Fry, Plantagenet Somerset. The Roman world 200 B.C.-A.D.300 / series editor and author: Plantagenet Somerset Fry ; [colour illustrations by John Flynn et al.] ; [line drawings by Nicholas Hall]. — London : Macmillan Children′s, 1980. — 45p : ill(some col.),maps,1facsim,ports ; 33cm. — (History in pictures ; bk.5)
Includes index
ISBN 0-333-25542-9 : £3.95 B81-06493

930′.4 — Ancient world, ca B.C. 560-B.C. 223 — *Early works*

The **Greek** historians : the essence of Herodotus, Thucydides, Xenophon, Polybius / selected and edited by M.I. Finley. — Harmondsworth : Penguin, 1977, c1959 (1980 [printing]). — 501p : 1map ; 18cm. — (The Viking portable library)
Translations from the Greek. — Originally published: New York : Viking Press, 1959 ; London : Chatto & Windus, 1960
ISBN 0-14-015065-x (pbk) : £2.50 B81-07116

930′.4 — Civilization, *ca B.C.546-A.D.100*

Yamauchi, Edwin M.. The world of the first Christians / Edwin Yamauchi. — Tring : Lion, 1981. — 128p : ill(some col.),col.maps ; 25cm
Ill on lining papers. — Also available as 4 separate booklets
ISBN 0-85648-163-7 : £5.95 B81-17014

930′.5 — Ancient world, *ca 1-100 — For study of Bible. N.T.*

Blaiklock, E. M.. The world of the New Testament / E.M. Blaiklock. — London : Ark, 1981, c1979. — 127p : ill,maps ; 21cm. — (Bible study commentary)
ISBN 0-86201-087-x (pbk) : Unpriced
B81-32450

931 — ANCIENT HISTORY. CHINA

931′.01 — China. Palaeolithic artefacts — *Illustrations*

Zhong guo gu ren lei hua ji = Atlas of primitive man in China / compiling group of the atlas [organized by] Institute of Vertebrate Paleontology and Paleoanthropology, Chinese Academy of Sciences. — Beiging : Science Press ; New York ; London : distributed by Van Nostrand Reinhold, 1980. — 174p : chiefly ill(some col.),col.maps ; 30cm
Chinese title transliterated. — Maps on lining papers
ISBN 0-442-20013-7 : £24.95
Also classified at 569′.9 B81-37693

931′.04 — Ancient China. Qin Shi Huang Di, *Emperor of China — Biographies*

Cotterell, Arthur. The first emperor. — London : Macmillan, Oct.1981. — [224]p
ISBN 0-333-32444-7 : £9.95 : CIP entry
B81-26749

932 — ANCIENT HISTORY. EGYPT

932 — Ancient Egypt. Social life — *For children*

Vernus, Pascal. Times of the pharaohs / Pascal Vernus ; [illustrations Yves Beaujard] ; [translated by Derek Lywood]. — St Albans : Hart-Davis, 1980. — 63p : ill(some col.),1col.map ; 27cm. — (Signposts series)
Translation of: Au temps des pharaons
ISBN 0-247-13033-8 : £3.50 B81-02405

932 — Ancient Egypt, *to B.C.30*

Newby, P. H.. Warrior pharaohs : the rise and fall of the Egyptian empire / P.H. Newby. — London : Faber, 1980. — 212p : ill(some col.),maps,ports(some col.) ; 25cm
Ill on lining papers. — Bibliography: p208-209. — Includes index
ISBN 0-571-11641-8 : £8.95 : CIP rev.
B80-18100

932 — Egypt. Ancient Egyptian pyramids

Edwards, I. E. S.. The pyramids of Egypt / I.E.S. Edwards ; illustrated by J.C. Rose. — Rev. ed., Repr. with minor revisions. — Harmondsworth : Penguin, 1980, c1961. — 319p,32p of plates : ill,2maps,plans,ports ; 18cm. — (Pelican books)
Previous ed.: 1947. — Bibliography: p299-312. — Includes index
ISBN 0-14-120168-8 (pbk) : £1.95 B81-01378

932 — Egypt. Gurob. Ancient Egyptian antiquities. Excavation of remains, *1888-1920*

Thomas, Angela P.. Gurob : a New Kingdom town / Angela P. Thomas. — Warminster : Aris & Phillips, c1981. — 2v.(vi,92p,59p of plates) : ill,maps ; 30cm. — (Egyptology today ; no.5 1981)
Includes index
ISBN 0-85668-131-8 (pbk) : Unpriced : CIP rev.
Primary classification 932 B80-22714

932 — Egypt. Qaṣr Ibrîm. Cemeteries. Ancient Nubian antiquities. Excavation of remains, *1961*

Mills, A. J.. The cemeteries of Qaṣr Ibrîm : a report of the excavations conducted by W.B. Emery in 1961. — London : Egypt Exploration Society, Jan.1982. — [94]p. — (Excavation memoirs, ISSN 0307-5109 ; 51)
ISBN 0-85698-078-1 : £60.00 : CIP entry
B81-38844

932 — Egypt. Valley of the Kings. Ancient Egyptian royal tombs. Excavations of remains

Romer, John. Valley of the kings / John Romer. — London : Joseph, 1981. — 293p,[16]p of plates : ill(some col.),maps,facsims,plans,ports ; 25cm
Ill on lining papers. — Bibliography: p282-286. — Includes index
ISBN 0-7181-2045-0 : £12.50 B81-39852

932 — Egypt. Valley of the Kings. Ancient Egyptian royal tombs: Tomb of Tutankhamun, *Pharaoh of Egypt*. Excavation of remains

Hoving, Thomas. Tutankhamun : the untold story / Thomas Hoving. — Harmondsworth : Penguin, 1980, c1978. — 384p,[8]p of plates : 3ill,1map,1plan,ports ; 20cm
Originally published: New York : Simon and Schuster, 1978 ; London : Hamilton, 1979. — Includes index
ISBN 0-14-005337-9 (pbk) : £2.50 B81-00663

932 — Egypt. Western Desert. Prehistoric antiquities

Wendorf, Fred. Prehistory of the eastern Sahara / Fred Wendorf, Romuald Schild. — New York ; London : Academic Press, c1980. — xviii,414p : ill,maps ; 19cm. — (Studies in archaeology)
Bibliography: p401-409. — Includes index
ISBN 0-12-743960-9 : £36.40
Also classified at 333.7′0932 B81-07525

932 — London. Camden *(London Borough)*. Museums: Petrie Museum. Exhibits: Ancient Egyptian antiquities from Gurob: Exhibits at Petrie Museum — *Catalogues*

Thomas, Angela P.. Gurob : a New Kingdom town / Angela P. Thomas. — Warminster : Aris & Phillips, c1981. — 2v.(vi,92p,59p of plates) : ill,maps ; 30cm. — (Egyptology today ; no.5 1981)
Includes index
ISBN 0-85668-131-8 (pbk) : Unpriced : CIP rev.
Also classified at 932 B80-22714

932′.005 — Ancient Egypt. Archaeological investigation — *Serials*

The **Journal** of Egyptian archaeology. — Vol.66 (1980). — London : Egypt Exploration Society, 1980. — 192p
ISSN 0307-5133 : £10.00 B81-09691

932′.006′041 — Ancient Egypt. Archaeological investigations. British organisations: Egyptian Exploration Society, *1882-1982*

Excavating in Egypt. — London : British Museum Publications, Feb.1982. — [192]p
ISBN 0-7141-0932-0 : £5.95 : CIP entry B81-35829

932′.0074′02134 — London. Camden *(London Borough)*. Museums: British Museum. *Department of Egyptian Antiquities, to 1980*

James, T. G. H.. The British Museum and Ancient Egypt. — London : British Museum Publications, Aug.1981. — [32]p
ISBN 0-7141-0930-4 (pbk) : £3.95 : CIP entry B81-18106

932′.0074′02142 — London. Camden *(London Borough)*. Museums: British Museum. Stock: Ancient Egyptian antiquities — *Catalogues*

British Museum. Catalogue of Egyptian antiquities in the British Museum. — London : British Museum Publications
5: Early dynastic objects. — Sept.1981. — [192]p
ISBN 0-7141-0927-4 : £25.00 : CIP entry B81-28201

933 — ANCIENT HISTORY. PALESTINE

933 — Israel, *to ca B.C.900* — *For schools*

Hughes, Gerald. The birth of a nation / Gerald Hughes and Stephen Travis. — Tring : Lion Publishing, 1981. — 32p : ill(some col.),col.maps ; 25cm. — (Introducing the Bible ; 1)
Cover title
ISBN 0-85648-263-3 (pbk) : £1.25 B81-16687

933 — Jews, *B.C.165-A.D.50* — *For schools*

Yamauchi, Edwin M.. The Jewish world / Edwin Yamauchi. — Tring : Lion, 1981. — 32p : ill (some col.),col.maps ; 25cm. — (The World of the first Christians ; 1)
Cover title
ISBN 0-85648-267-6 (pbk) : £1.25 B81-20678

933 — Jews, *B.C.500-A.D.73* — *For schools*

Hughes, Gerald. The end of an era / Gerald Hughes and Stephen Travis. — Tring : Lion Publishing, 1981. — p65-96 : ill(some col.),col.maps ; 25cm. — (Introducing the Bible ; 3)
Cover title
ISBN 0-85648-265-x (pbk) : £1.25 B81-16685

933 — Jordan. Khirbat Qumran. Antiquities, *B.C.125-A.D.68*

Discoveries in the Judaean desert. — Oxford : Clarendon Press, Sept.1981
7: Qumrân grotte 4
III. — [320]p
ISBN 0-19-826321-x : £25.00 : CIP entry B81-23880

933′.05 — Palestine. Jewish Rebellion, *66* — *Early works*

Josephus, Flavius. [De Bello Judaico. English]. The Jewish War / Josephus ; translated by G.A. Williamson. — Rev. ed. / revised with a new introduction, notes and appendixes by E. May Smallwood. — Harmondsworth : Penguin,, 1981, c1969. — 511p : maps,plans,1geneal.table ; 20cm. — (Penguin classics)
Translation of: De Bello Judaico. — Previous ed.: 1970. — Bibliography: p496-498. — Includes index
ISBN 0-14-044420-3 (pbk) : £3.95 B81-40008

934 — ANCIENT HISTORY. INDIA

934′.0072041 — India. Antiquities. Discovery by Britons, *1765-1927*

Keay, John. India discovered : the achievement of the British Raj / John Keay ; photographed by Clive Friend ; designed by Philip Clucas ; produced by Ted Smart and David Gibbon. — Leicester : Windward, 1981. — 288p : chiefly col. ill,1col.map,col.ports ; 33cm
Bibliography: p282-283. — Includes index
ISBN 0-7112-0047-5 : £10.95 B81-38118

935 — ANCIENT HISTORY. NEAR EAST

935 — Ancient Mesopotamia, *to ca 74*

Roux, Georges. Ancient Iraq / Georges Roux. — 2nd ed. — Harmondsworth : Penguin, 1980. — 496p,[16]p of plates : ill,maps ; 18cm. — (Pelican books)
Previous ed.: London : Allen & Unwin, 1964. — Includes index
£2.50 (pbk) B81-03605

935 — Ancient Mesopotamian antiquities. Excavation of remains, *1800-1979*

Lloyd, Seton. Foundations in the dust : the story of Mesopotamian exploration / Seton Lloyd. — Rev. and enl. ed.. — London : Thames and Hudson, c1980. — 216p : ill,maps,facsims,ports ; 25cm
Previous ed.: London : Oxford University Press, 1947. — Bibliography: p211-212. - Includes index
ISBN 0-500-05038-4 : £12.00 B81-05775

935 — Iran. Barlekin. Antiquities. Excavation of remains

Burton-Brown, T.. Barlekin / T. Burton-Brown. — Wootton Woodstock (Westend House, Wootton Woodstock, Oxon) : T. Burton-Brown, 1981. — xxi,138p,xp of plates : ill ; 21cm
Includes index
ISBN 0-9501925-3-8 (pbk) : £6.00 B81-16084

935 — Iran. Luristan. Archaeological investigation, *1963-1969* — *Personal observations*

Goff, Clare. An archaeologist in the making : six seasons in Iran / Clare Goff. — London : Constable, 1980. — 284p,[9]p of plates : ill,3maps,plans,ports ; 23cm
Includes index
ISBN 0-09-463380-0 : £9.95 : CIP rev. B80-14083

935 — Iraq. Nineveh. Excavation of remains, *1846*

Brackman, Arnold C.. The luck of Nineveh : in search of the lost Assyrian empire / Arnold C. Brackman. — New York ; London : Van Nostrand Reinhold, 1981, c1978. — viii,349p,[8]p of plates : ill,1map ; 23cm
Originally published: New York : McGraw-Hill, 1978 ; London : Eyre Methuen, 1980. — Includes index
ISBN 0-442-28260-5 (pbk) : £7.60 B81-37023

935′.03′05 — Assyrian culture — *Serials*

The **Assyrian** observer. — Issue no.1 (Winter 1978)-. — Slade Green (108 Alderney Rd, Slade Green, Kent DA8 2JD) : Assyrian Observer Incorporation, 1979. — v. : ill ; 21cm
Quarterly. — Continues: The Assyrian. — Description based on: Issue no.5 (Winter 1980)
ISSN 0144-7122 = Assyrian observer : £5.00 per year B81-05309

936 — ANCIENT HISTORY. EUROPE NORTH AND WEST OF ITALIAN PENINSULA

936 — Europe. Antiquities, *to ca B.C.1*

Phillips, Patricia. The prehistory of Europe / Patricia Phillips. — Harmondsworth : Penguin, 1981, c1980. — 314p,[16]pof plates : ill,maps ; 20cm. — (Pelican books)
Originally published: London : Allen Lane, 1980. — Bibliography: p297. — Includes index
ISBN 0-14-022102-6 (pbk) : £3.95 B81-21009

936 — Western Europe. Ancient Roman civilization, *300-400*

The **Roman** West in the third century : contributions from archaeology and history / edited by Anthony King and Martin Henig. — Oxford : B.A.R., 1981. — 2v.(538p) : ill,maps ; 30cm. — (BAR. International series ; 109)
Includes bibliographies
ISBN 0-86054-127-4 (pbk) : £20.00 B81-36618

936 — Western Europe. Beaker folk. Archaeological investigation

Harrison, Richard J.. The beaker folk : Copper Age archaeology in Western Europe / Richard J. Harrison. — London : Thames and Hudson, c1980. — 176p : ill,maps,plans ; 25cm. — (Ancient peoples and places ; v.97)
Bibliography: p167-170. - Includes index
ISBN 0-500-02098-1 : £12.00 B81-04514

936 — Western Europe. Megalithic monuments

Service, Alastair. [Megaliths and their mysteries]. A guide to the Megaliths of Europe / Alastair Service and Jean Bradbery. — London : Granada, 1981, c1979. — 284p : ill,maps ; 20cm. — (A Paladin book)
Originally published: London : Weidenfeld and Nicolson, 1979. — Map on inside cover. — Bibliography: p268-275. - Includes index
ISBN 0-586-08359-6 (pbk) : £2.95 B81-22282

936.1 — Great Britain. Ancient Roman forts

Wilson, Roger. Roman forts : an illustrated introduction to the garrison posts of Roman Britain / Roger Wilson. — London (31 Foubert′s Place, W.1) : Bergström & Boyle, c1980. — 96p : ill,1map,plans ; 23cm
Bibliography: p90-91. — Includes index
ISBN 0-903767-30-9 (cased) : £5.95
ISBN 0-903767-25-2 (pbk) : £3.95 B81-02316

936.1 — Great Britain. Antiquities

Muir, Richard, *1943-*. Riddles in the British landscape / Richard Muir. — London : Thames and Hudson, c1981. — 192p : ill,maps ; 26cm
Bibliography: p190. — Includes index
ISBN 0-500-24108-2 : £8.95 B81-16959

936.1 — Great Britain. Archaeology. Terminology

Adkins, Lesley. A thesaurus of British archaeology. — Newton Abbot : David & Charles, Nov.1981. — [288]p
ISBN 0-7153-7864-3 : £15.00 : CIP entry B81-30388

936.1 — Great Britain. Archaeology, *to 1980*

Hudson, Kenneth. A social history of archaeology : the British experience / Kenneth Hudson. — London : Macmillan, 1981. — viii,197p : ill,ports ; 25cm
Includes index
ISBN 0-333-25679-4 : £20.00 B81-37117

936.1 — Great Britain. Hill forts — *Festschriften*

Hill-fort studies : essays for A.H.A. Hogg / edited by Graeme Guilbert. — [Leicester] : Leicester University, 1981. — 216p : ill,maps,plans,1ports ; 26cm
Includes bibliographies and index
ISBN 0-7185-1200-6 : £19.00 : CIP rev. B81-04366

936.1 — Great Britain. Social life, *B.C.700-A.D.43*

Herdman, Margaret. Life in Iron Age Britain / Margaret Herdman. — London : Harrap, 1981. — 47p : ill,maps,plans ; 18x22cm. — (History in evidence)
ISBN 0-245-53534-9 (pbk) : £1.65 B81-17198

936.1'006 — Great Britain. Archaeology. Organisations — *Serials*

Council for British Archaeology. Archaeology in Britain / the Council for British Archaeology. — 1979. — London : The Council, c1980. — 107p
ISBN 0-900312-69-6 : Unpriced
ISSN 0305-8456 B81-04706

936.1'0088054 — Great Britain. Children. Social life, *to ca 43* — *For children*

Clarke, Amanda. Growing up in Ancient Britain / Amanda Clarke. — London : Batsford Academic and Educational, 1981. — 72p : ill ; 26cm
Bibliography: p69. — Includes index
ISBN 0-7134-3557-7 : £5.50 B81-24311

936.1'009'732 — Great Britain. Ancient Roman towns. Social life — *For schools*

Corbishley, Mike. Town life in Roman Britain / Mike Corbishley. — London : Harrap, 1981. — 49p : ill,maps,ports ; 18x21cm. — (History in evidence)
Text on inside cover. — Bibliography: p48
ISBN 0-245-53535-7 (pbk) : £1.65 B81-34912

936.1'01 — Great Britain, *ca B.C.3200-ca B.C.1200*

Burgess, Colin. The age of Stonehenge / Colin Burgess. — London : Dent, 1980. — 402p,[16]p of plates : ill,maps,plans ; 25cm. — (History in the landscape series)
Bibliography: p380-390. — Includes index
ISBN 0-460-04254-8 : £12.00 : CIP rev. B80-05733

936.1'01 — Great Britain. Lower Palaeolithic civilization & middle Palaeolithic civilization

Roe, Derek A.. The Lower and Middle Palaeolithic periods in Britain / Derek A. Roe. — London : Routledge & Kegan Paul, 1981. — xvi,324p,[16]p of plates : ill ; 26cm. — (Archaeology of Britain)
Bibliography: p285-300. — Includes index
ISBN 0-7100-0600-4 : £35.00 : CIP rev. B80-27642

936.1'01 — Great Britain. Megalithic circles. Sites — *Technical data*

Thom, A. (Alexander). Megalithic rings : plans and data for 229 monuments in Britain / A & A.S. Thom ; collated, with archaeological notes, by A. Burl. — Oxford : B.A.R., 1980. — 405p : ill,1map,plans ; 30cm. — (BAR. British series, ISSN 0143-3032 ; 81)
Includes index
ISBN 0-86054-094-4 (pbk) : £12.00 B81-36636

936.1'01 — Great Britain. Palaeolithic civilization & Mesolithic civilization. Archaelogical sources

Morrison, Alex. Early man in Britain and Ireland : an introduction to Palaeolithic and Mesolithic cultures / Alex Morrison. — London : Croom Helm, c1980. — 209p : ill,maps ; 24cm. — (Croom Helm studies in archaeology)
Bibliography: p174-203. - Includes index
ISBN 0-85664-084-0 (cased) : £12.95 : CIP rev.
ISBN 0-85664-089-1 (pbk) : £7.95 B80-11246

936.1'01 — Great Britain. Prehistoric antiquities, *to ca B.C.1000*

Laing, Lloyd. The origins of Britain / Lloyd and Jennifer Laing. — London : Routledge & Kegan Paul, 1980. — x,197p : ill,col.maps,ports ; 24cm
Bibliography: p193-194. - Includes index
ISBN 0-7100-0431-1 : £7.95 : CIP rev. B80-09924

936.1'01 — Great Britain, *to B.C.54* — *For schools*

Triggs, Tony D.. Ancient Britons / Tony D. Triggs. — Edinburgh : Oliver & Boyd, 1981. — 41p : ill,1map,1plan ; 19x25cm. — (Exploring history)
Text on inside covers. — Bibliography: p41. — Includes index
ISBN 0-05-003417-0 (pbk) : £1.25 B81-15327

936.1'04 — Great Britain. Ancient Roman antiquities

Wilson, Roger J. A.. A guide to the Roman remains in Britain / Roger J.A. Wilson ; with a foreword by J.M.C. Toynbee. — 2nd ed. — London : Constable, 1980. — xv,415p : ill,maps,plans ; 18cm
Previous ed.: 1975. — Maps on lining papers. — Bibliography: p389-407. — Includes index
ISBN 0-09-463260-x : £4.95 : CIP rev. B80-02985

936.1'04 — Great Britain. Ancient Roman towns

Bennett, Julian. Towns in Roman Britain / Julian Bennett. — Princes Risborough : Shire Publications, 1980. — 72p : ill,maps,plans ; 21cm. — (Shire archaeology series ; 13)
Bibliography: p35. - Includes index
ISBN 0-85263-495-1 (pbk) : £1.50 B81-07741

936.1'04 — Great Britain, *B.C.50-A.D.480*

Salway, Peter. Roman Britain / by Peter Salway. — Oxford : Clarendon, 1981. — xx,824p : maps ; 23cm. — (The Oxford history of England ; 1A)
Bibliography: p753-775. — Includes index
ISBN 0-19-821717-x : £19.50 B81-36153

936.1'04 — Great Britain, *B.C.55-A.D.400*

Todd, Malcolm, *1939-*. Roman Britain 55 B.C.-A.D.400 : the province beyond ocean / Malcolm Todd. — [London] : Fontana, 1981. — 285p : ill,maps,plans ; 18cm. — (Fontana history of England)
Bibliography: p274. — Includes index
ISBN 0-00-633756-2 (pbk) : £2.95 B81-25622

936.1'04 — Great Britain, *B.C.55-A.D.410*

Todd, Malcolm, *1939-*. Roman Britain : 55 BC-AD 400 : the province beyond ocean / Malcolm Todd. — Brighton : Harvester in association with Fontana Paperbacks, 1981. — 285p : ill,maps ; 23cm. — (Fontana history of England)
Bibliography: p274. — Includes index
ISBN 0-7108-0300-1 : £20.00 : CIP rev. B81-12809

936.1'04 — Great Britain. Social life, *B.C.55-A.D.410*

Birley, Anthony. Life in Roman Britain / Anthony Birley. — New ed. — London : Batsford, 1981. — xv,176p : ill,1map,ports ; 22cm
Previous ed.: 1964. — Bibliography: pxiii-xiv. — Includes index
ISBN 0-7134-3643-3 (pbk) : £5.95 B81-36704

Branigan, Keith. Roman Britain : life in an imperial province / Keith Branigan. — London : Reader's Digest, c1980. — 320p : ill(some col.),maps(some col.),1facsim ; 27cm. — (Life in Britain)
Maps on lining papers. — Includes index
£9.95 B81-04771

936.1'104'074029134 — Edinburgh. Museums: National Museum of Antiquities of Scotland. Stock. Ancient Roman antiquities — *Catalogues*

National Museum of Antiquities of Scotland. The Romans in Scotland : an introduction to the collections of the National Museum of Antiquities of Scotland / [compiled by] D.V. Clarke, D.J. Breeze & Ghillean Mackay. — Edinburgh ([Queen St., Edinburgh EH2 1JD]) : The Museum, 1980. — 79p,[4]p of plates : ill (some col.),maps ; 25cm
Bibliography: p77-79
ISBN 0-11-491637-3 (pbk) : £3.00 B81-02394

936.1'11 — Northern Scotland. Coastal regions & islands. Iron Age promontory forts

Lamb, R. G.. Iron Age promontory forts in the Northern Isles / R.G. Lamb. — Oxford : B.A.R., 1980. — 102,[12]p of plates : ill,maps,plans ; 30cm. — (BAR. British series ; 79)
Bibliography: p97-99. — Includes index
ISBN 0-86054-087-1 (pbk) : £4.00 B81-16556

936.1'13501 — Scotland. Shetland. Prehistoric antiquities

Fojut, Noel. A guide to prehistoric Shetland / by Noel Fojut. — Lerwick : Shetland Times, 1981. — xii,73p,4p of plates : ill,maps ; 22cm
ISBN 0-900662-32-8 (pbk) : Unpriced B81-33585

936.1'223 — Scotland. Grampian Region. Forres. Standing stones: Sueno's stone

Southwick, Leslie. The so-called Sueno's Stone at Forres / Leslie Southwick. — [Elgin] : Moray District Libraries, 1981. — 20p,[4]p of plates : ill,1map ; 22cm
Unpriced (pbk) B81-39355

936.1'423 — Scotland. Strathclyde Region. Bute. Antiquities — *Serials*

Transactions of the Buteshire Natural History Society. — Vol.21 (1980). — [Rothesay] ([c/o The Museum, Stuart St., Rothesay, Buteshire]) : [The Society], [1980]. — 115p
ISBN 0-905812-02-6 : Unpriced
Primary classification 574.9414'23 B81-25500

936.1'423 — Scotland. Strathclyde Region. Iona. Antiquities. Excavation of remains

Reece, Richard. Excavations in Iona 1964 to 1974 / by Richard Reece. — London (31 Gordon Sq., WCH1 0PY) : Institute of Archaeology, 1981. — vii,118p : ill,map,plans ; 30cm. — (Occasional publication / Institute of Archaeology, ISSN 0141-8505 ; no.5)
Includes bibliographies
ISBN 0-905853-09-1 (pbk) : Unpriced B81-29794

936.1'423 — Scotland. Strathclyde Region. Mid Argyll. Antiquities

Mackenna, F. S.. Pen sketches from mid-Argyll / F.S. Mackenna. — [Kilberry?] ([Kilberry, Kintyre, Central Region]) : Natural History & Antiquarian Society of Mid-Argyll, [1981]. — [28]p : ill,1map ; 23cm
Cover title. — Ill on inside cover
Unpriced (pbk) B81-18450

936.1'6'005 — Northern Ireland. Antiquities — *Serials*

Historic monuments / Department of the Environment for Northern Ireland. — 1979-1980. — Belfast : H.M.S.O., 1981. — 11p
ISBN 0-337-08166-2 : £1.20 B81-20336

936.2'009'732 — England. Towns. Archaeological investigation, *1976-1981*

Recent archaeological research in English towns / edited by John Schofield and David Palliser with Charlotte Harding. — London : Council for British Archaeology, 1981. — x,125p : 1map ; 30cm
Includes bibliographies and index
ISBN 0-906780-09-8 (pbk) : Unpriced B81-28221

936.2'02 — England. Iron Age hill forts

Dyer, James. Hillforts of England and Wales / James Dyer. — Aylesbury : Shire, 1981. — 64p : ill,maps ; 21cm. — (Shire archaeology ; 16)
Bibliography: p34. - Includes index
ISBN 0-85263-536-2 (pbk) : £1.95 B81-17558

936.2'04 — England. Invasion by Ancient Rome, *43*

Webster, Graham. The Roman invasion of Britain / Graham Webster. — London : Batsford Academic and Educational, 1980. — 224p,[16]p of plates : ill,maps,plans ; 24cm
Bibliography: p205. - Includes index
ISBN 0-7134-1329-8 : £8.95 B81-05105

936.2'04 — England. Political events, *48-58*

Webster, Graham. Rome against Caratacus. — London : Batsford, Nov.1981. — [224]p
ISBN 0-7134-3627-1 : £9.95 : CIP entry B81-30359

936.2'04'0922 — England. Ancient Romans — *Biographies*

Birley, Anthony. The Fasti of Roman Britain / Anthony R. Birley. — Oxford : Clarendon, 1981. — xii,476p ; 24cm
Bibliography: p436-443. — Includes index
ISBN 0-19-814821-6 : £30.00 B81-26235

936.2'12 — London *(City)*. **Antiquities. Excavation of remains,** *1973-1979*

Schofield, John. Archaeology of the City of London / [text by John Schofield and Tony Dyson] ; [with contributions by Brian Hobley et al.]. — London (c/o Museum of London, London Wall, EC2Y 5HN) : City of London Archæological Trust, 1980. — 75p : ill(some col.),maps(some col.),facsims,plans(some col.) ; 25cm
Maps on inside covers
ISBN 0-9506907-0-8 (pbk) : £3.25 : CIP rev. B80-08060

936.2'12 — London *(City)*. **Lower Thames Street. Antiquities. Excavation of remains,** *1974*

Jones, David M.. Excavations at Billingsgate buildings "Triangle", Lower Thames Street, 1974 / by David M. Jones ; with finds reports edited by Michael Rhodes. — [London] ([c/o Hon. Secretary, London & Middlesex Archaeological Society, Museum of London, 150 London Wall, RC2Y 5HN]) : [London & Middlesex Archaeological Society], 1980. — ix,169p,[2]folded leaves of plates : ill,maps ; 25cm. — (Special paper / London and Middlesex Archaeological Society ; no.4)
Bibliography: p165-168
ISBN 0-903290-20-0 (pbk) : Unpriced B81-20909

936.2'1204 — London *(City)*, *43-410*

Marsden, Peter. Roman London / Peter Marsden. — London : Thames and Hudson, c1980. — 224p : ill,maps,facsims,plans,2ports ; 25cm
Bibliography: p215-218. - Includes index
ISBN 0-500-25073-1 : £8.95 B81-05195

936.2'195 — London. Richmond upon Thames *(London Borough)*. **Twickenham,** *to 704*

Urwin, A. C. B.. Twickenham before 704 AD / by A.C.B. Urwin. — [Twickenham] ([59 Park House Gardens, Twickenham, Middx]) : [Twickenham Local History Society], 1980. — 21p : 1map ; 20cm. — (Paper / Borough of Twickenham Local History Society ; no.45)
Bibliography: p20
ISBN 0-903341-30-1 (pbk) : £0.75 B81-05604

936.2'262 — West Sussex. Chichester, *B.C.55-A.D.450*

Chichester, the Roman City / [researched and designed by members of the Chichester WEA local history workshop class]. — [Chichester] ([29 Little London, Chichester PO19 1PB]) : Chichester District Museum, [1979?]. — [8]p : ill,2maps,1plan ; 21cm
Bibliography: p7-8
£0.15 (unbound) B81-37216

936.2'313 — Wiltshire. Old Swindon Hill. Antiquities. Excavation of remains

Canham, Roy. The archaeology of Old Swindon Hill / by Roy Canham and Bernard Phillips. — [Swindon] ([Civic Offices, Euclid St., Swindon SN1 2JH]) : [Borough of Thamesdown Arts and Recreation Committee], [1980]. — [17]p : ill,maps,1plan ; 30cm. — (Swindon Archaeological Society report ; no.1)
Cover title
£0.25 (pbk) B81-04498

936.2'33 — Dorset. Antiquities

Osborn, George. Exploring ancient Dorset : car guide to nearly 50 of the county's key archaeological landmarks - hill-forts, burial chambers, Roman roads, ancient battlefields, cemeteries, stone circles and stone monuments / [George Osborn]. — Sherborne : Dorset Publishing, 1976. — 48p : ill,maps ; 19x25cm
Map on inside cover
ISBN 0-902129-25-2 (pbk) : £1.50 B81-21275

936.2'332 — Dorset. Hambledon Hill. Neolithic antiquities. Excavation of remains

Mercer, Roger. Hambledon Hill : a neolithic landscape / Roger Mercer. — Edinburgh : Edinburgh University Press, c1980. — vii,71p : ill,maps,plans ; 21cm
Bibliography: p68-71
ISBN 0-85224-406-1 (pbk) : £2.50 B81-04724

936.2'35604 — Devon. Exeter. Ancient Roman antiquities

Bidwell, Paul T.. Roman Exeter : fortress and town / by Paul T. Bidwell [for] Exeter City Council. — Exeter (Royal Albert Memorial Museum, Queen St., Exeter EX4 3RX) : Exeter Museum Service, 1980. — ix,96p : ill,maps,plans,1port ; 30cm
Bibliography: p90-94. — Includes index
ISBN 0-86114-270-5 (pbk) : £2.95 B81-04064

936.2'385 — Somerset. Carhampton. Antiquities. Sites

Dixon, Janet. Carhampton / by Janet Dixon ; supplemented and prepared for publication by Edward F. Williams. — Taunton (Taunton Castle, Taunton, Somerset) : Somerset Archaeological and Natural History Society, 1980. — 24p,7leaves : maps ; 30cm. — (Parish surveys in Somerset, ISSN 0141-5506 ; 3)
ISBN 0-902152-09-2 (pbk) : Unpriced B81-17263

936.2'389 — Somerset. Whitestaunton. Antiquities. Sites

Carter, Roger W. (Roger William), *1939-*. Whitestaunton / by Roger W. Carter ; fieldwork also by Mary Parmiter, Peter J. Wood. — Taunton (Taunton Castle, Taunton [Somerset]) : Somerset Archaeological and Natural History Society, 1981. — 18p,[8] leaves of plates : ill,maps ; 30cm. — (Parish surveys in Somerset, ISSN 0141-5506 ; 4)
Text, map on covers. — Bibliography: p17
ISBN 0-902152-11-4 (pbk) : Unpriced B81-27739

936.2'393'005 — Avon. Bristol. Antiquities — *Serials*

BARG review / Bristol Archaeological Research Group. — No.1(1980)-. — Bristol (Bristol City Museum, Queen's Rd, Bristol BS8 1RL) : The Group, 1980-. — v. : ill,maps ; 30cm
Annual. — Continues: BARG bulletin
ISSN 0144-6576 = BARG review : Unpriced B81-04493

BARG review / British Archaeological Research Group. — Issue no.2 (1981). — Bristol : The Group, [1981]. — 80p
ISSN 0144-6576 : Unpriced B81-33286

936.2'41 — Gloucestershire, *43-410*

McWhirr, Alan. Roman Gloucestershire. — Gloucester : Alan Sutton, July 1981. — [192]p
ISBN 0-904387-63-1 (cased) : £7.95 : CIP entry
ISBN 0-904387-60-7 (pbk) : £3.95 B81-19123

936.2'41'00750922 — Gloucestershire. Antiquities. Collectors, *1466-1954*

Gray, Irvine. Antiquaries of Gloucestershire and Bristol / by Irvine Gray. — Bristol (9 Pembroke Rd., Clifton, Bristol BS8 3AU) : Bristol and Gloucestershire Archaeological Society, 1981. — 210p : facsims ; 23cm
Includes index
ISBN 0-900197-14-5 : Unpriced B81-22095

936.2'44 — Hereford and Worcester. Herefordshire. Antiquities

Turner, J. H. (John Hopkins). Herefordshire register of countryside treasures / ... researched and the text prepared in the Countryside Section of the Hereford and Worcester County Planning Department by J.H. Turner during the period 1976-80 ; the photographs were taken by J.K. Cornelius and P. Parker (except where otherwise acknowledged) ; the maps were prepared by M. Baylis. — [Worcester] ([County Hall, Spetchley Rd., Worcester, WR5 2NP]) : County Council of Hereford and Worcester, 1981. — iii,vii,84p,[28]p of plates (some folded) : ill,col.maps ; 30cm
Includes index
£3.50 (pbk) B81-31218

936.2'44'005 — Hereford and Worcester. Worcestershire. Archaeological investigation — *Serials*

Transactions of the Worcestershire Archaeological Society. — 3rd ser. vol.7 (1980). — Worcester ([c/o 4 Orchard Rd, Malvern, Worcs.]) : The Society, [1980?]. — xiii,356p
ISSN 0143-2389 : Unpriced B81-35116

936.2'447 — Hereford and Worcester. Malvern Hills *(District)*. **Iron Age hill forts: Midsummer Hill. Excavation of remains**

Stanford, S. C.. Midsummer Hill : an Iron age hillfort on the Malverns : excavations carried out for the Malvern Hills Archaeological Committee 1965-1970 / by Stanley C. Stanford with reports by Eric L. Crooks ... [et al.]. — Leominster (Ashfield Cottage, Luston, Leominster, Herefordshire HR6 0EA) : S.C. Stanford, 1981. — 184p,[3]folded leaves of plates : ill,maps,plans ; 28cm
Bibliography: p169-171. — Includes index
ISBN 0-9503271-4-x (cased) : Unpriced
ISBN 0-9503271-3-1 (pbk) : Unpriced B81-28738

936.2'55 — Northamptonshire. Antiquities

Royal Commission on Historical Monuments (England). An inventory of the historical monuments in the County of Northampton / Royal Commission on Historical Monuments, England. — London : H.M.S.O.
Vol.3: Archaeological sites in north-west Northamptonshire. — 1981. — lv,222p,[42]p of plates(some folded) : ill(some col.),maps(some col.),plans ; 28cm
Map on folded leaf in pocket. — Includes index
ISBN 0-11-700901-6 : £40.00
ISBN 0-11-700900-8 (red binding) : Unpriced B81-39871

936.2'57'00723 — Oxfordshire. Archaeology. Field studies — *Serials*

[Field Section newsletter *(Oxfordshire. Department of Museum Services. Field Section)*]. Field Section newsletter / Oxfordshire County Museums. — 1979-. — [Woodstock] ([Fletcher's House, Woodstock, Oxon.]) : The Field Section, 1979. — v. : ill ; 30cm
Annual. — Continues: Archaeological and historical newsletter (Oxford City and County Museum)
ISSN 0260-6305 = Field Section newsletter — Oxfordshire County Museums : Unpriced B81-04941

936.2'59 — Buckinghamshire. Antiquities. Sites. Sources of evidence: Aerial photographs

Allen, Denise. Bucks archaeology from the air / by Denise Allen. — Aylesbury (Church St., Aylesbury) : Buckinghamshire County Museum, 1979. — 18p,[4]p of plates : ill,maps,plans ; 21cm
Bibliography: p18
ISBN 0-86059-197-2 (pbk) : Unpriced B81-17862

936.2'644 — Suffolk. Haverhill. Archaeology. Organisations: Haverhill and District Archaeological Group — *Serials*

[Journal *(Haverhill and District Archaeological Group)*]. Journal / Haverhill and District Archaeological Group. — Vol.1, no.1 (Aug. 1976)-. — Haverhill (c/o J. Ling, 27 Quendon Place, Haverhill, Suffolk) : The Group, 1976-. — v. ; 26cm
Two issues yearly. — Continues : Newsletter (Haverhill and District Archaeological Group). — Description based on : Vol.2, no.2 (Oct. 1979)
ISSN 0144-3968 = Journal — Haverhill and District Archaeological Group : Free to Group members only B81-02017

936.2'67 — Essex. Blackwater River region & Crouch River region. Prehistoric antiquities. Sites

Vincent, Stephen W.. Some prehistoric sites along the Rivers Blackwell and Crouch, Essex / by Stephen W. Vincent & William H. George. — [London] ([40 Credon Rd., Plaistow, E13 9BJ]) : [S.W. Vincent & W.H. George], [c1981]. — 15leaves : ill ; 30cm
Bibliography: leaf 15
£0.75 (pbk) B81-18264

936.2′67′005 — Essex. Archaeological investigation — *Serials*

Essex archaeology and history : the transactions of the Essex Archaeological Society. — 3rd ser. vol.11 (1979). — [Colchester] ([Colchester and Essex Museum, The Castle, Colchester CO1 1TJ]) : The Society, 1980. — 126p
ISSN 0308-3462 : Unpriced B81-31603

936.2′6723 — Essex. Colchester, *ca B.C.150-ca A.D.500.* **Archaeological sources**

Clarke, David T.-D.. Roman Colchester / [written by David T.-D. Clarke and G. Mark R. Davies]. — Colchester ([Town Hall, Colchester CO1 1PJ]) : Colchester Borough Council, Cultural Activities Committee, 1980. — 52p : ill(some col.),maps,plans,1geneal.table ; 30cm
Previous ed.: / by M.R. Hull. London : Society of Antiquarians, 1958. — Bibliography: p52
Unpriced (pbk) B81-06773

936.2′6752 — Essex. Springfield. Earthwork structures: Cursuses. Excavation of remains

Hedges, John D.. Springfield cursus : and the cursus problem / John D. Hedges and David G. Buckley. — Chelmsford (County Hall, Chelmsford, Essex CM1 1LF) : Essex County Council, 1981. — iv,37p,iip of plates : ill,1map,2plans ; 30cm. — (Occasional paper / Essex County Council, ISSN 0260-2369 ; no.1)
Cover title. — Text on inside cover. — Bibliography: p33-37
Unpriced (pbk) B81-37814

936.2′714 — Cheshire. Chester. Antiquities. Excavation of remains, *1974-1978*

Mason, D. J. P.. Excavations at Chester : 11-15 Castle Street and neighbouring sites 1974-8 : a possible Roman posting house (mansio) / D.J.P. Mason. — [Chester] ([27 Grosvenor St., Chester CH1 2DD]) : Chester City Council, Grosvenor Museum, [c1980]. — 95p : ill,plans (some col.) ; 30cm. — (Grosvenor Museum archaeological excavations and survey reports ; no.2)
Cover title. — Bibliography: p91-95
ISBN 0-903235-09-9 (pbk) : Unpriced
B81-09620

936.2′715 — Cheshire. Frodsham. Antiquities. Sites

Thompson, Patience. Frodsham : the archaeological potential of a town / Patience Thompson. — Chester (Commerce House, Hunter St., Chester CH1 1SN) : Cheshire County Council, 1980. — 10p,4leaves of plates : ill,4maps ; 30cm. — (Cheshire monographs ; 1)
Bibliography: p9
Unpriced (spiral) B81-21977

936.2′78 — Cumbria. Lake District. Antiquities

Clare, T.. Archaeological sites of the Lake District / T. Clare. — Ashbourne : Moorland, c1981. — 159p : ill,maps,plans ; 21cm
Includes index
ISBN 0-86190-015-4 (cased) : Unpriced : CIP rev.
ISBN 0-86190-014-6 (pbk) : £4.95 B81-08872

936.2′81′00222 — Yorkshire, *to ca 410* — *Illustrations*

Cole, Don. The picture story of prehistoric and Roman Yorkshire / by Don Cole & David Thornton. — Leeds (101 Blue Hill La., Leeds LS12 4NX) : D. & J. Thornton, [1981]. — 16p : ill,maps ; 21cm
ISBN 0-907339-02-6 (pbk) : £0.50 B81-22803

936.2′843 — North Yorkshire. York. Antiquities. Archaeological investigation

The **Archaeology** of York / [general editor P.V. Addyman]. — London : Published for the York Archaeological Trust by the Council for British Archaeology
Vol.14: The past environment of York. — 1980
Fasc.3: Environmental evidence from Roman deposits in Skeldergate / by A.R. Hall, H.K. Kenward and D. Williams with contributions by J. Allison ... [et al.]. — [2]p,p101-156 : ill,plans ; 25cm
English text, English, French and German summarics. — Bibliography: p155-156
ISBN 0-900312-56-4 (pbk) : Unpriced
B81-16026

The **Archaeology** of York. — London : Council for British Archaeology
Vol.17: The small finds
Fasc.3: Anglo-Scandinavian finds from Lloyds Bank, Pavement, and other sites. — Nov.1981. — [108]p
ISBN 0-906780-02-0 (pbk) : £4.20 : CIP entry
B81-35021

936.2′843 — North Yorkshire. York. Antiquities. Sites

Royal Commission on Historical Monuments (England). An inventory of the historical monuments in the City of York / Royal Commission on Historical Monuments, England. — London : H.M.S.O.. — xcviii,282p,[201]p of plates : ill(some col.),8col.maps,plans ; 28cm
ISBN 0-11-700992-x : £55.00
ISBN 0-11-700892-3 (red binding) B81-39868

936.2′857′005 — Cleveland. Hartlepool *(District).* **Antiquities. Archaeological investigation** — *Serials*

Heruteu : magazine of Hartlepool Archaeological and Historical Society. — Issue no.1-. — [Peterlee] ([c/o Mr E. Smith, 6 Girton Close, Peterlee, Co. Durham]) : The Society, [1980]-. — v. ; 30cm
Annual
ISSN 0261-801x = Heruteu : Unpriced
B81-33725

936.2′88 — Northumberland. National parks: Northumberland National Park. Antiquities. Sites — *For environment planning*

Archaeological sites and buildings in the Northumberland National Park. — Newcastle upon Tyne ([c/o] National Park Officer, Bede House, All Saints Centre, Newcastle upon Tyne) : [Northumberland National Park and Countryside Committee], 1976. — 14,xxivp : maps ; 30cm. — (Working paper / Northumberland National Park ; 8)
Bibliography: p14
Unpriced (spiral) B81-29615

936.2′881 — Northumberland. Corbridge, Chesterholm & Greenhead. Ancient Roman settlements

Graham, Frank, *1913-*. The Stanegate : Corbridge, Vindolanda and Carvoran in the days of the Romans / by Frank Graham ; illustrated by Ronald Embleton. — Newcastle upon Tyne : F. Graham, c1981. — 32p : ill (some col.),maps,plans ; 24cm
ISBN 0-85983-181-7 (pbk) : £1.00
Primary classification 388.1′09362′7 B81-21264

936.2′88104 — Northern England. Ancient Roman fortifications: Hadrian′s Wall, *to 1976*

Forde-Johnston, James. Hadrian′s wall / James Forde-Johnstone. — London : Book Club Associates, 1977. — 205p : ill(some col.),maps,plans,ports ; 26cm
Bibliography: p203. — Includes index
Unpriced B81-39171

936.2′901 — Cardiff. Museums: National Museum of Wales. Stock: Bronze Age Welsh artefacts — *Catalogues*

National Museum of Wales. Guide catalogue of the Bronze Age collections / [National Museum of Wales] ; by H.N. Savory. — Cardiff : National Museum of Wales, 1980. — 258p,x leaves of plates : ill(some col.),maps,1plan ; 25cm
Bibliography: p221-228. - Includes index
ISBN 0-7200-0219-2 (pbk) : £7.00 B81-04782

936.2′93′005 — Clwyd. Antiquities. Excavation of remains — *Serials*

Archaeology in Clwyd. — 1980. — Mold (c/o County Planner and Estates Officer, Shire Hall, Mold, Clwyd) : Clwyd County Council, [1981]. — 15p
Unpriced B81-33302

936.2′989 — South Glamorgan. Barry. Ancient Roman agricultural industries. Farms. Buildings. Excavation of remains, *1965-1970*

Jarrett, Michael G.. Whitton : an Iron Age and Roman farmstead in South Glamorgan / Michael G. Jarrett and Stuart Wrathmell. — Cardiff : Published on behalf of the Board of Celtic Studies of the University of Wales [by] University of Wales Press, 1981. — xiii,262p,[21]p of plates, 10 folded leaves of plates : ill(some col.),maps,plans ; 30cm
Bibliography: p255-262
ISBN 0-7083-0765-5 : Unpriced : CIP rev.
B80-22724

936.3 — Southern Poland. Neolithic settlements

Kruk, Janusz. The Neolithic settlement of southern Poland / Janusz Kruk ; edited by J.M. Howell and N.J. Starling ; translated by M. Hejwowska. — Oxford : B.A.R., 1980. — 129p : ill,maps ; 30cm. — (BAR. International series ; 93)
Translated from the Polish. — Bibliography: p112-129
ISBN 0-86054-107-x (pbk) : £6.00 B81-36622

936.4 — France. Berry. Bituriges Cubi human settlements, *to ca 500.* **Archaeological investigation**

Leday, Alain. La campagne à l′époque romaine dans le Centre de la Gaule : villas, vici et sanctuaires dans la Cité de Bituriges Cubi = Rural settlement in Central Gaul in the Roman period : villas, vici and sanctuaries in the civitas of the Bituriges Cubi / Alain Leday. — Oxford : B.A.R., 1980. — 2v.(435p,lxxxviiip of plates) : ill,maps,plans ; 30cm. — (BAR. International series, ISSN 0143-3067 ; 73)
French text and English translation. — Bibliography: p433-435
ISBN 0-86054-081-2 (pbk) : £15.00 B81-16548

936.4 — France. Frénouville. Necropolises. Antiquities. Excavation of remains, *1970-1972* — *French texts*

Pilet, Christian. La nécropole de Frénouville : étude d′une population de la fin du IIIe à la fin du VIIe siècle / Christian Pilet. — Oxford : B.A.R., 1980. — 3v. : ill,maps ; 30cm. — (BAR. International series ; 83)
ISBN 0-86054-096-0 (pbk) : £23.00 B81-36616

936.4 — France. Lyons region. Antiquities, *to 700.* **Archaeological investigation** — *French texts*

Récentes recherches en archéologie galloromaine et paléochrétienne sur Lyon et sa région / volume sous la direction de Stephen Walker. — Oxford : B.A.R., 1981. — 339p : ill,maps,plans ; 30cm. — (BAR. International series ; 108)
French text, English summaries. — Includes bibliographies
ISBN 0-86054-126-6 (pbk) : £12.00 B81-36620

936.4 — Switzerland. Lakes. Residences. Archaeological investigation

Harding, A. F.. The lake dwellings of Switzerland : retrospect and prospect / by A.F. Harding. — [Edinburgh] ([Old College, South Bridge, Edinburgh EH1]) : University of Edinburgh, Department of Archaeology, 1980. — 16p : 1map ; 30cm. — (Occasional paper / University of Edinburgh Department of Archaeology, ISSN 0144-3313 ; no.5)
Bibliography: p14-16
Unpriced (pbk) B81-09419

936.4′0074′02142 — London. Camden *(London Borough).* **Museums: British Museum. Exhibits: Celtic antiquities from France** — *Catalogues*

Stead, Ian. The Gauls. — London : British Museum Publications Ltd, May 1981. — [80]p
ISBN 0-7141-2008-1 (pbk) : £3.95 : CIP entry
B81-07429

936.4′01 — France. Magdalenian antiquities

Hemingway, M. F.. The initial Magdalenian in France / M.F. Hemingway. — Oxford : B.A.R., 1980. — 2v.(502p(2fold.)) : ill,maps ; 30cm. — (BAR. International series ; 90)
Bibliography: p477-502
ISBN 0-86054-104-5 (pbk) : £17.00 B81-36612

937 — ANCIENT HISTORY. ROME

937 — Ancient Roman civilization — *For children*

Romans / consultant editor Henry Pluckrose ; illustrated by Ivan Lapper. — London : Hamilton, 1981. — 28p : col.ill,1col.map,col.ports ; 21cm. — (Small world)
Includes index
ISBN 0-241-10628-1 : £2.50 B81-28742

937 — Ancient Roman civilization — *For schools*

Yamauchi, Edwin M.. The Roman Empire / Edwin Yamauchi. — Tring : Lion Publishing, 1981. — p65-96 : ill(some col.),col.maps,ports ; 25cm. — (The World of the first Christians ; 3)
Cover title
ISBN 0-85648-269-2 (pbk) : £1.25 B81-16681

937 — Ancient Rome. Frontiers — *Conference proceedings*

International Congress of Roman Frontier Studies *(12th : 1979 : University of Stirling).* Roman frontier studies 1979 : papers presented to the 12th International Congress of Roman Frontier Studies / edited by W.S. Hanson and L.J.F. Keppie. — Oxford : B.A.R., 1980. — 3v.(1111p) : ill,maps,plans ; 30cm. — (BAR. International series, ISSN 0143-3067 ; 71)
Includes chapters in French and German. — Includes bibliographies
ISBN 0-86054-080-4 (pbk) : £28.00 B81-16552

937 — Ancient Rome. Social life — *For children*

Feyel, Gilles. Times of the Romans / Gilles Feyel ; [translated from the French by Yvonne Messenger] ; [illustrated by Yves Beaujard]. — St.Albans : Hart-Davis, 1981. — 60p : ill(some col.),2col.maps,1col.plan ; 27cm. — (Signposts series)
Translation of: Au temps des Romains
ISBN 0-247-13036-2 : £3.50 B81-11568

937 — Ancient Rome. Social life — *For schools*

Jamieson, Jean M.. The Romans / Jean M. Jamieson ; drawings by Philip Page. — London : Edward Arnold, 1981. — 48p : ill,maps ; 20x26cm
Includes index
ISBN 0-7131-0505-4 (pbk) : £1.95 B81-25394

Yamauchi, Edwin M.. Roman life and beliefs / Edwin Yamauchi. — Tring : Lion Publishing, 1981. — p97-128 : ill(some col.),col.maps ; 25cm. — (The World of the first Christians ; 4)
Cover title
ISBN 0-85648-270-6 (pbk) : £1.25 B81-16680

937 — Italy. Antiquities. Excavation of remains

Lancaster in Italy and North Africa : archaeological research undertaken by the Dept. of Classics & Archaeology in 1980. — [Lancaster] : University of Lancaster, 1981. — 25p : ill,plans ; 30cm
Includes bibliographies
ISBN 0-901699-74-8 (pbk) : Unpriced
Also classified at 939′.73 B81-29457

937′.0072 — Ancient Roman antiquities. Archaeological investigation, *to 1980*

Todd, Malcolm, *1939-*. The rediscovery of the Roman Empire : an inaugural lecture delivered in the University of Exeter on 21 November 1980 / Malcolm Todd. — [Exeter] : University of Exeter, 1981. — 16p ; 21cm
ISBN 0-85989-192-5 (pbk) : £0.60 B81-25570

937′.0072024 — Ancient Rome. Historiography. Gibbon, Edward — *Critical studies*

Bennett, J. A. W.. Essays on Gibbon / by J.A.W. Bennett. — Cambridge (Magdalene College, Cambridge) : J.A.W. Bennett, 1980. — 85p : 1coat of arms ; 21cm
Unpriced (pbk) B81-08654

937′.0072024 — Ancient Rome. Historiography. Tacitus, Cornelius — *Critical studies*

Martin, Ronald. Tacitus / Ronald Martin. — London : Batsford Academic and Educational, 1981. — 238p ; 23cm
Bibliography: p269-277. — Includes index
ISBN 0-7134-2722-1 (corrected) : £14.95 B81-24970

937′.01 — Central Italian civilization, *to ca B.C.1000.* **Archaeological sources**

Barker, Graeme. Landscape and society : prehistoric Central Italy / Graeme Barker. — London : Academic Press, 1981. — xiv,281p : ill,maps ; 24cm. — (Studies in archaeology)
Bibliography: p238-263. — Includes index
ISBN 0-12-078650-8 : £13.80 B81-35423

937′.04 — Ancient Rome, *B.C.195-B.C.189.* **Livy. Ab urbe condita. Books 34-37** — *Commentaries*

Briscoe, John. A commentary on Livy, books xxxiv-xxxvii / by John Briscoe. — Oxford : Clarendon Press, 1981. — xx,442p : maps ; 23cm
Includes index
ISBN 0-19-814455-5 : £25.00 B81-18304

937′.04 — Punic War, *2nd.* **Military operations. Role of Hannibal**

Bath, Tony. Hannibal′s campaigns : the story of one of the greatest military commanders of all time / Tony Bath. — Cambridge : Stephens, 1981. — 144p : ill,maps ; 24cm
Bibliography: p144
ISBN 0-85059-492-8 : £7.50 : CIP rev. B81-14829

937′.05′0924 — Ancient Rome. Brutus, Marcus Junius — *Biographies*

Clarke, M. L.. The noblest Roman : Marcus Brutus and his reputation / M.L. Clarke. — London : Thames and Hudson, c1981. — 157p : 1geneal.table ; 23cm. — (Aspects of Greek and Roman life)
Includes index
ISBN 0-500-40040-7 : £10.00 B81-08296

937′.05′0924 — Ancient Rome. Pompey, *the Great, B.C.58-B.C.48* — *Biographies*

Greenhalgh, Peter, *1945-*. Pompey : the Republican prince / Peter Greenhalgh. — London : Weidenfeld and Nicolson, c1981. — xv,320p,[4]p of plates : ill,maps,ports ; 24cm
Bibliography: p304-309. - Includes index
ISBN 0-297-77881-1 : £18.50 B81-05465

937′.06 — Ancient Rome. Historiography. Gibbon, Edward. Decline and fall of the Roman Empire — *Critical studies*

Gossman, Lionel. The empire unpossess′d : an essay on Gibbon′s Decline and fall / Lionel Gossman. — Cambridge : Cambridge University Press, 1981. — xvi,160p : 1ill ; 24cm
Includes index
ISBN 0-521-23453-0 : £15.00 B81-26196

937′.07 — Ancient Rome, *14-284*

Millar, Fergus. The Roman Empire and its neighbours / Fergus Millar ; with contributions by Richard N. Frye ... [et al.]. — 2nd ed. — London : Duckworth, 1981, c1967. — xi,370p,[16]p of plates : ill,maps,facsims,plans ; 23cm
Translation of: Das Römische Reich und seine Nachbarn. — Previous ed.: London : Weidenfeld & Nicolson, 1967. — Bibliography: p337-353. — Includes index
ISBN 0-7156-1452-5 (cased) : £24.00 B81-28974

937′.07 — Ancient Rome, *B.C.44-A.D.14*

Rome, the Augustan age. — Oxford : Oxford University Press, Nov.1981. — [800]p
ISBN 0-19-872108-0 (cased) : £28.00 : CIP entry
ISBN 0-19-872109-9 (pbk) : £13.00 B81-30218

937′.07 — Ancient Rome. Political events, *14-37* — *Latin texts — Texts with commentaries*

Tacitus, Cornelius. [Annales]. The annals of Tacitus, Books 1-6 / edited with a commentary by F.R.D. Goodyear. — Cambridge : Cambridge University Press. — (Cambridge classical texts and commentaries ; 23)
Vol.1: Annals 1.55-81 and Annals 2. — 1981. — viii,490p ; 23cm
Latin text, English commentary. — Bibliography: p461-472. — Includes index
ISBN 0-521-20213-2 : £30.00 : CIP rev. B81-20639

937′.07 — Ancient Rome. Political events, *69* — *Latin texts — For schools*

Tacitus, Cornelius. [Histories. Books 1-2]. Tacitus ; Histories books I & II / edited by A.L. Irvine. — Letchworth : Bradda, 1981. — v,196p : 2maps,1plan ; 20cm
Latin text, introduction and notes in English. — Originally published: London : Methuen, 1952. — Includes index
£3.50 (pbk) B81-32613

937′.07′0924 — Ancient Rome. Fronto, Marcus Cornelius — *Biographies*

Champlin, Edward. Fronto and Antonine Rome / Edward Champlin. — Cambridge, Mass. ; London : Harvard University Press, 1980. — 185p ; 24cm
Includes index
ISBN 0-674-32668-7 : £8.40 B81-05453

937′.5 — Etruscan civilization, *ca B.C.1600-ca A.D.480*

Ridgway, David. The Etruscans / by David Ridgway. — Edinburgh (19 George Sq., Edinburgh, EH8 9JZ) : University of Edinburgh Department of Archaeology, 1981. — vii,45p : 2maps ; 30cm. — (Occasional paper / University of Edinburgh Department of Archaeology, ISSN 0144-3313 (corrected) ; no.6)
Bibliography: p37-45
Unpriced (pbk) B81-11323

937′.5 — Italy. Etruscan antiquities — *Personal observations*

Lawrence, D. H.. Mornings in Mexico ; and Etruscan places / D.H. Lawrence. — Harmondsworth : Penguin in assocation with William Heinemann, 1960 (1981 [printing]). — 214p,[16]p of plates : ill ; 18cm
Mornings in Mexico originally published: London : Martin Secker, 1927
ISBN 0-14-001513-2 (pbk) : £1.75
Primary classification 917.2′04822′0924 B81-27652

938 — ANCIENT HISTORY. GREECE

938 — Ancient Greece, *B.C. 478-B.C. 404*

Quinn, T. J.. Athens and Samos, Lesbos and Chios 478-404 B.C.. — Manchester : Manchester University Press, Nov.1981. — [96] p. — (Publications of the Faculty of Arts of the University of Manchester ; no.27)
ISBN 0-7190-1297-x : £10.00 : CIP entry B81-40274

938 — Ancient Greece, *B.C.350-B.C.100*

Walbank, F. W.. The Hellenistic world. — Brighton : Harvester Press, June 1981. — [288] p. — (Fontana history of the ancient world)
ISBN 0-7108-0310-9 : £18.95 : CIP entry B81-12807

938 — Ancient Greek civilization

Levi, Peter. Atlas of the Greek world / by Peter Levi. — Oxford : Phaidon, c1980. — 239p : ill (some col.),maps(some col.),plans(some col.),ports(some col.) ; 31cm
Maps on lining papers. — Bibliography: p227-228. - Includes index
ISBN 0-7148-2044-x : £15.00 : CIP rev. B80-23848

Porter, Eliot. The Greek world / [photographs by] Eliot Porter ; text by Peter Levi. — London : Aurum, 1981. — 144p : col.ill,2maps ; 31cm
ISBN 0-906053-24-2 : £15.00 B81-13057

938 — Ancient Greek civilization, *B.C.336-B.C.130*

Walbank, F. W.. The hellenistic world / F.W. Walbank. — [London] : Fontana Paperbacks, 1981. — 287p,[8]p of plates : ill,maps,ports ; 19cm. — (Fontana history of the ancient world)
Bibliography: p266-275. - Includes index
ISBN 0-00-635365-7 (pbk) : £2.95 B81-19345

Walbank, F. W.. The Hellenistic world / F.W. Walbank. — Brighton : Harvester Press in associaiton with Fontana, 1981. — 287p,[8]p of plates : ill,4maps ; 23cm. — (Fontana history of the ancient world)
Bibliography: p266-275. — Includes index
ISBN 0-391-02302-0 : £18.95 B81-29200

938 — Ancient Greek civilization, *ca B.C.500- ca B.C.300*

Dover, K. J.. The Greeks / Kenneth Dover ; from the BBC television series by Christopher Burstall and Kenneth Dover. — London : British Broadcasting Corporation, 1980. — xiii,146p,[12]p of plates : ill(some col.),maps ; 24cm
Maps on lining papers. — Includes index
ISBN 0-563-17805-1 : £7.95 B81-37808

938 — Ancient Greek civilization — *For children*

Ancient Greeks / consultant editor Henry Pluckrose ; illustrated by Ivan Lapper and John Flynn. — London : Hamilton, 1981. — 28p : col.ill,col.ports ; 21cm. — (Small world)
Includes index
ISBN 0-241-10629-x : £2.50 B81-28743

938 — Ancient Greek civilization, *to B.C.100 — For schools*

Amos, H. D.. These were the Greeks / H.D. Amos and A.G.P. Lang. — Amersham : Hulton, 1979. — 224p : ill,maps,plans,ports ; 25cm
Bibliography: p222-223. - Includes index
ISBN 0-7175-0789-0 (pbk) : £2.95 B81-05774

938 — Ancient Greek civilization, *to B.C.323 — For schools*

Jamieson, Jean M.. The ancient Greeks / Jean M. Jamieson ; drawings by Philip Page. — London : Edward Arnold, 1981. — 48p : ill,maps,ports ; 20x26cm
Includes index
ISBN 0-7131-0504-6 (pbk) : £1.95 B81-31869

938 — Ancient Greek civilization, *to ca B.C.500*

Finley, M. I.. Early Greece : the bronze and archaic ages / M.I. Finley. — New and rev. ed. — London : Chatto & Windus, 1981. — xiii,149p,ivp of plates : ill,maps,1plan ; 21cm. — (Ancient culture and society)
Previous ed.: 1970. — Bibliography: p142-146. — Includes index
ISBN 0-7011-2589-6 (cased) : £6.95
ISBN 0-7011-2545-4 (pbk) : £3.95 B81-17718

938 — Classical civilization

Lloyd-Jones, Hugh. Discipline and imagination : the classics in the modern world. — London : Duckworth, Feb.1982. — [184]p
ISBN 0-7156-1517-3 : £18.00 : CIP entry B81-36224

938 — Ionian culture, *to ca B.C.500*

Emlyn-Jones, C. J.. The Ionians and Hellenism : a study of the cultural achievement of the early Greek inhabitants of Asia Minor / C.J. Emlyn-Jones. — London : Routledge & Kegan Paul, 1980. — x,237p,[16]p of plates : ill,1map ; 23cm. — (States and cities of Ancient Greece)
Bibliography: p217-227. — Includes index
ISBN 0-7100-0470-2 : £10.50 : CIP rev. B80-22728

938′.005 — Classical civilization — *For schools — Serials*

[Omnibus *(London)*]. Omnibus. — 1st issue-. — London (31 Gordon Sq., WC1H 0PY) : J.A.C.T., 1981-. — v. : ill ; 30cm
ISSN 0261-507x = Omnibus (London) : Unpriced B81-29080

938′.007 — Classical studies, *to ca 1920*

Wilamowitz-Moellendorff, Ulrich von. History of classical scholarship. — London : Duckworth, Feb.1982. — [224]p
Translation of: Geschichte der Philologie
ISBN 0-7156-0976-9 : £18.00 : CIP entry B81-36975

938′.0072024 — Ancient Greece. Historiography. Herodotus — *Critical studies*

Hart, John. Herodotus and Greek history. — London : Croom Helm, Feb.1982. — [208]p
ISBN 0-7099-1224-2 : £14.95 : CIP entry B81-37558

938′.0072024 — Classical studies. Raven, J. E. — *Personal observations — Collections*

John Raven / by his friends ; edited by John Lipscomb and R.W. David. — Royston (Docwra′s Manor, Shepreth, Royston, Herts.) : Faith Raven, c1981. — x,96p : 1ill,1geneal.table,ports ; 23cm
ISBN 0-9507345-0-0 : Unpriced B81-19607

938′.01 — Ancient Greek civilization. Origins

Oliva, Pavel. The birth of Greek civilization / Pavel Oliva ; [translated by Iris Urwin Levitová]. — London : Orbis Publishing, 1981. — 200p : ill,maps ; 25cm
Translation from the Czech. — Bibliography: p188-193. — Includes index
ISBN 0-85613-321-3 : £7.95 B81-31143

938′.05 — Peloponnesian War. Historiography. Thucydides. History of the Peloponnesian War — *Critical studies*

Gomme, A. W.. A historical commentary on Thucydides / by A.W. Gomme, A. Andrewes and K.J. Dover. — Oxford : Clarendon Press
Vol.V: Bk.VIII. — 1981. — xv,502p : maps ; 23cm
Includes index
ISBN 0-19-814198-x : £25.00 : CIP rev. B80-07164

Pouncey, Peter R.. The necessities of war : a study of Thucydides′ pessimism / Peter R. Pouncey. — New York ; Guildford : Columbia University Press, 1980. — xv,195p ; 24cm
Bibliography: p187-190. - Includes index
ISBN 0-231-04994-3 : £10.80 B81-05211

Proctor, Dennis. The experience of Thucydides / Dennis Proctor. — Warminster : Aris & Phillips, c1980. — viii,264p ; 22cm
Bibliography: p226-231. — Includes index
ISBN 0-85668-153-9 : £12.00 : CIP rev. B80-06732

Rawlings, Hunter R. The structure of Thucydides′ History / Hunter R. Rawlings III. — Princeton ; Guildford : Princeton University Press, c1981. — xiv,278p ; 23cm
Bibliography: pxiii-xiv. — Includes index
ISBN 0-691-03555-5 : £14.80 B81-40275

938′.06 — Ancient Greece. Political events, *B.C.371-B.C.362*

Buckler, John. The Theban hegemony 371-362 B.C. / John Buckler. — Cambridge, Mass. ; London : Harvard University Press, 1980. — x,339p : ill,maps ; 15cm. — (Harvard historical studies ; v.98)
Bibliography: p325-333. - Includes index
ISBN 0-674-87645-8 : £15.00 B81-06234

938′.06 — Ancient Greece. Second Athenian League, *B.C. 378-B.C. 338*

Cargill, Jack. The Second Athenian League : empire or free alliance? / Jack Cargill. — Berkeley [Calif.] ; London : University of California Press, c1981. — xvii,215p : 1ill ; 25cm
Texts in Greek. — Includes index
ISBN 0-520-04069-4 : £17.25 B81-39773

938′.07 — Ancient Greece, *B.C.362-B.C.146 — Readings from contemporary sources*

The **Hellenistic** world from Alexander to the Roman conquest. — Cambridge : Cambridge University Press, Nov.1981. — [506]p
ISBN 0-521-22829-8 (cased) : £30.00 : CIP entry
ISBN 0-521-29666-8 (pbk) : £9.95 B81-31262

938′.07 — Military campaigns by Ancient Macedonian military forces, *B.C.336-B.C.323 — For war games*

Barker, Phil. Alexander the Great′s campaigns : a guide to Ancient political and military wargaming / Phil Barker. — Cambridge : Stephens, 1979 (1981 [printing]). — 160p : ill,maps,plans ; 24cm
Bibliography: p159-160
ISBN 0-85059-553-3 (pbk) : £3.95 B81-32617

938′.07′0924 — Ancient Macedonia. Alexander III, *King of Macedonia — Biographies*

Hammond, N. G. L.. Alexander the Great : King, commander and statesman / by N.G.L. Hammond. — London : Chatto & Windus, 1981. — x,358p : ill,maps,plans,ports ; 25cm
Map on lining papers. — Bibliography: p335-339. — Includes index
ISBN 0-7011-2565-9 : £14.95 B81-18229

938′.107′0924 — Ancient Macedonia. Philip II, *King of Macedonia — Biographies*

Philip of Macedon / edited by Miltiades B. Hatzopoulos, Louisa D. Loukopoulos. — London : Heinemann, 1981. — 254p : ill(some col.),col.maps,1facsim,1geneal.table ; 28cm
Originally published: Athens : Ekdotike Athenon, 1980. — Ill on lining papers. — Bibliography: p235. — Includes index
ISBN 0-435-36340-9 : £21.00 B81-28430

938′.4 — Ancient Megara, *to B.C.336*

Legon, Ronald P.. Megara : the political history of a Greek city-state to 336 B.C. / Ronald P. Legon. — Ithaca ; London : Cornell University Press, 1981. — 324p : ill,maps ; 24cm
Bibliography: p305-312. — Includes index
ISBN 0-8014-1370-2 : £15.00 B81-36567

938′.5 — Ancient Athenian civilization, *B.C.478-B.C.336 — Readings from contemporary sources*

Political and social life in the great age of Athens : a source book / edited by John Ferguson and Kitty Chisholm. — London : Ward Lock Educational in association with the Open University, 1978. — xxii,248p,[8]p of plates : ill ; 24cm
Includes index
ISBN 0-7062-3641-6 (cased) : £7.00
ISBN 0-7062-3628-9 (pbk £2.25) B81-05761

938′.5 — Greece. Athens. Acropolis. Ancient Greek temples: Parthenon, *to 1980*

Woodford, Susan. The Parthenon / Susan Woodford. — Cambridge : Cambridge University Press, 1981. — 48p : ill,1map,plans,1port ; 21x22cm. — (Cambridge introduction to the history of mankind. topic books)
ISBN 0-521-22629-5 (pbk) : £1.80 B81-27005

938′.503′0924 — Athenian Empire. Themistocles. Biographies: Plutarch. Lives. Themistocles — *Commentaries*

Frost, Frank J.. Plutarch′s Themistocles : a historical commentary / Frank J. Frost. — Princeton ; Guildford : Princeton University Press, c1980. — xiii,252p : 2maps,1geneal.table ; 23cm
Bibliography: p241-246. - Includes index
ISBN 0-691-05300-6 : £9.70 B81-03951

938′.8 — Greece. Sikyon. Ancient Greek antiquities. Excavation of remains

Griffin, Audrey. Sikyon. — Oxford : Oxford University Press, Nov.1981. — [288]p. — (Oxford classical and philosophical monographs)
ISBN 0-19-814718-x : £15.00 : CIP entry B81-33651

939.1 — ANCIENT HISTORY. AEGEAN ISLANDS

939′.18 — Greece. Crete. Knossos. Antiquities

Hood, Sinclair. Archaeological survey of the Knossos area / Sinclair Hood and David Smyth with a section on the physical environment of the Knossos area by Neil Roberts. — 2nd ed, rev. and expanded. — [London] : British School at Athens, 1981. — x,69p,[4]p of plates : ill,col.maps ; 30cm + 1map(col ; on sheet 108x88cm). — (Supplementary volume / British School at Athens ; no.14)
Previous ed.: 1958. — In slip case. — Includes index
ISBN 0-500-96015-1 (pbk) : £19.00 B81-20840

939′.18 — Greece. Crete. Knossos. Minoan palaces: Palace of Minos. Archaeological investigation, *1878-1978*

Hood, Sinclair. The Bronze Age palace at Knossos : plan and sections / Sinclair Hood and William Taylor. — [London] : British School at Athens, 1981. — xiv,34p,4[p] of plates : ill ; 30cm + 2folded sheets(plans ; 87x105cm). — (Supplementary volume / British School at Athens ; no.13)
In slip case. — Bibliography: pxi-xiv.. — Includes index
ISBN 0-500-96016-x (pbk) : £14.00 B81-20841

939′.18 — Minoan civilization

Cotterell, Arthur. The Minoan world / Arthur Cotterell. — London : Book Club Associates, 1979. — 191p : ill(some col.),maps,plans,ports ; 26cm
Bibliography: p187. — Includes index
Unpriced B81-39162

939.2 — ANCIENT HISTORY. ASIA MINOR

939′.2 — Hittite civilization

Gurney, O. R.. The Hittites / O.R. Gurney. — 2nd ed., Repr. with revisions. — Harmondsworth : Penguin, 1981. — 242p,32p of plates : ill,1map ; 18cm
Previous ed.: 1952. — Bibliography: p220-233. - Includes index
ISBN 0-14-020259-5 (pbk) : £2.50 B81-20663

939′.21 — Turkey. Attalid Kingdom, *ca.B.C.241-B.C.133*

Allen, R. E.. The Attalid Kingdom. — Oxford : Clarendon Press, Sept.1981. — [288]p
ISBN 0-19-814845-3 : £15.00 : CIP entry B81-23750

939′.24 — Turkey. Caria. Hellenization. Role of Mausolus, *B.C.377-B.C.352*

Hornblower, Simon. Mausolus. — Oxford : Clarendon, Feb.1982. — [384]p
ISBN 0-19-814844-5 : £20.00 : CIP entry B81-35804

939′.34 — Turkey. Aşvan Kale. Antiquities. Excavation of remains

Mitchell, Stephen, *1948-*. Aşvan Kale : Keban rescue excavations, Eastern Anatolia / Stephen Mitchell. — Oxford : B.A.R.
1: The Hellenistic, Roman and Islamic sites. — 1980. — 264p,[11]p of plates : ill,maps,plans ; 30cm. — (Monograph / British Institute of Archaeology at Ankara ; no.1) (BAR. International series ; 80)
Bibliography: p261-264
ISBN 0-86054-091-x (pbk) : £14.00 B81-36583

939′.34 — Turkey. Deve Hüyük. Cemeteries. Antiquities, *B.C.1000-B.C.1*

Moorey, P. R. S.. Cemeteries of the first millennium B.C., at Deve Hüyük, near Carchemish, salvaged by T.E. Lawrence and C.L. Wooley in 1913 : (with a catalogue raisonné of the objects in Berlin, Cambridge, Liverpool, London and Oxford) / P.R.S. Moorey. — Oxford : B.A.R., 1980. — ix,183p : ill,1map ; 30cm. — (BAR. International series ; 87)
Bibliography: p164-183
ISBN 0-86054-101-0 (pbk) : £8.00 B81-36582

939.37 — ANCIENT HISTORY. CYPRUS

939′.37 — Cyprus. Copper Age civilization. Archaeological sources — *Conference proceedings*

Chalcolithic Cyprus and Western Asia / edited by Julian Reade. — London : British Museum, 1981. — 74p : ill,maps,plans ; 30cm. — (Occasional paper / British Museum, ISSN 0142-4815 ; no.26)
Conference papers. — Bibliography: p69-74
ISBN 0-86159-026-0 (pbk) : Unpriced B81-21821

939′.37′007402496 — West Midlands *(Metropolitan County)*. **Birmingham. Art galleries: Birmingham Museums & Art Gallery. Exhibits: Ancient Cypriot antiquities,** *to ca 350 — Catalogues*

Birmingham Museums & Art Gallery. A catalogue of Cypriot antiquities in Birmingham Museum and Art Gallery / [catalogue by Edgar Peltenburg]. — [Birmingham] ([Chamberlain Sq., Birmingham B3 3DH]) : Birmingham Museum and Art Gallery, 1981. — 84p : ill,1map ; 20cm
Bibliography; p79-80
ISBN 0-7093-0064-6 (pbk) : Unpriced B81-37372

939.4 — ANCIENT HISTORY. SYRIA AND ARABIA

939′.4 — Syria. Jerablus. Tells: Carchemish. Excavation of remains, *1912-1977*

. Carchemish : report on the excavations at Jerablus on behalf of the British Museum conducted by D.G. Hogarth, R. Campbell Thompson and C. Leonard Woolley with T.E. Lawrence, P.L.O. Guy, and H. Reitlinger. — London : Published for the Trustees of the British Museum by British Museum Publications
Pt.3: The excavations in the inner town / by Sir Leonard Woolley. And, The Hittite inscriptions / by R.D. Barnett. — 1952, c1978 (1978 [printing]). — p158-290,[164]p of plates : ill,plans ; 33cm
Originally published: London : British Museum, 1952. — Includes index
ISBN 0-7141-1003-5 : £35.00 B81-39031

939′.4 — Syria. River Qoueiq valley. Antiquities. Archaeological investigation

The **River** Qoueiq, Northern Syria, and its catchment : studies arising from the Tell Rifa′t Survey 1977-79 / general editor John Matthers ; contributors Dominique Collon ... [et al.]. — Oxford : B.A.R., 1981. — 2v.(510p) : ill,maps,plans ; 30cm. — (BAR. International series ; 98)
Includes bibliographies
ISBN 0-86054-117-7 (pbk) : £23.00 B81-36617

939′.4004924 — Ancient Middle East. Jews, *to 66 — Early works*

Josephus, Flavius. Works / Josephus. — Cambridge, Mass. : Harvard University Press ; London : Heinemann. — (The Loeb classical library ; 456)
10: Jewish antiquities, Book 20 ; General index to volumes 1-10 / with an English translation by Louis H. Feldman. — 1981, c1965. — xi,382p,[3]folded leaves of plates : 3maps ; 18cm
Translation of: Ioudaikēs archaiologias. — Parallel Greek text and English translation. — This translation originally published: as part of vol.9 1965. — Bibliography: p156-157
ISBN 0-434-99456-1 : £5.00 B81-35365

939′.4′0072024 — Ancient Middle Eastern civilization. Theories of Velikovsky, Immanuel — *Serials*

[Workshop *(Society for Interdisciplinary Studies)*] . Workshop : members newsletter / Society for Interdisciplinary Studies. — Issue no.1 (Mar.1978)-. — Orpington (c/o D. Shelley-Pearce, 29 Cudham Lane North, Orpington, Kent BR6 6BX) : The Society, c1978-. — v. ; 30cm
Irregular. — Description based on: Issue no.4 (Feb.1979)
ISSN 0260-2806 = Workshop - Society for Interdisciplinary Studies : Unpriced B81-03274

939′.44 — Lebanon. Baalbek. Antiquities

Ragette, Friedrich. Baalbek / by Friedrich Ragette ; with an introduction by Sir Mortimer Wheeler. — London : Chatto & Windus, 1980. — 128p : ill,maps,plans ; 26cm
Plans on lining papers. — Bibliography: p125. - Includes index
ISBN 0-7011-2146-7 : £9.50 : CIP rev. B80-22730

939′.44 — Phoenician civilization

Harden, D. B.. The Phoenicians / Donald Harden. — Repr. with revisions and extended bibliography. — Harmondsworth : Penguin, 1980, c1971. — 317p,[48]p of plates : ill,maps,facsims,plans,1geneal.table ; 20cm. — (A Pelican book)
Originally published: London : Thames & Hudson, 1962. — Bibliography: p251-276. — Includes index
ISBN 0-14-021375-9 (pbk) : £3.25 B81-03609

939.5 — ANCIENT HISTORY. BLACK SEA AND CAUCASUS REGIONS

939′.55 — Urartian civilization, *to B.C.600*

Frankel, David. The ancient kingdom of Urartu / David Frankel. — London : British Museum Publications, c1979. — 32p : ill,1map ; 24cm
Cover title. — Ill on inside cover. — Bibliography: p32
ISBN 0-7141-1100-7 (pbk) : Unpriced B81-08121

939.6 — ANCIENT HISTORY. CENTRAL ASIA

939′.600481 — Central Asia. Indo-Greeks, *ca B.C.250-ca B.C.50*

Narain, A. K.. The Indo-Greeks / A.K. Narain. — Delhi ; Oxford : Oxford University Press, 1980. — x,201p,[16]p of plates : ill,maps,1geneal.table ; 23cm
Originally published: Oxford : Clarendon Press, 1957. — Bibliography: p182-190. - Includes index
ISBN 0-19-561046-6 : Unpriced B81-14281

939.7 — ANCIENT HISTORY. NORTH AFRICA

939′.7 — North African culture, *B.C. 146-A.D. 640*

MacKendrick, Paul. The North African stones speak / Paul MacKendrick. — London : Croom Helm, c1980. — xxi,434p : ill,maps,plans ; 24cm
Bibliography: p334-409. - Includes index
ISBN 0-7099-0394-4 : £10.95 : CIP rev. B80-06733

939′.73 — Tunisia. Carthage. Antiquities. Excavation of remains

Lancaster in Italy and North Africa : archaeological research undertaken by the Dept. of Classics & Archaeology in 1980. — [Lancaster] : University of Lancaster, 1981. — 25p : ill,plans ; 30cm
Includes bibliographies
ISBN 0-901699-74-8 (pbk) : Unpriced
Primary classification 937 B81-29457

939.8 — ANCIENT HISTORY. SOUTHEASTERN EUROPE

939′.8 — Romania. Rast. Neolithic antiquities. Excavation of remains

Dumitrescu, Vladimir. The Neolithic settlement at Rast : (South-West Oltenia, Romania) / Vladimir Dumitrescu ; translated from the Romanian by Nubar Hampartumian. — Oxford : B.A.R., 1980. — 133p,xci p of plates : ill,plans ; 30cm. — (BAR. International series, ISSN 0143-3067 ; 72)
ISBN 0-86054-076-6 (pbk) : £12.00
ISBN 0-86054-071-5 B81-20660

939′.8 — Romania. Tîrpeşti. Antiquities, *to 600*

Marinescu-Bîlcu, Silvia. Tîrpeşti : from prehistory to history in Eastern Romania / Silvia Marinescu-Bîlcu ; translated from the Romanian by Georgeta Bolomey. — Oxford : B.A.R., 1981. — 187p,[230]p of plates : ill,1maps,plans ; 30cm. — (BAR. International series ; 107)
Translated from the Romanian. — Includes bibliographies
ISBN 0-86054-125-8 (pbk) : £20.00 B81-36626

939′.8 — Thracian civilization

Hoddinott, R. F.. The Thracians / R.F. Hoddinott. — [London] : Thames and Hudson, c1981. — 192p : ill,maps,plans ; 25cm. — (Ancient peoples and places ; v.98)
Bibliography: p177-183. - Includes index
ISBN 0-500-02099-x : £12.00 B81-03316

940 — HISTORY. EUROPE

940 — Europe, *B.C.500-A.D.1915*

Lawrence, D. H.. Movements in European history / D.H. Lawrence. — Oxford : Oxford University Press, 1971 (1981 [printing]). — xxviii,336p : maps ; 20cm. — (Oxford paperbacks)
Originally published: under the name of Lawrence H. Davison, London : Mitford, 1921. — Includes index
ISBN 0-19-285113-6 (pbk) : £2.95 : CIP rev. B81-22559

940 — Europe. Castles

Castles : a history and guide / foreword by Sir John Hackett ; special consultant R. Allen Brown ; [main contributors] Michael Prestwich, Charles Coulson. — Poole : Blandford, 1980. — 192p : ill(some col.),facsims(some col.),maps (some col.),plans,ports ; 29cm
Bibliography: p188. — Includes index
ISBN 0-7137-1100-0 : £8.95 B81-02799

940 — Europe. Social conditions, *B.C.700-A.D.1970*

Everyman in Europe : essays in social history / [edited by] Allan Mitchell, Istvan Deak. — 2nd ed. — Englewood Cliffs ; London : Prentice-Hall, c1981. — 2v.(vi,234;vi,218p) ; 23cm
Previous ed.: 1974. — Includes bibliographies. — Contents: Vol.1. The pre industrial millenia — Vol.2. The industrial centuries
ISBN 0-13-293613-5 (pbk)
ISBN 0-13-293621-6 (v.2) : £6.45 B81-25057

940 — Europe, *to 1980* **—** *For schools*

Larkin, P. J. (Patrick John). European heritage / P.J. Larkin ; illustrated by Jennifer J. More. — Amersham : Hulton, 1981. — 63p : col.ill,colmaps ; 25cm
ISBN 0-7175-0882-x (pbk) : Unpriced B81-14340

940 — European civilization, *to 1980.* **Influence of Etruscan civilization —** *Sources of data: Etruscan antiquities*

Bonfante, Larissa. Out of Etruria : Etruscan influence north and south / Larissa Bonfante. — Oxford : B.A.R., 1981. — ii,173p,[84]p of plates : ill,maps,1plan ; 30cm. — (BAR. International series ; 103)
Bibliography: 135-160
ISBN 0-86054-121-5 (pbk) : £10.00 B81-36625

940 — European Community countries — *Humour*

Rushton, William. The reluctant Euro : Rushton versus Europe / William Rushton. — London : Queen Anne, 1980. — 96p : ill ; 26cm
ISBN 0-362-00527-3 : £4.95 B81-04780

Rushton, William. The reluctant Euro : Rushton versus Europe / William Rushton. — London : Macdonald Futura, 1981, c1980. — 96p : ill ; 21cm
Originally published: London : Queen Anne, 1980
ISBN 0-7088-2095-6 (pbk) : £1.50 B81-41008

940 — European Community countries. Rural regions. Social conditions — *Conference proceedings*

Rural response to the resource crisis in Europe : papers presented at a seminar 24-26 April 1981 / edited by Anne McLean Bullen and John Hosking. — Ashford, Kent : Wye College (University of London), 1981. — ii,ii,111p : ill ; 30cm. — (Seminar paper / CEAS, ISSN 0307-1111 ; no.13)
At head of title: Centre for European Agricultural Studies Association
ISBN 0-905378-40-7 (spiral) : £9.50 B81-38953

940 — North-western Europe. Waterfront structures, *45-1500.* **Archaeological investigation —** *Conference proceedings*

International Conference on Waterfront Archaeology in North European Towns *(1st : 1979 : Museum of London)*. Waterfront archaeology in Britain and Northern Europe : a review of current research in waterfront archaeology in six European countries, based on the papers presented to the First International Conference on Waterfront Archaeology in North European Towns held at the Museum of London on 20-22 April 1979 / edited by Gustav Milne and Brian Hobley. — London : Council for British Archaeology, 1981. — xi,156p : ill,maps,plans ; 30cm. — (CBA research report, ISSN 0589-9036 ; no.41)
Includes index
ISBN 0-906780-08-x (pbk) : Unpriced : CIP rev. B81-21586

940'.01 — European civilization. Theories of French intellectuals. Influence of World War 1

Cadwallader, Barrie. Crisis of the European mind : a study of André Malraux and Drieu la Rochelle / Barrie Cadwallader. — Cardiff : University of Wales Press, 1981. — xii,267p ; 22cm
Includes index
ISBN 0-7083-0759-0 : Unpriced : CIP rev. B80-10905

940'.04916 — Celtic civilization. Occult aspects — *Serials*

The new Celtic review : Celtic lore and druid philosophy / the G.S.O. Society. — [19--]-. — London (BM Oak Grove, WC1V 6XX) : Golden Section Order Society, [19--]-. — v. : ill,maps ; 42cm
Quarterly. — Description based on: Jan.1980 issue
ISSN 0144-8005 = New Celtic review : £1.00 (free to members) B81-04815

940'.04924 — Europe. Jews. Persecution, *ca 1900-1949*

Bauer, Yehuda. The Jewish emergence from powerlessness / Yehuda Bauer. — London : Macmillan, 1980, c1979. — xiv,89p ; 23cm
Originally published: Toronto : University of Toronto Press, c1979. — Includes index
ISBN 0-333-28175-6 : £12.00 : CIP rev. B79-37091

940'.07'1041 — Great Britain. Educational institutions. Curriculum subjects: European studies — *Serials*

Euroednews / UK Centre for European Education. — No.1 (Jan.1980)-. — London (University of London Institute of Education, Rm 301, 58 Gordon Sq., WC1H 0NT) : The Centre, 1980-. — v. ; 30cm
Three issues yearly
ISSN 0260-8979 = Euroednews : Unpriced B81-09052

940'.07'15 — Great Britain. Adult education. Curriculum subjects: European studies — *For teaching*

Liggett, Eric. The European studies syllabus : an EEC study guide for students / Eric Liggett. — Glasgow (The Gressingham Press, 34 Balfron Rd, Killearn, Glasgow G63) : E. Liggett, 1981. — 83leaves ; 30cm
Bibliography: leaves 71-77
ISBN 0-9507058-3-7 (pbk) : £2.85 B81-31935

940'.09'732 — Western Europe. Cities. Social life — *Case studies — Personal observations*

Ardagh, John. A tale of five cities : life in provincial Europe today / John Ardagh. — London : Secker & Warburg, 1979. — 457p : ill,maps ; 24cm
Bibliography: p457
ISBN 0-436-01748-2 : £8.95 B81-10774

940.1 — HISTORY. EUROPE, 476-1453

940.1 — European civilization, *ca 400-1500*

Le Goff, Jacques. Time, work, & culture in the Middle Ages / Jacques Le Goff ; translated by Arthur Goldhammer. — Chicago ; London : University of Chicago Press, 1980. — xvi,384p ; 24cm
Translation of: Pour un autre Moyen Age. — Includes index
ISBN 0-226-47080-6 : £13.50 B81-05410

940.1 — European civilization *related to* **Irish civilization,** *400-1200* **—** *Festschriften*

Ireland in early mediaeval Europe. — Cambridge : Cambridge University Press, June 1981. — [400]p
ISBN 0-521-23547-2 : £39.00 : CIP entry
Primary classification 941.5 B81-14958

940.1 — Western European civilization. Role of chivalry, *ca 1000-ca 1400*

Barber, Richard, *1941-*. The reign of chivalry / Richard Barber. — Newton Abbot : David & Charles, c1980. — 208p : ill(some col.),ports ; 29cm
Bibliography: p201. - Includes index
ISBN 0-7153-7740-x : £7.95 : CIP rev. B79-26084

940.1'2 — Ancient Rome. Provinces. Settlement by Germanic tribes, *418-584*

Goffart, Walter. Barbarians and Romans A.D. 418-584 : the techniques of accommodation / by Walter Goffart. — Princeton ; Guildford : Princeton University Press, c1980. — xv,278p : 2maps ; 23cm
Includes index
ISBN 0-691-05303-0 : £14.00 B81-12462

940.1'2 — Europe. Anglo-Saxon antiquities & Jutish antiquities — *Festschriften*

Angles, Saxons and Jutes : essays presented to J.N.L. Myres / edited by Vera I. Evison. — Oxford : Clarendon Press, 1981. — xxx,254p,[15]p of plates : ill,maps,2ports ; 26cm
Includes bibliographies and index
ISBN 0-19-813402-9 : £20.00 B81-26821

940.1'8 — First Crusade

Runciman, Steven. The First Crusade / Steven Runciman. — Abridged ed. — Cambridge : Cambridge University Press, 1980. — 240p : ill (some col.),maps,ports ; 26cm
Previous ed.: published as A history of the Crusades. Vol.1 : The First Crusade and the foundation of the Kingdom of Jerusalem. 1951. — Maps on lining papers. — Includes index
ISBN 0-521-23255-4 : £9.50 : CIP rev. B80-28891

940.1'84 — Fourth Crusade

Godfrey, John. 1204, the unholy Crusade / John Godfrey. — Oxford : Oxford University Press, 1980. — xi,184p,16p of plates : ill,maps,1facsim,2geneal.tables ; 25cm
Bibliography: p176-177. - Inlcudes index
ISBN 0-19-215834-1 : £12.50 : CIP rev. B80-19521

940.2 — HISTORY. EUROPE, 1453-

940.2 — Europe, *1870-1950* **—** *For Irish students*

Gray, E. C.. History : Europe 1870-1950 / E.C. Gray. — Dublin (Ballymount Rd., Walkinstown, Dublin 12) : Helicon, 1981. — 48p ; 21cm. — (Notes on Leaving Certificate)
Text on inside cover
Unpriced (pbk) B81-40901

940.2 — European culture, *1500-1800*

Burke, Peter. Popular culture in early modern Europe / Peter Burke. — London : Temple Smith, 1979, c1978. — 365p,[16]p of plates : ill,facsim,ports ; 22cm
Bibliography: p329-351. - Includes index
ISBN 0-85117-178-8 (pbk) : £4.50 B81-00665

940.2'1 — European civilization, *1300-1600*

Europe reborn : the story of Renaissance civilization / Robert Douglas Mead, series general editor ; [contributors Julian Mates et al.]. — New York : New American Library ; London : New English Library, [1975]. — 324p,[16]p of plates : ill,1map,1plan,1port ; 18cm + Teacher's manual(122p ; 18cm). — (A Mentor book)
Includes bibliographies and index
Unpriced (pbk) B81-11195

940.2'2'072 — Western Europe, *ca 1500-1799.* **Historiography**

Stone, Lawrence. The past and the present / Lawrence Stone. — Boston, Mass. ; London : Routledge & Kegan Paul, 1981. — xii,274p ; 23cm
ISBN 0-7100-0628-4 : £8.75 : CIP rev. B81-02377

940.2'32 — Europe, *1500-1600 — For schools*
Sixteenth-century Europe / [edited by] Katherine Leach. — Basingstoke : Macmillan Education, 1980. — vi,114p ; 22cm. — (Documents and debates)
Includes bibliographies
ISBN 0-333-27500-4 (pbk) : £1.95 : CIP rev.
B80-13143

940.2'4 — Thirty Years' War
Wedgwood, C. V.. The Thirty Years War. — London : Methuen, Nov.1981. — [544]p
Originally published: London : Cape, 1938
ISBN 0-416-32020-1 (pbk) : £5.95 : CIP entry
B81-30551

940.2'5 — European civilization. Influence of freemasonry, *1600-1800*
Jacob, Margaret C.. The radical enlightenment : Pantheists, Freemasons and Republicans / Margaret C. Jacob. — London : Allen & Unwin, 1981. — xiii,312p,[1]leaf of plates : ill ; 23cm. — (Early modern Europe today)
Includes index
ISBN 0-04-901029-8 : Unpriced : CIP rev.
B81-02547

940.2'53 — European culture, *1700-1800*
The **Enlightenment**. — Milton Keynes : Open University Press. — (Arts : a second level course)
At head of title: Open University
Unit 6: Architecture and landscape / prepared for the course team by Colin Cunningham and Gillian Perry. — 1980. — 78p : ill,plans ; 30cm. — (A204 ; 6)
Bibliography: p77-78
ISBN 0-335-07603-3 (pbk) : Unpriced
B81-39325

The **Enlightenment**. — Milton Keynes : Open University Press. — (Arts : a second level course)
At head of title: Open University
Unit 7: William Hogarth / prepared for the course team by Aaron Scharf. — 1979. — 74p : ill,facsims ; 30cm. — (A204 ; 7)
Bibliography: p73
ISBN 0-335-07604-1 (pbk) : Unpriced
B81-39326

The **Enlightenment**. — Milton Keynes : Open University Press. — (Arts : a second level course)
At head of title: Open University
Units 8-9: Hume's Enquiry concerning the principles of morals / prepared for the course team by Rosalind Hursthouse, Stuart Brown and P.N. Furbank. — 1979. — 71p : ill,facsims,ports ; 30cm. — (A204 ; 8-9)
Bibliography: p68-69
ISBN 0-335-07605-x (pbk) : Unpriced
B81-39327

The **Enlightenment**. — Milton Keynes : Open University Press. — (Arts : a second level course)
At head of title: Open University
Unit 29: French architecture / prepared for the course team by Stephen Bayley and Belinda Thomson. — 1980. — 54p : ill,facsims,plans,ports ; 30cm. — (A204 ; 29)
Bibliography: p54
ISBN 0-335-07615-7 (pbk) : Unpriced
B81-39328

The **Enlightenment**. — Milton Keynes : Open University Press. — (Arts : a second level course)
At head of title: Open University
Unit 30: Chardin / prepared for the course team by Francis Frascina. — 1980. — 72p : ill,facsims,ports ; 30cm. — (A204 ; 30)
Bibliography: p71
ISBN 0-335-07616-5 (pbk) : Unpriced
B81-39329

The **Enlightenment**. — Milton Keynes : Open University Press. — (Arts : a second level course)
At head of title: The Open University
Units 31-32: Dangerous acquaintances by Choderlos de Laclos / prepared for the Course Team by Graham Martin, with the assistance of Dorothy Goldman ... [et al.]. — 1980. — 55p : ill,1port ; 30cm. — (A204 ; 31-32)
Bibliography: p55
ISBN 0-335-07617-3 (pbk) : Unpriced
B81-13174

940.2'7 — Europe. Social conditions, *1789-1848*
Cook, Chris. European political facts 1789-1848 / Chris Cook and John Paxton. — London : Macmillan, 1981. — vi,195p ; 25cm
Includes index
ISBN 0-333-21697-0 : £20.00 : CIP rev.
B80-13226

940.2'7 — France. British prisoners of war. Escapes, *1803-1809 — Personal observations*
Hewson, Maurice. Escape from the French : Captain Hewson's narrative (1803-1809) / edited and with an introduction by Antony Brett-James. — Sevenoaks : Hodder and Stoughton in association with Webb & Bower, 1981. — 192p : ill,maps,facsims,ports ; 26cm
Bibliography: p191
ISBN 0-340-26240-0 : £8.95 B81-31868

940.2'7 — Napoleonic Wars. Army operations by German allies of France, *1800-1815*
Pivka, Otto von. Napoleon's German allies / text by Otto von Pivka. — London : Osprey. — (Men-at-arms series ; 106)
4: Bavaria / colour plates by Richard Hook. — 1980. — 40p,A-Hp of plates : ill(some col.),map,ports ; 24cm
English text, English, French and German captions to plates. — Bibliography: p2
ISBN 0-85045-373-9 (pbk) : £2.95 B81-13930

940.2'7 — Napoleonic wars. Peninsular campaign
Lachouque, Henry. Napoleon's war in Spain, 1807-1814. — London : Arms & Armour Press, Jan.1982. — [288]p
Translation of: Napoléon et la campagne d'Espagne
ISBN 0-85368-506-1 : £15.00 : CIP entry
B81-33778

940.2'7 — Napoleonic Wars. Peninsular campaigns *— Correspondence, diaries, etc. — Early works*
Aitchison, John, *1788-1875*. An ensign in the Peninsular War : the letters of John Aitchison / edited by W.F.K. Thompson. — London : Joseph, 1981. — 349p,[8]p of plates : ill,maps,1facsim,ports ; 24cm
Maps on lining papers. — Bibliography: p318-319. — Includes index
ISBN 0-7181-1828-6 : £15.95 B81-16666

940.2'7'0924 — Napoleonic Wars. Army operations by Great Britain. *Army. 95th (Rifle) Regiment — Personal observations*
Kincaid, *Sir* **John**. Adventures in the Rifle Brigade ; and, Random shots from a rifleman. — Glasgow (20 Park Circus, Glasgow G3 6BE) : Richard Drew, Nov.1981. — [304]p
Contents: Adventures in the Rifle Brigade. Originally published: London : s.n., 1830 — Random shots from a rifleman. Originally published: London : s.n., 1835
ISBN 0-904002-83-7 : £9.50 : CIP entry
B81-30892

940.2'8 — Europe, *1815-1871 - Welsh texts*
Jones, Marian Henry. Hanes Ewrop, 1815-1871. — Cardiff : University of Wales Press, June 1981. — 1v.
ISBN 0-7083-0801-5 : £9.95 : CIP entry
B81-12832

940.2'8 — Europe, *1815-1941*
Watson, Jack B.. Success in European history 1815-1941 / Jack B. Watson. — London : Murray, 1981. — 458p : ill,maps,ports ; 24cm. — (Success studybooks)
Bibliography: p437-439. — Includes index
ISBN 0-7195-3794-0 (pbk) : £3.95 B81-25166

940.2'8 — Europe. Revolutions, *1789-1917*
Taylor, A. J. P.. Revolutions and revolutionaries. — Oxford : Oxford University Press, Nov.1981. — [168]p. — (Oxford paperbacks)
Originally published: London : H. Hamilton, 1980
ISBN 0-19-285102-0 (pbk) : £2.95 : CIP entry
B81-31068

940.2'8'0222 — Europe. Royal courts, *ca 1860-1914 — Illustrations*
Finestone, Jeffrey. The last courts of Europe / Jeffrey Finestone ; introduction by Robert K. Massie. — London : Dent, 1981. — 256p : ill,ports,1geneal.table ; 30cm
Includes index
ISBN 0-460-04519-9 : £12.95 B81-40894

940.2'84 — Europe. Revolutions, *1848*
Jones, Peter S.. The 1848 revolutions. — London : Longman, Nov.1981. — [104]p. — (Seminar studies in history)
ISBN 0-582-35312-2 (pbk) : £1.85 : CIP entry
B81-30291

940.2'87 — Europe, *1870-1914*
Mayer, Arno J.. The persistence of the old regime : Europe to the Great War / Arno J. Mayer. — London : Croom Helm, 1981. — xi,367p ; 22cm
Bibliography: p33-349. — Includes index
ISBN 0-7099-1724-4 : £11.95 B81-33442

940.2'87'0924 — Europe. Intellectual life, *1880-1908 — Personal observations*
Symons, Arthur. The memoirs of Arthur Symons : life and art in the 1890s / edited by Karl Beckson. — University Park ; London : Pennsylvania State University Press, c1977. — 284p : 1port ; 24cm
Includes index
ISBN 0-271-01244-7 : Unpriced B81-19794

940.3 — HISTORY. WORLD WAR 1, 1914-1918

940.3 — World War 1
Everett, Susanne. World War 1 / Susanne Everett ; introduction by John Keegan. — London : Hamlyn, 1980. — 256p : ill(some col.),col.maps,3facsims,col.plans,ports(some.col) ; 32cm. — (A Bison book)
Includes index
ISBN 0-600-39480-8 : £6.95 B81-02524

940.3 — World War 1 *— For schools*
Evans, David, *1931-*. The Great War 1914-1918. — London : Edward Arnold, Apr.1981. — 1v.. — (Twentieth century world history)
ISBN 0-7131-0539-9 (pbk) : £1.75 : CIP entry
B81-06594

Morrison, Dorothy, *1932-*. The Great War 1914-18 / Dorothy Morrison. — Edinburgh : Oliver & Boyd, 1981. — 41p : ill,maps,facsims,ports ; 19x25cm. — (Exploring history)
Text on inside covers. — Bibliography: p41. — Includes index
ISBN 0-05-003416-2 (pbk) : £1.25 B81-15328

940.3'112 — World War 1. Responsibility of Germany
Hillgruber, Andreas. Germany and the two world wars / Andreas Hillgruber ; translated by William C. Kirby. — Cambridge, Mass ; London : Harvard University Press, 1981. — viii,120p ; 24cm
Translation of: Deutschlands Rolle in der Vorgeschichte der beiden Weltkriege. — Bibliography: p107-113. — Includes index
ISBN 0-674-35321-8 : £10.15
Also classified at 940.53'112 B81-39779

940.3'141 — World War 1. Peace. Negotiations. Role of British government, *1919-1923*
Dockrill, Michael L.. Peace without promise : Britain and the peace conferences 1919-23 / Michael L. Dockrill and J. Douglas Goold. — London : Batsford Academic and Educational, 1981. — 287p : maps ; 23cm
Bibliography: p275-280. - Includes index
ISBN 0-7134-2694-2 : £14.95 B81-15965

940.3'141 — World War 1. Peace. Treaties: Treaty of Versailles, *1919*
Mee, Charles L.. The end of order : Versailles 1919 / Charles L. Mee. — London : Secker & Warburg, 1981, c1980. — xviii,301p ; 25cm
Originally published: New York : Elsevier-Dutton, 1980. — Bibliography: p269-273. - Includes index
ISBN 0-436-27650-x : £8.95 B81-06238

940.3'141'0924 — World War 1. Peace. Negotiations. Role of House, Edward M.
Floto, Inga. Colonel House in Paris : a study of American policy at the Paris Peace Conference 1919 / Inga Floto. — Princeton ; Guildford : Princeton University Press, 1980. — ix,374p ; 25cm
Originally published: Aarhus : Universitetsforlaget i Aarhus, 1973. — Bibliography: p362-370. — Includes index
ISBN 0-691-04662-x : £9.10 B81-25975

940.3′1422 — World War 1. Reparation by Germany, *1922-1923*

Rupieper, Hermann J.. The Cuno government and reparations 1922-1923 : politics and economics / by Hermann J. Rupieper. — The Hague ; London : Nijhoff, 1979. — viii,289p ; 25cm. — (Studies in contemporary history ; vol.1)
Bibliography: p261-282. - Includes index
ISBN 90-247-2114-8 : Unpriced B81-16022

940.3′162′0941 — Great Britain. Left-wing peace movements, *1814-1918 compared with* **left-wing peace movements in Germany**

Carsten, F. L.. War against war. — London : Batsford, Feb.1982. — [336]p
ISBN 0-7134-3697-2 : £14.95 : CIP entry
Also classified at 940.3′162′0943 B81-37574

940.3′162′0943 — Germany. Left-wing peace movements, *1914-1918 compared with* **left-wing peace movements in Great Britain**

Carsten, F. L.. War against war. — London : Batsford, Feb.1982. — [336]p
ISBN 0-7134-3697-2 : £14.95 : CIP entry
Primary classification 940.3′162′0941 B81-37574

940.4′12′41 — World War 1. Army operations by Great Britain. *Army.* **Armoured combat vehicles: Tanks**

Foley, John. The boilerplate war / John Foley. — London : W.H. Allen, 1981, c1963. — xi,199p ; 18cm. — (War in the twentieth century) (A Star book)
Originally published: London : Muller, 1963. — Includes index
ISBN 0-352-30884-2 (pbk) : £1.95 B81-21754

940.4′12′41 — World War 1. Army operations by Great Britain. *Army.* **Bantam batallions**

Allinson, Sidney. The Bantams : the untold story of World War I / Sidney Allinson. — London : Howard Baker, 1981. — 287p,[8]p of plates : ill,ports ; 23cm
Includes index
ISBN 0-7030-0201-5 : £8.95 B81-08711

940.4′143′0924 — World War 1. Western Front. Army operations by Germany. *Heer. Feld-Artillerie Regiment, 63te — Personal observations — Correspondence, diaries, etc.*

Sulzbach, Herbert. With the German guns : four years on the Western Front 1914-1918 / by Herbert Sulzbach ; with a foreword by Terence Prittie ; translated from the German Zwei lebende Mauern by Richard Thonger. — London : Warne, 1981, c1973. — 256p,[12]p of plates : ill,ports ; 23cm. — (A Leo Cooper book)
Translation of: Zwei lebende Mauern. — Originally published: London : Cooper, 1973
ISBN 0-7232-2794-2 : £9.95 B81-21790

940.4′144 — World War 1. Western Front. Army operations — *Sociological perspectives*

Ashworth, Tony. Trench warfare 1914-1918 : the live and let live system / Tony Ashworth. — London : Macmillan, 1980. — xi,266p,[16]p of plates : ill,1map,2plans ; 23cm
Includes index
ISBN 0-333-25766-9 : £15.00 : CIP rev. B80-02264

940.4′144′05 — World War I. Western Front — *Serials*

Stand to! : the journal of the Western Front Association. — No.1 (Spring 1981)-. — South Croydon (c/o P.T. Scott, 6 Cranleigh Gardens, Sanderstead, South Croydon, Surrey CR2 9LD) : The Association, 1981-. — v. : ill,facsims ; 30cm
ISSN 0261-6548 = Stand to! : Unpriced B81-33715

940.4′144′0924 — World War 1. Western Front. Army operations by Great Britain. *Army. London Scottish Regiment — Personal observations*

Dolden, A. Stuart. Cannon fodder : an infantryman's life on the Western front 1914-18 / A. Stuart Dolden. — Poole : Blandford, 1980. — 185p,[8]p of plates : ill,1facsim,ports ; 23cm
Includes index
ISBN 0-7137-1108-6 : £4.95 B81-04651

940.4′144′0924 — World War 1. Western Front. Army operations by Great Britain. *Army — Personal observations*

Harbottle, George. Civilian soldier 1914-1919 : a period relived / by George Harbottle. — [Jesmond] ([Block 'A', Scottish Life House, Archbold Terrace, Jesmond, Newcastle upon Tyne NE2 1DA]) : G. Harbottle, [1981?]. — 132p : ill,maps,ports ; 21cm
Limited ed. of 100 copies. — Includes index
ISBN 0-907113-03-6 (pbk) : Unpriced B81-31857

940.4′144′0924 — World War 1. Western Front. Army operations by Great Britain. *Army. Royal Field Artillery. Brigade, 52nd, 1915-1917 — Personal observations*

Talbot Kelly, R. B.. A subaltern's odyssey : memories of the Great War 1915-1917 / R.B. Talbot-Kelly ; edited by R.G. Loosmore. — London : Kimber, 1980. — ill,maps,ports ; 24cm
Includes index
ISBN 0-7183-0247-8 : £8.50 B81-05258

940.4′15′0924 — World War 1. Arabian campaign & Dardanelles campaign — *Personal observations*

Crutchley, Charles. Shilling a day soldier / Charles Crutchley. — Bognor Regis : New Horizon, c1980. — 128p,[8]p of plates : ill,1map ; 21cm
ISBN 0-86116-598-5 : £4.75 B81-21779

940.4′2 — World War 1. Army operations by Great Britain Army. Australian and New Zealand Army Corps, *1914-1915*

Bean, C. E. W.. The story of Anzac : from the outbreak of war to the end of the first phase of the Gallipoli campaign, May 4, 1915 / C.E.W. Bean ; with introduction by K.S. Inglis. — St.Lucia, Qld. : University of Queensland Press in association with the Australian War Memorial ; Hemel Hampstead : Distributed by Prentice-Hall, c1981. — lxviii,662p,[84]p of plates : ill,maps,ports ; 23cm. — (The Official history of Australia in the war of 1914-1918, ISSN 0159-5261 ; v.1)
Facsim of: 3rd ed. Sydney : Angus & Robertson, 1942. — Includes index
ISBN 0-7022-1585-6 : £16.70
ISBN 0-7022-1586-4 (pbk) : Unpriced B81-40130

940.4′2 — World War 1. Army operations by Great Britain. *Army. Australian and New Zealand Army Corps, 1915-1916*

Bean, C. E. W.. The story of Anzac : from 4 May, 1915, to the evacuation of the Gallipoli Peninsula / C.E.W. Bean ; with an introduction by A.J. Hill. — St. Lucia. Qld. : University of Queensland Press in asociation with the Australian War Memorial ; Hemel Hempstead : Distributed by Prentice-Hall, c1981. — xxxix,975p,[124]p of plates : ill,maps,ports ; 22cm. — (The Official history of Australia in the war of 1914-1918, ISSN 0159-5261)
Facsim. of: ed. published: Sydney : Angus & Robertson, 1944. — Includes index
ISBN 0-7022-1603-8 (cased) : £16.70
ISBN 0-7022-1604-6 (pbk) : Unpriced B81-40129

940.4′21 — World War 1. Army operations by Great Britain. *Army. British Expeditionary Force, 1914 (August-November)*

Simpson, Keith. The Old Contemptibles. — London : Allen & Unwin, Aug.1981. — [176]p
ISBN 0-04-940062-2 : £9.95 : CIP entry B81-15868

940.4′25 — World War 1. Gallipoli campaign

Laffin, John. Damn the Dardanelles! : the story of Gallipoli / John Laffin. — London : Osprey, 1980. — 224p : ill,maps,ports ; 25cm
Bibliography: p220-221. — Includes index
ISBN 0-85045-350-x : £9.95 : CIP rev. B80-18104

940.4′3 — World War 1. Military operations, *1918*

Brook-Shepherd, Gordon. November 1918. — London : Collins, Nov.1981. — [300]p
ISBN 0-00-216558-9 : £8.95 : CIP entry B81-30322

940.4′31 — France. Étaples. Great Britain. *Army.* **Mutiny,** *1917.* **Role of Toplis, Percy**

Allison, William. The monocled mutineer / William Allison and John Fairley. — London : Quartet, 1979. — 199p,[8]p of plates : ill,ports ; 20cm
Originally published: 1978
ISBN 0-7043-3287-6 (pbk) : £2.50 B81-22980

940.4′34 — France. Calais. Great Britain. *Army.* **Mutiny,** *1918*

Killick, Alf. Mutiny! : an account of the Calais soldiers' mutiny in 1918 written by a leading participant / Alf Killick. — [London] ([1 Mentmore Terrace, E8 3PN]) : [Militant], [1976]. — 9p ; 30cm
£0.20 (unbound) B81-19554

940.4′4 — World War 1. Air operations

Campbell, Christopher. Aces and aircraft of World War I / Christopher Campbell ; illustrated by the author and John W. Wood. — Poole : Blandford, 1981. — 144p : ill(some col.),ports ; 31cm
Includes index
ISBN 0-7137-0954-5 : £9.95 : CIP rev. B80-04603

940.4′4943 — World War 1. Air operations by Germany. *Kriegsmarine. Marine-Luftschiffabteilung*

Robinson, Douglas H.. The Zeppelin in combat : a history of the German Naval Airship Division, 1912-1918 / Douglas H. Robinson. — 3rd ed. — Seattle ; London : University of Washington Press, 1971 (1980 [printing]). — xiv,417p,[34]p of plates (2fold.) : ill,plans,ports ; 23cm
Previous ed.: Henley-on-Thames : Foulis, 1971. — Bibliography: p370-377. — Includes index
ISBN 0-295-95752-2 : £15.00 B81-17893

940.4′514 — Steam liners: Lusitania *(Ship).* **Sinking,** *1915*

Hickey, Des. Seven days to disaster : the sinking of the Lusitania / Des Hickey and Gus Smith. — London : Collins, 1981. — 336p,[8]p of plates : ill,2maps,facsims,ports ; 23cm
Bibliography: p325-331. — Includes index
ISBN 0-00-216882-0 : £8.50 : CIP rev. B81-15894

940.4′514′0924 — World War 1. Dardanelles campaign. Naval operations by Great Britain. *Royal Navy, 1915-1916 — Correspondence, diaries, etc*

Denham, H. M.. Dardanelles. — London : Murray, Oct.1981. — [224]p
ISBN 0-7195-3858-0 : £11.00 : CIP entry B81-27350

940.4′54 — World War 1. Naval operations by Germany. *Kriegsmarine. Deutsches Ostasiatisches Kreuzergeschwader, 1914*

Hoyt, Edwin P.. Defeat at the Falklands : Germany's East Asia Squadron 1914 / Edwin P. Hoyt. — London : Hale, 1981. — 240p,[12]p of plates : ill,maps,ports ; 23cm
Bibliography: p234-235. — Includes index
ISBN 0-7091-8863-3 : £9.95 B81-23250

940.4′65′4427 — France. Roeux. Commonwealth World War 1 military cemeteries: Brown's Copse Cemetery. Graves — *Lists*

Great Britain. *Commonwealth War Graves Commission.* War graves of the British Commonwealth : the register of the names of those who fell in the Great War and are buried in Brown's Copse Cemetery, Rœux, France / compiled and published by order of the Imperial War Graves Commission, London. — Amended version. — Maidenhead : Commonwealth War Graves Commission, 1981. — 53p : 1map,1plan ; 26cm. — (France ; 604)
Previous ed.: 1928
Unpriced (pbk) B81-40802

940.4′81′41 — World War 1. Army operations by Great Britain. *Army, 1916-1918 — Personal observations*

Brown, Archie. Destiny / by Archie Brown. — Bognor Regis : New Horizon, c1979. — 125p,[11]p of plates : ill,facsims,ports ; 22cm
ISBN 0-86116-192-0 : £4.25
Also classified at 940.54′81′41 B81-17754

940.4′81′41 — World War 1. Army operations by Great Britain. *Army. Queen's Own Cameron Highlanders. Battalion, 8th, 1915-1918 — Personal observations*
Davies, Hugh. The compassionate war / by Hugh Davies. — [London] ([c/o Nene Way, Sutton, Peterborough, Cambs.]) : Abbotsbury Publications, 1980. — i,81p : port ; 21cm
Port. on inside front cover
Unpriced (pbk) B81-08438

940.4′81′41 — World War I. Army operations by Great Britain. *Army — Personal observations*
Griffith, Wyn. Up to Mametz / by Wyn Griffith. — London : Severn House, 1981. — 238p ; 21cm
ISBN 0-7278-0648-3 : £5.95 B81-17823

940.5 — HISTORY. EUROPE, 1918-

940.5 — Europe, *1900-1975 — For schools*
Evans, David, *1931-*. Europe in modern times 1900-1975 / David Evans. — London : Edward Arnold, 1981. — 224p : ill,maps,facsims,ports ; 25cm
Includes index
ISBN 0-7131-0472-4 (pbk) : £4.50 B81-40558

940.5 — Europe, *1914-1979*
Carr, Edward Hallet. From Napoleon to Stalin and other essays / by E.H. Carr. — London : Macmillan, 1980. — ix,277p ; 23cm
Includes index
ISBN 0-333-28941-2 : £20.00 : CIP rev. B80-24973

Hughes, H. Stuart. Contemporary Europe : a history / H. Stuart Hughes. — 5th ed ed. — Englewood Cliffs ; London : Prentice-Hall, c1981. — xv,620p : ill,maps,ports ; 25cm
Previous ed.: 1976. — Col.maps on lining papers. — Includes bibliographies and index
ISBN 0-13-170027-8 : £12.95 B81-21012

940.5 — Europe, *1919-1955 — For schools*
Twentieth-century Europe / [compiled by] Richard Brown, Christopher Daniels. — Basingstoke : Macmillan Education, 1981. — viii,120p : 1ill,plans ; 22cm. — (Documents and debates)
Includes 1 text in French. — Includes bibliographies
ISBN 0-333-27984-0 (pbk) : £2.45 : CIP rev. B80-13640

940.5 — European culture, *1900-1980*
Culture and society in contemporary Europe : a casebook / edited by Stanley Hoffmann, Paschalis Kitromilides. — London : Allen & Unwin, 1981. — 237p ; 26cm. — (Casebook series on European politics and society ; no.2)
ISBN 0-04-809014-x (cased) : Unpriced : CIP rev.
ISBN 0-04-809015-8 (pbk) : Unpriced B81-13448

940.53 — HISTORY. WORLD WAR 2, 1939-1945

940.53 — World War 2
Arnold-Foster, Mark. The world at war. — 2nd ed. — London : Thames Methuen, Oct.1981. — [340]p
Previous ed.: London : Collins, 1973
ISBN 0-423-00150-7 : £7.50 : CIP entry B81-28038

The **History** of the Second World War / editor-in-chief Sir Basil Liddell Hart. — London : Phoebus, c1980. — 464p : ill(some col.),facsims(some col.),col.maps,ports ; 31cm
Includes index
ISBN 0-7026-0063-6 : £12.95 B81-01379

Young, Peter, *1915-*. World War II / Peter Young. — London : Hamlyn, 1980. — 249p : ill(some col.),col.maps,1facsim,col.plans,ports (some col.) ; 32cm. — (A Bison book)
Includes index
ISBN 0-600-34171-2 : £6.95 B81-02622

940.5′3 — World War 2, *1941*
Collier, Richard. 1941 : Armageddon. — London : Hamilton, June 1981. — [352]p
ISBN 0-241-10611-7 : £9.95 : CIP entry B81-08905

940.53 — World War 2 — *For schools*
Monham, Kathleen. Growing up in World War II / Kathleen Monham. — Hove : Wayland, 1979. — 96p ; 24cm. — (Growing up in other times)
Bibliography: p96
ISBN 0-85340-636-7 : £3.50 B81-35175

940.53′03′21 — World War 2 — *Encyclopaedias*
The **Almanac** of World War II / edited by Peter Young. — London : Hamlyn, c1981. — 613p : ill,col.maps,ports ; 22cm. — (A Bison book)
Includes index
ISBN 0-600-34208-5 : £5.95 B81-37327

The **Historical** encyclopedia of World War II / edited by Marcel Baudot ... [et al.] ; translated from the French by Jesse Dilson ; with additional material by Alvin D. Coox, Thomas R.H. Havens. — London : Macmillan, 1981, c1980. — xxii,548p : ill,maps ; 26cm
Translation of: Encyclopedie de la Guerre 1939-1945. — Originally published: New York : Facts on File, 1980. — Bibliography: p545-548
ISBN 0-333-28211-6 : £15.00 B81-12766

Marshall Cavendish encyclopedia of World War II. — London : Marshall Cavendish, June 1981. — 11v.
ISBN 0-85685-948-6 : CIP entry B81-11928

940.53′112 — World War 2. Responsibility of Germany
Hillgruber, Andreas. Germany and the two world wars / Andreas Hillgruber ; translated by William C. Kirby. — Cambridge, Mass ; London : Harvard University Press, 1981. — viii,120p ; 24cm
Translation of: Deutschlands Rolle in der Vorgeschichte der beiden Weltkriege. — Bibliography: p107-113. — Includes index
ISBN 0-674-35321-8 : £10.15
Primary classification 940.3′112 B81-39779

940.53′113 — World War 2. Causes. Economic aspects
Kaiser, David E.. Economic diplomacy and the origins of the Second World War : Germany, Britain, France, and Eastern Europe, 1930-1939 / David E. Kaiser. — Princeton ; Guildford : Princeton University Press, c1980. — xvi,346p ; 25cm
Bibliography: p329-338. — Includes index
ISBN 0-691-05312-x (cased) : £14.00
ISBN 0-691-10101-9 (pbk) : £7.00 B81-12464

940.53′15′03924 — China. Shanghai. Jewish communities, *1938-1945.* **Political aspects**
Tokayer, Marvin. The fugu plan / Marvin Tokayer and Mary Swarty. — Feltham : Hamlyn Paperbacks, 1981, c1979. — 287p,[4]p of plates : ill,ports ; 18cm
Originally published: New York ; London : Paddington Press, 1979. — Includes index
ISBN 0-600-20176-7 (pbk) : £1.75
Also classified at 951′.8004924 B81-14606

940.53′15′03924 — Europe. Jews. Escapes. Role of Christians, *1939-1945 — Case studies*
Hellman, Peter. Avenue of the righteous / Peter Hellman. — London : Dent, 1981. — xviii,267p,[8]p of plates : ill,1facsim,ports ; 22cm
ISBN 0-460-04503-2 : £7.95 B81-08116

940.53′15′03924 — Jews. Genocide, *1939-1945*
Bayfield, Tony. Churban : the murder of the Jews of Europe / Tony Bayfield. — London : Michael Goulston Educational Foundation, 1981. — 192p : ill,maps,facsims,ports,1geneal.table ; 25cm. — (Jewish responses ; 3)
Maps on inside covers
ISBN 0-907372-00-7 (pbk) B81-40850

940.53′15′03924 — Poland. Jews: Hart, Kitty — *Biographies*
Hart, Kitty. Return to Auschwitz : the remarkable story of a girl who survived the Holocaust / Kitty Hart. — London : Sidgwick & Jackson, 1981. — 178p,[8]p of plates : ill,1plan,ports ; 25cm
Includes index
ISBN 0-283-98775-8 : £7.95 B81-30704

940.53′15′03924 — Poland. Warsaw. Jews, *1939-1946 — Childhood reminiscences*
Zuker-Bujanowska, Liliana. Liliana's journal : Warsaw 1939-1945 / Liliana Zuker-Bujanowska. — Loughton : Piatkus, 1981, c1980. — viii,162p,[8]p of plates : 1ill,1facsim,ports ; 23cm
Translated from the Polish. — Originally published: New York : Dial Press, 1980
ISBN 0-86188-057-9 : £6.50 B81-08285

940.53′15′039240924 — Eastern Europe. Jews. Genocide, *1939-1945 — Personal observations*
Trepman, Paul. Among men and beasts / Paul Trepman ; translated from the Yiddish by Shoshana Pena and Gertrude Hirschler. — South Brunswick : A.S. Barnes ; London : Yoseloff, c1978 (1979 printing). — 229p,[1]leaf of plates : 1port ; 22cm
ISBN 0-498-02168-8 : £5.00 B81-37481

940.53′163′0944 — World War 2. French collaboration
Gordon, Bertram M.. Collaborationism in France during the Second World War / Bertram M. Gordon. — Ithaca ; London : Cornell University Press, 1980. — 393p ; 24cm
Bibliography: p361-378. — Includes index
ISBN 0-8014-1263-3 : £11.75 B81-01941

940.53′22 — Great Britain. Foreign relations with France, *1939-1940*
Gates, Eleanor M.. End of the affair. — London : Allen & Unwin, Sept.1981. — [464]p
ISBN 0-04-940063-0 : £17.50 : CIP entry B81-20116

940.53′22′41 — Great Britain. Churchill, Winston S. (Winston Spencer), *1874-1965.* **Interpersonal relationships with Gaulle, Charles de,** *1940-1945*
Kersaudy, François. Churchill and De Gaulle / François Kersaudy. — London : Collins, 1981. — 476p,[8]p of plates : ports ; 24cm
Bibliography: p468-470. — Includes index
ISBN 0-00-216328-4 : £12.95 : CIP rev.
Primary classification 940.53′22′44 B81-20153

940.53′22′44 — France. Gaulle, Charles de. Interpersonal relations with Churchill, Winston S. (Winston Spencer), *1874-1965, 1940-1945*
Kersaudy, François. Churchill and De Gaulle / François Kersaudy. — London : Collins, 1981. — 476p,[8]p of plates : ports ; 24cm
Bibliography: p468-470. — Includes index
ISBN 0-00-216328-4 : £12.95 : CIP rev.
Also classified at 940.53′22′41 B81-20153

940.53′22′73 — United States. Foreign relation with Japan, *1941-45*
Iriye, Akira. Power and culture : the Japanese-American war, 1941-1945 / Akira Iriye. — Cambridge, Mass. ; London : Harvard University Press, 1981. — ix,304p : 1map ; 24cm
Bibliography: p287-295. — Includes index
ISBN 0-674-69580-1 : £13.20
Primary classification 940.53′24′52 B81-38272

940.53′24′52 — Japan. Foreign relations with United States, *1941-45*
Iriye, Akira. Power and culture : the Japanese-American war, 1941-1945 / Akira Iriye. — Cambridge, Mass. ; London : Harvard University Press, 1981. — ix,304p : 1map ; 24cm
Bibliography: p287-295. — Includes index
ISBN 0-674-69580-1 : £13.20
Also classified at 940.53′22′73 B81-38272

940.53′4 — Europe. Resistance movements, *1939-1945*
Healey, Tim. Secret armies : resistance groups in World War Two / Tim Healey. — London : Macdonald, 1981. — 48p : ill(some col.),col.maps,facsims,ports ; 31cm
Bibliography: p46. — Includes index
ISBN 0-356-06553-7 : £3.95 B81-38537

940.53′4′0922 — Western Europe. Resistance movements, *1939-1945 — Biographies*
Foot, M. R. D.. Six faces of courage / M.R.D. Foot ; with a preface by R.V. Jones. — Rev. ed. — [London] : Magnum, 1980, c1978. — 173p,[8]p of plates : ports ; 18cm
Originally published: London : Eyre Methuen, 1978
ISBN 0-417-04560-3 (pbk) : £1.50 B81-07109

940.53'422395 — Kent. Elham. Effects of World War 2, *1940 — Personal observations*

Knight, Dennis. Harvest of Messerschmitts : the chronicle of a village at war - 1940 / Dennis Knight : based on the diary of Mary Smith of Elham. — [London] : Warne, 1981. — 183p : ill,maps,ports ; 25cm
Includes index
ISBN 0-7232-2772-1 : £8.95 B81-39292

940.53'4234'0222 — Channel Islands. Occupation by German military forces, *1940-1945 — Illustrations*

Ramsey, Winston G.. The war in the Channel Islands : then and now / Winston G. Ramsey. — London : Battle of Britain Prints International, c1981. — 254p : ill,maps,facsims,plans,ports ; 31cm. — (An After the Battle publication)
Ill on lining papers
ISBN 0-900913-22-3 : £10.95 B81-25260

940.53'4234'0924 — Channel Islands. Occupation by German military forces, *1940-1945 — Personal observations*

Stroobant, Frank. One man's war / Frank Stroobant. — [London] : Corgi, 1981. — 173p,[4]p of plates : 1facsim,1plan,ports ; 18cm
Originally published: Guernsey : Guernsey Press, 1967
ISBN 0-552-11630-0 (pbk) : £1.25 B81-21399

940.53'42345'0924 — Sark. Social life. Effects of World War 2 *— Personal observations — Correspondence, diaries, etc.*

Tremayne, Julia. War on Sark : the secret letters of Julia Tremayne / introduction by Michael Beaumont. — Exeter : Webb & Bower, 1981. — 208p : ill,facsims ; 25cm
ISBN 0-906671-41-8 : £7.95 B81-23968

940.53'438 — Poland. Resistance movements, *1939-1945 — Polish texts*

Jurewicz, Lesław. Zbrodnia czy początek wojny domowej / Lesław Jurewicz. — Londyn : Poets' and Painters' Press, 1980. — 149p,[8]p of plates : 2maps,facsims,1port ; 22cm
Two maps attached to back cover. — Bibliography: p143-149
Unpriced (pbk) B81-14726

940.53'438 — Poland. Resistance movements: Armia Krajowa, *1939-1945 — Readings from contemporary sources — Polish texts*

Armia krajowa w dokumentach 1944-1945 / [komitet redakcyjmy : Halina Czarnocka ... et al.]. — Londyn [i.e. London] (11 Leopold Rd., W.5) : Studium Polski Podziemnej
Polish text, synopsis in English
Tom.5: Październik 1944-Lipiec 1945. — 1981. — xl,534p : 1facsim ; 24cm
Includes index
ISBN 0-9501348-4-8 : Unpriced B81-13984

940.53'438'0924 — Poland. Resistance movements: Armia Krajowa, *1939-1940.* **Nowak, Jan** *— Biographies — Polish texts*

Nowak, Jan. Kurier z Warszawy / Jan Nowak (Zdzisław Jeziorański). — Londyn (27 Hamilton Rd., Bedford Park, W4 1AL) : Odnowa, c1978. — 468p,[15]p of plates : ill,facsims,ports ; 16cm
Polish text. — Title on t.p. verso: Courier from Warsaw. — Includes index
ISBN 0-903705-37-0 (pbk) : Unpriced B81-21240

940.53'438'0924 — Poland. Resistance movements: Armia Krajowa. Okulicki, Leopold *— Biographies — Polish texts*

Krzyżanowski, Jerzy R.. Generał : opowieść o Leopoldzie Okulickim / Jerzy R. Krzyżanowski. — Londyn (27 Hamilton Rd., Bedford Park, W4 1AC) : Odnowa, 1980. — 243p ; 19cm
Title on t. p. verso: The general : a story on General Leopold Okulicki. — Bibliography: p241-242. - Includes index
ISBN 0-903705-35-4 (pbk) : £5.00 B81-21239

940.53'4384 — World War 2. Warsaw Uprising. Role of Armia Krajowa. *Baszta.* **Personnel** *— Lists — Polish texts*

Żołnierze Pułku Armii Krajowej 'Baszta' : 1. VIII. 1944-27. IX. 1944. — Buckhurst Hill (c/o Mr. W. Zlotnicki, 7 Bush Rd., Buckhurst Hill, Essex IG9 6ER) : Kolo Basztowcow i Mokotowiaków Londyn, [1981?]. — 99p ; 27cm
Unpriced (pbk) B81-40657

940.53'44 — France. Resistance movements, *1940-1944*

Schoenbrun, David. Soldiers of the night : the story of the French resistance / David Schoenbrun. — London : Hale, 1981, c1980. — xi,512p,[32]p of plates : ill,1map,1facsim,ports ; 25cm
Originally published: New York : Dutton, 1980. — Bibliography: p495-497. — Includes index
ISBN 0-7091-9070-0 : £9.95 B81-22107

940.53'44'0924 — France. Resistance movements, *1939-1945.* **Lionel, Frédéric** *— Biographies*

Lionel, Frédéric. Challenge : on special mission / by Frédéric Lionel ; with a foreword by Sir George Trevelyon. — Sudbury : Spearman, 1980. — iii,147p ; 23cm
Translation of: Un chemin sur la braise
ISBN 0-85435-354-2 : £4.50 B81-23269

940.53'448 — Southern France. Resistance movements, *1940-1944*

Leslie, Peter. The liberation of the Riviera : the resistance to the Nazis in the South of France and the story of its heroic leader, Ange-Marie Miniconi / Peter Leslie. — London : Dent, 1981, c1980. — 254p,[16]p of plates : ill,maps,facsims,ports ; 24cm
Originally published: New York : Wyndham, 1980
ISBN 0-460-04487-7 : £7.95 B81-11496

940.53'45 — Italy. San Marzano, Betty, *contessa di, 1943-1944 — Biographies*

Reid, Ian, *1915-*. A game called survival : the story of Betty di San Marzano and her children in wartime Italy / Ian Reid. — London : Evans, 1980. — 144p,[8]p of plates : ill,1map,ports ; 21cm
ISBN 0-237-45527-7 : £6.95 B81-08249

940.53'45'0924 — Italy. Resistance movements, *1944-1945 — Personal observations*

Whiting, Douglas. Prisoners, people, places, partisans and patriots / Douglas Whiting. — Bognor Regis : New Horizon, c1980. — 227p,[12]p of plates : ill,facsims,3ports ; 21cm
ISBN 0-86116-404-0 : £5.25 B81-21720

940.53'4585 — World War 2. Siege of Malta, *1940-1943*

Attard, Joseph. The Battle of Malta / Joseph Attard. — London : Kimber, 1980. — 252p.[12]p of plates : ill,2maps ; 24cm
Bibliography: p241. - Includes index
ISBN 0-7183-0028-9 : £9.95 B81-04460

940.53'495'0924 — Greece. Resistance movements: ELAS, *to 1945 — Personal observations*

Sarafis, Stefanos. ELAS : Greek Resistance Army / Stefanos Sarafis ; translated by Sylvia Moody ; biographical introduction and footnotes by Marion Sarafis. — London : Merlin, 1980. — ci,556p,[16]p of plates : ill,maps,music,facsims,ports ; 25cm
Translation from the Greek. — Maps on lining papers. — Two maps (1 folded sheet : 2 sides) attached to lining paper. — Bibliography: p537-538. - Includes index
£12.50 B81-09376

940.53'497'0924 — Yugoslavia. Resistance movements: Partizani, *1941-1945 — Personal observations*

Djilas, Milovan. Wartime : with Tito and the partisans / Milovan Djilas ; translated by Michael B. Petrovich. — London : Secker & Warburg, 1980, c1977. — x,470p,[16]p of plates : ill,1map,ports ; 20cm
Originally published: New York : Harcourt Brace Jovanovich ; London : Secker & Warburg, 1977. — Includes index
ISBN 0-436-12971-x (pbk) : £4.95 B81-03488

940.53'51'0924 — World War 2. Japanese campaign, *1941-1945 — Personal observations*

Guillain, Robert. I saw Tokyo burning. — London : J. Murray, Sept.1981. — [320]p
Translation of: La guerre au Japon
ISBN 0-7195-3862-9 : £9.50 : CIP entry B81-21539

940.53'561 — World War 2. Role of Turkey

Weber, Frank G.. The evasive neutral : Germany, Britain and the quest for a Turkish alliance in the Second World War / Frank G. Weber. — Columbia ; London : University of Missouri Press, 1979. — ix,244p ; 23cm
Bibliography: p221-232. — Includes index
ISBN 0-8262-0262-4 : £11.70 B81-16629

940.54 — Great Britain. Churchill, Winston S. (Winston Spencer), *1874-1965.* **Relations with generals of Allied Forces,** *1940-1945*

Pitt, Barrie. Churchill and the generals : an account of the events upon which the BBC-Le Vien TV play by Ian Curteis "Churchill and the generals" was based / by Barrie Pitt ; editorial consultant Jack Le Vien. — London : Sidgwick & Jackson, 1981. — 196p,[12]p of plates : ill,maps,ports ; 24cm
Includes index
ISBN 0-283-98744-8 : £8.95 B81-19741

940.54'012 — World War 2. Military operations by Allied forces. Strategy. Deceptions

Cruickshank, Charles. Deception : in World War II / Charles Cruickshank. — Enl. Oxford University Press pbk. ed. — Oxford : Oxford University Press, 1981. — xii,257p,[16]p of plates : ill,maps ; 20cm
Previous ed.: 1979. — Bibliography: p232. — Includes index
ISBN 0-19-285104-7 (pbk) : £2.95 B81-23526

940.54'05'094762 — World War 2. Katyn Massacre

Zawodny, J. K.. Death in the forest : the story of the Katyn Forest Massacre / by J. K. Zawodny. — Notre Dame ; London : University of Notre Dame, c1962 (1980 [printing]). — xv,235p : ill,1map ; 21cm. — (International studies of the Committee on International Relations)
Bibliography: p201-218. — Includes index
ISBN 0-268-00849-3 (cased) : Unpriced
ISBN 0-268-00850-7 (pbk) : £4.75 B81-14100

940.54'1 — World War 2. Army operations by Allied forces, *1939-1944.* **Armoured combat vehicles: Stuart tanks**

Perrett, Bryan. The Stuart light tank series / text by Bryan Perrett ; colour plates by David E. Smith. — London : Osprey, 1980. — 40p,[8]p of plates : ill(some col.) ; 25cm. — (Vanguard series ; 17)
ISBN 0-85045-370-4 (pbk) : £2.95 B81-07285

940.54'1 — World War 2. Army operations by Allied forces *— For children*

Kay, F. George. The Beaver book of war stories / George Kay ; illustrated by Peter Dennis. — London : Beaver, 1981. — 156p : ill,maps ; 18cm
ISBN 0-600-20362-x (pbk) : £0.95 B81-26158

940.54'12'41 — Great Britain. *Army. Kent Home Guard*

Gulvin, K. R.. Kent Home Guard : a history / by K.R. Gulvin. — Rochester (162 Borstal Rd., Rochester, Kent ME1 3BB) : North Kent Books, 1980. — 92p : ill,facsims,ports ; 22cm
Bibliography: p91
ISBN 0-9505733-3-7 : £3.75 B81-10525

940.54'12'41 — World War 2. Army operations by Great Britain. *Army. Armoured Division, 7th — Christian viewpoints*

Dow, A. C.. A padre's parables / A.C. Dow. — [Scotland?] : [s.n.], [1980?] (Greenock : Orr, Pollack & Co). — 75p ; 22cm
£1.50 (pbk) B81-10769

940.54'12'41 — World War 2. Military operations by British commandos

Butler, Rupert. Hand of steel : the story of the Commandos / Rupert Butler. — London : Severn House, 1981, c1980. — 261p ; 21cm
Originally published: Feltham : Hamlyn, 1980. — Bibliography: p261
ISBN 0-7278-0672-6 : £7.95 B81-09014

940.54'12'73 — World War 2. Army operations by United States. *Army. Infantry Division, 30th*

Hewitt, Robert L.. Work horse of the Western Front : the story of the 30th Infantry Division / by Robert L. Hewitt. — Nashville : Battery Press ; Walpole (Sunnybank, Halesworth Rd., Walpole, Suffolk) : P. Quorn [distributor], [1980]. — x,356p : ill,maps,plans,ports ; 24cm
Originally published: Washington : Infantry journal, 1946. — Maps on lining papers
ISBN 0-89839-036-2 : £12.50 B81-09927

940.54'12'73 — World War 2. Military operations by American military forces

Heiferman, Ronald. USA in World War II / Ronald Heiferman, Ward Rutherford, Thomas A. Siefring. — London : Hamlyn, c1980. — 384p : ill(some col.),col.maps,col.plans,ports (some col.) ; 31cm. — (A Bison book)
Includes index
ISBN 0-600-34154-2 : £7.95 B81-03328

940.54'13'43 — World War 2. Army operations by Germany. *Heer, 1939-1944.* **Armoured combat vehicles: PsKpfw IV tanks**

Perrett, Bryan. The Panzerkampfwagen IV / text by Bryan Perrett ; colour plates by David E. Smith. — London : Osprey, 1980. — 40p,[8]p of plates : ill(some col.) ; 25cm. — (Vanguard series ; 18)
ISBN 0-85045-371-2 (pbk) : £2.95 B81-07284

940.54'13'43 — World War 2. Army operations by Germany. *Heer, 1940-1945.* **Armoured combat vehicles: Tiger tanks**

Perrett, Bryan. The tiger tanks / text by Bryan Perrett ; colour plates by David E. Smith. — London : Osprey, 1981. — 40p,A-Hp of plates : ill(some col.),1plan,1port ; 24cm. — (Vanguard series ; 20)
English text, English, French and German captions to plates
ISBN 0-85045-389-5 (pbk) : £2.95 B81-13928

940.54'21 — Devon. Plymouth. Air raids by Germany. *Luftwaffe, 1940-1944*

Wintle, Frank. The Plymouth blitz / Frank Wintle with additional research by Nicholas Smith. — Bodmin : Bossiney, 1981. — 96p : ill,ports ; 21cm
Bibliography: p94
ISBN 0-906456-51-7 (pbk) : £1.75 B81-19668

940.54'21 — Germany. Berlin. Air raids by United States. *Army Air Force. Air Force, 8th, 1944 (March)*

Ethell, Jeffrey. Target Berlin : Mission 250: 6 March 1944 / Jeffrey Ethell & Alfred Price. — London : Jane's, 1981. — xii,212p,[32]p of plates : ill,maps,2facsims,ports ; 25cm
Bibliography: p164. — Includes index
£8.95 B81-37402

940.54'21 — Greece. Crete. Germany. *Heer.* **Kreipe, Karl. Capture by Allied forces,** *1944 — Personal observations*

Moss, W. Stanley. Ill met by moonlight / W. Stanley Moss. — Large print ed. — Bath : Chivers, 1981. — ix,249p : 2maps ; 23cm. — (A New Portway large print book)
Originally published: London : Harrap, 1950
ISBN 0-85119-123-1 : Unpriced B81-27554

940.54'21 — London. Bromley *(London Borough).* **Air raids by Germany.** *Luftwaffe, 1940-1945*

Blake, Lewis. Bromley in the front-line : the story of the London Borough of Bromley under enemy air attack in the Second World War told for the first time from official war records / Lewis Blake. — [Whitstable] ([c/o G.L. Dennington, 30 Pier Ave., Whitstable, Kent]) : L. Blake, c1980. — [88]p : ill,1map,ports ; 21cm
£1.50 (pbk) B81-06952

940.54'21 — West Germany. Hamburg. Bombing by Allied air forces, *1943 (July)*

Middlebrook, Martin. The Battle of Hamburg : Allied bomber forces against a German city in 1943 / Martin Middlebrook. — London : Allen Lane, 1980. — 424p,[24]p of plates : ill,maps,plans,ports ; 23cm
Bibliography: p415. — Includes index
ISBN 0-7139-1074-7 : £8.95 B81-01560

Musgrove, Gordon. Operation Gomorrah : the Hamburg firestorm raids / Gordon Musgrove. — London : Jane's, 1981. — xiv,197p,xxxiip of plates : ill,maps ; 25cm
Includes index
ISBN 0-7106-0079-8 : £8.95 B81-39446

940.54'21 — West Germany. Nuremberg. Air raids by Great Britain. *Royal Air Force. Bomber Command, 1944*

Middlebrook, Martin. The Nuremberg raid, 30-31 March 1944 / Martin Middlebrook. — Repr. with revisions. — London : Allen Lane, 1980. — xv,367p,[16]p of plates : ill,maps,facsims,ports ; 23cm
Originally published: 1973. — Bibliography: p358. — includes Index
ISBN 0-7139-0612-x : £8.95 B81-03601

940.54'21 — West Germany. Schweinfurt. Air raids by United States. *Army Air Force. Air Force, 8th, 1943 — Personal observations*

Bendiner, Elmer. The fall of fortresses : a personal account of one of the most daring and deadly air battles of the Second World War / by Elmer Bendiner. — London : Souvenir Press, 1981, c1980. — 258p,[8]p of plates : ill,ports ; 23cm
Originally published: New York : Putnam, 1980
ISBN 0-285-62478-4 : £7.50 B81-17700

940.54'21 — World War 2. Atlantic campaign. Naval operations by Great Britain. *Royal Navy.* **Battleships: Royal Oak** *(Ship).* **Sinking**

Weaver, H. J.. Nightmare at Scapa Flow : the truth about the sinking of H.M.S. Royal Oak / H.J. Weaver. — Peppard Common : Cressrelles, 1980. — 191p,[10]p of plates : ill,facsims,1map,ports ; 23cm
ISBN 0-85956-025-2 : £6.90 : CIP rev. B80-13642

940.54'21 — World War 2. Balkan campaigns & Italian campaigns. Army operations by Germany. *Heer.* **Tank units** *— Illustrations*

Panzers in the Balkans and Italy. — Cambridge : Stephens, May 1981. — [96]p. — (World War 2 photo albums ; no.19)
ISBN 0-85059-456-1 (cased) : £5.50 : CIP entry
ISBN 0-85059-457-x (pbk) : £3.95 B81-12823

940.54'21 — World War 2. Battle of Arnhem. Army operations by Great Britain. *Army. Airborne Division, 1st.* **Role of Great Britain.** *Army. Royal Army Medical Corps — Personal observations*

Mawson, Stuart R.. Arnhem doctor / Stuart Mawson ; foreword by Sir John Hackett. — London : Orbis Publishing, 1981. — 170p ; 23cm
ISBN 0-85613-324-8 : £6.95 B81-19058

940.54'21 — World War 2. Battle of Britain

Collier, Richard. Eagle Day : the Battle of Britain, August 6-September 15 1940 / Richard Collier ; picture research by Chaz Bowyer. — Re-illustrated ed. — London : Sphere, 1981, c1980. — 255p : ill,2maps,ports ; 24cm
Originally published: London : Dent, 1980. — Bibiography: p241-251. — Includes index
ISBN 0-7221-2480-5 (pbk) : £4.75 B81-33598

Deighton, Len. Battle of Britain / Len Deighton. — London : Cape, 1980. — 224p : ill(some col.),col.maps,facsims,1form,ports(some col.) ; 26cm
Includes index
ISBN 0-224-01826-4 : £8.50 : CIP rev. B80-13643

Tilbury, Ann. The Battle of Britain / Ann Tilbury ; illustrated by Michael Turner. — London : Macdonald, 1981. — 61p : ill(some col.),1 col.map ; 29cm. — (Macdonald living history)
Translation from the French. — Ill on lining papers. — Includes index
ISBN 0-356-06756-4 : Unpriced B81-38539

940.54'21 — World War 2. Battle of Britain. Air operations by Great Britain. *Royal Air Force. Fighter Command. Group, no.12*

Turner, John Frayn. The Bader Wing / John Frayn Turner. — Speldhurst : Midas Books, 1981. — 153p,[16]p of plates : ill,1form,ports ; 23cm
Includes index
ISBN 0-85936-279-5 : £6.50 B81-40319

940.54'21 — World War 2. Battle of Britain. Air operations in East Kent *— Correspondence, diaries, etc.*

Collyer, David G.. Battle of Britain diary : July-September 1940 / David G. Collyer. — [Deal] ([c/o David G. Collyer, 25 Pilot's Ave., Deal, Kent CT14 9HQ]) : Kent Defence Research Group, 1980. — 120p : ill,maps,1port ; 22cm
Bibliography: p114. — Includes index
ISBN 0-9507408-0-2 (pbk) : £2.50 B81-33681

940.54'21 — World War 2. Battle of Calabria & Battle of Spartivento *— Personal observations*

Smith, Peter C. (Peter Charles), *1940-*. Action imminent : three studies of the naval war in the Mediterranean theatre during 1940 / Peter C. Smith. — London : Kimber, 1980. — 352p,[24]p of plates : ill,maps,ports ; 24cm
Includes index
ISBN 0-7183-0277-x (corrected) : £11.95
Also classified at 940.54'5941'0924 B81-05295

940.54'21 — World War 2. Battle of Cassino

Majdalany, Fred. Cassino : portrait of a battle / by Fred Majdalany ; with an introduction by Sir John Hackett. — London : W.H. Allen, 1981, c1957. — ix,270p : maps ; 18cm. — (War in the twentieth century) (A Star book)
Originally published: London : Longmans, Green, 1957. — Includes index
ISBN 0-352-30839-7 (pbk) : £1.95 B81-21755

Piekalkiewicz, Janusz. Cassino : anatomy of the battle / Janusz Piekalkiewicz. — London : Orbis, c1980. — 192p : ill,1facsim,maps,plans,port ; 25cm
Map on lining papers. — Bibliography: p188-189. — Includes index
ISBN 0-85613-021-4 : £8.95 B81-02802

940.54'21 — World War 2. Battle of Crete

Simpson, Tony. Operation Mercury : the battle for Crete, 1941. — London : Hodder & Stoughton, Aug.1981. — [272]p
ISBN 0-340-23118-1 : £8.50 : CIP entry B81-15821

940.54'21 — World War 2. Dunkirk campaign. Evacuation of Great Britain. *Army. British Expeditionary Force, 1940*

Harman, Nicholas. Dunkirk. — London : Coronet, May 1981. — [304]p
Originally published: 1980
ISBN 0-340-26660-0 (pbk) : £1.95 : CIP entry B81-07625

940.54'21 — World War 2. French & German campaigns. Military operations by American military forces, *1944-1945*

Weigley, Russell F.. Eisenhower's lieutenants : the campaign of France and Germany, 1944-1945 / Russell F. Weigley. — London : Sidgwick & Jackson, 1981. — xviii,800p : ill,maps,ports ; 25cm
Maps and portraits on lining papers. — Includes index
ISBN 0-283-98801-0 : £12.50 B81-34765

940.54'21 — World War 2. Italian campaign, *1944 (January-June)*

Trevelyan, Raleigh. Rome '44. — London : Secker & Warburg, Oct.1981. — [364]p
ISBN 0-436-53400-2 : £7.95 : CIP entry B81-25323

940.54'21 — World War 2. Mediterranean campaign. Air operations by Germany. *Luftwaffe.* **Bomber aeroplanes** *— Illustrations*

German bombers over the Med : a selection of German wartime photographs from the Bundesarchiv, Koblenz / [compiled by] Bryan Philpott. — Cambridge : Stephens, 1980. — 94p : chiefly ill,1map,ports ; 25cm. — (World War 2 photo album ; no.13)
ISBN 0-85059-393-x (cased) : £4.95 : CIP rev.
ISBN 0-85059-394-8 (pbk) : £3.50 B80-02612

940.54'21 — World War 2. Normandy campaign

Belchem, David. Victory in Normandy / by David Belchem. — London : Chatto & Windus, 1981. — 192p : ill(some col.),maps (some col.),col.plans,ports(some col.) ; 26cm
Bibliography: p192. — Includes index
ISBN 0-7011-2546-2 : £9.95 : CIP rev. B81-11962

940.54'21 — World War 2. Normandy campaign. D-Day, *1944*. Combined operations by Allied forces

Paine, Lauran. D-Day / by Lauran Paine. — London : Hale, 1981. — 210p,[8]p of plates : ill ; 23cm
Bibliography: p205-206. — Includes index
ISBN 0-7091-8860-9 : £8.95 B81-27155

940.54'21 — World War 2. North Atlantic campaign. Naval operations by Germany. *Kriegsmarine*. Battleships: Tirpitz *(Ship)*

Kennedy, Ludovic. Menace : the life and death of the Tirpitz / Ludovic Kennedy. — London : Sphere, 1981, c1979. — 157p,[16]p of plates : ill,maps,ports ; 18cm
Originally published: London : Sidgwick and Jackson, 1979. — Bibliography: p152. — Includes index
ISBN 0-7221-5165-9 (pbk) : £1.25 B81-12208

940.54'21 — World War 2. Western European campaigns. Army operations by Allied armies, *7th June-31st August 1944*

Keegan, John. Six armies in Normandy. — London : Cape, Feb.1982. — [320]p
ISBN 0-224-01541-9 : £8.50 : CIP entry B81-40241

940.54'21 — World War 2. Western European campaigns. Army operations by Germany. *Heer, 1943-1945*

Seaton, Albert. The fall of fortress Europe 1943-1945 / Albert Seaton. — London : Batsford, 1981. — 218p,[16]p of plates : ill,maps,plans,ports ; 24cm
Bibliography: p209-212. — Includes index
ISBN 0-7134-1968-7 : £9.95 B81-27208

940.54'21 — World War 2. Western European campaigns. Army operations by Germany. *Heer. Gebirgsjäger*

Lucas, James. Alpine elite : German mountain troops of World War II / James Lucas. — London : Jane's, 1980. — 226p : ill,1map,plans,ports ; 24cm
Bibliography: p220. - Includes index
ISBN 0-7106-0063-1 : £8.95 B81-08305

940.54'21 — World War 2. Western European campaigns. Army operations by United States. *Army. Armored Division, 2nd, 1940-1945*

Katcher, Philip. US 2nd Armored Division 1940-45 / text by Philip Katcher ; colour plates by Mike Chappell. — London : Osprey, 1979. — 40p,A-Hp of plates : ill(some col.,ports ; 25cm. — (Vanguard series ; 11)
English text; notes on col. plates in French and German
ISBN 0-85045-331-3 (pbk) : £2.95 B81-26863

940.54'21 — World War 2. Western European campaigns. Combined operations by United States. *Army. Glider Infantry, 327/401, 1942-1945*

McDonough, James Lee. Sky riders : history of the 327/401 Glider Infantry / James Lee McDonough, Richard S. Gardner. — Nashville : Battery Press ; Walpole (Sunnybank, Halesworth Rd., Walpole, Suffolk) : Patrick Quorn [distributor], c1980. — xiii,162p : ill,1map,facsims,ports ; 24cm
ISBN 0-89839-034-6 : £10.00 B81-04794

940.54'21'0922 — World War 2. Battle of Cassino. Army operations by Poland. *Wojsko. Lwowski Batalion. Strzelców, 18-ty — Personal observations — Collections — Polish texts*

18 Lwowski Batalion Strzelców w bitwie o Monte Cassino ... / [redaktor C. Rodziewicz]. — [London] ([c/o West London Offset Co., 86 Lillie Rd, SW6]) : Wydawnictwo Kola Oddziałowego 18LBS, 1979. — 60p : ill,maps,plans,ports ; 24cm
Bibliography: p59
Unpriced (pbk) B81-22772

940.54'21'0922 — World War 2. Normandy campaign. D-Day, *1944*. Combined operations by Allied forces *— Personal observations — Collections*

Warner, Philip. The D Day landings / Philip Warner. — London : Kimber, 1980. — 309,[12]p of plates : ill,maps,ports ; 25cm
Bibliography: p285. - Includes index
ISBN 0-7183-0447-0 : £9.95 B81-04784

940.54'21'0924 — London. East End. Air raids by Germany. *Luftwaffe, ca 1940 — Personal observations*

Nixon, Barbara. Raiders overhead : a diary of the London blitz / by Barbara Nixon. — London : Scolar/Gulliver, 1980. — 176p : ill,1port ; 23cm
Previous ed.: London : Lindsay Drummond, 1943
ISBN 0-906428-06-8 : £6.95 : CIP rev. B80-12662

940.54'21'0924 — World War 2. Greek campaign & Yugoslav campaign. Role of Polish soldiers, *1941-1945 — Personal observations — Polish texts*

Vučković, Zvonimir. Sećanja iz rata / Zvonimir Vučković ; predgovor Ivana D. Pajića. — London (53 Hawthorn Drive, Harrow HA2 7NW) : Naše delo, 1980. — 228p,[4]p of plates : ill,maps,facsims,ports ; 22cm. — (Biblioteka Naše delo)
£3.00 (pbk) B81-29274

940.54'21'0924 — World War 2. Greek campaign, *1941-1942 — Personal observations*

Howell, Edward. Escape to live / by Edward Howell. — London : Grosvenor, c1981. — ix,217p : 2maps ; 19cm
ISBN 0-901269-56-5 (pbk) : £1.50 B81-24315

940.54'21'0924 — World War 2. Italian campaign. Army operations by Great Britain. *Army. Royal Irish Fusiliers. D Company, 1944 — Personal observations*

Horsfall, John, *1915-*. Fling our banner to the wind / John Horsfall. — Kineton : Roundwood, 1978. — xvii,225p,[13]p of plates : ill,maps,ports ; 24cm
Includes index
£4.25 B81-15012

940.54'21'0924 — World War 2. Normandy campaign. Army operations by Great Britain. *Army, 1944 — Personal observations*

How, J. J.. Normandy : the British breakout / J.J. How. — London : Kimber, 1981. — 238p : ill,maps,ports ; 25cm
Bibliography: p229-231. — Includes index
ISBN 0-7183-0118-8 : £8.95 B81-32957

940.54'21'0924 — World War 2. Normandy campaign *— Personal observations*

Rohmer, Richard. Patton's gap : an account of the Battle of Normandy 1944 / Richard Rohmer. — London : Arms and Armour, c1981. — 240p,[22]p of plates : ill,maps,ports ; 24cm
Bibliography: p237-240
ISBN 0-85368-118-x : Unpriced B81-36512

940.54'21'0924 — World War 2. Polish campaign *— Personal observations — Polish texts*

Paporisz, Romuald. Dokad? : strzepy dziennika / Romuald Pporisz. — Londyn (i.e. London) : Poets and Painters Press, 1981. — 159p ; 22cm
Unpriced (pbk) B81-17076

940.54'21'0924 — World War 2. Western European campaigns. Military operations by Great Britain. *Army, 1944-1945*. Cinephotographers *— Personal observations*

Grant, Ian, *1917-*. Cameramen at war / Ian Grant. — Cambridge : Stephens, 1980. — 192p : ill,ports ; 25cm
ISBN 0-85059-489-8 : £7.95 B81-29717

940.54'23 — World War 2. Battle of El Alamein

Strawson, John. El Alamein : desert victory / John Strawson. — London : Dent, 1981. — 191p : ill,plans,ports ; 24cm
Bibliography: p185-186. — Includes index
ISBN 0-460-04422-2 : £8.95 : CIP rev. B81-20611

940.54'23'0924 — World War 2. Army operations by Germany. *Heer. Afrikakorps, 1941-1942.* Rommel, Erwin

Heckmann, Wolf. Rommel's war in Africa / Wolf Heckmann ; translated from the German by Stephen Seago ; foreword by Sir John Hackett. — London : Granada, 1981. — xvi,366p,[16]p of plates : ill,maps,plans,ports ; 23cm
Translation of: Rommels Krieg in Afrika. — Bibliography: p355-357. — Includes index
ISBN 0-246-11157-7 : £9.95 B81-24960

940.54'23'0924 — World War 2. East African campaign. Military operations by Great Britain. *Army, 1940-1941 — Personal observations*

Crosskill, W. E.. The two thousand mile war / W.E. Crosskill ; foreword by Richard Turnbull. — London : Hale, 1980. — 224p,[24]p of plates : ill,maps,ports ; 23cm
Bibliography: p215. - Includes index
ISBN 0-7091-8591-x : £8.25 B81-04842

940.54'23'0924 — World War 2. North African campaign. Army operations by Great Britain. *Army. Long Range Desert Group — Personal observations*

Lloyd Owen, D. L.. Providence their guide : a personal account of the Long Range Desert Group 1940-45 / D.L. Lloyd Owen ; with a foreword by Sir John Hackett. — London : Harrap, 1980. — xviii,238p,[16]p of plates : ill,3maps,2facsims,ports ; 25cm
Maps on lining papers. — Includes index
ISBN 0-245-53603-5 : £9.50 B81-04509

940.54'25 — Hong Kong. Allied forces. Surrender, *1941*

Lindsay, Oliver. The lasting honour : the fall of Hong Kong, 1941 / [Oliver Lindsay]. — London : Sphere, 1980, c1978. — xii,226p,8p of plates : ill,maps,1facsim,ports ; 18cm
Originally published: London : Hamilton, 1978. — Bibliography: p213-215. — Includes index
ISBN 0-7221-5542-5 (pbk) : £1.25 B81-00667

940.54'25 — India *(Republic)*. Goa. Coastal waters. German merchant ships: Ehrenfels *(Ship)*. Sinking. Role of Great Britain. *Army. Calcutta Light Horse, 1943*

Leasor, James. Boarding party / James Leasor ; with a foreword by the Earl Mountbatten of Burma. — Large print ed. — Leicester : Ulverscroft, 1980, c1978. — 374p ; 23cm. — (Ulverscroft large print series)
Originally published: London : Heinemann, 1978
ISBN 0-7089-0502-1 : £4.25 : CIP rev. B80-11675

940.54'25 — Japan. Hiroshima & Nagasaki. Nuclear bombing, *1945*. Effects

Hiroshima-shi Nagasaki-shi Gembaku Saigaishi Hensho Iinkai. Hiroshima and Nagasaki : the physical, medical and social effects of the atomic bombing / the Committee for the Compilation of Materials on Damage Caused by the Atomic Bombs in Hiroshima and Nagaskai ; translated by Eisei Ishikawa and David L. Swain. — London : Hutchinson, 1981. — xlv,706p : ill,maps,ports ; 25cm
Translation of: Hiroshima Nagasaki no gembaku saiga. — Originally published: New York : Basic Books, 1981. — Bibliography: p641-680. — Includes index
ISBN 0-09-145640-1 : £20.00 : CIP rev. B81-20595

940.54'25 — Japan. Hiroshima. Nuclear bombing, *1945 — Campaign for Nuclear Disarmament viewpoints*

No more Hiroshimas : a second generation Youth CND pamphlet. — London (11, Goodwin St., N4 3HQ) : Campaign for Nuclear Disarmament, [1981]. — 7p : ill ; 30cm
£0.30 (unbound) B81-16646

940.54'25 — Japan. Nagasaki. Nuclear bombing, *1945.* **Survivors' experiences** — *Personal observations*

Akizuki, Tatsuichiro. Nagasaki 1945 : the first full-length eyewitness account of the atomic bomb attack on Nagasaki / Tatsuichiro Akizuki ; translated by Keiichi Nagata ; edited and with an introduction by Gordon Honeycombe. — London : Quartet, 1981. — 158p,[8]p of plates : ill,1port ; 20cm
Translation from the Japanese. — Previous control number ISBN 0704323044
ISBN 0-7043-3382-1 (pbk) : £2.50 : CIP rev. B81-16878

940.54'25 — Sino-Japanese War, *1937-1945.* **Air operations by Allied air forces**

Caidin, Martin. The ragged, rugged warriors / Martin Caidin. — London : Severn House, 1980, c1966. — xiv,366p : ill,maps ; 21cm
Originally published: New York : Dutton, 1966. — Includes index
ISBN 0-7278-0642-4 : £1.95
Primary classification 940.54'26 B81-01710

940.54'25 — World War 2. Singapore campaign

Holmes, Richard, *1946-.* The bitter end : the fall of Singapore 1941-1942. — Chichester (Strettington House, Strettington, Chichester) : Antony Bird, Feb.1982. — [250]p
ISBN 0-907319-03-3 : £9.50 : CIP entry B81-36055

940.54'25'0922 — Japan. Hiroshima. Nuclear bombing, *1945* — *Childhood reminiscences — Collections*

Children of Hiroshima. — [Japan] : Publishing Committee for 'Children of Hiroshima' ; London : Distribution by Taylor & Francis, c1980. — xxxv,333p,[2]leaves of plates(some folded) : ill,1map ; 22cm
Translated from the Japanese. — Includes index
ISBN 0-85066-216-8 (pbk) : Unpriced : CIP rev. B81-05146

940.54'25'0924 — Burma. Japanese military forces. Escapes of British soldiers, *1942* — *Personal observations*

Clifford, Francis. Desperate journey / Francis Clifford. — [London] : Corgi, 1981, c1979. — 190p : 1facsim ; 18cm
Originally published: London : Hodder & Stoughton, 1979
ISBN 0-552-11686-6 (pbk) : £1.35 B81-24305

940.54'25'0924 — World War 2. Burma campaign. Army operations by Great Britain. *Army, 1942* — *Personal observations*

Finnerty, John Tim. All quiet on the Irrawaddy / John 'Tim' Finnerty. — Bognor Regis : New Horizon, c1979. — 225p,[16]p of plates : ill,2maps,1facsim,1plan,ports ; 22cm
Map on lining paper
ISBN 0-86116-157-2 : £4.95 B81-11594

940.54'25'0924 — World War 2. Burma campaign. Army operations by Great Britain. *Army. South-East Asia Command. Special Force, 1944* — *Personal observations*

James, Richard Rhodes. Chindit / Richard Rhodes James. — London : Sphere, 1981, c1980. — 214p,[8]p of plates : ill,maps,ports ; 18cm
Originally published: London : John Murray, 1980. — Includes index
ISBN 0-7221-5102-0 (pbk) : £1.50 B81-38566

940.54'25'0924 — World War 2. Philippines campaign — *Personal observations*

Romulo, Carlos P.. [I saw the fall of Philippines]. Last man off Bataan / Carlos P. Romulo. — London : Sphere, 1969, c1943 (1981 [printing]). — 254p ; 18cm
Originally published: London : Harrap, 1943
ISBN 0-7221-7470-5 (pbk) : £1.50 B81-23333

940.54'26 — World War 2. Pacific campaigns, *1941-1945*

Costello, John. The Pacific war. — London : Collins, Nov.1981. — [736]p
ISBN 0-00-216046-3 : £9.50 : CIP entry B81-30214

940.54'26 — World War 2. Pacific campaigns. Air operations by Allied air forces, *1941-1942*

Caidin, Martin. The ragged, rugged warriors / Martin Caidin. — London : Severn House, 1980, c1966. — xiv,366p : ill,maps ; 21cm
Originally published: New York : Dutton, 1966. — Includes index
ISBN 0-7278-0642-4 : £1.95
Also classified at 940.54'25 B81-01710

940.54'26 — World War 2. Pacific campaigns. Air operations by United States. *Army Air Force*

Mondey, David. USAAF at war in the Pacific / David Mondey and Lewis Nalls. — London : Ian Allan, 1980. — 160p : ill,maps,ports ; 30cm
Maps on lining papers
ISBN 0-7110-1026-9 : £9.95 B81-04849

940.54'26 — World War 2. Pacific campaigns. Air operations by United States. *Army Air Force. Air Force, Seventh, 1942-1945*

Rust, Kenn C.. Seventh Air Force : story : - in World War II / Kenn C. Rust. — Temple City : Historical Aviation Album ; London : Hersant [distributor], 1979. — 64p : ill,1map ; 28cm. — (A Historical Aviation Album publication)
ISBN 0-911852-84-0 (pbk) : Unpriced B81-40690

940.54'26 — World War 2. Pacific campaigns. Military operations by United States. *Marine Corps, 1944*

Hoyt, Edwin P.. To the Marianas : war in the Central Pacific : 1944 / Edwin P. Hoyt. — New York ; London : Van Nostrand Reinhold, c1980. — xi,292p,[16]p of plates : ill,maps,ports ; 24cm
Bibliography: p279-281. — Includes index
ISBN 0-442-26105-5 : £9.70 B81-09913

940.54'26 — World War 2. Pacific campaigns. Naval air operations by United States. *Army Air Force* **& United States.** *Navy, 1942:* **Tokyo Raid**

Glines, Carroll V.. Doolittle's Tokyo raiders / by Carroll V. Glines. — New York ; London : Van Nostrand Reinhold, 1981. — 449p : ill,1map,ports ; 23cm
Originally published: 1964. — Includes index
ISBN 0-442-21925-3 (pbk) : £6.70 B81-26570

940.54'26 — World War 2. Pacific campaigns. Naval air operations by United States. *Navy.* **Grumman Hellcat aeroplanes**

Anderton, David A.. Hellcat / text by David A. Anderton ; illustrations by Rikyu Watanabe. — London : Jane's, 1981. — 56p : ill(some col.),1map ; 34cm
ISBN 0-7106-0036-4 : £4.95 B81-27536

940.54'26'0222 — World War 2. Pacific campaigns. Naval air operations by United States. *Navy.* **Aircraft carriers. Aeroplanes** — *Illustrations*

Sowinski, Larry. The Pacific War : as seen by US Navy photographers during World War 2 / by Larry Sowinski. — London : Conway Maritime, 1981. — 208p : ill(some col.),ports ; 31cm
Ill on lining papers
ISBN 0-85177-217-x : £12.50 B81-41005

940.54'26'0924 — World War 2. Pacific campaigns. Military operations by United States. *Marine Corps* — *Personal observations*

Manchester, William. Goodbye, darkness : a memoir of the Pacific war / William Manchester. — London : Joseph, 1981, c1979. — 401p : ill,maps,ports ; 24cm
Originally published: Boston, Mass. : Little, Brown, 1980. — Map on lining papers
ISBN 0-7181-2011-6 : £8.95 B81-18705

940.54'4 — Allied air forces. Aeroplanes. Losses, *1939-1945*

Philpott, Bryan. In enemy hands : revealing true stories behind wartime Allied aircraft losses / Bryan Philpott ; foreword by Sir Douglas Bader. — Cambridge : Stephens, 1981. — 89p : ill,ports ; 25cm
Ill on lining papers
ISBN 0-85059-499-5 : Unpriced : CIP rev. B81-18092

940.54'4 — Germany. Air raids by Allied forces, *1943-1944.* **Strategy**

Rostow, W. W.. Pre-invasion bombing strategy. — Farnborough, Hants. : Gower, Sept.1981. — [176]p
ISBN 0-566-00482-8 (cased) : £12.50 : CIP entry
ISBN 0-566-00483-6 (pbk) : £4.95 B81-21534

940.54'4 — World War 2. Air operations

Overy, R. J.. The air war 1939-1945 / R.J. Overy. — London : Europa, c1980. — xii,263p,[12]p of plates : ill ; 24cm
Bibliography: p240-256. — Includes index
ISBN 0-905118-53-7 : Unpriced B81-02768

World War II in the air / edited by James F. Sunderman. — New York ; London : Van Nostrand Reinhold, 1981, c1963. — 2v. : ill,1map,1facsim,ports ; 24cm
Originally published: New York : Watts, 1962-63. — Includes index
ISBN 0-442-20044-7 (pbk) : Unpriced
ISBN 0-442-20045-5 (Europe) : £6.70 B81-28465

940.54'4 — World War 2. Air operations by Allied air forces. B-24 Liberator aeroplanes

Bowman, Martin. The B-24 Liberator 1939-1945 / Martin Bowman. — Norwich (33 Orford Pl., Norwich) : Wensum, c1979. — 128p : ill(some col.),maps ; 31cm
ISBN 0-903619-27-x : £5.95 B81-13346

940.54'4'0922 — World War 2. Air operations by allied air forces. Bomber aeroplanes. Gunners

Bowyer, Chaz. Guns in the sky : the air gunners of World War Two / Chaz Bowyer. — London : Corgi, 1981, c1979. — ix,182p : ill,ports ; 24cm
Originally published: London : Dent, 1979. — Bibliography: p179-180. — Includes index
ISBN 0-552-98121-4 (pbk) : £2.95 B81-27840

940.54'43'42 — England. Great Britain. *Royal Air Force.* **Aerodromes,** *1939-1945*

Action stations. — Cambridge : Stephens
2: Military airfields of Lincolnshire and the East Midlands / Bruce Barrymore Halpenny. — 1981. — 217p : ill,maps,plans,ports ; 24cm
Ill on lining papers. — Includes index
ISBN 0-85059-484-7 : £8.95 B81-24469

Action stations. — Cambridge : Stephens
3: Military airfields of Wales and the North-West / David J. Smith. — 1981. — 217p : ill,maps,plans,ports ; 24cm
Ill on lining papers. — Includes index
ISBN 0-85059-485-5 : £8.95 B81-40061

940.54'43'4281 — Yorkshire. Air bases, *1939-1945*

Rapier, Brian J.. White Rose Base / Brian J. Rapier. — [2nd ed]. — [York] ([1 Driffield Terrace, The Mount, York YO2 2DD]) : [Air Museum York Publications], 1980. — 94p : ill,maps,facsims,ports ; 30cm
Previous ed.: Lincoln : Aero Litho Co. (Lincoln), 1972. — Includes index
ISBN 0-9507326-0-5 (pbk) : Unpriced B81-07379

940.54'4941 — World War 2. Air operations by Great Britain. *Royal Air Force.* **Armstrong Whitworth Albemarle aeroplanes, Supermarine Spitfire XII aeroplanes & Short Shetland flying boats**

Bowyer, Michael J. F.. Aircraft for the Royal Air Force / Michael J.F. Bowyer. — London : Faber, 1980. — 170p : ill ; 25cm
Includes index
ISBN 0-571-11515-2 : £9.50 : CIP rev. B80-09529

940.54'4941 — World War 2. Air operations by Great Britain. *Royal Air Force. Bomber Command*

Hastings, Max. Bomber Command / Max Hastings. — London : Pan, 1981, c1979. — 489p,[8]p of plates : ill,maps,ports ; 18cm
Originally published: New York : Dial / J. Wade ; London : Joseph, 1979. — Bibliography: p454-458. - Includes index
ISBN 0-330-26236-x (pbk) : £2.50 B81-19761

940.54'4941 — World War 2. Air operations by Great Britain. *Royal Air Force. Bomber Command. Group, No.5*
Bowyer, Chaz. Bomber Group at war / Chaz Bowyer. — London : Ian Allan, 1981. — 160p : ill,ports ; 30cm
Bibliography: p160
ISBN 0-7110-1087-0 : £9.95 B81-22778

940.54'4941 — World War 2. Air operations by Great Britain. *Royal Air Force.* **De Havilland Mosquito aeroplanes**
Bishop, Edward. The wooden wonder : the story of the de Havilland Mosquito / Edward Bishop. — 2nd rev. ed. — Shrewsbury : Airlife, 1980. — 189p : ill,ports ; 22cm
Previous ed.: London : Parrish, 1959. — Includes index
ISBN 0-906393-04-3 : £6.95 B81-39362

940.54'4941 — World War 2. Air operations by Great Britain. *Royal Air Force Squadron, 85*
Fighter squadron at war / [compiled by] A.J. Brookes. — London : Ian Allan, 1980. — 128p : ill,maps,facsims,ports ; 31cm
ISBN 0-7110-1083-8 : £9.95 B81-04409

940.54'4941 — World War 2. Naval air operations by Great Britain. *Royal Navy. Fleet Air Arm*
Winton, John. Find, fix and strike! : the Fleet Air Arm at war 1939-45 / John Winton. — London : Batsford, 1980. — 152p,[32]p of plates : ill,8maps,ports ; 25cm
Includes index
ISBN 0-7134-3488-0 : £9.95 B81-04558

940.54'4941'0924 — France. Great Britain. *Royal Air Force.* **Pilots. Escapes,** *1943 — Personal observations*
Griffiths, Frank. Winged hours / Frank Griffiths. — London : Kimber, 1981. — 192p,[8]p of plates : ill,3maps,ports ; 24cm
Includes index
ISBN 0-7183-0128-5 : £8.50 B81-25181

940.54'4941'0924 — World War 2. Air operations by Great Britain. *Royal Air Force, 1943-1944.* **Fighter aeroplanes** *— Personal observations*
White, Roger Henshaw. Spitfire saga : with a spell on Wellingtons / Roger Henshaw White. — London : Kimber, 1981. — 221p : ill,ports ; 24cm
Includes index
ISBN 0-7183-0058-0 : £8.75 B81-29582

940.54'4941'0924 — World War 2. Air operations by Great Britain. *Royal Air Force. Bomber Command, 1944-1945.* **Avro Lancaster aeroplanes** *— Personal observations*
Tripp, Miles. The eighth passenger : the experiences of a bomb-aimer in Lancaster bombers during the Second World War / Miles Tripp. — Milton Keynes : Robin Clark, 1979, c1969. — 188p : maps ; 18cm
Originally published: London : Heinemann, 1969. — Includes index
ISBN 0-86072-023-3 (pbk) : £1.50 B81-39721

940.54'4941'0924 — World War 2. Air operations by Great Britain. *Royal Air Force. Bomber Command. Group, No.2, 1938-1940 — Personal observations*
Passmore, Richard. Blenheim boy / Richard Passmore. — London ([13 Nicosia Rd., SW18 3NE]) : Thomas Harmsworth, 1981. — 254p,[16]p of plates : ill,2maps ; 23cm
ISBN 0-9506012-2-5 : £7.95 B81-28504

940.54'4941'0924 — World War 2. Air operations by Great Britain. *Royal Air Force.* **Fighter aeroplanes. Pilots** *— Personal observations*
Page, Geoffrey. Tale of a Guinea Pig / Geoffrey Page. — London : Pelham, 1981. — 218p,[8]p of plates : ill,ports ; 23cm
ISBN 0-7207-1354-4 : £6.95 : CIP rev. B81-16879

940.54'4941'0924 — World War 2. Air operations by Great Britain. *Royal Air Force.* **Supermarine Spitfire aeroplanes** *— Personal observations*
Smith, W. G. G. Duncan. Spitfire into battle / W.G.G. Duncan Smith. — London : Murray, 1981. — 235p,[17]p of plates : ill,maps,ports ; 23cm
Includes index
ISBN 0-7195-3831-9 : £9.50 : CIP rev. B81-27393

940.54'4941'0924 — World War 2. Naval air operations by Great Britain. *Royal Navy. Fleet Air Arm.* **Fairey Swordfish aeroplanes** *— Personal observations*
Kilbracken, John Godley, *Baron.* Bring back my Stringbag : Swordfish pilot at war 1940-45 / Lord Kilbracken. — London : Pan in association with Peter Davis, 1980, c1979. — 221p,[4]p of plates : ill,ports ; 18cm
Originally published: London : P. Davis, 1979
ISBN 0-330-26172-x (pbk) : £1.50 B81-20043

940.54'4941'0924 — World War 2. Night air operations by Great Britain. *Royal Air Force.* **Fighter aeroplanes** *— Personal observations*
Rawnsley, C. F.. Night fighter / C.F. Rawnsley and Robert Wright ; foreword by John Cunningham. — London : Corgi, 1957 (1980 [printing]). — 359p ; 18cm
Originally published: London : Collins, 1957
ISBN 0-552-11597-5 (pbk) : £1.35 B81-20053

940.54'4943 — England. Air raids by Germany. *Wehrmacht, 1944-1945.* **V-1 flying bombs**
Longmate, Norman. The doodlebugs : the story of the flying-bombs / Norman Longmate. — London : Hutchinson, 1981. — 548p,[16]p of plates : ill,1map,ports ; 23cm
Bibliography: p488-513. — Includes index
ISBN 0-09-144750-x : £12.95 B81-24524

940.54'4943 — London. Air raids by Germany. *Wehrmacht.* **V-1 flying bombs & V-2 rockets,** *1944-1945*
Johnson, David, *1950-.* V for vengeance : the second battle of London / David Johnson. — London : Kimber, 1981. — 203p : ill,maps,1facsim,ports ; 25cm
Includes index
ISBN 0-7183-0188-9 : £8.95 B81-32958

940.54'4943 — World War 2. Air operations by Germany. *Luftwaffe.* **Aeroplanes**
Cooper, Matthew. The German Air Force 1933-1945 : an anatomy of failure / Matthew Cooper. — London : Jane's, 1981. — v,406p,[32]p of plates : ill,maps,plans,ports ; 25cm
Bibliography: p396-399. — Includes index
ISBN 0-7106-0071-2 : £12.95 B81-27531

940.54'4943 — World War 2. Air operations by Germany. *Luftwaffe.* **Junkers Stuka aeroplanes**
Barker, A. J.. Stuka Ju-87 / A.J. Barker. — London : Arms and Armour, 1980. — 64p : ill (some col.),ports ; 29cm. — ([War planes in colour] ; 5) (A Bison book)
Bibliography: p64
ISBN 0-85368-474-x : £2.95 : CIP rev. B80-18108

940.54'4943 — World War 2. Night air operations by Germany. *Luftwaffe.* **Fighter aeroplanes** *— Illustrations*
The Defence of the Reich. — London : Arms and Armour, Jan.1982. — [232]p
Translation of: Die Deutsche Nachtjagd
ISBN 0-85368-414-6 : £9.95 : CIP entry B81-33783

940.54'4943'0222 — World War 2. Naval air operations by Germany. *Kriegsmarine.* **Aeroplanes** *— Illustrations*
German maritime aircraft : a selection of German wartime photographs from the Bundesarchiv, Koblenz / [compiled by] Bryan Philpott. — Cambridge : Stephens, 1981. — 94p : chiefly ill,1map ; 25cm. — (World War 2 photo album ; no.18)
ISBN 0-85059-445-6 (cased) : Unpriced : CIP rev.
ISBN 0-85059-446-4 (pbk) : £3.95 B80-22734

940.54'49438'0924 — World War 2. Air operations by Polish pilots *— Personal observations*
Gnyś, Wladek. First kill : a fighter pilot's autobiography / Wladek Gnyś. — London : Kimber, 1981. — 207p : ill,ports ; 24cm
Includes index
ISBN 0-7183-0397-0 : £8.50 B81-29577

940.54'4952 — World War 2. Air operations by Japan. *Navy. Air Services.* **Mitsubishi Zero aeroplanes**
Mikesh, Robert C.. Zero fighter / text by Robert C. Mikesh ; illustrations by Rikyu Watanabe. — London : Jane's, 1981. — 56p : ill(some col.) ; 34cm
ISBN 0-7106-0037-2 : £4.95 B81-27537

Willmott, H. P.. Zero A6M / H.P. Willmott. — London : Arms and Armour, 1980. — 64p : ill (some col.),2ports ; 29cm. — ([War planes in colour] ; 6) (A Bison book)
ISBN 0-85368-085-x : £2.95 : CIP rev. B80-18109

940.54'4973 — World War 2. Air operations by United States. *Army Air Force. Air Force, Twentieth.* **Boeing B29 aeroplanes**
Birdsall, Steve. Saga of the Superfortress : the dramatic story of the B-29 and the Twentieth Air Force / Steve Birdsall. — London : Sidgwick & Jackson, 1981, c1980. — 346p,[4]p of plates : ill(some col.),2facsims,ports ; 27cm
Originally published: New York : Doubleday, 1980. — Bibliography: p340. — Includes index
ISBN 0-283-98786-3 : £10.95 B81-33088

940.54'4973 — World War 2. Air operations by United States. *Army Air Force. Airborne Division, 17th*
Pay, D. R.. Thunder from heaven : story of the 17th Airborne Division 1943-1945 / D.R. Pay. — Nashville : Battery Press ; Walpole (Sunnybank, Halesworth Rd., Walpole, Suffolk) : P. Quorn [distributor], [1980]. — xii,179p : ill,facsims,plans,ports ; 27cm
Originally published: Birmingham, Mich.: Boots, 1947
ISBN 0-89839-037-0 : £11.25 B81-09928

940.54'4973 — World War 2. Air operations by United States. *Army Air Force. Bomber Command.* **Documents**
A Guide to the reports of the United States Strategic Bombing Survey. — Woodbridge : Boydell Press, Sept.1981. — [224]p. — (Royal Historical Society guides and handbooks. Supplementary series ; no.2)
ISBN 0-901050-71-7 : £15.00 : CIP entry B81-20602

940.54'4973 — World War 2. Air operations by United States. *Army Air Force.* **Mustang P-51 aeroplanes**
Grant, William Newby. P-51 Mustang / William Newby Grant. — London : Arms and Armour, 1980. — 64p : ill(some col.),ports(some col.) ; 29cm. — ([War planes in colour] ; 3) (A Bison book)
Bibliography: p64
ISBN 0-85368-454-5 : £2.95 : CIP rev. B80-18110

940.54'4973 — World War 2. Naval air operations by United States. *Navy.* **Aircraft carriers. Aeroplanes**
Kilduff, Peter. US carriers at war / Peter Kilduff. — London : Ian Allan, 1981. — 128p : ill,maps ; 30cm
Maps on lining papers. — Bibliography: p128
ISBN 0-7110-1077-3 : £10.95 B81-31992

940.54'4973'0924 — World War 2. Air operations by United States. *Army Air Force. Air Force, 8th — Personal observations*
McCrary, John R. Tex. First of the many : a journal of action with the men of the Eighth Air Force / by John R. (Tex) McCrary and David E. Scherman. — London : Robson, 1981, c1944. — xvi,241p,[129]p of plates : ill,facsims,ports ; 25cm
Originally published: New York : Simon and Schuster, 1944
ISBN 0-86051-129-4 : £12.50 B81-19710

940.54'5 — World War 2. Naval operations
Westwood, J. N.. Fighting ships of World War II / J.N. Westwood. — London : Sidgwick & Jackson, 1979, c1975. — 160p : ill ; 26cm
Originally published: 1975. — Includes index
ISBN 0-283-98530-5 (cased) : £6.95
ISBN 0-283-98287-x B81-04176

940.54′52 — World War 2. Allied naval blockades. Penetration by Axis merchant ships

Brice, Martin H.. Axis blockade runners of World War II / Martin Brice. — London : Batsford, 1981. — 159p,[16]p of plates : ill ; 24cm
Bibliography: p154-155. — Includes index
ISBN 0-7134-2686-1 : £9.95 B81-37843

940.54′5941 — Great Britain. Shipping services: Elder Dempster Lines. Ships. Sinking, ***1939-1945***

Cowden, James E.. The price of peace : Elder Dempster 1939-1945 / by James E. Cowden. — Liverpool (202 Cotton Exchange Building, Old Hall St., Liverpool L3 9LA) : Jocast, c1981. — 99p : ill,ports ; 21cm
ISBN 0-9507480-0-5 (pbk) : Unpriced B81-22143

940.54′5941 — Soviet Union. Convoys from Iceland, ***1942:*** **PQ17**

Irving, David. The destruction of convoy PQ.17 / David Irving. — Rev. and updated ed. — London : Kimber, 1980. — 314p,[24]p of plates : ill,2charts,ports ; 25cm
Previous ed.: London : Cassell, 1968. — Includes index
ISBN 0-7183-0477-2 : £12.50 B81-03559

940.54′5941 — World War 2. Naval operations by Great Britain. ***Royal Navy.*** **Supply ships: Glenearn** ***(Ship)***

Aiken, Alexander. In time of war / by Alex. Aiken. — Glasgow (48 Merrycrest Ave., Giffnock, Glasgow [G46 6BJ]) : A. Aiken, 1980. — xiv,430p : ill,maps,ports ; 22cm
Maps (4 folded sheets : 4 sides), plans (1 folded sheet : 1 side) in pocket
ISBN 0-9502134-4-6 : Unpriced B81-05725

940.54′5941′0924 — France. ***Marine. Force Y.*** **Shadowing by Great Britain.** ***Royal Navy. Force H, 1940 — Personal observations***

Smith, Peter C. (Peter Charles), *1940-*. Action imminent : three studies of the naval war in the Mediterranean theatre during 1940 / Peter C. Smith. — London : Kimber, 1980. — 352p,[24]p of plates : ill,maps,ports ; 24cm
Includes index
ISBN 0-7183-0277-x (corrected) : £11.95
Primary classification 940.54′21 B81-05295

940.54′5941′0924 — Great Britain. ***Royal Navy.*** **Destroyers: Intrepid** ***(Ship), 1937-1943 — Personal observations***

Mack, George. HMS Intrepid : a memoir / George Mack. — London : Kimber, 1980. — 208p : ill,1map,1plan,ports ; 24cm
Bibliogrphy: p201. — Includes index
ISBN 0-7183-0037-8 : £7.95 B81-07209

940.54′5941′0924 — World War 2. Naval operations by Great Britain. ***Royal Navy — Personal observations — Polish texts***

Wroński, Bohdan. Wspomnienia płyną jak okręty / Bohdan Wroński. — Londyn : Odnowa, 1981. — 191p : ill,facsims ; 22cm
ISBN 0-903705-38-9 (pbk) : Unpriced B81-40385

940.54′5943 — World War 2. Naval operations by Germany. ***Kriegsmarine.*** **Commerce raiders**

Muggenthaler, August Karl. German raiders of World War II / August Karl Muggenthaler. — London : Pan, 1980, c1977. — 319p,[4]p of plates : ill,maps,2ports ; 18cm
Originally published: Englewood Cliffs : Prentice-Hall, 1977 ; London : Hale, 1978. — Bibliography: p297-312. — Includes index
ISBN 0-330-26204-1 (pbk) : £1.95 B81-02737

940.54′5943 — World War 2. Naval operations by Germany. ***Kriegsmarine.*** **Destroyers & escort ships**

German destroyers and escorts. — Cambridge : Stephens, May 1981. — [96]p. — (World War 2 photo albums ; no.20)
ISBN 0-85059-458-8 (cased) : £3.95 : CIP entry
ISBN 0-85059-459-6 (pbk) : £3.95 B81-12824

940.54′5943′0222 — World War 2. Naval operations by Germany. ***Kriegsmarine.*** **Motor torpedo boats —** ***Illustrations***

E-boats and coastal craft : a selection of German wartime photographs from the Bundesarchiv, Koblenz, / [compiled by Paul Beaver]. — Cambridge : Stephens, 1980. — 94p : chiefly ill,1map ; 25cm. — (World War 2 photo album ; no.17)
ISBN 0-85059-443-x (cased) : Unpriced : CIP rev.
ISBN 0-85059-444-8 (pbk) : £3.95 B80-23887

940.54′5943′0924 — World War 2. Naval operations by Germany. ***Kriegsmarine.*** **Battleships: Bismarck** ***(Ship) - Personal observations***

Müllenheim-Rechberg, Burkard, *Freiherr von*. Battleship Bismarck. — London : Bodley Head, May 1981. — [288]p
This translation originally published: Annapolis : Naval Institute Press, 1980
ISBN 0-370-30390-3 : £7.95 : CIP entry B81-06038

940.54′5973 — World War 2. Naval operations by United States. ***Navy.*** **PT boats**

Johnson, Frank D.. United States PT-Boats of World War II in action / by Frank D. Johnson ; line illustrations by John Batchelor. — Poole : Blandford, 1980. — 159p : ill,ports ; 29cm
Includes index
ISBN 0-7137-1025-x : £6.95 : CIP rev. B80-00961

940.54′59931 — World War 2. Naval operations by New Zealand. ***Royal New Zealand Navy.*** **Cruisers: Achilles** ***(Ship)***

Harker, Jack S.. HMNZS Achilles / Jack S. Harker. — Auckland ; London : Collins, 1980. — 264p,[24]p of plates : ill,ports ; 22cm
Bibliography: p259. — Includes index
ISBN 0-00-216961-4 : £7.50 B81-05273

940.54′6 — Great Britain. ***Royal Marines*** **& Great Britain.** ***Royal Navy.*** **Awards of medals,** ***1939-1946:*** **Distinguished Service Medal —** ***Lists***

The **Distinguished** Service Medal 1939-1946 / compiled and edited by W.H. Fevyer. — Polstead : Hayward ; London (5 Buckingham St., W.C.2) : Distributed by London Stamp Exchange, 1981. — vi,163p : 2ill ; 25cm
Includes index
ISBN 0-903754-90-8 (corrected pbk) : Unpriced B81-40988

940.54′65′4336 — West Germany. Durnbach. Commonwealth World War 2 military cemeteries: Durnbach War Cemetery. Graves — ***Lists***

Great Britain. *Commonwealth War Graves Commission*. War dead of the British Commonwealth : the register of the names of those who fell in the 1939-1945 War and are buried in cemeteries in Germany : Durnbach War Cemetery, Part 1 (Abd-Gow) / Commonwealth War Graves Commission. — Amended version. — Maidenhead (2 Marlow Rd., Maidenhead, Berks. SL6 7DX) : The Commission, 1981. — xi,49p : 1map,1plan ; 27cm. — (Germany ; 15-17)
Previous ed.: 1958
Unpriced (pbk) B81-37637

Great Britain. *Commonwealth War Graves Commission*. War dead of the British Commonwealth : the register of the names of those who fell in the 1939-1945 War and are buried in cemeteries in Germany : Durnbach War Cemetery : Part III (Oak-Yth) : the Durnbach Cremation Memorial : minor cemeteries in Bavaria / compiled and published by order of the Imperial War Graves Commission. — Amended version. — Maidenhead : Commonwealth War Graves Commission, 1981. — xii,p99-148 : 1map ; 27cm. — (Germany ; 15-17)
Previous ed.: 1958
Unpriced (pbk) B81-37638

Great Britain. *Commonwealth War Graves Commission*. War dead of the British Commonwealth : the register of names of those who fell in the 1939-1945 War and are buried in cemeteries in Germany : Durnbach War Cemetery : Part II (Gra-Nxe) / compiled and published by order of the Imperial War Graves Commission. — Maidenhead : Commonwealth War Graves Commission, 1981. — xi,97p : ill,1map,1plan ; 27cm. — (Germany ; 15-17)
Originally published: London : Imperial War Graves Commission, 1958
Unpriced (pbk) B81-37639

940.54′65′43512 — West Germany. Kiel. Commonwealth World War 2 military cemeteries: Kiel War Cemetery. Graves — ***Lists***

Great Britain. *Commonwealth War Graves Commission*. War graves of the British Commonwealth : the register of names of those who fell in the 1939-1945 war and are buried in cemeteries in Germany : Kiel War Cemetery / compiled and published by order of the Imperial War Graves Commission. — Maidenhead : Commonwealth War Graves Commission, 1981. — xii,42p : ill,1map,1plan ; 26cm. — (Germany ; 12)
Originally published: London : Imperial War Graves Commission, 1957
Unpriced (pbk) B81-37694

940.54′65′4355 — West Germany. Cologne. Commonwealth World War 2 military cemeteries: Cologne Southern Cemetery. Graves — ***Lists***

Great Britain. *Commonwealth War Graves Commission*. War graves of the British Commonwealth : the register of the names of those who fell in the 1939-1945 War and are buried in cemeteries in Germany : Munster Heath War Cemetery, Cologne Southern Cemetery, minor cemeteries in north-west Germany / compiled and published by order of the Imperial War Graves Commission. — Amended version. — Maidenhead : Commonwealth War Graves Commission, 1981. — xiv,36p : 1map,2plans ; 26cm. — (Germany 3-5)
Previous ed.: London : Imperial War Graves Commission, 1957
Unpriced (pbk)
Also classified at 940.54′65′4359 B81-40397

940.54′65′4355 — West Germany. Kleve. Commonwealth World War 2 military cemeteries: Reichwald Forest War Cemetery. Graves — ***Lists***

Great Britain. *Commonwealth War Graves Commission*. War graves of the British Commonwealth : the register of the names of those who fell in the 1939-1945 War and are buried in cemeteries in Germany : Reichswald Forest War Cemetery : Part II (Cab-Dyt) / compiled and published by order of the Imperial War Graves Commission. — Amended version. — Maidenhead : Commonwealth War Graves Commission, 1981. — ix,p49-93,[1]p of plates : 1map,1plan ; 27cm. — (Germany ; 1)
Previous ed.: 1957
Unpriced (pbk) B81-37636

940.54′65′4359 — West Germany. Münster. Commonwealth World War 2 military cemeteries: Münster Heath War Cemetery. Graves — ***Lists***

Great Britain. *Commonwealth War Graves Commission*. War graves of the British Commonwealth : the register of the names of those who fell in the 1939-1945 War and are buried in cemeteries in Germany : Munster Heath War Cemetery, Cologne Southern Cemetery, minor cemeteries in north-west Germany / compiled and published by order of the Imperial War Graves Commission. — Amended version. — Maidenhead : Commonwealth War Graves Commission, 1981. — xiv,36p : 1map,2plans ; 26cm. — (Germany 3-5)
Previous ed.: London : Imperial War Graves Commission, 1957
Unpriced (pbk)
Primary classification 940.54′65′4355 B81-40397

940.54′65′438 — Poland. Commonwealth World War 2 military cemeteries. Graves — *Lists*

Great Britain. *Commonwealth War Graves Commission.* War graves of the Commonwealth : the register of the names of those who fell in the 1939-1945 War and are buried in cemeteries in Poland and Union of Soviet Socialist Republics : cemeteries in Poland and the Union of Soviet Socialist Republics / compiled and published by order of the Commonwealth War Graves Commission. — Amended version. — Maidenhead : Commonwealth War Graves Commission, 1981. — vii,56p : plans ; 27cm. — (Poland ; 1-3) (USSR ; 1-3)
Previous ed.: 1961
Unpriced (pbk)
Primary classification 940.54′65′47 B81-37820

940.54′65′44 — France. Commonwealth World War 2 military cemeteries. Graves — *Lists*

War dead of the British Commonwealth : the register of the names of those who fell in the 1939-1945 war and are buried in cemeteries in France. — Amended version. — Maidenhead ([2 Marlow Rd., Maidenhead, SL6 7DX]) : Commonwealth War Graves Commission
Previous ed.: 1958
France 857-912: Choloy War Cemetery and cemeteries in Meurthe-et-Moselle, Moselle, Bas-Rhin and Haut-Rhin. — 1981. — xxvi,47p : 1map,1plan ; 27cm
Unpriced (pbk) B81-38559

940.54′65′441 — North-western France. Commonwealth World War 2 military cemeteries. Graves — *Lists*

Great Britain. *Commonwealth War Graves Commission.* War graves of the British Commonwealth : the register of the names of those who fell in the 1939-1945 War and are buried in cemeteries in France : minor cemeteries in Nord-3 / compiled and published by order of the Imperial War Graves Commission. — Amended version. — Maidenhead : Commonwealth War Graves Commission, 1981. — xxii,35p : 2maps ; 26cm. — (France ; 112-162)
Previous ed.: 1958
Unpriced (pbk) B81-39941

940.54′65′4422 — France. St Charles de Percy & St Desir. Commonwealth World War 2 military cemeteries. Graves — *Lists*

Great Britain. *Commonwealth War Graves Commission.* War graves of the British Commonwealth : the register of the names of those who fell in the 1939-1945 War and are buried in cemeteries in France : St. Charles de Percy Cemetery, St. Desir War Cemetery / compiled and published by order of the Imperial War Graves Commission. — Amended version. — Maidenhead : Commonwealth War Graves Commission, 1981. — xxii,61p : 2maps,2plans ; 26cm. — (France ; 1074-1075)
Previous ed.: 1956
Unpriced (pbk) B81-39942

940.54′65′47 — Soviet Union. Commonwealth World War 2 military cemeteries. Graves — *Lists*

Great Britain. *Commonwealth War Graves Commission.* War graves of the Commonwealth : the register of the names of those who fell in the 1939-1945 War and are buried in cemeteries in Poland and Union of Soviet Socialist Republics : cemeteries in Poland and the Union of Soviet Socialist Republics / compiled and published by order of the Commonwealth War Graves Commission. — Amended version. — Maidenhead : Commonwealth War Graves Commission, 1981. — vii,56p : plans ; 27cm. — (Poland ; 1-3) (USSR ; 1-3)
Previous ed.: 1961
Unpriced (pbk)
Also classified at 940.54′65′438 B81-37820

940.54′72 — British prisoners of war. Royal Air Force personnel. Escapes, *1939-1945.* Escapes, *1939-1945*

Brickhill, Paul. Escape - or die : authentic stories of the RAF Escaping Society / Paul Brickhill ; with introduction by H.E. Bates ; and foreword by Sir Basil Embry. — London : Pan, 1981, c1952. — 189p ; 18cm
Originally published: London : Evans, 1952
ISBN 0-330-02098-6 (pbk) : £0.95 B81-13019

940.54′72′430924 — Austria. Karawanken Mountains. Road tunnels: Loibl Pass tunnel. Construction by prisoners of war, *1942-1945 — Personal observations*

Lacaze, André. The tunnel / André Lacaze ; translated from the French by Julian and Anne Gray. — London : Hamilton, 1980. — 471p ; 25cm
Translation of: Le tunnel
ISBN 0-241-10415-7 : £7.95 : CIP rev. B80-10907

940.54′72′430924 — East Germany. Colditz. Prisoners of war, *1940-1945 — Personal observations — Correspondence, diaries, etc.*

Platt, J. Ellison. Padre in Colditz : the diary of J. Ellison Platt / edited by Margaret Duggan. — London : Hodder and Stoughton, 1978 (1980 [printing]). — 318p ; 18cm
ISBN 0-340-25994-9 (pbk) : £1.95 : CIP rev. B80-24976

940.54′72′430924 — Germany. Australian prisoners of war, *1939-1945 — Personal observations*

Taylor, Geoff, *1920-.* Piece of cake / Geoff Taylor†. — [London] : Corgi, 1980, c1956. — 314p ; 18cm
Originally published: London : P. Davies, 1956
ISBN 0-552-11539-8 (pbk) : £1.50 B81-08216

940.54′72′430924 — Germany. Australian prisoners of war, *1942-1945 — Personal observations*

Younger, Calton. No flight from the cage / Calton Younger ; with an introduction by Sir John Hackett. — London : W.H. Allen, 1981, c1956. — 254p ; 18cm. — (War in the twentieth century) (A Star book)
Originally published: London : Muller, 1956
ISBN 0-352-30828-1 (pbk) : £1.95 B81-29368

940.54′72′430924 — Germany. Concentration camps, *1940-1945 — Personal observations — Polish texts*

Cudem ocaleni : wspomnienia z kacetów : praca zbiorowa. — London (4 Praed Mews, W2 1QZ) : Katolicki O′srodek Wydawniczy Veritas, 1981. — 327p ; 23cm
Includes index
Unpriced B81-21020

940.54′72′430924 — Germany. Concentration camps, *1943-1945 — Personal observations*

Wiesel, Elie. Night / Elie Wiesel ; translated from the French by Stella Rodway ; foreword by François Mauriac. — Harmondsworth : Penguin, 1981, c1960. — 126p ; 18cm
Translation of: La nuit. — Originally published: London : MacGibbon & Kee, 1960
ISBN 0-14-006028-6 (pbk) : £1.00 B81-35251

940.54′72′430924 — Poland. Oświęcim. Concentration camps: Auschwitz *(Concentration camp), 1940-1945 — Personal observations*

Kielar, Wieslaw. Anus mundi : five years in Auschwitz / Wieslaw Kielar ; translated from the German by Susanne Flatauer. — London : Allen Lane, 1981, c1980. — 312p : 2plans ; 24cm
Translation of: Anus mundi. — Originally published: New York : Times Books, 1980
ISBN 0-7139-1315-0 : £7.50 B81-14658

940.54′72′43094386 — Poland. Óswięcim. Concentration camps: Auschwitz *(Concentration camp).* Policies of governments of Allied countries, *1942-1945*

Gilbert, Martin. Auschwitz and the Allies / Martin Gilbert. — London : Joseph, 1981. — 368p,[16]p of plates : ill,maps,facsims,ports ; 25cm
Map on lining papers. — Includes index
ISBN 0-7181-2017-5 : £12.00 B81-40696

940.54′72′43094934 — Belgium. Malmédy. American prisoners of war. Massacres by Waffen-SS, *1944*

Whiting, Charles. Massacre at Malmédy / Charles Whiting. — London : Arrow, 1981, c1971. — x,245p : maps ; 18cm
Originally published: London : Cooper, 1971. — Bibliography: p245
ISBN 0-09-925430-1 (pbk) : £1.25 B81-18562

940.54′72′470924 — Poland. British prisoners of war, *1945 — Personal observations*

Young, Scotty. Descent into danger / [edited by] Gordon Thomas. — London : Arrow, 1981. — 240p ; 18cm
Author: Scotty Young. — Originally published: London : Wingate, 1954
ISBN 0-09-925940-0 (pbk) : £1.50 B81-26993

940.54′72′470924 — Poland. Population. Deportation by Soviet military forces, *1939-1945 — Personal observations*

Hadow, Maria. Paying guest in Siberia / Maria Hadow. — Maidstone (24 Week Street, Maidstone, Kent) : Londinium, 1978, c1959. — 127p : 1facsim ; 19cm
Originally published: London : Harvill, 1959
ISBN 0-906264-01-4 (pbk) : £0.80 B81-07703

940.54′72′470924 — Soviet Union. Polish prisoners of war, *1939-ca 1945 — Personal observations*

Thackeray, Alec. You′ll need a guardian angel / Alec Thackeray. — London : Arrow, 1981, c1979. — 268p ; 18cm
Originally published: London : Hamilton, 1979
ISBN 0-09-925540-5 (pbk) : Unpriced B81-36087

940.54′72′520924 — Hong Kong. British prisoners of war, *1941-1945 — Personal observations — Welsh texts*

Evans, Frank. Yn nwylo′r Nipon : atgofion carcharor rhyfel / Frank Evans. — Llandysul : Gwasg Gomer, 1980. — 107p,[12]p of plates : ill,maps,facsims,ports ; 19cm
ISBN 0-85088-613-9 (pbk) : £1.95 B81-04710

940.54′72′520924 — Philippines. Davao. American prisoners of war, *1942-1943 — Personal observations*

Mellnik, Stephen M.. Philippine war diary 1939-1945 / Stephen M. Mellnik. — Rev. ed. — New York ; London : Van Nostrand Reinhold, 1981. — 346p,[16]p of plates : ill,maps,1plan,ports ; 23cm
Previous ed.: published as Philippine diary, 1939-1945. 1969. — Includes index
ISBN 0-442-21258-5 (pbk) : £11.00 B81-37779

940.54′72′520924 — Singapore. Changi. American women prisoners of war, *1942-1945 — Personal observations — Correspondence, diaries, etc.*

Bloom, Freddy. Dear Philip : a diary of captivity, Changi 1942-45 / Freddy Bloom. — London : Bodley Head, 1980. — 157p,[1]leaf of plates : 1plan,ports ; 23cm
ISBN 0-370-30345-8 : £5.95 : CIP rev. B80-20059

940.54′72′520924 — South-east Asia. Australian prisoners of war, *1941-1944 — Personal observations*

Braddon, Russell. The naked island / Russell Braddon ; with drawings made in Changi prison camp by Ronald Searle. — London : Joseph, 1981, c1952. — 284p : ill,ports ; 23cm
Originally published: London : Laurie, 1952
ISBN 0-7181-1996-7 : £6.95 B81-07068

940.54′72′520959 — South-east Asia. Allied prisoners of war. Prison life, *1941-1945*

Lindsay, Oliver. At the going down of the sun : Hong Kong and South-East Asia 1841-1945 / Oliver Lindsay. — London : Hamilton, 1981. — ix,258p,[8]p of plates : ill,1map,ports ; 26cm
Bibliography: p250. - Includes index
ISBN 0-241-10542-0 : £9.50 B81-09837

940.54′72′94 — New South Wales. Cowra. Japanese prisoners of war. Escapes, *1944*

Gordon, Harry. Die like the carp! / Harry Gordon. — [London] : Corgi, 1980, c1978 (1981 [printing]). — 284p : plans ; 18cm
Originally published: Stanmore, N.S.W. : Cassell, 1978
ISBN 0-552-11665-3 (pbk) : £1.25 B81-21394

940.54′7541′0922 — World War 2. Military operations by British military forces. Voluntary aid detachments, *1939-1946 — Personal observations — Collections*

Once upon a ward : V.A.D.s′ own stories and pictures of service at home and overseas 1939-1946 / compiled by Doreen Boys ; foreword by Joy Fawcett. — Upminster (197 Corbets Tey Rd., Upminster, Essex) : D. Boys, c1980. — 207p : ill,ports ; 22cm
ISBN 0-9507221-0-3 : £4.95 B81-05594

940.54′7541′0924 — World War 2. Army operations by Great Britain. *Army. Royal Army Medical Corps — Personal observations*

Aylett, Stanley. Surgeon at war / Stanley Aylett. — Bognor Regis : New Horizon, c1979. — 186p,[30]p of plates : ill,facsims,ports ; 22cm
ISBN 0-86116-190-4 : £4.95 B81-26080

940.54′7541′0924 — World War 2. British nursing services *— Personal observations*

McBryde, Brenda. A nurse′s war / Brenda McBryde. — London : Sphere, 1980, c1979. — 184p,[8]p of plates : ill,1map,3ports ; 18cm
Originally published: London : Chatto and Windus, 1979. — Includes index
ISBN 0-7221-5774-6 (pbk) : £1.25 B81-00668

940.54′81′41 — World War 2. Army operations by Great Britain. *Army — Personal observations*

Brown, Archie. Destiny / by Archie Brown. — Bognor Regis : New Horizon, c1979. — 125p,[11]p of plates : ill,facsims,ports ; 22cm
ISBN 0-86116-192-0 : £4.25
Primary classification 940.4′81′41 B81-17754

940.54′81′438 — World War 2. Army operations by Poland. *Wojsko, 1938-1942 — Personal observations — Polish texts*

Czarnecki, Zygmunt Jerzy. Kataklizm : 1938-1942 / Zygmunt Jerzy Czarnecki. — London : Katolicki Ośrodek Wydawniczy Veritas, 1980. — 208p,[14]p of plates : ill,facsims,ports ; 20cm
Unpriced B81-20679

940.54′81′94 — World War 2 *— Australian viewpoints — Personal observations*

McKie, Ronald. Echoes from forgotten wars / Ronald McKie. — Sydney ; London : Collins, 1980. — 269p : maps ; 22cm
ISBN 0-00-216443-4 : £7.95 B81-06232

940.54′83 — Allied armies. Generals. Interpersonal relationships, *1943-1945*

Irving, David. The war between the generals / David Irving. — London : Allen Lane, 1981. — 446p,[32]p of plates : ill,1map,facsim,ports ; 24cm
Map on lining papers. — Includes index
ISBN 0-7139-1344-4 : £9.95 B81-26568

940.54′83 — Allied armies. Soldiers. Army life, *1940-1945*

Ellis, John, *1945-*. The sharp end of war : the fighting man in World War II / John Ellis. — Newton Abbot : David & Charles, c1980. — 396p,[32]p of plates : ill,2plans ; 24cm
Bibliography: p379-390. - Includes index
ISBN 0-7153-7775-2 : £8.95 : CIP rev.
B80-10908

940.54′83′54 — Great Britain. *Army. Indian Army.* **Soldiers,** *1939-1945*

Lever, J. C. G.. The sowar and the jawan : the soldiers of the former Indian army and their homelands / J.C.G. Lever. — Ilfracombe : Stockwell, 1981. — 160p ; 22cm
Bibliography: p160
ISBN 0-7223-1440-x : £7.15 B81-26567

940.54′85′09494 — Switzerland. Espionage, *1939-1945*

Garliński, Józef. The Swiss corridor : espionage networks in Switzerland during World War II / Józef Garliński. — London : Dent, 1981. — xviii,222p,[12]p of plates : ill,maps,1facsim,ports ; 24cm
Bibliography: p209-213. - Includes index
ISBN 0-460-04351-x : £9.95 B81-19746

940.54′86 — Netherlands. Amsterdam. Industrial diamonds. Rescue by Allied secret services, *1940*

Walker, David E.. [Adventure in diamonds]. Operation Amsterdam / David E. Walker. — London : Granada, 1974, c1962 (1980 [printing]). — 174p ; 18cm. — (A Mayflower book)
Originally published: London : Evans, 1962
ISBN 0-583-12233-7 (pbk) : £0.95 B81-01654

940.54′86 — World War 2. Military operations. Effects of possession by Allied forces of Axis forces′ Enigma cipher machines

Calvocoressi, Peter. Top Secret Ultra / Peter Calvocoressi. — London : Cassell, 1980. — 132p,[16]p of plates : ill,facsims,ports ; 23cm
Includes index
ISBN 0-304-30546-4 : £4.95 B81-01381

Garliński, Józef. Intercept : the Enigma war / Józef Garliński ; foreward by R.V. Jones. — [London] : Magnum, 1981, c1979. — xx,219p,[8]p of plates : ill,2maps,ports ; 20cm
Originally published: London : Dent, 1979. — Bibliography: p205-211. — Includes index
ISBN 0-417-05640-0 (pbk) : £1.75 B81-14233

940.54′86 — World War 2. Military operations. Effects of possession by Allied forces of Axis forces′ Enigma cipher machines *— Personal observations*

Calvocoressi, Peter. Top Secret Ultra / Peter Calvocoressi. — London : Sphere, 1981, c1980. — 152p,[8]p of plates : ill,facsims,ports ; 18cm
Originally published: London : Cassell, 1980. — Includes index
ISBN 0-7221-2291-8 (pbk) : £1.25 B81-35526

940.54′86 — World War 2. Military operations. Effects of possession by Allied forces of Axis forces′ Enigma cipher machines *— Polish texts*

Garliński, Józef. Enigma : tajemnica drugiej wojny światowej / Józef Garliński. — Londyn : Odnowa, 1980. — 255p,[16]p of plates : ill,maps,facsims,ports ; 22cm
Bibliography: p241-247. — Includes index
ISBN 0-903705-31-1 (pbk) : Unpriced
B81-21027

940.54′86′41 — Switzerland. British anti-German espionage, *1939-1945*

Read, Anthony. Operation Lucy : most secret spy ring of the Second World War / Anthony Read and David Fisher. — London : Hodder and Stoughton, 1980. — 254p,[8]p of plates : ill,ports ; 24cm
Bibliography: p239-241. — Includes index
ISBN 0-340-25902-7 : £8.50 : CIP rev.
B80-20061

940.54′86′410924 — Germany. Anti-German espionage by British prisoners of war, *1940-1945 — Personal observations*

Brown, John, *1908-1964*. In durance vile / by John Brown ; revised and edited by John Borrie. — London : Hale, 1981. — 160p,[8]p of plates : ill,port ; 23cm
Bibliography: p153. — Includes index
ISBN 0-7091-8980-x : £7.95 B81-24552

940.54′86′410924 — World War 2. Anti-German espionage *— Personal observations*

Fraser-Smith, Charles. The secret war of Charles Fraser-Smith / with Gerald McKnight and Sandy Lesberg. — London : Joseph, 1981. — 159p,[12]p of plates : ill ; 23cm
Includes index
ISBN 0-7181-2035-3 : £7.50 B81-40220

940.54′86′410924 — World War 2. Intelligence operations by Great Britain. *Royal Air Force. Administrative and Special Duties Branch, 1940-1946 — Personal observations*

Peskett, S. John. Strange intelligence : from Dunkirk to Nuremberg / S. John Peskett. — London : Hale, 1981. — 208p,[12]p of plates : ill,1map,1facsim,ports ; 23cm
Includes index
ISBN 0-7091-8978-8 : £7.95 B81-22295

940.54′86′410924 — World War 2. Intelligence operations by Great Britain. *Royal Air Force. Y Service — Officers′ personal observations*

Clayton, Aileen. The enemy is listening / Aileen Clayton. — London : Hutchinson, 1980. — 381p,[16]p of plates : ill,maps,1facsim,ports ; 23cm
Maps on lining papers. — Bibliography: p350-352. - Includes index
ISBN 0-09-142340-6 : £9.95 : CIP rev.
B80-11253

940.54′86′410924 — World War 2. Military operations by Great Britain. *Army. Special Operations Executive. French Section.* **Millar, George,** *to 1946 — Biographies*

Millar, George. Road to resistance : an autobiography / George Millar. — London : Arrow, 1981, c1979. — 411p : 1map ; 18cm
Originally published: London : Bodley Head, 1979
ISBN 0-09-925600-2 (pbk) : £1.95 B81-30662

940.54′86′4370924 — World War 2. Anti-German espionage. Moravec, Frantisek *— Biographies*

Moravec, Frantisek. Master of spies : the memoirs of General Frantisek Moravec. — London : Sphere, 1981, c1975. — xx,235p : 1map ; 18cm
Originally published: London : Bodley Head, 1975
ISBN 0-7221-6175-1 (pbk) : £1.50 B81-28987

940.54′86′4′81 — Norway. Gold reserves. Rescue by resistance movements, *1940*

Baden-Powell, Dorothy. Pimpernel gold. — Large print ed. — Anstey : Ulverscroft, Oct.1981. — [368]p. — (Ulverscroft large print series)
Originally published: New York : St. Martin′s Press ; London : Hale, 1978
ISBN 0-7089-0700-8 : £5.00 : CIP entry
B81-30365

940.54′87′430924 — World War 2. Anti-British espionage. Druid

Mosley, Leonard. The Druid. — London : Eyre Methuen, Jan.1982. — [256]p
ISBN 0-413-40280-0 : £7.50 : CIP entry
B81-34399

940.54′87′430981 — Brazil. Intelligence operations by German secret services, *1939-1945*

Hilton, Stanley E.. Hitler′s secret war in South America 1939-1945 : German military espionage and Allied counterespionage in Brazil / Stanley E. Hilton. — Baton Rouge ; London : Louisiana State University Press, c1981. — 353p : ill,1map,ports ; 24cm
Bibliography: p339-345. — Includes index
ISBN 0-8071-0751-4 : £12.00 B81-25432

940.54′886′41 — World War 2. British propaganda

Cruickshank, Charles. The fourth arm : psychological warfare 1938-1945 / Charles Cruickshank. — Oxford : Oxford University Press, 1981, c1977. — 200p,[16]p of plates : ill,facsims ; 20cm. — (Oxford paperbacks)
Originally published: London : Davis-Poynter, 1977. — Bibliography: p191. — Includes index
ISBN 0-19-285103-9 (pbk) : £2.95 : CIP rev.
B81-23882

940.55 — HISTORY. EUROPE, 1945-

940.55 — Europe. Political events, *1945-1980*

Jones, R. Ben. The making of contemporary Europe / R. Ben Jones. — London : Hodder and Stoughton, c1980. — 205p : ill,maps ; 24cm
Bibliography: p200-202. - Includes index
ISBN 0-340-25794-6 (cased) : £9.50 : CIP rev.
ISBN 0-340-25795-4 (pbk) : £4.50 B80-24977

940.55 — Western Europe. Political events, *1945-1980*

Urwin, Derek W.. Western Europe since 1945. — 3rd ed. — Harlow : Longman, July 1981. — [416]p
Previous ed.: 1972
ISBN 0-582-49071-5 (pbk) : £4.95 : CIP entry
B81-15935

940.55′8 — Europe. Social conditions *— For schools*

Barnes, Anthony. Europe : people and society / Anthony Barnes. — London : Harrap, 1980. — 48p : ill(some col.),col.maps,plan,ports ; 30cm. — (Harrap′s European studies course ; pt.4)
Map on inside front cover
ISBN 0-245-53482-2 (pbk) : £1.80 B81-12091

940.55′8′05 — Western Europe. Relations with Latin America — *Serials*
Europe and Latin America : an annual review of European-Latin American Relations / Latin America Bureau. — 1980-. — London (PO Box 134, NW1 4JY) : The Bureau, 1980-. — v. ; 21cm
Continues: Britain and Latin America
ISSN 0260-5023 = Europe and Latin America : £1.95
Also classified at 980′.038′05 B81-04447

941 — HISTORY. GREAT BRITAIN

941 — Great Britain, *60-1485 — For schools*
Page, Philip. Who? What? Why?. — London : Edward Arnold, Sept.1981
Bk.1: AD60 to 1485. — [32]p
ISBN 0-7131-0471-6 (pbk) : £1.00 : CIP entry B81-23833

941 — Great Britain, *1688-1901 — For schools*
History in close-up. — London : Cassell. — (Cassell history. Level 4)
Britain and Europe 1688-1901 / Leonard W. Cowie. — 1981. — 237p : ill,maps,facsims,ports ; 25cm
Includes index
ISBN 0-304-30644-4 (pbk) : £3.50 : CIP rev. B81-02649

941 — Great Britain. Abbeys & priories, *to 1979*
Wright, Geoffrey N.. Discovering abbeys and priories / Geoffrey N. Wright. — 2nd ed. — Aylesbury : Shire Publications, 1979. — 64p,[16]p of plates : ill,1plan ; 18cm. — (Discovering series ; no.57)
Previous ed.: 1969. — Includes index
ISBN 0-85263-454-4 (pbk) : £0.75 B81-05865

941 — Great Britain. Archives. Organisations: Historical Manuscripts Commission — *Serials*
Great Britain. *Royal Commission on Historical Manuscripts*. Secretary′s report to the Commissioners / the Royal Commission on Historical Manuscripts. — 1979-80. — London : H.M.S.O., 1980. — 24p
ISBN 0-11-440110-1 : £2.40 B81-01383

941 — Great Britain. Castles, *to ca 1852*
Johnson, Paul. The National Trust book of British castles / Paul Johnson. — London : Granada, 1981, c1978. — 235p,[40]p of plates : ill(some col.),facsims,plans,ports ; 20cm. — (A Panther book)
Originally published: London : National Trust : Weidenfeld & Nicolson, 1978. — Bibliography: p219-220. - Includes index
ISBN 0-586-05125-2 (pbk) : £3.95 B81-11465

941 — Great Britain. Country houses. Organisations: Historic Houses Association — *Serials*
The **Historic** Houses Association journal. — Vol.1, no.1 (Summer 1976)-. — Dunstable (Oldhill, London Rd, Dunstable, Bedfordshire) : ABC Historic Publications for the Association, 1976-. — v. : ill,ports ; 30cm
Irregular. — Description based on: Vol.4, no.2 (July 1980)
ISSN 0260-8707 = Historic Houses Association journal : Unpriced B81-20436

941 — Great Britain — *History — For schools*
Cowie, Evelyn E.. History in close-up. — London : Cassell
Britain and the world 1901-75. — Dec.1981. — [224]p
ISBN 0-304-30645-2 : £3.50 : CIP entry B81-31463

941 — Great Britain. Ley systems
Watkins, Alfred. The proof of ancient track alinement / by Alfred Watkins. — Cambridge (142 Pheasant Rise, Bar Hill, Cambridge CB3 8SD) : Institute of Geomantic Research, 1981. — 4p : ill ; 30cm
Unpriced (pbk) B81-33580

941 — Great Britain. Literary associations
Daiches, David. Literary landscapes of the British Isles. — 2nd ed. — London : Bell & Hyman, Sept.1981. — [287]p
Previous ed.: London : Paddington Press, 1979
ISBN 0-7135-1244-x : £7.95 : CIP entry B81-22522

941 — Great Britain. Local history — *For schools*
Lines, C. J.. The past around us / authors Clifford Lines, Laurie Bolwell. — London : Macdonald Educational, c1981. — 48p : ill (some col.),1col.map,plans(some col.),ports (some col.) ; 22cm. — (Town and around. History)
Cover title. — Text on covers
ISBN 0-356-07192-8 (pbk) : Unpriced B81-32718

941 — Great Britain. Muslims. Social life — *For schools*
Iqbal, Muhammad, *1938-*. Call from the minaret : a Muslim family in Britain / Muhammad Iqbal. — Sevenoaks : Hodder and Stoughton, c1980. — 56p ; 22cm
Bibliography: p50-52
ISBN 0-340-25682-6 (pbk) : £1.95 : CIP rev. B80-07169

941 — Great Britain. Property of national importance. Preservation
Our past before us. — London : Maurice Temple Smith, Sept.1981. — [288]p
ISBN 0-85117-219-9 (pbk) : £6.95 : CIP entry B81-28563

941 — Great Britain. Relations with Canada — *Conference proceedings*
Britain and Canada : a colloquium held at Leeds, October 1979 : papers and report / edited with an introduction by David Dilks. — London (Marlborough House, Pall Mall, S.W.1) : Commonwealth Foundation, 1980. — 109p ; 25cm. — (Occasional paper / Commonwealth Foundation, ISSN 0069-7087 / no.49)
Cover title
Unpriced (pbk)
Also classified at 971 B81-08049

941 — Great Britain. Residences. Historical sources
Hilton, John. Your house and its history / John Hilton. — Hadlow ([19 Lonewood Way,] Hadlow, Tonbridge, Kent) : J. Hilton, c1981. — 23p : ill,facsims,plans ; 22cm
£0.60 (pbk) B81-40293

941 — Great Britain. Royal weddings, *to 1981*
Ashdown, Dulcie M.. Royal weddings / Dulcie M. Ashdown. — London : Hale, 1981. — 208p,[24]p of plates : ill,ports ; 25cm
Bibliography: p184. — Includes index
ISBN 0-7091-9383-1 : £9.50 B81-27844

941 — Great Britain. Social conditions, *1066-1900 — For schools*
Lines, C. J.. Life in the past / authors Clifford Lines, Laurie Bolwell. — London : Macdonald Educational, 1981. — 48p : ill(some col.),map,col.ports ; 22cm. — (Town and around. History)
Cover title. — Text on covers
ISBN 0-356-07191-x (pbk) : Unpriced B81-29915

941 — Great Britain. Social conditions, *ca 1000-1979 compared with* **social conditions in France,** *ca 1000-1979*
Britain and France : ten centuries / edited by Douglas Johnson, François Crouzet and François Bédarida. — Folkestone : Dawson, 1980. — 379p ; 24cm
ISBN 0-7129-0831-5 : £20.00 : CIP rev.
Also classified at 944 B80-09603

941 — Great Britain. Social customs, *1780-1914*
Girouard, Mark. The return to Camelot. — London : Yale University Press, Sept.1981. — [320]p
ISBN 0-300-02739-7 : £12.50 : CIP entry B81-28808

941 — Great Britain. Social life, *1400-1750 — For schools*
Pollard, Michael, *1931-*. Traders and travellers 1400-1750 / Michael Pollard ; illustrated by Robert G. Hunter. — Glasgow : Blackie, 1981. — 94p : ill(some col.) ; 21cm. — (The Story of life ; 5)
ISBN 0-216-90734-9 (pbk) : £2.95 B81-29246

941 — Great Britain. Social life, *to 1500.* **Archaeological sources: Wood**
Taylor, Maisie. Wood in archaeology / Maisie Taylor. — Princes Risborough : Shire, 1981. — 56p ; 21cm. — (Shire archaeology series ; 17)
Bibliography: p55. — Includes index
ISBN 0-85263-537-0 (pbk) : £1.95 B81-40854

941 — Great Britain. Society. Permissiveness
Fletcher, Vera M.. Vera veritas / Vera M. Fletcher. — Bognor Regis : New Horizon, c1981. — 84p ; 21cm
ISBN 0-86116-439-3 : £3.50 B81-32567

941 — Great Britain. Stately homes
Scott, Amoret. Discovering stately homes / Amoret and Christopher Scott. — [New] ed. — Aylesbury : Shire, 1981. — 96p : ill,maps ; 18cm. — (Discovering series ; no.164)
Previous ed.: 1975. — Includes index
ISBN 0-85263-554-0 (pbk) : £1.25 B81-40742

941 — Great Britain. Structures of historical importance — *Questions & answers*
Jamieson, Alan. Castles, churches and houses / Alan Jamieson ; illustrated by Philip Page. — [Harmondsworth] : Puffin, 1981. — 63p : ill,forms ; 20cm. — (An Outdoors puzzle book)
ISBN 0-14-031315-x (pbk) : £0.80 B81-21120

941 — Great Britain, *to 1976 — For children*
Harris, Nathaniel. History around us / Nathaniel Harris. — London : Hamlyn, 1979. — 192p : ill(some col.),maps(some col.),ports(some col.) ; 19cm
Includes index
ISBN 0-600-39529-4 : £2.75 B81-01382

941 — Great Britain, *to 1979*
Places : an anthology of Britain / chosen by Ronald Blythe. — Oxford : Oxford University Press, 1981. — 238p : ill ; 24cm
Ill on lining papers. — Includes index
ISBN 0-19-211575-8 : £7.95 B81-22120

Randle, John. Understanding Britain : a history of the British people and their culture / John Randle. — Oxford : Basil Blackwell, 1981. — vi,222p : ill,maps,facsims,ports ; 25cm
Bibliography: p210-212. — Includes index
ISBN 0-631-12471-3 (cased) : £8.50 : CIP rev.
ISBN 0-631-12883-2 (pbk) : £2.95 B80-10570

941 — Great Britain, *to 1980*
The **Country** life book of the living history of Britain / consultant editor W.G.V. Balchin. — London : Country Life, 1981. — 256p : ill (some col.),maps(some col.),facsims(some col.),ports(some col.) ; 35cm
Bibliography: p249-251. — Includes index
ISBN 0-600-36783-5 : £15.00 B81-40808

941 — Great Britain, *to 1980 — For schools*
Openings in history. — London : Hutchinson
Tudors and Stuarts / David Kennedy. — 1981. — [64]p : ill,maps,ports,1geneal.table ; 30cm
ISBN 0-09-141301-x (pbk) : Unpriced : CIP rev. B80-09931

941′.0022′2 — Great Britain. Antiquities, *to 1700.* **Reconstruction drawings**
Sorrell, Alan. Reconstructing the past / Alan Sorrell ; edited by Mark Sorrell. — London : Batsford Academic and Educational, 1981. — 168p,4p of plates : ill(some col.) ; 26cm
Includes index
ISBN 0-7134-1588-6 : £8.95 B81-19642

941′.003′21 — Great Britain. Literary associations, *to 1980 — Encyclopaedias*
Eagle, Dorothy. The Oxford illustrated literary guide to Great Britain and Ireland / compiled and edited by Dorothy Eagle and Hilary Carnell. — [New ed.] / revised by Dorothy Eagle. — Oxford : Oxford University Press, 1981. — vi,312p,[47]p of plates : ill(some col.),maps(some col.),ports ; 29cm
Previous ed.: published as The Oxford literary guide to the British Isles. Oxford : Clarendon Press, 1977. — Includes index
ISBN 0-19-869125-4 : £12.50 : CIP rev.
Also classified at 820′.3′21 B81-02647

941'.003'21 — Great Britain. Local history — *Encyclopaedias*

Richardson, John, *1935-*. The local historian's encyclopedia / John Richardson. — New Barnet (Orchard House, 54 Station Road, New Barnet, Herts.) : Historical Publications, 1974 (1977 [printing]). — 312p : ill ; 20cm
Bibliography: p275-283. — Includes index
£2.50 (pbk) B81-05584

941'.003'21 — Great Britain, *to 1970* — *Encyclopaedias*

A **dictionary** of British history / editorial consultant J.P. Kenyon. — London : Secker & Warburg, 1981. — 410p : maps,1geneal.table ; 23cm
ISBN 0-436-23308-8 : £10.00 : CIP rev.
B81-21653

941'.003'21 — Great Britain, *to 1979* — *Encyclopaedias*

The **Illustrated** dictionary of British history / general editor Arthur Marwick ; contributing editors Christopher Harvie, Charles Kightly, Keith Wrightson. — [London] : Thames and Hudson, c1980. — 319p : ill,coats of arms,facsims,geneal.tables,maps,1plan,ports ; 26cm
ISBN 0-500-25072-3 : £8.95 B81-01898

941'.00451 — Great Britain. Italian immigrants. Social life — *Italian texts* — *Serials*

Londra sera. — [No.1, 1978?]-. — London : Editoriale Londra Sera ; London ([1 Benwell Rd, N7]) : Spotlight Magazine Distribution [Distributor], [1978?]-. — v. : ill,chart, ports ; 45cm
Irregular. — Description based on: April 1979 issue
ISSN 0260-4582 = Londra sera : £0.10
B81-04588

941'.004916 — Great Britain. Celtic civilization. Scottish literary sources & Welsh literary sources, *to 1100*

Hughes, Kathleen. Celtic Britain in the early Middle Ages : studies in Welsh and Scottish sources / by the late Kathleen Hughes ; edited by David Dumville. — Woodbridge : Boydell, c1980. — ix,123p,[4]p of plates : ill,facsims,ports ; 24cm. — (Studies in Celtic history ; 2)
Bibliography: p101-112. - Includes index
ISBN 0-85115-127-2 : £12.00 : CIP rev.
B80-22737

941'.0049185 — Great Britain. Polish exiles. Organisations: Związek Ziem Wschodnich Rzeczypospolitej Polskiej — *Regulations* — *Polish texts*

Związek Ziem Wschodnich Rzeczypospolitej Polskiej. Statut / Związku Ziem Wschodnich Rzeczypospolitej Polskiej. — London (43 Eaton Place, S.W.1) : Zarząd Główny Związku Ziem Wschodnich R.P., 1981. — [2],14p : ill,map,coat of arms ; 22cm
Cover title
Unpriced (pbk) B81-29626

941'.004924 — Great Britain. Jews: Solomon, H. N., *1795-1881* — *Biographies*

Baum, Jeffrey. A light unto my path : the story of H.N. Solomon of Edmonton / [by Jeffrey and Barbara Baum]. — [Enfield] ([37 Chase Court Gardens, Enfield, Middx.]) : Edmonton Hundred Historical Society, [1980?]. — 46p : ill,1map,1facsim,1port,geneal.tables ; 30cm. — (Occasional paper / Edmonton Hundred Historical Society ; no.43)
ISBN 0-902922-39-4 (pbk) : £0.60 B81-18913

941'.004924'05 — Great Britain. Jews — *Serials*

Koleinu. — Vol.1, no.1 (Sept.1980 = Tishrei 5741)-. — London (523 Finchley Rd, NW3 7BD) : British Dror/Habonim, 1980-. — v. : ill,ports ; 30cm
Irregular. — Merger of: Newsletter (Habonim) ; and, Igeret
ISSN 0260-6585 = Koleinu : Unpriced
B81-09134

941'.00496 — Great Britain. Negroes. Social life, *to 1958* — *Readings from contemporary sources* — *For schools*

File, Nigel. Black settlers in Britain 1555-1958 / Nigel File and Chris Power. — London : Heinemann Educational, 1981. — 92p : ill,facsims,ports ; 27cm
Bibliography: p90
ISBN 0-435-31173-5 (pbk) : £3.50 : CIP rev.
B80-34315

941'.0049921'05 — Great Britain. Filipino immigrants — *Serials*

Balita : pahayagan ng mga Pilipino. — Vol.1, no.1 (Nov.-Dec.1979)-. — London : P.O. Box 375, NW2 4HD : Balita, 1979-. — v. : ill ; 30cm
Monthly. — Text in English and Tagalog. — Subtitle varies. — Description based on: Vol.1, no.4 (Mar.-Apr.1980)
ISSN 0260-6690 = Balita : £3.80 per year
B81-07794

Pahayagan : news bulletin of the Pagkakaisa ng Samahang Pilipino. — Vol.1, no.1 (July 1980)-. — London (23 Derwent House, Southern Grove Rd, E3 4PU) : Pagkakaisa, 1980-. — v. : ill ; 42cm
Six issues yearly. — Text in English and Tagalog
ISSN 0260-6682 = Pahayagan : £2.70 for 12 issues B81-07793

941'.007'2 — Great Britain. Local history. Research — *Manuals*

Hoskins, W. G.. Fieldwork in local history. — 2nd ed. — London : Faber, Feb.1982. — [216]p
Previous ed.: 1967
ISBN 0-571-18051-5 (cased) : CIP entry
ISBN 0-571-18050-7 (pbk) : Unpriced
B81-38839

941'.0074'02 — Great Britain. Country life museums — *Directories*

Hudson, Kenneth. The Shell guide to country museums / Kenneth Hudson. — London : Heinemann, c1980. — xii,241p,[16]p of plates : ill(some col.),maps,ports ; 23cm
Includes index
ISBN 0-434-35370-1 : £6.50 B81-03940

941'.009'52 — Great Britain. Woodlands, *to 1975*

Rackham, Oliver. Trees and woodland in the British landscape / Oliver Rackham. — London : Dent, 1976 (1981 printing). — 204p,[8]p of plates : ill,maps ; 22cm. — (Archaeology in the field series)
Bibliography: p183-185. — Includes index
ISBN 0-460-02223-7 (pbk) : £4.95 B81-21850

941'.009'52 — Great Britain. Woodlands, *to 1980*

Harvey, Nigel. Trees, woods and forests / Nigel Harvey. — Princes Risborough : Shire, 1981. — 32p : 1map,facsims ; 21cm. — (Shire album ; 74)
Bibliography: p32
ISBN 0-85263-572-9 (pbk) : £0.95 B81-40857

941'.009'732 — Great Britain. Towns — *For schools*

Roberts, Frank, *1939-*. Our towns and cities / Frank and Bernie Roberts. — Basingstoke : Macmillan Education, 1981. — 31p : ill,maps,plans ; 30cm. — (Looking at Britain ; 1)
ISBN 0-333-28409-7 (pbk) : £1.35 B81-21371

941'.009'732 — Great Britain. Towns. Streets, *1900* — *For schools*

Purkis, Sallie. In the street in 1900 / Sallie Purkis. — Harlow : Longman, 1981. — 24p : ill ; 21cm. — (Into the past ; 2)
Cover title. — Text and ill on inside covers
ISBN 0-582-18435-5 (pbk) : £0.65 B81-30706

941'.009'732 — Great Britain. Urban regions. Social conditions — *For schools*

George, David. Living in cities / David George. — Harlow : Longman, 1981. — 46p : ill,maps,1facsims,1plan ; 24cm. — (Longman social science studies. Series 2)
Bibliography: p46
ISBN 0-582-22305-9 (pbk) : £1.45 B81-40703

941'.009'734 — Great Britain. Countryside

Freethy, Ron. The making of the British countryside / Ron Freethy. — Newton Abbot : David & Charles, c1981. — 256p : ill ; 24cm
Bibliography: p249-251. - Includes index
ISBN 0-7153-8012-5 : £7.95 B81-20810

In the country : Angela Rippon, Phil Drabble, Bernard Price, Ted Moult, Tom Weir, Elizabeth Eyden, Richard Mabey, Joe Henson and Gordon Beningfield / edited by Peter Crawford. — London : Macmillan, 1980. — 202p : ill(some col.),maps,ports(some col.) ; 24cm
Includes index
ISBN 0-333-29325-8 : £7.65 : CIP rev.
B80-21220

941'.009'734 — Great Britain. Countryside — *Encyclopaedias*

Book of the British countryside / [edited and designed by Drive Publications Limited]. — Repr. with amendments. — London : Drive Publications for the Automobile Association, 1981. — 535p : ill,maps ; 27cm
Previous ed.: 1973
£10.95 B81-15475

941'.009'734 — Great Britain. Countryside — *Serials*

Countryside monthly. — No.1005 (June 1981)-. — St Albans : Gilbertson & Page, 1981-. — v. : ill,ports ; 25cm
Continues: Gamekeeper and countryside
ISSN 0261-2208 = Countryside monthly : £6.60 per year B81-32701

941'.009'734 — Great Britain. Rural regions. Social conditions

Smith, Anthony, *1938-*. The Down your way book / Anthony Smith and Gay Search ; introduction by Brian Johnston. — London : Arthur Barker, 1981. — viii,190p : ill,1map,1facsim,ports ; 26cm
Ill on lining papers
ISBN 0-213-16787-5 : £6.95 B81-32307

941'.009'734 — Great Britain. Rural regions. Social conditions, *1837-1901*

The **Victorian** countryside / edited by G.E. Mingay. — London : Routledge & Kegan Paul, 1981. — 2v.(xvi,702p,[98]p of plates) : ill,facsims,plans,ports ; 26cm
Bibliography: p639-677. — Includes index
ISBN 0-7100-0736-1 : £40.00 (The set) (v.1) : £25.00 (v.2) : £25.00 B81-27776

941'.009'734 — Great Britain. Rural regions. Social life, *1900* — *For schools*

Merson, Elizabeth. In the country in 1900 / Elizabeth Merson. — Harlow : Longman, 1981. — 24p : ill ; 21cm. — (Into the past ; 4)
Cover title. — Text and ill on inside covers
ISBN 0-582-18437-1 (pbk) : £0.65 B81-27117

941'.009'92 — Great Britain. Kings & queens, *to 1980*

Delderfield, Eric R.. Kings and Queens of England and Great Britain. — 3rd ed. — Newton Abbot : David and Charles, Oct.1981. — [160]p
Previous ed.: 1970
ISBN 0-7153-8299-3 (pbk) : £1.95 : CIP entry
B81-30195

941'.009'92 — Great Britain. Kings. Mistresses, *1660-1936*

Hardy, Alan. The King's mistress / Alan Hardy. — London : Evans, 1980. — 189p,[16]p of plates : ill,ports ; 23cm
Bibliography: p182-183. — Includes index
ISBN 0-237-45526-9 : £7.95 B81-01384

941'.009'92 — Great Britain. Monarchs, *to 1977* — *For children*

Lewis, Brenda Ralph. Kings and queens of England / written by Brenda Ralph Lewis ; illustrated by John Leigh-Pemberton and Peter Robinson. — Loughborough : Ladybird, c1981
Bk.1. — 51p : col.ill,col.maps,1col.plan,1col.geneal.table ; 18cm
Text, ill on inside covers
ISBN 0-7214-0560-6 : £0.50 B81-39377

941'.009'92 — Great Britain. Monarchs, *to 1977 — For children* *continuation*

Lewis, Brenda Ralph. Kings and queens of England / written by Brenda Ralph Lewis ; illustrated by John Leigh-Pemberton and Peter Robinson. — Rev. ed. — Loughborough : Ladybird, c1981
Bk.2. — 51p : col.ill,1geneal.table ; 18cm
Text, ill on inside covers
ISBN 0-7214-0561-4 : £0.50 B81-39378

941'.009'92 — Great Britain. Royal families, *973-1976*

Plumb, J. H.. Royal heritage : the story of Britain's royal builders and collectors / by J.H. Plumb ; published in association with the television series written by Huw Wheldon and J.H. Plumb. — London : British Broadcasting Corporation, 1977 (1981 [printing]). — 360p : ill(some col.),facsims,ports(some col.) ; 30cm
Includes index
ISBN 0-563-17974-0 (pbk) : £8.50
Also classified at 708.2 B81-27707

941'.009'92 — Great Britain. Royal families, *to 1977.* **Local associations: Lancashire. Rossendale** *(District)*

Elliott, Jon, *1911-*. Royalty and Rossendale : a survey of Rossendale connections with the Crown from the earliest times : with a list of related exhibits in the Rossendale Museum / by Jon Elliott. — 2nd ed. — Rossendale ([Rawtenstall, Rossendale, Lancashire BB4 6RE]) : Rossendale Museum, 1981. — 22p : ill ; 16x21cm
Previous ed.: 1977
£0.30 (unbound) B81-37662

941'.009'92 — Great Britain. Royal families, *to 1979 — Questions & answers*

Litvinoff, Sarah. The Royal Family quiz book / compiled by Sarah Litvinoff. — London : Arrow, 1980. — 139p ; 18cm
ISBN 0-09-924760-7 (pbk) : £1.00 B81-02598

941'.009'92 — Great Britain. Royal families, *to 1980 — For children*

Hichens, Phoebe. The book of the Royal Family. — London : Macmillan, Sept.1981. — [128]p
ISBN 0-333-31562-6 : £4.95 : CIP entry B81-23945

941.01 — Great Britain. Colonisation by Norsemen, *ca 700-ca 1300.* **Influence,** *to 1980*

Leirfall, Jon. West over sea : reminders of Norse ascendency from Shetland to Dublin / Jon Leirfall ; translated by Kenneth Young from the Norwegian Vest i havet. — Sandwick : Thule Press, 1979. — 159p : ill,maps,coat of arms,port ; 22cm
ISBN 0-906191-15-7 : £4.95
ISBN 0-906191-11-4 (pbk) : Unpriced B81-18914

941.02 — Great Britain. Social life, *1100-1400 — For schools*

Pollard, Michael, *1931-*. Castles and Crusaders 1100-1400 / Michael Pollard ; illustrated by John Hunt. — Glasgow : Blackie, 1981. — 78p : ill(some col.) ; 21cm. — (The Story of life ; 4)
ISBN 0-216-90733-0 (pbk) : £2.75 B81-16195

941.06 — Great Britain, *1603-1714*

Farmer, D. L.. Britain and the Stuarts. — London : Bell and Hyman, Oct.1981. — [436]p
Originally published: 1965
ISBN 0-7135-0445-5 (pbk) : £5.50 : CIP entry B81-32086

941.06 — Great Britain. Political events, *ca 1620-1800*

Three British revolutions : 1641, 1688, 1776 / edited by J.G.A. Pocock. — Princeton : Guildford : Princeton University Press, c1980. — lx,468p ; 23cm. — (Folger Institute essays)
Includes index
ISBN 0-691-05293-x : £10.10
ISBN 0-691-10087-x (pbk£6.90)
Also classified at 973 B81-06957

941.06'2 — Great Britain, *1637-1660*

Into another mould : aspects of the Interregnum / edited by Ivan Roots. — Exeter : University of Exeter, 1981. — 75p ; 21cm. — (Exeter studies in history, ISSN 0260-8626 ; No.3)
Includes bibliographies
ISBN 0-85989-162-3 (pbk) : Unpriced B81-39597

941.06'8'0924 — Great Britain. Chandos, Cassandra Willoughby, *Duchess of - Biographies*

Johnson, Joan. Excellent Cassandra. — Gloucester : Alan Sutton, Sept.1981. — [160]p
ISBN 0-904387-76-3 : £7.95 : CIP entry B81-20571

941.07 — Great Britain, *1700-1800 — For schools*

Farnworth, Warren. Eighteenth century Britain. — London : Bell & Hyman, Oct.1981. — [80] p. — (History around us)
ISBN 0-7135-1288-1 (pbk) : £3.95 : CIP entry B81-25723

941.07 — Great Britain, *1760-1980 — For schools*

Lane, Peter. British politics and people 1760-1980 / Peter Lane. — London : Heinemann Educational, 1981. — iv,284p : ill,maps,facsims,ports ; 24cm
Includes index
ISBN 0-435-31550-1 (pbk) : £3.50 : CIP rev. B81-07944

941.07 — Great Britain, *1815-1851 — For schools*

Patrick, John. Waterloo to the Great Exhibition. — London : Murray, Dec.1981. — [96]p
ISBN 0-7195-3880-7 (pbk) : £1.95 : CIP entry B81-31534

941.07 — Great Britain. Social conditions, *1700-1980*

Walker, J. (James). British economic and social history 1700-1980 / J. Walker. — 3rd ed. / revised by C.W. Munn. — Plymouth : Macdonald and Evans, 1981. — 452p ; 22cm
Previous ed.: 1979. — Includes index
ISBN 0-7121-0288-4 (pbk) : £5.50 B81-15242

941.07'072 — Great Britain, *ca 1750-ca 1950.* **Historiology**

Great Britain 1750-1950 : sources and historiography. — Milton Keynes : Open University Press. — (Arts : a fourth level course)
At head of title: The Open University
Block 2: Popular politics 1750-1870 / prepared by the Course Team. — Rev. ed. — 1981. — 24p ; 30cm. — (A401 ; II, 3-6)
Previous ed.: 1974. — Contents: Units 3-6
ISBN 0-335-00957-3 (pbk) : Unpriced B81-13178

941.07'076 — Great Britain, *1760-1980 — Questions & answers — For schools*

Documents and questions / Peter Lane [editor]. — London : John Murray, c1981
1: British history 1760-1815. — 74p : ill,maps,facsims
ISBN 0-7195-3774-6 (pbk) : £1.95 B81-29691

Documents and questions / Peter Lane [editor]. — London : John Murray, c1981
2: British history 1815-1914. — 90p : ill,maps,facsims
ISBN 0-7195-3775-4 (pbk) : £2.25 B81-29692

Documents and questions / Peter Lane [editor]. — London : John Murray, c1981
3: British history 1914-1980. — 74p : ill,maps,facsims
ISBN 0-7195-3776-2 (pbk) : £1.95 B81-29690

941.07'076 — Great Britain. Social conditions, *1760-1980 — Questions & answers — For schools*

Rayner, E. G.. British social and economic history since 1760 / E. Rayner, R. Stapley, J. Watson. — Oxford : Oxford University Press, 1980. — 64p : ill,2maps,facsims ; 25cm. — (Evidence in question)
ISBN 0-19-913217-8 (pbk) : £1.00 B81-01385

941.07'0880623 — Great Britain. Working classes. Social life, *ca 1750-1980*

Ereira, Alan. The people's England / Alan Ereira. — London : Routledge & Kegan Paul, 1981. — xviii,285p : ill,maps,ports ; 24cm
Includes index
ISBN 0-7100-0596-2 : £9.50 B81-19831

941.07'092'2 — Great Britain. Prime ministers, *to 1979 — Biographies*

Thomson, George Malcolm. The Prime Ministers : from Robert Walpole to Margaret Thatcher / George Malcolm Thomson. — London : Secker & Warburg, 1980. — xxiv,260p,[16]p of plates : ill(some col.),2facsims,ports(some col.) ; 26cm
Bibliography: p259-260
ISBN 0-436-52045-1 : £10.00 B81-03635

941.07'2 — Great Britain, *ca 1740-ca 1780 — For schools*

Burrell, R. E. C.. England 1750 : an introduction to the series / R.E.C. Burrell. — Exeter : Wheaton, 1980. — 73p : ill,1facsim,maps,ports ; 21cm. — (The Making of the Industrial Revolution series)
ISBN 0-08-022209-9 (pbk) : £1.80 B81-01730

941.07'2 — Great Britain. Jacobite Rebellion, *1745.* **Role of France**

McLynn, F. J.. France : and the Jacobite rising of 1745 / F.J. McLynn. — Edinburgh : Edinburgh University Press, c1981. — 277p : ill,ports ; 22cm
Bibliography: p266-270. — Includes index
ISBN 0-85224-404-5 : Unpriced B81-36319

941.07'2 — Great Britain. Jacobite Rebellion, *1745.* **Suppression by Cumberland, William Augustus,** *Duke of, 1721-1765*

Speck, W. A.. The Butcher. — Oxford : Blackwell, Sept.1981. — [224]p
ISBN 0-631-10501-8 : £10.00 : CIP entry B81-21461

941.07'3'0880623 — Great Britain. Working classes. Social life, *ca 1700-ca 1900*

St Clair, Isla. The song and the story / Isla St Clair and David Turnbull. — London : By arrangement with the British Broadcasting Corporation [by] Pelham, 1981. — 90p : ill (some col.),music,ports(some col.) ; 24cm
ISBN 0-7207-1324-2 : £5.95 : CIP rev.
Also classified at 784.4'942 B81-15859

941.07'3'0924 — Great Britain. Devonshire, Georgiana Cavendish, *Duchess of — Biographies*

Masters, Brian. Georgiana : Duchess of Devonshire / Brian Masters. — London : Hamilton, 1981. — xii,324p,[8]p of plates : ill,ports ; 23cm
Bibliography: p316-317. — Includes index
ISBN 0-241-10662-1 : £15.00 : CIP rev. B81-15809

941.07'3'0924 — Great Britain. Politics. Castlereagh, Robert Stewart, *Viscount — Biographies*

Hinde, Wendy. Castlereagh / Wendy Hinde. — London : Collins, 1981. — 320p,[13]p of plates : ill,1map,ports ; 24cm
Bibliography: p303-307. — Includes index
ISBN 0-00-216308-x : £16.00 B81-33242

941.07'5'0924 — Great Britain. William IV, *King of Great Britain — Biographies*

Somerset, Anne. The life and times of William IV / Anne Somerset ; introduction by Antonia Fraser. — London : Weidenfeld and Nicolson, c1980. — 223p : ill(some col.),facsims,1geneal.table,ports(some col.) ; 26cm
Spine title: William IV. — Ill on lining papers. — Bibliography: p220. — Includes index
ISBN 0-297-77839-0 : £6.95 B81-01386

941.081 — British culture. Influence of Ancient Greek culture, *1800-1900*

Turner, Frank M.. The Greek heritage in Victorian Britain / Frank M. Turner. — New Haven ; London : Yale University Press, c1981. — xiv,461p,[10]p of plates : ports ; 25cm
Includes index
ISBN 0-300-02480-0 : £18.90 B81-23586

941.081 — Great Britain, *1815-1914 — For schools*

Helm, P. J.. Modern British history. — London : Bell & Hyman
Originally published: 1965
Pt.1: 1815-1914. — Nov.1981. — [269]p
ISBN 0-7135-1803-0 (pbk) : £2.75 : CIP entry B81-34714

Hill, C. P. (Charles Peter). British history 1815-1914 / C.P. Hill & J.C. Wright. — Oxford : Oxford University Press, 1981. — 313p : ill,maps,ports ; 23cm
Includes index
ISBN 0-19-913264-x (pbk) : £3.50 B81-25406

941.081 — Great Britain. Country houses. Social life, *1837-1910*

Victorian and Edwardian country-house life from old photographs / [compiled by] Anthony J. Lambert. — London : Batsford, 1981. — x,[110]p : chiefly ill,ports ; 26cm
ISBN 0-7134-1737-4 : £7.50 B81-05821

941.081 — Great Britain. Political events, *1815-1979*

Peacock, Herbert L.. A history of modern Britain : 1815 to 1979 / Herbert L. Peacock. — 4th ed. — London : Heinemann Educational, 1980. — 427p : ill,maps,facsims,ports ; 22cm
Previous ed.: 1976. — Bibliography: p415-418. — Includes index
ISBN 0-435-31718-0 (pbk) : £4.25 B81-05698

941.081 — Great Britain. Social conditions, *1800-1900 — For schools*

British social and economic history 1800-1900 / [edited by] Neil Tonge and Michael Quincey. — Basingstoke : Macmillan Education, 1980. — vii,120p ; 22cm. — (Documents and debates)
Includes bibliographies
ISBN 0-333-27452-0 (pbk) : £2.25 : CIP rev. B80-12733

941.08'1 — Great Britain. Social conditions, *1840-1980*

Social conflict and the political order in modern Britain. — London : Croom Helm, Jan.1982. — [224]p
ISBN 0-7099-0708-7 : £12.50 : CIP entry B81-34314

941.081 — Great Britain. Social conditions, *1900 — For schools*

Purkis, Sallie. At home in 1900 / Sallie Purkis. — Harlow : Longman, 1981. — 24p : ill ; 21cm. — (Into the past ; 1)
Cover title. — Text and ill on inside covers
ISBN 0-582-18436-3 (pbk) : £0.65 B81-27231

941.081'0886464 — Great Britain. Needlewomen. Social life, *1843-1890*

Walkley, Christina. The ghost in the looking glass : the Victorian seamstress / Christina Walkley. — London : Owen, 1981. — xi,137p : ill ; 24cm
Includes index
ISBN 0-7206-0561-x : £12.50 B81-32870

941.081'092'2 — Great Britain. Royal families, *ca 1800-1979*

Talbot, Godfrey. The Country life book of the royal family / Godfrey Talbot. — Richmond upon Thames : Country Life Books, 1980. — 207p : ill,facsims,ports(some col.),geneal.tables ; 31cm
Geneal.table on lining papers. — Includes index
ISBN 0-600-37648-6 : £10.00 B81-14262

941.081'092'4 — England. Nelson, Horatia — *Biographies*

Gérin, Winifred. Horatia Nelson / Winifred Gérin. — Oxford : Oxford University Press, 1981, c 1970. — xiv,350p,[30]p of plates : ill,facsims,ports,geneal.tables ; 22cm
Originally published: Oxford : Clarendon Press, 1970. — Bibliography: p339-341. — Includes index
ISBN 0-19-285112-8 (pbk) : £3.95 : CIP rev. B81-22611

941.081'092'4 — Great Britain. Albert, *Prince, Consort of Victoria, Queen of Great Britain — Conference proceedings*

Prince Albert and the Victorian Age : a seminar held in May 1980 under the auspices of the University of Bayreuth and the City of Coburg / edited by John A.S. Phillips. — Cambridge : Cambridge University Press, 1981. — xiv,152p : ill,1port ; 25cm
Includes 2 chapters in German
ISBN 0-521-24242-8 : £15.00 : CIP rev. B81-19107

941.08'1092'4 — Great Britain. Churchill, Randolph S. — *Biographies*

Foster, R. F.. Lord Randolph Churchill. — Oxford : Clarendon Press, Nov.1981. — [440]p
ISBN 0-19-822679-9 : £15.00 : CIP entry B81-28852

941.081'092'4 — Great Britain. Gladstone, W. E. Religious beliefs, *1809-1859*

Butler, Perry. Gladstone : church, state and Tractarianism. — Oxford : Clarendon Press, Feb.1982. — [230]p. — (Oxford historical monographs)
ISBN 0-19-821890-7 : £17.50 : CIP entry B81-35762

941.081'092'4 — Great Britain. Gladstone, W. E. (William Ewart) — *Biographies*

Stansky, Peter. Gladstone : a progress in politics / by Peter Stansky. — New York ; London : Norton, c1979. — xxii,201p ; 21cm
Bibliography: p191-194. — Includes index
ISBN 0-393-01418-5 : £5.95 : CIP rev. B80-18945

941.081'092'4 — Great Britain. Granville, Harriet Granville, *Countess — Biographies*

Askwith, Betty. Piety and wit : a biography of Harriet, Countess Granville, 1785-1862. — London : Collins, Feb.1982. — [195]p
ISBN 0-00-216258-x : £14.50 : CIP entry B81-37581

941.081'092'4 — Great Britain. Heckford, Sarah — *Biographies*

Allen, Vivien. Lady trader. — Large print ed. — Anstey : Ulverscroft, Dec.1981. — [496]p. — (Ulverscroft large print series)
Originally published: London : Collins, 1979
ISBN 0-7089-0728-8 : £5.00 : CIP entry B81-32037

941.081'092'4 — Great Britain. Victoria, *Queen of Great Britain.* **Local associations: Isle of Wight. East Cowes. Country houses: Osborne House**

Whittle, Tyler. Victoria and Albert at home / Tyler Whittle. — London : Routledge & Kegan Paul, 1980. — xvi,212p,[16]p of plates : ill,1geneal.table,plans,ports ; 25cm
Bibliography: p199-205. — Includes index
ISBN 0-7100-0541-5 : £7.95 : CIP rev.
Also classified at 941.081'092'4 B80-18113

941.081'092'4 — Great Britain. Victoria, *Queen of Great Britain.* **Local associations: Scotland. Grampian Region. Kincardine and Deeside** *(District).* **Castles: Balmoral Castle**

Whittle, Tyler. Victoria and Albert at home / Tyler Whittle. — London : Routledge & Kegan Paul, 1980. — xvi,212p,[16]p of plates : ill,1geneal.table,plans,ports ; 25cm
Bibliography: p199-205. — Includes index
ISBN 0-7100-0541-5 : £7.95 : CIP rev.
Primary classification 941.081'092'4 B80-18113

941.081'092'4 — Great Britain. Victoria, *Queen of Great Britain, to 1839 — Biographies*

Plowden, Alison. The young Victoria / Alison Plowden. — London : Weidenfeld and Nicolson, c1981. — viii,230p,[8]p of plates : ill,ports,geneal.tables ; 23cm
Bibliography: p219-221. — Includes index
ISBN 0-297-77868-4 : £9.95 B81-10787

941.08'13'0924 — Great Britain. Victoria, *Queen of Great Britain, 1878-1885 — Correspondence to Victoria, Empress, consort of Friedrich III, Emperor of Germany*

Victoria, *Queen of Great Britain.* Beloved mama. — London : Evans Bros., Oct.1981. — [224]p
ISBN 0-237-44997-8 : £10.95 : CIP entry
Also classified at 943.08'3'0924 B81-25777

941.082 — Great Britain, *1914-1979*

Thomson, David, *1912-*. England in the twentieth century : (1914-79) / David Thomson. — [2nd ed.] / with additional material by Geoffrey Warner. — Harmondsworth : Penguin, 1981. — xii,382p ; 19cm. — (The Pelican history of England ; v.9)
Previous ed.: 1965. — Includes index
ISBN 0-14-020691-4 (pbk) : £1.75 B81-37256

941.082 — Great Britain. Political events, *1918-1979*

Gilbert, Bentley B.. Britain since 1918 / Bentley B. Gilbert. — 2nd ed. — London : Batsford Academic and Ecucational, 1980. — 231p ; 23cm
Previous ed.: London : Batsford, 1967. — Bibliography: p229-231. — Includes index
ISBN 0-7134-2523-7 (cased) : £9.95 (pbk) : £4.95 B81-01558

941.082 — Great Britain. Social conditions, *1901-1914 — For schools*

Wood, Sydney. The Edwardians / Sydney Wood. — Edinburgh : Oliver & Boyd, 1981. — 40p : ill,maps,ports ; 19x25cm. — (Exploring history)
Text on inside cover. — Bibliography: p39-40. — Includes index
ISBN 0-05-003349-2 (pbk) : Unpriced B81-26546

941.082'022'2 — Great Britain. Social life, *1930-1953 — Illustrations*

Memory lane : a photographic album of daily life in Britain 1930-1953 / introduced by James Cameron ; photographic research by Harold Chapman ; captions by Joanna Smith. — London : Dent, 1980. — [304]p : ill,chiefly ports ; 25cm
ISBN 0-460-04457-5 : £9.95 : CIP rev. B80-18114

941.082'0880621 — Great Britain. Upper classes. Social life, *1920-1970*

Barrow, Andrew. Gossip : a history of high society from 1920 to 1970 / Andrew Barrow. — London : Pan, 1980, c1978. — 282p : ill,ports ; 25cm
Originally published: London : H. Hamilton, 1978. — Includes index
ISBN 0-330-26223-8 (pbk) : £3.95 B81-00669

941.082'0880623 — Great Britain. Working classes. Social life, *1889-1939 — Childhood reminiscences — Collections*

Humphries, Stephen. Hooligans or rebels?. — Oxford : Blackwell, Nov.1981. — [288]p
ISBN 0-631-12982-0 : £10.00 : CIP entry B81-30170

941.082'092'4 — England. Beaufort, Henry Somerset, *Duke of — Biographies*

Beaufort, Henry Somerset, *Duke of.* Memoirs / the Duke of Beaufort. — Richmond upon Thames : Country Life Books, 1981. — xiii,178p,[28]p of plates : ill,1map,1plan,ports ; 25cm
Includes index
ISBN 0-600-31574-6 : £8.95 B81-24190

941.082'092'4 — Great Britain. Churchill, Winston S. (Winston Spencer), *1874-1965, 1900-1939 — Biographies*

James, Robert Rhodes. Churchill : a study in failure 1900-1939 / Robert Rhodes James. — Harmondsworth : Penguin, 1973, c1970 (1981 [printing]). — xvi,478p ; 18cm
Originally published: London : Weidenfeld & Nicolson, 1970. — Bibliography: p447-451. — Includes index
ISBN 0-14-005974-1 (pbk) : £2.25 B81-33613

941.082'092'4 — Great Britain. Churchill, Winston S. (Winston Spencer), *1874-1965, 1940-1965 — Personal observations — Correspondence, diaries, etc.*

Colville, John, *1915-*. The Churchillians / John Colville. — London : Weidenfeld and Nicolson, c1981. — 222p,[8]p of plates : ill ; ports ; 23cm
Includes index
ISBN 0-297-77909-5 : £8.95 B81-14265

941.082'092'4 — Great Britain. Churchill, Winston S. (Winston Spencer), *1874-1965* **— *Biographies — For children***

Bailey, Eva. Churchill / Eva Bailey. — Hove : Wayland, 1981. — 72p : ill,facsims,ports ; 23cm. — (Wayland history makers)
Bibliography: p70. — Includes index
ISBN 0-85340-645-6 : £3.95 B81-24338

Butler, William Vivian. Winston Curchill : never surrender / William Vivian Butler. — London : Hodder and Stoughton, 1980. — 128p : ill,1map,facsims,ports ; 24cm. — (Twentieth century people)
Includes index
ISBN 0-340-24860-2 : £4.95 : CIP rev. B80-13146

941.082'092'4 — Great Britain. Churchill, Winston S. (Winston Spencer), *1874-1965.* **Political speeches —** *Collections*

Churchill, Winston S. (Winston Spencer), *1874-1965.* Churchill speaks : Winston S. Churchill in peace and war : collected speeches, 1897-1963 / editor Robert Rhodes James. — Leicester : Windward, 1981, c1980. — xv,997p : 1port ; 24cm
Originally published: New York : Chelsea House, 1980. — Includes index
ISBN 0-7112-0092-0 (pbk) : £8.95 B81-15657

941.082'092'4 — Great Britain. Cooper, Diana, *1892-* **—** ***Biographies***

Ziegler, Philip. Diana Cooper / Philip Ziegler. — London : Hamilton, 1981. — xii,336p,[16]p of plates : ill,ports ; 24cm
Bibliography: p320-321. — Includes index
ISBN 0-241-10659-1 : £9.95 : CIP rev. B81-23864

941.082'092'4 — Great Britain. Edward VII, *King of Great Britain.* **Interpersonal relationships with Langtry, Lillie**

Brough, James. The prince and the lily / James Brough. — Sevenoaks : Coronet, 1978, c1975. — 332p ; 18cm
Originally published: New York : Coward McCann and Geoghegan ; London : Hodder and Stoughton, 1975. — Includes index
ISBN 0-340-23384-2 (pbk) : £1.10 : CIP rev.
Primary classification 792'.028'0924 B78-23604

941.082'092'4 — Great Britain. Fairweather, Audrey — ***Biographies***

Fairweather, Audrey. Gran's war / Audrey Fairweather. — Bognor Regis : New Horizon, c1980. — 245p ; 21cm
ISBN 0-86116-209-9 : £6.25 B81-21719

941.082'092'4 — Great Britain. Leefe, Harry — ***Biographies***

Leefe, Tindall. A second pair of eyes / Tindall Leefe. — Woodford Green (32 St Albans Cres., Woodford Green, Essex IG8 9EH) : T. Leefe, [1980]. — x,167p ; 22cm
£2.00 (pbk) B81-10828

941.082'092'4 — Great Britain. Leslie, Anita — ***Biographies***

Leslie, Anita. The gilt and the gingerbread : an autobiography / Anita Leslie. — London : Hutchinson, 1981. — 201p,[12]p of plates : ill,ports ; 24cm
Includes index
ISBN 0-09-145630-4 : £8.95 : CIP rev. B81-20145

941.082092'4 — Great Britain. Mountbatten, *Louis, Earl Mountbatten, 1900-1979* **—** ***Biographies***

Hough, Richard. Mountbatten. — Large print ed. — Long Preston : Magna Print Books, Oct.1981. — [480]p
Originally published: London : Weidenfeld and Nicolson, 1980
ISBN 0-86009-362-x : £4.95 : CIP entry B81-27440

941.082'092'4 — Great Britain. Mountbatten, Louis Mountbatten, *Earl* **—** ***Biographies — For children***

Dobson, Julia. Mountbatten, hero. — London : MacRae, Feb.1982. — [48]p. — (Blackbird books)
ISBN 0-86203-062-5 : £2.75 : CIP entry B81-36046

Ross, Josephine. Lord Mountbatten / Josephine Ross ; illustrated by Peter Gregory. — London : Hamilton, 1981. — 63p : ports ; 22cm. — (Profiles)
ISBN 0-241-10593-5 : £3.25 B81-23223

941.082'092'4 — Great Britain. Mountbatten, Louis Mountbatten, *Earl* **—** ***Personal observations***

Smith, Charles, *1908-*. Fifty years with Mountbatten / Charles Smith. — [Feltham] : Hamlyn Paperbacks, 1981, c1980. — 176p,[8]p of plates : 2ill,facsims,ports ; 18cm
Originally published: London : Sidgwick and Jackson, 1980. — Includes index
ISBN 0-600-20403-0 (pbk) : £1.25 B81-26096

941.082'092'4 — Great Britain. Mounter, Donald — ***Biographies***

Mounter, Donald. One man's journey / Donald Mounter. — Bognor Regis : New Horizon, c1980. — 264p ; 22cm
ISBN 0-86116-563-2 : £6.25 B81-21809

941.082'092'4 — Great Britain. Politics. Astor, Nancy — ***Biographies***

Masters, Anthony. Nancy Astor : a life / Anthony Masters. — London : Weidenfeld and Nicolson, c1981. — 237p,[8]p of plates : ill ; 23cm
Bibliography: p229-230. - Includes index
ISBN 0-297-77704-1 : £7.95 B81-15181

941.082'092'4 — Great Britain. Politics. Bevin, Ernest — ***Biographies***

Stephens, Mark. Ernest Bevin - unskilled labourer and world statesman 1881-1951 / Mark Stephens. — London (Transport House, Smith Sq., SW1P 3JB) : Transport & General Workers Union, 1981. — 142p,[8]p of plates : ill,facsims,ports ; 18cm
Bibliography: p139-140. - Includes index
ISBN 0-907475-00-0 (pbk) : £0.95 B81-21261

941.082'092'4 — Great Britain. Politics. Wilkinson, Ellen — ***Biographies***

Vernon, Betty D.. Ellen Wilkinson. — London : Croom Helm, Jan.1982. — [272]p
ISBN 0-85664-984-8 : £12.95 : CIP entry B81-33773

941.082'092'4 — Great Britain. Saxton, James — ***Biographies***

Saxton, James. Something will come to me / James Saxton. — Ilfracombe : Stockwell, 1981. — 219p ; 22cm
ISBN 0-7223-1467-1 (pbk) : £2.50 B81-40454

941.082'092'4 — Great Britain. Spencer-Churchill, Clementine Churchill, *Baroness* **—** ***Biographies***

Soames, Mary. Clementine Churhill / by her daughter Mary Soames. — Harmondsworth : Penguin, 1981, c1979. — 790p,[8]p of plates : ill,facsims,geneal.table,ports ; 18cm
Originally published: London : Cassell, 1979. — Bibliography: p767-769. - Includes index
ISBN 0-14-005469-3 (pbk) : £2.50 B81-04001

941.082'092'4 — Great Britain. Sutherland, Millicent Fanny Egerton, *Duchess of* **—** ***Biographies***

Stuart, Denis. Dear Duchess. — London : Gollancz, Jan.1982. — [256]p
ISBN 0-575-03020-8 : £9.95 : CIP entry B81-35883

941.083 — Great Britain, *1914-1945*

Taylor, A. J. P.. English history 1914-1945 / A.J.P. Taylor. — Reprinted with rev. bibliography. — Harmondsworth : Puffin, 1981, c1975. — 875p,1folded leaf of plates : ill,maps ; 18cm
Originally published: Oxford : Oxford University Press, 1965. — Bibliography: p729-774. — Includes index
ISBN 0-14-021181-0 (pbk) : £3.50 B81-29155

941.083 — Great Britain, ***1929-1945 — Readings from contemporary sources***

Peterborough Newspaper columnist. All the best people — : the pick of Peterborough, 1929-1945 / chosen by Alex Faulkner and Tom Hartman ; with résumés of each year's events by Tom Hartman ; introduced by Michael Hogg ; illustrated by Timothy Jaques. — London : Allen & Unwin, 1981. — 321p : ill ; 23cm
Includes index
ISBN 0-04-808029-2 : Unpriced : CIP rev. B81-15871

941.083 — Scotland, *1914-1980*

Harvie, Christopher. 'No Gods and precious few heroes' Scotland 1914-1980. — London : Edward Arnold, Sept.1981. — [192]p. — (The New history of Scotland ; 8)
ISBN 0-7131-6318-6 (cased) : £9.95 : CIP entry
ISBN 0-7131-6319-4 (pbk) : £4.95 B81-23834

941.083'092'4 — Great Britain. Churchill, Winston S. (Winston Spencer), ***1874-1965, 1929-1939 — Biographies***

Gilbert, Martin. Winston Churchill : the wilderness years / Martin Gilbert. — London : Macmillan, 1981. — 279p : ill,1facsim,ports ; 25cm
Bibliography: p269-271. — Includes index
ISBN 0-333-32564-8 : £8.95 B81-40732

941.083'092'4 — Great Britain. Lloyd George, David — ***Biographies***

Morgan, Kenneth O.. David Lloyd George : 1863-1945 / Kenneth O. Morgan. — [Cardiff] : Gwasg Prifysgol Cymru, 1981. — 91p,[5]p of plates : ill,1map,ports ; 21cm
Parallel Welsh and English text. — Bibliography: p91
ISBN 0-7083-0790-6 (pbk) : £1.95 B81-15484

941.083'092'4 — Great Britain. Lloyd George, David — ***Illustrations***

Parry, Bryn. David Lloyd George / Bryn Parry, Emyr Price, Gareth Price. — [Caernarfon] ([County Offices, Caernarfon, Gwynedd LL55 1HS]) : Gwynedd Archives Service, c1981. — [60]p : ill,facsims,ports ; 21cm
Parallel Welsh and English text
ISBN 0-901337-28-5 (pbk) : £2.25 B81-38459

941.083'092'4 — Great Britain. Read, Jack, ***1916-1926 — Biographies***

Read, Jack. Ten years in the life of a country boy / Jack Read. — Bognor Regis : New Horizon, c1980. — 131p ; 21cm
ISBN 0-86116-364-8 : £4.25 B81-21728

941.084 — Great Britain. Social conditions, ***1935-1950 — Readings from contemporary sources***

McMillan, James. The way it happened, 1935-1950 : based on the files of Express Newspapers / James McMillan. — London : Kimber, 1980. — 269p,[16]p of plates : ill,facsims,ports ; 24cm
Includes index
ISBN 0-7183-0467-5 : £9.95 B81-04153

941.084'088042 — Great Britain. Women. Social life, *1939-1945*

Minns, Raynes. Bombers and mash : the domestic front 1939-45 / Raynes Minns. — London : Virago, 1980. — 236p : ill,facsims ; 25cm
Bibliography: p201-202. - Includes index
ISBN 0-86068-041-x (pbk) : £4.95
Also classified at 641.5941 B81-03349

941.084'088054 — Great Britain. Children. Social life, ***1939-1945 — For children***

Fyson, Nance Lui. Growing up in the Second World War / Nance Lui Fyson. — London : Batsford Academic and Educational, 1981. — 72p : ill,ports ; 26cm
Bibliography: p68. — Includes index
ISBN 0-7134-3574-7 : £5.95 B81-24310

941.084'092'2 — Great Britain. Social life, ***1939-1945 - Personal observations - Collections***

Longmate, Norman. The home front. — London : Chatto & Windus, June 1981. — [256]p
ISBN 0-7011-2553-5 : £9.50 : CIP entry B81-12386

941.084'092'4 — Great Britain. Elizabeth, *Queen, consort of George VI, King of Great Britain — Biographies*

Cathcart, Helen. The Queen Mother herself. — Large print ed. — Long Preston : Magna Print Books, Jan.1982. — [480]p
Originally published: London : W.H. Allen, 1979
ISBN 0-86009-366-2 : £5.25 : CIP entry B81-33770

Longford, Elizabeth. The Queen Mother / Elizabeth Longford. — London : Weidenfeld and Nicolson, c1981. — 184p : ill(some col.),facsims,ports(some col.),2geneal.tables ; 26cm
Includes index
ISBN 0-297-77976-1 : £7.95 B81-25273

941.084'092'4 — Great Britain. Windsor, Wallis Windsor, *Duchess of — Biographies*

Mosley, Diana. The Duchess of Windsor / Diana Mosley ; editorial consultant and illustrations editor Jack Le Vien. — London : Sidgwick & Jackson, 1980 (1981 [printing]). — 175p,[32]p of plates : ill,facsims,ports ; 18cm
Includes index
ISBN 0-283-98774-x (pbk) : £1.75 B81-28525

941.085 — Great Britain, *1945-1981*

Burnet, Alastair. The time of our lives : a pictorial history of Britain since 1945 / Alastair Burnet, Willie Landels. — London : Elm Tree, 1981. — 208p : ill(some col.),ports (some col.) ; 27cm
Includes index
ISBN 0-241-10666-4 : £9.95 : CIP rev. B81-30442

941.085 — Great Britain. Social change, *ca 1950-1980*

Martin, Bernice. A sociology of contemporary cultural change / Bernice Martin. — Oxford : Blackwell, 1981. — ix,272p : ill ; 24cm
Includes index
ISBN 0-631-12973-1 : £12.50 B81-31781

941.085 — Great Britain. Social conditions, *1945-1979*

Britain : progress and decline / edited by William B. Gwyn and Richard Rose for the British Politics Group. — London : Macmillan, 1980. — xiii,164p ; 23cm
Includes index
ISBN 0-333-24427-3 : £20.00 : CIP rev. B80-07240

941.085 — Great Britain. Social conditions, *1945-1980*

Heren, Louis. Alas, alas for England : what went wrong with Britain / Louis Heren. — London : Hamilton, 1981. — 177p ; 23cm
Includes index
ISBN 0-241-10538-2 : £7.95 B81-12468

941.085'092'2 — Great Britain. Charles, *Prince of Wales* **& Diana,** *Princess of Wales — Biographies*

Honeycombe, Gordon. Royal wedding / Gordon Honeycombe. — London : Joseph, 1981. — 191p : ill(some col.),facsims,ports(some col.),geneal.tables ; 29cm
ISBN 0-7181-2088-4 : £9.95 B81-37869

The **Prince** and Princess of Wales. — Norwich : Jarrold, c1981. — [36]p : chiefly col.ill,coat of arms,col.ports,2geneal.tables ; 28cm
Cover title. — Text, coat of arms, geneal.tables on inside covers
ISBN 0-85306-985-9 (pbk) : Unpriced B81-37868

Royal Wedding Day Souvenir, 29 July 1981. — London : Harmondsworth for Associated Newspapers Group, c1981. — 48p : ill(some col.),ports(some col.) ; 30cm. — (A Daily Mail publication)
Ports on inside covers
£1.25 (pbk) B81-37867

941.085'092'2 — Great Britain. Charles, *Prince of Wales.* **Engagement to Diana,** *Princess of Wales*

Arnold, Harry. Charles and Diana / Harry Arnold. — Large print ed. — Bath : Chivers Press, 1981. — 228p,[8]p of plates : ports ; 23cm. — (A Lythway book)
Originally published: [London] : New English Library, 1981
ISBN 0-85119-780-9 : Unpriced : CIP rev. B81-14782

The **Royal** wedding : all you need to know about the royal wedding day. — London : Mirror Books for Mirror Group Newspapers, 1981. — 26p : ill,1map,ports(some col.) ; 37cm
"A 'Sunday mirror' royal wedding souvenir". — One sheet (ports) as insert
ISBN 0-85939-267-8 (unbound) : £0.50 B81-28919

941.085'092'2 — Great Britain. Charles, *Prince of Wales.* **Engagement to Diana,** *Princess of Wales — Illustrations*

The **Love** story of Charles and Diana. — London : IPC Magazines, c1981. — [40]p : chiefly ill (some col.),ports(some col.) ; 30cm
£0.50 (unbound) B81-34773

941.085'092'2 — Great Britain. Charles, *Prince of Wales.* **Interpersonal relationships with Diana,** *Princess of Wales*

Whitaker, James, *1940-*. Settling down / James Whitaker. — London : Quartet, 1981. — 127p : ill(some col.),ports(some col.) ; 30cm
ISBN 0-7043-3385-6 (pbk) : £4.95 B81-33658

941.085'092'2 — Great Britain. Charles, *Prince of Wales.* **Interpersonal relationships with Spencer,** *Lady* **Diana**

Dunlop, Janice. Charles and Diana : a royal romance / Janice Dunlop. — Sevenoaks : Hodder and Stoughton, 1981. — 158p,[16]p of plates : ill,ports ; 18cm. — (Coronet books)
ISBN 0-340-27274-0 (pbk) : £0.95 : CIP rev. B81-12387

941.085'092'2 — Great Britain. Charles, *Prince of Wales.* **Marriage to Diana,** *Princess of Wales — For children*

Daly, Audrey. Royal wedding / by Audrey Daly ; photographs by John Scott. — Loughborough : Ladybird, 1981. — 50p : ill(some col.),ports ; 18cm
Text and ill on lining papers
ISBN 0-7214-0712-9 : £0.50 B81-39257

941.085'092'2 — Great Britain. Politics. Bevan, Aneurin & Lee, Jennie *— Biographies*

Lee, Jennie. My life with Nye / Jennie Lee. — London : Cape, 1980. — 277p,[16]p of plates : ill,ports ; 23cm
Includes index
ISBN 0-224-01785-3 : £8.50 : CIP rev. B80-24978

941.085'092'2 — Great Britain. Spencer, *Lady* **Diana. Engagement to Charles,** *Prince of Wales*

Diana, our future queen : special royal engagement souvenir. — London : IPC Magazines, c1981. — 30p : ill(some col.),ports (some col.),geneal.tables ; 30cm
£0.50 (unbound) B81-16090

Holden, Anthony. Their Royal Highnesses : the Prince & Princess of Wales / Anthony Holden. — London : Weidenfeld and Nicolson, 1981. — 160p,[32]p of plates : ill,facsims,ports(some col.),geneal.tables ; 26cm
Ports on lining papers. — Bibliography: p151-153. — Includes index
ISBN 0-297-77982-6 : £7.95 B81-26468

Keay, Douglas. Royal wedding / [written by Douglas Keay] ; [edited by Jane Reed and Douglas Keay]. — London : IPC Magazines, c1981. — 157p : ill(some col.),coat of arms,facsim,ports(some col.),2geneal.tables ; 28cm
ISBN 0-85037-382-4 (pbk) : £2.25 B81-25063

Prince Charles and Lady Diana. — Norwich : Jarrold, c1981. — [16]p : ill,ports,1geneal.table ; 19cm
Cover title. — Ports, geneal. table on inside covers
ISBN 0-85306-968-9 (pbk) : Unpriced B81-26131

941.085'092'4 — Great Britain. Andrew, *Prince, son of Elizabeth II, Queen of Great Britain — Biographies*

Fisher, Graham. Prince Andrew / Graham and Heather Fisher. — London : W.H. Allen, 1981. — 173p,[8]p of plates : ports,1geneal.table ; 23cm
Includes index
ISBN 0-491-02614-5 : £5.95 B81-08514

941.085'092'4 — Great Britain. Charles, *Prince of Wales — Biographies*

Campbell, Judith. Charles : a prince of our time / Judith Campbell. — London : Octopus, 1981. — 96p : col.ill,coats of arms,col.ports,1col.geneal.table ; 33cm
Ports on lining papers. — Includes index
ISBN 0-7064-0968-x : £3.95 B81-28252

Cathcart, Helen. Prince Charles : the biography / by Helen Cathcart. — Large print ed. — Bath : Chivers Press, 1981, c1976. — vii,269p,[8]p of plates : ill,ports ; 23cm. — (A New Portway large print book)
Originally published: London : W.H. Allen, 1976
ISBN 0-85119-148-7 : £5.95 : CIP rev. B81-12881

Charles, *Prince of Wales*. Charles in his own words / compiled by Rosemary York ; designed by Perry Neville. — London : W.H. Allen, 1981. — 125p : ill,ports ; 26cm
Originally published: London : Omnibus Press, 1981
ISBN 0-491-02676-5 : £4.95 B81-27073

Holden, Anthony. Charles, Prince of Wales / Anthony Holden. — London : Pan, 1980. — xiv,391p,[16]p of plates : ill,ports,geneal.tables ; 18cm
Originally published: London : Weidenfeld and Nicolson, 1979. — Bibliography.: p370-372. — Includes index
ISBN 0-330-26167-3 (pbk) : £1.95 B81-00670

Vickers, Hugo. Debrett's book of the Royal Wedding / Hugo Vickers. — London : Debrett's, 1981. — 176p : ill(some col.),ports (some col.),2geneal.tables ; 31cm
ISBN 0-905649-35-4 : £8.95 B81-21363

941.085'092'4 — Great Britain. Charles, *Prince of Wales — Biographies — For children*

Morrison, Ian A.. HRH Prince Charles / written by Ian A. Morrison. — Loughborough : Ladybird, 1981. — 51p : ill(some col.),ports (some col.) ; 18cm
Ill, geneal.table on lining papers
ISBN 0-7214-0692-0 : £0.50 B81-21154

941.085'092'4 — Great Britain. Foley, Winifred, *1945-1980 — Biographies*

Foley, Winifred. Back to the forest / Winifred Foley. — London : Macdonald, 1981. — 206p ; 23cm
ISBN 0-354-04354-4 : £7.50 B81-22195

941.085'092'4 — Great Britain. Margaret, *Princess, Countess of Snowdon — Biographies*

Dempster, Nigel. H.R.H. Princess Margaret. — London : Quartet Books, Oct.1981. — 1v.
ISBN 0-7043-2314-1 : £7.95 : CIP entry B81-31091

941.085'092'4 — Great Britain. Murphy, Joseph, *1945-1980 — Biographies*

Murphy, Joseph. Tears for Kathleen / by Joseph Murphy. — Bognor Regis : New Horizon, c1979. — 107p ; 21cm
ISBN 0-86116-095-9 : £2.50 B81-21726

941.085'092'4 — Great Britain. Philip, *Prince, consort of Elizabeth II, Queen of Great Britain — Biographies*

Fisher, Graham. Consort : the life and times of Prince Philip / Graham and Heather Fisher. — London : W.H. Allen, 1980. — 192p,[8]p of plates : 2geneal.tables,ports ; 22cm
Bibliography: p186. — Includes index
ISBN 0-491-02853-9 : £5.95 B81-01387

941.085'092'4 — Great Britain. Philip, *Prince, consort of Elizabeth II, Queen of Great Britain — Biographies* *continuation*

Fisher, Graham. Consort : the life and times of Prince Philip / Graham and Heather Fisher. — London : W.H. Allen, 1980 (1981 [printing]). — 192p,[8]p of plates : ports,2geneal.tables ; 18cm. — (A Star book)
Bibliography: p186. — Includes index
ISBN 0-352-30835-4 (pbk) : £1.50 B81-21752

Judd, Denis. Prince Philip : a biography / Denis Judd. — London : Joseph, 1980. — 270p,[32]p of plates : ill,1facsim,ports,geneal.tables ; 24cm
Geneal.tables on lining papers. — Bibliography: p262-264. — Includes index
ISBN 0-7181-1959-2 : £8.95 B81-00671

941.085'092'4 — Great Britain. Politics. Benn, Tony — *Biographies*

Jenkins, Robert. Tony Benn : a political biography / Robert Jenkins. — London : Writers and Readers Publishing Cooperative, 1980. — 291p,viiip of plates : ill,ports ; 23cm
Includes index
ISBN 0-906495-35-0 : £6.95 B81-22764

941.085'092'4 — Great Britain. Politics. Butler, Richard Austen Butler, *Baron — Biographies*

Cosgrave, Patrick. R.A. Butler : an English life / Patrick Cosgrave. — London : Quartet Books, 1981. — 166p ; 23cm
ISBN 0-7043-2258-7 : £6.95 B81-18655

941.085'092'4 — Great Britain. Politics. Foot, Michael — Biographies

Hoggart, Simon. Michael Foot. — London : Hodder & Stoughton, Sept.1981. — [224]p
ISBN 0-340-27040-3 (cased) : £8.95 : CIP entry
ISBN 0-340-27600-2 (pbk) : £5.95 B81-21581

941.085'092'4 — Great Britain. Politics. Healey, Denis, *to ca 1970 — Biographies*

Healey, Denis. Healey's eye : a photographic memoir / by Denis Healey. — London : Cape, 1980. — 191p : ill(some col.),ports(some col.) ; 25cm
Bibliography: p187. — Includes index
ISBN 0-224-01793-4 : £7.95 : CIP rev. B80-13647

941.085'092'4 — Great Britain. Politics. Redcliffe-Maud, *Lord — Biographies*

Redcliffe-Maud, *Lord*. Experience of an optimist. — London : Hamilton, July 1981. — [256]p
ISBN 0-241-10569-2 : £12.50 : CIP entry B81-19187

941.085'092'4 — Great Britain. Politics. Thomas, George - *Biographies*

Hunston, Ramon. "Order, order". — London : Lakeland, Apr.1981. — [160]p
ISBN 0-551-00882-2 (pbk) : £1.60 : CIP entry B81-08938

941.085'092'4 — Great Britain. Rice-Davies, Mandy — *Biographies*

Rice-Davies, Mandy. Mandy / Mandy Rice-Davies with Shirley Flack. — London : Joseph, 1980. — 223p,[16]p of plates : ill,ports ; 23cm
ISBN 0-7181-1974-6 : £6.95 B81-01388

941.085'5 — British culture, *1945-1960*

Hewison, Robert. In anger : culture in the Cold War 1945-60 / Robert Hewison. — London : Weidenfeld and Nicolson, c1981. — 230p,[8]p of plates : ill ; 22cm
Includes index
ISBN 0-297-77890-0 : £9.95 B81-16214

941.085'5'0924 — Great Britain. Eden, Anthony — *Biographies*

Carlton, David. Anthony Eden : a biography / David Carlton. — London : Allen Lane, 1981. — 528p,[8]p of plates : ill,ports ; 24cm
Bibliography: p509-514. — Includes index
ISBN 0-7139-0829-7 : £20.00 B81-32751

941.085'6'0924 — Great Britain. Political events, *1960-1963 — Personal observations — Correspondence, diaries, etc.*

Evans, Harold, *1911-*. Downing Street diary : the Macmillan years 1957-1963 / Harold Evans. — London : Hodder and Stoughton, 1981. — 318p,[8]p of plates : ill,ports ; 24cm
Bibliography: p305-306. - Includes index
ISBN 0-340-25897-7 : £9.95 B81-10531

941.085'6'0924 — Great Britain. Politics, *1964-1970.* Rose, Paul — *Biographies*

Rose, Paul. Backbencher's dilemma / Paul Rose. — London : Muller, 1981. — 198p ; 23cm
ISBN 0-584-10379-4 : £8.95 B81-17017

941.085'6'0924 — Great Britain. Politics. Stewart, Michael, *1906— — Biographies*

Stewart, Michael, *1906-*. Life and Labour : an autobiography / Michael Stewart. — London : Sidgwick & Jackson, 1980. — 288p,[8]p of plates ; 24cm
Includes index
ISBN 0-283-98686-7 : £12.50 B81-02285

941.085'7 — Great Britain. Social conditions, *1970-1979 — Conference proceedings*

British Association for the Advancement of Science. *Meeting (1979 : Heriot-Watt University).* The political economy of tolerable survival / [papers presented to Section F (Economics) of the British Association for the Advancement of Science] ; edited by Maxwell Gaskin. — London : Croom Helm, c1981. — 220p : ill ; 23cm
Includes bibliographies
ISBN 0-7099-0266-2 : £12.95 : CIP rev. B80-26570

941.085'7 — Great Britain. Social life, *1970-1979*

Booker, Christopher. The Seventies : portrait of a decade / Christopher Booker. — Harmondsworth : Penguin, 1980. — 349p ; 19cm
Originally published: London : Allen Lane, 1980
ISBN 0-14-005783-8 (pbk) : £1.50 B81-01733

Booker, Christopher. The seventies : portrait of a decade / Christopher Booker. — London : Allen Lane, 1980. — 349p ; 23cm
ISBN 0-7139-1329-0 : £7.50 B81-05710

941.085'7'0207 — Great Britain. Social life, *1970-1979 — Humour*

Mikes, George. How to be decadent / George Mikes ; Nicolas Bentley drew the pictures. — Harmondsworth : Penguin, 1981, c1977. — 87p : ill ; 18cm
Originally published: London : Deutsch, 1977
ISBN 0-14-004952-5 (pbk) : £1.00 B81-33611

941.085'7'0924 — Great Britain. Colquhoun, Maureen, *1974-1979 — Biographies*

Colquhoun, Maureen. A woman in the House / Maureen Colquhoun. — Shoreham-by-Sea : Scan, c1980. — 224p ; 23cm
Includes index
ISBN 0-906360-05-6 : £8.50 B81-08371

941.085'7'0924 — Great Britain. Thatcher, Margaret — *Biographies*

Murray, Patricia. Margaret Thatcher / Patricia Murray. — [New and rev. ed.]. — London : W.H. Allen, 1980. — 238p,[12]p of plates : ill,ports ; 23cm
Previous ed.: London : Star, 1978. — Includes index
ISBN 0-491-02882-2 : £5.95 B81-01389

941.085'7'0924 — Great Britain. Thatcher, Margaret — *Biographies — For children*

Levin, Angela. Margaret Thatcher / Angela Levin ; illustrated by Peter Wingham. — London : Hamilton, 1981. — 63p : ill,ports ; 22cm. — (Profiles)
ISBN 0-241-10596-x : £3.25 : CIP rev. B81-12820

941.085'8 — Great Britain. Country houses. Social life — *Case studies*

Young, John, *1934-*. The country house in the 1980s / John Young. — London : Allen & Unwin, 1981. — 150p : ill,ports ; 24cm
Includes index
ISBN 0-04-720022-7 : Unpriced : CIP rev. B81-12839

941.085'8 — Great Britain — *For schools*

Thompson, Kenneth. About Great Britain. — London : Cassell, Jan.1982. — [64]p. — (Skills in research series)
ISBN 0-304-30646-0 : CIP entry B81-34141

941.085'8 — Great Britain. Social conditions — *For schools*

Lines, C. J.. Modern Britain / authors Clifford Lines, Laurie Bolwell. — London : Macdonald Educational, 1981. — 48p : ill(some col.),1col.map ; 21cm. — (Town and around. Social studies)
Cover title. — Text on covers
ISBN 0-356-07195-2 (pbk) : Unpriced B81-29912

941.085'8 — Great Britain. Social life — *Soviet viewpoints*

Ovchinnikov, V. V.. Britain observed : a Russian's view / by V.V. Ovchinnikov ; translated from the Russian by Michael Basker. — Oxford : Pergamon, 1981. — 225p ; 22cm
Translation from the Russian. — Includes index
ISBN 0-08-023603-0 (cased) : £8.50 : CIP rev.
ISBN 0-08-023608-1 (pbk) : Unpriced B80-23890

941.085'8 — Great Britain. Society

Bivand, Roger. Britain : continuity and change / Roger Bivand and Ewa Siarkiewicz-Bivand. — Oxford : Pergamon, 1981. — xiv,108p,[24]p of plates : ill,maps,1facsim,ports ; 25cm. — (Language courses / Pergamon Institute of English (Oxford))
At head of half title: Pergamon Institute of English (Oxford). — Bibliography: p106. - Includes index
ISBN 0-08-025312-1 (pbk) : £3.95 : CIP rev. B80-12734

Madden, Deirdre. Home and community / Deirdre Madden. — Dublin : Gill and Macmillan, 1981. — 348p : ill ; 27cm
Includes index
ISBN 0-7171-0997-6 (pbk) : £5.40
Primary classification 640 B81-21406

941.085'8 — Great Britain. Society — *For school leavers*

Jones, Clive, *19---*. Lifetalk! : situations and tasks for social and life skills / Clive Jones ; edited by Chris Webb. — London : Macmillan, 1980. — 69p : ill,facsims,forms ; 24cm
ISBN 0-333-28682-0 (pbk) : £2.50 B81-06133

941.085'8 — Great Britain. Society — *For slow learning school leavers*

Armitage, Andrew. Do it yourself : practical guidance and exercises in social and life skills / Andrew Armitage ; illustrated by Angela Morgan. — London : Edward Arnold, 1981. — 133p : ill,1map,facsims,plans,forms
ISBN 0-7131-0520-8 (pbk) : £3.50 : CIP rev. B80-32996

Thomas, Mike. On our own two feet / Mike and Sally Thomas. — London : Heinemann Educational, 1981. — 3v. : col.ill,forms ; 30cm
Cover title. — Contents: Book 6 : Settling in — Book 7 : Safe & secure — Book 8 : Around and about
ISBN 0-435-50823-7 (pbk) : Unpriced B81-11694

941.085'8 — Great Britain. Society — *Practical information — For school leavers in Avon*

Work out? : your guide to survival after leaving school / [prepared by the County of Avon Careers Service in association with Bristol and West Building Society]. — [Bristol] ([P.O. Box 11, Avon House, The Haymarket, Bristol BS99 7DE]) : [County of Avon, Department of Public Relations and Publicity], c1981. — 32p : ill,1form ; 22cm
Cover title
ISBN 0-86063-117-6 (pbk) : Unpriced B81-33091

941.085'8'0246 — Great Britain. Society — *For technicians*
Carroll, Don, *19---*. General and communications studies : don't you believe it! / Don Carroll. — London : Macmillan, 1981. — 112p : ill,facsims,forms,ports ; 21x24cm. — (Macmillan technician series)
ISBN 0-333-29462-9 (pbk) : Unpriced B81-25995

941.085'8'05 — Great Britain — *Serials*
The **Book** of the year. — Sept.1979 to Sept.1980. — London : Ink Links Ltd., 1980. — 1v. : ill,ports ; 24cm
Only one issue published
Unpriced B81-36542

941.085'8'05 — Great Britain. Social conditions — *Direct Action Movement viewpoints — Serials*
Direct action : paper of the Direct Action Movement. — No.1-. — Manchester (164 Corn Exchange Buildings, Manchester M4 3BN) : The Movement, [1981]-. — v. : ill ; 28cm
Description based on: No.2
ISSN 0261-8753 = Direct action : £1.60 for 6 issues B81-33939

941.085'8'05 — Great Britain. Social conditions — *Serials*
Britain. / [Reference Division, Central Office of Information]. — 1981. — London : H.M.S.O., 1981. — 498p
ISBN 0-11-701004-9 : £11.00 B81-24117

941.085'8'0880621 — Great Britain. Upper classes. Social events
The **Debrett** season : a lighthearted romp through the social and sporting year / edited and compiled by Adam Helliker. — [London] : Debrett's Peerage, [1981]. — 219p : ill ; 23cm
ISBN 0-905649-47-8 (pbk) : £6.95 B81-19286

941.085'8'0924 — Great Britain. Countryside — *Personal observations*
Bell, Richard, *1951-*. Richard Bell's Britain. — London : Collins, 1981. — 192p : col.ill,col.map ; 26cm
Includes index
ISBN 0-00-219569-0 : £9.95 B81-20913

941.1 — HISTORY. SCOTLAND

941.1 — Scotland, *1470-1625*
Wormald, Jenny. Court, Kirk, and community : Scotland 1470-1625 / Jenny Wormald. — London : Edward Arnold, 1981. — viii,216p ; 20cm. — (The New history of Scotland ; 4)
Bibliography: p195-202. — Includes index
ISBN 0-7131-6310-0 (cased) : Unpriced : CIP rev.
ISBN 0-7131-6311-9 (pbk) : £4.95 B81-10019

941.1 — Scotland. Buildings of historical importance: National Trust properties
National Trust for Scotland. Treasures of Scotland / Magnus Magnusson. — [Edinburgh] : National Trust for Scotland, 1981. — 208p : ill(some col.),1map,ports ; 29cm
Ill on lining papers. — Includes index
ISBN 0-297-77898-6 : £10.95 B81-40204

941.1 — Scotland. Strathclyde Region. Glasgow. Art galleries: Kelvingrove Museum and Art Gallery. Exhibits: Archives. Special subjects. Western Scotland — *Catalogues*
Clyde men of the world : an exhibition of archives reflecting the world impact of Western Scotland, arranged to mark International Archives Week, 4-10 November 1979 [at Kelvingrove Museum and Art Gallery : catalogue / Strathclyde Regional Council. — [Glasgow] ([20 India St., Glasgow G2 4PF]) : The Council, c1979. — 54p,8p of plates : ill,facsims,ports ; 21x30cm
Unpriced (pbk) B81-14051

941.1 — Scotland, *to 1854*
Prebble, John. The lion in the North : a personal view of Scotland's history / John Prebble. — Harmondsworth : Penguin, 1973 (1981 [printing]). — 363p : 1map,geneal.tables ; 20cm
Originally published: London : Secker and Warburg, 1971. — Bibliography: p339-342. — Includes index
ISBN 0-14-005645-9 (pbk) : £2.75 B81-21117

941.1 — Scotland, *to 1980 — For schools*
Melvin, Eric. A new Scottish history / Eric Melvin, Ian Gould, John Thompson. — London : Murray
Book 2. — c1981. — x,270p : ill,maps,facsims,ports ; 25cm
Includes index
ISBN 0-7195-3639-1 (pbk) : £3.25 : CIP rev. B81-05550

941.1'009'734 — Scotland. Rural regions. Social conditions, *to 1780*
Dodgshon, Robert A.. Land and society in early Scotland. — Oxford : Clarendon Press, Feb.1982. — [400]p
ISBN 0-19-822660-8 : £22.50 : CIP entry B81-35761

941.1'009'92 — Scotland. Monarchs, *843-1714*
The **Kings** and queens of Scotland : from Kenneth mac Alpin to the Young Pretender / illustrations by Christopher Haddon. — Edinburgh : Canongate, 1980. — 95p : ill ; 19cm
ISBN 0-903937-78-6 (pbk) : £1.95 B81-01576

941.101 — Scotland, *to 843.* **Archaeological sources**
Ritchie, Graham. Scotland : archaeology and early history / Graham and Anna Ritchie. — London : Thames and Hudson, c1981. — 192p : ill,maps,plans ; 25cm. — (Ancient peoples and places ; v.99)
Bibliography: p183-186. - Includes index
ISBN 0-500-02100-7 : £10.50 B81-12147

941.101'0924 — Scotland. Macbeth, *King of Scotland — Biographies*
Ellis, Peter Berresford. MacBeth : High King of Scotland 1040-57 AD / Peter Berresford Ellis. — London : Muller, 1980. — xi,133p,[8]p of plates : ill,1geneal.table,1map ; 23cm
Bibliography: p124-126. — Includes index
ISBN 0-584-10464-2 : £7.95 : CIP rev. B80-10412

941.102 — Scotland, *1000-1306*
Barrow, G. W. S.. Kingship and unity : Scotland 1000-1306 / G.W.S. Barrow. — London : Edward Arnold, 1981. — 185p : 2maps,1geneal.table ; 20cm. — (The New history of Scotland ; 2)
Bibliography: p170-172. — Includes index
ISBN 0-7131-6306-2 (cased) : Unpriced : CIP rev.
ISBN 0-7131-6307-0 (pbk) : £4.95 B81-02385

941.103 — Scotland. Independence. Declarations, *1320 — Texts*
The **Declaratioun** o Arbroath 1320 / translated into Scots by John Law ; calligraphy by Janet Stewart. — Blackford : Ochils Publications, [1981]. — 1scroll ; 33x51 rolled to 36cm + 1 pamphlet(([4]p ; 30cm))
Translated from the Gaelic. — Title from container. — Limited ed. of 1000 signed and numbered copies. — In tube
Unpriced B81-12937

941.105 — Scotland. Social conditions, *1542-1587 — For schools*
Watson, Roger. At the time of Mary Queen of Scots / Roger Watson. — Harlow : Longman, 1981. — 64p : ill,maps,facsims,ports ; 24cm. — (Focus on history)
Text on inside covers. — Includes index
ISBN 0-582-18229-8 (pbk) : £1.15 B81-34936

941.105'092'4 — Scotland. Mary, *Queen of Scots — Biographies — For schools*
Jamieson, Bruce. Mary Stuart Queen of Scots / Bruce Jamieson. — Edinburgh : Oliver & Boyd, 1981. — 40p : ill,maps,facsims,ports ; 19cm. — (Exploring history)
Text and ill on inside covers. — Bibliography: p 39. — Includes index
ISBN 0-05-003415-4 (pbk) : £1.40 B81-40201

941.106'1 — Scotland, *1603-1625*
Lee, Maurice. Government by pen : Scotland under James VI and I / Maurice Lee, Jr.. — Urbana ; London : University of Illinois Press, c1980. — xiv,232p,[8]p of plates : ports ; 24cm
Bibliography: pxiii-xiv. - Includes index
ISBN 0-252-00765-4 : £9.60 B81-05089

941.107 — Scotland, *1746-1832*
Lenman, Bruce. Integration, enlightenment, and industrialization : Scotland 1746-1832. — London : Edward Arnold, Nov.1981. — [192] p. — (The New history of Scotland)
ISBN 0-7131-6314-3 (cased) : £9.95 : CIP entry
ISBN 0-7131-6315-1 (pbk) : £4.95 B81-30596

941.107'3 — Scotland, *1791-1799 — Early works — Facsimiles*
The **Statistical** account of Scotland 1791-1799 / edited by Sir John Sinclair. — Wakefield : EP Publishing
Facsimile of: 1st ed. Edinburgh : W. Creech, 1791-1799
Vol.17: Inverness-shire, Ross and Cromarty / with a new introduction by Malcolm Gray. — 1981. — liv,682p,[1]leaf of plates : 1map ; 23cm
Includes index
ISBN 0-7158-1017-0 : £35.00
ISBN 0-7158-1000-6 (set) : Unpriced B81-31476

941.107'3'0924 — Scotland. Politics. Muir, Thomas, *1765-1799 — Biographies*
Bewley, Christina. Muir of Huntershill / Christina Bewley. — Oxford : Oxford University Press, 1981. — 212p,[8]p of plates : ill,1map,ports ; 23cm
Bibliography: p202-208. — Includes index
ISBN 0-19-211768-8 : £8.50 B81-30939

941.1082'092'4 — Scotland. Fraser, Amy Stewart — *Biographies*
Fraser, Amy Stewart. Roses in December : Edwardian recollections / Amy Stewart Fraser. — London : Routledge & Kegan Paul, 1981. — ix,158p : ill,ports ; 23cm
Ill on lining papers. — Bibliography: p156
ISBN 0-7100-0823-6 : £6.95 : CIP rev. B81-05128

941.1085'092'4 — Scotland. Garvie, Sheila — *Biographies*
Garvie, Sheila. Marriage to murder : my story- / Sheila Garvie ; with an introduction and postscript by Laurence Dowdall. — Edinburgh : W & R Chambers, 1980. — 173p,[16]p of plates : ill,facsims,ports ; 23cm
ISBN 0-550-20356-7 : £6.95 B81-02295

941.1085'8 — Scotland. Social conditions. Effects of exploitation of petroleum deposits in North Sea
The **Social** impact of oil in Scotland : a contribution to the sociology of oil / edited by Ron Parsler and Dan Shapiro. — Farnborough, Hants. : Gower, c1980. — vii,176p ; 23cm
Conference papers. — Includes bibliographies
ISBN 0-566-00375-9 : £9.50 : CIP rev. B80-07241

941.1'1 — Scotland. Highlands & Islands, *1100-1500*
The **Middle** Ages in the Highlands. — Inverness ([Hazelbrae House, Glen Urquhart, Inverness]) : Inverness Field Club, 1981. — 179p : ill,maps,plans,geneal.tables ; 21cm
Editor: Loraine Maclean. — Includes index
ISBN 0-9502612-1-1 (pbk) : £5.50 B81-26611

941.1'1 — Scotland. Highlands & Islands. Social development — *Conference proceedings*
Island and coastal communities : economic and social opportunities : proceedings of a conference organized by the Fraser of Allander Institute at Kyle of Lochalsh, 26-28 April 1978 / edited by D.R.F. Simpson ; with a foreword by Sir Kenneth Alexander. — Glasgow (100 Montrose St., Glasgow G4 0LZ) : The Institute, 1980. — iv,134p : 2ill,1map ; 21cm. — (Research monograph / Fraser of Allander Institute ; no.9)
Includes bibliographies
ISBN 0-904865-25-8 (pbk) : £4.25 B81-19492

941.11 — Scottish culture, *to 1980*
A **Companion** to Scottish culture. — London : Edward Arnold, Sept.1981. — [448]p
ISBN 0-7131-6344-5 : £17.00 : CIP entry B81-22520

941.1′10858 — Scotland. Highlands & Islands — *For industrial development*

The Top country : develop in the Highlands and Islands of Scotland. — Inverness (Bridge House, Bank St., Inverness IV1 1QR) : Highlands and Islands Development Board, c1981. — 40p : col.ill,col.maps,ports(some col.) ; 30cm
Cover title. — Map on inside cover
Unpriced (pbk) B81-38374

941.1′2004395 — Scotland. Orkney, Shetland & Western Isles. Settlement by Vikings, *to 1100*

The Northern and Western Isles in the Viking world. — Edinburgh ([George IV Bridge, Edinburgh EH1 1EW]) : National Library of Scotland, 1981. — 20p : ill ; 25cm. — (Exhibition catalogue / National Library of Scotland ; no.17)
Includes bibliographies
ISBN 0-902220-39-x (pbk) : Unpriced B81-16302

941.1′32 — Scotland. Orkney, *to 1979*

Brown, George Mackay. Portrait of Orkney / George Mackay Brown ; with photographs by Werner Forman. — London : Hogarth, 1981. — 127p : ill(some col.),1map,facsims ; 20x27cm
Bibliography: p127
ISBN 0-7012-0513-x : £8.50 B81-12678

941.1′32 — Scotland. Shetland. Burra. Social change, *1971-1979*

Byron, Reginald. Burra fishermen : social and economic change in a Shetland community / by Reginald Byron. — [Glasgow] ([2 The Square, University of Glasgow, Glasgow G12]) : [North Sea Oil Panel of the Social Science Research Council], [1981?]. — 71p : 2maps ; 21cm. — (North Sea Oil Panel occasional paper ; no.9)
Bibliography: p71
ISBN 0-86226-066-3 (pbk) : £1.80 B81-38560

941.1′32071 — Scotland. Orkney. Lairds. Relations with Morton *(Earls of), 1700-1750*

Fereday, R. P.. Orkney feuds and the ′45 / R.P. Fereday. — Kirkwall ([Kirkwall, Orkney]) : Kirkwall Grammar School, 1980. — viii,176p : ill,maps,ports ; 23cm
Maps on lining papers. — Includes index
Unpriced B81-06241

941.1′35 — Scotland. Shetland. Dunrossness. Social change

Byron, Reginald. Social change in Dunrossness : a Shetland study / by Reginald Byron, Graham McFarlane. — [London] : [Social Science Research Council], c1980. — 150p in various pagings : 2maps ; 21cm. — (North Sea Oil Panel occasional paper ; no.1)
Bibliography: 2p
ISBN 0-86226-026-4 (pbk) : £1.80 B81-09957

941.1′35082 — Scotland. Shetland. Social life, *1880-1980*

Irvine, James W.. Footprints : aspects of Shetland life over the last 100 years / by James W. Irvine. — [Lerwick] ([Shetland Library, Lower Hillhead, Lerwick, Shetland ZE1 0EL]) : Education Committee, Shetland Islands Council, 1980. — 92p,[16]p of plates : ill ; 22cm
Unpriced (pbk) B81-32488

941.1′350858′0222 — Scotland. Shetland. Social life *— Illustrations*

Kidd, Tom. Life in Shetland / photographs by Tom Kidd ; with an introduction by James R. Nicolson. — Edinburgh : Harris, 1980. — [129]p of plates : chiefly ill,1map ; 21cm
ISBN 0-904505-97-9 : £6.95 B81-06664

941.1′350858′05 — Scotland. Shetland. Social life *— Serials*

Shetland life. — No.1 (Nov.1980)-. — Lerwick (Prince Alfred St., Lerwick, Shetland) : Shetland Times Ltd., 1980-. — v. : ill,ports ; 28cm
Monthly
ISSN 0260-5732 = Shetland life : £9.72 per year B81-08770

941.1′4 — Scotland. Western Isles. St Kilda — *Serials*

St. Kilda mail. — [No.1 (197-)?]-. — Edinburgh (c/o Mrs C. Erskine, National Trust for Scotland, 5 Charlotte Sq., Edinburgh, EH2 4DU) : St. Kilda Club, [197-]-. — v. : ill ; 21cm
Annual. — Description based on: No.5 (Mar.1981)
ISSN 0261-5541 = St. Kilda mail : Free to Club members B81-30828

941.1′402 — Scotland. Hebrides, *1016-1316 — Early works*

[Cronica regum Mannie & Insularum. *English & Latin*]. Cronica regum Mannie & Insularum = Chronicles of the kings of Man and the Isles : BL Cotton Julius Avii / transcribed and translated with an introduction by George Broderick. — [Douglas] : Manx Museum and National Trust, 1979. — xii,[95]p ; 30cm
Parallel Latin text and English translation
Unpriced (spiral)
Also classified at 942.7′9 B81-26125

941.1′4083′0924 — Scotland. Western Isles, *ca 1925 — Personal observations*

Gordon, Seton Paul. The immortal Isles / by Seton Paul Gordon ; with headpieces by Finlay Mackinnon and photographs by the author ; introduction by Adam Watson. — Perth (176, High St., Perth, Scotland) : Melven, 1979. — xx,227p,[32]p of plates : ill,1port ; 22cm
Facsim. reprint. Originally published: London : Williams and Norgate, 1926
ISBN 0-9505884-5-8 (pbk) : £4.95 B81-11262

941.1′40857′0924 — Scotland. Hebrides. Social life, *1970-1979 — Personal observations*

Brown, Jean, *1930-*. A song to sing and a tale to tell / Jean Brown. — Findhorn : Thule, 1981. — 174p : ill,1map,ports ; 21cm
Originally published: S.l. : s.n., 1979
ISBN 0-906191-62-9 (pbk) : £2.75 B81-36450

941.1′5 — Scotland. Highlands, *to 1979*

Brander, Michael. The making of the Highlands / Michael Brander. — London : Book Club Associates, 1980. — 240p : ill(some col.),maps,facsims,ports(some col.) ; 24cm
Ill. on lining papers. — Bibliography: p236. — Includes index
Unpriced B81-39168

941.1′5 — Scotland. North-west Highlands. Coastal regions. Social life, *ca 1975-ca 1980 — Personal observations*

Glasser, Ralph. Scenes from a Highland life / Ralph Glasser. — London : Hodder and Stoughton, 1981. — 175p,[8]p of plates : ill,1map ; 25cm
Map on lining papers
ISBN 0-340-25564-1 : £8.50 : CIP rev. B81-06060

941.1′5081′0924 — Scotland. Highlands. Social life, *1842-1882 — Personal observations*

Victoria, *Queen of Great Britain*. Queen Victoria′s Highland journals / [edited by] David Duff. — [Rev. ed.]. — Exeter : Webb & Bower, 1980. — 240p : ill(some col.),1map,1facsim,ports ; 26cm
Previous ed.: published as Victoria in the Highlands. London : Muller, 1968. — Includes index
ISBN 0-906671-11-6 : £9.95 : CIP rev. B80-08545

941.1′5083′0924 — Scotland. Highlands. Social life, *ca 1920-ca 1930 — Childhood reminiscences*

Miller, Christian. A childhood in Scotland / Christian Miller ; illustrated by Ray Evans. — London : John Murray, 1981. — 112p : ill ; 23cm
ISBN 0-7195-3830-0 : £6.50 B81-37464

941.1′72 — Scotland. Highland Region. Easter Ross. Social conditions, *1750-1850*

Mowat, Ian R. M.. Easter Ross 1750-1850 : the double frontier / Ian R.M. Mowat. — Edinburgh (138 St Stephen St, Edinburgh, EH3 5AA) : Donald, c1981. — ix,270p : maps ; 25cm
Bibliography: p214-235. - Includes index
ISBN 0-85976-063-4 : £15.00 B81-10389

941.1′72 — Scotland. Highland Region. Gairloch. Social life, *ca 1845-1920 — Personal observations*

Mackenzie, Osgood Hanbury. A hundred years in the Highlands / Osgood Hanbury Mackenzie of Inverewe. — New ed. / edited, and with an additional chapter by his daughter M.T. Sawyer of Inverewe. — Edinburgh (5 Charlotte Sq., Edinburgh EH2 LDU) : National Trust for Scotland in association with Bles, 1980. — 221p,[8] leaves of plates : ill,1map,facsims,ports ; 22cm
Originally published: London : Bles, 1949
ISBN 0-7138-0640-0 (pbk) : Unpriced B81-07018

941.2′1′009734 — Scotland. Grampian Region. Rural regions. Social life, *1700-1800 — Early works*

Alexander, William, *1826-1894*. Notes and sketches illustrative of Northern rural life : in the eigthteenth century / by William Alexander ; with an introduction by Ian Carter. — Limited 1981 ed. — Finzean (Haughend, Finzean, Aberdeenshire) : Callander, 1981. — xiv,176p : ill ; 22cm
Bibliography: p176
ISBN 0-907184-02-2 (pbk) : £4.50 B81-21851

941.2′23 — Scotland. Grampian Region. Elgin, *1900-1980 — Illustrations*

Elgin, past & present / compiled by Mike Seton ; photography by Pete Bonar. — Elgin ([c/o Director of Libraries], Elgin Public Library, Grant Lodge, Cooper Park, Elgin, IV30 1HS) : Moray District Libraries, 1980. — 48[i.e. 97]p : chiefly ill,1map ; 20x22cm
Bibliography: p97
Unpriced (pbk) B81-17801

941.2′23 — Scotland. Grampian Region. Gordonstoun. Public schools. Chapels: Michael Kirk, *to 1979*

Lightowler, Edward. The Michael Kirk, Gordonstoun : and its historical background / Edward Lightowler ; with a preface by H.R.H. The Prince of Wales. — Edinburgh : Harris, 1980. — 120p,[8]p of plates : ill,1port ; 23cm
ISBN 0-904505-96-0 : £6.00 B81-11367

941.2′4 — Scotland. Grampian Region. Kincardine and Deeside *(District)*. **Castles: Balmoral Castle. Social life,** *1842-1980*

Clark, Ronald W.. Balmoral : Queen Victoria′s highland home / Ronald W. Clark. — [London] : Thames and Hudson, c1981. — 144p : ill,maps,facsims,ports ; 25cm
Bibliography: p138-139. — Includes index
ISBN 0-500-25078-2 : £7.95 B81-39130

941.2′6 — Scotland. Tayside Region. Arbroath. Social life, *1860-1940 — Illustrations*

Arbroath Public Library. A prospect of Arbroath : photographs of Old Arbroath from the collections in Arbroath Public Library and Signal Tower Museum. — [Forfar] ([County Buildings, Forfar DD8 3LG]) : Angus District Libraries and Museums, c1981. — 83p : chiefly ill,ports ; 15x21cm
Unpriced (pbk) B81-29713

941.2′8 — Scotland. Tayside Region. Perth. Barnhill, Bridgend & Kinnoull, *to 1974*

Kinnoull, Bridgend and Barnhill / by pupils of Primary VII of Kinnoull School. — [Perth] : [Perth Civic Trust], [1976]. — 24p,[4]p of plates : ill ; 22cm
Unpriced (pbk) B81-09341

941.2′8 — Scotland. Tayside Region. Perth. Parks: Inches, *to 1979*

Fothergill, Rhoda. The Inches of Perth : a short account / by Rhoda Fothergill. — [Perth?] : [s.n.], [1980?] (Perth : Munro & Scott). — 31p,[4]p of plates : ill ; 22cm
Unpriced (pbk) B81-09344

941.2′9081′0222 — Scotland. Fife Region, *1837-1910 — Illustrations*

Victorian and Edwardian Fife from old photographs / [compiled by] Raymond Lamont-Brown and Peter Adamson ; foreword by Frank Muir. — Edinburgh (36 North Castle St., Edinburgh EH2 3BN) : Ramsay Head, 1980. — 114p : ill,ports ; 26cm
ISBN 0-902859-69-2 : £5.95 B81-05059

941.2'95 — Scotland. Fife Region. Glenrothes. Country houses: Pitcairn House. Excavation of remains

Reid, M. L.. Pitcairn House excavation 1980 / M.L. Reid. — Glenrothes (New Glenrothes House, North St., Fife KY7 5PR) : Glenrothes Development Corporation, [1980]. — 11p,[5] leaves of plates : ill,1plan ; 30cm
Bibliography: p10-11
Unpriced (pbk) B81-18899

941.2'95 — Scotland. Fife Region. Methil. Parish churches: Methil Parish Church, *to 1979*

Methil Parish Church history / [written by Mr. McGuire]. — [Methil] (c/o Rev. A.H. Gray, 14 Methilbrae, Methil, Leven) : Methil Parish Church, [1979]. — [8]p : ill,ports ; 21cm
Unpriced (unbound) B81-32485

941.2'98 — Scotland. Fife Region. Charlestown, Limekilns & Pattiesmuir, *to 1978*

Chesher, Susan. A short history of the villages : Charlestown, Limekilns and Pattiesmuir / written by Susan Chesher, Linda Foster and Laurence Hogben. — [Charlestown (Ardsheil, West Rd, Charlestown, Dunfermline, Fife]) : [N. Fotheringham for Charlestown, Limekilns and Pattiesmuir Community Council], [1979?]. — 21p : ill,1map,facsims,1port ; 30cm
Bibliography: p21
£1.40 (pbk) B81-13362

941.3'00491497 — South-east Scotland. Gypsies. Social life, *to 1944*

Gordon, Anne, *1927-*. Hearts upon the highway : gypsies in South-East Scotland / [by Anne Gordon] ; [illustrations by Anne Carrick]. — [S.l.] : [s.n.], [c1980] (Galashiels : McQueen Printers). — 139p : ill,maps,ports,geneal.table ; 20cm
Bibliography: p138-139
Unpriced (pbk) B81-29280

941.3'10858 — Scotland. Central Region. Rural regions. Social conditions — *For structure planning*

Central Region western rural area structure plan : consultative survey report. — [Stirling] ([Viewforth, Stirling FK8 2ET]) : Central Regional Council, Department of Planning, 1979. — 38p : ill,maps ; 30cm
Cover title
Unpriced (pbk) B81-12709

941.3'12 — Scotland. Central Region. Balquhidder region, *to 1980*

Beauchamp, Elizabeth. The braes o' Balquhidder : a history and guide for the visitor / by Elizabeth Beauchamp. — Glasgow : Heatherbank, 1981. — x,272p,[6]p of plates : ill,2maps ; 21cm
Previous ed.: 1978. — Text, map on covers. — Bibliography: p260-261. - Includes index
ISBN 0-905192-29-x (pbk) : £3.95 B81-22420

941.3'18 — Scotland. Central Region. Bo'ness. Churches: Kinneil Church

Hunter, R. L.. The kirk of Kinneil / by R.L. Hunter. — [Edinburgh] ([74, Trinity Road, Edinburgh EH5 3JT]) : [R.L. Hunter], [1981]. — 11p,1leaf of plates : ill,1map,1plan ; 22cm
Unpriced (pbk) B81-35438

941.3'18 — Scotland. Central Region. Falkirk, *1900-1914 — Illustrations*

Easton, Thomas. Easton's Falkirk : Victorian and Edwardian photographs / by Thomas Easton. — [Falkirk] ([Public Library, Hope St., Falkirk FK1 5AU]) : Falkirk District Council, Department of Libraries and Museums, [1981]. — 46p : chiefly ill,ports ; 15x21cm. — (Falkirk Museums publication)
Cover title
ISBN 0-906586-17-8 (pbk) : Unpriced B81-33578

941.3'18 — Scotland. Central Region. Falkirk, *to ca 1980*

Anderson, John M. (John Miller). This is my town : a series of letters to my grandchildren about the town of Falkirk, 1977-1980 / John M. Anderson. — Stirling (Old High School, Academy Rd., Stirling) : Educational Resources Unit, c1980. — 126p in various pagings : ill ; 21cm
Bibliography: p123-125
ISBN 0-906098-01-7 (pbk) : Unpriced B81-39375

941.3'4 — Edinburgh. Leith Walk. Social change, *to 1978*

Leith Walk and Greenside : a social history / Leith Walk Research Group, Department of Extra Mural Studies, University of Edinburgh, October 1978-1979. — [Edinburgh] ([11 Buccleuch Place, Edinburgh EH8 9JT]) : [The Group], [1979?]. — 23p,[1]leaf of plates : 1map ; 30cm
Cover title
Unpriced (pbk) B81-27845

941.3'4 — Edinburgh. Literary associations, *to 1979*

Royle, Trevor. Precipitous city : the story of literary Edinburgh / Trevor Royle. — Edinburgh : Mainstream, c1980. — 210p,[8]p of plates : ill,ports ; 23cm
Bibliography: p199-200. - Includes index
ISBN 0-906391-09-1 : £6.95 B81-03957

941.3'4 — Edinburgh. Newbridge & Kirkliston. Social conditions — *For environment planning*

Newbridge and Kirkliston local plan : report of survey. — [Edinburgh] ([City Chambers, High St., Edinburgh EH1 1YJ]) : City of Edinburgh District Council, Planning Department, 1980. — 8leaves ; 30cm
Unpriced (pbk) B81-12707

941.3'4 — Edinburgh. Queensferry. Social conditions — *For environment planning*

Queensferry local plan : report of survey. — [Edinburgh] ([City Chambers, High St., Edinburgh EH1 1YJ) : City of Edinburgh District Council, Planning Department, 1980. — 7leaves,2leaves of plates (some folded) : 2maps ; 30cm
Unpriced (pbk) B81-12711

941.3'5 — Scotland. Lothian Region. Mayfield & Newtongrange. Social conditions — *For environment planning*

Mayfield and Newtongrange local plan : survey and options / [prepared by Midlothian District Council, Department of Planning & Building Control]. — Roslin (7 Station Rd., Roslin, Midlothian [EH25 9PF]) : [The Department], 1981. — v,55p : ill,maps(some col.) ; 30cm
Map on 1 folded leaf in pocket
Unpriced (spiral) B81-17158

941.3'5 — Scotland. Lothian Region. Penicuik, *to 1979*

History of Penicuik. — [Midlothian] ([5 Knightslaw Place, Penicuik, Midlothian EH26 9EU]) : Penicuik Historical Society
Vol.1. — [1979]. — [40]p : ill ; 21cm
Includes bibliographies
£0.50 (unbound) B81-23220

History of Penicuik. — [Midlothian] ([5 Knightslaw Place, Penicuik, Midlothian EH26 9EU]) : Penicuik Historical Society
Vol.2. — 1979. — 68p : maps ; 21cm
Includes bibliographies
£0.50 (pbk) B81-23218

The History of Penicuik. — [Midlothian] ([5 Knightslaw Place, Penicuik, Midlothian EH26 9EU]) : Penicuik Historical Society
Vol.3. — [1980?]. — 38p ; 21cm
Includes bibliographies
£0.50 (pbk) B81-23219

941.3'6 — Scotland. Lothian Region. Cockenzie & Port Seton, *to 1980*

Turner, R.. One hundred years new : Cockenzie and Port Seton / written by R. Turner. — Edinburgh (25 Nicolson Sq., Edinburgh) : Sound & Visual Products, 1980. — 39p : ill,maps,ports ; 25cm
Unpriced (pbk) B81-37980

941.3'6 — Scotland. Lothian Region. North Berwick, *to ca 1940*

Ferrier, Walter M.. The North Berwick story / Walter M. Ferrier. — North Berwick (13 East Rd., North Berwick, East Lothian EH39 4LF) : Royal Burgh of North Berwick Community Council, 1980. — viii,102p,[36]p of plates : ill (some col.),maps,col.coat of arms,facsims,ports ; 22cm
Bibliography: p88-92. - Includes index
£5.85 B81-04647

941.3'7 — Great Britain. Tweed River region, *to 1979*

Thackrah, J. R.. The River Tweed / by John Richard Thackrah. — Lavenham : Terence Dalton, 1980. — viii,124p : ill,maps,ports ; 24cm
Maps on lining papers. — Bibliography: p123-124. - Includes index
ISBN 0-900963-98-0 : £6.95 B81-04502

941.3'7081'0222 — Scotland. Border country. Social life, *1860-1930 — Illustrations*

A Scottish border camera 1860-1930 / [the photographs of R. Clapperton, Selkirk] ; edited by Ian W. Mitchell. — Edinburgh (PO Box 506, SW Postal District, Edinburgh 10) : Moorfoot, [1981]. — [36]p : chiefly ill,ports ; 23cm
ISBN 0-906606-04-7 (pbk) : Unpriced B81-22138

941.3'7081'0222 — Scotland. Border country. Social life, *ca 1855-1910 — Illustrations*

The Victorian and Edwardian Borderland from rare photographs / [compiled by] Raymond Lamont-Brown and Peter Adamson ; foreword by the Lord Home of the Hirsel. — St. Andrews (52 Buchanan Gardens, St. Andrews KY16 9LX) : Alvie, 1981. — 123,[13]p : ill,ports ; 26cm
ISBN 0-9506200-1-7 : £6.80
Also classified at 942.8'8081'0222 B81-29725

941.3'82 — Scotland. Borders Region. Peebles, *1796-1815*

Scott, Sheila A.. Peebles during the Napoleonic Wars / [compiled by Sheila Scott]. — [Peebles] ([43 Rosetta Rd., Peebles EH45 8HH]) : S. Scott, 1980. — 11p : 1ill,2facsims,1ports ; 22cm
£0.25 (pbk) B81-09320

941.3'85 — Scotland. Borders Region. Blainslie region, *to 1980*

Oliver, W. H. (Winston Henry). The history of Blainslie, Roxburghshire / by W.H. Oliver. — Blainslie (Blain, Blainslie, Galashiels, TD1 2PR, Selkirkshire) : W.H. Oliver, c1981. — viii,72p : ill,maps,ports ; 22cm
Bibliography: p72. — Includes index
ISBN 0-9506354-0-5 (pbk) : Unpriced B81-25219

941.3'92 — Scotland. Cheviot Hills. Social life, *ca 1915-1930 — Childhood reminiscences*

Derwent, Lavinia. God bless the Borders! / Lavinia Derwent ; illustrated by Elizabeth Haines. — London : Hutchinson, 1981. — 143p : ill ; 23cm
ISBN 0-09-144780-1 : £5.95 : CIP rev. B81-02086

941.4'10858'072 — Scotland. Strathclyde Region. Social conditions. Research projects — *Directories — Serials*

Strathclyde. *Regional Council.* Register of research and data inventory / Strathclyde Regional Council. — 1980. — Glasgow (Strathclyde House [20], India St., Glasgow [G2 4PF]) : Department of Policy Planning, [1980]. — [110]p
Unpriced B81-08771

941.4'23 — Scotland. Strathclyde Region. Dunoon region, *to ca 1930*

Stirling, Nancy. Round and about Dunoon : by Nancy Stirling / line drawings by Ken Ashfield. — Rosemount (Park Rd., Kirn.) : Argyll Reproductions, [1980?]. — [44]p : ill,1map,1port ; 21cm
Unpriced (pbk) B81-09540

941.4'25 — Scotland. Strathclyde Region. Dumbarton. Social life, *1890-1959 — Illustrations*

Dumbarton : at work & play / [compiled] by Michael C. Taylor. — Dumbarton (Levenford House, Helenslee Rd., Dumbarton) : Dumbarton District Libraries, c1981. — 52p : ill,ports ; 21cm
ISBN 0-906927-05-6 (pbk) : £1.50 B81-23581

941.4'28 — Scotland. Strathclyde Region. Gourock, Inverkip & Wemyss Bay, *to 1980 — Illustrations*

Gourock, Inverkip and Wemyss Bay / [compiled by] Joy Monteith, Sandra Macdougall. — Greenock (Central Library, Clyde Sq., Greenock) : Inverclyde District Libraries, [1981]. — 60p : ill,1map ; 19x20cm
Map on inside cover. — Bibliography: p60
ISBN 0-9500687-2-1 (pbk) : £2.00 B81-23023

941.4'28 — Scotland. Strathclyde Region. Greenock, *ca 1860-1970 — Illustrations*

Monteith, Joy. Greenock from old photographs / Joy Monteith, Matt Anderson. — Greenock (Central Library, Clyde Sq., Greenock) : Inverclyde District Libraries, 1980. — 60p : chiefly ill,1map ; 20cm
Map on inside cover. — Bibliography: p59
ISBN 0-9500687-1-3 (pbk) : £1.75 B81-03136

941.4'28 — Scotland. Strathclyde Region. Greenock. Social conditions, *1842 — Inquiry reports*

Reports on the sanitary condition of the labouring population of Scotland : in consequence of an inquiry directed to be made by the Poor Law Commissioners, presented to both Houses of Parliament, by Command of Her Majesty, July 1842. — [Glasgow] ([Southbrae Drive, Jordanhill, Glasgow G13 1PP]) : [Jordanhill College of Education Local History Archives Group], 1978. — [14]p : facsim
Facsim of: edition published London : Clowes for HMSO, 1842
Unpriced (pbk) B81-40335

941.4'32 — Scotland. Strathclyde Region. Old Kilpatrick. Social conditions *— For environment planning*

Local plan : Old Kilpatrick : report of survey. — [Clydebank] ([District Council Offices, Rosebery Pl., Clydebank, G81 1UA]) : [Clydebank District Council], [1980?]. — 16leaves,[5]leaves of plates : ill,maps ; 30cm
Cover title
Unpriced (pbk) B81-12585

941.4'36 — Scotland. Strathclyde Region. Kirkintilloch. Social conditions *— For environment planning*

Strathkelvin District (Kirkintilloch area) local plan survey review : February 1977-January 1980. — Kirkintilloch ([P.O. Box 4, Council Chambers, Kirkintilloch, Glasgow G66 1PW]) : [Strathkelvin District Council], [1980?]. — 11leaves ; 30cm
Unpriced (spiral) B81-12586

941.4'36 — Scotland. Strathclyde Region. Kirkintilloch, *to 1979*

Martin, Don, *19---*. The story of Kirkintilloch / Don Martin. — [Glasgow] ([District Library H.Q., 170 Kirkintilloch Rd., Bishopbriggs, Glasgow, G64]) : Strathkelvin District Libraries & Museums, 1980. — 60p : ill,1coat of arms,facsims,ports ; 21cm. — (Auld Kirk Museum publications ; no.5)
Facsim on end papers. — Bibliography: p60
ISBN 0-904966-05-4 (pbk) : £1.30 B81-11541

941.4'360858 — Scotland. Strathclyde Region. Strathkelvin *(District).* **Social conditions** *— For environment planning*

District report / Strathkelvin District Council. — Bishopbriggs (1A Churchill Way, Bishopbriggs) : The Council, 1977. — i,28p : maps ; 30cm
Unpriced (pbk) B81-11856

941.4'41 — Scotland. Strathclyde Region. Lochwinnoch. Social life, *1939-1979 — Personal observations*

Jay, Charlie. Life in the valley / by Charlie Jay. — Paisley (18 Gordon St., Paisley PA1 1XB) : Paton, [1980?]. — 54p : ill,ports ; 21cm
Articles reprinted from the Paisley & Renfrewshire Gazette, 1975-1976
Unpriced (pbk) B81-05583

941.4'410858 — Scotland. Strathclyde Region. Renfrew *(District).* **Social conditions** *— For industrial development*

Renfrew District : industrial handbook. — [London] : [Burrow], [1981?]. — 64p : ill(some col.),maps(some col.) ; 30cm
£3.00 (pbk) B81-39346

941.4'43 — Scotland. Strathclyde Region. Glasgow. South Side *— Serials*

South side news and Glasgow advertiser. — June 1981-. — [Paisley] ([20 Gordon St., Paisley]) : [James Paton Ltd.], 1981-. — v. : ill,ports ; 40cm
Weekly. — Merger of: South side news ; and, Glasgow advertiser
ISSN 0262-1967 = South side news and Glasgow advertiser : £0.15 per issue
B81-39535

941.4'43 — Scotland. Strathclyde Region. Glasgow, *to 1980*

Lindsay, Maurice. Portrait of Glasgow / Maurice Lindsay. — 2nd ed. — London : Hale, 1981. — 252p,[24]p of plates : ill,1map,ports ; 23cm
Previous ed.: 1972. — Includes index
ISBN 0-7091-8872-2 : £8.95 B81-34731

941.4'430858 — Scotland. Strathclyde Region. Glasgow. Social conditions *— For environment planning*

Glasgow. *District Council.* Corporate plan : district profile / City of Glasgow District Council. — [Glasgow] ([84 Queen St., Glasgow G1 3DP]) : [The Council], [1980]. — [82]p : ill,maps ; 30cm
Unpriced (spiral) B81-28239

941.4'57 — Scotland. Strathclyde Region. Avondale, *to 1980*

Downie, William Fleming. A history of Strathaven and Avondale / by William Fleming Downie. — [Strathaven] ([10 Ryeland Street, Strathaven, Lanarkshire ML10 6DL]) : [W.F. Downie], 1979. — vii,339p,8p of plates : ill ; 22cm
Bibliography: p339
£5.50 (£4.00 pbk) (cased) B81-09548

941.4'610857 — Scotland. Strathclyde Region. Cunninghame *(District).* **Households. Social conditions,** *1978*

Household survey 1978 / Cunninghame District Council. — [Irvine] ([Cunninghame House, Irvine KA12 8EE]) : [The Council], [1981?]. — [101]leaves,[10]p,[14]leaves : maps,forms ; 30cm
Cover title
Unpriced (pbk) B81-20224

941.5 — HISTORY. IRELAND

941.5 — Ireland, *1600-1900*

Cullen, L. M.. The emergence of modern Ireland 1600-1900 / L.M. Cullen. — London : Batsford Academic, 1981. — 292p ; 23cm
Includes index
ISBN 0-7134-2747-7 : £17.50 B81-33068

941.5 — Ireland, *1603-1923*

Beckett, J. C.. The making of modern Ireland 1603-1923 / by J.C. Beckett. — London : Faber, 1981. — 514p,[6]p of plates : 3maps ; 21cm
Originally published: 1966. — Bibliography: p462-497. — Includes index
ISBN 0-571-18035-3 : £10.00 B81-17785

941.5 — Ireland. Political events, *1500-1980*

The **Troubles** / Richard Broad ... [et al.] ; editor Taylor Downing ; picture editor Isobel Hinshelwood. — London : Thames : Macdonald Futura, 1980. — 208p : ill,maps,1coat of arms,facsims,ports ; 26cm
Bibliography: p204. - List of films: p205. - Includes index
ISBN 0-354-04608-x (cased) : £7.50
ISBN 0-7088-1966-4 (pbk) : £4.95 B81-03734

941.5 — Ireland. Social conditions, *1600-1922 — Festschriften*

Irish population, economy and society. — Oxford : Oxford University Press, Jan.1982. — [300]p
ISBN 0-19-822499-0 : £17.50 : CIP entry
B81-34379

941.5 — Ireland. Social life, *to ca 1900*

Cullen, L. M.. Life in Ireland / L.M. Cullen. — London : Batsford, 1968 (1979 [printing]). — xiv,178p : ill,1 plan ; 22cm
Includes bibliographies and index
ISBN 0-7134-1449-9 (pbk) : £4.95 B81-02301

941.5 — Ireland, *to 1925*

Ranelagh, John. Ireland : an illustrated history / John Ranelagh. — London : Collins, 1981. — 267p : ill(some col.),maps(some col.),facsims,ports ; 28cm
Bibliography: p259-263. - Includes index
ISBN 0-00-216294-6 : £10.95 B81-15988

941.5 — Ireland, *to 1974*

Kee, Robert. Ireland : a history / Robert Kee. — London : Weidenfeld and Nicolson, c1980. — 256p,[16]p of plates : ill(some col.),maps,facsims,ports(some col.) ; 26cm
Bibliography: p249. - Includes index
ISBN 0-297-77855-2 : £9.95 B81-03984

941.5 — Irish civilization *related to* **European civilization,** *400-1200 — Festschriften*

Ireland in early mediaeval Europe. — Cambridge : Cambridge University Press, June 1981. — [400]p
ISBN 0-521-23547-2 : £39.00 : CIP entry
Also classified at 940.1 B81-14958

941.5 — Irish civilization, *to 1200*

Scherman, Katharine. The flowering of Ireland : saints, scholars and kings / by Katharine Scherman. — London : Gollancz, 1981. — xv,368p : ill ; 24cm
Bibliography: p354-357. — Includes index
ISBN 0-575-03010-0 : £8.50 B81-39085

941.5 — Irish civilization, *to ca 1965*

Irish history and culture : aspects of a people's heritage / [edited by H. Orel]. — [Portmarnock] ([98 Ardilaun, Portmarnock, Co. Dublin]) : Wolfhound, 1979, c1976. — ix,387p : ill,facsims,maps,ports ; 24cm
Originally published: Lawrence : University Press of Kansas, 1976. — Includes bibliographies and index
ISBN 0-905473-32-9 (cased) : Unpriced
ISBN 0-905473-33-7 (pbk) : Unpriced
B81-01390

941.5 — Irish culture *— History*

Irish studies. — 1. — Cambridge : Cambridge University Press, Apr.1981. — [176]p
ISBN 0-521-23336-4 : £16.50 : CIP entry
B81-03358

941.5

Wallace, Martin. A short history of Ireland. — Newton Abbot : David & Charles, Apr.1981. — [166]p
Originally published: 1973
ISBN 0-7153-6974-1 (pbk) : £2.95 : CIP entry
B81-07444

941.5'005 — Irish culture *— History — Serials*

Irish studies. — 1-. — London : Cambridge University Press, 1980-. — v. ; 23cm
Annual
ISSN 0260-8480 = Irish studies : £16.50
B81-11223

941.5'007'1041 — Great Britain. Educational institutions. Curriculum subjects: Irish studies *— Serials*

Irish studies in Britain. — No.1(Spring 1981)-. — London (83 Frithville Gardens, W12) : Addison Press in association with Irish Cultural Activities, London, 1981-. — v. : ill ; 29cm
Two issues yearly
ISSN 0260-8154 = Irish studies in Britain : £1.00 per year B81-32396

941.5'007'1241 — Great Britain. Secondary schools. Curriculum subjects: Ireland, *to 1980.* **Teaching**

Milne, Kenneth. New approaches to the teaching of Irish history / by Kenneth Milne. — London : Historical Association, c1979. — 47p ; 21cm. — (Teaching of history series ; no.43)
Bibliography: p43-47
ISBN 0-85278-203-9 (pbk) : £1.40 B81-23005

941.5'0072 — Ireland. Historiography

Irish historiography 1970-79 / edited by Joseph Lee. — Cork (University College, Cork, [Irish Republic]) : Cork University Press, 1981. — vii,238p ; 22cm
ISBN 0-902561-20-0 (pbk) : £8.00 B81-29508

941.503 — Ireland. Political events, *1318-1361*
Frame, Robin. English lordship in Ireland, 1318-1361. — Oxford : Clarendon Press, Feb.1982. — [360]p
ISBN 0-19-822673-x : £22.50 : CIP entry
B81-35760

941.505'092'4 — Ireland. O'Malley, Grace — *Biographies*
Chambers, Anne. Granuaile : the life and times of Grace O'Malley c.1530-1603 / Anne Chambers. — Portmarnock (98 Ardilaun, Portmarnock, County Dublin) : Wolfhound, 1979. — 213p : ill,maps,coats of arms,facsims,ports,geneal.tables ; 22cm
Bibliography: p206-207. — Includes index
ISBN 0-905473-31-0 : Unpriced B81-13600

941.505'092'4 — Ireland. Stanihurst, Richard — *Biographies*
Lennon, Colm. Richard Stanihurst the Dubliner 1547-1618 : a biography / Colm Lennon. — Blackrock : Irish Academic Press, c1981. — 186p : maps ; 23cm
Bibliography: p170-178. — Includes index. — Includes: On Ireland's past / Richard Stanihurst. — Translation of: De rebus in Hibernia gestis. Liber 1
ISBN 0-7165-0069-8 : Unpriced B81-31881

941.507'092'4 — Ireland. Politics. Tone, Theobald Wolfe — *Biographies*
Boylan, Henry. Theobald Wolfe Tone / Henry Boylan. — Dublin : Gill and Macmillan, 1981. — 145p ; 19cm. — (Gill's Irish lives)
Bibliography: p140-141. — Includes index
ISBN 0-7171-1090-7 (cased) : £8.50
ISBN 0-7171-1071-5 (pbk) : £2.60 B81-40895

941.5081 — Ireland. Political events, *1870-1921 — Trotskyist viewpoints*
Hadden, Peter. Divide and rule : Labour and the partition of Ireland / Peter Hadden. — Dublin (75 Middle Abbey St., Dublin 1) : MIM, 1980. — 73p ; 21cm
£0.60 (pbk) B81-19730

941.5081 — Ireland. Social conditions, *1800-1980*
Daly, Mary E.. Social and economic history of Ireland since 1800 / Mary E. Daly. — Dublin : Educational Co., 1981. — 236p : ill,maps ; 21cm
Bibliography: p223-231. — Includes index
Unpriced (pbk) B81-29572

941.5081 — Ireland. Social life, *1875-1925 — Readings from contemporary sources*
Faces of Ireland : 1875-1925 / [compiled by] Brian M. Walker, Art Ó Broin and Seán McMahon. — Belfast : Appletree, c1980. — 447p in various pagings : ill,facsims,ports ; 21cm
Includes items in Irish. — Originally published: in 4 vols. as Faces of the past. 1975 ; Faces of the west. 1976 ; Faces of Munster. 1977 ; Faces of old Leinster. 1978. — Ill. on lining papers. — Bibliography: p119-118. — Includes index
ISBN 0-904651-47-9 : Unpriced B81-27190

941.5081'022'2 — Ireland, *1842-ca 1910 — Illustrations*
Ireland from old photographs / introduction and commentaries by Maurice Gorham. — London : Batsford, 1971 (1979 [printing]). — [159]p : chiefly ill,ports ; 25cm
ISBN 0-7134-2195-9 (pbk) : £3.50 B81-08382

941.5081'03'21 — Ireland, *1800-1979 — Encyclopaedias*
Hickey, D. J.. A dictionary of Irish history since 1800 / D.J. Hickey, J.E. Doherty. — Dublin : Gill and Macmillan, 1980. — 615p ; 23cm
ISBN 0-7171-0895-3 : £20.00 B81-01912

941.5081'092'4 — Ireland. MacNeill, Eoin — *Biographies*
Tierney, Michael. Eoin MacNeill : scholar and man of action 1867-1945 / by Michael Tierney ; edited by F.X. Martin. — Oxford : Clarendon Press, 1980. — xxii,409p,[5]p of plates : ill,ports ; 22cm
Bibliography: p386-390. — Includes index
ISBN 0-19-822440-0 : £22.50 : CIP rev.
B80-18552

941.5081'092'4 — Ireland. O'Connell, Daniel — *Correspondence, diaries, etc.*
O'Connell, Daniel. The correspondence of Daniel O'Connell / edited by Maurice R. O'Connell. — Dublin (Airton Rd, Tallaght, Co. Dublin) : Blackwater for the Irish Manuscripts Commission
Vol. 7: 1841-1845. — [1978]. — viii, 366p ; 25cm
Bibliography: pvii-viii. — Includes index
ISBN 0-905471-03-2 : Unpriced B81-24267

O'Connell, Daniel. The correspondence of Daniel O'Connell / edited by Maurice R. O'Connell. — Dublin (Airton Rd, Tallaght, Co. Dublin) : Blackwater for the Irish Manuscripts Commission
Vol. 8: 1846-1847, with supplementary letters and series indexes. — c1980. — xvi,373p ; 25cm
Bibliography: pviii-xii. — Includes index
ISBN 0-905471-04-0 : Unpriced B81-24268

941.5081'092'4 — Ireland. Politics. O'Connell, Daniel — *Biographies*
O'Ferrall, Fergus. Daniel O'Connell / Fergus O'Ferrall. — Dublin : Gill and Macmillan, 1981. — 151p ; 19cm. — (Gill's Irish lives)
Bibliography: p144-149. — Includes index
ISBN 0-7171-1070-2 (cased) : £8.50
ISBN 0-7171-1041-9 (pbk) : £2.60 B81-40897

941.5082 — Ireland. Political events, *1940-1980 — British & Irish Communist Organisation viewpoints*
Neutrality and partition ... / British & Irish Communist Organisation. — Dublin : B & ICO (Dublin Branch), 1981. — 20p : ill ; 26cm
Unpriced (unbound) B81-21978

941.5082 — Irish culture, *1922-1979*
Brown, Terence. Ireland : a social and cultural history 1922-79 / Terence Brown. — [London] : Fontana, 1981. — 364p ; 18cm
Includes index
ISBN 0-00-635253-7 (pbk) : £3.50 B81-12004

941.5082'1 — Ireland, *1912-1922*
O'Connor, Ulick. A terrible beauty is born : the Irish troubles, 1912-1922 / Ulick O'Connor. — London : Granada, 1981, c1975. — 192p,[8]p of plates : ill,ports ; 18cm. — (A Panther Book)
Originally published: London : Hamilton, 1975. — Bibliography: p182-186. — Includes index
ISBN 0-586-05375-1 (pbk) : £1.50 B81-32920

941.5082'1'0922 — Ireland. Political events, *1916-1921 — Biographies*
O'Farrell, Padraic. Who's who in the Irish war of independence 1916-1921 / Padraic O'Farrell. — Dublin : Mercier, 1980. — 186p ; 22cm
£9.00 B81-14999

941.5082'1'0924 — Anglo-Irish War, *1920-1921 — Personal observations*
Barry, Tom. Guerilla days in Ireland / Tom Barry. — Dublin : Anvil, 1962 (1981 [printing]). — xi,242p,[16]p of plates : ill,2maps,ports ; 23cm
Originally published: Dublin : Irish Press, 1949. — Includes index
ISBN 0-900068-55-8 (cased) : £11.00
ISBN 0-900068-55-8 (pbk) : Unpriced
B81-39816

941.5082'1'0924 — Ireland. MacGill, Patrick — *Biographies*
MacGill, Patrick. Children of the dead end : the autobiography of a navvy / by Patrick MacGill. — Ascot : Caliban, 1980. — xiv,305p ; 21cm
Originally published: London : Jenkins, 1914
ISBN 0-904573-36-2 : £9.00 B81-16154

941.5082'1'0924 — Ireland. Political events, *1917-1921 — Personal observations*
Breen, Dan. My fight for Irish freedom / Dan Breen. — Rev. and enl. ed. — Dublin : Anvil, 1964 (1981 [printing]). — 208p,[16]p of plates : ill,ports ; 23cm
Previous ed.: Dublin : Talbot, 1924. — Includes index
ISBN 0-900068-56-6 (cased) : £11.00
ISBN 0-900068-58-2 (pbk) : Unpriced
B81-39817

941.5082'1'0924 — Ireland. Politics. Carson, Edward Henry Carson, Baron — *Biographies*
Stewart, A. T. Q.. Edward Carson / A.T.Q. Stewart. — Dublin : Gill and Macmillan, 1981. — 150p ; 19cm. — (Gill's Irish lives)
Bibliography: p139-142. — Includes index
ISBN 0-7171-1075-3 (cased) : £8.50
ISBN 0-7171-0981-x (pbk) : £2.60 B81-40896

941.5082'1'0924 — Ireland. Politics. Griffith, Arthur — *Biographies*
Younger, Carlton. Arthur Griffith / Carlton Younger. — Dublin : Gill and Macmillan, 1981. — 156p ; 19cm. — (Gill's Irish lives)
Includes index
ISBN 0-7171-1073-7 (cased) : £8.50
ISBN 0-7171-1011-7 (pbk) : £2.60 B81-40899

941.6081 — Northern Ireland. Social life, *1880-1915 — Readings from contemporary sources*
Walker, Brian Mercer. Faces of the past : a photographic and literary record of Ulster life 1880-1915 / by Brian Mercer Walker. — Belfast : Appletree, 1974 (1978 [printing]). — 111p : ill,ports ; 20cm
Ill on inside covers. — Bibliography: p109. - Includes index
ISBN 0-904651-00-2 (cased) : Unpriced
ISBN 0-904651-01-0 (pbk) : £2.50 B81-18498

941.6082 — Northern Ireland. Political events, *ca 1920-1974*
Buckland, Patrick. A history of Northern Ireland / Patrick Buckland. — Dublin : Gill and Macmillan, 1981. — 195p : 1map ; 22cm
Bibliography: p181-186. - Includes index
ISBN 0-7171-1123-7 (cased) : Unpriced
ISBN 0-7171-1069-9 (pbk) : £3.95 B81-18911

941.6082'092'4 — Northern Ireland. Shea, Patrick — *Biographies*
Shea, Patrick. Voices and the sound of drums : an Irish autobiography / Patrick Shea. — Belfast : Blackstaff, c1981. — 208p ; 23cm
Includes index
ISBN 0-85640-228-1 (cased) : £6.95
ISBN 0-85640-247-8 (pbk) : £3.50 B81-19774

941.6082'4 — Northern Ireland. Political events. Attitudes of Trades Union Congress — *Revolutionary Communist Group viewpoints*
TUC hands off Ireland! / Smash the Prevention of Terrorism Act Campaign. — London (BCM JPLTD, WC1N 3XX) : Junius, 1981. — 15p : facsims ; 21cm. — (Revolutionary Communist pamphlets, ISSN 0141-8874 ; no.8)
£0.30 (pbk) B81-17747

941.60824 — Northern Ireland. Social conditions, *1968-1975 — Psychological perspectives*
Fields, Rona M.. [Society under siege]. Northern Ireland : society under siege / Rona M. Fields ; foreword by Alfred McClung Lee. — New Brunswick ; London : Transaction Books, c1980. — xvi,267p : ill ; 23cm
Originally published: Philadelphia : Temple University Press, 1977. — Includes index
ISBN 0-87855-806-3 (pbk) : Unpriced
B81-31121

941.60824 — Northern Ireland. Social conditions, *1976-1979*
O'Dowd, Liam. Northern Ireland : between the civil rights and civil war / Liam O'Dowd, Bill Rolston, Mike Tomlinson. — London (55 Mount Pleasant, WC1X 0AE) : CSE Books, 1980. — 224p : ill,facsims,maps ; 21cm
Bibliography: p209-218. — Includes index
ISBN 0-906336-18-x (cased) : £12.00 : CIP rev.
ISBN 0-906336-19-8 (pbk) : £3.95 B80-13236

941.6'12081 — Antrim *(District).* **Antrim. Social life,** *ca 1865-ca 1880 — Childhood reminiscences*
Irvine, Alexander. The souls of poor folk. — Belfast : Appletree Press, Oct.1981. — [160]p
ISBN 0-904651-86-x : £4.50 : CIP entry
B81-30189

941.6'18 — Newtownabbey *(District).* **Carnmoney region. Agricultural industries. Farms: Sentry Hill. Social life,** *ca 1850-1917*
Walker, Brian Mercer. Sentry Hill. — Belfast : Blackstaff Press, Nov.1981. — [192]p
ISBN 0-85640-254-0 (pbk) : £5.95 : CIP entry
B81-34962

941.69′80824′05 — Cavan *(County) — Serials*
[Yearbook *(Cavan Association, Dublin)*].
Yearbook / Cavan Association, Dublin. — 1979-. — [Dublin] : [The Association], 1979-. — v. : ill,ports ; 30cm
Annual. — Description based on: 1980 issue
£1.50 B81-38523

941.7 — Western Ireland *(Republic) — Serials*
[Western news *(Galway)*]. Western news : incorporating Galway people and Western observer, West awake magazine. — Vol.2, no.8 (14 June 1980)-. — Galway (Mary St., Galway) : [S.n.], 1980-. — v. : ill,ports ; 44cm
Weekly. — Continues: West awake
£0.20p B81-05937

941.7082 — Ireland *(Republic).* **Political events,** *1917-1973*
De Valera, Eamon. Speeches and statements by Eamon de Valera, 1917-73 / edited by Maurice Moynihan. — Dublin : Gill and Macmillan, 1980. — xlvii,634p,[2]p of plates : facsims,ports ; 24cm
Includes some speeches in Irish. — Includes index
ISBN 0-312-22457-5 : £35.00 B81-04139

941.7082′1′0924 — Ireland *(Republic).* **Collins, Michael,** *1890-1922.* **Death**
Feehan, John M.. The shooting of Michael Collins / John M. Feehan. — Dublin : Mercier, 1981. — 125p : 1map ; 18cm
ISBN 0-85342-659-7 (pbk) : £2.30 B81-32460

941.7082′1′0924 — Ireland *(Republic).* **Lankford, Siobhán,** *1894-1923 — Biographies*
Lankford, Siobhán. The hope and the sadness : personal recollections of troubled times in Ireland / by Siobhán Lankford. — Cork (86 South Main St., Cork) : Tower Books, 1980. — 274p,[8]p of plates : ill,maps,ports ; 21cm
Map on lining papers
£6.60 B81-07833

941.70824′05 — Ireland *(Republic).* **Political events** *— Fine Gael viewpoints — Serials*
[National democrat *(Dublin)*]. National democrat : official Fine Gael journal. — Vol.1, no.1 (Apr.1978)-. — [Dublin] ([Fine Gael Rooms, Leinster House, Dublin 2]) : [Fine Gael], 1978-. — v. : ill ; 45cm
Monthly. — Description based on: Vol.3, no.4 (Sept. 1980)
Unpriced B81-06196

941.70824′05 — Ireland *(Republic).* **Social life** *— Serials*
Howarth, Peter H.. Rhymes & reasons / Peter H. Howarth. — [Vol.1, no.1 (1981)]-. — Castleisland (Castleisland, Co. Kerry) : P.H. Howarth, 1981-. — v. : ill ; 21cm
Monthly
Unpriced B81-29644

941.7′3 — Mayo *(County).* **Westport. Country houses: Westport House,** *to 1981*
Sligo, Denis Browne, *Marquess of.* Westport House and the Brownes. — Ashbourne : Moorland Publishing, Jan.1982. — [112]p
ISBN 0-86190-045-6 : £5.95 : CIP entry B81-38833

941.7′6 — Leitrim *(County).* **Ballinaglera. Social life,** *to 1979*
Clancy, Eileen. Ballinaglera parish, Co. Leitrim : aspects of its history and traditions / by Eileen Clancy and Patrick J. Forde. — Dublin (36 Dodder Park Rd., Rathfarnham, Dublin 14) : E. Clancy, 1980. — xiii,212p,[15]p of plates (some folded) : ill,maps,ports ; 21cm
Includes index
£5.00 (pbk) B81-23217

941.8′1506 — Westmeath *(County), ca 1600-ca 1680 — Early works — Facsimiles*
Piers, *Sir* **Henry.** A chorographical description of the county of West-Meath / by Sir Henry Piers ; with 12 illustrations by David Foster. — Tara (c/o Publications Secretary, Skryne Castle, Tara, Co. Meath) : Meath Archaeological and Historical Society, 1981. — xvi,120p[11]leaves of plates : ill,1map ; 22cm
Facsim. of: 2nd ed. Originally published in: Collectanea de rebus Hibernicis / edited by C. Vallancey. Dublin : s.n., 1786. — Includes index
ISBN 0-9500332-4-3 : £5.50 B81-10167

941.8′22′005 — Meath *(County) — History — Serials*
Riocht na Midhe : records of Meath Archaeological and Historical Society. — Vol.6, no.4 (1978-1979). — Tara (Mrs. E. Hickey, Publications Officer, Skyrne Castle, Tara, Co. Meath) : [The Society], [1980?]. — 129p
Unpriced B81-32691

941.8′35 — Dublin, *837-1978*
Somerville-Large, Peter. Dublin / Peter Somerville-Large. — London : Granada, 1981, c1979. — 330,[16]p of plates : ill,ports ; 20cm. — (A Panther book)
Originally published: London : Hamilton, 1979. — Bibliography: p299-304. — Includes index
ISBN 0-586-05236-4 (pbk) : £2.25 B81-24933

941.8′35 — Dublin, *1660-1860*
Craig, Maurice. Dublin 1660-1860 / Maurice Craig. — Dublin : Figgis, 1969 (1980 printing). — xxi,361p,[47] of plates : ill,maps,plans ; 21cm
Originally published: London : Cresset, 1952. — Bibliography: p342-352. — Includes index
ISBN 0-900372-91-5 (pbk) : Unpriced B81-03937

941.8′35004395 — Dublin. Vikings, *ca 900-950*
Smyth, Alfred P.. Scandinavian York and Dublin : the history and archaeology of two related Viking kingdoms / Alfred P. Smyth. — New Jersey : Humanities ; Dublin ([Tudor House, Taney Rd., Dundrum, Dublin 14]) : Templekieran
2. — c1979. — x,361p,[1]leaf of plates : ill,maps,plans,geneal.tables ; 22cm
Includes index
ISBN 0-391-01049-2 (pbk) : Unpriced
Primary classification 942.8′43004395
B81-20802

941.8′350822′0924 — Dublin. Social life, *ca 1940-1959 — Personal observations*
Corkery, Tom. Tom Corkery′s Dublin. — Dublin : Anvil Books, 1980. — 127p : ill ; 25cm
Unpriced (corrected) B81-12458

941.8′38 — Dublin *(County).* **Dún Laoghaire,** *to 1980*
Pearson, Peter. Dun Laoghaire/Kingstown. — Dublin : O′Brien Press, June 1981. — [160]p. — (Urban heritage series, ISSN 0332-1886 ; 2)
ISBN 0-905140-83-4 : £9.00 : CIP entry B81-12887

941.8′70824′05 — Laois *(County).* **Social life** *— Serials*
Laois Association yearbook. — 1978-. — Dublin (3, Lower Abbey St., Dublin 1) : Tara Publishing, 1978-. — v : ill,ports ; 30cm
£0.75 B81-04695

941.8′70824′06 — Laois *(County).* **Social life. Organisations: Laois Association** *— Serials*
Laois Association yearbook. — 1980. — Dublin (1 Poolbeg St., Dublin 2) : Carlton Pub., [1980?]. — 44p
Unpriced B81-09032

941.8′90824′05 — Kilkenny *(County) — Serials*
Kilkenny standard. — [Vol.1 (1980)?]-. — [Kilkenny] ([High St., Kilkenny]) : [Kilkenny standard], [1980?]-. — v. : ill,ports(some col.) ; 44cm
Weekly. — Text mainly in English, but also in Irish. — Description based on: Vol.2, no.28 (Friday 10th July 1981
Unpriced B81-39516

941.9′2 — Tipperary *(County).* **Toomevara,** *to 1980*
Toomevara : the unbroken chain / [compiled and edited by Tom Shanahan]. — [Toomevara] ([Toomevara, Nenagh, Co. Tipperary, Ireland]) : [T. Shanahan?], 1981. — 55p : ill,ports ; 30cm
Cover title
Unpriced (pbk) B81-17812

941.9′2081 — Ireland, *1800-1900 — Study regions: Tipperary (County)*
O′Shea, James. The priest, society and politics in nineteenth century Ireland. — Dublin : Wolfhound Press, Oct.1981. — [300]p
ISBN 0-905473-71-x : £12.00 : CIP entry B81-27477

941.9′4′00207 — Limerick *(County), to 1978 — Humour*
Lysaght, Paddy. The comic history of Limerick / Paddy Lysaght ; illustrations by J. English. — Dublin : Mercier, c1979. — 88p : ill ; 18cm
ISBN 0-85342-591-4 (pbk) : £1.60 B81-05993

941.9′5 — Cork *(County).* **Fermoy,** *1841-1890*
Brunicardi, Niall. Fermoy : 1841 to 1890 a local history / Niall Brunicardi. — [Fermoy] ([Duntaheen Rd., Fermoy, Co. Cork]) : Éigse Na Mainistreach, 1978. — p146-230 ; 33cm
Cover title
Unpriced (pbk) B81-21894

941.9′5 — Cork *(County).* **Fermoy,** *1891-1940*
Brunicardi, Niall. Fermoy : 1891-1940 a local history / Niall Brunicardi. — [Fermoy] ([Duntaheen Rd., Fermoy, Co. Cork]) : Éigse Na Mainistreach, 1979. — p231-320 ; 33cm
Cover title
Unpriced (pbk) B81-21893

941.9′5 — Cork *(County).* **West Cork. Rural regions. Social life,** *to ca 1920*
Crowley, Flor. In west Cork long ago / by Flor Crowley. — Dublin : Mercier, 1979 (1980 [printing]). — 127p ; 18cm
ISBN 0-85342-600-7 (pbk) : £1.80 B81-06754

941.9′50824′05 — Cork *(County) — Serials*
[Cork weekly examiner *(1981)*]. Cork weekly examiner. — No.1 (Thursday Apr.2, 1981)-. — Cork (95 Patrick St., Cork) : T. Crosbie, 1981-. — v. : ill,ports ; 60cm
Continues: Irish weekly examiner
Unpriced B81-32190

941.9′56081 — Cork *(County).* **Cork** *(City), 1850-1907*
Steps & steeples : Cork at the turn of the century / [compiled by] Colm Lincoln. — Dublin : O′Brien, 1980. — 148p : chiefly ill,maps ; 26cm. — (Urban heritage series, ISSN 0332-1886 ; 1)
Ill on lining papers. — Includes index
ISBN 0-905140-82-6 : £8.00 B81-09561

941.9′6 — Kerry *(County).* **Blasket Islands. Social life,** *1856-1935 — Personal observations — Collections*
Memoirs of the Great Blasket Island. — Oxford : Oxford University Press, [1981?]. — 3v. : ill,maps,ports ; 21cm
Title from container. — In slip case. — Contents: The islandman / by Tomás Ó Crohan. Originally published: Dublin : Talbot, 1934 - The western island, or, The Great Blasket 1944 - An old woman′s reflections / by Peig Sayers. Oxford : Oxford University Press, 1962
ISBN 0-19-281319-6 : £5.00 B81-22328

941.9′6 — Kerry *(County).* **Blasket Islands. Social life,** *1910-1930 — Personal observations — Irish texts*
Sayers, Peig. Machnamh seanmhná / Peig Sayers a cheap ; Máire Ní Chinnéide a chuir in eagar. — Eagrán nua / in eagar ag Pádraig Ua Maoileoin. — Baile Átha Cliath : Oifig an tSoláthair, 1980. — 142p : 1port ; 18cm
Previous ed.: 1939
£1.00 (pbk) B81-15187

941.9′6 — Kerry *(County).* **Blasket Islands,** *to 1979*
Stagles, Joan. The Blasket Islands : next parish America / Joan & Ray Stagles. — Dublin : O′Brien, 1980. — 144p : ill,maps,plans,ports ; 2lcm. — ([Island series], ISSN 0332-1932 ; [4])
Ill on lining papers. — Includes index
ISBN 0-905140-63-x : £8.80 B81-15266

941.9′6 — Kerry *(County).* **Castleisland,** *to 1980*
O′Shea, Kieran. Castleisland : church and people / Kieran O′Shea. — [Castleisland] ([College Rd. Castleisland, Co. Kerry. Ireland]) : [K. O′Shea], c1981. — 67p,[1]folded leaf of plates : ill,2maps,coat of arms,ports ; 22cm
Unpriced (pbk) B81-27101

942 — HISTORY. ENGLAND

942 — England, *410-1975*
Seaman, L. C. B.. A new history of England 410-1975 / L.C.B. Seaman. — Brighton : Harvester Press, 1981. — xxiii,576p ; 24cm
Includes index
ISBN 0-85527-697-5 : £12.95 B81-21421

942 — England, *446-1979*
Ridley, Jasper. The history of England / by Jasper Ridley. — London : Routledge & Kegan Paul, 1981. — xiv,331p : ill ; 24cm
Includes index
ISBN 0-7100-0794-9 : £7.95 : CIP rev. B81-21480

942 — England, *1307-1536*
Myers, A. R.. England in the late Middle Ages / A.R. Myers. — 8th ed. — Harmondsworth : Penguin, 1971 (1981 [printing]). — 284p,[24]p of plates : ill,2maps,1facsim,1geneal.table ; 18cm. — (Pelican history of England ; 4)
Previous ed.: 1969. — Bibliography: p263-269. - Includes index
ISBN 0-14-020234-x (pbk) : £1.95 B81-20378

942 — England, *1485-1837 — For schools*
Middleton, Geoffrey. Tudors, Stuarts and Georgians / Geoffrey Middleton ; illustrated with comtemporary pictures and by Peter Dennis and T.A.S. Limited. — Harlow : Longman, 1981. — 79p : ill(some col.),maps (some col.),facsims(some col.),ports(some col.) ; 27cm. — (History in focus ; 4)
Includes index
ISBN 0-582-18316-2 (pbk) : £2.10 B81-10170

942 — England. Anglo-Saxon cemeteries — *Conference proceedings*
Anglo-Saxon Symposium *(4th : 1979 : Oxford).* Anglo-Saxon cemeteries 1979 / the fourth Anglo-Saxon Symposium at Oxford ; edited by Philip Rahtz, Tania Dickenson and Lorna Watts. — Oxford : B.A.R., 1980. — xiii,389p : ill,maps ; 30cm. — (BAR. British series ; 82)
Includes bibliographies
ISBN 0-86054-095-2 (pbk) : £12.00 B81-36632

942 — England. Castles. Social life, *1000-1500 — For children*
Adams, Carol. How they lived in a medieval castle / Carol Adams ; illustrated by Gareth Adamson. — Guildford : Lutterworth, 1981. — 31p : ill(some col.) ; 23cm. — (How they lived ; 11)
Ill on lining papers. — Includes index
ISBN 0-7188-2439-3 : £1.95 B81-39067

942 — England *— History — For schools*
Pictorial history. — Huddersfield : Schofield & Sims
Bk.3. — Rev. ed. / by J.E. Allen ; drawings by W.M. Ireland and Neville Swaine. — c1981. — 94p : col.ill,ports(some col.) ; 25cm
Previous ed.: i.e. Rev. ed. in 8 v. by H.E. Hounsell and D.W. Airne, 1961-1962
ISBN 0-7217-1601-6 (pbk)
ISBN 0-7212-1596-6 (non-net) : £1.55 B81-27166

942 — England. Local history. Historical sources
Stephens, W. B.. Sources for English local history / W.B. Stephens. — Revised and expanded ed. — Cambridge : Cambridge University Press, 1981. — xv,342p ; 23cm. — (The Sources of history, studies in the uses of historical evidence)
Previous ed.: Manchester : Manchester University Press, 1973. — Includes index
ISBN 0-521-23763-7 (cased) : £25.00 : CIP rev.
ISBN 0-521-28213-6 (pbk) : £8.95 B81-25773

942 — England. National Trust properties — *Serials*
National Trust studies. — 1981. — London : published for Sotheby Parke Bernet Publications by Philip Wilson, 1980. — 160p
ISBN 0-85667-110-x : £12.50
ISSN 0142-3487 B81-07345

942 — England. Parish churches, *1086-1558*
Platt, Colin. The parish churches of medieval England / Colin Platt. — London : Secker & Warburg, 1981. — xvi,185p : ill,maps,plans ; 26cm
Includes index
ISBN 0-436-37553-2 (cased) : £15.00
ISBN 0-436-37554-0 (pbk) : £5.95 B81-19707

942 — England. Places of historical importance
Green, Howard. Let's visit history / Howard Green. — Bognor Regis : New Horizon, c1980. — 129p,[18]p of plates : ill,1facsim ; 21cmcm
ISBN 0-86116-532-2 : £5.75 B81-21721

942 — England. Rural regions. Working life, *to ca 1930*
Hartley, Dorothy. The land of England : English country customs through the ages / Dorothy Hartley ; with line drawing by the author. — London : Macdonald, 1979 (1980 [printing]). — x,374p,[20]p of plates : ill,maps ; 24cm
Includes index
£8.95 B81-07505

942 — England. Seaside resorts *— For children*
Healey, Tim. Let's go to the seaside / Tim Healy ; photography by Andreas Nicola. — London : Watts, c1981. — 32p : col.ill ; 22cm. — (Let's go series)
ISBN 0-85166-792-9 : £2.99 B81-21750

942 — England. Social conditions, *100-1450*
Peasants, knights and heretics : studies in Medieval English social history / edited by R.H. Hilton. — Cambridge : Cambridge University Press, 1976 (1981 [printing]). — vi,330p : ill ; 22cm. — (Past and present publications)
Includes index
ISBN 0-521-28019-2 (pbk) : £4.95 : CIP rev. B80-32999

942 — England, *to 1914 — Readings from contemporary sources*
English historical documents / [general editor David C. Douglas]. — 2nd ed. — London : Eyre Methuen
[Vol.2]: 1042-1189 / edited by David C. Douglas and George W. Greenaway. — 1981. — xxxi,1083p : ill,maps,geneal.tables ; 25cm
Previous ed.: London : Eyre & Spottiswoode, 1953. — Includes bibliographies and index
ISBN 0-413-32500-8 : £60.00 : CIP rev. B81-13518

942 — England, *to 1973*
Burke, John, *1922-*. An illustrated history of England / John Burke ; foreword by Arthur Bryant. — London : Book Club Associates, 1974 (1980 [printing]). — 349p : ill(some col.),1map,ports(some col.) ; 26cm
Originally published: London : Collins, 1974. — Ill. on lining papers. — Includes index
Unpriced B81-39170

942'.004924 — England. Jews. Readmission, *1603-1655*
Katz, David S.. Philo-semitism and the readmission of the Jews to England 1603-1655. — Oxford : Clarendon Press, Jan.1982. — [300]p. — (Oxford historical monographs)
ISBN 0-19-821885-0 : £17.50 : CIP entry B81-34388

942.007 — North-west England. Urban regions. Children. Social conditions, *1750-1850*
Cruickshank, Marjorie. Children and industry. — Manchester : Manchester University Press, Oct.1981. — [192]p
ISBN 0-7190-0809-3 : £16.50 : CIP entry B81-28053

942'.009'1734 — England. Rural regions. Social change, *1780-1850*
Horn, Pamela. The rural world 1780-1850 : social change in the English countryside / Pamela Horn. — London : Hutchinson, 1980. — 331p : ill,1facsim ; 24cm. — (Hutchinson social history of England)
Bibliography: p311-326. - Includes index
ISBN 0-09-141880-1 (cased) : £12.00 : CIP rev.
ISBN 0-09-141881-x (pbk) : £4.50 B80-06775

942'.009'52 — England. Woodlands, *to 1979*
Rackham, Oliver. Ancient woodland : its history, vegetation and uses in England / Oliver Rackham. — London : Edward Arnold, 1980. — xii,402 : ill,maps ; 29cm
Maps on lining papers. — Bibliography: p361-376. — Includes index
ISBN 0-7131-2723-6 : £50.00 : CIP rev. B79-33980

942'.00973'2 — England. Towns, *1500-1800*
Country towns in pre-industrial England. — Leicester : Leicester University Press, Sept.1981. — [256]p. — (Themes in urban history)
ISBN 0-7185-1175-1 : CIP entry B81-23850

942'.009'732 — England. Urban regions. Social life, *1500-1780*
English urban history 1500-1780. — Milton Keynes : Open University Press, 1977. — (Arts : a third level course)
At head of title: The Open University
[Block 1]: The urban setting
[Unit] 1, [Unit] 2 and [Unit] 3. — 110p : ill,maps ; 30cm. — (A300 ; 1, 2 and 3)
Includes bibliographies. — Contents: Unit 1: Introduction : defining the town / by Peter Clark - Unit 2: The European context / by Peter Burke - Unit 3: The English urban landscape / by Paul Slack
ISBN 0-335-05250-9 (pbk) : Unpriced B81-09635

English urban history 1500-1780. — Milton Keynes : Open University Press, 1977. — (Arts : a third level course)
At head of title: The Open University
[Block 1]: The urban setting
Unit 4: Towns and townspeople 1500-1780 : a document collection / prepared for the course team by Peter Clark and Philip Morgan. — 89p ; 30cm. — (A322 ; 4)
ISBN 0-335-05251-7 (pbk) : Unpriced B81-09634

English urban history 1500-1780. — Milton Keynes : Open University Press, 1977. — (Arts : a third level course)
At head of title: The Open University
[Block 2]: The fabric of the traditional community. — 159p : ill,maps,facsims,ports ; 30cm. — (A322 ; 5, 6, 7 and 8)
Includes bibliographies. — Contents: Unit 5: The economic and social structure / by Charles Phythian-Adams - Unit 6: Political organization in the sixteenth-century town / by Kevin Wilson - Unit 7: The cultural function of the traditional town / by Peter Clark - Unit 8: The cultural role of towns in the late sixteenth and seventeenth centuries / Peter Clark
ISBN 0-335-05252-5 (pbk) : Unpriced B81-09638

English urban history 1500-1780. — Milton Keynes : Open University Press, 1977. — (Arts : a third level course)
At head of title: The Open University
[Block 3]: The traditional community under stress. — 136p : ill,maps ; 30cm. — (A322 ; 9, 10, 11 and 12)
Includes bibliographies. — Contents: Unit 9: Urban crisis or urban change? / by Charles Phythian-Adams and Paul Slack - Unit 10: Economic growth and change in seventeenth-century English towns / by Penelope Corfield - Social problems and social policies / by Paul Slack - The triumph of civic oligarchy in the seventeenth century? / by Rosemary O'Day
ISBN 0-335-05253-3 (pbk) : Unpriced B81-09637

English urban history 1500-1780. — Milton Keynes : Open University Press, 1977. — (Arts : a third level course)
At head of title: The Open University
[Block 4]: The rise of the new urban society. — 120p : ill,maps ; 30cm. — (A322 ; 13, 14, 15 and 16)
Includes bibliographies. — Contents: Unit 13: London, 1660-1780 / by John Stevenson - Unit 14: Spas and seaside resorts, 1660-1780 / by John Barrett - Unit 15: The industrial towns before the factory, 1680-1780 / by Penelope Corfield - Unit 16: Conclusion / by Rosemary O'Day
ISBN 0-335-05254-1 (pbk) : Unpriced B81-09636

942'.009'734 — England. Countryside — *Illustrations*
Mannes-Abbott, Sheila. Fair seasons. — London : Eyre Methuen, Oct.1981. — [32]p
ISBN 0-413-39920-6 : £4.95 : CIP entry B81-27933

942'.009'734 — England. Rural regions, *1580-1800 — For historical geography*

Butlin, R. A.. The transformation of rural England c.1580-1800. — Oxford : Oxford University Press, Jan.1982. — [64]p. — (Theory and practice in geography)
ISBN 0-19-874046-8 (pbk) : £2.95 : CIP entry
B81-33903

942'.009'734 — England. Rural regions. Gentry. Social life, *1810-1820 — Illustrations*

Sperling, Diana. Mrs Hurst dancing : and other scenes from Regency life 1812-1823 / watercolours by Diana Sperling ; text by Gordon Mingay. — London : Gollancz, 1981. — xvi,[70]p,70leaves of plates : (col.ill) ; 23x25cm
ISBN 0-575-03035-6 : £8.50 B81-40219

942'.009'734 — England. Rural regions. Social conditions, *1066-1348*

Hallam, H. E. (Herbert Enoch). Rural England 1066-1348 / H.E. Hallam. — [London] : Fontana, 1981. — 309p ; 18cm. — (Fontana history of England)
Includes index
ISBN 0-00-635607-9 (pbk) : £3.50 B81-25620

942'.009'734 — England. Rural regions. Social life, *1900-1914*

Thomas, Edward, *1878-1917*. Edward Thomas on the countryside : a selection of his prose and verse / edited by Roland Gant. — London : Faber, 1977 (1981 [printing]). — 183p ; 20cm. — (Faber paperbacks)
Bibliography: p181-183
ISBN 0-571-11779-1 (pbk) : £2.25 : CIP rev.
B81-23760

942'.009'734 — England. Rural regions. Social life, *ca 1500-1950 — Readings from contemporary sources*

Change and tradition in rural England : an anthology of writings on country life / chosen and edited by Denys Thompson. — Cambridge : Cambridge Unversity Press, 1980. — x,291p,[12]p of plates : ill,4ports ; 23cm
Bibliography: p285-288. — Includes index
ISBN 0-521-22546-9 : £10.50 : CIP rev.
B80-30508

942'.009'734 — England. Rural regions. Women. Social life, *1500-1900*

Fussell, G. E.. The English countrywoman : her life in farmhouse and field from Tudor times to the Victorian age / G.E. & K.R. Fussell. — London : Orbis, 1981. — 221p,[64]p of plates : ill ; 24cm
Originally published: London : Melrose, 1953. — Includes index
ISBN 0-85613-336-1 : £10.00 B81-26614

942'.009'734 — England. Villages. Social life

Jenkins, Alan C.. A village year / Alan C. Jenkins. — Exeter : Webb & Bower, 1981. — 160p : ill(some col.) ; 26cm
Includes index
ISBN 0-906671-38-8 : £8.95 : CIP rev.
B81-25888

942.01 — Anglo-Saxon civilization, *ca 900-ca 1100*

Whitelock, Dorothy. History, law and literature in 10th-11th century England / Dorothy Whitelock. — London : Variorum Reprints, 1981. — 368p in various pagings : 1port ; 24cm. — (Collected studies series ; 128)
Includes index
ISBN 0-86078-074-0 : £22.00 B81-15562

942.01 — Anglo-Saxon civilization, *to 1066*

Whitelock, Dorothy. The beginnings of English society / Dorothy Whitelock. — 2nd ed., Repr. with revisions. — Harmondsworth : Penguin, 1972, c1954 (1981 [printing]). — 256p ; 18cm. — (The Pelican history of English ; 2)
Previous ed.: 1952. — Bibliography: p244-248. - Includes index
ISBN 0-14-020245-5 (pbk) : £1.75 B81-12148

942.01 — Anglo-Saxon civilization, *to 1066.* **Archaeological sources**

Wilson, David M.. The Anglo-Saxons / David Wilson. — 3rd ed. — Harmondsworth : Penguin, 1981. — 188p,[40]p of plates : ill,maps,plans ; 20cm. — (Pelican Books) (The Pelican history of England)
Previous ed.: 1971. — Bibliography: p165-167. — Includes index
ISBN 0-14-021229-9 (pbk) : £2.25 B81-35511

942.01 — Anglo-Saxon culture, *to 1066*

The **Anglo-Saxons**. — Oxford : Phaidon, Oct.1981. — [272]p
ISBN 0-7148-2149-7 : £19.50 : CIP entry
B81-30468

942.01 — England, *60-1086*

Wood, Michael, *1948-*. In search of the Dark Ages / Michael Wood. — London : British Broadcasting Corporation, 1981. — 244p : ill,maps,2facsims,ports,geneal.table ; 26cm
Bibliography: p237. — Includes index
ISBN 0-563-17835-3 : £8.95 B81-16435

942.01 — England. Anglo-Saxon antiquities

The **Archaeology** of Anglo-Saxon England / edited by David M. Wilson. — Cambridge : Cambridge University Press, 1981, c1976. — xvi,532p,[22]p of plates : ill,maps,plans ; 26cm
Originally published: London : Methuen, 1976. — Bibliography: p463-511. — Includes index
ISBN 0-521-28390-6 (pbk) : £9.95 : CIP rev.
B81-14985

942.01'05 — England, *450-1066 — Serials*

Anglo-Saxon England. — 9. — Cambridge : Cambridge University Press, 1981. — ix,318p
ISBN 0-521-23449-2 : £23.50 : CIP rev.
B81-04306

Anglo-Saxon England. — 10. — Cambridge : Cambridge University Press, Feb.1982. — [324]p
ISBN 0-521-24177-4 : £25.00 : CIP entry
B81-40272

942.01'4'088054 — England. Children. Social life, *ca 470-ca 690 — For schools*

Lewis, Brenda Ralph. Growing up in the Dark Ages / Brenda Ralph Lewis. — London : Batsford Academic and Educational, 1980. — 72p : ill,1facsim ; 26cm
Bibliography: p70. — Includes index
ISBN 0-7134-3362-0 : £4.50 B81-01910

942.01'53'0924 — England. Oswald, *King of Northumbria — Biographies*

Lavery, Pamela. Oswald, saint of kings / Pamela Lavery. — Bognor Regis : New Horizon, c1980. — 180p ; 21cm
ISBN 0-86116-338-9 : £4.75 B81-22096

942.01'6 — England, *832-900 — Old English texts — Early works*

[**Saxon Chronicle**. *Selections*]. The Parker chronicle 832-900 / edited by A.H. Smith. — Rev. ed. / with a bibliography compiled by M.J. Swanton. — [Exeter] : University of Exeter, 1980. — viii,71p : 1map ; 20cm. — (Exeter medieval English texts)
Anglo-Saxon text, English notes. — Previous ed.: London : Methuen's Old English Library, 1935. — Bibliography: p53-55. - Includes index
ISBN 0-85989-099-6 (pbk) : £1.50 B81-12140

942.01'8 — England, *1013-1042.* **Encomium Emmae Reginae** — *Critical studies*

John, Eric. The Encomium emmae reginae : a riddle and a solution / by Eric John. — Manchester : John Rylands University Library of Manchester, 1980. — p58-94 ; 25cm
£1.75 (pbk) B81-35544

942.01'9'0924 — England. Edward, *King of England — Biographies*

Barlow, Frank. Edward the Confessor / Frank Barlow. — London : Eyre Methuen, 1970 (1979 [printing]). — xxiv,375p,[16]p of plates : ill,maps,facsims,1geneal.table ; 24cm. — (English monarchs)
Genealogical table on folded leaf attached to inside cover. — Bibliography: p345-357. — Includes index
ISBN 0-413-45950-0 (pbk) : £4.95 B81-14299

942.02 — England, *1066-1307*

Stenton, Doris Mary, *d.1971*. English society in the early Middle Ages (1066-1307) / Doris Mary Stenton. — 4th ed. — Harmondsworth : Penguin, 1965 (1981 [printing]). — 319p ; 18cm. — (Pelican history of England ; 3)
Previous ed.: 1962. — Bibliography: p301-303. — Includes index
ISBN 0-14-020252-8 (pbk) : £2.25 B81-16986

942.02 — England, *1066-ca 1200 — Conference proceedings*

Battle Conference on Anglo-Norman Studies *(2nd : 1979)*. Proceedings of the Battle Conference on Anglo-Norman Studies, II, 1979 / edited by R. Allen Brown. — Woodbridge : Boydell, 1980. — xiii,210p : ill,maps,plans ; 25cm
Includes index
ISBN 0-85115-126-4 : £14.00 : CIP rev.
B80-06244

Battle Conference on Anglo-Norman Studies *(3rd : 1980)*. Proceedings of the Battle Conference on Anglo-Norman Studies, III, 1980 / edited by R. Allen Brown. — Woodbridge : Boydell, 1981. — 241p : ill,maps,plans,geneal.tables ; 25cm
Includes index
ISBN 0-85115-141-8 : £17.50 B81-33747

942.02 — England. Social conditions, *1066-1348*

Hallam, H. E. (Herbert Enoch). Rural England : 1066-1348 / H.E. Hallam. — Brighton : Harvester in association with Fontana Paperbacks, 1981. — 309p ; 23cm. — (Fontana history of England)
Includes index
ISBN 0-7108-0099-1 : £20.00 : CIP rev.
B81-12806

942.02'1 — England. Norman Conquest

Wise, Terence. 1066 : year of destiny / Terence Wise. — London : Osprey, 1979. — 232p : ill,3maps,2plans,1geneal.table ; 26cm
Bibliography: p223-228. - Includes index
ISBN 0-85045-320-8 : £7.50 : CIP rev.
B79-24139

942.03 — England, *1150-1500 — For schools*

Nichol, Jon. The Middle Ages / Jon Nichol and David Downton. — Oxford : Blackwell, 1981. — 64p : ill,maps,coats of arms,1facsim,plans,1geneal.tables ; 30cm. — (Evidence)
ISBN 0-631-93390-5 (pbk) : £1.95 B81-29686

942.03'1'0922 — England. Henry II, *King of England.* **Disputes with Becket, Thomas,** *Saint.* **Historical sources: Correspondence**

Duggan, Anne. Thomas Becket : a textual history of his letters / Anne Duggan. — Oxford : Clarendon Press, 1980. — xxii,318p ; 23cm
Bibliography: pxiv-xxii. - Includes index
ISBN 0-19-822486-9 : £17.50 : CIP rev.
B79-34634

942.03'1'0924 — England. Becket, Thomas, *Saint — Biographies — French texts*

Foreville, Raymonde. Thomas Becket dans la tradition historique et hagiogrphique / Raymonde Foreville. — London : Variorum Reprints, 1981. — 347p : ill,maps,1port ; 24cm. — (Collected studies series ; 130)
Includes index
ISBN 0-86078-076-7 : £22.00 B81-16966

942.03'5'0924 — England. Edward I, *King of England — Biographies*

Chancellor, John. The life and times of Edward I / John Chancellor ; introduction by Antonia Fraser. — London : Weidenfeld and Nicolson, c1981. — 224p : ill(some col.),maps,facsims (some col.),ports(some col.),geneal.tables ; 26cm
Ill on lining papers. — Bibliography: p220. — Includes index
ISBN 0-297-77840-4 : £6.95 B81-09588

942.03'7 — England. Political events, *1272-1377*

Prestwich, Michael. The three Edwards : war and state in England, 1272-1377. — London : Methuen, Dec.1981. — [352]p
Originally published: London : Weidenfeld and Nicolson, 1980
ISBN 0-416-30450-8 (pbk) : £4.95 : CIP entry
B81-31713

942.03'7 — English culture. Patronage by middle classes, *ca 1300-ca 1500 — Festschriften*

Profession, vocation and culture in later medieval England. — Liverpool : Liverpool University Press, Dec.1981. — [238]p
ISBN 0-85323-324-1 : £15.00 : CIP entry
B81-31512

942.03'8 — England, *1381-1394 — Early works*

The **Westminster** Chronicle, 1381-1394. — Oxford : Clarendon Press, Nov.1981. — [648]p. — (Oxford medieval texts)
ISBN 0-19-822255-6 : £48.00 : CIP entry
B81-30324

942.03'8 — England. Peasants' Revolt

Foot, Paul. This bright day of summer : the Peasants' Revolt of 1381 / by Paul Foot. — London (265 Seven Sisters Rd., N4 2DE) : Produced and distributed for the SWP by Socialists Unlimited, 1981. — 23p ; 21cm
ISBN 0-905998-22-7 (unbound) : £0.35
B81-32749

Fryde, E. B.. The Great Revolt of 1381 / E.B. Fryde. — London : Historical Association, c1981. — 36p ; 22cm. — (General series / Historical Association ; 100)
Bibliography: p35-36
ISBN 0-85278-239-x (pbk) : Unpriced
B81-32840

Morton, A. L.. When the people arose : peasants' revolt of 1381 / by Al.L. Morton. — London : Communist Party of Great Britain, 1981. — 32p : ill,1map ; 21cm. — (A Communist Party pamphlet)
ISBN 0-86224-012-3 (pbk) : £0.50 B81-26651

942.03'8 — England. Peasants' Revolt — *Conference proceedings*

Past and Present Society. *Conference (1981 : Burlington House).* Past and Present Society Conference : the English rising of 1381 : [held] Wednesday 1 July 1981 at the Geological Society of London, Burlington House, Piccadilly, London W1V 0JU. — Oxford (Corpus Christi College, Oxford [OX1 4JF]) : The Society, 1981. — 208p in various pagings : 2maps ; 30cm
Includes one paper in French. — Cover title
£6.00 (pbk) B81-29889

942.04 — England, *1400-1500*

McFarlane, K. B.. England in the fifteenth century. — London (35 Gloucester Ave., NW1 7AX) : Hambledon Press, Oct.1981. — [320]p. — (History series ; 5)
ISBN 0-9506882-5-8 : £15.00 : CIP entry
B81-27367

942.04 — Wars of the Roses

Goodman, Anthony. The Wars of the Roses : military activity and English society, 1452-97 / Anthony Goodman. — London : Routledge & Kegan Paul, 1981. — 294p : ill,maps,1geneal.table ; 23cm
Bibliography: p284-289. — Includes index
ISBN 0-7100-0728-0 : £12.95 : CIP rev.
B81-15931

942.04'3 — England. Political events, *1422-1461*

Griffiths, Ralph A.. The reign of King Henry VI : the exercise of royal authority, 1422-1461 / Ralph A. Griffiths. — London : Benn, 1981. — xxiv,968p,[32]p of plates : ill,maps,ports,geneal.tables ; 25cm
Bibliography: p907-933. — Includes index
ISBN 0-510-26261-9 : Unpriced : CIP rev.
B81-04192

942.04'3'0924 — England. Henry VI, *King of England — Biographies*

Wolffe, B. P.. Henry VI / Bertram Wolffe. — London : Eyre Methuen, 1981, c1980. — 400p,[25]p of plates : ill,maps,coats of arms,facsims,plans,ports,1geneal.table ; 25cm. — ([English monarchs])
Bibliography: p375-384. — Includes index
ISBN 0-413-32080-4 : £19.95 B81-13992

942.04'3'0924 — England. Talbot, John, *Earl of Shrewsbury — Biographies*

Talbot, Hugh, *1909-*. The English Achilles : an account of the life and campaigns of John Talbot, Ist Earl of Shrewsbury (1383-1453) / by Hugh Talbot ; with an introduction by C.V. Wedgwood. — London : Chatto & Windus, 1981. — 205p : ill,maps,plans,ports,geneal.tables ; 23cm
Bibliography: p190-191. — Includes index
ISBN 0-7011-2574-8 : £8.95 B81-27577

942.04'4'0924 — England. Clarence, George Plantagenet, *Duke of — Biographies*

Hicks, M. A.. False, fleeting, perjur'd Clarence : George, Duke of Clarence 1449-78 / M.A. Hicks. — Gloucester (17a Brunswick Rd., Gloucester GL1 1HG) : Alan Sutton, 1980. — 270p : ill,coat of arms,facsims,ports,geneal.tables ; 22cm
Bibliography: p248-255. - Includes index
ISBN 0-904387-44-5 : £7.95 : CIP rev.
B80-22745

942.04'6'0924 — England. Richard III, *King of England*

Ross, Charles. Richard III. — London : Eyre Methuen, Oct.1981. — [416]p. — (English monarchs)
ISBN 0-413-29530-3 : £15.00 : CIP entry
B81-28833

942.04'6'0924 — England. Richard III, *King of England — Biographies — Early works*

Halsted, Caroline A.. Richard III : as Duke of Gloucester and King of England / by Caroline A. Halsted. — Gloucester (17a Brunswick Rd., Gloucester, GL1 1HG) : Sutton, 1977 (1980 [printing]). — 2v.(xi,457p;xii,570p) : ill,1coat of arms,1facsim,1port,geneal.tables ; 22cm
Facsim. of ed. published: London : Longman, Brown, Green and Longmans, 1844
ISBN 0-904387-41-0 (cased) : £16.00 set
ISBN 0-904387-14-8 B81-12050

942.05 — England. Tudor *(House of) — For schools*

Nichol, Jon. The Tudors / Jon Nichol. — Oxford : Blackwell, 1981. — 62p : ill,maps,ports ; 30cm. — (Evidence in history)
Text and maps on inside covers
ISBN 0-631-93370-0 (pbk) : £1.95 B81-17715

942.05'1 — England, *1485-1509*

Alexander, Michael Van Cleave. The first of the Tudors : a study of Henry VII and his reign / by Michael Van Cleave Alexander. — London : Croom Helm, 1981, c1980. — x,280p : 1port ; 25cm
Originally published: Totowa, N.J. : Rowman and Littlefield, 1980. — Bibliography: p245-260. — Includes index
ISBN 0-7099-0503-3 : £12.95 B81-07986

942.05'2'0924 — England. More, *Sir Thomas, Saint, 1518-1532 — Biographies*

Guy, J. A.. The public career of Sir Thomas More / J.A. Guy. — Brighton : Harvester, 1980. — xii,220p ; 25cm
Includes index
ISBN 0-85527-963-x : £20.00 : CIP rev.
B80-14087

942.05'2'0924 — England. Politics. Russell, John, *Earl of Bedford — Biographies*

Willen, Diane. John Russell, first Earl of Bedford : one of the King's men / Diane Willen. — London : Royal Historical Society, 1981. — xi,145p,1 leaf of plates : 1port ; 23cm. — (Royal Historical Society studies in history series ; no.23)
Includes index
ISBN 0-901050-60-1 : £13.00 B81-12005

942.05'2'0924 — England. Wolsey, Thomas — *Biographies*

Harvey, Nancy Lenz. Thomas Cardinal Wolsey / by Nancy Lenz Harvey. — New York : Macmillan ; London : Collier Macmillan, c1980. — xiv,258p,[8]p of plates : ill,ports ; 25cm
Bibliography: p229-232. — Includes index
ISBN 0-02-548600-4 : £8.95 B81-22916

942.05'5 — England, *1558-1603 — For schools*

Lane, Peter. Elizabethan England / Peter Lane. — London : Batsford Academic and Educational, 1981. — 96p : ill,maps,fascims,ports,1geneal.table ; 26cm. — (Visual sources series)
Includes index
ISBN 0-7134-3566-6 : £5.95 B81-24301

942.05'5 — England. Buildings. Social life, *1558-1603*

Birt, David. Elizabeth's England / David Birt ; line drawings by Joyce Fogg ; photographs by Deryn Birt. — London : Longman, c1981. — 225p : ill,1map ; 22cm. — (Longman travellers series)
Includes index
ISBN 0-582-50287-x : £7.50 B81-23987

942.05'5 — England. Social life, *1558-1603 — For schools*

Reynoldson, Fiona. The Elizabethans / Fiona Reynoldson. — London : Heinemann Educational, 1980. — 59p : ill,maps,plans,ports ; 28cm
ISBN 0-435-31730-x (pbk) : £2.25 B81-02785

942.05'5 — England. War with Spain, *1588.* **Spanish Armada**

Howarth, David, *1912-*. The voyage of the Armada : the Spanish story / David Howarth. — London : Collins, 1981. — 256p,[13]p of plates : ill,maps,1facsim,ports ; 24cm
Bibliography: p248-249. - Includes index
ISBN 0-00-211575-1 : £8.95 B81-26462

942.05'5 — England. War with Spain, *1588.* **Spanish Armada** *— Readings from contemporary sources — Spanish texts*

State papers relating to the defeat of the Spanish Armada, anno 1588. — Havant : K. Mason
Originally published: London : Navy Records Society, 1895
Vol.1. — Sept.1981. — [369]p
ISBN 0-85937-264-2 : £15.00 : CIP entry
B81-26685

State papers relating to the defeat of the Spanish Armada, anno 1588. — Havant : K. Mason
Originally published: London : Navy Records Society, 1895
Vol.2. — Sept.1981. — [420]p
ISBN 0-85937-265-0 : £15.00 : CIP entry
B81-26696

942.05'5 — English civilization, *1580-1642*

Hill, Christopher, *1912-*. Intellectual origins of the English revolution / Christopher Hill. — Repr. with corrections. — Oxford : Clarendon Press, 1980, c1965. — ix,333p ; 19cm
Includes index
ISBN 0-19-822635-7 (pbk) : £4.95 B81-01391

942.05'5'0202 — England, *1579-1581 — Chronologies*

Kirton, J. P.. Chronological record of Elizabethan era : 1579-1581 / by J.P. Kirton. — [Bromley] ([67 Oxhawth Cres., Bromley, Kent, BR2 8BN]) : Marlowe Society, [1981]. — 45p : 1map,ports ; 21cm
Unpriced (pbk) B81-11332

942.05'5'0922 — England. Elizabeth I, *Queen of England.* **Interpersonal relationships with Essex, Robert Devereux,** *Earl of*

Strachey, Lytton. Elizabeth & Essex : a tragic history / Lytton Strachey ; introduced by Michael Holroyd. — Oxford : Oxford University Press, 1981. — xv,187p ; 20cm. — (Oxford paperbacks)
Originally published: London : Chatto & Windus, 1928. — Bibliography: p178-179. — Includes index
ISBN 0-19-281310-2 (pbk) : £2.95 : CIP rev.
B81-25790

942.05'5'0924 — England. Elizabeth I, *Queen of England — Biographies — For children*

Zamoyska, Betka. Queen Elizabeth I / Betka Zamoyska. — Harlow : Longman, 1981. — 69p : ill(some col.),facsims,ports(some col.),geneal.table ; 25cm. — (Longman great lives)
Genealogical table on lining papers. — Bibliography: p68. — Includes index
ISBN 0-582-39031-1 : £3.95 B81-39666

942.05'5'0924 — England. Leicester, Robert Dudley, *Earl of — Biographies*

Kendall, Alan, *1939-*. Robert Dudley Earl of Leicester / Alan Kendall. — London : Cassell, 1980. — xi,259p,[16]p of plates : ill,facsims,ports ; 25cm
Includes index
ISBN 0-304-30442-5 : £8.95 B81-27841

Wilson, Derek. Sweet Robin : a biography of Robert Dudley, Earl of Leicester 1533-1588 / Derek Wilson. — London : Hamilton, 1981. — xi,355p,[8]p of plates : ill,ports,1geneal.table ; 25cm
Bibliography: p342-347. — Includes index
ISBN 0-241-10149-2 : £18.00 B81-20838

942.05'5'0924 — England. Unton, *Sir Henry, ca.1557-1596 — Biographies*

Cox, Angela. Sir Henry Unton, Elizabethan gentleman. — Cambridge : Cambridge University Press, Dec.1981. — [45]p. — (Cambridge introduction to the history of mankind)
ISBN 0-521-22549-3 (pbk) : £1.95 : CIP entry B81-33883

942.06 — England, *1603-1660*

The **Age** of Milton : backgrounds to seventeenth-century literature / C.A. Patrides, Raymond B. Waddington, editors. — Manchester : Manchester University Press, 1980. — x,438p,[8]p of plates : ill,music,ports ; 24cm
Bibliography: p393-427. — Includes index
ISBN 0-7190-0770-4 : £22.50 : CIP rev.
Primary classification 820.9'003 B80-06532

942.06 — England, *1603-1714*

Coward, Barry. The Stuart age : a history of England 1603-1714 / Barry Coward. — London : Longman, 1980. — xii,493p : maps ; 22cm. — (A History of England)
Bibliography: p461-472. — Includes index
ISBN 0-582-48279-8 (cased) : £13.00
ISBN 0-582-48833-8 (pbk) : £7.50 B81-00672

942.06 — England, *1618-1689*

Seventeenth-century England : a changing culture, 1618-1689. — Milton Keynes : Open University Press. — (Arts : a second level course)
At head of title: The Open University
[Block 1]: A different world / prepared for the course team by Christopher Hill and Kevin Wilson. — 1980. — 71p : ill,maps,facsims,ports ; 30cm. — (A203 ; block 1)
Bibliography: p69
ISBN 0-335-11035-5 (pbk) : Unpriced B81-13175

Seventeenth-century England : a changing culture, 1618-1689. — Milton Keynes : Open University Press. — (Arts : a second level course)
At head of title: The Open University
[Block 2]: A changing culture / prepared for the course team by Tim Benton ... [et al.]. — 1981. — 98p : ill,plans ; 30cm. — (A203 ; block 2)
Includes bibliographies
ISBN 0-335-11036-3 (pbk) : Unpriced B81-27600

Seventeenth-century England : a changing culture, 1618-1689. — Milton Keynes : Open University Press. — (Arts : a second level course)
At head of title: The Open University
[Block 3]: A divided society / prepared for the course team by Colin Chant, Christopher Hill and Anne Laurence. — 1981. — 83p : ill,1map,facsims,ports ; 30cm. — (A203 ; block 3)
Includes bibliographies
ISBN 0-335-11037-1 (pbk) : Unpriced B81-27598

Seventeenth-century England : a changing culture, 1618-1689. — Milton Keynes : Open University Press. — (Arts : a second level course)
[Block 4]: The revolution and its impact / prepared for the course team by Christopher Hill ... [et al.]. — 1981. — 86p : ill,maps,facsims,ports ; 30cm. — (A203 ; block 4)
Includes bibliographies
ISBN 0-335-11038-x (pbk) : Unpriced B81-27599

Seventeenth-century England : a changing culture, 1618-1689. — Milton Keynes : Open University Press. — (Arts : a second level course)
At head of title: The Open University
The development of prose / prepared for the course team Joan Bellamy and Simon Eliot. — 1981. — 30p : facsims,ports ; 30cm. — (A203 ; PD)
Bibliography: p30
ISBN 0-335-11047-9 (pbk) : Unpriced B81-13177

Seventeenth-century England : a changing culture, 1618-1689. — Milton Keynes : Open University Press. — (Arts : a second level course)
At head of title: The Open University
Illustration book 1. — 1980. — 56p of ill (some col.) : facsims,plans,ports ; 30cm. — (A203 ; IB (1))
Cover title
ISBN 0-335-11045-2 (pbk) : Unpriced B81-13176

942.06'0880621 — England. Country houses. Social life, *1603-1714 — For children*

Ellenby, Jean. The Stuart household / by Jean Ellenby ; illustrated by Juliet Stanwell-Smith. — Cambridge : Published for the National Trust by Dinosaur, c1981. — 32p : col.ill ; 23cm
ISBN 0-85122-221-8 (pbk) : £0.80 : CIP : rev. B80-18117

942.06'092'4 — England. Evelyn, John, *1620-1706 — Biographies*

Bowle, John, *1905-*. John Evelyn and his world : a biography / John Bowle. — London : Routledge & Kegan Paul, 1981. — xvii,277p,8p of plates : ports ; 24cm
Includes index
ISBN 0-7100-0721-3 : £12.50 B81-21001

942.06'1'0924 — England. Buckingham, George Villiers, *Duke of, 1592-1628 — Biographies*

Lockyer, Roger. Buckingham : the life and political career of George Villiers, first Duke of Buckingham 1592-1628 / Roger Lockyer. — London : Longman, 1981. — xix,506p,[8]p of plates : ill,maps,facsims,ports,geneal.tables ; 24cm
Bibliography: p476-486. — Includes index
ISBN 0-582-50296-9 : £14.95 : CIP rev. B81-13535

942.06'1'0924 — England. James I, *King of England — Biographies*

Bingham, Caroline. James I of England / Caroline Bingham. — London : Weidenfeld and Nicolson, 1981. — 236p,[8]p of plates : ports,1geneal.table ; 23cm
Bibliography: p213-217. — Includes index
ISBN 0-297-77889-7 : £9.95 B81-09590

942.06'1'0924 — England. Politics. Naunton, *Sir Robert — Biographies*

Schreiber, Roy E.. The political career of Sir Robert Naunton 1589-1635 / Roy E. Schreiber. — London : Royal Historical Society, 1981. — viii,190p ; 23cm. — (Royal Historical Society studies in history series ; no.24)
Bibliography: p174-178. — Includes index
ISBN 0-901050-79-2 : £9.33 B81-30786

942.06'2 — England. Intellectual life, *1640-1660*

Hill, Christopher, *1912-*. Some intellectual consequences of the English Revolution / Christopher Hill. — London : Weidenfeld and Nicolson, c1980. — 100p ; 23cm
Includes index
ISBN 0-297-77780-7 : £5.95 B81-01931

942.06'2 — English Civil War

Young, Peter, *1915-*. Civil War England / Peter Young ; live drawings by Stephen Beck. — London : Longman, 1981. — 185p : ill,maps,facsims,ports ; 22cm. — (Longman travellers series)
Bibliography: p178-180. — Includes index
ISBN 0-582-50286-1 : £7.95 B81-36287

942.06'2 — English Civil War. Army operations by England and Wales. *Army, 1642-1649*

Hutton, Ronald. The royalist war effort 1642-1646. — London : Longman, Oct.1981. — [208]p
ISBN 0-582-50301-9 : £12.00 : CIP entry B81-27978

942.06'2 — English Civil War. Battle of Marston Moor

Newman, Peter, *19---*. The Battle of Marston Moor, 1644 / Peter Newman. — Chichester : Bird, 1981. — 156p,[4]p of plates : maps,ports ; 24cm
Bibliography: p147-149. — Includes index
ISBN 0-907319-00-9 : £9.95 B81-37722

942.06'2 — English Civil War. Battle of Naseby — *For wargaming*

Asquith, Stuart A.. The campaign of Naseby 1645 / text by Stuart A. Asquith ; colour plates arranged by Peter Gilder ; colour map by Christine Howes. — London : Osprey, 1979. — 40p,A-Hp of plates : ill(some col.),1facsim,plans(some col.) ; 24cm. — (Wargames series ; 1)
ISBN 0-85045-337-2 (pbk) : £2.95 B81-13929

942.06'2 — English Civil War. Battle of Roundway

Colman, Pamela. Devizes in the Civil War / Pamela Colman & Bryan Coupe. — Devizes (5 Trafalgar Place, Bath Rd., Devizes, Wilts.) : Downwriter, [1981?]. — [8]p : ill,maps,plans,ports ; 30cm
Bibliography: p[8]
Unpriced (unbound) B81-32788

942.06'2 — English Civil War. Causes, *1642*

Woods, T. P. S.. Prelude to Civil War 1642 : Mr. Justice Malet and the Kentish petitions / T.P.S. Woods ; with an introduction by Ivan Roots. — Salisbury : Michael Russell, 1980. — xi,244p,[8]p of plates : ill,2facsims,1plan,ports ; 24cm
Bibliography: p205-218. - Includes index
ISBN 0-85955-070-2 : £8.95 B81-09929

942.06'2 — English Civil War. Oxfordshire campaign, *1642-1646*

Carter, Andrew, *1947-*. The Oxfordshire area in the Civil War / by Andrew Carter and John Stevenson. — [Oxford] : BBC Radio Oxford, [197-?]. — 23p : ill,1map ; 22cm
Cover title
Unpriced (pbk) B81-36840

942.06'2 — English Civil War. Parliamentarian forces. Raising — *Early works*

England and Wales. *Parliament*. A declaration of the Lords and Commons assembled in Parliament, for the raising of all power, and force, as well trained bands as others, in several counties of this kingdom. — Mount Durand : Toucan, 1981. — 6p ; 21cm
Facsim. of: ed. published London : For Thomas Banks and William Ley, 1642?
ISBN 0-85694-245-6 (pbk) : Unpriced B81-30794

942.06'2 — English Civil War. Siege of Chichester

The **Civil War** : and mid-17th century Chichester / [researched and designed by members of the Chichester WEA local history workshop class]. — [Chichester] ([29 Little London, Chichester PO19 1PB]) : Chichester District Museum, [1979?]. — [8]p : ill,1map ; 21cm
Bibliography: p8
£0.15 (unbound) B81-37221

942.06'2'0924 — England. Charles I, *King of England — Biographies*

Gregg, Pauline. King Charles I / Pauline Gregg. — London : Dent, 1981. — 496p,[16]p of plates : ill,1facsim,ports ; 24cm
Bibliography: p461-485. — Includes index
ISBN 0-460-04437-0 : £12.50 B81-33419

942.06'7 — England. Political events. Role of England and Wales. *Army, 1685-1688*
Childs, John. The Army, James II and the Glorious Revolution / John Cholds. — Manchester : Manchester University Press, c1980. — xix,226p : 1port ; 25cm
Includes index
ISBN 0-7190-0688-0 : £14.95 B81-03339

942.07 — England, *1688-1978*
Webb, R. K.. Modern England : from the eighteenth century to the present / R.K. Webb. — 2nd ed. — London : Allen & Unwin, 1980. — xiv,685p : 6maps ; 24cm
Previous ed.: New York : Dodd, Mead, 1968 ; London : Allen and Unwin, 1969. — Bibliography: p658-662. — Includes index
ISBN 0-04-942166-2 : £14.00
ISBN 0-04-942167-0 (pbk) : £6.95 B81-01935

942.07 — England, *1714-1801 — For schools*
Lane, Peter. Georgian England / Peter Lane. — London : Batsford Academic and Educational, 1981. — 96p : ill,2maps,1facsim,ports ; 26cm. — (Visual sources series)
Includes index
ISBN 0-7134-3358-2 : £5.95 B81-08615

942.07 — England. Social conditions, *1760-1939*
Larkin, P. J. (Patrick Jones). English economic and social history 1760-1939 : background and documents / P.J. Larkin. — Amersham : Hulton, 1979, c1980. — 445p : ill,maps,1facsim,ports ; 21cm
Bibliography: p442-445
ISBN 0-7175-0823-4 (pbk) : £3.90 B81-05218

942.07 — England. Social conditions, *ca 1800-1979*
Perkin, Harold. The structured crowd : essays in English social history / Harold Perkin. — Brighton : Harvester, 1981. — xi,238p ; 23cm
Includes index
ISBN 0-85527-413-1 : £20.00 : CIP rev. B80-21453

942.07 — England. Social life, *1714-1837 — Readings from contemporary sources*
An **Age** of elegance : life in Georgian England : an anthology / [compiled by] A.F. Scott. — Old Woking : Gresham in association with Ahrend, 1979. — xii,260p : ill,ports ; 21cm
Bibliography: p260
ISBN 0-905418-78-6 : £7.50 B81-03927

942.07'0880621 — England. Rural regions. Upper class households. Social life, *ca 1715-ca 1830 — For children*
Ellenby, Jean. The Georgian household / by Jean Ellenby ; illustrated by Juliet Stanwell-Smith. — Cambridge : Published for the National Trust by Dinosaur, c1980. — 32p : col.ill ; 23cm
ISBN 0-85122-222-6 (pbk) : £0.80 : CIP rev. B80-07621

942.07'3 — England. Social life, *1758-1802 — Correspondence, diaries, etc.*
Woodforde, James. The diary of a country parson : the Reverend James Woodforde / edited by John Beresford. — Oxford : Oxford University Press, 1968 (1981 [printing]). — 5v. : ill,ports ; 23cm
Originally published: London : Humphrey Milford, 1924-31. — Includes index
ISBN 0-19-811485-0 : £65.00 B81-28459

942.07'3'0924 — England. Davies, Scrope — *Biographies*
Burnett, T. A. J.. The rise and fall of a regency dandy : the life and times of Scrope Berdmore Davies / T.A.J. Burnett ; with a foreword by Bevis Hillier. — London : Murray, 1981. — 256p,[12]p of plates : ill,ports ; 23cm
Bibliography: p234-238. — Includes index
ISBN 0-7195-3864-5 : £9.50 : CIP rev. B81-21519

942.081 — England. Country estates. Social life, *ca 1900 — For children*
Graham-Cameron, M. G.. Life on a country estate / by M.G. Graham-Cameron ; illustrated by Helen Herbert. — Cambridge : Published for the National Trust by Dinosaur, c1978. — 32p : col.ill ; 23cm
ISBN 0-85122-155-6 (pbk) : £0.60
ISBN 0-85122-157-2 B81-30771

942.081 — England. Intellectual life, *1830-1870*
Heyck, T. W.. The transformation of intellectual life in Victorian England. — London : Croom Helm, Nov.1981. — [256]p. — (Studies in society and history)
ISBN 0-7099-1206-4 : £11.95 : CIP entry B81-30536

942.081'0880622 — England. Middle classes. Social life, *1860-1920*
Watt, Jill. Grannie Loosley's kitchen album 1860-1920 : at home with an English family / Jill Watt. — London : Sidgwick and Jackson, 1980. — 129p : ill,facsims,geneal.table,ports ; 28cm
Ill on lining papers. — Includes index
ISBN 0-283-98704-9 : £6.95 B81-01587

942.081'0924 — England. Countryside, *ca 1860-ca 1880 — Personal observations*
Jefferies, Richard. The open air. — London : Wildwood House, Aug.1981. — [288]p
ISBN 0-7045-0422-7 (pbk) : £2.95 : CIP entry B81-25125

942.081'092'4 — England. Rural regions. Social life, *1872-1891 — Personal observations*
Jefferies, Richard. The toilers of the field / Richard Jefferies. — London : Macdonald Futura, 1981. — 215p ; 18cm. — (Heritage)
Originally published: London : Longmans, 1892. — Bibliography: p10-11
ISBN 0-7088-2068-9 (pbk) : £1.60 B81-33210

942.082'092'2 — England. Social life, *1901-1910 — Childhood reminiscences — Collections*
Edwardian childhoods / [compiled by] Thea Thompson. — London : Routledge & Kegan Paul, 1981. — xiii,232p,[32]p of plates : ill,ports ; 24cm
ISBN 0-7100-0676-4 : £9.75 B81-08287

942.082'092'4 — England. Burge, Henrietta — *Biographies*
Burge, Henrietta. I remember / Henrietta Burge. — Bognor Regis : New Horizon, c1979. — 232p ; 21cm
ISBN 0-86116-099-1 : £2.95 B81-21711

942.082'092'4 — England. Dowden, Harry Clifford — *Biographies*
Dowden, Marjorie A. E.. Harry Clifford Dowden, M.Sc., F.R.I.C. 1899-1959 / Marjorie A.E. Dowden. — [Bedford] ([4 Lansdowne Rd, Bedford MK40 2BU]) : [M.S.E. Dowden], 1980. — 22p ; 20cm
Unpriced (pbk) B81-30769

942.082'092'4 — England. Dowding, Muriel Dowding, *Baroness — Biographies*
Dowding, Muriel Dowding, *Baroness*. Beauty — not the beast : an autobiography / Muriel, the Lady Dowding. — St. Helier : Spearman, 1980. — x,275p : ill,ports ; 23cm
ISBN 0-85978-056-2 : £6.50 B81-31327

942.082'092'4 — England. Fish, Vera K. — *Biographies*
Fish, Vera K.. Past remembering / by Vera K. Fish ; edited by Beryl J. Read. — London : Regency Press, [1980]. — 64p : ill,ports ; 22cm
ISBN 0-7212-0695-6 : £3.00 B81-07902

942.082'092'4 — England. Griffin, J. B. — *Biographies*
Griffin, J. B.. This is my life / J.B. Griffin. — Bognor Regis : New Horizon, c1979. — 186p,[15]p of plates : ill,facsims,ports ; 21cm
ISBN 0-86116-082-7 : £3.50 B81-21712

942.082'092'4 — England. Griffiths, Dora M. — *Biographies*
Griffiths, Dora M.. Through a vicarage window / Dora M. Griffiths. — Bognor Regis : New Horizon, c1979. — 277p ; 22cm
ISBN 0-86116-108-4 : £3.50 B81-21702

942.082'092'4 — England. Griffiths, George — *Biographies*
Griffiths, George, *1909-*. Sixty five years in six hours / George Griffiths. — Bognor Regis : New Horizon, c1980. — 324p,[6]p of plates : ill ; 21cm
ISBN 0-86116-573-x : £6.75 B81-21763

942.082'092'4 — England. Sapley, Merielle — *Biographies*
Sapley, Merielle. A child at risk / Merielle Sapley. — Bognor Regis : New Horizon, c1978. — 138p ; 22cm
ISBN 0-86116-020-7 : £3.50 B81-39179

942.082'092'4 — England. Social life, *1914-1979 — Personal observations*
Dobrin, Nancy. Happiness : a twinge of conscience is a glimpse of God / by Nancy Dobrin. — London : Regency, c1980. — 175p ; 23cm
ISBN 0-7212-0665-4 : £5.00 B81-05626

942.082'092'4 — England. Wells, Lucy — *Biographies*
Wells, Lucy. Sunshine and shadow : an autobiography / Lucy Wells. — [East Grinstead] ([43 Crescent Rd, East Grinstead, Sussex RH19 1HR]) : L. Wells, [1981?]. — 219p : ill,ports ; 21cm
Unpriced (pbk) B81-08088

942.083'092'4 — England. Playden, Annie. Interpersonal relationships with Apollinaire, Guillaume
Adlard, John. One evening of light mist in London : the story of Annie Playden and Guillaume Apollinaire / by John Adlard. — Edinburgh : Tragara, 1980. — 33p,[2]leaves of plates : ill,ports ; 23cm
Limited ed.: of 145 numbered copies
Unpriced (pbk)
Primary classification 841'.912 B81-14745

942.083'092'4 — England. Rural regions. Social life, *1934-1935 — Personal observations — Correspondence, diaries, etc.*
White, T. H.. England have my bones / T.H. White. — London : Macdonald Futura, 1981. — vii,306p : ill ; 18cm. — (Heritage)
Originally published: London : Collins, 1936
ISBN 0-7088-2070-0 (pbk) : £2.25 B81-33211

942.083'092'4 — England. Social life, *1920-1945 — Personal observations*
Wright, Lilian. The Mack sisters / Lilian E. Wright. — Bognor Regis : New Horizon, c1981. — 323p ; 19cm
ISBN 0-86116-593-4 : £6.75 B81-37162

942.084'092'4 — England. McShane, Yolande — *Biographies*
McShane, Yolande. Daughter of evil : the true story / Yolande McShane. — London : Star, 1980. — 252p ; 18cm
ISBN 0-352-30563-0 (pbk) : £1.50 B81-04429

942.084'092'4 — England. Social life, *1943-1944 — Personal observations*
Dobie, J. Frank. A Texan in England / by J. Frank Dobie. — Austin ; London : University of Texas Press, 1980, c1972. — xiii,285p ; 21cm
Originally published: London : Hammond, 1946. — Includes index
ISBN 0-292-78034-6 (pbk) : £4.15 B81-19548

942.085'6'0924 — England. Social life, *1960-1969 — Personal observations*
Gosling, Ray. Personal copy : a memoir of the sixties / Ray Gosling. — London : Faber, 1980. — 223p ; 23cm
ISBN 0-571-11574-8 : £7.95 B81-01900

942.085'7 — England. Social life, *1970-1979*
Miller, John, *1940 Aug.23-*. Roots of England / John Miller & Sid Waddell. — London : British Broadcasting Corporation, 1980. — 208p,[8]p of plates : ill(some col),ports(some col.) ; 24cm
Bibliography: p207-208
ISBN 0-563-17792-6 : £7.45 B81-02619

942.085'8'0924 — England. Countryside — *Personal observations*
'BB'. The quiet fields / 'BB' ; illustrated by D.J. Watkins-Pitchford. — London : Joseph, 1981. — 205p : ill ; 23cm
ISBN 0-7181-2039-6 : £7.50 B81-36127

Edwards, Percy. Percy Edwards' country book / illustrations by David Edwards. — London : Arthur Barker, c1980. — 167p : ill ; 23cm
ISBN 0-213-16762-x : £5.95 B81-11598

942.085'8'0924 — England. Countryside — *Personal observations* *continuation*

Jenkins, Alan C.. A countryman's year / Alan C. Jenkins ; illustrated by Peter Barrett. — Exeter : Webb & Bower ; Leicester : WHS Distributors, 1980. — 208p : ill(some col.) ; 26cm
Includes index
ISBN 0-906671-17-5 : £8.95 : CIP rev.
B80-18112

942.1/8 — HISTORY. ENGLAND. SPECIAL LOCALITIES

942.1 — England. Thames River. River crossings

Phillips, Geoffrey. Thames crossings. — Newton Abbot : David and Charles, Nov.1981. — [288]p
ISBN 0-7153-8202-0 : £12.95 : CIP entry
B81-30591

942.1 — London. Buildings of historical importance

Dalzell, W. R.. The Shell guide to the history of London / W.R. Dalzell. — London : Joseph, c1981. — 496p,[32]p of plates : ill(some col.),maps,1plan,ports ; 26cm
Bibliography: p485. — Includes index
ISBN 0-7181-2015-9 : £12.50 B81-34515

942.1 — London. Socially disadvantaged inner areas *compared with* **socially disadvantaged inner areas in Paris**

Madge, Charles. Inner city poverty in Paris and London / Charles Madge and Peter Willmott. — London : Routledge and Kegan Paul, 1981. — xi,133p ; 23cm. — (Reports of the Institute of Community Studies) (Routledge social science series)
Bibliography: p129-131. — Includes index
ISBN 0-7100-0819-8 : £8.50 : CIP rev.
Also classified at 944'.36 B81-21481

942.1 — London. Thames River region, *to 1980*

Bates, L. M.. The spirit of London's river : memoirs of the Thames waterfront / L.M. Bates. — Woking : Gresham in association with the Europa, 1980. — xiii,183p,[26]p of plates : ill,2ports ; 22cm
Includes index
ISBN 0-905418-43-3 : £7.95 B81-25094

942.1'004924 — London. Jews. Social life, *ca 1930-1942 — Personal observations*

Bloch, Sidney, *1924-*. No time for tears : childhood in a rabbi's family / Sidney Bloch. — London : Kimber, 1980. — 176p ; 23cm
ISBN 0-7183-0497-7 : £5.50 B81-04526

942.1'074'0924 — London. Social life, *1826-1839 — Personal observations — Early works*

Tristan, Flora. Flora Tristan's London journal : a survey of London life in the 1830s / a translation ... by Dennis Palmer and Giselle Pincetl. — London : Prior, 1980. — xx,259p,[16]p of plates : ill,1facsim,1map ; 23cm
Translation of: Promenade dans Londres. — Map on lining papers
ISBN 0-86043-404-4 : £7.50 : CIP rev.
B80-14089

Tristan, Flora. The London journal of Flora Tristan, 1842. — London : Virago, Jan.1982. — [320]p
Translation of: Promenades dans Londres
ISBN 0-86068-214-5 (pbk) : £3.95 : CIP entry
B81-33764

942.1'081 — London. Social conditions, *1869 — Early works*

Greenwood, James. The seven curses of London. — Oxford : Blackwell, Jan.1982. — [288]p
Originally published: London : S. Rivers, 1869
ISBN 0-631-12778-x : £12.00 : CIP entry
B81-34292

942.1'081'0222 — London. Social life, *ca 1840-ca 1915 — Illustrations*

A **London** album : early photographs recording the history of the city and its people from 1840 to 1915 / [compiled by] Roger Whitehouse. — London : Secker & Warburg, 1980. — [164],xxvi p : all ill,2maps,1facsim,3plans,ports ; 31cm
Includes index
ISBN 0-436-57090-4 : £12.50 B81-04561

942.1'081'0924 — London. Social life, *1870-1879 — Childhood reminiscences*

Hughes, M. V.. [A London child of the seventies]. A London child of the 1870s / M.V. Hughes. — Large print ed. — Bath : Chivers, 1980, c1977. — 233p ; 23cm
ISBN 0-85997-474-x : £5.50 : CIP rev.
B80-18121

942.1'081'0924 — London. Social life, *1880-1890 — Childhood reminiscences*

Hughes, M. V.. [A London girl of the eighties]. A London girl of the 1880s / M.V. Hughes. — Large print ed. — Bath : Chivers, 1980, c1979. — 403p : ill ; 23cm
ISBN 0-85997-475-8 : £5.50 : CIP rev.
B80-18122

942.1'081'0924 — London. Social life, *1890-1899 — Personal observations*

Hughes, M. V.. [A London home in the nineties]. A London home in the 1890s / M.V. Hughes. — Large print ed. — Bath : Chivers, 1980. — 336p ; 23cm
ISBN 0-85997-476-6 : £5.50 : CIP rev.
B80-18120

942.1'081'0924 — London. Social life, *1890-1900 — Childhood reminiscences*

Farjeon, Eleanor. A nursery in the nineties / Eleanor Farjeon. — Oxford : Oxford University Press, 1980, c1935. — 534p,[8]p of plates : music,ports ; 20cm
Facsim. of: edition published London : Gollancz, 1935
ISBN 0-19-281308-0 (pbk) : £3.95 : CIP rev.
Also classified at 929'.2'0942 B80-12667

942.1'083'0924 — London. Social life, *1920-1939 — Personal observations*

Hughes, M. V.. A London family between the wars / M.V. Hughes. — Large print ed. — Bath : Chivers, 1980, c1979. — 232p ; 23cm
Originally published: London : Oxford University Press, 1940
ISBN 0-85997-477-4 : £5.50 : CIP rev.
B80-18123

942.1'0857 — Urban regions. Social life — *Study regions: London, 1970-1979*

Raban, Jonathan. Soft city / Jonathan Raban. — [London] : Fontana, 1975, c1974 (1981 printing). — 253p ; 18cm
Originally published: London : Hamilton, 1974. — Bibliography: p251-253
ISBN 0-00-636429-2 (pbk) : £1.95 B81-40133

942.1085'8 — London. Graffiti — *Illustrations*

Charoux, Jac. London -graffiti- / photographed by Jac Charoux ; introduction by John Cooper Clarke. — London : W.H. Allen, 1980. — 96p : chiefly ill(some col.) ; 25cm
ISBN 0-491-02813-x : £5.95 B81-00673

942.1085'8'05 — London — *Serials*

The **Free** weekEnder. — Mar.6 1981. — London (28-30 Little Russell St., WC1) : C & E Publications, 1981-. — v. : ill,ports ; 32cm
Weekly
ISSN 0261-605x = Free weekEnder : Free
B81-32296

942.1'2 — London *(City).* **Smithfield,** *to 1980*

Forshaw, Alec. Smithfield : past & present / Alec Forshaw & Theo Bergström. — London : Heinemann, 1980. — 191p : ill,maps,1facsim,1plan,ports ; 25cm
Bibliography: p187-188. — Includes index
ISBN 0-434-26902-6 : £7.50 B81-04726

942.1'32 — London. Covent Garden — *Serials*

The **Covent** Garden courier. — Vol.1, no.2 (Apr.1981)-. — London (43 St John St., EC1M 4AN) : Woodpecker Publications, 1981-. — v. : ill,ports ; 41cm
Monthly. — Continues: Covent Garden news (London : 1981)
ISSN 0261-8796 = Covent Garden courier : Unpriced B81-33937

The **Covent** Garden magazine. — No.1 (May 1981)-. — London (7 Neal St., WC2H 9PU) : Covent Garden Magazine Ltd., 1981-. — v. : ill,ports ; 28cm
Monthly
ISSN 0260-8030 = Covent Garden magazine : £7.50 per year B81-33721

942.1'32 — London. Covent Garden, *to 1980*

Woodiwiss, Audrey. The history of Covent Garden : Covent Garden through the years / Audrey Woodiwiss. — London : R. Conway for the Covent Garden General Store, 1980. — 115p : ill,ports ; 18cm
ISBN 0-9507132-0-1 (pbk) : Unpriced
B81-17772

942.1'32 — London. Westminster *(London Borough).* **Bond Street,** *to 1978*

Desebrock, Jean. The book of Bond Street Old and New / by Jean Desebrock ; partly based on material compiled by H.B. Wheatley. — London : Tallis, c1978. — 165p : ill,2maps,facsims,ports ; 29cm
£5.00 B81-05187

942.1'32 — London. Westminster *(London Borough).* **Government buildings: Palace of Westminster,** *to 1979*

Boyne, *Sir* **Harry**. The Houses of Parliament / Sir Harry Boyne ; photographs by Adam Woolfitt. — London : Batsford, 1981. — 95p : col.ill,col.ports ; 31cm
Includes index
ISBN 0-7134-2365-x : £7.95 B81-27546

Cormack, Patrick. Westminster Palace & Parliament / by Patrick Cormack ; with an introduction by George Thomas. — London : Warne, 1981. — 180p : ill,facsims,ports ; 25cm
Includes index
ISBN 0-7232-2681-4 : £9.95 B81-09582

942.1'32 — London. Westminster *(London Borough).* **Palaces**

Nash, Roy. Buckingham Palace : the place and the people / Roy Nash. — London : Macdonald, 1980. — 192p,[16]p of plates : ill (some col.),facsims,1plan,ports(some col.) ; 27cm
Ill on lining papers. — Bibliography: p183-184. — Includes index
ISBN 0-354-04529-6 : £9.95 B81-04739

942.1'32 — London. Westminster *(London Borough).* **Palaces: Buckingham Palace,** *to 1980*

Nash, Roy. Buckingham Palace : the place and the people / Roy Nash. — London : Macdonald, 1980 (1981 [printing]). — 192p.[16]p of plates : ill(some col.),1facsim,1plan,ports(some col.) ; 26cm
Bibliography: p183-184. — Includes index
ISBN 0-354-04820-1 (pbk) : £4.95 B81-31290

942.1'32 — London. Westminster *(London Borough).* **Westminster,** *to 1980*

Hunting, Penelope. Royal Westminster : a history of Westminster through its Royal connections / researched and written by Penelope Hunting. — [London] : [Royal Institution of Chartered Surveyors], c1981. — 224p : ill(some col.),maps (some col.),facsims,col.plan,ports ; 25cm
Published for the exhibition 'Royal Westminster'. Created and organized by the Royal Institution of Chartered Surveyors. — Bibliography: p198-202. — Includes index
ISBN 0-85406-128-2 (cased) : £16.00
ISBN 0-85406-127-4 (pbk) : £5.00 B81-40486

942.1'32074'0924 — London. Westminster *(London Borough).* **Lower middle classes. Social life,** *1826-1830 — Personal observations — Correspondence, diaries, etc*

Pocock, John Thomas. The diary of a London schoolboy : 1826-1830 / by John Thomas Pocock ; edited by Marjorie Holder and Christina Gee. — London (28 Willoughby Rd., NW3 1SA) : Camden History Society, 1980. — xvii,87p,[6]p of plates : ill,1coat of arms,maps,1geneal.table,ports ; 21cm
Includes index
ISBN 0-904491-15-3 (pbk) : £3.00 B81-05595

942.1'34 — London. Kensington and Chelsea *(London Borough).* **Chelsea. Social life,** *ca 1920-ca 1940 — Childhood reminiscences*

Gamble, Rose. Chelsea child / Rose Gamble. — Large print ed. — Bath : Chivers, 1980, c1979. — 369p ; 23cm. — (New Portway)
Originally published: London : British Broadcasting Corporation, 1979
ISBN 0-85997-481-2 : £5.50 : CIP rev.
B80-22749

942.1'42 — London. Camden *(London Borough).* **Hampstead,** *1902-1928 compared with* **Hampstead,** *1980 — Illustrations*
Hampstead as it was / compiled by Clive R. Smith. — London (62 Greyhound Hill, N.W.4) : C.R. Smith, [1981]. — 30p : chiefly ill,2ports ; 22x31cm
Cover title
ISBN 0-904595-05-6 (pbk) : £1.50 B81-29506

942.1'42 — London. Camden *(London Borough).* **Hampstead,** *to 1980*
Norrie, Ian. Hampstead. — London : Wildwood House, July 1981. — [208]p
ISBN 0-7045-3060-0 : £7.95 : CIP entry B81-15903

942.1'43 — London. Islington *(London Borough), to 1810 — Early works — Facsimiles*
Nelson, John, *fl.1811.* [The history, topography and antiquities of the parish of St Mary, Islington, in the county of Middlesex]. The history of Islington / John Nelson. — Rev. ed. / together with 79 additional illustrations and an introduction by Julia Melvin. — London : Philip Wilson, 1980. — xv,viii,417p[76]p of plates : ill,maps,coats of arms,ports ; 28cm
Facsim. of: 1st ed., London : Russell, 1811. — Limited ed. of 1,000 copies. — Includes index
ISBN 0-85667-104-5 : £30.00 B81-05201

942.1'43 — London. Islington *(London Borough).* **Towers: Canonbury Tower,** *1509-1980*
Canonbury Tower : a brief guide / [based on Richard Oakley's Brief history of Canonbury Tower] ; [edited by Wilmot Bennitt and Roger Green]. — London (Canonbury Tower, Canonbury Pl. N1 2NQ) : Tavistock Repertory Company (London), c1980. — 16p : ill,plans,ports ; 21cm
Cover title
Unpriced (pbk) B81-12510

942.1'430858'0222 — London. Islington *(London Borough) — Illustrations*
Usborne, Ann. A portrait of Islington. — London (4 Canonbury Mansions, N.1.) : Damien Tunnacliffe, Oct.1981. — [64]p
ISBN 0-9506284-1-7 : £3.95 : CIP entry B81-30513

942.1'44 — London. Hackney *(London Borough).* **Hoxton. Social conditions,** *1851-1871 — Sources of data: Census data*
Knott, Bettie. The hub of Hoxton : Hoxton Street 1851-1871, based on a study of the censuses / by Bettie Knott. — [London] : London Borough of Hackney Library Services, 1981. — viii,88p : 1map ; 30cm
Cover title. — Bibliography: p87-88
Unpriced (pbk) B81-36097

942.1'44082'0924 — London. Hackney *(London Borough).* **Austrian Jewish refugees. Lang, Martha** *— Biographies*
Lang, Martha. The Austrian cockney / Martha Lang. — London (136 Kingsland High St., E8) : Centreprise, c1980. — 67p : ill,2facsims,ports ; 21cm
ISBN 0-903738-49-x (pbk) : £1.00 B81-10770

942.1'440858 — London. Hackney *(London Borough).* **Social conditions**
Report from Hackney : a study of an inner city area / Michael Young ... [et al.]. — London : Policy Studies Institute, 1981. — 62p ; 21cm
ISBN 0-85374-188-3 (pbk) : £2.50 B81-09963

942.1'5 — London. Tower Hamlets *(London Borough).* **Brick Lane. Political events,** *1978.* **Racial factors**
Leech, Kenneth, *1939-.* Brick Lane 1978 : the events and their significance / Kenneth Leech. — Birmingham (1 Finch Rd., Lozells, Birmingham B19 1HS) : AFFOR, 1980. — 28p : ill,1map ; 26cm
ISBN 0-907127-03-7 (pbk) : £1.00 B81-22244

942.1'5 — London. Tower Hamlets *(London Borough).* **Poplar. Social life,** *ca 1914-ca 1935 — Childhood reminiscences*
Scannell, Dorothy. Mother knew best. — Large print ed. — Bath : Chivers, Oct.1981. — [320] p. — (A New Portway large print book)
Originally published: London : Macmillan, 1974
ISBN 0-85119-139-8 : £5.70 : CIP entry B81-25799

942.1'5 — London. Tower Hamlets *(London Borough).* **Rothschild Buildings. Jewish communities. Social life,** *1887-1920*
White, Jerry. Rothschild Buildings : life in an East End tenement block 1887-1920 / Jerry White ; foreword by Raphael Samuel. — London : Routledge & Kegan Paul, 1980. — xviii,301p,[16]p of plates : ill,3maps,facsims,1plan,ports ; 23cm. — (History Workshop series)
Includes index
ISBN 0-7100-0429-x (cased) : £11.50 : CIP rev.
ISBN 0-7100-0603-9 (pbk) : £6.95 B80-18124

942.1'5 — London. Tower Hamlets *(London Borough).* **Stepney. Sidney Street Siege**
Rogers, Colin, *1918-.* The battle of Stepney : the Sidney Street Siege : its causes and consequences / Colin Rogers. — London : Hale, 1981. — 222p,[6]p of plates : ill,maps,1facsim,1plan,ports ; 23cm
Includes index
ISBN 0-7091-9146-4 : £7.95 B81-38915

942.1'5004924 — London. East End. Jews, *1840-1939 — Conference proceedings*
The **Jewish** East End 1840-1939 : [proceedings of the conference held on 22 October 1980 jointly by the Jewish Historical Society of England and the Jewish East End Project of the Association for Jewish Youth] / [edited and prepared by Aubrey Newman]. — London (33 Seymour Place, W1H 5AP) : The Jewish Historical Society of England, 1981. — xi,358p,[2]leaves of plates : ill,1map ; 21cm
Bibliography: p357-358
ISBN 0-902528-14-9 (pbk) : Unpriced B81-36842

942.1'5'007 — London. East End. Information sources *— Directories*
Marcan, Peter. An East End directory : a guide to the East End of London with special reference to the published literature of the last two decades / compiled and edited by Peter Marcan ; with contributions by John Dixon and Agnes Valentine ; photography by Nancy Holzman. — High Wycombe (31 Rowliff Rd., High Wycombe, Bucks.) : Peter Marcan, 1979. — 143p,10p of plates : ill,maps ; 30cm
Includes index
ISBN 0-9504211-2-x (pbk) : Unpriced B81-29349

942.1'50858'05 — London. East End *— Serials*
East End news. — Summer special (1980); Issue no.1 (Friday Mar.13 1981)-. — London (17 Victoria Park Sq., E2 9PE) : Trailglow, 1980-. — v. : ill,facsims,ports ; 43cm
Weekly. — Pre-publication no. issued Summer 1980. — Description based on: Issue No.1 (Friday Mar.13 1981)
ISSN 0261-6270 = East End news : £0.10 per issue B81-32208

942.1'62 — London. Greenwich *(London Borough).* **Woolwich region** *— Serials*
Woolwich mercury. — 1980-. — London (116 Deptford High St., SE8) : South East London & Kentish mercury, 1980-. — v. : ill,ports ; 42cm
Weekly. — Continues in part: South East London and Kentish mercury. — Description based on: No.8822 (Wednesday Apr.15 1981)
ISSN 0261-6696 = Woolwich mercury : Unpriced B81-32251

942.1'620858'05 — London. Greenwich *(London Borough) — Serials*
Greenwich & Bexley advertiser. — Vol.2, no.1 (week ending 7th Mar.1981)-. — [London] (124 Woolwich SE18) : Moadford (Newspapers) Ltd., 1981-. — v. : ill,ports ; 37cm
Weekly. — Merger of: Greenwich Borough advertiser ; and Bexley Borough advertiser. — Description based on: Vol.2, no.8 (week ending 25th Apr.1981)
ISSN 0261-6955 = Greenwich & Bexley advertiser : Unpriced
Also classified at 942.1'770858'05 B81-32246

Greenwich mercury. — 1980-. — London (116 Deptford High St., SE8 4NS) : South East London & Kentish Mercury, 1980-. — v. : ill,ports ; 42cm
Weekly. — Continues in part: South East London and Kentish mercury. — Description based on: No.8822 (Wednesday Apr.15th 1981)
ISSN 0261-622x = Greenwich mercury : £0.12 B81-32245

942.1'63 — London. Lewisham *(London Borough).* **Lee,** *ca 1600-1970*
Birchenough, Josephine. Some farms and fields in Lee / Josephine Birchenough with John King. — [London] (116 Manor La., SE12 8LR) : J. Birchenough, c1981. — vi,38p : maps ; 21cm
Cover title. — Includes index
ISBN 0-9507525-0-9 (pbk) : Unpriced B81-26127

942.1'630858'05 — London. Lewisham *(London Borough) — Serials*
Deptford and Peckham mercury. — 1980-. — London (116 Deptford High St., SE8) : South East London & Kentish mercury, 1980-. — v. : ill,ports ; 42cm
Weekly. — Continues in part: South East London and Kentish mercury. — Description based on : No 8822 (Wednesday Apr.15 1981)
ISSN 0261-6742 = Deptford and Peckham mercury : £0.12 per issue
Also classified at 942.1'640858'05 B81-32250

Lewisham mercury. — 1980-. — London (116 Deptford High St., SE8 4NS) : South East London & Kentish mercury, 1980-. — v. : ill,ports ; 42cm
Continues in part: South East London and Kentish mercury
ISSN 0261-6238 = Lewisham mercury : £0.12 B81-32259

942.1'64 — London. Southwark *(London Borough).* **Bermondsey,** *1939-1945*
Stewart, James D.. Bermondsey in war 1939-1945 / by James D. Stewart. — [London] ([c/o London Borough of Southwark Library Services, 20/22 Lordship La., SE22 8HN]) : [Bermondsey and Rotherhithe Society], [1981]. — ii,95p : ill ; 21cm
ISBN 0-9507462-0-7 (pbk) : Unpriced B81-15117

942.1'64 — London. Southwark *(London Borough).* **Rotherhithe,** *to 1979 — For schools*
Boast, Mary. The story of Rotherhithe / [text by Mary Boast] ; [illustrated by David Burch]. — [London] ([c/o Dulwich District Libraries, Lordship La., SE22 8NB]) : Council of London Borough of Southwark, 1980. — 28p : ill,1map,1coat of arms,1port ; 21cm. — (Neighbourhood histories / London Borough of Southwark ; no.6)
ISBN 0-905849-03-5 (pbk) : Unpriced B81-18721

942.1'64 — London. Southwark *(London Borough).* **Walworth. Social life,** *1905-1927 — Personal observations*
Bennett, H. J.. I was a Walworth boy / H.J. Bennett. — London (13 Peckham High St., S.E.15) : Peckham Publishing Project, c1980. — 92p : ill,1map,facsims,ports ; 21cm
ISBN 0-906464-71-4 (pbk) : £1.50 B81-18983

942.1'640858'05 — London. Southwark *(London Borough) — Serials*
Deptford and Peckham mercury. — 1980-. — London (116 Deptford High St., SE8) : South East London & Kentish mercury, 1980-. — v. : ill,ports ; 42cm
Weekly. — Continues in part: South East London and Kentish mercury. — Description based on : No 8822 (Wednesday Apr.15 1981)
ISSN 0261-6742 = Deptford and Peckham mercury : £0.12 per issue
Primary classification 942.1'630858'05 B81-32250

942.1'65 — London. Lambeth *(London Borough).* **Brixton. Events,** *1981 — South London Workers Against Racism viewpoints*
Police out of Brixton! / South London Workers Against Racism. — [London] ([BM RCT Ltd, WC1V 6XX]) : Junius Publications, 1981. — 15p : ill,ports ; 21cm. — (Revolutionary communist pamphlets, ISSN 0141-8874 ; no.10)
Cover title
£0.30 (pbk) B81-23361

942.1'65 — London. Lambeth *(London Borough).* **Public open spaces,** *to 1976*
Draper, Marie P. G.. Lambeth's open spaces : an historical account / by Marie P.G. Draper. — [London] (Directorate of Amenity Services, 4 Knights Hill, SE27 2HY) : London Borough of Lambeth, 1979. — 96p : ill,maps,facsims,ports ; 30cm
Includes index
ISBN 0-905208-03-x (pbk) : Unpriced
B81-14549

942.1'65 — London. Lambeth *(London Borough).* **Streatham,** *to 1979*
Gower, Graham. A brief history of Streatham / by Graham Gower. — London (50 Staplefield Close, S.W.2) : Streatham Society, 1980. — 34p,[4]p of plates : ill,2maps ; 21cm. — (Local history booklet / Streatham Society ; n.1)
Bibliography: p33
Unpriced (pbk) B81-12151

942.1'66 — London. Wandsworth *(London Borough).* **Putney** — *Serials*
Putney chronicle. — 1 (Friday Apr.3 1981)-. — London (Newpaper House, Windslow Rd, W6 9SF) : London & Westminster Newspapers Ltd., 1981-. — v. : ill,ports ; 45cm
Weekly
ISSN 0261-6327 = Putney chronicle : £0.10 per issue B81-32209

942.1'66081'0222 — London. Wandsworth *(London Borough), 1870-1930 — Illustrations*
The **Way** we were, 1870-1920 : scenes of the Borough of Wandsworth : a selection from the Wandsworth Libraries local history collection / compiled by Anthony Shaw. — [London] : Wandsworth Borough Council Libraries and Arts, c1980. — 48p : chiefly ill ; 30cm
ISBN 0-902837-10-9 (pbk) : £1.95 B81-38882

942.1'770858'05 — London. Bexley *(London Borough) — Serials*
Greenwich & Bexley advertiser. — Vol.2, no.1 (week ending 7th Mar.1981)-. — [London] (124 Woolwich SE18) : Moadford (Newspapers) Ltd., 1981-. — v. : ill,ports ; 37cm
Weekly. — Merger of: Greenwich Borough advertiser ; and Bexley Borough advertiser. — Description based on: Vol.2, no.8 (week ending 25th Apr.1981)
ISSN 0261-6955 = Greenwich & Bexley advertiser : Unpriced
Primary classification 942.1'620858'05
B81-32246

942.1'78 — London. Bromley *(London Borough).* **County houses: Camden Place,** *to 1979*
Wilson, Ken, *1923-*. Camden Place, Chislehurst : the story of a country house in words and drawings / by Ken Wilson. — Bromley : Bromley Library Service, 1981. — [35]p : ill,1map,plans,ports ; 15x22cm
Bibliography: p[3]
ISBN 0-901002-04-6 (pbk) : £1.00 B81-40810

942.1'780858'05 — London. Bromley *(London Borough) — Serials*
Bromley borough news : incorporating Biggin Hill news. — No.1/287 (Saturday Mar.7th 1981)-. — [Westerham] ([152 Main Rd, Biggin Hill, Westerham, Kent]) : [s.n.], 1981-. — v. : ill ; 42cm
Fortnightly. — Continues: Biggin Hill news
ISSN 0261-6106 = Bromley borough news : Unpriced B81-32292

942.1'84 — London. Ealing *(London Borough).* **Southall. Peach, Blair. Death**
The **Death** of Blair Peach : the supplementary report of the unofficial committee of enquiry / chairman, Michael Dummatt. — London : Published for the committee by the National Council for Civil Liberties, 1980. — 53p : 1map ; 22cm
ISBN 0-901108-91-x (pbk) : £1.50 B81-12755

942.1'84 — London. Ealing *(London Borough).* **Southall,** *to 1965*
Kirwan, Paul. Southall : a brief history / by Paul Kirwan. — Repr. with index. — Ealing ([Central Library, Walpole Park, Ealing W5]) : London Borough of Ealing Library Service, 1980. — vi,62p,[4]p of plates : ill ; 21cm
Originally published: 1965. — Bibliography: p53-54. — Includes index
ISBN 0-86192-003-1 (pbk) : Unpriced
B81-27605

942.1'85 — London. Brent *(London Borough).* **Wembley Stadium,** *to 1980*
Bass, Howard. Glorious Wembley : the official history of Britain's foremost entertainment centre. — Enfield : Guinness Superlatives, Feb.1982. — [176]p
ISBN 0-85112-237-x (pbk) : £5.95 : CIP entry
B81-38829

942.1'86 — London. Harrow *(London Borough).* **Pinner. Social life,** *to 1979*
A **Pinner** miscellany / [edited by] P.J. Snell. — Pinner (21 Cecil park, Pinner, Middlesex) : Pinner Local History Society, 1980. — 36p,[12]p of plates : ill,maps ; 30cm
Unpriced (pbk) B81-06447

942.1'87 — London. Barnet *(London Borough).* **Hendon & Mill Hill** — *History — Serials*
[Transactions *(Mill Hill and Hendon Historical Society)*]. Transactions / Mill Hill and Hendon Historical Society. — No.1 (New series) (1979)-. — [London] (c/o Mr J.W. Collier, 47 Longfield Ave., NW7 7EH) : The Society, 1979-. — v. ; 22cm
Irregular
ISSN 0260-7867 = Transactions - Mill Hill and Hendon Historical Society : Unpriced
B81-06902

942.1'87081 — Great Britain. Victoria, *Queen of Great Britain.* **Golden jubilee celebrations,** *1887* **& diamond jubilee celebrations,** *1897:* **Celebrations in Barnet** *(London Borough)*
Victorian Jubilees : some events which took place in 1887 and 1897 in the Borough of Barnet / editor Edward Sammes. — London (88 Temple Fortune Lane, NW11 7TX) : Hendon & Distrit Archaeological Society, 1977. — 48p : ill,facsims ; 22cm. — (Occasional paper / Hendon and District Archaeological Society ; no.4)
ISBN 0-9503050-2-2 (pbk) : £0.50 B81-29799

942.1'870858'05 — London. Barnet *(London Borough) — Serials*
Hendon-Edgware independent. — No.1 (Apr.1981)-. — [Harrow] (386 Kenton Rd, Kenton, [Harrow, Middx HA3 9HG]) : [Billington & Wright], 1981-. — v. : ill,ports ; 44cm
Weekly. — Description based on: No.2 (16th Apr.1981)
ISSN 0262-2319 = Hendon-Edgware independent : £0.03 per issue B81-39512

942.1'88 — London. Haringey *(London Borough).* **Tottenham. Parish churches: Tottenham Parish Church,** *to 1979*
Dalby, Mark. Tottenham parish church and parish : a brief history and guide / Mark Dalby. — 2nd and rev. ed. — [London] ([Priory Flats, Church La., N17 7HH]) : [M.Dalby], 1980. — 89p : ill ; 21cm
Previous ed.: 1979. — Bibliography: p89-90
Unpriced (spiral) B81-15112

942.1'89'006 — London. Enfield *(London Borough).* **Historiology. Organisations: Edmonton Hundred Historical Society** — *Serials*
[Chronicle *(Edmonton Hundred Historical Society)*]. Chronicle / Edmonton Hundred Historical Society. — No.1 (Oct.1978)-. — [London] ([c/o J. Baum, 25 Harington Terrace, Edmonton, N18 1JX]) : The Society, 1978-. — v. ; 30cm
Ten issues yearly. — Description based on: No.22 (Nov.1980)
ISSN 0260-9355 = Chronicle — Edmonton Hundred Historical Society : Unpriced
B81-10568

942.1'8902 — London. Enfield *(London Borough).* **Social conditions,** *1086-1400*
Pam, D. C.. The hungry years : the struggle for survival in Edmonton and Enfield before 1400 / by David Pam. — [London] ([Southgate Town Hall, Green Las., Palmers Green, N13]) : Edmonton Hundred Historical Society, 1980. — 31p : ill,2maps,1facsim ; 30cm. — (Occasional paper. New series / Edmonton Hundred Historical Society ; no.42)
ISBN 0-902922-38-6 (pbk) : £0.95 B81-11054

942.1'91 — London. Croydon *(London Borough).* **Parks: Norwood Grove,** *to 1979*
Mojon, Daphne. Norwood Grove / by Daphne Mojon. — London (50 Staplefield Close, S.W.2) : Streatham Society, 1980. — 12p,[4]p of plates : ill,2maps ; 21cm. — (Local history booklet / Streatham Society ; no.3)
Cover title. — Map on cover
Unpriced (pbk) B81-12156

942.1'91082'0222 — London. Croydon *(London Borough), 1901-1919 — Illustrations*
Edwardian Croydon illustrated : photographs for the period 1901 to 1919 / editor John B. Gent. — Croydon (96a Brighton Rd., South Croydon CR2 6AD) : Croydon Natural History and Scientific Society, 1981. — 48p : chiefly ill,1map,ports ; 30cm
Map on inside cover. — Bibliography: p48
ISBN 0-9501310-8-3 (pbk) : £1.95 B81-21329

942.1'92 — London. Sutton *(London Borough).* **Country houses: Carshalton House,** *to 1974*
Jones, A. E.. The story of Carshalton House / A.E. Jones. — Sutton (Central Library, St. Nicholas Way, Sutton, Surrey) : London Borough of Sutton Libraries and Arts Services, 1980. — vi,137p : ill,maps,plans,ports ; 21cm
Bibliography: p129-130. — Includes index
ISBN 0-907335-01-2 (pbk) : Unpriced
B81-05513

942.1'93 — London. Merton *(London Borough).* **Wimbledon. Social life,** *1906-1918 — Childhood reminiscences*
Fawcett, Patrick. Memories of a Wimbledon childhood 1906-1918 / by Patrick Fawcett ; with a foreword by Richard Milward. — London (26 Lingfield Rd., S.W.19) : John Evelyn Society, c1981. — 32p : ill,1col.plan,ports ; 21cm. — (A John Evelyn Society publication)
Text on inside cover
ISBN 0-9502405-5-9 (pbk) : £1.00 B81-36575

942.1'940858'05 — London. Kingston upon Thames *(London Borough) — Serials*
The **Kingston** informer : Kingston, Surbiton, New Malden, Tolworth, Thames Ditton, Hampton, Teddington. — [Vol.?]1, (1979)-. — Kingston upon Thames (78 Richmond Rd, Kingston upon Thames, Surrey KT2 5EL) : Kingston Informer Ltd., 1979-. — v. : ill,ports ; 46cm
Weekly. — Description based on: Vol.3, no.29 (Thursday July 16th 1981)
ISSN 0261-8699 = Kingston informer : Unpriced B81-39520

942.1'95 — London. Richmond upon Thames *(London Borough).* **Teddington,** *ca 1560-1910 — Illustrations*
Teddington as it was / researched and compiled by members of the Teddington Society. — Nelson : Hendon Publishing, c1980. — [48]p : chiefly ill,1map,ports ; 21x29cm
Text, ill on inside covers
ISBN 0-86067-058-9 (pbk) : £2.30 B81-07155

942.1'95 — London. Richmond upon Thames *(London Borough).* **Twickenham,** *1600-1900*
Twickenham 1600-1900 : people and places. — [Twickenham] ([59 Park House Gardens, Twickenham, Middx.]) : [Twickenham Local History Society], 1981. — 55p : ill,1map,ports ; 20cm. — (Borough of Twickenham Local History Society paper ; no.47)
Published to accompany an exhibition organised by Richmond upon Thames Library Department and the Borough of Twickenham Local History Society, 1981
ISBN 0-903341-32-8 (pbk) : £1.00 B81-26120

942.1'950858'05 — London. Richmond upon Thames *(London Borough) — Serials*
[Reflections *(London)*]**Reflections** : the Richmond magazine. — Vol.1, no.1 (Dec./Jan. 1980/81)-. — London (5 Porchester Place, W2 2BS) : [s.n.], 1980-. — v. : ill,ports ; 30cm
Six issues yearly
ISSN 0260-8499 = Reflections (London) : Unpriced B81-10249

942.2 — England. Lower Thames River Basin, *to 1970*
Astbury, A. K.. Estuary : land and water in the lower Thames basin / by A.K. Astbury. — London (9 Lancashire Court, New Bond St., W.1) : Carnforth, c1980. — 326p,[48]p of plates : ill,2maps,1facsim ; 23cm
Map(1 folded sheet) attached to inside back cover. — Includes index
ISBN 0-9507246-0-2 : £8.75 B81-10663

942.2′005 — Southern England - *History. Periodicals*
Southern history. — Vol.3. — Gloucester (17a Brunswick Rd, Gloucester GL1 1HG) : Alan Sutton, May 1981. — [272]p
ISBN 0-904387-65-8 (cased) : £12.50 : CIP entry
ISBN 0-904387-66-6 (pbk) : £7.50
ISSN 0142-4688 B81-12370

942.2′009′46 — Southern England. Coastal regions — *For schools*
Border, Rosemary. The South Coast / Rosemary Border. — London : Harrap, 1981. — 48p : ill,maps,ports ; 19x22cm. — (The Regions of Britain)
ISBN 0-245-53566-7 (pbk) : £1.50 B81-27839

942.2′01′07402262 — West Sussex. Chichester *(District).* **Museums: Chichester District Museum. Exhibits: Items associated with Saxons in South-east England,** *to 1066 — Catalogues*
The **South** Saxons : a temporary exhibition Chichester District Museum May 29th-August 25th 1979 / text by Martin G. Welch ... [et al.] ; line drawings by Susan J. England, Fred Aldsworth. — [Chichester] ([29 Little London, Chichester]) : Chichester District Museum, [1979?]. — [32]p : ill ; 22cm
Bibliography on inside cover
Unpriced (pbk) B81-37465

942.2′1′005 — Surrey — *History — Serials*
Surrey yesterdays. — No.1-. — Maidstone (109 Week St., Maidstone, Kent ME14 1RB) : South Eastern Magazines, 1980-. — v. : ill,ports ; 21cm
Quarterly
ISSN 0260-0978 = Surrey yesterdays : £0.95 per issue B81-05635

942.2′12 — Surrey. Sunbury Common. Parish churches: St. Saviour′s Church *(Sunbury on Thames), to 1980*
Heselton, Kenneth Y.. The Parish of St. Saviour : the story of Sunbury Common & its church / by K.Y. Heselton ; with a contribution by A.F.P. Brown. — Sunbury-on Thames (c/o The Vicarage, 205 Vicarage Rd., Sunbury-on-Thames, Middx) : Parochial Church Council of St. Saviour, Upper Sunbury, 1981. — 66p : ill ; 22cm
£0.75 (pbk)
Also classified at 942.2′12 B81-29233

942.2′12 — Surrey. Sunbury Common, *to 1980*
Heselton, Kenneth Y.. The Parish of St. Saviour : the story of Sunbury Common & its church / by K.Y. Heselton ; with a contribution by A.F.P. Brown. — Sunbury-on Thames (c/o The Vicarage, 205 Vicarage Rd., Sunbury-on-Thames, Middx) : Parochial Church Council of St. Saviour, Upper Sunbury, 1981. — 66p : ill ; 22cm
£0.75 (pbk)
Primary classification 942.2′12 B81-29233

942.2′12 — Surrey. Sunbury-on-Thames. Country houses: Sunbury Court, *to 1980*
Heselton, Kenneth Y.. A history of Sunbury Court / by Kenneth Y. Heselton. — Sunbury-on-Thames (12 Heathcroft Ave., Sunbury-on-Thames, Middx) : Sunbury and Shepperton Local History Society, 1981. — 16p ; 22cm. — (Occasional publications / Sunbury and Shepperton Local History Society ; no.6)
Bibliography: p16
Unpriced (pbk) B81-33336

942.2′13 — Surrey. Frimley. Social life, *ca 1870-ca 1950 — Personal observations*
Hills, Daisy. Old Frimley : including the old Warren Estate, St. Peters Church and other stories / by Daisy Hills. — [Frimley] : [D. Hills], 1978. — 142p,[8]p of plates : ill,ports ; 21cm
Unpriced (pbk) B81-04990

942.2′142 — Surrey. Woking, *to ca 1870*
Locke, Arthur. A short history of Woking / by Arthur Locke. — Woking (Chapel St., Woking, Surrey) : Nancy Leigh Bookshop, 1980. — 57p ; 22cm
ISBN 0-9507315-0-1 (pbk) : £1.25 B81-06668

942.2′1420858′05 — Surrey. Woking *(District) — Serials*
Woking & Byfleet herald. — Thursday Feb.12th 1981-. — Chertsey (31 Windsor St., Chertsey, Surrey) : Rawlings & Walsh, 1981-. — v. : ill,ports ; 60cm
Weekly. — Continues: Woking herald
ISSN 0261-6114 = Woking & Byfleet herald : £0.10 B81-32294

942.2′145 — Surrey. Walton-on-Thames. Parish churches: St. Mary′s with St. John′s *(Church : Walton-on-Thames), to 1979*
Alward, Marion E.. Historical notes / by Marian E. Alward and Irene R. Sandells. — Walton-on-Thames ([Church St., Walton-on-Thames, Surrey]) : St Mary′s with St John′s, [1980?]. — 40p : ill ; 21cm
Unpriced (pbk) B81-11099

942.2′162 — Surrey. Guildford, *1830-1940 — Illustrations*
Alexander, Matthew. Vintage Guildford / by Matthew Alexander. — Nelson : Hendon Publishing, c1981. — [44]p : ill,2facsims,ports ; 21x29cm
Text, ill on inside covers
ISBN 0-86067-070-8 (pbk) : £2.60 B81-40692

942.2′19 — Surrey. Badshot Lea, *to ca 1980*
Hewins, Maurice. Badshot people / Maurice Hewins. — [Farnham] ([c/o Maurice Hewins, 31 Badshot Park, Badshot Lea, Farnham, Surrey]) : [Badshot Lea Village Hall Trust], [1981]. — 34p : ill,1map,1facsim,ports ; 30cm
Cover title
£1.50 (pbk) B81-27613

942.2′19 — Surrey. Frensham region, *ca 1890 to 1977 — Illustrations*
A **Frensham** heritage : photographs and drawings / [Frensham and Dockenfield Local History Group] ; with an introduction by John Chuter. — [Frensham] ([Kennel Farm, Frensham, Surrey]) : The Group, 1977. — 48p : chieflyill,facsims,ports ; 30cm
Ill on inside covers
Unpriced (pbk) B81-09240

942.2′19 — Surrey. Frensham region, *to 1977*
Hickling, Robert. A Frensham history / by Robert Hickling. — [Frensham] ([Kennel Farm, Frensham, Surrey]) : Frensham and Dockenfield Local History Group, 1978. — 32p : ill,1map,ports ; 21cm
Cover title. — Includes index
Unpriced (pbk) B81-09239

942.2′3′00946 — Kent. Coastal regions, *to 1979*
Hillier, Caroline. The bulwark shore : Thanet and the Cinque Ports / Caroline Hillier ; with photographs by John Mosley. — London : Eyre Methuen, 1980. — 317p,[16]pofplates : ill,maps,ports ; 23cm
Map on lining papers. — Bibliography: p301-306. — Includes index
ISBN 0-413-39580-4 : £7.95 : CIP rev.
Also classified at 942.2′5′00946 B80-18553

942.2′301 — Kent, *410-866*
Mirams, Michael David. Ethelbert′s kingdom : the story of the Jutish and Saxon kings of Kent / by Michael David Mirams. — Rochester (162, Borstal Rd., Rochester, Kent) : North Kent Books, 1981, c1980. — 79p,[1]leaf of plates : ill,maps,facsims,2plans,geneal.tables ; 21cm
Bibliography: p75
£2.40 (pbk) B81-40177

942.2′3082′0924 — Kent. Rural regions. Social life, *1910-1980 — Personal observations*
Ellerby, Charles M.. Time after time / by Charles M. Ellerby ; sketches by the author. — [Dartford] : [C.M. Ellerby], 1980 (Gravesend : P. Ness). — 140p : ill ; 19cm
Unpriced B81-04698

942.2′312 — Kent. Dartford — *Serials*
Gravesend & Dartford advertiser. — Vol.1 (1981)-. — [London] (124 Woolwich, SE18) : Moadford (Newspapers) Ltd., 1981-. — v. : ill,ports ; 37cm
Weekly. — Continues: Gravesend & Dartford Borough advertiser. — Description based on: Vol.1, no.100 (week ending 25th Apr.1981)
ISSN 0261-6718 = Gravesend & Dartford advertiser : Unpriced
Also classified at 942.2′315 B81-32253

942.2′315 — Kent. Gravesend — *Serials*
Gravesend & Dartford advertiser. — Vol.1 (1981)-. — [London] (124 Woolwich, SE18) : Moadford (Newspapers) Ltd., 1981-. — v. : ill,ports ; 37cm
Weekly. — Continues: Gravesend & Dartford Borough advertiser. — Description based on: Vol.1, no.100 (week ending 25th Apr.1981)
ISSN 0261-6718 = Gravesend & Dartford advertiser : Unpriced
Primary classification 942.2′312 B81-32253

942.2′323 — Kent. Halling, *to 1978*
Gowers, E. S.. Across the low meadow : Halling, a village on the Meadway / by E.S. Gowers and Derek Church. — Maidstone (45 Scott St., Maidstone, Kent) : Christine Swift, 1979. — 134p,[37]p of plates : ill,maps,facsims,ports ; 22cm
Maps on lining papers. — Bibliography: p133-134. - Includes index
£5.95 B81-18925

942.2′323 — Kent. Rochester. Riverine regions, *to 1930*
Harris, Edwin. The riverside : an itinerary of the Medway within the City of Rochester and memories it recalls / by Edwin Harris. — Rochester (162 Borstal Rd., Rochester, [Kent ME1 3BR]) : North Kent Books, [1980?]. — [50]p,[12]p of plates : ill,ports ; 22cm
Originally published: Rochester : E. Harris, 1930. — Limited ed. of 500 copies
ISBN 0-9505733-2-9 (pbk) : £2.00 B81-09251

942.2′330858′05 — Kent. Swale *(District) — Serials*
Sheerness & Sittingbourne advertiser. — Vol.1, no.1 (1980)-. — Maidstone (121 Week St., Maidstone ME14 1RB) : Moadford (Newspapers) Ltd., 1980-. — v. : ill,ports ; 37cm
Weekly. — Description based on: Vol.1, no.45 (week ending 25th Apr.1981)
ISSN 0261-670x = Sheerness & Sittingbourne advertiser : Unpriced B81-32252

942.2′34 — Kent. Canterbury. Cathedrals: Canterbury Cathedral — *Serials*
Canterbury Cathedral Chronicle. — No.75(1981). — Canterbury (11b The Precincts, Canterbury [Kent]) : The Friends of Canterbury Cathedral, 1981. — 64p
Unpriced B81-32279

942.2′34 — Kent. Canterbury. Cathedrals: Canterbury Cathedral, *to 1979*
Keates, Jonathan. Canterbury Cathedral / Jonathan Keates & Angelo Hornak. — London : Summerfield Philip Wilson, 1980. — 96p : col.ill,col.facsims,2plans,col.ports ; 28cm
ISBN 0-85667-088-x (cased) : £6.95 (pbk) : £2.95 B81-09166

942.2′36 — Kent. Crockenhill. Graveyards: Old Burying Ground, *to 1980*
Black, Shirley Burgoyne. The old burying ground, Crockenhill, Kent / by Shirley Burgoyne Black. — Sevenoaks (33 Tudor Drive, Otford, Sevenoaks, Kent TN14 5QP) : Darenth Valley, c1981. — 19p : ill,1plan ; 21cm
ISBN 0-9507334-0-7 (pbk) : £0.95 B81-20824

942.2′36 — Kent. Edenbridge — *History — Serials*
Aspects of Edenbridge. — No.1-. — Edenbridge (c/o J. Willsmer, Little Hatch, Crouch House Rd, Edenbridge [TN8 5EL]) : Edenbridge and District Historical Society, 1980. — v. : ill,maps ; 21cm
ISSN 0261-8850 = Aspects of Edenbridge : £0.95 per issue B81-34034

942.2′36 — Kent. Otford. Houses: Chantry, ***The, to 1540***

Stoyel, Anthony D.. Otford′s medieval court hall : an account of the origin of The Chantry, Otford, Kent / Anthony D. Stoyel. — Sevenoaks (52 Tudor Drive, Otford, Sevenoaks, Kent TN14 5QR) : Sevenoaks District Architectural History, 1980. — 26p ; 21cm
£0.50 (pbk) B81-04759

942.2′372 — Kent. East Malling, ***to 1978***

McNay, Michael. Portrait of a Kentish village : East Malling 827-1978 / Michael McNay. — London : Gollancz, 1980. — 144p,[8]p of plates : ill,facsims,maps ; 24cm
Maps on lining papers. — Includes index
ISBN 0-575-02876-9 : £8.95 B81-01901

942.2′372 — Kent. East Peckham, ***ca 1900-1979 — Illustrations***

Remember East Peckham / [compiled] by Margaret Lawrence. — [Tonbridge] ([c/o Barnsfield, Church La., East Peckham, Tonbridge, Kent]) : P. Morgan, 1979. — [40]p : ill,ports ; 21x30cm
£2.00 (pbk) B81-07838

942.2′375 — Kent. Boughton Monchelsea. Social life, ***1900-1940 — Personal observation — Collections***

Boughton Monchelsea 1900-1940 : a village remembered / compiled and edited by Denis Tye. — Kent : Kent County Council County Library, 1980. — 56p : ill ; 21cm
Cover title
Unpriced (pbk) B81-24380

942.2′375 — Kent. Maidstone, ***to 1980***

Watson, Hilary C.. The book of Maidstone : Kent′s county town / by Hilary C. Watson. — Buckingham : Barracuda, 1981. — 144p : ill,maps,facsims,ports ; 24cm
Maps on lining papers. — Includes index
ISBN 0-86023-121-6 : £9.95 B81-40021

942.2′392 — Kent. Ashford. Social life, ***1600-1700***

Seventeenth-century Ashford : life in the Kentish market town / research by members of the Ashford Local History Group ; editor W.R. Briscall. — Ashford [Kent] (187 Canterbury Rd., Kennington, Ashford, Kent TN24 9QH) : LRB Historical Publications, 1980. — 44p : ill,4maps,2coats of arms,2ports ; 30cm. — (Ashford history series ; 3)
Includes index
ISBN 0-905511-02-6 (pbk) : Unpriced B81-22389

942.2′395 — Kent. Folkestone & Hythe — ***Serials***

Folkestone & Hythe advertiser. — Vol.1, no.1 (1981)-. — Maidstone (121 Week St., Maidstone, Kent) : Moadford (Newspapers), 1981-. — v. : ill,ports ; 37cm
Weekly. — Description based on: Vol.1, no.5 (Apr.21 1981)
ISSN 0261-6211 = Folkestone & Hythe advertiser : Unpriced B81-32263

942.2′395 — Kent. Folkestone region — ***Serials***

Folkestone & Hythe pictorial. — Feb.1981-. — Folkestone (The Bayle, Folkestone, Kent) : South Kent Newspapers (Westminster Press Limited), 1981-. — v. : chiefly ill,ports ; 45cm
Monthly
ISSN 0261-6300 = Folkestone & Hythe pictorial : £0.12 per issue B81-32201

942.2′5′005 — East & West Sussex — ***History — Serials***

Sussex yesterdays : [history and heritage of the county]. — No.1-. — Maidstone (109 Week St., Maidstone, Kent ME14 1RB) : South Eastern Magazines, 1980-. — v. : ill ; 21cm
Quarterly
ISSN 0144-6878 = Sussex yesterdays : £0.95 per issue B81-26386

942.2′5′00946 — East Sussex. Coastal regions, ***to 1979***

Hillier, Caroline. The bulwark shore : Thanet and the Cinque Ports / Caroline Hillier ; with photographs by John Mosley. — London : Eyre Methuen, 1980. — 317p,[16]pofplates : ill,maps,ports ; 23cm
Map on lining papers. — Bibliography: p301-306. — Includes index
ISBN 0-413-39580-4 : £7.95 : CIP rev.
Primary classification 942.2′3′00946 B80-18553

942.2′501 — East & West Sussex. Settlement by Saxons, ***450-1066***

The South Saxons in the Chichester district / [researched and designed by members of the Chichester WEA local history workshop class]. — [Chichester] ([29 Little London, Chichester PO19 1PB]) : Chichester District Museum, [1979?]. — [8]p : ill,1plan ; 21cm
Bibliography: p7-8
£0.05 (unbound) B81-37220

942.2′5083′0924 — East & West Sussex. Social life, ***1906-ca 1920 — Childhood reminiscences***

Gaster, Harold. A morning without clouds / Harold Gaster. — London : Cape, 1981. — 143p ; 23cm
ISBN 0-224-01964-3 : £5.50 : CIP rev.
B81-20626

942.2′51 — East Sussex. Pevensey, ***to 1980***

Sacret, G. C.. Guide to Pevensey and its Court House / [researched and written by G.C. Sacret]. — [Pevensey] ([Lyons Close, High St., Pevensey, E. Sussex]) : [Pevensey Town Trust], [1981?]. — 16p : 1plan ; 21cm
Text and plan on inside covers
Unpriced (pbk) B81-29623

942.2′54 — East Sussex. Portslade, ***to 1980***

Elliott, A. G.. A second portrait of Portslade and Brighton / by A.G. Elliot. — Portslade ([22 Hurst Cres., Portslade, E. Sussex BN4 1SG]) : A.G. Elliot, 1981. — 32p : chiefly ill ; 22cm
ISBN 0-9506387-4-9 (pbk) : £1.10
Also classified at 942.2′56 B81-18630

942.2′540858′05 — East Sussex. Hove — ***Serials***

Brighton & Hove leader : incorporating the Advertiser. — Thursday, June 25, 1981-. — [Brighton] ([Robert St., Brighton BN1 1RX]) : [Southern Publishing], 1981. — v. : ill,ports ; 42cm
Weekly. — Continues: Advertiser (Brighton)
ISSN 0262-1681 = Brighton & Hove leader : Unpriced
Primary classification 942.2′560858′05
B81-39537

942.2′56 — East Sussex. Brighton, ***to 1980***

Elliott, A. G.. A second portrait of Portslade and Brighton / by A.G. Elliot. — Portslade ([22 Hurst Cres., Portslade, E. Sussex BN4 1SG]) : A.G. Elliot, 1981. — 32p : chiefly ill ; 22cm
ISBN 0-9506387-4-9 (pbk) : £1.10
Primary classification 942.2′54 B81-18630

942.2′56073 — East Sussex. Brighton, ***1740-1820***

Farrant, Sue. Georgian Brighton 1740 to 1820 / by Sue Farrant. — Brighton : Centre for Continuing Education, University of Sussex, 1980. — 60p : maps ; 22cm. — (Occasional papers / University of Sussex Centre for Continuing Education, ISSN 0306-1108 ; no.13)
ISBN 0-904242-15-3 (pbk) : £1.25 B81-09416

942.2′56084′0924 — East Sussex. Brighton. Social life, ***1932-1943 — Childhood reminiscences***

Dallaway, Enid. Sunshine, sand and sea / Enid Dallaway. — Bognor Regis : New Horizon, c1980. — 205p,[16]p of plates : 2ill,ports ; 21cm
ISBN 0-86116-169-6 : £5.25 B81-25985

942.2′560858′05 — East Sussex. Brighton — ***Serials***

Brighton & Hove leader : incorporating the Advertiser. — Thursday, June 25, 1981-. — [Brighton] ([Robert St., Brighton BN1 1RX]) : [Southern Publishing], 1981. — v. : ill,ports ; 42cm
Weekly. — Continues: Advertiser (Brighton)
ISSN 0262-1681 = Brighton & Hove leader : Unpriced
Also classified at 942.2′540858′05 B81-39537

942.2′57 — East Sussex. Lewes, ***1859-1913 — Illustrations***

Brent, Colin E.. Victorian Lewes / compiled by Colin Brent & William Rector. — London : Phillimore, 1980. — [96]p : chiefly ill,ports ; 25cm
ISBN 0-85033-355-5 : £5.95 B81-01614

942.2′57 — East Sussex. Peacehaven & Telscombe Cliffs — ***Serials***

Meridian post : community newspaper for Peacehaven & Telscombe Cliffs area. — Vol.1, no.1 (Feb./Mar.1981)-. — Peacehaven (c/o 103 South Coast Rd, Peacehaven, [East Sussex]) : Meridian Post Steering Committee, 1981-. — v. : ill ; 44cm
ISSN 0260-8766 = Meridian post : Unpriced
B81-00705

942.2′58 — East Sussex. Eastbourne. Houses: Greys, ***The , to 1910***

Davies, Hereward. ′The Greys′ Eastbourne / Hereward Davies. — Ilfracombe : Stockwell, 1981. — 91p,[4]p of plates : 1ill,1facsim,ports ; 19cm
ISBN 0-7223-1447-7 : £3.75 B81-16774

942.2′5801 — East Sussex. Eastbourne, ***to 1086.*** **Archaeological sources**

Heys, Geoffrey. Early settlement in Eastbourne / by Geoffrey Heys. — [Eastbourne] ([21 King′s Drive, Eastbourne, Sussex BN21 2NX]) : F.G. Heys, c1980. — iv,59p : maps ; 21cm
£1.70 (pbk) B81-06153

942.2′59 — East Sussex. Hastings, ***to 1980***

Powys, John F. C.. Hastings / [by John F.C. Powys]. — Lewes (44 St. Anne′s Crescent, Lewes, East Sussex BN7) : East Sussex County Library, 1981. — 12p : ill ; 22cm. — (An East Sussex County Library brief history)
Cover title. — Bibliography: p12
ISBN 0-86147-028-1 (pbk) : £0.50 B81-26650

942.2′61 — West Sussex. Crawley, ***to 1914***

Crawley : Victorian new town / edited by John Lowerson. — Brighton : Centre for Continuing Education University of Sussex, c1980. — 44p : maps,1facsim ; 22cm. — (CCE occasional paper, ISSN 0306-1108 ; no.12)
Cover title
ISBN 0-904242-14-5 (pbk) : £0.90 B81-09417

942.2′610858′05 — West Sussex. Crawley — ***Serials***

The new Crawley observer. — Thursday Jan.22 1981-. — Crawley (12 The Boulevard, Crawley, Sussex RH10 1XY) : Sussex Express and County Herald, 1981-. — v. : ill,ports ; 42cm
Weekly. — Continues: Crawley & district observer
ISSN 0261-6181 = New Crawley observer : £0.12 B81-32288

942.2′62 — West Sussex. Chichester ***(District), to 1980***

The Story of the district / Chichester District Museum ; [illustrations by Susan J. England]. — [Chichester] ([29 Little London, Chichester PO19 1PB]) : [The Museum], [1981?]. — 15p : ill(some col.),maps,1col.plan,1col.port ; 21cm
£0.15 (unbound) B81-37214

942.2′62 — West Sussex. Chichester. Parks: Priory Park. Antiquities

McCann, Alison. A short history of Chichester Greyfriars and Priory Park / by Alison McCann and Timothy J. McCann. — [Chichester] ([29 Little London, Chichester PO19 1PB]) : Chichester District Museum, [1981?]. — [16]p : ill,2plans ; 22cm
Cover title
£0.40 (pbk) B81-37217

942.2′680858′05 — West Sussex. Worthing — ***Serials***

Worthing and district advertiser : for Worthing, Lancing, Sompting, Ferring and Findon. — No.1 (Wednesday May 13 1981)-. — Worthing (21 Chatsworth Rd, Worthing [W. Sussex] BN11 1NA) : Beckett Newspapers, 1981-. — v. : ill,ports ; 46cm
Weekly
ISSN 0261-6459 = Worthing and district advertiser : Unpriced B81-32202

942.2′680858′05 — West Sussex. Worthing — *Serials* *continuation*
Worthing gazette & herald. — No.3178 (Friday May 15 1981)-. — Worthing (21 Chatsworth Rd., Worthing, East Sussex) : Beckett Newspapers, 1981-. — v. : ill,ports ; 46cm
Weekly. — Merger of: Worthing gazette; and, Worthing herald
ISSN 0261-6122 = Worthing gazette & herald : £0.12 B81-32295

942.2′69 — West Sussex. Henfield, *1939-1946 — Readings from contemporary sources*
Bishop, Lucie. Henfield in battledress. — Henfield (Highfield, Henfield, West Sussex) : L. Bishop, Dec.1981. — [120]p
ISBN 0-9507841-0-9 (pbk) : £2.95 : CIP entry B81-34967

942.2′7′009734 — Hampshire. Villages, *to 1979*
Brode, Anthony. The Hampshire village book / Anthony Brode ; with illustrations by R.E. Gasman. — Newbury (3 Catherine Rd., Newbury, Berks.) : Countryside, 1980. — 185p : ill,1map ; 22cm
Bibliography: p180-181. — Includes index
ISBN 0-905392-06-x (pbk) : £3.95 B81-01726

942.2′725 — Hampshire. Aldershot, *to 1980*
Cole, Howard N.. The story of Aldershot : a history of the civil and military towns / by Howard N. Cole. — Updated & enl. ed. — Aldershot (4 Grosvenor Rd, Aldershot, Hants.) : Southern, Books, 1980. — xxx,480p,[128]p of plates : ill,maps,coats of arms,1facsim,ports ; 22cm
Previous ed.: Aldershot : Gale and Polden, 1951. — Bibliography: p461-463. — Includes index
ISBN 0-9507147-0-4 : Unpriced B81-08070

942.2′732 — Hampshire. Andover, *ca 1880-1980 — Illustrations*
Andover : seen and remembered / [compiled by] Edward Kendall & Derek Dine. — [Winchester] ([81 North Walls, Winchester, SO23 8BY]) : Hampshire Country Library, c1980. — 49p : chiefly ill,facsims ; 18x23cm
Bibliography: p49
ISBN 0-901406-04-x (corrected : pbk) : £2.15 B81-06669

942.2′732 — Hampshire. Andover — *History — Serials*
Lookback : official journal of the Andover Local History Society. — [No.1]. — Andover (c/o [Mr A.C. Raper] Andover Public Library, Chantry Way, Andover, Hants. SP10 1LT) : The Society, [1980]-. — v. : ill ; 21cm
Continues: Test Valley & Border anthology
ISSN 0144-5898 = Lookback : Unpriced B81-01392

942.2′7320858′05 — Hampshire. Test Valley *(District) — Serials*
The **Test** Valley advertiser. — [Issue 1 (1981)?]-. — Winchester (79 Parchment St., Winchester, Hampshire) : Test Valley advertiser, [1981?]-. — v. ; 46cm
Weekly. — Description based on: Issue 21 [(Thursday 21st May 1981)]
ISSN 0262-1924 = Test Valley advertiser : Unpriced B81-39518

942.2′735 — Hampshire. Winchester. Political events, *1642 — Correspondence, diaries, etc. — Facsimiles*
The **Kings** Majesties message to the inhabitants of the City of Winchester concerning the late battaile : also their answer to the aforesaid message : likewise a true relation of a famous victory obtained by the inhabitants of Manchester against the Lord Strange ... — Mount Durand : Toucan, 1981. — [8]p ; 21cm
ISBN 0-85694-243-x (pbk) : Unpriced B81-26843

942.2′735 — Hampshire. Winchester, *to 1979*
Turner, Barbara Carpenter. Winchester / by Barbara Carpenter Turner. — Southampton : Paul Cave, 1980. — xii,220p : ill(some col.),2maps,ports ; 26cm
Includes index
ISBN 0-86146-013-8 : £9.50 B81-11312

942.2′74 — Hampshire. Petersfield, *1515-1597*
Yates, E. M.. Petersfield in Tudor times / written for the Petersfield Area Historical Society ; by E.M. Yates. — Petersfield (c/o Mrs. D. Grainger, Maple Lodge, Tilmore Rd., Petersfield) : The Society, c1979. — 48p : ill,1map,1coat of arms,1facsim ; 21cm. — (Petersfield papers, ISSN 0308-9266 ; no.5)
Ill on inside covers. — Bibliography: p42
£1.50 (pbk) B81-13657

942.2′74 — Hampshire. Petersfield. Social life, *1660-1715*
Thomas, James H. (James Harry). Petersfield under the later Stuarts : an economic and social study / written for the Petersfield Area Historical Society by James H. Thomas. — Petersfield (c/o Mrs. J. Gard, 14 Lynton Rd, Petersfield) : Petersfield Area Historical Society, c1980. — 56p : ill,1map,facsims ; 22cm. — (Petersfield papers, ISSN 0308-9266 ; no.6)
Ill on inside covers
£1.50 (pbk) B81-09961

942.2′75 — Hampshire. Totton, *1837-1914*
Southgate, Michael. Old Tolton / by Michael Southgate. — Southampton : Paul Cave, 1979. — 56p : ill,ports ; 20cm
Ill on inside covers
ISBN 0-86146-006-5 (pbk) : Unpriced B81-08549

942.2′76 — Hampshire. Southampton. Buildings of historical importance, *to 1979*
Money, R. A.. Southampton town of antiquity / by R.A. Money. — Southampton : G.F Wilson, 1980. — 39p ; 21cm
ISBN 0-900810-28-9 (pbk) : Unpriced B81-22805

942.2′76 — Hampshire. Southampton. Woolston, *1900-1980 — Illustrations*
Focus on Woolston : a brief history of the area told in photographs covering the period 1900-1980 / [compiled] by Audrey Cleverley. — [Southampton] ([18 Longmore Ave., Woolston, Southampton SO2 9FZ]) : [A.J. Cleverley], 1981. — 62p : chiefly ill,1map,1coat of arms,facsims,ports ; 30cm
ISBN 0-9507584-0-x (pbk) : Unpriced B81-27181

942.2′76083 — Hampshire. Southampton. Social conditions, *1920-1929*
Gadd, Eric Wyeth. Southampton in the ′twenties / by Eric Wyeth Gadd. — Southampton : Cave Publications, 1979. — 72p : ill,ports ; 21cm
Ill, ports on inside covers
£1.00 (pbk) B81-34898

942.2′772 — Hampshire. Hedge End, *to 1979*
Blyth, Joyce B.. The changing face of Hedge End : Hampshire / by Joyce B. Blyth. — Hedge End (The Willows, Nursery Grove, Hedge End, Southampton) : J.B. Blyth
£1.20 (pbk) B81-27828

Blyth, Joyce B.. The changing face of Hedge End, Hampshire / Joyce B. Blyth. — Southampton (The Willows, Nursery Grove, Hedge End, Southampton [S03 4ND]) : J.B. Blyth
Pt.2. — 1981. — 28p : ill ; 26cm
Bibliography: p28
Unpriced (pbk) B81-32733

942.2′82 — Isle of Wight. Newport & Carisbrooke, *to 1979 — Illustrations*
Newport past & present / [compiled] by Timothy Blackmore & Ian Orton. — 2nd ed. — Newport, Isle of Wight (Parkhurst Rd., Newport, Isle of Wight PO30 5TX) : Isle of Wight County Library, 1980. — [60]p : col.ill,ports ; 15cm
Previous ed.: 1979
ISBN 0-906328-04-7 (pbk) : £1.45 B81-34897

942.2′91 — Berkshire. Thatcham, *to 1979*
Allen, Peter, *1948-*. A popular history of Thatcham / by Peter Allen. — [Thatcham] ([13 Elmhurst Rd., Thatcham, Berks. RG1 3DQ]) : [P. Allen], [1980]. — 127p,[12]p of plates : ill,1maps ; 22cm
Bibliography: p127
£3.00 (pbk) B81-10680

942.2′93 — Berkshire. Reading region, *to 1979*
Phillips, Daphne. The story of Reading : including Caversham, Tilehurst, Calcot, Earley and Woodley / Daphne Phillips. — Newbury (3 Catherine Rd., Newbury, Berks.) : Countryside Books, 1980. — 188p : ill,3maps,ports ; 22cm
Bibliography: p180-181. — Includes index
ISBN 0-905392-07-8 (pbk) : £3.95 B81-07678

942.2′96 — Berkshire. Cookham, *1800-1947*
Parkes, Roger. Alice Ray Morton′s Cookham : a Victorian view of Village, Rise and Dean / by Roger Parkes ; sketches redrawn by Vesla Stranger ; original notes and recollections discovered by The Cookham Society ; scrapbook and album recreated by Alan Walker. — Buckingham : Barracuda Books, c1981. — 120p : ill(some col.),col.maps,1facsim,ports ; 24cm
Ill on lining papers. — Includes index
ISBN 0-86023-145-3 : £9.95 B81-21914

942.2′96 — Berkshire. Datchet, *to 1980*
Gameson, F. H.. The changing village : a history of Datchet / Felix Gameson. — Datchet (Datchet, Berks.) : Manor Publishing, 1981. — 74p : ill,facsims,1port ; 21cm
ISBN 0-86290-001-8 (pbk) : Unpriced B81-28897

942.2′96 — Berkshire. Windsor, *1640-1660*
South, Raymond. Royal castle, rebel town : puritan Windsor in Civil War & Commonwealth / by Raymond South. — Buckingham : Barracuda, 1981. — 112p : ill,maps,coats of arms,facsim,ports ; 24cm
Ill on lining papers. — Includes index
ISBN 0-86023-131-3 : £8.95 B81-17636

942.2′96 — Berkshire. Windsor. Castles. Collegiate churches: Windsor Castle. *St. George′s Chapel.* **Organisations: Society of the Friends of St. George′s and the Descendants of the Knights of the Garter** *— Serials*
Society of the Friends of St. George′s and the Descendants of the Knights of the GarterReport of the Society of the Friends of St George′s and the Descendants of the Knights of the Garter. — Vol.6, no.1 (1979-1980). — [Windsor] ([The Curfew Tower, Windsor Castle, Windsor, Berks.)) : The Society, [1981]. — 40p
£0.50 (free to members) B81-17473

942.3 — South-west England. Antiquities, *to ca 1979*
Pearce, Susan M.. The archaeology of South West Britain / Susan M. Pearce. — London : Collins, 1981. — 287p : ill,maps ; 24cm. — (Collins archaeology)
Bibliography: p273-282. — Includes index
ISBN 0-00-216219-9 : £13.50 B81-29581

942.3 — South-west England. Buildings of historical importance, *1550-1750*
Brown, Patrick. Buildings of Britain 1550-1750 : South-West England. — Ashbourne : Moorland Publishing, Oct.1981. — [160]p
ISBN 0-86190-030-8 : £8.95 : CIP entry B81-28024

942.306 — England. Social conditions, *1580-1680*
Wrightson, Keith. English society, 1580-1680. — London : Hutchinson Education, Nov.1981. — [272]p. — (Hutchinson social history of England)
ISBN 0-09-145170-1 (cased) : £12.00 : CIP entry
ISBN 0-09-145171-x (pbk) : £5.95 B81-28794

942.3′1′005 — Wiltshire — *History — Serials*
The **Wiltshire** archaeological magazine. — Vols.70/71 (1975/1976)-. — Gloucester : Produced for the Society by Alan Sutton, 1978-. — v. ; 25cm
Annual. — Continues: The Wiltshire archaeological and natural history magazine. Part B, Archaeology and local history. — Description based on: Vols.72/73 (1977/1978)
ISSN 0309-3476 = Wiltshire archaeological magazine : Free to Society members
B81-01393

942.3'1081'088636 — Wiltshire. Shepherds. Social life, *1800-1900*

Hudson, W. H.. A shepherd's life / W.H. Hudson ; foreword by Phil Drabble. — London : Macdonald Futura, 1981. — 223p : maps,ports,facsims ; 27cm
Originally published: London : Methuen, 1910. — Maps on lining papers. — Includes index
ISBN 0-354-04650-0 : £9.95 B81-22085

942.3'13 — Wiltshire. Highworth, *to 1980*

A **History** of Highworth. — Highworth : Highworth Historical Society, [1980?]
Pt. 1. — Highworth : Highworth Historical Society, [1980?]. — 148p,[1]leaf of plates : ill,maps,ports ; 30cm
ISBN 0-9507355-1-5 (pbk) : Unpriced
ISBN 0-9507355-0-7 (set) : Unpriced
B81-40371

942.3'13 — Wiltshire. South Marston. Social life, *ca 1885-ca 1900 - Personal observations*

Williams, Alfred. In a Wiltshire village. — Gloucester : Alan Sutton, Sept.1981. — [192]p
ISBN 0-904387-62-3 (pbk) : £3.95 : CIP entry
B81-20570

942.3'13 — Wiltshire. Swindon. Social life, *1930-1940 — Childhood reminiscences*

Ausden, Ken. Up the crossing / Ken Ausden ; illustrated by Phillida Gili. — London : British Broadcasting Corporation, 1981. — 237p : ill ; 22cm
ISBN 0-563-17902-3 : £6.50 B81-22762

942.3'15 — Wiltshire. Bradford-on-Avon, *to 1980*

Niblett, Bertram Sidney. Memories of Bradford-on-Avon / by Bertram Sidney Niblett. — Trowbridge ([Bythesea Rd., Trowbridge, Wiltshire]) : Wiltshire Library & Museum Service, 1981. — ill,1port ; 21cm
ISBN 0-86080-077-6 (pbk) : £2.00 B81-26472

942.3'15 — Wiltshire. Trowbridge — *Serials*

Trowbridge star. — 1 (Wednesday 1 April 1981)-. — Trowbridge (15 Duke Street, Trowbridge, Wiltshire) : B. Lansdown, 1981-. — v. : ill,ports ; 42cm
Weekly
ISSN 0261-6092 = Trowbridge star : Unpriced
B81-32297

942.3'17 — Wiltshire. Seend, *to 1980*

Bradby, Edward. Seend : a Wiltshire village past and present. — Gloucester : Alan Sutton, Nov.1981. — [256]p
ISBN 0-904387-74-7 (cased) : £6.95 : CIP entry
ISBN 0-904387-81-x (pbk) : £3.95 B81-32590

942.3'3 — Dorset, *to 1979*

Cullingford, Cecil N.. A history of Dorset / Cecil N. Cullingford ; drawings by Ralph Sharpe ; cartography by John Britton. — London : Phillimore, 1980. — 128p,[24]p of plates : ill (some col.),facsims(some col.),maps,ports ; 26cm. — (The Darwen county history series)
Bibliography: p123-124. — Includes index
ISBN 0-85033-255-9 : £6.95 B81-01921

942.3'3084'0924 — Dorset, *ca 1930-1945 — Childhood reminiscences*

Barnes, Tim. My Dorset days / Tim Barnes. — Sherborne : Dorset Publishing, 1980. — 80p : ill,1port ; 21cm
ISBN 0-902129-37-6 (pbk) : £2.20 B81-17811

942.3'31 — Dorset. Piddle Valley. Social life, *to 1979*

The **Piddle** Valley book of country life / edited by Muriel Pike ; flower drawings by Elizabeth Bairstow, other illustrations by Caroline Pike. — London : Hutchinson, 1980. — 159p : ill,music ; 23cm
ISBN 0-09-142520-4 : £4.95 : CIP rev.
B80-13650

942.3'31 — Dorset. Sherborne. Social life, *1901-1950 — Personal observations*

Fudge, Dorothy. Sands of time : the autobiography of Dorothy Fudge / edited by Frank Alcock. — [Wimborne] ([23, Beaucroft La., Colehill, Wimborne, Dorset BH21 2PE]) : [Word and Action], [1981]. — 39p : ill,1facsim,ports ; 21cm
Facsim. on inside covers
ISBN 0-904939-27-8 (pbk) : Unpriced
B81-20826

942.3'31 — Dorset. Sherborne, *to 1980*

Gibb, J. H. P.. The book of Sherborne / by J.H.P. Gibb. — Buckingham : Barracuda, 1981. — 144p : ill,maps,facsims,plans,ports ; 27cm
Maps on lining papers. — Bibliography: p139. — Includes index
ISBN 0-86023-081-3 : £12.50 B81-33675

942.3'31 — Dorset. Trent. Social conditions — *For environment planning*

Trent study : planning for change in a rural community / a comprehensive rural study and management programme commissioned by the Ernest Cook Trust and undertaken by Graham Moss Associates. — Richmond : Graham Moss Associates, 1980. — viii,119p : ill,maps,facsims,plans ; 21x30cm
Unpriced (pbk) B81-09445

942.3'32 — Dorset. West Stour, *to 1980*

Ash, John, *1906-*. West Stour in Dorset : a journey through the centuries / by John Ash. — West Stour (West Stour, Dorset SP8 5RL) : J. Ash, c1980. — xiii,162p : ill,1map,ports ; 21cm
Map on folded sheet attached to cover. — Bibliography: p162. — Includes index
ISBN 0-9506956-0-2 (pbk) : £3.50 B81-05609

942.3'36 — Dorset. Brownsea Island, *1890-1935 — Illustrations*

Memories of old Poole / compiled from postcards of Poole and district by Andrew Hawkes. — Poole (99 High St., Poole, Dorset BH15 1AP) : A. Hawkes, 1981. — p220-235 : chiefly ill ; 21cm
Cover title: Brownsea Island. — Includes index
ISBN 0-9506404-6-8 (pbk) : £1.35 B81-29701

942.3'37 — Dorset. Poole. Sandbanks, *1900-1930 — Illustrations*

Memories of old Poole / compiled from postcards of Poole by Andrew Hawkes. — Poole (99 High St., Poole, Dorset, BH15 1AP), A.D. Hawkes, 1980. — 186-216p : chiefly ill ; 21cm
Cover title: Sandbanks. — Includes index
ISBN 0-9506404-5-x (pbk) : £1.45 B81-08290

942.3'38 — Dorset. Bournemouth. Talbot Village, *to 1975*

Gillett, Mildred. Wanderings in Talbot village : a study of philanthropy in the mid-nineteenth century / by Mildred Gillett. — 3rd ed. — Bournemouth ([Teachers' Centre, 40 Lowther Rd., Bournemouth]) : Bournemouth Local Studies Publications, 1981. — 34p : ill,maps ; 21cm
Previous ed. i.e. Rev. ed.: 1978
ISBN 0-906287-29-4 (pbk) : £0.50 B81-10729

942.3'38081 — Dorset. Bournemouth. Residents & visitors, *1800-1920*

Popham, Rita M.. They came to Bournemouth : some famous residents and visitors / by Rita M. Popham. — Bournemouth (The Teachers' Centre, 40 Lowther Rd., Bournemouth [Dorset]) : Bournemouth Local Studies Publications, 1981. — 44p : ill,2ports ; 21cm
Includes index. — Publisher's no.: 660
ISBN 0-906287-36-7 (pbk) : £0.50 B81-33119

942.3'38082 — Dorset. Bournemouth, *1902-1905*

Parsons, J. F.. County Borough of Bournemouth, Beale mayor 1902-1905 / by J.F. Parsons. — Bournemouth (Teachers' Centre, 40 Lowther Rd., Bournemouth) : Bournemouth Local Studies Publications, 1981. — 51p : ill ; 22cm. — (J.E. Beale and the growth of Bournemouth ; pt.2)
Bibliography: p51
ISBN 0-906287-33-2 (pbk) : £0.50 B81-18935

942.3'41 — Jersey, *to 1980*

Croad, George W.. A Jersey album / by George W. Croad ; with a foreword by Sir Martin Le Quesne. — [St Brelade's Bay] ([The Close, St Brelade's Bay, Jersey]) : [G.W. Croad], [1981]. — xxvi,237p,[68]p of plates : ill(some col.),facsims,ports,(some col.)geneal.tables ; 27cm
Facsims on lining papers. — Includes index
B81-34435

942.3'41073 — Jersey. Invasion by French military forces, *1781*

Mayne, Richard, *1929-*. The battle of Jersey / by Richard Mayne. — London : Phillimore, 1981. — xii,116p,[21]p of plates : ill(some col.),maps,1facsim,ports ; 26cm
Maps on lining papers. — Includes index
ISBN 0-85033-381-4 : £8.95 B81-19372

942.3'42084'0924 — Guernsey. Social life, *1940-1945 — Personal observations*

Roussel, Leslie E.. Evacuation / Leslie E. Roussel. — Bognor Regis : New Horizon, c1980. — 108p ; 21cm
ISBN 0-86116-441-5 : £3.50 B81-21724

942.3'5 — Devon, *to 1979.* **Archaeological sources**

Archaeology of the Devon landscape : essays on Devon's archaeological heritage / by Peter Beacham ... [et al.]. — Exeter (County Hall, Topsham Rd., Exeter EX2 4QH) : County Planning Department, Devon County Council, c1980. — 142p : ill,maps,plans ; 24cm
Bibliography: p140-141
ISBN 0-86114-286-1 (pbk) : £2.00 B81-29892

942.3'5 — Devon, *to 1981*

My Devon / Hugh Caradon ... [et al.]. — Bodmin : Bossiney, 1981. — 104p : ill ; 21cm
ISBN 0-906456-56-8 (pbk) : £1.95 B81-39062

942.3'5'005 — Devon — *History — Serials*

[Report and transactions *(Devonshire Association for the Advancement of Science, Literature and Art)*]. Report and transactions / the Devonshire Association for the Advancement of Science, Literature and Art. — Vol.112 (1980). — Exeter (7 The Close, Exeter EX1 1EZ) : The Association, 1980. — xxix,280p
ISSN 0309-7994 : £5.00 B81-10555

942.3'5'00946 — Devon. Coastal regions, *to 1979*

Coastlines of Devon. — Exeter (County Hall, Exeter EX2 4QH) : Devon County Council, Planning Department, 1980. — 113p : ill,1map ; 23cm
Cover title. — Includes bibliographies
ISBN 0-86114-282-9 (pbk) : £1.75 B81-04047

942.3'5081'0222 — Devon. Social life, *1845-1914 — Illustrations*

Victorian and Edwardian Devon from old photographs / introduction and commentaries by Brian Chugg. — London : Batsford, 1975 (1979 [printing]). — [128]p : ill,ports ; 25cm
ISBN 0-7134-2113-4 (pbk) : £3.50 B81-02258

942.3'52 — Devon. Barnstaple, *ca 1860-ca 1960 — Illustrations*

Barnstaple yesterday : over 160 photographs of Barnstaple from 1860's onwards / [compiled] by Julia & Jonathan Baxter. — [Bristol] (Feeder Rd., Bristol BS2 3TJ) : H.J. Chard, c1980. — [91]p : chiefly ill,1map,facsims,ports ; 25cm
ISBN 0-9507330-0-8 (pbk) : £2.75 B81-06870

942.3'52 — Devon. Lynton & Lynmouth, *1850-1980*

Delderfield, Eric R.. The book of Lynton & Lynmouth : a brief history of the romantic villages with illustrations and maps / by Eric Delderfield. — Exmouth : ERD, 1981. — 59p : ill,3maps ; 19cm
ISBN 0-900345-34-9 (pbk) : £0.60 B81-21741

942.3'52'009734 — North Devon. Rural regions — *Illustrations*

Ravilious, James. The heart of the country / James & Robin Ravilious ; with a foreword by Ronald Blythe. — London : Scolar, 1980. — [127]p : ill,ports ; 28cm
ISBN 0-85967-590-4 (cased) : £10.95 : CIP rev.
ISBN 0-85967-627-7 (pbk) : £5.95 B80-10911

942.3′56′0810222 — Devon. Exeter, *ca 1880-ca 1935* **—** *Illustrations*

Old Exeter. — 2nd ed. — Exeter : Webb and Bower, Nov.1981. — [176]p
Previous ed.: Plymouth : Baron Jay Ltd, 1977
ISBN 0-906671-66-3 : £7.95 : CIP entry
B81-34209

942.3′57 — Devon. Sidmouth. Fishing communities. Social life, *1900-1905* **—** *Personal observations*

Reynolds, Stephen. A poor man′s house / by Stephen Reynolds. — [London] : London Magazine Editions, 1980. — xvi,320p ; 18cm
Originally published: London : Macmillan, 1908
ISBN 0-904388-35-2 : £5.50 B81-26668

942.3′7 — Cornwall. Castles, *to 1979*

Price, Mary, *1946-*. Castles of Cornwall / Mary & Hal Price. — Bodmin : Bossiney, 1980. — 117p : ill,1 map,ports ; 22cm
ISBN 0-906456-46-0 (cased) : £3.75
ISBN 0-906456-47-9 (pbk) : £1.75 B81-03921

942.3′7 — Cornwall, *to 1980*

Du Maurier, Daphne. Vanishing Cornwall / Daphne du Maurier ; photographs by Christian Browning. — [New] ed. — London : Gollancz, 1981. — 208p : ill(some col.),1col.map,col.ports ; 26cm
Previous ed.: 1967. — Bibliography: p208
ISBN 0-575-02844-0 : £7.50 B81-24177

942.3′7085′0924 — Cornwall. Prynn, Edward — *Biographies*

Prynn, Edward. A boy in hob-nailed boots : the story of his life, part 1 / Edward Prynn ; edited by Jo Park. — Padstow (11 Church) : Tabb House, 1981. — 78p,[16]p of plates : ill,ports ; 21cm
ISBN 0-907018-07-6 (pbk) : £2.95 B81-34424

942.3′7′08570924 — Cornwall. Rural regions. Social life — *Personal observations*

Tangye, Derek. Sun on the lintel. — Large print ed. — Bath : Chivers, Jan.1982. — [312]p. — (A New Portway large print book)
Originally published: London : Michael Joseph, 1976
ISBN 0-85119-152-5 : £5.35 : CIP entry
B81-33814

942.3′71 — Cornwall. Launceston, *to 1980*

Rendell, Joan. Gateway to Cornwall / Joan Rendell. — St. Teath : Bossiney, 1981. — 104p : ill,2facsims,ports ; 21cm
ISBN 0-906456-48-7 (pbk) : £1.50 B81-15309

942.3′78 — Cornwall. Carrick *(District).* **Roseland,** *to 1977*

O′Toole, Laurence. The Roseland : between river and sea / Laurence O′Toole. — Padstow : Lodenek, 1978. — 173p : ill,2maps,facsims ; 26cm
Bibliography: p173
ISBN 0-902899-71-6 (cased) : Unpriced
ISBN 0-902899-70-8 (pbk) : £3.75 B81-25905

942.3′81 — Somerset. Axbridge region — *History — Serials*

[Journal *(Axbridge Archaeological and Local History Society)*]. Journal / Axbridge Archaeological and Local History Society. — [No.1] (1978)-. — Axbridge (King John′s Hunting Lodge Museum, The Square, Axbridge, Somerset) : The Society, 1978-. — v. : ill ; 27cm
Irregular. — Continues in part: Journal (Axbridge Caving Group and Archaeological Society)
Unpriced B81-05681

942.3′83 — Somerset. Frome, *to 1976*

McGarvie, Michael. The book of Frome : a history / by Michael McGarvie. — Basingstoke : Barracuda, 1980. — 147p : ill,maps,facsims,plans,ports,geneal.table ; 27cm
Map on lining papers. — Bibliography: p143-144. — Includes index
ISBN 0-86023-097-x : £11.50 B81-04072

942.3′83 — Somerset. Glastonbury. Abbeys: Glastonbury Abbey, *to ca 1140* **—** *Early works*

William, *of Malmesbury*. [De antiquitate Glastonie Ecclesie. English]. The early history of Glastonbury. — Woodbridge : Boydell & Brewer, Oct.1981. — [256]p
Translation of: De antiquitate Glastonie Ecclesie
ISBN 0-85115-154-x : £20.00 : CIP entry
B81-25748

942.3′83 — Somerset. Mendip region. Buildings of historical importance

Reid, R. D.. Some buildings of Mendip / R.D. Reid. — [Winscombe] : [Mendip Society] ; [Bristol] ([14 Downy Sq., Bristol 8]) : [Distributed by Radcliffe Press], [1979]. — x,67p : ill(some col.),map ; 25cm
Includes index
ISBN 0-905459-16-4 (pbk) : Unpriced
B81-30014

942.3′87 — Somerset. Bishops Lydeard, *to 1981*

Discovering Bishops Lydeard. — [Bishops Lydeard] ([Stones Turow, Bishops Lydeard, Taunton]) : [D. Smith], [1981]. — 20p : ill,map ; 22cm
Text on inside covers
£0.40 (pbk) B81-38393

942.3′89 — Somerset. Langport, *to 1921*

Warbis, A. T.. A short history of Langport / by A.T. Warbis. — St Peter Port : Toucan, 1981. — p165-188 : ill ; 26cm. — (Ilchester and district occasional papers, ISSN 0306-6010 ; no.27)
Facsim of: edition published Yeovil : s.n., 1922
ISBN 0-85694-185-9 (unbound) : Unpriced
B81-39035

942.3′9′005 — Avon. Local history — *Serials*

Avon past : the joint journal of Avon Archaeological Council and Avon Local History Association. — Issue no.1 (Oct.1979)-. — Bristol (c/o Mrs. L. Hamid, ′Avon Past′, Avon Community Council, 209 Redland Rd, Bristol 6) : The Archaeological Council, 1979-. — v. : ill ; 21cm
Two issues yearly. — Merger of: Newsletter (Avon Archaeological Council); and, Newsletter (Avon Local History Association). — Description based on: Issue no.3 (Autumn 1980)
ISSN 0260-2954 = Avon past : £2.00 per year
B81-14366

942.3′9′009734 — Avon. Villages. Social conditions

Village life in Avon : a study of Winford, Wickwar, Hinton Blewett and Timsbury / [Working Group on Village Community Life]. — Bristol (P.O. Box 11, Avon House, The Haymarket, Bristol BS99 7DE) : Avon County Council Public Relations Department, [1981]. — 44p : ill,1 col.map,plans ; 20x21cm
ISBN 0-86063-114-1 (pbk) : £1.50 B81-23295

942.3′91 — Avon. Filton, *to 1980*

Harris, W. L.. Filton, Gloucestershire : some account of the village and parish / by W.L. Harris. — [Bristol] (42 Gloucester Road North, Filton Park, Bristol) : W.L. and L.N. Harris, c1981. — 318p : ill,1map,facsims,ports,1geneal.table ; 23cm
Includes index
ISBN 0-9507387-0-0 : £8.50 B81-27819

942.3′93 — Avon. Avonmouth, *to 1981*

Thomas, Ethel. Down the ′mouth : a history of Avonmouth / Ethel Thomas. — New ed. — Bristol (55 Cook St., Avonmouth, Bristol BS11 9JY) : E. Thomas, 1981. — 128p : ill,1map,ports ; 23cm
Previous ed.: 1977. — Includes index
ISBN 0-9507477-0-x : £5.50 B81-40826

942.3′93 — Avon. Bristol. Hospitals: St. Bartholomew′s Hospital *(Bristol),* **to 1530. Excavation of remains**

Price, Roger, *19---*. Excavations at St. Bartholomew′s Hospital Bristol / Roger Price. — Bristol (14 Dowry Sq., Bristol 8) : Published for the Bristol Threatened History Society by Redcliffe, 1979. — 24p : ill,plans ; 21cm
Bibliography: p24
ISBN 0-905459-20-2 (pbk) : £0.70 B81-10786

942.3′930855′0222 — Avon. Bristol, *1953-1956* **—** *Illustrations*

Winstone, Reece. Bristol as it was 1953-1956 / the photographs taken and collected by, and the book written, designed and published by Reece Winstone. — 2nd ed. — Bristol (23 Hyland Grove, Bristol 9) : R. Winstone, 1979. — 68p : chiefly ill,ports ; 26cm
Previous ed.: 1969. — Includes index
ISBN 0-900814-56-x : £5.80 B81-08069

942.3′98 — Avon. Bath. Country houses: Bailbrook, *to 1978*

Little, Bryan. Bailbrook. — Southall (Aeradio House, Hayes Rd., Southall, Middx.) : IAL, c1979. — 37p : ill(some col.),col.coat of arms,facsims,plan,ports ; 17x22cm
Author: Bryan Little. — Limited ed
ISBN 0-906452-01-5 : Unpriced B81-18845

942.3′98 — Avon. Bath. Social life, *1680-1850*

Neale, R.S.. Bath 1680-1850 : a social history, or, a valley of pleasure, yet a sink of iniquity / R.S. Neale. — London : Routledge & Kegan Paul, 1981. — xiv,466p : ill,maps,facsims,ports ; 23cm
Map on lining papers. — Includes index
ISBN 0-7100-0639-x : £18.00 : CIP rev.
B81-06591

942.3′980858′05 — Avon. Bath — *Serials*

[Bath herald *(Bath : 1980)*]. Bath herald. — No.1 (Friday Oct.3 1980)-. — Bath (34 Westgate St., Bath BA1 1EW) : [Wessex Newspapers Ltd.], 1980-. — v. : ill ; 44cm
Weekly. — Continues: Bath weekly chronicle. — Description based on: No.14 (Friday, Jan.2 1981)
ISSN 0261-1937 = Bath herald (Bath. 1980) : Unpriced B81-16819

942.4′083′0924 — England. Midlands. Agricultural industries. Farms. Social life, *ca 1905-ca 1925* **—** *Personal observations*

Waine, M. E.. All our own horses / by M.E. Waine. — Wolverhampton (Mount Pleasant, Beamish La., Albrighton, Wolverhampton WV7 3JJ) : Mooley, 1981. — 68p : ill ; 22cm
Unpriced B81-20795

942.4′1 — Gloucestershire. Country houses owned by British royal families, *to 1980*

Samders, Geoffrey. Royal homes in Gloucestershire. — Gloucester (17a Brunswick Rd., Gloucester, GL1 1HG) : Alan Sutton, June 1981. — [36]p
ISBN 0-904387-89-5 (pbk) : £1.95 : CIP entry
B81-19122

942.4′1′005 — Gloucestershire. Local history — *Serials*

Gloucestershire local history newsletter / Gloucestershire Community Council. — No.1 (Autumn 1979) ; No.1 (Autumn 1980)-. — Gloucester (Community House, 15 College Green, Gloucester GL1 2LZ) : The Council, 1980. — v. ; 33cm
Two issues yearly. — Supplement to: Local history bulletin (Gloucestershire. Community Council). — Introductory no., called no.1, issued Autumn 1979
ISSN 0260-5139 = Gloucestershire local history newsletter : Unpriced B81-04540

942.4′107′0924 — Gloucestershire. Social life, *1783-1854* **—** *Personal observations — Correspondence, diaries, etc.*

Witts, F. E.. The diary of a Cotswold parson / [F.E. Witts] ; chosen, edited and introduced by David Verey. — Gloucester (17a Brunswick Rd., Gloucester GL1 1HG) : Alan Sutton, 1978 (1980 printing). — 189p : ill,1map,1facsim,ports,1geneal.table ; 22cm
Text and map on inside covers. — Includes index
ISBN 0-904387-33-x (cased) : Unpriced
ISBN 0-904387-19-4 B81-21287

942.4′14 — Gloucestershire. Gloucester. City walls. Gates: East Gate, *to 1980*

Heighway, Carolyn M.. The East Gate of Gloucester / by Carolyn Heighway. — [Gloucester] ([Brunswick Rd., Gloucester]) : Gloucester City Museum and Gloucester Civic Trust, c1980. — 127p,[4]p of plates : ill,plans ; 21cm
Text on covers. — Bibliography: [1]p
£0.75 (pbk) B81-06475

942.4'16 — Gloucestershire. Cheltenham, *to 1980*

Hart, Gwen. A history of Cheltenham. — 2nd ed. — Gloucester : Alan Sutton, Nov.1981. — [352]p
Previous ed.: 1965
ISBN 0-904387-87-9 : £12.00 : CIP entry
B81-32589

942.4'17 — England. Northern Cotswolds — *Serials*

North Cotswold standard : Bourton on the Water, Stow on the Wold, Moreton in the March, Chipping Norton, Chipping Campden. — Wednesday, June 10, 1981-. — [Stow-on-the-Wold] ([2 Digbeth St., Stow-on-the-Wold, Glos.]) : Cirencester Newspaper Co., 1981-. — v. : ill,ports ; 40cm
Weekly
ISSN 0262-169x = North Cotswold standard : Unpriced B81-39533

942.4'19 — Gloucestershire. Cam, *1870-ca 1960* **& Dursley,** *1870-ca 1960 — Illustrations*

Dursley & Cam. — Gloucester : Alan Sutton, Nov.1981. — [128]p
ISBN 0-904387-88-7 (pbk) : £3.95 : CIP entry
B81-32591

942.4'19 — Gloucestershire. Eastcombe, *to 1980*

Lambert, M. D.. The unknown Cotswold village : Eastcombe 1500-1980 / M.D. Lambert and Juliet Shipman with contributions by Linda Hall and F.T. Hammond. — Eastcombe (The Yews, Eastcombe, Stroud, Glos.) : M.D. Lambert, 1981. — 62p : ill,maps,facsims,plans,ports,1geneal.table ; 28cm
ISBN 0-7049-0491-8 (pbk) : Unpriced
B81-28448

942.4'4'005 — Hereford and Worcester. Herefordshire — *History — Serials*

Transactions of the Woolhope Naturalists' Field Club, Herefordshire. — Vol.43, Part 1 (1979). — Hereford (40 Stanhope St., Hereford) : The Club, 1979. — 83p
Unpriced B81-10250

942.4'41 — Hereford and Worcester. Bewdley, *to 1977*

Marsh, Jean, *1897-*. Bewdley : a Cxv sanctuary town / Jean Marsh ; edited and produced by Harold Parsons. — Stourbridge (1 Cedar Gardens, Kinver, Stourbridge) : Halmar, 1979. — 24p : ill,map ; 22cm
ISBN 0-9502565-2-8 (pbk) : £0.80 B81-29279

942.4'44 — Hereford and Worcester. Leominster *(District).* **Kington** *— History — Serials*

[Papers *(Kington History Society)*]. Papers / Kington History Society. — 1977-1978-. — Kington (c/o Mr. R.J. Jenkins, [5 Wishlades Row, Kington, Herefordshire]) : The Society, 1978-. — v. ; 30cm
Annual. — Description based on : 1978-1979 issue
ISSN 0260-583x = Papers — Kington History Society : £0.60 (free to Society members)
B81-04757

942.4'45 — Hereford and Worcester. Ross-on-Wye region. Agricultural industries. Farms. Social life, *1796-1797 — Diaries*

Hughes, Anne. Anne Hughes, her boke / edited by Mollie Preston ; introduced by Michael Croucher ; linocuts by Tony Evora. — London : Folio Society, 1981. — 176p : ill ; 20cm
Originally published: in the Farmers weekly. 1937. — In a slip case
£7.25 B81-31968

942.4'47 — Hereford and Worcester. Whitbourne, *to 1978*

Williams, Phyllis. Whitbourne : a bishop's manor / Phyllis Williams. — Whitbourne (Hamish Park, Whitbourne, Herts.) : P. Williams, 1979. — xii,186p,[76]p of plates : ill,maps,facsims,ports ; 24cm
Includes index
ISBN 0-9506853-0-5 (pbk) : Unpriced
B81-09381

942.4'48 — Church of England. *Diocese of Worcester.* **Ecclesiastical estates. Social conditions,** *680-1540*

Dyer, Christopher. Lords and peasants in a changing society : the estates to the Bishopric of Worcester, 680-1540 / Christopher Dyer. — Cambridge : Cambridge University Press, 1980. — xiv,427p : ill,maps ; 23cm. — (Past and present publications)
Bibliography: p390-412. - Includes index
ISBN 0-521-22618-x : £22.50 B81-08283

942.4'49 — Hereford and Worcester. Ashton-under-Hill. Social life, *1911*

Archer, Fred, *1915-*. When Adam was a boy. — London : Hodder & Stoughton, Sept.1981. — [224]p. — (Coronet books)
Originally published: London : Hodder & Stoughton, 1979
ISBN 0-340-27104-3 (pbk) : £1.50 : CIP entry
B81-22537

942.4'5 — Shropshire, *to 1980*

Bailey, Brian J.. Portrait of Shropshire / by Brian J. Bailey. — London : Hale, 1981. — 175p,[24]p of plates : ill,1map ; 23cm
Bibliography: p159-160. — Includes index
ISBN 0-7091-9340-8 : £7.95 B81-40932

942.4'53 — Shropshire. Baschurch, *1980*

Baschurch Domesday book 1980. — [Shrewsbury] ([Linley, Church Rd., Baschurch, Shrewsbury, Shropshire SY4 2EE]) : [Baschurch Women's Institute], [1980]. — 36p,folded leaf : 1plan ; 26cm
Limited ed. of 250 copies. — Cover title
£1.00 (pbk) B81-40709

942.4'53 — Shropshire. Myddle. Social life, *1634-1700 — Early works*

Gough, Richard. [Human nature displayed in the history of Myddle]. The history of Myddle / Richard Gough ; edited with an introduction and notes by David Hey. — Harmondsworth : Penguin, 1981. — 224p : 1map,facsims,plans ; 20cm
Originally published: London : s.n., 1834
ISBN 0-14-005841-9 (pbk) : £2.50 B81-11528

942.4'53 — Shropshire. Myddle. Social life, *1642-1699*

Gough, Richard. [Human nature displayed in the history of Myddle]. The history of Myddle / Richard Gough. — London : Macdonald Futura, 1981, c1979. — xxxvii,213p : 1map ; 18cm. — (Heritage)
Originally published: as Human nature displayed in the history of Myddle. London : s.n., 1834. — Includes index
ISBN 0-7088-2072-7 (pbk) : £1.60 B81-33212

942.4'54 — Shropshire. Shrewsbury, *ca1860-1935 compared with* **Shrewsbury,** *1978-1981 — Illustrations*

The Changing face of Shrewsbury : second series : a second selection of old photographs and their modern counterparts which appeared in the Shrewsbury chronicle between 1978 and 1981. — Shrewsbury : Shrewsbury Chronicle, 1981. — [84]p : chiefly ill ; 18x23cm
ISBN 0-903802-16-3 (pbk) : £2.00 B81-37340

942.4'57 — Shropshire. Ludlow, *1860-1920 — Illustrations*

Webb, BillA Ludlow album : a collection of old photographs / compiled by Bill Webb. — Shrewsbury (7 London Rd., Shrewsbury) : Shropshire Libraries, 1981. — [68]p : chiefly ill ; 18x23cm
ISBN 0-903802-15-5 (pbk) : £2.20 B81-26569

942.4'57 — Shropshire. Ludlow. Broad Street, *to 1979*

Lloyd, David, *1935-*. Broad Street : its houses and residents through eight centuries / by David Lloyd ; with illustrations by Stanley Woolston ; Foreword by Alec Clifton-Taylor. — Birmingham (58 Lower Tower St., Birmingham B19 3NE) : Studio Press, 1979. — 71p : ill,maps,facsims,plans ; 30cm. — (Ludlow research paper, ISSN 0142-4548 ; no.3)
Plan on inside cover. — Includes index
Unpriced (pbk) B81-05406

942.4'62 — Staffordshire. Ashley, *to ca 1900*

Ashley : a history / edited by Tony Lancaster. — [Market Drayton] ([c/o Mrs J.M. Butcher, Whirlow, Chapel La., Hookgate, Market Drayton, Shropshire]) : [Ashley Local History Society], [1981]. — 54p : ill,1 map ; 22cm
Includes index
Unpriced (pbk) B81-17784

942.4'62 — Staffordshire. Betley, *to 1980*

Betley : a village of contrasts / edited by Robert Speake. — Keele (The University, Keele, Staffs. ST5 5BG) : Department of Adult Education, [University of Keele], 1980. — 225,[20]p of plates : ill,maps,facsims,plans,forms,ports,geneal.tables ; 22cm. — (Department of Adult Education, University of Keele local history publications. Series no.3, ISSN 0144-140x)
Includes index
£3.95 (pbk) B81-23360

942.4'63 — Staffordshire. Stoke-on-Trent. Abbeys: Hulton Abbey. Excavation of remains, *1960-1980*

Hulton Abbey, Stoke-on-Trent : history. — [S.l] : [S.n], [1981?]. — 3p : 1plan ; 21cm + 1plan (33x21cm folded to 21x17cm)
£0.02 (unbound) B81-37074

942.4'6307'0222 — Staffordshire. Stoke-on-Trent, *ca 1750-1978 — Illustrations*

Warrillow, Ernest J. D.. A lantern lecture on Stoke-on-Trent / by Ernest J.D. Warrillow ; with 133 illustrations by and from the author's collection of photographs. — Stoke-on-Trent (c/o Students' Bookshops, Raymond St., Shelton, Stoke-on-Trent ST1 4DP) : Etruscan Publications, c1980. — 278p : ill(some col),1map,1plan,2col ports ; 30cm
£12.75 B81-03575

942.4'64 — Staffordshire. Stafford. Parish churches: St. Bertelin's *(Church : Stafford),* **St. Chad's** *(Church : Stafford)* **& St. Mary's** *(Church : Stafford), to 1980*

Three Stafford churches. — [Stafford] ([P.O. Box 11, County Buildings, Martin St., Stafford ST16 2LH]) : Staffordshire County Council, [1980]. — 44p : ill,plans ; 30cm. — (Local history source book / Staffordshire County Council Education Department, ISSN 0306-5820 ; L.39)
Unpriced (pbk) B81-13358

942.4'640858'05 — Staffordshire. Stafford *(District) — Serials*

Stafford & Stone trader. — No.1 (Thursday May 21 1981)-. — Wolverhampton (Queen St., Wolverhampton) : Express and Star, 1981-. — v. : ill,ports ; 45cm
Weekly
ISSN 0261-6084 = Stafford & Stone trader : Unpriced B81-32298

942.4'65 — Staffordshire. Uttoxeter region — *Serials*

[**Staffordshire post** *(Uttoxeter)*]. Staffordshire post : for Uttoxeter, Cheadle and districts. — Issue no.1-. — Uttoxeter (5 The Square, Uttoxeter) : [Glenn Publications], [1979]-. — v. : ill ; 42cm
Fortnightly. — Continues: Uttoxeter and Ashbourne promotor. — Description based on: Issue no.22
ISSN 0144-8315 = Staffordshire post (Uttoxeter) : Free B81-02039

942.4'66 — Staffordshire. Brewood, *to 1958*

Greenslade, M. W.. A history of Brewood / by M.W. Greenslade & L. Margaret Midgley. — Stafford (Friars Terrace, Stafford, ST17 4AY) : Staffordshire County Library, 1981. — p.18-48 : ill,plans ; 30cm
Originally published in The Victoria history of the county of Stafford, vol.5, edited by L. Margaret Midgley : Oxford : Oxford University Press for the University of London Institute of Historical Research, 1959
ISBN 0-903363-09-7 (pbk) : £1.00 B81-17799

942.4'87 — Warwickshire. Kenilworth, *1826-1979*

Drew, John H.. Yesterday's town : Kenilworth : a town built around a castle / by John H. Drew. — Buckingham : Barracuda, 1980. — 128p : ill,facsims,plans,ports ; 27cm
Ill. on lining papers. — Also published in a numbered ed. — Includes index
ISBN 0-86023-103-8 : £10.50 B81-05620

942.4'87 — Warwickshire. Leamington Spa. Social life, *1890-1979 — Personal observations — Collections*

More looking back : a collection of memories of Leamington / by members and friends of the Leamington Literary Society. — [Leamington Spa] ([Hon. Sec., 3 Guyscliff Rd., Leamington Spa CV32 5BZ]) : Leamington Literary Society, c1980. — vii,181p,[1] leaf of plates : ill,maps,ports ; 23cm
ISBN 0-9507175-1-7 : Unpriced
ISBN 0-9507175-0-9 B81-06987

942.4'89 — Warwickshire. Stratford-upon-Avon. Social life, *1878-1920 — Personal observations*

Hewins, George. The Dillen : memories of a man of Stratford-Upon-Avon / edited by Angela Hewins. — London : Elm Tree, 1981. — xi,180p : ill,1plan,ports,1geneal.table ; 24cm
Transcribed from tapes of interviews with George Hewins
ISBN 0-241-10558-7 : £7.95 : CIP rev.
B81-02365

942.4'91 — West Midlands *(Metropolitan County).* **Woverhampton. Parks: West Park,** *to 1981 — Illustrations*

Wolverhampton West Park 1881-1981. — [Wolverhampton] ([Civic Centre, St Peters Sq. Wolverhampton WV1 1RG]) : Wolverhampton Borough Council, 1981. — [20]p : ill,2facsim ; 30cm
(unbound) B81-39764

942.4'92 — West Midlands *(Metropolitan County).* **Walsall** *(District).* **Darlaston & Willenhall,** *1850-1955*

Willenhall and Darlaston yesterdays. — Walsall (Central Library, Lichfield St., Walsall, West Midlands WS1 1TR) : Walsall Metropolitan Borough Archives Service, 1981. — 30leaves,[30]leaves of plates : ill ; 15x21cm
ISBN 0-9502318-6-x (pbk) : Unpriced
B81-26026

942.4'920858'05 — West Midlands *(Metropolitan County).* **Walsall** *(District) — Serials*

Walsall trader : including Aldridge, Pelsall, Darlaston, Bloxwich. — No.1 (Thursday May 14 1981)-. — Wolverhampton (Queen St., Wolverhampton [W. Midlands]) : Express and Star Group, 1981-. — v. : ill,ports ; 45cm
Weekly
ISSN 0161-6343 = Walsall trader : Unpriced
B81-32210

942.4'930858'05 — West Midlands *(Metropolitan County).* **Dudley** *(District) — Serials*

Dudley evening mail : circulating throughout Dudley, Stourbridge, Halesowen & Brierley Hill. — Oct.1980-. — Dudley : Birmingham Post and Mail Ltd. for BPM Holdings, 1980-. — v. : ill,ports ; 43cm
Daily. — Description based on: Monday, Apr.13, 1981
ISSN 0261-8613 = Dudley evening mail : £0.10 per issue B81-33706

942.4'940858'05 — West Midlands *(Metropolitan County).* **Sandwell** *(District) — Serials*

Sandwell trader : incorporating West Bromwich, Wednesbury, Tipton, Great Bridge & Oldbury. — No.1 (Thursday Feb.12 1981)-. — Wolverhampton (Queen St., Wolverhampton [W. Midlands]) : Express and Star Group, 1981-. — v. : ill,ports ; 44cm
Weekly
ISSN 0261-6335 = Sandwell trader : Unpriced
B81-32211

942.4'96 — West Midlands *(Metropolitan County).* **Birmingham. Castles: Weoley Castle,** *to 1929*

Hall, R. H. (Ralph Hunter). Weoley Castle and its families / Ralph H. Hall. — [Birmingham] ([85 Church Rd., Northfield, Birmingham B31 2LB]) : Northfield Society, 1981. — 16p : ill,1map,1geneal.table ; 30cm. — (Occasional papers / Northfield Society, ISSN 0142-9965 ; no.12)
Cover title. — Bibliography: p16
Unpriced (pbk) B81-33335

942.4'96 — West Midlands *(Metropolitan County).* **Birmingham. Selly Oak** *— Serials*

SOAP : Selly Oak alternative paper. — Issue no.1-. — [Birmingham] ([c/o Ms. B. Fay, 64 Oak Tree La., Selly Oak, Birmingham]) : [s.n.], 1980-. — v. : ill ; 28cm
Quarterly (1980), six issues yearly (1981-). — Description based on: Issue no.4
ISSN 0261-1953 = SOAP. Selly Oak alternative paper : £0.10 per issue B81-17463

942.4'96004924 — West Midlands *(Metropolitan County).* **Birmingham. Jews. Social conditions,** *1749-1914*

Birmingham Jewry 1749-1914. — [Leicester] ([c/o Dr. A. Newman, Unversity Rd., Leicester, LE1 7RH]) : [University of Leicester]
Vol.1. — 1980. — 135p : ill,maps,facsims,ports ; 30cm
Bibliography: p129-190. — Includes index
Unpriced (pbk) B81-19344

942.4'98 — International reconciliation. Role of Coventry

Rose, W. E.. Sent from Coventry : a mission of international reconciliation / by W.E. Rose. — London : Wolff, c1980. — 108p,[4]p of plates : ill,ports ; 20cm
Bibliography: p103-104. - Includes index
ISBN 0-85496-211-5 (pbk) : £3.50 : CIP rev.
B80-30809

942.5'0858'0222 — England. Chilterns *— Illustrations*

Gedling, Alan. Chiltern keepsakes / drawings by Allan Gedling. — [Cheltenham] : Thornhill, [1981]. — [21]leaves of plates : chiefly ill ; 22x31cm : 1map
Map on outside cover
ISBN 0-904110-72-9 (pbk) : £1.50 B81-40195

942.5'1 — Derbyshire. Buildings of historical importance

Merrill, John N.. [Famous Derbyshire homes]. Historical buildings of Derbyshire / by John N. Merrill ; line drawings and maps by Paul Boyes. — Winster (Winster, Derbyshire) : Walking Boots, 1981. — 88p : ill,maps ; 21cm
Originally published: Clapham, N. Yorkshire : Dalesman, 1973. — Includes index
ISBN 0-907496-00-8 (pbk) : £1.50 B81-19728

942.5'11'005 — England. South Pennines *— History — Serials*

Pennine magazine. — Vol.1, no.1 (Oct./Nov.1979)-. — Hebden Bridge (The Birchcliffe Centre, Hebden Bridge, West Yorkshire HX7 8DG) : Pennine Development Ltd., 1979-. — v. : ill ; 30cm
Six issues yearly. — Description based on: Vol.2, no.3 (Feb./Mar.1981)
ISSN 0261-2836 = Pennine magazine : £4.00 per year B81-20426

942.5'13 — Derbyshire. Abney, *to 1980*

Tomlinson, Tom D.. Ye ancient parish of Habenai (Abney) / by Tom Tomlinson. — [Hathersage] ([The Vicarage, Hathersage, Sheffield S30 1AB]) : [Hathersage Parochial Church Council], [1980]. — 12p : ill,maps ; 22cm
Cover title
£0.40 (pbk) B81-18660

942.5'13 — Derbyshire. Hathersage. Parish churches: St. Michael and All Angels *(Church : Hathersage), to 1980*

St Michael and All Angels, Hathersage. — [Hathersage] ([The Vicarage, Hathersage, Sheffield S30 1AB]) : [Hathersage Parochial Church Council], [1980]. — 1folded sheet : ill (some col.),1port ; 21x44cm folded to 21x15cm
£0.30 B81-19089

942.5'14 — Derbyshire. North East Derbyshire *(District).* **Country houses: Hardwick Hall,** *1587-1591*

. [Chatsworth House, MS.6. Selections]. The building of Hardwick Hall / edited by David N. Durant and Philip Riden. — Chesterfield (18 Mill La., Wingerworth, Chesterfield, Derbys.) : Derbyshire Record Society
Pt.1: The Old Hall, 1587-91. — 1980. — xlii,152p,[3]p of plates : ill,1facsim,1plan ; 22cm
ISBN 0-9505940-6-7 : Unpriced B81-32336

942.5'14 — Derbyshire. Unstone, *to 1935*

Battye, Kathleen M.. Unstone : the history of a village / by Kathleen M. Battye. — [Unstone] ([Siscar House, Unstone, Sheffield S18 5AL]) : [K.M. Battye], c1981. — iii,154p,[1]folded leaf of plates : ill,maps,coats of arms,facsims ; 22cm
Includes index
ISBN 0-9507560-0-8 (pbk) : £6.50 B81-28223

942.5'15 — Derbyshire. South Normanton. Social life, *1920-1930 — Personal observations*

James, Nora. A Derbyshire life / Nora James. — South Normanton (c/o South Normanton Community Arts Project, South Normanton Community Centre, Mansfield Rd., South Normanton, Derbyshire) : Post Mill Press, c1981. — iv,47p,[4]p of plates : ill ; 21cm
ISBN 0-907569-00-5 (pbk) : Unpriced
B81-31972

942.5'17 — Derbyshire. Allestree, *to 1980*

Eisenberg, Elizabeth. Allestree / by Elizabeth Eisenberg. — Derby (20 Evans Ave., Allestree Park, Derby DE3 2ET) : E. Eisenberg, 1981. — 16p : ill,1map,1coat of arms ; 21cm
£0.65 (pbk) B81-22436

942.5'17 — Derbyshire. Derby. Local authority housing estates: Mackworth Estate. Social conditions, *to 1979*

Mackworth Estate. Mackworth Estate jubilee : a social history / compiled by Mackworth Townswomen's Guild. — [Mackworth] ([126 Greenwich Drive South, Mackworth, Derby DE3 4AG]) : [The Guild], [1980]. — 19 leaves,[1] leaf of plates : ill ; 17x21cm
Cover title
£0.25 (pbk) B81-06831

942.5'17 — Derbyshire. Derby, *to 1979*

Rippon, Anton. The book of Derby : from settlement to city / by Anton Rippon. — Buckingham ([Meadows House, Well St., Buckingham]) : Barracuda, 1980. — 140p : ill,maps,1coat of arms,facsims,ports ; 27cm
Ill on lining papers. — Bibliography: p135. — Includes index
ISBN 0-86023-073-2 : £11.50 B81-05395

942.5'19 — Derbyshire. Swadlincote *— Serials*

Swadlincote times. — No.1 (Friday Apr.3rd 1981)-. — Coalville (Bridge Rd, Coalville, Leicestershire) : Trident Midland Newspapers, 1981-. — v. : ill,ports ; 43cm
Weekly
ISSN 0261-6076 = Swadlincote times : £0.10
B81-32289

942.5'21 — Nottinghamshire. Clayworth. Personal property. Probate inventories, *1670-1710 — Collections*

Village life from wills & inventories : Clayworth parish 1670-1710 / edited by Elizabeth R. Perkins. — Nottingham (Publications Unit, Department of Adult Education, 14 Shakespeare St., Nottingham NG1 4FJ) : Centre for Local History, University of Nottingham, c1979. — 25,xxxix p : ill ; 30cm. — (Record series / Centre for Local History, University of Nottingham ; 1)
Unpriced (pbk)
Primary classification 929'.342521 B81-09831

942.5'24 — Nottinghamshire. Newark *(District).* **Country parks: Rufford Park,** *to 1980*

Rufford : past and present. — Nottingham (Trent Bridge House, Fox Rd., West Bridgford, Nottingham) : Nottinghamshire County Council Leisure Services, 1980. — 24p : ill (some col.),map,plans,ports,1geneal.table ; 21x30cm
Cover title
ISBN 0-902751-12-3 (pbk) : Unpriced
B81-26304

942.5'27073'0924 — Nottinghamshire. Nottingham. Upper middle classes. Social life, *1751-1810 — Personal observations — Correspondence, diaries, etc.*

Gawthern, Abigail. The diary of Abigail Gawthern of Nottingham 1751-1810 / edited by Adrian Henstock. — Nottingham (Bromley House, Angel Row, Nottingham) : Thoroton Society of Nottinghamshire, 1980. — viii,175p,[8]p of plates : ill,facsims,maps ; 24cm. — (Record series / Thoroton Society ; v.33)
Includes index
ISBN 0-902719-06-8 (pbk) : £4.75 B81-05597

942.5'28 — Nottinghamshire. Arnold, *to 1977*
The **Arnhals** of Sherwood Forest : a history of Arnold. — Bognor Regis : New Horizon, c1978. — xii,166p,[8]leaves of plates : ill,1map ; 22cm
Includes index
ISBN 0-86116-088-6 : £3.50 B81-21778

942.5'29 — Nottinghamshire. Ratcliffe on Soar, *to 1978*
Collins, H. H.. The village of Ratcliffe on Soar : an account of times past in a small Nottinghamshire village / H.H. Collins. — Ratcliffe on Soar (Vikings, Ratcliffe on Soar, Notts.) : H.H. Collins, 1979. — 109,[11]p of plates : ill,1map,1port,geneal.tables ; 21cm
£1.50 (pbk) B81-15179

942.5'3'00946 — Lincolnshire. Coastal regions, *to 1980*
Robinson, David N.. The book of the Lincolnshire seaside : the story of the coastline from the Humber to the Wash / by David N. Robinson. — Buckingham : Barracuda, 1981. — 172p : ill,maps,2coats of arms,facsims,ports ; 27cm
Maps on lining papers. — Bibliography: p164-166. — Includes index
ISBN 0-86023-122-4 : £12.50 B81-33674

942.5'3'009734 — Lincolnshire. Rural regions. Social conditions
Rural facilities survey 1980 : general findings. — [Lincoln] ([County Offices, Lincoln LN1 1YJ]) : Lincolnshire County Council, 1981. — 33p : 1map ; 21cm
Unpriced (unbound) B81-19563

942.5'306 — Lincolnshire, *1600-1700*
Holmes, Clive. Seventeenth-century Lincolnshire / by Clive Holmes. — Lincoln (47 Newland, Lincoln) : History of Lincolnshire Committee for the Society for Lincolnshire History and Archaeology, 1980. — xiv,279p,[9]p of plates : ill,maps,coat of arms, plan,ports ; 24cm. — (History of Lincolnshire ; 7)
Bibliography: pxii-xiv. - Includes index
ISBN 0-902668-06-4 : Unpriced B81-10168

942.5'32 — Lincolnshire. Binbrook. Agricultural industries. Farms. Social life, *1871-1875 — Correspondence, diaries, etc*
Stovin, Cornelius. Journals of a Methodist farmer 1871-1875. — London : Croom Helm, Dec.1981. — [276]p
ISBN 0-7099-2324-4 : £12.50 : CIP entry B81-31431

942.5'32 — Lincolnshire. Louth, *to 1980*
Robinson, David N.. The book of Louth : the story of a market town / by David N. Robinson. — Buckingham : Barracuda, 1979. — 156p : ill,maps,facsims,ports ; 27cm
Bibliography: p150-151. — Includes index
ISBN 0-86023-094-5 : £11.50 B81-40004

942.5'34 — Lincolnshire. Doddington, *1560-1830*
Doddington : the prospect of a village, 1560-1830 / edited by Ian S. Beckwith ; based upon work carried out by students at Bishop Grosseteste College of Education. — Lincoln : Bishop Grosseteste College, 1977 (1979 printng). — ii,21p : ill,1map ; 21cm
Bibliography: p21
Unpriced (pbk) B81-22170

942.5'34016 — Lincolnshire. Lincoln. Flaxengate. Timber buildings, *ca 875-ca 1200.* **Excavation of remains**
Perring, Dom. Early medieval occupation at Flaxengate, Lincoln. — London : Council for British Archaeology for the Lincoln Archaeological Trust, Sept.1981. — [47]p. — (The Archaeology of Lincoln ; v.9-1)
ISBN 0-906780-10-1 (pbk) : £9.00 : CIP entry B81-23794

942.5'38 — Lincolnshire. Colsterworth, *to 1977*
Baird, Kenneth. Colsterworth village history / by Kenneth Baird. — [Colsterworth] (Twyford House, [22 Bourne Rd.,] Colsterwoth, [Grantham, Lincs. NG33 5JE]) : K. Baird, [1980?]. — 28p,[2]folded p of plates : 2maps ; 21cm
Cover title
£0.50 (pbk) B81-05582

942.5'38 — Lincolnshire. Grantham, *to 1979*
Bygone Grantham. — Grantham (78 Barrowby Rd., Grantham, Lincs. NG31 8AF) : Bygone Grantham. — (The Bygone series)
Vol.3 / by Michael Painter and Malcolm G. Knapp. — 1978. — 36p : ill,facsims ; 21x22cm
ISBN 0-906338-07-7 (pbk) : £1.20 B81-20377

942.5'42 — Leicestershire. Leicester. Castles: Leicester Castle, *to ca 1930*
Chinnery, G. A.. Leicester Castle & the Newarke / G.A. Chinnery. — Leicester (96 New Walk, Leicester LE1 6TD) : Leicestershire Museums, Art Galleries & Records Service, 1981. — 16p : ill ; 15x21cm. — (Leicestershire Museums publications)
ISBN 0-85022-069-6 (pbk) : Unpriced B81-22801

942.5'44 — Leicestershire. Market Harborough, *1835-1942*
Davies, J. C. (John Christopher). Yesterday's town : Victorian Harborough / by J.C. Davies ; illustrations by Michael C. Brown. — Buckingham : Barracuda, 1980. — 128p : ill,maps,1facsim,ports ; 27cm
Maps on lining papers. — Includes index
ISBN 0-86023-118-6 : £10.50 B81-11237

942.5'45'005 — Leicestershire. Rutland *(District) — History — Serials*
Rutland record : journal of the Rutland Record Society. — No.1 (1980)-. — Uppingham (Secretary, Colley Hill, Lyddington, Uppingham, Rutland, LE15 9LS) : The Society, 1980-. — v. : ill,maps,ports ; 30cm
Annual
Unpriced B81-06105

942.5'46 — Leicestershire. Melton Mowbray, *1800-1900*
Brownlow, Jack. Melton Mowbray, queen of the shires / Jack Brownlow. — Wymondham (Wymondham, Melton Mowbray, Leics.) : Sycamore, c1980. — 271p : ill,facsims,ports ; 29cm
Includes index
ISBN 0-905837-08-8 : £15.00 B81-01394

942.5'46 — Leicestershire. Melton Mowbray, *to 1977*
Hunt, Philip E.. The story of Melton Mowbray / Philip E. Hunt. — 2nd ed. rev. — [Leicester] : Leicestershire County Council Libraries & Information Service, 1979. — 153p,[8]p of plates : ill,1map ; 18cm
Previous ed.: Grantham : Palmer Publishing & Printing Co., 1957. — Includes index
ISBN 0-85022-049-1 (pbk) : £1.50 B81-33548

942.5'49 — Leicestershire. Groby *— Serials*
Groby flyer. — Issue 1 (Sept.1980)-. — Groby (6 Whitehouse Close, Groby, Leicestershire LE6 0GW) : The Groby Flyer, 1980-. — v. : ill,ports ; 42cm
Quarterly. — Description based on: Issue 2 (Dec.1980)
ISSN 0261-2542 = Groby flyer : Unpriced B81-21351

942.5'590858'05 — Northamptonshire. South Northamptonshire *(District) — Serials*
[The Advertiser *(Buckingham)***]**. The Advertiser : circulating in North Bucks and South Northants. — No.6016 (Friday, Apr.3, 1981)-. — Buckingham (2 Market Hill, Buckingham) : Buckingham Advertiser, 1981-. — v. : ill,ports ; 42cm
Weekly. — Merger of: Buckingham advertiser ; and, Towcester and Brackley advertiser
ISSN 0261-2879 = Advertiser (Buckingham) : £0.10 per issue
Also classified at 942.5'91 B81-32189

942.5'6 — Bedfordshire, *1660-1920*
Miscellanea. — Bedford (County Record Office, County Hall, Bedford) : Bedfordshire Historical Record Society, 1980. — 133p ; 21cm. — (The Publications of the Bedfordshire Historical Record Society ; v.59)
Includes index
ISBN 0-85155-041-x (pbk) : £4.00 B81-14508

942.5'6 — Bedfordshire, *ca 1100-ca 1940 — Festschriften*
Worthington George Smith and other studies / presented to Joyce Godber. — Bedford (County Record Office, County Hall, Bedford) : Bedfordshire Historical Record Society, 1978. — 243p : ill,maps,facsims,ports ; 22cm. — (The Publications of the Bedfordshire Historical Record Society ; v.57)
Includes index
ISBN 0-85155-038-x (pbk) : £5.00 B81-14509

942.5'6'009734 — Bedfordshire. Countryside
Bedfordshire : landscape & wildlife. — [Bedford] ([County Hall, Bedford, MK42 9AP]) : [Bedfordshire County Council, County Planning Department], [1980?]. — 39p : ill,col.maps ; 20cm
Unpriced (pbk) B81-12590

942.5'61 — Bedfordshire. Bedford, *to 1979 — Illustrations*
Bedford : in times past / [compiled by] A.E. Baker & N.C. Wilde. — Chorley : Countryside, c1980. — 48p : ill ; 22x20cm
ISBN 0-86157-034-0 (pbk) : £2.00 B81-21072

942.5'610858'05 — Bedfordshire. North Bedfordshire *(District) — Serials*
[Bedfordshire journal *(North Beds edition)***]**.
Bedfordshire journal. — North Beds ed. — [No.1 (197-)]-. — Bedford (18 St. Pauls Sq., Bedford) : Narieway, [197-]-. — v. : ill ; 42cm
Weekly. — Continues: Bedfordshire journal. — Description based on: Thursday Feb.12 1981
ISSN 0261-6262 = Bedfordshire journal. North Beds edition : £0.10 per issue B81-32204

942.5'630858'05 — Bedfordshire. Mid Bedfordshire *(District) — Serials*
[Bedfordshire journal *(Mid Beds edition)***]**.
Bedfordshire journal. — Mid Beds ed. — [No.1 (197-)]-. — Bedford (18 St. Pauls Sq., Bedford) : Narieway, [197-]-. — v. : ill,ports ; 42cm
Weekly. — Continues: Bedfordshire journal (East Beds edition). — Description based on: Friday Feb.13 1981
ISSN 0261-6254 = Bedfordshire journal. Mid Beds edition : £0.10 per issue B81-32205

942.5'65 — Bedfordshire. Dunstable, *1100-1550*
Evans, Vivienne. A brief history of Dunstable with the Priory 1100-1550 / Vivienne Evans. — [Dunstable] ([184 West St., Dunstable, Beds.]) : [V. Evans], [1980]. — 42p : ill,maps,coats of arms,1plan ; 30cm
Cover title
Unpriced (pbk) B81-28338

942.5'7 — Oxfordshire, *to 1980 — Conference proceedings*
The **Oxford** region : papers presented to a conference to mark 100 years of adult education in Oxford / edited by Trevor Rowley. — Oxford : Oxford University, Department for External Studies, c1980. — vii,258p : ill,maps,1facsim,plans,ports ; 30cm
ISBN 0-903736-10-1 (pbk) : Unpriced B81-05914

942.5'7'005 — Oxfordshire *— History — Serials*
Oxfordshire local history. — Vol.1, no.1 (Autumn 1980)-. — Oxford (c/o Miss C. Moore, 86 Lonsdale Rd, Oxford) : Oxfordshire Local History Association, 1980-. — v. ; 21cm
Two issues yearly
ISSN 0260-7565 = Oxfordshire local history : £5.00 per year B81-20454

942.5'71 — Oxfordshire. Witney, *1837-1944 — Illustrations*
Witney as it was / [compiled] by Tom Worley. — Nelson : Hendon Publishing, c1981. — [44]p : chiefly ill,ports ; 21x29cm
Text on inside covers
ISBN 0-86067-068-6 (pbk) : £2.60 B81-25998

942.5'74 — Oxfordshire. Oxford. Inland waterway communities. Social conditions, *1500-1900*
Prior, Mary. Fisher Row : fishermen, bargemen and canal boatmen in Oxford, 1500-1900. — Oxford : Clarendon Press, Dec.1981. — [416]p
ISBN 0-19-822649-7 : £22.50 : CIP entry B81-32045

942.5'74081'0922 — Oxfordshire. Oxford. Eccentrics, *1842-1975*

Marriott, Paul J.. Oxford characters / by Paul J. Marriott. — Oxford (41 Canning Cres., Oxford OX1 4XA) : P.J. Marriott, 1979. — 28p : ports ; 21cm
Text on inside covers
£0.85 (pbk) B81-37645

942.5'76 — Oxfordshire. Lyford, *to 1974*

Howse, Violet M.. Lyford : a parish record / by Violet M. Howse. — [Faringdon] ([Rosemary House, Church Green, Stanford-in-the-Vale, Faringdon, Oxon]) : [V.M. House], 1981. — 58p,[14]p of plates,[10]leaves of plates(4 folded) : ill,maps,1coat of arms,1facsim,geneal.tables ; 24cm
Unpriced (pbk) B81-14142

942.5'79 — Oxfordshire. Brightwell-cum-Sotwell, *to 1980*

Heyworth, F. V.. Brightwell-cum-Sotwell : some aspects of its history / by F.V. Heyworth. — [Wallingford] ([Middle Farm, Church La., Brighton-cum-Sotwell, Wallingford OX10 0SD]) : [K. Owen], c1981. — 27p ; 21cm
Unpriced (pbk) B81-35503

942.5'79 — Oxfordshire. Henley-on-Thames, *1791-1815*

Phillips, Robert. Henley and its volunteer forces : the town at the time of the Napoleonic Wars / by Robert Phillips. — [Henley-on-Thames] : Cressrelles, 1980. — 47p : ill,facsims ; 21cm
Bibliography: p41
ISBN 0-85956-060-0 (pbk) : Unpriced
B81-10864

942.5'8 — Hertfordshire, *to ca 1975*

A **Hertfordshire** sampler / compiled by James Coutts Smith ; illustrated by David Baker. — [Stevanage] ([c/o East Division Library Headquaters, 38 High St., Stevenage SG1 3HD]) : Hertfordshire Publications, 1980. — 157p : ill,music ; 22cm
Bibliography: p155-157
ISBN 0-901354-18-x (pbk) : Unpriced
B81-11834

942.5'8 — Southern Hertfordshire — *Serials*

[Review *(St. Albans)*]. Review : St. Albans, Harpenden, Welwyn Garden City, Hatfield, Radlett. — 1981-. — St. Albans (The Lawns, Mount Pleasant, St. Albans, Herts.) : SDH Publications, 1981-. — v. : ill,maps,ports ; 46cm
Weekly. — Continues: Review & express. — Description based on: No.408 (Thursday July 23 1981)
ISSN 0261-8737 = Review (St. Albans) :
Unpriced B81-39517

942.5'8038 — Hertfordshire. Peasants' Revolt — *Conference proceedings*

The **Peasants'** Revolt in Hertfordshire : the rising and its background : a symposium. — Stevenage Old Town (c/o East Division Library Headquaters, 38 High St., Stevenage Old Town, Hertfordshire) : Hertfordshire Publications, 1981. — 189p : ill,maps,2facsims ; 24cm
Bibliography: [8]p. — Includes index
ISBN 0-901354-19-8 (pbk) : Unpriced
B81-34349

942.5'81 — Hertfordshire. Hitchin, *to 1980*

Foster, Anthony M.. The book of Hitchin / by Arthur M. Foster ; illustrations selected and described by the staff of Hitchin Museum and Art Gallery and the author. — Buckingham : Barracuda, 1981. — 132p : ill,maps,1coat of arms,plans,facsims,ports ; 27cm
Maps on lining papers. — Bibliography: p125. — Includes index
ISBN 0-86023-138-0 : £11.95 B81-12509

942.5'83 — Hertfordshire. Hertford, *1830-1938* — *Illustrations*

Yesterday's town : Hertford : a century of progress / [compiled] by Cyril Heath. — Buckingham : Barracuda, c1981. — 108p : chiefly ill,facsims,ports ; 27cm
Facsims. on lining papers. — Bibliography: p104. - Includes index
ISBN 0-86023-119-4 : £10.95 B81-17125

942.5'84 — Hertfordshire. Dacorum *(District).* **Estates: Ashridge Estate,** *to 1979*

Coult, Douglas. A prospect of Ashridge / by Douglas Coult. — London : Phillimore, 1980. — ix,262p,[25]p of plates : ill(some col.),facsims,plans,ports(some col.),1geneal.table ; 23cm
Includes index
ISBN 0-85033-360-1 : £7.50 B81-19508

942.5'840858'05 — Hertfordshire. Dacorum *(District)* — *Serials*

Berkhamsted and Tring mail : also covering Hemel Hempstead. — No.471 (Wednesday, July 2 1980)-. — Luton (75 Castle St., Luton LU1 3AH) : Home Counties Newspapers, 1980-. — v. : ill,ports ; 46cm
Weekly. — Merger of: Berkhamsted mail ; and, Tring advertiser
ISSN 0144-851x = Berkhamsted and Tring mail : Unpriced B81-04638

942.5'86 — Hertfordshire. Welwyn, *to 1980*

Welwyn : a village appraisal / [the Welwyn Planning and Amenity Group]. — [Welwyn] ([48 Carleton Rise, Welwyn, Herts. AL6 9RG]) : [The Group], [1981]. — 20p : ill,1col.map ; 21x30cm
Cover title. — Limited ed. of 500 copies
£1.00 (pbk) B81-39974

942.5'860858'02471 — Hertfordshire. Welwyn Hatfield *(District).* **Social conditions** — *For environment planning*

Report of studies 1980 : the Welwyn Hatfield district plan. — Welwyn Garden City (A.G. Swanson, Controller of Technical Services, Council Offices, The Campus, Welwyn Garden City, Herts. AL8 6AE) : Welwyn Hatfield District Council, [1981?]. — 179p[33]leaves of plates(some folded) : ill,maps,plans ; 30cm
Unpriced (spiral) B81-38583

942.5'87 — Hertfordshire. Cheshunt, *1900-1960* — *Illustrations*

Cheshunt past : a selection of old photographs / with notes by Jack Edwards. — Cheshunt (48, Albury Ride, Cheshunt, Waltham Cross, EN8 8XF) : J. Edwards, 1980. — [43]p : chiefly ill,ports ; 30cm
Cover title
Unpriced (pbk) B81-07572

942.5'87 — Hertfordshire. Cheshunt region — *Serials*

Cheshunt & Waltham telegraph. — No.6, 145 (Friday, Jan.16, 1981)-. — Waltham Cross (241 High St., Waltham Cross, Herts. EN8 7BD) : Enfield Newspapers, 1981-. — v. : ill,ports ; 60cm
Weekly. — Merger of: Cheshunt telegraph ; and, Waltham telegraph
ISSN 0262-1835 = Cheshunt & Waltham telegraph : £0.10 per issue B81-39534

942.5'87 — Hertfordshire. Waltham Cross, *1860-1948* — *Illustrations*

Waltham Cross past : a selection of old photographs and engravings with notes / [compiled] by Jack Edwards. — Waltham Cross (69 Millcrest Rd., Goff's Oak, Waltham Cross EN7 5NU) : J. Edwards, [1980]. — [63]p : all.ill,facsims,ports ; 30cm
£2.50 (pbk) B81-30658

942.5'88 — Hertfordshire. Watford. Museums: Watford Museum. Stock: Items associated with Rickmansworth — *Catalogues*

Parrott, E. V.. The Rickmansworth Collection in the Watford Museum / by E.V. Parrott. — [Rickmansworth] ([66, The Queens Drive, Rickmansworth, Herts.]) : E.P. Publications, [1981]. — [8]p ; 19cm
Cover title
£0.50 (pbk) B81-15414

942.5'91 — Buckinghamshire. Wolverton. Social life, *1940-1945* — *Personal observations*

White, Doris, *1922-*. D for Doris, V for Victory / by Doris White. — Milton Keynes (109 Church St., Wolverton, Milton Keynes MK12 5LD) : Oakleaf Books in association with People's Press of Milton Keynes, 1981. — 81p,[4]p of plates : ill,2ports ; 21cm
ISBN 0-907524-00-1 (cased) : Unpriced
ISBN 0-907524-01-x (pbk) : Unpriced
B81-22931

942.5'91 — Northern Buckinghamshire — *Serials*

[The Advertiser *(Buckingham)*]. The Advertiser : circulating in North Bucks and South Northants. — No.6016 (Friday, Apr.3, 1981)-. — Buckingham (2 Market Hill, Buckingham) : Buckingham Advertiser, 1981-. — v. : ill,ports ; 42cm
Weekly. — Merger of: Buckingham advertiser ; and, Towcester and Brackley advertiser
ISSN 0261-2879 = Advertiser (Buckingham) : £0.10 per issue
Primary classification 942.5'590858'05
B81-32189

942.5'93 — Buckinghamshire. Aylesbury region — *Serials*

Bucks advertiser : incorporating the Thame gazette and Aylesbury news. — No.7611 (Friday, July 4 1980)-. — Luton (Castle St., Luton) : Home Counties Newspapers, 1980-. — v. : ill,ports ; 46cm
Weekly. — Continues: Bucks advertiser and Aylesbury news
ISSN 0144-784x = Bucks advertiser :
Unpriced B81-02068

942.5'95 — Buckinghamshire. Marlow — *Serials*

Marlow free press : a localised edition of the Bucks free press. — May 1981-. — [High Wycombe] ([Gomm Rd, High Wycombe, Bucks.]) : [Bucks Free Press], 1981-. — v. : ill,ports ; 60cm
Weekly. — Local ed. of: Bucks free press. — Description based on: Friday, May 29, 1981
ISSN 0262-2300 = Marlow free press : £0.15 per issue B81-39513

942.5'950858'05 — Buckinghamshire. Wycombe *(District)* — *Serials*

Wycombe district news. — Autumn 1978-. — High Wycombe (Gomm Rd, High Wycombe) : Bucks Free Press, 1978-. — v. : ill,maps,plans,ports ; 43cm
Two issues yearly. — Published on behalf of: Wycombe District Council. — Description based on: Summer 1980 issue
ISSN 0260-4566 = Wycombe district news :
Unpriced B81-03284

942.5'98 — Buckinghamshire. Hedgerley, *to 1979*

A **South** Bucks village : the history of Hedgerley / compiled by Michael Rice. — [Hedgerley] ([12 Stevenson Rd, Hedgerley, Bucks, SL2 3YE]) : Hedgerley Historical Society, c1980. — 111p : ill,1map,ports ; 21cm
Unpriced (pbk) B81-10356

942.6'083'0924 — East Anglia. Orphans. Social life, *1916-1936* — *Childhood reminiscences*

Hitchman, Janet. The King of the Barbareens / Janet Hitchman. — Harmondsworth : Puffin, 1981, c1960. — 220p ; 19cm
Originally published: London : Putnam, 1960
ISBN 0-14-031365-6 (pbk) : £1.25 B81-20959

942.6'084 — East Anglia. Social conditions, *1939*

Brown, R. Douglas. East Anglia 1939 / by R. Douglas Brown. — Lavenham : Terence Dalton, 1980. — viii,200p : ill,facsims, 1map,ports ; 24cm
Text on lining papers. — Bibliography: p202. - Includes index
ISBN 0-86138-000-2 : £7.95 B81-04522

942.6'1'009734 — Norfolk. Rural regions. Social life — *Stories, anecdotes*

Douglas, Peter, *1932-*. About this village / Peter Douglas. — [London] : Corgi, 1981, c1980. — 175p : ill ; 18cm
Originally published: Woodbridge : Boydell, 1980
ISBN 0-552-11671-8 (pbk) : £0.95 B81-21396

Douglas, Peter, *1932-*. Down the village street / Peter Douglas ; illustrations by Martin Honeysett. — [London] : Corgi, 1980, c1978 (1981 [printing]). — 156p : ill ; 18cm
Originally published: Woodbridge: Boydell, 1978
ISBN 0-552-11256-9 (pbk) : £0.95 B81-25436

942.6'10858'05 — Norfolk — *Serials*

[**Norwich mercury** *(Wymondham & county edition)*]. Norwich mercury. — Wymondham & county ed.. — No.7086 (Friday May 1 1981)-. — Norwich (Prospect House, Rouen Rd, Norwich NR1 1RE) : Eastern Counties Newspapers Group, 1981-. — v. : ill,ports ; 40cm
Weekly. — Continues in part: Norwich mercury, Norfolk news and journal
ISSN 0261-6319 = Norwich mercury. Wymondham & county edition : Unpriced
B81-32206

942.6'12 — Norfolk. Cromer, *to 1966*

Holden, C. Crawford. Cromer : the cutting of the gem / by C. Crawford Holden. — Cromer ([4A Chesterfield Villas, West St., Cromer, Norfolk NR27 9ED) : Poppyland, 1967 (1979 [printing]). — 24p : ill(some col.) ; 21cm
Text and ill on inside covers
ISBN 0-9504300-3-x (pbk) : £0.80 B81-21862

942.6'12 — Norfolk. Holkham. Estates: Holkham *(Estate), 1800-1910*

Martins, Susanna Wade. A great estate at work : the Holkham estate and its inhabitants in the nineteenth century / Susanna Wade Martins. — Cambridge : Cambridge University Press, 1980. — xiv,289p : ill,1geneal.table,maps,plans,ports ; 24cm
Bibliography: p283-284. — Includes index
ISBN 0-521-22696-1 : £24.00 B81-01826

942.6'12 — Norfolk. Sheringham, *to 1979*

Brooks, Peter, *1927-*. Sheringham - the story of a town / Peter Brooks. — Cromer ([4A Chesterfield Villas, West St., Cromer, Norfolk NR27 9ED]) : Poppyland, 1980. — 24p : ill (some col),1map,1plan ; 22cm
Text and ill on inside covers
ISBN 0-9504300-5-6 (pbk) : £0.90 B81-21863

942.6'15 — Norfolk. Norwich, *to 1975*

Corfield, P. J.. Towns, trade, religion, and radicalism : the Norwich perspective on English history / by P.J. Corfield. — Norwich (Norwich NR4 7TJ) : Centre of East Anglian Studies, University of East Anglia, c1980. — 40p : ill,maps,facsims,1plan,ports ; 21cm. — (The First Helen Sutermeister memorial lecture)
ISBN 0-906219-07-8 (pbk) : £1.50 B81-18396

942.6'15 — Norfolk. Norwich, *to 1980*

Historic Norwich : with city-centre map. — Norwich : Jarrold Colour Publications, c1981. — [32]p : ill(some col.),1col.map,ports ; 25cm
English text, English, French and German introduction and captions. — Cover title. — Ill, ports, text on inside covers
ISBN 0-85306-945-x (pbk) : Unpriced
B81-21897

942.6'15 — Norfolk. Norwich, *to ca 1900*

Solomons, Gerald. Stories behind the plaques of Norwich / by Gerald Solomons. — Norwich (17 Cantley La., Norwich [NR4 6TA]) : Capricorn Books, 1981. — 74p : ill ; 24cm
Includes index
ISBN 0-9507484-0-4 (pbk) : £2.50 B81-17783

942.6'17 — Norfolk. South Walsham, *to 1980*

Amos, G. S.. A history and description of South Walsham, Norfolk / G.S. Amos. — [South Walsham] ([Field View, South Walsham, Norwich, Norfolk]) : [G.S. Amos], 1981. — 68p : ill,maps,1plan ; 30cm
Cover title
£3.00 (spiral) B81-28741

942.6'17081'0222 — Norfolk Broads, *1880-1890 — Illustrations*

The **Broadland** photographers / compiled by C.S. Middleton. — Norwich (33 Orford Place, Norwich NR13) : Wensum Books, 1978. — [95]p : ill,ports ; 22cm
Bibliography: [p95]
ISBN 0-903619-23-7 (pbk) : £2.95 B81-12281

942.6'18 — Norfolk. Great Yarmouth, *to 1979*

Lewis, Charles, *1944-*. Great Yarmouth : history, herrings and holidays / [Charles Lewis]. — Cromer ([4A Chesterfield Villas, West St., Cromer, Norfolk NR27 9ED]) : Poppyland, 1980. — 23p : ill(some col.),maps(some col.) ; 21cm
Text and ill on inside covers
ISBN 0-9504300-4-8 (pbk) : £0.90 B81-21864

942.6'19 — Norfolk. Woodton, *to 1979*

History of Woodton, Norfolk. — [Lowestoft] ([c/o W.J. Goode, 8 Amberley Court, Oulton Broad, Lowestoft, Suffolk NR32 4RL]) : Friends of the Round Tower Churches Society, [1980]. — 46p : geneal.tables ; 26cm
Cover title
£0.75 (pbk) B81-06483

942.6'4'00952 — Suffolk. Small woodlands — *For environment planning*

Small woods in Suffolk 1980 survey report. — [Ipswich] ([c/o E. E. Barritt, County Planning Officer, County Hall, Ipswich IP4 2JS]) : Suffolk County Council, 1981. — 22p : ill,map ; 30cm
ISBN 0-86055-073-7 (unbound) : Unpriced
B81-28895

942.6'4043'0924 — Suffolk. Hopton, John — *Biographies*

Richmond, Colin. John Hopton : a fifteen century Suffolk gentleman / Colin Richmond. — Cambridge : Cambridge University Press, 1981. — xix,267p : 3maps,2geneal.tables ; 23cm
Includes index
ISBN 0-521-23434-4 : £17.50 B81-15732

942.6'46 — London. Camden *(London Borough)*. **Museums: British Museum. Stock: Anglo-Saxon antiquities from Sutton Hoo** — *For teaching*

The **Sutton** Hoo ship burial : illustrated notes for teachers / British Museum Education Service. — [London] : [British Museum], [1981?]. — 19p : ill ; 30cm
Cover title
Unpriced (pbk) B81-17142

942.6'46 — Suffolk. Dunwich, *to 1826*

Parker, Rowland. Men of Dunwich : the story of a vanished town / Rowland Parker. — London : Granada, 1980, c1978. — 272p : ill,maps ; 20cm. — (A Paladin book)
Originally published: London : Collins, 1978. — Bibliography: p267. - Includes index
ISBN 0-586-08330-8 (pbk) : £1.95 B81-05215

942.6'46 — Suffolk. Kesgrave, *to 1974*

Ponting, Gerald. The story of Kesgrave : stability and growth in a Suffolk parish / Gerald and Margaret Ponting. — Callanish (Callanish, Isle of Lewis) : G. & M. Ponting, c1980. — ix,183leaves,[10]leaves of plates : ill,maps,plans, ; 30cm
ISBN 0-9505998-2-4 (spiral) : Unpriced
B81-16570

942.6'46 — Suffolk. Melton, *to 1980*

Bentham, Cecil. Melton and its churches / by Cecil Bentham. — Ipswich : East Anglian Magazine, c1981. — 64p : ill,1port ; 21cm
ISBN 0-900227-54-0 (pbk) : £1.95 B81-34519

942.6'46 — Suffolk. Sutton Hoo. Anglo-Saxon antiquities. Excavation of remains, *1966-1970*

Longworth, I. H.. Sutton Hoo excavations 1966, 1968-70 / I.H. Longworth and I.A. Kinnes. — London : British Museum, 1980. — 63p : ill,maps ; 30cm. — (Occasional paper / British Museum, ISSN 0142-4813 ; no.23)
Bibliography: p63
ISBN 0-86159-021-x (pbk) : Unpriced
B81-08673

942.6'460856'0922 — Suffolk. Suffolk Coastal *(District)*. **Villages. Social life,** *ca 1965 — Personal observations — Collections*

Blythe, Ronald. Akenfield : portrait of an English village / Ronald Blythe. — Harmondsworth : Penguin, 1972 (1980 [printing]). — 336p ; 18cm
Originally published: London : Allen Lane, 1969
ISBN 0-14-003461-7 (pbk) : £1.50 B81-29156

942.6'5'005 — Cambridgeshire. Local history — *Serials*

The **conduit** : a six-monthly bulletin for the exchange of information and views between local history, archaeological and conservation groups in the county of Cambridgeshire / prepared and circulated by the Cambridge Antiquarian Society. — No.1 (Sept.1980)-. — Cambridge (University Archives, University Library, West Road, Cambridge CB3 9DR) : The Society, 1980-. — v. ; 21cm
ISSN 0144-8439 = Conduit : £0.50 (free to members) B81-06830

942.6'54 — Cambridgeshire. Ramsey, *1540-1881 — Early works*

Wise, John, *fl.1881*. Ramsey Abbey : its rise and fall, taken from the Ramsey History or Chronicle, and other reliable sources ; also an account of the Manor & Parish since the Dissolution ... / by John Wise, W. Mackreth Noble. — Fenstanton (12 Church St., Fenstanton, Huntingdon) : Grasshopper Press, 1981. — 226,viip,[5]leaves of plates : ill ; 18cm
Facsim of: 1st ed., Huntingdon : Ellis & Cooper, 1882. — Includes index
ISBN 0-904701-10-7 (pbk) : £3.95
Primary classification 942.6'54 B81-28318

942.6'54 — Cambridgeshire. Ramsey. Abbeys: Ramsey Abbey, *to 1540 — Early works*

Wise, John, *fl.1881*. Ramsey Abbey : its rise and fall, taken from the Ramsey History or Chronicle, and other reliable sources ; also an account of the Manor & Parish since the Dissolution ... / by John Wise, W. Mackreth Noble. — Fenstanton (12 Church St., Fenstanton, Huntingdon) : Grasshopper Press, 1981. — 226,viip,[5]leaves of plates : ill ; 18cm
Facsim of: 1st ed., Huntingdon : Ellis & Cooper, 1882. — Includes index
ISBN 0-904701-10-7 (pbk) : £3.95
Also classified at 942.6'54 B81-28318

942.6'54 — Cambridgeshire. St Ives, *ca 1890-1970 — Illustrations*

Portrait of St. Ives / [compiled by] Valerie Kendall. — St. Ives, Cambs. (Norris Library and Museum, The Broadway, St. Ives, Huntingdon, Cambs. PE17 4BX) : Friends of Norris Museum, 1981. — 51p : chiefly ill,1map,ports ; 15x21cm. — (Occasional publications / Friends of the Norris Museum ; no.2)
Map on inside cover. — Bibliography: p52
ISBN 0-9507209-1-7 (pbk) : Unpriced
B81-34448

942.6'57 — Cambridgeshire. Landbeach & Waterbeach. Social conditions — *For structure planning*

Survey ; analysis : and suggestions for action : Waterbeach and Landbeach district plan. — Cambridge (1 South Cambridgeshire Hall, Hills Rd., Cambridge CB2 1PB) : Planning Department, Cambridgeshire District Council, 1980. — 40p : maps ; 30cm
Cover title
Unpriced (pbk) B81-17882

942.6'590858'05 — Cambridgeshire. Cambridge — *Serials*

Cambridge weekly news. — No.1 (Thursday Feb.5 1981)-. — Cambridge (51 Newmarket Rd, Cambridge CB5 8EJ) : Cambridge Newspapers Ltd., 1981-. — v. : ill ; 42cm
Continues: Cambridge independent press and chronicle
ISSN 0261-1872 = Cambridge weekly news : £0.12 per issue B81-16818

942.6'69 — Suffolk. Ipswich. Personal property. Probate inventories, *1583-1631 - Texts*

The **Ipswich** probate inventories, 1583-1631. — Woodbridge : Boydell Press, July 1981. — [144]p. — (Suffolk Records Society ; v.22)
ISBN 0-85115-148-5 : £12.00 : CIP entry
B81-14907

942.6'712 — Essex. Saffron Walden, *1850-1973 — Illustrations*

Saffron Walden in old photographs / [compiled by] H.C. Stacey. — Saffron Walden : Daniel, c1980. — [190]p : chiefly ill,1 facsim,ports ; 24cm
ISBN 0-85207-148-5 (pbk) : £4.95 B81-05548

942.6'715 — Essex. Braintree & Bocking, *to 1899*
Quin, W. F.. A history of Braintree and Bocking / W.F. Quin. — [Brentwood] ([15 Westbury Drive, Brentwood, Essex]) : [W.F. Quin], c1981. — vi,242p : ill(some col.),maps,facsims,ports ; 24cm
Bibliography: p242
ISBN 0-9507378-0-1 : £7.50 B81-23375

942.6'715 — Essex. Braintree & Bocking, *to 1980*
Baker, Michael, *1957-*. The book of Braintree and Bocking / by Michael Baker. — Buckingham : Barracuda, 1981. — 148p : ill,maps,facsims,ports ; 27cm
Maps on lining papers. — Bibliography: p145. — Includes index
ISBN 0-86023-134-8 : £11.95 B81-33676

942.6'723 — Essex. Colchester, *500-1400.* **Archaeological sources**
Crummy, Philip. Aspects of Anglo-Saxon and Norman Colchester / by Philip Crummy ; with contributions by Nina Crummy ... [et al.]. — London : Council for British Archaeology, 1981. — viii,91p : ill,maps,plans ; 30cm. — (Colchester archaeological report ; 1) (CBA research report, ISSN 0589-9036 ; no.39)
Includes index
ISBN 0-906780-06-3 (pbk) : Unpriced : CIP rev. B81-07454

942.6'725 — Essex. Walton-on-the-Naze, *1800-1867*
Boyden, Peter B.. Walton 1800-1867 : a history of the nineteenth century town to the coming of the railway / by Peter B. Boyden. — Walton-on-the-Naze (2 Mill 6a., Walton-on-the-Naze, Essex, CO14 8PE) : Walton-on-the-Naze Records Office, c1981. — iv,42p ; 26cm
Includes index
£0.75 (pbk) B81-31217

942.6'73 — Essex. Harlow. Development, *1947-1980*
Gibberd, Frederick. Harlow : the story of a new town / Frederick Gibberd, Ben Hyde Harvey, Len White and other contributors ; foreword by Lord Greenwood of Rossendale. — Stevenage : Publications for Companies, 1980. — xx,414p,[8]p of plates : ill(some col.),maps (some col.),1facsim,plans,ports ; 24cm
Bibliography: p395-399. — Includes index
ISBN 0-904928-11-8 (cased) : £11.90 (pbk) : £5.95 B81-10304

942.6'74 — Essex. Theydon Bois. Social life, *1927-1972 — Personal observations*
Farmer, Jack. Theydon Bois as I knew it / by Jack Farmer. — Theydon Bois (65 Theydon, Park Rd., Theydon Bois, Epping, Essex CM16 7LR) : J.R. Farmer, 1980. — 183p : ill,ports ; 21cm
ISBN 0-9507367-0-8 (pbk) : £4.00 B81-05696

942.6'756 — Essex. Dengie region, *to 1953*
Bruce, Kevin. Dengie : the life and the land / by Kevin Bruce. — [Chelmsford] : Essex Record Office in collaboration with the Burnham and District Local History and Amenity Society, 1981. — [40]p : ill,1map ; 21cm. — (Essex Record Office publication ; no.82)
Bibliography: p[40]
ISBN 0-900360-58-5 (pbk) : £1.50 B81-40022

942.6'76 — Essex. Brentwood — *Serials*
Brentwood and Billericay post and argus. — No.628 (Wednesday June 18 1980)-. — [Brentwood] ([23 Crown St., Brentwood, Essex]) : Greater London & Essex Newspapers, 1980-. — v. : ill ; 42cm
Weekly. — Continues: Brentwood & Billericay argus
ISSN 0144-8528 = Brentwood and Billericay post and argus : £0.10 per issue
Also classified at 942.6'772 B81-03579

942.6'772 — Essex. Billericay — *Serials*
Brentwood and Billericay post and argus. — No.628 (Wednesday June 18 1980)-. — [Brentwood] ([23 Crown St., Brentwood, Essex]) : Greater London & Essex Newspapers, 1980-. — v. : ill ; 42cm
Weekly. — Continues: Brentwood & Billericay argus
ISSN 0144-8528 = Brentwood and Billericay post and argus : £0.10 per issue
Primary classification 942.6'76 B81-03579

942.6'775 — Essex. Rayleigh. Castles: Rayleigh Castle. Excavation of remains, *1959-1961*
Helliwell, Leonard. Documentary evidence and report on excavations 1959-1961 / on behalf of the Rayleigh Mount Local Committee of the National Trust by L. Helliwell and D.G. Macleod. and Report on excavations 1969-70 / sponsored by the Ministry of Public Buildings and Works ; by D.G. Macleod. — [Benfleet] ([c/o Hon. Sec., 9 Netherlands, Thundersley, Benfleet, Essex]) : The Committee, 1981. — 72p,[4]p of plates : ill,2maps,plans ; 26cm
ISBN 0-7078-0081-1 (pbk) : Unpriced B81-38607

942.6'795081 — Essex. Southend-on-Sea. Social life, *ca 1850-1910*
Everritt, Sylvia. Southend seaside holiday / Sylvia Everritt. — London : Phillimore, c1980. — x,130p,[24]p of plates : ill,2maps,facsims,ports ; 23cm
Bibliography: p127-128. — Includes index
ISBN 0-85033-334-2 : £5.95 B81-01945

942.6'7950858'05 — Essex. Southend-on-Sea — *Serials*
Standard recorder. Southend. — Friday July 17, 1981-. — Basildon (Newspaper House, Chester Hall La., Basildon, Essex) : John H. Burrows and Sons, 1981-. — v. : ill,port ; 42cm
Weekly
ISSN 0262-1843 = Standard recorder. Southend : £0.08 per issue B81-39536

942.7'009'92 — Northern England. Persons, *to ca 1928*
Dane, Rebecca. More true tales : of the famous and the Courageous : from the Lake District and the Northern Counties / Rebecca Dane and Craig MacNeale. — Darlington ([P.O. Box 38, Darlington, Co. Durham DL3 7TR]) : Nordales (Five Counties), [c1981]. — 48p : ill,ports ; 21cm. — (Around the North series)
Cover title
ISBN 0-9504314-8-6 (pbk) : Unpriced B81-22307

942.702 — Northern England. Effects of Norman Conquest, *to 1135*
Kapelle, William E.. The Norman conquest of the North : the region and its transformation, 1000-1135 / by William E. Kapelle. — London : Croom Helm, 1979. — 329p : ill,geneal.tables,maps ; 24cm
Bibliography: p295-313. — Includes index
ISBN 0-7099-0040-6 : £14.95 : CIP rev. B79-36605

942.7'1 — Cheshire, *to 1980*
Sylvester, Dorothy. A history of Cheshire / Dorothy Sylvester ; drawings by Grace Corbett ; cartography by Geoffrey Barber and Fred Castle. — 2nd ed. — London : Phillimore, 1980. — 127p,[24]p of plates : ill(some col.),maps,coats of arms,facsims,ports ; 26cm. — (The Darwen county history series)
Previous ed.: Henley-on-Thames : Darwen Finlayson, 1971. — Bibliography: p119-122. - Includes index
ISBN 0-85033-384-9 : £6.95 B81-19371

942.7'13 — Cheshire. Middlewich, *to 1900.* **Archaeological sources**
Thompson, Patience. Middlewich : the archaeological potential of a town / Patience Thompson. — Chester (c/o County Planner, Commerce House, Hunter St., Chester) : Cheshire County Council, 1981. — 15p : maps ; 30cm. — (Cheshire monographs ; 2)
Bibliography: p13-14
ISBN 0-906767-03-2 (spiral) : Unpriced B81-22418

942.7'14 — Cheshire. Chester, *1272-1377*
Booth, Paul Howson William. The financial administration of the Lordship and county of Chester 1272-1377. — Manchester : Manchester University Press, June 1981. — [192]p. — (Publication / Chetham Society ; vol.28)
ISBN 0-7190-1337-2 : £12.50 : CIP entry B81-10455

942.7'14 — Cheshire. Chester, *ca 1850-1910 — Illustrations*
Chester as it was / [compiled] by T.E. Ward. — Nelson : Hendon Publishing, c1980. — [48]p : chiefly ill ; 21x29cm
Text, ill on inside covers
ISBN 0-86067-062-7 (pbk) : £2.30 B81-07154

942.7'140857 — Cheshire. Chester *(District).* **Households. Social conditions,** *1979*
Redfern, J. T.. Cheshire household survey 1979 : Chester District report / [J.T. Redfern, G.A. Hamilton, A.J. Orman]. — Chester (County Treasury, County Hall, Chester) : Research and Intelligence Section, Central Policy & Research Unit, Cheshire County Council, 1981. — 78,xvp : ill,maps,forms ; 30cm. — (People & houses of Cheshire ; 11)
ISBN 0-904073-10-6 (spiral) : £5.00 B81-36847

942.7'16 — Cheshire. Macclesfield — *Serials*
Macclesfield express advertiser and times and courier. — No.1 (Thursday, Aug.6, 1981]-. — Stockport (Wood St., Hollywood, Stockport [SK3 0AB]) : Lancashire and Cheshire County Newspapers, 1981-. — v. : ill,ports ; 60cm
Weekly. — Merger of: Macclesfield advertiser ; and, Macclesfield express
ISSN 0262-2297 = Macclesfield express advertiser and times and courier : £0.15 per issue B81-39541

942.7'16 — Cheshire. Poynton — *History — Serials*
Poynton Local History Society newsletter. — Issue no.1 (May 1980)-. — [Poynton] ([c/o W.H. Shercliff, 2 Hazel Drive, Poynton, Stockport, Cheshire SK12 1PX]) : The Society, 1980-. — maps ; 30cm
Two issues yearly
ISSN 0261-8818 = Poynton Local History Society newsletter : Unpriced B81-35090

942.7'160858'05 — Cheshire. Macclesfield *(District) — Serials*
Wilmslow express advertiser and Alderley and Knutsford. — No.1 (Thursday, Aug.6, 1981)-. — Stockport (Wood Street, Hollywood, Stockport [SK3 0AB]) : Lancashire and Cheshire County Newspapers, 1981-. — v. : ill,ports ; 60cm
Issued twice a week. — Merger of: Wilmslow and Alderley and Knutsford advertiser ; and, Wilmslow county express
ISSN 0262-2289 = Wilmslow express advertiser and Alderley and Knutsford : £0.10 per issue B81-39540

942.7'17 — Cheshire. Ellesmere Port and Neston *(District), to 1980*
Burnley, Kenneth. Portrait of Wirral / by Kenneth Burnley. — London : Hale, 1981. — 238p : ill,1map ; 23cm
Bibliography: p225-227. — Includes index
ISBN 0-7091-9409-9 : £7.95
Also classified at 942.7'51 B81-40931

942.7'17 — Cheshire. Neston & Parkgate, *ca 1850-ca 1940 — Illustrations*
Yesterday's Wirral : Neston, Parkgate & Heswall / [compiled by Ian & Marilyn Boumphrey]. — [England] : [I. & M. Boumphrey], c1980. — [60]p : chiefly ill,ports ; 30cm
Bibliography: p[60]
ISBN 0-9507255-0-1 (pbk) : £2.30
Also classified at 942.7'51 B81-06997

942.7'19 — Cheshire. Lymm, *1895-1974 — Sources of data: Lymm. Urban District Council. Minutes*
Thomas, G. H. (Gareth Hugh). The minutes tell the story : Lymm 1895-1974 / G. H. Thomas. — [Lymm] ([c/o 3 Hazel Drive, Lymm, Cheshire]) : Lymm and District Local History Society, [1981]. — 43,[12]p : ill,2maps ; 21cm
Unpriced (pbk) B81-37653

942.7'32 — Greater Manchester *(Metropolitan County).* **Brindleheath,** *to 1980*
Chapman, Ike. Brindleheath : a Salford village / Ike Chapman. — Swinton (375 Chorley Rd., Swinton M27 2AY) : Neil Richardson, [1981]. — 32p : ill,maps,facsims,plans ; 30cm
£1.75 (pbk) B81-36192

942.7'32 — Greater Manchester *(Metropolitan County).* **Salford,** *1962-1979*

The **Continuing** conurbation : change and development in Greater Manchester / edited by H.P. White. — Farnborough, Hants. : Gower, c1980. — 207p : ill,maps,1plan ; 26cm
ISBN 0-566-00248-5 : £10.50 : CIP rev. B80-12670

942.7'32 — Greater Manchester *(Metropolitan County).* **Salford** *— Serials*

Salford city reporter and advertiser. — No.1 (Friday Aug.7 1981)-. — Salford (496 Liverpool St., Salford 6) : Lancashire and Cheshire County Newspapers Ltd., 1981-. — v. : ill,ports ; 60cm
Weekly. — Continues: Salford city reporter
ISSN 0261-8729 = Salford city reporter and advertiser : £0.14 per issue B81-39519

942.7'33 — Great Manchester *(Metropolitan County).* **Manchester. Inner areas. Social conditions** *— Serials*

Inner city focus : news, views and information about Inner Manchester. — No.1(Mar. 1981)-. — [Manchester] ([c/o S. Howarth, 19 Meade Grove, Longsight, Manchester]) : [Manchester Conference Communications Group], 1981-. — v. ; 30cm
Monthly. — Description based on: No.2(May 1981)
ISSN 0261-6491 = Inner city focus : Unpriced B81-32394

942.7'34 — Greater Manchester *(Metropolitan County).* **Stockport. Hillgate. Social life,** *1914-1939 — Personal observations*

Hooley, Jim. A Hillgate childhood / myself when young ; by Jim Hooley. — [Stockport] ([Town Hall, Stockport SK1 3XE]) : Age Concern Stockport, c1981. — [44]p : ill ; 21cm
ISBN 0-9507670-0-x (pbk) : Unpriced B81-37337

942.7'340858'05 — Greater Manchester *(Metropolitan County).* **Stockport** *(District) — Serials*

Express advertiser : Cheadle, Cheadle Hulme, Bramhall, Gatley, Heald Green. — No.1 (Thursday, Aug.6, 1981)-. — Stockport (Wood St., Hollywood, Stockport [SK3 0AB]) : Lancashire and Cheshire County Newspapers, 1981-. — v. : ill,ports ; 60cm
Weekly. — Continues: Stockport express. Cheadle, Cheadle Hulme, Bramhall, Gatley, Heald Green ; and in part, Stockport advertiser
ISSN 0262-1975 = Express advertiser : £0.15 per issue B81-39542

Stockport express advertiser. Bredbury, Romiley, Woodley, Marple, High Lane, Disley. — No.1 (Thursday, Aug.6, 1981)-. — Stockport (Wood St., Hollywood, Stockport [SK3 0AB]) : Lancashire and Cheshire County Newspapers, 1981-. — v. : ill,ports ; 60cm
Weekly. — Continues: Stockport express. Bredbury, Marple, Romiley, High Lane, Disley ; and in part, Stockport advertiser
ISSN 0262-1991 = Stockport express advertiser. Bredbury, Romiley, Woodley, Marple, High Lane, Disley : £0.15 per issue B81-39544

Stockport express advertiser. Town edition. — No.1 (Thursday, Aug.6, 1981)-. — Stockport (Wood St., Hollywood, Stockport [SK3 0AB]) : Lancashire and Cheshire County Newspapers, 1981-. — v. : ill,ports ; 60cm
Weekly. — Continues: Stockport express. Town edition ; and in part, Stockport advertiser
ISSN 0262-1983 = Stockport express advertiser. Town edition : £0.15 per issue B81-39543

942.7'35 — Greater Manchester *(Metropolitan County).* **Hyde,** *1887-1947 — Illustrations*

Hyde in old photographs / [compiled] by Alice Lock. — [Ashton-under-Lyne] ([Stamford House, Jowett's Walk, Ashton-under-Lyne, Lancs. OL7 0EP]) : Libraries and Arts Committee, Tameside Metropolitan Borough, 1981. — [48]p : all ill,ports ; 21x29cm
ISBN 0-904506-06-1 (pbk) : £1.95 B81-25231

942.7'35 — Greater Manchester *(Metropolitan County).* **Stalybridge. Country houses: Stayley Hall,** *to 1980*

Summers, Eric. The history and architecture of Stayley Hall 1580-1980 / written and illustrated by Eric Summers. — S.l. : E. Summers, 1981. — 24p : ill ; 21cm. — (Local heritage series ; v.1)
ISBN 0-9507460-0-2 (pbk) : Unpriced B81-16569

942.7'36073'0222 — Great Manchester *(Metropolitan County).* **Wigan** *(District), 1760-1830 — Illustrations*

Those dark satanic mills : an illustrated record of the Industrial Revolution in South Lancashire / [compiled by Alastair Gillies assisted by R.J. Bond]. — Leigh : Wigan Record Office, c1981. — 110p : ill,facsims,ports ; 30cm
ISBN 0-9507643-0-2 (pbk) : £2.50 B81-40057

942.7'37 — Greater Manchester *(Metropolitan County).* **Bolton** *— Serials*

The **Bolton** express : including Westhoughton and Farnworth. — No.1 (1978)-. — [Bolton] ([Mealhouse Lane, Bolton BL1 1DE]) : St Regis Newspapers Ltd, 1978-. — v. : ill,ports ; 41cm
Weekly. — Description based on: No.101 (Friday Mar.6 1981)
ISSN 0261-6289 = Bolton express : Unpriced B81-32203

942.7'392 — Greater Manchester *(Metropolitan County).* **Heywood,** *ca 1860-1975 — Illustrations*

Bygone Heywood : a photographic record / compiled by John Cole and Grahame Fish. — [Rochdale] ([P.O. Box 15, Town Hall, Rochdale OL16 1AB]) : Rochdale Metropolitan Borough Council, 1981?. — [40]p : chiefly ill,1facsim,ports ; 23x29cm
Text on inside covers
ISBN 0-906960-02-9 (cased) : Unpriced
ISBN 0-906960-01-0 (pbk) : Unpriced B81-27180

942.7'393 — Greater Manchester *(Metropolitan County).* **Oldham,** *to 1980*

Oldham pastimes / [compiled] by Dennis Ball. — [Manchester] ([7a Cherwell Ave., Heywood, Greater Manchester OL1Q 4SE]) : [D. Ball], [1981]. — 88p : ill,1map,facsims ; 22cm
£2.00 (pbk) B81-15696

942.7'51 — Merseyside *(Metropolitan County).* **Heswall,** *ca 1900-ca 1950 — Illustrations*

Yesterday's Wirral : Neston, Parkgate & Heswall / [compiled by Ian & Marilyn Boumphrey]. — [England] : [I. & M. Boumphrey], c1980. — [60]p : chiefly ill,ports ; 30cm
Bibliography: p[60]
ISBN 0-9507255-0-1 (pbk) : £2.30
Primary classification 942.7'17 B81-06997

942.7'51 — Merseyside *(Metropolitan County).* **Wallasey,** *1760-1930 — Illustrations*

Wallasey of yesteryear / [text by] Carol E. Bidston. — Birkenhead (Central Library, Borough Rd., Birkenhead, Merseyside) : Department of Leisure Services, Libraries and Arts, Metropolitan Borough of Wirral, 1980. — [33]p : ill,maps,coat of arms ; 21x30cm
Maps on inside covers. — Bibliography: p[33]
ISBN 0-904582-01-9 (pbk) : Unpriced B81-07881

942.7'51 — Merseyside *(Metropolitan County).* **Wirral** *(District), to 1980*

Burnley, Kenneth. Portrait of Wirral / by Kenneth Burnley. — London : Hale, 1981. — 238p : ill,1map ; 23cm
Bibliography: p225-227. — Includes index
ISBN 0-7091-9409-9 : £7.95
Primary classification 942.7'17 B81-40931

942.7'53073'0924 — Merseyside *(Metropolitan County).* **Liverpool. Roscoe, William** *— Biographies*

Murphy, Graham, *1946-.* William Roscoe : his early ideals and influence / by Graham Murphy. — [Liverpool] ([31 Highville Rd., Liverpool L16 9JE]) : [G. Murphy], c1981. — 35p : 1ill,facsims,2ports ; 21cm
Bibliography: p35
£0.75 (pbk) B81-35548

942.7'53083'0924 — Merseyside *(Metropolitan County).* **Liverpool. Working class communities. Social life,** *1930-1932 — Childhood reminiscences*

Forrester, Helen. Twopence to cross the Mersey / Helen Forrester. — London : Fontana, 1981, c1974. — 223p ; 18cm
Originally published: London : Cape, 1974
ISBN 0-00-636168-4 (pbk) : £1.75 B81-14268

942.7'54 — Merseyside *(Metropolitan County).* **Huyton & Roby,** *to 1979*

Colwell, Andrew G.. Beautiful Huyton with Roby : 'a charming residential suburb' / by Andrew G. Colwell. — [Wirral] ([37 Kirkway, Greasby, Wirral, Merseyside L49 2ND]) : [A.G. Colwell], c1980. — 122p : ill,maps,facsims,ports ; 31cm
Cover title. — Map and ill on inside covers. — Bibliography: p122
£3.25 (pbk) B81-23591

942.7'57 — Merseyside *(Metropolitan County).* **Newton-le-Willows,** *1900-1920 — Illustrations*

Frost, Arthur. Photographs of Newton-le-Willows from 1900-1920 / Arthur Frost ; commentary by his daughter Eileen M. Gaskell. — [Newton-le-Willows] ([87 Ashton Rd., Newton-le-Willows, Merseyside WA12 0AH]) : [E.M. Gaskell], [1981]. — 48p : all ill,ports ; 24cm
Cover title
Unpriced (pbk) B81-34930

942.7'6 — Lancashire, *to 1980*

Gooderson, P. J.. A history of Lancashire / P.J. Gooderson. — London : Batsford, 1980. — 192p : ill,coats of arms,maps ; 25cm
Bibliography: p179-184. — Includes index
ISBN 0-7134-2588-1 : £5.95 B81-01909

Lancashire pride. — Clapham [N. Yorkshire] : Dalesman, 1981. — 96p : ill ; 21cm
ISBN 0-85206-634-1 (pbk) : £2.50 B81-22919

942.7'607 — Lancashire. Social life, *1700-1980*

Jones, Patricia P.. Lancashire lattice / Patricia P. Jones. — Ormskirk : Hesketh, 1981. — 57p : ill ; 21cm
ISBN 0-905777-20-4 (pbk) : £2.90 B81-39802

942.7'623 — Lancashire. Blackburn *— Serials*

The **Blackburn** citizen. — Oct. 1978-. — Blackburn (Refuge Assurance Buildings, Ainsworth St., Blackburn, [Lancs.]) : Citizen Newspapers, 1978-. — v. : ill,ports ; 42cm
Weekly. — Description based on: Thursday, July 16, 1981
ISSN 0262-1827 = Blackburn citizen : Unpriced B81-39538

942.7'623 — Lancashire. Darwen *— Serials*

The **Darwen** citizen. — May 24 1979-. — Blackburn (Refuge Assurance Buildings, Ainsworth St., Blackburn, [Lancs.]) : Citizen Newspapers, 1979-. — v. : ill,ports ; 42cm
Weekly. — Description based on: Thursday, July 16, 1981
ISSN 0262-1959 = Darwen citizen : Unpriced B81-39539

942.7'6250858'05 — Lancashire. Hyndburn *(District) — Serials*

The **Hyndburn** citizen. — 1979-. — Blackburn (Refuge Assurance buildings, Ainsworth St., Blackburn, [Lancs.]) : Citizen Newspapers, 1979-. — v. : ports ; 42cm
Weekly. — Description based on: Thursday July 16 1981
ISSN 0262-1878 = Hyndburn citizen : Unpriced B81-39521

942.7'642 — Lancashire. Burnley. Top o' th' Town, *to ca 1980*

Frost, Roger, *1947-.* Top o' th' town Burnley / by Roger Frost with the help of the Urban Studies Group of Burnley Teachers' Centre. — [Burnley] ([Grimshaw St., Burnley BB11 2BD]) : Lancashire County Council Library and Leisure Committee, 1981. — 87p : ill,maps,1facsim,1port ; 21c
Ill on inside covers. — Bibliographies: p86
ISBN 0-902228-39-0 (pbk) : £1.50 B81-27610

942.7′642′005 — Lancashire. Burnley *(District)* — *History — Serials*

[Retrospect *(Burnley)*]. Retrospect : the journal of Burnley and District Historical Society. — Vol.1 (1980)-. — [Burnley] ([The Hon. Secretary, c/o Central Library, Burnley, Lancs.]) : The Society, 1980-. — v. ; 30cm
Annual
ISSN 0261-5061 = Retrospect (Burnley and District Historical Society) : Unpriced
B81-30010

942.7′6650858′05 — Lancashire. Preston *(District)* — *Serials*

The **Preston** citizen. — 1980-. — Preston (85 Fishergate, Preston [Lancs.]) : Preston citizen, 1980-. — v. : ill,ports ; 42cm
Weekly. — Description based on: Thursday July 16 1981
ISSN 0262-1894 = Preston citizen : Unpriced
B81-39524

942.7′67 — Lancashire. Leyland region — *Serials*

The **Leyland** citizen. — Mar.1981-. — Preston (85 Fishergate, Preston, [Lancs.]) : Preston citizen, 1981-. — v. : ill,ports ; 42cm
Weekly. — Description based on: Thursday July 16 1981
ISSN 0262-1886 = Leyland citizen : Unpriced
B81-39525

942.7′682 — Lancashire. Poulton-le-Fylde, *1835-1975 — Illustrations*

Wiseman, David, *1940-*. Poulton-le-Fylde in bygone days / David Wiseman. — Chorley : Countryside Publications, c1981. — 72p : ill,1facsim,ports ; 20x21cm
ISBN 0-86157-050-2 (pbk) : Unpriced
B81-40882

942.7′69 — Lancashire. Lancaster. Buildings of historical importance

Morrish, Alison V.. Buildings of Lancaster / by Alison V. Morrish. — Rev. and repr. / rev. by E. Tyson. — [Lancaster] ([Old Town Hall, Market Sq., Lancaster]) : [Lancaster City Museum and Art Gallery], 1981. — 18p ; 30cm. — (A Lancaster Museum monograph)
Cover title. — Previous ed.: 1975. — Bibliography: p18
£0.20 (pbk) B81-28302

942.7′69 — Lancashire. Whittington. Country estates: Whittington Estate, *to 1980*

Copeland, B. M.. Whittington : the story of a country estate / B.M. Copeland. — Leeds (Hudson Rd., Leeds LS9 7DL) : Maney, 1981. — x,166p,[20]p of plates : ill,maps,ports ; 26cm
Ill and map on lining papers. — Bibliography: p157-159. - Includes index
£10.75 B81-22427

942.7′8 — Cumbria. Lake District. Social life, *to ca 1970*

Rollinson, William. Life & tradition in the Lake District / by William Rollinson ; drawings by David Kirk. — Re-set with minor corrections / foreword by Melvyn Bragg. — Clapham [N. Yorkshire] : Dalesman, 1981. — 237p,[72]p of plates : ill,facsims,plans,ports ; 24cm
Originally published: London : Dent, 1974. — Bibliography: p229-231. — Includes index
ISBN 0-85206-635-x (pbk) : £6.50 B81-22926

942.7′806 — Cumbria. Social life, *1600-1700*

Macfarlane, Alan. The justice and the mare's ale : law and disorder in seventeenth century England / Alan Macfarlane in collaboration with Sarah Harrison. — Oxford : Blackwell, 1981. — xii,238p : ill,maps,facsims,ports ; 25cm
Ill on lining papers. — Includes index
ISBN 0-631-12681-3 : £8.50 B81-17662

942.7′8081 — Cumbria. Social conditions, *1830-1950*

Marshall, J. D.. The Lake Counties : from 1830 to the mid-twentieth century : a study in regional change / J.D. Marshall and John K. Walton. — Manchester : Manchester University Press, c1981. — xii,308p : ill,maps,facsims,ports ; 24cm
Includes index
ISBN 0-7190-0824-7 : £13.50 B81-22905

942.7′80858′0222 — Cumbria. Lake District. Social life — *Illustrations*

A **Lakeland** camera / [compiled by] David Jones. — Salisbury : Michael Russell, 1980. — 96p : ill,ports ; 31cm
ISBN 0-85955-080-x : £6.95 B81-09930

942.7′83 — Cumbria. Cartmel, *to 1880*

Dickinson, J. C.. The land of Cartmel : a history / by J.C. Dickinson. — Kendal (28 Highgate, Kendal, Cumbria) : Titus Wilson, 1980. — xii,112p,16p of plates : ill ; 26cm
Bibliography: p107-108. — Includes index
ISBN 0-900811-12-9 : £5.95 B81-11419

942.7′84 — Cumbria. Wasdale, *to 1979*

Wasdale : a celebration in words and pictures / chosen by Ruth Eversley. — Beckermet : Michael Moon, 1981. — xiv,149p : ill,maps,facsims,ports ; 23x26cm
ISBN 0-904131-25-4 : £8.50 B81-28243

942.7′9 — Isle of Man, *1016-1316 — Early works*

[Cronica regum Mannie & Insularum. *English & Latin*]. Cronica regum Mannie & Insularum = Chronicles of the kings of Man and the Isles : BL Cotton Julius Avii / transcribed and translated with an introduction by George Broderick. — [Douglas] : Manx Museum and National Trust, 1979. — xii,[95]p ; 30cm
Parallel Latin text and English translation
Unpriced (spiral)
Primary classification 941.1′402 B81-26125

942.7′9′0074 — Isle of Man. Ramsey. Museums: Grove, The *(Museum of rural life) — Visitors' guides*

A **Guide** to 'The Grove' rural Life Museum, Ramsey, Isle of Man : a branch of the Manx Museum and National Trust. — Douglas : Manx Museum and National Trust, 1981. — 31p : ill ; 21cm
£0.60 (pbk) B81-26805

942.8′004924 — North-east England. Jewish communities, *1755-1980*

Olsover, Lewis. The Jewish communities of North-East England 1755-1980 / by Lewis Olsover. — Gateshead (Summerfield, Saltmeadows Rd., Gateshead, Tyne and Wear NE8 3AJ) : Mark, 1981, c1980. — 357p : ill,facsims,ports ; 22cm
Bibliography: p344-345. - Includes index
ISBN 0-9506224-4-3 : £7.95 B81-20794

942.8′081 — North-east England. Social conditions, *1800-1980*

Stephenson, John, *1935-*. God save the pit / John Stephenson. — [Eppleton] ([All Saints Vicarage, Eppleton, Sunderland, Tyne & Wear]) : [J. Stephenson], [1981]. — [72p : ill,facsims ; 21cm
Cover title
Unpriced (pbk) B81-18222

942.8′1 — West Yorkshire *(Metropolitan County).* **Antiquities,** *to 1500.* **Sites. Archaeological investigation**

West Yorkshire : an archaeological survey to A.D. 1500 / [edited by M.L. Faull and S.A. Moorhouse]. — Wakefield ([County Hall, Wakefield WF1 2QW]) : W. Yorkshire Metropolitan County Council, 1981. — 4v. : maps(some col.) ; 30-42cm
Bibliography: (41p). — Includes index
ISBN 0-86181-001-5 (pbk) : £39.00 B81-23264

942.8′1 — Yorkshire. Buildings of historical importance, *1550-1750*

Hey, David. Yorkshire / David Hey. — Ashbourne : Moorland, c1981. — 165p : ill,1map,plans ; 25cm. — (Buildings of Britain 1550-1750)
Ill on lining papers. — Bibliography: p161. — Includes index
ISBN 0-86190-021-9 : £8.95 : CIP rev.
B81-15838

942.8′1 — Yorkshire, *ca 50-ca 1920*

Pocock, Michael. A history of Yorkshire / by Michael Pocock. — Clapham [N. Yorkshire] : Dalesman, 1978. — 128p : ill ; 21cm
Bibliography: p127-128
ISBN 0-85206-451-9 (pbk) : £1.95 B81-22917

942.8′1 — Yorkshire. Manor houses, *to 1700*

Ambler, Louis. The old halls & manor houses of Yorkshire. — Ashbourne : Moorland Publishing, Nov.1981. — [256]p
Facsim. of 1st ed. London : Batsford, 1913
ISBN 0-86190-025-1 : £13.95 : CIP entry
B81-30383

942.8′1 — Yorkshire, *to 1980*

Yorkshire pride : an illustrated selection of prose and verse. — Clapham [N. Yorkshire] : Dalesman, 1981. — 95p : ill ; 21cm
ISBN 0-85206-633-3 (pbk) : £2.50 B81-22918

942.8′1′0076 — Yorkshire, *to 1980 — Questions & answers*

Kellett, Arnold. Know your Yorkshire / by Aronld Kellett. — Clapham, N. Yorkshire : Dalesman, 1980. — 48p : ill,1map,1facsim,ports ; 19cm
ISBN 0-85206-615-5 (pbk) : £0.85 B81-06745

942.8′1083 — West Yorkshire *(Metropolitan County).* **Social life,** *1900-1935*

Mitchell, W. R. (William Reginald). Yorkshire mill town traditions / by W.R. Mitchell ; with drawings by Ruth Blackburn. — Clapham, N. Yorkshire : Dalesman, 1978. — 80p : ill ; 21cm
ISBN 0-85206-483-7 (pbk) : £1.40 B81-13391

942.8′10858′0924 — Yorkshire. Rural regions. Social life, *ca 1980 — Personal observations*

Drysdale, Ann. Faint heart never kissed a pig. — London : Routledge & Kegan Paul, Feb.1982. — [170]p
ISBN 0-7100-0972-0 : £5.95 : CIP entry
B81-37577

942.8′12 — West Yorkshire *(Metropolitan County).* **Cornholme. Social life,** *1851*

Cornholme. — [Halifax] ([c/o J. Harber, 1 Stafford Place, Halifax]) : [Workers' Education Association Yorkshire North District], [1980]. — 28p : ill,maps,1facsim ; 21cm
Cover title
£0.20 (pbk) B81-09539

942.8′12 — West Yorkshire *(Metropolitan County).* **Cornholme. Social life,** *1901-1914*

Edwardian Cornholme / [written and produced collectively by Neil Arnold ... et al.]. — [Leeds] ([7 Woodhouse Sq., Leeds LS3 IAD]) : [Workers' Educational Association Yorkshire North District], [1981]. — 28p : ill,ports ; 21cm. — (Pamphlet / Workers' Educational Association. Yorkshire North District ; no.2)
Cover title. — Text on inside covers
£0.45 (pbk) B81-32744

942.8′12 — West Yorkshire *(Metropolitan County).* **Halifax** — *Serials*

Halifax free press. — No.1 (Jan.1981)-. — Halifax (1 Stafford Pl., Halifax) : Free Press, 1981-. — v. : ill ; 31cm
Monthly
ISSN 0261-2526 = Halifax free press : £0.20 per issue B81-21352

942.8′12 — West Yorkshire *(Metropolitan County).* **Heptonstall,** *1700-1800*

Heptonstall township in the eighteenth century / Hebden Bridge W.E.A. branch. — Halifax (17 Bankhouse Lane, Salterhebble, Halifax) : J. Harber, [1981]?. — 39p : maps,facsims ; 21cm
Cover title
£0.30 (unbound) B81-38394

942.8′13 — West Yorkshire *(Metropolitan County).* **Colne Valley** — *Serials*

The **valley** voice : Colne Valley's new monthly newspaper. — No.1 (Apr.1981)-. — Marsden (16 Peel St., Marsden) : Colne Valley Press, 1981-. — v. : ill,ports ; 31cm
Cover of first issue reads: Not! the Colne Valley news ... introducing the Valley voice. — Continues: Colne Valley news
ISSN 0261-6890 = Valley voice : £0.12
B81-34061

942.8′13 — West Yorkshire *(Metropolitan County).* **Lockwood,** *to 1979*

Clarke, Brian, *1935-*. The history of Lockwood and North Crosland / compiled by Brian Clarke. — Lockwood (Thornfield Avenue, Lockwood, West Yorkshire) : B. Clarke, [1980?]. — 168p : ill,maps ; 22cm
£2.90 (pbk) B81-10651

942.8'19 — West Yorkshire *(Metropolitan County).* **Cookridge. Social conditions,** *to 1980*

Cole, Don. Cookridge : the story of a Yorkshire township / written and illustrated by Don Cole. — Leeds (101 Blue Hill La., Leeds, LS12 4NX) : D. & J. Thornton. — (The Local library series)
Part 2. — 1981. — 48p : ill,maps ; 21cm
ISBN 0-907339-03-4 (pbk) : £1.00 B81-33105

942.8'19 — West Yorkshire *(Metropolitan County).* **Garforth** — *Serials*

Garforth shopper. — 1980-. — Leeds (Lambert's Yard, Rothwell, Leeds [W. Yorkshire]) : Rothwell Advertiser Press, 1980-. — v. : ill ; 45cm
Monthly. — Description based on: July issue 1981
ISSN 0262-1908 = Garforth shopper : Unpriced B81-39523

942.8'19 — West Yorkshire *(Metropolitan County).* **Garforth,** *to 1980*

A **Short** history of Garforth. — [Garforth] ([c/o The Secretary, 2 Moorland Terr., Garforth, Yorks.]) : [Garforth Historical Society], [1981]. — 77p : ill,maps,1coat of arms ; 22cm
Map on folded leaf attached to inside cover. — Bibliography: p70. - Includes index
Unpriced (pbk) B81-17643

942.8'19 — West Yorkshire *(Metropolitan County).* **Horsforth** — *Serials*

Horsforth shopper. — Thursday July 23 1981-. — Leeds (Lambert's Yard, Rothwell, Leeds [W. Yorkshire]) : Rothwell Advertiser Press, 1981-. — v. : ill,ports ; 45cm
Fortnightly
ISSN 0262-1916 = Horsforth shopper : Unpriced B81-39522

942.8'19 — West Yorkshire *(Metropolitan County).* **Leeds,** *1700-1979*

A **History** of modern Leeds / Derek Fraser, editor. — Manchester : Manchester University Press, c1980. — xiii,479p : ill,maps,ports ; 24cm
Ill on lining papers. — Includes index
ISBN 0-7190-0747-x : £17.50 : CIP rev. B80-23901

942.8'19 — West Yorkshire *(Metropolitan County).* **Leeds** — *Serials*

The **Leeds** and Harrogate graphic : [social, sporting & industrial life of Leeds & Harrogate]. — June 1980-. — Leeds (11 Vinery Rd, Leeds LS4 2LB) : [Wiltonfield], 1980-. — v. : ill ; 30cm
Monthly. — Continues: Leeds graphic
ISSN 0260-2733 = Leeds and Harrogate graphic : £0.40 per issue
Also classified at 942.8'42 B81-02016

942.8'19 — West Yorkshire *(Metropolitan County).* **Yeadon,** *to 1940*

Yeadon, Yorkshire / edited by T. Illingworth. — [Horsforth] ([14 Airedale Grove, Horsforth, Leeds LS18 5EF]) : T. Illingworth, 1980. — xiv,222p : ill,maps,2facsims,ports ; 23cm
£5.95 (pbk) B81-05028

942.8'21 — South Yorkshire *(Metropolitan County).* **Sheffield. Jewish communities,** *ca 1920-1980*

Krausz, Armin. Sheffield Jewry : commentary on a community / by Armin Krausz. — Ramat-Gan : Bar-Ilan University (British Friends, London) ; Sheffield (EMI House, Matilda St., Sheffield 1) : Naor, 1980. — xiv,418p,[12]p of plates : ill,facsims,ports ; 24cm
Bibliography: p401-404. — Includes index
£10.50 B81-08523

942.8'21 — South Yorkshire *(Metropolitan County).* **Sheffield region** — *Serials*

[The Star weekly *(Sheffield)***]**. The Star weekly : Sheffield's own newspaper. — No.1 (1979)-. — Sheffield (York St., Sheffield S1 1PU) : Sheffield Newspapers, 1979-. — v. : ill,ports ; 41cm
Description based on: No.96 (Thursday Apr.2, 1981)
ISSN 0261-8605 = Star weekly (Sheffield) : Unpriced B81-33703

942.8'23 — South Yorkshire *(Metropolitan County).* **Aston & Brinsworth** — *Serials*

Aston & Brinsworth advertiser. — 1981?-. — [Rotherham] ([42 Effingham St., Rotherham]) : [H. Garnett] 1981?-. — v. : ill,ports ; 66cm
Weekly. — Description based on: Friday Feb.6th 1981 issue
ISSN 0261-6165 = Aston & Brinsworth advertiser : £0.12 B81-32291

942.8'23 — South Yorkshire *(Metropolitan County).* **Rawmarsh & Mexborough** — *Serials*

Rawmarsh & Mexborough advertiser. — 1981?-. — [Rotherham] ([42 Effingham St., Rotherham]) : [H. Garnett], 1981?-. — v. : ill,ports ; 66cm
Weekly. — Description based on: Friday Feb.6th 1981 issue
ISSN 0261-6173 = Rawmarsh & Mexborough advertiser : £0.12 B81-32290

942.8'230858'05 — South Yorkshire *(Metropolitan County).* **Rotherham** *(District)* — *Serials*

Dinnington & Kiveton advertiser. — Firday Feb.6th 1981-. — Rotherham (42 Effingham St., Rotherham, [S. Yorkshire]) : Hy. Garnett and Co., 1981-. — v. : ill,ports ; 65cm
Weekly. — Continues in part: Rotherham & South Yorkshire advertiser (B editiom)
ISSN 0261-6475 = Dinnington & Kiveton advertiser : £0.12 per issue B81-32200

Maltby & Wickersley advertiser. — Friday Feb.6th 1981-. — Rotherham (45 Effingham St., Rotherham [S. Yorkshire]) : Hy. Garnett and Co., 1981-. — v. : ill,ports ; 65cm
Weekly. — Continues in part: Rotherham & South Yorkshire advertiser (B edition)
ISSN 0261-6483 = Maltby & Wickersley advertiser : £0.12 per issue B81-32199

Thrybergh & Dalton advertiser. — Friday Feb.6th 1981-. — Rotherham (42 Effingham St., Rotherham [S. Yorkshire]) : Hy. Garnett and Co., 1981-. — v. : ill,ports ; 65cm
Weekly. — Continues in part: Rotherham & South Yorkshire advertiser (B edition)
ISSN 0261-6467 = Thrybergh & Dalton advertiser : £0.12 per issue B81-32198

942.8'3 — North Humberside. Country houses, *1750-1850*

Allison, K. J.. 'Hull gent. seeks country residence' 1750-1850 / by K.J. Allison. — Beverley : East Yorkshire Local History Society, 1981. — 65p : maps,1plan ; 22cm. — (E.Y. local history series ; no.36)
Bibliography: p64-65. — Includes index
ISBN 0-900349-36-0 (pbk) : £1.75 B81-27883

942.8'30858 — Yorkshire Wolds. Social life — *Stories, anecdotes*

Johnson, Herbert. Tales from the Wolds / by Herbert Johnson. — Driffield (16 Howl La., Hutton, Driffield YO25 9QA) : Hutton, 1980. — 96p : ill,1port ; 21cm
Bibliography: p95
ISBN 0-907033-02-4 (pbk) : Unpriced B81-27864

942.8'32 — Humberside. Barrow-on-Humber. Social life, *1804-1910* — *Personal observations*

Borrill, Dora M.. Charlotte / by Dora M. Borrill ; illustrations by Roy Turner ; photographs by George Schofield. — [Barow-on-Humber] ([The Gables, Barrow-on-Humber, S. Humberside DN19 7DQ]) : [D.M. Borrill], [1981?]. — 84p : ill(some col.),ports ; 21cm
Unpriced (pbk) B81-33584

942.8'32 — Humberside. Barton-upon-Humber — *Serials*

Barton star. — Jan.30 1981-. — Barton (40 High Str., Barton, Lincs.) : LSG Newpapers, 1981-. — v. : ill,ports ; 42cm
Weekly. — Continues: Humber and Barton star
ISSN 0261-6246 = Barton star : £0.15 B81-32699

942.8'32 — Humberside. Elsham. Country houses: Elsham Hall, *to 1980*

Elsham. — [Derby] : [English Life Publications], [1981]. — 19p : ill ; 24cm
Cover title
ISBN 0-85101-180-2 (pbk) : £0.60 B81-40141

942.8'32 — Humberside. Winteringham, *1761-1871*

A **History** of a village : Winteringham 1761-1871 / by Winteringham Local History Group. — [Hull] ([39 High St., Hull]) : [Bradley], 1980. — 145p : ill,maps,facsims,plans ; 31cm
Unpriced B81-05040

942.8'34 — Humberside. Grimsby, *to 1981*

Kaye, David, *1929-*. The book of Grimsby : the story of borough, town and port / by David Kaye. — Buckingham : Barracuda Books, 1981. — 136p : ill,maps,facsims,ports ; 27cm
Maps on lining papers. — Bibliography: p129-130. — Includes index
ISBN 0-86023-137-2 : £11.95 B81-26075

942.8'34082'0924 — Humberside. Grimsby. Social life, *ca 1910* — *Paersonal observations*

Sparkes, J. H.. The life and times of a Grimsby street urchin / by J.H. Sparkes. — Ilfracombe : Stockwell, 1981. — 41p ; 19cm
ISBN 0-7223-1512-0 (pbk) : £1.99 B81-39663

942.8'35 — Humberside. Bubwith, *to 1978*

Bubwith : an East Yorkshire parish / [contributors W.F. Atkinson ... et al.] ; [edited by S. Gilby, J. Henley] ; [with illustrations by E. Fisk]. — North Ferriby ([c/o] Lockington Publishing Co., The Studio, Railway Station, North Ferriby) : Bubwith Village Trust, 1979. — 80p,[6]p of plates : ill,1facsim,maps,1plan
Bibliography: p80
ISBN 0-905490-08-8 : Unpriced B81-33125

942.8'37 — Humberside. Hull, *to 1979*

Gillett, Edward. A history of Hull / Edward Gillett and Kenneth A. MacMahon. — Oxford : Published for the University of Hull by the Oxford University Press, 1980. — x,428p,12p of plates : ill,maps,ports ; 23cm. — (University of Hull publications)
Includes index
ISBN 0-19-713436-x : £12.00 : CIP rev. B80-23902

942.8'39 — Humberside. Garton on the Wolds. Towse *(Family).* **Estates,** *1537-1800*

Towse, Clive. An account of an estate in Garton in the East Riding, the property of the Towse family, 1537-1800 : with a note on the Somerset branch of the family / by Clive Towse. — [Cardiff] ([30 Twyn-y-Fedwen Rd., Cardiff CF4 1HU]) : Privately printed for C.K. Towse, 1980. — 31p : 1geneal.table
Limited ed. of 150 copies
£2.80 (21cm) B81-05674

942.8'39 — Humberside. Great Driffield. Buildings — *Illustrations*

Sargeant, Gary. Sketches of Driffield / drawings by Gary Sargeant ; text by Christine Clubley. — Driffield (16 Howl La. Hutton, Driffield YO25 9QA) : Hutton, 1980. — [39]leaves : ill ; 21x30cm
ISBN 0-907033-03-2 (spiral) : £5.50 B81-27863

942.8'4 — North Yorkshire. Dales. Buildings of historical importance, *to ca 1900*

Raistrick, Arthur. Buildings in the Yorkshire Dales : who built them, when and how? / by Arthur Raistrick. — Clapham [N. Yorkshire] : Dalesman, 1976 (1981 [printing]). — 88p : ill,plans ; 21cm
Bibliography: p88
ISBN 0-85206-367-9 (pbk) : £2.25 B81-22923

942.8'4 — North Yorkshire. Dales. Social life, *to ca 1965*

Hartley, Marie. Life & tradition in the Yorkshire Dales / by Marie Hartley and Joan Ingilby. — Re-set with minor corrections. — Clapham [N. Yorkshire] : Dalesman, 1981. — 207p,[96]p of plates : ill,1map,ports ; 25cm
Originally published: London : Dent, 1968. — Includes index
ISBN 0-85206-632-5 (pbk) : £6.50 B81-22921

942.8'4 — North Yorkshire. Derwent Valley, *1740-1980*

Cooper, Brian. Transformation of a valley. — London : Heinemann Educational, Sept.1981. — [272]p
ISBN 0-435-32973-1 : £13.50 : CIP entry B81-22637

942.8'4 — North Yorkshire. Foss River, *to 1973*

Fife, Michael G.. The river Foss : from Yearsley village to York its history and natural history / by Michael G. Fife and Peter J. Walls. — York : Sessions, 1973 (1981 [printing]). — iii,68p : ill,maps,col.plans ; 24cm
Text on inside covers. — Bibliography: p68
ISBN 0-900657-17-0 (pbk) : £1.50 B81-15311

942.8'41 — North Yorkshire. Skipton, *ca 650-1700*

Williams, David, *1952-*. Medieval Skipton / David Williams. — [Skipton] ([Town Hall, Skipton, North Yorks, BD23 1AH]) : Craven Museum, [1981?]. — 30p : ill,maps,plans ; 30cm
Unpriced (pbk) B81-37466

942.8'42 — North Yorkshire. Harrogate — *Serials*

The **Leeds** and Harrogate graphic : [social, sporting & industrial life of Leeds & Harrogate]. — June 1980-. — Leeds (11 Vinery Rd, Leeds LS4 2LB) : [Wiltonfield], 1980-. — v. : ill ; 30cm
Monthly. — Continues: Leeds graphic
ISSN 0260-2733 = Leeds and Harrogate graphic : £0.40 per issue
Primary classification 942.8'19 B81-02016

942.8'43004395 — North Yorkshire. York. Vikings, *ca 900-950*

Smyth, Alfred P.. Scandinavian York and Dublin : the history and archaeology of two related Viking kingdoms / Alfred P. Smyth. — New Jersey : Humanities ; Dublin ([Tudor House, Taney Rd., Dundrum, Dublin 14]) : Templekieran
2. — c1979. — x,361p,[1]leaf of plates : ill,maps,plans,geneal.tables ; 22cm
Includes index
ISBN 0-391-01049-2 (pbk) : Unpriced
Also classified at 941.8'35004395 B81-20802

942.8'43081 — North Yorkshire. York, *1831-1981*

York 1831-1981 : 150 years of scientific endeavour and social change / editor Charles Feinstein. — York : Sessions, 1981. — xii,340p : ill,maps,plans,ports ; 21cm
Includes bibliographies and index
ISBN 0-900657-55-3 (cased) : Unpriced
ISBN 0-900657-56-1 (pbk) : Unpriced
B81-26348

942.8'45 — North Yorkshire. Tadcaster. Country houses: Hazlewood Castle, *to 1980 — Illustrations*

Thornton, David, *1935-*. Hazlewood Castle : a pictorial record / written by David Thornton ; with photographs by Harry Royston. — Leeds (101 Blue Hill La., Leeds LS12 4NX) : D. & J. Thornton, [1981]. — [32]p : ill,1plan ; 15x21cm
Plan on inside cover
£1.00 (pbk) B81-27092

942.8'47 — North Yorkshire. Eskdale. Social life, *ca 1900-1973*

Cockcroft, Barry. [Sunley's daughter]. The ways of a Yorkshire dale / by Barry Cockcroft. — Clapham [N. Yorkshire] : Dalesman, 1981, c1974. — 112p : ill,ports ; 21cm
Originally published: London : Dent, 1974
ISBN 0-85206-619-8 (pbk) : £2.75 B81-13395

942.8'47 — North Yorkshire. Robin Hood's Bay, *1885-ca 1930 — Illustrations*

Robin Hood's Bay as it was : a pictorial history / [compiled] by J. Robin Lidster. — Nelson : Hendon Publishing, c1981. — 44p : ill,1map,1plan,ports ; 29cm
Text on inside cover
ISBN 0-86067-063-5 (pbk) : £2.60 B81-22847

942.8'48 — North Yorkshire. Richmond, *to 1900*

Wenham, L. P.. A Richmond miscellany / by L.P. Wenham and C.J. Hatcher. — [Northallerton] ([c/o County Archivist, County Record Office, County Hall, Northallerton, N. Yorks. DL7 8AD]) : North Yorkshire County Council, 1980. — 106p : ill,maps ; 31cm. — (North Yorkshire County Record Office publications ; no.25)
Includes index
ISBN 0-906035-14-7 (pbk) : Unpriced
B81-32150

942.8'49 — North Yorkshire. Stokesley region, *to 1900*

Historical glimpses of the town of Stoxley and the parishes of Wiruletun, Billesdala, Kirkebie cum Broctun, Childale, Hoton-juxta-Rudbie : a miscellany. — [Whitby] (c/o Bleach Mill Farm, Kildale, Whitby, N. Yorkshire]) : [Stokesley & District Local History Study Group], [c1981]. — 45p : ill ; 22cm
Cover title
Unpriced (pbk) B81-36147

942.8'54 — Cleveland. Coatham & Redcar. Piers, *1871-1979 — Illustrations*

The **End** of the pier book : a pictorial record of Redcar and Coatham piers / [compiled] by Peter Sotheran. — Redcar : Sotheran, c1981. — 26p : ill ; 20x22cm
ISBN 0-905032-12-8 (pbk) : £1.00 B81-29897

942.8'54 — Cleveland. Coatham & Redcar, *to 1945*

Cockroft, Janet. Redcar and Coatham : a history to the end of World War II / by Janet Cockroft ; edited by Peter Sotheran ; line drawings by M. John Hallisell. — 2nd ed., rev. and enl. — Redcar : Sotheran, c1980. — 144p,12p of plates : ill,maps,1coat of arms,facsims ; 23cm
Previous ed.: 1976. — Bibliography: p142-144
ISBN 0-905032-08-x (cased) : Unpriced
ISBN 0-905032-09-8 (pbk) : £1.95 B81-29898

942.8'62 — Durham *(County).* **Byers Green,** *to 1979*

Stephenson, John, *1935-*. The bonny backstreets of Byers Green / John Stephenson. — [Houghton] ([All Saints Eppleton, Vicarage, Houghton, Tyne-Wear]) : [J. Stephenson], [1981]. — 68p : ill,facsims ; 22cm
Cover title
Unpriced (pbk) B81-15419

942.8'63 — Durham *(County).* **Cockerton,** *1851*

Cockerton in 1851. — [Darlington] ([c/o Audlt Education Centre, Bennett Hse., Darlington]) : [Workers' Educational Association], [1981?]. — 32p : ill,maps,1facsim ; 30cm
Cover title. — Map on inside cover
£0.75 (pbk) B81-13966

942.8'63 — Durham *(County).* **Darlington,** *to 1980*

Chilton, J. Douglas. Jottings over a lifetime in and around Darlington / J. Douglas Chilton. — [Darlington] ([4 Southend Ave., Darlington, Co. Durham]) : [J.D. Chilton], 1981. — 107p : ill,1map,2ports ; 21cm
Unpriced (pbk) B81-24893

942.8'65 — Durham *(County).* **Durham. City walls,** *1072-1854*

Johnson, Margot. The walls and towers of Durham / [Margot Johnson] ; [prepared by Anthony R.N. Scott]. — [Durham] ([c/o County Planning Officer, County Hall, Durham DH7 5UF]) : Council of the City of Durham, 1980. — [4]p : col.map ; 30cm
Unpriced (unbound) B81-30812

942.8'73 — Tyne and Wear *(Metropolitan County).* **Gateshead —** *Serials*

Midweek post. — No.1 (1979)-. — Gateshead (191 High St., Gateshead, Tyne and Wear) : Bensham Press, 1979-. — v. : ill,ports ; 45cm
Weekly. — Description based on: No.90 (21st July 1981)
ISSN 0261-8702 = Midweek post : Unpriced
B81-39526

942.8'750858'05 — Tyne and Wear *(Metropolitan County).* **South Tyneside** *(District) — Serials*

South Tyneside post. — No.1 (1980)-. — Gateshead (191 High St., Gateshead, Tyne and Wear) : Bensham Press, 1980-. — v. : ill,ports ; 45cm
Weekly. — Description based on: No.66 (July 22nd 1981)
ISSN 0261-8710 = South Tyneside post : Unpriced B81-39527

942.8'76 — Tyne and Wear *(Metropolitan County).* **Newcastle upon Tyne. Benwell. Social conditions,** *to 1980*

West Newcastle in growth and decline / Benwell Community Project. — Newcastle (85 Adelaide Terrace, Newcastle upon Tyne NE4 8BB) : Benwell Community Project, 1981. — 92p : ill,maps,facsims,ports ; 30cm. — (Benwell Community Project final report series ; no.11)
ISBN 0-906316-10-3 (pbk) : £3.00 B81-33411

942.8'76 — Tyne and Wear *(Metropolitan County).* **Newcastle upon Tyne. Jesmond Vale. Social life,** *1910-1945 — Personal observations*

Ellison, Emley L.. Memories of Jesmond Vale / by Emley L. Ellison ; compiled by Cora Sanderson. — Gosforth (41, Church Rd., Gosforth, Tyne & Wear NE3 1VE) : Geordieland, c1980. — 32p : ill,maps,ports ; 22cm
Maps on inside covers
ISBN 0-9503539-6-5 (pbk) : £0.75 B81-22086

942.8'760858'0222 — Tyne and wear *(Metropolitan County).* **Newcastle upon Tyne —** *Illustrations*

Coult, Terry. Sketches of Newcastle / Terry Coult. — Durham ([Anchor & Hope Cottage, Cove Hill, Perran-ar-Worthal, Truro, Cornwall TR3 7QQ]) : Corbett, c1980. — [32]p : all ill ; 21x30cm
ISBN 0-904836-10-x (pbk) : £1.50 B81-05413

942.8'760858'05 — Tyne and Wear *(Metropolitan County).* **Newcastle upon Tyne —** *Serials*

[City news *(Newcastle upon Tyne. Information and Publicity Department)***]**. City news / City of Newcastle upon Tyne. — Issue no.51 (April 1981)-. — Newcastle upon Tyne (Civic Centre, Newcastle upon Tyne, Newcastle upon Tyne NE1 8QN) : Newcastle Information and Publicity Department, 1981-. — v. : ill,ports ; 40cm
Eight issues yearly. — Continues: Newcastle city news
ISSN 0261-3964 = City news (Newcastle upon Tyne) : Unpriced B81-27913

942.8'79 — Tyne and Wear *(Metropolitan County).* **Cullercoats, Monkseaton & Whitley Bay,** *to 1890 — Early works*

Tomlinson, William Weaver. Historical notes on Cullercoats, Whitley and Monkseaton : with a descriptive memoir of the coast from Tynemouth to St. Mary's Island / by William Weaver Tomlinson. — Newcastle-upon-Tyne : Frank Graham, 1980. — lx,164p : ill,2maps,1port ; 19cm
Facsim of: ed. published London : W. Scott, 1893. — Includes index
ISBN 0-85983-171-x (pbk) : £3.50 B81-07144

942.8'8 — Northumberland. National parks: Northumberland National Park. Social conditions *— For environment planning*

The **local** community. — Newcastle upon Tyne ([c/o] National Park Officer, Bede House, All Saints Centre, Newcastle upon Tyne) : [Northumberland National Park and Countryside Committee], 1976. — 15p,[5]p of plates : maps ; 30cm. — (Working paper / Northumberland National Park ; 6)
Unpriced (spiral) B81-29617

942.8'8081'0222 — England. Border country. Social life, *ca 1855-1910 — Illustrations*

The **Victorian** and Edwardian Borderland from rare photographs / [compiled by] Raymond Lamont-Brown and Peter Adamson ; foreword by the Lord Home of the Hirsel. — St. Andrews (52 Buchanan Gardens, St. Andrews KY16 9LX) : Alvie, 1981. — 123,[13]p : ill,ports ; 26cm
ISBN 0-9506200-1-7 : £6.80
Primary classification 941.3'7081'0222
B81-29725

942.8'8081'0222 — Northumberland. Social life, *1860-1950 — Illustrations*

Northumberland memories : an album of photographs of life in Northumberland between 1860 and 1950 / edited for the Association of Northumberland Local History Societies by Robin Gard. — Newcastle upon Tyne : Frank Graham, 1981. — [64]p : all ill,ports ; 24cm
ISBN 0-85983-191-4 (pbk) : £2.25 B81-24968

942.9 — HISTORY. WALES

942.9œb98 — Gwent. Chepstow, *1870-1970 — Illustrations*

Chepstow Museum. Chepstow in old photographs / compiled by Jane Pearson. — Chepstow (Bridge St., Chepstow) : Chepstow Museum, [1981?]. — [60]p : ill ; 15x21cm
ISBN 0-9503295-4-1 (pbk) : Unpriced B81-21962

942.9′041 — Wales. Rebellions, *1400-1412*

Allday, D. Helen. Insurrection in Wales : the rebellion of the Welsh led by Owen Glyn Dwr (Glendower) against the English Crown in 1400 / by D. Helen Allday. — Lavenham : Terence Dalton, 1981. — xii,182p,[24]p of plates : ill,maps,geneal.tables ; 23cm
Map on lining papers. — Bibliography: p175. — Includes index
ISBN 0-86138-001-0 : £6.95 B81-24042

942.9′07 — Wales, *1780-1980*

A **People** and a proletariat : essays in the history of Wales 1780-1980 / edited by David Smith. — London : Pluto in association with Llafur, The Society for the Study of Welsh Labour History, 1980. — 239p ; 21cm
Includes bibliographies
ISBN 0-86104-322-7 (cased) : £10.00
ISBN 0-86104-321-9 (pbk) : £4.95 B81-04017

942.9′081 — Wales. Social change, *1850-1870*

Jones, Ieuan Gwynedd. Explorations and explanations : essays in the social history of Victorian Wales / Ieuan Gwynedd Jones. — Llandysul : Gwasg Gomer, 1981. — 338p,[3] folded leaves : ill,maps ; 22cm
Bibliography: p321-330. — Includes index
ISBN 0-85088-644-9 : £9.75 B81-40042

942.9′082 — Wales, *1880-1980*

Morgan, Kenneth O.. Rebirth of a nation : Wales 1880-1980 / by Kenneth O. Morgan. — Oxford : Clarendon, 1981. — x,463p : 2maps ; 24cm. — (The History of Wales ; [v.6])
Bibliography: p422-445. - Includes index
ISBN 0-19-821736-6 : £15.00 : CIP rev. B80-12672

942.9′0858′05 — Wales *— Serials*

[Arcade *(Cardiff)***]**. Arcade : Wales fortnightly. — No.1 (Oct.31 1980)-. — Cardiff (43 Lower Cathedral Rd, Cardiff CF1 8LW) : Arcade Publications, 1980-. — v. : ill,ports ; 32cm
ISSN 0261-538x = Arcade (Cardiff) : £0.40 B81-32266

942.9′0858′072 — Wales. Social conditions. Research sponsored by Great Britain. *Welsh Office — Serials*

Great Britain. *Welsh Office*. Research, Wales / Welsh Office. — 7th report (1979-80). — Cardiff : H.M.S.O., 1980. — 16p
ISBN 0-11-790152-0 : £4.00 B81-08787

942.9′0858′0924 — Wales. Rural regions. Social life *— Personal observations*

Craig, Thurlow. The Sunday express Up country yearbook / Thurlow Craig ; illustrations by Bill Martin. — London : Corgi, 1981, c1979. — 216p : ill ; 20cm
Originally published: London : A. Barker, 1979
ISBN 0-552-98120-6 (pbk) : £1.35 B81-27832

942.9′10856′0924 — North Wales. Rural regions. Social life, *1965-1974 — Personal observations*

West, Elizabeth. Garden in the hills / Elizabeth West. — London : Corgi, 1981, c1980. — 204p : 1plan ; 18cm
Originally published: London : Faber, 1980
ISBN 0-552-11707-2 (pbk) : £1.25 B81-27831

942.9′23 — Gwynedd. Eifionydd. Social life *— Personal observations — Welsh texts*

Jones, Elis Gwyn. Hunaniaeth Eifionydd / gan Elis Gwyn Jones. — Caernarfon ([Maesincla, Caernarfon, Gwynedd LL55 1LH]) : Gwasanaeth Llyfrgell Gwynedd, 1981. — 26p : 1port ; 22cm. — (Darlith flynyddol Eifionydd ; 1981)
"Darlith a dreddodwyd yng Ngwesty′r Marine, Cricieth, Tachwedd 14eg, 1980"
ISBN 0-904852-21-0 (pbk) : £0.30 B81-18620

942.9′23 — Gwynedd. Lleyn Peninsula. Social life, *1910-20 — Childhood reminiscences — Welsh texts*

Roberts, Griffith T.. Pan oeddwn fachgen- : darlith flynyddol Llŷn 1979 / gan Griffith T. Roberts. — Caernarfon (Llyfrgell Arfon/Dwyfor, Maesincla, Caernarfon, Gwynedd LL55 1LH) : Cyngor Sir Gwynedd Gwasanaeth Llyfrgell, 1979. — 27p : 1port ; 19cm
ISBN 0-904852-15-6 (pbk) : Unpriced B81-07335

942.9′25 — Gwynedd. Bethesda. Social life, *ca 1930 — Personal observations — Welsh texts*

Williams, R. M. (Robert Maurice). Hon ydyw′r afon : darlith a draddodwyd yng Nghapel Jerusalem, Bethesda, Mawrth 14, 1979 / gan R.M. Williams. — Caernarfon (Llyfrgell Arfon/Dwyfor, Caernafon, Gwynedd Llyfrgell Gwynedd), 1979. — 32p : 1port. — (Darlith flynyddol Llyfrgell Bethesda ; 1979)
ISBN 0-904852-14-8 (pbk) : Unpriced B81-09525

942.9′29 — Gwynedd. Blaenau Ffestiniog. Social life, *1940-1950 — Childhood reminiscences — Welsh texts*

Thomas, Gwyn, *1936-*. Yn blentyn yn y Blaenau : darlith a draddodwyd ym Mhlas Tanybwlch, Maentwrog, Mawrth 6, 1981 / gan Gwyn Thomas. — [Caernarfon] ([Maesincla, Caernarfon, Gwynedd LL55 1LH]) : Cyngor Sir Gwynedd, Gwasanaeth Llyfrgell, 1981. — 25p : 1port ; 21cm. — (Darlith flynyddol Llyfrgell Blaenau Ffestiniog ; 1981)
Unpriced (pbk) B81-17048

942.9′31 — Clwyd. Uwchaled, *to 1979 — Welsh texts*

Awelon o Uwchaled / golygydd Gwilym G. Jones. — Y Bala ([County Press Buildings, Bala, Gwynedd LL23 7PG]) : Llyfrau′r Faner, 1980. — v,157p : ill,ports ; pbk
£1.50 B81-10284

942.9′37 — Clwyd. Llangollen. Butler, *Lady* **Eleanor & Ponsonby, Sarah** *— Biographies*

Mavor, Elizabeth. The ladies of Llangollen : a study in romantic friendship / Elizabeth Mavor. — Harmondsworth : Penguin, 1973, c1971 (1981 [printing]). — xxi,242p,[16]p of plates : ill,facsims,ports ; 18cm
Originally published: London : Joseph, 1971. — Includes index
ISBN 0-14-003708-x (pbk) : £1.95 B81-25449

942.9′390858′05 -- Clywd. Wrexham Maelor *(District) — Serials*

The **Wrexham** express. — No.1 (Oct.1980)-. — Wrexham (Express House, Lord St., Wrexham [Clwyd] LL1 1LR) : St Regis Newspapers, 1980-. — v. : ill,ports ; 40cm
Weekly. — Description based on: No.22 (Thursday Mar.5 1981)
ISSN 0261-6297 = Wrexham express : Unpriced B81-32207

942.9′61 — Dyfed. Llanarth. Social life, *ca 1930 — Personal observations — Welsh texts*

Davies, Joan. Pen y mwdwl / Joan Davies. — [Caernarfon] ([c/o Calvinistic Methodist Book Agency, Heol Ddewi, Cearnerfon LL55 1ER]) : Gwasg Pantycelyn, c1980. — 117p ; 19cm
Unpriced (pbk) B81-09523

942.9′61 — Dyfed. Soar-y-mynydd. Social life, *to 1979*

Jones, Evan, *1895-*. Cymdogaeth Soar-y-mynydd / Evan Jones. — Abertawe : C. Davies, c1979. — 132p : ill,ports ; 19cm. — (Cyfres cynefin ; 1)
ISBN 0-7154-0493-8 (pbk) : £1.75 B81-13971

942.9′61083′0924 — Dyfed. Ceredigion *(District)*. **Social life,** *ca 1920-ca 1930 — Childhood reminiscences — Welsh texts*

Davies, T. J.. Pencawna / T.J. Davies. — Abertawe, C. Davies, 1979. — 1107p,[8]p of plates : ports ; 22cm
ISBN 0-7154-0517-9 (pbk) : £2.25 B81-09524

942.9′62 — Dyfed. St. David′s. Cathedrals: St. David′s Cathedral, *to 1981*

Evans, J. Wyn. Eglwys Gadeiriol Ty DDewi, 1181-1981 = St. David′s Cathedral, 1181-1981. — St. David′s (St. David′s, Dyfed) : Yr Oriel Fach, July 1981. — [160]p
ISBN 0-905421-02-7 : £12.95 : CIP entry B81-21599

942.9′62 — Dyfed. St David′s. Social life, *to 1977*

James, David W. (David William), *1910-*. St. David′s and Dewisland : a social history / David W. James. — Cardiff : University of Wales Press, 1981. — xxiv,228p,[8]p of plates : ill,facsims,2maps ; 23cm
Bibliography: p225-227
ISBN 0-7083-0797-3 : Unpriced : CIP rev. B81-12834

942.9′65 — Dyfed. Laugharne. Castles: Laugharne Castle. Excavation of remains, *to 1980*

Interim reports of excavations at Laugharne Castle, Dyfed, 1976-1980 by Richard Avent and Dryslwyn Castle, Dyfed, 1980 by Peter Webster. — [Cardiff] ([University College Cardiff, 40 Park Place, Cardiff CF1 3BB]) : [Department of Extra-Mural Studies], 1981. — 54p : ill,maps,plans ; 30cm
(pbk)
Also classified at 942.9′68 B81-38881

942.9′65′005 — Dyfed. Carmarthenshire *— History — Serials*

The **Carmarthenshire** historian. — Vol.17. — Carmarthen (Dark Gate Chambers, Red St., Carmarthen) : Dyfed Rural Council, [1980]. — 84p
£1.00 B81-13095

942.9′650857′0924 — Dyfed. Carmarthen *(District)*. **Rural regions. Social life,** *1976-1979 — Personal obsevations*

Cragoe, Elizabeth. Sweet nothings : a country commonplace book / by Elizabeth Cragoe. — London : Hamilton, 1980. — 181p ; 23cm
ISBN 0-241-10495-5 : £6.95 : CIP rev. B80-23905

942.9′68 — Dyfed. Llandeilo. Castles: Dryslwyn Castle. Excavation of remains, *1980*

Interim reports of excavations at Laugharne Castle, Dyfed, 1976-1980 by Richard Avent and Dryslwyn Castle, Dyfed, 1980 by Peter Webster. — [Cardiff] ([University College Cardiff, 40 Park Place, Cardiff CF1 3BB]) : [Department of Extra-Mural Studies], 1981. — 54p : ill,maps,plans ; 30cm
(pbk)
Primary classification 942.9′65 B81-38881

942.9′7 — Glamorgan, *ca 1500-1960*

Stewart Williams′ Glamorgan historian. — Barry : Stewart Williams
Vol.12 / edited by Roy Denning. — [1981]. — 208p : ill,maps,1facsim,ports ; 23cm
Includes index
ISBN 0-900807-43-1 : £7.95 B81-36194

942.9′71 — Mid Glamorgan. Gilfach Goch. Social life, *1916-1980 — Personal observations — Welsh texts*

Pritchard, Katie Olwen. Y glas a′r coch / gan Katie Olwen Pritchard. — Caernarfon (Llyfrgell Arfon/Dwyfor, 'Maesincla', Caernarfon, Gwynedd) : Cyngor Sir Gwynedd Gwasanaeth Llyfrgell, 1981. — 42p : 1port ; 18cm. — (Darlish flynyddol Llyfrgell Penygroes ; 1980/81)
ISBN 0-904852-22-9 (pbk) : £0.60 B81-28898

942.9′72 — Mid Glamorgan. Ystradyfodwg. Social life, *1734-1753*

Lewis, William. 18th century Rhondda and the Red Priest / William Lewis ; English translation by G. Llewellyn. — [Rhondda] ([c/o Mr. G. Llewellyn, 1 Mill St., Ystrad Pentre, Rhondda, Mid Glam. CF41 7SQ]) : [Rhondda Society], c1980. — 16p : 1map ; 22cm
Translation of: Cwm Rhondda a′r Ffeirad Coch. — Cover title
ISBN 0-9507338-0-6 (pbk) : Unpriced B81-23335

942.9′73083′0924 — Mid Glamorgan. Cynon Valley. Coal mining communities. Social life, *ca 1925-1946 — Personal observations*
Morgan, Robert, *1921-*. My lamp still burns / Robert Morgan. — Llandysul : Gomer, 1981. — 141p ; 22cm
ISBN 0-85088-944-8 : £5.75 B81-40039

942.9′75 — Mid Glamorgan. Merthyr Tydfil, *to 1980*
Merthyr Tydfil : 1500 years / edited with an introduction by Huw Williams. — [Merthyr Tydfil] : Merthyr Tydfil Local History Group ; [Dowlais] ([17 Morlais St., Dowlais, Merthyr Tydfil, M. Glam. CF48 3AY]) : H. Williams [distributor], [1980]. — 87p : ill,1map,1facsim,1plan,ports ; 22cm
£1.00 (pbk) B81-01395

942.9′78 — Mid Glamorgan. Llantwit Fardre, *to 1980 — Illustrations*
Lewis, Dillwyn. Under the parish lantern : Llanilltud Faerdref parish in pictures / by Dillwyn Lewis. — Pontypridd (12 Llantrisant Rd, Beddau, Pontypridd, Mid Glamorgan CF38 2BB) : D. Lewis, 1981. — 33p,[240]p of plates : chiefly ill,facsims,ports ; 22cm
ISBN 0-9500567-2-3 : Unpriced B81-27748

942.9′87081′0222 — Cardiff, *1880-1980 — Illustrations*
Stewart Williams′ Cardiff yesterday / [compiled by Stewart Williams]. — Barry : Stewart Williams
Bk.2 / foreword by Bill Barrett. — 1981. — [220]p : chiefly ill,facsims,ports ; 24cm
Facsims on lining papers
ISBN 0-900807-44-x : £5.95 B81-20803

Williams, Stewart. Stewart Williams′ Cardiff yesterday. — Barry : Stewart Williams
Bk.3 / foreword by Dannie Abse. — 1981. — [120]p : chiefly ill,1facsim,ports ; 25cm
Facsims on lining papers
ISBN 0-900807-46-6 : £5.95 B81-40047

942.9′89 — South Glamorgan. Cadoxton. Parish churches: St. Cadoc′s *(Church : Cadoxton), to 1980*
Luxton, Brian C.. St. Cadoc′s : a history of the old village church Cadoxton-juxta-Barry / by Brian C. Luxton. — Barry (12 Coldbrook Rd., Barry [CF6 7NF]) : B. Luxton, 1980. — 82p : ill,1map,1plan,1port ; 22cm
Unpriced B81-09943

942.9′89 — South Glamorgan. Cowbridge, *to 1980*
Robinson, David M. (David Martin). Cowbridge : the archaeology and topography of a small market town in the Vale of Glamorgan / David M. Robinson for the Glamorgan-Gwent Archaeological Trust. — Swansea (6 Prospect Pla., Swansea SA1 1QP) : Glamorgan-Gwent Archaeological Trust, 1980. — xiii,85p : ill,maps,plans(some col.) ; 30cm. — (Town survey ; no.1)
Includes index
ISBN 0-9506950-1-7 (pbk) : £4.50 B81-02771

942.9′89 — South Glamorgan. Penarth, *1841-1871*
Benjamin, E. Alwyn. Penarth, 1841-1871 : a glimpse of the past / by E. Alwyn Benjamin. — Cowbridge ([Cowbridge, S. Glam.]) : D. Brown, 1980. — 182p : ill,maps,facsims,ports ; 22cm
Includes index
ISBN 0-905928-11-3 (pbk) : £4.30 B81-02722

942.9′89 — South Glamorgan. St Andrews Major. Social life, *1840-1880*
Griffiths, Matthew. Portrait of a parish : St Andrews Major and Dinas Powys in the mid-nineteenth century / by Matthew Griffiths. — Cardiff (38 Park Place, Cardiff [CF1 3PP]) : University College, Cardiff, Department of Extra-Mural Studies, 1980. — viii,52p,4p of plates : ill,maps ; 21cm. — (Park Place papers ; no.8)
Bibliography: p52
£1.00 (pbk) B81-04642

942.9′91 — Gwent. Caerleon, *to 1980*
Hockey, Primrose. Caerleon past and present / Primrose Hockey. — Risca : Starling Press, 1981. — 147p,[73]p of plates : ill,1map,facsims,ports ; 22cm
ISBN 0-903434-43-1 : £5.00 B81-22390

942.9′91 — Gwent. Newport. Social life — *Illustrations*
Newport survey / edited by Sir Tom Hopkinson. — Newport, Gwent : Gwent College of Higher Education
Part 1-1980: The family. — c1980. — 57p : ill,ports ; 42cm
ISBN 0-9507317-0-6 (pbk) : £2.00 B81-07533

942.9′93 — Gwent. Risca, *to 1900*
Jones, Alan Victor. Risca — its industrial and social development / Alan Victor Jones. — Bognor Regis : New Horizon, c1980. — 128p,[18]p of plates : ill,maps,1facsim ; 22cm
Bibliography: p123-128
ISBN 0-86116-472-5 : £4.50 B81-21703

942.9′95 — Gwent. Abertillery, *1890-1972 — Illustrations*
Old Abertillery in photographs / [compiled] by Keith Thomas ; foreword by Jeffrey Thomas. — Barry : Stewart Williams, 1981. — [121]p : chiefly.ill,ports ; 26cm
ISBN 0-900807-45-8 : £5.95 B81-25218

942.9′95 — Gwent. Blaina, Brynmawr & Nantyglo. Social life, *1851-1974 — Illustrations*
Old Brynmawr, Nantyglo & Blaina in photographs / [compiled] by Trevor Rowson and Edwin Jones ; foreword by Peter J. Law. — Barry : Stewart Williams, 1980. — [120]p : all ill,1facsim,ports ; 26cm
ISBN 0-900807-42-3 : £5.95 B81-03130

942.9′95 — Gwent. Ebbw Vale, *1844-1976 — Illustrations*
Old Ebbw Vale : in photographs / [compiled] by Keith Thomas. — Barry : Stewart Williams
Vol.2 / foreword by J.H. Powell. — 1980. — [120]p : all ill,facsims,ports ; 26cm
ISBN 0-900807-41-5 : £5.95 B81-19887

942.9′95 — Wales. Mining villages. Social life — *Study regions: Gwent. Six Bells — For children*
Broomfield, Stuart A Welsh mining village / Stuart Broomfield ; photographs by Chris Fairclough. — London : Black, 1981. — 25p : ill,1map,1plan,ports ; 22cm. — (The Strands series ; 10)
ISBN 0-7136-2084-6 : £2.50 : CIP rev.
B80-18947

942.9′97 — Gwent. Llantarnam. Abbeys: Llantarnam Abbey, *to 1979*
Mahoney, Teresa A.. Llantarnam Abbey : 800 years of history / Teresa A. Mahoney. — [Cwmbran] ([Llantarnam Abbey, Cwmbran, Gwent, NP44 3YJ]) : [Sisters of St Joseph], [1981]. — vii,238p : 1geneal.table ; 26cm
Limited ed. of 200 copies. — Bibliography: p195-205
Unpriced (pbk) B81-40665

942.9′98 — Gwent. Chepstow region, *1860-1980 — Illustrations*
Waters, Mercedes. In and around Chepstow / Mercedes Waters. — Chepstow (41 Hardwick Ave., Chepstow, Gwent NP6 5DS) : Moss Rose, 1981. — [41]p : all.ill ; 23x30cm
ISBN 0-906134-13-7 (pbk) : Unpriced
B81-24531

942.9′98 — Gwent. Llanthony. Abbeys: Llanthony Abbey, *to ca 1850*
Hopkins, Gordon. Llanthony Abbey and Walter Savage Landor / by Gordon Hopkins. — [s.l.] : C.H.G. Hopkins ; Cowbridge ([Prebends Gate Cottage, Quarry Heads La., Durham DH1 3DZ]) : D. Brown [distributor], 1979. — 48p : 1ill,1map ; 21cm
ISBN 0-905928-04-0 (pbk) : £0.90
Also classified at 828′.709 B81-09536

942.9′98 — Gwent. Raglan. Castles: Raglan Castle
Durant, Horatia. Raglan Castle / by Horatia Durant. — 2nd ed. — Risca ([Tredegar St.,] Risca, Newport, Gwent NP1 6YB) : Starling, 1980. — 100p,[14]p of plates : ill,1col.coat of arms,ports ; 22cm
Previous ed.: Pontypool : Hughes and Sons, 1966. — Includes index
ISBN 0-903434-41-5 (pbk) : £3.00 B81-04103

942.9′98 — Gwent. Tintern. Abbeys: Tintern Abbey, *to 1981*
Kelley, Frank. 850th anniversary of the foundation of Tintern Abbey / [by Frank Kelley]. — [Abergavenny ([The Rectory, Llanddewi Ysgyryd, Abergavenny, Gwent NP7 8AG]) : [Tintern Festival Organising Committee], [1981?]. — 8,[4]p : ill ; 21cm
Cover title
Unpriced (pbk) B81-31982

943 — HISTORY. CENTRAL EUROPE, GERMANY

943 — Germany. Ley systems
Gerlach, Kurt. Leys of the German Empire / by Kurt Gerlach ; translated by Michael Behrend. — Cambridge (142 Pheasant Rise, Bar Hill, Cambridge) : Institute of Geomantic Research, [1980?]. — 24p,[2]p of plates : maps ; 30cm
Translation of essays originally appearing in 'Germanien' between 1940-1943. — Cover title
Unpriced (pbk) B81-39689

943′.0003′21 — Holy Roman Empire — *Encyclopaedias*
The **Holy** Roman Empire : a dictionary handbook / edited by Jonathan W. Zophy. — Westport ; London : Greenwood Press, 1980. — xvi,551p : maps ; 25cm
Bibliography: p507-512. — Includes index
ISBN 0-313-21457-3 : £27.90 B81-23456

943′.004924 — Germany. Jews — *Serials*
[Year book *(Leo Baeck Institute)*]. Year book / Leo Baeck Institute. — 25, (1980). — London : Secker & Warburg for the Institute, c1980. — xii,490p
ISBN 0-436-24433-0 : £9.00 B81-01396

943′.07 — Germany, *1800-1914*
Sagarra, Eda. An introduction to nineteenth century Germany / Eda Sagarra. — Harlow : Longman, 1980. — vii,312p : ill,maps,ports ; 22cm
Bibliography: p299-304. — Includes index
ISBN 0-582-35137-5 (cased) : Unpriced
ISBN 0-582-35138-3 (pbk) : £4.50 B81-08462

943.08 — Germany, *1860-1979*
Calleo, David. The German problem reconsidered : Germany and the world order, 1870 to the present / David Calleo. — Cambridge : Cambridge University Press, 1980, c1978. — xi,239p ; 24cm
Bibliography: p211—231. - Includes index
ISBN 0-521-29966-7 (pbk) : £4.95 B81-11192

943.08 — Germany, *1866-1945*
Craig, Gordon A.. Germany 1866-1945 / by Gordon A. Craig. — Oxford : Oxford University Press, 1981. — xv,825p : 1map ; 20cm
Originally published: Oxford : Clarendon Press, 1978. — Bibliography: p774-809. - Includes index
ISBN 0-19-285101-2 (pbk) : £6.95 : CIP rev.
B80-13653

943.08 — Germany, *1914-1945*
Germany in the age of total war / edited by Volker R. Berghahn and Martin Kitchen. — London : Croom Helm, c1981. — 266p ; 23cm
Bibliography: p258-260. - Includes index
ISBN 0-7099-0119-4 : £13.95 B81-17853

943.08′092′4 — Germany. Political events in role of Bismark, Otto, *Fürst von, 1851-1898*
Mitchell, Ian R.. Bismarck and the development of Germany / Ian R. Mitchell. — Edinburgh : Holmes McDougall, 1980. — v,142p : ill,maps,ports ; 19x25cm
Bibliography: p137-138. — Includes index
ISBN 0-7157-1793-6 (pbk) : £2.95 B81-10783

943.08′092′4 — Germany. Politics. Windthorst, Ludwig — *Biographies*
Anderson, Margaret Lavinia. Windthorst : a political biography / by Margaret Lavinia Anderson. — Oxford : Clarendon, 1981. — xi,522p,[1]leaf of plates : 1port ; 23cm
Bibliography: p481-500. — Includes index
ISBN 0-19-822578-4 : £25.00 : CIP rev.
B81-06040

943.08′2 — Franco-Prussian War

Howard, Michael, *1922-*. The Franco-Prussian War : the German invasion of France, 1870-1871 / Michael Howard. — London : Methuen, 1981, c1961. — ix,512p : maps,plans ; 21cm
Originally published: London : Hart-Davis, 1961. — Bibliography: p.459-473. — Includes index
ISBN 0-416-30750-7 (pbk) : Unpriced
B81-34711

943.08′3′0924 — Germany. Victoria, ***Empress, consort of Friedrich III, Emperor of Germany, 1878-1885 — Correspondence to Victoria, Queen of Great Britain***

Victoria, *Queen of Great Britain*. Beloved mama. — London : Evans Bros., Oct.1981. — [224]p
ISBN 0-237-44997-8 : £10.95 : CIP entry
Primary classification 941.08′13′0924
B81-25777

943.08′4 — Germany. Frederick III, ***Emperor of Germany - Biographies***

Van der Kiste, John. Frederick III. — Gloucester (17a Brunswick Rd, Gloucester GL1 1HG) : Alan Sutton, May 1981. — [240]p
ISBN 0-904387-77-1 : £8.95 : CIP entry
B81-08933

943.08′4′0924 — Germany. Wilhelm II, ***Emperor of Germany — Critical studies***

Kaiser Wilhelm II : new interpretations. — Cambridge : Cambridge University Press, Feb.1982. — [324]p
ISBN 0-521-23898-6 : £19.50 : CIP entry
B81-36950

943.085 — Germany. Nationalsozialistiche Deutsche Arbeiter-Partei. ***Schutzstaffel, to 1945***

Höhne, Heinz. The order of the death′s head : the story of Hitler′s SS / Heinz Höhne ; translated from the German by Richard Barry. — London : Pan, 1972, c1969 (1981 [printing]). — xxx,655p,[13]p of plates : ill,maps,ports ; 20cm
Translation of: Der Order unter dem Totenkopf. — Originally published: London : Secker and Warburg, 1969. — Bibliography: p619-635. — Includes index
£2.95 (pbk) B81-26332

943.085 — Germany. Nationalsozialistische Deutsche Arbeiter-Partei. ***Schutzstaffel, to 1945***

Reitlinger, Gerald. The SS : alibi of a nation 1922-1945 / Gerald Reitlinger ; with a new foreword by Martin Gilbert. — London : Arms and Armour, 1981. — xi,502p,[16]p of plates : ill,maps,ports ; 23cm
Originally published: London : Heinemann, 1956. — Bibliography: p455-460. - Includes index
ISBN 0-85368-187-2 : £8.95 B81-21265

943.085 — Germany. Political events, ***1919-1945 — For schools***

Gray, Ronald. Hitler and the Germans. — Cambridge : Cambridge University Press, Nov.1981. — [45]p. — (Cambridge introduction to the history of mankind)
ISBN 0-521-22702-x (pbk) : £1.95 : CIP entry
B81-32525

943.085 — Germany. Political events, ***1924-1932***

Abraham, David. The collapse of the Weimar Republic : political economy and crisis / by David Abraham. — Princeton ; Guildford : Princeton University Press, c1981. — 366p : ill ; 25cm
Bibliography: p328-349. — Includes index
ISBN 0-691-05322-7 (cased) : £16.70
ISBN 0-691-10118-3 (pbk) : £7.00
ISBN 0-691-09356-3 B81-29487

943.085 — Germany. Social change, ***1918-1933***

Social change and political development in Weimar Germany / edited by Richard Bessel and E.J. Feuchtwanger. — London : Croom Helm, c1981. — 297p : ill ; 23cm
Includes index
ISBN 0-85664-921-x : £13.95 B81-07129

943.086 — Germany. Nationalsozialistische Deutsche Arbeiter-Partei. ***Waffenschutzstaffel. Totenkopfdivision, 1933-1945***

Höhne, Heinz. The Order of the Death′s Head : the story of Hitler′s SS / Heinz Höhne ; translated from the German by Richard Barry. — [London] : Nationwide Book Service, 1980, c1969. — xii,690p : maps ; 24cm
Translation of: Der Orden unter den Totenkopf. — Originally published: London : Secker & Warburg, 1969. — Bibliography: p659-672. — Includes index
ISBN 0-436-20065-1 : £12.00

943.086′092′2 — Germany, ***1933-1945 — Personal observations — Collections***

Lang, Daniel. A backward look : Germans remember / by Daniel Lang. — New York ; London : McGraw-Hill, 1979 (1981 [printing]). — 112p,[18]p of plates : ill,ports ; 21cm
ISBN 0-07-036241-6 (pbk) : £3.50 B81-37862

943.086′092′4 — Germany. Heydrich, Reinhard — ***Biographies***

Graber, G. S.. The life and times of Reinhard Heydrich / G.S. Graber. — London : Hale, 1981. — 245p,[8]p of plates : ill ; 22cm
Includes index
ISBN 0-7091-8869-2 : £7.95 B81-16956

943.086′0924 — Germany. Hitler, Adolf — ***Biographies***

Stone, Norman. Hitler. — London : Hodder and Stoughton, Jan.1982. — [240]p
Originally published: 1980
ISBN 0-340-27538-3 (pbk) : £1.25 : CIP entry
B81-34137

943.086′092′4 — Germany. Hitler, Adolf. Influence of occultism

Suster, Gerald. Hitler and the age of Horus / Gerald Suster. — London : Sphere, 1981, c1980. — xviii,231p,[8]p of plates : ill,ports ; 18cm
Bibliography: p215-216. — Includes index
ISBN 0-7221-8287-2 (pbk) : £1.50 B81-25433

943.086′092′4 — Germany. Koehn, Ilse, ***to 1945 — Biographies***

Koehn, Ilse. Mischling, second degree : my childhood in Nazi Germany / Ilse Koehn. — Harmondsworth : Puffin, 1981, c1977. — 221p ; 18cm. — (Puffin plus)
Originally published: New York : Greenwillow Books, 1977 ; London : H. Hamilton, 1978
ISBN 0-14-031356-7 (pbk) : £1.25 B81-25206

943.087 — West Germany, ***1945-1979***

Childs, David. West Germany : politics and society / David Childs and Jeffrey Johnson. — London : Croom Helm, c1981. — 231p ; 23cm
Includes bibliographies and index
ISBN 0-7099-0701-x (cased) : £10.95 : CIP rev.
ISBN 0-7099-0702-8 (pbk) : £6.95 B80-18130

943.087 — West Germany, ***1945-1980***

The **West** German model. — London : Cass, Aug.1981. — [184]p
ISBN 0-7146-3180-9 : £12.50 : CIP entry
B81-18034

943.087′4 — Germany, ***1945-1952***

Mann, Anthony. Comeback : Germany 1945-1952 / Anthony Mann. — London : Macmillan, 1980. — x,242p,[8]p of plates : ill,maps,ports ; 23cm
Includes index
ISBN 0-333-27499-7 : £9.95 B81-04032

943.6 — HISTORY. AUSTRIA

943.6′04 — Austria. Habsburg ***(House of), 1809-1918***

Taylor, A. J. P.. The Hapsburg monarchy 1809-1918 : a history of the Austrian Empire and Austria-Hungary / A.J.P. Taylor. — Harmondsworth : Penguin, 1981, c1948. — 304p ; 20cm
Originally published: London : Macmillan, 1941. — Bibliography: p292-295. — Includes index
ISBN 0-14-022304-5 (pbk) : £2.95 B81-17822

943.6′04′0924 — Austro-Hungarian Empire. Political events. Role of Seton-Watson, R. W., ***1900-1920***

Seton-Watson, Hugh. The making of a new Europe : R.W. Seton-Watson and the last years of Austria-Hungary / Hugh and Christopher Seton-Watson. — London : Methuen, 1981. — x,458p : maps,1port ; 24cm
Maps on lining papers. — Bibliography: p443-445. - Includes index
ISBN 0-416-74730-2 : £25.00 B81-19865

943.6′1304 — Austrian culture: Viennese culture, ***ca 1850-1914***

Schorske, Carl E.. Fin-de-siècle Vienna : politics and culture / Carl E. Schorske. — Cambridge : Cambridge University Press, 1981, c1979. — xxx,378p : ill(some col.),maps,plans,col.ports ; 24cm
Originally published: New York : Knopf, 1979. — Includes index
ISBN 0-521-28516-x (pbk) : £6.95 B81-27902

943.7 — HISTORY. CZECHOSLOVAKIA

943.7′042 — Czechoslovakia. Political events, ***1945-1948***

Myant, M. R.. Socialism and democracy in Czechoslovakia 1945-1948 / M.R. Myant. — Cambridge : Cambridge University Press, 1981. — ix,302p ; 23cm. — (Soviet and East European studies)
Bibliography: p275-291. — Includes index
ISBN 0-521-23668-1 : £20.00 : CIP rev.
B81-23754

943.8 — HISTORY. POLAND

943.8 — Poland, ***1772-1980***

Giertych, Jędrzej. In defence of my country / Jędrzej Giertych. — London (175 Carlingford Rd., N15 3ET) : J. Giertych, 1981. — 748p,2folded leaves of plates : ill,maps(some col.),facsims ; 23cm. — (Publications of Roman Dmowski Society ; no.19)
Includes index
£12.00 (pbk) B81-34922

943.8 — Poland, ***to 1980***

Davies, Norman. A history of Poland. — Oxford : Clarendon Press, Apr.1981
Vol.1: The origins to 1795. — [560]p
ISBN 0-19-822555-5 : £32.50 : CIP entry
B81-01397

Davies, Norman. A history of Poland. — Oxford : Clarendon Press, Apr.1981
Vol.2: 1795 to the present. — [672]p
ISBN 0-19-822592-x : £32.50 : CIP entry
B81-03139

943.8 — Polish culture, ***to 1980***

The **Tradition** of Polish ideals : essays in history and literature / by W.J. Stankiewicz. — London : Orbis, 1981. — 288p,[16]p of plates : ill,facsims,ports ; 21cm
Includes index
ISBN 0-901149-18-7 (pbk) : Unpriced
B81-34444

943.8′005 — Poland — ***History — Serials***

Antemurale / Institutum Historicum Polonicum Romae. — 24. — Romae [Rome] : Institutum Historicum Polonicum Romae ; London : Orbis (London Ltd.) [[distributor]], 1980. — 325p
£8.50 B81-32217

943.8′04 — Poland. Independence. Implications of Treaty of Versailles, ***1919 — Polish texts***

Wieczór wersalski : w sześćdziesięciolecie podpisania traktatu wersalskiego / [redaktor Józef Płoski]. — Londyn ([8 Alma Terrace, Allen St., W8 6QY]) : [Instytut Romana Dmowskiego w Londynie, 1980. — 46p,[8]p of plates : ill,1map,ports ; 18cm
At head of title: Instytut Romana Dmowskiego w Londynie. — Bibliography: p43-46
Unpriced (pbk) B81-21995

943.8′04′0924 — Poland. Haendel, Wilhelm — ***Biographies***

Haendel, Wilhelm. The last battle and fall of the Austrian Monarchy / Wilhelm Haendel. — Bognor Regis : New Horizon, c1980. — 142p ; 21cm
ISBN 0-86116-608-6 : £5.25 B81-21772

943.8'04'0924 — Poland. Intellectual life, *1920-1957 — Personal observations — Interviews — Polish texts*

Wat, Aleksander. Mój wiek : pamiętnik mówiony / Aleksander Wat ; przedmowa Czesława Miłosza. — Wyd. drugie popr. / do druku przygotowała Lidia Ciołkoszowa. — Londyn : Polonia Book Fund, 1981. — 372,386p : ports ; 20cm
Previous ed.: 1977. — Includes index
ISBN 0-902352-11-3 (pbk) : £12.00 B81-19087

943.8'05'0924 — Poland. Wyhowska De Andreis, Wanda *— Biographies — Polish texts*

Wyhowska De Andreis, Wanda. Między Dnieprem a Tybrem / Wanda Wyhowska De Andreis. — Londyn : Polska Fundacja Kulturalna, 1981. — 200p,[2]p of plates : 1ill,1map ; 18cm
Unpriced (pbk) B81-35508

943.8'053'0924 — Poland, *1940-1942 — Personal observations — Correspondence, diaries, etc. — Polish texts*

Krzysztoporska, Maria. Ze wspomnień tułaczych / Maria Krzysztoporska. — London (4 Praed Mews, W2 1QZ) : Katolicki Ośrodek Wydawniczy Veritas, c1981. — 142p : 1port ; 19cm
Includes index
Unpriced (pbk) B81-21024

943.8'053'0924 — Poland. Social life, *1944-1946 — Personal observations — Correspondence, diaries, etc. — Polish texts*

Bogusławska, Anna. Na ruchomym gruncie : pamiętnik młodej polki 1944-1946 / Anna Bogusławska. — Londyn : Polska Fundacja Kulturalna, 1980. — 226p ; 19cm
Unpriced (pbk) B81-10546

943.8'054 — Poland, *1954 — Correspondence, diaries, etc. — Polish texts*

Tyrmand, Leopold. Dziennik 1954 : 1-2 / Leopold Tyrmand. — London (10 Queen Anne's Gardens, W4 1TU) : Polonia, 1980. — 364p : 1port ; 22cm
ISBN 0-902352-15-6 (pbk) : £8.25 B81-14727

943.8'055 — Poland. Social change *— Trotskyist viewpoints*

Posadas, J.. The process of the permanent revolution in Poland / J. Posadas. — London (24 Cranbourn St., W.C.2.) : Revolutionary Workers Party (Trotskyist), 1981. — 26p ; 21cm. — (A European Marxist review publication ; no.3/81)
£0.30 (pbk) B81-30067

943.8'055 — Poland. Society

Brandys, Kazimierz. A question of reality / Kazimierz Brandys ; translated form the French by Isabel Barzun. — London : Blond & Briggs, 1981, c1980. — 180p ; 23cm
Translation of: Nierzeczywistosc. — Originally published: New York : Scribner, 1980
ISBN 0-85634-114-2 : £5.95 B81-11804

943.8'055'0207 — Poland. Political events, *1980 — Cartoons*

Polskie lato 1980 : (w karykaturze) / [zebrał i opracował Andrzej J. Chilecki]. — Londyn : Polonia, 1980. — 40p : all ill ; 21cm
£1.00 (pbk) B81-20674

943.9 — HISTORY. HUNGARY

943.9'052'0922 — Hungary. Invasion by Soviet Union, *1956 — Personal observations — Collections*

Eye-witness in Hungary : the Soviet invasion of 1956 / edited by Bill Lommax [i.e. Lomax]. — Nottingham : Spokesman, 1980. — 183p ; 22cm
Bibliography: p182-183
ISBN 0-85124-291-x : £8.50 B81-04747

944 — HISTORY. FRANCE

944 — France. Social conditions, *1300-1800*

Le Roy Ladurie, Emmanuel. The mind and method of the historian / Emmanuel Le Roy Ladurie ; translated from the French by Siân and Ben Reynolds. — Brighton : Harvester, 1981. — v,310p ; 23cm
Translation of selections from: Le territoire de l'historien, vol.2
ISBN 0-85527-928-1 : £20.00 B81-31479

944 — France. Social conditions, *ca 1000-1979 compared with* **social conditions in Great Britain,** *ca 1000-1979*

Britain and France : ten centuries / edited by Douglas Johnson, François Crouzet and François Bédarida. — Folkestone : Dawson, 1980. — 379p ; 24cm
ISBN 0-7129-0831-5 : £20.00 : CIP rev.
Primary classification 941 B80-09603

944'.01 — France, *ca 820-ca 880 — Conference proceedings*

Charles the Bald : court and kingdom : papers based on a colloquium held in London in April 1979 / edited by Margaret Gibson and Janet Nelson with the assistance of David Ganz. — Oxford : B.A.R., 1981. — xii,400p : ill,maps ; 30cm. — (BAR. International series ; 101)
Includes 2 papers in German and 1 in French. — Includes index
ISBN 0-86054-115-0 (pbk) : £15.00 B81-36621

944'.021 — France, *987-1328*

Hallam, Elizabeth M.. Capetian France 987-1328 / Elizabeth M. Hallam. — London : Longman, 1980. — xiii,366p : maps,geneal.tables ; 24cm
Bibliography: p334-341. — Includes index
ISBN 0-582-48909-1 : £18.15 : CIP rev.
B80-22769

944'.021 — France. Cathedrals, *1150-1280*

Dunlop, Ian. The cathedrals' crusade. — London : H. Hamilton, Feb.1982. — [256]p
ISBN 0-241-10689-3 : £12.50 : CIP entry
B81-35792

944'.024'0924 — France. Philippe IV, *King of France — Biographies*

Strayer, Joseph R.. The reign of Philip the Fair / by Joseph R. Strayer. — Princeton ; Guildford : Princeton University Press, c1980. — xvi,450p,[4]p of plates : ill,1map,facsims ; 25cm
Bibliography: p425-438. — Includes index
ISBN 0-691-05302-2 (cased) : £19.20
ISBN 0-691-10089-6 (pbk) : £7.50 B81-01553

944'.025 — France, *1300-1500 — French texts*

Contamine, Philippe. La France au XIVe et XVe siècles : hommes, mentalités, guerre et paix / Philippe Contamine. — London : Variorum Reprints, 1981. — 360p in various pagings : ill,maps,1port ; 24cm. — (Collected studies series ; CS144)
Includes 2 papers in English. — Includes index
ISBN 0-86078-091-0 : £24.00 : CIP rev.
B81-21528

944'.025 — France, *1325-1400.* **Froissart, Jean. Chroniques** *— Critical studies*

Froissart : historian / edited by J.J.N. Palmer. — Woodbridge : Boydell, 1981. — xi,203p : maps ; 24cm
Bibliography: p184-194. - Includes index
ISBN 0-85115-146-9 : £20.00 : CIP rev.
B81-06579

944'.026'0924 — France. Joan, *of Arc, Saint — Biographies*

Jeffery, Colin. Joan of Arc / Colin Jeffery & Paul Dunn ; illustrations by Sister Teresa Margaret. — London : Catholic Truth Society, [1979]. — [16]p : col.ill ; 19cm
ISBN 0-85183-299-7 (pbk) : £0.40 B81-00674

944'.026'0924 — France. Joan, *of Arc, Saint - Biographies*

Scott, Leonard E.. Joan of Arc. — Oxford (107 Marlborough Rd., Oxford, OX1 4LX) : Alder, Aug.1981. — [128]p
ISBN 0-907162-01-0 (cased) : £8.95 : CIP entry
ISBN 0-907162-02-9 (pbk) : £4.95 B81-17518

944'.026'0924 — France. Joan, *of Arc, Saint — Biographies*

Warner, Marina. Joan of Arc : the image of female heroism / Marina Warner. — London : Weidenfeld and Nicolson, 1981. — xxvi,349p,[24]p of plates : ill(some col.),1map,facsims(some col.),ports(some col.) ; 25cm
Bibliography: p277-333. — Includes index
ISBN 0-297-77638-x : £9.95 B81-34794

944'.028 — France, *1500-1600*

Salmon, J. H. M.. Society in crisis : France in the sixteenth century / J.H.M. Salmon. — London : Benn, 1975 (1980 [printing]). — 384p,[12]p of plates : ill,maps,ports,geneal.tables ; 24cm. — (A Benn study. History)
Bibliography: p352-369. — Includes index
ISBN 0-510-26352-6 : £12.95 : CIP rev.
B79-37590

944'.028 — France, *1515-1547*

Knecht, R. J.. Francis I. — Cambridge : Cambridge University Press, Feb.1982. — [458]p
ISBN 0-521-24344-0 : £25.00 : CIP entry
B81-36952

944'.028 — French civilization, *1500-1600*

Febvre, Lucien. Life in Renaissance France / Lucien Febvre ; edited and translated by Marian Rothstein. — Cambridge, Mass. ; London : Harvard University Press, 1977 (1979 [printing]). — xx,163p : 1map ; 23cm. — (A Harvard paperback)
Translation from the French. — Includes index
ISBN 0-674-53180-9 (pbk) : £2.80 B81-32508

944'.028 — French culture, *1530-1607*

Grendler, Paul F.. Culture and censorship in late Renaissance Italy and France / Paul F. Grendler. — London : Variorum Reprints, 1981. — 318p in various pagings : facsims,1port ; 24cm
Includes index
ISBN 0-86078-084-8 : £24.00 : CIP rev.
Primary classification 363.3'1'0944 B81-22670

944'.028 — French culture, *1534-1573*

Kelley, Donald R. (Donald Reed). The beginning of ideology : consciousness and society in the French Reformation / Donald R. Kelley. — Cambridge : Cambridge Universiy Press, 1981. — xv,351p ; 24cm
Includes index
ISBN 0-521-23504-9 : £24.00 B81-21688

944'.03 — France, *1589-1661*

Bonney, Richard. The King's debts. — Oxford : Clarendon Press, Oct.1981. — [384]p
ISBN 0-19-822563-6 : £22.50 : CIP entry
B81-26704

944'.033 — France, *1600-1700*

Treasure, G. R. R.. Seventeenth century France / by G.R.R. Treasure. — 2nd ed. — London : Murray, 1981. — 579p ; 22cm
Previous ed.: London : Rivingtons, 1966. — Includes index
ISBN 0-7195-3823-8 (pbk) : £7.50 : CIP rev.
B81-08901

944'.035'0924 — France. Marie Antoinette, *Queen, consort of Louis XVI, King of France — Biographies*

Seward, Desmond. Marie Antoinette / Desmond Seward. — London : Constable, 1981. — 297p,[1]leaf of plates : ports ; 23cm
Bibliography: p279-281. — Includes index
ISBN 0-09-463360-6 : £8.95 B81-26848

944'.035'0924 — France. Politics. Lafayette, Marie Joseph Paul Yves Roch Gilbert du Motier, *marquis de, 1776-1790 — Correspondence, diaries, etc.*

Lafayette, Marie Joseph Paul Yves Roch Gilbert du Motier, *marquis de.* Lafayette in the age of the American Revolution : selected letters and papers, 1776-1790 / Stanley J. Idzerda editor ... — Ithaca ; London : Cornell University Press
Vol.3: April 27, 1780-March 29, 1781. — 1980. — xxxix,577p : ill,maps,facsims,ports,1geneal.table ; 24cm
Includes the French texts of some letters and papers. — Bibliography: pxxix-xxxii. — Includes index
ISBN 0-8014-1335-4 : £18.00 B81-27509

944.04 — France. Political events, *1789-1799*
Hibbert, Christopher. The French Revolution / Christopher Hibbert. — London : Allen Lane, 1980. — 351p,[24]p of plates : ill,2maps,ports ; 25cm
Bibliography: p336-341. — Includes index
ISBN 0-7139-1151-4 : £8.95 B81-01607

944.04 — France. Political events, *1789-1799.* **Historiography**
Furet, François. Interpreting the French Revolution. — Cambridge : Cambridge University Press, Oct.1981. — [204]p
Translation of: Penser la Révolution française
ISBN 0-521-23574-x (cased) : £15.00 : CIP entry
ISBN 0-521-28049-4 (pbk) B81-25816

944.04′01′9 — France. Political events, *1789-1800.* **Psychological aspects**
Le Bon, Gustave. The French Revolution and the psychology of revolution / Gustave LeBon ; with a new introduction by Robert A. Nye. — New Brunswick ; London : Transaction, c1980. — l,337p ; 24cm. — ([Social science classics series])
Translation of: La révolution française et la psychologie des révolutions. — Originally published: as The psychology of revolution. London : T.F. Unwin, 1913. — Includes index
ISBN 0-87855-310-x : £11.75
ISBN 0-87855-697-4 (pbk) : £4.25
Also classified at 322.4′2′019 B81-04122

944.04′092′4 — France. Napoléon I, *Emperor of the French, to 1796 — Biographies*
Ratcliffe, Bertram. Prelude to fame : an account of the early life of Napoleon up to the Battle of Montenotte / Bertram Ratcliffe. — London : Warne, 1981. — vii,112p,[8]p of plates : maps,ports ; 23cm
Bibliography: p107-108. - Includes index
ISBN 0-7232-2682-2 : £7.95 B81-20961

944.05′092′4 — Europe. Social change. Role of Napoléon I, *Emperor of the French, 1789-1815*
Holtman, Robert B.. The Napoleonic revolution / Robert B. Holtman. — Baton Rouge ; London : Louisiana State University Press, 1978, c1967. — 225p : ill,maps ; 22cm
Originally published: Philadelphia : Lippincott, 1967. — Includes index
ISBN 0-8071-0487-6 (pbk) : £2.40 B81-16625

944.05′092′4 — France. Napoléon I, *Emperor of the French — Biographies — For children*
Drouet, Augustin. Napoleon / Augustin Drouet ; illustrated by Daniel Poicard ; [tanslated by Merle Philo]. — St. Albans : Hart-Davis, 1981. — 30p : col.ill,1col.map ; 25cm. — (Junior histories)
Translation of the French
ISBN 0-247-13215-2 : £2.95 B81-39468

Masters, Anthony. Napoleon / Anthony Masters. — Harlow : Longman, 1981. — 69p : ill(some col.),facsims,col.map,ports(some col.) ; 25cm. — (Longman great lives)
Map on lining papers. — Bibliography: p68. — Includes index
ISBN 0-582-39040-0 : £3.95 B81-39668

944.06′1′0924 — France. Louis XVIII, *King of France — Biographies*
Mansel, Philip. Louis XVIII / Philip Mansel. — London : Blond & Briggs, c1981. — x,497p,[16]p of plates : ill,2maps,ports,2geneal.tables ; 24cm
Bibliography: p464-481. - Includes index
ISBN 0-85634-093-6 : £18.95 B81-06767

944.07 — French civilization, *1848-1945*
Zeldin, Theodore. France 1848-1945 : taste & corruption / by Theodore Zeldin. — Oxford : Oxford University Press, 1980. — 426p ; 20cm
Bibliography: p415-417. - Includes index
ISBN 0-19-285100-4 (pbk) : £3.95 : CIP rev. B80-13655

Zeldin, Theodore. France 1848-1945. — Oxford : Oxford University Press, May 1981. — (Oxford paperbacks)
Originally published: as the Third section of France 1848-1945. Vol.2 : Intellect, taste and anxiety : Oxford : Clarendon Press, 1977
Anxiety & hypocrisy. — [448]p
ISBN 0-19-285106-3 (pbk) : £4.50 : CIP entry B81-06609

944.08 — France, *1870-1976 — For schools*
Williams, Barry, *1932-*. Modern France 1870-1976 / Barry Williams. — London : Longman, 1980. — 140p : ill,maps,facsims,ports ; 21cm. — (Modern times)
Maps on inside covers. — Includes index
ISBN 0-582-22246-x (pbk) : £1.30 B81-02961

944.08 — France, *1918-1980*
Tint, Herbert. France since 1918 / Herbert Tint. — 2nd ed. — London : Batsford, 1980. — 221p ; 23cm
Previous ed.: 1970. — Bibliography: p215-216. - Includes index
ISBN 0-7134-3455-4 (cased) : £8.95
ISBN 0-7134-3448-1 (pbk) : £4.50 B81-04795

944.081′4 — France, *1914-1918.* **Psycholinguistic aspects**
Slater, Catherine. Defeatists and their enemies. — Oxford : Oxford University Press, Nov.1981. — [192]p. — (Oxford modern language and literature monographs)
ISBN 0-19-815776-2 : £12.50 : CIP entry B81-30565

944.081′5 — France. Political events, *1933-1958 — Trotskyist viewpoints*
Grant, Ted, *19---*. [France in crisis]. The rise of De Gaulle and the class struggle / by Ted Grant. — London (1 Mentmore Terrace, E8 3PN) : Militant, 1980. — 41p ; 21cm
Originally published: 1958
ISBN 0-906582-00-8 (pbk) : £0.30 B81-19731

944.083 — France. Social conditions, *1968-1980*
Social movement and protest in France. — London : Frances Pinter, Jan.1982. — [270]p
ISBN 0-86187-213-4 : £14.75 : CIP entry B81-40255

944.083′7 — France. Political events, *1972-1979*
Frears, J. R.. France in the Giscard presidency / J.R. Frears. — London : Allen & Unwin, 1981. — xii,224p : 1ill ; 23cm
Bibliography: p216-219. — Includes index
ISBN 0-04-354025-2 (cased) : £19.95 : CIP rev.
ISBN 0-04-354026-0 (pbk) : £4.95 B81-13765

944.083′7 — French civilization, *ca 1970-ca 1980*
France today : introductory studies / edited by J.E. Flower. — 4th ed. — London : Methuen, 1980. — viii,222p ; 22cm
Previous ed.: 1977. — Includes bibliographies and index
ISBN 0-416-74010-3 (pbk) : £4.25 : CIP rev. B80-19537

944.083′7′0924 — France. Social life, *1979 — Personal observations*
Bernen, Robert. In the heat of the sun / Robert Bernen. — London : Hamilton, 1981. — 133p ; 23cm
ISBN 0-241-10521-8 : £7.95 B81-08616

944.083′8 — France *— For children*
Rutland, Jonathan. Let′s go to France / Jonathan Rutland. — London : Watts, c1980. — 32p : col.ill,2col.maps ; 22cm
ISBN 0-85166-860-7 : £2.99 B81-02759

This is France / illustrated by Toni Goffe. — London : Transworld, 1981. — 31p : col.ill,1col.map ; 28cm. — (A Carousel book)
Text, ill on inside covers
ISBN 0-552-54178-8 (pbk) : £0.95 B81-32967

944.083′8 — France *— For schools*
Houldsworth, Peter. All about France. — London : Hodder & Stoughton, Feb.1982. — [128]p
ISBN 0-340-25595-1 (pbk) : £2.25 : CIP entry B81-37589

944.083′8′076 — France *— Questions & answers — For schools*
Houldsworth, Peter. Find out about France. — London : Hodder & Stoughton, Feb.1982. — [32]p
ISBN 0-340-25596-x (pbk) : £0.45 : CIP entry B81-37590

944′.13 — France. Vannetais. Social conditions, *ca 1730-1793*
Le Goff, T. J. A.. Vannes and its region : a study of town and country in eighteenth century France / by T.J.A. Le Goff. — Oxford : Clarendon Press, 1981. — vii,445p : ill,maps ; 22cm
Bibliography: p389-421. - Includes index
ISBN 0-19-822515-6 : £25.00 : CIP rev. B80-18175

944′.25 — France. Rouen. Effects of Wars of Religion, *to 1594*
Benedict, Philip. Rouen during the Wars of Religion / Philip Benedict. — Cambridge : Cambridge University Press, 1981. — xix,297p : ill,maps,1coat of arms ; 24cm. — (Cambridge studies in early modern history)
Bibliography: p265-287. - Includes index
ISBN 0-521-22818-2 : £24.00 : CIP rev. B80-26345

944′.36 — France. Paris. Socially disadvantaged inner areas *compared with* **socially disadvantaged inner areas in London**
Madge, Charles. Inner city poverty in Paris and London / Charles Madge and Peter Willmott. — London : Routledge and Kegan Paul, 1981. — xi,133p ; 23cm. — (Reports of the Institute of Community Studies) (Routledge social science series)
Bibliography: p129-131. — Includes index
ISBN 0-7100-0819-8 : £8.50 : CIP rev.
Primary classification 942.1 B81-21481

944′.36081 — Paris. *Commune*
Tombs, Robert. The war against Paris 1871. — Cambridge : Cambridge University Press, Dec.1981. — [272]p
ISBN 0-521-23551-0 : £22.50 : CIP entry B81-32598

944′.360812 — France. Paris. Political events, *1870-1871*
Horne, Alistair. The fall of Paris : the siege and the commune 1870-71 / Alistair Horne. — Harmondsworth : Penguin, 1981, c1965. — 540p,[8]p of plates : ill,maps, ports ; 20cm
Text on inside cover. — Originally published: London : Macmillan, 1965. — Bibliography: p515-520. — Includes index
ISBN 0-14-005210-0 (pbk) : £3.95 B81-16975

944′.36′0816 — France. Paris. Social life, *1940-1944*
Pryce-Jones, David. Paris in the Third Reich. — London : Collins, Aug.1981. — [320]p
ISBN 0-00-216645-3 : £12.50 : CIP entry B81-15896

944′.360837′0222 — France. Paris, *1979 — Illustrations*
Garnett, Bill. Paris / written by Bill Garnett ; picture researcher Kathy Brandt ; commissioned photography by Bill Garnett. — London : Marshall Cavendish, 1978. — 97p : ill(some col.),1map ; 28cm. — (The World′s cities)
Ill on lining papers
ISBN 0-85685-501-4 : £3.95 B81-03656

944′.360838 — France. Paris *— For children*
Barillot, Sylvie. Living in Paris / Sylvie Barillot. — Hove : Wayland, 1981. — 52p : ill,1port ; 22cm. — (Living in famous cities)
Bibliography: p51. — Includes index
ISBN 0-85340-813-0 : £3.75 B81-23258

944′.54 — France. Villages. Social life *— Study regions: Monts — For schools*
Wright, Adrian. Looking at a French village / Adrian Wright. — Sevenoaks : Hodder and Stoughton, c1980. — 22p : ill(some col.),1col.map,col.facsims ; 25cm
ISBN 0-340-23496-2 (unbound) : £0.95 : CIP rev. B80-10912

944′.72 — France. Dordogne, *to 1979*
Law, Joy. Dordogne / Joy Law. — London : Macdonald Futura, 1981. — 221p,[16]p of plates : ill,maps,ports ; 24cm
Map on lining papers. — Bibliography: p193-196. — Includes index
ISBN 0-354-04602-0 : £8.95 B81-15321

944′.88 — France. Montaillou. Social life, *1294-1324*

Le Roy Ladurie, Emmanuel. Montaillou : Cathars and Catholics in a French village / Emmanual Le Roy Ladurie ; translated by Barbara Bray. — Harmondsworth : Penguin, 1980, c1978 (1981 [printing]). — xvii,381p : 3maps ; 20cm
Translation of: Montaillou. — Originally published: London : Scolar, 1978. — Bibliography: p357-358. — Includes index
ISBN 0-410-05471-5 (pbk) : £2.95 B81-25079

944′.949 — Monaco. Monte Carlo — ***Serials***

[Society ***(London : 1981)*****]**. Society : the magazine of the Société des bains de mer, Monte Carlo. — Vol.1, no.1 (Spring/Summer 1981)-. — London (25 Manchester Sq., W1) : Guest Publications, 1981-. — v. : ill(chiefly col.),facsims,ports(some col.) ; 30cm
Text in English and French
ISSN 0261-653x = Society (London. 1981) : Unpriced B81-33717

944′.98 — France. Romans. Rebellions, *1579-1580*

Le Roy Ladurie, Emmanuel. Carnival in Romans : a people's uprising at Romans 1579-1580 / Emmanuel Le Roy Ladurie ; translated by Mary Feeney. — Harmondsworth : Penguin, 1981, c1979. — xvii,416p : ill,maps,1coat of arms,facsims ; 20cm
Translation of: Le carnaval de Romans. — Originally published: New York : Braziller, 1979. — Bibliography: p382-397. — Includes index
ISBN 0-14-005609-2 (pbk) : £3.25 B81-25086

945 — HISTORY. ITALY

945 — Italy. City republics, *ca 1000-ca 1600*

Martines, Lauro. Power and imagination : city-states in Renaissance Italy / Lauro Martines. — London : Allen Lane, 1980, c1979. — xii,513p,[12]p of plates : ill,maps ; 24cm
Originally published: New York : Knopf, 1979. — Bibliography: p475-484. — Includes index
ISBN 0-7139-1314-2 : £12.00 B81-05280

945 — Italy. Intellectual life, *ca 1700-1910*

Jacobitti, Edmund E.. Revolutionary humanism and historicism in modern Italy / Edmund E. Jacobitti. — New Haven ; London : Yale University Press, c1981. — xii,248p ; 24cm
Bibliography: p219-233. — Includes index
ISBN 0-300-02479-7 : £11.30 : CIP rev. B81-12366

945 — Italy. Political events, *400-1000*

Wickham, Chris. Early medieval Italy : central power and local society 400-1000 / Chris Wickham. — London : Macmillan, 1981. — xl,238p : 6maps,2geneal.tables ; 23cm. — (New studies in medieval history)
Bibliography: p195-208. — Includes index
ISBN 0-333-26671-4 (cased) : Unpriced : CIP rev.
ISBN 0-333-26672-2 (pbk) : Unpriced B80-21238

945′.006′042132 — London. Westminster ***(London Borough)*****. Italian cultural institutions: Istituto Italiano di cultura nel Regno Unito —** ***Serials — Italian texts***

[Anno di attività 1 Gennaio ... 31 Dicembre ... ***(Istituto Italiano di cultura nel Regno Unito)*****]**. Un anno di attività, 1 Gennaio ... — 31 Dicembre ... / Istituto Italiano di cultura nel Regno Unito. — 1976-. — Londra (39 Belgrave Sq., SW1) : The Institute, 1976-. — v. ; 21cm
Annual. — Description based on: 1979 issue
ISSN 0260-6577 = Anno di attività — Istituto Italiano di Cultura nel Regno Unito : Unpriced B81-08436

945′.0072 — Italian antiquities, *to 1830.* **Archaeological investigation**

Archaeology and Italian society : prehistoric, Roman and medieval studies / edited Graeme Barker and Richard Hodges. — Oxford : B.A.R., 1981. — 342p : ill,maps,plans ; 30cm. — (Papers in Italian archaeology ; 2) (BAR. International series ; 102)
Includes bibliographies
ISBN 0-86054-120-7 (pbk) : £14.00 B81-36624

945′.05 — Italian civilization, *ca 1300-ca 1600*

Burckhardt, Jacob. The civilization of the Renaissance in Italy. — 2nd ed. — Oxford : Phaidon, Aug.1981. — [462]p. — (Landmarks in art history)
Translation of: Die Kultur der Renaissance in Italien. — Previous ed. of this translation: 1945
ISBN 0-7148-2140-3 (pbk) : £7.50 : CIP entry B81-18115

945′.05′0321 — Italian civilization, *ca 1320-1600 — Encyclopaedias*

A Concise encyclopaedia of the Italian Renaissance / edited by J.R. Hale. — [London] : Thames and Hudson, 1981. — 360p : ill,maps,facsims,music,ports,geneal.tables ; 22cm
Bibliography: p360
ISBN 0-500-23333-0 : £9.50 B81-40576

945′.06 — Italian culture, *1530-1607*

Grendler, Paul F.. Culture and censorship in late Renaissance Italy and France / Paul F. Grendler. — London : Variorum Reprints, 1981. — 318p in various pagings : facsims,1port ; 24cm
Includes index
ISBN 0-86078-084-8 : £24.00 : CIP rev.
Primary classification 363.3′1′0944 B81-22670

945′.08 — Italy. Risorgimento, *to 1870*

Beales, Derek. The Risorgimento and the unification of Italy. — London : Longman, Dec.1981. — [176]p
Originally published: London : Allen & Unwin, 1971
ISBN 0-582-49217-3 (pbk) : £3.95 : CIP entry B81-31825

945.09 — Italy. Political events, *1870-1930*

Gramsci and Italy's passive revolution / edited by John A. Davis. — London : Croom Helm, c1979. — 278p : 3maps ; 23cm
Includes index
ISBN 0-85664-704-7 : £12.50 : CIP rev. B79-15153

945.092′7 — Italy. Society, *1970-1980*

Contemporary Italian sociology : a reader / edited, translated and with an introduction by Diana Pinto. — Cambridge : Cambridge University Press, 1981. — xiii,233p ; 24cm
Includes index
ISBN 0-521-23738-6 (cased) : £20.00
ISBN 0-521-28191-1 (pbk) : Unpriced B81-39905

945.092′8 — Italy. Society. Political aspects

Fraser, John, *1939-*. Italy : society in crisis/society in transformation / John Fraser. — London : Routledge & Kegan Paul, 1981. — vii,307p ; 23cm
Bibliography: p296-299. — Includes index
ISBN 0-7100-0771-x : £10.95 : CIP rev. B81-13730

945′.31 — Italy. Venice, *1405-1797*

Norwich, John Julius. Venice : the greatness and the fall / John Julius Norwich. — [London] : Allen Lane, 1981. — 400p,[16]p of plates : ill,maps,facsims,ports ; 24cm
Bibliography: p383-387. — Includes index
ISBN 0-7139-1409-2 : £12.00 B81-35738

945′.31 — Italy. Venice. Political events, *1508-1511*

Gilbert, Felix. The Pope, his banker and Venice / Felix Gilbert. — Cambridge, Mass. ; London : Harvard University Press, 1980. — vi,157p,[4]p of plates : ill,2maps,ports ; 22cm
Includes index
ISBN 0-674-68975-5 : £7.50 B81-06972

945′.31 — Venetian Empire, *to ca 1800*

Morris, Jan. The Venetian empire : a sea voyage / Jan Morris. — London : Faber, 1980. — 192p,[16]p of plates : ill(some col.),maps,ports ; 25cm
Maps on lining papers. — Bibliography: p188. - Includes index
ISBN 0-571-09936-x : £9.50 : CIP rev. B80-18948

945′.51 — Italy. Florence. Social life, *1200-1400*

Holme, Timothy. Vile Florentines / Timothy Holme. — London : Cassell, 1980. — 193p ; 21cm
Includes index
ISBN 0-304-30323-2 : £7.95 B81-22850

945′.51 — Italy. Florence. Society, *1280-1530*

Trexler, Richard C.. Public life in Renaissance Florence / Richard C. Trexler. — New York ; London : Academic Press, c1980. — xxvi,591p : ill,maps ; 25cm. — (Studies in social discontinuity)
Maps on lining papers. — Bibliography: p556-572. - Includes index
ISBN 0-12-699550-8 : £25.20 B81-19332

945′.63206 — Italian civilization: Roman civilization, *1450-1550*

O'Malley, John W.. Rome and the Renaissance : studies in culture and religion / John W. O'Malley. — London : Variorum Reprints, 1981. — 319p in various pagings : 1port ; 24cm. — (Collected studies series ; 127)
Text in English and Latin. — Includes index
ISBN 0-86078-073-2 : £22.00 B81-15559

945′.634 — Vatican, *to 1979*

Mayer, Fred. The Vatican / photographed by Fred Mayer ; text by Peter Hebblethwaite ... [et al.]. — Dublin : Gill and Macmillan, 1980. — 226p : chiefly col.ill,col.facsims,1plan,col.ports ; 35cm
ISBN 0-7171-1083-4 : £18.00 B81-05912

945′.6340928 — Vatican. Social life

Bull, George. Inside the Vatican. — London : Hutchinson, Sept.1981. — [272]p
ISBN 0-09-140070-8 : £8.50 : CIP entry B81-17515

945′.67706 — Italy. Urbino ***(Duchy)*****. Social conditions,** *1450-1550*

Clough, Cecil H.. The Duchy of Urbino in the Renaissance / Cecil H. Clough. — London : Variorum Reprints, 1981. — 390p in various pagings : facsims,2ports ; 24cm. — (Collected studies series ; 129)
Includes index
ISBN 0-86078-075-9 : £24.00 B81-15561

945′.700441 — Southern Italy. Normans, *962-1268 — French texts*

Ménager, L.-R.. Hommes et institutions de l'Italie normande / L.-R. Ménager. — London : Variorum Reprints, 1981. — 372p in various pagings : geneal.tables ; 24cm. — (Collected studies series ; 136)
Includes index
ISBN 0-86078-082-1 : £22.00 B81-15560

945′.700441 — Southern Italy. Normans, *1060-1200*

Norwich, John Julius. The Normans in the South. — London (100 Harbord St., SW6 6PH) : Solitare Books, July 1981. — [372]p
Originally published: London : Longmans, 1967
ISBN 0-907387-00-4 (pbk) : £4.50 : CIP entry B81-14410

945.85 — HISTORY. MALTA

945′.85 — Malta. Naval operations, *1798-1979*

Elliott, Peter, *1922-*. The cross and the ensign : a naval history of Malta 1798-1979 / Peter Elliott. — Cambridge : Stephens, 1980. — 217p : ill,maps ; 24cm
Bibliography: p210-213. — Includes index
ISBN 0-85059-425-1 : £8.95 B81-29716

946 — HISTORY. IBERIAN PENINSULA, SPAIN

946 — Iberian civilization, *ca 1400-ca 1700 — Festschriften*

Mediaeval and Renaissance studies on Spain and Portugal in honour of P.E. Russell / edited by F.W. Hodcroft ... [et al.]. — Oxford : Society for the Study of Mediaeval Languages and Literature, 1981. — viii,226p ; 23cm
Bibliography: p223-226
ISBN 0-907570-00-3 : £8.00 : CIP rev. B81-27987

946′.004933 — Spain. Moors, *to 1492*

Brett, Michael, *1934-*. The Moors : Islam in the West / text by Michael Brett ; photographs by Werner Forman. — London : Orbis, c1980. — 128p : col.ill,col.facsims ; 31cm. — (Echoes of the ancient world)
Bibliography: p126. - Includes index. — Maps on lining papers
ISBN 0-85613-279-9 : £7.95 B81-01398

946′.04 — Spain, *1516-1700*
Lynch, John, *1927-*. Spain under the Habsburgs / John Lynch. — 2nd ed. — Oxford : Basil Blackwell
Vol.1: Empire and absolutism 1516-1598. — 1981. — xi,399p : ill,maps,ports ; 23cm
Previous ed.: 1964. — Bibliography: p376-383. — Includes index
ISBN 0-631-12692-9 (cased) : £17.50
B81-40312

Lynch, John, *1927-*. Spain under the Habsburgs / John Lynch. — 2nd ed. — Oxford : Basil Blackwell
Vol.2: Spain and America 1598-1700. — 1981. — viii,327p : ill,maps,1port ; 23cm
Previous ed.: 1969. — Bibliography: p307-314. — Includes index
ISBN 0-631-12702-x (cased) : £17.00
B81-40313

946′.05 — Spain, *1598-1750*
Stradling, R. A.. Europe and the decline of Spain : a study of the Spanish system, 1580-1720 / R.A. Stradling. — London : Allen & Unwin, 1981. — 222p : maps ; 23cm. — (Early modern Europe today)
Bibliography: p1-23. — Includes index
ISBN 0-04-940061-4 : Unpriced : CIP rev.
B81-15869

946′.053 — Spain, *1665-1700*
Kamen, Henry. Spain in the late seventeenth century, 1665-1700 / Henry Kamen. — London : Longman, 1980. — xiii,418p : ill,maps,1geneal.table ; 25cm
Bibliography: p395-408. - Includes index
ISBN 0-582-49036-7 : £17.50 : CIP rev.
B80-10417

946.08 — Spain. Political events, *1868-1979*
Carr, Raymond. Modern Spain 1875-1980 / Rayond Carr. — Oxford ; Oxford University Press, 1980. — xvii,201p : 1map ; 20cm. — (OPUS)
Bibliography: p182-188. — Includes index
ISBN 0-19-215828-7 (cased) : £7.50 : CIP rev.
ISBN 0-19-289090-5 (pbk) : Unpriced
B80-10913

946.081 — Spanish Civil War
Fraser, Ronald, *1930-*. Blood of Spain : the experience of civil war, 1936-1939 / Ronald Fraser. — Harmondsworth : Penguin, 1981, c1979. — 628p : maps ; 20cm
Originally published: London : A. Lane, 1979. — Bibliography: p595-599. — Includes index
ISBN 0-14-005480-4 (pbk) : £4.95 B81-05532

946.081 — Spanish Civil War, *1936-1937 — Trotskyist viewpoints*
Trotskiĭ, L.. Lessons of Spain / by Leon Trotsky ; with the original 1938 introduction. — London (1 Mentmore Terrace, E8 3PN) : Militant, 1980. — 24p : 1ill ; 21cm
Originally published: London : Strachan, 1938
ISBN 0-906582-07-5 (pbk) : £0.30 B81-19729

946.081 — Spanish Civil War. Military operations by International Brigades. British units — *Personal observations — Collections*
The **Road** to Spain : anti-fascists at war 1936-1939 / introduced and edited by David Corkill and Stuart J. Rawnsley. — Dunfermline : Borderline, 1981. — xix,164p ; 21cm
ISBN 0-906135-03-6 (pbk) : £4.95
Also classified at 335.6 B81-40413

946.082 — Spain, *1938-1977*
Carr, Raymond. Spain : dictatorship to democracy / Raymond Carr and Juan Pablo Fusi Aizpurua. — 2nd ed. — London : Allen & Unwin, 1981. — xxi,288p ; 23cm
Previous ed.: 1979. — Includes index
ISBN 0-04-946015-3 (corrected) : £12.50 : CIP rev.
ISBN 0-04-946014-5 (pbk) : £4.95 B81-09493

946.082 — Spain. Republican fugitives, *1939-1976 — Case studies*
Torbado, Jésus. The moles / Jésus Torbado, Manuel Leguineche ; translated by Nancy Festinger. — London : Secker & Warburg, 1981. — xii,226p : 1map,ports ; 22cm
Translation of: Los topos
ISBN 0-436-52600-x : £8.95 B81-37487

946.083 — Spain — *For children*
Rutland, Jonathan. Let′s go to Spain / Jonathan Rutland. — London : Watts, c1980. — 32p : col.ill,col.maps ; 22cm
ISBN 0-85166-861-5 : £2.99 B81-03466

This is Spain / illustrated by Chris Masters. — London : Transworld, 1981. — 32p : col.ill,col.maps ; 28cm. — (A Carousel book)
Text on inside covers. — Includes index
ISBN 0-552-54181-8 (pbk) : £0.95 B81-32966

946′.1083 — Spain. Galicia — *For schools*
Chambers, Keith. Galicia / Keith Chambers. — London : Harrap, 1981. — 32p : ill,maps,1facsim ; 14x22cm. — (Discovering Spain)
ISBN 0-245-53418-0 (pbk) : £0.95 B81-34914

946′.41 — Spain. Madrid. Palaces: Buen Retiro Palace, *to 1643*
Brown, Jonathan. A palace for a king : the Buen Retiro and the court of Philip IV / Jonathan Brown and J.H. Elliott. — New Haven ; London : Yale University Press, 1980. — xvi,296p : ill,facsims,plans,ports,1geneal.table ; 27cm
Bibliography: p281-287. - Includes index
ISBN 0-300-02507-6 : £15.00 : CIP rev.
B80-22772

946′.41 — Spain. Madrid. Social life — *For children*
Sainz, Elena. Living in Madrid / Elena Sainz. — Hove : Wayland, 1981. — 52p : ill,1col.map,facsims,1port ; 22cm. — (Living in famous cities)
Bibliography: p51. — Includes index
ISBN 0-85340-816-5 : £3.75 B81-24336

946′.60826 — Spain. Basque Provinces. Political events. Role of Euzkadi ta Askatasuna, *to 1980*
Janke, Peter. Spanish separatism : ETA′s threat to Basque democracy / Peter Janke. — London : Institute for the Study of Conflict, c1980. — 20p : 2maps ; 30cm. — (Conflict studies, ISSN 0069-8792 ; no.123)
Cover title. — Bibliography: p20
£2.00 (pbk) B81-04767

946′.81 — Spain. Andalusia. Alpujarras. Social life, *1920-1935 — Personal observations*
Brenan, Gerald. South from Granada / by Gerald Brenan. — Cambridge : Cambridge University Press, 1980, c1957. — xii,282p,[10]p of plates : ill,1maps,ports ; 23cm
Originally published: London : Hamilton, 1957
ISBN 0-521-28029-x (pbk) : £3.95 : CIP rev.
B80-11693

946′.89 — Gibraltar. Foreign relations between Great Britain & Spain — *Inquiry reports*
Great Britain. *Parliament. House of Commons. Foreign Affairs Committee.* Seventh report from the Forign Affairs Committee : session 1980-81 : Gibraltar: the situation of Gibraltar and United Kingdom relations with Spain : together with appendices thereto, the proceedings of the Committee relating to the report, and the minutes of evidence taken before the Committee on 18,25 February, 18,25 March and 6 May, with appendices. — London : H.M.S.O., [1981]. — lxviii,143p : 1map ; 25cm. — ([HC] ; 166)
Includes some appendices in Spanish with English translation
ISBN 0-10-216681-1 (pbk) : £7.65 B81-39917

947 — HISTORY. EASTERN EUROPE, SOVIET UNION

947 — Eastern Europe, *1740-1980*
Okey, Robin. Eastern Europe 1740-1980. — London : Hutchinson, Sept.1981. — [256]p
ISBN 0-09-145000-4 (cased) : £10.00 : CIP entry
ISBN 0-09-145001-2 (pbk) : £4.95 B81-22667

947 — Eastern Europe. Social conditions — *Marxist viewpoints*
Bahro, Rudolf. The alternative in Eastern Europe / Rudolf Bahro ; translated by David Fernbach. — London : Verso, 1981. — 463p ; 21cm
Translation of: Die Alternative. — Originally published: London : NLB, 1978. — Includes index
ISBN 0-86091-734-7 (pbk) : £4.50 : CIP rev.
B81-03717

947 — Russia, *987-1917*
Massie, Suzanne. Land of The firebird : the beauty of old Russia / Suzanne Massie. — London : Hamilton, 1980. — 493p,[34]p of plates : col.ill,ports ; 25cm
Originally published: New York : Simon & Schuster, 1980. — Bibliography: p461-472. — Includes index
ISBN 0-241-10517-x : £12.50 B81-16102

947 — Soviet Union, *to 1975*
An **Introduction** to Russian history / edited by Robert Auty and Dimitri Obolensky with the editorial assistance of Anthony Kingsford. — Cambridge : Cambridge University Press, 1980. — xiii,403p,[3]p of plates : maps,2geneal.tables ; 23cm. — (Companion to Russian studies ; 1)
Originally published: 1976. — Includes bibliographies and index
ISBN 0-521-20893-9 (pbk) : £7.95 B81-34267

947′.0005 — Eastern Europe — *Serials*
Oxford Slavonic papers. New series. — Vol.14. — Oxford : Clarendon Press, Dec.1981. — [144]p
ISBN 0-19-815657-x : £15.00 : CIP entry
B81-31449

947′.0005 — Eastern European culture — *History — Serials*
Irish Slavonic studies : the journal of the Irish Slavists′ Association. — No.1 (1980)-. — Belfast (The Editorial Secretary, Department of Slavonic Studies, Queen′s University, Belfast BT7 1NN) : The Association, 1980-. — v. ; 21cm
Annual
ISSN 0260-2067 = Irish Slavonic studies : £2.00 B81-04438

947′.009′732 — Russia *(RSFSR)*. **Urban regions. Social life —** *Case studies — For schools*
Rostas, Cathy. Life in a Russian town / Cathy Rostas. — London : Harrap, 1981. — 95p : ill,1map ; 22cm
ISBN 0-245-53507-1 (pbk) : £2.50 B81-19458

947′.043′0924 — Russia. Ivan IV, *Tsar of Russia — Biographies*
Carr, Francis, *1924-*. Ivan the Terrible / Francis Carr. — Newton Abbot : David & Charles, 1981. — 220p : ill,1map,ports,1geneal.table ; 24cm
Bibliography: p215. — Includes index
ISBN 0-7153-7958-5 : £10.50 B81-21069

947′.05′0924 — Russia. Peter I, *Tsar of Russia — Biographies*
Massie, Robert K.. Peter the Great : his life and world / Robert K. Massie. — London : Gollancz, 1981, c1980. — xii,909p,[24]p of plates : ill(some col.),maps,ports(some col.),geneal.table ; 25cm
Originally published: New York : Knopf, 1980. — Maps on lining papers. — Bibliography: p863-867. — Includes index
ISBN 0-575-01557-8 : £9.95 B81-03400

947′.06′05 — Russia, *1700-1800 — Serials*
[Newsletter, Study Group on Eighteenth-Century Russia]. Newsletter. — No.8 (Sept. 1980). — [S.l.] (c/o School of Modern Languages and European History, University of East Anglia, Norwich NR4 7TJ) : The Group, 1980. — 106p
ISSN 0306-8455 : £4.00 B81-15438

947′.063 — Russia. Social conditions, *1762-1796*
De Madariaga, Isabel. Russia in the age of Catherine the Great / Isabel de Madariaga. — London : Weidenfeld and Nicolson, c1981. — xii,698p : maps ; 24cm
Bibliography: p653-675. - Includes index
ISBN 0-297-77394-1 : £20.00 B81-15632

947'.063'0924 — Russia. Catherine II, *Empress of Russia — Biographies*

Troyat, Henri. Catherine the Great / Henri Troyat ; translated by Emily Read. — London : Granada, 1981, c1978. — 394p : 1port ; 20cm. — (A Panther book)
Translation of: Catherine la Grande. — Originally published: Henley-on-Thames : A. Ellis, 1979. — Bibliography: p383-386. — Includes index
ISBN 0-586-05301-8 (pbk) : £2.95 B81-27051

947'.07 — Crimean War

. Crimea, 1854-56. — Thame (103, High St., Thame, Oxfordshire OX9 3D2) : Hayes Kennedy, June 1981. — [200]p
ISBN 0-86269-001-3 : £15.00 : CIP entry
B81-14469

947'.073 — Crimean War. Army operations by Great Britain. *Army. Regiment of Foot, 4th — Personal observations — Correspondence, diaries, etc.*

Hall, Jasper. Letters from the Crimea : Captain Jasper Hall of the 4th (or King's own) Regiment of Foot, to his sister and father / transcribed and annotated with an introduction by Edith Tyson. — [Lancaster] ([Old Town Hall, Market Sq., Lancaster LA1 1HT]) : [Lancaster City Council, Museum and Art Gallery], [1981?]. — 26,vip,[2]p of plates : 1ill,2maps ; 30cm. — (A Lancaster Museum monograph)
Unpriced (unbound) B81-22984

947.08 — Russia, *1812-1980*

Westwood, J. N.. Endurance and endeavour : Russian history 1812-1980. — 2nd ed. — Oxford : Oxford University Press, June 1981. — [464]p. — (The Short Oxford history of the modern world)
Previous ed.: 1976
ISBN 0-19-822855-4 (cased) : £17.50 : CIP entry
ISBN 0-19-822856-2 (pbk) : £7.95 B81-18065

947.08'3 — Russia. Political events, *1914-1917*

Hasegawa, Tsuyoshi. The February Revolution : Petrograd, 1917 / Tsuyoshi Hasegawa. — Seattle ; London : University of Washington Press, c1981. — xxii,652p,[8]p of plates : ill,maps,ports ; 24cm. — (Publications on Russia and Eastern Europe of the School of International Studies ; vol.9)
Map on lining papers. — Bibliography: p603-624. — Includes index
ISBN 0-295-95765-4 : Unpriced B81-39881

947.08'3 — Soviet Union. Political events, *1900-1924 — For schools*

Aylett, J. F.. Russia in revolution / J.F. Aylett ; illustrations by Val Saunder. — London : Edward Arnold, 1981. — 47p : ill,maps,ports ; 24cm. — (Links)
Bibliography: p47. — Includes index
ISBN 0-7131-0522-4 (pbk) : £1.75 B81-25988

947.084 — Soviet Union, *1917-1953*

Carrère d'Encausse, Hélène. A history of the Soviet Union 1917-1953. — London : Longman
Vol.1: Lenin : revolution and power. — Dec.1981. — [320]p
Translation of: Lénine, la révolution et le pouvoir
ISBN 0-582-29559-9 (pbk) : £4.95 : CIP entry
B81-31821

Carrère d'Encausse, Hélène. A history of the Soviet Union 1917-1953. — London : Longman
Vol.2: Stalin : order through terror. — Feb.1982. — [288]p
Translation of: Staline, l'ordre par la terreur
ISBN 0-582-29560-2 (pbk) : £4.95 : CIP entry
B81-37601

947.084 — Soviet Union, *1917-1979 — Soviet viewpoints*

Ponomarev, B. N.. Selected speeches and writings / by P.N. Ponomarev. — Oxford : Pergamon, 1981. — xv,372p ; 22cm
Includes index
ISBN 0-08-023606-5 : £19.75 : CIP rev.
Also classified at 335'.009 B80-18949

947.084 — Soviet Union, *1917-1980*

McCauley, Martin. The Soviet Union since 1917. — London : Longman, Nov.1981. — [352]p. — (The Longman history of Russia ; v.7)
ISBN 0-582-48979-2 (cased) : £12.00 : CIP entry
ISBN 0-582-48980-6 (pbk) : £6.50 B81-31083

947.084 — Soviet Union. Political events, *1917-1973*

Nove, Alec. Stalinism and after / Alec Nove. — 2nd ed. — London : Allen & Unwin, 1981. — 207p : maps ; 22cm
Previous ed.: 1975. — Bibliography: p201-202. — Includes index
ISBN 0-04-320144-x (pbk) : Unpriced : CIP rev. B81-25140

947.084 — Soviet Union. Political events, *1917-1980 — Dissident viewpoints*

Turchin, V. F.. The inertia of fear : and the scientific worldview / Valentin Turchin ; translated by Guy Daniels. — Oxford : Robertson, 1981. — xii,300p ; 24cm
Translation from the Russian. — Originally published: New York : Columbia University Press, 1980. — Includes index
ISBN 0-85520-400-1 : £12.50 : CIP rev.
B81-05131

947.084 — Soviet Union. Social conditions, *1917-1978*

Nove, Alec. Political economy and Soviet socialism / Alec Nove. — London : Allen & Unwin, 1979. — xii,249p ; 22cm
Includes index
ISBN 0-04-335037-2 (corrected : cased) : £10.00 : CIP rev.
ISBN 0-04-335039-9 (pbk) : £4.95 B78-35876

947.084'092'4 — Soviet Union. Ginzburg, Evgenii͡a Semënovna *— Biographies*

Ginzburg, Evgenii͡a Semënovna. Within the whirlwind / Eugenia Ginzburg ; translated by Ian Boland ; introduction by Heinrich Böll. — London : Collins and Harvill, 1981. — xix,423p : maps ; 25cm
Translation of: Krutoi marshrut
ISBN 0-00-262366-8 : £9.95 B81-27165

947.084'1'0924 — Soviet Union. Lenin, V. I. — *Biographies*

Lenin : the revolutionary / [contributors V.P. Filatov ... et al.]. — Moscow : Progress ; [London] : Distributed by Central Books, c1980. — 215p,[31]p of plates : ill,port ; 18cm
Translation of: Lenin
ISBN 0-7147-1605-7 : £1.50 B81-27752

947.084'1'0924 — Soviet Union. Lenin, V. I. — *Chronologies*

Weber, Gerda. Lenin : life and works / Gerda and Herman Weber ; edited and translated by Martin McCauley. — London : Macmillan, 1980, c1974. — 224p ; 23cm. — (Macmillan chronology series)
Translation of: Lenin-Chronik. — Bibliography: p199-202. — Includes index
ISBN 0-333-28467-4 (cased) : £10.00
ISBN 0-333-28468-2 (pbk) : £3.95 B81-05693

947.084'2 — Soviet Union. Political events. Role of revolutionary military forces, *1921-1940* **compared with role of China.** *Zhong guo ren min jie fang jun* **in political events in China,** *1945-1971*

Adelman, Jonathan R.. The revolutionary armies : the historical development of the Soviet and the Chinese people's liberation armies / Jonathan R. Adelman. — Westport ; London : Greenwood Press, 1980. — x,230p ; 22cm. — (Contributions in political science, ISSN 0147-1066 ; no.38)
Bibliography: p199-223. - Includes index
ISBN 0-313-22026-3 : Unpriced
Also classified at 951.05 B81-06514

947.084'2'0924 — Soviet Union. Borodin, M. M. — *Biographies*

Jacobs, Dan N.. Borodin : Stalin's man in China / Dan N. Jacobs. — Cambridge, Mass. ; London : Harvard University Press, 1981. — viii,369p,[8]p of plates : ill,facsim,ports ; 24cm
Bibliography: p331-346. — Includes index
ISBN 0-674-07910-8 : £15.00 B81-38140

947.085 — Soviet Union, *1945-1979 — Soviet viewpoints*

Kosygin, A. N.. Selected speeches and writings / by A.N. Kosygin. — Oxford : Pergamon, 1981. — vii,320p ; 22cm
Translation from the Russian. — Includes index
ISBN 0-08-023610-3 : £19.50 : CIP rev.
B81-10446

947.085 — Soviet Union, *1945-1980*

Mooney, Peter. The Soviet superpower. — London : Heinemann Education, Oct.1981. — [224]p. — (Studies in modern history)
ISBN 0-435-31600-1 (cased) : £10.50 : CIP entry
ISBN 0-435-31601-x (pbk) : £4.50 B81-28078

947.085 — Soviet Union, *1953-1979*

The **Soviet** Union since Stalin / edited by Stephen F. Cohen, Alexander Rabinowitch, Robert Sharlet. — London : Macmillan, 1980. — viii,342p ; 25cm
Conference papers. — Originally published: Bloomington : Indiana University Press, c1980. — Includes index
ISBN 0-333-30867-0 (cased) : £12.50
ISBN 0-333-30868-9 (pbk) : Unpriced
B81-13401

947.085 — Soviet Union. Attitudes of Western world, *1940-1979*

Solzhenit͡syn, Aleksandr. The mortal danger : how misconceptions about Russia imperil the West / Alexander I. Solzenitsyn ; translated form the Russian by Michael Nicholson and Alexis Klimoff. — 2nd ed. — London : Bodley Head, 1981. — 130p ; 20cm
Previous ed.: published in Foreign affairs, Vol.58, No.4, Spring 1980
ISBN 0-370-30903-0 (pbk) : £2.50 B81-28461

947.085'3 — Soviet Union

Medish, Vadim. The Soviet Union / Vadim Medish. — Englewood Cliffs ; London : Prentice-Hall, c1981. — xiv,367pp : ill,maps,ports ; 23cm
Includes bibliographies and index
ISBN 0-13-823567-8 (pbk) : £6.45 B81-12517

947.085'3 — Soviet Union. Political events — *Forecasts*

Amal'rik, Andreĭ. Will the Soviet Union survive until 1984? / Andrei Amalrik. — Rev. and expanded ed. / edited by Hilary Sternberg. — Harmondsworth : Penguin, 1980. — 223p : ill ; 20cm. — (A Pelican book)
Translated from the Russian. — Previous ed.: New York : Harper & Row, 1970 ; London : Allen Lane, 1970
ISBN 0-14-022190-5 (pbk) : £2.50 B81-10281

947.085'3'0924 — Soviet Union. Brezhnev, L. I. — *Biographies*

Murphy, Paul J.. Brezhnev : Soviet politician / Paul J. Murphy. — Jefferson, N.C. : McFarland ; Folkestone : distributed by Bailey & Swinfen, 1981. — vii,363p : ill,1facsim,ports ; 24cm
Includes index
ISBN 0-89950-002-1 : £19.95 B81-37036

947'.3120853 — Russia *(RSFSR).* **Moscow —** *For children*

Harding, Ron. Living in Moscow / Ron Harding. — Hove : Wayland, 1980. — 52p : ill,1map,1col.plan ; 22cm. — (Living in famous cities)
Bibliography: p51. — Includes index
ISBN 0-85340-698-7 : £3.50 B81-01953

947'.710842'0924 — Ukraine. Social life, *1942-1945 — Childhood reminiscences*

Skyba, Alex. Drastic changes in my life / Alex Skyba. — Bradford (Bolton Royd, Manningham La., Bradford 8) : Bradford Literary Group, c1981. — 14p : ill ; 22cm. — (B.L.G. ; no.003)
£0.50 (pbk) B81-36435

947'.714 — Ukraine. Kiev region. Political events, *1880-1930 — Personal observations — Collections — Polish texts*
Czwarty, Tom. Pamiętnik kijowski / Tom Czwarty. — London : Orbis Books, [1980]. — 212p,[24]p of plates : ill,maps,1facsim,ports ; 22cm
Maps on lining papers
ISBN 0-901149-19-5 : Unpriced B81-40387

948 — HISTORY. SCANDINAVIA

948'.02 — Viking children. Social life — *For children*
Ferguson, Sheila. Growing up in Viking times / Sheila Ferguson. — London : Batsford Academic and Educational, 1981. — 72p : ill,maps ; 26cm
Bibliography: p70. — Includes index
ISBN 0-7134-2730-2 : £5.50 B81-24309

948'.02 — Viking civilization, *ca 800-1200.* **Archaeological sources**
Economic aspects of the Viking Age / edited by David M. Wilson and Marjorie L. Caygill. — London : British Museum, 1981. — 56p : ill,2maps ; 30cm. — (Occasional paper / British Museum, ISSN 0142-4815 ; no.30)
Includes bibliographies
ISBN 0-86159-030-9 (pbk) : Unpriced B81-34552

948'02 — Viking civilization, *to 1050*
Simpson, Jacqueline. The Viking world / Jacqueline Simpson. — London : Batsford, 1967 (1980 [printing]). — 192p : ill(some col.),maps ; 26cm
Originally published: as Everyday life in the Viking age. 1967. — Bibliography: p187-188. - Includes index
ISBN 0-7134-0777-8 : £7.95 B81-05667

948'.02 — Vikings
Graham-Campbell, James. The Vikings / James Graham-Campbell and Dafydd Kidd. — London : Published for the Trustees of the British Museum by British Museum Publications Limited, c1980. — 200p : ill(some col.),maps(some col.),plans(some col.) ; 29cm
Published to accompany an exhibition at the British Museum, 1980. — Bibliography: p189. - Includes index
ISBN 0-7141-1352-2 (cased) : £8.95 : CIP rev.
ISBN 0-7141-1353-0 (pbk) : £3.95 B79-37592

948'.02 — Vikings — *For children*
Vikings / consultant editor Henry Pluckrose ; illustrated by Ivan Lapper. — London : Hamilton, 1981. — 28p : col.ill,1col.map ; 21cm. — (Small world)
Includes index
ISBN 0-241-10503-x : £2.50 B81-38531

948.9 — HISTORY. DENMARK AND FINLAND

948.9'01 — Denmark, *909-1134 — Early works*
Saxo Grammaticus. Danorum regum heroumque historia books x-xvi : the text of the first edition with translation and commentary in three volumes / Saxo Grammaticus ; [translated by] Eric Christiansen. — Oxford : B.A.R.. — (BAR. International series ; 84)
Vol.1: Books X,XI,XII and XIII. — 1980. — [17],347p : maps,geneal.tables ; 30cm
Parallel English translation and Latin text. — Bibliography: p8-17 prelim. pages
ISBN 0-86054-097-9 (pbk) : £12.00 B81-36610

948.97 — HISTORY. FINLAND

948.97'02 — Finland, *1808-1914*
Paasivirta, Juhani. Finland and Europe : international crises in the period of autonomy 1808-1914. — London : C. Hurst, Nov.1981. — [288]p
Translation of: Suomi ja Eurooppa : Autonomiakausi ja Kansainväliset kriisit (1808-1914)
ISBN 0-905838-55-6 : £12.50 : CIP entry B81-30973

949.2 — HISTORY. LOW COUNTRIES, NETHERLANDS

949.2'04 — War of the League of Augsburg. Battle of Beachy Head
Armstrong, Robert, *1940-*. The Battle of Beachy Head / by Robert Armstrong. — [Eastbourne] ([20 Pevensey Rd., Eastbourne, E. Sussex]) : [Sound Forum], [1979]. — [38]p : 1 ill ; 19cm
£0.35 (unbound) B81-04861

949.2'07'0924 — Netherlands. Grotenberg, Wim — *Biographies*
Grotenbreg, Wim. No time to die / Wim Grotenbreg's story as told to Kay Hunter. — London : Regency Press, c1980. — 103p,[5]p of plates : ill,2facsims,ports ; 23cm
ISBN 0-7212-0640-9 : £3.00 B81-07804

949.3 — HISTORY. BELGIUM

949.3'043 — Belgium — *For schools*
Barnes, Anthony. Introducing Belgium / written by Anthony Barnes. — London : Harrap, 1981. — 88p : ill,map,1coat of arms,1facsims,ports,1geneal.table ; 19x22cm
ISBN 0-245-53501-2 (pbk) : £3.15 B81-29579

949.4 — HISTORY. SWITZERLAND

949.4'073 — Switzerland — *For schools*
Pargeter, Joan. Introducing Switzerland / written by Joan Pargeter. — London : Harrap, 1981. — 81p : ill,2maps ; 19x21cm
ISBN 0-245-53502-0 (pbk) : £3.15 B81-37990

949.5 — HISTORY. GREECE

949.5 — Byzantine Empire. Political events, *to ca 1400*
Karlin-Hayter, Patricia. Studies in Byzantine political history : sources and controversies / Patricia Karlin-Hayter. — London : Variorum Reprints, 1981. — 336p in various pagings ; 24cm. — (Collected studies series ; CS141)
Eleven papers in French, 7 in English. — Facsimile reprints of: 18 articles in French and English published between 1962 and 1981. — Includes index
ISBN 0-86078-088-0 : £24.00 : CIP rev. B81-21525

949.5 — Byzantine Empire, *to 1453*
Byzantium : an introduction / edited by Philip Whitting. — New ed. — Oxford : Blackwell, 1981. — xiii,178p,[8]p of plates : ill,maps,2plans ; 22cm
Includes bibliographies and index
ISBN 0-631-12772-0 (pbk) : £4.95 B81-11472

949.5 — Greece, *1800-1980*
Clogg, Richard. Modern Greece / Richard Clogg. — London : Historical Association, c1981. — 36p : 1map ; 22cm. — (General series / Historical Association ; 101)
Bibliography: p35-36
ISBN 0-85278-244-6 (pbk) : Unpriced B81-31492

949.5 — Greece, *ca 400-ca 1460*
Cheetham, Nicolas. Mediaeval Greece / Nicolas Cheetham. — New Haven ; London : Yale University Press, 1981. — viii,341p : 2maps,geneal.tables ; 22cm
Bibliography: p328-332. — Includes index
ISBN 0-300-02421-5 : £12.00 B81-18212

949.5'0074'02262 — West Sussex. Chichester. Museums: Chichester District Museum. Exhibits: Byzantine antiquities — *Catalogues*
The **Byzantine** world : A.D.330-1453 / edited by Tim Boatswain and Loraine Knowles. — [Chichester] ([29 Little London, Chichester PO19 1PB]) : Chichester District Museum, [1978]. — 36p : ill ; 21cm
Published to accompany an exhibition held at Chichester District Museum, 1978. — Bibliography: p35
£0.10 (pbk) B81-37222

949.5'009'734 — Greece. Islands. Villages. Children. Social life — *Case studies — For children*
Matthews, Carola. Dimitra of the Greek islands / written by Carola Matthews ; illustrated by Gordon Stowell. — Guildford : Lutterworth, 1980. — 32p : col ill,2 maps ; 23cm. — (How they live now ; 3)
Maps on lining papers. — Includes index
ISBN 0-7188-2404-0 : £2.50 B81-03914

949.5'01 — Byzantine civilization, *500-600*
Cameron, Averil. Continuity and change in sixth-century Byzantium / Averil Cameron. — London : Variorum Reprints, 1981. — 338p in various pagings : ill,1port ; 24cm. — (Collected studies series ; CS143)
Includes index
ISBN 0-86078-090-2 : £24.00 : CIP rev. B81-21527

949.5'01 — Byzantine Empire. Social conditions, *ca 300-1000 — French texts*
Patlagean, Evelyne. Structure sociale, famille, chrétienté à Byzance : IVe-XIe siècle / Evelyne Patlagean. — London : Variorum Reprints, 1981. — 345p in various pagings : ill ; 24cm. — (Collected studies series ; 134)
Includes index
ISBN 0-86078-080-5 : £22.00 B81-15558

949.5'03 — Byzantine civilization, *1071-1167*
Browning, Robert, *1914-*. Church, state and learning in twelfth century Byzantium / by Robert Browning. — London : Dr. Williams's Trust, 1981. — 24p ; 22cm. — (Lecture / Friends of Dr. Williams's Library ; no.34)
At head of title: Friends of Dr. Williams's Library
£0.80 (pbk) B81-11545

949.5'04 — Byzantine Empire. Social conditions, *1204-1453 — Critical studies*
Ševčenko, Ihor. Society and intellectual life in late Byzantium / Ihor Ševčenko. — London : Variorum Reprints, 1981. — 374p in various pagings : facsims,1port ; 24cm. — (Collected studies series ; CS137)
Includes texts in classical Greek and 1 paper in French. — Facsimile reprints of: 15 articles in English and French. — Includes index
ISBN 0-86078-083-x : £24.00 : CIP rev.
Primary classification 949.5'04 B81-22500

949.5'04 — Byzantine Empire. Social conditions, *ca 1200-1453*
Ševčenko, Ihor. Society and intellectual life in late Byzantium / Ihor Ševčenko. — London : Variorum Reprints, 1981. — 374p in various pagings : facsims,1port ; 24cm. — (Collected studies series ; CS137)
Includes texts in classical Greek and 1 paper in French. — Facsimile reprints of: 15 articles in English and French. — Includes index
ISBN 0-86078-083-x : £24.00 : CIP rev.
Also classified at 949.5'04 B81-22500

949.5'074 — Greece, *1933-1945 — Correspondence, diaries, etc.*
NacVeagh, Lincoln. Ambassador MacVeagh reports : Greece 1933-1947 / edited by John O. Iatrides. — Princeton, N.J. ; Guildford : Princeton University Press, c1980. — xi,769p : ports ; 25cm
Includes index
ISBN 0-691-05292-1 : £19.20 B81-03749

949.5'074 — Greece. Political events, *1940-1949 — Conference proceedings*
Greece : from resistance to civil war / edited by Marion Sarafis ; introduced by Nicos Svoronos. — Nottingham : Spokesman, 1980. — 142p ; 22cm
Conference papers. — Includes index
ISBN 0-85124-289-8 (cased) : £7.50
ISBN 0-85124-290-1 (pbk) : £2.95 B81-06281

949.5'2 — Greece. Peloponnesus. Helos Plain. Rural regions. Human settlements, *to 1980*
Wagstaff, J. M.. The development of rural settlements. — Amersham : Avebury Publishing, Sept.1981. — [162]p
ISBN 0-86127-302-8 (pbk) : £12.00 : CIP entry B81-21522

949.5'506'0222 — Greece. Ionian Islands, *ca 1860 — Illustrations — Facsimiles*
Lear, Edward. Views in the Seven Ionian Islands : a facsimile of the original edition published in 1863 by the artist / by Edward Lear. — Oldham : Broadbent, c1979. — 2p,[45]leaves : chiefly col.ill ; 51cm
Limited ed. of 1000 numbered copies
ISBN 0-904848-04-3 : Unpriced B81-32949

949.6 — HISTORY. BALKAN PENINSULA

949.6 — Balkan countries. Foreign relations between Germany & Great Britain, *1911-1914*

Crampton, R. J.. The hollow detente : Anglo-German relations in the Balkans, 1911-1914 / by R.J. Crampton. — London : Prior, [1980]. — 255p : 5maps ; 24cm
Bibliography: p223-240. — Includes index
ISBN 0-86043-400-1 : £8.95 : CIP rev. B80-05160

949.6 — Balkan countries. Social conditions, *1800-1850*

Balkan society in the age of Greek independence / edited by Richard Clogg. — London : Macmillan in association with the Centre of Contemporary Greek Studies, King's College, University of London, 1981. — vi,253p ; 25cm
Conference papers. — Includes index
ISBN 0-333-31580-4 : £15.00 B81-25350

949.6 — Balkan Peninsula. Revolutions, *1566-1945*

Djordjević, Dimitrije. The Balkan revolutionary tradition / Dimitrije Djordjevic and Stephen Fischer-Galati. — New York ; Guildford : Columbia University Press, 1981. — xv,271p ; 22cm
Includes index
ISBN 0-231-05098-4 : £11.55 B81-14738

949.65 — HISTORY. ALBANIA

949.6'5 — Albania, *to 1975*

Pollo, Stefanaq. The history of Albania : from its origins to the present day / Stefanaq Pollo and Arben Puto with the collaboration of Kristo Frasheri and Skender Anamali ; English translation by Carol Wiseman and Ginnie Hole. — London : Routledge & Kegan Paul, 1981. — xiii,322p,[32]p of plates : ill,coat of arms,1facsim,ports ; 25cm
Translation of: L'histoire de l'Albanie. — Bibliography: p294-304. — Includes index
ISBN 0-7100-0365-x : £18.95 : CIP rev. B80-11695

949.7 — HISTORY. YUGOSLAVIA

949.7'01 — Yugoslavia. Unification, *1914-1918 — Conference proceedings*

The **Creation** of Yugoslavia 1914-1918 / edited by Dimitrije Djordjevic. — Santa Barbara ; Oxford : Clio, c1980. — viii,228p : 2maps ; 24cm
Conference papers. — Includes index
ISBN 0-87436-253-9 : £7.85 B81-05080

949.7'021'0924 — Yugoslavia. Paul, *Prince of Yugoslavia — Biographies*

Balfour, Neil. Paul of Yugoslavia : Britain's maligned friend / by Neil Balfour and Sally Mackay. — London : Hamilton, 1980. — 335p,[12]p of plates : ill,1map,ports,3geneal.table ; 23cm
Bibliography: p328-329. - Includes index
ISBN 0-241-10392-4 : £15.00 : CIP rev. B80-10914

949.7'023'0924 — Yugoslavia. Tito, Josip Broz — *Biographies*

Djilas, Milovan. Tito : the story from inside / by Milovan Djilas ; translated by Vasilije Kojić and Richard Hayes. — London : Weidenfeld and Nicolson, 1981. — 185p,[8]p of plates : 2ill,ports ; 23cm
Translation from the Serbo-Croatian. — Originally published: New York : Harcourt, Brace, Jovanovich, 1980
ISBN 0-297-77885-4 : £7.95 B81-15183

Maclean, Fitzroy. Josip Broz Tito : a pictorial biography / Fitzroy Maclean. — London : Macmillan, c1980. — 127p : ill(some col.),maps (some col.),facsims,ports ; 27cm
Includes index
ISBN 0-333-31003-9 : £7.95 B81-19783

949.7'023'0924 — Yugoslavia. Tito, Josip Broz — *Biographies — For children*

Gibson, Michael, *1936-*. Tito / Michael Gibson. — Hove : Wayland, 1981. — 72p : ill,1map,ports ; 22cm. — (Wayland history makers)
Bibliography: p70. — Includes index
ISBN 0-85340-844-0 : £3.95 B81-37697

949.7'023'0924 — Yugoslavia. Tito, Josip Broz — *Croatian texts*

Djilas, Milovan. Druženje s Titom / Milovan Djilas. — Harrow (c/o 53 Hawthorn Drive, Harrow, Middlesex, HA2 7NU) : Aleksa Djilas, [1981]. — 167p ; 19cm
Includes index
Unpriced (pbk) B81-14724

949.77 — HISTORY. BULGARIA

949.7'703'0924 — Bulgaria. Zhivkov, Todor — *Biographies*

Zhivkov, Todor. Statesman & builder of new Bulgaria. — Oxford : Pergamon, Dec.1981. — [325]p. — (Leaders of the world)
ISBN 0-08-028205-9 : £10.00 : CIP entry B81-35889

949.8 — HISTORY. ROMANIA

949.8'03 — Romania. Political events, *1977-1980*

Michael-Titus, C.. Romania under pressure : report II / C. Michael-Titus. — Upminster (c/o 44 Howard Rd., Upminster RM14 2UF) : Panopticum Press London, 1981. — 43p : facsims,ports ; 21cm
ISBN 0-907256-04-x (pbk) : Unpriced B81-11522

949.8'101 — Romanian civilization: Moldavian civilization, *400-1100.* **Archaeological sources**

Teodor, Dan Gh.. The East Carpathian area of Romania in the V-XI centuries A.D. / Dan Gh. Teodor ; translated from the Romanian by Nubar Hampartumian. — Oxford : B.A.R., 1980. — 126p,64p of plates : ill,1map ; 30cm. — (BAR. International series ; 81)
ISBN 0-86054-090-1 (pbk) : £11.00 B81-36588

950 — HISTORY. EURASIA, ASIA

950 — Central Asia. Political events. Foreign relations between Great Britain & Russia, *1805-1895*

Morgan, Gerald. Anglo-Russian rivalry in Central Asia, 1805-1895. — London : Cass, Sept.1981. — [272]p
ISBN 0-7146-3179-5 : £12.50 : CIP entry B81-21487

950'.049159 — Asia. Baluchis & Pathans, *to 1980*

Wirsing, Robert G.. The Baluchis and Pathans / by Robert G. Wirsing. — London (36 Craven St., WC2N 5NG) : Minority Rights Group, 1981. — 23p : 2ill ; 30cm. — (Report / Minority Rights Group, ISSN 0305-6252 ; no.48)
Bibliography: p19
£1.20 (pbk) B81-27061

950'.07'1142142 — London. Camden *(London Borough).* **Universities. Colleges: University of London.** *School of Oriental and African Studies — Serials*

University of London. *School of Oriental and African Studies.* Calendar for the ... session / School of Oriental and African Studies, University of London. — 65th (1980-81). — London : The School, [1980?]. — 220p
ISBN 0-7286-0077-3 : £2.00
ISSN 0305-6260 B81-03793

950'.074'02649 — Ipswich. *Department of Recreation and Amenities.* **Stock: Asian artefacts**

Ipswich. *Department of Recreation & Amenities.* Asia : a guide to the Ipswich collections / [author D.L. Jones]. — Ipswich ([Civic Centre, Civic Drive, Ipswich IP1 2EE]) : Ipswich Borough Council, Department of Recrteation & Amenities, [1980?]. — [39]p : ill ; 18x25cm
Cover title
ISBN 0-906688-02-7 (pbk) : Unpriced B81-10224

950'.1 — Asian civilization, *ca 500-1500*

Pritsak, Omeljan. Studies in medieval Eurasian history / Omeljan Pritsak. — London : Variorum Reprints, 1981. — 375p in various pagings : 1map,1port,geneal.tables ; 24cm. — (Collected studies series ; 132)
Text in English and German. — Includes index
ISBN 0-86078-078-3 : £22.00 B81-17963

950'.427'0924 — East Asia, *1975-1978 — Personal observations*

Williams, Maslyn. Faces of my neighbour : three journeys into East Asia / Maslyn Williams. — Sydney ; London : Collins, 1979. — 312p ; 22cm
ISBN 0-00-216435-3 B81-09010

950'.428'05 — Asia. Political events — *Serials*

[Asian digest *(London)*]. Asian digest. — Aug.1980-. — London : 139 Fonthill Rd, N4 3HF : Hansib Pub., 1980-. — v. : ill,ports ; 28cm
Monthly
ISSN 0144-9753 = Asian digest (London) : £5.00 per year B81-02333

950'.428'05 — Asia — *Serials*

Asian and African studies. — 17 (1981). — London : Curzon Press, Nov.1981. — [360]p
ISBN 0-7007-0145-1 : £6.00 : CIP entry
ISSN 0571-2742
Also classified at 960'.328'05 B81-39229

The **Far** East and Australasia. — 12th ed. (1980-81). — London : Europa, c1980. — xxiv,1365p
ISBN 0-905118-51-0 : Unpriced : CIP rev.
ISSN 0071-3791 B80-28929

The **Far** East and Australasia. — 13th ed. (1981-82). — London : Europa, Oct.1981. — [1385]p
ISBN 0-905118-66-9 : CIP entry
ISSN 0071-3791 B81-27349

Owen's commerce and travel and international register. — 28th ed. (1981). — London : Owen's Commerce & Travel Ltd, c1981. — 1051p
ISBN 0-900576-12-x : Unpriced
Also classified at 960'.328'05 B81-28379

951 — HISTORY. CHINA AND ADJACENT AREAS

951 — China. Social life, *to 1979 — Readings from contemporary sources*

Chinese civilization and society : a sourcebook / edited by Patricia Buckley Ebrey. — New York : Free Press ; London : Collier Macmillan, c1981. — xxxiii,429p : 1map ; 24cm
Bibliography: p418-422. - Includes index
ISBN 0-02-908760-0 (pbk) : £6.95 B81-19595

951'.025 — China, *1260-1370*

China under Mongol rule / edited by John D. Langlois, Jr. ; contributors Hok-lam Chan ... [et al.]. — Princeton ; Guildford : Princeton University Press, c1981. — xvi,487p,[8]p of plates : ill,facsims,ports ; 25cm
Includes index
ISBN 0-691-03127-4 (cased) : £17.50
ISBN 0-691-10110-8 (pbk) : £7.30 B81-25514

951'.026 — China, *1587*

Huang, Ray. 1587 : a year of no significance : the Ming dynasty in decline / Ray Huang. — New Haven ; London : Yale University Press, c1981. — xiii,278p,[17]p of plates : ill,ports ; 25cm
Bibliography: p261-265. - Includes index
ISBN 0-300-02518-1 : £12.60 B81-16155

951'.03 — China. International relations with Japan, *1800-1945*

The **Chinese** and the Japanese : essays in political and cultural interactions / edited by Akira Iriye ; contributors Madeleine Chi ... [et al.]. — Princeton ; Guildford : Princeton University Press, c1980. — xi,368p ; 25cm
Includes index
ISBN 0-691-03126-6 (cased) : £13.70
ISBN 0-691-10086-1 (pbk) : £5.45
Also classified at 952'.025 B81-04737

951'.03 — China. Modernisation. Role of overseas activities of Chinese business firms, *1893-1911*

Godley, Michael R.. The Mandarin-capitalists from Nanyang : overseas Chinese enterprise in the modernization of China 1893-1911 / Michael R. Godley. — Cambridge : Cambridge University Press, 1981. — viii,222p : 1map ; 24cm. — (Cambridge studies in Chinese history, literature and institutions)
Bibliography: p206-211. — Includes index
ISBN 0-521-23626-6 : £19.50 B81-32081

951′.03′0924 — China. Yuan, Shikai — *Biographies*

MacKinnon, Stephen R.. Power and politics in late Imperial China : Yuan Shi-kai in Beijing and Tianjin, 1901-1908 / Stephen R. MacKinnon. — Berkeley ; London : University of California Press, c1980. — xii,260p : 1map,1port ; 24cm
Bibliography: p239-253. — Includes index
ISBN 0-520-04025-2 : £11.00 B81-27207

951.04 — China, *1911-1971*

MacDonald, Malcolm, *1901-*. Inside China / by Malcolm MacDonald ; with photographs by William MacQuitty. — London : Heinemann, 1980. — 208p : ill(some col.),maps,ports(some col.) ; 26cm
Ill on lining papers. — Includes index
ISBN 0-434-44040-x : £9.50 B81-01892

951.04 — China. Political events, *1900-1949 — For schools*

Denning, Michael, *1954-*. China 1900-49 / Michael Denning. — London : Edward Arnold, 1981. — 31p : ill,maps,ports ; 25cm. — (Links : twentieth century world history books)
Bibliography: p31. — Includes index
ISBN 0-7131-0537-2 (pbk) : £1.50 B81-36872

951.04 — China. Political events, *1926-1949*

Zhou, Enlai. Selected works. — Oxford : Pergamon, May 1981. — [430]p. — (Leaders of the world)
ISBN 0-08-024550-1 (cased) : £12.00 : CIP entry
ISBN 0-08-024551-x (pbk) : £5.95 B81-04290

951.04′0924 — China. Wang, Fanxi, *to 1949 — Biographies*

Wang, Fanxi. Chinese revolutionary : memoirs 1919-1949 / Wang Fan-hsi ; translated and with an introduction by Gregor Benton. — Oxford : Oxford University Press, 1980. — xxi,282p ; 23cm
Translation of: Shuang shan hui yi lu. — Includes index
ISBN 0-19-211746-7 : £15.00 : CIP rev. B79-01657

951.04′1 — China. Intellectual life, *1915-1927*

Lin, Yü-sheng. The crisis of Chinese consciousness : radical antitraditionalism in the May Fourth Era / Lin Yü-sheng. — Madison ; London : University of Wisconsin Press, 1979. — xiv,201p ; 24cm
Bibliography: p165-179. - Includes index
ISBN 0-299-07410-2 : £15.00 B81-09324

951.04′1 — China. Political events. Role of foreign banks, *ca 1900-1925*

Dayer, Roberta Allbert. Bankers and diplomats in China 1917-1925 : the Anglo-American relationship / Roberta Allbert Dayer. — London : Cass, 1981. — xxvii,295p : 1map ; 23cm
Bibliography: p254-276. — Includes index
ISBN 0-7146-3118-3 : £16.00 : CIP rev. B79-06168

951.04′2 — Sino-Japanese War, *1937-1945*

Wilson, Dick. When tigers fight. — London : Hutchinson, Oct.1981. — 1v.
ISBN 0-09-146571-0 : £9.95 : CIP entry B81-26767

951.04′2′0924 — China, *1928-1949 — Personal observations*

Snow, Edgar. Edgar Snow′s China : a personal account of the Chinese Revolution compiled from the writings of Edgar Snow / by Lois Wheeler Snow. — London : Orbis, c1981. — xx,284p : ill,maps,ports ; 29cm
Includes index
ISBN 0-85613-364-7 : £7.95 B81-25095

951.05 — China — *For schools*

Pask, Raymond. China. — London : Heinemann Educational, Jan.1982. — [64]p
ISBN 0-435-34689-x (pbk) : £2.80 : CIP entry B81-34497

951.05 — China. Political events, *1958-1979*

Leys, Simon. The chairman′s new clothes : Mao and the cultural revolution / Simon Leys ; translated by Carol Appleyard and Patrick Goode. — Rev. ed. — London : Allison & Busby, 1981. — 272p ; 20cm
Translation of: Les habits neuf du president Mao. — Previous ed.: 1977. — Includes index
ISBN 0-85031-435-6 (pbk) : £3.95 B81-36321

951.05 — China. Political events. Role of China. *Zhong guo ren min jie fang jun, 1945-1971 compared with* **role of revolutionary military forces in political events in Soviet Union,** *1921-1940*

Adelman, Jonathan R.. The revolutionary armies : the historical development of the Soviet and the Chinese people′s liberation armies / Jonathan R. Adelman. — Westport ; London : Greenwood Press, 1980. — x,230p ; 22cm. — (Contributions in political science, ISSN 0147-1066 ; no.38)
Bibliography: p199-223. - Includes index
ISBN 0-313-22026-3 : Unpriced
Primary classification 947.084′2 B81-06514

951.05′092′4 — China. Alley, Rewi — *Biographies*

Chapple, Geoff. Rewi Alley of China. — London : Hodder & Stoughton, July 1981. — [230]p
ISBN 0-340-25687-7 : £8.95 : CIP entry B81-21649

951.05′092′4 — China. Mao, Zedong — *Biographies — For children*

Kolpas, Norman. Mao / Norman Kolpas. — Harlow : Longman, 1981. — 69p : ill(some col.),col.maps,ports(some col.). — (Longman great lives)
Map on lining papers. — Bibliography: p69. — Includes index
ISBN 0-582-39032-x : £3.95 B81-39667

951.05′092′4 — China. Mao, Zedong — *Biographies — For schools*

Dures, Alan. Mao Tse-tung / Alan and Katharine Dures. — London : Batsford Academic and Educational, [1980]. — 80p : ill,1map,1plan,ports ; 26cm. — (World leaders in context)
Bibliography: p4. — Includes index
ISBN 0-7134-1923-7 : £4.95 B81-00675

951.05′5 — China. Political events, *1942-1962*

Brugger, Bill. China : liberation and transformation 1942-1962 / Bill Brugger. — London : Croom Helm, 1981. — 288p : 1map ; 22cm
Bibliography: p268-279. — Includes index
ISBN 0-7099-0605-6 (pbk) : Unpriced : CIP rev.
ISBN 0-7099-0606-4 (pbk) : £6.95 B80-20071

951.05′6 — China. Political events, *1962-1979*

Brugger, Bill. China : radicalism to revisionism 1962-1979 / Bill Brugger. — London : Croom Helm, 1981. — 275p : 1map ; 22cm
Bibliography: p256-267. — Includes index
ISBN 0-7099-0610-2 (cased) : Unpriced
ISBN 0-7099-0611-0 (pbk) : £5.95 B81-08977

951.05′7 — China, *1976-1979*

China since Mao / edited by Kwan Ha Yim. — London : Macmillan, 1980. — 202p : 1map ; 24cm
Includes index
ISBN 0-333-28589-1 : £10.00 : CIP rev. B79-37103

Garside, Roger. Coming alive : China after Mao / Roger Garside. — London : Deutsch, 1981. — viii,458,[8]p of plates : ill,1plan,ports ; 24cm
Bibliography: p44-447. — Includes index
ISBN 0-233-97295-1 : £8.95 B81-25148

951.05′7 — China. Social conditions, *1970-1980*

Bonavia, David. [The Chinese today]. The Chinese / David Bonavia. — London : Allen Lane, 1981, c1980. — x,290p,[16]p of plates : ill,1map ; 23cm
Originally published: New York : Lippincott & Crowell, 1980. — Includes index
ISBN 0-7139-1377-0 : £7.95 B81-04775

951.05′7′0924 — China. Social life, *1977-1979 — Personal observations*

Fraser, John, *1944-*. The Chinese : portrait of a people / John Fraser. — Toronto ; London : Collins, 1980. — 463p,[16]p of plates : ill,1map,1facsim,ports ; 24cm
ISBN 0-00-216817-0 : £7.95 B81-17252

951.05′8 — China — *For children*

Mason, Sally. Let′s go to China / text and photographs by Sally Mason ; [maps by Brian and Constance Dear, and Tony Payne]. — London : Watts, 1981. — 32p : col.ill,2col.maps ; 22cm
Includes index
ISBN 0-85166-928-x : £2.99 B81-22933

This is China / illustrated by Chris Masters. — London : Transworld, 1981. — 31p : col.ill,col.maps ; 28cm. — (A Carousel book)
Text on inside covers. — Includes index
ISBN 0-552-54180-x (pbk) : £0.95 B81-32965

951.05′8 — China. Social life — *For children*

Jullien, Claire. Life in China / Claire Jullien, Jean-Louis Boissier ; [translated by Denis Grayson] ; [edited by Catherine M. Dell]. — St. Albans : Hart-Davis, 1981. — 62p : ill(some col.),ports ; 27cm. — (Signposts series)
Translation from the French
ISBN 0-247-13037-0 : £3.50 B81-39611

951.05′8′0222 — China. Social life — *Illustrations*

Arnold, Eve. In China / Eve Arnold. — London : Hutchinson, 1980. — 201p : chiefly col.ill ; 31cm
ISBN 0-09-143550-1 : £16.00 : CIP rev. B80-23911

951.05′8′05 — China — *For Western businessmen — Serials*

China-international business : an information and research series / the China-International Business Project. — Vol.1, no.1 (1981)-. — New York ; Oxford : Pergamon Press for the Project, 1981-. — v. ; 23cm
Six issues yearly. — Description based on: Vol.1, no.2 (1981)
ISSN 0270-7446 : Unpriced B81-27920

951.05′8′0922 — China. Persons — *Biographies*

Bartke, Wolfgang. Who′s who in the People′s Republic of China = Zhong hua ren min gong he guo ren ming lu / by Wolfgang Bartke ; [English translation by Franciscu Verellen]. — Brighton : Harvester, 1981. — xii,729p : ill,ports ; 32cm
Translated from the German
ISBN 0-7108-0320-6 : £50.00 : CIP rev. B81-13545

951′.13 — China. Jiangsu *(Province).* **Jiading. Confucian loyalists,** *to 1645*

Dennerline, Jerry. The Chia-ting loyalists : Confucian leadership and social change in seventeenth-century China / Jerry Dennerline. — New Haven ; London : Yale University Press, c1981. — xix, 389p : ill,maps,ports,geneal.tables ; 25cm. — (Yale historical publications. Miscellany ; 126)
Bibliography: p367-378. — Includes index
ISBN 0-300-02548-3 : £22.00 : CIP rev. B81-12365

951′.13204 — China. Shanghai, *1919-1979*

Shanghai : revolution and development in an Asian metropolis / edited by Christopher Howe. — Cambridge : Cambridge University Press, 1981. — xvii,444p : ill,maps ; 23cm. — (Contemporary China Institute publications)
Includes index
ISBN 0-521-23198-1 : £30.00 : CIP rev. B80-28931

951′.132042 — China. Shanghai. Political events, *1927-1937*

Coble, Parks M.. The Shanghai capitalists and the Nationalist government, 1927-1937 / Parks M. Coble, Jr. — Cambridge, Mass. : Council on East Asian Studies, Harvard University ; Cambridge, Mass. ; London : Harvard University Press [distributor], 1980. — xiv,357p ; 24cm. — (Harvard East Asian monographs ; 94)
Bibliography: p325-337. — Includes index
ISBN 0-674-80535-6 : £9.00 B81-16533

951'.1403 — China. Shantung *(Province)*. Peasants. Rebellions, *1774*
Naquin, Susan. Shantung rebellion : the Wang Lun uprising of 1774 / Susan Naquin. — New Haven ; London : Yale University Press, c1981. — xvii,228p : ill,maps,plans ; 22cm
Bibliography: p211-219. — Includes index
ISBN 0-300-02638-2 : £14.00 : CIP rev.
B81-23799

951'.156057'0924 — China. Peking. Social life, *1973-1977 — Personal observations*
Fisher, Lois. Go gently through Peking : a Westerner's life in China / Lois Fisher. — Large print ed. — Leicester : Ulverscroft, 1980, c1979. — 421p ; 23cm. — (Ulverscroft large print)
Originally published: London : Souvenir Press, 1979
ISBN 0-7089-0559-5 : £4.25 ; CIP rev.
B80-35586

951'.156058 — China. Peking. Social life — *For children*
Peng, Wenlan. Living in Peking / Wenlan Peng. — Hove : Wayland, 1981. — 52p : ill,1col.map ; 22cm. — (Living in famous cities)
Bibliography: p51. — Includes index
ISBN 0-85340-815-7 : £3.75 B81-37702

951'.18 — China. Loyang, *493-534*
Jenner, W. J. F.. Memories of Loyang : Yang Hsüan-chih and the lost capital (493-534) / by W.J.F. Jenner. — Oxford : Clarendon Press, 1981. — xii,310p : 3maps ; 23cm
Bibliography: p285-295. — Includes index
ISBN 0-19-821568-1 : £25.00 B81-35520

951'.2505'05 — Hong Kong — *Serials*
Hong Kong. — 1981. — Hong Kong : Government Printer ; London (6 Grafton St., W1X 3LB) : Hong Kong Government Office [distributor], 1981. — 307p
£4.00 B81-30739

951'.5 — Tibet. Social life, *1942-1943*
Tung, Rosemary Jones. A portrait of lost Tibet / Rosemary Jones Tung ; ornamental art by Zlatko Paunov. — London : Thames and Hudson, 1980. — xvi,224p : ill,1map,ports ; 25cm
Bibliography: p223-224
ISBN 0-500-54068-3 : £8.95 B81-05429

951'.5 — Tibetan civilization, *to 1980*
Zwalf, W.. Heritage of Tibet. — London : British Museum Publications, Oct.1981. — [144]p
ISBN 0-7141-1420-0 : £5.95 : CIP entry
B81-28001

951'.5 — Tibetan civilization, *to 1980 — Festschriften*
International Seminar on Tibetan Studies *(1979 : Oxford)*. Tibetan studies : in honour of Hugh Richardson : proceedings of the International Seminar on Tibetan Studies, Oxford 1979 / edited by Michael Aris and Aung San Suu Kyi. — Warminster : Aris & Phillips, c1980. — xx,348p : ill,facsims,1port ; 25cm. — (Aris and Phillips central Asian studies)
ISBN 0-85668-190-3 (pbk) : £12.00 : CIP rev.
B80-34366

951'.73042'0924 — Mongolia *(People's Republic)*. Polish exiles. Social life, *1940-1942 — Personal observations — Polish texts*
Dubanowiczowa, Magdalena. Na mongolskich bezdrożach : wspomnienia z zesłania 1940-1942 / Magdalena Dubanowiczowa. — 2gie wyd. — Londyn : Nakładem Polskiej Fundacji Kulturalnej, 1980. — 286p : 1port ; 19cm
Previous ed.: 1974
Unpriced (pbk) B81-10552

951'.8004924 — China. Manchuria. Jewish communities. Establishment. Policies of Japanese government, *1934-1941*
Tokayer, Marvin. The fugu plan / Marvin Tokayer and Mary Swarty. — Feltham : Hamlyn Paperbacks, 1981, c1979. — 287p,[4]p of plates : ill,ports ; 18cm
Originally published: New York ; London : Paddington Press, 1979. — Includes index
ISBN 0-600-20176-7 (pbk) : £1.75
Primary classification 940.53'15'03924
B81-14606

951.9'504 — South Korea. Social conditions, *1945-1975*
The **Economic** and social modernization of the Republic of Korea / Edward S. Mason ... [et al.] with Leroy Jones ... [et al.]. — Cambridge, Mass. : Council on East Asian Studies, Harvard University ; Cambridge, Mass. ; London : Harvard University Press [distributor], 1980. — xxxii,552p : ill,maps ; 24cm. — (Harvard East Asian monographs. Studies in the modernization of the Republic of Korea, 1945-1975 ; 92)
Bibliography: p525-534. - Includes index
ISBN 0-674-23175-9 : £12.00 B81-16610

952 — HISTORY. JAPAN

952 — Japan, *1800-1980*
Beasley, W. G.. The modern history of Japan / W.G. Beasley. — 3rd ed. — London : Weidenfeld and Nicolson, 1981. — ix,358p : maps ; 22cm
Previous ed.: 1973. — Bibliography: p333-340. — Includes index
ISBN 0-297-77961-3 (cased) : £12.95
ISBN 0-297-77962-1 (pbk) : £6.95 B81-26060

952 — Japan. Influence of Western world, *1600-1980*
Jansen, Marius B.. Japan and its world : two centuries of change / Marius B. Jansen. — Princeton ; Guildford : Princeton University Press, c1980. — xii,128p : ill,ports ; 23cm. — (The 1975 Brown & Haley lectures)
Bibliography: p117-123. - Includes index
ISBN 0-691-05310-3 : £5.30 B81-08657

952 — Japan, *to 1867*
Totman, Conrad. Japan before Perry : a short history / Conrad Totman. — Berkeley ; London : University of California Press, c1981. — xv,246p : ill ; 23cm : 1map
Bibliography: p239-240. — Includes index
ISBN 0-520-04132-1 (pbk) : £12.00 B81-36414

952 — Japan, *to 1980*
Macintyre, Michael. The Shogun inheritance : Japan and the legacy of the Samurai / Michael Macintyre. — London : Collins, 1981. — 215p : col.ill,1map,col.ports ; 29cm
ISBN 0-00-216350-0 : £12.95 : CIP rev.
ISBN 0-563-17942-2 (BBC) B81-20154

952 — Japanese civilization, *to 1978*
Milward, R. S.. Japan : the past in the present / R.S. Milward ; with an introduction by G.C. Allen. — Tenterdan : Norbury, 1979. — xi,132p ; 21cm
Includes index
ISBN 0-904404-28-5 (cased) : £4.95
ISBN 0-904404-29-3 (pbk) : Unpriced
B81-40324

952'.007'047 — Soviet Union. Japanese studies
Kirby, E. Stuart. Russian studies of Japan : an exploratory survey / E. Stuart Kirby. — London : Macmillan, 1981. — xv,226p ; 23cm
Bibliography: p151-217. — Includes index
ISBN 0-333-28166-7 : £20.00 B81-23077

952'.02 — Japan. Social conditions, *1500-1650 — Conference proceedings*
Japan before Tokugawa : political consolidation and economic growth, 1500 to 1650 / [based on a conference sponsored by the Joint Committee on Japanese Studies of the Social Science Research Council and the American Council of Learned Societies and by the Japan Society for the Promotion of Science] ; edited by John Whitney Hall, Nagahara Keiji and Kozo Yamamura. — Princeton ; Guildford : Princeton University Press, c1981. — xiv,392p : maps ; 23cm
Includes index
ISBN 0-691-05308-1 : £12.60 B81-25962

952'.025 — Japan. International relations with China, *1800-1945*
The **Chinese** and the Japanese : essays in political and cultural interactions / edited by Akira Iriye ; contributors Madeleine Chi ... [et al.]. — Princeton ; Guildford : Princeton University Press, c1980. — xi,368p ; 25cm
Includes index
ISBN 0-691-03126-6 (cased) : £13.70
ISBN 0-691-10086-1 (pbk) : £5.45
Primary classification 951'.03 B81-04737

952.03'1 — Japan. Political events, *1868-1912*
Bowen, Roger W.. Rebellion and democracy in Meiji Japan : a study of commoners in the popular rights movement / Roger W. Bowen. — Berkeley ; London : University of California Press, c1980. — xv,367p : 1ill,maps ; 25cm
Bibliography: p347-359. - Includes index
ISBN 0-520-03665-4 : £15.00 B81-03066

952.04'8 — Japan — *For children*
Ashby, Gwynneth. Let's go to Japan / text and photographs by Gwynneth Ashby ; general editor Henry Pluckrose. — London : Watts, c1980. — 32p : col.ill,col.maps ; 22cm
ISBN 0-85166-863-1 : £2.99 B81-01947

952.04'8 — Japan. Society
Inside Japan / [edited by Howard Smith]. — London : British Broadcasting Corporation, 1981. — 224p : ill(some col.),maps,ports(some col.) ; 24cm
Bibliography: p217-222. — Includes index
ISBN 0-563-16300-3 : £7.50 B81-26997

952.04'8'0222 — Japanese artefacts — *Illustrations*
Japan style : essays / by Mitsukuni Yoshida ... [et al.] ; [translation J.V. Earle]. — London (10 Parkfields, SW15 6NH) : Serindia, 1980. — 148p : ill(some col.) ; 26x27cm
Published to accompany an exhibition at the Victoria and Albert Museum, London, 1980. — Translation from the Japanese
ISBN 0-906026-03-2 : £6.95 B81-07042

952.04'8'088054 — Japan. Children. Social life — *Case studies — For children*
Piggott, Juliet. Kiku of Japan / written by Juliet Piggott ; illustrated by Gordon Stowell. — Guildford : Lutterworth, 1980. — 31p : ill (some col.),2maps ; 23cm. — (How they live now ; 1)
Maps on lining papers. — Includes index
ISBN 0-7188-2389-3 : £2.50 B81-02872

953 — HISTORY. ARABIAN PENINSULA AND ADJACENT AREAS

953 — Arabia, *to 1980*
Serjeant, R. B.. Studies in Arabian history and civilisation / R.B. Serjeant. — London : Variorum Reprints, 1981. — 350p in various pagings : ill,1map,ports ; 24cm. — (Collected studies series ; CS145)
Includes texts in Arabic. — Includes bibliographies and index
ISBN 0-86078-092-9 : £24.00 : CIP rev.
B81-21529

953'.004927 — Arabia. Rwala. Social conditions
Lancaster, William. The Rwala Bedouin today / William Lancaster. — Cambridge : Cambridge University Press, 1981. — x,179p : ill,1map,ports,geneal.tables ; 23cm. — (Changing cultures)
Bibliography: p172-174. — Includes index
ISBN 0-521-23877-3 : £17.50
ISBN 0-521-28275-6 (pbk) : £5.95 B81-38287

953'.04 — Arabian civilization. Attitudes of English persons, *ca 1800-1975*
Tidrick, Kathryn. Heart-beguiling Araby / Kathryn Tidrick. — Cambridge : Cambridge University Press, 1981. — xii,244p : ill,2maps,ports ; 24cm
Bibliography: p231-238. — Includes index
ISBN 0-521-23483-2 : £12.50 B81-30789

953'.04 — Egyptian-Wahhabi war
Sabini, John. Armies in the sand : the struggle for Mecca and Medina / John Sabini. — London : Thames and Hudson, c1981. — 233p : ill,1map,ports ; 25cm
Includes index
ISBN 0-500-01246-6 : £7.95 B81-11564

953'.1053'0924 — Egypt. Sinai. United Nations. *Emergency Force, 1966-1967 — Personal observations*
Rikhye, Indar Jit. The Sinai blunder : withdrawal of the United Nations Emergency Force leading to the Six-Day War of June 1967 / Indar Jit Rikhye. — London : Cass, 1980. — xii,240p,[8]p of plates : ill,maps,ports ; 23cm
Includes index
ISBN 0-7146-3136-1 : £13.50 : CIP rev.
Primary classification 956'.046'0924 B79-15158

953′.1054 — Egypt. Gaza Strip & Sinai. Occupation by Israel, *1967-1980*

Harris, William Wilson. Taking root : Israeli settlement in the West Bank, the Golan and Gaza-Sinai, 1967-1980 / William Wilson Harris. — Chichester : Research Studies Press, c1980. — xxii,223p : ill,maps ; 29cm. — (Geographical research studies series ; 1)
Bibliography: p199-207. — Includes index
ISBN 0-471-27863-7 (pbk) : £16.50 : CIP rev.
Also classified at 956.91′4 ; 956.95 B80-35587

953′.35 — Yemen *(People′s Democratic Republic), 1900-1980*

Peterson, J. E.. Yemen. — London : Croom Helm, Jan.1982. — [208]p
ISBN 0-7099-2003-2 : £11.95 : CIP entry
B81-33892

953′.35 — Yemen *(People′s Democratic Republic).* **Aden,** *1839-1872*

Kour, Z. H.. The history of Aden 1839-72 / Z.H. Kour. — London : Cass, 1981. — 240p : 3maps ; 23cm
Bibliography: p233-234. — Includes index
ISBN 0-7146-3101-9 : £15.00 : CIP rev.
B79-06169

953′.5 — Oman. Dhofar. Military operations by Great Britain. *Army. Special Air Service Regiment, 22nd, 1971-1976 — Personal observations*

Jeapes, Tony. SAS : Operation Oman / Tony Jeaps. — London : Kimber, 1980. — 247p,[12]p of plates : ill,maps,1facsim,ports ; 25cm
Includes index
ISBN 0-7183-0018-1 : £8.95 B81-03650

953′.53′009734 — Oman. Rural regions. Social life *— For children*

Dutton, Roderic. Arab village / Roderic Dutton ; photographs by John B. Free. — London : Black, c1980. — 25p : col.ill,2col.maps ; 22cm. — (BEANS. Geography)
Ill on lining papers
ISBN 0-7136-2036-6 : £2.50 : CIP rev.
B80-14096

953′.5305 — Oman, *1932-1979*

Clements, Frank A.. Oman : the reborn land / F.A. Clements. — London : Longman, 1980. — 182p,[13]p of plates : ill(some col.),1col.map,2ports ; 23cm
Bibliography: p169-175. — Includes index
ISBN 0-582-78300-3 : £9.95 B81-03551

953′.57 — Dubai. Social life *— Personal observations*

Robinson, Janet, *1941-*. Dubai Arabia / Janet Robinson. — Bognor Regis : New Horizon, 1981. — 179p,[82]p of plates : ill,maps,ports ; 22cm
ISBN 0-86116-700-7 : £9.95 B81-24947

953′.57 — United Arab Emirates. Social conditions, *to 1980*

Heard-Bey, Franke. From Trucial States to United Arab Emirates. — London : Longman, Jan.1982. — [320]p
ISBN 0-582-78032-2 : £12.75 : CIP entry
B81-34287

953′.6 — Persian Gulf countries, *to 1978*

The **Persian** Gulf States : a general survey / Alvin J. Cottrell, general editor ; C. Edmund Bosworth ... [et al.], editors. — Baltimore ; London : Johns Hopkins University Press, c1980. — xxxiv,695p : ill,maps,facsims ; 27cm
Includes bibliographies and index
ISBN 0-8018-2204-1 : £20.00 B81-05266

953′.65 — Bahrain, *to 1979*

Khuri, Fuad I.. Tribe and State in Bahrain : the transformation of social and political authority in an Arab State / Fuad I. Khuri. — Chicago ; London : University of Chicago Press, 1980. — xiii,289p : ill,2maps,geneal.tables ; 24cm. — (Publications of the Center for Middle Eastern studies ; no.14)
Bibliography: p281-284. — Includes index
ISBN 0-226-43473-7 : £9.60 B81-21180

953′.67053 — Kuwait

Sapsted, David. Modern Kuwait / David Sapsted. — London : Macmillan, 1980. — 186p : col.ill ; 25cm
Includes index
ISBN 0-333-31098-5 : £10.00 B81-23073

953′.8 — Saudi Arabia. Hā'il, *to 1980*

Ward, Philip. Hail : oasis city of Saudi Arabia. — Cambridge : Oleander Press, Dec.1981. — [350]p. — (Arabia past & present ; v.11)
ISBN 0-900891-75-0 : £24.75 : CIP entry
B81-31541

953′.804 — Saudi Arabia, *1901-1932*

Helms, Christine Moss. The cohesion of Saudi Arabia : evolution of political identity / Christine Moss Helms. — London : Croom Helm, c1981. — 313p : maps ; 23cm. — (Croom Helm series on the Arab world)
Bibliography: p291-303. — Includes index
ISBN 0-7099-0441-x : £14.95 B81-03924

953′.805 — Saudi Arabia. Royal families, *1900-1980*

Lacey, Robert. The kingdom. — London : Hutchinson, Oct.1981. — [450]p
ISBN 0-09-145790-4 : £8.95 : CIP entry
B81-26796

953′.8053′088054 — Saudi Arabia. Children. Social life *— Case studies — For children*

Freeth, Zahra. Rashid of Saudi Arabia / written by Zahra Freeth ; illustrated by Gordon Stowell. — Guildford : Lutterworth, 1980. — 30p : col.ill,2maps ; 23cm. — (How they live now ; 2)
Maps on lining papers. — Includes index
ISBN 0-7188-2390-7 : £2.50 B81-02873

954 — HISTORY. SOUTH ASIA, INDIA

954 — India. Political events, *ca 1860-1980 — For schools*

Tames, Richard. India and Pakistan in the twentieth century / Richard Tames. — London : Batsford Academic and Educational, 1981. — 96p : ill,3maps,facsims,ports ; 26cm. — (Twentieth century world history)
Bibliography: p94. - Includes index
ISBN 0-7134-3415-5 : £5.95 B81-15963

954 — India. Portuguese colonies. Social conditions, *ca 1630-ca 1670*

Boxer, C. R.. Portuguese India in the mid-seventeenth century / C.R. Boxer. — Delhi ; Oxford : Oxford University Press, 1980. — x,57p : maps ; 22cm
Maps on lining papers. — Includes index
ISBN 0-19-561200-0 (pbk) : £4.50 B81-14283

954 — India *(Republic).* **Palaces**

Gaekwad, Fatesinghrao, *Maharaja of Baroda*. The palaces of India / Maharaja of Baroda ; with photographs by Virginia Fass. — London : Collins, 1980. — 245p : ill(some col.),maps (some col.),ports(some col.) ; 32cm
ISBN 0-00-211678-2 : £25.00 B81-03622

954 — India *(Republic), to 1980*

Lall, Arthur. The emergence of modern India / Arthur Lall. — New York ; Guildford : Columbia University Press, 1981. — viii,260p ; 24cm
Includes index
ISBN 0-231-03430-x : £10.45 B81-27115

954′.005 — South Asia *— History — Serials*

Purvadesh. — Vol.1, no.1 (Summer 1980)-. — London (125 Harold Rd, E13 0SF) : A.N. Banger, 1980-. — v. ; 21cm
Two issues yearly
ISSN 0144-946x = Purvadesh : £6.00 per year
B81-01399

954.02′5′0924 — Moghul Empire. Gulbadan, *Princess, daughter of Bābar, Emperor of Hindustan — Biographies*

Godden, Rumer. Gulbadan : portrait of a rose princess at the Mughal court / by Rumer Godden ; picture research by Helen Topsfield. — London : Macmillan, 1980. — 153,[6]p : col.ill,1map,1facsim,1geneal.table ; 23cm
Bibliography: p[5]
ISBN 0-333-30434-9 : £7.95 B81-02687

954.02′9′0924 — India. Suraj Mal, *Maharaja — Biographies*

Natwar-Singh, K.. Maharaja Suraj Mal - 1707-1763 : his life and times / by K. Natwar-Singh. — London : Allen & Unwin, 1981. — xiv,136p,[9]p of plates : ill(some col.),2maps,ports,geneal.tables ; 23cm
Bibliography: p130-132. - Includes index
ISBN 0-04-923072-7 : Unpriced B81-21266

954.03′1′0924 — India. Social life, *1837-1854 — Personal observations — Correspondence, diaries, etc.*

Lawrence, Honoria. The journals of Honoria Lawrence : India observed 1837-1854 / edited by John Lawrence and Audrey Woodiwiss. — London : Hodder and Stoughton, 1980. — 253p,[8]p of plates : ill,maps,facsims,ports ; 25cm
Includes index
ISBN 0-340-23919-0 : £10.95 : CIP rev.
B80-13163

954.03′5′0924 — India. Politics. Kitchlew, Saifuddin *— Biographies*

Kitchlew, F. Z.. Freedom fighter : the story of Dr. Saifuddin Kitchlew / F.Z. Kitchlew. — Bognor Regis : New Horizon, c1979. — 107p,[4]p of plates : ill,ports ; 21cm
ISBN 0-86116-126-2 : £4.50 B81-21911

954.03′53′0924 — India. Lytton, Robert Bulwer Lytton, *Earl of — Biographies*

Raymond, E. Neill. Victorian viceroy : the life of Robert, the first Earl of Lytton / by E. Neill Raymond. — London : Regency Press, c1980. — 317p,[8]p of plates : ill,2maps,ports ; 23cm
Maps on lining papers. — Bibliography: p313-317. - Includes index
ISBN 0-7212-0599-2 : £8.00 B81-05081

954.03′57′0924 — India. Social life, *ca 1920-ca 1930 — Personal observations*

Battye, Evelyn. Costumes and characters of the British Raj. — Exeter : Webb & Bower, Oct.1981. — [64]p
ISBN 0-906671-42-6 : £6.95 : CIP entry
B81-30475

954.03′58′0924 — India. Prendergast, John *— Biographies*

Prendergast, John. Prender′s progress : a soldier in India, 1931-47 / John Prendergast. — London : Cassell, 1979. — 256p,[16]p of plates : ill,1map,3plans,ports ; 23cm
ISBN 0-304-30471-9 : £7.95 B81-01400

954.03′58′0924 — India. Social life, *1929-1947 — Personal observations*

Rowntree, John. A chota sahib : memoirs of a forest officer / by John Rowntree. — Padstow (11 Church St., Padstow, Cornwall) : Tabb House, 1981. — 110p,[8]p of plates : ill,maps,ports ; 21cm
ISBN 0-907018-04-1 (pbk) : £2.95 B81-21244

954.04′2′0924 — India *(Republic).* **Nehru, Jawaharlal** *— Correspondence, diaries, etc.*

Nehru, Jawaharlal. Jawaharlal Nehru : an anthology / edited by Sarvepalli Gopal. — Delhi ; Oxford : Oxford University Press, 1980. — xxi,662p : 1port ; 23cm
Includes index
ISBN 0-19-561220-5 : £11.00 B81-21162

954.05′2 — Indian culture. Influence of Western tourists

Mehta, Gita. Karma cola / Gita Mehta. — London : Collins, 1981, c1979. — 210p ; 18cm
Originally published: New York : Simon and Schuster, 1979 ; London : Cape, 1980
ISBN 0-00-636092-0 (pbk) : £1.50 B81-12006

954.05′2′0222 — India *(Republic) — Illustrations*

MacQuitty, William. The glory of India. — London : Collins, Feb.1982. — [64]p
ISBN 0-00-216635-6 (pbk) : £5.95 : CIP entry
B81-37591

954.05′2′0882945 — India ***(Republic).*** **Hindu children. Social life** — *Case studies — For children*

Hardy, Aruna. Ravi of India / written by Aruna Hardy ; illustrated by Gordon Stowell. — Guildford : Lutterworth, 1980. — 31p : col.ill,2maps ; 23cm. — (How they live now ; 4)
Maps on lining papers. — Includes index
ISBN 0-7188-2419-9 : £2.50 B81-02874

954′.2 — India ***(Republic).*** **Oudh. Political events,** *1720-1801*

Barnett, Richard B.. North India between empires : Awadh, the Mughals, and the British 1720-1801 / Richard B. Barnett. — Berkeley ; London : University of California Press, c1980. — xvii,276p : ill,maps,ports ; 25cm
Bibliography: p255-272. - Includes index
ISBN 0-520-03787-1 : £15.00 B81-15973

954′.4052′0222 — India ***(Republic).*** **Rajasthan** — *Illustrations*

Raghubir Singh. Rajasthan : India′s enchanted land / introduction and 80 colour photographs by Raghubir Singh ; foreword by Satyajit Ray. — London : Thames and Hudson, c1981. — 32p,80p of plates : chiefly col.ill,1map,col.ports ; 25x28cm
ISBN 0-500-54070-5 : £16.00 B81-10520

954′.52 — India ***(Republic).*** **Simla,** *1820-1940*

Barr, Pat. Simla : a hill station in British India. — London : Scolar Press, Feb.1982. — [148]p
Originally published: 1978
ISBN 0-85967-659-5 (pbk) : £7.50 : CIP entry B81-39231

954′.5600421 — India ***(Republic).*** **Delhi. Britons. Social life,** *1848-1850 — Correspondence, diaries, etc.*

Bayley, Emily, ***Lady.*** The golden calm : an English lady′s life in Moghul Delhi : reminiscences / by Emily, Lady Clive Bayley and by her father, Sir Thomas Metcalfe ; edited by M.M. Kaye. — Exeter : Webb & Bower ; Leicester : WHS Distributors, 1980. — 217p : col.ill,facsims,1col.port ; 26cm
Text, ill on lining papers. — Includes index
ISBN 0-906671-19-1 : £9.95 : CIP rev. B80-18134

954′.792035′0924 — India. Maharashtra. Political events. Role of Ranade, Mahadev Govind, *1850-1897*

Tucker, Richard P.. Ranade and the roots of Indian nationalism / Richard P. Tucker. — Chicago ; London : University of Chicago Press, 1972 (1976 [printing]). — xiii,259p : 1map ; 23cm
Bibliography: p241-254. — Includes index
ISBN 0-226-81532-3 (pbk) : £7.70 B81-38147

954′.82 — India. Tamil Nadu ***(State).*** **Coimbatore & Karadibavi. Social life,** *1917-1933 — Childhood reminiscences*

Sreenivasan, Kasthuri. Climbing the coconut tree : a partial autobiography / Kasthuri Sreenivasan. — Delhi ; Oxford : Oxford University Press, 1980. — xiii,163p,[16]p of plates : ill,1facsim,ports ; 23cm
Includes index
ISBN 0-19-561242-6 : £5.50 B81-04930

954.91 — HISTORY. PAKISTAN

954.9′124 — Pakistan. North-West Frontier Province. Waziristan. Mahsuds. Relations with government of Great Britain

Howell, Evelyn. Mizh : a monograph on Government′s relations with the Mahsud tribe / by Evelyn Howell ; with a foreword by Akbar S. Ahmed. — Karachi ; Oxford : Oxford University Press, 1979. — xii,119p,1leaf of plates : 1col.map ; 23cm. — (Oxford in Asia historical reprints)
Originally published: Simla : Government of India Press, 1931
ISBN 0-19-577269-5 (geneal.tables) : £6.50 B81-27569

954.92 — HISTORY. BANGLADESH

954.9′2 — Bangladesh. Political events. Role of Christian missions, *to 1979*

Hussain, Asaf. Birth of Bangladesh : political role of missions / Asaf Hussain. — Leicester : Islamic Foundation, c1980. — 16p ; 30cm. — (Situation report / Islamic Foundation ; no.7) (Study paper / Islamic Foundation ; no.3)
English text, English and Arabic introduction
ISBN 0-86037-086-0 (pbk) : Unpriced B81-34743

954.9′205 — Bangladesh. Political events, *1971-1979*

Rahman, Matiur. Iron bars of freedom / by Matiur Rahman and Naeem Hasan. — London (33 Stroud Green Rd., N4 3EF) : News and Media for Research and Documentation, c1980. — 288p ; 22cm
Bibliography: p276-283. — Includes index
ISBN 0-906172-07-1 (cased) : Unpriced
ISBN 0-906172-06-3 (pbk) : unpriced B81-05721

954.9′205 — Bangladesh. Political events, *1975-1980*

The **Eclipse** of secular Bangladesh. — London (317 Seely Rd., SW17 9RB) : Radical Asia Books, 1981. — 66p ; 15x21cm
ISBN 0-907546-00-5 (pbk) : £1.00 B81-26071

954.9′22 — Bangladesh. Dacca. Social life — *For children*

Petersen, Palle. Boy in Bangladesh / Palle Petersen. — London : A. & C. Black, c1981. — 25p : col.ill,col.maps ; 22cm. — (Beans. Geography)
Translation of: Ali er kuli. — Includes index
ISBN 0-7136-2119-2 : £2.95 : CIP rev. B81-03171

954.93 — HISTORY. SRI LANKA

954.9′3 — Sri Lanka, *to 1980*

De Silva, K. M.. A history of Sri Lanka. — London : Hurst, July 1981. — [660]p
ISBN 0-905838-50-5 : £13.50 : CIP entry B81-14407

954.9′3′009734 — Sri Lanka. Rural regions. Social life — *For children*

Bennett, Gay. Sri Lanka / Gay Bennett ; photographs by Christopher Cormack. — London : Black, c1980. — 25p : col.ill,2col.maps ; 22cm. — (Beans) (BEANS. Geography)
ISBN 0-7136-2076-5 : £2.50 : CIP rev. B80-14097

954.94′054 — Israel — *For children*

Rutland, Jonathan. Let′s go to Israel / text and photographs by Jonathan Rutland ; [maps by Brian and Constance Dear and Tony Payne]. — London : Watts, 1981. — 32p : col.ill ; 22cm
Includes index
ISBN 0-85166-921-2 : £2.99 B81-22932

954.98 — HISTORY. BHUTAN

954.9′8 — Bhutan, *1783 — Illustrations*

Davis, Samuel. Views of medieval Bhutan. — London (10 Parkfields, SW15 6NH) : Serindia Publications, Jan.1982. — [128]p
ISBN 0-906026-10-5 : £18.00 : CIP entry B81-34642

954.9′8 — Bhutan, *to ca 1700*

Aris, Michael. Bhutan : the early history of a Himalayan kingdom / Michael Aris. — Warminster : Aris & Phillips, c1979. — xxxiv,344p : ill(some col.),maps,ports,geneal.tables ; 22cm. — (Aris & Phillips Central Asian studies)
Maps on lining papers. — Bibliography: p275-288. - Includes index
ISBN 0-85668-082-6 : Unpriced B81-03083

955 — HISTORY. IRAN

955′.05 — Iran. Political events. Role of Great Britain, Soviet Union & United States, *ca 1900-1979*

Fatemi, Faramarz S.. The U.S.S.R. in Iran : the background history of Russian and Anglo-American conflict in Iran, its effect on Iranian nationalism, and the fall of the Shah / Faramarz S. Fatemi. — South Brunswick : Barnes ; London : Yoseloff, c1980. — 219p : 1map ; 22cm
Bibliography: p201-205. - Includes index
ISBN 0-498-02340-0 : £6.95 B81-05976

955′.03 — Iran, *1501-1736*

Savory, R. M.. Iran under the Safavids / Roger Savory. — Cambridge : Cambridge University Press, 1980. — x,277p : ill,1map,plans,ports ; 24cm
Includes index
ISBN 0-521-22483-7 : £15.00 B81-04556

955′.03 — Iran, *1800-1980*

Keddie, Nikki R.. Roots of revolution. — London : Yale University Press, Nov.1981. — [316]
ISBN 0-300-02606-4 (cased) : £21.00 : CIP entry
ISBN 0-300-02611-0 (pbk) : £4.15 B81-35023

955′.04 — Iran. Social conditions, *1797-1979*

Keddie, Nikki R.. Iran : religion, politics and society : collected essays / Nikki R. Keddie. — London : Cass, 1980. — ix,243p ; 23cm
ISBN 0-7146-3150-7 (cased) : £13.50 : CIP rev.
ISBN 0-7146-4031-x (pbk) : £6.95 B80-17567

955′.053 — Iran, *1954-1980*

Heikal, Mohamed. The return of the Ayatollah. — London : Deutsch, Sept.1981. — [240]p
ISBN 0-233-97404-0 : £8.00 : CIP entry B81-20607

955′.053′0924 — Iran. Mohammed Reza Pahlavi, *Shah of Iran — Biographies*

Mohammed Reza Pahlavi, ***Shah of Iran.*** The Shah′s story / Mohammed Reza Pahlavi ; translated from the French by Teresa Waugh. — London : Joseph, 1980. — 239p,[8]p of plates : ports ; 24cm
Translation of: Réponse à l′histoire. — Includes index
ISBN 0-7181-1944-4 : £8.50 B81-02478

955′.053′0924 — Iran. Political events, *1978-1979 — Personal observations*

Hunt, Paul. Inside Iran / Paul Hunt. — Tring : Lion Publishing, 1981. — 159p : ill,ports ; 18cm
ISBN 0-85648-378-8 (pbk) : £1.50 B81-14118

955′.053′0924 — Iran. Political events. Role of Mohammed Reza Pahlavi, *Shah of Iran, 1953-1979*

Saikal, Amin. The rise and fall of the Shah 1941-1979 / Amin Saikal. — London : Angus & Robertson, 1980. — xiv,279p, [8]p of plates : ill,maps,ports ; 23cm
Originally published: Princeton, N.J. : Princeton University Press, 1980. — Bibliography: p247-268. — Includes index
ISBN 0-207-14412-5 : £7.95 B81-01584

955′.053′0924 — Iran. Political events. Role of United States. *Central Intelligence Agency, 1953 — Personal observations*

Roosevelt, Kermit. Countercoup : the struggle for the control of Iran / Kermit Roosevelt. — New York ; London : McGraw-Hill, c1979. — x,217p,[8]p of plates : ill,facsims,1map,ports ; 24cm
Includes index
ISBN 0-07-053590-6 : £6.95 B81-03189

955′.054 — Iran. Wars with Iraq, *1980-.* **Causes**

Aziz, Tariq. Tariq Aziz on the Iraqi-Iranian conflict. — [London] (177 Tottenham Court Rd., W.1) : Iraqi Cultural Centre, [1981]. — 16p ; 30cm
Unpriced (unbound) B81-18449

956 — HISTORY. MIDDLE EAST

956 — Middle East, *1900-1979 — For schools*

Lawless, Richard I.. The Middle East in the twentieth century / Richard I. Lawless with Heather Bleaney, Anne Findlay and David Imrie. — London : Batsford, 1980. — 96p : ill,maps,ports ; 26cm. — (Twentieth century world history)
Bibliography: p94. - Includes index
ISBN 0-7134-2494-x : £4.95 B81-02259

956 — Middle East. Arab countries, *to 1978*

Hourani, Albert. The emergence of the modern Middle East / Albert Hourani. — London : Macmillan in association with St Antony's College, Oxford, 1981. — xx,243p ; 23cm. — (St Antony's/Macmillan series)
Includes index
ISBN 0-333-26949-7 : £20.00 : CIP rev.
B79-30457

956 — Middle East. Cultural processes, *to 1980*

Eickelman, Dale F.. The Middle East : an anthropological approach / Dale F. Eickelman. — Englewood Cliffs ; London : Prentice-Hall, c1981. — xiv,336p : ill,maps,ports ; 23cm. — (Prentice-Hall series in anthropology)
Includes index
ISBN 0-13-581629-7 (pbk) : £7.75 B81-16651

956 — Middle East. Political events, *1914-1979 — Readings from contemporary sources*

The **Middle** East, 1914-1979 / [compiled by] T.G. Fraser. — London : Edward Arnold, 1980. — xviii,205p : 3maps ; 20cm. — (Documents of modern history)
Bibliography: p197-198. - Includes index
ISBN 0-7131-6292-9 (pbk) : £4.95 : CIP rev.
B80-14098

956 — Middle East. Social conditions, *ca 1910-1980 — Festschriften*

Change and development in the Middle East : essays in honour of W.B. Fisher / edited by John I. Clarke and Howard Bowen-Jones. — London : Methuen, 1981. — xiii,322p : ill,maps,1port ; 24cm
Includes bibliographies and index
ISBN 0-416-71080-8 : £18.50 B81-30816

956 — Middle East. Social conditions, *to 1960*

Baer, Gabriel. Fellah and townsman in the Middle East. — London : Cass, Oct.1981. — [344]p
ISBN 0-7146-3126-4 : £15.00 : CIP entry
B81-24671

956 — Middle East, *to 1979*

Keddie, Nikki R.. The Middle East and beyond. — London : Cass, May 1981. — [248]p
ISBN 0-7146-3151-5 : £12.50 : CIP entry
B81-08856

956'.004927 — Middle East. Palestinian Arabs, *1917-1980*

Gilmour, David. Dispossessed : the ordeal of the Palestinians 1917-1980 / David Gilmour. — London : Sidgwick & Jackson, 1980. — 237p,[24]p of plates : ill,maps,ports ; 25cm
Bibliography: p219-223. — Includes index
ISBN 0-283-98687-5 : £12.50 B81-01401

956'.004927 — Middle East. Palestinian Arabs. Policies of United States government, *to 1980*

Shadid, Mohammed K.. The United States and the Palestinians / Mohammed K. Shadid. — London : Croom Helm, c1981. — 252p : ill,maps ; 23cm
Bibliography: p225-246. - Includes index
ISBN 0-7099-0364-2 : £12.95 B81-20785

956'.04 — Arab-Israeli War, *1969-1970*

Bar-Siman-Tov, Yaacov. The Israeli-Egyptian war of attrition, 1969-1970 : a case study of limited local war / Yaacov Bar-Siman-Tov. — New York ; Guildford : Columbia University Press, 1980. — xi,248p : ill ; 22cm
Includes index
ISBN 0-231-04982-x : £10.80 B81-04657

956'.04 — Arab-Israeli War. Army operations by armoured combat vehicles, *1948-1978*

Zaloga, Steven J.. Armour of the Middle East wars 1948-78 / text and colour plates by Steven J. Zaloga. — London : Osprey, 1981. — 40p,A-Hp of plates : ill(some col.),1map ; 24cm. — (Vanguard series ; 19)
English text, English, French and German captions to plates
ISBN 0-85045-388-7 (pbk) : £2.95 B81-13932

956'.04 — Middle East. Air operations by Great Britain. *Royal Air Force, 1945-1972*

Lee, *Sir* **David**, *1912-*. Flight from the Middle East : a history of the Royal Air Force in the Arabian peninsula and adjacent territories 1945-1972 / by Sir David Lee. — London : H.M.S.O., 1980. — xvi,339p,[46]p of plates (some folded) : ill(some col.),maps(some col.),ports ; 23cm
At head of title: Ministry of Defence : Air Historical Branch (RAF). — Includes index
ISBN 0-11-772356-8 : £9.75 B81-14690

956'.04 — Middle East. Petroleum exporting countries

Fisher, W. B.. The oil states / W.B. Fisher. — London : Batsford Academic and Educational, 1980. — 71p : ill,maps,facsims,ports ; 26cm. — (Today's world)
Includes index
ISBN 0-7134-2477-x : £4.95 B81-01557

956'.04 — Middle East. Political events, *1945-1980.* **International politico-economic aspects** — *Conference proceedings*

The **Middle** East in world politics / edited by Mohammed Ayoob. — London : Croom Helm in association with the Australian Institute of International Affairs, c1981. — 217p ; 23cm
Conference papers. — Includes index
ISBN 0-7099-0502-5 : £10.95 B81-13347

956'.04 — Middle East. Political events, *1948-1980*

Riad, Mahmoud. The struggle for peace in the Middle East. — London : Quartet, Oct.1981. — [416]p
ISBN 0-7043-2297-8 : £11.95 : CIP entry
B81-25709

956'.04 — Middle East. Political events, *1973-1979*

Crisis management and the super-powers in the Middle East / edited by Gregory Treverton. — Farnborough, Hants. : Published for the International Institute for Strategic Studies by Gower, c1981. — vi,183p ; 23cm. — (Adelphi library ; 5)
Includes index
ISBN 0-566-00347-3 : £11.50 B81-11620

956'.04 — Middle East. Political events, *1973-1980*

Peace-making in the Middle East / edited by Lester A. Sobel ; contributing editor, Hal Kosut. — Oxford : Clio Press, c1980. — 286p ; 24cm. — (Checkmark books)
Originally published: New York : Facts on File, 1980. — Includes index
ISBN 0-87196-267-5 : £8.60 B81-15271

956'.04 — Middle East. Political events. Role of Soviet Union, *1970-1978*

Sella, Amnon. Soviet political and military conduct in the Middle East / Amnon Sella. — London : Macmillan, 1981. — xiii,211p : maps ; 23cm
Bibliography: p192-196. — Includes index
ISBN 0-333-27093-2 : £15.00 : CIP rev.
B80-18951

956'.04 — Middle East. Social life

Abdallah, Maureen Smallwood. The Middle East / by Maureen Smallwood Abdallah. — London : Macdonald Educational, 1980. — 61p : col.ill,col.maps,ports(some col.) ; 29cm. — (Macdonald countries specials)
Col.ill, col.map on lining papers. — Includes index
ISBN 0-356-06777-7 (cased) : £3.50
ISBN 0-356-06776-9 (pbk) : £2.25 B81-01544

956'.04'05 — Middle East — *Serials*

The **Middle** East and North Africa. — 27th ed. (1980-81). — London : Europa, 1980. — xx,985p
ISBN 0-905118-50-2 : Unpriced : CIP rev.
ISSN 0076-8502
Also classified at 961'.048'05 B80-18135

The **Middle** East and North Africa. — 28th ed. (1981-82). — London : Europa, Sept.1981. — [1005]p
ISBN 0-905118-65-0 : CIP entry
ISSN 0076-8205
Also classified at 961'.048'05 B81-20494

Middle East contemporary survey / the Shiloah Center for Middle Eastern and African Studies, Tel Aviv University. — Vol.1 (1976-77)-. — New York ; London : Holmes & Meier, 1978-. — v. : ill,maps ; 24cm
Annual. — Description based on: Vol.3 (1978-79)
ISSN 0163-5476 = Middle East contemporary survey : Unpriced B81-34020

Middle east yearbook. — 1979. — London (63, Long Acre WC2 9JH) : IC Magazines, c1979. — 240p
ISBN 0-905268-07-5 : Unpriced
ISSN 0308-1699 B81-12399

956'.04'05 — Middle East. Social conditions — *Serials*

Middle east annual review. — 1979. — Saffron Walden (21 Gold St., Saffron Walden, Essex CB10 1EJ) : World of Information, c1978. — 432p
ISBN 0-904439-04-6 : £11.50
ISSN 0305-3210 B81-03663

Middle east annual review. — 1980. — Saffron Walden (21 Gold St., Saffron Walden, Essex CB10 1EJ) : World of Information, c1979. — 430p
ISBN 0-904439-10-0 : £11.50
ISSN 0305-3210 B81-09158

956'.04'0924 — Peace. Negotiations between Israel & Egypt, *1977-1979 — Personal observations*

Dayan, Moshe. Break-through : a personal account of the Egypt-Israel peace negotiations / Moshe Dayan. — London : Weidenfeld and Nicolson, c1981. — 368p,[16]p of plates : maps,ports ; 24cm
Includes index
ISBN 0-297-77916-8 : £10.95 B81-26467

956'.046 — Mediterranean Sea. United States. *Navy.* **Warships: Liberty** *(Ship).* **Attack by Israeli military forces,** *1967*

Taylor, Jim, *1924-*. Pearl Harbour II 3b the true story of the sneak attack by Israel upon the U.S.S. Liberty, June 8, 1967 / by Jim Taylor. — London : Regency Press, 1980. — 235p,[4]p of plates : ill,1chart,maps,facsims ; 23cm
Bibliography: p233-235
ISBN 0-7212-0592-5 : £5.00 B81-06003

956'.046'0924 — Arab-Israeli War, *1967 — Personal observations*

Rikhye, Indar Jit. The Sinai blunder : withdrawal of the United Nations Emergency Force leading to the Six-Day War of June 1967 / Indar Jit Rikhye. — London : Cass, 1980. — xii,240p,[8]p of plates : ill,maps,ports ; 23cm
Includes index
ISBN 0-7146-3136-1 : £13.50 : CIP rev.
Also classified at 953'.1053'0924 B79-15158

956'.048'0924 — Arab-Israeli War, *1973.* **Army operations by Israel.** *Tseva haganah le-Yisrael — Personal observations*

Adan, Avraham. On the banks of the Suez : an Israeli general's personal account of the Yom Kippur war / Avraham (Bren) Adan. — London : Arms and Armour Press, c1980. — xii,479p,[16]p of plates : ill,maps,ports, ; 24cm
Translated from the Hebrew. — Ill on lining papers. — Includes index
ISBN 0-85368-177-5 : £9.95 B81-04109

956.1 — Turkey, *1900-1980*

Berberoglu, B.. Turkey in crisis. — London : Zed Press, July 1981. — [128]p
ISBN 0-905762-56-8 : £9.95 : CIP entry
B81-18060

956.1 — Turkey, *to 1967*

Davison, Roderic H.. Turkey. — Beverley (42 Northgate, Walkington, Beverley, North Humber, HU17 8ST) : Eothen Press, Dec.1981. — [181]p
Originally published: Englewood Cliffs : Prentice-Hall, 1968
ISBN 0-906719-02-x (cased) : £9.95 : CIP entry
ISBN 0-906719-03-8 (pbk) : £5.50 B81-35896

956.1'01 — Byzantine Empire. War with Seljuk Empire. Battle of Manzikert

Friendly, Alfred. The dreadful day : the Battle of Manzikert, 1071 / Alfred Friendly. — London : Hutchinson, 1981. — 256p : maps ; 23cm
Bibliography: p241-246. - Includes index
ISBN 0-09-143570-6 : £10.95 B81-08148

956.1'038 — Turkey. Political events. Role of Turkish military forces, *1980-1981*

Mackenzie, Kenneth, *19---.* Turkey under the generals / Kenneth Mackenzie. — London (12 Golden Sq., W1R 3AF) : Institute for the Study of Conflict, c1981. — 31p : 1map ; 25cm. — (Conflict studies, ISSN 0069-8792 ; no.126)
£3.50 (pbk) B81-10098

956.2 — Turkey. Ephesus, *262-1863*

Foss, Clive. Ephesus after antiquity : a late antique, Byzantine and Turkish city / Clive Foss. — Cambridge : Cambridge University Press, 1979. — x,218p : ill,1map,plans ; 26cm
Ill on lining papers. — Bibliography: p199-211. - Includes index
ISBN 0-521-22086-6 : £15.00 B81-09819

956.45'04 — Cyprus. Political events, *1960-1980*

Polyviou, Polyvios G.. Cyprus : conflict and negotiation 1960-1980 / Polyvios G. Polyviou. — London : Duckworth, 1980. — ix,246p : maps ; 24cm
Includes index
ISBN 0-7156-1522-x (pbk) : £9.80 B81-01402

956.45'04'0924 — Cyprus. Makarios III, *Archbishop of Cyprus — Biographies*

Mayes, Stanley. Makarios : a biography / Stanley Mayes. — London : Macmillan, 1981. — xii,303p,[8]p of plates : ill,ports ; 23cm
Bibliography: p287-289. — Includes index
ISBN 0-333-28127-6 : £15.00 : CIP rev. B80-13659

956.54 — Israel, *ca 1850-1980*

Cragg, Kenneth. This year in Jerusalem. — London : Darton, Longman & Todd, Sept.1981. — [192]p
ISBN 0-232-51534-4 (pbk) : £5.95 : CIP entry B81-20476

956.6'2 — Armenian civilization, *to 1977*

Lang, David Marshall. Armenia : cradle of civilization / by David Marshall Lang. — 3rd ed corrected. — London : Allen & Unwin, 1980. — 320p,[8]p of plates : ill(some col.),facsims,1geneal.table,maps,ports ; 26cm
Previous ed.: 1978. — Maps on lining papers. — Bibliography: p297-307. - Includes index
ISBN 0-04-956009-3 : £15.00 B81-08483

956.6'7 — Turkey. Elazig. Armenians. Social life, *1890-1910 — Childhood reminiscences*

Totovents, Vahan. Scenes from an Armenian childhood / Vahan Totovents ; translated from the Armenian with a foreword by Mischa Kudian. — London : Mashtots, 1980. — ix,182p ; 23cm
Originally published: London : Oxford University Press, 1962
ISBN 0-903039-07-9 : £6.50 B81-05613

956.7'043 — Iraq. Political events, *1968-1974 — Socialist viewpoints — Conference proceedings*

Ḥizb al-Baʻth al-ʻArabī al-Ishtirākī (Iraq). *Congress (8th : 1974).* The 1968 revolution in Iraq : experience and prospects : the political report of the Eighth Congress of the Arab Baʻth Socialist Party in Iraq, January 1974. — London : Ithaca, 1979. — 176p ; 23cm
Translated from the Arabic
ISBN 0-903729-45-8 (cased) : £6.00
ISBN 0-903729-46-6 (pbk) : £2.50 B81-40193

956.7'043 — Iraq. Political events, *1968-1980*

Iraq. — London : P.O. Box 210, N16 5PL : CARDRI, 1981. — 25p : ill,1map,ports ; 22cm
£0.50 (pbk) B81-23107

956.7'043'05 — Iraq. Political events — *CARDRI viewpoints — Serials*

Iraq solidarity voice / Committee Against Repression & for Democratic Rights in Iraq (CARDRI). — No.1 [(197-?)]-. — London (P.O. Box 210, N16 5PL) : CARDRI, [197-?]-. — v. : facsims,ports ; 30cm
Description based on: No.6 (Feb.1981)
ISSN 0261-3840 = Iraq solidarity voice : Unpriced B81-32393

956.7'043'05 — Iraq — *Serials*

[Iraq *(London. 1980)***].** Iraq : weekly bulletin of the Iraqi Press Office. — No.1 (1980)-. — London ([177 Tottenham Court Rd, W1]) : The Office, 1980-. — v. : ill,ports ; 42cm
ISSN 0261-6769 = Iraq (London. 1980) : Unpriced B81-32705

956.9 — Jerusalem *(Kingdom), to 1291*

Prawer, Joshua. Crusader institutions / Joshua Prawer. — Oxford : Clarendon, 1980. — xv,519p : 3maps ; 23cm
Includes index
ISBN 0-19-822536-9 : £30.00 : CIP rev. B79-25518

956.91'042 — Syria. Political events. Role of power elites, *1961-1980*

Dam, Nikolaos van. The struggle for power in Syria : sectarianism, regionalism and tribalism in politics, 1961-1980 / Nikolaos van Dam. — London : Croom Helm, c1981. — 169p : 1map ; 23cm
Originally published: 1979. — Bibliography: p152-163. — Includes index
ISBN 0-7099-2601-4 : £10.95 B81-13356

956.91'4 — Syria. Golan Heights. Occupation by Israel, *1967-1980*

Harris, William Wilson. Taking root : Israeli settlement in the West Bank, the Golan and Gaza-Sinai, 1967-1980 / William Wilson Harris. — Chichester : Research Studies Press, c1980. — xxii,223p : ill,maps ; 29cm. — (Geographical research studies series ; 1)
Bibliography: p199-207. — Includes index
ISBN 0-471-27863-7 (pbk) : £16.50 : CIP rev.
Primary classification 953'.1054 B80-35587

956.94 — Palestine. Political events, *to 1980 — Socialist viewpoints*

Debate on Palestine / edited by Fouzi-el-Asmar, Uri Davies, Naim Khader. — London : Ithaca, 1981. — 151p : ill ; 23cm
Bibliography: p151
ISBN 0-903729-64-4 (cased) : £7.50
ISBN 0-903729-65-2 (pbk) : Unpriced B81-16106

956.94'001 — Palestine. Zionism

Said, Edward W.. The question of Palestine / Edward W. Said. — London : Routledge & Kegan Paul, 1981, c1979. — xix,265p ; 22cm
Originally published: New York : Times, 1979 ; London : Routledge & Kegan Paul, 1980. — Bibliography: p239-242. - Includes index
ISBN 0-7100-0777-9 (pbk) : £3.95
Primary classification 956.94'004927 B81-07543

956.94'001 — Zionism, *1897-ca 1910*

Vital, David. Zionism. — Oxford : Clarendon Press, Dec.1981. — [450]p
ISBN 0-19-827443-2 : £17.50 : CIP entry B81-31455

956.94'001 — Zionism. Attitudes of communists, *1917-1973 — Readings*

The Left against Zion : Communism, Israel and the Middle East / edited by Robert S. Wistrich. — London : Vallentine, Mitchell, 1979. — xv,309p ; 23cm
ISBN 0-85303-193-2 (cased) : £11.50 : CIP rev.
ISBN 0-85303-199-1 (pbk) : £4.95 B78-35792

956.94'001 — Zionism. Policies of British government, *1900-1922*

Hardie, Frank. Britain and Zion : the fateful entanglement / by Frank Hardie and Irwin Herrman. — Belfast : Blackstaff, c1980. — x,117p : maps,1facsim ; 23cm
Bibliography: p102-105. - Includes index
ISBN 0-85640-229-x : £7.95 B81-12224

956.94'001'0924 — Zionism. Herzl, Theodor — *Biographies*

Stewart, Desmond. Theodor Herzl : artist and politician / Desmond Stewart. — London : Quartet, 1981, c1974. — ix,395p : 2maps,1geneal.table ; 22cm
Originally published: London : Hamilton, 1974. — Bibliography: p379-385. - Includes index
ISBN 0-7043-3352-x (pbk) : £4.95 B81-18236

956.94'001'0924 — Zionism. Role of Namier, *Sir Lewis*

Rose, Norman. Lewis Namier and Zionism / Norman Rose. — Oxford : Clarendon, 1980. — vii,182p ; 23cm
Bibliography: p177-178. — Includes index
ISBN 0-19-822621-7 : £9.95 : CIP rev. B80-12676

956.94'004924 — Palestine. Jewish settlements, *to 1980 — Palestine Liberation Organisation viewpoints*

Facts about Israeli settlements. — London (52 Green St., W1) : Palestine Liberation Organisation, [1981]. — 15p : 2maps ; 21cm
Unpriced (unbound) B81-18642

956.94'004927 — Palestine. Palestinian Arabs

Said, Edward W.. The question of Palestine / Edward W. Said. — London : Routledge & Kegan Paul, 1981, c1979. — xix,265p ; 22cm
Originally published: New York : Times, 1979 ; London : Routledge & Kegan Paul, 1980. — Bibliography: p239-242. - Includes index
ISBN 0-7100-0777-9 (pbk) : £3.95
Also classified at 956.94'001 B81-07543

956.94'03 — Palestine. Social conditions, *1880-1946*

Graham-Brown, Sarah. Palestinians and their society 1880-1946 : a photographic essay / Sarah Graham-Brown. — London : Quartet, 1980. — 184p : ill,maps,facsims,ports ; 26cm
Bibliography: p183-184
ISBN 0-7043-2225-0 (cased) : Unpriced
ISBN 0-7043-3343-0 (pbk) : £4.95 B81-08403

956.94'03'0222 — Palestine, *1856-1860 — Illustrations*

Frith, Francis. Egypt and the Holy Land in historic photograph : 77 views / by Francis Frith ; introduction & bibliography by Julia Van Haaften ; selection & commentary by Jon E. Manchip White. — New York : Dover Publications ; London : Constable, 1980. — xxv,77p : chiefly ill,1port ; 31cm
'The photographs are a selection from those that originally appeared in the four-volume series published by William Mackenzie, London ca.1862, with the titles (I) Sinai and Palestine ; (II) Lower Egypt, Thebes, and the Pyramids ; (III) Upper Egypt and Ethiopia ; (IV) Egypt, Sinai, and Palestine. Supplementary Volume' - T.p. verso. — Bibliography: pxxiii-xxiv
ISBN 0-486-24048-7 (pbk) : £4.55
Primary classification 962'.03'0222 B81-30113

956.94'04 — Palestine. Political events, *1917-1978 — Palestine Liberation Organisation viewpoints*

This is Zionism. — London ([52 Green St., W1]) : PLO, [1981]. — [6]p ; 21cm
Unpriced (unbound) B81-18647

956.94'04 — Palestine. Political events, *1917-1980 — Palestine Liberation Organisation viewpoints*

Do you know? : twenty basic facts about the Palestinian question. — London ([52 Green St., W1]) : PLO, [1981]. — 1folded sheet ; 30x21cm folded to 11x21cm
Unpriced (unbound) B81-18641

Facts of Israeli expansion. — London (52 Green St., W1) : Palestine Liberation Organisation, [1981]. — [12]p : col.maps ; 20cm
Cover title
Unpriced (pbk) B81-18640

956.94'05'0924 — Israel, *1948-1978 — Personal observations*

Laffin, John. The Israeli mind / John Laffin. — London : Cassell, 1979. — 243p : 1map ; 23cm
Includes index
ISBN 0-304-30399-2 : £5.95 B81-03099

956.94'054 — Israel. Social conditions

Frankel, William. Israel observed : an anatomy of the state / William Frankel. — [London] : Thames and Hudson, c1980. — 288p ; 24cm
Bibliography: p280-283. — Includes index
ISBN 0-500-01247-4 : £7.95 B81-01403

Studies of Israeli society. — New Brunswick, N.J. ; London : Transaction. — (Publication series of the Israel Sociological Society)
Bibliography: p255-296
Migration, ethnicity and community / editor Ernest Krausz. — c1980. — 308p : maps ; 23cm
ISBN 0-87855-369-x (pbk) : Unpriced B81-13619

956.94'054 — Palestine — *Palestine Liberation Organisation viewpoints*

Who are the Palestinians? : profile of a nation. — London ([52 Green St., W1]) : Palestine Liberation Organisation, [1981]. — 1folded sheet ; 41x31cm folded to 11x21cm
Unpriced (unbound) B81-18643

956.94'054 — Palestine. Political events. Attitudes of United Nations

Nuseibeh, Hazem Zaki. Palestine and the United Nations / Hazem Zaki Nuseibeh. — London : Quartet Books, 1981. — 200p : maps ; 24cm
ISBN 0-7043-2289-7 : £7.95 B81-33671

956.94'054 — Palestine. Political events. Attitudes of United Nations — *Palestine Liberation Organisation viewpoints*

Palestine and international opinion. — London (52 Green St., W1) : Palestine Liberation Organisation, [1981]. — [10]p ; 21cm
Unpriced (unbound) B81-18645

956.94'054 — Palestine. Political events. Attitudes of Zionists — *Palestine Liberation Organisation viewpoints*

Zionist mythinformation : the PLO replies. — London (52 Green St., W1) : Palestine Liberation Organisation, [1981]. — 11p ; 21cm
Unpriced (unbound) B81-18646

956.94'054 — Palestine — *Socialist viewpoints*

Watkins, David, *1925-*. The world and Palestine / David Watkins. — [London] ([21 Collingham Rd, SW5 0NU]) : Labour Middle East Council, [1980]. — 27p ; 21cm
£0.65 (pbk) B81-01991

956.94'4 — Jerusalem. Political events, *to 1979 — Conference proceedings*

Jerusalem : the key to world peace. — London (16 Grosvenor Crescent, SW1X 7EP) : Islamic Council of Europe, 1980. — xix,333p : ill ; 23cm
Conference papers
ISBN 0-907163-30-0 (cased) : £10.00
ISBN 0-907163-35-1 (pbk) : £4.95 B81-18589

956.94'404 — Jerusalem. Political events, *1917-1979*

Cattan, Henry. Jerusalem / Henry Cattan. — London : Croom Helm, c1981. — 229p : maps ; 23cm
Includes index
ISBN 0-7099-0412-6 : £12.50 : CIP rev. B80-22778

956.94'405 — Jerusalem. Political events, *1948-1980*

Prittie, Terence. Whose Jerusalem? / Terence Prittie. — London : Muller, 1981. — x,246p,[22]p of plates : ill,maps ; 24cm
Bibliography: p225-227. — Includes index
ISBN 0-584-10440-5 : £9.95 : CIP rev. B81-06025

956.94'4054 — Jerusalem — *For children*

Paul, Geoffrey D.. Living in Jerusalem / Geoffrey D. Paul ; photographs by Gemma Levine. — Hove : Wayland, 1981. — 52p : ill ; 22cm. — (Living in famous cities)
Bibliography: p51. — Includes index
ISBN 0-85340-812-2 : £3.75 B81-23257

956.95 — Jordan. West Bank. Occupation by Israel, *1967-1980*

Harris, William Wilson. Taking root : Israeli settlement in the West Bank, the Golan and Gaza-Sinai, 1967-1980 / William Wilson Harris. — Chichester : Research Studies Press, c1980. — xxii,223p : ill,maps ; 29cm. — (Geographical research studies series ; 1)
Bibliography: p199-207. — Includes index
ISBN 0-471-27863-7 (pbk) : £16.50 : CIP rev.
Primary classification 953'.1054 B80-35587

956.95'2 — Jerusalem. Holy places: Noble Sanctuary, *to 1969*

Duncan, Alistair. The Noble Sanctuary : portrait of a holy place in Arab Jerusalem / by Alistair Duncan. — 2nd ed. — London ([73, Riverview Gardens, London SW13J]) : Middle East Archive, 1981. — 80p : col.ill,1col.map,1col.plan ; 23x25cm
Previous ed.: Harlow : Longmans, 1972. — Ill on lining papers. — Bibliography: p80
ISBN 0-9507453-0-8 : Unpriced B81-33663

957 — HISTORY. ASIATIC SOVIET UNION, SIBERIA

957'.0841'0924 — Russia *(RSFSR).* **Siberia. Political events. Role of Kolchak, Aleksandr Vasil'evich,** *1918-1920*

Cracknell, Brian. The failure of Admiral Kolchak / by Brian Cracknell. — Harrow : Eureditions, 1978. — 42p : maps ; 21cm
Bibliography: p39
ISBN 0-906204-06-2 : Unpriced B81-26992

957'.0842'0924 — Russia *(RSFSR).* **Siberia. Polish exiles. Social life,** *1941-1946 — Childhood reminiscences*

Hautzig, Esther. The endless Steppe / Esther Hautzig. — Harmondsworth : Puffin Books in association with Hamilton, 1981, c1968. — 186p ; 18cm
Originally published: New York : Crowell, 1968 ; London : Hamilton, 1969
ISBN 0-14-031369-9 (pbk) : £0.95 B81-33039

958 — HISTORY. CENTRAL ASIA

958 — Central Asia, *1866 — Early works*

Central Asia 1866. — Letchworth (P.O. Box 1, Letchworth, Herts.) : Short-Run Reprints, 1981. — 47p ; 20cm. — (Reprints for researchers ; no.2)
Originally published: in Quarterly review, Vol.120. London : J. Murray, July & Oct.1866
£0.90 (pbk) B81-22266

958 — Central Asia. Political events. Role of Russia, *1865 — Early works*

The Russians in central Asia in 1865. — Letchworth (P.O. Box 1, Letchworth, Herts.) : Short-Run Reprints, 1981. — 57p : 1map ; 20cm. — (Reprints for researchers ; no.1)
Originally published: in Quarterly review, Vol.118. London : J. Murray, July & Oct.1865
£0.90 (pbk) B81-22261

958'.1 — Afghanistan, *to 1980*

Griffiths, John C. (John Charles). Afghanistan : key to a continent / John C. Griffiths. — London : Deutsch, 1981. — 225p,[8]p of plates : ill,maps ; 23cm
Includes index
ISBN 0-233-97350-8 : £7.95 B81-26283

958'.1 — Afghanistan, *to 1980 — For children*

Gilfond, Henry. Afghanistan / by Henry Gilfond. — New York ; London : Watts, c1980. — 64p : col.ill,1map ; 23cm. — (A First book)
Bibliography: p61. — Includes index
ISBN 0-531-04157-3 : £2.99 B81-05067

958'.103 — Afghan Wars

Heathcote, T. A.. The Afghan Wars 1839-1919 / T.A. Heathcote. — London : Osprey, 1980. — 224p : ill,maps,ports,2geneal.tables ; 24cm
Bibliography: p218-219. — Includes index
ISBN 0-85045-354-2 : £9.95 : CIP rev. B80-18136

958'.1044 — Afghanistan. Political events, *1978-1981*

Afghanistan in crisis / edited by K.P. Misra. — London : Croom Helm, 1981. — 150p ; 26cm
Bibliography: p120-150
ISBN 0-7099-1727-9 : £10.95 B81-41019

958'.1044 — Afghanistan. Political events, *ca 1975-1980*

Newell, Nancy Peabody. The struggle for Afghanistan / Nancy Peabody Newell, Richard S. Newell. — Ithaca ; London : Cornell University Press, 1981. — 236p : ill,map ; 22cm
Includes index
ISBN 0-8014-1389-3 : £9.00 B81-36453

958'.1044'0222 — Afghanistan — *Illustrations*

Michaud, Roland. Afghanistan / Roland and Sabrina Michaud. — London : Thames and Hudson, 1980. — 23p,98p of plates : chiefly col.ill,1map ; 27x31cm
Translation of: Mémoire de l'Afghanistan
ISBN 0-500-54067-5 : £18.00 B81-05209

958'.1044'05 — Afghanistan. Political events — *Islamic viewpoints — Serials*

Afghan voice. — Vol.1 no.1 (May 1980)-. — London (PO Box 164, WC2N 4EV) : Afghan Muslims, 1980-. — v. : ill ; 43cm
Irregular
ISSN 0261-0388 = Afghan voice : £0.10 B81-13092

958'.40853'0924 — Soviet Central Asia. Social life — *Personal observations*

Fax, Elton C.. Hashar / Elton C. Fax. — Moscow : Progress ; [London] : Central Books [Distributor], 1980. — 206p,[60]p of plates : ill,maps,ports ; 21cm. — (Impressions of the USSR series)
Maps on lining papers
ISBN 0-7147-1625-1 : £1.95 B81-29308

958'.45085'0924 — Kazakhstan. Social life, *1945-1970 — Personal observations — Polish texts*

Bukowiński, Władysław. Wspomnienia z Kazachstanu / Władysław Bukowiński. — London (26 Pont St., S.W.1) : Spotkania, c1979. — 78p : ill,port ; 22cm. — (Biblioteka Spotkań)
Unpriced (pbk) B81-29277

959 — HISTORY. SOUTH-EAST ASIA

959 — South-east Asia, *to 1978*

Hall, D. G. E.. A history of South-east Asia. — 4th ed. — Basingstoke : Macmillan, Apr.1981. — [1072]p
Previous ed.: 1968
ISBN 0-333-24163-0 : £12.95 : CIP entry
ISBN 0-333-24164-9 (pbk) : £5.95 B81-02094

959'.053 — South-east Asian culture *related to* **industrialisation** — *Conference proceedings*

Culture and industrialization : an Asian dilemma / Rolf E. Vente, Peter S.J. Chen (eds.). — Singapore ; London : Published for the Institute of Asian Affairs [by] McGraw-Hill, c1980. — viii,295p ; 22cm
Conference papers. — Bibliography: p271-284. - Includes index
ISBN 0-07-099655-5 : £7.50
Primary classification 338.0959 B81-13662

959'.053'05 — South-east Asia. Political events — *Serials*

Southeast Asian affairs. — 1980. — Singapore : Institute of Southeast Asian Studies ; London : Heinemann Educational, 1980. — 367p
ISBN 0-435-83757-5 : £18.00 B81-03314

959.3 — HISTORY. THAILAND

959.3'04 — Thailand. Political events, *1930-1980*

Girling, John L. S.. Thailand : society and politics / John L.S. Girling. — Ithaca, N.Y. ; London : Cornell University Press, 1981. — 306p : 2maps ; 22cm. — (Politics and international relations of Southeast Asia)
Bibliography: p289-295. — Includes index
ISBN 0-8014-1130-0 : £15.00 B81-39832

959.3'044 — Thailand. Rebellions, *1965-1980*

Randolph, R. Sean. Thai insurgency : contemporary developments / R. Sean Randolph, W. Scott Thompson ; foreword by Ray S. Cline. — Beverly Hills ; London : Sage [for] the Center for Strategic and International Studies, c1981. — 88p : 2maps ; 22cm. — (The Washington papers ; vol.ix, 81) (A Sage policy paper)
Bibliography: p87-88
ISBN 0-8039-1608-6 (pbk) : £2.50 B81-29262

959.5 — HISTORY. MALAYSIA, BRUNEI, SINGAPORE

959.5'1 — Malaysia. Johor. Mohamed Salleh bin Perang, *Datuk Bentara Luar Johor — Biographies*

Sweeney, Amin. Reputations live on : an early Malay autobiography / Amin Sweeney. — Berkeley ; London : University of California Press, c1980. — x,167p : ill,maps,1facsim,ports,geneal.tables ; 23cm
Translation and study of the Tarikh Datuk Bentara Luar Johor / Mohamed Salleh bin Perang. — Bibliography: p155-158. — Includes index
ISBN 0-520-04073-2 : £12.00 B81-27867

959.51 — West Malaysia. Selangor. Carey Island. Ma' Betisék. Cultural processes

Karim, W.. Ma' Betisék concepts of living things. — London : Athlone Press, Nov.1981. — [200] p. — (Monographs on social anthropology, ISSN 0077-1704 ; 54)
ISBN 0-485-19554-2 : £18.00 : CIP entry B81-30560

959.5'705 — Singapore. Social conditions

Knights, Ian E.. Singapore : an outline guide for expatriate contract employees / [author Ian E. Knights for the] Royal Commonwealth Society. — [16th rev. ed.]. — London : Information Bureau, [The Society], 1981. — 17p,[1]p of plates : 2maps ; 30cm. — (Notes on conditions)
Previous ed.: 1978. — Bibliography: p15-17
ISBN 0-905067-90-8 (unbound) : Unpriced B81-31500

959.5'705 — Singapore. Social life

Dutton, Geoffrey. Impressions of Singapore / Geoffrey Dutton ; photographs by Harri Peccinotti. — London : Macmillan in association with Mobil Oil Singapore, 1981. — 152p : col.ill,1map ; 26cm
Map on lining papers
ISBN 0-333-33723-9 : £9.95 B81-38800

959.6 — HISTORY. CAMBODIA

959.6'04 — Cambodia, *1976-1979*

Burchett, Wilfred. The China, Cambodia, Vietnam triangle. — London : Zed Press, Jan.1982. — [256]p
ISBN 0-86232-085-2 (pbk) : £4.95 : CIP entry B81-37549

959.6'04'05 — Cambodia. Political events — *Serials*

Kampuchea bulletin / British Kampuchea Support Campaign. — No.1 [(1980?)]-. — Sheffield (c/o The Editor, 92 Carsick Hill Rd, Sheffield S10 3LX) : The Campaign, [1980?]-. — v. : ill ; 30cm
Six issues yearly. — Description based on: No.2 (July/Aug.1980)
ISSN 0261-4022 = Kampuchea bulletin : £2.50 per year B81-29090

959.7 — HISTORY. VIETNAM

959.7 — Vietnam. My Thuy Phuong. Political events, *1885-1979*

Trullinger, James Walker. Village at war : an account of revolution in Vietnam / James Walker Trullinger, Jr.. — New York ; London : Longman, c1980. — xviii,235p,[12]p of plates : ill,3maps ; 24cm
Bibliography: p214-222. — Includes index
ISBN 0-582-28181-4 : £11.95 B81-23676

959.7'03 — Vietnam. Political events. Role of United States government, *1940-1956*

Patti, Archimedes L. A.. Why Viet Nam? : prelude to America's albatross / Archimedes L.A. Patti. — Berkeley ; London : University of California Press, c1980. — xx,612p,[8]p of plates : ill,maps,ports ; 24cm
Maps on lining papers. — Bibliography: p571-576. - Includes index
ISBN 0-520-04156-9 : £11.75 B81-15970

959.704 — Vietnam. Political events, *1945-1977 — Soviet viewpoints*

Divil'kovskiĭ, S.. The road to victory : the struggle for national independence, unity, peace and Socialism in Vietnam / S. Divilkovsky, I. Ognetov ; [translated from the Russian by Yuri Sviridov]. — Moscow : Progress ; [London] : Distributed by Central Books, c1980. — 269p ; 20cm
Translation of: Put' k pobede
ISBN 0-7147-1610-3 (pbk) : £1.95 B81-27751

959.704'092'4 — Indo-China. Political events, *1940-1979 — Personal observations*

Scholl-Latour, Peter. Death in the ricefields : thirty years of war in Indochina / Peter Scholl-Latour ; translated by Faye Carney. — London : Orbis, 1981. — 383p,[1]folded leaf of plates : 1map ; 22cm
Translation of : Der Tod im Reisfeld. — Includes index
ISBN 0-85613-342-6 : £6.95 B81-38938

959.704'32 — North Vietnam. Political events. Role of United States government, *1964-1968*

Thies, Wallace J.. When governments collide : coercion and diplomacy in the Vietnam conflict 1964-1968 / Wallace J. Thies. — Berkeley ; London : University of California Press, c1980. — xix,446p ; 25cm
Bibliography: p431-438. — Includes index
ISBN 0-520-03962-9 : £12.00 B81-05799

959.704'32 — Vietnamese wars. Policies of United States government *compared with* **policies of governments of China & Soviet Union,** *1964-1975*

Papp, Daniel S.. Vietnam : the view from Moscow, Peking, Washington / by Daniel S. Papp. — Jefferson, N.C. : McFarland ; Folkestone : Distributed by Bailey & Swinfen, 1981. — v,257p : ill,ports ; 24cm
Includes index
ISBN 0-89950-010-2 : £14.35 B81-37665

959.704'342 — Vietnamese Wars. Army operations by United States. *Army, to 1972.* **Armoured combat vehicles**

Starry, Donn A.. [Mounted combat in Vietnam]. Armoured combat in Vietnam / Donn A. Starry. — Poole : Blandford, 1981, c1980. — xii,250p : ill,maps ; 25cm
Originally published: Washington : Dept. of the Army, 1978. — Includes index
ISBN 0-7137-1166-3 : £6.95 B81-08126

959.8 — HISTORY. INDONESIA

959.8 — Indonesia, *to 1980*

Legge, J. D.. Indonesia / J.D. Legge. — 3rd ed. — Sydney ; London : Prentice-Hall of Australia, c1980. — viii,214p : 1map ; 21cm
Previous ed.: 1977. — Bibliography: p195-205. — Includes index
ISBN 0-7248-0637-7 (cased) : Unpriced
ISBN 0-7248-0636-9 (pbk) : Unpriced B81-18629

959.8'3'030924 — Borneo. Social life — *Personal observations*

Barclay, James. A stroll through Borneo. — Large print ed. — Anstey : Ulverscroft, Jan.1982. — [505]p. — (Ulverscroft large print series : non-fiction)
Originally published: London : Hodder and Stoughton, 1980
ISBN 0-7089-0742-3 : £5.00 : CIP entry B81-33955

959.8'5 — Indonesia. South Moluccas. Political events. Role of Netherlands, *1817-1955*

Kaam, Ben van. The South Moluccans : background to the train hijackings / Ben van Kaam ; translated from the Dutch by Marguerite Isaacs-Jonathon. — London : Hurst, c1980. — viii,151p : 1map ; 23cm
Translation of: Ambon door de Eeuwen. — Bibliography: p145-146. — Includes index
ISBN 0-905838-24-6 : £10.00 B81-06818

959.8'6 — Indonesia. East Timor. Political events, *1975-1979 — British Campaign for an Independent East Timor viewpoints*

Integration never! : East Timor's struggle against Indonesian aggression. — London (40 Concanon Rd, S.W.2) : British Campaign for an Independent East Timor, [1981]. — 20p : ill,1map ; 21cm. — (A BCIET publication)
Unpriced (pbk) B81-10357

959.8'6 — Indonesia. East Timor, *to 1979*

Suter, Keith. West Irian, East Timor and Indonesia / by Keith Suter. — London (36 Craven St., WC2N 5NG) : Minority Rights Group, 1979. — 27p : 3maps ; 30cm. — (Report / Minority Rights Group, ISSN 0305-6252 ; no.42)
Bibliography: p27
£0.75 (pbk)
Primary classification 995'.1 B81-05182

959.8'6 — Indonesian culture: Balinese culture, *1891-1908*

Geertz, Clifford. Negara : the theatre state in nineteenth century Bali / Clifford Geertz. — Princeton ; Guildford : Princeton University Press, c1980. — xii,295p,1 leaf of plates : ill (some col.),maps,1plan ; 25cm
Bibliography: p267-288. - Includes index
ISBN 0-691-05316-2 (cased) : Unpriced
ISBN 0-691-00778-0 (pbk) : Unpriced B81-08586

959.9 — HISTORY. PHILIPPINES

959.9'046 — Philippines. Political events, *1972-1979*

Turpin, Alex. New society's challenge in the Philippines / Alex Turpin. — London (12 Golden Sq., W1R 3AF) : Institute for the Study of Conflict, 1980. — 23p : 1map ; 30cm
Cover title. — Bibliography: p23
£2.00 (pbk) B81-04697

959.9'1 — Philippines. Ifugao. Cultural processes — *Illustrations*

Conklin, Harold C.. Ethnographic atlas of Ifugao : a study of environment, culture, and society in northern Luzon / Harold C. Conklin with the special assistance of Puggūwon Lupāih and Miklos Pinther, cartographer. — New Haven ; London : Published with the cooperation of the American Geographical Society of New York [by] Yale University Press, 1980. — vii,116p : ill,col.maps ; 41x47cm
Bibliography: p38-39. - Includes index
ISBN 0-300-02529-7 : £47.00 B81-09390

959.9'1 — Philippines. Northern Luzon. Ilongots. Cultural processes

Rosaldo, Michelle Z.. Knowledge and passion : Ilongot notions of self and social life / Michelle Z. Rosaldo. — Cambridge : Cambridge University Press, 1980. — xv,286p : ill,2maps ; 24cm. — (Cambridge studies in cultural systems ; 4)
Bibliography: p275-279. — Includes index
ISBN 0-521-22582-5 (cased) : £17.50
ISBN 0-521-29562-9 (pbk) : £4.95 B81-24490

960 — HISTORY. AFRICA

960 — Africa - *History*

The **Cambridge** history of Africa. — Cambridge : Cambridge University Press, Apr.1981
Vol.1: From the earliest times to c.500 BC. — 1v.
ISBN 0-521-22215-x : CIP entry B81-04307

960 — Africa, *to 1979 — For East African students*

Singh, Malkiat. African history : a revision course for primary and junior secondary classes / Malkiat Singh ; [illustrations by Ray Martin]. — London : Evans, 1980. — 202p : maps ; 21cm
ISBN 0-237-50441-3 (pbk) : £1.70 B81-01404

960′.09′734 — Africa. Villages. Children. Social life — *For children*

Lewin, Hugh. Jafta / story by Hugh Lewin ; pictures by Lisa Kopper. — London : Evans, c1981. — [24]p : ill ; 20x23cm. — (Jafta's family series)
ISBN 0-237-45543-9 : £2.50 B81-23666

960′.09′734 — Africa. Villages. Fathers. Social life — *For children*

Lewin, Hugh. Jaffa — my father / story by Hugh Lewin ; pictures by Lisa Kopper. — London : Evans, 1981. — [24]p : ill ; 20x23cm. — (Jaffa's family series)
ISBN 0-237-45545-5 : £2.50 B81-26033

960′.09′734 — Africa. Villages. Mothers. Social life — *For children*

Lewin, Hugh. Jafta — my mother / story by Hugh Lewin ; pictures by Lisa Kopper. — London : Evans, 1981. — [24]p : ill ; 20x23cm. — (Jafta's family series)
ISBN 0-237-45544-7 : £2.50 B81-23665

960′.09′734 — Africa. Villages. Social life — *For children*

Lewin, Hugh. Jaffa — the wedding / story by Hugh Lewin ; pictures by Lisa Kopper. — London : Evans, 1981. — [24]p : ill ; 20x23cm. — (Jaffa's family series)
ISBN 0-237-45546-3 : £2.50 B81-26032

960′.2 — Africa, *1840-1914 - For East African students - For schools*

Tidy, Michael. A history of Africa, 1840-1914. — London : Hodder and Stoughton, Aug.1981
Vol.2: 1880-1914. — [224]p
ISBN 0-340-24411-9 (pbk) : £3.25 : CIP entry B81-18066

960′.22 — Africa, *1400-1800*

Oliver, Roland. The African Middle Ages 1400-1800 / Roland Oliver, Anthony Atmore. — Cambridge : Cambridge University Press, 1981. — viii,216p : maps ; 22cm
Includes index
ISBN 0-521-23301-1 (cased) : £15.00
ISBN 0-521-29894-6 (pbk) : £5.50 B81-26191

960′.23 — Africa, *1800-1980*

Oliver, Roland. Africa since 1800 / Roland Oliver, Anthony Atmore. — 3rd ed. — Cambridge : Cambridge University Press, 1981. — xii,372p : maps ; 23cm
Previous ed.: 1972. — Bibliography: p354-357. — Includes index
ISBN 0-521-23485-9 (cased) : £17.50 : CIP rev.
ISBN 0-521-29975-6 (pbk) : £5.95 B81-07579

Thatcher, Paul. Students' notes on the history of Africa in the 19th and 20th centuries / Paul Thatcher. — Harlow : Longman, 1981. — 138p : maps ; 22cm
ISBN 0-582-60362-5 (pbk) : £1.30 B81-40308

960′.3 — Africa, *1900-1980 — For schools*

Campling, Elizabeth. Africa in the twentieth century / Elizabeth Campling. — London : Batsford Academic and Educational, 1980. — 96p : ill,7maps,ports ; 26cm. — (Twentieth century world history)
Includes index
ISBN 0-7134-2492-3 : £4.95 B81-01405

960′.328 — Africa. Social life — *For children*

Laurent, André. Life in Africa / André Laurent ; [translated by Penny Hayman]. — St. Albans : Hart-Davis, 1981. — 62p : ill(some col.) ; 27cm. — (Signposts series)
Translation from the French. — Includes index
ISBN 0-247-13038-9 : £3.50 B81-39609

960′.328′05 — Africa — *Serials*

[Africa now *(London : 1981)*]. Africa now. — Feb. 1981 ; 1 (Apr. 1981)-. — [London] ([50 Pall Mall, SW1Y 5JQ]) : [Pan-African Publishers], 1981-. — v. : ill,ports ; 27cm
Monthly. — Pre-publication no. issued Feb. 1981
ISSN 0261-5908 = Africa now (London. 1981) : £0.70 per issue B81-31568

Asian and African studies. — 17 (1981). — London : Curzon Press, Nov.1981. — [360]p
ISBN 0-7007-0145-1 : £6.00 : CIP entry
ISSN 0571-2742
Primary classification 950′.428′05 B81-39229

Owen's commerce and travel and international register. — 28th ed. (1981). — London : Owen's Commerce & Travel Ltd, c1981. — 1051p
ISBN 0-900576-12-x : Unpriced
Primary classification 950′.428′05 B81-28379

960′.328′05 — Africa. Social conditions — *Serials*

Africa guide. — 1978. — Saffron Walden (21 Gold St., Saffron Walden, Essex CB10 1EJ) : Africa Guide Co., c1977. — 360p
ISBN 0-904439-02-x : £11.50
ISSN 0308-678x B81-03764

Africa guide. — 1979. — Saffron Walden (21 Gold St., Saffron Walden, Essex CB10 1EJ) : World of Information, c1978. — 366p
ISBN 0-904439-05-4 : £11.50
ISSN 0308-678x B81-03765

Africa guide. — 1980. — Saffron Walden (21 Gold St., Saffron Walden, Essex CB10 1EJ) : World of Information, c1979. — 430p
ISSN 0308-678x : £11.50
ISBN 0-904439-10-0 B81-09132

961 — HISTORY. NORTH AFRICA

961′.048′05 — North Africa — *Serials*

The **Middle** East and North Africa. — 27th ed. (1980-81). — London : Europa, 1980. — xx,985p
ISBN 0-905118-50-2 : Unpriced : CIP rev.
ISSN 0076-8502
Primary classification 956′.04′05 B80-18135

The **Middle** East and North Africa. — 28th ed. (1981-82). — London : Europa, Sept.1981. — [1005]p
ISBN 0-905118-65-0 : CIP entry
ISSN 0076-8205
Primary classification 956′.04′05 B81-20494

961.2 — HISTORY. LIBYA

961′.2 — Libya, *to 1981*

Wright, John. Libya. — London : Croom Helm, Nov.1981. — [288]p
ISBN 0-7099-2733-9 : £14.95 : CIP entry B81-30539

961′.204 — Libya. Social conditions. Effects of petroleum industries

Allan, J. A.. Libya : the experience of oil / J.A. Allan. — London : Croom Helm, c1981. — 328p : ill,maps ; 23cm
Bibliography: p317-323. — Includes index
ISBN 0-7099-0420-7 : £14.95 : CIP rev. B81-12829

962 — HISTORY. EGYPT

962 — Egypt, *1805-1966*

Modern Egypt : studies in politics and society / edited by Elie Kedourie and Sylvia G. Haim. — London : Cass, 1980. — 136p ; 23cm
Incorporates the studies published in a special number of Middle Eastern studies
ISBN 0-7146-3168-x : £13.50 : CIP rev. B80-12186

962′.03′0222 — Egypt, *1856-1860 — Illustrations*

Frith, Francis. Egypt and the Holy Land in historic photograph : 77 views / by Francis Frith ; introduction & bibliography by Julia Van Haaften ; selection & commentary by Jon E. Manchip White. — New York : Dover Publications ; London : Constable, 1980. — xxv,77p : chiefly ill,1port ; 31cm
'The photographs are a selection from those that originally appeared in the four-volume series published by William Mackenzie, London ca.1862, with the titles (I) Sinai and Palestine ; (II) Lower Egypt, Thebes, and the Pyramids ; (III) Upper Egypt and Ethiopia ; (IV) Egypt, Sinai, and Palestine. Supplementary Volume' - T.p. verso. — Bibliography: pxxiii-xxiv
ISBN 0-486-24048-7 (pbk) : £4.55
Also classified at 956.94′03′0222 B81-30113

962′.04′0924 — Egypt. Social life, *1889-1902 — Childhood reminiscences*

Hussein, Taha. An Egyptian childhood : the autobiography of Taha Hussein / translated by E.H. Paxton. — London : Heinemann, 1981. — 85p ; 19cm. — (African writers series ; 228)
Translated from the Arabic. — Originally published: London : Routledge, 1932
ISBN 0-435-90228-8 (pbk) : £1.50 B81-16280

Hussein, Taha. An Egyptian childhood : the autobiography of Taha Hussein / translated by E.H. Paxton. — London : Heinemann, 1981. — 85p ; 19cm. — (Arab authors ; 16)
Translated from the Arabic. — Originally published: London : Routledge, 1932
ISBN 0-435-99416-6 (pbk) : £2.25 B81-16281

962′.054′0924 — Egypt. Political events. Role of Sadat, Anwar el-, *1970-1981*

Shoukri, Ghali. Egypt : portrait of a President. — London : Zed Press, Dec.1981. — [512]p
ISBN 0-86232-072-0 (pbk) : £8.95 : CIP entry B81-35867

962′.054′0924 — Egypt. Sadat, Anwar el- — *Biographies*

Hirst, David. Sadat. — London : Faber, Nov.1981. — [320]p
ISBN 0-571-11690-6 : £8.50 : CIP entry B81-35866

962.4 — HISTORY. SUDAN

962.4′004963 — Sudan. Dinka, *to 1974 — Interviews*

Deng, Francis Mading. Dinka cosmology / by Francis Mading Deng. — London : Ithaca, 1980. — 348p ; 23cm
ISBN 0-903729-29-6 : £12.50 B81-06835

962.4′03 — Sudan. Mahdiyah, *1881-1898*

Holt, P. M.. The Mahdist State in the Sudan : 1881-1898 : a study of its origins, development and overthrow / by P.M. Holt. — 2nd ed. — Nairobi ; Oxford : Oxford University Press, 1979, c1970. — xv,295p,[5]p of plates : maps ; 32cm
Originally published: Oxford : Clarendon, 1970. — Bibliography: p267-277. — Includes index
ISBN 0-19-572451-8 (pbk) : £2.25 B81-34940

962.4′04 — Sudan. Political events, *1956-1980*

Malwal, Bona. People & power in Sudan : the struggle for national stability / by Bona Malwal. — London : Ithaca, 1981. — v,277p ; 23cm
ISBN 0-903729-78-4 : Unpriced B81-35260

962.4′04 — Sudan. Political events, *1969-1980*

Bashier, Zakaria. The national reconciliation in the Sudan and its aftermath / Zakaria Bashier. — Leicester : Islamic Foundation, c1981. — 20p ; 30cm. — (Seminar papers / Islamic Foundation ; 12)
ISBN 0-86037-092-5 (pbk) : Unpriced B81-35079

962.6′2 — Sudan. Omdurman. Women. Social life

Cloudsley, Anne. The women of Omdurman : victims of circumcision / Anne Cloudsley. — London (4 Craven Hill, W2 3DS) : [A. Cloudsley], [c1981]. — vii,140p,[12]leaves of plates : ill,maps,geneal.tables ; 21cm
Bibliography: p139-140
ISBN 0-9507398-0-4 (pbk) : £3.50 B81-17727

963 — HISTORY. ETHIOPIA

963′.02 — Ethiopia, *1270-ca 1850*

Abir, Mordechai. Ethiopia and the Red Sea : the rise and decline of the Solominic dynasty and Muslim-European rivalry in the region / Mordechai Abir. — London : Cass, 1980. — xx,251p : maps ; 23cm
Bibliography: p237-243. - Includes index
ISBN 0-7146-3164-7 : £13.50 : CIP rev. B80-18137

963′.06 — Ethiopia. Political events, *1974-1980*

Molyneux, Maxine. The Ethiopian revolution. — London : New Left Books, Oct.1981. — [300]p
ISBN 0-86091-043-1 (cased) : £12.00 : CIP entry
ISBN 0-86091-741-x (pbk) : £4.50 B81-30146

963′.06′05 — Ethiopia. Political events — *Serials*
STORM : newsletter of the Somali, Tigray & Oromo resistance movements. — No.1 (Nov.1980)-. — London ([87 Gower St., WC1E 6AA]) : STORM, 1980-. — v. ; 30cm
Quarterly. — Subtitle varies
ISSN 0261-409x = STORM. Somali, Tigray & Oromo resistance monitor : Unpriced
B81-31055

963′.506 — Ethiopia. Eritrea. Civil war, *1961-1979*
Behind the war in Eritrea / edited by Basil Davidson, Lionel Cliffe and Bereket Habte Selassie. — Nottingham : Spokesman, 1980. — 150p ; 22cm
Conference papers
ISBN 0-85124-301-0 (cased) : £10.50
ISBN 0-85124-302-9 (pbk) : £3.50 B81-04709

964 — HISTORY. MOROCCO

964′.003′21 — Morocco, *788-1979 — Encyclopaedias*
Spencer, William. Historical dictionary of Morocco / by William Spencer. — Metuchen ; London : Scarecrow, 1980. — xliv,152p : 1map ; 23cm. — (African historical dictionaries ; no.24)
Bibliography: p113-152. — Includes index
ISBN 0-8108-1362-9 : £7.70 B81-05298

964′.02 — Morocco, *1510-1903*
Yahya, Dahiru. Morocco in the sixteenth century : problems and patterns in African foreign policy / Dahiru Yahya. — Harlow, Longman, 1981. — xvi,224p : 2maps,geneal.tables ; 23cm. — (Ibadan history series)
Bibliography: p201-217. — Includes index
ISBN 0-582-64670-7 : £17.50 B81-38265

964′.02′0202 — Morocco, *1665-1756 — Chronologies — Early works*
al-Qādirī, Muhammad. Muhammad al-Qādirī's Nashr al-mathānī, The chronicles / [edited by] Norman Cigar. — London : For the British Academy by Oxford University Press, 1981. — lxxi,320p,[2]leaves of plates : ill,maps,facsims ; 23cm. — (Fontes historiae Africanae. Series Arabica ; 6)
Arabic text, English translation and notes. — At head of title: Union académique internationale. — Bibliography: p273-286. — Includes index
ISBN 0-19-725994-4 (pbk) : £18.00 B81-36459

964.8 — HISTORY. WESTERN SAHARA

964′.8 — Western Sahara. Political events. Role of Morocco & Mauritania, *1934-1975*
Thompson, Virginia, *1903-*. The Western Saharans : background to conflict / Virginia Thompson and Richard Adloff. — London : Croom Helm, c1980. — 348p : maps ; 23cm
Bibliography: p325-340. - Includes index
ISBN 0-7099-0369-3 : £3.95 : CIP rev.
B80-22780

964.9 — HISTORY. CANARY ISLANDS

964′.9 — Canary Islands, *to 1980*
Mercer, John, *1934-*. The Canary Islanders : their prehistory, conquest and survival / John Mercer. — London : Collings, 1980. — xvii,285p,[16]p of plates : ill,1coat of arms,maps ; 24cm
Bibliography: p272-280. — Includes index
ISBN 0-86036-126-8 : £15.00 B81-01406

965 — HISTORY. ALGERIA

965′.003′21 — Algeria, *to 1980 — Encyclopaedias*
Heggoy, Alf Andrew. Historical dictionary of Algeria / Alf Andrew Heggoy with Robert R. Crout. — Metuchen ; London : Scarecrow, 1981. — x,237p : maps ; 23cm. — (African historical dictionaries ; no.28)
Includes index
ISBN 0-8108-1376-9 : £9.45 B81-18856

965′.02 — Algeria, *1500-1830*
Wolf, John B.. The Barbary Coast : Algiers under the Turks 1500 to 1830 / John B. Wolf. — New York ; London : Norton, c1979. — xii,364p : ill,ports ; 22cm
Bibliography: p339-351. - Includes index
ISBN 0-393-01205-0 : £10.95 B81-03962

965′.04 — Algeria. Political events, *1954-1962*
Talbott, John. The war without a name : France in Algeria, 1954-1962 / John Talbott. — London : Faber, 1981. — xii,305p : 2maps ; 22cm
Originally published: New York : Knopf, 1980. — Bibliography: p290-297. - Includes index
ISBN 0-571-11671-x : £6.95 B81-10617

966 — HISTORY. WEST AFRICA

966 — West Africa, *830-1350 — Readings from contemporary sources*
Corpus of early Arabic sources for West African history : translated by J.F.P. Hopkins / edited and annotated by N. Levtzion & J.F.P. Hopkins. — Cambridge : Cambridge University Press, 1981. — xx,492p : 2ill,1map,1geneal.table ; 24cm. — (Fontes historiae Africanae. Series Arabica ; 4)
Bibliography: p434-440. - Includes index
ISBN 0-521-22422-5 : £35.00 B81-09628

966 — West Africa, *1000-1980 — For West African students*
Thatcher, Paul. West African history. — New ed. / Paul Thatcher. — Harlow : Longman, 1980. — 119p : maps ; 22cm. — (Study for success) (Certificate notes)
Previous ed.: published as Topics in West African history / A.A. Boahen. 1974
ISBN 0-582-60398-6 (pbk) : £1.05 B81-19093

966 — West Africa, *1800-1979*
Webster, J. B.. The revolutionary years : West Africa since 1800. — New ed. / J.B. Webster, A.A. Boahen with Michael Tidy. — London : Longman, 1980. — ix,406p : ill,maps,ports ; 22cm. — (The growth of African civilisation)
Previous ed.: 1967. — Bibliography: p390-393. - Includes index
ISBN 0-582-60332-3 (pbk) : Unpriced : CIP rev. B80-02277

966.1 — HISTORY. MAURITANIA

966′.1′00321 — Mauritania, *to 1980 — Encyclopaedias*
Gerteiny, Alfred G.. Historical dictionary of Mauritania / by Alfred G. Gerteiny. — Metuchen, N.J. ; London : Scarecrow Press, 1981. — xv,98p : 1map ; 23cm. — (African historical dictionaries ; no.31)
Bibliography: p83-96
ISBN 0-8108-1433-1 : £7.00 B81-36519

966.23 — HISTORY. MALI

966′.23 — Mali. Jenne. Prehistoric antiquities. Archaeological investigation, *1977*
McIntosh, Susan Keech. Prehistoric investigations in the region of Jenne, Mali : a study in the development of urbanism in the Sahel / Susan Keech McIntosh and Roderick J. McIntosh. — Oxford : B.A.R., 1980. — 2v.(541p) : ill,maps ; 30cm. — (Cambridge monographs in African archaeology ; 2) (BAR. International series ; 89)
Bibliography: p510-541
ISBN 0-86054-103-7 (pbk) : £20.00 B81-36619

966.25 — HISTORY. UPPER VOLTA

966′.25 — Upper Volta. Liptako, *1800-1900.* **Historical sources: Oral traditions**
Irwin, Paul. Liptako speaks : history from oral tradition in Africa / Paul Irwin. — Princeton ; Guildford : Princeton University Press, c1981. — xxiv,221p : ill,2maps ; 23cm
Bibliography: p203-218. — Includes index
ISBN 0-691-05309-x : £10.80 B81-26855

966.3 — HISTORY. SENEGAL

966′.3′00321 — Senegal, *to 1980 — Encyclopaedias*
Colvin, Lucie Gallistel. Historical dictionary of Senegal / Lucie Gallistel Colvin. — Metuchen ; London : Scarecrow, 1981. — xiv,339p : maps ; 23cm. — (African historical dictionaries ; no.23)
Bibliography: p293-339
ISBN 0-8108-1369-6 : £12.25 B81-17378

966.4 — HISTORY. SIERRA LEONE

966′.4 — Sierra Leone, *to 1980 — For schools*
Fyle, C. Magbaily. The history of Sierra Leone : a concise introduction / C. Magbaily Fyle. — London : Evans, 1981. — x,150p : maps ; 22cm
Bibliography: p145-150
ISBN 0-237-50508-8 (pbk) : Unpriced
B81-26004

966′.404 — Sierra Leone. Social conditions
Knights, Ian E.. Sierra Leone : an outline guide for expatriate contract employees / [Ian E. Knights]. — 15th rev. ed. — London : Royal Commonwealth Society, 1979. — 18p : 2maps ; 30cm. — (Notes on conditions)
Previous ed.: 1977. — Bibliography: p17
ISBN 0-905067-73-8 (unbound) : Unpriced
B81-37761

966.57 — HISTORY. GUINEA-BISSAU

966′.5702 — Guinea-Bissau. Political events, *1963-1980*
Davidson, Basil. No fist is big enough to hide the sky : the liberation of Guinea Bissau and Cape Verde. — London : Zed, July 1981. — [225]p
ISBN 0-905762-93-2 : £12.95 : CIP entry
Also classified at 966′.5802 B81-18047

966.58 — HISTORY. CAPE VERDE ISLANDS

966′.5802 — Cape Verde Islands. Political events, *1963-1980*
Davidson, Basil. No fist is big enough to hide the sky : the liberation of Guinea Bissau and Cape Verde. — London : Zed, July 1981. — [225]p
ISBN 0-905762-93-2 : £12.95 : CIP entry
Primary classification 966′.5702 B81-18047

966.9 — HISTORY. NIGERIA

966.9′00973′2 — Nigeria. Southern states. Urban regions. Yorubaland. Social life - *For children*
Barker, Carol. Kayode and his village in Nigeria. — Oxford : Oxford University Press, June 1981. — [40]p
ISBN 0-19-279737-9 : £4.50 : CIP entry
B81-12338

966.9′03′0924 — Nigeria. Hausa. Baba, *of Karo — Biographies*
Baba, *of Karo*. Baba of Karo : a woman of the Muslim Hausa. — London : Yale University Press, Oct.1981. — [304]p
Originally published: New York : Praeger, 1954
ISBN 0-300-02734-6 : £7.50 : CIP entry
B81-32084

966.9′05′0924 — Nigerian Civil War — *Personal observations*
Ọbasanjọ, Ọluṣẹgun. My command : an account of the Nigerian Civil War 1967-1970 / Ọluṣẹgun Ọbasanjọ. — Ibadan ; London : Heinemann, 1980. — xiii,177p : ill,maps,ports ; 23cm
Includes index
ISBN 0-435-96533-6 : £8.50 B81-02051

Ọbasanjọ, Oluṣẹgun. My command : an account of the Nigerian civil war 1967-1970 / Olusegun Obasanjo. — London : Heinemann, 1980 (1981 [printing]). — xiii,177p : ill,maps,ports ; 19cm. — (African writers series ; 249)
Includes index
ISBN 0-435-90249-0 (pbk) : £1.50 B81-20839

966.9′4 — Nigeria. Niger delta. Prehistoric settlements. Economic conditions. Archaeological investigation
Nzewunwa, Nwanna. The Niger Delta : aspects of its prehistoric economy and culture / Nwanna Nzewunwa. — Oxford : B.A.R., 1980. — 267p : ill,maps ; 30cm. — (Cambridge monographs in African archaeology ; 1) (BAR. International series, ISSN 0143-3067 ; 75)
Bibliography: p249-267
ISBN 0-86054-083-9 (pbk) : £10.00 B81-16550

967 — HISTORY. CENTRAL AFRICA

967 — Africa south of the Sahara. Cultural processes
Schneider, Harold K.. The Africans : an ethnological account / Harold K. Schneider. — Englewood Cliffs ; London : Prentice-Hall, c1981. — x,278p : ill,maps ; 23cm. — (Prentice-Hall series in anthropology)
Bibliography: p255-264. — Includes index
ISBN 0-13-018648-1 (pbk) : £6.45 B81-14101

967 — Africa south of the Sahara. Influence of developed countries
Marnham, Patrick. [Fantastic invasion]. Dispatches from Africa / Patrick Marnham. — [London] : Abacus, 1981, c1980. — xii,241p : 4maps ; 20cm
Originally published: London : Cape, 1980
ISBN 0-349-12280-6 (pbk) : £1.95 B81-39872

967 — Africa south of the Sahara. Role of Scottish persons: Grampian Region persons, *ca 1780-ca 1980*
Hargreaves, John D.. Aberdeenshire to Africa. — Aberdeen : Aberdeen University Press, Dec.1981. — [150]p
ISBN 0-08-025764-x : £9.00 : CIP entry B81-31358

967 — Central Africa & East Africa. Prehistoric settlements. Archaeological investigation
Hodder, Ian R.. Symbols in action. — Cambridge : Cambridge University Press, Feb.1982. — [244]p. — (New studies in archaeology)
ISBN 0-521-24176-6 : £19.50 : CIP entry B81-36953

967'.005 — Africa south of the Sahara — *Serials*
Africa south of the Sahara. — 10th ed. (1980-81). — London : Europa, 1980. — xxiv,1372p
ISBN 0-905118-49-9 : Unpriced : CIP rev.
ISSN 0065-3896 B80-12678

Africa south of the Sahara. — 11th ed. (1981-82). — London : Europe, Aug.1981. — [1412]p
ISBN 0-905118-64-2 : CIP entry
ISSN 0065-3896 B81-16915

New African yearbook. — 1979. — London (63, Long Acre, WC2) : IC Magazines, c1979. — 400p
ISBN 0-905268-09-1 : Unpriced
ISSN 0140-1378 B81-12553

New African yearbook. — 1980. — London (63, Long Acre, WC2) : IC Magazines, c1980. — 415p
ISBN 0-905268-19-9 : Unpriced
ISSN 0140-1378 B81-12554

967'.0072 — Africa south of the Sahara, *1800-1900*. Historical sources
Robinson, David, *1938-*. Sources of the African past : case studies of five nineteenth-century African societies / David Robinson and Douglas Smith. — London : Heinemann, 1979. — xiv,203p : ill,maps ; 26cm
Includes bibliographies and index
ISBN 0-435-94248-4 (cased) : Unpriced
ISBN 0-435-94249-2 (pbk) : £3.95 B81-40666

967'0072 — Africa south of the Sahara. Historical sources: Oral traditions — *Study examples: Bantu*
The **African** past speaks : essays on oral tradition and history / edited by Joseph C. Miller. — Folkestone : Dawson, 1980. — xii,284p : ill,maps,geneal.tables ; 23cm
Includes index
ISBN 0-7129-0951-6 : £17.00 : CIP rev. B79-37598

967'.009'94 — Africa south of the Sahara. Political events, *1950-1979* — *Personal observations*
Scott, David, *1919-*. Ambassador in black and white : thirty years of changing Africa / David Scott. — London : Weidenfeld and Nicolson, 1981. — xii,258p,[8]p of plates : ill,1map,ports ; 24cm
Bibliography: p250-251. - Includes index
ISBN 0-297-77865-x : £10.95 B81-22409

967.11 — HISTORY. CAMEROON

967'.11 — Cameroon. Meiganga. Gbaya. Social change
Burnham, Philip. Opportunity and constraint in a savanna society : the Gbaya of Meiganga, Cameroon / Philip Burnham. — London : Academic Press, 1980. — xix,324p,viip of plates : ill,maps,1plan ; 24cm. — (Studies in anthropology)
Bibliography: p304-310. — Includes index
ISBN 0-12-146060-6 : £16.00 : CIP rev. B80-22912

967.21 — HISTORY. GABON

967'.21'00321 — Gabon, *to 1980* — *Encyclopaedias*
Gardinier, David E.. Historical dictionary of Gabon / by David E. Gardinier. — Metuchen, N.J. ; London : Scarecrow Press, 1981. — xxv,254p : maps ; 23cm. — (African historical dictionaries ; no.30)
Bibliography: p198-254
ISBN 0-8108-1435-8 : £10.50 B81-36521

967.24 — HISTORY. CONGO

967'.2401'0924 — Congo. Colonisation by France. Role of Brazza, Pierre Savorgnan de, *1875-1885*
Nwoye, Rosaline Eredapa. The public image of Pierre Savorgnan de Brazza and the establishment of French imperialism in the Congo, 1875-1885 / by Rosaline Eredapa Nwoye ; with an academic memoir by Roy C. Bridges and John D. Hargreaves. — [Aberdeen] : Aberdeen University African Studies Group, 1981. — xiv,161p : 1map,ports ; 30cm
Ports on inside cover. — Bibliography: p153-161
Unpriced (pbk) B81-36469

967.3 — HISTORY. ANGOLA

967'.3'00321 — Angola, *to 1979* — *Encyclopaedias*
Martin, Phyllis M.. Historical dictionary of Angola / Phyllis M. Martin. — Metuchen ; London : Scarecrow, 1980. — xxi,174p : 3maps ; 23cm. — (African historical dictionaries ; no.26)
Bibliography: p94-165. — Includes index
ISBN 0-8108-1322-x : £7.70 B81-02757

967'.304 — Angola. Political events. Role of United States
Holness, Marga. Memorandum on the Clark Amendment : the U.S. threat to destabilise Angola / by Marga Holness. — London (34 Percy St., W1P 9FG) : Mozambique, Angola & Guiné Information Centre, 1981. — 5p ; 30cm
£0.40 (unbound) B81-34697

967.41 — HISTORY. CENTRAL AFRICAN REPUBLIC

967'.41'00321 — Central African Republic, *1800-1979* — *Encyclopaedias*
Kalck, Pierre. Historical dictionary of the Central African Republic / by Pierre Kalck ; translated by Thomas O'Toole. — Metuchen ; London : Scarecrow, 1980. — xlii,152p : maps ; 23cm. — (African historical dictionaries ; no.27)
Translation from the French. — Bibliography: p137-152
ISBN 0-8108-1360-2 : £7.00 B81-09564

967.43 — HISTORY. CHAD

967'.4304 — Chad. Political events, *1960-1980*
Thompson, Virginia, *1903-*. Conflict in Chad / Virginia Thompson and Richard Adloff. — London : Hurst for the Institute of International Studies, Berkeley, Calif., c1981. — vii,180p ; 23cm
Bibliography: p159-173. — Includes index
ISBN 0-905838-70-x (pbk) : £7.50 : CIP rev. B81-30412

967.51 — HISTORY. ZAIRE

967.5'1 — South-east Zaire. Luba, *to 1891*
Reefe, Thomas Q.. The rainbow and the kings : a history of the Luba Empire to 1891 / Thomas Q. Reefe. — Berkeley ; London : University of California Press, c1981. — xx,286p : ill,maps ; 23cm
Bibliography: p247-261. — Includes index
ISBN 0-520-04140-2 : £15.00 B81-34461

967.6 — HISTORY. EAST AFRICA

967.6 — East Africa, *ca 1900-1980*
Nabudere, D. Wadada. Imperialism in East Africa. — London : Zed, Sept.1981
Vol.1: Imperialism and exploitation. — [240]p
ISBN 0-905762-99-1 : £12.95 : CIP entry B81-20522

967.61 — HISTORY. UGANDA

967.6'1 — Uganda. Political events, *1885-1979*
Nabudere, D. Wadada. Imperialism and revolution in Uganda / D. Wadada Nabudere. — London (86 Lauriston Rd., E9 7HA) : Onyx, 1980. — viii,376p ; 23cm
Bibliography: p362-365. - Includes index
ISBN 0-906383-06-4 (cased) : £14.25 : CIP rev.
ISBN 0-906383-07-2 (pbk) : Unpriced B79-23708

967.6'1004914 — Uganda. Asian communities. Social life — *Stories, anecdotes*
Patel, Kirit T.. In search of tomorrow / Kirit T. Patel. — Bognor Regis : New Horizon, c1979. — 110p ; 21cm
ISBN 0-86116-120-3 : £2.95 B81-39473

967.6'103 — Uganda, *1888-1980*
Jørgensen, Jan Jelmert. Uganda : a modern history / Jan Jelmert Jørgensen. — London : Croom Helm, c1981. — 381p : 1map ; 23cm
Bibliography: p355-370. — Includes index
ISBN 0-85664-643-1 : £13.95 B81-25151

967.6'104'0924 — Uganda. Amin, Idi, *to 1979* — *Biographies*
Kamau, Joseph. Lust to kill : the rise and fall of Idi Amin / Joseph Kamau and Andrew Cameron. — [London] : Corgi, 1979. — 351p,[16]p of plates : ill,ports ; 18cm
ISBN 0-552-11058-2 (pbk) : £1.25 B81-17773

967.62 — HISTORY. KENYA

967.6'2 — East Africa. Masai. Social life
Ole Saibull, Soloman. Herd and spear : the Maasai of East Africa / Soloman ole Saibull and Rachel Carr ; foreword by Edward Moringe ole Sokaine. — London : Collins and Harvill, 1981. — 141p,[16]p of plates : ill,1map,ports ; 22cm
ISBN 0-00-262303-x : £8.95 B81-26101

967.6'2'00321 — Kenya, *to 1980* — *Encyclopaedias*
Ogot, Bethwell A.. Historical dictionary of Kenya / by Bethwell A. Ogot. — Metuchen, N.J. ; London : Scarecrow Press, 1981. — xvii,278p : 1map ; 23cm. — (African historical dictionaries ; no.29)
Bibliography: p219-276
ISBN 0-8108-1419-6 : £11.20 B81-36522

967.6'201 — Kenya, *to 1850*
Spear, T.. Kenya's past. — London : Longman, Jan.1982. — [240]p
ISBN 0-582-64695-2 (cased) : £9.95 : CIP entry
ISBN 0-582-64696-0 (pbk) : £4.95 B81-34556

967.6'203 — Kenya. Social change, *1905-1970* — *Marxist viewpoints*
Kitching, G. N.. Class and economic change in Kenya : the making of an African petite bourgeoisie 1905-1970 / Gavin Kitching. — New Haven ; London : Yale University Press, 1980. — xx,479p : ill,maps ; 24cm
Bibliography: p462-467. — Includes index
ISBN 0-300-02385-5 : £15.00 : CIP rev. B80-21418

967.6'203'0924 — Kenya. Fisher, Suzanne — *Biographies*
Fisher, Suzanne. We lived on the verandah / Suzanne Fisher. — Bognor Regis : New Horizon, c1980. — 201p,[6] of plates : ill,ports ; 22cm
ISBN 0-86116-381-8 : £5.50 B81-21706

967.6'204 — Kenya. Society — *For Kenyan students*
Ayot, Henry Okello. Primary social studies / Henry Okello Ayot, Daniel Mutungi Kiminyo. — London : Macmillan Ecucation
Pupil's bk.2: The Highland people. — c1980. — 44p : ill(some col.),1col.plan ; 25cm
ISBN 0-333-30952-9 (pbk) : £0.85 B81-20014

967.6'204'0924 — Kenya. Mboya, Tom — *Biographies*

Goldsworthy, David. Tom Mboya. — London : Heinemann Educational, Jan.1982. — [320]p
ISBN 0-435-96275-2 : £13.00 : CIP entry B81-34569

967.6'204'0924 — Kenya. Ricciardi, Mirella — *Biographies*

Ricciardi, Mirella. African saga. — London : Collins, Nov.1981. — [320]p
ISBN 0-00-216191-5 : £9.95 : CIP entry B81-30261

967.6'26 — Kenya. Thika. Social life, *1913-1925 — Childhood reminiscences*

Huxley, Elspeth. The flame trees of Thika : memories of an African childhood / Elspeth Huxley. — Harmondsworth : Penguin Books in association with Chatto & Windus, 1962, c1959 (1981 [printing]). — 280p ; 19cm
Originally published: London : Chatto & Windus, 1959
ISBN 0-14-001715-1 (pbk) : £1.50 B81-40096

967.6'27 — Kenya. Amboseli region. Sites. Archaeological investigation

Foley, Robert. Off-site archaeology and human adaptation in Eastern Africa : an analysis of regional artefact density in the Amboseli, Southern Kenya / Robert Foley. — Oxford : B.A.R., 1981. — 265p : ill,maps ; 30cm. — (Cambridge monographs in African archaeology ; 3) (BAR. International series ; 97)
Bibliography: p204-216
ISBN 0-86054-114-2 (pbk) : £10.00
ISBN 0-86054-109-6 B81-40115

967.6'2704 — Kenya. Lake Turkana region. Social life

Amin, Mohamed. Cradle of mankind. — London : Chatto and Windus, Sept.1981. — [192]p
ISBN 0-7011-2587-x : £14.95 : CIP entry B81-23746

967.7 — HISTORY. DJIBOUTI (REPUBLIC), SOMALIA

967'.7 — Horn of Africa. Political events, *1884-1979*

Selassie, Bereket Habte. Conflict and intervention in the Horn of Africa / Bereket Habte Selassie. — New York ; London : Monthly Review Press, c1980. — x,211p : maps ; 21cm
Includes index
ISBN 0-85345-534-1 : £8.00 B81-06007

967'.7103 — Djibouti *(Republic).* **Social conditions,** *1967-1977*

Tholomier, Robert. Djibouti : pawn of the horn of Africa / Robert Tholomier ; an abridged translation and postscript by Virginia Thompson and Richard Adloff. — Metuchen ; London : Scarecrow, 1981. — x,163p : 1map ; 23cm
Translation from: A Djibouti avec les Afars et les Issas. — Bibliography: p149-155. — Includes index
ISBN 0-8108-1415-3 : £7.00 B81-32560

967'.73 — Somalia, *to 1978*

Lewis, I. M.. A modern history of Somalia : nation and state in the Horn of Africa / I.M. Lewis. — Revised ed. — London : Longman, 1980. — ix,279p : maps ; 21cm
Previous ed.: published as 'The modern history of Somaliland from nation to state'. London : Weidenfeld and Nicolson, 1965. — Includes index
ISBN 0-582-64657-x (pbk) : £4.50 : CIP rev. B79-31443

967'.7305 — Somalia. Cultural processes

Lewis, I. M.. Somali culture, history and social institutions : an introductory guide to the Somali Democratic Republic / I.M. Lewis. — London : London School of Economics & Political Science, 1981. — 54p,[3]p of plates : maps ; 21cm
Bibliography: p41-45
ISBN 0-85328-071-1 (pbk) : £2.00 B81-17723

967.8 — HISTORY. TANZANIA

967.8'26 — Tanzania. Iraqw. Cultural processes

Thornton, Robert J.. Space, time and culture among the Iraqw of Tanzania / Robert J. Thornton. — New York ; London : Academic Press, c1980. — xxiv,275p : ill,maps,plans ; 24cm
Bibliography: p259-266. — Includes index
ISBN 0-12-690580-0 : £19.20 B81-15122

967.8'28 — Tanzania. Wanyamwezi. Cultural processes

Abrahams, R. G.. The Nyamwezi today : a Tanzanian people in the 1970s / R.G. Abrahams. — Cambridge : Cambridge University Press, 1981. — xiv,145p : ill,1map ; 23cm. — (Changing cultures)
Bibliography: p140-142. — Includes index
ISBN 0-521-22694-5 : £15.00
ISBN 0-521-59619-6 (pbk) : £4.95 B81-19011

967.9 — HISTORY. MOZAMBIQUE

967'.96 — Mozambique. Quelimane region. Social conditions. Effects of capitalism, *ca 1850-1975*

Vail, Leroy. Capitalism and colonialism in Mozambique : a study of Quelimane district / Leroy Cail and Landeg White. — London : Heinemann, 1980. — xii,419p : ill,facsims,3maps ; 23cm
Includes index
ISBN 0-435-94870-9 : £19.50 : CIP rev. B80-13228

968 — HISTORY. SOUTHERN AFRICA

968 — South Africa. Bantu Homelands. Social conditions

Rogers, Barbara. Divide & rule : South Africa's Bantustans / by Barbara Rogers. — Rev. and enl. ed. — London (104 Newgate St., EC1A 7AP) : International Defence and Aid Fund for Southern Africa, 1980. — 135p,[8]p of plates : ill,1map ; 21cm
Previous ed.: 1976. — Bibliography: p133. - Includes index
ISBN 0-904759-40-7 (pbk) : £2.00 B81-11523

968 — South Africa, *to 1980*

Gann, L. H.. Why South Africa will survive : a historical analysis / L.H. Gann and Peter Duignan. — London : Croom Helm, 1981. — 312p : maps ; 23cm
Includes index
ISBN 0-7099-0223-9 : £14.95 : CIP rev. B80-27696

968 — Southern Africa, *to 1980 — For Southern African students*

Junior certificate history of southern Africa. — London : Heinemann Educational
Bk. 2: Southern Africa in the late nineteenth and twentieth centuries / Boleswa History Project ; editor Leonard Ngcongco ; writing team N. Bhebe ... [et al.]. — 1981. — xviii,126p : ill,maps,ports ; 22cm
Bibliography: p120. — Includes index
ISBN 0-435-94161-5 (pbk) : £2.40 B81-40377

968 — Southern Africa, *to 1981 — For East African students — For schools*

Parker, Graham. History of Southern Africa. — 2nd ed. — London : Bell & Hyman, Jan.1982. — [308]p
Previous ed.: 1975
ISBN 0-7135-1215-6 (pbk) : £5.95 : CIP entry B81-33836

968.04 — South Africa. Social conditions, *ca 1800-1914*

Economy and society in pre-industrial South Africa / edited by Shula Marks and Anthony Atmore. — London : Longman, 1980. — 385p : 2ill,maps ; 23cm
Includes index
ISBN 0-582-64655-3 (cased) : Unpriced : CIP rev.
ISBN 0-582-64656-1 (pbk) : £3.95 B80-09993

968.04'092'4 — South Africa. Social life, *1864-1901 — Personal observations — Correspondence, diaries, etc.*

Turner, Sidney. Portrait of a pioneer : the letters of Sidney Turner from South Africa 1864-1901 / selected and edited by Daphne Child. — Johannesburg ; London : Macmillan, 1980. — xi,144p,[16]p of plates : ill,map,facsim,ports ; 24cm
Bibliography: p143
ISBN 0-86954-095-5 : £9.95 B81-22854

968.04'8 — Boer War

The **South** African War : the Anglo-Boer War 1899-1902 / general editor Peter Warwick ; advisory editor S.B. Spies. — Harlow : Longman, 1980. — 415p : ill(some col.),maps (some col.),facsims,plans,ports ; 27cm
Bibliography: p404-407. — Includes index
ISBN 0-582-78526-x : £12.50 : CIP rev. B80-11699

968.04'8 — Boer War. British military forces. Officers. Casualties — *Lists — Early works*

Dooner, Mildred G.. The "Last post" : being a roll of all officers (naval, military or colonial) who gave their lives for their Queen, King and country in the South African War, 1899-1902 / by Mildred G. Dooner. — Polstead (The Old Rectory, Polstead, Suffolk) : Hayward, c1980. — vii,446p : 1ill ; 21cm
Facsim of: 1st ed. London : Simpkin, Marshall, 1903
ISBN 0-903754-92-4 : Unpriced B81-22232

968.04'8 — Boer War. Great Britain. *Army. Natal Field Force.* **Casualties —** *Lists*

The **South** African War casualty roll : the Natal Field Force, 20th Oct. 1899-26th Oct. 1900. — Polstead : Hayward, c1980 ; London (5 Buckingham St., W.C.2) : London Stamp Exchange [Distributor]. — 237p ; 32cm
ISBN 0-903754-90-8 (pbk) : Unpriced B81-22763

968.05 — South Africa, *1915-1980 — South African Communist Party viewpoints*

South African communists speak : documents from the history of the South African Communist Party 1915-1980. — London (39 Goodge St., W.1.) : Inkululeko, c1981. — xx,469p : 2ports ; 22cm
Bibliography: px. — Includes index
ISBN 0-9504225-2-5 : Unpriced B81-40660

968.05 — South Africa. Political events, *1914-1978 — Conference proceedings*

Southern African research in progress : papers given at the Centre for Southern African Studies, University of York / edited by Anne V. Akeroyd and Christopher R. Hill. — [York] : The Centre, c1980. — ii leaves, 175p : 1ill ; 25cm. — (Collected papers / University of York. Centre for Southern African Studies ; 5)
Includes bibliographies
ISBN 0-905055-05-5 (pbk) : £3.00 B81-27018

968.05 — Southern Africa. Political events, *1945-1978*

Southern Africa : the continuing crisis / edited by Gwendolen M. Carter and Patrick O'Meara. — London : Macmillan, 1979. — xii,404 : 1ill,maps. — (Contemporary African issues series)
Originally published: Bloomington : Indiana University Press, 1979. — Bibliography: p363-381. — Includes Index
ISBN 0-333-27495-4 (pbk) : £1.95 : CIP rev. B79-18842

968.05'092'4 — South Africa. Duncan, Patrick — *Biographies*

Driver, C. J.. Patrick Duncan : South African and Pan-African / C.J. Driver. — London : Heinemann, 1980. — xiv,326p,[12]p of plates : ill,maps,ports ; 24cm
Includes index
ISBN 0-435-96200-0 : £19.50 : CIP rev. B79-30459

968.05'092'4 — South Africa. Matthews, Z. K. — *Biographies*

Matthews, Z. K.. Freedom for my people : the autobiography of Z.K. Matthews : southern Africa 1901 to 1968 / [edited with a] memoir by Monica Wilson. — London : Collings in association with David Philip, Capetown, 1981. — ix,253p,[8]p of plates : ill,ports ; 23cm
Bibliography: p238-244. — Includes index
ISBN 0-86036-147-0 : £12.50 B81-10634

968.06'2 — South Africa. Political events, *1976*

Brooks, Alan, *1940-*. Whirlwind before the storm : the origins and development of the uprising in Soweto and the rest of South Africa from June to December 1976 / by Alan Brooks and Jeremy Brickhill. — London (104 Newgate St., EC1A 7AP) : International Defence and Aid Fund for Southern Africa, 1980. — 367p,[20]p of plates : ill,5maps ; 21 cm
Includes index
ISBN 0-904759-36-9 (cased) : £8.00
ISBN 0-904759-37-7 (pbk) : £4.00 B81-29028

968.06'2 — South Africa. Political events, *1976-1980*

Carter, Gwendolen M.. Which way is South Africa going / Gwendolen M. Carter. — Bloomington ; London : Indiana University Press, c1980. — xii,162p : 2maps ; 25cm
Includes index
ISBN 0-253-10874-8 : £7.80 B81-01407

968.06'2 — South Africa. Social change. Political aspects

Hanf, Theodor. South Africa : the prospects of peaceful change : an empirical enquiry into the possibility of democratic conflict regulation / Theodor Hanf, Heribert Weiland and Gerda Vierdag in collaboration with Lawrence Schlemmer, Rainer Hampel and Burkhard Krupp. — London : Collings, c1981. — xviii,492p : ill ; 24cm
Translation of: Südafrika, friedlicher Wandel?. — Bibliography: p475-485. — Includes index
ISBN 0-253-35394-7 : £15.00 B81-39657

968.06'2 — Southern Africa. Political events, *1976-1980*

Callinicos, Alex. Southern Africa after Zimbabwe / Alex Callinicos. — London : Pluto, 1981. — 186p : 1map ; 20cm
Includes index
ISBN 0-86104-336-7 (pbk) : £2.95 B81-16483

968.1'1 — Botswana. Serowe. Social life, *1875-1980 — Personal observations — Collections*

Head, Bessie. Serowe : village of the rainwind / Bessie Head. — London : Heinemann, 1981. — xxiv,200p : 2maps,ports ; 19cm. — (African writers series ; 220)
Bibliography: p199-200
ISBN 0-435-90220-2 (pbk) : £2.95 B81-27015

968.1'102 — Botswana. Political events, *1885-1899*

Maylam, Paul. Rhodes, the Tswana, and the British : colonialism, collaboration, and conflict in the Bechuanaland Protectorate, 1885-1899 / Paul Maylam. — Westport, Conn. ; London : Greenwood Press, 1980. — x,245p : maps ; 25cm. — (Contributions in comparative colonial studies ; no.4)
Bibliography: p225-234. — Includes index
ISBN 0-313-20885-9 : £19.50 B81-23466

968.1'601'0924 — Lesotho. Sotho. Moshoeshoe, *Chief of the Basotho — Biographies — For schools*

Grant, Neville. Moshoeshoe : founder of a nation / Neville Grant. — London : Longman, 1981. — 66p : ill,1map ; 20cm. — (Makers of African history)
ISBN 0-582-60367-6 (pbk) : £0.65 B81-40199

968.1'603 — Lesotho. Social conditions

Lesotho / Commonwealth Institute. — London : The Institute, [1980]. — 12p : 2col.maps ; 30cm. — (Commonwealth fact sheet, ISSN 0306-3801)
Bibliography: p11
ISBN 0-900906-81-2 (unbound) : Unpriced B81-01408

968.2'04 — South Africa. Transvaal, *1834-1902*

Cartwright, A. P.. The old Transvaal 1834-1899 / A.P. Cartwright, Nat Cowan. — Cape Town ; London ; Purnell, c1978. — 151p : ill,2maps,facsims,ports ; 30cm
Maps on lining papers
ISBN 0-86843-020-x : £12.75 B81-02312

968.2'21054'0924 — South Africa. Johannesburg region. Coloured persons. Social life, *1920-1939 — Childhood reminiscences*

Abrahams, Peter, *1919-*. Tell freedom / by Peter Abrahams. — London : Faber, 1954 (1981 [printing]). — 311p ; 20cm
ISBN 0-571-11777-5 (pbk) : Unpriced
ISBN 0-571-11778-3 (pbk) : Unpriced (non-net) B81-12559

968.2'21062 — South Africa. Johannesburg. Social life *— For children*

Gibbs, Richard. Living in Johannesburg / Richard Gibbs. — Hove : Wayland, 1981. — 52p : ill,1col.map ; 22cm. — (Living in famous cities)
Bibliography: p51. — Includes index
ISBN 0-85340-843-2 : £3.75 B81-24335

968.4'045 — Zulu War

Barthorp, Michael. The Zulu War : a pictorial history / Michael Barthorp. — Poole : Blandford, 1980. — ix,181p : ill,plans,ports ; 26cm
Bibliography: p177. — Includes index
ISBN 0-7137-1005-5 : £8.95 : CIP rev. B80-14099

968.8'02 — Namibia. Political events, *1904-1907*

Bridgman, Jon M.. The revolt of the Hereros / Jon M. Bridgman. — Berkeley ; London : University of California Press, c1981. — 184p,[14]p of plates : ill,8maps,ports ; 23cm. — (Perspectives on Southern Africa ; 30)
Includes index
ISBN 0-520-04113-5 : £9.00 B81-27494

968.8'03 — Namibia, *1900-1980*

Namibia. — London : Longman, Apr.1981. — [350]p
ISBN 0-582-59734-x : £9.95 : CIP entry
ISBN 0-582-59735-8 (pbk£4.50) B81-02113

968.8'03 — Namibia. Political events, *1960-1980 — International Defence and Aid Fund viewpoints*

Namibia : the facts. — London (104 Newgate St., EC1 7AP) : International Defence & Aid Fund, 1980. — 100p,[8]p of plates : ill,maps,1facsim,1port ; 21cm
Map on inside cover. — Bibliography: p97-78. - Includes index
ISBN 0-904759-41-5 (pbk) : £1.50 B81-05776

968.8'03 — Namibia. Political events, *ca 1970-1982 — Christian viewpoints*

Namibia in the 1980's. — London : Catholic Institute for International Relations, Oct.1981. — [64]p
ISBN 0-904393-58-5 (pbk) : CIP entry B81-31179

968.8'03'05 — Namibia. Political events — *SWAPO viewpoints — Serials*

[Information & comments *(SWAPO)***]**.
Information & comments / SWAPO of Namibia. — Vol.1, no.1 (1979)-. — London (188 North Gower St., NW1) : SWAPO Western Europe Office, 1979-. — v. ; 30cm
Irregular. — Description based on: Vol.1, no.4
ISSN 0260-3411 = Information & comments - SWAPO : Unpriced B81-04650

968.91 — HISTORY. ZIMBABWE

968.91 — Zimbabwe. Political events, *1890-1980*

Meredith, Martin. The past is another country : Rhodesia : UDI to Zimbabwe / Martin Meredith. — Rev. and extended ed. — London : Pan, 1980. — 429p : ill,2maps ; 18cm. — (Pan world affairs)
Previous ed.: London : Deutsch, 1979. — Bibliography: p412-414. — Includes index
ISBN 0-330-26268-8 (pbk) : £2.50 B81-03100

968.91 — Zimbabwe, *to 1980*

Hudson, Miles. Triumph of tragedy? : Rhodesia to Zimbabwe / by Miles Hudson. — London : Hamilton, [1981]. — 252p : maps ; 23cm
Bibliography: p245-246. — Includes index
ISBN 0-241-10571-4 : £9.95 : CIP rev. B81-10415

Martin, David, *1936-*. The struggle for Zimbabwe : the Chimurenga War / David Martin and Phyllis Johnson. — London : Faber, 1981. — xvii,378p,[16]p of plates : ill,2maps,ports ; 23cm
Includes index
ISBN 0-571-11066-5 : £10.95 : CIP rev. B81-02371

968.91'01 — Zimbabwe. Shona, *900-1850*

Beach, D. N.. The Shona & Zimbabwe 900-1850 : an outline of Shona history / D.N. Beach. — London : Heinemann, 1980. — xiv,422p,10p of plates : ill,maps ; 22cm
Bibliography: p392-410. - Includes index
ISBN 0-435-94505-x : £12.50 B81-06868

968.91'04 — Zimbabwe. Political events

Hills, Denis. Rebel people / by Denis Hills. — London : Allen & Unwin, 1978. — 248p : maps ; 23cm
ISBN 0-04-920056-9 : £6.50 : CIP rev. B78-32641

968.91'04 — Zimbabwe. Political events, *1820-1980*

Elliott, Hugh P.. Dawn in Zimbabwe / [Hugh P. Elliott]. — London : Grosvenor, 1980. — 23p : 1map,ports ; 15x21cm
ISBN 0-901269-57-3 (pbk) : £0.50 B81-07127

968.91'04 — Zimbabwe. Political events, *1979-1980*

Hills, Denis. The last days of white Rhodesia / Denis Hills. — London : Chatto & Windus, 1981. — 187p : 1map ; 23cm
ISBN 0-7011-2554-3 : £8.50 : CIP rev. B81-03162

968.94 — HISTORY. ZAMBIA

968.94 — Zambia. Copperbelt. Social conditions, *1950-1956*

Epstein, A. L.. Urbanization and kinship. — London : Academic Press, Dec.1981. — [300]p
ISBN 0-12-240520-x : CIP entry B81-31337

969 — HISTORY. INDIAN OCEAN ISLANDS

969'.8203'05 — Mauritius *— For expatriate Mauritians — Serials*

Voice of Mauritians. — 15th anniversary issue (1979). — London (c/o Mr. J.K. Lee, 135 Mitcham Rd, SW17 9PE) : Association for the Promotion of the Welfare of Mauritians in the U.K., 1979. — 28p
£0.25 B81-09188

Voice of Mauritians. — Spring 1980. — London (c/o Mr. J.K. Lee, 135 Mitcham Rd, SW17 9PE) : Association for the Promotion of the Welfare of Mauritians in the U.K., 1980. — 27p
£0.25 B81-09189

970 — HISTORY. NORTH AMERICA

970.004'97 — Alaska. Wainwright. Eskimos. Social life

Nelson, Richard K.. Shadow of the hunter : stories of Eskimo life / Richard K. Nelson ; illustrations by Simon Koonook. — Chicago ; London : University of Chicago Press, c1980. — xiii,282p : ill ; 23cm
ISBN 0-226-57179-3 : £7.50 B81-05214

970.004'97 — Apaches, *to ca 1900*

Apache Indian. — New York ; London : Garland. — (American Indian ethnohistory. Indians of the Southwest)
8. — 1974. — 269p : 1map ; 23cm
Includes bibliographies. — Contents: The Jicarilla Apache Indians : a history 1598-1888 / by Alfred Barnaby Thomas — Anthropological material on the Jicarilla Apaches / by Jean Ware Nelson — The Jicarilla Apaches 1601-1849 / by Elizabeth V. Atwater
ISBN 0-8240-0710-7 : Unpriced B81-25522

970.004′97 — Apaches, *to ca 1900*
continuation

Apache Indians. — New York ; London : Garland. — (American Indian ethnohistory. Indians of the Southwest)
2. — 1974. — 361p : ill,maps,facsims ; 23cm
Includes bibliographies. — Contents: The Ascarate grant / by Jocelyn J. Bowden — An ethnological study of Tortugas, New Mexico / by Alan James Oppenheimer
ISBN 0-8240-0716-6 : Unpriced B81-25526

970.004′97 — California. Siskiyou County. Karok Indians. Social life, *1908-1909 — Personal observations*

Arnold, Mary Ellicott. In the land of the grasshopper song : two women in the Klamath River Indian country in 1908-09 / by Mary Ellicott Arnold and Mabel Reed. — Lincoln [Neb.] ; London : University of Nebraska Press, 1980, c1957. — 313p,[16]p of plates : ill,1map,ports ; 21cm. — (Bison book)
Originally published: New York : Vantage Press, 1957
ISBN 0-8032-1804-4 (cased) : Unpriced
ISBN 0-8032-9703-7 (pbk) : £3.55 B81-12607

970.004′97 — Eastern North America. North American Indians. Cultural processes, *1600-1800 — Readings from contemporary sources*

The **Indian** peoples of Eastern America : a documentary history of the sexes / edited by James Axtell. — New York ; Oxford : Oxford University Press, 1981. — xx,233p : 1map ; 24cm
Bibliography: p229-233. — Includes index
ISBN 0-19-502740-x (cased) : £7.50
ISBN 0-19-502471-8 (pbk) : Unpriced B81-23696

970.004′97 — North American Indian artefacts, *to 1979*

Feest, Christian F.. Native arts of North America / Christian F. Feest. — London : Thames and Hudson, c1980. — 216p : ill(some col.),1map ; 22cm. — ([The World of art library])
Bibliography: p198-208. — Includes index
ISBN 0-500-18179-9 : £5.95 B81-21954

970.004′97 — North American Indian children. Social life, *to ca 1890 — For schools*

Hodgson, Pat. Growing up with the North American Indians / Pat Hodgson. — London : Batsford Academic and Educational, 1980. — 72p : ill,1map,1port ; 26cm
Bibliography: p70. — Includes index
ISBN 0-7134-2732-9 : £4.50 B81-21958

970.004′97 — North American Indians, *ca1740-1979 — Biographies*

American Indian leaders : studies in diversity / edited by R. David Edmunds. — Lincoln, Neb. ; London : University of Nebraska Press, 1980. — xiv,257,[8]p of plates : maps,ports ; 21cm
Includes index
ISBN 0-8032-1800-1 (cased) : £11.70
ISBN 0-8032-6705-3 (pbk) : £3.60 B81-21952

970.004′97 — North American Indians, *to 1980*

The **American** Indian, past and present. — 2nd ed. / edited by Roger L. Nichols. — New York ; Chichester : Wiley, c1981. — xii,283p ; 23cm
Previous ed.: Waltham, Mass. : Xerox College Publications, 1971. — Bibliography: p277-283
ISBN 0-471-06321-5 (pbk) : £5.00 B81-23694

Hodge, William H.. The first Americans : then and now / William H. Hodge. — New York ; London : Holt, Rinehart and Winston, c1981. — xx,551p : ill,maps,ports ; 25cm
Map on lining papers. — Includes bibliographies and index
ISBN 0-03-056721-1 : £10.95 B81-23693

970.004′97 — Oklahoma. Five Civilized Tribes, *1865-1907.* **Social life** *— Personal observations — Collections*

Perdue, Theda. Nations remembered : an oral history of the five civilized tribes, 1865-1907 / Theda Perdue. — Westport, Conn. ; London : Greenwood Press, 1980. — xxiv,221p : ill,maps ; 22cm. — (Contributions in ethnic studies, ISSN 0196-7088 ; no.1)
Bibliography: p201-209. — Includes index
ISBN 0-313-22097-2 : £15.50 B81-23690

970.004′97 — South Dakota. American Indian reservations: Rosebud Reservation. Brulé Indians. Cultural processes

Grobsmith, Elizabeth S.. Lakota of the Rosebud : a contemporary ethnography / Elizabeth S. Grobsmith. — New York ; London : Holt, Rinehart and Winston, c1981. — xii,120p : ill,maps ; 24cm. — (Case studies in cultural anthropology)
Bibliography: p115-120
ISBN 0-03-057438-2 (pbk) : £3.25 B81-23388

970′.0074′02649 — Ipswich. *Department of Recreation and Amenities.* **Stock: North & South American artefacts**

Ipswich. *Department of Recreation & Amenities.* The Pacific, Australia and the Americas : a guide to the Ipswich collections / [author D.L. Jones]. — Ipswich ([Civic Centre, Civic Drive, Ipswich IP1 2EE]) : Ipswich Borough Council, Department of Recreation & Amenities, [1980?]. — [36]p : ill ; 18x25cm
Cover title
ISBN 0-906688-03-5 (pbk) : Unpriced
Primary classification 990′.074′02649
B81-10223

970.01′5′0924 — North America. Exploration. Colón, Cristóbal *— Biographies — For children*

Duchet-Suchaux, Gaston. Christopher Columbus / Gaston Duchet-Suchaux ; illustrated by Eduardo T. Coelho ; [translated by Merle Philo]. — St. Albans : Hart-Davis, 1981. — 30p : col.ill,1col.map ; 25cm. — (Junior histories)
Translation of the French. — Text on lining paper
ISBN 0-247-13217-9 : £2.95 B81-39463

970.02 — America. Social life, *ca 1550-1800 — Case studies*

Struggle and survival in colonial America / edited by David G. Sweet and Gary B. Nash. — Berkeley ; London : University of California Press, c1981. — 398p : ill,maps ; 24cm
Includes bibliographies and index
ISBN 0-520-04110-0 : £17.00 B81-36457

970.053′6′0924 — North America. Polish immigrants. Social life, *1959-1963 — Personal observations — Polish texts*

Świdzińska, Halina. Drogi i bezdroża : wspomnienia i opowieści o ludziach i zdarzeniach / Halina Świdzińska. — Londyn : OPiM, 1981. — 238p,[3]leaves of plates : 3ports ; 22cm
£4.00 (pbk)
Also classified at 891.8′537 B81-18265

971 — HISTORY. CANADA

971 — Canada. French speaking persons, *1760-1980*

Legendre, Camille. French Canada in crisis : a new society in the making? / Camille Legendre. — London (36 Craven St., WC2N 5NG) : Minority Rights Group, 1980. — 20p : 1map ; 30cm. — (Report / Minority Rights Group, ISSN 0305-6252 ; no.44)
Bibliography: p17
£0.75 (pbk) B81-05637

971 — Canada. Relations with Great Britain *— Conference proceedings*

Britain and Canada : a colloquium held at Leeds, October 1979 : papers and report / edited with an introduction by David Dilks. — London (Marlborough House, Pall Mall, S.W.1) : Commonwealth Foundation, 1980. — 109p ; 25cm. — (Occasional paper / Commonwealth Foundation, ISSN 0069-7087 ; no.49)
Cover title
Unpriced (pbk)
Primary classification 941 B81-08049

971′.00497 — Canada. North American Indians

Price, John A.. Indians of Canada : cultural dynamics / John A. Price. — Scarborough ; London : Prentice-Hall, c1979. — 261p : ill,map,ports ; 23cm
Bibliography: p239-253. — Includes index
ISBN 0-13-456962-8 (pbk) : £5.80 B81-21953

971.01′8 — Canada. English persons. Capture by Eskimos, *ca 1725 — Early works — Facsimiles*

Hofland, Barbara. Little Manuel, the captive boy / Barbara Hofland. — New York ; London : Garland, 1978. — 120p in various pagings,[1] folded leaf of plates : ill,facsims ; 19cm. — (The Garland library of narratives of North American Indian captivities ; v.44)
Facsimile reprints. — Contents: Little Manuel, the captive boy / Barbara Hofland — Seizure of the ship industry. Originally published: London : T. Tegg, 1830 - St Maur, or, The captive babes recovered. Originally published: New York : J. Emory and B. Waugh, 1830
ISBN 0-8240-1668-8 : Unpriced
Also classified at 976.4′02 B81-23691

971.063 — Canada. Political events, *1945-1980*

Bothwell, Robert. Canada since 1945 : power, politics, and provincialism / Robert Bothwell, Ian Drummond, John English. — Toronto ; London : University of Toronto Press, c1981. — xii,489,[14]p of plates : ill,ports ; 24cm
Bibliography: p461-467. — Includes index
ISBN 0-8020-2417-3 : £18.00 B81-34328

971.064′3 — Canada. Social conditions *compared with* **social conditions in United States,** *1964-1974*

Michalos, Alex C.. North American social report : a comparative study of the quality of life in Canada and the USA from 1964 to 1974 / by Alex C. Michalos. — Dordrecht ; London : Reidel
Vol.3: Science, education and recreation. — c1981. — xv,219p : ill ; 23cm
Includes index
ISBN 90-277-1257-3 (pbk) : Unpriced
Also classified at 973.923 B81-27729

971.064′6 — Canada. Social life

Nach, James. Canada in pictures / by James Nach and others. — New York : Sterling ; London : Oak Tree, 1980. — 64p : ill,1map,ports ; 27cm. — (Visual geography series)
Originally published: 1966. — Includes index
ISBN 0-7061-2199-6 : £2.50 B81-00676

971.6′13 — Nova Scotia. Pictou region. Settlement by Scottish immigrants, *1793-1830*

Mackay, Donald, *19---*. Scotland farewell : the people of the Hector / Donald Mackay. — Toronto : McGraw-Hill Ryerson ; Edinburgh : Paul Harris, c1980. — xxvi,229p,[8]p of plates : ill,maps,1facsim,1port ; 23cm
Bibliography: p216-218. - Includes index
ISBN 0-86228-016-8 : £7.50 B81-03085

972 — HISTORY. MIDDLE AMERICA, MEXICO

972 — Chicanos, *to 1980*

Vigil, James Diego. From Indians to Chicanos : a sociocultural history / James Diego Vigil. — St. Louis ; London : Mosby, 1980. — xv,245p : ill,maps,facsims ; 24cm
Includes bibliographies and index
ISBN 0-8016-5230-8 (pbk) : £8.00 B81-09763

972 — Maya civilization

Social process in Maya prehistory : studies in honour of Sir Eric Thompson / edited by Norman Hammond. — London : Academic Press, 1977. — xiv,609p,6pofplates : ill(some col.),maps,ports ; 26cm
Includes bibliographies and index
ISBN 0-12-322050-5 : £39.60 B81-39564

972 — Mexican civilisation, *to 1979*

Gyles, Anna Benson. Of gods and men : Mexico and the Mexican Indian / Anna Benson Gyles and Chloë Sayer. — London : British Broadcasting Corporation, 1980. — 232p,[16]p of plates : ill(some col.),2maps ; 23cm
Maps on lining papers. — Bibliography: p222-228. — Includes index
ISBN 0-563-17804-3 : £10.50 B81-01600

972′.003′21 — Mexico, *to 1980 — Encyclopaedias*

Briggs, Donald C.. Historical dictionary of Mexico / by Donald C. Briggs and Marvin Alisky. — Metuchen ; London : Scarecrow, 1981. — xiv,259p ; 23cm. — (Latin American historical dictionaries ; no.21)
Bibliography: p237-259
ISBN 0-8108-1391-2 : £10.50 B81-22990

972'.01'088054 — Aztec children. Social life — *For schools*

Lewis, Brenda Ralph. Growing up in Aztec times / Brenda Ralph Lewis. — London : Batsford Academic and Educational, 1981. — 72p : ill,maps,1port ; 26cm
Bibliography: p70. - Includes index
ISBN 0-7134-2734-5 : £5.50 B81-12558

972'.02 — Mexico, *1519-1810*

MacLachlan, Colin M.. The forging of the cosmic race : a reinterpretation of colonial Mexico / Colin M. MacLachlan, Jaime E. Rodriguez O. — Berkeley ; London : University of California Press, c1980. — xiv,362p,[24]p of plates : ill,maps,2ports ; 24cm
Maps on lining papers. — Bibliography: p339-351. — Includes index
ISBN 0-520-03890-8 : £15.00 B81-07675

972'.02'0924 — Mexico. Conquest by Spain. Cortés, Hernándo

Prescott, William H.. The conquest of Mexico / W.H. Prescott ; introduction by Thomas Seccombe. — London : Dent, 1909 (1978 [printing]). — xix,436p : 1map ; 19cm. — (Everyman's library ; no.397)
Originally published in 2 vols.. — Bibliography: pxiii.. — Includes index
ISBN 0-460-00397-6 (cased) : £5.95
ISBN 0-460-01397-1 (pbk) : Unpriced B81-13997

972.08'1 — Mexico, *1910-1920*

Henderson, Peter V. N.. Félix Díaz, the Porfirians, and the Mexican Revolution / by Peter V.N. Henderson. — Lincoln [Neb.] ; London : University of Nebraska Press, c1981. — xi,239p : 1port ; 23cm
Bibliography: p221-231. — Includes index
ISBN 0-8032-2312-9 : £2.00 B81-25649

972'.37 — Mexico. Naranja. Social conditions, *1885-1926*

Friedrich, Paul. Agrarian revolt in a Mexican village : with a new preface and supplementary bibliography / Paul Friedrich. — Chicago ; London : University of Chicago Press, 1977. — xiv,162p : ill,maps,ports,geneal.tables ; 23cm. — (A Phoenix book)
Originally published: Englewood Cliffs ; Hemel Hempstead : Prentice Hall, 1970. — Bibliography: p151-162
ISBN 0-226-26481-5 (pbk) : £3.70 B81-38143

972.84 — HISTORY. EL SALVADOR

972.84'052 — El Salvador. Political events, *1980 — Tricontinental Society viewpoints*

El Salvador : the development of the people's struggle : documents and interviews from Popular Liberation Forces - FPL - 'Farabundo Marti' and the Popular Revolutionary Bloc (BPR). — London (P.O. Box Tricontinenal, 29 Islington Park Street, N1) : Tricontinental Society, [1980]. — 37p : ill,maps ; 30cm
Cover title. — Text on inside covers
£0.50 (pbk) B81-32319

972.85 — HISTORY. NICARAGUA

972.85'052 — Nicaragua. Political events, *1979-1980*

Black, George. Triumph of the people : the Sandinista revolution in Nicaragua. — London : Zed, Nov.1981. — [320]p
ISBN 0-86232-036-4 (pbk) : £5.50 : CIP entry B81-30342

972.85'052 — Nicaragua. Political events, *ca 1970-1980*

Weber, Henri. The Nicaraguan revolution. — London : New Left Books, Oct.1981. — [180]p
Translated from the French
ISBN 0-86091-044-x (cased) : £9.00 : CIP entry
ISBN 0-86091-742-8 (pbk) : £3.25 B81-30147

972.86 — HISTORY. COSTA RICA

972.86'052 — Costa Rica, *1948-1979 — Society of Friends viewpoints*

Bird, Leonard A.. Costa Rica : a country without an army / by Leonard A. Bird. — Extended ed.. — Leeds (30 Gledhow Wood Grove, Leeds LS8 1NZ) : Northern Friends Peace Board, [1981]. — 21p : 1col.map ; 21cm
Cover title. — Previous ed.: 197-?
£0.50 (pbk) B81-09316

972.87 — HISTORY. PANAMA

972.87'402 — Panama. Caledonia Bay. Antiquities, *1515-1800.* **Archaeological investigation**

Horton, Mark. Caledonia Bay, Panama, 1979 : a preliminary report on the archaeological project of Operation Drake / by Mark Horton. — London (210 Euston Rd.) : Operation Drake, 1980. — 36p,[17]p of plates : ill,maps ; 30cm
Unpriced (unbound) B81-15116

972.9 — HISTORY. WEST INDIES

972.9'03 — West Indies. Sugar plantations. Social conditions, *to 1807 — For schools*

Grant, Alison. Bristol and the sugar trade / Alison Grant ; illustrated from contemporary sources. — Harlow : Longman, 1981. — 96p : ill,maps,1plan,ports ; 20cm. — (Then and there series)
Includes index
ISBN 0-582-21724-5 (pbk) : £0.85
Primary classification 382'.41361'0942393 B81-35310

972.91'064'0924 — Cuba. Castro, Fidel — *Biographies*

Humphrey, Paul. Castro / Paul Humphrey. — Hove : Wayland, 1981. — 72p : ill,1facsim,1map,ports ; 22cm. — (Wayland history makers)
Bibliography: p70. — Includes index
ISBN 0-85340-828-9 : £3.95 B81-37699

972.91'064'0924 — Cuba. Politics. Role of Castro, Fidel, *1964-1968*

Halperin, Maurice. The taming of Fidel Castro / Maurice Halperin. — Berkeley ; London : University of California Press, c1981. — x,345p : maps ; 24cm
Includes index
ISBN 0-520-04184-4 : £11.50 B81-34186

972.92'06'05 — Jamaica — *Serials*

The **Weekly** gleaner. — Vol. 1521 (Wednesday July 23rd 1980)-. — Kingston, Jamaica : Gleaner Co. ; Maidstone (Larkfield, Maidstone, Kent) : Printed, distributed and serviced in the UK by the Kent Messenger Group, 1980-. — v. ; 37cm
Continues: Jamaican weekly gleaner
ISSN 0250-7773 = Weekly gleaner : £0.15 per issue B81-00677

972.93'04 — Dominican Republic, *1844-1979*

Bell, Ian. The Dominican Republic / Ian Bell. — Boulder, Colo. : Westview ; London : Benn, 1981. — xv,392p : ill,maps,ports ; 24cm. — (Nations of the modern world)
Bibliography: p371-374. — Includes index
ISBN 0-510-39042-0 : £12.95 : CIP rev. B80-08566

972.94'03 — Haiti. San Domingo. Slaves. Rebellion, *1791-1803*

Geggus, David Patrick. Slavery, war, and revolution. — Oxford : Clarendon Press, Dec.1981. — [480]p
ISBN 0-19-822634-9 : £25.00 : CIP entry B81-31741

972.96 — Bahamas. Social life — *For schools*

Berryman, John. The Bahamas : a social studies course for secondary schools / John Berryman. — [London] : Macmillan Caribbean, 1980. — 100p : ill,maps,1coat of arms,1geneal.table ; 25cm
Bibliography: p100
ISBN 0-333-29222-7 (pbk) : £2.25 B81-07019

972.96 — Bahamas. Windsor, Edward, *Duke of, 1940-1945 — Biographies*

Pye, Michael, *1946-*. The King over the water / Michael Pye. — London : Hutchinson, 1981. — 280p,[12]p of plates : ill,1map,ports ; 23cm
Bibliography: p278-280
ISBN 0-09-144660-0 : £7.95 : CIP rev. B81-01409

972.98'304 — Trinidad and Tobago. Social conditions — *For schools*

Mitchell, Nikola. Trinidad and Tobago : a social studies course for secondary schools / Nikola Mitchell. — London : Macmillan Caribbean, 1981. — 92p : ill,1coat of arms,maps,ports ; 25cm
Bibliography: p92
ISBN 0-333-31482-4 (pbk) : £1.90 B81-40517

973 — HISTORY. UNITED STATES

973 — American civilization, *to 1980*

Introduction to American studies / edited by Malcolm Bradbury and Howard Temperley. — London : Longman, 1981. — xiii,331p : maps ; 22cm
Bibliography: p296-316. — Includes index
ISBN 0-582-48903-2 (cased) : Unpriced : CIP rev.
ISBN 0-582-48904-0 (pbk) : £5.50 B80-26356

973 — United States. Americans. Capture by North American Indians, *1690-1870 — Early works*

Milet, Pierre1635-1709. Captivity of Father Milet / Pierre Milet. — New York ; London : Garland, 1978. — 225p in various pagings : ill ; 23cm. — (The Garland library of narratives of North American Indian captivities ; v.96)
Facsimile reprints. — Contents: Capitivity of Father Milet / Pierre Milet — Capitivity among the Oneidas of Father Milet / Pierre Milet — Lost and found / Ole T. Nystel — Wehman's book on the scalping knife / Henry J. Wehman — Left by the Indians / Emeline J. Fuller
ISBN 0-8240-1720-x : £40.00 B81-23692

973 — United States. Political events, *ca 1630-1830*

Three British revolutions : 1641, 1688, 1776 / edited by J.G.A. Pocock. — Princeton : Guildford : Princeton University Press, c1980. — lx,468p ; 23cm. — (Folger Institute essays)
Includes index
ISBN 0-691-05293-x : £10.10
ISBN 0-691-10087-x (pbk£6.90)
Primary classification 941.06 B81-06957

973 — United States, *to 1976 — For schools*

Baydo, Gerald. USA : a synoptic history of America's past / Gerald Baydo. — New York ; Chichester : Wiley, c1981
Includes bibliographies and index
Vol.1. — viii,320,A16,I6p : ill,maps,ports ; 23cm
ISBN 0-471-06433-5 (pbk) : £4.90 B81-13079

Baydo, Gerald. USA : a synoptic history of America's past / Gerald Baydo. — New York ; Chichester : Wiley, c1981
Includes bibliographies and index
Vol.2. — viii,p290-648,A16,I11 : ill,maps,ports ; 23cm
ISBN 0-471-06431-9 : £4.90 B81-13080

973'.004924 — United States. Jews. Social life, *to 1975*

Grinstein, Hyman B.. A short history of the Jews in the United States / by Hyman B. Grinstein. — London : Soncino, c1980. — 208p : ill,facsims,ports ; 24cm. — (The Jewish library ; 7)
Bibliography: p185-186. - Includes index
£10.00 B81-06211

973'.004951 — United States. Chinese. Social life, *ca 1865-1975*

Kingston, Maxine Hong. China men / Maxine Hong Kingston. — London : Pan, 1981. — 300p ; 20cm. — (Picador original)
Originally published: New York : Knopf, 1980
ISBN 0-330-26367-6 (pbk) : £1.50 B81-14993

973′.00496073 — United States. Urban regions. Negroes. Social life, *to 1979*

In search of the promised land : essays in black urban history / edited by Theodore Kornweibel, Jr. — Port Washington ; London : National University Press : Kennikat, 1981. — x,227p ; 23cm. — (Interdisciplinary urban series)
Bibliography: p220-227
ISBN 0-8046-9267-x : £14.85 B81-29476

973′.00496073′00321 — United States. Negroes — *Encyclopaedias*

Encyclopedia of black America / W. Augustus Low, editor ; Virgil A. Clift, associate editor. — New York ; London : McGraw-Hill, c1981. — xix,921p : ill,maps,facsims,ports ; 29cm
Includes bibliographies and index
ISBN 0-07-038834-2 : £18.75 B81-32120

973′.009′734 — United States. Rural regions. Social conditions

Carlson, John E.. Rural society and environment in America / John E. Carlson, Marie L. Lassey, William R. Lassey. — New York ; London : McGraw-Hill, c1981. — xxii,425p : ill,maps,facsims ; 24cm
Bibliography: p392-404. — Includes index
ISBN 0-07-009959-6 : £13.50 B81-23962

973′.01′9 — United States, *to ca 1980 — Psychological perspectives*

Our selves/our past : psychological approaches to American history / edited by Robert J. Brugger. — Baltimore ; London : Johns Hopkins University Press, c1981. — xiii,416p ; 24cm
Bibliography: p405-414
ISBN 0-8018-2312-9 (cased) : £18.50
ISBN 0-8018-2382-x (pbk) : Unpriced
B81-40024

973′.0491497 — United States. Gypsies. Social life

McLaughlin, John B.. Gypsy lifestyles / John B. McLaughlin. — Lexington : Lexington, c1980 ; [Farnborough, Hants] : Gower, 1981. — xvi,105p ; 24cm
Includes index
ISBN 0-669-03754-0 : £9.50 B81-14215

973′.072024 — United States. Historiography. Adams, Henry — *Critical studies*

Blackmur, R. P.. Henry Adams / R.P. Blackmur ; edited with an introduction by Veronica A. Makowsky ; foreword by Denis Donoghue. — London : Secker and Warburg, 1980. — xxvii,354p,[1] leaves of plates : 1port ; 21cm
Bibliography: p.346-348. - Includes index
ISBN 0-436-05060-9 : £9.95 B81-07722

973′.09′92 — United States. Presidents, *to 1981 — Biographies*

Cook, Denys. Presidents of the U.S.A. / Denys Cook. — Newton Abbot : David & Charles, c1981. — 288p ; 23cm
Includes index
ISBN 0-7153-8067-2 : £9.50 : CIP rev.
B81-09976

973.2 — American civilization, *1620-1778 — For children*

Palmer, Ann. Growing up in colonial America / Ann Palmer. — Hove : Wayland, 1979, c1978. — 95p : ill,2facsims ; 24cm. — (Growing up in other times)
Bibliography: p93. - Includes index
ISBN 0-85340-547-6 : £2.95 B81-09934

973.2 — United States, *1585-1776*

Simmons, R. C.. The American colonies : from settlement to independence / R.C. Simmons. — Harlow : Longman, 1976 (1981[printing]). — vii,438p : maps ; 20cm
Bibliography: p389-415. - Includes index
ISBN 0-582-49201-7 (pbk) : £5.95 B81-19097

973.2 — United States. Social life, *ca 1600-1775*

Bridenbaugh, Carl. Early Americans / Carl Bridenbaugh. — New York ; Oxford : Oxford University Press, c1981. — xii,281p : 3ill,2maps ; 22cm
ISBN 0-19-502788-4 : £12.00 B81-32545

973.2′092′4 — United States. Politics. Franklin, Benjamin — *Biographies*

Davies, Eryl. Benjamin Franklin : experimenter extraordinary / Eryl Davies. — Hove : Wayland, 1981. — 72p : ill,1chart,facsims,ports ; 24cm. — (Pioneers of science and discovery)
Bibliography: p70. — Includes index
ISBN 0-85340-825-4 : £3.95 B81-37698

973.2′092′4 — United States. Politics. Franklin, Benjamin — *Stories, anecdotes*

Ben Franklin laughing : anecdotes from original sources by and about Benjamin Franklin / edited with an introduction by P.M. Zall. — Berkeley ; London : University of California Press, c1980. — 204p : 1port ; 24cm
Includes index
ISBN 0-520-04026-0 : £7.75
Primary classification 818′.102′08 B81-27618

973.2′4 — United States, *1660-1685*

Sosin, J. M.. English America and the Restoration Monarchy of Charles II : transatlantic politics, commerce, and kinship / J.M. Sosin. — Lincoln, Neb. ; London : University of Nebraska Press, c1980. — 389p ; 24cm
Includes index
ISBN 0-8032-4118-6 : £16.50 B81-25427

973.3′072073 — War of American Independence. American historiography, *to 1787*

Cohen, Lester H.. The revolutionary histories : contemporary narratives of the American revolution / Lester H. Cohen. — Ithaca ; London : Cornell University Press, 1980. — 286p ; 23cm
Bibliography: p231-232. - Includes index
ISBN 0-8014-1277-3 : £9.00 B81-07274

973.3′1 — War of American Independence. Political aspects

The **Revolution** that wasn't : a contemporary assessment of 1776 / edited with an introduction by Richard M. Fulton. — Port Washington ; London : Kennikat, 1981. — viii,247p ; 22cm. — (Series in American studies)
ISBN 0-8046-9259-9 : £16.55 B81-13295

973.3′13 — United States. Declaration of Independence

Wills, Garry. Inventing America : Jefferson's Declaration of Independence / Garry Wills. — London : Athlone, 1980, c1978. — xxvi,398p ; 23cm
Originally published: Garden City, N.Y. : Doubleday, 1978. — Includes index
ISBN 0-485-11201-9 : £12.50 : CIP rev.
B80-11702

973.3′13′01 — United States. Declaration of Independence. Influence of philosophy

White, Morton. The philosophy of the American revolution / Morton White. — Oxford : Oxford University Press, c1978 (1981 [printing]). — xiv,299p ; 21cm. — (A Galaxy book)
Includes index
ISBN 0-19-502891-0 (pbk) : Unpriced
B81-37943

973.3′8 — War of American Independence — *Personal observations — Collections*

The **Revolution** remembered : eyewitness accounts of the War for Independence / edited by John C. Dann. — Chicago ; London : University of Chicago Press, 1980. — xxvi,446p : ill,facsims,ports ; 25cm. — (Clements Library bicentennial studies)
Includes index
ISBN 0-226-13622-1 : £12.00 B81-01683

973.4′092′4 — United States. Politics. Lyon, Matthew — *Biographies*

Austin, Aleine. Matthew Lyon : "new man" of the democratic revolution, 1749-1822 / Aleine Austin ; foreword by Richard B. Morris. — University Park ; London : Pennsylvania State University Press, c1981. — xii,192p : ill ; 24cm
Bibliography: p175-184. — Includes index
ISBN 0-271-00262-x : £10.70 B81-34200

973.4′1′0924 — United States. Washington, George — *Biographies — For children*

Clark, Philip, *1944-*. Washington / Philip Clark. — Hove : Wayland, 1981. — 72p : ill,1map,ports ; 23cm. — (Wayland history makers)
Bibliography: p69. — Includes index
ISBN 0-85340-845-9 : £3.95 B81-24377

973.4′6′0924 — United States. Jefferson, Thomas — *Biographies — Welsh texts*

Maelor, Thomas William Jones, *Baron*. Thomas Jefferson : trydydd Arlywydd America / gan yr Arglwydd Maelor. — [Denbigh] : Gwasg Gee, 1980. — 80p,[4]p of plates : ill,1port ; 23cm
Bibliography: p71
£2.50 B81-01994

973.5 — United States. Social life, *ca 1830-ca 1860*

Saum, Lewis O.. The popular mood of pre-Civil War America / Lewis O. Saum. — Westport, Conn. ; London : Greenwood Press, 1980. — xxiv,336p ; 25cm. — (Contributions in American studies ; no.46)
Bibliography: p291-323. — Includes index
ISBN 0-313-21056-x : £19.50 B81-23469

973.6 — United States. Wars with North American Indians, *1848-1865*

Utley, Robert M.. Frontiersmen in blue : the United States Army and the Indian, 1848-1865 / by Robert M. Utley. — Lincoln, [Neb.] ; London : University of Nebraska Press, 1981, c1967. — xv,384p,[32]p of plates : ill,maps,ports ; 24cm
Originally published: New York : Macmillan ; London : Collier Macmillan, 1967. — Bibliography: p350-362. — Includes index
ISBN 0-8032-4550-5 (cased) : Unpriced
ISBN 0-8032-9550-2 (pbk) : £7.00 B81-38246

973.6′092′4 — United States. Erwin, Margaret Johnson — *Correspondence, diaries, etc.*

Erwin, Margaret Johnson. Like some green laurel : letters of Margaret Johnson Erwin 1821-1863 / John Seymour Erwin. — Baton Rouge ; London : Louisiana State University Press, c1981. — xxiii,154p,[12]p of plates : ill,3plans,ports ; 23cm. — (The Library of Southern civilization)
Bibliography: p145-149. — Includes index
ISBN 0-8071-0761-1 : £7.75 B81-25561

973.7′092′4 — United States. Lincoln, Abraham — *Biographies — For children*

Kolpas, Norman. Abraham Lincoln / Norman Kolpas. — Harlow : Longman, 1981. — 69p : ill(some col.),col.maps,facsims,ports(some col.) ; 25cm. — (Longman great lives)
Map on lining papers. — Bibliography: p69. — Includes index
ISBN 0-582-39030-3 : £3.95 B81-39669

973.7′092′4 — United States. Wars with Dakota Indians, *1862-1863 — Personal observations*

M'Conkey, Harriet E. Bishop. Dakota war whoop / Harriet E. Bishop M'Conkey. — New York ; London : Garland, 1978. — 304p,[6] leaves of plates : ports ; 19cm. — (The Garland library of narratives of North American Indian captivities ; v.78)
Facsimile of: edition published Saint Paul : Merrill, 1863
ISBN 0-8240-1702-1 : Unpriced B81-25525

973.7′1 — United States. Political events, *1861-1865*

Rawley, James A.. The politics of union : northern politics during the Civil War / James A. Rawley. — Lincoln [Neb.] ; London : University of Nebraska Press, 1980, c1974. — xiv,202p ; 21cm. — (A Bison book)
Originally published: Hinsdale, Ill. : Dryden Press, 1974. — Bibliography: p190-197. - Includes index
ISBN 0-8032-3856-8 (cased) : Unpriced
ISBN 0-8032-8902-2 (pbk) : £2.40 B81-17367

973.7′11 — American Civil War. Causes

Collins, Bruce. The origins of America's Civil War / Bruce Collins. — London : Edward Arnold, 1981. — 169p : 2maps ; 22cm. — (Foundations of modern history)
Bibliography: p159-164. — Includes index
ISBN 0-7131-6337-2 (cased) : Unpriced
ISBN 0-7131-6330-5 (pbk) : £4.75 B81-24954

973.7′82 — American Civil War. Army operations by Confederate States of America. *Army. Texas Cavalry Regiment, 24th, 1863-1865 — Personal observations — Correspondence, diaries, etc.*
Foster, Samuel T.. One of Cleburne′s command : the Civil War reminiscences and diary of Capt. Samuel T. Foster, Granbury Texas Brigade, CSA / edited by Norman D. Brown. — Austin ; London : University of Texas Press, c1980. — xlvii,192p : ill,facsims,maps ; 24cm
Includes index
ISBN 0-292-76014-0 : £9.70 B81-35523

973.7′82 — American Civil War - *Confederate viewpoints - Correspondence, diaries, etc*
Chesnut, Mary Boykin. Mary Chesnut′s civil war. — London : Yale University Press, Apr.1981. — [960]p
ISBN 0-300-02459-2 : £18.85 : CIP entry B81-09984

973.7′82 — Confederate States of America. *Army.* **Army life,** *to 1865 — Personal observations — Facsimiles*
Dawson, Francis W.. Reminiscences of confederate service : 1861-1865 / Francis W. Dawson ; edited by Bell I. Wiley with an introduction, appendix, and notes. — Baton Rouge ; London : Louisiana State University Press, c1980. — xv,214p ; 24cm. — (The Library of Southern civilization)
ISBN 0-8071-0689-5 : £8.95 B81-06255

973.7′83 — United States. *Army.* **Soldiers. Army life,** *1861-1865*
Wiley, Bell Irvin. The life of Billy Yank : a common soldier of the Union / Bell Irvin Wiley. — Baton Rouge ; London : Louisiana State University Press, 1978, c1971. — 454p,[26]p of plates : ill,ports ; 23cm
Originally published: Indianapolis : Bobbs Merrill, 1952. — Includes index
ISBN 0-8071-0477-9 (cased) : Unpriced
ISBN 0-8071-0476-0 (pbk) : £4.50 B81-09323

973.8′6 — United States. Wars with Teton Indians. Battle of Wounded Knee Creek
Smith, Rex Alan. Moon of Popping Trees / Rex Alan Smith. — Lincoln, [Neb.] ; London : University of Nebraska Press, 1981, c1975. — xii,219p : maps ; 21cm
Originally published: New York : Reader′s Digest, 1975. — Bibliography: p205-207. — Includes index
ISBN 0-8032-4123-2 (cased) : Unpriced
ISBN 0-8032-9120-5 (pbk) : £2.30 B81-38211

973.8′9 — Spanish-American War
Trask, David F.. The war with Spain in 1898 / David F. Trask. — New York : Macmillan ; London : Collier Macmillan, c1981. — xiv,654p : maps ; 24cm. — (The Macmillan wars of the United States)
Includes index
ISBN 0-02-932950-7 : £18.95 B81-38654

973.9′092′2 — United States. Social life, *ca 1900-1979 — Personal observations — Collections*
Terkel, Studs. American dreams : lost and found / Studs Terkel. — London : Hodder and Stoughton, 1981, c1980. — xxv,470p ; 25cm
Originally published: New York : Pantheon, 1980
ISBN 0-340-26701-1 : £8.95 : CIP rev. B81-13576

973.9′092′4 — United States. Astor, Brooke — *Biographies*
Astor, Brooke. Footprints : an autobiography / Brooke Astor. — London : Weidenfeld and Nicolson, 1980. — 175p,[16]p of plates : ill,ports ; 23cm
Originally published: Garden City, N.Y. : Doubleday, 1980
ISBN 0-297-77863-3 : £10.00 B81-01410

973.9′092′4 — United States. Heiresses: Hutton, Barbara, *1912 Nov.14- — Biographies*
Van Rensselaer, Philip. Million dollar baby : an intimate portrait of Barbara Hutton / by Philip Van Rensselaer. — London : Hodder and Stoughton, 1980, c1979. — 285p,[16]p of plates : ill,ports ; 23cm
Originally published: New York : Putnam, 1979
ISBN 0-340-25606-0 : £6.95 : CIP rev. B80-10424

973.91′5′088055 — United States. Young persons. Social life, *1920-1929*
Fass, Paula S.. The damned and the beautiful : American youth in the 1920′s / Paula S. Fass. — Oxford : Oxford University Press, 1977 (1979 [printing]). — xii,497p : ill ; 21cm
Includes index
ISBN 0-19-502492-3 (pbk) : £3.50 B81-02845

973.917 — United States. Society, *1938-1978*
Polenberg, Richard. One nation divisible : class, race, and ethnicity in the United States since 1938 / Richard Polenberg. — Harmondsworth : Penguin, 1980. — 363p ; 18cm. — (The Pelican history of the United States ; v.7)
Originally published: New York : Viking, 1980. — Includes index
ISBN 0-14-021246-9 (pbk) : £1.95 B81-11540

973.917′092′4 — United States. Longworth, Alice Roosevelt — *Interviews*
Teague, Michael. Mrs. L : conversations with Alice Roosevelt Longworth. — London : Duckworth, Oct.1981. — [224]p
ISBN 0-7156-1602-1 : £8.95 : CIP entry B81-24633

973.917′092′4 — United States. Roosevelt, Franklin Delano — *Biographies — For children*
Butler, William Vivian. Franklin D. Roosevelt. — London : Hodder & Stoughton Children′s Books, Jan.1982. — [128]p. — (Twentieth century people)
ISBN 0-340-27097-7 : £5.50 : CIP entry B81-34160

973.918′092′4 — United States. Social life, *1946-1951 — Personal observations*
Cooke, Alistair. Letters from America, 1946-1951 / Alistair Cooke. — Harmondsworth : Penguin, 1981. — 203p ; 19cm
Originally published: London : Hart-Davis, 1951
ISBN 0-14-005763-3 (pbk) : £1.50 B81-25082

973.92′092′4 — United States. Social life, *1951-1968 — Personal observations*
Cooke, Alistair. Talk about America : 1951-1968 / Alistair Cooke. — Harmondsworth : Penguin, 1981, c1968. — 271p ; 18cm
Originally published: London : Bodley Head, 1968
ISBN 0-14-005764-1 (pbk) : £1.50 B81-40780

973.92′092′4 — United States. Social life, *1969-1979 — Personal observations*
Cooke, Alistair. The Americans : letters from America on our life and times, 1969-79 / Alistair Cooke. — Harmondsworth : Penguin, 1980, c1979. — 287p ; 19cm
Originally published: London : Bodley Head, 1979
ISBN 0-14-005691-2 (pbk) : £1.50 B81-01632

973.922′092′4 — United States. Exner, Judith — *Biographies*
Exner, Judith. My story / Judith Exner as told to Ovid Demaris. — London : Futura, 1978, c1977. — 299p ; 18cm. — (A Circus book)
Originally published: New York : Grove Press, 1977
ISBN 0-7088-1513-8 (pbk) : £0.95 B81-04789

973.922′092′4 — United States. Kennedy, John F. *— Biographies*
Campling, Elizabeth. Kennedy / Elizabeth Campling. — London : Batsford Academic and Educational, [1980]. — 96p : ill,ports ; 26cm. — (World leaders in context)
Bibliography: p94. - Includes index
ISBN 0-7134-1920-2 : £4.95 B81-12642

973.923 — United States. Social conditions *compared with* **social conditions in Canada,** *1964-1974*
Michalos, Alex C.. North American social report : a comparative study of the quality of life in Canada and the USA from 1964 to 1974 / by Alex C. Michalos. — Dordrecht ; London : Reidel
Vol.3: Science, education and recreation. — c1981. — xv,219p : ill ; 23cm
Includes index
ISBN 90-277-1257-3 (pbk) : Unpriced
Primary classification 971.064′3 B81-27729

973.924′092′4 — United States. Nixon, Richard, *to 1974 — Biographies*
Longford, Frank Pakenham, *Earl of.* Nixon : a study in extremes of fortune / Lord Longford. — London : Weidenfeld and Nicolson, c1980. — ix,205p,[8]p of plates : ports ; 23cm
Bibliography: p196-198. — Includes index
ISBN 0-297-77708-4 : £8.95 B81-00678

973.924′092′4 — United States. Politics. Liddy, G. Gordon — *Biographies*
Liddy, G. Gordon. Will : the autobiography of G. Gordon Liddy. — London : Sphere, 1981, c1980. — 486p ; 18cm
Originally published: New York : St. Martin′s Press, 1980. — Includes index
ISBN 0-7221-5549-2 (pbk) : £1.75 B81-26823

Liddy, G. Gordon. Will : the autobiography of G. Gordon Liddy. — London : Severn House, 1981, c1980. — 374p ; 24cm
Originally published: New York : St. Martin′s Press, 1980. — Includes index
ISBN 0-7278-2014-1 : £7.95 : CIP rev. B81-12850

973.927 — United States — *For children*
This is the U.S.A. / illustrated by Toni Goffe. — London : Transworld, 1981. — 32p : col.ill,col.maps ; 28cm. — (A Carousel book)
Text on inside covers. — Includes index
ISBN 0-552-54179-6 (pbk) : £0.95 B81-32968

973.927 — United States. Social change — *Forecasts*
Ferguson, Marilyn. The Aquarian conspiracy : personal and social transformation in the 1980s / by Marilyn Ferguson ; foreword by Max Lerner. — London : Routledge & Kegan Paul, 1981, c1980. — 448p ; 24cm
Originally published: Los Angeles : J.P. Tarcher ; New York : distributed by St. Martin′s Press, 1980. — Bibliography:p429-437. — Includes index
ISBN 0-7100-0829-5 : £12.95 : CIP rev. B81-11964

973.927′05 — United States — *Serials*
World almanac & book of facts. — 1981. — New York : Newspaper Enterprise Association ; [London] : Windward, c1980. — 976p
ISBN 0-7112-0068-8 : £1.95
ISSN 0084-1382 B81-17468

973.927′092′4 — United States. Reagan, Nancy - *Biographies*
Reagan, Nancy. Nancy. — London : Robson Books, June 1981. — [224]p
ISBN 0-86051-143-x : £6.95 : CIP entry B81-12907

973.927′092′4 — United States. Reagan, Ronald — *Biographies*
Reagan, Ronald. [Where′s the rest of me?]. My early life, or, Where′s the rest of me? / by Ronald Reagan with Richard G. Hubler. — London : Sidgwick & Jackson, 1981. — 316p,[8]p of plates : ill,ports ; 23cm
Originally published: New York : Duell, Sloan and Pearce, 1965. — Includes index
ISBN 0-283-98771-5 : £7.95 B81-19373

Reagan the man, the president / Hedrick Smith ... [et al.]. — Oxford : Pergamon, 1981, c1980. — vi,201p,[32]p of plates : ports ; 24cm. — (Leaders of the world)
ISBN 0-08-027916-3 : £5.95 B81-11505

974 — HISTORY. UNITED STATES. NORTH-EASTERN STATES

974 — New England, *to 1950 — Readings from contemporary sources*
Strand, Paul. Time in New England : photographs / by Paul Strand ; text selected and edited by Nancy Newhall ; preface by Paul Metcalf ; afterword by Beaumont Newhall. — Millerton, N.Y. : Aperture ; Oxford : Phaidon [distributor], c1980. — 256p : ill ; 31cm
Originally published: New York : Oxford University Press, 1950. — Also available in a limited ed. of 450 copies numbered and signed by Mrs Paul Strand and Beaumont Newhall, accompanied by an original hand-pulled, dust-grain gravure Iris 1928 signed by Mrs Paul Strand
ISBN 0-89381-060-6 : £21.50
Primary classification 779′.9974043′0924
B81-19006

974′.00497 — New England. North American Indians. Social life, *to 1620*
Russell, Howard S.. Indian New England before the Mayflower / Howard S. Russell. — Hanover, N.H. ; London : University Press of New England, 1980. — xi,284p : ill,maps,1plan,1port ; 24cm
Bibliography: p237-270. — Includes index
ISBN 0-87451-162-3 : £10.50 B81-21957

974′.01 — New England. North American Indian antiquities, *to ca 1600.* **Archaeological investigation**
Snow, Dean R.. The archaeology of New England / Dean R. Snow. — New York ; London : Academic Press, c1980. — xiv,379p : ill,maps ; 25cm. — (New world archaeological record)
Bibliography: p345-362. — Includes index
ISBN 0-12-653950-2 : £18.20 B81-24013

974′.01 — United States. Eastern states. Prehistoric antiquities
Morgan, William N.. Prehistoric architecture in the Eastern United States / William N. Morgan. — Cambrige, Mass. ; London : MIT, c1980. — xxxix,197p : ill,maps,plans ; 18x25cm
Bibliography: p173-179. - Includes index
ISBN 0-262-13160-9 : £15.50 B81-08581

974′.02′0922 — New England. North American Indians. White settler captives, *1676-1724 — Personal observations — Collections*
Puritans among the Indians : accounts of captivity and redemption 1676-1724 / edited by Alden T. Vaughan & Edward W. Clark. — Cambridge, Mass. ; London : Belknap Press of Harvard University Press, 1981. — x,275p : ill,maps,facsims,1 port ; 24cm
Bibliography: p247-267. — Includes index
ISBN 0-674-73901-9 : £14.00 B81-39827

974′.043′0924 — United States. Eastern states. Social life, *1973-1976 — Personal observations*
Jenkins, Peter, *1951-*. A walk across America / Peter Jenkins. — Tring : Lion, 1980, c1979 (1981 [printing]). — 320p : ill,1map,ports ; 18cm
Originally published: New York : Morrow, 1979
ISBN 0-85648-358-3 (pbk) : £1.50 B81-19670

974.7′043 — New York *(State).* **Social life** *— For children*
Sandeman, Christine. New York family / Christine Sandeman ; photographs by Chris Fairclough. — London : A. & C. Black, c1981. — 25p : col.ill,1col.map ; 22cm. — (Beans. Geography)
ISBN 0-7136-2120-6 : £2.95 : CIP rev.
B81-03172

974.7′1004924 — New York *(City).* **Jews. Social conditions,** *1900-1979*
Moore, Deborah Dash. At home in America : second generation New York Jews / Deborah Dash Moore. — New York ; Guildford : Columbia University Press, 1981. — xiii,303p : ill,plans,ports ; 24cm. — (The Columbia history of urban life)
Bibliography: p265-287. - Includes index
ISBN 0-231-05062-3 : £8.80 B81-11751

974.7′1043 — New York *(City).* **Social life** *— For children*
Donvan, John. Living in New York / John Donvan. — Hove : Wayland, 1980. — 52p : ill,1col.map ; 22cm. — (Living in famous cities)
Bibliography: p51. — Includes index
ISBN 0-85340-696-0 : £3.50 B81-03125

974.7′1043′0222 — New York *(City) — Aerial photographs*
Fried, William. New York in aerial views : 68 photographs / by William Fried ; with identifications by Edward B. Watson. — New York : Dover ; London : Constable, 1980. — [142]p : chiefly ill ; 30cm
ISBN 0-486-24018-5 (pbk) : £4.25 B81-28930

974.7′45 — New York *(State).* **Sharon Springs,** *1825-1979*
Durlach, Hansi. The short season of Sharon Springs : portrait of another New York / original photographs by Hansi Durlach ; text by Stuart M. Blumin in collaboration with Deborah Adelman Blumin. — Ithaca ; London : Cornell University Press, 1980. — 128p : ill,2facsims,ports ; 29cm
ISBN 0-8014-1303-6 : £11.95 B81-10959

974.8′1103 — Pennsylvania. Philadelphia. Social conditions, *1800-1975*
The **Divided** metropolis : social and spatial dimensions of Philadelphia, 1800-1975 / edited by William W. Cutler, III and Howard Gillette, Jr. — Wesport, Conn. ; London : Greenwood Press, 1980. — xviii,308p : ill,maps ; 25cm. — (Contributions in American history ; no.85)
Bibliography: p285-298. — Includes index
ISBN 0-313-21351-8 : Unpriced B81-05510

974.8′11041′0222 — Pennsylvania. Philadelphia. Social life, *1839-ca 1900 — Illustrations*
Library Company of Philadelphia. Nineteenth-century photography in Philadelphia : 250 historic prints from the Library Company of Philadelphia / [selected] by Kenneth Finkel. — New York : Published in cooperation with the Library Company of Philadelphia by Dover ; London : Constable, c1980. — xxviii,226p : chiefly ill,ports ; 29cm
Bibliography: p221. - Includes index
ISBN 0-486-23932-2 (pbk) : £5.65 B81-04858

975 — HISTORY. UNITED STATES. SOUTH-EASTERN STATES

975′.00496073 — United States. Southern states. Negroes, *1863-1877*
Litwack, Leon F.. Been in the storm so long : the aftermath of slavery / Leon F. Litwack. — London : Athlone Press, 1980, c1979. — xvi,651p ; 25cm
Originally published: New York : Knopf, 1979. — Bibliography: p627-635. — Includes index
ISBN 0-485-11218-3 : £14.50 : CIP rev.
B80-26358

975′.00496073 — United States. Southern states. Negroes. Social life *— Childhood reminiscences*
Wright, Richard, *1908-*. Black boy / Richard Wright. — Walton-on-Thames : Nelson, 1980. — 285p ; 19cm. — (Panafrica library)
Originally published: London : Harper, 1945
ISBN 0-17-511616-4 (pbk) : £1.95 : CIP rev.
B80-18500

975′.00497 — United States. Southern states. North American Indians, *to 1840*
Wright, J. Leitch. The only land they knew : the tragic story of the American Indians in the Old South / J. Leitch Wright, Jr. — New York : Free Press ; London : Collier Macmillan, c1981. — xi,372p,[16]p of plates : ill,maps,facsims,ports ; 25cm
Bibliography: p335-357. — Includes index
ISBN 0-02-935790-x : £9.95 B81-39021

975.2′6 — Maryland. Baltimore, *to 1979*
Olson, Sherry H.. Baltimore : the building of an American city / Sherry H. Olson. — Baltimore ; London : Johns Hopkins University Press, c1980. — ix,432p : ill,maps ; 29cm
Includes index
ISBN 0-8018-2224-6 : £13.75 B81-03946

975.3′02′0222 — Washington, D.C., *1846-1932 — Illustrations*
Old Washington, D.C. in early photographs 1846-1932 / [compiled] by Robert Reed. — New York : Dover ; London : Constable, 1980. — x,165p : ill ; 30cm
Includes index
ISBN 0-486-23869-5 (pbk) : £4.45 B81-03968

975.6′175 — North Carolina. Roanoke Island. Settlement by English, *1585-1609*
Durant, David N.. Ralegh's lost colony / David N. Durant. — London : Weidenfeld and Nicolson, c1981. — xvii,188p,[8]p of plates : ill,maps,facsims,ports ; 23cm
Includes index
ISBN 0-297-77867-6 : £10.00 B81-08618

975.8′043′0924 — Georgia *(State).* **Political events. Role of Carter, Jimmy,** *1972-1977*
Fink, Gary M.. Prelude to the Presidency : the political character and legislative leadership style of Governor Jimmy Carter / Gary M. Fink. — Westport, Conn. ; London : Greenwood Press, 1980. — xxvi,225p : ill ; 22cm. — (Contributions in political science, ISSN 0147-1066 ; no.40)
Bibliography: p213-217. - Includes index
ISBN 0-313-22055-7 : Unpriced B81-06021

975.9′063′02491 — Florida *— For British tourists — Serials*
Florida world news. — No.1 (June 1980)-. — London (56 Wigmore St., W1) : Print Out, 1980-. — v. : ill ; 42cm
Monthly
ISSN 0260-602x = Florida world news : Unpriced B81-08354

976 — HISTORY. UNITED STATES. SOUTH CENTRAL STATES

976.3′03 — Louisiana. Purchase by United States. Influence of foreign relations, *ca 1630-1805*
DeConde, Alexander. This affair of Louisiana / Alexander DeConde. — Baton Rouge ; London : Louisiana State University Press, 1978, c1976. — x,325p,[12]p of plates : ill,1map,ports ; 23cm. — (Louisiana paperbacks in history)
Originally published: New York : Scribner, 1976. — Bibliography: p279-314. — Includes index
ISBN 0-8071-0497-3 (pbk) : £4.55 B81-32501

976.4 — Texas, *to 1980*
Richardson, Rupert Norval. Texas : the lone star state. — 4th ed. / Rupert Norval Richardson, Ernest Wallace, Adrian N. Anderson. — Englewood Cliffs ; London : Prentice-Hall, c1981. — x,485p : ill,maps(some col.),ports ; 24cm
Previous ed.: 1970. — Map, text on lining papers. — Includes bibliographies and index
ISBN 0-13-912444-6 : £12.30 B81-25169

976.4′02 — Texas. Spanish boys. Capture by North American Indians, *ca 1820 — Early works — Facsimiles*
Hofland, Barbara. Little Manuel, the captive boy / Barbara Hofland. — New York ; London : Garland, 1978. — 120p in various pagings,[1] folded leaf of plates : ill,facsims ; 19cm. — (The Garland library of narratives of North American Indian captivities ; v.44)
Facsimile reprints. — Contents: Little Manuel, the captive boy / Barbara Hofland — Seizure of the ship industry. Originally published: London : T. Tegg, 1830 - St Maur, or, The captive babes recovered. Originally published: New York : J. Emory and B. Waugh, 1830
ISBN 0-8240-1668-8 : Unpriced
Primary classification 971.01′8 B81-23691

976.4′04′0924 — Mier Expedition *— Personal observations*
McCutchan, Joseph D.. Mier expedition diary : a Texan prisoner's account / by Joseph D. McCutchan ; edited by Joseph Milton Nance ; foreword by Jane A. Kenamore. — Austin ; London : University of Texas Press, c1978. — xxiv,246p,[8]p of plates : ill,1map,facsims,plan,ports ; 24cm. — (The Elma Dill Russell Spencer Foundation series ; no.8)
Map on lining papers. — Bibliography: p217-225. - Includes index
ISBN 0-292-74006-9 : £9.00 B81-18858

976.4′157 — Texas. Big Thicket. Social life *— Personal observations — Collections — Interviews*
Big Thicket legacy / compiled and edited by Campbell and Lynn Loughmiller ; foreword by Francis E. Abernethy. — Austin ; London : University of Texas Press, c1977 (1980 printing). — xxiv,222p : ill,ports ; 26cm
ISBN 0-292-70733-9 (pbk) : £6.30 B81-38244

976.4'93061'0924 — Texas. Big Bend region. Social life, *1909-1913 — Personal observations*
Langford, J. O.. Big Bend : a homesteader's story / by J.O. Langford with Fred Gipson ; photographs by Henry B. Du Pont and Joe W. Langford ; drawings by Hal Story. — 2nd ed. — Austin ; London : University of Texas Press, c1973 (1980 printing). — 159p,[24]p of plates : ill,ports ; 23cm
Previous ed.: 1952. — Includes index
ISBN 0-292-70734-7 (pbk) : £4.90 B81-38243

976.4'96 — Texas. El Paso. Mexicans, *1880-1920*
García, Mario T.. Desert immigrants : the Mexicans of El Paso, 1880-1920 / Mario T. García. — New Haven ; London : Yale University Press, c1981. — xii,316p,[15]p of plates : ill,maps,1port ; 25cm. — (Yale Western Americana series ; 32)
Bibliography: p283-300. - Includes index
ISBN 0-300-02520-3 : £14.50 B81-16153

977 — HISTORY. UNITED STATES. NORTH CENTRAL STATES

977'.00497 — North America. Great Lakes region. North American Indian antiquities
Mason, Ronald J.. Great Lakes archaeology / Ronald J. Mason. — New York ; London : Academic Press, 1981. — xxiii,426p : ill,maps,plans ; 25cm. — (New World archaeological record)
Bibliography: p407-420. — Includes index
ISBN 0-12-477850-x : £22.80 B81-38904

977.1'73042'0924 — Ohio. Dayton. Social life, *1940-1945 — Childhood reminiscences*
Bailey, Anthony. America, lost & found / Anthony Bailey. — London : Faber, 1981, c1980. — 152p,[8]p of plates : ill,facsims,ports ; 22cm
Originally published: New York : Random House, 1981
ISBN 0-571-11714-7 : £6.95 B81-19841

977.3'463 — Illinois. Jacksonville, *to 1870*
Doyle, Don Harrison. The social order of a frontier community : Jacksonville, Illinois 1825-70 / Don Harrison Doyle. — Urbana ; London : University of Illinois Press, c1978. — xiii,289p,[16]p of plates : ill : maps ; 24cm
Bibliography: p273-282. — Includes index
ISBN 0-252-00685-2 : £7.80 B81-05617

977.5'043'0924 — Wisconsin. Politics. Role of McCarthy, Joseph
O'Brien, Michael, *1943-*. McCarthy and McCarthyism in Wisconsin / Michael O'Brien. — Columbia, Mo. ; London : University of Missouri Press, 1980. — ix,269p ; 24cm
Bibliography: p250-259. — Includes index
ISBN 0-8262-0319-1 : £14.30 B81-29587

977.7'17 — Iowa. Cherokee. Antiquities. Excavation of remains
The **Cherokee** excavations : Holocene ecology and human adaptations in northwestern Iowa / edited by Duane C. Anderson, Holmes A. Semken, Jr. — New York ; London : Academic Press, c1980. — xvi,277p : ill,1map ; 25cm. — (Studies in archaeology)
Includes bibliographies and index
ISBN 0-12-058260-0 : £13.00 B81-17421

977.8'66 — Missouri. St Louis, *to 1975 — Readings from contemporary sources*
St. Louis / edited by Selwyn K. Troen and Glen E. Holt. — New York ; London : New Viewpoints, 1977. — xxxiii,220p : ill ; 22cm. — (Documentary history of American cities)
Includes index
ISBN 0-531-05393-8 (cased) : Unpriced
ISBN 0-531-05603-1 (pbk) : £4.50 B81-04117

978 — HISTORY. UNITED STATES. WESTERN STATES

978 — North America. Rocky Mountains. Passes, *1540-1950*
Sprague, Marshall. The great gates : the story of the Rocky Mountain passes / by Marshall Sprague. — Lincoln, [Neb.] ; London : University of Nebraska Press, 1981, c1964. — 468p,[16]p of plates : ill,maps ; 21cm
Originally published: Boston : Little, Brown, 1964. — Includes index
ISBN 0-8032-4122-4 (cased) : Unpriced
ISBN 0-8032-9119-1 (pbk) : £5.80 B81-38210

978'.02 — United States. Western states, *ca 1770-ca 1900*
The **West** : an illustrated history / edited by Henry Steele Commager with Marcus Cunliffe, Maldwyn A. Jones. — London : Orbis, 1980, c1976. — 288p : ill(some col.),col.maps,facsims,ports ; 29cm
Originally published: Danbury : Grolier, 1976?. — Ill on lining papers. — Bibliography: p277-279. — Includes index
ISBN 0-85613-307-8 : £7.50 B81-01411

978'.02'05 — United States. Western states. Social life, *1880-ca 1920 — Serials*
[Western magazine *(London)***].** Western magazine. — No.1 (Oct.1980)-. — London : IPC Magazines, 1980-. — v. : ill,ports ; 29cm
Monthly
ISSN 0144-848x = Western magazine (London) : £0.70 per issue
Primary classification 823'.0874'08 B81-04761

978'.02'088636 — United States. Western states. Cattle drovers. Social life, *to 1890*
Worcester, Donald E.. The Chisholm Trail : high road of the cattle kingdom / Don Worcester. — Lincoln [Neb.] ; London : Published for Amon Carter Museum of Western Art by University of Nebraska Press, c1980. — xx,207p : ill,1map,port ; 23cm
Bibliography: p189-199. — Includes index
ISBN 0-8032-4710-9 : £9.40 B81-29363

978'.02'0924 — United States. Western states. Fitzpatrick, Thomas *— Biographies*
Hafen, LeRoy R.. Broken Hand : the life of Thomas Fitzpatrick : mountain man, guide and Indian agent / by LeRoy R. Hafen. — [Rev. ed.]. — Lincoln, [Neb.] ; London : University of Nebraska Press, 1981, c1973. — xiii,359p : ill,1map,ports ; 21cm. — (A Bison book)
Originally published: Denver, Colo. : Old West Pub. Co., 1973. — Includes index
ISBN 0-8032-7208-1 (pbk) : £3.90 B81-22816

978'.02'0924 — United States. Western states. Wootton, Richens Lacy *— Biographies*
Conard, Howard Louis. Uncle Dick Wootton : the pioneer frontiersman of the Rocky Mountain region / by Howard Louis Conard ; edited by Milo Milton Quaife. — London : [Neb.] ; London : University of Nebraska Press, 1980. — xxiii,462p : 1map ; 21cm. — (A Bison book)
Originally published: 1890. — Includes index
ISBN 0-8032-1408-1 (cased) : £13.50 (pbk) : £4.50 B81-07873

978.6'663 — Montana. Madison River Valley. Livestock: Sheep. Production. Ranches. Social life, *1920-1942 — Personal observations*
Call, Hughie. Golden fleece / by Hughie Call ; illustrated by Paul Brown. — Lincoln, [Neb.] ; London : University of Nebraska Press, 1981. — xvii,250p : 1map ; 21cm
Originally published: Boston, Mass. : Houghton Mifflin, 1942
ISBN 0-8032-1413-8 (cased) : Unpriced
ISBN 0-8032-6308-2 (pbk) : £3.60 B81-38245

979 — HISTORY. UNITED STATES. PACIFIC COAST STATES

979.1'04'0924 — Arizona. Frontier life, *1900-1914 — Personal observations*
Faunce, Hilda. Desert wife / by Hilda Faunce ; introduction by Frank Water ; with illustrations by W. Langdon Kihn. — Lincoln, Neb. ; London : University of Nebraska Press, 1981, c1961. — xiv,304p : ill ; 21cm
Originally published: Boston, Mass. : Little, Brown, 1934
ISBN 0-8032-1957-1 (cased) : Unpriced
ISBN 0-8032-6853-x (pbk) : £3.60 B81-23112

979.4'00497 — Californian Indians. Cultural processes
Heizer, Robert F.. The natural world of the California Indians / Robert F. Heizer and Albert B. Elsasser. — Berkeley ; London : University of California Press, 1980. — 271p,[8] of plates : ill(some col.),maps ; 21cm. — (California natural history guide ; 46)
Bibliography: p259-264 — Includes index
ISBN 0-520-03895-9 (cased) : £7.75 B81-21956

979.4'04 — California. Gold mining communities. Sociocultural aspects, *1849-1850*
Fender, Stephen. Plotting the Golden West. — Cambridge : Cambridge University Press, Jan.1982. — [256]p
ISBN 0-521-23924-9 : £15.00 : CIP entry B81-34327

979.4'04'088622 — California. Gold prospectors. Social life, *1848-1849*
Jackson, Donald Dale. Gold dust : the California gold rush and the forty-niners / by Donald Dale Jackson. — London : Allen & Unwin, 1980. — x,361p : ill,2maps,ports ; 25cm
Bibliography: p335-345. - Includes index
ISBN 0-04-973012-6 : £8.95 : CIP rev. B80-07188

979.4'053'0924 — California. Chinese immigrants. Social life, *ca 1940-ca 1955 — Childhood reminiscences*
Kingston, Maxine Hong. The woman warrior : memoirs of a girlhood among ghosts / Maxine Hong Kingston. — London : Pan, 1981, c1977. — 185p ; 20cm. — (Picador)
Originally published: New York : Knopf, 1976 ; London : Allen Lane, 1977
ISBN 0-330-26400-1 (pbk) : £1.50 B81-14992

979.4'61051 — California. San Francisco. Earthquakes, *1906*
Thomas, Gordon. [The San Francisco earthquake]. Earthquake : the destruction of San Francisco / Gordon Thomas and Max Morgan-Witts. — London : Arrow, 1981, c1971. — 301p ; 18cm
Originally published: New York : Stein and Day ; London : Souvenir, 1971. — Bibliography: p279-291. - Includes index
ISBN 0-09-924450-0 (pbk) : £1.35 B81-05249

979.5'00497 — London. Westminster *(London Borough).* **Museums: British Museum.** *Department of Ethnography.* **Stock: Pacific Northwest Coast Indian artefacts** *— Catalogues*
King, J. C. H.. Artificial curiosities from the northwest coast of America. — London : British Museum Publications, July 1981. — [216]p
ISBN 0-7141-1562-2 : £30.00 : CIP entry B81-22574

980 — HISTORY. SOUTH AMERICA

980 — Latin America, *to 1979*
Crow, John A.. The epic of Latin America / John A. Crow. — 3rd ed., expanded and updated. — Berkeley ; London : University of California Press, c1980. — xxvi,929p : maps ; 24cm
Previous ed.: Garden City, N.Y. : Doubleday, 1971. — Maps on lining papers. — Bibliography: p899-900. - Includes index
ISBN 0-520-04107-0 : £18.00 B81-03746

980'.003'21 — Latin America. Social conditions *— Encyclopaedias*
Rossi, Ernest E.. The Latin American political dictionary / Ernest E. Rossi, Jack C. Plano. — Santa Barbara ; Oxford : ABC-Clio, c1980. — xi,261p ; 24cm
Includes index
ISBN 0-87436-302-0 : £13.75 B81-28958

980'.004'96 — Latin American negro civilization *— Encyclopaedias*
Nuñez, Benjamin. Dictionary of Afro-Latin American civilization / Benjamin Nuñez with the assistance of the African Bibliographic Center. — Westport ; London : Greenwood Press, 1980. — xxxv,525p : maps,facsims ; 25cm
Bibliography: p505-512. — Includes index
ISBN 0-313-21138-8 : £27.90 B81-23461

980'.004'98 — Central Brazil. Suya. Cultural processes
Seeger, Anthony. Nature and society in central Brazil : the Suya Indians of Mato Grosso / Anthony Seeger. — Cambridge, Mass. ; London : Harvard University Press, 1981. — ix,278p : ill ; 25cm
Bibliography: p269-273. — Includes index
ISBN 0-674-60485-7 : £16.50 B81-38276

980'.004'98 — Inca civilization — *For children*
Millard, Anne. The Incas / [Anne Millard] ; [illustrator Richard Hook]. — London : Longman, 1980. — 44p : col.ill,1col.map ; 29cm. — (Great civilisations ; 7)
Text on lining papers. — Includes index
ISBN 0-582-39071-0 : £2.75 : CIP rev. B80-09545

980'.02'0924 — London. Westminster *(London Borough).* **Houses: Canning House. Exhibits: Items associated with Bolívar, Simón** — *Catalogues*
Simón Bolívar 1783-1830 : commemorative exhibition 10-21 June, 1974, Canning House. — London : Hispanic & Luso Brazilian Council, [1974]. — [8]p : ill ; 21cm
Unpriced (unbound) B81-29204

980'.03 — Latin America. Rural regions. Social change, *ca 1900-1979*
Environment, society, and rural change in Latin America : the past, present, and future in the countryside / edited by David A. Preston. — Chichester : Wiley, c1980. — xi,256p : ill,maps ; 24cm
Includes bibliographies and index
ISBN 0-471-27713-4 : £14.50 : CIP rev. B80-21457

980'.031 — Latin America, *1800-1900*
Burns, E. Bradford. The poverty of progress : Latin America in the nineteenth century / E. Bradford Burns. — Berkeley ; London : University of California Press, c1980. — 183p,[8]p of plates : ill,1map,ports ; 23cm
Maps on lining papers. — Includes index
ISBN 0-520-04160-7 : £7.75 B81-11247

980'.033 — Latin America, *1939-1945*
Humphreys, R. A. (Robert Arthur). Latin America and the Second World War. — London : Athlone Press, Aug.1981. — (University of London Institute of Latin American Studies monographs, ISSN 0776-0846 ; 10)
Vol.1: 1939-1942. — [256]p
ISBN 0-485-17710-2 : £16.00 : CIP entry B81-19174

980'.038'05 — Latin America. Relations with Western Europe — *Serials*
Europe and Latin America : an annual review of European-Latin American Relations / Latin America Bureau. — 1980-. — London (PO Box 134, NW1 4JY) : The Bureau, 1980-. — v. ; 21cm
Continues: Britain and Latin America
ISSN 0260-5023 = Europe and Latin America : £1.95
Primary classification 940.55'8'05 B81-04447

980'.038'05 — Latin America — *Spanish texts — Serials*
Correo Latinoamericano. — Año 1, no.1 (30 de abr./6 de mayo)-. — Londres [London] (1 Cambridge Terrace, Regents Park WC1) : New America Publications : Londres (1 Benwell Rd., N7) : Spotlight Magazine Distribution [distributor], 1981-. — v. : ill,ports ; 42cm
Weekly
ISSN 0262-2335 = Correo Latinoamericano : £20.00 per year B81-39514

981 — HISTORY. BRAZIL

981'.06 — Brazil. Frontier life, *1930-1980.* **Politico-economic aspects**
Foweraker, Joe. The struggle for land : a political economy of the pioneer frontier in Brazil from 1930 to the present day / Joe Foweraker. — Cambridge : Cambridge University Press, 1981. — xxi,258p : maps ; 23cm. — (Cambridge Latin American studies ; 39)
Bibliography: p235-255. — Includes index
ISBN 0-521-23555-3 : £20.00 B81-37998

981'.3063 — North-east Brazil. Social conditions — *Conference proceedings*
The Logic of poverty : the case of the Brazilian Northeast / edited by Simon Mitchell. — London : Routledge & Kegan Paul, 1981. — ix,189p : 1ill ; 24cm
Conference papers
ISBN 0-7100-0637-3 (pbk) : £7.95 B81-03217

981'.5105 — Brazil. Diamantina. Social life, *1893-1895 — Childhood reminiscences*
Morley, Helena. The diary of 'Helena Morley' / translated from the Portuguese by Elizabeth Bishop. — London : Virago, 1981, c1979. — xxxvii,281p : ill ; 20cm
Originally published: New York : Farrar, Straus and Cudahy, 1957 ; London : Gollancz, 1958
ISBN 0-86068-200-5 (pbk) : £3.50 : CIP rev. B81-14438

982 — HISTORY. ARGENTINA

982'.00421 — Argentina. Britons. Social life, *to 1980*
Graham-Yooll, Andrew. The forgotten colony : a history of the English-speaking communities in Argentina / Andrew Graham-Yooll. — London : Hutchinson, 1981. — 317p,[8]p of plates : ill,facsims,ports ; 23cm
Bibliography: p275-306. — Includes index
ISBN 0-09-145310-0 : £12.95 : CIP rev. B81-12319

982'.04'0924 — Argentina. Rosas, Juan Manuel de — *Biographies*
Lynch, John, *1927-.* Argentine dictator : Juan Manuel de Rosas 1829-1852 / by John Lynch. — Oxford : Clarendon, c1981. — 414p,[1]leaf of plate : 1port ; 22cm
Bibliography: p389-404. — Includes index
ISBN 0-19-821129-5 : £22.50 : CIP rev. B81-13829

982'.062 — Argentina. Political events. Role of Argentina. *Ejército, 1945-1962*
Potash, Robert A.. The Army & politics in Argentina 1945-1962 : Perón to Frondizi / Robert A. Potash. — London : Athlone, 1980. — ix,418p,[8]p of plates : ports ; 24cm
Originally published: Stanford : Stanford University Press, 1980. — Bibliography: p385-404. — Includes index
ISBN 0-485-11205-1 : £15.00 B81-03930

982'.064'0924 — Argentina. Perón, Eva — *Biographies*
Fraser, Nicholas. Eva Perón / Nicholas Fraser and Marysa Navarro. — London : Deutsch, 1980. — 192,[22]p,[12]p of plates : 2ill,ports ; 23cm
Bibliography: p[14]-[18]. - Includes index
ISBN 0-233-97236-6 : £6.95 B81-01412

982'.70049166 — Argentina. Patagonia. Welsh communities. Social life, *ca 1860-1979 — Personal observations — Collections — Welsh texts*
Atgofion o Batagonia : ysgrifau gan rai o'r Gwladfawyr sydd yno heddiw / wedi eu golygu gan R. Bryn Williams. — Llandysul : Gwasg Gomer, 1980. — 133p : ill,maps,ports ; 22cm
ISBN 0-85088-653-8 (pbk) : £2.25 B81-03939

983 — HISTORY. CHILE

983'.005 — Chile — *History — Serials — Spanish texts*
Nueva historia / Asociación de Historiadores Chilenos (U.K.). — Año 1, no.1-. — Londres (c/o Institute of Latin American Studies, 31 Tavistock Sq., WC1H 9HA) : La Asociación, 1981. — v. : maps ; 23cm
Three issues yearly
ISSN 0261-2909 = Nueva historia : Unpriced B81-37240

983'.064 — Chile. Political events, *1900-1978 — Trotskyist viewpoints*
Martinez, Jorge. Lessons of Chile / by Jorge Martinez. — London (1 Mentmore Terrace, E8 3PN) : Militant, 1980. — 40p : ill,ports ; 28cm
"First published by 'Nuevo Claridad' Apartaode Correos 35.124. Madrid, Spain"
ISBN 0-906582-05-9 (pbk) : £0.50 B81-21260

984 — HISTORY. BOLIVIA

984'.052 — Bolivia, *1952-1980*
Dunkerley, James. Bolivia : coup d'état / [written by James Dunkerley]. — London (PO Box 134 NW1 4JY) : Latin America Bureau, c1980. — 88p : ill,1map ; 21cm. — (Latin America Bureau special brief)
Bibliography: p84
ISBN 0-906156-11-4 (pbk) : £1.50 B81-08969

985 — HISTORY. PERU

985'.01'088054 — Inca children. Social life — *For schools*
Lewis, Brenda Ralph. Growing up in Inca Times / Brenda Ralph Lewis. — London : Batsford Academic and Educational, 1981. — 72p : ill,1map,ports ; 26cm
Bibliography: p70. - Includes index
ISBN 0-7134-2736-1 : £5.50 B81-12557

985'.25 — Peru. Lima. Shanty towns. Social conditions — *Study regions: Medalla Milagrosa*
Lloyd, P. C.. The 'young towns' of Lima : aspects of urbanization in Peru / Peter Lloyd. — Cambridge : Cambridge University Press, 1980. — ix,160p : 4maps ; 24cm. — (Urbanization in developing countries)
Bibliography: p146-156. — Includes index
ISBN 0-521-22871-9 (cased) : £15.00 : CIP rev.
ISBN 0-521-29688-9 (pbk) : £4.50 B80-25214

986.1 — HISTORY. COLOMBIA

986.1'0632 — Colombia. Political events, *1946-1966*
Oquist, Paul. Violence, conflict, and politics in Colombia / Paul Oquist. — New York ; London : Academic Press, c1980. — xiv,263p : 1map ; 24cm. — (Studies in social discontinuity)
Bibliography: p239-251. — Includes index
ISBN 0-12-527750-4 : £14.00 B81-17714

989.5 — HISTORY. URUGUAY

989.5'061'0924 — Uruguay. Batlle y Ordóñez, José, *1907-1915 — Biographies*
Vanger, Milton I.. The model country : José Batlle y Ordonẽz of Uruguay 1907-1915 / Milton I. Vanger. — Hanover, N.H. ; London : Published for Brandeis University Press by University Press of New England, 1980. — xii,436p : ill,ports ; 24cm
Includes index
ISBN 0-87451-184-4 : £15.00 B81-12008

990 — HISTORY. OCEANIA, ATLANTIC OCEAN ISLANDS, POLAR REGIONS, ETC

990 — Pacific Islands. Cultural processes, *1768-1779*
Cook's voyages and peoples of the Pacific / edited by Hugh Cobbe. — London : Published for the Trustees of the British Museum and the British Library Board by British Museum Publications, c1979. — 143p,[8]p of plates : ill (some col.),charts,maps,facsims,ports ; 26cm
Published to accompany an exhibition. — Bibliography: p143
ISBN 0-7141-1550-9 (cased) : £8.95 : CIP rev.
ISBN 0-7141-1551-7 (pbk) : £3.95
Primary classification 910'.09164 B78-40594

990'.074'02649 — Ipswich. *Department of Recreation & Amenities.* **Stock: Australasian artefacts & Oceanic artefacts**
Ipswich. *Department of Recreation & Amenities.* The Pacific, Australia and the Americas : a guide to the Ipswich collections / [author D.L. Jones]. — Ipswich ([Civic Centre, Civic Drive, Ipswich IP1 2EE]) : Ipswich Borough Council, Department of Recreation & Amenities, [1980?]. — [36]p : ill ; 18x25cm
Cover title
ISBN 0-906688-03-5 (pbk) : Unpriced
Also classified at 970'.0074'02649 B81-10223

993 — HISTORY. MELANESIA, NEW ZEALAND

993.1 — New Zealand, *to 1979*
A **Book** of New Zealand. — Rev. and enl. [ed.], edited by J.C. Reid and P. Cape. — Auckland ; London : Collins, 1979. — xx,292p,[32]p of plates : ill(some col.),1port ; 22cm
Previous ed.: / edited by J.C. Reid, 1964. — Includes index
ISBN 0-00-216942-8 : £6.95 B81-02938

993.1 — New Zealand, *to 1980*
The **Oxford** history of New Zealand / edited by W.H. Oliver with B.R. Williams. — Oxford : Clarendon, 1981. — xiii,572p : ill,maps ; 25cm
Bibliography: p513-551. — Includes index
ISBN 0-19-558062-1 (cased) : £18.50
ISBN 0-19-558063-x (pbk) : Unpriced B81-40581

993.1'004994 — New Zealand. Maoris, *to 1980*
Houghton, Philip. The first New Zealanders. — London : Hodder and Stoughton, May 1981. — [156]p
ISBN 0-340-25241-3 : £6.95 : CIP entry B81-04238

993.103'2 — New Zealand. Political events, *1936-1940 — Correspondence, diaries, etc.*
Lee, John A.. The John A. Lee diaries 1936-1940 / with a foreword, commentary and afterword by John A. Lee. — Christchurch [N.Z.] ; London : Whitcoulls, 1981. — 237p : ports ; 25cm
Includes index
ISBN 0-7233-0638-9 : Unpriced B81-34929

993.103'2'0924 — New Zealand. Politics. Locke, Elsie — *Biographies*
Locke, Elsie. Student at the gates / Elsie Locke. — Christchurch, N.Z. ; London : Whitcoulls, 1981. — 180p,[8]p of plates : ill,ports ; 22cm
ISBN 0-7233-0658-3 : Unpriced B81-34944

993.103'2'0924 — New Zealand. Social life, *ca 1920-ca 1940 — Childhood reminiscences*
Dunstan, Peggy. A fistful of summer / Peggy Dunstan ; illustrated by Jean Oates. — Christchurch [N.Z.] ; London : Whitcoulls, 1981. — 142p : ill ; 22cm
ISBN 0-7233-0633-8 : Unpriced B81-27816

993.12'004994 — New Zealand. North Island. Maoris. Social life, *1900-1979 — Personal observations*
Stirling, Eruera. Eruera : the teachings of a Maori elder / Eruera Stirling ; as told to Anne Salmond. — Wellington ; Oxford : Oxford University Press, c1980. — 288p : ill,maps,facsims,ports,geneal.tables ; 25cm
English and Maori text. — Bibliography: p279-283. — Includes index
ISBN 0-19-558069-9 (cased) : £20.50
ISBN 0-19-558070-2 (pbk) : Unpriced B81-26239

993.12'2 — New Zealand. Auckland. Social life — *Illustrations*
Barriball, Martin. Auckland / photography Martin Barriball ; text Gordon McLauchlan. — Wellington ; London (11 Southampton Row, WC1 5HA) : A.H. & A.W. Reed, c1978. — 120p : col.ill,2ports ; 26cm
ISBN 0-589-01198-7 : £6.95 B81-15352

993.15 — New Zealand. South Island. Western coastal regions — *Illustrations*
Burford, John. The coast and the coasters / John Burford. — Christchurch [N.Z.] ; London : Whitcoulls, 1981. — 78p : all col.ill,1map,col.ports ; 29cm
ISBN 0-7233-0634-6 : Unpriced B81-23176

993'.5 — Solomon Islands. Malaita. Kwaio. Massacres by Europeans, *1927*
Keesing, Roger M.. Lightning meets the west wind : the Malaita massacre / Roger M. Keesing, Peter Corris. — Melbourne ; Oxford : Oxford University Press, 1980. — xv,219p : ill,maps,ports ; 23cm
Maps on lining papers. — Includes index
ISBN 0-19-554223-1 : £11.95 B81-05940

993'.6 — Papua New Guinea. Karavar. Cultural processes
Errington, Frederick Karl. Karavar : masks and power in a Melanesian ritual / Frederick Karl Errington. — Ithaca ; London : Cornell University Press, 1974. — 259p : ill,1map ; 22cm. — (Symbol, myth and ritual series)
Bibliography: p255-256. — Includes index
£15.75 B81-22066

994 — HISTORY. AUSTRALIA

994'.0049915 — Australia. Colonisation by European countries. Attitudes of aborigines, *1788-1980*
Broome, Richard. Aboriginal Australians. — London : Allen & Unwin, Jan.1982. — [224]p. — (The Australian experience)
ISBN 0-86861-043-7 : £10.00 : CIP entry B81-33931

994'.0049915 — Australian aborigines — *For children*
Aborigines / consultant editor Henry Pluckrose ; illustrated by Maurice Wilson. — London : Hamilton, 1981. — 28p : col.ill ; 21cm. — (Small world)
Includes index
ISBN 0-241-10630-3 : £2.50 B81-38532

994'.0049915'0924 — Australian aborigines. Social life, *1803-1835 — Personal observations*
Morgan, John, *fl.1852.* The life and adventures of William Buckley : thirty-two years a wanderer amongst the aborigines of the unexplored country round Port Phillip / John Morgan. — Firle : Caliban, 1979. — 238p : ill,ports ; 19cm
Originally published: Hobart : Macdougall, 1852
ISBN 0-904573-12-5 : £7.50
Primary classification 919.4'042'0924 B81-32621

994.04'092'4 — Australia. Edwin, John — *Biographies*
Edwin, John. I'm going - what then? / John Edwin. — Bognor Regis : New Horizon, c1978. — 167p ; 21cm
Includes index
ISBN 0-86116-060-6 : Unpriced B81-21781

994.04'1'0924 — Australia. Fisher, Andrew — *Biographies*
Andrew Fisher : 1862-1928 / [compiled by John Malkin]. — S.L. : s.n., [1980] (David : Walker & Connell Ltd. printers). — 40p, : ill,ports,geneal.table ; 24cm
Cover title
Unpriced (pbk) B81-14739

994.05 — Australia. Attitudes of returned Italian immigrants in Italy, *1960-1970*
Thompson, Stephanie Lindsay. Australia through Italian eyes : a study of settlers returning from Australia to Italy / Stephanie Lindsay Thompson. — Melbourne ; Oxford : Oxford University Press, 1980. — xxi,271p : ill,maps ; 23cm
Map on lining papers. — Bibliography: p261-263. - Includes index
ISBN 0-19-550570-0 : £17.50 B81-08578

994.05'092'4 — Australia. Menzies, *Sir* **Robert,** *1894-1978 — Biographies*
Hazlehurst, Cameron. Menzies observed / Cameron Hazlehurst. — Sydney ; London : Allen and Unwin, 1979. — 392p : ill,1facsim,ports ; 26cm
ISBN 0-86861-320-7 : £10.00 B81-01724

994.06'3 — Australia — *For children*
Truby, David W.. Let's go to Australia / David Truby. — London : Watts, c1980. — 32p : col.ill,2col.maps ; 22cm
ISBN 0-85166-862-3 : £2.99
ISBN 0-531-00988-2 (U.S.) B81-03563

994.4'10049915 — New South Wales. Sydney region. Australian aborigines, *1788-1860*
Willey, Keith. When the sky fell down : the destruction of the tribes of the Sydney region 1788-1850s / Keith Willey. — Sydney ; London : Collins, 1979. — 231p,[12]p of plates : ill(some col.),1map,ports ; 22cm
Bibliography: p221-223. - Includes index
ISBN 0-00-216434-5 : £5.95 B81-06233

994.5'1 — Australia. Victoria. Melbourne. Port Phillip. Upper classes. Social life, *1836-1851*
De Serville, Paul. Port Phillip gentlemen and good society in Melbourne before the gold rushes / Paul de Serville. — Melbourne ; Oxford : Oxford University Press, 1980. — 256p,[14]p of plates : ill,map,ports ; 23cm
Bibliography: p238-245. — Includes index
ISBN 0-19-554212-6 : £19.00 B81-01928

995 — HISTORY. NEW GUINEA

995'.1 — Indonesia. Irian Jaya, *to 1979*
Suter, Keith. West Irian, East Timor and Indonesia / by Keith Suter. — London (36 Craven St., WC2N 5NG) : Minority Rights Group, 1979. — 27p : 3maps ; 30cm. — (Report / Minority Rights Group, ISSN 0305-6252 ; no.42)
Bibliography: p27
£0.75 (pbk)
Also classified at 959.8'6 B81-05182

995'.3 — Papua New Guinea. Social conditions
Baker, Leigh R.. Papua New Guinea : an outline guide for expatriate contract employees / [author Leigh R. Baker] ; [edited by Ian Knights for the] Royal Commonwealth Society. — [2nd rev. ed.]. — London : Information Bureau, [The Society], 1981. — 14p,[3]p of plates : maps ; 30cm. — (Notes on conditions)
Previous ed.: published in Hong Kong, Trinidad and Papua New Guinea / Ian Knights. 1979. — Bibliography: p13-14
ISBN 0-905067-91-6 (unbound) : Unpriced B81-31496

995'.5 — Papua New Guinea. Eastern Highlands. Cultural processes. Regional variations — *Case studies*
Pataki-Schweizer, K. J.. A New Guinea landscape : community, space, and time in the eastern highlands / K.J. Pataki-Schweizer. — Seattle ; London : University of Washington Press, c1980. — xxii,165p : ill,maps ; 24cm. — (Anthropological studies in the Eastern Highlands of New Guinea ; v.4)
Bibliography: p148-160. — Includes index
ISBN 0-295-95656-9 : £24.00 B81-05063

996 — HISTORY. POLYNESIA

996'.18 — Easter Island. Cultural processes
McCall, Grant. Rapanui : tradition and survival on Easter Island / Grant McCall. — Sydney ; London : Allen & Unwin, 1981, c1980. — 197p : ill,2maps,ports ; 23cm
Maps on lining papers
ISBN 0-86861-274-x : £12.50 B81-26681

996'.81'00222 — Kiribati. Social life — *Illustrations*
Whincup, Tony. Nareau's nation : a portrait of the Gilbert Islands / Tony Whincup. — London : Stacey International, 1979. — 227p : chiefly ill(some col.),col.maps ; 30cm
ISBN 0-905743-16-4 : £5.00 B81-09585

997 — HISTORY. ATLANTIC OCEAN ISLANDS

997'.11 — Falkland Islands, *to 1980*
Strange, Ian J.. The Falkland Islands / by Ian J. Strange. — 2nd ed. — Newton Abbot : David & Charles, c1981. — 256p : ill,maps ; 23cm
Previous ed.: 1972. — Bibliography: p242-245. — Includes index
ISBN 0-7153-8133-4 : £8.50 : CIP rev. B81-19167

997'.3 — St Helena, *to 1979*
Cross, Tony. St. Helena : including Ascension Island and Tristan da Cunha / Tony Cross. — Newton Abbot : David & Charles, c1981. — 192p : ill,maps ; 23cm
Bibliography: p187-188. — Includes index
ISBN 0-7153-8075-3 : £4.95 B81-08699

998 — HISTORY. POLAR REGIONS

998'.2 — Greenland. Social life, *1957-1963 — Correspondence, diaries, etc.*
Frederiksen, Thomas. Eskimo diary / Thomas Frederiksen ; foreword by Emil Rosing ; English translation by Jack Jensen and Val Clery ; caligraphy by Mel Potek. — London : Pelham, 1981, c1980. — 148p : col.ill,col.maps,ports ; 26cm
Parallel Greenlandic text and English translation of the Danish publication Gronlandske dagbogsblade
ISBN 0-7207-1311-0 : £7.95 B81-15322